The Warmth of Other Suns

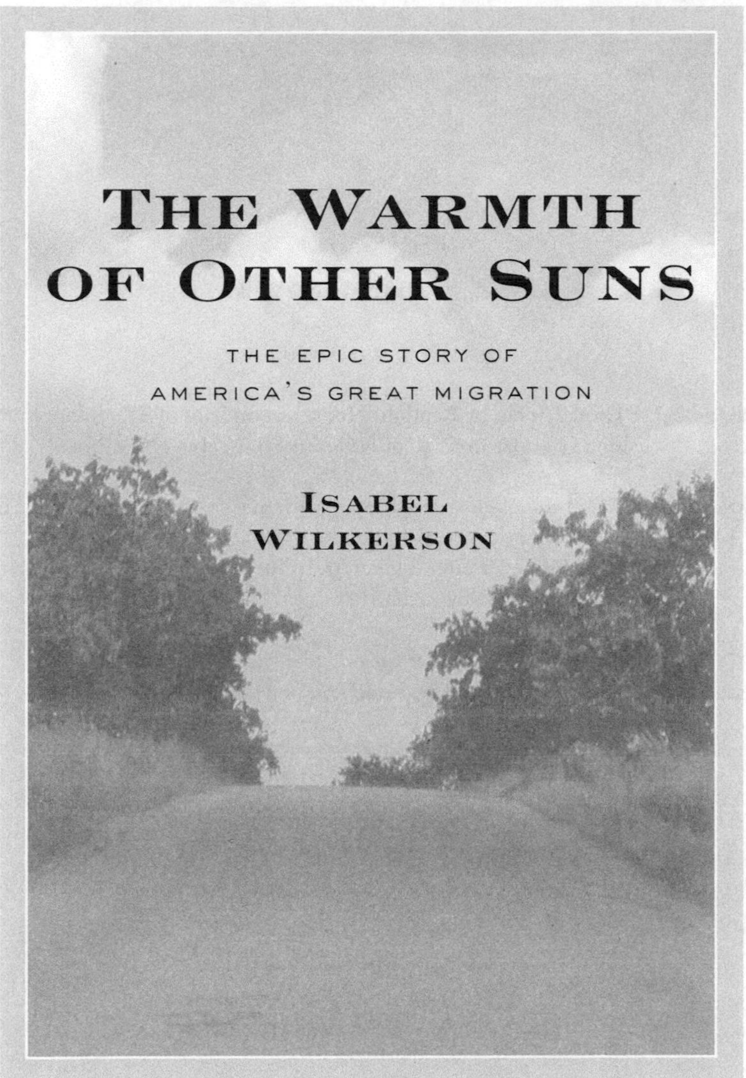

RANDOM HOUSE NEW YORK

Published in the United States by Random House, an imprint of The Random House Publishing Group, a division of Random House, Inc., New York.

Random House and colophon are registered trademarks of Random House, Inc.

Our title *The Warmth of Other Suns* is taken from the final pages of the unrestored edition of *Black Boy* by Richard Wright. Used by permission.

Permissions acknowledgments for previously published material can be found beginning on page 621.

ISBN 978-0-679-44432-9
eBook ISBN 978-0-679-60407-5

Printed in the United States of America

www.atrandom.com

10 12 14 16 18 17 15 13 11

Book design by Christopher M. Zucker

To my mother and
to the memory of my father,
whose migration made me possible,
and to the millions of others like them
who dared to act upon their dreams

I was leaving the South
To fling myself into the unknown. . . .
I was taking a part of the South
To transplant in alien soil,
To see if it could grow differently,
If it could drink of new and cool rains,
Bend in strange winds,
Respond to the warmth of other suns
And, perhaps, to bloom.

—Richard Wright

Contents

PART ONE

In the Land of the Forefathers

Our mattresses were made
of corn shucks
and soft gray Spanish moss
that hung from the trees. . . .
From the swamps
we got soup turtles
and baby alligators
and from the woods
we got raccoon,
rabbit and possum.
—Mahalia Jackson, *Movin' On Up*

Leaving

This land is first and foremost
his handiwork.
It was he who brought order
out of primeval wilderness . . .
Wherever one looks in this land,
whatever one sees that is the work of man,
was erected by the toiling
straining bodies of blacks.
—David L. Cohn, *God Shakes Creation*

They fly from the land that bore them.
—W. H. Stillwell

I

CHICKASAW COUNTY, MISSISSIPPI, LATE OCTOBER 1937

IDA MAE BRANDON GLADNEY

THE NIGHT CLOUDS were closing in on the salt licks east of the oxbow lakes along the folds in the earth beyond the Yalobusha River. The cotton was at last cleared from the field. Ida Mae tried now to get the children ready and to gather the clothes and quilts and somehow keep her mind off the churning within her. She had sold off the turkeys and doled out in secret the old stools, the wash pots, the tin tub, the bed pallets. Her husband was settling with Mr. Edd over the worth of a year's labor, and she did not know what would come of it. None of them had been on a train before—not unless you counted the clattering local from Bacon Switch to Okolona, where, "by the time you sit down, you there," as Ida Mae put it. None of them had been out of Mississippi. Or Chickasaw County, for that matter.

There was no explaining to little James and Velma the stuffed bags and chaos and all that was at stake or why they had to put on their shoes and not cry and bring undue attention from anyone who might happen to see them leaving. Things had to look normal, like any other time they might ride into town, which was rare enough to begin with.

Velma was six. She sat with her ankles crossed and three braids in her hair and did what she was told. James was too little to understand. He was three. He was upset at the commotion. *Hold still now, James. Lemme put your shoes on,* Ida Mae told him. James wriggled and kicked. He did not like shoes. He ran free in the field. What were these things? He did not like them on his feet. So Ida Mae let him go barefoot.

Miss Theenie stood watching. One by one, her children had left her and gone up north. Sam and Cleve to Ohio. Josie to Syracuse. Irene to Milwaukee. Now the man Miss Theenie had tried to keep Ida Mae from marrying in the first place was taking her away, too. Miss Theenie had no choice but to accept it and let Ida Mae and the grandchildren go for good. Miss Theenie drew them close to her, as she always did whenever anyone was leaving. She had them bow their heads. She whispered a prayer that her daughter and her daughter's family be protected on the long journey ahead in the Jim Crow car.

"May the Lord be the first one in the car," she prayed, *"and the last out."*

When the time had come, Ida Mae and little James and Velma and all that they could carry were loaded into a brother-in-law's truck, and the three of them went to meet Ida Mae's husband at the train depot in Okolona for the night ride out of the bottomland.

2

WILDWOOD, FLORIDA, APRIL 14, 1945
GEORGE SWANSON STARLING

A MAN NAMED ROSCOE COLTON gave Lil George Starling a ride in his pickup truck to the train station in Wildwood through the fruit-bearing scrubland of central Florida. And Schoolboy, as the toothless orange pickers mockingly called him, boarded the Silver Meteor pointing north.

A railing divided the stairs onto the train, one side of the railing for white passengers, the other for colored, so the soles of their shoes would not touch the same stair. He boarded on the colored side of the railing, a final reminder from the place of his birth of the absurdity of the world he was leaving.

He was getting out alive. So he didn't let it bother him. "I got on the car where they told me to get on," he said years later.

He hadn't had time to bid farewell to everyone he wanted to. He stopped to say good-bye to Rachel Jackson, who owned a little café up on what they called the Avenue and the few others he could safely get to in the little time he had. He figured everybody in Egypt town, the colored section of Eustis, probably knew he was leaving before he had climbed onto the train, small as the town was and as much as people talked.

It was a clear afternoon in the middle of April. He folded his tall frame into the hard surface of the seat, his knees knocking against the seat back in front of him. He was packed into the Jim Crow car, where the railroad stored the luggage, when the train pulled away at last. He was on the run, and he wouldn't rest easy until he was out of range of Lake County, beyond the reach of the grove owners whose invisible laws he had broken.

The train rumbled past the forest of citrus trees that he had climbed since he was a boy and that he had tried to wrestle some dignity out of and, for a time, had. They could have their trees. He wasn't going to lose his life over them. He had come close enough as it was.

He had lived up to his family's accidental surname. Starling. Distant cousin to the mockingbird. He had spoken up about what he had seen in the world he was born into, like the starling that sang Mozart's own music back to him or the starling out of Shakespeare that tormented the king by speaking the name of Mortimer. Only, George was paying the price for tormenting the ruling class that owned the citrus groves. There was no place in the Jim Crow South for a colored starling like him.

He didn't know what he would do once he got to New York or what his life would be. He didn't know how long it would take before he could send for Inez. His wife was mad right now, but she'd get over it once he got her there. At least that's what he told himself. He turned his face to the North and sat with his back to Florida.

Leaving as he did, he figured he would never set foot in Eustis again for as long as he lived. And as he settled in for the twenty-three-hour train ride up the coast of the Atlantic, he had no desire to have anything to do with the town he grew up in, the state of Florida, or the South as a whole, for that matter.

3

MONROE, LOUISIANA, EASTER MONDAY, APRIL 6, 1953

ROBERT JOSEPH PERSHING FOSTER

IN THE DARK HOURS OF THE MORNING, Pershing Foster packed his surgery books, his medical bag, and his suit and sport coats in the trunk, along with a map, an address book, and Ivorye Covington's fried chicken left over from Saturday night.

He said good-bye to his father, who had told him to follow his dreams. His father's dreams had fallen apart, but there was still hope for the son, the father knew. He had a reluctant embrace with his older brother, Madison, who had tried in vain to get him to stay. Then Pershing pointed his 1949 Buick Roadmaster, a burgundy one with whitewall tires and a shark-tooth grille, in the direction of Five Points, the crossroads of town.

He drove down the narrow dirt roads with the ditches on either side that, when he was a boy, had left his freshly pressed Sunday suit caked with mud when it rained. He passed the shotgun houses perched on cinder blocks and hurtled over the railroad tracks away from where people who looked like him were consigned to live and into the section where the roads were not dirt ditches anymore but suddenly level and paved.

He headed in the direction of Desiard Street, the main thoroughfare, and, without a whiff of sentimentality, sped away from the small-town bank buildings and bail bondsmen, the Paramount Theater with its urine-scented steps, and away from St. Francis Hospital, which wouldn't let doctors who looked like him perform a simple tonsillectomy.

Perhaps he might have stayed had they let him practice surgery like he was trained to do or let him walk into the Palace and try on a suit like anyone else of his station. The resentments had grown heavy over the years. He knew he was as smart as anybody else—smarter, to his mind—but he wasn't allowed to do anything with it, the caste system being what it was. Now he was going about as far away as you could get from Monroe, Louisiana. The rope lines that had hemmed in his life seemed to loosen with each plodding mile on the odometer.

Like many of the men in the Great Migration and like many emigrant men in general, he was setting out alone. He would scout out the New World on his own and get situated before sending for anyone else. He drove west into the morning stillness and onto the Endom Bridge, a tight crossing with one lane acting like two that spans the Ouachita River into West Monroe. He would soon pass the mossback flatland of central Louisiana and the Red River toward Texas, where he was planning to see an old friend from medical school, a Dr. Anthony Beale, en route to California.

Pershing had no idea where he would end up in California or how he would make a go of it or when he would be able to wrest his wife and daughters from the in-laws who had tried to talk him out of going to California in the first place. He would contemplate these uncertainties in the unbroken days ahead.

From Louisiana, he followed the hyphens in the road that blurred together toward a faraway place, bridging unrelated things as hyphens do. Alone in the car, he had close to two thousand miles of curving road in front of him, farther than farmworker emigrants leaving Guatemala for Texas, not to mention Tijuana for California, where a wind from the south could blow a Mexican clothesline over the border.

In our homes, in our churches,
wherever two or three are gathered,
there is a discussion of what is best to do.
Must we remain in the South
or go elsewhere? Where can we go
to feel that security which other people feel?
Is it best to go in great numbers or only in several families?
These and many other things are discussed over and over.

—A COLORED WOMAN IN ALABAMA, 1902

THE GREAT MIGRATION, 1915–1970

THEY FLED as if under a spell or a high fever. "They left as though they were fleeing some curse," wrote the scholar Emmett J. Scott. "They were willing to make almost any sacrifice to obtain a railroad ticket, and they left with the intention of staying."

From the early years of the twentieth century to well past its middle age, nearly every black family in the American South, which meant nearly every black family in America, had a decision to make. There were sharecroppers losing at settlement. Typists wanting to work in an office. Yard boys scared that a single gesture near the planter's wife could leave them hanging from an oak tree. They were all stuck in a caste system as hard and unyielding as the red Georgia clay, and they each had a decision before them. In this, they were not unlike anyone who ever longed to cross the Atlantic or the Rio Grande.

It was during the First World War that a silent pilgrimage took its first steps within the borders of this country. The fever rose without warning or notice or much in the way of understanding by those outside its reach. It would not end until the 1970s and would set into motion changes in the North and South that no one, not even the people doing the leaving, could have imagined at the start of it or dreamed would take nearly a lifetime to play out.

Historians would come to call it the Great Migration. It would become perhaps the biggest underreported story of the twentieth century. It was vast. It was leaderless. It crept along so many thousands of currents over so long a stretch of time as to be difficult for the press truly to capture while it was under way.

Over the course of six decades, some six million black southerners left the land of their forefathers and fanned out across the country for an uncertain existence in nearly every other corner of America. The Great Migration would become a turning point in history. It would transform urban America and recast the social and political order of every city it touched. It would force the South to search its soul and finally to lay aside a feudal caste system. It grew out of the unmet promises made after the Civil War and, through the sheer weight of it, helped push the country toward the civil rights revolutions of the 1960s.

During this time, a good portion of all black Americans alive picked up and left the tobacco farms of Virginia, the rice plantations of South Carolina, cotton fields in east Texas and Mississippi, and the villages and backwoods of the remaining southern states—Alabama, Arkansas, Florida, Georgia, Kentucky, Louisiana, North Carolina, Tennessee, and, by some measures, Oklahoma. They set out for cities they had whispered of among themselves or had seen in a mail-order catalogue. Some came straight from the field with their King James Bibles and old twelve-string guitars. Still more were townspeople looking to be their fuller selves, tradesmen following their customers, pastors trailing their flocks.

They would cross into alien lands with fast, new ways of speaking and carrying oneself and with hard-to-figure rules and laws. The New World held out higher wages but staggering rents that the people had to calculate like a foreign currency. The places they went were big, frightening, and already crowded—New York, Detroit, Chicago, Los Angeles, Philadelphia, and smaller, equally foreign cities—Syracuse, Oakland, Milwaukee, Newark, Gary. Each turned into a "receiving station and port of refuge," wrote the poet Carl Sandburg, then a Chicago newspaper reporter documenting the unfolding migration there.

The people did not cross the turnstiles of customs at Ellis Island. They were already citizens. But where they came from, they were not treated as such. Their every step was controlled by the meticulous laws of Jim Crow, a nineteenth-century minstrel figure that would become shorthand for the violently enforced codes of the southern caste system. The Jim Crow regime persisted from the 1880s to the 1960s, some eighty years, the average life span of a fairly healthy man. It afflicted the lives of at least four generations and would not die without bloodshed, as the people who left the South foresaw.

Over time, this mass relocation would come to dwarf the California Gold Rush of the 1850s with its one hundred thousand participants and the Dust Bowl migration of some three hundred thousand people from Oklahoma and Arkansas to California in the 1930s. But more remarkably, it was the first mass act of independence by a people who were in bondage in this country for far longer than they have been free.

"The story of the Great Migration is among the most dramatic and compelling in all chapters of American history," the Mississippi historian Neil McMillen wrote toward the end of the twentieth century. "So far reaching are its effects even now that we scarcely understand its meaning."

Its imprint is everywhere in urban life. The configuration of the cities as we know them, the social geography of black and white neighborhoods, the spread of the housing projects as well as the rise of a well-scrubbed black middle class, along with the alternating waves of white flight and suburbanization—all of these grew, directly or indirectly, from the response of everyone touched by the Great Migration.

So, too, rose the language and music of urban America that sprang from the blues that came with the migrants and dominates our airwaves to this day. So, too, came the people who might not have existed, or become who they did, had there been no Great Migration. People as diverse as James Baldwin and Michelle Obama, Miles Davis and Toni Morrison, Spike Lee and Denzel Washington, and anonymous teachers, store clerks, steelworkers, and physicians, were all products of the Great Migration. They were all children whose life chances were altered because a parent or grandparent had made the hard decision to leave.

The Great Migration would not end until the 1970s, when the South began finally to change—the whites-only signs came down, the all-white schools opened up, and everyone could vote. By then nearly half of all black Americans—some forty-seven percent—would be living outside the South, compared to ten percent when the Migration began.

"Oftentimes, just to go away," wrote John Dollard, a Yale scholar studying the South in the 1930s, "is one of the most aggressive things that another person can do, and if the means of expressing discontent are limited, as in this case, it is one of the few ways in which pressure can be put."

By the time it was over, no northern or western city would be the same. In Chicago alone, the black population rocketed from 44,103 (just under three percent of the population) at the start of the Migration to more than one million at the end of it. By the turn of the twenty-first century, blacks made up a third of the city's residents, with more blacks living in Chicago than in the entire state of Mississippi.

It was a "folk movement of incalculable moment," McMillen said.

And more than that, it was the first big step the nation's servant class ever took without asking.

The passenger train came wheezing through the north Georgia mountains after the colored school let out, and when it passed through the hill town of Rome, Georgia, back during the Depression, a little girl would run down the embankment and wait for it to rush past the locust trees. She would wave to the people in the metal boxes on wheels, the important people, their faces looking away, and dream of going wherever it was they were rushing to.

Years later, she got on a train herself, heading north. The railcar was filled with the expectant faces of people hoping for all the rights and privileges of citizenship. She stepped off at Union Station in the border city of Washington, D.C. It was the start of the North, filled as it was with grand squares and circles named after northern heroes of the Civil War—Ulysses S. Grant, William Tecumseh Sherman, George Henry Thomas, David G. Farragut—names, to this day, reviled in the South. She made her way to the address she had been given and settled onto the fold-out sofa in the front room of a second cousin she barely knew. Soon afterward, she performed a ritual of arrival that just about every migrant did almost without thinking: she got her picture taken in the New World. It would prove that she had arrived. It was the migrant's version of a passport.

The picture is sepia, two by three inches, from the forties. Two young women sit on the front steps of a row house on R Street in Washington, looking very Bette Davis. Stacked heels and padded shoulders, wool coats brushing their knees. They are new in town. Childhood friends from Georgia meeting up now in the big city. Their faces give no hint of whatever indignities the South had visited upon them. That was over now. Their faces are all smiles and optimism. The one in the pearls used to greet the train when she was little and dream of going with it. She would become a teacher and, years later, my mother.

As a girl, I found the picture in a drawer in the living room, where many of those artifacts of migration likely ended up. I stared into the faces, searched the light in their eyes, the width of their smiles for clues as to how they got there.

Why did they go? What were they looking for? How did they get the courage to leave all they ever knew for a place they had never seen, the will to be more than the South said they had a right to be? Was it a braver thing to stay, or was it a braver thing to go? What would have happened if she had not gone north and met and married the Tuskegee Airman from Virginia, a migrant himself, who would become my father? Would I (and millions of other people born in the North and West) have even existed? What would have happened had all those people raised under Jim Crow not spilled out of the South looking for something better? If they had not gone north, what would New York look like? What would Philadelphia, Detroit, Pittsburgh, Chicago, Los Angeles, Washington, and Oakland look like? What, for that matter, would the South look like? Would it have changed on its own? Or did the black exodus force the South to face itself in ways no one could ever have thought possible?

"What would have happened if I'd stayed?" my mother asked out loud, repeating a question put to her one day. "I don't even want to think about that."

She never used the term "Great Migration" or any grand label for what she did nor did she see her decision as having any meaning beyond herself. Yet she and millions of others like her were right in the middle of it. At one point, ten thousand were arriving every month in Chicago alone. It made for a spectacle at the railroad platforms, both north and south.

"I went to the station to see a friend who was leaving," Emmett J. Scott, an official at Tuskegee Institute in Alabama, wrote shortly after the Migration began. "I could not get in the station. There were so many people turning like bees in a hive."

Those millions of people, and what they did, would seep into nearly every realm of American culture, into the words of Ralph Ellison and Toni Morrison, the plays of Lorraine Hansberry and August Wilson, the poetry and music of Langston Hughes and B. B. King, and the latter-day generation of Arrested Development and Tupac Shakur. It all but consumed the work of Richard Wright, the bard of the Great Migration. He gave voice to the fears and yearnings of his fellow migrants through his novel *Native Son* and his autobiography, *Black Boy.* He had been a sharecropper's son in Natchez, Mississippi. He defected to the receiving station of Chicago, via Memphis, in December 1927, to feel, as he put it, "the warmth of other suns."

Yet for all of its influence, the Migration was so vast that, throughout history, it has most often been consigned to the landscape, rarely the foreground. Scholars have devoted their attention to the earliest phase of the Migration, the World War I era. "Less has been written about the more massive sequence of migration that began during World War II," the historian James N. Gregory wrote in 2005, "and a comprehensive treatment of the century-long story of black migration does not exist."

This book addresses that omission. The stories in this book are based on the accounts of people who gave hundreds of hours of their days to share with me what was perhaps the singular turning point in their lives. They were among more than twelve hundred people I interviewed for this book in New York, Chicago, Los Angeles, Milwaukee, and Oakland. All of them journeyed from the South during the Great Migration, and it is their collective stories that inform every aspect of this book.

For the three main characters—Ida Mae Brandon Gladney, George Swanson Starling, and Robert Joseph Pershing Foster—and for others like them, the circumstances of their migrations shaped who they were and defined the course of their fortunes or misfortunes and the lives of their descendants. The events were thus easily recounted when the participants were called upon to do so. Official records corroborated those details that were indeed verifiable. But it is the larger emotional truths, the patient retelling of people's interior lives and motivations, that are the singular gift of the accounts in this book. With the passing of the earliest and succeeding generations of migrants, it is these stories that have become the least replaceable sources of any understanding of this great movement of people out of the South to the American North and West.

This book covers a span of some one hundred years. As the narrative moves through time, the language changes to retain the authenticity of each era. The word "colored" is used during the portion of the book in which that term was a primary identifier for black people, that is, during the first two-thirds of the twentieth century, as evidenced by the colored high schools the people attended and the signage that directed them to segregated facilities. As the narrative moves into the 1960s, it shifts to the use of the term "black," after it gained popularity during the civil rights era, and then to both "black" and "African American" in the current era.

Over time, the story of the Great Migration has suffered distortions that have miscast an entire population. From the moment the emigrants set foot in the North and West, they were blamed for the troubles of the cities they fled to. They were said to have brought family dysfunction with them, to more likely be out-of-work, unwed parents, and on welfare, than the people already there.

In the past twenty years, however, an altogether different picture has emerged from ongoing research by scholars of the Great Migration. Closer analysis of newly available census records has found that, contrary to conventional thought, black migrants were actually more likely to be married and to raise their children in two-parent households, and less likely to bear children out of wedlock. "Compared with northern-born blacks," writes the sociologist Stewart E. Tolnay, a leading expert on the Migration, "southern migrants had higher rates of participation in the labor force, lower levels of unemployment, higher incomes, lower levels of poverty and welfare dependency." The lives of the people in this book bear out this more complex understanding of the Great Migration and, based on the new data, represent the more common migrant experience than many previous accounts.

Despite the overlapping of time and place in the text, the three main people in this narrative never met or knew one another. Their paths never crossed except through their experiences with me and metaphorically through the interlocking chapters of this book. The narrative portrays the phenomenon through people unknown to one another, in the way that migrants moving along different currents would not have intersected, their anonymity a metaphor for the vast and isolating nature of the Migration itself.

The actions of the people in this book were both universal and distinctly American. Their migration was a response to an economic and social structure not of their making. They did what humans have done for centuries when life became untenable—what the pilgrims did under the tyranny of British rule, what the Scotch-Irish did in Oklahoma when the land turned to dust, what the Irish did when there was nothing to eat, what the European Jews did during the spread of Nazism, what the landless in Russia, Italy, China, and elsewhere did when something better across the ocean called to them. What binds these stories together was the back-against-the-wall, reluctant yet hopeful search for something better, any place but where they were. They did what human beings looking for freedom, throughout history, have often done.

They left.

PART TWO

BEGINNINGS

This was the culture
from which I sprang.
This was the terror
from which I fled.
—RICHARD WRIGHT,
Black Boy

Ida Mae Brandon Gladney

CHICAGO, 1996

FROM THE OPEN DOOR IN THE VESTIBULE, I see her. She is sitting in a cotton housedress on a baby blue, plastic-covered easy chair by the window. She is looking through a parting of the curtains at the street circus below. There they are, all scuffling beneath her: urban drug dealers, falling-down sweatpants pooling at their feet, now bent over the driver's-side window of a late-model sedan from the suburbs; fourth-graders doing lookout for men who could be their fathers; young girls with their stomachs swelling already; middle-aged men living out of their Pontiacs; gangsters who might not make it to the weekend.

She lives on the second floor of a three-flat on the South Side of Chicago. She taps her foot and moves closer to the sill. This is not what she had come to Chicago for, nor was it what she expected it to be. But here she is, and this is what it has become, a place so dangerously absurd that it is living entertainment in her old age. She knows the street names and the code words for all the hustlers and pushers playing out their lives beneath her window, and even though they may have just shot a rival or just got out on parole, they look out for her and greet her kindly—*you watch yourself now, Grandma*—because there is something sweet and kind about her, and she is from the Old Country and has survived a life of fear and privation they will never know.

She has an endearing gap in her teeth, which go just about any which way they please, and her hair is now as soft and white as the cotton she used to pick not particularly well back in Mississippi. She is the color of sand on a beach, which she had heard of growing up but had never seen for herself until she arrived in Chicago half a lifetime ago. She has big searching eyes that see the good in people despite the evil she has seen, and she has a comforting kind of eternal beauty, her skin like the folds of a velvet shawl.

Her name is Ida Mae, and she is a long way from where she started back in the hard soil of the eastern foothills of Mississippi during the century's adolescence. She leans forward and adjusts herself for a long conversation. Her hazel eyes grow big as she begins to tell her story.

VAN VLEET, MISSISSIPPI, 1928
IDA MAE BRANDON GLADNEY

IT BEGAN, LIKE MANY STORIES DO, with a man.

Actually, two men. They both came calling in the quiet hours of the hot season, when the cotton lay gestating in the field. Ida Mae had just sprouted into a woman of fifteen, and the suitors were out front clutching their hats to their chests.

They descended from opposite corners of old Chickasaw County, down the dirt roads that became mud rivers in the wet season and dust clouds in the dry but were the only route to the bottomland by the Natchez Trace and an audience with Ida Mae, who was amused by it all.

David McIntosh came after church on a tall red horse, the sun slanting heat through the hackberry trees, and he was always the first one there. He sat stiff in his Sunday clothes and sugar-talked the daughter in an old chair in the front room while her mother, Miss Theenie, stood peeping by the door. When he had said all he had to say, which was never soon enough for Miss Theenie, he climbed back on his horse and, as the daughter suspected, rode off to another girl he was weighing, named Sallie.

George Gladney walked three or four miles past the salt licks of Long Creek and over the railroad tracks to see Ida Mae. It took him longer than it took David McIntosh, and by the time he got there, his shirt was wet with perspiration and brown from the dust clouds stirred up on the road. Sometimes David's horse was still tied out front. George was a quiet, austere man and felt a certain proprietorship toward Ida Mae. He waited for David to finish before going in himself. He stood outside and watched David mount his horse and gallop away before walking up the plank steps of the porch. Coming in second would give him more time to win the girl over and assess her fitness as a wife.

Miss Theenie was not particular about either one of them. To begin with, they were too old for Ida Mae, trotting up the porch in their twenties when Ida Mae hadn't long turned fifteen. David was barely as tall as Ida Mae, and both of them were too dark by Miss Theenie's reckoning. She had little assurance of her daughters' upward mobility in a world where most colored women were sharecroppers' wives, but she could hope for the more favorable economic prospects of a lighter man, based on his acceptability to white people and even kinship to them, maybe, which would be all the better.

Ida Mae didn't go for that kind of talk and didn't pay it much attention. One color of wildflower was no better than another to her, so she made no distinctions whatsoever. She had a way of looking past the outer layer of people and seemed to regard everyone she met with a kind of searching intensity, as if this were the first person she had ever seen.

In any case, Miss Theenie's protests were likely just an excuse. Whatever his attributes, Miss Theenie was not inclined to like any man that came courting her second girl. Miss Theenie gave birth to her in a little wood house on Cousin Irie's land and named her Mae Ida after her husband's mother, Ida.

It was March 5, 1913, some three years after the start of the Great Migration that Ida Mae would unwittingly become a part of. There was a spark inside of her, and, when she got big enough, she told people to call her Ida Mae instead of Mae Ida. She would later say it sounded less old-timey to her, but it was an early indication that she could think for herself when she chose to.

She was a small-framed girl with a chiseled face the color of nut butter and her dark brown hair in plaits most of the time. It turned out she was fearless and spirited and liked doing the kinds of things men are known for doing. She was no good in the field, but she could chop wood and kill snakes and didn't mind doing it, and that was a good thing for Miss Theenie.

By the time men started showing up on the porch for Ida Mae, Miss Theenie was a widow, left to tend the land they lived on all by herself. She stood eye to eye with most men and suffered no fools, but she had little help now. Her oldest daughter, Irene, had gone off and gotten married. Her two grown sons, Sam and Cleve, had fled north to Ohio like more and more colored boys chafing in the South seemed to be doing. Her husband, Joseph, had just about run them off before he died. Joseph would beat them for any little thing, since they weren't his blood like the girls were. And that didn't make them want to stay either. So they went up north. That left Miss Theenie with her youngest daughters—Josephine, who was able to work but wouldn't, and Talma, who was too young to work—and her second, the tomboy, Ida Mae.

On her way home from school, Ida Mae climbed up the hickory and walnut trees on the side of the road and shook them down. She picked the skittle bumps off the ground and cracked them on her teeth. She saw how her brothers relieved themselves in the woods at the side of a tree and tried it herself. Being a girl, it didn't work as well when she tried it standing up.

Sam and Cleve, before they left, had to shoo her away when they went out hunting rabbit. She crouched behind the trees, and they heard her rustling near them and threw tap sticks at her, the sticks they took to kill the rabbits with. Sometimes she spotted a rabbit sleeping and popped it with a tap stick, and, along with whatever her brothers took in, they would eat well that night.

Sometimes her brothers didn't want to be bothered. So they gave her a quarter and let her plow in their place so they could go to a pickup baseball game. She'd get behind the mule and go up and down the field cutting lines in the earth as if it were the most important job in the world. The kids started calling her Tom because she acted more like a boy.

They lived on the curving land in the hill country of northeast Mississippi. It was a voluptuous place, more beautiful than the Delta land along the Great River, and like anything beautiful, had a tendency to break grown people's hearts. It was not meant to work as hard as it was made to when it came to sowing cotton, and, of the two regions, it had the more difficult birthing pains.

Joseph Brandon had come into ownership of a piece of bottomland, where he planted cotton and grew hogs. The land that colored men managed to get was usually scratch land nobody wanted. Still, he courted the land every spring. He cut lines in the earth with an old till, a swayback mule, and a horse named Jim. He planted cottonseed in the topsoil and tried to conjure rain. When the land turned green, he chopped the unwanted leaves that got in the way of the buds trying to grow.

By late summer, if the rains had come but not rotted the seed, if the sun had burned long enough by day and the dew had descended by night, dry snow sprang from the earth at the tips of low scrub that came to bud with his prayers and sweat. The land would be salted with white confetti that spread out to the tree line. Then he had to bend down in the beating sun to pick the bolls and crouch and crawl to reach the lowest buds.

Before she was big enough to see over the cotton, Ida Mae followed her father out to the field. He gave her a flour sack to keep her occupied, and she tagged behind him and gathered cotton bolls even though what little she brought in was not of much use. It turned out she had no talent whatsoever for the field and didn't like the chore of picking. But her father was always out there, and picking gave her time with him.

"That's how come I know about the field," she would say half a life later. "Wherever he went, I went."

When he wasn't nursing the cotton, he was tending the hogs. Sometimes the hogs ran off and got stuck in the creek water swollen up after the gully washers that poured from the sky in the spring. Ida Mae followed her father down to the creek and watched him slosh in the water to save his drowning hogs. The rains brought moccasin snakes to the surface and left them alive on the creek bank when the water fell back. Ida Mae took sticks to pick them up with and played with them like toys.

The rains beat down on Mississippi in May of 1923. The hogs went down to the creek and got stuck like they always did, but when her father slogged in after them, he had trouble bringing them in for all the floodwater that had risen up. He got sick from exposure and never recovered. He was forty-three years old.

He was diabetic, and the grown people said he was dead. But Ida Mae sat at the side of his bed and touched him, and he was warm. No doctor ever tended to him. There were no colored doctors around. The white ones were all in town, and the family would have had to meet them halfway, if they were going to see them at all, because the doctors in town didn't know the backwoods. Even if they had been inclined to come, the roads were too muddy from the rains to get through.

Ida Mae thought the grown people should give him more time; maybe he would come out of the spell he was in. Years later, she learned that educated people had a name for what her father appeared to be in. They called it a coma. But in that world and in that time, nobody could know for sure and nobody would pay a little girl any attention, and so they set the date for the burial.

She and her sisters Irene and Josie and Talma didn't have any shoes and went trailing behind their mother in their bare feet to the funeral. Nobody felt sorry for them because most other people didn't have shoes either.

When they closed the casket, Ida Mae thought for sure that her father was alive in there. "I still say today he wasn't dead," she would say three-quarters of a century later. "At that time, they didn't have a way to know."

Not long after the funeral, Ida Mae was sitting on the bin where they stored the hay and corn, in an enclosure they called a crib. She looked up and saw what looked to be her father walk in. It was both startling and natural. He reached his hand out to her and took her hand in his and held it. When she realized what was happening, she ran out screaming and went to get Miss Theenie.

"Daddy's in the crib!" she cried. "I saw him!"

"Girl, get away from me with that lying," Miss Theenie said. "Joseph wouldn't scare you."

"I held his hand, just as plain as day," Ida Mae said.

She never saw him again. As the summer wore on, it sank in that he wasn't coming back, and she started resenting the world and the people who had fathers. She started fighting and picking fights with people for no reason.

School was out because colored children only went to school when they were not needed in the field. Ida Mae and other colored children in rural Mississippi didn't start school until the cotton was picked, which meant October or November, and they stopped going to school when it was time to plant in April. Six months of school was a good year.

She was still grieving when it was time to go back the next fall. She walked a mile of dirt road past the drying cotton and the hackberry trees to get to the one-room schoolhouse that, one way or the other, had to suffice for every colored child from first to eighth grade, the highest you could go back then if you were colored in Chickasaw County.

The children formed a walking train to get there. It started with the child farthest away and picked up more children as it moved in the direction of the schoolhouse until just about the whole school was in a cluster at the front door.

Ida Mae was easily distracted by the nut trees along the way and had a hard time keeping up. "I be lagging behind hollering and crying, 'cause they run off and leave me," she said.

When the rains came and the water got too high for the children to pass through the hog wallows in places like where Ida Mae lived, the old people cut down a tree and trimmed the limbs so the children could cross over the log to get to school.

The school was a narrow frame cabin with wood benches and long windows, run by a teacher who was missing a leg. Amos Kirks was a source of unending curiosity and whispers among the children. He was of an age where he might have lost his leg in World War I, but none of the children knew for sure. He walked into the schoolroom, hobbling on crutches, in a suit and with a stern face. He rotated the grades as if the room were a railroad switch yard, calling the second- and third-graders to the front when it was their turn, while the other children moved to the back to do their lessons.

He towered above them and always wore a tie. But all the children could see was the left pant leg pinned up at the knee and air where a calf and foot should have been.

One day Mr. Kirks came in, and his pant leg wasn't pinned at the knee. He had a new leg. But he couldn't walk on it like a real one. "He throwed the leg, like it was tiresome to him," Ida Mae said. "And it would swing. He kind of swing it around."

It was the talk of the schoolyard.

"He finally got him a leg!" the children whispered to each other.

When Mr. Kirks wasn't looking, Ida Mae tried to tug at his pant cuff. "I sat side of him," Ida Mae said years later. "I try to do all I know how to get up under there and see how that leg look. I'd sat by him, and I just rub and do. He couldn't feel it no way. And I could see the clear foot in the shoe."

Ida Mae had to make sure Mr. Kirks didn't catch on. For the slightest infraction, Mr. Kirks would send some boys out to the woods to get branches off a tree. Then the child who was talking out of turn or drawing when he should be listening was called up front for lashings with the switch.

Ida Mae knew how that felt. In the fall after her father died, they were in the middle of a spelling lesson. One of the words was a city in the North called Philadelphia. Mr. Kirks called on Ida Mae to spell it. Some words, the children turned into jingles to help them remember. For geography, it was *George Eat O Gray Rat At Poor House Yesterday.* For Mississippi, it was *M eye crooked-letter crooked-letter eye crooked-letter crooked-letter eye humpback humpback eye.*

Ida Mae had heard about the North but didn't know Philadelphia or any ditties for it. She stumbled over the word. Mr. Kirks thought she was acting up. He told some boys to go out to the woods and get him a switch. He held the branches over the fire and told Ida Mae to come up front. He told her to bend over. He drew his arm back, and, in front of all the other children, he whipped her. And each time the switch snapped her back, he shouted a letter: P-H-I-L-A-D-E-L-P-H-I-A.

She was hurt to be singled out that day. She wasn't saying she hadn't done a devilish thing in her life. She was just thinking to herself all she had done was miss the word, and the whipping wasn't called for. After school, she went up to Mr. Kirks and told him so.

"If I had a daddy, you wouldn'ta whoop me," Ida Mae told him. "You whoop me 'cause I don't have a daddy."

He never whipped her again.

She seemed to be more aware of how life was harder now. Things she wouldn't have paid attention to before, she seemed to be noticing.

On her way to and from school, she passed the farm of a man named Mr. Bafford. His wife had left him to raise their son by himself, and he seemed to take out his grief on those around him. He had a yard full of trees that bore more fruit than he could ever consume or pick fast enough to sell. The peaches and apples and pears were some of the biggest and sweetest in the bottoms. They ripened and fell to the ground, and still he dared anyone to come onto his land to get any.

Ida Mae figured out a way to get some. She stopped by and talked with Mr. Bafford and made sure to keep him talking. And if he ever looked away, she reached down and slipped a pear or an apple into her dress. "You know they fall off, he coulda give us some of 'em," she said. "Every time I got a chance, I got me some."

It was approaching Christmas, the first Christmas since her father had died. One day when Ida Mae stopped to see Mr. Bafford, she started wondering aloud whether Santa Claus was going to come this year, what with her daddy gone and all.

"That's the first thing they teach y'all, a lie," Mr. Bafford said. "Ain't no such thing as Santa Claus."

It crushed Ida Mae to hear him say that. She was ten, and, even in the gaunt world she lived in, she still believed in Santa Claus. She started crying when Mr. Bafford said it.

"That taken all the joy out of life then," she said.

There would be no Christmas that year. "I'm not able to pay Santa Claus to come to us," Miss Theenie told the girls. Ida Mae began to resent everybody now. She was getting into more scrapes coming and going to school and getting ornery without cause.

A boy named Henry Lee Babbitt used to ride his horse to school every day and brought corn to feed him with. Ida Mae lived farther than Henry Lee did and had to walk. Something got into Ida Mae one day, and she told Henry Lee she was going to set his horse loose. She went up to the horse and reached for the bridle bit that tied the horse to the hitching post.

"Tom, you bet not turn my horse aloose," Henry Lee said.

"What if I do?" Ida Mae shot back.

"You do, I beat your brains out."

The two of them stood there next to the horse, Ida Mae holding the bridle bit and threatening to pull it off and Henry Lee trying to keep her from doing it.

"I dee-double-dog-dare you to pull that bridle," Henry Lee said. "You take that there, and you take a nickel off a dead man's eye."

She yanked the bridle off the horse and dropped it to the ground. "And down the road we went, me and the boy there, fighting," she said years later.

Henry Lee reached down and grabbed the bridle bit from where she left it and raised it up against her. "He took it and nearly beat me to death," she said. "I got a knot in back of my head now where he hit me with that bridle bit."

Without her half brothers and her father around, she was on her own. "You had to fight," she would later say. "Them boys would mess with you. You couldn't whoop 'em. But you did what you could."

Within a few years, the boys would not want to fight with her anymore. They wanted to sit and hold her hand and talk. The spark that made her fight them drew the quiet ones to her when it came time for courting. She was fifteen when two in particular started showing up at the front porch with those intentions.

On a Sunday after service in the summer of 1928, the church mothers at New Hope Baptist set out the hot platters of corn bread and collards and salted hams. Whoever made the collards worried if they were tender enough. Whoever baked the pound cake prayed that people would favor her cake over somebody else's potato pie.

It was the time of the year they called the lay-by, when the people left the cotton alone and waited for it to sprout. The people had turned the benches up and spread the food on the tables outside the little frame church. They called the event Children's Day, in the spirit of Men's Day and Women's Day other times of the year. An event like this was all there was on colored people's off day in the backwoods of Chickasaw County. People came in from Buena Vista, or Bewnie as they called it, and from over near Houston, the county seat, and even Okolona, arriving in their wagons and surreys.

These were the times when sharecroppers and servants could recede into a world of their own making, where Jim Crow didn't bother to enter. They could forget that there was such a thing as colored or white and just be. Sundays like this turned the churchyard into courting grounds for marriageable girls and young men looking for wives or diversions.

George Gladney showed up with a bunch of other young men from across the creek in somebody's old Model T Ford. He was twenty-two, stern-faced, and serious even then. "He wasn't no smiling man," Ida Mae said.

He was from around Bewnie, which was seven or eight miles south of Van Vleet. He was among the last of twelve to fifteen children. (No one alive knows for sure how many there were; his father had children by several wives, who died young or at least before he did.) George's mother died before he acquired much to remember her by. He was raised by an older brother, Willie, and the weight of his circumstances seemed to show in his face.

It was getting to the time when he should settle down. So he walked up to Ida Mae that afternoon. She was eating on the grass in her Sunday dress. He introduced himself, but she didn't pay him much attention. Her mind was on someone else, and she was mad at the moment. A boy by the name of Alfonso Banks had shown up at church that day with another girl.

Alfonso was the love of her short life. He was friends with her brothers, older and sure of himself in a way that drew the girls to him. No one had really taken her anywhere her whole life, and she felt grown up and free when he did. Excitement seemed to follow him even when he had nothing to do with it. One time he took her to a church revival, which was the country equivalent of a night on the town. It was Alfonso and Ida Mae and Ida Mae's big sister, Irene, and another young man who was escorting Irene that night. They drove up to the church and got out of the car, all of them young and giddy. They attracted the attention of a man named Bay-Bay, who had designs on Ida Mae's sister. He saw them and got enraged.

"Who is this out here laughing?" he said to them.

They ignored him. They started up the steps, and as they walked toward the church door, Bay-Bay pulled out a gun and shot at them six times, aiming at Irene or her escort or both. He was a bad shot and didn't hit anybody. But it was exciting and the talk of the woods and further proof to Ida Mae that Alfonso Banks sure knew how to show a girl a good time, even though he had nothing to do with it.

She had been out with Alfonso enough to feel a kind of ownership that was implied if not outright said. When she saw Alfonso come to Children's Day with another girl, she went up and spoke her mind.

"What'd you bring her here for?" Ida Mae said.

"I brought her for Children's Day."

"Unh-huh."

Something rose up in her. She took the umbrella in her hand and knocked it across his head. "Boy, I loved that boy," she said years later. "And he come bringing that girl over there. And I hit him all cross the head. My mother hit me with a poker when I got home. Everybody was talking about it. You know how folks talk. Said I was wrong. Had no business hitting him cross the head on church grounds."

When George showed up that day, she was distracted and didn't give this new face much thought. But he seemed to have made up his mind about her and started coming by her house on Sunday afternoons, giving her time to see the light.

He endured the stone face of Miss Theenie's disapproval and the teasing curiosity of Josie and Talma to spend time with Ida Mae. When he felt he was on firm enough ground to do so, he began making noises about the other young men: David McIntosh, Alfonso Banks, and another one, Freddie McClendon. He didn't like them coming around, and it showed on his face.

The other men must have noticed an intensity of purpose in George that they could not have fully understood, and they avoided running into him. It got to the point where, during his final visits, David McIntosh, sensing the hour growing late, would say, "Well, I guess I better go 'fore Gladney get here."

George's steadfastness won her over, and she finally agreed to marry him and be free of life under her mother. But she and George had to keep it to themselves. Miss Theenie wouldn't allow it if she knew. She never liked any of the boys courting Ida Mae, and she didn't like George.

"He's old enough for your daddy," Miss Theenie used to say of George, who was by now twenty-three to Ida Mae's sixteen.

In the middle of October 1929, George made arrangements for them to run off and get married. He found a preacher and a place near Bewnie outside her mother's circle. He went into Houston and bought a yellow dress with a blouson waist low on the hip, as was the style back in the twenties, for Ida Mae to wear.

The morning of October 14, 1929, Ida Mae fed the chickens and did her chores like any other day and kept a lookout for George to come and take her to a new life. But before he could get there, a neighbor man pulled up to their cabin and went in to see her mother.

"I heard your daughter gettin' married in Bewnie tonight," the man said.

Miss Theenie started cursing and went looking for Ida Mae. Ida Mae knew she would pay for plotting under her mother's nose. She ran and hid under the bed and wondered how she would get out when George came for her. Now that Miss Theenie knew George was on his way, Miss Theenie would be ready for him.

Josie and Talma and Miss Theenie looked out in the crib and out by the cows and called out to her in the little wood house and couldn't find her. The search for Ida Mae must have touched something in Miss Theenie. Something must have told her it was time for Ida Mae to leave her. She got through cursing, and Ida Mae felt safe to come out.

Miss Theenie went up to her second daughter and told Ida Mae her decision about the wedding.

"Well, I give you tomorrow," Miss Theenie said, "providing all us can go with you."

The next day, October 15, 1929, they all went to the minister's house.

Ida Mae put on the yellow dress with the blouson waist that George had chosen for her. The yard was filled with people as they stood on the porch steps and George Gladney and Ida Mae Brandon were declared man and wife.

"We wish you much joy," the people in the yard said.

George took her to the Edd Pearson plantation, a few miles away, where he would sharecrop cotton and she would learn to be a wife. Two weeks later, something called the stock market crashed, and things would get harder than they ever knew they could. Because, if the planters suffered, so much more would the sharecroppers under them.

An invisible hand ruled their lives and the lives of all the colored people in Chickasaw County and the rest of Mississippi and the entire South for that matter. It wasn't one thing; it was everything. The hand had determined that white people were in charge and colored people were under them and had to obey them like a child in those days had to obey a parent, except there was no love between the two parties as there is between a parent and child. Instead there was mostly fear and dependence—and hatred of that dependence—on both sides.

The particulars of all this eluded Ida Mae. White people were everywhere around her, but they were separate from her, in a separate schoolhouse, on separate land on the other side of a firewall that kept white and colored from occupying the same sidewalk. Colored people had to step off the curb when they passed a white person in town, and if the minutest privilege could be imagined, the ruling class claimed it. Ida Mae lived only a few towns away from Calhoun City, Mississippi, where there were white parking spaces (the ones closest to the bank in the town square) and colored parking spaces (on the other side of the street) well into the 1950s. There were no signs for them; it was just the work of the invisible hand.

Neither Miss Theenie nor George ever took Ida Mae into Houston or Okolona, where white people transacted their business affairs, and, growing up, Ida Mae had few direct dealings with white people. When she did, it was in the service of them and their whims whether she wished it or not, and, in the short time she was in their presence, it seems they made sure to remind her what her place was in their eyes even when she was too young to understand it.

She was about six or seven years old when one day her father told her to take a small section of plow to get sharpened at the blacksmith. That way, he wouldn't have to quit working to go himself. She rode the horse down the dirt path through the hackberry trees to the blacksmith's house.

The blacksmith was a kind and middle-aged white man with two grown sons. The blacksmith pulled the plow sweeps off the horse and went into the back to sharpen them. As Ida Mae stood waiting, the blacksmith's two sons came up to her. They were in their twenties and, with their father occupied, were looking to have some fun.

"We gon' put her in the well," they said to each other and laughed.

Each man took an arm, and as she screamed for them to let her go, they dragged her to a well with a wall around it and dangled her over the mouth of it. Ida Mae could see down the black hole of the well, her legs hanging over the rim. She fought and kicked and screamed at the men to let her go. She looked around and saw nobody there to help her. The men's father was still working on the plow bits.

The men watched her squirm and laughed at the sight of her squirming. They held her over the well until the fun wore off. Then they put her down, and she ran to where the blacksmith was and waited for him to come out with the freshly sharpened sweeps.

Her father used to send her there all the time. After that, he never sent her anymore. When it came down to it, there was nothing he could do to keep it from happening again. Decades later, she would think about how they could have dropped her, even by accident, and how she would have died and nobody would have known where she was or how she'd gotten there.

"They wouldn't have never told," she said.

Ida Mae soon discovered that, when it came to white people, there were good ones and bad ones like anything else and that she had to watch them close to figure out the difference. She was too good-natured to waste energy disliking them no matter what they did but looked upon them as a curiosity she might never comprehend. She learned to give them the benefit of the doubt but not be surprised at anything involving them. This alone probably added decades to her life.

A white lady named Miss Julie McClenna lived across the pasture, and she was nice to Ida Mae. After Ida Mae's father died, Miss McClenna paid Ida Mae to gather up eggs in the henhouse. Sometimes she took her into town to help her carry eggs to sell. She gave Ida Mae live chickens and leftover food, knowing that Ida Mae's mother had just been left a widow.

After school, Ida Mae walked a mile to the big house across the pasture to gather eggs for Miss McClenna in the evenings. She always hoped for a lot of eggs. If there were too many for Miss McClenna to carry herself, she would take Ida Mae into Okolona with her. It was the only chance Ida Mae got to go into town.

Ida Mae gathered more than usual one time, and Miss McClenna took her into Okolona to help her sell them to the white people in town. They delivered the eggs to customers' houses, straight to their doors, and Miss McClenna had Ida Mae carry the basket of eggs for her.

The day had gone well until they knocked on one woman's door to make a delivery. Ida Mae stood with the basket behind Miss McClenna as Miss McClenna prepared to step inside.

"You can't bring that nigger in," the woman said from her front door as soon as she saw Ida Mae.

Miss McClenna knew what that meant. She motioned for Ida Mae to go to the back door to deliver the eggs while Miss McClenna stepped inside to complete the transaction.

On the way back home, Miss McClenna seemed unsettled by it.

"Did you hear what she called you?" Miss McClenna asked Ida Mae.

"Yeah, but I ain't pay it no attention," Ida Mae said. "They call you so many names. I never pay it no attention."

The incident jarred Miss McClenna. The "hardware of reality rattled her," as the artist Carrie Mae Weems would say decades later of such interactions.

What few people seemed to realize or perhaps dared admit was that the thick walls of the caste system kept everyone in prison. The rules that defined a group's supremacy were so tightly wound as to put pressure on everyone trying to stay within the narrow confines of acceptability. It meant being a certain kind of Protestant, holding a particular occupation, having a respectable level of wealth or the appearance of it, and drawing the patronizingly appropriate lines between oneself and those of lower rank of either race in that world.

An attorney's wife in Alabama, for instance, was put on notice one day at a gathering at her home for the upper-class women in her circle. Between the hors d'oeuvres and conversation, one of the clubwomen noticed, for the first time apparently, a statuette of the Virgin Mary on a cabinet in the hostess's living room. The guest cattily remarked upon it. *Why, she never knew that the hostess and her family were Catholics!*

The attorney's wife was shaken by the accusation, and quickly replied that *of course not, they were Methodists and she thought everyone knew that. She only had the statuette because she happened to like it.*

But after the party was over and the guests were gone, the accusation haunted her, and she fretted over the implication that she might be seen as a member of a lesser tribe. That day, the attorney's wife took down the statuette of Mary that she liked so much and put it away for good. She could not afford even the appearance of having stepped outside the bounds of her caste.

Neither could Miss Julie McClenna. As far as Ida Mae knew, Miss McClenna never sold eggs to that lady again. But that was also the end of her brief employment with Miss Julie McClenna and the end of the trips into Okolona. "She never did take me no more after that," Ida Mae said.

In the bottoms where Ida Mae grew up, it was a crazy enough world that they could almost time the weekends by a white farmer who lived down the road.

He was fine when he was sober and actually liked colored people. But he got drunk on Fridays and came staggering on his old horse to the colored people's cabins. They could hear the hoof steps and hollering as he rode in waving his gun.

"I'm coming through!" he shouted.

Grown people dropped their buckets and went running. Children hid under the cabins on the dirt floor between the stilts, while he huffed and cussed and tried to smoke them out.

"I'm a shoot y'all!" he hollered. "I'm a kill y'all!"

There was always a commotion and a panic whenever he came through. It could happen day or night. There was never much warning, and they had to scramble to escape his ragged gunshots. Then they had to lie perfectly still. "We'd run under the house, and, wherever he hear a bump, he would shoot," Ida Mae said.

One day when he came through, Ida Mae was outside and couldn't get under the house in time. Josie and Talma had scattered already, and she didn't see where they had gone. The man had wobbled off his horse and was coming through, firing his gun.

A barrel of cornmeal was right next to her, and she saw it and jumped inside. She sank into the grit cushion of meal with her chin digging into her knees. All the while, the man hollered and grunted around her, and the bullets made the pinging noises of metal against tin. She pulled the top over her head and tried not to breathe. She stayed in the barrel until the shooting and the cussing stopped.

He was drunk and a bad aim and never actually hit anybody as far as Ida Mae knew. No sheriff or police were ever called in. There would have been no point in calling. And so the drunk farmer could go on shooting and scaring the Brandons and other colored people in the bottoms whenever he felt like it.

"He call hisself having fun," Ida Mae said.

As she grew older, she learned that there was more to the southern caste system than verbal slights and the antics of a crazy white farmer. In the summer of 1926, when she was thirteen, a cloud passed over the grown people, and it showed in their faces. She could overhear them whispering about something that had happened in town, some terrible thing they didn't want the children to know about. It had to do with two colored boys—the Carter brothers, as she heard it—and a white woman.

"They said something to the white lady," she said.

And, as best as Ida Mae could make out, the white people had taken the boys and hanged them in Okolona that morning. Ida Mae would always remember it because that was the day her cousin was born and they named the baby Thenia after Ida Mae's mother. The grown people wept in their cabins.

After the funeral, the surviving Carters packed up and left Mississippi. They went to a place called Milwaukee and never came back.

In three years' time, Ida Mae and George would move to the Pearson plantation, and things would unfold in such a way that Ida Mae would eventually follow the Carters up north. Although she didn't see how it might apply to herself at the time, the Carter migration was a signal to Ida Mae that there was, in fact, a window out of the asylum.

The Stirrings of Discontent

Everybody seems to be asleep
about what is going on right under our noses.
That is, everybody but those farmers
who have wakened up on mornings recently
to find every Negro over 21 on his place gone—
to Cleveland, to Pittsburgh,
to Chicago, to Indianapolis. . . .
And while our very solvency
is being sucked out beneath us,
we go about our affairs as usual.

—EDITORIAL, *The Macon Telegraph,*
SEPTEMBER 1916

SELMA, ALABAMA, EARLY WINTER 1916

NO ONE KNOWS WHO was the first to leave. It was sometime in the middle of World War I. The North faced a labor shortage and, after centuries of indifference, cast its gaze at last on the servant class of the South. The North needed workers, and the workers needed an escape. No one knows exactly when or how it commenced or who took the first actual step of what would become the Great Migration.

One of the earliest references came on February 5, 1916, and was seen as an isolated, random event. It merited only a paragraph in the *Chicago Defender,* the agitator and unwitting chronicler of the movement, and was likely preceded by unremarked-upon departures months before. Railroads in Pennsylvania had begun undercover scouting of cheap black labor as early as 1915. But few people noticed when, in the deep of winter, with a war raging in Europe and talk of America joining in, several hundred black families began quietly departing Selma, Alabama, in February 1916, declaring, according to the *Chicago Defender*'s brief citation, that the "treatment doesn't warrant staying."

Ida Mae Brandon was not yet three years old. George Starling, Pershing Foster, and millions of others who would follow in the footsteps of those first wartime families from Selma had not yet been born. But those early departures would set the stage for their eventual migration.

The families from Selma left in the midst of one of the most divisive eras in American history—the long and violent hangover after the Civil War, when the South, left to its own devices as the North looked away, dismantled the freedoms granted former slaves after the war.

The plantation owners had trouble imagining the innate desires of the people they once had owned. "I find a worse state of things with the Negroes than I expected," wrote General Howell Cobb, a Georgia planter, shortly after the slaves were freed. "Let any man offer them some little thing of no real value, but which looks a little more like freedom, and they catch at it with avidity, and would sacrifice their best friends without hesitation and without regret."

"They will almost starve and go naked," wrote a planter in Warren County, Georgia, "before they will work for a white man, if they can get a patch of ground to live on and get from under his control."

For all its upheaval, the Civil War had left most blacks in the South no better off economically than they had been before. Sharecropping, slavery's replacement, kept them in debt and still bound to whatever plantation they worked. But one thing had changed. The federal government had taken over the affairs of the South, during a period known as Reconstruction, and the newly freed men were able to exercise rights previously denied them. They could vote, marry, or go to school if there were one nearby, and the more ambitious among them could enroll in black colleges set up by northern philanthropists, open businesses, and run for office under the protection of northern troops. In short order, some managed to become physicians, legislators, undertakers, insurance men. They assumed that the question of black citizens' rights had been settled for good and that all that confronted them was merely building on these new opportunities.

But, by the mid-1870s, when the North withdrew its oversight in the face of southern hostility, whites in the South began to resurrect the caste system founded under slavery. Nursing the wounds of defeat and seeking a scapegoat, much like Germany in the years leading up to Nazism, they began to undo the opportunities accorded freed slaves during Reconstruction and to refine the language of white supremacy. They would create a caste system based not on pedigree and title, as in Europe, but solely on race, and which, by law, disallowed any movement of the lowest caste into the mainstream.

The fight over this new caste system made it to the U.S. Supreme Court. Homer A. Plessy, a colored Louisianan, protested a new state law forbidding any railroad passenger from entering "a compartment to which by race he does not belong." On June 7, 1894, Plessy bought a first-class ticket on the East Louisiana Railroad, took an empty seat in the white-only car, and was arrested when he refused to move. In 1896, in the seminal case of *Plessy v. Ferguson,* the Supreme Court sided with the South and ruled, in an eight-to-one vote, that "equal but separate" accommodations were constitutional. That ruling would stand for the next sixty years.

Now, with a new century approaching, blacks in the South, accustomed to the liberties established after the war, were hurled back in time, as if the preceding three decades, limited though they may have been, had never happened. One by one, each license or freedom accorded them was stripped away. The world got smaller, narrower, more confined with each new court ruling and ordinance.

Not unlike European Jews who watched the world close in on them slowly, perhaps barely perceptibly, at the start of Nazism, colored people in the South would first react in denial and disbelief to the rising hysteria, then, helpless to stop it, attempt a belated resistance, not knowing and not able to imagine how far the supremacists would go. The outcomes for both groups were widely divergent, one suffering unspeakable loss and genocide, the other enduring nearly a century of apartheid, pogroms, and mob executions. But the hatreds and fears that fed both assaults were not dissimilar and relied on arousing the passions of the indifferent to mount so complete an attack.

The South began acting in outright defiance of the Fourteenth Amendment of 1868, which granted the right to due process and equal protection to anyone born in the United States, and it ignored the Fifteenth Amendment of 1880, which guaranteed all men the right to vote.

Politicians began riding these anti-black sentiments all the way to governors' mansions throughout the South and to seats in the U.S. Senate.

"If it is necessary, every Negro in the state will be lynched," James K. Vardaman, the white supremacy candidate in the 1903 Mississippi governor's race, declared. He saw no reason for blacks to go to school. "The only effect of Negro education," he said, "is to spoil a good field hand and make an insolent cook."

Mississippi voted Vardaman into the governor's office and later sent him to the U.S. Senate.

All the while, newspapers were giving black violence top billing, the most breathless outrage reserved for any rumor of black male indiscretion toward a white woman, all but guaranteeing a lynching. Sheriff's deputies mysteriously found themselves unable to prevent the abduction of a black suspect from a jailhouse cell. Newspapers alerted readers to the time and place of an upcoming lynching. In spectacles that often went on for hours, black men and women were routinely tortured and mutilated, then hanged or burned alive, all before festive crowds of as many as several thousand white citizens, children in tow, hoisted on their fathers' shoulders to get a better view.

Fifteen thousand men, women, and children gathered to watch eighteen-year-old Jesse Washington as he was burned alive in Waco, Texas, in May 1916. The crowd chanted, "Burn, burn, burn!" as Washington was lowered into the flames. One father holding his son on his shoulders wanted to make sure his toddler saw it.

"My son can't learn too young," the father said.

Across the South, someone was hanged or burned alive every four days from 1889 to 1929, according to the 1933 book *The Tragedy of Lynching,* for such alleged crimes as "stealing hogs, horse-stealing, poisoning mules, jumping labor contract, suspected of killing cattle, boastful remarks" or "trying to act like a white person." Sixty-six were killed after being accused of "insult to a white person." One was killed for stealing seventy-five cents.

Like the cotton growing in the field, violence had become so much a part of the landscape that "perhaps most of the southern black population had witnessed a lynching in their own communities or knew people who had," wrote the historian Herbert Shapiro. "All blacks lived with the reality that no black individual was completely safe from lynching."

In this atmosphere, *The Clansman,* a 1905 novel that was the basis of the 1915 film *Birth of a Nation,* became a national bestseller. It fed whites' panic over freed blacks in their midst and inspired people in Georgia to revive the Ku Klux Klan the year the film was released. Soon Klansmen in full regalia were holding public parades before cheering white crowds across the South like celebrations of the Fourth of July, the Klan then seen not as a rogue outlier but as the protector of southern tradition. Thus the fragile interdependence between the races turned to apprehension and suspicion, one race vowing to accept no less than the total subjugation of the other.

The planter class, which had entrusted its wives and daughters to male slaves when the masters went off to fight the Civil War, was now in near hysterics over the slightest interaction between white women and black men. It did not seem to matter that the danger to white women of rape by a black man, according to the white South Carolina–born author Wilbur Cash, "was much less, for instance, than the chance that she would be struck by lightning."

White citizens, caught up in the delirium in the decades following Reconstruction, rioted in Georgia, North and South Carolina, Tennessee, Florida, Texas, Arkansas, and central Illinois. They killed colored residents and set fire to their homes on rumors of black impropriety, as authorities stood by or participated.

In the darkest hours of this era, the abolitionist Frederick Douglass saw his health fade just as everything he spent his life fighting for was falling apart. He said, in his last great public lecture, delivered in Baltimore in January 1894, a year before his death, "I hope and trust all will come out right in the end, but the immediate future looks dark and troubled. I cannot shut my eyes to the ugly facts before me."

It was during that time, around the turn of the twentieth century, that southern state legislatures began devising with inventiveness and precision laws that would regulate every aspect of black people's lives, solidify the southern caste system, and prohibit even the most casual and incidental contact between the races.

They would come to be called Jim Crow laws. It is unknown precisely who Jim Crow was or if someone by that name actually existed. There are several stories as to the term's origins. It came into public use in the 1830s after Thomas Dartmouth Rice, a New York–born itinerant white actor, popularized a song-and-dance routine called "the Jim Crow" in minstrel shows across the country. He wore blackface and ragged clothes and performed a jouncy, palsied imitation of a handicapped black stable hand he had likely seen in his travels singing a song about "Jumping Jim Crow." Jim Crow was said to be the name of either the stable hand or his owner living in Kentucky or Ohio. Rice became a national sensation impersonating a crippled black man, but died penniless in 1860 of a paralytic condition that limited his speech and movement by the end of his life.

The term caught the fancy of whites across the country and came to be used as a pejorative for colored people and things related to colored people, and, by 1841, was applied to the laws to segregate them. The first such laws were passed not in the South, but in Massachusetts, as a means of designating a railcar set apart for black passengers. Florida, Mississippi, and Texas enacted the first Jim Crow laws in the South right after the Confederates lost the Civil War—Florida and Mississippi in 1865 and Texas in 1866. The northerners who took over the South during Reconstruction repealed those hastily passed laws. The Federal Civil Rights Act of 1875 explicitly outlawed segregation. But the northerners who were there to enforce the law retreated by the late 1870s and left the South to its own devices. As the twentieth century approached, the South resurrected Jim Crow.

Streetcars, widely in use from the 1880s, had open seating in the South, until Georgia demanded separate seating by race in 1891. By 1905, every southern state, from Florida to Texas, outlawed blacks from sitting next to whites on public conveyances. The following year, Montgomery, Alabama, went a step further and required streetcars for whites and streetcars for blacks. By 1909, a new curfew required blacks to be off the streets by 10 P.M. in Mobile, Alabama. By 1915, black and white textile workers in South Carolina could not use the same "water bucket, pails, cups, dippers or glasses," work in the same room, or even go up or down a stairway at the same time.

This new reality forced colored parents to search for ways to explain the insanity of the caste system to their uncomprehending children. When two little girls in 1930s Florida wanted to know why they couldn't play on a swing like the white children or had to sit in a dirty waiting room instead of the clean one, their father, the theologian Howard Thurman, had to think about how best to make them understand. "The measure of a man's estimate of your strength," he finally told them, "is the kind of weapons he feels that he must use in order to hold you fast in a prescribed place."

All told, these statutes only served to worsen race relations, alienating one group from the other and removing the few informal interactions that might have helped both sides see the potential good and humanity in the other.

Now the masses of black workers cast about on their own in a buyer's labor market with little in the way of material assets or education or a personal connection to even the coldest slave master, who would have shown a basic watchfulness if only to protect his financial investment. Their lives were left to the devices of planters with no vested interest in them and, now, no intimate ties to ease the harshness of their circumstances or to protect them, if only out of paternalism, from the whims of night riders, a hell-bent jury, or poor whites taking out their resentment at their unwitting competitors for work.

David L. Cohn, in the 1935 book *God Shakes Creation,* wrote that, for a colored man without a white sponsor, "his fate is in the lap of the gods."

Each year, people who had been able to vote or ride the train where they chose found that something they could do freely yesterday, they were prohibited from doing today. They were losing ground and sinking lower in status with each passing day, and, well into the new century, the color codes would only grow to encompass more activities of daily life as quickly as legislators could devise them.

Thus, those silent parties leaving Selma in the winter of 1916 saw no option but to go. Theirs would become the first volley of a leaderless revolution. There was no Moses or Joshua or Harriet Tubman, or, for that matter, Malcolm X or Martin Luther King, Jr., to organize the Migration. The best-known leader at the start of it, Booker T. Washington, was vehemently against abandonment of the South and strongly discouraged it. Frederick Douglass, who saw it coming but died before it began, was against the very thought of it and considered an exodus from the South "a premature, disheartening surrender."

Those entreaties had little effect.

"The Negroes just quietly move away without taking their recognized leaders into their confidence any more than they do the white people about them," a Labor Department study reported. A colored minister might meet with his deacons on a Wednesday, thinking all was well, and by Sunday find all the church elders gone north. "They write the minister that they forgot to tell him they were going away."

Ordinary people listened to their hearts instead of their leaders. At a clandestine meeting after a near lynching in Mississippi, a colored leader stood before the people and urged them to stay where they were.

A man in the audience rose up to speak.

"You tell us that the South is the best place for us," the man said. *"What guaranties can you give us that our life and liberty will be safe if we stay?"*

The leader was speechless.

"When he asked me that, there was nothing I could answer," the leader said afterward. "So I have not again urged my race to remain."

Any leader who dared argue against leaving might arouse suspicion that he was a tool of the white people running things. Any such leader was, therefore, likely to be ignored, or worse. One Sunday, a colored minister in Tampa, Florida, advised from the pulpit that his flock stay in the South. He was "stabbed the next day for doing so."

In the years leading up to and immediately following the turn of the twentieth century, a generation came into the world unlike any other in the South. It was made up of young people with no personal recollection of slavery—they were two generations removed from it. The colored members of this generation were free but not free, chafing under Jim Crow and resisting the studied subservience of their slave parents and grandparents. They had grown up without the contrived intimacy that once bound the two races. And it appeared that young whites, weaned on a formal kind of supremacy, had grown more hostile to blacks than even their slaveholding ancestors had been.

"The sentiment is altogether different now," William C. Oates, the old-guard former governor of Alabama, said in 1901 of the newer generation of white southerners. "When the Negro is doing no harm, why, the people want to kill him and wipe him from the face of the earth."

The colored people of this generation began looking for a way out. "It is too much to expect that Negroes will indefinitely endure their severe limitations in the South when they can escape most of them in a ride of 36 hours," the Labor Department warned. "Fifty years after the Civil War, they should not be expected to be content with the same conditions which existed at the close of the war."

Younger blacks could see the contradictions in their world—that, sixty, seventy, eighty years after Abraham Lincoln signed the Emancipation Proclamation, they still had to step off the sidewalk when a white person approached, were banished to jobs nobody else wanted no matter their skill or ambition, couldn't vote, but could be hanged on suspicion of the pettiest infraction.

These were the facts of their lives:

There were days when whites could go to the amusement park and a day when blacks could go, if they were permitted at all. There were white elevators and colored elevators (meaning the freight elevators in back); white train platforms and colored train platforms. There were white ambulances and colored ambulances to ferry the sick, and white hearses and colored hearses for those who didn't survive whatever was wrong with them.

There were white waiting rooms and colored waiting rooms in any conceivable place where a person might have to wait for something, from the bus depot to the doctor's office. A total of four restrooms had to be constructed and maintained at significant expense in any public establishment that bothered to provide any for colored people: one for white men, one for white women, one for colored men, and one for colored women. In 1958, a new bus station went up in Jacksonville, Florida, with two of everything, including two segregated cocktail lounges, "lest the races brush elbows over a martini," *The Wall Street Journal* reported. The president of Southeastern Greyhound told the *Journal,* "It frequently costs fifty percent more to build a terminal with segregated facilities." But most southern businessmen didn't dare complain about the extra cost. "That question is dynamite," the president of a southern theater chain told the *Journal.* "Don't even say what state I'm in."

There was a colored window at the post office in Pensacola, Florida, and there were white and colored telephone booths in Oklahoma. White and colored went to separate windows to get their license plates in Indianola, Mississippi, and to separate tellers to make their deposits at the First National Bank of Atlanta. There were taxicabs for colored people and taxicabs for white people in Jacksonville, Birmingham, Atlanta, and the entire state of Mississippi. Colored people had to be off the streets and out of the city limits by 8 P.M. in Palm Beach and Miami Beach.

Throughout the South, the conventional rules of the road did not apply when a colored motorist was behind the wheel. If he reached an intersection first, he had to let the white motorist go ahead of him. He could not pass a white motorist on the road no matter how slowly the white motorist was going and had to take extreme caution to avoid an accident because he would likely be blamed no matter who was at fault. In everyday interactions, a black person could not contradict a white person or speak unless spoken to first. A black person could not be the first to offer to shake a white person's hand. A handshake could occur only if a white person so gestured, leaving many people having never shaken hands with a person of the other race. The consequences for the slightest misstep were swift and brutal. Two whites beat a black tenant farmer in Louise, Mississippi, in 1948, wrote the historian James C. Cobb, because the man "asked for a receipt after paying his water bill."

It was against the law for a colored person and a white person to play checkers together in Birmingham. White and colored gamblers had to place their bets at separate windows and sit in separate aisles at racetracks in Arkansas. At saloons in Atlanta, the bars were segregated: Whites drank on stools at one end of the bar and blacks on stools at the other end, until the city outlawed even that, resulting in white-only and colored-only saloons. There were white parking spaces and colored parking spaces in the town square in Calhoun City, Mississippi. In one North Carolina courthouse, there was a white Bible and a black Bible to swear to tell the truth on.

These were the facts of their lives—of Ida Mae's, George's, and Pershing's existence before they left—carried out with soul-killing efficiency until Jim Crow expired under the weight of the South's own sectarian violence: bombings, hosing of children, and the killing of dissidents seeking basic human rights. Jim Crow would not get a proper burial until the enactment of federal legislation, the Civil Rights Act of 1964, which was nonetheless resisted years after its passage as vigorously as Reconstruction had been and would not fully take hold in many parts of the South until well into the 1970s.

And so what started as a little-noticed march of the impatient would become a flood of the discontented during World War II, and by the tail end of the Migration, a virtual rite of passage for young southerners—brothers joining brothers, nieces joining aunts, as soon as they got big enough to go.

Many of the people who left the South never exactly sat their children down to tell them these things, tell them what happened and why they left and how they and all this blood kin came to be in this northern city or western suburb or why they speak like melted butter and their children speak like footsteps on pavement, prim and proper or clipped and fast, like the New World itself. Some spoke of specific and certain evils. Some lived in tight-lipped and cheerful denial. Others simply had no desire to relive what they had already left.

The facts of their lives unfurled over the generations like an overwrapped present, a secret told in syllables. Sometimes the migrants dropped puzzle pieces from the past while folding the laundry or stirring the corn bread, and the children would listen between cereal commercials and not truly understand until they grew up and had children and troubles of their own. And the ones who had half-listened would scold and kick themselves that they had not paid better attention when they had the chance.

And in this way, the ways of the South passed from one generation to the next in faraway cities by the Pacific Ocean and on the shores of the Great Lakes and along the Hudson and Potomac and Allegheny rivers. These are the stories of the forgotten, aggrieved, wishful generations between the Harlem Renaissance and the civil rights movement, whose private ambition for something better made a way for those who followed. Of the three whose lives unfold in these pages, Ida Mae Brandon Gladney left first, in the 1930s, George Swanson Starling in the 1940s, and Robert Joseph Pershing Foster in the 1950s, in a current that swept up millions of others like them.

George Swanson Starling

NEW YORK CITY, 1996

HIS WORLD IS THE BASEMENT of a brownstone on 132nd Street west of Lenox Avenue, a shaft of light streaking through the burglar bars on a single window. Outside, there is Harlem—Tupac on boom boxes, street preachers on soap crates. Crack addicts scrounging for change. There are middle-aged volunteers planting beds of impatiens in a footprint of earth in the concrete, German tourists pressed against bus windows to see the Apollo Theater and the Abyssinian Baptist Church.

He has lived here so long that not much of this fazes him anymore. He is a widower now. He walks lean and upright, and he towers over you as he leads you to the one room he keeps for himself out of the whole brownstone he owns. It is the product of all the hustling and saving he had to do when he arrived here a country boy from the South. His apartment is a cluttered storeroom, really, with a single bed, a couple of chairs, a dresser with a picture of his grandmother, Annie the root doctor, on it, and half-open boxes of his accumulated highs and regrets.

The knees that used to climb suckling tree limbs to pick grapefruit back in Florida and worked the train aisles up and down the East Coast all those years are giving way to arthritis now. He takes a seat by the bed and talks in a monotone without taking a breath, there is so very much to say. He has catalogued in his mind every character who ever passed his way, can mimic their toothless drawl with wicked precision, recall every good and bad thing he has ever done or that has ever been done to him, every laughable contrivance of Jim Crow, every grievance and kind turn, all the people who made a way out of no way in that world growing up.

George Swanson Starling came from the featureless way station of citrus groves and one-star motels between the Georgia border and Orlando, Florida, a place of cocksure southern sheriffs, overworked pickers, root doctors, pool hustlers, bootleggers, jackleg preachers, barely a soul you could trust, and a color line as hard as Mississippi's. It comes back to him, one image after another, how Jim Crow had a way of turning everyone against one another, not just white against black or landed against lowly, but poor against poorer and black against black for an extra scrap of privilege. George Starling left all he knew because he would have died if he had stayed.

His face is long and creaseless. He was handsome in his day, a basketball player in high school, good with numbers, a ladies' man. He holds out a crate of Florida oranges like the ones he used to pick and offers you one, says, even after all that picking and all that it cost him, they're better than the ones from California. A smile lifts his face at the absurdities of the world he left, and which, in some ridiculous way, he still loves. Then his eyes well up over all that they have seen.

EUSTIS, FLORIDA, 1931

BEHIND THE ST. JAMES A.M.E. Church over at Prescott and MacDonald was an old orange tree that turned out oranges with dimpled skin as green as saw grass on the outside but inside sweet as sugarcane by September. To look at it, no one would know the fruit was ripe unless they climbed up and tried one, which George Starling and some other boys did once they made the discovery.

The tree was taller than a telephone pole, and it was hard for the boys to pass it by knowing what they did about those oranges. They waited for nightfall, when church would start and the deacons would light the kerosene lamps by the pews.

The boys climbed the twenty-foot tree and picked the oranges by the sanctuary light as the church people sang about Jesus. They steadied themselves in the crook of a limb and stuffed their shirts and trouser pockets until the buttons gaped. Then they turned back home, peeling and slurping, a trail of orange hulls following them all the way down MacDonald Avenue.

The church people tried to wait for the fruit to turn orange. But George and the other boys picked the tree clean before the church people could get to it. And so it went, George Starling and others in his impatient generation outwitting the old folks they saw as too content in their spirituals and their place in that world.

Here they were in Eustis, Florida, in the interior Citrus Belt of the state, hemmed into the colored part of town called Egypt. It was the haphazard cluster of dirt yards and clapboard bungalows, juke joints and corner churches where the colored people lived and conducted their affairs. It was unofficially policed by a man named Henry McClendon, a steward at another church in town. He lived across the street from St. James and saw George and his friends Sam Gaskin and Ernest Sallet sneak around the side of the church as he sat on his front porch one night.

When the boys got up into the tree, he started probing the limbs with a flashlight.

"Come down outta that tree in the name of the law!" he said.

The boys froze and hoped he would go away.

"I'm gonna come and tell your daddies. Y'all 'round here stealing these oranges, and y'all 'bout the same ones been stealing the wood from on the back porch."

"Man, we don't eat no wood. We been getting these oranges from around here for years. Ain't nobody want no wood."

"Oh yeah, y'all 'bout stole the wood. I'm coming out there, and I'm a tell your daddy."

The boys scrambled out of the tree and got on their knees because the worst thing that could happen to a colored child in the South was for a parent to hear that a child was acting up. There would be no appeals, the punishment swift and physical. The arbitrary nature of grown people's wrath gave colored children practice for life in the caste system, which is why parents, forced to train their children in the ways of subservience, treated their children as the white people running things treated them. It was preparation for the lower-caste role children were expected to have mastered by puberty.

For a young colored boy in the South, "the caste barrier is an ever-present, solid fact," John Dollard, an anthropologist studying the region's caste system, wrote at the time. "His education is incomplete until he has learned to make some adjustment to it. . . . The Negro must haul down his social expectations and resign himself to a relative immobility."

Indeed, breaking from protocol could get people like George killed. Under Jim Crow, only white people could sit in judgment of a colored person on trial. White hearsay had more weight than a colored eyewitness. Colored people had to put on a show of cheerful subservience and unquestioning obedience in the presence of white people or face the consequences of being out of line. If children didn't learn their place, they could get on the wrong side of a white person, and the parents could do nothing to save them.

"The question of the child's future is a serious dilemma for Negro parents," wrote J. W. Johnson around the time George and his friends got caught picking those oranges. "Awaiting each colored boy and girl are cramping limitations . . . ; and this dilemma approaches suffering in proportion to the parents' knowledge of and the child's innocence of those conditions."

There was no time for childish ideals of fair play and equality. *Oh, you calling them grown folks a lie?* George remembered parents saying. *Them grown folks wouldn't a said it if they didn't see you doing it.*

So the boys pleaded with Mr. McClendon that night. "We make a promise. You don't tell our daddies. We won't come back here to get no more fruit. We won't bother the oranges no more."

George didn't actually believe this as he said it. He knew they were wrong, but he didn't like how the grown people wouldn't believe him no matter what he said, and he didn't see the punishment as fitting the crime. He was getting to be a teenager now. He was learning that you didn't have a right to stand up for yourself if you were in his position, and he wasn't liking it.

George Starling was a fairly new boy in town. He had spent most of his short life circling north-central Florida as his parents hunted for work.

He was born on a tobacco farm out by the scrub oaks and wire grass near Alachua, Florida, halfway between Jacksonville and the Gulf of Mexico, on June 1, 1918. Lil George and his father—called Big George to distinguish him from the son—his mother, Napolean, and his half brother, William, all lived with a cast of uncles, aunts, and cousins headed by a hard-bitten curmudgeon of a grandfather, a man named John Starling.

John Starling was a sharecropper who smoked a corncob pipe and had few good words for anybody. Once he kicked the cat into the fire when it tried to rub his leg. He was from the Carolinas, where the plantation owner he worked for used to come down to the field and flog the workers with a horsewhip if they weren't going fast enough, as a rider might snap a whip at his mule. One day, the owner came down with the horsewhip, and the sharecroppers killed him. They swam across the river and never went back. That's all the grandfather would say.

It was before the turn of the twentieth century, and instead of going north, where there would have been no place for a colored farmer like him, John Starling went south to the warm, rich land of the Florida interior. There, Big George and the rest of that generation were born, and the family acquired its surname. Originally, they were Stallings. But nobody could pronounce it right. When they first joined their little country church, the preacher welcomed the newcomers every Sunday with a different mispronunciation.

"And we're glad to have the Stallions here with us today," the preacher announced during service.

"Stallings! Stallings!" John protested.

He eventually settled on Starling, which was a close enough compromise to suit him and the people around them.

By the time little George was born, John was working for a planter by the name of Reshard. He was living a hard enough life as it was and had other grandchildren in his care for whom he had little patience. He liked to put cotton between their toes and light it to wake them up in the morning. But the grandfather and his second wife, Lena, took a liking to little George. He was the only child of John's firstborn (George's half brother, William, had a different father), and Lena used to grab him close.

"Come up here, boy, give your grandma some sugar."

He could see a bulge in her cheeks from the snuff in her mouth and snuff juice dripping down her chin. George tightened his face and twisted his head, but that didn't stop her from planting a snuff-scented wet one right on the lips.

They were farming tobacco and cotton, among other things, and the grandfather liked to take little George out to the field with him and out to the boiler when he went to fire up the tobacco. He would let George sleep on top of the boiler shed when he got tired. He'd have George right by him and seemed to make a show of it, which only made life tougher for little George, propped up as he was distinct from his cousins.

"My cousins would be out there with their fists shaking at me," he remembered.

There were aunts and uncles all around. One of the younger aunts, called Sing, was married to a short-tempered man named Sambo. Sing attracted the attention of men without trying, and Sambo could never get used to it. As it was, colored men had little say over their wives since the days when slave masters could take their women whenever they pleased and colored men could do nothing about it. Planters were known to take the same liberties the slave masters had, and the contradictions were not lost on colored men: white men could do to colored women what colored men could be burned alive for doing to white women. In this sexual testing of wills, Sambo was overcautious toward his wife. He told her if she kept it up with what he saw as flirting, he was going to kill her one day. She just laughed. He was always talking like that. Big George told his sister not to make light of her husband. But she didn't pay it any mind.

One day, Sambo went to John's house and told Big George he was going rabbit hunting and needed some shells. Big George went and got the shells for Sambo. A few minutes later, he heard a shot from the woods.

"I guess Sambo done got him a rabbit," Big George said.

Sambo had just killed Big George's little sister.

These became some of Lil George's earliest memories. Each year, he saw his grandfather return from the planter's house after another dispiriting settlement and recount to the family what had transpired.

At the end of every harvest, the planter would call John Starling up to the big house. John would knock on the back door, the only door colored people were permitted to enter, according to southern protocol. He and the planter met in the planter's kitchen.

"Come on in, John," the planter said. "Come here, boy. Come here. Have a seat. Sit down here."

The planter pulled out his books. "Well, John," the planter began. "Boy, we had a good year, John."

"Yes, sir, Mr. Reshard. I'm sure glad to hear that."

"We broke even. You don't owe me nothing. And I don't owe you nothing."

The grandfather had nothing to show for a year's hard toiling in the field.

"This is all he ends up, 'We broke even,' " George would say years later. "He has no money, no nothing for his family. And now he's ready to start a new year in the master's debt. He'll start all over again. Next year, they went through the same thing—'We broke even.' "

The following year, the grandfather went to the big house and got the same news from Reshard.

"Well, by God, John, we did it again. We had another good year. We broke even. I don't owe you nothin, and you don't owe me nothin."

George's grandfather got up from the table. "Mr. Reshard, I'm sho' glad to hear that. 'Cause now I can go and take that bale of cotton I hid behind the barn and take it into town and get some money to buy my kids some clothes and some shoes."

The planter jumped up. "Ah, hell, John. Now you see what, now I got to go all over these books again."

"And when he go over these books again," George said long afterward, "he'll find out where he owed that bale. He gonna take that bale of cotton away from him, too."

John had no choice but to tell Reshard about that extra bale of cotton. In the sharecropping system, it was the planter who took the crops to market or the cotton to the gin. The sharecropper had to take the planter's word that the planter was crediting the sharecropper with what he was due. By the time the planter subtracted the "furnish"—that is, the seed, the fertilizer, the clothes and food—from what the sharecropper had earned from his share of the harvest, there was usually nothing coming to the sharecropper at settlement. There would have been no way for George's grandfather to sell that one extra bale without the planter knowing it in that constricted world of theirs. In some parts of the South, a black tenant farmer could be whipped or killed for trying to sell crops on his own without the planter's permission.

Even though John wouldn't be able to keep the extra bale, Reshard was considered "a good share, a good boss, a good master," in George's words, " 'cause he let us break even."

Most other sharecroppers ended deeper in debt than before. "They could never leave as long as they owed the master," George said. "That made the planter as much master as any master during slavery, because the sharecropper was bound to him, belonged to him, almost like a slave."

The anthropologist Hortense Powdermaker, studying the sharecropping system back in the 1930s, estimated that only a quarter to a third of sharecroppers got an honest settlement, which did not in itself mean they got any money. "The Negro farm hand," a colored minister wrote in a letter to the *Montgomery Advertiser* in Alabama, "gets for his compensation hardly more than the mule he plows, that is, his board and shelter. Some mules fare better than Negroes."

There was nothing to keep a planter from cheating his sharecropper. "One reason for preferring Negro to white labor on plantations," Powdermaker, a white northerner, observed, "is the inability of the Negro to make or enforce demands for a just statement or any statement at all. He may hope for protection, justice, honesty from his landlord, but he cannot demand them. There is no force to back up a demand, neither the law, the vote nor public opinion. . . . Even the most fair and most just of the Whites are prone to accept the dishonest landlord as part of the system."

That did not keep some sharecroppers from trying to get what they were due after a hard year's labor. During the lull before harvest time, one of George's uncles, Budross, went to the little schoolhouse down in the field and learned to read and count. When it came time to settle up over the tobacco George's grandmother Lena had raised, the uncle stood by while the planter went over the books with her. When they got through, George's uncle spoke up.

"Ma, Mr. Reshard cheatin' you. He ain't addin' them figures right."

The planter jumped up. "Now you see there, Lena, I told you not to send that boy to school! Now he done learn how to count and now done jumped up and called my wife a lie, 'cause my wife figured up these books."

The planter's men came and pistol-whipped the uncle right then and there.

The family had to get him out that night. "To call a white woman a lie," George said, "they came looking for him that night. They came, fifteen or twenty of them on horseback, wagon."

George's grandparents knew to expect it. "We got to get you away from here 'cause you done call Mr. Reshard a lie. And you know they ain't gon' like that."

George was too young to understand what was happening but heard the grown people talk about it in whispers. It was the middle of the 1920s, and George never knew exactly where the uncle went. The particulars were never spoken.

"They hid him out" was all George would say. "He left from out of there."

Lil George and his parents didn't stay in Alachua much longer after that. They fled to St. Petersburg on the Gulf of Mexico, where they would no longer be under a field boss or overseer. They could work in the big high-rise hotels going up, and with all the tourists from up north and the building boom in the beach towns on the coast, they could be free of the farm and find plenty of work.

They were living in a row house off Fifth Avenue in the colored district. The father found work in construction, and things were good. But by the late 1920s, when the Great Depression descended on the country, things weren't so good. Big George took to drinking and would lie in wait on the porch for Lil George's mother to get back from church on Sunday. Once, instead of coming straight back, she stopped a few doors down to chat with a neighbor. Big George saw her dawdling, and that set him off.

"You making plans to meet some other man," Big George said.

He jumped on her and started hitting her. Lil George and his half brother, William, were sitting on the porch and could see it.

It wasn't the first time. Lil George cried over it. He was torn between the two of them. Sometimes William, who had a different father and was two years older than Lil George, would throw rocks at Big George to make him stop. Lil George hated it when William did that. He adored his parents. This time, Lil George got mad. The two boys went and got a brick from under a wash pot in the kitchen and hit Big George with it. Then they ran down the street to get away. Big George was hurt more by the pain he had caused his son than by the brick itself and went calling after his namesake. *Son, come back here. I'm not gonna bother you.*

The marriage gave out after that, and the family split up. The mother kept William on the Gulf Coast with her. And Big George headed east to the town of Eustis, where he said he would send for Lil George after he got established. For the time being, Lil George was sent to live with his mother's mother in Ocala, a town in the scrublands midway between Alachua and Eustis.

The grandmother was a root doctor named Annie Taylor who was a big-boned woman as tall as a man. She lived on a corner lot and grew pole beans alongside the fence. She was already raising one daughter's two boys, and here came another one from another daughter, Napolean, now that she had quit her husband.

Annie set George to work right away. She took him and his cousins out to the woods and showed them which twigs and roots to dig up: sassafras, sulfur, and goldenrod. They would tramp behind her through the scrub and wire grass back to the house—George and his cousins James and Joseph, whom they called Brother. She would stir the roots into foul-smelling potions that people bought to thin their blood, cut a fever, shush a hacking cough. She knew all the roots and could identify them, and she knew what they were good for.

The boys were her nearest patients, and every season brought a new torture. Sulfur and cream of tartar at the first sign of spring to thin the blood for the summer. Castor oil to clean your system out in the winter. Balls of asafetida hung around the neck to ward off flu and tuberculosis, the asafetida resin rolled up like flour dough and smelling only slightly worse than cow dung. She put the asafetida paste into little sacks and made necklaces for the boys to wear (which they took off and put in their pockets as soon as they got from around her). In between, she plied them with goldenrod for fever, asafetida with whiskey for a bad cold, and any number of bitter-tasting concoctions that made the boys hate to get sick.

If she detected a cold in the chest, she unscrewed the top of the kerosene lamp, tipped it over a spoonful of sugar, and let four or five drops of kerosene saturate the sugar. Then she stuck the spoon into their tight faces for them to swallow. There was no point in trying to run and hide. "You better not be talking about no run-and-hide," George said years later. "She didn't play that. 'Now you gonna get a whippin' on top of it.' "

The three little boys were left in Annie Taylor's care because there was a great churning among the young people of working age like her daughters. Her oldest girl, George's mother, was off on the Gulf Coast. And her two youngest girls, Annie (whom they called Baby) and Lavata (who actually was the baby but whom they called Date), were up in New York. Baby couldn't keep little James and Brother in New York with her, so she left them with her mother to raise, like a lot of migrants did when they went up north.

Young people like them weren't tied to a place like their slave grandparents had been forced to, and they weren't content to move from plantation to plantation like their parents. Ever since World War I had broken out and all those jobs had opened up in the North, there had been an agitation for something better, some fast, new kind of life where they could almost imagine themselves equal to the white people. And so they had gone off to wherever the money seemed to be raining down—to the Gulf Coast rising up in a construction boom or the orange groves at picking season or the turpentine camps if they couldn't manage anything else; or, if they had nerve in the early days of the Migration, they'd hop a train to the edge of the world, straight up the coast, past Georgia and both Carolinas and straight through Virginia and up to New York, where people said you could get rich just mopping floors.

To the old folks who stayed, the young people looked to be going in circles, chasing a wish. Some went crossways to someplace in Alabama or Georgia, where they heard things were better, only to find the South to be the South wherever they went. Some went north, high and mighty, and came back south, low and broke. Some people's pride wouldn't let them come back at all. So they shoehorned themselves into tenements and made like they were rich or just plain made do and dazzled the folks back home with all the money they wired back.

Some people back home came to depend on that money, to half expect it, and they got agitated when it didn't come. They figured the people who left were making all that money up north and just about owed it to them, especially if they left children behind. Baby and Date kept up fairly regular payments to their mother to cover Baby's two little boys. George's father sent money for George, too. At first. But after a while, it got to the place where he wouldn't send any money, and the grandmother had to stretch what her daughters sent for two into enough to take care of all three of them.

Sometimes George heard his grandmother fretting about how she was running out of money and hadn't heard from Big George. It was the Depression, and sometimes even the daughters got slow sending money for the two which had stretched to three, and the grandmother had a problem on her hands. The daughters had gotten themselves out in that big world way up north—who knew what kind of fix they were in?—and here she was left with the little ones.

When the money got low, Annie Taylor got in her rocking chair on the porch and rocked back and forth. She hummed and sang as she rocked. *Guide me o'er, thou Great Jehovah, pilgrim to this barren land. I am weak, but thou art mighty. Guide me with thy loving hand.*

George and James and Brother heard her humming.

"Grandma humming that song again," George told James. "Somethin' gonna happen soon."

The palm of her hand started to itch, or so she said. And before long, a Western Union man came rolling up the street, announcing a telegram for Miss Annie Taylor.

"Somebody would be done wired us some money," George would say years later. "Yes, sirree."

The waiting and hoping went on for two years, and then it was decided that it was best for George to be with his father, and he joined his father in Eustis.

Big George worked at the loading dock of a packinghouse and ran a one-room convenience store over on Bates Avenue. He sold baked goods and castor oil to the fruit pickers and day workers and the children on their lunch break from the colored high school across the street in a citrus farming town in the underdeveloped midsection of a still-isolated state.

Lake County and the rest of central Florida were far from the lights of Miami and the palm-tree version of paradise that tourists came for. This was the Florida that had entered the Union as a slave state, where a Florida slaveholder could report without apology, in 1839, that he worked his slaves "in a hurrying time till 11 or 12 o'clock at night, and have them up by four in the morning." Florida went farther than some other slave states in the creativity of its repression: Slaves could not gather together to pray. They couldn't leave their plantations, even for a walk, without written permission from their owner. If they were accused of wrongdoing, "their hands were burned with a heated iron, their ears nailed to posts," or their backs stripped raw with seventy-five lashes from a buckskin whip. The few free blacks in the state had to register with the nearest probate court or could be automatically enslaved by any white person who stepped forward to claim possession.

As the country neared the point of collapse over the issue of a state's right to slavery, Florida, in the early winter of 1861, became one of the first to secede from the Union in the months leading up to the Civil War. Florida broke away on January 10, 1861, three weeks after the first rebel state of South Carolina, and a day after Mississippi. Florida heartily joined a new country whose cornerstone, according to the Confederacy's vice president, Alexander Hamilton Stephens, was "the great truth that the negro is not equal to the white man; that slavery—subordination to the superior race—is his natural and normal condition." This new government, Stephens declared, "is the first, in the history of the world, based upon this great physical, philosophical, and moral truth."

Thus began the bloodiest war on American soil, after four years of which the Confederates fell in the spring of 1865. Immediately, Florida, Mississippi, and Texas took steps to begin imposing a formal caste system, becoming the first in the South to do so. They hastened to pass laws restricting the newly freed people barely before the cannons had cooled. Florida's 1865 law set forth, among other things, that "if any negro, mulatto or other person of color shall intrude himself into any railroad car or other public vehicle set apart for the exclusive accommodation of white people," he would be sentenced to "stand in pillory for one hour, or be whipped, not exceeding thirty-nine stripes, or both, at the discretion of the jury."

Florida was shut off from the rest of the world by its cypress woods and turpentine camps. It was another country, with its own laws and constitution. And all through the 1920s, when George was a toddler and then in grade school, the grown people hung their heads over the violence that descended over them and passed the stories among themselves and to the children when they got old enough to understand.

They talked about the white mob that burned down the colored section of Ocoee, over by Orlando, when a colored man tried to vote back in 1920, how the man was hanged from a tree and other colored people were burned to death and the remaining colored people packed up and never returned. They whispered about the time the white people burned and leveled Rosewood, a colored settlement by the Gulf of Mexico, halfway between St. Petersburg and Tallahassee, because a white woman said a colored man had attacked her. It was where, a survivor said, "anything that was black or looked black was killed." That was in 1923.

And then, in the fall of 1934, when George was a teenager and old enough to take note of such things, perhaps the single worst act of torture and execution in twentieth-century America occurred in the panhandle town of Marianna, Florida, a farm settlement halfway between Pensacola and Tallahassee.

That October, a twenty-three-year-old colored farmhand named Claude Neal was accused of the rape and murder of a twenty-year-old white woman named Lola Cannidy. Neal had grown up across the road from Lola Cannidy's family. He was arrested and signed a written confession that historians have since called into question. But at the time, passions ran so high that a band of more than three hundred men armed with guns, knives, torches, and dynamite went searching for Neal in every jail within a seventy-five-mile radius of Marianna.

The manhunt forced the authorities to move Neal across the panhandle, from Marianna to Panama City by car, to Camp Walton by boat, to Pensacola by car again, with the mob on their trail at every turn. Finally, the Escambia County sheriff, fearing that his jail in Pensacola was too dilapidated to withstand attack, decided to take Neal out of state altogether, to the tiny town of Brewton, Alabama, fifty-five miles north of Pensacola. Someone leaked Neal's whereabouts, and a lynching party of some one hundred men drove several hours on Highway 231 in a thirty-car caravan from Florida to Alabama. There the men managed to divert the local sheriff and overtake the deputy. They stormed the jail and took Neal, his limbs bound with a plow rope, back to Marianna.

It was the early morning hours of October 26, a Friday. Neal's chief abductors, a self-described "committee of six," an oddly officious term commonly used by the leaders of southern lynch mobs, set the lynching for 8 P.M., when most everyone would be off work. The advance notice allowed word to spread by radio, teletype, and afternoon papers to the western time zones.

Well before the appointed hour, several thousand people had gathered at the lynching site. The crowd grew so large and unruly—people having been given sufficient forewarning to come in from other states—that the committee of six, fearing a riot, took Neal to the woods by the Chipola River to wait out the crowds and torture him before the execution.

There his captors took knives and castrated him in the woods. Then they made him eat the severed body parts "and say he liked it," a witness said.

"One man threw up at the sight," wrote the historian James R. McGovern.

Around Neal's neck, they tied a rope and pulled it over a limb to the point of his choking before lowering him to take up the torture again.

"Every now and then somebody would cut off a finger or toe," the witness said. Then the men used hot irons to burn him all over his body in a ritual that went on for several hours.

"It is almost impossible to believe that a human being could stand such unspeakable torture for such a long period," wrote the white undercover investigator retained by the NAACP.

The crowd waiting in town never got to see Neal die. The committee of six decided finally to just kill him in the woods. His nude body was then tied to the back of a car and dragged to the Cannidy house, where men, women, and children stabbed the corpse with sticks and knives. The dead girl's father was angry that Neal was killed before he could get to him. "They done me wrong about the killing," the father said. "They promised me they would bring him up to my house before they killed him and let me have the first shot. That's what I wanted."

The committee hanged the body "from an oak tree on the courthouse lawn." People reportedly displayed Neal's fingers and toes as souvenirs. Postcards of his dismembered body went for fifty cents each. When the sheriff cut down the body the next morning, a mob of as many as two thousand people demanded that it be rehanged. When the sheriff refused to return it to the tree, the mob attacked the courthouse and rampaged through Marianna, attacking any colored person they ran into. Well-to-do whites hid their maids or sent cars to bring their workers to safety. "We needed these people," said a white man who sat on his porch protecting his interests with a loaded Winchester. Florida Governor David Sholtz had to call in the National Guard to quell the mob.

Across the country, thousands of outraged Americans wrote to President Franklin D. Roosevelt demanding a federal investigation. The NAACP compiled a sixteen-page report and more files on the Neal case than any other lynching in American history. But Neal had the additional misfortune of having been lynched just before the 1934 national midterm elections, which were being seen as a referendum on the New Deal itself. Roosevelt chose not to risk alienating the South with a Democratic majority in Congress at stake. He did not intervene in the case. No one was ever charged in Neal's death or spent a day in jail for it. The Jackson County grand jury, in the common language of such inquests, reported that the execution had occurred "at the hands of persons unknown to us."

Soon afterward, it was learned that Neal and the dead girl, who had known each other all their lives, had been lovers and that people in her family who discovered the liaison may have been involved in her death for the shame it had brought to the family. Indeed, the summer after Neal was lynched, the girl's father was convicted of assault with intent to kill his niece because he suspected that that side of the family had had a hand in his daughter's death.

In sentencing the father to five years in prison for attacking the relative, the judge said, "I hate to pass this sentence on an old man such as you, but I must do it. To be perfectly fair with you, I don't believe you have any too many brains."

The father replied, "Yes, judge. I am plumb crazy."

Thereafter, Florida continued to live up to its position as the southernmost state with among the most heinous acts of terrorism committed anywhere in the South. Violence had become such an accepted fact of life that, in 1950, the Florida governor's special investigator, Jefferson Elliott, observed that there had been so many mob executions in one county that it "never had a negro live long enough to go to trial."

The grown people's whispers of unspeakable things seeped into George's subconscious like a nursery rhyme, even though he was too young to know the particulars or understand the meaning of it all. Surrounded as he was by the arbitrary violence of the ruling caste, it would be nearly impossible for George or any other colored boy in that era to grow up without the fear of being lynched, the dread that, in the words of the historian James R. McGovern, "he might be accused of something and suddenly find himself in a circle of tormentors with no one to help him."

By the time Lil George was old enough to notice, it seemed as if the whole world was crazy, not because of any single event but because of the slow discovery of just how circumscribed his life was turning out to be. All this stepping off the sidewalk, not looking even in the direction of a white woman, the sirring and ma'aming and waiting until all the white people had been served before buying your ice cream cone, with violence and even death awaiting any misstep. Each generation had to learn the rules without understanding why, because there was no understanding why, and each one either accepted or rebelled in that moment of realization and paid a price whichever they chose.

No one sat George down and told him the rules. His father was quiet and kept his wounds to himself. George's teachers were fear and instinct. The caste system trained him to see absurdity as normal.

Like the time George went for an ice cream cone at the pharmacy in downtown Eustis. He wouldn't be able to sit at the counter, he knew that going in. Anytime a white customer walked up, he had to step back and wait for him or her to be served first. George had learned this, too, by now. The pharmacist had a dog, a little terrier. And when George walked up to the counter, three or four white men who were standing around looked at one another and then at the pharmacist. The owner called out to the dog. And the dog jumped up onto the counter.

When the pharmacist had everyone's attention, he turned to the dog.

"What would you rather do?" the pharmacist asked the dog. "Be a nigger or die?"

The dog rolled over on cue. It flipped onto its back, folded its legs, shut its eyes, and froze. The grown people at the counter and up front near George shook with laughter.

George was a teenager and outnumbered. He was the only one of his kind in this place. All he could do was stand there and take it. Any other response would require an explanation. *What's the matter with you, boy? You don't like it?* he could hear them saying.

All kinds of thoughts went through his mind. "A whole lot of things," he said. "How you'd like to kill all of 'em, for one thing."

On its face, it looked to be a black-and-white world, but George learned soon enough that the caste system was a complicated thing that had a way of bringing out the worst in just about all concerned. Sometimes it seemed that loyalty didn't stand a chance against suspicion and self-preservation. Even on the lowest rung, some people would squeeze what little they could even when nobody had anything.

Reverend J. W. Brinson was a jackleg preacher who ran the colored grocery store on MacDonald in Egypt town. The store had a slot machine that took customers' nickels and dimes but gave hardly any back. People went in and played the dime machine for an hour or two, and everybody could see that the machine was ready to deliver. That's when Reverend Brinson would step in and close up shop. "He figure that machine is getting hot and is gonna start paying off," George recalled. "And he run everybody out the store."

George and his friends walked out as told. Then they watched old man Brinson take the slot machine to his house next door. "We would tip up on the porch," George said, "and we could hear him in there in the bedroom and hear that slot machine just ringing. And he just be burning it up trying to get that jackpot for himself."

On top of that, the merchandise in the grocery store was unjustly high, to hear George tell it, and he and his friends resented it. They found a way to get back what they figured they had overpaid.

They noticed that Reverend Brinson went into town the same time every day, leaving the store in the care of his wife, Mary, who was a sweet woman but couldn't count. One day the boys sat under a big old oak tree and waited for Reverend Brinson to pull away. Then they went in and played nice to Miss Brinson.

"Hi, Miss Brinson."

"Hello, boys. How y'all?"

"We wanna get something, Miss Brinson."

"Yeah, alright. What y'all want?"

"We want ten cent worth of bologna."

The Brinsons had a scale in the back of the store where the icebox was, which required Miss Brinson to go back in the icebox, get the roll of bologna, and bring it to the butcher block near the counter. She carved enough slices until it looked about right, cutting less than she needed so as not to waste slices the customer didn't want. Then she went back to the scales to weigh the bologna as the boys watched.

"Oh, Miss Brinson, you ain't quite got ten cent worth up there yet. You got to get some more."

"Yeah, that's right," she said, admitting the discrepancy.

She hauled the loaf of bologna back to slice some more, leaving the slices she had already cut on the counter, two or three of which the boys slipped into their mouths. She came huffing back with the extra slices, only to learn it still wasn't enough.

"Oh, you ain't got it yet, Miss Brinson."

Back and forth she went, the loaf shrinking and the scale not budging, until the boys were full from the extra slices they'd eaten.

"Aw, that's alright, Miss Brinson. That's close enough. Just wrap it up."

Come summer, the Brinsons set watermelons out on the bare floor in front of the counter. George and the other boys saw them there and decided to go in one day. They lined up along the counter and started looking around. One pointed to a jar of pickles on the very top shelf.

"Miss Brinson, how much is that jar of pickles up there?"

"Well. Let me see now. Which one?"

Miss Brinson went to get the ladder and climbed up to check. And as she stretched herself to reach the last jar, one of the boys took his foot and started a watermelon rolling. He kicked it to the next boy, who kicked it to the next boy, until the melon had rolled and creaked down the wood plank floor toward the front screen. The last boy was positioned to kick it outside, none of them for a second taking his eyes off Miss Brinson, still reaching for the jar of pickles. They would get two or three watermelons that way.

Poor Reverend Brinson must have suspected that they stole from him, and he kept his prices high, which only encouraged more pilfering. It was George's and the other boys' way of getting justice in an unjust world. And so it went in Egypt town, the poor at odds with the broke.

George was a boy interested in the things boys are interested in and not particularly wanting to live the life the preachers set out at Gethsemane Baptist Church. Not then, anyway. There wasn't much to do around Eustis when school was out. Sure, they could fish and swim awhile in one of the lakes. But there weren't any jobs, and so they got into the things that boys get into, like picking green oranges while the church people sang about Jesus.

He was friends with a bootlegger's brother who lived behind the poolroom. Grown men roosted on the benches out front like crows on a fence, and there were big trees all around. The boys shot pool when the grown men let them and then made off with a pint of the bootlegger's moonshine. They poured water in place of the liquor and put the bottle back where they found it. They figured they weren't hurting anybody. The bootlegger was breaking the law anyway. They figured it was like taking something that wasn't supposed to exist in the first place.

George was growing taller and bigger and was in high school now. He grew to over six feet and started playing basketball at Curtright. He was walking taller and straighter. One day he went up to Ocala to see his grandmother the root doctor. He liked to surprise her, so he didn't let her know that he was coming. But she knew anyway. "You think you slipped up on me," she said once. "I knew you was coming 'cause my nose was itching. I just told somebody, 'Somebody's coming to see me.' "

She saw the change in him, how he was wearing grown folks' clothes, walking taller, straighter, suddenly aware of how he looked in a mirror. It always happened that the young people got to a certain age and thought they were the best thing that ever walked the earth. "I see George got you in long pants now," she said. "You must be smelling yourself."

It's true that George got into his share of devilment, but, fortunately for him, it turned out that he had a thing for numbers and words. He could remember just about anything that was set in front of him, and school came easy to him. He devoured books even though they were the white schools' leftovers and had pages missing. He started to think about how he could escape this place, maybe even go to college.

The kids noticed and looked to George to help them with their lesson. But they seemed to wish they didn't have to ask. They would turn around and tease him for doing what they should have been doing.

"So what you doing tonight, George?"

"Getting my lesson."

"Yeah, you go on and get your lesson, and we'll get the girls."

George couldn't abide the teasing and didn't believe they were doing all they said they were anyway. He would finish his homework and tip over to the house of whatever girl they said they were having their fun with. He would sweet-talk the girl, and since he was tall and not, as they say, hard on the eyes, he managed to do quite well, in his estimation.

The next day in school, the boasting would commence.

"They brag about how they were with this girl last night," George said years later. "I say to myself, 'I know you lying.' But I couldn't tell them. I used to walk the back roads. Nobody would see me."

George was always observing the developments around him, and here was a lesson in the underhanded nature of some human relations. "I know they would be telling lies on the girls," he said years later, " 'cause I be setting up there with that same girl in her house. That's how I found out how the boys lie on girls."

He didn't want them knowing his business. He indulged them instead.

"What'd you do last night, Lil George?"

"Man, I had so much work. I was getting my lesson."

By the time they got old enough to work, most of the kids had dropped out of school altogether. By graduation day, there were only six seniors in the Class of 1936 at Curtright Vocational Training School, and George Swanson Starling was valedictorian. He got accepted to Florida Agricultural and Mechanical State College in Tallahassee. His father did not really understand why he would want to go when he could be making a little money picking in the groves. But he sent him anyway.

George came home with better than decent grades. But a year passed and then another whole six months with other people working and George just reading books. His father didn't see the point of it. In the middle of George's sophomore year, his father told him he had gotten enough schooling and it was time for him to work. Maybe he could pick it up later.

Big George didn't see where it made much difference anyway, hardly anybody they knew went to college. The father had only gone to fifth grade, and he was doing alright, running the store and packing fruit at the Eichelberger Packing Company.

"With two years of college, you should be able to be president of the United States," his father figured.

"But I'm taking a four-year course number, and you dropping me in the middle of the stream. I'm not prepared to do anything because I'm only halfway there."

George had made valedictorian at Curtwright and, just as significant to him, was the only one from his high school to finish the first year of college without failing any subject. He thought he deserved better.

But his father had made up his mind. Lil George was his namesake, but he wasn't his only concern. Big George had remarried since coming to Eustis. He had a wife now and two stepsons to think about. He had that little store to keep up and dreams of a little orange grove of his own for his old age. He wasn't willing to spend what money he had to send George back to school to study Socrates and polynomials. It was an outrageous indulgence when everybody else was working the groves every day.

A few days later, George was looking for some papers. Rummaging through a dresser drawer, he found some postal receipts for deposits his father had made in a savings account at the post office.

"He had a drawer full of them where he was saving in the post office," George said years later. "But he was telling me he didn't have any money. And that made me angry, and I couldn't sense it into him that I needed to go on and get the other two years. So I just got angry and evil, and I decided I would do something to hurt him."

George had gotten around with the girls, but he always seemed to come back to one in particular. Inez Cunningham was a girl from the backwoods with full cheeks and a narrow waist who had endured an even more unsettled childhood than he had. Her parents had died young and left her in the care of a Pentecostal aunt who trotted her to late-night church meetings with holy rollers talking in tongues. She spent so much of her girlhood in the quaking pews of the Pentecostal church that she swore she would never join a church again if she got free. She kept her word and never did.

She wore plaits and plain dresses and didn't have the pomaded hair some other girls had or the stockings and jewelry that made certain girls look more refined. But she had a way of smiling and tilting her head to the side and some kind of simpatico, outsider way of looking at the world that appealed to a young man like George who felt life had never cut him a fair deal.

She had graduated from high school and was doing the common and necessary job of cleaning white people's homes. But with George up in Tallahassee around those well-turned-out coeds training to be teachers, she fixated on her deficiencies. She imagined her competition in high heels and straight hair, their dignified talk turning George's head. She convinced herself he would choose one of them over her and told him as much.

Big George didn't want Inez around his son either. She was from the backwoods and, in the pecking order that emerged even on the lowest rung—people with house notes versus people who paid rent, factory workers versus servants—Big George saw Inez as lower than the Starlings.

During spring break of his sophomore year, the subject of school came up again. George asked his father if he would send him back, and again the answer was no. George was incensed and decided to do something about it. It was April 19, 1939. He took his father's car and drove up to the house where Inez lived.

"Come on, let's take a ride," he said.

"What you doing?"

"Come on, let's ride."

"Well, where you going?"

"Oh, just a ride."

She hopped in, and he drove south for five miles to Tavares, the county seat. He drove around to the back of the courthouse, where the jail was, and slowed to a stop.

"Where you going?" Inez asked, alarmed now.

He grabbed her hand. "Come on. I want to show you something."

He led her upstairs and into the magistrate's office.

"Well, what can I do for ya, boy?" the magistrate said.

"We come to get married," George said.

Inez nearly fainted. She looked to George to explain himself.

"Well, you been pressuring me about gettin' married. You're telling me that I'm gonna end up marrying one of those college girls that's getting a schoolteacher's education. And you're not gonna be good enough for me. And I keep telling you that that wouldn't make any difference. But you can't seem to believe that, and you don't want to wait. I wanted to show you that you the only one that I wanted. So we just gonna get married now."

Inez stood there with her mouth open. "I—I didn't know" was all she could manage.

She was wearing whatever dress she happened to put on that morning, and he had on whatever he'd thrown on, too.

"Now, you know that'll cost you a dollar fifty, boy," the county judge, A. S. Herlong, said. "A dollar for the license. Fifty cent for a witness."

"Yes, sir."

The judge went through the vows and declared them man and wife. She was twenty-one. He was twenty and not legally old enough to marry.

"I told the man I was twenty-one," George later said. "They didn't care. If you black, they don't care nothin' about Negroes. They didn't check it out. I would be twenty-one in a couple of months. But anyway, we got married."

As they drove back to Eustis, George told Inez his plan.

"You gon' have to continue to stay with your people. We got to keep this secret until I find out whether I'm going back to school or not."

George left out a crucial bit of information in what he told Inez, although it wouldn't take her long to figure it out. "I didn't tell her my ulterior motive," he said years later. Now, in all fairness, he said, "I was in love with her. But I didn't have no intention of getting married, not at that stage, until I got mad with my daddy. He didn't even want me to be courting this girl, much less talking about marrying her.

"So I figured that would fix him up good 'cause he won't send me back to school," he said. "I got in all that trouble for a dollar fifty cents."

George hadn't really thought his revenge scheme through to completion. He held out hope that his father would change his mind. George would spring the news about Inez on him only if his father didn't come around. The two of them kept their secret through the spring and into the summer, when George went to New York like a lot of college students from the South to make spending money for school.

He worked at a dry cleaner's in Flatbush and lived with the aunts who had sent money to his grandmother, the root doctor in Ocala. Toward the end of the summer, he wrote his father: *I have my money for my books and everything. I bought what clothing I'll need. Are you going to be able to pay my tuition?*

Lil George didn't know it, but the people back home had been grumbling in Big George's ear. The father had already done more than he had to. Nobody else was spending all that money for school. None of them had gone off to college, and they had made out alright. Their kids were working in the groves and bringing in good money. What was Lil George doing? His father wrote him back: *No, I just won't be able to do it. You'll have to work this year, and we'll see how things are next year.*

The summer was almost over. The semester would be starting soon. George had run out of time. He realized his dream was over. He wrote his father again. He wanted to get back at him now: *Well, that's alright, don't worry about it 'cause I'm married anyhow. I'm married to Inez.*

George waited for the fireworks. But they never came. He caught the bus back home, and the old people who hadn't seen him in months recognized him as he walked from the bus station. They called out to him from their front porches.

"Hey, ain't that Lil George Starling?"

"Yes, ma'am, this is me."

"Come here, boy. Lord have mercy, what is wrong with you? You done gone plumb fool. They tell me you done jumped up and married that Cunningham girl. And your daddy said, he was here gettin' ready to send you back to school."

George couldn't speak. The old people went on.

" 'Cause your daddy said he was gettin' ready to send you back to school, and, before he know anything, you come writing him about you done got married."

The word had spread all across Egypt town, and everybody knew about the ingrate son who had ruined his chance at college, marrying some girl from the wrong side of town.

Dog, the ole man done tricked me, George thought to himself. He knew how they talked. And in the old people's sweet scolding, he could hear how the story got repackaged in the telling, people in town with nothing better to do, who never had the chance at college themselves, maybe never tried or even wanted to go, delighting in the confusion and goading Big George over it.

"George, where is that boy? Is he going to school?"

"No, you know what that devilish boy done? I'm here gettin' ready to send him back to school, and here he come writing me the other day tellin' me about he married."

"Well, I declare! You mean to tell! Now, I know that boy ain't done nothin' like that! And hard as you workin' trying to send him to school!"

And so it went. If the father had ever intended on sending him back, he now had a publicly acceptable excuse for not doing so, and he had come out the hero in the deal.

As for Lil George, no colleges near Eustis nor any state universities in Florida, for that matter, admitted colored students. The closest colored colleges were hours away. He had a wife to support now. So he would have to do precisely what his father had intended all along. It looked as if he might never make it back to school.

And he would have to live with vows made in anger for the rest of his life. It would not be happy because he knew and she knew how it had come to be. But they would both try to make the best of it now that the deed was done.

Robert Joseph Pershing Foster

LOS ANGELES, 1996

THE PANELED DOOR RISES a story high and would befit a museum or government office but is actually the front door of a Spanish Revival south of Wilshire. The door opens, and there stands a onetime bourbon-swilling army captain and deft-handed surgeon who, now in his later years, is a regular at the blackjack tables and the trifectas at Santa Anita. But he is, at the heart of it all and perhaps most important, a long-standing, still bitter, and somewhat obsessive expatriate from the twentieth-century South, the heartbreak Jim Crow land he chose to reject before it could reject him again.

He is a Californian now, this Robert Joseph Pershing Foster. He is the color of strong coffee and has waves in his hair, which he lets grow as untamed as Einstein's but then brushes back like the boys in the band. He's wearing a white cotton island shirt, loose slacks, and sandals, the uniform of the well-to-do L.A. pensioner. He has the build and bearing of a Sammy Davis, Jr., and not a little of the showmanship and delightful superficiality that seem to grow on people in certain circles of L.A.

He walks straight-backed and slew-footed into the foyer, past the curved, faux–*Gone With the Wind* staircase and the East Asian pottery. He gestures toward the living room, an imposing museum of a space that dwarfs him in its volume, fairly frozen in the sea foam carpet and hot pink tulip chairs out of a sherbety Doris Day movie from the fifties. The whole effect is as starched and formal as the tuxedos he used to wear to the parties he threw for himself back when his wife, Alice, was alive and the money was raining down like confetti. He seems accustomed to people fawning over the place and, with the prim air of leading men of his favorite movies from back in the forties, insists on serving his guests a slice of lemon pound cake and vanilla ice cream on Rosenthal china, whether they would like to have it or not.

His heavy-lidded eyes look straight into those of his listener and have a distractingly thick fringe of lashes like those seen on babies and starlets.

He is a physician—or was for most of his adult life and, by most accounts, a very good one—and is prone to pontificate like a man of his years and accomplishments. But he is just as likely to interrupt himself and check the time to see if he can still make the one o'clock at the Hollywood Park racetrack.

His photo albums are filled with an unlikely assortment of bookies and blues singers and dentists and fraternity men and surgeons and society people whose approval he craved even though he knew they were too pretentious to matter, really. He doesn't say it because it would be gauche and hardly worth mentioning from his point of view, but there happen to be a lot of little Roberts around town, due to the fact that, over the years, he delivered a number of baby boys whose mothers were so grateful for his firm hand and calming reassurances at the precise moment of truth that they named their sons not after their husbands, but after the doctor who delivered their babies.

Before he begins his story, he tells you it's a long one and you can't get it all. He's lived too many lives, done too much, known too many people, ridden so high and so low that there's no point in fooling yourself into thinking you can capture the whole of it.

You could try, of course, and he agrees to give as much as he can.

"I love to talk," he says, a smile forming on his still-chiseled face as he sits upright in his tulip chair. "And I am my favorite subject."

MONROE, LOUISIANA, 1933

IT WAS SATURDAY. Pershing Foster, the teenage son of ambitious but barely paid schoolteachers, began to stir in the thin light of morning. He lived across the railroad tracks from the rest of Monroe, in the worn colored section mockingly known as New Town despite its dirt roads and old shotgun houses on stilts. He pulled out his good pants with the three-inch waistband and the buttons on the side. A few hours from now, the Paramount Theater would go dark, and Jean Harlow or Errol Flynn or some other airbrushed and porcelain movie star would appear out of nowhere, big as a building.

Pershing wanted to be there when the curtain went up and escape his segregated cell of a life, if only for ninety-four minutes. But his father reminded him he couldn't leave just yet. The cows had to be brought in from the grazing pasture and milked before he could go.

Morning after morning, his father had tried to teach him how to milk. Each time, Pershing bent down and pulled hard on the teats, but he could never get the hang of it, nor, truth be told, really wanted to. One time, the cow kicked over the bucket, and the milk spilled everywhere, which only proved to Pershing, who didn't want to be there in the first place, that he wasn't cut out for this line of work.

"I told you that cow didn't like me," Pershing said.

His father couldn't afford to lose a whole bucket of milk. Madison Foster was the principal of the colored high school—a misnomer because it included every grade from the first through the eleventh, but, in any case, paid him a fraction of what the state openly and unapologetically paid his white counterparts and left him and his family only slightly better off than the colored servants in town. He needed that milk to supplement his wages, and he didn't have milk to waste.

"Let him go," his father finally conceded to his wife, Ottie. "Unloose him. Unloose him."

Pershing got his way. He was the last child Ottie would ever bear, and, to the degree that a colored child could be spoiled when so much of the world was cut off to him, he was.

There were three children above him. Madison was the oldest and away most of the time, off in medical school. He was going to be the first doctor in the family, as Ottie, who set her sights higher than the teacher that she was, liked to say of her firstborn. Leland, the second son, was a star pitcher at Morehouse College in Atlanta. His parents had big plans for Leland, naming him as they did after their alma mater, Leland College in New Orleans. People were saying Leland had a shot at the Negro Leagues. He had to fight the girls off him as it was. He had a sculpted mahogany face and waves in his hair. He had the best mind of all the four children but, to his mother's great sorrow, was a regular at the pool hall and the juke joints, despite her best efforts. The women called him Woo, which is what they whispered when they saw him.

There was a sister named Emlyn. They called her Gold owing to the sunset cast to her skin and her place as the only surviving girl. Her twin, Evelyn, had died as an infant. Everybody fussed over Gold and told her how beautiful she was, which she was.

The table seemed set before Pershing was even born, and he couldn't see how to stand out on his own or figure out how he fit in as the youngest. A few years before, when he was about ten, he hit upon something that he thought he could do. He was in fifth grade, and when the school bell rang, he ran to meet his mother in her seventh-grade classroom. He told her his discovery as they walked home together.

"Mama, I believe I can play the piano."

"You think you can?"

"Yes, Mama, I know I can."

"What makes you know?"

"Mama, all you got to do is do like this," he said, banging his fingers on an invisible keyboard as he walked, "and hum the song, and it'll come out."

"You think so, baby?"

"Yes, Mama."

"Well, tomorrow after school, you go down, and you try it on the piano, and you let me know how you come out."

The next day, he did as she said. Noise came out of the piano instead of the music in his head, and that was the end of his short career as a pianist. He never spoke of it again. And, seeing that he didn't bring it up, neither did his mother.

The day the cow kicked over the bucket, they let Pershing have his way. He was a teenager now and off to the Paramount. It sat gaudy and beautiful on the other side of the Missouri Pacific Railway tracks from the colored section of town. He stepped out of the white frame bungalow with his pants creased to a knife edge, the crinkled waves in his hair pomaded and patted down, and proceeded down the dirt roads leading downtown. He went past the little plank houses that stood on cinder blocks due to the rains and floods and jumped over the dirt ditches that made grass islands of every yard around.

He picked up paper-shell pecans that fell in people's yards like litter. Soon he came to the places where the white people lived. The streets were paved and smooth now. In New Town, the roads were earthen humps with a ditch on either side to catch the bayou when it ran out of places to go. Whenever it rained, the streets turned to mud, and Pershing and the other children jumped in the ditches and splashed around as if the ditches were a swimming pool. They didn't know what a real pool was like because the only one in town didn't allow children who looked like them.

Trucks rumbled down the road and flung dust on the porches and through the screens and into the front rooms of the houses on Pershing's side of town. The mud and dust were an affront to Pershing, and he defied it the best he could. He made a game out of proving he could outwit his lower-caste world.

"It was my personal pride to wait till a rainy day and polish my black-and-white shoes," he said, "and wear them when the rain had stopped and jump over puddles and not get a spot of anything on them."

Those dirt roads were the reason he never learned to skate, and he could never forget that.

"We could buy skates," Pershing would remember even as an old man. "But we couldn't buy sidewalks."

Downtown was called Five Points, the intersection of Eighteenth and Desiard, and when Pershing got there, he walked further down Desiard Street past Piccadilly's restaurant, where the white people ate, and on to the Paramount straight ahead. He could see the double glass doors in front and a crowd forming outside. He knew to ignore the front entrance. It was off-limits to people like him.

He went to get his ticket. It was a more complicated affair than it had to be, owing to the whims and peculiarities of how Jim Crow played out in a particular town or establishment. For a time, there was a single ticket agent working both booths—the window for the colored and the one for the white. The agent swiveled between the two openings to sell the movie tickets, a roll to the white line and then a pivot to the colored. It created unnecessary confusion and waiting time for one line or the other, the waiting borne more likely by the colored moviegoers than the white, as waiting to be served after colored people would have been unacceptable to the white clientele. By the time Pershing was nearly grown, the swiveling ticket agent was dispensed with in favor of altogether separate windows and ticket sellers, which would cost a little more but would move the white and colored lines along more quickly and was more in keeping with the usual protocols of Jim Crow.

The Paramount fancied itself like one of the great opera houses of Europe with its crimson velvet curtains and pipe organ rising from the orchestra pit. A double-wide staircase ushered theatergoers to its box seats. But Pershing would not be permitted near them. He followed the colored crowd to the little door at the side entrance, while the white people passed through the heavy glass doors on Desiard. He saw Jimmy and Clarence and Nimrod and just about every other kid from New Town on his way in.

The side door opened onto a dark stairway. Pershing mounted the steps, anxious to get a seat before the lights went dim. He went up one flight, two flights, three, four, five flights of stairs. The scent of urine told him he was getting closer to the colored seats.

At the top of the stairs, there was Bennie Anderson, the colored ticket taker, ready to take his stub. The urine aroma was thick and heavy now. The toilet was stopped up most of the time, and the people did what they had to. Some relieved themselves on the way up. Pershing thought they did it on purpose—a protest maybe for the condition of the place, not registering that it was other colored people who had to suffer for it. He could understand it, but he didn't much approve.

Pershing sat hard in the wooden seat and tried not to notice the stuffed upholstery on the main floor below. Sometimes the kids would rain popcorn and soda pop on the white people. At last, the place went dark, and Pershing left Monroe. He was on a bright veranda with Myrna Loy and Tyrone Power out in California. It was a perfect world, and he could see himself in it.

The only way that someone as proud and particular as Pershing could survive in the time and place he was in was to put his mind somewhere else. He grew up watching his parents exercise exquisite control over the few things they were permitted to preside over in life. Their domain was the Monroe Colored High School, where Madison was principal and Ottie taught seventh grade. It was a small brick building with 1,139 pupils and a teacher for each grade, from kindergarten to eleventh, and run with the precision of a military institution.

Madison James Foster was a short man partial to vested suits and Bible scripture. He had had a hard, orphan-like childhood which he kept to himself other than to say that he had been raised not by his parents but by white people in New Iberia, down by the Gulf. As a boy in the 1880s, he showed a gift for reciting verse, and his white guardians had him perform for their guests as parlor entertainment. There he stood in the middle of a Victorian front room, white guests gathered around him, and was told to recite scripture for their amusement. They saw that he had a facile mind and, when the time came, offered him some assistance to get a degree. He landed at an old colored school called Leland College in New Orleans, where he met a preacher's daughter named Ottie. They graduated from Leland in 1905 and married the same year. They had big plans for themselves just as Jim Crow was closing doors on them.

They set out to teach far from New Orleans, in a moated land of cotton gins and oak trees dripping plant feathers between the Ouachita River and the bayou. An opportunity had arisen in Monroe, an old mill town near the upper brim of the Louisiana boot, not far from where the shoelaces would be. Monroe was three counties west of Mississippi, seventy-five miles from Vicksburg. It was closer to the cotton fields of the Delta than the bons-temps-rolling high life of New Orleans, where the two of them had met. To the north was the tenant-farming Ozark land of warm springs and hard living in Arkansas, where an attempt by sharecroppers to unionize in the town of Elaine would be crushed with bloody efficiency in 1919. To the west was Texas, the wide-open grazing and cotton land of vigilante justice and lynching spectacles that drew people by the thousands and made the newspapers all over the country.

In the midst of this violence, Monroe was a quietly hierarchal town with its two castes remaining in their places and separated by two sets of railroad tracks. The town had been founded by French traders in the nineteenth century and became a mill town serving the nearby cotton plantations and lumber concerns by the time the Fosters got there.

The town came into its own in the 1920s with the arrival of a crop-dusting outfit out of Macon, Georgia, the company having decided to move to the more strategically located town of Monroe, closer to the Mississippi Delta. In 1928, a businessman named C. E. Woolman purchased what was then known as Huff Daland Dusters. He switched from crop dusting and began running the first passenger flights between Mississippi and Texas, via Monroe and Shreveport, in 1929. The company would later come to be known as Delta Air Lines, named after the region it originally served. Delta's presence in Monroe was little more than a distant point of pride to the colored people there, as they could not have become pilots, stewardesses, or gate agents for the airline and might glean only the ancillary benefits of cleaning the airport and serving the now wealthier and well-positioned white people working there. Delta would remain headquartered in Monroe until 1941, when it relocated to Atlanta with the United States's entry into World War II.

It was in Monroe that Madison and Ottie Foster spent their honeymoon hoping to prosper despite the limits of their era, a time when Jim Crow was closing in on them and mutating all over the South. Madison took a position as principal and she as a teacher of the colored children who spilled out of the shotgun houses on the colored side of the Kansas City Southern and Union Pacific railroad tracks. They eventually bought a white frame bungalow on Louise Anne Avenue surrounded by icemen, barbers, sawmill workers, and domestics. The colored people took to calling the husband "Professor Foster" out of an overinflated respect for his bachelor's degree and the position he held over them. It came out " 'Fessor Foster," though, by the time people got through saying it.

He cut a tight-buttoned bearing in his Kuppenheimer suits and Arrow shirts with detachable white collars and cuff links, always gold cuff links. By the late twenties, he was in a position of some prestige among colored people in town, the president of the Louisiana Colored Teachers Association, and was regularly mentioned in the Louisiana News section of the *Chicago Defender* for attending or speaking at some important colored meeting or convention.

He rose early to open his school and greeted the people on their porches as he passed. He had authority of some sort over practically every child in New Town. Some Sundays, he preached at Zion Traveler Baptist Church. It was a world unto itself. The striving colored people in town, stooped and trodden the rest of the week, invested their very beings into the church and quarreled over how things should be run and who should be in charge of the one thing they had total control over.

In the summer of 1932, the church actually split into two rival factions as to who should be the pastor. One side was backing the Reverend W. W. Hill, an old-school preacher who had just been ousted; the other was supporting Professor Foster, a starched man with a standoffish wife and brilliant children whom some people saw as having enough influence as it was, seeing as how he already ran the school. The church grew so divided that people were no longer speaking. Enemy lines were drawn. The church had to shut down for two whole months. The authorities in Monroe took away the keys.

The church reopened the first Sunday in September 1932, along with the wounds and hostilities that were no closer to healing than the day the church was shuttered. That morning, Sunday school had barely begun when "there arose a contention between the two factions as to who was in charge of the church," the *Chicago Defender* reported.

There was a question as to whether the apparent victor, Professor Foster, should speak, the Hill people saying it was perhaps best that he not, the anti-Hill faction urging him to go forward.

Professor Foster was accustomed to running things. He arose and stood stiff and pious and was reading Bible scripture, when four women walked up to the pulpit and demanded he stop preaching, as if to suggest he had no right to be taking over as he had.

It was an outrageous, unheard-of disruption, practically blasphemous, and the church broke into an uproar. Several men rushed the pulpit and began fighting. A deacon backed out of the door, hitting back at those who pursued him and falling down in the street. A parishioner named James Dugans, who was either a supporter of Professor Foster or merely enraged at the show of disrespect, picked up a chair, drew a pistol, and started shooting. A bullet struck a woman named Patsy Daniels in the stomach. Incensed, her father ran to a house next door and got a pistol of his own. The father came back to a fight that had now spilled out to the front of the church.

When the first gunman, Dugans, saw the woman's now-armed father, he shot him in the chest. The bleeding father continued firing as he fell, killing Dugans and wounding three other parishioners. Patsy Daniels died from her wounds. In all, as many as seven people were left wounded, including the dead woman's father. Professor Foster and his family managed to escape unharmed—physically, in any case. The Monroe police again had to take the keys of the church. Until the congregation could settle its dispute, "the doors of the church were securely nailed up," the *Atlanta Daily World* reported.

Pershing was thirteen. He would now end up seeing the world as a beleaguered and underappreciated Foster, a member of a resented clan in a small, clannish subculture inside a segregated pressure cooker of a life. The incident was so unseemly and beneath him that he never spoke of it. But he carried the sense of betrayal and insecurity with him and in some ways would spend the rest of his life both running from those who rejected his family and craving their acceptance.

After the melee, neither Reverend Hill nor Professor Foster would ever muster the full support of the congregation or get to run Zion Traveler Baptist Church. In time, life somehow returned to some version of normalcy, and Professor Foster instead took comfort in his place as the leading black educator in town. On school mornings, he stood at the front steps of the school with a pocket watch in one hand and a paddle in the other. Sometimes the students came running across the school yard late and out of breath.

"The trains cut us off, 'Fessor Foster," the children would tell him.

"I'm gon' cut *you* off," he'd say, raising his paddle. "Get up early. Get up early."

He held chapel before class started, quoting the Old Testament in the auditorium for an hour every morning, and he believed in sparing neither the rod, paddle, or switch. He half waited for some child to get out of line so he could make an example out of him. But as anybody who grew up in that world could tell you, he was no better or no worse than any colored schoolmaster in the South when it came to such things.

His wife, Ottie Alberta Wright Foster, was a prim and ambitious woman, who made the society pages of the colored papers as president of the Golden Seal Embroidery Club and for hosting such things as a wedding breakfast for a bridal party in what the *Defender* called a "lovely home . . . prettily decorated for the occasion." Ottie was raised in New Orleans, a magic circus of a place compared to Monroe, braided with openly mixed-race Creole people and their patois and jambalaya. She brought the food and ways with her and spent hours on the roux for her gumbo when things were good. To be reputed to be Creole was enough to make her exotic to some colored people, whether she was actually Creole or not—which no one ever established for sure but most assumed was true.

She was a small woman with skin the color of chestnuts and wavy black hair. It was said she would have been considered quite a beauty if it weren't for the tight bun she wore low on her head with the severe center part at her forehead and the fact that she seemed rarely to smile at anyone other than her children.

All of the children were bright. But in the family hierarchy, there was not much Pershing could do to distinguish himself with one big brother off in medical school and another a star athlete. He played softball with the neighborhood kids, where they used broomsticks for bats and made their own rules because nobody had seen an official baseball game. But he wasn't especially good at it.

Pershing looked for a way to prove himself. There were three fig trees in their yard, and he picked the figs and sold them to the neighbors, thirty-five cents for a gallon bucket. He gave them a broad smile and charmed them into believing they needed the figs for breakfast or for preserves or to can for the coming winter.

He practiced smiling in the mirror and writing with his left hand even though he didn't need to. He lived for the pat on the head from his father but especially his mother for washing out the washtub or any little thing that he did. He took to cleaning the house to make them happy and to keep the compliments coming, but it only felt good as long as he did it before they could ask.

He was crushed whenever he fell short. His parents punished him by making him go to the back steps and sit there. He sat hugging his dog and cried. Sometimes his mother got tired of him sitting on the steps and called him in. Otherwise, he couldn't leave until his father said so.

"Alright," Professor Foster would say. "Come back in."

It was true he couldn't milk a cow, but he didn't mind churning. He churned the milk as it soured and clabbered. Ottie skimmed the butter off, and he proceeded to go door to door, selling the butter and the buttermilk in a lard bucket with a cultivated earnestness and the crisp airs he was beginning to master.

Mrs. Poe, don't you wanna buy some milk from me? Can I start bringing you milk on Thursdays?

He found that he could get people to like him and that if people liked him he could get what he wanted.

For each grade there was one teacher. And when Pershing got to the seventh grade, Mama taught him. She stood at the front of the room and drilled math and verse into him and the rest of the class without humor or partiality. Sometimes Pershing got restless and leaned over to talk to Moses Potter or Nimrod Sherman or maybe Jimmy Peters. When he did, Ottie stopped in the middle of the lesson and glared down hard at him.

"Pershing, be quiet."

She stood by the blackboard and waited.

"Pershing, be quiet."

He didn't hear her, engrossed as he was. She marched over to his desk. He felt her shadow looming over him and continued to talk. She raised her left hand and smacked him in front of the class.

The other children laughed and laughed. Pershing put his head down and knew not to test Mama anymore. He could get away with less with his mother than with any other teacher in the school.

It seemed to him that for every good thing about being the teacher and principal's son there was a bad thing to it. If he was caught running down the street, somebody would stick her head out the window and remind him who he was.

"Boy, get on out the street. I'm a tell Miss Foster on you."

To further complicate his life, the Fosters were bookish, small-boned people and the children of the sawmill hands towered over Pershing. The days when he didn't walk home with Mama, when he was alone on the streets of New Town, some of the boys lay in wait for him. They surrounded him and taunted him for the way he carried himself and the half inch of extra privilege he had over them.

"You think you somebody 'cause you 'Fessor Foster's boy. You think you better than anybody else 'cause you a Foster."

They made a circle around him and felt bigger because of it. If Professor Foster had whipped the boys with his strap that day, Pershing paid for it that afternoon. They beat him and had a good time doing it. He took it because he had to and fighting wasn't in him. Telling his father would have made things worse. Professor Foster knew no other way to keep errant children in line and would have beat the boys again if he knew what they'd done to his youngest boy, which would have only made life harder for Pershing. So he kept it to himself.

As Pershing got to be a teenager, he started venturing out into the neighborhood, poking his head into the juke joints and the pool hall where the hip cats drank late into the night. It was where the men slapped Woo on the back as they poured him another shot of whiskey. But whenever Pershing poked his head inside, he got the same wave of the hand from the proprietor and the men lining the wall.

"Boy, get outta here. You ain't got no business in here. 'Fessor Foster wouldn't want you in here."

Woo wouldn't have minded and never told him not to come in, but the word had spread somehow that Professor Foster and his wife had a different life in mind for Pershing.

There were pressures coming at him from every direction—his high-minded parents trying to make up in a single generation all that they had been denied through generations of slavery; bullying kids who taunted him and resented his station, tentative though it was; neighborhood people watching his every move. Then there were the reminders that no matter what he did or how smart he might be, he would always be seen as inferior to the lowliest person in the ruling caste, which only meant he had to work even harder to prove the system wrong because it had been drilled into him that he had to be better than the system construed him to be.

He lived under the accumulated weight of all these expectations.

"People in the town demanded more of us," he said years later, "and we had to give it. I respected what they told me. And anything I didn't want them to see, I kept it out of their sight."

Every few years, a teacher from Monroe Colored High loaded a band of students onto the flat bed of a pickup truck and rattled across the Missouri Pacific Railway tracks. They passed the rich people's porticos and pulled up to the back entrance of the white high school in town. The boys jumped out and began stacking the truck bed with the books the white school was throwing away. That is how Monroe Colored High School got its books. The boys loaded the truck with old geography and English texts, some without covers and with pages torn out and love notes scrawled in the margins, and headed back to their side of town.

By the time he was old enough to understand where the books came from, Pershing was fast putting together the pieces of the world he lived in. He knew there was a dividing line, but it was hitting him in the face now. He was showing a talent for science and was getting to the point that he needed reference books to do his lesson. But it was against the law for colored people to go to the public library. "And the library at the Colored High School did not live up to its name," he said years later.

He was in the eighth grade when word filtered to his side of the tracks that Monroe was getting a new high school. It wouldn't replace the old building that Monroe Colored High was in. It was for the white students, who already had a big school. It would be called Neville High. The colored people could see it going up when they ventured to the other side of the tracks. It rose up like a castle, four stories of brick and concrete with separate wings and a central tower, looking as if it belonged at Princeton or Yale. It opened in 1931 on twenty-two acres of land. The city fathers made a fuss over the state-of-the-art laboratories for physics and chemistry, the 2,200-seat balconied auditorium, the expanded library, and the fact it was costing $664,000 to build.

As the new high school took shape across town, Pershing watched his father rise in the black of morning to milk the cows and walk the mile and a half to open his building the size of a grade school. His father, his mother, and the other teachers at Monroe Colored High School were working long hours with hand-me-down supplies for a fraction of the pay their white counterparts were getting. In Louisiana in the 1930s, white teachers and principals were making an average salary of $1,165 a year. Colored teachers and principals were making $499 a year, forty-three percent of what the white ones were.

Pershing's parents could console themselves that they were faring better than colored teachers in other southern states, a reflection not necessarily of their superior performance but that there were states even worse than Louisiana when it came to teachers' pay. In neighboring Mississippi, white teachers and principals were making $630 a year, while the colored ones were paid a third of that—$215 a year, hardly more than field hands. But knowing that didn't ease the burden of the Fosters' lives, get their children through college, or allow them to build assets to match their status and education.

The disparity in pay, reported without apology in the local papers for all to see, would have far-reaching effects. It would mean that even the most promising of colored people, having received next to nothing in material assets from their slave foreparents, had to labor with the knowledge that they were now being underpaid by more than half, that they were so behind it would be all but impossible to accumulate the assets their white counterparts could, and that they would, by definition, have less to leave succeeding generations than similar white families. Multiplied over the generations, it would mean a wealth deficit between the races that would require a miracle windfall or near asceticism on the part of colored families if they were to have any chance of catching up or amassing anything of value. Otherwise, the chasm would continue, as it did for blacks as a group even into the succeeding century. The layers of accumulated assets built up by the better-paid dominant caste, generation after generation, would factor into a wealth disparity of white Americans having an average net worth ten times that of black Americans by the turn of the twenty-first century, dampening the economic prospects of the children and grandchildren of both Jim Crow and the Great Migration before they were even born.

For now, each day, Pershing's parents and the families whose children they taught had to live with the reality that they had to do more with less. Southern states made no pretense as to the lopsided division of resources to white and colored schools, devoting as much as ten dollars per white student for every dollar spent on a colored student and showing little interest beyond that meager investment.

"The money allocated to the colored children is spent on the education of the white children," a local school superintendent in Louisiana said bluntly. "We have twice as many colored children of school age as we have white, and we use their money. Colored children are mighty profitable to us."

When a fire broke out in the basement of Monroe Colored High School, destroying classroom furniture and equipment, the city refused to so much as replace the desks and teaching supplies that had burned to ashes, as the *Monroe News Star* reported. The tax dollars were earmarked for Neville. The colored parents, already strapped, would have to raise the money themselves. That would be just one more thing weighing on Professor Foster. As it was, he wasn't making half of what the Neville High School principal made. Nobody in New Town would be allowed in the new building when it opened, other than to clean it, and the idea of Pershing attending it, no matter how smart he was, was unthinkable.

It was not something the Fosters would have wanted to dwell on, as it would have done them no good, but their very existence, their personal aspirations, and the purpose of their days were in direct opposition to the white ruling-class policy on colored education—that is, that colored people needed no education to fulfill their God-given role in the South.

"If these Negroes become doctors and merchants or buy their own farms," a southern woman told the celebrated journalist Ray Stannard Baker, "what shall we do for servants?"

The unfairness started to eat at Pershing. It was a curse to be able to see it. Better not to know. But the older he got, the more he was starting to want. And the more he wanted, the harder it was to accept that he might never get it—all because of a chemical in his skin that some people resented and felt superior to and that no one on this earth could change. To make matters worse, he had the misfortune of having developed exquisite taste and what little he was exposed to only fed his ambitions.

"Everything you wanted was white and the best," he said.

Pershing had started to notice the girls, and they started to notice him. They were getting to an age where they would walk home from school together, meet at the Paramount for the picture show, and eventually end up in a park or a field somewhere. Somebody would get a car from an uncle or someone or other, and they would drive up to where the new Neville High was, shiny new and perched high on a hill. It was lush and secluded, and when they had finished with the girls, they whirred past the grounds and flung their spent condoms on the green.

"That's how we showed our resentment," he said years later. "Don't think we were blind."

Just before dark, when the sky is neither blue nor black but purple, Pershing stepped out of the tin tub to get ready for a Saturday night. He put on long pants and cheap cologne and walked in the direction of the Miller and Roy Building on the colored side of Five Points, about a mile from the center of town.

It was in the shadow of downtown in a world of its own. The axis was Eighteenth and Desiard. Across from the office building was the drugstore. Behind the drugstore was a café. Behind the café was a liquor store. Across from the liquor store was the pool hall.

He had his shirt buttoned low and open as he strutted down Desiard. He was two blocks from the Miller and Roy Building when a car pulled up to the curb. The exhaust spit and coughed. A white man leaned out of the window.

"Hey, boy."

Pershing kept walking. He hated being called boy even though he was one. They barked it at the sawmill hands and at bent-over, old colored men and even upstanding men like his father. He was fourteen, and it was already beginning to grate on him.

"Hey, boy!"

Pershing stopped and consoled himself: *You can answer him because you are a boy. You're not twenty-one yet. Technically you're still a boy. That makes it okay for him to address you as boy.*

He turned toward the car and kept it to "Yes," instead of "Yes, sir."

"Boy, I'll pay you if you get me a nice, clean colored girl."

Pershing breathed deep. Ever since his sister, Gold, had hit puberty, he could hardly walk down the street with her without white men with snuff in their mouth yelling out what they would do to her. It made him want to vomit. She kept her head up and held his hand tight and walked through it. He could never defend her, never stand up to a gang of them on a street corner. "That was death," he would say years later.

Pershing knew it from the sheer insanity all around him. When he was eleven years old, a white mob burned down the courthouse across the border in Sherman, Texas.

It started with a colored man accused of raping a white woman, a confession extracted, a trial hastily set. But just as the trial opened, a mob stormed the courtroom and torched the building to get to the defendant, George Hughes. Court officials fled through a second-story window and left Hughes in a steel vault with a bucket of water.

Firefighters tried to save the courthouse, but the mob slashed the water hoses to keep the blaze going. The mob then dynamited the vault where Hughes had been left. The mob found him dead, crushed by the explosion, the water bucket almost empty. The courthouse then burned to the ground.

Disappointed that they had not gotten to Hughes before he died, the people in the mob hanged his body from a cottonwood tree and set it on fire with furniture they looted from a nearby colored hotel. Then they torched the colored district, as the colored people of Sherman fled to the homes of white friends or left town. A half-dozen colored homes escaped the torching only because a white man told the mob the houses belonged to him.

This was the world Pershing was growing up in. He had learned the rules early in life. Now he was standing at a vacant curb, just him and a white man out prowling. He had never seen the man before, imagined he must have come in from the country and made a beeline for the colored section with one thing in mind, as was his prerogative. Not just any colored girl. *A nice, clean colored girl.*

The man waited, and Pershing assessed the situation. He was on the colored side of town, a block from the rooming house. He knew every turn and alley. He was in the majority around here.

He looked at the man. "A nice, clean colored girl," he said, calculating the risks of what he might say next. "Let me see. I tell you what. You get your mama for me, and I'll get you one."

He didn't wait for the man's reaction. Pershing vanished into the colored alleys of Five Points. He couldn't believe what had come out of his mouth. His face was flushed, and his hands shook. He could get hanged for that. Nothing more needed to happen to remind him who had the power over him and what they could do if they wanted.

"You lived with it," Pershing said years later. "But it wasn't that you liked the taste of it."

And I'd whisper to myself that someday
the sun was going to shine down on me
way up North in Chicago or Kansas City
or one of those other faraway places that
my cousin . . . always talked about. . . .
I felt the same restlessness in me.

—Mahalia Jackson, *Movin' On Up*

THE SOUTH, 1915 TO THE 1970S

AT EASTER AND AROUND THE FOURTH OF JULY, the people from the North came. They looked like extras out of a movie at the Saturday matinee. They wore peplums and bergamot waves. Even the wind moved aside as they walked.

They flashed thick rolls of cash from their pockets—the biggest bills on the outside covering the ones and fives. They said they were making all kinds of money. But they didn't have to say it because the cars and the clothes did the talking. They had been wiring more money to their families back home than they truly could spare and had been saving up all year for those gloves and matching purse. But they weren't telling the people in the South that.

They made sure to show up at their mother-churches, where everyone would see them: at Gethsemane Baptist Church in Eustis, Florida, where Lil George went; at Thankful Baptist Church in Rome, Georgia, where my mother saw the people visiting from the North; at New Hope Baptist Church in Chickasaw County, Mississippi, where Ida Mae lived.

Even at Zion Traveler Baptist Church in Monroe, Louisiana, where Pershing grew up, the partisans set aside their rivalries and sat upright in the pews when the people from the North came. The pastor would ask the visitors to rise, and it was then that the people from up north or out west stood up in their butterfly hats and angel dresses and in suits upholstered to the tall men's frames. People who hadn't seen them in ages now craned their necks to see how Willie and Thelma looked and if they had changed any. And the pastor went on about how this one was building cars in Detroit and that one was doing us proud in Oakland.

They were received like visiting dignitaries. They had once been just like the people who stayed. Now they were doing important-sounding work for the government in Washington, in the hotels on Michigan Avenue in Chicago, in the garment district in New York or in the apartments of the rich people on Riverside Drive. They wore the protective coating of the North. They lived in big cities too distracted to care what the colored people did as long as they did it to themselves, and that was the greatest blessing of all.

At night when the junebugs came out, the children sat at the knees of the people from the North and heard stories of doing unimaginable things like sitting in the front of a trolley car and saying "Yes" instead of "Yes, sir" to a white person and living to tell it.

In Grenada, Mississippi, two little boys couldn't wait for their big sister Francie to come visit from Ohio. Gilbert and Percy Elie would crouch at her feet and listen to her.

"We would sit on the porch in the moonlight," Gilbert remembered, "and she would tell us about the North."

Then she went back to Ohio. And life returned to the way it was for Gilbert and Percy, living as they were in the altogether different country of the Mississippi Delta.

They and Ida Mae and George and Pershing and children all over the South were growing up, trying to comprehend the caste they were born into, adjusting or resisting, lying in bed at night and imagining a world that was different and free, and knowing it was out there because they had seen it in the casual airs, the haughtiness even, and the clothes and the stories of the people from the North. Now nothing around them made sense, and everything that happened to them imprinted itself into their psyches and loomed larger because they had glimpsed what was possible outside the bars of their own existence.

Yet they were too young to escape. So they had to endure their peculiar station in the feudal world they were consigned to and the madness that could intrude at any given moment.

Like the night back in the 1940s, "a moon-shining night, bright, like it's almost day," when little Gibert and Percy were sitting on the front porch steps of their family's cabin.

The boys could hear voices coming from the woods. The voices echoed through the trees in the night. The boys got quiet and still and tried to make out what was happening. They could hear the crackle of a whip and a hollow wailing coming from the woods. A colored man was being lashed in the pine scrub beyond their cabin.

The boys heard the man cry out with each blow.

"Alright, we gonna take a break," some voices finally said.

There was silence. Then the men took up the task again.

"We gonna kill you," the voices said from the woods.

"Please, *please,* don't," the colored voice said. "Before y'all do, will you let me pray?"

The man began to pray. "The man prayed a prayer like a Baptist preacher," Gilbert remembered decades later. "I ain't never heard a man pray like that man."

"Father, forgive them, for they know not what they doing," Gilbert remembered the man praying. "I lived a good life for you, if you never done nothing for me, Lord, please . . ."

"Alright, that's enough," the other voices said.

The man continued to pray. The beating and wailing commenced again. Then the wailing stopped.

"The sonabitch dead," came a voice from the woods.

Gilbert could never get the man's cries out of his head. "We don't know who he was," Gilbert said some fifty years later, "or what he was supposed to have done."

The seeds of Gilbert's departure from Mississippi were sown that night. More seeds were planted another day, when he and his father and brother were walking home from the movie theater in town.

The street was little more than an alley, barely wide enough for two people to walk astride. Gilbert was about twelve. He was reading a comic book and not paying attention. Three white boys not much older than Gilbert came in their direction. Gilbert's father and brother instinctively jumped out of the way. Gilbert was looking at his comic book and bumped into one of the boys.

The boy grabbed Gilbert by the collar.

"Who do you think you are?" Gilbert remembered the boy asking him.

The boy spat at him, and Gilbert hit the boy back. Gilbert's father was shaking with fear. He begged forgiveness from the boy who spat on his son. Then he turned to his son and upbraided him.

"Boy, what's the matter with you?" his father said. "Are you crazy?"

The father fumed at him. "All the way home, he didn't talk to me," Gilbert remembered decades later.. "I got home, he didn't say a word."

That night, Gilbert could hear his father confiding to his mother through the cardboard-thin walls of their cabin. "Sugar, that one son we got, Gilbert, I'm afraid for him," the father whispered. "That boy'll never live if he stays in Grenada."

Gilbert knew that. He shared his dreams with Percy when they worked in the field hoeing and plowing and weighing up the cotton.

"We would plow side to side," Gilbert remembered. "He'd have a row, and I'd have a row. We would talk. We would talk about school or what I'm gonna do when I get to be grown, when I leave here."

His big sister's stories of life up north had seeped into him, and one day when he got big enough, he told himself, he was going to follow her to Ohio. And he did.

Hundreds of miles away, out in the country near Jackson, North Carolina, a family named DeBreaux was in a tizzy whenever cousin Beulah was expected in from New York. The mother cooked all day. The daughters, Virginia and Lee, cleaned and swept and tried to imagine how she would look. It was as if the queen of England were coming.

Beulah blew into town in the latest silk dresses, her high heels click-clacking on the pavement. Her hair was pressed and shiny and swung when she turned her head. The girls touched it to see how it felt.

"If we could just look like that," Virginia told her sister.

Virginia started dreaming then and there. *Someday, I'm going to New York.*

She sat and planned the whole thing out with her little brother. She wouldn't have to pick cotton anymore or feel the spike of frost on the wet grass going barefoot to the outhouse in the morning.

In the early 1940s, she did, in fact, join the multitudes. The day she left, her mother made fried chicken and broke down crying. Her father was too hurt to speak. He stayed in the house as they left. "He did not bid us good-bye," she said. She ended up in Brooklyn, where the elevated train shook the apartment and looked as if it were coming straight into the window, and where she would get her hair pressed and wear high heels click-clacking on the pavement like Beulah.

Sometimes, the young people had little choice but to leave, sooner than they had imagined. Such was the case with my mother's older brother. He was a teenager in Rome, Georgia, working as a driver and office boy for an upstanding white man in town during the Depression. He would drive the man from Georgia to Miami for the man's business trips, alone with him in the car for hours at a time. He liked the man because he let him keep the big new shiny car after dropping the man off at the white hotel. It was one of the few company jobs accorded colored teenagers in the South at that time and was thought to be a good one.

One day, he was straightening the man's office when he opened a drawer and saw something white folded inside. He pulled it out and unfurled the fabric.

It was a white robe and hood.

Trembling, he put it back in the drawer, and had to reconsider everything he thought he knew about the man he had trusted and the world in which he lived. That night, he went home and told his parents and little sisters that he was leaving Georgia for Detroit, one of the receiving stations for people from that part of the South. He had made his decision, was shocked into it, really. He would get a job at Chrysler like a cousin of theirs. He was joining the Great Migration for the most personal and profound of reasons, and, without knowing it, planting a seed in my mother's imagination, knowing as she did why her big brother had fled.

Several seeds were planted, too, in Ida Mae, Lil George, and Pershing. Ida Mae heard about this one or that one going north to freedom after a lynching or a raw deal at settlement. Her big brothers, Sam and Cleve, had fled to Toledo, her big sister Irene was talking about going to Milwaukee, and, as Ida Mae came of age, she saw the cloche hats and unobtainable finery of city living in the pages of the Sears, Roebuck catalogue out of Chicago.

Lil George watched the Blye brothers, Babe and Reuben, older boys who'd gone north to New York, come back to Eustis in their zoot suits and fedoras. They talked about all the money they were making building the 9W highway up in Jersey, about the skyscrapers and streetlights, the dance halls in Harlem, the parties in Corona, and the boulevards paved where the colored people lived.

"We used to sit up all night," George remembered, "and listen to Babe and M.B. and Reuben and Freeman and all them talkin' about New York. And I said, 'Boy, that sounds just like heaven. I wanna see some of that. *New York*. I'm sure going to New York soon as I get big enough.'"

And in Monroe, Louisiana, if Mantan Moreland passed through town, there was a stir in the pews and talk in the pool hall. Everyone wanted to sit down with the native son who had made it to Hollywood, even if it was only as a shuffling sidekick in the movies.

Pershing saw the parade of people from the North and the movie scenes at the Paramount of life beyond Louisiana and began dreaming of escape, too. When he was still small enough to fit in the crawl spaces of the houses on cinder-block stilts, he played pretend with a girl down the street named Clara Poe. They peeked out from under the floor joists and waited for a car to rumble down Louise-Anne Avenue and fought over whose it was. *It's my car. No, it's my car.* Then they pretended they were in the car leaving.

Clara always said she was going to Chicago, where her uncles were. But no matter how many times Clara said Chicago, Pershing said he was going to California. He didn't have any family there. All he knew was that, one day, somehow, whenever he got big and whatever it took, he was going.

A Burdensome Labor

This land is first and foremost
his handiwork. . . .
Wherever one looks
in this land,
whatever one sees
that is the work of man,
was erected by the
toiling straining bodies of blacks.
—David L. Cohn, *God Shakes Creation*

But the Egyptians
mistreated
and oppressed us,
assigning us a
burdensome labor.
—Deuteronomy 26:6

CHICKASAW COUNTY, MISSISSIPPI, 1929
IDA MAE BRANDON GLADNEY

IDA MAE'S NEW HUSBAND took her to live in a little wood cabin on Edd Pearson's plantation on a clearing past the Natchez Trace. Ida Mae was sixteen. In the morning, the sun poked at them through the gaps in the roof. At night, they could see the stars through the ceiling cracks over their bed. It just about rained inside as much as out.

They set about working cotton for Mr. Edd. All around them, the land was in a state of being cotton or becoming cotton, brown and rutted for planting, green shoots willed into rows of coddled bushes until the land was white out to the tree line. Every so often, a wood cabin broke the clearing, raw and thrown-together, built uneasily on a footprint of land that was a fraction of what was devoted to the field.

The people who lived in the cabins gave the best hours of their days to cotton, working until the sun went behind the trees and they couldn't see their hands anymore.

Early morning, the mist rose over the fields and made a halo on the surface of the earth. Ida Mae's new husband and the sharecroppers working other sections of Pearson's land tried to pick as much as they could before the sun got high.

Edd Monroe Pearson was a decent boss man, as decent as could be expected from a planter in Mississippi in the 1920s. He presided over the lives of some dozen families who grew his crops, as Ida Mae would recall, and he took half of whatever they produced, whether it was cotton or turkeys or hogs. At the end of the season, he deducted the debts he said they owed—cottonseed, fertilizer, implements, ginning fees, cornmeal, salt pork—the "furnish," as it was called, of their half of the harvest. Money rarely changed hands between planter and sharecropper, as the entire system was built on credit. The sharecroppers owed the planters, the planters owed the merchants, the merchants owed the banks, and the banks were often beholden to some business concern in the North, where most of the real money was in the first place.

Unlike some planters, Mr. Edd actually gave George and Ida Mae a few dollars when settling time came at the end of the harvest, although they never knew whether they would get anything or how much it might be or if it was actually what they were due, nor could they complain if it wasn't. Edd Pearson was about the best boss man a colored sharecropper could hope for.

But he was a ranking member of the dominant caste and felt it within his right to involve himself in the private affairs of his serfs.

He came through the field on his horse one day and saw George bent over picking through the rows. George and Ida Mae had been out for hours and the sun had cooked their backs. Ida Mae had no gift for picking like her new husband did and had fallen farther and farther behind, stooping from the weight of the sack.

George had called out to her, but she was too far back and too beat from the sun to catch up. After a few dozen pounds, her knees gave way.

She saw a clear path up ahead and dropped onto her sack, collapsed in the dirt aisle between the cotton rows.

Mr. Edd rode up to George and questioned him about it.

"Your wife don't do nothing, do she, but sit down," Mr. Edd said to George.

George would have liked to have said it was his business and not Mr. Edd's, but colored men could not say such things to a white man in Mississippi and get away with it in 1929.

When Mr. Edd was gone, George went back to Ida Mae.

"See can't you try and do a little bit better," George said, caught between the two of them.

She said she would try, but there was no use pretending. She was not going to be of much help in the field. She had never been able to pick a hundred pounds. One hundred was the magic number. It was the benchmark for payment when day pickers took to the field, fifty cents for a hundred pounds of cotton in the 1920s, the gold standard of cotton picking.

It was like picking a hundred pounds of feathers, a hundred pounds of lint dust. It was "one of the most backbreaking forms of stoop labor ever known," wrote the historian Donald Holley. It took some seventy bolls to make a single pound of cotton, which meant Ida Mae would have to pick seven thousand bolls to reach a hundred pounds. It meant reaching past the branches into the cotton flower and pulling a soft lock of cotton the size of a walnut out of its pod, doing this seven thousand times and turning around and doing the same thing the next day and the day after that.

The hands got cramped from the repetitive motion of picking, the fingers fairly locked in place and callused from the pricks of the barbed, five-pointed cockleburs that cupped each precious boll. The work was not so much hazardous as it was mind-numbing and endless, requiring them to pick from the moment the sun peeked over the tree line to the moment it fell behind the horizon and they could no longer see. After ten or twelve hours, the pickers could barely stand up straight for all the stooping.

Ida Mae had watched people do it all her life and knew how it was done. But when it came time to actually go out and pick it, she would look up and see everybody else far down the row. At weighing time, she would empty her sack on the scale and never get three digits.

Above her was an entire economy she could not see but which ruled her days and determined the contours of her life. There were bankers, planters, merchants, warehouse clerks, fertilizer wholesalers, seed sellers, plow makers, mule dealers, gin owners. A good crop and a high price made not much improvement to the material discomforts of Ida Mae's existence but meant a planter's wife could "begin to dream of a new parlor carpet and a piano" and a salesman of farm implements could be "lavish with more expensive cigars than he smoked last year." On Wall Street, there were futures and commodities traders wagering on what the cotton she had yet to pick might go for next October. There were businessmen in Chicago needing oxford shirts, socialites in New York and Philadelphia wanting lace curtains and organdy evening gowns. Closer to home, closer than one dared to contemplate, there were Klansmen needing their white cotton robes and hoods.

In the half light of morning, when the mist hung low and the dew was thick on the bolls, the pickers set out to the field as their slave foreparents had done year in and year out for two centuries. *"The first horn was blown an hour before daylight as a summons for work hands to rise."* Each one looked out across the field to infinity. The quarry was spread over acres and rows far from the starting plant, and they could not see the end of what they were expected to pick.

On large fields during the height of the season—which began in August in south Texas and moved eastward, reaching the Carolinas by early fall—the star pickers sped like fan blades through the cotton, a blur of fingers and bolls, arms and torsos switching from the left row to the right, picking on both sides of them and tossing the cotton like feathers into their sack. The sacks were strapped over their shoulders and dragged in the dirt behind them like an extra limb, the sacks weighing as much as a human adult by the end of the day and making them stoop all the more.

They picked until they were hypnotized by the picking. By midday, the fast ones and the slow ones were far from the center, the stars way up ahead and not looking back, the slow ones trailing behind, the most watchful of everyone's placement. The field was flat and unbroken by trees, and there was no escape from the hundred-degree heat. The sun bore down on them through the head rags and the Panama hats and made the cotton field shimmer like the ocean. Pickers thought they saw things, like people who had died and come back, and waved a handkerchief in the air to call the water boy from under a shade tree. He was usually a picker's child, the one designated to fetch the bucket of well water when they needed it, half the water splashing out of the bucket and onto the ground as the water boy trudged down the rows.

Throughout the cotton kingdom, the act of picking cotton was the same. But in the hills, the cotton was sparser and shorter, not thick and shoulder high like cotton in the Delta. It was harder to get a hundred, much less more. You had to pick a wider field and stoop to pick the lowest bolls to reach the same benchmark.

There were ways to make life easier or harder for yourself when it came to picking cotton. Experienced pickers knew to pick in a rapid, flowing motion, trancelike and efficient. The strongest of the men, men like George, could pick two or three times their weight in cotton—four hundred pounds gave a man bragging rights in anybody's field. A woman could hold her head up if she picked a hundred.

It was a mean enough world that people got desperate. For one thing, for day pickers, there was the money. For another, there was their pride. And then there was the fact that they did not want to be there in the first place. Some people collected rocks, hid them in their pockets, and threw them into their sack at weighing time to make a heavier load. Some people picked the stalk and all to add extra weight. Some were the first out in the morning, picking early while the dew was on the bud, which meant much of the weight was water. It was a trick they could get away with unless the planter set the cotton out in the sun to dry it out, which some did. When those who were so inclined didn't outright lard their sacks, they helped themselves to the peaches and berries on the edges of the boss's cotton and gave themselves a raise for breaking their backs in the field.

Many years later, the people would stand up to water hoses and sheriffs' dogs to be treated as equal. But for now the people resisted in silent, everyday rebellions that would build up to a storm at midcentury. Rocks stuffed into cotton sacks in Mississippi at weighing time. The COLORED ONLY signs pulled from the seat backs of public buses and converted into dartboards in dorm rooms in Georgia. Teenagers sneaking into coffee shops and swiveling on the soda fountain stools forbidden to colored people in Florida and then running out as fast as they'd come in before anybody could catch them. Each one fought in isolation and unbeknownst to the others, long before the marches and boycotts that were decades away.

Sometime in the 1930s, a crew of pickers had been assembled to harvest a wide field of cotton near Brookhaven, Mississippi, some two hundred miles south of Chickasaw County, where Ida Mae lived. On the crew was a big man who had just gotten out of Parchman Prison. Word spread through the field that the man had killed somebody, but no one knew for sure. It was clear from the start that the man could pick. He was used to picking with a gun to his back. He could pick like a machine when he got paid for it.

People could hardly pick for watching the man. One of the slower pickers was a teenager who figured if he could just stick behind the prisoner, he could make more money for himself. So he got behind him and did what he did, or tried to anyway. The prisoner did not speak. He just picked until he was a faint figure in the distance. The slow picker fell behind, and when dusk approached, he knew from his sack that he was underweight. The other pickers headed to the scales. But the slow picker dragged his sack behind a tree. He looked to his left and to his right and in front of him to see that no one was watching. Then he pulled down his coveralls. He opened the sack that represented a day's worth of work and his bent back and the pennies he would get for this bent back because he knew it did not amount to a hundred pounds. That was when he positioned the sack just so and relieved himself in the boss man's cotton for spite and the extra dime because he didn't like having to pick cotton anyway.

Ida Mae grew up isolated in the hills and never heard about these things until it was too late to do her any good. So she and her husband worked the piece of Pearson land apportioned to them with duty and resignation.

She herself could not afford a dress made out of the cotton that ruled their days. What she wore was pieced together from flour sacks that she boiled for hours until the flour company's name finally faded away. Burlap scratching her skin and the sun hunting her down, she dragged a sack behind her and plucked and picked, not figuring she was clothing a small piece of the world and never giving much thought to where the contents would land.

All around her in raw cabins leaning in different corners of the plantation were offshoots of her husband's family: half brothers, whole sisters, uncles, cousins, and their wives and husbands and children. A nephew, Robert Pulliam, whom they called Saint, helped them pick cotton sometimes. A cousin named Joe Lee was willing to help, but nobody much wanted him around because he was known for taking things that weren't his. A neighbor named Addie B. raised turkeys on the half for Mr. Edd and fretted over them when they went roosting in the woods. George's brother Willie was the patriarch because he was the oldest of them all.

Ida Mae tried to learn who all these people were and set about trying to become a wife. Willie's daughter, Callie Mae, showed her how to roll dough and make blackberry cobbler and tomato pie. They went picking blackberries on the running vine up and down the ditch bank to bake their cobblers with. George liked his greens with fatback or hog maws, and she learned how to cook them like he liked. She got up early and chopped wood as well as a man for the cooking fire. She put the meat on, and before the meat was brown and near ready to fall off the bone, she stuffed the greens in the pot and they cooked down and swam in pot liquor so good it made you want to swallow your tongue, as they used to say in their highest compliment to a cook. George would never just come out and say he liked it; he just ate, and that's how she knew he did.

Saturday was for washing and ironing. She hauled water in from the well and washed their clothes in the iron kettle. Sunday was for church. The rest of the time, she was out in the field beside George, hoeing or chopping or picking cotton around the army worms that nested in the leaves. It took fourteen hundred pounds to make a bale, and George needed to make a bale every two or three days in the picking season. Mr. Edd took half. "You know he comes first," Ida Mae would say years later.

They saved a little piece of land behind the house to plant corn and collards and peanuts and sweet potatoes. George hauled Ida Mae out to plant and till their little garden in the off hours, but Ida Mae didn't much want to be out there. They had been working all day and were planting the last of the corn. George dug a trough in the earth and told her to come behind him and scatter the kernels in the trench he made, which she did until she got tired of it. She had a pail full of seeds left. She threw the whole pail of kernels into the hole he dug and told him she was just fresh out of seeds.

In the fall, the corn came up. It was full and dense in one spot of land, the corn stalks elbowing one another in the row. George and Ida Mae ate well that season. George didn't have much to fuss about.

There were things she was good at and things she was not so good at, and she saved herself a lot of aggravation by knowing the difference between the two. She was good at raising chickens, and she kept one in a coop to press into service whenever she needed it. "If I wanted it for breakfast, I'd kill it in the morning," she said. "I go out there wring the neck off, have my hot water scalding, cut him up, and fry him for breakfast."

Nothing scared her. Like that morning at picking time when George had already left for the field. She lay in bed and heard a rattling in the kitchen. *"I know ain't nobody in that kitchen,"* she told herself, rising to see what it was. A speckler—a snake as long as a broom handle—had slithered over the edge of a bucket and was helping itself to the drinking water she had hauled in from the well. She backed out of the door and got the pitchfork and stuck it through him. She held up the pitchfork with the snake dangling from it and dropped it into the dirt yard. Then she took a stick and beat it until it stopped making *S*'s with its body. The snake was full of guinea eggs it had swallowed from the guinea nest, and it hadn't had a chance to wrap itself around a tree to break the eggs in it yet. The eggs broke when she killed it.

She told George about it when he dragged in from the field. He didn't praise her for her bravery or say much of anything. "I been seeing 'em all day" was all he said.

It was getting to be the 1930s. It was a hurting time, and the farm people almost couldn't give the cotton away. The value of what they harvested, the worth of their hard labor and the measure of their days, plummeted after the crash of 1929. A bale of cotton had gone for nearly thirty cents in the mid-1920s and for nearly seventeen cents in the late 1920s. By 1931, the planters couldn't get six cents for the same bale of cotton. The people in New York and Boston were not ordering up new seersucker suits and cotton pillowcases like they did just a few years before. The cotton ripened in the bud, but there was nobody to buy it. So the boss men went without new Model T Fords. The sharecroppers went without shoes.

Ida Mae fed the chickens and worked the field barefoot. She watched George haul in cotton with no assurance of what, if anything, the planter might give him for it and tried not to worry her mind over what she could not fix. Before long, she started feeling full around her belly. She didn't think much of it. She went about her chores and rode horseback when she went to visit her kin people. No horse was fast enough for Ida Mae, and she raced now like she always did. It wasn't good for the life that was growing inside her, and she miscarried riding those horses before she knew she was expecting.

Her belly got full again, and she didn't ride horses this time. She hated waddling into church with her flour sack dress pulling tight across the front and her belly sticking out. She was in the field when the thunder came. It started as a light knocking deep inside her. She ran into the house, and the thunder got violent. It shot to the top of the ceiling and hurled itself back into her. She got up and started walking, walking in a circle around the bed. The midwife came and watched her rock from foot to foot.

"I could see the pain comin' down on the top of the house and keep comin'," she said.

The men don't know what the women go through, was what she was thinking, don't feel the stab of lightning inside.

"Oughta be so they could," Ida Mae said.

She stopped her pacing and squatted beside the bed. She was on her knees. The life force reached out of her and into the light.

It was a girl. Ida Mae never wanted a girl. She was still thinking like a tomboy wanting to climb a tree. The baby had big eyes and a brown, narrow face like her husband's. They named her Velma. In time, Ida Mae took to her and held her close.

Within a year or so, she started feeling full again. It was another girl. They named her Elma but called her Baby Sis. Ida Mae took them to the field with her when it was time to plant. She set them both down in the shade of a plum tree. It got too hot for them out in the field. They were toddlers now. Ida Mae told them to sit still and then took her place behind her husband at the turnrow.

The sun bore down on Ida Mae and George, and soon they heard crying near the plum tree. It was Velma wailing and Baby Sis lying sick with half-eaten plums beside her. Velma had reached up and gotten her some, and Baby Sis ate them and got the flux, as the country people called whatever stomach ailment, poison, or virus had got into the baby. It was a perilous world in the early 1930s, even without Jim Crow. Dysentery, typhus, malaria all thrived in the backwoods of the Deep South before penicillin or common vaccines were invented. There were no doctors nearby, and, by the time they got Baby Sis to one, it was too late. They buried her in a little box at the church cemetery near Bewnie.

Ida Mae told herself that day that she would never leave a child of hers alone again.

In September of 1935, she finally got the boy she wanted. He had the brown, narrow face of her husband. When it came time to name him, a neighbor girl stepped forward. The girl looked after Velma when Ida Mae was in the field and took care of a little white boy in town when she was summoned to do so. His name was James Walter. George and Ida Mae had never laid eyes on the boy, but they named their son after him and hoped maybe good fortune would rain down on their son like it seemed to fall on the white people.

Not long after he had begun walking, something took over little James. He began rearing back and shaking all of a sudden. It could happen anytime, and it so worried Ida Mae that she went looking for advice.

"Next time he has a seizure," a neighbor lady told her, "whatever he got on, pull it off."

George had managed to scrape together a pair of shoes and socks and pants for his only son and was still paying on them. On a Sunday after church, when George was out in the field somewhere, little James had a shaking fit. Ida Mae pulled off his shoes and tore off his socks as the neighbor lady told her to do. Off came his little shirt and pants. She made a wood fire and held little James tight as she threw his clothes into the flames.

George got home, and she gave him the good news that she had cured little James. But that's not what stood out in George's mind.

"Whatchu doing burning up his shoes?" George asked her. George didn't have a decent pair himself.

Reason can't explain it, except that maybe little James outgrew whatever afflicted him or maybe it wasn't really seizures in the scientific sense of the word or maybe her belief that she had exorcised the thing actually killed it. In any case, whatever James had, it never came back after she burned his clothes to cinders.

A new year rang in. It was 1937. It looked to be no better than the year before. They were calling it the Depression now. People took to begging and scraping to eat. A man down the road started stealing hogs to sell and eat as his own. He was white and a friend, so to speak, to George. He rounded up somebody's hogs one day and came by George and Ida Mae's to get George to help skin them.

George didn't want to get blamed for somebody else's misdeeds. He could get killed for stealing a white man's hogs. He told the man to do it himself. The man didn't like hearing no. George and the man argued, and the man stormed off.

"I'll be back," he said. "I'm a fix you."

Chickasaw County had a sheriff, but calling him would have never crossed George's mind. No sheriff would take a colored man's side against a white man, no matter who was right. George called out to Ida Mae.

"Ida Mae, you take the kids and go on in the house," he said. "I'm a sit right here till they come back."

He sat on the porch waiting with his shotgun on his knee. He looked out for an open-bed truck trailing dust in the road or a car packed with men looking for trouble. Ida Mae crouched down and tried to still little James and Velma. George waited and waited. But they never came. "The next day or two," Ida Mae said, "him and George back friends again, I reckon, getting the hogs."

People learned to want less and live with whatever they had. The boss men said there was little to nothing to give at settlement time. They told the day pickers they wouldn't be needing them. The cast-off croppers and field hands moved from place to place. They walked to the next farm up the road to see if they could use an extra hand and to the relatives who might make a place for them in their cabin. Mr. Edd kept George and Ida Mae on. They were good workers, Ida Mae's picking notwithstanding, and he was an optimist. But now there were five people in their little sharecropper cabin. Besides them and Velma and James, they had taken in a boarder, so to speak. It was George's sister Indiana. She helped with the picking of crops and the raising of turkeys, and she slept by the door in the front room.

In the spring, when George and Ida Mae planted cotton and prayed for rain, the turkey hen laid her eggs. "She'd set there and set there," Ida Mae said. "Just sit there about three or four weeks. She'd get up, shake herself off, and go get her some water, dust water all over her and do round and all, take a bath, I reckon, what it was. She'd be setting while we planted cotton."

By the time the cotton was in the ground, the chicks poked out of their shells and required Ida Mae's attention. Ida Mae and Addie B. and other women on the Pearson plantation scooped up the chicks and tended them for Mr. Edd. He would be coming back just before Thanksgiving to take half of however many turkeys each woman managed to raise.

Ida Mae pulled off the beak crust that they came into the world with and crushed corn for them to eat because they were too little to eat feed corn. The hawks circled overhead, waiting for her to leave, ready to swoop down and pick off a baby chick and fly back into the air before you knew it.

Ida Mae didn't worry about the hawks. She knew the hens moved in a flock and didn't leave their babies like humans do.

"You know a hen will take up for her chickens more so than people will take up for one another," Ida Mae said. "Whenever a old hawk would come along—you heard talk how a hawk will hover and all the chicks run under her wing—she hugs them and she sticks up for 'em and keep a funny noise, and you knew that hawk was somewhere around."

She trusted God and nature more than any man and learned to be a better person watching the lower creatures of the earth. "The ant see a crumb, he can't carry it himself," Ida Mae said. "Don't you know another ant will come and help him? They better than people."

Addie B. and the other women fretted over their turkeys, worried when they went off and when they took forever coming back because Mr. Edd was going to want his turkeys soon. Ida Mae let her turkeys run free and pick after bugs and ants and twigs in the dirt. They went exploring out in the woods and roosted wherever they pleased. And when they came back, she threw corn at their feet.

The turkeys grew big and plump as September approached, and the land was turning white with cotton.

EUSTIS, FLORIDA, 1939
GEORGE SWANSON STARLING

A FLATBED TRUCK creaked down a highway through rattlesnake scrub and okra growing wild in the field. George Starling should not have been on that truck. He should have been in a college classroom up in Tallahassee. But his father said he'd had enough schooling, and schools nearby did not allow colored students. So Lil George went and got himself a wife out of spite and love, too, and had to feed her now, and so was sitting on a flatbed truck en route to the groves instead of in the library stacks at a college in the state capital.

The truck was on its way between the groves on a chill morning at picking season. It was hauling men to pick fruit for fresh juice and frozen concentrate, for gift boxes of temple oranges and ruby grapefruit, and the perfect balls of citrus stacked high on grocery shelves for people in New York to pick through.

The owners of the groves rode their dogs in the covered front seats safe from the wind. The pickers rode on the flatbed truck with the frost cutting their faces. Twenty or thirty men hunched on the open barge, their legs dangling over the sides of it and a stack of ladders tied loose along the rim.

George sat pinned between the regular pickers, who were missing teeth and taking liberties with the language and knew more about picking than he ever cared to know. They got a kick out of bouncing over potholes, grove to grove, next to the college boy. They looked to be the smart ones now, hadn't had to squint over any textbooks or waste time in somebody's high school. And here they were carrying a bushel sack in the same flatbed truck as Lil George. Back when he was still in school and picking only during semester break, they started calling him "Schoolboy."

"Schoolboy," one of them said, "I don't know whatchu goin' to school fuh. You right out'chere with us. I ain't went so far as the sixth grade, and I can pick more fruit in one hour than you pick all day. You ain't had to go no twelfth grade to learn how to do this."

"Yeah, you right," George said. "But the difference between you and me, is I can leave from out here, and you can't. When the opportunity presents itself, I can leave."

That was easy to say when he was back and forth to Tallahassee, calling himself a freshman and then a sophomore and looking like he could do anything in the world. Now he was picking because he had to, no different from them.

He told himself that this picking situation was a temporary setback and kept himself busy doing whatever came up. Some days, the high school had him substitute for a sick teacher. He had more education than most colored people in town anyway. He sold insurance on the side to the colored people out in the woods. But the groves were all there was most days, and he climbed the flatbed like every other colored citizen who could use the money, which was just about all of them at one time or another.

Fruit was the currency of central Florida. The land was given over to citrus trees, groves of them spanning the low hills from Eustis up to

Ocala and down to Orlando. Tourism hadn't yet bloomed the way it would decades later in central Florida, and Eustis, Ocala, and even Orlando were just places to pass through on the way to Miami. Each year in the late thirties and early forties, some two million tons of oranges and grapefruit were coming out of the state, most of it from the region where George lived.

The people who picked the fruit and the big owners of the groves were often at odds with each other, one side poor, one side landed, one needing more money than the other was willing to give. But they agreed on one thing: they wanted the trees heavy with oranges and the people of the North flush and hungry because then there would be work enough for everyone.

So they pampered the trees like infants. When a hard freeze afflicted the groves, the people burned logs and rubber tires and lit the oil heaters to keep the orange trees warm. They prayed for a miracle like the one at a grove they called Ole Natural. A big freeze had settled in back in 1895, and most of the other groves looked as if they had been set on fire after it left. But Ole Natural survived the big freeze, and its orange trees came back on their own.

Lake County held a high place in the Citrus Belt and once was the orange capital of the world. But Lil George never took it that seriously and never got but so good at picking. He could never claim to have picked the most bushels in the least amount of time. It was piecework, and the winners of the race were not necessarily the quickest minds but the fastest hands. George had a quick mind.

In the late fall, a crowd gathered before the sun came up, when the fog hung close to the earth. The people stood watching at the corner of Bates and Palmetto and in front of the pool hall over in East town, near Egypt. They waited in the wet dark for the flatbed truck to roll up. The foreman climbed down and picked out the best pickers for his crew. The foremen were the middlemen between the packinghouses and the pickers, and both sides might have cause to distrust them now and then. They chose the pickers and oversaw the picking and each had their own way of supervising. It might be Oscar Lipscomb or Uncle John Fashaw or a man they called Mr. Pat choosing his pickers for the season.

George hoped to get on the Blye brothers' crew. They were ten years older than he was. They knew their way around the juke joints and the raccoon woods around Eustis. One of them was named Arnette, but they called him Whisper because he had got his throat cut and could speak no louder than that.

The other brother, Reuben, towered over the tallest of men. He had a stone face, a long series of wives, and had seen just about everything. When he was a little boy, an uncle told him to come help him with an errand. The two of them rode out into the woods and came to a stop at a tree. A colored man was hanging dead from a limb. The uncle needed Reuben's help cutting the rope and getting the limp, lynched body down. Reuben was ten years old. He would never forget that.

When Reuben got big, he fled to New York, worked at a tombstone factory in Brooklyn, on the 9W highway through Kingston up into Albany. He worked crushing tomatoes at a ketchup factory and had seen so many of the unmentionable things that got mangled into the ketchup that he never ate ketchup again. Now he was back in Eustis working as a foreman in the groves. He looked straight at you and through you and had a way of making women forget their husbands when they saw him.

It was a buyer's market in the picking world. There were always plenty more people who wanted to pick than there was room or need for in the groves. The lucky ones loaded onto the truck, their legs dangling from the rim of the flatbed.

At the grove, they each picked a number out of a hat and went to the row with that number. They got paid by how many boxes of fruit they picked by sunset and had to keep up with little tickets to prove what they had picked. If the row was thick with fruit, it would be a good day. They could stand at the underskirt and fill a two-bushel box. If it was sparse, they had to climb into two or three trees to get that much.

It tempted good people to try to outtrick one another. You looked for a way out. You learned to watch everybody and the rows coming up. The rule was that when you finished yours, you moved in order to the next row available. If it was a dud row like the one you were working, you did your best to avoid it.

"If that next row is a bad row," George said, "and you on a bad row, and here's somebody else by you on a bad row, you lag back, you keep watching them. You let them get through first, ahead of you, so they can get that bad row. Then you hurry up and get through."

If the next one up was thick with fruit and "you on a bad row, you run through it," George said. "But you be sure they done moved over before you leave your row. You get cagey. It's little tricks in all this."

Some men could pick a hundred boxes a day. They called them high rollers. George never managed more than sixty-five or seventy. He never cared enough about it to get proficient.

They set the ladders in the tree, ladders sixteen and twenty feet high, sometimes spliced like extension cords and leaning forty feet up, a full four stories, along the spine of the tree. They had to set them so the ladder wouldn't kick when they reached the top and wouldn't split the tree in two, which was liable to happen with a ladder set in the fork of a young bud. They learned to plant their ladders deep in the soil.

The trees were wet from the rain, and George and the pickers had to balance themselves on the slick limbs of the old seedlings. They disappeared into the branches with a bushel sack on their shoulders and a clipper in their hand and only came down when the sack was full and their shoulders ached and they were sick from the sight of fruit. Tangerines, tangelos, temple oranges, navel oranges, Valencia oranges, seeded grapefruit, seedless grapefruit, red navels, ruby reds, lemons, and kumquats. If he had to pick, which he did, George would rather pick grapefruit because they filled a box quicker. But the packinghouses knew that, too. So they paid less for grapefruit than just about anything else.

Up and down the ladders they went, working top to bottom, snipping fruit and filling boxes. Sometimes they heard a voice cry out way down the grove; a picker had come across a wasp nest and pulled at it instead of an orange. Every now and then, they heard a thud and then a cry. A limb had snapped. Somebody fell out of a tree, broke an arm or leg or neck.

George climbed the high limbs of four or five grown seedlings one morning and was climbing deep into the next. The foreman that day was an old colored man named Deacon John Fashaw. They called him Uncle John. George knew him from Gethsemane Baptist Church. The deacon oversaw the harvest of some of the groves at the Eichelberger Packing Company. He called George out of the tree in the middle of the grove.

"Number fourteen!" he yelled.

Deacon Fashaw presided over his pickers with a suckle from an orange tree. It looked like a switch a mother whipped her children with. He called George over to him with the suckle in his hand.

"Now, number fourteen," the deacon said, looking up into the limbs at George.

"Yes, sir."

"Come down here. Bring ya ladder."

"Dog, what Uncle John want?" George said under his breath and then, out loud, "I'll be there, Uncle John."

If he didn't move fast, next thing he'd know, Deacon Fashaw would be there shaking his ladder from under the tree.

"Come down, young man. Come down."

George climbed down, and Deacon Fashaw swooshed the switch at him. Anybody else, and George would have had him on the ground. But it was Deacon Fashaw, and the men respected his position too much to fight him.

"Now, you bring your ladder back here. I told you to bring your ladder back here."

George ran back to get the ladder and followed Deacon Fashaw back to the first tree he had picked.

"Now, you see that orange up there in the top of the tree?"

"Yeah, Uncle John."

"Well, you know they want that orange in New York, and you done left it up there in that tree. And I don't like it. And Mr. Eichelberger don't like it. Mr. Eichelberger don't like it, and I ain't gon' have it. Now, you put that ladder back in that tree, and you go right on up there and pick that orange right now."

Deacon Fashaw stood and watched George position his ladder and climb into the tree for that one orange as the other pickers peered through the branches. It was all part of Uncle John's plan. "He let you get four or five trees away so you have to drag that back," George said. "You probably done lost five or six boxes while you doing that. You do that two or three times, you soon get the message that 'I'm gonna be sure I clean my tree before I leave it.' I mean clean it."

They moved from grove to grove in a single day. The flatbed truck rumbled down a highway past the bean fields and the turpentine stills. Midday, they finished one grove and were moving to the next. The truck reached an intersection and swung a hard left. The ladders broke from their lashes and shifted under the men. The loose ladders pushed the men off the open bed of the truck and onto the rough surface of the highway as if they had been shot from a gun.

George felt himself thrown to the gravel. His heels nearly hit his back, and he tried to break the fall with his elbow and knee. Half the workers were on the ground. Some had fallen onto their heads and were lying unconscious. A man named Nathan Bailey was never able to work again. He got two hundred dollars for his injuries after the men petitioned the packing company for help. George got twelve dollars and forty-eight cents for his swollen knee and elbow, which he would remember for as long as he lived; they sent him two payments of six dollars and twenty-four cents each.

Most of the men took it and were grateful. George wasn't. The work was hard, and now it was dangerous. "You not getting anything to begin with, you know, at the best," he said.

George had some schooling, and the old men who teased him for it put their pride in their sack when they thought the packinghouse was cheating them.

"Schoolboy, look a here," a man said. "Tell me how much I got for my work. Here my envelope."

George took it and looked at it and turned to the man. "How many boxes of oranges did you pick?" George asked. "How many boxes of tangerines did you pick? How many boxes of grapefruit?"

The man told him what he thought he had picked, and George did the math.

"No, you three dollars short. They done cheated you out of three dollars somewhere 'cause if you picked the number of boxes you say you picked, you didn't get paid for all of it."

Two or three days' pay had disappeared. It was hard to keep up. Each kind of fruit paid a different rate—four cents a box for grapefruit one day, ten cents a box for tangerines the next, six cents a box for oranges. If they didn't know how much they picked of each kind of fruit or lost the little ticket that said what they had picked or if the foreman added the numbers on the ticket wrong, whether on purpose or by accident, the pickers didn't get what little they were due.

"Sometimes they would tell you that they paying one thing and when you get your pay, you got less," George said. "And if you couldn't figure, you didn't know the difference. They were very good at that. They promise you four cents for a box of grapefruit, and you get two cents."

The pickers took whatever they got. Some asked about the difference but didn't dare press it. Some wrote it off, blamed themselves, said they must have been the ones who'd lost their ticket. There was no point in protesting. There wasn't enough work as it was. It was the Depression. And for every man waiting at the corner of Bates and Palmetto in the black wet morning at picking time, hoping to board a truck to the groves, there were ten more out there hoping he would miss it.

MONROE, LOUISIANA, 1935
ROBERT JOSEPH PERSHING FOSTER

PERSHING WAS SIXTEEN and making his first trip out of Monroe on his own on a bus ticket his brother Madison had given him for graduation. Pershing had just finished the eleventh grade, which was as far as you could go if you were colored in Louisiana, and he was beside himself with anticipation.

The sign on the front of the bus said ST. LOUIS and Pershing climbed on board with his suitcase in his hand and his back propped straight as if he were stepping onto the *Queen Mary* and going to France. He dusted the folds of his tweed suit and headed down the central aisle of the bus in search of a seat. The bus was not going to take him to the Big North of southern dreams but to a modest city in a border state where his brother was serving out his medical residency, and well enough out of the South.

He scanned the aisle to find a place for himself. His eye caught the wooden shingle with the metal prongs on the bottom, the shingle that said COLORED on one side and WHITE on the other. It was set into holes at the top of a seat back toward the latter half of the bus. He didn't like seeing it, but he knew to expect it. He took a seat behind the wooden shingle and looked out the window at the view.

Those white and colored shingles were as much a part of the southern landscape as cotton growing in the field. Each state and city had a different requirement or custom to signal how the races were to be separated and to what extent the races were to be divided. In North Carolina, white and colored passengers could not occupy "contiguous seats on the same bench." Virginia prohibited the two races from sitting side by side on the same bench unless all other seats were filled. Several states required that the placard saying WHITE OR COLORED be "in plain letters, not less than two inches high." In Houston, the race to which the seat belonged was posted on the back of the seat. In Georgia, the penalty for willfully riding in the wrong seat was a fine of a thousand dollars or six months in prison. Colored passengers were assigned to the front of the railcar on the train but to the rear of other conveyances to, in the words of the mayor of Birmingham, do "away with the disagreeable odors that would necessarily follow the breezes."

The bus headed north along the Mississippi River into Arkansas, picking up more people at stops along the way. The seats began to fill. More white passengers than colored seemed to be boarding. They had taken up some of the seats in the very front and were spreading further back. Now, each time new white people got on, they picked up the wooden shingle and inserted it in the seat back where Pershing was sitting. It seemed only the white people could touch the shingle and set the musical chairs in motion.

"Go 'head, boy. Move on back," the driver told him.

Pershing rustled himself up from the seat he was in. Gathered his things. Looked for an empty space behind him. Moved back a row. Sometimes the new passenger took up a whole row by himself, forcing Pershing back just so the newcomer wouldn't have to sit next to anyone else.

At every stop, they had to move again until the colored passengers were now crowded into a few seats in the back and Pershing found himself in the very last row.

It was early summer, and road dust flew into the windows and rushed to the back seat, where Pershing in his brand-new tweed suit was pressed among the other colored passengers.

The dust coated the tweed and his skin and his hair, and Pershing found it unbearable, packed as he was like livestock.

"I was dressed as good as I could be," Pershing said years later. "And I felt very down that I had to submit to this."

He looked around him at the other colored passengers to his left and to his right, grown people, beaten down, hunched in their seats. They dropped their eyes, and he dropped his.

"Some have endured, and that's all they've known," Pershing said. "They don't expect anything better, and nobody's demanding anything better. You wouldn't have survived if you had done too much demanding anyway."

It was a long ride, there was no toilet on the bus, and the back seats took every bump on the road. Before Pershing could make it to St. Louis, he passed his urine and sat in his soaked tweed pants and felt lower than he had in his entire short life.

St. Louis was a blur. Madison carted Pershing all over St. Louis, took him into Homer G. Phillips Hospital, where Madison was a resident and where the nurses fawned over the cute little brother with the thick eyelashes and waves in his hair. Madison reminded him it was time to get ready for college. For a while, when he was thirteen or fourteen, Pershing actually thought he didn't have to go. He told his mother that one day.

"Mama, I'm gonna stop school."

He didn't realize how impossible that was, his father being principal and all.

Ottie indulged him.

"Baby, why are you gonna stop school?"

"I want some of the things the other boys got."

"Like what?"

"Like clothes."

"Well, what do you want?"

Pershing couldn't think of much in particular that he didn't already have.

"I want a suit. I want a pair of shoes."

"Now, I tell you what you do," his mother said. "You save your little money you get from the milk. Now, get you a little job after school or in the summer, and you work and save your money. And when you got half of whatever it cost, I'll give you the other half."

Pershing listened.

"And you don't pay down on anything," she told him. "You can keep your money as well as that white man can."

The nearest college was right in Monroe, across the railroad tracks from where they lived. Northeast Louisiana College had a brand-new campus with reasonable fees, built with taxpayer money, to which his parents' meager salaries contributed. Students who looked like Pershing weren't permitted there. So the family debated where Pershing would go.

His mother wanted him at Morehouse, the most prestigious college in the country for colored men. It was in Atlanta, which might as well have been Paris, and she wanted the biggest she could get for her baby. All these years she had saved up her teaching money, kept it in a chifforobe with a key, which the children knew not to touch. It would be their future. The last time she opened the chifforobe, it was to send Leland to Morehouse. It was expensive, and he had not fared well. Professor Foster blamed the school, but anyone who knew Leland knew the trouble was with Leland, whom the women called Woo and who was brilliant, beloved, and weak to life's temptations. They had wasted their precious, second-class, colored teacher's wages on Leland at Morehouse. Now Ottie was trying to send Pershing there, and Pershing wanted to go.

"No, you don't go to Morehouse," Professor Foster said.

"You'll go to Morehouse," his mother said.

So it was settled. He would go to Morehouse. But the family had to save up the extra money it would take. Pershing would have to spend two years at the lesser-known alma mater of his parents, Leland College, before living out his mother's dream.

The summer after his freshman year at Leland, he needed a job. He heard the furniture store downtown needed janitors. He dressed and went down and got in line with all the other colored boys wanting to work.

The white foreman called him to the front when it was his turn for an interview.

"Boy, do you go to school?" the foreman asked.

"Yes, sir, I do," he said. "I just completed my first year at Leland College."

"Boy, if you go to college, you don't need a job as a janitor."

Few people, white or black, in Ouachita County had the chance to go to college. Resentments ran deep, especially when it came to a colored boy getting to go when some southerners were still debating whether colored people were worth educating at all. Too many educated colored people, and it would upset the whole balance of power in the caste system and give other colored people ideas.

The man turned to some other boys in line, who weren't in school and didn't need tuition, and hired them. Pershing had a long memory, and he would nurse that wound for years. Here he was trying to make something of himself, and the invisible hand was punishing the ambitious, and rewarding the servile to keep colored people in their place.

Later in the summer, he went looking for work at the sawmill.

He saw a classmate there from high school and was told the work wasn't too hard. It was stacking wood staves to make barrels. Pershing asked the foreman for a job. There was nothing available, he was told. He was getting desperate. He spotted his friend stacking staves.

"Show me how to do this."

The friend showed him what to do, and Pershing worked beside him. He looked up and saw the foreman watching him. Pershing pretended not to see him, worked even harder. The foreman left, and, when he came back, Pershing was still at work. At the end of the day, the foreman hired him. Pershing finished out the summer stacking staves, not minding the hard work and not finding it demeaning.

"Sometimes," he said, "you have to stoop to conquer."

Morehouse was a heavenly place. Colored boys racing straight-backed and self-important in their sweater vests, hair brushed back with a hint of a center part. Arriving at chapel to sit with their respective fraternities and daring not take the wrong row. There was a sister school, Spelman, the women sealed off in their cloistered dormitories and emerging in fitted dresses and gloves to be paired with Morehouse men, who were the only men worthy of them. There was the graduate school, Atlanta University, where the brightest of both schools were expected to go to take their master's and doctorates. It was all too perfect for words.

Whatever future there was for colored America, they believed themselves to be it, and they carried themselves accordingly. Then there was Atlanta. Too many colored doctors and lawyers and businessmen to count, living in brick houses set back from the road and with staircases inside, driving fancy cars and not apologizing for it.

"I saw blacks living like people ought to live," Pershing would say years later.

Atlanta was big enough to get lost in. Enough colored people to be anonymous. The colored people drew a fence around themselves and manufactured a world so grand they told themselves they didn't want whatever Jim Crow was keeping from them.

Pershing was at peace. It was the fall of 1937.

After the first homecoming game, Pershing and a science classmate by the name of Morris Williams took two girls out dancing. They both chipped in the money they needed and bought sloe gin for the four of them and whiled away the night.

They took the girls home and were walking back to the dormitory. As they crossed the intersection of Fair and Ashby, Pershing slowed down to a stop in the middle of the street. He was wobbling from the gin. He stood and looked around. He was in Atlanta in the middle of the night, far from the stooping and yessums of Monroe. He was surrounded by a whole campus of somebodies like him and doing whatever he pleased.

He stood in the street, half drunk and half dreaming. Cars slowed and honked, and he paid them no mind.

"Boy, come on," his friend said. "Get out the street. That car's gon' hit you, you drunk fool."

"Yes, I'm drunk," Pershing said. "I ain't in Monroe, don't nobody know me, and I don't give a damn.

"I'm free," he said.

Pershing did not know precisely where he would end up or how. But he knew at that moment that he would never live in another country Jim Crow town again. He would do whatever it took to get as far away as he could.

"That bug got in me," Pershing would later say. "I wanted, I wanted to get out."

Shadows still hung over him. His big brother Leland was rarely in class but was a four-letter man at Morehouse and a star pitcher on the baseball team. The Spelman women called out his name on the yard. And then there was Madison, his oldest brother. Madison still hung over him from afar. Madison was a doctor. Madison sang. Madison dressed. The women loved Madison.

"So you hit school," Pershing would remember years later, "and 'That's Foster's brother. That's Foster's brother.' It's hard to be the little one. You fightin' for identity. And everybody discussing everything you did. And when it was bad, they blew it up."

Pershing threw himself into the one thing that brought him the most attention. He had a voice as rich as an organ, so he joined the school choir. He started singing solo at the Christmas concert at Sisters Chapel at Spelman and made a name for himself. In time, people didn't ask about Leland and baseball as much anymore or about his brother the doctor.

In his senior year, sometime in 1939, Pershing arrived for choir practice one day when the head of the music department, a man by the name of Harold Stotford, called him over. They stood in the rehearsal room as students gathered to practice.

"Foster, wait here a minute," Professor Stotford said. "I want you to meet this young lady."

A young woman of modest dress and perfect manners stepped forward. She was a gifted pianist and a newer member of the choir. She was the color of the buttermilk he used to make with his mother and had brown hair brushing her shoulder. She looked out from wire-rimmed glasses that were an accurate barometer of how studious she was.

Pershing recognized her instantly. She could have been a celebrity on campus had she not had the breeding and sweet nature not to make a fuss of her position. She was the beloved only daughter of the president of Atlanta University, the campus's graduate school, and was well known to anyone with the least awareness of social standing.

Her name was Alice Clement.

She was a sophomore at Spelman. Her family lived in a mansion high on a hill on university grounds. It was redbrick with black shutters. The estate was called Hickory Hill and looked like Mount Vernon. Her father, President Rufus Clement, had a car and driver. Her cotillions and bridge parties were chronicled in the society pages of the *Atlanta Daily World,* the colored newspaper in town. She was bookish and would not likely have been made Miss Spelman had she even cared to run, but she would know how to throw a dinner party for twelve. She was the embodiment of most everything an ambitious colored man of the day was trained to want.

"This is the daughter of President Clement," Professor Stotford said, "who happens to be that gentleman there. President of Atlanta University. I want you to meet Alice Clement."

"How do you do?" Pershing said. He made a mental note to himself to make the most of his good fortune.

At the next choir rehearsal, he made it his business to start a conversation with her in the hope that something might come of it. She finally asked him to take her to a party. He was all too happy to oblige.

He put on his wittiest, most charming self, and soon the boy from Monroe, Louisiana, was courting the quiet and self-contained daughter of a university president. Pershing escorted her to parties, took her to dances with a foursome. He was spending more time up at Hickory Hill and gaining automatic admission to the world of the most influential colored people in all of Atlanta.

Pershing Foster was not what Rufus Early Clement would have had in mind for his only daughter. Clement had risen from a bellhop and delivery boy in Kentucky to become the head of one of the most elite colored universities in the country and its longest-serving president. He was a square-jawed, politically astute academic who rarely smiled and wore a look of professorial detachment at both the lectern and the many social engagements that demanded his attendance. He met regularly with the likes of Eleanor Roosevelt and Paul Robeson in his capacity not only as a university president but as a leading figure among the colored bourgeoisie in the South.

Clement gained a reputation as a cautious and incurious steward whom history will record as the man who ousted W. E. B. Du Bois, the leading black intellectual of his time, from a professorship at Atlanta University after years of clashing egos and temperaments.

W. E. B. Du Bois arrived at Atlanta University, already in his seventies and with plans for an ambitious study on race relations, at around the same time that Clement was confronted with this new boy interested in his only daughter. Clement would be at odds with Du Bois almost from the start, perhaps threatened by the long shadow of his celebrity or put off by the elder man's impertinent disregard for Clement, who was thirty years younger than Du Bois. But it was just as likely a contest between the accommodating pragmatism of the southern-born Clement and the impatient radicalism of the northern-bred Du Bois. The two men were the very embodiment of the North-South divide among black intellectuals.

In any case, Clement blocked Du Bois's every move, even standing in the way of a thousand-dollar grant Du Bois was pursuing, according to Du Bois's biographer David Levering Lewis. Du Bois suspected Clement of sabotaging him and said he "regretted the necessity of having to work with a president who seemed incapable of appreciating the great opportunity facing the university." For his part, Clement complained that Du Bois "had become extremely difficult" and that he believed Du Bois's age was impairing him. In 1943, Clement found a way to get rid of Du Bois altogether by invoking, with the support of the board of trustees he had lobbied, an arbitrary loophole requiring compulsory retirement at sixty-five. He informed Du Bois that he would be retired when his contract ended at the close of the school year.

"The result of this action was disastrous," Du Bois wrote in his autobiography. "Not only was a great plan of scientific work killed at birth, but my own life was thrown into confusion." Du Bois "fought back in despair" against his termination, Lewis wrote. Students from Morehouse, Spelman, Clark, and Atlanta University rose up in support of Du Bois in a scornful letter to President Clement: "Our regret," they wrote, "is that we did not have more courses under him, and the students who follow us will not have the opportunity which we have had in absorbing his rich experience and inspiration."

Du Bois was beside himself. "There was no earthly reason why this wish of mine should not have been granted and applauded," he said.

His northern friends thought they knew what the trouble was. "He's buried himself in the South too long," Arthur Spingarn, the NAACP president, concluded, "protecting ideas nobody but he understands, and raising hope for change which may be comprehended in a hundred years."

Du Bois returned north, to New York, where he took a position as director of special research at the NAACP, the organization he had cofounded thirty-four years before, and moved into an apartment on Sugar Hill in Harlem.

For his part, Rufus Clement had proven that, even if out of his own insecurities and desire for control, he could be a cunning and formidable adversary. He had prevailed in the short run, regardless of the consequences or of which side of history he would ultimately fall on.

As for this new young man at his doorstep wanting to court his only daughter, Clement was still sizing him up. Pershing was respectful and well mannered, as Dr. Clement would have expected of any Morehouse man. He was a math major—smart, clearly. But on the face of it, Pershing was just another student who had worked waiting tables at the cafeteria and who was just now making a name for himself as a soloist in the choir. He had come from some country town out in Louisiana. Someone said his parents taught school or something. Dr. Clement had never heard of the Fosters, nor had he any reason to recognize Monroe.

No young man with the courage to come courting his daughter would have had an easy time of it. Worse still, this was not looking like a move up in Dr. Clement's estimation, so he looked judgingly through his spectacles.

But Pershing told of the great plans he had for himself. He talked about pursuing his doctorate in biology at Atlanta University. Or maybe going to a graduate school up north, like the University of Michigan or the University of Chicago. Pershing figured that southern elites always loved those northern status symbols even if they didn't care to live there themselves. Maybe he would get a scholarship to go. Then he would apply for a fellowship in New York, maybe. His brother was a doctor, internal medicine, and he was considering that, too, by the way.

Pershing was talking the president's language, the vocabulary of upward mobility. He had potential. He was ambitious, if nothing else. And Alice—quiet, demure Alice—had taken to him. He had a street wit about him that made her laugh. He was the life of the party she never was, and she seemed content to bask in his light.

Pershing graduated Morehouse with a major in math and a minor in biology in the spring of 1939 and sang solo at commencement. He took up graduate studies at Atlanta University while Alice completed her time at Spelman. He was moving into a world where great things were expected of him. Dr. Clement looked for him to make good on his promise to become someone worthy of his daughter. Madison wanted his baby brother to follow in his footsteps. His mother, too, wanted a second doctor in the family and knew her youngest had it in him. So he applied to Meharry Medical College in Nashville and was accepted. His mother sent him the registration fee.

"I sat awake all night," he said. "Do I want to go? Or don't I want to go?"

If he could have done anything in the world at that moment, he would have dropped it all and gone up north to New York or out west to California. He'd always had a thing for California. He would go into show business, maybe, and sing and perform onstage. The audiences would love him, and he would be who and where he was meant to be. But he kept his dreams to himself and did what was expected of him. He sent in the registration fee and would start medical school in the South, in the state of Tennessee, a place far from his dreams, in the fall.

A Thin Light Far Away

In the winter of 1919, when Ida Mae was trailing her father out to the field, George and Pershing were learning to crawl, and the first wave of migrants was stirring to life, an astronomer made a startling discovery. The astronomer, named Edwin Hubble, working out of the University of Chicago, looked through one of the most powerful telescopes of his time.

What he saw would eventually become the most significant astronomical find of the century and would come to parallel the awakening of an isolated people in his own country. It would confirm what for generations had been whispered of but dismissed as impossible. It occurred near the start of a long pilgrimage of Americans seeking to escape their own harsh, known world.

Hubble identified a star that was far, far away and was not the same sun that fed life on Earth.

It was another sun.

And it would prove for the first time in human history that there were galaxies other than our own, that the universe was much bigger than humans had ever imagined, that there were, in fact, other suns.

The Awakening

You sleep over a volcano,
which may erupt at any moment.

—Laura Arnold, describing the South in a debate on the merits of migration, two weeks before she herself left North Carolina for Washington, D.C.

I am in the darkness
of the south
and I am trying
my best to get out.
O please help me
to get out of
this low down county
I am counted no more thin a dog
help me please help me.

—an unidentified letter writer from Birmingham, Alabama

CHICKASAW COUNTY, MISSISSIPPI, LATE SEPTEMBER–EARLY OCTOBER 1937

ADDIE B., who lived down the road on the same plantation as Ida Mae, rose early to feed the turkeys at her cabin across the field. Addie B. always fretted about her turkeys. She looked all over and called out to them. But there was no clucking or nipping or kicking of dust. The yard was barren. The turkeys were gone. Mr. Edd, the boss man over all of them, would be coming for his turkeys soon, to sell in time for Thanksgiving. There would be no explaining the disappearance to Mr. Edd. The economics were simple. The turkeys were money when money was the one thing nobody had. The punishment—she did not want to think about the punishment. Besides, she had an idea of what happened to her inventory. She decided to tell Mr. Edd her suspicions before he could ask. Mr. Edd rounded up some men.

Later that night, around nine or ten o'clock, the pounding started on Ida Mae's door. It was like the sound of wild dogs trailing raw meat. It seemed far away at first, and then it drew closer, mad fists beating the bare face of the cabin. The cabin was dark, and Ida Mae was asleep. She was alone in the house with little Velma and James and her sister-in-law Indiana, who was meek and of little help. Her husband was not yet back from his errands in town. She threw back the coverlet and fingered the sides of the walls to get to the front door. She stumbled past the two little ones, who were, by some miracle, still asleep, stepped around the hearth and between the two beds on each side of the door. Indiana, in the bed closest to the ruckus, got up to follow her and stood behind her and watched.

Ida Mae cracked open the door and saw the men, four or five of them with chains and shotguns. She recognized the boss man, Mr. Edd. And she recognized his friend Mr. Willie Jim, another planter, but could not make out the faces of the others standing before her in the middle of the night.

She tried to dispense with them, told them her husband wasn't in and she didn't know when he would be back. That wasn't why they were there. Willie Jim stepped forward to speak for them all. They wanted to know if Joe Lee was in her house.

Joe Lee was her husband's cousin, who lived further down the road and would have had no business there that time of night, which is what she told them. He worked the land like the rest of them and, though well into his twenties, still lived on his father's farm. He had a reputation for taking things that weren't his. She said she hadn't seen him.

"Joe Lee is in there. And we want him outta there."

"What'd he do?"

"That's alright, we want him outta there."

They had searched the other sharecropper cabins. Somebody said they saw Joe Lee escape to her house. Willie Jim was getting agitated, thought she was ornery, disputing them like she was, and raised up his chain and drew it back to hurl at her. Mr. Edd stepped forward and told him not to. He liked George and Ida Mae, and he needed that cotton out of the field.

"Don't you hit her," Mr. Edd said.

"That's alright. Let 'em hit me," Ida said, stiffening herself.

"No, he ain't gon' hit you now," he told her.

Willie Jim stepped back, reminded of what they had come for. The men fanned out, their heavy boots clomping the old wood boards on the porch. They surrounded the house and ran toward the back door of the kitchen, the cabin's only other way out, and caught Joe Lee trying to get away. He had fled into the house as Ida Mae slept. He had darted past Indiana as she lay in bed in the front room. But Indiana was too afraid to tell anybody.

"Why ain't you tell me you saw Joe Lee come through here?" Ida Mae asked her afterward. Then she thought about it and realized that if they had caught her in a lie, it would have been worse. And so the two of them concluded it was best that Indiana knew but didn't tell and that Ida Mae didn't know and didn't lie.

Ida Mae couldn't go back to sleep, and she couldn't wait for her husband to get back home. Finally, she heard a motor rumbling outside. She ran out to get him.

"Get out. I got something to tell you."

"What is it?"

"They come and got Joe Lee out the house."

"Who?"

"Your boss."

"I know Mr. Edd ain't did that."

"They caught him trying to step out the back door."

They stood absorbing what it meant and not knowing why it happened.

"What way they went with him?" George asked.

A part of him wanted to go and set things straight, try to talk some sense into his boss man. Ida Mae didn't want him to go. No good could come of it. She didn't see which way they went anyway, black as it was. And they had been gone a good while.

EUSTIS, FLORIDA, DECEMBER 1941
GEORGE SWANSON STARLING

ON THE OTHER SIDE OF THE EARTH, at a harbor in Hawaii, a bomb exploded. It was at a naval base. Pearl Harbor. People heard it on the radio, not knowing what it meant.

The United States was joining the war over in Europe. George Starling got notice to report for an army physical. But the doctor looked him over and disqualified him on account of what the doctor said was a weak heart. George was scared he would die at any minute. But the minutes turned into weeks and then months, and he figured either the doctor didn't know what he was talking about or his heart had recovered.

In the spring, there would be no work after the fruit was picked from the trees. George was hearing talk of war jobs up in a place called Detroit. The factories that made cars were rolling out planes and weapons twenty-four hours a day. He did not particularly want to go to Detroit. He didn't have people there, nor did he know much about it. But they were paying a ridiculous sum of money—dollars an hour instead of pennies a box. He could make enough in a couple of months to last him a year. He heard they were so desperate you could get a job right off the bus. He floated the idea to his wife.

Inez didn't want him to go. For most of their marriage, they had been living with Big George at his house on Bates Avenue. She spent her days sweeping up after the white family she had inherited from her mother and aunt and from her grandmother before them. She was scrubbing toilets when what she really wanted to do, she told George, was to go to beauty school in Tampa, the Angelo Beauty College, it was called, and learn how to fix hair.

She hardly ever saw George as it was. When he wasn't out picking fruit, he was out in the backwoods selling insurance. Lately, he had taken to ferrying people around in his old car as if he were a cab driver. There were no taxis for colored people, so he took people to town for groceries or picked them up after the show to make a little extra money. Friday nights, all day Saturday, and into Sunday evening, George was gone, carrying other people to the things he and Inez could be doing together.

He called himself saving for the future. He had it all planned out. He would save enough money to put her through beauty school. Then she would start working and help him finish college in Tallahassee. That would be their freedom.

So he gave his weekends to his passengers. Sometimes they just showed up at his house for him to take them somewhere. Inez was stirring the grits for breakfast when Lil George came into the kitchen one morning.

"Well, I'm a run this guy downtown to do his shopping," George said. "I'll be back by the time you get breakfast ready."

He took the man downtown and dropped him off with his groceries. On his way home, somebody else flagged him down.

"Hey, Lil George, whatchu doin'?"

"I'm not doing anything."

"How 'bout running me downtown?"

He would start his morning with the best of intentions and not get back until dark. "But all the while I'm away from home, I'm working," George said.

He knew he would be in for a fight as soon as he stepped in the door. "My wife would be swole up big as this room by then 'cause I'm gone all day."

George figured as much and tried to soften her up.

"I know you thought I wasn't never coming back," he said.

She grunted, fuming still.

He told her what had happened and how people had flagged him down in the street and had no way to get their groceries and how one thing had led to another and you know there was no way to reach you because there weren't any phones to call from and, anyway, look at what I got.

Fifty cents on this trip, a dollar on that one, and at the end of the day, George pulled in five, ten, twenty, sometimes thirty dollars in change.

"See how much money I made while I was out. I made all of this."

He dumped it all on the bed, quarters, halves, and paper money. Inez was too mad to look at it.

"Well, all of this goes toward your going to school. That's what I'm scuffling for. So you can go to school."

She kept quiet. So he went on.

"I'm a let you save it now," he said. " 'Cause you know I was sincere. You put it in the trunk so you know where it is. So when you get enough to go you can go."

But she wouldn't get over all those lost weekends so easily. If he took her wants for granted, she would do the same for his. She stood there as if she hadn't heard him. So George went and put the money away himself. Soon he had Mason jars full of quarters and halves, fruit jars filled with nickels and change rattling in tin cans, the start of a future in bottles all over the house.

It was the start of 1943. When the picking season was over and it was nearing spring, everybody's money went dry. The people needing rides trailed off. George saw it coming and started talking again about going to Detroit for the summer to make enough for them to go to school. He made a note to himself: 1943 was the year for Inez to go to beauty school.

"When it gets a little bit warmer, when the fruit season is over," he told her, "I'm going to Detroit to work. Then I could send you to school. It's nothing to do around here during the summer. Ain't no working. I can't even make no money hustling. So I'm going out to Detroit and work and send you to school."

George had it all worked out. Inez just listened. The neighbors had been telling her to watch after her husband. He wasn't going to Detroit to work, they said, he was going to be with some woman, probably one of those schoolteachers he went to school with up in Tallahassee. *Heard one of them was up in D.C. Bet he's going up there to be with her. He's not going to Detroit.*

Inez was quiet. So he repeated himself.

"This year, you going to Tampa. I want you to go to school."

"I don't want to go to no school. I changed my mind. I want to go to Detroit with you."

"What you talking 'bout? You been preaching about Angelo Beauty School, now you want to go to Detroit? You go on to beauty school, where you wanted to go. You can always see the world. You can't always go to school. You're not going to Detroit with me. That's it."

The neighbors would surely talk now. Some came up to George himself. "Why you not letting your wife go with you? They say you not going to Detroit. You going to D.C."

He paid them no mind and caught a bus up to Detroit with his friends Sam Gaskin and Charlie Bollar, whom they called Mud.

The day he left, Inez was too mad and too hurt to say good-bye.

She headed to work. "I hope you all take care of yourselves" was all she could manage.

They made B-29 cargo planes at a plant in Hamtramck. George arrived in the late spring of 1943, and they put him to work on a jig making frame covers for the hatch doors and rudders of the cargo planes. They applied chemicals to the covers to make them strong but light. The chemicals were so flammable that anyone caught with a cigarette in his pocket was fired on the spot.

George set about learning the job and adjusting to a gray concrete city he wasn't particular about when a cousin of his wife's showed up unannounced. That was the point. Inez had sent him to see if George was really there and not with some other woman. The cousin reported back that George was doing what he said he was, and only then could Inez feel halfway good about going on to Tampa to take a short course in beauty culture.

George worked nights drilling holes around hatch door frames to attach the covers with screws. He had to bend or lie flat or get on his knees and twist himself to drill the holes straight.

The place was swimming with Communist sympathizers and alleged saboteurs, or so people said, in the hothouse of wartime. Because spies were believed to be inside the plants themselves, any missing or wrongly placed screws were enough to draw suspicion and reprisals in an already cheerless endeavor.

"This made it a nervous, nerve-racking situation," George would say years later. "You know, you drilling all kind of ways and you trying at your very best, and every now and then, you gonna get a hole angle, it's not gonna be right. But if you got too many of them, then you were in trouble."

And every minute, George was scared the whole place would blow up from all the chemicals and paranoia.

Then on the humid night of Sunday, June 20, 1943, a fight broke out between several hundred white and colored men on Belle Isle, a park extending into the Detroit River on the east side of town. The fighting spread north, south, and west as rumors circulated among blacks that white men had killed a colored woman and thrown her baby into the Detroit River and, among whites, that colored men had raped and killed a white woman in the park.

Neither rumor turned out to be true, but it was all that was needed to set off one of the worst riots ever seen in the United States, an outbreak that would mark a turning point in American race relations. Until the 1943 uprising in Detroit, most riots in the United States, from the 1863 Draft Riots in New York to the riots in Tulsa in 1921, to Atlanta in 1906 to Washington, D.C., to Chicago, Springfield, and East St. Louis, Illinois, and Wilmington, North Carolina, among others, had been white attacks on colored people, often resulting in the burning of entire colored sections or towns.

This was the first major riot in which blacks fought back as earnestly as the whites and in which black residents, having become established in the city but still relegated to run-down ghettos, began attacking and looting perceived symbols of exploitation, the stores and laundries run by whites and other outsiders that blacks felt were cheating them. It was only after Detroit that riots became known as primarily urban phenomena, ultimately centered on inner-city blacks venting their frustrations on the ghettos that confined them.

The Detroit riots went on for close to a week, ending in thirty-four deaths and more than one thousand wounded. The Sunday night the riots began, as many as five thousand people joined in the stoning, stabbing, beating, and shooting, so many people injured that the municipal hospital was admitting riot victims at a rate of one a minute.

George was living at 208 Josephine near Hastings and Woodward and heard the mayhem in the streets and on the radio all through the night. He was living in the middle of the crowded colored quarter mockingly called Paradise Valley, where blacks were stoning the cars of passing whites, whites were beating up blacks as they emerged from the all-night theaters on Woodward, and an inspector on the scene reported to the police commissioner that the situation was out of control.

The rioting continued into the next morning. It was now Monday, the start of the work week. A co-worker of George's called him up.

"Hey, Starling, what you gonna do?"

"Do 'bout what?"

" 'Bout going to work."

"I'm going."

"Man, you must be crazy."

"What you talking about?"

"Don't you know? Where you been? You didn't know it was a riot going on?"

"Yeah, but I ain't got nothin' to do with it. I ain't in no gang."

"This ain't no gang fight. This is a riot."

"Well, they ain't gonna bother me. I ain't done nothing to nobody. I'm going on to work."

"You gonna get yourself killed."

George had to take two trolleys to get to Hamtramck. He boarded the first in a colored neighborhood and instantly knew something was wrong. The colored people were sitting up straight; the white people were crouched in their seats so they couldn't be seen out the window.

Wonder why these people down on the floor like they are? he asked himself.

The trolley made its way to a white neighborhood, and now the colored people crouched down and the white people sat up.

Well, what in the devil is going on? he said to himself.

The trolley pulled into the intersection. A mob two blocks long stood cursing outside the trolley.

What's wrong with all them people? he thought.

The mob became a single organism descending on the trolley. The trolley operator moved fast. "He went back the other way," George said. "That's the only thing that saved us. And that's when I began to realize the seriousness of this thing."

He managed to make it to work that day. But the trouble wasn't over. The rioting continued all day Monday and into a second night. When he got back home to Hastings Street that evening, a mob was approaching from Woodward, howling and turning over cars.

"I ran so fast till my heels were hittin' my back," he said.

And as he rounded the corner onto Josephine, he could see a colored mob forming. "They were turning over white cars," he said, "dumping the people out like you dump ashes out an ashtray and setting the cars on fire."

Some colored men in his block stood on the sidewalk, trying to figure out what to do. They had gathered the empty bottles in their flats to throw at people if it came to that. "We were wondering how it was gonna end up," George said.

A white undertaker in the block joined the colored men contemplating the situation. He did not leave when the other white people fled. He fixed his feet on the ground with the neighbors who happened to be colored and let it be known where he stood. He might need their protection if it came to that.

"You know, them white folks raising hell over there on Woodward Avenue," the white undertaker started to say.

"Yeah, they sure are," George said.

The white undertaker drew closer and into their circle. "But us colored folks is giving 'em hell over on Hastings," he said.

The colored men welcomed a new brother, and they all laughed at the meaning of that.

George stood on the porch and watched the National Guard tanks with machine guns on top parade through the streets. He sat up all night looking out the window as they passed.

He heard windows smashing and then saw a man with a sofa on his back. Another one had a shoulder of meat. A third had about five or six loaves of bread in his arm.

One morning, as the riots wore on, he passed a Florsheim shoe store while heading to work. People were grabbing shoes through the broken glass and running in the morning sun.

A co-worker was with him and ran over to the store.

"Come on, let's get some," he said.

"Man, I don't want no shoes," George said. "I don't need no shoes like that."

The friend went in without him, grabbed two shoes, and went tearing down the street. He was giddy until he looked at what he had. He had made off with two left shoes.

"Now he gonna go back and try to find the mates," George said. George told him he was crazy.

"No, man, these *good* shoes," his friend said. "If I find the mate to these shoes, I don't have to buy no more shoes for a good while."

He went back in the store, and in that instant the police showed up and caught him in the act. They fired shots, and one hit him in the stomach. He later landed in jail.

The looters took over after the mob cleared out. Within days, the freight trucks rolled up to Hastings and Josephine and all over Detroit and came to a stop in front of suspect stoops. Out came men in overalls pushing dollies, coming for the stolen merchandise. Minutes later,

George saw a sofa come out of a two-flat. Somebody had seen the tenants looting and told.

When the time came to go back to work, George rounded the corner to get to the entrance and felt sick. "I got the feeling like I was walking into Alcatraz or Sing Sing," he said, "to begin a lifetime sentence."

At the plant he learned that several men he worked with had gotten shot in the rioting. One or two had been killed. Between the riot and the anti-Communist paranoia and the plant itself, it was time to go.

"Look, I can't take it," George told his foreman. "I can't come in here another day."

"Well, you know you are frozen on this job."

"But I'm defrosting. I cannot, I cannot come in here no more. Now, you can take it any way you want. I'm just not coming back."

"You know, if you walk out of here, you subject to be in the army in the next twenty-four hours."

"I can't help that," George said, knowing he'd already been rejected for army duty. "I'm gone."

"You have to wait till the pay period to get your money."

"I want my money now. I'm a sit right here. I ain't goin' nowhere until y'all give me all of my money. Now, y'all can do what you want. I'm leaving."

Finally they cut him a check. "And I left the next day."

It was late summer now and going into autumn. There were only two places he knew of to go and live. One was New York, where he had aunts and uncles and no job. The other was Florida, where he had a wife, a father, the dim hope of going back to school, and a patched-together work life of whatever came up.

He caught a bus home to Florida with a sense of dread and defeat. He had gone to college and gone up north and now was returning to exactly the same place he had left. He went back to picking fruit. But instead of hundreds of men in their prime standing at the corner of Bates and Palmetto hoping to board the truck, a small cluster gathered there—old men and women, errand boys and domestics, children, too, who would never have made the cut before the war, along with the few young men like Charlie "Mud" Bollar, and Sam Gaskin and George, who hadn't been chosen to go off to fight.

With the high rollers gone, the three of them reveled in their good fortune. Here they were the only strong pickers left. The trees heavy with fruit. The fruit rationed and prized like never before. The packinghouses helpless to get the fruit out of the trees and, not knowing how long the situation, meaning the war, would drag on, forced to pay an extra nickel a box to entice anybody who could crawl to get on the truck to come pick.

George, Mud, and Sam boarded the truck with the newcomers and rode out thirty, forty miles into the grove. Only it was different this time. George was seeing the world in a new light after being in Detroit. The three of them had gotten used to fair wages for their hard work up north and walked with their backs straight now. George, in particular, never had the constitution to act subservient, and his time up north, where colored people didn't have to step off the sidewalk, only made him more impatient with the role the southern caste system assigned him.

He had gotten used to carrying himself in a different way, talking to white people as equals in Detroit. Now that he was back in Eustis, he made a point to do whatever he could to keep from addressing white people as "sir" or "ma'am." "They'd say, 'So and so and so, boy,' " he said. "I would never say, 'Yes, sir' or 'No, sir.' I'd say, 'That's right.' 'Sure.' 'Certainly.' "

"What you mean by *certainly*?" would come the indignant reply. "You don't know how to say, 'Yes, sir'?"

A colored teacher who had finished the University of Michigan ran into the same trouble in Mississippi at around the same time. He needed to send a wire to a colleague and went into a drugstore to do so. The drugstore owner asked where the wire was going.

"Do they have a phone there?" the druggist asked.

"Yes, they do," the colored teacher replied.

"Do they have a phone there?" the druggist asked again.

"Yes, they have a phone," the colored teacher said, wondering why the druggist hadn't understood him the first time.

"Goddamn it, when you talk to a white man, you say, 'sir'!"

The teacher, to avoid further escalation, addressed him as "sir" and walked out the door. There he saw a group of white men waiting. The teacher jumped into his car. "I didn't run," the teacher said, "but I made haste to my car and left that town just as fast as I could."

George knew that the minutest breach of protocol could be risky but had a hard time submitting to it. The North had changed him, and Mud and Sam, too, and they couldn't go back to the way they were before. The three of them had a plan. They were tired of having to take whatever pennies the packinghouses decided to pay them, and with the war on and not enough pickers, this was one of the few times the workers had any leverage.

George, Mud, and Sam decided to make the most of the situation and stand up for themselves like men. They took to strolling the grove and assessing it themselves before setting their ladders in a tree. Sam and Mud walked the grove as if they were the foremen and looked over the density of the fruit to see what they were in for.

George stayed with the crew of old men and women warming themselves by a fire in the fog. The workers wanted to know when they could start picking. George stood with them and told them the plan.

"Now, look," he said. "Everybody sit down till we get the price straight. Nobody go to work."

"What about the foreman?"

"I don't care what the foreman say. Nobody go to work until we give the word."

The old men and women were used to cleaning white yards and cooking in white kitchens ten or twelve hours a day for seventy-five cents, maybe a dollar. George told them if they could get a good price, they could make that much in an hour or two. Sounded like voodoo talk to them.

"We got to take what the white folks tells us," they told him. "You can't do no different."

George looked back down the row for Mud and Sam to show up and back at his skeptical army.

"I don't want to hear that stuff," George said. "I been listening to that all my life."

The old men and women worried what would happen if they didn't get their price and worried all the more if they got it. With the war on, it was a new day, George told them.

"We got a chance to kind of get back at them," he said, trying to inspire them to stand up for themselves. "I ain't thinking about no future. I'm thinking about right now."

Besides, Sam and Mud had already tried to scare the pickers into submission.

"Anybody put a ladder up under them trees," Mud told them, "we gonna snatch it from under you and stomp you when you hit the ground!"

The pickers waited. Mud and Sam emerged from deep in the grove.

"Well, what it looks like?" George asked.

"It's pretty good over here in one spot," they said.

"Well, what do you think?"

"We'll do it for twenty-two cents."

George spoke for the group since he was the one who had been to school. He went to the foreman to start the unthinkable act of negotiating with a white man.

"What you paying for this?" George asked the foreman.

"Well, you know, this is good fruit, boy," the foreman said. "Now, you can get well in here. These oranges big as grapefruit."

"How much you paying?"

"We paying good. That's fifteen cents a box."

"That ain't good enough. Nope. We can't pick it for that. We want twenty-two cents a box."

"Naw, we can't give you that."

George thought it over.

"Okay, we'll do it for twenty-two cents. Straight through, good and the bad."

"Naw, we can't."

"Well, we can't pick it, then."

"We forty miles from town."

"I know. We still not gonna pick it."

"Well, y'all pick a load. I don't want to send the truck driver back empty. So y'all pick enough so he can take a load into the packinghouse. Then I'll send word to the boss and tell him what y'all wantin' to do."

"No, we not gonna pick one. You can send the truck back to town, and we'll wait. Got nothing to do."

"Y'all just doing us this way because y'all got the advantage over us. This war ain't gon' last forever, and, by God, y'all gon' pay for this."

"We already paid," George said. "All these years we couldn't even ask how much you were paying for a box of fruit or we'd get fired. You gave us what you wanted to give us. You promised us one thing and give us another. You put the payday off whenever you get ready. Sometime you didn't pay us, period. So now, far as I'm concerned, this is reckoning day. And I ain't worried about after the war. You can pay us what we want, or else your fruit gonna hang out there. And they want it in New York. They want it all over the world, and you ain't got nobody to pick it."

The foreman needed the fruit out of the trees. He left with the truck driver and before long was back from the packinghouse. He told them to go to work. He would pay them twenty-two cents. This time.

The old men and women set their ladders in the trees and commenced picking, and by nightfall, they and these cocksure boys had made more in a day than they would have otherwise made in a week.

People could buy stew meat now and put Sunday suits on will-call at Ferran's. The Mason jars of quarters Lil George was saving up multiplied. He knew the wages they were making out in the groves couldn't last forever. Everything depended on the supply and demand created by the war, and who knew how much more time they had? He decided to make the most of it while he could. The way things were going, he could earn enough money for college and then some. Until then, while the money was flowing, he thought it was time to rent a place of their own and get out from under his father. Maybe that was what he and Inez needed, now that she was back from her short course in beauty culture.

"Go downtown and look in Thompson's," he told her. "Pick out some things you think you would like to have for the house, so we know what we're doing when we move."

"I don't want to go down there and ain't got no money," she said. George always had these grand ideas, planning their future in his head. "How you gon' buy any furniture?" she asked. "You ain't got no money to buy no furniture with."

"Don't worry about it. Just go and look. You never can tell what might take place."

One day he just took her by the hand. "Come on," he said. "I'm a take you down to Thompson's, and you gonna pick out some furniture."

"Pick it out? What you gon' pay for it with?"

"Get your coat and come on, let's go." George scooped up seven or eight jars of quarters and halves, and they went to Thompson's.

"What you see in here that you like?" he asked her.

She saw a bed, a sofa, a dining room set.

"How much is that?" George asked the clerk, a white man.

"You could pay two dollars down and seventy-five cents a week on it," the clerk said.

"I don't want to know all of that. I want to know how much does it cost, and if I pay cash for it, how much can I get off?"

"Cash?" the clerk asked. "You gon' pay cash for all this, boy?"

"I just might."

"Let me see now."

The clerk gave him a figure. George did some adding himself and figured the quarters and halves would cover it.

"Okay, I'll take it."

"Well, you know this is for cash, you know."

"Yeah, I'll take it."

George went out to the car and came back with a box of Mason jars and set the jars on the counter.

"You got a can opener?" George asked. He had glued the tops on to keep the money from falling out or a thief from getting in. They cut the tops off, and George dumped the quarters and halves out on the counter. The coins clinked and rolled, and George started counting.

Inez stood looking first at the money and then at George. The clerk ran out into the street.

"By God, y'all come in here. You ain't gon' believe this. This damn boy in here got over three hundred dollars in jars."

They counted out quarters and halves until George paid him for every bit.

"And when I left out of there," George said, "he was still shaking his head." Inez too.

The pickers had more money in their pockets than they were raised to think they had a right to, and times were the best they had ever been, which said more about how meager the past had been than how great the present was. There was a war going on, after all. They hated that there was a war, but they knew that it made them indispensable for once, and deep inside they wished it would never end.

ATLANTA, 1941

ROBERT JOSEPH PERSHING FOSTER

THINGS WERE SPINNING FAST AROUND PERSHING, and, before he knew it, he had allowed himself to be pulled completely into the bourgeois world that he had become besotted with and that would be his ticket out of the world he had come from. He had been squiring around the daughter of the president of Atlanta University for two years now. The daughter, Alice Clement, finished Spelman on June 4, 1941, and it was decided that it was time the two be married. Shortly after commencement, a breathless announcement ran in the *Chicago Defender:*

> *Enlisting widespread interest is the engagement of Miss Alice Clarissa Clement, charming and attractive daughter of President and Mrs. Rufus E. Clement of Atlanta University, to Robert Joseph Pershing Foster, son of Mr. and Mrs. Madison James Foster of Monroe, La.*
>
> *The announcement was made on Thursday evening at a party honoring Miss Clement.*

That December, on the evening of the twenty-third, a Tuesday, and not by coincidence the anniversary of Dr. and Mrs. Clement's own wedding twenty-two years before, Robert Joseph Pershing Foster married Alice Clarissa Clement and entered the insular and parallel universe that was colored society. Dr. Benjamin Mays, the president of Morehouse College and a celebrated figure of the day, married them. The groom was two days shy of his twenty-third birthday. The bride was twenty-one.

The Japanese had attacked Pearl Harbor just a few weeks before. But the troubles of the outside world were put aside that night. It was the social event of the season, played up in the *Atlanta Daily World,* the *Chicago Defender,* and the *New York Amsterdam News;* and here was Pershing right in the middle of it.

"The wedding—" Pershing began many years later. "Can I brag a little? It was a monster. If you can visualize a Gothic chapel. Stained-glass windows. Long mahogany benches. Then a balcony. Pipe organs up the wall. A master organist."

There were eight bridesmaids and a maid of honor in floor-length white taffeta and with tiaras on their heads. They carried long-stemmed red roses, heavy in their arms. There were eight groomsmen, including Pershing's brothers Madison and Leland, in white tie and tails.

"White kid gloves," Pershing continued. "Patent-leather shoes. We were clean as chitlins."

As he recounted that day half a century later, he would not for some reason speak of the bride as much as the details of the spectacle itself. The *Atlanta Daily World* reported that she wore a gown of ivory satin, its neckline embroidered with seed pearls, and a floor-length veil that "fell from a crown of orange blossoms." The altar was "banked with palms and ferns," "numerous sixteen branch candelabra and three huge urns of gladioli and lilies," in what the paper called "a setting of splendor and beauty."

One of the groomsmen, Jimmy Washington, would always remember the night they got married. Because it was beautiful, he said years later, and it rained in sheets that night.

There would not be much of a honeymoon. School took them in opposite directions. Alice went off to New York to study music at Juilliard, an extraordinary thing for a young colored woman of the day. Pershing prepared to go to Nashville to attend Meharry Medical College, and the two saw each other when they could. It was wartime, and it seemed everybody was separated from their sweethearts.

Alice completed a year at Juilliard, and then it was decided that it was better for her to stay with her parents and teach in Atlanta than to live in Nashville with Pershing, who was caught up in his medical studies. She would be in familiar surroundings in Atlanta. Her father could secure an ideal position at a public school there for her, and neither she nor Pershing would have to trouble themselves with the messy details of keeping house at this stage in their lives.

By the time Pershing found out, it had all been decided. Pershing had no choice but to go along with it. What money he and Alice had was coming from Dr. Clement, and he was calling the shots. So Alice taught in Atlanta and visited Nashville when she could.

After a visit in the early spring of 1943, Alice discovered she was pregnant. She gave birth to a girl that December. They named her Alberta Ann, after Pershing's beloved mother, Ottie Alberta. She had a brown velvet Gerber baby face. They wrapped her in baby bunting and began to call her Bunny, a name that would stick for as long as she lived.

Pershing finished Meharry in 1945 and moved to St. Louis to serve out his residency at Homer G. Phillips Hospital, the colored facility where Madison had served his. Alice was expecting their second child now, and her parents argued against her trying to raise two babies in St. Louis with Pershing working three and four nights straight as a resident.

"Why do that when you can live here?" they asked.

"See, they can show you a million reasons to keep that daughter and granddaughter at home," Pershing said years later. "They were logical reasons. And you couldn't beat 'em."

That October, the second girl was born. Pershing named her Alice Emlyn, after his wife and the beloved sister he could never protect from the white men who called out to her in Monroe. Little Alice inherited her father's big eyes and sharp nose and looked like a lighter incarnation of him. Everyone came to call her Robin, similar to Pershing's actual first name, Robert.

She was born in Atlanta surrounded by the Clements while Pershing was working the ward twenty-four hours straight, until he was cross-eyed and crazy from it.

"In the evening when you got through work," Pershing said, "you said, *'Whew, thank God.'* And you run upstairs, taking your clothes off on the elevator. Run to the shower. Get you a gulp, throw your whiskey, and get you two, three shots. Towel around you and hit the shower. And get out and get a cab and hit the streets. Anywhere. It didn't matter where you went. *Let me get away from this.* And then you had to come home sober. And you had to sleep fast 'cause you had to get up the next morning looking bright-eyed and bushy-tailed in a crisp, clean uniform and white shoes. And you had to *'Good morning, Mr. So-and-So.'* "

A resident ahead of him noticed his work and suggested he go up for a surgery residency when the time came.

"You think I can do it?" Pershing asked.

"Yes," the resident said. "Try."

Pershing did as he said and started a new round of training that would last several more years and take him to hospitals in North Carolina and New York City to train in surgery.

Soon he began getting disturbing reports from home. His mother had taken ill.

It was cancer. Her kidney. He left to be with her. She had prayed to God every night to let her see her baby become a doctor. There he sat, a doctor in training now, reading aloud the *Reader's Digest* to her. She tried to stand up to go over to him. But she couldn't.

"What's the matter?" he asked her.

He got up to kiss her on the cheek. She tried to speak. She was worried what would become of her son in this bourgeois world he was entering.

"Baby," she said, "always be independent. You don't want to be dependent all your life and have to depend on someone else for a drink of water."

Pershing kept those words inside of him. In a few years, he completed his training, and, though she would not live to see it, he would become a surgeon at last.

For a time, Madison was the only colored physician in all of Ouachita County, Louisiana, after a doctor by the name of Chandler died. Years before, two colored doctors had been forced out of Monroe, the author Ray Stannard Baker reported, "because they were taking the practice of white physicians."

So Madison learned to step judiciously in his practice. He tended to the students at a colored college out from town and the poor people out in the country where the white doctors would not go. The country people paid him with the side of a freshly killed hog until they could get the money, which some never did. When Madison's patients needed to go to the hospital, Madison could not admit them. He was not allowed in the hospital to practice. So he carried a hospital in his medical bag and made the front room of every shotgun cabin an operating room.

Madison had his hands full, and he enlisted Pershing's help with his patients out in the countryside when Pershing was on break from his residency. Pershing was glad to help. But he did not want to be a country doctor. And he was thinking even then that he would have to get out of Monroe to be the doctor and the man he knew he could be. He wanted the shiny fixtures of a modern hospital and a staff of nurses at his side that he could direct like an orchestra.

Pershing was visiting once when someone sent for him to deliver a baby out in the country. He arrived with his satchel. Someone met him at the door.

"Doc, I think she's ready."

The fireplace was spitting ashes. The woman's kinfolk stood drinking strong coffee and waiting for the woman to pass the baby.

Pershing saw her splayed flat on a cot, looking ready to burst. He set down his satchel and went over to her. He reviewed in his head the principles of the obstetrics course he had only recently completed. There was no point in pining for the trappings of a modern hospital or the equipment he was used to in medical school. He would have to make do with whatever was in the cabin and his medical bag. They would get through it somehow.

He reached toward her and felt for the hard surface of a human head at the beginning of life. The woman bore down and grunted. He in turn made note of the contractions and the baby's position. He tried to help her bear down. But the baby didn't come.

The woman had been through more births than Pershing had and could sense the tentative touch of a book-learned delivery. All this analysis, and still no baby.

"That's alright, Doc," she finally said. "Get on out the way."

She rolled her round body off the edge of the cot. She grunted and squatted on the bare surface of the floor and pushed hard. Pershing watched and did as she said.

"Come on, now," she said. "Catch it."

He moved into position. A few grunts more, and the baby plopped into his hands. *Shoop, bingo.*

The woman paid what she could, which in the usual currency was not much more than food and a promise but was beyond calculating when it came to wisdom. He learned that all the book knowledge and equipment in the world didn't make you a good doctor if you didn't know what you were doing or listen to your patients. He learned a lesson that night that would stay with him for the rest of his life and would pay off in ways he couldn't imagine.

Things appeared to be looking up for Pershing. He had traveled across the South for his degrees, been to St. Louis, spent summers picking tobacco in Connecticut with other Morehouse students, visited New York, seen the differences between North and South, and now, having deferred his military duty during medical school, was reporting to Fort Sam Houston, Texas, for a training course for army medical officers about to begin their tours. He would be called Captain Foster, and it was from his short time in the army that he would plot the rest of his life.

He was bright and earnest, and, while that didn't always get him what he wanted or deserved in the Jim Crow South, he was getting a break now, it seemed. The colonel, impressed with him, pulled him aside and suggested that Pershing could well make chief of surgery at his new posting.

"Foster, you're the only colored officer with surgical training here," the colonel said. "You don't get this often, but I'm going to give you first choice."

Pershing threw his shoulders back.

"Thank you, Colonel," Pershing said. "Alright. Now what are my choices?"

World War II was over, and another, smaller one was brewing in Korea. He could go on to Korea, stay in the South at Fort Sam Houston, or go to Austria, a base of the European theater. The colonel encouraged him to go to Austria, and that's what Pershing chose.

Thousands of colored soldiers had preceded him overseas during the two great wars—more than a million in World War II alone—and that service had been a defining experience for many of them. They were forced into segregated units and often given the most menial tasks or the most dangerous infantry tours. But they also experienced relief from Jim Crow in those European villages, were recognized as liberating Americans rather than lower-caste colored men, and felt pride in what their uniform represented.

They returned home to a Jim Crow South that expected them to go back to the servile position they left. Most resented it and wanted to be honored for risking their lives for their country rather than attacked for being uppity. Some survived the war only to lose their lives to Jim Crow.

In the spring of 1919, a colored soldier named Wilbur Little returned home to Blakely, Georgia, after a tour of duty in World War I. A band of white men saw him at the train station in his uniform. They ordered him to take it off and walk home in his underwear. He refused. Soon anonymous notes were warning him to leave town if he wanted to wear his uniform. Days later, a mob attacked him as he greeted friends congratulating him on his achievements. He was found beaten to death on the outskirts of town. He was wearing his uniform. He had survived the war only to be killed at home. Cases like that were cause enough for some men to go north.

Pershing put those things aside and chose to revel in the idea that he could actually be chief of surgery. Alice was elated. They had been married for eight years now and had never lived together more than a few weeks at a time. The two girls, Bunny and Robin, were just about school age now. Alice had been rearing them in Atlanta with her parents while Pershing did his medical training in different parts of the South. Now the four of them could be a family.

They arrived just outside Salzburg, and Pershing went straight to his new commanding officer. He wanted to make a good impression.

"Captain Foster has reported for duty, sir," he said.

The new colonel was from Mississippi, and, in an instant, Pershing found himself hurled back to the South. The colonel had not expected his new surgeon to be colored, nor had he been told that this colored surgeon was supposed to be in charge—or, if he did know, he chose to ignore it. He told Pershing he had nothing for him to do.

"Why don't you go out?" the colonel said. "Can't you go somewhere? Come back in a week."

"Well, I don't have any money," Pershing said. "I've come all the way from Fort Houston, and the next payday hasn't come, Colonel."

The southern colonel had no assignment for him, so Pershing had no choice but to wait until the following week. When he returned, he learned there would be no leadership position for him. A white officer would be chief of surgery, as it had always been. Pershing would have no title other than staff doctor. Jim Crow had followed him across the Atlantic, and it was hitting him that he would never get ahead as long as these apostles of Jim Crow were over him.

Still, he dutifully made his rounds when it was his turn, tending to the basic needs of the soldiers, itching to do something more in keeping with his credentials. It turned out that many of the patients were soldiers' wives with gynecological and obstetrical complications that called for interventions that by now he was well equipped to handle. But for one reason or another, a superior officer always seemed to intervene and never let him treat the white ones.

One day a patient was in labor on his watch. The nurse thought it might be time. Pershing said it was still too soon.

"She's not quite ready yet," he told the nurse. "Watch her close, now."

Other doctors tended to deliver when it was most convenient, pump general anesthesia into the patient and get it over with, he recalled years later. Cesarean sections were all the rage. But Pershing had learned from the woman in the cabin back in Louisiana that everything had its own time. He liked to let a baby come when it was ready. Others said he let the labor go on too long. But he thought it was a more welcoming way for one to enter the world if one were not rushed into it. So, while other doctors relied on general anesthesia, he preferred local for the sake of the mother and the baby.

A white doctor of his same rank caught wind of the delay. He stepped in over Pershing's head and delivered the baby as Pershing watched, too hurt to speak and not daring to.

Never was there a rule written down somewhere, but that was how it played out. "You make the rounds," Pershing said years later, "and you're standing behind other doctors, and they're talking about your patient."

He was noticing it more and more, like how, whenever a white woman needed surgery, they never let him in the operating room. They sent him over to operate on the men. It was Jim Crow all over again, and he thought again about his short- and long-term prospects. It was reminding him that he had a decision to make. When he got out of the army, he would get as far away from Jim Crow's disciples as he could.

For now he had no choice. He was under these people and had to make the best of it. He pushed the hurt and anger inside himself and decided that if all they would let him do was take somebody's pulse, he would take it better than any doctor there. And so he doted on the few patients he got.

"I treated every white boy like he was the king of Siam," he said, "and didn't lose dignity. It's a fine art."

It all changed one day when a woman in labor suddenly stopped contracting. It was another doctor's patient, the one who had intervened when he thought Pershing had let a labor go on too long. The doctor was getting second opinions and let Pershing come in this time. Pershing saw the woman on the operating table in preparation for a C-section.

He looked the patient over and gave his diagnosis.

"She's in uterine inertia," Pershing said. "The uterus is tired. It's stopped pushing. You need to start a glucose drip of Pitocin to make the uterus start contracting."

The doctor decided to try it. The nurses later went to Pershing and gave him the news.

"The baby's crawling," they said. "The baby came."

One evening soon afterward, he and Alice were at dinner in the officers' club. The waiter asked what they were drinking and soon reappeared with another round.

"Compliments of the lieutenant over there," the waiter said.

Pershing reached for Alice's hand. They danced their way over to the table where the lieutenant, a white man from Kentucky, was sitting with his wife.

"You wouldn't remember me," the wife said. "But I'm the patient whose baby you just delivered. I must give you a kiss for saving me from a C-section."

She gave him a kiss in front of everyone.

"You were the talk of the commissary," she said.

People were taking notice. He was young, charming, and brilliant. People saw him in line and tittered about him.

"I hear we got a new doctor, and he's colored," people were saying.

"Would you have a colored doctor deliver your baby?" somebody else would throw in.

CHICKASAW COUNTY, MISSISSIPPI, FALL 1937

IDA MAE BRANDON GLADNEY

THE MEN WHO pounded on Ida Mae's door that black night, who raised a chain up to her, frightening her and the children and her sister-in-law Indiana, who slept by the door, went and hunted down her husband's cousin Joe Lee over the turkeys that had disappeared.

They tied Joe Lee's hands behind him with hog wire and took him to the woods out by Houston, a few miles away.

They tied him up for stealing Addie B.'s turkeys, which belonged to Mr. Edd.

Joe Lee did not work for Mr. Edd—his father had a piece of land he farmed on his own. But it didn't matter because any boss man in the ruling class could claim jurisdiction when he pleased. A colored man, a few miles west of here, was whipped when he asked a storekeeper for a receipt. If what Addie B. said was true, Joe Lee had committed a serious crime against Mr. Edd, and it didn't matter who he worked for.

So they took him out to the woods.

They laid him across a log by the schoolhouse. They beat him with the chains that Willie Jim had raised up to Ida Mae. And when he said he didn't know anything about any turkeys, they paid it no mind. They beat him until his coveralls turned red with blood and stuck to the surface of his skin as if with adhesive. Then they took him to the Chickasaw County jail and left him bleeding alone in the cell.

The next morning, Addie B.'s turkeys wandered back on their own to her cabin across the field. They had been roosting in the countryside and came cawing and clucking before George and Ida Mae knew why Joe Lee was captured in the first place or what had become of him. There were no apologies. Sometimes they just got the wrong man. Joe Lee was known for taking what wasn't his, but this was one time when he hadn't.

George went to Mr. Edd first thing in the morning to find out what happened and where his cousin was and to register his discontent. Ida Mae didn't want him going in the state of mind he was in and told him to mind his words. He had to walk a thin line between being a man and acting a slave. Step too far on one side, and he couldn't live with himself. Step too far on the other, and he might not live at all.

He got there and asked Mr. Edd what happened.

"Where is Joe Lee?" George asked.

"We tried to wait till you got there," Mr. Edd said.

George thought it best not to press the matter of what happened to Joe Lee. All these years he had been loyal to Mr. Edd, and Mr. Edd had been fair with him. So he spoke only as a husband and father, which he felt was within his right.

"Very idea you upsettin' my family," he said, looking down as he prepared to leave and not quite knowing what else to do.

Joe Lee survived the night. The boss man told George to go get him at the jail. George, Willie, Saint, and the other colored men on the plantation took grease to peel the overalls off him, just as their slave forefathers had done after whippings generations before. They carried Joe Lee back to his father's farm in the fresh clothes they put on him, and the people went back to picking cotton. The lash wounds on Joe Lee's back healed in time. But Joe Lee was never right again, people said. And, in a way, neither was George.

On the drive back home, George searched himself, hard and deep. This wasn't the first beating, and it wouldn't be the last. Joe Lee had lived, but he just as easily could have died. And there was not a thing anybody could do about it. As it was, Ida Mae felt George was in danger for asking Mr. Edd about it at all. Next time, it could be him. George had a brother in Chicago. Ida Mae's big sister, Irene, was in Milwaukee and had been agitating for them to come north.

He made up his mind on the way back. He drove into the yard and went into the cabin to break the news to Ida Mae.

"This the last crop we making," he said.

EUSTIS, FLORIDA, 1944
GEORGE SWANSON STARLING

WORD SPREAD THROUGH THE CITRUS GROVES that a cell of pickers had taken to demanding twenty-two cents a box and refusing to pick if they didn't get it. It was a miracle wage, and soon other pickers were trying to join Lil George's roving union. But some got scared at the way George talked to the white people like he was equal and never went picking with him again.

The foremen who assembled the crews and oversaw the citrus harvest knew they were in for a long day when they saw George, Mud, and Sam awaiting pickup with other hungry workers at the corner of Bates and Palmetto. Most foremen had little sympathy for the pickers. Their job was to get the fruit out of the trees as fast as they could, and this back-and-forth over pay was wasting time. Even worse, these boys had no business telling white men what to do. Most foremen told the pickers to take whatever the packinghouses were offering.

The Blye brothers were different. They were among the few colored foremen around and had grown up with most of the pickers. Reuben, who towered over most men and had a way of making women forget their husbands; Babe, who liked to gamble and hunt possum; and Whisper, who could speak no louder than that because he had got his throat cut, had been pickers themselves and knew the packinghouses could pay more if they wanted to. Florida growers were grossing fifty million dollars a year from that fruit back in the forties, and the brothers felt the pickers deserved better.

After assessing a grove, George and the Blye brothers conferred on the price the pickers should ask for. Then the brothers went and told the packinghouse it looked like the pickers flat-out wouldn't work if they didn't get their price, and they didn't know what had got into them. The Blye brothers hoped to convince the packinghouses that, with the war on, there weren't enough good pickers to choose from and they were stuck with whoever was left, crazy though these pickers may be, that the packinghouses needed to think about paying more if they wanted the fruit out of the trees, at least for now. Of course, the Blye brothers, being colored and walking a fine line themselves, didn't put it like that. They just said the pickers were refusing and they didn't know what in the world had got into them.

Back in the groves, the brothers confided to George, Mud, and Sam that they were within their rights to ask and that there was room to maneuver. The packinghouses were wringing the most they could out of all of them, including the Blye brothers, who had reason to believe they themselves weren't getting paid what the white foremen were, this being the South in the 1940s.

The grove owners and their packinghouses had a near monopoly on the growing and selling of citrus. They were among the richest men in central Florida; their European vacations and their daughters' cotillions and the visits of their children from the best boarding schools in the South were all chronicled in the local papers that everyone, including workers like the Blye brothers and George, could read. It was a multimillion-dollar industry fed by the demands of wealthy and middle-class families from Chicago to Long Island who expected orange juice with their toast and coffee every morning.

The brothers urged the three men and their frightened, thrown-together crew of pickers to stand their ground.

"Man, sock it to 'em, sock it to 'em," Reuben told George, knowing how much the grove owners were making off the fruit and that they were likely cheating them all.

"Don't pick it no less," Whisper said. "Don't pick it no less than twenty-two cents. Goddammit, I'm a tell the man y'all ain't gon' do it."

Most times George, Mud, and Sam got their price right there on the spot. But sometimes they didn't. They couldn't depend on getting the Blye brothers as their foremen every time. And when they didn't, some foremen just said no without telling the packinghouse at all. Some went to the packinghouse but accepted whatever the packinghouse told them. Others went ahead and sent the truck back to the packinghouse empty of fruit and waited to see what the owners said. Sometimes the packinghouses relented. But sometimes the driver would come back from the packinghouse saying, "Well, they say they not gon' pay that."

The pickers dragged back to the truck when that happened for the empty-handed ride back to town. George started to climb up with them. But most foremen weren't like the Blye brothers and wouldn't let him on the truck if he told the crew not to pick.

"You big with your big-mouth self," one foreman said. "You get back to town best way you can."

And so George had to thumb a ride for thirty or forty miles after facing down a foreman while his followers rumbled past him on the flatbed of the truck.

He was developing a reputation for stirring up trouble in the groves. These walkouts were beginning to look something like a union. The grove owners didn't like unions, didn't allow unions, and weren't going to stand for it, especially from a band of colored pickers trying to take advantage of the war. Inez was scared for her husband but too disgusted to let it show. Didn't he realize that he was colored in the South? Why couldn't he be satisfied like everybody else?

Big George had been working with them when Lil George stood up to a foreman in Orlando.

The next day, Big George begged off. "I ain't going with you," he said. "Y'all too crazy."

He knew, and everyone else knew, that every time George went out to the groves standing up to packinghouses, he was pushing the limits of what a colored man in Florida in the 1940s was allowed to get away with.

In the months that George had been rousing up the pickers, their world had grown even more dangerous due to the state's desperate wartime need for labor. From the panhandle to the Everglades, Florida authorities were now arresting colored men off the street and in their homes if they were caught not working. Charged with vagrancy, the men were assessed fines of several weeks' pay and made to pick fruit or cut sugarcane to work off the debt if they did not have the money, which few of them did and as the authorities fully anticipated. Those captured were hauled to remote plantations or turpentine camps, held by force, and beaten or shot if they tried to escape.

It was an illegal form of contemporary slavery called debt peonage, which persisted in Florida, Georgia, Alabama, and other parts of the Deep South well into the 1940s. Federal investigations into neoslavery in Florida uncovered numerous abuses of kidnapping and enslavement and led to a 1942 indictment and trial of a sugar plantation company in the Everglades.

Lake County, too, needed as many workers as could be rounded up and in 1944 elected a new sheriff to see to it. He was Willis Virgil McCall, the six-foot-tall son of a dirt farmer who policed the county with a ten-gallon hat, size thirteen boots, and a Winchester rifle he did not hesitate to cock. He was openly linked to white supremacists and would be implicated in the deaths and abuse of dozens of blacks in what would become a twenty-eight-year reign. As soon as he took office, he set to work. He arrested forty pickers for vagrancy, including a man from Deacon Fashaw's crew, in late January and early February 1945.

They were arrested for not working on a Saturday, at a time when George, Sam, and Mud were leading actual strikes in the groves.

Each day, the danger was drawing closer, and there was now even more pressure on George's pickers to work no matter how much George managed to win for them. McCall stepped up his arrests. In February, he showed up at the home of a picker from a crew in Leesburg, fifteen miles west of Eustis. The picker, Mack Fryar, had already worked that week, but, to the sheriff's way of thinking, the picker had no business being at home on a Saturday instead of out in the groves. McCall ordered Fryar to come with him. When he asked why, McCall replied, "None of your damn jaw, just come on with me." McCall struck the picker in the head with a blackjack for such impudence, knocking him unconscious in front of the picker's wife and fourteen-year-old son. He then hauled the picker to the Lake County jail.

The FBI began an investigation, and an agent was seen visiting the picker's wife, Annie. Local whites got wind of it and began plotting mob action because they saw her as "stirring up trouble for the sheriff and the county" by talking to the FBI. Neighbors warned the wife, and upon the picker's release, the Fryars fled to Harlem, "leaving all their possessions, except some money from the sale of her chickens."

George, now an unintended union organizer, somehow managed to stay under the radar screen for months, or so it appeared, in the eleven hundred square miles of citrus land being policed by Sheriff McCall. But that could not go on forever. The orange groves had become a battlefield over more than just fruit but over the rights of the people lowest down in the citrus world and the caste system itself, and the only thing that couldn't be known was how far George, Mud, and Sam could push it.

For several days late in the picking season, no rain fell from the sky. The limbs of the tangerine trees shrank in response. The stems became a tough rubber, harder to cut.

Lil George and his crew landed in a tangerine grove out in Sanford in the middle of this unpleasant development. They hated picking tangerines. The fruit was small, and it took more of them to fill a box. The very properties that made them easy to peel made them harder to pick. The rind broke and bruised almost at the touch, meaning it was harder to get a box of perfect tangerines. They had to be clipped flush without scraping the fruit, all while the picker was reaching between the branches and trying to steady himself on a limb. Then they had to be packed just so in the crate so the stem of each tangerine wouldn't injure the rest.

However difficult they were to pick, tangerines were big sellers at market. Growers in Lake County were known for holding down their production costs, and thus netting "returns to the grower considerably above the state average," according to a newspaper report.

To do that, the grove owners were holding the pickers to nickels on a box. But, with the war on, tangerines were selling an average of four dollars and forty cents a box at auction in 1944, nearly twice the going rate before the United States entered World War II. Across the state, tens of thousands of tangerines were being shipped out every week, a good portion of them coming out of Lake County. There were 2.6 million citrus trees in Lake County, the third most in the state next to Polk and Orange counties.

George's crew arrived at the tangerine grove out in Sanford that morning. The foreman said the packinghouse would pay ten cents a box. George said that wasn't enough what with all they had to do and how hard it was to pick fragile tangerines in the best of conditions, which, after the lack of rain, these weren't.

The price was always in flux depending on the circumstances anyway. This was one time where the pickers saw more work for themselves and thought the price should reflect that. So, no, they needed twenty cents. The foreman held his ground. Lil George started to round up the pickers to head back home, to see if twenty cents sounded better to the foreman than no tangerines at all. George told his crew to get back on the truck, *we're going back to town.*

"Well, we done come all this far now," they said. "We may as well work today, and then we won't come back tomorrow."

This was always the hard part. The pickers liked the miracle money on the days when the foreman gave in. But when the foreman turned them down, they were scared to leave with ill will in the air. *What was the point of antagonizing the boss man? Let's go on and work while we're out here.*

But George knew that walking out was the only leverage they had.

"No, we not gonna work today," George told the pickers. "We are *not* going to work today. Now, you made enough money yesterday. You already made more in one day than you make in a week doing day's work. You ain't never made over six dollars a week. Yesterday, you made seven, eight, nine dollars. So you not losing anything. You gaining. So you can afford to go home and sit down today. Now, we *not* picking."

The pickers didn't move.

"What are you worried about?" George asked them. "Just take it easy."

"Well, we done warmed our pail."

"So now you don't have to cook. Just take that on back home and eat."

Word got back to the owner of the grove that there was trouble in the tangerine stands, and he came out to the field himself. He demanded to know why they were standing there not picking.

"We not gonna pick tangerines for less than twenty cents a box," George told him.

The man cursed and called them names. He had a gun on him like many a man, colored and white, in those parts at that time and told them he would use it if he had to. George, Mud, and Sam knew from hunting squirrel and possum how to handle a gun, too, and told him as much. The pickers, too frightened to speak, watched the standoff between George and the grove owner, not knowing how far either of them would take this thing or how all of them would manage to get out of this.

The men came to no agreement. The owner stormed back to his truck and sped away in a cloud of dust down an alley of his unpicked tangerine trees. George tried to step onto the flatbed truck to head back to town with his pickers. The foreman pushed him off.

"No, boy," he said. "Y'all can't work, you ain't gon' ride. These others can go back on here, but you ain't going back on there."

The pickers were scared to get on the truck and scared not to.

"Y'all go 'head," George said. "Don't worry about me. Go on and get in the truck. You ride. I'll get back to town. Don't worry about me. Just get on the truck."

He hitched a ride back to town and wondered how long his little union would hold.

Fear spread among Lil George's band of pickers after that losing day in the tangerine groves. The owner had come out and seen them not picking. All these walkouts, and there might come a time when the packinghouse wouldn't let them work at all. The boss men might blame them for the fruit hanging unpicked in the trees. A picker would end up hanging from a tree himself before long, if this kept up.

They talked among themselves when George, Mud, and Sam weren't around. They didn't like how George, in particular, had a way of being what they considered impudent with white people in a way that made everyone nervous.

Things had gone too far, as the other pickers saw it. These boys had been up north and were going to get all of them killed. That night, after the defeat over the tangerines, they went in secret to the owners of the grove.

"Us come by to tell y'all how come us didn't work today," they said. "Them boys, Sam and Mud and Lil George. You know them is bad. Them boys is bad. We know y'all is always done a good part by us colored folks, and we wanted to work. But them boys told us if we put a ladder in that tree, they gonna snatch the ladder up and stomp us when we hit the ground. So we scared. We know y'all is good white folks and has always done a good part by us. And it wasn't none a us."

Sometime later, a young man was tending the grove owner's yard. He was clearing debris around the garage when he heard voices inside. They were the voices of grove owners talking among themselves about people on the colored side of town, something about the trouble some men were causing in the groves.

The yard man recognized the name of Lil George Starling. Schoolboy had helped him fill out ration papers for sugar and gasoline. It was wartime, and he wouldn't have gotten any if he didn't have papers, and he wouldn't have had papers if George hadn't filled them out for him.

That night after work, the yard man went to Lil George.

"Lil George, I come to tell you what I heard them saying about you boys today in the garage up there," he said.

George looked at him and listened.

"I heard them plottin' that they gon' take you boys out," he said. "Say if they get rid a you three, that the rest of them they could handle. Say 'cause y'all got a big influence over them others. And so they scared a y'all. So they planning to get rid a y'all."

The yard man said he heard mention of a cypress swamp eighteen miles out from town.

"They talking 'bout taking y'all out to Blackwater Creek," he said. "They talking 'bout giving y'all a necktie party. They gon' take y'all out there and hang y'all in one of them cypress trees."

Something in George half expected as much. The man went on.

"I thought I would tell you 'cause you always were nice to me," he said. "When I had papers to fill out, I would bring my papers to you.

You would always do it for me. You never charged me anything. And I wanted you to know. I came out here to tell you y'all better watch yourself."

"I appreciate that," George told him, not wanting to betray the churning in his stomach. "Man, I ain't studyin' 'bout them people."

Inside was a different story. "I couldn't rest comfortable," he said.

Leaving was his only option. He went to tell his father. Big George was trying to set out a little grove of his own at a place called Grand Island five or six miles out from town. He had just put his orange trees in the ground and had to haul water out to them to soak them so they could catch root.

Lil George helped him haul lake water in barrels. Together, they poured the pails of water at the roots of the trees every evening.

Out in the grove that night, Lil George told him his plans.

"After today, I'm not gonna be able to help you haul no water," he said. "I'll help you water these trees. Then I'm gonna get my clothes together, and I'm gonna take on off. Because I'm not gonna change."

He told his father what his father already knew. Men had been hanged for far less than what George was orchestrating. And there would be no protecting him if he stayed. In Florida and in the rest of the Deep South, "the killing of a Negro by a white man ceased in practice even to call for legal inquiry," a white southerner observed in the early 1940s.

George and his father lived with that reality every day of their lives, and now it was right before them.

"So the best thing for me to do," George told his father, "is to get on out from around here."

FORT POLK, LOUISIANA, EARLY 1953
ROBERT JOSEPH PERSHING FOSTER

BY THE TIME his tour of duty in Austria was over, Pershing had worked his way to a position of esteem if not authority and won awards for his medical skills. He had worked long hours, odd hours, building up his reputation, but it had left him no further ahead. Most southern hospitals wouldn't allow him inside an operating room no matter how gifted he was or what he'd done in the army. There was simply no place for a high-minded colored surgeon who thought he was as good as, or, to hear him tell it, better than most anybody else. He was now discharged to Fort Polk, Louisiana, and, with no job prospects and a family to support, was plotting his escape from the world he had known. But where? And to what?

He stayed awake at night weighing the options. All this education and no place to practice and live out his life as he imagined it to be. The only assurance of a job was back home in Monroe. Madison would be overjoyed to have his little brother join his small-town practice. But Louisiana was out of the question. In the time Pershing had been away, the Fosters had lost their place as the leading and often resented colored family in Monroe. His mother, Ottie, had passed away. His father, Professor Foster, had been edged out of his position as principal of Monroe Colored High School, to which he had devoted most of his adult life and identity. He had been forced into retirement and had to watch as a younger rival from his own faculty, Henry Carroll, not only ascended to the principal's desk but also, through carefully tended connections to a former governor of Louisiana, James A. Noe, managed to get a new colored high school built and named after himself.

Robert watched the school go up and grieved for his heartbroken father. Just being a Foster in Monroe was like being in exile now. Besides, Alice had no interest in that small town. She wouldn't stand for it, and Pershing couldn't bear it.

He could return to Alice's home in Atlanta. The Clements would be beside themselves. And that was the problem. Dr. Clement could surely set him up in practice, and Alice and Pershing could join colored society as the daughter and son-in-law of a distinguished university president. They would have a place card calligraphied for them whenever dignitaries came to visit—Eleanor Roosevelt, the Rockefellers, and so forth. They would have everything they aspired to. But at what price? He imagined he couldn't so much as choose the seasoning on the roast with Dr. Clement down the street.

As it was, Dr. Clement was growing in prominence in Atlanta, looming larger than ever before, running for the Board of Education, seeking to become the first colored holder of a major office since Reconstruction.

Back in medical school, Pershing had begun suspecting he had lost his place as the man in his family. While he was away learning to be a doctor, the family grew accustomed to Pershing's absence, had settled into routines and ways of being that could not be turned off overnight.

Alice and the girls were living in President Clement's brick Georgian mansion with its circular driveway and Doric-columned veranda, its groundskeepers and servants, its chintz draperies and damask upholstery in grand parlors and receiving rooms. There, dignitaries gathered for tea and, in the evenings, Dr. Clement read to his beloved granddaughters in a club chair by the fireplace, pictures of the girls on the mantel next to the porcelain figurines. The Clements and Alice would gather the girls around the baby grand to sing along as Alice played.

Bunny and Robin had become adorable little girls in pigtails and ribbons and patent-leather shoes, but Pershing didn't truly know them. He had missed the milestones in their lives, their first steps, their first words, their first day of school. It was the Clements who dried their tears when they fell and went over their homework with them.

Pershing could not blame anyone for what had become of his role in the family. He had agreed to the arrangement. Now he decided he needed to get as far from the Clements as he could to take possession of the family that was slipping from his influence. Atlanta was in the South, anyway. Atlanta was off the list.

He sat down and tried to figure out—*where else did he know anybody?* There must be someplace outside the South he could go. In the years since World War I, a large colony of colored people from Monroe had established themselves in Detroit. Faroker Johnson was one hometown man he knew. He was a dentist who had preceded him at Meharry and was practicing up in River Rouge. Then there was his boyhood friend Nimrod Sherman. He was a psychiatrist up in Detroit and doing alright for himself. But Detroit didn't have the sophistication Pershing was looking for, and he didn't consider it for very long. Same for St. Louis, where he had done his residency, and even Chicago, which was cold besides.

What he wanted was New York, where they never turned the lights out and had the best of anything you could think of. But he didn't know anybody there. That wasn't the natural route people from Louisiana took to get out of the South. They went where the railroad took them, straight north to Chicago and Detroit. Or west to California, where the climate was more to their liking.

So Pershing would have to think West, which was not a difficult thing to do. He had been hearing about California all his life, played pretend with Clara Poe and always said he was going to California before he even knew what it was. Seemed like everybody who left Monroe was talking California. There was a contingent up in Oakland, a branch down in Los Angeles, spreading out to Fresno and over to San Bernardino. He had names, lots of names. More than enough to make a practice out of. Not only was it out of the South, it was about as far as you could get from the South and the Clements, too.

He began to get excited at the very thought. No more stepping to the side door to get your meal like a hog at a trough. No more operations in somebody's kitchen and lynchings in the next county. He could dress like he wanted, act like he wanted, be who he wanted and how he wanted to be it. He would not have to try to protect his daughters from some planter with snuff in his mouth and know he couldn't. In California, he could stand up straight and not apologize for it. He would know what white people's water tasted like and drink it whenever he wanted. It wasn't one thing. It was everything. He was going to be a citizen of the United States, like the passport said.

He told Alice his decision. They could start out fresh in California, the four of them. He would go first and see it for himself. She and the girls would stay in Atlanta for now, and she could start packing their belongings. He would send for them after he got settled. All he had to do now was save a little money. And figure how best to get out.

AMERICA, 1915–1970

A SERIES OF UNPREDICTABLE EVENTS and frustrations led to the decisions of Ida Mae Gladney, George Swanson Starling, and Robert Pershing Foster to leave the South for good. Their decisions were separate and distinct from anything in the outside world except that they were joining a road already plied decades before by people as discontented as themselves. A thousand hurts and killed wishes led to a final determination by each fed-up individual on the verge of departure, which, added to millions of others, made up what could be called a migration.

If there was a single precipitating event that set off the Great Migration, it was World War I. After all, blacks had tried to escape the South with limited degrees of success from the time the first slaves arrived in Virginia in 1619. The Underground Railroad spirited hundreds of slaves out of the South and as far north as Canada before the Civil War. Later, in 1879, Benjamin "Pap" Singleton, a former slave who made coffins for colored lynching victims and was disheartened by the steadiness of his work, led a pilgrimage of six thousand ex-slaves, known as Exodusters, from the banks of the Mississippi River onto the free soil of Kansas.

In the ensuing decades, a continuous trickle of brave souls chanced an unguaranteed existence in the unknown cities of the North. The trickle became a stream after Jim Crow laws closed in on blacks in the South in the 1890s. During the first decade of the twentieth century, some 194,000 blacks left the coastal and border states of the South and settled in relative anonymity in the colored quarters of primarily northeastern cities, such as Harlem in New York and in North Philadelphia. Some were domestics for wealthy northerners; others were musicians, intellectuals, and exiled politicians of the Reconstruction era who would inspire colored people in the South by their very existence.

But the masses did not pour out of the South until they had something to go to. They got their chance when the North began courting them, hard and in secret, in the face of southern hostility, during the labor crisis of World War I. Word had spread like wildfire that the North was finally "opening up."

The war had cut the supply of European workers the North had relied on to kill its hogs and stoke its foundries. Immigration plunged by more than ninety percent, from 1,218,480 in 1914 to 110,618 in 1918, when the country needed all the labor it could get for war production. So the North turned its gaze to the poorest-paid labor in the emerging market of the American South. Steel mills, railroads, and packinghouses sent labor scouts disguised as insurance men and salesmen to recruit blacks north, if only temporarily.

The recruiters would stride through groupings of colored people and whisper without stopping, *"Anybody want to go to Chicago, see me."* It was an invitation that tapped into pent-up yearnings and was just what the masses had been waiting for. The trickle that became a stream had now become a river, uncontrolled and uncontrollable, and about to climb out of its banks. Some 555,000 colored people left the South during the decade of the First World War—more than all the colored people who had left in the five decades after the Emancipation Proclamation, which promised the freedoms they were now forced to pursue on their own.

At first the South was proud and ambivalent, pretended that it did not care. "As the North grows blacker, the South grows whiter," the *New Orleans Times-Picayune* happily noted.

Then, as planters awoke to empty fields, the South began to panic. "Where shall we get labor to take their places?" asked the *Montgomery Advertiser,* as southerners began to confront the reality observed by the *Columbia State* of South Carolina: "Black labor is the best labor the South can get. No other would work long under the same conditions."

"It is the life of the South," a Georgia plantation owner once said. "It is the foundation of its prosperity. . . . God pity the day when the negro leaves the South."

"With all our crimes of omission and commission, we still retain a marked affection for the Negro," wrote David L. Cohn in the 1935 book *God Shakes Creation.* "It is inconceivable to us that we should be without him."

The Macon Telegraph put it more bluntly: "We must have the negro in the South," it said. "It is the most pressing thing before this State today. Matters of governorships and judgeships are only bagatelle compared to the real importance of this negro exodus."

Yet as reality sank in, nobody could agree on what to do about it, debating to the point of exasperation. "Why hunt for the cause when it's plain as the noonday sun?" wrote a white reader in the *Montgomery Advertiser.* "He doesn't want to leave but he knows if he stays here he will starve. They have nothing to eat, no clothes, no shoes, and they can't get any work to do and they are leaving just as fast as they can get away. . . . If the Negro race could get work at 50 cents a day he would stay here."

And a newspaper in Columbia, South Carolina, put this question to the ruling caste: "If you thought you might be lynched by mistake," the paper asked, "would you remain in South Carolina?"

When the South woke up to the loss of its once guaranteed workforce, it tried to find ways to intercept it. Southern authorities resurrected the anti-enticement laws originally enacted after the Civil War to keep newly freed slaves from being lured away, this time, however, aimed at northern companies coveting the South's cheapest and most desperate workers.

"Conditions recently became so alarming—that is, so many Negroes were leaving," wrote an Alabama official, that the state began making anyone caught enticing blacks away—labor agents, they were called—

pay an annual license fee of $750 "in every county in which he operates or solicits emigrants" or be "fined as much as $500 and sentenced to a year's hard labor."

Macon, Georgia, required labor agents to pay a $25,000 fee and to secure the unlikely recommendations of twenty-five local businessmen, ten ministers, and ten manufacturers in order to solicit colored workers to go north. But by the middle of World War I, those laws were useless. Northern industries didn't need to recruit anymore. Word had spread, and the exodus took on a life of its own. "Every Negro that makes good in the North and writes back to his friends, starts off a new group," a Labor Department study observed.

So the South tried to choke off the flow of information about the North. The chief of police in Meridian, Mississippi, ordered copies of the *Chicago Defender* confiscated before they could be sold, fearing it was putting ideas into colored people's heads.

When the people kept leaving, the South resorted to coercion and interception worthy of the Soviet Union, which was forming at the same time across the Atlantic. Those trying to leave were rendered fugitives by definition and could not be certain they would be able to make it out. In Brookhaven, Mississippi, authorities stopped a train with fifty colored migrants on it and sidetracked it for three days. In Albany, Georgia, the police tore up the tickets of colored passengers as they stood waiting to board, dashing their hopes of escape. A minister in South Carolina, having seen his parishioners off, was arrested at the station on the charge of helping colored people get out. In Savannah, Georgia, the police arrested every colored person at the station regardless of where he or she was going. In Summit, Mississippi, authorities simply closed the ticket office and did not let northbound trains stop for the colored people waiting to get on.

Instead of stemming the tide, the blockades and arrests "served to intensify the desire to leave," wrote the sociologists Willis T. Weatherford and Charles S. Johnson, "and to provide further reasons for going."

To circumvent the heavy surveillance, some migrants simply bought tickets to cities two or three stations away where they would not be recognized or where there was less of a police presence. There, under less scrutiny, they bought tickets to their true destination. Those who had somehow gotten on the wrong side of somebody in the ruling class had to go to unusual lengths to get out, one man disguising himself as a woman to flee Crystal Springs, Mississippi, for Chicago in the 1940s.

Chastened by their losses, some businessmen tried conciliation, one delegation going so far as to travel to Chicago to persuade former sharecroppers that things had changed and it was time they came back. (The sharecroppers showed no interest and instead took the opportunity to complain about being cheated and whipped while in their employ.) In the 1920s, the Tennessee Association of Commerce, the Department of Immigration of Louisiana, the Mississippi Welfare League, and the Southern Alluvial Land Association all sent representatives north to try to bring colored workers back. They offered free train tickets and promised better wages and living conditions. They returned empty-handed.

When these efforts didn't work, some planters increased wages, if only temporarily, and tried easing up on their workers to induce them to stay. "Owing to the scarcity of labor," the Labor Department reported, "a Georgia farmer near Albany this year laid aside his whip and gun, with which it is reported he has been accustomed to drive his hands, and begged for laborers."

Oblivious to the hand-wringing, trainloads of colored people took their chances and crowded railroad platforms. Men hopped freight trains and hoboed out of the South in grain bins. Women walked off cotton fields in Texas, hiding their Sunday dresses under their field rags, bound for California. A granite quarry in Lithonia, Georgia, had to shut down because its workers had vanished. "One section gang left their tools on the spot, not stopping to get their pay," Arna Bontemps wrote of one work site.

All the while, in the places they left, the weeds grew up over the cotton, the rice and tobacco lay fallow and unpicked, and the mules wandered the pastures because, as the historian James R. Grossman noted, there was no one to hitch them to a plow.

Breaking Away

I was leaving without a qualm,
without a single backward glance.
The face of the South that I had known
was hostile and forbidding,
and yet out of all the conflicts
and the curses . . . ,
the tension and the terror,
I had somehow gotten the idea
that life could be different. . . .
I was now running more away
from something than toward something. . . .
My mood was:
I've got to get away;
I can't stay here.

—Richard Wright, *Black Boy*

CHICKASAW COUNTY, MISSISSIPPI, OCTOBER 1937

IDA MAE BRANDON GLADNEY

IN A DAY, the world had changed. Everything was in a commotion, but George and Ida Mae could not let it show. Joe Lee had been beaten half dead over a false accusation about some turkeys that had run off. He had been left in a jail cell, barely conscious, his clothes sticking to his bloodied skin, and nothing was done about it. Ida Mae and George bent their heads and prayed for light. Then they went out in the field the next day. They picked long and hard and more urgently than before. They decided they would leave as soon as they got the cotton out of the ground.

They would give Mr. Edd no cause to suspect their intentions or to withhold their pay. They needed whatever was due at settlement to get out of Mississippi.

They could not risk telling anyone but Saint and Miss Theenie and the one or two other relatives they needed to help them get out. And so they continued to gather the cotton. The land went from white to brown as they made their way across it. They began selling off their possessions, one by one, so as not to attract attention. The cows. The hogs. The chickens. The feather beds and quilts. The tin tub. The wash pots. The rusted old Model T Ford. The double-blade axes Ida Mae used to chop wood and kill snakes with. They went into town and sold what livestock was theirs and not Mr. Edd's. What they didn't sell they gave away or left with Saint to dispense with.

And if anybody asked what was going on, they knew to say, "We just running out of room."

For some reason, Ida Mae was dragging more than usual. But there was so much to do and so little time, there was no point in mentioning it. They needed to get out before people started speculating about what it was they were doing. The way people talked, it wouldn't take long to get back to Mr. Edd. Someone would love to curry favor, alert him to a sharecropper trying to leave. There were spies and Toms all over the place, setting up fellow colored men and sending them to their deaths for an extra privilege or two. Planters did not like to lose good help. They had ways of keeping sharecroppers under them, claimed they owed money when they didn't, that they had to work off the debt, which meant they were working for free and made fugitives of them if they left. The planters kept the books, and, even if a sharecropper had the nerve to keep his own, a colored man's numbers didn't count.

If George and Ida Mae didn't get out, life could be harder than it already was. The quicker they got the cotton out of the ground, the better off they would be.

It was already late in the season, and before long they had picked their last bale. George had to figure out how best to leave. He decided first to get off Mr. Edd's land. They quietly gathered up what little they were taking and carried it over to Miss Theenie's after the cotton was picked. They would leave from the house where George had courted Ida Mae.

George wanted to settle with Mr. Edd as soon as possible and prepared to go see him. After what happened to Joe Lee, Ida Mae worried whenever George went out.

"George, be careful," she said.

"I ain't gon' be careful. I ain't done nothing to him."

George went up to Mr. Edd like it was any other end-of-the-season settlement. He gave no indication that it was his fervent hope never to see him again in life or ever again to set foot in the state of Mississippi.

He looked over the list of credits and debits Mr. Edd had tallied—the bales of cotton he and Ida Mae had gathered, the seed and cornmeal they had consumed. It didn't matter what he thought of it. He couldn't dispute it no matter what it said. At the bottom of the page was a figure that showed he had a few dollars coming to him for a year's worth of labor.

It was not much, but it was more than many sharecroppers got. Fewer than one out of five sharecroppers ever saw a profit at the end of the year. Of the few who got anything, their pay came to between $30 and $150 in the 1930s for a year of hard toil in the field, according to a leading Yale anthropologist of the era, or between nine and forty-eight cents a day. The remaining eighty percent either broke even, meaning they got nothing, or stayed in debt, which meant they were as bound to the planter as a slave was to his master.

There was no place to appeal. "How a man treats his tenants is not felt to be a matter of public concern," the anthropologist Hortense Powdermaker wrote, "but is as much his private affair as what brand of toothpaste he uses."

George did the math in his head and saw that, along with what he had managed to save up to this day, it was enough for four tickets north on the Illinois Central Railroad.

Mr. Edd handed him the bills, and George completed the transaction without so much as a smile, which was his way. He tucked the money in his pocket and thought about what next to say. There before him stood his boss man and overseer of close to ten years. Mr. Edd was a man a full head taller than George and partial to ten-gallon hats. Whatever he may have done to other colored people in the name of the white man's law, Mr. Edd had been honorable in his dealings with him. He had never raised a hand to him or Ida Mae, and George gave him no cause to do so.

George could have left after settlement without saying a word. It was a risk to say too much. The planter could rescind the settlement, say he misfigured, turn a credit into a debit, take back the money, evict the family or whip the sharecropper on the spot, or worse. Some sharecroppers, knowing they might not get paid anyway, fled from the field, right in midhoe, on the first thing going north.

The planters could not conceive of why their sharecroppers would want to leave. The dance of the compliant sharecropper conceding to the big planter year in and year out made it seem as if the ritual actually made sense, that the sharecropper, having been given no choice, actually saw the tilted scales as fair. The sharecropper's forced silence was part of the collusion that fed the mythology.

And so it came as a shock to many planters when their trusted sharecroppers expressed a desire to leave. Like one planter in Florence, Alabama. Year after year, he would go down the list of staples he said his sharecropper, Jack Fowler, owed:

I LB FLOUR

I LB RICE

I LB CORN MEAL

I LB COFFEE

The planter scanned the page and decided to add a few more pounds of coffee, increasing Fowler's debt to him. One year, the sharecropper finally spoke up, careful not to suggest the planter was a liar or an outright cheat.

"Mr. Perry, you know I don't drink coffee."

With that, the planter added another pound of coffee to the list. The sharecropper could do nothing but watch.

One year, the planter's son happened to come in during settlement and spoke up himself.

"Pa, you know Jack don't drink coffee."

And, for once, the sharecropper didn't have to pay for something he had never consumed in the first place.

Sometime after settlement, he went to tell his boss man he was leaving for a place called Lake Forest, Illinois. The planter had already settled with Jack Fowler and had no rational excuse to keep the sharecropper on his plantation, which didn't mean he couldn't have if he wanted to. Instead, the planter tried to scare the sharecropper out of leaving.

"Jack, you gonna go up there and freeze your brains," the planter told his sharecropper. "And who is going to handle my horses when you leave?"

Knowing the dangerous and arbitrary rules of the world he was in, George stood before Mr. Edd and weighed what he should say. Mr. Edd had already paid him, so George thought he was safe. They had agreed that George did not owe him and was not in the planter's debt. Mr. Edd had always been a man of his word, and George trusted him to keep it now. George made the calculation that the truth would serve him better than if he were later caught in a knowing omission. He prayed and breathed deep before speaking.

"Well, this'll be my last crop with you, Mr. Edd," George said. He told him he and Ida Mae were moving to Milwaukee.

Mr. Edd did not see it coming.

"Oh, you ain't gon' leave, George," Mr. Edd said.

George was a quiet man who could pick a whole field by himself without complaint. He took whatever was given him and knew not to question. Yet he had a way of walling off his family that even a segregationist could respect. George was the kind of sharecropper a planter could depend on, and Mr. Edd showed his appreciation by letting him clear a few dollars most years. Mr. Edd didn't want to lose George. He wanted to know what he was leaving for. George told him he didn't like what happened to Joe Lee.

"Oh, you ain't gon' leave for that," Mr. Edd said. "It wasn't none a you."

"I know," George said. "It wouldn't been me."

Ida Mae was gathering their belongings while George settled with Mr. Edd. She lumbered as she went about her packing. Miss Theenie looked at her hard. She saw something that nobody else would notice, how Ida Mae loped now, the way the burlap tugged across the front of her.

"Look to me like you pregnant," she said.

"Oh, no, I ain't."

"What you goin' up there for pregnant?"

"I ain't pregnant."

She was a couple of months along now and had kept it to herself. George might tell her to stay in Mississippi, leave her and the children with Miss Theenie, say he would send for her like the other men who say they're going to send for their wives and don't, get up to the big city and forget all about what they left. If Miss Theenie knew, she would kick up a fuss and scare George into leaving Ida Mae there. So she lied to Miss Theenie, denied up and down that she was expecting, and Miss Theenie couldn't prove it but knew that time would tell and prove her right.

There was no way for Ida Mae to know what was transpiring between her husband and Mr. Edd at settlement. George had prayed over it and had hoped Mr. Edd would remain a man of his word. If all went well, George told Ida Mae, he would go to the train station in Okolona ahead of them. He wanted to get the tickets right away. He had arranged in advance for one of his brothers to take Ida Mae and the children to the station to meet him. The plan was for them to leave that night.

EUSTIS, FLORIDA, APRIL 1945
GEORGE SWANSON STARLING

LIL GEORGE BROKE THE NEWS to Inez that he was getting out of Eustis on the next train out of Wildwood. The grove owners had it in for him because he had roused up the pickers. The pickers had turned on him out of fear for themselves. He had no choice but to get out. He told Inez he was going up to Harlem, where his aunts were.

He started gathering his things right away. There was no time to waste. The yard boy who warned him about the grove owners' meeting didn't seem to know any more than what he'd happened to overhear—that the grove owners were plotting to take George and Mud and Sam out to the cypress swamps over at Blackwater Creek and hang them at "a necktie party," that the owners were bent on teaching them a lesson for stepping out of their place, demanding an extra dime for the fruit they picked, and turning the heads of the faithful other pickers who had been content with whatever the owners gave them.

There was no telling whom the grove owners might have enlisted, when or how they might round the boys up, whether it would be the new big-hat sheriff, some crew foremen, or Klansmen currying favor, whether it might be somebody George would recognize right away after all these years or not know at all. He went about his last-minute arrangements, watchful of everybody and careful to mind his steps.

He could not be seen anywhere near the groves again. It was dangerous enough just being in Eustis during the hours it took to get out. There were so many things he wanted or needed to do—he was leaving forever, after all—but he was running out of time.

He dashed off a letter to his aunts, Annie and Lavata, to alert them to his situation. They would need to know to expect him.

He tried to reassure Inez that everything would work out, but she was still seething over the fact that he had turned their lives upside down and put all of them in danger. She hadn't approved of what he had been doing anyway and didn't know why he couldn't make himself satisfied like everybody else.

"What did you expect from a bunch of handkerchief heads?" she asked him. "What do you expect?"

"I guess I expect the unexpectable," he said, "because they don't look at things like the way I do."

Here he was running for his life, and the two of them were arguing over what couldn't be undone. George didn't ask Inez what he should do. He didn't consult her as to where he should go or whether she would join him. He just told her he was going up to where his aunts were.

"I'm going to New York and get situated," he said. "And when I get situated, I'll send for you."

Their anniversary, April 19, was coming up in a few days, but if everything worked according to plan, he would be gone by then. He felt there was no time for debating and thought he should be the judge of what would happen to him. "After all," he would say years later, "it was my neck on the block."

Inez heard the magic words—"I'll send for you"—and did not put up much more of a fuss. He had not taken her to Detroit, but he would bring her to New York, and that was good enough for now. She warmed to the idea and felt better and better about it. She thought less now of the danger of the circumstances than of their new life up north. A chance to start over in a new place together.

He told Mud and Sam he was leaving. They were leaving, too. Sam was talking Washington, D.C., where he had a brother. Mud was talking about a place he had heard of called Rochester, New York. Then Lil

George said good-bye to Inez and good-bye to his father, who, if he was worried, kept it to himself.

"Yeah, well," Big George said, "I think this will be the best. I guess if you gonna still act that way, it's best for you to go."

MONROE, LOUISIANA, MARCH 1953
ROBERT JOSEPH PERSHING FOSTER

PERSHING WAS WORKING AT FORT POLK, an hour's drive from Monroe, for the singular purpose of saving up the money to go to California. His heart was already gone. His mother had died. His widowed father, Professor Foster, had been forced out as principal of the school to which he had devoted his life, by one of his own teachers. The coup left Professor Foster a leader in exile. He watched the new colored high school he had always dreamed of rise up under the name of his rival. Pershing grieved for his father and all that had happened in a caste system that seemed to rely on pitting the lowliest people against one another.

He drove between Monroe and Fort Polk at the edge of spring, blind to the wild grasses that blushed on either side of the Bayou Desiard. The bayou cut through town and bent toward the west, and the land was thick with crimson clover crawling up the folds in the land.

It was beautiful, but it didn't matter. Pershing was thirty-four years old. His life was in front of him, and he was not going to live it out in a one-stoplight town in the South.

On that, he and Alice had agreed, and she would wait for him to send for her and the girls once he got situated. Still, his brother Madison tried to get him to stay, reclaim the family's former glory. Madison had a small practice there and was ready to etch Pershing's name beside his on the door. The two of them could work out of Madison's second-floor office on Desiard. They could travel the parish in their portable hospital and tend to the colored schoolteachers and the women who took in washing, the athletes out at Grambling and the sharecroppers who might pay with buttermilk or the side of a freshly killed hog.

But Pershing did not want to be paid with buttermilk or the side of a freshly killed hog and did not want to deliver babies in somebody's kitchen.

There was a respectable hospital in town. St. Francis. It was a brick building that stood with the color and trim efficiency of a manila folder. It had white beds in one wing and colored beds in another and was closed to colored doctors. Pershing put St. Francis out of his mind and figured he would work at Fort Polk until he had the money to leave.

One day he went into town and walked into the old clothing shop of a white storekeeper. He had known the man since he was a little boy picking up clothes for his father.

"I'm M. J. Foster's boy. I think you have a suit for him," he used to go in and say.

Pershing was grown up now. He was in uniform with his captain's bars and medical caduceus. The storekeeper noticed and asked what he was going to do when he got out of the army.

"Well, I'm going to go into practice, private practice," Pershing said.

"Are you gonna come here with your brother?"

"No, I'm going to California and start my practice there when I get out of Fort Polk. And this is what I plan to do."

"What's wrong with St. Francis?"

Pershing shook his head. The man had lived there since before Pershing was born, and a central fact of colored people's existence hadn't registered after all these years.

"You know that colored surgeons can't operate at St. Francis, Mr. Massur."

The man looked startled and caught himself. White-only and colored-only signs were all over town, but the storekeeper had not thought about how segregation applied to the hospital. The storekeeper had watched Pershing grow into an upstanding young man and had known the Fosters for years. For a split second, the storekeeper seemed to see Pershing as no different than any other bright young physician. But Pershing's words brought him back to reality: the rest of the white world did not see Pershing the way the storekeeper did, and that gave the storekeeper an uncomfortable glimpse of the burdens on one of his best customers.

There was a moment of awkwardness between the two men. And as the realization hit the storekeeper, the truth hit Pershing, too. He stepped outside himself and considered the absurdity that he was doing surgery for the United States Army and couldn't operate in his own hometown.

The man tried to recover, offer advice and encouragement. "Well, why don't you all build a hospital, you and your brother?"

"Mr. Massur, do you realize that we are doctors and not businessmen? The cost of building a hospital and operating one would be astronomical."

There was very little to say after that. Even the storekeeper could see the impossibility of the situation. He wished Pershing well in whatever he did, and Pershing went on his way.

Mr. Massur had meant well. Still it made no sense to Pershing that one set of people could be in a cage, and the people outside couldn't see the bars. But he told himself it didn't matter anyway because he was through with Monroe, through with small towns and small minds and particularly small-minded small towns in the South.

He didn't like how you couldn't get your teeth cleaned without everybody knowing it. He didn't like how the white people couldn't quite manage to call him "Dr. Foster" but spat out "Doc" as if they were addressing the cook. He didn't like how his brother Madison denied himself certain twentieth-century conveniences to avoid submitting to the indignities of Jim Crow.

Madison never went to the side window of a white restaurant, never sat in the back of the Paramount Theater like other colored people. Because he never went. He drove his son, little Madison James, to the theater and watched the colored people climb the back stairs and pack the balcony to see whatever was playing. But he never went inside himself.

In the 1940s, Madison had petitioned St. Francis Hospital for a position on staff. The hospital rejected him. But he refused to leave town, and he didn't let it stop him from working. If he couldn't practice at a hospital, he would carry a hospital in his trunk. He had a portable operating table built especially for his patients and lugged it into their shotgun houses when it was time to do surgery or deliver their babies.

He didn't suffer the humiliation of seeing a suit he wanted to try on in a store but couldn't because colored people weren't allowed that courtesy. He just never went. He sent his wife, Harriet, instead. The two of them would drive up and down Desiard Street from Hanes to the Palace, the finest men's stores in town. Madison sat in the car and waited while Harriet went from store to store and came out with an armload of clothes. She held up each suit on its hanger. He inspected the weave and the cut from the car window and told her which ones to buy. And that is how Madison got his wardrobe.

Pershing wouldn't stand for that. Pershing wanted to walk right into the Palace and try on a suit if he pleased and sit in a corner booth at The Lounge if he wanted. He was restless for a basic kind of freedom that was crazy at best and arrogant at worst for a colored man in that place at that time, and the two brothers knew it.

One last time, each made his pitch to the other. Pershing tried to get Madison to go with him to California, set up practice there. After all, they practically had a clientele waiting for them. Half of colored Monroe was already out there. Madison tried to get Pershing to stay. Louisiana was home, and things would never change if everyone gave up and left. What did Pershing know about starting a practice in California? He had never set foot in California. Running away meant Jim Crow had won, and Madison wasn't going to give the rascals that. And besides, there was no guarantee Jim Crow wasn't out in California.

It was getting to be early April. The brothers made a necessary peace. Pershing decided to leave the day after Easter with Madison's blessing, if not approval, and readied for the round of formal good-byes.

The Covingtons, who lived down the street from Madison, heard Pershing was leaving and planned the going-away party for the Saturday night before Easter. The Hills, the Browns, January the Tailor, and all the better-off colored people in New Town gathered at the Covingtons' white frame bungalow with the azaleas out front at the corner of Eleventh and Louise Anne Avenue.

Ivorye Covington cooked all day for the Fosters—fried chicken and waffles and collard greens and corn bread. The place was prim with white tablecloths and upholstery and smoky from the Camels and Chesterfields.

Pershing, the bon vivant in sport coat and ruler-creased trousers, made the rounds through the dining room and living room and Ivorye's yellow kitchen with a shot of bourbon in his hand. He was leaving first thing Monday morning, he told everyone, heading southwest to Houston on his way west to first stop by and see a Dr. Anthony Beale—*you remember Anthony Beale, who used to go out with my sister, Gold; he's practicing in Houston now, and he said he could help me get started there, but I said thank you very much, but I'm set on California.*

Late into the evening, Ivorye's husband, N.E., turned down the record player in the front room, clearing the haze of chatter and bebop. The dancing by the credenza came to a stop. And Napoleon Brown and

Pless Hill, Big Madison and Harriet and the rest raised their glasses to Pershing, who was joining the Migration without them.

Pershing looked out into the faces and could not for the life of him figure out why these people were frittering away their lives in a place like this.

"How in the world can you stay in Monroe," he finally said, "and live in this Jim Crow situation?"

It was pompous, as he was at times known to be, and perhaps out of place at so well meaning a send-off. But he had convinced himself it was crazy to stay and wrong if he left without coming right out and saying it.

"How can you stay here and take the crumbs?" he said. "Come go to Heaven with me. To California."

He knew no more about California than they did, and he won no immediate converts that night. But he had planted the seed and would follow up once he had seen the state for himself.

I pick up my life
And take it with me
And I put it down in
Chicago, Detroit,
Buffalo, Scranton . . .
I pick up my life
And take it on the train
To Los Angeles, Bakersfield,
Seattle, Oakland, Salt Lake,
Any place that is
North and West—
And not South.

—LANGSTON HUGHES,
"ONE-WAY TICKET"

AMERICA, 1915–1975

AS THEY SUMMONED THE WILL TO LEAVE, it would never have occurred to Ida Mae, George, and Pershing, or the millions of others who continued to flee the South over the decades of the Great Migration, that it was supposed to have ended in World War I, when they were just coming into the world. They joined a flight already in progress when the narrow straits of their lives compelled them to do so. Theirs is a kind of living testimony that migrations fed by the human heart do not begin and end as neatly as statisticians might like.

The Great Migration in particular was not a seasonal, contained, or singular event. It was a statistically measurable demographic phenomenon marked by unabated outflows of black émigrés that lasted roughly from 1915 to 1975. It peaked during the war years, swept a good portion of all the black people alive in the United States at the time into a river that carried them to all points north and west.

Like other mass migrations, it was not a haphazard unfurling of lost souls but a calculable and fairly ordered resettlement of people along the most direct route to what they perceived as freedom, based on railroad and bus lines. The migration streams were so predictable that by the end of the Migration, and, to a lesser degree, even now, one can tell where a black northerner's family was from just by the city the person grew up in—a good portion of blacks in Detroit, for instance, having roots in Tennessee, Alabama, western Georgia, or the Florida panhandle because the historic rail lines connected those places during the Migration years.

"Migratory currents flow along certain well-defined geographical channels," wrote E. G. Ravenstein, a British historian, in his landmark 1885 study of human migration. "They are like mighty rivers, which flow along slowly at the outset and after depositing most of the human beings whom they hold in suspension, sweep along more impetuously, until they enter one of the great . . . reservoirs."

The Great Migration ran along three main tributaries and emptied into reservoirs all over the North and West. One stream, the one George Starling was about to embark upon, carried people from the coastal states of Florida, Georgia, the Carolinas, and Virginia up the eastern seaboard to Washington, Philadelphia, New York, Boston, and their satellites. A second current, Ida Mae's, traced the central spine of the continent, paralleling the Father of Waters, from Mississippi, Alabama, Tennessee, and Arkansas to the industrial cities of Cleveland, Detroit, Chicago, Milwaukee, Pittsburgh. A third and later stream carried people like Pershing from Louisiana and Texas to the entire West Coast, with some black southerners traveling farther than many modern-day immigrants.

The chronology of this Great Migration, as is the case in many immigrant experiences, was sometimes a more circuitous affair than might be expected and has at times been reported. Some participants of the Great Migration made trips outside the South before their actual and final leaving, which suggests that a great deal of ambivalent churning preceded a fair number of departures. Many served overseas during wartime, in the First and Second World Wars and in the conflict in Korea. Some managed to visit relatives up north; some tried to make a go of it in one city before trying out another. These trips often exposed them to the freedoms they were denied back home, served as way stations where they could earn enough money for the next leg of their journey, or otherwise emboldened them and fed their desire to migrate. Thus, leaving the South was not always a direct path but one of testing and checking of facts with those who had left ahead of them, before making the great leap themselves.

Yet the hardened and peculiar institution of Jim Crow made the Great Migration different from ordinary human migrations. In their desperation to escape what might be considered a man-made pestilence, southern blacks challenged some scholarly assumptions about human migration. One theory has it that, due to human pragmatism and inertia, migrating people tend to "go no further from their homes in search of work than is absolutely necessary," Ravenstein observed.

"The bulk of migrants prefers a short journey to a long one," he wrote. "The more enterprising long-journey migrants are the exceptions and not the rule." Southern blacks were the exception. They traveled deep into far-flung regions of their own country and in some cases clear across the continent. Thus the Great Migration had more in common with the vast movements of refugees from famine, war, and genocide in other parts of the world, where oppressed people, whether fleeing twenty-first-century Darfur or nineteenth-century Ireland, go great distances, journey across rivers, deserts, and oceans or as far as it takes to reach safety with the hope that life will be better wherever they land.

PART THREE

EXODUS

There is no mistaking
what is going on;
it is a regular exodus.
It is without head, tail, or leadership.
Its greatest factor is momentum,
and this is increasing,
despite amazing efforts on the part
of white Southerners to stop it.
People are leaving their homes
and everything about them,
under cover of night,
as though they were going
on a day's journey—
leaving forever.

—*The Cleveland Advocate,*
APRIL 28, 1917

We look up at
the high southern sky. . . .
We scan the kind black faces
we have looked upon
since we first saw the light of day,
and, though pain is in our hearts,
we are leaving.

—RICHARD WRIGHT,
12 Million Black Voices

The Appointed Time of Their Coming

Even the stork
in the sky knows
her appointed seasons,
and the dove,
the swift and the thrush
observe the time
of their migration.
—Jeremiah 8:7

NEAR OKOLONA, MISSISSIPPI, LATE AUTUMN 1937
IDA MAE BRANDON GLADNEY

IDA MAE AND THE CHILDREN rumbled over curled ribbons of dirt road in a brother-in-law's truck from Miss Theenie's house to the train depot in Okolona. Piled high around them were all the worldly possessions they could manage to carry—the overalls and Sunday clothes, the cook pots and kerosene lamps, a Bible and the quilts that Ida Mae and Miss Theenie had sewn out of used-up remnants of the clothes they had worn out tilling the Mississippi soil. Miss Theenie had not wanted them to go and had prayed over them and with them and then watched as her second-born daughter left the rutted land of the ancestors. *"May the Lord be the first one in the car," Miss Theenie had whispered about the train they were hoping to catch, "and the last out."*

Heading to the depot through the dust hollows and the cotton fields and away from the only place she had ever lived, Ida Mae did not know what would become of them or if her husband could actually pull this thing off. She did not know if Mr. Edd would let them go or stand in their way, if her husband would get anything from Mr. Edd at settlement, if they would be better off up north or, if they failed, worse off for having the nerve to try to leave—and if, in the end, they would truly make it out of Mississippi at all.

But there at the depot was her husband, the taciturn man who kept his emotions to himself, who had courted her and won her over despite Miss Theenie's objections, and who had decided that he did not want his family under the mercurial thumb of Mississippi for one more hour. He had not asked Ida Mae what she thought about leaving or whether she wanted to go. He had merely announced his decision as the head of the family, as was his way, and Ida Mae had gone along with it, as was hers.

She had not wanted to leave Miss Theenie and her sister Talma and all the people she had ever known, but her lot was with her husband, and she would go where he thought it best. Both she and Miss Theenie could take comfort in knowing that Ida Mae's sister Irene would be there to receive them in Milwaukee and that half her husband's siblings were up north in Beloit, Wisconsin, and in Chicago, and so Ida Mae would not be alone in that new land.

Mr. Edd had been a man of his word. He did not try to keep George and Ida Mae from leaving. George had gotten a few dollars from Mr. Edd and managed to secure four train tickets to Milwaukee via Chicago, having likely secured them not in Houston, where he might have been recognized, but in Okolona, where he was less likely to be noticed and where they would be leaving from.

And so the family—Ida Mae, George, Velma, James, and the little one still forming in Ida Mae's belly—boarded a train in Okolona. They were packed in with the baggage in the Jim Crow car with the other colored passengers with their babies and boxes of fried chicken and boiled eggs and their belongings overflowing from paper bags in the overhead compartment. The train pulled out of the station at last, and Ida Mae was on her way out of Chickasaw County and out of the state of Mississippi for the first time in her life.

EUSTIS, FLORIDA, APRIL 14, 1945
GEORGE SWANSON STARLING

GEORGE HAD NO TIME for formalities or the seeking of advice or reassurance. He had to go. There was no point in discussing it, and no one he told tried to argue him out of leaving, except for Inez, who wasn't so concerned that he was going but that he wasn't taking her with him. He hadn't had time to figure out what to do with Inez. All he knew was he had to get himself out of Lake County, Florida, before the grove owners got to him first.

All three of the men who had stirred up the commotion in the groves were heading out quick: George to New York, Charlie to Rochester, Sam to Washington, D.C. They each had to figure out where they knew somebody up north and the most direct route to wherever the people they knew were located. They did not so much choose the place as the place presented itself as the most viable option in the time they had to think about it. They did not dare travel to the train station together or allow themselves to be seen together once it was clear they had to get out.

George would be traveling fast and light—a few books, some papers, a change of clothes. He got a man most people wouldn't associate him with but whom he felt he could trust, old Roscoe Colton, to drive him to the train station at Wildwood, a good forty-five minutes' drive on the two-lane gravel roads from Eustis. They rode through the groves that George had picked and that he knew the names of and were the reason he was forced to leave. But he wasn't feeling sentimental about it. He had to get out of the county first. The two of them had to make sure they didn't attract attention to themselves, didn't get stopped along the way, and weren't being followed.

They went west with the sun, rambling along the southern edge of Lake Eustis, passing the county seat of Tavares, where George and Inez had gotten married at the courthouse almost exactly six years before, and crossing into Sumter County between Lake Deaton and Lake Okahumpka. Roscoe Colton's truck pulled up to the depot at Wildwood, and George, tight and sober-faced, walking slow and deliberate so as not to look like the fugitive he had unwittingly become, climbed the colored steps onto the Silver Meteor, headed for New York.

MONROE, LOUISIANA, THE MONDAY AFTER EASTER 1953
ROBERT JOSEPH PERSHING FOSTER

IN THE DARK HOURS OF THE MORNING, Pershing Foster pulled away from his father and brother, the house on Louise Anne Avenue, and his caged existence in the caste-bound, isolated South. The night clouds crawled eastward, the sky itself floating in the opposite direction from him in the damp, cool air. He pointed his Buick Roadmaster to the west, away from Monroe, and settled into the tufted bench seat for the nearly two thousand miles of road ahead of him, the distance that now stood between him and California, between Jim Crow and freedom.

He was setting out on a course that was well trodden by 1953. In the years before Pershing's migration, many hundreds of people from Monroe and thousands more from the rest of Louisiana had joined the river to California. Mantan Moreland, a minor Hollywood figure who made a name for himself as the fumbling manservant and loyal incompetent of black-and-white comedies and Charlie Chan capers, left Monroe for Los Angeles during the Depression. It spread around New Town that he had been on his way to shining shoes in West Monroe and passed a tree with a colored man hanging from it. He left that day and headed to California.

A toddler named Huey Newton was spirited from Monroe to Oakland with his sharecropper parents in 1943. His father had barely escaped a lynching in Louisiana for talking back to his white overseers. Huey Newton would become perhaps the most militant of the disillusioned offspring of the Great Migration. He founded the Black Panther Party in 1966 and reveled in discomfiting the white establishment with his black beret, rifle, and black power rhetoric.

Another boy from Monroe who migrated with his parents to Oakland took an entirely different path. He would go on to become one of the greatest basketball players of all time. Bill Russell was born in Monroe in 1934 and watched his parents suffer one indignity after another. His father once went to a gas station only to be told he would have to wait for the white people to get their gas first. He waited and waited, and, when his turn seemed never to come, he started to pull off. The owner came up, put a shotgun to his head, and told him he was not to leave until all the white people had been served.

"Boy, don't you ever do what you just started to do," the station owner said.

As for Russell's mother, a policeman once grabbed her on the street and ordered her to go and take off the suit she was wearing. He said that she had no business dressing like a white woman and that he'd arrest her if he ever saw her like that again. Bill Russell watched his mother sit at the kitchen table in tears over the straits they were in.

Soon afterward, his parents packed up the family and moved to Oakland, where a colony of people from Monroe had fled. Russell was nine years old. He would get to go to better schools, win a scholarship to the University of San Francisco, and lead his team, the Dons, to two NCAA championships, a first for an integrated basketball team, collegiate or professional. He would join the Celtics in 1956 and lead Boston to eleven championships in his thirteen seasons. He would become perhaps the greatest defensive player in NBA history and the first black coach in the NBA. There is no way to know what might have happened to Bill Russell had his parents not migrated. What is known is that his family had few resources and that he would not have been allowed into any white college in Louisiana in the early 1950s, and thus would not have been in a position to be recruited to the NBA. The consequences of his absence from the game would now be unimaginable to followers of the sport.

In Pershing's own circle, a funeral director named John Dunlap went to Oakland. Pershing's boyhood friend Jimmy Marshall had been out in Los Angeles since the war. A friend named Limuary Jordan moved out to L.A. in 1950. By the time Pershing turned the corner of Desiard Street for good, more than 462,000 colored people, many of them from Louisiana and Texas, were already out in California, most of them people he never knew but who had joined the march before him.

World War II had set off a virtual stampede. In all of California, there had been only 124,306 colored people in 1940, before the United States entered the war. But during the rest of that decade, the population almost quadrupled—337,866 more hopeful souls flooded into California for the shipyard jobs and the defense industry jobs and the ancillary jobs that came with the wartime and postwar economy. More colored people migrated to California in the 1940s than had come in all the previous decades put together. And so, heading out as he was in 1953, Pershing left with the feeling that the Great Migration had passed him by, that he was playing catch-up with a tide that had already rolled away. He drove with a sense of urgency, not knowing that he was, in fact, right in the middle of a wave that was more than fifteen years from ebbing. Another 340,000 colored people would go to California in the fifties, the decade he left Louisiana. Another quarter million would follow in the sixties.

For now, he imagined there was a whole world just waiting for him to get there, people living the high life in Los Angeles and building businesses in Oakland. He had no idea which city he would end up in. He was partial to Los Angeles, based on what he knew of it from the movies he had seen at the Paramount, but there were more people from Monroe in Oakland. He decided not to worry about that now. He would visit them both and decide once he got there. The thing he knew for sure was he was going to California.

He drove west and slightly south in the direction of Houston, where he would visit a Dr. Anthony Beale and knew he could be assured of a place to rest for the night. The sun rose behind him in his rearview mirror. He drove alone with only the radio to keep him company, stations moving in and out like guests at a party. As soon as he got used to one, another would break in and take its place, often the new one not nearly so engaging as the last.

He had nothing but time, time to think, and, as he drove, he knew this was the time to shed his southern self for good, starting with the name. *Pershing.* It was stiff and archaic and not him at all. It was for another man and time. His mother had meant well when she named him after John J. Pershing, the World War I general. It was the fall of 1918. She was growing full with her last son forming inside her, and General Pershing was pushing the Germans past the Argonne Forest when an armistice ended the Great War. The general was a household name at the time, an American hero, and she decided to add the name to the list she had in mind for her unborn child.

The baby was delivered by a midwife on Christmas Day 1918. His full name would be Robert Joseph Pershing Foster. His mother called him Pershing after the general and insisted that everyone else do the same.

A name was a serious undertaking. It was the first and maybe only thing colored parents could give a child, and they were often sentimental about it. They had a habit of recycling the names of beloved kinpeople, thus ending up with three or four Lou Dellas in one or two generations. Out of the confusion it created, children got nicknames like Boo or Pip or Sweet, which after repeated use meant nobody knew anybody's given name until they got married or died. It left mourners at southern funerals not knowing for sure who was in the casket unless the preacher called out "Junebug" in the eulogy. *Oh, that's Junebug that died!*

Sometimes parents tried to superimpose glory on their offspring with the grandest title they could think of, or, if they were feeling especially militant, the name of a senator or president from the North. It was a way of affixing acceptability if not greatness. It forced everyone, colored and white, to call their janitor sons Admiral or General or John Quincy Adams, whether anybody, including the recipient, liked it or not. White southerners who would not call colored people Mr. or Mrs. were made to sputter out Colonel or Queen instead.

And so, growing up, he was called not by his first name, Robert, but by the more imperial-sounding Pershing. The problem was that by the time he got to grade school nobody in Monroe knew or cared much about the feats of an ancient general way off in Europe somewhere. It had no meaning to the people around him, and he was the only Pershing they knew. The colored children in New Town had a hard time pronouncing it. They called him *Percy, Purly, Persian, Putty,* which made an ill-fitting name even less bearable and a mockery of his mother's intentions.

He was starting over now. His mother was gone. What he would be called would be up to him. In California, he would be Robert or, better yet, Bob. Bob with a martini and stingy-brim hat. It was modern and hip, and it suited the new version of himself as the leading man in his own motion picture. He had tested it out in Atlanta, and it had caught on. The people in California who knew him back home would get used to it in time. *Bob.* Simple and direct and easy to remember. He rolled the word around in his mind, and he liked it.

ON THE ILLINOIS CENTRAL RAILROAD, OCTOBER 1937

IDA MAE BRANDON GLADNEY

IDA MAE SAT UP and watched Mississippi blur past her through the film of soot on the train window. By some miracle, she and her husband had managed to keep their secret from most of the plantation throughout the picking season and left whole branches of the family and people they had known since childhood in the dark as to what they were up to. They couldn't chance it and had no choice. "You didn't go around telling neighbors and everybody else in the farm. A lot of 'em didn't know we was gone," she said, "till we was gone."

The two of them, along with little James and Velma, boarded a screeching metal horse on wheels, heading north and slightly west on the Mobile and Ohio Railroad, a feeder line to the main rail. They rode in the darkness on an old train called The Rebel, a mule-headed relic of the Confederate South, rattling toward something they had never seen and did not know. Over the course of the next twenty-four hours, they would have to collect their belongings and change trains in Jackson, Tennessee, to board the Illinois Central Railroad, the legendary rail system that, for a great portion of the twentieth century, carried upward of a million colored people from the Deep South up the country's central artery, across the Mason-Dixon Line, and into a new world called the Midwest. It carried so many southern blacks north that Chicago would go from 1.8 percent black at the start of the twentieth century to one-third black by the time the flow of people finally began to slow in 1970. Detroit's black population would skyrocket from 1.4 percent to 44 percent during the era of the Migration.

It would not have occurred to them that they were riding history. They were leaving as a family, not as a movement, on the one thing going north. But as it happened, the Illinois Central, along with the Atlantic Coast Line and Seaboard Air Line railroads, running between Florida and New York, and the Union Pacific, connecting Texas and California, had become the historic means of escape, the Overground Railroad for slavery's grandchildren. It hurtled its passengers along the same route and under the same night sky as the Underground Railroad, the secret network of safe houses leading north that had spirited slaves to freedom the previous century.

Even before the first anxious sharecroppers boarded the Illinois Central, sometime in the early stages of World War I, the railroad had a pedigree that made it inadvertently synonymous with freedom to black southerners who could manage to secure a ticket. The Illinois Central Railroad was founded in 1850 as a connector between Chicago and Cairo, a river town at the southern tip of the state, adding steamboats down the Mississippi and ultimately rail lines to New Orleans and the Gulf of Mexico. For a time, Mark Twain piloted the railroad's steamboats up and down the Mississippi, and Abraham Lincoln was a rising attorney on retainer to the railroad before his election to the White House.

The Civil War brought an end to regular passenger use, and the railroad was pressed into the service of the Union Army, funneling troops and supplies from the North to the South for the war effort. At war's end, the railroad laid or acquired tracks into the more isolated precincts of Mississippi, Arkansas, Tennessee, and Louisiana and unwittingly made the North a more accessible prospect for black southerners desperate to escape. Each train route of the Illinois Central had a name of its own. The trains were called The Planter, The Creole, The Diamond, The Panama Limited, and, most famous of all, the one that Ida Mae rode, The Louisiane, later renamed The City of New Orleans, which went straight up the country's spine from the Mississippi Delta to the flat wheat prairie land and Chicago itself.

The Illinois Central brought more than merely the chance to leave. It brought parcels from the North that became accidental marketing brochures—the catalogues from Sears, Roebuck, the lovingly wrapped boxes of hand-me-downs from relatives who had made it north, and the discreetly bound copies of the *Chicago Defender,* the colored newspaper that was virulently anti-South and for that reason virtually banned in the region. Pullman porters smuggled the paper into the luggage holds during their regular runs between Chicago and the Deep South, hurling them out by the bundle at strategic points along their routes and thus spreading the word about the possibilities of the North. This makeshift distribution system helped make the *Chicago Defender* one of the most widely circulated black newspapers in the country by the end of World War I and its founder, a migrant from Georgia named Robert Sengstacke Abbott, one of the richest colored men in the country.

The Illinois Central sped past the pine woods and the cotton fields, and in time the railroad's cars were packed with the peasant caste of the South, "the huddled masses yearning to breathe free" in their own country and, save for their race and citizenry, not unlike the passengers crossing the Atlantic in steerage with the intention of never returning to the old country.

Ida Mae and her family boarded the Illinois Central in the middle of the Great Migration, during the statistical lull between the peak outflows of colored southerners during the world wars, unaware of the enormity of the thing and what it might mean beyond themselves.

ON THE SILVER METEOR, APRIL 14, 1945
GEORGE SWANSON STARLING

GEORGE WAS STUFFED into a hardback seat in the baggage car on the Silver Meteor up the East Coast. He was packed in with other colored passengers breaking open their cold chicken and hard-boiled eggs and shushing their children. He didn't pay them much mind. He was still too mad thinking about why he was on that train in the first place.

"I was angry," he said later, conjuring up emotions of fifty years before. "I was angry with my people. We caused them to earn more money in one day than they ever earned in a whole week. And they would complain, 'us not lettin' them work' one or two times. It was only about two or three occasions where we didn't work because we didn't get the price we asked for. And they go to the man's house at night and complain. They made it even worse for us. They couldn't see that we were helping them till after we all scattered."

For once he was riding in the front of something, as opposed to the customary back of everything else. On the railroad, the Jim Crow car was usually the first car behind the coal-fired locomotive that belched soot, fumes, and engine noise. It was the car that would take the brunt of any collision in the event of a train wreck. It was where the luggage and colored passengers were placed, even though their train fare was no different from what white passengers in the quieter rear of the train paid for the same class of service. He and the other colored passengers just had to live with it. George gave it little thought because he was on his way out.

EAST TEXAS, APRIL 1953
ROBERT JOSEPH PERSHING FOSTER

THE LAND WAS CHANGING now as Robert passed over into Texas, the two-lane road fringed yellow with buttercups, the pine stands giving way to cattle ranches and barbecue joints in Panola County. He passed Fish Lake Slough and Flat Fork Creek north of Timpson. The air was moist and heavy now. As he drew near to Splendora County and on to Houston, there was a drizzle in the air and fog on the ground that hid the trees behind a gray veil.

He would eventually follow the country's southern hemline along the Rio Grande. He could have taken the worn Mother Road of the Dust Bowl itinerants and young easterners in their convertibles with the wind whipping their Elvis pompadours. He could have joined Route 66 early on in Oklahoma City, due northwest of Monroe, or in Elk City, Oklahoma, or in Amarillo, Texas.

But that was not considered the most direct route to Los Angeles, and all along he had planned to stop in Houston, where he could stay with Dr. Beale, his friend from back in medical school. And as he never did anything ordinary and as he wanted to cross into another country if only by a few yards to say that he had tasted the tequila, he took a circuitous route to Nuevo Laredo on the Mexican border, which would satisfy his craving for adventure and for doing whatever he did with style and grandiosity.

He pulled into Houston and up to Dr. Beale's house feeling good about his decision and the world. The trip so far had been smooth, as of course it would be in that Buick Roadmaster. He didn't know when he had ever been so happy as the day he bought that car. It made a good impression wherever it went, which is exactly what he wanted.

"If you had seen it, you would have wanted it, too," he would say years later. "They just took chrome and splashed it on that car when they made it, the Roadmaster Buick. And it rode like a chariot. I bought it in St. Louis and drove through a housing project, and I can hear the little kids screaming now, *'Good Lord, look at that car.'* "

Dr. Beale knew he was coming and took it upon himself to show Robert around Houston. They relived their medical school days, and Dr. Beale repeated his offer to help Robert set up practice there if Robert was willing to consider it. But Robert's heart was set on California. He was trying to get away from the South. Texas, with its segregation and cotton fields, never stood a chance. And so Robert declined the offer and, after thanking his friend for the hospitality, set off in the direction of the nearest border town, Laredo.

There he crossed the bridge over the Rio Grande into Nuevo Laredo in Mexico. He drove past the clay storefronts where they sold garlic cloves and pictures of Jesus. The music cried out from second-floor windows, and the streets felt like alleys. He slowed near the places that peddled *vinos y licores* and came to a stop near the cantinas with their gringo girlie posters and red vinyl-top bar stools off Guerrero Street.

He got there in time to sample the margaritas before nightfall and, though he enjoyed the tequila, thought it best to head back before too long. He crossed the Rio Grande again and awaited clearance at U.S. customs. He waited longer than he thought he should, which might have been trivial under normal circumstances but was an eternity to him at the time.

He had a long drive ahead of him. There were 766 miles between Laredo and a town called Lordsburg, New Mexico, where friends had assured him he'd find safe lodging. That meant he had fifteen hours of driving without sleep, and that was only if he managed to keep an ambitious pace of fifty miles an hour on those two-lane highways winding through every whistle stop en route.

Robert was anxious to get back on the road. His turn in line had finally come, and here were the border patrolmen smoking and chatting it up with each other.

"I shouldn't have to wait this long for you to check me clear," he finally said.

"If you want to cross the border, you better shut up," a patrolman said.

Night was forming and Robert needed to get on his way. He didn't have the luxury of checking into a hotel that night as long as he was in the state of Texas. He didn't need any further delay. So he did as they said. They waved him through.

He was more tired now than before. He had more than half of Texas in front of him and a couple of hours of margaritas in his veins. There were roadside motels on both sides of the highway, but he drove past them and gave them no thought. There was no point in asking for a room. They didn't take colored people, and it did no good to think about it. They might as well not have existed.

He reassured himself with the advice he'd gotten that there was a motel in Lordsburg, New Mexico, that took in colored people. He drove over dry riverbeds and through the Stockton Plateau and came parallel to the Texas Pecos Trail near Del Rio.

He was leaving the wet green land for the dry dust land, and there were times he couldn't go any further. The eyelids grew heavy, and the road seemed to blur. He would look for a safe place, the next town maybe, a mile or ten miles or twenty miles down the road, a place not so isolated and alone but quiet enough to be still. He would have to keep himself awake until he found such a place. He would pull over into an empty filling station or a wedge in the road and shut his eyes to rest.

He wouldn't sleep in another bed until he got out of the state of Texas.

The long and thinly populated stretches were the hard gasp of the journey. Every fifty or sixty miles, you saw a crippled Hudson or Pontiac, overheated, engine trouble, out of gas. It reminded you of the treachery of it all and how lucky you were still to be moving. In west Texas, there were fewer and fewer towns, and what towns there were, were smaller and farther apart. If you got stranded, you could only sit and hope that help arrived before the next meal. There was no assurance of a telephone and no way to reach anyone in the event of an emergency. If a tire went flat or a fan belt broke or the car let out a strange crackle or groan, your fate was in the hands of the gods. You could go an hour without seeing another car on the road.

At night, when you couldn't see, you were grateful for the occasional truck wheezing up the hill ahead of you and lighting your path. You might piggyback him even though he was going slower than you would like.

There developed a code of the road among colored people making the crossing. When you got sleepy, there were places you stopped and places you didn't. You stopped at a filling station and asked if the owner minded if you parked there. If you saw a car or two stopped on the side of the road, you might pull up. Somebody else might pull up behind you and do the same.

You tried to stay awake until you found such a place. It might take fifteen minutes. It might take an hour. Before stopping, you ran your eyes over the resting car's bumper and rear windshield, checked for a Confederate flag. You would be crazy to pull up behind one of those. If you saw a pack of cars, you were wary. If you had to stop, you wanted to stop behind one car resting, someone tired and alone like yourself.

The next morning, not having been able to check into a motel, you might stop at a gas station and slap water on your face in the restroom or gargle with ginger ale or fountain water under a colored-only sign.

It called for exquisite planning and a certain surrender to whatever lay ahead. In making the crossing two years before, Limuary Jordan, whom Robert knew back in Monroe, loaded up on bread and lunch meat at the grocery store for himself and his family. They stopped only once, at a colored motel in El Paso. They would drive their DeSoto for three full days and three full nights.

They carried with them twenty-five pounds of ice in a lard bucket as a makeshift air conditioner—or for the radiator if it overheated, an affliction so many of those wheezing old jalopies were prone to suffer—along with a copy of the 121st Psalm:

I raise my eyes toward the mountains.
From where will my help come?
My help comes from the Lord,
the maker of heaven and earth.
God will not allow your foot to slip;
your guardian does not sleep. . . .
By day the sun cannot harm you,
nor the moon by night.
The Lord will guard you from all evil,
will always guard your life.
The Lord will guard your coming and going
both now and forevermore.

Robert was not a particularly religious man, but he was a determined one. He might not have known the blessing for pilgrims making a dangerous trek, the Old Testament prayer some other migrants carried with them, but the spirit of it would follow him nonetheless, and, whether he knew it or not, he would come to need its reassurance and protection for the long, lonely journey into the desert.

ON THE ILLINOIS CENTRAL RAILROAD, OCTOBER 1937
IDA MAE BRANDON GLADNEY

THE RAILCARS CLATTERED ALONG THE TRACKS, and Ida Mae and her family swayed with every rocking motion as the train wound north in the pitch black of night. The countryside gave way, and they passed out of Mississippi into Tennessee and away from the Pearson Plantation and the arbitrary rules they had lived under. They did not know precisely what they would do for work in the North, but they would never again drag another sack of cotton on their backs through a hot, bearing-down field.

From the overcrowded seats in the Jim Crow car, Ida Mae could not have imagined what finery filled the buffet lounges and Pullman cars where the white people sat and would not have let her mind dwell on it even if she had. While the Illinois Central and its counterparts on the East Coast and along the Rio Grande were effectively freedom trains for colored people, deliverance out of the South did not come without its own humiliations, which could eat away at the spirit if one let it. There was no guarantee, for instance, that they could get food on the long ride in either direction because the great bulk of the dining car was reserved for whites and partitioned off by an insistent green curtain.

There was rarely enough room for the many people in steerage. My father would remember trying to get from Washington to Tuskegee, Alabama, where he was a pilot during World War II, and having trouble just getting food. "I rode the train from Washington to North Carolina standing up," he said decades later, "waiting to get into the dining car." The line was several cars long, and there were only four seats in a back corner of the dining car where colored people could sit. For that reason, colored people learned to pack their own food to avoid needing what they couldn't get—cold fried chicken, hard-boiled eggs, and biscuits in a shoe box—which Ida Mae and thousands of others carried on board and which led people to call the migration trains "the Chicken Bone Special."

Still, just being on the train set them apart from the people they left behind. These great creatures on tracks were as big as buildings and longer than roads. They had grand, triumphant-sounding names—Silver Meteor, Broadway Limited—and took people to grand, triumphant-sounding places, and just a little bit of that prestige could rub off on them, and they could walk a little taller in their overalls knowing they were going to freedom.

The train rumbled toward the western tip of Kentucky, wending north toward Illinois. There, on the stiff seats of the colored car, they sat bundled together, George, stoic and straight-backed, keeping whatever apprehensions he had to himself, Ida Mae, wide-eyed and homesick at the same time, Velma's head pressing against her arm, James wriggling in her lap, and another one restless in her belly.

ON THE SILVER METEOR,
SOMEWHERE IN THE CAROLINAS, APRIL 15, 1945
GEORGE SWANSON STARLING

GEORGE HAD BEEN RIDING for close to half a day, only it was the dark hours of the morning of the day after he left Eustis, Florida. The hard, upright seats made it tough to get any sleep. He looked out the window at the blur of countryside and the train depots where they stopped to collect and deposit passengers. The train passed from South Carolina into North Carolina, and with each mile that moved him closer to New York, he began to get exhilarated.

The further north the train got, the more he started thinking about this new life ahead of him and what he had been through. "I was hoping that the conditions would be better," he said. "But I know one thing, I was sick of them gossiping, lying Negroes in Eustis, and I wasn't never coming back there no more. I was never gonna put my foot back there no more in life because they had spoiled my experience. And I was finished."

SOMEWHERE EAST OF EL PASO, APRIL 1953
ROBERT JOSEPH PERSHING FOSTER

ROBERT CROSSED WEST TEXAS through the dry sandpaper fields, past the blur of oil drills and ranches set back from the road and the yucca plants with flower stems like fishing poles. There would appear on either side of the road a drive-in theater with pink cursive lettering or a pit stop that sold liquor and ammo.

The land was red now. Bulls grazed on the scratch land to the south. The red suede hills began a slow roll at Uvalde, and he found himself driving through cuts in the rise of the hills. Now and again, he passed over another dry river waiting for the rain to come home.

He drove parallel to the Rio Grande. The hills became washboard steppes in Hudspeth County. He was almost at El Paso, the last southern town heading west, a border town. Under the circumstances, borders could be deceptive. They are a blend of the two lands they straddle, not fully one or the other, ripe for ambiguity and premature assumptions. El Paso, the unspoken border between the Jim Crow South and the free Southwest, was no different.

Heading to California, Jim Crow was no longer the law after El Paso. The signs that said COLORED above the railcar doors went blank, a metaphor for crossing into a land without segregation. Colored rail passengers heading west were free to move to the seats in the white cars for the remainder of the ride to California. Apparently few ever did, too afraid to push convention, and with good reason. In border towns, freedom was arbitrary and unpredictable. Not every restaurant was open to colored people, hotel access still dependent on local convention and the owner's whim. A colored traveler could never be sure where rejection might greet him. Thus the real border stretched farther than by law it had a right to.

Heading back from California, the South officially began in El Paso. There, Jim Crow laws took over again for any colored person crossing into the state of Texas. There began the spectacle of colored passengers moving to their places from the integrated cars to the Jim Crow cars. The colored and white signs went back up. The colored people knew to gather their things a few stops ahead and move before being told to, to spare themselves the indignity.

It was a spectacle played out in one way or the other on every train coming into or out of the South until Jim Crow died a violent death in the 1960s. At particular stops, which had less to do with the old Mason-Dixon Line than with the psychological border claims of the South, the train cars would undergo a similar transformation.

Up and down the East Coast, the border crossing for Jim Crow was Washington, D.C., which was technically south of the Mason-Dixon Line but was effectively the honorary North, as it was the capital of the Union during the Civil War. Later, it was the first stop on the migration route up the East Coast, the place where colored southerners could escape the field or kitchen and work indoors for the government and sit where they liked on the buses and streetcars. But to blacks in the Deep South, Washington had a significance beyond perhaps any other city in the North. A colored tailor in Georgia told the author Ray Stannard Baker that he was leaving the South for Washington because he wanted "to be as near the flag as I can."

Between Alabama and Detroit, the dividing line was the Ohio River, as it had been during slavery, where, once across it, blacks were free if they only could manage to get there. Between Mississippi and Chicago, Jim Crow went out of effect in Cairo, Illinois, at the southern tip of the state. For a time in the 1920s, the ride to Chicago was interrupted after the train crossed the Ohio River into Cairo, as if the train were passing from Poland into the old Soviet Union during the Cold War. Once over the river and officially in the North, the colored cars had to be removed in a noisy and cumbersome uncoupling and the integrated cars attached in their place to adhere to the laws of Illinois. Colored passengers had to move, wait, reshuffle themselves, and haul their bags to the newly attached integrated cars. Going south, the ritual was reversed. The railroad men now had to reattach the colored-only cars and remove the integrated cars in a clamorous ordeal to meet the laws of Kentucky. Colored passengers had to gather up their things and take their second-class seats, reminded, in that instance, that they were now reentering the South. Such was the protocol of a border crossing.

Colored travelers needed to be aware of these borders whether they were riding the rails or not. The border sentiments spilled over into a general protocol that colored people had to live by. It determined whether or how easily they might find a room or food. They could look silly asking for a colored restroom in a border town that felt more northern than southern and presumptuous in a town that felt the opposite.

"How a colored man, or a white man either, for the matter, can be expected to know all the intricacies of segregation as he travels in different parts of the country is beyond explanation," wrote Robert Russa Moton, the black scholar who succeeded Booker T. Washington as president of Tuskegee Institute in Alabama. "The truth of the matter is, he is expected to find out as best he can."

Usually, colored travelers wanted to avoid insult at all cost and protected themselves by assuming that segregation was the rule whenever they needed a place to eat or sleep. But heat and fatigue could make people do anything to get out of the fix of driving for days without sleep.

Around the same time that Robert was making his way across the country, a family from Beaumont, Texas, near the Louisiana border, was making the same drive. The patriarch of the family was doing the driving. With him were his wife, his grown daughter, and her three children—two boys, between eight and ten, and a girl, about five or six. They had piled into a '49 Chevrolet and were rumbling across Texas en route to California.

They had driven all day and had come into night, and they reached the border city of El Paso. The man could not drive any farther and, as this was the border and he was almost out of Texas, decided to stop and ask if the motel took colored people.

As could be expected, the answer was no. But he was tired. He had the three grandkids, the wife, and the grown daughter with him. And he was colored but was different from the majority of colored people. He had straight hair and pale skin. He looked white, and so did his wife and daughter and two of her three children.

He decided to try another motel. He had been honest, and it hadn't gotten him anywhere.

"Well, I know what to do here," the grandfather said.

This time he would not ask about a room for colored people. He would just ask for a room, like a white person would.

But the family had a problem. One of the grandchildren, a boy, about ten at the time, did not look white. His skin was brown. His hair had a tight curl. He would blow their cover. There would be no way to explain it.

For the plan to work, the motel must not know about the boy, and for that to happen, the grandfather needed the children's cooperation. They were playing in the back seat, counting the stars and pointing out the window at the Big Dipper in the sky. The grandfather needed them to be quiet and to keep their heads down. He told them to pretend to be asleep.

"Now, don't get up, don't get up," he said as he and his wife prepared to go to the front desk. "Don't y'all raise your head up. Somebody come over here, don't raise your head up. Stay down."

The instructions were primarily meant for Jules, the ten-year-old who looked like what he was. But the grandfather told all the children in the hope that what one did, they all would do.

The children could sense his fear and were afraid to move. "You scared, somebody talking to you like that," Pat Botshekan, then the little granddaughter in the back seat, said almost half a century later.

The grandfather and his wife walked up to the front desk, and he asked for a room as a white person would. The clerk checked him in and gave him the key and pointed him in the direction of the room.

Now he had a place for the night, but he also had a problem. They had to get Jules into the room without the front desk discovering what Jules was.

They went back to the car to gather their things. The grandfather got his wife and daughter and the two children who looked white out of the car. It was late at night now, and the grandfather, tired from the drive and the stress of the moment, scrambled to sneak Jules out of the car without detection.

For the plan to work, Jules would have to do what was not natural for a ten-year-old boy. He would have to keep still and be perfectly quiet and not let his arms and legs stick out or rear up his head out of the blanket or let anybody see him. There was no time to explain why they had to hide him and not the other children, or why he was the only one who couldn't under any circumstances be seen while the others would walk in like normal. Somehow he had to understand how imperative it was that he not let a patch of his brown skin show.

Everywhere the family went, little Jules stood out from the rest of the family, and that was hard enough. Now he was being sneaked into a strange place in the middle of the night as if he were contraband.

The grandfather put the blanket over Jules, sitting in the back seat. He tucked the little boy's brown arms and legs under the blanket to make sure they didn't show. He lifted the little boy in his arms like a bag of groceries and carried him into the room. That is how they managed to get a bed for the night. But it was said that the memory stayed with Jules and that he was not quite ever the same after that.

Like most colored people making the journey, Robert could not pass for white and was not in a position to try to fool his way into a room, which is not to suggest that all who could did. In fact, he found it sad and equally humiliating to have to deny who you were to get what you deserved in the first place.

No, for him and for most people in his predicament, you were not free till you had cleared the gate. But even a border's borders are not always clear. Where is it safe to assume you are out of one country and well into another? When can you sigh a sigh of relief that you have passed from the rituals of one place into those of the other side?

Robert took nothing for granted. He assumed he was not out of the South until he was a safe distance from El Paso. He gave himself breathing room and was more cautious than most. He did not want to subject himself to the indignities of being colored any more than he had to and so would make no attempt to stop and inquire until he was all but certain he had a shot at a room.

He crossed into New Mexico and drove some more until he reached Lordsburg, some four hours past the border on those old two-lane roads.

Lordsburg was a dusty old frontier town with saloons famous for fistfights and a Southern Pacific Railroad track paralleling Main. He would have had no reason to stop there if it didn't happen to be the only place in New Mexico he had been told that he could be assured of a place to sleep.

The rooming house in Lordsburg was part of a haphazard network of twentieth-century safe houses that sprang up all over the country, and particularly in the South, during the decades of segregation. Some were seedy motels in the red-light district of whatever city they were in. There were a handful of swanky ones, like the Hotel Theresa in Harlem. But many of them were unkempt rooming houses or merely an extra bedroom in some colored family's row house in the colored district of a given town. They sprang up out of necessity as the Great Migration created a need for places where colored people could stop and rest in a world where no hotels in the South accepted colored people and those in the North and West were mercurial in their policies, many of them disallowing blacks as readily as hotels in the South.

Thus, there developed a kind of underground railroad for colored travelers, spread by word of mouth among friends and in fold-up maps and green paperback guidebooks that listed colored lodgings by state or city.

Colored travelers, hoping to plan their journeys in advance and get assurance of a room, carried the guidebooks in their glove compartments like insurance cards. But the books were often out of date by the time they were printed, the accuracy of their entries based on the fortunes of "hoteliers" who may have only been renters themselves. A colored traveler had to prepare for the possibility that he might arrive at a place in the guidebook only to find that the proprietor had been gone for years and then have to take up the search for a room all over again. Still, the mere presence of the guidebooks and of word-of-mouth advice about places to stay gave a sense of order and dignity to the dispiriting prospect of driving cross-country not knowing for sure where one might lay one's head.

The rooming house in Lordsburg was forgettable and left no impression on him other than it was like all the other rooming houses that took in colored people. A bedroom with no assurance of a key, an old toilet down the hall, sheets the previous guest may have slept on. The rooming houses that catered to a colored trade usually had no competition, and their clientele had no choice.

And so neither would Robert. The only bed he knew between Houston and Lordsburg was the bench seat of the Buick. Lordsburg was the first chance in a thousand miles of road to sleep and was the only certain sleep and shower before Los Angeles. He made the most of it. He was fussy about such things as the proper shave and a well-pressed shirt, so he took his time the next day. He got a later start than he should have.

He had known that there were no guarantees for the first half of the journey, meaning the South, except for his Buick and Dr. Beale back in Houston. Now he was crossing over into the land of the free. He had known the rules in the South. He hadn't liked them, but he had expected them. "There were no hotels taking blacks then," Robert remembered years later. "No. None. So if you had a friend who would take you in, you went there, period, and you were through. And then you worried about the next stop."

He was putting that all behind him now. He drove toward Arizona, confident that this was one thing he didn't have to worry about anymore.

Crossing Over

Do you remember any good stopping places
in Arizona or western Texas?
Anything in Phoenix or El Paso?
And what is the best route from here to the coast?
I have never driven it, you know.

—THE POET ARNA BONTEMPS IN A LETTER TO THE POET LANGSTON HUGHES BEFORE A CROSS-COUNTRY TRIP FROM ALABAMA TO CALIFORNIA

WESTERN NEW MEXICO, APRIL 1953

ROBERT JOSEPH PERSHING FOSTER

LATE AFTERNOON. The desert was different from anything he had seen before. Great bowl of sky. Fringe of mountain in the distance. He was soon in Arizona. The desert began playing tricks on the eyes. It seemed he was driving and standing still at the same time. Road signs began warning of dust storms. Gas stations sold bags of water for people to placate their overheated radiators. He couldn't wait to get to California.

He drove through the dry earth and yucca as heat vapor stirred at the surface. He soon entered the flat plains of the Salt River Valley. The dry land sprouted fields of sorghum and soybeans. Crop dusters flew low in the distance.

Night moved in from behind. The mountains were now crisp against the light of the falling sun.

The next big city was Phoenix, and he drove in anticipation of it. As he drew nearer, a curtain of night cloud fell behind him to the east. He could see it coming in his rearview mirror. The sky turned navy, then black. He soon saw the outline of Phoenix off to his right, north of the highway.

But the road would not take him where he wanted to go. It veered away from the lights and continued south and west along the outskirts of town. The fifteen hundred miles of driving caught up with him now. His eyelids grew heavy, and his head filled with the fog of the onset of sleep.

It occurred to him that he had squandered his energy on the easiest leg of the journey, on the closely set hamlets with their billboards and ranch signs, the distractions and margaritas at the Mexico border, even gassing up and eating in Lordsburg. He did not regret it, but he was paying for it now. Ahead was the long stretch of aloneness in the desert.

He thought he'd better stop now. If he looped back to Phoenix, he could poke around for a colored boardinghouse and be in a bed of uncertain hygiene in a couple of hours. But the highway continued away from the lights and into a vast darkness. He could lose an hour just trying to find his way back to town.

He considered the options. He was a safe distance from the South, long past Texas and well beyond New Mexico. This far west, he wouldn't have to wander the city and hunt down the first colored person he saw for directions to where the colored people board. He was free now, like a regular American.

Up ahead, a bank of neon signs popped up in the distance and fought one another over guests for the night. The motels sat low to the ground at angles from the road, little more than stretch trailers with rhinestone facades. He pulled up to the parking lot of the first one he came to.

The car kicked up gravel dust as it crawled up to the vacancy sign that blinked the promise of a decent night's sleep. He noticed a white Cadillac convertible pulling into the parking lot, its mirror-slick chrome and the headlights shining onto the building. A man who could have been in a Brylcreem commercial was at the wheel and next to him a blond lady friend. The man was laughing. The woman had her head on his shoulder. They were in their own world as they stepped out of the car and floated into the motel in front of him. It was a scene right out of the movies and Robert's kind of place. He felt even better about this new citizenship he was acquiring.

He had been driving since noon and was wrinkled from the ride. He was a formal man in a formal age, and so he couldn't go in like this. He brushed his fingers along the sleeves of his shirt and ironed the front with his palm. He got his sport coat, shook the dust out of it, and afterward straightened his tie. He didn't have a comb within reach; he hadn't thought that far ahead. So he smoothed the top and sides of his head with his hand.

He caught sight of his face in the mirror and the dark wood finish of his skin. The skin was moist and glistened in the blinking neon of the vacancy sign. *Good lord.* He had been sweating in the heat all day. They might think he was a common laborer. He felt his pockets for a handkerchief. He took it and wiped the shine off his nose, off his cheeks and chin, and mopped the sweat from his forehead. It was not his best presentation, but it would have to do.

When he got out of the car, he dusted his coat sleeves and checked for wrinkles again. He stood up as if there were a brace strapped to his back. Then he walked up to the front desk for a room. At reception, he took a deep breath and put on the most charming rendition of himself.

"I'd like to get a room for the night, please," he said.

The man looked flustered. "Oh, my goodness," the man at the front desk said. "We forgot to turn off the vacancy sign."

Robert tried to hide his disappointment.

"Oh, thank you," Robert said.

He climbed back into the car and drove away from the motel and the vacancy sign that continued to blink. He had been in the South long enough to know when he had been lied to. But there were plenty of motels on the road, and it didn't matter what one man thought of him.

He wasn't thinking rights and equality. "I thought a bed and a shower and something to eat," he would say years later.

He drove to the next motel in the row, a hundred or so yards away.

"I'd like to get a motel room," he said, stiffer than before. He was cautious now, and the man must have seen his caution.

"I'm sorry," the man said, polite and businesslike. "We just rented our last room."

Robert looked into the face, tried to read it. He noticed that "the face was awkward, trying to be loose and matter of fact. All calm and uncomfortable."

He thanked the man anyway, tried to prove himself even in rejection. "Usually when we try to fit in, we're above them," Robert thought to himself, sad and indignant at the same time. "If we're going to be nice, we're nicer than they would be to each other."

Knowing that wasn't helping him now. He was getting anxious. The pulse was racing. He was agitated, sweating on a cool desert night.

He went to a third motel and was sweetly rejected a third time. It was fully night now, the sky black and dense. He should have been in bed hours ago. His was the only car on the road now. The motel lots were quiet and still. The lamp lights on bedside tables were clicking off, that young couple in the Cadillac all situated now. The road was getting darker, lonelier, as the world settled in for the night.

Anybody looking for a room had one by now. Any leftover rooms would go empty. And still they were turning him away.

He replayed the rejections in his mind as he drove the few yards to the next motel. Maybe he hadn't explained himself well enough. Maybe it wasn't clear how far he had driven. Maybe he should let them know he saw through them, after all those years in the South. He always prepared a script when he spoke to a white person. Now he debated with himself as to what he should say.

He didn't want to make a case of it. He never intended to march over Jim Crow or try to integrate anybody's motel. He didn't like being where he wasn't wanted. And yet here he was, needing something he couldn't have. He debated whether he should speak his mind, protect himself from rejection, say it before they could say it. He approached the next exchange as if it were a job interview. Years later he would practically refer to it as such. He rehearsed his delivery and tightened his lines. "It would have been opening-night jitters if it was theater," he would later say.

He pulled into the lot. There was nobody out there but him, and he was the only one driving up to get a room. He walked inside. His voice was about to break as he made his case.

"I'm looking for a room," he began. "Now, if it's your policy not to rent to colored people, let me know now so I don't keep getting insulted."

A white woman in her fifties stood on the other side of the front desk. She had a kind face, and he found it reassuring. And so he continued.

"It's a shame that they would do a person like this," he said. "I'm no robber. I've got no weapons. I'm not a thief. I'm a medical doctor. I'm a captain that just left Austria, which was Salzburg. And the German Army was just outside of Vienna. If there had been a conflict, I would have been protecting you. I would not do people the way I've been treated here."

It was the most he'd gotten to say all night, and so he went on with his delivery more determinedly than before. "I have money to pay for my services," he said. "Now, if you don't rent to colored people, let me know so I can go on to California. This is inhuman. I'm a menace to anybody driving. I'm a menace to myself and to the public, driving as tired as I am."

She listened, and she let him make his case. She didn't talk about mistaken vacancy signs or just-rented rooms. She didn't cut him off. She listened, and that gave him hope.

"One minute, Doctor," she said, turning and heading toward a back office.

His heart raced as he watched her walk to the back. He could see her consulting with a man through the glass window facing the front desk, deciding in that instant his fate and his worth. They discussed it for some time and came out together. The husband did the talking.

He had a kind, sad face. Robert held his breath. "We're from Illinois," the husband said. "We don't share the opinion of the people in this area. But if we take you in, the rest of the motel owners will ostracize us. We just can't do it. I'm sorry."

By now, if they had agreed to it, Robert would have been willing to check out before dawn, before anybody could see him, if that's what it took. It was a long shot, but some white proprietors had been known to sneak a colored traveler in on occasion, harbor them like a fugitive or a runaway slave, so long as he was out before the neighbors got wind of it. Robert would have accepted that even if he didn't like it.

In his delirium, he imagined the exchange between husband and wife in the back office minutes before, the woman arguing his case, the husband skeptical, wary.

"Nobody'll see him anyway," the wife's whispering.

"Yes, they will," the husband's responding.

"How will they know?"

"Somebody might see him when he drives out of here. Or somebody might see his car. Where he's been before, the people that turned him down. They'd know we let him stay here."

And so the answer was no. Robert thanked them anyway, especially the woman. If it had been up to her, he would have had the room. "I believe that with everything that's in me," Robert said when he was older and grayer. "This thing I've analyzed three thousand times."

Somehow Robert made it back to the car. He was in the middle of the desert and too tired to go on and too far along not to keep going. His mind took him back to Monroe, to the going-away party they gave him just a few nights ago. His own words rose up and laughed at him. *How in the world can you stay here in this Jim Crow situation? Come go to Heaven with me, to California.*

He drove, erratic, in the direction of the road and, thus, California, although he was nowhere near California, and saw the lights of a filling station. He needed gas and could use some coffee if he was to make it through the desert and the night. He drove into the station and stopped at a pump.

The owner, a middle-aged white man, came right out.

"May I help you?"

Robert couldn't answer. The man repeated himself.

"Hey, fella, what's wrong? What's the matter? Are you sick?"

"No," Robert said, unable to manage much more.

The man sensed something. He put his hand on Robert's shoulder, and Robert tried to tell him what had happened. The man shook his head as if he understood.

Something in the voice, in the way the man looked into his eyes and touched his shoulder and tried in the middle of a cool desert night to console him, made Robert feel all the sadder. It confirmed he wasn't crazy, and that made him feel utterly alone. Yes, there was an evil in the air and this man knew it and the woman at the motel knew it, but here he was without a room and nobody of a mind to do anything had done a single thing to change that fact. And that made the pain harder, not easier, to bear.

Robert broke down. The exhaustion, the rejection, the unwinding of his dreams in a matter of minutes, it all caught up with him at once. He had driven more than fifteen hundred miles, and things were no different. In fact, it felt worse because this wasn't the South. It wasn't even close to the South. He sat unable to speak for longer than is comfortable in front of a total stranger. His voice cracked as the story tumbled out of him.

"I came all this way running from Jim Crow, and it slaps me straight in the face," Robert said. "And just think, I told my friends, why did they stay in the South and take the crumbs? *'Come to California.'* "

The man listened with the helplessness of the well-intentioned and tried to cheer him up.

"Come on, let me get you a cup of coffee. Where are you going anyway?"

"Los Angeles."

"Well, I went to USC, and I hate to disappoint you, but Los Angeles ain't the oasis you think it is."

Robert was feeling sick now. It was too late to turn back, and who knew what he was heading into? The man told him to gear himself up. The man didn't use the term, and nobody had bothered to tell Robert ahead of time, but some colored people who had made the journey called it *James* Crow in California.

"You will see it, and it'll hit where it hurts," the man said. "What are you in?"

"I'm a doctor."

"Well, you're going to find it in the hospitals going to work."

Robert was thinking fast, reconsidering, weighing, and waking up. The dream looked to be over before he could even get to California. The man brought him a cup of coffee and filled his tank. Robert got back on the highway and drove into the black hole of night. Soon he came to a fork in the road and saw a sign that made his heart sink:

LOS ANGELES 380 MILES
SAN DIEGO 345 MILES

He knew he couldn't drive a mile farther than necessary in this condition, and so San Diego it would be. "I could just see numbers in my mind now," he said many years later. "Los Angeles this way and San Diego that way. And the number was far less distance, and I chose that."

In the absolute darkness he found himself in, he could not see the will of the road. He went on faith that he was not driving off into a ravine.

Every cell wanted sleep. He bit his tongue to keep his eyelids from sneaking shut. He sang, sang anything, to keep his mind from turning in for the night. Now when he needed the radio, there was no radio, just a crackle of white noise from someplace far away.

Suddenly, somewhere around Gila Bend, the road got mean, turned without warning, a sharp left, then a sharper, uglier right, back and forth, and all over again. The car tilted upward, gaining elevation and resisting the climb as any car would. It forced him into an alertness his body wasn't prepared for and that he hadn't anticipated.

The road shot more curves at him, one right after the other, so that he was going north and south as much as west, and he had to slow down to absorb the blind hooks and horseshoes coming at him. He knew he wasn't the best driver in the world, hadn't done that much of it really. And so he would have to brake to a crawl if he was going to make it.

Before it hadn't mattered much that this was a two-lane road with no reflector lights and no guardrails to catch him. Now it did. Interstate highways didn't exist yet. Dwight D. Eisenhower, the president who would go on to build them, had only recently taken office. Of course, Robert didn't know that, and knowing it wouldn't have helped him.

The mountains closed in on him. He couldn't make out the earth from the sky. The sky was black, the road was black. He could see the black shape of saguaro cactus standing helpless as he passed. He drove into the cave of night, more alone now than ever.

It got to the point where he could go no further, and he pulled over to the side of the road. He unfolded himself from behind the wheel and caught an hour of half sleep. He would have to stop again two or three times that night. Each time, it left him not much more refreshed than before. He had no choice but to start the engine and take up the task again.

He wound through rock canyons and crossed Fortune Wash near the Gila River. A film stuck to his skin and to his wrinkled shirt and trousers. He had not had a chance to wash yesterday off. He opened the windows and vents to get air.

Another hour passed, and ahead was a valley, a black velvet plain with diamonds on it. It was the city of Yuma. He saw motel signs with amusing desert names. He gave them no thought. He knew better now.

Soon he came upon the Colorado River. A road sign said he had reached the California line. But he was too beat down now to pay it much attention.

His back pinched from days and nights of driving. His fingers were sore from clutching the steering wheel. His wrists ached, and still there was more road. The road would not end.

Just past Felicity came the warnings of the desert: CHECK YOUR RADIATOR. LAST CHANCE FOR WATER. LAST CHANCE FOR GAS STATIONS. STRONG WINDS POSSIBLE.

What was this place he was going to? What was he doing behind the wheel in the middle of the pitch-black desert by himself? Could it be worth all this? It had seemed so clear back in Monroe. Now he fought with himself over the fear and the doubt. He couldn't bear to hear the I-told-you-so's. If he turned back now, if he changed his mind or lost his nerve, the I-knew-its would ring in his ear. Dr. Clement would be the first to say it.

He was dreading the place already. "But there was no turning back," he would say years later. "I had to get here. I had to try."

He blinked at oncoming headlights, willing himself awake. Orion stretched over the highway and made an arc across the sky. It filled the windshield and stayed with him until the sun came back.

Near the Tecate Divide, the pink light of morning came in from behind. He was in San Diego County. Another fifty miles to the coast. The sun was on his back as he pulled away for good from the South and the center of gravity.

ON THE ILLINOIS CENTRAL AT THE ILLINOIS BORDER, OCTOBER 1937

IDA MAE BRANDON GLADNEY

IN THE DARK HOURS OF THE MORNING, Ida Mae and her family crossed the Mason-Dixon Line, at the Ohio River, the border between Kentucky and Illinois, between the provincial South and the modern North, between servitude and freedom, without comment.

The black night pressed against the windows and looked no different in the New World than in the Old. It was as thick and black in Illinois as it was in Kentucky or Tennessee. From the railcar window, the land looked to be indistinguishable, one state from another, just one big flat plain, and there was nothing in nature that one could see that said colored people should be treated one way on one side of the river and a different way on the other.

Crossing the line was a thing of spiritual and political significance to the guardians of southern law and to colored people escaping it who knew they were crossing over. But going north, most migrants would have been asleep or unable to see whatever the line looked like if they even knew where it was.

On the red-eye going north, the railroad would not likely have disrupted the entire train just so colored people could sit with white people now that they legally could. Ida Mae had no memory of such a commotion in any case, only that they'd made it out of Mississippi. They crossed into Illinois at *Cairo* and passed through *Carbondale* and *Centralia.* Then *Champaign. Kankakee. Peotone. Matteson. Grand Crossing. Woodlawn. Hyde Park. Oakland. Twenty-second Street. Twelfth Street Station. Chicago.*

They would have to change trains yet again to continue on to Milwaukee, where Ida Mae's sister Irene lived and where they could set about finding work to sustain them in the New World.

ON THE SILVER METEOR, NORTHERN NEW JERSEY, APRIL 15, 1945
GEORGE SWANSON STARLING

AT DAYBREAK, the Silver Meteor wound its way into Pennsylvania Station at Newark, New Jersey. The conductor called out the name of the station and the city, and after so long a ride through the night and now into day, some passengers from the South gathered their things and stepped off the train, weary and anxious to start their new lives and relieved to have made it to their destination at last.

"Newark." It sounded so tantalizingly close to "New York," and maybe, some assumed, was the way northerners, clipping their words as they did, pronounced New York. It was confusing to have their intended destination preceded directly by a city with such a similar name and with an identically named station. And as they had been riding for as many as twenty-four hours and were nervous about missing their stop, some got off prematurely, and, it is said, that is how Newark gained a good portion of its black population, those arriving in Newark by accident and deciding to stay.

George Starling knew better. He had been to New York before, just not on the train. He remained in his seat until he arrived at the real New York, where the aunts who had sent money to his grandmother, the root doctor, to help raise him and his cousins were waiting for him at their Harlem doorsteps.

SAN DIEGO COUNTY, APRIL 1953
ROBERT JOSEPH PERSHING FOSTER

IT WAS EARLY IN SAN DIEGO. Robert Foster could see the concrete skyline and the headlights of a city waking up. He drew closer to the heart of town. Trolley cars clanked past the palm trees on C Street. The Pacific Ocean was up ahead. He was finally on the other side of the desert. He was hours from Los Angeles but well into California, the end of the line when it came to the Migration. It was more a relief now than a wonder.

His eyes scanned the pedestrians for pigment. He stopped at the curb and flagged down the first colored person he saw. He had not talked to a soul during his night in the desert. This would be the first encounter in this new adopted land. His heart sank as he uttered the words that seemed an admission of failure.

"Pardon me," he said, edgily, to the man. "Where can you find a colored hotel?"

"What do you mean, a *colored* hotel?" the man said with the casual annoyance of an urbanite interrupted by a tourist. "I can tell you where a hotel is. There's a hotel right there."

"No, I don't want that," Robert said. "Just tell me where most of the colored folks stay."

Robert was too tired to argue. Three states without sleep. He had a stubble of beard on his face that he would otherwise never be seen in public with. He could not bear rejection again.

"I could not," he began, still searching for the right words decades later, "the thought—it was overwhelming—of me being turned down again. I couldn't do that."

Robert repeated himself to the man. The man assured him he didn't have to stay in a place like that in San Diego but gave him the name of a small, featureless hotel anyway, a place for colored people, since he was so insistent on that.

Robert found the place. He slept and showered and shaved for the first time since New Mexico. When he opened his eyes hours later, there he was in a segregated hotel. A week on the road, and he was in the exact same place, it seemed, that he left.

Later in the day, he headed north past the Joshua trees. Los Angeles was another 121 miles from San Diego. He didn't know which city would be the right one for him—Los Angeles or Oakland—or where he would work or how he would set up a practice wherever he ended up. He had just come out of the desert, in every sense of the word, and the details of his future were too much to think about right now.

He drove north toward whatever awaited him. Billboards popped up on both sides of the highway. They whizzed past him as he drove. They had women in rouge and lipstick and men with stingy-brim hats with the cord above the brim selling lager beer and cigarettes. The people in the billboards were smiling and happy. They looked out onto the highway and straight into the cars.

They kept him company, and, although they weren't talking to him, he told himself they were. "I played a game that it was for me," he later said.

Soon one billboard stood out from the others. IT'S LUCKY WHEN YOU'RE IN CALIFORNIA, it said cheerfully. It was hawking Lucky lager beer to every car that passed. Robert repeated those words in his mind.

"It's gonna be lucky for me in California. It's gonna be good."

It had to be. He said it over and over to himself until he actually started to believe it.

THE SOUTH, 1915–1975

FROM THE MOMENT the first migrants stepped off the earliest trains, the observers of the Great Migration debated what made millions of rural and small-town people turn their backs on all they knew, leave the land where their fathers were buried, and jump off a cliff into the unknown.

Planters blamed northern recruiters, who were getting paid a dollar a head to deliver colored labor to the foundries and slaughterhouses of the North. But that only held for the earliest recruits, usually young men, field hands, with nothing to lose. Others said the *Chicago Defender* seduced them. But they could only be seduced if there was some passion already deep within them.

Economists said it was the boll weevil that tore through the cotton fields and left them without work and in even greater misery, which likely gave hard-bitten sharecroppers just one more reason to go. Still, many of them picked cotton not by choice but because it was the only work allowed them in the cotton-growing states. In South Carolina, colored people had to apply for a permit to do any work other than agriculture after Reconstruction. It would not likely have been their choice had there been an alternative. And besides, many of the migrants, people like George Starling and Robert Foster and many thousands more came from southern towns where they did not pick cotton or from states less dependent on it and thus would have made their decisions with no thought of the boll weevil or the pressure on cotton prices.

The Chicago Commission on Race Relations, an investigative body created after the World War I wave of migration, decided to ask migrants why they had left. A few of their responses were these:

- Some of my people were here.
- Persuaded by friends.
- For better wages.
- To better my conditions.
- Better conditions.
- Better living.
- More work; came on visit and stayed.
- Wife persuaded me.
- Tired of the South.
- To get away from the South.

The earliest departures were merely the first step in a divorce that would take more than half a century to complete. At the time it was misunderstood as a temporary consequence of war and declared over when the war ended. But the people who before had been cut off from the North now had the names of neighbors and relatives actually living there. Instead of the weakening stream that observers predicted, the Great Migration actually gathered steam after World War I.

It continued into the twenties with the departure of some 903,000 black southerners, nearly double the World War I wave. It did not stop in the thirties, when, despite the Depression, 480,000 managed to leave. Among them was Ida Mae Gladney. World War II brought the fastest flow of black people out of the South in history—nearly 1.6 million left during the 1940s, more than in any decade before. George Starling was one of them. Another 1.4 million followed in the 1950s, when Robert Pershing Foster drove out of Louisiana for good. And another million in the 1960s, when, because of the more barefaced violence during the South's desperate last stand against civil rights, it was actually more treacherous to leave certain isolated precincts of the rural South than perhaps at any time since slavery.

The numbers put forward by the census are believed by some historians to be an underestimate. Unknown numbers of migrants who could pass for white melted into the white population once they left and would not have been counted in the Migration. Colored men fearful of being extradited back to the South over purported debts or disputes would have been wary of census takers. And overcrowded tenements with four or five families packed into kitchenettes or day workers rotating their use of a bed would have been hard to accurately account for in the best of circumstances. "A large error in enumerating southern blacks who went North," wrote the historian Florette Henri, "was not only probable but inescapable."

The journey north was a defining moment for the people embarking upon it. Many years later, most everyone would remember how they chose where they went, the name of the train they took, and whom they went to stay with. Some would remember the exact day they departed and the places the train stopped on the way to wherever they were going. A man named Robert Fields, who as a teenager hid in the freight cars to flee Yazoo City, Mississippi, remembered arriving in Chicago on the day Rudolph Valentino died, which would make it August 23, 1926, because the news of Valentino's death was on the front page of every newspaper and was all anyone was talking about that day.

Robert Pershing Foster would remember leaving right after Easter, which, unbeknownst to him, was a popular time to leave. Given a choice, southerners preferred not to go north facing winter, and leaving at Easter gave them plenty of time to adjust to the North before the cold set in. George Starling would remember that he left Florida on April 14, 1945, as if it were his birthday, which in a way it was.

Decades after she left, Ida Mae Gladney would remember that they got the cotton clean out of the field before they left, which would make it mid- to late October, and that she was pregnant with her youngest child but not yet showing, which would make it 1937.

Well after Ida Mae, George, and Robert made their way out of the South, a man by the name of Eddie Earvin would always remember how he left because he went to such great lengths to escape the Mississippi Delta. It was the spring of 1963.

Many of the observers and participants of the first wave of the Migration had passed away, having concluded that the phenomenon was long over. They would not have imagined that someone like Earvin might have a harder time leaving than many before him.

But in the early 1960s, secluded regions of the rural South—Alabama and Mississippi in particular—had become war zones in the final confrontation between segregationists and the civil rights movement. Spies and traitors were everywhere, the violence raw and without apology, the segregationists standing more boldfaced, clamping down harder as outsiders tried to force integration on them. No one was exempt—not well-to-do white northerners like Andrew Goodman and Michael Schwerner, not upstanding family men like Medgar Evers, or even four little middle-class girls in church on a Sunday morning in Birmingham in 1963.

Earvin's story is evidence of just how long the Great Migration stretched across a hard century, how universal were the impulses of those who left, and how treacherous it could be to try to leave certain remote and Victorian pockets of the American South throughout the sixty-odd years the Great Migration lasted.

Eddie Earvin was twenty in the spring of 1963. He was a day picker at a plantation in Scotts, Mississippi, walking with pieces of cardboard tied to his one pair of shoes to cover the bottoms of his feet. "We were still in slavery, like," he would say years later.

He started picking when he was five and chopping weeds off the cotton at six. And when he was seven or eight, a boy named Charles Parker was skinned alive for opening a door for a white woman and speaking to her in a way she didn't like, as the grown folks told it. Eddie would never forget that.

He picked because he had to and crawled on his knees to cut spinach because spinach is low to the ground. He got ten cents for a fifty-pound basket of spinach. He could pick only two or three baskets a day because spinach is light.

One day when he was out cutting spinach, he sliced into his finger but was afraid to leave the field. It was six miles to the doctor in town. He worked two more days and on the third day decided to walk to town to see the doctor. The boss man passed him on his way back to the field and jumped out of his truck.

"Don't you know you don't go nowhere unlessen I tell you to?" the boss man said.

He pulled a Winchester rifle out of the truck. "Maybe I ought to kill you right now," he said.

The man put the rifle to Eddie's head.

"You don't go nowhere unlessen I tell you to go," he told him.

Eddie was seventeen. He decided that, somehow or other, he would find a way out. When he was twenty, he made his plans. A bus ticket to Chicago was twenty-one dollars, as he remembered it. It took him six or seven months to save up for it. But that was the easy part. Now he had to find out how to use it without calling attention to himself in that little town where everybody knew everybody and it seemed everyone was watching.

There was a bus that stopped near him, but he couldn't catch that bus or inquire about it. "Everybody knew what you'd be trying to do if you caught that bus," he said. And you had to walk six miles to get to it.

There was another little bus stop in a town nearby. It did not post the bus schedule, and he was not in a position to ask. "They didn't tell you the schedule," he would say years later. "A lot of things you'd want to know, you couldn't ask."

So he went to the station at different times of the day. Each time, he sat and waited for the bus to leave, and when it belched out of the depot, he looked at the station clock and made a note of it. Sometimes the bus left early, he found. Sometimes it left late. He tried to get an average time so he would not miss it on the day he wanted to go. That was how he learned the bus schedule.

"We had been checking for months," he said.

He decided to leave in May 1963 and take his sister and her two children with him. He didn't tell anyone what he was doing. "You didn't talk about it or tell nobody," he said. "You had to sneak away."

That day, he acted as if it were any other day. He went up to a man named Eason and casually asked him if he could give them a ride.

"We going to Greenville today," he told Eason. "Could you take us?"

He didn't tell Eason he was leaving Mississippi for good or that he needed to catch a bus pulling out at a certain time or that this was the moment of truth after planning this in his mind for most of his short adult life. The man might not have taken them if he knew. So Eddie kept it to himself.

The four of them got in the car with nothing but a few clothes in a paper bag. When they got to Greenville, they paid the man three or four dollars. Eason figured out what they were up to when he saw where they wanted to be dropped off.

"What do you call yourself doing?" he asked them.

"We getting out of town," Eddie said. The man got scared himself after that.

Eddie and his sister and her two kids got on the bus, and before anybody knew it, they were out of the county with everything they had in a shopping bag wrapped in a rope of sea grass.

They sat in the back and kept their mouths shut. "The white folks could talk," he would say years later. "You sit and be quiet. Where we came from, we didn't move from the back. We just sat there. We weren't the type to move around. We wasn't sure we could move. So we didn't move. That fear."

He had learned that fear when he was little and once passed the white people's church. The kids came out of the church when they saw him. They threw rocks and bricks and called him the vilest names that could spring from a southern tongue. And he asked his grandparents, "What kind of god they got up inside that church?"

He was getting away from all that now. He looked out at the lights and the billboards. The driver announced that they were passing out of Mississippi and into Tennessee. He was out for sure now and on his way to Illinois, and at that moment he could feel the sacks of cotton dropping from his back. Years later, he would still tremble at the memory and put into words the sentiments of generations who went in search of a kinder mistress.

"It was like getting unstuck from a magnet," he said.

PART FOUR

The Kinder Mistress

The lazy, laughing South
With blood on its mouth. . . .
Passionate, cruel,
Honey-lipped, syphilitic—
That is the South.
And I, who am black, would love her
But she spits in my face. . . .
So now I seek the North—
The cold-faced North,
For she, they say,
is a kinder mistress.
—Langston Hughes, "The South"

Chicago

Timidly, we get off the train.
We hug our suitcases,
fearful of pickpockets. . . .
We are very reserved,
for we have been warned not to act green. . . .
We board our first Yankee street car
to go to a cousin's home. . . .
We have been told
that we can sit where we please,
but we are still scared.
We cannot shake off three hundred years of fear
in three hours.

—Richard Wright, *12 Million Black Voices*

CHICAGO, TWELFTH STREET STATION, OCTOBER 1937

IDA MAE BRANDON GLADNEY

THE LEAVES WERE THE COLOR of sweet potatoes and of the summer sun when it sets. They had begun to fall from the branches and settle in piles at the roots of the elm trees. The leaves had begun to fall when Ida Mae and George walked into the cold light of morning for the very first time in the North.

Ida Mae and her family had ridden all through the night on the Illinois Central and had arrived, stiff and disheveled, in a cold, hurrying place of concrete and steel. People clipped past them in their wool finery and distracted urgency, not pausing to speak—people everywhere, more people than they had maybe seen in one single place in their entire lives, coming as they were from the spread-out, isolated back country of plantations and lean-tos. They would somehow have to make it across town to yet another station to catch the train to Milwaukee and cart their worldly belongings to yet another platform for the last leg of their journey out of the South.

Above them hung black billboards as tall as a barn with the names of connecting cities and towns and their respective platforms and departure times—Sioux Falls, Cedar Rapids, Minneapolis, Omaha, Madison, Dubuque—footfalls, redcaps, four-faced clocks, and neon arrows pointing to arrivals and track numbers. The trains were not trains but Zephyrs and Hiawathas, the station itself feeling bigger and busier than all of Okolona or Egypt or any little town back home or anything they could possibly have ever seen before.

They would have to ride the La Crosse and Milwaukee Railroad for three more hours to get to their final stop in their adopted land. They could not rest easy until they had made it safely to Ida Mae's sister's apartment in Milwaukee. In the end, it would take multiple trains, three separate railroads, hours of fitful upright sleep, whatever food they managed to carry, the better part of two days, absolute will, near-blind determination, and some necessary measure of faith and just plain grit for people unaccustomed to the rigors of travel to make it out of the land of their birth to the foreign region of essentially another world.

The great belching city she passed through that day was the first city Ida Mae had ever laid eyes on. That first glimpse of Chicago would stay with her for as long as she lived.

"What did it look like at that time, Chicago?" I asked her, half a life later.

"It looked like Heaven to me then," she said.

New York

A blue haze descended at night
and, with it, strings of fairy lights
on the broad avenues. . . .
What a city! What a world! . . .
The first danger I recognized . . .
was that Harlem would be
too wonderful for words.
Unless I was careful,
I would be thrilled into silence.

—THE POET ARNA BONTEMPS UPON
FIRST ARRIVING IN HARLEM, 1924

NEW YORK CITY, PENNSYLVANIA STATION, APRIL 15, 1945
GEORGE SWANSON STARLING

IN THE SPACE OF TWENTY-FOUR HOURS, George Starling had put behind him the slash pines and cypress swamps of his former world and was finally now stepping out of Pennsylvania Station. He walked beneath the Corinthian columns and the iron fretwork of its barrel-vaulted ceiling and into the muted light of a spring morning in Manhattan. He could see a blur of pedestrians brushing past him and yellow taxicabs swerving up Eighth Avenue. Concrete mountains were obscuring the sky, steam rising from sewer grates, the Empire State Building piercing the clouds above granite-faced office buildings, and, all around him, coffee shops and florists and shoe stores and street vendors and not a single colored- or white-only sign anywhere.

This was New York.

He had made it out of Florida and was now reaching into his pocket for the address and telephone number of his aunt Annie Swanson, the one they called Baby, who lived up in Harlem. But he couldn't find the slip of paper with her number on it, and, in his fatigue and confusion and the upset of all he had been through, couldn't remember precisely where she lived even though he had been there before, and so he made his way to the apartment of the only friend whose Harlem address he could remember and who just happened to be home.

"He took me in, and I sat there, and I tried to think," George said. "The more I tried to think, the more confused I got."

All the streets were numbered. What number street was she on? All the tenements looked the same. Which tenement was she in? She had moved so much. Where was she the last time he was here?

"Don't worry about it," the friend said. "It'll come to you eventually. I'm a let you take you a good, hot bath, lay down, and relax a while."

George got in the tub, and it came to him. "Oh shoot, I know where my aunt lives," he said, and he hurried out of the tub. "Now I remember it. Now it has come to me. Maybe I needed to relax."

He had crossed into another world and was feeling the weight of it all. "I think I was overtired," he would say years later, "from getting ready to leave and getting out of there."

The friend directed him to Aunt Baby's three-room apartment on 112th Street between Fifth and Lenox, where he would sleep on the sofa in the front room until he could find work and a place of his own.

He set his things down just inside her front door, and, at that moment, he became a New Yorker, because, unlike on his other visits to the North, this time, he planned to stay. He would have to get accustomed to a concrete world with the horizon cut off by a stand of brownstones, to a land with no trees and where you couldn't see the sun. Somehow, he would have to get used to the press of people who never seemed to sleep, the tight, dark cells they called tenements. He would quicken his steps, learn to walk faster, hold his head up and his back stiff and straight, not waving to everyone whose eyes he met but instead acting like he, too, had already seen and heard it all, because in a way, in a life-and-death sort of way, he had.

Curiously enough, one thing was for sure. He didn't see himself as part of any great tidal wave. "No," he said years later. "I just knew that

I was getting away from Florida. I didn't consider it like it was a general movement on and I was a part of it. No, I never considered that."

He could only see what was in front of him, and that was, he hoped, a freer new life for himself. "I was hoping," he said years later. "I was hoping I would be able to live as a man and express myself in a manly way without the fear of getting lynched at night."

Los Angeles

Maybe we can start again,
in the new rich land
—in California,
where the fruit grows.
We'll start over.
—John Steinbeck, *The Grapes of Wrath*

LOS ANGELES, APRIL 1953

ROBERT JOSEPH PERSHING FOSTER

ROBERT DROVE UNDER A GRAY GAUZE SKY through the thicket of shark-fin taillights, up Crenshaw and Slauson and Century, the stickpin palms arched high above him. He went screeching and lurching with the distracted urgency of a man meeting a blind date, picturing the first glance and dreading the faint chance of disappointment.

He drove into the white sun. Everything was wide open and new. The city unfurled itself, low and broad, the boulevards singing Spanish descriptions, *La Cienega, La Brea, La Tijera.* There were orange trapezoid signs staked high above the diners and auto dealerships and neon lights at the coin-op laundries.

The farther he went, the better it got. The trees were not trees anymore but Popsicles and corncobs. The lawns spread out like pool tables, and you could cut yourself on the hedgerows. Everything was looking like a villa or a compound now, statues and gumdrop trees marching down overdone driveways and Grecian urns set out on the porticoes.

The whole effect was like a diva with too much lipstick, and he loved it. The too-muchness of it all.

He was drawing near the Wilshire district and was looking for St. Andrews Place, where a Dr. William Beck, an old professor from medical school, now lived.

Dr. Beck started practicing medicine when Robert was just learning to crawl. However hard Robert thought he had it, Dr. Beck had had it rougher. It began with why Dr. Beck had become a doctor in the first place. Decades before, his father had tuberculosis. There were no colored doctors around, and no white doctors would come out to the farm. The father died, and so the son decided he would be the doctor that didn't exist when they needed one. He specialized in tuberculosis and diseases of the lung and would spend the rest of his life fighting what took his father away.

No colored man out on a farm was going to die abandoned if he could help it. He took a job teaching at Meharry and on the weekends went out into the country making house calls on colored families who couldn't make it into Nashville. Every Sunday he drove the back roads to the sharecropper shacks and the shotgun houses in his crisp suits and late-model car. Some of the white people accused him of being uppity and not knowing his place. Threats and shots were fired. One afternoon, some roughnecks pulled him from his car and beat him. From then on, his wife, Reatha, and their two young children, William, Jr., and Vivian, rode with him whenever he went.

"They would drive out as a family, figuring that they wouldn't kill him in front of them," his granddaughter, Reatha Gray Simon, said years later.

Mrs. Beck was prominent in her own right in the South's distorted world of colored privilege. Her father, a dentist, was said to have been an outside child of an Alabama governor, a condition that afforded the family land and means when the son decided to set up house outside Monroe, Louisiana. The son had thirteen children, and all of them went to college in the days when most colored people did not make it to high school.

Dr. and Mrs. Beck were in their fifties now, Robert's parents' generation. They themselves had arrived in Los Angeles only six years before. They were part of the postwar flood of colored Louisianans that was turning Los Angeles into New Orleans west. Dr. Beck arrived as an elder statesman who had taught many of the colored doctors practicing there, and Mrs. Beck arrived the very picture of a doctor's wife. She was a beauty of the Lena Horne variety, who had never spent a day at work and was accustomed to maids and cooks and would thus not know what to do with either a typewriter or a mop. When they first arrived, they noticed to their dismay that most colored people were living on the more congested east side of town, east of Main Street and far from the circular driveways of Beverly Hills.

They looked further west and found a house more in keeping with their vision of themselves. It was a four-bedroom peach stucco mansion set back from the road on St. Andrews between Pico and Country Club. The address was 1215 St. Andrews. It had a wide portico with balustrades like the bridges of Paris. It was surrounded by houses that were equally grand. And they wanted it.

But the neighborhood was all white, and there was a covenant on the house that forbade the owners from selling to colored people. Still a real estate agent managed to secure the house for them in spite of the restriction. During the early testing of limits that presaged the white flight from northern and western cities in the 1960s, realtors found ways around the covenants by buying properties themselves and selling them at a higher price to colored people, by arranging third-party transfers that hid the identity of the true purchasers, or by matching defiant or desperate white sellers with equally anxious colored buyers, which together were just about the only way colored people could get into certain neighborhoods. In any case, Dr. and Mrs. Beck, bourgeois though they were, waited until after dark to move into 1215 St. Andrews Place. But someone must have seen them. That night, as they began unpacking, an orange light danced in front of the picture window. The palm tree on their manicured lawn was on fire. It was not unlike the crosses that burned in the South, except this was California.

They were not new to this kind of hostility, and they decided not to run from it. They had survived the South during far uglier days. And they considered themselves upstanding people that anyone should be proud to live next to. They went to court to challenge the covenant and defend the means by which they had acquired the house; and, when it was over, they had won the right to stay. The white people emptied out of the block within months.

On a spring afternoon six years later, Robert Pershing Foster drew near the vicinity of the peach stucco house that his mentor had to sue to live in, to begin his own life in California.

Robert had arrived in one of the last receiving stations of the twentieth-century migration out of the South. For most of the state's history, the distance between California and the old Confederacy had discouraged all but the most determined of black pioneers. The people were of so little means that they could scarcely take a chance on someplace so far away in the decades before the Great Migration. There was already an abundance of unskilled labor from China, Japan, and Mexico, which gave California industries little need to recruit cheap black labor from the South, had they been so inclined.

Still, a small contingent of blacks had lived in California since the eighteenth century. There were two blacks among the forty-four settlers who founded Los Angeles on September 4, 1781. Some arrived over the ensuing decades, when slaveholders who moved west brought their slaves with them. Others worked as fur traders, scouts, cowboys, and miners. But even before the end of the Civil War, California, like other states outside the South, strongly discouraged the migration of freed slaves across its border. The state constitutional convention seriously considered prohibiting colored people from living in California. The measure did not pass but was a reflection of the fear and intolerance directed toward them.

By 1900, there were only 2,131 black people in the city of Los Angeles out of a total population of 102,479, and only 11,045 in the entire state of California. The numbers rose slowly but steadily over the years but did not take off during the labor shortage of World War I as in the North. California had not been as dependent on European labor as had other parts of the country, and Los Angeles, the state's largest city, did not then have an industrial base as did the cities of the North.

But even in the low-status laborer and domestic positions that were the caste-ordered preserve of colored people in the South, colored migrants to California faced stiff competition from the many immigrants already there, the Mexicans and Filipinos working the loading docks, the Europeans in personal service to the glamorous and the wealthy.

"Even the seeming inapproachable shoe-shining field was competed for by the Greeks," observed a report by the Works Progress Administration in the 1930s on the challenges facing black workers in Los Angeles. "Trained English servants succeeded them as valets and butlers."

The polyglot nature of Los Angeles made it harder for colored migrants to figure out this new terrain, where competition was coming from every direction and each minority was pitted against the others. "In certain plants, Mexicans and whites worked together," the Works Progress Administration reported. "In some others, white workers accepted Negroes and objected to Mexicans. In others, white workers accepted Mexicans and objected to Japanese. White women worked with Mexican and Italian women, but refused to work with Negroes. . . . In the General Hospital, Negro nurses attended white patients, but were segregated from white nurses in dining halls: in a manufacturing plant white workers refused to work with Negroes, but worked under a Negro foreman."

Into this world arrived the migrants from the South, looking for a place for themselves far from home, not knowing what to expect in a city with a whimsical caste system and no rules that anyone could see.

The Becks were expecting him. Word had reached them that he was heading to California, although Robert did not alert them himself or assume he could stay with them. Driving in the middle of a foreign city, it hit him that he had arrived in Los Angeles without any assurance of anything. It was not clear who would take him in or for how long. The nearest relative was two thousand miles away. And he suddenly started to feel alone and uncertain again. "I knew I could find a place to sleep in any hotel I knew would take me in," he would say years later, "but I didn't know what my future was."

He decided to look up Dr. Beck's office and go by there first. He didn't want to give the impression that he expected to live off the Becks. "These were not relatives I was going to see," Robert said. "I didn't know the Becks would take me in."

He found the address in the phone book. It was an office building on South Figueroa, number 4240. It turned out Dr. Beck was delighted to see him.

"Come here, boy," Dr. Beck said greeting him. "Of course you'll be staying with us. We've got a big house, plenty of room."

Robert regaled the Becks with the story of his journey. And he told them that it was not yet over, that he was going up to Oakland to see about the prospects there.

"Now, when you get through looking it over," Dr. Beck said, "come on back here, and I'll give you all the surgery out of my practice."

Robert was relieved and knew that Dr. Beck had the best of intentions. But he also knew he couldn't make a living on one man's referrals alone. So he made plans to drive up to Oakland and to see if it better suited him. In the meantime, he would take in L.A.

Johnny Warmsley, an old schoolmate from Morehouse, took him around, brought in another guy they knew from Atlanta, Wilbur Pew Beulow, who owned a gas station now, and showed him Hollywood and Vine, which actually meant something in those days, and Beverly Hills, the hills in general, the colored nightclubs on Central Avenue, the department stores on Wilshire, the palm trees, the billboards, the people dressed like Dean Martin and Doris Day, the broad silver sidewalks, and the mansions the color of cotton candy.

They rode and rode, and Robert drank it in. He saw what he had driven all this way for and had had in his mind for as long as he could remember, and there it was laid out before him better than a dream.

"I loved it," Robert said. *"I loved it, loved it, loved it, loved it."*

You could drive for hours and still not see the end of it. He could get lost in a town like this, be whoever he wanted to be. It was a blank canvas waiting for him to start painting on it. "Big, open, hustle and bustle," he said. "It was big, big, big. It was the cleanest city I'd ever seen. It was clean enough to eat breakfast off the sidewalk. *Beautiful.* I loved it."

Johnny Warmsley gave him the verbal map of the city.

"Now, Los Angeles is divided into East and West by Main Street," Johnny told him. "All the boulevards go this way, and the streets go that way. The colored neighborhoods are mostly east. There are very few of us west of Crenshaw." That meant most of the places you heard about in the movies: Bel-Air, Brentwood, Beverly Hills, Malibu. They were off-limits to colored people, Johnny Warmsley told him.

Robert would have expected as much after his ordeal in Arizona and was too excited to muster much disappointment. After all, the Becks were living west of Crenshaw, the lawsuit notwithstanding, and that gave him hope that Los Angeles was making as much progress as most any city he might choose.

Johnny and Wilbur were happy to take him to where the movie stars lived and maybe make a sighting. But Robert said he didn't care about that. He had already seen Barbara Stanwyck once. It was when he was based in Austria for the army and the colonel from Mississippi, rather than giving Robert an assignment, ordered him to make himself scarce. The Clements gave him and Alice the money for a trip. They went all over Europe and when they were in Venice, they were standing in St. Mark's Square when they saw Barbara Stanwyck and whoever her husband was at the time.

"And she whispered to him, 'Look at the blacks over there,'" Robert remembered. "I read her lips. She didn't say it in a demeaning manner, but I saw him look over to where we were. And they were giving false grins for all the populants of the city. If you see a celebrity, sure, I want to see the celebrity. But I'd seen enough not to go gaga over it."

He woke up from the city's spell. The glamour was all well and good, but he had other things on his mind.

"I was thinking of more urgent things," he said. "What will I do? *What will I do?* I had to think about surviving."

And so something compelled him several hundred more miles through the mountains, a fear that he was on his own now, far from home, that failure was a distinct but unbearable possibility and that everyone was watching and ready to comment on how things turned out. There was a dread deep within him that he might not make it in L.A., however besotted he was. And so he prepared to drive to Oakland in order to settle on a city for good.

He was weighing every nuance and eventuality, and the stars seemed to have preordained Oakland. It had more people from Monroe than any other place on the coast. He would have a ready-made clientele. He would be looking up his old friend John Dunlap, who had been in the mortuary business in Monroe, knew everybody from back home, and had assured him of plenty of patients. It was as if Oakland were sitting there waiting for him. He could not rest until he had seen it.

He rode at God's knee between the two great cities of California and saw the clouds search out folds in the mountains. He made his way across the San Francisco Bay and into Oakland, which by the early 1950s had become a satellite of colored Louisiana. The shipyards and the loading docks and the railroad jobs had called out to the southerners running from Jim Crow and had given them haven and jobs paying more than a dollar an hour. They settled in the foothills of west Oakland and Richmond, far from the wealthy white cliff-side mansions and nearer to the shipyards. They planted their collards and turnip greens, and let chickens forage out back.

Robert drove into west Oakland, past the fussy Victorian row houses and the worker cottages, turreted and marching in lockstep, barely a foot between them, roosters and pole beans growing in some of the postage stamp yards. It was looking familiar. It was looking like Monroe, which was perhaps one reason why people from Monroe had gravitated there in the first place and made a colony for themselves. It was precisely what Robert was looking to get away from. It was not living up to his glamour vision of California. It felt as if he had driven all this way for the same place he had left.

He was searching for Forty-second and Lusk, where John Dunlap lived. Dunlap, as Robert called him, had moved to Oakland at the height of the war, in 1943, not knowing a soul. The climate agreed with him. He got a room and sent for his wife. From then on, he saw southerners like Robert show up in Oakland looking for something they couldn't name. "They started coming every week," Dunlap said decades later. "They were coming in carloads."

Dunlap had married into a family of morticians and so had taken up the trade himself. Robert was counting on Dunlap to show him around and help him build a clientele. Morticians were always good people to know. Having seen the villas in Los Angeles, Robert was expecting a spread befitting someone with the guaranteed customer base a mortician enjoys. But he pulled up to Lusk and found the little white worker cottage belonging to Dunlap.

Dunlap was glad to see him and showed Robert where he would be sleeping—on a makeshift bed in the front room. He apologized for not being able to take Robert around. But he was working hard to make ends meet in this new world and was too beat at the end of the day to be of much help. It turned out Dunlap hadn't found work as a mortician in Oakland. He and other middle-class migrants from the South, it turns out, were not unlike the immigrant taxi drivers you hear about who had been doctors or engineers back in Pakistan. Dunlap had been somebody back home, but it didn't translate at his destination. And so he had taken a job as a laborer at the shipyard.

Dunlap pointed Robert in the direction of the hospitals he knew of and the people Robert might like to see from back home in Monroe. Robert set out in the morning for the hospitals and clinics he'd heard about. He went to Kaiser, the big industrialist-shipping conglomerate, to see what possibilities there might be for a medical position. He came back empty.

"I'm not finding what I want," he told Dunlap.

Dunlap knew what that meant. Not only was Robert having no luck finding a place to practice, he wasn't liking Oakland. As Dunlap saw it, Dr. Beck had gotten to Robert first. Los Angeles had seduced him. And Oakland did not stand a chance. Robert made up his mind and phoned Alice and the Clements about his decision. And as soon as he did, he drove back to Los Angeles to start living for the first time in his life.

The Things They Left Behind

There were no Chinaberry trees. No pecan trees. . . .
Never again would I pick dew berries
or hear the familiar laughter from the field truck.
This was my world now, this strange new family
and their cramped quarters over the tiny grocery store
they grandly called the "confectionery."

—Clifton Taulbert, *The Last Train North*

IN THE NORTH AND WEST, 1915–2000

WHEN THEY FLED, there were things they left behind. There were people they might not see again. They would now find out through letters and telegrams that a baby had been born or that a parent had taken ill or passed away. There were things they might not ever taste or touch or share in again because they were hundreds of miles from all that they had known. From this moment forward, it would take great effort and resources merely to sit and chat over salt pork and grits with a beloved mother or sister who had chosen not to go. Perhaps the greatest single act of family disruption and heartbreak among black Americans in the twentieth century was the result of the hard choices made by those on either side of the Great Migration.

The South was still deep within those who left, and the sight of some insignificant thing would take them back and remind them of what they once were. For my mother, a vase of Casablanca lilies far from home took her back to the memory of this:

Once a year on a midsummer night that could not be foretold, a curious plant called the night-blooming cereus would decide to undrape its petals. It was said, among the colored people in the small-town South who followed such things and made a ritual of its arrival, that if you looked hard enough, you could see the face of the baby Jesus in the folds of the bloom.

My mother's mother, who sang to her camellias and made showpieces of the most recalcitrant and unlovable of plants—the African violets and Boston ferns that died when other people just looked at them—did not want to leave the land of her ancestors, the drawl of small-town convention, the hard soil she had willed into a cutting garden. There was chaos in the Jim Crow world outside her picket fence. But inside, there was peace and beauty, and she insulated herself in her perennial beds.

She grew a night-blooming cereus on the front porch of her yellow bungalow. Its gangly branches coiled out of its pot and snaked along the porch planks. It was an unpleasant-looking orphan of a plant that was only worth growing for the one night in the year when its white, lily-like petals managed to open for a few hours when nobody would be up to see it.

My mother's mother tended its homely stalks all through the year. She watched it close and made note when the buds were plump and ready to unfurl. As soon as she was certain, she alerted the neighbors as they passed her front yard with its roses the size of saucers, which she sold after some cajoling for a dollar apiece, and its crape myrtles the color of cotton candy.

"My night-blooming cereus is going to open tonight," she told them.

Amanda Poindexter, Miss Lilybell Nelson, who lived up the hill and sang like a bird, Mrs. Jacobs next door, and a few other neighbor ladies on Gibbon Street would arrive at my grandmother's front porch at around midnight. They drank sweet tea and ate freshly churned vanilla ice cream. They rocked in the porch swing, which creaked as they rocked, and they waited. As a young girl, my mother sat watching on the porch steps, mystified by the grown people's patience and devotion.

The opening took hours. Sometime around three in the morning, the white petals spread open, and the women set down their sweet tea to crane their necks over the blossom. They inhaled its sugary scent and tried to find the baby Jesus in the cradle in the folds. Most exclaimed that they saw it; my mother said she never did. But she would remember the wait for the night-blooming cereus, the Georgia heat stifling and heavy, and take the memory with her when she left, though she would never share in the mystery of that Gibbon Street ritual again.

As best they could, the people brought the Old Country with them—a taste for hominy grits and pole beans cooking in salt pork, the "sure enoughs" and "I reckons" and the superstitions of new moons and itchy palms that had seeped into their very being.

In the New World, they surrounded themselves with the people they knew from the next farm over or their Daily Vacation Bible School, from their clapboard Holiness churches, from the colored high schools or the corner store back home, and they would keep those ties for as long as they lived. The ones from the country fired their shotguns into the night air on New Year's Eve like they did back home in Georgia and Mississippi and ate black-eyed peas and rice for good luck on New Year's Day. The people from Texas took Juneteenth Day to Los Angeles, Oakland, Seattle, and other places they went. Even now, with barbecues and red soda pop, they celebrate June 19, 1865, the day Union soldiers rode into Galveston, announced that the Civil War was over, and released the quarter-million slaves in Texas who, not knowing they had been freed, had toiled for two and a half years after the Emancipation Proclamation.

Whole churches and social rituals in the North and West would be built around certain southern towns or entire states. Well into the 1990s, at the Bridge Street Church in Brooklyn, for instance, when people from South Carolina were asked to stand and make themselves known, half the flock would rise to its feet. To this day, people still wear sequins and bow ties to the annual Charleston Ball in Washington, where a good portion of the Carolinas went.

It turned out they were not so different from Sicilians settling in Little Italy or Swedes in Minnesota.

In the New World, colonies organized themselves into Mississippi and Arkansas Clubs in Chicago; Florida Clubs in Harlem; Carolina Clubs in Brooklyn and Philadelphia; and numerous Texas Clubs, general Louisiana Clubs, several New Orleans Clubs, and, among others, a Monroe, Louisiana, Club and a Lake Charles, Louisiana, Club in Los Angeles.

They met over oxtails and collard greens well into the turn of the new century or for as long as the original migrants lived to recall among their dwindling membership the things they'd left behind: the ailing parents and scuffling siblings and sometimes even their own children; the courtly tipping of one's hat to a stranger; the screech owls and whip-poorwills wailing outside their windows foretelling an imminent death; paper-shell pecans falling to the ground; mimosa trees, locust trees, dogwood trees, and chinaberries; the one-room churches where the people fanned themselves through parching revivals and knelt by the ancestors buried beside the sanctuary light. These things stayed with them even though they left, because a crying part of them had not wanted to leave.

"If I were half as well treated home as here," a migrant in Pittsburgh told the economist Abraham Epstein early in the Migration, "I would rather stay there."

They wired money back home, as expected, and sent a larger share of their straining paychecks than they could truly afford to the people they left behind. In his study of the Migration, Epstein found that eighty percent of the married migrants and nearly half of the single ones were sending money home, most sending five dollars per week and some sending ten or more dollars per week out of weekly wages of fifteen dollars back then for unskilled laborers, as many of them would have been.

There was something earnest and true-hearted about them. They greeted people on northern sidewalks a little too quickly and too excitedly for the local people's liking and to the stricken embarrassment of their more seasoned cousins and northern-born children. They talked of a lush, hot-blooded land to children growing up fast and indifferent in a cold place too busy to stop and visit.

Transplanted in Alien Soil

Should I have come here?
But going back was
impossible. . . .
Wherever my eyes turned,
they saw stricken,
frightened black faces
trying vainly to cope
with a civilization
that they did not understand.
I felt lonely.
I had fled one insecurity
and embraced another.
—Richard Wright,
Black Boy

MILWAUKEE, WISCONSIN, NOVEMBER 1937
IDA MAE BRANDON GLADNEY

IDA MAE REUNITED WITH HER BIG SISTER, Irene, at the train station in Milwaukee, and it was clear to both sisters that Ida Mae and George had a long way to go before they could survive on their own in the North. Ida Mae had made it out of Mississippi, but her task had just begun. Irene took them to her walk-up apartment in a two-flat off Reservoir on the North Side of the city. The sister had been in Milwaukee only a couple of years herself, having followed her husband, the third one, Richard, there in 1935. Ida Mae and her family camped out in Irene's front room with all their worldly belongings while Ida Mae's husband went out hunting for work.

Ida Mae had landed in Milwaukee because her sister had migrated there along a not altogether random route established at the start of the movement, back when the two of them were just little girls. It was one of the by-products of the Great Migration that particular southern counties became feeder lines to specific destinations in the North, based on where the earliest migrants went and established themselves, which in turn was often based on something as random as where the northern companies recruiting southerners in World War I just happened to be based. Irene had followed one of those tributaries.

A map of the crosscurrents of migration would link otherwise completely unrelated southern counties and towns with seemingly random northern cities that, other than the train lines and sometimes in spite of them, made little practical sense but nonetheless made sister cities of the unlikeliest of pairings: Palestine, Texas, and Syracuse, New York; Norfolk, Virginia, and Roxbury in Boston; Brookhaven, Mississippi, and Bloomington, Illinois. Small colonies of migrants from Chickasaw County, Mississippi, ended up in Toledo, Ohio, where Ida Mae's older brothers fled, and in Kalamazoo, Michigan, when the call came for workers.

But for most sharecroppers in Chickasaw County, the Promised Land was, oddly enough, a place called Beloit, Wisconsin, on the Rock River seventy-five miles southeast of Milwaukee, which, along with Chicago, because of the *Chicago Defender* and the mail-order catalogues, would have figured prominently in their minds.

The foundries and metalworking factories in Beloit and the steel mills and manufacturers of farm implements in Milwaukee went to northeast Mississippi to hire workers used to hard labor for little money back during World War I. With so many northerners nosing around the South for cheap black labor, the recruiters had to work undercover and spread themselves out among the targeted states to escape detection, arrest, or fines that could run into the thousands of dollars.

Ultimately, southern protectionism had limited effect, and neighbors and cousins of Ida Mae's husband made their way from Okolona to Beloit, some later fanning out to Milwaukee and Chicago. And so, arriving as she did deep into the Depression, Ida Mae's sister, Irene, followed a quiet but well-trod rivulet from Chickasaw County to Milwaukee.

The city's colored population had not skyrocketed as it had in Detroit, which rose sevenfold from 5,741 to 41,000, or Gary, which shot up from 383 to 5,300, during World War I. But the number of colored people in Milwaukee had risen from a mere 980 in 1910 to 2,229 by 1920, an increase of 127 percent, and continued to rise in the 1920s and 1930s.

Once Irene got to Milwaukee, it didn't take her long to start sending gift boxes of clothes from the North and talking up Wisconsin—not pressuring Ida Mae, who was too easygoing to take anything too seriously anyway, but just telling her flat out, "If I was you, I just wouldn't stay down there."

Milwaukee was a frank and clattering workhorse of a town, a concrete smokestack of a place with trolley cars clanking against a web of power lines and telephone cables filling the sky. Curls of steam rose from the rooftops and factory silos and from the gray hulk of the Schlitz brewery over by the Cherry Street Bridge.

It was the other side of the world from the wide-open, quiet land of the cotton fields. Ida Mae saw things she never imagined, bridges that lifted into the air to let ships pass through, traffic lights and streetlamps and flocks of white-robed women—nuns, she was told they were—their habits fluttering in the wind and their crisp headdresses making a stiff halo around their faces. Ida Mae had never seen anyone like them before. She felt drawn to them, and she liked to watch them float by, regal and otherworldly.

There were unknown tongues and aromas drifting out of the beer gardens and delicatessens. There were Germans, Poles, Slavs, Hungarians, Irish, Italians, Greeks, and Russians who had come here, as Ida Mae and her husband had, willing to work their way up from the bottom and make a life for themselves in a freer place than the one they had left. Before World War I, Milwaukee had not extended itself to the laboring caste of the South, nor had it needed to, with the continuing supply of European immigrants to work its factories.

But, as in the rest of the industrial North, the number of Europeans immigrating to Milwaukee plummeted from 22,508 in the first decade of the twentieth century to a mere 451 during all of the 1920s because of the war. Factories that had never before considered colored labor came to see the advantages of colored workers from the South, even if some of the so-called advantages were themselves steeped in stereotype. "They are superior to foreign labor because they readily understand what you try to tell them," one employer reported. "Loyalty, willingness, cheerfulness. Quicker, huskier, and can stand more heat than other workmen."

Most colored migrants were funneled into the lowest-paying, least wanted jobs in the harshest industries—iron and steel foundries and slaughtering and meatpacking. They "only did the dirty work," a colored steelworker said of his early days in Milwaukee, "jobs that even Poles didn't want."

But it was now the fall of 1937, and even those jobs were disappearing. George and Ida Mae arrived in Milwaukee as the city was falling deeper into the Depression. The automotive, farm, and heavy machinery sectors suffered crushing layoffs in August 1937, two months before they arrived, layoffs that would continue well into the following year. The kinds of jobs George was looking for and that most colored men performed—unskilled labor that was often hot, tedious, backbreaking, or dangerous—plunged by seventy percent, from 1,557 such jobs in 1930 to only 459 at the end of the decade, around the time George and Ida Mae arrived.

With jobs scarce, the old tendency toward intolerance and exclusion reasserted itself. Hiring managers at A. O. Smith Company, a tank and auto frame factory, said there was no use in colored people applying for jobs there because the company "never did and didn't intend to employ Negroes." Company guards knew to stop colored job seekers at the gates.

Still, the urge to get out of the South was so strong that by the mid-1930s, Milwaukee's North Side, a neighborhood of tenements and two-flats just above the city's central business district, was already becoming the colored side of town. Since World War I, it had been filling each day with more and more colored people from the South, so much so that in some grade-school classrooms, nearly every child was from Mississippi, Tennessee, or Arkansas, and those born in the North were in the minority. The way things looked, Ida Mae's children would add three more to that demographic equation.

By now Ida Mae couldn't hide the fact that she was pregnant and was already making plans to head back to Mississippi to give birth. She didn't quite trust whatever it was they did to people in hospitals. She had never been inside one but had heard that they strapped women down during delivery, and so she decided to surrender herself to a Mississippi midwife as she and everybody she knew had always done.

It was calculated that the baby was due sometime in the late spring, so she would be heading back to Mississippi in three or four months. George hadn't found steady work yet, and Ida Mae would have to leave him with her sister and brother-in-law while he continued to hunt for work. Ida Mae's return to Mississippi delayed her adjustment to the New World, planning as she was to leave nearly as soon as she arrived. But her decision had assured her that she wouldn't end up like so many other wives, left down south waiting for a husband who might never get around to sending for them.

HARLEM, SPRING 1945
GEORGE SWANSON STARLING

GEORGE HAD THE GOOD FORTUNE to have made it out of Florida and to have arrived in New York well into World War II, and was thus able to find a job right away. It was a job doing the one thing, whether he sought it or not, that would keep him tied to the South. It was a job on the railroad, the Seaboard Air Line, it was called, which would keep him on the rails up and down the East Coast for days and weeks at a time, expose him to the temptations of women and drink, and do little to help his already colicky marriage to Inez.

He was overqualified and overeducated for the job as a coach attendant, hauling luggage into the baggage car and helping people stow their carry-ons in the overhead bins for a dime or a nickel tip. But it was a step up from what they had wanted him to do when they first got a look at him.

"We need some big, tall, husky boys like you to carry the trays in the dining room," the manager told him.

"Well, you need some big husky boys to carry the bags on the coaches too," George said.

"We need waiters."

"But I don't want to wait no tables."

The war was on and labor was short, so George got the job as coach attendant. He wouldn't get paid what his white counterparts were getting even in the enlightened North. He would be getting more than he ever had as a fruit picker down south, which was not particularly a great triumph but was a fact known to anyone, including and perhaps especially railroad management, as it was a convenient way to explain away the lower pay scale for black employees. *At least you're making more than you did down south,* they could say.

The job meant working twenty-four- and forty-eight-hour runs up and down the East Coast on trains called the Silver Comet, the Silver Star, and the Silver Meteor, the very train he rode when he migrated north. He would work the Jim Crow car and the white car behind it, stacking trunks and suitcases up to the ceiling, getting ice, and polishing shoes. He would make close to a hundred dollars every two weeks for it.

In attending to the needs of his white clientele, he would be addressed as "boy," as was the custom when he was working the white cars, even though by now he was twenty-seven years old and towered over most everyone who addressed him as such.

They could call him what they wanted on the train. He didn't like it, but it didn't define him. He lived in Harlem now and was free.

He had avoided the racial turf wars that characterized other cities during the Great Migration. In Manhattan, those fights had been settled long before World War II, when George got there.

The first blacks in Harlem were actually a small group of seventeenth-century slaves of the Dutch West India Company. They built the original road between lower Manhattan and Harlem and worked the farms and estates of what was then undeveloped marshland and countryside.

As more Africans were shipped in to build the colony, the majority were concentrated in lower Manhattan, where the first eleven African captives had landed on the island in 1625. They and those that followed were imported by the Dutch to clear timber and construct the city's roads and buildings. They worked in captivity for two hundred years, until New York abolished slavery in 1827. Emancipation set free ten thousand slaves in Manhattan. But they found their economic conditions little changed, confined as they were to the lowliest positions and facing steep competition from newly arrived immigrants.

Their tenuous condition and the state of race relations in general reached a nadir in the city during the Civil War Draft Riots of 1863, when Irish immigrants launched a five-day assault on freed slaves in lower Manhattan.

The trouble began when the federal government announced it would start drafting men to serve in the Union Army. Wealthy men could avoid the draft by paying three hundred dollars or hiring a substitute. Anger rose among Irish working-class men, in particular, who couldn't afford to buy their way out of a war they felt they had no stake in. They saw it as risking their lives to defend southern slaves, who would, in their minds, come north and only become competition for them. As it was, the Irish were already competing with former slaves in New York, whose very presence undercut the wages of working-class whites because blacks had little choice but to accept lower pay for whatever work they did.

The draft began July 11, 1863. Two days later, on the morning of July 13, mobs began assaulting blacks on the streets. They attacked a fruit vendor and a nine-year-old boy in lower Manhattan and set fire to a colored orphanage in Midtown. They attacked white women married to colored men and burned boardinghouses and tenements where colored people lived, stripping the clothes off the white property owners. They dragged a black coachman out of his home, hanged him from a lamppost, and then dragged the body through the streets by the genitals.

In five days of rioting, anti-war mobs lynched eleven black men and drove the colony of former slaves in lower Manhattan into a continual search for housing. Black residents moved steadily north from one unestablished and unsavory neighborhood to the next, from lower Manhattan to Greenwich Village to the coldwater flats of the Tenderloin District and finally to pockets of upper Manhattan, in the emerging district north of Central Park known as Harlem.

By the late nineteenth century, Harlem was no longer isolated farmland but, due to the rise in immigration from eastern and southern Europe and the completion of new subway routes, was now a fashionable district of middle-class Germans, Russians, Jews, and Irish living in recently built brownstones on broad boulevards and of newly arrived Italians living in the more working-class outskirts of East Harlem. It was where Oscar Hammerstein bought and sold property during the boom years at the turn of the twentieth century and it was the district represented by Fiorello La Guardia in the U.S. House of Representatives during the Depression.

As a stream of colored people trudged north from other parts of Manhattan and from the countryside of the American South, the Italians and Jews ceded much of Harlem to the new arrivals in the early decades of the twentieth century for the greener hamlets of Westchester, Queens, and the Bronx or the stylish apartments on Riverside Drive.

By 1930, some 165,000 colored people were living in Harlem, packed so densely that some tenants had to sleep in shifts—"as soon as one person awoke and left, his bed was taken over by another," the historian Gilbert Osofsky wrote. Harlem had become majority black, its residents having built institutions like the Abyssinian Baptist Church, regaling white audiences at the Cotton Club, reciting poetry at private salons, running numbers rackets, and baptizing themselves in the Harlem and East Rivers.

Even during the Depression, people continued to pour in by the tens of thousands, such that the Reverend Adam Clayton Powell, Sr., wrote, "There was hardly a member of Abyssinian Church who could not count on one or more relatives among the new arrivals."

The changeover in Harlem was not a smooth one and went to the very heart of the basic difference between the North and South, between the authoritarian control over colored lives under Jim Crow and the laissez-faire passivity in the big, anonymous cities of the North and West.

The receiving stations of the Great Migration were no more welcoming of the colored migrants than the South was—in fact, the arrival of colored migrants set off remarkable displays of hostility, ranging from organized threats against white property owners who might sell or rent to blacks to firebombing of houses before the new colored owners could even move in.

White Harlemites banded together into committees to fight what they openly called "a growing menace," an "invasion" of "black hordes," and a "common enemy," using what Gilbert Osofsky called "the language of war." They formed organizations like the Save-Harlem Committee and the Harlem Property Owners Improvement Corporation to protect against "the greatest problem Harlem has had to face."

Panicked property owners drafted restrictive covenants in which they swore not to let colored people into their properties for fifteen years or "till when it was thought this situation . . . will have run its course." Some covenants covered entire blocks and went so far as to limit the number of colored janitors, bellboys, butlers, maids, and cooks to be employed in a Harlem home or business. White leaders tried to segregate churches, restaurants, and theaters, the Lafayette Theater on Seventh Avenue permitting colored people to sit only in the balcony, no different from Mississippi.

White leaders warned colored real estate agents not to seek housing on certain streets and tried to negotiate a boundary line that colored people would agree not to cross. On the other side of the color line, they took recalcitrant white neighbors to court if they broke down and rented to colored people against the rules of the covenants.

In the end, none of these things worked, not because anti-black forces gave up or grew more tolerant but because of the more fluid culture and economics of the North—the desire of whites to sell or rent to whomever they chose whether for profit or out of fear, necessity, or self-interest, or the temptation of higher rents that could be extracted from colored tenants with few other places to go.

Just as significantly, these things didn't work because of what might be called the dispassion of the indifferent. The silent majority of whites could be frightened into lockstep solidarity in the authoritarian South but could not be controlled or willed into submission in the cacophonous big cities of the North.

The Great Migration forced Harlem property owners to make a choice. They could try to maintain a whites-only policy in a market being deserted by whites and lose everything, or they could take advantage of the rising black demand and "rent to colored people at higher prices and survive," Osofsky wrote. Most were pragmatic and did the latter.

The flood of colored migrants soon broke down the last of the racial levees in Harlem, and signs went up all over the place, alerting people to the opening up of the market. The following notice, one among many, was posted in front of a Harlem tenement in 1916, at the start of the Great Migration:

NOTICE

We have endeavored for some time to avoid turning over this house to colored tenants, but as a result of . . . rapid changes in conditions . . . this issue has been forced upon us.

The posted concessions, addressed to white neighbors with a sense of defeat and resignation, offered a glimpse into the differences between the North and South. The South, totalitarian and unyielding, was at that very moment succeeding at what white Harlem leaders were so desperately trying to do, that is, controlling the movements of blacks by controlling the minds of whites.

"The basic collapse of all organized efforts to exclude Negroes from Harlem was the inability of any group to gain total and unified support of all white property owners in the neighborhood," Osofsky wrote. "Landlords forming associations by blocks had a difficult time keeping people on individual streets united."

The free-spirited individualism of immigrants and newcomers seeking their fortune in the biggest city in the country thus worked to the benefit of colored people needing housing in Harlem. It opened up a place that surely would have remained closed in the straitjacketed culture of the South.

By the 1940s, when George Starling arrived, Harlem was a mature and well-established capital of black cultural life, having peaked with the Harlem Renaissance, plunged into Depression after the 1929 stock market crash, climbed back to life during World War II, and, unbeknownst to the thousands still arriving from Florida, the Carolinas, Georgia, and Virginia, not to mention Jamaica and the rest of the Caribbean when George got there, was at that precise moment as rollickingly magical as it was ever likely to be.

Seventh Avenue was the Champs-Élysées, a boulevard wide and ready for any excuse for a parade, whether the marches of the minister Father Divine or several thousand Elks in their capes and batons, and, on Sunday afternoons, the singular spectacle called The Stroll. It was where the people who had been laundresses, bellmen, and mill hands in the South dressed up as they saw themselves to be—the men in frock coats and monocles, the women in fox stoles and bonnets with ostrich feathers, the "servants of the rich Park and Fifth Avenue families" wearing "hand-me-downs from their employers," all meant to evoke startled whispers from the crowd on the sidewalk: *"My Gawd, did you see that hat?"*

Virtually every black luminary was living within blocks of the others in the elevator buildings and lace-curtained brownstones up on Sugar Hill, from Langston Hughes to Thurgood Marshall to Paul Robeson, Duke Ellington, and W. E. B. Du Bois, on and off, to Richard Wright, who had now outgrown even Chicago, and his friend and protégé Ralph Ellison, who actually lived in Washington Heights but said it was close enough to be Harlem and pretty much considered it so.

Of course, George, having just arrived from Florida, was nowhere near the Sugar Hill set. He was, however, good with money and managed to save up enough fairly quickly to find a more than decent place to live. He located a brownstone on 132nd Street off Lenox in what the people on Sugar Hill called the Valley, which accounted for most of what would be considered Harlem and was thought of as perfectly respectable, even admirable, for someone like George. Now that he had a place and had put a down payment on it, he was in a position to send for Inez. In the meantime, he made the most of his free, new self.

When he wasn't on the rails, he was at the Savoy Ballroom, the rum-boogie emporium that took up a whole city block at Lenox and 140th Street. It had a marble staircase and a cut-glass chandelier in the lobby, settees for guests to rest on between dances, two bands alternating so the music never stopped. Anyone might be there, from a shoeshine boy to Greta Garbo or the Prince of Wales. For a time, Ella Fitzgerald was the house vocalist, Benny Goodman or Jimmy Lunceford might be there on any given night, and if you stayed there long enough—which, having come all this way, George, of course, did—you were bound to run into someone from back home in the South—someone from Durham, Charleston, Richmond, Augusta, or, to George's delight, Eustis, Florida.

Gussie Robinson, Louis and Cleo Grant, "Babe" Blye—old Reuben's brother—John Burns, Mary McClendon, and a whole bunch of the Youngs. All of them might show up at the Savoy or at a place called Big George's or the Monte Carlo out in Corona, where a colony of Eustis people were living, which meant that pretty much every weekend, there was a Great Migration convention, a reunion of onetime fruit and cotton pickers, yard boys and house girls and country schoolteachers who had left all the sirring and ma'aming behind. They were jitterbugging on a floating wood floor in the sequins and Florsheims they now could afford, toasting themselves in another world altogether, a world of their own making in the North—if only for a Saturday night.

LOS ANGELES, 1953
ROBERT JOSEPH PERSHING FOSTER

ROBERT WAS HEADING BACK to Los Angeles sometime in the late spring of 1953 with the relief and uncertainty of a discriminating man having finally made the decision of his life. He would no longer be a visitor here. For better or for worse, it was home now, and yet he knew little of it. It was as if he had married a perfect stranger and was now confronting the enormity of getting to know her after the deed was done. He had to convince himself that he had made the right choice, that, after all, there really had been no choice for an educated and ambitious colored man like him at the time.

He had driven clear across the country and more than halfway up the California coast and back, with an unsatisfying flirtation with Oakland in between. But his task had just begun.

What little he had when he set out from Louisiana had now dwindled to almost nothing. He pulled into Los Angeles with all of a dollar and a half in his pocket. Now it somehow had to be converted into enough money to buy equality, meaning, to him, enough to go anywhere, do anything, buy the best of whatever he might want. He could not erase half a lifetime of sirring and stepping off the sidewalk, but he would have a good time trying.

He did not have enough to put a security deposit on an apartment, so he had to return to Dr. Beck, who put him up in the guest room of his house and made good on his promise to throw some surgery his way.

Dr. Beck called Robert into his office early on.

"I want you to examine this lady," Dr. Beck told him, starting to describe the patient. "This is Mrs. Brown. I think she has a tumor. Check her out. Tell me what she needs."

Dr. Beck had already examined the patient and knew precisely what she needed, but it was his way of easing Robert into this part of his practice. "That would feed you," Robert said years later. "It wouldn't give me quail, but it would feed me."

He needed to find a place so he could send for Alice and the girls. He was itching to be on his own and make a name for himself. He couldn't do that sitting in somebody else's office waiting for a patient to need surgery.

He heard that the Golden State Mutual Life Insurance Company, the largest colored insurance company in the West (founded by William Nickerson, Jr., a migrant from Texas; George Allen Beavers, a migrant from Georgia; and Norman Oliver Houston, a native Californian, in 1925), was hiring doctors to go house to house to collect urine samples and do routine examinations of customers seeking coverage. Years later, this kind of work would be performed by people with a fraction of his education, and it would be unthinkable for a doctor to show up at a patient's house for any reason, much less to collect urine samples.

It was beneath him, and it was exactly the kind of thing he was running from in Louisiana. He never wanted to be a country doctor going out to people's shotgun houses with a satchel in his hand. Now he would be a city doctor going out to people's bungalows with a satchel in his hand, and not to deliver babies or patch wounds but to take people's blood pressure, of all things. There was no way he could let the people back in Monroe, and, Heaven forbid, his in-laws, the Clements, know how humble his existence was and how desperate he had become.

But he needed the money and had no choice. He was better off than most other new arrivals from the South, who didn't have his credentials. So he made himself grateful for the $7.50 he got for each exam and for the extra $2.50 for the cup of urine.

It was as if he were a young boy again, going door-to-door as he had in Monroe, asking people if they wanted some figs to can for the coming winter. As he had before, he tried to make the best of the situation. He learned to ingratiate himself to the customers while making sure not to miss anything lest he not get paid. But he never knew what he was in for, because here, unlike in Monroe, he was a small person in a big place, a colored man who had memorized the rules of the South and was now in a place with no rules, none that he could see anyway, and where the Foster name could not help him.

One day he showed up at the modest home of a colored couple in their fifties somewhere in South Central. The wife met him at the door and called her husband to the front room.

"John, the doctor's here," the wife said before disappearing into the kitchen.

Robert checked off the answers the husband gave about preexisting conditions, fractures, and surgeries. He gave the man a cup to collect the urine in and later began the physical.

He put a blood pressure cuff on the man's arm and began listening for the systolic pressure. Just then the wife walked in and turned the television on so loud that Robert couldn't hear the beat.

"Could you ask your wife to please cut the television off?" Robert asked. "I can't do my examination."

The woman complied, and soon Robert was finished with the husband.

"Now," Robert said, "I also have a form to examine your wife."

"Alright," the husband said. "Baby, come on. The doctor's ready to do your physical."

The wife came out. She was a large woman in a housedress and apron. She had her hands on her hips. And Robert was unprepared for what she had to say.

"I told you I wasn't going to let no nigger doctor examine me."

Robert was beside himself. There were many things one could say about the South, but he had never experienced rejection by patients of his own kind and hadn't anticipated such a thing in this new place. Colored doctors in the South were revered because there were so few of them and because they were the only ones who could be counted on to go into the country to tend to colored people. They were greeted like Union soldiers come to free the slaves. Because of the great chasm between blacks and whites, colored doctors also had a virtual monopoly on colored patients.

He realized he had entered a more complicated universe than he had imagined. Colored people in California didn't have to go to colored doctors if they didn't want to. They had choices colored people in the South couldn't dream of. To make matters worse for a colored doctor new in town, the very system that instilled privilege and superiority in southern whites also instilled a sense of inferiority in their colored workers, and when the latter got the chance to get all that had been denied them, some sought out whatever they were convinced was superior—and thus white.

In that one exchange, Robert experienced a by-product of integration that would affect nearly every black business and institution when the doors of segregation flung open—rejection by a black customer base for the wide-open new world. It didn't take Robert long to realize that he would have to work doubly hard to win over his own people and get any patients at all. But at the moment, he was so hurt and rattled by the woman's rejection that he couldn't think straight.

"It frightened me so," Robert said years later, "I threw all my things in my bag and dashed out of the house to leave."

"I'm sorry, Doctor," the husband was saying.

"That's alright, that's alright," Robert said, the door closing behind him.

Robert got into his car and only then realized that, in his haste, he had forgotten something.

"Oh, my gosh, I've undergone this embarrassment," he thought to himself, "and I don't have the urine specimen. I'll only get $7.50."

He needed every nickel, so he had no choice. "I cut the motor off," he said, "swallowed my pride, and went back and got the urine specimen."

The woman never let him examine her, and it was just as well. The experience had begun to shape his vision of this new world. "To think that I had come all the way from the Deep South," he would say many years later, "out here to this Land of Milk and Honey and Opportunity and Intelligence, to find that one of my own color was disrespecting me."

He endured such slights for years, and drove all over South Central Los Angeles doing perfunctory examinations and collecting urine as if he were a traveling salesman and not a surgeon with military awards, and he did it because he had to. "That's the cut that you took to get your foot in the door," he would say years later.

The ready-made clientele of old Louisianans he had imagined in his more cocksure moments in Monroe did not materialize. The people were there, alright. He saw them spilling onto Jefferson after Mass on Sunday mornings and packing into the clubs and cafés on Central Avenue and shopping on Crenshaw. But he had no easy way to get to them. Some were going to white doctors over in Leimert Park. Some were going to colored doctors they already knew. Specialists like him often built a practice through referrals, but few doctors knew him well enough to refer patients to him, and they seemed content with the surgeons already on their roster. Los Angeles was turning out to be bigger than he thought, and it was harder to make inroads.

Even the people he knew from back in Monroe were slow to seek him out for treatment. Some people acted different when they got out to the New World. Some changed their names, no longer wanted to be called Boo but by their given name, Henry or William, as Robert himself had done. Some were anxious to leave the South and the past behind and preferred doctors from California, because people from California were seen as better educated, more sophisticated, untainted by the South, and just "better." Some people disappeared completely—the palest Creoles passed into white society, never to be seen again in the colored world. But mostly, the same cliques and assumptions people had had back home had migrated with them to the New World. Some people had resented Robert and the Fosters back in Monroe and brought the feelings with them. And some just couldn't bear the idea of little Pershing from back home examining them.

"All that crowd over there, and then some," Robert said. "They didn't come. My father taught half of 'em. There's enough people in this town to give me the biggest practice in the world that I went to grade school with."

He learned he would have to make do without them. He was feeling anxious and slightly desperate and could not bear the thought of failure. Big Madison was back in Monroe, looking to hear how his little brother was handling all those patients he bragged about. Alice and the girls were awaiting word as to when they would join him in what everyone expected would be a fabulous new home. And his father-in-law was surely expecting a progress report on how his practice was faring in Los Angeles, a city the father-in-law had argued against in the first place.

As it was, the Clements were beside themselves with excitement over developments back in Atlanta. President Clement had decided to make a historic bid to become the first colored member of the Atlanta Board of Education. Colored people could not vote in most of the South and could lose their lives for even trying to register, and here was Clement running for public office in the biggest city in the South. It was such a long shot that Robert was too weary to pay it much attention.

Somehow Robert had to find a way out of this new desert he was in. So he wasted no time seeking out prospects wherever he could. Rather than bemoan his lowered position as a traveling hack for an insurance company, he started viewing every insurance customer needing a physical as a potential patient. He dug deep into himself and resurrected the earnest little boy selling figs and buttermilk back in Monroe. He put on his most charming self and tried to win over whoever was placed before him, no matter how surly or resistant or lowly the patient was.

"If people saw you and liked you," he began, "it's your job to charm 'em, show how efficient you were."

He spent many lonely hours crisscrossing neighborhoods in South Central Los Angeles, far from the Becks' and the manicured places he wanted to be, conducting those insurance examinations.

Then, in May, a month after he had arrived in Los Angeles, he got word from Atlanta: President Clement had beaten the longest of odds and been elected to the Board of Education. He had defeated an incumbent, 22,259 votes to 13,936 votes, in an election in which Red-baiting detractors tried to get him disqualified in the eleventh hour and his opponent, who had been on the board since 1927, had been so confident that he didn't even campaign.

"I didn't think the people were ready for this," his opponent, J. H. Landers, told *The Atlanta Constitution.*

The win made Clement the first colored man to win a major office in Georgia since Reconstruction and was significant enough to merit a story in *The New York Times* and articles in *Time* and *Newsweek*. "For the first time since Reconstruction days," the *Times* wrote, "a Negro won nomination to Atlanta's Board of Education."

The news filtered back as Robert was knocking on doors collecting urine samples and still boarding with the Becks. He was feeling even more isolated and alone and could not let on to anyone back home the truth of his situation. Just as he was needing to muster more faith than ever, the South chose a rare instance to let slip a colored victory—and to President Clement, no less, the man who had never thought Robert measured up, who had taken over his role as the head of his own family, and who second-guessed his every decision, even his choice to leave the South. Robert was struggling with that choice at that very moment and now could not escape his father-in-law's triumph because it was national news.

Robert was now feeling the accumulated weight of all the pressure he was under. With the Clements unwittingly gaining a greater hold on Alice and the girls as President Clement rose in stature, Robert fretted over his options. He had to get himself established, and soon. He devised a new plan to gain a foothold in Los Angeles: he now decided to canvass physicians door-to-door to try to build up referrals. He would market himself at the big middle-class churches in town. He would court potential patients wherever he could and dress in such a way that they wouldn't forget him.

So, in between insurance exams, he went from building to building, office to office, up and down Jefferson Avenue and off Vermont and Figueroa, tracking down physicians like a homeless man looking for change. He knocked on glass doors with a doctor's name etched on them as he dreamed his, too, would be one day. He sucked in his pride and took in a deep breath and tried introducing himself to physicians who knew or thought little of him to get into their good graces. He showed them his surgery credentials and asked if they wouldn't mind referring cases to him if they didn't do surgery themselves.

"That was met with poor success," Robert said. Here he was, a perfect stranger from someplace down south—Louisiana, was it?—asking for a favor. The big-city doctors who happened to beat him to California or had grown up there didn't take to it kindly. "So you took a lump in the jaw and kept on to the next office."

He made his pitch again and again and got the same response. "All the cordiality in the world," Robert said. "They would say, 'I've been using Dr. XYZ for all these years. Show me one good reason I should change to you.' "

He didn't have an answer then, but he was determined that one day he would. So he set about trying to make a name for himself the best he knew how. He started going to churches even though he was rarely seen in them otherwise. He decided to put on his loudest, most ostentatious suit and tie so the people would remember him. He made a show of dropping more than he really could afford when the collection plate came his way, enough for the church people to be sure to notice. He asked the ministers if they would introduce him to their congregations from the pulpit as they did politicians and visitors from back South.

"I didn't have any responses," he said.

But Golden State Insurance kept sending him out, and those after-hours insurance examinations were adding up. So he decided to turn his attention to the people themselves. He was doing more and more of those exams, and the anonymous working-class colored people of South Central L.A., many newly arrived from Texas or Arkansas or parts of Louisiana that Robert did not know, began to notice this smooth-talking physician, who looked more like a high roller than a doctor in his loud, tailored suits and stingy-brim hats and who made you feel as though you were the most important person in the world.

He conducted enough of those examinations and collected enough of those critical vials of urine to move into an apartment west of Crenshaw, near the Becks. He had been in Los Angeles a couple of months, getting himself set up, and could send for Alice and the girls now. His name was now forming on the lips of cleaning ladies and laborers, gamblers and seamstresses, postal workers and stevedores scattered all over South Central who wanted a doctor they could relate to, the humble and exuberant people who would eventually become the foundation of everything he would ever do in Los Angeles and among the most loyal people ever to enter his life.

Divisions

I walked to the elevator and rode down with Shorty.
"You lucky bastard," he said bitterly.
"Why do you say that?"
"You saved your goddamn money and now you're gone."
"My problems are just starting."
—Richard Wright, *Black Boy/American Hunger*

THE NORTH AND WEST, 1915 TO THE 1970S

UNKNOWINGLY, the migrants were walking into a headwind of resentment and suspicion. They could not hide the rough-cast clothes ill suited for northern winters or the slow syrup accents some northerners could not decipher. They carried with them the scents of the South, of lye soap and earthen field. They had emerged from a cave of restrictions into wide-open, anonymous hives that viewed them with bemusement and contempt. They had been trained to walk humbly, look down when spoken to. It would take time to learn the ways of the North.

What they could not have realized was the calcifying untruths they would have to overcome on top of everything else. As soon as the North took note of the flood of colored people from the South, sociologists and economists began studying the consequences of their arrival and drawing conclusions about who these people were and why they were coming.

"With few exceptions," wrote the economist Sadie Mossell of the migration to Philadelphia, "the migrants were untrained, often illiterate, and generally void of culture."

"The inarticulate and resigned masses came to the city," wrote the preeminent sociologist E. Franklin Frazier of the 1930s migration to Chicago, adding that "the disorganization of Negro life in the city seems at times to be a disease."

In 1965, Daniel Patrick Moynihan, then an official in the U.S. Department of Labor, called the inner cities after the arrival of the southern migrants "a tangle of pathology." He argued that what had attracted southerners like Ida Mae, George, and Robert was welfare: "the differential in payments between jurisdictions *has* to encourage *some* migration toward urban centers in the North," he wrote, adding his own italics.

Their reputation had preceded them. It had not been good. Neither was it accurate. The general laws of migration hold that the greater the obstacles and the farther the distance traveled, the more ambitious the migrants. "It is the higher status segments of a population which are most residentially mobile," the sociologists Karl and Alma Taeuber wrote in a 1965 analysis of census data on the migrants, published the same year as the Moynihan Report. "As the distance of migration increases," wrote the migration scholar Everett Lee, "the migrants become an increasingly superior group."

Any migration takes some measure of energy, planning, and forethought. It requires not only the desire for something better but the willingness to act on that desire to achieve it. Thus the people who undertake such a journey are more likely to be either among the better educated of their homes of origin or those most motivated to make it in the New World, researchers have found. "Migrants who overcome a considerable set of intervening obstacles do so for compelling reasons, and such migrations are not taken lightly," Lee wrote. "Intervening obstacles serve to weed out some of the weak or the incapable."

The South had erected some of the highest barriers to migration of any people seeking to leave one place for another in this country. By the time the migrants made it out, they were likely willing to do whatever it took to make it, so as not to have to return south and admit defeat. It would be decades before census data could be further analyzed and bear out these observations.

One myth they had to overcome was that they were bedraggled hayseeds just off the plantation. Census figures paint a different picture. By the 1930s, nearly two out of every three colored migrants to the big cities of the North and West were coming from towns or cities in the South, as did George Starling and Robert Foster, rather than straight from the field. "The move to northern cities was dominated by urban southerners," wrote the scholar J. Trent Alexander. Thus the latter wave of migrants brought a higher level of sophistication than was assumed at the time. "Most Negro migrants to northern metropolitan areas have had considerable previous experience with urban living," the Taeuber study observed.

Overall, southern migrants represented the most educated segment of the southern black population they left, the sociologist Stewart Tolnay wrote in 1998. In 1940 and 1950, colored people who left the South "averaged nearly two more years of completed schooling than those who remained in the South." That middle wave of migrants found themselves, on average, more than two years behind the blacks they encountered in the North.

But by the 1950s, those numbers would change. As the Migration matured, the migrants would arrive with higher levels of education than earlier waves of migrants and thus greater employment potential than both the blacks they left behind and the blacks they joined. A 1965 study of ninety-four migrants to Chicago, most of them from Mississippi and Arkansas, found that thirteen percent were illiterate (defined as having five or fewer years of schooling), compared to forty-five percent of the people in the southern counties they came from. The migrants and the blacks they encountered in the poor west side neighborhood of North Lawndale had roughly the same amount of schooling—an average of about eight years, the study found. "There is no support," the sociologist Frank T. Cherry wrote, for the notion of "a less-well-educated" pool of migrants entering Chicago "than it already has."

A seminal study that would be published that same year went even further. Across the North as a whole, the post–World War II migrants "were *not* [italics in original] of lower average socioeconomic status than the resident Negro population," the Taeubers wrote in their 1965 census analysis of migrants arriving north from 1955 to 1960. "Indeed, in educational attainment, Negro in-migrants to northern cities were equal to or slightly higher than the resident *white* population."

Against nearly every assumption about the Migration, the 1965 census study found that the migrants of the 1950s—particularly those who came from towns and cities, as had George Starling and Robert Foster—had more education than even the northern white population they joined. The percentage of postwar black migrants who had graduated from high school was as high as or higher than that of native whites in New York, Cleveland, Philadelphia, and St. Louis and close to the percentage of whites in Chicago.

As for blacks who had the advantage of having come from the urban South, the percentage who had graduated from high school was higher than that of the whites they joined, by significant margins in some cases, in each of the seven northern cities the study examined.

In Philadelphia, for instance, some thirty-nine percent of the blacks who had migrated from towns or cities had graduated from high school, compared with thirty-three percent of the native whites. In Cleveland, forty percent of migrants from the urban South were high school graduates compared to thirty-one percent of the native whites. This was the case for George Starling, Robert Foster, and hundreds of thousands of other colored migrants from the small-town South, who, it turns out, often had as much as or more education than those they met, colored or white, in the cities to which they fled, though they were often looked down upon.

Indeed, when it came to their black counterparts, the Taeuber study found that, in every major city the migrants fled to, a higher percentage of migrants had completed at least one year of high school than the black population they joined—sixty-one percent of migrants compared to fifty-three percent of native blacks in New York, fifty-six percent of migrants compared to fifty-two percent of native blacks in Chicago, sixty-three percent of migrants compared to fifty-four percent of native blacks in Cleveland, sixty-six percent of migrants compared to fifty-four percent of black natives in Washington, D.C., sixty percent of migrants compared to forty-eight percent of native blacks in Philadelphia, and so on.

The migrants, the Taeubers found, "resemble in educational levels the whites among whom they live," and they tended to be "of substantially higher socioeconomic status, on the average, than the resident Negro population." The researchers added that "these findings are at variance with most previous discussions of Negro migration."

The misconceptions about the migrants carried over to their presumed behavior upon arrival. Contrary to popular convention, the migrants were more likely to be married and remain married, less likely to bear children out of wedlock, and less likely to head single-parent households than the black northerners they encountered at their destinations. They were more likely to be employed, and, due to their willingness to work longer hours or more than one job, they actually earned more as a group than their northern black counterparts, despite being relegated to the lowliest positions.

"Black men who have been out of the South for five years or more are, in every instance, more likely to be in the labor force than other black men in the North," wrote Larry H. Long and Lynne R. Heltman of the Census Bureau in 1975. They found that, among young black men in the North, fifteen percent of those born in the North were jobless as against nine percent of the southern migrants they studied. "The same pattern applies to all other age groups and to the West," the census found.

Whatever their educational level, the migrants "more successfully avoided poverty," wrote Long and his colleague Kristin A. Hansen of the Census Bureau, "because of higher rates of labor force participation and other (unmeasured) characteristics."

There developed several theories as to why. One was that, because of the migrants' hard-laboring lives in the South, they had "a stronger attachment to the labor force as a result of their work-oriented values," Long and Hansen wrote. Another explanation pointed to disadvantages facing the northern-born blacks in the migrants' destinations—"exposure to drugs, crime and other conditions in big cities that may be handicaps in obtaining and holding jobs."

There is yet another possible reason—that the migrants who would make it out of the South and outlast others who gave up and returned home were a particularly resilient group of survivors. "The migration of blacks out of the South has clearly been selective of the best educated," Long and Hansen wrote. "It is possible that the least capable returned, leaving in the North a very able and determined group of migrants."

Those who would tough it out in the North and West were "not willing to risk relocation in the South because of possible greater advantages in their current location," wrote the sociologists Wen Lang Li and Sheron L. Randolph in a 1982 study of the migrants.

This would suggest that the people of the Great Migration who ultimately made lives for themselves in the North and West were among the most determined of those in the South, among the most resilient of those who left, and among the most resourceful of blacks in the North, not unlike immigrant groups from other parts of the world who made a way for themselves in the big cities of the North and West.

There appeared to be an overarching phenomenon that sociologists call a "migrant advantage." It is some internal resolve that perhaps exists in any immigrant compelled to leave one place for another. It made them "especially goal oriented, leading them to persist in their work and not be easily discouraged," Long and Heltman of the Census Bureau wrote in a 1975 report. In San Francisco, for instance, the migrants doubled up like their Chinese counterparts and, as in other cities, tended to "immigrate as groups and to remain together in the new environment for purposes of mutual aid," wrote the sociologist Charles S. Johnson.

The willingness to do whatever it took to survive appeared to offer some protection from the ills surrounding them, North and South. The San Francisco study found that the migrants were half as likely to be separated, divorced, or widowed as the blacks they encountered upon arrival. Overall, wherever they went, they tended to be "more family-stable compared both to those they left behind at their origin and those they encountered at their destination," the sociologist Thomas Wilson wrote in 2001. "They are less likely to bear children outside of marriage and less likely to be divorced or separated from their spouses."

The findings, he wrote, "are once again clearly at odds with earlier claims that family dysfunction was carried north by southern migrants."

Still, the stereotypes persisted despite the evidence and extended to even the youngest migrants. The children, having emerged from one-room schoolhouses with their southern English, were often labeled retarded by northern school officials, regardless of their native abilities. Segregation was not the law, but northerners would find creative ways to segregate the migrant children from the white children when so inclined.

"Colored pupils sometimes occupy only the front seats or the back seats," wrote the researcher W. A. Daniel in 1928. "They are grouped on one side, or occupy alternate rows; sometimes they are seated without regard to race; or they share seats with white pupils, a method used regularly by one teacher for punishing white pupils."

The absurdities of the South seemed to follow the migrants north despite their efforts to escape. One migrant child faced altogether different seating and circumstances in each classroom he entered. In this case, the student, Daniel wrote, "is literally forced to take the back seat" in one classroom. "In another room, he is the president of his class, and in another the editor of the paper, in another in charge of the tool room, while in another he is expected to do more than his share of menial tasks."

It was in the early 1920s that a little boy named James Cleveland Owens migrated with his sharecropper parents from Oakville, Alabama, to Cleveland, Ohio, when he was nine years old. The city of Cleveland was the Promised Land to colored people in his part of Alabama, as reflected by his middle name. The parents had debated for months over whether to leave, the mother anxious to do so, the father, having been beaten down by sharecropping, worried and fearful. As they prepared to leave, the little boy happened to bump into his father while they were packing for the train. The father put both hands on his son's shoulders to steady himself but quickly removed them out of embarrassment. Only then did the boy realize that his father's hands were "shaking with fright."

The boy's first day of school in the North, he was assigned to a grade lower than the one he'd been in where he had come from, and the teacher couldn't understand his southern accent. When she asked him his name, he said he was called J.C. The teacher misheard him and, from that day forward, called him Jesse instead. So did everyone else in this new world he was in. He would forever be known as Jesse Owens, not by his given name. He would go on to win four gold medals at the 1936 Olympics in Berlin, becoming the first American in the history of track and field to do so in a single Olympics and disproving the Aryan notions of his Nazi hosts.

It made headlines throughout the United States that Adolf Hitler, who had watched the races, had refused to shake hands with Owens, as he had with white medalists. But Owens found that in Nazi Germany, he had been able to stay in the same quarters and eat with his white teammates, something he could not do in his home country. Upon his return, there was a ticker-tape parade in New York. Afterward, he was forced to ride the freight elevator to his own reception at the Waldorf-Astoria.

"I wasn't invited to shake hands with Hitler," he wrote in his autobiography. "But I wasn't invited to the White House to shake hands with the President either. I came back to my native country, and I could not ride in the front of the bus. I had to go to the back door. I couldn't live where I wanted. Now, what's the difference?"

It would take the arrival of millions of more migrants and many more decades of perseverance on their part and on the part of protesters for human rights before they would truly become accepted.

But his father, a man of few words who had come north with the greatest reluctance and worry, was overcome with the enormity of the moment and how it had come to be. His son had had the chance to go to good schools, run on real tracks, and be coached at Ohio State University, rather than spend his life picking cotton. "My son's victories in Germany," Henry Owens said, "force me to realize that I made the best move of my life by moving out of the South."

CHICAGO, AUGUST 1938
IDA MAE BRANDON GLADNEY

MISS THEENIE HAD BEEN RIGHT about her daughter. Ida Mae was expecting when she left Mississippi with her husband and two little ones in the fall of 1937. That spring, she returned south for the express purpose of having the baby in the familiar hands of a midwife. She had heard that up north, doctors strapped women down when they went into labor, and she wasn't going to submit to that kind of barbarity. So she gave birth to her last child in Miss Theenie's house, on May 28, 1938. It was a baby girl, and Ida Mae named her Eleanor, like the first lady of the land, Eleanor Roosevelt.

She kept the baby in Mississippi until she was plump and strong and then carried her and little James and Velma north on the Illinois Central sometime in August to rejoin her husband. Only this time, Ida Mae didn't return to Milwaukee. She got off in Chicago, the city of skyscrapers and Montgomery Ward that she had thought was Heaven when she first set foot in the North.

While she was away giving birth, George had left Milwaukee, having found little work and given up on the prospects of making a living there. One of his brothers had settled in Chicago. So George turned to the bigger city with its steel mills, blast furnaces, slaughterhouses, and tanneries. He would have been willing to take just about anything to feed his family, having stooped to pick cotton all his life, but what he found first was a job on another man's ice wagon.

Up and down the rutted streets they went, steering the horse and wagon in the early-morning hours, delivering ice to the colored people in their cold-water flats on the South Side.

"Iceman! Iceman!" they shouted as they steered.

"Bring me fifty pounds!" someone would yell from the window of a three-flat.

"Bring me a hundred!" came an order from another.

George slung a rug across his shoulders and hoisted a block of ice on his back to carry it up the tenement steps. He was used to hauling a hundred pounds of cotton in a day for fifty cents. Now he could make that with each fifty-pound block of ice. And he was delivering a lot of it. Ice melted fast in the summer heat. Some people needed to replenish their iceboxes every day. He was already making more money than in Mississippi, and not under the shotgun scrutiny of a planter. It was stoop labor, and he couldn't do it forever. But it would have to do for now.

By the time Ida Mae got back with the baby and little James and Velma, he had secured for his family a one-room basement apartment among the frail tenements and dilapidated lean-tos in the roped-off colored section of town.

It was a kitchenette in a two-flat in the low Forties off St. Lawrence. Preceding waves of European immigrants had lived there before them in creaking buildings from the nineteenth century, the streets now pockmarked and piled so high with rubbish that ice wagons couldn't get through some of them. It was only a few miles south but a world away from the boulevards and skyscrapers Ida Mae had seen when she first arrived, gray and weed-strewn as this new place of hers was.

They were confined to a little isthmus on the South Side of Chicago that came to be called "Bronzeville," the "black belt," "North Mississippi." It was "a narrow tongue of land, seven miles in length and one and one half miles in width," as the midcentury historians St. Clair Drake and Horace Cayton described it, where a quarter-million colored people were packed on top of one another by the time Ida Mae and her family arrived.

Up and down Indiana and Wabash and Prairie and South Parkway, across Twenty-second Street and down to Thirty-first and Thirty-ninth and into the low Forties, a colored world, a city within a city, rolled out from the sidewalk, the streets aflutter with grocers and undertakers, dressmakers and barbershops, tailors and pressers, dealers of coal and sellers of firewood, insurance agents and real estate men, pharmacists and newspapers, a YMCA and the Urban League, high-steepled churches—Baptist, Holiness, African Methodist Episcopal churches practically transported from Mississippi and Arkansas—and stacked-heeled harlots stumbling out of call houses and buffet flats.

There were temptations a southern sharecropper couldn't have known existed and that could only catch root when so many people were packed into one place, the police could be bought, and the city looked away: reefer pads, card sharks, gangsters and crapshooters. The so-called mulatto queen of the underworld running poker games. Policy kings running the numbers racket, ready to take a migrant's newly earned dollar fresh from the slaughterhouse. The migrants could see Ma Rainey at the Regal or just melt into the neon anonymity of city life without a watchful uncle or jackleg preacher knowing about it.

This was the landing place in Chicago for most colored people just in from the South. They had left the wide-open spaces and gravel roads of the cotton fields and had to watch their every step. Ida Mae and George, in particular, pious and churchly as he was, wanted nothing to do with the devilment crowding in on them but had to make the best of it and just be thankful for having made it out of Mississippi alive.

By the time Ida Mae and her family arrived, Chicago was a major terminus of the Great Migration of colored people out of the South and of latter-day immigrants from central and eastern Europe. It had first been settled in 1779 by a black man named Jean Baptiste Point DuSable in what was then wilderness. He was a fur trader who built a "rude cabin on the sandpoint at the mouth of the river."

Ida Mae found the living conditions not much better than those back home and, in some cases, worse. "A few goats and an occasional pig" roamed alleyways that reeked of rotting vermin. Front doors hung on single hinges. The sun peeked through cracks in the outer walls. Many rooms sat airless and windowless, packed with so many people that some roomers had to sleep in shifts, all of which made a mockery of city codes devised to protect against these very things.

"Families lived without light, without heat, and sometimes without water," observed Edith Abbott, a University of Chicago researcher who studied tenement life in Chicago in the 1930s, the time when Ida Mae arrived. "The misery of housing conditions at this time can scarcely be exaggerated."

They were living in virtual slave cabins stacked on top of one another, wives, like Ida Mae, cooking on hot plates and hanging their laundry out the window, if they had a window at all, unable to protect themselves or their children from the screams and conversation and sugar talk and fighting all around them. It was as if all of them were living in one room without space for their own thoughts or for their dreams of how best to get out.

Ida Mae soon discovered that there really was no getting out, not right off anyway. "Negro migrants confronted a solid wall of prejudice and labored under great disadvantages in these attempts to find new homes," Abbott wrote. The color line in Chicago confined them to a sliver of the least desirable blocks between the Jewish lakefront neighborhoods to the east and the Irish strongholds to the west, while the Poles, Russians, Italians, Lithuanians, Czechs, and Serbs, who had only recently arrived themselves, were planting themselves to the southwest of the colored district.

With several thousand black southerners arriving each month in the receiving cities of the North and no extra room being made for them, "attics and cellars, store-rooms and basements, churches, sheds and warehouses," according to Abraham Epstein in his study of the early migration, were converted to contain all the new arrivals. There was "rarely a place in these rooms for even suitcases or trunks."

People like Ida Mae had few options, and the landlords knew it. New arrivals often paid twice the rent charged the whites they had just replaced for worn-out and ill-kept housing. "The rents in the South Side Negro district were conspicuously the highest of all districts visited," Abbott wrote. Dwellings that went for eight to twenty dollars a month to white families were bringing twelve to forty-five dollars a month from black families, those earning the least income and thus least able to afford a flat at any rent, in the early stages of the Migration. Thus began a pattern of overcharging and underinvestment in black neighborhoods that would lay the foundation for decades of economic disparities in the urban North.

Ida Mae tried never to worry about things she couldn't change and so made do with what they could get. She wasn't the only one. "Lodgers were not disposed to complain about the living conditions or the prices charged," Epstein wrote. "They were only too glad to secure a place where they could share a half or at least a part of an unclaimed bed."

The story played out in virtually every northern city—migrants sealed off in overcrowded colonies that would become the foundation for ghettos that would persist into the next century. These were the original colored quarters—the abandoned and identifiable no-man's-lands that came into being when the least-paid people were forced to pay the highest rents for the most dilapidated housing owned by absentee landlords trying to wring the most money out of a place nobody cared about.

It would soon come to be that anyone living in any American city would know exactly where these forgotten islands were, if only to make sure to avoid them: under the viaduct along a polluted stream in Akron, Ohio; in the Hill District in Pittsburgh; Roxbury in Boston; the east side of Cincinnati; the near east side of Detroit; nearly all of East St. Louis; whole swaths of the South Side of Chicago and South Central in Los Angeles; and much of Harlem and Bedford-Stuyvesant in New York.

Like other migrants with limited options, Ida Mae and her family moved from place to place, from one unacceptable flat to a slightly larger and less odious option a few blocks away, not unlike sharecroppers moving from farm to farm looking for a less exploitive arrangement with, they hoped, a fairer planter. Soon they were living on the top floor of a three-flat at Thirty-sixth and Wabash. It was well into the Great Depression, and a man took to sleeping at odd hours of the day on the little landing outside their kitchen door.

"I open the door and put garbage out there, and he still be sleep," Ida Mae remembered. "I don't know who he was. He stayed there winter and summer. He didn't bother nobody. He was sleeping like he was in a bed. He had his little cover out there."

Did he ever wake up when you went out there? I asked her once. "No," she said. "Because I reckon he done did his devilment all night."

Ida Mae didn't know it, but, with the Great Depression deepening, she and her family had arrived in a city unprepared for and utterly resistant to the continuing influx of migrants. City fathers and labor experts had expected the Great Migration to end with World War I. Jobs and housing were scarcer now. White unions were refusing colored workers membership, keeping colored wages low, restricting the work that migrants could do, and leaving them unprotected during cutbacks.

The colored old-timers who were already there were not especially happy to see them. Even as the Migration was a bonanza for colored storekeepers and businessmen, it meant more competition for the already limited kinds of jobs blacks were allotted and made the black presence in the city more conspicuous and threatening to the city's racial alchemy.

As it was, the city was still recovering from the tensions of one of the worst race riots in American history. The riots had set the city on edge and hardened race lines that would persist for generations.

The trouble began after an incident only blocks from the three-flat at Thirty-sixth and Wabash where Ida Mae's family would live exactly two decades later. It was the summer of 1919. World War I, the stimulus of the first wave of the Great Migration, was over. Munitions plants had shut down, the factories that lured black southerners were now letting workers go, the country was on the verge of recession, not able even to imagine the actual Depression that was brewing. The migrants, hemmed in and living on top of one another, even as more of them arrived, pressed against the white neighborhoods on their borders and were met with death threats and bombings when they ventured to the other side.

The demilitarized zone was a moving target that no one could see but that everyone knew in his bones. Blacks were finding more things off-limits than it would otherwise appear, defined by custom and whites' discomfort rather than by law. Even the beaches of Lake Michigan were segregated. Everyone was feeling the strain of a declining economy. Whites saw the migrants as competition for a scarcer pool of jobs and took to attacking them along the western boundary of the black belt.

Then on Sunday, July 27, 1919, a seventeen-year-old black boy named Eugene Williams, swimming along the shore of Lake Michigan, drifted past an invisible line in the lake into the white side of the Twenty-ninth Street beach.

As was common in the North, there were no white or colored signs. It was merely understood that whites entered and used the beach at Twenty-ninth Street and blacks were to stay near the Twenty-seventh Street entrance two blocks north. The imaginary color line stretched out into the water. Swimming as he was, the boy couldn't see the line where the white water began because the water looked the same.

Carl Sandburg, the future poet who was then a reporter for the *Chicago Daily News,* recounted it this way: "A colored boy swam across an imaginary segregation line. White boys threw rocks at him and knocked him off a raft. He was drowned."

Blacks demanded that the white police officer on the scene arrest the whites they said had hurled rocks at Williams. The officer refused, arresting, instead, a black man in the crowd "on a white man's complaint."

Within hours, tensions reached a boil on both sides, and a riot was in full cry. Whites dragged black passengers from streetcars and beat them. Blacks stabbed a white peddler and a white laundryman to death. Two white men were killed walking through a black neighborhood, and two black men were killed walking through a white neighborhood.

White gangs stormed the black belt, setting houses on fire, hunting down black residents, firing shotguns, and hurling bricks.

All told, the riots coursed through the south and southwest sides of the city for thirteen days, killing 38 people (23 blacks and 15 whites) and injuring 537 others (342 blacks, 178 whites, the rest unrecorded) and not ending until a state militia subdued them.

Contrary to modern-day assumptions, for much of the history of the United States—from the Draft Riots of the 1860s to the violence over desegregation a century later—riots were often carried out by disaffected whites against groups perceived as threats to their survival. Thus riots would become to the North what lynchings were to the South, each a display of uncontained rage by put-upon people directed toward the scapegoats of their condition. Nearly every big northern city experienced one or more during the twentieth century.

Each outbreak pitted two groups that had more in common with each other than either of them realized. Both sides were made up of rural and small-town people who had traveled far in search of the American Dream, both relegated to the worst jobs by industrialists who pitted one group against the other. Each side was struggling to raise its families in a cold, fast, alien place far from their homelands and looked down upon by the earlier, more sophisticated arrivals. They were essentially the same people except for the color of their skin, and many of them arrived into these anonymous receiving stations at around the same time, one set against the other and unable to see the commonality of their mutual plight.

Thus these violent clashes bore the futility of Greek tragedy. Yet the situation was even more complicated than the black migrants could have imagined. As they made their way north, so did some of the poorer whites from the South, looking not for freedom from persecution but for greater economic rewards for their hard work. Slavery and sharecropping, along with the ravages of the boll weevil and floods, had depressed the wages of every worker in the South. The call of the North drew some of the southern whites the migrants had sought to escape.

Initially, they came to the North in greater numbers, but they were much more likely to return south than colored southerners were—fewer than half of all white southerners who left actually stayed in the North for good, thus behaving more like classic migrant workers than immigrants. Still, many brought their prejudices with them and melted into the white working-class world of ethnic immigrants to make a potent advance guard against black inroads in the North.

As a window into their sentiments, a witness to the Detroit riots in 1943 gave this description of a white mob that had attacked colored people in that outbreak. "By the conversation of the men gathered there, I was able to detect that they were Southerners and that they resented Negroes working beside them and receiving the same amount of money," the informant said, adding that these southern whites believed that the black migrants "ought to be 'taken down a peg or two.' "

Perhaps the earliest indication of what the migrants were unknowingly up against came from an outbreak directly related to the Great Migration, or rather to how the North reacted to the newcomers from the South. These were the riots that erupted in East St. Louis, Illinois, in the summer of 1917 after companies being struck by white workers hired colored migrants to replace them. The migrants were flocking to the city at a rate of a thousand a month, some eighteen thousand having arrived that spring, and they instantly became the perfect pawns, an industrialist's dream: they were desperate to leave the South, anxious for work, untutored in union politics or workers' rights—as most could not have imagined unionizing themselves as field hands, thus uncomprehending of the idea of a worker making demands and unlikely to complain about whatever conditions they might face.

Once the strike was over, the colored migrants, resented by the unions and unprotected by the plants that had hired them, paid the price. One union wrote its members that "the immigration of the southern Negro into our city for the past eight months has reached a point where drastic action must be taken" and demanded that the city "retard this growing menace, and devise a way to get rid of a certain portion of those who are already here."

On the night of July 1, a carload of whites fired shots into colored homes. The colored residents fired back when a second car filled with whites passed through, killing two policemen. The next day, full-scale rioting began. Colored men were "stabbed, clubbed and hanged from telephone poles." A colored two-year-old "was shot and thrown into the doorway of a burning building."

"A black skin was a death warrant on the streets of this Illinois city," wrote an observer shortly afterward.

The police, charged with quelling the riot, in some cases joined in, as did some in the state militia sent in to restore order, actions that resulted in seven courts-martial. All told, thirty-nine blacks and eight whites were killed, more than a hundred blacks were shot or maimed, and five thousand blacks were driven from their homes.

After the two riots, city leaders in Chicago could see no end to the racial divisions without intervention and a public appeal for tolerance. A white-led, biracial commission set up to investigate the climate and circumstances leading to the riots produced a 672-page report, *The Negro in Chicago*. It stands to this day as one of the most comprehensive examinations of both the early stages of the Great Migration and race relations in a northern American city.

With a sense of urgency, it set out fifty-nine recommendations for improving race relations. It urged that the police rid the city's colored section of the vice and prostitution that plagued the black belt; that the schools hire principals with an "interest in promoting good race relations"; that white citizens seek accurate information about blacks "as a basis of their judgments"; that restaurants, stores, and theaters stop segregating when they weren't supposed to; that companies "deal with Negroes as workmen on the same plane as white workers" and stop using them as strikebreakers and denying them apprenticeships; that labor unions admit colored workers when they qualified; that employers "permit Negroes an equal chance with whites to enter all positions for which they are qualified by efficiency and merit"; that the press avoid using epithets in referring to blacks and treat black stories and white stories with the same standards and "sense of proportion."

With the commission having no authority to enforce its recommendations and a good portion of the citizenry not likely even to have seen them, much of its counsel went unheeded. So Ida Mae arrived in a world that was perhaps even tenser than before the riots. In the ensuing decades, the color line would only stiffen. The South Side would become almost totally black and the North Side almost totally white. Ida Mae's adopted home would become one of the most racially divided of all American cities and remain so for the rest of the twentieth century.

NEW YORK, SUMMER 1945
GEORGE SWANSON STARLING

GEORGE FINALLY BROUGHT INEZ to New York in June of 1945 to begin life on their own for the first time in their marriage. Now that he had a decent job on the railroad, he was hoping she could now get a job as a beautician like she had trained for and they could make a go of it in New York.

But Inez was still nursing a grudge over how little time they had spent together since they'd been married, how he'd gone off to Detroit without her, how he had taken so long to send for her, and now, here he was, likely to be gone half the time working the rails.

He was always the one with big dreams, and he had them now. He wanted to make up for all they didn't have and couldn't have back in Florida. He located a little beauty shop around the corner from the brownstone where they lived that had six available booths for her to use.

"Inez, this is your chance," he told her. "We can rent this place, and you can do hair in one booth and rent out the other five booths. You can build you up a business here, and then after a while you don't have to do no hair at all, just supervise."

But Inez wasn't of a mind to do much of what he said, given all they had been through, so she decided to forgo hairdressing after all. She would never work at it a day in her life. Instead she took a short nursing course and got a job at a hospital to show her independence, to spite him, or both.

George had escaped Florida but could not run away from the frustrations of an impulsive, ill-advised marriage. Inez had arrived in Harlem, but nothing had changed. They were getting along no better than before. So when he wasn't on the rails, he began to fall under Harlem's spell like many of the new arrivals suddenly free of the South. Between the people he knew from back in Florida and the co-workers he met riding the rails, he had a ready-made set of diversions every night of the week in a place that never shut down and was spilling over with people.

It was said that Harlem was one of the most crowded places in all of the country. Some half a million colored people were crammed into a sliver of upper Manhattan that was about fifty blocks long and only seven or eight blocks wide. A 1924 study by the National Urban League confirmed what colored tenants already knew: that colored renters paid from forty to sixty percent higher rents than white tenants for the same class of apartment. So colored people in Harlem took in boarders and worked second and third jobs.

Beginning in World War I, as many as seven thousand people were estimated to be living in a single block in Harlem. The crush of people begging for space forced rents even higher in what became a landlord's paradise. Cash-strapped renters looked for new ways to make their rent. They began throwing end-of-the-month parties, "where they drank bathtub gin, ate pig knuckles and danced with the lights off," as Arna Bontemps wrote. They called them rent parties. They charged twenty-five cents admission for a few hours of smoke-hazed, gin-juiced, tom-tom caterwauling, and poker playing with people from back home and with worldly-wise northerners they did not know just to help make that month's rent.

Up and down the side streets off Lenox and Seventh Avenues, people flung open their apartment doors the Saturday night before the rent was due. They served pork chops and pigs' feet and potato salad just like down south, except that the food and spirits were for sale, and they put Count Basie on the record player to give people something to dance to. Total strangers looking for a good time could stroll down the block looking for a red, pink, or blue light in a window and listening for the rabble of a rent party in progress. Signs went up inviting anybody willing to pay. One read:

There'll be brown skin mammas
High Yallers too
And if you ain't got nothing to do
Come on up to Roy and Sadie's
West 126 St. Sat. Night May 12th.
There'll be plenty of pig feet
An lots of gin
Jus ring the bell
An come on in.

Tenants stood to make the most money if they got the partygoers playing poker, and George was all for it. There were some people from

Eustis, Florida, living up on Seventh Avenue, between 146th and 147th Streets. They lived right next door to each other and started running their parties simultaneously.

"We just go from one house to the other," George said. "We get tired of playing over to Freeman's, or we get mad with him about something, and we go over to M.B.'s. We go from one house to the other. We would be gambling the whole weekend."

When they got tired of the people on Seventh Avenue, they went over to the Bronx, where the Blye brothers had a sister named Henry living over at Third Avenue and Seventeenth Street, and played some more.

The wives and girlfriends served the gin and bourbon and the grits and eggs and biscuits and smoked pork from the pork store down the street, the big poker players never getting up from the table, shoveling forkfuls of grits into their mouths between hands.

They were playing five-card stud, and sometimes there were so many people there'd be two or three games running, people just in or visiting from Eustis and Ocala, people who had been in Harlem for years, hustlers who made a life out of circulating at the gambling tables of the rent parties to beat the tenants out of their own rent money. It was an open invitation, after all.

George saw the money they were making—some of them were pulling in hundreds of dollars a weekend—and decided to throw some parties himself.

He went in with his friend Babe Blye, one of the Blye brothers from back home in Florida (there were nine brothers in all, plus three girls that the parents had given boys' names to, but that's another story). Babe was working as an auto painter for General Motors in New York and was living upstairs from George and Inez in the brownstone George was buying. Sometimes Inez served food, sometimes she wouldn't. Sometimes she would stay down in their apartment. Working the rails mostly for tips, George could use the extra money for the house note and went in with Babe to run some poker parties.

George figured out the system. "If you stay outta the game, and if you run a game for four or five hours or more, you gonna have most of the money," George said. "You're gonna have most of the money and the cut. Because most of the players are going to lose."

Trouble was, Babe couldn't just sit back and watch. "See, that was our weakness," George said. "Babe couldn't stay outta the game. He just had to get in the game, and he'd lose pretty near everything that we take in."

Like most migrants from the South, George had surrounded himself with the people he knew from back in the Old Country, but the Old Country was still in the people no matter where they went, and George found that, as much as he loved the people from back home, he could never truly move up with the country people still acting country. He never put it in so many words, but he didn't keep his resentment to himself.

"We done sat up here all night, and you done gambled all the money out of the cut box," he told Babe. "We just set this whole thing up for nothing. And now we got to clean up and see how many cigarette spots somebody done burned in the furniture. And we don't have a thing to show for it."

Then one night, George had had enough. They were gambling upstairs in Babe's apartment. They had a big game going, and Babe and George were both in the game. George looked to be winning the pot when Babe called him. Two men they didn't know and who looked to have been in Harlem much longer than George and Babe were in the game, as often happened when the migrants threw open their doors to make extra money to make ends meet. George caught Babe dealing off of the bottom of the deck. He hit himself from the bottom with an ace, giving himself a better hand than everyone else.

Babe had cheated to win the pot, but it did not appear that the two other men had caught on. "I couldn't say anything because of the other guys in the game," George said. "If they caught you cheating, some of them guys would kill you right on the spot. So I had to sit there and let Babe go with that. I lost thirty dollars down the deal."

George made a show of borrowing thirty dollars from the pot.

"Well, I'm borrowing thirty dollars," he said to no one in particular, figuring Babe would get the message that George was onto his cheating and wanted him to stop.

"That was for the benefit of the other guys around the table, not to become suspicious," George said.

When the game was over, George headed downstairs. Babe called out to him.

"Hey, son. You know you owe me thirty dollars."

"I do?" George asked. "Let me tell you one thing. I will never in life play with you again. Because you dealt yourself off the bottom with an ace that beat my hand, and the only reason I let you go, I didn't want you to get me and you both killed because there were other people in the game. And you know the rule is, if you caught cheating, you in trouble.

Now, I don't want no killing in the house. It might have been me. So I had to let you go with that."

George wasn't finished.

"Didn't you hear me saying, 'I'm borrowing thirty dollars out the pot?' I took my money out that I lost. I don't owe you nothing. You owe me your life 'cause if I had squawked about you dealing off the bottom, you and I both might have got killed."

He told Babe, who was, after all, his tenant, that he was through with him when it came to gambling. "I ain't gon' never pay you," George said. "And, furthermore, I ain't gon' never gamble with you no more. If you can't gamble with your friends without being cheated, who can you gamble with?"

That was the end of George's short, unhappy career running a gambling den. He wasn't making money, and now it was dangerous.

The city had a way of bringing out the best and now the worst in everyone. People got up to the big city and either forgot where they came from and took on the meanest aspects of a hard life or kept a kind of sweet country blindness and fell victim to what looked to be city charms but could be traps if you weren't wise to them. Or they somehow managed to keep the best of both worlds, keep the essential goodness of the old culture and the street wit of the new. George had to learn to recognize that admixture in the people who surrounded him, even as he tried, sometimes successfully, sometimes not, to do the same himself.

LOS ANGELES, JUNE 1953
ROBERT JOSEPH PERSHING FOSTER

ROBERT HAD BEEN IN CALIFORNIA for a couple of months now, taking whatever work Dr. Beck threw his way and doing physicals for Golden State Insurance. He had set aside some of what he had been making and was starting to feel he could pull a practice together, what with all the people he was meeting through Golden State.

He decided it was time he got an office of his own. He could never get ahead on those ten-dollar physicals, and he wouldn't be able to make the most of Dr. Beck's referrals or treat any patients without an office they could come to. Besides, Alice and the girls were wanting to know when they could come out to California, and the Clements, just waiting for him to fall short, wanted to know what was taking him so long since he had raved so much about the place before he had seen it.

Robert didn't want an office in the predictable places where colored businesses went. He didn't want to be in Compton or Watts or South Central. He wanted to be as far north as he could afford, which wouldn't be but so far north given his resources and wouldn't be practical anyway, given where his current roster of potential patients was living. He wanted a location with some prestige so he could live out the California dream he had in his head and justify the fees he thought he deserved, not knowing that a shot of penicillin generally went for five dollars no matter where you were.

He went driving around the west side looking for the right kind of place for himself. He found an office to let at 959 West Jefferson, well west of Central Avenue, right across the street from the University of Southern California campus. He could always say he was near Southern Cal, and he liked the sound of that.

It was a ground-floor suite at the front of an office building with a dentist upstairs and a doctor and an Asian import-export company on the ground floor with him. The office directly behind his was occupied by an internist from Los Angeles who was neither willing to nor interested in extending himself to this newcomer just in from the South, as seemed to be the distancing and disdainful attitude of many of the people who happened to have gotten to the North or West first or had the advantages of having grown up outside the walls of Jim Crow.

The internist had come from a completely different world, an integrated world that Robert both distrusted and envied, a world he could only hope his young daughters could grow to master and benefit from but not completely lose themselves in one day.

The building was just a few blocks south of the apartment on Ellendale he had secured for himself and his family until they could afford the house everyone expected of him. Everything finally seemed to be coming together.

That office was where he would start his new life. "And it was a beautiful building," Robert said. "It had a nice marquee in front of it. My office was at the front of the building, and my name was on the window, beautifully etched."

He put a deposit on an X-ray machine and the draperies for the office, a desk in the waiting room, chairs for the patients he hoped to attract. Now that he was nearly established, the people from Monroe turned out. Limuary Jordan and his wife, Adeline, came and helped him set up the office.

"We built his operating table in a room over there," Limuary would remember.

Howard Beckwith, a friend from back home, built furniture and opened his line of credit for Robert to use to get on his feet. Limuary loaned him money, too. They all made sure he ate.

"Come on, Doc, you can't practice on your empty stomach," they said. "You gotta eat."

Mrs. Beck and her daughter, Vivian, planned an open house for that July. They supplied the linens, the lace tablecloths, the crystal punch bowls. They made the punch and refreshments and served as hostesses in their cinched-waist dresses and pumps.

"I spent my last dime buying whiskey at Mick's for the open house," Robert said. "We had two fifths of whiskey."

He invited twenty people. The friends from Morehouse and Spelman and Atlanta University all came out, and Robert was in business.

He called Alice to say it was time. He was ready for them to join him in Los Angeles. They had been waiting in Atlanta for him to give them the word. The girls were growing up fast, and he had missed most of it. Bunny was nine already, and Robin was seven. He was all packed and ready to receive them. He would move out of the Becks' and into an apartment a few blocks north of his new office.

But when it came time to actually move in, the manager told him she was sorry but it was already rented to somebody else.

"That was my introduction to the deception of California," he said.

Alice and the girls had come all this distance, and he didn't have a place for them. He had to scramble to find something else before word got back to the Clements. He heard about a Dr. Anderson he knew from back in Louisiana, who happened to be moving out of his apartment. It was on St. Andrews Place, near the Becks'. It had two bedrooms. It was a far cry from Hickory Hill, the president's mansion back at Atlanta University, where Alice and the girls had been living. But the family would be together for the first time since Austria.

"And he rented it to me for my family," Robert said.

Alice set about making the apartment a home, while Robert began building a practice. He discovered he was having trouble attracting his most obvious patient base. For some reason, even with the new office on the fashionable side of town, the people from back home—from Monroe and from his days at Morehouse and Alice's days at Spelman—weren't coming. They had shown up for the hors d'oeuvres and whiskey at the open house, but they weren't coming in for appointments.

"Some were going to white doctors," he would say years later. "But not all of them went to white doctors. I really don't know who they were going to. I wasn't really interested in who they were going to. I wanted them to come to me."

He figured he was a hometown patient's dream. He was board-certified in surgery but was doing family practice, knew their family histories, could talk their language, and, as he had done all his life, would do just about anything to please them.

But among the gumbo recipes and family Bibles they brought to California were the petty rivalries from back in Louisiana. People had long memories, and if Professor Foster had taken a switch to them without cause or Robert's mother had been too hard on them in the seventh grade or if one of the Fosters had happened not to speak to them at Zion Baptist Church one Sunday back in 1932, they remembered it and carried it with them across the desert to California.

And that wasn't all. Some of the middle-class people from back in Monroe—the insurance agents and teachers and salesclerks—seemed to resent even the early signs of success and the fact that he was wanting people to call him Robert instead of Pershing after all these years.

They seemed to be second-guessing him more than his other patients did. They questioned the motives of his every instruction and stood up to him like they did when they were back in the third grade, especially when it came to surgery.

"See, they got lots of time before they get on the table," Robert remembered. "They can think a whole lot. They can get another consultation. They'd be quick to say, 'I'll get another consultation.' Or somebody would say, 'What you tryin' to do? Buy a mink coat for Alice?' Now, that slaps you. People can be little."

The rejection hurt him and gnawed at him. It stayed with him for decades. He set out to prove he could make it without them. He would be the very best doctor he knew how. He would focus not on the grudging people from Monroe but on the people who wanted him as their doctor. He would put on a show so they wouldn't forget him. He would pull in more of the cooks and laborers from Texas and the Mardi Gras–celebrating people from New Orleans and Baton Rouge, who would appreciate his loud suits and stingy-brim hats and folksy, one-of-the-people bedside manner.

The people from Monroe would learn how wrong they had been.

To Bend in Strange Winds

I was a Southerner,
and I had the map of Dixie on my tongue.
—Zora Neale Hurston, *Dust Tracks on a Road*

CHICAGO, LATE 1938
IDA MAE BRANDON GLADNEY

There was a knock on the door at Ida Mae's tiny flat one afternoon when she was at home alone taking care of the children. It was a neighbor lady who had taken notice of the new family just up from Mississippi, seen that the young mother was by herself with the little ones much of the time, the husband likely off to work somewhere, and the neighbor lady was saying she had come to introduce herself.

Ida Mae thought it was awfully nice of the lady to drop by. She hadn't been in Chicago long, as the woman likely knew. George had secured the apartment while Ida Mae was in Mississippi giving birth to Eleanor.

On days when there was no work to be had, Ida Mae was cooped up in the kitchenette apartment, far from home, in a big, loud city she didn't yet know. She was used to wide-open spaces, trees everywhere, being able to see the sun set and rise and the sky stretched out over the field. She was used to killing a chicken if she needed one, not lining up at a butcher and paying for it in pieces with money she didn't have. As much as she hated picking cotton, she missed her sisters-in-law and the other families on the plantation and her mother and younger sister. She didn't know too many people in Chicago yet and was isolated with only little James and Eleanor with her during the day, as Velma was off in grade school.

So Ida Mae welcomed the neighbor lady and invited her in to sit a while. The lady had brought something with her. It was a bottle of homemade wine. Ida Mae had never had wine before. George didn't believe in it, and Ida Mae never had occasion to try it.

The woman opened the bottle and poured some for the two of them to drink while they talked. Ida Mae took a few sips and started feeling woozy as the woman asked her how she'd gotten there. The woman learned all about how Ida Mae's family first tried Milwaukee and how Ida Mae went back to Mississippi to have the baby when George told her he was going to try Chicago. The woman poured more wine, and Ida Mae got giddy and light-headed. She had never felt this way before.

The woman was from Mississippi but had been in Chicago for some time, had gotten to know the city's virtues and vices and how a city resident, which Ida Mae now was, should comport oneself. She told Ida Mae that now that she was in the North, she shouldn't wear her head scarf out in public—that was for back when she was in the field; that she shouldn't hang her wet laundry out the front window, even though there was no place else to let the linens dry out in the open sun like back home; that she should make sure the kids had shoes on when they went out, even though the kids hated shoes and shoes cost money they didn't have.

Ida Mae told the lady she appreciated that advice, but soon she wasn't comprehending much of anything the neighbor lady was saying. When the bottle of wine was finished, the lady said she'd better be heading back home.

George came home soon after the neighbor lady left. He found Ida Mae giggling and slurring her words, talking gibberish, and the children needing to eat and get their diapers changed. She told him that a nice neighbor lady had stopped by and that she had tried some of the wine the lady brought.

George was furious. The devilment of the city had come right into his home, as hard as he tried to protect his family from it. Ida Mae was too sweet-natured to recognize when someone might be taking advantage and wasn't wise to the machinations of the people who had preceded them to Chicago. She wouldn't have noticed if they made fun of them, looked down on them, or took pleasure in seeing the simple country people fall under the city's spell. He had to make it clear to Ida Mae that she was not to just let anybody in—this was Chicago, after all. He told her he didn't want that lady coming around anymore and that Ida Mae wasn't to drink any more wine, which was a sin in his estimation anyway.

When Ida Mae came to her senses, she was shamefaced about what had happened. She was waking up to the ways and the people of the North. She soon learned that the colored people who had gotten there before her and had assimilated to the city didn't look too kindly upon her innocent country ways.

In the receiving cities of the North and West, the newcomers like Ida Mae had to worry about acceptance or rejection not only from whites they encountered but from the colored people who arrived ahead of them, who could at times be the most sneeringly judgmental of all.

The northern-born colored people and the long-standing migrants, who were still trying to keep their footing in the New World, often resented the arrival of the unwashed masses pouring in from the very places some of the old-timers had left. As often happens with immigrant groups, some of the old-timers would have preferred to shut the door after they got there to protect their own uncertain standing.

The small colony of colored people already in the New World had made a place for themselves as an almost invisible minority by the time the Migration began. Many were the descendants of slaves the North had kept before Abolition or of slaves who fled the South on the Underground Railroad or were among the trickle of pioneers who had migrated from the South in the decades after the Civil War.

A good portion were in the servant class—waiters, janitors, elevator operators, maids, and butlers to the wealthiest white families in the city. But some had managed to create a solid though tenuous middle class of Pullman porters, postal workers, ministers, and businessmen who were anxious to keep the status and gains they had won. The color line restricted them to the oldest housing in the least desirable section of town no matter what their class, but they had tried to make the best of it and had created a world within a world for themselves.

From this group came the letters and newspaper stories about the freedoms of the North that helped inspire blacks to leave the South in the first place. The Great Migration brought in many a northerner's sweetheart, aunts, uncles, siblings, nieces, nephews, parents, and children. It also delivered hundreds of thousands of new customers, voters, readers, patients, and parishioners to the black institutions that stood to profit and be forever changed by the influx.

"They have been our best patrons," a colored physician in Chicago told researchers studying the Migration in the 1930s. "We have increased from five to two hundred and fifty doctors. We are living in better homes, and have more teachers in the schools; and nearly every colored church has benefitted."

Businessmen jumped at the opportunity. They opened restaurants serving hog maws and turnip greens. A man named Robert Horton opened Hattiesburg Shaving Parlor in a five-block stretch along Rhodes Avenue where some 150 families from that Gulf Coast town were huddled together. A few blocks away, there sat the Mississippi Coal and Wood Company, the Florida East Coast Shine Parlor to pull in the Floridians, and the Carolina Sea Island Candy Store for those who'd made it from there.

The Migration made giddy landlords of some of the old-timers. It gave them the chance to get extra money and bragging rights, too, by renting their spare rooms and garages to the new people. In Los Angeles and Oakland, it became a status symbol to have the wherewithal to take in roomers.

"I got a sharecropper," a woman in Los Angeles was heard boasting.

"Honey, I got me three sharecroppers!" another one said.

The churches stood to gain the most, and did. They ran notices in the *Defender* proclaiming, "Strangers welcome." Walters African Methodist Episcopal Church in Chicago tripled in membership. The city's Olivet Baptist Church got five thousand new members in the first three years of the Migration, making it one of the largest Baptist churches and one of the first megachurches in the country. A migrant from Alabama said she couldn't get in the first time she went. "We'd have to stand up," she said. "I don't care how early we'd go, you wouldn't get in."

But soon the cultural and class divisions between the newcomers and the old-timers began to surface. Many of the migrants, seeking the status and security they could not get back home, filled the stained-glass sanctuaries of the mainline churches. Others were overwhelmed by the size of the congregations and the austerity of their services. One migrant said she "couldn't understand the pastor and the words he used" at Olivet and couldn't get used to the singing. "The songs was proud-like," she said.

A migrant from Louisiana felt out of place at Pilgrim Baptist, another big, old-line church. "Nobody said nothing," the migrant said. "But there were whispers all over the place."

The migrants did as much moving around from church to church as they did from flat to flat. They tended to favor smaller storefront churches opened up by ministers fresh from the South, where they could sing the spirituals, catch the spirit, and fan themselves like they were used to. The reason one woman left a mainline church was because it was "too large—it don't see the small people."

The migrants brought new life to the old receiving stations. But by their sheer numbers, they pressed down upon the colored people already there. Slumlords made the most of it by subdividing what housing there was into smaller and smaller units and investing as little as possible in the way of upkeep to cash in on the bonanza. It left well-suited lawyers and teachers living next to sharecroppers in head scarves just off the Illinois Central. The middle-class and professional people searched for a way out.

"They tried to insulate themselves by moving further south along the narrow strip that defined the gradually expanding South Side Black Belt," wrote the historian James Grossman. "But the migrants inevitably followed."

Unlike their white counterparts, the old settlers had few places to go and were met with hostility and violence if they ventured into white neighborhoods. The color line hemmed them in—newcomers and old-timers alike—as they all struggled to move up. "The same class of Negroes who ran us away from Thirty-seventh Street are moving out there," a colored professional man said after moving further south to Fifty-first Street ahead of the migrants. "They creep along slowly like a disease."

The fate of the city people was linked to that of the migrants, whether they liked it or not, and the city people feared that the migrants could jeopardize the status of them all. A colored newspaper called *Searchlight* chastised them for boarding the streetcars in soiled work clothes after a day at the stockyards and accused them of threatening the freedoms colored people had in the North. "Don't you know that you are forcing on us here in Chicago a condition similar to the one down South?"

A survey of new migrants during World War II found that an overwhelming majority of them looked up to the people who were there before them, admired them, and wanted to be as assured and sophisticated as they were. But a majority of the colored people already in the New World viewed the newcomers in a negative light and saw them as hindering opportunities for all of them.

The anxious old settlers were "like German Jews who in the late nineteenth century feared that the influx of their coreligionists from eastern Europe would endanger their marginal but substantial foothold in gentile Chicago," wrote the historian James R. Grossman.

"Those who have long been established in the North have a problem," the *Chicago Defender* acknowledged. "That problem is the caring for the stranger within their gates."

It turned out that the old-timers were harder on the new people than most anyone else. "Well, their English was pretty bad," a colored businessman said of the migrants who flooded Oakland and San Francisco in the forties, as if from a foreign country. To his way of looking at it, they needed eight or nine years "before they seemed to get Americanized."

As the migrants arrived in the receiving stations of the North and West, the old-timers wrestled with what the influx meant for them, how it would affect the way others saw colored people, and how the flood of black southerners was a reminder of the Jim Crow world they all sought to escape. In the days before Emancipation, as long as slavery existed, no freed black was truly free. Now, as long as Jim Crow and the supremacy behind it existed, no blacks could ever be sure they were beyond its reach.

One day a white friend went up to a longtime Oakland resident named Eleanor Watkins to ask her what she thought about all the newcomers.

"Eleanor," the woman said, "you colored people must be very disgusted with some of the people who have come here from the South and the way they act."

"Well, Mrs. S.," Eleanor Watkins replied. "Yes, some colored people are very disgusted, but as far as I'm concerned, the first thing I give them credit for is getting out of the situation they were in. . . . Maybe they don't know how to dress or comb their hair or anything, but their children will and *their* children will."

In the early years of the Migration, the *Chicago Defender* took it upon itself to help correct the country people it had helped lure to the North to better fit the city people's standard of refinement. "It is our duty," the *Defender* wrote, "to guide the hand of a less experienced one, especially when one misstep weakens our chance for climbing."

The *Defender* ran periodic lists of "do's and don'ts" that recirculated over time and were repeated to newcomers like Ida Mae:

> Don't hang out the windows.
>
> Don't sit around in the yard and on the porch barefoot and unkempt.
>
> Don't wear handkerchiefs on your head.
>
> Don't use vile language in public places.
>
> Don't allow children to beg on the streets.
>
> Don't appear on the street with old dust caps, dirty aprons and ragged clothes.
>
> Don't throw garbage in the backyard or alley or keep dirty front yards.

The Chicago Urban League, which helped direct migrants to temporary shelter, rental options, and jobs, was the closest the migrants got to Customs in the North. It held what it called "Strangers Meetings" to help acclimate the newcomers, and its members went door-to-door, passing out leaflets advising the migrants as to their behavior and comportment. To the *Defender*'s do's and don'ts, the Urban League distributed cards adding the following admonishments:

1. Do not loaf. Get a job at once.
2. Do not live in crowded rooms. Others can be obtained.
3. Do not carry on loud conversations in street cars and public places.
4. Do not keep your children out of school.
5. Do not send for your family until you get a job.

Ida Mae didn't take it personally when people pointed these things out to her, like the neighbor lady who had brought the wine. Ida Mae wouldn't likely have seen her again because the family moved so much in those early months in Chicago. But she thanked people like her and a lady who mentioned her head scarf on the bus one day. She was grateful for the advice and, in fact, took most of it.

But there were some things she was not ever going to do. She was never going to change her name to something citified and highfalutin. She was never going to take on northern airs and name-drop about the pastor she knew from this or that church or the alderman who stopped to greet her at the polls, even though she would come to know famous people who made good up in the North because she had known their kin people back in Mississippi. She was never going to forget the folks back home and how she loved them so. She was never going to change her Mississippi drawl, not in the least, not even after she had spent more of her life in the North than in the South, not even when some northerners still had trouble understanding her decades after she'd been there; though she wasn't trying to be difficult and was just being herself, she simply didn't care what anybody thought. It didn't matter, because people seemed to love her for it.

She decided to keep the things that made her feel like home deep within herself, where nobody could judge her, and inside the walls of their kitchenette apartment where she made turnip greens and peach cobbler and sweet potato pie flecked with nutmeg and sang spirituals like in Mississippi as often as she liked.

NEW YORK, JANUARY 1947
GEORGE SWANSON STARLING

IT TOOK EIGHT YEARS OF MARRIAGE, broken by fearsome silences and fitful separations due to George's work on the railroad and the circumstances under which he had to migrate north. But finally George and Inez had a baby. It was a boy. He was born in January 1947, and they named him Gerard. There were already enough Georges in the family, and Gerard was close enough.

"I was the happiest man in the world when this boy came," George said. "I thought we weren't gonna never have no children."

George couldn't stop taking pictures of the baby. And the arrival of their son gave Inez a new purpose. She threw herself into motherhood. That was a good thing, because, soon after the baby was born, George had to take to the road again to care for his growing family.

In no time George was back on the rails, working the legendary trains that followed the East Coast route of the Great Migration. His job put him in the middle of one of the biggest population shifts in the country's history. He saw firsthand the continuing stream of people pouring out in front of him. He helped them carry their cardboard boxes tied with string, the hand-me-down suitcases, the hatboxes and steamer trunks. Some came north with only a cotton sack or a paper bag with all they owned or were able to get out with.

"Time they get their seat and their bags up, here come the shoe boxes," he said. Fried chicken, boiled eggs, crackers, and cakes.

He was working the Silver Comet from New York to Birmingham, the Silver Spur from New York to Tampa, and the other Great Migration trains. His job was to help people load their bags, direct them to their seats, warm their babies' milk, and generally attend to their needs and clean up after them. The ride could last as long as twenty-eight hours from the southernmost stop to Pennsylvania Station in Manhattan.

George walked up and down the train aisles, helping people board or disembark at every stop along the way. He rarely got a chance to sit down, much less sleep. The pay was lower than it might otherwise have been because he was expected to get tips to compensate for it. But when he was working the Jim Crow car, he was mostly servicing the lowliest, poorest-paid workers in the South—or in the country, for that matter. Many of them had never been on the train before and knew nothing about the protocol of gratuities.

They gave him food instead. "Want some fried chicken?" the colored passengers would ask him. "I give you some fried chicken. You already gettin' paid."

He had come from the place they were leaving and knew not to expect a tip or hold it against them. He knew the fear and uncertainty in their hearts because he had felt it himself. He had ridden the night train north just as they had and spoke their language and could read the worried optimism in the faces.

When the train approached Washington, D.C., the dividing line between the Jim Crow South and the free North, and rode deeper into the Promised Land, his role took on an unexpected significance.

As they neared the final stops, it became necessary for George to become more than a baggage handler, but tutor and chaperone to nervous charges arriving in the New World. At the moment of the migrants' greatest fear and anxiety, it fell to him to ease them into the Promised Land, tell them whatever he knew about this new place, which bus or subway to take, how far the station was from their cousin's apartment, to watch out for panhandlers and hustlers who might take what little change they had left, and usher them and their luggage off to whatever the future held for them.

It was his tap on the shoulder that awakened them as the train neared their stop and alerted them to their new receiving city. He and other colored porters were men in red caps and white uniforms, but they functioned as the midwives of the Great Migration, helping the migrants gather themselves and disembark at the station and thus delivering to the world a new wave of newcomers with each arriving train.

It seemed to George that the moment they stepped on the train going north, they became different people, started acting like what they imagined the people up north to be. Some started talking their version of a northern accent, sitting up straighter, eating their chicken wings with their pinkie out, becoming more like the place they were heading to. "A lot of them pretending to be always northerners," George said, knowing full well the difference.

Heading south, it was a quiet and sober train, filled with the people of the North returning home, in their finest suits and hats, and southern visitors having just seen the big city for themselves.

Heading north, the trains were more festive and anxious, filled with people migrating out with all their worldly goods and the people from the North returning to their adopted cities with all they could manage to take with them that they missed from back home in the South.

George could tell the people from the North. The bags that were empty heading south were now heavy with ham and hog head cheese and turnip roots and sweet potatoes and any little thing they cherished from back home and had a hard time getting in the North or that, if they could get it in the North, just didn't taste the same.

One day at a little station somewhere in South Carolina, George helped his passengers get their bags up onto the luggage rack above the seats on the Silver Comet as he always did. The train then left the station, and George was in the back of the colored railcar. He always liked to stand in the back so he could observe the passengers and see who might need his help.

"They wanted to assign us seats in the front," George said of the bulkhead crew seats, "but I never liked sitting in front of my people. I couldn't see how I could be helpful in the car, sitting in front of everybody. I like to sit behind them so I can see what's happening."

That day after the train left the station in South Carolina, he began to notice the sound of a slow drip hitting the floor of the railcar and the seats below. He looked up and saw that it was coming from a bag up on the luggage rack. Whatever the liquid was, it was red and looked to be blood, and as he got closer he discovered that it was in fact blood dripping out of the bag.

"They must have just killed a hog or something, cut him up and put him in the bag," George said. "I keep hearing something dripping, and I look up, and here's this bag with blood just drippin' all out of this bag. They done butchered up somebody's chicken or hog and had him in the bag. They must have done it on the way to the train, and they didn't get rid of all the blood, they were still draining in the bag rack."

George was used to people bringing all kinds of things, live chickens and rabbits, a whole side of a pig. But this was the first time someone brought something they hadn't even finished butchering. George took the bag and sat it on the floor. He wiped it down and mopped up the blood that had dripped from it. He never did see whose bag it was or what kind of animal was inside it, given all that he had to do tending to the train and the other customers. And no passenger claimed the bloody bag for the duration of the trip. In the commotion of arrival at one of the stations up north, the bag just disappeared into the disembarking crowd, its owner having claimed it in anonymity.

After a while, nothing surprised George, but he dreaded the work he was in for on the rides north. The bags were so heavy he could barely lift them from the ground. His knees were bad from all the basketball he used to play in high school, and the people, having morphed into northerners just by stepping onto the Silver Comet, were expecting the full rights of citizenship, to begin with George picking up their overloaded bags.

They carried jars of fig preserves, pole beans, snap peas, and peaches, whole hams, whatever the folks back home were growing on the farm and other treasured pieces of the South they could carry back with them.

One passenger came on with a big hatbox that looked innocent enough, but when George tried to pick it up, the front end flew up and he could feel something moving inside. When he tried to steady the hatbox, the other side flew up.

"I could feel it going to the front," he said. "She had a big old watermelon in there rolling down in the bag. That's why it was flopping back and forth."

A man with a trunk boarded at a tiny station somewhere near Abbeville, South Carolina, bound for New York. George saw him and jumped down from the train.

"I need some help with my bag," the man said.

George reached down to grab the trunk and fell trying to lift it.

"Hey, man," George said. "What do you *have* in this bag?"

"Clothes, daddy, clothes," the man said. "You know I been down here for two weeks. I had to have something to change in."

"Yeah," George said. "Okay, then, if you want your clothes up on this train, you better give me a hand with this bag. 'Cause I can't lift it off the ground."

Together they pushed it up the steps and shoved it onto the train. The train rocked from side to side as George struggled to drag the trunk down the aisle.

It was dark by now, and George managed to push the trunk to the back. He held up one end by the handle to position it in a corner away from the other passengers. Then he dropped it.

"And when it hit the floor, the latches flew off," George said.

And out came the contents.

"The potatoes rolled out that bag, and the engineer is hitting these curves," George said, "and you could hear 'em rolling all over the floor."

The man whose trunk it was got alarmed.

"Hey, daddy, you gotta flashlight?" he asked.

"I don't have no flashlight that's gonna last long enough for you to find all your clothes," George said. " 'Cause they rolling all over the train. And I need my flashlight. I'm sorry, man."

The train lurched from side to side and from one curve into the next and with each curve came the rumbling sound of mud-caked Carolina sweet potatoes. The colored car was in an uproar, the man's trunk flung open, its latch broken, the man running down the aisle in the dark after the contents, and the fifty-one other passengers rolling with laughter and very likely helping themselves to sweet potatoes they hadn't managed to bring aboard themselves but that would make a nice sweet potato pie once they got back to Harlem.

LOS ANGELES, 1954
ROBERT JOSEPH PERSHING FOSTER

ALICE BEGAN SETTING UP HOUSE in the walk-up apartment Robert had scrambled to secure for his family after the apartment he wanted mysteriously fell through. It was nowhere near the space Alice was accustomed to and had few of the amenities and not a whiff of the grandeur of her parents' brick Georgian estate back in Atlanta.

As she began to arrange what furniture they had, shop for groceries, dust, and clean, which she had never in her life really had to do before, and direct their two little girls, it soon hit Alice and Robert: they had been married for twelve years but had never lived together as husband and wife, other than their short tour of duty in Austria, where they had not so much kept house as camped out. Such was the life of ambitious black southerners trying to find a place for themselves in a not altogether welcoming world. Robert had been in medical training for much of those twelve years of marriage, and the Clements had thought it best that Alice stay with them while Robert pursued his internships and residencies and tried to figure out and save up for where he wanted to migrate.

Over the years, they had seen each other when they could. But they had both settled into their own ways of doing things, essentially living out their lives on their own. Now that they were finally all together in Los Angeles, it hit them that they didn't really know each other.

Alice didn't know how Robert liked his food cooked or that he was prone to work late hours. Robert had to learn how to be a father to two daughters who had been raised by socialite grandparents and who were missing the only world they had ever known.

He came to that realization when he was out with his older daughter, Bunny, one day. She saw a toy she wanted and was insisting that her father buy it for her. Robert had just opened his practice and was watching every nickel. Bunny had been raised like a princess back in Atlanta, and Robert thought she had more than enough toys and dolls as it was.

"Why, you don't need that," Robert told her.

"Well, if you don't give it to me, Granddaddy will."

Robert discovered that his whole family was really the Clements' and not his, and he had to figure out how to reclaim his status in the household. He and Alice began fighting over her cooking, which had become a symbol of their class differences and the variation in southern culture, depending upon which state you happened to be from.

Robert wanted oxtails and turnip greens and red-peppered gumbo like he grew up with in Louisiana. Alice had never really cooked for him before. And what she cooked was what any well-born 1950s homemaker would prepare for her family—the soufflés and casseroles of the upper classes of the day. She went to a great deal of trouble to make these Betty Crocker–era meals. But Robert didn't like them, and he took her style of cooking as a repudiation of his tastes.

"It needs some more seasoning in it," he said.

"The children don't like it that way," Alice told him.

"Children eat what their mama give 'em," Robert said. "And you give 'em the food the way I like it to be cooked."

But it was already too late. The children had become set in their expectations, the family system already established. Robert and Alice fought and fought over it. They were paying a price for the sacrifices they had made to get established outside the South. Every day, they were confronted with a difference they hadn't noticed before, something so basic as a meal suddenly becoming a metaphor of the different worlds they came from. The dinner table became a testing of wills over which culture would prevail, the high-toned world of black elites in Atlanta or the hardscrabble but no less proud black middle class of small-town Louisiana, and, more important, who was going to run the family—the Clements from afar or Robert, who was working long hours to take care of them now.

It exposed a chasm between the two of them that would never be fully resolved but that both would have to live with. "That was a big hurdle," Robert said.

As it was, they were living in a cramped apartment with temporary furniture and tacked-down rugs and trying to make the best of it.

"We were not defined by where we lived," Robert said. "We felt we'd make it in time. And we lived that way."

So long as they were in a walk-up apartment, Alice put off her socialite yearnings. She wanted to wait to make her presence known to the colored elite in Los Angeles. She wanted to wait until they could secure a house more befitting her station. She took a position teaching third grade in the Los Angeles public school system to help them save up for the house they would need before she could announce herself to L.A. society.

Robert didn't see the point of waiting. She was the same person now as she would be when they got a house. But Alice knew the value of a proper entrance when one was coming in as an outsider, as any southerner new to California would be. Robert kept asking anyway. It would be good for business to start making connections, and she was all but assured of acceptance to those patrician circles by birth alone.

"Well, when you gonna join?" he'd ask her.

"It's too expensive for us out here now," she'd say. "The time's not right."

From Atlanta, her mother had signed her up with the Links, perhaps the most elite of the invitation-only, class- and color-conscious colored women's societies of the era.

But Alice wouldn't activate her membership until they got a house. "We're not ready, Robert," she said. "No, we're not ready."

It was a reminder to Robert that he had not yet lived up to her and her family's expectations. The shadow of Rufus Clement loomed over him from across the continent. The family he was just now getting to know was used to living on an estate with formal gardens and servants, and here they were, cramped together with him in a walk-up apartment like waitstaff.

Robert was not in a position to duplicate what they had back in Atlanta. So he set out to prove himself in other ways. If Alice wasn't ready to go Hollywood, Robert was. His practice was just beginning to take off, and he had an idea of what he needed to cap off the image he was trying to create. He went to Dr. Beck for advice.

"Doctor, I wanna buy a Cadillac," Robert said, announcing his desire for the most coveted car on the market in those days. "Do you think I'd hurt myself if I bought a Cadillac?"

"Can you meet the notes, boy?"

"Yes, I can."

"Go buy it, then."

Alice was against it and said so. "How'd you like a Cadillac parked in front of an upstairs apartment? Don't you think you're a little premature?"

"Yes, but I want one."

"You don't wanna buy a Cadillac, and you live in a walk-up apartment," Alice said. "You don't have a garage to put it in."

But Robert had made up his mind. He thought he could attract more patients with it. Patients half expected their doctor to be driving a Cadillac. It would make them respect him more, give them something to brag about. And if they were bragging about him, more patients might come his way. Besides, there was something deep inside him that had to prove to the world and to himself that he had made it.

So he went downtown to Thomas Cadillac to buy himself one. But the salesclerk took him past the showroom of new Cadillacs to the dealership's used car lot.

"I told him I wanted a new car, and he kept showing me used cars," Robert said, exasperated but by now picking up on the subtleties of his interactions in the New World.

"I thanked him and went home," Robert said.

Then he wrote a letter to General Motors, Cadillac division, in Detroit: *"I'm a young black physician, just getting started,"* he wrote. *"All my life I dreamed Cadillac, and when I had enough money to go down and get one, the man insults me by showing me used cars."*

Soon after he wrote the letter, he got a call from the dealership. "We have instructions," Robert remembered the man saying, "to deliver to you a Cadillac to your liking. What day would you like to come down and select it?"

It was 1955, so he headed right over to pick out a 1955 model. "A white Cadillac," he said years later, a smile forming on his face, "with blue interior and whitewall tires. Yes, indeedy. See what you can get when you step on the right feet?"

Some of the people from Monroe thought the car pretentious and over the top. They were still having a hard time even picturing him a doctor. But just putting the key in the ignition made him feel like he had moved up in the world.

"And I learned that lesson from Dr. Beck's advice," Robert said years later. "To hell with what people think of me. Go on and do what you wanna do. They gonna do what they wanna do anyhow, say what they wanna say anyway."

He mulled over his words. "That's right," he said. "And you get more if they feel you ain't suffering."

He was already plotting new ways to prove himself to the naysayers, black and white, in Louisiana and in L.A. "My lifestyle'll blow 'em outta the water," Robert would say. "Just blow 'em outta the water, 'cause I'll go on and do what I wanna do."

The Other Side of Jordan

We cannot escape our origins,
however hard we might try,
those origins contain the key
—could we but find it—
to all that we later become.
—James Baldwin,
Notes of a Native Son

CHICAGO, NOVEMBER 1940
IDA MAE BRANDON GLADNEY

THE CROWDS GATHERED early at the fire station at Thirty-sixth and State on the morning of November 5, 1940. It was election day. President Franklin D. Roosevelt was in a tighter-than-expected race against a maverick businessman, Wendell Willkie. Europe was at war, the United States was in Depression despite the gains of the New Deal, and Roosevelt was now the first president in history to seek a third term, which his Republican opponent was using against him.

For weeks, precinct captains and ward volunteers had canvassed the tenements and three-flats on the South Side of Chicago. They had passed out palm cards and campaign flyers to the domestics and factory workers and to untutored potential voters like Ida Mae.

Illinois was considered crucial to Roosevelt this election, so much so that the Democrats held their national convention in Chicago that year. He had been elected twice before by landslides against Herbert Hoover and Alf Landon, and he now needed the Midwest and Chicago, in particular, to turn out for him if he were to stay in the White House.

Ida Mae didn't know what was at stake, but suddenly everyone around her was talking about something she'd never heard of back in Mississippi. The precinct captain for her area, a Mr. Tibbs, had been out in the neighborhood rousing the people to register for the upcoming election. She had seen him and gotten the slip his workers handed out and was curious about all the commotion.

Back home, no one dared talk about such things. She couldn't vote in Mississippi. She never knew where the polls were in Chickasaw County. And even if she had had the nerve to go, she would have been turned away for failing to pay a poll tax or not being able to answer a question on a literacy test for which there was no answer, such as how many grains of sand there were on the beach or how to interpret an obscure article of the Mississippi constitution to the election registrar's satisfaction. She and most every other colored person in the South knew better than even to try.

So she never thought about her senator or congressman or state representative or about Theodore Bilbo, an admitted Klansman and a famous Mississippi governor. Bilbo had been one of the most incendiary segregationists of the era, yet she didn't pay him much mind because she had nothing to do with his getting into office and couldn't have voted against him even if she knew when and how to do it.

Bilbo made it to the governor's mansion without citizens like Ida Mae or Miss Theenie having any say as to his getting into or remaining in office. He later ascended without them to the U.S. Senate, where, in 1938, the year Ida Mae finally migrated to Chicago, he helped lead one of the longest filibusters in the history of the Senate, the one to thwart a bill that would have made lynching a federal crime.

At one point in the filibuster, he rose to speak on behalf of his constituents—not the entire state of Mississippi but the white voters there—and in opposition to the interests of half the state. He spoke in defense of the right to kill black citizens as white southerners saw fit.

"If you succeed in the passage of this bill," Bilbo told his Senate colleagues, *"you will open the floodgates of hell in the South. Raping, mobbing, lynching, race riots, and crime will be increased a thousand fold; and upon your garments and the garments of those who are responsible for the passage of the measure will be the blood of the raped and outraged daughters of Dixie, as well as the blood of the perpetrators of these crimes that the red-blooded Anglo-Saxon white Southern men will not tolerate."*

Ida Mae hadn't bothered to know what politicians like Bilbo were doing because it wouldn't have done her any good. Nobody she knew had even tried to vote. Nobody made note of election day whenever it came. It was as if there were an invisible world of voting and elections going on about its business without her.

Now it was 1940, and she was in Chicago. All around her were new arrivals like herself who had never voted before and were just getting the hang of elections after a lifetime of being excluded. Suddenly, the very party and the very apparatus that was ready to kill them if they tried to vote in the South was searching them out and all but carrying them to the polls. To the Democrats in the North, each new arrival from the South was a potential new vote in their column. It was in the Democrats' best interest to mobilize these people, who, now given the chance to vote, might go Republican. The Republicans, after all, had been the party of Lincoln and of Reconstruction. The Republicans had opposed the segregationists who had held the migrants down in the South. But now the migration trains were delivering brand-new voters to the hands of whoever got to them first.

Chicago was a Democratic town, and the Democrats had the means to make the most of this gift to the party. They were counting on the goodwill Roosevelt had engendered among colored people with his New Deal initiatives. Still, the precinct captains took no chances. They went door-to-door to talk up the New Deal and to register the people. They asked them about their kids and jobs and convinced them that the Democrats in the North were different from those in the South. They printed up party slates and passed out palm cards—political crib notes that would fit in the palm of the hand—so the people would know whom to vote for when they got inside the booth.

On election day, Ida Mae walked up to the fire station around the corner from her flat at Thirty-sixth and Wabash to vote for the first time in her life. The sidewalks were teeming with volunteers to usher neophytes into the station and to the correct sign-in tables. Inside, election judges, clerks, a policeman or two monitored the proceedings.

Ida Mae was not certain what to do. She had never touched an election ballot. She walked in, and a lady came over and directed her to where she should go. Ida Mae stepped inside a polling booth for the first time in her life and drew the curtain behind her. She unfolded the palm card she had been given and tried to remember what the lady had told her about how to punch in her choices for president of the United States and other political offices. It was the first time she would ever have a say in such things.

"She showed me how to do it," Ida Mae said.

What was unthinkable in Mississippi would eventually become so much a part of life in Chicago that Mr. Tibbs would ask Ida Mae to volunteer at the polls the next time. She had a pleasant disposition, and Mr. Tibbs put her to work helping other people learn how to vote. She would stand outside the firehouse, directing newcomers who were clutching their palm cards and looking as puzzled as she had been her first time at the polls.

She did not see herself as taking any kind of political stand. But in that simple gesture, she was defying the very heart of the southern caste system, and doing something she could not have dreamed of doing—in fact, had not allowed herself even to contemplate—all those years in Mississippi.

But she had seen for herself the difference it could make the first time she had stepped inside a voting booth. Ida Mae's first vote and George's first vote and those of tens of thousands of other colored migrants new to the North were among the 2,149,934 votes cast for President Roosevelt in Illinois that day in 1940. Ida Mae's new home was a deeply divided swing state that year, and this was among the tightest of races. It turned out for Roosevelt that it was a good thing the migrants had come. The ballots cast by Ida Mae and other colored migrants up from the South were enough to help give Roosevelt the two percent margin of victory he needed to carry the state of Illinois and, by extension, the United States—to return him to the White House.

ON THE SILVER COMET, MID- TO LATE 1940S
GEORGE SWANSON STARLING

THE TRAIN HAD ROLLED OUT OF BIRMINGHAM and was wending its way toward New York. It would stop in Wattsville, Ragland, Ohatchee in Alabama, in Cedartown, Rockmart, Atlanta, Athens, Elberton in

Georgia, on its way to the Carolinas and up the East Coast. George was working the train as a railcar attendant and was settling into a twenty-three-hour workday of hauling bags, sweeping and dusting, tending and picking up after the fifty-two passengers in his car.

Somewhere along the route, he looked out of the vestibule door by the draft gears between the railcars. The train leaned into a sharp bend in the track. The railcars spread apart to take the full curve. And suddenly, George could see the figure of a man standing between the railcars, clinging to the edge by the door. The man stood as still as a piece of furniture. With the railcars spread open as they were, the man could no longer hide. He looked into George's face and did not speak. His eyes begged George not to turn him in.

It is not known how many migrants made it out of the South by hopping a freight or passenger train as this man did. They called what this man was doing "hoboing." It was one of the ways some men and boys, often the most desperate, the poorest, the most adventurous, or those who got on the wrong side of a planter or a sheriff, got out.

Years before, in 1931, a boy by the name of Johnson plotted his way out of Lake Charles, Louisiana, with three of his friends. They were hoping to make it to Los Angeles. All over the South, there were colored boys like him dreaming of hopping a train. They practiced how to jump on and off the freight cars when the trains passed through Yazoo City, Mississippi, or Bessemer, Alabama, or any number of small towns. They would ride a couple hundred feet and jump off until they got the hang of it.

Johnson and his friends talked about escaping Lake Charles, Louisiana, for months. They planned the day of departure, only to put it off because one boy's mother got sick or another lost his nerve. Finally they set a date and met at the rail yard one night in 1931. They had nothing but the clothes they were wearing and a couple dollars in their pockets. The four of them grabbed the side of a car and hopped aboard as the train wound along the tracks.

The passenger trains would have been a surer way to get out. The freights were not marked and did not announce their destinations like the passenger trains did. Anyone riding them couldn't be certain where he was headed. But scheduled trains were riskier because the passengers, the conductors, the porters, and attendants like George might see them and turn them in. So most stowaways hopped a freight train, lonely with its grain and cotton bins. If they found a car open, they hid inside. Sometimes they had no choice but to ride on top of the car, holding tight against the wind kicked up by a train going seventy miles an hour.

Johnson and his friends made it onto the freight train and were headed out of Louisiana and into Texas. But what they hadn't realized was that the freight trains had police, men who patrolled the freight cars and were on the lookout for stowaways like them. The patrolmen were called railroad bulls, and they were hired to do whatever it took to get stowaways off the train. They were known to beat or shoot anyone they caught or to send stowaways to a chain gang, where they might never be seen again. The bulls had names like "Denver Bob" and "Texas Slim."

Johnson and his friends were positioning themselves on a freight car and dreaming of California when a bull caught sight of them. It was harder to go undetected when there were four people rather than one. The bulls started hurling rocks and the boys had no choice. They jumped sixteen or seventeen feet from a moving freight train, not knowing where they were or when the next freight was coming or if whatever came through was going to California.

Now they were lost somewhere in Texas. They had to wait for hours before another train rumbled through. They hopped on it, not knowing where it was headed. Suddenly it stopped on a trestle bridge suspended two stories above a ravine. The bulls liked to stop on high bridges to force stowaways off the train. It left the boys with nowhere to hide. They could stay and face a beating from the bulls or risk injuring themselves in yet another jump.

They jumped. They tumbled downhill in the darkness. They were still in Texas, crawling through weeds, the bulls' flashlights searching the scrub brush.

In all the commotion, Johnson got separated from the other three as they rolled down the ravine. He was alone in the brush as he heard the train rattle away from him. He crawled in the brambles, hungry, lost, and jarred by the escape. He crawled toward the light of a settlement in search of food.

He came to a fire where real hoboes, men who rode trains for the thrill of it, were gathered near the tracks of the freight train. The hoboes were sitting around a pot over a fire, one man with a potato, another with a skinned rabbit over the flame. The men were covered in soot. This was what they called the hobo jungle, where they slept and cooked their food, which was whatever the group of them had managed to rustle up, before taking to the trains again.

"What'd you bring to put in the pot?" they asked the boy.

He didn't have anything. He was not of their world.

"You better go and look for something," they told him.

The boy walked further toward the light of the settlement in search of food to bring back to the strangers by the fire.

He approached a house. A white woman answered. She didn't seem surprised. The people in the settlement had seen a lot of boys and men hopping trains like him.

"Madame," he said, "I'm hoboing." He asked if she had food she could spare. "Anything you have."

She gave him bread and chicken. With that, he returned to the hobo jungle, handed over what he had gotten, and was finally able to eat. At daybreak, he hopped the first train that came through. He rode not knowing where he was headed and not, of course, able to ask.

The train was not going west to California. It was going north toward Chicago. There, the next morning, he hopped a train going west with the sun. The boy would make it to California and become an extra in the movies, an officeholder in the Lake Charles, Louisiana, Club, and a respectable accountant in South Central Los Angeles.

George had heard about these boys and men hoboing out of the South but had never seen one for himself until that day on the northbound train. He was as startled as the disheveled, soot-covered man in front of him.

"I can't believe what I'm looking at," George thought to himself. "I can't believe I'm seeing what I see."

The man must have sneaked onto the train as it sat boarding passengers or run alongside it and jumped up as the train either slowed to a stop or pulled out of a station.

And now he was clinging to the sides of the railcar as it rocked at top speed, the wind rushing between the cars as they rumbled and turned.

George never knew what became of the man or the others he saw hoboing on the trains. They never spoke. He himself had stared death in the face in Florida and felt sadness and awe at whatever drove them to steal onto a train this way.

"They were standing there like statues," George said. "Like they were part of the equipment. I couldn't tell whether they were living or dead there for a while."

Sometimes he would see the same few coming back and forth, as if that were the only way they could manage to go north or south. It was nerve-jangling to George to see them because he was supposed to turn them in. But he just couldn't bring himself to do it.

"I would never give them up," he said. "I'd pretend I didn't see them. One or two occasions, I'd sneak a sandwich or something out of the diner."

And after he did that, they would always disappear.

LOS ANGELES, SUMMER 1955

ROBERT JOSEPH PERSHING FOSTER

AFTER TWO YEARS OF HARD WORK, Robert managed to attract enough patients needing some sort of surgery that he was finally able to secure admitting privileges at a hospital in Los Angeles. It was nowhere near Cedars Sinai or UCLA Medical Center but was a little place called Metropolitan Hospital over at Twenty-first and Hoover Street, near his office. It had a mostly colored patient load and a mostly white staff of doctors. There were only a few colored doctors, and Robert was one of them.

They did most of their surgeries in the morning, and around noon they broke for lunch. They sat in the lounge to eat or read the newspapers and waited for their next cases to come up.

But Mondays were different. Monday was the day when the white doctors came back from the weekend, regaling one another with their exploits at the casinos and their triumphs on the golf courses in Palm Springs or Las Vegas. Robert dreaded Mondays.

One Monday, they turned and looked at him.

"Bob, have you been to Caesars?"

"No, I haven't seen it," Robert said, looking down. "I've never been there."

Robert hated to admit that. He wanted more than anything to be able to go to Vegas. He was born for Vegas. By now he had the money to go. That was what he came out here for—to be a full citizen, do whatever people of his station did, regardless of what color they were.

He began avoiding the other doctors on Mondays. He made himself busy, buried himself in his newspaper, and avoided eye contact so they wouldn't engage him in conversation during their animated recaps. But he couldn't escape hearing their tales from the casinos.

He sat there having to listen to them talk about Vegas for months, seething and saying nothing. They seemed to have caught on that he didn't want to join in and left him alone as they compared notes among themselves.

"Then, every now and then," Robert remembered, "somebody would make a mistake and ask to confirm or give your feeling about a club or gambling in Las Vegas."

One day, he spoke up.

"Listen, I'm tired of you guys asking me about Las Vegas," he said. "You know colored people can't go to the hotels there or the casinos. It's a thorn in my side, so don't ask me about that."

The doctors fell silent. "That embarrassed all those who heard it," Robert remembered years later. "They had a guilt feeling that they were a part of that. This is the way I perceived it anyway. Maybe they didn't give a nickel. I don't know."

The doctors stopped asking him about Vegas, but that didn't mean he stopped thinking about it, wishing for it.

Over time, Robert began hearing rumors about blacks protesting their exclusion from Las Vegas and that the city might be opening up. He went to two doctor friends of his, one a brother of his classmate Dr. Beale back in Houston, and another, Dr. Jackson, who had both gotten into hospital management and seemed always to know the latest.

He asked them what they'd heard about Vegas.

"Is it true that blacks can go there now?"

"I ain't heard that, Bob," Dr. Jackson said.

They had, however, heard that there was a colored man in Vegas who people said was helping get colored people into a few of the hotels and casinos.

"I tell you what you do," Dr. Jackson said. "Why don't you call Jimmy Gay?"

"Who's Jimmy Gay?"

James Arthur Gay was perhaps the most influential colored man in the still-segregated world of Las Vegas. He had migrated there from Fordyce, Arkansas, after World War II and found himself locked out of both the mortuary trade, for which he had been trained, and the resort industry, to which he aspired. College degree in hand, he worked his way up from a cook at a drive-in to become one of the first colored executives at a casino, the Sands, at a time when stars like Nat King Cole and Sammy Davis, Jr., were not permitted to stay in hotels on the Strip. Knowing how hard it had been for him to cross the color line in Vegas, he took it upon himself to help spirit other colored people in wherever he could, risking his own tenuous standing to do so.

Over time, he became the contact person, a secret agent of sorts, the one connection in an almost underground network in Las Vegas, where a colored visitor could not otherwise be assured of getting a room at a mainline hotel. Jimmy knew who to talk to in order to secure rooms for colored people at the Vegas hotels and knew how to do it discreetly, and he was in a position to screen, through word of mouth in that insular circle of colored people for whom he would perform such a service.

So Robert called him.

"This is Bob Foster, Jimmy," Robert said. "Jackson and Beale told me to call you and find out if this was true. Have they opened Las Vegas up?"

"You planning to come up?"

"If we can go. Can we go? Could we come?"

"Well, how many in your party? When are you planning to come? Get your party together and call me, and I'll see what I can do."

Robert couldn't wait to tell his friends about it. It took them some time to get it together. A total of thirteen people signed up to go in what would be an early foray past the color line in Vegas: doctors, doctors' wives, a school principal. They started planning right away. They made their plane and train reservations. They read up on the casinos and the shows they wanted to see. The women shopped for what seemed like weeks.

"They had three different outfits for every day," Robert said. *"Three completely different outfits."*

Jimmy had arranged for them to stay at the Riviera Hotel. Robert couldn't wait. It was the first high-rise in Vegas. It had cost ten million dollars to build and had just opened that spring to worries that it was so big that the desert sand might sink under its weight. It was right on the Strip, its name in big letters on a V-shaped marquee above the sign for the Starlight Lounge. Dean Martin was part owner. Liberace played there. It would become the set for *Ocean's Eleven.* It was so very Rat Pack, and Robert could just picture himself at a dinner show in the Clover Room. All summer, a jingle was running on the radio stations in Los Angeles about "The Riv," as it came to be called, like it was the hottest thing going in Vegas. *There's a new high in the Las Vegas sky, the Riviera Hotel.* Robert used to sing along with the jingle and only got more excited.

"You heard it a million times a day," Robert said. "And, oh, I'd just be thinking about the trip we were going to have."

The people who flew in piled into several taxicabs at the Vegas airport and pulled up to the canopied driveway of the Riviera with enough luggage for a celebrity road tour. They walked into the marble lobby, chatting and giddy.

"Now, we all dressed to the fingertips," Robert said, "sharp as sharp could be. Everybody."

Robert saw bellmen all around but noticed that no one stepped forward to get the luggage. Someone in the group asked for help. At last a bellman came and brought their luggage in, loads of it, to the front desk.

In the lobby, Robert's group met up with the couple who had caught the train and had arrived ahead of them. The wife was named Thurma Adams. She jumped up and ran toward Robert and the others and began acting out of sorts. She was humming under her breath as if to warn them of something, but it was in a childlike code that Robert had trouble deciphering.

She was skipping as she sang, *"La de, da, de, da, la de da, de da!"*

"Thurma, Thurma, Thurma," Robert said. "Have you lost your mind?"

"Just go on over to that desk," she told him. "You'll see."

Robert understood instantly. "And chills went through me," he remembered. "A wave of nausea."

Phoenix again.

"Oh hell, we ain't gonna get this room," he thought to himself. "The same story, 'There's no room in here.' "

Here they were, thirteen travelers just arrived in a place they thought had opened up to people like them. They couldn't have been sure of it but wanted so much to believe that they had taken the chance anyway, and now they were being told there were no accommodations for them, and they're standing there in the gilded lobby like refugees, homeless in their tailored suits and sequins and with enough luggage for a European holiday.

Robert tried to calm himself and salvage the situation. He went over to the front desk just as he had in Phoenix, but more assured this time because he had been through this before and besides, he was a Californian now.

"This is Dr. Robert Foster," he began. "We have a party of thirteen people from Los Angeles. We are supposed to have room reservations."

"Who made them?" the clerk asked.

"Mr. Jimmy Gay made them," Robert answered.

"Who's Jimmy Gay?"

"Jimmy Gay knows somebody here. I didn't get the name of the person who made them for me."

The front-desk clerk called the reservations supervisor, and he came out.

"And they looked, and they looked and they looked and they looked," Robert remembered.

"They looked for what they knew wasn't there. And I know that one, too."

The front desk said it could find no reservation for any of them, made no offer to accommodate them, and made no suggestions nor showed any interest in where else they might possibly go.

"So I'm standing there fuming," Robert said many years later. "*How do I get out of this? How we gonna get out this hotel with all this luggage?* Humiliation galore. I felt everybody in the place looking at us. I felt as if the shower door had fallen, and I looked up and saw I had an audience of fifty people. I just felt that they could see clear through me that we had been rejected. And that was what I felt at that desk."

He decided to call Jimmy Gay from a phone booth in the hotel. Maybe that would clear things up. Fortunately, Jimmy was home.

Jimmy told him that he would check on it and that Robert should stay by the phone booth.

"Don't let anybody use the phone you on," Jimmy said. "Block it. Leave the line open. I want to make a phone call, and I'll call you right back. Stay by the phone."

Jimmy couldn't locate the reservations clerk he had talked to at the Riviera, late as it was. So he came up with an alternative.

"Go to the Sands Hotel," he instructed. He told them who to ask for when they got there. "He'll take care of you and the party."

So Robert and the twelve others once again loaded into several cabs and went to the Sands Hotel. Because Jimmy had made reservations at the Riviera and not the Sands, the Sands didn't have enough rooms for the entire party that night. The Sands made arrangements for them to stay at yet another hotel, the Flamingo Capri, further down on the Strip.

"We'll come and get you tomorrow," the front-desk clerk said. The

Sands kept its word, and the next morning they were, at last, all unpacking their things at the Sands.

"I got a warm spot with Sands for what they did for us," Robert would say years later.

Jimmy Gay and his wife, Hazel, puddle-hopped them from nightclub to nightclub where Jimmy knew they would be accepted. They heard Pearl Bailey in the lounge. They made three shows a night. And Robert got to go inside the casinos he had heard his fellow physicians brag and goad him about for months and that he dreaded hearing mention of. But now he didn't have to dread it anymore.

"We lived the part," Robert said.

He remembered one night in particular. He was wearing a black mohair suit he ordered specifically for the occasion from the tailor who dressed Sammy Davis, Jr., and Frank Sinatra. He wore a black tie with a burgundy stripe, a white tab-collar shirt, gold cuff links, black shoes, black silk socks, and a white handkerchief with his initials, *RPF,* embroidered in silver.

All the humiliation melted away, the white doctors' idle chatter, the rejection at the Riviera.

He was finally in the world he belonged in, living out a dream like an honorary member of the Rat Pack. Jim Crow, the South, Louisiana, Monroe, Phoenix, the downside of L.A.—all gone for now. He was in a casino out of a movie. Dean Martin could have walked in any minute, or so it seemed, and here was Robert, right in the middle of it, acting as if he'd been to it.

"And I am playing the roulette. And I'm enjoying myself, and I'm having a good time, and I'm standing up betting over some other people there, and I hit my number, and I eased the buttons loose on the coat, and I hit number eleven, and I reached over like this to pick up my chips and open my coat and show my blood red silk lining.

"People said, 'Oh, look at that!' A white woman said that. She had never seen a red lining in a suit. That was very avant-garde. All this conservative stuff outside. And this red satin lining inside."

For once he would not be dreading lunchtime at the hospital that Monday.

CHICAGO, EARLY 1939
IDA MAE BRANDON GLADNEY

GEORGE AND IDA MAE had been in the North for close to two years. They had three little ones to feed and were still having trouble finding work. They had arrived in the depths of the Great Depression with the fewest skills any migrant could have but with the most modest of expectations and the strongest of backs. They had taken their chances and found even the most menial jobs hard to come by.

Anything with the least amount of status or job security seemed reserved for people who did not look like them and often spoke with an accent from a small eastern European country they had never heard of. They were running into the same sentiment, albeit on a humbler level, that a colored man in Philadelphia faced when he answered an ad for a position as a store clerk. "What do you suppose we'd want of a Negro?" the storekeeper asked the applicant.

George had been struggling since he arrived. He had worked on a coal truck, dug ditches for the Works Progress Administration, delivered ice to the tenements on the South Side, and been turned away from places that said they weren't hiring or just had nothing for him. He would just keep looking until he found something.

Finally, he landed a job that suited his temperament on the soup-making line at the Campbell Soup plant, a place so big there was bound to be some work for him if the people were open to hiring him, which, fortunately for him, they were. The plant was on twenty-two acres at Thirty-fifth and Western by the panhandle tracks, where they mixed several thousand tomatoes and oxtails at a time to make soup for customers west of the Mississippi. He had been working all his life, but this was the first indoor job he had ever had.

His days would now turn on the directions of foremen and the spinning of machinery, the orderly and finite ticking of the company punch clock instead of the rhythms of the field, where he and Ida Mae used to work according to what an anthropologist once called "the great clocks of the sky."

The plant turned out six thousand cans of soup a minute along three miles of tracks and switches. He was entering the world of assembly-line factory culture, the final destination of many unskilled black southerners once they got established in the North. Whatever reception he got, good or bad, he kept it to himself, as was his way, and he carried out whatever duties he was to perform without complaint, whatever kind of soup was coming down the vats in his direction.

Like so many others, he had gone from the mind-numbing sameness of picking cotton to the mind-numbing sameness of turning a lever or twisting a widget or stoking a flame for one tiny piece of a much larger thing he had no control over. He had moved to a different part of the country but was on the same rung of the ladder. It was, in some ways, not all that different from picking cotton. The raw bolls went off to some mill in Atlanta or Massachusetts to be made into something refined and unrecognizable from what he saw of it, from the poorly remunerated kernel of the thing that represented George's and other sharecroppers' contribution to the final product intended for someone far better off than he. Except now, in Chicago, he would get paid.

Just by being able to keep his job, which he would for many years, George would be spared the contentious relations at so many plants in the North, where the migrants were scorned if they were hired at all, or outright turned away. Most migrants like George were hired into either menial labor—janitors or window cleaners or assembly-line workers—or hard labor—longshoremen, coal miners, stokers of foundries and diggers of ditches, which is what he had done before landing the assembly-line job at Campbell Soup.

Many companies simply didn't hire colored workers at all but for altogether different reasons from the South. It wasn't because of an explicit Berlin Wall of exclusion, written into law and so engrained as to not need to be spelled out for people on either side, as in the South. Instead, in the North, companies and unions said that, however much they might want to hire colored people, their white workers just wouldn't stand for it. And, for the sake of morale, the companies and unions weren't going to force the issue.

A glass plant in Pittsburgh tried to hire colored workers, but the white workers ran them out, the researcher Abraham Epstein reported, by cursing them and "making conditions so unpleasant they were forced to quit." At a steel mill there, the white bargemen threatened to walk out "because black workers were introduced among them." The white workers at the mill were appeased only "by the provision of separate quarters" for the colored workers.

A factory in Chicago reported that after it hired colored workers, there was "friction in the washrooms" and that "for every colored girl employed, we lost five white girls."

"I find a great resentment among all our white people," the manager of a wholesale millinery in Chicago reported. "I couldn't overcome the prejudice enough to bring the people in the same building, and had to engage outside quarters for the blacks. . . . We thought it would be nice if we would start a school for machine operators. . . . I received a delegation from our sewing hall who said they resented the idea. They wouldn't listen to it at all, and I had to abandon the project. Their argument was: 'If you let them in it won't be long until we are out entirely.' The attitude against the colored is only the same as it was against the Slavs or the foreign races when they first intruded the field."

Somehow the migrants persisted, partly because they had little choice and could only hope that open-minded whites might see past the preconceptions. A Chicago laundry, for instance, reported that when it hired its first colored girl, "the white girls threatened to quit. The manager asked them to wait a week and, if they still objected, he would let her go." As it turned out, the white girls grew to like the colored girl, and she was permitted to stay.

Overall, however, what was becoming clear was that, north or south, wherever colored labor was introduced, a rivalrous sense of unease and insecurity washed over the working-class people who were already there, an unease that was economically not without merit but rose to near hysteria when race and xenophobia were added to preexisting fears. The reality was that Jim Crow filtered through the economy, north and south, and pressed down on poor and working-class people of all races. The southern caste system that held down the wages of colored people also undercut the earning power of the whites around them, who could not command higher pay as long as colored people were forced to accept subsistence wages.

The dynamic was not lost on northern industrialists, who hired colored workers as strikebreakers and resorted to them to keep their labor costs down just as companies at the end of the twentieth century would turn to the cheap labor of developing nations like Malaysia and Vietnam. The introduction of colored workers, who had long been poorly paid and ill treated, served as a restraint on what anyone around them could demand.

"Their presence and availability for some of the work being performed by whites, whether they are actually employed or not," wrote the sociologist Charles S. Johnson, "acts as a control on wages."

By the time George managed to find steady work, he was joining the forty percent of black men doing unskilled or semiskilled work in

Chicago in the 1940s. Another thirty-four percent of black men were working as servants, meaning that, for three out of four black men, the only work they could get was work that nobody else wanted—lowly and menial or hard, dangerous, and dirty. Nearly the inverse was true for white men, the majority of whom—some sixty percent—were doing skilled, clerical, business, or professional work, clean indoor jobs.

The ceiling was even lower and the options fewer for colored women, a situation that was making it even harder for Ida Mae to find work. By 1940, two out of every three colored women in Chicago were servants, as against seventeen percent of white women (most of those newly arrived immigrants). Only a fraction of colored women—a mere seven percent—were hired to do clerical work—common and upstanding positions for women of the day—compared to forty-three percent of white women.

Under these conditions, Ida Mae and George found themselves at the bottom looking up at the layers of immigrants, native-born white people, and even northern-born black people who were stacked above them in the economic hierarchy of the North. It was all well and good that George now had a job at Campbell Soup. But they would never be able to get settled in Chicago until Ida Mae found reliable work. So Ida set out to look whenever George wasn't at work and, the rest of the time, took care of the children.

By now it was winter in Chicago, and the cold was beginning to get to her. She had never felt anything like it before. It was a supernatural kind of cold that burned the tips of her fingers and hunted her down through the layers of sweaters to the half inch of skin that happened to have been left unprotected.

On the streets, there were perils at every turn. The sidewalks were glazed with ice, and she had to climb over hills of unmelted snow. She looked up and saw spears of icicles hanging from the gutters and soffits of the buildings. The icicles were as big as a human leg and pointed toward the sidewalk like swords. She heard that sometimes the icicles broke from the buildings and killed people. It was like being on a different planet.

"You spit, and it would be froze," she said.

She didn't complain about it. She just did what she had to do. She trudged through the snow to take baby Eleanor to the clinic at Forty-third and State for the immunizations the city said the baby had to have.

She wrapped Eleanor in so much swaddling you couldn't tell there was a baby inside.

At the clinic, the nurse gave her instructions.

"Mother," the nurse said, "take the baby's clothes off."

Ida Mae thought that was the craziest thing in the world, cold as it was outside. She didn't want Eleanor exposed like that.

"All that snow out there," Ida Mae said. "I ain't takin' my baby's clothes off."

"The doctor has to see her," the nurse told her.

Ida Mae balked but soon learned there was no point in protesting. This was the way they did things here on this new planet she was on.

NEW YORK, DECEMBER 1951
GEORGE SWANSON STARLING

NO MATTER HOW SETTLED the migrants got or how far away they ran, the South had a way of insinuating itself, reaching out across rivers and highways to pull them back when it chose. The South was a telegram away, the other end of a telephone call, a newspaper headline that others might skim over but that hurtled them back to a world they could never fully leave.

George had been in New York for six years when the South came back to haunt him. Sometime in late December 1951, he got word that something terrible had happened to an old acquaintance back in Florida.

It was someone he knew from his days as a substitute teacher at the colored school in Eustis during the lulls in the picking season. George had only a couple years of college, but it was more education than most colored people in town, which was why they called him Schoolboy with his proper-sounding talk. So George was a welcome and natural fill-in for the regular teachers when they took sick or went away.

He loved imparting whatever wisdom he had acquired in his twenty-odd years. But he soon came to realize that colored teachers were making only a fraction of what the white teachers were making in Florida.

He was always alert to any hint of injustice, and here was yet another example of the double-sided world he was living in. He would later lead a series of strikes in the groves, which would force him out of Florida for good, but before that time, while he was substitute teaching, he got pulled into a different crusade.

Harry T. Moore, a churchly schoolteacher from an old place called Mims over on the Atlantic Coast, was the NAACP's chief organizer for all of Florida back in the 1930s and 1940s. He wore out three cars crisscrossing the state in his stiff suit and tie, teaching colored people how to vote before Florida granted them the right to, investigating lynchings, and protesting segregated schools and unequal pay for colored teachers. He did much of this work as a volunteer, driving alone in the backwoods and small towns of Florida, "where no restaurant would serve him, no motel would house him, and some gas stations wouldn't let him fill his tank, empty his bladder or even use the phone," his biographer Ben Green wrote.

These were the dark early days of the civil rights movement, before it even had a name: Martin Luther King, Jr., was still in grade school, Rosa Parks was a young bride, and the NAACP was an underground organization in the South. It was still building a base there among its fearful constituents, and segregationists were viewing it as an uppity troublemaker meddling in the private affairs of the southern order of things. It took courage even to be associated with it in those days, let alone be its field secretary in one of the most violent states in the South. Between 1882 and 1930, vigilantes in Florida lynched 266 black people, more than any other state, so many, in fact, that, after white men killed a black man with a hatchet one day, a newspaper could smugly and correctly report, "It is safe to predict that nothing would be done about it." The same could be said for the hundreds of blacks driven out of town in that same era, their homes shot up and set afire in the all-black settlements of Rosewood and Ocoee. "We are in the hands of the devil," a black Floridian said.

It was here that Harry T. Moore began his quiet crusade. He wore out typewriter ribbons and worked a hand-cranked ditto machine to produce his measured entreaties to governors and legislators in cases of brutality or injustice in the courts, often facing ridicule or outright rejection. One case in particular spurred him to action. A young colored boy sent a Christmas card to a white girl, who showed the card to her father. A posse of white men captured the boy, hogtied him, and forced the boy's father to watch as they tortured the boy and drowned him in the river. The posse would later say the boy jumped into the water on his own.

Moore then stepped up his letters, circulars, and broadsides and threw himself into more dangerous terrain, the fight against lynching and police brutality. He began conducting his own one-man investigations into every lynching in Florida, interviewing the victims' families and writing to the government on their behalf.

When he wasn't working to hold officials to their oaths of duty, he was going door-to-door, town to town, trying to recruit people to join his cause. It was in this way that George Starling met Harry T. Moore.

The men were not friends. They only met once. But both he and George shared an outrage over the treatment of colored people when it came to the schools. Florida school boards, each its own little fiefdom, had a habit of shutting down the colored schools weeks or months before the school year was supposed to end, blaming the closures on budget shortfalls that for some reason did not affect class time at the white schools. It was a way for county school boards to save on both the cost of running colored schools and having to pay colored teachers for the already foreshortened school year colored schools had.

Even when the teachers got to work a full year under the colored school schedule, they were paid a salary of $542 a year, compared to $1,146 per year for white teachers in the late 1930s, forty-seven percent of what the white teachers were making. There was nothing the colored teachers or parents could do about it until Harry T. Moore, himself the principal at a grade school in Brevard County, started a petition to protest it.

George Starling met Moore sometime in the early 1940s when the civil rights worker arrived in Eustis to enlist colored teachers in the effort. Moore had been making his way around an unwelcoming state and was now seeking to make inroads in Lake County in the state's central interior. Moore wanted to start a local chapter in Eustis to build up state membership and widen support for the cause. He needed people on the ground to help him discreetly canvass the colored district of Eustis, allay people's fears, and take on the forbidding task of convincing them to join the NAACP.

Moore gathered the colored people of Eustis together at Gethsemane Baptist Church one Sunday after service. Moore, along with his wife, Harriette, laid out his plan to petition the state to raise colored teachers' pay and said he needed someone to lead the NAACP registration drive in Eustis. The principal of the colored school, a Mr. J. S. Pinckney, expressed support for the cause; after all, he was being cheated by the pay gap too. Everyone in town knew how vocal George could be, and the principal nominated him to lead the registration effort.

"I didn't want to do it," George said years later. But the principal assured him that he wouldn't be going it alone.

"I'll help you," the principal said. "We need somebody that knows how to organize people, how to approach people."

"So I let him talk me into doing it," George said years later. "And I started first working with the teachers."

Sunday evenings after church, George went door-to-door to try to persuade them in private to join the NAACP. Membership dues were a dollar. Sometimes the principal went with him. But George was having little success.

"I couldn't get one single teacher to join," he said years later. "And I was tight with most all the teachers out there."

The teachers were making all kinds of excuses and were flat-out saying they just couldn't do it. George thought something wasn't adding up. These were intelligent, reasonable people, people he had known all his life and worked with at school when he was a substitute. They were the ones who would benefit most from the changes the NAACP was seeking.

So one day, he cornered one of the teachers he was closest to and asked her what was going on.

"Look, now," he said. "Something is not right. Why is it that I can't get any teacher to join the NAACP? We all tight together, but I can't get none of y'all to sign up."

The teacher didn't want to talk about it. But George persisted.

"I'm not gonna take 'no' for no answer today," he said. "I wanna know what's happening."

So she told him.

"Well, the principal held a faculty meeting," she began, "and he told all the teachers that any teacher that joins the NAACP, he would personally see that they don't ever teach in this county no more."

The principal had given the impression to the colored people in town and to Harry Moore himself that he was all for progress and the NAACP. But he was undercutting the effort in private, knowing George's every move and every person George was talking to and in the perfect position to manipulate the results.

When George approached the principal, he discovered the nature of the contradictions and the compromising position the principal was in, not that George thought it was right. First, to George's surprise, the principal joined the NAACP for himself and his wife.

But he gave George a warning.

"Now, don't put my name on there," the principal said. "We'll pay our membership fee, but you don't have to put our names on the list."

Then George discovered the real problem. Word had gotten back to the county school board that Harry T. Moore, who was by then known and despised by white officials all over the state, was stirring up trouble among the colored teachers in Lake County. If the principal didn't get the situation under control and the NAACP out of the schools, he could lose his job or worse. The principal assured the board that he would take care of it, and he did.

"I told my teachers if they join that fight, I'll fire 'em all," the colored principal reported to white school board officials. "I said, not near one a y'all better not join the NAACP."

"Yeah, Pinckney, you a good man," a white school board official said, as the story was told among the colored people in Eustis. "You a good man."

Any teacher caught working with the NAACP could face retaliation in Florida. Firing teachers was a common tool of the authorities to undercut efforts to equalize their pay. In due course, the authorities fired NAACP leader Harry T. Moore from his principal's position and banned him from ever teaching in Florida again. Without work and with two young daughters to support, Moore struck a deal to work full-time for the NAACP, but he had to raise some of the money for his salary himself.

He did not let that stop him, and his biggest fight was only beginning. It involved the sheriff in the county where George grew up and would make national headlines.

It started on the morning of Saturday, July 16, 1949, when a seventeen-year-old white woman accused four black men of raping her and attacking her husband on an isolated road in Lake County, near the town of Groveland. A manhunt led to the arrests of three young black men, one of whom had been in police custody at the time the girl said the rape occurred, but was still considered a suspect. The authorities shot and killed a fourth suspect before he could be taken to jail.

Tensions ran so high that the 350 colored residents of Groveland had to be evacuated to Orlando, where the Red Cross, the Salvation Army, and colored and white churches put them up.

The three young men were reportedly beaten with rubber hoses while in police custody, with Lake County Sheriff Willis McCall, an imposing figure in a Stetson hat, announcing that a confession had been extracted from them. By then the case had become so emotionally charged that the court had a hard time finding a lawyer to represent the defendants. The one who finally agreed, Alex Akerman, said he "had no desire to handle the case," and said to himself, as he drove toward Lake County for the trial, that he knew this would be "the end" of his career.

The three suspects were luckier than many other black men accused of raping a white woman. They actually lived long enough to hear the jury's conviction. Two were sentenced to death. The one who had been in police custody at the time of the rape was shown mercy and sentenced to life in prison.

The trial had been so tense that the judge took it upon himself to show the defense team—Akerman and the NAACP lawyers, along with two northern reporters covering the case—the safest door from which to exit after the verdict was read. They would all have to get out of town quick. They hoped the verdict would be handed down before nightfall. It wasn't. They followed the judge's warning and headed out the side door into the Florida night after the verdict, convicting the men, was read. As they drove out of town, they could see the headlights of two unidentified cars tailing them. The NAACP lawyer floored the accelerator, barely able to keep ahead of the menacing headlights bearing down on them through hairpin country roads. The two cars hunted them into the darkness. The defense team finally made it to the county line and crossed over into another jurisdiction. Only then did the cars tailing them back away.

This was the world Harry T. Moore operated in and that George knew all too well.

The Groveland case, as it came to be known, roused Moore to action. He fired off letters of protest to the governor, to the FBI, to the U.S. attorney general. The pressure he and the NAACP headquarters put on the courts won the men a second trial. (The one who had been shown mercy because he had been in police custody at the time of the rape was advised to be grateful for his life sentence and not seek further redress through a second trial.)

The night before the trial was to begin, for reasons that remain unclear and known only to him, Sheriff McCall decided to move the prisoners to another jail. He handcuffed them together and drove them himself in his patrol car. At one point, he moved the two men to the front seat with him. Minutes later, he was calling for backup. He said the handcuffed men had attacked him and tried to escape. He said he had defended himself by shooting them, emptying his .38 Smith and Wesson in the process.

The shootings and the photographs of the two black men, their bodies splayed on the ground still handcuffed together, attracted national headlines and criticism of the sheriff, the governor, and the Florida legal system from all over the country. The heat ratcheted up further when it turned out that one of the two men had actually survived the shooting by pretending to be dead so the sheriff would stop shooting him.

Harry Moore began calling for an investigation of the shootings and for Sheriff McCall's ouster. Either the sheriff had shot two shackled men without cause or he had shown recklessness and lack of forethought in transporting the men alone, as Moore saw it. Moore was doing what no colored men dared to do in those days of southern apartheid: he was standing up to the most powerful man in all of Lake County. He was attracting more attention from white supremacists, who had resented him in the past but were incensed at him now. He began getting death threats and for the first time started carrying a gun with him on those lonely drives into the country.

At the same time, unbeknownst to the local whites who deplored him, Moore was losing the support of NAACP headquarters in New York, an organization Moore had worked hard for but which had its own national ambitions and was at that very moment seeking changes in the Florida operation Moore had built. Now that Florida was on the map, in civil rights terms, headquarters wanted to capitalize on the publicity of the Groveland case for its broader goals. It pushed for greater membership and for centralized county chapters rather than the small colonies Moore had nurtured in places like Eustis. Headquarters could not have known the tensions on the ground in those isolated hamlets or the fear in the people George tried to sign up in Eustis all those years ago, or recognize that country people couldn't risk being seen outside their homes at a countywide NAACP meeting that would attract life-threatening attention. Not then anyway.

Moore and the NAACP remained at odds through the fall and into Thanksgiving of 1951. At a statewide meeting in early December, national officers finally managed enough votes to oust Moore, who had virtually given his life to the cause. His very strength was his undoing that night. The chapters in the small hamlets that were so loyal to him, because they knew more than anyone the dangers he faced just getting there to see them, did not have the resources to send delegates to that meeting. Thus the meeting was dominated by the delegates from Miami, Tallahassee, Jacksonville, big-city groups that had their own politics and looked down upon the country teacher from a small town on the Mosquito Coast none of them had been to.

Now, despite his hard work, Moore was no longer the head of the Florida NAACP. But the white supremacists he had challenged all those years wouldn't have known that. To them he was still the NAACP's man on the ground and a target of their anger. Soon white men from outside his county started asking people in town where that colored NAACP fellow lived. There was a mysterious break-in at the Moores' house, which sat isolated on a country road surrounded by orange groves.

And then on Christmas night 1951, the Moores' twenty-fifth wedding anniversary, a bomb exploded under the floorboards beneath their bed as they slept. It hurled furniture into the air and crushed the bed into a crater in the earth. The force of the blast could be heard the next town over. Harry and Harriette Moore suffered grave internal injuries. Relatives rushed them to the nearest hospital, some thirty-five miles away. But, as was the common dilemma for colored patients in the South, they had to wait for the only colored doctor in town to get there to attend them. Harry T. Moore was dead by the time the colored doctor arrived. Harriette, saying she did not want to live without her husband, survived for eight days before succumbing herself.

The county, the state, and the FBI conducted a months-long investigation. It was determined that the Klan, specifically the Orlando Klavern, was behind the bombing. But as the investigation narrowed its focus, the Klansmen closed rank. At their meetings, they now began requiring everyone to recite the Klan oath of secrecy as the investigation closed in on them. The chief suspects all said they had been at a barbecue with twenty or thirty other members at the time of the attack, a convenient alibi for most anyone who would come under suspicion. Ultimately, no one was ever charged or spent a day in jail for the murder of Harry and Harriette Moore, considered by some the first casualties of the modern civil rights movement.

News of the bombing reached George up in Harlem, and he found it both shocking and half expected, knowing what he did about that land of raccoon woods and cypress swamps thick with fear and secrets.

When he spoke of Harry T. Moore, he spoke matter-of-factly, without emotion, flat and to the point. It was as if nothing in the world could surprise him. He had just about heard and seen it all.

Years later, when George was an old man, he would find God, become a deacon, and join the choir at a Baptist church in Harlem. People always said he had a beautiful voice. He was a tenor baritone. He knew all the words to just about any Baptist hymn. Whenever he stood up and sang, there he was, towering over all the sopranos and tenors, his voice rising up above the others but his eyes welling up and tears falling in droplets down the sides of his cheeks. It happened whenever he sang.

LOS ANGELES, MID- TO LATE 1950S
ROBERT JOSEPH PERSHING FOSTER

ROBERT WAS MAKING a bigger name for himself now. He was getting a reputation not just for making a show of his every arrival but for being the kind of doctor who could just look at somebody and tell that the problem was with the spleen.

The people from Monroe began taking notice. They started coming around, tentative and curious at first. Robert never knew what to expect when they showed up. Jimmy Marshall's mother had tried to make herself go and see Robert, but for the longest time she just couldn't get used to his being a doctor. She still hadn't adjusted to the idea of calling him Robert. She kept slipping and couldn't bring herself to say it.

"I can't believe little Pershing Foster is a doctor!" she once exclaimed.

He was becoming so popular that she finally went to see him. But she was appalled at what he asked of her at her first appointment. "How dare you tell me to take my clothes off!" she told Robert as he prepared for the examination.

"Bob got so tickled," Jimmy remembered. "Then, after he treated her, she had to admit, 'He's a good little doctor.' "

Robert's office was well situated on West Jefferson, a fashionable black business district closer to Beverly Hills than South Central, and he now had admitting privileges at several hospitals. He was getting to know other doctors but, oddly enough and just as important, was popular with the orderlies and charge nurses and even the people in the cafeteria, the kind of people other doctors ignored. And they started showing up at his office, too.

"My patients loved me," he said matter-of-factly years later. "They could tell me anything. They'd tell you in a minute, 'I can talk to you.' "

They waited for hours to see him. Many were people who back in Texas or Louisiana or Arkansas might have only rarely seen a physician, who were used to midwives and root doctors and home remedies they handed down and concocted for themselves. Here was a doctor who was as science-minded and proficient as any other but who didn't make fun of their down-home superstitions and knew how to comfort them and translate modern medicine into a language they could understand.

"It was twenty people deep on Saturdays," Malissa Briley, a patient of his, remembered. "They would come early, sign up, then leave, go shopping and run errands, come back three or four hours later and still have to wait."

Any number of times he'd ask, "How long you been waiting?"

"Don't even ask me," she'd say. "You know how long I been waiting."

People would complain among themselves. "They would sit up in the office and fuss and carry on about how he's never on time," Briley said. "And the very next time you go, you see the same people waiting."

And after hours of sitting and passing the time, when they finally made it into his office, he would light a cigarette and throw his feet up on his desk and ask them what was going on in their lives.

"Tell me about it," he would say.

Husbands shared suspicions about their wives. Mothers brought their children in.

"Doctor, I believe she's pregnant," a mother told Robert. "Make her tell you whose baby it is."

He loved it so much, he practically gave his life over to the worries and fixes his patients got themselves into.

"If you got sick and had a complication," he said, "I didn't leave your bed until you showed signs of improvement, if it took all night long. If you had tubes down your nose and through your stomach and intravenous going, I'd stay there and be sure that they worked. Then I'd get up and go home, shave, dress, get as sharp as I could get, and come back at visiting hours. And walk over to the bed, feel the pulse."

"Miss Brown, you feel any better?" he'd say.

"Baby, this is my doctor," the patient would tell her husband.

Sometimes the discussion was with the relative in the room.

"Hey, Doc. He's sick as he can be," a patient's relative might say.

It got to the point that it seemed people could tell when he stepped out of the elevator and onto the floor, and it reassured people and they almost started feeling better at the sight of him. This spread to the friends and relatives visiting the patient and to the people who weren't his patients, seeing him dote on someone else.

"You know some other doctor's patient," he said, "and they call me in to do the surgery or whatever it was. And then I wouldn't go back until the man is better. When I *know* he looks better. And I'm sharp, got on the latest fashions. I put the show on so you wouldn't forget. They called me 'the Jitterbug Doctor.' Think I'm kidding, don't you? Straight, straight just like it is. But the point was that they would not forget me. And others would see you in the room with them. And they would remember you outside the room. They'd get your card and call you."

Sometimes he'd hear from patients' relatives, people coming in from out of town or just new to California who were feeling under the weather and worried what it might be. Someone would hand them Robert's number with no more explanation than this: "If you just call this number, and tell him 'I'm sick,' he'll tell you what to do."

One of the people who called him one day was a cook from east Texas working the cafeteria line at the old hospital on Hoover Street. She had seen the jitterbug doctor, liked him, and told him she had a cousin she thought could use his help. The cook sent her cousin to see Robert for a physical and an assessment of her medical problems.

The cook's cousin was a woman named Della Beatrice Robinson. People called her Della Bea. She was a singer who had not long since migrated from Texas. Della Bea took her cousin's suggestion and made an appointment.

Della Bea was so pleased with the treatment and with the southern, down-home way about this doctor, something comforting and familiar about him, that she kept coming back. She also had another idea.

"My husband needs to come in to see you," she said after a few visits.

She said her husband would need the last appointment of the day and that his name was Ray Charles Robinson—Ray Charles to most of the world.

"So there I got Ray Charles," Robert would say years later. "The rest was up to me and Ray, and it flew."

Both men were from the South and had come to Los Angeles chasing a dream, Ray having migrated in 1950, three years before Robert. Both were more ambitious, controlling, and meticulous than the gaudy, juke-joint side of them might suggest. Both moved in highfalutin circles but were most at ease with plainspoken common folk, which is what they really were deep inside. They were both on the verge of making it big in their respective worlds. And neither could truly put behind them the hurts each had endured in the South or overcome the excesses of those fixations. The two would be friends from that day on.

With all these new patients, Robert's practice was taking off. He was now ready to move his family into a house more befitting their station. From his in-laws' perspective, it was about time. The Clements were living in the president's mansion, pretty much an estate, back at Atlanta University, and they felt their daughter and granddaughters had been holed up long enough in that walk-up apartment off Jefferson. It was enough that Robert had taken the three of them away from Atlanta and the Clements as it was. When was he ever going to make good on his potential, all his talk, and give Alice and the girls the luxuries to which the Clements had made them accustomed? It had been eighteen months already.

Robert found a way out. He located a house on an exclusive block of Georgians and avant-garde contemporaries with putting-green lawns and bougainvillea draping the sides of vanilla stucco walls. The block was in a neighborhood known as West Adams, just south of Pico, a few minutes' drive from Wilshire, and on the western side of Crenshaw. It already had a few colored people living there—the fights over restrictive covenants had occurred a decade before, so he wouldn't have to make a political statement just to move into a house, which, apolitical as he was, would not have interested him. He chose not to try to integrate a new neighborhood, although, by then, he could have afforded most any he wanted. Two court rulings—*Shelley v.* and *Barrows v.*—had struck down restrictive covenants by the time he arrived, but whites were still resisting black incursions into the strongholds of Glendale, Canoga Park, Hawthorne, South Gate, and through most of the San Fernando Valley. There was a bombing near Culver City and cross burning in Leimert Park.

Some neighborhood groups went so far as to buy up properties themselves, "even at a financial loss, to prevent blacks from moving in," wrote the historian Josh Sides.

But the San Fernando Valley suburb of Pacoima got especially creative when a black government worker named Emory Holmes moved in with his family in 1959. The neighbors put their heads together and decided to make calls to every business in town posing as Holmes or his wife. The first week in the neighborhood, the Holmeses were flooded at odd times of the day with visits from "a life insurance sales representative, a milk delivery service, a drinking water company, three repair services, several taxis, an undertaker, a *Los Angeles Times* newspaper carrier, a veterinarian, a sink repair service, a termite exterminator, a pool installer," Sides wrote. Finally, the neighbors threw rocks through their windows and spray-painted their garage: BLACK CANCER IS HERE. DON'T LET IT SPREAD!

Robert wasn't going to put himself through that. He found a safe place that suited him. Not only were black people there already, but they were among the finest and most socially connected in all of old Los Angeles. The house was a white Spanish Revival at 1680 Victoria Avenue, right next door to the most prominent colored architect in Los Angeles and maybe the country, Paul Williams. The street had physicians and dentists and socialites on it, people who regularly made the society pages of *The Los Angeles Sentinel.*

The family moved in on Palm Sunday 1956, three years after Robert's lonely drive through the desert. The girls each chose a room. The sofas and cocktail tables and dining room suite arrived. Now Alice could finally join the Links and host her bridge parties and socials, and they could all take up their rightful place, wherever it might lead them, in this bright new city of theirs. In the meantime, shortly before moving into their new home, Robert and Alice got a welcome surprise: a third daughter arrived in December 1955. They named her Joy.

Complications

What on earth was it, I mused,
bending my head to the wind,
that made us leave
the warm, mild weather of home
for all this cold,
and never to return,
if not for something worth hoping for?
—Ralph Ellison, *Invisible Man*

CHICAGO, 1939–1940

IDA MAE BRANDON GLADNEY

THINGS HAD GROWN DESPERATE, and, although she had three little ones at home, Ida Mae had to find some kind of work if they were to survive another year. The options for colored women fresh from the field were limited up north—mainly, to cleaning white people's homes, doing laundry, or working a factory line, if the factory was short of men or of white women. For Ida Mae, domestic work was the likeliest option for now.

It was still the Depression, and it seemed as if the North just didn't know what to do with colored women who were still learning the ways of the cities. Even in the best of times, many industries, while accepting black men for their strong backs, and then only in limited numbers, refused to hire black women, seeing no need to have them around. Throughout the North and West, black women migrants were having the hardest time finding work of all the people pouring into the big cities, harder than Polish and Serbian immigrants to Chicago, harder than Italian and Jewish immigrants to New York, harder than Mexican and Chinese immigrants of either gender in California. They were literally at the bottom of the economic hierarchy of the urban North, the least connected by race and gender to the power brokers in their adopted lands and having to stand in line to hire out scrubbing floors when times got hard during the Depression years.

Some employers started requiring them to have college degrees, which neither they nor the vast majority of other unskilled laborers could have been expected to have. Some demanded that black women take voice tests to weed out those from the South, tests that Mississippians just up from the plantation would have been all but assured of failing. Even those lucky enough to land in a training course for assembly-line work found that they were often shunted to "positions in either the cafeteria or bathrooms."

Entire companies and classes of work were closed off to them without apology. A few years after Ida Mae arrived, a plant in Ohio, for instance, sent out a call for five hundred women, specifying that they be white. The plant had to alter its age limits, lower its requirements, and go to neighboring states like Illinois to get enough white women, who were more likely than colored women to be able to stay at home with their children. Even when it was unable to fill its quota, the plant still refused to hire colored women.

Thus colored women were left to fight for even the most menial of jobs, facing intense competition from the Irish, German, and Scandinavian servant girls preferred by some of the wealthier white families.

There emerged several classes of domestics. Those on the lowest rung resorted to "slave markets" where colored women gathered on street corners from as early as six in the morning and waited for white housewives from the Bronx and Brooklyn in New York or from Hyde Park or Pill Hill in Chicago to bid on them for as little as fifteen cents an hour.

Twenty-five such markets were active in New York City alone by 1940. One was by a five-and-dime at 167th and Gerard near the Grand Concourse in the Bronx, where the lowliest women from Harlem sat on crates waiting to be picked. Another was a few blocks north at 170th and Walton, the waiting women a little better clothed and slightly less desperate, knowing that the Bronx housewives had to pass them first before getting to the market at Gerard. In Chicago, there was a crowded market at Twelfth and Halsted, where colored women jockeyed over the white housewives who were looking them over, the whole enterprise having the effect of bidding down the colored domestics' wages. One woman at the Chicago slave market reported making fifty cents a day, what she would have made picking cotton in the field.

If she were desperate enough, a colored woman needing work would just show up in a white neighborhood, the wealthier the better, and simply walk down the street. "Someone would invariably call out the window," wrote the sociologist Barbara Clegg Gray, and hire the woman on the spot to clean the toilets or scrub the floors or whatever the white housewife discovered she needed for maybe a dollar or two.

In Los Angeles, due to the "great horde of jobless domestics, white families in one of the wealthiest cities in the country could hire colored domestics for as little as five dollars a week" in the 1930s. For that sum, families got someone who would work ten or twelve hours a day doing anything from washing dishes and clothes to cooking and scrubbing floors for not much more than she could have made picking cotton back in Texas.

One colored woman in Los Angeles said she thought getting her high school diploma would make a difference. She kept trying to find different work. Jobs on assembly lines, running elevators, clerking in stores, filing in offices, were typical jobs open to unskilled women in those days. "But everywhere I went," she said, "they wanted to keep me working as a domestic."

The randomness of this kind of work, hiring oneself out to total strangers with no standards in duties or wages, opened domestics to all kinds of exploitation for very little pay. They could never know for sure what they would be asked to do, how long they would be expected to do it, or if they would be paid what was promised.

It seemed everyone was trying to wring the most out of whatever they had, some white housewives even turning back the hands of the clock to keep from paying a domestic for all the hours she actually worked. Older domestics took to forewarning the new ones to take their own clock to work with them and to prepare for any indignity. One housewife ordered a domestic to eat her lunch out of the pet's bowl, not wanting the help to eat from the same dishes as the family.

In many cases, the housewives were neither accustomed to hired help nor familiar with colored people, harboring assumptions and prejudices of the day due to lack of exposure. The housewives and their domestics brought differing expectations, and frequently each side felt somehow aggrieved. While an employer could go out and hire someone else, some employees, having no legal recourse, took their frustrations out on their madames' homes when not paid or otherwise exploited, slashing the draperies they had just ironed or defacing the floors they had scrubbed.

Aside from these sources of friction, colored domestics could not know what perils they might face from opportunistic sons or husbands assuming that younger domestics would do more than just clean. As it was, the very act of walking the streets for work came awfully close in appearance to how prostitutes plied their trade—except that the domestics were working at the whim of Janes instead of Johns.

The expectation that any colored woman walking in the white section of town was available to scrub floors and wash windows would continue into the 1960s, such that a colored professional woman appearing in a white neighborhood in the North had to be prepared to be called out to just because she was black. "Say, girl," a woman called out to my mother in the late 1950s when she was on her way, in her tailored suit and heels, to decorate and fit slip covers in Cleveland Park, a wealthy neighborhood in Washington, D.C. "Could you come up here and clean my bathroom?"

"I'm looking for someone to clean mine," my mother yelled back to the woman.

Ida Mae's husband would not have stood for his wife to walk the streets for work, and in any case, Chicago had grown so segregated that the wealthy white neighborhoods were far from where they lived. But one day Ida Mae got word of a job from someone she knew from back home in Mississippi, and that felt a little safer.

A girl who was doing day's work for a well-to-do couple on the North Side needed someone to fill in for her. It would be temporary, Ida Mae's friend told her, but would have to do for now.

"Miss Gladney will work in your place," Ida Mae's friend told the girl.

The job was more than an hour away on the streetcar, farther north of the Loop than she lived south, almost up near Evanston. The regular girl who mopped floors and folded laundry for the family would be away for a week. The job was paying something like four or five dollars a day. Ida Mae didn't hesitate.

"I was glad to take her place," she would say years later.

She dressed for the job and took a change of clothes with her. It turned out to be a man and his wife living in a grand apartment above a shoe store the wife ran.

Ida Mae took the elevator up and went into a glorious apartment, where she found the husband alone in the couple's bedroom. He was still asleep, which seemed odd to Ida Mae, so she began looking for things to do. The husband roused himself and told Ida Mae what he expected of her.

"Get in the bed with me," he said.

He told her the regular girl stayed in bed with him all day long. He reassured Ida Mae not to worry, he'd do the cleaning later. He figured that was a fair exchange and good deal for her, a cleaning girl not having to clean at all and still getting paid for it.

Ida Mae was in her midtwenties, a mother of three by then, married to a pious man who wouldn't stand for another man touching his wife. She knew white men in the South took whatever liberties they wanted with colored women, and there was nothing the women or their husbands could do about it. All her life in Mississippi, she had managed to avoid unwanted advances because she had rarely worked in white people's homes. Now here she was in Chicago, a white man expecting her to sleep with him as if that were what any colored woman would just naturally want to do. And no matter what happened, she would have no legal recourse. There would be no witnesses. It just would be a privileged man's word against hers.

She was thinking fast. She was as mad at the girl who sent her without warning her of what the job really entailed as she was at the man expecting her to climb into bed with him with his wife just a floor below. She started to leave. But she had come all this way, had spent the train fare, and she needed the money.

Her body stiffened, and she backed away from the man.

"Just show me what you want cleaned," Ida Mae said.

Somehow, something in the way she stood or looked straight at him as she said it let the man know she meant business. He didn't press the matter. He left her alone.

"He didn't say no more 'cause he seen I wasn't that type of person," Ida Mae said years later.

And perhaps in that moment Ida Mae discovered one difference between the North and South. She would not likely have gotten out of it in Mississippi. Her refusal would have been seen as impudence, all but assuring an assault. And there would have been nothing done about it. Here, the northern man seemed to view such a conquest as a hoped-for fringe benefit rather than a right. That, along with Ida Mae's indignation over the whole thing, appeared to keep her safe.

That day, she cleaned the bathroom, the kitchen, the bedroom, and changed the linens as she had gone there to do. The man stayed in his room. She never went back.

She missed out on the rest of the week's pay, which she desperately needed. Later, she confronted the regular girl who worked for the couple.

"So you don't do nothin' but stay in the bed all day, huh?" Ida Mae said. "Don't ask me to go back up there again."

The girl paid Ida Mae out of the money she was making off the couple. The whole sordid affair stayed with Ida Mae for years. She couldn't see how the girl could live with herself.

"I just don't know," Ida Mae would say years later. "Supposing the wife came back home? I just couldn't see how she did it."

With five mouths to feed, the family couldn't go much longer unless Ida Mae found a job. In the fall of 1939, something finally opened up at Inland Steel, over at Sixty-third and Melvina, on the city's southwest side. George had a brother working there. At this point, Ida Mae didn't much care what it was as long as it wasn't day's work cleaning toilets and fighting off the madame's husband.

It was her first real job in Chicago. They called her a press operator. She was in the canning department, where her job was to work the presser that attached the curved tops that cover cans as they came down the assembly line. She had to fit the tops on, her arms going up and down and up and down, over and over and over again.

She was excited at first but then found it to be a nerve-jangling endeavor. The factory was loud, the noise a little like being inside a car engine. The mechanical arms that she operated were sharp and heavy and were known to slice off people's fingers and hands.

She was on the line one day when another worker, a colored woman, got some of her fingers cut off. Ida Mae was a couple of machines down from her.

There wasn't much of a commotion, as Ida Mae remembered it.

"They stopped everybody for a while," she said. "Then they went out with her so fast. And she never did come back."

Ida Mae quit soon after that. A line job turned up at Campbell Soup, where George was working. It wouldn't last long either, after a woman stole her coat that winter. She got a job at a printing press, and it looked to be a good one. But in time she would get a job at a hospital, Walther

Memorial on the West Side of Chicago, working as a hospital aide. She sterilized instruments, cheered up patients, which was her specialty, and organized the gauzes, bandages, and intravenous lines in central supply.

It took her a while to learn how everything worked and how to get the little scissors and scalpels cleaned just so.

"I wash tray by tray and put the instruments back in there till I learned it," Ida Mae said. "And I learned all them instruments. Some of them I couldn't call the name, but you better believe I know where they went."

Sometimes she would poke her head in during surgery when she dropped off a tray of instruments she had sterilized. She liked to see the babies come into the world, and the doctors let her stay sometimes.

She had been through it four times herself and still marveled at the sight and sound of a new life making its entrance. "They always come out hollering," she said. Just like her babies had.

"You know, that's amazing, ain't it?" she said.

With Ida Mae working, the family could move out of the one-room apartment at Twenty-first and State and into a flat big enough for everyone. In the coming years, they would live all over the black belt.

Now that they were getting situated, people from back home in Mississippi started to make their way north to stay or to visit and see what it was like.

Saint, who had helped them move their things from Edd Pearson's plantation and get out of Mississippi, came up with his wife, Catherine, and their children, and stayed for good. Ida Mae's brother-in-law Aubrey, her younger sister Talma's husband, came up for a while to see if he would like it, but he didn't and moved back to Mississippi, where the people tipped their hat to you as they passed and looked up to him because of his family's long years in the South, where he had made peace and found a way to get along with the white people and benefit from it. Joe Lee, whose flogging was the reason George and Ida Mae had left, even came up and lived there for a while. But he was never quite right after all he had been through. He never married and did not make out very well or live too long, and nobody cared to talk about him very much.

One time, George's brother Winston, whom everyone called Win, came up from the plantation just for a visit and wasn't ashamed to look up at the tall buildings reaching for the sky.

George took him around the first day, and at the end of it they settled in for the night. Win got ready for bed and then started calling for his brother.

"Come help me," Win said. "I can't blow this light out."

George found him standing by the bulb. Win had been blowing on the bulb until he was almost out of breath.

"Win, you can't blow it out, you got to turn it off," George told him, reaching for the light switch and shaking his head. It hadn't been that long ago that he, too, had been callow to the New World.

"George showed him how to cut it off," Ida Mae said, "and we never had no more trouble with him."

They were becoming Chicagoans now. They would talk about Win and that lightbulb for years.

It was only a matter of time before just about every colored family in the North, unsettled though they might have been, got visitors as George and Ida Mae did. There was a back-and-forth of people, anxious, giddy, wanting to come north and see what all the fuss was about. And whenever a colored guest paid a visit while the Migration was on, and even decades later, he or she could be assured of finding the same southern peasant food, the same turnip greens, ham hocks, corn bread in Chicago as in Mississippi.

But the visitors were a curiosity to the children of the North. The uncles and cousins from the South often had a slow-talking, sweetly alien, wide-openness about them that could both enchant and startle some of the more reserved nieces and nephews who barely knew them, as was the case with a character from Mississippi visiting relatives in Pittsburgh in August Wilson's *The Piano Lesson* in the following exchange:

> BOY WILLIE: *How you doing, sugar?*
>
> MARETHA: *Fine.*
>
> BOY WILLIE: *You was just a little old thing last time I seen you. You remember me, don't you? This your Uncle Boy Willie from down South. That there's Lymon. He my friend. We come up here to sell watermelons. You like watermelons?*
>
> (MARETHA *nods.*)
>
> *We got a whole truckload out front. You can have as many as you want. What you been doing?*
>
> MARETHA: *Nothing.*

BOY WILLIE: *Don't be shy now. Look at you getting all big. How old is you?*

MARETHA: *Eleven. I'm gonna be twelve soon.*

BOY WILLIE: *You like it up here? You like the North?*

MARETHA: *It's alright.*

BOY WILLIE: *That there's Lymon. Did you say hi to Lymon?*

MARETHA: *Hi.*

LYMON: *How you doing? You look just like your mama. I remember you when you was wearing diapers.*

BOY WILLIE: *You gonna come down South and see me? Uncle boy Willie gonna get him a farm. Gonna get a great big old farm. Come down there and I'll teach you how to ride a mule. Teach you how to kill a chicken, too.*

NEW YORK, 1950S

GEORGE SWANSON STARLING

GEORGE WAS JUST BACK ONE EVENING from a forty-eight-hour turnaround from New York to Florida and to New York again and had gotten his check and cashed it. Rather than head straight home to Inez, he thought he'd stop and get a drink at a bar near Penn Station.

He was with another colored railroad attendant, chugging his beer as the bar filled up. He and his co-worker barely noticed that everyone else at the bar happened to be white as they regaled each other with stories from riding the rails. When it was time to go, they paid their tab and put their glasses down.

The bartender had said very little to them the whole time they were there. Now the bartender calmly picked up their glasses, and instead of loading them into a tray to be washed, he took them and smashed them under the counter. The sound of glass breaking on concrete startled George and his co-worker, even though this wasn't the first time this had happened to them, just not at this bar, and it attracted the attention of other patrons.

"They do it right in front of us," George said. "That's the way they let us know they didn't want us in there. As fast as you drink out of a glass and set it down, they break it."

There were no colored or white signs in New York. That was the unnerving and tricky part of making your way through a place that looked free. You never knew when perfect strangers would remind you that, as far as they were concerned, you weren't equal and might never be. It was just the prerogative of whoever happened to be in a position to keep you from getting what the law said you had a right to, because nobody was going to enforce it anyway.

And so the glass he drank from went crashing under a counter in Manhattan.

It was hitting George in all directions. At sudden and unexpected times like these in New York, in crude and predictable ways when he went back south for his job, and now on the train itself. He was a stickler for rules and regulations and businesslike comportment even if it was only for lifting and loading bags. He was in uniform and was representing not just the railroad but himself and colored people, and he took the job of attending to his passengers seriously.

His formal bearing did not sit well with some of the southern conductors he worked for, who considered him acting above his station, which to his mind he was. He still saw himself as the college boy, someone who read the newspapers, kept up with world affairs, and knew as much as most anyone he was serving. The white southerners he worked with didn't like it any more than the grove foremen did.

"They kept me at a hardship," George said.

Somehow, without trying, he managed to get on the bad side of a southern conductor out of Tampa.

The conductor liked to tease and joke with the colored attendants, one in particular. The conductor would nudge and kick the colored attendant, and the colored attendant, knowing his place, would jump and laugh and, to George's mind, put on a show for the conductor.

"Hah, hah, don't do that, Cap!" the colored attendant would josh the conductor in mock protest.

George stood stone-faced and made no attempt to hide his disdain.

Now the conductor began making extra demands on them all. He liked to make the rail attendants wipe the railcar steps while the train was moving. He got a kick out of that.

He wanted the attendants to drop the traps of the bottom step and wipe the steps down so he wouldn't get dirt on him when he got off to direct passengers at the station. Usually, it was something the attendants did once the train had stopped. The conductor didn't want that. He liked to see them bending over, dangling along the side, and struggling to wipe the bottom step while the train was running twenty-five, thirty miles an hour.

George resisted wiping the steps until he thought it was safe. The other car attendant did as the conductor ordered. George stood to the side, his face pinched and frowning, as his co-worker tried to hold on and clean the step with the train rocking toward the station and the conductor chortling at the sight of it.

One day the conductor confronted George.

"What's the matter with you, boy? You can't laugh?"

"Yes, sir, I have a good sense of humor," George said. "But I don't see anything funny about what y'all are doing."

The conductor began singling out George from that day on, blocking him in the aisles, jabbing him as he passed. There was little George could do about it and still keep his job. George had been through worse things in the South and figured it was just one more thing he would have to watch out for.

But it got to the point that, when George saw him coming down the aisle to check tickets, he had to step between the seats to avoid a confrontation.

"He got to the place when he get along about where I was," George said, "and he would step out of the aisle in between the seats and step on my foot, like that. And then he'll walk back and look at me."

George thought to himself, *"I don't know how I'm a deal with this 'cause he gonna do this one day and I'm a try to kill him."*

"I was praying that I never had to reach that point," he said.

One afternoon, they were pulling out of Clearwater on the Silver Star, a sleek, steel-encased all-reserve train that was the pride of the Seaboard Air Line Railroad. It went up the west coast of Florida along the Gulf of Mexico en route to New York. It had only the finest and highest-class people on it, as George remembered, and he had worked his way up to that route.

As the train gained speed as it headed out of the station, George was helping an elderly white lady with her two bags. He had gotten one bag into the rack overhead and was heaving the second bag over the edge of the compartment.

"And just as I went up with the next bag and set it up in the rack," George said, "something hit me from behind like a truck. *Boom!*"

The conductor, a sturdy and heavyset man, had knocked into George as George tried to steady himself on the moving train while holding the bag overhead. George's knees were bad from all the basketball he had played in high school, and, standing on the train rocking as it was, he was off balance and had nothing to hold on to.

"He come up from behind me like a football player blocking the line," George said.

The conductor shoved George into the seat where the passenger was. George managed to drop the bag onto the rack and not onto the elderly white passenger. But the force of the conductor's weight knocked George over onto the lady, a precarious situation for a colored man in the South.

The train rumbled from side to side as George stood and tried to straighten himself. He suspected he knew what had happened but looked around anyway and saw the conductor in the aisle grinning. This feud was escalating to a point that was getting dangerous for George. If the passenger were hurt or frightened by a colored man sprawled over her as he was, George would be the one to take the fall for it, and the conductor knew it. If the passenger grew hysterical and accused George of attacking her, there would be nothing George could do, and far worse could happen to him.

But it was a fortunate thing for George that the white woman saw that he had been pushed and did not let it rattle her.

"Well, what's wrong with him?" she asked George.

"Miss, you know what he was trying to do?"

She shook her head no.

"He was trying to make me drop that bag on your head. He's just that mean, and he just don't like nobody. He did that to try to make me drop that bag on your head."

"What is wrong with him?"

George started telling his story about how the conductor had been harassing him all this time, and now the conductor had pushed him and didn't even seem to care about the passengers' safety, and she listened because she had seen it for herself.

"Well, something needs to be done about that."

"Yes, ma'am. But they just don't pay me no attention if I try to do anything about it."

He paused. "But you could do something about it."

"Well, who do I write?"

"You just write it, and I'll send it," he said, not wanting to risk her forgetting about it or just not getting around to it. "You write it, and give it to me."

And so the woman wrote up her complaint and gave the letter to George. He, in turn, attached a letter of his own and sent it to the superintendent in Jacksonville, Florida, who was over that route at that time.

George never heard from the superintendent's office about the harassment he had endured.

"But when they saw her letter, they immediately went into action," he said.

The office called the conductor in to question him about the white woman's complaint and suspended him for sixty days. It wasn't long before the conductor found out that it was George who had had a hand in the suspension, and, of course, that did not sit well with him.

George only heard the outcome from other attendants and never got a response himself. Still, it could be said that he had emerged victorious. And that only created more trouble for him. He had expected as much and had prepared for it. When he dropped off the woman's letter, he decided to do it on the way north, so that by the time it got into the superintendent's hands, George would be well out of Florida and out of the conductor's orbit.

Back in New York, he went straight to the railroad office to get a route change.

"Look, I'm not going back to the west coast anymore," George told the dispatcher. "I had an incident down there with a conductor. I know it's gonna be rough. And I'm not going back down there."

George proposed switching with another attendant who had always wanted the coveted all-reserve train to Tampa–St. Petersburg but didn't have George's seniority. George was willing to take a less desirable route to avoid any more trouble.

"No, you can't do that," the dispatcher told him.

"Look, I just told you I had an incident down there. I'm not going back down there 'cause I know what they're contemplating. I'm not going back."

"Well, I don't know what to tell you. You can't change."

George decided to call the other attendant himself.

"Look, you been raving you wanna run to St. Petersburg. I tell you what, when we come out Saturday, you set up in my car in the west coast and I'll set up in your car going to Miami. We'll just switch. You can go to St. Pete, and I'll take your run to Miami."

The attendant took George's old route, was happy to take it, and, when George's stand-in got to Tampa, a group of white men met him at the train.

"Yeah, which one of you boys is that nigger boy called Starling? You George Starling?"

"No, sir, I ain't no George Starling."

"Why, by God, where is he?"

"Well, he's not on here."

"Well, by God, we gonna find him. He done got Captain Wills put in the street for sixty days, and we gonna teach him a lesson."

When the car attendant who traded routes with George got back from that first run to Tampa, he went to George and told him what had happened.

"Boy," he said, "I don't know what you did down there, but they mad with you down there. Don't you go back down there."

"Why you think I switched with you?" George asked. "You tell them, don't worry, I'm not coming back down there no time soon."

George didn't go back to Tampa for five years. New conductors and managers came in, and it was only then that George felt it safe to go back.

LOS ANGELES, 1961
ROBERT JOSEPH PERSHING FOSTER

IT WAS WELL INTO THE NIGHT of March 20, 1961, when the telephone rang at the Foster house on Victoria, and Robert took the call. A nearly hysterical voice was coming at him, and Robert tried to make out the facts tumbling out from the other end of the line. It was the wife of a man who had somehow stumbled and sliced his left hand on the edge of a glass table, severing an artery. The man was hemorrhaging and losing consciousness. The man would need to be seen right away.

Robert would drop everything for any of his patients and had done so countless times, to the detriment of his own family. But this injury got his attention more than most. It was a disoriented Ray Charles, who was facing the loss of the use of his left hand, a disaster for the piano-playing singer, or, with all the bleeding he sustained, the loss of more than that.

The circumstances of the fall were unclear and only made the situation more delicate. For several days, Ray had been under pressure to write a playbook of songs for a big tour coming up. He had put in long hours, dictating the music in his head to a collaborator writing the songs down on paper. He had been up most of the previous night, had worked all day and into a second night. He was finding it hard to stay alert, and he was running out of time. He had turned to drugs before and so now summoned his heroin dealer to help him get through the night, according to his biographer Michael Lydon.

After the dealer's last visit to Ray's house near Baldwin Hills, Ray went thrashing about alone in his den, knocking into walls and furniture, out of his mind. Ray would later say the episode had less to do with drugs than fatigue, although he was candid about his drug use. "I didn't see how the dope was hurting," he said in his 1978 autobiography, *Brother Ray*. "I don't mean I wasn't sick now and then in those years, 'cause I was. I'd hit a dry period and go through the same convulsions as any other junkie."

As for the events leading up to that night, he said, "I'm sure that sometime during that day—like all days—I had my little fix and maybe it was stronger than usual."

That night, as he remembered it, he collapsed from exhaustion and "somehow, in my state of unconsciousness, I slammed my hand against a glass table top and sliced it to ribbons." His hand went numb. He was so high, exhausted, or just out of it, the injury didn't register with him. And he just lay there, "bleeding like a hog."

It was around that time that his son, Ray, Jr., ventured into the den. Little Ray was six years old and wanted to say good night to his father. The boy opened the door to his father's den and found him with his shirt covered in blood and blood on the walls.

Ray's writing partner and his drummer rushed in to help him. They wrapped his hand in beach towels, soaking up two quarts' worth of blood, and tried to get him walking to keep him from losing consciousness.

They chose not to call an ambulance under the circumstances. His wife, Della Bea, then eight months pregnant, instead called Robert, who told them to meet him at his clinic at once. Ray arrived at Robert's office on West Jefferson Avenue bleeding so heavily that he went into convulsions. Robert quickly sewed the wound and admitted Ray into the hospital, where Ray required a transfusion of four pints of blood.

There Robert examined Ray more closely and discovered that Ray had not only sliced an artery but severed a tendon as well. Robert would have to perform emergency surgery to reconnect the tendon if Ray was to regain use of his hand. After the surgery, Robert told Ray he was not to use the hand for six weeks.

"Naturally, I refused," Ray said years later. His big tour was starting the next week, so he told Robert he would just play with one hand. A publicist had already devised an explanation for the public. They would say he had slipped in the bathtub.

Robert could not have been pleased with Ray's insistence but knew him well enough not to be surprised. With Ray determined to go on tour against doctor's orders, Robert insisted on going along with him to attend to the wound should anything happen to it, which, naturally, it did.

Robert put a cast on the hand to protect it, but that only seemed to attract attention and endanger it more. "Everyone I met couldn't resist touching it or shaking it," Ray recalled. "The hand did get infected, but Bob was there to keep me straight."

The tour was a dream of Ray's from back when he had gotten his start in those Jim Crow towns in Florida, where he could just see himself leading a big band like Duke Ellington's—with trombones, trumpets, saxophones, guitars, him on piano, of course, and the Raelettes, his doo-wopping backup singers in their form-fitting sequins and stilettos.

Robert traveled with them to St. Louis, checking on his most famous patient's most precious instrument and loving his front-row seat to smoke-filled celebrity. The tour continued on to Detroit, where Ray struck up his orchestra and somebody decided to bring a blind teenager onto the stage. It was said that the teenager had been signed up by a new outfit called Motown and could sing and play the harmonica. It was Stevie Wonder, "Little Stevie," as he was known back then, who, not surprisingly, idolized Ray Charles and got the chance to play a few songs with him that spring night in Detroit.

Ray's hard-driving life of drugs and women was beginning to catch up with him—he would end up arrested for drug possession in Boston and would end up fathering a total of twelve children, only three of them by his wife, Della Bea, who divorced him in 1977.

But it occurred to him as he was writing his biography that he did not want to leave the wrong impression about his physician, a man he described as "one of the dearest people I've ever known."

He said: "I must say something about Bob, though, before anyone gets the wrong idea. Although he was my personal friend, and although he traveled with me for about ten days during the time my hand was in the cast, I never let him do anything illegal for me. I liked him too well for that. If you really love a person, you won't get him involved in something which might hurt him."

The hand began to heal, and after a week and a half on the road, Robert felt it safe to return to Los Angeles and to his practice. "He sewed up my hand so smoothly that you can barely detect the cuts today," Ray said years later. "He's the man who got me through the crisis with my hand, and for a piano player, that's some serious business."

It was time for Robert to leave the tour for another reason. Not only did he have a life and practice back in Los Angeles, he had another patient to attend to. Ray's wife, Della Bea, was expecting her third child and wanted Robert to deliver her baby. She had had a difficult delivery with her first son before she had heard of Robert Foster and had now come to rely on him.

The baby was born in May of 1961. It was a boy. After all that had happened in the preceding month and the time spent tending them before that, the couple decided to name the new baby Robert.

THE NORTH, 1915–1975

FROM THE VERY BEGINNING, scholars would debate the effects of the Migration, whether it was a success or a failure, whether the people who left had done better by leaving or would have been better off staying, whether the poorest among them merely imported the disorganized family systems inherited from slavery and carried into sharecropping or whether the anonymous, overpacked cities merely brought out the worst in the weaker souls. Usually these were macroeconomic, sociological questions as to the effect of the North or South on the people who left or stayed.

But back when the Migration first began, the venerable Chicago

Commission on Race Relations, convened after World War I, chose to ask the migrants themselves about their perceptions of how they were faring in the North. These were a few of their responses:

Do you feel greater freedom and independence in Chicago? In what ways?

- *Yes. Feel free to do anything I please. Not dictated to by white people.*
- *Yes. Can vote; no lynching; no fear of mobs; can express my opinion and defend myself.*
- *Yes. Feel more like a man. Same as slavery, in a way, at home. I don't have to give up the sidewalk here for white people.*
- *Sure. Feel more freedom. Was not counted in the South; colored people allowed no freedom at all in the South.*

What were your first impressions of Chicago?

- *When I got here and got on the street car and saw colored people sitting by white people all over the car I just held my breath, for I thought any minute they would start something. Then I saw nobody noticed it, and I just thought this was a real place for colored people.*
- *Was completely lost, friend was to meet me but didn't and I was afraid to ask anyone where to go; finally my friend came; was afraid to sleep first night—so much noise; thought the cars would finally stop running so I could rest.*
- *Always liked Chicago, even the name before I came.*
- *Didn't like it; lonesome, until I went out.*
- *Liked Chicago from the first visit made two years ago; was not satisfied until I was able to get back.*

In what respects is life harder or easier here than in the South?

- *Easier, you can make more money and it means more to you.*
- *Find it easier to live because I have more to live on.*
- *Earn more money; the strain is not so great wondering from day to day how to make a little money do.*
- *Harder because of increased cost of living.*

WHAT DO YOU LIKE ABOUT THE NORTH?

- *Freedom and opportunity to acquire something.*
- *Freedom allowed in every way.*
- *Freedom of speech, right to live and work as others. Higher pay for labor.*
- *Freedom; privileges; treatment of whites; ability to live in peace; not held down.*
- *Freedom of speech and action. Can live without fear, no Jim Crow.*
- *The schools for the children, the better wages, and the privileges for colored people.*
- *The people, the freedom and liberty colored people enjoy here that they never before experienced.*

WHAT DIFFICULTIES DO YOU THINK A PERSON FROM THE SOUTH MEETS IN COMING TO CHICAGO?

- *Getting accustomed to cold weather and flats.*
- *Rooming and "closeness" of the houses.*
- *Growing accustomed to being treated like people.*
- *Getting used to the ways of the people; not speaking or being friendly; colder weather, hard on people from the South.*
- *I know of no difficulties.*

ARE YOU ADVISING FRIENDS TO COME TO CHICAGO?

- *Yes. People down there don't really believe the things we write back; I didn't believe myself until I got here.*
- *No. I am not going to encourage them to come, for they might not make it, then I would be blamed.*
- *Wish all the colored folks would come up here where you ain't afraid to breathe.*

The River Keeps Running

"Why do they come?" I asked a Negro minister in Philadelphia. "Well, they're treated more like men up here in the North," he said, "that's the secret of it. There's prejudice here, too, but the colour line isn't drawn in their faces at every turn as it is in the South. It all gets back to a question of manhood."

—Ray Stannard Baker, *Following the Color Line*

"Every train, every bus, they were coming."

—Manley Thomas, *a migrant from Tennessee to Milwaukee*

WHITFIELD, MISSISSIPPI, FEBRUARY 7, 1958
IDA MAE BRANDON GLADNEY

IT WOULD BECOME LEGEND in Chicago among the migrants and their children, the lengths to which some colored people would go to get out of the South. The Great Migration was now into its fourth decade. People who were children when it began were well into middle age. And back in Mississippi, people were still trying to escape. Ida Mae would hear about these people and pray for them.

One of the most desperate souls was a perfectly well man named Arrington High, who had been consigned to the Mississippi State Hospital for the Insane for protesting the southern order of things. The hospital and its hundred or so outbuildings, originally called the Mississippi Lunatic Asylum, took up some three thousand isolated acres in the pine woods southeast of Jackson, near Terrapin Skin Creek, in a place called

Whitfield, some 170 miles from where Ida Mae was born. From the time it opened in 1935, anyone saying, "They took him to Whitfield," meant nobody ever expected to see the person again.

What got Arrington High in trouble was a weekly newsletter he published that argued for integration. He had been editor of a two-page mimeographed broadside, the *Eagle Eye,* for some fourteen years and had made a name for himself protesting the treatment of colored people in central Mississippi. What got him declared insane, however, was exposing the segregationists who were consorting with prostitutes at a colored brothel that catered only to white politicians. It was a death wish of a crusade that actually may have fit the legal definition of insanity for a colored man in Mississippi at the time.

High was taken into custody and committed to the insane asylum in October 1957. It was a sentence that would shut him off, at age forty-seven, from the rest of the world and his wife and four children for the remainder of his life. He was held in confinement deep in the woods, surrounded by guards and hospital personnel, a good fifteen miles from the nearest city. It amounted to a total silencing of a revered dissident of the Mississippi order of things and a slow death in a crazy place where he would be subjected to whatever indignities his keepers devised.

The world of Mississippi and the world of Chicago were intertwined and interdependent, and what happened in one did not easily escape the notice of the other from afar. Word of his capture made it to Chicago. Ida Mae, a faithful reader of the *Chicago Defender* even in the days when it was well past its prime, would take note of people like Arrington High back in her home state and wish them safety.

A colored physician that Ida Mae and most everyone from Mississippi knew through word of mouth, a man named T. R. M. Howard, also made note of what happened to Arrington High. Dr. Howard had founded the Mississippi Regional Council of Negro Leadership, a local precursor to the civil rights groups that would become household names in the 1960s. He organized protests from his base in the all-black town of Mound Bayou in the Delta. But his activities forced him to escape Mississippi a few years before Arrington High was committed to the asylum. From Chicago, Dr. Howard tried to figure out a way to help his friend.

The asylum put patients to work in the dairy and truck farms and the orchards run by the state. Some of the patients had to be up at dawn to work the farms. Arrington High got up at 5 A.M. on February 7, 1958, a Friday, to milk the cows, which was one of his chores.

It was still dark outside, and instead of heading to pasture, he scurried down a deserted path on the hospital grounds and came upon a row of five cars that were parked at the side of a quiet stretch of road.

A door in the second car opened, and he got inside the only car with a colored driver. That car and the four other cars, driven by white men, inched their way to the exit so as not to kick up any more dust or engine noise. There, the white man driving the lead car in the caravan motioned to the hospital guard at the front gate. The guard waved the processional through with a tilt of his flashlight.

Arrington High was out of the asylum but not out of danger. The motorcade took the highway, careful not to drive too fast or too slow as to attract attention. They drove 105 miles through Pelahatchie, Hickory, Meridian, and Toomsuba, Mississippi, to the Alabama line. It would take them more than two hours to get there, and they had to watch for cars tailing them and sheriffs hunting them, as surely by now the asylum officials knew that High had gone missing.

At the Alabama line, the drivers took no chances. They did not cross the state border themselves with their Mississippi license plates. Instead they took Arrington High to the state line and instructed him to get out of the car and walk over into Alabama. There a caravan of five other cars, all with Alabama license plates, were waiting for him. As before, there were four white drivers and one colored driver. The caravan would attract less attention if two colored men were driving together than it would if Arrington High were riding with a white man.

He was in Alabama but still not safe. He was still in the South and within siren call of any Mississippi sheriff. The cars took him to a predetermined location. There waiting for him was a pine coffin. He was told to get inside. The coffin had breathing holes in it for him to get air. The men sealed him in the coffin and loaded it onto a hearse. On top of the coffin, the men placed a load of flowers so that it would appear that the coffin had just been driven from a funeral.

The hearse drove to a railroad station, where the coffin was loaded on a train bound for Chicago. He lay still and quiet, unable to turn over or adjust himself for the fifteen-hour ride to the North.

The moment the train pulled out of the station in Alabama bearing

Arrington High's coffin, Dr. Howard, awaiting word in Chicago, got a long-distance telephone call.

"The Eagle has flown the coop," the voice on the line said.

High made his escape in a ritual of last resort that, in some way or another, had been used to deliver black people out of the South from the time of the Underground Railroad, the slaves using whatever means they had at their disposal. Men disguised themselves as women, women dressed as men to elude detection.

A century before High was nailed into his coffin, a man named Henry Brown, a slave on a tobacco plantation near Richmond, Virginia, began plotting his escape the moment he saw his wife and three young children carted away in chains to some unknown part of North Carolina. His master had sold them off. Brown did not know they were being sold, did not get to hold them one last time, did not know where they were being taken, and would have been flogged or worse if he tried to search for them in North Carolina. He chose to leave the South and the "whips and thumbscrews" altogether. He prayed over it, and it came to him that he should pack himself into a box and get himself "conveyed as dry goods to a free state."

He had a carpenter build a crate of a size commonly sent on the railcars. The box was three feet, one inch wide by two feet, six inches high and had three little gimlet holes for air. Brown then went to a white man he thought he could trust. The man asked if the box was for Brown's clothes. Brown said, no, he was going to get into it himself. The five-foot, six-inch Brown would have to fold himself into the fetal position and remain that way for the twenty-odd hours it would take to reach the North. His white friend did not think it safe and did not want to seal Brown inside the box.

"I insisted upon his placing me in it, nailing me up," Brown wrote in his autobiography, "and he finally consented."

The friend had promised to accompany the box to protect it on the journey, but at the last minute decided against it. Brown would have to go it alone. The friend sent a telegram to an acquaintance in Philadelphia "that such a box was on its way to his care."

The morning of March 29, 1849, the friend carried the box, with Brown folded inside with a few small biscuits, to the express office. There, it was later placed upside down, which left Brown sitting on his head, even though the box explicitly said, THIS SIDE UP WITH CARE. From the express office, the box went to the train depot and "tumbled roughly into the baggage car" where it happened to fall right side up, only to be put on a steamboat upside down again and left that way for close to two hours.

Brown was in agony but dared not moan. He waited for death and prayed. Then he heard the men say, "We have been here two hours and have traveled twenty miles. Let us sit down and rest ourselves." In so doing, the men happened to turn the box over.

The box then arrived at the depot in Washington. There he heard a voice say, "There is no room for this box. It will have to remain behind."

Brown, stiff and contorted and now fearful, had to keep silent. He felt a man's hands reach for the box and squeeze it onto the railcar, his head pointing down again, until someone righted it at the next stop. He arrived in Philadelphia at three in the morning. He had been doubled up in the box for twenty-six hours.

Before daylight, a wagon drove up and a white man got out and inquired about the box. He carried the box to an office on North Fifth Street. Several abolitionists had gathered to witness the opening of the parcel.

They locked the door behind them. But once the box was placed before them, the men seemed afraid to open it. Finally one of them said, "Let us rap upon the box and see if he is alive."

Someone then tapped on the sides of it.

"Is all right within?" the voice asked, trembling.

"All right," Brown replied.

The people were joyful. And Brown was free. He would go on to Boston, which was judged to be safer, and for the rest of his life he would go by the name of Henry *Box* Brown, in light of how he had gained his freedom.

Some one hundred years after Henry Brown shipped himself north, the train bearing Arrington High's coffin arrived at the Twelfth Street station in Chicago. Dr. Howard, the friend who had helped organize the escape, met the train at the station that had come to symbolize the Great Migration itself. The coffin would now have to be transported by hearse to a funeral home. There, a group of men opened the lid and welcomed Arrington High to the receiving city of Chicago. The people were joyful.

How many people fled the South this way during the Great Migration is impossible to know, due to the very nature of the mission. For the operation to work, it required the highest level of secrecy, coordination and planning worthy of the Secret Service, the active and willing participation of sympathetic white southerners, the cooperation of funeral homes in both the departure and receiving states, the complete trust of the person being ferried out by friends and loved ones willing to put themselves in danger to save a single soul, and a good measure of courage and faith on everyone's part.

It would appear from the precision of the Arrington High escape that this was not the first time the people involved in its execution had carried out an operation such as this. To this day, many funeral directors refuse to discuss the matter, admit their involvement, or bring unwanted attention to it—in case, it would seem, it might need to be used again.

"That underground is as effective today in the South," Arrington High told the *Chicago Defender* after his arrival, "as it was during the days of slavery."

It was Dr. Howard who, with the help of more than a dozen others, arranged for his colleague's escape and greeted him upon arrival. He knew what it meant to flee for your life. He did not have to imagine what Arrington High had been through during that dark, cramped ride to Chicago. He himself had to be spirited from Mississippi only a few years before.

NEW YORK, 1957

GEORGE SWANSON STARLING

GEORGE STARLING WAS RUNNING the rails up and down the East Coast, and, as he did, he was in a way running from Inez. George loved Inez. But Inez was not an easy woman to love. There was a storm inside her that nobody seemed able to calm.

It had started long before, when she and her toddler sister were left orphaned right after Inez was born. They were raised by poor, put-upon, Bible-thumping Pentecostal aunts, who couldn't afford two more mouths to feed, and by a Victorian grandmother, who thought the only way to break a girl as stubborn as Inez was to beat her the way the overseers beat their foreparents. They hauled Inez and her older sister to their Holiness church, where the aunts and the grandmother caught the spirit and talked in tongues. Inez's sister did not let it get to her. Inez rebelled from the start.

George had taken a liking to Inez back in Eustis, maybe because she was as headstrong as he was and knew what it was like to feel tossed about as a child by the people charged with caring for her. He hadn't given much thought to the consequences of marrying her, hadn't given much thought to marriage at all. But now he found himself bound to her, with a young son she adored, and as principled and stubborn as he was, he wasn't going to admit defeat no matter how blue and ornery she could be.

There were happy times, when the folks from back home paraded up from Florida. George could regale them with stories from the railroad, and Inez could show off how well they had made out in New York, how much better things were there than down south, how the little country orphan girl was living in a brownstone in the biggest, brightest city in maybe the whole world.

In the summer, it seemed as if there was someone from Eustis coming up every weekend. If George wasn't on the rails, he would throw some ribs on the grill. Babe Blye, who lived upstairs from George and Inez in the second-floor apartment, would drive out to the woods, out to Westchester or Connecticut, and bring back some possum or run to the corner store and get the whiskey and chitlins. Inez and Babe's wife, Hallie Q., would cook up the possum and the chitlins and stir up some collard greens, make the potato salad, and there would be a Florida reunion in the middle of Harlem. Everybody who came up to New York from Eustis knew to stop by George and Inez's place.

Soon, after so many years with just the three of them, their household expanded further. They had a little girl in 1954. She looked just like George and had his temperament. They named her Sonya. Now they had two little ones to raise.

Then, one day in 1957, word arrived about a death in the family that would bring more changes to the household. Inez's sister had taken ill and died back in Florida. She left behind a teenage daughter named Pat, who was bright but distraught and who everyone feared was headed for trouble.

Like many people who had come up from the South, George and Inez sent for the girl to come live with them. Inez wasn't especially happy about her niece coming. Life was hard enough in New York. Inez had put Eustis behind her and was working hard to take care of her own children. She and George had to leave the children alone more than they wanted to as it was in order to meet the house note and the property taxes, the utilities, and everything else that seemed to be high just because this was New York.

But George saw something in the girl, a quick mind and a good heart, and thought they could help her. Besides, he knew that most migrant families that moved up north took in a relative or two at some point or other. It was how a lot of newcomers got situated in the New World, and was the right and southern thing to do.

There were people in Eustis who never left and never wanted to leave and couldn't see why anybody would go up north with all the crime and drugs and devilment. They felt sorry for the sheltered teenager whose mother had taken ill and died in her arms and who now was being shipped up north to live with an aunt and uncle she barely knew in a city she had never seen.

"All the people in my little town saw doom for me," Pat said years later. "Uncle George took me in."

George knew firsthand how the folks in Eustis could be. He told Pat she needed to make the most of the mind God had given her and warned her that there would be people pitying her and expecting her to fail.

"You must not fail," George told Pat, "because they're expecting you to."

But when Pat arrived, George was hardly ever around, working the rails as he was. Inez couldn't hide her resentment, and it was just the two of them, aunt and niece, in the first floor of their brownstone sometimes. Inez told her she would give her a week, and then Pat would have to start paying rent.

Pat protested that her mother had just died, that she didn't have a job yet, she didn't know the city well enough. Inez didn't need to be told how rough life could be. She had never had the chance even to know her mother. She had little sympathy and didn't want her around.

Inez got worried about the money it was costing to have Pat there and would lock the kitchen to control who could get in. Pat would have to sneak in there when the kitchen was open.

"I would go in there and snatch everything I could outta there," Pat said.

One day, soon after she arrived, George and Inez left for work, and Gerard, now twelve, and little Sonya, who was about six, were left alone in the house with Pat, who was still getting used to all the lights and the noise and the perils of the big city.

About ten boys showed up at the front door. Gerard let them in, and they all headed straight for the kitchen.

"They had this white stuff, and they were doing something with it," Pat remembered. She had never seen this in Eustis before. The boys were doing drugs, she later learned.

It was summer, and, each day, after George and Inez left, the boys would show up and head for the kitchen.

"They would come there to roll that stuff and then hit the door," Pat remembered.

The temptations of the city had seeped into George and Inez's house when they weren't looking, when they were out trying to make a living to stay in the city that was swallowing up their son. Pat eventually got the nerve to confront Gerard.

"I'm gonna tell Inez," she warned him.

Gerard knew how much his mother adored him and dared Pat to say anything.

Pat got up the courage to tell Inez. She told her that when she went off to work, Gerard was letting in a bunch of boys, and they were doing dope in the kitchen.

Inez grew enraged.

"How dare you say that about Gerard!" she told Pat.

George wasn't around. He was on the train. And Inez told Pat she wanted her out of the house.

"I don't appreciate you talking about my son taking drugs," she said.

Pat was between jobs, was just a teenager, and had no money. But she was too proud to argue with her aunt.

"Well, if that's what you want me to do," she said.

She gathered what few things she had and started walking, not knowing where she was going. She got to a shoe-shine stand and asked the man if he knew of anyone with rooms for rent.

He took her to the apartment of a sweet old couple. The wife sang with a gospel group, and Pat stayed there until she got on her feet.

George got back from the rails, not knowing what had happened to Pat or where she was. He didn't intercede because Pat was Inez's blood relative, not his. It was only some time later that she saw George and told him what had happened.

"Pat, I had no idea," George said. "I didn't know where you were. She told me you had just left. I had no idea that she had done that."

Inez was her aunt, but it was George she would always be closer to, like a second daughter to him.

"The man cared more about me than she did," Pat said. "Had he been there that day, I would have waited and told him. My pride wouldn't let me."

Pat's warnings turned out to be prophetic. Gerard would only sink deeper into drugs and watch his friends die from overdoses of heroin. One of them they found dead in an elevator. Gerard would go on to steal televisions and radios and cash from his parents, anything of value that they hadn't locked up or hidden away or could be easily carried out the door. He would bring sadness and heartbreak to Inez and especially to George, who could rarely even bring himself to talk about his son. He had come all this way from Florida, and here was something that had turned out worse in ways he couldn't have thought possible.

Gerard would get himself together for a time but would never truly get on his feet. And during those moments of victory, his father preached at him.

"You owe God," he'd tell Gerard. "You owe it to him to go around and tell your generation the evil of dealing in drugs and how he rescued you."

Inez, who had adored and indulged Gerard, retreated into herself and seemed to take the sorrows out on those around her. She had a coat that Pat used to beg her to let her wear.

"A little coat that I loved," Pat said.

Pat had come up from the country with few clothes of her own, and when it got cold she wanted to wear one of Inez's coats, that one in particular. Pat was always talking about that coat.

"Uncle George knew I liked it," Pat said. "Everybody knew I liked it."

One day, after she had moved out, she saw her Uncle George.

"Pat, I got some bad news for you."

"What is it?"

"Your aunt threw that coat you so loved in the garbage can today," he said. "I begged her not to, but she did it anyway."

Pat went to their house and looked in the trash can for it.

"By the time I went there, it was gone," Pat said.

It all came back to Pat, the things the family used to say about Inez, that they could never make sense of "how when she was a little baby, how stubborn she was and how their grandmother would whip them and she refused to bow."

Pat would eventually make peace with her aunt. She would grow up, get married, have a family of her own, and join a church, which was what all of them had been raised to do. Inez never joined a church in New York. It reminded her too much of the hard life she'd had in Eustis and of a little girl's imaginings of how different life might have been if her mother had lived, the mother who died bringing Inez into the world.

Pat managed to convince Inez to go with her on occasion.

And every time, Pat remembered, "she would break down crying, and she'd have to leave the church."

LOS ANGELES, MAY 1962
ROBERT JOSEPH PERSHING FOSTER

THE SONG HIT the *Billboard* charts in May 1962. It stayed there for seven weeks and peaked at Number 20.

The song was by a famous migrant from Albany, Georgia, Robert's most high-maintenance patient, Ray Charles. It was about Robert or, rather, an idealized version of him in a smoke- and drug-filled world of airless recording studios, martini nightclubs, cross-country road tours, and shimmying, wig- and rouge-wearing backup-singer love triangles that was the life of Ray Charles in the sixties and which Robert entered unavoidably and not unhappily as his personal physician during the peak of both men's careers. The song was called "Hide Nor Hair," and the chorus went like this:

Well, I called my Dr. Foster and when the girl answered the phone,
I got a funny feeling, the way she said Dr. Foster had gone.
She said, "He left with a lady patient, about 24 hours ago."
I added two and two, and here's what I got: I got I'll never see that girl no more.

I ain't seen hide nor hair of my baby, since she went away.
If Dr. Foster has got her, then I know I'm through,
Because he's got medicine and money, too.
I ain't seen hide nor hair of my baby, since that day.

Robert knew Ray was working on a song about him, or about a doctor at least. Ray asked Robert's permission to use his name before recording it. Coming as it did just months after Robert had put his hand back together and delivered his son, it was Ray's way of thanking a man he had come to depend on. Robert, always craving approval and enamored of show business, gave him the go-ahead.

Robert wasn't looking to be the subject of a song and really didn't need it. Years later, he didn't talk about it much and, the times he did, it was rather like a footnote. But when it first hit the airwaves back in 1962, his practice took off like never before. He could see the effects of the Migration in his waiting room—former sharecroppers from east Texas, schoolteachers from Baton Rouge, gamblers from Arkansas, Creoles from New Orleans. He ended up with more patients than he could handle, more than was really fair to him or to the patients, seeing as how he liked to spend so much time with each one, get to know them and their lives and desires, and seeing how much they took to that kind of attention. He had more business than he ever could have imagined back when he was dreaming of getting out of Louisiana, trying to convince himself as much as everybody else that he really could make it in California.

It reached the point where the hallway outside his office began to look like some of the train stations during the Migration. Patients started lining up hours before he got there, a reunion of Texans and Louisianans and migrants from Arkansas, spilling out of the reception room and into the outer corridor, patients sitting cross-legged on the floor, heads tilted back against the wall, all waiting to hear their names called. They knew he might still be at the racetrack or just in from Vegas. He'd step over the dangling legs and watch out for their feet as he waded through the crowd to get to his office door.

Some would end up waiting all day to see him, and somehow he made each one feel as if he or she were the only patient in the world. He would stay until ten or eleven at night or until he had seen the very last patient.

It got so crowded, like a Saturday-night rent party, that some people just couldn't take the waiting anymore, no matter how good he was. Reatha Gray Simon, his mentor Dr. Beck's granddaughter, had a brief falling-out with him over the fact that she practically had to block out a whole day to see him.

"I knew he was sometimes in surgery," she said, "but sometimes he was at the track. The waiting room was like the neighborhood barbershop."

That was just how he wanted it. Gambling and medicine were basically his life. He could lose himself in both and had a hard time walling off his professional and personal lives. He doted on his patients and sometimes went gambling with them. He didn't look down his speculum at the cooks and mailmen he treated and made sure to invite them to the parties he gave.

"Some wouldn't come for whatever reason," he said. The house was practically a mansion, and Robert threw out the red carpet, literally. "Most of them probably didn't feel comfortable. But I was gracious as I could be if they came. I'd bend over backwards to make them come."

The Prodigals

[My father], along with
thousands of other Negroes,
came North after 1919
and I was part of that generation
which had never seen the landscape
of what Negroes sometimes call the Old Country.
James Baldwin, *Notes of a Native Son*

'Sides, they can't run us all out.
That land's got more of our blood in it than theirs.
Not all us s'posed to leave. Some of us got to stay,
so y'all have a place to come back to.
—a sharecropper who stayed in
North Carolina, from Marita
Golden, *Long Distance Life*

SOMEWHERE NEAR CARTERSVILLE, GEORGIA, SUMMER 1956

THE ROAD SIGNS were warning that the 1956 Pontiac with the shark-tooth grille and chrome racing stripes on the hood was drawing closer to the hill town of Rome, Georgia. My mother was driving, only it was clear from everything about her that she wouldn't become my mother for a while. She would have been wearing a poodle skirt with a cinched waist, a scarf folded Marilyn Monroe–style atop her head and knotted breezily at the neck, pressed curls peeking out from the sides. Dark, movie star sunglasses dwarfed her face and shielded her eyes, the eyes scanning for the one thing she needed, could not put off, had to do before pulling into her old hometown of Rome.

The car was brand-new, blue, the color of the flag, as my mother would remember it, with whitewall tires and white side panel trim. But it was dusty from the drive, its windshield spotted and speckled, and not looking anywhere close to the four thousand dollars she'd paid for it. Her sister Theresa, who had followed her up north, was with her, and they couldn't roll into town like that. No migrant could, none would dare let on that their new life was anything less than perfect; they had to prove that their decision to go north was the superior and right thing to do, that they were living the dream and everything was out of a Technicolor movie set.

Besides, the people back home would be disappointed if they didn't put on a show, and so they did. So she would have to find a car wash before she could get so close to town that some neighbor might see her in a dusty old automobile and conclude that things weren't nearly as swell up north as they had been claiming. If she did not find a car wash, it would be all over North Rome before she turned onto Gibbon Street to greet her mother and nieces, who, at that very moment, were praying she was running late because they weren't finished waxing the floors and shining the windows with old pages of the *Rome News Tribune,* hadn't smoothed out the chenille blankets with the cotton-ball fringe in the guest bedroom, the corn bread hadn't risen yet, the African violets needed watering, and what if she pulled up just now?

My mother delayed her arrival and the moment she would see her own beloved mother to stop in Cartersville to get the Pontiac washed and polished. That was the most important thing, after all. She had driven to Rome before, but it was in a Chevrolet, a used one at that. She had not long before started a new job teaching school, bought herself a row house in an all-white block in Northwest Washington, and now had this new car. But it wouldn't mean as much unless the people back home could see the manifestation of all this for themselves.

"We wanted to arrive in the daytime so people would come out looking at us," my mother remembered of the trip she made with her sister. "We tooted the horn, and Mother came out. I don't know why we went to Rome. To show off the car, I guess."

The car, with its precious Washington, D.C., license plates, would cause a commotion, like a UFO from another planet, which is just what she wanted, and all the little children would look at that shiny, chrome-plated car and inspect the tags and ask, "What is a 'District of Columbia'?"

At holidays and in summer, the migrants came home. They would leave a trail of Cadillac dust on Highway 61 in the Delta or along Route 1 through the Carolinas and Georgia. They had prepared all year for this moment of glory, and there were times when in some church parking lots in Grenada or Greenville, there were more Illinois license plates than those from Mississippi.

They had gone off to a new world but were still tied to the other. Over time, the language of geographic origin began to change; the ancestral home no longer the distant Africa of unknown forebears but the more immediate South of uncles and grandparents, where the culture they carried inside them was pure and familiar.

The homesick migrants loaded up their sleepy children in the dark hours of the morning for the long drive to the mother country when there was a death in the family or a loved one needing tending or just to show off how well they were making out up north. When they saw the cold airs of the New World seeping into their northern-bred children, they sent them south for the summer so the children would know where they came from. The migrants warned their children to be on their best behavior, especially when it came to the white people they might encounter.

But the children did not have the internalized deference of their southern cousins. They got into scrapes with the other children and couldn't remember all the rules. One migrant's son, Emmett Till, on a visit from Chicago to Mississippi in 1955, was killed for breaking protocol in some way that will probably never be known for sure, except that everyone agreed it involved something he had said to a white woman, which only served to remind those who left of the rightness of their decision and those who stayed how foolhardy it could be to forget for a moment where you were when you crossed into the very different country of the South.

Ida Mae did not go back often, not because she was afraid but because she had a family to tend to in Chicago. She went back for illnesses and funerals—when her mother, Miss Theenie, took ill and died, and years later, when her baby sister, Talma, got sick and died. Her husband,

George, went back only once—for the funeral of the brother who had raised him, Willie. And even then he did not stay the night; he left for Chicago right away.

Robert Foster did not go back often either. His goal was to get as many of his loved ones from Monroe to move out to California, and he went back only when he had to. Alice had no interest in going, and he did not insist on Alice or the girls visiting Monroe. They would grow up knowing little of their father's small-town Louisiana roots. When he returned home, he put on a show, as would have been expected of him, and made sure it was clear that he was now more California than Louisiana.

It would be a long time before George Starling would feel safe returning to Eustis, Florida, seeing how he had left. Southern sheriffs and planters were known to have long memories and even to go after migrants who had fled north. Some white southerners tried to convince the workers who had fled that conditions had improved. Some extradited people for whatever reason they saw fit.

"Even in the North, refugees were not always safe," wrote Arna Bontemps and Jack Conroy in the 1945 book *Anyplace but Here*. "One hard-working migrant was astonished when a detective from Atlanta approached him and informed him that he was wanted back home for 'spitting on the sidewalk.' "

So George was not inclined to linger in the vicinity of Eustis, Florida. His job on the railroad took him south, but on a line that usually veered west toward Birmingham. The times he worked a train that happened to take him through Florida, he did not leave the station or request permission to go home. The few relatives he trusted drove thirty or forty miles from Eustis or Alachua to meet him at the Wildwood station, bearing gossip, good wishes, and hams. George, in his porter's cap and uniform, leaned out of the coach door to see them and left weighed down with homemade cakes or fresh fish they had caught for him to take back up north.

"Where they stop the train and fuel up, they had to stop there a good little while," George's Uncle Andrew "Jack" Johnson said. "We'd go there and meet him. And most of the time we carry him something. Give him his handout, such as we had."

It was a measure of their pride and devotion that the uncle and his wife drove close to two hours in thunderstorms and waited for however long it took the train to get there for the few minutes they'd get to see him. "He'd have time enough to speak and pass a few words," the uncle remembered, "while the train was fueling up."

One time, George was hauling luggage at the train stop at Wildwood, when up stepped the most feared man in all of Lake County and one of the most notorious sheriffs in the South, Willis V. McCall. The sheriff was just one more reason that George went no closer to his hometown of Eustis than the depot at Wildwood.

McCall was the lawman who had shot two handcuffed prisoners, killing one, as he transported them from one jail to another for an upcoming trial in the Groveland rape case back in 1949. The trial and the subsequent shootings attracted nationwide attention partly because one of the men McCall thought he had killed had actually survived to tell what happened to him. The NAACP field secretary Harry T. Moore and his wife had died from a bomb placed under Moore's bed after Moore had accused McCall of police brutality in the case.

Over the years, McCall would be accused, implicated, or indicted in dozens of cases of prisoners dying under suspicious circumstances while in his custody. He patrolled the colored section in his ten-gallon hat, interrogating and pistol-whipping colored men for any suspicion and putting colored fruit pickers in jail if he caught them not working on a Saturday.

The colored people of Eustis and the rest of Lake County lived in fear of his patrol car crawling through their gravel streets.

"Here come the Big Hat Man," the people would say when they saw him approaching.

People scurried from the street. They cleared the benches on McDonald Avenue and fled behind the storefronts when they saw him coming.

"That bench would be cleared in two seconds," George said.

The sheriff had free rein and used to come into Big George's corner store and drink his sodas without paying.

"Well, see you, George," McCall would tell Big George, slurping on a soda to which he had helped himself.

The day Lil George saw Sheriff McCall, George was loading baggage on a train heading north. The sheriff was there to get an escaped prisoner from one of the railcars. The sheriff saw George on the station platform and recognized him from George's father's convenience store.

"Hey, don't I know you?"

"I guess you do."

"What's your name?"

"My name is George Starling, Jr."

"Oh, you George's boy, heh?"

"I'm George's son."

That was the only time in all the years that Willis McCall was sheriff that George actually spoke with him. George felt safe because he was about to jump up on the train, and so he spoke his mind as he never would have in Eustis.

"I was biggity then," George said. "And he got a little red in the face, and he kind of grinned a little bit."

McCall regained his composure.

"Well, when you coming home?"

"I ain't," George told him. "I live in New York. I ain't coming back to Eustis."

George turned away and hopped up on the train. "I ain't, not long as you still living," he said under his breath.

Emmett Till was perhaps the most memorialized black northerner ever to go south, if only because he never made it back alive and because of the brutal reasons that he didn't. His mother had sent her only child south for the summer in 1955 to spend time with his great-uncle in Mississippi. She never saw him alive again. He was bludgeoned and shot to death a month after his fourteenth birthday. Three days later, two fishermen found his body in the Tallahatchie River. Against the advice of those around her, his mother, Mamie Till, decided to hold the funeral with an open casket, so people could see what Mississippi had done to him.

Mourners and the curious clogged Fortieth and State Streets to line up and see his swollen, disfigured body inside the old barrel-vaulted Roberts Temple Church of God. Many of the people paying their respects had come from Mississippi like Emmett Till's family, had lived and escaped the violence, and here it was being brought back to Chicago in the form of a fourteen-year-old boy. It could just as easily have been one of their children lying there lifeless. How many of them had sent their children south to be with their cousins and grandparents, giving them the same warnings Mamie Till had given her son—that they mind themselves around white people?

Ida Mae went to Roberts Temple Church of God that day in early September and stood in line with the thousands of others waiting to see him. She felt she had to. It took hours to reach the casket. She was unprepared for what confronted her when she leaned over the glass-covered coffin. The undertakers had done what they could, but an eye was out of its socket and the face so disfigured that it did not resemble a human being's. She had to look away.

George said he didn't want to go, and he didn't. He had lived it and seen enough.

Disillusionment

Let's not fool ourselves,
we are far from the Promised Land,
both north and south.
—Dr. Martin Luther King, Jr.

It was a hoax if you ask me. . . .
They're packed tight
into the buildings,
and can't do anything,
not even dream of going North,
the way I do
when it gets rough.
—a colored man who never left Alabama, quoted in *The New York Times* in 1967

CHICAGO, 1951
IDA MAE BRANDON GLADNEY

BY MIDCENTURY, the receiving cities of the Great Migration strained under the weight of millions of black southerners trying to situate themselves as tens of thousands more alighted from Pontiacs and railroad platforms each week. In the spring of 1951, a colored bus driver and former army captain named Harvey Clark, and his wife, Johnetta, faced an impossible living situation.

It was a dilemma confronting Ida Mae and her family and just about every colored household up from the South. There was not enough housing to contain them, and the white neighborhoods bordering the black belt were barricading themselves further, not flinching at the use of violence to keep the walls in place.

Ida Mae and her family moved from flat to flat within those walls. Once they lived in an apartment over a funeral home, where little Eleanor played among the caskets and rode with the undertaker to pick up bodies. As it was, Chicago was trying to discourage the migration of any more colored people from the South. In 1950, city aldermen and housing officials proposed restricting 13,000 new public housing units to people who had lived in Chicago for two years. The rule would presumably affect colored migrants and foreign immigrants alike. But it was the colored people who were having the most trouble finding housing and most likely to seek out such an alternative. And it was they who were seen as needing to be controlled, as they had only to catch a train rather than cross an ocean to get there. Nothing had worked before at keeping the migrants out once the Migration began, and this new plan wouldn't either. But it was a sign of the hostility facing people like Harvey Clark and Ida Mae, as white home owners stepped up pressure on the city to protect their neighborhoods.

"They don't want the Negro who has just moved out of rural Dixie as their neighbor," a city official told the *Chicago Defender* in a story that described what it called a "2-Year City Ban on Migrants."

With close to half a million colored people overflowing the black belt by 1950, racial walls that had been "successfully defended for a generation," in the words of the historian Allan Spear, were facing imminent collapse, but not without a fight. Chicago found itself in the midst of "chronic urban guerilla warfare" that rivaled the city's violent spasms at the start of the Migration, "when one racially motivated bombing or arson occurred every twenty days," according to the historian Arnold Hirsch.

Harvey Clark was from Mississippi like Ida Mae and brought his family to Chicago in 1949 after serving in World War II. Now that they were in the big city, the couple and their two children were crammed into half of a two-room apartment. A family of five lived in the other half. Harvey Clark was paying fifty-six dollars a month for the privilege, up to fifty percent more than tenants in white neighborhoods paid for the same amount of space. One-room tenement life did not fit them at all. The husband and wife were college-educated, well-mannered, and looked like movie stars. The father had saved up for a piano for his eight-year-old daughter with the ringlets down her back but had no place to put it. He had high aspirations for their six-year-old son, who was bright and whose dimples could have landed him in cereal commercials.

The Clarks felt they had to get out. By May of 1951, they finally found the perfect apartment. It had five rooms, was clean and modern, was closer to the bus terminal, and cost only sixty dollars a month. That came to four dollars a month more for five times more space. It was just a block over the Chicago line, at 6139 West Nineteenth Street, in the working-class suburb of Cicero. The Clarks couldn't believe their good fortune.

Cicero was an all-white town on the southwest border of Chicago. It was known as the place Al Capone went to elude Chicago authorities back during Prohibition. The town was filled with first- and second-generation immigrants—Czechs, Slavs, Poles, Italians. Some had fled fascism and Stalinism, not unlike blacks fleeing oppression in the South, and were still getting established in the New World. They lived in frame cottages and worked the factories and slaughterhouses. They were miles from the black belt, isolated from it, and bent on keeping their town as it was.

That the Clarks turned there at all was an indication of how closed the options were for colored families looking for clean, spacious housing they could afford. The Clarks set the move-in date for the third week of June. The moving truck arrived at 2:30 in the afternoon. White protesters met them as the couple tried to unload the truck.

"Get out of Cicero," the protesters told them, *"and don't come back."*

As the Clarks started to enter the building, the police stopped them at the door. The police took sides with the protesters and would not let the Clarks nor their furniture in.

"You should know better," the chief of police told them. "Get going. Get out of here fast. There will be no moving in that building."

The Clarks, along with their rental agent, Charles Edwards, fled the scene.

"Don't come back in town," the chief reportedly told Edwards, "or you'll get a bullet through you."

The Clarks did not let that deter them but sued and won the right to occupy the apartment. They tried to move in again on July 11, 1951. This time, a hundred Cicero housewives and grandmothers in swing coats and Mamie Eisenhower hats showed up to heckle them. The couple managed to get their furniture in, but as the day wore on, the crowds grew larger and more agitated. A man from a white supremacy group called the White Circle League handed out flyers that said, KEEP CICERO WHITE. The Clarks fled.

A mob stormed the apartment and threw the family's furniture out of a third-floor window as the crowds cheered below. The neighbors burned the couple's marriage license and the children's baby pictures. They overturned the refrigerator and tore the stove and plumbing fixtures out of the wall. They tore up the carpet. They shattered the mirrors. They bashed in the toilet bowl. They ripped out the radiators. They smashed the piano Clark had worked overtime to buy for his daughter. And when they were done, they set the whole pile of the family's belongings, now strewn on the ground below, on fire.

In an hour, the mob "destroyed what had taken nine years to acquire," wrote the historian Stephen Grant Meyer of what happened that night.

The next day, a full-out riot was under way. The mob grew to four thousand by early evening as teenagers got out of school, husbands returned home from work, and all of them joined the housewives who had kept a daylong vigil in protest of the Clarks' arrival. They chanted, "Go, go, go, go." They hurled rocks and bricks. They looted. Then they firebombed the whole building. The bombing gutted the twenty-unit building and forced even the white tenants out. The rioters overturned police cars and threw stones at the firefighters who were trying to put out the blaze.

Illinois Governor Adlai Stevenson had to call in the National Guard, the first time the Guard had been summoned for a racial incident since the 1919 riots in the early years of the Migration. It took four hours for more than six hundred guardsmen, police officers, and sheriff's deputies to beat back the mob that night and three more days for the rioting over the Clarks to subside. A total of 118 men were arrested in the riot. A Cook County grand jury failed to indict any of the rioters.

Town officials did not blame the mob for the riot but rather the people who, in their view, should never have rented the apartment to the Clarks in the first place. To make an example of such people, indictments were handed down against the rental agent, the owner of the apartment building, and others who had helped the Clarks on charges of inciting a riot. The indictments were later dropped. In spite of everything, the Clarks still felt they had a right to live in a city with good, affordable housing stock. But the racial hostility made it all but impossible to return.

Walter White, the longtime leader of the NAACP, kept close watch of the case. He had been challenging Jim Crow since the 1920s and compared the hatred he saw in the Cicero mob to the lynch mobs he had seen in the South. "It was appalling to see and listen to those who were but recently the targets of hate and deprivations," he said, "who, beneficiaries of American opportunity, were as virulent as any Mississippian in their willingness to deny a place to live to a member of a race which had preceded them to America by many generations."

It was the middle of the Cold War, and the famous columnist and broadcaster of the day Walter Winchell weighed in on what he called the "bigoted idiots out there," who "did as much for Stalin as though they had enlisted in the Red Army."

That fall, Governor Stevenson, who would go on to become the Democratic nominee for president the following year, told a newly convened state commission on human rights that housing segregation was putting pressure on the whole system. "This is the root of the Cicero affair," the governor said, "the grim reality underlying the tension and violence that accompany the efforts of minority groups to break through the iron curtain."

The Cicero riot attracted worldwide attention. It was front-page news in Southeast Asia, made it into the *Pakistan Observer,* and was remarked upon in West Africa. "A resident of Accra wrote to the mayor of Cicero," according to Hirsch, "protesting the mob's 'savagery' and asking for an 'apology to the civilized world.' "

It was U.S. Attorney Otto Kerner whose job it was to prosecute the federal case against the Cicero officials accused of denying the Clarks their civil rights. Kerner's name would later become linked to one of the most cited reports on race relations in this country. President Lyndon Johnson chose him to head a federal investigation into the racial disturbances of the 1960s. The commission's findings, released in February 1968 as the *Report of the National Advisory Commission on Civil Disorders,* would come to be known as the Kerner Report. Its recommendations would be revisited for decades as a measure of the country's progress toward equality, its stark pronouncement invoked many times over: *"Our nation is moving toward two societies,"* the report said, *"one black, one white—separate and unequal."*

Well into the twentieth century, Cicero would remain synonymous with intolerance and corruption. It would come to be seen in the same light as other symbolic places, like Ocoee, Florida, or Forsyth County, Georgia, where many blacks dared not think of living and thought twice before even driving through, well into the 1990s. By then Cicero was racked by a series of scandals involving a mayor who would ultimately serve prison time on federal corruption charges. Even white immigrant families were leaving Cicero, ceding it to Mexican immigrants. In 2000, the U.S. Census found that, of Cicero's population of 85,616, just one percent of the residents were black, nearly half a century after the riots that kept the Clarks from moving in.

It was an article of faith among many people in Chicago and other big cities that the arrival of colored people in an all-white neighborhood automatically lowered property values. That economic fear was helping propel the violent defense of white neighborhoods.

The fears were not unfounded, but often not for the reasons white residents were led to believe, sociologists, economists, and historians have found. And the misunderstanding of the larger forces at work and the scapegoating of colored migrants, those with the least power of all, made the violence all the more tragic.

Contrary to conventional wisdom, the decline in property values and neighborhood prestige was a by-product of the fear and tension itself, sociologists found. The decline often began, they noted, in barely perceptible ways, before the first colored buyer moved in.

The instability of a white neighborhood under pressure from the very possibility of integration put the neighborhood into a kind of real estate purgatory. It set off a downward cycle of anticipation, in which worried whites no longer bought homes in white neighborhoods that might one day attract colored residents even if none lived there at the time. Rents and purchase prices were dropped "in a futile attempt to attract white residents," as Hirsch put it. With prices falling and the neighborhood's future uncertain, lenders refused to grant mortgages or made them more difficult to obtain. Panicked whites sold at low prices to salvage what equity they had left, giving the homeowners who remained little incentive to invest any further to keep up or improve their properties.

Thus many white neighborhoods began declining before colored residents even arrived, Hirsch noted. There emerged a perfect storm of nervous owners, falling prices, vacancies unfillable with white tenants or buyers, and a market of colored buyers who may not have been able to afford the neighborhood at first but now could with prices within their reach. The arrival of colored home buyers was often the final verdict on a neighborhood's falling property value rather than the cause of it. Many colored people, already facing wage disparities, either could not have afforded a neighborhood on the rise or would not have been granted mortgages except by lenders and sellers with their backs against the wall. It was the falling home values that made it possible for colored people to move in at all.

The downward spiral created a vacuum that speculators could exploit for their own gain. They could scoop up properties in potentially unstable white neighborhoods and extract higher prices from colored people who were anxious to get in and were accustomed to being overcharged in the black belt.

"The panic peddler and the 'respectable' broker earned the greatest profits," Hirsch wrote, "from the greatest degree of white desperation."

It seemed as if little had changed from the hostilities of the early years of the Migration, when colored tenants on Vincennes Avenue got the following notice: *"We are going to blow these flats to hell and if you don't want to go with them you had better move at once. Only one warning."* The letter writers carried out their threat. Three bombs exploded over the following two weeks.

Thirty years later, things were no better and may actually have been worse, as the black belt strained to hold the migrants still pouring in even as the borders with white neighborhoods were being more vigorously defended.

By the late 1950s, Ida Mae and George, now both working blue-collar jobs and their children now adults and with blue-collar jobs of their own, were dreaming of finding a place where they could pool their incomes and live together under one roof. But it would be some time before they were in a position to act or could find a safe and affordable place to go.

At the same time, an urban turf war had risen up around them. Bombings, shootings, riots, or threats greeted the arrival of nearly every new colored family in white-defended territory. The biggest standoffs came between the groups with the most in common, save race: the working-class white immigrants and the working-class black migrants, both with similar backgrounds and wanting the same thing—good jobs and a decent home for their families—but one group not wanting to be anywhere near the other and literally willing to fight to the death to keep the other out.

It was a chilling parallel to the war playing out at the very same time in the South, from the arrest of Rosa Parks in 1955 for refusing to give up a bus seat in Alabama to white troops blocking nine colored students in 1957 on their first day of school in Little Rock, Arkansas, after the Supreme Court said they had the right to enroll.

After World War II, Chicago, Detroit, Cleveland, and other northern and western cities would witness a fitful migration of whites out of their urban strongholds. The far-out precincts and the inner-ring suburbs became sanctuaries for battle-weary whites seeking, with government incentives, to replicate the havens they once had in the cities.

One such suburb was Dearborn, Michigan, just outside Detroit. By the mid-1950s, Dearborn was swelling with white refugees from the city. The suburb's mayor, Orville Hubbard, told the *Montgomery Advertiser* in Alabama that the whites had been "crowded out of Detroit by the colored people." He was more than happy to welcome these new white residents and said, to the delight of southern editorialists, "These people are so anti-colored, much more than you in Alabama."

Having already fled the cities, the newcomers were not going to let colored people into their new safehold. "Negroes can't get in here," Mayor Hubbard told the southerners. "Every time we hear of a Negro moving in, we respond quicker than you do to a fire."

Decades later, the message would still hang in the air, the calculus pretty much the same. By the end of the twentieth century, blacks would make up more than eighty percent of the population of Detroit. Just across the Ford Expressway, the black population of the suburb of Dearborn, the 2000 census found, was one percent.

NEW YORK, 1963
GEORGE SWANSON STARLING

EVERY NIGHT, the violence came into George Starling's living room. He had been watching the nightly news, the grainy black-and-white images of colored teenagers standing up to southern sheriffs, and he could see himself as a young man again, pressing against the barbed wall of the caste system in Florida. Sheriff's deputies were pounding the young people with fire hoses and beating them with batons. This was the South he left. He wondered if it would ever change.

He was on the subway one morning heading to work at Pennsylvania Station in the midst of this southern assault. He got settled in his seat and opened the newspaper. "I looked at the front page," he said, "and there's all these black people down on the ground, and dogs jumping all over them and the cops standing over them with billies and beating on them down in Alabama on a march."

Something welled up in George. Everything raced before him: the cheating foremen in the groves, his running for his life, the hangings and burnings, the little southern dog that would rather die than be black, the bomb going off on Christmas Day under the bed of a good man trying to bring justice to Florida. And then there was New York. Wide open and stifling at the same time. Yes, he was alive, but it was a slow death in a hard city. He was a baggage handler for all intents and purposes and would be no more than that no matter how much potential he had.

The city was pressing down on him and swallowing up his children. It never failed to remind him that he was seen as alien, the Yankee bartender taking the trouble to break the glass George had drunk from rather than use it again. There was no place else to run. And now the heat was turning up in the South again. Hosing and police dogs and people watching it as if it were a made-for-TV movie and the blacks just having to take it like they had for generations.

"I had the paper in front of my face," he said. *"And I got so mad. I dropped the paper down. And when I dropped the paper, I'm looking right in a white man's face just sitting across from me. I had never seen the man before, didn't know him from Adam, but he was white. And the hatred just surged up in me after looking at this thing in the paper. I just wanted to hurt somebody white. And I had to just really restrain myself to keep from just getting up. And that*

was the thing that went on during the whole campaign," as he called the civil rights movement.

George got hold of himself. He pulled himself back from the edge. This thing was driving him crazy, and there was nothing he could do about it. The white man probably never had a clue. George would go about his job on the train, and no one would know the difference. But the despair did not leave him. He still had loved ones in the South. "I was worried about all my family and friends," he said. "I had a lot of people there. My father and mother were living. My brother and all the kids that I went to school with and my wife's people. There were a lot of people that I was concerned with."

He saw the fear firsthand on the faces of colored passengers heading north and in his tense interactions with white southerners when he worked the rails going south. As bad as it was, and as bad as it had been all those decades before, some of the most boldfaced terrors of the civil rights movement were yet to come—the bombing deaths of four little girls just before a Sunday church service in Birmingham, the assassinations of civil rights workers, black and white, Andrew Goodman, James Chaney, and Michael Schwerner and Medgar Evers, the confrontation on a bridge in Selma, Alabama. Those would not come until Jim Crow's fitful last hours.

George kept close contact with the people back home and, like many migrants in the North, sent money to support the protests because the migrants knew more than most anyone what the people back home were up against.

One day in 1962, in the middle of the civil rights movement, he heard something that set him off again. By civil rights standards it was a relatively small thing, and that is what drew him to it. For some reason nothing seemed as fate-tempting and blasphemous as someone setting fire to three defenseless colored churches, as in Georgia in September 1962. They were razed to the ground by white supremacists bent on keeping colored people from something as basic as signing up to vote. George was raised in the church and felt it hallowed and sanctified and the only safe place even the old slaveholders had dared not enter. It represented a breach of the most private, holy space.

He read in the *New York Amsterdam News* that there was a drive on to raise money to rebuild the churches. He started a collection himself. He went to the underpaid cooks and baggage men and redcaps and porters working the rails with him. He got fifty cents here and a dollar there from people like Walter Watkins from Washington, D.C., Ralph Covington from Brooklyn, Van Truett from the Bronx, G. T. Craig from Baltimore, J. E. Aaron of Brooklyn, and thirty-eight other co-workers. It took him four weeks to raise forty-one dollars. In January 1963, he walked over to the office of the *Amsterdam News* and handed a check in that amount to a rebuilding fund the paper was sponsoring.

With George, it was never the money when it came to these things but the sense of indignation over the injustice of it all and about doing something, anything, and getting other people as roused up about it as he was, just like he did back in the orange groves in Florida all those years ago. He had been in Harlem and working for the railroad for eighteen years now and knew he and his co-workers could raise more than a few dollars to help fight bigotry in the region they left.

The *Amsterdam News* soon closed the fund, figuring it had raised all it was going to get. The churches in Georgia had already begun rebuilding with donations that had come in from all over the country. But George hadn't stopped collecting money. He kept a ledger of all the men who contributed and what they contributed, each fifty-cent and dollar increment from Percy Brown of Mount Vernon, Yace Brown of Queens, Adolph Thomas of Philadelphia. In March, George showed up again at the newspaper office with a check for forty-four dollars more.

"I wanted to help in the only way I know," he told the *Amsterdam News*.

LOS ANGELES, AUGUST 1961
ROBERT JOSEPH PERSHING FOSTER

ROBERT WAS IN REGULAR CONTACT with the folks back home, and in one of his phone calls to Monroe, his big brother Madison mentioned that he was due for some upcoming surgery, what seemed on the face of it to be fairly routine, the problem being his gallbladder. But Robert, a surgeon of many years now, knew that nothing involving surgery was routine and urged his brother to come out to California, where he could get the best of medical care. Robert would make all the arrangements, and Madison wouldn't have to submit to the small-town, probably proficient, but still segregated medicine back in Louisiana.

"Come," Robert told him. "I don't want those white doctors in Monroe operating on you. You come out here so I'll know what kind of care you're getting."

Madison had heard about the state-of-the-art facilities in Los Angeles. He knew his brother would see to it that he got the very best—that was just the way Robert was and he couldn't help himself. So, although the trip out west would be taxing, he decided to leave his wife, Harriet, and son, Madison James, in Monroe and follow his little brother's advice and come to L.A.

"He had confidence in me," Robert said.

Robert set about planning the best medical care for his brother. He handpicked the surgeon—board-certified, it went without saying—who was one of his most trusted friends. On the day of the operation, Robert was there in his scrubs in the operating room, serving as second assistant and watching every move.

"And when he picked the knife up to make the incision," Robert remembered, "I closed my eyes and flinched. I felt it. I couldn't assist with that attitude. So the surgeon said, 'Bob, you let Palmer Reed move up, and you step back so I can sponge.' And I settled down."

Robert stayed for the duration of the surgery. "I saw everything, and it was a flawless operation. It was beautiful. There was no mistake made. None."

He felt proud and vindicated that he had insisted that his big brother come out to California and that things had gone so well. To Robert, it was just one more way to prove to the brother who had stayed in the South that he had made the right decision to migrate and that things really were better in California.

Robert was in a great mood and started joking with his brother that maybe he should recuperate at Robert's house or with their sister, Gold, who by now Robert had lured to California, too.

"You wasting money in a private room," Robert said. "Come to my house or go live with Gold."

"Okay," Madison said. "I'll be ready to go. I just don't feel good right now."

Three or four days after surgery, Madison was still saying he didn't feel good. He started sending out for antacids to relieve his abdominal pressure. But he wasn't complaining.

"And he didn't have any symptoms that would make us want to do anything special," Robert later said. "We know there's a certain amount of discomfort you gonna have. He was taking soft foods, and he was up. He was ambulated the next day after surgery. Temperature was flat. He was doing fine."

After several more days, a nurse woke Robert up one morning.

"Dr. Foster, this is Miss Smart. I'm calling you about Dr. Madison Foster."

"Yes."

"He went to the bathroom, Dr. Foster."

Robert heard the gravity in her voice, the succinctness of her message, and knew what it meant, could read her shorthand. Madison must have strained himself and, in the straining, dislodged some plaque that could be anywhere in his body, in his heart, his lungs, his brain. There was no telling where it could be. Robert got straight to the point.

"Is he alive?"

The nurse told him, yes, and that they had called in several doctors to attend to him.

"Fine," Robert said, suspecting that it wasn't.

At once he began calling in the specialists he knew, and then he rushed to the hospital. Madison's hospital room was full of doctors. They were surrounding his bedside, all working on him.

"And I'll never forget the look in his eyes," Robert said, his head down now. "And he's looking at me. And that look in his eye was saying, *'Is this it?'* Little Bubba, he called me. *'Little Bub, is this it?'* He was so worried. And I'm crying and talking."

Robert tried to comfort him.

"Don't worry, Bubba," Robert said. "It's alright. It's gonna be alright."

Madison was a physician himself and knew that it wasn't.

"He knew I was only reassuring him," Robert would later say, "because why would I be crying?"

Robert got on the phone with Madison's wife, Harriet, who was still awaiting word back in Monroe about how the gallbladder surgery had gone. "I gave her an hour-to-hour report," he said. "And that went on all day."

Instead of saving his brother in California, Robert would end up sending Madison back home in a casket, the people in Monroe clucking over Robert's so-called Promised Land and what a shame it all was. Harriet would hold it against him for years. Madison had died of a blood clot; that had been the source of his discomfort, and nothing, it seemed, could have prevented it. Robert would have been the first to blame the doctors if it had happened in the South, but this had been in California, and he had chosen the surgeons and seen the operation with his own eyes. Robert would blame himself for as long as he lived, torture himself with *"What would have happened if . . . ,"* and would never truly get over it.

REVOLUTIONS

I can conceive of no Negro native to this country
who has not, by the age of puberty, been irreparably scarred
by the conditions of his life. . . .
The wonder is not that so many are ruined
but that so many survive.

—JAMES BALDWIN, *Notes of a Native Son*

CHICAGO, 1966
IDA MAE BRANDON GLADNEY

ONE DAY IN 1966, something hopeful called to Ida Mae, who was now fifty-three and a grandmother. She scuttled past the dime stores and beauty shops on Sixty-third Street with Eleanor's little children, Karen and Kevin, in tow. They were rushing in the direction of a quavering voice on a loudspeaker. Up ahead, she could see a crowd of onlookers, the faithful and the curious, packed in the street and on the sidewalks near Halsted and sober-faced police officers circling the crowd on horseback.

She arrived late and out of breath. Years later, all she would remember was the voice saying something about "little white children and little colored children," or so she thought, and all the people, hordes of them, straining to hear but tense from the police scrutiny and the vaguely dangerous nature of the moment.

Dr. Martin Luther King, Jr., was there in person and speaking before them. It was one of his rare appearances in Ida Mae's neighborhood during his first major attempt to bring the civil rights movement to the

North. Ida Mae almost missed it. She arrived too late to get anywhere near the podium. Neither she nor Karen or Kevin could see over the crowd that had gathered long before them.

"They had him way up on something high," she said decades later. "And you could hear his voice talking through those horns."

Ida Mae wanted to move closer to see him. That was what she had come for, after all. "I never did get close enough," she said. "I didn't want to push through the crowd. Everybody was so touchy. And I had kids, you see, and I just couldn't pull them up in there. I never did get to see him good."

Ida Mae was taken in by the sheer presence of the man, who by then had already won the Nobel Peace Prize, led the March on Washington, witnessed the signing of the 1964 Civil Rights Act, and overseen his epic battles against Jim Crow in places like Selma and Montgomery.

But Chicago was a turning point for King. His movement was aging, its actions drawing greater skepticism and its successes leaving him with fewer obvious dragons to slay. It was a campaign looking for a cause. The inroads into southern segregation gave King a greater awareness of the unresolved tensions in the North in the wake of the Great Migration.

"Negroes have continued to flee from behind the Cotton Curtain," King told a crowd at Buckingham Fountain near the Loop, testing out a new theme in virgin territory. "But now they find that after years of indifference and exploitation, Chicago has not turned out to be the New Jerusalem."

Yet the very thing that made black life hard in the North, the very nature of northern hostility—unwritten, mercurial, opaque, and eminently deniable—made it hard for King to nail down an obvious right-versus-wrong cause to protest.

Blacks in the North could already vote and sit at a lunch counter or anywhere they wanted on an elevated train. Yet they were hemmed in and isolated into two overcrowded sections of the city—the South Side and the West Side—restricted in the jobs they could hold and the mortgages they could get, their children attending segregated and inferior schools, not by edict as in the South but by circumstance in the North, with the results pretty much the same. The unequal living conditions produced the expected unequal results: blacks working long hours for overpriced flats, their children left unsupervised and open to gangs, the resulting rise in crime and drugs, with few people able to get out and the problems so complex as to make it impossible to identify a single cause or solution.

King was running headlong into what the sociologist Gunnar Myrdal called the Northern Paradox. In the North, Myrdal wrote, "almost everybody is against discrimination in general, but, at the same time, almost everybody practices discrimination in his own personal affairs"—that is, by not allowing blacks into unions or clubhouses, certain jobs, and white neighborhoods, indeed, avoiding social interaction overall.

"It is the culmination of all these personal discriminations," he continued, "which creates the color bar in the North, and, for the Negro, causes unusually severe unemployment, crowded housing conditions, crime and vice. About this social process, the ordinary white Northerner keeps sublimely ignorant and unconcerned."

Thus any civil rights campaign in the North would not be an attack on outrageous laws that, with enough grit and fortitude, could be overturned with the stroke of a pen. Instead, King would be fighting the ill-defined fear and antipathy that made northern whites flee at the sight of a black neighbor, turn away blacks at realty offices, or not hire them if they chose. The "enemy" was a feeling, a general unease that led to the flight of white people and businesses and sucked the resources out of the ghettos the migrants were quarantined into. No laws could make frightened white northerners care about blacks enough to permit them full access to the system they dominated.

"So long as this city is dominated by whites, whether because of their numbers without force or by their force if they were in the minority," the *Chicago Tribune* once wrote, "there will be limitations placed on the black people."

Still, despite the odds, King was compelled to go north—was called to it, he said—as had a good portion of his people in the still-unfolding Migration. He had made the journey himself when he went to Boston University for graduate school and while there met his wife, Coretta, another southerner. King's campaign in the North was "in one sense simply reacting to a major shift in the epicenter of black America," the historian James R. Ralph wrote. "It was following the great demographic flow of black Americans from the rural South to the urban North."

King actually moved into an apartment in the most hardscrabble section of town, the West Side neighborhood of North Lawndale, where the poorest and most recent arrivals from the South had shakily established themselves. He had a chesslike series of encounters with Mayor Richard J. Daley, the mayor-boss of Chicago, who managed to outwit the civil rights leader at nearly every turn. For one thing, Daley knew not to make the same mistakes as his southern counterparts. He met with King, appearing cooperative rather than ignoring him or having him thrown into jail. He vowed to protect the marchers with a heavy police presence that sometimes outnumbered the marchers. It worked so well that the protesters rarely had the chance to contrast their peaceable courage against foaming-at-the-mouth supremacists because Daley's police force didn't let any white mob get near them, which kept the protests off the news and kept the movement from gaining traction, just as Daley had hoped.

That is until, after months of buildup, King went to march against housing segregation in a neighborhood called Marquette Park on the city's southwest side. This was a working-class neighborhood of Poles, Lithuanians, Germans, and Italians who had not long since gotten their starter bungalows and were standing their ground against the very thought of colored people moving in.

It was August 5, 1966. A fist-shaking crowd of some four thousand residents had gathered in advance. Upon his arrival, they cursed King with epithets from a knoll overlooking the march. Many people in the crowd waved Confederate flags. Some wore Nazi-like helmets. One placard read KING WOULD LOOK GOOD WITH A KNIFE IN HIS BACK.

The march had barely begun when a heckler hurled a rock as big as a fist at King, striking him in the head, just above the right ear. He fell to his knees, and, as he tried to get up, the crowd pelted the demonstrators with bottles, eggs, firecrackers, and more rocks. Some in the crowd turned and smashed rocks into cars and buses that passed with colored people in them. Some twelve hundred police officers and two hundred plainclothesmen had gathered in anticipation of trouble, but this was one of the rare occasions that they were outnumbered by white residents primed for confrontation.

As the eight hundred King supporters tried to carry on the march, they passed men, women, and children on their front stoops, who called the marchers "cannibals," "savages," and worse. A column of three hundred jeering white teenagers sat in the middle of the street to block the marchers' path. The police dispersed the youths with nightsticks waving, and the march was able to resume. But the teenagers repositioned themselves half a block down and sat in the street again. It took a second charge from the police to break up the young hecklers.

When the march wound down, the mob chased the buses carrying King's people away. Rising in agitation that lasted for hours, the mob smashed an effigy of King, overturned a car on Marquette Road, stoned other cars, and fought police trying to clear the place out, requiring reinforcements to beat the mob back with clubs and shots fired into the air. In the end, some thirty people were injured and forty were arrested.

Some of King's aides had warned him not to go to Chicago. He said he had to. "I have to do this," he said as he tried to steady himself after the stoning, "to expose myself—to bring this hate into the open."

He had marched in the deepest corners of Alabama but was unprepared for what he was in for in Chicago. "I have seen many demonstrations in the South," he said that violent day in the Promised Land. "But I have never seen anything so hostile and so hateful as I've seen here today."

Ida Mae watched it on the news that night and worried for the man she so badly had wanted to see. She expected this in Mississippi, not in the North. "No," she would say decades afterward, "some places I just trusted more than others."

NEW YORK, PENNSYLVANIA STATION, MID-1960S
GEORGE SWANSON STARLING

THE WORLD WAS CHANGING, and George, without trying, was on the front lines. In the South, the trains had been segregated for as long as most people had been alive. Now he was in the uncomfortable position of enforcing new laws that were just now filtering into everyday practice.

There he was, scanning the crowds on the railroad platform as the southbound Silver Comet stretched down the track, belching and ready to board. The train would pull out of the station at 12:45 en route to Birmingham with some twenty-eight stops in between. Passengers packed the railway platform, suitcases, hatboxes, overnighters, trunks, briefcases, and Gimbel's shopping bags at their feet.

George went about his job of getting their luggage and helping them to their seats, but this time, he looked the passengers over in a way he never did before. He looked to see if they were in prim Sunday clothes or loud juke-joint get-ups, if the people seeing them off were self-contained New Yorkers bidding people good-bye or excitable southerners still new to the spectacle. He checked to see if they haughtily took to their reserved seats in the integrated railcar as if they owned it or if they were wide-eyed and tentative about sitting in the same section as the white passengers.

George was paying close attention because this was the mid-1960s. The trains in the North had always been integrated, but blacks had to move to separate cars before being permitted into the South. During the run between New York and Alabama, it had been George's job to move the colored passengers from their seats in the white section and into the Jim Crow car before crossing from Washington into the segregated state of Virginia.

But after the sit-ins and marches in the South, things were beginning to change. President Lyndon B. Johnson signed the Civil Rights Act on July 2, 1964, 101 years after Abraham Lincoln signed the Emancipation Proclamation granting rights that would have to be spelled out again long after Lincoln was gone. Now blacks were entitled to the same privileges as any other citizens. They were not to be segregated in any sphere in life. But it would take time, up to a decade or more, for the message to sink in to those who chose not to recognize the new law.

In addition, it was not as if a copy of the Civil Rights Act went out to every black household. Some didn't know what their new rights were exactly and had lived under the old order for so long that they were tentative about testing out the new one. In public conveyances, it fell to workers like George Starling, if they were so inclined—which it so happened he was—to alert their fellow migrants to rights they weren't certain they could assert. On the train, it meant negotiating the tricky business of reorienting the black passengers when the train passed into or out of what had been Jim Crow territory.

For as long as most anyone alive could remember, this was the way things had worked on the railroad: a black passenger boarding a southbound train at, say, Pennsylvania Station in New York would be assigned a seat anywhere on the train and could sit there without a second thought until the train reached the border city of Washington, D.C. From the time of Reconstruction in the 1870s, Washington had been the dividing line between the free North and the segregated South. Black passengers getting off in Washington had nothing to worry about. But for those continuing south, the crews who ran the train, the porters who helped passengers on and off, and the black passengers themselves knew to gather their things and move to the Jim Crow car up front to make sure the races were separated when the train crossed into the state of Virginia.

The civil rights legislation of the mid-1960s changed all that, or was intended to. But custom had a way of lingering well after the ink was dry. So in the transition to integration, black passengers were not automatically granted the right to keep their seats no matter what their ticket or President Johnson said.

George was on the front lines in these early days of integration, when some conductors, many of them southern, held close the old traditions and ordered porters like George to move the colored passengers into the Jim Crow car, no matter the law. Some conductors, like many other southerners, resented the new laws that had been forced upon them. Others could always say that white southerners boarding the train below Washington were still not comfortable riding in the same coach as black people and might kick up a fuss.

As the train drew closer to Washington, the conductor gave George a passenger manifest identifying the passengers he wanted moved to the old Jim Crow car, meaning all the black passengers traveling below Washington.

George knew it wasn't right and began discreetly approaching colored passengers as the train pulled out of Baltimore en route to Washington. He tried to alert them to what was about to happen and let them know they had a right to stay where they were. But it was a perilous act on his part. The passengers might get scared and turn him in. He might be accused of inciting the passengers and disrupting the orderly relocation of passengers who didn't mind moving. It was especially dangerous because he was not heading north on the train but south into what might be considered enemy territory. Either way, he could be fired for what he was doing.

He knew he couldn't be seen openly advising black passengers to defy the conductor's orders. So from the moment he boarded the train in New York and began waiting on the black passengers in his charge, he paid close attention to them, scrutinized them to see which ones might be more receptive.

Then, as the train rumbled toward Union Station in Washington, and when he had made certain that the conductor wasn't around, he began approaching colored passengers, one by one. He leaned over the seat and began speaking in whispers.

"Look," he told them, "what I want to say to you is confidential, between you and me. If you don't think you can keep it confidential, let me know now, and I won't say any more. But it's to your benefit."

"Okay, okay."

Then he would explain the situation.

"Well, now, going below Washington," he would tell them, "they want us to move y'all up front in the Jim Crow car. But you have paid for a seat to wherever you're going. You paid an extra fee to reserve this seat, and you're entitled to keep this seat to your point of destination. But they not gonna tell you that. They gonna tell you, you got to move up front."

He waited for their response, checked for a show of interest and curiosity instead of fear and distrust. Then he would know whether to proceed. If he felt safe, he would go on.

"What you do," he continued, "is tell them that you don't care to move. Just tell them that."

Then he told them what to expect and gave them a little script. "They're gonna give you an argument," he said. "But just tell 'em, 'Look, I have a reserved seat here from New York to Jacksonville. Washington isn't my destination, and I'm not moving anywhere. Now, if you want me to move, you get the cops and come and move me. I'm not voluntarily moving anywhere.' "

He reassured them that they were within their rights. "They're not gon' bother you," he told them. "Because they know if you got nerve enough to tell 'em that you're not gonna move and if they force you to move, that they have a suit on their hands."

But it occurred to him that he needed to protect himself. He couldn't give any appearance of undermining the conductor's orders or inspiring the black passengers to do something that would otherwise never occur to them. So he admonished them further. "And don't go telling them, 'Well, the attendant told me I didn't have to move,' " George said. "Or you'll get me killed. Just tell 'em you're not gonna move. They not gonna move you."

Some of them got scared at that kind of talk. So George gave them an out. "If you feel more comfortable, and you think you should go up to that Jim Crow car when you have paid to ride like everybody else, then you go," he said. "I'll move you."

He forewarned them that if they decided to take the chance, they should know that he would have to feign indifference, pretend to have no knowledge of the matter if the conductor got involved. "He's gonna be telling me to take you up front, and you gonna be tellin' him that you're not going, and I'm gonna just be standing there. I'm gonna be saying, 'Naw, I ain't got nothin' to do with it.' "

By the time the train got halfway to Washington, he had a good idea of who he had in the railcar with him and which of them might be safe to approach.

"You could tell just by who brings them to the station," he said, "how they depart, the conversations."

But sometimes he would misjudge a passenger and come close to getting caught. Some passengers would loud-talk him.

"What? What the hell you talkin' 'bout?" they'd ask, not comprehending his plan.

George would speak in an even quieter whisper to get their voices down, which only meant they couldn't hear him and made them ask more questions, even louder than before.

"What? I don't have to move? How come I don't have to move?"

George would just shake his head and step away. "You know to leave them alone," he said.

What gave George the greatest sense of defeat were the people who went up to the Jim Crow car anyway. "They move anyway to avoid trouble," he said. "Quite a few would move up because the other attendants—they wouldn't tell the people. They wouldn't go to 'em like I would. Some of them would even support the conductor in telling them, 'You better move. You gotta move.' "

George didn't see it that way, and after all he had been through in the South, and even in the North, he felt it his duty to let the people know. It was the same George who tried to rouse the fruit pickers some twenty years before, to get them to stand up for what was due them.

In this case, on the train, George was fortunate. "None of them ever exposed me," he said.

And what's more, of the cases he saw, the people who resisted got to stay in their rightful seats. "Every incident that came up," George said, "they left them alone."

CHICAGO, SPRING 1967
IDA MAE BRANDON GLADNEY

IT HAD BEEN CLOSE TO THIRTY YEARS since Ida Mae and her family had come up north. The children were grown now. And by the late 1950s, the first generation born in the North had arrived. Eleanor, who had come north in Ida Mae's belly, had gotten married right out of high school and had two kids. James and his wife, Mary Ann, soon followed with four kids of their own. Ida Mae held the babies close and prayed for the first members of the family born free in the Promised Land.

There were different branches now, and they were getting by, but still renting and not settled in a place of their own. From flat to flat, in and around the straining borders of the South Side, Ida Mae and her family had moved more in Chicago than they had when they were sharecroppers in Mississippi, as they had never moved in Mississippi like some of the people they knew because they had always stayed with their one planter, Mr. Edd.

They had lived at Twenty-first and State, Thirty-third and State, Forty-fifth and St. Lawrence, and were now in the 700 block of West Sixty-sixth Place. They had been all over the South Side.

They felt they had been in Chicago long enough without owning something. George had been at Campbell Soup for years. Ida Mae was working as a nurse's aide at Walther Memorial Hospital. Velma was teaching, James was driving a bus for the Chicago Transit Authority. Eleanor was a ticket agent for the elevated train. So together, they had enough to put something down on some property.

Not unlike many immigrant families, they wanted to stay together and wanted a place big enough for all of them. Their search led them to a beige brick three-flat in a long-contested but, they believed, newly opened-up neighborhood called South Shore on the southern tip of the black belt. It was a few blocks west of Lake Michigan. The street was lined with oak trees along the sidewalk and brick bungalows and multiflats with little patches of yard in front.

They went to see the place at night.

An Italian car salesman and his family lived there. It had room enough for James and his family on the first floor, Ida Mae and her husband on the second, Eleanor and her kids on the third, or if necessary, a tenant to help with the house payments. Ida Mae and her family didn't have enough furniture to fill the flat. They wanted the place and everything in it: the plastic-covered upholstery, the marble-topped coffee table, the lamps, the dining room table, the breakfront and buffet, and the baby blue draperies over the front windows.

The Italian car salesman said he liked them and wanted them to have it. The family paid thirty thousand dollars and moved in without incident. There was the little matter of a bullet hole in one of the windows in the front room, but Ida Mae didn't let it bother her as it appeared the shot had been fired sometime before they moved in. Thirty years after they arrived in the New World with little more than their kids and the clothes on their backs, Ida Mae and her husband were finally homeowners in Chicago.

"It was beautiful," Ida Mae said years later. "Trees everywhere, all up and down the block."

Weeks passed. Ida Mae went to work one morning and came back that evening on the streetcar over on Exchange. She walked down Colfax in the neighborhood of brick apartment buildings, barbershop storefronts, and frame bungalows along a route that she was just beginning to learn.

It was then that she noticed something missing across the street from her three-flat. A house had vanished. The people across from her had moved it, or so it appeared. There was now a small crater in the earth where, just that morning, a house used to be.

It was a wonderment to Ida Mae and to James and Eleanor and the grandkids. Why would their nice white neighbors move their house clear off the street? Where did they go? What did this mean?

They would never see them again to get the answers. They would never fully know for sure what had happened or why. It would become part of their family lore, one of the things they would tell over and over again, shaking their heads and hunching their shoulders as they looked out their second-floor window at the sociology unfolding beneath them.

As it was, too much was happening anyway. Within weeks of the disappearing house, moving vans clogged Colfax Street. More people were vanishing, but those people left their houses behind. They took their sofas and upright pianos and were gone.

"Lord, they move quick," Ida Mae said years later. "And then blacks started moving in. Oh, Lord."

The whites left so fast Ida Mae didn't get a chance to know any of them or their kids or what they did for a living or if they liked watching

The Ed Sullivan Show like she did Sunday nights. They didn't stick around long enough to explain. But some of the whites who left the South Side in a panic would talk about it years later and, to tell the truth, never got over the loss of their old neighborhoods.

"It happened slowly, and then all of a sudden, *boom,*" said a white homemaker who fled Ida Mae's neighborhood around that time and was quoted by the writer Louis Rosen, who had been a teenager when his parents fled South Shore, in the book *South Side.* "Everyone was gone. Everything changed. Before you know it, this one, that one. And then you heard, 'So-and-so's moving.' People didn't want to be the last."

A white father told Rosen, "I fought the good fight. I couldn't stay there with my three kids—my oldest was only fourteen at the time. I made a judgment. I did the best I could."

"It was like sitting around with a big group," said a white husband. " 'Okay, guys, in the next year, we're all going.' "

"It was who found a house first," the wife chimed in.

"Exactly. And we all went," the husband said.

To the colored people left behind, none of it made any sense. "It was like having a tooth pulled for no reason," said a black resident who moved his family in, only to watch the white neighbors empty out.

By the end of the year, the 7500 block of Colfax and much of the rest of South Shore went from all white to nearly totally black, which in itself might have been a neutral development, except that many houses changed hands so rapidly it was unclear whether the new people could afford the mortgages, and the rest were abandoned to renters with no investment or incentive to keep the places up. The turnover was sudden and complete and so destabilizing that it even extended to the stores on Seventy-fifth Street, to the neighborhood schools and to the street-sweeping and police patrols that could have kept up the quality of life. It was as if the city lost interest when the white people left.

The ice cream parlor closed. The five-and-dime shut down. The Walgreens on the corner became a liquor store. Karen and Kevin enrolled in Bradwell Elementary School and remember being, along with two other kids, the only black children in the entire school in 1968. By the time they graduated four years later, the racial composition had completely reversed: only four white children were left. South Shore would become as solidly black as the North Shore was solidly white. Ida

Mae's neighborhood never had a chance to catch up with all the upheaval and was never the same again.

South Shore was one of the last white strongholds on the South Side, the completion of a cycle that had begun when the migrants first arrived and started looking for a way out of the tenements. There were fifty-eight bombings of houses that blacks moved into or were about to move into between 1917 and 1921 alone, bombings having become one of the preferred methods of intimidation in the North. In neighborhood after neighborhood, with the arrival of black residents the response during the Migration years was swift and predictable.

It happened to ordinary people like Ida Mae and to celebrities like Mahalia Jackson, the leading gospel singer of her day. When she began looking for a house in a well-to-do section of the South Side, people held meetings up and down the block. A Catholic priest rallied his parishioners and told them not to sell to her.

"You'd have thought the atomic bomb was coming instead of me," the singer said.

She got calls in the middle of the night, warning her, "You move into that house, and we'll blow it up with dynamite. You're going to need more than your gospel songs and prayers to save you."

She bought the house. It was a sprawling red brick ranch and the house of her dreams, coming as she had from the back country of Louisiana. A doctor had broken ranks and sold it to her. As soon as she moved in, the neighbors shot rifle bullets through her windows. The police were posted outside her house for close to a year.

"One by one," she said, "they sold their houses and moved away. As fast as a house came on the market a colored family would buy it."

Even Hyde Park, an island of sophistication just north of Ida Mae's working-class neighborhood of South Shore, succumbed to the same fears and raw emotion that overtook the rest of the city's South Side.

"Shall we sacrifice our property for a third of its value and run like rats from a burning ship," said a handbill circulated among white residents trying to keep blacks on the other side of State Street, "or shall we put up a united front to keep Hyde Park desirable for ourselves?"

Oddly enough, Hyde Park was one of the very few places where the alarmist rhetoric did not completely take. It was home to the venerable University of Chicago, which had its own interest in maintaining stability, and the neighborhood was blessed with some of the finest residential architecture in the city, giving many whites compelling and overriding reasons to stay. The neighborhood was one of the most expensive on the

South Side, so blacks who moved there had to have the means just to get in. Thus Hyde Park actually became a rare island of integration despite the initial hostilities.

Still, it was surrounded by all-black neighborhoods in a deeply divided city. Entire communities like the suburb of Cicero remained completely off-limits to blacks, and whites would avoid so much as driving through whole sections of the south and west sides for the remainder of the century.

By the time the Migration reached its conclusion, sociologists would have a name for that kind of hard-core racial division. They would call it hypersegregation, a kind of separation of the races that was so total and complete that blacks and whites rarely intersected outside of work. The top ten cities that would earn that designation after the 1980 census (the last census after the close of the Great Migration, which statistically ended in the 1970s) were, in order of severity of racial isolation from most segregated to least: (1) Chicago, (2) Detroit, (3) Cleveland, (4) Milwaukee, (5) Newark, (6) Gary, Indiana, (7) Philadelphia, (8) Los Angeles, (9) Baltimore, and (10) St. Louis—all of them receiving stations of the Great Migration.

NEW YORK, LATE SUMMER 1967
GEORGE SWANSON STARLING

THERE CAME A TIME in the lives of many migrants' children when the parents sent them south for the summer to protect them from the uncaring streets of the Promised Land or to learn the culture of their family of origin or of the Old Country itself. It was a ritual practiced more or less by most families to ensure that their children knew where they came from.

George and Inez Starling sent their daughter, Sonya, down to Eustis when she was thirteen. What happened there was the last thing they expected: she got pregnant.

"It almost killed my wife," George said.

It was devastating after all they had been through and was the beginning of the most trying season of their lives. They had been married for twenty-eight years. Theirs had not been a happy union, but at least they had a family and had made out okay in New York, almost in spite of themselves, because they were hard workers and deep down good and decent people.

They had the highest hopes for their children, raised in a world free of the hardships they had endured in Florida. And now, it was as if the South and the backbiting country town they had left had reached back and punished them for having had the nerve to leave.

George had made a winless bargain. He had taken a job that kept him away from the very people he was working so hard to take care of, and he could not undo the damage already done. His absence only created a bigger gulf between him and Inez and left the children without a father most of the time and a mother with demons of her own to raise them practically by herself.

When they learned of Sonya's pregnancy, George would not admit his pain. He reacted with resignation and had little sympathy for the despair Inez felt, just as, all those years before, she had had little sympathy for his earnestness in organizing the pickers in the citrus groves.

The wounds they both carried had hardened and calcified, and the crisis over Sonya—*What would become of her? What kind of future would she have? How would they manage to raise the baby?*—only widened the chasm. Each blamed the other and themselves.

When he finally spoke, George's words cut deep. He said Sonya was no different from Inez. "It wasn't on account of your purity," he told her with the barbed edge that seemed to characterize more and more of their interactions, "that it didn't happen to us. You can't deny it 'cause you were doing it with me."

Sonya gave birth to a baby boy she named Bryan. It was 1968. She was fourteen.

George, fatalistic now after all that they had been through, said all he could do was laugh. The sins of the father were visiting the children. He thought back to when he was in the tenth grade and a girl in his class turned up pregnant.

"She named me the father," he said.

His first reaction was how did she know that he was the father, that just about anybody could have been the father. His second reaction was that there went his future. For the rest of his life, he would be picking fruit during the citrus season and digging up palmetto roots the rest of the time, pretty much the only work around.

"Let me finish the eleventh grade," he remembered telling the grown folks. "I'd just like to finish out the eleventh grade. I don't mind doing the right thing."

The baby was born dead. "I was so relieved," George said. "I never tried to find out if it was mine."

Now his daughter had come to him with the same news the girl he dallied with in high school had broken to her family all those years ago.

"Now you know," he thought to himself. *"Now you know how that mother felt when her daughter said she was pregnant by you."*

And so when the crisis over Sonya came up, George could only laugh through his tears at how much of what he had sown he appeared to be reaping. "I never did tell my wife," George said. "I didn't try to tell my wife why I was laughing. It was retribution."

It was retribution on several fronts. At around the same time that Sonya got pregnant, so did another woman. It was a woman George had been going out with behind Inez's back. As their marriage strained under the weight of unspoken resentments, he gave in to temptation. It only made unpleasant matters even worse and life nearly unbearable for Inez, the discovery of two pregnancies she never would have imagined or wished for.

The sadness and irony seemed to be turning in on itself, and it all seemed to point back to the rash and fateful day that George tried to get back at his father by marrying Inez in the first place. It appeared in the end he was only getting back at himself.

The other woman gave birth to a son. The boy was named Kenny. He was born a few months after Sonya's baby was born.

Kenny would grow up as an outside son, knowing his father, George, from afar and valuing him more than perhaps anyone else on earth because he was in some ways more like his father than anyone else and loved what little he knew of him.

LOS ANGELES, 1967
ROBERT JOSEPH PERSHING FOSTER

RUFUS CLEMENT AND HIS SON-IN-LAW, Robert Foster, were at opposite ends of the Great Migration. They represented the two roads that stood before the majority of black people at the start of the century. One man had stayed in the South. One had left it behind. Both had worked long and hard and had all the material comforts most any American could dream of. Yet both men wanted to prove to the other and to everyone else that his was the wiser choice, his life the more meaningful one.

President Clement was the tight-buttoned scion of the southern black bourgeoisie. Robert was a brilliant but tortured free spirit who had run from the very strictures Clement stood for. Clement was a distinguished accommodationist in the Jim Crow South—a beneficiary of it, in fact. He was not unlike the colored university president in Ralph Ellison's *Invisible Man,* whose allegiance was, above all, to the institution he ran, which had become an extension of himself. He was a pragmatist who had learned the fine art of extracting whatever he needed from guilt-ridden northerners or poorly credentialed but powerful segregationists who wouldn't want him living next to them but might grant him a concession or donate to his cause, the colored graduate school Atlanta University. He was so vigilant as to his place in the colored hierarchy that he kept a card file near his desk, *Time* magazine reported, on every black person in the United States that he considered "worthy of a high position in Government and education" in case he got a query from Washington.

Without trying, Rufus Clement had become an unwitting rival of Robert, not only for the affections of Robert's wife and children but in both men's unspoken effort to prove that where each man had ended up was the better place for colored people.

Robert had made out well as a noted surgeon in Los Angeles. But it did not rate with his father-in-law, Rufus Clement, who had staked his claim in the South and prospered. President Clement had avoided the messy confrontations of the civil rights era, saying at one point that he had been disturbed, as any right-thinking southerner might be, by the sit-ins but recognized that "this is the way in which they have tried to dramatize the way in which the American Negro has to live in his own country." He reassured white southerners that "we don't want to sit beside you, we just want to sit when we eat, like other people sit. We don't want to intermarry with your people. We simply want to get a drink of water where there is a drinking fountain available."

His patient and deferential ambitions paid off in 1953, when, against the longest of odds, he was elected to the Atlanta Board of Education—a first for a colored person there, while Robert, by contrast, was doing physicals and collecting urine samples for Golden State Insurance in what then seemed an unpromising start in California.

The Clements hovered over Robert and pulled at his wife and daughters from afar. And as they did, Robert retreated further into the world of his patients, his bookies, and the B-list musicians he liked to hang around with. He was drinking more and coming in late. He had fallen hard for Vegas and now had discovered horse racing. He joined the club room at Santa Anita, since now he could well afford it, and liked to catch the trifectas at Hollywood Park racetrack down in Inglewood.

He would go to Vegas whenever the spirit hit him and could play long and well. "I don't need to eat and rarely need to go to the bathroom," Robert would say. "I can go thirty-six hours." He liked the Sands Hotel and the Las Vegas Hilton. He went so often and bet so much that the hotels started comping him rooms and meals. Some trips, he brought back tens of thousands of dollars. Some trips, he lost that much. But he was hooked.

While he was out betting heavy and looking for something that did not exist and that nobody could give him, Alice set about establishing herself as a proper surgeon's wife. She joined the Links and the auxiliary of doctors' wives and hosted teas and bridge parties for the same kind of social set she had grown accustomed to back in Atlanta. The girls took piano and voice lessons and came out at their cotillions in white princess gowns. They were living parallel lives, and Alice and the girls tried not to notice that Robert, whose long hours helped finance their ball gowns and socials, was trying to fill some hole that could not be filled and was hardly ever around.

At one point, Alice had had enough. She packed up the girls and moved back to Atlanta with the Clements, who surely had not approved of how their daughter and granddaughters were faring with Robert. Somehow Alice and Robert made up, and she came back to Los Angeles. But nothing really had changed. They had both come into their own and seemed less suited in some ways than before. Perhaps they had always been ill suited for each other but were just beginning to realize it, now that they had a life and a family and reputations to protect.

They reached a kind of understanding and came together on the shining occasions when their mutual love of hosting and socializing happened to intersect at the grand parties they threw and the costumes they wore.

It was a ritual, and they had an understanding. Robert dressed Alice. Robert bought the clothes. Robert chose the clothes. Dressing Alice was his personal project. He studied her as a surveyor would study an isthmus, knew her assets and liabilities as far as tailoring went, and accompanied her not so much as an advocate for her tastes but as a guardian of his own reputation.

When Alice started moving up in the Links and had more cotillions to go to, he was happy for her and wanted her to look good. But it was a defensive kind of happiness. He wanted Alice to outdress the other women. "I didn't want those women to say my wife had anything less than the best," Robert said.

In the early days, he would prep her before a big formal. *"You got to go out there first, baby,"* he would tell her. *"You represent me."*

Every entrance was a production. They would approach the doorway of a ballroom. Robert would adjust himself and pause to let his wife go before him. "I'd walk two paces to the right and the rear and just watch her make that entrance," he said. "And she could walk."

Before every big occasion, the ritual was the same: the two heading to the store's back room, the salesclerk bringing in dresses that Robert knew were all wrong for Alice, and Robert saying, "Pick what you like." Alice would try on a dress. Robert inspected her and directed her movements.

"Walk," he told her. And she would begin.

"Come to me." She moved toward him.

"Sit." She would find an ottoman and position herself.

"Stand." She lifted herself up.

"Turn." And she would do so.

"If the dress didn't talk to me, it wasn't her dress," he said. "The salespeople go crazy. 'Who is this man? Who *is* he?' "

Over time, he began to sort the big moments of his life by whatever Alice was wearing. It seemed as if he remembered the gown if he remembered nothing else. Those gowns got people talking, and it was exactly what he wanted to hear: *Foster, you dress your women well.* "I couldn't be betting a hundred dollars on a horse and skimping on my wife," he told me many years later. "I know I'm bragging, and I'm enjoying it."

Sometimes the Clements would come out to visit them in Los Angeles, and Robert would put on his most charming performance to prove how well he had made out in the Promised Land. He invited the colored men of importance in the city to meet with his father-in-law and alerted the *Los Angeles Sentinel* so that the visit could be captured for posterity, as the Clements would have expected. The two men would never be close, but Robert knew how to put on a show when he had to.

By 1966, President Clement had risen to such a level of esteem at Atlanta University that a building was named in his honor. Clement Hall, an august red brick classroom building on the campus promenade, had its formal dedication on October 16, 1966. Alice and Robert's youngest daughter, Joy, in bangs and a white headband, cut the ribbon with her grandfather right behind her. Alice stood watching in a pillbox hat and tailored dark suit and corsage. Bunny was there in a tweed peacoat and gloves, with her Jackie-Kennedy-in-the-White-House bob and beautifully chiseled sixties cover-girl face, in a show of support for her grandfather. Robert did not attend.

The man who had managed to oust W. E. B. Du Bois from Atlanta University by lobbying the university's board of trustees all those years ago was in New York in early November 1967 for the regular meeting of that same board of trustees.

On the afternoon of Tuesday, November 7, during a break in the board's proceedings, Clement collapsed in his suite at the Roosevelt Hotel. He died of an apparent heart attack. He was sixty-seven years old.

He and his wife, Pearl, had planned to embark on a round-the-world tour after the board meeting. Instead, plans for interment were made. Pearl would have to move out of the president's mansion at Atlanta University, which had been her home and decorated to her liking for most of her adult life. She would have to move in with her next of kin, her beloved only daughter, Alice, in Los Angeles. Robert would have a wing with a bedroom and sitting area built for his mother-in-law and would try to make the best of it.

News reports of Rufus Clement's death appeared in the *Atlanta Daily*

World, the *New York Amsterdam News,* the *Los Angeles Sentinel,* and elsewhere. The *New York Amsterdam News* wrote that, "in addition to his widow, he is survived by a daughter, Mrs. Robert Foster of Los Angeles." Robert himself went unmentioned.

CHICAGO, FEBRUARY 1968
IDA MAE BRANDON GLADNEY

A POLICE WAGON pulled up to a West Side hospital over at Division and Kedzie, amid a rabble of placard-waving protesters on strike against the hospital, Walther Memorial. The strikers marched at the entrance in the biting cold. They were picketing for higher wages for the orderlies and nurse's aides who did the kinds of things nobody notices until they go undone.

Inside the police wagon, bundled up with coats and purses, looking wide-eyed at the people protesting in circles along the sidewalk, were Ida Mae and her co-worker and friend Doris McMurray. For several weeks in February 1968, that was how Ida Mae went to work each day.

Ida Mae respected the strikers, knew them by name, had worked right beside them, and got along with most of them, but she wasn't going to stand out there and strike with them. She had been working since she was big enough to get behind a plow. She had had all kinds of backbreaking, mind-numbing, sometimes dangerous and usually thankless jobs and had finally come into a position as a hospital aide. She had gotten the job in 1949, after more than a decade of scuffling from domestic to steel worker to press operator. She had finally come into a job she liked and that suited her temperament. She had come a long way from the cotton fields in Mississippi for the chance to work indoors with people rather than outdoors with crops and to get paid for the job and feel some dignity doing it. She had never stood up to a boss or refused to work or tried to petition for more money, even though she surely could have used it and more than likely deserved it. She had faith that whatever she needed would eventually come to her. The concept of not working a job one had agreed to do was alien to Ida Mae.

So when her union local announced it was going on strike at the beginning of 1968, Ida Mae and her friend Doris never considered that they would stop going to work. Decades earlier, colored migrants, unaccustomed to unions and not understanding labor politics, had been brought in by northern industrialists specifically to break up strikes. White union members resented the migrants and beat them for breaching the picket lines they had unwittingly been brought in to cross.

Ida Mae was not schooled in the protocols of union organizing, but she knew she couldn't afford to lose her job and couldn't see how not working was going to help her keep it. She was under more pressure than ever. She and George had just bought their first house, the three-flat in South Shore, and had new and different bills coming at them than ever before—from the mortgage to the utilities to property taxes and hazard insurance.

"My pastor was just begging me," Ida Mae remembered. "Please don't cross that picket line."

Her children were worried for her. "They didn't want me to go," Ida Mae said. "But I wasn't studyin' them."

George was his usual contained self. If he was scared for her, he didn't let on. The idea of not going to work was as foreign to him as it was to Ida Mae. "I don't reckon he ever knowed no different," Ida Mae said.

She made no apology for doing what she felt was living up to her responsibilities. Even the union boss teased her and said he knew why Ida Mae couldn't strike.

"She can't stay off," he said. "She got to pay for that three-flat building. She got to pay that house note."

"You right," Ida Mae said.

When Ida Mae and Doris told management they were going to keep working, the hospital arranged for a driver to pick them up at a designated location and escort them into the building.

One day, the strikers beat up the hospital driver after he had dropped the women off, and, for the first time, Ida Mae realized the seriousness of this thing. Then the hospital came up with another way to get Ida Mae and Doris to work: it arranged for a police wagon to pick up the two women at a designated bus stop.

"It was just like we were going to jail," Ida Mae said.

They would climb out of the police wagon at the entrance to the hospital, and the police would walk them past the pickets into the building.

"Scabs!" some of the picketers, shivering on the cold sidewalk, would yell at Ida Mae and Doris.

"You a scab," Ida Mae would shoot back, not knowing the labor union meaning of the word but hurling it anyway because, to her, everybody should have been working.

Ida Mae couldn't let a heckler go unanswered, and it frightened Doris.

"Shut up, Ida," Doris whispered. *"Ida, hush."*

The two of them were working on the sixth floor in surgery and on their breaks could look out the window and see the pickets below. After so many hours outside, the strikers had to find ways to protect themselves from the freezing wind. They would scurry to their cars and sit for a while, and they would use buckets instead of the toilet in the building because the hospital wouldn't let them in.

The strikers never threw anything but names at Ida Mae and Doris, and when the two of them looked back on it years later, they marveled that they had never gotten hurt.

"I wouldn't do that now," Doris said.

Ida Mae turned to Doris. "Well, I didn't really understand," Ida Mae said. "We all supposed to be working."

CHICAGO, NEW YORK, LOS ANGELES, AND MEMPHIS, APRIL 1968

THE EVENING WAS unusually cool for Memphis in April. It was shortly before six o'clock, and Martin Luther King, Jr., was heading to dinner before attending a rally for striking sanitation workers. He was standing on the second-floor balcony of the Lorraine Motel on Mulberry Street just outside his room, room 306. A half dozen of his aides were with him, gathering themselves to leave. Someone reminded King of how chilly it was getting. He agreed and went to get his topcoat.

At the precise moment that he turned back to his room, a minute past six on April 4, 1968, a single .30-caliber bullet was fired into the balcony. The rifle shot, thought to have come from a flophouse across the street through the bare branches of the mimosa trees, struck him in the neck and severed his spinal cord. King was pronounced dead at St. Joseph's Hospital at 7:05 P.M., Central Time. Within hours, the poor, colored sections of more than a hundred cities went up in flames.

That night, George Starling was rounding the corner at 131st Street and St. Nicholas Avenue in Harlem. He was returning home from a night out with the guys and saw the fires rising up ahead. He was trying to get to 132nd and Lenox, not yet knowing what had happened to set the people off. The whole thing was a blur, and he was looking for a way to get around the mayhem.

"It was in the direction of St. Nicholas Avenue," he said. "It could have been on Broadway, St. Nicholas, or Amsterdam. It was up on that hill. They were burning everything up there. The sky was lit up like it was the end of time."

He made his way home, and it was "only when I got into the house and turned on the radio that I heard the news that Martin Luther King had been shot in Memphis."

The evening of the assassination, Ida Mae would cup her face in disbelief at the news playing out in a scratchy, continuous, uncomprehensible loop on the AM radio dial and the family's black-and-white television set. She would pray for the soul of the man she so admired and had once almost seen during his Chicago campaign two years before as he had tried to free the people who had fled to the North.

On the other side of town, over on the West Side, police sirens wailed and rocks crashed through the plate-glass windows of grocers and liquor stores. Whole blocks went up in smoke in Chicago and on the streets of Newark, Detroit, Boston, Kansas City, Baltimore, Washington, D.C., and elsewhere. The receiving stations of the Great Migration would burn all through the night after Martin Luther King, Jr., was assassinated. And when it was over, some neighborhoods, the old places the migrants had packed into when the Migration began, would look like Berlin after an air strike during the Second World War.

The dispossessed children of the Great Migration but, more notably, the lifelong black northerners broken by the big cities let out a fury that made a mockery of the free harbor the North was reputed to be. A presidential commission examining the disturbances found that more black northerners had been involved in the rioting than the people of the

Great Migration, as had mistakenly been assumed. "About 74 percent of the rioters were brought up in the North," wrote the authors of what would become known as the Kerner Report. "The typical rioter was a teenager or young adult, a lifelong resident of the city in which he rioted." What the frustrated northerners "appeared to be seeking was fuller participation in the social order and the material benefits enjoyed by the majority of American citizens," the commission found.

The discontent of the young people unsettled the migrant parents who had fled the violence of the South. They could do little to dissuade their children from whatever role they might play in the outburst. It was too late to try to get them jobs at now-closed factories or the education they missed if they gave up on school, or, maybe most of all, the grounding and strength they themselves had acquired after having endured so much. The parents had come from the Old Country, had been happy to have made it out alive and make a few dollars an hour. *What did they know of the frustration of the young people who had grown up in the mirage of equality but a whole different reality, in a densely packed world of drugs and gangs and disorder, with promises that seemed to have turned to dust?*

Ida Mae saw the destruction on the news and, as usual, tried not to worry about things she could not control. George Starling managed to negotiate his way through the burning streets of Harlem. They had long since left the South where Dr. King had been killed. And yet they were pulled into the aftermath. In the North, the migrants grieved for the man who had worked miracles in the land of their birth and thus for them from afar.

It was Thursday, a workday, and across the country, Robert Foster, workaholic that he was, would have been in his office attending his usual overflow of patients at what would have been late afternoon on the West Coast.

His office on Jefferson and his house in West Adams were comfortably situated far from Watts, where the fires had burned three years before. Ever conscious of appearances and propriety, he would be nearly as incensed at the violence as he was stunned at the assassination. To him, spite never settled anything. It only gave your detractors more ammunition and, as it had back when the colored people in Monroe had urinated in the colored section of the Paramount Theater, only ended up hurting the people themselves.

To Robert, the whole world had just about gone mad. A few years before King's death, Robert had been beside himself when he learned that Bunny, a student at Spelman College in Atlanta caught up in the zeitgeist of the movement, was talking about maybe picketing, too, as only a bourgeois daughter of the upper class would. It would not be trying to register poor people to vote in the backwoods of Mississippi—that was out of the question—but by, say, protesting Rich's department store in downtown Atlanta with a white-gloved delegation of other colored college girls.

On this, Rufus Clement and Robert agreed: Bunny simply could not be seen being arrested with the riffraff, all because Rich wouldn't let colored girls try on hats. Of course, Robert understood the indignity, had lived it after all, which is why he had raised her in Los Angeles and taken her to Beverly Hills for whatever she and Alice and the other girls might ever think they wanted.

It wasn't that he was against the civil rights movement. He was all for standing up for one's rights. It was just that, to his way of thinking, the way to change things was to be better than anybody at whatever you did, wear them down with your brilliance, and enjoy the heck out of doing it. So he had no patience for these sit-in displays, at least for his daughters anyway, much less actual violence. The day King died was a dark day all around.

It was around midnight that George encountered the destruction in Harlem. It wasn't all the people out in the streets that got his attention. It wasn't unusual for a lot of people to be out on the streets of Harlem if it were the least bit warm. What caught his eye were the flames.

That Thursday evening in April, George had been hanging out with the guys over on Prospect Avenue. He was talking baseball and downing boilermakers—a shot of Smirnoff's with orange juice and a chaser of beer. He was trying to escape the disappointments of an underutilized mind and a sand trap of a marriage he was too loyal and upright to leave.

The men were so distracted by the vodka and the joshing over the Yankees and the Mets and the Dodgers, who had years before left Brooklyn for Los Angeles, and over the baseball season that was to begin the very next week, that they failed to register the assassination of one of the most influential figures in American history.

It was only when George finally made it into his car and back into Harlem that he realized that something terrible had happened.

"The sky lit up," he remembered. "When I turned into 131st Street, as soon as I looked, I saw: 'The whole sky is on fire.' "

George Starling knew what it meant to stare an enemy down in a life-and-death sort of way and had respect for Dr. King. But by the time King was assassinated, George was unable to marshal much emotion. He had grown up with that kind of violence against people fighting the system and half expected it. No, what had really shaken him was the assassination five years earlier of John F. Kennedy, the president so many blacks had placed their hopes in, Kennedy having come from the North and from what they saw as a more enlightened generation than previous presidents.

George was in Florida in November 1963. "I used to go down every October or November. I had just passed through Ocala, on the way to Gainesville, and it was in the afternoon," George remembered.

"And I turned the radio on, and I heard them say, *'And the President of the United States has been assassinated. He was shot, and he did not survive.'* Or something like that. And I said, 'Now, what kind of joke is that?' And then it came back on. You know they wouldn't have risked repeating it over and over. And when I realized that Kennedy had really been killed, assassinated, that thing hit me. When I knew anything, I had run off the road. I don't know what I was doing. And it just so happened that the shoulder was grassy. It wasn't that much traffic. It was in the midafternoon, and I just brought the car to a stop, and I just sat there, and I cried like a baby."

For some reason it was different with King than with Kennedy. Perhaps the losses were piling up and George couldn't muster the same shock and pain anymore. "I didn't cry," he said. "I was just astonished. I was just numb. I couldn't believe it. Then I thought about his speech. He predicted his own death whether he knew it or not. He told it. *'I've been to the top of the mountain, and I've looked over, and I've seen the Promised Land. I may not make it there with you, but you will get to the Promised Land.'* "

James Earl Ray, a forty-year-old drifter and prison escapee, would be convicted of the murder. Ray left a trail of evidence that he had been stalking King for months, but, until his own death in 1998, left questions as to what role he had actually played in the assassination.

Ray was not from the South, as the migrants who left it might have expected. He was from Alton, Illinois.

Precisely a week after King's death, and two years after King's brokered and dispiriting effort to end housing segregation in Chicago, President Lyndon Johnson signed the Fair Housing Act of 1968, banning discrimination on the basis of race, color, religion, or national origin in the renting or selling of property. King's bruising fight for the people in the North would not be won until King had died.

The Fullness of the Migration

And so the root
Becomes a trunk
And then a tree
And seeds of trees
And springtime sap
And summer shade
And autumn leaves
And shape of poems
And dreams
And more than tree.
—Langston Hughes

THE NORTH AND WEST, 1970

THIS WAS THE YEAR that demographers called the turning point in the exodus of black Americans out of the South. It was the year that the revolutions of the 1960s began to bear fruit and black children were entering white schools in the South without death threats or the need for the National Guard. The people from the South continued to go north in great waves because nobody told them the Migration was over, but fewer were leaving than in previous decades and nearly as many blacks in the North and West, particularly the children of the original people of the Great Migration, began to contemplate or act upon a desire to return south, now that things appeared to be changing.

Ida Mae, the sharecropper's wife from Chickasaw County, Mississippi, was not among them. She was like the majority of the original migrants, people who were not really migrants at all but who had left for good and didn't look back. She was fifty-seven years old now, a grandmother, and had been in Chicago for more than half her life. The elevated train, the three feet of snow falling in April when it had no business falling, the all-white neighborhood that had turned black in an eye blink—it was all part of her now.

Her life revolved around family, church, and work, really no different than the order of things would have been in Mississippi, except that the city that brought freedom also brought unforeseen hazards and heartbreak.

She had gotten used to the concrete and congestion, the press of buildings in place of the expanse of field. She had learned to quicken her step as she walked to or from work, but she still smiled at people on the bus or reached out to help young mothers balancing babies and strollers. She was even getting to know the gangbangers who had begun to position themselves on the street corners to establish their turf and organize their drug inventory. She spoke to them and they spoke back to her, calling her "Grandma" and watching out for her, to the dismay of her own children, whose objections she largely ignored because the gangbangers and their little lookouts were God's children too, to her way of thinking.

She was in the city but not fully wise to it, nor seeking to be.

One day, coming home from work, she stepped off the curb at the green light for pedestrians to cross Eighty-seventh Street at the Dan Ryan Expressway. The right turn on red had just been made legal. A man in a late-model sedan pulled out in front of the bus just as she was trying to cross. She fell onto the hood and then tumbled to the concrete.

"That was a good fall," she said. She was sore but not much else.

The man who hit her was worried for her and drove her to Jackson Park Hospital, where she was declared fine, save for a few bruises to her legs, arms, and ego. They called her husband to tell him what had happened.

"Oh, he fussed," she said, which looked to be the only way he knew to show he cared.

"You should have watched where you were going!" he told her when she got home. The idea of losing Ida Mae seemed to incite as much anger as worry in him.

There was already a sense of lingering sadness in the house. Their beloved Velma, the little girl Ida Mae hadn't wanted at first but whom she had held close and cherished and who had ridden next to her, along with little James, on the train ride north, was gone now. There had been a car accident a few years before. The details of the crash somehow didn't matter so much in the eternity between getting the call and making it to the hospital. Ida Mae saw her firstborn trying to hold on to life and then slip away. Ida Mae almost fell apart. Decades later, it would be the one thing she rarely talked about, as if not talking about it made it less real. And even though she knew full well that it was, she couldn't bear to let the thought of it slip into her subconscious. She acted as if it had never happened, and if it came up, her voice went uncharacteristically flat, and she quickly found something else to talk about. *"The police," she would say, "they was riding last night. . . ."*

Ida Mae and her husband had settled into whatever they were going to be in the North. They were blue-collar, churchgoing, taxpaying home owners with now two, instead of three, grown children. Ida Mae now had six little grandchildren, all of whom had been born within the bonds of holy matrimony, even though Eleanor's didn't manage to last, which perfectly reflected the demographics of the times. Ida Mae's husband was a deacon in the church whose pastime was cheering the White Sox on television with their grandson Kevin and instructing him on the strategies of the game. Ida Mae and her husband were never going to go to college or rise much beyond where they were, but they had come a long way from where they had started, and that was an accomplishment in itself.

Many years later, people would forget about the quiet successes of everyday people like Ida Mae. In the debates to come over welfare and pathology, America would overlook people like her in its fixation with the underclass, just as a teacher can get distracted by the two or three problem children at the expense of the quiet, obedient ones. Few experts trained their sights on the unseen masses of migrants like her, who worked from the moment they arrived, didn't end up on welfare, stayed married because that's what God-fearing people of their generation did whether they were happy or not, and managed not to get strung out on drugs or whiskey or a cast of nameless, no-count men.

There were two sets of similar people arriving in Chicago and other industrial cities of the North at around the same time in the early decades of the twentieth century—blacks pouring in from the South and immigrants arriving from eastern and southern Europe in a slowing but continuous stream from across the Atlantic, a pilgrimage that had begun in the latter part of the nineteenth century. On the face of it, they were sociologically alike, mostly landless rural people, put upon by the landed upper classes or harsh autocratic regimes, seeking freedom and autonomy in the northern factory cities of the United States.

But as they made their way into the economies of Chicago, Detroit, Cleveland, Milwaukee, and other receiving cities, their fortunes diverged. Both groups found themselves ridiculed for their folk ways and accents and suffered backward assumptions about their abilities and intelligence. But with the stroke of a pen, many eastern and southern Europeans and their children could wipe away their ethnicities—and those limiting assumptions—by adopting Anglo-Saxon surnames and melting into the world of the more privileged native-born whites. In this way, generations of immigrant children could take their places without the burdens of an outsider ethnicity in a less enlightened era. Doris von Kappelhoff could become Doris Day, and Issur Danielovitch, the son of immigrants from Belarus, could become Kirk Douglas, meaning that his son could live life and pursue stardom as Michael Douglas instead of as Michael Danielovitch.

A name change would have had no effect in masking the ethnicity of black migrants like Ida Mae, George, and Robert. It would have been superfluous, given that their surnames, often inherited from the masters of their forebears, were already Anglo-Saxon. They did not have the option of choosing for themselves a more favored identity. They could not easily assimilate whether they sought to or not. They could send their children to northern schools that were superior to anything back south, acquire a northern accent, save up for suits to replace the overalls and croker sack dresses of the field, but they would never be mistaken for an English or Welsh arriviste the way a Czech or Hungarian immigrant could if so inclined. Black migrants did not have the same shot at craft unions or foreman jobs or country clubs or exclusive cul-de-sac lace-curtain neighborhoods that other immigrants could enter if they were of a mind to do so.

A daughter of white ethnics could instantly escape the perceived disadvantages of her origins by marrying a man of northern or western European descent and taking his surname. She and whatever children she bore could thus assume the identity of a more privileged caste. With the exception of extraordinarily light-skinned blacks passing into the white world for these very same privileges, the daughter of the average black migrants would gain no such advantage by intermarrying. She would still be seen as black and be subject to the scrutiny of the outside world, no matter whom she married or whose name she took.

Even without trying to pass oneself off as anything other than what he or she was, an ethnic immigrant would not likely be distinguishable from any other white person boarding a train, lining up for a foreman's job, or waiting for a loan officer at a bank—public situations that opened black migrants to immediate rejection but that white ethnic immigrants were protected from by virtue of their skin color.

Ultimately, according to the Harvard immigration scholar Stanley Lieberson, a major difference between the acceptance and thus life outcomes of black migrants from the South and their white immigrant counterparts was this: white immigrants and their descendants could escape the disadvantages of their station if they chose to, while that option did not hold for the vast majority of black migrants and their children. The ethnicity of the descendants of white immigrants "was more a matter of choice, because, with some effort, it could be changed," Lieberson wrote, and, out in public, might not easily be determined at all.

The hierarchy in the North "called for blacks to remain in their station," Lieberson wrote, while immigrants were rewarded for "their ability to leave their old world traits" and become American as quickly as possible. Society urged them to leave Poland and Latvia behind and enter the mainstream white world. Not so with their black counterparts like Ida Mae, Robert, and George.

"Although many blacks sought initially to reach an assimilated position in the same way as did the new European immigrants," Lieberson noted, "the former's efforts were apt to be interpreted as getting out of their place or were likely to be viewed with mockery." Ambitious black migrants found that they were not able to get ahead just by following the course taken by immigrants and had to find other routes to survival and hoped-for success.

Contrary to common assumptions about childbearing and welfare, many black migrants compensated for the disadvantages they faced by cutting back in every way they could, most notably by having fewer children than the eastern and southern Europeans arriving at the same time. Ida Mae, for example, bore no more children after the one she carried in her belly from Mississippi at the age of twenty-five, despite the many fertile years she spent in the North. She and her husband could not afford another mouth to feed.

It turned out that, during the first three decades of the Great Migration, fertility rates for black women migrants from the South were actually among the lowest of all newer arrivals to the North, according to Lieberson's compilation of census data. In 1940, for the fifteen-to-thirty-four age group, Ida Mae's at the time, there were 916 children per thousand black women, as against 951 for Austrians, 1,030 for Russians, 1,031 for Poles, 1,176 for Hungarians, and 1,388 for Italians. Czech women were virtually tied with black women at 923 children per thousand women. The disparities only widened with age. Among those in the forty-five-to-fifty-four age group, central and eastern European immigrant women had borne, in some cases, twice as many children per thousand as black migrant women in the North in 1940, with the Russians having borne 3,111, the Hungarians 3,305, the Austrians 3,683, the Czechs 4,045, the Poles 4,192, and the Italians 4,638 compared to 2,219 children having been born to black women by the same point in their lives in the North.

Clyde Vernon Kiser, a political scientist at Columbia University, studying the black migration from south Georgia to the Northeast in the 1930s, also found fertility to be "significantly reduced by migration" among black couples who went to both New York and Boston.

"The differences in most cases are of a massive nature," Lieberson reported.

Blacks, though native born, were arriving as the poorest people from the poorest section of the country with the least access to the worst education. Over the decades of the Migration, they came with every disadvantage and found themselves competing not only with newcomers like themselves but with second- and third-generation European immigrants already established in apprenticeships and factory jobs that were closed off to black migrants, the immigrants and their children permitted into the very trade unions that prohibited black citizens from joining.

Because they were largely excluded from well-paying positions in even unskilled occupations and were concentrated in servant work and other undesirable jobs, blacks were the lowest paid of all the recent arrivals. In 1950, blacks in the North and West made a median annual income of $1,628, compared to Italian immigrants, who made $2,295, Czechs, who made $2,339, Poles, who made $2,419, and Russians, who made $2,717.

"There is just no avoiding the fact that blacks were more severely discriminated against in the labor market and elsewhere," Lieberson wrote. They "had to work more hours to earn less money than anyone else," the historian Gilbert Osofsky wrote.

The people of the Great Migration had farther to climb because they started off at the lowest rung wherever they went. They incited greater fear and resentment in part because there was no ocean between them and the North as there was with many other immigrant groups. There was no way to stem the flow of blacks from the South, as the authorities could and did by blocking immigration from China and Japan, for instance. Thus, blacks confronted hostilities more severe than most any other group (except perhaps Mexicans, who could also cross over by land), as it could not be known how many thousands more might come and pose a further threat to the preexisting world of the North.

The presence of so many black migrants elevated the status of other immigrants in the North and West. Black southerners stepped into a hierarchy that assigned them a station beneath everyone else, no matter that their families had been in the country for centuries. Their arrival unwittingly diverted anti-immigrant antagonisms their way, as they were an even less favored outsider group than the immigrants they encountered in the North and helped make formerly ridiculed groups more acceptable by comparison.

Ida Mae was so isolated, living as she was in the all-black neighborhood of South Shore, that she had little contact with other immigrant groups except perhaps at work. She tried to make the best of it since she had no control over who had gotten to Chicago before she did or how they lived or what they thought of her. Her world was small, purposely so, built around her family and the people she knew from back home in Mississippi, and that was the way she and her husband preferred it.

NEW YORK, 1970
GEORGE SWANSON STARLING

THIS IS WHAT GEORGE STARLING'S LIFE had become at its midpoint.

He had made it up north, alright, as he had dreamed so long ago. But he had an unhappy wife who could not be made happy and two teenage children who were good at heart but had been swallowed up by the worst aspects of the North and South while he and his wife were out working long hours to give the kids a life they themselves had never had. He had a two-year-old by another woman that he had to support and a decent-paying but dead-end job as essentially a servant to railroad passengers needing help with their luggage, directions to their seats, another pillow, their shoes shined.

He turned fifty-two in 1970. He had been in the North for a quarter of a century. He would never be the chemist or accountant he had seen for himself in his mind, would never work a white-collar job or any kind of job that would make use of his intellect. And, by an accident of birth, he had managed to suffer the terror and injustice of Jim Crow but just missed the revolution that opened up the best in education and unheard-of career opportunities for black people with the passage of the civil rights laws of the 1960s. The revolution had come too late for him. He was in his midforties when the Civil Rights Act was signed and close to fifty when its effects were truly felt.

He did not begrudge the younger generation their opportunities. He only wished that more of them, his own children, in particular, recognized their good fortune, the price that had been paid for it, and made the most of it. He was proud to have lived to see the change take place.

He wasn't judging anyone and accepted the fact that history had come too late for him to make much use of all the things that were now opening up. But he couldn't understand why some of the young people couldn't see it. Maybe you had to live through the worst of times to recognize the best of times when they came to you. Maybe that was just the way it was with people.

He did not dwell on this long or let it get him down. He stood as straight-backed now as he had when the South told him he didn't have a right to. He started going to church and found solace in that. He started singing in the choir. He had a way of sitting back and shaking his head at absurdities—whether segregationists training their terriers to mock black people in the South or black people with no hope or home training shooting each other over a nickel bag in the North.

The young people were letting their hair grow out and wearing Afros that his generation would never have been seen out in public with. They were living together—shacking up, they called it—in a flouting kind of way that even now, tortured as his marriage was, he couldn't bring himself to do. They were taking things farther than he ever would have had the nerve to contemplate, preaching black power, calling the white man a devil, walking arm in arm down the street with white women, all of those things that would have gotten him killed when he was their age.

The young people picked up on something strong and unnameable in him. They never bothered him as he climbed the stairs out of his basement apartment with his creaky and now-arthritic knees, heading to work at Pennsylvania Station or returning late at night from a forty-eight-hour run.

He knew more than most people of his generation precisely what he had missed out on, and what his life could have been. He had had a taste of college, knew he could do the work, and was convinced he could have succeeded.

How complicated had the ending of his college career been. Looking back on it, the course of his life had turned on that moment. He would not have been working in the citrus groves or had the standoff with the grove owners that had forced him to flee to the North if he had stayed in school. That moment would gnaw at him for as long as he lived. What if his father hadn't gotten it into his head that George had had enough schooling, if his father had helped out with the tuition George needed, if his father hadn't had a new family to support and chosen that obligation over college for his son? Then there was segregation. What if colored students had been allowed to attend the state schools near Eustis in George's day, as they could after the civil rights movement, where it would have been easier for George to make a go of it, work and go part-time if he had to?

Then there was George himself. At midlife, George had to search his soul and live with the regrets of his own missteps. If only he hadn't rushed to get back at his father by marrying a woman from the other side of the tracks, giving his father further reason to withhold his support and leaving George with a wife to take care of besides, perhaps he would have gotten the education that would have allowed him to fulfill his potential. As it was, he had only to look at Inez to be reminded of what could have been.

"It was spite," George would say of the decisions he made at that moment in his life.

He took every chance he got to warn young people not to make his mistakes, not knowing if they heard him but feeling he had to get it out.

"That's why I preach today, *Do not do spite,*" he said. "Spite does not pay. It goes around and misses the object that you aim and comes back and zaps you. And you're the one who pays for it."

LOS ANGELES, 1970

ROBERT JOSEPH PERSHING FOSTER

ON CHRISTMAS DAY 1970, Robert P. Foster turned fifty-two years old. He had been in Los Angeles for seventeen years. But, for some reason, he was unable to fill up on what he had acquired any more than he could carry fog in his satchel.

He had a practice that minted money. With all those migrants from Texas and Louisiana, he had patients spilling out of his office and into the hall, sitting like refugees on the floor all day, waiting for him to check their blood pressure.

By then he found it hard to walk down a hospital ward without orderlies and scrub nurses hailing him from closing elevator doors, *"Hey, Doc! Remember me?"* from some long-ago operation, and his feigning recollection so as not to disappoint them.

He was comfortably situated. There was the well-born wife, the three beautiful daughters, and the 3,600-square-foot house west of Crenshaw—if only by a block—with the white Cadillac in the driveway. He was famous even. Ray Charles's song about him, "Hide Nor Hair," spent seven weeks on the *Billboard* charts back in 1962. But he woke up that morning with the feeling that nothing mattered but the events that were about to unfold that day.

Until this moment, he had lived his life with the perpetual sense of watching a reception through a keyhole, of arriving too late and without the proper documentation. There he would be at the front gate, all dressed and superior to the people inside but afraid of being denied admittance. He craved acceptance from those most determined to withhold it from him and met slights and rejections at nearly every turn. The small-minded people in that Jim Crow town. Rufus and Pearl Clement scrutinizing his every move since the day he married Alice. The colonel from Mississippi who wouldn't let him operate on white women. The motel clerks in Phoenix who denied him a room. The colored people who happened to have gotten to L.A. first and wouldn't lend a newcomer a hand. That hotel in Vegas.

After all this time, he still couldn't shake these things. Rufus Clement had been dead for years. The run-in with the motel clerks in Phoenix—that was seventeen years ago. The colonel farther back than that. All the good and extraordinary things that had happened to him seemed never to make up for the rejection he had endured, and he set out to prove that he was better than what they took him for, even though the people who haunted him would never see it, no matter what he did.

Because of the fifty-one previous years of his life, he had a number of complexes. He had a Napoleon complex, a southern complex, a baby-of-the-family complex. He had both a superiority complex and an inferiority complex, and, because he was born on Christmas Day, a Christmas baby complex.

He had never had much of a birthday party, a fate known to just about anyone who enters the world on Christmas. His mother had tried to give him a birthday party once when he was a young boy in Monroe. She invited all the children in New Town. Only four came.

That would not happen this time. He finally had all the pieces in place to celebrate his having arrived. In a few hours, he would give a gala in honor of himself. It would make up for all the parties he'd never had, all the slights he had ever suffered. It would prove to everyone that he had put Monroe and the South behind him and made it in L.A. He had worked it all out in his head.

He would have guests from back east and up the coast and from all over the country. Monroe, too, of course. The best hams and the finest heavy bond paper for the invitations. Anything that anyone had ever thought of for a party, he would have. It would cost in the thousands, like the major motion picture wrap parties over in Beverly Hills, and he wanted the guests to see every dime of it. He had rehearsed the whole thing in his mind.

That morning he woke up early, just like when he was a teenager back in Monroe racing to lose himself in the celluloid illusion of California sophisticates from the colored balcony of the Paramount. Now he was in California, finally a sophisticate himself, and the urine-scented steps of the Paramount were from another lifetime.

But as he rewound a tape that had yet to be recorded, a thunderstorm gathered in his stomach. He could hear the sounds of a party forming on the first floor. Footsteps on linoleum, the help skittering between the refrigerator and the sink and around the avocado green Formica island back to the refrigerator again. The low screech of high chairs being positioned at the bar, the setting down of serving pieces and highball glasses, the opening and closing of the heavy front door with the arrival of roses and ice. He had done all he could, and now it was up to the workers, who, sweet though they might be, could not possibly understand how crucial it was that there be only cashews and almonds and, for God's sake, no peanuts in the nut bowls.

The sound of urgent disorder rose up the staircase and into his room. Rather than being pleased that all was going more or less according to plan, he was sickened at the prospect that, for all his preparation, things might be less than perfect.

He could hear the assembling of a party. The storm grew worse in his stomach.

For most of 1970, Robert had devoted himself to the second job of planning his own arrival party. He had told his wife, Alice, and daughter Joy and his mother-in-law, Pearl, as soon as the thought had occurred to him. He told Bunny and Robin in Chicago to be in Los Angeles that Christmas and sent them checks for their gowns with instructions to start shopping immediately. He told his nephew, Madison, a graduate student at the University of Michigan, that he expected him in from Ann Arbor. He told Madison's mother, Harriet, that he wanted her in from Monroe.

He alerted the members of his wedding party, the former groomsmen in black tails and white kid gloves and the bridesmaids with tiaras planted over their Bette Davis curls, so they could mark Friday, December 25, 1970, on their calendars. Leo, the maître d' at L'Escoffier, a French restaurant at the Beverly Hilton, would oversee the whole affair. The date fell within weeks of Alice's fiftieth birthday, as well as Bunny's and Gold's birthdays. But the party would be essentially for him.

Robert began devising the guest list as if it were a state dinner. He began thinking menu and decor. A tent over the patio. Belgian lace for the tablecloths. Open bar with unpronounceable top-shelf spirits. He slept with the thought of it. He carried it in his head to work. During breaks in the day, he would think aloud to a nurse about this or that entrée or particular band, not necessarily because he wanted a second opinion—he would not have turned to them for that—but because he assumed everyone was as captivated as he was.

In fact, some were. At the office one day, a patient overheard him buzzing about the party. The patient joined in and offered to help. He said he did a little printing work and could make Doc Foster some nice invitations for the party. Robert was horrified at the notion and thought it should be obvious that no ordinary printer would do for a party of this caliber.

"Thank you very much," Robert said, "but they're already taken care of."

In truth, he had not begun looking. But he was grateful for the reminder and would track down an engraver immediately. "It had to be the best person in the city," he would say years later. "And I knew the best couldn't be a patient of mine."

He dispatched his mother-in-law to get on it right away. Her southern socialite airs would come in handy about now. It would give her something to occupy her mind and less time to scrutinize him. She spent an entire month choosing between white and ecru and the proper weight for the card stock. They found the invitations at the old Bullock's Wilshire in Beverly Hills, off Rodeo Drive. They had them engraved on Crane's paper, white with red lettering and a red border along the edge. "Etiquettely," he said, "it was perfect."

The invitations read:

Doctor and Mrs. Robert P. Foster
At Home
Friday, the twenty-fifth of December
At nine o'clock in the evening
1680 Victoria Avenue
Regrets Only *Cocktails—Dancing*

Two hundred invitations went out, and as Robert was at the peak of his practice and popularity, 194 accepted. "We counted all but six R.S.V.P.'s," he said, "and the six that declined were all out of town."

That raised the stakes for everything else, beginning with the costumes for the principals. He was the star and would have to look it. He went to the Beverly Hills couturiers, the tailors to Sammy Davis, Jr., who, from across a blackjack table some people said he favored, and found a suit to his liking. Crushed velvet had just hit the scene, very Fifth Dimension, Age of Aquarius, and all that. So that's what he would wear. Black crushed velvet suit. Black crushed velvet bow tie. Black velvet Bally slippers with a gold medallion above the instep. The suit had a red lining to match the red silk handkerchief in his breast pocket, and the shirt cuff fell precisely one inch below the jacket sleeve, just as it should.

Finding something for Alice would take more time. He was the show-off, just waiting for somebody to say, *Bob Foster, you too much.* They went all over Beverly Hills, to the back rooms of the designer floors of the finest department stores, Robert watching, advising, critiquing, and, for one reason or another, dismissing and rejecting as Alice tried on hanger after hanger of dresses.

One night after work, rather than heading straight home or to the track, Robert drove north and west from his medical office toward Beverly Hills. He went directly to the French Room at Bullock's Wilshire, which he had been known to keep open in search of the right attire. They had been there already, but he wanted to check again.

This time, he saw an organza gown loaded with beadwork. It was gaudy like New Orleans, and the skirt looked as if somebody had thrown rubies on the sidewalk. Robert told the salesclerk to wrap it up immediately. He carried it home and ran up the steps to show Alice. It was late, and he woke her up.

"Try it on, baby," he said.

She got up, and he positioned himself three feet to the right and rear in a corner of the yellow-trimmed bedroom to watch her move in it.

Walk.

Turn.

Come to me.

"It became alive when she walked," he said.

In Ann Arbor, his nephew, Madison, awaited word on the big party between sociology colloquia and trying to take over the administration building at the University of Michigan. He was a three-piece-suited militant who knew how to use a fish fork. Robert had given him a year's notice about the party. All year long, if the phone rang and it was Robert, he knew what it was about. *I'm having Mrs. Williams roast the nuts for the party. Hampton Hawes has agreed to do the jazz set. I'm flying the Smithfield hams in from Virginia.*

From the moment they accepted, he and the 194 other people on the guest list (and the guests they were bringing with them) were on a low-grade state of alert whether they liked it or not. Anyone deemed close enough to be invited also knew that Robert would expect them to look and act the part he assigned them. He wanted them to have a good time, of course, but he would also be sure to make note of the cut of their jackets and where a dress hem fell in relation to the ankle or knee. He would be judging them all. It was just how he was, and he couldn't help it.

Madison felt the heat as much as anyone. He was the only child of Robert's deceased oldest brother. Theirs was the closest that either had to a father-son relationship. They were the only Foster men left after all the deaths in the family. Big Madison, when he was alive, had made a point of not leaving the South, not running away and chasing a dream as Robert and millions of others had done, but staying and making the most of the angst and subtle shifts in sentiment of southern whites watching their meal ticket disappear on north- and westbound trains. Little Madison had thus been raised in the South, with the pride and insecurities that came with it, and, despite his father's decision to stay, looked up to his Uncle Robert, who had made good out west.

A visit from Robert was a cause of great anxiety. Robert once visited Michigan in the midsixties. Madison did his best to impress him. He took him to the fanciest place he could afford. It took some time for the guests to figure out what they wanted from the menu. But they ordered and had a fine time. On the ride back, Robert gave his assessment of the evening.

"That was B+," he said.

Madison sank into his seat and waited to hear what he had missed.

"You shouldn't have let your guests struggle with the menu," Robert told him.

Madison never really got over it. Almost forty years later, and he was still second-guessing the evening. "I didn't preorder the food," he would say long afterward. "It was a painful lesson. I learned it."

He was southern and did everything he could to prove himself. He tried to pull Robert's daughters back to their Louisiana roots, but they looked upon him as their country cousin from back in Monroe, a place they cared little about, growing up as they did in California.

Madison was a graduate student when Robert's oldest daughter, Bunny, got her master's at the University of Iowa. He didn't have the money for a new suit. He flew in anyway. At the commencement, Robert pulled him aside.

"Your suit pants are shiny," Robert said. "You shouldn't go out like that."

Madison would not let that happen again.

He had a year's notice on the party and made use of it. He went to a tailor and had two suits cut for the occasion, hoping that one of them might meet Robert's exacting standards.

December 25, 1970. A Friday. The florists draped pine leaf garlands down the railing of the front staircase. To the branches they fastened red plastic birds with glitter on the wing tips so that every four feet there was a little bird in flight.

The caterers moved the dining room table in front of the gold draperies. They covered it with $250 worth of white Belgian lace and set sterling candelabras on each end, as the Clements would have done. The Smithfield hams arrived from Virginia. The shrimp gumbo was set out with instructions that it never hit empty.

The barkeep lined the liquor bottles behind the highball glasses at the bar. "I told the bartender to give everybody two shots whether they wanted it or not," Robert said.

All day, the heavy front door opened and closed with the arrival of supplies, and the telephone rang on and off, people just landing at LAX, people needing directions. Dusk fell, and the time drew near. Robert began to feel sick. The thunderstorm grew worse in his stomach. He felt weak and exhausted. His knees gave way. He fell back, collapsed. He had to be helped upstairs, lie down, gather himself. He lay there staring at the yellow walls in the master bedroom, fretting and unable to face the possibility of imperfection.

He closed his eyes. He tried to rest. Soon, outside his window, he could hear the rumble of car engines rounding St. Charles Place and turning up South Victoria. The screeching came to a stop. The creak of the passenger door of a Cadillac opening and the thud of its closing. The engine shutting down and the valet taking the keys. The first guests had arrived and were walking down the red-carpeted sidewalk he conceived of months ago.

Round the corner and down the stairs, he could hear muffled conversation, a party being born. He reminded himself why he had spent the better part of a year and really all of his life planning for this moment. He got up, steadied himself. He checked himself in the mirror, practiced his smile, and straightened his crushed-velvet tie.

"Let's get on with it," he said to himself, liking what he saw. "It's on."

He is wearing mutton-chop sideburns, flecked gray, and an Afro shaped like a mushroom cap. Hip as you got in those days. He greets his guests with a cigarette between his fingers and his legs purposely slew-footed, as if he were posing for Esquire. *It will make better pictures for the photographer he has hired to trail him and the guests all night.*

Soon the set piece begins to take shape. There's Joe Luellen, who hit town back in the thirties and played in The Great White Hope. *And three men standing together in velvet suits that forewarn the fashion crimes of the seventies.*

On a foot-high stand above the crowd, Sweets Edison is on trumpet under the green-striped tent over the patio. Hampton Hawes is playing piano with his head reared back. Everybody has a glass of something in one hand and a cigarette in the other like jewelry.

There's his mother-in-law near the hot pink tulip-upholstered love seat, in a four-hundred-dollar gown and a solid gold bracelet he bought her and which he complained she never gave him credit for. And she's greeting and upstaging as if she paid for the whole shebang. ("I ignored it, I ignored it," he would say years later, betraying that he most certainly had not.)

There are two or three wet bars, help everywhere, dressed in maid's uniforms and monkey suits, people checking coats, people parking cars, people pouring martinis, people picking up dishes before they have a chance to clink the top of an end table.

There's Bunny sticking her tongue out at the camera. And Ray Charles under the tent over the patio by the band. And Robert's bookie. And a judge. A postmaster. And a dentist. Robert's sister, Gold, in pink chiffon on a barstool, holding a pack of Marlboros. Keisha Brown, a gospel rock singer, sweating on stage in blood-red velvet. Madison, in a three-piece suit that thankfully met Robert's approval, doing the funky chicken with a woman in white bell-bottoms. Alice in her cat-eye glasses, posing for pictures, calm and dignified in that heavy beaded dress by the staircase.

The following Thursday, December 31, 1970, a breathless review ran on page C2 of the *Los Angeles Sentinel,* declaring it "certainly 'The Party of the Year,' without a doubt" (phrasing that unwittingly introduced the very doubt it sought to dispel). The column ran without pictures and began like this:

> *One of the Angel City's most fabulous parties to date was given by the Robert Fosters on Christmas Day, at their home on Victoria Avenue. The prominent physician and his wife, who is president of the L.A.*

Chapter of the Links, had their large back yard area tinted [sic] *for the occasion, and the View Park decorators had a field day. . . .*

For her party, Alice wore a Malcolm Star original that fairly sparkled with jewels. . . . Mrs. Rufus E. Clement, formerly of Atlanta, and Louisville, Ky., now makes her home in L.A. with her daughter and son-in-law, and assisted in receiving the 400 guests.

Who was there? Well, we could easily say the Who's Who of L.A. Society. . . . And believe it or not, at times there were as many as 200 beautiful people, milling, sipping, and just having a marvelous time on Christmas Day at the Robert Fosters. . . . This was certainly "The Party of the Year," without a doubt.

Robert had a photo album made of the night's festivities. It was made of brown leather, and etched onto the front was "Robert's Birthday" in gold italics. Over the succeeding decades, he would pull out the party album before he would his wedding pictures or his medical degree. The brown leather got worn in spots from the viewing. Usually, he would not bother to mention the *Sentinel* story nor the party itself so much as what went into it.

"For some reason, it drops," he told me years later when I asked him about the particulars. "It's not any less valuable or delicious. But for some reason, it didn't seem as important as when I was putting it together."

Some of the guests he never saw again. Some died. Some lost touch. It was a wrap, and everyone was marvelous.

He took comfort in any sign of the night's immortality. One day he passed the stationery department at Bullock's. The invitations to his party were mounted and on display. "I went in once and told the lady, 'That's mine,' " he said. "She looked at me like I was a fool. I just smiled."

Talking about it kept the party going, and so it never really ended in his mind. He did not wait for reviews, he solicited them. He called Jimmy Marshall, one of his oldest friends from back in Monroe, right after the party.

"Jimmy, did I wig 'em?" he asked.

"Yeah, you hit it," Jimmy said.

What are they saying, what are they thinking? Robert asked Jimmy. Everyone was bowled over, of course. Jimmy didn't want to say it, but the Monroe people thought he had gone too far. The black maid in the black-and-white dress and white bow in the foyer was over the top even for Robert.

"We've been maids long enough," Jimmy told Robert. "People didn't go for that."

Robert didn't take it too well. "Either he answered or cussed," Jimmy said decades later, "which I didn't care, in either case."

As long as the two had known each other, Robert's fixations never made sense to Jimmy. "He always sought approval," Jimmy said. "And I never understood it because he had it all."

PART FIVE

AFTERMATH

The migrants were gradually absorbed
into the economic, social, and political life of the city.
They have influenced and modified it.
The city has, in turn, changed them.

—ST. CLAIR DRAKE AND HORACE H. CAYTON,
Black Metropolis

In the Places They Left

The only thing
we are proud of
in connection with
the South
is that we left it.

—Jefferson L. Edmonds, the publisher of *The Liberator,* one of the first colored newspapers in Los Angeles

CHICKASAW COUNTY, MISSISSIPPI, 1970

IDA MAE BRANDON GLADNEY

THE RAW WOOD CABINS and gravel roads that broke the clearings in the bottomlands of Chickasaw County did not change much in the thirty years after Ida Mae and millions of other black people left the South in a migration that was now slowing down as Mississippi began fitfully opening up. Mr. Edd, whose land Ida Mae and her husband had sharecropped, died of a heart attack back in 1945, a few years after Ida Mae went north. Willie Jim, who came with Mr. Edd looking for Joe Lee that night all those years ago over the missing turkeys, was still alive. He ran a thousand-acre plantation with up to two hundred hoe hands and forty sharecropper families well into the 1960s.

The land was still devoted to cotton, but big combines and mechanical harvesters now did most of the work. The people who had not gone north now worked in factories, textile mills, and hardware plants, factories that made poly foam and felt for the manufacture of furniture, and factories that made trailers, sewer pipes, corrugated boxes, shipping crates.

The county and the rest of Mississippi and the old Confederacy had come out on the other side of a second civil war, the war over civil rights for the servant caste of the South. Chickasaw County had not been in the middle of it, had not been a focus of Martin Luther King or the freedom riders. It was too sparsely populated and too out of the way. But it was no less resistant to change, especially when it came to black people voting (where "intemperate individuals of both races created incidents best forgotten," the Chickasaw County Historical and Genealogical Society wrote dismissively of the era), and when it came to the integration of the schools, which had been segregated for longer than most anyone had been alive.

It was in 1954 that the Supreme Court ruled on *Brown v. Board of Education of Topeka,* declaring segregated schools inherently unequal and therefore unconstitutional. In a subsequent ruling in 1955, the Court ordered school boards to eliminate segregation "with all deliberate speed."

Much of the South translated that phrase loosely to mean whenever they got around to it, which meant a time frame closer to a decade than a semester. One county in Virginia—Prince Edward County—closed its entire school system for five years, from 1959 to 1964, rather than integrate.

The state funneled money to private academies for white students. But black students were left on their own. They went to live with relatives elsewhere, studied in church basements, or forwent school altogether. County supervisors relented only after losing their case in the U.S. Supreme Court, choosing finally to reopen the schools rather than face imprisonment.

It would take more than fifteen years before most of the South conceded to the *Brown* ruling and then only under additional court orders.

"This was passionately opposed," wrote the Chickasaw Historical Society, "not only by most of the whites—but by some of the blacks as well." That sentiment, if true, would have been explained away by the blacks who left as an indication that the blacks who stayed may have been more conciliatory than many of the people in the Great Migration.

It wasn't until the 1970–71 school year that integration finally came to Chickasaw County, and then only after a 1969 court order, *Alexander v. Holmes,* that gave county and municipal schools in Mississippi until February 1970 to desegregate. But even that deadline would be extended for years for particularly recalcitrant counties.

All the marching and court rulings did little to change some southerners' hearts. A 1968 survey found that eighty-three percent of whites said they preferred a system with no integration. And they acted on those preferences. By 1970, 158 new white private schools had opened up in Mississippi. By 1971, a quarter of the white students were in private schools, the white families paying tuition many could scarcely afford. Mothers went back to work to help cover tuition, "spent all their savings and forfeited luxuries and necessities in life," some splitting their children up and enduring the "expense and inconvenience of transporting the children long distances to and from school," according to the Mississippi-born scholar Mark Lowry, to avoid having their children sit in the same classroom with black children.

In the meantime, in the middle of the turmoil over what would become of the children of Mississippi, dozens of school districts forwent federal funding rather than integrate their schools. During the worst of things, at least one school superintendent, Lowry wrote, committed suicide.

EUSTIS, FLORIDA, 1970
GEORGE SWANSON STARLING

LAKE COUNTY, FLORIDA, began to join the rest of the free world in the late 1960s and early 1970s, six decades into the Great Migration, when black children and white children, for the first time in county history, began sitting in the same buildings to learn their cursive and multiplication tables.

Change did not come without incident. The first sign of trouble was a fight at the newly integrated high school between a white boy and a black boy. It fell to the black assistant principal, who had been demoted from principal of the colored high school to an assistant at the reconstituted school, to intervene. It was unclear who started what, but the black assistant principal ruled in favor of the white student to the outcries of reverse favoritism from the black parents.

"The black people could not understand why he should discipline this black kid that had an altercation with the white kid, and they been dogging us all our lives," George Starling, who had been keeping close contact, said years later. The assistant principal was his stepbrother in that small world of Eustis, Florida.

The black parents felt the white student had started the fight by provoking the black student and that the assistant principal should have ruled accordingly. But in the tinderbox of what was still very much an experiment in caste integration, he had little choice.

"We're crying out against prejudice and mistreatment," George said. "If you want it eliminated, you have to do unto others as you want them to do unto you."

When the next big fight broke out, Willis McCall rode up with his police dog to go after the black student. This time, the black parents rose up and protested. A church load of them, emboldened by the civil rights gains and the counterbalancing effect of all the people they knew up north, rode over to the county seat of Tavares, got a Reverend Jones to speak for them, and protested to the Lake County School Board.

"The people let Willis McCall know that they weren't scared of him or his dog," Viola Dunham, a long-time resident with three boys in school at the time, remembered. "We let him know he does not run the school system. We let them know we didn't want Willis McCall raising our children. And we did not back down that time."

Since the 1940s, Willis McCall had cast a long shadow over Lake County. His handling of the Groveland case, in which a white woman accused four black men of raping her back in 1949, had made national headlines and put Lake County on the map as a symbol of racial injustice. McCall had shot two shackled defendants while transporting them the night before their second trial. One of the men, Walter Irvin, actually survived the shooting and lived to tell how McCall had taken the backwoods, stopped in a remote location, told them to get out, and shot them.

After being hospitalized for his wounds, Irvin was retried, reconvicted, and once again sentenced to death. A few years later, a new governor, LeRoy Collins, reviewed his case and, in 1955, commuted Irvin's death sentence to life imprisonment. It was a stunning decision at that time in the Jim Crow South and one handed down against the vehement opposition of Sheriff McCall and other white Floridians.

The governor, a segregationist but otherwise a moderate by southern standards, was disturbed by the many shortcomings in the case. "My conscience told me it was a bad case, badly handled, badly tried and now, on this bad performance, I was asked to take a man's life," Collins later said. "My conscience would not let me do it."

His death sentence commuted, Walter Irvin would be imprisoned for eighteen years for a crime he maintained his whole life he had not committed. DNA testing was not yet in use to prove or disprove his claim. In 1969, he was paroled on the condition that he never set foot in Lake County again. But the following year, he was granted permission to visit his family there for a single day. Soon after he got there, "he dropped dead while sitting on a front porch." He was forty-two years old. Officials like McCall said he had a heart attack. But after all that had preceded Irvin's death, some black people in town believed it was no accident.

Into the early 1970s, Willis McCall was still the sheriff of Lake County. He was still wearing his ten-gallon hats. The Groveland case had made him something of a celebrity among Florida segregationists. He would become the center of case after case of alleged abuse and misconduct against black people in the county. He would be investigated forty-nine times and survive every one of them.

As the world began to change around him, he stood his ground in defense of the old order of things. When President John F. Kennedy was assassinated in November 1963, "the only public building in the United States that refused to lower its flag to half-staff was McCall's jail in Tavares," the Lake County seat, according to the author Ben Green.

COLORED ONLY and WHITE ONLY signs were coming down all over the South during the 1960s. But Sheriff McCall did not take down the COLORED WAITING ROOM sign in his office until September 1971, and then only under threat of a federal court order. He may have been the last elected official in the country to remove his Jim Crow sign, Green said.

McCall was reelected seven times, that is, until 1972, when Florida Governor Reubin Askew stepped in and suspended him after yet another violent assault on someone in his custody. This time, McCall was indicted for second-degree murder for allegedly kicking a black prisoner to death. The prisoner was in jail for a twenty-six-dollar traffic ticket. McCall was acquitted.

But he lost the election that November. Blacks were now able to vote, and they turned out in force to defeat him the first chance they got.

"We sent cars out and taxicabs," Viola Dunham, a longtime resident and a sister-in-law of George Starling, remembered. "We started getting these people out to vote."

Then, too, a new generation of whites had entered the Florida electorate, the younger people who may have identified with the young freedom riders in Mississippi and Alabama even if they would not have participated themselves, and the snowbirds, the white northerners who were buying up vacation homes or retiring to central Florida with the boom that came with the arrival of Disney World and who couldn't relate to the heavy-handedness of a small-town southern sheriff. And now it seemed that even the most steadfast traditionalists had finally tired of the controversies and felt it was time for him to go.

The defeated sheriff retreated to his ranch on Willis V. McCall Road in Eustis, where he tended his citrus grove, welcomed his partisans, and held forth on his decades of lordship over Lake County. He could take comfort in the fact that, for better or for worse, Lake County would not soon forget him, and he took pride in his role of protecting southern tradition.

The times might have changed, but he never would or sought to. Displayed in his home was the COLORED WAITING ROOM sign that once hung in his office and that he was forced to take down under threat of a court order. Nobody in the world was going to tell him what he could do or what he could hang in his own home on Willis V. McCall Road.

MONROE, LOUISIANA, EARLY 1970S
ROBERT JOSEPH PERSHING FOSTER

THE FOSTERS HAD ALWAYS had a complicated relationship with their hometown of Monroe—or rather, with the few other ambitious and educated black people maneuvering among themselves for the few spoils allowed them in a segregated world. The rivalries would pass from one generation to the next until it no longer mattered because most of the Foster descendants had died or, like Robert, migrated away. As prominent as the Fosters had been, there would be no direct descendants living there by the 1970s, and the rivalries would play out from afar.

In the time since Robert drove away from Monroe for good, Robert's father had died, his brother Madison had visited Los Angeles for surgery and died from complications there, his brother Leland had moved to the Midwest, his sister, Gold, had followed Robert to L.A. in the 1960s, and his nephew, Madison James, was in graduate school at the University of Michigan and not likely to move back.

But even before Robert migrated west, the Fosters had begun to languish like deposed monarchs on the outskirts of influence in town. By the 1950s, Professor Foster had been edged out of his principalship and a new colored high school had gone up to replace the old one the Fosters had run for decades.

There was a time when hardly any black child in Monroe could get through high school without getting past a Foster. Now a whole new generation was growing up not knowing who they were. Not only had many of the Fosters left, but the Migration had drained away many of the people who remembered them. It was the price they paid for migrating.

Some old-timers expected that the new high school would be named after Professor Foster for all his years of service. He had taught, overseen, or influenced the education of most every black person in Monroe from the 1920s to the 1940s. But there were not enough partisans to push the case.

The new high school would take the name of a family that had stayed in Monroe, had not run north or west or forsaken Monroe for the so-called Promised Land. The Carrolls had been in Ouachita Parish since Reconstruction, and, like others who stayed, moved into greater prominence as possible competitors migrated away. When the new school went up, it was named after one of the Carrolls—Henry Carroll, who had become the first black member of the Monroe Board of Education—rather than the retired and nearly forgotten Professor Foster. Robert's father had to watch from the sidelines as the new school he had always dreamed of rose up in the name of a rival.

"Papa was hurting, dying inside," Robert said. "But he never let you know it."

The next year, the Foster name was affixed to something the Fosters would not, in principle, have been against but would not have otherwise chosen for themselves, given their preoccupation with high-minded achievement. The Fosters lost out with the high school, but as a consolation prize, a public housing project was named after Professor Foster, the Foster Heights Homes on Swayze Street, a few blocks from the new high school. It was as if all that Professor Foster had endured and devoted his life to had been boiled down to an assemblage of low-rise apartments of pink brick and struggling lawn. Every shooting or drug bust or robbery that might happen there and make it to the evening news ("Last night, in a drug raid at the Foster Heights Homes . . .") would resurrect the Foster name in a way that was counter to everything the family stood for.

Robert didn't want to go back to see the housing project with his surname on it, but he did and found it neatly spread out, rather like a roadside motel. He would have to go back to bury his father and big brother and sister-in-law Harriet.

Each visit was a time of melancholy. Finally, no immediate family was left. There were still no sidewalks in New Town, and the streets were still unpaved, just as they were when he was a boy. It only confirmed that he could not have lived out his life in this place.

By the early 1970s, integration was beginning to filter into everyday life in Monroe. So, after visiting the graves of his mother and father and his big brother Madison, Robert decided to walk into a diner that used to be only for white people. It was a place he could only have dreamed of entering as a young man. He sat down without incident, ordered and ate, and nobody commented on it one way or the other. It was nothing special and, in fact, underwhelming after all those years of being denied entrance and dreaming of being inside. How could it be that people were fighting to the death over something that was, in the end, so very ordinary? He had crossed into territory forbidden him growing up, and now the circle was complete. It was much like returning to a building that had seemed so imposing when you were a child but was, in fact, small and forgettable when seen through the eyes of an adult.

Before leaving Monroe, he passed the big new colored high school on Renwick Street and could not help but think of his father walking to his old schoolhouse in the dark of morning to open up Monroe Colored High with its used books from the white school and secondhand desks. The new Carroll High School was something Professor Foster could only have dreamt of in those early days, and, for as long as he lived, Robert would remain convinced that it should rightly have carried his name.

Robert returned to L.A. and again tried to put Monroe behind him. He would never fully be able to. And so he worked harder at everything he did. He gave all of himself to whatever was his fancy at the moment.

Each December 23, he put aside his patients and gambling to devote himself to commemorating his marriage to Alice. He made the reservations and all the arrangements. Every year, the plan was exactly the same.

Robert and Alice would go to Scandia on Sunset Boulevard. The maître d' would make a show of the appetizer and subsequent courses. There would be a gift immediately following the entrée—a diamond ring or a fur coat. There would be some grand gesture at the end and a toast to however many years it had been.

But things did not always go according to plan—not in any huge, irreversible way, but in the little ways that could easily rattle Robert, who was easily rattled anyway.

One anniversary, the maître d' happened to seat them at a table in a darkened corner in the back.

"I couldn't stand it," Robert said.

He fumed and sulked. He could barely enjoy the anniversary he was supposed to be celebrating. When he could stand it no longer, he summoned the maître d'.

"Please move me to another table," Robert said. "It's too dark."

(*"I tipped him, and that will work wonders. You have to be careful not to overdo it. Then you show your ignorance."*)

Another year, the maître d' sat them at a booth. It was in the right place in the room. But something was wrong. The booth sank in where Robert was sitting.

"When I sat down in the booth, my wife was taller than I," he said. "I didn't like that."

He told Alice to switch places with him, "so that I wouldn't be shorter than she was." Alice, having already settled on her side of the booth, had to collect her purse. The two got up and circled each other to take the other's seat.

Only then could the evening commence.

"Leo, what are we going to eat tonight?"

There came the courses, and he would watch with pride and amazement as Alice negotiated whatever elaborate or towering concoction was put before her.

Then came the part Robert liked the most, the part he put the most ritual and planning into.

The morning of the dinner, he had called the florist.

"I want red roses and baby's breath," he had told the florist. "I want to be able to see over the table."

The florist fretted over what that meant for the arrangement, precisely what the dimensions should be.

"Alright, get me the width and the length of the table," Robert said. Someone called the restaurant and got the measurements for the particular table Robert had reserved for this particular anniversary, and the roses and ferns could then be cut and arranged.

"Each year I added one red rose to that bouquet," he said.

It was their thirty-third anniversary. "We're in the center of the dining room," Robert remembered. The maître d' came out with "thirty-three long-stemmed roses with white baby's breath and fern and ribbon," he remembered. "Each anniversary, one more ribbon."

Losses

It occurred to me that no matter where I lived,
geography could not save me.

—Jacqueline Joan Johnson,
who migrated from Charleston,
South Carolina, to New York in 1971

LOS ANGELES, DECEMBER 1974
ROBERT JOSEPH PERSHING FOSTER

WITHIN FOUR YEARS of Robert's big party of a lifetime, Alice, who had married him to the unspoken disappointment of her upper-crust parents, had followed him to Austria and Los Angeles and Vegas, allowed herself to be his mannequin and muse, given legitimacy to his aspirations and become his ticket to high society, which he both coveted and resented, Alice with her cat-eye glasses and teacher's solemnity, had fallen gravely ill and died.

Again, like his brother Madison, here was another family member passing away, and his medical certifications and surgical expertise could do nothing to stop it. She died of cancer, as had Robert's mother, on December 8, 1974, at the age of fifty-four. Her passing and burial rites were both headlined in the *Chicago Defender* and the *Atlanta Daily World,* the black newspaper that had charted her every coming and going for most of her life.

The *Defender,* taking interest from half a continent away, described her as "one of Los Angeles' most prominent civic and social figures," "wife of noted surgeon, Dr. Robert Pershing Foster," and "a tireless worker in numerous civic and philanthropic organizations."

She was interred far from the tinseled veneer of Los Angeles in Louisville, Kentucky, at her father's burial site, reclaimed in death as a Clement, not a Foster. They had been married thirty-three years, not one of them in Monroe. On that, they had both agreed.

As quiet and self-contained as she was, the house felt empty and unbearably silent after she was gone. The girls were all off on their own, two now married and living back east, the youngest away at college. Robert, along with Alice's mother, Pearl, returned disheartened from the interment and took up their positions in their respective corners of the echoing mansion. As big as it was, it was feeling too small for two people so different from each other, who had put up an appearance of cordiality only to appease the one thing they had in common—sweet and devoted Alice. Neither had liked how the other seemed to control her, and now the reason they endured each other was gone and not coming back.

Each missed her more than they could have possibly anticipated. Even Robert—who had directed her choice of clothing, dissected her every attribute and deficit, stayed out late tending his patients and his vices, and taken for granted that she would be there whenever he needed her—felt her absence perhaps more than her presence now that he no longer had it.

With each passing day, Pearl grew angrier and more resentful. Of all the people in her life and all the people she had known and loved, here she was left with the one she least wanted to be around. How was it that the two of them had survived? It would never have occurred to her when she moved to Los Angeles, a widow from Atlanta, into the new wing Robert had built for her that her daughter would precede both of them in death and that so full a house would come down to just these two.

Now Robert was asking her to contribute a little in rent each month, which she took as an insult, given how the Clements had helped them in the early years of their marriage and how she had just now lost her only child. Robert thought it was only fair, given that he had vowed to take care of her daughter, not her, but still had done so, even building a wing for her, from the time Rufus Clement had died seven years before. He knew that Pearl had the money to share the household expenses from Clement's pension and estate. And, besides, Robert said, "I had given her anything she wanted." They could come to no agreement, and matters only grew worse.

The gambler and the socialite were marooned in a house that was big, but not big enough to escape each other. They were the oddest of couples and each was all that the other had. Day after day, he went to his office, hoping to avoid her on the way out. Day after day, she was stuck in the house where every lamp and figurine reminded her of the daughter she had lost.

She had never wanted to be part of the Great Migration or come out to California. She had lived her whole life in the South and was in Los Angeles only because her daughter's husband had been so insistent on fleeing the South and had taken Alice and the girls with him. Now, with Alice gone, she was alone in a city she had never wanted to be in. She had little to fill the hours. Robert and Pearl ground through their days in slow motion and tried to pretend the other wasn't there.

It wasn't long until she realized she couldn't take it anymore. She could no longer hold in the resentment. One day, she broke the silence.

"Why did you have to be the one to live, and not my daughter?" she finally said.

She had gotten it out, and there was nothing left to say after that. The tension had likely been building up from the moment they'd met. Her time in the house couldn't last much longer. She packed her belongings and moved back to Kentucky, where her late husband and daughter were buried. And Robert was alone in the house and with himself for the first time in his life.

CHICAGO, FEBRUARY 1975
IDA MAE BRANDON GLADNEY

IDA MAE'S SISTER IRENE, the one who had urged Ida Mae to come north in the first place, saying, *"I just wouldn't stay down there if I was you,"* and whom they moved in with upon arrival, was having eye surgery. She hoped Ida Mae would come up to Milwaukee to help her while she recovered. Ida Mae wanted to go but wasn't sure she would be able to.

There was so much going on in Ida Mae's household with everybody either coming or going to work and trying to take care of the grandkids, who were teenagers now, and get to church on time and pay the light bill and the house note. Ida Mae couldn't drive and didn't have a way to get there. And it was the darkest days of winter.

George and Ida Mae were not the youthful innocents fleeing the hard soil of the South for Chicago as they had been all those years ago. They were in their sixties now—George was sixty-eight and Ida Mae was sixty-two. They had lived in Chicago for longer than they had been in Mississippi and were still working, which they had been doing in one form or the other from the time they could pick up a hoe or reach over a wash pot.

They had reached the point in life where everyone around them seemed to be succumbing to something—high blood pressure, diabetes, which they called sugar, cancer, stroke, hysterectomies, heart attacks, or some combination of them all.

Ida Mae had had to go back to Mississippi some years before to see about her ailing mother. Miss Theenie had collapsed from a stroke and, isolated in the country as she was, had lain out in her yard, unable to move, for more than a day until someone happened to pass by on that lonely gravel road and see her. Miss Theenie did not live too much longer after that. Ida Mae went down to the funeral in the spring of 1959 and grieved mightily over it, but she had a family of her own to tend to.

Ida Mae herself had finally gotten over her fear of hospitals and had the hysterectomy her doctor said she needed. George had an enlarged heart and had already suffered two heart attacks. Each time, the family managed to get him to go to the hospital. But, stubborn as he was and disbelieving and suspicious of northern medicine, he wouldn't submit to any surgery or medication upon release—the nitroglycerin or beta-blockers that would have been standard at the time. To him that was just some kind of northern trickery and against his faith in God.

"He didn't have no medicine 'cause if he had it, he wouldn't take it," Ida Mae said. "He would never believe nothin' was wrong with him. He didn't believe in no doctors."

Whatever he was feeling, he just said it was indigestion. Once when he went to the hospital, the triage nurse was asking him about his symptoms.

"Don't ask so many questions," he told her. "Just do something for me and ask questions later."

Now her beloved big sister Irene was needing her, and Ida Mae was trying to figure out how to get to her. George told her she should stay home, tend to the family, and go to church. But it turned out that a friend named Evelyn happened to be heading to Milwaukee at around the same time, and Ida Mae's daughter Eleanor told her she should make up her own mind and go see about her sister. Eleanor agreed to go with her.

They helped Irene as best they could. When they arrived back in Chicago and pulled up to the house, they knew something was wrong. It was a Sunday, midday, and George's Chevrolet was still parked out front when he should have been at church.

Ida Mae and Eleanor walked into the vestibule. James came right out. He told them George had had another heart attack while Ida Mae was away. It was the third one her husband had had. It struck him that morning. This time he didn't come back from the hospital.

James broke the news to Ida Mae and Eleanor that George had passed away. "They had to pick both of us up off the floor of the vestibule," Ida Mae said.

She thought back to the start of the weekend. How she had chosen to see about her sister instead of staying home. How, the night before she left, the cat had slapped her in the face.

"I should have known then," Ida Mae said.

She remembered George's warning her over and over, "Now you work and make your own money," he used to say, " 'cause one day I ain't gon' be here."

She thought about his last heart attack. "The doctor said he'd never pull out of another one," she remembered.

Even Irene said she knew something was about to happen, although it wasn't clear exactly how. "Ida Mae, I started to tell you to go back home," Irene said after she learned that George had died.

James said he had found him.

"His arm was as hard as this seat."

"No, I found him," his wife, Mary Ann, said.

"No, you didn't," James said. "You fell out in the hallway."

"I should have been there," Ida Mae said in one of her rare displays of regret. For forty-five years, she had been the dutiful wife of a hardworking and stoic man, cooking and cleaning after him and obeying him—most of the time—like the pastor had said to do. And here, when he needed her, in his last moments on this earth, she wasn't there.

She tried to remind herself why she had gone. "Eleanor said I was always doing what he said to do," she remembered. "She said I should go on up and see about my sister. I ain't saying he'd a lived. George went to a funeral that Saturday. Something told me, 'Ida Mae, you better stay here.' . . . You think about these things."

She mulled this over in the days after his death. Then Ida Mae dried her tears and consoled herself with something her husband used to say.

"He always said the Lord wasn't gon' let him suffer," Ida Mae said. He had suffered enough in his life. He had been a good provider, and he had kept his faith that God, who had delivered them from Mississippi, would look after him in the end.

He was right. He was the one who used to open up the church. He had set out his suit, shirt, shoes, and tie well in advance so he would be ready that Sunday. "He died in his sleep," Eleanor said, "with his hand over his heart like somebody had placed it there."

NEW YORK, 1978
GEORGE SWANSON STARLING

ALL THE SORROWS caught up with Inez. There would be scientific and medical explanations for what befell her. But those who knew her could see the storm whirling inside her, which she had tried to suppress, a thousand little heartaches since coming into the world just as her mother left it and being hooked now into a marriage born of adolescent love but mostly of spite.

Her churlishness had managed to alienate so many people, perhaps without intending to, but people didn't tend to stay around long enough to figure out the motivation. The one thing she categorically loved most in this life, her firstborn, Gerard, had broken her heart with his addictions. The drugs had turned him into a stranger and stolen her son from her.

She would never fully get over it. And as Gerard sank further and, by some miracle, came out of it, only to sink back again, she and George moved further apart. George practically had a second family, distant though he was, now that he had a son by another woman. But he stayed in the marriage out of a distorted sense of honor and duty rather than truly wanting to be there, and Inez had to live with that, too. The New World had been a land of milk and honey, of a hard-won measure of freedom and working-class achievements—the Harlem brownstone, the insurance policies and certificates of deposit, the upstairs tenants who brought in extra income, the furniture, cars, and appliances, the steady if monotonous jobs that impressed the folks back home—but they had come at a steep price.

Inez suffered under the weight of her disappointments and the mirage of what, from Florida, looked like a well-lived life in the North. By early 1978, the heartaches caught up with her. She was diagnosed with breast cancer and succumbed later that year.

Even as her body failed her and she had little time left on this earth, she and George circled each other, could not break through the hurts and recriminations that had built up over the decades since he had grabbed her by the hand and ushered her into the magistrate's office back in Florida to get back at his father. Her passing lent a finality to that error in judgment. They had lived with it but had not been happy, and the marriage ended more sorrowfully than either of them could have ever imagined that spring day back in Florida in 1939.

LOS ANGELES, 1978
ROBERT JOSEPH PERSHING FOSTER

WHEN ALICE DIED, so did the highbrow social theater she and Robert had shared in Los Angeles. Robert would no longer keep open the private salons of the finest department stores to find some heavily beaded gown for Alice. The invitations to this or that black-tie function evaporated. The phone didn't ring as much. With Pearl gone back to Kentucky, he had the whole house to himself.

Even the office didn't feel the same. What was he raking in all this money for if he couldn't spend it on someone he could show off and brag about? He was going on sixty now, and it was time he started thinking about letting his private practice go and taking a more predictable position at a hospital somewhere. He wouldn't have to worry about managing an office or patients needing him in the middle of the night. He could spend more time out in Vegas or at the track, doing what he wanted to do, what he came out to California for in the first place.

He decided to take a staff position at the Veterans Hospital in Brentwood. It would allow him to focus on medicine and his patients, not on rent, utilities, and payroll. It seemed a perfect fit. He was a veteran after all.

His life would now revolve around carpools to the hospital, treating the same kind of people he treated when he was in the army in Austria—rather like going back in time. And then there were the trips to Vegas whenever he could get away.

It was nothing for him to catch a plane to Vegas after work, gamble all night, fly back the next morning, and make it to his office just in time for his first patient.

"It was a sickness," said Limuary Jordan, who knew him in Monroe and in Los Angeles and had little patience for him. "I know for a fact that here's a man who could make five hundred or six hundred dollars a day in his office back in the seventies and still had to go and gamble in Vegas, go play his blackjack."

He would arrive at the Las Vegas Hilton and, unlike his first trip back in the fifties, would be ushered to one of the best rooms in the house. "The room was comp," Robert said.

"The meals were comp." He was betting so much money, the casino at the Hilton could be assured it would get the cost of them back, and more.

Robert would head to the casino and start playing blackjack or the roulette wheel. Mostly blackjack. Of course, there were no clocks or windows. None of the gamblers knew whether it was day or night. It didn't matter to Robert because he could play for almost twenty-four hours straight anyway.

"I don't know when to get up," Robert said.

There were times, lots of times, when he lost, in a matter of minutes, more than some people made in three or four years on a fairly decent job. And when he lost, he just kept playing, feeling it in his bones that the next hand, the next game, would be the one to turn things around.

He could rise out of the hole and get back in it for hours or days. He could get away with losing great sums of money because the casino knew he was good for it.

During one particularly rough stretch, he had a run of good luck and then sudden, heart-stoppingly bad luck. He was betting heavy and winning at first. He got cocky enough to tell the man in the casino cage that he was going to give him ten percent of whatever he won. He got to ten thousand, eleven thousand, twelve thousand, thirteen thousand dollars, and started attracting the attention of other gamblers around him.

Then nothing seemed to go his way.

He usually took someone with him—a nurse, a patient, another gambling buddy—to keep track of his winnings so he could concentrate on his game. When he hit it big, whoever was with him could count on getting a few thousand dollars from him to take back to Los Angeles. When he was losing, they sat helpless and watching. His nurse from the office was with him this time. As Robert's fortunes rose and fell by the hundreds with each bet, she started to notice something and tried to bring it to his attention.

"You know," the nurse began, "seems like every time you get to thirteen thousand dollars, you start losing."

That would not have been enough to stop him. It was not one of his better trips. But it was Vegas, and there was always another day. He was always playing to the crowd, knew all the casino workers, and loved it. Whatever he lost, he figured he would make it up tomorrow.

One time, Jimmy Gay, the man who had introduced Robert to Vegas and had been a boyhood friend of Limuary's in the small world of southerners in the L.A.-Vegas circuit, ran into Robert after a big win.

Robert had forty or fifty thousand dollars in front of him, and Jimmy wanted to intercede to keep him from losing it.

"Bob, let me go put it up for you," Jimmy said.

"No, I can handle my money," Robert shot back. "I'm a grown man. I don't need nobody to handle my money."

A couple hours later, Robert came back, wanting to borrow two thousand dollars.

"He done lost that fifty thousand and wanted two thousand to get it back," Limuary remembered. "Bob squandered a fortune."

But he seemed only to remember the times when he hit it big. It was what he lived for. Like the time when a friend who went with him had to keep up with the kind of money you only heard of in bank robberies.

"We brought back fifty-three thousand dollars," Robert said of one trip in the 1970s.

"He came back with a paper sack full of money," Limuary remembered, "and everybody knew his business on the job, and he'd pay all the people he owed."

But it was never really about the money for Robert. He had plenty coming in to begin with. It was hard really to know what it was about, except that he was weak for it and that deep inside him was a southerner with still a lot to prove. Gambling drew him, and he couldn't stay away. When he couldn't make it to Vegas, he bet on the horses at Santa Anita or played blackjack in a bare gymnasium of a space over by the Hollywood Park racetrack, anywhere he could escape into the nerve-jangling uncertainty and the rare seconds of elation that lasted only long enough to reel him back in.

He was handling sums of money that people back in Monroe could not fathom. "He won and lost several fortunes of a lifetime," Jimmy Marshall, his fellow migrant and friend, said.

In the midnineties, Robert, never a good driver to begin with, had a car accident, rammed into a median strip over on Crenshaw. He tore up his Cadillac. Someone came to help him out of the car.

"Are you hurt?" the man asked.

"No, I'm alright," Robert said.

"Did you get your bottle?" the man asked, figuring, why else would someone ram into a median strip?

"No, I don't drink," Robert told the man. Not anymore, anyway.

He would not be able to drive anymore. He shouldn't have been driving in the first place, his friends would say. But that wasn't going to stop him from getting to wherever he needed to gamble, even in a city of expressways and little in the way of public transportation.

He figured what he would do. *"I'll take a taxi to the racetrack," he thought to himself.*

One day, he summoned a cab to his house on Victoria. He got in and directed the driver to Hollywood Park racetrack. Then it hit him. Why go to Hollywood Park when he knew where he really wanted to go?

"How much would it be to take me to Vegas?" he asked.

The cab driver told him the fare. He told the driver to head to Vegas. That time, he won big, which he would have needed to in order to get home, and flew back to Los Angeles with a sack full of money—triumph and self-esteem in a sack, to his mind.

More North and West Than South

I could come back down to New Orleans
for wonderful visits with my people,
but I couldn't stay.
Chicago and the North, where
I was used to Negroes being more free,
was where I belonged.
—Mahalia Jackson, *Movin' On Up*

CHICAGO, 1978
IDA MAE BRANDON GLADNEY

IDA MAE SETTLED INTO HER ROLE as the sweet-natured but no-nonsense matriarch of the family now that her husband was gone. She had managed to re-create the village of extended family that existed on the plantations down south, her grown children and grandchildren surrounding her in the three-flat they had been in now for more than a decade.

The neighborhood had changed around them, had become all black and significantly poorer and more crime-ridden than it had been when they arrived. She and her family looked inward and lived their lives in the compound they created—her son, James, and his wife, Mary Ann, and their young children living on the first floor; Ida Mae living with Eleanor and her two children on the second floor; and a tenant named Betty, who was almost like a daughter to her, on the third floor.

There was always a commotion now that Kevin and Karen were out of high school and just starting their lives and Eleanor was divorced but with a full social schedule of house parties and lady friends from back in high school and new boyfriends, the phone always ringing for Eleanor.

Someone was always coming or going, wanting to know if the mail had arrived, if a job had come through, if a sweetheart had called yet, if a friend had said what time the party was, all of them expecting Ida Mae to keep up with this information since she was retired and home most of the time, and bending down and giving her a peck on the cheek as they got their coat and headed for the door again.

If they were all home at the same time, Kevin might be watching the White Sox in his room, Eleanor catching the news in hers, and Ida Mae watching a game show in the living room while keeping an eye on the drug busts and prostitutes on the street, which was usually better than any show on television anyway. There was a time back in Mississippi when nobody had a television—it hadn't been invented yet—and now everyone had one and retreated into his or her separate world.

Holidays brought everyone together, especially Thanksgiving. It's not clear whether anybody gave it any thought, but turkeys had been one of the reasons they were in Chicago in the first place. Maybe they would have come to Chicago anyway, it was just meant to be. In any case, in the fall of 1977, Ida Mae's family was chosen out of all the families on the South Side to represent the typical Chicago family at Thanksgiving. Someone at Jewel, the Chicago supermarket chain, knew someone who knew Ida Mae's family, knew James and Mary Ann, knew they were good solid people and that Ida Mae was beloved by all who came in contact with her.

Jewel brought a camera crew to their three-flat in South Shore. The dining room table was draped with white lace and candles, filled with platters of green beans and cranberry sauce and sweet potato pie and a roasted turkey at the head of the table. James with a mustachioed grin and his mother's narrow face, Mary Ann in auburn curls and a white silk blouse, and three of their four children sat smiling and happy as if in dinnertime conversation around the dining room table. A photographer captured the moment.

The picture ran as a full-page ad for Jewel Food Stores in the *Chicago Metro News* on Saturday, November 26, 1977. The headline read "Platters Full of Plenty Thanks." Near the center of the picture was Ida Mae with a platter full of salad, standing at the head of the table in a polyester dress, her white hair in a French twist, her big goggle glasses taking up most of her face. Her eyes looked directly into the camera and she smiled as if unburdened and free despite the turmoil outside her front windows. For now, she was taking up a whole page in an ad out of Norman Rockwell in a city that had resisted people like her coming north, and, for one brief holiday weekend, had made it to the big time in Chicago.

NEW YORK, 1978
GEORGE SWANSON STARLING

INEZ WAS GONE, but the churchwomen bearing homemade pound cakes held little interest for George Starling. Inez was the only woman he would ever consider as a wife, however unhappy they had been. Now that she was gone, he was left to watch helplessly as the children he was not around enough to raise got themselves into fixes. He would try to impart wisdom from what he had learned from his own mistakes to children and grandchildren who did not appear anxious to hear it. He was getting to be looked upon as just an old man from the South. What did he know of the frustrations of being young and black and wanting to be somebody and all the temptations and obstacles they faced and what it took to survive?

He had been the one to set the course of their lives by migrating to New York before they were born. The parts of the city that black migrants could afford—Harlem, Bedford-Stuyvesant, the Bronx—had been hard and forbidding places to raise children, especially for some of the trusting and untutored people from the small-town South. The migrants had been so relieved to have escaped Jim Crow that many underestimated or dared not think about the dangers in the big cities they were running to—the gangs, the guns, the drugs, the prostitution. They could not have fully anticipated the effects of all these things on children left unsupervised, parents off at work, no village of extended family to watch over them as might have been the case back in the South. Many migrants did not recognize the signs of trouble when they surfaced and so could not inoculate their children against them or intercede effectively when the outside world seeped into their lives.

George's two children would come to resent the overcrowding and the vice and concrete, the people on top of one another and the perils all around. Both Gerard and Sonya would succumb to them in one form or another then run from the toxic influences that caught root in the city. They would move to Florida, the Old Country, by the 1980s, Sonya to Eustis, of all places, which she found smaller and, after the death of Jim Crow, more welcoming, and Gerard to Miami, where he made unheard-of sums of money dealing drugs during the cocaine boom, falling deeper into the drug world he was initiated into as a boy in New York.

Gerard blamed New York for the road he had taken, and he hated the city for it, unable to own up to the choices he himself had made.

"If I hadn't been born and raised in New York," he once told his cousin Pat, "I never would have been on drugs. I wouldn't have lived the life that I lived. I hate New York."

Both of George's children went in the opposite direction from the one George had taken, went back to the place he had left and made decisions he couldn't understand. It was as if their return was a rebuke to his attempt to spare them the pain he had endured and to give them chances at decent schools and work options other than fruit picking, choices he himself had never had growing up.

George would rarely talk about his children, so great was his disappointment.

The one constant in his life was the job on the railroad that took him along the path of the Great Migration he had made himself back during the war. Down and back, South and North, New York to Florida and New York again. He was sixty years old and had been working the rails for thirty-five years. How many times had he plied this route, passed through Wildwood, Jacksonville, Savannah, Raleigh, Richmond, and Washington and on up to New York, again and again? How many thousands of migrants had he helped up the train steps carrying their luggage? How much history had he seen unfolding in the faces of the people boarding those trains?

He was nearing retirement and was doing precisely the same thing now that he was when he was twenty-five. He had not moved up or been promoted in all those years. He had tried to propose to his superiors improvements in service since he was in a position to see up close exactly what the passengers needed. But nothing ever came of it. He learned to accept his lot, and it got to the point where he just stopped applying for positions, like conductor or ticket taker, that it was clear he wasn't going to get. Toward the end of his career, he got to be in charge of the luggage in the club cars. But it was really not much different than before.

As he had done when he first started, he would walk from one end of the train to the other all night long. He could rarely sit and never sleep during a twenty-four-hour run. All through the night, he had to take people's luggage at every stop and put it away and reposition it and pull out the luggage for passengers disembarking. He walked back and forth, up and down.

Sometimes he would take Inez's niece Pat with him on those night runs. He would get her settled in her seat and go to work.

"There never was a time that I saw him sleep," she remembered. "He never complained. It wasn't a gravy job, and it was beneath his dignity. He never got a chance to use his mind. When he first started, it was an honor to be a porter on that train at that time. But in reality, it wasn't nothin' but hard labor."

The Great Migration had played out before his very eyes. Now it was coming to a close from a demographic, macroeconomic point of view. On the ground, it was maturing, the migrants and their families situated in the North, no longer nervous and starry-eyed, missing their stop or getting off too early or by accident in Newark. Now he was watching and helping the grown children and grandchildren of the Migration make their way back to the Old Country. The ways of the North had settled into most of them. Many of his passengers were born and raised in the North and were making their first visits to the South, rather than returning to a place they had known.

He could tell the original migrants. They were requiring more help getting up the steps, beginning to need canes, many still speaking in their southern accents. They were the ones sitting up straighter, more alert, their memories awakened, when they passed the fields of tobacco and cotton, the small church-steepled towns along the way and the groves of orange trees that George knew so well, because, mean and ornery as it may have been, the South was still the Old Country, the land where their fathers and mothers were buried, and these original migrants were heading home to it, at least for now.

LOS ANGELES, 1978
ROBERT JOSEPH PERSHING FOSTER

ROBERT, a widower nearing sixty now, had landed what would seem the perfect position. He was doing precisely what had been denied him back in Louisiana. He was on staff at a hospital. And not just any hospital. He was physician to the staff of the West Los Angeles Veterans Administration Medical Center in Brentwood. It took up twenty-two acres between UCLA and the Brentwood Country Club. Its curving drives were named after the great generals of history—MacArthur, Patton, Pershing, the name he had gone by for the first half of his life. It was bigger and better than St. Francis, the small-town hospital that had rejected doctors who looked like him during the days of Jim Crow and had given him one more reason to leave the South. It would be vindication for all that he had endured back home.

He would make less than when he was in private practice, when he was limited only by the hours in the day and the energy he could muster. But he no longer had to concern himself with patient billing and office leases and could concentrate on what he loved most—doting on his patients, the employees at the VA hospital. Immediately, he set about getting to know everyone.

Some of the staff took to him right away, especially the few black ones who had migrated from the South like he had. Before long, he was carpooling with some of them to get to work. They quickly learned that his other love was gambling, and they could tell when he had just gotten back from Vegas. They would drive up to his mansion early in the morning and toot the horn. Robert would scramble down the walkway, silk suit pressed and necktie in place, limping in his stocking feet with his dress shoes in his hand.

He brought his crushed velvet, jitterbug demeanor to the gray, humorless bureaucracy of a government hospital. He put his feet up on his desk as he always had and asked about his patients' complaints and worries before pulling out his stethoscope. He had built an entire practice on understanding his patients' personal troubles so that he could get to the bottom of their medical ailments, as he saw one as being connected to the other.

Migrants from the South treasured his bedside manner and had made up the majority of the patients in his private practice. But Robert was now in a world more like the one he worked in as an army doctor in Austria during the Korean War. Most of the patients, meaning the hospital staff members, were bureaucrats or military and not of his background. Some had come from the South in the parallel migration of whites seeking their own fortune in the wide-open world of California during the years of the Great Migration.

The whole enterprise was an adjustment for Robert. He was used to being in charge and the center of attention, running his office as he pleased. Now he had to be at work by eight in the morning. Bureaucrats wouldn't put up with what his adoring working-class patients would accept. They wouldn't put up with him coming in on a morning flight from Vegas, rushing in late with his silk suits and sacks full of money. He couldn't charm his way into everyone's good graces by offering to pick up everybody's lunch tab with his winnings.

"That didn't work when you working for another man," said Limuary Jordan's wife, Adeline, one of Robert's sometime critics. "You got to follow his orders. You just don't come and walk over them like that."

His breezy airs did not sit well with some of the bureaucrats and their assistants. His being one of the few blacks in authority could have put him under perhaps even greater scrutiny. The bureaucrats began complaining about him, and soon he clashed with one hospital worker in particular. It may never be known precisely what happened. The military would not disclose details of the dispute, and Robert took the Hippocratic oath so literally that he rarely spoke of the specifics of any one patient. There were no legal charges against him, and he received workers' compensation for the distress he suffered. But trouble flared, his colleagues said, after a white woman patient at the hospital complained about an examination. Robert had managed to survive decades in the Jim Crow South without crossing a white woman and had actually won the gratitude of one from Kentucky when he interceded in her delivery and helped her avoid a cesarean section.

Now, decades later, after he had built a name for himself and had taken a job he did not need, he was running into the very thing he had come to California to escape. There were whispers within the hospital of professional incompetency, perhaps the one thing he had never been accused of in his life.

Robert refused to give up his position. But it would be only a Pyrrhic victory. The hospital, he reported, moved him from the offices that he and the white doctors who preceded him had worked out of. It transferred him to an older building "in a cramped examining room next to a loud lavatory reeking with urine and feces," he wrote in the mid-1990s in a letter of complaint to the Labor Department.

It was as if he had been hurled back fifty years to the Paramount Theater back in Monroe. It was nearing the eve of the twenty-first century, and it seemed as if Jim Crow would not die. His every move was scrutinized and the stress of the isolation weighed on him more heavily than anything in his life. He had made it to the paradise he had so believed in all those decades ago that he had bragged about it before even seeing it. Now, it had betrayed him in ways he could not have imagined.

He told his friends and family of his plight and the plight of coworkers who had also migrated from the South and were now helpless as they witnessed what was happening to him. He was so incensed that he complained to the Labor Department about the "personal isolation, professional and personal slights, rumors, [and] professional slander" he was enduring. He described "a continuous racist and stressful environment," language that he rarely used in all his descriptions of life in the South.

He had given his life over to his patients to the detriment of his own family, a decision that would weaken his ties to his daughters and grieve him later in life when his choices could not be undone. He had sat at the bedside of patients who loved him for his devotion. And now a new one had turned on him and threatened the reputation that had taken him a lifetime to build.

Things only got worse. In seeking workers' compensation, Robert was required to be evaluated by a psychiatrist with ties to the VA hospital. The psychiatrist seemed to dismiss what Robert told him and directed Robert to prove to him the difference in the size of Robert's old office and the smaller one to which he had been demoted.

The psychiatrist "proceeded to command me to step forward," Robert wrote, "pick up a commercial tape from his desk and stoop down in a servile manner to measure his office for square footage." Something about a surgeon being commanded by anyone to stoop to the floor and take measurements brought back memories of the sirring and ma'aming back in the South and made him feel lower than at any time since perhaps his migration through the desert.

"I am humiliated and ensnared in an evaluation process which is untenable," Robert wrote.

He had never wanted to make a federal case out of the times in his life he had been ill-treated because of the caste into which he had been born and the era in which he lived. But here he was making a plea to the government as he fought for his good name. The stress forced him to seek treatment from a cardiologist and from vascular and orthopedic surgeons and a psychiatrist. They told him he needed to quit to protect his health, but Robert did not want to go out that way, not after all he had been through, proving himself at every turn, starting with the decision to migrate in the first place.

The only good thing about the situation was that Rufus Clement had not lived to see it. Surely he would have told him that this was proof of what Clement had believed all along, that Robert would have been better off casting his lot in the South. Better, too, that big Madison hadn't lived to see it either. Surely, he would have shed a tear for his little brother who so loved medicine and worked so hard at pleasing everyone.

The dispute dragged on for years as Robert sought relief through workers' compensation for the toll the situation had taken on his health. One day in the middle of this episode in his life, he was walking down the red-carpeted aisle toward the club room at Santa Anita when it felt as if he were being stabbed in the chest. He was suffering a heart attack. He would require bypass surgery and would see his life slow down considerably.

He would soon take his own physicians' advice and retire from the VA hospital. It was not how he wanted to end his career. The memory of what he felt was a forced ouster in his adopted home would stay with him for the rest of his life. He had seen roadblocks to black progress even in his beloved California. "And it's harder and heavier the higher the paycheck," he said.

As for Robert's reputation, the one he fought so hard to maintain during his dispute with the hospital, it remained as it had always been. Patients from the VA hospital continued to see him, dropping by the house on Victoria to seek his advice. And many years later, the State Medical Board in Sacramento showed the record of Dr. Robert P. Foster to be free of any sanctions during the forty-four years he was licensed to practice medicine in the state of California.

But he would never see California the same. He would have many moments of joy from the old patients who consulted him and brought their children for him to examine and allay their worries long after he had retired. But he would never get over what befell him.

"He was dying on the inside," his friend and patient Malissa Briley said.

Redemption

For our light
and momentary troubles
are achieving for us
an eternal glory
that far outweighs them all.
—2 Corinthians 4:17

I

CHICAGO, SUMMER 1996

IDA MAE GLADNEY IS EIGHTY-THREE YEARS OLD when I first meet her. She is a churchgoing pensioner with time on her hands. She spends most of her days alone while everyone else is out working. She does word puzzles and crosswords, whole paperback books of them, to keep her mind sharp. She collects the funeral programs of the people she knew and loved in Mississippi and Chicago, who are, one by one, passing away, getting extras for other mourners the way young people collect business cards and email addresses. It is the currency of the old. In the meantime, she manages to keep up with the job pursuits and love lives of her grandchildren and great-grandchildren.

She has little interest in soap operas and doesn't need to watch police dramas on television. She has one right outside her window. Hers is a bow-front window, curved like a movie screen. She can monitor the street day or night from her box seat, which is actually a baby blue, plastic-covered easy chair by the front window, on the second floor of her three-flat. Things are happening that she never saw growing up in Mississippi, and she isn't always certain of exactly what it is she is looking at. She is watching the street from her window the afternoon I meet her.

A man is selling drugs out of a trash can. She can see, plain as day, where he puts them and how he gets them out of the trash for the white customers in their SUVs with suburban license plates. Another hides his stash in his mouth. And when customers come up, he pulls a piece of his inventory from his tongue to sell to them. The police are on to it, too. "The police put flashlights down their mouth," she says. "Sometimes the police make them stoop over."

A man is climbing out of an old Pontiac he sleeps in. He and the car have been outside her house for weeks. A teenage mother has just popped her son for something Ida Mae can't make out because a car passes by just when the mother yells something at the boy. Usually it's "M—f—" or "G—d—," Ida Mae says, and it hurts her to see people do that to their children.

The other night, she says, she was setting out the trash and saw a woman on her knees in the alley doing something to a man who was up against the garage. "I was looking for her head, and I never did see it," Ida Mae says. She didn't know exactly what the woman was doing but she knew they shouldn't have been doing it and knew better than to say anything and thought it best to go back inside. "I just can't get it out of my mind," she says.

When the police aren't around, the people are out in the street like characters in a cable television drama and the drug dealers are up and down the block but mostly at the corner where there was once an ice cream parlor, back when she first moved here.

These are the lost grandchildren of the Migration who have grown hard in the big city and did not absorb the lessons of the past or the good to be found in the steadying rituals and folk wisdom of the South. Ida Mae and James and Eleanor can't understand how they do the things they do, how they would rather trawl the streets than go to work every day and be able to hold their heads high.

Something about too many people packed together and nothing to guide them makes the children worse than they used to be, to her mind. At the moment, the city is in a crisis because two grade-schoolers, one of them only seven, have been accused of killing another child. Nobody knows for sure what happened and she certainly couldn't say, but she knows one thing for sure: "They curse like sailors, they throw rocks, they do everything they big enough to do. They ain't got no home training, and they mama can't do nothing 'cause she on drugs. That seven-year-old, they say he was the ringleader. He know more than he telling. But they shouldn't put them in the penitentiary. They too young. They not gone ever forget it."

She keeps going. "I know kids 'cause I been one," she says. "I used to tease this girl that her mama was dead. I think about that a lot sometimes. She held that against me the rest of her life. She used to cry when I said it. I didn't know what it was to lose a mother. I had lost my father. I thought everyone should die. I was nine or ten years old. I was bad. Now they double worse. What go in the wash come out in the rain. *Watch what I say, now.* You got to start working on those little ones early. I ain't got much education, but I sho' know folks. I ain't scared of these kids but I stay out of their way."

The craziness has Ida Mae hemmed in on all sides. When she leaves to go to church, if she goes to buy groceries, if she takes a walk to get some exercise, the drug dealers and lookout boys greet her as she leaves and welcome her when she gets back. When she hears sirens or gunshots, she runs to the window to see what has happened now. She is an eyewitness to a war playing out on the streets below her. Staying on top of everything is how she makes peace with the craziness she cannot escape.

She would never dream of going outside at night by herself. But it is not because she is afraid of the gangbangers and the drug dealers. She speaks to them and prays for them, and in turn they look out for her. They call her "Grandma" and tell her not to come out on certain days.

"You better stay in the house," they tell her. "Because we don't know what time we gon' start shootin'."

On a July afternoon, she is telling her story about the ride up north and making her way in Chicago in those early days. We are in the middle of a conversation when something crashes outside the window. It rattles me, and I look toward the window to see what it might be. Ida Mae does not flinch. She has learned the difference between danger and mischief, between a gunshot and a rock through a window. Whatever it was, it's as if it didn't happen.

"Did you hear that?" I ask her. "Sounds like some glass broke."

"Honey, they does that. They throw bottles at each other."

"You didn't even look up."

"I hear too much of it," she says. "I'd be lookin' all day." She lets out a big laugh.

Every day, there is something or other. On an otherwise quiet afternoon, we look out the window and see two police officers leading a black man in a white windbreaker and baseball cap, hands cuffed, down the sidewalk in front of the apartment building next door.

"That's the janitor," she tells me. "He works there. Wonder what did he do?"

He lopes along, head up, scanning the street like a politician on a tour of his district. He looks both ways before stepping off the curb to cross the street to the patrol car. He nods his respects to the teenage girls walking past.

Ida Mae doesn't know what he has done, but figures she'll find out in due course.

"People talk," she says. "You don't have to ask."

She has an idea of what it was. There was a raid in the building a few weeks before. The police took seventeen or eighteen people out in handcuffs.

"Did it at night," she says. "They carried them all out tied together. I got tired of counting. You know that still ain't stop them? They still up in there. I don't know what'll stop 'em. I guess the Lord knows."

She watches and makes note of what's going on around her. Every month, there's a neighborhood crime watch meeting, and she is sure to attend. Trouble is, she believes some of the police are not much better than the criminals. "The detectives are the ones doing the dirt," she says. Somehow, some of the dealers are onto the police or get forewarning of their arrival. "They have a phone," she says. "They know when the police coming."

Still, she manages to stay out of everybody's way. She may be stuck in her own home, but she has too much faith or stubbornness to let fear take over.

"I ain't gone live nowhere scared," she says. "I ain't calling the police. Long as they don't bother me. If I know what's going on, they do, too."

And she refuses to put bars on the windows. "My husband say, he never be behind no bars," she says. "And neither am I."

2

HARLEM, 1996

IT REQUIRES descending down a narrow set of stairs into an airless vestibule in the basement of a three-story brownstone to get to where the owner lives. He has taken the dankest, darkest space for himself and given over the rest of the building, the rooms with light and space, to whatever tenants he has.

George Starling never cared about creature comforts and finery but about getting a square deal, which he on occasion achieved, and the right to exercise the free will he was not permitted in the South. His life is scattered in boxes all over his room, file folders stuffed with pictures of him and Inez as teenagers in Florida, mimeographed copies of his lawyerly letters to the railroad or union leaders about this or that provision or instance of inequity, and the funeral programs of loved ones who have passed away.

He is seventy-eight now, a grandfather and great-grandfather, a deacon in the church. He sits upright and stoic. He enunciates each syllable in this early conversation and speaks in the deliberate and formal manner of the professor he once wanted to be. But the longer he talks, the more comfortable he gets and the more he sounds like the southerner he is inside.

He feels it his responsibility to share what he knows and takes it upon himself to explain whatever he says in the greatest detail. He talks for forty-five patient and exacting minutes about what it takes to pick string beans and describes the difference between the walking buds, the junior buds, the uncle buds, and seedling trees he used to pick back in Florida.

A car pulls up. It's his pastor, Reverend Henry Harrison, dropping by to see Deacon Starling. The pastor, hearing the topic of the South and the Migration, begins telling the story of how his father escaped from a labor camp in South Carolina by swimming through a swamp, and, eventually, in 1930, finding his way to New York.

Both men start to lament the changes all around them, the sadder effects of the big city of the North on the people of the South. George waxes on about the days when "people would come down to 135th

Street with their house chairs, and they would baptize people in the Harlem River.

"We used to have a boat ride off 125th Street in the Dyckman section," he says.

"Spread the blankets out. Midsummer, people didn't have air-conditioning. People would stay up there all night and play card games.

"Things were so much different," he says. "Drugs wasn't heard of where I came from. When I came to New York, I didn't know what a reefer was."

"We got to being Americanized," Reverend Harrison is saying. "It got to where we don't help each other."

George has children and grandchildren and even a great-grandchild now, but there is an aloneness to the character of his life. He seems content in the solitude of his room with its dust-covered floor, barely made bed, and no sign of a woman's touch. He seems on a mission to sort through the paperwork of his life, find some meaning in all the railroad pamphlets and official letters he wrote on behalf of workers' rights that were politely dismissed or not acted upon.

His face turns ashen and he looks away when the subject turns to his children and grandchildren. His son by Inez had squandered the very opportunities George had left the South for, and he had limited contact with the now-grown son he had outside his marriage.

Then there was the daughter, Sonya. She was sweet but unsettled, too, back and forth between Florida and New York. George had been having heart trouble and had just come out of triple bypass surgery when he got word that Sonya had died in a car accident down in Eustis.

He flew down to Florida for the funeral. The people who had stayed in the South gathered around to console him.

"We would be in a room with a crowd of people," his niece Pat said, "and he would get up and leave the room. He'd come back and just carry on the conversation. You knew he had been crying."

He buried his daughter next to his wife.

3

LOS ANGELES, SPRING 1996

THIS IS THE 1970S set piece known as Dr. Robert Foster's living room. It is a room that is little changed, you learn, from the time when his wife, Alice, was alive. You are encased in cream and raspberry upholstery, sea foam carpet, and harvest gold draperies cascading down from ten-foot ceilings, more space than one person could possibly need and, by that measure alone, the very picture of success in California.

The host has momentarily disappeared down a hall and into the avocado green and harvest gold kitchen. He emerges, taking care with his steps, with a tray of lemon pound cake with vanilla ice cream, which you would really prefer not to take, since you have only just eaten; but it is clear from the formality with which he presents it and then watches as you pick up the fork that there is no choice but to accept this gesture of hospitality.

In a bookcase, there are volumes of Tolstoy, Freud, Goethe, and Herodotus. On his face is a smile of satisfaction at the interest being taken in a life he loves to talk about.

You learn the basics of what he wishes you to know about his growing up in Monroe, marrying the daughter of a university president, leaving the South for California, about the three daughters and now the grandchildren, the gambling and the current state of his health and how he views the world as a southern émigré in California. Those things will be fleshed out in due time over the course of several months.

You learn that right now he has heart problems, has already had bypass surgery. "The chest pain is growing more frequent," he says. "But I'm not going to have another operation. If anything happened to me tomorrow, I wouldn't have any regrets. I have lived. I've done it all. The world don't owe me nothin'."

He is retired from the practice of medicine and spends most of his time at the blackjack tables or on the phone dispensing free medical advice to former patients and old friends or ordering around a gardener who indulges his every whim as to precisely where the begonias should be. Years before, Robert woke up the morning of his oldest daughter's wedding, and, instead of taking his time dressing in his tuxedo, he got out and had the front yard dug up to plant flowers to match Bunny's wedding bouquet.

Now, on this late spring afternoon, he was fretting over the backyard. "Now turn it a little more," he was telling the gardener one day about a particular pot of geraniums. "Not to the left! To the right! To the right!"

He has come all this way and is living in a 3,600-square-foot monument to his success in California. But the most enduring accomplishments you cannot see: the cooks and teachers and postal workers all over southern California who would do just about anything for him because he had saved their lives or brought them into the world or repaired some broken piece of themselves. And the three daughters whom he spared from having to go to segregated schools in the South and who grew up free with their cotillions in California.

The daughters lead upper-middle-class lives, had married well if not long, and have children who can only be said to be brilliant. Bunny is now working as an artists' agent in Chicago. Robin is a city manager who is living outside Washington with her second husband and her son, who is being courted by the Ivies. The youngest daughter, Joy, is a physician—a radiologist—married to a day trader, and has two precocious young children in Long Beach, about thirty miles south of Robert.

Alice never got to see the fruits of her labor, and, at weddings and holidays, it falls to Robert to be mother and father, neither of which he is naturally suited for. But he rises to the occasion when called upon to do so. When Joy brought home a young man she appeared to be serious about, Robert stepped forward as a father protecting his youngest.

He asked the young man, Lee Ballard, to go out for a drive to the dry cleaners with him. He made it sound like a request, which, of course, it was not. Lee climbed into Robert's white Cadillac, and Robert began driving, erratic as usual. Then Robert began his inquiries.

"How do you like California?" he asked Lee once they were on their way. "And how do you plan to take care of my daughter?"

The drive lasted two hours. The beau survived the drive and ended up marrying Robert's youngest daughter. The marriage would last longer than those of the other girls.

The telephone rings. It's the third or fourth time in the space of a couple of hours. The phone usually starts ringing around three or four o'clock, after people get home from seeing their new doctors. Robert excuses himself to take the call in the kitchen. It's another friend and former patient calling about an ailment and how best to treat it and to check to see if his new doctor is prescribing the right medication. Robert indulges the man, addresses his worries, gives him advice.

"Demerol is the name of it," Robert is telling the person on the other end of the line. "Now, put something in your stomach."

The person has more questions for Robert about what he's been prescribed.

"Percodan? Any of those things nauseate the heck out of you," Robert tells him. "Take as little medicine as you can—"

The person interrupts, and Robert listens.

"Take your aspirin," Robert tells him.

The person cuts in again, still expressing concern. Robert reassures him.

"Sounds like you going to be alright, Phil. God bless you."

EUSTIS, FLORIDA, JULY 1996
GEORGE SWANSON STARLING

SOME FIFTY-ONE YEARS have passed since the standoff in the central Florida citrus groves that almost got George Starling killed. He has lived out his life in New York. The grove owners he stood up to are long dead, as is the high sheriff, old Willis McCall, who lorded over Lake County with a Smith and Wesson and a ten-gallon hat.

George has felt it safe to come back to visit and is now sitting at a diner out by Ocala with his old friend Reuben Blye, who was one of George's picking foremen back in the forties. They both had lived up north. Reuben, at age eighty-nine, is now living back in Florida with his sixth wife, having survived the treachery of the South and the temptations of the North and is at this moment reliving those days with George, who is back in town for a high school reunion.

"Do you know a Florida man got more sense than a born New Yorker, George?" Reuben asks, not really looking for George to answer. "You know that?"

"I had never given it a thought that way."

"One that's been around like us, George. We know our way around better than some of them up there."

"Well, you had to have a lot of sense to learn how to survive down here during those times to stay out of trouble, you know."

"George, you done run that railroad so long up and down from coast to coast on the train," Reuben says. "And look how we travel. Look at Rube, done travel, done made thirty-seven states. I already had it in my head. You don't get me every day."

As torn as George was about his time in Florida, he had never truly left it in his mind. Ever since his father had died, he had kept a little piece of property in Eustis, vacant land with live oaks and scrub brush near the house where his father had run the little convenience store. He never knew exactly what he would do with it and had no plans to live there ever again. He just liked the idea of having control over something in a place that had controlled his every step for so long.

"When I left, I swore that I would never come back under no circumstances anymore," he said. "When I left, I was just that bitter. I didn't intend to come back at all."

Ten years passed before he felt it safe to return. The deaths and illnesses lured him back and he began to see how the South seemed to be changing, in small ways and big ways, right before his eyes. "I never thought I would live to see the day," he said of some of the strides being made. "If anybody told me that there would be a black mayor in Birmingham, I would have told them they were crazy. Now they have black mayors all over the place down south. How many black mayors we got up north?"

He had once seen a black man and a white woman walking down the street in downtown Tavares, the county seat and the domain of old Willis McCall. George was having a hard time getting used to seeing what could have gotten him killed in his day.

"I never thought I'd see the day when a black man would walk down the street holding hands with a white woman," he said. "It amazes me when I see the intermingling. When I was a boy down here, when you went through the white neighborhood you had to be practically running. Now black people are living in there. They all mixed up with the whites right there in Eustis."

We are riding through Eustis and out to the orange groves near Sanford and the train station in Wildwood where the relatives would come to greet George when his train passed through. He and Reuben are returning to the places where they picked oranges and okra, the places they could and couldn't go and where the black people lived. Reuben does most of the directing because he has been living back in Florida for several years now. George sits up and starts pointing when he sees something he recognizes.

"They used to baptize us down here," George says as we wind past Lake Eustis. "To the left are the water oak trees."

We drive farther out. The land is wild scrub brush broken by stands of domed trees, the citrus that ruled their lives growing up.

"Over to the right, over here was woods," George says, "just like you see to the right, but they cleared that up."

"Here go the seedling groves," Reuben says.

"Is that Lake Ale there?"

"That Lake Ale. Those seedling groves right in here had all them pecan trees."

"Was this the Natural?" George asks of the legendary grove that has withstood the worst winters and hardest of freezes.

"The Natural's out there by Emaraldi Island."

"I told you Reuben would know where everything is," George says, turning in my direction.

"If you dropped an orange in the Natural Grove, five minutes and it would just be hittin' the ground. You could get up in one of those trees and look all over this south Florida."

"This is Ole Jones' place."

"I picked in that grove where I had a thirty-six-foot ladder spliced with a twenty-six-foot ladder, and it just reached the bottom limb."

"That's right. All us here, Charlie, Mud, me, we used to hunt coons and possum 'long here."

We drive further and further out.

"This here is Ole Cannon Grove."

"This is not the way it looked before the last big freeze," George says. "This is new. They reset, they put new trees there."

"All this here was froze out."

"Nineteen eighty-nine, it snowed in Florida. Had two and three inches of snow."

"Have you ever seen a forest that would burn out with a fire?" George asks me. "Well, that's just the way those trees look. Them trees looked just like somebody went through there with a flamethrower."

George comes back to Eustis every two years for the biennial reunion of Curtwright Colored High School. He always comes down on the train he once worked. It's owned by Amtrak now and, as a pensioner with thirty-five years of service, he gets to ride for free. He can finally sit like the passengers he served and look out the window to see what they saw, reliving with each trip the migration he made all those years ago.

When George returns to Eustis, he is looked upon with a distant kind of respect. He was one of them once, but he chose a different path, knows things they couldn't know, survived in a place where they're not sure they could make it. He's been gone so long that whatever he knows about Eustis is either frozen in the 1940s or distorted through the secondhand recounting in long-distance phone calls and letters and rumor. He's fuzzy on some of the names of the people who live there now.

Whole generations have been born since he left, and he searches out his connections to them, the ways he might know them—through a grandparent, great-aunt, or second cousin of theirs whom he grew up with but who may not be around anymore. He stays with Viola, the widow of his deceased stepbrother, and spends much of his time visiting with the few people who were around when he was here, reliving those days, and catching up on the things he has missed. When people hear that he's in town, they head over to Viola's bungalow and remove their hats before they walk in to see a prodigal son of Eustis.

It is Sunday on the July weekend of the high school reunion, and George puts on his burgundy polyester suit, burgundy tie, burgundy socks, and white straw hat to worship at the church he grew up in as a boy and where the doomed Harry T. Moore recruited him in the early drive for equal rights. Seventy parishioners take their places in the dark wood pews affixed to orange carpet.

Pastor William Hawkins beseeches the congregation to take up a special plate for the black churches that have recently been burned throughout the South. It is as if it is 1963 again.

"We ought to do something to assist them," he says. "And this is one of the reasons we better secure our own church."

People pull out money to give to the other churches and pray that they won't be next. The choir motions for George to come forward and sing the solo for the collection.

"What you give, what more He gives to you," he sings.

Then the pastor turns to George. "We are always glad to see our member from New York," Reverend Hawkins says, motioning to George to come to the pulpit to speak.

George stands before the congregation of mostly new faces, the descendants of those he knew, and looks around at a church that was as much a part of him as the South itself.

"Needless to say, I am grateful to be in your midst," he says. "I look over and see my father and my mother and my daughter. And it always makes me a little full. So if I become emotional, I hope you will understand."

He then sings a hymn, *"Without God I could do nothing . . . without him, I would fail. . . ."*

The congregation claps after he finishes, and he takes his glasses off and wipes the tears with his handkerchief before walking back to his seat at the side of the church. He takes his place and sits upright in a pew next to the pulpit with a silver cane beside him and tears escaping from his eyes.

LOS ANGELES, NOVEMBER 23, 1996
ROBERT JOSEPH PERSHING FOSTER

THE REGULARLY SCHEDULED BIMONTHLY MEETING of the Monroe, Louisiana, Club of Los Angeles, California, is not so much called to order as roused to life when ten of the sixteen surviving and currently active members trickle into the bungalow of Leo and Era Davis on Ninety-third Street east of Crenshaw. They gather in the Davises' den with the circular metal staircase and prepare to catch up with one another and with news from back home in Monroe.

It is surely one of the smallest Louisiana clubs in the city, not to mention its being overshadowed by all the Texas Clubs around town. "We're a dying breed," says Limuary Jordan, a club member who left Louisiana in his DeSoto more than half a century before. "It's a fact. Everybody in the club is over sixty. And without any new Monroe people . . . there are Monroe people here, but they don't affiliate with us. They don't belong to no club. So we are of a particular time."

"A lot of them don't have anything to do with the South," his wife, Adeline, says. "A lot of them, when they left, they were gone."

The few members who are still active approach the club with a sense of formality and ritual. Robert Foster had to secure approval beforehand to invite a guest, who brings the attendance at today's meeting to eleven. As the graying expatriates from Monroe begin to take their seats, I explain my presence as his guest and tell them about my work on the Great Migration. They listen without emotion or much in the way of comment, not seeing exactly what the Migration has to do with them, even though they had all been right in the middle of it. At the appointed hour, John Collins, whom they just call Collins, stands up like a proper reverend and prays stiffly in his black suit and gray vest and fedora.

"Lord, we thank you for this food we are about to receive, and we thank you for another day," he begins. "We pray for the lady visitor and the book she's trying to put together. Give her knowledge and wisdom and watch over her. In Jesus' name. Amen."

Spread out before the assembled are oxtails, collard greens, corn bread, sweet potatoes, potato salad, red beans and rice, and pound cake on an orange tablecloth in the wood-paneled dining room.

It is a time of unaccustomed quiet in the city after so much upheaval. The Rodney King beating, police acquittals, and ensuing riots were only a few years back, the business districts of South Central still in recovery. The people have been divided and whipsawed by the O. J. Simpson trial, the saga of a once-loved black football player acquitted of killing his white wife and her friend, the people by now just wishing the whole thing would go away but unable to escape it, billboards and headlines in every direction.

That very day, Robert passed a newspaper box with a poster about the O.J. trial. "I'm so sick of O.J.," he said, "I don't know what to do. They have choked us with this."

No one in the Monroe Club wants to talk about it. Instead, as if on cue, the never-ending loop of how people are faring back home and in Los Angeles and what they have been through in both places picks up where it left off from the last meeting as if it were fresh and new and has never come up before.

"If you look at it," Howard Beckwith begins, "we in the same instance as in the South. They throwing them in jail just like the South. The jails filled with colored people. The South has made a desperate change. Things you couldn't do in the South, you can do now. You can walk down the street with a white woman. The mayor is black."

"Who's that?" someone asks.

"You know Dr. Pierce what run the drugstore," Beckwith says. "One of his sons."

"No, it's not," someone breaks in, one-upping Beckwith and trying to prove who has the better connections to a place they still feel tied to even if nobody else cares about the distinctions. "It's one of Dr. Pierce's *cousin's* sons. The cousin of Dr. Pierce, one of his sons."

"That's Eliza Davis's son," a woman whispers to me by way of explanation. *"She was my classmate,"* she wants me to know.

Somehow the line of conversation reminds Collins about being black in the South and the talk turns to a kind of testifying rather than an interaction, each member reciting an experience independent from the others and at times seemingly unrelated. Here it is, fifty years after most of them left, and they can't stop talking about the South. They are exiles with ties to two worlds, still obsessed with the Old Country, and have never let it go.

Collins tells them about the time a white man slapped a ladle of water out of his hand as he was taking a drink. A woman describes being home from college and a policeman coming up and asking why she wasn't picking cotton or in the kitchen. Someone else mentions the movable sign on the trolley car and how "you had to sit and look at that sign that said 'Colored.' " Everyone nods in recognition.

Marshall brings up the segregated lines and the swiveling ticket agent at the Paramount Theater again. "The woman in the ticket counter swiveled to the white side to sell tickets and then swiveled to the colored," he says. "We walked up all those flights of stairs."

"That's all over the South," Beckwith says. "You didn't know nothing different."

Robert breaks in, momentarily distracted by the meal. "Era, what did you do with the oxtail? It's out of sight."

"Cake and ice cream? Cake and ice cream?" Mrs. Davis asks with a sugar voice, cake held up high.

Marshall then remembers an incident at Woolworth's, a seemingly small thing that let him know he was not meant to stay in the South.

"A white girl waited on me and gave me a token for my change," Marshall begins. "I went to tell on the woman, that she had taken my money and given me a token back that was worthless. All I got was the satisfaction of telling the man and of telling my mother when I got home."

He recounted what his mother told him: "You're going to have to leave this place, you keep that up."

Which is why Marshall ended up in California.

Then Robert joins in. "I had taken my bath in the tin tub," he begins. "I was clean."

"Was that the Saturday-night bath?" Beckwith's wife, Isabel, asks.

Everyone laughs in recognition. Like most black people in the South, none of them had had indoor plumbing back then, and Saturday was the one night in the week when they could manage the time-consuming ritual of boiling water from the well and filling a tin tub so everyone in a given family could take a bath.

They knew just what Robert meant. They let him finish his story.

"A white man called me over," Robert goes on. " 'Hey, boy, I'll pay you if you can tell me where I can find a clean colored girl.' "

He pauses for effect.

"I told him, 'I'll get you one if you get me your mother.' "

"Foster, did you really say that?"

"So help me God."

"You lucky to be alive."

And, Perhaps, to Bloom

Most of them care nothing whatever about race.
They want only their proper place in the sun
and the right to be left alone,
like any other citizen of the republic.
—James Baldwin, *Notes of a Native Son*

CHICAGO, 1997
IDA MAE BRANDON GLADNEY

IDA MAE SETS HONEY on the window screen in her yellow-tiled kitchen to feed the bees. She gives away tiny seeds of four-o'-clocks and morning glories. They are a wonder to her, waking up as they do at the same time every day, more reliable than the best-intentioned people.

In her kitchen, she cooks no differently than if she were in Mississippi, folding the eggs and sugar, butter and nutmeg into softened sweet potatoes to make sweet potato pie, boiling her collards and mustard greens with ham hocks until they are rich and satiny and then making the corn bread to go with them. She has no use for recipes. It's all in her memory from what Miss Theenie taught her and her sisters-in-law back in Mississippi. She sifts cornmeal, white flour, a little baking powder, and a palmful of salt into a tin pan. She stirs in six eggs, sprinkles in a little sugar, and spreads a pool of vegetable oil in the baking pan before pouring in the batter.

Not too long ago, Eleanor went down south with a friend and came back reporting that the people were using self-rising meal for their corn bread in Mississippi now. Ida Mae didn't know what to make of it. She would have to rethink what she was doing. It was a revolutionary break from how they did things when she was there. For generations, they had used plain old cornmeal, back to slavery days, when that was all that they had. Everything in the recipes in their heads called for it. For years, they'd had self-rising meal in the North, but Ida Mae never tried it because that's not what they used down south when she was coming up. It wouldn't be authentic. But Ida Mae thought she might as well try it if that was the way they were doing things now. So she and Eleanor went out and bought some self-rising meal, and Ida Mae tried it. But the corn bread rose up like a pound cake. She wasn't sure if it was this newfangled meal or how she used it, but she never did try it again.

On this day, she puts the corn bread, made the way it was when she was coming up, into the oven and waits for it to bake. The corn bread grows plump and golden, and Ida Mae pulls it out when it is ready.

"Now you put you some butter and some buttermilk on it," she says, "and it make you want to hurt yourself."

At this stage of her life, the kitchen, where she whips up from memory the staples of the South, and the living room, where she monitors the streets of the North, are the center of her everyday world. Lately the invitations she gets are not to the weddings and baby showers of the young but to the funerals and wakes of her dwindling generation. It seems as though every week someone is admitted to the hospital or being eulogized. As she's the healthiest one in her circle of friends and the oldest member of her extended family, everyone expects to see her in their moments of grief.

She has just heard that another sister-in-law, Dessie, has died, and Ida Mae is getting ready to go to her funeral. The news hurls her back to the Pearson plantation in Mississippi, she and Dessie stopping to pick blackberries and Dessie teaching her how to make blackberry cobbler and tomato pie. She remembers being a young bride in a strange world, of all her husband's people on the plantation, all the brothers and their wives, the sisters and their kids, and how they took to her and brought her into their family.

"All them dead now," she says of her husband's generation of brothers and sisters.

The descendants want her to speak at the funeral since she is the oldest one left. Ida Mae doesn't like to dwell on the past or get mired in sadness. She doesn't want to do it.

"It's nothing I can say," she says. "Nothing I can say can bring her back."

She's beginning to dread funerals altogether but will go to this one and do what is expected of her. She will console the living, but it's getting harder and harder.

"I don't like going to funerals anymore," she says. "If it's sad, it just tears me to pieces."

One day she gets word that her beloved nephew Robert, whom they call Saint and who helped her and her family get out of Mississippi sixty years ago, has suffered a stroke. What is worse, his wife, Catherine, had a stroke just before he did. He had gone to the hospital every day to check on his wife before being stricken himself and each time was heartbroken over her blank stares and unmovable limbs. Now the two of them are separated for the first time in their marriage, she in the hospital, he in rehab. Ida Mae has to visit them both.

Today she is going to see Saint at a rehabilitation center at Ninety-fifth and Cicero. Saint had helped Ida Mae and her husband sell the things they didn't have time to dispense with or that, had they tried, would have attracted unwanted attention as they plotted their escape. He ended up following them up to Chicago with his wife and family in 1943, and they stayed with Ida Mae and George, as was the tradition among people migrating from the South, until they could get on their feet.

"I decided to come up because I had people up here," he is saying, sitting in his wheelchair. "People were coming up. I got in the crowd."

Saint and Ida Mae start reminiscing about the people they know from back home, how they are faring, who's a deacon now, who's moved into a nursing home, who's moved in with their grown kids out in the suburbs.

"It's a shame we all here and don't see each other," Robert says.

Then it hits him that he can't see his wife either. He starts to look down, and his eyes get moist. It's been the saddest of years, his wife taking sick and now him in a wheelchair from a stroke just like she had. His eyes well up.

Ida Mae looks at him, sorrowful and sad, too. This is her nephew by marriage. She is not much older than he is. She has known him for some sixty-five years. She owes him in part for her safe passage out of the South. His wife, Catherine, is one of the sweetest people she has ever known. And they call the man before her Saint for a reason. He wants to be with his wife, but he can't. The whole thing is breaking Ida Mae's heart too. But then she catches herself, stiffens her back, and makes up her mind to have none of that pity.

"Now, we not going to do that," she says staring at the floor, not able to look Saint in the face. "God don't make no mistakes. Either you gon' get better or you not. He's gon' see about you and do what he want. Now, you be thankful you did all you could. You didn't miss a day."

She's older than all of them but fit and modern in her mint green pantsuit and black pumps and copper mesh hat with her white curls peeking from beneath it, while the younger nephew is bound for the moment to a wheelchair.

She changes the subject, tries to lighten the heaviness in the air. "The kids fuss at me," she tells him about how she eats everything put before her. "They say, 'She don't let no food pass her mouth.' I say, 'Be a time you won't have to worry about me eatin'.' They say, 'There she go again.' "

"I told my kids, I'm doing pretty good to be seventy-seven years old," Saint says.

Ida Mae looks at him and smiles.

"That ain't old," she tells him.

On a late winter afternoon, Ida Mae is going through some old funeral programs like other people go through family photo albums. She starts to thinking about all the funerals she has been to, and one stands out in her mind. It was of a nephew of her husband. The nephew had been gay, and his companion, who was white, was distraught beyond words.

As she is recounting the story, Betty, the tenant from upstairs, happens to be there for a visit. Ida Mae describes how the companion was so torn up about her nephew's death that he nearly climbed into the casket.

"It was a white fella he was living with," she says. "And when they closed the casket, that white boy *fell* out. He said, 'Don't close the casket!' He took care of him to the end. Wouldn't let him go.

"I guess he musta really loved him," she says.

"That's not love," Betty breaks in. "God didn't mean for no man to be with no other man. They can't love. They don't know what love is."

"You don't think they can love each other?" Ida Mae asks her.

"Can't no man love another man. Only men and women can love each other."

Ida Mae just looks straight ahead toward the couch. She knows what she saw. There are husbands who don't show out like that for their wives and wives looking relieved and near-gleeful at their husbands' funerals.

Ida Mae shakes her head. "Well, I don't know what it is," she says. "But it sure is something there."

Ida Mae is the last of her sisters and brothers still alive. The last one to go was Irene, the sister who urged her to come up north in the first place and whom she and her family stayed with in Milwaukee for a time.

Irene died in 1996, and it fell to Ida Mae to manage her affairs. It meant periodic trips to Milwaukee that Ida Mae took on without a great show of sentiment as just part of her duty as a sister.

It is the middle of October 1997. We are driving north toward Milwaukee on Lake Shore Drive along the curves of Lake Michigan. It is a blue glass sea with white waves like the ocean.

It has been a year since Irene's death, and still Ida Mae has business she must attend to. I had offered to drive Ida Mae and Eleanor to Milwaukee, and we are on our way on a steel gray morning. A storm gathers as we head north on the Edens Expressway. The rain beats down in sheets. Cars are having to slow to a crawl, and you can barely see ahead of you. The trip is going to take much longer than expected. This will cut into the time she will have to take care of things.

"It's really coming down," I say. "Of all days. I hope it won't be like this all day long."

This sets off an automatic response in Ida Mae, and she reframes the moment for everyone.

"Now, we ain't got nothing to do with God's business," she says, sitting back in her seat.

She adjusts herself and straightens her scarf, contenting herself with whatever the day has in store.

NEW YORK, 1997
GEORGE SWANSON STARLING

THERE IS A STIRRING among the original migrants and their children. The question is whether they should go back south again. Some haven't been back since they left and see no reason to go back now. Some go back and forth all the time and have already picked out a plot of land. George is somewhere in the middle.

He has diabetes now, and his knees are failing him. People in his circle from back in Florida are dying off or moving away. He's now under some pressure to move back to Florida from people who see the reconstituted South as the next refuge. People who left decades before, and even more likely their children, can't help but consider the prospects of a changed South, whether they act on it or not.

"Two more years, and I'll be able to retire and I'm gone," some of the people who came north have been saying. They say they are weary of the confined spaces, the cost of living, the crime, just the stress of living among so many millions of people.

"I don't know why you staying up here," some of them have been telling George. *"Better get out from here while you can."*

It reminds George of how people talked during the Migration. "People saying the same thing they said before, just in the reverse," he says.

But there are fundamental differences, as he sees it, between those who went north and those who stayed in the South, the people and the place he would be returning to if he chose to do so, and he doesn't see that changing. "Those who didn't leave learned to accept it," he says.

He never did.

"I think about leaving the North," he says. "But I would be a stranger down there. I've lived in New York for fifty-two years. I've spent more time here than there. I'm a New Yorker now. Almost all the ones I grew up with are in nursing homes. If I went back, what would I do?"

There is an unspoken fear among some migrants to the North that, no matter how much better you could live in the South on those northern pensions, going home is somehow moving backward, a retreat, an admission of failure or at worst something that, like retirement itself, could signal the end of the full part of life and perhaps the end of life itself.

It was making George think back to what had happened to his old friend Babe Blye.

Babe was George's best friend and upstairs tenant who had worked with him in the orange groves when they were young men. Babe had come to New York in 1932 with his brother Reuben, well before George, and had gone back and forth between New York and Florida until George came up. For years, the two of them had lived in George's brownstone together with their wives, like the Ricardos and the Mertzes on *I Love Lucy*.

Babe so loved New York that he didn't go back to Florida "unless somebody was sick or died," Reuben said.

For years he worked at a car-painting factory in New York, caught possum in the Connecticut woods for their barbecues, and ran poker parties with George that almost got them killed. When Babe got sick, he went to George and told him he was going home. He asked George, whom he always called Son, a favor before he left.

"Son," Babe said. "I ain't gon' live long, Son. I'm going back. But I want you to sing 'Peace in the Valley' at my funeral."

"Babe, I ain't got no guarantee I'm a outlive you."

"Oh, yeah, you gon' outlive me."

"Well, close as we've been, I don't know if I can sing that."

"Goddammit, I want you to sing 'Peace in the Valley' now," Babe said. "Goddammit, I want you to promise me 'fore I go. You gon' sing 'Peace in the Valley'?"

"Okay. Yeah, Babe, I'm a sing 'Peace in the Valley.' "

In his heart he knew he couldn't. They were too close, like brothers, Babe and his wife, Hallie Q., upstairs from George and Inez all those years.

Babe left New York and went back to Eustis to live out his final years. He didn't live terribly long after that, a couple of years, as George and Reuben recalled.

He knew he was sick when he left. "He didn't tell me everything," George said. "But he knew something was wrong. And all of a sudden, he got it on his mind he wanted to go back home."

Babe died in 1976. The funeral was at the St. James Methodist Church, where George and Sam and Mud had eaten all those oranges back when they were little boys.

George went back for the funeral but didn't think he could get through a song about his friend and onetime crew foreman who had protected him in the orange groves. He figured he wouldn't have to, what with Babe being gone and no one there to make him do it.

Apparently Babe had told his wife, Hallie Q. She went up to George at the funeral.

"George, you supposed to sing 'Peace in the Valley,' " she said.

"Q., I can't do it."

"You promised Babe."

Somehow George got through the song Babe loved so much. George had to take his handkerchief and wipe his eyes at the end of it. The original Migration people were falling away.

LOS ANGELES, AUTUMN 1996
ROBERT JOSEPH PERSHING FOSTER

ROBERT'S FRIENDS and former classmates are getting up in years and facing one ailment or another, which puts Robert in almost as much demand as he was when he had a full-time practice. A friend called to complain about a cough and thought he might need to go to the hospital. Robert calmed him down and told him to give the antibiotics a chance to work.

Today he has gotten word that an old classmate from Morehouse is in the hospital, and Robert wants to go by and see him. We drive to a hospital in South Central. As we walk out of the elevator to get to the man's room, someone runs toward us.

"Dr. Foster, Dr. Foster!" the man is exclaiming.

It's an orderly who recognizes Robert from years ago and comes over to him out of breath.

"Don't you remember me from that appendectomy over on Hoover?"

"Why, of course, I do," Robert says, not remembering the man exactly but not letting on.

The orderly gets Robert caught up on what he has been doing the past few years, excitedly trying to impress him, and Robert wishes him well.

"You take care, Dr. Foster."

"And you as well."

Back at the house, he boils water for tea. He seems calm and at peace, distant now from the multiple recountings of the hard trek he made to get to California. He has thought things through and seems to have figured out his thinking now.

"I wanted to prove to them that I was worthy of a room," he says of his rejection along his journey. "I was not sure that I was good enough to be admitted. What good had it done me to get all this education and work as a surgeon in the army?"

"Have you ever been back through that stretch?" I ask him.

"Never," he shoots back. "I drove back south, but I went through Oklahoma."

He pauses and considers the effect his migration had on how he lived out the rest of his life and how he raised his daughters. He had demanded more of them than might have been necessary. He became obsessed with appearances and spent a fortune on their clothes and breeding so that there would be no reason for them to be rejected as he had been.

"I gave my daughters ballet so they could know how to walk," he said, "and create the picture I wanted. I wanted them to have an excellent education. I didn't want them to suffer the pains of racism. I didn't want them to have to sit in the back of the bus, suffer the unwelcome attention of low-class whites. I didn't want them to be open to being molested."

Unlike other parents raised in the South, he had never drilled into his children the hardships he had endured or dwelled on the limits of what they could or could not do based on the color of their skin. It was a strategy that worked beautifully in producing young women of grace and refinement but left them knowing little about the rituals and folk wisdom and history of the South or, in the end, that part of their father.

He remade himself in California and still does not fully know what to make of the place.

"It seemed like a fairyland the way they painted the picture," he says, "and I bought it."

"What do you think now?" I ask him.

"It's not the oasis that I thought it was," he says, "but I've got over that, too."

He pauses and considers the options of a stifled life under the deadly combination of Jim Crow and "little-townism," as he calls it, if he had stayed in Monroe or even Atlanta.

"I don't think I could have done any better," he finally says.

Robert has a taste for collard greens and corn bread, and we go to his favorite soul food restaurant in Inglewood, over by Crenshaw and Manchester, run by some people from Mississippi. He orders up yams and collards and smothered chicken and remembers that it was here that he sat when the riots over the Rodney King verdict broke out in May 1992. He remembers telling the waitress to wrap everything up.

"Let me get out of here," he told her. He turned north on Crenshaw and raced to get back home.

On this day four years later, the streets of his beloved adopted city are quiet, and Robert is momentarily back in the South with the comfort food of his youth. When it's time to leave, I prepare to take him home, but he tells me he'd rather be dropped off somewhere else. He wants to go to Hollywood Park racetrack, which all too conveniently happens to be right around the corner from the restaurant. He assures me he will have a way to get home. On the short ride to the track, he talks about how it feels, just going into a casino, which, for him, is more than a casino, but freedom itself.

"I walk into a casino," he says, "and I act like I own it."

Walking in like that attracts just the kind of attention he craves.

"What kind of surgeon *are* you?" a man asked him once, having heard he was a doctor.

"A damn good one," Robert told the man with a smile.

We arrive at the track, and Robert gets out of the car in his windbreaker and pensioner's slacks. He looks up at the exterior of the track, which looms high above him like a coliseum. He is a regal man, small-boned and slight in stature, and he looks out of place given his bearing and pedigree. But he quickens his step the closer he gets to the entrance. I watch him to make sure he gets in alright until he disappears into the crowd. He does not look back but straight ahead, as if he owns the place.

The Winter of Their Lives

That the Negro American has survived at all is extraordinary —a lesser people might simply have died out, as indeed others have.
—Daniel Patrick Moynihan, *The Negro Family*

NEW YORK, 1997
GEORGE SWANSON STARLING

THE HARLEM THAT GEORGE STARLING FLED to in 1945 no longer exists. The Savoy Ballroom closed its doors in 1958. Small's Paradise closed in 1986, its patrons now frail and the children of the Migration not dressing up and dancing the Lindy Hop late into the night. The Sunday stroll died off with the top hat. The black elites—the surgeons and celebrities who would have made their homes on Sugar Hill in previous generations—can now move wherever they want. Many of them live in Westchester or Connecticut now.

The magnificent brownstones are aging and subdivided. Urban pioneers have only recently begun to turn them around. The streets have been given over to teenagers with boom boxes, to crack dealers and crack addicts, prostitutes and soapbox preachers, wig shops and liquor stores, corner stores selling single cigarettes for a nickel apiece and homeless people pushing their worldly possessions in shopping carts down what is no longer Lenox Avenue but Malcolm X Boulevard.

George Starling has lived in Harlem for half a century and knows and loves it in spite of itself. Many of the people who came up from the

South have passed away. There are fewer and fewer old-timers left. Still he makes his way around with a sense of ownership and belonging. He has lived there for longer than most of the people around him have been alive.

It has gotten to the point that his mind is still sharp but he can't drive anymore on account of his eyesight, and his knees fairly creak as he negotiates the steps to the basement apartment of his brownstone on 132nd Street.

When he returns home in the evening from church or the grocery store, and if someone happens to stop to talk to him, someone who, say, maybe has not been seen on the block before, a voice might holler out from across the street in the dark. It is a neighbor watching out for him.

"You alright, Mr. G.? Everything alright, Mr. George?"

"Yeah, I'm alright."

"Okay. We just want to be sure."

Back in 1950, on the occasion of Harlem's fiftieth anniversary as a black community, the *New York Age* asked residents why they had moved to Harlem and why they stayed.

An ice vendor was one of the people who responded. "I know everybody in my block," he said, "and I don't think I want to go anywhere else to live, until I go to heaven."

George Starling knows how the ice vendor felt. As hard as the going has been up in Harlem, he has been free to live out his life as he chooses, been free to live, period, something he had not been assured of in Florida in the 1940s. He has made his mistakes, plenty of them, but he alone has made them and has lived with the consequences of exercising his own free will, which could be said to be the very definition of freedom.

A neighbor passes and yells, "Hey, Mr. George!" He smiles and nods and lifts his hand in the neighbor's direction.

Despite all the changes, it is still a neighborhood with its own sense of order and kinship.

"The people around here know more what's going on over here than I do," he says of his brownstone.

Anyone coming up to his door might face an inquiry.

"He know you?" somebody might ask on George's behalf.

When he was still driving, the crack addicts and prostitutes—or, more precisely, the addicts who were prostituting themselves to get more cocaine—would approach him as he pulled up to the curb.

"You need some company tonight?"

"No, darling, I don't need no company tonight."

Sometimes they come to him with good news, knowing how upright he carries himself.

"I'm going to school now, Mr. G.," they'll say. "Can you give me two dollars for some cigarettes?"

He looks them over and sees that they are only telling him what they think he wants to hear. "They come up, and they look like they just came out a garbage can," he says, shaking his head.

School is something he takes seriously because he hadn't been able to complete his own education. He calls them on it.

"Yeah? How long you been in school?"

They might not have an answer, but he gives them a couple dollars anyway.

"I give it to you Tuesday," they assure him.

"You don't owe me," George tells them. " 'Cause I don't want to get mad with you when you don't pay me back."

Sometimes they come up to him to report their progress, as if he were everybody's grandfather, and they feel the need to prove themselves to him.

"I just dropped out of rehab, but I'm going right back," they'll say, even though George can see full well that they can't be in rehab if they are running up and down the street as they have been all these months.

From his front stoop George Starling watches a most desperate parade. On these streets, there were once people gliding down the boulevard as if on a Paris runway, the men in overcoats and fedoras, the women in mink-collared swing coats and butterfly hats, all rushing to work for the rich white people or the manufacturers of paint or hats or lampshades. Now there are the hooded and disheveled descendants of the least able of the migrants living out their lives on the streets.

"I'm sitting out front now," he is saying to me over the telephone, *"and I see them ducking down these drug holes. They come here so beautiful, and in a few weeks look like they climbed out of a garbage can. We're the ones that's killing ourselves. I don't see one white person in this block selling drugs. They got the nerve to be mad at the blue-eyed devil. You don't have to take those drugs and sell 'em. Nobody's making you sell drugs. We're the ones that's killing ourselves. They won't learn in this century and maybe not in the next one."*

He wishes he could take all of them aside and warn them of the path they are taking. And, to those willing to listen, he does. But he has seen so much, it has begun to affect how he looks at them.

One time, a few years back, his door bell rang at two in the morning. He got up to see who or what it was.

"What do you want? You know what time it is?"

There before him was an addict, probably trying to sell him another trinket out of the trash that he didn't need.

"You know it's two in the morning?" George asked the addict.

"Your lights burning," the addict said. "The lights on your car, Mr. G. I'm sorry, Mr. G., but your lights're on in your car."

George thanked him. He rushed out to turn off the lights and promised himself he wouldn't prejudge these people anymore.

"I just thank the Lord," he says, "that, by his grace, it's not me."

LOS ANGELES, WINTER 1997
ROBERT JOSEPH PERSHING FOSTER

BY THE CLOSE OF 1996, Robert's body began to fail him. Everything that happened to him he knew precisely what it was because he had diagnosed it in everyone else, divined it before they or their other doctors even knew they had it. It was a gift to those who turned to him for help, a curse when applied to oneself. He calculated the symptoms and risks of whatever he saw happening to him, second-guessed his doctors, naturally, and then surrendered to whatever they suggested, depending on if he agreed with them.

His biggest frustration was not the natural breakdown of his body but not being able to reach his doctors when he wanted. He had always coddled his patients, brought a southern courtliness to his practice. He checked on them when they didn't expect it, went over impending procedures four or five times to make sure they understood because he felt they would come out of the procedure better if they went into it in the right state of mind. Now, aging and ill in an anonymous city out west, he can go days or weeks without hearing from a doctor. Test results come not with the reassuring words or stroke on the shoulder from his physician but in a form letter from some laboratory out in Riverside.

He has already had a heart attack and bypass surgery. Now his kidneys have succumbed, and he has to endure dialysis several times a week. He is growing frailer but is still sound of mind. He has a live-in nurse now, a sweet woman of good humor named Barbara Lemmons, who is from the South like most everybody else in his life and who indulges his idiosyncrasies.

He has taken care of everyone else, outlived his brothers Madison and Leland and his sister, Gold, the only one he had managed to lure out to California and then only after her marriage broke up. He misses them terribly, but especially Gold, whom he had tried to protect as a young boy back in Monroe and couldn't. Even when he had grown up, his money and status couldn't protect her from herself. She had taken to drinking, a Foster weakness, as their nephew Madison would put it. "She liked the parties, liquor, men," Madison said, "and broke up many a marriage." Robert couldn't protect her from her Billie Holiday of a life. And now she was gone.

His mentor, Dr. Beck, who took him in when he first got to Los Angeles, and Dr. Beck's son, William, who was almost like a brother to him, have passed away, along with so many others, Alice first among them. He has four grandchildren whom Alice did not live to see—Bunny's son and Robin's son, who are practically grown up and far away besides, and Joy's two little ones, who are growing up in Long Beach but whom he sees mainly at birthdays and holidays.

His world has grown smaller, and he is losing control, bit by bit, over his physical self. He seems to savor all the more the little joys in life—a perfectly broiled porterhouse steak, geraniums planted just so in the backyard, a call from a beloved patient.

There is a long list of things he is not supposed to have anymore—fatback and ham hocks, watermelon and barbecue sauce, biscuits, corn bread, tomatoes, and sweet potatoes—just torture to a southerner. But Barbara and his friends manage to slip him some corn bread with the collards anyway because it makes him so happy, and what is the point of living if you can't have a bit of joy in your life?

Every morning she gets up at eight, opens the drapes, and turns on the sprinklers. She invariably finds him at the side of his bed on the telephone. He comes into the kitchen. She gives him grits, which are on the approved list, but with a little salt, which is not. No matter what the list says, he refuses to give up his bacon.

He loves fried catfish, which is not approved, and he could eat that every day. "I know it's not on the list," he says. "But I don't care. Let's cook it."

She puts a chopping board onto the Formica-top island by the Thermador oven near the avocado green Frigidaire. She positions a chair so that he can watch her dust the fish in cornmeal and fry it.

When it is time to get dressed, she pulls some things from the closet for him to wear even if he is not expecting to see anyone that day.

"Yeah, that's fine, but run the iron over those pants," he'll say.

He has nothing but time on his hands, and he frets over the garden with its camellias and hollyhocks that he can no longer manage to his liking. He gets Barbara out there planting the annuals and worries over the placement and composition. They'll be watching the news and he'll be thinking about where he is going to put the begonias. They'll be having their grits and bacon at breakfast, and all of a sudden Robert will blurt out an idea.

"How do you think the geraniums would look over there in that corner?" he asks her. "I'm going to need some impatiens." And the two of them tramp out to the backyard to position them just so.

Robert has just gotten out of the hospital again, and the phone is ringing like mad. One time, Barbara picked up the phone and heard a gravel voice that sounded familiar.

"This is Ray Charles," the man said. "Let's speak to the old man. I'm calling to see if he wants some steaks."

Barbara was holding the receiver to her ear and the cradle to her hip. She whispered to Robert, "Ray Charles is on the phone!"

Robert took the receiver, and Ray got straight to the point.

"You gon' be at home?" Ray asked him. "You want these steaks? I'll be over there with them."

Barbara was in a panic. Ray Charles was on his way. She had just cleaned the living room, but she hadn't gotten to the kitchen or vacuumed the orange carpet in the den where Robert spent most of his day, when it occurred to her, what was the point of rushing?

He can't see anyway, she said to herself. *He won't know what room he's in.*

She calmed herself down. When the doorbell rang and Ray Charles arrived, she sent him through the kitchen. "You just say step up or step down," she later recounted. "Why should I let him trample through the living room I just finished vacuuming? He wasn't dressed up, and he don't know the difference."

Ray Charles came bearing ten or twelve steaks that Robert was not supposed to have but that no one in the world could stop Ray Charles from giving him—all New York cut and porterhouse, no T-bone, just as Robert liked it.

Ray chided Robert for not letting him know what hospital he had been in.

"Now, I had to call all over town, every hospital, looking for you," Ray said. "Where in the hell did you go? Why did you go way out there? I'm a shoot you if you go off again and don't let me know where you are."

The cancer diagnosis came in a form letter. He turned to Barbara and said, "Look at this." He would never have allowed a patient of his to discover such news this way.

"All he would do is look at it," Barbara remembered.

Now that he needed her more than ever, she would not be with him much longer. She already had high blood pressure and an enlarged heart. Now a blood clot had formed in her chest. It broke apart and traveled to her leg. "My leg felt like jelly," she said. "It felt like it wasn't there."

Barbara would no longer be able to work for Robert. By the late spring, a succession of nursing aides would come and go, but nothing would be the same after Barbara left.

Without her to keep him company and indulge his whims as his body grew weaker, he was finding fewer reasons to keep going.

Earlier in the year, he had received the most wonderful news about one of his grandchildren. Robin's son, Daniel Moss, a brilliant boy who took after all of his ambitious forebears, had been in the enviable position of having turned down early admission to Harvard and an offer from Princeton. He had chosen Yale, where he would be a goalie on the soccer team. He had been spared the pain of Jim Crow and the second-class schooling in the South because his mother had been spared it when Robert had moved the family to California.

Robert was too ill to fully enjoy the news about his grandson but could not help but contemplate how over the moon his mother, Ottie, would be if she were alive. All those years of scraping to send her four children to segregated colleges and never seeing her youngest son become the surgeon she so dreamed of. The idea of her great-grandson turning down Harvard and Princeton would have been beyond her comprehension.

His daughters were preparing a trip back east for Daniel's high school graduation. It was around the time of Father's Day. Robert had hoped to go but was not well enough to make the trip. And that made him all the sadder. While everyone else was at Daniel's graduation, a triumphant moment for the family and for Robert as the patriarch, he felt more alone than perhaps ever before. He started refusing to go to dialysis, knowing full well the consequences.

I visited him and found him inconsolable. I asked him if he wanted to go for a drive and get some sunshine. He shook his head no. I told him I had brought him some mangos and angel food cake. He looked away. "I hate to see you like this," I told him. "What can I do to cheer you up?" He stared out the patio door at the begonias growing unattended and a lawn that was not as it should be or would have been if he had been well.

It got to the point that the only way he would go to dialysis was if someone insisted upon it. He was up and ready when I arrived to take him one day. His dark pants hung like draperies from his disappearing frame, and he took slow, labored steps as if he were walking in mud. He walked toward the stairs leading up to the landing above the den where the current aide, Renee, and I were setting up the wheelchair. As he neared the stairs, the hem of his pants got caught under his shoe and he teetered forward, reaching for my arm but missing it as he stumbled in a half-second fall on the top step. We rushed toward him and grabbed him at the waist and arm to lift him to an upright sitting position on the edge of the stairs. He sat flustered and defeated, his eyes lowered and looking at the floor in disbelief at his lot.

The dialysis center was at San Vicente and Third Street. He sat sinking into the passenger's seat, pointing to direct me to the center, his finger wagging becoming more rapid and insistent when I took a turn he did not think right. He shook his head to show his disapproval and struggled to clear his throat to say no, make a right at this corner. His mind was sharp. He knew exactly where we were going and how best to get there.

It was getting to be late June. "I'm getting weaker and weaker," he told me. "As soon as I put the walker on the landing to the den, it slid beneath me. I hit the landing hard. I called the nurse. She didn't hear me. I tried three times. I took a hammer and banged on the coffee table to get her to help me."

He turned his thoughts to more pleasant things, the visitors who had stopped by to see him that day. "I just know so many beautiful people," Robert said.

Just the other day, he had told some friends, "I would give anything for a piece of watermelon," which he conveniently did not say he was not supposed to have.

Sylvester Brooks, the president of the Monroe Club and a faithful admirer, came by and brought Robert the watermelon he so craved. He sat on a bar stool and told Robert what folks in the club were up to.

Robert's old friend from back home Beckwith, who helped him set up his first office and even built furniture for it, stopped by to check on him. Robert was happy to see him. But it was a painful visit and did not last long.

"As well as I know him," Robert said, "we had so little to say. He was not completely comfortable. But that doesn't matter. No, it doesn't matter."

Then a man from back in Monroe, a man named Charles Spillers, dropped by. He had caught the bus from Slauson and Normandie in the center of South Central to see his old physician from the VA hospital.

He had heard of Dr. Foster before he'd ever gone to see him at the VA. He remembered Ray Charles's song about him. *"Dr. Foster got medicine and money too,"* the man sang to himself. "I said, that must be some doctor, that Dr. Foster."

Robert had been concerned about this new patient before him.

"You losing too much weight," Robert had told him. "You're sick. You need help."

The man had been a deckhand on a dredge and done ground maintenance at the VA hospital. He had dug up old graves, the graves of people who had died of tuberculosis, and he had dug them without a mask. He had worked in fields that leaked uranium, where some of his co-workers had died within weeks of exposure.

He was from the Old Country of Louisiana, believed in root doctors, and was suspicious after all he had seen in the South and West. He had pulled for Robert back at the VA, and he worried about what would happen to him after his trouble at the hospital.

"I'm not sure his kidneys went out on their own," Spillers confided to me. "You have to watch a rattlesnake if you get in the bed with him."

Charles Spillers felt he owed a debt to Robert as his physician even though he was too religious and superstitious to do some of what Robert told him. It was more that he felt inspired by him and appreciated Robert's forewarnings, which Spillers promptly used as a cue to go see his root doctor.

"If it wasn't for him, I would have been gone," Spillers said.

He remembered the first time he went to see Robert in his office. "You're just fading away right before me," Robert had told him during the exam. "I'm going to admit you to the hospital."

Spillers trusted the doctor but not the hospital and did not go. "The Holy Spirit came and told me don't go to the hospital," he said.

The man went to a root doctor instead, a woman from back south who was now in L.A. She plied him with root tea and Epsom salts in water. She made a fire in the house, even though it was August, and covered him with quilts until he sweated out the virus she believed to be in him. The fever broke, and he began to eat again and put weight back on.

Robert didn't take it personally or prejudge the man. He had grown up in the South and knew and accepted its ways. And that endeared Robert to the man all the more. He felt he had Robert to thank for alerting him to the problem and for saving his life.

"He meant so much to so many people," Spillers said. "I owe him so much."

He had ridden the bus to see his doctor, who was now sick himself. He sat with him for a while and then prepared to leave. As he headed toward the door to catch the bus back home—not knowing how long the wait would be; this was, after all, L.A.—he turned to his old doctor and friend from the VA hospital with a mixture of worry and gratitude, and the sweet folk spirit of the ancestral South.

"Dr. Foster," he said with heavy eyes, *"I'm lighting seven candles for you."*

By the summer of 1997, Robert Foster was finding his world constricted and fewer reasons to wake up in the morning. The things he loved to do, he could no longer do. He couldn't make it to the racetrack. Vegas was out of the question. His mansion on Victoria had become a glorious prison. The things he loved to eat, he could no longer get. His beloved nurse was ailing herself and no longer there to sneak him a half strip of bacon or a spoonful of peach cobbler. Then there were the twice-weekly trips to dialysis, which made him dread the start of every new week.

In late July, he went into the hospital for repair of a vein damaged by dialysis. He returned home weaker than before. Then, a few days later, on Sunday morning, August 3, he did not respond when called for breakfast. His left arm was motionless. He had suffered a massive stroke. He fell into a coma.

Word spread rapidly through the dwindling corps of original migrants from Monroe who had come out to California all those decades before.

Reatha Beck Smith, the widow of his old mentor Dr. Beck, who put Robert up when he first arrived in Los Angeles and who helped him get on his feet and open his office, rushed to the hospital as soon as she heard the news. She herself was in her nineties now and had her family and old friends from Louisiana with her. She saw him there lying motionless, the central and unforgettable figure of so many parallel worlds, who had saved so many lives but could not save his own.

"We went to see him at the hospital," she remembered. *"He wouldn't open his eyes. We called out our names, each one. And we could feel him squeezing our hand, each one."*

He never came out of the coma. He took his last breath on Wednesday, August 6, 1997. He was seventy-eight years old.

The memorial was the following Monday at the church where he had walked his three daughters down the aisle at their weddings but where he was rarely seen after Alice died.

Along the front pews sat the fruits of his labors and the embodiments of whatever dreams he carried with him while driving through the desert decades before: his eldest daughter, Bunny, now an artist's agent in Chicago, trim and regal in a black sculpted suit and with an upright bearing being consoled by her son Woodie White; his middle daughter, Robin, now a city manager in San Jose, sitting with her husband, Alan Christianson, and son, Daniel Moss, the pride of the family, who, having turned down Harvard and Princeton, would start at Yale a few weeks from now. Robert had lived long enough to know that. Then came Robert's youngest daughter, Joy, a radiologist, seated with her husband, Lee, a day trader, and their two small children, Lia and Adam.

The pews were filled with people from back in Monroe, old classmates from Morehouse, the people he knew from the racetrack, the people he had worked with at the VA hospital, the people whose gallbladders and appendixes he had removed and whose babies he had delivered and the babies that he had brought into the world and who were now grown men and women with gray hair and children of their own.

All of them showed up, their faces glazed and empty, to pay their respects. The daughters had had Robert cremated, which caused some grumbling among those who had wished to see him once more or who were grieving that they had not made it by to see him in time or who knew that it had simply not been the way southerners put away their dead.

The service was a tightly scripted affair.

"We gather in the faith and hope of Jesus Christ," the minister, who had not known Robert, intoned. "We come to comfort and support each other in our common loss—Robert Joseph Parish Foster."

Nobody remarked on the mispronunciation of "Pershing" in his final hour. Few people in California likely knew the name anyway. He had dispensed with it on his way to California for that very reason.

His nephew, Madison, read a scripture assigned to him from Ecclesiastes: "For everything there is a time, a time to be born and a time to die . . . "

Robert's gambling buddy Romie Banks rose and addressed his friend and those assembled: "Robert, you have fought so many battles, been a champion for so many people. He was a perfectionist at everything he did except winning at the racetrack."

Robert's son-in-law Lee went to the altar. "He let you know which way the wind was blowing," the son-in-law said, "whether you liked it or not."

The Morehouse alumni stood when asked to make themselves known.

Easter Butler, who had met Robert at the racetrack, declared simply, "Dr. Foster was one of the greatest men I ever knew."

Afterward, the people assembled back at the house on Victoria. Now, the street, unlike the last few weeks of his life when he was in his weakest, loneliest state, was crowded, overcome by cars—Mercedes, Cadillacs, sport utility vehicles, German and Japanese cars.

The people gathered around the crushed-velvet armchairs and the orange shag rug and the Zenith television console in the den, the room where Robert had thrown so many parties and had lived out the last months of his life.

A copy of *Life* magazine with Coretta Scott King in mourning sat in the bookcase, along with *Roots* by Alex Haley, surgery and gynecology textbooks, a book entitled *Difficult Diagnosis,* and, sitting alone, the brown desk plate that read, ROBERT P. FOSTER, MD.

The mourners partook of the honeydew and cantaloupe, cheesecake, lemon cake, and ham spread out on the dining room table. The testimonials continued all afternoon.

Della Bea Robinson, Ray Charles's ex-wife, showed up to pay her respects because "Bob delivered my son," she said. "My husband named our son after him."

The moment made Della Bea think about what a perfectionist Robert had been, which was a good thing to have in a surgeon. "We were going to a concert," she remembered, "and Alice came down the steps and couldn't find the right gloves. She put on a pair of gloves she found. Bob saw her when she came out. 'Something is wrong. The gloves are off,' he said. He noticed everything."

Leah Peterson, who had worked at the VA hospital with him, remembered turning to him for advice. "I used to go up and talk to him," she said. "I told him what I wanted to do with my years. Bob started buying me books."

A realtor named Nick White said simply, "He delivered me."

Madison, his nephew, left the memorial repast early and brooded over a glass of ice water at a restaurant over in Santa Monica. He was feeling alone as the only Foster left from that era and isolated from what he saw as the bourgeois pretensions of the day's proceedings, which, to him, did not reflect his uncle's southern joie de vivre. "He didn't get as good as he gave," Madison said after the funeral, "and he gave the best."

Madison was the self-described country cousin and one of Robert's biggest champions, a living reminder of the South that Robert had put behind him. Madison thought about all the things Robert had been through in the South and out west, the rejections despite the triumphs and never feeling good enough. These things made him an exacting, infuriating, insecure perfectionist who left a mark on everyone he met. The people around him knew to smooth their tie, check their hem, reach a little higher, do a little more because Robert Foster demanded it of them. He made everybody crazy and better for the sky-high expectations he had of them for even the smallest of things.

"If you bought him a melon," Madison said, "you couldn't just buy a melon. You had to stop and think about that melon. That's how he was with everything."

Madison thought back to how Robert had tried to get all of Monroe to come to Los Angeles. "Bob would say, 'You want some Monroe? Plenty Monroe out here. You can have Monroe in California.' "

Then Madison remembered the trips he had made to Los Angeles, his feeling tentative and unsure, being from small-town Louisiana as he was but exhilarated to be out in California with his uncle.

"Come on, chief," Bob would say. "Let's go to Beverly Hills and have breakfast on the veranda. Put your chain out. Put that gold chain out. You ain't on no college campus now. Put your chain out. That's why I gave you that damn chain."

This was Robert's Promised Land. He walked around as if he had been born to it. "You didn't have a care in the world," Madison remembered. "All your problems were gone. Nothing could happen to you. You were with Uncle Bob. He lightened a room. He created another world for you. The man had a certain magic to him."

The story of Robert Joseph Pershing Foster of Monroe, Louisiana, and Los Angeles, California, did not end with his death. Years later, people were still trying to decipher the meaning of his life. Some people were too distraught to speak of him with anyone outside their circle. Others could not stop referring to him in the present tense.

For some of his patients, Robert was the only doctor they had ever been to. They remember him making hospital rounds at midnight, stepping in with free medical advice upon hearing that an acquaintance of somebody's co-worker was in the least bit of trouble.

Perhaps it could be said that gambling was his mistress, medicine his beloved. Another migrant named Malissa Briley did not fully grasp it until she had to go into surgery herself. She was in her midforties at the time, a social worker in L.A. who had gone to Spelman with Alice. She was anxious about going into the hospital.

Robert did the surgery, and the surgery went well. But later that night, her blood pressure shot out of control. She was on the verge of having a stroke, which could have killed her or left her paralyzed. The hospital tried to get her blood pressure down but had no success. At midnight, the hospital called Robert to report the turn of events. He rushed over right away. He tried to lower her blood pressure, but he couldn't get it down either.

The next morning, Briley awoke to see Robert in a chair by her bed. She was stunned to see him there. It was early winter, the quiet time of the morning, so early that the hospital hadn't brought the breakfast tray yet. He was in his street clothes and uncharacteristically wrinkled. He hadn't shaved, had bags under his eyes.

"What are you doing here this early?" she asked him.

He told her she had gone through a crisis the night before and that neither he nor the hospital could get her blood pressure down.

"What did you do?" she asked.

"Well, I got to the point I couldn't do nothing but pray," he said.

He had stayed by her hospital bed all night. He had sat upright in a chair in his street clothes. Any patient he lost, he took it personally and especially hard. He took it as a sign of his own failure. So he had fought back sleep watching over this patient and praying for her to live.

By morning, her blood pressure had returned to a safe range. He made sure her vital signs were stable, gave instructions to the nurse to call him immediately should there be any change. Then he left to see about the rest of his patients.

"He had stayed through the night," she said forty years later, still almost in disbelief. "I woke up, and there he was. That I'll never forget, as long as I live."

Robert Foster did not want to return to Louisiana, in life or in death. Nor did he choose to be interred with the Clements in Kentucky. He paid down on a place for himself at a cemetery in Los Angeles.

His body was cremated and placed in an urn in a granite mausoleum with rows of bronze plaques lining the wall like identical file cabinets. His sits in a corner high on the wall with a vase of purple silk roses. IN LOVING MEMORY OF ROBERT P. FOSTER, M.D., 1918–1997, the plaque reads.

The mausoleum is high on a hill at Inglewood Park Cemetery. The urns face a picture window with a view of the cemetery's manicured gardens and, beyond that, Hollywood Park racetrack. It is the closest

Robert could get to the track he so loved. Every so often one can see, settled along a curb of the cemetery road, a crumpled copy of the *Daily Racing Form* blown over from the track, and, if listening closely, hear the clomping roar of a horse race in progress over at Hollywood Park. Beloved California.

CHICAGO, AUGUST 1997
IDA MAE BRANDON GLADNEY

THE TRANSFORMATION of the South Shore section of Chicago from an all-white neighborhood to a near totally black one was complete by the time the Great Migration ended in the mid-1970s. But there was a less visible change that made life more difficult still for people like Ida Mae.

Had a study, like the 1968 Kerner Report on the state of race in America, been conducted of Ida Mae's adopted neighborhood, it might have concluded that there were, in fact, two neighborhoods—one, hardworking and striving to be middle class, the other, transient, jobless, and underclass; one, owners of property, the other, tenants and squatters; one, churchgoing and law-abiding, the other, drug-dealing and criminal—both coexisting on the same streets, one at odds with the other.

Ida Mae lived in the former world but had to negotiate the latter. The transformation had been so rapid that the city had not had a chance to catch up with it. Politicians came and went, but the problems were bigger than one local official could solve. The problems were social, economic, geographic, perhaps even moral. A succession of mayors had appeased or looked away from the troubles of South Shore, it was but one of some fifty identifiable neighborhoods in the city and not anywhere close to the worst. In fact, it had had a storied past as the home of the South Shore Country Club, a columned and grand clubhouse with its own golf course and riding stables that in its heyday had drawn celebrities like Jean Harlow and Amelia Earhart. By the time the neighborhood turned black in the mid-1970s, its membership had dwindled, and it was taken over by the Chicago Park District.

Mayors Richard J. Daley, Michael Bilandic, and Jane Byrne all relied on the votes of solidly Democratic South Shore to be elected, but life grew no better for Ida Mae. Ida Mae and other black residents had the highest hopes that their concerns might be heard when Harold Washington was elected mayor in 1983, but his election was so fraught with racial tension and his tenure so embattled that they could not look to him for much more than historic symbolism, which had a certain value but did not make their streets safer. Then Washington died unexpectedly at the start of his second term.

Thus the stalwart property owners of South Shore learned to rely on themselves to monitor the crime and mayhem around them. They formed block clubs and neighborhood watch groups, and, on the second Thursday of every month, the most dedicated believers turn out for police beat meetings to report what they are seeing, hear what the police are doing, and make their voices heard. The meetings are part of a community policing plan known as the Chicago Alternative Policing Strategy, or CAPS.

These days, Ida Mae goes to the beat meetings with the regularity and sense of obligation with which some people go to church. She never misses one because there is always so much to report. She and James and their friend and tenant Betty put on their coats and gather themselves for each meeting regardless of whether the problems are solved, which they frequently are not.

The four of us are in the car heading to a beat meeting one November when we see teenagers on the corner north of their three-flat.

"They're out there again," James says.

I ask him what they're doing.

"Drugs," he says matter-of-factly. "They're selling drugs."

Night is falling as a handful of people gathers for the meeting of Police Beat 421 at the South Shore Presbyterian Church. The people descend the steps to the church basement, where a man sits at a table in the back with a stack of flyers and neighborhood crime lists, called hot sheets, laid out in neat piles.

The hot sheets are like a neighborhood report card and are the first things the people reach for. They rifle through them, scanning for their street and block number to see the details of whatever crimes have been reported, if the knifing or carjacking they saw was ever called in, what the police say they are doing about it, and whether there have been any arrests.

About twenty people, including Ida Mae, James, and Betty, are still going over their hot sheets as they take their seats in the gray metal folding chairs in a basement with yellow cinder-block walls and a red-painted concrete floor, when the meeting is called to order.

The moderator asks what new problems there are. James and several others reach for the index cards being distributed to write out the things they have witnessed. The residents often do not put their names on the cards for fear of reprisal. Ida Mae rarely speaks up because she is convinced the gangs send moles to the meetings, which are public after all, to see who is snitching.

In the meeting, the people learn that Beat 422 held a march against gangs and crime, but they are not certain if they can muster such a march.

"We're at the last stand here," the moderator says. "We don't have any other alternative. If we don't do something, they will take us over."

Everyone knew who she meant by "they."

Someone brings up a worrisome but low-end priority: prostitution is getting worse over at Seventy-ninth and Exchange.

"We know that, okay," the moderator says. "That's a hot spot," she admits and quickly moves on to the robberies, shootings, and drug dealing.

After the meeting adjourns, Ida Mae pulls a policeman over to report one of the more benign sightings, but a measure of the general unruliness around them. "They pull up a truck and take the stoves out," Ida Mae says of theft going on in the building next door.

The police officer stares straight ahead. It's barely worth his time. He walks away to another conversation.

"They don't know nothing," Ida Mae says.

She buttons her coat and walks over to her son. "We ain't done nothing here," she says.

"The important thing is to keep coming," James says.

It is mid-May, the start of the crazy season in South Shore. The weather will be warm soon, and the kids will be out of school, roaming the streets with nothing to do. This time, a gang officer, a big, bearded man in a blue Nike sweatshirt and jeans, is there to brief the beat meeting.

"You have two gangs operating in 421," the officer is telling residents. "The Black Stones and the Mickey Cobras."

The residents listen, but they know they have a gang problem. They start to rattle off street names they want the police to check.

The officer jumps in. "We been hitting that area hard," the officer says. "Every day we've been locking someone up new. We're hitting Colfax, Kingston, Phillips real hard. They know our cars. They got so many guys out there doing lookout, hypes who work for them. They whistle when we get close."

He tells the residents to report whatever they see. "I call the police enough, they should know my name," a middle-aged woman in a brown beret says. "We got some terrible kids over where we are. It be raining and sleeting and they coming and going. And the girls are worse than the boys."

"Amen," Ida Mae chimes in.

The next meeting begins with a sober announcement: "We had a shooting of one of our CAPS members at Seventy-eighth and Coles."

"Did they catch the offender?" a resident asks.

"No, not as of yet." The people look down at their hot sheets.

The beat meetings attract all kinds of visitors—city hall bureaucrats, politicians running for reelection, people heading rape crisis centers or collecting names for this or that petition. This time, the visitor is a legal advocate in a beard and corduroy pants who doesn't live in the neighborhood. He rises to speak and tries to get the group to join him in opposing a city ordinance that would clamp down on loitering.

"It will make open season on all black youth," the man says of what he believes will happen if the ordinance were to pass.

The residents want the ordinance anyway, anything to bring them relief.

A man in his sixties stands up as if to speak for them all.

"We live in this neighborhood," the man says. "We own houses and pay taxes. We're scared to go outside. Practically every evening there's a shooting. I don't care about their rights. Maybe you have to get the good ones to get the bad."

This being Chicago, famously local in its politics, the residents of South Shore have learned where to get their immediate needs met—a broken hydrant fixed, a pothole patched, a house condemned. The alderman is the closest politician to turn to. Most Chicagoans know their alderman by sight or even personally and will call upon him without hesitation if they think he can help.

When Ida Mae's alderman, William Beavers, shows up at her beat meeting, there is great anticipation because he is one of the most powerful black politicians in the city and everyone knows him. He has been the Seventh Ward alderman for fourteen years. He arrives in a brown double-breasted suit and has cameras and lights and a television crew with him, which only adds to the sense of the drama of his visit.

"The area is coming back," he announces to the residents. He then lists what he's doing for the ward: "We got a new field house. We're building a senior home at Seventy-fourth and Kingston. We have a new shopping center at Ninety-fifth and Stoney."

Then he gets to what matters to them most, the crime, says he's seen it himself, especially the prostitutes over on Exchange Street. "They're on Exchange all day and all night," he says. "They be waving, 'Hey, Alderman Beavers!' "

A woman raises her hand with a complaint that is right up his alley. "There's no curb across the street for us," she says.

"I put them on the other side," he says without apology. "I put them where the people vote."

He then leaves them with a hotline number to call to report crime: the number, he says, is 1-800-CRACK-44.

South Shore is in Police Beat 421, Ward Seven, State Representative District 25, and State Senate District 13. The officeholders of the latter two districts rarely figure into the daily concerns of most people in Chicago. The state legislators are just low enough on the political food chain to go unrecognized, focused as they are on approving budgets and legislation. They are just lofty enough, however, to be seen as of little help in an immediate crisis as when, say, a drug dealer sets up shop in front of your house. It could be argued that many people could not name their state legislators off the top of their heads. As for state senators, there are fifty-nine of them, they meet in Springfield, and they are not usually household names, as would be the mayor or even one's alderman.

So when, in 1996, a young constitutional lawyer and community activist from Hyde Park ran for the Illinois State Senate seat in District 13, Ida Mae, voting her usual straight Democratic ticket, would become among the first people ever to have voted for the man. She would not have to give it much thought. He did not have Chicago roots and the name was unusual—Barack Obama. But he was running unopposed, having edged out the woman who had asked him to run in her place before changing her mind. His wife, Michelle, had grown up in South Shore, in the more stable section of bungalows further to the west. So

Ida Mae and an overwhelming majority of the Democratic stronghold of predominantly black South Shore voted him into office as their state senator.

On August 14, 1997, exactly one month before Alderman Beavers shows up with cameras and lights at Ida Mae's beat meeting, Barack Obama makes an appearance. He is introduced as the state senator for the district, which not everyone in the room could be expected to know, as he has only been in office since January. He is tall, slight of build, formal in speech and attire, looks like a college student, and he arrives without lights, cameras, or entourage.

He stands before them and gives a minilecture to these bus drivers, secretaries, nurse's aides, and pensioners about what state legislators do. He says that while the state legislature is not responsible for the police department, it passes laws that the police have to enforce. He describes the role of the legislature in education policy and in health care. And he invites those assembled to call his office anytime.

"Sometimes a call from the senator's office," he says like the professor he once was, "may be helpful in facilitating some issues that you have concerns about. Sometimes a call from my office will be answered much more quickly so we can move through some of the bureaucracy a little bit faster."

Ida Mae and the rest of the people listen politely and with appreciation. But, as this is just another meeting, they sit in anticipation of the reason they are here tonight: the discussion with police about the latest shootings, stabbings, and drug deals, the immediate dangers they will face just getting back home.

The thirty-six-year-old freshman state senator finishes his presentation to Beat 421. The people clap with gratitude as they always do and then turn back to their hot sheets.

That night, as he bounded up the steps and out of the church basement, nobody in the room could have imagined that they had just seen the man who, a decade from now, would become the first black president of the United States.

NEW YORK, SPRING 1998

THE TROUBLE BEGAN with a mysterious dark spot on the back of George Starling's foot. One of his grandsons had been the first to notice it. George was a diabetic and knew not to take chances with such things. He made an appointment to see his doctor right away.

The doctor admitted him to the hospital for tests. There was fear the foot might need to be amputated. "All these tests," Pat, the niece who used to live with him and Inez, said.

Pat came in from Washington, where she was now living, and her brother came in from New Jersey to see about their uncle. There was relief when it turned out that the foot would not need to be amputated. But George was now requiring dialysis. The knees that had always given him trouble could not be relied upon now to hold him up, and he was having a harder time keeping his balance.

Pat and her brother helped George get up when they were there. But after they and his other visitors left, George slipped and fell in the hospital. In time, he appeared to be recovering and was looking to go home.

"Well, they not gonna keep me no longer," he told Pat.

"Okay, now," Pat said. "I'll be up there to see about you."

But he was instead transferred to a nursing home for rehabilitation. While there, he lost his balance and fell again. This time he hit his head.

By now, Gerard, his firstborn, had been alerted in Florida as to his father's condition. The two had long been at odds. Gerard's lifestyle was counter to everything George had worked for. Gerard had been a drug hustler operating out of Miami and Gainesville. He had had money, homes, cars, women. Wherever he showed up, he gave everybody a hundred dollars just because he could. But in recent years, he had been down on his luck. He had diabetes, like his father, and was on dialysis and insulin.

Hearing that his father was in the hospital, he made plans to come up to New York. "We were all waiting on Gerard with great anticipation," Pat remembered.

It was while Gerard was trying to figure out what day to come to New York that George fell and hit his head. He suffered a cerebral hemorrhage and slipped into a coma. By the time Gerard made it to New

York, George was unconscious and hooked up to machines to sustain him on the chance he might come out of the coma.

Pat took Gerard to the hospital to see his father. "The moment he walked in and saw him, he broke down crying," Pat said.

Gerard had to leave the room. He said he couldn't stand to see his father that way. They didn't stay much longer.

Gerard had not realized how grave his father's condition was. He decided to head back to Florida, seeing as how there was nothing he could do to change things.

"Do you want to go and see him one more time before you get ready to go?" Pat asked him.

No, he said, he couldn't bear it.

Gerard drove back to Florida weak and in despair. He had missed several rounds of dialysis and had used cocaine in the interim, Pat discovered. When he got back to Gainesville, he still did not go to dialysis.

"He had already given up," Pat said.

Within days of seeing his father, Gerard suffered a massive seizure and died. He was fifty-one years old. His father was not conscious enough to know that he had lost his firstborn son. George, barely alive himself, was now the last one left of the nuclear family that had begun with him and Inez some sixty years before in Eustis.

There was no one in the hospital room when I went to see George Starling. The monitors attached to him beeped and flashed the minutest change in his vital signs. The robust onetime porter who could regale people for hours with his stories of the South and of the Great Migration was silent and motionless. He looked to be asleep, whatever wisdom or stories left now locked up inside of him. As much living as he had done, his seemed a life of missed chances and incompletion. Here was someone who had been born too early and in the wrong place to reach his true potential, had left to make a better way for himself, but had seemed to carry the sorrows of the South with him, without complaint.

I reached for his hand and squeezed it lightly and told him I had come from Chicago to see him. His face showed no reaction. His hand managed to press back into mine.

George Swanson Starling never came out of the coma. He died on September 3, 1998, a Thursday. Because he had migrated out of the South, lived most of his life in the North but remained connected to both, two funeral services were required. One was in New York, at the

Baptist House of Prayer on 126th Street in Harlem, on September 17; the other in Florida, at Gethsemane Baptist Church in Eustis, two days later.

In the North, in Harlem, where he had found refuge from the South, the people turned out to see him one last time. The Deacon Board, the Pastor's Aide Club, the 132nd Street Block Association, the neighbors who had looked out for him from across the street all packed into the church. The choir sang for him and shook the floor from the choir box as the fans whirred and oscillated around them.

One by one, people came forward to say they would miss his opening the church doors Sunday mornings, miss the sight of him reading the dictionary, and would remember him as "a gentleman of the first order."

A man, tentative in his steps and taking in the measure of the sanctuary, had arrived an hour early. He had a shaved head and full beard. He sat alone in the third pew as the church began to fill. His eyes were red. He stared at the silver casket, then leaned onto the pew in front of him and buried his face in his arms. When Pat arrived, she went over and sat beside him. It was Kenny, George's younger son, whose conception had broken Inez's heart. And that heartbreak kept him from feeling part of the family or ever truly knowing his father.

Before George took ill, Kenny went to George and let him know how he was doing. Kenny was married, had kids, was living in the Bronx. He told him he had converted to Islam, had changed his name to Amjad Mujaahid, which means, he said, "One who is noble, a warrior in the cause of God."

"Daddy," Kenny told George, "that name is in memory of you."

"That's real nice, son," Kenny remembers George saying. "I'm still calling you Kenny."

Now the man he wished he'd had more time to get to know was dead. The service was a blur of song and testimonials. He took off his glasses and used a handkerchief to wipe his eyes, as his father had done whenever he sang.

It was hurricane season at the time of George Starling's death. Hurricane Bonnie and Hurricane Danielle had gathered east of the Leeward Islands that August. By mid-September, when George Starling was transported back to the state of Florida for the last time, a new hurricane had formed and was nearing the Florida coast. The National Weather Service had named it Hurricane Georges.

Back in Eustis, the southern funeral commenced at Gethsemane Baptist Church. But Viola Dunham, the sister-in-law he used to stay with whenever he visited, could not bring herself to go. "It's killing me," she said. "I want to remember him sitting in my kitchen eating breakfast and running his mouth."

A cousin named Lila Mae went and spoke for the people who had stayed in the South, remembering him as the hometown boy who made good in the North with his railroad job and dignified bearing.

"As he journeyed to New York and became a porter," she began, "nothing was finer than to see this good-looking cousin come into Wildwood station and to bring him some sausage. All of his splendor and grace. It was something to see. Little George never forgot where he came from."

Reuben Blye, who'd known George most of his life, sat staring out into the sanctuary in a gray suit and tie in a front pew. Sam Gaskin, who had stood up with him against the grove owners back in the forties, was there, too. A processional of eight or ten cars led by a white hearse passed through town near the corner where George had stood and waited for the open-bed truck to take pickers to the citrus groves some sixty years before.

The cortege turned off a main thoroughfare and crept down a dirt path to a clearing of wild grass scattered with the headstones of nearly all the black people who had ever lived and died in Eustis. The cars crossed a pebbled, pitted clearing and came to a stop at a green tent pitched before two juniper bushes in the middle of Mount Olive Cemetery. A dozen people took their places before the casket. The pastor stood and said his last words: *"From dust thou art . . ."*

That evening, the sun fell behind the horizon and made what looked like streaks of fire across the sky after George Starling was returned for the last time to the Florida earth he had fled.

THE EMANCIPATION OF IDA MAE

My presence will go with you. And I will give you rest.
—EXODUS 33:14

CHICAGO, OCTOBER 15, 1998
IDA MAE BRANDON GLADNEY

IDA MAE WAS GOING BACK to visit Mississippi. It was early autumn, the same time of year she had left sixty-one years before. It would be her first time on Mississippi soil since her sister Talma had died in Tupelo in 1983. Ida Mae had gone down when she got word that her youngest sister had taken ill. She sat at the side of her sister's bed for her last hours on this earth.

Ida Mae remembered she had been watching Talma, and Talma had been trying to speak.

"Don't you see all them people in white singing?" Talma had said, delirious. "They just singing away."

Ida Mae looked in the direction Talma was facing and tried to see the people in white but couldn't. Days later, at Talma's funeral, the choir sang in all white.

"She saw them before," Ida Mae said, convinced of it.

Ida Mae and I are driving along Route 8, heading east toward Vardaman in the direction of Chickasaw County. We pass a cotton gin and bales of cotton bound in the field and covered with tarp. The bales are packed high and tight and look like cubes of Styrofoam the size of a school bus from a distance.

We cross a gravel road with cotton on either side of it. "That cotton's loaded," Ida Mae said, her eyes growing big. "Let's go pick some."

"You sure that's alright?" I ask. "That's somebody's cotton. What if they see us?"

"They not gon' mind what little bit we pick," she says, pushing open the passenger door.

She jumps out and heads into the field. She hasn't picked cotton in sixty years. It's as if she can't wait to pick it now that she doesn't have to. It's the first time in her life that she can pick cotton of her own free will.

I follow her out, and she starts pulling at the bolls, and I pull at them too. No cars or trucks pass by, and we are surrounded by cotton.

We carry a bouquet of cotton buds back to the car and head to her sister-in-law Jessie Gladney's house. Along the route, there are no streetlights, traffic lights, or stop signs. There are no street signs to identify what road you are on. The directions to the house call for looking for a cotton gin, passing and keeping count of five or six bridges that are merely dirt mounds over dry creek beds, making a right at a Baptist church, and looking for the sister-in-law's off-white double-wide on the right-hand side of the road, assuming we're on the correct one.

Jessie is Ida Mae's sister-in-law twice over, in the small, insular circles of rural Mississippi. She was married to Ida Mae's husband's brother Ardee, and she is the sister of the man Ida Mae's sister Talma married. Jessie moved up to Chicago in 1946 but recently returned to Mississippi, where her brother Aubrey lives. She went back south with her husband, but he was ill and not particular about moving back to Mississippi and did not live long after they had arrived. That left Jessie widowed and alone in the isolated double-wide with her sweet nature and bad knees.

Ida Mae and Jessie greet and hug each other like sisters, and Ida Mae rests herself in Jessie's recliner with a throw over it and starts talking about the cotton she and I picked by the side of the road.

"Ooh, it was so much cotton," she says. "Cotton everywhere."

"The highest I ever picked was one hundred eighty-seven pounds," Jessie says.

"I just couldn't do it," Ida Mae says. "I'd pick and cry. I ain't never liked the field."

The two of them catch up on the latest with the kids and nieces and nephews, and then Ida Mae starts talking about life back up in the North.

"You see everything up there, Jessie," she says. "Seem like they choose this block to do all they dirt. They sell drugs there. They open their mouths and put it down their throat. That's where they keep it. One lady died from swallowing it. It must have got hung up in her lung. I missed her and asked about her. She used to sit under the tree out there. She was in her fifties, and she died from it."

Ida Mae pauses and looks away. "I reckon people who've passed on wouldn't want to come back if they could. They couldn't take what's going on now days."

Jessie mostly listens. She's having trouble with her legs, and her husband's death is still weighing on her heart.

Which reminds Ida Mae of her husband. "I waited on George forty-seven years," she says. "And I mean I waited on him. When he come home from work, and when he wanted his breakfast, lunch, and dinner, I give it to him. I served him. They expect too much. When he passed, I wasn't thinking about no other husband. I laugh and talk with them, but that's as far as it go."

The next day we are riding through the curving hills of Chickasaw County, rising and sinking along the red dirt road. We are retracing the corners Ida Mae and her family lived and sharecropped and looking for anyone she might know who is still around. We drive through pine woods draped in kudzu and through tumbling fields down a gravel road that kicks up dirt as we pass.

Every now and then, the hills are broken by a cabin with a chicken-wire fence around it and a pickup truck at the side. The land is quiet, at peace, as if the bloodshed of the twentieth century never happened. There appears a black man riding high up on a tractor as it inches down a gravel road in a cloud of gravel dust, and he tips his hat as he passes us, a courtly gesture from another century that one would never see in Chicago.

Ida Mae's brother-in-law Aubrey, who was married to her late sister Talma, is leading her from place to place. He knows the land because he returned to Mississippi decades ago after trying Chicago and not liking it.

Aubrey tries to find Miss Theenie's house, the one where the men came courting Ida Mae on the front porch. They spot a weathered shack leaning on its side. They stop to inspect it and conclude that it might have been Miss Theenie's but they couldn't say for sure. Falling-down shacks look pretty much the same.

"Been so long," Ida Mae says.

In the car, Ida Mae looks out at all the cotton, the cotton that ruled her days and that she's free from now.

Aubrey points to a machine off in the distance.

"That machine can pick fifteen to twenty bales of cotton in a day," Aubrey says proudly of the advancements made since Ida Mae left.

"Sho' 'nough?" Ida Mae says blankly. She looks out with vague interest at the blur of field. Then she turns the conversation to the old friends she wants to see and how different things look to her now.

She is getting a little disoriented, one hill indistinguishable from another, nothing but trees or cabins as guideposts and the terrain seeming wilder than before. "I don't remember so many crooks and turns," she says of the land and the gravel road we are on.

She is having trouble with the heat after being in Chicago so long. "It's a different kind of hot down here," she says. And she's feeling a little sick, as people do when they drink the water they are warned about when they visit developing countries. Later in the day she will put some nutmeg in the palm of her hand and lick it to settle her stomach, and not draw the least attention to herself among the people in Mississippi, which is, after all, where she learned it.

In and around the settlements of Chickasaw County, Ida Mae visits with a succession of people who knew her. They greet her like a loved one they just discovered happens to be alive after all. She visits Isolena Harris, Marcelle Barr, Doretta Boston, a lady named Azaline.

Aubrey has taken charge and takes great pride in being the one to ask bewildered home folks, "You know who this is?"

The people inspect Ida Mae's face. She was a young mother in her twenties the last time some of them saw her. Now she's a great-grandmother. They look hard and see the pointed nose of her sister Talma or the nut butter coloring of Miss Theenie. Some catch on right away and startle themselves in the recognition.

"You know I know Miss Ida Mae! I declare! How you doing!" one lady says, after figuring it out, grabbing Ida Mae, and smothering her in hugs.

She stops by to see an old classmate named Castoria.

"You know who this is?" Aubrey asks again.

Castoria says she can't place her, doesn't know her.

"Yes, you do," Aubrey insists. "This is Ida Mae."

Castoria's face brightens. The two of them embrace each other and let out gap-toothed smiles.

"Girl, I ought to whoop you good!" Castoria says. "Lord have mercy on me. When have I seen Ida Mae?"

"It's been years and years and years," Ida Mae says. "I went to school with you. Just a few of us living now."

"Lord have mercy on my soul!" Castoria says, still staring at Ida Mae.

Aubrey takes her to the church cemetery where many of the black people of Chickasaw County are buried. She finds her mother, Miss Theenie, and some cousins and aunts, but not the father she loved so dearly.

One of the headstones appears to be testimony to the hard times the people faced under Jim Crow.

It reads simply: THY TRIAL'S ENDED.

Aubrey scans the headstones of all the people they once knew.

"Ida Mae, you gonna be buried down here?" Aubrey asks her.

"No, I'm gonna be in Chicago," she tells him.

We pull up to a frame house with a pickup truck and farm implements in the yard. It's where David McIntosh lives. He was the suitor who rode on horseback to court Ida Mae had when she was a young girl and who lost out to the man who married Ida Mae and carried her off to Chicago.

Had things turned out differently, had she not married George, this might be where Ida Mae would be living: on a Chickasaw County farm with chickens and pole beans in walking distance from where she grew up. She would never have lived in Chicago, might never have seen it. She wouldn't have been able to vote all those years or work in a big city hospital, to ride the elevated train and taste Polish sausage and be surrounded by family and friends most everywhere she went because most everyone she knew moved north like she did. Her children—James, Eleanor, Velma—not to mention the grandchildren, might not have existed or would surely have been different from what they were if they had. It's almost incomprehensible now.

David comes out of the house in his baseball cap. He has not seen her in half a lifetime. He recognizes her instantly. He breaks into a smile.

"How you, Ida Mae?"

"I'm blessed," she says, smiling back.

He is a compact man in soiled denim and bifocals, not much taller than Ida Mae. He stayed in Mississippi and lived his life close to the land, the opposite of how Ida Mae ended up. He studies her face across the decades and reaches out and grabs her hand.

Just then, David's wife, in white braids, comes out to see who is visiting, and Ida Mae and David keep it to a warm hug and a few words.

Ida Mae climbs into the car, still looking back at David, and he still looking at her.

"Bless his heart," Ida Mae says, as the car backs out of his dirt yard. "I knew him the minute I saw him."

That turned out to be the last time they would see each other. He died the next year, and she would not mourn so much as contemplate the meaning of what might have been and what their lives had turned out to be.

CHICAGO, MARCH 5, 1999
IDA MAE BRANDON GLADNEY

IDA MAE'S LIVING ROOM had a pink glow to it. The new venetian blinds she dreamed of had finally arrived. Their pink slats cast a rose-colored light in the room. It was just how she liked to see the world, and she was happier for it. She was all dressed up, her hair in cotton white Shirley Temple curls, pink lipstick on, smiling and free. It was her eighty-sixth birthday.

A thick snow was falling outside and coated the trees. Betty, who lived upstairs, waited with her for the guests to arrive.

The news was on. There was a report about a white man who had gotten the death penalty for dragging a black man to death in Jasper, Texas. But this was Ida Mae's birthday, and no one wanted to think about black men being dragged to death. They had lived it, and it hadn't gone away, and there was nothing they could do about it. Plus, that was Texas, not Mississippi. They were from Mississippi.

Outside, a man was parking his truck in front of the empty lot next to Ida Mae's house. She heard the screeching of the brakes and turned toward the window to see what was going on.

"He needs to move that truck," Ida Mae said. "That rusted-back truck is blocking my view."

Eleanor's daughter Karen arrived with a new boyfriend named Mike. He had a square jaw and specks of gray in his hair, looked to be late forties to midfifties. When Mike came in, Ida Mae noticed him right away. "I don't know who that is," she said, "but he sho' ain't bad on the eyes."

Their old friend Wilks Battle walked in and took a seat next to Ida Mae. He had just come from the hospital. His mother had been diagnosed with liver cancer. The doctor said there was no more they could do. He said it could be two months or two days, they just didn't know. He bent his head down, eyes cast to the carpet.

Ida Mae looked wide-eyed into his face with wonder and sympathy. All the people she had lost and buried, and still she listened as if this were the first she had heard of death and the first she had seen of grief.

"Well," she said in a low and gentle voice, "God don't make no mistakes."

"Yes, ma'am, I know," he said, looking away.

"No, God don't make no mistakes."

The meal was fish—"cat" and "buffalo" that Eleanor fried—coleslaw, and hush puppies. Mary Ann made the tuna macaroni salad and apple muffins. Karen brought a yellow layer cake with strawberries on top and the potato salad she was still refusing to divulge the recipe for no matter how much people begged.

The ten or so people gathered for Ida Mae's birthday that night stood in a circle around the dining room table as Mary Ann prayed, "Dear God, thank you for Grandmother . . ."

Ida Mae made sure to sit across the dining room table from Mike, her granddaughter notwithstanding, and proceeded to tell her story.

"I been in Chicago sixty-two years," she began. "I came here in 1937. Well, I came to Milwaukee first. I came when Eleanor was three month old and James was three year old. In them days on the train, everybody had shoe boxes full of food."

"The ways we got here . . . ," Mike said, shaking his head.

He had come up late, in 1969.

"I came up as a young man from Macomb, Mississippi," he said. "I guess it was coming to an end then. People stopped coming when things got better in the South."

A heavy snow fell outside. In a symbolic kind of way, snow was to Chicago what cotton was to Mississippi. It blanketed the land. It was inevitable. Both were so much a part of the landscape of either place that where you saw snow you by definition would not see cotton and vice versa. Coming to Chicago was a guarantee that you would not be picking cotton. The people sitting at the dining room table this late winter night had chosen snow over cotton.

It was a new century now. Ida Mae had never expected to see it. But here she was about to celebrate another birthday. She didn't know how many more she might live to see, and she didn't worry about it. It was March 2002. She was in a new chair by the window now. It was a gold velveteen recliner that could swivel and pivot, and she could watch the world play out beneath her from whatever angle she chose. She had replaced the baby blue carpet and the baby blue plastic-covered furniture she inherited from the nice Italian people when she bought the three-flat some thirty-five years ago. She had hung new draperies and kept the new blinds at half-mast to frame her view of the mayhem below. It was better than a movie.

"The police," she'd say, "they riding tonight. When it's a shooting, they ride for a good week. They been riding hard lately."

That meant the street might be quiet for a change. She lived with the daughter she had carried in her belly to the New World, the daughter who was now a grandmother herself, and with the daughter's son, whose quick mind and good nature couldn't protect him from the will of the streets. Just about every evening, James, the son who had balked at the shoes she had tried to put on him for the migration north and who was now a grandfather, his hair flecked with gray, would come up from the first floor to watch *Wheel of Fortune* with her on the Magnavox.

She had outlived her proud and stoic husband; her two oldest daughters; the suitor she might have married who would have kept her in the South; the hot-headed Willie Jim, who raised his chains up to her that night in Mississippi; old Mr. Edd, who was a decent boss man but still made life harder than it had to be down south; Miss Julie McClenna, blind and sweet though she was; and even the more tortured souls like Robert Foster and George Starling, whom she never knew but who, along with several million others, were on the train out of the South with her in spirit if not in fact.

Ida Mae Gladney, Robert Foster, and George Starling each left different parts of the South during different decades for different reasons and with different outcomes. The three of them would find some measure of happiness, not because their children had been perfect, their own lives without heartache, or because the North had been particularly welcoming. In fact, not a single one of those things had turned out to be true.

There had been sickness, disappointment, premature and unexpected losses, and, among their children, more divorces than enduring marriages, but at least the children had tried. The three who had come out of the South were left widowed but solvent, and each found some measure of satisfaction because whatever had happened to them, however things had unfolded, it had been of their own choosing, and they could take comfort in that. They believed with all that was in them that they were better off for having made the Migration, that they may have made many mistakes in their lives, but leaving the South had not been one of them.

Ida Mae outlasted them all. Here she was, well into a new millennium no one ever thought she would live to see, eighty-nine going on ninety, and dancing some old version of the black bottom that the old people wouldn't let her dance eight decades before. She was snapping her fingers to B. B. King, who had come north from Mississippi like her, from a place called Itta Bena. She was singing along with the words: *"To know you is to love you, is to see you being free as the wind . . . "*

Mississippi was deep inside her, but she gave no thought to ever living there again. Home was wherever she planted herself, and that happened to be Chicago. She had been there for sixty-six years, longer than some people get to live.

There were several dozen people in Chicago, Milwaukee, Beloit, and Toledo, descended from the original sharecroppers who had left the clay hills of northeastern Mississippi back in the 1930s and 1940s, including, among the descendants, Ida Mae's two surviving children, six grandchildren, seven great-grandchildren, and assorted nieces and nephews. Of those descendants, there were bus drivers, secretaries, teachers, administrators, a bank teller, a lawyer, a customer service representative, government workers.

Ida Mae was the only original migrant left in the family. She was held in high esteem in her white suit and with her cottony white hair combed into a French twist at annual reunion dinners at, say, a Holiday Inn on the outskirts of one of the arrival cities. She had a niece and a brother- and sister-in-law back in Mississippi. And that was pretty much all that was left back home.

She was a Chicagoan now but had seen and heard so much, so many wondrous, sad, and unspeakable things in her life, that there still wasn't time enough to tell all that she had witnessed.

"The half ain't been told," she said.

She put the disappointments in a lockbox in the back of her mind and lived in the moment, which is all anybody has for sure. She had learned long ago, when things were so much harder in the Old Country she left behind, that, after all she had been through, every day to her was a blessing and every breath she took a gift.

Epilogue

Because we have tasted
the bitter swill
of civil war and segregation,
and emerged from that dark chapter
stronger and more united,
we cannot help but believe
that the old hatreds shall someday pass;
that the lines of tribe shall soon dissolve;
that, as the world grows smaller,
our common humanity
shall reveal itself. . . .

—Barack Obama,
Presidential Inaugural Address,
January 20, 2009

By the time the Great Migration was over, few Americans had not been touched by it. The descendants of those who left the South were raised in a world their ancestors could not have comprehended. Those who stayed had relatives up north or out west that they could boast about and options they had not had before if they, too, wanted to leave. In parts of old Abbeville County, South Carolina, for instance, "there is not one family that does not have close relatives in Philadelphia," wrote the scholar Allen B. Ballard. "It's always Philadelphia." Their world—the former Confederacy—was made better in part because of the pressures put upon it by those who made the sacrifice to leave it. The blacks who arrived from Africa and the Caribbean entered a country where people of African descent could breathe freer for all that had come before them.

They lived next to and did business with the great mass of people who had migrated from the South. So, too, did other immigrants and native whites who employed the migrants and their children, rented to them, sold goods to them, fled from them, or befriended them. And people the world over were enriched by the music the migrants carried north with them and, through translation, became—from Louis Armstrong to Miles Davis to Aretha Franklin to the Rolling Stones to Tupac Shakur, and many others—essentially the soundtrack of the twentieth century.

With all that grew out of this mass movement of people, did the Great Migration achieve the aim of those who willed it? Were the people who left the South—and their families—better off for having done so? Was the loss of what they left behind worth what confronted them in the anonymous cities they fled to?

Throughout the Migration, social scientists all but concluded that the answer to those questions was no, that the Migration had led to the troubles of the urban North and West, most scholars blaming the dysfunction of the inner cities on the migrants themselves. The migrants were cast as poor illiterates who imported out-of-wedlock births, joblessness, and welfare dependency wherever they went.

"Masses of ignorant, uncouth, and impoverished migrants flooded the city," the sociologist E. Franklin Frazier wrote of the migration to Chicago, "and changed the whole structure of the Negro community."

The presence of the migrants "in such large numbers crushed and stagnated the progress of Negro life," the economist Sadie Mossell wrote early in the migration to Philadelphia.

Newly available census records suggest the opposite to be true. According to a growing body of research, the migrants were, it turns out, better educated than those they left behind in the South and, on the whole, had nearly as many years of schooling as those they encountered in the North. Compared to the northern blacks already there, the migrants were more likely to be married and remain married, more likely to raise their children in two-parent households, and more likely to be employed. The migrants, as a group, managed to earn higher incomes than northern-born blacks even though they were relegated to the lowest-paying positions. They were less likely to be on welfare than the blacks they encountered in the North, partly because they had come so far, had experienced such hard times, and were willing to work longer hours or second jobs in positions that few northern blacks, or hardly anyone else for that matter, wanted, as was the case with Ida Mae

Gladney, George Swanson Starling, Robert Foster, and millions of others like them.

"The Southerners had their eye out for something," an old settler, Arthur Fauset, was quoted as saying in a book on the migration to Philadelphia. "These shrewd South Carolinians came here as if they knew there was something they could get and they went after it."

It could not have been imagined in the early decades of the Great Migration that some of those unwashed masses yearning to breathe free would end up leading the very cities that had rejected them upon arrival.

The first black mayors in each of the major receiving cities of the North and West were not longtime northern native blacks or those having arrived from the Caribbean but participants or sons of the Great Migration. Carl Stokes, whose parents migrated from Georgia to Ohio during World War I, would be elected, in 1967, mayor of Cleveland, the first black to hold that office in any major American city. Tom Bradley, the son of sharecroppers, whose family fled central Texas for California when he was six years old, would become, in 1973, the first black mayor of Los Angeles. Coleman Young, whose parents brought him north from Tuscaloosa, Alabama, would become, in 1974, mayor of Detroit. Harold Washington, whose father migrated from Kentucky to Illinois, would, in 1983, be elected, contentiously so, mayor of Chicago. Wilson Goode, the son of sharecroppers from North Carolina, would become, in 1984, the mayor of Philadelphia. David Dinkins, the son of a barber who migrated from Newport News, Virginia, to Trenton, New Jersey, would, in 1990, become mayor of New York. And Willie Brown, a onetime farmhand who left the cotton fields of east Texas for northern California, would become mayor of San Francisco in 1996, after having served as the Speaker of the California Assembly, the first black to do so. Many of these men would serve multiple, if often difficult, terms in office, but each had exceeded anything their origins would have foretold.

Over time, the Migration would transform American music as we know it. The three most influential figures in jazz were all children of the Great Migration. Miles Davis was born in Alton, Illinois, after his family migrated from Arkansas. Thelonious Monk migrated with his family from North Carolina when he was five. John Coltrane left High Point, North Carolina, for Philadelphia in 1943, when he was sixteen. Coltrane had never owned a saxophone before his mother bought him a used one once he got north. "He would just sit there all the time and practice and smoke cigarettes," a friend said. The neighbors complained, and a minister decided to give Coltrane the key to a Philadelphia church where he could play his sax whenever he wanted, which was often enough that his friends thought it bordered on the maniacal.

Such may be the sheer force of determination of any emigrant leaving one repressive place for something he or she hopes will be better. But for many of the migrants from the South, the stakes were especially high—there was no place left to go, no other refuge or other suns to search for, in their own country if they failed. Things had to work out, whatever it took, and that determination showed up in the statistics.

"Upon their arrival in northern cities, the recent southern migrants actually enjoyed greater family stability than their northern-born neighbors," the sociologists Stewart Tolnay and Kyle Crowder wrote in 1999.

"Compared with northern-born blacks," Tolnay wrote in 2003 as a result of his continuing research, "southern migrants had higher rates of participation in the labor force, lower levels of unemployment, higher incomes, lower levels of poverty and welfare dependency."

Something deep inside helped push them past the improbability of survival in a strange land and even past many people already there. "Whether one considers poverty status, earnings, or total income," the census analysts Larry H. Long and Lynne R. Heltman wrote, "independent studies are in unanimous agreement with the present finding that southern-born blacks are more economically successful in the North than northern born blacks."

In cases where things went awry, it turned out that the longer the migrants were exposed to the northern cities, the more vulnerable some became to the troubles of the preexisting world they had entered. If anything, the scholars found, the migrants who stumbled were brought down by the conditions of the northern cities, not the other way around.

"Instead of thinking of southern migrants as the 'culprits' in changes that have occurred in the urban black family during this century," Tolnay and Crowder wrote, "it may be more accurate to think of them as the 'victims' of their new residential milieu."

Just to leave, the migrants had to draw upon their inner reserves, transcend the limits of caste and geography and the station to which they had been assigned. The beneficiaries, despite the casualties, were many. The migrants would seem to be the prime beneficiaries of their actions. But they were the ones who had to face the unsettled in-betweenness of their emigrant status. Their individual actions, added together, benefited their children, their grandchildren, and even those they left behind in the South as much as if not more than themselves.

The Migration helped other people of color—the later arrivals from Asia, South and Central America, and the Middle East—whose worlds opened up further as the country liberalized its views of diversity. The Migration exposed white Americans outside the South to black culture and created an opportunity—much of it missed—to bridge the races in the New World. The Migration changed American culture as we know it. The migrants brought the blues and birthed whole genres of music—jazz, rock, rhythm and blues, hip-hop. The Migration would influence the language, food, dance, and dress we take for granted. The Migration "led to higher earnings, an influential black electorate and a black middle class," wrote the preeminent sociologist Reynolds Farley.

Regardless of their formal education, those who persevered in the New World, on the whole, enjoyed greater economic success than they would have otherwise. "Black migrants who left the South and did not return had higher incomes than those who never left or those who returned," the census analysts Larry H. Long and Kristin A. Hansen wrote. And, as the Migration spread the issue of race relations across the United States, forcing the entire country to face its centuries-old demons, it also helped inspire and pressure other racial regimes such as that of South Africa and, thus, was a gift to other parts of the world.

In their own lives, whatever individual success each migrant found was in part a function of how he or she adapted to the New World and made peace, or not, with the Old. Each of the three people in this book represented some aspect of the emigrant psyche, of the patterns of adjustment facing anyone who has ever left one place for another, desperate to make a go of it.

Robert Foster found financial success and walked taller in a land more suited to him. But he turned his back on the South and the culture he sprang from. He rarely went back. He plunged himself fully into an alien world that only partly accepted him and went so far as to change his name and assume a different persona to fit in. It left him a rootless soul, cut off from the good things about the place he had left. He put distance between himself and his own children, hiding his southern, perhaps truest, self. He sought to overcome his emigrant insecurities by trying to prove himself at the casinos, proving instead how much one could lose in so short a time. In later life, he hungered for any news or reminder of home, like many an exile. He became as obsessed with outward appearances as the city he fled to and nursed ancient wounds until the day he died. But he would have had it no other way.

George Starling succeeded merely by not being lynched. Just living was an achievement. He managed to reach a level of material solvency he might never have known in the South, assuming he had survived. He paid a price. He enjoyed the fruits of the North and the South but grieved over how he had to leave and what might have been. He was as northern as he was southern, biregional, one might say, not fully one or the other. His ultimate success was psychological freedom from the bonds of his origins. Leaving the South and working the railroads gave him a view of the world he might otherwise never have had. He became a master observer of people and events. And in the end, the thing he wanted most of all, the education denied him early in life, came to him perhaps without his realizing it. He got an education, not the formal one of his dreams, but one he could not have imagined, a fuller one, perhaps, for having left the limited world of his birth.

Ida Mae Gladney had the humblest trappings but was the richest of them all. She had lived the hardest life, been given the least education, seen the worst the South could hurl at her people, and did not let it break her. She lived longer in the North than in the South but never forsook her origins, never changed the person she was deep inside, never changed her accent, speaking as thick a Mississippi drawl in her nineties as the day she caught the train out of Okolona sixty-odd years before. She was surrounded by the clipped speech of the North, the crime on the streets, the flight of the white people from her neighborhood, but it was as if she were immune to it all. She took the best of what she saw in the North and the South and interwove them in the way she saw fit. She followed every jump shot of the Chicago Bulls and knew how to make sweet potato pie like the best of them in the Delta. She lived in the moment, surrendered to whatever the day presented, and remained her true, original self. Her success was spiritual, perhaps the hardest of all to achieve. And because of that, she was the happiest and lived the longest of them all.

From the moment the first migrants set foot in the North during World War I, scholars began weighing in on the motivations of people like Ida Mae, George, and Robert—whether it was the pull of the North or the push of the South, whether they were driven by economics or by injustice and persecution, whether changes in cotton production started the Migration or merely hastened what was already under way, and whether the Migration would end, as some wrongly anticipated, with World War I.

Scholars widely disagreed over the role of lynchings in sparking a particular wave of migration. Some scholars saw no connection between lynching and an exodus of blacks from a given community, suggesting that the people might have been too afraid to leave or had simply accepted violence as a part of life in the South. Others found evidence that blacks did, in fact, leave as might be expected after those public executions. Given the enormity of the Migration, it is quite possible that both observations could have been true, that blacks might have found it more daunting or were not in a position to leave in the immediate aftermath of a lynching but that such violence might have planted the seeds of a departure that may have taken months to actually pull off, as in the case of Ida Mae Gladney.

In any case, the turmoil in the South could be felt in the North. "Black school principals in Philadelphia," wrote the scholar Allen B. Ballard, could tell that "something had happened in a particular section of the South by the concentration of refugees from a certain place."

At the same time, the exodus forced change in the South, albeit a slow and fitful one, almost from the start: the number of lynchings in the South declined in each successive decade of the Great Migration as the number of black departures went up. Though the violence would continue into the 1960s and there were many factors that figured into that form of vigilantism, it took less than a decade of migration to begin making a difference. "Since 1924"—some eight years into the Great Migration—"lynchings have been on a marked decline," *The Montgomery Advertiser* of Alabama observed in 1959, four decades after the Migration began. "Lynchings have reached a vanishing point in recent years."

For decades, it was argued that the Great Migration was triggered by changes in cotton farming: the boll weevil infestation of the 1920s and the early mechanical cotton harvester unveiled in the 1940s. But whatever cotton's role in the Migration, it could, at best, account for only the subset of migrants who were picking cotton in the first place. Changes in cotton farming could not account for the Great Migration as a whole or for the motivations of the people who came from Virginia, Kentucky, Tennessee, North Carolina, western Texas, and Florida, for instance, where cotton was not the main industry, or for those in the cotton states who happened to be doing work other than picking cotton. Nor could it account for those who were in the industry but left for other reasons.

The timing of the Great Migration alone raises questions as to whether changes in cotton harvesting caused the Migration or whether it was the Migration that in fact set off changes in cotton production. The mechanical cotton picker did not exist when the exodus began. The Migration had been under way for some thirty years before the first viable prototypes were actually in use in the fields.

The Migration had siphoned off half a million black workers by 1920 alone. Not all of them were cotton pickers, but there was enough fretting over the loss of labor that the South began searching for a mechanical replacement for the workers the plantations were losing. The exodus of black southerners accelerated the drive toward finding a machine that could do what the pickers did. In the race toward an alternative, inventors registered nearly five hundred patents between 1901 and 1931, the early decades of the Migration, for some version of a hoped-for machine to pick cotton. That amounted to more than all the patents that had been issued in the entire second half of the nineteenth century, when the South did not have to worry about blacks leaving en masse.

Still, many planters were slow to accept the idea of such a machine or the implications of the growing black exodus. Nor did they welcome the sizable investment the new machines would require. Into the mid-1940s, the machines were plagued by imprecision, pulling up the stalks and all, and were seen as producing an inferior grade of cotton than what came from human hands. Thus, many planters did not then consider the machines a viable alternative.

It took World War II and the even bigger outflow of blacks to awaken them to what some agricultural engineers working on a mechanical harvester already knew: "Much of this labor is not returning to the farm," Harris P. Smith, the chief of agricultural engineering at Texas A&M University, wrote in 1946. "Therefore, the cotton farmer is forced to mechanize." As for the connection between the Migration and the machine, Smith concluded that "instead of the machines displacing labor, they were used to replace the labor that had left the farm."

It was not until the 1950s—close to two generations after the Great Migration began—that cotton harvesters were in wide enough use to do what human hands had done for centuries. But by then, some four million black people had already left.

In interviews with more than twelve hundred migrants across the country about their decisions to migrate, none mentioned the boll weevil or the economics of cotton. This in itself does not mean these things were not unseen forces in their lives, only that they were not thinking of them as they made their decision, or in hindsight. It appeared that when it came to a life-altering change of such gravity, it was not one thing; it was many things, some weighing more heavily in one migrant's heart than another but all very likely figuring into the calculus of departure.

All told, perhaps the most significant measure of the Great Migration was the act of leaving itself, regardless of the individual outcome. Despite the private disappointments and triumphs of any individual migrant, the Migration, in some ways, was its own point. The achievement was in making the decision to be free and acting on that decision, wherever that journey led them.

"If all of their dream does not come true," the *Chicago Defender* wrote at the start of the Great Migration, "enough will come to pass to justify their actions."

Many black parents who left the South got the one thing they wanted just by leaving. Their children would have a chance to grow up free of Jim Crow and to be their fuller selves. It cannot be known what course the lives of people like Toni Morrison, James Baldwin, Diana Ross, Aretha Franklin, Michelle Obama, Jesse Owens, Joe Louis, Jackie Robinson, Serena and Venus Williams, Bill Cosby, Condoleezza Rice, Nat King Cole, Oprah Winfrey, Berry Gordy (who founded Motown and signed children of the Migration to sing for it), the astronaut Mae Jemison, the artist Romare Bearden, the performers Jimi Hendrix, Michael Jackson, Prince, Sean "P. Diddy" Combs, Whitney Houston, Mary J. Blige, Queen Latifah, the director Spike Lee, the playwright August Wilson, and countless others might have taken had their parents or grandparents not participated in the Great Migration and raised them in the North or West. All of them grew up to become among the best in their fields, changed them, really, and were among the first generation of blacks in this country to grow up free and unfettered because of the actions of their forebears. Millions of other children of the Migration grew up to lead productive, though anonymous, lives in quiet, everyday ways that few people will ever hear about.

Most of these children would attend better schools than those in the South and, as a whole, outperform their southern white counterparts and nearly match the scores of northern-born blacks within a few years of arrival. Studies conducted in the early 1930s found that, after four years in the North, the children of black migrants to New York were scoring nearly as well as northern-born blacks who were "almost exactly at the norm for white children," wrote Otto Klineberg, a leading psychologist of the era at Columbia University.

"The evidence for an environmental effect is unmistakable," he reported. He found that the longer the southern-born children were in the North, the higher they scored. The results "suggest that the New York environment is capable of raising the intellectual level of the Negro children to a point equal to that of the Whites." Klineberg's studies of the children of the Great Migration would later become the scientific foundation of the 1954 Supreme Court decision in the school desegregation case, *Brown v. the Board of Education,* a turning point in the drive toward equal rights in this country.

In the end, it could be said that the common denominator for leaving was the desire to be free, like the Declaration of Independence said, free to try out for most any job they pleased, play checkers with whomever they chose, sit where they wished on the streetcar, watch their children walk across a stage for the degree most of them didn't have the chance to get. They left to pursue some version of happiness, whether they achieved it or not. It was a seemingly simple thing that the majority of Americans could take for granted but that the migrants and their forebears never had a right to in the world they had fled.

A central argument of this book has been that the Great Migration was an unrecognized immigration within this country. The participants bore the marks of immigrant behavior. They plotted a course to places in the North and West that had some connection to their homes of origin. They created colonies of the villages they came from, imported the food and folkways of the Old Country, and built their lives around the people and churches they knew from back home. They took work the people already there considered beneath them. They doubled up and took in roomers to make ends meet. They tried to instill in their children the values of the Old Country while pressing them to succeed by the standards of the New World they were in.

As with immigrant parents, a generational divide arose between the migrants and their children. The migrants couldn't understand their impatient, northern-bred sons and daughters—why the children who had been spared the heartache of a racial caste system were not more grateful to have been delivered from the South. The children couldn't relate to the stories of southern persecution when they were facing gangs and drive-by shootings, or, in the more elite circles, the embarrassment of southern parents with accents and peasant food when the children were trying to fit into the middle-class enclaves of the North.

And though this immigration theory may be structurally sound, with sociologists even calling them immigrants in the early years of the Migration, nearly every black migrant I interviewed vehemently resisted the immigrant label. They did not see themselves as immigrants under any circumstances, their behavior notwithstanding. The idea conjured up the deepest pains of centuries of rejection by their own country. They had been forced to become immigrants in their own land just to secure their freedom. But they were not immigrants and had never been actual immigrants. The South may have acted like a different country and been proud of it, but it was a part of the United States, and anyone born there was born an American.

The black people who left were citizens, and many of their forebears had been in this land before the country was founded. They were among the first nonnative people to set foot in the New World, brought by the Europeans to build it from wilderness and doing so without pay and by force from the time of the first arrivals in 1619 to their emancipation 246 years later. For twelve generations, their ancestors had worked the land and helped build the country. Into the twentieth century, their fourth century in America, they still had had to step aside and fall further down the economic ladder with each new wave of immigrants from all over the world, after generations as burden bearers.

It is one of those circular facts of history that, in the three great receiving cities to which southern blacks fled—the cities that drew Ida Mae, George, and Robert—blacks had been among the first nonnatives to set foot on the soil and to establish settlements centuries before. Black *mestizos* were among the forty-four Mexican settlers arriving in 1781 at the pueblo that would become Los Angeles. Jean Baptiste Point DuSable, a fur trader born of an African slave woman in Haiti, built, in 1779, the first permanent settlement in what is now known as Chicago. Jan Rodrigues, a sailor of African descent working for and later abandoned by Dutch merchants on an untamed island in the New World, created the first trading post on what is now known as Manhattan, in 1613.

And so when blacks who had migrated north and west showed resentment at being considered immigrants, it was perhaps because they knew in their bones that their ancestors had been here before there was a United States of America and that it took their leaving the South to achieve the citizenship they deserved by their ancestry and labors alone. That freedom and those rights had not come automatically, as they should have, but centuries late and of the migrants' own accord.

With the benefit of hindsight, the century between Reconstruction and the end of the Great Migration perhaps may be seen as a necessary stage of upheaval. It was a transition from an era when one race owned another; to an era when the dominant class gave up ownership but kept control over the people it once had owned, at all costs, using violence even; to the eventual acceptance of the servant caste into the mainstream.

The Great Migration was the final break from an abusive union with the South. It was a step in freeing not just the people who fled, but the country whose mountains they crossed. Their exodus left a still imperfect but far different landscape than before the Migration began.

It was, if nothing else, an affirmation of the power of an individual decision, however powerless the individual might appear on the surface. "In the simple process of walking away one by one," wrote the scholar Lawrence R. Rodgers, "millions of African-American southerners have altered the course of their own, and all of America's, history."

Over the decades, perhaps the wrong questions have been asked about the Great Migration. Perhaps it is not a question of whether the migrants brought good or ill to the cities they fled to or were pushed or pulled to their destinations, but a question of how they summoned the courage to leave in the first place or how they found the will to press beyond the forces against them and the faith in a country that had rejected them for so long. By their actions, they did not dream the American Dream, they willed it into being by a definition of their own choosing. They did not ask to be accepted but declared themselves the Americans that perhaps few others recognized but that they had always been deep within their hearts.

Notes on Methodology

I began this work because of what I saw as incomplete perceptions, outside of scholarly circles, of what the Great Migration was and how and why it happened, particularly through the eyes of those who experienced it. Because it was so unwieldy and lasted for so long, the movement did not appear to rise to the level of public consciousness that, by any measure, it seemed to deserve.

The first question, in my view, had to do with its time frame: what was it, and when precisely did it occur? The Great Migration is often described as a jobs-driven, World War I movement, despite decades of demographic evidence and real-world indicators that it not only continued well into the 1960s but gathered steam with each decade, not ending until the social, political, and economic reasons for the Migration began truly to be addressed in the South in the dragged-out, belated response to the Civil Rights Act of 1964.

The second question had to do with *where* it occurred. The migration from Mississippi to Chicago has been the subject of the most research through the years and has dominated discussion of the phenomenon, in part because of the sheer size of the black influx there and because of the great scholarly interest taken in it by a cadre of social scientists working in Chicago at the start of the Migration. However, from my years as a national correspondent at *The New York Times* and my early experiences growing up in a world surrounded by people who had come to the mid-Atlantic region during the latter half of the migration from all over the southeastern seaboard, I knew it to be a farther-reaching national resettlement than had been described by most studies of it.

Third, as most studies of the Migration focused on the important questions of demographics, politics, economics, and sociology, I wanted to convey the intimate stories of people who had dared to make the crossing. I wanted to capture the enormity of the phenomenon by tracking unrelated people who had followed the multiple streams of the Great Migration over the course of the decades it unfolded. I wanted to reach as many as I could of this dwindling generation in the spirit of the oral history projects with the last surviving slaves back in the 1930s.

Therefore, in the mid-1990s, I set out on a search for people who had migrated from the South to the North and West during the Great Migration. That search led me to Mississippi Clubs, Masonic lodges, class reunions, and union meetings of retired postal workers, bus drivers, transit workers, and other retirees on the South Side of Chicago; to quilting clubs, Baptist churches, and senior centers in Manhattan and Brooklyn; to Louisiana Clubs, Texas Clubs, Sunday Masses, Creole luncheons, and Juneteenth Day celebrations (commemorating the day the last slaves in Texas learned they were free, two years after Emancipation) in Los Angeles; to senior centers, libraries, and community meetings in Oakland; and to funerals and family reunions in Milwaukee. In these and dozens of other places frequented by seniors in these cities, I collected names and stories, interviewing more than twelve hundred people who shared with me preliminary versions of their experiences. I conducted follow-up interviews with three dozen of the most promising former migrants and settled on three complementary subjects through whose lives I hoped to re-create the broad sweep of the movement.

The book is essentially three projects in one. The first was a collection of oral histories from around the country. The second was the distillation of those oral histories into a narrative of three protagonists, each of whom led a sufficiently full life to merit a book in his or her own right and was thus researched and reported as such. The third was an examination of newspaper accounts and scholarly and literary works of the era and more recent analyses of the Migration to recount the motivations, circumstances, and perceptions of the Migration as it was in progress and to put the subjects' actions into historical context.

As might be expected, the participants in the Migration had keener memories of their formative years and of the high and low points of their lives—the basis of this book—than of the more mundane and less relevant aspects of their retirement years. Some subjects recalled certain moments of their lives with greater detail than did other subjects recounting the same point in their own trajectory, which is reflected in the text. Furthermore, in their wisdom and commitment to an accurate rendering of events, they frequently declined to speculate or press beyond what they recollected. Where possible, I confirmed or clarified their accounts through interviews with the dwindling circle of surviving witnesses, cohorts, and family members; through newspaper accounts in the South and North dating back to 1900; and through census, military, railroad, school, state, and municipal records.

The primary subjects and many of the secondary informants were interviewed for dozens, if not hundreds, of hours, most of the interviews tape-recorded and transcribed. I returned to their counties of origin to interview the surviving people who knew them and to retrace their lives in the South. I then reenacted all or part of each subject's migration route, devoting most of my time to the migration of Robert Foster, which meant driving from Monroe, Louisiana, to Houston and Laredo, Texas, to Lordsburg, New Mexico, Phoenix, San Diego, Los Angeles, and on to Oakland, as Dr. Foster described in bitter detail, with my parents as generational tour guides for most of the journey. My father took notes and my mother offered commentary as I tried to re-create the experience of one person driving the entire distance through the desert night.

"You know he must have been ready to cry right about in here," my mother said as the car I had rented, a new Buick as was his when he made the crossing, hurtled into hairpin curves in total darkness with hundreds of miles yet to go. As it turned out, I was not able to reenact to the letter one of the most painful aspects of the drive. I was nearly ready to fall asleep at the wheel by the time we reached Yuma, Arizona. My parents insisted that we stop. We got a hotel room with, of course, no trouble at all, the one thing he had been so desperate for all those decades ago but that was denied him over and over again that long night in 1953.

The seeds of this project were sown within me years ago, growing up with parents who had migrated from the South and who sent me to an affluent white grade school that they themselves could never have dreamed of attending. There, classmates told of ancestors coming from Ireland or Scandinavia with little in their pockets and making something of themselves in the New World. Over time, I came to realize that the same could be said of my family and of millions of other black Americans who had journeyed north during the Great Migration.

I gravitated to the children of recent immigrants from Argentina, Nepal, Ecuador, El Salvador, with whom I had so much in common as the children of newcomers: the accents and folkways of overprotective parents suspicious of the libertine mores of the New World and our childish embarrassment at their nervous hovering; the exotic, out-of-step delicacies from the Old Country that our mothers lovingly prepared for our lunchboxes; the visits to my parents' fellow "immigrant" friends—all just happening to be from the South and exchanging the latest about the people from back home; the gentle attempts at instilling Old World values from their homelands, my father going so far as to nudge me away from city boys and toward potential suitors whose parents he knew from back home in Petersburg, Virginia, who were, to him, upstanding boys by definition and who would make a fine match in his view, which all but guaranteed that I'd have little interest in them.

Thus I grew up the daughter of immigrants, "a southerner once removed," as the Mississippi-born poet Natasha Trethewey once called me. My parents bore the subtle hallmarks of the immigrant psyche, except they were Americans who had taken part in an internal migration whose reach and nuances are still little understood.

The research into the world of the Great Migration required wading through dozens of scholarly works of the era, which were a revealing commentary on the attitudes and conditions the migrants lived under before and after their departures. Some of the works were benignly patronizing. Many betrayed such unquestioning bigotry as to be nearly unreadable. All were useful in some way or another. Yet, throughout my research, I was at times struck by the wisdom and compassion of otherwise detached social scientists, many of them white, privileged, and exhibiting unavoidable prejudices of the day but still often rendering prescient and even-handed conclusions. At the start of its 672-page report on the 1919 Chicago Riots, the sober, white-led Chicago Commission on Race Relations, presaging the sentiments of a yet-to-be-born African-American president, whose rise would have been beyond imagination at the time, admonished in 1922:

It is important for our white citizens always to remember that the Negroes alone of all our immigrants came to America against their will by the special compelling invitation of the whites; that the institution of slavery was introduced, expanded and maintained by the United States by the white people and for their own benefit; and they likewise created the conditions that followed emancipation.

Our Negro problem, therefore, is not of the Negro's making. No group in our population is less responsible for its existence. But every group is responsible for its continuance. . . . Both races need to understand that their rights and duties are mutual and equal and their interests in the common good are identical. . . . There is no help or healing in appraising past responsibilities or in present apportioning of praise or blame. The past is of value only as it aids in understanding the present; and an understanding of the facts of the problem—a magnanimous understanding by both races—is the first step toward its solution.

Afterword

Ida Mae Gladney died peacefully in her sleep after a brief onset of leukemia in September 2004. Her family was so distraught that her children and grandchildren kept her room precisely as it was for years. The door remained closed in memoriam to her, and no one had the heart or strength to touch it.

ACKNOWLEDGMENTS

This book is the culmination of many years of research and distillation and could not have come to be without the faith and encouragement of critical people and institutions at crucial moments in its gestation.

I wish first to express gratitude for my parents—my mother and my late father, who gave me my earliest understanding of the Great Migration through their lives and experiences and through what they passed on to me, and who were the inspiration for what I did not know was possible when I first began pursuing the idea.

Thank you to the people who helped to create the groundwork necessary for my intuitions to become a reality: Denise Stinson, who believed in the book from the start, and Michael Winston, for his wise counsel.

I wish to thank my editors at Random House—Ann Godoff, who acquired it, Jonathan Karp, who cheered it on, and, most of all, Kate Medina, who embraced it, championed it, and brought it into the world. I also benefited from the support and insights of Lindsey Schwoeri, Millicent Bennett, Jonathan Jao, Amelia Zalcman, Sally Marvin, Carol Schneider, London King, Ashley Gratz-Collier, and Steve Messina and his team, among many others at Random House. Thank you ever so much.

During the course of the research, I was fortunate to have been able to rely on support from a fellowship from the John Simon Guggenheim Foundation; an Edith Kreeger Wolf endowed lectureship at Northwestern University; a semester as Ferris Professor of Journalism at Princeton University; and various lectures and seminars I delivered at such places as Brown University, the Nieman Foundation at Harvard University, the narrative journalism conference in Aarhus, Denmark, the University of Nevada at Reno, the University of Mississippi at Oxford, and, for three years, as the James M. Cox Professor of Journalism at Emory University. I am grateful to Boston University, where I now am on faculty, for its role in promoting narrative nonfiction such as this book and for the support of David Campbell, Thomas Fiedler, Louis Ureneck, Mitchell Zuckoff, Robert Manoff, Richard Lehr, Robert Zelnik, Caryl Rivers, Safoura Rafeizadeh, and James Brann.

I was on leave from *The New York Times* for much of the time I was researching the book with the good wishes of three executive editors, Bill Keller, Joseph Lelyveld, and Howell Raines, who showed patience and understanding as I pursued this calling, as well as the good cheer of Soma Golden Behr.

This has been a personal journey that, due to the nature of the work and the loss of the primary subjects, transformed me out of necessity from journalist to unintended historian. I am grateful for the insights of historians who have made rigorous examination of the American past, particularly of the Jim Crow era, their life's work. In particular, I wish to thank Leon Litwack, who shared with me his wisdom and made sure I left Berkeley with the books I needed from his favorite used book store, the old Cody's near campus.

Beyond these, I thank God for the will and fortitude to make it through this journey. But also for their encouragement at critical moments, I am grateful to Alex Reid, Jonathan Schwartz, Rick Jones, Gwendolyn Whitt, Fannye Jolly, Michael Elliston, D. J. Page, D. M. Page, Laleh Khadivi, Pat Harris, Marcia Lythcott, Debora Ott, and, for their belief in me over the years, Frances Ball, Gladys Pemberton, Beatrice Judge, Lawrence Kaggwa, Ronald Richardson, and the Taylor family of Richmond and Petersburg, Virginia. Thank you to Eva Harvey, Robert K. Watts, and Joseph Beck for sharing their memories of the Jim Crow South; and my sincerest gratitude to those who assisted in the research: Christine Savage in the final throes of production, Christine Li, Emily Truax, Sarah Stanton, and, especially, Kathryn Wilson for her hard work in the early years of the project.

I am deeply grateful for the time and contributions of the more than twelve hundred people who shared their stories in preliminary interviews in the first year and a half of the research and whose experiences, while not explicitly cited in the text, helped shape its direction. They were my initial teachers in the world of Jim Crow and the unseen chorus that validated the final narrative. For going out of their way to help identify people who had migrated from the South as they had done, I am grateful for the kindness shown me by Wilks Battle, Bennie Lee Ford, Aline Heisser-Ovid, and, especially, Almeta Washington.

I wish to thank the subjects' families for allowing me into their lives and entrusting me with their loved ones on trips both long and short that we made to the places they worked and lived and, for two of them, back to the Old Country. In particular, I want to thank Eleanor Smiley, James and Mary Ann Gladney, Karen Smiley, Kevin Smiley, Madison James Foster II, Bunny Fisher, Joy Foster, and Patricia George for their warmth and encouragement, and Amjad "Kenny" Mujaahid for his inspiring letters of support.

Finally, I reserve the greatest measure of gratitude for Ida Mae Gladney, George Swanson Starling, and Robert Pershing Foster, the people who gave so much of themselves to a book they would never see. They believed in me and in this project perhaps more than anyone else, perhaps, at times, even more than I did. Their unfailing faith in this work carried me through when I doubted what was possible. Meeting and sharing with them their final years on this earth has been one of the great joys and honors of my life, and I have been inspired and made better for having known them.

ISABEL WILKERSON
June 2010

SELECTED INTERVIEWS AND SOURCES

CALIFORNIA
Dr. Robert P. Foster
Cathryn Covington Baker
Lee Ballard
Romie Banks
Mrs. J. M. Beard
Howard and Isabelle Beckwith
Pat Botchekan
Malissa Briley
Sylvester Brooks

Claire Collins
John Collins
Joseph Cooper
Ivorye Covington
Leo DeJohn
John Dunlap
Dallas Evans
Sherman Ferguson
Bennie Lee Ford
Joy Foster
Warren Hollingsworth
Jessie Holmes
Charles Honore
Marilyn Hudson
Robert Johnson
Carrie Jones
Limuary and Adeline Jordan
Barbara Lemmons
Marguerite Lewis
Nellie Lutcher
Carl Kendall
James Marshall
Leola McMearn
Cleo Pierre
John Rachal, Sr.
Vera Roberts
Della B. Robinson
De Willow Sherman
Reatha Gray Simon
Reatha Beck Smith
Ida Bryant Spigener
Barbara Starks
Ruby Thomas
Melba Thompson
Almeta Washington
Inette Weasel
Betty S. White

FLORIDA

Reuben Blye
Viola Dunham
Watson Dunham
Cleave Frink
Patricia George
Reverend William Hawkins
Andrew "Jack" Johnson
Carla Mitchell
Virginia Sallet

GEORGIA

Joseph Beck
Sharon Seay
James C. Washington

ILLINOIS

Ida Mae Brandon Gladney
Laura Addison
Ruby Barnes
Wilks Battle
Bessie Baugard
Homer Betts
Erma Bien-Aimee
Marie Billingsley
Barbara Bowman
Isiah Bracy
Albert Brooks
George Brown
Joe L. Brown
Herbert Bruce
Albert Sidney Burchett
Tony Burroughs
Florine Burton
Betty Caldwell
Orlando Campbell
Joseph Chapman
James Clark
Elwood Crowder
Austin Cunningham
Grady Davis
Henrietta Dawson

John Harold Earl
Arthur Ellis
Lisa Ely
Mildred Elzie
Eddie Ervin
Robert David Fields
Bunny Fisher
Myrtis Francis
Lasalle Frelix
Phlenoid Gaiter
James and Mary Ann Gladney
Walter Goudy
Ruth Hamilton
Aaron Henderson
Leon "Jack" Hillman
James Hobbs
Spurgeon Holland
Karyne Islam
Urelle Jackson, Sr.
Isabel Joseph Johnson
Willie Johnson
Lola Jones
Spencer Leak
Emma Leonard
Clinton Lewis
Hollis Lewis
Carl Little
Ruth McClendon
Doris McMurray
Charles Mingo
Irene Nelson
Clara Piper
Raymar Pitchfork
Robena Porter
Robert Pulliam
Edna Robertson
William G. Samuels
James Seahorn
Eleanor Smiley
Karen Smiley
Kevin Smiley
Coy F. Smith
Ruby W. McGowan Mays Smith
Laura Starks
Howard Stephenson
Roma Stewart
Bennie Therrell
Riley Tubbs
John Valson
Mamie Westley
Mary Louise Wiley
Delores Woodtor

LOUISIANA

Joella Burton
Madison James Foster II
Faroker Johnson
Clara Poe
B. D. Robinson
Rosalie Taylor
Florence Todd
Clyde Walker

MISSISSIPPI

Marcelle Barr
Doretta Boston
Gilbert Elie
Aubrey Enochs
Gloria Enochs
Jessie Gladney
Isolena Harris
David McIntosh

NEW YORK

George Swanson Starling
Dees Abraham
Nathaniel M. Baker
Maxie Broughton
Bennie Brown
Gary Byrd

Franklin Caldwell
John Carter
Christine Chambers
Virginia DeBreaux Hall
Petite Bell Hammond
Reverend Henry V. Harrison
James Hobbs
Clarence Jerrell
Julia Johnson
Gardenia Joyner
Aurilla Moore
Ulysses Morris
Amjad "Kenny" Mujaahid
Onie Bell Carter Norwood
Donald Payne
Delphine Smith Peterman
Henry Roberts
Ruth Rudder
Jerry Ward
Robert K. Watts
Monifa White
Manier E. Webber
Eva Mae Williams

Tennessee
Richard Jarvis Enochs

Wisconsin
Jerome Hervey
Freddie Knox
Manley Thomas

Partial list of organizations that offered support and access to migrants

California
Betty Hill Recreation Center, Senior Line Dancing
East Texas Club of Los Angeles
Estelle Van Meter Senior Center
Grambling Alumni Association, Los Angeles
Independent Square Senior Center
Jefferson Council
Jim Gilliam Senior Center
Lake Charles, Louisiana, Club
LA–LA (Louisiana to Los Angeles), Inc.
Monroe, Louisiana, Club
Mount Carmel Senior Center
People Coordinated Services
St. Andrew's Senior Group
St. Bernadette Senior Center
Slauson Senior Recreation Center
Theresa Lindsay Senior Center
Vineyard Recreation Senior Center
Watts Senior Center
Xavier College Alumni Club of Los Angeles

Florida
Gethsemane Baptist Church, Eustis
NAACP, South Brevard Chapter

Georgia
National Funeral Directors and Morticians Association

Illinois
Ada S. Niles Senior Center
African-American Police League
Afro-American Genealogical and Historical Society of Chicago

AFSCME, Chicago District Council
Atlas Senior Center, Chicago Area Agency on Aging
Bethel Terrace Senior Center
Brookhaven, Mississippi, Club
Carter Funeral Home
Chicago Housing Authority Senior Housing
Chicago Pensioners Club
Chicago Urban League
Chicago Usher Board
Cotton Plant, Arkansas, Club
DuSable High School
Fourth District, Beat 414, South Chicago
Greater St. John's AME Church
Greenville, Mississippi, Club
Greenwood, Mississippi, Club
Grenada, Mississippi, Club
Happy Action Seniors, St. Joachim Church
Historic Pullman Foundation
Latney Funeral Home
Leak and Sons Funeral Home
Local 241/Chicago Transit Authority Bus Drivers Union
Metro Seniors in Action
National Alliance of Postal and Federal Employees, Chicago Branch, Retirees' Division
Neptune Seniors
Newton, Mississippi, Club
Old Friends of Chicago
Pastors of Englewood, Seventh District
Police Beat 713, Boulevard Arts Center
Prince Hall Masonic Lodge of the State of Illinois
Senior Advisory Committee, Third District
Senior Advisory Committee, Fourth District
Senior Steppers' Set at Mr. G's
Tabernacle Baptist Church
Third District, Beat 312, Grand Crossing
Third District, Beat 322, Grand Crossing
Third District, Beat 323, Grand Crossing
UBA A. Philip Randolph Center
Vicksburg, Mississippi, Club
Willa Rawls Manor
WBEZ-FM
WGCI-AM
WVON-AM

New York

African American Quilting Club, Brooklyn
Baptist House of Prayer, Harlem
Bridge Street Baptist Church, Brooklyn
Central Harlem Senior Center
First Baptist Church, Brooklyn
Lagree Baptist Church, Harlem
Metropolitan A.M.E. Church, Harlem
New York City Department of Aging
Wilson Major Morris Senior Center, Harlem
WLIB-AM

Notes

vii **I was leaving the South:** Richard Wright, *Black Boy* (New York: HarperCollins, 1993, a reissue of Wright's autobiography, originally published in 1945 by Harper and Brothers). This passage is from a last-minute insertion in a restructuring of the book, which originally had been titled *American Hunger.* For its release in 1945, the title was changed to *Black Boy* and the second half of the book, describing Wright's adjustment in the North, was deleted at the behest of the Book-of-the-Month Club. Wright chose to insert this passage as a compromise ending to the revised autobiography. Because this passage was not part of the original manuscript, it is not included in the text of the modern-day version. The passage instead appears in the footnotes of the 1993 reprint, p. 496.

Part I: In the Land of the Forefathers

1 **Our mattresses were made:** Mahalia Jackson with Evan McLeod Wylie, *Movin' On Up* (New York: Hawthorn Books, 1966), pp. 22, 25.

Leaving

3 **The land is first:** David L. Cohn, *God Shakes Creation* (New York: Harper and Brothers, 1935), pp. 32, 33.

3 **They fly from the land:** W. H. Stillwell, "Exode," *Chicago Inter-Ocean,* March 12, 1881. The stanza reads: "They fly from the land that bore them, as the Hebrews fled the Nile; from the heavy burthens [*sic*] o'er them; from unpaid tasks before them; from a serfdom base and vile."

5 **A man named Roscoe Colton:** Jonathan Rosen, "Flight Patterns," *The New York Times Magazine,* April 22, 2007, pp. 58–63.

THE GREAT MIGRATION, 1915–1970

8 **In our homes:** "The Negro Problem," *Independent* 54: 2221. The colored Alabama woman interviewed for this 1902 article requested that her name not be used, fearing retribution for expressing a desire to leave. The fear of being identified was common among southern black letter writers to the *Chicago Defender* inquiring about opportunities in the North and others discussing or considering migration. Often they explicitly pleaded that their identities not be revealed.

8 **"They left as though":** Emmett J. Scott, *Negro Migration During the War* (New York: Oxford University Press, 1920), p. 44.

9 **Over the course:** Estimates vary for the number of blacks who left the South during the Great Migration. Some have put the number at well over six million. The historian Jeffrey S. Adler writes that "the total for the three-decade period after 1940 exceeded 4.3 million" alone. David R. Colburn and Jeffrey S. Adler, eds., *African-American Mayors: Race, Politics, and the American City* (Urbana: University of Illinois Press, 2001), p. 4. Definitions vary as to which states make up the South, with the border states of Maryland, Delaware, and the District of Columbia often included. This book uses a definition based on the states that made up the Confederacy and the definitions and perceptions of the migrants who left the South. The migrants' decision to escape to those border regions and those states' participation in the Civil War on the Union side suggest that politically, psychologically, and demographically they were not southern but rather part of the North to which the migrants fled. Those states had net inflows of blacks in a dramatic departure from the states the migrants perceived of as the South. The estimate, just over five and a half million, used in this book is a conservative one and derives from data compiled from Public Use Microdata Sample (PUMS) Tapes of U.S. Census figures for out-migration of African Americans from the former Confederate states of Alabama, Arkansas, Florida, Georgia, Louisiana, Mississippi, North Carolina, South Carolina, Tennessee, and Virginia, along with Kentucky and Oklahoma, to the former Union states that attracted the bulk of the migrants, namely, New York, New Jersey, Connecticut, Massachusetts, Pennsylvania, Michigan, Indiana, Ohio, Illinois, Iowa, Wisconsin, Minnesota, Kansas, California, Nevada, Oregon, and the District of Columbia, along with the border states of Delaware, Maryland, and Missouri and the state of Washington, which was not admitted to the Union until after the Civil War. The number is considered to be an underestimate. "One estimate places the net under-enumeration of Negro males [alone] at about 20 per cent," wrote the sociologists Karl E. Taeuber and Alma F. Taeuber in "The Changing Character of Negro Migration," *The American Journal of Sociology* 70, no. 4 (January 1965), p. 433.

9 **"receiving station":** Carl Sandburg, *The Chicago Race Riots, July 1919* (New York: Harcourt, Brace and Howe, 1919), p. 60.

10 **Over time:** See Nicholas Mirkowich, "Recent Trends in Population Distribution in

California," *Geographical Review* 31, no. 2 (April 1941), pp. 300–307, for a general discussion of Gold Rush and Dust Bowl migrations.

10 **for far longer:** Blacks were enslaved in this country for 244 years, from 1619 to 1863. As of 2010, they have been free for 147 years.

10 **"The story of":** Neil R. McMillen, "The Migration and Black Protest in Jim Crow Mississippi," in *Black Exodus: The Great Migration from the American South,* ed. Alferdteen Harrison (Jackson: University Press of Mississippi, 1991), p. 81.

10 **By then nearly half:** U.S. Bureau of the Census, *Historical Statistics of the United States, Colonial Times to 1970, Part 1* (Washington, D.C.: U.S. Government Printing Office, 1975), table A, pp. 177–194; 1970 State Form 2 IPUS sample. From James N. Gregory, *The Southern Diaspora: How the Great Migrations of Black and White Southerners Transformed America* (Chapel Hill: University of North Carolina Press, 2005). See also Reynolds Farley and Walter Allen, *The Color Line and the Quality of Life in America* (Washington, D.C.: Russell Sage Foundation, 1987), pp. 112–13. Cited by Dernoral Davis in "Portrait of Twentieth-Century African-Americans," in *Black Exodus,* ed. Harrison, p. 12. See also John D. Reid, "Black Urbanization of the South," *Python* 35, no. 3 (1974), p. 259, for reference to the South's being 53 percent black in 1970, the end of the Migration.

10 **"Oftentimes, just to go":** John Dollard, *Caste and Class in a Southern Town* (New Haven, Conn.: Yale University Press, 1937), p. 302.

11 **In Chicago alone:** U.S. Census Bureau, Census 2000 Redistricting Data (Public Law 94-171) Summary File, Table PL1. In 2000, the black population was 1,084,221 in the city of Chicago and 1,033,809 in the state of Mississippi.

11 **"folk movement":** McMillen, "The Migration and Black Protest in Jim Crow Mississippi," p. 81.

11 **Farragut:** Union naval officer David G. Farragut, who rose to admiral, led the capture of the South's largest city during the Battle of New Orleans in April 1862.

12 **ten thousand:** Allan H. Spear, *Black Chicago: The Making of a Negro Ghetto, 1890–1920* (Chicago: University of Chicago Press, 1967), p. 209.

12 **"I went to the station":** Scott, *Negro Migration During the War,* p. 41.

12 **into the words of:** Lawrence R. Rodgers, *Canaan Bound: The African-American Great Migration Novel* (Urbana: University of Illinois Press, 1997), pp. x, xiii. The author notes that, among scholars, "the Great Migration, for many years, remained primarily an academic sideshow displaying only limited signs of penetrating the realm of national popular discourse and culture." However, in the arts, the Great Migration and the resulting issues of "movement and identity have, over the entire history of published black literature, occupied the center of African American consciousness." On p. 3, he adds, "As one of the most widely shared experiences of black America, migration, whether through force or volition, has remained a central subject of black literature and folklore." Blyden Jackson, professor of literature emeritus at the University of North Carolina at Chapel Hill, wrote that "no event, large or small, . . . has had an impact equal in mass or gavity upon the consciousness of black writers." Blyden Jackson, "Introduction," in *Black Exodus,* p. xv.

13 **"Less has been written":** Gregory, *The Southern Diaspora,* p. 5.

13 **the language changes:** Writers navigating the language of intolerance often struggle with how to convey old attitudes and norms with the authenticity the work demands but with the grace and sensitivity required to reach current and future generations. On issues of race and ethnicity, the debate often centers on how best to describe black Americans when the names for the group change with the political fashions of the times and with the origins and intentions of the speaker regarding whatever term is at issue. Based on my many interviews with people from the era, the term "colored" was the most common word they used among themselves. This is not to say that prominent blacks of the day did not use the term "Negro," many arguing that its capitalization bestowed greater status on a group hungry for recognition. But ordinary blacks seemed to wince at how the word could be so easily corrupted by the ruling class, coming out "nigra" instead of the more formal-sounding "Negro," and thus they tended to use the term somewhat derisively in everyday conversation. As for the N-word itself, I have chosen to use it only where required for context, which turned out to be rarer than might be assumed. I chose to use great care out of an acknowledgment of the violence and loss of life that often accompanied its utterance. On the whole, I found that people who had most felt the sting of the word and the violence that undergirded it were less likely to use the word in casual speech than people who had never had to step off a sidewalk because of the color of their skin.

14 **"Compared with northern-born":** Stewart E. Tolnay, "The African American 'Great Migration' and Beyond," *Annual Review of Sociology* 29 (2003): 219.

PART II: BEGINNINGS

17 **This was the culture:** Richard Wright, *Black Boy* (New York: HarperCollins, 1993), p. 303.

IDA MAE BRANDON GLADNEY

19 **From the open door:** Unless otherwise indicated, all references to Ida Mae Gladney are based on continual interviews and conversations with her from May 1996 to August 2004.

31 **Calhoun City, Mississippi:** Interview with Jarvis Enoch, Ida Mae's nephew and a professor at Tennessee State University, in September 1998 in Nashville, about his experiences growing up in Calhoun City, Mississippi, in the 1940s and 1950s.

33 **"hardware of reality":** Carrie Mae Weems, *Constructing History: A Requiem to Mark the Moment,* a film directed and narrated by Weems (Atlanta: Savannah College of Art and Design with the National Black Arts Festival, 2008).

THE STIRRINGS OF DISCONTENT

36 **Everybody seems to be:** *Macon Telegraph,* Editorial, September 15, 1916, p. 4.

36 **One of the earliest:** "Race Labor Leaving," *Chicago Defender,* February 5, 1916, p. 1. Though this is what scholars have cited as the earliest known reference to a group of colored people leaving the South during World War I, it can logically be assumed that other parties left before them in the early stages of the war without telling any-

one of their intentions. The full headline was "Race Labor Leaving. Much Concern over Possible Shortage of Labor—Exodus Steady—Treatment Doesn't Warrant Staying." The paragraph read: "Selma, Ala., Feb. 4—The white people of the extreme South are becoming alarmed over the steady moving of race families out of the mineral belt. Hundreds of families have left during the past few months and the stream is continuing. Every effort is being made to have them stay, but the discrimination and the race prejudice continues as strong as ever. Not many years ago there was a dearth of labor in this part of the country and the steerage passengers from Europe were sought. They cannot do the work of the race men, as they do not understand. Local editorials in white papers are pleading with the business men to hold the race men if possible."

37 **"treatment doesn't warrant staying":** Ibid.

37 **the long and violent hangover:** Some historians have termed the period between Reconstruction and the early twentieth century the Nadir. See Rayford Logan, *The Negro in American Life and Thought, The Nadir: 1887–1901* (New York: Dial Press, 1954).

37 **"I find a worse state":** Robert Preston Brooks, *The Agrarian Revolution in Georgia, 1865–1912,* doctoral dissertation (Madison: University of Wisconsin, 1914; reprinted New York: AMS Press, 1971), pp. 413–14.

37 **"They will almost":** "Laborers Wanted," *Southern Cultivator,* March 1867, a letter from a writer identified by the initials G.A.N. of Warrenton, Georgia, dated February 2, 1867, APS Online, p. 69.

38 **The fight over:** Harvey Fireside, *Separate and Unequal: Homer Plessy and the Supreme Court Decision That Legalized Racism* (New York: Carroll & Graf, 2004).

38 **Fourteenth Amendment:** The Fourteenth Amendment to the Constitution, of 1868, enacted to establish the rights of freed slaves after the Civil War, reads as follows: "All persons born or naturalized in the United States, and subject to the jurisdiction thereof, are citizens of the United States and of the State wherein they reside. No State shall make or enforce any law which shall abridge the privileges or immunities of citizens of the United States; nor shall any State deprive any person of life, liberty, or property, without due process of law; nor deny to any person within its jurisdiction the equal protection of the laws."

38 **Fifteenth Amendment:** The Fifteenth Amendment to the Constitution, of 1880, granting freed slaves the right to vote, reads: "The right of citizens of the United States to vote shall not be denied or abridged by the United States or by any State on account of race, color, or previous condition of servitude."

39 **"If it is necessary":** Ray Stannard Baker, *Following the Color Line* (New York: Doubleday and Page, 1908), p. 245 for Hoke Smith quotation, p. 246 for Vardaman remark on lynching.

39 **"The only effect":** *Jackson* (Mississippi) *Weekly Clarion-Ledger,* July 30, 1903, quoted in *The Oratory of Southern Demagogues,* ed. Calvin McLeod Logue and Howard Dorgan (Baton Rouge: Louisiana State University Press, 1981), p. 73.

39 **Fifteen thousand:** "Summary Punishment Administered by Mob," *Hobart* (Oklahoma) *Republican,* May 16, 1916, p. 1.

39 **"My son can't learn":** "Waco Horror Stirs to Action," *Savannah Tribune,* July 8, 1916, page 4. "Supreme Penalty for Murder Paid by Negro Ghoul," *Monroe News-Star,* March 5, 1935, p. 1—an example of newspaper headlines of the Migration era in the town where Pershing Foster grew up.

39 **someone was hanged:** Arthur F. Raper, *The Tragedy of Lynching* (Chapel Hill: University of North Carolina Press, 1933), p. 36.

39 **"insult to a white person":** Ibid.

39 **stealing seventy-five cents:** Baker, *Following the Color Line,* p. 176.

39 **"perhaps most":** Herbert Shapiro, *White Violence and Black Response: From Reconstruction to Montgomery* (Amherst: University of Massachusetts Press, 1988), p. 32.

40 **Soon Klansmen:** *Documented History of the Incident Which Occurred at Rosewood, Florida, in January 1923,* an investigation submitted to the Florida Board of Regents, December 22, 1993, p. 2. This seventy-nine-page report, commissioned by the State of Florida and conducted by a team of historians from the University of Florida, the State University of Florida, and Florida A&M University, provides a detailed account of the mob attack on the colored town of Rosewood and of the political and racial climate leading to the massacre, including the rebirth and rise to prominence of the Klan.

40 **"was much less":** Wilbur J. Cash, *The Mind of the South* (Garden City, N.Y.: Doubleday, 1941), pp. 124–25.

40 **White citizens, caught up:** The years and locations of the major riots of this era were: Wilmington, North Carolina (1898); Atlanta (1906); Springfield, Illinois (1908); East St. Louis, Illinois (1917); and Charleston; Nashville; Omaha; Elaine, Arkansas; Longview, Texas; Chicago; and Washington, D.C., among other places, in 1919, the year following the end of World War I.

40 **"I hope and trust":** Frederick Douglass, "The Lessons of the Hour," an address to the Metropolitan A.M.E. Church, Washington, D.C., delivered January 9, 1894 (Baltimore: Press of Thomas & Evans, 1894), p. 23.

40 **It was during that time:** See Gilbert Thomas Stephenson, "The Separation of the Races in Public Conveyances," *The American Political Science Review* 3, no. 2 (May 1909): 181 on the origins of the term "Jim Crow" and the first Jim Crow laws in Massachusetts, 1841. See also Ronald L. F. Davis, "Creating Jim Crow," http://www.jimcrowhistory.org/history/creating2.htm, as well as David Hinckley, "Natural Rhythm: Daddy Rice and the Original Jim Crow," New York *Daily News,* May 27, 2004. Mississippi, in 1865, required separate seating for all colored people except those "traveling with their mistresses, in the capacity of nurses." Florida, in 1865, made no such allowances and punished people of either race with standing in a "pillory for one hour" or a whipping "not exceeding thirty nine stripes." Texas, in 1866, simply required every railroad company to "attach to each passenger train run by said company one car for the special accommodation of Freedmen."

41 **Streetcars:** C. Vann Woodward, *The Strange Career of Jim Crow* (New York: Oxford University Press, 1966), pp. 97–102.

41 **"The measure of":** Howard Thurman, *The Luminous Darkness: A Personal Interpretation of the Anatomy of Segregation and a Ground of Hope* (New York: Harper and

Row, 1965), pp. 70–71. Thurman, a prominent theologian in the mid–twentieth century and a migrant himself, was born in Daytona Beach, Florida, in 1899. He was the dean of Rankin Chapel at Howard University and later the dean of Marsh Chapel at Boston University, where he became a mentor of Martin Luther King, Jr., while King was a seminary student at the university.

42 **"his fate":** David L. Cohn, *God Shakes Creation* (New York: Harper and Brothers, 1935), p. 156.

42 **"a premature":** Philip S. Foner, ed., *The Life and Writings of Frederick Douglass,* vol. 4, specifically from "The Negro Exodus from the Gulf States, an Address Before Convention of the American Social Science Association, Saratoga Springs, New York, September 12, 1879" (New York: International Publishers, 1955), p. 336.

42 **"The Negroes just quietly":** U.S. Department of Labor, Division of Negro Economics, *Negro Migration in 1916–17* (Washington, D.C.: U.S. Government Printing Office, 1919), p. 95.

43 **"You tell us":** Ibid., p. 31.

43 **"stabbed the next day":** Ibid., p. 95.

43 **"The sentiment":** *Proceedings of the Constitutional Convention of Alabama,* 1901, 4, p. 4441.

43 **"It is too much":** U.S. Department of Labor, *Negro Migration in 1916–17,* p. 13.

44 ***These were the facts:*** See Baker, *Following the Color Line,* pp. 29–36, for description of segregated elevators, waiting rooms, libraries, parks, and saloons and streetcar protocols. See Bertram Wilbur Doyle, *The Etiquette of Race Relations in the South: A Study in Social Control* (Port Washington, N.Y.: Kennikat Press, 1937), p. 147 (rules on amusement parks, theaters, and playhouses); p. 148 (rules on boarding and exiting streetcars); pp. 149–150 (rules on waiting rooms at depots and the protocol of colored people being served at ticket windows); p. 151 (different hours at colored and white schools, segregated ambulances); p. 152 (segregated hearses and cemeteries). See William H. Chafe, Raymond Gavins, and Robert Korstad, eds., *Remembering Jim Crow* (New York: New Press, 2001), p. 110, on separate windows for car license plates in Indianola, Mississippi.

44 **In 1958, a new:** Cal Brumley, "Segregation Costs: Dixie Firms Find Them More a Burden as Racial Tension Grows," *The Wall Street Journal,* December 17, 1957, p. 1.

44 **separate tellers:** See *Chicago Defender,* March 21, 1931, p. 3, on separate teller for colored people at an Atlanta bank.

44 **Colored people had:** Stetson Kennedy, *Jim Crow Guide to the U.S.A.* (Westport, Conn.: Greenwood Press, 1959), p. 227.

44 **the conventional rules:** Charles S. Johnson, *Patterns of Negro Segregation* (New York: Harper and Brothers, 1943), pp. 124–26. Johnson devoted an entire section to racial etiquette on the highway. "When driving their own cars," he wrote, "they were expected to maintain their role as Negros and in all cases to give whites the right-of-way." He later added, "If there is any doubt about whose turn it is to make a move in traffic, the turn is assumed to be the white person's."

44 **If he reached:** Hortense Powdermaker, *After Freedom: A Cultural Study of the Deep*

South (New York: Viking Press, 1939), p. 49. See also Kennedy, *Jim Crow Guide to the U.S.A.,* pp. 221–23.

45 **In everyday interactions:** Hugh Stephen Whitaker, "A Case Study in Southern Justice: The Emmett Till Case," unpublished dissertation for the Graduate School of Florida State University, August 1963. See p. 11 for description of taboos between blacks and whites in the South through the 1960s.

45 **The consequences:** James C. Cobb, *The Most Southern Place on Earth: The Mississippi Delta and the Roots of Regional Identity* (New York: Oxford University Press, 1992), p. 213.

45 **It was against the law:** Woodward, *The Strange Career of Jim Crow,* pp. 117–18, on Arkansas law on segregated racetrack betting and Birmingham ban on integrated playing of checkers.

45 **At saloons in Atlanta:** Baker, *Following the Color Line,* p. 36.

45 **There were white parking spaces:** "Confusion with Jim Crow Bible," *The Raleigh Evening Times,* March 29, 1906, p. 1. The story describes an incident during the trial of a black schoolteacher accused of disposing of a mule on which there was a mortgage. A defense witness, who was colored but looked white, took the stand and was being sworn in when the judge told the sheriff the man had been given the wrong Bible. "That one over this is the one for the use of the white people," Judge Amistead Jones said. "Not that I am a stickler about such matters, but if there are to be different Bibles kept for the races, then you must not get them mixed that way. Have a different place for them, and keep them there. Then such mistakes as this will not be made." Also practiced in Atlanta, and thus likely elsewhere in the South, as described by Baker in *Following the Color Line,* p. 36.

George Swanson Starling

47 **His world is the basement:** Unless otherwise indicated, all references to George Starling are based on numerous interviews and conversations with him from June 1995 to June 1998.

50 **"the caste barrier":** John Dollard, *Caste and Class in a Southern Town* (New Haven, Conn.: Yale University Press, 1937), p. 65.

50 **"The question of":** J. W. Johnson, *Along This Way* (New York: Viking Press, 1933), p. 56.

53 **In some parts:** Nell Irvin Painter, *Exodusters: Black Migration to Kansas after Reconstruction* (New York: Knopf, 1977), p. 83; original citation: Henry Adams, *Senate Report 693,* 2, p. 104.

54 **only a quarter:** Hortense Powdermaker, *After Freedom: A Cultural History of the Deep South* (New York: Viking Press, 1939), p. 86.

54 **"The Negro farm hand":** "The Negro Exodus," *Montgomery Advertiser,* a letter from J. Q. Johnson, pastor of St. Paul A.M.E. Church in Columbia, Tennessee, April 27, 1917, p. 4.

54 **"One reason for preferring":** Powdermaker, *After Freedom,* p. 86.

58 **"in a hurrying time":** Theodore Dwight Weld, *American Slavery as It Is: Testimony of a Thousand Witnesses (*New York: The American Anti-Slavery Society, 1839), p. 38.

58 **Florida went farther:** See Julia Floyd Smith, *Slavery and Plantation Growth in Antebellum Florida, 1821–1860* (Gainesville: University Press of Florida, 1973), p. 102, on punishment for slaves; p. 121 on law requiring free blacks to register or face arbitrary reenslavement.

59 **Florida, in the early winter:** The southern states did not all secede at the same time. There were two waves of secession following the November 1860 election of Abraham Lincoln and a Republican majority in Congress, portending abolition of a state's right to, among other things, maintain or expand slavery. The first wave of secession included seven slave states, beginning with South Carolina on December 20, 1860, followed by Mississippi on January 9, 1861; Florida on January 10, 1861; Alabama on January 11, 1861; Georgia on January 19, 1861; Louisiana on January 26, 1861; and Texas on February 1, 1861. The second wave of secession came after the outbreak of war at Fort Sumter, South Carolina, in April 1861. In the second wave were the marginally more moderate, previously fence-sitting slave states of Virginia, April 17, 1861; Arkansas, May 6, 1861; Tennessee, May 7, 1861; and North Carolina, May 20, 1861. The Confederacy also claimed portions of modern-day Oklahoma, New Mexico, and Arizona, as well as the support of Missouri and Kentucky, slaveholding border states that did not formally secede.

59 **"the great truth":** "The Southern Confederacy. Slavery the Basis of the New Government, An Official Manifesto. Speech of Vice-President Stephens," *The Philadelphia Inquirer,* March 28, 1861, p. 1. Stephens delivered this extemporaneous speech in Savannah, Georgia, on March 21, 1861, after the first Confederate states had seceded from the Union and drafted the Confederate Constitution. That document was largely based on the U.S. Constitution, setting forth three branches of government with duties nearly identical to those in the Union. The Confederate Constitution states in Part 4, Section 9: "No bill of attainder, ex-post facto law, or law denying or impairing the right of property in negro slaves shall be passed." The constitution was adopted by what was known as the Congress of the Confederate States (at the time, South Carolina, Mississippi, Florida, Alabama, Georgia, Louisiana, and Texas) at a joint meeting in Montgomery, Alabama, on March 11, 1861, precisely one week after Lincoln took the oath of office on March 4, 1861.

59 **"if any negro":** Gilbert Thomas Stephenson, "The Separation of the Races in Public Conveyances," *The American Political Science Review* 3, no. 2 (1909): 181.

59 **"anything that was black":** *Documented History of the Incident Which Occurred at Rosewood, Florida, in January 1923* (submitted to the Florida Board of Regents, December 22, 1993), p. 19.

59 **single worst act:** James R. McGovern, *Anatomy of a Lynching: The Killing of Claude Neal* (Baton Rouge: Louisiana State University Press, 1982), pp. 52–66.

60 **It was the early morning:** "Group Kills Negro; Disappoints Crowd," Associated Press, October 28, 1934; appeared in *The New York Times,* October 28, 1934.

60 **The crowd grew so large:** See *The Lynching of Claude Neal* (New York: National Association for the Advancement of Colored People, 1934), p. 2, for an account of the lynching. Also McGovern, *Anatomy of a Lynching,* pp. 79–90, for details of mob behavior, the lynching, and the rioting by whites after Neal's death.

61 **Soon afterward:** "Lynch Victim's Innocence Apparent as Father of Girl Is Sentenced," *Pittsburgh Courier,* June 15, 1935, p. A4. The Neal lynching cast a lingering cloud over race relations in Jackson County, Florida, decades after the killing. James R. McGovern, a historian examining the case in the early 1980s, found people who had clear memories of the lynching and its aftermath but were reluctant to speak about it out of fear of reprisal. This was especially true of black residents, one of whom, in finally relenting to give an interview, said, "Well, if I am going down, it will be for a good cause." McGovern, *Anatomy of a Lynching,* p. xi.

62 **"never had a negro":** Ben Green, *Before His Time: The Untold Story of Harry T. Moore, America's First Civil Rights Martyr* (New York: Free Press, 1999), p. 244.

62 **"he might be accused":** McGovern, *Anatomy of a Lynching,* p. 6.

Robert Joseph Pershing Foster

72 **The paneled door:** Unless otherwise indicated, all references to Robert Pershing Foster are based on numerous interviews and visits with him from April 1996 to July 1997.

77 **1,139 pupils:** See "Louisiana States," *Chicago Defender,* October 10, 1931, p. 19, regarding the number of students at Monroe Colored High.

80 **the church broke into an uproar:** "Two Murdered in Baptist Church Riot: Four Others Wounded During Free for All Fight," *Chicago Defender,* September 17, 1932, p. 1.

80 **"the doors of the church":** "Eight Wounded, One Killed in Church Fight," *Atlanta Daily World,* September 8, 1932, p. 2.

85 **In Louisiana in the 1930s:** D. T. Blose and H. F. Alves, *Biennial Survey of Education in the U.S., Statistics of State School Systems, 1937–38,* U.S. Office of Education Bulletin, 1940, no. 2, p. 137. Cited in Charles S. Johnson, *Patterns of Negro Segregation* (New York: Harper and Brothers, 1943), p. 16.

85 **The disparity in pay:** Thomas M. Shapiro, *The Hidden Cost of Being African-American: How Wealth Perpetuates Inequality* (New York: Oxford University Press, 2004), p. 47.

85 **lopsided division of resources:** W. D. Weatherford and Charles S. Johnson, *Race Relations: Adjustment of Whites and Negroes in the United States* (Boston: D. C. Heath, 1934), pp. 358–59, on disparity of investment in white schools and colored schools in the South.

86 **"The money allocated":** Robert A. Margo, *Race and Schooling in the South, 1880–1950: An Economic History* (Chicago: University of Chicago Press, 1990), p. 44, citing Carleton Washburne, *Louisiana Looks at Its Schools* (Baton Rouge: Louisiana Educational Survey Commission, 1942), p. 111.

86 **"If these Negroes become":** see Ray Stannard Baker, *Following the Color Line* (New York: Doubleday, Page, 1908), p. 295, for quote lamenting the effect of education for black southerners.

88 **Sherman, Texas:** Arthur F. Raper, *The Tragedy of Lynching* (Chapel Hill: University of North Carolina Press, 1933; reprinted Mineola, New York: Dover Publications, 2003), pp. 319–55.

89 **And I'd whisper:** Mahalia Jackson with Evan McLeod Wylie, *Movin' On Up* (New York: Hawthorne Books, 1966), p. 36.

90 **Gilbert and Percy Elie:** Interview with Gilbert Elie, who migrated from Grenada, Mississippi, to Akron, Ohio. Conducted in Grenada, Mississippi, May 29, 1996.

92 **Hundreds of miles away:** Interview with Virginia Hall, a migrant from North Carolina, in Brooklyn, New York, February 22, 1998.

A BURDENSOME LABOR

97 **"one of the most backbreaking":** Donald Holley, *The Second Great Emancipation: The Mechanical Cotton Picker, Black Migration and How They Shaped the Modern South* (Fayetteville: University of Arkansas Press, 2000), p. xii.

97 **It took some seventy:** See ibid., p. 9, for a description of the basic mechanics of picking and the number of bolls per pound of seed cotton.

98 **"begin to dream":** Rupert B. Vance, *Human Factors in Cotton Culture* (Chapel Hill: University of North Carolina Press, 1929), p. 135, quoting the author Henry K. Webster from "Slaves of Cotton," *American Magazine,* July 1906, p. 19.

98 ***"The first born":*** Ulrich B. Phillips, in Vance, *Human Factors in Cotton Culture,* p. 47.

99 **Sometime in the 1930s:** Interviews with Lasalle Frelix, a migrant from Brookhaven, Mississippi, in Chicago, 1996.

102 **A bale of cotton:** William C. Holley and Lloyd E. Arnold, *Changes in Technology and Labor Requirements in Crop Production: Cotton,* National Research Project Report no. A-7 (Philadelphia: Works Progress Administration, September 1937), pp. 19–54. Also Ronald E. Seavoy, *The American Peasantry: Southern Agricultural Labor and Its Legacy: A Study in Political Economy, 1850–1995* (Westport, Conn.: Greenwood Press, 1998), pp. 37–47, cited in Holley, *The Second Great Emancipation,* p. 56.

109 **The other brother:** Interviews with Reuben Blye in Eustis, Florida, July 1997 and July 1998.

113 **In North Carolina:** Gilbert Thomas Stephenson, "The Separation of the Races in Public Conveyances," *The American Political Science Review* 3, no. 2 (May 1909): 200–201.

120 **standing in the way:** David Levering Lewis, *W. E. B. Du Bois: The Fight for Equality and the American Century, 1919–1963* (New York: Henry Holt, 2000), pp. 491–92.

120 **"The result of this action":** Ibid., p. 495; Arnold Rampersad, *The Art and Imagination of W. E. B. Du Bois* (Cambridge: Harvard University Press, 1976), p. 22; W. E. B. Du Bois, *The Autobiography of W. E. B. Du Bois: A Soliloquy on Viewing My Life from the Last Decade of Its First Century* (New York: International Publishers, 1968), p. 323.

120 **"There was no earthly":** Lewis, *W. E. B. Du Bois,* pp. 493–95.

121 **His northern friends thought:** Ibid., p. 495, citing Shirley Graham Du Bois, *His Day Is Marching On: A Memoir of W. E. B. Du Bois* (Philadelphia: J. B. Lippincott, 1971), p. 71.

123 **In the winter of 1919:** Richard Panek, "The Loneliness of the Long-Distance Cosmologist," *The New York Times,* July 25, 1999, available at www.nytimes.com.

123 **It would confirm:** Alexander S. Sharov and Igor D. Novikov, *Edwin Hubble, the*

Discoverer of the Big Bang Universe, trans. Vitaly Kisin (Cambridge, England: Cambridge University Press, 1993), pp. 9, 10, 29–35.

The Awakening

124 **You sleep over a volcano:** Glenda Elizabeth Gilmore, *Gender and Jim Crow: Women and the Politics of White Supremacy in North Carolina, 1896–1920* (Chapel Hill: University of North Carolina Press, 1996), pp. 132–33. Gilmore recounts a debate on a summer night in 1901 in Charlotte, North Carolina, between two well-educated young women, Addie Sagers and Laura Arnold, on the topic "Is the South the Best Home for the Negro?" Sagers argued against going north, where, she said, the only jobs open to blacks were "bell boy, waiter, cook or house maid," and where northern unions excluded blacks from their ranks. Arnold, her debate opponent, railed against the violence, segregation, and disenfranchisement of blacks in the South. She agreed that "the unknown was frightening," but added, "if the Puritans could cross the oceans in small boats, surely North Carolina's African-Americans could board northbound trains." Gilmore notes that Arnold's "received more points than any other speech that night." Two weeks later, Arnold "took her own advice and moved to Washington, D.C."

124 **I am in the darkness:** Emmett J. Scott, "Additional Letters of Negro Migrants, 1916–1918," *The Journal of Negro History* 4, no. 4 (October 1919): 412–45, quote on p. 440. This letter, dated May 13, 1917, was one of several hundred letters from anxious black southerners, written primarily to the *Chicago Defender* and collected and published by Emmett Scott in two series of articles at the end of World War I.

130 **a fight broke out:** Alfred McClung Lee and Norman D. Humphrey, *Race Riot* (New York: Dryden Press, 1943), p. 26.

131 **The Detroit riots:** Ibid., p. 28.

135 **A colored teacher:** William H. Chafe, Raymond Gavins, and Robert Korstad, eds., *Remembering Jim Crow: African Americans Tell About Life in the Segregated South* (New York: New Press, in association with Lyndhurst Books of the Center for Documentary Studies of Duke University), p. 201.

140 **Enlisting widespread interest:** "Alice Clarissa Clement to Wed Robert Foster: She Is a Spelman 1941 Graduate," *Chicago Defender,* June 21, 1941, p. 18.

140 **The *Atlanta Daily World*:** "Miss Clement Is Wed to Robert P. Foster Tuesday," *Atlanta Daily World,* December 25, 1941, p. 3.

143 **"because they were taking":** Baker, *Following the Color Line*, p. 250.

145 **In the spring of 1919:** "Army Uniform Cost Soldier His Life," *Chicago Defender,* April 5, 1919, p. 1.

147 **Pitocin:** The use of pitocin, a synthetic form of the hormone oxytocin, has grown more controversial in the decades since the Korean War, as more women seek natural childbirth with as few artificial inducements as possible. The emphasis on natural childbirth was not the prevailing view during the time of Pershing Foster's army service and was in fact considered the slower, more natural, and perhaps more progressive alternative to the cesareans preferred and commonly performed by many doctors of the era.

150 **fifty million dollars a year:** *Citrus Growing in Florida,* Bulletin no. 2, New Series, State of Florida, Department of Agriculture, October 1941, p. 5.

152 **It was an illegal form:** Terrell H. Shofner, "The Legacy of Racial Slavery: Free Enterprise and Forced Labor in Florida in the 1940s," *The Journal of Southern History* 47, no. 3 (August 1981): 414–16. The case against the Sugar Plantation Company in the Everglades was ultimately unsuccessful in the southern court system, which was sympathetic to the planters and hostile to the federal government, and may have in fact emboldened some planters to continue forcing colored people to work against their will. But it offered evidence and made public the extent of the alleged abuses. The company managed to evade prosecution when a Florida judge quashed the indictment.

152 **Willis Virgil McCall:** John Hill, "A Southern Sheriff's Law and Disorder," *The St. Petersburg Times,* November 28, 1999. See also Greg Lamm, "Willis V. McCall: Blood, Hatred, Fear: The Reign of a Traditional Southern Sheriff," *Leesburg* (Fla.) *Commercial,* May 20, 1987, p. A1.

153 **In February:** Shofner, "The Legacy of Racial Slavery," pp. 421–422.

153 **McCall struck:** "Terrorism Being Used to Frustrate Justice," *The Atlanta Daily World,* June 30, 1945, p. 1.

153 **"leaving all their possessions":** "Harlem Pair Tells of McCall's Acts," *New York Amsterdam News,* November 24, 1951, p. 1.

154 **"returns to the grower":** "Lake County Growers Shown Management Theories in Grove Tour," *The Sunday Orlando Sentinel Star,* December 21, 1941, p. 22.

154 **four dollars and forty cents:** Ibid., pp. 30–36.

154 **2.6 million citrus trees:** "Citrus Shipments Up 15% over Last Week; Tangerines in Van," *The Sunday Orlando Sentinel Star,* November 30, 1941, p. 10. See also "Growing Conditions," *The Sunday Orlando Sentinel Star,* December 28, 1941, p. 19. For ranking of citrus industry by county, see *Fruit and Vegetable Crops of Florida: A Compendium of Information on the Fruits and Vegetables Grown in Florida* (Tallahassee: Florida State Department of Agriculture, August 15, 1945).

157 **"the killing of a Negro":** Wilbur J. Cash, *The Mind of the South* (Garden City, N.Y.: Doubleday, 1941), p. 129.

161 **Later, in 1879:** Nell Irvin Painter, *Exodusters: Black Migration to Kansas After Reconstruction* (New York: Knopf, 1977), pp. 109–10, 184–85.

161 **Immigration plunged:** Florette Henri, *Black Migration: Movement North, 1900–1920* (Garden City, N.Y.:Anchor Press/Doubleday, 1975), p. 52. Original data on immigration of 1,218,480 in 1914 plunging to 110,618 in 1918 from the U.S. Census.

161 **So the North:** David L. Cohn, *God Shakes Creation* (New York: Harper and Brothers, 1935), p. 335.

161 **The recruiters would stride:** James R. Grossman, *Land of Hope* (Chicago: University of Chicago Press, 1989), p. 70.

162 **"As the North":** "Why the Negroes Go North," *Literary Digest* 77, no. 7 (May 19, 1923): 14, quoting *The Times-Picayune* (New Orleans). Appears in Grossman, *Land of Hope,* p. 43.

162 **"Where shall we get":** *Montgomery Advertiser,* quoted in "Negro Moving

North," *Literary Digest* 53, no. 15 (October 7, 1916): 877; from Grossman, *Land of Hope,* p. 40.

162 **"Black labor":** *Columbia State,* quoted in Emmett J. Scott, *Negro Migration During the War* (New York: Oxford University Press, 1920), p. 156, and Grossman, *Land of Hope,* p. 40.

162 **"It is the life":** *Report of the Industrial Commission on Agriculture and Agricultural Labor,* vol. 10 (Washington, D.C.: U.S. Government Printing Office, 1901), pp. 382–83, 518; cited in Gilbert Osofsky, *Harlem: The Making of a Ghetto* (New York: Harper and Row, 1963), p. 27.

162 **"With all our crimes":** Cohn, *God Shakes Creation,* p. 205.

162 **"We must have":** *The Macon Telegraph,* September 15, 1916, p. 4.

162 **"Why hunt for the cause":** *Montgomery Advertiser,* a letter in response to "Exodus of the Negroes to Be Probed," September 1916.

162 **"If you thought":** George Brown Tindall, *Emergence of the New South, 1913–1945* (Baton Rouge: Louisiana State University Press, 1967), p. 149; cited in Henri, *Black Migration,* p. 75.

162 **"Conditions recently":** U.S. Department of Labor, Division of Negro Economics, *Negro Migration in 1916–1917* (Washington, D.C.: U.S. Government Printing Office, 1919), p. 63.

163 **Macon, Georgia, required:** St. Clair Drake and Horace R. Cayton, *Black Metropolis: A Study of Negro Life in a Northern City* (Chicago: University of Chicago Press, 1945), p. 59.

163 **"Every Negro":** U.S. Department of Labor, *Negro Migration in 1916–1917,* p. 12.

163 **The chief of police:** Grossman, *Land of Hope,* p. 44.

163 **In Brookhaven, Mississippi:** Scott, *Negro Migration During the War,* p. 77.

163 **In Albany, Georgia:** U.S. Department of Labor, *Negro Migration in 1916–17,* p. 110.

163 **In Summit, Mississippi:** Grossman, *Land of Hope,* p. 48, from Junius B. Wood, *The Negro in Chicago* (Chicago: Chicago Daily News, 1916), p. 9; Scott, *Negro Migration,* p. 73; *Chicago Defender,* August 26, 1916; Emmett J. Scott, "Additional Letters of Negro Migrants of 1916–1918," *Journal of Negro History,* October 1919, p. 451; William F. Holmes, "Labor Agents and the Georgia Exodus," *South Atlantic Quarterly* 79 (1980), pp. 445–46, on dispersal of Georgia migrants at train station.

163 **"served to intensify":** Willis D. Weatherford and Charles S. Johnson, *Race Relations: Adjustment of Whites and Negroes in the United States* (Boston: D. C. Heath, 1934), p. 339.

163 **some migrants:** Scott, *Negro Migration During the War,* p. 77.

163 **one man disguising himself:** Interviews with Ruby Lee Welch Mays Smith, Chicago, January–October 1996.

163 **one delegation:** David L. Cohn, *Where I Was Born and Raised* (South Bend, Ind.: University of Notre Dame Press, 1967), pp. 340–45. Managers at King and Anderson plantation went to Chicago to convince sharecroppers to come back in the 1940s; cited in Nicholas Lemann, *The Promised Land* (New York: Knopf, 1991), pp. 47–48.

164 **In the 1920s:** Chicago Commission on Race Relations, *The Negro in Chicago: A Study*

of Race Relations and a Race Riot (Chicago: University of Chicago Press, 1922), p. 104.

164 **"Owing to the scarcity":** U.S. Department of Labor, *Negro Migration in 1916–17,* p. 96.

164 **Men hopped freight trains:** Grossman, *Land of Hope,* p. 40.

164 **"One section gang":** Arna Bontemps and Jack Conroy, *Anyplace but Here* (Columbia: University of Missouri Press, 1945), p. 164.

164 **the weeds grew up:** Grossman, *Land of Hope,* p. 40.

Breaking Away

165 **I was leaving:** Richard Wright, *Black Boy* (New York: HarperCollins, 1993), p. 493.

167 **Of the few who got:** Hortense Powdermaker, *After Freedom: A Cultural Study of the Deep South* (New York: Viking Press, 1930), pp. 86–87.

167 **"How a man treats":** Ibid., p. 86.

168 **Like one planter:** Based on a letter sent to me by Ruth McClendon of Waukegan, Illinois. She heard me speaking about the Great Migration on WBEZ-FM, the public radio station in Chicago. The letter, dated August 17, 1995, was three pages, handwritten on yellow legal paper. In it, she shared the story of her grandparents leaving Alabama for Illinois during World War I.

172 **Pershing was working:** Ozeil Fryer Woolcock, "Social Swirl," *Atlanta Daily World,* March 8, 1953, p. 3, and March 15, 1953, p. 18. Both stories are useful in that they confirm the general timing of Robert Foster's departure. They note that he went to see his wife and daughters in Atlanta in early to mid-March before his migration trip to California. On Friday, March 13, 1953, the latter story notes, he was feted with "a small impromptu party by his wife, Alice Clement Foster, who invited a few former college mates in for an evening of dancing and chatting. The residence was most colorful with the St. Patrick motif, assisting Mrs. Foster was her mother, Mrs. Rufus E. Clement." The story said that Robert was to leave Atlanta that Tuesday, which would have been March 17. Robert would head back to Monroe one last time before his migration, as he would have to pass through Louisiana en route to California. There, he had at least two weeks to spend time with his own family and friends and to prepare for the long journey ahead. When he later recounted the time leading up to his departure, he went on at length about his final weeks in Monroe and the pre-Easter send-off given him by his close friends and family in his hometown, marking the beginning of his journey out of the South. He never mentioned the visit to Atlanta or the party given him by his in-laws, which suggests it did not figure into his definition of his migration journey or the moment of his emotional break from the South. It also reflected how he viewed the more formal, socially correct world of the Clements compared to the humbler circles of his origins, which seemed to have greater meaning to him.

177 **I pick up my life:** Langston Hughes, *One-Way Ticket* (New York: Knopf, 1949), p. 61.

178 **"Migratory currents flow":** E. G. Ravenstein, "The Laws of Migration," *Journal of the Royal Statistical Society,* no. 2 (June 1889): 284.

178 **"They are like":** Ibid., p. 280.

178 **Some participants:** Joe William Trotter, Jr., *Black Milwaukee: The Making of an Industrial Proletariat, 1915–1945* (Urbana: University of Illinois Press, 1985). Trotter recounts the especially convoluted migration of a man, identified as J.H., who was "born in Canton, Mississippi. At 16, he went to Memphis, Tennessee. From Memphis he went to Sapulpa, Oklahoma. From Sapulpa he went to the army and to France. After the war [World War I] he settled in Kansas City. From Kansas City [he migrated to] Chicago and then Milwaukee at the age of 40. He has lived in Milwaukee for six years." The account was originally published by the Milwaukee Urban League in its 1942–1943 Annual Report.

179 **"go no further":** Ravenstein, "Laws of Migration," p. 250.

179 **"The more enterprising":** Ibid., p. 279.

Part III: Exodus

181 **There is no mistaking:** *The Cleveland Advocate,* April 28, 1917.

181 **We look up at:** Richard Wright, *12 Million Black Voices* (New York: Viking Press, 1941), p. 92.

The Appointed Time of Their Coming

186 **A toddler named Huey Newton:** Dennis Hevesi, "Huey Newton Symbolized the Rising Black Anger of a Generation," *The New York Times,* August 23, 1989, p. 37.

186 **Another boy from Monroe:** Bill Russell, *Second Wind: The Memoirs of an Opinionated Man* (New York: Fireside, 1979), pp. 24–27.

190 **It carried so many:** Hollis R. Lynch, *The Black Urban Condition: A Documentary History, 1866–1971* (New York: Crowell, 1973), pp. 425–32. The black population of Chicago rose from 30,150 in 1900 to 44,103 in 1910, the last census before the Migration statistically began, and rose to 1,102,620 in 1970. In Detroit, the black population rose from 4,111 in 1900 to 5,741 in 1910 and 660,428 in 1970.

190 **the Illinois Central:** John F. Stover, *History of the Illinois Central Railroad* (New York: Macmillan, 1975), p. 15 on its founding, p. 89 on Lincoln's role.

200 **Later, it was the first stop:** Ray Stannard Baker, *Following the Color Line* (New York: Doubleday, Page, 1908), p. 113.

200 **"How a colored man":** Robert Russa Moton, *What the Negro Thinks* (Garden City, N.Y.: Doubleday, Doran, 1929), p. 82. See also Bertram Wilbur Doyle, *The Etiquette of Race Relations in the South: A Study in Social Control* (Port Washington, N.Y.: Kennikat Press, 1937), p. 156. Doyle was a professor of sociology at Fisk University.

201 **a family from Beaumont:** Interview with Pat Botshekan in Los Angeles, March 18, 1996.

Crossing Over

205 **Do you remember:** Charles H. Nichols, ed., *Arna Bontemps–Langston Hughes Letters, 1925–1967* (New York: Dodd, Mead, 1980), p. 24.

217 **In South Carolina:** Graham Russell Hodges, *Studies in African History and Culture* (New York: Garland, 2000), p. 155.

217 **Some of my people:** Chicago Commission on Race Relations, *The Negro in Chicago: A Study of Race Relations and a Race Riot* (Chicago: University of Chicago Press, 1922), pp. 97–98.

217 **The earliest departures:** Emmett J. Scott, *Negro Migration During the War* (New York: Oxford University Press, 1920), p. 13.

217 **Instead of the weakening stream:** E. G. Ravenstein, "The Laws of Migration," *Journal of the Royal Statistical Society* 52, no. 2 (1889), p. 278. "The most striking feature of the northern migration was its individualism," Emmett J. Scott wrote in 1920, as if the Migration were over.

218 **"A large error":** Florette Henri, *Black Migration: Movement North, 1900–1920* (Garden City, N.Y.: Anchor/Doubleday, 1975), p. 72.

218 **Robert Fields:** Interview with Robert Fields in Chicago, 1995.

219 **Eddie Earvin:** Interview with Eddie Earvin in Chicago, May 1995, after having been given his name at a reunion at DuSable High School.

Part IV: The Kinder Mistress

223 **The lazy, laughing South:** Langston Hughes, "The South," *The Crisis,* June 1922.

Chicago

225 **Timidly, we get:** Richard Wright, *12 Million Black Voices* (New York: Viking Press, 1941), pp. 99–100.

New York

227 **A blue haze:** Arna Bontemps, "The Two Harlems," *American Scholar,* Spring 1945, p. 167.

Los Angeles

230 **Maybe we can start again:** John Steinbeck, *The Grapes of Wrath* (New York: Viking Press, 1939; updated edition New York: Penguin Books, 1997), p. 89.

232 **They went to court:** "Covenant Suit Arguments on August 22," *Los Angeles Sentinel,* July 31, 1947, p. 3, gives an overview of the case as it is about to go before the court.

233 **a small contingent:** Lawrence Brooks de Graaf, "Recognition, Racism and Reflections on the Writing of Western Black History," *Pacific Historical Review* 44, no. 1 (February 1975): 23.

233 **strongly discouraged:** Lawrence Brooks de Graaf, "Negro Migration to Los Angeles, 1930–1950," dissertation submitted to the University of California, Los Angeles, May 1962, p. 14.

233 **By 1900:** Ibid., p. 16.

233 **"Even the seeming":** Octavia B. Vivian, *The Story of the Negro in Los Angeles County* (Washington, D.C.: Federal Writers' Project, Works Progress Administration, 1936), p. 31.

234 **"In certain plants":** Ibid., p. 33.

THE THINGS THEY LEFT BEHIND

238 **There were no Chinaberry:** Clifton Taulbert, *The Last Train North* (Tulsa, Okla.: Council Oaks Books, 1992), pp. 43–44.

240 **had toiled:** It is not known precisely why there was a two-and-a-half-year delay in getting word to the slaves in Texas. One theory was that a messenger bearing the news of freedom was murdered on his way to Texas. Another was that slave masters deliberately withheld the news to keep their unpaid labor for as long as they could. Another was that there simply weren't enough Union troops in Texas to enforce the Proclamation, which was dated January 1, 1863. The announcement read by the Union troops in the form of General Order no. 3 was as follows: *"The people of Texas are informed that in accordance with a Proclamation from the Executive of the United States, all slaves are free. This involves an absolute equality of rights and rights of property between former masters and slaves, and the connection heretofore existing between them becomes that between employer and free laborer"* (available at www.juneteenth.com). Also see "An Obscure Texas Celebration Makes Its Way Across the U.S.," *The New York Times,* June 18, 2004.

241 **"If I were half":** Abraham Epstein, *The Negro Migrant in Pittsburgh* (New York: Arno Press, 1969 reissue of 1918 original), p. 27.

241 **Epstein found:** Ibid., p. 24.

TRANSPLANTED IN ALIEN SOIL

242 **Should I have come:** Richard Wright, *Black Boy* (New York: HarperCollins, 1993), pp. 306–7.

243 **A map:** Arna Bontemps and Jack Conroy, *Anyplace but Here* (Columbia: University of Missouri Press, 1945), p. 164.

243 **Beloit, Wisconsin:** Morton Rubin, "Migration Patterns from a Rural Northeastern Mississippi Community," *Social Forces* 39, no. 1, Oct. 1, 1960–May 1961, pp. 59–66. See also Paul Geib, "From Mississippi to Milwaukee: A Case Study of the Southern Black Migration to Milwaukee, 1940–1970, *The Joural of Negro History* 83, no. 4 (Autumn 1998): 229–48.

244 **Gary:** The Jackson Family of singers, including Michael and Janet, probably the most famous natives of Gary, Indiana, had roots in the South like most other black people born in Gary in the past century. The singing group's father, Joseph, was born in Fountain Hill, Arkansas, in 1929 and went to Chicago, just west of Gary, when he was eighteen. The group's mother, the former Katherine Scruse, was born in Barbour County, Alabama, and brought to East Chicago, Indiana, by her parents when she was four. Joseph and Katherine met in the Chicago area and married in November 1949. Their nine surviving children were born in Gary.

244 **But, as in the rest:** Joe William Trotter, Jr., *Black Milwaukee: The Making of an Industrial Proletariat, 1915–1945* (Chicago: University of Chicago Press, 1985), p. 42.

244 **"They are superior":** Ibid., p. 55.

245 **"only did the dirty work":** Ibid., p. 47.

245 **even those jobs:** Ibid., p. 152.

245 **"never did":** Ibid., p. 167.

247 **The first blacks in Harlem:** James Riker, *Revised History of Harlem (City of New York): Its Origin and Early Annals* (New York: New Harlem Publishing, 1904), p. 189; cited in Gilbert Osofsky, *Harlem: The Making of a Ghetto: Negro New York, 1890–1930* (New York: Harper and Row, 1963), p. 83.

248 **The trouble began:** Iver Bernstein, *The New York City Draft Riots: Their Significance for American Society and Politics in the Age of the Civil War* (New York: Oxford University Press, 1990); cited in Leslie M. Harris, *In the Shadow of Slavery: African Americans in New York City, 1826–1863* (Chicago: University of Chicago Press, 2003).

249 **By 1930:** Osofsky, *Harlem,* p. 130 on population, p. 139 on sleeping in shifts, p. 129 for Adam Clayton Powell quote.

249 **"a growing menace":** *Harlem Magazine,* February 1914, p. 21; cited in Osofsky, *Harlem,* p. 107.

249 **Panicked property owners:** Osofsky, *Harlem,* pp. 105–7.

249 **White leaders tried:** *The New York Age,* August 29 and November 14, 1912; January 9, 1913.

249 **White leaders warned:** Osofsky, *Harlem,* p. 108.

250 **"rent to colored":** Ibid., p. 110.

250 **NOTICE:** New York Urban League, "Twenty-four Hundred Negro Families in Harlem: An Interpretation of the Living Conditions of Small Wage Earners," typescript, Schomburg Collection, 1927, p. 7; cited in Osofsky, *Harlem,* p. 110.

251 **"The basic collapse":** Osofsky, *Harlem,* p. 109.

251 **"servants of the rich":** Jervis Anderson, *This Was Harlem, 1900–1950* (New York: Farrar, Straus and Giroux, Noonday Press, 1981), pp. 321–22.

252 **It had a marble:** Ibid., pp. 308–9.

253 **Golden State Mutual Life Insurance Company:** John N. Ingham and Lynne B. Feldman, *African-American Business Leaders: A Biographical Dictionary* (Westport, Conn.: Greenwood Press, 1994), pp. 58–65. William Nickerson, one of the founders of Golden State Mutual Life Insurance, left Houston, Texas, for Los Angeles in 1921 and attributed his migration to the fact that "things were happening in the state, one of which was the riot [Longview, Texas, in 1919 and perhaps Tulsa in 1921]. So becoming disgusted," he said, "I decided to take my wife and eight children and move to California." Four years later, he would become one of the founders of the largest black-owned insurance company in the state.

258 **"I didn't think":** Jim Pinson, "City School Board Seat Won by Negro," *The Atlanta Constitution,* May 15, 1953, p. 1.

258 **"For the first time":** "Negro Is Victor in Atlanta Vote; Defeats White School Board Member, 22,259 to 13,936—Mayor Renominated," *The New York Times,* May 15, 1953; "Atlanta Negro Is Elected to Board of Education," *New York Herald Tribune,* May 15, 1953, p. 1.

Divisions

260 **I walked to the elevator:** Richard Wright, *Black Boy* (New York: HarperCollins, 1993), p. 303.

260 **"With few exceptions":** Sadie Tanner Mossell, "The Standard of Living Among One

Hundred Negro Migrant Families in Philadelphia," *Annals of the American Academy of Political and Social Science* 98 (November 1921): 216.

261 **"The inarticulate and resigned masses":** E. Franklin Frazier, *The Negro Family in Chicago, 1939* (Chicago: University of Chicago Press, 1932), pp. 80, 84.

261 **"a tangle of pathology":** Daniel Patrick Moynihan, *The Negro Family: The Case for National Action* (Washington, D.C.: Office of Policy Planning and Research, United States Department of Labor, 1965), p. 23.

261 **"the differential in payments":** Daniel Patrick Moynihan, "The Crisis in Welfare," *The Public Interest,* Winter 1968, pp. 3–29.

261 **"It is the higher":** Karl E. Taeuber and Alma F. Taeuber, "The Changing Character of Negro Migration," *The American Journal of Sociology* 70, no. 4 (January 1965): 429–41.

261 **"As the distance":** Everett S. Lee, "A Theory of Migration," *Demography* 3, no. 1 (1966): 57.

261 **"Migrants who overcome":** Ibid., pp. 55–56.

262 **"The move to northern":** J. Trent Alexander, "The Great Migration in Comparative Perspective: Interpreting the Urban Origins of Southern Black Migrants to Depression-Era Pittsburgh," *Social Science History,* Fall 1998, pp. 358–60. Alexander's analysis of census data found that, in 1940, only thirty-seven percent of black migrants to northern cities were from rural areas. Two-thirds were from towns with populations of 2,500 or more (p. 365).

262 **"Most Negro migrants":** Taeuber and Taeuber, "The Changing Character of Negro Migration," pp. 430–32.

262 **"averaged nearly two more years":** Stewart E. Tolnay, "Educational Selection in the Migration of Southern Blacks, 1880–1990," *Social Forces,* December 1998, pp. 492–97.

262 **A 1965 study:** Frank T. Cherry, "Southern In-Migrant Negroes in North Lawndale, Chicago, 1949–1959: A Study of Internal Migration and Adjustment," unpublished dissertation, University of Chicago, Department of Sociology, September 1965, p. 71.

262 **"There is no support":** Ibid., p. 98.

262 **"were *not* of lower":** Taeuber and Taeuber, "The Changing Character of Negro Migration," pp. 429–41.

262 **the 1965 census study:** Ibid., p. 439.

263 **"resemble in educational levels":** Ibid., pp. 436–39.

264 **"Black men who have been":** Larry H. Long and Lynne R. Heltman, "Migration and Income Differences Between Black and White Men in the North," *The American Journal of Sociology* 80, no. 6 (May 1975): 1396–97.

264 **"more successfully avoided poverty":** Larry H. Long and Kristin A. Hansen, "Selectivity of Black Return Migration to the South," *Rural Sociology* 42, no. 3 (Fall 1977): 318. Based on a paper presented at the annual meeting of the Southern Sociological Society, Atlanta, March 30–April 2, 1977.

264 **"not willing to risk":** Wen Lang Li and Sheron L. Randolph, "Return Migration and Status Attainment Among Southern Blacks," *Rural Sociology* 47, no. 2 (Summer 1982): 395.

264 **It made them "especially goal oriented":** Larry H. Long and Lynne R. Heltman, "Migration and Income Differences between Black and White Men in the North," *The American Journal of Sociology* 90, no. 6 (May 1975): 1406.

265 **In San Francisco, for instance:** Charles S. Johnson, Herman H. Long, and Grace Jones, *The Negro Worker in San Francisco* (San Francisco: YWCA, the Race Relations Program of the American Missionary Association, and the Julius Rosenwald Fund, May 1944), pp. 15–23.

265 **"more family-stable":** Thomas C. Wilson, "Explaining Black Southern Migrant Advantage in Family Stability: The Role of Selective Migration," *Social Forces* 80, no. 2 (December 2001): 555–71.

265 **"Colored pupils sometimes occupy":** W. A. Daniel, "Schools," in *Negro Problems in the Cities,* ed. T. J. Woofter (College Park, Md.: McGrath Publishing, 1928), p. 183.

265 **"is literally forced":** Ibid.

265 **James Cleveland Owens:** William J. Baker, *Jesse Owens: An American Life* (New York: Free Press, 1986), p. 16.

266 **The boy's first day:** Ibid., p. 19.

266 **It made headlines:** Larry Schwartz, "Owens Pierced a Myth," http://espn.go.com/sportscentury/features/00016393.html.

266 **"I wasn't invited":** Susan Robinson, "A Day in Black History: Jesse Owens," www.gibbsmagazine.com/Jessie%20Owens.htm.

267 **"My son's victories":** Donald McRae, *Heroes Without a Country: America's Betrayal of Joe Louis and Jesse Owens* (New York: Ecco, 2002), p. 168.

268 **"a narrow tongue":** St. Clair Drake and Horace Cayton, *Black Metropolis: A Study of Negro Life in a Northern City* (Chicago: University of Chicago Press, 1945), p. 12.

269 **There were temptations:** Ibid., p. 438. See Frazier, *The Negro Family in Chicago*, p. 103, on the mulatto woman running the biggest poker games on the South Side.

269 **This was the landing place:** Drake and Cayton, *Black Metropolis,* pp. 610–11.

269 **"rude cabin":** A. T. Andreas, *History of Chicago: From the Earliest Period to the Present Time* (Chicago: A. T. Andreas, 1884), pp. 70, 71.

269 **"A few goats":** Edith Abbott, *The Tenements of Chicago, 1908–1935* (Chicago: University of Chicago Press, 1936), pp. 121–23.

269 **"Families lived without light":** Ibid., p. 126.

270 **"Negro migrants confronted":** Ibid., p. 117.

270 **"attics and cellars":** Abraham Epstein, *The Negro Migrant in Pittsburgh* (New York: Arno Press, 1969), p. 13. Originally published by the University of Pittsburgh in 1918.

270 **New arrivals often paid:** Chicago Commission on Race Relations, *The Negro in Chicago: A Study of Race Relations and a Race Riot* (Chicago: University of Chicago Press, 1922), p. 93.

270 **"The rents in the South Side":** Abbott, *The Tenements of Chicago,* p. 125.

270 **Dwellings that went:** Thomas Jackson Woofter, *Negro Problems in Cities* (New York: Harper and Row, 1928), p. 127.

270 **"Lodgers were not disposed":** Epstein, *The Negro Migrant in Pittsburgh,* p. 8.

272 **Whites saw the migrants:** Chicago Commission on Race Relations, *The Negro in Chicago,* p. 3.

272 **"A colored boy swam":** Carl Sandburg, *The Chicago Race Riots* (New York: Harcourt, Brace and Howe, 1919), p. 3.

272 **"on a white man's complaint":** Chicago Commission on Race Relations, *The Negro in Chicago,* p. 4.

272 **Blacks stabbed a white peddler:** Ibid., p. 10.

272 **Two white men:** Ibid., p. 11.

273 **White gangs stormed:** Ibid., pp. 1–6.

273 **Initially, they came:** James N. Gregory, *The Southern Diaspora: How the Great Migrations of Black and White Southerners Transformed America* (Chapel Hill: University of North Carolina Press, 2005), p. 16.

274 **"By the conversation":** Alfred McClung Lee and Norman D. Humphrey, *Race Riot* (New York: Dryden Press, 1943), p. 81.

274 **"the immigration":** U.S. Department of Labor, Division of Negro Economics, *Negro Migration in 1916–17* (Washington, D.C.: Government Printing Office, 1919), p. 131.

274 **"stabbed, clubbed and hanged":** Oscar Leonard, "The East St. Louis Pogrom," *Survey,* July 14, 1917, p. 331; cited in Herbert Shapiro, *White Violence and Black Response: From Reconstruction to Montgomery* (Amherst: University of Massachusetts Press, 1988), p. 116.

274 **The police:** Chicago Commission on Race Relations, *The Negro in Chicago,* pp. 71–78.

275 **With a sense of urgency:** Ibid., pp. 640–51.

277 **"where they drank":** Arna Bontemps, "The Two Harlems," *The American Scholar,* Spring 1945, p. 168.

277 **There'll be brown skin mammas:** Frank Byrd, "Rent Parties," in *A Renaissance in Harlem: Lost Essays of the WPA,* ed. Lionel C. Bascom (New York: Amistad Press, 1999), pp. 59–67.

To Bend in Strange Winds

285 **I was a Southerner:** Zora Neale Hurston, "Backstage and the Railroad," *Dust Tracks on a Road* (Philadelphia: J. B. Lippincott, 1942), p. 98.

288 **"They have been our best":** E. Franklin Frazier, *The Negro Family in Chicago* (Chicago: University of Chicago Press, 1932), pp. 108–9.

288 **Businessmen jumped:** James R. Grossman, *Land of Hope: Chicago, Black Southerners, and the Great Migration* (Chicago: University of Chicago Press, 1989), p. 155.

288 **"I got a sharecropper":** Josh Sides, *L.A. City Limits: African American Los Angeles from the Great Depression to the Present* (Berkeley: University of California Press, 2003), p. 50.

288 **they ran notices:** Grossman, *Land of Hope,* pp. 156–57, on the effects of the Migration on churches in the North.

289 **"They tried to insulate":** Ibid., p. 139.

289 **"The same class of Negroes":** Frazier, *The Negro Family in Chicago,* p. 112.

289 **A colored newspaper:** Chicago Commission on Race Relations, *The Negro in Chicago: A Study of Race Relations and a Race Riot* (Chicago: University of Chicago Press, 1922), p. 304.

289 **A survey of new migrants:** Charles S. Johnson, Herman H. Long, and Grace Jones, *The Negro Worker in San Francisco* (San Francisco: YWCA, the Race Relations Program of the American Missionary Association, and the Julius Rosenwald Fund, May 1944), p. 19 on how migrants and nonmigrants viewed one another.

290 **"like German Jews":** Grossman, *Land of Hope,* p. 144.

290 **"Those who have long been":** "Our Part in the Migration," *Chicago Defender,* March 17, 1917, p. 9.

290 **"Well, their English":** Douglas Henry Daniels, *Pioneer Urbanites: A Social and Cultural History of San Francisco (*Philadelphia: Temple University Press, 1980), p. 171.

290 **"Eleanor":** Ibid., p. 175.

291 **"It is our duty":** *Chicago Defender,* March 17, 1917, and January 18, 1918, cited in Grossman, *Land of Hope,* pp. 144–45.

291 **Don't hang out the windows:** "A Few Do's and Don'ts," *Chicago Defender,* July 13, 1918, p. 16.

291 **Don't use vile language:** "Some Don'ts," *Chicago Defender,* May 17, 1919, p. 20.

291 **1. Do not loaf:** Grossman, *Land of Hope,* pp. 146–47.

The Other Side of Jordan

302 **We cannot escape:** James Baldwin, *Notes of a Native Son* (Boston: Beacon Press, 1955), p. 20.

303 ***"If you succeed": Congressional Record,*** 75, Session 3, pp. 893, 873.

310 **James Arthur Gay was perhaps:** Ed Koch, "Pioneering Civic Leader, Hotel Executive Gay Dies at 83," *Las Vegas Sun,* September 13, 1999, http://www.lasvegassun.com/news/1999/sep/13/pioneering-civic-leader-hotel-executive-gay-dies-a/.

315 **"What do you suppose":** Scott Nearing, *Black America* (New York: Schocken Books, 1929), p. 78; original reference: H. G. Duncan, *The Changing Race Relationship in the Border and Northern States* (Philadelphia, 1922), p. 77.

315 **Campbell Soup plant:** "Business & Finance: Soup," *Time,* September 2, 1929, www.time.com/time/magazine/article/0,9171,7737779,00.html.

315 **"the great clocks of the sky":** Robert Redfield, *Tepoztlán, A Mexican Village: A Study of Folk Life* (Chicago: University of Chicago Press, 1930), p. 83. Redfield describes the daily rhythms of life in his ethnography of a village in the Yucatán. His description could apply to rural people the world over who spend their days working the land. "In Tepoztlán," he writes, "as in other simple societies, the pulse of life is measured more directly than it is with us by the great clocks of the sky."

315 **The plant turned out:** Al Chase, "Chicago to Have One of the World's Largest Soup Factories," *Chicago Daily Tribune,* November 20, 1927, p. C1.

316 **"making conditions so unpleasant":** Abraham Epstein, *The Negro Migrant in Pittsburgh* (New York: Arno Press, 1969), p. 32.

316 **"friction in the washrooms":** Chicago Commision on Race Relations, *The Negro in*

Chicago: A Study of Race Relations and a Race Riot (Chicago: University of Chicago Press, 1922), p. 395.

317 **"I find a great resentment":** Ibid., pp. 394–95, on resistance to black workers at a millinery and on white women threatening to quit a laundry that introduced a black woman among them.

317 **"Their presence and availability":** Charles S. Johnson, *A Preface to Racial Understanding* (New York: Friendship Press, 1936), pp. 38–39.

318 **By 1940:** St. Clair Drake and Horace R. Cayton, *Black Metropolis: A Study of Negro Life in a Northern City* (Chicago: University of Chicago Press, 1945), p. 227, Figure 16 from the 1940 Census.

320 **"where no restaurant":** Ben Green, *Before His Time: The Untold Story of Harry T. Moore, America's First Civil Rights Martyr* (New York: Free Press, 1999), p. 5.

320 **These were the dark:** Paul Ortiz, *Emancipation Betrayed: The Hidden History of Black Organizing and White Violence in Florida from Reconstruction to the Bloody Election of 1920* (Berkeley: University of California Press, 2005), p. 61.

320 **"It is safe to predict":** Green, *Before His Time,* p. 43, citing a quote in the *Tampa Morning Tribune.*

320 **"We are in the hands":** "Florida Topics," *New York Freeman,* June 25, 1887.

321 **Florida school boards:** Charles Johnson, *Patterns of Negro Segregation* (New York: Harper and Brothers, 1943), p. 16.

323 **the authorities fired:** Green, *Before His Time,* p. 85.

324 **The three young men:** Ibid., p. 91.

324 **The trial had been so tense:** Ibid., pp. 103–6, for a detailed account of the car chase after the Groveland trial.

330 **Both men were from:** Ray Charles and David Ritz, *Brother Ray: Ray Charles' Own Story* (New York: Da Capo Press, 1978), p. 165.

331 **"even at a financial loss":** Josh Sides, *L.A. City Limits: African American Los Angeles from the Great Depression to the Present* (Berkeley: University of California Press, 2003), pp. 101–6.

Complications

332 **"What on earth was it":** Ralph Ellison, *Invisible Man* (New York: Vintage, 1995), p. 294 (reissue; originally published by Random House, New York, 1952).

333 **"positions in either":** Kimberley L. Phillips, *AlabamaNorth: African-American Migrants, Community and Working-Class Activism in Cleveland, 1915–1945* (Urbana: University of Illinois Press, 1999), pp. 241–42.

333 **Entire companies and classes:** Charles S. Johnson, *To Stem This Tide: A Survey of Racial Tension Areas in the United States* (Boston: Pilgrim Press, 1943), pp. 11–12.

333 **Those on the lowest rung:** Brenda Clegg Gray, *Black Female Domestics During the Depression in New York City, 1930–1940* (New York: Garland Publishing, 1993), pp. 57, 58.

333 **One was by:** Vivian Morris, "Slave Market" and "Domestic Price Wars," in *A Renaissance in Harlem: Lost Essays of the WPA,* ed. Lionel C. Bascom (New York: Amistad Press, 1999), pp. 146–57.

333 **In Chicago:** St. Clair Drake and Horace H. Cayton, *Black Metropolis: A Study of Negro Life in a Northern City* (Chicago: University of Chicago Press, 1945, reprinted 1993), pp. 245–46.

334 **"Someone would invariably":** Gray, *Black Female Domestics,* p. 51.

334 **One colored woman:** Keith Collins, *Black Los Angeles: The Maturing of the Ghetto, 1940–1950* (Saratoga, Calif.: Century Twenty One Publishing, 1980), pp. 53–54, cited in Kevin Leonard, *Years of Hope, Days of Fear: The Impact of World War II on Race Relations in Los Angeles,* pp. 40, 41.

334 **turning back the hands:** Morris, "Slave Market," p. 150.

334 **One housewife:** Gray, *Black Female Domestics,* p. 61.

334 **In many cases:** Ibid., p. 67.

339 **Boy Willie:** August Wilson, *The Piano Lesson* (New York: Penguin Books, 1990), p. 20.

340 **The bartender:** "Restaurant Keeper Who Breaks Dishes He Uses in Serving Negroes, Will Have to Get New Supply if This Plan Works," *The Pittsburgh Courier,* February 14, 1931, p. A7, a story about black resistance to the practice of restaurants breaking the dishes used by blacks.

346 **For several days:** Michael Lydon, *Ray Charles: Man and Music* (New York: Riverhead Books, 1998), p. 197. Ray Charles and David Ritz, *Brother Ray* (New York: Dial Press, 1978), p. 201.

346 **After the dealer's:** Charles and Ritz, *Brother Ray,* p. 201.

346 **It was around that time:** Lydon, *Ray Charles,* p. 197.

346 **They chose not to call:** Charles and Ritz, *Brother Ray,* p. 202; Lydon, *Ray Charles,* p. 198. These accounts differ in the timing and nature of Ray's arrival at the hospital. His biographer's account is more consistent with the sense of obligation and protocol with which Robert Foster was known to have treated his patients. Foster, honoring the patient-doctor privilege, did not speak in detail about individual patients.

347 **"Naturally, I refused":** Charles and Ritz, *Brother Ray,* p. 202.

347 **"Everyone I met":** Ibid.

347 **The tour was a dream:** Lydon, *Ray Charles,* p. 198.

348 **"one of the dearest":** Charles and Ritz, *Brother Ray,* p. 202.

349 **"Do you feel greater freedom":** Chicago Commission on Race Relations, *The Negro in Chicago: A Study of Race Relations and a Race Riot* (Chicago: University of Chicago Press, 1922), pp. 98–101.

The River Keeps Running

351 **"Why do they come?":** Ray Stannard Baker, *Following the Color Line* (New York: Doubleday, Page, 1908), p. 133.

351 **"Every train, every bus":** Interview with Manley Thomas, who migrated from Jackson, Tennessee, to Milwaukee in September 1950. Interview conducted June 26, 1998, in Milwaukee.

351 **Arrington High:** Dan Burley, "Mississippi Escapee Yearns to Return," *Chicago Defender,* February 24, 1958, p. A4.

354 **Henry Brown:** Henry Box Brown, *Narrative of the Life of Henry Box Brown* (Man-

chester, England: Lee and Glynn, 1851; reprint, Chapel Hill: University of North Carolina Press, 2008), p. 84.

355 **Brown was in agony:** From the account by William Still from *The Underground Rail Road* on the arrival of Henry Box Brown at the Pennsylvania Anti-Slavery Society offices. Cited in Appendix B of the 2008 reprint of *Narrative of the Life of Henry Box Brown,* pp. 160–63.

355 **They locked the door:** Henry Box Brown, *Narrative of Henry Box Brown, Who Escaped from Slavery Enclosed in a Box 3 Feet Long and 2 Wide. Written from a Statement Made by Himself. With Remarks upon the Remedy for Slavery by Charles Stearns* (Boston: Brown and Stearns, 1849); cited in Alan Govenar, *African American Frontiers: Slave Narratives and Oral Histories* (Santa Barbara, Calif.: ABC-CLIO, 2000), pp. 9–16.

356 **many funeral directors:** Interviews with black funeral directors in Chicago and at an annual National Funeral Directors Association meeting in Norfolk, Virginia, yielded polite changes of subject when directors were asked about the issue of funeral home involvement in these escapes out of the South.

356 **"That underground":** Burley, "Mississippi Escapee Yearns to Return."

The Prodigals

364 **[My father], along with:** James Baldwin, *Notes of a Native Son* (Boston: Beacon Press, 1955), p. 72.

364 **'Sides, they can't run us:** Marita Golden, *Long Distance Life* (New York: Doubleday, 1989), p. 39.

367 **"Even in the North":** Arna Bontemps and Jack Conroy, *Anyplace but Here* (Columbia: University of Missouri Press, 1945), p.170.

Disillusionment

371 **Let's not fool ourselves:** Speech by Martin Luther King, Jr., May 17, 1956, MLK speech file, MLK Library, cited in James R. Ralph, Jr., *Northern Protest: Martin Luther King Jr., Chicago and the Civil Rights Movement (*Cambridge, Mass.: Harvard University Press, 1993), p. 30.

371 **It was a hoax:** Robert Coles, "When the Southern Negro Moves North," *The New York Times Magazine,* September 17, 1967, pp. 25–27.

372 **"They don't want":** L. Alex Wilson, "Plan 2-Year Ban on Migrants," *Chicago Defender,* July 1, 1950, p. 22.

372 **"successfully defended":** Allan H. Spear, *Black Chicago: The Making of a Negro Ghetto, 1890–1920* (Chicago: University of Chicago Press, 1967), p. 223.

372 **"chronic urban guerilla warfare":** Arnold R. Hirsch, *Making of the Second Ghetto: Race and Housing in Chicago, 1940–1960* (Chicago: University of Chicago Press, 1983), p. 41.

373 **The moving truck arrived:** "Justice Department Probes Case of Negro Kept Out of Home," *Atlanta Daily World,* July 11, 1951, p. 1.

373 **The Clarks did not let:** "Truman May Act in Cicero Case," *Chicago Defender,* September 29, 1951, p. 1.

374 **A mob stormed the apartment:** Stephen Grant Meyer, *As Long as They Don't Move Next Door: Segregation and Racial Conflict in American Neighborhoods* (Lanham, Md.: Rowman and Littlefield, 2000), pp. 118–19. Details of the mob's destruction of the Clarks' apartment and belongings from *Chicago Defender,* August 11, 1951, p. 7; *Chicago Defender,* July 21, 1951, p. 5; *Atlanta Daily World,* July 13, 1951, p. 1; "Ugly Nights in Cicero," *Time,* July 23, 1953.

374 **The next day:** "Chicago Called Guard for 1919 Riots," *Chicago Defender,* July 21, 1951, p. 5, for reference to National Guard in racial incidents. "Truman May Act in Cicero Case," *Chicago Defender,* September 29, 1951, p. 1, on arrests of 118 people in the Cicero rioting and the grand jury's decision not to indict.

375 **"It was appalling":** Walter White, "Probe of Cicero Outbreaks Reveals Rioters Not Red but Yellow," *Chicago Defender,* July 28, 1951, p. 7.

375 **"bigoted idiots":** "Support Is Growing for Cicero Riot Victims," *Atlanta Daily World,* p. 1.

375 **"This is the root":** "Illinois Gov. Blames Housing Shortage for Riot in Cicero," *Atlanta Daily World,* October 21, 1951, p. 1.

375 **"A resident of Accra":** Hirsch, *Making of the Second Ghetto,* p. 53.

375 ***"Our nation is moving":*** *Report of the National Advisory Commission on Civil Disorders* (New York: E. P. Dutton, 1968), p. 1. The 609-page report, issued by a commission chaired by Otto Kerner, then governor of Illinois, and at the behest of President Lyndon B. Johnson, examined the causes of a national outbreak of violence in twenty-three cities in the mid-1960s. The commission stated: "This is our basic conclusion: Our nation is moving toward two societies, one black, one white—separate and unequal."

377 **"The panic peddler":** Hirsch, *Making of the Second Ghetto,* pp. 31–35.

377 ***We are going to blow:*** "Bomb Explosion Wrecks Flat Building; Lives Imperiled When Angry Whites Hurl Dynamite: Police Failed to Protect Homes," *Chicago Defender,* September 28, 1918, p. 1.

378 **"crowded out of Detroit":** Meyer, *As Long as They Don't Move Next Door,* p. 122.

380 **He read in:** See "RR Employes Give to Church Fund," *New York Amsterdam News,* January 5, 1963, p. 24, for George Starling raising money to help rebuild churches in Georgia.

381 **In March, George:** See "Airline Workers Still Helping Razed Church," *New York Amsterdam News,* March 16, 1963, p. 5, for George Starling handing over the second check to help rebuild churches in Georgia.

Revolutions

385 **I can conceive:** James Baldwin, *Notes of a Native Son* (Boston: Beacon Press, 1955), p. 59.

386 **"Negroes have continued":** James R. Ralph, Jr., *Northern Protest: Martin Luther King Jr., Chicago and the Civil Rights Movement* (Cambridge, Mass.: Harvard University Press, 1993), p. 35.

387 **"almost everybody is against":** Gunnar Myrdal, *An American Dilemma: The Negro Problem and Modern Democracy,* vol. 2 (New York: Harper and Brothers, 1944), p. 1010.

387 **"So long as this city":** "White and Black in Chicago," *Chicago Tribune,* August 3, 1919, p. F6. The editorial also said, "We admit frankly that if political equality had meant the election of Negro mayors, judges, and a majority of the city council, the whites would not have tolerated it. We do not believe that the whites of Chicago would be any different from the whites of the south in this respect. . . . Legally a Negro has a right to service anywhere the public generally is served. He does not get it. Wisely, he does not ask for it. There has been an illegal, nonlegal or extra legal adjustment founded upon common sense which has worked in the past, and it will work in the future."

387 **"in one sense":** Ralph, *Northern Protest,* p. 34.

388 **It was August 5, 1966:** Gene Roberts, "Rock Hits Dr. King as Whites Attack March in Chicago," *The New York Times,* August 6, 1966, p. 1.

388 **The march had barely begun:** Ibid. on where the rock hit King. Ralph, *Northern Protest,* on the size of the rock.

388 **As the eight hundred:** Roberts, "Rock Hits Dr. King as Whites Attack March in Chicago."

389 **Some of King's aides:** See Ralph, *Northern Protest,* p. 33, for attempts by top advisers to dissuade King from going north. The advisers argued that their work in the South was far from complete, that the North would be unreceptive, and that such efforts would hurt northern support for their cause. "King thought otherwise, and rejected this counsel just as he would subsequent warnings," according to Ralph.

389 **"I have to do this":** "Dr. King Is Felled by Rock: 30 Injured as He Leads Protesters; Many Arrested in Race Clash," *Chicago Tribune,* August 6, 1966, p. 1.

389 **"I have seen many demonstrations":** Ibid.

396 **"It happened slowly":** Louis Rosen, *The South Side: The Racial Transformation of an American Neighborhood* (Chicago: Ivan R. Dee, 1998), p. 118.

396 **"I fought the good fight":** Ibid., p. 147.

396 **"It was like sitting around":** Ibid., p. 120.

396 **"It was like having":** Ibid., p. 26.

397 **Mahalia Jackson:** Mahalia Jackson and Evan McLeod Wylie, *Movin' On Up* (New York: Hawthorne Books, 1966), p. 119.

397 **"Shall we sacrifice":** Arna Bontemps and Jack Conroy, *Anyplace but Here* (Columbia: University of Missouri Press, 1945), p. 176.

398 **The top ten cities:** Isabel Wilkerson, "Study Finds Segregation in Cities Worse than Scientists Imagined," *The New York Times,* August 5, 1989, an article on the findings of a five-year study of 22,000 census tracts conducted by University of Chicago sociologists Douglas S. Massey and Nancy A. Denton.

401 **kept a card file:** "The Extracurricular Clout of Powerful College Presidents," *Time,* February 11, 1966, p. 64.

405 **"in addition to his widow":** "Dr. Rufus Clement of AU Dies Here," *New York Amsterdam News,* November 11, 1967, p. 45.

407 **The evening was unusually cool:** Earl Caldwell, "Martin Luther King Is Slain in Memphis; White Is Suspected; Johnson Urges Calm: Guard Called Out; Curfew

Ordered in Memphis, but Fires and Looting Erupt," *The New York Times,* April 5, 1968, p. 1.

409 **"About 74 percent":** *Report of the National Advisory Commission on Civil Disorders* (New York: Bantam Books, 1968), p. 6.

The Fullness of the Migration

413 **And so the root:** Langston Hughes, "For Russell and Rowena Jelliffe," *Cleveland Call and Post,* April 6, 1963, p. B1.

415 **There were two sets:** Stanley Lieberson, *A Piece of the Pie: Blacks and White Immigrants Since 1880* (Berkeley and Los Angeles: University of California Press, 1980), pp. 32–33.

416 **white immigrants:** Ibid., p. 34.

417 **"called for blacks":** Ibid., p. 35.

418 **fertility rates for black women:** Ibid., pp. 193–97. See also Clyde Vernon Kiser, *Sea Island to City* (New York: AMS Press, 1967), pp. 204, 205. This study from the 1930s found that the Migration "significantly reduced" fertility rates. In New York, "twenty-four out of forty wives married 1–10 years had borne no children. Five of the fourteen married 10–20 years were childless, as were the two wives married 20–30 years."

418 **blacks were the lowest paid:** Lieberson, *A Piece of the Pie,* pp. 292–93; Gilbert Osofsky, *Harlem: The Making of a Ghetto* (New York: Harper and Row, 1968), p. 16.

418 **"There is just no avoiding":** Ibid., p. 369.

Part V: Aftermath

433 **The migrants were gradually absorbed:** St. Clair Drake and Horace H. Cayton, *Black Metropolis: A Study of Negro Life in a Northern City* (Chicago: University of Chicago Press, 1945, reprinted 1993), p. 75.

In the Places They Left

435 **The only thing:** Lonnie G. Bunch III, "The Greatest State for the Negro: Jefferson L. Edmonds, Black Propagandist of the California Dream," in *Seeking El Dorado: African Americans in California,* ed. Lawrence B. de Graaf, Kevin Mulroy, and Quintard Taylor (Los Angeles: Autry Museum of Western Heritage in association with University of Washington Press, Seattle, 2001), p. 132. Jefferson Lewis Edmonds was a farmer, teacher, and state legislator in Mississippi during Reconstruction. He left Mississippi for Los Angeles in 1886, shortly after an incident in which whites, fearing that a group of colored residents were about to walk into the Carrollton County courthouse, opened fire on the unarmed people, killing twenty of them. Edmonds became editor of *The Liberator,* a colored newspaper in Los Angeles.

435 **Mr. Edd, whose land:** Chickasaw County Historical and Genealogical Society, *Chickasaw County History,* vol. 2 (Dallas: Curtis Media, 1997), p. 430 on Willie Jim Linn and p. 497 on Edd Monroe Pearson.

436 **The people who had not gone:** Ibid., p. 10.

436 **"intemperate individuals":** Ibid.

437 **"spent all their savings":** Mark Lowry II, "Schools in Transition," *Annals of the Association of American Geographers* 63, no. 2 (June 1973): pp. 173, 178.

437 **In the meantime:** Ibid., p. 176.

439 **"My conscience told me":** Ben Green, *Before His Time: The Untold Story of Harry T. Moore, America's First Civil Rights Martyr* (New York: Free Press, 1999), pp. 206–7.

439 **"he dropped dead":** Ibid., p. 207.

439 **"the only public building":** Ibid., pp. 206–8.

439 **But Sheriff McCall did not:** Ibid., p. 207.

440 **McCall was reelected:** Ibid., p. 208. See also Ramsey Campbell, "Lake's Willis McCall Is Dead," *Orlando Sentinel,* April 29, 1994, p. A1.

441 **The new high school:** *Contributors of Ouachita Parish: A History of Blacks to Commemorate the Bicentennial of the United States of America* (The Black Bicentennial Committee of Ouachita Parish, 1976), p. 10.

Losses

445 **It occurred to me:** Jacqueline Joan Johnson, *Rememory: What There Is for Us,* cited in Malaika Adero, *Up South* (New York: New Press, 1993), p. 108.

445 **"one of Los Angeles' ":** "Rites Held for L.A. Socialite Mrs. Alice Clement Foster, 54," *Chicago Defender,* December 17, 1974, p. 4.

More North and West Than South

455 **I could come back:** Mahalia Jackson with Evan McLeod Wiley, *Movin' On Up* (New York: Hawthorne Books, 1966), p. 117.

456 **"Platters Full of Plenty Thanks":** An advertisement appearing in *Chicago Metro News,* November 26, 1977, p. 18.

462 **"personal isolation":** Based on an undated, registered letter written by Robert Foster to Edward Bounds, director of the U.S. Labor Department in San Francisco, as part of a workers' compensation claim filed as a result of a dispute with the West Los Angeles Veterans Administration Medical Center in Brentwood.

And, Perhaps, to Bloom

481 **Most of them care nothing:** James Baldwin, *Notes of a Native Son* (Boston: Beacon Press, 1955), p. 21.

The Winter of Their Lives

491 **That the Negro American:** Daniel Patrick Moynihan, *The Negro Family: The Case for National Action* (Washington, D.C.: United States Department of Labor, Office of Policy Planning and Research, 1965), p. 23.

492 **"I know everybody":** "Why Do You Live in Harlem? Camera Quiz," *New York Age,* April 29, 1950.

Epilogue

527 **"there is not one family":** Allen B. Ballard, *One More Day's Journey* (New York: McGraw-Hill, 1984), p. 13.

528 **"Masses of ignorant":** E. Franklin Frazier, *The Negro Family in the United States* (New York: Dryden Press, 1948), p. 285. Originally published by the University of Chicago Press, 1939.

528 **"in such large numbers":** Sadie Tanner Mossell, "The Standard of Living Among One Hundred Negro Migrant Families in Philadelphia," *Annals of the American Academy of Political and Social Science* 98 (November 1921): 216.

528 **better educated:** Stewart E. Tolnay, "Educational Selection in the Migration of Southern Blacks, 1880–1990," *Social Forces* (December 1998): 489–508. "The educational differences between southern migrants and native northerners were considerably smaller than the corresponding difference between migrants and their relatives and neighbors remaining in the South," Tolnay writes. Because a disproportionate number of educated blacks migrated out of the South, the number of years of schooling for migrants on the whole was higher than might otherwise have been expected and not far from the educational levels of blacks already in the North, a difference of one and a half years by 1950. The quality of their southern education, however, was generally considered inferior.

529 **"The Southerners had their eye":** Allen B. Ballard, *One More Day's Journey* (New York: McGraw Hill, 1984), p. 191.

529 **John Coltrane:** Lewis Porter, *John Coltrane: His Life and His Music* (Ann Arbor: University of Michigan Press, 1998), p. 33.

530 **"Upon their arrival":** Stewart E. Tolnay and Kyle D. Crowder, "Regional Origin and Family Stability in Northern Cities: The Role of Context," *American Sociological Review* 64 (1999): 109.

530 **"Compared with northern-born blacks":** Stewart E. Tolnay, "The African American 'Great Migration' and Beyond," *Annual Review of Sociology* 29 (2003): 219. See also Larry H. Long and Lynne R. Heltman, "Migration and Income Differences Between Black and White Men in the North," *The American Journal of Sociology* 80, no. 6 (May 1975): 1395–1407.

530 **Something deep inside:** Long and Heltman, "Migration and Income Differences Between Black and White Men in the North," p. 1395.

530 **"Instead of thinking":** Tolnay and Crowder, "Regional Origin and Family Stability in Northern Cities," p. 109.

531 **"led to higher earnings":** Reynolds Farley, "After the Starting Line: Blacks and Women in an Uphill Race," *Demography* 25, no. 4 (November 1988): 477.

531 **"Black migrants who left":** Larry H. Long and Kristin A. Hansen, "Selectivity of Black Return Migration to the South," *Rural Sociology* 42, no. 3 (Fall 1977): 325. Based on a paper presented at the annual meeting of the Southern Sociological Society, Atlanta, March 30–April 2, 1977.

533 **"Black school principals":** Allen B. Ballard, *One More Day's Journey,* p. 186.

533 **"Since 1924":** "4,733 Mob Action Victims Since '82, Tuskegee Reports," *Montgomery Advertiser,* April 26, 1959.

534 **The mechanical cotton picker:** Donald Holley, *The Second Great Emancipation: The Mechanical Cotton Picker, Black Migration, and How They Shaped the Modern South* (Fayetteville: University of Arkansas, 2000), pp. 38–40.

534 **Still, many planters:** Ibid., p. 101.

534 **"Much of this labor":** Harris P. Smith, "Late Developments in Mechanical Cotton Harvesting," *Agricultural Engineering,* July 1946, p. 321. Smith, the chief of the division of agricultural engineering at the Texas Agricultural Experiment Station, presented this paper at a meeting of the American Society of Agricultural Engineers at Fort Worth, Texas, in April 1946. See also Gilbert C. Fite, "Recent Changes in the Mechanization of Cotton Production in the United States," *Agricultural History* 24 (January 1950): 28, and Oscar Johnston, "Will the Machine Ruin the South?" *Saturday Evening Post* 219 (May 31, 1947): 37.

535 **"If all of their dream":** "Our Part in the Exodus," *Chicago Defender,* March 17, 1917, p. 9.

535 **Toni Morrison:** Toni Morrison's parents migrated from Alabama to Lorraine, Ohio. Diana Ross's mother migrated from Bessemer, Alabama, to Detroit, her father from Bluefield, West Virginia. Aretha Franklin's father migrated from Mississippi to Detroit. Jesse Owens's parents migrated from Oakville, Alabama, to Cleveland when he was nine. Joe Louis's mother migrated with him from Lafayette, Alabama, to Detroit. Jackie Robinson's family migrated from Cairo, Georgia, to Pasadena, California. Bill Cosby's father migrated from Schuyler, Virginia, to Philadelphia, where Cosby was born. Nat King Cole, as a young boy, migrated with his family from Montgomery, Alabama, to Chicago. Condoleezza Rice's family migrated from Birmingham, Alabama, to Denver, Colorado, when she was twelve. Thelonious Monk's parents brought him from Rocky Mount, North Carolina, to Harlem when he was five. Berry Gordy's parents migrated from rural Georgia to Detroit, where Gordy was born. Oprah Winfrey's mother migrated from Kosciusko, Mississippi, to Milwaukee, where Winfrey went to live as a young girl. Mae Jemison's parents migrated from Decatur, Alabama, to Chicago when she was three years old. Romare Bearden's parents carried him from Charlotte, North Carolina, to New York City. Jimi Hendrix's maternal grandparents migrated from Virginia to Seattle. Michael Jackson's mother was taken as a toddler from Barbour County, Alabama, by her parents to East Chicago, Indiana; his father migrated as a young man from Fountain Hill, Arkansas, to Chicago, just west of Gary, Indiana, where all the Jackson children were born. Prince's father migrated from Louisiana to Minneapolis. Sean "P. Diddy" Combs's grandmother migrated from Hollyhill, South Carolina, to Harlem. Whitney Houston's grandparents migrated from Georgia to Newark, New Jersey. The family of Mary J. Blige migrated from Savannah, Georgia, to Yonkers, New York. Queen Latifah's grandfather migrated from Birmingham, Alabama, to Newark. Spike Lee's family migrated from Atlanta to Brooklyn. August Wilson's mother migrated from North Carolina to Pittsburgh, following her own mother, who, as the playwright told it, had walked most of the way.

536 **"almost exactly at the norm":** Otto Klineberg, *Negro Intelligence and Selective Migration* (New York: Columbia University Press, 1935), pp. 43–45. The IQ tests were of

ten-year-old girls in Harlem, divided on the basis of how long they had lived in New York. Those in New York for less than a year scored 81.8, those in New York one to two years scored 85.8, those in New York for three to four years scored 94.1, and those born in New York scored 98.5. Other studies—of boys or with the use of other measurements—found what Klineberg described as an "unmistakable trend" of improved intellectual performance the longer the children were in the North.

536 **Klineberg's studies:** "Otto Klineberg, Who Helped Win '54 Desegregation Case, Dies at 92," *The New York Times,* March 10, 1992.

537 **Jean Baptiste Point DuSable:** Bessie Louise Pierce, *A History of Chicago,* vol. 1 (New York: Knopf, 1937), pp. 12, 13. Pierce describes Point DuSable as having been the son of a man from "one of France's foremost families" and says "that his mother was a Negro slave." Christopher R. Reed, "In the Shadow of Fort Dearborn: Honoring DuSable at the Chicago World's Fair of 1933–1934," *Journal of Black Studies* 21, no. 4 (June 1991): 412.

537 **Jan Rodrigues:** Leslie M. Harris, *In the Shadow of Slavery: African Americans in New York City, 1626–1863* (Chicago: University of Chicago Press, 2003), pp. 12–13.

538 **"In the simple process":** Lawrence R. Rodgers, *Canaan Bound: The African American Great Migration Novel* (Urbana: University of Illinois Press, 1997), p. 186.

Notes on Methodology

543 **It is important:** Chicago Commission on Race Relations, *The Negro in Chicago: A Study of Race Relations and a Race Riot* (Chicago: University of Chicago Press, 1922), pp. xxiii, xxiv.

Index

Permissions Acknowledgments

Grateful acknowledgment is made to the following for permission to reprint previously published material:

BEACON PRESS. Excerpts from *Notes of a Native Son* by James Baldwin, copyright © 1955 and copyright © renewed 1983 by James Baldwin. Reprinted by permission of Beacon Press, Boston.

DUTTON SIGNET, A DIVISION OF PENGUIN GROUP (USA) INC.: Excerpt from Act 1, Scene i, from *The Piano Lesson* by August Wilson, copyright © 1988, 1990 by August Wilson. Reprinted by permission of Dutton Signet, a division of Penguin Group (USA) Inc.

JOHN HAWKINS & ASSOCIATES, INC., AND THE ESTATE OF RICHARD WRIGHT: Excerpts from *12 Million Black Voices* by Richard Wright, copyright © 1940 by Richard Wright. Reprinted by permission of John Hawkins & Associates, Inc., and the Estate of Richard Wright.

HARPERCOLLINS PUBLISHERS: Excerpt from *Dust Tracks on a Road* by Zora Neale Hurston, copyright © 1942 by Zora Neale Hurston, copyright renewed 1970 by John C. Hurston. Excerpts from *Black Boy* by Richard Wright, copyright © 1937, 1942, 1944, 1945 by Richard Wright, copyright renewed 1973 by Ellen Wright. Reprinted by permission of HarperCollins Publishers.

ALFRED A. KNOPF, A DIVISION OF RANDOM HOUSE, INC., AND HAROLD OBER ASSOCIATES INCORPORATED: Excerpt from "For Russell and Rowena Jelliffe," excerpt from "One-Way Ticket," and an excerpt from "The South" from *The Collected Poems of Langston Hughes*, copyright © 1994 by the Estate of Langston Hughes. Reprinted by permission of Alfred A. Knopf, a division of Random House, Inc. Additional rights by permission of Harold Ober Associates Incorporated.

THE PHI BETA KAPPA SOCIETY: Excerpt from "The Two Harlems" by Arna Bontemps, *American Scholar*, Volume 14, No. 2, Spring 1945, p. 167, copyright © 1945 by The Phi Beta Kappa Society. Reprinted by permission of The Phi Beta Kappa Society.

RAY CHARLES MARKETING GROUP: Excerpt from "Hide Nor Hair" by Percy Mayfield and Morton Craft, copyright © Tangerine Music Corporation. All rights reserved. Reprinted by permission. Under license from the Ray Charles Marketing Group on behalf of Tangerine Music Corporation.

UNIVERSITY OF NORTH CAROLINA PRESS: Excerpt from *Gender and Jim Crow: Women and the Politics of White Supremacy in North Carolina, 1896–1920* by Glenda Elizabeth Gilmore, copyright © 1996 by the University of North Carolina Press. Reprinted by permission of the publisher, www.uncpress.unc.edu.

VIKING PENGUIN, A DIVISION OF PENGUIN GROUP (USA) INC.: Excerpt from Chapter 9 from *The Grapes of Wrath* by John Steinbeck, copyright © 1939, copyright renewed 1967 by John Steinbeck. Reprinted by permission of Viking Penguin, a division of Penguin Group (USA) Inc.

About the Author

Isabel Wilkerson won the 1994 Pulitzer Prize for Feature Writing for her reporting as Chicago bureau chief of *The New York Times.* The award made her the first black woman in the history of American journalism to win a Pulitzer Prize and the first African American to win for individual reporting. She won the George Polk Award for her coverage of the Midwest and a John Simon Guggenheim Fellowship for her research into the Great Migration. She has lectured on narrative writing at the Nieman Foundation at Harvard University and has served as Ferris Professor of Journalism at Princeton University and as the James M. Cox Jr. Professor of Journalism at Emory University. She is currently Professor of Journalism and Director of Narrative Nonfiction at Boston University. During the Great Migration, her parents journeyed from Georgia and southern Virginia to Washington, D.C., where she was born and reared. This is her first book.

About the Type

This book was set in Granjon, a modern recutting of a typeface produced under the direction of George W. Jones, who based Granjon's design upon the letter forms of Claude Garamond (1480–1561). The name was given to the typeface as a tribute to the typographic designer Robert Granjon.

A "blank wall" for J. Robert Oppenheimer
Supreme Court outlaws school segregation

1955 The Davy Crockett craze
Enter the beat generation
Formosa resolution
Geneva summit
Ike's heart attack

1956 Grace Kelly becomes a princess
Hungary, Suez, and Ike's reelection
Montgomery bus boycott

1957 Little Rock
Russia launches its first sputnik
The Edsel disaster
U.S. rocket fiasco at Cape Canaveral

1958 Hula hoop craze
Eisenhower Doctrine in Mideast
Nixon mobbed in Caracas
Sherman Adams's vicuña coat
John Birch Society founded

1959 Charles Van Doren unmasked
Nixon in Moscow; Khrushchev in U.S.

1960 FDA approves Enovid — the Pill
Black sit-ins start in Greensboro, N.C.
U-2 incident; Geneva summit collapses
Kennedy elected President by an eyelash

1961 Alan Shepard's fifteen minutes in space
Freedom riders in Dixie
The Bay of Pigs
Kennedy vs. Khrushchev in Vienna
LBJ visits Saigon, pledges support
Taylor-Rostow mission to Vietnam

1962 Grossinger's first Singles Only weekend
John Glenn orbits earth
James Meredith at Ole Miss
SDS organized
Cuban missile crisis

1963 *Who's Afraid of Virginia Woolf?*
Beatles tour U.S.
Birmingham and Bull Connor
Wallace stands in the schoolhouse door
March on Washington
Diem brothers assassinated in Saigon
Death in Dallas

1964 Tonkin Gulf
The first of the long hot summers
Mario Savio and the Free Speech Movement

[illegible]sissippi
[illegible]
Medicare; the "Xerox Congress"
LBJ commits U.S. ground troops in Vietnam
Herald Tribune coins "credibility gap"
Selma march; Watts
Electricity blackout blankets Northeast

1966 Nudity becomes chic
America scarred by 43 race riots
"Black power!" — and backlash

1967 The great year of the hippy
Operations Cedar Falls and Junction City
Ghetto violence peaks

1968 Loss of the U.S.S. *Pueblo*
Tet
RFK and Martin Luther King die
Columbia campus blows
Jacqueline Kennedy remarries
My Lai
Nixon elected in a cliffhanger

1969 Apollo 11 lands on moon
Woodstock
Chappaquiddick
Charles Manson
M Days for peace
Chicago Seven trial

1970 Women's Lib and hotpants
Cambodia and Kent State
Judge Carswell rejected
X-rated movies sweep country
Angela Davis and George Jackson
Postal strike
White House hires Plumbers

1971 U.S. ping-pong players visit China
"Mayday Tribe" in Washington
Pentagon Papers leaked
A second-story job on Dr. Fielding
ITT, Vesco, and the milk fund
Phase One and Phase Two
Attica

1972 Bobby Fischer and Clifford Irving
Nixon in Peking and Moscow
Giap's offensive
Watergate and cover-up
McGovern: a disaster for the Democrats
Kissinger: "Peace is at hand"
Saturation bombing and a cease-fire
Dead ahead: Watergate exposure

THE GLORY AND THE DREAM

A Narrative History of America

1932–1972

WILLIAM
MANCHESTER

THE GLORY AND THE DREAM

A Narrative History of America 1932–1972

VOLUME TWO

LITTLE, BROWN AND COMPANY
BOSTON – TORONTO

Acknowledgments of permission to reprint excerpted material appear on pages 1641–1643.

Portions of this book were first published in slightly altered form in the *New York Times Magazine* and *New York* magazine.

Published simultaneously in Canada by Little, Brown & Company (Canada) Limited

PRINTED IN THE UNITED STATES OF AMERICA

Contents

PART II
Sacrifice and Transformation
1941–1950

PART III
Sowing the Wind
1951–1960

PART IV
Reaping the Whirlwind
1961–1968

PART V
Nixon, After All
1969-1972

THE GLORY AND THE DREAM

A Narrative History of America

1932–1972

Twenty-one

MR. CHAIRMAN, MR. CHAIRMAN

LATER THE SPECTER of Dienbienphu would loom ever larger in the American consciousness, but at the time it was something that was happening to somebody else. Its downfall wasn't the only major event of 1954, or even one of the top stories. That was a newsy year in the United States. In January the world's first atomic submarine, *Nautilus,* had steamed out of the Navy boatyard in Groton, Connecticut, under its own power. Six weeks later in Detroit six leaders of the Communist Party in Michigan were found guilty of conspiring to overthrow the U.S. government. Confronted by indisputable evidence of an approaching recession, the President decided in his March 12 cabinet meeting to call it a "rolling readjustment."

The Easter 1954 issue of *McCall's* introduced "togetherness," a concept which quickly became so popular that it took on overtones of a social crusade and became almost a national purpose of the 1950s. The Air Force Academy was created on April 1; its first class was sworn in at Lowry Air Force Base, Denver, Colorado. Rejecting a lower British bid, Secretary of Defense Charles E. Wilson awarded contracts for construction of the Chief Joseph Dam in the state of Washington to an American firm, and both houses of Congress approved the St. Lawrence Seaway.

Julius and Ethel Rosenberg were executed June 19 after a demonstration outside the White House in which picketers protesting the sentence were accosted by noisy young demonstrators bearing placards which read TWO FRIED ROSENBERGERS COMING RIGHT UP. Admiral Robert B. Carney, Chief of Naval Operations, contributed to cold war tensions by telling reporters that he and his staff expected a Chinese Communist attack on the offshore islands of Quemoy and Matsu within a month. "They have information I do not have," said the President. Nevertheless, he warned that any assault on Formosa "will have to run over the Seventh Fleet." The cabinet was elated at its July 23 meeting to learn that economic indicators would soon turn upward, ending the rolling readjustment. August's Hurricane Carol blew down the steeple of Boston's historic Old North Church. Other hurricanes named Edna and Hazel followed in September.

Eisenhower and Churchill conferred in Bermuda on world peace. The Atomic Energy Commission on October 5 approved a contract under which a West Memphis power plant would be built for the TVA by a southern utility group headed by Edgar H. Dixon and Eugene A. Yates. President Eisenhower described his administration's political philosophy as "dynamic conservatism," then as "progressive, dynamic conservatism," then as "progressive moderation," then as "moderate progressivism," and then as "positive progressivism." On December 21, 1954, Dr. Samuel H. Sheppard, a Cleveland osteopath, was convicted of murdering his wife Marilyn on July 4. Sir Edmund Hillary, conqueror of Mount Everest, was thrilling lecture audiences in the Middle West, and nationwide circulation was given to the first authoritative reports linking cigarette smoking and heart disease.

Playboy was selling for fifty cents, competing on newsstands with such other publications of the decade as *Flair* (fifty cents), *Confidential*, "Uncensored and Off the Record" (a quarter), *Mad* (a dime), and, at fifteen cents, the most successful periodical of the 1950s, *TV Guide*, which by the end of the decade would be running fifty-three regional editions for seven million subscribers.

America's drug culture lay far in the future, but the roots of its idiom could be heard at bebop sessions where one heard the esoteric jazz of such maestros as Miles Davis and Thelonious Monk. They called money bread and girls chicks. To understand was to flip; something which in the past had been fabulous was now crazy. Superlatives of crazy were cool, groovy, the end, and far out (later to become out of sight). To be appreciative was to be hip, and someone who was so hip that he had passed into an ecstatic trance would soon be called a hippy.

Better known then, and a source of amusement in intellectual circles throughout the decade, was advertising cant. As society became more aware of advertisers, and as they became more clever, their instant clichés briefly became part of the language. In 1954 the reigning platitude was the suffix "wise," meaning "with regard to," "in respect of," or "in the manner of." Battered by overuse, it became an all-purpose word. Instead of saying "This year's cars are all chrome," you said, "Stylewise, this year's cars are all chrome." Moneywise, a tycoon was rich. Sequencewise, a loser was last. Agewise, a girl was young; clotheswise, she might be chic; and personalitywise, she would be attractive. Boozewise, you might have a big night. Headwise, you would feel terrible in the morning, but jobwise, you would make it to the office.

On the other side of the island from Madison Avenue lay Tin Pan Alley, and there sovereignty still rested in the clammy hands of the balladeers. The biggest hit of 1954 was Kitty Kallen's "Little Things Mean a Lot." Runners-up included Perry Como's "Wanted," Frank Sinatra's "Young at Heart," and the Crew Cuts' (only classical musicians wore their hair long then) "Sh-Boom." Archie Bleyer's "Hernando's Hideaway" was another memorable ditty that year. The Four Aces' "Three Coins in the Fountain" was from the motion picture of the same name, a Cinemascope production in De Luxe Color starring Dorothy McGuire, Clifton Webb, and Jean Peters. Waterfront corruption in New York was a running story throughout 1954—on April 15 Albert Anastasia was deprived of his citizenship—and the Academy of Motion Picture Arts and Sciences awarded its Oscar for the best picture of the year to *On the Waterfront*. Other honored films were *The Caine Mutiny, The Country Girl, Seven Brides for Seven Brothers, Sabrina, Executive Suite, Dial M for Murder, Rear Window,* and Disney's *20,000 Leagues Under the Sea*. Movies still weren't making much money, but for the time being the big talent was staying in Hollywood.

Variety listed as 1954's most popular television programs *I Love Lucy, Dragnet,* and the mixed bags of Groucho Marx and Ed Sullivan. The only really bright hour of TV comedy, Sid Caesar and Imogene Coca's Saturday evening *Your Show of Shows*, folded in 1954 after 160 performances; the network blamed lack of audience interest. Above all, 1954 was the year of the quiz show: *I've Got a Secret, Stop the Music, Place the Face, Name That Tune,* and *What's My Line*. The big money quiz programs, *Twenty-one* and

The $64,000 Question, were in the wings. TV spectaculars—long, lavish, one-performance extravaganzas—were more interesting. *Amahl and the Night Visitors,* a Christmas Eve opera written for television by Gian-Carlo Menotti in 1951, had been acclaimed everywhere. As it happened, 1954's chief spectacular, *Satins and Spurs,* was so terrible that its star, Betty Hutton, retired from show business. Next year promised to be much better, though. Contracts were out for Mary Martin's superb *Peter Pan,* to be telecast March 7, 1955.

Obviously television was having an immense impact on American mores, but defining the nature of the impact was difficult. Some thought the networks were too wide-open, too permissive. TV fare was more violent than radio, and franker about sex. Plunging necklines, an exciting development of the early 1950s, left little doubt that female performers were mammary and proud of it. When Desi Arnaz impregnated his wife and costar, Lucille Ball, the producers of *I Love Lucy* took it as an opportunity; each week's episode offered late bulletins on Lucy's condition, and Desi was even depicted suffering from sympathetic morning sickness.

In reality TV was merely noting a trend here, one whose implications would not emerge until another decade. The medium itself would never be a pace-setter. Like the life-styles of the 1950s of which it was so faithful a mimic, it was bland, innocuous, noncontroversial. Its most familiar themes were charming but irrelevant to real issues: the bromides Loretta Young read at the end of each program, Dave Garroway's "Peace," and the "Ho-Ho Song" to which Red Buttons danced offstage.

Commercial? Absolutely: the profit motive was as sacred as togetherness. Sneering at it was almost prima facie evidence of subversion. Everybody was selling something, and Americans approved; the diversity of their marketplace was the marvel of the world. A confidential survey made for the Republican National Committee by Batten, Barton, Durstine, and Osborn reported that foreign policy was the number one issue for American voters, with Communist infiltration in the U.S. second, but it was untrue. The agency was telling its clients what they wanted to hear. Prosperity was what Americans wanted, and they had it, were getting fat with it, and enjoyed reading the scales. It was a bull market that was going to get bullier. Detroit was counting on Chevrolet's Dinah Shore to be especially alluring in 1955. The automotive industry's confident—and justifiable—expectation was that nearly eight million cars would be sold, nearly a million more than in any previous year.

In February 1954 over 7,500 Republicans descended on Washington to eat fried chicken box lunches in the Ellipse and observe Lincoln Day by singing "God Bless America." The President came out for a few brief remarks. At the moment he wasn't toying with "moderate progressivism" or any of that; he used the simple term "conservative," paused, then added firmly: "And don't be afraid to use that word." They cheered. Middle-class Republicans were feeling their oats. They were proud to be conservative, prosperous, conformist, and vigilant defenders of the American way of life, and they wanted no truck with crackpots, Reds, heretics, Bohemians, radicals, nuts, Bolsheviks, loonies, pinkos, fellow travelers, galoots, geezers, or screwballs. Eggheads were subjects of particular scorn. No wild-eyed college professors were going to be allowed to gum up the works. On April 13, 1954, James Reston reported in the *New York Times* that the Atomic Energy Commission, at the direction of President Eisenhower, had withdrawn the security clearance of Dr. J. Robert Oppenheimer pending an investigation of charges that he had, among other things, "worked tirelessly from January 21, onward, to retard the United States H-bomb program."

The accusation had been lodged five months earlier by William L. Borden, former executive secretary of the Joint Congressional Committee on Atomic Energy and senior assistant to Senator Brien McMahon. Borden had written J. Edgar Hoover on November 7, 1953, that "more probably than not J. Robert Oppenheimer is an agent of the Soviet Union." A bill of particulars followed, including charges that prior to April 1942 "He was contributing substantial monthly sums to the Communist Party," that "His wife and younger brother were Communists," and that "He had no close friends except Communists."

Borden's motives are obscure. He had nothing new. The government had long known that Oppenheimer had been a freewheeling left-of-center ideologue in the 1930s. It hadn't affected his work. Lately he hadn't had much to do with Washington anyhow. At one time he had been a member of no fewer than thirty-five government committees, but in July 1952 he had resigned as chairman of the AEC General Advisory Commission, and since the beginning of the Eisenhower administration he had been devoting most of his energies to the Institute for Advanced Study in Princeton, of which he was the director. As a government consultant he retained his top-secret Q clearance, but he never used it. At the time of Borden's accusations Oppenheimer wasn't even in the country. He had been chosen to deliver the BBC's prestigious Reith Lecture for 1953, and while he was in Britain Oxford decided to award him his sixth honorary degree. It was a question of who was more honored by the occasion, Oppenheimer or Oxford. By this time America's most eminent scientist had been elected to every learned society in Europe. Prizes, awards, and foreign decorations had been showered upon him. At home he had been chosen for everything from the American Academy of Arts and Sciences to the *Popular Mechanics* Hall of Fame.

Now Borden said he was a Russian spy. What is far more likely is that he was a victim of scientific politics. A savage dispute was raging between nuclear physicists belonging to two schools of thought named for America's two great nuclear laboratories, Los Alamos and Livermore. The Los Alamos group, comprising Oppenheimer's colleagues and protégés, held that nuclear missiles should be only one of many kinds of weapons in the American arsenal. This was called "finite containment." The Livermore, or Teller, group believed that the nation's security depended upon the unlimited development of nuclear striking power. That was "infinite containment." Most scientists took the finite view, but an administration that advocated "massive retaliation" was plainly thinking in infinite terms. The Livermore men were in power, and this, in fact, was one reason Oppenheimer had withdrawn to Princeton. But that wasn't enough for his adversaries. The debate had turned some men of science into fanatics—which is not really surprising, since the issue could determine the future of the human race—and certain admirers of Edward Teller were determined to discredit Oppenheimer. Almost certainly they were behind Borden.

Borden, however, merely wrote a letter. Washington desks were covered with such letters then. There was no reason why an official should pay attention to a new smear, unless, of course, he thought there was something in it. That was true in this instance. J. Edgar Hoover had been suspicious of J. Robert Oppenheimer for a long time. In 1947 Hoover had done all he could to tag Oppenheimer as a security risk. The *Herald Tribune* reported that the FBI file on Oppenheimer was four feet six inches high. Borden could hardly have sent his letter to a more receptive addressee, and the chances are that he knew it.

Hoover spent the next three weeks preparing an inch-thick digest of the Oppenheimer file. On November 30 he sent it to the White House. Copies went to Lewis A. Strauss at the Atomic Energy Commission and Charlie Wilson at the Pentagon. After reading his, Wilson phoned the President; he wanted Oppenheimer barred from all military installations at once. Eisenhower called it "very disturbing" (which of course it was, however you felt about Oppenheimer) and called an emergency meeting to weigh the charges. Had the scientist ever been confronted with them? he asked. Told he hadn't, Ike ordered a hearing. Meantime, he said, he wanted a "blank wall" put between Oppenheimer and all government secrets. It was an arresting phrase, and although only Wilson, Strauss, Brownell, and Robert Cutler of the National Security Council had been present, word of the decision reached the Washington gossips and, through them, the Capitol Hill home of Senator Joseph R. McCarthy.

Upon returning from England Oppenheimer found a message to call Admiral Strauss. Strauss urged him to come to the capital at once; the matter was pressing and couldn't be discussed over the telephone. On the afternoon of December 21 the scientist entered the AEC's gleaming marble building on Constitution Avenue, and in room 236, the admiral's large, paneled office, he found Strauss in conference with Major General Kenneth D. Nichols, the commission's general manager. They asked him to join them at a conference table. There, after an exchange of pleasantries and news of mutual friends, Strauss told Oppenheimer, as gracefully as you can tell a man such a thing, that he was suspected of treason. Eisenhower's directive was explained to him, and then the possibility of a graceful exit was discussed. Oppenheimer refused to take it.

On Christmas Eve a special indignity was visited upon him. Security men from the AEC arrived in Princeton to confiscate all classified material in his possession. The hearing was then scheduled for April. Reston knew of it. He intended to publish nothing until a decision had been reached, but since McCarthy was planning to announce it in the Senate to claim that he had forced the administration's hand, Reston went ahead. The news was sensational, and the determination to avoid further sensationalism gave the subsequent hearing a furtive air. The sessions, closed to the press and public, were held in temporary building T-3, a shabby relic of OPA's wartime bureaucracy. To hoodwink any reporters who might learn of the location, Oppenheimer used a back door. The trial—for that is what it amounted to—was held in T-3's room 2022, a 24- by 12-foot office which had been converted to its temporary purpose by an arrangement of tables, chairs, and a seedy old leather couch. Oppenheimer used the couch; afterward a participant would recall that the scientist "leaned back lazily, sometimes as though his thoughts were elsewhere, on the sofa which had been turned into a dock for the occasion."

A bench had been set up at the opposite end of the room. There sat Oppenheimer's judges: Gordon Gray; Thomas A. Morgan, a retired industrialist; and Ward V. Evans, emeritus professor of chemistry at Northwestern. The AEC was represented by Robert Robb, counsel to its Personnel Security Board. Robb contributed to the inquisitional aura by adopting the abrasive manner of a prosecuting attorney. His attitude toward Oppenheimer was one of contempt. A stranger entering room 2022 would never have guessed that the man under interrogation had been director of the laboratory that had perfected the atomic bomb. Robb used all the timeworn trial tricks, including keeping the sunlight in the defendant's eyes by putting his own back to a window. The 992-page transcript of the hearings bristles with his disdain.

Periodically Oppenheimer's disembodied voice would be heard over a portable public address system—recordings of wartime G-2 telephone taps which had been made without his consent or even knowledge. It was humiliating; at times it was almost unbelievable. When André Malraux read the record of the proceedings he expressed astonishment that Oppenheimer, who after all was a free man, had remained to hear Robb's studied insults. Malraux said, "He ought to have stood up and shouted, 'Gentlemen, *I* am the atomic bomb.'" But Oppenheimer was too diffident, too introverted for that, and he had suffered much brooding over the destruction of Hiroshima; he felt, as he told a friend, that "We did the devil's work."

After taking testimony from forty witnesses, the tribunal retired to write its opinion. The allegation that Oppenheimer had been an enemy agent was rejected: "We have given particular attention to the question of his loyalty and we have come to the clear conclusion, which should be reassuring to the people of this country, that he is a loyal citizen." Indeed, the panel observed, "It must be said that Dr. Oppenheimer seems to have had a high degree of discretion reflecting an unusual ability to keep to himself vital secrets." Evans, the only scientist on the tribunal, wanted to restore Oppenheimer's security clearance, but Gray and Morgan wouldn't go that far. They didn't like some of Oppenheimer's friends. It was their opinion that his "associations have reflected a serious disregard for the requirements of the security system." Then there was his troubling lack of enthusiasm for the superbomb:

> We find his conduct in the hydrogen bomb program sufficiently disturbing as to raise a doubt as to whether his future participation, if characterized by the same attitudes in a government program relating to the national defense, would be clearly consistent with the best interests of security.

Oppenheimer appealed the two-to-one decision to the AEC, which upheld it in a four-to-one vote. Commissioner Henry D. Smyth urged the others to see that Oppenheimer's "loyalty and trustworthiness emerge clearly," that in the light of his distinguished attainments "his services could be of great value to the country in the future," and that "the security system has . . . neither the responsibility nor the right to dictate every detail of a man's life." But it was precisely there that the others parted company with him; a man of great achievements might be forgiven much, and the commissioners were less rigid than the Gray board in passing judgment on Oppenheimer's mixed feelings about thermonuclear weapons, but failure to repudiate friends and relatives with unorthodox political persuasions could not be overlooked.

Ironically, the effect of purging Oppenheimer was the exact opposite of what his enemies had intended. In martyrdom he acquired new stature. Teller, on the other hand, became something of an outcast. The plotters had expected him to become the new wise man of nuclear physics. Instead he was ostracized. The only established scientist who had spoken against Oppenheimer, he was looked upon as an FBI informer, a turncoat who had betrayed both a fellow scientist and science itself. At scientific meetings he was snubbed by the others; when he protested they walked away. Eventually he came to be tolerated, but he was never really trusted again; in panel discussions and conversations his fellow physicists were formal and guarded. He appealed to Enrico Fermi, now near death, and the great Italian scientist supported him in an article in the magazine *Science,* but to Teller's critics this was just one more breach of ethics. They put him down as a publicity seeker and continued to ignore him. In the world of science his Dr. Strangelove image had already formed.

Meantime the human condition which would be symbolized by Strangelove had been brought into focus by a chance wind in the western Pacific Ocean, giving Americans a brief but terrible glimpse of what they were doing to themselves and to the world. On March 1, when Robb was preparing his case against Oppenheimer, the AEC had exploded its second hydrogen bomb on Bikini atoll, just east of Eniwetok. Outstripping all expectations, it ripped open the coral reef with a force of some 18 million to 22 million tons of TNT—the equivalent of 900 to 1,000 Hiroshima bombs. Then the wind picked up the fallout. Meteorologists had predicted a stiff breeze to the north. Instead, it blew southward until, 120 miles from Bikini and far from the danger zone marked by the bomb testers, it dropped clouds of radioactive dust on a Japanese trawler grimly misnamed the *Lucky Dragon No. 5.* The startled Japanese fishermen at first thought themselves to be in the world's first tropical snowstorm. By the time they reached their home port of Yaizu, the ghastly truth had begun to emerge. All twenty-three of them were sick and had to be hospitalized. Subsequently one, the wireless operator, died. Meanwhile sensitive devices had picked up traces of radioactivity from rainfall in Japan, Australia, the United States, Europe, and even in the oil in airliners which had been flying over India.

This brought a new term to the vocabulary of death: strontium 90, or radiostrontium, a heavy radioactive isotope of strontium with a half-life of 25 years. That was what had been in the lethal blizzard which had struck the *Lucky Dragon No. 5.* Deposited in the bones, like calcium, and combined with radioactive iodine, which had been discovered in the thyroid glands of the fishermen, strontium 90 was a cause of cancer. It was further believed to threaten posterity, though its impact there could not be measured for several generations. Admiral Strauss called the scientists who warned of these dangers, "appeasers" and "alarmists." He dispatched his own teams of technicians around the world, and their findings appeared to justify his name for the project, "Operation Sunshine." Other investigators were gloomy. A. H. Sturtevant, emeritus professor of biology at Cal Tech, said that "the bombs already exploded will ultimately result in the production of numerous defective individuals." Curt Stern, professor of genetics at Berkeley, said, "By now everyone in the world harbors in his body small amounts of radioactivity from past H-bomb tests," and physicist Ralph Lapp, a consultant for the Bikini tests and head of the Office of Naval Research nuclear branch, predicted that at some time in the 1970s the buildup of radioactive material in the stratosphere would exceed the maximum permissible amount and begin to affect the health of everyone on earth.

At the distance of twenty years this issue may seem to transcend all others of that spring—the uproar over the Bricker amendment, the crisis in Indochina, the fall of Oppenheimer—but at the time it, like them, was overshadowed by a question so absurd, so petty, so devoid of significance or even seriousness as to cast grave doubts upon the ability of democratic institutions to survive the challenges of the second half of the twentieth century. Incredible as it seems now, for thirty-five days the nation was engrossed in a dispute which began as a quarrel over who had granted a routine promotion, from captain to major, to a left-wing Army dentist named Irving Peress.

"Who promoted Peress?" Senator McCarthy demanded over and over. He never found out, and the truth is that he wasn't much interested. Peress merely gave him an excuse to wade into the Army. Actually the dentist's majority had come to him not because any of his superiors approved it, but because he was entitled to it under automatic provisions of the Doctor Draft Law, a measure meant to correlate military pay with civilian earnings—and one which McCarthy had approved. Peress had entered the Army in October 1952. He received his bronze oak leaves a year later. Next it developed that he had belonged to the American Labor Party, then tantamount to being a Communist. In testifying before McCarthy's subcommittee at Camp Kilmer, New Jersey, on January 30, 1954, he invoked the Fifth Amendment. The Office of the Adjutant General had already instructed the First Army to discharge him, and three days later it did, but that wasn't good enough for the junior senator from Wisconsin. McCarthy thought the Army should have court-martialed Peress. He took its failure to do so as proof that Communists had infiltrated the War Department, a situation which he meant to remedy by means of his investigative powers.

McCarthyologists reasoned that there must be more to it than that, and in fact there was much more. To be sure, as a nihilist Joe McCarthy was opposed to the Army for no better reason than that it represented established authority. His first appearance as a Washington mischief-maker, predating his discovery of Communism, had pitted him against the Army. During the Battle of the Bulge seventy-three SS troopers had murdered 150 captured American GIs at Malmedy. After the war they had been sentenced to death, and in 1949 Joe had taken up the SS cause. The furor had brought the senator the sort of headlines he craved (MCCARTHY HITS BRUTALITY; MCCARTHY HINTS AT MYSTERY WITNESS; MCCARTHY CHARGES WHITEWASH). The Germans' lives had been spared, and nothing that had happened since then suggested that he would be reluctant to take on the Pentagon again. Yet he bore it no grudge. There was no conflict between his interests and the Army's. In early 1954 he had stronger motives for attacking other institutions. The decision to attack the Army was not really his; it was made for him by two remarkable young men, two members of McCarthy's staff who might be called the Leopold and Loeb of the 1950s. Their names were Roy M. Cohn and G. David Schine.

Cohn typified young political militants of his generation, just as Mario Savio and Mark Rudd would later typify theirs. Short, dark, insensitive, and haughty, he also possessed a photographic memory. His drooping eyelids and his curiously sensual mouth gave him a sullen, vulpine expression. Like McCarthy, he loved a quarrel for its own sake. The fact that Cohn always kept his dark hair combed was just about the only sign that he came from a good family. His father—a Democrat—was a judge in the appellate division of the New York Supreme Court. Roy's mother worshipped him. Once in his childhood, when he was invited on an excursion to be supervised by the father of one of his friends, the father had a phone call from Mrs. Cohn. She said, "You're in for a great treat. Roy's going with you. He's such a smart boy and knows so much about so many things. I'm sure you'll get a lot of pleasure out of him and probably learn a lot from him, too."

Certainly he was precocious. At twenty he was graduated from Columbia Law School; he had to loiter around Manhattan waiting to turn twenty-one before he could be admitted to the bar. On that day he was sworn in as an Assistant U.S. Attorney. He became a specialist in what was called subversive activities, working on, among other cases, the Remington and Rosenberg trials. At twenty-three he was an inside source for Walter Winchell and George Sokolsky, and while he was scratching their backs, they scratched his with flattering references which gave him a start on his next goal: appointment as special assistant to U.S. Attorney General James McGranery. He reached it in September 1952. Cohn's first day in Washington was a portent: he was sworn in in McGranery's private office, although no new oath was necessary; he held a press conference to announce his duties but forgot to reveal his title, held a second press conference to correct the oversight, demanded a private cable address and a private telephone line to his former boss in New York, and was turned down both times but somehow managed to have three other junior lawyers evicted from the office they shared so that it could become his private office. In December he prepared the indictment which charged Owen Lattimore with perjury. That case collapsed, but by then Cohn didn't care; on January 14, 1953, he had resigned from the Justice Department to become chief counsel for Senator Joseph R. McCarthy's Permanent Investigations Subcommittee.

Schine was the sleeker of the two, a fair, languid youth with the face and physique of a fledgling Greek god. Born to wealth, he was a graduate of Andover and Harvard, '49. In Cambridge he had been conspicuous for his valet and his big black convertible with a two-way phone-radio. The Harvard *Crimson* took note of his way of arriving at parties:

> This consisted of phoning from his car and saying, "This is G. David Schine. I'm now driving through Copley Square. Could you direct me a little further," and then later, "This is G. David Schine. I'm now at Kenmore Square. Could you give me more directions please."

Like Cohn, he became interested in Communism. In school he wrote a paper about it which he afterward published as a six-page pamphlet, *Definition of Communism.* After Schine became famous *Time* called it "remarkably succinct." The *New Yorker,* more critical, reported that "It puts the Russian Revolution, the founding of the Communist Party, and the start of the First Five Year Plan in years when these things did not happen. It gives Lenin the wrong first name. It confuses Stalin with Trotsky. It confuses Marx with Lenin. It confuses Alexander Kerensky with Prince Lvov. It confuses fifteenth-century Utopianism with twentieth-century Marxism." By then copies of it had become extremely rare, but when it first appeared, *Definition of Communism* could be found beside the Gideon Bible in every Schine hotel—the Roney Plaza in Miami Beach, the Ten Eyck in Albany, the Ambassador in Los Angeles, the Ritz Carlton in Atlantic City, and the Boca Raton in Boca Raton. One guest who read it with pleasure was a certain Rabbi Benjamin Schultz, the director of something called the American Jewish League Against Communism. Rabbi Schultz sought Schine out and introduced him to George Sokolsky. Through Sokolsky, Schine met Cohn, and through Cohn he met McCarthy.

Putting a multimillionaire on the subcommittee payroll would have been ridiculous. Besides, Schine didn't have any qualifications, as the word is understood on Capitol Hill. Early in 1953 Cohn persuaded McCarthy to appoint his new friend chief consultant on psychological warfare. There was no such position. Cohn made it up. Schine was delighted to serve without pay. In New York the two young men set up temporary headquarters in the Waldorf Towers, where Schine had a permanent suite, and there they planned an ingenious investigation of the Voice of America. Voice employees were quietly urged to put the finger on fellow workers with odd ideas or habits—it was these informants McCarthy had in mind when he talked of his "Loyal American Underground"—and after televised hearings under klieg lights there was general agreement in the press that the Senator's exuberant protégé had demoralized the Voice program. Cohn and Schine were still only twenty-six. There was no limit to how far they might go.

They flew to Europe, surfacing in Paris on Easter Sunday, April 4. Eighteen days of madness followed: in-and-out trips to European capitals during which they strutted and posed for the press and exercised, to the greatest possible degree, their rights and prerogatives as representatives of the U.S. Congress. And wherever they went they were trailed by a gleeful corps of correspondents who chanted:

Positively, Mr. Cohn!
Absolutely, Mr. Schine!

Or sang:

Oh, the Cohn Schines east!
The Cohn Schines west!
McCarthy knows
Where the Cohn Schines best!

By late 1953 McCarthy's hostility toward the White House was apparent to all around him. Two days before Thanksgiving he made it public. In a November 16 broadcast Harry Truman had referred scathingly to "McCarthyism." Joe had demanded equal time to reply. Like the administration, the networks were trying desperately to appease him, and the request was granted. But after the first few minutes the senator turned his wrath from Truman to Eisenhower. At a press conference the week before Ike had said he didn't know what McCarthyism meant. He would soon find out, Joe said ominously. Ike had also expressed confidence in his ability to rid the government of security risks; in next year's congressional elections, he said, the issue would be a dead one. Far from it, the senator told his radio and television audience. The "raw, harsh, unpleasant fact" was that "Communism is an issue and will be an issue in 1954."

Of course, he said patronizingly, the Republican administration was doing "infinitely" better than the Democrats in this respect. But there were "a few cases where our batting average is zero—we struck out." As always he got down to cases: names, dates, figures, dossiers—the wrong ones, though his listeners couldn't tell that. Joe said that was shameful, it was disgraceful, it made McCarthy sick way down deep inside. But there was worse. Despite admonitions from him, Eisenhower, like Truman before him, persisted in adhering to mutual aid treaties with Britain while the British insulted the memory of American boys who had fallen in Korea by trading with Peking. McCarthy's voice rose nasally:

"Are we going to continue to send perfumed notes? . . . it is time that we, the Republican Party, liquidate this blood-stained blunder . . . we promised the American people something different. Let us deliver—not next year or next month—let us deliver now. . . . We can do this by merely saying to our allies and alleged allies, 'If you continue to ship to Red China . . . you will not get one cent of American money.' "

Eisenhower was furious. C. D. Jackson and Paul Hoffman urged him to repudiate McCarthy as a Republican at the next presidential press conference. Hagerty agreed; so did Bryce Harlow and four other presidential assistants. But Nixon said the real victim in such a showdown would be the Republican party. It was decided that Dulles should answer McCarthy at his own press conference on December 1 with a statement that Eisenhower would approve word by word. McCarthy, the secretary said, had attacked "the very heart of U.S. foreign policy." That policy was to treat other nations as sovereign, not to pick their trade partners or "make them our satellites." As a real anti-Communist hard-liner—unlike McCarthy—Dulles observed that the United States must always be prepared "to retaliate with a devastating blow against the vitals of Russia," and that it retained the capacity to do this "only because we share the well-located bases of other friendly countries."

McCarthy was now on favorite turf. He liked nothing better than a slugging match with a Secretary of State, and he hadn't had one for nearly a year. Besides, this was an exceptionally good time to do mischief. Eisenhower was about to confer with Churchill in Bermuda. An emotional televised appeal to the American people on the eve of the conference could go a long way toward sabotaging it and embarrassing the President. And that was in fact Joe's next move. On the evening of December 3, as Ike was leaving for the meeting, McCarthy took the air to cry out against Englishmen who fattened their bankrolls by dealing with the murderers of U.S. soldiers. He implored "every American who feels as I do about this blood trade with a mortal enemy to write or wire the President . . . so he can be properly guided." Five days later the White House acknowledged that over fifty thousand messages had been received. No one in Washington had been deceived by the moonshine about guidance. This was a straight-out contest between the two men, and the presidential spokesman who reported the mail count did not pretend otherwise. McCarthy won among letter writers, he announced, while Eisenhower held the edge among those who had sent telegrams. Since the White House receives comparatively few wires, this was an artful way of saying that the senator had overwhelmed the President.

It was at this point that it became fashionable in Washington to describe McCarthy as the second most powerful man in the country. Certainly any demagogue who could trigger that sort of response had become formidable. There were other indications that McCarthyism was approaching a new crest. In the next month, January 1954, Gallup reported that public approval of the senator had risen sixteen percentage points in the past six months. Fewer than three Americans in every ten disapproved of him. It is improbable that one in ten knew what a mountebank he was, so dexterous had he become in his manipulation of the press, but if the reactions of the man on the street can be put down to ignorance—and they probably can—those of the U.S. Senate cannot. Nowhere else was his wickedness so well known, yet in February, when the time came to vote on a $214,000 appropriation for his permanent subcommittee, the membership of the Senate was reduced to quivering jelly. Exactly one senator, Fulbright of Arkansas, had the courage to vote against it. Among those who did not find it possible to join Fulbright were Kennedy of Massachusetts, Johnson of Texas, Humphrey of Minnesota, Kefauver of Tennessee, Mansfield of Montana, Magnuson of Washington, Russell of Georgia, Long of Louisiana, Williams of Delaware, Kuchel of California, Douglas of Illinois, Lehman of New York, and Margaret Chase Smith of Maine. All were resolute, their characters were strong, they were enormously popular with their constituents. But they had never before encountered a prodigy like Joseph R. McCarthy.

Who believed him? Where was his strength? Who were the hard-core McCarthyites? They were Legionnaires, Minute Women, Texas millionaires, and people who felt threatened by fluoridation of public reservoirs and campaigns for mental health. They belonged to organizations like the DAR, the Sons of I Shall Return, We the Mothers Mobilize, the Nationalist Action League, and the Alert Council for America. They were anti-eggheads like Louis Bromfield, John Chamberlain, Max Eastman, James Burnham, and William F. Buckley Jr. ("McCarthyism," Buckley wrote, ". . . is a movement around which men of good will and stern morality can close ranks.") They were fugitives from lost battles against Roosevelt legislation, the alliance with western Europe, the United Nations, the communications revolution, anti-anti-Semitism, the egalitarian passion, racial equality, the great internal migration of the 1940s, and social upheavals which were destroying the lines between the classes and the sexes, and widening those between the generations. At McCarthy rallies they sang reedily, "Nobody Loves Joe but the People," and politicians were convinced that dark masses of troubled voters stood behind them. It was believed on Capitol Hill, in the winter of 1953–54, that eight men in the Senate owed their presence there to McCarthy support.

As the second year of the Eisenhower administration began, the junior senator from Wisconsin stood on an awesome pinnacle, and Roy M. Cohn was right up there with him. G. David Schine was missing. He had been drafted. His absence was thought unimportant in Washington. Schine wasn't bright, like Cohn. In fact, McCarthy had secretly found him a pain in the neck. He hadn't mentioned this to Cohn, because McCarthy needed Cohn. What he was just discovering was that Cohn needed someone, too. Cohn needed Schine.

Schine's greeting from the Army had arrived in July. Apparently the blow was unexpected; he seems to have forgotten that he had even registered. Until then he and Cohn had been busy having a lively time—adjoining rooms in the Statler from Monday to Friday, merry weekends in Manhattan, and the anticipatory pleasure of planning antic forays into stodgy bureaucratic agencies. Joe, a lazy demagogue, had left the running of the subcommittee to them. They had felt, and had seemed to be, invulnerable. If no one in the capital dared strike back at them, who would? The answer was Schine's Gloversville draft board. There was irony here. The good citizens of Gloversville were too far from the power structure to know of Schine's mighty friends. They were also safe from a political fix: the one thing Washington feared more than McCarthy was a selective service scandal.

Cohn's first thought was that his friend should be commissioned immediately. It was impossible; the Army, Navy, and Air Force in turn rejected Schine as unqualified. Cohn then summoned to his office Brigadier General Miles Reber, the Army's chief of liaison on the Hill. Later Joseph N. Welch, special Army counsel, was to question Reber about that.

WELCH: Were you actually aware of Mr. Cohn's position as counsel for this committee?

REBER: I was, Mr. Welch.

WELCH: Did that position . . . increase or diminish the interest with which you pursued the problem?

REBER: . . . I feel that it increased the interest.

WELCH: Disregarding the word "improper" influences or pressure, do you recall any instance comparable to this in which you were put under greater pressure?

REBER: . . . I recall no instance in which I was put under greater pressure.

The Pentagon hadn't taken this lightly. Indeed, to outsiders the most remarkable aspect of the Schine case was not the pressure from Cohn, but the favoritism which the military establishment had voluntarily displayed over a rich young McCarthy protégé who was, after all, only one of nearly a half-million Americans to be drafted that year. Schine's situation had been studied by the Secretary of Defense, the Secretary of the Army, two Army chiefs of staff, a vice chief of staff, the adjutant general of the Army, the commanding general of the Transportation Corps, the Air Force major general directing legislative liaison, and the judge advocate of the Navy.

At the direction of Secretary of the Army Robert T. Stevens, a New York textile manufacturer whose role in the affair would soon grow, two full colonels and a lieutenant colonel were ordered to reconsider the possibility that Schine might be officer material. Meanwhile the young applicant himself had begun to take an interest in the matter. The first time General Reber interviewed him, Schine was ready to raise his right hand and be sworn in as an officer right there. He was put out when Reber explained that there was more to it than that. As the general later testified, "he apparently felt that the business of filling out forms and going through with the processing was an unnecessary routine step."

On November 3, 1953, Schine went into uniform, and after fifteen days of temporary duty in New York ("to complete committee work") he was assigned to Company K, Fort Dix, New Jersey, for four weeks of basic training. Thanks largely to Cohn's persistence, the case remained open. Indeed, it grew even more interesting. The Army cannot be said to have been inflexible. Unlike other recruits, Schine was given a pass almost every weekend. His limousine was allowed inside the camp to pick him up and bring him back. He was released from drill for no fewer than 250 long-distance telephone calls. One rainy day, when everybody else was on the rifle range, Company K's commander found Private Schine goldbricking. Schine threw a comradely arm over the captain's shoulder and explained that he had been studying logistics "to remake the military along modern lines"—an excuse which actually was accepted. Schine's unusual ideas about how he might serve his country might, in fact, have been taken more seriously had not McCarthy, in his own talks with the Pentagon, let it be known that he did not share Cohn's unqualified enthusiasm for Schine. In a monitored call to Stevens the senator asked the secretary, as a "personal favor," not to assign

"Dave . . . back on my committee." He said that Schine was "a good boy but there is nothing indispensable about him . . . it is one of the few things I have seen Roy completely unreasonable about."

John G. Adams, counselor for the Department of the Army, was now receiving the brunt of Cohn's anger. In his phone conversations with Schine, at the camp, Cohn would learn of little ways in which his friend's life might be made easier. He would then call Adams at any hour. Once he phoned Amherst College, where Adams was speaking, in an effort to have Schine relieved from KP duty the following day. If his suggestions were rejected, he became cross. During a heated discussion in New York he ordered Adams out of his car in the middle of three lanes of traffic, at Park Avenue and Forty-sixth Street, and on January 14, 1954, when Adams told him that Schine, like 90 percent of all inductees, would probably draw overseas duty, Cohn said this would "wreck the Army" and cause Stevens to be "through as Secretary of the Army."

By now the bizarre situation was being whispered about. In mid-December Drew Pearson ran an account of the Schine story. The following week the *Baltimore Sun* carried a long piece about it, and a *New York Post* article appeared in January. At the same time, McCarthy's view of the Army was darkening. Goaded by Cohn, wrathful over the discharge of Peress, and spurred, perhaps, by his need for daily victories, he erupted at a subcommittee hearing in New York on February 18. The unlucky witness at the time was Brigadier General Ralph W. Zwicker, a hero of the Bulge and the commanding officer of Camp Kilmer in New Jersey. McCarthy told Zwicker that he was "not fit to wear that uniform," that he should "be removed from any command," and that he did not have "the brains of a five-year-old child." When word of this reached the Pentagon, Stevens, under pressure from Ridgway, told the press that McCarthy would not be given the names of officers answerable for the discharge of Peress. Stevens deplored the "humiliating treatment" and "abuse" of Zwicker. He ordered the general not to appear before the subcommittee again, and said that he would testify instead. The secretary promptly received a phone call from McCarthy. "Just go ahead and try it, Robert," the senator said menacingly. "I am going to kick the brains out of anyone who protects Communists! . . . You just go ahead . . . I will guarantee you that you will live to regret it."

This was followed on February 24 by what became celebrated as "the chicken luncheon" in Dirksen's Senate office, an attempt by senior Republicans to close the widening breach between McCarthy and the Army. Stevens found himself facing McCarthy, Dirksen, Karl Mundt and Charles Potter; Nixon was in an adjoining office. The secretary, as one reporter put it, was like a goldfish in a tankful of barracuda. Believing himself safe in the hands of these genial, sympathetic fellow Republicans, Stevens lowered his guard. All he wanted, he said, was to live and let live. Sure, he would be glad to put his name on a statement to that effect. He then did. The next thing he knew, the doors opened to admit a crowd of newspapermen. Mundt waded into them, distributing copies of the "memorandum of understanding," which was what Stevens, disarmed by the senatorial bonhomie all around him, had just signed. Now in anguish he found that in neglecting to read the fine print he had capitulated to virtually all McCarthy's demands. Among other things, the memorandum stipulated:

> There is complete agreement that the Secretary . . . will give the committee the names of everyone involved in the promotion and honorable discharge of Peress and that such individuals will be available to appear before the committee. If the committee decides to call General Zwicker . . . General Zwicker will be available.

In the Pentagon next morning officers greeted one another by waving handkerchiefs. "Private Schine," said one of them, "is the only man left in the Army with any morale." The *Times* of London commented that "Senator McCarthy achieved today what General Burgoyne and General Cornwallis never achieved—the surrender of the American Army." Herblock depicted Eisenhower whipping a white feather from a scabbard and saying to McCarthy, "Have a care, sir!" Palmer Hoyt of the *Denver Post* telegraphed Sherman Adams: FROM HERE IT LOOKS AS THOUGH STEVENS' COMPLETE CAVE-IN HAS SPATTERED MORE MUD ON THE U.S. ARMY UNIFORM THAN HAVE ALL OUR ENEMIES IN ALL OUR WARS. A story going the rounds in Washington went, "Stevens didn't mean to surrender to the senators. He just thought they wanted to look at his sword," and McCarthy, brutal in triumph, told a reporter that Stevens could not have yielded "more abjectly if he had got down on his knees."

For the next two weeks matters drifted. Republicans were huddling all over the capital. National Chairman Leonard W. Hall, having called McCarthy a "great asset" less than a month earlier, now criticized his conduct with Stevens. The President praised Zwicker at his March 3 press conference and said his administration would not stand having any official "submit to any kind of personal humiliation when testifying before congressional committees or elsewhere." Extraordinary efforts continued to be made in the hope of accommodating Joe. All that was required of him at this point was that he show the same spirit of compromise. He wouldn't do it. Instead he taunted the Pentagon, calling Peress the "sacred cow of certain Army brass" and saying that his investigation of the case had established "beyond any possibility of a doubt" that "certain individuals in the Army have been promoting, covering up, and honorably discharging known Communists."

"Just damn tommyrot," Defense Secretary Wilson replied. McCarthy was ridiculed in the Senate for the first time, by Ralph E. Flanders of Vermont: "He dons his warpaint. He goes into his war dance. He emits his warwhoops. He goes forth to battle and proudly returns with the scalp of a pink Army dentist. We may assume that this represents the depth and seriousness of the Communist penetration in the country at this time." Senator John Sherman Cooper of Kentucky congratulated Flanders, and the President wrote to him: "I was very much interested in reading the comments you made in the Senate today. I think America needs to hear from more Republican voices like yours." Attacking McCarthy still took courage, but it had begun, and the Army took heart. The senator's impact on the military had been fearful, Hanson Baldwin wrote in the *New York Times:* "Its morale is depressed; discipline and efficiency leave much to be desired." Now it was ready to go over to the counteroffensive, and the weapon it chose was the Schine affair. A strong case could be made that McCarthy and Cohn had been punishing the Army for allowing Cohn's friend to be drafted; it was probably true, and in any event it was the weakest spot in Joe's armor. On March 11 the Army leaked (through a Democrat) a chronology of the Schine case, including Cohn's threat to "wreck the Army."

Next day McCarthy countercharged that the Army had attempted to "blackmail" him into calling off his "exposure of Communists" by holding Schine as a "hostage." Plainly a full-dress congressional investigation was needed to hear both sides. The White House hoped it would be made by the Senate Armed Services Committee —McCarthy influence was relatively weak there—but the chairman, Leverett Saltonstall of Massachusetts, was up for reelection in November and wanted no part of it. A mazurka of parliamentary moves followed. The Democrats tried to have it assigned to the full Senate Committee on Government Operations; their own senators there, with Margaret Chase Smith, would outnumber McCarthy's men. The Republicans wouldn't stand for that, however, and the only solution acceptable to all parties was foolish: the conduct of McCarthy and Cohn was to be investigated by their own subcommittee. McCarthy agreed to step down as chairman; Mundt, one of his most ardent admirers, would preside. Cohn was similarly unqualified to serve as chief counsel. The task of finding a successor for him seemed insurmountable; what was needed was an able attorney who had not expressed an opinion about McCarthy. Dirksen came up with Ray Jenkins, a Knoxville, Tennessee, trial lawyer. Procedural questions followed. Dirksen protested against public hearings, but Lyndon Johnson successfully demanded televised sessions, and McCarthy won the right of cross-examination—one he had adamantly denied to witnesses when he sat in the chair.

The hearings opened in the floodlit Corinthian splendor of the Senate Caucus Room shortly after 10:30 on the morning of April 22, 1954. Everything seemed to be in order. Jenkins was at the microphone. The gavel was in Mundt's hand. McCarthy sat far to his left, at the very end of the coffin-shaped table. Nine months earlier Democratic members of the committee had begun boycotting its meetings in protest against McCarthy's tactics, but now they were back with their minority counsel, twenty-eight-year-old Robert F. Kennedy, then known chiefly for his hostility to Cohn. Mundt exchanged banalities with John McClellan of Arkansas, the ranking Democrat;* then he rapped for order. Mundt said, "Our counsel, Mr. Jenkins, will call the first witness." Jenkins opened his mouth—it was enormous—but before he could speak there was an interruption. The record reads:

> McCarthy: A point of order, Mr. Chairman; may I raise a point of order?

According to H. M. Robert's *Rules of Order*, a chairman may be interrupted on a point of order, provided that the question is one

* McClellan followed details of the privileges which had been extended to Private Schine with great interest. He had lost two of his three sons in World War II.

of propriety under the rules. McCarthy had something else in mind. His resonant voice rose.

> McCarthy: I have heard from people in the military all the way from generals with the most upstanding [*sic*] combat records down to privates recently inducted and they indicate they are very resentful of the fact that a few Pentagon politicians attempting to disrupt our investigations are naming themselves the Department of the Army. . . . The Department of the Army is not doing this. It is three civilians in the Army and they should be so named.

An impartial chairman would have gaveled McCarthy into silence the moment it became clear that, far from raising a procedural matter, he was making a speech. Mundt let him make it. Placidly he agreed to a preposterous McCarthy proposal: that judgment be withheld on whether the Secretary of the Army represented the Army. With that as an opening, McCarthy interrupted to make the same speech again. "Mr. Chairman, Mr. Chairman," he sang out in that tight whine. Mundt looked down the table and nodded, and Joe made his point again:

> McCarthy: I maintain it is a disgrace and a reflection upon every one of the million outstanding men in the Army to let a few civilians who are trying, trying to hold up an investigation of Communists labelling themselves as the Department of the Army.

McClellan quietly pointed out that the 46 countercharges against the Army had been signed for the subcommittee by "Joe McCarthy, Chairman," but Mundt ruled in favor of the Wisconsin senator. A pattern was forming. Joe would dominate the hearings as surely as though he were in the chair. Between his "points of order" and his cross-examinations, he would say everything he wanted to say. Mundt was his man, and so, it developed, was Ray Jenkins. Chosen for his supposed impartiality, the subcommittee's special counsel openly encouraged McCarthy's excesses, swearing him in and asking him to explain "just what the set-up of the Communists is." To the dismay of those who had been through this so many times before, Joe produced maps mounted on easels and a pointer. At the end of his lecture he said, "There are many people who think that we can live side by side with Communists." Eagerly Jenkins said, "What do you say about that, sir?" The answer consumed most of that afternoon. Even so, Jenkins was not done with encouraging Joe:

JENKINS: Senator McCarthy. . . . it is about closing time. . . . Now, while you have an audience of perhaps twenty or thirty million Americans . . . I want you to tell . . . what each individual American man, woman and child can do . . . to do their bit to liquidate the Communist party.

McCarthy's critics were in despair. The senator seemed invincible. Nothing, not even the U.S. Army, was a match for him. By the force of his personality he was turning each session into a McCarthy melodrama, with doctored photographs, phony FBI reports, memoranda lifted from Pentagon files by the Loyal American Underground, and savage little McCarthy homilies, such as the bit of advice he attributed to one of his childhood mentors, someone called Indian Charlie, to the effect that "if one was ever approached by another person in a not completely friendly fashion, one should start kicking at the other person as fast as possible below the belt until the other person was rendered helpless." The moment any testimony unfavorable to him began to get interesting he would rumble into the record with one of his vibrant calls for "A point of order," or "Mr. Chairman, Mr. Chairman," and then he would be off with a digression about how "sick and tired" he was of "sitting down here" and hearing all these "packs of lies." So one-sided were the hearings becoming that the Caucus Room audience, which had come to see a fight, grew restive and cheered Symington just for having the courage to talk back to Joe: "You said something about being afraid. I want you to know from the bottom of my heart that I'm not afraid of anything about you or anything you've got to say any time, any place, anywhere."

No one else around the table seemed prepared to go farther than that, and of all of them the man who appeared least likely to bell the McCarthy tiger was the Army's special counsel. Tall, portly, and birdlike, Joseph N. Welch was sixty-three, a lifelong Republican and a senior partner in the eminently respectable Boston firm of Hale and Dorr. He had undertaken this assignment for no fee. And that, said reporters, must have been why he had been chosen. Hour after hour he sat quietly with an elbow on the table, his chin in the palm of his hand or his fingers tracing the furrows on his forehead. He might have been another spectator. He let McCarthy browbeat his client, Stevens, without an objection. The few remarks he did make were almost comic in their grave courtesy. With his green bow ties, his fussy manner, and his high-pitched voice, Welch seemed more like a Dickensian solicitor than a successful American trial lawyer.

Rarely had the capital seen a man whose appearance was more deceptive. He knew the impression he conveyed and was content; at times, he had found, it was useful to be underestimated. Life on Beacon Hill and Boston Common had not prepared him for the McCarthy demimonde of bluster, intimidation and transparent lies, so Welch cocked his head and listened. His hands deep in his pockets, his toes pointed outward, he could be seen during recesses lurking on the fringes of groups, taking everything in. And when he spoke up at the hearings, as in time he did, the contrast between him and McCarthy could not have been greater. As Michael Straight put it in his *Trial by Television*, "McCarthy never forgot the vast audience. Welch seemed not to remember it. McCarthy spoke with contempt for the mob. Welch seemed to be conversing respectfully with one individual, and so he gained the audience's devotion to the end."

Bit by bit those watching Welch for this first time sensed the steel in him. He and McCarthy were the real duelists here, and their first significant encounter came on the ninth day of the hearings, when Welch cross-examined the senator over a confidential FBI letter which had found its way into McCarthy's hands. Along the way it had been retyped, an important point because under the law the retyping of a classified document amounted to publication. Joe crouched over the microphone, tense and swarthy. Under the klieg lights a roll of flesh beneath his dark eyebrows gave his upper eyelids a slanted, demonic expression. Welch let him wait awhile. The Bostonian lolled almost puckishly on an elbow, finger crooked on the purplish veins of his cheek, his brow wrinkled as though he were looking for the first time at something which was quite incredible. Now he was ready.

WELCH: Senator McCarthy, when you took the stand you knew of course that you were going to be asked about this letter, did you not?

MCCARTHY: I assumed that would be the subject.

WELCH: And you, of course, understood that you were going to be asked the source from which you got it.

MCCARTHY: . . . I won't answer that. . . .

WELCH: Have you some private reservation when you take the oath that you will tell the whole truth that lets you be the judge of what you will testify to?

McCARTHY: The answer is that there is no reservation about telling the whole truth.

WELCH: Thank you, sir. Then tell us who delivered the document to you!

McCARTHY: The answer is no. You will not get the information.

Jenkins came to the senator's rescue with the amazing opinion that McCarthy's position was justified because he was a "law enforcing officer . . . ferreting out crime," and the committee members turned to other matters. Only gradually did they and their audience realize what Welch had done. He had exposed McCarthy as an outlaw. In acknowledging his possession of the purloined letter the senator had violated a federal statute, and by refusing to answer Welch's questions he had put himself in contempt of Congress. There was something else. His defiance of the Boston attorney had been somehow familiar. Comparing impressions at the end of that session they realized why. For four years the country had watched McCarthy bully witnesses who refused to respond to his own interrogations. He had held these people up to public scorn as "Fifth Amendment Communists," reducing the Bill of Rights to an epithet. Now he was behaving in the same way.

Demagogues are conspicuously vulnerable to ridicule, but masters of derision are rare. Since the emergence of Cohn and Schine there had been speculation over whether their relationship was an unusual one, but no one could think of the right way to touch upon this very delicate subject. Welch found a way to do it. He had been honing the rapier of his wit since the hearings began, waiting to thrust it under McCarthy's bludgeon. The opportunity arose in an exchange over a cropped photograph. Cohn had given Jenkins, in proof of an obscure point, what appeared to be a picture, taken at Maguire Air Force Base, of Stevens beaming at Schine. Then the original turned up. In it Stevens was smiling at someone else, who had been cropped out to produce the fake. There was a thoughtful silence in the Caucus Room. Cohn strenuously denied knowing that this picture had been cropped. He said he didn't even know where it had come from. Welch innocently asked the witness at the time, another member of McCarthy's staff, "Do you think it came from a pixie?"

There was a rumbling at the end of the table. The bludgeon was being raised. McCarthy asked, "Will the counsel for my benefit define—I think he might be an expert on that—what a pixie is?"

Welch's rapier flashed: "Yes, I should say, Mr. Senator, that a pixie is a close relative of a fairy."

The chuckles were suppressed, but the giant had been wounded. From that moment forward McCarthy reserved his most venomous tones for Welch and searched for a way of retribution. On June 9, in the eighth week of testimony, he thought he had it. Cohn was in the chair at the time. Welch was asking him about the subcommittee's hunt for subversives among Army Signal Corps employees at Fort Monmouth in New Jersey.

WELCH: Mr. Cohn, if I told you now that we had a bad situation at Monmouth, you'd want to cure it by sundown if you could, wouldn't you?

COHN: Yes, sir.

WELCH: May I add my small voice, sir, and say whatever you know about a subversive or a Communist or a spy, please hurry! Will you remember these words?

McCarthy's voice rose, tense and vibrant.

MCCARTHY: Mr. Chairman, in view of that question—

MUNDT: Do you have a point of order?

MCCARTHY: Not exactly, Mr. Chairman, but in view of Mr. Welch's request that the information be given once we know of anyone who might be performing any work for the Communist Party, I think we should tell him that he has in his law firm a young man named Fisher . . . who has been for a number of years a member of an organization which was named, oh years and years ago, as the legal bulwark of the Communist Party. . . .

Welch looked stricken. A hush had fallen over the table. Smiling, licking his lips, his words freighted with sarcasm, McCarthy went on:

MCCARTHY: . . . Knowing that, Mr. Welch, I just felt that I had a duty to respond to your urgent request. . . . I have hesitated about bringing that up. But I have been rather bored with your phony requests to Mr. Cohn here that he personally get every Communist out of government before sundown. Therefore we will give you the information about the young man in your own organization. . . .

And he did, while Welch, obviously desolate, sat with his head in his hands, staring at the table before him. By now it was clear that something had gone wrong. Cohn, still at the microphone, was staring at the senator and shaking his head in silent entreaty. If anything, he seemed more distressed than Welch. But McCarthy went on to the end, shredding the reputation of someone whose very existence had not been a matter of public knowledge until now.

> McCarthy: . . . Whether you knew he was a member of that Communist organization or not I don't know. I assume you did not, Mr. Welch, because I get the impression that while you are quite an actor, you play for a laugh, I don't think you have any conception of the danger of the Communist Party. I don't think you would ever knowingly aid the Communist cause. I think you are unknowingly aiding it when you try to burlesque this hearing in which we are trying to bring out the facts, however.

He snickered. In that silence it was eerie. The room awaited Welch's reply. It was long in coming; once while McCarthy was still speaking the Bostonian's lips had formed the mute word "stop," but now he seemed to be groping for words. To Mundt he said, leaning forward, "Mr. Chairman, under these circumstances I must have something approaching a personal privilege." Mundt said quickly, "You may have it, sir. It will not be taken out of your time." He, too, was upset. Everyone at the table appeared to be affected, with the exception of McCarthy, who was talking loudly to one of his aides. Welch had to begin three times before he could attract the senator's attention. "I can listen with one ear," McCarthy said to him. "This time," said the Bostonian, "I want you to listen with both." McCarthy ordered the aide to bring a clipping showing that Frederick G. Fisher had belonged to the Lawyers Guild, the proscribed organization. "I think," said the senator, "that should be in the record."

> Welch: You won't need anything in the record when I have finished telling you this. Until this moment, Senator, I think I never really gauged your cruelty or your recklessness. Fred Fisher is a young man who went to the Harvard Law School and came into my firm and is starting what looks to be a brilliant career with us.

He then told the television audience what insiders at the hearings already knew. Welch's one misgiving about coming to Washington had been the possibility that because of him, someone at Hale and Dorr might be slandered. In talking to the two young assistants he had planned to bring to the capital with him he learned that one of them—Fred Fisher—had briefly belonged to the Lawyers Guild after leaving law school.* On learning more about it, he had resigned. Welch had left Fisher in Boston, and McCarthy and Cohn, who knew of him, had agreed not to mention his name. In 1954 few worse things could happen to a man than being identified over national television as a subversive. That was what McCarthy, to pay off a score, had done to Fisher. Welch now told the full story. At the end of it he turned back to the senator.

> WELCH: . . . Little did I dream you could be so reckless and so cruel as to do an injury to that lad. It is true he is still with Hale and Dorr. It is true that he will continue to be with Hale and Dorr. It is, I regret to say, equally true that I fear he shall always bear a scar needlessly inflicted by you. If it were in my power to forgive you for your reckless cruelty I would do so. I like to think that I am a gentle man, but your forgiveness will have to come from someone other than me.

McCarthy afterward told a friend that as Welch spoke he could feel knots in his stomach. It wasn't contrition. He was probably incapable of that. What he grasped was that he had stumbled badly, that Welch had outwitted him again. Trying desperately to regain his footing, he growled that Welch had no right to mention cruelty because he had "been baiting Mr. Cohn here for hours."

> WELCH: Senator, may we not drop this? We know he belonged to the Lawyers Guild, and Mr. Cohn nods his head at me.

Cohn, in evident agony, was indeed nodding at Welch. He was also biting his lips and trembling visibly.† He had crushed too many witnesses himself not to see what Welch was doing to McCarthy. To Cohn Welch said: "I did you, I think, no personal injury, Mr. Cohn."

> COHN: No, sir.
>
> WELCH: I meant to do you no personal injury and if I did I beg your pardon.

* The other was James D. St. Clair, who became counsel to President Nixon during the House of Representatives impeachment inquiry twenty years later.

† Writing in the February, 1968, *Esquire*, Cohn revealed that McCarthy had consented not to bring up Fisher if Welch promised not to explore Cohn's lack of a military record. Welch had kept his word. Thus Cohn had reason to be concerned over his leader's violation of the agreement.

Again Cohn nodded. Again McCarthy tried to shape a reply, and again Welch turned him away.

> WELCH: . . . Let us not assassinate this lad further, Senator. You have done enough. Have you no sense of decency, sir, at long last? Have you no sense of decency?

The senator stared into his lap, looked up, and tried one more time. He tried to ask Welch if it was not true that Fisher had been his assistant. This time the Bostonian silenced him with superb disdain.

> WELCH: Mr. McCarthy, I will not discuss this with you further. You have sat within six feet of me and could have asked me about Fred Fisher. You have brought it out. If there is a God in heaven it will do neither you nor your cause any good. I will not discuss it further. I will not ask Mr. Cohn any more questions. You, Mr. Chairman, may, if you will, call the next witness.

But there would be no more testimony that day. The audience was struggling to its feet, cheering Welch. Even Mundt was with them. He put down his gavel, and six policemen, who had been told at the opening of each session to eject anyone who applauded, stood impassive. McCarthy's face was grim; he was breathing hard. Welch moved toward the door, and a woman there touched his arm and then began to cry. As he stepped into the hall the press corps surged after him. Suddenly everyone broke for the door. It was as though someone had yelled, "Fire!" They couldn't wait to get out, and presently McCarthy, who had not left his chair, was left with the guards and the television technicians. He looked around, stretching his neck, trying to catch someone's eye. At first no one would look at him, then one man did. The senator turned his palms up and spread his hands. He asked, "What did I do?"

After thirty-six days of testimony the Army-McCarthy hearings ended on June 17. The subcommittee then studied the 7,400 printed pages of testimony and issued a report blaming both sides. At first the extent of the damage done to McCarthy was unknown. He had been exposed before and had recovered quickly each time. His physical stamina was unimpaired, he retained the loyalty of eight to ten key senators, his influence with the Republican legislative leadership continued to be great, and with his customary vigor he announced new investigations of Communists in the Army, the defense industry, and the CIA.

All died stillborn. New voices were being heard in the land on the subject of McCarthy, and old voices spoke in different tones. From Nebraska, Republican leader Jim Schramm wrote Sherman Adams that every member of the Republican State Central Committee felt that GOP candidates had been hurt by the "public spectacle" of the hearings. In Colorado Palmer Hoyt said, "It is now time for the Republican party to repudiate Joe McCarthy before he drags them down to defeat," and in Ohio conservative Republican congressman George Bender, campaigning for Taft's Senate seat, declared that "McCarthyism has become a synonym for witch-hunting, star-chamber methods, and the denial of those civil liberties which have distinguished our country in its historic growth." Cohn, it was generally agreed, had been discredited. With every subcommittee member except McCarthy against him, he resigned July 19. ("A great victory for the Communists," Joe said bitterly.) Since the first open rupture between the senator and the Army, at the beginning of the year, poll takers had been observing a vast change in the public's view of McCarthy. By late August some 22 percent of the adult population had revised their opinion of him downward. Over 24 million Americans now looked upon him with disfavor.

Ralph Flanders didn't wait until all the evidence was in. Two days after McCarthy's disastrous attack on Fisher, the Vermont Republican introduced a resolution calling on the Senate to strip its junior member from Wisconsin of his chairmanships. McCarthy said, "I think they should get a net and take him to a good quiet place." The measure was given little chance then. Knowland denounced it next day at a hurriedly called press conference, and southern Democrats let it be known that they were wary of a precedent which might threaten the seniority system. Debate opened on Friday, June 30. That evening Flanders, shifting tactics, substituted a simple motion of censure: "Resolved, That the conduct of the Senator from Wisconsin, Mr. McCarthy, is contrary to senatorial traditions, and tends to bring the Senate into disrepute, and such conduct is hereby condemned." Knowland proposed that it be referred to a select committee of three Republicans and three Democrats. That seemed safe. The members, chosen by Knowland and Lyndon Johnson, were all conservatives. Their chairman was Utah Republican Arthur V. Watkins. The McCarthy men felt they had won.

They misjudged Watkins. Determined to avoid another carnival, the chairman banned television from the new hearings and laid down strict ground rules. Even smoking was forbidden. Either Joe or his attorney would be allowed to cross-examine witnesses, but not both. Since McCarthy was a poor courtroom lawyer, this meant that he had to yield the center of the stage. At the first session he tested Watkins with cries of "Mr. Chairman, Mr. Chairman." The chairman's gavel came down like an executioner's ax. He said crisply, "The Senator is out of order. . . . We are not going to be interrupted by those diversions and sidelines. We are going straight down the line." McCarthy bolted into the corridor, where the television crews were waiting, and spluttered into a microphone, "I think this is the most unheard of thing I ever heard of." Unimpressed, the select committee reported out the Flanders resolution with the recommendation that McCarthy be censured, and the full Senate agreed 67 to 22—this in a chamber which had produced exactly one anti-McCarthy vote, Fulbright's, the previous January.

Vice President Nixon, exercising his prerogative as presiding officer of the Senate to alter the title of a measure, struck out the word "censure," changing it to "Resolution relating to the conduct of the Senator from Wisconsin, Mr. McCarthy." He was trying to help Joe, and McCarthy's admirers sought semantic solace in that. McCarthy himself was undeceived. "Well," he told reporters, "it wasn't exactly a vote of confidence." He said, "I'm glad to have this circus ended so I can get back to the real work of digging out Communism, crime, and corruption." In the White House Eisenhower greeted his cabinet with a slow grin. "Have you heard the latest?" he asked. "McCarthyism is McCarthywasm."

So it was. Missing the stimulus of Cohn, Joe became listless, flabby, and easily depressed. His devoted followers had formed a Committee of Ten Million Americans Mobilizing for Justice, with a retired rear admiral as "chief of staff," to protest the censure; they delivered to the Capitol, in an armored truck, a petition bearing 1,000,816 signatures. In New York thirteen thousand attended a "Who Promoted Peress?" rally. Its sponsors included Governor Bracken Lee of Utah, Alvin M. Owsley of the American Legion, Mrs. Grace Brosseau of the DAR, a former governor of New Jersey, and a former ambassador to Russia. A high school band played "On, Wisconsin." A rock singer intoned that he would "shake, rattle, and roll" for their leader, and Cohn told the crowd that "Joe Mc-

Carthy and I would rather have American people of this type than all the politicians in the world." But Joe himself wasn't there. He had hurt his arm shaking hands with a voter. In what some saw as a symbolic act, the other man had inadvertently shoved Joe's elbow through a glass table top. The senator went into Bethesda Naval Hospital and emerged with a sling.

McCarthy's successor as chief Republican campaigner was Richard Nixon. The Democrats said they couldn't see much difference. Nixon charged that their party was "bending to the Red wind." When Adlai Stevenson observed that the American economy appeared to be in the doldrums, Nixon accused him of "spreading pro-Communist propaganda." If the Democrats endorsed by Stevenson were elected, he said, "the security risks which have been fired by the Eisenhower administration will all be hired back," and he urged patriotic Democrats to "put their party in their pocket and vote for an Eisenhower Congress" because "we recognize the Communist menace and this administration is determined to crush that menace." The Communist party, he warned, was battling "desperately and openly" against Republicans because "the candidates running on the Democratic ticket are, almost without exception, members of the Democratic party's left-wing clique which has been so blind to the Communist conspiracy and has tolerated it in the United States."

"By golly," said Eisenhower, "sometimes you sure get tired of all this clackety-clack." Nixon was weary of it, too; "I'm tired, bone tired, my heart's not in it," he told a friend. Barnstorming the country seemed particularly fatiguing this time, but the President's decision not to campaign actively left Nixon as the party's highest-ranking politician, and he believed that much was at stake. "The election of a Democratic Eighty-fourth Congress in November," he told the Ohio Republican state convention in Columbus, "will mean the beginning of the end of the Republican party. It is that simple." To stave it off he delivered 204 speeches, held over a hundred press conferences, flew 26,000 miles, and visited 95 cities in 31 states. By the end of it he had become the country's second most controversial figure. "McCarthyism in a white collar," said Stevenson of his tactics. Walter Lippmann went further. He described the Vice President as a "ruthless partisan" who "does not have within his conscience those scruples which the country has a right to expect in the President of the United States."

It was characteristic of the 1950s that even Eisenhower's adversaries were anxious to believe the best of him, and he was not held responsible for Nixon's speeches. How he could have avoided knowing about them was unexplained. The *Herald Tribune,* whose most loyal subscriber he was, played them on its front page. Somehow it was felt, as James Reston wrote, that the President would never imply that the Democrats had winked at treason, "but things are done in his name he knows not of." To be sure, Nixon's style was not Eisenhower's style. Ike wanted to be regarded, he said, as "President of all the people," and invective wasn't his forte anyway. Nevertheless, he wanted the candidates of his party to win, believed Nixon was helping them, and cheered him accordingly.

Both men had hoped that Republicans could stow campaign rhetoric and run on the administration's record. "The time, the right time to start winning the 1954 elections is *now,*" Nixon had told the cabinet in April 1953. Eisenhower believed that his 1954 legislative accomplishments were worth boasting about. It had been a good session, despite the sideshow in the Senate Caucus Room. He had signed into law bills extending the federal housing program and reciprocal trade agreements, liberalizing the Atomic Energy Act, broadening unemployment insurance and social security, simplifying customs procedures, establishing a new farm program, authorizing two billion dollars for federal highways, and providing more than a billion dollars in tax relief. He calculated that his "batting average" had been .830 and was delighted. The *Congressional Quarterly,* figuring differently, put it at .646; even so, he had done well, and Democratic predictions that a Republican administration would bring back the Depression—as irresponsible, in their way, as Nixon's Red issue—had been exposed as myth.

But the twenty-year trend toward Democratic voter registrations had given the party out of power the same advantage that the Republicans once had. All other things being equal, the man in the middle tended to favor the Democrats. Eisenhower and Nixon were also fighting history; the party in power has nearly always lost strength in off-year elections. Furthermore, postwar prosperity had paused to catch its breath. There were no breadlines in 1954, but farm prices had taken a downward lurch, and the recession had given some employers the jitters.

In view of the hurdles ahead, party councils had decided that a Republican hatchet man was needed. The Vice President had been chosen because he handled hatchets well, because using this one would endear him to the rank and file of his party, and because, as Eisenhower pointed out, it would add to his fame. Nixon was game —"Every campaign has to have someone out front slugging," he said —but he was also unenthusiastic. It wasn't pleasant to return to Whittier as commencement speaker, which he did in the spring of 1954, to find that two reception lines had been set up, one for students who didn't want to shake his hand. His wife liked strife even less than he did, and in mid-February, after a long talk, they had discussed the possibility of his retirement from public life when his present term ended in 1956. According to Murray Chotiner, Nixon weighed the relative merits of opening his own law practice and joining an established firm while flying back to Washington on election eve. As the plane entered its glide pattern he handed Chotiner seven pages of notes. "Here's my last campaign speech," he said. "You may want it as a souvenir, I'm through with politics."

The results of the election were perplexing. The Democrats did regain control of Congress, whereupon Nixon had to admit that the survival of Republicanism hadn't been at stake after all. McCarthy called it "a bad defeat" and held the administration responsible for waging "jungle warfare among those of us who were trying to expose and root out Communists." But it wasn't bad at all. The Republican edge in the 83rd Congress had been so slight that realists had conceded its loss in advance. After the dust had cleared the Democrats had recaptured twenty House seats—they had expected fifty —and in the Senate they had won just two. "The administration," the *Washington Post and Times-Herald* concluded two days later, "has experienced neither victory nor overwhelming defeat at the polls."

Nixon interpreted the returns for the cabinet that same day. What they showed, he said, was "really a dead heat." He thought he knew a way to improve performance. The key to future campaigns, he said, was a good public relations program. The American people had to be "sold." The party with the best image would win elections; the secret to control of 1600 Pennsylvania Avenue would lie not on Main Street or Wall Street, but on Madison Avenue. Parties would invest in catchy jingles, not pretentious campaign songs. How a candidate looked on the television screen would be as important as what he had to say. It would all be one big package, Nixon told them, and he offered to show them the gist of it. Reaching into his pocket he drew out a mechanical toy drummer, wound it up, and sent it clattering down the polished table past the astonished President and his secretaries. The Vice President said, "Just keep beating that goddamned drum."

The most memorable singing commercial of that year, as evocative of the Army-McCarthy hearings as Joe's sonorous "Mr. Chairman, Mr. Chairman," went:

When the values go up, up, up,
And the prices go down, down, down,
Robert Hall this season
Will show you the reason,
*Low overhead, low overhead!**

Robert Hall, clothier, was a precursor of the discount houses which had begun to rise, like vast gymnasiums, on the outskirts of metropolitan areas and in suburban shopping centers. The first of them, E. J. Korvette, had opened its doors in 1948. It had been an instant success. In the past, discounting had been largely confined to shabby little factory annexes, difficult to find and seldom clean. Labels had been removed from wares; the wholesaler didn't want the retailer to know that he was competing with him. Now an entirely new approach to merchandising was emerging. Businessmen had begun to grasp the implications of America's automotive economy. In the 1930s and 1940s, when the greater part of customers had arrived on buses and streetcars, downtown streets lined with retail stores had made sense. But now public transportation had begun to atrophy. The typical urban shopper of the 1950s came in a car and had no place to put it. Downtown parking had become almost impossible. Millions of meters were being installed, but the results were disappointing; as often as not a Main Street merchant, blind to his own interests, would allow his clerks to occupy the spaces in front of his store and feed the meters every hour while potential customers cruised up and down.

Shopping centers were the obvious solution. Planners provided them with ample parking facilities, great tracts paved with ma-

* Copyright 1946, 1954, 1963, and 1972 by Robert Hall Clothes, Inc. Reprinted by permission.

cadam. Nationwide firms began erecting discount wonderlands: Korvette's, Topp's, Bradlee's, Grant's, King's, etc. By selling directly to the consumer there, manufacturers avoided the retailers' overheads. Those Main Street merchants who could afford suburban annexes built them. The rest joined a long, slow decline into what sociologists began to call "inner-city blight."

Meantime the discount marts were acquiring problems of their own. Shoplifting grew to epidemic proportions, encouraged by the discounters' practice of substituting checkout counters for aisle clerks. After hours, shopping center parking areas were often inhabited by restless teen-agers. Mobile like their parents, they needed a place to rendezvous. Unfortunately, police discovered, the paved expanses became staging areas for gang fights and drag racing.

Fueled by affluence, the teen subculture continued to develop its separate identity in the 1950s, with its own customs, status symbols, stigmata, rites, and fads—the ducktail haircuts and sleeves rolled up to a prescribed length for boys, and, for girls, poodle cuts and pop-it necklaces that could be changed from chokers to waist-length. Long hair and peculiar modes of dress lay a decade away, but the new language which would go with them was already developing. Like the bop musicians they admired, teen-agers frequently used the term cool, though for them the emphasis was different; it meant pretty much what keen, neat, swell, snazzy, or smooth had meant twenty years earlier. "Like" had become an all-purpose pauseword and modifier.

Scram had been replaced by blast-off, and a drip was now a drag. The draggiest were variously described as spastics, turkeys, nerds, yo-yos, or—the most popular of all pejoratives—square. A teen-ager would say, "She's a —," switching to mimicry and drawing a square in the air with his index finger. It was considered tactful, if the square was present, to refer to her obscurely as an "L7" (because the letter and the numeral could form a crude square). The ultimate in squares was the cube. Wits would say that he was so square he could block his own hat. That might elicit a grudging laugh, but as a rule joking with teen-agers of that period was a risky business; they would often riposte with a withering "Hardeeharhar."

Every adolescent familiar with the facts of life, as they were still called, knew that a drive-in movie was a passion pit. Admittance to these arenas of foreplay was restricted, of course, to those with automobiles (wheels), but almost every boy in the great middle class either had wheels or knew someone who could get them; the Allstate Insurance Company found that nationally 75 percent of all high school juniors had driver's licenses and nearly 60 percent had access to the family car for "social purposes." The auto was so fundamental a part of the subculture that teen-age argot was often almost indistinguishable from hot-rod slang (also called jive), though subtle distinctions could be detected. To a pure hot-rodder, drag, for instance, had nothing to do with social acceptability; it was a race, from a standing start, between motor vehicles powered by souped-up engines. The hot-rod itself was also known as a hack, a stormer, a bomb, a screamer, or a draggin' wagon. Substantial alterations, a sure way to acquire greater prestige within the peer group, were chopping (lowering the roof) and raking (lowering the front end). Tires were skins; whitewalls, snowballs. Driving around for the sheer joy of the trip was bombing or spooking.

That was for lovers of speed, which did not then mean amphetamines. The vast majority of adolescents were much more interested in exploring sexual diplomacy. Unless he had been grounded—enjoined from the use of the family car—a young male who had taken his date to the passion pit would attempt to make out (the equivalent of the long-gone pitching woo) under cover of darkness. The eternal scourge of seducers and the most common of all female complaints was still known almost universally as the curse, or the monthly, though girls' boarding schools in New England clung to the more proper, and more engaging, "off the sports list." This could be frustrating for the fledgling roué, unless the date was a blind one and had been revealed to him, during a moment under a strong light, as a dog, or a beast. Of course, the girl also had discriminatory rights. If she reached the conclusion that her escort was a drag, she might incinerate him with "DDT" (drop dead twice). That was the ultimate insult. His position would then be extremely uncomfortable, or, to use his word for it, hairy.

Teen-agers and their younger brothers and sisters were emerging as a major target group for national advertisers. They not only had their fashions; increasingly they had a voice in what their parents bought. David Riesman observed: "One must listen to quite young children discussing television models, automobile styling, or the merits of various streamliners to see how gifted they are as consumers . . . their influence in family councils must not be underestimated." Eugene Gilbert, who was then establishing a consulting firm to advise businessmen on marketing policies for young customers, told his clients:

> An advertiser who touches a responsive chord in youth can generally count on the parent to finally succumb to purchasing the product. . . . It is not to be denied that a parent subjected to requests from the youngster who thinks he is in dire need of an item, witnessed on television, may find it easier to "give in" rather than dispute rationally with a highly emotionalized child.

A survey found that 94 percent of the mothers interviewed said that their children had asked them to buy goods they had seen on television. Testers of small children discovered that they could recognize the word "detergent" before they could even read. Exposed to TV while still in their playpens and then put in front of the tube to keep them quiet, they looked upon the world of goods with a sophisticated awareness new to their generation. *American Girl,* the magazine of the Girl Scouts, noted that their subscribers "use their first lipstick, wear their first nylons and first bra sooner than girls ten years ago." Brassiere styles for twelve-year-olds were named Allowance, Freshman, Little Angel and Littlest Angel—"the bra that expands as a girl develops." Bernice Fitz-Gibbon, merchandising consultant for *Seventeen* magazine, told advertisers attending a "fashion clinic" that "Your fashion department is the wooing chamber. Get the teen-age fly to come into your parlor and little by little the web will be spun. Then when the girl marries you haven't lost a customer. You've gained a goldmine." Miss Fitz-Gibbon advised her audience to lure "the teen tycoons, not in the sweet by-and-by, but in the much sweeter now-and-now." She described young girls as "women of means."

Often they were women of very substantial means. *Teen Times,* the magazine of the Future Homemakers of America, put weekly spending by seventh-graders at 30 cents to $8.50 and by high school seniors at $1.65 to $19.50, but in some cases it was much more. In a pictorial essay *Life* described the expenditures of a suburban seventeen-year-old girl who was given $4,000 each year. Among her budget items were $1,300 for bedroom decorations, $1,500 for clothes (including seven bathing suits), and $500 for entertainment, not counting "a jaunt to Hawaii for having survived high school." *Life* noted that "more and more teen-agers will be moving into Suzie's bracket." It ended on what was meant to be a cheerful note:

"Her parents' constant indulgence has not spoiled Suzie. She takes for granted all the luxuries that surround her because she has had them all her life."

National statistics on this emerging leisure class of youth were awesome. As the flood of war and postwar babies approached puberty the new market expanded until there were between eighteen and twenty million of the new consumers in the country. Their annual purchases rose to 10 billion dollars, then to 25 billion. Gilbert reported that girls between fourteen and seventeen were spending 773 million dollars on "back to school" outfits alone. In one year of the 1950s, *Teen Times* found, the average American adolescent spent $555 "for goods and services, not including the necessities normally supplied by their families."

Entire industries retooled to accommodate the young. The phonograph record business offered them two lines, "singles" (45 rpm) for subteens and "albums" (33⅓ rpm) for the teen-age market. Together they bought 43 percent of all records sold in the United States. Adolescent purchases accounted for 53 percent of movie admissions, 44 percent of camera sales, 39 percent of new radios bought, and 9 percent of new automobile sales. Each year the fifteen-to-nineteen group was spending 20 million dollars on lipstick, 25 million on deodorants, and 9 million on home permanents. The total spent annually on toiletries by teen-agers of both sexes was almost a third of a billion dollars.

Some parents raised in the austere 1930s were becoming accustomed to such phenomena as a twelve-year-old daughter's weekly trip to the hairdresser, or a fourteen-year-old son engrossed in a brochure on retirement insurance written for his age bracket. In certain places the younger generation had its own credit accounts, with such enticing names as the 14 to 21 Club, the Campus Deb Account, and the Starlet Charge Account. They might order merchandise over Princess phones in their own rooms, or exchange Going Steady rings ($12.95, "nothing down, payments of 50 cents a week") with boyfriends or girlfriends. In California one firm built a $2,500,000 teen-age shopping center, with six stores, a milk bar, a swimming pool, an ice-skating rink, and a bank.

On the evening of December 15, 1954, Walt Disney touched off a children's craze that showed the whole country how very young consumers could be successfully wooed. *Disneyland* was then the high point of Wednesday TV for 40 million viewers, most of them youngsters and their parents, and that week's program was the first in a series on Davy Crockett. As played by twenty-nine-year-old Fess Parker, a hitherto unknown actor, Davy was a hero of irresistible charm. Mesmerized by his folksiness, tiny America was easy prey for hawkers of Crockett pseudomemorabilia. By the following spring every playground and supermarket seemed to be populated by five-year-olds wearing coonskin caps. The price of coonskins jumped to $8 a pound. Before the boom ended the following summer 100 million dollars' worth of coons had been marketed, not to mention Davy Crockett sweat shirts, sleds, blankets, snowsuits, toothbrushes, school lunch boxes, swing sets, playhouses, sandboxes, stools, toy guns, and bicycles. An entrepreneur overstocked with 200,000 pup tents stenciled "Davy Crockett" on them and sold them all in two days. Some adults were pushed past endurance; a department store buyer said, "The next person who says Davy Crockett to me gets a Davy Crockett flintlock over his head," and it was a rare mother who didn't want to stop her ears after the thousandth rendering of Fess Parker's "Ballad of Davy Crockett," which sold four million copies during his six-month hegemony:

Born on a mountain top in Tennessee,
Greenest state in the Land of the Free,
Raised in the woods so's he knew ev'ry tree,
Kilt him a b'ar when he was only three.

Davy, Davy Crockett,
King of the wild frontier!

Fred M. Hechinger of the *New York Herald Tribune* feared that a "passion for possession" might be putting a spiritual blight on youth. In that regard two forms of entertainment introduced in 1954 were troubling. The new music of Bill Haley and the Comets, billed as "the first R 'n' R Pop Smash," gave rise to fears that the children of the new prosperity, like those of the Twenties, might be seduced into a mindless hedonism. To this Stanley Kramer's *The Wild One* added a prophecy of savage violence. Marlon Brando played the title character, Johnny, the apelike "president" of a scruffy motorcycle club whose members wore skin-tight jeans and black leather jackets with a skull and crossbones painted on the back. In the film Brando's gang rides into a quiet town on a lazy Saturday afternoon and, for want of anything else to do, takes the place apart. Obviously the movie was an indictment, but of what? Youth? Permissiveness? Disrespect for law and order? Most critics wrote that Kramer was showing a seamy side of postwar opulence, of crass acquisitiveness run amuck. Some, repelled by the movie's brutality—in that gentler time it *was* rough—suggested that such censure might be carried too far.

One small group of youthful Bohemians thought that no indictment of materialism could be strong enough. To them affluence was an outrage. They had grappled with it and lost. Now they conceded that they were beaten, or, more succinctly, beat. The beat generation first surfaced in the early 1950s amid the peeling billboards and crumbling stucco of Los Angeles's seedy Venice West. Nurtured in dimly lit coffeehouses there, the movement then leaped 350 miles north and found a Mecca at 261 Columbus Avenue in San Francisco, soon to be famous throughout the movement as the City Lights Bookshop. The store's colorful co-owner was Lawrence Ferlinghetti, a bearded native of Paris who had served in the Navy, worked at *Time* as a mail boy, and taken degrees at Columbia and the Sorbonne. In 1953 he and Peter D. Martin founded their emporium as the first all-paperback bookstore in the United States. Ferlinghetti took the name from the Chaplin film. Expanding, he established City Lights Books, a publishing house. The first poet on its list was himself. The title of one of Ferlinghetti's poems, "Tentative Description of a Dinner to Promote the Impeachment of President Eisenhower," gives some idea of how far he was from the typical merchant of the 1950s.

The City Lights Bookshop served as an address for certain authors who had no fixed address of their own. They were unusual, even in their profession. Gregory Corso had been captured in 1946 for trying to seize New York City by carrying out a series of elaborate robberies with his friends; when arrested, Corso was attempting to coordinate the attempt with a walkie-talkie. After three years in prison he educated himself in Harvard's Widener Library and wrote such poems as "Marriage," in which he advised a young man planning an evening with his fiancée:

Don't take her to movies but to cemeteries tell all about
werewolf bathtubs and forked clarinets then desire her
and kiss her and all the preliminaries and she going just
so far and I understanding why not getting angry saying
You must feel! It's beautiful to feel!

The ages of beat writers put them in the swing generation, though they had now opted out of it. As social prophets they advocated spontaneous expression, travel, Oriental mysticism, singing folk ballads, playing the guitar, the blues, sex in all its forms, and their version of the American dream. Some of them became celebrities. The most famous was a husky French-Canadian who had played football at Columbia, served as a merchant seaman during World War II, and taught at the New School for Social Research in the late 1940s. Born Jean-Louis Kerouac, he changed his first name to Jack for his first book, *The Town and the City,* in 1950. Kerouac rebuked commentators who called him and other new renaissance authors negative. He insisted that they were in fact passionately affirmative. On television Ben Hecht asked him why he didn't write more about "what's wrong with this country." Kerouac wrote afterward:

> . . . all he wanted me to do was speak out my mind AGAINST people, he sneeringly brought up Dulles, Eisenhower, the Pope, all kinds of people like that . . . No, I want to speak FOR things, for the crucifix I speak out, for the Star of Israel I speak out . . . for sweet Mohammed I speak out, for Lao-tse and Chuang-tse I speak out, for D. T. Suzuki I speak out . . . why should I attack what I love out of life. This is Beat. Live your lives out? Naw, LOVE your lives out. When they come and stone you at least you won't have a glass house, just your glassy flesh.

His *On the Road* was written in three weeks. Truman Capote said of it, "It isn't writing at all—it's typing." Yet it told people something they wanted to hear; they bought 500,000 copies. *On the Road's* wenching episodes were dull, the visions of the characters were puerile, and for all their expeditions back and forth across the country they never seemed to get anywhere or find anything, not even themselves. But perhaps that was the point. At least Kerouac's people were looking; they refused to be encapsulated by things they owned. The Beats were honest men offended by the sterile myths of their decade. Allen Ginsberg, a more powerful writer than Kerouac, was devastating on the cold war:

> *America you don't really want to go to war.*
> *America it's them bad Russians.*
> *Them Russians them Russians and them Chinamen. And them Russians.*

The Russia wants to eat us alive. The Russia's power mad.
She wants to take our cars from out our garages.
Her wants to grab Chicago. Her needs a Red Reader's Digest. Her wants our auto plants in Siberia. Him big bureaucracy running our fillingstations.
That no good. Ugh. Him make Indians learn read. Him need big black niggers. Hah. Her make us all work sixteen hours a day. Help.
America this is quite serious.
America this is the impression I get from looking in the television set.
America is this correct?
I'd better get right down to the job.
It's true I don't want to join the Army or turn lathes in precision parts factories, I'm nearsighted and psychopathic anyway.
America I'm putting my queer shoulder to the wheel.

Ginsberg wasn't really demented, but a year of psychotherapy had changed his life. That was in 1954 and early 1955. It ended his career as a fledgling market research consultant. Coming off the couch he turned out "Howl" in a nonstop frenzy. San Francisco policemen confiscated it as obscene, but a judge found "redeeming social importance" in the long poem, and Ginsberg joined Kerouac, Corso, Ferlinghetti, and other stars in the beat firmament.

No sooner had they arrived than prim admirers tried to sanitize them. Entranced English teachers averted their eyes from Ginsberg's homosexuality and Kerouac's amorality. Beat, they said, was short for "beatitude"; these poets were blessed. The beats were understandably nettled. Whatever the intrinsic value of their work, and it is probably slight, they did succeed in their social purpose of raising doubts about thoughtless conformity. Denying them would have turned them into literary eunuchs. But there was little chance of the attempt succeeding; the continuing uproar over them assured that.

Twenty years later the only odd aspect of their movement would be that it had been so controversial. It was never revolutionary. Its poets were yea-sayers and minstrels, not challengers of the social order. They broke no windows, planted no bombs, profaned no faiths, and were no threat to the establishment—a word which, in its later sense, did not then exist in the American language. Kenneth Rexroth, at fifty their senior citizen, did declaim sardonically, "I write poetry to seduce women and overthrow the capitalist system." In reality, however, Rexroth was married, the father of two children, the proud holder of several literary awards, and, as a former popcorn salesman, something of an entrepreneur. So, in fact, was Kerouac; in *The Subterraneans* he ingenuously describes the hero's disappointment and frustration when he learns that another beat writer has received a larger publisher's advance than his own. Elsewhere Kerouac said, "We love everything—Billy Graham, the Big Ten, Rock and Roll, Zen, apple pie, Eisenhower—we dig it all." They didn't, of course, and he didn't expect to be taken seriously, but the beats were incapable of militance. The thought of them marching on the Pentagon or stoning National Guardsmen is ludicrous. They would have been startled by anyone who called policemen pigs, and the closest any of them came to a demonstration was Ginsberg wearing a sandwich board that said SMOKE POT.

But that was enough to affront convention then. Smoking marijuana was believed to be wicked beyond imagining. In addition, beats were known to use foul language, sometimes in public. It was an intolerant time. Exotic life-styles were suspect. The mere fact that members of the movement said they were different put them beyond the pale. "Beatnik" was coined as a term of opprobrium. Male beatniks wore khaki trousers, sandals, and beards. (Their hair, however, was short.) The movement's females could be distinguished by their tousled hair and black leotards. Though they scorned lipstick, they put so much make-up around their eyes that they were sometimes called "raccoons." Beatniks were said to live in what they called "pads," surrounded by unwholesome books and records. They didn't pick up after themselves. The beds were unmade—did not, in fact, have proper bedclothes. Reportedly they slept naked on bare mattresses and did disgraceful things in the dark, even when they weren't married. Some had actually advocated bearing children out of wedlock.

Eisenhower's America was horrified. Fathers told daughters that they could not date beatniks. Ronald Reagan told jokes about football players in sandals. Slick magazine writers described beatnik debauchery. Commuters exchanged stories about beatnik orgies. Hollywood cranked out morality tales with beatnik villains. Even Helen Trent acquired a beatnik character. In Middletown, Connecticut, teen-agers in a convertible tried to run down a bearded man on a bicycle because they thought that such a defier of conventions must be beat. And at the bottom of all this commotion was nothing more sinister than a few romantic poets who recoiled from the prevailing life-style. They were individualists, and in that sense their claim to be the real Americans was valid. They asked only to secede from the majority, and they expounded nothing more than the eternal bohemia, as in this passage from *On the Road:*

> . . . they danced down the street like dingledodies, and I shambled after as I've been doing all my life after people who interest me, because the only people for me are the mad ones, the ones who are mad to live, mad to talk, mad to be saved, desirous of everything at the same time, the ones who never yawn or say a commonplace thing, but burn, burn, burn like fabulous yellow roman candles exploding like spiders across the stars and in the middle you see the blue centerlight pop and everybody goes "Awww!"

That was what passed for nonconformity then. The alarm next time would be triggered by the real thing.

Montage: The Mid-Fifties

DAISY: You the policeman?
JOE: Yes ma'am (Shows ID) My name's Friday. . . .
This is Frank Smith.
FRANK: Hello.

not a recession, said the White House, but a "rolling readjustment"

Best actress of 1955: Anna Magnani in The Rose Tattoo

The Man With the Golden Arm   Bad Day at Black Rock   East of Eden
Mister Roberts   Diabolique   The Desperate Hours

"*Sincerity*," said Vice President Nixon, "*is the quality that comes through on television.*"

And here is the best part
You have a head start
If you are among
The very young
At heart

She's the sweetest little rosebud that Texas ever knew
Her eyes are bright as diamonds, they sparkle like the dew
You may talk about your Clementine and sing of Rosalee
But the yellow rose of Texas is the only girl for me

AFL, CIO TO MERGE

Better dead than Red

See the U.S.A. in your Chevrolet

According to Nancy Mitford, "England" is U and "Britain" non-U, and "dentures" is non-U for false teeth.

"A Classic"
— Brooks Atkinson
New York Times
KURT WEILL'S
THE THREE-PENNY OPERA
English adaptation of book and lyrics by
MARC BLITZSTEIN
Original text by
BERT BRECHT
THEATRE DE LYS
121 Christopher Street
WAtkins 4-8782

MARTY (in a low, intense voice): *You don't like her. My mother don't like her. She's a dog, and I'm a fat, ugly little man. All I know is I had a good time last night. I'm gonna have a good time tonight. If we have enough good times together, I'm going down on my knees and beg that girl to marry me.*

McCALL'S
The magazine of Togetherness

When it seems that everything is lost
I will smile and never count the cost
If you love me, really love me,
Let it happen, darlin', I won't care

EINSTEIN DEAD

BEST SELLERS: Nonfiction
Gift from the Sea by Anne Morrow Lindbergh
Life Is Worth Living by Fulton J. Sheen
MacArthur 1941-1951 by Major General Charles A. Willoughby and John Chamberlain
Call to Greatness by Adlai E. Stevenson
The Scrolls from the Dead Sea by Edmund Wilson

Best actor of 1954: Marlon Brando in On the Waterfront
Best actress of 1954: Grace Kelly in The Country Girl

BEST SELLERS: Fiction
Not As a Stranger by Morton Thompson
Marjorie Morningstar by Herman Wouk
Andersonville by Mackinlay Kantor
The Man in the Gray Flannel Suit by Sloan Wilson
Something of Value by Robert Ruark

"In the opinion of the Joint Chiefs, MacArthur's strategy would involve us in the wrong war, at the wrong place, at the wrong time and with the wrong enemy."

Seven Brides for Seven Brothers   Three Coins in the Fountain
Twenty Thousand Leagues Under the Sea   Dial M for Murder
Executive Suite   Rear Window   Mr. Hulot's Holiday

two doctors working together, Gregory Pincus of the Worcester Foundation for Experimental Biology and John Rock of the Reproductive Study Center in Brookline, Mass., have discovered a drug which, when taken as a pill by a woman, interrupts the process of ovulation.

Hey there you with the stars in your eyes
Love never made a fool of you
You used to be too wise

Better Red than dead

Mama   *Make Room for Daddy*   *Our Miss Brooks*   *Mr. Peepers*
Burns and Allen Show   *December Bride*   *Leave It To Beaver*
Father Knows Best   *The Phil Silvers Show*   *Ozzie and Harriet*
Dobie Gillis   *The Honeymooners*   *Goodnight, Mrs. Calabash*

Twenty-two

WITH ALL DELIBERATE SPEED

THE AVERAGE AMERICAN MALE in 1954 stood five feet nine inches tall and weighed 158 pounds, according to Dr. George Gallup's Institute of Public Opinion, a diligent collector of such Americana. The average female was five feet four and weighed 132. Husbands thought the knack of running a smooth, orderly household was more important in a wife than anything else, and most of them—55 percent—felt that American women were spoiled.

In announcing these and other results of an elaborate study of American life, the institute observed that "Throughout history, races and nations have sometimes been remembered for their small human quirks rather than for their great deeds and battles. Here," it said, "are some of the small things that 'homo Americanus' may be famous for in 1,000 years' time." In fact they have become of interest after only twenty years' time, and although some are frivolous, it is interesting, and sometimes even significant, to know the little details of everyday life—what people thought of themselves and others, what they worried about, and how they lived. Already some of the findings of this survey seem quaint.

No audible voices protested the traditional distinctions between the sexes. Wives believed that men drank too much and that one of the chief faults of husbands was "just not paying enough attention," but nothing was said about chauvinism. The typical woman said she preferred marriage to a career. She wanted the word "obey" taken out of the wedding ceremony—it is rather astonishing that it was still there—but in other ways she accepted the double standard. For example, 61 percent of all women agreed that a wife should never open her husband's mail, even if a letter arrived in a scented envelope addressed in feminine handwriting, and when asked, "Should a wife's adultery be more condemned than a husband's?" an overwhelming majority of women—four out of every five—replied, "Yes, of course it should."

Most people listed money as their greatest worry; only 21 percent checked "the threat of world war, keeping the peace." Confidence in the United States and pride of country ran high. Generosity was voted the most conspicuous American characteristic, followed by friendliness, understanding, piety, love of freedom, and progressivism. The American faults listed were petty: shallowness, egotism, extravagance, preoccupation with money, and selfishness.

There were still enough farmers for them to be treated as a separate category. They were the first to rise in the morning; 69 percent of them were out of bed before 6 A.M. The typical American, on the other hand, got up at 6:30 A.M. weekdays and 8 A.M. Sundays. (Women, surprisingly, rose a bit later than men.) The average bedtime was 10 P.M. weekdays and 11 P.M. Saturdays. The typical breakfast was served at 7 A.M., the typical lunch at noon, and the typical supper or dinner at 6 P.M. The postwar custom of a fifteen-minute coffee break was catching on, but less than half of the population enjoyed it; to the question, "At your place of work are employees given time off for coffee, refreshments, or rest?" 51 percent checked "No." Farmers suffered more from the well-named common cold than any other group. The peak month for colds was February, when 15 percent of the adult population, or 15 million people, had them. The low point was July, but even then 5 percent, or five million, were coughing and sneezing and generally miserable.

Even without a war or scandal to divide the country, living was a strain. Every other adult complained of trouble getting to sleep. It was a greater problem for women than men, worse for the unmarried than the married, greatest for the divorced and the widowed. The main cause given was "nervous tension." Sedatives had not achieved wide acceptance; most insomniacs just tossed and turned. Among other complaints, one American in three said his feet hurt, one in five had trouble hearing, two in seven were worried about being overweight, and two out of three wore glasses, half of them all the time.

By gourmet standards their eating habits were dull. If allowed to order anything for dinner, regardless of cost, they said they would choose fruit cup, vegetable soup, steak and french fried potatoes, peas, rolls and butter, apple pie à la mode, and coffee. Three million Americans were vegetarians. Nearly six in ten drank wine, beer or liquor, but they didn't drink much; fewer than one in five had something every day. Their favorite sport was bowling. A startling eight million bowled at least once a week, and there were three occasional bowlers for every golfer or ping-pong player, the second and third most popular recreations. Only 52 percent of all adults knew how to swim, a reflection of the fact that opportunities for swimming were fewer then, for vacations were shorter and less frequent. Over 15 million, or 15 percent of all adults, had not been more than 250 miles from home—the equivalent, then, of one day's ride in an automobile. After Sunday dinner half of all families with cars took an afternoon pleasure ride, but they didn't go far. One American in four had not seen either the Atlantic Ocean or the Pacific.

Nine out of ten adults had been on a train, and four in ten had spent at least one night on a Pullman sleeper. Trips by air, though rising in frequency, were still preferred by a minority. Cars were used for short trips, but traffic was lighter than it has since become. One reason was that there were about 50 million fewer people living in the country. Farmers excluded, the average worker lived two miles from his job, and he could get there in about eighteen minutes. One man in three went home for lunch. Less than one-third of all families said grace at meals, but 95 percent said they believed that prayer helped "in one way or another," 94 percent believed in God, and 68 percent in life after death; 69 percent were in favor of adding the phrase "under God" to the pledge of allegiance, which was done on June 14, 1954. The highest proportion of Bible readers was in the South, the lowest in New England and the Middle Atlantic states. America's two favorite mottoes were "Do unto others as you would have them do unto you," and "Live and let live."

In winter the average family with a house kept it heated at 70 degrees in the daytime and 60 degrees at night. The smallest amount of money a family of four needed to get along in an average U.S. community was $60 a week. (In 1937 it had been $30 a week.) The impression fostered by movies and television was that twin beds had become increasingly popular, but only one couple in eight had them; the rest still slept in double beds. Men preferred showers to bathtubs. Women favored tubs, three to one. The average family had a pet, with dogs outnumbering cats two to one. Most Americans said they liked and trusted their neighbors. Prudence with money, instilled during the Depression, was habitual. If suddenly given $10,000, the average American said, he would buy a home. The next largest group would pay off debts, put the money in a bank, or invest in securities. Only a few said they would take life easy, travel, or go on a spending spree. A twenty-three-year-old Chicago stenographer replied that she would get married right away. Another working girl answered that she would move to California, "where there are plenty of men."

On the whole, America remained a nation of optimists. In spite of grousing about high taxes and high prices—though even then they were considered high—a clear majority said they believed they were better off than their parents had been. The average American wanted to live to be a hundred, and more men than women wanted it, though women, with their longer life expectancy, had a greater chance of reaching it. Asked to single out the age he would most like to live over again, the typical adult chose twenty-one. Nearly half of all those polled had a pet superstition. The superstitions named most often were knocking on wood, avoiding black cats when walking, and throwing spilled salt over the shoulder. Women were more superstitious than men.

Most people thought the ideal family had three youngsters. Mothers felt that the first child should not arrive until the second year of marriage. Parental opinions of 1954's young people were high; they were regarded as more sensible and level-headed than the parents had been at that age. But the children were more critical: only one in five had no complaints about his father or mother. Nearly all adult Americans felt that a child ought to have an allowance, even though fewer than three out of ten parents had had one when young. While disturbed about juvenile delinquency, which had been rising since World War II and was already a source of anxiety, most adults took the position that parents, not youngsters, were chiefly to blame for it. Typical parents of that time thought a girl should not begin dating until she was sixteen.

Mixed marriages, a term which then meant marriages between Christians of different religious faiths, were a subject of lively discussion. Slightly more than half the people—54 percent—approved of them, but only one American in four believed they had much chance of turning out successfully. Marriages between Gentiles and Jews were statistically insignificant. Unions between whites and Negroes, as blacks were then called, were unknown to the great middle class. Their possibility wasn't even discussed.

Negroes still did not exist as people for mainstream America. In popular entertainment they were more like pets. Stepin Fetchit, Hattie McDaniel, Butterfly McQueen, and Eddie Anderson—these were good for the nudge and the guffaw but they weren't looked upon as human beings. If Hollywood wanted to portray human feelings in a man with a black face, it put burnt cork on the face of somebody like Al Jolson. Black America was unnoticed by white America. "I am an invisible man," cried the hero of Ralph Ellison's 1953 novel. ". . . I am invisible, understand, simply because other people refuse to see me. I can hear you say, 'What a horrible, irresponsible bastard!' And you're right. . . . But to whom can I be responsible, when you refuse to see me?"

Now, after three centuries of black submission and black servitude, "the long habit of deception and evasion," as Ellison once called it, was about to end. The Supreme Court of the United States had pondered the matter and concluded that Negroes were real people after all, and that as such they must become visible to their white compatriots and treated as equals everywhere, beginning in the public schools.

By the U.S. Supreme Court clock it was 12:52 P.M., May 17, 1954. A concealed hand parted the red velour draperies at the front of the Court's magnificent chamber, and nine men robed in black, stepping past the gleaming Ionic columns, seated themselves in the leather chairs at the long mahogany bench. Editors all over the world were awaiting what was already being called the greatest moment in the Court's history since the Dred Scott decision of 1857. Associate Justice Robert Jackson, who was convalescing from a heart attack, had left his hospital bed that morning so that the full Court, including its three southerners, would be present for the occasion. In a departure from custom, newsmen had not been given advance copies of the decision. They had no inkling of which way it would go. The new Chief Justice had been on the bench only six months. At the time of his appointment lawyers had been appalled by his total lack of judicial experience, and few in Washington had been willing to predict how he would stand in this case of Brown v. Board of Education of Topeka. Earl Warren was no racist, but he had the reputation of being a staunch believer in states' rights.

Wire service reporters who cover Court sessions scribble bulletins in longhand at the press table, just below the bench, and send them on their way in pneumatic tubes. At 12:57 the Associated Press A wire came alive:

> Chief Justice Warren today began reading the Supreme Court's decision in the public school segregation cases. The Court's ruling could not be determined immediately.

Delivery of an opinion by the Chief Justice meant that he sided with the majority. This was Warren's first important ruling, and for a while all that spectators could be sure of was that he was taking an unconscionable amount of time to say what the decision was. Instead of delivering a brisk text he was meandering, stopping to cite such psychologists and sociologists as Kenneth Clark and Gunnar Myrdal on the mental development of Negro children. At 1:12 the exasperated AP correspondent dispatched a second bulletin. Warren was clearly opposed to segregation on principle, he said, but "the Chief Justice had not read far enough in the court's opinion for newsmen to say that segregation was being struck down as unconstitutional."

The decision's constitutional pivot was the Fourteenth Amendment: "Nor shall any state deny to any person the equal protection of the laws . . . ," but there was no judicial precedent for this application of it. The Supreme Court had never ruled on the issue of school segregation. In 1896 it had laid down a "separate but equal" doctrine in a case involving segregation of train passengers. Since then it had found against segregated housing and railroad transportation and ordered Negro students admitted to graduate schools of six southern and border state universities. Now at 1:20 P.M. Warren came to the climax of the ruling:

> To separate [Negro children] from others of similar age and qualifications solely because of their race generates a feeling of inferiority as to their status in the community that may affect their hearts and minds in a way never to be undone . . . We conclude that in the field of public education the doctrine of "separate but equal" has no place. Separate educational facilities are inherently unequal.

Segregation in schools, then, was unconstitutional: against the law. And the decision was unanimous, a special triumph for the National Association for the Advancement of Colored People and its scholarly counsel, Thurgood Marshall, himself a graduate of Jim Crow schools. Acknowledging that compliance would take time, the Court said it would withhold further instructions until its fall term. Meanwhile all sides were asked to prepare arguments on when segregation should be abolished and who—a special master or the federal district courts—should establish and enforce the terms under which it would end.

In the white South there was gloom. No greater blow to its social structure could be imagined. In seventeen states and the District of Columbia public school segregation was required by law, and four other states permitted it. Altogether, schools with a total population of twelve million children were affected. The first reactions of the authorities responsible for them varied according to their geographical location. In Kansas and Oklahoma, border states, officials were calm; they predicted that the change would be made with little commotion, if any. In Austin Governor Allan Shivers said Texas would submit, though he warned that full compliance might "take years." After studying the full opinion, Virginia's Governor Thomas Stanley told the press: "I shall call together . . . representatives of both state and local governments to consider the matter and work toward a plan which will be acceptable to our citizens and in keeping with the edict of the court."

The Deep South was more hostile. South Carolina's Governor James F. Byrnes, now seventy-five, said he was "shocked." He could scarcely claim to be surprised. In the hope of intimidating the Court, South Carolina had amended its constitution to allow for abandonment of the public school system. The question now was whether it would carry out its threat. Georgia had taken the same step, and its leaders were fiercer. Senator Richard Russell argued that racial matters were in the jurisdiction of the legislative, not the judicial, branch of government, and he accused the Warren Court, as some were already calling it, of "a flagrant abuse of judicial power." Governor Herman Talmadge delivered a diatribe: "The United States Supreme Court . . . has blatantly ignored all law and precedent . . . and lowered itself to the level of common politics . . . The people of Georgia believe in, adhere to, and will fight for their right under the U.S. and Georgia constitutions to manage their own affairs." They would, he said, "map a program to insure continued and permanent segregation of the races."

By autumn there was a lot of that sort of rhetoric as local candidates in southern elections fell to quarreling over who would be the greater defender of white supremacy. The Court, wary of civil disorder, set no rigid schedule for compliance. At the same time the justices let it be known that having laid down the law, they meant to see that it was enforced. Federal courts and local school districts were directed to evaluate their situations and study administrative problems. Then they were to take steps toward a "prompt and reasonable start" in carrying out the decision with "all deliberate speed" as soon as was "practicable."

President Eisenhower was troubled by all this. He knew there was a certain inevitability in it—that the end of European colonialism in Africa and Asia was bound to be matched in the United States by rising protests against discrimination, and that Americans were increasingly aware that the country's position of world leadership was being jeopardized by racism at home. Still, his innate conservatism distrusted sudden change. Privately he called the Warren appointment "the biggest damfool mistake I ever made." While believing in eventual integration, he argued that "if you try to go too far too fast . . . you are making a mistake." Nixon disagreed. He said that he felt strongly that "civil rights is primarily a moral rather than a legal question." But Ike remained reticent on this very delicate issue. To one of his advisers he said emphatically: "I am convinced that the Supreme Court decision set back progress in the South at least fifteen years. . . . It's all very well to talk about school integration—if you remember you may also be talking about social *dis*integration. Feelings are deep on this, especially where children are concerned. . . . We can't demand perfection in these moral questions. All we can do is keep working toward a goal and keep it high. And the fellow who tries to tell me that you can do these things by force is just plain nuts."

Still, as an old soldier he knew that orders must be obeyed. The Court had interpreted the Constitution; the chief executive had to carry out its instructions. At his direction all District of Columbia schools were integrated at once. He ended segregation on all Navy bases where it was still practiced—Truman had abolished it on Army posts—and overnight, literally over one night, the COLORED and WHITE signs over drinking fountains and rest room doors disappeared from naval installations. Lois Lippman, a Boston Negro, became the first black member of the White House secretarial staff; a few months later another Negro, E. Frederic Morrow, was appointed an administrative assistant to the President. Hagerty saw to it that all these facts reached the press; no one would say that Eisenhower wasn't practicing what he expected of others.

Over the next several months Oklahoma, Texas, Kentucky, West Virginia, Maryland, Tennessee, Arkansas, and Delaware reported partial integration in 350 school districts. Elsewhere the picture was less encouraging. Legislatures in Virginia and the Deep South passed complex measures designed to lead to long, involved court battles and circumvent the Supreme Court's ruling. Their governors were speaking stubbornly of "state sovereignty," "nullification," and the "interposition" of state authority to balk enforcement of federal laws—antebellum expressions which had not been heard since the death of John C. Calhoun. Encouraged by the warlike stance of their leaders, southerners on the lower rungs of the social ladder were reviving the Ku Klux Klan and organizing White Citizens' Councils to resist integration. Tempers were short throughout the white South.

But there could be no turning back now. Blacks had tempers, too. Over a century earlier de Tocqueville had predicted that once Negroes "join the ranks of free men, they will be indignant at being deprived of almost all the rights of citizens; and being unable to become the equals of the whites, they will not be slow to show themselves their enemies." That was the alternative to substantial integration. The Court had stirred hope in Negro hearts, and it is hope, not despair, that is the fuel of social action. J. Edgar Hoover reported to the White House that the sale of small arms had increased all over the South. In some communities it was up by as much as 400 percent. The most volatile rhetoric was coming from whites, but it was also notable that throughout the winter of 1954–55 the Black Muslims, with their gospel of inverted racism and retaliatory violence, were expanding rapidly.

Americans found, to their consternation, that they were rapidly moving into an era of racial incidents. Given the deeply held convictions at either end of the spectrum, such episodes were unavoidable. Militant whites vowed to defend the racial status quo, which the NAACP and the new Negro organizations springing up around it were bound to challenge. As often as not the officials in the middle simply came apart. With Thurgood Marshall as her adviser a twenty-six-year-old black woman, Autherine Lucy, announced her intention to enroll at the University of Alabama. The university trustees were distraught. After three days of unruly crowds at Tuscaloosa, during which her car was stoned and pelted with rocks, Miss Lucy reached the registrar's office, only to be handed this telegram from the trustees: FOR YOUR SAFETY AND THE SAFETY OF THE STUDENTS AND FACULTY MEMBERS OF THE UNIVERSITY, YOU ARE HEREBY SUSPENDED FROM CLASSES UNTIL FURTHER NOTICE. Marshall led her to a court, which lifted the suspension. The trustees then met that night, accused Miss Lucy of making "false, defamatory, impertinent, and scandalous charges" against the university authorities—and ordered her permanent expulsion.

Frustration ran high on both sides in such episodes. With the power of the federal courts behind her, Autherine Lucy was bound to win in the end, and the trustees knew it. Only a bullet could stop her—a haunting possibility. Not only were guns and gunmen all around; it was possible, and indeed in some cases probable, that such a killer would go free. The same Constitution which required desegregation entitled a defendant to trial before a jury of his peers. His peers, in large areas of the South, were likely to acquit him. This happened. The first such incident occurred in Greenwood, Mississippi, in August 1955. Emmett Till, a fourteen-year-old black youth from Chicago, was visiting relatives there. Rumor spread that he had insulted a white woman, and three white men dragged him from his relatives' home and drowned him. Witnesses identified two of the three killers to federal agents, but an all-white jury acquitted them. The two—they were half-brothers—were then charged with kidnapping by a U.S. attorney, but a grand jury refused to indict them, and the FBI, which had painstakingly assembled irrefutable evidence, reluctantly closed its file.

By the first anniversary of the Supreme Court decision, racism lay like an ugly blight across much of the South. Rabble-rousers stirred up mobs which frightened, and sometimes attacked, blacks insisting on their constitutional rights. The cruelest incidents were in the grade schools, where children, most of them too small to understand the savage struggle being waged over them, were subjected to intimidation and outright terror. The return to school each September is a familiar American ritual. Mothers dress youngsters in new clothes, brush their hair, give them pencil cases, and send them off to their new classrooms. It is at precisely this time that boards of education introduce whatever changes in regulations there are to be—such as desegregation. Beginning the year after the Supreme Court decision and extending to the end of the 1950s, American front pages each fall carried accounts of ghastly demonstrations in front of bewildered pupils. Sometimes there was violence.

Two representative incidents erupted almost simultaneously in one week of 1956. In Clinton, Tennessee, mob hysteria was whipped up by John Kasper, a racist zealot from Washington, D.C. (He saw no irony in his charge that desegregation was the work of "outside agitators.") Until Kasper arrived, Clinton had been a quiet backwater town of four thousand people, where twelve black students were preparing to enroll in the local high school. Goaded by him, a thousand Clinton citizens disrupted the school, blocked traffic, battered the cars of Negroes who happened to be passing through, and then threw themselves on the eight-man Clinton police force shouting, "Let's get the nigger lovers! Let's get their guns and kill them!" After a night of fear 100 state troopers, 633 National Guardsmen, and seven M-41 tanks put down what looked like an incipient revolution. That was a lot of law enforcement for one township, but the country was learning how vulnerable to hotheads schools were. Mansfield, Texas, with a population of 1,450, was even smaller than Clinton. There a federal district court had ordered the integration of three blacks with three hundred white high school students. On registration day four hundred men barged into the school waving placards that read DEAD COONS ARE THE BEST COONS and $2 A DOZEN FOR NIGGER EARS. The three Negro students quickly withdrew. A fourteen-year-old white girl told a reporter: "If God wanted us to go to school together He wouldn't have made them black and us white."

It was easy for Americans outside the South to be scornful of it, but it wasn't necessarily fair. The fact that racist vigilantes could disrupt the peace did not make them a majority. In the aftermath of the Clinton disorders the town looked like a stronghold of bigotry. Kasper, arrested on charges of instigating a riot, was freed. In a current election campaign the White Citizens' Council there nominated its own candidate for mayor. Bumper stickers urging his election seemed to be everywhere. In the school students wearing Confederate flags sewn on their sweaters stoned black boys, shouted

"Nigger bitches" and "Dirty nigger whores" at black girls, and poured ink over the blacks' books. On the morning of election day a white minister attempting to escort the Negro children past a mob outside the school was badly beaten; so were two people who tried to come to his assistance. The principal expelled a thirteen-year-old white boy for assaulting a black girl and then, after he himself had been threatened, announced that the school was being closed "because of lawlessness and disorder." At that point, just as Clinton seemed lost to decency, the tide shifted. On orders from Attorney General Brownell, the FBI arrested sixteen of the mob's ringleaders. Fifty white high school students, led by the seventeen-year-old football captain, asked people to comply "with the federal court order to provide an education for all the citizens of Anderson County who desire it." Then came a surprise, even to those who thought they knew the town well. The polls closed, the votes were counted—and every segregationist candidate for local office was defeated by a margin of nearly three to one.

That year a new phrase was on the lips of public speakers: "the winds of change." The expression came out of Morocco, where French troops transferred from Vietnam were fighting another losing battle against anticolonialists, but it also seemed applicable to the United States. The Warren Court in particular appeared to be a storm center for winds of change. In time its reinterpretations of the Constitution would bar prayer from classrooms, expand defendants' rights to counsel (notably in Miranda v. Arizona), extend freedom of speech and freedom of the press to moviemakers, strike the bonds of censorship from pornographers, and lay down guidelines for legislative apportionment in the states.

Diehard conservatives dug in. IMPEACH EARL WARREN billboards went up all over the South. The Chief Justice had become the most controversial figure in the government since Franklin Roosevelt; all turmoil and racial tensions were laid at his door. Yet the Supreme Court was but one of many federal institutions which were acting to alter the system. Congress was fashioning the first of what would eventually be five civil rights acts. The Civil Service Commission was speeding up the advancement of black workers, and federal regulatory agencies were taking a sudden interest in charges of discrimination. One of them, the Interstate Commerce Commission, was weighing a proposal to forbid the interstate segregation of travelers on trains, buses, and in waiting rooms when a black seamstress in Montgomery, Alabama, anticipated it.

Her name was Rosa Parks, she was forty-two years old, and on Thursday, December 1, 1955, she was very tired. She found a seat on a Montgomery bus, but when the bus filled up the driver told her to stand so a white man could sit there. It was an old southern custom for Negroes to surrender their seats to whites. It was also against the law for anyone to disobey a bus driver's instructions. Mrs. Parks thought about it for a moment and then said she wouldn't move. At that moment, Eldridge Cleaver later wrote, "somewhere in the universe a gear in the machinery had shifted."

Arrested at the next stop, she was charged with a misdemeanor, found guilty, and fined ten dollars. That made Mrs. Parks's friends angry, and she was a popular woman; within forty-eight hours mimeographed pamphlets being distributed in Negro neighborhoods called for a one-day boycott of all city transportation. The boycott was so spectacular a success that leaders of Montgomery's black community started asking one another larger questions. The city's 25,000 blacks accounted for 75 percent of the bus company's patronage. Suppose they extended the boycott and set terms for an end to it? Eventually the management would either yield or go bankrupt.

That was how it started. The company was told that it would have no more black passengers until Negroes were seated on a first come first served basis and allowed to keep their seats. In addition the Negro leaders demanded that drivers be ordered to treat blacks courteously and that black drivers be hired for buses in Negro districts. The management replied that white drivers would be polite, but that was all. So the passenger strike continued. It was 95 percent effective, and as the weeks passed with no compromise on either side, the determination of the blacks simply increased. The rest of Alabama began to watch Montgomery; then the rest of the country; and then the world. The segregationists were led by W. A. Gayle, Montgomery's mayor. Gayle and his fellow members of the city commission ceremoniously joined the local White Citizens' Council. Then he declared that the city would never capitulate to the boycotters. He said, "We have pussyfooted around long enough and it has come time to be frank. There seems to be a belief on the part of the Negroes that they have the white people hemmed in a corner and they are not going to give an inch until they can force the white people of the community to submit to their demands."

Gayle's chief adversary, the leader of the blacks, was Martin Luther King, an unknown twenty-six-year-old clergyman. King had come to Montgomery the year before to become pastor of the Dexter Avenue Baptist Church. The white South paid grudging respect to black clergymen, but King was one of the new Negroes, and he lay outside the southern white experience. He was a Ph.D., a product of Harvard, and a genuine scholar. In his sermons he dwelt less on the river Jordan than on the wisdom of Socrates, Aristotle, Shakespeare, Galileo, and Toynbee. Writing in his small white Montgomery bungalow to the soft accompaniment of classical music, he had fused Christianity, Hegelianism, and Gandhiism into a philosophy teaching strength through struggle and harmony out of pain. Gandhi's satyagraha—passive resistance and noncooperation as a way of opposing mistreatment—had become King's "soul force." He showed his congregation films of the Indian mahatma and said of the boycott:

> This is not a tension between the Negroes and whites. This is only a conflict between justice and injustice. We are not just trying to improve Negro Montgomery. We are trying to improve the whole of Montgomery. If we are arrested every day; if we are exploited every day; if we are triumphed over every day; let nobody pull you so low as to hate them.

He taught the Dexter Avenue church's worshippers the meaning of "victory over your enemies through love," and he inspired them with rousing old Baptist hymns and camp-meeting tunes, sometimes with new words:

Deep in my heart,
I do believe
We shall overcome
One day.

Hard-core segregationists were derisive. One described King as "just another rabble-rouser the Communistic N-double-A-C-P is sending down here to stir up our decent Nigras." Not all whites felt that way. Mayor Gayle was discovering that families accustomed to Negro help were giving rides to their cooks and handymen or paying their taxi fares. He protested that the domestics "are fighting to destroy our social fabric just as much as the Negro radicals who are leading them," and he said, "The Negroes are laughing at white people behind their backs. They think it's very funny that whites who are opposed to the Negro boycott will act as chauffeur to Negroes who are boycotting the buses."

After three months of deadlock the city attorney produced a 1921 state anti-labor law enjoining restraint of trade. Under it a grand jury indicted King and 114 other black leaders. "In this state," the indictment read, "we are committed to segregation by custom and law; we intend to maintain it." The defendants were fingerprinted and freed on $300 bond each. Late in March King became the first of them to come to trial on the charge of conspiring "without a just cause or legal excuse" to hinder a company in its conduct of business. Black witnesses testified that they certainly did have just cause. One told how a bus driver had shut the door on her blind husband's leg and then stepped on the accelerator. A second described a Negro being forced from a bus at pistol point because he did not have correct change. A third said his pregnant wife had been compelled to surrender her seat to a white woman, and a fourth said a driver had called her an "ugly black ape."

King, who had waived a jury trial, pointed out that the boycott had begun spontaneously and that he had become its spokesman only after it was in full swing. The judge nevertheless found him guilty; he was ordered to pay $1,000 in fines and court costs and released on bond pending appeal. If the verdict was meant to intimidate Montgomery's Negroes, its effect was the exact opposite. They promptly held a rally on the lawn outside the courthouse. One black shouted, "We ain't going to ride the buses now for sure." A middle-aged woman pushed through the crowd to tell King, "My heart and my pocketbook are at your disposal." A mass prayer meeting was scheduled for that evening. One man called to the others, "Are you going to be there?" They called back, "Yes!" He asked, "Are you going to ride the buses?" and they roared, "No!"

And they didn't. Spring passed, summer passed, and still the spirit of the blacks showed no signs of flagging. The mayor confided to friends that he had never dreamed that Negroes could be this determined. The bus company sank into debt. Drivers drifted into other jobs or left the city. The Negroes showed every sign of being able to survive without them. Some had become accustomed to walking to work, some had bicycles, and for the others King had organized a vast car pool with two hundred automobiles. The mayor announced that this was illegal. In the twelfth month of the customer strike King and the other black leaders were arrested for running a business enterprise without a franchise. They were on trial in state circuit court when electrifying news arrived. The Supreme Court, which had already overturned the "separate but equal" doctrine for recreational facilities as well as in schools, had now killed it in public transportation. Discrimination on buses was now a violation of federal law. Martin Luther King was free. He was in addition a world celebrity. The unprecedented boycott had dealt Alabama segregation a devastating blow. American Negroes everywhere had found new hope, and the young black preacher had been catapulted into the first rank of the struggle for civil rights.

King did not gloat. He advised his flock to act with dignity and without pride. He said, "We have been going to the back of the bus for so long that there is danger that we will instinctively go straight back there again and perpetuate segregation." At the same time, he continued, "I would be terribly disappointed if any of you go back to the buses bragging, 'We, the Negroes, won a victory over the white people.' If you do, our struggle will be lost all over the South. Go back with humility and meekness."

He would have been less than human if he hadn't ridden a bus himself when the boycott ended, 381 days after Rosa Parks had started it. The driver said to him, "Is this the Reverend?" The clergyman said, "That's right. How much?" It was fifteen cents—up a nickel from the year before—and putting the coins in the slot he took a front seat. He said afterward, "It was a great ride." Most Montgomery whites were relieved to have it all over, and some were in good humor. A bank teller wryly told a reporter, "They'll find that all they've won in their year of praying and boycotting is the same lousy service I've been getting every day." On one bus a white man said to nobody in particular, "I see this isn't going to be a white Christmas." A nearby black smiled. "Yes sir," he said. "That's right."

Long after an event has passed, its place in the scheme of things becomes clear, but at the time it often seems insignificant. Doubtless the driver who told Mrs. Parks to stand merely thought he was dealing with one uppity Nigra; had he known that his own grandchildren would one day study the incident in school, he might have been more circumspect. Presidents are more conscious of history than bus drivers, but they, too, may be blind to the consequences of their decisions. Dwight Eisenhower was above all a man of peace. That and his respect for congressional prerogatives had caused him to stop other members of his administration from making unwise commitments on Indochina. Yet in the same year that Rosa Parks altered destiny, Ike took the country a step down the long road toward madness in Vietnam.

It was not the first such step. Any assessment of the growth in presidential war-making powers should note the precedents set by Franklin Roosevelt in 1941 and 1942. Before then, congressional authority in this area was intact. It was shakier afterward; FDR, with his brilliant display of political legerdemain, had used executive agreements to create a situation in which the Axis powers were virtually compelled to attack the United States. Then came Korea. Cabell Phillips, Harry Truman's biographer, observes that "His decision to intervene in Korea . . . came close to pre-empting the right to declare war . . . all Presidents are now armed with the Truman precedent to strike swiftly on their own, wherever and with whatever force is necessary, when they believe the national interest demands it."

The last steps in the erosion of congressional authority, and the accompanying executive ascendancy, were to be taken by Lyndon Johnson and Richard Nixon against the backdrop of Southeast Asia, but each link in the chain of precedent deserves notice. The Formosa resolution of 1955 was one of them. It was a special consequence of the cold war, but its implications for the future were broad and grave.

Dean Acheson had wanted to wait "until the dust has settled" in China before formulating a new policy there. By 1955 it was as settled as it would ever be, yet the eastern edge of the picture remained murky. The Communists controlled the mainland and the Nationalists Formosa, but the status of Formosa Strait, which separated them, was unresolved. Here and there the 115-mile-wide sound was sprinkled with tiny, barren islands whose only real significance, in 1955, was as a bone of contention between the Peoples Republic of China, on the one hand, and Chiang and his American allies on the other.

The islands varied in size and proximity to larger land masses. One group of sixty-four islets, the Pescadores, was thirty miles from Formosa and was considered a part of it; the White House let it be known that any attack on the Pescadores would be interpreted as preliminary to an invasion of Formosa and as such would be resisted by the Seventh Fleet. Congressional approval was not needed for a defense of the Pescadores because they had been captured from Japan in World War II; under international law the United States was entitled to protect them. The situation on the far side of the strait was different. The islands there were Quemoy, Matsu, and the Tachen group, each of which was more than a hundred miles from Formosa and within five to ten miles of the mainland. As Adlai Stevenson pointed out, they lay "almost as close to the coast of China as Staten Island does to New York," had "always belonged to China," and were properties to which neither the U.S. nor the Nationalists on Formosa had any legal claim. Walter Lippmann underscored the implications of this: ". . . were we to intervene in the offshore islands, we would be acting on Chinese territory in a Chinese civil war."

Nothing would have given John Foster Dulles greater satisfaction. He was ready to fight for the offshore islands any time, and he complained to Sherman Adams about the inability of the British and other U.S. allies to understand "the tremendous shock that a retreat from Quemoy and Matsu would be to the free people of East Asia." That was how Dulles saw the world. He conjured up visions of mass meetings in places like Sumatra and Tibet, with millions of stern peasants gathered under banners reading FREE PEOPLE OF EAST ASIA UNITE and SUPPORT COLLECTIVE SECURITY. The Chinese Communists knew of Dulles's intractability and liked to twit him. While he was in Manila signing the Southeast Asia Treaty Organization protocols in September 1954 they had bombarded Quemoy, and the following January 18 they occupied the islet of Yikiang in the Tachens. Since Yikiang was so microscopic that it wasn't even shown on State Department maps, and since the Tachens were two hundred miles north of Formosa, the threat to Chiang's Nationalists was obscure. Nevertheless, the Joint Chiefs went into emergency session. A majority was hawkish. Admiral Radford, Admiral Carney, and General Nathan F. Twining felt that it was time to take a stand against the Communists and bring about a showdown once and for all.

General Ridgway was the lone dissenter. He advised the President that "Such an action would be almost impossible to limit. It would bring us into direct conflict with the Red Chinese. It could spread to full and all-out war, employing all the terrible weapons at our command." Even if China were conquered, Ridgway went on, the situation would still be highly unsatisfactory; the United States would have created "by military means a great vacuum. Then we would have to go in there with hundreds of thousands of men to fill that vacuum—which would bring us face to face with Russia along a seven-thousand-mile frontier."

With Ridgway the only dove, the Joint Chiefs voted to move against the Reds. Dulles agreed; so did Senator Knowland. But Eisenhower concluded that Ridgway was right. Once again he refused to be drawn into a war on the Asian mainland. The war fever abated. Nevertheless, Dulles did succeed in persuading Ike that face was involved. After the seizure of Yikiang the Peking radio had declared that the thrust showed a "determined will to fight for the liberation of Taiwan." If under these circumstances America did nothing, Dulles warned, Asians would conclude that the U.S. was a paper tiger. The President agreed to do something. He would ask Congress for a resolution.

His message of January 24 was unprecedented in American history. Ike was asking Congress for something more and something less than a declaration of war. He wanted it to let him decide when and where America would fight. He said:

> The situation has become sufficiently critical to impel me, without awaiting action by the United Nations, to ask the Congress to participate now, by specific resolution, in measures designed to improve the prospects for peace. These measures would contemplate the use of the armed forces of the United States, if necessary, to assure the security of Formosa and the Pescadores.

The President then suggested that whether or not a Chinese attack off the offshore islands invited retaliation depended upon the character of the assault. If they just wanted Quemoy and Matsu he might let them have it. If they had a leap toward Formosa in mind, he might not. He wanted Congress to let him read the Communist mind and take whatever action he thought appropriate.

For a measure which was meant to remove doubts, this one bewildered a lot of people. Liberal Democrats contended that Ike already had authority to take the steps he had in mind. As champions of Roosevelt-Truman foreign policy, they were believers in a strong Presidency. His constitutional power as commander in chief, they insisted, permitted him to deploy American military might any way he wished. Some of the arguments spun that winter make curious reading today. Vietnam was destined to become the graveyard of many U.S. policies, none more so than this one. As in the struggle over the Bricker amendment, conservatives wanted to keep the prerogative of making great decisions abroad on Capitol Hill, while liberals insisted that it belonged in the White House. The absolutist nature of the liberal position was most clearly stated by Richard H. Rovere. On March 19, 1955, he wrote that:

> . . . the President's power to defend Formosa does not rest on the hastily composed resolution that Congress passed in January. As President of the United States he has the right to take whatever action he deems necessary in any area he judges to be related to the defense of this country, regardless of whether it is related to the defense of Formosa or anything else.

Eisenhower himself was uncertain over whether he was giving Congress something or taking it away. Before sending the message to the Capitol he made one change. It had read, "The authority I request may be in part already inherent in the authority of the Commander-in-Chief." He crossed this out and wrote in its place, "Authority for some of the actions which might be required would be inherent in the authority of the Commander-in-Chief." Congress was no surer of itself than he was. The most common interpretation there was that the administration was looking for a way to get off the hook on the offshore islands.

Hubert Humphrey tried in vain to tack on an amendment which would have restricted the grant of power to Formosa and the Pescadores. Others in Congress were worried that the United States might be trapped into a war over some obscure place that had nothing to do with American security. Senator Ralph E. Flanders went further. "We have had intimations from the highest quarters," he said, "that it would be militarily advisable to prevent the massing of troops and equipment gathered for the purpose of making an assault on the islands. Put in plain English, this is preventive war. And it is seriously proposed as a possible action pursuant to the purposes of this resolution."

Opposition receded when Senator George threw his great weight behind the bill, saying, "I hope no Democrat will be heard to say that because the President of the United States came to Congress he is thereby subject to criticism." The resolution passed the Senate 85 to 3 and the House 410 to 3. Eisenhower signed it on January 29. That happened to be George's seventy-seventh birthday, and a great fuss was made over the senator when he arrived for the ceremony. Yet in less than a month the Seventh Fleet seemed to show how pointless the whole debate had been by evacuating fourteen thousand Chinese Nationalist troops from the Tachens. So much for the Formosa resolution, Washington said, assuming that it would now become a meaningless scrap of paper. But one man saw it differently. Adlai Stevenson observed that the President had asked for, and had received from Congress, a "blank check." That is precisely what it was. One day Eisenhower or another occupant of his office could present it for payment without consulting Congress further. The delicate balance of constitutional powers had shifted again; another restraint on the chief executive had been removed.

Eisenhower's greatest foreign policy coup, which came six months later, was a public relations triumph. To achieve it he had to all but run over John Foster Dulles. For ten years the Republican Old Guard had resolutely opposed any meeting with the Soviet leaders. Winston Churchill had been proposing a top-level meeting for some time—he called it a "summit"—but for American conservatives the mere suggestion that an American President might clink cocktail glasses with the Russians was like a Pavlovian bell. It set them to protesting against another Yalta or Potsdam, to them synonyms for sellout. Dulles agreed; as an anti-Communist fundamentalist he recoiled from any bargaining with men as steeped in sin as the Soviets.

He couldn't come right out and say that, because the President had repeatedly declared that he would meet anyone, anywhere, in the name of peace. Therefore Dulles tried to establish impossible prerequisites for such a meeting. Before it could be seriously considered, he said, Moscow must show by its deeds that the Soviet Union belonged to the comity of nations and would cooperate in settling differences. When pressed for an example of such a deed, he would reply with vague generalities. He gave the impression that he might be impressed by a withdrawal of all Russian troops from eastern Europe, say, or free elections throughout Russia under U.N. supervision. Sometimes he implied that he would expect handsome apologies from them, too, for their transgressions in the past.

To mollify him and the Republican ultras, Eisenhower called in key senators and congressmen and promised them that he would not be party to "another Yalta." He assured them that no commitments would be made without their approval. Dulles, who was there, said he wouldn't put it past the Russians to make some grandstand play in the name of world peace. He would be on the lookout for it, he said grimly.

Eisenhower had said nothing when Dulles spoke scornfully of dramatic peace proposals. Inwardly, however, he must have been troubled. He himself had that very thing in mind. Nothing definite had been decided, but the draft of a fresh approach to disarmament lay on his desk. In March the President had appointed Nelson Rockefeller chairman of a panel of experts in arms control and psychological warfare. He had given Rockefeller office space at the Marine Corps base at Quantico and asked him to come up with new recommendations which might be produced at a summit meeting. Dulles heard about the task force, but he didn't know its mission. All the same, he was suspicious. To Sherman Adams he said of Rockefeller, "He seems to be building up a big staff. He's got them down at Quantico, and nobody knows what they're doing."

They were studying European opinion surveys. People in the NATO nations, they learned, were weary of the alliance, unenthusiastic about the American bases on the continent, and in favor of banning nuclear weapons. That was disturbing. Lacking Russia's huge standing army, America needed the bombs and the bases as a deterrent. Some way must be found to keep them and still convince Europeans that the U.S. was seeking peace. The Quantico group's answer was a proposal for aerial inspection—in a felicitous phrase, "Open Skies." The idea was not new. Aerial inspection had been suggested as early as 1946 in a Bernard Baruch plan for the international control of atomic energy, and later it had appeared in the report of a U.N. disarmament commission and an Acheson plan for "international disclosure and verification" of all armed forces and weapons. Until now, though, it had been overlooked. Eisenhower thought it both appealing and practical. He hadn't made up his mind over whether to present it at the summit, but on the way to the *Columbine*, his plane, he stuffed it in his briefcase.

The *Columbine*'s destination was Geneva. There he unpacked in the fifteen-room Château Creux de Genthod, which the wife of a Swiss perfume tycoon had placed at his disposal. Meantime Plane No. 001 of the Ilyushin fleet landed and discharged down its ramp Stalin's two successors, Nikita Khrushchev and Nikolai Bulganin, the first looking like a labor union boss and the second bearing an uncanny resemblance to Colonel Sanders, the fried chicken magnate of the early 1970s. Later that afternoon, Anthony Eden and French Premier Edgar Faure arrived to complete the roster of participants in the Big Four talks, or, in the neat Swiss phrase, the Conférence à Quatre. Already the Spirit of Geneva, the newsmen's name for it, was casting a magic spell, attracting crowds of tourists and some celebrities. Pastor Martin Niemöller was there to hold a press conference, and an American clergyman, Billy Graham, was presiding over a revival in the Parc des Eaux-Vives.

In the Palais des Nations Dulles looked disconsolate. Ike, by contrast, was in fine form. At first he tried to match Dulles's stony expression, agreeing with the secretary that it would be unwise to raise false hopes that might be quickly dashed if the meetings were unfruitful. But Eisenhower was too genial, too optimistic, too bursting with good spirits to stay gloomy. He allowed himself to tell the press that "a new dawn may be coming," and in chairing the opening session on Monday, July 18, he spent the first quarter-hour greeting Marshal Zhukov.

The Russians, for their part, seemed more relaxed than at any time since the war. Khrushchev assured his listeners that "neither side wants war," and back home *Pravda* and *Izvestia* were telling the Russian people the same thing—a major shift in the party line, which until now had held that the rest of the world was implacably against them. Khrushchev, Bulganin, and Zhukov rode around Geneva in open cars and took long walks without bodyguards, something of an embarrassment to the Americans, because Eisenhower's every move was screened by Secret Service details and monitored by men in helicopters overhead.

Nevertheless, it was Ike who dominated the Conférence à Quatre. His smile, his candor, and his obvious concern for all mankind captivated the Europeans. *Le Monde* of Paris, usually anti-American, observed that "Eisenhower, whose personality has long been misunderstood, has emerged as the type of leader humanity needs today." Addressing himself to the Soviets, he said earnestly: "The American people want to be friends with the Soviet people. There are no natural differences between our peoples or our nations. There are no territorial or commercial rivalries. Historically, our two countries have always been at peace." He then proposed freer communications between East and West, disarmament, and a united, democratic Germany.

Despite their better manners, the Russians were still Russians when the chips were down. They had a few favorable words to say about peaceful coexistence, but in exchange for it they wanted nothing less than the dissolution of NATO. They dusted off and presented a plan which all those present had heard before: America, Russia, and China would each limit itself to 1,500,000 soldiers; Britain and France would have 650,000 each; and all nuclear weapons would be banned. When they laid that on the table the talks bogged down. After a two-hour huddle of the Americans in the château, Stassen went off to draw up a general disarmament proposal while the President himself drafted an Open Skies presentation. He continued to be undecided about submitting it; he wanted to hear what Bulganin had to say in the morning. Bulganin said nothing new. Not much was expected from Ike, either; this was the fourth day of the conference, and the others assumed that he had already spoken his mind. His first words were familiar: the United States was "prepared to enter into a sound and reliable agreement making possible the reduction of armaments." Then he paused, squared his shoulders against the high windows looking out over Lake Geneva, took off his glasses, and laid them down. He said:

> I should address myself for a moment principally to the delegates from the Soviet Union, because our two great countries admittedly possess new and terrible weapons in quantities which do give rise in other parts of the world, or reciprocally, to the fears and dangers of surprise attack.
>
> I propose, therefore, that we take a practical step, that we begin an arrangement, very quickly, as between ourselves—immediately. These steps would include:
>
> To give each other a complete blueprint of our military establishments, from beginning to end, from one end of our countries to the other; lay out the establishments and provide the blueprints to each other.
>
> Next, to provide within our countries facilities for aerial photography to the other country—we to provide the facilities within our country, ample facilities for aerial reconnaissance, where you can make all the pictures you choose and take them to your own country to study; you to provide exactly the same facilities for us and we to make these examinations, and by this step to convince the world that we are providing as between ourselves against the possibility

> of great surprise attack, thus lessening danger and relaxing tension.
>
> Likewise we will make more easily attainable a comprehensive and effective system of inspection and disarmament, because what I propose, I assure you, would be but a beginning. . . .
>
> The United States is ready to proceed in the study and testing of a reliable system of inspections and reporting, and when that system is proved, then to reduce armaments with all others to the extent that the system will provide assured results.
>
> The successful working out of such a system would do much to develop the mutual confidence which will open wide the avenues of progress for all our peoples.

During the translation a blinding flash of lightning filled the room, thunder rolled across the lake, and all the electricity in the Palais des Nations went dead. Ike chuckled. He said, "I didn't mean to turn the lights off." They flickered on again, revealing a dumbfounded Russian delegation. The Soviet Union was still in the grip of Stalinist paranoia. Diplomats in Moscow were shadowed, foreign correspondents were limited in their movements, the telephones of foreigners were tapped, and any Soviet citizen seen in conversation with them was closely questioned. The idea of providing the Americans with detailed maps of their military bases and then allowing U.S. photographers to fly over and take all the pictures they liked was stupefying. Khrushchev and his fellow delegates didn't know what to say. They just stared.

The Europeans were overjoyed. They hailed the proposal as a diplomatic masterstroke. Premier Faure said, "I wish the people of the world could have been in this conference room to hear the voice of a man speaking from great military experience. Had this been possible, they would believe that something had changed in the world in the handling of this question of disarmament. I am sure that this conference has scored its first victory over skepticism." Next morning newspaper editorials all over western Europe echoed Faure. Opening the skies was something everyone could understand. It was simple and direct, and only a President whose country had nothing to hide could have proposed it.

In practice it was impossible, as out of the question for Americans as for Russians. Ike's military advisers knew that. They had read the fine print he had skipped in his extemporaneous delivery—Open Skies was described there as a suggestion to "instruct our representatives in the Subcommittee on Disarmament in discharge of their mandate from the United States to give priority effort to the study of inspection and reporting"—and they had concluded that he was talking about a distant goal, something that could become practical only after a great many other agreements had been reached and tested. The Pentagon was not paranoid, but it did have a great many hoops through which anyone must jump before he could look at classified material. A government that withheld data from J. Robert Oppenheimer wasn't going to turn it over to the NKVD. This was still the McCarthy era. The senator might be discredited, and the country might be willing to forgive the promoters of Peress, but that was a far cry from filling the sky over Los Alamos with MIGs.*

At the end of the conference Bulganin drew the President aside and said, "Don't worry—this will come out all right." Ike left Geneva convinced that the Soviet leaders, especially Zhukov, were persuaded that he had been sincere. In the following months they treated Open Skies gingerly, mindful, perhaps, of the enthusiasm which had greeted it elsewhere. As late as March 1, 1956, Eisenhower was writing Bulganin to propose the merger of Open Skies and another plan, for the peaceful use of atomic energy. By then, however, Bulganin was being shouldered aside by Khrushchev, who wasn't interested in conciliatory gestures. He preferred to deliver speeches about "wars of national liberation." The Spirit of Geneva was dead. There had been no detente. The conference had achieved nothing that lasted, and is now remembered only for the warmth of Ike's grin and the density of the ice which it didn't melt.

Mercifully, disillusionment was slow to emerge. As the President flew home, Geneva was being acclaimed as a thundering success. Gallup reported that 84 percent of the American people could not think of a single thing in the Eisenhower administration that deserved criticism. The *Columbine* brought the President home in the early hours of Sunday, July 24. It was still dark, the Washington National Airport was drenched in rain. Nevertheless, people were there to cheer him as he descended the ramp, and others lined the roads to the White House. It was a peak in his Presidency, one of the great moments of the 1950s. He had left determined to lessen world ten-

* Assuming, that is, that the Russian photographers would have been in Russian planes. They could have been carried in American transports while the American photographers flew over the Soviet Union in Russian planes. Eisenhower hadn't made that clear, and no one asked him. Perhaps even elated Europeans knew in their hearts that Open Skies were too redolent of BBD&O.

sions, he was returning in apparent triumph, and now he looked forward to a long golfing vacation in Denver.

On September 23, 1955, President Eisenhower awoke early on Byers Peak Ranch outside Denver, where he was the guest of Aksel Nielsen, a Colorado banker, and cooked his own breakfast: beef bacon, pork sausage, fried mush, and flapjacks. He stopped off at the stucco administration building at Lowry Air Force Base, spent two intensive hours working with aides, and then drove to the Cherry Hills Country Club for eighteen holes of golf. He shot 84, which was better than it seemed because twice his game had been interrupted by urgent phone calls, one of them from Dulles about the Soviet responses to Open Skies.

The President lunched on hamburger and raw onions, then golfed another nine holes. On the eighth hole he paused, frowning, and rubbed his chest. To the club pro he said, "Maybe I can't take those onions any more. They seem to be backing up on me. I seem to have a little heartburn." The rest of his afternoon was spent in the basement of his mother-in-law's Lafayette Street home painting; he was copying a photograph of an Argentine woman in the July 11 issue of *Life*. Then George and Mary Allen arrived for dinner. Over roast lamb, potatoes, and vegetables Ike mentioned being troubled by the onions earlier, but then he appeared to forget it. At 10 P.M. he retired to his second-floor bedroom. Mamie's bedroom was directly across the hall.

She awoke at 2:30 A.M. and heard him tossing about. Crossing the corridor, she found him asleep but restless. "What's the matter, Ike?" she asked. "Are you having a nightmare or something?" No, he mumbled; he was fine; she left. But he wasn't fine. And he couldn't get back to sleep. Suddenly an agonizing pain gripped his chest. He rose and crossed the hall to her. He couldn't speak; he rubbed his chest to show where it hurt. Remembering the onions, she gave him milk of magnesia. She was troubled. This was something new; he had never complained of a pain there before. Picking up the phone, she called Major General Howard McC. Snyder, the President's personal physician, at Lowry's bachelor officers' quarters four miles away. She told him what was happening and said, "You'd better come over."

Snyder didn't need to be told. Those symptoms would alarm any doctor. Flinging his clothes over his pajamas, he told his driver,

"Seven-fifty Lafayette Street, and step on it." They raced through red lights all the way; at 3:12 the doctor was at the President's bedside. Ike was flushed, sweating, and in extreme discomfort. His pulse was rapid and his blood pressure was high. Listening to his chest with a stethoscope, Snyder reached a diagnosis within minutes. The President had been stricken by a coronary thrombosis. His heart had been damaged; how much, Snyder could not tell. He administered amyl nitrate, papaverine hydrochloride to dilate Ike's arteries, and morphine for shock. Then he gave him a shot of heparin to prevent clotting. At 3:45 he administered a second injection of morphine. Ike fell into a deep sleep. His crisis was passing, but Snyder decided that for the time being he would tell no one of it, not even Mrs. Eisenhower. There was nothing they could do, and the commotion of an alarmed household would only decrease the President's chances.

For nearly four hours the doctor sat alone by the bed. A little before 7 A.M., when others in the gray brick house began to waken, he sent for Ann Whitman. The President was indisposed, he told the secretary; it was a digestive upset. At 10:30 this word was given to the press and flashed around the world. By then, however, Snyder knew he couldn't withhold the truth much longer. He quietly informed Mrs. Eisenhower of it and called the chief of cardiology at Fitzsimons General Hospital, just outside Denver, asking him to bring an electrocardiograph. Ike awoke at 11:45. He was conscious but feeble. The tracing of the electrocardiograph, when spread out on Mrs. Doud's dining room table, confirmed the diagnosis, and Snyder told Ike what had happened. He said, "We would like to take you to Fitzsimons." Then he said that an ambulance would not be necessary. The President nodded and asked him to inform the Secret Service. Assisted down the stairs and into a limousine waiting in the driveway, Ike was driven nine miles to the hospital. There a wheelchair took him to a special suite and an oxygen tent.

At 2:30 P.M. a press aide at Lowry told the White House correspondents there: "The President has just had a mild anterior—let's cut out the word 'anterior'—the President has just had a mild coronary thrombosis. He has just been taken to Fitzsimons General Hospital. He was taken to the hospital in his own car and walked from the house to the car."

His last words were drowned by pandemonium.

In Washington, where it was 4:30 P.M., Jim Hagerty had returned from vacation that morning. Informed by phone of the heart attack shortly before the announcement to the press in Denver, he immediately put through a call to Vice President Nixon's white brick home in Washington's fashionable Spring Valley neighborhood. The Nixons had just returned from a wedding, and the Vice President was reading the *Washington Evening Star*'s brief account of Eisenhower's digestive upset. Hagerty asked him, "Dick, are you sitting down?" Nixon said he wasn't, and then the President's press secretary, speaking very slowly, told him what happened. He said, "The press will be told about it in a half-hour or so." Nixon said, "My God!"

Hanging up, the Vice President walked into his living room in a daze and sat down. According to his later recollection, he said nothing for at least five minutes. After the shock had worn off he phoned William Rogers, then deputy attorney general, and asked him to come at once. By the time Rogers's taxi drew up, the news had been broken in Denver. Nixon's phone was ringing constantly. Outside, a crowd was gathering: neighbors, reporters, photographers. Determined to say nothing to newspapermen, Nixon remained inside as long as he could. By the time he had finished dinner, however, the din outside had become alarming, and he decided to hide out in Rogers's Bethesda home. It was like a movie escape. Rogers called his wife and told her to come and park a block away, keeping the motor running. Then, while nine-year-old Tricia Nixon distracted the crowd on the lawn, the two men darted out a side door, raced down an alley, and jumped into the car.

In Prestwick, Scotland, the weather was cold and drizzly as Sherman Adams, the assistant to the President, checked into headquarters of the U.S. base there with Colonel Andrew J. Goodpaster. Adams had just completed a four-week tour of U.S. installations in Europe; he was meeting General Gruenther for a return flight to Washington that night. Before they could exchange a word the commanding officer of the base darted up and told them that he had just learned the President had been hospitalized in Denver with a heart attack. No details were available. Fleetingly Adams wondered whether Denver's elevation of five thousand feet would be good for a mending heart. Then it occurred to him that if Eisenhower had to be ill, this was a good time for it. Congress was in recess, Ike had no pending obligations as head of state, presidential duties were at a minimum, and planning for the coming year's program, then in its early stages, would not require the President's attention for some time.

Wall Street did not know that. The stock market, which is a kind of fun-house mirror exaggerating ups and downs in the American mood, opened nervously Monday morning as the plane bearing Adams approached the U.S. coast. Then stocks dove. The Dow Jones average plummeted to 444.56; losses were estimated at twelve billion dollars; it was the Street's worst day since the Crash.

The extent of Ike's illness was the only topic of conversation at 1600 Pennsylvania Avenue that noon when Adams arrived in time to lunch with Nixon, Rogers, and Jerry Persons. Halfway through the meal a call came from Denver. Dr. Paul Dudley White, the eminent Boston heart specialist, had completed his first examination of the President and was surprisingly optimistic. Ike's condition was satisfactory, he said, and his morale was good. He would be able to meet a light schedule in two weeks if all went well, and could probably return as a full-time President within a few months. Indeed, Dr. White said, barring the unforeseen, Eisenhower ought to be able to run for reelection. The stock market, delighted with this prognosis, surged back on Tuesday, and administration leaders lunched again, this time in the office of Secretary Humphrey in the Treasury Building, to consider ways of carrying on in the chief's absence.

All that week Washington buzzed with rumors of mistrust and misunderstandings on the highest levels of the government, and all of them were false. Eisenhower's much maligned staff system worked smoothly while he himself lay on a hospital bed 1,551 miles away. On Thursday the cabinet met with Nixon presiding. He read the morning bulletin from Denver—the President had had an excellent night, his first one out of the oxygen tent—and after a review of the diplomatic fronts by Dulles, Brownell led a discussion on the delegation of powers. As things worked out in the days ahead, Nixon signed some papers "in behalf of" the President while Adams really ran the office. Once a week during the rest of Eisenhower's convalescence Adams flew to Denver to report on meetings of the cabinet and the National Security Council. Only urgent problems were brought to the President's bedside. There were few of those; the one topic of substance was the coming State of the Union message, and that wasn't due until January.

In Adams's opinion, "the real key figure in the government" that autumn was Paul Dudley White. By the end of September Dr. White had become the most famous physician in the country. His candid medical briefings reassured the press and the country, and with his encouragement—sometimes, in fact, at his insistence—presidential aides overcame their reluctance to burden the hospitalized chief executive. "Look," White said to Hagerty, "he's not so much of an invalid as he is the President of the United States lying in there. He wants to do his job." On October 14 Ike told Adams he felt fine. "Funny thing," he said. "If the doctors didn't tell me differently, I would think this heart attack belonged to some other guy."

That was his sixty-fifth birthday, and sacks of congratulatory mail were piled high in the hospital auditorium. Over and over the President told visitors how moved he was by them; to Mamie he said, "It really does something for you to know that people all over the world are praying for you." The White House correspondents gave him his gayest moment of the day. Their gift was a suit of fire-engine red pajamas with five tiny gold stars embroidered on each collar tab and "Much Better, Thanks" embroidered over the breast pocket. To complete the gaudy costume, Merriman Smith of the United Press and Laurence H. Burd of the *Chicago Tribune* had contributed a 39-cent black cowboy tie tricked out with silver sequins. Ike was delighted. He told Dr. White these were the most marvelous pajamas he had ever owned. The doctor encouraged him to wear them as often as possible. They were more important than they seemed, White privately told the presidential staff; one of the worst aspects of a heart attack was the depression that accompanied recovery.

For a time it seemed that Ike might be spared that. Discharged from Fitzsimons after a fluoroscopic examination, he returned to Washington on November 11 for a long White House weekend, and on November 14 he drove to his Gettysburg farm with Mrs. Eisenhower. Seven thousand Pennsylvanians greeted him there, waving placards saying GLAD YOU'RE HOME, IKE and WELCOME HOME, IKE AND MAMIE. On November 22 he presided over a cabinet meeting, his first since the attack, at Camp David. All of those present noticed that he had lost weight, but his spirits appeared to be fine. He had seen an editorial expressing surprise that the cabinet could work well without him, he said. In fact, he said with a smile, there were hints that it had worked better. Adams noted: "He was quick, decisive, and keen. I could see that the Cabinet liked what they saw. Some of them were openly astonished by the President's fast recovery and all of them were agreeably surprised."

Then, back in Gettysburg, gloom struck. December was dark, cold, and wet; the putting green at the farm was brown and soggy. Cooped up indoors, he faced, as Hagerty put it, "the sheer, God-awful boredom of not being President." For five terrible weeks he stalked around the farmhouse using a golf club as a cane, suffering in that special hell known only to victims of severe depression. In the two months since his coronary neither he nor anyone close to him had seriously supposed that he might run for another term. Now he began to have second thoughts. Paul Dudley White saw no reason why he shouldn't stay in the White House. It was, the President told those around, something to think about.

Newspapermen raised the question on January 8, 1956, at a Key West press conference. Ike had flown down for a few days of work and exercise. After a thirty-minute stroll he faced the reporters and was asked about his political future. He replied: "All the considerations that apply to such things are complicated. Naturally I will want to confer with my most trusted advisers." He noted that the Presidency was probably the most tiring job in the world but that "it also has, as I have said before, its inspirations." Afterward newsmen asked one another what that had meant. By a margin of nearly five to one they concluded that Ike would retire at the end of this term.

The minority wasn't so sure; they were picking up persistent rumors that the President was scheduling a meeting to weigh that very question. It was true, and the meeting was held that same week. Puckishly Ike called it for the evening of Friday, January 13, and made out place cards for exactly thirteen men. Mrs. Eisenhower joined them for dinner in the Mansion's state dining room and retired when they withdrew into the second-floor Trophy Room. Sitting with his back to the fireplace, Ike explained that he wanted each of them to speak out frankly on the question of whether he should try for another term and why. There was, of course, little doubt about which way the wind would blow. As Adams dryly observed afterward, "I don't imagine that the President expected to get a cross-fire of pro-and-con arguments from a group like that one. . . . If Eisenhower was looking for cogent reasons for leaving his office, he would have hardly sought them from his own appointees."

Adams, Humphrey, Dulles, Hagerty, Summerfield, Lodge, Persons, Len Hall, Brownell, Howard Pyle, Tom Stephens—one by one they told him how indispensable he was. Then Milton Eisenhower, who didn't want his brother to run again, summed up the arguments on both sides. The President made no decision then. He appeared to be undecided as late as February 13. That morning he reminded a cabinet meeting that he had wanted to put into his inaugural address his intention of remaining in office for only one term. He had been dissuaded, he said, and now he regretted it. Adams, however, was already proceeding on the assumption that they would be in the White House for another four years. While the President had been in Key West his chief assistant had called in government carpenters to shorten the office of the presidential appointments secretary, thereby creating a small room adjacent to the office large enough for a cot and a lounging chair—a retreat where Ike could rest before lunch, as Paul Dudley White had recommended. Adams counted on continuing strong support from the doctor for a second term, and he wasn't disappointed; on February 14, in his last medical briefing, White was able to remove the last traces of doubt about his patient's stamina. X-rays of his heart now and before the attack were almost identical, showing that there had been no enlargement of it since he had resumed normal activity in January. If the President ran again, White said, he would vote for him.

The following day the President flew to Secretary Humphrey's Georgia plantation and tested his strength golfing and hunting. He felt fine, and that convinced him: he was going to run. At 4 P.M. Tuesday he told Adams, Nixon, Persons, and Hall, and at 10:37 A.M. on Wednesday, February 29, he announced the news to the press in the Indian Treaty Room. If asked to make the race again, he said, "My answer will be positive, that is, affirmative."

The radio networks broadcast their first bulletin at 10:52, and in the next moment the House Armed Services Committee was given a startling glimpse of the postwar revolution in communications. A witness there was reciting a long list of statistics. Congressmen were dozing, reporters doodling. Only Chairman F. Edward Hebert of Louisiana was bright-eyed. Suddenly he whacked his gavel and cried, "Gentlemen, the President has just announced his candidacy for reelection!" After the excitement had died down a colleague from Illinois asked Hebert how he had known. The telephone hadn't rung, no notes had been passed, no one had entered the room.

Shamefacedly, Hebert confessed; instead of listening to the witness he had been tuned in to one of the tiny new transistor radios, tucked inside the pocket of his coat and hooked up with an earphone that looked like a hearing aid.

In a telecast that evening from the oval office Ike told an audience estimated at 65 million: "I wanted to come into your homes this evening because I felt the need of talking to you directly about a decision I made today after weeks of the most careful and devoutly prayerful consideration. . . . I have decided that if the Republican party chooses to nominate me I shall accept the nomination. Therefore, if the people of this country should elect me I shall continue to serve them in the office I now hold. I have concluded that I should permit the American people to have the opportunity to register their decision in this matter."

Beforehand, he had been chatting with television adviser Robert Montgomery when a network assistant asked him about an inch-high plaque on his desk bearing the Latin motto *Suaviter in Modo, Fortiter in Re,* and the translation "Gently in Manner, Strongly in Deed." The President chuckled and said, "Maybe I'd better hide that; it proves I'm an egghead."

The country's ranking egghead was also in a witty mood. Asked about the President's decision, Adlai Stevenson said, "The real reason Eisenhower is running again is that he can't afford to retire to his farm at Gettysburg while Benson is Secretary of Agriculture."

In the high summer of 1956 the corn stood tall from Mount Rushmore to the panhandle. America seemed to have returned, momentarily at least, to the frivolous 1920s, to wonderful trivia, hot music, placid politics, glamorous athletes, and automobile worship. General Motors president Harlow Curtice was *Time*'s Man of the Year. The compact Rambler was Detroit's current success; Republicans were wondering whether George Romney of American Motors might make a future President.

President Eisenhower's contribution to the American landscape, the interstate highway system, was just getting under way; ultimately it would provide 41,000 miles of new roads—high-speed, limited access, nonstop travel arteries. It was going to be the biggest public works project in the nation's history; the cost was expected to run somewhere between 33 and 41 billion dollars. (It came to 76 billions.) Landlocked cities in the Middle West would be opened to new commerce. The driving time between Chicago and Indianapolis alone would be cut from six hours to three. Roadside services would become a billion-dollar industry, and people and goods would move quickly and safely across the country on well-engineered ribbons of concrete.

It was appropriate that in 1956 Oregon miler Jim Bailey was clocked at 3:58.6, the first under-four-minute mile run in the United States. Americans were not only moving toward new horizons; they could hardly wait to get there. The Gross National Product was 400 billion dollars' worth of goods and services that year, and inflation was still negligible, though a warning of what lay ahead came in February, when after twenty-four years of unchanged postal rates, first-class mail went from three cents to four and airmail from six cents to seven.

Businessmen pointed with pride to the increase in productivity, and sermons and editorials viewed with alarm the frantic pace of American life. Popular misconceptions to the contrary, however, America did not lead the world in suicides. According to the World Health Organization, the U.S. suicide rate was 10.8 per 100,000 (16.1 for men and 4.3 for women), which put it far down the list, below Denmark (24.1), Austria, Switzerland, Japan, Sweden, West Germany, Finland, France, and England and Wales. Of course, psychiatric help was now more available for Americans, and beginning in 1956 jittery executives could find peace with meprobamate, an exceptionally effective tranquilizer better known by its trade name, Miltown. *Time* called Miltown "Don't-Give-a-Damn Pills." Their first big markets were Madison Avenue and Hollywood. In Hollywood, a drugstore at Sunset and Gower pasted a huge red sign across its display window: "Yes, we have Miltown!" Milton Berle said, "I'm thinking of changing my name to Miltown Berle." It was a poor year for humor.

Popular athletes of the 1940s were entering the cruel twilight of their trade: Joe DiMaggio was in his forties, and now that Floyd Patterson was heavyweight champion, Joe Louis, overweight and slow, was stumbling into the oblivion of professional wrestling. Jackson Pollock died and Liberace arrived, accompanied by his ubiquitous mother. Grace Metalious and Françoise Sagan also emerged, edifying nobody, and so did a new minstrel of youth whose voice seemed to be everywhere, singing, "Hi luh-luh-luh-luv yew-hew," or

Awopbopaloobop! alopbamboom!
Tutti Frutti! Aw rutti!
Tutti Frutti! Aw rutti!

Elvis Aaron Presley made his movie debut that fall in *Love Me Tender*. He sang four songs in a secondary role, and his curious amalgam of rock 'n' roll, bluegrass, and boogie dominated the show. All year he toured the South and West, fighting off hysterical teen-agers in pedal pushers and boosting his first LP album—it went straight to the top of *Billboard's* weekly ratings—and such singles as "Don't Be Cruel" and "Heartbreak Hotel," each of which sold over a million copies.

Presley shocked the parents of young girls. Drape-suited and tight-panted, his petulant eyes glassy and his pouting lips hanging open, he would grip the microphone, crouch, and then buck his hips against his dangling guitar. Television producers refused to show him below the waist. They called him lewd, and they were right; that was the secret of his appeal. Teen-aged girls carved his name on their forearms with pen knives while older women bestowed gifts upon him and tried to lure him away. In Amarillo a reporter asked him if he was contemplating marriage. He replied, "Why buy a cow when you can get the milk through the fence?"

Offstage Presley could be refreshingly straightforward. Unlike Liberace, Presley had no musical pretensions. He recalled that he had been given a guitar when he was twelve. "I beat on it for a year or two," he said. "Never did learn much about it." Tired of driving trucks, he had taken the guitar to a recording studio. "It sounded like somebody beatin' on a bucket lid," he said, "but the engineer at this studio had a recording company called Sun, and he told me I had an unusual voice, and he might call me up sometime." When Presley records started to sell, he acquired a manager who said, "He may not sound like a hillbilly, but he gets the same response."

The pervasive vulgarity of Elvis the Pelvis was part of his appeal. He liked to spend hours at amusement parks riding dodgem cars, wore $10,000 gold lamé suits, and bought a fleet of Cadillacs painted in pastels. Obsessed with his hair—it was turning prematurely gray—and guarded by a ratpack of muscular young men who doubled as companions, he settled down in a garish estate ringed with sentry boxes. When he wanted to go nightclubbing word would be phoned ahead, so that precautions could be taken. Like royalty, he carried no cash. Then, like G. David Schine, he was drafted. In Germany, where he was stationed, he received much attention from the local press, in which he was identified as a symbol of American culture.

Presley in the flesh wasn't much different from the comic opera roles he played on the screen. In this he was supremely a man of the time. There was little room in the ambiance of 1956 for genuine tragedy. Sober events were ignored or externalized. It is significant that on July 20, 1956, one of the most important dates in American history, headline writers were enthralled by the fact that Eisenhower had at last balanced a budget. None noted that on that day, according to the Geneva agreement of 1954, free elections were to be held in Vietnam. The failure to hold them would produce the Viet Cong, civil war, and American intervention; but commentators had no time for its implications then.

The catastrophes that did attract attention were explicit, obvious; the kind that tabloids feed on. It was a time of sensations. Victor Riesel, a New York labor columnist, was blinded by a man who threw acid in his face. Dr. Jesús de Galíndez disappeared outside a Manhattan subway station; presumably he was kidnapped by henchmen of Rafael Trujillo, the dictator of the Dominican Republic, and murdered. On Parris Island, South Carolina, a Marine Corps drill instructor led 74 recruits into a treacherous tidal stream; six of them drowned. In Boston the FBI solved a $2,775,000 Brink's robbery, and the great Hungarian uprising was encouraged by Radio Free Europe in an act of criminal irresponsibility.

In June of 1956 Phyllis Brown, an editor at the Research Institute of America, entertained Wisconsin bankers at their annual convention with a charming little talk on the innate frailties of her sex. Never tell a woman she is being illogical, she said: "The average woman starts off on the premise that the way she feels about something is itself a most compelling argument." Miss Brown further recommended that they praise women more than men and remember that women always take things personally.

Time reprinted this Aunt Tom's remarks with a manly good humor. In another issue *Time*'s editors put a woman of intellectual pretensions in her place by reporting that "Like many of her sisters in what she bitterly refers to as the Second Sex, France's Simone de Beauvoir would rather talk than eat." Women's magazines, edited by men, treated their subscribers with similar condescension. A *Ladies' Home Journal* editor explained to a writer, "If we get an article about a woman who does anything adventurous, out of the way, something by herself, you know, we figure she must be terribly aggressive, neurotic." At the peak of feminine achievement the *Journal* introduced to its readers a Texas housewife who had her face made up an hour after breakfast and could say, "By 8:30 A.M., when my youngest goes to school, my whole house is clean and neat and I am dressed for the day, I am free to play bridge, attend club meetings, or stay home and read, listen to Beethoven, and just plain loaf."

There were signs, for those who could read them, that not all of her sisters were satisfied with bridge or club meetings. In 1956 *McCall's* published an innocent little piece called "The Mother Who Ran Away" and was dumbfounded to find that it drew more readers than anything they had ever carried. Later *Redbook* ran an article on "Why Young Mothers Feel Trapped." Young mothers who felt that way were encouraged to write in—and more than twenty-four thousand of them did. But the notion that a woman should aspire to become something other than a fetching housewife was too heretical to take hold. The altar remained the only acceptable destination for single girls, and those who managed to reach it with a prize groom in tow became celebrities. Memorable brides of 1956 included Mrs. E. Clifton Daniel Jr., née Margaret Truman, and the former Odile Rodin, who became the fifth wife of Porfirio Rubirosa. (Her predecessors were Danielle Darrieux, Doris Duke, Barbara Hutton, and the daughter of Rafael Trujillo.) The ultimate prize, however, was won that year by a pretty actress from Philadelphia who, after being wooed by dress designer Oleg Cassini and actor Jean-Paul Aumont, hooked the most eligible bachelor in Europe: Prince Rainier III of Monaco. How Grace Kelly did it was a secret to be pondered by the wives of America as they loaded their automatic washing machines and scoured the blades of their husbands' electric carving knives. All her father would say was: "Grace met him when she was on the French Riviera. She went there to make a picture called *To Catch a Thief*—and look what she came back with."

The father, a Philadelphia contractor and politician who had been national sculling champion and therefore something of a catch himself, recalled that when the prince first called at the Kelly mansion, "I was under the impression he was going to stay just a couple of hours. But he stayed and stayed and stayed." Kelly was wary. ("I don't generally approve of these oddballs she goes out with.") Then Rainier asked for Grace's hand. This being too important a matter for her, she was sent off while the menfolk conferred. In a speech which might be memorized by every American tycoon whose daughter is being courted by a sovereign, Kelly warned Rainier to beware the occupational weaknesses of his class: "I told the prince that royalty didn't mean a thing to us. I told him that I certainly hoped he wouldn't run around the way some princes do, and I told him that if he did, he'd lose a mighty fine girl." Mrs. Kelly sold her as-told-to memoirs to Hearst (*My Daughter Grace Kelly, Her Life and Romances*). The *Chicago Tribune*, in an allusion to Monaco's Monte Carlo, complained, "She's too well-bred a girl to marry the silent partner in a gambling parlor." Aristotle Onassis, who virtually owned Monte Carlo and would continue to pay no French taxes if Grace presented her husband with an heir, cried, "I am mad with joy," and gave the Monaco Red Cross a million francs.

The Kelly-Rainier wedding was an MGM press agent's dream, one reason being that the MGM publicity department had a hand in it. On April 12 the American Export liner *Constitution* hovered off the French coast and set Grace on the deck of the prince's white yacht *Deo Juvante II*. Accompanying her were 80 wedding guests, 24 columnists, four trunks, 20 hatboxes, 36 other pieces of luggage, and the bride's black French poodle, Oliver. Overhead, an aircraft from Onassis's private squadron bombarded the yacht with red and white carnations. From the shore came a din: klaxons, sirens, rockets, and cannon firing 21-gun salutes. The dock was literally black with newspapermen—1,500 of them from all over the world, more than had covered the Geneva summit the year before. Ashore and with Grace beside him in his green Chrysler Imperial, Rainier discovered that his way was temporarily blocked by fifty photographers. Everyone seemed to be in Monaco except the ones the couple most wanted: Europe's more famous crowned heads. Elizabeth II had declined to come, and other members of European royalty had followed her example. England was represented in Monaco by a minor diplomat and Randolph Churchill, who yelled in a moment of pique, "I didn't come here to meet vulgar people like the Kellys."

If Elizabeth was wary of being exploited by the world press, others with famous names didn't mind at all. President Eisenhower was represented at the wedding by Conrad Hilton, the hotel magnate. The Aga Khan was there with his begum. Somerset Maugham led Monte Carlo's literary contingent, and former King Farouk of Egypt, now obese and besotted, distressed the wedding marshals by waddling up the central staircase of St. Nicholas Cathedral, supposedly reserved for the bridal party. He was whisked aside and the principals arrived. Grace said "*Je veux,*" thereby becoming twice a princess, four times a duchess, nine times a baroness, eight times a countess, four times a marchioness, and once a viscountess. Her wedding gifts included a quarter-million dollars in diamonds alone. Pickpockets at the festivities made off with $150,000, but to Onassis, who kept picking up tabs, it was all worth it. In August Rainier disclosed that his wife was pregnant. Monaco celebrated the announcement with fireworks, trumpets, bonfires, and dancing in the street and the *New York Daily Mirror* used a line it had been saving almost a year: MONACO WEATHER FORECAST: A LITTLE RAINIER IN FEBRUARY.

In the four years since Farouk had fled Cairo, taking his priceless collection of pornography with him, Egypt had become the stronghold of a military clique. Lieutenant Colonel Gamal Abdel Nasser emerged in June 1956 as the leader of the junta. John Foster Dulles believed he had Nasser's number, and he decided to teach him a lesson. The upshot was a minor war and, ironically, a tremendous boost for President Eisenhower in his campaign for reelection.

As a neutral in the cold war, Nasser was naturally anathema to Dulles. The United States had been trying to coax Egypt into the western camp. With that in view, Washington had told Cairo the previous winter that it would loan the Egyptians 56 million dollars for their three-mile Aswan High Dam on the Nile. But Nasser was ungrateful. He recognized Red China, tried to break up the Baghdad Pact, announced plans to visit Moscow, and traded 200 million dollars' worth of cotton for Czechoslovakian guns. Thereupon Dulles, on July 19, publicly canceled the American loan. Foreign service officers on the State Department's Middle Eastern desk had warned that Nasser might seize the Suez Canal in retaliation. He did. He cried, "I look at Americans and say: may you choke to death on your fury!" He said, "We shall build the high dam as we desire. The annual income of the Suez Canal is 100 million dollars. Why not take it ourselves?" Then: "We shall rely on our own strength, our own muscle, our own funds. And it will be run by Egyptians! Egyptians! Egyptians!"

The full weight of this blow fell not upon the United States, but on Britain and France. At the urging of anticolonialists in Washington, the British had withdrawn the last of their troops from Suez in June. Now Nasser had cut Anglo-French industry off from its chief source of petroleum. Of the 1.5 million barrels of oil that passed through the canal each day, 1.2 million went to western Europe. Suez provided two-thirds of the fuel the continent needed for heat and production, and the other third came overland through pipes that could easily be sabotaged by the Arabs. Therefore this was a real crisis for London and Paris. It would have taxed the gifts of a Disraeli, and the householder at 10 Downing Street was no Disraeli. He was Sir Anthony Eden, once Churchill's great foreign secretary and now worn to a shadow. The office of prime minister was simply too much for him. Struggling along with less than five hours sleep a night, he became addicted to amphetamines. Years later medical scientists discovered that amphetamines could rob a sensible man of his good judgment, and that was what happened to Eden in 1956.

Blaming Dulles for their plight, Eden and Guy Mollet, the French premier, turned their backs on Washington. They decided to tackle the problem in their own way—or, to be precise, in the way advocated by David Ben-Gurion. To the Israeli premier, this seemed a perfect time to settle accounts with the hated Egyptians. Russia was preoccupied by a developing crisis in Hungary, the United States was in the middle of a national election, and the British and the French, furious at Nasser, were spoiling for a fight. Ben-Gurion reminded them that under certain circumstances an Anglo-French expeditionary force could act in the Middle East under a cloak of legitimacy. The Tripartite Declaration of 1950 provided that Britain and France could reoccupy the Suez Canal if war erupted between Israel and Egypt. Ben-Gurion said he would be delighted to provide that excuse, and Eden and Mollet endorsed the plan.

In the last week of October the CIA received troubling reports. Israel was mobilizing. More than 100,000 Israeli troops were poised along their border with Egypt, and Israeli tanks were in position for a lunge westward. Whitehall and the Quai d'Orsay had lapsed into a studied silence. To Washington the very correctness of their behavior was puzzling. They were like men building up an alibi. It was hard to believe that they could be plotting with Jerusalem, though. Eisenhower, who was in Walter Reed for a physical checkup on Sunday, October 28, rejected the idea. Drafting notes to Ben-Gurion between trips up and down hospital corridors for tests, Ike said wryly, "Israel and barium make quite a combination."

The Israelis struck the next day. At 3 P.M. Washington time teletypes chattered out the first bulletin: Israeli forces were crossing into Egyptian territory. Eden and Mollet now had their justification. They went through the motions of sending ultimatums to Jerusalem and Cairo demanding that both sides lay down their arms. In the House of Commons Eden said, "We have asked the Egyptian government to agree that Anglo-French forces should move temporarily into key positions." If the request was ignored, he said, British and French troops would intervene in Suez "in whatever strength may be necessary."

Eisenhower had left the hospital to campaign in the South. Now he rushed back to Washington. At 7 P.M. that Monday, as dusk began to gather in the capital, his limousine entered the southwest gate of the White House grounds. After conferring with Adams, Radford, Persons, and the Dulles brothers, he authorized a statement from Hagerty: "At the meeting the President recalled that the United States, under this and prior administrations, had pledged itself to assist the victim of any aggression in the Middle East. We shall honor our pledge."

On Wednesday British bombers based in Cyprus attacked Egyptian airfields. Ike said, "I just don't know what got into those people. It's the damnedest business I ever saw supposedly intelligent people get themselves into." But: "We cannot subscribe to one law for the weak, another for those allied with us." In a Wednesday telecast he told the American people just that. The British and the French, who held Dulles responsible for the whole mess, were furious. Eden let it be known that he would reject any U.N. cease-fire proposal. On Saturday Dulles, exhausted and distraught, collapsed; an ulcer had penetrated his abdominal wall; he was taken to Walter Reed for two and a half hours of surgery. The world seemed very near war that weekend. On Sunday the White House learned that British and French troops were boarding transports at Cyprus for an invasion of Suez. Early Monday British paratroopers began landing on the north end of the canal. That evening Bulganin warned Eden,

Mollet, and Ben-Gurion that unless they withdrew immediately they would become targets for Red missiles loaded with nuclear warheads. At the same time Bulganin proposed to Eisenhower that the United States and the Soviet Union form an alliance to stop the invasion. Ike was indignant. To an aide he said, "Those British—they're still my right arm!" He told Bulganin that Russo-American intervention was "unthinkable" and accused the Soviet premier of trying to divert attention from Hungary, where the Red Army "at this very moment is brutally repressing the human rights of the Hungarian people."

This was more than cold war rhetoric. Ike was right: the Russians were also guilty of atrocities that week. Afterward the Communists would remember Suez while the West remembered Hungary; in fact the two were equally ugly. On Wednesday, the day of the first RAF raids on the canal zone, anti-Soviet rioters in Budapest had made Imre Nagy premier of Hungary. By Saturday the entire country had risen. Nagy denounced the Warsaw Pact, which made Hungary a Soviet satellite. Russian troops withdrew from Budapest and then regrouped to crush the revolt. The streets were carpeted with the bodies of Budapest's martyrs, Joseph Cardinal Mindszenty took refuge in the besieged American embassy, and the Hungarian delegation to the United Nations begged the U.N. to intervene. Lodge introduced a measure which would do that. The Russians vetoed it. Eisenhower spent twenty million dollars in Mutual Security funds on food and medicine for Hungary. He ordered that 21,500 Hungarian refugees be admitted to the United States and told his staff to see to it that the administration found homes and jobs for them, and he sent protests to Bulganin. The Soviet premier coldly replied that Russia and Hungary would settle their differences without outside help.

On the morning of Tuesday, November 6, 1956, French infantry seized the east side of the canal, Russian troops captured Nagy, the U.N. General Assembly condemned Soviet aggression, and 61,616,938 Americans went to the polls. War was on everyone's mind, and the country's most famous general was on the ballot. The conclusion that the voters put the two together is inescapable. Perhaps they were right to do so. Certainly Ike retained his poise throughout that terrible week. Adams was with the President in his oval office when Eden phoned. Eisenhower said heartily, "Well, Anthony, how *are* you?"

It was a question, Adams dryly observed, which, "it seemed to me at the time, would have required a long and involved answer."

Afterward there is a certain inevitability to political landslides, and this one was no exception. Eisenhower would have been reelected if Nasser had kept his hands off Suez and Hungary had remained servile. No Democratic candidate could have driven him from office, and to those who enjoy hindsight it may seem surprising that a man as intelligent as Adlai Stevenson didn't realize that. Gallup figures showed that the President retained the confidence of better than seven out of every ten Americans. In his first term he had accomplished much that had seemed unattainable four years earlier. The Korean War had been ended, and without a depression. McCarthy had been routed. The Bricker amendment was a dead issue. Knowland stood isolated in the Senate. The Republican party was now committed to the United Nations, and except for Styles Bridges no Republican with a safe seat was advocating the invasion of China or a preventive war against Russia. Furthermore, Ike's management of domestic problems suggested that he was a wiser politician than he appeared to be. His federal highway program was outspending the WPA. Inflation had been checked. Labor was getting a larger share of the national income. Social security had been extended. The administration had built a sound antitrust program, and its soil bank, by appeasing farmers, had robbed the Democrats of a major issue.

The President had still other assets, less tangible but very real, which could be redeemed at the polls. His personality was gilt-edged political capital. Joseph Alsop wrote that "Eisenhower's greatest single contribution has been bringing us back to a sense of the true American style—setting the style, in fact, by his own example and in the most trying circumstances," and Richard H. Rovere concluded that "when Eisenhower has spoken for the nation, he has . . . in general appeared before the world as a not unworthy successor to those few American presidents whom the world has known and respected."

This account is, of course, incomplete. If those had been the only issues, the Democrats would not have battled so hard for the nomination. To them the administration seemed highly pregnable. The GOP was more than ever the party of big business. The schism between liberal Republicans and the Old Guard continued to be unsightly. Dulles's performance abroad had been less than brilliant, as the mess in the Middle East demonstrated. Apart from these, there were three overriding major points at issue: the President's health, Vice President Nixon, and the eloquence and charm of the Democratic nominee.

Hopes for Dwight Eisenhower's longevity were at best precarious. If reelected he would be seventy before he left office. Only a year ago he had suffered a massive heart attack, and he himself had observed that the Presidency was the most demanding job in the world. Moreover, there was worry about more than his heart. Less than ten weeks before the national conventions he was stricken with another ailment, taken from the White House in an ambulance, and subjected to a two-hour ordeal on the operating table.

At first the Denver scenario seemed to be repeating itself. In the small hours of June 9 Dr. Snyder was awakened in his Connecticut Avenue apartment by an anxious Mamie Eisenhower. The President was tossing and turning. He complained of stomach pains. What should she do? Milk of magnesia was ineffective, and Snyder hurried to the Executive Mansion. After breakfast Hagerty issued a brief statement: "The President has an upset stomach and headache. Dr. Snyder has been with him since early this morning. There is nothing wrong with his heart." But that was far from reassuring. The Denver crisis had also begun with a "digestive upset." A second statement was more specific: "The President has had an attack of ileitis (inflammation of the lower portion of the small intestine)." As a "precaution" he was entering Walter Reed Hospital.

It was a wretched day for Hagerty. He kept telling reporters that ileitis wasn't serious while appearances indicated that it was. The ambulance left the Mansion behind a screen of motorcycles with screaming sirens. Paul Dudley White appeared. ("They wanted me on hand in case anything needed to be done," he said.) Another specialist was stopped by state policemen in South Carolina and hurried aboard a jet trainer for a supersonic trip to Walter Reed, where a dozen surgeons were examining the lower part of the President's digestive system. Surgery was necessary—without it the condition could lead to gangrene of the bowel—but Hagerty had been right, there was nothing to worry about. Afterward Dr. Leonard D. Heeton, the leading surgeon, was asked whether he thought Ike should decline to run for reelection. He said, "I certainly do not." Of the President's life expectancy Snyder said, "We think it improves it." The physicians estimated that he would be back on the job in four to six weeks, and headlines across the country read OKAY FOR IKE TO RUN SAY DOCTORS.

Kenneth S. Davis, Stevenson's biographer, believed afterward that the frailty of Eisenhower's health, "far from being a hazard to his reelection, was probably a political asset. Having passed through the valley of the shadow of death, he was now a greater hero, more beloved of the populace than before." Davis thinks this was due to Ike's personal qualities, "to the perfection with which he expressed the dominant mood of the country and to the warm affection he personally inspired." Democrats were aware of Eisenhower's appeal and treated him gingerly.

Nixon was another matter. The leaders of the party out of power had noted with grim pleasure that he had reconsidered and decided to run again. They took it as an article of faith that the rest of the country despised the Vice President as much as they did, and they went for him with sandbags. Stevenson called the Vice President "shifty," "rash," "inexperienced," and a "man of many masks," and in Minneapolis on November 5 he told listeners that Nixon "has put away his switch-blade and now assumes the aspect of an Eagle Scout." The Vice President, he reminded them, had recently declared in their city that there would be no war in the Middle East. Like many other Democrats, Stevenson honestly thought that a Nixon succession to the Presidency would be a catastrophe.

Nixon could ignore the opposition, and he did. The critics in his own party were more serious. Ironically, the GOP leader of the "Dump Nixon movement," as it was called, was Harold Stassen, Nixon's first political idol. Not without reason, Stassen believed that the President wouldn't be heartbroken if the movement succeeded. To an adviser Ike expressed doubts about Nixon's stature and then said: "Well, the fact is, of course, I've watched Dick a long time, and he just hasn't grown. So I just haven't honestly been able to believe that he is presidential timber."

At that point the party's rank and file took a hand. Republican voters, always strong for Nixon, let their wishes be known; in the New Hampshire and Oregon primaries 52,202 of them wrote his name in under Ike's. That impressed Nixon, if not Stassen. On April 26 the Vice President asked for an appointment with the President and told him he would be happy to make the race again. Eisenhower rang for Hagerty, who came in to find the two running mates of 1952 grinning at each other. According to Hagerty's recollection, the President said, "Jim, Dick just told me he would be happy to be on the ticket, and he has made up his mind that he would like to run again with me." Adams and Persons came in, and after they had the news Ike said to Hagerty, "What do you think we ought to do on the announcement?" The press secretary suggested that Nixon make it to White House correspondents right now. Eisenhower nodded and said, "Jim, you go with him, and after he finishes his announcement, you say I was delighted to hear this news from the Vice President."

That was the end of serious attempts to dump Nixon in 1956, and for all practical purposes it was the end of Harold Stassen's political career. His arguments had convinced only one delegate, an eccentric Nebraskan named Terry Carpenter who had been identified with the Coughlin-Townsend fringe in the 1930s. In the roll call of states Carpenter expressed his displeasure with Nixon by casting one vice-presidential vote for a mythical "Joe Smith," thereby providing the San Francisco convention with one of its two memorable moments. The other one came when Eisenhower paused in his acceptance speech to berate liberal columnists. That brought the delegates to their feet, roaring. For as long as they could remember they had suffered the barbs and quips of publicists who had small use for them and their party, and now their President gave them a chance to get a little of their own back. Next day the political writers filled columns with passionate defenses of freedom of the press. In the long run it made no difference. The resentment of political journalists was in the open now, and in a later Republican administration Nixon and his own Vice President would build it into a major issue.

Four years earlier Governor Stevenson had won the admiration of the commentators by his dignity and grace in defeat. This was his second time round, and it was too much to expect that he could repeat that sparkling performance. He didn't. He dulled the memory of it. Musing over the tactics which had won in 1952, the Democratic standard-bearer succumbed to the fatal charms of the media manipulators. He allowed himself to be drawn into discussions of the relative merits of the "old" Stevenson and the "new" Stevenson, as if there were two of him running around, and there was a lot of mindless chatter in his entourage about the "blurring" of his "image."

"The campaign of 1956 was curious and special," a veteran Democrat later told Emmet John Hughes. "It was nearly a classic of its kind. For it's almost impossible to recall anything you people did wrong—and nearly as hard to remember anything we did right." The worst thing was Truman's emergence from retirement. Trying to secure the nomination for Governor Averell Harriman of New York, he drew Stevenson into a wasting intraparty fight for political survival, and when he found he couldn't rule the convention he seemed bent upon ruining Stevenson's hopes. In his anger the former President gave the Republicans ammunition beyond their wildest hopes. He called Stevenson a "conservative" who followed the "counsel of hesitation" and lacked "the kind of fighting spirit we need to win."

Stevenson had other handicaps. He should have been dueling with Eisenhower, not Truman and Nixon. But the President had taken a lofty stance above the battle. Like President Roosevelt, he wouldn't let his opponent come to grips with him. When not preoccupied with the deepening crises abroad, he ran serenely on the GOP's bland campaign slogan, "Peace, Progress, Prosperity." Nixon, meantime, had discovered what would later become one of his most familiar political stratagems. Confronted by alternatives, he would choose the popular one while insisting that it was really the harder of the two. It would be "easy," he said, for him to endorse an end to hydrogen bomb testing, as Stevenson was urging. Then, his voice vibrating, the Vice President announced that his conscience compelled him to defy public opinion and call for continuing tests. Actually it was Stevenson who was taking the hard road; few votes were lost that year by demanding bigger and better bombs. Nixon was having it both ways, pleasing the majority while winning marks for audacity.

The professionals in Stevenson's camp warned that the testing issue would alienate large blocs of Democrats, especially in ethnic and blue-collar neighborhoods. He knew it, and his decision to plunge ahead anyway, insisting that what he had to say needed saying, was an example of true political courage. In such moments the gallant candidate of 1952 could still be seen. He hadn't lacked heart then and didn't now. His difficulties were with shrewdness and native cunning—small virtues, perhaps, but essential in a political leader.

To laymen, Eisenhower's testing argument—that improved bombs must be built so that the U.S. could "negotiate" from a "position of strength rather than weakness," that "the only way to win World

War III is to prevent it"—sounded persuasive. While time would later vindicate Stevenson, elections are not won by such moral victories. The cold war was still a formidable reality in 1956. Stevenson misjudged its impact, and not only on the question of testing. In the middle of one address he declared that it was time to take a "new look" at American defenses and to consider "ending the draft." So many voices were raised in protest that he was thrown on the defensive, never a good stance for the challenger.

As November approached, Stevenson's campaign became wobbly. He was tired, he was careless, and in his election eve telecast he was guilty of bad taste. Repugnant as the matter was, he said, "I must say bluntly that every piece of scientific evidence we have, every lesson of history and experience, indicates that a Republican victory tomorrow would mean that Richard M. Nixon would probably be President of the country within the next four years." It was true. Saying it in a nationwide broadcast was another matter. It jarred Stevenson's followers, and it was an unhappy note upon which to end a brave battle against odds.

The dimensions of the second Eisenhower avalanche were awesome. He won 457 electoral votes to Stevenson's 72, amassing a triumphant margin of nearly ten million votes. For the first time in a quarter of a century, Negroes were voting Republican. The President had won two-thirds of the nonunion labor vote and 45 percent of the votes of union members. He had swept all the new suburbs. His plurality was 16 percent, just two points behind Hoover's in 1928.

This time Eisenhower celebrated in the presidential suite of Washington's Sheraton Park. By 9 P.M. what little suspense there had been was over. Sherman Adams was sitting on the floor staring rapturously at a small TV tube. Jerry Persons called out in his Alabama accent: "I want all of you to know that the cradle of the Confederacy—Montgomery, Alabama—has just voted for a Republican for the first time in its history!" Ike led the cheering. To Emmet Hughes he said, "There's Michigan and Minnesota still to see. You remember the story of Nelson—dying, he looked around and asked, 'Are there any of them still left?' I guess that's me. When I get in a battle, I just want to win the whole thing . . . six or seven states we can't help. But I don't want to lose any more. Don't want any of them 'left'—like Nelson. That's the way I feel."

All in all it had been a tedious election. Yet there had been one exciting moment at the Democratic convention. Declining to select his running mate, Stevenson had announced that the delegates would make the choice, and in the ensuing turmoil the watching nation had been given a glimpse of the future.

The scramble was between Estes Kefauver, Albert Gore, Robert Wagner, John F. Kennedy, and—the only man who had come to Chicago as an avowed vice-presidential candidate—Hubert Humphrey. Kefauver won, but Kennedy, in nearly beating him, had made a greater impression on the watching audience. The nomination had seemed to be in his grasp after Senator Lyndon Johnson came out for him, shouting tremulously, "Texas proudly casts its vote for the fighting sailor who wears the scars of battle," but at that moment Missouri switched from Gore to Kefauver. Next day the *New York Herald Tribune*'s convention story began, "The famous Kennedy luck ran out today." Actually, losing the vice-presidential nomination was the luckiest thing that had ever happened to Kennedy. He had appeared on the rostrum to make a short, charming speech of concession, and his winning manner had created an instant Kennedy constituency. The country was now aware of him. As James MacGregor Burns noted, "Kennedy's near-victory and sudden loss, the impression he gave of a clean-cut boy who had done his best and who was accepting defeat with a smile—all this struck at people's hearts in living rooms across the nation."

That was half of it. The other half was that since he hadn't made the ticket, its subsequent defeat couldn't be blamed on him or, more especially, on his Catholicism, which had been regarded as a crushing political handicap since Hoover's rout of Al Smith in 1928. Shortly after the election Kennedy was told that he would easily win the vice-presidential nomination in 1960. "I'm not running for Vice President any more," he said crisply. "I'm now running for President."

Twenty-three

THE PURSUIT OF HAPPINESS

THE EISENHOWER SIESTA, as it may be called, extended from the Korean armistice in 1953 to the autumn of 1957, when Americans who had assumed that their technical supremacy would never be challenged were dismayed to learn that rocketeers in the Soviet Union had stolen a long march on them. After that, the country's self-confidence was never the same. Ahead lay a frantic hundred-billion-dollar scramble to reassert the U.S. technological lead by exploring the stars while, year by year, disheartening developments on earth were causing a new and different erosion of American pride. To those who had cherished it, the 1953–57 breather would come to be remembered as an uncomplicated, golden time, mourned as lost childhoods are mourned and remembered, in nostalgia, as cloudless.

If it was never that splendid, neither was it as flatulent as its intellectuals made it out to be. In their view these were dreary, complacent years of an all-out, pedal-to-the-floor materialistic binge in which mass society bred alienation, conformity, facelessness, and moral emptiness; a frivolous boredom and a joyless vulgarity; a time of rootlessness, when small-town hotels were being replaced by 41,000 motels, at the more pretentious of which you could, for a quarter, lie on a bed and have your erogenous zones jiggled. The disillusioned saw America as a country in which religion had been reduced to Dial-a-Prayer, *Modern Screen*'s series on "How the Stars Found Faith," and prepackaged sixty-second solutions for every spiritual problem. In this judgment the mid-1950s were entirely lacking in merit, with status being represented by the key to the executive washroom, virility by the Mennen After-Shave Club, democracy by a vote for Miss Rheingold, decor by the knotty pine rumpus room, and economics by You Auto Buy Now.

There *were* a lot of gadgets. Technological change had never held a greater fascination for Americans. Men talked wonderingly of transistors, those slivers of germanium or silicon no bigger than a shoelace tip which, when not running tiny radios like Congressman Hebert's, were powering hearing aids so small that they could fit in the frames of spectacles and lightening the load of fighter planes by 1,500 pounds. But all the gadgetry wasn't necessarily bad. Only an ascetic crank could despise the Simmons Company for promoting king- and queen-sized Beautyrest mattresses. If it was absurd to find strips of paper across motel toilet seats reading "This seat has been sterilized for your protection," the fact remained that too much cleanliness was preferable to too little. And after Los Alamos and all that it was rather engaging to find that American technologists were now making life more comfortable.

There was nothing inherently wrong with the innovations, though their sheer number was sometimes bewildering: central vacuuming, vinyl flooring, push-button phones, stereo FM sets, washer-dryers, automatic transmissions, drive-in shopping malls, air-conditioned buses, electric blankets, electric floor polishers, electric pencil sharpeners, electric can openers, and electric floor waxers, to name only the most conspicuous. One by one they appeared, were assimilated into the general experience, and became a part of the average middle-class American's routine. And little by little the more practical innovations altered everyday existence. At one time or another in the mid-1950s millions of men and women of the swing generation realized that in countless little ways life had become easier, more tolerable, more convenient, more interesting—in a word, more livable. At about the same time they remembered the Depression. With a sense of awe they realized: *It's gone.*

And so it had. Evidence of a surge to abundance was everywhere. The boom arose from many springs; natural resources, global politics after World War II, demography, the altered economy of Western Europe, and Americans' love of work. The United States was producing half of the world's goods. Since the war the Gross National Product had doubled. (By the early 1970s it would double again.) U.S. investment abroad had increased from twelve billion dollars to eighty billions. The budget of one firm, General Motors, had grown to the size of Poland's.

The consequence of all this was a standard of living beyond the comprehension of the rest of the world. Nearly 60 percent of all American families were reporting wages in the middle-class brackets. Just since the late 1940s the median family income had risen from $3,083 to $5,657; even when corrected for inflation this meant a rise of 48 percent. America, in Adolf A. Berle's phrase, was in the throes of "galloping capitalism." The proletariat was being transformed. Assembly line workers with working wives were driving expensive new automobiles and buying stocks. *Fortune* in May 1954 suggested that it was "time to change the stereotype of the American middle-class consumer. He is not, and has not been for some years, a small landlord or drugstore proprietor. If any stereotype at all is meaningful, it might be the machinist in Detroit."

No sooner had the Depression survivor comprehended the new prosperity than he became obsolescent. Economic prosperity had been the impossible dream of his youth. His fiscal instincts were timid, defensive; if he could get a hundred dollars together, he squirreled it away. But thrift had suddenly become old-fashioned. Americans who had come of age since World War II, who had no memory of the lean years, were spending every cent they could lay their hands on together with other income they wouldn't earn for a long time to come. "Big spender" became a term of approbation. The spenders were living on credit and buying on margin like the speculators of 1929, except that they were acquiring consumer goods, not securities. Life for them was life on the installment plan. Between 1952 and 1956 consumer debt in the United States increased from 27.4 billion dollars to 42.5 billions, or 55 percent. Installment credit grew 63 percent and that for automobiles almost 100 percent. Though these were boom years, disposable income for individuals increased by merely 21 percent. The new Americans were in hock to the future, and they were plainly enjoying it. They spoke with easy confidence of "debt consolidation" and revolving credit plans. A new profession, debt counseling, sprang up to advise them on ways of handling their credit.

Even the big earners among the new suburbanites saved little. In both Long Island's Levittown and Illinois's Park Forest, the average bank deposit was about $300. Accustomed to tax withholding and packaged mortgages, the young couples were indifferent to rates of interest. Installment buyers asked of a new purchase only the size of the monthly payments. They actually seemed to find security in the entrapment of bank loans, in the obligations of coupon books with specified payments and debts. And the banks were delighted to oblige them. "Instead of merchandising the idea of saving," William H. Whyte Jr. observed, they were providing "the apparatus of it."

Grasshoppers, their scandalized parents called them. Older brothers and sisters were also shocked. Over and over one heard couples in their thirties say of those in their twenties, "When we were that age we wouldn't have dreamed of going into debt." But in the past Americans had lacked the protection of such institutions as hospital insurance and expanded social security. There were fewer reasons for nest eggs now. In a short-term emergency the new people could always float another loan. That clearly violated the precepts of rugged individualism—what Max Weber called the Protestant ethic—but it was individualism, the young hedonists in the developments pointedly replied, which had led to the Depression. In ads one noted a decline in the very vocabulary of the Protestant ethic: such verbs as "compel," "force," "climb," and "control" had become unfashionable. Spending was not only more fun, the young argued; it was more sensible. Some thought it more patriotic, too. One radio station recorded a five-voice choir singing a jingle which ended, "Buy, buy something that you need today" and played it seventy times a day.

Even if you didn't need what you bought, you were still fueling the boom. Any tendency to go the other way was considered alarming. One New York newspaper reported that a "rise in thrift" was "disturbing the administration." Madison Avenue quoted Samuel Butler—"All progress is based upon a universal desire on the part of every organism to live beyond its income"—and a researcher for the J. Walter Thompson agency came up with an indulgent quotation from, of all people, Benjamin Franklin: "Is not the hope of being one day able to purchase and enjoy luxuries a great spur to labor and industry? . . . May not luxury therefore produce more than it consumes, if, without such a spur, people would be, as they are naturally enough inclined to be, lazy and indolent?" (In the ad citing this reflection the agency said that it "appears to be a mature afterthought, qualifying his earlier and more familiar writings on the importance of thrift.")

John Kenneth Galbraith maintained that talk of customer sovereignty had become nonsense. Demand was managed; consent was engineered; the public was being subjected to organized bamboozlement. This was consumership, as essential to an understanding of the evolving new economy as Dullesship was to an understanding of American policy abroad. In the packaged suburbs it was called the "good life." It meant the gratification of acquisitive desires—the split-level home, two cars in the two-car garage, a boat, a place at the beach, more new possessions as old ones wore out or became unfashionable (which was often, thanks to the wizards of planned obsolescence), and, somewhere in the nebulous future, college educations for the children, who would then begin to repeat the process. But the prosperity psychology was not confined to the suburbanites. It was meant to include everyone in the growing middle class. It had to be; mass production assumed mass consumption. Farther down the status ladder, Americans whose lower incomes would not permit a move to the Park Forests, Park Merceds, and Drexelbrooks (that is, an income below $4,800 to $5,200) participated by buying other wares, notably those hawked in television commercials: beers, dentifrices, pain-killers, rinses, cake mixes, laxatives, detergents, razor blades, skin conditioners, cigarettes, and—the big purchase for most families—new cars. In the relentless propaganda for goods in general, viewers were ceaselessly urged to be on the lookout for advertised brands, to get them, to incur debt with approved finance companies if that was necessary, and to participate in the huckstered vision of the good life or risk the loss of everything they prized, including their own sense of identity.

The concepts of consumer exploitation and manipulation were not new to the mid-1950s, but widespread awareness of them was. Motivational research, with all it implied, was becoming highly sophisticated. Its seductive presence was felt in virtually every walk of life. The candor of advertising's chief legerdemainists was sometimes breathtaking. They gloried in building empires on the smell of soap, the texture of its suds, the whiteness of textiles. At their wish, they boasted—and they had polls and sales figures to confirm them—buyers from Oregon to Cape Cod switched to Marlboros, discarded their undershorts for jockey shorts by Fruit of the Loom, or made pilgrimages to the loan companies so their wives and daughters could answer affirmatively the famous question which, Philip Wylie had said, was inherent in all ads beamed at American women: "Madam, are you a good lay?"

Of the creative pitchmen A. C. Spectorsky said:

> These people, God save us all, set the styles, mold the fashions, and populate the dreams of the rest of the country. What they do will be done, a few weeks or months later, by their counterparts in Lake Forest and Santa Barbara and on the Main Line. What they decree, via such esoteric channels as the "People Are Talking About . . ." feature in *Vogue,* will all too often be picked up and actually talked about, in Beverly Hills, Grosse Pointe, and Sewickley. What they tell us to buy, by God, we buy.

Spectorsky was fascinated by these transactions. Others were more judgmental. The deliberate encouragement of irrational behavior and impulse buying constituted an invasion of privacy, they said; people were being victimized. The creation of wants was a form of enslavement, and the critics believed that they could detect symptoms of profound disturbance beneath the prosperous surface of Eisenhower America. The figures on alcoholism and addiction to the new tranquilizers were alarming. By 1957 drug sales had increased sevenfold since the end of the war. There was much more shoplifting. In one Illinois community the average shoplifter was not, as might be expected, a figure of destitution or even want. She was, the chief of police said, a housewife married to a junior executive making $8,000 a year; she was a churchgoer, active in the PTA, a member of a bridge club, and a consumer with about $50 a week to spend.

Galbraith was troubled by society's double standard: "Anything which increases production from given sources is good and implicitly important; anything which inhibits or reduces output is, *pro tanto,* wrong." The prophets of self-indulgence and accumulation applauded private goods but recoiled from public services—education, public health, crusades against urban blight. According to that reasoning, Galbraith contended, it was "unquestionably more rewarding, in purely pecuniary terms, to be a speculator or a prostitute than a teacher, preacher or policeman." The younger generation was being "prevulgarized," Louis Kronenberger wrote, "as materials are said to be preshrunk." Edmund Wilson wrote: "Production, consumption and profit have come to play the role that religion played in our grandfather's generation." Such things, he said, could not even be discussed, since "they have taken the place of the Book of Genesis and the divinity of Jesus Christ." To some observers the admen seemed to be stockbrokers in neuroses. Walter Lippmann scorned them as "new barbarians," and Galbraith, in a striking passage, indicted consumerism and at the same time provided later writers with a bench mark against which to measure the very different society of the late 1960s and early 1970s:

> These are the days in which even the mildly critical individual is likely to seem like a lion in contrast with the general mood. These are the days when men of all social disciplines and all political faiths seek the comfortable and the accepted; when the man of controversy is looked upon as a disturbing influence; when originality is taken to be a mark of instability; and when, in minor modification of the scriptural parable, the bland lead the bland.

An understanding of the social revolt that came fifteen years later is impossible without some grasp of the 1950s life-style which arose from the new prosperity. Here, as elsewhere, the character of the time is most easily discerned in the new suburbs. They were not representative of all America (hardly anyone ever died there, for example, and there were almost no unmarried adults) but they did represent what America was becoming. It was there that junior executives unwound after each day, there that their wives honored what Betty Friedan would call the "feminine mystique"—and there that future hippies and straights roamed the community playgrounds.

The vast internal migration of the early 1940s had continued, in a somewhat lower key, in the postwar period. Throughout the 1950s over a million farmers were leaving their farms each year—17 million altogether for the postwar era by the 1960s. At the same time the centers of the cities, once so splendid, were being deserted—to become ghettos of the poor and bastions of the rich. The rest fled and camped outside. Even in so settled a prewar suburb as Stratford, Connecticut, commutation tickets had doubled and then tripled, and in the new cities the figures comprised virtually the entire male population. Every weekday morning now hundreds of thousands of white-collar workers rode or drove into Manhattan; every evening they returned home. At the end of the 1950s the population of the island south of City Hall was over a million by day—and about two thousand at night. During the decade more than a million New Yorkers left the city to live in the postwar communities ringing it. The suburbs, John Brooks wrote, were "draining downtown of its nighttime population, except for night watchmen and derelicts; it was becoming a part-time city, tidally swamped . . .

when the cars and commuter trains arrived and abandoned again at nightfall when the wave sucked back—left pretty much to the thieves, policemen, and rats."

It was the same in all American metropolises. Of the thirteen million new homes which were built in settled areas in the ten years before 1958, about eleven million—85 percent—were outside the inner cities. Refugees from both the farms and the central cities were converging on townships which hadn't even existed on V-J Day. The loss of metropolitan vigor was especially significant. In the past it had served as a magnet for the young and ambitious. Now it was flowing into the rising communities on the perimeters of the cities, to the curving superblocks, garden duplexes, and red brick labyrinths and manicured lawns of suburbia. There stood the dormitories of the new people, the swing generation and its younger cousins. In these developments the new life-style flourished.*

Its most conspicuous quality was a tremendous emphasis on social skills. Rural and small-town America had been strongholds of what David Riesman called "inner-directed" men and women. The source of their direction—he compared it to a gyroscope—was planted early in life by parents and never wavered afterward. The classic example of inner direction was the Englishman who dressed for dinner in the jungle. In the suburbs an entirely different type was gaining ascendancy: the "other-directed Americans." Their impetus came from an insatiable need to be liked. Riesman likened this to radar picking up impulses. The response was an adjustment to what the group wanted. In the Hillendales and Gardenvilles the accolade was to be called "well-adjusted."

These characteristics were not new to the postwar United States. Seymour Martin Lipset argues persuasively that Americans, with their lack of an autocracy and their emphasis on egalitarianism, have always been other-directed, and Alexis de Tocqueville found supportive evidence more than a hundred years ago. Though Americans took great pride in talking about their individualism, he noted, their special genius—and the source of their greatest potential weakness—lay in their ways of cooperation with each other. If America ever lost that drive, he predicted, it would be through strengthening social virtues at the expense of all others, creating a dictatorship of the majority. "In times of equality," he wrote, "no matter what political

* The word "development" has since come to mean a publicly financed housing project. Here it is used in its earlier sense, as a tract of developed land.

laws men devise for themselves, it is safe to foresee that trust in common opinion will become a sort of religion, with the majority as its prophet." The danger in this was that the individual might be "overwhelmed by the sense of his insignificance and weakness."

This is precisely what such critics as William Whyte thought they saw emerging in the suburbs of the 1950s. The great stress on behavior acceptable to the team was inhibiting to the individual, they believed; it was thwarting natural leaders and creating a new breed of yes-men. In some ways that was inevitable. Small business was going under everywhere. Americans increasingly were employed by bureaucracies, both private and public. In 1956 the country passed a milestone as important, in its way, as the closing of the frontier in 1890: the number of blue-collar workers (people producing things) was surpassed by that of white-collar workers (in middle-class, service occupations). Increasingly the representative wage earner became the pencil pusher working for a large, impersonal entity. In the newly developed areas it sometimes seemed that everyone was employed by a vast floating cooperative. The swing generation had become a generation of technicians, of interchangeable parts. Its members knew it—and for the most part they liked it.

To be sure, they often spoke of life as a treadmill, but their despair was a mock despair; if they felt imprisoned, their prison was the most comfortable in history, as they would have been the first to point out. Paternalism had become benevolent. The most modest example was RCA's issuance of company neckties. Other corporations went farther. Richfield Oil erected model homes and IBM built country clubs; Reynolds Tobacco engaged company chaplains and Eastman Kodak and Du Pont employed staff psychiatrists. To junior executives who spent their weekdays in such corporate wombs, a carryover of organizational principles in the home neighborhood was only natural.

"It seemed to me," John Steinbeck wrote of the newly organized, "that they looked at me for a place to insert a coin." That was unfair. There was nothing inherently wrong in Park Merced's employment of uniformed attendants to cut the grass, or in Drexelbrook's annual Christmas decoration contest for its 1,223 garden apartments, in which the rivalry between garden courts became so imaginative that a hundred thousand Philadelphians drove out every year to see it. Life in the developments was in many ways an improvement over the life its dwellers had known as children in the 1930s, and not just because everyone was now prosperous. Even as modern business kept all ways of advancement open in order that any junior executive might graduate one day to Westchester, Bull Valley, or Bloomfield Hills, so were the new suburbs free, unstructured, and genuinely hospitable to anyone from any background except blacks, whose time had not yet come. Families moving in found that their new neighbors were eager to help them unpack, take care of their children, and feed them until they had settled down. Even William Whyte conceded that the young suburbanites had achieved "a pretty high quotient of kindliness and fundamental decency."

They owned their own homes, and that was important; it satisfied an old American yearning. Their sense of community was rooted in the American past, too; the pioneers had also been generous and hospitable. The new people were relaxed and informal, almost to a fault. Sport shirts and denim pedal pushers replaced collars and hose. Mother wouldn't have dreamed of going downtown without dressing; now her daughter went with her hair in curlers, and if anyone thought the kerchief over it suggestive of the babushkas worn by the peasant women of eastern Europe, she didn't care. Her concern was the attitude of the other girls in her neighborhood. They did the same thing and would have been disappointed in her if she had done anything else.

Children in the developments exchanged toys and clothes almost as though they were community property, which they almost were. If little Bobby had outgrown his playsuit, it went to little Billy across the way. It wasn't unusual for a mother to recognize a familiar garment on a strange child long afterward; since she had given it away it had passed through several households. Bikes and scooters were also exchanged. Front doors were unlocked; neighbors felt free to enter without knocking. Doors inside were disappearing. So were the massive overstuffed chairs of the Thirties, the heavy rugs and the inside walls; the formal dining room mother had dusted every day and used only for big meals had been replaced by a single living-dining-kitchen area, and the suburbanites saw little reason to mourn its loss, even when guests came. The sitdown dinner had been succeeded by casserole dinners, served buffet style. Sometimes they were awkward, but no one seemed to mind. This way a hostess could enjoy her own party.

The host usually mixed the drinks beforehand, which in 75 percent of the dwellings were martinis. If there was an uprising in the nursery he hurried off to suppress it. Suburban fathers took a livelier interest in their children; home had become a place for companionship and recreation. Nearly two-thirds of all American husbands were helping with housework by 1954, and in the developments the percentage was higher. In addition, and to a degree which often amazed their own parents, the young fathers there were pitching in to help with the dishes, the cooking, and the diapering of the babies. Russell Lynes complained that the young wives were beginning to treat their husbands as part-time servants or as the latest new appliance, but to the new men there was nothing emasculating about stopping at the supermarket for extra groceries on the way home from work, or filling in at the laundromat, or pushing the stroller around the block. They believed it was good for them and good for their families. Spock was the grandfather clock by which the new fathers set their watches, and he approved, and that made it right.

Suburban mothers, in the togetherness vanguard, seemed very young and often were. During the 1950s the age at which U.S. women married dropped from twenty-two to twenty and into the teens. High school marriages became an accepted phenomenon. Children began going steady in junior high school. Girls began thinking about their weddings then or even earlier; a *New York Times* advertisement for a child's dress said, "She Too Can Join the Man-Trap Set."

Being a successful man-trap entailed being desirable—a good lay, in Wylie's phrase; ideally, a great lay. To achieve this happy state females of all ages invested in wardrobes, cosmetics, and exotic perfumes whose makers claimed that they incited rape. Since 1939 the average woman had shrunk three or four sizes. Instead of shopping for a dress her size, she now found one she liked and then dieted to fit it. Metrecal made its appearance and found an eager mass market. So did a new Clairol slogan: "If I have only one life, let me live it as a blonde." Some social scientists and aging suffragettes worried about women's reckless haste to abandon their hard-won independence, but their voices were muffled. *Life* applauded the mass movement of girls into the home, and in a cover story on the suburban wife *Time* reported that wives were "having too good a time . . . to believe that they should be unhappy." The truth, Carl N. Degler wrote, was that "American society in general, which includes women, shuns like a disease any feminist ideology."

By the late 1950s the U.S. birth rate was approaching India's. The number of U.S. mothers who had given birth to three or more children had doubled in twenty years. The increase was most spectacular among college women; they were abandoning careers to bear four, five, and six or more children. The percentage of females in the American college population (35 percent) was lower than that in any European country and smaller than the prewar figure on U.S. campuses (40 percent). Nearly two-thirds of matriculating girls dropped out before graduation, while more than half the men stayed. Many coeds left the classroom to take menial jobs, supporting their partners, who remained on campus; this was called the degree of "Ph.T." (Putting Husband Through). Other women quit because they had *not* acquired spouses. Deans' offices found that coeds were leaving at the end of the first year or two because they had found the pickings slim and wanted to try their luck elsewhere.

To ambitious junior executives hanging their hats in Levittown and casting covetous eyes on Westchester, the right spouse was as important as a hearty chuckle and a sincere necktie. Corporations set up training programs to show company wives what they should and should not do, and *Fortune* found in interviews that the wives, especially the young ones, approved of the idea. They felt that women should become gregarious if they were shy, and, if they were smarter than men, learn to hold their tongues. Several movies of the time dramatized their situation, among them *Executive Suite* and *Woman's World.* The theme in each was a corporation's search for the right man to fill a big job and how a wise mate could help her man by wearing the right dress, hiring the right interior decorator, choosing the right friends, and serving the boss his favorite menu when he came to dinner.

The very anonymity of the big corporation served to sap confidence and independence in men and women dependent on it. So did their own lack of roots. In the front office, where employees were so many pins on a map, personnel chiefs seemed to move them about with reckless abandon. Each relocation meant farewells to friends and the search for new ones elsewhere. The *Wall Street Journal* reported that a Montgomery Ward executive and his family had been moved twenty-eight times in twenty-six years of marriage. Growing mobility was a fact of suburban life. According to Atlas Van Lines, the average corporate manager now moved fourteen times in his lifetime, once every two and a half years. For him the ability to adjust to new circumstances was important to a degree beyond the comprehension of men who live their lives in one place. Though the premium on socialization in the developments sometimes became excessive, the alternative—a family dependent upon its own emotional resources—was considered worse.

Suburbia was superbly equipped to meet the needs of newcomers. Its inhabitants had little reason to feel lonely. The American compulsion to join every association on sight found its ultimate expression there. Meetings were scheduled by one organization or another at every hour from breakfast to late in the evening. Partners were always available for bridge, canasta, poker and bowling. Camera, bird-watching, gun, embroidering, archery, and ping-pong clubs flourished; so did PTAs, the League of Women Voters, the ADA, the Minute Women and, beginning in 1958, the John Birch Society.

Many Americans who would later rise in public life began to acquire their political expertise in suburbia's constant shuffle of adjustment. Here they were likelier to be Republican than in their old neighborhoods. Socially ambitious couples arriving from the inner cities switched their party affiliations—much as they abandoned other lower-class ways. Their parents had contributed to the Democratic party's huge great urban majorities. They didn't. Now that they had made it, they wanted to pull the ladder up behind them. In Europe the postwar expansion of labor unions was leading to the formation of a large, militant, class-conscious force. Not here; although eighteen million industrialized U.S. workers were now unionized, their craving for middle-class status, and the frequency with which it was being satisfied, created instead a large new middle group. Uneasy in their new roles, distrustful of liberalism, and deeply hostile toward further social reforms, they constituted a neoconservative force which would become increasingly significant as the old Roosevelt coalition faltered.

The most common indictment of suburbia's life-style was that it was oppressive. Its passion for informality was so intense that preference for privacy was treated almost as a sign of malaise. Picture windows became windows for looking in. Couples who wanted to lock out the neighbors occasionally were expected to provide an explanation afterward. The group felt it had a right to know everything—"Did you have your period yesterday?" or "Who was that woman you were talking to at Stop and Shop?" or "Your Roger was looking daggers when he left for the office this morning. What's his problem?"

The term "polite society" fell into disuse because society wasn't polite any more. The increasing use of first names was extraordinary. Once it had been limited to family and friends. Then it was extended to colleagues at work and the neighborhood. At office parties and neighborhood cocktail parties finding out who you were talking to became increasingly difficult. Last names were used only in introductions; afterward everyone was Al, Debby, Chuck, or Beth. Eventually the circle of first-namers widened to include virtually everyone who knew who you were: doctors, tradesmen, the children of others, etc. The suburbanite who arrived home to find her bathroom being used by a strange boy might be greeted, "Hi, Doris." In suburbia this was looked upon as just friendliness. Any objection to it would be regarded as snobbish and resented.

One option closed to the suburbanite was scolding someone else's child—in the idiom of earlier generations, "correcting" him. Any correction had to come from his own parents, and there wasn't much of it. Children were special people in the new communities. Whether or not they benefited from their status was a question which would later be debated nationally. Certainly they weren't neglected. Permissiveness took time and patience, and the parents in the developments were among the most permissive in the country. Children made other demands on their time. A mother was expected to plan her youngster's activities and then chauffeur him to them. At times this required the energy and ingenuity of a Grossinger's social director, for suburbia's children were busy all the time. Sociologists were struck by the remarkable degree to which their lives were organized for them. After school and on Saturdays, hurrying station wagons crisscrossed suburbia, carrying their charges to dancing lessons, Little League practice, tennis lessons, sailing lessons, play groups, parties, piano lessons, Cub Scouts, dramatic school—schedules which returned them home just in time for dinner and evenings in front of the television set. So occupied were they, Henry A. Murray protested in *Daedalus*, that their chances of growing into individuals were being curtailed sharply, if not crushed altogether; "parents make their babies play with other babies," he wrote, "as soon as they can toddle." The swing generation wasn't much interested in individuality. Though older executives still paid lip service to it, their juniors were more anxious to raise children who, as they put it, could "get along with other people." They admired that quality in one another, sought to develop it in themselves, and saw it becoming the key to success in the next generation.

The upshot was that millions of pupils approached the age of awareness equipped with marvelous radar but no gyroscopes. They were well instructed about society's need for morale but hadn't been told what it produced; they knew a great deal about achieving popularity but very little about achieving anything else. "Give me a boy for the first seven years and he will be a Catholic for life," a prelate had said. The apostles of adjustment had more than seven years, and it is doubtful that even the church could have done a more thorough job than they did. First mothers instilled in children the necessity for wooing their peers. Next came practice workouts in sandboxes and on swing sets. Activities followed: Brownies, Little Leagues, etc. The propaganda for good fellowship was relentless. Sunday schools in the modern churches taught that God was really just a pal; that religion was fun, like the movie nuns who played softball and rode around in helicopters. Any fledgling Luther who felt inclined to cultivate his own identity was exhorted not to by the mass media, while the last layers of goodguymanship polish were zealously applied in the new suburban schools.

The character and quality of classroom instruction in America varied from one community to another. In some, McGuffey readers and rote memorization were still prevalent. One-teacher public elementary schools were on the way out, however; their number dropped from 143,391 in 1932 to 59,652 in 1950, and at the end of the Eisenhower era they would be down to 20,213. The leaders in the profession, honored at teachers' conventions and teachers colleges and extolled by the National Education Association, were advocates of what was called progressive education. It wasn't really progressive. It had been that, in its beginnings as a movement, when it was dedicated to freeing the imaginative child from lockstep classroom discipline and encouraging him to develop his own individuality. Then, as educators became more enthusiastic about developing social skills, teachers replaced the old stress on intellectual attainments with the even greater constraints involved in turning a child into what Gesell profiles suggested he should be.

Pupils in these schools were not told what they must learn. They were asked to choose their own electives. To avoid fixed standards of performance ("straitjackets," they were called), grades were often limited to "satisfactory" and "unsatisfactory." Courses in "family living" replaced algebra, geometry, grammar, and foreign languages. At times the attitude of the new educators toward the traditional academic disciplines bordered on outright hostility. Eric Baber, superintendent of the Park Forest, Illinois, high school, which in 1954 was chosen one of the five winners in the "All America Schools" contest of the National Municipal League, deplored the stubbornness with which college admissions offices clung to entrance requirements. "The so-called 'bright student,'" he said, "is often one of the dumbest or least apt when he gets away from his textbooks and memory work. This is evidenced by the fact that many $20,000-to-$100,000 jobs in business, sales, sports, radio . . . are held by persons with I.Q.s of less than ninety."

Alert to signs of what was denigrated as "maladjustment," teachers in schools participated in their pupils' choices of friends, their games at recess, their very fantasies. Instead of visiting national monuments, classes visited dairies or grocery stores. Learning to become consumers, they gathered information that, they were told, would be useful to them in later life. In such "doing" sessions, supervisors explained at PTA meetings, pupils were participating in actual situations. Abjuring what was called "elitism," they were concentrating not on what changes might be made in life, but how to make them "without upsetting human relationships." "Ours is an age of group action," Dr. Baber told a teachers' workshop, stressing the need to emphasize the extroverted side of their pupils' nature. So the children were taught, and so they learned to be "well-rounded"—people who understood that the goals of the individual and the goals of society were identical. If uncertain about a problem, they polled one another.

Some parents objected. They wanted to bring back Latin, chemistry, integral calculus—courses that colleges and universities also wanted. Smiling principals shook their heads and replied, "We teach the child, not the subject." They believed that in preparing pupils for participation in the consumer world they were taking a practical, realistic, hardheaded approach which would be vindicated by the future.

On October 4, 1957, Tass, the Soviet news agency, had an interesting item for the American public. "The first artificial earth satellite has now been created," it announced. "This first satellite was successfully launched in the USSR . . . Artificial earth satellites will pave the way for space travel and it seems that the present generation will witness how the freed and conscious labor of the people of the new socialist society turns even the most daring of man's dreams into reality."

To grasp the full impact of this announcement, it must be remembered that in 1957 the United States was still regarded as the home of scientific innovation. It was a running joke of the postwar years that from time to time Moscow would announce that this or that Russian—usually some Ivan or Ilya no one had ever heard of—was responsible for a discovery which everyone outside the Soviet Union knew had been made in the United States. Americans had grown up believing they held a virtual monopoly on technological ingenuity. Now the proud were fallen. In addition they were mortified. Nikita Khrushchev was crowing, "People of the whole world are pointing to the satellite. They are saying that the U.S. has been beaten." And so they were. Tass called the space vehicle a *sputnik;* literally a "traveling companion" or, more appropriately, a "fellow traveler." It instantly won the attention of the world. To the United States it came as a shock on the order of the Crash.

Montage: Eisenhower At Flood Tide

Best actor of 1956: Yul Brynner in The King and I
Best actress of 1956: Ingrid Bergman in Anastasia

Stevenson, Stevenson
If you vote for Stevenson
He will be, easily,
President next year
Help him win, get him in
Now the fight's begun
Gotta be, gotta be, gotta be
Believe in Stevenson!

ALTHEA GIBSON WINS WIMBLEDON TROPHY

La Strada

SCOTT paper has WET STRENGTH

A white sport coat and a pink carnation
I'm all dressed up for the dance
A white sport coat and a pink carnation
I'm all alone in romance

Around the World in 80 Days

Dear Modern Screen:

I think you had a hand in the reconciliation of the Dean Martins. You wrote on "open letter" in Modern Screen telling Dean and Jeanne how silly they were to stay apart when they really love one another. I read your words, and I bet they did, too.

Maria, New York

The wedding day burst fair and warm; Margaret Truman walked out of the 91-year-old house a last time on the arm of her ever-punctual, this time solemn father. "She looks beautiful, Mr. Truman," called a voice from the crowd. "Thank you, thank you very much," said the father of the bride. "I think so, too."

YOUTHFUL INSURGENTS ATTACK BATISTA'S PALACE: 46 DIE

And after this fling
Who could blame Mr. Bing
If he shipped Madam Callas to Dallas?

BEST SELLERS: Fiction
Don't Go Near the Water by William Brinkley
By Love Possessed by James Gould Cozzens
The Last Hurrah by Edwin O'Connor
Auntie Mame by Patrick Dennis
Peyton Place by Grace Metalious

Shortly after 8 o'clock on Sunday night, Staff Sergeant Matthew C. McKeon limped into the barracks of Platoon 71 at the U.S. Marine Corps Recruit Depot, Parris Island, S.C.... The 74 boots of Platoon 71 followed him toward the salt tidal marshes of Parris Island, where death was waiting.

U.S. INTERSTATE HIGHWAY SYSTEM TO BE LAUNCHED

The Catered Affair

PLEASE INFORM EUROPE AND THE AUSTRIAN GOVERNMENT . . . THEY OPENED FIRE ON EVERYBODY . . . A FEW HUNDRED TANKS ATTACKED BUDAPEST . . . THERE IS HEAVY FIGHTING . . . I STAY OPEN AND CONTINUE WITH THE NEWS . . . WE SHALL INFORM THE WORLD ABOUT EVERYTHING. LONG LIVE HUNGARY AND EUROPE. THE RUSSIANS ARE USING PHOSPHORUS BULLETS. ANY NEWS ABOUT HELP? QUICKLY, QUICKLY, WE HAVE NO TIME TO LOSE. NO TIME TO LOSE. I AM RUNNING OVER TO THE WINDOW IN THE NEXT ROOM TO SHOOT BUT I WILL BE BACK. WE WILL HOLD OUT TILL THE LAST DROP OF BLOOD. GOOD-BYE FRIENDS. GOOD-BYE FRIENDS. GOD SAVE OUR SOULS. THE RUSSIANS ARE TOO NEAR.

The Edsel performs fine, rides well, and handles good.

WEST SIDE STORY
Book by Arthur Laurents
Music by Leonard Bernstein
Lyrics by Stephen Sondheim
WINTER GARDEN

Try *Zest* — the soapless soap

BEST SELLERS: Nonfiction
Arthritis and Common Sense by Dan Dale Alexander
Kids Say the Darndest Things by Art Linkletter
The Search for Bridey Murphy by Morey Bernstein
Profiles in Courage by John F. Kennedy
Too Much, Too Soon by Diana Barrymore and Gerold Frank

Just walking in the rain gettin' soaking wet
Torturing my heart by trying to forget
Just walking in the rain so alone and blue
All because my heart still remembers you

Make me feel real loose
Like a long-necked goose
Oh, baby, that's what I like

By ABIGAIL VAN BUREN
DEAR ABBY
The funniest questions, and the wittiest and wisest answers, from the famous "Dear Abby" column

Standing on the corner watching all the girls go by
Standing on the corner watching all the girls go by
Brother you don't know a nicer occupation
Matter of fact neither do I
Than standing on the corner watching all the girls
watching all the girls watching all the girls
go by

You ain't nothin' but a hound dawg

My baby rocks me with a steady roll

Bus Stop

Where there's life — there's BUD

Twenty-four

BEEP BEEP

THE FIRST WORD that a Russian sphere the size of a beachball was circling the earth once every 96.2 minutes, traveling at a speed of 18,000 mph and emitting beeping sounds as it did so, had reached Washington, quite by chance, during a cocktail party in the Soviet embassy at 1125 Sixteenth Street. Scientists from twenty-two countries were observing 1957–58 as an International Geophysical Year, or IGY as they called it—a general sharing of data—and Russian diplomats were entertaining fifty IGY luminaries that historic Friday evening when one of the guests, Walter Sullivan of the *New York Times*, was called away for an urgent telephone call. At the phone he learned of the Tass announcement. He hurried back and whispered to an American scientist, Dr. Lloyd Berkner, who rapped on the hors d'oeuvre table until the hubbub quieted. "I wish to make an announcement," he said. "I am informed by the *New York Times* that a satellite is in orbit at an elevation of 900 kilometers.* I wish to congratulate our Soviet colleagues on their achievement."

The room burst into applause. Eminent scientists are indifferent to national loyalties, and the Americans there were particularly generous. Dr. Joseph Kaplan, chairman of the U.S. IGY program, called the Russian achievement "tremendous" and added, "If they can launch one that heavy, they can put up much heavier ones." The White House, however, was momentarily speechless. The advent of the first sputnik astounded U.S. intelligence even though the So-

* Approximately 559 miles.

viets had made no great secret of their satellite plans. At an IGY planning conference in Barcelona Russian delegates had spoken openly and confidently of their plans to launch a space vehicle. As early as November 1954, Defense Secretary Wilson had been asked whether he was concerned over the possibility that the USSR might win the satellite race. He had snorted, "I wouldn't care if they did."

That continued to be the Republican line now that Sputnik was an accomplished fact. Administration spokesmen seemed to suggest that the press was making molehills out of molehills. Hagerty issued a statement describing the satellite as a matter "of great scientific interest" but adding that "we never thought of our program as one which was in a race with the Soviet's." Wilson, now in retirement, called the Russian feat "a nice technical trick." Rear Admiral Rawson Bennett, chief of the Office of Naval Research, wondered why there was so much fuss over a "hunk of iron almost anybody could launch." White House adviser Clarence Randall described the space vehicle as "a silly bauble"—thereby infuriating the President—and Sherman Adams said disparagingly that the government wasn't interested in "an outer-space basketball game." (In his memoirs Adams regretted this. "I was only trying to reflect the President's desire for calm poise," he wrote, "but I had to admit on reflection that my observation seemed to be an overemphasis of the de-emphasis.")

Others in Washington were in no mood to dismiss Sputnik so lightly. Trevor Gardner, who as former Assistant Secretary of the Air Force had tried to mediate interservice quarrels over who should run the American space program, said bitterly, "We have presently at least nine ballistic missile programs, all competing for roughly the same kind of facilities, the same kind of brains, the same kind of engines and the same public attention." Electronics and air-frame experts recalled Wilson's casual attitude toward space research. "The basic reason we're behind the Russians," a major defense contractor said, "is that we haven't gone all out." One of the President's closest aides said he felt an urge to "strangle" Budget Director Percival Brundage. Knowland privately warned Ike that the worldwide impact of the Soviet accomplishment had all but nullified the value of America's Mutual Security program, and some publicists were actually suggesting a negotiated peace with the Russians "before it is too late."

The Democrats, predictably, were indignant. Senator Henry Jackson of Washington wanted the President to proclaim "a week of shame and danger." Missouri's Symington demanded a special session of Congress. Fulbright of Arkansas said, "The real challenge we face involves the very roots of our society. It involves our educational system, the source of our knowledge and cultural values. And here the Administration's program for a renaissance of learning is disturbingly small-minded." Majority Leader Johnson saw cosmic implications in the Russian success. "The Roman empire controlled the world because it could build roads," he said. "Later—when men moved to the sea—the British Empire was dominant because it had ships. Now the Communists have established a foothold in outer space. It is not very reassuring to be told that next year we will put a 'better' satellite into the air. Perhaps," he concluded sarcastically, "it will even have chrome trim—and automatic windshield wipers."

This was more than partisan oratory. Periodically Americans feel a need to agonize over why the country has gone soft. The last time it had happened had been in the spring of 1940, when France was falling and the older generation thought American youth too engrossed in swing to hear the Nazi jackboots. Now, as then, the press was aroused. "It is downright terrifying with [Sputnik] staring down at us," the Portland *Oregonian* said, and *Time* said that "the U.S. takes deep pride in its technical skills and technological prowess, in its ability to get things done—first. Now, despite all the rational explanations, there was a sudden, sharp national disappointment that Americans had been outshone by the Red moon." John Kenneth Galbraith had been awaiting publication of *The Affluent Society*. Neither he nor his publishers had expected much of a sale. "Then, in the autumn of 1957," he wrote in an introduction to the second edition, "the Soviets sent up the first Sputnik. No action was ever so admirably timed. Had I been younger and less formed in my political views, I would have been carried away by my gratitude and found a final resting place beneath the Kremlin Wall. I knew my book was home."

Americans were learning humility—and humiliation. They had become an international laughingstock. At a scientific conference in Barcelona Leonid I. Sedov, Russia's chief space scientist, taunted a U.S. colleague: "You Americans have a better standard of living than we have. But the American loves his car, his refrigerator, his house. He does not, as we Russians do, love his country." Anti-Americans were derisive. RUSSIANS RIP AMERICAN FACE, read a headline in Bangkok's *Sathiraphab,* and a Beirut professor said dryly of his students, "You would have thought they launched it themselves." The editors of London's *Economist* saw the Russians scoring a brilliant psychological triumph in the Afro-Asian world. French journalists saw the catch, the price the Soviet masses had paid. Thierry Maulnier wrote in *Le Figaro,* "The Russian people can . . . . see in the sky a brilliant star which carries above the world the light of Soviet power, thanks to millions of pots and shoes lacking," and *Combat* commented: "We ourselves would like it if the Russians would put some of their pride into the evolution of a better world—an end to the world of concentration camps." But in all Europe only the London *Express,* faithful to Britain's old ally, predicted that somehow the United States would muddle through: "The result will be a new drive to catch up and pass the Russians in the sphere of space exploration. Never doubt for a moment that America will be successful."

Americans themselves had plenty of doubts, and the more they knew about the implications of the Soviet achievement the more apprehensive they became. In those first days virtually all the details about the man-made star came from Tass and *Pravda;* the Smithsonian Institution was building an astrophysical observatory in Cambridge to track precisely this sort of phenomenon, but it was unfinished and unable even to correlate visual observations being phoned to it by widely scattered moonwatchers. The Russians disclosed that their first sputnik was a polished steel ball twenty-two inches in diameter, weighing 184.3 pounds and equipped with four radio antennas. Its orbit was higher than U.S. scientists had thought possible. Because of that height it would avoid the atmosphere and could keep circling the earth for years. Sputnik's weight was also stunning; the directors of America's Vanguard Project, still in the theoretical stage, had been hoping to send a 21.5-pound Navy Viking research projectile to a maximum of 300 miles. That would have required 27,000 pounds of rocket thrust. The Russian catapult had used 200,000 pounds—an incredible figure, clearly indicative of a new source of power.

As new data came in and were digested by MIT computers, American appreciation of Soviet technical virtuosity soared. The orbit was stunning. It was elliptical, of course, carrying the sputnik from an apogee 583 miles above the earth to a perigee 143 miles down, but since both of these distances were added to the radius of the earth (3,960 miles) the ellipse was almost a circle, showing that the Russians had precise control as well as power. Moreover, the launch had been daring. The simplest way to orbit the satellite would have been to aim it eastward from the equator, taking advantage of the earth's rotation to give the object about 1,000 mph of free speed—in effect, a tailwind. Vanguard's planners had expected to do this; according to their calculations the Viking rocket, rising due east from Florida, would have had a 914 mph boost. But Vanguard rocketeers working under lights those first nights were astounded to learn that the Russian course was 65 degrees the other way. That indicated that they had power to burn. It had another significance. Vanguard's course would have kept it south of Europe and most of Russia. Sputnik's journey took it over most of the inhabited earth, meaning most of the world's peoples could see it, as well as hear it and read about it—a propaganda coup in itself.

Americans would be among the last to have a clear view of it, owing, perhaps, to a sly bit of Muscovite humor. The launch had been timed so that during its first weeks the satellite would pass over the United States during the day, when it would be invisible against the glare of the sun, or at night, when the shadow of the earth would hide it. The curious—and there were tens of thousands of them—had to peer up at daybreak and twilight, when the object could be briefly glimpsed against the gray sky. That would change. The orbit was shifting around the earth at four degrees a day, Dr. Joseph A. Hynek of the Smithsonian observatory explained; on about October 20 the sputnik would come into view overhead for those with binoculars or small telescopes. But Americans, impatient as always, wanted to know everything now. They had been huddling over their radios and television sets since that Friday night when an NBC commentator had told them, "Listen now for the sound which forevermore separates the old from the new." Then they had heard it for the first time, alternating between 20 and 40 megacycles—an eerie A-flat beeping from outer space.

It was generally assumed in those early days that the object was sending back signals in cipher, and CIA cryptographers worked in shifts to break the code. A man who could enlighten them happened to be right there in Washington; he was General Anatoly Arkadievich Blagonravov, chief of the three-man delegation Moscow had sent to the IGY conference. There was no code, the general said. The designers had put the beeps in to track the sputnik and reassure themselves that the satellite was still out there. There was nothing in the steel ball except the transmitter and the batteries. The power of the signal was one watt—just about enough for a conversation between hams in Australia and the United States. In about three weeks the batteries would be exhausted, Blagonravov said, and the beeping would stop. A likely story, Americans snorted. Who could trust a Russian general? There was something fishy about those signals. "Many believe that the whole story has not been told," *Time* noted darkly. The CIA had better get to the bottom of it, the man on the street muttered, or the U.S. taxpayer would know the reason why.

Sputnik I dealt the coup de grace to Ford's fading Edsel, which had been introduced to the public the month before, and which was now widely regarded as a discredited symbol of the tinny baubles Americans must thrust aside. There were other scapegoats. The administration was one. It was M. Robert Bendiner who suggested that until now the Republican idea of a scientist had been a man who tore and compared cigarettes on television. Public education was another conspicuous target and did, in fact, have much to answer for. American parents were angered to learn that while their children were being taught "life adjustment," Russian education had been acquiring a reputation for being tough and competitive, ruthlessly winnowing out mediocrities beginning in the fourth grade and awarding to outstanding students the laurels which, in the United States, were reserved for athletes and baton-twirling, tail-twitching cheerleaders.

Parental wrath would grow with the publication of John Gunther's *Inside Russia Today*, then in galleys. Gunther reported that "In the schools which prepare for college, the Soviet child must absorb in ten years what an American child gets in twelve—perhaps more." Russian pupils, he said, went to school six hours a day, six days a week, attending classes 213 days a year as against 180 in the United States, and in the last two years of schooling four hours of homework were assigned each day. Gunther continued:

> . . . the main emphasis is on science and technology, for both boys and girls, and herein lies the greatest challenge to our system. In addition to ten solid years of mathematics, every child must take four years of chemistry, five of physics, six of biology. By contrast, only about half of American high schools have *any* physics, and

only 64 percent have *any* chemistry. An American authority told me that the average Soviet boy or girl graduating from the tenth grade (our twelfth) has a better scientific education—particularly in mathematics—than most American college graduates!

Emphasis on science came early in Soviet schools; pupils began studying optics and quantum theory in grade school. By the mid-1950s the USSR was graduating twice as many scientists and engineers as the United States, and in a sixty-four-page report the National Science Foundation estimated that 14 percent of all Soviet scientists were allowed to pursue basic research—that is, inquiries which may or may not have practical significance. Such work often seems pointless at the time, but it is the restless search for answers by the laboratory man with insatiable curiosity which makes possible the technological miracles of the next generation. Thomas Edison could not have developed the incandescent lamp without Henry Cavendish and Michael Faraday; the atomic bomb became a reality because in 1905 Albert Einstein had published an obscure volume setting forth the proposition, then wholly inapplicable, that energy is encompassed in every bit of matter; and the H-bomb was created by men who had been studying the stars. Charles E. Wilson thought basic research ridiculous. As Secretary of Defense he had once mocked it as finding out "what makes grass green and fried potatoes brown," a remark scientists now remembered and quoted bitterly. The number of Americans in long-range studies was fractional, and the funds allotted to them—about 450 million dollars a year—represented only one-tenth of one percent of the national income.

Now scientists were beginning to speak up. Norbert Wiener had something to say about science and society. Wiener blamed the tight lid government had clamped on research, beginning with radar and the Manhattan Project. The consequence, he said, was that the individual scientist was often not only unaware of the vast problem he was dealing with, but even worse, that his scientific inquisitiveness was frequently discouraged. Physicists pointed out that the Soviets had an 8.3-billion electron-volt particle accelerator (atom smasher), better than America's best, the University of California's betatron, and UCLA's Joseph Kaplan, the U.S. IGY chairman, said, "In oceanography, meteorology, and upper-atmosphere physics, the indications are that they are certainly as good as we are."

Edward Teller also spoke up. Though still a pariah among most of his fellow physicists, Teller remained a brilliant and prescient scholar. His Pentagon friends pointed out that in last April's issue of *Air Force* magazine, six months before the first beep, he had gloomily written: "Ten years ago there was no question where the best scientists in the world could be found—here in the U.S. . . . Ten years from now the best scientists in the world will be found in Russia." In the Soviet Union, he had pointed out, science was almost a religion; its ablest men were singled out and treated as a privileged class while their underpaid American colleagues lacked status in their society and could offer few incentives to bright protégés. His appeal for respect for the dignity of scientific inquiry was well taken. The number of cartoons about mad scientists dropped sharply. There were also fewer jokes about them. And it was extraordinary how quickly the word egghead dropped out of the language.

For some time Walter Lippmann had been urging his countrymen to consecrate themselves to a national purpose. Few had grasped what he had in mind, but now they knew: the national purpose was to rescue education and, with it, America's next generation. Suddenly Rudolf Flesch's *Why Johnny Can't Read—and What You Can Do About It,* which had come out in 1955 without making much of a dent, was on everyone's best-seller list. Hardly anyone had a good word for schools as they were except people like Dr. Ruth Strang of Teachers College, Columbia, and she and TC were in disgrace. Social critics' heaviest guns trained on just such educators, or, as they were derisively christened, "educationists." Chancellor Lawrence A. Klimpton of the University of Chicago explained how the Strangs and the William Heard Kilpatricks had distorted and misrepresented the ideas of John Dewey. Dewey had held that thinking begins in an interest, or a concern. But this had been twisted into an insistence that teachers must amuse, or entertain, pupils.

Herbert Hoover said that the Communists "are turning out twice or possibly three times as many" scientists "as the U.S." He scorned the "too prevalent high-school system of allowing a thirteen- or fourteen-year-old kid to choose most of his studies." That same week another distinguished engineer from whom more would be heard on this score observed in Detroit that one root of the trouble lay in the "misconception of the worth" of the American high school. "We have always overvalued it," said Rear Admiral Hyman G. Rickover, the man responsible for America's atomic submarines. "It comes out," he continued, "that we have many more children in high school and in college than [Europeans] have in secondary schools and universities, and this makes us proud. But all these comparisons are meaningless because the European secondary school graduate has learned more than most of our college graduates. As to the high school diploma," he added heavily, "the less said about it the better."

Even resolute Republicans were uneasy. Clare Boothe Luce, in other ways a steadfast defender of the status quo during the Eisenhower years, found complacency on this issue impossible. She called the sputnik's beep an "outer-space raspberry to a decade of American pretensions that the American way of life is a gilt-edge guarantee of our national superiority." Her husband was also troubled by heretical thoughts. "Turning to Washington for reassurance," *Time* said nervously, "the U.S. saw administrative confusion, sensed a crisis in leadership and demanded action." The stock market tobogganed dizzily downward that week, and with Russia's man-made moon flashing across the skies all America seemed depressed. A contagion of black humor cropped up—proposals to change Project Vanguard's name to Project Rearguard and a story about a Washington reporter who called the U.S. Space Agency, asked how the program was going, and was asked by the girl on the phone, "Sir, are you calling *for* information or *with* information?"

Sputnik I's beeps died away in the last week of October, as General Blagonravov had predicted. It was still there and could be tracked, but at least you couldn't hear it any more. Then, just as Americans had begun to catch their breath, Sputnik II went up on November 3. In some ways it was a more breathtaking achievement than its predecessor. The new satellite weighed 1,120.29 pounds—making it six times as heavy as Sputnik I—and its orbit carried it 1,056 miles away from the earth. "The unfathomed natural processes going on in the cosmos," Moscow radio proclaimed, "will now become more understandable to man." It was true; American scientists were envious. A space vehicle that large would house a maze of instruments radioing back data on cosmic rays, solar radiation above the atmosphere, atmospheric temperature and composition, the danger of meteors, the earth's gravitation, its magnetic field, its electric charge, and the cloud patterns of its weather. The Russians had another surprise. There was a little dog of the *laika* breed aboard, strapped with contrivances which would provide other information about the ability of fauna to survive in space.

It was another luckless day for administration image makers. Ideally news of the event should have found the leaders of the government at their desks furiously striving to catch up. As it happened, Eisenhower was just returning from a West Point class of '15 reunion and homecoming football game, while a Big Ten game had taken Charlie Wilson's successor, the new Secretary of Defense, Neil McElroy, to Columbus.

The United States was in an uproar. The presence of the dog in Sputnik II clearly meant that eventually the Russians intended to put a man on the moon. Most people in the U.S. were determined to beat them there, and they were becoming impatient with the composure of their President. *Time* said: "The storm showed promise of being the most serious that Dwight Eisenhower had ever faced." A headline in the *Pittsburgh Press* begged: SHOOT THE MOON, IKE.

Ike wasn't going to do it. He refused to be stampeded. Unlike the three Presidents who followed him in the White House, he had grave doubts about the wisdom of investing the national resources in space exploration. He was General Eisenhower now, pondering what he saw as a military threat. He knew he was falling in public esteem. To Gallup's question, "Do you approve of the way Eisenhower is handling his job as President?" only 57 percent now answered affirmatively. Previously the figure had rarely dropped below 71 percent. The present decline was greatest in the South, where it had dropped from 72 percent the previous January to an all-time low of 36 percent.* No President enjoys an erosion of popularity, and Ike valued public esteem more than most. But on matters of national security he was the expert, and he had regarded rocketry from the first as a military matter. He suspected his opinion was shared in the Kremlin, and from mid-October on he was certain of it, largely thanks to a remarkable interview with Nikita Khrushchev by James Reston of the *New York Times*.

The first secretary of the Soviet Communist party was in an expansive mood. Elated by the triumphs of his scientists, he boasted that the space satellites were only the beginning of Russia's rocket

* Much of the loss here was attributable to the Little Rock crisis. See pages 978–91.

wonders. "When we announced the successful launching of an Intercontinental Ballistic Missile," he gloated, "some American statesmen did not believe us. Now that we have successfully launched an earth satellite, only technically ignorant people can doubt this. The U.S. does not have an intercontinental ballistic missile; otherwise it would also have easily launched an earth satellite of its own." The West, he said, might as well scrap its B-52s and abandon its airfields: "If you study our latest proposals you will no longer find any mention of control posts at airfields* . . . It is useless to create control posts to watch obsolete airplanes." In another interview that same week with two visiting British M.P.s he said even more vividly: "Bombers are obsolete. You might as well throw them on the fire. You cannot send human flesh and blood to fight things like that." A few days later the Russians announced that they had successfully tested a new hydrogen warhead for a guided missile. To General Eisenhower there could be but one interpretation of all this. The skeptics of Russian advances in rocketry had been wrong. Khrushchev had to be believed now. Manned bombers might not yet be obsolete, but they were becoming obsolete. The Soviet Union had in fact developed the dreaded ICBM. The touch of one button in Moscow and Washington would vanish.

The danger then confronting the United States is evident in retrospect:

June 5, 1957 An Army Jupiter travels over 1,500 miles from Cape Canaveral, the first successful flight of an intermediate range weapon (IRBM) for the United States.

August 26, 1957 The USSR reports that it has successfully tested a multistage ICBM.

November 28, 1958 An American Atlas completes a 6,325-mile flight from Cape Canaveral to Ascension Island, the first full-range flight for a U.S. ICBM.

Thus Soviet rocketry held a clear lead for fifteen perilous months. The U.S., to be sure, was hardly defenseless. Despite Khrushchev's jeers at bombers, at every hour of the day and night the vigilant Strategic Air Command had fleets of B-52 jets in the air in a state of readiness with nuclear warheads on board, and the Jupiter IRBMs, poised on NATO bases ringing the Soviet Union, were a powerful deterrent to Russian aggression. Nevertheless, the fact re-

* Control posts: radar installations.

mained that America had fallen behind in the vital ICBM race and would remain there for well over a year.

In the seclusion of the presidential mansion, Ike was very different these days from the cool-headed, almost tranquil chief executive who exasperated the White House press corps. "Although Eisenhower maintained an official air of serenity," Sherman Adams later wrote, "he was privately as concerned as everybody else in the country by the jump ahead that the Russians had made in scientific enterprise." Even before the ascent of Sputnik II he had ordered McElroy, sworn in only the day before, to undertake an immediate, urgent review of the country's missile program, and when Emmet John Hughes suggested to him that popular concern could be an advantage, winning support for new programs, the President quickly replied, "Oh, absolutely. Anything that will get us out of this complacency—and make this next Congress realize how serious things are—that's all to the good."

His problem was more complicated than that. If he had revealed the real stakes in this contest with the Russians, Congress and the people would not only have lost their complacency, they might very well have lost their perspective, or even their minds. The previous spring the President had asked H. Rowan Gaither Jr., then chairman of the board of the Ford Foundation, to evaluate the nation's state of defense readiness with the cooperation and guidance of the National Security Council. The results were submitted in November, just after Sputnik II went into orbit. They were so shocking that the President decided to suppress them. The Gaither Report endorsed a proposal for a nationwide nuclear bomb shelter program. The shelter plan was financially impossible, Ike concluded, and he saw no point in publication of a text which would merely terrify the people without offering any hope of a solution.

He believed a solution could be found, however. The answer was to draw ahead, or at least abreast, of the Soviet missile achievements. As he saw it, that was the task before the country, not exploits in outer space. It was as great a challenge as any President had ever faced, and because of it he had no difficulty in keeping his eyes off the stars, though not many in the country, or even in his own administration, could resist the fascination of space travel. Knowland couldn't; Ike had to tell him curtly that he had no intention of being "pushed into an all-out effort in every one of these glamour performances without any idea of their eventual cost." The

President's determination to keep all rocket programs in the Defense Department, at least for the present, was also challenged, by Vice President Nixon and President James R. Killian of MIT, whom Ike appointed special assistant to the President for science and technology on November 7. Eisenhower said to both that the mechanics of launching space rockets and long-range missiles were virtually the same; a costly duplication of effort made no sense to him. Killian was doubtful, and Nixon, supporting Killian, argued that America's image abroad would be more favorable if the peaceful aspects of space exploration were handled by an agency without ties to the country's military establishment. The President, less concerned with image than with survival, replied that he would rather have "one good Redstone nuclear-armed missile than a rocket that could hit the moon." He added pungently, "We have no enemies on the moon."

His wisdom is apparent to a generation accustomed to nuclear weapons housed in hardened silos, Polaris submarines, and fail-safe mechanisms—all the horrid realities of the future from which Ike flinched but which he nevertheless faced. ICBMs, which the Russians had, and the inferior IRBMs, which America had, had not yet found their way into the language. Even the sophisticated had not come to terms with the implications of joining H-bomb warheads to unmanned missiles capable of traversing oceans and continents at speeds even greater than Sputnik I's 18,000 mph. All that was beyond the mind of the average American in 1957. A paragraph in the October 28 *Time* gives some idea of the innocence of the well-informed then. It was headed "What About Armed Satellites?" and it might have been written by Jules Verne:

> Many imaginative military planners have dreamed of satellite fortresses armed with nuclear missiles to shoot at the earth below. All space vehicles must be lightly built to conserve weight. They would therefore be vulnerable, and since they are forced to move on predictable orbits, they should not be too hard to shoot down. One suggested method of dealing with a hostile satellite is to shoot a modest rocket into its orbit, but moving in the opposite direction. The warhead would burst and fill the orbit with millions of small particles. Any one of these, hitting the satellite with twice its orbital speed (36,000 mph) would have the effect of a meteor, punching a hole and sending a blast of flame and shock into its interior.

That was in 1957, with a Soviet projectile in orbit and fresh information about the phenomenon accumulating hourly. Another five months would pass before *Time* reported: "A word coming more and more into Pentagon usage is 'overkill'—a blunt but descriptive term implying a power to destroy a military target many times more than necessary." By then the country was learning fast. But when Eisenhower had taken office the very theory of guided missiles had been almost as remote as the atomic bomb concept when Einstein's famous letter reached FDR's desk in October 1939. During the eight years after V-J Day government spending on long-range ballistic missile projects had averaged less than a million dollars a year. In 1954 American physicists advised Washington that they now believed they could design a hydrogen warhead small enough to be carried in the nose of a missile. The administration then gave the green light to ballistic missile development. But the United States was already behind—the Russians had decided to push on with missile research without knowing whether one would ever be capable of carrying a warhead—and the lag grew greater after a fateful recommendation of the U.S. IGY committee.

In 1954 Wernher von Braun, the Nazi V-2 scientist who was to become a naturalized U.S. citizen the following year, had persuaded the Army and the Navy to share in a joint venture under his leadership. Von Braun planned to soup up the Army's tested Redstone missile with booster rockets and send a tiny (five-pound) satellite into orbit. The endeavor was christened Project Orbiter. It was coming along nicely until October of that year, when an International Geophysical Year panel meeting in Rome proposed earth satellite launchings during the IGY—from July 1957 to December 1958. The Americans on the panel agreed. They recommended that the United States undertake a satellite project as part of the country's IGY contribution. The White House consented. At the same time certain administration policy makers insisted that any appearance of using an IGY undertaking for military purposes must be avoided. Their reasoning was the same as that set forth three years later by Killian and Nixon; neutral governments might misunderstand and become offended. It made sense to the National Security Council, which thereupon separated satellite research from military ballistic work. This decision, ending von Braun's Project Orbiter, was reached in mid-1955, when, as it happened, up in Dearborn the

Ford Motor Company was deciding to produce the starcrossed Edsel.

After Sputnik I went up, I. M. Levitt, director of Philadelphia's Fels Planetarium, called the separation of the rocketeers and the missilemen an "astonishing piece of stupidity." Army projectile engineers echoed him. In 1955 progress on their Jupiter IRBM had been sufficiently advanced for it to launch a satellite; in September 1956 a modified Jupiter-C reached a height of 650 miles, higher than Sputnik I's orbit, and sailed on for a distance of 3,500 miles. There was no appeal from the National Security Council, however. Orbiter's rocket men were transferred to Project Vanguard, its successor. Vanguard was then assigned to the Navy on the ground that the Navy's Vikings and Aerobees represented greater advances in high-altitude missile research than similar enterprises in the other services. There Vanguard had languished. As a first step under the new management, Director John P. Hagen, the Canadian astronomer now at the helm, announced his intention of launching a 20-pound satellite—one-eighth the weight of Sputnik I—late in 1954. But then there were snags, delays, postponements. Hagen issued a revised schedule, under which the first 21½-pound satellite would go up in the spring of 1958, provided the 27,000-pound thrust of its Viking launcher worked perfectly. Hagen and his colleagues were still working on this when Soviet scientists began hurtling Red moons across the skies.

In Eisenhower's mind the distinction between scientific inquiry and military necessity continued to be sharply defined, and he drew it in his first press conference after the launching of Sputnik I. Vanguard was a scholarly undertaking, he said, "merely an engagement on our part to put up a vehicle of this kind." It was all very well in its way; if the ambitions for it were realized, mankind's knowledge would be enriched with information about "temperatures, radiation, ionization, pressures." But it had nothing to do with any race to the moon, and he didn't know where that idea had started, and he wished someone would tell him.

The launching of the sputnik, Ike said, was something else again. It meant Soviet possession "of a very powerful thrust in their rocketry, and that is important." Unfortunately the figures he had received up to now were militarily meaningless: "I don't know anything about their accuracy, and until you know something about their accuracy, you know nothing at all about their usefulness in warfare." He acknowledged that he was deeply concerned: "I wish we were farther ahead and knew more as to accuracy and to the erosion and to the heat-resistant qualities of metals, and all the other things we have to know about. I wish we knew more about it at this moment."

It was Russian weaponry, he explained, that was the source of his anxiety. The administration had spent $110 million on its satellite project and would spend more. All the same, missile research and development would continue to have priority over it. Almost disdainfully he said: "So far as the satellite itself is concerned, that does not raise my apprehensions, not one iota."

Over at the Vanguard offices, Dr. Hagen and his staff appeared to be equally tranquil. They acknowledged some obstacles, some disappointments, but that was always the way of things on the drawing boards and in the labs. Nodding and puffing thoughtfully on his pipe, the soft-spoken Hagen conceded that his launching vehicle was still undergoing tests, but neither he nor his colleagues admitted to any sense of failure. They had promised to put a satellite in orbit before IGY's end, and that was over a year away. Time, they gently reminded journalists, has little meaning in basic research.

> *fau-bus* (faw-bus), v.i.; FAUBUSED, FAUBUSING. 1. To commit an error of enormous magnitude through malice and ignorance. 2. To make a serious error, to commit a fault through stupidity or mental confusion. Syn. Blunder, err, bollix.

Thus Jack Mabley of the *Chicago Daily News* proposed, in October 1957, that the name of Arkansas Governor Orval Faubus be added to the language. The suggestion never caught on, partly because Faubus's period of notoriety, though great, was brief, and also because under it all he was really quite colorless. If Faubus had not existed it would not have been necessary to invent him. All over the South white politicians were campaigning against the Supreme Court's three-year-old decision striking down the concept of separate but equal education. In Alabama alone four gubernatorial candidates were pledging unyielding opposition to school integration, one of them vowing he would go to jail for segregation and another going one better by swearing that he would die for it. The difference between them and Faubus was that he was already in office and therefore able to attract and hold national attention by official action. In that tumultuous fall he moved in counterpoint with the momentous developments at Cape Canaveral and in outer space, his parochialism juxtaposed against their promises of glory.

There was never any doubt about Faubus's motives. In Arkansas he faced an uphill fight for reelection. The state had a strong tradition against a third-term governor, and his popularity was waning; he had offended liberal constituents by approving rate increases for utilities and railroads and disillusioned others by raising taxes. His strategy was to build a new base in red-neck, racist eastern Arkansas. On August 20, 1957, he made his first move, calling on Deputy Attorney General William Rogers in Washington to ask what the government would do to prevent violence when Little Rock schools opened in September. This was the first time anyone had intimated that violence might come to Little Rock. All the signs indicated that integration would proceed smoothly. On the initiative of Mayor Woodrow W. Mann the city had worked out a model seven-year integration program, carefully picking black pupils likely to do well. Startled by Faubus's question, Rogers replied that local disorders were usually handled by local police.

To be certain that federal officials were still abreast of developments there, the deputy attorney general sent the head of the Justice Department's civil rights division to Little Rock. The official, himself a native of Arkansas, explained to Faubus how federal injunctions could pinion conspirators. He asked the governor why he expected trouble. Faubus's answer was evasive; his evidence, he said, was "too vague and indefinite to be of any use to a law-enforcement agency." Back in Washington, the official reported that he believed the governor intended to play racial politics with schoolchildren.

Faubus's next step confirmed him. On August 29 the governor asked a state court to block the city's integration schedule on the ground that it would lead to bloodshed. The local judge gave him his injunction and was promptly overruled by U.S. District Judge Ronald Davies. The board of education proceeded with its integration arrangements. They were modest enough; nine black pupils were to be enrolled with the two thousand whites in Little Rock's Central High School. There were still no signs of unrest, but to be safe Mayor Mann and his 175-man police force worked out tactics for controlling possible demonstrations.

It was a waste of time. The governor had no intention of consulting the mayor. His plan was rather to call out the National Guard and order it to stop the nine Negro children from registering. Getting wind of this on September 1, Arkansas's most famous citizen, Winthrop Rockefeller, hurried to the statehouse and for two hours begged Faubus not to do it. The governor refused. He said, "I'm sorry, but I'm already committed. I'm going to run for a third term, and if I don't do this, Jim Johnson and Bruce Bennett"—racists who would oppose him in the primary—"will tear me to shreds." At 9 P.M. on September 2, the evening before schools would reopen, National Guardsmen carrying M-1s with fixed bayonets set up a perimeter defense around Central High while their leader, a major general in the Air National Guard, set up his command post in the principal's office. An hour later Faubus appeared on Little Rock's KTHV-TV and announced that he had called out the militia "to maintain or restore the peace and good order of this community." The city, he said, was on the brink of riot: "the evidence of discord, anger, and resentment has come to me from so many sources as to become a deluge!"

Little Rock was astonished. The mayor said, "There was no indication whatever. We had no reason to believe there would be violence." The governor had said that the city's stores were running out of knives (sold "mostly to Negro youths"), but an FBI check of 100 stores revealed that the sale of knives and guns was below normal. The only weapons in sight were those of the National Guard. There had been every reason to believe that the capital of the state would follow the pattern of three other Arkansas communities—Fort Smith, Ozark, and Van Buren—which were quietly integrating that same day. Now the nine black youngsters, arriving at Central High in a group, were turned away by National Guardsmen who said, "Governor Faubus has placed this school off limits to Negroes." One fifteen-year-old black girl tested the perimeter. The Guardsmen raised their rifles against her, and as she retreated a spectator called out, "Go home, you burr head"; then the white-haired wife of a teacher shielded the child and led her to a bus stop. That was the extent of Faubus's "violence," and Judge Davies denied a new petition for further delay of integration.

At the judge's request, fifty FBI agents had roamed Little Rock, looking once more for signs of racial tension. Their 500-page report disclosed not a shred of evidence to support the claim that the peace was threatened. Accordingly, Davies summoned the governor to appear in court September 20 and show cause why he should not be enjoined from interfering with the school board's program. Faubus had retired to the salmon-pink gubernatorial mansion and ringed it with Guardsmen, but a U.S. marshal easily penetrated this screen and handed him the summons on the executive lawn. For the first time the governor looked worried. He wired President Eisenhower, complaining that he was being investigated by federal agents, that his telephone was being tapped, and that he had learned of a scheme to take him "into custody, by force." He asked for a presidential assurance of "understanding and cooperation." Eisenhower replied, "The only assurance I can give you is that the federal constitution will be upheld by me by every legal means at my command."

Representative Brooks Hays, Little Rock's congressman, thought Eisenhower and Faubus ought to sit down together and talk things over. It was arranged; on September 14, the eleventh day of the crisis, they met at the summer White House in Newport, Rhode Island. Sherman Adams's impression of Faubus was that "he would not be unreasonable or difficult to deal with," and Eisenhower thought Faubus seemed confused about the course he should take. Both were wrong. The governor continued to stonewall, and the situation was unchanged six days later when Judge Davies called from his bench, "Civil case no. 3113 on a Motion for preliminary injunction." He was handling the hearing like any other, but it was historic. The governor of a state was being brought to justice in a federal court.

Faubus himself was not there. Ever since calling out the National Guard he had dodged questions about his evidence of violence by promising to produce it in open court, but the evidence wasn't there, either. In place of it were three Arkansas lawyers representing him. They filed motions asking first that Davies disqualify himself because of personal bias, and second that charges against the governor be dismissed here because they should be heard by a three-judge court. Davies quietly overruled them. Speaking from notes, their chief counsel then said, "The position of the respondent, Governor Faubus, and his military officers must be firm, unequivocal, unalterable: that the governor of the state of Arkansas cannot and will not concede that the United States in this court or anywhere else can question his discretion and judgment."

The attorney asked if he and his colleagues might be excused from the hearings, the judge nodded, and they walked out. The governor's defense had rested without summoning a witness. His argument was that federal courts had no jurisdiction over him in Arkansas. That issue had been raised in 1861 and presumably settled in 1865.

The U.S. attorney had planned to call nearly two hundred witnesses. Now eight were enough. They included the mayor, the police chief, and the superintendent of schools. All testified to the city's racial peace. Summing up the evidence afterward, the judge said it showed that the school board's integration program had been "thwarted by the governor of Arkansas by the use of National Guard troops," adding, "It is equally demonstrable from the testimony here today that there would have been no violence in carrying out the plan of integration." He thereupon issued orders that Faubus and the National Guard were to stop their interference. Asked to comment, Faubus scrawled a statement for reporters. He noted that his attorneys had not been present, omitting the fact that they had left on his instructions. He declared: "Now comes the crucifixion. There will be no cross-examination, no evidence presented for the other [his own] side. So now, by the use of carefully selected witnesses, the Justice Department's case can be continued. The results are a foregone conclusion." That night he issued a milder statement, attacking Davies's "unwarranted action" but saying that he would comply with the court order until its "certain reversal on appeal." The militia was withdrawn from Central High, and as the troops marched away Faubus and his wife Alta left Little Rock for a Southern Governors' Conference in Sea Island, Georgia. On the way they stopped to see a Georgia-Texas football game in Atlanta. Afterward a fellow governor told the press, "He's really lapping up the glory. There were 33,000 people at the game, and every time they cheered a play, Faubus got up and bowed."

That evening he was the cynosure of all eyes in the Silver Room of Sea Island's Cloister Hotel, signing autographs, drinking bourbon and Seven-Up, and dancing. His partners included Mrs. James Karam, who was accompanying the governor's party. Her husband had been unable to make the trip. "Jimmy the Flash" Karam, as he was known in Little Rock, was one of the governor's closest friends. A former football player and professional strikebreaker, Karam was now head of the Arkansas State Athletic Commission. As such he had intimate knowledge of the world of locker rooms, sparring partners, and bullyboys. That was what was keeping him home. He had a special assignment from the governor, and it began at daybreak the following morning. While the Faubuses and his wife lay asleep in Sea Island recovering from the festivities in the Silver Room, Karam was deploying a force of husky young men outside Central High, whispering here, nodding there, and ducking in and out of a filling station phone booth.

At 6 A.M. seventy Little Rock policemen arrived swinging nightsticks and erected sawhorse barricades around the school. Three weeks earlier that would have been enough to keep the peace, but now the crisis had been building too long; Faubus's prediction of trouble was about to become self-fulfilling, especially with Karam there to rally faint hearts. Afterward the mayor blamed what happened on "professional agitators" and an assistant police chief said that "half the troublemakers were from out of town." Civic pride kept them from pointing out that many of the leaders were figures in Little Rock sports and therefore friends of the policemen. Some cops, sympathetic with them, were defensive about being here. "Do you think I like this?" one of them told spectators. "I'm just trying to do my job."

At 8:45 the Central High class bell sounded. In the next instant a yell went up: "Here come the niggers!" These blacks weren't schoolchildren. They were four Negro newspapermen who had arrived together. Retreating, they were pursued by about twenty bullyboys, who cut them off and began systematically beating them. One cop climbed on a car to get a better look. Others moved in to stop the mayhem, and as they did Jimmy Karam cried angrily, "The niggers started it!" A powerfully built youth hurried up to him and said, "Get me five or six boys and get them over there where the nigger kids came in last time." Karam rounded up five of the biggest and led them there. He was too late; while the mob had been watching the attack on the black reporters, the nine Negro children had arrived in two cars and walked into the school. Once there, they seemed safe. Most of the white students looked at them curiously. Some made friendly overtures. None appeared to be hostile.

Nevertheless, the position of the newcomers was untenable. The scene outside was rapidly deteriorating. Radio and television descriptions of the melee had attracted toughs from surrounding towns. The throng doubled and redoubled, until nearly a thousand men were milling around, spoiling for a fight. The ineffectual police response to the assault on the Negro newsmen had taught them that hooliganism would go unpunished. Looking for new targets, they settled on white journalists. Three *Life* men were mauled. Every reporter without a southern accent was in danger. So were the policemen and the state troopers who had answered their appeals for help. In the turmoil the sawhorse barricades were demolished. Surging toward Central High, the crowd was at its very doors when, at 11:50 A.M., Mayor Mann capitulated and ordered the black children withdrawn from the school. The toughs dispersed, chortling. Jimmy Karam darted into the filling station booth and put through a call. Shortly afterward Governor Faubus called a press conference in Sea Island. "The trouble in Little Rock," he said, "vindicates my good judgment."

President Eisenhower was in Washington that morning, speaking before the International Monetary Fund. All that week he had been depressed by the growing crisis in Arkansas. He told Sherman Adams that he was well aware that the Warren Court's resolution of Brown v. Board of Education was "cutting into established customs and traditions in such communities as Little Rock," and "You cannot change the hearts of people by law." Later in the week he would tell four moderate southern governors, "I have never said what I thought about the Supreme Court decision—I have never told a soul." He added, "But how I feel about it is immaterial. The fact is that it is the law, and as the President of the United States I have the responsibility of seeing to it that it is enforced." He had been about to leave the Monetary Fund meeting after speaking when he received an urgent call from Brownell. The attorney general gave him a terse account of the disorders outside Central High. The President then approved a tough statement:

> The federal law and orders of a United States District Court . . . cannot be flouted with immunity by any individual or any mob of extremists. I will use the full power of the United States including whatever force may be necessary to prevent any obstruction of the law and to carry out the orders of the Federal Court.

He was hoping to shake some sense into Faubus. But it was too late. He had barely returned to Newport when a second call from Brownell came in over the maximum-security telephone in his personal quarters. Reports from U.S. marshals in Arkansas disclosed that law enforcement had broken down on both the state and local levels. A mob had ruled at Central High. Moreover, Little Rock was asking Washington to intervene; School Superintendent Virgil Blossom had just called the Justice Department and said, "Mayor Mann wants to know who to call to get federal help." He had been put through to Brownell, who, after hanging up, had drafted a proclamation setting forth the traditional authority and responsibility of the President, reaching back to 1795, to use troops to enforce the federal law. If approved by Eisenhower, it would open the way to sending in the Army. Ike listened to it over the phone. He said, "I want you to send up that proclamation. It looks like I will have to sign it, but I want to read it."

He studied it that evening on the sun porch of his living quarters and went to bed leaving it unsigned. The prospect appalled him, he told Adams; using U.S. soldiers against U.S. citizens would never be "a wise thing to do in this country." But events in Little Rock had acquired a momentum of their own. It is doubtful that even Orval Faubus and Jimmy Karam could have controlled them now. Only strict obedience of the court order would keep the Army out, and a crowd which has successfully defied policemen obeys nobody. Walking to his Newport office just before eight o'clock the following morning, Ike squinted at the horizon and said, "There's a cold wind blowing up." It was an omen. In less than an hour Brownell was on the line again with bad news from Central High. The mob was even bigger today; pushing and shoving, it jeered cops who tried to break it up. The nine Negro students had stayed home. In the opinion of the U.S. marshals, only their absence had saved the school from an invasion. This time Mayor Mann had sent Washington a telegram formally requesting presidential intervention. Eisenhower hung up and signed the proclamation, and that evening he went on national television to explain: "The very basis of our individual rights and freedoms rests upon the certainty that the President and the executive branch of government will support and insure the carrying out of the decisions of the federal courts, even, when necessary, with all the means at the President's command. Unless the President did so, anarchy would result."

That morning, responding to the proclamation, Secretary of Defense Wilson had placed the Arkansas National Guard in federal service, beyond the reach of Governor Faubus, and General Maxwell Taylor, the Army chief of staff, had assigned the 327th Battle

Group of the 101st Airborne Division to bring peace to Central High. Eight C-130 and C-123 transport planes had carried the paratroopers from Fort Campbell, in Kentucky, to Arkansas. As Eisenhower spoke to the nation the first trucks drew up in front of the school. For the first time since Reconstruction days southern intransigence on the issue of race had brought Army rule.

The difference between these troops and the militia was striking. Both wore the same uniform, but the resemblance ended there. The National Guard was made up of weekend soldiers, easygoing, casual in dress, and slow to obey. The 101st Airborne was a crack outfit, professional in all ways. While salty officers carrying swagger sticks barked commands, disciplined men spilled out of the trucks and formed ranks on the school grounds. Jeeps were parked just so, in a line. Immaculate tents, each the same distance from the others, rose in a field beyond Central High's tennis courts. Field telephone wires were strung from oaks in the school yard, and before dawn walkie-talkies crackled with the code names of communications men: "Hello, Defiance, this is Crossroads Six. Come in, Roadblock Alpha."*

Roadblock Alpha was the scene of the day's most dramatic incident. The barrier had been thrown up in an intersection a block east of Central High. There, in the first olive moments of Tuesday morning, ringleaders began organizing their men. A lanky, lantern-jawed major watched them from beside a sound truck. His voice rasped over the loudspeaker: "Please return to your homes or it will be necessary to disperse you." They didn't budge. "Nigger lover," one of them muttered, and another called, "Russian!" A man in a baggy brown suit shouted to the others, "They're just bluffing. If you don't want to move, you don't have to."

The major ripped out a command. Twelve paratroopers with fixed bayonets formed a line and braced their rifle butts against their hips in the on-guard position for riot control; it brought each bayonet on a line with the crowd's throats. Again the major snapped an order, and the soldiers moved forward. The mob retreated. The man in the brown suit held his ground until the last moment; then he broke and ran. He didn't run far, however. The Army had won the

* The officer responsible for this impressive display, the 101st's commander, was Major General Edwin Walker. Later he was retired for circulating John Birch Society material among his men; later still, he was on the wrong side in a racial incident and was arrested. He retired in Dallas, where he flew the American flag upside down. In Little Rock his conduct was above reproach.

first skirmish, but the showdown was yet to come. The black children hadn't even reached the school.

That moment arrived in a crisp, swiftly executed maneuver. Central High's 8:45 bell rang. Simultaneously the barricade at Park Avenue and Sixteenth Street opened to admit a lead jeep, an Army station wagon, and a rear guard jeep. They braked together in front of the school, and the Negro children emerged from the station wagon as three platoons of paratroopers ran up on the double with rifles at port arms and formed a semicircle, shielding the children with a hedge of bayonets. A fourth platoon, lining up on either side of the black students, escorted them up the steps. The crowd watched in stunned silence. Then a woman cried brokenly, "Oh my God! The niggers are inside!" Others shouted, "They're in! They're in!" Another woman screamed and tore at her hair. The crowd shifted, tilting forward.

At Roadblock Alpha the throng had thickened. Again the major said harshly, "Let's clear this area right now. This is the living end! I'll tell you, we're not going to do it on a slow walk this time." Nothing happened, and he ordered the paratroopers to resume their advance. As they came on, the crowd recoiled, hopping, to the front lawn and then to the veranda of a private home, all the time yelling that this was private property, that the troopers had no right to come after them on it. The soldiers didn't miss a step. Up on the porch they came, and then across it as the mob scrambled backward from the bayonets.

Those who hesitated were being methodically pushed off the piazza when one of them struck back. He was C. E. Blake, a Missouri-Pacific switchman who had been among the most active agitators during the past two days. Blake seized a soldier's rifle barrel and dragged him down. As they sprawled together another paratrooper reversed his M-1 and clouted the switchman's head with the steel butt. Blood streaming from his scalp, he crawled away on all fours shouting at photographers, "Who knows the name of that lowlife son of a bitch who hit me?" Without a glance in his direction the troopers continued to move out while a stony-eyed sergeant called, "Keep those bayonets high—right at the base of the neck."

Back from Sea Island, Orval Faubus joked with the press ("I feel like MacArthur. I've been relieved of my job") and asked the networks for equal time to answer President Eisenhower. ABC-TV gave it to him; the other two turned him down because he refused to answer questions afterward. In the Faubus version of what had happened, Blake had been "a guest in a home." Troopers had run wild with "wholesale arrests." High school girls had been "taken by the FBI and held incommunicado for hours of questioning while their frantic parents knew nothing of their whereabouts." Young white southern womanhood was very much on the governor's mind; he held up a photograph for just a moment and said, "Evidence of the naked force of the federal government is here apparent in these unsheathed bayonets in the backs of schoolgirls." Again, he cried that he had returned from Georgia to find paratroopers "bludgeoning innocent bystanders, with bayonets in the backs of schoolgirls, and the warm, red blood of patriotic Americans staining the cold, naked, unsheathed knives." At the end he cried: "In the name of God, whom we all revere, in the name of liberty which we hold so dear, which we all cherish, what is happening in America?"

What was happening in Little Rock bore little relationship to his speech. Blake, of course, had been no one's guest. Only eight arrests had been made; four of the men had been fined for loitering, and the other four had been released at the police station. The FBI hadn't questioned anyone; J. Edgar Hoover said the governor was "disseminating falsehoods." As for the bayonets in girls' backs, the picture, which Faubus had quickly whipped out of sight, was of girls walking—and giggling—past a group of soldiers.

Those were the facts, and they testified to the good judgment of the troops from Fort Campbell. It continued to go unrecognized by Faubus. Two weeks later he descended to what the *Washington Post and Times-Herald* called "the lavatory level," charging that troopers were entering the girls' locker room at Central High and staying to leer at their nudity. Reporters asked Faubus for eyewitness accounts or documentary proof. He replied, "I do not choose to release them at this time." Actually he never produced evidence to support any of his accusations. In November the Army withdrew all but a token force from the school, and the black children began attending Central High unescorted. By the following May the incident belonged to history. It had been a skillful if expensive use of force; keeping the nine Negro students in school had cost the federal government $4,051,000.

But the country paid another, far higher price for the events that autumn in Arkansas. The real significance of Little Rock lay in its impact on the white South. Deep in the southern consciousness lay tales of the Civil War and its aftermath, told to them in childhood by their grandparents, and the trouble at Central High evoked the martyred ghosts of that terrible era. On this subject they were beyond the reach of reason. Their reaction was compounded of the Stars and Bars, the strains of "Dixie," Jackson at Bull Run, Lee at Appomattox, and the dead on the field at Antietam. It rendered them blind to Faubus's clumsy lies. Northern soldiers on southern soil meant just one thing to them—an evil, loathsome presence to be attacked in righteous wrath, sounding a rebel yell that drowned out voices of sanity. Senator Richard Russell of Georgia accused Eisenhower of "applying tactics that must have been copied from the manual issued to the officers of Hitler's storm troopers."* Senator Olin Johnson of South Carolina said, "If I were Governor Faubus, I'd proclaim an insurrection down there, and I'd call out the National Guard, and I'd then find out who's going to run things in my state." Senator James O. Eastland of Mississippi charged, "Eisenhower has lit the fires of hate," and Senator Herman Talmadge of Georgia said, "We still mourn the destruction of Hungary. Now the South is threatened by the President of the United States using tanks [*sic*] and troops in the streets of Little Rock. I wish I could cast one vote for impeachment right now." Alabama's Governor James E. "Kissin' Jim" Folsom promised that he would disband his state's National Guard before he would let Eisenhower federalize it, and Governor James Bell Timmerman of South Carolina resigned his U.S. Navy reserve commission so he could not be called into service.

They were the leaders. In a thousand ways private southerners made it known that they regarded Faubus as their hero and the President as their enemy. Gallup found that while only 10 percent of the people in northern and western states thought Eisenhower had been wrong in sending the troopers to Central High, only a third of the southerners thought he had been right. In Jacksonville, Florida, an Air Corps veteran mailed his four Air Medals and six battle stars to the White House for distribution among the paratroopers. In Marshall, Texas, a speaker at a Kiwanian luncheon said,

* The President, indignant, wired Russell: "I must say I completely fail to understand your comparison of our troops to Hitler's storm troopers. In one case military power was used to further the ambitions of a ruthless dictator; in the other to preserve the institutions of free government."

"This is the darkest day in Southern history since the reconstruction"; the Kiwanians then refused to pledge their allegiance to the flag. Near Dover, Delaware, two Negroes in business suits were ordered to leave a Howard Johnson restaurant by a waitress who said, "Colored people are not allowed to eat in here," thereby embarrassing the State Department; one of the men was the finance minister of Ghana, who had entertained Richard Nixon in his home, and the other was his secretary. As always in the South, the raising of the racial issue was accompanied by intimations of terror. In Albany, Georgia, night riders put a college for Negroes to the torch, and at the height of the Little Rock crisis six Alabamans trapped a black named Judge Aaron on a lonely country road, took him to a deserted shack, castrated him with a razor blade, and poured turpentine into the wound. None of them had known Aaron; one of them said afterward, "We just wanted some nigger at random."

The subsequent career of Orval Faubus was a measure of southern feeling. The governor had played his role in full view of Arkansas voters. Elsewhere biased reporting may have clouded the judgment of readers, but not in Faubus's home state; one of the bravest chapters in American journalism was written by Harry Scott Ashmore of the *Arkansas Gazette*, who won a Pulitzer Prize for his superb coverage of the turmoil at Central High. Not all of his subscribers were appreciative. Ashmore's phone rang around the clock with threatening calls; Faubus denounced him as "an ardent integrationist"; Little Rock's racist Capital Citizens Council called him the state's "Public Enemy No. 1," and a statewide boycott cost the *Gazette* 3,000 subscriptions. He continued to print the truth, whereupon the people of Arkansas swept Faubus back into the statehouse in 1958 for a third term—he received 255,086 votes; the man who ran second got 56,966—and continued to reelect him by massive majorities in subsequent elections. In 1967, after twelve years in the executive mansion, he retired.

Outside the South, and indeed beyond the United States, was another matter. The struggle to put the nine black children in Central High had global ramifications. Little Rock, an editor wrote at the time, had become "a name known wherever men could read newspapers and listen to radios, a symbol to be distorted in Moscow, misinterpreted in New Delhi," and "painfully explained in London." Americans solicitous of good opinion in foreign capitals were chagrined. They recognized the principles at stake in Arkansas, and saw them being flouted; and they felt shame.

And yet they had virtually nothing to say about the human dimensions of the episode. In perspective that silence is deafening. The voice of the American Negro was still unheard. The word southerner meant white southerner. There was no term for the South's blacks, and U.S. newspapers there and elsewhere seldom carried day-by-day news about them. The true meaning of the Howard Johnson episode was that a victim of racial discrimination had to be a cabinet member in a foreign country before the country's conscience was stirred, and even then it regretted not the wrong done, but the damage to America's image.

Black adults, bred to passivity, accepting the system because for so long there had been no alternative, turned inward as they always had, transmuting what should have been righteous anger into despair. For every American Negro who felt elation when the 101st Airborne triumphed in Arkansas there were dozens who feared—justifiably—the rage of aroused whites; who read of Judge Aaron and knew that there, but for the grace of God, went they. But their children reacted differently. Coming after the Montgomery bus boycott and the Supreme Court decisions outlawing discrimination, the confrontation at Central High confirmed the hope that the stereotypes of the past might be broken. It was in this sense, in the fall of 1957, that Little Rock left a profound impression on such young blacks as Stokely Carmichael, who was sixteen; Cassius Clay, fifteen; H. Rap Brown, thirteen; and Angela Davis, twelve.

In the first fortnight of November those who thought it their duty to cheer up America examined the bleak clouds that had been gathering, and in search of silver linings concentrated on repairing the havoc that had been wreaked upon U.S. morale by the sputniks. Von Braun told the press that the United States could launch a satellite with equipment already available. To the surprise of everyone, including those who had been working on it, Secretary McElroy announced that Vanguard was back on schedule. Emissaries from *Time*, dispatched to take soundings in 33 cities, found stout hearts in the president of the Kansas City Stock Yards Company, a Florida congressman, a group of bankers in Lincoln, Nebraska, and a Los Angeles sales engineer ("Six weeks ago I'd walk into an aircraft plant and it would look as if everybody from the chief engineer to the draftsmen was taking a coffee break at once. When I made my rounds this week, the recreation rooms were empty. Everybody was working.")

"Upward" was the inspirational title of a *Reader's Digest* article by Beirne Lay Jr., who suggested that "a Supreme Being" was America's silent ally in the space quest. By then the administration was responding to aroused public opinion. Rocket crews worked feverishly at Cape Canaveral, and at Nixon's urging the President reluctantly agreed that he must do something more to brighten the country's mood. After his appointment of Killian as special assistant for science and technology (to Ike's annoyance the press changed this to "missile czar") he named a Pentagon coordinator to crack down on interservice rivalries. Then he decided to deliver a series of five presidential TV talks. Much was expected of these, and the first went well. In it he displayed the four-foot nose cone of a retrieved Jupiter. He explained: "One difficult obstacle on the way to producing a long-range weapon is that of bringing a missile back from outer space without its burning up like a meteor . . . This one here in my office is the nose cone of an experimental missile. It has been hundreds of miles into outer space and back. Here it is, completely intact." It was his conviction, he said, that "as of today the overall military strength of the free world is distinctly greater than that of the Communist countries." ICBMs were on their way. Meantime SAC's B-52 jet bombers stood vigil.

The mail response was encouraging. His second chat was equally successful, and he set to work on a draft of the third, to be telecast from Cleveland. It was slow going; he had a lot on his mind. The seasonal load of the Presidency is always at its heaviest between Labor Day and Christmas. On December 16 he was scheduled to preside over a NATO meeting in Paris. Before then he had to complete his legislative program for the coming year and explain it to the congressional leadership. The massive federal budget for the coming fiscal year demanded presidential attention, the new State of the Union address would be due in January, and it now appeared that the country was entering a major recession.

Still, restoring the nation's self-confidence was the most urgent issue before the President, and he was determined to complete the remaining TV talks. He didn't do it. On November 25, 1957, for the third time in twenty-six months the President of the United States was in bed, prostrate, unable to meet the simplest of his obligations. Dr. Snyder diagnosed his illness as a "vascular spasm." To the rest of the country it was a stroke.

That Monday before Thanksgiving, awaiting the arrival of Morocco's King Mohammed V on a state visit, the President had stood bareheaded in a raw autumn wind at Washington National Airport. Back in his White House office, Ike said he felt a chill coming on. He was afraid he might be catching the flu. It was graver than that. Dictating to Ann Whitman, his secretary, he was dismayed to find that the words wouldn't come. Near tears, she went to Sherman Adams. "The President has gone back to the house," she said. "He tried to tell me something but he couldn't express himself. Something seemed to have happened to him all of a sudden. And just now he gave up and went home. I can't imagine what's wrong with him."

In the presidential apartment upstairs, Adams found the President in pajamas. Snyder, on his way, had telephoned instructions for his patient to go to bed. Eisenhower smiled at his assistant. He said, "I suppose you are dis–" He couldn't finish it. Hesitating, he stammered: ". . . talking about the dinner tonight." Frustrated and angry over his inability to talk about plans for entertaining the African king, he struggled to say, "There's nothing the matter with me! I am perfectly all right!" But plainly he was having trouble forming words. As he continued to falter, he repeatedly came out with a word or syllable that had no relation to the word that was in his mind. In dismay Mrs. Eisenhower said to Adams, "We can't let him go down there in this condition." Adams agreed. He told the President that Nixon could take his place at the dinner. Ike shook his head violently. He managed to say, "If I cannot attend to my duties, I am simply going to give up this job. Now that is all there is to it."

Then the doctor arrived. On hearing a single word from Eisenhower—"international," which came out "internatt-nl"—Snyder reached his diagnosis. Ike's stroke had affected the speech center of the brain. He was suffering from aphasia, an impairment of the power to use words as symbols of ideas. It was impossible to say whether the lesion would heal, and if it did, how quickly. The doctor called Walter Reed and Adams called Nixon, who agreed to preside at the banquet. For the time being nothing was said to the press. Hagerty was in Paris advancing the NATO trip. When word of the President's illness reached him there, he wept.

But it was not an occasion for grief after all. Eisenhower's recovery was both speedy and miraculous. His improvement was noted in a matter of hours. Even as a Hagerty assistant briefed reporters on the findings of four neurological specialists ("an occlusion" accompanied by "slight difficulty in speaking"), the President was back in the White House watching Wyatt Earp on television. The next morning he awoke at 7:40 A.M., showered, and made his own breakfast. He painted awhile, picking up where he had left off on a portrait of Britain's Princess Anne. Feeling much better, he received his aides and the Moroccan king, worked on state papers for a half-hour, and signed or initialed a dozen of them. On Thursday, Thanksgiving, he went to church and shrugged off the helping hand of the pastor. In the Mansion he carved a forty-pound Thanksgiving turkey. Then, with Snyder as their house guest, the Eisenhowers drove to the Gettysburg farm. Saturday they watched the Army-Navy game. With Snyder's approval, Ike planned to return to a full schedule on Monday and preside over a cabinet meeting. The doctor told the press, "The President's progress continues to be excellent."

At Cape Canaveral, Vanguard scientists looked forward to giving the convalescing President's spirits a boost by putting an American sputnik in orbit on December 6. Everything seemed ready that Friday morning. The tall, three-stage, black-and-silver Navy Test Vehicle 3, or TV-3, stood in a spider-web gantry. Sunlight sparkled on a rime of frost crystals from its liquid oxygen fuel. TV-3 had been hurried along on orders from Washington; it was expected to throw into outer space a U.S. satellite the size of a small bowling ball—not much, to be sure, but a symbol of fine workmanship and American determination to enter and then win the space race. To reap a propaganda harvest the administration had made certain that the entire world knew what was coming. Although the Martin rocket had never been tested before, its performance was expected to be flawless. Pentagon PR men had kept 127 American and foreign journalists posted on latest developments, including details on the countdown, usually highly classified information. U.S. READY TO FIRE SATELLITE, said a *New York Times* head. The *Pittsburgh Sun-Telegram* predicted: MOON—MINUTES TO GO. The Associated Press distributed an advance story to member papers for release the moment the satellite went into orbit. In a thousand press rooms it was in type, ready to go:

> Cape Canaveral, December 6 (AP)—The radio-signalling baby moon circling the earth is the U.S.'s reply to Russia that it too can stake a claim to the space frontier.

After several postponements because of valve leaks, Cape Canaveral hoisted the red ball signifying that Vanguard blast-off was imminent. Observation planes—two old World War II B-17s and a new Cessna—took off and rose swiftly to gain altitude. They looked down on a multitude of spectators. None were allowed within three miles of the launching pad, but enormous crowds were watching from the barriers there. Children had been dismissed from schools throughout Florida's Canaveral peninsula; factories and offices had let their workers out; the streets, yards, and public beaches were dense with anticipative Americans awaiting the historic event.

At 10:42 A.M. the gantry was wheeled away; it was wheeled back fifty minutes later and then at last rolled away for good. The last cable connecting TV-3 to the disconnect pole dropped away at 1:44. Within seconds the first whiffs of white-hot vapor emerged from the rocket's base. In Washington the voice of Vanguard's deputy director, J. Paul Walsh, could be heard over an open phone. He called: "Zero! . . . *Fire!* . . . First ignition! . . ."

The massive rocket stirred and rose cumbersomely from the pad a foot, then two feet, then three. At that point, two seconds after launch time, it appeared to stand motionless, fixed in space. Suddenly Walsh cried, "*Explosion!*" A long orange flame spurted from beneath the doomed rocket, shot downward, and then surged upward in a billowing sheet of fire that enveloped TV-3's right side. Overhead one of the B-17 pilots was shouting: "There it goes! There is an explosion! Black smoke is now over the entire area—We do not see the rocket that is carrying our satellite—The rocket may not have gotten off—There is a very large black smoke cloud—a very large black area around the location that the explosion occurred."

The smoke was caused by streams of water and carbon dioxide from automatic extinguishers. As it drifted away the rocket's nose cone could be seen leaning against the disconnect pole. Here and there fires continued to burn. The charred and mutilated tail jutted into the pad. One part of the assembly was intact: the coconut-sized satellite had been thrown clear and lay on the ground, sending steady signals on its assigned frequency, 108 megacycles.

It was a public relations disaster. The scientists protested in vain that this had only been a test. Having summoned the world's attention in anticipation of its applause, the United States now had to endure its scorn and derision. Grinning Russians at the U.N. advised Americans to apply for Soviet technical assistance to backward nations. In London a calypso balladeer sang over the BBC, "Oh, from America comes the thought/ Their own little Sputnik won't go off," and the wits of five continents rechristened TV-3 the flopnik, sputternik, goofnik, dudnik, oopsnik, puffnik, stallnik, and kaputnik. Lyndon Johnson wailed in the Senate, "How long, how long, oh God, how long will it take us to catch up with Russia's two satellites?" Confronting a gloomy press conference in Washington, Vanguard's Dr. Hagen, had a one-word comment: "Nuts." Editorial writers sought a new scapegoat—they settled on the public relations men, who joined the progressive educators in disgrace—and a professor in Pittsburgh said, "It's our worst humiliation since Custer's last stand."

In the age of instant communications the debacle seemed to be worse than it was. The fallen rocket wasn't the only one in the U.S. arsenal. Within a month, as soon as Cape Canaveral's launch pad could be repaired, the Navy would be ready for another satellite shot. The very week of the TV-3 fiasco the Air Force successfully retested Thor and Atlas missiles, and by March the Army would have eight Jupiter-Cs ready for the space program, each of them larger and more dependable than the Vanguard. The President had ordered the Jupiters withheld from civilian scientists because of military testing's absolute priority, but now he rescinded that order. Soon the people would forget the shame of December 6. The politicians would not forget, however. To them the risk of another such public roasting was unthinkable. From this point forward a succession of adminstrations would be committed to staying in the space race until it was won. No excuse for dropping out would be acceptable. Other calls upon the nation's resources, whatever their urgency—and by the late 1960s the need for some of them would be desperate—would have to wait until the Stars and Stripes had been firmly planted on the moon.

Portrait of an American

THE EDSEL

CONCEIVED IN 1948, the car was meant to solve a problem, not to become one. Satisfied Ford owners who grew more prosperous were ignoring the firm's Mercurys and trading up instead to Buicks, Pontiacs, and Oldsmobiles. "We have been growing customers for General Motors," said a Ford executive. Six years later company planners began investing a quarter-billion dollars on a new medium-price ($2,400 to $4,000) automobile. They knew they had to sell at least 200,000 in the first year to make money, but they were confident they could do it.

Lacking a name, they called it the E-Car, the E standing for "Experimental." Nothing was spared in its development. The mid-1950s were the salad days of motivational research, and among the advisers to the E-Car's stylists was the Columbia University Bureau of Applied Social Research, which appraised the "personalities" of other medium-priced cars, concluding, among other things, that the Buick was the wife of a professional man and the Mercury was sexy. After poring over this data, one of the Dearborn executives wrote: "The most advantageous personality for the E-Car might well be THE SMART CAR FOR THE YOUNGER EXECUTIVE OR PROFESSIONAL FAMILY ON ITS WAY UP," and added in explanation, "On Its Way Up: 'The E-Car has faith in you, son; we'll help you make it!'"

On August 15, 1955, the corporation's general staff, headed by Henry Ford II and Ernest R. Breech, witnessed the unveiling of a full-size clay model of the car, with tinfoil substituted for aluminum and chrome. They applauded. The stock market was booming that summer, and so was the medium-price market. Times seemed propitious for the E-Car. It already had the external features which were to become famous: the flaring gull-wing tail and the pinched-in oval radiator grille. Inside, it was to be what one designer called "the epitome of the push-button era."

After the motivational people had turned up 6,000 possible names, all of them alphabetized and cross-referenced, Breech christened it the Edsel, after Henry II's father, on a hunch. E-Day was set for September 4, 1957. On E minus 51 the first Edsels began rolling off assembly lines, but only a few people, all carefully screened, were allowed to see them. A tremendous aura of mystery was created by the car's promoters. Ads showed it as a blur, or as a shapeless hulk beneath canvas. Edsel buildings were fitted with special locks that could be changed in fifteen minutes should a key fall into the hands of Chrysler or General Motors spies. In July word was leaked that a model had been conveyed in a closed truck to Hollywood, where Cascade Pictures photographed it in a locked studio while armed guards patrolled outside. ("We took all the precautions we take for our AEC films," a Cascade spokesman said.) Ford's test track was encircled by barbed wire and camouflaged sentry boxes. In Dearborn telescopes kept watch on nearby roofs and hills for any competitors' agents who might be lurking there.

Business Week called the launching of the Edsel the most expensive such venture in the history of commerce. The stakes were enormous. Ford's Edsel division had its own plant, with 800 executives and 15,000 workers; 60 highly paid copywriters were turning out advertising copy, and nearly 1,200 auto dealers across the nation had surrendered profitable franchises for other makes to sell Edsels. They would become rich if it proved popular—and would lose their shirts if it failed.

In the last week of August Ford spent $90,000 on a three-day press conference at which 250 newsmen were shown the four main Edsel lines, which would be available in eighteen models. The affair was not an unqualified success. Daredevil drivers at the wheels of souped-up Edsels scared the daylights out of the reporters, and the music stands of a band hired for the occasion bore, in memory of Glenn Miller, the initials GM. These matters were slight but ominous. The new car appeared to be unlucky. Still, the public's curiosity was undoubtedly aroused. By the weekend that followed E-Day, almost three million people had entered dealers' showrooms to see what all the fuss was about. On E-Day itself, over 6,500 had bought Edsels. Dearborn was elated. If just one in fifteen of the remainder signed up, the car would finish its first year in the black.

It didn't happen. For one thing, the golden age of the medium-price car had begun to wane. In July the stock market had broken sharply, signaling the onset of the 1957–58 recession; *Automotive News* reported that dealers were experiencing the second worst season for sales in the history of the industry. More important, on E plus 30—October 4, 1957, a date which will live in infamy at the Ford Motor Company—the Russians sent their first sputnik into orbit. Styles Bridges's thundering rhetoric in the Senate was typical of the American reaction: "The time has clearly come to be less concerned about the depth of pile on the new broadloom rug or the height of the tailfin on the new car and to be more prepared to shed blood, sweat, and tears." In this new climate of opinion *Business Week* called Dearborn's latest spawn "a nightmare." *Consumer Reports* said it represented "the many excesses" with which Detroit was "repulsing more and more potential car buyers," and *Time* wrote that it was "a classic case of the wrong car for the wrong market at the wrong time" and "a prime example of the limitations of market research, with its 'depth interviews' and 'motivational' mumbo-jumbo."

But there was more to it than that. The Edsel was a failure by other standards. The oval grille set vertically in the front end, with the aluminum letters EDSEL emblazoned in it, was not a success. Its designer had adopted the idea from contemporary European automobiles in the hope that it would give the car cachet. It didn't, partly because it was inconsistent with the rest of the front design, and the public's negative reaction to it was the first blow against the auto's success. One writer likened it to an egg. Others described it as a horse collar, Bugs Bunny, and—this may have been inspired by malicious counter public relations of General Motors or Chrysler—a toilet seat.

Even worse, fully half of the first Edsels to go on the market were lemons. Brakes failed, push buttons didn't work, oil pans fell out, trunks wouldn't open, hoods stuck, transmissions froze, paint peeled, hubcaps fell off, batteries died, doors wouldn't close—the list of defects seemed to have no end.

On E plus 3 the theft of an Edsel occurred in North Philadelphia. There were virtually no others. It was a sign of the car's diminishing glamour that it didn't even seem to be worth stealing. After the bloom wore off nationwide sales plummeted until the sales chart in Dearborn resembled a ski slope. Dealers were selling fewer than one-fifth of the number necessary if they were to break even. The promotion became defensive, frantic:

> 1959 Edsel. Looks right! Built right! Prices right! Makes history by making sense. Exciting new kind of car! A full-size practical beauty. Roomy without useless length. Soundly engineered. Powered to save. And priced with the most popular three!

On January 14, 1958, the Ford Motor Company merged its Edsel and Lincoln-Mercury departments. The new car had lost 400 million dollars. It was finished, and the entire country knew it. The time had come to throw in the towel. Unfortunately that was not yet possible. Just as new cars need a long lead time, so does a cessation of production. The Edsel's new models had been designed long ago; the steel dies had been cut, and the 1959s were plonking down at the end of their assembly lines. Finally, having sold fewer than 1 percent of the cars bought during their time on the market, the Edsel's manufacturers discontinued manufacture on November 19, 1959. Viewers of *Wagon Train,* a Western TV series sponsored by the car's advertising agency, were invited to participate in a contest. The purpose was promotional, but the prizes weren't Edsels. They were ponies.

Twenty-five

THE CRUSADE FALTERS

In 1958 Mike Todd's *Around the World in Eighty Days* entered its third year as the movie industry's greatest box office sensation since the arrival of the tube. Part of its appeal lay in the realization that in the late 1950s, as in Jules Verne's early 1870s, transportation was big news. The globe was growing noticeably smaller, and not only because of the satellites. British Overseas Airways Corporation introduced jet airliners for trans-Atlantic flights on October 4, 1958, and two months later, on December 10, U.S. jetliners made their first domestic appearance on the National Airlines New York to Miami run. The St. Lawrence Seaway was opened to traffic on April 25, 1959. U.S.S. *Wisconsin,* the U.S. Navy's last battleship, was put in mothballs as Mamie Eisenhower christened N.S. *Savannah,* the first atom-powered merchant ship. Nuclear submarines surpassed Verne's wildest, 20,000-leagues-deep dream, circling the globe underwater and crossing the North Pole by passing beneath the Arctic ice cap. In June 1959 the world's largest sub, the 110-million-dollar *George Washington,* slid stern first into the Thames River at Groton, Connecticut, carrying sixteen solid-fuel Polaris missiles, a guarantee that Russia could never level all U.S. nuclear bases in a sneak ICBM attack.

The American Telephone and Telegraph Company now had 100 million telephones in service, half the world total. Direct distance dialing (DDD), which had been introduced in Englewood, New Jersey, on November 10, 1951, was now being extended to overseas calls. Ocean telephone cables, radiophone, and over-the-horizon radio—soon to be joined by Telstar, the Bell System's first experimental communications satellite—linked Americans with 190 nations and territories overseas. Mark Cross, manufacturer of alligator handbags, provided some insight into the global character of modern American business when it announced a grant of financial aid to Zululand for the propagation of the crocodile species. At the same time, shrinking trade routes brought American auto dealers new competition from abroad. Foreign cars were accounting for 10 percent of all automobile sales in the United States. The leaders were West Germany's Volkswagen (1958 sales were 102,035), France's Renault (47,567), Italy's Fiat (23,000), and Britain's Hillman (18,663). Japan, Sweden, and Holland were about to enter the American market with other small cars, and Detroit, in a gesture toward reality, at last prepared to make little American autos. To distinguish them from automobiles made overseas they were to be called "compacts."

Asked what Americans might expect to find when they reached the moon, Edward Teller replied grimly, "Russians." In early January 1959 the Soviets launched Lunik I, a spectacular 3,245-pound satellite that came within 5,000 miles of the moon. Their head start in space exploration continued to be a tremendous advantage, though the United States had begun to take the first steps toward catching up. Cape Canaveral crews finally put a tiny American satellite in orbit with an Army Jupiter-C rocket. The National Defense Education Act of 1958 provided federal aid for improved teaching in science, mathematics, and foreign languages. In 1958 Congress also created the National Aeronautics and Space Administration (NASA). To test human endurance in space, Air Force Captain Joe Kittinger took the longest parachute jump in history, bailing out at 76,400 feet, falling twelve miles before a barometric device on his parachute blew it open, and landing safely in the New Mexican desert. Front pages on April 10, 1959, introduced the country to a new category of celebrities—the Project Mercury astronauts. All were veteran test pilots aged thirty-two to thirty-seven. Their names were Alan Shepard, Walter Schirra, Virgil Grissom, John H. Glenn Jr., Scott Carpenter, Gordon Cooper, and Donald Slayton. Each was white, a father, a native of small-town America, and a Protestant. Six of the seven had crew cuts.

The oceans on either side of the United States, which had been so comforting to isolationists in the 1930s, seemed at times to have shrunk to fordable streams. In August 1958 scientists debating the threat of fallout agreed that the bones of all Americans could be affected to some extent by any nuclear explosion anywhere on earth. Remote Indochina became less remote on July 10, 1959, when two American military advisers were killed and a third wounded at Bien Hoa, Vietnam, twenty miles north of Saigon. They had been watching a Jeanne Crain film, *The Tattered Dress*, on a home projector in a mess hall. Terrorists had surrounded the building, and when a sergeant switched on the lights to change reels, they had opened fire.

The first Eisenhower administration now belonged to the past, and some notable figures had vanished with it. Joe McCarthy died of drink on May 2, 1957. ("He was discouraged," George Sokolsky wrote. "He regarded himself as betrayed. He particularly felt that he was betrayed by Vice President Nixon, whom he had always trusted.") His widow, Jean Kerr McCarthy, continued to live in Washington; four years later she married a member of the Civil Aeronautics Board. Frank Lloyd Wright died at eighty-nine, leaving a time bomb of controversy over his last major work, New York City's three-million-dollar Solomon R. Guggenheim museum. Deaths in the entertainment world included Errol Flynn, Mario Lanza, Maxwell Anderson, and Lou Costello. John L. Lewis resigned as president of the United Mine Workers. Dave Beck of the Teamsters went to jail, leaving his successor, Jimmy Hoffa, locked in a desperate struggle with John F. Kennedy, a member of a Senate investigating committee, and Robert F. Kennedy, the committee's chief counsel. Maria Callas, thirty-five, left an Italian millionaire, Giovanni Meneghini, for the shipping czar Aristotle Socrates Onassis. Some gossips thought that at fifty-three Onassis was too old for her.

Increasingly the decade was being compared with the 1920s. Zany as they were, the 1950s had witnessed nothing comparable to the ukulele or flagpole sitting until 1958, when the deficiency was spectacularly remedied by two young toymen in San Gabriel, California. Richard Knerr and Arthur Melin, co-owners of an enterprise called the Wham-O Manufacturing Company, had started making slingshots after World War II with less than $1,000 capital. In 1957 they had racked up their first big score with Frisbees, light plastic saucers which could be skimmed slowly through the air from one thrower to another. At a New York toy fair in March 1958 an acquaintance told them that large wooden hoops had achieved swift and startling popularity in Australia; children rotated them on their hips. Back at Wham-O, Knerr and Melin went into production with wooden hoops. After twenty or so they stopped; they didn't like wood and wanted to experiment with plastics. In May they had what they wanted: three-foot hoops of gaudy polyethylene tubing which could be marketed at ninety-three cents each, representing a 16 percent gross profit. Wham-O's new toy was christened the hula hoop.

Patenting the hoops was impossible and by Labor Day a dozen other firms were turning out imitations under other trademarks. Even so, by early September Wham-O had sold two million hula hoops for a net profit of over $300,000. Then adults started using them for calisthenics. Wham-O's bookkeeper couldn't keep up with the production figures. Workers went into three shifts. Counting the copiers at home and abroad, hula hoop sales that autumn were reckoned in the tens of millions. So widespread was their use that European medical journals warned of injuries which might be sustained by enthusiasts. It was a long list. In Leiden, Holland, a Dutch woman was being wheeled into surgery for removal of her appendix when her physician found that what was really wrong with her was a torn abdominal muscle, the result of strenuous gyrations inside a hoop. In England, where a quarter-million hulas had been sold, the British Medical Association cautioned, "No one with a known heart disease should try it, and anyone who is out of training should not go hard at it right away." Japanese emergency wards were filling up with hoopers suffering from slipped discs and dislocated backbones. After a child was killed chasing a runaway hula the hoops were banned from Tokyo streets. Nevertheless sales there passed the three million mark. Lines of Japanese waiting to buy more stretched down the Ginza for blocks, and Premier Nobusuke Kishi received one as a gift on his sixty-second birthday.

Queen Mother Zaine of Jordan, returning from a visit to Europe, included a hula in her luggage. That should have been a guarantee of respectability, but some toymakers were nervous just the same. One of hooping's attractions for adult spectators was its suggestiveness on some hips. An unexpected pleasure at football games that autumn was a view of winsome drum majorettes pumping their loins in a frenzy of excitement as thousands cheered. A French manufacturer of hoops, Jacques de Saint-Phalle, was afraid the church might notice and object. Saint-Phalle had a reputation to safeguard; in hoopless times he made his living manufacturing plastic tubing for hospitals and laboratories. To protect himself he persuaded French celebrities to be photographed hooping. Finland solved the same problem by staging marathons in which participants had to keep three hulas going, at the neck, hips, and knees.

Elsewhere the American fad swept on, whatever watchers with coarse minds thought. In Germany it was popularized by the prizefighter Max Schmeling and his wife Anny Ondra. Germans who had no children, and therefore no easy explanation for buying toys, avoided embarrassment by having stores deliver them, wrapped, at night. A party of Belgian explorers leaving for the South Pole disclosed that twenty hoops were in their baggage; the expense was charged to morale. In some countries hoop shortages were serious. Correspondents in Johannesburg, where hulas were retailing at sixty-five cents, reported that only white customers could afford them; the natives were restless until charitable organizations started distributing free hoops. *Het Vrije Volk* of Amsterdam noted that Dutch industries requiring plastic tubing were at a standstill, and in Warsaw a weekly newspaper for young Poles observed, "If the Ministry of Light Industry and the Chamber of Artisans do not embark upon the production of hoops, we will be seriously delayed in hula hoop progress, especially on the international level." The ministry and the chamber continued to be dilatory, so hulas were smuggled in through East Germany.

The craze receded as quickly as it had spread. By the summer of 1959 discarded hoops had begun to pile up in city dumps, but the rage had been a singular illustration of how great a grasp even the trivia of American mass culture had on the rest of the world.

In Europe, Whitehall and the Quai d'Orsay had blamed Dulles for the Suez disaster; in Washington, a number of members of the Eisenhower administration were inclined to agree with them. Given the Mideast as it was after Suez, however, there were no two minds about what Washington's next move should be. It was an article of cold war faith that every desirable part of the world must belong to either the Communist world or the Free World. Sherman Adams wrote in 1961:

> The defeat of the attempt by Britain and France to settle the Suez Canal controversy by military force temporarily destroyed the prestige and political power of those two nations in the Middle East

> . . . Unless the United States undertook to fill the vacuum and made clear to the world the intention to do so, the President said, the Soviets could be counted upon to move into the Middle East and we would find ourselves in an intolerable situation.

The President told the congressional leadership, "I just do not believe that we can leave a vacuum in the Middle East," and to a joint session on the Hill he asked for authority to use U.S. troops there "to secure and protect the territorial integrity and political integrity and political independence of . . . nations requesting such aid against overt armed aggression from any nation controlled by International Communism." This was the Eisenhower Doctrine. Like FDR's undeclared war of 1940–41, Truman's decision to send American soldiers to Korea without consulting Congress, and the Formosa resolution of 1955, the doctrine was another long step toward presidential authority to use U.S. armed forces anywhere.

Adams put his finger on one weakness in the Eisenhower Doctrine. "The difficulty in any American attempt to stop the spread of Communism abroad," he wrote, "was in trying to prove that an internal upheaval which posed as a nationalist struggle was really under the direction of Moscow." The resolution supporting the doctrine passed the House easily but ran into trouble in the Senate. As in the Formosa resolution debate, critical senators were divided. Some believed the White House was trying to share responsibility for what should be an executive decision; others thought Eisenhower was asking for the right to make war. Richard Russell of Georgia and Fulbright of Arkansas were particularly apprehensive. Russell told Dulles, "We are being asked to buy a pig in a poke." Dulles replied that the issue was one of loyalty. He said to Russell, "If we are going to pinpoint everything, if Congress is not willing to trust the President . . . we can't win this battle."

But where was the battle? Britain and France having laid down their arms, the only Mideast danger spots were disputes between Arabs and Israel in the Gaza Strip and the Gulf of Aqaba. After two months of debate the Senate approved the resolution 72 to 19. "During the following year," Adams wrote, "there were a series of explosive developments in Jordan, Syria, and Lebanon, and all involved, directly or indirectly, the application of the Eisenhower Doctrine." In reality they mostly involved its inapplicability. Trouble in Jordan arose in a classic Mideastern form: anti-Israel Arabs rocked Amman, forcing the resignation of young King Hussein's premier. The king then appealed to Eisenhower, claiming that the crisis was "the responsibility of international Communism and its followers." Dulles endorsed this motion, and the President sent the Sixth Fleet to make a whiff-of-grape demonstration in the eastern Mediterranean. In the shadow of the guns Hussein selected a loyal government. The rioters having dispersed, the new premier survived. There is no evidence that the outcome would have been different without the warships.

The Syrian blowup came next, and it had an *opéra bouffe* air. Dulles was eager to show the flag in Damascus, but the Syrians weren't buying that. The government favored the Soviet Union; the opposition consisted of anti-American officers; each preferred to be left alone with the other. King Saud of Saudi Arabia assured Eisenhower that ideology had nothing to do with the feud, that no true Arab could be a Communist. The President replied that he had heard that one before; de Gaulle had told him that "no true Frenchman could be a Communist." "Obviously, the turmoil was Communist-inspired," Adams wrote, "but, in contrast to the situation in Jordan, the Syrian government wanted nothing to do with any assistance from the West, and there was therefore little that Eisenhower could do about it. This was an example of the weakness of the Eisenhower Doctrine."

On the morning of July 14, 1958, Washington awoke to learn that the Middle East was in the throes of one of its periodic convulsions. During the night pro-Nasser Arab nationalists in Iraq had seized the Baghdad radio station, post office, cable office, and the bridges over the Tigris River. Advancing on the royal palace, they put the king and the crown prince to the sword. Premier Nuri as-Said tried to escape disguised as a woman, but he, too, was captured and slain. This knocked out the central prop holding up Dulles's Baghdad Pact, which was only six months old.* It also panicked President Camille Chamoun of Lebanon. Earlier Chamoun had accused Arab Communists of a massive infiltration of his regime. Secretary General Dag Hammarskjöld had personally led a United Nations observation team investigating the charge. They had found no evidence supporting Chamoun's fears. Now, convinced that he was next

* Citing the Eisenhower Doctrine, Dulles had assured member countries that the United States would shield them from subversion with a "mobile power of great force." After the Baghdad coup the alliance was re-created, omitting Iraq, as the Central Treaty Organization (CENTO), with headquarters in Ankara, Turkey.

on Nasser's list, he formally requested the dispatch of American troops to Beirut. Eisenhower consented.

This was 1930s isolationism turned on its head, the far swing of the interventionist pendulum. By no stretch of the imagination could American security be said to be in jeopardy. After 9,000 U.S. Marines had been put ashore under the watchful eye of 70 Sixth Fleet warships and 420 fighter planes, until then the greatest concentration of American armed might ever assembled in peacetime, the President issued a statement explaining that "The mission of these forces is to protect American lives—there are about 2,500 Americans in Lebanon," but there was not a shred of proof that any Americans (or Lebanese, for that matter) were in danger. Moreover, by raising that issue the President in effect conceded that the Eisenhower Doctrine was irrelevant. Dulles tried to convince the congressional leadership that it was. If the United States did not act on Chamoun's request, the Secretary of State warned, "our prestige is gone; nobody will take our word again—ever. If we get there first, there might not be Communist intervention." Fail to act, he said, and the free world would lose not only the Mideast and nearly three-fourths of the free world's oil reserve with it, but also Africa and non-Communist Asia. This catechism was to be recited by cold-warriors as a justification for the use of force in every international crisis down to and including Vietnam. Eisenhower had resisted it in 1954. This time resistance came from the leaders on the Hill. They made it plain that they wanted no share in the responsibility for the Lebanese move.

To all intents and purposes, that was the end of the Eisenhower Doctrine. Four months later Chamoun was replaced by a neutralist president and premier, and at their request the marines were withdrawn. The episode had been "a frustrating and unhappy experience for Eisenhower," Adams concluded. Its implications were graver than they seemed at the time; the President had warned the senators and representatives that he might have to risk war in the Mideast without prior discussion in Congress—"In this case," he said, "if there has to be a public debate about the course of action, there would be no use in taking it at all"—thereby adding to the sanction of precedent under which presidential power to make war was expanding.

Gunboat diplomacy on the other side of the globe was something new for the United States. It suggested an imperial presence, and that is precisely what such Europeans as Reiner Hellman, author of *Amerika auf dem Europe Markt*, and J.-J. Servan-Schreiber of *Le Défi Américain* (*The American Challenge*) believed they saw rising on the western rim of their horizon. To prewar Europeans the old America had appeared to be a land of affluence and ballyhoo, where everyone looked like Gary Cooper and Ginger Rogers and had children like Mickey Rooney and Ann Rutherford. That U.S.A. had been idealistic and innocent, the wonder and secret envy of the world. Except in time of natural disasters, when Americans were Good Samaritans, they had played virtually no role in world affairs.

Now they were all over the globe. Missionaries of Point Four, ECA, and technical assistance programs had fanned out across Africa and Asia. Congress had chartered the Development Loan Fund for underdeveloped countries, Fulbright scholarships, and Smith-Mundt exchanges for forty-two countries not covered by the Fulbright program. The number of American tourists abroad was increasing 12 percent annually; there were more than two million U.S. tourists in far lands in the late 1950s, and they were spending more than two billion dollars a year there.

It was not always spent wisely and gracefully. For every European who said with Churchill, "I love these Americans. They have behaved so generously," there was one or more who shared the contempt of Jean-Paul Sartre: "*Les Américains ne comprendront jamais rien à existentialisme.*" Defenders of older cultures on the continent and in Asia felt threatened by the spread of Americanization. They were alarmed by the appeal of America's teen-age culture, especially its music, for the world's youth. Jazz could be heard almost everywhere. The young king of Thailand was writing songs for a Broadway musical called *Peep Show*, and the king of Cambodia taught himself to play a hot saxophone. And then there were the American soft drinks. In Bangkok the prime minister was the Coca-Cola concessionaire and the police chief had the Pepsi-Cola franchise; Adlai Stevenson called their rivalry "the ice cold war." Coke was ahead there and everywhere else. The sun never set on it. Every day people abroad consumed fifty billion bottles of it, enough Coke to float a light cruiser.

"What we are faced with," Servan-Schreiber wrote, "is not classic imperialism driven by a desire for conquest, but an overflow of power due to the difference in 'pressure' between America and the rest of the world." U.S. industry was in the process of investing 57.5 billion dollars in overseas plants, with a gross output of about 100 billion dollars a year. "One by one," Servan-Schreiber warned, "American firms are setting up headquarters to coordinate their activities throughout Western Europe."

As the American giants grew larger and stronger, Europeans, Asians and Africans became more curious about the quality of life in the United States. Not everything they heard was accurate and balanced. Admirers of the Soviet Union and the new China came down hard on racial discrimination, picturing the Montgomery bus boycott and Little Rock as race riots. Most accounts of American society emphasized the high standard of living; it was becoming a source of bitterness. The gap between the American standard and that of the rest of the world, particularly in the emerging countries, was steadily widening. In 1950 Premier Liaquat Ali Khan of Pakistan said on a visit to the United States: "As I let myself ponder over this, I suddenly see the United States of America as an island—a fabulously prosperous island. And all around this island I see the unhealthy sea of misery, poverty, and squalor in which millions of human beings are trying to keep their heads above water. At such moments I fear for this great nation as one fears for a dear friend."

U.S. embassies, USIS libraries, and cultural centers around the globe became targets in forty major riots. Spontaneous attacks on the American flag were now a common phenomenon, the reason in most cases being a long-smoldering anti-Americanism among the demonstrators which, for one reason or another, had reached the flash point. There were five such disturbances in Indonesia alone. They were by no means confined to nations whose leaders were critical of the United States. Demonstrations occurred in neutral capitals—Algiers, Cairo, and Khartoum among them—and even in those of U.S. allies, including Rio de Janeiro, Athens, Saigon, Taipeh, and Panama City.

Americans were puzzled. They had thought of themselves as being generous with foreign aid programs, unaware that, as Leon Keyserling wrote, the actual percentage of America's Gross National Product that flowed into international economic cooperation and assistance was "so imperceptible that one blushes to mention it." The American man in the street suspected that the rioters had been misled by agitators. If they understood the benefits of free enterprise, he thought, they would want it, too. In his naiveté he omitted the many other factors that made the U.S. mix so successfully, natural resources and the temperate climate being among them. He thought that if men in other lands only knew how prosperous the U.S. was, they would cheer the Stars and Stripes, not defile it. It never occurred to him that documenting that prosperity would be regarded as intolerable gloating.

It didn't occur to his leaders, either. In boning up for visits abroad, Vice President Nixon memorized charts and graphs showing how much better off Americans were than less fortunate people. After one of the visits he described how, in discussions with citizens in host countries, he had awaited an opening and then rammed his points home:

> I cited figures to show that the 44 million families in America own 56 million cars, 50 million television sets, 143 million radio sets, and that 31 million of those families own their own home. Then I made the point that so many people overlook. What these statistics dramatically demonstrate is this: that the United States, the world's largest capitalist country, has from the standpoint of the distribution of wealth come closest to the ideal of prosperity for all in a classless society.

By midpoint in the second Eisenhower administration, a considerable number of people overseas had heard this line of reasoning. President Eisenhower had taken to sending Mr. and Mrs. Nixon abroad a lot. In the interests of international good will the Vice President had endured diarrhea in Indonesia, Afghanistan, and Ethiopia, picketing in Burma, insults in Casablanca, and a sweaty hour trapped in a defective Mexico City elevator.

These efforts were to be capped, in the spring of 1958, by a strenuous eighteen-day tour of South America with stops in Uruguay, Colombia, Argentina, Paraguay, Bolivia, Ecuador, Peru, and Venezuela. It was to be a neighborly gesture, and Nixon expected it to be boring. Afterward he wrote: "Of all the trips I made abroad as Vice President the one I least wanted to take was my visit to South America in 1958—not because I thought it would be difficult but because I thought it would be relatively unimportant and uninteresting compared with the assignments I had in Washington at that time." The CIA had assured him that the trip would be uneventful. To newspapermen who were hesitant about covering it he said that they would probably miss little if they stayed home.

There wasn't much in the beginning. South Americans of the ruling classes, who welcomed the Nixons to Montevideo, Buenos Aires, Asunción, and La Paz, were accustomed to North American policy makers taking them for granted. Under Assistant Secretary Henry Holland, who kept watch on Latin America for Dulles, the State Department fought all proposals for U.S. loans to countries there on the ground that if liberals came to power they might try to regulate businessmen, thus depressing business morale. The elite in the first countries Nixon visited knew that, appreciated it, and had no intention of rocking the boat.

Here and there on street corners intense young men held up signs calling the *yanqui* Vice President "Racist," "Imperialist," and "Son of a Dog." One placard advised him to "Go back to the U.S.A. where you enjoy the lynchings of Negroes and massacres of Indians." As a forthright politician, he paused wherever possible to explain that he wasn't a racist, an imperialist, or a son of a dog; that he didn't enjoy lynchings or massacres and had not, in fact, participated in any of them. But these incidents didn't amount to much. The number of pickets at his early stops were so few he didn't notice them. For every hostile placard there were greeters to welcome him with the Latin *abrazo,* a good-natured bear hug. He heard some students chanting "*Fuera Nixon.*" His translator told him it meant "Go home, Nixon." He said smilingly that he didn't want to go; people were much friendlier here.

No one later could remember exactly when and where the chants changed to "*Muera Nixon*"—death to Nixon. He was jeered in Buenos Aires on the fifth day and booed in Asunción on the sixth, but on the whole the crowds remained cordial. Bolivians showered him with flying confetti; there were no visible signs of danger there. Actually he had been lucky. An attack on him had been narrowly averted in Bolivia by blowing up a railroad track to isolate a mining town where protesters wearing bandoliers of dynamite sticks had assembled. Elsewhere police vigilance had turned away men bent on violence. Such good fortune couldn't favor the Nixons all the way, and it didn't. Their first inkling that disaster might lie ahead came in Lima, Peru, on Wednesday, May 7, their eleventh day away from home.

The reception at Lima Airport was gracious, but as the motorcade entered the city Nixon observed that there were not many people on the streets and most of those who were there "did not seem to be aware" of who he was. The Peruvian official in his car explained that the motorcade route had not been published, to avoid "incidents." This, Nixon was to recall, was "somewhat disquieting since I had not anticipated any incidents in friendly Peru."

Little is known about the leaders of the mobs which were to confront Nixon there and later in Venezuela. They are shadowy figures, made more so by Nixon's later insistence that all his troubles could be traced to a centrally controlled Communist conspiracy. Upon his arrival at Lima's majestic Grand Hotel Bolívar, he wrote afterward, the extent of the plot was revealed to him: "It was apparent that the Communists, after the failure of their efforts to disrupt my tour in Uruguay, Argentina, or Bolivia, had decided to make an all-out effort to embarrass me and the United States at San Marcos University, an institution so well known throughout Latin America that whatever happened there would be front-page news everywhere." Watching the demonstrators, he thought, "How are they able to stir the people up to this pitch? Then I realized as this was going on that right here was the ruthlessness and the determination, the fanaticism of the enemy that we face. That was what I saw in the faces of the mob. This is really Communism as it is." Noting the youth of the crowds, he wrote, "My reaction was a feeling of absolute hatred for the tough Communist agitators who were driving children to this irrational state."

This is largely conjecture. Undoubtedly there were Communists in the forces which were forming against him in Peru and Venezuela, and clearly people were inflamed by the *Tribuna Popular*, the Communist weekly, which ran a front-page picture of him retouched so that his teeth looked like fangs and his expression was that of a madman. But to infer from this that all the Latin-American demonstrators protesting his trip were being manipulated and coordinated by agents of the Cominform is, to put it mildly, rich. The CIA was far from omniscient in these years—the agency had been caught napping by the Iraqi coup—but it is hard to believe that it would have missed something that big. A more reasonable interpretation is that poor people, regarding themselves as victims of injustice, saw an opportunity to express their hatred of the wealthy and—understandably—took it. Communists and extremists of other persuasions then added fuel to the flames of anti-American rage that had sprung up on their own.

The mobs in Lima were ugly, but there was a respite for the vice-presidential party afterward. Four days in Ecuador and Colombia provided an opportunity to regain the strength needed for the last and most risky stop: Caracas. The situation in Venezuela was volatile, the mood in the streets was ugly, and the ruling junta, which had been in power less than four months, had not taken the vigorous measures needed to suppress the troublemakers. Unwilling to acknowledge its helplessness, the new government responded to periodic inquiries from the American embassy with assurances that it foresaw no serious incidents for the Vice President and that it was prepared to deal with any which might arise.

Caracas was the one city in which Communist plotting against Nixon was probably a factor. South American Communists are proud of their ability to organize, and the Venezuelan mobs awaiting him had been well prepared. As the vice-presidential aircraft entered its glide pattern over Maiquetía Airport on the morning of Tuesday, May 13, five crowds took up strategic positions. One was at the air terminal. Three others lay in wait for the motorcade on the twelve-mile road between the airfield and the Panteón Plaza in the center of Caracas, where Nixon was scheduled to lay a wreath on the tomb of Simón Bolívar. The last and largest of the crowds, in the plaza itself, was armed with Molotov cocktails. At one place or another, the ringleaders expected Nixon to be torn to pieces and burned. In Venezuela that is regarded as the most degrading death possible. The previous January it had been the fate of policemen defending the outgoing regime, and the fresh memory of that doubtless accounts for the reluctance of surviving police officers to come to Nixon's aid.

Official laxity went beyond that, however, and some aspects of it are still puzzling. American correspondents covering the Vice President's tour landed before he did and found that five hundred anti-Nixon teen-agers had been bused to the airfield and deployed on the terminal's observation deck. Obviously they were there to make trouble. Already they were shaking fists and shouting insults at the plane overhead. Yet when Secret Service agents asked the Venezuelan security chief to make them move, he refused, saying, "They are harmless. They have a right to demonstrate." He then ordered the motorcade to form in the street beyond the terminal instead of at the customary place on the field. That meant the Nixons would have to walk another hundred yards, through demonstrators. His subsequent explanation—that the sleek motorcade limousines would have detracted from the splendor of the honor guard—was preposterous.

Other suspicious figures that day included the bandleader at the airport, who knew that whenever he struck up the American or Venezuelan national anthem the Vice President would have to stand at attention, and the authorities responsible for safeguarding the motorcade route. These last were the most derelict of all. They told Americans responsible for the Vice President's safety that all traffic on it had been halted an hour before his arrival. This was untrue; heavy traffic on it continued. In addition, men and material for the three ambushes had been assembled at points where even a casual inspection would have revealed them. Junta complicity in the plot is unthinkable, but hope for a newsworthy episode is not. Latin American editors had noted that the disorders in Lebanon and elsewhere had attracted American attention and aid. If shaking the Vice President up would end U.S. complacency about its southern neighbors, they implied it would not be wholly deplorable. Nixon later found this explanation for the poor security persuasive. He noted, with commendable restraint, that those responsible cannot have known much about mobs.

In descending an airplane ramp he customarily sized up a crowd to see what kind of reception he might expect. One glance at these shrieking youths told him, as he put it afterward, that "here was one place where we would have an altogether different situation than we ever had in any country I visited." The interpreter said, "They aren't friendly, Mr. Vice President." Nixon didn't have to understand Spanish to know that; the din was so great that he could scarcely hear the national anthems and the 19-gun salute for him. Before the last 105 shells had been fired he decided to skip the other airport formalities, notably the greeting to him and his response. To the interpreter he said, "Look, we're not going to do the mike scene," and to Venezuela's foreign minister, Oscar García Lutín, "Let's dispense with the customary speeches here and go directly to our cars. No one could possibly hear what we said over the noise of this mob."

It was then that he missed the limousines. He turned to where they should have been and discovered instead that the red carpet ran all the way to the terminal building, through it, and out the other side. There in the distance the cars gleamed. In between angry teen-agers were forming ranks and brandishing gamy fruit and other refuse. The bayonets of the honor guard might have been useful, but their commander was nowhere to be found.

The situation was rapidly deteriorating when the Americans found unexpected allies: thirty aircraft mechanics at the field. They cheered him as the others booed, making themselves so conspicuous that they briefly distracted the crowd. That gave the Americans time to slip into the terminal building. Coming out of it, Nixon and his wife were just below the observation deck when the bandleader decided to replay the Venezuelan national anthem. The Nixons froze. The Vice President had what he afterward called "the sensation that rain was falling"; then he realized that it was spittle. The saliva was coming from the crowd overhead, and some of it, from tobacco chewers, fell on the new red suit Pat Nixon had bought for the trip, staining it with splotches of a dirty brown. A rubber noisemaker struck Nixon on the face. The music ended. He took Pat's arm and they waded into the throng, toward the cars, following a flying wedge of Secret Service agents and Americans from the embassy.

With a sudden lurch the wedge shoved the Vice President into the first car and Pat into the second. Secret Service agents and interpreters followed. As they rapidly rolled up windows and wiped the saliva from their faces and clothes, they were joined by their host and hostess, Foreign Minister García Lutín in Nixon's limousine and Señora García Lutín in Mrs. Nixon's. Both were mortified. García Lutín, a gentle, mild-mannered man, tried to clean the worst of the spittle from the Vice President's suit. "Don't bother," Nixon said sharply. "I am going to burn these clothes as soon as I can get out of them." The foreign minister then tried to explain. He said, "The Venezuelan people have been without freedom so long that they tend now to express themselves more vigorously perhaps than they should. In our new government we do not want to do anything which would be interpreted as a suppression of freedom." Nixon replied, "If your new government doesn't have the guts and good sense to control a mob like the one at the airport, there soon will be no freedom for anyone in Venezuela."

The ride into Caracas was hair-raising. Led by a police escort and a press truck, they were going 40 mph on the Autopista, a modern dual-lane highway, while demonstrators on motorcycles and motor scooters zigzagged in and out of the motorcade, shouting, spitting, and throwing rotten fruit at the lead car. The windows had to remain closed. The air inside—there was no air-conditioning—became stifling. Approaching the city, Nixon noticed that the sidewalks were deserted and the shops locked and shuttered. He was about to remark that this was ominous when he heard a dull thud. Momentarily he thought the driver had hit a pothole. Then he heard another thud and then another; the car was being hit by flying rocks. Simultaneously the chauffeur slammed on his brakes and skidded to a halt. They had reached the city limits and the first ambush. A tattered mass of people of all ages and descriptions came boiling out of a dingy alley nearby and rushed into the street hurling heavy stones. The roadblock here was unfinished, and the driver found a way around it, but a few minutes later he braked again. On a slope where the Autopista curves into the city and becomes the lower end of the Avenida Sucre, a six-lane roadway with a center divider, it bisects one of the poorest neighborhoods in Caracas, and the second trap was there. A huge dump truck and several buses and cars had been parked in the street and abandoned. Another ragged throng carrying placards and clubs came howling down on the stalled motorcade. There were more rocks here, and several wild-eyed demonstrators flung themselves at Nixon's limousine.

Here, too, a detour was found, and the motorcade raced on, tense and silent, until, in the very center of Caracas and almost at their destination, the way was blocked by the most elaborate barricade yet. Three banks of buses, trucks, and automobiles had been parked directly in the path of the motorcade. The chauffeur could not cross the center island because there the traffic was one-way, toward them, and it was hopelessly jammed anyhow. For a few seconds nothing happened. The silence was eerie. Then Agent Jack Sherwood said under his breath, "Here they come."

Later estimates of this mob put it between two and five hundred. Running full tilt and spitting as they came, the demonstrators brandished axes, poles, and sections of pipe. Watching from the motorcade's press car, Earl Mazo of the *New York Herald Tribune* thought the spectacle looked "like a scene from the French Revolution." This was the ultimate in mobs, a killer mob. The saliva streaming down the windshield was so thick that the driver turned on the windshield wiper. The leaders rode pickaback, shouting instructions and leading the chant: "Muera Nixon! Muera Nixon!" Their obvious aim was to get the Vice President and drag him out, by opening the doors if possible, by smashing the windows if not. A large stone hit one window and stuck in the special glass, spraying splinters from it into García Lutín's face. He cried, "It's in my eye! My eye!" Another window, the one by the interpreter, was hit by a length of iron pipe. It did not give way entirely, but pieces of it struck the interpreter's mouth. Sherwood, hit, began to bleed. Fragments struck Nixon in the face. Another piece of pipe, thrust through the opening, wobbled toward him.

The foreign minister, almost hysterical, sobbed, "This is terrible, terrible." Nixon looked out the back window. As he remembered afterward, he was relieved to see that Pat was chatting away with Señora García Lutín, "as though the trouble was no worse than an afternoon traffic jam on the Hollywood Freeway." Her driver had showed presence of mind by pushing his front bumper against the front limousine, so that the mob couldn't get at the Vice President through the rear window. The demonstrators, Nixon saw, were not interested in Pat's car. Those were the only bright spots, however. The violence had continued here for twelve minutes, and now it seemed that it could have but one outcome.

Inside the limousine they heard one of the pickaback commanders outside shout an order. The car began to rock. To those who knew the ways of mobs—as all here did—this was the most frightening development yet. Rioters unable to get in an automobile rock it, trying to turn it over and set it afire, cremating the occupants. The window beside Nixon gave way. Sherwood and another agent, in the front seat, drew their guns.

At that moment, about 12:45 P.M. on May 13, 1958, Richard Nixon's chances of surviving the afternoon were even slighter than he knew. Four blocks away at the Bolívar Tomb an American scouting party, which included a Secret Service agent, the embassy's military attachés, and the Vice President's administrative assistant, had arrived early to appraise the situation for the wreath-laying ceremony. They were aghast. Between six and eight thousand angry people were milling around. Here, as at the airport, police protection had disappeared. In the place of law officers, surly demonstrators were waiting at strategic corners on the Avenida Sucre. Their hostility toward Americans was obvious. The attachés being in uniform, they were kicked, spat upon, and manhandled, and a window in an embassy station wagon was broken. Thoroughly alarmed, the scouting party sent back three separate warning messages in code over a prearranged radio network centered at Caracas police headquarters.

At the third barricade the motorcade was disintegrating. Drivers behind the leading cars who could find a way clear were wheeling out of line and racing away down side streets, leaving the embattled American Vice President and his escorts to their fate. So chaotic had the situation become that to this day there is confusion over how Nixon escaped. According to his recollection, the driver of the truck carrying the correspondents who were covering the tour "somehow . . . edged his way into the oncoming lane of traffic, clearing a path for us like a football blocker leading a ball carrier. Our driver took us down the wrong side of the street with Mrs. Nixon's car following behind us." Mazo of the *Herald Tribune* was on that truck, however, and in his memory, just as the violence seemed to be reaching a murderous climax, "some Venezuelan soldiers showed up. They made a narrow opening in the traffic tie-up. Mrs. Nixon's car followed close behind."

The limousines at that time were still headed for the Panteón Plaza. In the last block before reaching it the Vice President told the chauffeur to swerve down an alley and take off in the opposite direction. The foreign minister cried, "We can't leave our protection!" Nixon said, "If that's the kind of protection we're going to get, we're better off going it alone." Once they were safe on another main boulevard he ordered a stop so that he could talk to Pat and take stock. The lead car was a wreck; all its windows were broken and its fenders smashed, and everyone in it had been scratched or cut. At the same time, no one had been seriously injured. The ladies were unhurt and the way ahead was clear. They drove directly to the U.S. embassy residence, located on the top of a steep, easily defensible hill in Caracas's exclusive Las Lomas neighborhood. Nixon took his first nap in twelve years of public life, sleeping the sleep of the exhausted; the rest of the men turned the hill into a fortress. The embassy's marine detachment and the Secret Service agents were reinforced by sixty American military men who were in the country as instructors of the Venezuelan armed forces. All messages, packages, and letters coming to the embassy were screened by security men. Plans were secretly drawn to leave Caracas at 3 P.M. the following day, nine hours ahead of schedule, and at Maiquetía Airport other guards prepared to defend the vice-presidential aircraft against possible attack.

Meanwhile, back in Washington, orders had been cut for a fantastic rescue mission. Lacking information about the Nixon party and warned to expect the worst, President Eisenhower had dispatched to Venezuela six destroyers, a guided-missile cruiser, and an aircraft carrier equipped to land marines by helicopter. A thousand marines and paratroopers were suiting up at Guantánamo Bay and on Puerto Rico, and Air Force fighters and bombers had been alerted to stand by. Nixon himself knew nothing of this. Dulles had cabled him the details, but this message, like the others that day, never reached its destination. The Nixons were dining alone in the privacy of their room at the embassy when the ambassador interrupted them. Word of the sensational new development had just reached him via a news report. The Pentagon had announced it at 6:05 P.M., explaining in a communiqué that "The movement is being undertaken so these troops will be in a position to cooperate with the Venezuelan government if assistance is requested."

This was an unexpected propaganda gift to the Venezuelan extremists responsible for the mobs. They had been in disgrace, but now they were almost forgotten as all Latin America protested the armada, which awakened in them the worst fears of North American imperialism. Nixon and the ambassador quickly issued a joint statement explaining that everyone was safe and there was no need for outside help. Next morning, when communications had been restored, the President was able to telephone the Vice President, who reassured him.

At Washington National Airport fifteen thousand people cheered Nixon as he came down the ramp. Eisenhower was there, accompanied by his entire cabinet. Nixon spoke briefly, saying that the best part of going away was coming home and that most of the people he had seen in his South American travels had been friendly.

Lima and Caracas had tested the Vice President and tempered him, but the effect of the incident on Nixon's popularity was as brief as it was immense. In June 1958, a month later, the Gallup poll showed him leading Adlai Stevenson for the first time and running a dead heat with Kennedy. It was the high point of his popularity in the 1950s. By the end of autumn it would be a memory. The Republicans were in trouble, and as their ranking politician he was, too.

Society knows few greater satisfactions than the discovery of a puritan caught practicing what he has preached against, and rarely does it happen so startlingly as in the month after Richard Nixon's return from Venezuela. The scandal was accompanied by a symbol as memorable as any in the influence-peddling 1940s. For 1958 not only produced the hula hoop, the big TV quiz shows, and Alec Guinness in neighborhood theaters showing the Japs how to build that bridge over the River Kwai; it was also the year of the vicuña coat. Before that summer possibly one American in ten thousand could have told you that the vicuña is a small fleet-footed hoofed mammal found in the Andes from Ecuador to Bolivia and much hunted for the wool of its fine lustrous undercoat, which is woven into fine cloth. By July 4 every taxpayer knew that a vicuña topcoat was to men what mink was to women—warm, handsome, stylish, and a status symbol. The taxpayer knew, if for no other reason, because every Democrat running for office was telling the vicuña story.

It is a curious fact that no one ever cleared up the question of how much vicuña wool there was in the vicuña coat, although that was one reason the government had brought the manufacturer, Bernard Goldfine, to book; he had been putting a "90% wool, 10% vicuña" label on cloth that actually contained some nylon. This and all other aspects of the story were eclipsed by testimony that the White House had intervened in Goldfine's behalf and that he, in appreciation, had seen to it that one of his top-quality, five-hundred-dollar coats hung in the closet of the assistant to the President of the United States, the former governor of New Hampshire, Sherman Adams. Other expressions of Goldfine's gratitude had included the gift to Adams of a $2,400 Oriental rug from Macy's and picking up the tab on twenty-one occasions between 1955 and May 1958 when members of the Adams family had stayed at Boston's elegant Sheraton Plaza Hotel, running up bills totaling $3,096.56. He had also paid for Adams's stays at the Waldorf Astoria in Manhattan. Goldfine had then claimed all of these expensive favors as business expenses on his tax returns.

They were deductible, under Internal Revenue regulations, provided some "ordinary and necessary" benefit or advantage had flowed to Goldfine businesses from the expenditure. It had, and he could prove it. The two men were very close. Subpoenaed telephone records were to reveal that over a six-month period Goldfine had placed 43 long distance calls to Adams, about one every four days. Adams had made countless others to the textile manufacturer and in his behalf. On December 30, 1953, the President's chief of staff had called Federal Trade Commission chairman Edward F. Howrey —who owed his appointment to Adams—to ask the source for the complaint against Goldfine for mislabeling textiles. On April 14, 1955, when the manufacturer was again under investigation for the same charge, Adams used his influence to get Goldfine an appointment with Howrey. During it, Goldfine wielded the name of his friend in a heavy-handed manner. "Please get me Sherman Adams on the line," he ordered a secretary in a voice loud enough to be heard in the next office. "Sherm, I'm over here at the FTC," he said on the phone. "I was well treated over here."

The following year Adams had asked Gerald Morgan, the White House special counsel, to ask Security and Exchange lawyers for confidential information about an SEC investigation of Goldfine's East Boston Company—a violation of the commission's rules. Later John Fox, publisher of the *Boston Post*, was an especially damaging witness. He testified that Goldfine regarded his friendship with the President's assistant as a license to make deals. "He told me," Fox said in one of his less plausible moments, "that as long as he had Sherman Adams in his pocket he could do it." Fox further testified, "I asked Mr. Goldfine just what his trouble . . . was and he told me they had accused him of mislabeling." Later, "as a matter of idle curiosity," Fox asked if Adams had taken care of the FTC matter, and Goldfine "told me that he had."

On that rare afternoon in June when the first choice Adams-Goldfine revelations were entered into the record of the House Special Subcommittee on Legislative Oversight, the presidential aide was delivering a baccalaureate address to the Holderness School for boys in New Hampshire on "the questions the Bible tells us shall be asked on Judgment Day." Adams had long been interested in what was going to happen to sinners on that Day. Democrats knew him as the stern moralist who had decried minks, freezers, and influence peddling during Truman's tenure, calling that administration an "Augean stables" in a memorable January 1952 speech and promising that Eisenhower would end such corruption. "Here is the man to do it," he said. "The kind of people with whom he has surrounded himself is answer enough for that."

Conservative Republicans also resented Adams. They remembered his accusations that Taft was stealing GOP delegate votes in Texas. "Thou shalt not steal," he had cried, wagging a finger at them. To them he was the man who had delivered a ruthless judgment against Air Force Secretary Harold Talbott because he had solicited business for his efficiency-engineering firm on official Air Force stationery. One of the bitterest ironies of the Goldfine disclosures was that White House secretaries, one of whom worked within seventy-five feet of President Eisenhower's desk, had accepted cash gifts from the textile manufacturer ranging from $35 to $150. Until now that would have been enough to bring instant dismissal from Eisenhower's chief of staff, who had warned them to be on the lookout for improper requests for influence. Now they could not even be reprimanded. In the West Wing of the White House members of the President's staff moved on tiptoe and spoke in whispers, as though someone in the First Family were gravely ill.

How had it happened? All his life Adams had been, as his eighty-two-year-old father put it, "sound as a dollar and square as a brick." His wife Rachel fondly called him "the Great Stone Face." In the White House he scrupulously paid for office stamps he put on personal letters and insisted that he be billed for personal phone calls. Until recently he had still used stationery headed "Sherman Adams, Governor of New Hampshire," with "ex-" typed in. He was always at his desk by 7:30 in the morning—that had been true in New Hampshire, too, where he had been known to wade through blizzards to get to work on time—and any member of the staff who came in after the office had opened would hear his sharp call: "You're late to work this morning!" In using the telephone he refused to waste valuable time saying "Hello" or "Good-bye." He began talking the instant the other person picked up the receiver, and when he had said his piece he promptly hung up, cutting off the other fellow in mid-sentence. No man had ever been more trusted by a President. He checked out every piece of paper, every visitor, and every decision headed for Eisenhower's desk, giving Ike clear options for choice, as in a short list of men eligible for a cabinet post. "Whatever I have to do," the President had told a press conference, "he has in some measure to do." Adams had never betrayed that enormous trust. How, then, had he wound up in the sticky embrace of a man like Bernard Goldfine?

Much of the answer lies in the fact that there were two Bernard Goldfines. One of them was a cheap, devious manipulator, always in and out of trouble with the government and capable of exploiting any relationship. That was the Goldfine who had attracted the interest of the House committee. But Adams had never met that man. The Goldfine he had known ever since the war was a self-made, humble, eager-to-please immigrant, a diamond in the rough eager to use his wealth in good causes. In Adams's words he was "an upright and honest citizen, trustworthy and reliable." The suggestion that he would stoop to underhanded practices was absurd. He didn't need to be underhanded; he was already rich. The Goldfine empire consisted of six textile mills in Maine, Vermont, New Hampshire, and Massachusetts and two real estate firms, East Boston Company and the Boston Port Development Company. Each year he gave $50,000 to charities. He, his wife, and his four children lived in a fashionable home in Boston's Chestnut Hill suburb.

Adams had been introduced to him by Norris Cotton, U.S. Senator from New Hampshire, as a public-spirited millionaire who refused to follow other textile manufacturers in the exodus south to cheap southern labor and taxes. Adams made inquiries and found that Goldfine was known to be a sound businessman with a good reputation in his trade; he treated his employees well, paid good wages, and had never been in trouble with the textile union. Once he had held a good-will conference between representatives of labor and management. It had been attended by the governors of Maine, New Hampshire, Vermont, and Massachusetts. His friends and admirers included Cotton, Senator Frederick Payne of Maine, Speaker of the House John McCormack, Mayor John Hynes of Boston, and John Steelman and Maurice Tobin of the Truman administration.

The congressional investigation of Goldfine's manipulations revealed that some of these friendships had seamy sides. He owned the house in which Cotton lived, and he had made Payne's purchase of a home possible by lending him $3,500 for a down payment without interest, which had never been repaid. His relationship with Fox had begun when he had taken the extraordinary step of extendng $400,000 credit to the *Post* in exchange for an editorial endorsement of Massachusetts Governor Paul A. Dever's campaign for reelection. Recently the Goldfine-Fox friendship had soured, which may account for the incriminating passages in Fox's testimony.

Goldfine and Adams had become and remained steadfast friends. Rachel Adams and Charlotte Goldfine were also close to one another. The four of them often spent weekends together—in his memoirs Adams describes Goldfine as "a man with a lot of good fun in him"—and when young Solomon Goldfine almost failed at Dartmouth, "Uncle Sherm" sternly lectured him and put him on the right track. In this context the gifts become more understandable. They went both ways; the Goldfines had an oil painting from Rachel, and Goldfine wore a gold Le Coultre wristwatch inscribed "To B.G. from S.A. Jan. 20, 1953." Adams was startled to learn that Goldfine had deducted the hotel bills on his tax returns. He had been under the impression that the suites were rented permanently by one of Goldfine's companies and would have been empty if Adams hadn't used them. As for the favors he had done for Goldfine, they weren't at all improper, he said. He hadn't guided him. Nor had he known that he had violated an FTC rule by making information available to his friend. In any event, that had been the extent of the accommodation. He would have done the same for any businessman bewildered by Washington bureaucracies.

White House correspondents hammered at Hagerty: "Does this indicate a departure from the administration's previous attitude toward freeloading by high officials?" He ducked: "I don't know what you mean by that. . . . This is a personal friend, if that's what you're talking about." They relentlessly pursued him: "It's all right for a personal friend?" He dodged again: "I stick with the letter that the governor issued. The facts are as they are."

The presidential assistant's failure to grasp the interpretation which others might put on his relationship with Goldfine stemmed in part from an inability to see himself as others might see him. Adams knew Adams to be honest; that was that. So was his friend; it couldn't be otherwise. Those close to the former governor believed that he had been flattered by the admiration of the Lithuanian immigrant who had followed the Horatio Alger course to the top. Adams's bedrock New England upbringing prevented him from being free with his own money, but he could not resist the lavish attentions of an openhanded big spender. Thus he had drifted thoughtlessly across a line.

Testifying before the subcommittee on June 7, a full week after the disclosure of his relationship with Goldfine, Adams acknowledged that he had been "imprudent." He said, "If . . . I have in any way so conducted myself as to cast any semblance of doubt upon such conduct, I can only say that the error was one of judgment and certainly not of intent." The question was whether that concession from him was adequate now. He had made it only after he had found that it was not enough to sit behind the White House gates and issue a statement attacking the "unwarranted and unfair insinuations" of his accusers. Newspaper editors, vigilant as always on the issue of morality in public servants, were reminding their readers that on May 4, 1956, President Eisenhower had said:

> If anyone ever comes to any part of this government . . . claiming some privilege . . . on the basis that he is part of my family or of my friends, that he has any connection with the White House, he is to be thrown out instantly . . . I can't believe that anybody on my staff would ever be guilty of an indiscretion. But if ever anything came to my attention of that kind, any part of this government, that individual would be gone.

Now, two years and fifty-five days later, Eisenhower faced 257 reporters in the Indian Treaty Room and doggedly declared that "Anyone who knows Sherman Adams has never had any doubt of his personal integrity and honesty. No one has believed that he could be bought." Adams had been accused of imprudence, and he had used that word himself. Ike said, "Now, the utmost prudence must necessarily be used by everyone attached to the White House . . . Carelessness must be avoided." But a valuable presidential aide should not be lost because he had skidded once, especially in these circumstances:

> I personally like Governor Adams. I admire his abilities. I respect him because of his personal and official integrity. I need him.
>
> Admitting the lack of that careful prudence in this incident . . . I believe with my whole heart that he is an invaluable public servant doing a difficult job efficiently, honestly, and tirelessly.

Ike had gone over the statement with Hagerty, who had approved it, believing that it would take the pressure off Adams. Only afterward did the presidential press secretary see the three damaging words leap from the pages: *I need him.* In a stroke the President had allowed his critics to depict him as a weak old man who could not govern without the help of an indispensable man and had permitted an exception to the White House rule that anyone on his staff involved in improper conduct should be fired.

The President, then, had gone bail for Adams's faith in his friend and benefactor Bernard Goldfine. Much would now depend upon the manner of the man with whom he had been imprudent. That came next and it destroyed Adams. The ensuing sessions on Capitol Hill turned into a burlesque. It began when Goldfine strode into the hearing room of the House subcommittee brandishing a twenty-five-page introductory statement. He had already angered the committee by releasing the text to the press at 7 A.M., three hours before he was scheduled to testify. Unperturbed and jaunty in a dark blue suit, wearing a blue silk tie initialed BG, he took the chair to read it. Then he removed his gold watch and passed it to the committeemen ("providing I get it back"), explaining, "The watch I am wearing now, on the back of it is written 'to B.G.'—that means Bernard Goldfine—'from S.A.'—that's Governor Sherman Adams—dated 'Jan. 20, 1953,' and we all know that date. That is the inauguration date President Eisenhower was inaugurated." In the visitors' section Rachel Adams winced. She had just realized that that was how their friend had been introducing himself to strangers, including federal officials, all these years.

In the spectacle that followed, the star millionaire was assisted by a worshipful secretary named Mildred Paperman; an entourage of lawyers headed by Roger Robb, who had been the heavy-handed cross-examiner of J. Robert Oppenheimer; Tex McCrary, a Manhattan press agent; and a press headquarters in Washington's Sheraton-Carlton Hotel featuring caviar, free whiskey, and "Press Receptionist" Bea Duprey, a Boston Venus whose most conspicuous activity was urging reporters to get her measurements (35-22-35) right. There was also a New York flack named Jack Lotto, who identified himself as "a former ace reporter for INS" and who, in his press releases, spelled his client's name "Bernard Goldfein." Late one night Lotto caught two spies bugging the office from the next room. One of them was a private detective, Baron (name, not title) Ignatius Sacklette, who had been working for the subcommittee. He was instantly dismissed. The other was Drew Pearson's legman, Jack Anderson. Pearson refused to fire Anderson. He said, "I need him."

On the first page of Goldfine's opening statement McCrary had printed in block letters the message: YOU WILL BE GREAT! In reality Goldfine was awful. McCrary had also underlined words to be emphasized. Instead of stressing them, Goldfine yelled them. Periodically McCrary had written "Glass of water." Unfortunately he had neglected to check out the committee room. There were no glasses there, only floppy paper cups, with the result that from time to time his client peered around in confusion. But neither McCrary nor any of the others was responsible for the devastating impression Goldfine made. He appeared to be a sleazy, amoral, double-shuffle con man because he was, in fact, a sleazy, amoral, double-shuffle con man.

His voice rasping and his tone belligerent, he told how he had clawed his way upward in New England's savage textile and real estate world. It was a world of which Eisenhower and Adams knew little. Whenever they thought of a businessman they thought of George Humphrey. Goldfine was of a different breed. Waving the watch and calling Fox a character assassin, he backpedaled frantically when committee counsel questioned him about his troubles with federal regulatory agencies. No, he had no records; "Paperwork has been out of my line." Ask his secretary; "After all, I'm not a bookkeeper. She is." Loyal Miss Paperman, seated a few feet away, piped up at this point in an attempt to explain why there were no records, and Robb snarled, "Keep quiet, keep quiet, keep *quiet!*" Begging the congressmen for understanding, Goldfine explained that Adams had merely given him directions to "these giant federal agencies where a little man gets lost without some kind of guidance from a friend."

At this juncture the subcommittee trapped him in a lie. In his opening statement he had flatly said, "The first difficulty that any of my mills ever had with the Federal Trade Commission was in November . . . 1953. Neither I nor anyone else in our companies had had prior experience with the FTC in matters of this type." His point, essential to his case and Adams's plausibility, was that when the FTC charged him with mislabeling in November 1953 he was so mystified that he needed Sherman Adams to explain what it was all about. Now subcommittee investigators produced proof that Goldfine had been inundated in 1942 and every year thereafter with FTC complaints accusing him of using labels that made his products appear to be of a higher quality than they were. At the hearing he answered weakly that this was just more paperwork and, besides, that they were "minor matters" and therefore not likely to get to his level. The congressmen didn't challenge him. They knew what else was coming.

Among the topics that Goldfine and Paperman were keeping quiet about, on the ground that they had no files, was a sum of $776,879.16, all of it in treasurer's checks and cashier's checks dating back to 1941 and, as of May 8, 1958, still uncashed. People in shady enterprises like money that way because, among other things, such checks have no time limit. Also, the name of a bank official, not that of the person footing the bill, appears on them. Finally, public officials fearful of cashing them because of the possibility of scandal may put them up as prime collateral for loans.

Goldfine refused to answer questions about his treasurer's and cashier's checks, saying that they were irrelevant. The committee counsel countered that they could hardly be called that, inasmuch as thirty of those which had been cashed had been given to legislative aides on Capitol Hill. The names of men close to John McCormack and Styles Bridges entered the transcript. Goldfine replied: "At Christmas time these are all checks that we have sent at different times to some of the poor workers who work in different offices at Christmas time. If that is something that is bad, I would like to be told about it."

He was told that it was bad to ease in and out of firms through dummy organizations and straw men, bad to match loans, bad to disregard federal and state regulations designed to protect the public, bad to subsidize a pack of big and little politicians who thus became indebted to him, and bad to build an incredible record of litigation, including 89 lawsuits in the Boston area alone. It was bad, and it was also criminal, to plunder his own companies, thereby defrauding fellow shareholders, and there had been a lot of that.

As the hearings progressed, Goldfine played more and more to the gallery, blustering and shouting his answers. He tried to argue that his infractions of the law had been insignificant, that he was the victim of legalisms—neglecting to file an annual report with the Vermont secretary of state, in one instance, and failure to take up his legal responsibilities as a company officer in others. As in most cases of financial skulduggery, the path of guilt was sometimes hard to follow, but plenty of Goldfine swindles were easy to understand. Operating through his secretary, who held key posts as treasurer and director in his firms, he repeatedly helped himself to generous sums of stockholder money. The pretenses for taking it varied. It would be called a loan, a sales commission, or repayment for nonexistent expenses ($25,475 in the case of a local firm dealing in real estate). Sometimes there was no excuse at all. The cash just disappeared. Neither he nor Miss Paperman could account for some $89,000 taken out in the late 1940s. She blandly suggested that the bank had "made mistakes in the past, and these can be an error." It was hard to pin down exchanges because she and her employer were dealing every day with hundreds of thousands of dollars in liquid assets. In one respect ominous for Goldfine, however, the particulars didn't matter. Whatever had happened, he clearly owed the government far more than he had claimed on his tax returns.*

Afterward Adams wrote of his relationship with Goldfine that "I knew little or nothing about the details of his business dealings. I did not learn of his tax arrears until some of the facts began to unravel as a result of the hearings by the Legislative Oversight Committee; nor did I know about his troubles with his East Boston Company's financial operations." No one, of course, had suggested that he had. The question was one of judgment. The unavoidable conclusion was that Eisenhower's chief of staff had been gulled and the office of the Presidency demeaned. He would have to step down. It was both a public and a private tragedy. Adams had brought a rare talent to the White House, and one wonders how he could have fashioned an enduring social relationship with a cheat. Goldfine's indifference to the implications of his conduct is astonishing. Even after Adams had set up his appointment with the chairman of the FTC, he let matters drift until three of his firms had been slapped with "cease and desist" orders for label violations. His concept of friendship appears to have been a lopsided swap. In return for a rug, a coat, and payment of some $3,000 in hotel bills, he had compromised Adams's honor. A friend said of Goldfine, "He's a name dropper and a Scotch drinker, and he had a weakness of talking too much, dropping too many names and things." Now he had set in motion a chain of events which could only end in the dropping of Adams's name from the White House roster.

* Goldfine was sentenced to a year in jail and fined $1,000 for contempt of Congress following the 1958 hearings. The sentence was suspended and he was placed on probation.

It didn't happen at once. Ike's executive officer was too valuable; he wouldn't give him up without a struggle. Another member of the White House staff explained, "Adams has been with the President since 1952, and he knows how he thinks better than any other man. He has talked with the President about policy more than any other man. The governor has got tucked away in his head all the policy decisions the President has ever made, all the policy questions that have been laid aside for the right time, all the questions that have been rejected. It would be impossible for any new man to operate like Adams operates. And the new man could never accumulate the knowledge that Adams has."

After the second week of the crisis—for that is what it amounted to—Ike and Adams persuaded themselves that the problem would go away. The President told Hagerty to announce meaningfully that "the Governor is back at his desk at White House business." In other words, Adams was staying.

Then came the Goldfine circus. When the House of Representatives voted August 13 to cite Adams's friend for contempt, the governor was through. A vast army of editorial writers and cartoonists, led by those who had supported Eisenhower in his two presidential campaigns, was waging an all-out war on him, and as the summer waned it grew more intense. That was the noisiest threat to Adams. It was secondary, however. The heart of the problem was political.

Democratic indignation was almost ritualistic—"I am tired of pious preaching from Sherman Adams," Adlai Stevenson said—but Republican censure came as a surprise to Eisenhower and Adams. It shouldn't have. This was an election year. Knowland, fighting a desperate battle for the California governorship, suggested that the President "should carefully weigh as to whether Adams has so hurt his usefulness that it might be harmful." Arthur Watkins of Utah was more blunt. "In the light of the record as measured by the high standards of ethics set by both the President and Mr. Adams," he said, "there seems to be no other possible conclusion than that Mr. Adams' usefulness is seriously impaired, if not completely destroyed."

The first test at the polls in 1958 came on September 8, when Maine voted. The Democratic slogan there was "Payne of Maine is mainly on the wane." If that was so, it was important; the results would be regarded as a measure of voter reaction to Goldfinian ethics. The Maine senator had never provided a convincing explanation of how he had acquired the $3,500 from Goldfine six years earlier, and his opponent, forty-four-year-old Governor Edmund S. Muskie, had made that the chief issue. The results made terrible reading in the White House. An incredible 20,000 registered Republicans had stayed home. Not only did Muskie become Maine's first popularly elected Democratic senator; his plurality was twice as large as he had predicted. The GOP slate had gone down with Payne. The Democrats had captured the statehouse, two of Maine's three congressional seats, and twelve seats in the state legislature. Senator Margaret Chase Smith said, "We took a shellacking." Hagerty said, "The President views it as I do. We took a beating," and Meade Alcorn, Republican national chairman, said that the results should "alert every Republican in the land to the urgency of an all-out effort on November 4."

Mainly it inspired them to redouble their insistence that Eisenhower dismiss Adams. "As Maine goes, so goes Adams," the Washington press corps prophesied. Alcorn's phone rang constantly. Goldwater said he was afraid that "the harm has already been done." Knowland, lagging now in the opinion polls, declared that Ike's assistant should resign "immediately," and New York's Congressman Kenneth Keating, running for the Senate, added that "the good of the country" required it.

Adams was a marked man, and he knew it. The pressure became intolerable, and he took a few days off for a fishing trip in southeast Canada with Rachel and Jerry and Alice Persons. They were up there in the stark beauty of the Miramichi valley when the boom was lowered upon him.

Nixon had called upon Ike with a painful message from virtually all Republicans running for Congress; Adams, they felt, was a sea anchor dragging them down. The President had promised to reconsider the subject. Then Alcorn reported that the party's big donors were keeping their checkbooks closed until "the Adams mess" had been cleaned up. The Republican National Committee was meeting in Chicago. Eisenhower asked Alcorn to make one more appraisal of party opinion. When the chairman returned shaken—Richard Simpson of Pennsylvania was threatening to lead a mutiny if Adams stayed another week—the President capitulated. He called it "the most hurtful, the hardest, the most heartbreaking decision" of his Presidency, and he refused to do the firing himself. He told

Alcorn, "You've got to handle it. It's your job, the dirtiest I can give you."

Adams, meantime, was finding that not even the lonely Miramichi country was remote enough to hide him; Canadian reporters were asking him when he would resign. It seemed to be the only question people asked him any more. Then Gerry Morgan phoned from the White House and, according to Adams's recollection, said "he thought I ought to come back to Washington because Nixon and Meade Alcorn . . . wanted to talk with me." He knew why: "So I went." At 8 A.M. the following day he was at his desk, ready for the blindfold and the last cigarette.

Nixon told him that most Republican candidates and political leaders would, as a matter of self-preservation, repudiate him, and that would make his position impossible. Alcorn spoke for an hour, mostly about GOP contributions drying up and the incipient revolt within the National Committee. Adams sat impassively in his great leather chair, his head thrown back, staring at the ceiling and nibbling a stem of his glasses. Then, with a weary nod, he agreed to go.

In *Six Crises* Nixon recalled how the 1958 election served "to virtually erase the public memory of my success in Caracas and put in its place an image of failure with which my name was associated." Friends urged him to avoid the campaign, since a Republican defeat was inevitable; Dewey said, "You have done enough for Republican candidates." But Eisenhower told him, "I would give a year of my salary if we could win either the House or the Senate." The President, "by personal and political inclination," did not want to become enmeshed in political battles which could destroy his ability to work constructively with Congress, Nixon wrote; therefore, "if anyone was to carry the major load for political cross-country campaigning, I was the one who had to do it."

> I could not stand aside and see my fellow Republicans go down to disastrous defeat. I had to risk my political prestige to avoid a disaster, if possible, knowing full well, as in 1954, we would probably lose, and I would be the big-name target for the defeat. . . . I ended up stumping more than 25,000 miles in twenty-five states.

What this account omits is the character of the Republican campaign and the zeal with which the President joined it in the last two weeks. Nixon's line of attack was narrow and highly partisan. The Democratic party, he warned, was a haven for "socialism" and "left-wing extremists." He accused the Democrats of "retreat and appeasement," scorned "the Acheson foreign policy" that "resulted in war," and rejoiced in the "military strength and diplomatic firmness" of the Republican administration. The President, appalled at first, told White House correspondents that he deplored "this kind of thing." That stirred up conservative protests, which turned him around so completely that he publicly praised his bellicose Vice President: "No one can do this more effectively than you." By the end of October Ike was sharing Nixon's mood. He vowed that "there will be no appeasing Communist aggression while I am President," declared that "the so-called missile gap is being rapidly filled," and called the Democrats "political radicals" and "self-styled liberals" with "the irresistible impulse . . . to squander money—your money."

On November 4 the roof fell in on the Republicans. They lost twelve seats in the Senate, forty-eight seats in the House, and thirteen of the twenty-one contests for governor. Knowland went down, and so, unexpectedly, did John Bricker in Ohio. Even rock-ribbed Republican Vermont was lost; for the first time in one hundred and six years a Democrat would represent it in Congress. Nixon summed up the nationwide results: "It was the worst defeat in history ever suffered by a party having control of the White House."

Three races were of national interest. In Massachusetts John F. Kennedy's margin was 874,608—the largest ever for a candidate for any office in the state, and the largest in any senatorial race in 1958. Barry Goldwater ran against the Democratic tide in Arizona and was reelected decisively. And Rockefeller, even more impressively, rolled up a landslide plurality of a half-million votes. A TV commentator observed, "The big winner in this election is Nelson Rockefeller; the big loser, Richard Nixon." On November 9 New York's Governor-elect flew south to rest on his Venezuelan estate. At Maiquetía Airport, where the Nixons' baptism of Caracas spit had begun six months earlier, reporters asked him about Nixon. Rockefeller replied, "*No tengo nada que ver con Nixon*"—"I have nothing to do with Nixon."

Late Fifties Montage

Best actor of 1958: David Niven in *Separate Tables*
The Horse's Mouth *The Inn of the Sixth Happiness*
The Long Hot Summer *The Brothers Karamazov*

Come and click with Dick
The one that none can lick
He's the man to lead the U.S.A....
So let's all click with Dick

CRISIS IN FRANCE FADES AS DE GAULLE TAKES HELM

Best actor of 1959: Charlton Heston in Ben-Hur
Best actress of 1959: Simone Signoret in Room at the Top

Just you wait, 'Enry 'Iggins, just you wait
You'll be sorry, but your tears will come too late
You'll be broke and I'll have money
Will I 'elp you? Don't be funny
Just you wait, 'Enry 'Iggins, just you wait

THE STATUS SEEKERS
An exploration of class behavior in America and the hidden barriers that affect you, your community, your future
VANCE PACKARD
Author of *The Hidden Persuaders*

Now — Zenith brings you portable TV's biggest picture . . . 21" Super Screen

Babies are FRAGILE — Handle with JOHNSON'S

Some Like It Hot
Pillow Talk
North by Northwest
The Nun's Story
On the Beach
Anatomy of a Murder

The Apartment *Inherit the Wind* *Sunrise at Campobello*
I'm All Right, Jack *Hiroshima, Mon Amour*

GET RID OF TIRED BLOOD! Take Geritol. It builds iron power in your blood fast.

MAXWELL HOUSE coffee: *TASTES* as good as it *SMELLS*

DURKEE'S Instant Minced Onion

BEST SELLERS: Nonfiction
The Rise and Fall of the Third Reich by William L. Shirer
Only in America by Harry Golden
Born Free by Joy Adamson
How I Made $2,000,000 in the Stock Market by Nicholas Darvas
Aku, Aku by Thor Heyerdahl

"Funniest Musical in Years"
—*N.Y. News*
BYE BYE BIRDIE
CHITA RIVERA DICK VAN DYKE
54th Street Theater
150 West 54th Street

Best actor of 1960: Burt Lancaster in *Elmer Gantry*
Best actress of 1960: Elizabeth Taylor in *BUtterfield 8*

K-E-Double-N-E-D-Y
Jack's the nation's favorite guy
Everyone wants to back Jack
Jack is on the right track

BEST SELLERS: Fiction
Doctor Zhivago by Boris Pasternak
Exodus by Leon Uris
Advise and Consent by Allen Drury
The Ugly American by William J. Lederer and Eugene Burdick
Lolita by Vladimir Nabokov

BAN takes the worry out of being close

noisiest potato chips in the world

1ST CLASS POSTAGE UP FROM 3c to 4c

little old wine-maker me

MOSCOW, NEW YORK START JET PASSENGER SERVICE

Hang down your head, Tom Dooley
Hang down your head and cry
Hang down your head, Tom Dooley
Poor boy, you're bound to die

POWER FAILURE HITS 500,000 NEW YORKERS: ANOTHER BIG BLACKOUT IS TERMED UNLIKELY

	1950	1960
U.S. homeowners	23,600,000	32,800,000
Powers mowers sold	1,000,000	2,600,000
Automatic washing machine sales	1,700,000	2,600,000
Children five to fourteen	24,300,000	35,500,000
Little Leagues	776	5,700
Girl Scouts, Brownies	1,800,000	4,000,000
Bowling lanes	52,500	108,000
Gallons of gin	6,000,000	19,000,000
Gallons of vodka	100,000	9,000,000
Pounds of aspirin	12,000,000	18,000,000

Things Go Better with **Coke**

Buy Beech-Nut, by Gum.

Any thirst you can get **7-UP** can quench

REAL GUSTO
In a Great Light Beer
SCHLITZ

Twenty-six

TATTOO FOR THE GENERAL

H. L. Mencken once observed that journalism is an inexact science. The last years of the Eisenhower era were rich in proof of it.

Six weeks after the Democrats' off-year sweep a special Arkansas legislative committee disclosed that it had "definitely proved that there was Communist influence" in the Little Rock integration dispute. The chairman, Representative Paul Van Dalsen, said that the committee's three-day public hearing had alerted Arkansas to the threat of Communism, and a colleague of Van Dalsen confidently predicted that American Negroes would reject invitations to join any new demonstrations instigated by the National Association for the Advancement of Colored People and "backed by the Communist Party." Racial peace, he said, lay dead ahead.

Clark Kerr, newly installed as the president of the University of California, took a close look at college students in 1959 and said, "The employers will love this generation. . . . They are going to be easy to handle. There aren't going to be any riots."

That November the Roman Catholic bishops of the United States, in opposing the use of federal money to promote artificial birth control at home and abroad, ridiculed the assertion that American Catholics would gradually come to accept contraception.

NBC, looking for a clean-cut young American to counterbalance Elvis Presley, chose Charles Van Doren, a $4,400-a-year Columbia University instructor who had just won $129,000 in fourteen spectacular weeks on the network's biggest quiz show, *Twenty-one.*

Hired at $50,000 a year as an NBC consultant and *Today* show commentator, he edited an inspirational anthology, *Letters to Mothers.* In his own mail, three of every four letters were from parents or teachers grateful to him for the shining example he was setting for the country's youth. Late in 1958, when a New York County grand jury began looking into charges that quiz shows were rigged, reporters converged on his smart Greenwich Village home. He scorned the idea. "I never got any kind of hint or help," he said, "and as far as I know, nobody else ever did on the program." When they persisted he said sternly, "It is an insult to keep asking me these questions."

Whereupon Negroes, college students, Catholics, and Charles Van Doren proceeded to surprise those who thought they knew them.

The hope that black militancy would go away died a sudden death on February 1, 1960, when four black students at the North Carolina Agricultural and Technical College entered an F. W. Woolworth store on South Elm Street in nearby Greensboro, made several small purchases, took seats at the lunch counter, and ordered coffee. In conformity with the southern laws and tradition requiring segregation, the management ignored them. They stayed in silence until closing time, and the next morning they appeared at the counter again, this time with five black friends. They called it a sit-in. Each succeeding day there were more of them. Calm and well-behaved, ignoring catcalling white youths who dangled Confederate flags in front of them and flipped cigarette butts at them, the young blacks let it be known that they were going to stay until they got their coffee.

If it had been up to the store's Greensboro employees, they would never have been served. But Woolworth is a nationwide chain, and that was what they were counting on. In North Carolina the movement spread to Durham, Winston-Salem, Charlotte, Raleigh, and High Point, and outside the state lunch counters were occupied in Nashville, Chattanooga, Tallahassee, Richmond, and Rock Hill, South Carolina. Over the next fortnight blacks staged Woolworth sit-ins in fifteen cities, and in Boston four hundred students from Harvard, Brandeis, Boston University, and MIT picketed twelve Woolworth stores. That pleased the Greensboro blacks. What happened next astonished them and the country. Demonstrators appeared at Walgreen, S. H. Kress, W. T. Grant, and Liggett lunch counters. Englewood, New Jersey, sympathizers took up a collection to back the demonstrators. Yale Divinity School students marched through downtown New Haven in support. Exasperated dime store managers raised their coffee prices to a dollar a cup for Negroes, unscrewed the seats, and threatened to close the lunch counters. Nothing worked; the demonstrators met them at every turn with new forms of passive resistance. Then the movement leaped from the stools to every segregated facility in society. There were sleep-ins in motel lobbies, play-ins in parks, read-ins in public libraries, watch-ins in movie theaters, bet-ins in bingo halls, sweat-ins in Turkish baths, and, when spring approached, swim-ins on restricted beaches.

On May 10 the blacks scored their first victory when lunch counters were desegregated in six Nashville stores, the first such general action in any southern state except Texas. All spring battles of attrition were fought throughout the South, with the color bar moving a foot here, a yard there, and pressure on the diehards mounting. On June 5 the blacks' Southern Regional Council reported desegregated counters in nine scattered border cities; there had been no violence in any of them, and none of the merchants had been hurt by the threat of retaliatory boycotts by angry whites. Virginia felt the opening wedge on June 23, when its Hot Shoppes were opened to Negroes. Knoxville stores ended lunch counter segregation July 18. July 25 was a day of black jubilation; the Woolworth and Kress stores in Greensboro, where it had all started six months earlier, were integrated. That same day four Virginia stores in the Norfolk-Portsmouth area also ended discrimination. After that the going was rougher. The never-say-die Deep South was digging in. On October 19 Atlanta policemen arrested fifty-one sit-in demonstrators led by Martin Luther King. They refused to put up bail and were jailed. The great sit-in blitz of 1960 was over, and the blacks paused to consolidate their gains. But even the Arkansas legislature now knew that the respite would only be temporary. A Negro nation of 18,871,831 was stirring. American blacks were becoming visible at last.

The future was revealed to Clark Kerr on the cloudless afternoon of Friday, May 13, 1960. The House Committee on Un-American Activities, still tenaciously investigating California Communists after all these years, was holding hearings in San Francisco's rococo city hall. Among those subpoenaed were several public schoolteachers and a Berkeley sophomore, all of them rumored to be active leftists. Several busloads of Berkeley students arrived to give them moral support. No demonstrations had been contemplated; in that innocent day few undergraduates knew how to demonstrate. They merely wanted seats in the hearing room. But the building was already crowded. Policemen barred the door at the top of the steps. Somebody started to push. One cop lost his footing; afterward it was said that he was beaten. Nightsticks appeared, and then hoses. At the end of a wild half-hour twelve people were casualties and fifty-two were on their way to jail. Jessica Mitford of Oakland reported in the *Nation* that "the current crop of students has gone far to shake the label of apathy and conformity that had stuck through the Fifties." She predicted that in the coming decade they would be dedicated to "shaping the future of the world." One beaten undergraduate told a reporter, "I was a political virgin, but I was raped on the steps of city hall." To the country's 3,610,000 students the message from Berkeley was a challenge. Impatient faculty members had long been goading them to make a political commitment. Now they knew how to do it.

During those same tumultuous months, as black pride and collegiate political awareness grew, the curtain was rising on another instrument of social change. On May 9, 1960, the U.S. Food and Drug Administration announced that it had approved an oral contraceptive as safe.* The Pill was Enovid, made by G. D. Searle & Company, Chicago, which said it had proved to be 100 percent effective in a four-year test by 1,500 women. Twenty pills a month, obtainable by prescription, would provide assurance against pregnancy at a cost of $10 to $11 a month. This chemical form of birth control, combined with the new intrauterine devices and an increase in the acceptance of surgical birth control, offered women escape from the fear of pregnancy, the restraint that had inhibited their sexual activity since the beginning of time. Now, it seemed, they could go to bed as freely as men. Physicians and pharmaceutical houses were overwhelmed by the demand from millions of women for the Pill. Never had so many people taken a potent drug regularly for any purpose other than the control of a disease. And the Roman Catholic bishops were dismayed when Monsignor Irving A. LeBlanc, director of the National Catholic Family Life Bureau,

* The *New York Times* carried the story on page 75 of its May 10 issue.

reported that Catholic women were taking it as regularly as non-Catholics. As recently as November 1959 the bishops had reproved "some representatives of Christian bodies"—Protestant clergymen—for not practicing continence. Now even Catholic priests, and indeed some sisters in holy orders, were reappraising their vows in the light of the altered facts of life.

The clay figure of Charles Van Doren began to crumble in August 1958, when one Herbert M. Stempel, a CCNY student who had won $49,500 on *Twenty-one* before losing to Van Doren, took his troubled conscience to Manhattan District Attorney Frank Hogan and the *New York World-Telegram and Sun.* Stempel told them that the show was a fake. He said that contestants were given the answers in advance until their popularity began to wane; then they had to take a dive. He had been ordered to lose to Van Doren, who, like him, had been coached in facial expressions, lip-biting, brow-mopping, and stammering as he agonized over a question in the glass-walled isolation booth on camera. Rehearsed by the show's producer, Van Doren had then amazed 25 million televiewers by such feats as naming the only three baseball players to have collected more than 3,500 hits ("Ty Cobb, Cap Anson and . . . Tris Speaker!"), identifying the singer of the aria "Sempre libera" in *La Traviata* ("She sings it right at the end of the party given by . . . What's her name! Soprano. Her name is . . . Violetta!"), and spitting out the names of the Seven Dwarfs ("Sleepy, Sneezy, Dopey, Happy"—pause—"the grouchy one—ah, Grumpy—Doc—ah, the bashful one—Bashful!").

Stempel and other contestants on *Twenty-one* and CBS's *The $64,000 Challenge* told their story to a New York grand jury. Van Doren denied it under oath, and Judge Mitchell Schweitzer, deeply offended by the slandering of a contemporary American folk hero, impounded the record on the ground that it contained accusations which had not been proved. Outside the jury room, Van Doren told the press that he was "sad" and "shocked" by the lies about him. He repeated that he had played "honestly. . . . At no time was I coached or tutored."

The trouble with perjury is that those who commit it have no way of knowing whether there is someone who can prove they were lying. There is always the possibility that a Whittaker Chambers has the truth socked away in a pumpkin, and that is what happened to Van Doren. One James Snodgrass, an artist and a *Twenty-one* winner, produced registered letters that he had mailed to himself one to three days before the programs he was on, containing the questions and answers involved. These were then opened by the House Subcommittee on Legislative Oversight, the same stern tribunal which had been Bernard Goldfine's, and thus Sherman Adams's, downfall. The letters confirmed Snodgrass, and the committee, taking up where the Manhattan grand jury had left off, began building a trap of testimony and exhibits for that winning, handsome, loose-limbed, Ivy-clothed son of a distinguished literary family named Charles Van Doren.

They sprung it in October 1959. Van Doren, playing the outraged patrician like Hiss before him, wired the subcommittee a categorical denial of all the charges maligning him, declaring that he had not been "assisted in any form" and that he would be "available" to the subcommittee whenever it wished to question him. Back came a telegram inviting him to appear before the congressmen voluntarily, at which time he vanished. A formal subpoena was issued, but the process server could not find him. For six days the American people did not know whether he was alive or dead. On the seventh day, October 14, he materialized by prearrangement in New York's Roosevelt Hotel, accepted the subpoena, and confronted a packed press conference. He read a prepared statement. "Distressed" by the course of events, he said, he had taken a leave of absence from Columbia and gone with his wife to New England, "to gather my thoughts . . . in the October beauty of the region." He hadn't known he was wanted. The reporters boggled. How could he have been unaware of the subpoena when it was the lead story in every newspaper and news broadcast? Smiling wanly, he said out of respect for the U.S. Congress he would have no further comment until he appeared in the "appropriate forum," which was to say, its hearing room.

He surfaced there next on November 2, conservatively dressed and obviously tense as he confessed. "I would give almost anything I have to reverse the course of my life in the last three years. . . . I've learned a lot about good and evil. They are not always what they appear to be. I was involved, deeply involved, in a deception . . . I was almost able to convince myself that it did not matter what I was doing because it was having such a good effect on the national attitude toward teachers, education, and the intellectual life."

In time he became "terribly uncomfortable," he continued, and "very much afraid." He begged the producers "several times" to let him lose. They replied that it would have to be done in "a dramatic manner." At last a glamorous blonde lawyer became a contestant, and one of the producers "told me that . . . I would be defeated by her. I thanked him." When the public began to learn that the show had been a fraud, Van Doren said, he had been "horror-struck. . . . I simply ran away. . . . Most of all, I was running away from myself." There was "one way out which I had, of course, often considered, and that was simply to tell the truth." But "emotionally" this was not "possible." Then the subpoena was served upon him. ". . . it was a small thing that tipped the scales. A letter came to me from a woman, a complete stranger, who had seen me on the Garroway show and who said she admired my work there. She told me that the only way I could ever live with myself, and make up for what I had done—of course, she, too, did not know exactly what that was—was to admit it, clearly, openly, truly. Suddenly I knew she was right." Next morning, Van Doren went on, he summoned up the courage to phone his lawyer, who, when he had heard all, said, "God bless you." And that was the end of his statement. Putting it down, he turned to the attorney and smiled at him.

It was preposterous. It was the subpoena, not an unknown woman, which had forced him to own up. Furthermore, if he had really been "terribly uncomfortable" on the show there had been no need to plea for release from the producers; all he had to do was give a wrong answer to one question on the air. A Republican member of the subcommittee, Steven B. Derounian of New York, saw through Van Doren's fraudulence. He said to him, "I don't think an adult of your intelligence ought to be commended for telling the truth." But that was just what the other congressmen proceeded to do. Chairman Oren Harris said he wanted to "compliment" him on his candor. Representative William E. Springer of Illinois expressed the hope that Columbia would not "prematurely" dismiss him from its faculty, and Representative Peter F. Mack of Illinois said he trusted that NBC would forgive him. Others said they wanted to "commend" him for his "fortitude," and for the "forthrightness" of his "soul-searching" statement. Five hours later Columbia, seeing things differently, announced that it was dispensing with Van Doren's services; NBC discharged him the next day. But that was not a popular reaction. The crowd at the hearing had been with Van Doren, applauding him and his admirers on the subcommittee and greeting Congressman Derounian's comment with stony silence. Columbia students held a rally to protest his ouster. A poll showed that three of every four Americans felt that faced with the same situation "most people" would have done what he had done, and NBC's mail favored him, five to one.

No sooner had Van Doren and thirteen other celebrities been indicted in New York for perjury than the Harris subcommittee turned up new evidence of TV fraud. Dick Clark, the number one disc jockey in the teen-age subculture, admitted that he chose records in which he had a financial interest. This was called "payola." Chairman John C. Doerfer of the FCC in effect defended it. Nobody was harmed by it, he argued, and any attempt at regulation would "tamper with our cherished freedom of speech." At that point it was discovered that Doerfer himself had accepted payola from one of the big broadcasters he was supposed to be watching. Eisenhower accepted his resignation, but here, too, the public seemed to be indifferent. It is not surprising that viewers who showed no concern over any of this should have accepted the networks' tasteless programming in 1960. If 1959 had been the Year of the Quiz Show, *Variety* suggested, 1960 was the Year of the Western. There were eight such programs on CBS, nine on NBC, and eleven on ABC—a total of twenty-four and a half hours of prime viewing time every week.

After seven years of basking in Eisenhower sunshine, the nation's opinion makers, including those who had supported the President, were becoming restless. As early as 1958 the *Chicago Daily News* had asked, "Things are in an uproar. But what is Eisenhower doing? All you read about is that he's playing golf. Who's running the country?" Subscribers, however, remained apathetic. While the President was in Europe, the Vice President scored a personal triumph in negotiating the end of a 116-day steel strike. Opinion polls were virtually unaffected; the public hadn't been watching. The newly freed Congo was bleeding in a tragic civil war, and rebellious Laotian soldiers led by Captain Kong Lee overturned the pro-Western government of Premier Tiao Samsonith; the average American couldn't have found either country on a map. At home a newspaper strike halted publication of all New York papers, there was a rash of prison riots, and another of bombs smuggled aboard airliners, including one planted by a greedy youth who thereby blew up his airborne mother, with everybody else on the flight, for her insurance. A survey reported that front pages were unread; readers preferred the comics and sports. When Caryl Chessman was executed in California after eight reprieves, opponents of capital punishment objected, but there were comparatively few of them, and the general lethargy seemed to be unaffected by a series of particularly brutal, senseless killings. One of them at this time was the murder of a Kansas farmer named Herbert Clutter with his wife, son, and daughter. *Time*'s account of the crime appeared in the news magazine's November 30, 1959, issue. Its headline was "In Cold Blood," and its readers included a writer named Truman Capote.

The instant cliché that year was the use of the word "bit" as an all-purpose verbal punctuation mark. Greensboro's blacks were doing "the protest bit." Romance was "the love bit," Metrecal "the diet bit," and Alfred Hitchcock's *Psycho* "the thrill bit." The commonplace cropped up almost everywhere, but it was never applied to one department of the federal government. No one ever said John Foster Dulles was doing "the diplomacy bit." It would have been unseemly, and it would also have been inappropriate, for Dulles belonged to an earlier age, to a craft of statesmanship fashioned by foreign ministers in cutaways and striped pants. His haughty moralizing and simplistic "massive retaliation" had been outmoded by the statistics of Soviet rocket thrust, and in the early months of 1959, as he hobbled back and forth to Walter Reed Hospital in the agony of his last illness, he seemed to realize that the rigidity of the East-West posture which he had done so much to perpetuate was about to become obsolete. He defended it to the last. Grimacing with pain as he left Washington on his final journey to Europe, he told a friend, "If it isn't cancer, then I feel the trip is too important to be put off. If it is cancer, then any additional discomfort doesn't fundamentally matter anyway."

It was cancer. Blasted daily by million-volt X-rays in Walter Reed Hospital or resting in the Florida sun on Jupiter Island, the secretary became preoccupied with his desperate, losing battle with death, and as he struggled the reins of statecraft slipped at last from his hands. Outwardly the world's balance of power was unchanged. The United States was still committed by treaty to the defense of forty-two nations, and Dulles, to use another emerging cliché, was still a man with tremendous clout. American editorial writers paid tribute to the "wise counsel" and "single-minded strength" of this "indispensable man." Whitehall sent him word that it was "extraordinarily sorry," the Quai d'Orsay expressed concern over "the greatest possible loss for the West," and Bonn regretted that "a spoke" had been "torn from the wheels of Western policy making." But that was all diplomatic cant, and Dulles must have known it. Although he kept in close touch with the White House and his own office by telephone, alert for any sign of cold war heresy, to those who could read the signs—and he was one who could—it was clear that moves toward a detente between Washington and Moscow awaited only his departure from the scene. "The clenched fist of Dulles," Emmet John Hughes wrote, was about to be replaced by "the outstretched hand of Eisenhower."

In the aftermath of the GOP's off-year election defeat, Hagerty had put together a long memorandum looking toward the 1960 election, in which Eisenhower, campaigning for a Republican successor, would stand on his record as a man of peace. Based on conversations with the President, it set forth as goals everything Dulles had resisted in his six years at Foggy Bottom. Its frank assumption was that the time had arrived for diplomatic flexibility. The President must take the center of the international stage, the Eisenhower-Hagerty memo held, as a peacemaker. Continuing, it declared that he must play this role in appearances at the United Nations, in journeys to the far corners of the world, including neutral India, and in a hospitable attitude toward suggestions that he participate in summit conferences and conversations with Russia's Khrushchev.

The Soviet premier was ready for such overtures. In welcoming Premier Anastas Mikoyan home from a U.S. tour on January 26, 1959, Khrushchev had said that "the possibility of a thaw" in Russo-American relations was "not excluded." "Everything possible" must be done to improve relations between the two superpowers, he said, for thermonuclear war was unthinkable; those in the West who said that Khrushchev was "more frightened of war than anyone else" were absolutely correct. As always, Dulles had replied that any meeting would have to be preceded by Soviet demonstrations of good faith, and that he doubted that there would be any, for the USSR, in his opinion, was committed to winning the cold war, not ending it. But this time another administration spokesman had expressed a different view. Vice President Nixon said that the United States also wanted a thaw, "because we realize that if there is none we will all be eventually frozen in the ice so hard that only a nuclear bomb will break it."

On May 24 the death watch at Walter Reed ended with the bulletin: MR. JOHN FOSTER DULLES DIED QUIETLY IN HIS SLEEP AT 7:49 E.D.T. THIS MORNING. Already Undersecretary Christian A. Herter was running the State Department. His first priority was the most recent of the long, dreary series of crises over Berlin. Khrushchev had delivered an ultimatum to the western powers: if they weren't out of the city in six months, the Red Army would throw them out. The characteristic Dulles response would have been a counter ultimatum and a show of strength, forcing a showdown on the brink of war. Eisenhower had taken a different tack. The President read a careful statement to a press conference declaring that if there was any shooting in Berlin it would be "to stop us from doing our duty. We are not saying that we are going to shoot our way into Berlin. We say we are just going to go and continue carrying out our responsibilities to those people. So that if we are stopped, it will be somebody else using force." Herter treated the ultimatum as a maneuver in presummit bargaining, and that, it developed, was exactly what it was.

Once Dulles was in his grave, events moved with almost unseemly haste. Five weeks later, on June 28, Soviet Deputy Premier Frol R. Koslov led a delegation of Russian officials to New York to open a Soviet Exhibition of Science, Technology, and Culture. On July 11 Eisenhower personally drafted an invitation to Khrushchev to visit the United States. And on July 23, two months to the day after Dulles's death, the Vice President of the United States was in Moscow to open an American National Exhibition in Sokolniki Park, thus paying what Eisenhower called a "return courtesy" for the New York visit of the Soviet officials.

What followed can hardly be called a contribution to the slackening of East-West tensions, but it did provide some insight into the combative instincts of Nikita Khrushchev and Richard Nixon. The exhibition's most interesting display was a six-room model ranch house with a central viewing corridor, permitting visitors to see all its furnishings. The Soviet leader had worked himself into a rage over it. It touched a sensitive nerve; Russia's sputniks had been built at the expense of consumer products and services. The opening of the fair was being televised in the USSR, and Khrushchev felt that he had been somehow outmaneuvered. He was spoiling for a fight. Nixon was the man to give it to him. The ceremony was to appear on American television, too. He expected to be the Republican presidential nominee next year, and whatever Hagerty's views on campaign strategy, Nixon had plans of his own which did not include allowing himself to be bullied on TV by an angry Communist. The result was what the press called the "kitchen debate" or the "Sokolniki Summit."

It began when they paused at the model home's sleek, gadget-stocked kitchen. Nixon declared that this was a typical American house, and that almost any U.S. workman could afford it or one like it. The Soviet premier bridled.

KHRUSHCHEV: You think the Russians will be dumbfounded by this exhibit. But the fact is that all newly built Russian homes will have this equipment. You need dollars in the United States to get this house, but here all you need is to be born a citizen. If an American citizen does not have dollars he has the right to . . . sleep on the pavement. And you say we are slaves of Communism!

NIXON: . . . We don't think this fair will astound the Russian people, but it will interest them just as yours interested us. To us diversity, the right to choose, the fact that we have a thousand different builders, that's the spice of life. We don't want to have a decision made at the top by one government official saying that we will have one type of house. That's the difference—

KHRUSHCHEV (*cutting in*): On political differences, we will never agree. If I follow you, I will be led astray by Mikoyan. He likes spicy soups and I don't. But that doesn't mean we differ.

NIXON: Isn't it better to be talking about the relative merits of our washing machines than the relative strength of our rockets? Isn't this the kind of competition you want?

KHRUSHCHEV (*pushing his thumb against Nixon's chest*): Yes, that's the kind of competition we want, but your generals say they are so powerful they can destroy us. We can also show you something so you will know the Russian spirit. We are strong, we can beat you. But in this respect we can also show you something.

NIXON (*wagging his finger at Khrushchev*): To me, you are strong and we are strong. In some ways, you are stronger than we are. In others, we are stronger. . . .

Pausing at a table of California wines, they scored their final points. Khrushchev proposed a toast "To peace and the elimination of all military bases on foreign lands."

NIXON (*without raising his glass*): Let us just drink a toast to peace.

A RUSSIAN BYSTANDER: One hundred years to Premier Khrushchev!

NIXON: I will drink to that. We may disagree with your policy, but we want you to be of good health. May you live to be one hundred years old.

KHRUSHCHEV (*after the toast*): At ninety-nine years of age we shall discuss these questions further. Why should we be in haste?

NIXON (*he has the last word*): You mean that at ninety-nine, you will still be in power, with no free elections?

It was a curious exchange, less a debate than a quarrel between two aggressive men, each of them determined to impress the audience as more peaceful than the other. Both suffered from a self-imposed handicap. In a thousand speeches, the Soviet leader had created a crude stereotype of the typical capitalist politician as a Wall Street lackey, and Nixon didn't fit it. Nixon's handicap was a mirror image of Khrushchev's. His archetype of the evil Communist boss had as much substance as a man of straw, as much life as a Sunday supplement demon. The American Vice President had scored more forensic points, but the Russian premier had come across as warm, direct, and perhaps as better suited to his role. Nixon emerged as a man who liked ideas, Khrushchev as one who loved his people and would go to great lengths to champion them. As if to confirm that, he overlooked Nixon's insolence—plainly he regarded it as that—and accepted Eisenhower's invitation to visit America once Nixon had returned home. "I am prepared to turn out my pockets to show that I am harmless," he said in his disingenuous way. "In the old times people used to leave their weapons in the hall when they went in to talk peace. We should do that now, and there should be no saber rattling." With that, he quietly scuttled his Berlin ultimatum.

One reason Dulles had given for opposing such summitry had been his concern that U.S. allies might feel that they were being abandoned. To reassure them, the President flew to Europe at the end of August for two weeks of talks with Konrad Adenauer, Harold Macmillan, and Charles de Gaulle. It was an amazing trip. In

Washington it was easy to forget the tremendous affection Europeans felt for Dwight D. Eisenhower. Their feeling for him was unclouded by partisanship or ideology. To them he was the kindly, straightforward, low-key American general who had led the victorious crusade to free them from Nazi rule. The Germans seemed as grateful as the British and French. As Eisenhower's Mercedes-Benz entered Bonn an estimated 315,000 people, twice the population of the city, lined the route, cheering him and holding up banners proclaiming, WE TRUST YOU and WE RELY ON YOU. In London his car was a dove-gray Rolls-Royce. There the shouts—from a crowd numbered in the hundreds of thousands—were "Glad to see you, Ike," and "Good for you, Ike," and as the motorcade entered Grosvenor Square, from which General Eisenhower had directed the coalition of armies that had routed Hitler, reporters saw tears in his eyes.

De Gaulle, now entering his difficult period, would have preferred that Parisians show more restraint, but it was impossible. At Le Bourget Airport the two generals-become-presidents exchanged tributes; then the throng's cry of "Ike!" which in French came out "Eek!" drowned out everything else. It never died out completely during Eek's two days in Paris, not even when he placed a wreath of pink lilies and red roses on the tomb of France's unknown soldier, beneath the Arc de Triomphe, or during his response to the continuing ovation at the Hôtel de Ville: "When the heart is full, the tongue is very likely to stumble. I have one small French phrase that, I think, expresses my feelings—*Je vous aime tous.*" Obviously it was impractical to conduct serious talks against such a background. De Gaulle did press his plan for a NATO guided by a three-power directorate. Eisenhower warded him off with a promise to keep in closer touch over the transatlantic phone. ("I know he's a stubborn man," Ike told an aide, "but as long as he's stubborn on our side, everything's all right.") After a weekend at Scotland's Culzean Castle, where he occupied a nine-room apartment given to him by the Scottish people after V-E Day, the President flew home September 7. There he told a welcoming crowd: "I am quite certain that for the moment, at least, everything is going splendidly."

Nikita Khrushchev's barnstorming of the United States was to be the next stage in the slackening of world tensions. On September 15, at Andrews Field in Maryland, Soviet Ambassador Mikhail Menshikov called to a ramp, "Nikita Sergeyevich, I salute you on American soil," and as American spectators blinked in disbelief, down the steps he came, short, bald, and stocky, wearing three small medals on his black suit and accompanied by his shy wife, Nina Petrovna, his daughters Julia and Rada, his son Sergei, and a retinue of sixty-three Russian bureaucrats. President Eisenhower formally welcomed them, and then they were off on a two-week guided tour of the United States with U.N. Ambassador Henry Cabot Lodge as their host.

On the whole it was a successful journey. Americans are partial to curmudgeons, and this one was as salty as Thomas Edison and Henry Ford. In speeches before American businessmen, tours of rural Iowa, and luncheons with Mayor Robert Wagner of New York and Mayor Norris Poulson of Los Angeles, Khrushchev came on as shrewd, eccentric, and unscrupulous, but very human and determined to live in peace with his neighbors. Inevitably there were incidents. Khrushchev won an argument with Sypros P. Skouras, president of Twentieth Century–Fox, and lost one to Walter Reuther and his six union vice presidents. (He then denounced them as "agents for capitalists" and was puzzled when Reuther laughed.) After a Hollywood troupe had performed a cancan for him, the premier revealed a priggish streak, calling the dance "immoral" and adding, "A person's face is more beautiful than his backside."

At Camp David, the presidential retreat on Maryland's Catoctin Mountain, Khrushchev was on his best behavior. He said nothing offensive. In fact, he said almost nothing beyond vague generalities. His concept of discretion seemed to preclude getting down to brass tacks. Midway in the second day of their talks Eisenhower turned to him with a personal appeal: "You have the opportunity to make a great contribution to history by making it possible to ease tensions. It is within your hands." But the Russian leader refused to be pinned down. He praised American roast beef, enjoyed a western movie with Ike, and, after a helicopter hop to Gettysburg, admired the President's prize herd of Black Angus cattle. For the time being, that was going to be the extent of his contribution to a detente.

After their third day together the two leaders issued a joint statement. They had agreed that general disarmament was the most important question facing the world, that negotiations on the Berlin issue should be "reopened with a view to achieving a solution which would be in accordance with the views of all concerned and in the interest of the maintenance of peace," that "all outstanding international questions should be settled not by the application of force but by peaceful means through negotiation," and that President Eisenhower would visit the Soviet Union next year.

For a while the newspapers made much of "the spirit of Camp David." Briefly it seemed almost as substantive as the Roosevelt-Churchill Atlantic Charter. A turning point, men thought, had been reached in U.S.-USSR relations at last. It was all illusion. The President and the premier hadn't even touched upon the basic and critical problems arising from different views over the future of Germany and the world. The benign mood eventually turned out to be evanescent. In time it soured and was succeeded by disenchantment. Among the participants who resolved that a firmer groundwork should be prepared before any new conferences with the Russians was Richard Nixon.

Nixon did not, however, feel that the disappointing outcome vindicated Dulles's implacable opposition to meetings at the top. The world's statesmen had embarked on what *Time* called "the new global game of personal diplomacy," and none of them wanted a return to the arctic past. Their orchestrated journeys were now following a definite plot leading toward a desirable ending. The next step would be what was being called the "Western Summit," a kind of semifinal conference whose participants would be Eisenhower, Macmillan, Adenauer, and De Gaulle. These four would renew their vows to keep Berlin free and hammer out a joint approach for the final conference, which would be between them and Khrushchev.

The semifinal was held in Paris in December. Eisenhower was not going to limit the December trip to France, though. The ventures in personal diplomacy, made endurable by the new Boeing 707 jet airliners, were encouraging. The rousing welcome given him in the capitals of western Europe had given rise to a naive hope that the enthusiasm of the crowds that cheered motorcades could somehow be transformed into enduring good will and better international relations. With this in mind, and with Hagerty's memorandum before him, the President decided that as long as he was abroad he might as well call on the rulers of Italy, Turkey, Pakistan, Afghanistan, India, Iran, Greece, Tunisia, Spain, and Morocco. Before leaving on this 19-day, 19,500-mile trip to eleven nations on three continents, he delivered a televised report to the country. "During this mission of peace and good will," he said, "I hope to promote a better understanding of America and to learn more of our friends abroad."

Whether it led to a greater understanding is moot. It did provide staggering new evidence of the President's popularity, however. In Italy, where Romans stood in drenching rains for a glimpse of him—here "Ike" came out "Eekay"—a journalist wrote in *Corriere Della Sera*, "We welcome this man who speaks to us with the accent of Kansas farmers who cultivate fields of wheat as vast as seas, of pioneers who went West not long before his birth. He speaks without rhetoric before the imminent peril as he calls for 'Peace, peace.'" Turkey was next. Eisenhower himself called his welcome to Ankara "the most stupendous I have ever seen." Over 750,000 Pakistanis welcomed him to Karachi, and in New Delhi he said he was "completely overwhelmed" by the crowds, as well he might have been: a million shouting Indians held aloft banners acclaiming him as, among other things, "Eisenhower, Prince of Peace," and they threw so many flowers at his open car that he stood a foot deep in blossoms. It was the same in every country. There were 750,000 cheering Iranians in Teheran, where he addressed a joint session of the Shah's parliament; 500,000 enthusiastic Athenians outside when he spoke to Greece's Chamber of Deputies; 500,000 Spaniards when Generalissimo Francisco Franco welcomed him to Madrid, and 500,000 to greet him in Casablanca.

It was numbing, and it was also rather baffling. Applause in western Europe could be traced back to World War II, but the only nation on this trip to have been in the war was Italy, and the Italians had been on the other side. Why should Indian untouchables walk forty miles to see the American President, or Afghan tribesmen spend days weaving floral tributes to lay before the wheels of his limousine? Part of the explanation seemed to lie in the recurring chants, in every tongue, of "Peace, peace." War was recognized everywhere as mankind's greatest scourge, even among peoples that had never heard gunfire. But that wasn't all that lay behind these awesome demonstrations. Clearly America was more beloved than Americans knew. Anti-Americans made more noise, but the vast majority in these countries seemed to admire and trust the United States.

Eisenhower returned home on December 22. That Christmas was a high point in his Presidency and in the history of U.S. diplomacy. In his annual Christmas message to the nation—beamed overseas this time in twenty-eight languages—he said of his journey: "My purpose was to improve the climate in which diplomacy might work more successfully; a diplomacy that seeks . . . peace with justice for all men." The test of his accomplishment lay less than five months away, when he and the three leaders of western Europe would confront Khrushchev in the summit of summits. It was scheduled to open on May 16, 1960, in Paris.

From time to time in the later 1950s subscribers to the *New York Times* read, under the byline of Herbert L. Matthews, captivating accounts of bearded young Cuban revolutionaries hiding out in the tangled jungles of that island's Sierra Maestra range. Their leader was a hulking, verbose lawyer in his early thirties, Fidel Castro Ruz. Castro had landed in Cuba on Christmas of 1956 with just twelve men. Taking to the hills before dictator Fulgencio Batista's soldiers could seize them, they unfurled the red and black flag of their 26th of July movement, so named for a desperate attack led by Castro on Santiago Batistianos on July 26, 1953, and called on Cuban lovers of freedom to join them.

In those early years Castro's movement was very popular in the United States. Batista's Cuba was a police state run by terrorists and corrupt bureaucrats who made fortunes in prostitution, gambling, and raids on the public till. Havana University was padlocked to suppress mutinous students; dissenters were murdered; their corpses were dismembered and sent to their parents, or dumped in gutters like garbage. Washington was elated at the prospect of a truly democratic Cuba. As early as March 1958 all deliveries of U.S. arms to Batista were halted. American correspondents like Matthews wrote sympathetic stories depicting Castro and his *barbudos*, or bearded rebels, as selfless Robin Hoods who wanted to give their countrymen liberty and justice. The reporters erred, but the error was common then, and it was shared by most members of the Cuban middle class and a great many influential Cuban army officers who were fed up with Batista. That was Batista's undoing. Castro had fewer than two thousand *barbudos* to put against forty thousand superbly equipped Batistianos, but businessmen and landowners were financing him, and the middle class was acclaiming the rebels, who were, for the most part, middle-class themselves—young professional men and intellectuals like Fidel, his brother Raul, and

Major Ernesto "Che" Guevara, the Argentine physician who had become Castro's Trotsky.

In the last weeks of 1958 Guevara routed three thousand government troops in the province of Las Villas, one hundred and fifty miles from the capital, and captured the provincial capital, Santa Clara. A trainload of troops sent by Batista refused even to get out of the railroad cars. The old regime was through, and Batista knew it. On New Year's Day he flew off into exile. Castro then began a seven-day, six-hundred-mile march of triumph down Cuba's Central Highway. Fidel's men fired their pistols and tommy guns at the sky. In affection they called their leader "El Caballo," the horse. He was Gargantuan, a charismatic figure before the concept became popular. His personal life was ascetic. There were no women in it. Except for fifty-cent Montecristo cigars, he never indulged himself. Getting him to change his grimy green field jacket was next to impossible.

"Power does not interest me, and I will not take it," Castro said. "From now on the people are entirely free." He restored Cuba's lost pride, gave it a national identity, rooted out corruption, and launched vast programs to educate Cuba's children and inspire their parents. When whispering voices tried to spread reports that he was a Communist, the general reaction was scorn. Reactionaries always called reformers Reds; men like Matthews of the *Times* could remember their doing it in Spain twenty years earlier and they said so.

To demonstrate that he was a good neighbor to the United States, Fidel flew to Washington with a hundred cases of good-will rum. He lunched on steak and champagne with Acting Secretary of State Christian Herter—he wore his field jacket even there—and talked to eighteen congressmen in the Senate Foreign Relations Committee room. "The July 26 movement is not a Communist movement," he told them. "Its members are Roman Catholics, mostly." Asked about American investments in Cuba, he replied, "We have no intention of expropriating United States property, and any property we take we'll pay for." He was charming. To be sure, there was one sour note. After a three-hour conference with Castro, Vice President Nixon wrote a twelve-page confidential memorandum for distribution to the CIA, the State Department, and the White House, in which he said that he was convinced that Cuba's new leader was "either incredibly naive about Communism or under Communist discipline." But the CIA pigeonholed it, State ignored it, and Eisenhower waved it away. The administration was getting a little tired of Nixon's seeing Communist bogeymen everywhere.

The rude awakening of the Americans, and the subsequent deterioration of U.S.-Cuban relations, came in that spring and summer of 1959. Castro's hatred of dictators vanished, it seemed, when the name of the dictator was Castro. His indifference to power also disappeared. With a ruthlessness that would have startled Batista, Fidel suspended habeas corpus, established military tribunals all over the island, and decreed an end to the right of convicted defendants to appeal their sentences. By September he was careening leftward. He recognized Red China, called the United States a "vulture . . . feeding on humanity," renounced Cuba's 1952 military pact with the U.S., and dared the *yanquis* to invade Cuba.

The idealists and visionaries of the 26th of July movement had been betrayed. When they realized it, all Cuba rocked with their thwarted rage. Over a hundred of them were jailed, and the others fled north to Florida. Manuel Ray, a radical young engineer who had commanded Castro's Havana underground, was one. Two were famous liberals: Mio Cardona, whom Castro had chosen to be the first premier of his new government, and Manuel Urrutia, also handpicked, the regime's first president. Others who felt that they had been sold to the Reds included brave officers like José Peréz ("Pepe") San Román, Erneido Oliva, and Huber Matos, one of the 26th of July heroes of the Sierra Maestra. Some were incredulous when they first heard of Castro's treachery. They said they wouldn't believe until they saw it. Some literally witnessed it. Dr. Manuel Francisco Artime, the brilliant young manager of Oriente province, heard Castro himself outline his plan to communize Cuba within three years. "I realized," Artime later said, "that I was a democratic infiltrator in a Communist government."

Such men could not compromise with what they regarded as total evil. If they wanted to call their souls their own, they had to escape through what American reporters were calling "the cane curtain" in the hope that one day they could reclaim their homeland. Cubans have a certain style about them, and some of their escapes were dashing. Artime's was one. He wrote a personal note to Castro declaring that he was quitting the movement because he had "heard from your lips the complete plans to communize Cuba." Dressed as a priest and carrying a pistol inside a missal, he walked into the

American embassy. There he was introduced to a certain man called "Williams," who saw to it that he sailed north in a secret compartment on a Honduran freighter. On the Tampa pier Artime was met by a tall American who identified himself as "Mr. Burnett, a friend of Williams." In Miami, which soon had so many refugees that it took on the air of a Cuban city, other friends of Williams and Burnett appeared and introduced themselves as "Jimmy," "Sonny," "Seabee," "Don," etc. All of them, Artime eventually discovered, were operatives of the United States Central Intelligence Agency.

They did not identify themselves as CIA agents, of course. Neither did they admit it if asked. Their cover story was that they were employed by a great American corporation which was determined to solve the Cuban problem. Their leader was particularly anxious to preserve this facade. He was tall and expensively dressed, and he was the only agent with a first and last name: "Frank Bender." "Remember, Manolo," Frank kept reminding Artime, "I am not a member of the United States government. I have nothing to do with the United States government. I am only working for a powerful company that wants to fight Communism." Later the Americans tried to give the impression that a Cuban millionaire was backing them. The Cubans winked at one another and joked that the "millionaire" was named "Uncle Sam." "At that time we were so stupid," one of them said long afterward. "We thought that Uncle Sam was behind us. He wanted to do this secretly. That was all right because he was Uncle Sam, and he is strong." The CIA agents solemnly told them that they all risked jail if the FBI found out what was going on. That, they explained, was why they could not disclose their real names. It was also given as the reason for a great deal of such hokey-pokey as blindfolds, passwords, and countersigns. The Americans were haunted by the fear that the operation might be penetrated by double agents. The Cubans were required to submit to lie detector tests, Rorschach tests, and lengthy interrogations by a genial, bespectacled psychiatrist with a heavy German accent. (He was "Max.") Those who passed were dispatched on mysterious errands—typically, one of them entailed flying to New York, registering at the Statler Hilton as "George L. Ringo," and following telephoned instructions from a series of callers—until their hosts' suspicions were allayed.

Those who had passed muster were divided into two groups. The younger men, who would do the actual fighting, were recruited for a brigade—La Brigada, as it was henceforth known. In Miami the older group formed a united political front, the Frente, which would eventually replace Castro's government. As an effective apparatus the Frente was a sieve, but it couldn't reveal much about its young soldiers because it wasn't told much. Not that that would have mattered. Had Fidel been told the strength of the tiny force to be sent against him, he wouldn't have believed it. He assumed it must have about 20,000 men. As late as November 1960 the actual figure was 450, and it never exceeded 1,200. To deceive the enemy if prisoners were taken, serial numbers began with 2500. When one recruit died in training, the brigade took its name from his number, 2506. Its emblem was the figure 2506 superimposed on a cross. They wore this on their uniforms and on a battle flag.

Later, after the agents' cover had been blown, it turned out that the operation had been guided by orders from the highest levels in Washington. Day-by-day supervision was the responsibility of the CIA's director, Allen Dulles; overall planning came from what was called "the special group"—a high command of officials from the White House, the Department of State, the Joint Chiefs of Staff, and the CIA. President Eisenhower did not attend their meetings, but he knew of them, and when Castro rejected the administration's last attempt to reach an understanding on March 17, 1960, the President approved a recommendation that the Cuban exiles be trained for possible use against Castro.

Many of La Brigada's operational details might have been lifted from one of Ian Fleming's bizarre spy novels about James Bond, which were then coming into vogue. The American officers who supervised the training of the exiles were borrowed from the Army and Marine Corps more or less on an old boy basis; frequently decorated in World War II and Korea, they tended to be high in personal courage and low in good judgment. Selecting sites for the training seems to have been almost haphazard. At first one of the Cubans used CIA money given to him by Frank Bender to lease the resort island of Useppa in the Gulf of Mexico; the Cubans were comfortably billeted at the Useppa country club, and the golfers among them improved their strokes. Next a C-54 transport plane flew them to the U.S. Army jungle warfare training camp at Fort Gulick in the Panama Canal Zone. They weren't supposed to know where they were, but one of their CIA instructors left a Panama City newspaper around, and the canal itself was clearly visible from a hill in the camp.

After eight weeks of lessons in guerrilla warfare—skills which, they were told, they would teach to a Cuban liberation army—they were transferred again, this time to Guatemala. Here, too, it was intended that they would be kept ignorant of their location. Leaving Panama, they were given only the code name of their destination, "little farm." But they knew what it meant soon after the two buses carrying them left Guatemala's San José Airport. The level of trainee sophistication was high. Many of them had traveled widely. The cobblestone streets and dirty adobe buildings in the Indian villages bespoke Central America, and the profusion of signs of American influence—Coca-Cola and Pepsi-Cola signs along the highway, and the number of filling stations selling Texaco, Shell, American or Esso gasoline—could only mean Guatemala. Soon the buses began climbing through the tropical foliage of the surrounding mountains, the Sierra Madre ridge on the Pacific coast of Guatemala. They were on their way to a vast coffee plantation, a *finca* belonging to Roberto Alejos, the brother of the Guatemalan ambassador to Washington. Alejos had given CIA operatives permission to use part of it for training after Miguel Ydígoras, the president of Guatemala, had agreed to look the other way. (In a sordid epilogue to the operation, Ydígoras would insist that the United States had agreed to press his claim for territory in British Honduras; Washington would vehemently deny it.) The camp there was christened Base Trax. It was characteristic of the operation that it was in the least desirable part of the *finca*. The volcano Santiaguito, still active, could be seen from base headquarters, and the camp's soil was volcanic ash. In some places the ash was six feet deep. Rainfall turned it into a thin porridge. The rains that year were the heaviest in memory. Much of the time the Cubans wallowed around in slime.

At this point some of them began to wonder aloud about the CIA's omniscience. They were hooted down by the others. The majority's trust in their *yanqui* advisers was complete. Surely, they reasoned, the mighty conquerors of Nazi Germany and Imperial Japan *must* know what they were doing. They agreed that La Brigada's strength was slight, but Castro, after all, had started his 26th of July movement with only a dozen guerrillas. At that time the parallel between them and him could be justified; their CIA advisers were planning to divide them into small guerrilla bands, each of which would be trained to infiltrate one of Cuba's six provinces. They were to be ready to go before the American presidential election; the deadline was September 19. It might have worked. Even if it hadn't, the consequences would have been bearable. Defeated bushfighters can usually fade away; small stigma is attached to their failure. Castro would be hard put to prove that the United States was behind them, and they might return to fight another time.

In August the special group in Washington began to doubt the wisdom of establishing guerrilla forces in the new Cuba. Castro's troops were far more formidable than Batista's had been. State Department figures put them at about 400,000 troops and militiamen, ten times his strength. A long bushwhacker campaign directed from the Sierra Maestra no longer seemed feasible. Moreover, Castro's men had been superbly equipped by his new friends in Moscow and Peking; the State Department study estimated that they had sent him 28,000 tons of military supplies. On top of all this, the vigilance and disposition of his coast watchers and aircraft spotters indicated that he had profited from Batista's mistakes in that regard, so that supplying guerrilla forces by airdrops now would be exceedingly difficult.

If these reasons were sound—and events the following year were to prove that they were, eminently so—then it would seem that they ought to have discouraged *any* military expedition. Not so; the men directing the operation from Washington began weighing the advantages of an amphibious landing by the Brigada with tactical air support provided by Cubans in American warplanes. Ship-to-shore invasions had been very effective in Europe and the Pacific in World War II, it was pointed out, and MacArthur had ravaged the North Korean supply lines by landing the 1st Marine Division at Inchon. No one appears to have pointed out to the group that La Brigada was the size of an American infantry battalion, and that no major amphibious operation had been attempted with fewer than nine battalions backed by artillery, air supremacy, and an armada of warships—1,200 of them at Okinawa, World War II's last ship-to-shore attack.

Confident that the key to victory had been found, Washington abandoned plans for guerrilla activity, certain that once La Brigada had established a bridgehead all Cuba would flock to its standard. In a long cable to Base Trax, CIA headquarters in Langley, Virginia, ordered that the number of bushfighters be reduced to sixty; the agents in Guatemala were to "use conventional arms and training for everyone else." The Cubans took this to mean that once they were ashore an American army would land behind them, that being the only circumstance, they reasoned, which could justify the change. Their CIA advisers not only failed to correct them; "Frank Bender," the leader, told Pepe San Román and his fellow Cuban officers that they were "going to have protection by sea, by air, and even from under the sea." All the CIA operatives were enthusiastic about the new plan, and from that day forward they made it plain that they looked upon expression of doubt that it would succeed as a sign of weakness. Frank Bender came to believe that it superseded his loyalty to the President of the United States. He told Pepe San Román that powerful figures in Washington were trying to call off the invasion, and that it was conceivable that orders to that end might arrive from the White House. "If this happens," he said, "you come here and make some kind of show, as if you were putting us, the advisers, in prison, and you go ahead with the whole plan, even if we are your prisoners." To make sure that the amazed Cuban understood him, he became more specific. He explained that they would have to put an armed member of La Brigada at the door of each CIA adviser, cut communications with Washington, and go ahead with the invasion. He would tell them when and how to leave Base Trax for the staging area. He laughed and said, "In the end we will win."

Doubtless Frank's superiors in Washington knew nothing of this. Like everyone else who was involved, they couldn't piece together the whole picture until long afterward. To varying degrees it was a muddle to Dwight Eisenhower in the White House, Fidel Castro in Havana, Allen Dulles in Virginia, Frank Bender in Guatemala, the Joint Chiefs in the Pentagon, the Frente in Miami, and the brave men drilling on the coffee plantation beneath the Sierra Madre. Communication was faulty. The special group had neglected to tell Eisenhower of the switch from guerrilla tactics to plans for an amphibious landing. The Cubans in La Brigada continued to believe that they would constitute only the first wave of an invasion, and the Frente had understood the Americans to say that no attack would be mounted with fewer than five thousand men.

The CIA was trying to recruit as many fighters as possible. Wages were paid—$175 a month for a man, $50 for his wife, and $25 for each child. In this situation it was inevitable that security would be compromised. The word was out, and it was out everywhere. Castro was regularly predicting the imminent arrival of the "mercenaries," but his people didn't need him to tell them it was coming. The lowliest *guajiro* cutting sugar cane knew that counterrevolutionaries were on their way. Articles about La Brigada appeared in the city of Guatemala in *La Hora* and had been reprinted in most of the Spanish-language press, including some newspapers circulating in Cuba. Militiamen of the new Cuba slept with their rifles, and artillerymen beside their guns.

Americans could read accounts in English in the *Miami Herald* and the *New York Times,* though on the whole people in the United States were less interested than Cubans in the coming battle. They knew that something was going on down there, but they were distracted by other matters. It was not their country which was going to be invaded. They were likelier to be preoccupied by the dramatic struggle for the Democratic presidential nomination and the approaching climax to Eisenhower's White House years—the great Paris summit, to be followed by his tour of the Soviet Union. Advance parties of Secret Service men were already checking security arrangements in the Elysée Palace when, on May 1, sixteen days before the conference was to begin in France, a strange aircraft appeared high in the skies over Sverdlovsk, an industrial complex in the Ural Mountains some 1,200 miles inside Russia. Like the brigade in Guatemala, the flight was part of a CIA operation; the airplane had been built to CIA specifications by Lockheed. Its official designation was U-2. Presently the entire world would know it as "the spy plane."

Long and black, with a high tail, wide wings, and a single turbojet engine, the U-2 was piloted from a one-man cockpit. In the strict sense of the word, it was not a warplane. There were no guns. Instead it was equipped with sensitive infrared cameras aimed through seven portholes under the fuselage. They could photograph a strip of earth 125 miles wide and 3,000 miles long, producing prints in 4,000 paired frames. The detail was almost unbelievable. Photo interpreters studying huge enlargements could actually read a newspaper headline that had been nine or ten miles below the aircraft. Other instruments could test the air for evidence of secret nuclear tests and measure the efficiency of Russian radar. The U-2's protection was its height. Efficient cruising performance at very high altitudes had been achieved by careful aerodynamic and structural details; it was believed to be beyond the reach of Soviet radar. All in all it was the most sophisticated espionage device the world had ever seen. Its pilot that May Day was named Francis Gary Powers.

Powers was one of a new breed of soldiers of fortune. He flew, not for love of country, but for money. It was a job to him, and a good one; he was earning $30,000 a year as against an $8,400 combined income for him and his wife before he went to work for the CIA. That had been four years earlier, when he had been a twenty-seven-year-old Air Force first lieutenant. Beefy, thickset, and with a crew-cut, he looked like a professional football player—a defensive tackle, perhaps, with diligence and reliability, but little imagination.

He was not stupid, however. Earlier in the year he had asked an intelligence officer, "What if something happens and one of us goes down over Russia? That's an awfully big country and it could be a hell of a long walk to a border. Is there anyone there we can contact? Can you give us any names and addresses?" According to Powers this was the first time the question had been asked, despite the fact that Operation Overflight, as it was called, was about to enter its fifth year. The reply was "No, we can't." He persisted: "All right, say the worst happens. A plane goes down and the pilot is captured. What story does he use? Exactly how much should he tell?" It is Powers's recollection—and no one has corrected him—that the intelligence officer's exact words were: "You may as well tell them everything because they're going to get it out of you anyway."

The lack of a well-rehearsed cover story is by no means the least credible aspect of the affair. Sherman Adams had been in the White House when Operation Overflight began in 1956, and he knew that none of the flights were made without the President's approval. Visiting Eisenhower after the Powers debacle, he asked him about it. "You're right," Ike said. "I made the decision, just as I have known about and personally approved every one of those flights. When they brought me the plan for this particular flight over Russia, I approved it as one among several within an intelligence policy already adopted. I had no thought of it having any possible bearing upon the summit meeting or on my forthcoming trip to Moscow.

Except for unforeseen circumstances, it would not have had any."

Doubtless Eisenhower believed that, but it is untrue. The circumstances were foreseeable, or, at any rate, sufficiently within the range of possibilities to be weighed carefully. Powers's last trip was not routine. It was the first of two overflights after a long period without any, and it was the first attempt to cross the entire Soviet Union. From an American base in Peshawar, Pakistan, Powers was to fly 3,800 miles to Bodo, Norway. Taking off from one country and landing in another required two ground crews. That, too, was unprecedented. It was judged to be worth chancing because, by going deeper into Russia than ever before, the U-2 would pass over important targets never before photographed.

There was considerable speculation among the U-2 pilots over the timing of the mission. One theory was that the Russians were on the verge of a missile guidance breakthrough and that the CIA was trying to crowd in as many targets as possible beforehand. Another was that Eisenhower wanted the latest available data before sitting down with Khrushchev, and still another that an approaching detente with the Russians would make any covert operations unwise in the future. The fliers were well aware that they were part of a shady business. The suspicion had been growing among them that Soviet radar had been developed to the point where it was possible to track them. The possibilities of mechanical failure were also discussed. "One loose screw, in just the right place," as Powers put it, "could bring an aircraft down." In fact, this had happened. A U-2 had crash-landed near Tokyo the previous autumn. A Japanese journalist had inspected it, concluded that its mission was espionage, and reported that finding at length in the next issue of his magazine.

The designers of the plane had known it would run unusual risks, and they had equipped it with timed destruction mechanisms. Later the "granger," a device designed to throw off radar, had been installed as a further precaution. Despite the intelligence officer's rather casual answer to Powers's question about contingency planning, some thought had been given to forced landings. Colonel William M. Shelton, the Air Force officer commanding the Operation Overflight unit, told Powers that if he found he was running low on fuel over the Soviet city of Landalaksha, in the Murmansk region, he could take a shortcut to alternate landing fields in Finland

and Sweden. He added, "Any place is preferable to going down in the Soviet Union."

The CIA had even considered the advantages of suicide for a downed pilot. Apparently the agency hadn't been able to make up its mind. The decision had been left with the fliers themselves. Cyanide tablets were available for those who wished them, and later they were shown a small device that looked like a good-luck charm. It was a silver dollar with a metal loop that permitted it to be fastened to a key chain or a chain around the neck. The loop unscrewed. Inside there was a straight pin, which in turn was a sheath that could be removed to expose a thin needle. Toward the end of the needle were tiny grooves. In the grooves was a sticky brown substance—curare, one prick of which brought instant death. Most of the pilots, including Powers, had decided against carrying either cyanide or curare, but when Colonel Shelton asked him during preparations for his last flight, "Do you want the silver dollar?" he changed his mind. He thought the deadly needle might make an effective weapon. "O.K.," he said, and slipped it into the pocket of his outer flight suit. He also carried a shaving kit, civilian clothes, a half-smoked packet of filter cigarettes, pictures of his wife, some German marks, Turkish liras, and Russian rubles; some gold coins, watches, and rings (to be used for bribery or barter if in need of help); about a hundred dollars in U.S. currency, some U.S. postage stamps, a Defense Department I.D. card, a NASA certificate, instrument rating cards, U.S. and international driver's licenses, a Selective Service card, a social security card, and an American flag poster that had "I am an American" printed on it in fourteen languages, including Russian. Long afterward Powers recalled that when he got into trouble he was asked whether he was an American. "It seemed," he said, "pointless to deny it."

The CIA facilities in Pakistan were surprisingly primitive; the airmen slept on folding cots and cooked their own food from rations. But they weren't there much. Most of the time they played poker and loafed at the U.S. Air Force base near Adana, Turkey. (A favorite topic in bull sessions was the coming summit meeting and how it could dispel world tension.) By March of 1960 they were champing at the bit. The number of flights had been drastically reduced now for nearly two years, and the fewer there were, the more apprehensive they became over the next one. Then, after a long pause, the two 1960 flights had been scheduled for April. Powers was the backup pilot for the first, April 9. It went smoothly. The second was to be his.

Things started to go wrong when, on arriving in Pakistan, he was told that the U-2 which had been reserved for this flight—it was the best they had—would be unavailable, having been grounded for a maintenance check. In its place he would fly a substitute, U-2 No. 360. This was bad news; No. 360 was a lemon; a "dog," they called it. There was always something going wrong with it. Its most recent malfunction was in the fuel tanks. Sometimes they wouldn't feed fuel to the engine. Colonel Shelton had them in mind when he authorized Powers to land in Finland or Sweden if necessary.

If the tanks behaved, and everything else went well, Powers's course would resemble a huge zigzag. Taking off from Peshawar, he would cross Afghanistan and the Hindu Kush, an extension of the Himalayas, and enter the Soviet Union near Stalinabad. Then he would pass over the Aral Sea, the Tyuratam Cosmodrome, Chelyabinsk, Sverdlovsk, Kirov, Archangel, Kandalaksha and Murmansk on the Kola peninsula; after Russia would come the Barents Sea and the northern coast of Norway to Bodo—some of the bleakest land in the world. The flight would take about nine hours. Three-fourths of it, 2,900 miles, would be inside the USSR. After the take-off he would break radio contact with the Mobile Control Officer. The rest of the trip would be made in complete silence. It was, Powers said, "a lonely feeling."

For three agonizing days it seemed that the flight would never get off the ground. Washington was hemming and hawing over last-minute instructions. Thursday, April 28, was fixed as the departure date when Colonel Shelton, Powers, and eighteen other specialists and crew members flew down to Peshawar from Turkey. Powers went to bed at 4 P.M. Wednesday. At 2 A.M. Thursday he was awakened and told that the takeoff had been postponed twenty-four hours. The next night was the same. This time he was up and "on the house"—breathing oxygen—when word came of another twenty-four-hour wait. Saturday there was a third twenty-four-hour delay. Somebody at 1600 Pennsylvania Avenue couldn't make up his mind.

At last, at 5:30 A.M. Sunday, May 1, Powers climbed into the plane for the preflight check. There the delay continued. The scheduled departure time was 6 A.M. It came and went without the signal to go. The cockpit was fiercely hot; his long underwear was drenched with perspiration when Colonel Shelton came out to explain. They were awaiting final approval from the White House. This had never happened before. Presidential approval had always come through before the pilot was locked in his seat and ready to go. The wait lasted twenty excruciating minutes. Then Powers was given the green light. He roared off and, once up, completed his flight log entries: the aircraft number, 360; the sortie number, 4154, and the time. It was 6:26 A.M. local time, 1:26 Greenwich mean time, and 8:26 P.M. in Washington. In Moscow it was 3:26 A.M.

Crossing into Russia the cloud cover was solid. That didn't matter here; the CIA wasn't interested in this area. The sky cleared over the Aral Sea, and glancing down he glimpsed the condensation trail of another single-engine jet plane, moving parallel to his course but in the opposite direction. Shortly afterward he saw another contrail, this one moving in the opposite direction. Probably it was the same machine. He assumed that Soviet spotters had spotted him on their radar screens and were sending up scouts. He wasn't worried. The trails were so far below him that the Russian pilot couldn't possibly see him.

Some thirty miles to the east he passed over the Tyuratam Cosmodrome, Russia's Cape Canaveral, and looked down on the pads from which the Soviet sputniks and ICBM's had been launched. He flipped switches, turning on the cameras. The cloud cover thickened again; he switched them off. Fifty miles south of Chelyabinsk the skies cleared, giving him a good view of the snow-topped Ural mountain range, once considered the dividing line between Asia and Europe, and at that point the aircraft started giving him trouble. The autopilot had gone haywire; the U-2 was pitching nose-up. He turned the autopilot off, drove the plane manually for a while, and turned the autopilot on again. Again it pitched. He considered turning back to Pakistan—in an abort situation the decision was up to the pilot—but he had already crossed 1,300 miles of Russia and the visibility ahead was excellent. He decided to continue, flying manually. Passing over an enormous oil storage area and an industrial complex, he zigged toward Sverdlovsk, the Soviet Ruhr. There, at an altitude of 65,000 feet, he made a 90-degree turn for a zag northward. He was making log entries of the altitude, time, speed, exhaust-gas temperature and engine instrument readings when he felt a dull thud. The plane bucked forward, and a blinding flash of orange light flooded the cockpit.

It was about a half-hour after midnight in the White House. In the Kremlin it was 7:30 A.M. Powers thought: "My God, I've had it now!"

Out of control, the machine started to go down. He reached for the destruction switches and changed his mind; he wanted to get into position to use the ejection seat first. He couldn't quite make it. The metal canopy rail was pinning his legs. Ejecting in this position, he would lose both legs, each severed about three inches above the knee. He was down to 34,000 feet and losing altitude fast. Fleetingly he thought of the destruction switches again, but first he wanted to release his seat belt. He did, and the force of gravity pulled him halfway out of the plane. Now the oxygen hoses were holding him back. He had forgotten to unfasten them. Near panic, he kicked and squirmed away from them. He floated free and was thinking about pulling the parachute ripcord when he felt a tremendous jerk. At 15,000 feet it had opened automatically. Suddenly his plane passed him; it was intact, and hurling downward. He thought of the silver dollar. Unscrewing the loop of it, he slipped out the suicide needle and considered pricking himself. Then he dropped it into his pocket. He wanted to live.

That was on a Sunday. The following Thursday Nikita Khrushchev addressed the Supreme Soviet for three and a half hours. His remarks on the U-2, coming at the end, set off two weeks of pandemonium.

	USSR	U.S. AND ALLIES
MAY 5	Khrushchev says: "I am duty bound to report to you on the aggressive acts . . . by the United States of America." Announces Russian gunners have shot down a U.S. aircraft over Soviet territory but does not say where. Charges that the mission of the operation was "one of aggressive provocation aimed at wrecking the summit conference." Is careful to exonerate Eisenhower of blame.	U.S. Aeronautics and Space Administration reports that a weather observation plane is missing over Turkey after pilot reported oxygen trouble. NASA says the pilot may have strayed over the Russo-Turkish border.

	USSR	U.S. AND ALLIES
MAY 6		Lincoln White, State Department spokesman: "There was absolutely no—N-O—deliberate intention to violate the Soviet air space, and there has never been." NASA identifies the "weather" pilot as Francis G. Powers. This is what Khrushchev has been waiting for.
MAY 7	Khrushchev tells the Supreme Soviet that Powers has been captured "alive and kicking," that a Russian rocket brought the U-2 down from an altitude of 65,000 feet, and that at that time the plane was 1,300 miles from the Soviet-Afghan border. Powers, he says, has made a complete confession.	State Department admits it lied yesterday. Says these "surveillance" flights date from Soviet rejection of Ike's "open skies" proposal at Geneva in 1955.
MAY 8		Consternation among allies over timing of flights, the fact that U.S. has been caught in lie, and the implication that the President has been unaware of something so important.
MAY 9	Khrushchev warns that Soviet rockets will attack countries that allow U.S. spy planes to use their territory.	Secretary of State Herter says Ike approved the program but specific flights are not subject to presidential approval. U-2 flights will continue.
MAY 10	Soviet formally protests U-2 operation and states that Powers will be tried.	
MAY 11		President Eisenhower assumes personal responsibility for the U-2 flights.

	USSR	U.S. AND ALLIES
	Speaking at a display of the U-2 wreckage, Khrushchev says, "The Russian people would say I was mad to welcome a man who sends spy planes over here."	
MAY 12		Eisenhower tells congressmen that he still plans to fly to Moscow unless the invitation is withdrawn.
MAY 14	Hopes that the summit can be retrieved rise when Khrushchev, arriving in Paris, pledges himself to work for its success.	
MAY 15	Khrushchev says he will not participate in the summit talks unless U.S. ends all U-2 flights, apologizes for past "aggressions," and punishes those responsible for the flights.	Eisenhower says the flights have been suspended and will not be resumed.
MAY 16	*Khrushchev, Eisenhower, President de Gaulle, and Harold Macmillan meet in Elysée Palace in Paris for the opening session of the conference. The atmosphere is frigid.*	
	Khrushchev takes the floor. He is curt and rude. He suggests that the summit be postponed for six months, accuses Ike of "treachery" and "bandit" acts, and cancels the invitation for the reciprocal Eisenhower visit to Russia.	Ike, grim, says that the overflights are over, but that Khrushchev's "ultimatum" is unacceptable to the U.S.

	USSR	U.S. AND ALLIES
	Khrushchev stalks from the palace, leaving behind the shambles of Ike's hopes for a detente and world conciliation.	Eisenhower returns to the U.S. embassy in Paris shaking with rage.
MAY 17	Khrushchev boycotts the meeting. One of his aides telephones the Elysée Palace to ask whether Ike is ready to apologize for the U-2 and punish those responsible.	De Gaulle and Macmillan make last-ditch efforts to save the conference. At 3 P.M. Eisenhower, de Gaulle, and Macmillan meet for the conference's first business session. Eisenhower: no apologies, no punishment.
	5 P.M.: *The summit ends.*	
MAY 18	In a chaotic press conference attended by 3,000 people, Khrushchev denounces the U.S. as "thief-like," "piratical," and "cowardly." The Soviet Union will now solve the Berlin problem by signing a separate treaty with Communist East Germany.	
MAY 25		General Thomas D. White, the U.S. Air Force chief of staff, says that the U-2 gamble was needless and that had he known about it he would have recommended suspension of the overflights before the summit.

On the way home Eisenhower landed in Lisbon; he had chosen this peculiar time to honor Antonio de Oliveira Salazar, Portugal's septuagenarian dictator. While strolling through the formal gardens of Queloz Palace he came upon an American reporter who was idly tossing French coins into a fountain. Wearily the President asked, "That how you're keeping busy?"

"No, sir," said the reporter. "This is just for luck."

Turning away, Eisenhower said, "Then you'd better throw some in for all of us."

But the President was not rid of the U-2 jinx. Japan, America's strongest Asian ally, was to be the last destination in his odyssey of personal diplomacy. Had the summit gone well, it would have been a triumphal tour. Now it became a desperate opportunity to patch up presidental prestige. Even that was denied him. Japan was known to be the Asian base for U-2 overflights. Three of the now notorious spy planes were there, and Japanese leftists, taking their cue from Khrushchev, made them an excuse for rioting. On June 11 Jim Hagerty landed at Tokyo's Haneda Airport to make arrangements for the visit. Like Nixon in Caracas, he was lucky to escape with his life. For over an hour a mob of twenty thousand kept him and Ambassador Douglas MacArthur II imprisoned in their automobile. They had to be rescued by a marine helicopter.

Eisenhower was in Manila when the Japanese cabinet, meeting in emergency session, asked him to stay away for the sake of his own safety. Humiliated, he went to Formosa instead, convoyed by 125 warships and 500 aircraft of the Seventh Fleet. The ships raced through the water at speeds exceeding thirty knots, not because they didn't want to keep Chiang Kai-shek waiting but as a precaution against unfriendly submarines. On the Chinese mainland Radio Peking was denouncing the President as a "god of plague." To give him some idea of how they felt, they battered the offshore island of Quemoy with its heaviest shelling in years. It could be heard abroad his Seventh Fleet armada. Wry correspondents said that he was the only chief of staff ever to get an eighty-thousand-gun salute.

When Eisenhower landed back in Washington on June 27, his travels were over. In eighteen months he had covered 60,000 miles in pursuit of peace, and he had come home empty-handed. Surveying the wreckage and looking for the cause, he said wanly, "After all, Communists will act like Communists." Emmet John Hughes wrote sorrowfully:

> All the gleam of political promise in his fantastic global journeys now was gone beyond recapturing. He had given unstintingly of his energy and his personality. He had been repaid in popular coin—the voices of millions yelling lusty ovations, the hands of millions waving gaudy banners. He had invested all this amassed political capital in the two great chances—one in Paris, one in Tokyo. Now it was spent—all of it.

The cold war was closing in again on all fronts. Travel to the Soviet Union became difficult. There were incidents at Checkpoint Charlie in Berlin. After the summit debris had been swept away, a ten-nation East-West disarmament conference, which had been going well all spring, resumed in Geneva; it, too, collapsed when Valerian A. Zorin, the chief Soviet delegate, denounced the West for ninety minutes and walked out. In July the Russians shot down an American RB-47 reconnaissance plane over international waters and vetoed a United States-sponsored U.N. resolution calling for an impartial investigation of it.

Then, in August, during the lull after the Democratic and Republican national conventions in the United States, Americans relived the mortification of the U-2 when Francis Gary Powers was convicted of espionage in Moscow. Powers had landed on a large state farm. Taking his pistol away from him, the farmers had held him at gunpoint until officers of the KGB—the Committee for State Security, the secret police—arrived to take him into custody. He told the Soviet court that he understood that the summit conference and Eisenhower's planned visit to the USSR had been called off because of his flight and that it had increased world tension. "I am sincerely sorry that I had anything to do with this," he said. He was sentenced to ten years in prison.*

During his last months in office the President became reflective. Government spending by his administration made Franklin Roosevelt's pump priming seem puny—the total cost of government, including state and local expenditures, was now 170 billion dollars, almost one-third of the Gross National Product—and he was chagrined by his party's failure to convert young independent voters who had supported him into Republicans. "What happened," he asked Sherman Adams when his former assistant returned to 1600 Pennsylvania Avenue for a visit, "to all those fine young people who sailed balloons and rang doorbells for us in 1952?"

He had one final word for his constituents, and he gave it the following January, three days before he left the White House. During the 1950s the Pentagon, and especially the Air Force, had fostered a growing band of corporations whose leaders were retired generals and admirals. Eisenhower warned of the dangers in this.

* After seventeen months the Russians exchanged him for Colonel Rudolf Abel, a Soviet spy who had been convicted in an American court. Lockheed gave Powers a job as a test pilot until 1970, when he was laid off.

In his farewell radio and television address to the American people he observed that "Disarmament, with mutual honor and confidence, is a continuing imperative. Because this need is sharp and apparent, I confess I lay down my official responsibilities in this field with a definite sense of disappointment." He continued, "I wish I could say tonight that a lasting peace is in sight. Happily, I can say that war has been avoided." He spoke of the prodigious growth of companies manufacturing munitions. Then:

"This conjunction of an immense military establishment and a large arms industry is new in the American experience. . . . We recognize the imperative need for this development. Yet we must not fail to comprehend its grave implications. . . . In the councils of government we must guard against the acquisition of unwarranted influence, whether sought or unsought, by the military-industrial complex. The potential for the disastrous rise of misplaced power exists and will persist."

It was a remarkable speech, but forces favoring an arms race between the United States and the Soviet Union were too strong. Despite their many differences they were, in essence, the world's two largest industrial nations. By 1966 the size of the American military-industrial complex, and its dependence on congressional appropriations, would become staggering. In that year Boeing and General Dynamics sold 65 percent of their output to the government; Raytheon sold 70 percent, Lockheed sold 81 percent, and Republic Aviation sold 100 percent. As Galbraith admonished readers of *The New Industrial State* six years later, a company developing a new generation of fighter aircraft, to cite but one example, was "in an admirable position to influence the design and equipment of the plane. It can have something to say on the mission for which it is adapted, the number of planes required, their deployment, and, by implication, on the choice of the enemy toward which it is directed."

The presidential election of 1960 shaped up as a classic duel. Both nominees were from the swing generation and had been young naval officers in World War II, each had entered public life in the months after World War II, and both were now vigorous men in their forties. Richard Nixon believed at the outset, in January 1960, that the coming race would be the closest presidential election in America up to that time. It was; but that was just about the only prediction about it which proved correct.

The United States was not the same country that Dwight D. Eisenhower and Adlai E. Stevenson had stumped in 1952, and it was even less like the country that had gone to war in Korea two years before that. By 1960 the wave of migrants to the new suburbia was at floodtide. The nation was richer. Washington, the new census revealed, had become the first American city with a black majority—54 percent as against 35 percent in 1950. By 1960 40 million American families, or 88 percent of them, owned at least one television set. Fully aware of the hundred million viewers, the two candidates were pondering ways to beguile them. Afterward it was widely believed that the tube helped Kennedy most. Marshall McLuhan thought he knew why. Kennedy, he said, had projected the image of a "shy young sheriff" in a TV western, while Nixon resembled "the railway lawyer who signs leases that are not in the best interests of the folks in the little town." What McLuhan overlooked was that as Americans became more prosperous they were increasingly conservative; more of them were investing in the railway, and were therefore on the lawyer's, not the sheriff's, side.

Each candidate followed a strategic plan. Kennedy appealed to the young, to the blue-collar vote, and to the liberal constituency which Roosevelt had drawn into the Democratic party in the 1930s. The two great Kennedy bases were the Democratic South—holding it was to be the task of his running mate—and the industrial northeast. His campaign would be largely directed at nine big states: Massachusetts, California, New York, Texas, New Jersey, Illinois, Ohio, Michigan, and Pennsylvania. If they could be carried, they would give him 237 of the 269 electoral votes he needed to be elected. His techniques included the mass registration of seven million unregistered voters—seven of every ten new registrants now were Democrats—the articulation of ideas from an Ivy League brain trust—Schlesinger, Galbraith, et cetera—and the brilliant tactics of his young Irish-Americans from Massachusetts, led by Lawrence F. O'Brien and Kenneth O'Donnell.

Kennedy's built-in advantages were support from organized labor, his father's great wealth, his Pulitzer Prize, a friendly press corps, his charisma—reporters were beginning to call it the Kennedy "style"—and his membership in the majority party.

His disadvantages were long memories of his father's support of appeasement twenty years earlier, his youth—forty-three to Nixon's forty-seven—his inexperience, and the widely held conviction, dating from Al Smith's candidacy in 1928, that a Roman Catholic could not be elected President.

Kennedy meant to run as hard as he could as far as he could as long as he could. Nixon took a different tack. He believed that a political campaign had high tides and low tides, and that to ignore them was to risk boring, and therefore alienating, the electorate. The object, in his view, was to "peak" a campaign—to bring it to a climax—on election day. Like Kennedy, Nixon planned to zero in on key states, seven of them in his case: New York, California, Michigan, Texas, Pennsylvania, Ohio, and Illinois. He also promised to campaign in each of the other forty-three states—a pledge he later regretted. He had no brain trust; now, as always, Nixon was a loner, a solitary, brooding introvert. While the theme of Kennedy's drive was that American prestige was slipping and that Americans must move ahead, the Republican nominee preached the virtues of free enterprise, individual responsibility, hard-nose anti-Communism, and Eisenhower peace with prosperity.

Nixon's built-in advantages were support from big businessmen, his greater experience (for example, in the steel strike settlement during the President's illness, and in his kitchen debate with Khrushchev), his strong middle-class roots, and Eisenhower's occupancy of the White House.

His disadvantages were recollections of Hoover in the White House, still vivid in the minds of older voters; his reputation as a dirty fighter—the "old Nixon"—the bad luck which was to plague him throughout this campaign, and his membership in the minority party.

Each year there were fewer Republicans in the United States. GOP candidates had won 49 percent of the votes cast in the off-year elections of 1950. In 1954 the figure was 47 percent; in 1958, 43 percent. A Gallup poll published in 1960 traced the decline of Republican loyalties in various occupational groups over the past eight years. Asked which party "best served" their interests, 28 percent of the farmers had said the Republicans in 1950. In 1960 only 18 percent said so. Among white-collar workers the drop had been even sharper, from 44 to 29 percent. Everybody liked Ike in the White House, but that affection wasn't transferable to Republicans playing supporting roles, and the rate of attrition among the party's lesser figures was alarming.

Eisenhower's effect on the 1960 race was further blurred by his equivocal feelings about his Vice President. He clearly preferred him to Kennedy, whom he regarded as a young upstart ("that boy," he called him), but he had told too many people that "Dick just isn't presidential timber"; the word was out. Eisenhower's insensitivity in this regard was puzzling. He slighted Nixon again and again. Discussing possible successors in his second term, he came down hard in favor of his last Secretary of the Treasury, Robert Anderson —"Boy, I'd like to fight for him in 1960!" Making a mental list, he added "some good new other fellows," including Attorney General William Rogers. He loyally included Sherman Adams, "although he'll be sixty-one in 1960, and that's pretty old for this job." Only at the end did he say, ". . . and Dick Nixon." On August 24, 1960, Eisenhower dealt Nixon the worst blow in the campaign. He was asked in a press conference, "What major decisions of your administration has the Vice President participated in?" The President's almost unbelievable reply was, "If you give me a week, I might think of one." Nixon wrote in *Six Crises* that Eisenhower had telephoned to apologize, saying that he had merely meant to be "facetious." The justification is odd, and he never offered any public explanation.

In a trial heat taken by Gallup after the 1958 off-year election, the voters chose Kennedy over Nixon, 59 to 41 percent. Just before the Vice President's visit to Moscow in July 1959, it was Kennedy 61 to Nixon 39—a greater margin than Eisenhower over Stevenson in 1956. After that trip the figures were Kennedy 52 to Nixon 48. In November 1959 Nixon moved ahead for the first time, 53 to 47. On the eve of the first presidential primary on March 8 that six-point margin held steady.

Between New Hampshire and the Democratic national convention in Los Angeles four months later, Kennedy captured the Democratic nomination by proving himself unbeatable. Other Democrats who had pursued it were Hubert Humphrey, Lyndon Johnson, Stuart Symington and—his last hurrah—Adlai Stevenson. Humphrey had led the challengers in the primaries. Kennedy bent Humphrey's lance in Wisconsin on April 5, taking 56 percent of the vote, and then destroyed him in supposedly anti-Catholic West Virginia on May 10, outpolling him three to two. At that point Humphrey quit; he had run out of money. Then the Kennedy bandwagon picked up momentum, winning in Maryland, in Indiana, and Oregon. By June 27, when Kennedy addressed the Montana legislature, in search of support, he had 550 of the 761 delegate votes needed for the nomination.

On the eve of the Democratic convention, Gallup had him leading Nixon 52 percent to 48 percent.

When he moved into his Los Angeles command post, suite 8315 of the Biltmore Hotel, the young Irish-American senator from Massachusetts had 600 delegate votes. Like all Democratic conventions, this one was boisterous, and rich in political talent. Chicago's retiring boss, Jake Arvey, was there with his successor, Dick Daley, and the most eloquent speech was that of Senator Eugene McCarthy, nominating Stevenson. Eleanor Roosevelt was for Stevenson; so was Marian Schlesinger. (Bob Kennedy scrawled a note to her husband: "Can't you control your wife—or are you like me?") The Stevenson people were well organized. They had packed the galleries, and their placard carriers were numerous on the convention floor; included among them was one whose sign delighted her candidate: an enormously pregnant woman, she carried a placard reading, STEVENSON IS THE MAN.

The Stevenson movement was exciting, at times it was even gallant, but it altered nothing. John F. Kennedy was nominated on the first ballot with 806 votes; Wisconsin's 15 had put him over the top. He chose Lyndon Johnson for the bottom of the ticket—no two men who were there can agree exactly how it was done, but Kennedy knew he needed November support in the South, and Johnson was the man likeliest to give it to him. In his acceptance speech Kennedy spoke of "a New Frontier—the frontier of the 1960s—a frontier of unknown opportunities and perils—a frontier of unfulfilled hopes and threats." He warned, "the New Frontier of which I speak is not a set of promises—it is a set of challenges. It sums up, not what I intend to offer the American people, but what I intend to ask of them." At the end he said, "Now begins another long journey, taking me into your cities and homes all over America. Give me your help"—the crowds cheered—"give me your hand"—they cheered again—"your voice and your vote"; they gave him a standing ovation, cheering on and on.

Gallup figures after the Democratic convention showed Kennedy leading 55 to 45.

After Nixon's nomination at the Republican national convention the following week, he took the lead in Gallup's report, 51 to Kennedy's 49. The week after that he lengthened the lead, 53 to 47. Late in August the two were running neck and neck. In September the number of undecided voters pushed both candidates below the 50 percent mark, but Nixon remained in front, 49 to Kennedy's 46.

This was the low point in the Democratic campaign. Lyndon Johnson, convinced that he would be the party's nominee, had scheduled a special session of Congress in which he expected to shine. Kennedy was now trapped in it while Nixon jubilantly opened his first tour in Atlanta on August 26. Six days later the special session ended and Kennedy took off for Maine. Gallup's new figures were Nixon 50, Kennedy 50.

Luck now intervened. On the third day of his southern trip Nixon struck his right kneecap on an automobile door in Greensboro, North Carolina. The injury did not heal. At Walter Reed Hospital he was told that it had become infected with hemolytic *Staphylococcus aureus*. Unless he remained at Walter Reed for two weeks of intensive antibiotic treatment, he was told, the cartilage of the joint would be destroyed. Thus he lay on his back from August 29 to September 9 with his leg in traction, wretched at the thought of the lost time. Back in action, he caught cold in St. Louis. His voice grew hoarse. To compound his misery, the religious issue emerged at this time under the worst possible circumstances for him.

Nixon had repeatedly instructed his staff not to discuss Kennedy's religion with anyone, under any circumstances. Unfortunately he could not control Dr. Norman Vincent Peale, the best-known Protestant clergyman in the country and a Nixon friend. Dr. Peale led a group of ministers issuing a statement expressing doubt that a Roman Catholic President could free himself from the influence of the church hierarchy in Rome. Nixon couldn't attack Dr. Peale, though he came close to it on that Sunday's *Meet the Press* program. Kennedy, meanwhile, had seized the chance to deal with this most delicate of issues, one that he had known he must confront sooner or later. The Greater Houston Ministerial Association had just invited him to discuss his faith on September 12 in Houston's Rice Hotel. He accepted. With dignity and lucidity he told them that he firmly believed in the complete separation of church and state, and that if he could not solve a conflict between his conscience and his office, he would resign. They applauded.

Two weeks later Gallup announced that voter preferences were again narrowing. The figures were Nixon 47 and Kennedy 46, with 7 percent undecided.

The race was approaching the critical period. In two September weeks both candidates stumped the country from coast to coast. Nixon had now traveled fifteen thousand miles in twenty-five states, addressing crowds exceeding two million voters, but he realized, as he later put it, that "no matter how big the crowds or how extensive the local coverage, it was a drop in the bucket: the effect up to September 25 would be infinitesimal compared with the first joint debate for all-network coverage the next evening, Monday, September 26."

There were to be four debates—the others were on October 7, October 14 and October 21—but the first one was the most important. It drew the largest audience, some seventy million Americans, twenty million more than the others, and it was a Kennedy triumph. That was dismaying for Nixon, and it came as a surprise. He was a skillful debater. Watching Kennedy's acceptance speech on television—unaware that Kennedy was exhausted—he had thought that his rival spoke too rapidly, that his voice was too high-pitched, and that his concepts were too complicated for the average American. That was why Nixon had accepted the challenge of the debates. Both men had crammed for the first debate as though they were boning up for a bar exam. In words and ideas it was a standoff. But that in itself was a victory for Kennedy. Until that evening Nixon had been the more famous of the two, holding as he did the higher office. But here they stood toe to toe with Howard K. Smith as referee, and Kennedy held his own. More important, he *looked* better. Those who heard them on radio thought both did well, but the larger television audience saw the senator as tanned and fit. Nixon, on the other hand, had lost five pounds in Walter Reed. He was haggard, and he wore a shirt collar a half size too large for him. He slouched, his expression was grim, and his complexion was pasty, a consequence of ill-advisedly coating his face with Lazy Shave, a pancake make-up meant to hide afternoon beard growth.

Gallup's new poll showed that Kennedy had moved ahead 49 to 46; 5 percent were undecided.

Drinking four chocolate milk shakes a day on his doctor's instructions, Nixon regained his lost weight. In subsequent debates he looked as fit as his rival. He scored more debating points, too. It was all to no avail; millions had seen all they wanted, and their minds were made up.

After the last debate, and before Nixon's last-minute surge, Gallup's findings were Kennedy 51, Nixon 45; 4 percent were undecided.

Two key incidents affected the Negro vote as the campaign approached the home stretch. Speaking in Harlem on October 12, Lodge, without consulting anyone, said: ". . . there ought to be a Negro in the Cabinet . . . It is part of our program and is offered as a pledge." Nixon angrily denied that it was part of any program of his—which unfairly but inevitably offended blacks. A week later, on October 19, a Martin Luther King sit-in once more collided with Georgia law. Arrested in an Atlanta department store for refusing to leave the store restaurant, King was sentenced to four months at hard labor. When reporters asked Nixon for an opinion, he answered that he had none. Privately he thought that King's constitutional rights had been violated, and he called Attorney General Rogers to ask for a Justice Department inquiry. Rogers agreed, but Eisenhower wanted no part of it and the matter was dropped. The Kennedys had reacted differently. The Democratic candidate put through a person-to-person call to Coretta King telling her of his sympathy and his desire to help in any way he could. Next he conferred with his brother. Bob phoned the Georgia judge who had sentenced King, and on the following day the black clergyman was out on bail. At the time the press was unaware of all this, but Mrs. King told other black leaders about it. They spread the word, which undoubtedly contributed to the tremendous majorities Kennedy rolled up in northern cities on November 8. One of the voters who switched was Martin Luther King's father. He told reporters that he never thought he could cast his ballot for a Catholic, but a call from his daughter-in-law had won him over. Kennedy murmured, "Imagine Martin Luther King having a bigot for a father." Then he added, "Well, we all have fathers, don't we?"

In the last days of October Gallup concluded that the race was too close for prediction. The Elmo Roper, Lou Harris, and Claude Robinson polls agreed, and Lawrence O'Brien told Kennedy that it was "a toss-up." It wasn't a dead heat all the way, though. Political writers and politicians on both sides agree that two trends counterbalanced in October. A decided shift toward Kennedy two weeks before the election was followed by a last-minute surge to Nixon. Nixon subsequently took this to be confirmation that Kennedy had "peaked" too early, but there is another interpretation. The switch in momentum accompanied President Eisenhower's entry into the campaign. Neither the U-2 nor the Japanese humiliation had diminished Ike's tremendous popularity in the country, but Nixon's relationship with him had continued to be difficult, which explains the Vice President's failure to ask for his help until Monday, October 21. The President plunged in then and turned the campaign around. Conceivably another week or even a few more days could have reversed the result.

Toward the end the election seemed to blur into a montage of sights and sounds: Kennedy reminding audiences in his cool clipped accents that Castro had put Communists "eight jet minutes from Florida," Nixon saying that America could not afford to use the White House "as a training ground for a man who wants to learn how to be President, at the expense of the United States of America," Kennedy repeating over and over, almost as an incantation, "This is a great country. But I think it can be greater. I think we can do better. I think we can make this country move again," Truman's profanity and Nixon's response, vowing never to sully the Presidency by using blasphemy while in the White House, Eisenhower reciting Republican accomplishments in the last eight years: a 48 percent increase in personal income, a 45 percent growth in the Gross National Product, the expansion of social security, the St. Lawrence Seaway, 41,000 miles of interstate highways—"My friends, never have Americans achieved so much in so short a time"—the teen-age girl "jumpers" in motorcade crowds, bobbing up for a glimpse of the candidate, the Vice President promising that a Nixon administration would never allow Red China into the U.N., thus giving "respectability to the Communist regime which would immensely increase its power and prestige in Asia, and probably irreparably weaken the non-Communist governments in that area," the enthusiasm on college campuses when Kennedy spoke of the years ahead, "the challenging, revolutionary Sixties," Nixon favoring a resumption of atom bomb tests, Kennedy's calloused hand bursting with blood near the end when a Pennsylvania admirer squeezed it too hard, Nixon charging that Kennedy, by declaring that American prestige was at an all-time low, was "running America down and giving us an inferiority complex," the smiles of the women whenever Kennedy mentioned his pregnant wife, and Nixon urging audiences: "Vote for the man you think America and the world needs in this critical period. Whatever that decision is, it is the one that I know will be best for America. It is one that we will all abide by; one that we will all support."

Abruptly it was over. Bright weather and the closeness of the contest brought forth the largest turnout in history—68,832,818 votes, 11 percent more than 1956. After voting, Nixon relaxed by driving three friends down the California coast and showing them Tijuana, the Mexican border town; Kennedy spent the day playing touch football in the family compound in Hyannisport. Elaborate electronic gear had been installed on the sun porch of Bob Kennedy's home there, and it was there that the Democratic candidate watched the results that night and Wednesday morning.

An IBM-CBS computer enlivened the early evening by predicting, on the basis of data available at 7:15 P.M., that Nixon would win—its incredible odds were 100 to 1—with 459 electoral votes to Kennedy's 68. Then, as hard figures poured in, the country appeared to be going Democratic in a landslide. Kennedy took Connecticut, always the first state with complete returns, by 90,000. He was winning New York City by a huge margin and carrying Philadelphia by 331,000, 68.1 percent of the vote. Cook County, under the watchful eye of Dick Daley, was giving the Democratic ticket a lead that seemed to place it beyond the reach of downstate Republican Illinois. At 10:30 Kennedy's popular vote plurality was 1,500,000. He was then being projected as the winner by 4,000,000 or 5,000,000. The IBM-CBS machine was giving him 311 electoral votes; NBC's RCA-501 computer was putting it at 401. Viewers in the eastern United States were switching off their sets and going to bed, believing that it was all over. Jacqueline Kennedy whispered to her husband, "Oh, Bunny, you're President now!" He replied quietly, "No . . . no . . . it's too early yet."

It was indeed. Kennedy's high-water mark came shortly after midnight. His margin then exceeded 2,000,000, and the first returns from Los Angeles County indicated that he might carry California by 8,000,000. It was at precisely that point that the ticket began to run into trouble. Something unexpected was happening on the far side of the Appalachians. In the swing county of Lexington, Kentucky, for example, Kennedy was running behind Stevenson in 1952 and far behind Truman in 1948. Early Kansas returns put Nixon ahead or abreast of Eisenhower in 1956. Over the next two hours the picture cleared. It was not reassuring to the watchers in Hyannisport. The GOP ticket was sweeping: Kansas by 60.4 percent, South Dakota by 58.3, North Dakota by 55.4, Nebraska by 62.1. Wisconsin, conceded to Kennedy in all the polls, was going Republican by over 60,000 votes and the Democratic lead in California was disappearing as returns came in from the Los Angeles suburbs. Nationally, Kennedy's popular vote margin dwindled to 1,700,000 to 1,600,000 to 1,100,000. Plainly it was going to be less than a million. It might vanish altogether.

By 3 A.M. the country knew that Nixon was going to carry more states than Kennedy. That was small comfort to the Republicans, though; their ticket had virtually no chance of winning the 269 electoral votes needed for a Nixon triumph. The larger question was whether Kennedy would make it. Four big states hung in the balance: Illinois (27 electoral votes), Michigan (20), California (32), and Minnesota (11). Nixon could become President only if he carried all four, at that point a very remote possibility. Any two would cinch the election for Kennedy. But if he took only one of them, he would fall short. His triumph would be thwarted by 14 or 15 Dixiecrat electors, and the winner would be chosen by the House of Representatives.

By dawn everyone in Hyannisport had gone to bed except Bob Kennedy, who kept vigil over the teletypes, the television sets, and the telephone. (The Kennedy phone bill for that night was $10,000.) At 9:30 Michigan's Republicans threw in the towel, having concluded that Kennedy's 67,000 vote lead there would hold. The ticket was also carrying Minnesota and Illinois. That was good enough for U. E. Baugham, chief of the U.S. Secret Service. Baugham put through a call from Washington to a team of sixteen of his agents registered at Hyannis's Holiday Heath Inn, and they moved in on the Kennedy compound. The campaign belonged to history. Kennedy was now President-elect Kennedy.

Official returns in December gave him 34,226,925 to Nixon's 34,108,662—a margin of 112,881, less than two-thirds of one percent of the popular vote. For Nixon it was a heartbreaker. A change of a half-vote per precinct would have given him the decision. He had run nearly five percentage points ahead of GOP congressional candidates, and of the country's eight geographic regions—New England, the mid-Atlantic states, the South, the farm states, the Rocky Mountain states, the industrial Midwest, the five Pacific states, and the border states—he had carried all but the first three. Some of his advisers wanted him to challenge the outcome. There was sufficient evidence of fraud in Illinois and Texas, among other states, to suggest the possibility of a turnaround. He was tempted, but decided against it. The barriers were too formidable. In Cook County, for example, a recount would have taken a year and a half, and there was no recount procedure at all in Texas. Meantime the country would have to be governed.

In January the U.S. Constitution played a cruel trick on this intense, driven man. Article II, Section 2, provides that after the presidential electors have cast their ballots, "the President of the Senate shall, in the presence of the Senate and House of Representatives, open all the certificates and the votes shall then be counted." The President of the Senate is the Vice President of the United States. Once before, in 1861, a Vice President, then John C. Breckinridge, had to attest thus to his defeat, then at the hands of Abraham Lincoln. Nixon solemnly announced the result, 303 to 219, with 15 Dixiecrats for Harry Byrd. He took the occasion to deliver a short, graceful speech congratulating Kennedy and Johnson and paying tribute to the stability of the American political process. In response the Congress gave him an ovation.

After he left an inaugural day luncheon at the F Street Club, his chauffeur gently reminded him that this was the last day that he, as Vice President, would have a limousine at his disposal. That evening Nixon rode to Capitol Hill. In the darkness the city seemed briefly deserted. He later wrote, "I got out of the car and looked once again down what I believe is the most magnificent vista in the world—the Mall, now completely snow-covered, with the Washington Monument and the Lincoln Memorial in the distance."

Here, as so often in his life, he found comfort in sententious reflections. "Defeat is a greater test of character than victory" was one. Another was in a handwritten letter from Robert O. Reynolds, the former Stanford All-American and Detroit Lions star who went on to become one of the owners of the Los Angeles Rams. "Sometimes one loses a battle to win the war," Reynolds wrote Nixon. Quoting one of his college professors, he explained:

> . . . defeats are poison to some men. Great men have become mediocre because of inability to accept and abide by a defeat. Many men have become great because they were able to accept and abide by a defeat. If you should achieve any kind of success and develop

> superior qualities as a man, chances are it will be because of the manner in which you meet the defeats that will come to you just as they come to all men.

Nixon liked that, and he remembered it while packing to go home to California and start all over again.

IV

REAPING THE WHIRLWIND

1961–1968

Twenty-seven

A NEW GENERATION OF AMERICANS

BITTER COLD had set in that week of Richard Nixon's farewell to Washington, and on Thursday, January 19, the day before Kennedy's inauguration, new snow began to fall. By late afternoon, when the government offices let out, streets and pavements were covered. Softly through the long blue winter twilight it sifted down in great powdery layers, and by 8 P.M., when the President-elect and his wife attended a concert in Constitution Hall, the District lay frozen under a thick coverlet which dismayed even hardy New Frontiersmen. Still it continued to fall, speckling the pink faces of soldiers using flamethrowers to melt the caked ice around the inauguration stand on the east side of the Capitol, deepening in the Capitol's many squares and circles, stitching the eaves of the Executive Office Building and the federal triangle complex with the same shimmering thread. Open fires were lit along the Mall in an attempt to keep it clear for traffic, but the flames had to be kept too low to help much, for the snow was accompanied by a wind that howled in from the Potomac and the Tidal Basin, sending the hard white silt scudding before its raw gusts. Shortly after 3:45 A.M., when the President-elect returned to his Georgetown home, the snow died away, but the cold continued to hold the city in its frigid grip. Drifts hung in the alleys of the Negro ghetto in northeast Washington, and there was an epidemic of broken oil burners in Cleveland Park.

At noon Friday the temperature was twenty degrees above zero; the winds were still punishing. Twenty minutes later the shivering crowd saw the new President appear on the stand and cheered, hoping to hear his speech soon. It didn't for a while. Instead it shivered some more while Richard Cardinal Cushing honked his way through an invocation that seemed endless. Like so many other chapters in John Kennedy's life, the inaugural was beginning in disarray. As the cardinal finished, smoke began to curl up from a short circuit in the wires under the lectern. Momentarily the horrified chief of the Secret Service envisaged the whole stand going up in flames. Three times he started to order it cleared and checked himself. Then the smoke stopped, only to be succeeded by another setback. Rising to read a poem, Robert Frost was blinded by the sun glaring on the snow; he had to put it away and recite a poem from memory. At last Chief Justice Warren administered the oath at 12:51. And with that, everything changed. Hatless and coatless, his voice frosting in the air, and his starchy vowels redolent of Boston, the vigorous young President set the tone of the new administration:

"Let the word go forth from this time and place, to friend and foe alike, that the torch has been passed to a new generation of Americans . . . tempered by war, disciplined by a hard and bitter peace, proud of our ancient heritage."

"That speech he made out there," Sam Rayburn said afterward, "was better than Lincoln." It was an occasion for extravagant remarks. After the tranquil, healing years under Eisenhower, the capital was witnessing the commencement of an innovative administration, the first since Franklin Roosevelt's. Now, as then, the accent was on youth. The new First Lady, who had been born the year of the Crash, was a young woman of stunning beauty. Joining her husband in the Capitol after his speech, she softly touched his face and said in her breathy way, "Oh, Jack, what a day!"

Subsequent days in those first weeks were equally radiant. Writing of Kennedy years afterward in a memoir on the swing generation, Joan Swallow Reiter said, "He was *our* President, the first born in our century, the youngest man ever elected to the office and, we were sure, certain to be one of the best." Among New Frontiersmen that faith was absolute: never had men picked up the symbols of command with greater confidence.

John Fitzgerald Kennedy had been chosen President by 34,221,463 Americans, or 49.7 percent of those who had voted. After his death in November 1963 a nationwide poll reported that 65 percent recalled casting their ballots for him, which meant that over ten million of his constituents had altered their memories of that election day. But they had been changing them even before he went to Dallas. In June 1963 another poll had found that 59 percent said they had voted Democratic three years earlier.

The phenomenon was not an accident. Kennedy had entered office determined to broaden his support in the country. During the interval between his election and his inauguration he had read Richard E. Neustadt's scholarly *Presidential Power*, in which Neustadt wrote that the public's impression of a chief executive "takes shape for most constituents no later than the time they first perceive him being President (a different thing from seeing him as a candidate)." Kennedy was determined that the first time Americans saw him as President he would be at the post and pulling away.

Noticing that there were no blacks among the Coast Guard cadets in the inaugural parade, he started an official inquiry on the spot. The next morning he was in his bare office early, witnessing the swearing in of his cabinet, pumping Harry Truman's hand—Truman was in the White House for the first time since his last day as tenant—and firing off Executive Order No. 1, to double the food rations of four million needy Americans. In the weeks which followed the new President continued to vibrate with energy. He would pace corridors while dictating rapidly, read on his feet, dart out for brisk constitutionals, and return in a fast walk that was almost a sprint, restlessly snapping his fingers. "He did everything today except shinny up the Washington Monument," James Reston wrote of one of those typical early days.

The rest of Washington was expected to keep pace with him. In the Kennedy administration, said Arthur J. Goldberg, the new Secretary of Labor, "the deadline for everything is day before yesterday." Charles E. Bohlen said, "I never heard of a President who wanted to know so much." Some members of the government were so hard-pressed by the new chief executive that routine work suffered. A committee chairman from the Hill complained, "*He* may have two hours to spend, but *I* don't," and Llewellyn Thompson, ambassador to Russia, who had seldom been alone with Eisenhower for more than ten minutes, had four two-hour sessions with Kennedy. The talk wasn't small talk. "When you see the President," a senator remarked, "you have to get in your car and drive like blazes back to the Capitol to beat his memo commenting on what you told him."

One day a hundred people were counted entering his West Wing office. One meeting there produced seventeen separate directives, and two months after taking the oath Kennedy had issued thirty-two official messages and legislative recommendations (Eisenhower had issued five in his first two months) while delivering twelve speeches, promulgating twenty-two executive orders and proclamations, sending twenty-eight communications to foreign chiefs of state, and holding seven press conferences. Reporters were fascinated: more of them came than for the press conferences of any other President before or since. A Washington wit observed that the new President seemed determined to be not only his own Secretary of State but his own Mrs. Roosevelt too. No detail seemed too small for him. At one early press conference he answered in a knowledgeable way a question about a proposal to ship $12,000,000 in Cuban molasses to the United States—information which had appeared four days earlier near the bottom of a departmental report. Noting that Army Special Forces troops had been deprived of their green berets, he ordered that they be returned. Conferring with generals about strategy in Southeast Asia, he tested the carbines being shipped to Vietnam, and as his first presidential spring approached he even detected crabgrass on the greening White House lawn and told the gardeners to get rid of it.

He was out to expand his all-important base. The people he needed were watching him, and he wanted to be sure they liked what they saw. The hatless, coatless vigor helped. Americans approve of self-starters. It was useful for reporters to report that the new President was very much in charge; useful, for example, to let the word get around that Dean Acheson had been given just four days to hammer out a detailed NATO report. The first televised sessions with the White House press corps were, of course, crucial. One of them—the third—was watched by some sixty-five million people in twenty-one and a half million homes. These performances were live. Kennedy had to be not only his own Mrs. Roosevelt but also his own Robert Montgomery. He did it; McLuhan acclaimed him as a virtuoso. And presently the wisdom of the Neustadt approach was reflected in studies by opinion samplers. Kennedy's racing start had converted an enormous segment of the electorate. These were Nixon voters who had changed their minds and would soon convince themselves that they had been for Kennedy all along. It was something of a political miracle: the new chief executive's base was as big as Ike's.

"Presidents, like great French restaurants, have an ambiance all their own," Douglass Cater observed. The Kennedy image was forming, an amalgam of, among other things, Jacqueline Kennedy's camellia beauty, three-year-old Caroline's Kate Greenaway charm, the elegant rhetoric of the President's speeches, the football on the attorney general's desk, and the new idealism. Gone were the former administration's flannel phrases—"bigger bang for a buck," "rolling readjustment," "agonizing reappraisal." Instead, the country learned, there was to be a dynamic policy of action, typified by the new Secretary of Labor, who settled a strike during his first twenty-four hours in office. Like the harassed senator, everyone in the new cabinet appeared to be driving like blazes, working twelve-hour days and displaying signs of Kennedy hypomania. It was mostly illusion, of course, and later there was bound to be some disillusion, but at the time it was undeniably impressive. One secretary was observed simultaneously signing his mail, carrying on a telephone conversation, and relaying instructions to an aide by crude semaphore; a second was said to be training himself to carry on with only six hours of sleep; and a third member of the cabinet, Robert McNamara, startled Pentagon guards by showing up at 7:30 each morning.

Restoration of green berets to the Special Forces reflected Kennedy's belief in excellence. Later David Halberstam would write of those first days that the members of the Kennedy team "carried with them an exciting sense of American elitism"—elitism was not yet a term of opprobrium—"a sense that the best men had been summoned forth from the country to harness this dream to a new American nationalism, bringing a new, strong, dynamic spirit to our historic role in world affairs." Examples abounded, particularly in the recruiting of distinguished scholars. An astonishing number of them came from Cambridge, Massachusetts; a mot of the time offered a new definition of a failure: a Yale man driving an Edsel with a Nixon sticker on it. Asked how he happened to be chosen Secretary of Agriculture, Orville Freeman said, "I'm not really sure, but I think it had something to do with the fact that Harvard does not have a school of agriculture." Freeman did indeed lack a Harvard degree, but what was more important in this administration was that at Minnesota he had been graduated magna cum laude and elected to Phi Beta Kappa. A Mauldin cartoon depicted a Phi Beta Kappa key as the new key to the capital. Disdain and even contempt for intellectuals, so conspicuous in Washington eight years earlier, had vanished. In cultivating this image, New Frontiersmen soft-pedaled certain inconvenient facts—their President loved golf, for example, and his two favorite songs, "Bill Bailey" and "Heart of My Heart," were anything but classical. Yet picturing him as a Brahmin was not inaccurate. As Truman had admired generals and Eisenhower tycoons, Kennedy turned to academics. Among his advisers were fifteen Rhodes scholars, led by the Secretary of State, and four professional historians. The Secretary of Defense, the Commissioner of Internal Revenue, the chairman of the Civil Service Commission, and the ambassadors to India, Japan, and Yugoslavia were former college teachers. The President's expert on gold was a professor. Even the President's military adviser, General Maxwell D. Taylor, came to him from the Lincoln Center for the Performing Arts, and for the first time in history the White House had a cultural coordinator.

The Best and the Brightest, Halberstam would later call them in a bitter reckoning of their foreign policy failures. His appraisal came eleven years later and was largely an indictment of their role in Vietnam. Unquestionably that was the worst of their handiworks, but it was not their only disaster, a fact to be weighed in putting the Kennedy years in perspective. The new administration had stumbled earlier. The responsibility for their first outstanding nonsuccess was far from theirs alone. They were executing a plan drawn up by the outgoing administration. Nevertheless, they should have been more skeptical of it. The fact that they were not is illustrative of how fallible the cleverest politicians can be. Their error lay in confusing image and reality. Looking back on those first weeks in power, Robert Kennedy would observe almost wistfully, "Those were the days when we thought we were succeeding because of the stories on how hard everybody was working." Their discovery of their mistake was a spin-off of one of American history's most farcical misadventures, which took its name from Cuba's Bahía de Cochinos, the Bay of Pigs.

Of that debacle Halberstam was to write: "How a President who seemed so contemporary could agree to a plan so obviously doomed to failure, a plan based on so little understanding of the situation, was astounding." Afterward Kennedy himself asked Ted Sorensen, "How could I have been so far off base? All my life I've known better than to depend on the experts. How could I have been so stupid, to let them go ahead?" Again and again, Arthur Schlesinger noted, the remorseful President would "recur incredulously to the Bay of Pigs, wondering how a rational and responsible government could ever have become involved in so ill-starred an adventure."

All that, of course, was after the fact. In the beginning the scheme had not seemed so harebrained. President-elect Kennedy had first learned of it from Allen Dulles on November 29, 1960. Two days after the inaugural, Dulles and General Lyman Lemnitzer, chairman of the Joint Chiefs, briefed the leading members of the new administration—Rusk, McNamara, Robert Kennedy. On January 28 the President called the first White House meeting to discuss the future of La Brigada. Schlesinger observed that Kennedy was "wary and reserved in his reaction." The CIA men told their new chief not to worry. There were no loose threads, they assured him; every base was covered.

Kennedy at that time had been President one week. He wanted time to mull the thing over, but the CIA said he couldn't have much of it. For La Brigada it was now or never. Castro was about to receive crated MIGs from Russia. By June 1 enough of them would be assembled and in service, piloted by Cuban fliers who were being trained in Czechoslovakia, to wipe out the brigade on the beaches. In addition, President Ydígoras said the trainees couldn't stay in Guatemala after April. By then the rainy season would turn the Sierra Madre into one vast bog. Further training there would be impossible. The CIA reported that La Brigada was fit and eager to fight. The liberation of Cuba awaited a word, a single word, from the President.

Still he hesitated. The pressure mounted. Allen Dulles bluntly put it to him: either he approved the plan or he would be refusing to allow freedom-loving exiles to deliver their homeland from a Communist dictatorship, encouraging Cuba to undermine democratic governments throughout Latin America, and creating an ugly '64 campaign issue as the disbanded, disillusioned brigade toured the United States under Republican auspices, revealing how Kennedy had betrayed them and the cause of anti-Communism. Dulles asked the President whether he was ready to tell this "group of fine young men" who asked "nothing other than the opportunity to try to restore a free government in their country" that they would "get no sympathy, no support, no aid from the United States?"

Kennedy asked what the chances of success were. Dulles reminded him that in June 1954 the CIA had overthrown Guatemala's Marxist government. He said, "I stood right here at Ike's desk, and I told him I was certain our Guatemalan operation would succeed, and, Mr. President, the prospects for this plan are even better than they were for that one." The Joint Chiefs unanimously endorsed it. Late in February Kennedy asked for a second opinion from the Chiefs. They sent an inspection team to the Guatemalan base. After reading the report and studying La Brigada's tactical plan, General Lemnitzer again predicted that it would succeed, and Admiral Arleigh Burke, chief of naval operations, seconded him. Looking for still another opinion, the President ordered to Guatemala a veteran Marine Corps colonel with a brilliant combat record. The result was this evaluation:

> My observations have increased my confidence in the ability of this force to accomplish not only initial combat missions, but also the ultimate objective, the overthrow of Castro. The Brigade and battalion commanders now know all details of the plan and are enthusiastic.* These officers are young, vigorous, intelligent and motivated by a fanatical urge to begin battle. . . .
>
> They say they know their own people and believe that after they have inflicted one serious defeat upon the opposition forces, the latter will melt away from Castro, whom they have no wish to support. They say it is a Cuban tradition to join a winner and they have supreme confidence they will win against whatever Castro has to offer.
>
> I share their confidence.

At that, Kennedy yielded, conceding that there was some logic in the argument that an administration which was prepared to send U.S. troops to fight Communism in Laos, on the other side of the world, could not ignore an aggressive Communist regime ninety miles south of Florida. Yet even then he expressed misgivings. Schlesinger later believed that if one senior adviser had spoken out against the expedition, it would have been canceled. Only he and Senator William Fulbright protested. (Chester Bowles and Edward

* The record shows that at that point the CIA had not shown any of them the plan.

R. Murrow knew of it and were against it, but as their sources of information were unofficial, they couldn't appeal to the White House.) Schlesinger asked Kennedy, "What do you think about this damned invasion?" Kennedy replied dryly, "I think about it as little as possible."

On Monday, April 10, the brigade was moved by truck to its point of embarkation, Puerto Cabezas, in Nicaragua. Thursday the men boarded the boats. On Friday their CIA leaders told them their objectives: the capture of three beaches in the Bay of Pigs, with brigade paratroops seizing key points in the great marshy swamp—Cienaga de Zapata—that lay between the island proper and the sea. At noon Sunday the expedition passed the point of no return. The rebels, their armada, and their tiny air force were committed.

The real nature of that commitment and the plan Kennedy thought he had approved were not the same thing, however. The President had been assured that the brigade comprised 1,400 elite troops who had been trained as guerrillas. Their objective in the Bay of Pigs, he—and they—had been told, was a remote, abandoned beach whose only signs of habitation were deserted resort houses. Landing at night, the briefers explained, the rebels' presence would be unknown to Castro. CIA intelligence further assured the President that the Cuban dictator would be unable to act for at least seventy-two hours. Even then he would be bewildered; to divert him, 168 brigade commandos would make a diversionary landing on the coast of Oriente province over three hundred miles away.

Dulles, Richard Bissell—chief architect of the CIA plan—and their advisers, including E. Howard Hunt Jr., were confident that enough Cubans were disillusioned with Castro to guarantee the success of the main landing. They reported that 2,500 of them belonged to resistance organizations, that another 20,000 sympathized with the resistance, and that 25 percent of the population, at the very least, was prepared to give the insurgents active support. This was essential, for both in private and in public Kennedy had emphasized that the American military would play no part in an assault on Castro. He was locked in on this. At an April 12 press conference he said that "there will not be, under any conditions, any intervention in Cuba by United States forces, and this government will do everything it possibly can—and I think it can meet its responsibilities—to make sure that there are no Americans involved in any actions inside Cuba . . . The basic issue in Cuba is not one between the United States and Cuba; it is between the Cubans themselves."

Should the exiles fail to establish a beachhead in the Bay of Pigs and hold it, he was told, they would break off the action and "melt into the hills." With that, the President thought that all bets had been covered. Believing such a diversion would alter the plan from one for a spectacular amphibious assault to a low-key infiltration, he felt that any chance that U.S. credibility and prestige might be damaged had been eliminated.

He was mistaken. The CIA to the contrary, none of the exiles had received any instruction in guerrilla warfare since November 4, 1960, at which time their force had numbered just 300 men. Many of the more recent recruits were not fit for an arduous jungle campaign. Only 135 members of the brigade were really soldiers. The rest were clerks, lawyers, bankers, physicians, geologists, teachers, cattlemen, newspapermen, musicians, draftsmen, engineers, artists, and mechanics. Three were Catholic priests and one was a Protestant clergyman. Crack troops should be young, in their late teens or early twenties. The average age of these men was twenty-nine; some of them were in their sixties, and some of the late arrivals had not learned to fire a rifle.

That was only the beginning of Kennedy's misapprehensions. Actually the question of how the rebels would fare in the hills was never tested, because, incredibly, the nearest range was the Escambray Mountains, eighty miles inland and separated from the Bay of Pigs by a hopeless tangle of swamps. Being Cubans, the exiles might have pointed that out. The difficulty was that nothing had been said to them about the possibility of melting away there or anywhere else. On its own, without consulting either the President or the Joint Chiefs, the CIA had decided to withhold the alternative plan from the insurgents. Its reasoning was that if the exiles knew of it, their determination to fight might be weakened; they might be tempted to abandon their beachhead while they still had a good chance of winning.

Everything possible was done to build up the insurgents' morale, and that included making promises that could not be kept. Frank Bender said to them: "You will be so strong, you will be getting so many people to your side, that you won't want to wait for us. You will go straight ahead. You will put your hands out, turn left, and go straight into Havana." Furthermore, the CIA agents assured the exiles that if they foundered Americans would rescue them. Long afterward their leader, José Pérez San Román, learned of the option, the last resort of flight to the hills. He said bitterly, "We were never told about this. What we were told was, 'If you fail *we* will go in.'" In Miami, Manuel Ray of the Frente believed that U.S. troops would come in as a second wave. He said later, "We were told that the landings would be followed up by all necessary support. We were even told that ten to fifteen thousand men would be available."

The first setback came in the air, and it was crucial. CIA appraisals of the Cuban air force had been scornful. Its combat efficiency was rated "almost nonexistent," its planes "for the most part obsolete and inoperative," and its leadership "entirely disorganized." Castro had fifteen B-26 bombers, ten Sea Furies, and four fast T-33 jet trainers. To knock them out, the CIA scheduled a strike against Cuban airfields on Saturday, April 15, two days before the landing. Eight exiles were to fly World War II prop-driven B-26s; afterward two of them would identify themselves in Miami as defectors from the Cuban air force. It wasn't good enough. Castro, after all, knew who was deserting from him and who wasn't, and to assure confusion among the Americans a *real* defector chose this awkward time to land in Jacksonville. The lumbering B-26s were slow, unwieldy, and plagued by engine trouble. Saturday evening Frank Bender sent a message to Pepe San Román. The bombing mission had been a success, he said; nearly all Castro aircraft had been destroyed on the ground—twelve at his Santiago de Cuba airfield, six to eight at Ciudad Libertad, and eight to ten at San Antonio. This would have been marvelous if it were true, but it wasn't; the Cuban air force had been left with six B-26s, two Sea Furies, four fighters and, most important, two T-33 jets. Unaccountably, both the CIA and the Joint Chiefs had assigned no value to the T-33s because they were trainer planes. They were jets all the same, and as such could fly circles around the insurgents' B-26s. Armed with 50-caliber machine guns, they would hop on the tails of the B-26s. Moreover, the bombers were particularly vulnerable to attack from the rear. As flown in World War II, B-26s had been defended by tail gunners, but the CIA had eliminated tail guns in these planes to put in extra gas tanks, giving the fliers more time in the air over Cuba. Now the exiled fliers were doomed. Air mastery would belong to Castro. Always important in an amphibious operation, this was especially so for this one because of another CIA error. For reasons which have never been explained, the agents had ordered all the supplies for the first ten days of fighting—the ammunition, gasoline, food, hospital equipment—loaded on one ship.

The name of the vessel was the *Río Escondito*. It was one of five hulking old World War II troop transports and two escort ships bearing the cover name García Line for this operation, and in a way it was a symbol of the entire undertaking. Unpainted and covered with rust, its engines temperamental and its hold reeking of foul odors, the *Río* listed like *The African Queen*. The exiles were appalled by it. One of them, Enrique Ruiz-Williams, a mortarman with some knowledge of the sea, was shocked—it gave him what he later described as "a cold feeling"—and Erneido Oliva felt "a great deception when we got over to the ships. It was something we didn't expect. That was not what we were waiting for." The idea that such a boat had been chosen for a mission of stealth was ludicrous. Its hoists and winches shrieked when used. Its rust-caked loading machinery was even noisier. The *Río* was already in trouble. Moving down the Mississippi to the Gulf of Mexico, one of its propellers had struck a log. Brigade frogmen found it completely bent. Its maneuverability sharply limited, it limped onward on its way to a duel with enemy aircraft.

Kennedy's understanding that young Cuban patriots would be landed quietly on an isolated coast were first jarred by a Manhattan public relations firm. Without a word to the White House or anyone else, including the Cuban Frente, whose authority was being preempted, the CIA had hired Lem Jones Associates to issue press releases in the name of the "Cuban Revolutionary Council." The bulletins were being telephoned to Jones's Madison Avenue office by CIA agents and then distributed to the press. One, "for immediate release," reported: "The principal battle of the Cuban revolt against Castro will be fought in the next few hours. Action today was largely of a supply and support effort." At the end it called for "a coordinated wave of sabotage and rebellion."

In Washington administration insiders were beginning to wonder whether it wasn't the exiles who were being sabotaged. Everything was going wrong for them. The landing craft assigned to their assault waves turned out to be fourteen-foot open boats with no protection for those aboard. The 50-caliber machine guns on them were improperly sighted and aimed in the wrong direction. The boats were powered by outboard motors; at the peak of the coming action one of the invaders, jumping from his ship, struck a pilot and knocked him overboard, leaving the landing craft to drift in aimless circles. There were other mishaps; aboard the transport *Atlántico* three insurgents were practicing with a 50-caliber machine gun when it tore loose from its mounting and fired wildly in all directions, killing one of their comrades and wounding two others. More ominous for the outcome of the operation, the force of rebel commandos who were supposed to draw Castro's mission away from the Bay of Pigs by a feint in Oriente province never reached the shore. Twice they boarded their landing craft and twice returned to reembark on their ship, *La Playa*. The CIA agents accompanying them sent back word that the diversion had been "aborted primarily because of bad leadership." The leaders had been chosen by the CIA.

The Oriente landing was to have been part of a cunning design meant to throw Castro off balance. Even more important were plans for a general uprising in Cuba by the anti-Castro underground. President Kennedy had been told that the underground movement was vital to the success of the mission. The Joint Chiefs had agreed. The behavior of the CIA, however, had been curiously ambivalent. The underground was part of the overall strategy. Agents had been in touch with Rogelio Gonzáles Corso, the almost legendary leader of the movement, known throughout Cuba under his code name, "Francisco." He and his men were on the alert. At the proper time they were to be told to create disorders and create a general air of insurgency which would then be capitalized upon by Radio Swan, the exiles' propaganda station; Radio Swan broadcasts would tell the populace how to help La Brigada, how to join its ranks, how to blow up power stations, and so on. This looked fine on paper, but in practice it raised a basic question of priorities. The difficulty was one of timing. The uprisings conflicted with the air strike meant to wipe out Castro's air force. Whichever one came first would alert him to the other. Command of the air was judged to be more important. It came first and it failed. The following night Radio Swan broadcast orders for the underground to rise. They were in code and lyrical in the most florid Howard Hunt prose:

> Alert! Alert! Look well at the rainbow. The first will rise very soon. Chico is in the house. Visit him. The sky is blue. Place notice in the

tree. The tree is green and brown. The letters arrived well. The letters are white. The fish will not take much time to rise. The fish is red.

The strangest thing about this message was that it seems to have beamed toward the wrong people. It was picked up by the Columbia and National broadcasting networks and by several Florida stations, none of which could fathom its meaning. But although it was repeated over and over, it reached none of the listeners for whom it was intended—the brigade, the commandos, the Frente, the infiltration teams, and the saboteurs in Cuba. In reality it didn't much matter, though. Castro, warned by the air attack the day before, had ordered a roundup of all Cubans whose loyalty to him was suspect. Instantly, in the words of nineteen-year-old Félix Rodríguez, one of those who was waiting to revolt, "The roads were closed, the houses were surrounded, and they were arresting thousands of people. I cried." In Havana alone more than two hundred thousand men and women were arrested and lodged in baseball parks, public buildings, theaters, and auditoriums. Thus the underground audience wasn't tuned in. It was being held at gunpoint. On the next day, D-day, Monday, April 17, 1961, Francisco himself was found guilty of treason and executed.

At 7:45 P.M. the previous evening the five rusty cargo ships and two escorts of the exiles' task force had arrived in the Bay of Pigs and cast anchor. One by one the subplots meant to support the insurgents on board had failed—the Oriente deception, the sabotage, Radio Swan's instructions, the rising of the underground—and now the amphibious landing would go in with as little subtlety as at Anzio. The men didn't know that. Like assault troops in all wars, they had been told as little as possible. They waited below deck dressed for combat, dozing fitfully. At 11 P.M. Pepe San Román, their commander, came topside for a breath of air. What he saw stunned him. The shore, which he had been told would be forsaken, glittered with lights. His briefers had described the Bay of Pigs as it had been three years earlier, before Castro seized power. Since then the government had decided to turn this strip of coast into a public park. Modern roads now crossed the swamps, which the CIA thought were still impassable. Three tourist centers were in advanced stages of construction. One of them dominated the brigade's first objective, the town of Girón. Motels, snack bars, and bathhouses—nearly two hundred buildings altogether—were almost ready; they would accommodate a thousand Cubans at a time. The grand opening was scheduled for May 20, less than five weeks away. Every weekend since Three Kings' Day in January sightseers by the thousands had been driving down from Havana to inspect the progress. This being a Sunday, the last cars had left only a few hours before the brigade's transports sighted land. There were still people moving around on the beach; construction workers putting the finishing touches on the new buildings were living in Girón with their families. It was as though Russian conspirators had planned a hostile landing on Coney Island or Jones Beach. When Kennedy found out he was openmouthed. He remembered that Eisenhower had been in the White House when this venture was planned, and he said, "My God, the bunch of advisers we inherited. . . . Can you imagine being President and leaving someone like all these people there?"

That may have been the worst of it, but it wasn't all. If there was one kind of operation the American military had mastered in the past twenty years, it was the amphibious landing. From North Africa to Normandy, from Guadalcanal to Inchon, fighting men had been put ashore with practiced skill. Tide tables, underwater obstacles, undertow, surf, riptides—all obstacles had been overcome by brilliant seamanship, special landing craft, and ingenious amphibious techniques. Veterans of those operations were now CIA strategists. If they remembered anything, it should have been that no American commander in those battles had been foolhardy enough to increase the odds against him by scheduling a landing at night. Yet that was what they had laid out for the Cuban exiles. In addition, they had neglected to note a vital feature of the Bay of Pigs: every approach to it was guarded by sharp coral reefs just beneath the surface.

The first insurgents to go in were frogmen, former officers in the Cuban navy whose job was to place landing lights. (Despite Kennedy's order to the contrary, Americans were leading them.) Coming upon the reefs, they realized that they would have to chart a way through. At midnight their first flashing beacon, a guide to the troops who would be coming ashore, was placed beside a concrete pier. No sooner had it been switched on than the headlights of a jeep appeared on the beach. It was a militia patrol. The jeep swerved and stopped, its lights on the frogmen. They opened fire on it. Next a truck carrying armed Castro militia raced up to join the jeep. Gunners aboard one of the troopships, the *Blagar,* silenced that threat, but it was small comfort; the first wave of exiles hadn't even left the transports and already the element of surprise—the sole justification for a night landing—had been lost.

Now the frogmen set to work in earnest trying to find lanes through the coral for LCVPs and the wider, tank-bearing LCUs. In some cases it was impossible. Men halted as far as 150 yards from the shore, waded through surf carrying weapons and radios which became inoperable in the salt water. The reefs knocked propellers off some boats. Impatient soldiers who leaped into deep water sank like stones because of heavy equipment lashed to them; comrades dragged them to safety. Some men yearned for dawn and even prayed for it, but daybreak, it became apparent, would only increase the odds against them. The officer who discovered that was Erneido Oliva. At 2:30 A.M., Oliva later testified, he reached the shore. The first building he saw was a shack with the antenna of a microwave station on top. He captured it at once, but as he said afterward, "You could see that they had transmitted from there recently." At 6 A.M. two more microwave stations had been discovered in Girón. In each the equipment was still warm. The failure of CIA intelligence to warn of them was one of the greatest oversights in the entire operation. Because of those sets, Castro knew they were here. Now he would be coming after them.

At 3:15 A.M. the bearded dictator had been roused in Havana and told that the enemy was landing troops at Girón and nearby Playa (beach) Larga. Wary of a trap, he asked for details. Operators at the microwave stations replied that they were under attack from naval gunfire, 50-caliber machine guns, bazookas, and recoilless cannons. Then they went off the air, obviously overrun. A beachhead had been established; at any moment a provisional government might be landed and recognized by the United States, creating a political problem. Castro was determined to throw the rebels into the sea.

It says much for the state of his defenses throughout Cuba that he had in that area, ready to march, a sufficient force to repel a landing much larger than this: a battalion commanded by Osmani Cienfuegos, his minister of public works; a battalion of militia armed with three mortar batteries; an infantry battalion; three battalions of reserves to guard the roads through the swamps, and several detachments of armed militia. Altogether 20,000 men barred the exiles' way out of the Zapata peninsula. In addition Castro still had his air force. At sunrise he ordered his six B-26s, each carrying a full bomb load, to take off from San Antonio de Los Baños airfield with a fighter escort and attack the ships at anchor in the Bay of Pigs.

There was a great deal of confusion on the beachhead that morning, part of it arising from the error of exiles on the ground who opened fire on their own planes. When Castro's pilots arrived over the beach the most vulnerable unit beneath them was La Brigada's heavy gun battalion. The frogmen had finished mapping a route through the coral at 6 A.M., and at 6:25 these big weapons began to come ashore. It was slow going, and it stopped altogether when the enemy swooped down from above. Briefly the action shifted to dogfights in the sky—the brigade's fliers were up there, too—but the T-33 jet trainers chased away the rebel aircraft. Then Castro's bombers zeroed in on the rusty cargo ships. The first to be lost was the *Houston,* loaded with ammunition and gasoline; twenty-six of her men drowned. Then came the *Río Escondido* and the ten days of supplies aboard her. A Sea Fury fighter put a rocket in the *Río,* which simply disintegrated in a blinding sheet of flame. That was enough for the task force commander. His crews, mostly Cubans with no strong political loyalties, were on the verge of mutiny. He notified Pepe San Román that although less than 10 percent of the brigade's ammunition had been unloaded, he and the surviving vessels were leaving now, immediately, at flank speed. He promised to come back that night.

In Washington the conflicting stories coming from Cuba at first seemed very far away. Cuba dominated the news that morning, however. In the United Nations Raúl Roa, Castro's foreign minister, had charged that in Saturday's air raid by rebel pilots in B-26s he detected the fine hand of the Central Intelligence Agency. Adlai Stevenson, disturbed, sent a query to Harland Cleveland. Cleveland called the Bureau of Inter-American Affairs, which called the CIA, which solemnly denied the charge, thereby betraying America's most respected spokesman in foreign affairs. On the strength of that, Stevenson told the U.N. that the President had vowed "to make sure that no American participates in an action against Cuba." He then read from a bogus statement by a phony defector in Miami, which Stevenson believed to be true. He said, "These pilots and certain other crew members have apparently defected from Castro's tyranny." He added: "No United States personnel participated. No

United States aircraft of any kind participated. These two planes, to the best of our knowledge, were Castro's own air force planes and, according to the pilots, they took off from Castro's own air force fields."

He held up a picture of one of the B-26s and said, "It has the marking of Castro's air force on the tail, which everyone can see for himself. The Cuban star and the initials F.A.R., *Fuerza Aerea Revolucionaria,* are clearly visible." Roa replied that anyone could have painted the insignia on, which of course was what had happened. The American ambassador assured him: "Steps have been taken to impound the Cuban planes and they will not be permitted to take off for Cuba."

There were to be no such steps. Already the CIA's cover story was becoming unstuck, leaving a humiliated Stevenson to extricate himself from the tangle of lies as best he could. As Robert F. Kennedy said afterward, "Things were beginning to surface." By Monday evening the worst was known. Kennedy's admirers abroad were dismayed. "In one day," said the *Cordiere della Sera* of Milan, "American prestige collapses lower than in eight years of Eisenhower timidity and lack of determination." The *Frankfurter Neue Presse* declared that "Kennedy is to be regarded as politically and morally defeated." In the U.N. General Assembly diplomats from African and Asian countries, remembering John Foster Dulles's charges that neutralism was immoral, were having a field day. Stevenson said dryly that he wasn't sure who was attacking Cuba, but he knew who was attacking the United States.

The 6 P.M. edition of Monday's *Miami News* bore the headline: CUBAN NAVY IN REVOLT; INVASION FORCE MOVES IN. The story disclosed that the navy's mutiny bore the imaginative code name "Bounty," and that the exiles were slicing up Castro's disintegrating forces with gigantic pincer attacks. "Various accounts" were cited as sources for the claim that the invaders had "hit the beaches in four of Cuba's six provinces, sparing only Havana Province and Camaguey in Eastern Cuba." The accounts were all wrong. There was no operation called "Bounty"; the navy remained loyal to a man; and the only action was on the shores of the Bay of Pigs, where the 20,000 defenders of Castro's regime had the exiles trapped with their backs to the sea.

Deserted by their ships, the invaders were in a hopeless position. Yet they were fighting magnificently. The paratroopers, though they had been dropped in the wrong place, were beating back militia attacks. Outnumbered thirteen to one or more, facing an enemy with heavy artillery and tactical air support, the brigade had lost fewer than a hundred men that first day while holding every position. Oliva's command, just 370 rebels, had thrown back 2,100 Castro soldiers and twenty tanks. They had sustained fewer than a hundred casualties while inflicting on the government—the figures are from a Castro doctor—five hundred dead and over a thousand wounded.

They were exultant. Their overall plight was known only to their leaders, who clung to hope because they were being encouraged by radio messages from CIA agents on the dispersed troopships. ("Hello, Pepe. I want you to know that we will never abandon you, and if things are very rough there we will go in and evacuate you.") Afterward there was much controversy about these exchanges. There can be no doubt that by heartening the men on the beach the agents prolonged their resistance and thereby added to the bloodshed. It was generally believed by CIA critics that strategists in the agency had convinced one another that Kennedy wouldn't let the invasion fail, whatever his earlier position—that once he realized that American prestige was at stake he would intervene with U.S. might. Here, as in so many other ways, they were wrong. He meant what he had said. "What is prestige?" he asked those around him in the White House that day. "Is it the shadow of power or the substance of power? We are going to work on the substance of power. No doubt we will be kicked in the can for the next couple of weeks, but that won't affect the main business."

Most Americans seemed to understand, and to sympathize. The bitterness which was to divide them later in the 1960s lay ahead. The country had not yet split into hostile camps. As Robert F. Kennedy was to write afterward in *Thirteen Days*, "We had virtual unanimity at the time of the Bay of Pigs." Editor John Fischer expressed the general view when he observed in *Harper's* that "Every President needs about twelve months to get his executive team organized, to feel his way into the vast and dangerous machinery of the bureaucracy. . . . While [Kennedy] was still trying to move in the furniture, in effect, he found the roof falling in and the doors blowing off." The Gallup poll showed that 82 percent of his countrymen approved of the way he was handling his job. "It's just like

Eisenhower," Kennedy said dourly. "The worse I do, the more popular I get."

To be sure, opinion wasn't unanimous. On the right were such hard-liners as Richard Nixon, who was to reveal in the November 1964 *Reader's Digest* that he had advised Kennedy to "find a proper legal cover and . . . go in." But that was expected. What was surprising was the emergence at this time, and on this issue, of an abrasive New Left. Schlesinger noted that many "on the left, more than one would have thought, now saw full vindication of their pre-election doubts about Kennedy." Their placards demanded "Fair Play for Cuba." They filled Manhattan's Union Square with demonstrators. Norman Mailer joined them. Outside the White House a sandwich board worn by a tall woman poet reproached the First Lady: JACQUELINE, VOUS AVEZ PERDU VOS ARTISTES. The Fair Play movement found recruits on many campuses, especially in the humanities and the social sciences; H. Stuart Hughes, a member of the Harvard history department and an early New Left militant, led seventy college teachers who signed an open letter to the President demanding that the administration "reverse the present drift towards American military intervention in Cuba." Barrington Moore Jr., a sociologist, predicted "a militarist and reactionary government that covers its fundamental policies with liberal rhetoric," and from a hospital bed C. Wright Mills, author of *The Power Elite*, telegraphed a Fair Play rally in California:

> Kennedy and company have returned us to barbarism. Schlesinger and company have disgraced us intellectually and morally. I feel a desperate shame for my country. Sorry I cannot be with you. Were I physically able to do so I would at this moment be fighting alongside Fidel Castro.

Actually Castro wasn't fighting. It wasn't necessary. At the Bay of Pigs his subordinates had the situation well in hand, and he stood to one side, a spectator for once, while they relentlessly reduced the perimeter of the rebel beachhead. Latin America had never seen weapons like those of the government troops. Monday morning four batteries of their Soviet 122-mm howitzers started to rake the beach; the exiles who had been in the target area stumbled around in a daze. Rebel tank commanders fought gallantly, but the Russian T-34 tanks outgunned them. By Monday evening the exiles were desperately short of ammunition. "The night came and we were expecting the ships," Pepe San Román later told Haynes Johnson. "Everybody turned their faces to the sea waiting for the ships. We knew that without the ships we could not make it." Midnight came and there was nothing. In despair Pepe boarded an open boat with his radio operator and cruised six miles out, trying to reach the CIA boats with his signal. Then he returned to his command post and sent another officer out to keep trying to reach the captains, whose mutinous crews had rendered them impotent. Hour after hour the message went out from the open boat: DOLORES. THIS IS BEACH. DOLORES. THIS IS BEACH. I AM TRYING TO FIND YOU. WE NEED YOU. WE NEED YOU.

At dawn Tuesday six of La Brigada's remaining B-26s tried to bomb the Cuban air force planes at San Antonio de Los Baños. Castro's luck held; cloud cover blanketed the field; there was no damage. On the ground at Girón, massed T-34s stood in a solid line, firing point-blank into the beachhead. Within the narrowing perimeter all omens were bad. The lack of air cover had been the exiles' undoing. Now they couldn't even be evacuated without it.

In the White House Tuesday evening the President was called away from the Mansion's annual congressional reception. Incongruously dressed in white tie and tails, he stood over a map in his office while Rusk, McNamara, two of the Joint Chiefs, and Richard Bissell of the CIA told him that only the U.S. air force could save the brigade from Castro's kangaroo courts. He compromised, authorizing a flight of six unmarked jets from the carrier *Essex*, on duty in the Caribbean off the Bay of Pigs. For one hour—from 6:30 A.M. to 7:30 A.M. Wednesday—the U.S. planes would keep the sky over the beachhead clear of Castro planes while the rebels' remaining B-26s attacked the government troops on the perimeter.*

The last act of the Bay of Pigs tragicomedy followed. The rebel fliers' base was at Puerto Cabezas in Nicaragua, a three-hour-and-twenty-minute flight from Cuba. They were exhausted by their previous missions; only two of them had the strength for another effort. Four American advisers, believing that jets from the *Essex* would protect them, volunteered to pilot the other B-26s. They then made the last and least plausible of all the CIA mistakes in the blunder-studded operation. Nicaragua and Cuba are in different time zones. The pilots forgot to reset their watches. They arrived over Girón

* In *Give Us This Day* E. Howard Hunt Jr. has the effrontery to charge that Kennedy's failure to fill the sky with American warplanes was to blame for the failure of the Bay of Pigs expedition.

an hour early, while the jets which were to shield them were still on the flight deck of the *Essex*. Castro's T-33s swarmed up and made short work of them; the four Americans were killed.

Only the final agony was left now. Pleas from Girón for reinforcements, tanks, and ammunition became fainter. Messages were terse: FIGHTING ON BEACH. SEND ALL AVAILABLE AIRCRAFT NOW. And: IN WATER. OUT OF AMMO. ENEMY CLOSING IN. HELP MUST ARRIVE IN NEXT HOUR. The last stand began Tuesday night. Encircled by Castro's artillery and tanks, the exiles' leader sent his last message at 4:32 P.M. Wednesday: AM DESTROYING ALL MY EQUIPMENT AND COMMUNICATIONS. TANKS ARE IN SIGHT. I HAVE NOTHING TO FIGHT WITH. AM TAKING TO THE WOODS. I CANNOT WAIT FOR YOU.

The woods could provide only temporary shelter. Lacking the fallback plan, the rebels stumbled into enemy hands one by one. Castro's triumph was complete. He had broken the invasion in less than seventy-two hours, turning it into what Haynes Johnson in his excellent study of the battle calls "perhaps the most heavily publicized of the many bungled, poorly planned operations since the Light Brigade charged into oblivion at Balaklava." Ahead for the survivors in the brigade lay the humiliation of a public trial in Havana's Sports Palace and an imprisonment which was not to end until Christmas 1962, when Robert F. Kennedy and James B. Donovan led a successful movement to ransom them.

In the mid-1960s contemporary historians tended to believe that in the long run the Bay of Pigs was really a blessing; that because of it Kennedy became disillusioned with experts and was better equipped to face the Cuban missile crisis eighteen months later. Seen from the 1970s, the debacle at Girón, and his reaction to it, have a very different look. On Thursday of that week, the day after the invasion collapsed, the President spoke before the American Society of Newspaper Editors at the Statler-Hilton Hotel in Washington. He took a fighting stance. He was letting Castro go this time, he said, but he wanted the record to show that "our restraint is not inexhaustible." The United States was ready to act, "alone, if necessary," to "safeguard its security," and he warned Moscow that "should that time ever come, we do not intend to be lectured on intervention by those whose character was stamped for all time on the bloody streets of Budapest."

This was cold war rhetoric at its most bleak. Implicit in it was the assumption that the only danger to America lay outside the country's borders. The country's one adversary was monolithic international Communism, whose forces were "not to be underestimated in Cuba or anywhere else in the world." The governments and peoples of the Western Hemisphere were exhorted to "take an ever closer and more realistic look at the menace of external Communist intervention and domination in Cuba," for it was "clearer than ever before that we face a relentless struggle in every corner of the globe that goes far beyond the clash of armies and even nuclear armaments."

The great liberal turning of the 1960s still lay ahead then. Once it had been taken, the threats to the nation would be viewed as internal—racism, militarism, pollution, technology, bureaucracy, the population explosion, "the establishment." But in the Kennedy years all that lay ahead. The liberal hero of the hour, who in the 1930s had been the angry young workman, in the 1940s the GI, and in the 1950s the youth misunderstood by his mother, had become, in the early 1960s, the dedicated Peace Corpsman battling hunger, disease—and Communism—with tools of peace. As an American liberal of the time, Kennedy believed that the basic reasons for the revolutionary movements in underdeveloped countries were poverty and ignorance, which were being exploited by Communists for their own ends. He was sure that once those conditions had been changed by Point Four programs, the appeal of Communism would vanish. That was what the appeal of the Alianza was all about. A Latin America allied with the United States in pursuit of progress, it was held, would reject overtures from the Comintern.

These beliefs were deeply held. There was, perhaps for the last time, a liberal conviction that man would be able to solve his problems. The young idealist of the early 1960s was a pragmatist, to use a word much in vogue then. The hour of Ralph Nader, the liberal model of the next decade, had not yet struck. In the Kennedy years liberals believed, as they had believed since the years of Franklin Roosevelt, that the remedy for social wrongs lay in big government and stronger presidential powers. Later their disenchantment would shake the very foundations of the republic.

Kennedy's speech in the Statler-Hilton that Thursday might have been delivered in the Eisenhower years, perhaps even by John Foster Dulles. There were many differences in style, but not much in substance. Like all cold warriors Kennedy invoked the name of Munich toward the end, reminding his listeners of its meaning: that democracies which failed to stand up to totalitarian dictators were doomed; that "our security may be lost, piece by piece, country by country, without the firing of a single missile or the crossing of a single border." He intended "to profit by this lesson," he said, and he concluded: "History will record the fact that this bitter struggle reached its climax in the late 1950s and the early 1960s. Let me then make clear as the President of the United States that I am determined upon our system's survival and success, regardless of the cost and regardless of the peril."

Thus one of the worst guesses ever of what history would say. That address was Kennedy's public response to the Bay of Pigs. Back at the White House he took another, more symbolic step. McGeorge Bundy's status as national security adviser was sharply upgraded. He was moved from the relatively humble Executive Office Building, on the other side of West Executive Avenue, to the West Wing. There, much closer to the President's oval office, Bundy began presiding over regular morning meetings of his National Security Council staff. In addition he extended his sway over the White House war room, with its huge maps and brightly colored telephones. Next time the forces of world Communism plotted a blow at the free world, the United States would be on guard. If they dared subvert the anti-Communist government of another weak little country anywhere, they would meet a firmer will. The White House was ready. Bundy was ready. The war room was ready. The hot lines were plugged in. The aggressors would be taught a lesson they would never forget.

Among the thoughtful readers of reports from Cuba was Nikita Sergeyevich Khrushchev. The Chairman wasn't much impressed by cold war oratory, having delivered a lot of it himself. What interested him was that the new President, young and inexperienced, had stumbled badly. Kennedy seemed unsure of himself. This looked like a good time to pounce on him.

The White House knew that in the Kremlin this would be the interpretation of the debacle. It was the chief reason for Washington's dismay after taking stock of the wreckage of confidence left by the Bay of Pigs. In February a meeting between Kennedy and Khrushchev had been scheduled for early June, in Vienna. On May 12 the Chairman wrote that the invitation was still open. Kennedy thought of suggesting a postponement. But that, he decided, would be interpreted as a further sign of weakness. Better the summit, he said, than the brink. Instead of staying away he would redouble his preparations for the Vienna conference. He had been told that the Chairman had been disdainful of Eisenhower's failure to bone up on his homework before his two summits with Khrushchev; whenever a tough question came up, Ike had had to turn to aides for answers. Kennedy decided that the important talks there would be just the two of them and an interpreter.

Like him, Khrushchev was under pressure from hard-liners at home, Stalinists who believed that the only way to get what you wanted from the other side was to demand it, to grab it, to be coarse and abusive and intimidating. There was a lot of this in Khrushchev himself. Stalin had admired it in him. It was what gave him his aura of primitive power. The previous autumn he had provided the U.N. General Assembly with a memorable demonstration of it. The Congo in these years was a graveyard for the reputations of geopoliticians. Khrushchev, already frustrated by the U-2 incident, the aborting of the Geneva summit with Eisenhower, and the end of his hopes for a Soviet-American detente, had been maddened at fresh humiliations in Katanga. He had blamed Dag Hammarskjöld, calling him a tool of colonial powers. Demanding that the post of secretary general of the U.N. be abolished, he had proposed that it be replaced by an executive body of three men representing the three groups of nations, western, Communist, and neutral. He had called it a "troika," after the Russian wagon drawn by three horses abreast. For emphasis, he had removed his shoe and pounded his desk in rhythm. The General Assembly was in an uproar. Trying to restore order, the Irishman who was presiding at the time banged the gavel so hard that he broke it. The chaos delighted the Chairman. Returning to Moscow, he crowed, "How shaky the United Nations is! It's the beginning of the end."

On January 6, 1961, Khrushchev countered the American liberals' policy toward underdeveloped countries—a dual plan of economic aid, with military intervention if necessary—with what was to be Communism's great challenge of the 1960s: "unlimited support" to "peoples fighting for their liberation" in "just" wars. Six weeks later Patrice Lumumba, his Congolese ally, was murdered in Katanga. The infuriated Russian called the assassination "the crowning achievement of Hammarskjöld's criminal activities" and again demanded the secretary general's immediate removal.

The Russian right had other grievances for which Khrushchev was the spokesman. Laos, which had appeared to be about to drop into their lap, was veering toward a neutral course. Red Army hard-liners wanted a resumption of nuclear tests, suspended in the Soviet Union since the fall of 1958; they now had 20-, 30-, 50-, and 100-megaton weapons, and were eager to try them out. These were daily irritants, symptoms of the cold war which kept the diplomatic climate chilly without creating a world crisis. But for them one issue was vital, and transcended the others. Khrushchev had variously described it as a "bone stuck in the throat," "a sort of cancerous tumor requiring a surgical operation," and a "Sarajevo" likely to lead toward another world war. It was divided Berlin.

For fifteen years the Russians had regarded the presence of the West in the former German capital as unbearable. Stalin had tried to evict Allied troops in 1948 and had been thwarted by the great airlift. When the first sputnik raised Soviet stock, Khrushchev had seized the opportunity to demand that Berlin be made a demilitarized "free city." He had given the Allies a six-month deadline then, and he had postponed it only when Eisenhower had made that a condition of Khrushchev's trip to the United States. Ike had made certain concessions. He had agreed that the Berlin situation was "abnormal." He had offered to negotiate the size of the western garrison there and the extent to which the city would serve as a base for West German propaganda and intelligence activities.

Now Khrushchev was stalking Kennedy with the same issue. In his wars-of-liberation speech the Chairman had come down hard on Berlin. He had openly threatened Kennedy. If "the imperialists" refused "to take into consideration the true situation," he had said, the Soviet Union would "take firm measures" and "sign a peace treaty with the German Democratic Republic." Thus Kennedy faced the demon Eisenhower had exorcised. Khrushchev made it clear that such an agreement would include guarantees that any "violation" of East Germany's frontiers would be considered "an act of aggression" against all members of the Warsaw Pact—meaning that the West would have to forsake Berlin or go to war. Did he mean it? Charles de Gaulle was doubtful. He urged the President to hold firm ("*tenir le coup*"). If Kennedy held fast and made plans for a new airlift, he said, the Chairman would back off. Looking to Vienna, Averell Harriman agreed, though he recommended different tactics. Khrushchev, he predicted, would be fierce. He would try to frighten the young President. The best response would be to turn him aside, but it should be done gently. And Kennedy mustn't overestimate his adversary. Khrushchev would be nervous too, Harriman said. The Chairman's only other trip to the West had failed. Furthermore, American Kremlinologists agreed that he had never forgotten his lowly origins. Inevitably there would be tension in Vienna. The Chairman would be offensive as only he knew how to be. The President, Harriman suggested, should rise above it and laugh it off.

This advice reached Kennedy in Paris, on the eve of his flight to Austria. The French leg of the trip had turned into a triumph for the young First Lady. Eleven years earlier, she had been a student here at the Sorbonne. Now she arrived with two truckloads of luggage, a blinding array of jewels, and a retinue that included Europe's leading hairdresser. De Gaulle could scarcely take his eyes off her. The French press cried "*Ravissante!*" "*Charmante!*" and "*Apothéose!*" Arriving at a press conference, the President said, "I do not think it altogether inappropriate for me to introduce myself. I am the man who accompanied Jacqueline Kennedy to Paris."

Vienna was different. Mrs. Kennedy teased Khrushchev—"Oh, Mr. Chairman, don't bore me with statistics"—but the gloomy pall was too heavy to be laughed away, even by her. Almost from the moment Khrushchev's black, Russian-built Chaika drove past the barbwire and up to the massive stone and stucco building that served as the U.S. embassy residence in the Austrian capital, the mood was as ugly as the weather. To an aide Kennedy described his adversary as a combination of external jocosity and "internal rage." During the two days of talks the rage was external, too. James Reston had asked to interview the President after the final encounter. Kennedy was wearing a hat that day, and as he entered the room where the reporter was waiting and sank down on a couch, he pushed the hat over his eyes and uttered a great sigh. Reston thought he seemed in a state of semi-shock. He asked the President, "Pretty rough?" Kennedy replied, "Roughest thing in my life."

Afterward Reston wrote:

> He [the President] came into a dim room in the American Embassy shaken and angry. He had tried, as always, to be calm and rational with Khrushchev, to get him to define what the Soviet Union would and would not do, and Khrushchev had bullied him and

> threatened him with war over Berlin. . . . Kennedy said just enough in that room to convince me of the following:
>
> Khrushchev had studied the events of the Bay of Pigs; he would have understood if Kennedy had left Castro alone or destroyed him; but when Kennedy was rash enough to strike at Cuba but not bold enough to finish the job, Khrushchev decided he was dealing with an inexperienced young leader who could be intimidated and blackmailed.

In their talks, Kennedy told Reston, the Chairman had been rude, savage; at times he had seemed to be about to lunge at Kennedy. On only one issue was he reasonable: Laos, which he regarded as unimportant. In discussing everything else his manner was vicious, sneering. Hammarskjöld had to go, he insisted; he must be replaced by the troika. Similarly, three executives from the world's three political camps would be needed to administer any disarmament agreement between the United States and the USSR. In vain Kennedy argued that an arrangement would be rendered impotent by a veto—"Even the Russian troika has but one driver." On the matter of Berlin Khrushchev delivered an ultimatum. The bone, he said, must be removed from the Soviet throat. With or without an American agreement, he would sign a treaty with East Germany before the end of the year. If the United States wanted to go to war on this question, there was nothing he could do about it. Madmen who sought war deserved only straitjackets.

During their last private meeting, held at Kennedy's request, the President desperately tried to dissuade him from so rash a step. Khrushchev bluntly refused. "I want peace," he said, "but if you want war that is your problem." His treaty decision was irreversible. He would sign it in December. As they parted Kennedy said, "It will be a cold winter."*

To Reston Kennedy said: "I've got two problems. First, to figure out why he did it, and in such a hostile way. And second, to figure out what we can do about it. I think the first part is pretty easy to explain. I think he did it because of the Bay of Pigs. I think he thought anyone who was so young and inexperienced as to get into a mess like that could be taken, and anyone who got into it,

* In *Khrushchev Remembers* the Chairman commented: ". . . I was genuinely pleased with our meeting in Vienna. Even though we came to no concrete agreement, I could tell that he was interested in finding a peaceful solution to world problems. . . . He was a reasonable man, and I think he knew that he wouldn't be justified in starting a new war over Berlin."

and didn't see it through, had no guts. So he just beat hell out of me. So I've got a terrible problem. If he thinks I'm inexperienced and have no guts, until we remove those ideas we won't get anywhere with him. So we have to act."

Khrushchev's credibility would be watched, too, and he knew it. Returning to Moscow, he ordered publication of the two aides-mémoire he had handed the President on nuclear testing and Berlin. Sharp eyes in the State Department saw that here there was no time limit attached to the Berlin demands, but it hardly mattered now. The whole world knew of the Russian ultimatum. Since then Khrushchev had increased the Soviet military budget by 3.144 billion rubles and had delivered a series of chauvinistic speeches.

Kennedy escalated with him. On June 25 he made a telecast report to the American people. "If war breaks out," he said, "it will have been started in Moscow and not in Berlin. . . . Only the Soviet government can use the Berlin frontier as a pretext for war." He asked Congress to approve authorization of $3,247,000,000 for the Pentagon, calling up reserves, tripling draft calls, raising the ceiling for combat troops, and reconditioning planes and ships which were in mothballs. Dean Acheson wanted him to declare a state of emergency, and Vice President Lyndon Johnson agreed. Kennedy preferred to leave the door open to negotiations. He hesitated to make an atomic bluff because it might be called. His chief fear, he told an editor of the *New York Post,* was that the Chairman "wants to rub my nose in the dirt," in which case "it's all over."

Pressure built up for both leaders. To reassure Germans in the old capital that they would not be abandoned, Kennedy sent his Vice President there with General Clay, the hero of the airlift. Khrushchev warned the world that the USSR could now create a bomb with an explosive power equal to 100 million tons of TNT and had rockets capable of delivering it. As though to prove his point, a second Soviet astronaut, Major Gherman S. Titov, was launched into orbit and circled the earth seventeen times. Kennedy urged Americans to build bomb shelters. Meanwhile Berlin was in an uproar. During July, 30,444 refugees flowed into the western part of the city. In the first ten days of August another 16,500 crossed. On the twelfth alone 4,000 were counted, among them a high proportion of physicians, technicians, and skilled workers—the very people necessary for the Five-Year Program of the First Secretary of East Germany's Communist party, Walter Ulbricht.

At a half-hour past midnight on August 13, sirens screamed down the dark and deserted streets as squat tanks—T-34s and T-54s—led East German military convoys to the twenty-five-mile border that separated the western part of the city from the east. Trucks of steel-helmeted Vopos, East Berlin policemen, took up positions in the major intersections. Troops unloaded wooden horses, concertinas of barbed wire, concrete posts, stone blocks, and picks and shovels. Four hours later, at sunrise, the beginning of a wall was visible. Four days later it was complete, imprisoning the Germans who remained in East Berlin.

The western powers had been caught off balance. Kennedy was away from Washington. It took the State Department four days to deliver a formal protest in Moscow. Then, on September 1, Khrushchev gave the screw another turn. U.S. seismographs recorded unmistakable evidence that the Russians had resumed testing. Kennedy and Macmillan appealed to the Chairman to stop, citing the extent and toxicity of the new fallout. Khrushchev ignored them. Detection devices picked up a second test, and a third. Over the next month the Soviets detonated thirty major devices, nearly all of them in the atmosphere. At the end of the series the Russians had become responsible for more radioactive poison in the air than the Americans, the British, and the French combined. In a speech before the Communist Twenty-second Congress the Chairman announced the imminent explosion of a 50-megaton bomb—2,500 times as large as the one which had been dropped on Hiroshima and five times the size of all high explosives used in all the wars in history. He drew laughter from the delegates at the next session when he told them that the resulting blast "proved somewhat bigger than the 50 megatons that the scientists had calculated," but that they would not be punished for the "mistake."

Kennedy decided that if this constituted Khrushchev's only answer to western proposals for an atmospheric test ban, he had to authorize a resumption of U.S. tests, though he approved only those underground, which had no fallout. In view of the acts of the Soviet government, he said, "we must now take those steps which prudent men find essential." It was now September 8, the peak of the crisis. The wall was complete, a corral of brick and jagged cement cutting through the heart of Berlin. Since August 22 all but one of the crossing points had been closed to the Allies, and there the Vopos insisted upon inspecting soldiers' papers. Any approach to the border closer than 100 meters (91 yards) was prohibited. Next notes to Paris, Bonn, and Washington formally demanded that West German leaders be forbidden to enter Berlin by plane. At that, the West stiffened. On September 8 Khrushchev's insistence that West German flights into Berlin should be controlled was curtly rejected. Ten days later, when Kennedy was about to leave Hyannisport to return to Washington, he was handed a grim note. Dag Hammarskjöld had been killed in a Congolese plane crash which has never been clearly explained. War had not seemed so close since V-J Day.

Two weeks later Khrushchev began to back away from the brink. To the Belgian diplomat Paul-Henri Spaak, who was visiting Moscow, he said, "I realize that contrary to what I had hoped the western powers will not sign the peace treaty. . . . I'm not trying to put you in an impossible situation; I know very well that you can't let yourself be stepped on." The bone in the throat wasn't intolerable, after all. "You know," he continued to the Belgian, "Berlin is not such a big problem for me. What are two million people among a billion Communists!" Nor was there any hurry now. He had given Kennedy an ultimatum—"by the end of the year"—but to Spaak he said, "I'm not bound by any deadline." Having built his wall, he now appeared to be trying to wring concessions from the West which would allow him to save face. He made several gestures intended to ease tensions, including generous comments about Kennedy's maturity and evident wisdom. When there was no response to them, he threw in his hand anyhow. Speaking once more to the Communist Party Congress, he declared on October 17, "The western powers are showing some understanding of the situation and are inclined to seek a solution to the German problem and the issue of West Berlin." He concluded, "If that is so, we shall not insist on signing a peace treaty absolutely before December 31, 1961."

With that, the confrontation ended. It seemed to be a victory for the Americans. Later the real price paid began to emerge. Given the attitude of Moscow, the Berlin question, and the resumption of nuclear testing, Schlesinger would write, "the President unquestionably felt that an American retreat in Asia might upset the whole world balance." Kennedy believed that there he must provide his adversaries with additional proof of fearlessness and backbone. To James Reston he observed that the only place where Communists were challenging the West in a shooting war was in Indochina, so "now we have a problem in trying to make our power credible, and Vietnam looks like the place."

This was a cheerless time for Lyndon Johnson. The year before, he had been the mighty majority leader of the U.S. Senate, and now, as Vice President, he occupied the emptiest, most exasperating position in the government. Every day Johnson's relative insignificance was driven home to him in countless ways. He was allowed only one parking place at the White House, and just one White House phone extension. (Attorney General Robert Kennedy had three.) His wife had never seen the inside of the presidential aircraft. He himself had been aboard, though not by invitation. Three times Kennedy aides had found him poking around its cabins alone. Inasmuch as they had been there because the President was about to use the plane, they had been obliged to ask him to leave. Each encounter should have been daunting, but he kept returning, fascinated, it seemed, by the symbols of real power.

Kennedy men treated Johnson people as outsiders. With the exception of Walter Jenkins, members of the vice-presidential staff were total strangers to the glamorous presidential advisers. Several lacked credentials to enter the White House and had seen it only as tourists. The obscurity even enveloped Secret Service agents assigned to the Johnson detail. Officially they were full equals of the men who guarded the President. In practice they were ostracized by the White House detail—excluded from their cars, their offices, their social functions. Most of them were philosophical about it. They knew there was nothing personal about the snubs. They had been banished by the elite because the man they were guarding was—there is no other word for it—unimportant.

Kennedy was largely unaware of this. Like most Presidents he kept the man next in line at arm's length. The occupants of America's first and second elective offices have never been congenial, for reasons rooted in historical precedent and, perhaps, in human nature. Some Vice Presidents who have been close to their chief executives in earlier years have been hurt to find friendship replaced by icy aloofness. They forget that to a President a Vice President is a daily reminder of his own mortality. He is more. Though individuals may contemplate the grave serenely, they are not constantly shadowed by understudies. Those who expect Presidents to provide Vice Presidents with detailed briefings rarely weigh the implications of it. To grasp it, one must understand the meaning of the Presidency, the legacy the second man stands to inherit. The head of a family may make out his will without flinching, but he would blanch if told that the man next door would, in the event of his death, become father to his children and husband to his wife.

Beyond this institutional difficulty lies another. It is a fact of political life that presidential campaign tickets are "balanced" by pairing two candidates from different parts of the country who appeal to different constituencies and whose make-ups may be antithetical. The husband, in short, must choose as his possible replacement a man who doesn't look like him, dress like him, talk like him, or share his values. Franklin Roosevelt and Harry Truman bore only the faintest resemblance to one another. The same was true of Eisenhower and Nixon, and of Kennedy and Johnson. To Kennedy, Johnson was a marvelous and often comical prodigy. His self-aggrandizement was shameless and exuberant; on trips abroad he would telephone his Washington office daily for reports on how his activities were being played in the American press. He was always campaigning—"My God!" gasped an American doctor in Pakistan. "He's shaking hands with a leper!"—and his decision to transform a Karachi camel driver into an ambassador of good will delighted the country. "We have come to see you and your camel," he told the astonished Bashir Ahmed. "Our President wants to see your camel. He has plans to make things better for you." He had no such thing, and the stunt seemed certain to backfire. Yet in the end it didn't. Ahmed's trip to the United States was an enormous success. Kennedy was impressed. "If it had been me," he said, "I'd have wound up with camel shit on the White House lawn."

Knowing how unhappy the Vice President was, the President went out of his way to honor Johnson and invent missions abroad for him. Later some of them became important. It is ironic that the two which appealed to him the least in advance loom largest in retrospect. The first was to Berlin. He was glum before it, but he spoke well there and was on hand to greet the first U.S. reinforcements to enter the city. His hosts believed that his visit was a turning point for the beleaguered city, and he returned home deeply affected.

The other trip, that May, was to Saigon. In the end it was of even greater significance, although that wasn't apparent then. The journey was a tour of southern Asia. The Vice President was expected to bolster the confidence of non-Communist regimes. He was not, as he had been in Berlin, a symbol of America's resolve to fight alongside them. At that time U.S. commitments there had not gone that far. Nevertheless, his pledge to Saigon was very strong. Greatly taken with Ngo Dinh Diem, he publicly hailed him as "the Winston Churchill of south Asia." After the party had left Vietnam, Stan Karnow, a writer for the *Saturday Evening Post*, asked him whether he really believed that. "Shit, man," the Vice President replied, "he's the only boy we got out here."

The Winston Churchill of south Asia was a dark, stubby, chain-smoking bachelor whose most striking trait was his seeming inability to end a conversation. Survivors would emerge from his big yellow stucco Freedom Palace after nonstop Diem monologues that were said to last six, seven, even twelve hours. But he didn't have many other weaknesses. At sixty he was decisive, dedicated, and firm in purpose. Diem was an archetype of the strong man in power. His title was president, yet he didn't think much of democracy. He was more of an Oriental despot, or at any rate an aloof mandarin who firmly believed that it was the duty of his people to respect and to obey him. His rivals were sent to concentration camps. Under him there was no freedom of the press and no real reform. Army officers were political appointees, chosen for their loyalty, not their ability, and though Diem himself was honest, the halls of his palace swarmed with the corrupt and the ambitious. Rigid and inflexible, he seemed to feel that Roman Catholics should be privileged for no other reason than that he himself was a Catholic. To an astonishing degree, his responsibilities were undelegated—company commanders couldn't move their men without his permission, and until late in his regime, no passport was valid unless it bore the signature of Diem himself. With each passing month he held the reins of authority more tightly, consulting only a few trusted aides and the members of his family, particularly an aggressive brother, Ngo Dinh Nhu and Nhu's lovely, venomous wife, known to American foreign correspondents as "the Dragon Lady." "If we open the window," Madame Nhu once said, explaining the Ngo philosophy of government, "not only sunlight but many bad things will fly in."

Little went in and not much came out. This was especially true of information. The lack of hard facts explains one of the two great mysteries about the Vietnam War: why it became a graveyard for the reputations of experts from the West. Rarely in history have so many eminent men been so singularly wrong about such an important event. Right down to October 1972, when Henry Kissinger fell flat on his face by prematurely announcing a settlement of it, soldiers and statesmen misjudged the character of the war and its probable course. On April 6, 1954, a New England senator had diverted his colleagues by reciting some earlier appraisals of it: "the military situation appears to be developing favorably" (Dean Acheson, 1952), "In Indochina we believe the tide now is turning" (Assistant Secretary of State Walter Robertson, 1953), a French victory "is both possible and probable" (Secretary of Defense Charles E. Wilson, 1954), and "the French are going to win" (Admiral Radford, 1954). The French lost, having sacrificed 19,000 Frenchmen in seven years.* That would seem to have vindicated the skeptical New England senator, who was John F. Kennedy. Then Kennedy, too, became trapped. In the White House his policy toward Vietnam came to be based on such Lewis Carroll appraisals as a 1960 Senate committee report which predicted that "on the basis of the assurances of the head of the military aid mission in Vietnam . . . the U.S. military . . . can be phased out of Vietnam in the forseeable future," and early in 1961 President Kennedy approved an aid plan based on the assumption that the war would be won in eighteen months.

The second Vietnam mystery is why Americans of so many persuasions, including four Presidents, two Republican and two Democratic, felt obliged to rescue the Saigon government. The country was, after all, in Asia, five thousand miles away, a primitive land of rice paddies and dense jungle curled around the remote Indochinese peninsula. Yet for over a decade administrations in Washington battled desperately to keep questionable men in power in there, even at the risk of domestic tranquillity at home. The American effort in Vietnam was ill-starred from the outset. Kennedy should have seen that. He was one of the few who had diagnosed the trouble in the beginning. As a congressman, he had toured Vietnam in 1951. "Without the support of the native population," he had said on *Meet the Press* on his return, "there is no hope of success in any of the countries of Southeast Asia." Later he, too, fell

* Compared with 45,882 Americans lost between 1961 and 1972. The usual figure given for French casualties is 92,000, but that includes Foreign Legionnaires, Africans, and Vietnamese who fought under the French flag. France, unlike the United States, sent no draftees to Vietnam.

under the spell of cold war rhetoric. America had "lost" China, cold-warriors held; now it must not "lose" Indochina.

The original American commitment to Saigon had been made in 1954 and renewed in 1957. In a letter to Diem after the Geneva agreements had been signed, President Eisenhower pledged U.S. support "to assist the Government of Viet-Nam in developing and maintaining a strong, viable state, capable of resisting subversion or aggression through military means." Ike made this agreement with the understanding that it would be accompanied "by performance on the part of Viet-Nam in undertaking needed reforms." The purpose of his assurance was to "discourage any who might wish to impose a foreign ideology on your free people."

"Ike has made a promise," Lyndon Johnson would say of Vietnam during his years in the White House. "I have to keep it." But he didn't. This wasn't a pact. The Senate had nothing to do with it. It lacked even the legitimacy of an executive order. Yet both Johnson and Kennedy felt bound by it. To have withdrawn U.S. support, Theodore C. Sorensen wrote, would have caused "the world to wonder about the reliability of this nation's pledges." Arthur Schlesinger went further:

> Whether we had vital interests in South Vietnam before 1954, the Eisenhower letter created those interests. Whether we should have drawn the line where we did, once it was drawn we became every succeeding year more imprisoned by it. Whether the domino theory was valid in 1954, it had acquired validity seven years later, after neighboring governments had staked their own security on the ability of the United States to live up to its pledges to Saigon. Kennedy . . . had no choice but to work within the situation he had inherited.

"The cause in Vietnam," Theodore H. White wrote in *The Making of the President 1968,* was "the cause of America for half a century, a cause made clear to the world. . . . If there is any fragile form of world order today, 400,000 American battle deaths in four wars in this century have created that world order." President Johnson argued that to "cut and run," would have been to "say to the world in this case that we don't live up to our treaties and don't stand by our friends." *Time* explained to those who felt otherwise that:

> . . . South Vietnam must be defended at all costs. . . . If the U.S. cannot or will not save South Viet Nam from the Communist

assault, no Asian nation can ever again feel safe in putting its faith in the U.S.—and the fall of all of Southeast Asia would only be a matter of time.

The consequences of such a withdrawal were considered unthinkable. In support of sending American draftees to Vietnam, Robert McNamara and the Joint Chiefs of Staff flatly declared that the alternative was serious deterioration throughout that part of the world. General Lyman L. Lemnitzer, speaking for the Chiefs, predicted that in the event of a Viet Cong victory, "We would lose Asia all the way to Singapore," and General Maxwell Taylor, confident of success against the guerrilla enemy—North Vietnam was "extremely vulnerable to conventional bombing," he said—told President Kennedy that a "U.S. military task force" was "essential."

There was no sense in any of this. If the Kennedy administration hadn't felt bound to evacuate the Cuban brigade from its doomed beachhead, then it owed Diem nothing. Furthermore, the Eisenhower letter had no validity now because Diem had openly flouted the obligation of introducing "needed reforms." He had also refused to hold all-Vietnam elections in 1956. For him to have invoked the sanctity of treaties would have been absurd, even if the United States had been bound to him by a treaty, which of course it wasn't.

The real pressures binding Washington to Saigon were political. McCarthy was dead, but both Democrats and Republicans were haunted by the nightmarish possibility that Diem might become a second Chiang Kai-shek. It is all the more ironical, then, that they repeated the very mistake Americans counseling Chiang had made; though the problem was political there, too, the aid they gave was military. One reason for their error was the attitude of powerful figures on Capitol Hill who had great faith in the Joint Chiefs and little trust in the political officers on the State Department's Asian desk. Another explanation lay in the character of the two cabinet members advising the White House on Vietnam in the early 1960s. McNamara was decisive and forceful, Rusk was timid and vague; inevitably the more persuasive voice came from the Pentagon.

Vietnam had been comparatively placid in the latter Eisenhower years. Eight hundred U.S. military advisers and three hundred million dollars in military aid a year had sufficed to preserve the status quo. Then, in December 1960, the month before Kennedy's inaugural, Diem's adversaries announced the formation of a National Liberation Front. In Freedom Palace their rivals christened the NLF the Viet Cong (literally, "Vietnamese Communists"). Diem wasn't worried by it at first. The previous autumn he had easily turned back an attempted coup, and when Vice President Johnson asked him if he wanted some American soldiers, he said he didn't. But though ground troops weren't necessary then, he admitted needing some help. President Kennedy approved the dispatch of a 400-man Special Forces group (the Green Berets) for training missions. For the first time the American commitment included troops.

Early in May 1961 a new U.S. ambassador, Frederick E. Nolting Jr., arrived in Saigon. His predecessor had tried to reason with Diem, and as a result had become, in effect, *persona non grata*. Nolting was resolved not to repeat that mistake. By now Viet Cong depredations were so obvious that even the mandarin president had to acknowledge them. The situation in the countryside was deteriorating. Guerrilla bands roamed at will, assassinating village chieftains. A U.S. intelligence estimate reported that an "extremely critical period" lay "immediately ahead" and warned that the Saigon regime's "reliance on virtually one-man rule" and "toleration of corruption" led many to "question Diem's ability to lead in this period."

In Washington the White House was being urged to step into the Vietnamese breach of its various bureaucratic constituencies. Deputy Undersecretary of State U. Alexis Johnson asked Kennedy to accept "defeat of the Vietcong" as a "real and ultimate" objective. The Joint Chiefs assured the President that 40,000 U.S. troops would "clean up the Vietcong threat," and that another 128,000 would be enough to turn back possible North Vietnam or Chinese Communist intervention. Roswell W. Gilpatric, McNamara's deputy at Defense, proposed talks with Diem on the "possibility of a defensive security alliance," and William P. Bundy, also in the Pentagon at that stage, urged "early and hard-hitting" American intervention in the war. Bundy gave it a 70 percent chance of success.

Kennedy authorized further studies, agreed to expand the 685-man U.S. military advisory group in Saigon, and approved plans to equip and pay 20,000 more Vietnamese troops for Diem (for a total of 150,000). Like Ike, he wanted aid contingent upon domestic reforms and mobilization of South Vietnamese resources against the Viet Cong, but he wasn't emphatic about it. He was preoccupied with Berlin and nuclear testing at the time. Schlesinger doubts that he ever gave Vietnam "his full attention." Observers attuned to the cold war continued to be baffled by Vietnam. "The situation gets worse almost week by week," Theodore H. White wrote in August 1961. White found that "guerrillas now control almost all the Southern delta—so much so that I could find no American who would drive me outside Saigon in his car even by day without military convoy." He reported a "political breakdown of formidable proportions." Then he wrote: ". . . what perplexes hell out of me is that the Commies, on their side, seem to be able to find people willing to die for their cause." The revolutionary spirit has often perplexed those not imbued with it.

The following month guerrillas captured a provincial capital and executed the governor. Diem's troops were in retreat everywhere. Reluctantly he summoned Nolting and asked for a bilateral defense treaty. Washington was in a responsive mood. All summer support had been coalescing around the Lyndon Johnson approach to Southeast Asia. The Vice President was voicing the classic liberal position: the real enemies in Vietnam, he had written on his return from there, were "hunger, ignorance, poverty, and disease." He believed that Americans "must—whatever strategies we evolve—keep those enemies the point of our attack, and make imaginative use of our scientific and technological capacity."

The President responded by sending to Saigon a high-level mission comprising two of his most trusted advisers, General Maxwell Taylor and Walt W. Rostow. Thus a general and a militant civilian —for Rostow, first to last, was the most uncompromising of the hawks—were to be the President's eyes and ears in Vietnam at this critical juncture. The absence of any American diplomat of stature was significant. It reflected, as Sorensen later wrote, "the State Department's inability to compete with the Pentagon." The result was further emphasis on military objectives at the expense of political considerations.

The Taylor-Rostow report marked one of the great turning points in the Vietnam War. To arrest the decline in Diem's fortunes, Kennedy was urged to send him a large contingent of American advisers, and—more important—American infantry: 8,000 at once and more as needed. Taylor, the dominant member of the team, wanted Vietnam to be the subject of a major presidential telecast. Some of his arguments for intervention were curious. In coming down hard on the side of an expeditionary force, for example, he compared Vietnam with Korea, "where U.S. troops learned to live and work without too much effort." Actually Korea and Vietnam were very different. The first was a conventional struggle, with enemy formations crossing a border and engaging Americans in fixed battles on terrain relatively familiar to U.S. soldiers. The second was irregular warfare in dense tropical jungle. Most important of all, the native population in South Korea wanted the Americans there. In Vietnam they didn't; Vietnamese villagers tended to regard U.S. Caucasian troops as successors to the French, and the Viet Cong as heroes.

Some members of the administration subcabinet—Chester Bowles, George Ball, and Averell Harriman among them—were appalled by this recommendation. The only senior man to question it, however, was Kennedy himself. He refused to go to the people on TV because that would confer upon Vietnam the status of Berlin. He also noted pointedly that Taylor and Rostow, unlike the Joint Chiefs, were optimistic about the effectiveness of U.S. intervention only if the North Vietnamese were prevented from infiltrating South Vietnam, and that they had no ideas for accomplishing that. What dismayed him most was the proposal to send soldiers. Sorensen wrote: "All his principal advisors on Vietnam favored it, calling it the 'touchstone' of our good faith, a symbol of our determination. But the President in effect voted 'no'—and only his vote counted." Kennedy told an aide: "They want a force of American troops. They say it's necessary in order to restore confidence and maintain morale. But it will be just like Berlin. The troops will march in; the bands will play; the crowds will cheer; and in four days everyone will have forgotten. Then we will be told we have to send more troops. It's like taking a drink. The effect wears off, and you have to take another."

Nevertheless, he was being manipulated. He vetoed U.S. troops but yielded on other points, and a buildup of U.S. strength in Vietnam began in December 1961. Like Eisenhower seven years earlier, the President affirmed the arrangement in a public exchange of letters with Diem. It wasn't all one-way; Diem conceded the need for reforms and acknowledged the need for more leadership and better morale in his army. But no limits were set for the amount of U.S. assistance or when it would end, other than when the Viet Cong had been pacified and the North Vietnamese driven out. Taylor saw no great peril in that. "The risks of backing into a major Asian war by way of South Vietnam," he cabled the President from the Philippines, "are present but not impressive." George Ball, on the other hand, was apprehensive. Diem wouldn't stop pressing until he got the administration to send infantrymen, he said. That was what Diem really wanted; it would allow him to stabilize his regime while the Americans did his fighting for him. Ball predicted that if that commitment was made it would not stay small. Within five years, he told the President, there would be 300,000 U.S. troops in Vietnam. Kennedy laughed and said, "George, you're crazier than hell."

One factor in the coming acceleration—which would vindicate Ball and then some—was the character of the Americans making decisions in Saigon. From early 1962 until the end of Kennedy's thousand days in power the two key figures were Ambassador Nolting and General Paul D. Harkins, the new head of the U.S. Military Assistance Advisory Group (MAAG), who reached Vietnam in February. The choice of both was tragic. Nolting, a member of an old Virginia family, was a traditionalist who knew nothing about Asia. His appointment had been recommended by the anti-Communist hard-liners in the State Department. In any crisis he would back Diem, and when Kennedy really needed him he would be found to be off cruising on the Aegean Sea on an extended vacation. Harkins was worse. He was the maverick son of a cultivated Boston family, a high school dropout who had risen in the Army solely because he was a good cavalryman, a spirited polo player, and a horsy companion for George S. Patton when Patton wanted to relax. In World War II Harkins had been Patton's deputy chief of staff; his nickname then had been "the ramrod" because of the way he drove Patton's orders home. Like Patton, he sometimes had trouble taking orders himself. This was to be particularly true when his instructions required him to send the President candid reports on how the war was going. Kennedy had made it plain that he wanted to know everything, the good news and the bad. But Harkins didn't like to relay bad news. He thought it might reflect on him. Instead he acted as though his mission were to make things look good on the surface. When he arrived in Saigon he told American correspondents that he was an optimist and liked to have optimists around him. Henceforth, he disclosed, the daily situation appraisal for Washington would be called "The Headway Report." He intended to leave no doubt that under him the fight against the Viet Cong would be making headway.

Nolting and Harkins agreed that Diem was the answer to all problems, that nothing could be done without him, and that since criticism of his regime would only anger him, there would be none of it. In the phrase of Homer Bigart of the *New York Times*, this became the policy of "Sink or Swim with Ngo Dinh Diem." Diem quickly realized that there was no limit to the ways he could take advantage of these two Americans.

The first drive against the Viet Cong after Harkins's arrival was called, appropriately, Operation Sunrise. Harkins told reporters that he was planning construction of a chain of fortified "strategic hamlets" which would be manned by home defense units; his co-planner was the Vietnamese president's brother Nhu. The next thing Washington knew, strategic hamlets were a thundering success, with over one-third of the total rural population living in them. The war seemed to be turning around. All the reports from Saigon were good. Skeptics could check Harkins's appreciations with those from Nolting, which also glowed.

In reality the experiments with the fortified hamlets were a failure. Nothing had changed except the men at the top. They were waging war through public relations releases. Reports from the field were being rewritten by Harkins, with pessimism and unwelcome information deleted and outright fiction substituted. Colonels and majors who objected—and some did, most memorably Lieutenant Colonel John Paul Vann—were transferred to unwelcome assignments with notations in their records that ended their military careers. When another general, junior to Harkins, toured the front and found a situation very different from that being depicted in the MAAG commander's self-serving dispatches, he gave Harkins an appraisal telling the truth about the war. Harkins scribbled in the margin—"Lies," "Lies," "More lies"—and stuck it in the back of a file cabinet. The real lies were his own, but the only sources to contradict him were the stories in American newspapers cabled back from correspondents in Vietnam. Harkins explained them away by calling the reporters sensation-mongers or, worse, traitors. When occasional reverses were acknowledged it was because Harkins had an ulterior motive. He wanted more men, more guns, more choppers. Failure to supply them, he warned, would mean that civilians were letting down the army, and anybody who remembered China knew what *that* would mean.

Had there been a Tet offensive or any other eruption in Viet Cong activity, this press-agentry might have been exposed in the beginning. As it happened, there was a drop in guerrilla activity. That was all the manipulators of news needed. Operation Sunrise, they declared, had brought blue skies over the battlefield. They were elated, and in Washington their elation was infectious. Maxwell Taylor said he sensed "a great national movement" in Vietnam to crush the Viet Cong. McNamara said, "Every quantitative measurement we have shows we're winning this war." President Kennedy, surprised and pleased, authorized an expansion of the Saigon command from 2,000 men to 16,000, and the U.S. Military Assistance Advisory Group (MAAG) was upgraded to the Military Assistance Command, Vietnam (MACV).

Montage: The Early Sixties

Michael row the boat ashore
Hal — le — lu —— jah
Michael row the boat ashore
Hal — le — lu —— jah

NEWBURGH MAYOR CUTS RELIEF TO MAKE UNEMPLOYED FIND JOBS

Are you smoking more and enjoying it less?

Margaret Mead, commenting on Mary Quant dresses which actually climb *above* the knee, observed, "We are going through a period of extreme exhibitionism."

VOTE HERE FOR MISS RHEINGOLD!

You gotta shake, rattle, 'n' roll

The Twist's origins are obscure, according to *Billboard.* It is said to have grown out of a dance called the Madison which originated in Philadelphia and was based on Rock 'n' Roll music. Nineteen-year-old Chubby Checker and twenty-two-year old Joe Dee are often considered the fathers of the Twist.

bug out

Good night, David
Good night, Chet

Maximilian Schell
in
JUDGMENT AT NUREMBERG

David Niven Anthony Quinn
in
THE GUNS OF NAVARONE

FICTION

Advise and Consent, Drury
Hawaii, Michener
The Last of the Just, Schwarz-Bart
Decision at Delphi, MacInnes
The Agony and the Ecstasy, Stone
To Kill a Mockingbird, Lee
The Winter of Our Discontent, Steinbeck
Mila 18, Uris
The Carpetbagger, Robbins
A Burnt-Out Case, Greene.

HAL — LE — LU —— JAH

NONFICTION

The Rise and Fall of the Third Reich, Shirer
The Waste Makers, Packard
The New English Bible
A Nation of Sheep, Lederer
Born Free, Adamson
The Snake Has All the Lines, Kerr
Nobody Knows My Name, Baldwin
The Making of the President 1960, White
The Politics of Upheaval, Schlesinger
The Conscience of a Conservative, Goldwater

I like your thinkin'

You still using that greasy kid's stuff?

the *way* people get information, rather than the information itself, is the key fact in history; the *medium* is the message.

LORD'S PRAYER BANNED IN SCHOOLS

The river Jordan is deep and wide
Hal — le — lu —— jah

CUBA SI, YANQUI NO

ROCKY'S SON LOST IN NEW GUINEA

2,990,513 JOBS IN FEDERAL GOVT.

Hey, fun-ny

ASTRONAUT PROBES SPACE IN A B. F. GOODRICH SUIT

And today motoring is safer than ever before because the tubeless tire, originated by B.F. Goodrich, provides protection against bruise blowouts.

Just think how much you're going to be missing. You won't have Nixon to kick around any more, because, gentlemen, this is my last press conference.

Elizabeth Taylor and Richard Burton
WHO'S AFRAID OF VIRGINIA WOOLF?
from the play by Edward Albee
Directed by Mike Nichols

scrambles back to pass he's in trouble

always use Gillette. Closest, fastest, safest razor you can buy

doctor coming on the field

Gillette gives you your money's worth

bringing out a stretcher

So act sharp, feel sharp
with Gillette blue blades

I mean he's really hurt

This land is my land
This land is your land

HAL — LU — LU —— JAH

Hey, getcha cold bean!
Hey, getcha Ballantine!

making out

LA DOLCE VITA

Twenty-eight

NOW THE TRUMPET SUMMONED US AGAIN

In 1961 the troubled years of the decade lay in the future. The disorders at home would not begin until the summer of 1964, eight months after President Kennedy's death. Later this would encourage the myth that if only he had lived none of it would have happened. In fact, his responsibility for the coming turmoil was substantial. The Vietnam buildup was one of two major steps he took toward it. The second step was his decision to mount a program aimed at putting a man on the moon before the end of the 1960s. Because Kennedy committed the country to the spending of vast sums on space exploration—over 56 billion dollars before Apollo 11 reached the moon, and even that wasn't the end of it—successive administrations lacked the resources to provide imaginative, far-reaching responses to the ghetto upheavals which rocked the nation from Watts to Harlem. Those riots, combined with anguished demonstrations against the U.S. role in Vietnam, weakened the fabric of American society to an extent unknown since the Civil War a hundred years earlier.

Kennedy agonized over both the Vietnam and space issues. In the first of them he may even have been on the verge of withdrawing from Indochina. Kenneth O'Donnell, his chief of staff, has said that he planned to get out in his second term, and before flying to Texas on his last journey the President had issued an order to bring back the first 1,000 U.S. military advisers. (According to O'Donnell, Lyndon Johnson quietly rescinded the order after the return from

Dallas.) There are other signs that Kennedy was moving toward disengagement. David Halberstam, who cannot be called a friendly critic on this issue, believes that Kennedy had made up his mind but "did not want to rush too quickly, to split his administration unnecessarily. There was always time."

Space exploration is another matter. Here there are no extenuations. Whatever the glory or lack of it attending that decision, all must go to Kennedy, and with each passing year the scales tip farther against him. By 1961 the space race no longer had any bearing on national security. Paradoxically, the very fact that the Russians had larger rockets was evidence of their technological inferiority. Americans had found a way to design H-bomb warheads which were only a fraction of their former size and weight. Therefore they had no need of powerful rockets to send them toward their targets. Soviet scientists required enormous boosters—over 800,000 pounds of thrust—because their H-bombs remained crude and big. That meant that in this early phase of space exploration they had power to burn, charges which could hurl much heavier satellites into orbit, but that was all it meant, and it wasn't much. In later phases the superiority of American technology would pay off. Everyone in the White House knew it; so did everyone in the Kremlin.

The man on the street did not know it. As far as he could see, the Russians were showing America their heels, and somehow that was menacing to the free world. It was useless to explain to him that three out of every four satellites now in orbit were American, that in contrast to the clumsy Sputniks and Luniks the United States had launched whole families of Vanguards, Discoverers, Explorers, Pioneers, Samoses, Tiroses (weather), Transits (navigational), Midases (infrared detector of missiles), and Echos (communications). What counted in the public's eye was that the Russians were more spectacular. They had been first in orbit, the first to hit the moon and then to photograph it, the first to put a satellite in orbit around Venus with devices to radio back information about it. It was now clear that they were going to beat U.S. scientists to manned space flight. They had already put dogs into orbit, and now the first vehicle to put a man up was standing by on a launch pad near the Aral Sea, the site Francis Gary Powers had been trying to photograph on his ill-starred flight the year before.

This had nothing to do with either American security or the pursuit of knowledge. It was a matter of face or, as someone unkindly called it, of astropolitics. Given Kennedy elitism there was probably no question that the United States would have risen to the challenge anyhow, but the cold war had a lot to do with it. Like Acheson and Dulles—and Richard Nixon—Kennedy believed that the whole world was watching the rivalry between the two superpowers, and that destiny hung on the outcome of every contest between them. The thought that the Soviet Union might be more admired by the emerging nations in Africa and Asia was unbearable. In some vague way the freedom of mankind was at stake. This is clear from the memoirs of Theodore C. Sorensen. To Kennedy, Sorensen writes, the "space gap" which the new administration had inherited symbolized the country's lack of "initiative, ingenuity, and vitality."

> He was convinced that Americans did not fully grasp the worldwide political and psychological impact of the space race. With East and West competing to convince the new and undecided nations which way to turn, which way was the future, the dramatic Soviet achievements, he feared, were helping to build a dangerous impression of unchallenged world leadership generally and scientific preeminence particularly.

In this view, the fact that the United States had superior weapons systems didn't count for much, because they didn't *seem* superior: "Other nations . . . assumed that a Soviet space lead meant a missile lead as well; and whether this assumption was true or false, it affected their attitudes in the cold war." Here, surely, was the triumph of image, the notion that in the huts and villages of the Third World peasants, weighing which way they would turn, were awaiting the latest word from outer space. The extraordinary implication was that Soviet rocketeering feats, if unchallenged, would be a greater blow to American prestige than anything else—greater, say, than oppressed American Negroes wrecking the centers of U.S. cities in riots of frustration.

This wasn't much of an improvement on the fantasies of John Foster Dulles, and Sorensen makes it clear that in this instance, unlike that of Vietnam, Kennedy was no reluctant convert: "The President was more convinced than any of his advisers that a second-rate, second-place space effort was inconsistent with this country's security and with the New Frontier spirit of discovery." Like Cuba, this had been one of his major themes in 1960. Campaigning in Manhattan, he had said: "These are entirely new times, and they require new solutions. The key decision which this [Eisenhower's] administration had to make in the field of international policy and prestige and power and influence was their recognition of the significance of outer space. . . . The Soviet Union is now first in outer space." In Pocatello, Idaho, he had charged: "They [other nations] have seen the Soviet Union first in space. They have seen it first around the moon, and first around the sun. . . . They come to the conclusion that the Soviet tide is rising and ours is ebbing. I think it is up to us to reverse that point." And in Oklahoma City five days before his election he had cried: "I will take my television black and white. I want to be ahead of them in rocket thrust."

On Monday of the second week in April, UPI began to move a story on the persistent Moscow rumor that Soviet rocketeers had sent a man into space and recovered him. Although that was premature, Tuesday evening the CIA reported that the flight was scheduled for that night. As Washington slept, Moscow's radios greeted the new day there with the slow, moving strains of the Russian patriotic anthem, "How Spacious Is My Country." It was followed by the momentous announcement: "The world's first spaceship, *Vostok*, with a man on board, has been launched on April 12 in the Soviet Union on a round-the-world orbit." To follow it, Russian children were released from classrooms, clerks from shops, workmen from factories. In the beginning they were silent, stunned. It seemed incredible that somewhere above them a fellow countryman could be soaring past the stars at 18,000 mph.

His name was Yuri Alekseyevich Gagarin, a twenty-seven-year-old Soviet major who had been chosen to be Russia's first "cosmonaut." Gagarin had been launched at 9:07 A.M. Moscow time—1:07 A.M. in Washington—and at the time his niche in history appeared to be somewhat greater than it was. There are events whose chief significance lies in the popular response they evoke at the time. The reaction to the Orson Welles Martian broadcast of 1938 was one; so were the Wanna-Go-Home riots of 1946 and the support for the Bricker amendment in the early 1950s. Now people, and not just Russian people, were hungry for heroes. The Soviet Union gave them Gagarin. After 108 hours of flight, 89 of which were spent actually in orbit, he descended from his altitude of 188 miles to become a prized propaganda asset. Standing on the tomb of Lenin, he received a twenty-gun salute. A Moscow square was named after him, then a glacier. Soviet artists set to work designing a commemorative stamp bearing his picture. In Russian newspapers his name was printed in red. Adoring Soviet journalists christened him Gaga. One wrote breathlessly of him that "his eyes were shining as though still reflecting spatial starlight." In Red Square Khrushchev made a speech comparing him to Columbus. A nationwide Soviet radio broadcast carried a conversation between Khrushchev and the cosmonaut, whose most improbable revelations were "While in outer space I was thinking about our party and our homeland," and "When I was going down, I sang the song, 'The Motherland Hears, the Motherland Knows.'"

Americans gnashed their teeth. "Kennedy could lose the 1964 election over this," a space administrator said, and a NASA scientist said, "Wait until the Russians send up three men, then six, then a laboratory, start hooking them together and then send back a few pictures of New York for us to see." At Cape Canaveral a bitter astronaut told a reporter, "We could have got a man up there. We could have done it a month ago if somebody at the top two years ago had simply decided to push it." At four o'clock that afternoon Kennedy faced a tumultuous press conference in the new State Department auditorium. He was asked: "Mr. President, a member of Congress said today he was tired of seeing the United States second to Russia in the space field. I suppose he speaks for a lot of others. . . . What is the prospect that we will catch up with Russia and perhaps surpass Russia in this field?" The reply was defensive: "However tired anybody may be, and no one is more tired than I am, it is a fact that it is going to take some time [to catch up] . . . We are, I hope, going to go in other areas where we can be first, and which will bring perhaps more long-range benefits to mankind. But we are behind." Columnist Hugh Sidey commented that this "seemed hardly in the spirit of the New Frontier." One news magazine reported that the nation's mood was one of "frustration, shame, sometimes fury," and predicted: "Only a spectacular and extremely difficult bit of rocketeering, say a manned trip around the moon, will top Russian spacemen in the eyes of the world."

In fact, Kennedy learned that evening, it had to be the moon or nothing; on lesser objectives the Soviet lead was too great to overcome. The President had called a 7 P.M. meeting in the Cabinet Room to search for alternatives. One by one his advisers spoke up—Jerome Wiesner; James Webb, NASA head; Dr. Hugh Dryden,

Webb's distinguished deputy; David Elliot Bell, director of the Bureau of the Budget; and Sorensen. The scientists had Kennedy at a disadvantage. Space was not his forte. He knew less about this issue than any other, hadn't been briefed on the projects at Cape Canaveral, and lacked the science background necessary to sort out scientific options and priorities. After Wiesner, Webb, and Dryden had spoken the President muttered gloomily, "We may never catch up." He said, "Now let's look at this. Is there any place we can catch them? What can we do?" He did know that three half-built U.S. rockets would produce over a million pounds of thrust each when finished. He asked of them: "What about Nova and Rover? When will Saturn be ready? Can we leapfrog?"

Dryden told him there was only one hope, and it would take a crash program similar to the Manhattan Project. That might put an American on the moon in ten years. It would be a gamble, though. And it would cost at least twenty billion dollars—perhaps twice that. The President was silent. Then he said, "The cost, that's what gets me." He looked hopefully at Bell, but there was no comfort there; Bell said that exploring space was a very expensive business. Kennedy asked, "Can't you fellows invent some other race here on earth that will do some good?" But nothing else had the fascination of a flight to the moon, and after drumming his fingernails on his teeth he asked Wiesner and the NASA men to take another look at the figures. Rising to go, he said, "When we know more, I can decide if it's worth it or not. If somebody can just tell me how to catch up. Let's find somebody—anybody. . . . There's nothing more important."

Three weeks later the American people showed that their judgment confirmed his. After twenty-eight months of delays and breakdowns, the first vehicle in NASA's Project Mercury rose from the gantries at Cape Canaveral. As a hundred million viewers held their breath, a tall, slender white Redstone rocket slowly climbed into the sky, emitting a widening vapor trail. Its passenger was naval Commander Alan B. Shepard Jr. The country was elated. On turnpikes and freeways drivers pulled over to the shoulder and turned up their car radios. An Indianapolis judge declared a recess so everyone in the courthouse could watch the picture on a television set which police had seized as part of a burglar's booty. The nation was eavesdropping on the exchanges between *Freedom 7*, as Shepard's space capsule was called, and his control in Florida. He was in outer space for fifteen minutes. His flight was nothing like Gagarin's complex trajectory, but for the moment Americans didn't care. As his capsule descended beside the carrier *Lake Champlain,* swinging widely beneath its parachute, the sailors cheered wildly. "It's a beautiful day," were his first words back on earth. "Boy, what a ride!" His ride to glory had only begun. New York gave him its biggest ticker tape welcome in history as of then. A new school in Deerfield, Illinois, was named for him. Greeting cards went on sale for admirers to send Shepard. Derry, New Hampshire, his home town, with a population of 6,987, staged a parade in his honor. People came from all over New England to march in it; Army, Navy, Marine Corps, Air Force, and National Guard troops passed in review while jet fighters roared overhead. Senator Styles Bridges in an eloquent speech described New Hampshire's pride in the new hero. Legislators debated renaming Derry "Spacetown, U.S.A."

None of this was lost on the White House, just then smarting from the Bay of Pigs defeat. On May 25 the President stood before Congress with a special message on "urgent national needs," his second State of the Union address in four months. He wanted "an estimated seven to nine billion dollars additional over the next five years" for the space program. He knew he was asking a lot, he said, but "These are extraordinary times. We face an extraordinary challenge." To him the issue was a matter of patriotism: "I am here to promote the freedom doctrine." He said: "I believe that this nation should commit itself to achieving the goal, before this decade is out, of landing a man on the moon and returning him safely to earth."

Congress approved by a thundering margin. Simultaneously ground was broken for expansion of facilities at Cape Canaveral and a mission control center in Houston. The aerospace industry was on its way.

In July, Air Force Captain Virgil I. Grissom completed a flight similar to Shepard's. The Russians sent Major Gherman S. Titov whirling around the earth seventeen times in August, and in November NASA orbited a male chimpanzee and recovered him after two trips around the earth; while up, the chimp responded to various lights by pulling levers which released sips of water or banana-flavored pellets. NASA then announced that the pilot of the first U.S. human orbital flight would be the oldest of the seven astronauts who had been chosen from 110 candidates, Marine Lieutenant

Colonel John H. Glenn Jr. By then the tremendous popularity of the Mercury Project had been established. It was evident that if Glenn made it back he would be America's first aerospace superstar, a second Lindbergh. Teams of journalists explored his childhood in the tiny hamlet of New Concord, Ohio, and returned with reams of data which captivated the nation. As a boy he had been an avid reader of *Buck Rogers*. He had admired Glenn Miller and had played a loud trumpet himself in the New Concord band. As strict Presbyterians the Glenns had held that cigarettes were sinful, and New Concord was a Presbyterian stronghold; boys from surrounding towns called it "Saint's Rest." Glenn and his chums had taken a pledge never to use profanity. Once while singing "Hail, Hail, the Gang's All Here," one besotted boy, throwing caution to the winds, had recklessly continued with the phrase, "What the hell do we care?" Now, a quarter-century later, the blasphemer told eager journalists how the future astronaut had rounded on him: "Johnny came up to me, white-faced and righteous, and told me to stop. I think he was ready to knock my block off." In 1962 Glenn's faith remained strong; he assured interviewers that he believed in "a power greater than I am that will certainly see that I am taken care of."

After ten frustrating postponements he lifted off the pad at 10 A.M., Tuesday, February 20, 1962. His departure was like Shepard's, but magnified many times. A great spurting gout of yellow-white flame licked out from the Atlas D rocket, casting weird shadows on the flat, sandy scrubland of Cape Canaveral. For four incredible seconds the rocket just hung there, balanced over its gantry. Then it ascended, gaining in momentum until it disappeared into the deep blue overarching sky. Glenn said, "Lift-off. The clock is operating. We're under way." From the Project Mercury Control Center the deep, calm voice of Lieutenant Colonel John "Shorty" Powers, NASA's public affairs officer, explained the next step to the country. It was the separation of the rocket and the capsule, *Friendship 7*, at the precise angle which would put Glenn in orbit. As it happened Glenn cried: "Capsule is turning around. Oh, that view is tremendous! I can see the booster doing turnarounds just a couple of hundred yards behind. Cape is go and I am go."

The temperature in the capsule had risen to 108 degrees, he noted, but the air-conditioning in his suit kept him cool. He had been instructed to explain his every sensation—the audience, after all, was paying for the trip—and he began by reporting that he had no feeling of speed. It was "about the same as flying in an airliner at, say, 30,000 feet, and looking down at clouds at 10,000 feet." Over the Atlantic he spotted the Gulf Stream, a river of blue in the gray sea. Over the West Coast he made out California's Salton Sea and the Imperial Valley, and he could pick out the irrigation canals near El Centro, where he had once lived. His first twilight was awesome: "As the sun goes down it's very white, brilliant light, and as it goes below the horizon you get a very bright orange color. Down close to the surface it pales out into a sort of blue, a darker blue, and then off into black." The stars were spectacular. "If you've been out on the desert on a very clear, brilliant night when there's no moon and the stars just seem to jump out at you, that's just about the way they look." Approaching Australia he radioed, "Just to my right I can see a big pattern of light, apparently right on the coast." From a tracking station below, Astronaut Gordon Cooper explained to him that this was the Australian city of Perth. Its 82,000 inhabitants had turned on all their light switches, to welcome him and test his night vision. Glenn replied, "Thank everybody for turning them on, will you?"

Glenn made other tests himself, exploring his weightless state. He swallowed some nutritious tablets and some applesauce which he squeezed out of a tube. No problems there, he reported: "It's all positive action. Your tongue forces it back in the throat and you swallow normally. It's all a positive displacement machine all the way through." He jiggled around as best he could to see if he could bring on giddiness or space sickness. There was none of it; "I have no ill effects at all from zero G. It's very pleasant, as a matter of fact. Visual acuity is still excellent. No astigmatic effects. No nausea or discomfort whatever." An amateur photographer, Glenn had brought a camera along. Instead of putting it on a shelf after he had taken some pictures through his window, he just stuck it out in the air, and there it stayed, suspended. Changing rolls, he let the film slip. He quickly reached for it, but as he explained to the enchanted millions, "instead of clamping onto it, I batted it and it went sailing around behind the instrument panel, and that was the last I saw of it."

Sometimes he ran out of words. "I don't know what you can say about a day in which you have seen four beautiful sunsets," he said. It was at that point that he forgot his travelogue commentary. So did his listeners. He was having trouble. As he passed over Mexico a small jet, meant to keep his capsule steady, developed a malfunction. He reported to the control center that the vehicle "drifts off in yaw to the right at about one degree per second. It will go to 20 degrees and hold at that." That was the end of the tests; the flight now commanded his entire attention; he had to take over the controls and fly it himself. That wasn't the end of his difficulties. During his second pass over the Pacific, his gyroscopes went out. The capsule began "rolling"—turning on its horizontal axis. Glenn eliminated that by skillful handling of the controls. Then, in his second orbit, he developed what looked like real trouble. An ominous light flashed on the control board at Cape Canaveral. It meant that *Friendship 7*'s fiberglas heat shield had come ajar. If the shield came off at any time before the capsule reentered the atmosphere, Glenn would be instantly incinerated. As it turned out, the fault was in the warning light, not the shield, but neither the astronaut nor his mentors on the ground knew that then. They made adjustments to change the reentry procedure, retaining the vehicle's retro-rockets—which were to be jettisoned—in the hope that their metal bands might help keep the shield in place. Then they prayed.

Glenn knew that this was the moment of maximum peril. His braking rockets were fired in sequence, and he braced himself. As the pressure on him mounted, *Friendship 7* shimmied. He gasped, "It feels like I'm going clear back to Hawaii." The G forces were mounting, squeezing him against his contour couch. He was coming down, and the heat shield was disintegrating, breaking up into growing fragments. Later he said, "You could see the fire and the glow from them—big flaming chunks." He couldn't explain it at the time because he had lost radio contact. That was to be expected; he was in the delicate process of reentering. The blackout lasted seven minutes and fifteen seconds. As it ended he could be heard shouting, "That was a real fireball!" At 2:43 P.M. the glowing capsule hit the waters of the Atlantic and was instantly enveloped in clouds of sizzling steam. At 3:01 the carrier *Noa* rescued Glenn. A steward handed him a glass of iced tea. Glenn said, "It was hot in there."

Idolatry awaited him. His footprints on the carrier deck were traced in white paint for later exhibition in the Smithsonian Institution. Cameramen recorded the fact that his eyes were full at the moment of reunion with his wife and children, and after he had wiped his eyes the handkerchief was set aside so it, too, would be preserved. As he fielded questions from the press, reporters noted that in speaking of himself and *Friendship 7* he often said "We"—just like Lindy at Paris's Le Bourget Field thirty-five years earlier. Vice President Johnson was there to greet him. Johnson said, "In my country we'd say you're pretty tall cotton. Were you very tense at takeoff?" Glenn replied that he supposed so. LBJ said, "You were about as near the Lord's end as a person ever is."

At Cape Canaveral one banner read: WELCOME TO EARTH. There the Vice President was replaced by the President, who had just flown over from Palm Beach. There was a bit of byplay as Glenn tried to put a hard hat on Kennedy and failed—JFK had once seen a picture of Calvin Coolidge in an Indian headdress and had vowed never to pose in a funny hat—and then the country's first astronaut was off to address a joint session of Congress. "Usually the honor is reserved for heads of state," Johnson told him, "but in this case the whole country has elected you." A gala parade in New York was next, featuring Glenn, the other six of the original astronauts, and a star-studded cast of big-name scientists. After that Glenn flew abroad to tour other continents, telling America's allies and the uncommitted peoples that truly great achievements were possible in a free society. *Time* commented: "In terms of national prestige, Glenn's flight put the U.S. back in the space race with a vengeance, and gave the U.S. and the entire free world a huge and badly needed boost."

"This is a new ocean," said Kennedy, "and I believe the U.S. must sail on it." At Cape Canaveral American rocketeers, confident once more, talked enthusiastically of launching two-man capsules by 1964; of giant, solid-propellant boosters to lift great payloads off the earth; and of plans for Project Apollo, aimed at putting three men on the moon and bringing them back, perhaps as soon as 1968. A passionate interest in space travel took on the proportions of a national rage. It was the theme of that year's Century 21 Exposition, in Seattle. "Orbit" entered Madison Avenue's vocabulary as a noun and as a verb. Small boys launched water-propelled toy satellites that landed in trees, like kites before them. Wernher von Braun, whose skills had played a major part in the success of the Atlas, became a national celebrity. ("He aimed for the stars," Mort Sahl said of his earlier years, "and often hit London.") Europeans of all convictions were tremendously impressed. Even Pablo Picasso, no Americanophile, said of Glenn, "I am as proud of him as if he were my brother." Presently all sorts of people were launching satellites —American Tel & Tel, for example, put up Telstar, and even the Canadians sent a small vehicle into orbit.

In August the Soviet Union's second cosmonaut, Major Gherman S. Titov, circled the earth seventeen times. This was seized upon as a new evidence for the need to mobilize America's industrial and technological might in a great effort to surpass the Russians once and for all. By now there were some dissenters, particularly on the campuses and in the U.S. intellectual community. The President answered them in September. Speaking at Rice University in Houston he said:

"But why, some say, the moon? . . . And they may well ask, why climb the highest mountain? Why, thirty-five years ago, fly the Atlantic? Why does Rice play Texas? . . . Many years ago the great British explorer George Mallory, who was to die on Mount Everest, was asked why did he want to climb it, and he said, 'Because it is there.' Well, space is there, and . . . the moon and the planets are there, and new hopes for knowledge and peace are there."

The black problem was also there, however, and it was much closer. In retrospect Kennedy's underreckoning of it seems astonishing. He was, after all, a northern liberal and an admirer of Martin Luther King. But the liberals, and even King, were about to be pressed hard by militant young northern blacks. While America's eyes had been turned upward toward the stars, they had been searching for ways to distract the country. The first attempt, and it was memorable, came in the spring of 1961. On May 4, three weeks after Gagarin's flight, seven black and six white members of the Congress of Racial Equality (CORE) left Washington by bus for an expedition through the Deep South. Their purpose was to challenge segregation in interstate bus terminals in defiance of local custom—in waiting rooms, restaurants, and toilets. They called themselves freedom riders.

The course they had charted zigzagged across Dixie: south through Virginia, North Carolina, and South Carolina; southwestward to Atlanta; westward through Alabama, and then on across Mississippi and down to New Orleans. It was bound to be a memorable trip. Their flouting of the customs of the region was breathtaking. After four years Little Rock was all but forgotten, and Arkansas was a border state anyway. Here in the real southland the relationships between the races were still very precise and had scarcely changed in the ninety years since the departure of the last carpetbagger. In that respect there were almost no southern liberals as the term was understood above the Mason-Dixon line. The WPA guidebook to Alabama, written by native New Dealers in 1941, pictured the sort of welcome wayfarers might expect in Montgomery, one of the state's three largest cities:

> The atmosphere of measured dignity tempered by cordiality is matched nowhere else in Alabama. A Negro boy—his face wreathed in smiles—usually accosts the traveler with, "You don't have to tote that grip, boss man; I'll do it cheap"; and a resident will willingly give directions and accompany the stranger a block or more to set him on the right road.

That was not an accurate description of the greeting awaiting the freedom riders, a fact so obvious that they can be fairly said to have been looking for trouble. The nature of their sponsorship was less clear. Under the leadership of James Farmer CORE was an independent, self-supporting organization and had been active since 1942. But in the seething days ahead many southern leaders and southern editorials would charge that the administration ("the Kennedys") was behind them or had at least encouraged them to come. The truth was that no one in the government had known of their journey until they had left on it. CORE had sent an advance copy of a press release about the trip to the Department of Justice, but it had wound up on the desk of Burke Marshall, chief of the Civil Rights Division, who was out with the mumps. Newspaper accounts of the departure had been buried on the inside pages. The White House first heard of it when the story erupted on front pages, and then its reaction was anger—directed at the riders.

From the administration's point of view, the timing was dreadful. Not only had the Russians just won the race for the first manned space flight to encircle the earth; the week after that the Cuban brigade had been overwhelmed on the beach. On June 3, less than a month away, Kennedy would meet Khrushchev in Vienna. The new President needed a victory or, if that was impossible, the absence of a fresh defeat. The last thing he wanted was an ugly racial incident. The Russians were still exploiting Little Rock for propaganda directed at the Third World, portraying America as racist. Any episode which could be interpreted as evidence of that would be a humiliation for the United States. That was how the White House first regarded the rides—as an embarrassment. Later John Kennedy, and particularly Robert Kennedy, would see the civil rights struggle as a moral imperative, but in their first months in office it was not yet that. An understanding of their position then is important, because it was shared by most liberal Democrats, including some who thought themselves to be very advanced.

Their commitment to end prejudice was total. It was a wrong, and they were determined to right it. It was intolerable to them that the Negro condition should be unchanged in the world's oldest and greatest democracy. Throughout that campaign John Kennedy had reminded audiences that "The Negro baby born in America today, regardless of the section of the nation in which he is born, has about one-half as much chance of completing high school as a white baby born in the same place on the same day, one-third as much chance of completing college, one-third as much chance of becoming a professional man, twice as much chance of becoming unemployed, about one-seventh as much chance of earning $10,000 a year, a life expectancy which is seven years shorter, and the prospects of earning only half as much." As President he had pledged himself to support programs aiming at correcting that injustice. What more could the blacks ask?

The first thing they asked was that liberals stop thinking of blacks as statistics. After that they expected an end to gradualism. They realized that the spring of 1961 was an awkward time for the government to deal with the freedom riders. Every season for the past century had been awkward, and so they had waited and waited and waited. What they expected their white sympathizers to understand was that to the new Negro, freedom for his people was more important than any issue in Vienna—or in Vietnam, or Cuba, or outer space.

In 1961 it was considered political bravery just to endorse equality before the law in front of an audience of southern whites. That was what Robert Kennedy did in his first major speech as attorney general, and he did it in Athens, Georgia, on May 6, two days after the departure from Washington of the freedom riders, of whose existence, however, he was still unaware. The occasion was Law Day at the University of Georgia. He went to explain to them that it was his sworn duty to uphold the law, a circumstance of which one might suppose law students would already be aware, but on this issue, in this part of the country, nothing could be assumed. "We are maintaining the orders of the courts," he told them. "We are doing nothing more nor less. And if any one of you were in my position, you would do likewise, for it would be required by your oath of office. You might not want to do it, you might not like to do it, but you would do it." This was hardly a passionate affirmation of the rights of an oppressed race, and there was even a hint in it that on this issue Robert Kennedy might be doing his duty against his better judgment, but there were no weasel words at the end: "Our position is clear. We are upholding the law. . . . In this case—in all cases—I say to you today that if the orders of the court are circumvented, the Department of Justice will act. We will not stand by or be aloof. We will move."

In civil rights, as in the Third World, liberals of the early 1960s believed in the eventual triumph of right. This perhaps more than anything else sets the Kennedy years apart from what lay ahead and makes them seem almost naive now. Send surplus wheat to an emerging nation, send Peace Corpsmen, send a Chester Bowles as the American ambassador, the catechism read, and you will have a bright new democracy, a credit to the free world and a potential ally in the eternal struggle against the powers of darkness in Moscow. So at home: strong leadership and the fundamental sense of decency in the American people would overcome the bigotry implanted by generations of ignorance. Integration was just good sense, and Americans were above all sensible; it was just a matter of showing them the light; if Eisenhower had taken a stand he could have accomplished it in the 1950s.

The notion that there were dark places in the American mind was illiberal and therefore rejected. The liberal vision had no explanation for the phenomenon of the McCarthyism, the most recent instance in which decency and good sense had been scorned by masses of Americans, but in 1961 nobody talked about McCarthy any more. Optimism was almost a requirement on the New Frontier. General Harkins had the right idea, his body counts were certainly encouraging, and why couldn't those American correspondents in Saigon join the team? On the domestic front good liberals would fight the good fight until the Negro baby born in America had just as much chance of completing his education as the white baby, no more chance of becoming unemployed, as much chance of earning $10,000 a year, and the same life expectancy.

However, these things took *time*. They mustn't expect it all *now*.

But the freedom riders wanted it all now.

Richmond, Petersburg, Lynchburg—here they stopped, stretched their legs, had a bite together at lunch counters under signs reading "White" and ignored the toilets designated "Colored" with no more than a few ugly looks and muttered obscenities from bystanders. Then stories about the trip began appearing in the newspapers of cities farther along on their route. They weren't big news yet, not important enough to attract the attention of an attorney general or a governor; all they warranted was a couple of sticks, a squib or two, something to wrap around the ads. But that was enough to alert gas station attendants leafing through the inside pages in search of the comics, enough for ticket clerks in the bus terminals, for sheriff's deputies passing by and the kind of men who hang around stations and depots waiting for something to happen.

The first incident was in Charlotte, North Carolina: a black freedom rider strolled into the bus station barbershop and refused to leave. He was arrested for trespassing and the others proceeded without him. It wasn't much, but the word was sent ahead, passed on as such news is always passed, by a phone call, or another driver, or police radio. It doesn't matter. It was inevitable and they expected it; that was why they had come. Still, the tension on the bus grew. When they saw the crowd at the station in Rock Hill, South Carolina, they knew the violence had begun to escalate. Three of them were beaten; then the Rock Hill police intervened. Again in Winnsboro, thirty-seven miles to the south, police stepped in before anything could start and arrested two riders. Next came another quiet stretch: Sumter and Camden, South Carolina; Augusta and Atlanta, Georgia. Atlanta was an important stop. They divided there into two groups for the ride to Birmingham, one going on a Trailways bus and the other by Greyhound. There was no trouble here—Georgia troopers were everywhere—but after Rock Hill and Winnsboro they were on page one of every newspaper in the South. It was a Sunday, the day papers are read most. They assumed that the population of Alabama would know all about them. It did.

Today travelers between Atlanta and Birmingham cruise easily across eastern Alabama on Interstate Route 20, but in 1961 that was still under construction, and they had to follow the tortuous curves of U.S. 78 through a succession of remote crossroads communities virtually untouched by postwar change. This was "upcountry" Alabama, an untamed region clothed with scrub pine—mostly high, with elevations of nearly 1,800 feet in the Raccoon and Lookout ranges, the southernmost spurs of Appalachia. Coming down off their slopes to the Cumberland plateau, the road descended to fields soybean farmers had reclaimed after the devastations of the boll weevil, to the coal region, and, beyond, to the Black Belt. Cleburne County, Calhoun County—these were an old breeding ground of wool-hats and red-necks, the strongholds of the camp meeting and the revival, and it was here, six miles from Anniston on U.S. 78, that a gang of Ku Klux Klansmen armed with blackjacks, clubs, and tire chains ambushed the Greyhound bus. A rock sailed through one window, followed by an incendiary bomb. As it burst into flame the riders fled. Twelve of them were being methodically beaten when policemen arrived and fired pistols into the air. Ambulances carried away the injured. Then Birmingham blacks who had heard of the battle arrived in cars and rescued the others.

The riders on the Trailways bus escaped the Klan trap, but in Anniston eight young toughs boarded the bus, dragged them into the aisles, and began punching them. Anniston cops drove them off. Birmingham, the destination of the bus, was worse. A crowd of men carrying lengths of pipe had surrounded the Trailways terminal at Nineteenth Street and Sixth Avenue North. An informer had warned the FBI about them. Incredibly, the FBI had not relayed the information to Burke Marshall's Civil Rights Division or to the attorney general's office. Instead it passed the tip along to the Birmingham police, whose chief, Police Commissioner T. Eugene "Bull" Connor, pigeonholed it. Although Connor's headquarters were only two blocks from the terminal, he sent no one over. The hoodlums there dragged the riders into the station and clouted them for thirty minutes, injuring three seriously enough to require hospitalization. The next morning the *Birmingham News,* which had denounced the *New York Times* the year before for saying that fear and hatred stalked the streets of Birmingham, now admitted that "fear and hatred did stalk Birmingham's streets yesterday." But Alabama officials had no apologies. Governor John Patterson said, "I cannot guarantee protection for this bunch of rabble-rousers," and Bull Connor said, "Our people of Birmingham are a peaceful people, and we never have any trouble here unless some people come into our city looking for trouble." Asked why there had been no policemen at the terminal, Connor said he had been shorthanded because it was Mother's Day. It was a joke.

The Sunday beatings brought the freedom riders to the attention of the Justice Department for the first time, and Burke Marshall called Bob Kennedy at home to tell him of it. Bob thought he might be able to resolve the situation with a phone call. He knew Patterson, who had been the first southern governor to support John Kennedy for President and had stayed with him even after his delegation had gone over to Lyndon Johnson. He called the governor Monday morning and asked him to protect the buses. Passengers on them had a right to travel between the states, and local authorities had a clear responsibility to guarantee their safe passage. Patterson agreed. Then he called back and said he had changed his mind. He had been elected with Klan support, and now the Klansmen were cashing in their credit.

This was the first of several strange long distance exchanges the two Kennedy brothers were to have with southern governors on the race issue, and like the others it was exasperating. Bob tried to phone Patterson again. He was told that the governor couldn't come to the phone. He tried again on Tuesday, on Wednesday, and on Thursday. Each time aides expressed their regrets. The most they could do, they said, was take a message, and they couldn't guarantee that it would reach the governor. They couldn't be sure, but they thought he was "out on the Gulf"—unreachable in any case. Meanwhile the situation in Birmingham was deteriorating. The original group of freedom riders, battered and frightened, had flown on to New Orleans, but their places had been taken by volunteers from Fisk University in Nashville, from Martin Luther King's Southern Christian Leadership Conference, and from the younger civil rights organizations, one such newcomer being a cool nineteen-year-old immigrant from Trinidad named Stokely Carmichael. In Washington, Attorney General Kennedy issued a statement asking for restraint from both the freedom riders and their opposition. He said, "In order to insure that innocent people are not injured, maimed, or even killed, I would call upon all people who have paramount interest in the future of our country to exercise restraint and judgment over their activities in the next few weeks or the next few days." There was a sense of unreality in this. He seemed to be trying to play the role of an impartial arbiter between two equally responsible, equally strong adversaries. The riders solemnly promised not to attack Alabamans; the Alabamans said nothing. Then Kennedy issued another statement saying, "What is needed now is a cooling-off period." A CORE spokesman tartly commented that what was needed was an end to cooling off, that black Americans had been cooling off for a hundred years. By Friday, when the new freedom riders prepared to continue the journey that the others had started, it was clear that they would be heading into fresh trouble. At his brother's request, President Kennedy put in a call to Governor Patterson. He was told that the governor was "out of town and still unreachable." He did get through to the lieutenant governor, who after several hours said he could arrange a meeting between the governor and a personal representative of the President.

The Kennedys chose John Seigenthaler, a handsome and brave young Tennessean and the attorney general's best friend. Seigenthaler was on a plane within an hour. At first his mission seemed successful. After he and Patterson had conferred for two hours they phoned Bob Kennedy. While Patterson listened and nodded Seigenthaler reported that he had been assured that Alabama had, as Patterson put it, "the means, ability, and the will to keep the peace without outside help." The governor said that he could protect everyone in the state, both Alabamans and visitors, in the cities and on the highways, and he said he would do it. Bobby then called Floyd Mann, the chief of Alabama's highway patrol, who backed up the governor's guarantee. With that, a biracial group of twenty-one students voted to board a Birmingham to New Orleans bus in the morning. An unexpected hitch developed when no driver could be found. Getting one required a long, abrasive phone conversation between the attorney general and George E. Cruit, the Greyhound representative in Birmingham, but in the end Cruit produced a man and the riders departed for Montgomery, which turned out to be even worse than Birmingham.

The trip there was uneventful. Mann's Highway Department did its part; both U.S. 65 and U.S. 31 were clear. The FBI had alerted the Montgomery police to the arrival of the bus, and when it was about fourteen miles from the city Mann radioed a second warning to Montgomery's police commissioner, Lester B. Sullivan. But Sullivan was no more ready than Connor to run interference for uppity blacks and renegade whites. He ignored the messages, and there were no policemen when the bus arrived at the Union Bus Terminal to confront a throng estimated at between a thousand and three thousand. The attorney general's office had a blow-by-blow account of what happened next because John Doar, second in command to Burke Marshall in the Civil Rights Division, was in the U.S. Attorney's office across the street from the terminal.* Doar had just put through a call to Kennedy when the bus drew up at the terminal. Kennedy and his deputy attorney general, Byron White, heard him say:

"The bus is in. The people are just standing there, watching. . . . Now the passengers are coming off. They're standing on a corner of the platform. Oh, there are fists, punching! A bunch of men led by a guy with a bleeding face are beating them. There are no cops. It's terrible. It's terrible. There's not a cop in sight. People are yelling, 'Get 'em, get 'em.' It's awful. . . . The cops are there now."

They were state troopers, not Montgomery policemen. ("We have no intention of standing police guard for a bunch of trouble-makers coming into our city," Sullivan told reporters.) And the troopers were too few to be effective. Mann saved one black by pulling his pistol, but the rest of the riders were beyond help. So were several bystanders who were unconnected with them, and who seem to have been attacked on general principle. One boy's leg was broken. A group of young whites poured inflammable liquid on another boy and set him on fire. One Montgomery woman held up her child so that he could reach out and beat on a black man with his fists. Other women swore at two white girls who had been among the riders and then slapped them with their purses. The girls begged a passing motorist for help. He said, "You deserve what you get. I hope they beat you up good." Another man in a rented car pulled over. "Come on, I'll help you," he called to the girls, "I'm a federal man." Before he could do anything, however, he was dragged to the pavement and slugged. He was John Seigenthaler, the President's personal envoy to the governor of Alabama, and he lay unconscious in his own blood on the sidewalk for twenty-five minutes before an ambulance arrived. Commissioner Sullivan later explained that no ambulance had been called for Seigenthaler because "every white ambulance in town reported their vehicles had broken down."

Bob Kennedy, livid, put Byron White on the next plane to Mont-

* On December 21, 1973, Doar became legal adviser to the House Judiciary Committee's inquiry into the possibility of impeachable offenses by President Nixon.

gomery with Jim McShane, U.S. marshal for the District of Columbia. After Little Rock, Attorney General William P. Rogers had instituted riot training for U.S. marshals and their deputies to provide a federal law enforcement force other than the Army. At Maxwell Air Force Base outside Montgomery, Byron White now assembled four hundred men who had been so trained—revenue agents, border patrolmen, and guards from federal prisons—and who could be swiftly deputized for the occasion. Meanwhile Doar appeared in U.S. District Court and obtained an injunction enjoining the Ku Klux Klan and the National States' Rights Party, the two organizations most heavily represented in the mob, from interfering with interstate travel by bus. Governor Patterson then appeared at long last to protest that these moves were unconstitutional. Besides, he said, federal officers were unnecessary. On that he was simply proved wrong.

That Saturday afternoon the most famous civil rights activist, Martin Luther King, flew into Montgomery. At the home of the Reverend Ralph Abernathy he announced that he would speak that evening to a rally in the First Baptist Church. This presented the Ku Kluxers and their allies with a prize beyond their most vicious dreams. For a while King didn't seem to be an insurable risk. Byron White was supervising the preparations of the marshals when he received a startling phone call: Governor Patterson had called a meeting of Alabama law enforcement officers and was instructing them to arrest any federal men who broke state laws. White went to the meeting alone. It was open to the press, which took down the tense exchange between him and the governor. Patterson asked the deputy attorney general to share the government's information about CORE. "No," said White. Then the governor asked for information about the freedom riders. "No," White said again. Then:

PATTERSON: You know where some of these freedom riders are, don't you?

WHITE: Yes, in the hospital.

PATTERSON: Do you know where the others are?

WHITE: No, I don't.

PATTERSON: If you knew where some of these people are, would you inform us?

WHITE: I will never know where these people are.

At that moment they were in the First Baptist Church with Martin Luther King. By nightfall some fifteen hundred Birmingham Negroes had arrived for the rally. It had scarcely begun when an ugly crowd began to gather in a park across the street. Learning that the local police were again absent, White dispatched his marshals by every conveyance he could find—postal delivery trucks, private automobiles, and a prison truck. They were wearing business suits and brassards and were armed with pistols, nightsticks, and tear gas guns. About a hundred of them had formed a skirmish line outside the church when the mob charged, hurling stones and broken bottles. With that, the governor declared marshal law. The marshals' skirmish line held until crucial reinforcements arrived: Floyd Mann at the head of his troopers, and Henry Graham, a National Guard major general, with a detachment of his men. Even so, before the attack of the mob was blunted the marshals had to fire several volleys of tear gas. The gas seeped into the hot, overcrowded church. At times the blacks there were close to panic. If the church had been put to the torch, which was the mob's intention, undoubtedly the loss of life would have been great. As it was, they were well shielded by the mixed force of state and federal law enforcement officers.

Governor Patterson phoned Attorney General Kennedy to protest that Alabama was being invaded.

"John, John," Bob said quietly. "What do you mean, you're being invaded? Who's invading you, John? You know better than that."

Patterson accused him of sending the freedom riders into the state and blamed him for the violence.

"Now John," Bob said. "You can say that on television. You can tell that to the people of Alabama, but don't tell me that. Don't tell me that, John."

Nevertheless Patterson did it again, repeating every word. Then he said that the National Guard would defend the church and the congregation inside, but could not guarantee the safety of King.

"I don't believe that," said Kennedy. "Have General Graham call me. I want to hear a general of the United States Army say he can't protect Martin Luther King."

By now the governor was yelling. He shouted shrilly that he was giving his opinion, not the general's. He cried that sending federal marshals had created "a very serious political situation" and shrilled, "You're destroying us politically!"

"John," Kennedy said in the same quiet tone. "It's more important that these people in the church survive physically than for us to survive politically."

That ended the threat of violence against the freedom riders. In the north, Patterson was regarded as the heavy loser in the episode. Southerners took a different view, however. Lost causes have had a special appeal to them since Appomattox. They rallied to his side, sent him money and encouragement, and promised to join the fight against integration. That was ominous; it committed them. Keeping the vow became a matter of honor, and by June it had been taken publicly by virtually every politician in Dixie, including George Corley Wallace, who the following year was elected to succeed Patterson.

Nevertheless, as such things go, the freedom riders were counted a success. No one had been killed, and Jim Crow had been routed. Enforced segregation in interstate travel, theoretically outlawed by the Supreme Court in 1950, now ended in fact. Bob Kennedy petitioned the Interstate Commerce Commission to issue regulations requiring desegregation in all interstate terminals, including airports and train depots, and four months later, on September 22, it did. A few cities cited local laws as an excuse for not complying; the Justice Department brought suit against them. By the end of 1961 Negroes could travel coast to coast without seeing "White" or "Colored" in waiting rooms.

Countless bastions of segregation remained, of course, and the most formidable of them were in Mississippi. In 1931 H. L. Mencken and Charles Angoff ran a two-part series in the *American Mercury* ranking the states from good to bad, "from civilized to barbaric." Their criteria included wealth, literacy, education, entries in *Who's Who in America*, symphony orchestras, crime, voter registration, infant mortality, transportation, and availability of medical attention. In the final standing Mississippi was last, behind the rest of the Deep South, and its situation hadn't changed in 1962; indeed, when John Bererdt repeated the Mencken-Angoff survey for the magazine *Lifestyle* ten years later, in November 1972, Mississippi was again on the bottom, just below Alabama.* The average Mississippian had less than nine years' schooling. Over a third of the people were poor, as the Department of Commerce *Statistical Abstract of*

* In 1931 Massachusetts was first. In 1972 Connecticut had replaced it.

the United States defines poverty. One in four households lacked plumbing and 29 percent telephones; only 24 percent read a daily newspaper and only 3 percent a news magazine. "The Closed Society," Professor James W. Silver of the University of Mississippi called the state in 1964, and it became clear as the 1960s progressed that an astonishing number of its people, white and black, were actually unaware of the civil rights movement. There were no attacks on the freedom riders there because the state police didn't allow them the freedom of movement necessary to be mobbed. Their buses were met at the Alabama border and escorted to Jackson, and when they ignored the discriminatory signs in the terminal there, they were arrested and led to jail. Eventually federal courts overturned their convictions, but the rulings meant little to individual prisoners, who had served their time by then.

Burke Marshall, almost alone in the Justice Department, understood the inflexibility of Mississippi white supremacy. He knew that its prophets regarded the present period as a second Reconstruction. If they were just as single-minded in their resistance to it as their great-grandfathers had been, they thought, the federal challenge would fail and the problem would go away. But in 1961 most of the rest of the Justice Department (with the exception of Doar) wasn't on Marshall's wavelength. At the end of the year the attorney general submitted a report to his brother, the President, on civil rights progress. It almost sang with hope, and in a Voice of America broadcast a week after the confrontation at the First Baptist Church, Bob declared that racism was ebbing in the United States. He actually predicted that a black man could be elected President before the end of the century.

A brief conversation with one Mississippi black, James Meredith, would have tempered his optimism. Meredith was a nine-year veteran of the Air Force and one of ten children of a farmer in the midstate town of Kosciusko. Inspired by President Kennedy's inaugural address, Meredith had written to the University of Mississippi the same evening he heard it, requesting an application for admission. He returned the completed form with an explanatory note: "I am an American-Mississippi-Negro citizen. With all of the occurring events regarding changes in our educational system taking place in our country in this new age, I feel certain that this application does not come as a surprise to you. I certainly hope that this matter will be handled in a manner that will be complimentary to the University and to the state of Mississippi."

Ole Miss, as the university at Oxford was known throughout the South, rejected him for complex academic reasons, but Meredith wasn't discouraged that easily, and he found a powerful ally in Medgar Evers, the state director of the NAACP. In June 1961 NAACP lawyers filed suit for Meredith in the federal district court, charging that he had been turned down solely because of his race. The litigation which followed is unique in the history of American jurisprudence. A district court judge ruled against Meredith twice. In June 1962 the court of appeals for the Fifth Circuit reversed the judge; then Judge Ben Cameron of the Fifth Circuit reversed the reversal. The appeals court vacated Cameron's order, but he promptly issued another. This went on until, after his fourth stay, he had made it clear that he intended to continue along this line indefinitely. The NAACP appealed for sanity to Supreme Court Justice Hugo Black. In September Black, a native Alabaman, upheld the court of appeals and ordered the university to admit Meredith at once. "Never!" cried Governor Ross Barnett, and two days later he went on statewide television to declare: "We will not surrender to the evil and illegal forces of tyranny."

Apart from his age—he was sixty-four in the autumn of 1962—Ross Barnett was more like Meredith, whom he was about to engage in a duel by proxy, than he would have acknowledged. Like him he had been one of ten children, and had come to manhood in the hardscrabble clay wasteland of central Mississippi, the barren soil familiar to explorers of Yoknapatawpha County, the creation of William Faulkner, whose nephew Murry Falkner would play a key role in the unfolding crisis just ahead. Like Meredith, Barnett was also a prisoner of the past, a fundamentalist who took the Old Testament to be the literal truth and believed it proscribed racial "mixing." In another time, under other stars, the two men might have become friends. Barnett would have liked that, for he was naturally warm and gentle, ready to do almost anything for someone in distress, including Negroes. But if the man was black he had to know his place. On the strength of his vow to keep the Merediths of Mississippi where they were, Barnett had been elected governor two years earlier with the endorsement of the state's White Citizens' Councils. As an elector in the last presidential election, he had bolted the Kennedy-Johnson ticket to vote for Harry Byrd. He was, in short, representative of his kind and his region: charming, ignorant, friendly, suspicious, blindly loyal to the lost Confederacy, appalled by the present and frightened of the future. Martyrs are made of just such stuff, and only one trait kept Barnett from becoming one. He was a coward. Under great pressure he would look for a way out, a deal. His tragedy, which became Mississippi's, was that he just didn't know how to find or make one.

If Barnett resembled Meredith, his antithesis was Robert F. Kennedy, who completely misread him. On the strength of the fact that Mississippi's highway patrol had effectively convoyed the freedom riders to safety, Bob assumed that the authorities there believed in law and order. He mistook the patrol's commander, the felicitously but inaccurately named Colonel T. B. Birdsong, for another Floyd Mann. All the situation seemed to need was a plan, and Bob was very good at plans. On Saturday, September 15, he called Barnett and explained crisply how it would all be managed. He understood, of course, that as a southern governor Barnett would have to offer token resistance. Therefore Meredith would be escorted by several marshals brandishing court orders. The governor could throw up his hands and the university officials, bowing to the inevitable, would then enroll Meredith. Kennedy asked if Barnett understood, if there were any questions. In what should have been recognized as a sign of how far apart they were, the governor said, "That will take about a year."

It took just five days. The following Thursday Meredith, accompanied by the marshals, appeared in Oxford to register. He was met by Barnett, who was attempting to shield the university administration by appearing himself in the role of a "special registrar." While two thousand white students chanted, "We want Ross, we want Ross," and "Glory, glory, segregation," the governor read a decree barring Meredith from the campus "now and forevermore." Then he handed it to him and said, "Take it and abide by it." One of the men from the Justice Department said, "Do you realize you are placing yourself in contempt of court?" Barnett said, "Are you telling me this or does it take a judge?"

His legal position, and he thought it unassailable, was what is called interposition—interposing himself, as a representative of the states' rights, between the administration in Washington and the people of Mississippi. He had asked his legislature to give him that authority, and it had complied. When American historians learned of that, they were incredulous. Interposition had been discredited as a doctrine before the Civil War. In fact, when John C. Calhoun had tried to invoke it in 1832, the Mississippi legislature of that time had rejected it as "a heresy, fatal to the existence of the Union . . . contrary to the letter and spirit of the Constitution and in direct conflict with the welfare, safety and independence of every state." Now, one hundred and thirty years later, the governor was trying to breathe life into the same dead dogma. The Fifth Circuit in New Orleans, undeceived and unwilling to recognize Barnett as a special registrar, ordered university officials to appear the following Monday and show cause why they should not be cited for contempt. Barnett protested bitterly to the press at the speed of the courts. Mississippi's Senator James Eastland phoned Bob Kennedy to say, "The governor thinks you can back down a little, and I think so, too." Bob replied, "You don't really believe that, Senator. You've been in the Senate too long to believe that."

In court the university officials promised to admit Meredith by 4 P.M. the next day. Barnett still refused to budge. Saying that he was "shocked" at the officials' "surrender," he announced that anyone from the Department of Justice who interfered with Mississippians doing their duty would be arrested and jailed. Kennedy phoned him to point out that the people of Mississippi, including their governor, were citizens of the United States of America and subject to its laws. Barnett said, "I consider the Mississippi courts as high as any other court and a lot more capable. . . . Our courts have acted too, and our legislature has acted too. I'm going to obey the laws of Mississippi!" His attorney general, Joe Patterson, then issued a statement saying that freedom had been dealt "a staggering blow. . . . The constitutional rights of over 5,000 students have been ignored to gratify the pretended constitutional rights of one."

Meredith made his second attempt to register the next day in Jackson, at the office of the university trustees. John Doar and Jim McShane were with him. They were met by Barnett, Colonel Birdsong, and a jeering crowd of onlookers. The university officials couldn't keep the commitment made yesterday in New Orleans, the governor said, because they had been subpoenaed by a legislative committee investigating un-Mississippian activities. Doar tried to serve court papers on the governor; Barnett put his hands in his pockets. Doar asked, "Do you refuse to let us through that door?" Courtly as always, the governor said, "Yes, sir, I do so politely."

Doar said, "And we leave politely." The crowd was not polite. As Meredith and his escort departed there were cries of "Go home, nigger," and "Communists!"

Bob Kennedy had been trying to keep Barnett's name out of the court proceedings because he remembered how Faubus had made political capital in Little Rock, but this was too much. The successive failures to admit Meredith were conveying the impression, in Mississippi at least, that the white supremacists were winning. Kennedy decided to ask for a Fifth Circuit order showing the governor in contempt. He phoned Barnett to tell him he was going to do it. He said further that Meredith would appear in Oxford in the morning, ready to attend classes. Barnett was aggrieved. Didn't that boy know when he wasn't wanted? As governor he had other duties, he said; he couldn't keep "running all over the State of Mississippi" for one Mississippian, and a Negro at that. Kennedy thought Meredith's enrollment would work. He said, "Why don't you try it for six months and see how it goes?"

"It's best for him not to go to Ole Miss," Barnett said.

Bob replied softly, "But he likes Ole Miss."

On campus alarmed faculty members noted a growing swell of visitors from all over Dixie, hard-bitten men with brush-fire eyes who were often armed and who asked, "Where will the nigger come from?" Their leader was General Edwin A. Walker, now of Dallas. On Wednesday, September 26, the day before the confrontation in Jackson, the general had issued a somewhat incoherent radio appeal to those who shared his convictions: "It is time to move. We have talked, listened, and been pushed around far too much by the anti-Christ Supreme Court. Rise to a stand beside Governor Barnett at Jackson, Mississippi. Now is the time to be heard. Ten thousand strong from every state in the union. The battle cry of the republic. Barnett, yes; Castro, no. Bring your flags, your tents, and your skillets. . . . The last time in such a situation I was on the wrong side. . . . This time I am out of uniform and I am on the right side and I will be there."

That day Barnett went into temporary seclusion. When Meredith and his escorts approached the campus in Oxford they were turned back by Lieutenant Governor Paul Johnson, backed by detachments of state troopers and county sheriffs. This time there was some jostling as the federal men tried to walk around Johnson in the hope that, having resisted, he would bow to the inevitable. He didn't bow. It was clear that force would be required to get past him. The marshals had been told to stop short of that, and there weren't enough of them anyway. Meredith was turned back again.

By this point every civil rights leader in America and most of official Washington thought that the Justice Department was being too patient, that the dignity of the federal government was in jeopardy. Robert Kennedy knew it, but he had sensed fear in Ross Barnett. The governor, he thought, would welcome an opportunity to save face; he seemed to be learning the peril of continuing to defy a federal court. On the phone the next morning, Thursday, Bob suggested that they explore the possibility of finding a way out. He had been right; the governor instantly agreed. If he had been as able a politician as George Wallace, the crisis might have been resolved then. But he wasn't able. His sense of timing (or Bob's timing in waiting this long to close with him) was wrong; too many hopes of total victory had been raised in diehard segregationists, emotions were running too high, too many Mississippians were calling for resistance "regardless of the cost in human life"—a phrase heard everywhere there. Most important, the governor didn't know how to strike a bargain. He knew he would have to sacrifice something to make peace, but he couldn't decide how much he would give up, how much resistance he could show for the sake of appearances and still remain below the flash point of violence.

Their first attempt to reach an understanding ended in ludicrous failure. They talked of Barnett and Lieutenant Governor Johnson at the campus gate, flanked by unarmed state troopers, facing McShane and thirty marshals. McShane would draw an unloaded pistol. The Mississippians would then step aside, and Meredith would pass through the gate and be registered. Barnett said one revolver wasn't enough. He wanted all thirty marshals to draw; that way, he could say he yielded to avoid bloodshed. Bobby proposed that the other marshals just slap their holsters. That wasn't sufficiently realistic for the governor, and so it was settled that all thirty guns would be drawn.

Earlier in the week this might have been enough, but now it would be dangerous. The fact that the troopers were unarmed was irrelevant; they would be counterbalanced by the guns carried by General Walker's followers in Oxford. In addition, Barnett was the only man on his side who knew of the deal. He might be the only one to step aside. The realization of this came to him while he was waiting for Meredith at the campus gate. The black Air Force veteran was then proceeding toward him in a thirteen-car convoy which was in radio contact with Washington. At 3:35 P.M. Mississippi time, 5:35 in Washington, Barnett called Kennedy to say that he couldn't control the crowd, it was too big and in too ugly a temper. That ended the showdown scenario. The convoy turned back. Meredith had been denied registration four times now, and that evening at the university white students held a wild demonstration.

But there would be no more failures. Bob Kennedy was conferring with General Maxwell Taylor, chairman of the Joint Chiefs, and his principal commanders, General Earle G. Wheeler and Major General Creighton W. Abrams. At the Justice Department an assistant attorney general was drafting documents for President Kennedy's signature putting Mississippi's National Guard in federal service, alerting U.S. infantry units at Fort Benning for action, and warning civilians in the streets of Oxford to go home and stay there. Another assistant attorney general was flying down to assume command of a growing force of marshals. From New Orleans came word that the Fifth Circuit had found Barnett guilty of contempt, ruling that if Meredith were not registered by Tuesday—it was now Friday—the governor would be fined $10,000 a day; for Lieutenant Governor Johnson, if Johnson took his place, it would be $5,000 a day.

The only card the government hadn't played was presidential prestige, and that was committed Saturday afternoon when the White House put through a call to the statehouse in Jackson. President Kennedy had already requested television time at 8 P.M. to lay the matter before the American people. He canceled it when Barnett proposed that Meredith be admitted secretly in Jackson on Monday while the governor was diverting the mob in Oxford. His manner didn't inspire confidence, however; hanging up, the President turned to the others and asked in wonder, "Do you know what that fellow said? He said, 'I want to thank you for your help on the poultry program.'"

At ten o'clock that evening the lack of confidence was justified. Barnett phoned the Justice Department to say that he had changed his mind. The agreement was off; he wouldn't go through with his part of it. Again the President requested television time, for 7:30 the following evening, Sunday, September 30. Sunday morning the governor called Robert Kennedy. It was another fruitless, frustrating conversation, and in the middle of it Bob lost his temper. He said his brother was going on TV to tell the country how Barnett had reached an agreement "with the President of the United States" and had then broken his word.

Alarmed, the governor said in a high-pitched voice, "That won't do at all."

"You broke your word to him."

"You don't mean the President is going to say that tonight?"

"He is."

Barnett, breathing hard, suggested flying Meredith in "this afternoon."

That seemed to be the end of it. Meredith, it appeared, would be enrolled that same day, and without bloodshed. He would be admitted quietly while state troopers kept the peace. Afterward Barnett would issue a furious statement saying that it had been done behind his back, that he was yielding to irresistible force but would fight it in the courts. Deputy Attorney General Nick Katzenbach flew down to supervise the details. At 5 P.M. Mississippi time, accompanied by Colonel Birdsong, he led four hundred marshals onto the Ole Miss campus, now almost deserted, through the little-used west gate. Meredith was taken quietly to Baxter Hall, at one end of the grounds, while Katzenbach and the marshals established a command post at the other end in the lovely old red brick Lyceum Building, the university's administration building. The President delayed his television address until 10 P.M. in the belief that the crisis would be all over by then. But this Sunday, like every other day in the Meredith case, seemed jinxed. Almost at once communications with Washington broke down, and they remained out until Monday morning. Even after Army units arrived on the scene, the Signal Corps was unable to establish a link to the White House. Throughout this, the height of the crisis, with the eyes of the nation and much of the world on Ole Miss, the President of the United States and the attorney general, his brother, received crucial reports from Katzenbach, who was dropping dimes into a pay phone in a campus booth.

As the sun sank over Mississippi it became evident that somehow word of what had happened was spreading in Oxford. A crowd of about a thousand quickly gathered outside the Lyceum. Meredith's whereabouts were unknown to them; throughout the coming nightmare he remained concealed a mile away, guarded by twenty-four marshals who had doffed their white helmets and orange vests so that they, too, would be inconspicuous. There can be little doubt about what would have happened to him, and possibly to them, if his presence in Baxter Hall had become known to the mob. Like Richard Nixon in Caracas, he was in very real danger of being torn apart. The marshals (all of whom were white southerners themselves) were being taunted with "Kill the nigger-loving bastards," "Go to Cuba, nigger lovers," and a chant: "Two-four-one-three, we hate Kennedy!" The evening deepened. The crowd doubled, and redoubled. Its shouts became obscene. The marshals were pelted with stones, then rocks, then lighted cigarettes. A Texas newsman and his wife were beaten by men swinging pieces of pipe. Many of the state troopers on the scene were unhelpful. Some stood aside with folded arms and did nothing.

It was 7:30 P.M. in Mississippi when the FBI monitored a radio signal ordering the state troopers to withdraw entirely and leave Meredith and the marshals to the mob. Later efforts to find out who had sent it were unsuccessful. Katzenbach phoned Bob Kennedy to tell him of it. In the background Bob could make out the ragged sounds of riot. Then—it was at 7:58—he heard that thumping sound of gas grenades. Katzenbach said, "Bob, I'm very sorry to report we've had to fire tear gas. We had no choice."

In Washington the President went on television unaware of the latest developments. To the best of his knowledge then, Barnett was keeping his word to maintain order with the troopers. He explained to the national audience that Meredith was on the campus, explained the need to enforce court order, spoke glowingly of the heroism of Mississippi men in the country's wars, and appealed to Ole Miss undergraduates: "The honor of your university and state are in the balance. I am certain that the great majority of the students will uphold that honor."

In Oxford the students watching him jeered. General Walker was moving among them purposefully. A fire engine and a bulldozer were seized by men who used them to try to crash through the line of marshals and into the Lyceum; well-lobbed grenades drove them off. The attackers hurled Molotov cocktails fashioned from Coca-Cola bottles. Campus benches were demolished to make jagged concrete projectiles, iron bars and bricks from construction sites were thrown, and here and there the crack of rifles could be heard as invisible snipers zeroed in on the Lyceum. Two men were killed, a French foreign correspondent and an Oxford spectator. Over a third of the marshals—166—were injured, and 28 were wounded by snipers' bullets. The marshals carried sidearms; they were under fire; it seemed right to return it. They repeatedly asked for permission to do so, and Katzenbach relayed the requests to Washington. The Kennedy brothers rejected the appeals. There would be no federal use of live ammunition, they ruled, unless Meredith was in danger. The marshals, exhausted and bloodied, held out with only their black, stubby tear gas guns to protect them.* Edwin Guthman was in the Lyceum, on the phone with Bob Kennedy. Bob asked, "How's it going down there?" Ed answered, "Pretty rough. It's sort of like the Alamo." Bob said, "Well, you remember what happened to those fellows."

At ten o'clock in Oxford, Katzenbach reluctantly told Washington that troops were necessary. In three-quarters of an hour the first unit arrived, sixty National Guardsmen of Troop E, 108th Armored Cavalry, under the command of Captain Murry C. Falkner. Before daybreak sixteen of them would become casualties, among them Captain Falkner, two of whose bones were broken by a brickbat. To the exasperation and then the fury of the Kennedys, nearly five hours passed before regular Army contingents, who had been alerted, reached the scene. Three times the marshals almost ran out of tear gas. When the soldiers did arrive, they had to fight their way to the campus. Forty of them were hit by missiles or shotgun blasts. Most of the attackers vanished in the night. The 503rd Military Police Battalion, arriving with the main body of troops from Memphis, arrested over two hundred members of the mob, including General Walker. Only twenty-four of them were students; the others came from all over Dixie—Georgia, Alabama, Louisiana, Tennessee, and Texas, as well as Mississippi. At dawn the campus was seen to be littered with chunks of cement, tear gas canisters, wrecked vehicles, rocks, smashed window glass, and green chips from thousands of pulverized Coke bottles. Governor Barnett blamed the riot on "inexperienced, nervous, trigger-happy" marshals.

* "One would remember them," Ed Guthman wrote nine years later, "in the racial riots and wild campus demonstrations of the latter half of the 1960s and at Kent State and at Jackson State universities in 1970, when lawmen, with far, far less provocation and injury than the marshals endured, gunned people down."

Shortly before eight o'clock Monday morning Jim McShane and two other marshals accompanied Meredith to the battered Lyceum. There, at last, he was admitted by Robert Byron Ellis, the stony-faced registrar. There was no resistance in the administration building, only resignation and studied courtesy. Meredith listed his academic goal as a degree in political science. With credits from extension courses already taken he would graduate in three semesters. As he left the Lyceum another student yelled, "Was it worth two lives, nigger?"

Booked and fingerprinted, Major General Edwin A. Walker was charged with assaulting an officer, resisting arrest, insurrection, and conspiracy. The charges were dropped three months later after he had been given a psychiatric examination at Parkland Memorial Hospital in Dallas, and on an April evening three months after *that* a sniper standing on his lawn and aiming a cheap mail order rifle tried to kill him. In December 1963 ballistics experts found that the owner of that rifle, and presumably the man who had fired it, was Lee Harvey Oswald, who, among other things, had become since then an active supporter of the Fair Play for Cuba Committee and the assassin of John F. Kennedy. The confusion of the radical left and radical right is puzzling unless one grasps that President Kennedy, supremely a man of the center, was hated by both. Their feelings for him had begun to harden at the time of the Bay of Pigs, when one extreme denounced him for backing the invasion of Castro Cuba while the other condemned him for not going all the way and wiping Castro out. By the end of his second year in office it was clear that among those at either end of the political spectrum Kennedy had become the most scorned President since Franklin Roosevelt.

The New Left had begun to organize for the long pull in June 1962, when forty-five quiet, neatly dressed young people met at an old UAW-CIO summer camp at Port Huron, Michigan, to found the Students for a Democratic Society. The SDS then was but a shadow of its future self. The principal activity at the meeting was discussion of a moderate, sixty-two-page manifesto drafted by a weedy, pock-marked twenty-two-year-old University of Michigan undergraduate named Tom Hayden. Hayden cited, as the two greatest challenges to society, racism and "the enclosing fact of the cold war, symbolized by the presence of the Bomb." He proposed "that we as individuals take the responsibility for encounter and resolution."

There was nothing new in the diagnosis or the prescription for cure: "We would replace power rooted in possession, privilege, or circumstances by power and uniqueness rooted in love, reflectiveness, reason and creativity." Hayden specifically renounced what would later become an SDS trademark—violence as catalyst for change—on the ground that it "requires generally the transformation of the target, be it a human being or a community of people, into a depersonalized object of hate."

The right was much farther along. The John Birch Society, the SDS's mirror image, was four years old and flourishing. His membership in it had been the reason for General Walker's dismissal from the Army, and the Kennedy brothers had increased its fame by damning it, the attorney general calling it "ridiculous" and the President warning that it was an inept adversary of Communism. Robert Welch, "The Founder," as he called himself, continued to mastermind Birch activities from a two-story brick building in the Boston suburb of Belmont. He seemed to enjoy publicity and was doubtless aware that it helped recruit new Birchers. The basic unit in the society was the chapter, which was frankly based on the Communist cell. (Welch was fascinated by Communism and imitated it slavishly.) Each chapter numbered between ten and twenty members. By the early 1960s there were reported to be chapters in thirty-four states and the District of Columbia with a total membership of about one hundred thousand. Birch ranks were increased by what The Founder called "fronts," such as the Patrick Henry Society, the Sons of the American Revolution, and the Minute Women and Minutemen. In many communities the Birchers were treated as a joke, but it was no joke in places like Shreveport, Tampa, Houston, and Dallas, where, as the *New York Times* reported, "businessmen, management executives, physicians, lawyers, and other 'solid' people have joined chapters."

As the decade grew older the New Left would emerge as the greater threat to democratic institutions, but that was not apparent in the Kennedy years. The resources of the right overshadowed anything at the other extreme; during the Kennedy Presidency outlays by ultraconservative organizations rose from five million dollars a year to over fourteen million, while the national budget for a liberal enterprise like the Americans for Democratic Action ran to a mere $150,000. The worst the left could do then was an occasional ill-tempered remark—C. Wright Mills was reported to have said on his deathbed that he was "ashamed to be an American, ashamed to have John F. Kennedy as his President"—while Senator Fulbright uncovered a working political arrangement between ultraconservative organizations and career officers in the regular Army. When Fulbright held hearings to bring it to light, he was all but drowned out by charges that he was trying to "muzzle the military."

Among the more conspicuous activities of the ultras in those years were Dallas's National Indignation Convention, first convened in 1961 and again in 1963. In its first session the 1,800 delegates to the convention roared their approval of a speaker who protested that the chairman was becoming moderate—"All he wants to do is impeach Warren—I'm for hanging him." Two years later the convention counteracted United Nations Day by holding a "United States Day"—an event blessed by Governor John B. Connally Jr. with an official proclamation.

Under the ultra umbrella were gathered such groups as the Reverend Billy James Hargis's Christian Crusade and Dr. Fred Schwarz's Christian Anti-Communism Crusade. The farthest reaches of the right wing were dismissed as a refuge for impotent crackpots. It is true that George Lincoln Rockwell's American Nazi Party never threatened American liberties, but elsewhere ultras were both respectable and influential. C. D. Jackson, publisher of *Life*, bore reluctant witness to this. After an issue of his magazine had treated Schwarz with disdain the flak from powerful advertisers was so great that Jackson flew to a Schwarz rally in the Hollywood Bowl to eat crow: "I believe we were wrong, and I am profoundly sorry. It's a great privilege to be here tonight and align *Life* magazine with Senator Dodd, Representative Judd, Dr. Schwarz and the rest of these implacable fighters against Communism."

Extremists of both left and right were characterized by what Benjamin DeMott has called "the Spirit of Overkill." Susan Sontag wrote in the *Partisan Review* that "the white race is the cancer of history." The *Berkeley Barb* flatly declared, "The professors have nothing to teach. . . . We can learn more from any jail than we can from any university." An off-Broadway cast chanted, "The middle class/ Are just like pigs . . . The middle class/ Are just like pigs," and in 1961 Bertrand Russell said, "We used to call Hitler wicked for killing off the Jews, but Kennedy and Macmillan are much more wicked than Hitler. . . . They are the wickedest people who ever lived in the history of man and it is our duty to do what we can against them." On the opposite horizon The Founder of the Birchers said of the United States that "the whole country is one vast insane asylum and they're letting the worst patients run the place," while Dean Noebel, a Christian Crusade prophet, maintained that agents in the bowels of the Kremlin had formed a "Commie-Beatle Pact"—"the Communists have contrived an elaborate, calculating, and scientific technique directed at rendering a generation of American youth useless through nerve-jamming, mental deterioration, and retardation. . . . The destructive music of the Beatles . . . reinforces . . . mental breakdown."

John Kennedy was very much aware of both varieties of irreconcilables. At the University of Seattle in November of 1961 he suggested that it was the very insolubility of the day's problems which engendered a yearning for simple answers. "There are two groups of these frustrated citizens," he said. "It is a curious fact that each . . . resembles the other. Each believes that we have only two choices: appeasement or war, suicide or surrender, humiliation or holocaust, to be either Red or dead." When possible he pricked them with wit. At a White House gathering, E. M. "Ted" Dealey of the morning *Dallas News* said, "We need a man on horseback to lead this nation, and many people in Texas and the southwest think that you are riding Caroline's tricycle." The editor of the evening paper in Dallas, the *Times Herald*, wrote Kennedy to say that Dealey did not speak for Texas. The President wrote back, "I'm sure the people of Dallas are glad when afternoon comes."

Ultra humor tended to be black humor. In milder versions it was innocuous. The sign on the marquee outside a Georgia theater showing *PT-109*, the story of the President's World War II heroism, read, "See How the Japs Almost Got Kennedy." A riddle ran, "If Jack, Bobby, and Teddy were on a sinking boat, who would be saved?" The answer: "The country." A mimeographed, widely circulated leaflet set forth plans for a Kennedy monument in Washington: "It was thought unwise to place it beside that of George Washington, who never told a lie, nor beside that of F. D. Roosevelt, who never told the truth, since John cannot tell the difference."* It continued:

> Five thousand years ago, Moses said to the children of Israel: "Pick up thy shovels, mount thy asses and camels, and I will lead you to the Promised Land." Nearly five thousand years later, Roosevelt said: "Lay down your shovels, sit on your asses, and light up a

* Many Roosevelt haters believe that there is an ostentatious FDR monument in the capital. In fact, Roosevelt had requested only that after his death a small plaque be placed on a rock outside the National Archives building on Pennsylvania Avenue, and that it bear simply his name and the dates of his birth and death. This was done in 1965. It is modest; few passersby notice it.

Camel; this *is* the Promised Land." Now Kennedy is stealing your shovels, kicking your asses, raising the price of Camels, and taking over the Promised Land.

From there to the outer limits of the lunatic fringe, however, ultra wit became increasingly unprintable. As in the Roosevelt years it was often preoccupied with unusual sexual practices, and it involved not only the Kennedy men and women, but also their children and even their pets. The sons of men who had mimicked FDR's upper-class accent now mimicked JFK's while telling stories about hot lines running from the Pope's toilet and the sewers of Rome to the White House, about the strange ways he spent his father's money, about a woman who claimed to be his first wife—Joe Kennedy was supposed to have bought an annulment—and even about his illnesses. Arthur Schlesinger noted that virtually every aspect of Kennedy fed resentment: "His appearance, his religion, his wealth, his intelligence, his university, his section of the country, his wife, his brothers, his advisers, his support of the Negroes, his determination to de-emotionalize the cold war, his refusal to drop the bomb." The ultras simply hated everything they read about the President.

That was a lot. News of the First Family and its various affiliates at times seemed to have preempted the attention of the communications industry. Kennedy lore was featured in films, on television, on the Broadway stage, and in musical tributes. Every bookshop had its department of Kennedy books, of which by 1962 there were already over a hundred; book collectors were paying small ransoms for signed copies of *Profiles in Courage*. The fact that Lord David Cecil's biography of Melbourne was the President's favorite book was enough to turn what had been a book of limited appeal into a best seller; a report that Kennedy had enjoyed Ian Fleming's *From Russia With Love* made Fleming a millionaire. Caroline Kennedy's picture was on the cover of *Newsweek*, and three screen magazines adopted the rule that *every* cover, every issue, must feature a photograph of Caroline's mother.

Once it became known that the President had learned to read 1,200 words a minute at a speed-reading course, the number of such courses increased tenfold. Courses at hairdresser schools gave instruction in how to imitate the First Lady's bouffant coiffures. Because her husband usually appeared bareheaded, Danbury, Connecticut, the center of the hatting industry, entered a severe recession. The White House press revealed that his favorite cocktail was a daiquiri; suddenly bottled daiquiri mixes appeared on the shelves of package stores. Jackie believed it was smart to have small dinner parties at home. As a result, the names of the great party givers of the Eisenhower years—Pearl Mesta, Gwen Cafritz, etc.—went into eclipse. The word went out that busy as they were, such key figures in the administration as Robert McNamara and General Taylor were finding time to improve their minds at "Hickory Hill University," the evening and weekend seminars at Robert Kennedy's Virginia home. The idea spread to Alexandria and Arlington, to Georgetown and Cleveland Park, and presently such firms as Johnson & Johnson were offering self-improvement courses for their executives.

The Kennedys were very outdoorsy. Not since Theodore Roosevelt had so ardent an advocate of the strenuous life lived in the White House. There was touch football, and sailing off Hyannisport, and Jackie's water-skiing. One or another of them was enthusiastic about nearly every sport: tennis, swimming, horseback riding, badminton, golf, softball, isometrics, skiing at Aspen, and hiking before breakfast. The fact that Pierre Salinger, the White House press secretary, had a stocky build which was growing stockier made him an apostate, almost un-American, and the President tried to redeem him by challenging him to push-up matches. With Pierre in mind, Kennedy at one time asked everyone on his staff to lose five pounds each. The President himself faithfully went through special back exercises in the miniature White House gym, in hotel rooms on trips, and on the floor of *Air Force One*.

At times the preoccupation with keeping fit became obsessive. The Hyannisport version of touch football was a rough sport; catching a pass in the rose bushes could be dangerous; Jackie quit playing after she broke a leg. When Kennedy appointed Red Fay Undersecretary of the Navy, Red, a balding friend from PT days, toured Navy bases taking on gobs in push-up contests. Guests at Hickory Hill were expected to play at least one set of tennis before breakfast, and after the President saw his Green Beret guerrilla fighters master an almost unbelievable obstacle course at Fort Bragg, he told his three middle-aged military aides that he wanted them to do it, too.

The most memorable physical education exploit of those days became known as the Great Hike. It began with General David M.

Shoup, commandant of the Marine Corps and a Kennedy favorite. Shoup unearthed a 1908 Theodore Roosevelt directive which had required Marine Corps company officers to march fifty miles in twenty hours, double-timing the last seven hundred yards. He sent a memo about it to the President, who after a little research wrote back: "President Roosevelt laid down such requirements not only for the officers of the Marine Corps but, when possible, for members of his own family, members of his staff and Cabinet, and even for unlucky foreign diplomats." Kennedy then challenged the Marine Corps. He asked Shoup whether today's marines could do as well as the marines of 1908. They could and did, but that was only the start of it. Robert Kennedy hiked the length of the C & O Canal path; assistant attorneys general and Justice Department secretaries followed him. The story reached the papers and engendered a craze. Walking long distances became the latest thing. People who seldom strolled farther than the distance from the armchair to the martini pitcher were on the road. Alarmed physicians pointed out that over-enthusiasm in exercise was dangerous. At their behest the President warned against overdoing it, and Salinger, who had rashly agreed to lead the White House press corps fifty miles, gratefully backed down.

Salinger was pitched into the Hickory Hill swimming pool fully dressed at the end of an uproarious lawn party there, and on impulse Ted Kennedy dove in after him. When stories of the incident found their way into print the frowns on the faces of Kennedy haters deepened. For some reason the episode seemed particularly decadent to them. Private swimming pools were an affront to the Protestant ethic anyhow; entering them wearing anything except a bathing suit was almost a perversion. But those who felt that way received an even ruder shock. June 17, 1962, was the attorney general's twelfth wedding anniversary. He and Ethel gave a party to celebrate it. Tables were set around the pool; Ethel was at a table that teetered on an impromptu catwalk which actually crossed the pool. Arthur Schlesinger and a partner decided to dance between courses. That was a mistake. Their weight on the catwalk tilted it. The hostess's chair started to slide, and, splash, there was Ethel, in the drink. Schlesinger, mortified, plunged in after her. They put on dry clothes and the party continued, but that wasn't the way the Kennedy haters told it; in their accounts the cavorting around the pool had stopped just shy of Babylon. For the next year Ethel had to set new guests straight on what had really happened, and sometimes she had the uneasy feeling that they didn't believe her.

Like FDR, President Kennedy came to realize that the very intemperance of those who spread malicious stories about him and his family was a political asset. It offended decent Americans and thus redounded to his advantage. He expected Barry Goldwater to run against him in 1964, and he wanted to be sure that the country understood the difference between his centralism and Goldwater's extremism. In a speech he never lived to deliver—it was in his pocket when he died—he scorned those who confused "rhetoric with reality" and assumed "that vituperation is as good as victory." And earlier he had said of them:

> They look suspiciously at their neighbors and their leaders. They call for a "man on horseback" because they do not trust the people. They find treason in our churches, in our highest court, in our treatment of water. . . . Unwilling to face up to the danger from without [they] are convinced that the real danger is from within.

Despite C. Wright Mills and H. Stuart Hughes, Communism was then a threat to American security, and despite Robert Welch and the Christian Crusaders, the threat came from the Soviet Union and not fluoridated water. The tensions of the cold war were powerful enough to generate one more convulsion of terror. It would bring the country and the world to the very brink of nuclear oblivion, and it came, anomalously, in a month of unsurpassed autumnal glory, October 1962.

Ordinarily Senator Kenneth Keating of New York was not a suspicious man, but reports from Cuban refugees reaching Florida that summer had troubled him. Fidel Castro's brother Raúl, Cuba's war minister, was known to have been in Moscow on July 2. Late in that same month activity in Cuban harbors picked up sharply; large numbers of Soviet freighters from the Black Sea began arriving at Mariel, a deepwater port on the northern coast of Pinar del Río province. Their cargoes were unknown, and puzzling. The ships rode high in the water and were distinguished by very wide hatches. Equally odd, each vessel brought with it large teams of Soviet technicians.

By the end of August more than five thousand Russians were in Cuba, and refugees being questioned at the CIA interrogation center at Opa-Locka, Florida, reported seeing truck convoys hauling long tubular objects swathed in tarpaulins. A CIA agent reaching Opa-Locka from Cuba had seen the tailpiece of one object and had a sketch of it. That same week Castro's personal pilot boasted in a Havana bar that Cuba now had long-range missiles with atomic warheads. On October 3 word reached Opa-Locka of activity "probably connected with missiles" in Pinar del Río. How much of this information reached Senator Keating is unknown, but in a series of speeches that month he warned of a Soviet military buildup. On October 10 he said that according to his informants, who had been "100 percent reliable," six intermediate-range missile sites were being constructed on the island.

The administration was skeptical. The Soviets had never put missiles in other countries, not even in bordering eastern European satellites bound to them by the Warsaw Pact. On both sides of the Iron Curtain Castro was regarded as an unstable leader and an unreliable ally. It was inconceivable that Khrushchev would entrust such a man with weapons which could destroy the world. The Kremlin had not recognized Cuba as a member of the Soviet bloc, though Castro had so proclaimed it. Cuba was far from the Soviet Union; transportation and communication lines between them could be quickly cut by the United States. Finally, the Russians could be sure that any such move would trigger a violent reaction in Washington.

At 3 P.M. Sunday, October 14, McGeorge Bundy was interviewed on television by Edward P. Morgan and John Scali of the American Broadcasting Company. As the President's special assistant for national security, he was asked to comment on Keating's charges. He replied: "I know there is no present evidence, and I think there is no present likelihood, that the Cubans and the Cuban government and the Soviet government would, in combination, attempt to install a major offensive capability." That was the opinion of almost everyone in the CIA. Keating, they thought, was being had. Cuban informants were notoriously unreliable. The tubular objects were doubtless SAMs—surface-to-air missiles of the kind that shot down Francis Gary Powers's U-2 twelve hundred miles within the Soviet Union. The Russians had provided Egypt and Indonesia with them, and other SAMs were known to be on their way to Castro. They were defensive weapons, nothing to worry about.

One man disagreed with the majority: John A. McCone, the CIA director. Returning to the capital after a wedding trip, McCone learned that there had been no aerial reconnaissance of western Cuba for a month. The reason was that SAM installations had been discovered there. No one had been willing to risk the loss of another U-2 to SAMs. McCone said that the gamble would have to be taken. On October 4 he called for the immediate photographing of the entire island, with special vigilance over its western end. After various delays because of clouds over the target areas and instructions for new U-2 pilots, October 14 dawned cloudless, and two Air Force majors took off for western Cuba. They had been told to expect ground fire, but the SAM crews were either absent or dozing; their sweep was a milk run. On their return their film magazines were dispatched to Washington and developed at processing laboratories. At the interpretation center in the Pentagon skilled specialists began studying enlargements of each frame.

By Monday afternoon they had seen enough to vindicate Keating. A field near San Cristóbal had been laid out in a trapezoidal pattern which until now had been seen only in U-2 photographs of the Soviet Union. There were SAM sites at each corner of the field, guarding a launch pad. No ballistic missiles were in sight, but the analysts had identified missile transporters, erectors, and the launchers. The evidence was not conclusive, but it certainly required immediate attention on the highest levels of the American government. Secretary McNamara had left the Pentagon earlier than usual—he was attending a seminar at Hickory Hill University—so the commanding general at the Defense Intelligence Agency put through a hot-line call to the Washington apartment of Deputy Secretary of Defense Roswell Gilpatric. It was a few minutes after 7 P.M., Monday, October 15, 1962.

Gilpatric, dressing for dinner and overdue at General Taylor's Fort McNair quarters, decided that he would be even later than he had expected. He said he wanted to see the photographs. Two analysts brought them. After looking at them and issuing appropriate orders he continued on to the general's dinner, where the principal guests were already being called to the telephone, one by one, and given whispered information which, they were cautioned, could not be shared with their wives. Reports for the President would be channeled through McGeorge Bundy, who was giving another dinner for Charles E. Bohlen, the newly appointed ambassador to France. Bundy received his call, from the deputy director of the

CIA, at 8:30. He decided not to tell the President until the next day. There was nothing Kennedy could do that was not already being done except lose a night's sleep. "So," he explained to the President in a subsequent memo, "I decided that a quiet evening and a night of sleep was the best preparation you could have in the light of what you would face in the days ahead."

Dean Rusk, presiding at a third formal dinner on the eighth floor dining room at the State Department, was chatting with his guest of honor. Foreign Minister Gerhard Schroeder of West Germany, when he was called to a phone in the butler's pantry. The caller was Assistant Secretary of State Roger Hilsman. Rusk listened a moment, then said, "Do you, personally, think this is it?" Hilsman replied, "There has only been a preliminary analysis, but from what I can get over the phone there doesn't seem to be much doubt." Any unusual behavior by the Secretary of State would set loose a flood of rumors. Rusk, though wretched, saw no alternative to observing the amenities. He returned to his guest, and the thirteen-day crisis began the next morning.

Tuesday, October 16, 1962

Analysts have been up all night reexamining the photographs of San Cristóbal; McNamara sees them at 7:30 A.M., Bundy at eight. Bundy goes directly to the President's bedroom, where Kennedy is reading the morning papers, and breaks the news: "Mr. President, there is now hard photographic evidence, which you will see a little later, that the Russians have offensive missiles in Cuba." The President directs Bundy to summon key members of the administration to an 11:45 A.M. meeting in the Cabinet Room. Then he calls his brother.

In addition to the Kennedys, those present at the 11:45 meeting, or subsequent sessions of it, include Gilpatric, Bundy, McNamara, Rusk, O'Donnell, Lyndon Johnson, McCone, Maxwell Taylor, General Marshall Carter of the CIA, Sorensen, George Ball, Gilpatric's counterpart at the State Department; Secretary of the Treasury Dillon; Edward Martin, Assistant Secretary of State for Latin America; Ambassadors Bohlen, Llewellyn Thompson, and Adlai Stevenson; U. Alexis Johnson, Paul Nitze, and three men no longer in the government: Dean Acheson, John J. McCloy, and Robert A. Lovett. These men will enter history as the Executive Committee of the National Security Council, or simply the Ex Comm.

Reports from technicians indicate that the San Cristóbal site will be ready for firing in about ten days, and that completion will cut the warning time for an attack on the United States from fifteen minutes to between two and three minutes. Robert Kennedy makes a note of the dominant feeling: "shocked incredulity." There is a general awareness that any American response might worsen the situation, but that not challenging Khrushchev would be the worst course of all.

The President orders a sharp increase in U-2 overflights. Other Ex Comm members will investigate possible choices—in Rusk's phrase, they will "box the compass." The State Department will explore the chances of support from Latin America and U.S. allies in Europe; the Defense Department will investigate the time factor, the kinds of units, and the number of men necessary for various military alternatives. At this point a majority feels that there is only one option: an air strike against the missile sites. Robert Kennedy passes a note to his brother: "I now know how Tojo felt when he was planning Pearl Harbor."

Wednesday, October 17

To maintain an appearance of calm, the President keeps a promise to campaign for Democratic candidates in Connecticut. He is away from the capital until midnight. The Ex Comm meets all day and most of the evening in George Ball's conference room on the seventh floor of the State Department. There is new U-2 evidence, and it is chilling. The Soviet technicians are working around the clock. Missiles are now visible in the photographs. Sixteen, and possibly thirty-two, sites may be ready for firing within a week. In addition to definite proof of medium-range missiles (1,000 miles) at San Cristóbal, there are intermediate-range sites (2,200 miles) in the Guanajay area, between San Cristóbal and Havana, and at Remedios in eastern Cuba. The intermediate-range weapons will be ready by December 1. They are what the military call "first-strike" weapons. With them, the U.S. Intelligence Board estimates, the USSR will be able to fire an initial salvo of forty nuclear warheads on targets in the United States as far west as Montana.

In the absence of his brother, Bob Kennedy emerges as the Ex Comm discussion leader. Majority opinion still favors an air attack—the euphemism for it is a "surgical operation." Bundy and Acheson are its chief advocates. McNamara proposes an alternative: a naval blockade of Cuba. Bombing and blockading are both acts of war, but the blockade has the advantage of avoiding bloodshed, at least in its first stages. An air strike would kill about 25,000 Cubans and an undetermined number of Soviet technicians. If Russians die, total war with the Soviet Union will be almost inevitable.

During the day six options, or "tracks," are pondered. Track A is to do nothing now. Track B would send an emissary to Khrushchev and try to settle matters quietly. Track C would hale the Russians before the U.N. Security Council. (Unfortunately Valerian Zorin of the USSR is chairman of the council this month.) Track D, known in the Ex Comm as "the slow track," is the blockade, Track E the air attack, and Track F an invasion of Cuba. Track F is put aside for restudy later; it cannot be weighed now because it must be preceded by elaborate preparations. However, these are under way.

Thursday, October 18

The U.S. intelligence community estimates that the weapons now in Cuba constitute about half the ICBM capacity of the entire Soviet Union. Photo analysis indicates that they are being aimed at specific American cities. If they are fired, eighty million Americans will be dead within a few minutes. According to the latest Intelligence Board reports, presented at the 11 A.M. session of the Ex Comm, the first missiles could be ready for launching in eighteen hours. The President says to Acheson, "This is the week I better earn my salary." While he is meeting with the Ex Comm, General Shoup says, "You are in a pretty bad fix, Mr. President." Kennedy replies swiftly, "You are in it with me."

The President has an appointment of long standing to receive Andrei Gromyko. He keeps it, talking with Gromyko for over two hours, giving him every opportunity to bring up the matter of missiles, but Gromyko misses all his cues. (Later there will be doubt that Gromyko knew what had been happening in Cuba.) Meanwhile, Rusk is suggesting to the Ex Comm that it regard Tuesday, October 23, as the deadline for action. If by then missile pads are still being built, he says, force should be used to remove them.

Air Force Chief of Staff Curtis LeMay joins the group and argues forcefully that a military attack is essential. The President asks LeMay what the Russian response might be. LeMay assures them that there would be none. Kennedy is skeptical: "They, no more than we, can let these things go by without doing something. They can't, after all their statements, permit us to take out their missiles, kill a lot of Russians, and then do nothing. If they don't take action in Cuba, they certainly will in Berlin." McNamara continues to build support for a blockade. A legal adviser from the State Department recalls Franklin Roosevelt's "quarantine-the-aggressor speech" and suggests it might be better if the blockade were called a quarantine. The weight of opinion is moving toward this option. Robert Kennedy is strongly in favor of it. With the memory of Pearl Harbor, he says, the United States cannot launch a surprise air attack in which thousands of innocent people would die. For a hundred and seventy-five years we have not been that kind of country, he says; surprise raids are not in the American tradition.

The evening session of the Ex Comm is held directly beneath a Rusk dinner for Gromyko on the eighth floor of the State Department Building. Reporters seeing the Secretary of Defense and the director of the CIA arriving sense something unusual. They are led to believe that McNamara and McCone are going to the dinner. To avoid another confrontation with the press, at the end of the meeting nine Ex Comm members—whose cars bear easily recognized license plates—pile into the attorney general's limousine. Their destination is the White House, where the President learns that the trend toward a blockade is continuing. Deputy Attorney General Katzenbach, a former professor of international law, is told to explore the legal basis for a blockade of Cuba.

Friday, October 19

Because the security lid is still on tight, the President leaves Washington again to honor an obligation, this time a commitment to campaign in Chicago. In the capital the Joint Chiefs put the Atlantic and Caribbean commands on alert at 1:20 P.M. The Pentagon announces that McNamara has asked the Chiefs to remain in Washington for six weeks to consult on "budget planning." Katzenbach reports that in his opinion a unilateral order for a blockade can be legally justified under the circumstances. The President decides to make a televised report to the American people Monday evening—the earliest time possible if all necessary steps are to be taken first.

The Ex Comm is in continuous session all day Friday and all Friday night. Now that there is a clear majority for the blockade,

Acheson withdraws. The others split into groups to write out their recommendations and then exchange papers. Out of this the outline of a definite plan begins to emerge. The most important of Friday's developments is the decision to ask for an endorsement of the blockade by the Organization of American States (OAS). A two-thirds majority of twenty voting American republics will be necessary. If achievable it will be invaluable, the Kremlinologists believe, because the Russians are impressed by legalisms. As an adjunct to this, Ball gives the bare facts of the crisis to Don Wilson, deputy to ailing Edward R. Murrow at the United States Information Agency. Wilson asks a Bell Telephone executive to clear lines to Spanish-language radio stations without telling the stations why.

Saturday, October 20

Robert Kennedy phones his brother at the Sheraton Blackstone Hotel in Chicago: the Ex Comm is ready with a plan of action. The President summons Salinger to the presidential suite at the Sheraton Blackstone and hands him a slip of paper: "Slight upper respiratory [infection]. 1 degree temperature. Weather raw and rainy. Recommended return to Washington." At 9:35 Chicago time Salinger makes the announcement to the press. Aboard *Air Force One* he asks Kennedy, "There's nothing wrong with your health, is there, Mr. President?" Kennedy replies, "If you know nothing about it, you're lucky."

The presidential aircraft reaches Andrews Field at 1:37 Eastern Standard Time; Robert Kennedy meets it. The afternoon session of the Ex Comm begins at 2:30 in the oval study on the second floor of the Executive Mansion. The President makes the final decision in favor of the blockade. The last small lingering doubt in his mind is removed when the commanding general of the U.S. Tactical Air Command tells him that even a major surprise air attack could not be certain to destroy all the missile sites and nuclear weapons in Cuba.

Adlai Stevenson, down for the day, suggests a deal. He proposes that the President tell the Russians that if they withdraw their missiles from Cuba, the United States will withdraw its missiles from Turkey and give up the American naval base at Guantánamo Bay. The general reaction is vehemently negative, a bitter aftertaste of which will stay with Stevenson until his death.

Elsewhere progress is smooth. Alexis Johnson has turned out a master scenario schedule of everything which must be done before the President's 7 P.M. speech Monday—instructions to U.S. embassies abroad, congressional briefings, etc. Acheson, recalled, agrees to tell Macmillan, de Gaulle, and Adenauer. Edward Martin prepares for the OAS meeting. As detailed arrangements are made and legal justifications marshaled, however, more and more government officials are brought into the discussions. As a consequence, word that something big is coming has begun to seep through to the press. Too many trips have been canceled, too many announcements made for odd reasons, too many lights have been burning late in unexpected places, too many high officers in the government have failed to appear at dinner parties or, having appeared, have left, murmuring excuses. James Reston of the *New York Times* and Alfred Friendly, managing editor of the *Washington Post,* have begun to stalk the truth, and Reston has most of the essential facts. At the President's personal request, both agree to publish less than they know until Tuesday.

The Navy has deployed 180 ships in the Caribbean. The B-52 bomber force has been ordered into the air fully loaded with atomic weapons; as one plane lands, another immediately takes its place in the air. Late Saturday night the 1st Armored Division begins to move out of Texas headed for embarkation ports in Georgia. Five other divisions are placed on alert.

Sunday, October 21

A golden fall day. In the State Department forty-three letters to heads of government and to Mayor Willy Brandt, mayor of West Berlin, are drafted for the President's signature. In addition, the President is writing a letter to Khrushchev; it will be delivered with a copy of his speech. American embassies and consulates abroad are warned to prepare for demonstrations and riots. U.S. ambassadors will receive explanatory telegrams at 6 P.M. tomorrow, an hour before Kennedy speaks. The U.S. Passport Office opens on a Sunday for one traveler—Dean Acheson's passport must be validated.

The secret won't keep much longer. An air of crisis hangs over Washington. The entire press corps now knows that something is afoot. The *New York Herald Tribune* spikes the story at McNamara's request, but other papers may be expected to divulge it at any time; the British embassy has found out what is coming, and the rest of the diplomatic corps have begun checking rumors. Sunday evening Dean Rusk advises his staff to get some sleep. "Gentlemen," he says, "by this time tomorrow we will be in a flaming crisis."

Monday, October 22

At noon Salinger announces that the President will speak on television at 7 P.M. The topic will be "of the greatest urgency."

Lawrence F. O'Brien phones twenty congressional leaders of both parties; the President wants to see them at 5 P.M. Those who can't make it by commercial airlines are picked up by Air Force planes—in some cases, jet fighters. The meeting turns out to be the most difficult of the crisis for Kennedy. The leaders condemn the quarantine-blockade as too weak. He leaves the room in a rage. Later, with his brother, he is more philosophical, recalling that though the congressional reaction is now more militant than his, it is close to what his was when he first learned of the missiles six days ago.

The diplomatic orchestration is flawless. Following the master scenario, separate briefings are given to forty-six allied diplomats, to Latin American ambassadors, and to envoys from the emerging nations. De Gaulle tells Acheson, "It is exactly what I would have done." At 6 P.M. Rusk sees Dobrynin, the Soviet ambassador; twenty-five minutes later Dobrynin emerges grim and shaken. (U.S. officials will come to believe afterward that Dobrynin had not known of the missiles in Cuba.) In France Acheson lays the matter before the NATO leadership. Adlai Stevenson delivers to Zorin of the USSR a request to convene a special meeting of the Security Council to deal with "the dangerous threat to the peace and security of the world by the secret establishment in Cuba" of missiles "capable of carrying thermonuclear warheads to most of North and South America."

The initial response to these moves is heartening, even among the governments of neutral nations. The Russians appear stunned. Only one allied leader is suspicious of the Americans: John Diefenbaker of Canada.

Kennedy's speech begins at 7 P.M. on all TV channels and on the Spanish language network:

"Good evening, my fellow citizens. The Government, as promised, has maintained the closest surveillance of the Soviet military buildup on the island of Cuba. Within the past week, unmistakable evidence has established the fact that a series of offensive missile sites is now in preparation on that imprisoned island. The purpose of these bases can be none other than to provide a nuclear strike capability against the Western Hemisphere."

He recites the Russian assurances, now revealed as "deliberate deception," and pledges that it will be his "unswerving objectives" to remove the nuclear menace. The quarantine, he says, is only an initial step; it will be followed by stronger measures if that is necessary. The Organization of American States is meeting in emergency session to consider the threat, and U-2 flights over Cuba are being intensified. He warns Khrushchev: any missile launched from Cuba will be regarded as an attack by the Soviet Union on the United States, requiring full retaliatory response against the USSR. Any vessels attempting to run the blockade will be sunk by the U.S. Navy.

After his speech he is handed a confidential report from McNamara listing the resources being marshaled for further military action: warplanes capable of flying 2,000 sorties against targets in Cuba, 90,000 marines and paratroopers forming an invasion force, and 250,000 troops backing them up. An estimate of American casualties in the event of invasion puts the expected figure at over 25,000.

Unexpectedly, there is a light note in this. The Pentagon reports to the President that the Russians and Cubans have inexplicably lined up their planes wing tip to wing tip, ready to be destroyed, like the American planes at Pearl Harbor twenty-one years earlier. Kennedy asks General Taylor to put a U-2 photographic mission over the U.S. air bases in Florida. "It will be interesting if we have done the same thing," he says. We have. The Air Force hastily disperses them.

Tuesday, October 23

George Ball, who has spent the night in troubled sleep on his office couch, awakens to see Dean Rusk looking down on him, smiling for the first time in a week. "We have won a considerable victory," Rusk says. "You and I are still alive." The worst fears have not, in fact, materialized. The Russians have not bombed U.S. bases in the Middle East, blockaded Berlin, or moved to close the Dardanelles. Soviet strategy, whatever its intended thrust, has been checked by the President's challenge.

In Moscow there is no reaction for thirteen hours. Then the American ambassador there is handed a note accusing the United States of "piracy" and denying that the missiles in Cuba are intended for military purposes. The note is interpreted as betraying uncertainty; Khrushchev, caught off guard, appears to be playing for time to think things through. Even so, there is little time for maneuver. President Kennedy has signed the blockade proclamation; it will go into effect tomorrow morning. In it, contraband is defined as covering offensive missiles, their warheads and electronic equipment, and bomber aircraft. Already the Navy is tracking Russian submarines in the Caribbean. The twenty-five Soviet merchant ships on the way to Cuba have not changed course. They are receiving an extraordinary number of coded messages from Russia.

The Organization of American States meeting opens at 9 A.M., with Dean Rusk in the United States chair. The resolution supporting the quarantine must win fourteen Latin American votes, a two-thirds majority. Edward Martin believes that it will get exactly fourteen. The Secretary hopes that his participation will widen the margin. It does—a few minutes after five o'clock the measure carries unanimously, 18-0, with only Uruguay abstaining. The Russians are reported to be astounded. At the same time, American ambassadors in Jamaica and Trinidad, Guinea, and Senegal report success in excluding the possibility that Soviet warheads might be flown to Cuba; their host governments have agreed to deny landing rights for Soviet bloc planes on their way there. Still another encouraging word comes from the U.N.: Stevenson has the support of seven of the eleven nations on the Security Council.

At the President's request, Robert Kennedy calls on Ambassador Dobrynin at the Russian embassy. Dobrynin spreads his hands; as far as he knows, there are no missiles in Cuba. Back at the White House, Bobby learns that the President has shortened the line of interception for the quarantine from eight hundred miles to five hundred miles, giving the Russians more time. McNamara phones from the Pentagon—the latest U-2 photographs show work continuing on the sites in Cuba.

President Kennedy has begun to show the tension. He talks rapidly, in staccato bursts, and his eyes are screwed up tight, as though he is squinting at the sun. A telegram arrives from Bertrand Russell:

YOUR ACTION DESPERATE. . . . NO CONCEIVABLE JUSTIFICATION. WE WILL NOT HAVE MASS MURDER. . . . END THIS MADNESS. Kennedy replies, "I think your attention might well be directed to the burglars rather than to those who have caught the burglars."

Wednesday, October 24

Ten A.M.: the blockade line is drawn. Since Monday afternoon an American fleet, designated Task Force 136, has been racing at flank speed—27 knots—to close off all five navigable channels through which ships from the mid-Atlantic can approach Cuba. Now they have reached their stations in a great arc five hundred miles out to sea from the eastern tip of Cuba. On the forward picket line there are thirteen destroyers; then two cruisers, each flanked by two more cruisers—nineteen ships altogether. Bearing down on them are the twenty-five Russian merchantmen, each of which has been spotted by Navy reconnaissance planes. Two of the vessels, the *Gagarin* and the *Komiles,* are within a few miles of the picket line. A Russian submarine has moved into position between them. In Washington the Ex Comm awaits the first interception, probably before noon.

Aerial photographs from special low-level reconnaissance missions of Cuba, supplementing the U-2s, show that feverish work continues on the ground there. Eight to ten bases are situated near the cities of San Cristóbal, Remedios, Guanajay, and Sagua la Grande. Each base has about four launchers. At least thirty missiles with nuclear warheads are in Cuba, and there are over twenty crated IL-28 (Ilyushin) jet light bombers capable of delivering nuclear bombs on American or Latin American cities. In the new photos the launching pads, the missiles, and the nuclear storage bunkers are clearly defined. Within a few days several of the launching pads will be ready for war.

At the U.N., Secretary General U Thant sends identical letters to Kennedy and Khrushchev urging suspension of the blockade and arms shipments for two to three weeks. Kennedy refuses to negotiate until the Russians agree to dismantle and remove the missile bases. In Moscow William Knox, an American industrialist, is invited to the Kremlin, where he finds Khrushchev in a state of near-exhaustion. The Soviet premier says he has a message for Washington. He looks like a man who has not slept all night; at times he is almost incoherent; the message is unimportant.

On his way to an Ex Comm session President Kennedy says to

his brother, "It looks really mean, doesn't it? But then, really there was no other choice. If they get this mean on this one in our part of the world, what will they do on the next?" Bob tells him, "I just don't think there was any choice, and not only that, if you hadn't acted, you would have been impeached." The President says, "That's what I think—I would have been impeached."*

The first sign of hope comes at 10:32 A.M. Twenty Russian ships have stopped dead in the water. Six, then twelve, turn around. Rusk nudges Bundy and says softly, "We're eyeball to eyeball and I think the other fellow just blinked."

Thursday, October 25

At 8 A.M., twenty-two hours after the quarantine proclamation, the first interception of a Russian ship occurs at sea. She is the tanker *Bucharest.* Identifying herself by radio and declaring that her only cargo is petroleum, she is allowed to proceed through the line of American warships. At 8:35 A.M. the East German passenger ship *Völkerfreund,* carrying twenty students, also passes. The President has ordered that the captain of each vessel must be permitted sufficient time to consult Moscow.

The situation is still grave. In Cuba work on the missile sites continues at an extraordinarily rapid pace. The IL-28 bombers are also being uncrated and assembled. Kennedy keeps the pressure. To all offers of compromise he replies that the missiles and bombers must be removed; nothing else will do.

In the U.N. Security Council, Valerian Zorin makes the mistake of challenging Adlai Stevenson to produce evidence of the missiles. As millions of Americans watch—it is during the dinner hour—Stevenson turns on him with superb scorn. He says he has proof, but first he asks Zorin to deny that the missiles are there. "*Yes* or *no*?" he snaps. "Don't wait for the translation, *yes* or *no*?" Zorin says

* In *Thirteen Days* Robert Kennedy wrote that this Wednesday and the following Saturday were the worst days of the crisis. Of that moment when they were awaiting the naval confrontation at sea on Wednesday, Bob wrote: "I think these few minutes were the time of gravest concern for the President. Was the world on the brink of a holocaust? Was it our error? A mistake? . . . His hand went up to his face and covered his mouth. His face seemed drawn, his eyes pained, almost gray. We stared at each other across the table. For a few fleeting seconds, it was almost as though no one else was there and he was no longer the President. Inexplicably, I thought of when he was ill and almost died; when he lost his child; when we learned that our oldest brother had been killed; of personal times of strain and hurt."

he is not in an American courtroom. Stevenson says, "You are in the courtroom of world opinion right now and you can answer *yes* or *no*." Zorin, retreating, says, "You will have your answer in due course." Stevenson closes in: "I am prepared to wait for my answer until hell freezes over, if that's your decision. And I am also prepared to present the evidence in this room." With that, he unveils easels which have been shrouded, revealing blown-up photos of the sites.

Friday, October 26

At 7 A.M. the American destroyer *Joseph P. Kennedy Jr.*, hails the freighter *Marulca* in the open sea about 180 miles northeast of Nassau. The *Kennedy* hoists the international signal "Oscar November," meaning "Heave to," and the *Marulca* does so. In less than an hour an armed boarding party of American sailors is searching her. There is no contraband; the ship is allowed to continue. The inference, which is encouraging, is that Moscow has instructed Soviet captains to submit to searches.

Nevertheless the Ex Comm is glum. In Cuba the Russians continue to work feverishly. The first missiles will be ready for firing in a matter of hours. At a White House press conference Salinger takes note of this and observes that the Soviet technicians are clearly trying to achieve "full operational capability as soon as possible." A State Department spokesman says ominously that if this continues, "further action" by the President "will be justified." Robert Kennedy tells Ambassador Dobrynin that the President cannot hold off more than forty-eight hours.

The first real break in the crisis comes at 1:30 P.M. It is highly unconventional. John Scali, a TV commentator who covers the State Department for the American Broadcasting Company, receives a telephone call from an acquaintance at the Soviet embassy. The caller is Alexander S. Fomin, a counselor at the embassy who is believed to be a colonel in the KGB, the Soviet secret police. Scali says he is busy. Fomin, highly agitated, says, "It's very important. Meet me at the Occidental in ten minutes." At the Occidental Restaurant on Pennsylvania Avenue, Fomin says he wants to know whether the State Department would discuss an agreement with three provisions: the removal of the missiles in Cuba under U.N. supervision, a promise from Castro to accept no offensive weapons in the future, and an American pledge not to invade Cuba. Scali says he will find out. At 7:35 the two men meet again in the coffee shop of the Statler Hilton. Scali, having talked to Rusk, informs the Russian that the United States government is definitely interested. Fomin rushes off.

At 6 P.M. (1 A.M. in Moscow) a long, emotional letter from Khrushchev starts coming through over the teletype linking the State Department with the American embassy in Moscow. The Soviet premier acknowledges for the first time that there are Russian missiles in Cuba. His proposal, he says, is this: no more weapons will go to Cuba, and those within Cuba will be either withdrawn or destroyed if Kennedy agrees not to attack Cuba. Essentially, these are Fomin's terms. At 10 P.M. the Ex Comm meets to consider the offer. The decision is to accept it as though it were a formal note and reply in the morning, pending a careful examination during the night by Kremlinologists at the State Department. The Fomin conditions will be studied at the same time. For the first time in ten days the President goes to bed believing that a peaceful solution may be found.

Saturday, October 27

The height of the crisis. Even as the reply to Khrushchev is being drafted, Radio Moscow broadcasts a second Khrushchev letter to Kennedy. This one is unacceptable. As a condition for withdrawal of the missiles he demands that NATO missile bases in Turkey be dismantled. The Ex Comm has already weighed the possibility of such a swap and rejected it. Though the bases in Turkey now have little military value (and will, in fact, be phased out soon), the Turks regard them as symbols of the American commitment. To bargain away the weapons of an ally in exchange for the security of the United States would, it is believed, shake, and perhaps shatter, the western alliance. This second letter is different in more than content; it lacks Khrushchev's style, and reads as though drafted by a committee. The FBI reports that Soviet diplomats in New York are preparing to destroy their documents. The bridges to sanity seem to be crumbling. On top of this there is another blow. An American U-2 pilot is shot down over Cuba, meaning that the SAM bases on the missile sites are operational; the missiles themselves will be next. The Joint Chiefs join the Ex Comm meeting. They recommend an air strike Monday, to be followed by an invasion of Cuba. With one exception the Ex Comm believes that there is no other course. The exception is the President. He says: "It isn't the first step that concerns me . . . but both sides escalating to the fourth and fifth step—and we don't go to the sixth because there is no one around to do so. We must remind ourselves we are embarking on a very hazardous course."

Robert Kennedy sees a way out. He proposes that they ignore the second letter and answer the first. Various drafts along these lines are submitted by Dean Rusk, George Ball, McGeorge Bundy, and Llewellyn Thompson. Bob doesn't like any of them. His brother tells him, "If you disagree so violently, go draft one yourself." Bob and Ted Sorensen leave the meeting to do just that. By choosing the terms they like best in each of the two letters and in the Fomin proposal, they agree to a proposal Khrushchev never made. The President approves it, sends it to Khrushchev at 8:05 P.M.—and tells the world he has accepted the Russian conditions. Bob then phones Dobrynin and asks him to come to the Justice Department. He tells the Soviet ambassador that they are running out of time. Only a few hours are left. The President must have a reply the next day. Dobrynin is pessimistic; the Kremlin, he says, is deeply committed to Castro.

At the White House the President remarks that the outcome seems to him to be touch and go, that it can now go "either way." McNamara, glancing at the sky on his way back to the Pentagon, wonders aloud how many more sunsets he will see. Thompson tells his wife that if he does not come home, he will let her know where she and the children will join him should the capital be evacuated.

Sunday, October 28

Another magnificent October day. A few minutes before 9 A.M. (4 P.M. in the Russian capital) Radio Moscow announces that an important announcement will be broadcast on the hour. This is the very last chance for peace. If Khrushchev rejects Kennedy's terms the American attack will go in. McNamara's estimate of U.S. casualties is now 40,000 to 50,000.

The Soviet announcer begins reading the Russian answer. The key to it is in the third paragraph:

> In order to eliminate as rapidly as possible the conflict which endangers the cause of peace . . . the Soviet government . . . has given a new order to dismantle the arms which you described as offensive, and to crate and return them to the Soviet Union.

Castro, who has not been consulted, declares that he has been betrayed, that he will ignore the settlement. But while he can delay the end of the crisis, he cannot stop it; though the missiles are on Cuban soil, they are in Russian hands, and there are no Cubans who know how to fire them anyhow. At 1:30 P.M. the Joint Chiefs signal Task Force 136: there will be no more boarding of ships, no show of force. The Ex Comm is jubilant, but the President speaks of how difficult it must have been for Khrushchev to back down; he warns them that there must be no claims of an American victory. He writes the Soviet premier a careful letter ending:

> I think we should give priority to questions relating to the proliferation of nuclear weapons, on earth and outer space, and to the great effort for a nuclear test ban.

That evening the Kennedy brothers review the thirteen days of crisis. At the end the President says, "Maybe this is the night I should go to the theater." Both of them laugh uproariously. Then Bob says, "If you go, I want to go with you."

Portrait of an American

PETER CARL GOLDMARK

BORN IN BUDAPEST on December 2, 1906, he was one of that generation of brilliant Hungarian scientists which included Edward Teller, John von Neumann, and Eugene Paul Wigner. But while they dedicated their talents to the technology of death, he became a leader in the communications revolution. They gave America the Bomb. He gave it the long-playing record, color television, and the promise of a whole new world of sight and sound.

His was a creative family. One great-uncle, Karl Goldmark, was one of the nineteenth century's most gifted composers of opera. Another great-uncle, Joseph Goldmark, discovered red phosphorus, essential to the manufacture of kitchen matches. Joseph defied the government of Austria-Hungary, fled to America, fought in the Civil War, and contributed to the defeat of Lee by inventing percussion caps for the Union Army.

Peter was a precocious child. Showing the Joseph in him, he exasperated his parents by taking over the family bathroom for his experiments, and before the onset of adolescence he had assembled a huge motion-picture projector. Later in his youth he told his teachers that he had found a mistake in a paper by Britain's most celebrated physicist, Ernest Rutherford. They were amused—until he reconstructed the experiment for them and proved himself right.

In a magazine he read an article by an eccentric Scotch stocking salesman, John Logie Baird, who devised a primitive television system in the early 1920s, convinced the Royal Society that it would work, and talked the BBC into transmitting experimental broadcasts. The article told how to assemble a receiver and advertised a kit. Peter sent for one. Years afterward he described the result: "The picture came through in postage-stamp size. You could hardly make it out, it flickered so. It was also in color—all red. But it was the most exciting thing in my life."

It remained so. He took an engineering degree at the Berliner Technische Hochschule and a doctorate in physics at the University of Vienna, where he displayed the Karl Goldmark in him at a series of concerts in which he performed as a pianist and cellist. But Baird had captured his imagination; his dissertation, "A New Method for Determining the Velocity of Ions," which he read before the Academy of Science in Vienna, laid much of the groundwork for television projection. When his faculty advisers urged him to continue as a physicist, he politely declined, packed his cello, and sailed for England.

Hired by Pye Radio, Ltd., in Cambridge, he built a mechanical TV transmitter. Although it worked, the Pye studios seemed indifferent to its possibilities, and after two years he left Cambridge with savings of $250 and boarded a boat for New York. There he applied for American citizenship and a job at RCA. To the subsequent chagrin of David Sarnoff, Sarnoff's underlings at NBC turned the slight Hungarian scientist away. CBS then hired him.

The next thing Peter's new superiors knew, he was glimpsed atop the Chrysler Building putting up a television antenna. Four relatively fallow years followed. Then, while visiting Canada in the spring of 1940, he happened to drop in at a theater showing the

Technicolor *Gone With the Wind.* Stunned by the beauty of the color, he said later, he came away with "an inferiority feeling about television in black and white." He developed color television in just three months.

His color system was built around a revolving disc with transparent color segments of green, blue, and red. The disc spun in front of the camera tube. When a picture representing, for example, the green in a scene was being sent out, the green transparency was in front of the camera; in the viewer's set another spinning disc, synchronized with the one in the camera, turned the picture into the right color, and the colors followed each other so rapidly that the viewer's eye mixed them together. In August 1940 Peter put on a demonstration for CBS executives. They saw an experimental set project, in succession, a lovely zinnia, black-eyed Susans, red sails in a sunset, a brunette with a red scarf, a blonde chasing a colorful beach ball into surf, and at the end—like a vaudeville show—an American flag waving in a spanking breeze.

Then war intervened. Peter led a team of engineers making devices to jam Nazi radar. In 1945 he turned again to color television. When the FCC held trials at the end of the decade, his pictures were beautiful, while RCA's, to the humiliation of David Sarnoff, showed green monkeys eating blue bananas. The FCC adopted the CBS system. Sarnoff hired a hundred expensive technicians, gave them a budget of 130 million dollars, and told them to develop better color. Meanwhile Peter came up with an improvement of his own called the shadow-mask tube. The FCC approved of RCA color, but RCA needed the shadow-mask tube for proper color projection—and had to pay CBS royalties for it. Later the Soviet Union and NASA's Apollo flights used Peter's original system.

One postwar evening he and several friends were listening to a record of Horowitz playing Brahms. "Suddenly," as he recalled afterward, "there was a click. The most horrible sound man ever invented, right in the middle of the music. Somebody rushed to change records. The mood was broken. I knew right there and then I had to stop that sort of thing."

After three years he had the 33⅓ rpm microgroove record as we know it, stamped from Vinylite to reduce surface noise. The old 78 rpm records had from 85 to 100 grooves to an inch; Peter increased this to from 224 to 300, which meant that 45 minutes of music could be played on the two sides of a 12-inch record—a whole concerto, or an entire symphony. Sarnoff announced that RCA had a 45-rpm record and ridiculed the notion that a slower speed was needed. But Columbia's first LP album was a tremendous success, offering everything from Bach to Harry James at prices ranging from $2.85 for a 10-inch popular disc to $4.85 for one of its 12-inch Masterworks, and RCA's challenge failed.

By Peter's fiftieth birthday CBS had assigned one executive to be his full-time factotum. (He was known as the "Vice President in Charge of Peter.") Then Peter was designated president of CBS laboratories, and the network built a workshop for him on a grassy knoll overlooking a Stamford thoroughfare not far from his home. Stanton later said, "The smartest thing we ever did was to build Peter a lab in the country to play with." From it CBS acquired patents on over a hundred of his inventions. One was the Reverbatron, which reproduces the vibrations of a large concert hall, adding depth to sound. Others included a record player for the blind and a miniature color television camera to transmit pictures for surgeons from inside the stomach, developed by Peter in one of his several roles—professor of medical electronics at the University of Pennsylvania. Perhaps his most extraordinary creation was EVR (Electronic Video Recording), a tiny device enabling the viewer to play programs on his home set without commercials—a seven-inch reel of tiny film covering a half-hour of color or an hour of black-and-white that would drop in place like a phonograph record and rewind automatically when finished.

In suburban Connecticut legends about him accumulated: stories of his musical evenings with Benny Goodman, a neighbor; his chess playing; his fantastic LP library; the speakers cunningly concealed about his house which could convert it into a church, with a choir singing in every corner. If a secretary came to work late and said her car was defective, Peter would repair it on the spot. Fastidious about his own Mercedes-Benz, he would clean up after the filling station attendants who serviced it. And he worked all hours, calling assistants at 3 A.M. or 5 A.M., saying, "Just thought of something, meet me at the lab," and hanging up.

There were tales about his temper, too. Yet he was one of the few scientists of his time with a social conscience, finding work for jobless blacks, heading the Stamford antipoverty office, and putting in long hours crusading for the use of educational television in public schools. He gave Stamford's Riverview Elementary School a complete television studio. Thanks in part to his efforts, by the time he retired in 1971 the teachers in nearly one-third of American schools were using film strips, projectors, or other visual teaching aids.

It was a measure of Peter's genius that CBS was very nervous about his retirement. The network offered him $75,000 a year for ten years to do nothing. He refused. Instead he threw his vast energies into a scheme for establishing as many as forty coast-to-coast TV channels by uniting domestic satellites and cable television. In his vision of the future there were nationwide chains of movie theaters of the air, free TV access to the voters for campaigning politicians, home instruction for students, and national facsimile newspapers delivered through television sets.

Once in the late 1960s a radio interviewer asked him whether he thought mental telepathy would ever replace TV. Peter paused, adjusted his glasses, and said it was conceivable that undiscovered radiation from the brain might be used someday. He added: "But that's a long way off."

There was a protracted silence in the studio. With Peter you couldn't be sure.

Twenty-nine

DON'T LET IT BE FORGOT

NOW IN THE THIRD YEAR of the Kennedy Presidency a fundamental change loomed in the character of the civil rights movement. Beginning with the Montgomery bus boycott in 1955 and extending through Little Rock, the freedom rides, and Oxford, Mississippi, the struggle for racial equality had been in the form of a serial drama, with whites in the role of bullies and blacks as martyrs. The conscience of the nation's great white middle class had been aroused, and its indignation had become a solvent eroding barriers of law and custom which had endured for generations. But that era was about to end. Angrier, fiercer, more headstrong blacks were fighting their way to the center of the stage. The established black leadership was discovering that young Negroes were approaching the end of their patience. The emergence of the eye for an eye trend foreshadowed a new, darker period in the struggle for integration, but first there were a few more episodes in the serial to be played out. The bully who made black martyrs best was the police commissioner of Birmingham, T. Eugene "Bull" Connor, who had first come to the nation's attention during the freedom rides. Two years had passed; he was about to assume a star role.

Martin Luther King had called Birmingham "the most segregated city in the United States." Connor liked to quote him on that; he wore his bigotry like a badge of pride. For twenty-three years the commissioner had used terror and brutality to cow Negro leaders, always with success. Not only were Birmingham's schools completely segregated; so were its public toilets, drinking fountains, theaters, parks, playgrounds, restaurants, and even churches. Federal rulings prohibiting discrimination did not intimidate Bull Connor. To him they were just contrivances for disrupting law and order in Birmingham and, as such, opposition to be ruthlessly crushed. Until the spring of 1963 civil rights leaders tried to stay clear of him; he was running for mayor, and racial demonstrations would merely give him more white votes. In April the election was over. He had lost, which made him meaner, but they were ready for him.

King's campaign opened April 2 with sit-ins and marches. Connor retaliated swiftly, arresting over four hundred Negroes on charges of parading without a permit, loitering, or trespassing. King then sent groups to worship in white churches, defying the police to seize them there. Connor refused to be drawn. He counted on Birmingham's white Christians to draw the color line, and most of them did; four churches admitted the Negroes, seventeen turned them away. King called for a protest march on Good Friday, April 12. Connor obtained an injunction forbidding it. Burke Marshall urged the black leaders hold off until the inauguration of Albert Boutwell, the moderate mayor-elect. Little could be expected from Arthur Hanes, the outgoing mayor, who said of Robert Kennedy, "I hope that every drop of blood that's spilled he tastes in his throat, and I hope he chokes on it," and of King, "This nigger has got the blessing of the Attorney General and the White House." But the black leadership had no choice. Their people were ready to march without them. The demonstrations were held in defiance of the injunction, and the inevitable arrests, including King's, followed.

On May 2 about five hundred Negroes were locked up—high school students, most of them, carried to jail in school buses. Other students paraded in protest the next day. White spectators pelted them with brickbats and bottles. King held a mass meeting in the New Pilgrim Baptist Church to protest; a thousand blacks came, and Connor threw police lines around the church. There were no incidents then, but when twenty-five hundred Negroes surged into downtown Birmingham the following day in another demonstration, Connor met them with police dogs and fire hoses. The dogs were trained to rip clothing with their teeth, and the hoses, with 700 pounds of pressure, smashed the blacks against buildings or to the ground. On May 4 newspaper readers around the world were shocked by a brutal photograph showing a huge, snarling dog lunging at a frightened Negro woman. President Kennedy said the picture made him "sick," and he said, "I can well understand why the Negroes of Birmingham are tired of being asked to be patient." An ADA delegation asked him to intervene, but at this point there was little he could do under the Constitution. He did send Burke Marshall down to open the channels of communications. In quiet talks with Birmingham businessmen Marshall negotiated a fragile truce which lasted five days. On May 11 the home of a Negro leader and a desegregated hotel were bombed. The next day, Mother's Day, enraged blacks again erupted into the streets, and this time they were too much for the policemen, the dogs and the hoses. After a night of riots and fires Connor asked the new governor, George C. Wallace, for reinforcements.

This was the first the rest of the nation heard of Wallace. He had been expecting something of this sort, and he was ready with a motley force—seven hundred deputy sheriffs, game wardens, liquor agents, and highway patrolmen. Shouting threats, they stomped around the city shoving blacks into doorways and snapping the safety catches of their guns menacingly. The blacks weren't surprised. They distrusted Wallace, and with good reason; he had already told the press that he would use the power of his office to suppress King. Of Marshall's truce he said that he would not be party to any "compromise on the issues of segregation." It was his avowed purpose to sabotage Marshall, and the only thing that stopped him was the decision of President Kennedy to fly three thousand troops to an air base near Birmingham. "This government," the President said, "will do whatever must be done to preserve order, to protect the lives of its citizens, and to uphold the law of the land." Any misuse of force by the governor's officers now would bring in an overwhelming counterforce. Mayor Hanes denounced "bayonet brotherhood." Wallace, furious, filed suit with the Supreme Court, charging that the President's action was "unconstitutional and void." The governor said, "This military dictatorship must be nipped in the bud." The Justice Department quietly replied that as commander in chief of the nation's armed forces the President could move troops to any base he wished.

Marshall reconciled the black and white leaders once more, and this time a lasting peace returned to the littered but integrated streets of Birmingham. The outcome was clearly another triumph for Martin Luther King. Its implications were discernible far beyond the city; again the conscience of the country's white middle class had been stirred, and elsewhere protesting Negroes were marching in Selma, Alabama; Albany, Georgia; Cambridge, Maryland; Raleigh and Greensboro, North Carolina; Nashville and Clinton, Tennessee; Shreveport, Louisiana; Jackson and Philadelphia, Mississippi; and, in the north, in Chicago. "The fires of frustration and discord," the President said, "are burning in every city . . . where legal remedies are not at hand." In a phrase which would be remembered, Ken O'Donnell predicted "a long, hot summer." Before autumn ended fourteen thousand demonstrators would be in southern jails.

The next chapter in Wallace's burgeoning gubernatorial career put him in the path of Attorney General Kennedy. Robert Kennedy didn't want the conflict, and in the beginning he thought it might be avoidable. He had come to believe that the Mississippi crisis might have ended differently if he had cultivated Ross Barnett earlier. He hoped to do better with Wallace, though the prospects could hardly have been called auspicious. Not only had Wallace been elected as a racist; it had been, and still was, his only issue. In his campaign he had repeatedly vowed to stand in the doorway of any white Alabama school to drive away Negro children, and he had ended his florid inaugural address with the incendiary passage: "In the name of the greatest people that have ever trod on this earth, I draw the line in the dust and toss the gauntlet before the feet of tyranny. And I say: Segregation now! Segregation tomorrow! Segregation forever!" Still, Bob Kennedy thought a man-to-man exchange with him might prevent future grief. The fact that he thought that is curious. Demagogues have never been responsive to the voices of reason, and Bob's manner did not encourage moderation in those who differed with him. But he never saw himself as others saw him. He thought he might bring George Wallace around to his way of thinking.

His suit bogged down from the very beginning. Like his predecessor in Montgomery's executive mansion, Wallace was almost impossible to reach from Washington by telephone. Intermediaries arranged a meeting, and Bob did everything he could to make it seem casual, even scheduling other appointments in Alabama to make it seem one of many calls there. But Wallace had other ideas. He wanted his constituents fully informed about his battles for white supremacy, and to that end he did everything but greet the attorney general at the airport with a band playing "Dixie." The statehouse was ringed by state troopers. Pickets carried placards reading: CHRISTIANS AWAKE, "COME OUT FROM AMONGST THEM AND BE YE SEPARATE," and KOSHER TEAM: KENNEDY KASTRO KHRUSHCHEV. The place where Jefferson Davis was sworn in as President of the Confederacy was marked by a fresh wreath, and a Daughter of the Confederacy clad in spotless white stood guard there with folded arms, presumably to prevent Kennedy from defiling it. Inside, Wallace greeted him by turning on a tape recorder "as a precaution." It was a waste of electricity; nothing of substance was said. The most urgent racial problem in Alabama, which Bob hoped Wallace would share with him, arose from court orders ruling that the state university must admit black applicants. Over and over he told Wallace that the law must be enforced, that it was their sworn duty to do so; over and over Wallace said that this would mean violence and that the blood would be on Kennedy's hands. At the end of the conference the governor called in the press to announce that nothing which had been said altered his vow to stand in the schoolhouse door. Kennedy said he hoped local authorities would discourage mob violence. Ed Guthman, who was with him, thought that "Bob was dumbfounded by Wallace's attitude. It was the closest I ever saw him come to throwing up his hands in despair."

The Kennedys were determined to prevent another Oxford. They had the campus photographed with the same reconnaissance planes which had been used over Cuba, and troop commanders used the photos to map maneuvers. Flying down to Muscle Shoals, the President spoke from the same platform as Wallace and elliptically warned him not to defy the law. Again the governor told reporters that his mind was unchanged. They were moving rapidly toward confrontation. Under the terms of a court order three Negroes had been declared eligible for the university's summer term, beginning June 10, one of them to an extension course and two to the main campus at Tuscaloosa. These two, Vivian J. Malone and Jimmy A. Hood, were in the same situation as James Meredith twenty months earlier. Wallace, more audacious than Barnett, announced that he intended not only to bar Hood and Miss Malone from the Tuscaloosa campus; he also meant to force federal officers to arrest Alabama's governor. After a U.S. District Court enjoined him with interfering with their enrollment, he declared: "The action I am going to take involves even my personal freedom, but I intend to carry it out, regardless of what risk I take."

As Bob Kennedy's deputy, Nick Katzenbach was again cast in his difficult Oxford role, leading the federal officers at Tuscaloosa. In the name of states' rights Wallace had mobilized his seven hundred deputy sheriffs, game wardens, liquor agents, and state troopers, plus several National Guard companies. Unlike Barnett, Wallace wasn't taking university administrators into his confidence. They didn't know whether he planned to seal off the campus, issue guns, or what. The situation had comic aspects. The administrators reported to Katzenbach that Al Lingo, the state patrol chief, had painted a white line on the pavement in front of Foster Auditorium, where students would register. Wallace was occupying an office just inside the entrance. He had installed two air-conditioners, and there, as the sweating deputy attorney general tried to guess what he was up to, the bantam governor of Alabama sat coolly reading the *Montgomery Advertiser*. In the White House the President and his brother listened to Katzenbach's running analysis on an open telephone line and watched events develop on television.

They decided to let Wallace have his show. Katzenbach's plan, which was adopted, was to make the governor look ridiculous by robbing his doorway stand of meaning. Katzenbach would drive Miss Malone and Hood to the campus. Parking the car and leaving them in it, he would confront Wallace himself, telling the governor that going through the door was unimportant, that the government considered the two students enrolled, and that they would begin classes in the morning. The President would federalize the 31st National Guard division if Wallace continued to obstruct them.

That is more or less what happened. Katzenbach told the press that the two blacks would arrive at 10 A.M. Wallace appeared at 9:53 escorted by towering state policemen in combat gear—helmets, side arms, gas guns, and truncheons. When Katzenbach and the two Negroes drove up, accompanied by marshals in mufti, Wallace's public relations man darted out with a lectern and put it in front of the white line. The temperature was almost 100 degrees. The heat seemed to rise from the pavement in waves, and reporters and troopers tried to crowd in the building's shadow as Wallace took his stand. He raised his right arm like a traffic policeman. Katzenbach walked up with a marshal on either side and halted in front of him. He said, "I have a proclamation from the President of the United States ordering you to cease and desist from unlawful obstructions." Wallace replied by reading a proclamation of his own excoriating "the unwelcome, unwarranted and force-induced intrusion upon the campus of the University of Alabama of the might of the central government." He concluded: "Now, therefore I, George C. Wallace, as governor . . . do hereby denounce and forbid this illegal and unwarranted action by the central government."

Arms folded, Katzenbach answered mildly that all this was about two students who simply sought an education—"a simple problem scarcely worth this kind of attention." He asked the governor to reconsider, and, when Wallace refused to reply, he returned to the car and drove the two Negroes to dormitories which the administration had already assigned to them. Four hours later a brigadier general in the National Guard drove up. He saluted Wallace, who saluted back; he told him that the Guard had been federalized and asked him to "please stand aside so that the order of the court may be accomplished." After a last bitter volley at Yankee justice Wallace walked away.

The Kennedys thought he had been made to look ludicrous, and that the country would see his posturing for the absurdity it was. Millions of Americans agreed, and since more than three hundred blacks enrolled in the university after Hood and Malone without incident—indeed, without a word or even a glance from the statehouse—it appeared that the governor had been outwitted. George Wallace didn't see it that way, however, and neither did his admirers. He declared, "I stood eyeball to eyeball with them and they turned back." So they had, on television; all that viewers of the news had seen was the exchange of statements between him and Katzenbach and Katzenbach's departure. The registration of the two blacks had occurred off camera, and Wallace, then an underrated politician, had seen that in the eyes of the easily manipulated, his show in apparently staring down a federal official would carry more weight. In his book *Wallace* Marshall Frady wrote that the Alabama governor had "discovered a dark, silent, brooding mass of people whom no one—the newspapers, the political leaders, the intellectuals—no one but Wallace had suspected were there."

The race issue had emerged as one of the great themes of the 1960s. Already the civil rights movement was being described as revolutionary. In a televised speech on the evening of that June 10, the day of the Wallace-Katzenbach confrontation, President Kennedy called it "a moral issue"—"as old as the Scriptures and . . .

as clear as the American Constitution." "A great change is at hand," he said, "and our task, our obligation, is to make that revolution, that change, peaceful and constructive for all." To that end he was asking Congress to enact a broad, sweeping civil rights bill committing it to the premise "that race has no place in American life or law."

Medgar Evers was returning that night to his home in Jackson, Mississippi, after attending a civil rights rally in a church. As the NAACP field secretary in that state, Evers had been James Meredith's friend and adviser, and that had marked him for Klansmen and the state's White Citizens' Councils. As he walked from his car he was murdered by a sniper lying in ambush. Discouraged and gloomy, the President said to Arthur Schlesinger, "I don't understand the South. I'm coming to believe that Thaddeus Stevens was right. I had always been taught to regard him as a man of vicious bias. But when I see this sort of thing I begin to wonder how else you can treat them."

When civil rights leaders told him that they were planning an enormous peaceful demonstration in Washington, he was appalled. "We want success in Congress," he said, "not just a big show." He was afraid it might get out of hand, or create "an atmosphere of intimidation." A. Philip Randolph, head of the Brotherhood of Sleeping Car Porters, answered him. The march was Randolph's idea. He had proposed it to Franklin Roosevelt twenty years earlier, and Roosevelt, equally apprehensive, had promised to establish a federal Committee on Fair Employment Practices if Randolph would call it off.* That had been the end of it then, but this time Randolph was determined to go ahead. "The Negroes are already in the streets," he said. "It is very likely impossible to get them off." He argued that it would be better that they be led by responsible leaders than by others who would exploit them and encourage violence.

The March on Washington, held on August 28, was a high point for those who believed that the grievances of the blacks could be redressed by working within the system. "We subpoenaed the conscience of the nation," Martin Luther King said. Nothing like it had ever been seen in the country—over two hundred thousand Americans, the largest crowd ever to gather in the capital, and all of them orderly. Most were Negroes, but thousands of whites came, too, led

* See Vol. I, page 297.

by Walter Reuther. They sang hymns and spirituals, and "We shall overcome," and they carried placards reading: EFFECTIVE CIVIL RIGHTS LAWS—NOW! INTEGRATED SCHOOLS—NOW! DECENT HOUSING—NOW!

Their self-discipline was a marvel. The District's fifty-nine hundred policemen had nothing to do but direct traffic; four thousand soldiers and marines who were standing by were never called. While the march was in progress the President received its leaders—among them King, Randolph, Reuther, Roy Wilkins, Whitney M. Young, Jr., Chairman John Lewis of the Student Nonviolent Coordinating Committee, and Floyd B. McKissick of CORE. Kennedy said he had been "impressed with the deep fervor and the quiet dignity" of the demonstration. They left and he watched the rest of it on television. The most memorable moment came when Martin Luther King spoke at the Lincoln Memorial:

"I have a dream that one day this nation will rise up, live out the true meaning of its creed: 'We hold these truths to be self-evident, that all men are created equal.' I have a dream that one day on the red hills of Georgia sons of former slaves and the sons of former slaveowners will be able to sit down together at the table of brotherhood. I have a dream that one day even the state of Mississippi, a state sweltering with the heat of injustice . . . will be transformed into an oasis of freedom and justice. I have a dream that my four little children will one day live in a nation where they will not be judged by the color of their skin but by the content of their character."

"Dream some more!" cried his delighted listeners. Yet there were other Americans who were not delighted. Ward leaders in the great ethnic neighborhoods of the northern cities, keystones in the Democratic coalition Roosevelt had built, were stirring angrily. The Poles, the Irish, and the Italians, all of whom had given Kennedy wide margins in the election three years earlier, had struggled up from the bottom without the help of the government. Negroes, they argued, should do the same. They pointed out that congressmen who urged integration had withdrawn their own children from Washington classrooms and put them in private schools, and that a California study reportedly showed that outspoken liberals privately opposed Negroes in their schools and neighborhoods. A Lou Harris survey revealed that the administration's handling of the race issue had alienated over four million Democrats. In the South, naturally, the deterioration was greatest. "K.O. the Kennedys" was a political slogan in Mississippi. The governor of moderate North Carolina said that if an election were held then, Kennedy would lose it, and in Birmingham a Lubell poll found only one white voter who had supported Kennedy and didn't regret it.

The tragic fact is that this was a reaction to what had been, on the whole, exemplary black behavior. White Americans who were offended by the rhetoric of Martin Luther King and who thought James Meredith uppity were in for a shock. The same Negroes they regarded as upstarts were being called Uncle Toms by some black audiences. In Harlem young Negroes threw eggs at King, and in Chicago they booed Meredith. Their new heroes were Muslim leaders Jeremiah X, Malcolm X, and Elijah Mohammed, who preached the innate wickedness of the white race and dismissed nonviolence as folly. "The day of nonviolent resistance is over," Malcolm X told them. "If they have the Ku Klux Klan nonviolent, I'll be nonviolent. If they make the White Citizens' Councils nonviolent, I'll be nonviolent. But as long as you've got somebody else not being nonviolent, I don't want anybody coming to me talking any nonviolent talk."

The first administration figure to encounter the new blacks was Robert Kennedy. He was impressed by a James Baldwin article in the *New Yorker* in which Baldwin wrote of the Negro's past of:

> . . . rope, fire, torture, castration, infanticide, rape; death and humiliation; fear by day and night, fear as deep as the marrow of the bone; doubt that he was worthy of life, since everyone around him denied it; sorrow for his women, for his kinfolk, for his children, who needed his protection, and whom he could not protect; rage, hatred and murder, hatred for white men so deep that it often turned against him and his own and made all love, all trust, all joy impossible.

Baldwin believed that "the price of the liberation of the white people is the liberation of the blacks," and he quoted a Negro spiritual: *"God gave Noah the rainbow sign:/ No more water, the fire next time!"*

The comedian Dick Gregory suggested to Burke Marshall that the attorney general ought to meet Baldwin. Marshall passed the recommendation along, and the two men had breakfast together at Hickory Hill. Their talk was brief but amiable, and Kennedy proposed that they continue it in New York the next day in his father's

Manhattan apartment. Burke Marshall would be with him. They wanted opinions about what the government should be doing, and they hoped that other blacks would join them. Baldwin said he would bring Kenneth B. Clark, the psychologist; Lorraine Hansberry, the writer; Lena Horne, Harry Belafonte, and Jerome Smith, a twenty-four-year-old CORE chairman who had been beaten and jailed during the freedom rides. Kennedy expected a serious discussion, the kind of talks he had had with Roy Wilkins and Martin Luther King. The first thing he got was a tirade from Smith, who said that being in the same room with Bob Kennedy made him feel like vomiting. From then on the meeting deteriorated.

Kennedy tried to explain what the government had done and was doing, and what its new bill would do. They didn't care. Baldwin didn't even know that a presidential civil rights message was before Congress. He said that the only reason the President had acted in Alabama was that a white man had been stabbed, and when Marshall protested that he had consulted Martin Luther King, they burst into laughter. This went on for three hours. Bob said afterward, "It was all emotion, hysteria. They stood up and orated. They cursed. Some of them wept and walked out of the room." Toward the end of it a young black said that he would not fight for the United States, and when Bob asked how he could say such a thing the youth repeated it.

The irony was that Bob's reason for coming to New York was to confer with several chain store executives over ways to end Jim Crow in their southern stores. That didn't impress the angry blacks either, and another attorney general might have become disenchanted with them. This one was different. He was resentful at the time; back in Washington, repeating the remark about refusing to defend the country, he added wonderingly, "Imagine anyone saying that." But later in the week he said thoughtfully, "I guess if I were in his shoes, if I'd gone through what he's gone through, I might feel differently about this country." It was the beginning of his real conversion to the movement, the realization that a rage that deep must have profound origins, and that if nothing was done about it the consequence would in fact be a fire next time.

On May 29 the President became forty-six years old. His staff had planned a surprise birthday party for him, getting him to it on the pretext that a call awaited him on the scramble phone in the situation room, but not much surprised this President, and he was grinning broadly when Mac Bundy led him into the White House mess. Pierre Salinger, the emcee, handed Kennedy a speech. "We know you usually write your speeches, Mr. President," he said, "but here is one written by a ghost writer, and we would like you to read it." It began, "Twoscore and six years ago there was brought forth at Brookline, Massachusetts . . ." Kennedy was handed a satellite model with a card reading, "Hope you have a good trip, Barry," and Jackie, teasing her husband over his pride in the new flower garden outside his office, gave him an enormous basket of dead grass. "From the White House Historical Society," the card read, "Genuine Antique Grass from the Antique Rose Garden." The evening was lovely. They spent it cruising down the Potomac in the presidential yacht, the *Honey Fitz*.

It was high tide for the Kennedy regime, but they didn't know that. They thought they had another five years in the White House, and when the President moved out he planned to start a new Washington newspaper. It would be a great one; the best newspapermen in the country would want to work for it. But that was a long way off, and they were not of an age to brood about the future. Youth continued to be a dominant theme in the administration. Their life-style in many ways was that of what were then called "the young marrieds." The three Kennedy wives, Jackie, Ethel, and Joan, were all pregnant that spring. Baby carriages and playpens had become familiar furniture in the homes of senior government officials who, in other years, would have been in their late fifties or sixties. That was part of the Kennedy era; like the Peace Corps it reminded young Americans that this was their President. To be sure, he had other constituencies, the intellectual community among them. Celebrating the end of his six-year term as a member of Harvard's board of overseers, he gave a stag dinner at the Executive Mansion for distinguished Harvard men. But even then he was conscious of his age. "It is difficult to welcome you to the White House," he said, "because at least two-thirds of you have attended more stag dinners here than I have."

His popularity, like that of any President, fluctuated. After the missile crisis in 1962 Gallup reported that 83 percent of the people approved of him; over the next ten months the figure fell to 61 percent and then 59. In September 1963, when the Senate ratified the nuclear test ban treaty with the Russians, the Gallup curve turned up. He had predicted that. The right-wingers, he believed, were misreading the country's mood. They made much of what they called a swing to conservatism on the campuses. They held that Admiral Lewis Strauss spoke for millions when he said, at the test ban hearings, "I am not sure that the reduction of tensions is necessarily a good thing," and that Edward Teller was reflecting the alarm of the entire middle class when he said at the same hearings, "If you ratify this treaty . . . you will have given away the future safety of this country." Kennedy didn't accept that. At Billings, Montana, and at Salt Lake City—in the very heart of what was thought to be Goldwater country—he was given standing ovations when, at midpoint in prepared speeches, he left his text to speak of his pride in the test ban. To friends he said that the treaty was the essence of his foreign policy; if he lost to Goldwater next year he would be willing to pay that price.

The signs of the coming detente were now unmistakable. The test ban, and the expressions of approval Kennedy heard across the country when it became an accomplished fact, had been possible because in Cuba the Russians had finally accepted the principle of verifying missile sites. The world had heard the last of the troika. In East Berlin Khrushchev said that the Wall had diminished the need for a separate German peace treaty. He had learned to live with the bone in his throat. Then Kennedy, speaking at American University on June 20, held out an olive branch to the Russians: "Our problems are man-made; therefore they can be solved by man . . . Some say that it is useless to speak of world peace . . . until the leaders of the Soviet Union adopt a more enlightened attitude. I hope they do. I believe we can help them do it. But I also believe that we must reexamine our own attitude."

The speech was largely ignored in the American press—his civil rights address, which came the following evening, preempted editorial attention—but the *Manchester Guardian* called it "one of the great state papers of American history," and Khrushchev, genuinely impressed, later told Harriman that it was "the greatest speech by an American President since Roosevelt."

On August 30 the Department of Defense announced that a hot line linking the White House and the Kremlin had gone into operation that same day. In October, when Russia's rift with China came into the open, Khrushchev said he did not share Mao's willingness to sacrifice millions of lives in a nuclear showdown with the West.

Kennedy then authorized a sale of surplus wheat to the Soviet Union as "one more hopeful sign that a more peaceful world is both possible and beneficial to all."

The radical right was furious, but he relished its fury. He delighted in building a record as a liberal President. Kennedy chuckled when Ike, baffled by Keynesian economics, cried out in a magazine article: "What can those people in Washington be thinking about? Why would they deliberately do this to our country?" What Kennedy was doing to the country's economy, with the help of Douglas Dillon and Walter Heller, was producing the longest peacetime expansion in history, resulting in an annual increase in the Gross National Product of 5.6 percent a year. And if Congress would go along with his recommendation for a tax cut, he believed, there would be no recession in 1964, either.

That was by no means certain. The 88th Congress was mulish. The President was far ahead of its conservative instincts with his liberal program calling for Medicare, massive grants to encourage the rebuilding of decaying urban slums, a more sensible farm plan, the development and conservation of national resources, improved social security, his broad civil rights bill, and a growing commitment to the Alianza. At the time, critics gave him low marks in his struggle for legislation. Looking back, it is surprising that he did as well as he did. Of 107 recommendations he had sent to the 87th Congress, 73 had been enacted into law, and the early legislative victories of his successor were programs Kennedy had sent to the 88th.

Addressing the Irish Parliament in June, he recalled a line from George Bernard Shaw's *Back to Methuselah:* "You see things; and you say 'Why?' But I dream things that never were; and I say 'Why not?' "* That was the Kennedy outlook at its best, a blend of social prophecy and political vision. He was not always on that plane. At times he seemed to be looking toward wrong horizons. A decade later his pledges to support manned space flight and supersonic transport would be seen as dubious ventures. But even his errors of exuberance seemed preferable to the stagnation of the 1950s. Like Franklin Roosevelt he was using politics to expand the limits of the possible at home and abroad. In that context his triumphant ten-day tour of Europe five months before his death, of which the Irish visit was a part, is important to an understanding of him. More

* Later this was attributed to him, and then to Robert Kennedy. But it was Shavian.

than anything else he resembled the statesmen of the European left, and they knew it. In him they saw their own idealized self-images. Willy Brandt in Germany, Gaston Defferre and Pierre Mendès-France in France, Harold Wilson in Britain, Pietro Nenni in Italy—all of them praised him, quoted him, and to some extent patterned their political styles after his. "Nenni, the old firebrand Socialist, cannot now contain his praise for Kennedy," Anthony Sampson wrote in the London *Observer*. ". . . There is hardly a word of anti-Americanism, except on the far right." As a liberal, Kennedy had, among other things, no patience with those who thought men should wear blinders to shield them from evil. Jailing students who wanted to see Castro's Cuba seemed to him absurd. "Why shouldn't they go?" he asked. "If I were twenty-one years old, that's what I would like to do this summer." And in Amherst on October 26, 1963, he spoke words which would be cherished by historians of his period:

"It may be different elsewhere. But democratic society—in it, the highest duty of the writer, the composer, the artist is to remain true to himself and to let the chips fall where they may. In serving his vision of the truth, the artist best serves his nation."

At such times John Kennedy seemed inevitable. But there was another aspect of him. Astronomers are familiar with the phenomenon of the dark star, a star so feebly luminous as to be invisible, one which follows another star and eclipses it sporadically. Kennedy had a dark star, a shadow of imminent tragedy which was never far from him and those he loved and which would intervene unexpectedly to obscure their most splendid moments. It happened now. In early August Jacqueline Kennedy gave birth to a second son, who arrived five and a half weeks prematurely and with a lung ailment. Christened Patrick Bouvier Kennedy, the baby struggled for thirty-nine hours before expiring. The President, desolate, tried to lift the little coffin at the services to carry it to the grave; then Cardinal Cushing gently drew him away.

To lift his wife's spirits Kennedy suggested that she accept an invitation from Aristotle Onassis, the Greek shipping tycoon, for an Aegean cruise on his majestic yacht, the *Christina*. Later she would remember early October as an unreal time, two dazzling weeks of sunshine between the loss of Patrick and the catastrophe that awaited in November. Dispatches from the Mediterranean traced her progress from Istanbul to Lesbos, Crete, Delphi, Marrakesh, and to an island in the Ionian Sea that Onassis owned. Royalty, beginning with the king and queen of Greece, entertained her and her sister Lee Radziwill; they toasted her, admired her, and gave her exotic gifts. When she returned to the White House on October 17, one member of the White House staff said, "Jackie has stars in her eyes—Greek stars." The President asked her if she would join him for a short campaign trip. She said fine, and she asked where, and he said Texas.

If there was any one place where things had seemed to be going exceptionally well for Kennedy earlier in the year, it was Saigon. Opening his State of the Union message on January 14, 1963, the President had reported: "The spearhead of aggression has been blunted in Vietnam." A Pentagon spokesman announced that "we have turned the corner in Vietnam," and General Harkins said that the war would be won "within a year." On April 22 Rusk said that the American effort in Saigon was "producing excellent results," and Ngo Dinh Diem and the Republic of Vietnam were "on their way to success." U. Alexis Johnson, Rusk's deputy undersecretary for political affairs, was particularly encouraged by "the intangible knitting together of government and people" in Vietnam and by the strategic hamlet program, which he called "the most important reason for guarded optimism."

Afterward this seemed puzzling. The fact that these prophets had been wildly wrong was bad enough; why had they been so eager to put themselves on the record? The answer was that they were trying to drown out other members of the government who were convinced that President Ngo Dinh Diem and everyone with him was doomed. The terms hawk and dove were not yet fashionable, but the administration was split along those lines. The chief hawks, or advocates of American involvement in the war, were the generals, including Maxwell Taylor, and McCone of the CIA, Rusk, Rostow, Ambassador Nolting in Saigon, and at this point McNamara, who was impressed by the force and precision of the reports from Saigon. Ranged against them were Robert Kennedy, George Ball, Averell Harriman, Roger Hilsman, Michael Forrestal, Richard Helms at the CIA, the American colonels in the field with Vietnamese troops, and American war correspondents, who sang to the tune of "Twinkle, Twinkle, Little Star":

We are winning, this we know.
General Harkins tells us so.

In the delta, things are rough.
In the mountains, mighty tough.
But we're winning, this we know.
General Harkins tells us so.
If you doubt this is true,
McNamara says so too.

As the third year of the Kennedy Presidency opened, no one could be said to be winning the war, because hardly anyone was fighting it. The Viet Cong was husbanding its strength, waiting to pounce, and the Republic of Vietnam's overcautious commanders had no intention of stirring them up. The calm was deceptive. The country was seething with resentment, and not all of Diem's critics were in the Viet Cong. Because he represented what might be called the Vietnamese establishment, the conservative, upper-class mandarins who spoke French and worshipped God as Roman Catholics, his natural adversaries in the non-Communist community were the young Buddhist priests and monks, who were poor, militant, middle- and lower-class, radical, and distrustful of everything western. Their religious faith was that of the majority, and they bitterly resented the privileges accorded the Catholics. Both sides were in a belligerent mood, needing only an incident to kindle a struggle between them.

It came in early May 1963. The Buddhists were celebrating Buddha's 2587th birthday in the ancient imperial city of Hue when officers commanding government troops ordered a group of them to disperse. They refused and the soldiers fired into the crowd, killing nine. Diem refused to express regrets—he said privately that he would lose face—and on June 11 a Buddhist monk, Quang Duc, protested with a spectacular demonstration of self-immolation. Sitting on the pavement, he waited patiently while his fellow monks drenched him with gasoline; then he struck a match and went up in flames. Other suicidal Buddhists followed his example, providing the press (which was notified in advance each time) with outstanding photographs. The newspaper-reading American public was appalled, but the government in Saigon was unmoved. President Diem at this point was almost entirely under the influence of his brother, Ngo Dinh Nhu, who was usually under the influence of opium. Madame Nhu demonstrated the ruling family's genius for public relations by telling reporters that she gaily clapped her hands each time one of these "so-called holy men" put on a "barbecue show."

Under great American pressure Diem tentatively agreed on June 15 to meet some of the Buddhist demands. Almost immediately it became clear that he had no intention of following through. On June 30 the Buddhist demonstrations were renewed. Students rioted in Vietnam schools, and American correspondents who were writing about the turmoil were attacked in the streets and beaten. This was too much for President Kennedy. The cold war thaw had provided him with a new incentive for wanting the shooting in Vietnam stopped. A truce was necessary before he could offer the world what he had called a "strategy of peace" at American University: "Not a *Pax Americana* enforced on the world by American weapons of war . . . not merely peace for Americans, but peace for all men; not merely peace in our time but peace for all time."

Apart from other considerations—such as corruption and ineffectuality—the rigid anti-Communism of Diem and the Nhus had no place in these plans for a new foreign policy. Kennedy wanted to take a strong hand with them, and when he discovered in early July that Nolting was absent on a two-month cruise in the remote Aegean, he decided that his first step should be to dispatch a new envoy to Saigon. Rusk picked the man, Henry Cabot Lodge. It was an excellent choice. Liberals in the administration were uneasy at first, fearing that as a patrician Lodge might favor South Vietnam's aristocracy. They didn't understand that as a Boston Brahmin Lodge expected the well-born to be gentlemen, which Diem and Nhu definitely were not. Among other things, gentlemen do not betray their friends. Whatever else may be said of Nolting's tenure, he had been a good friend to Diem, and they were about to repay him with an act of shocking treachery.

In a farewell speech at the airport Nolting spoke of bonds between the two countries: "humility and tolerance, respect for others and a deep sense of social justice." Correspondents thought these strange words in Vietnam, but Nolting believed them to be justified; the South Vietnamese president had just given him his word that there would be no more attacks on the Buddhists. Six days later Diem sent his secret police out on a midnight raid to seize the pagodas, arrest the priests and monks, and terrorize their followers. The raiders tried to camouflage their identity by wearing regular army uniforms, but the truth emerged forty-eight hours later after Madame Nhu, in a reference to a gang of cutthroats, which had been rooted out several years before, said that the sally had brought her "the happiest day in my life since we crushed the Binh Xuyen in 1955."

Lodge arrived in Saigon the following evening. He saw the raid as a studied act of scorn for the Americans. It was, in fact, a new low for Diem, and it marked the beginning of his isolation from other Vietnamese conservatives. His foreign minister quit in protest and shaved his head like a Buddhist monk. In Washington Madame Nhu's father, South Vietnam ambassador to the U.S., disowned his daughter. The Voice of America placed the blame for the storming of the pagodas squarely on the Nhus. Diem's generals, wanting no part of the atrocity, began plotting against him. Lodge cabled Washington that the plotters wanted to know what the American attitude would be if a coup was successful. What should he tell them?

The answer said much about the fissure in the Kennedy administration over the Vietnam question. It was August 24, a Saturday. The President was in Hyannisport. McNamara and McCone were on vacation, Rusk was out of town, and General Taylor could not be reached. Their key deputies were Gilpatric in the Pentagon, Helms at the CIA, and Ball at State, all critics of the regime in Saigon. The cable they approved was drafted by Ball, Harriman, Hilsman, and Forrestal, and it bluntly told the American ambassador that the Nhus must go. Afterward, when everyone was back in Washington, there were bitter recriminations, but when the President decided to put everyone on record no one was willing to take the responsibility for repudiating it.

The generals now had a green light from Lodge. On August 29 he cabled Rusk, "We are launched on a course from which there is no respectable turning back: the overthrow of the Diem government." Everything seemed set for it. Days passed, and then weeks, with no coup. The plotters appeared to have lost their nerve. The crackdown on the pagodas had cramped their style, sidelining several of their leaders, and Diem had tightened his control of the troops around Saigon. The State Department asked Lodge what was the matter with the generals. He said, "Perhaps they are like the rest of us, and afraid to die."

Encouraged by Diem's survival, the hawks in the administration took on new life. The need now, McNamara said at a council of war on August 31, was to reopen conversations with Diem. Rusk agreed, saying that this much was clear: the American presence must remain in Vietnam until the Viet Cong war was won, and the United States could not approve of a coup. General Taylor said they were both right. George Ball and Averell Harriman thought that this was absurd. Autumn was approaching, and each day the division between the two camps in Washington was wider. It became an abyss in September, when the National Security Council sent another fact-finding mission to Saigon. The investigators were Major General Victor H. "Brute" Krulak of the Marine Corps and, from the State Department, Joseph A. Mendenhall, a senior foreign service officer of comparable rank with experience in Vietnam. On their return President Kennedy reconvened the National Security Council, and each presented his report. General Krulak said that the war was being won and Diem's performance could hardly be improved upon. Mendenhall said that the Diem regime was at the point of collapse. There was a silence. Then the President said, "Were you two gentlemen in the same country?"

During all this the relationship between Lodge and General Harkins in Vietnam was deteriorating. Both were from Boston, and their families were old friends, but now they scarcely spoke to one another. Late in September McNamara and General Taylor arrived in Saigon on one more attempt to find out what was going on. At the airport Lodge, determined to reach McNamara first, detailed two of his men to obstruct Harkins's way. ("Please, gentlemen! Please let me through to the secretary!") Apart from that, Harkins was as cheerful as ever. His optimism was reflected in the opening paragraph of the subsequent McNamara-Taylor report, which declared that Diem's army "has made great progress and continues to progress." Because Diem's troops were victorious on all fronts, the appraisal continued, the first thousand American soldiers could be withdrawn before Christmas, and all of them would be home by the end of 1965. At the same time the report dealt a glancing blow to the heretical suggestion of Robert Kennedy that the Americans pull out now. McNamara and Taylor took what would be the Pentagon line to the bitter end:

> The security of South Vietnam remains vital to United States security. For this reason, we adhere to the overriding objective of denying this country to Communism and of suppressing the Vietcong insurgency as promptly as possible.

But this view was now definitely losing support in the administration. The President himself was moving away from it. Interviewed on CBS-TV by Walter Cronkite on September 2, he had said pointedly that if the Republic of Vietnam was to be successful in its struggle against the Viet Cong it needed "changes in policy, and perhaps in personnel." He had then said: "I don't think the war can be won unless the people support the effort, and in my opinion, in the last two months the government has gotten out of touch with the people. . . . In the first analysis, it is their war. They are the ones who have to win it or lose it. We can help them, we can give them equipment, we can send our men there as advisers, but they have to win it, the people of Vietnam."

Early in October a ten-million-dollar-a-month program for Diem was quietly suspended. He and the Nhus angrily denounced Kennedy, and Madame Nhu arrived in California to open a lecture tour of the United States, condemning Kennedy with the support of right-wing groups. From the outset the trip was a fiasco. Official Washington boycotted her. When she attempted to call on her estranged father, Tran Van Chuong, she found the door locked and bolted; the ex-ambassador was in Manhattan speaking on what he called "the trail of stench" left by his daughter. She tried to follow him. At La Guardia Field she was met by a city official who curtly denied that he was greeting her; "I'm just here to see that the lady has sufficient police protection," he said. Madame Nhu snapped that she didn't need protection. "God is in my corner," she said. She never did find Tran. Speaking at Harvard, she was picketed by about five hundred students carrying such signs as NHU DEAL IS NHU DIEM GOOD. They pounded on the door of the lecture hall, spattered the side of the building with eggs, and rattled the windows as she spoke. After Cambridge, her crowds dwindled. Apart from ultraconservative claques, virtually the only people who turned out to see her were reporters.

Back in Saigon the government seemed to be losing its grip on reality. Nhu was threatening to form an alliance with Hanoi to drive the Americans out of the country. Diem's secret police, having purged the Buddhists, were attacking the country's schools. In a series of incomprehensible raids they jailed college students, then high school pupils, and finally children in the elementary schools. Even Catholics weren't safe from persecution. Vietnamese of all faiths and persuasions were appealing to General Duong Van Minh, "Big" Minh, the most prestigious officer in the army, begging him to oust Diem and Nhu. Minh approached John Richardson, the

CIA station chief, and asked him for his advice. Bypassing General Harkins, Richardson arranged a meeting between Minh and Lodge. The ambassador told Minh that the Americans would do nothing to impede a coup, and that if it was successful U.S. aid would go to another anti-Communist government. This position was relayed to the White House, which approved it. Everyone in Washington and Saigon seemed to be aware of the coming revolt except Diem, Nhu, and General Harkins, who assured the President that there would be no coup, that it was all talk, that he had checked the rumors and found them to be groundless. Nothing could happen, Harkins said, without his knowing of it. It could, though. David Halberstam of the *New York Times* and another reporter had already received slips of paper with the message, "Please buy me one bottle of whisky at the PX"—the signal that the uprising was imminent.

Diem's hour struck at 1 P.M. Vietnamese time (1 A.M. in Washington) on Friday, November 1, All Saints' Day. In Saigon it was siesta time on a day of stupefying heat. The president and his brother had retired to their bedrooms in Gia Long palace, where they were presumably protected by the palace guard and seven-foot fences topped by barbed wire. But as they slept, truckloads of rebel marines wearing red kerchiefs had already launched an attack on their defenses while other soldiers threw up roadblocks at key intersections. The insurgents quickly seized the airport, the police station, navy headquarters on the banks of the Saigon River, and the government radio station, which broadcast a declaration in the name of fourteen generals and seven colonels: "Soldiers in the army, security service, civil defense force, and people's force! The Ngo Dinh Diem government, abusing power, has thought only of personal ambition and slighted the fatherland's interests. . . ."

That evening the siege of the palace began with a mortar and artillery barrage. In the early hours of the next morning a force of eighteen tanks began blowing holes in the fences. At 6:15 A.M. a rebel general ordered a five-minute cease-fire and called on Diem and Nhu to surrender. A white flag appeared in a first floor window, but Diem and Nhu were not there. They had fled through a secret tunnel to the Chinese suburb of Cholon, from which they sent word to the victorious junta that they were ready to open negotiations. Exactly what happened after that is unknown. Reportedly they accepted offers of safe conduct out of the country, but it was a ruse; they who had deceived so many were now betrayed themselves.

Picked up by rebel soldiers, they were killed, on orders from the generals, in the back of an armored personnel carrier. Their bodies were found there, riddled with bullets and dressed in Roman Catholic priests' robes in which they had hoped to escape if nothing else worked. Diem had also been stabbed repeatedly.

Awakened with the news in the Beverly Wilshire Hotel in Beverly Hills, Madame Nhu sobbed that President Kennedy was to blame. The President was in fact shaken, depressed for the first time since the Bay of Pigs; whatever Diem's faults, he said, he had not deserved to be slain. Elsewhere in the administration the news was accepted with resignation, even relief. There was one significant exception. Vice President Johnson was bitter. The Vice President had given Diem his hand, had been his friend, and in Johnson's view the friendship had symbolized the American commitment to Diem. The same officials who had been Diem's critics in the administration were also critical of the Vice President. He knew it, and knew who they were, and he had long since come to despise them and everything about them, right down to their Cardin shirts and PT-109 tie clasps. On other issues Johnson admired Kennedy, but not here.

The people of Saigon did not share Johnson's view. They had turned the day into a holiday, dancing in the streets; statues of Diem, his brother, and his sister-in-law were smashed and posters of them were torn down, until the only likeness of the late President in the capital was on one-piaster coins. The triumphant generals were showered with confetti everywhere they went, and Lodge became the first American within recent memory to be cheered in public. Hope was running high in the U.S. embassy; the factions which had been united against the ruling family seemed popular enough to give the country a stable government.

A week passed, and then two weeks; the autumn days grew shorter, and President Kennedy's spirits rose. The McNamara-Taylor report, dated October 2, was still on his desk, but he felt no sense of urgency about the need to deal with it. As David Halberstam later wrote:

> He knew Vietnam was bad and getting worse, that he was on his way to a first-class foreign policy problem, but he had a sense of being able to handle it, of having time, that time was somehow on his side. He could afford to move his people slowly; too forceful a shove would bring a counter-shove. It was late 1963, and since 1964 was an election year, any delay on major decisions was healthy; if the Vietnamese could hold out a little longer, so could he.

On November 13 he summoned a conference of his chief strategists for the coming campaign. Meeting in the Cabinet Room late that Wednesday afternoon, they agreed that prospects for a landslide victory against Goldwater were encouraging. The economy was flourishing. The annual Gross National Product had grown 100 billion dollars since his inaugural; its rate of growth was greater than that of either Russia or Europe. The huge new Saturn rocket, which would be launched next month, would at last put the United States ahead of the Soviet Union in the manned spacecraft race. Except for Vietnam the world was calm, and to get more perspective on that the President cabled Ambassador Lodge suggesting that he come home for a long talk. Lodge replied that he was making arrangements to leave Saigon as soon as possible. That would be on Thursday, November 21.

Richard M. Nixon, then an attorney representing Pepsi-Cola, left Dallas, Texas, aboard American Airlines Flight 82, bound for New York, at 9:05 A.M. on November 22, 1963, thus missing President Kennedy's arrival there aboard *Air Force One* by about two and a half hours. Mr. Nixon had spent the past two days at a Pepsi-Cola Bottlers Association meeting. He was just beginning to learn the ropes as a corporation lawyer. He had filed a petition for admission to the New York State bar only last Friday, and his name was not yet on his office door, because he would not become a full partner in the law firm of Mudge, Stern, Baldwin & Todd until January 1, 1964.

It was expected to remain there a long time. Earlier in the week during a televised interview Dwight Eisenhower had spoken of Nixon's chances in the next presidential election, but his remark is chiefly memorable as vintage Eisenhowerese: "Now, if there should be one of those deadlocks, I would think he would be one of the likely persons to be examined and approached, because he is, after all, a very knowledgeable and a very courageous type of fellow." Hardly anyone agreed with Ike. Certainly the American Broadcasting Company didn't. Not only had the network called a broadcast about him *The Political Obituary of Richard M. Nixon;* the program, filmed the year before, had featured an interview with, of all people, Alger Hiss. Two companies tried to cancel their advertising contracts with ABC because of it, but FCC Chairman Newton N. "Wasteland" Minow turned them down with the cold observation that broadcasting must be free from censorship by "those few, fearful advertisers who seek to influence the professional judgment of broadcast newsmen." President Kennedy said he agreed. Those were golden days for effete snobs.

Aboard Flight 82 a stewardess offered her distinguished passenger a selection of current periodicals, and if one could return in time from the mid-1970s to that fateful Friday, one of the differences to be noted in the American scene would be the wider choice of magazines, *Look, Life,* and the *Saturday Evening Post* then being alive, well, and on the stands. (The long retreat from mass circulation was already well advanced among newspapers, however, and four weeks earlier, on October 16, the *New York Mirror* had folded. Before the end of the decade 163 magazines and 160 daily newspapers, including the *Indianapolis Times,* the *San Francisco News-Call-Bulletin,* the *Boston Traveler,* the *Portland Reporter,* and the *Houston Press* would end publication.)

Nixon may well have picked *Time,* for he knew he would be in it. The first news page carried an informal picture of him—he was fifty and looked a young forty then—and in an accompanying interview he was quoted on the political consequences of the Saigon coup: "If this Viet war goes sour, Viet Nam could be a hot issue next year. If all goes well, it won't be. It's strange to me, when we are fawning over Tito, catering to Kadar, accommodating Khrushchev, we don't even have the decency to express our sympathy to a family which was a real foe of Communism."

Barry Goldwater, who rarely fawned over Communists, was the front runner for the 1964 Republican presidential nomination, Nelson Rockefeller having diminished his chances by marrying Happy Murphy the previous May. In that third week of November Goldwater had just scored a fresh triumph with one of his natural constituencies by telling a Better Business Bureau banquet in Chicago that the New Frontier had produced "1,026 days of wasted spending, wishful thinking, unwarranted intervention, wistful theories, and waning confidence."

Each time the Arizona senator tore into Kennedy reporters asked the President to reply. "Not yet," he would say, grinning; "not yet," but plainly he relished the prospect of running against him.

Among his valuable campaigners this time would be the First Lady. The Secret Service hoped Mrs. Kennedy could persuade her husband to be more careful in crowds. Eschewing SS advice the week before the Texas trip, he had ordered his driver to leave his car's motorcycle escort and detour through crowded downtown Manhattan. While the presidential limousine was halted at the traffic light an amateur photographer had darted up and fired a flash bulb at Kennedy's side of the car. A New York police official had told reporters, "She might well have been an assassin."

It was a year of technological innovations. Kodak introduced the Instamatic camera and Polaroid brought out color packs. Polyethylene appeared. Detroit's fall models featured sleekly sloping rear windows—"fastbacks," they were called; the one on the Sting Ray was particularly dramatic. On July 1, 1963, the Post Office Department, while announcing an increase in first-class postage from four cents to five, sprang the zip code system on a stunned and resentful public. The triumph of the digits moved one step closer with the conversion of the White House telephone number from NAtional 8-1414 to 456-1414. On the Bell systems' master map the hatched areas indicating switchovers to direct distance dialing were spreading like a vast cancer; DDD reached 44.2 Bell subscribers in 1963. Students at liberal arts colleges displayed decals reading, "I Am a Human Being—Do Not Fold, Spindle, or Mutilate."

The sale of Barbie dolls reached its initial peak in 1963, and Barbie, who had acquired a boyfriend, Ken, two years earlier, was now joined by her "best friend," Midge. (Barbie's "black is beautiful" friend, Christie, would not appear in the Mattel sales line until 1968. In 1963 black beauty, like black power, was waiting to be discovered.) The question of how lifelike female dolls should be was still sparking lively debates among toymakers. A considerable number of parents objected to Barbie's firm little breasts. The public attitude in such matters remained comparatively conservative. In the matter of premarital intercourse it continued to hold that "Nice girls don't," although Gael Greene, researching *Sex and the College Girl* in 1963, was finding that more and more nice girls *did.* (A memorable passage in Miss Greene's book, startling at the time, described a sorority girl pretending to climb a wall in mock agony while crying out in frustration, "You don't know how long it's been since I got screwed.")

Few of collegiate America's mothers had any idea how casually some of their daughters were accustomed to being bedded. Parents would later rise up in righteous indignation to protest coed dorms, only to reel back when confronted by the new facts of campus life.

One stunning fact was in a report of the infirmary at the University of California in Berkeley to the effect that venereal disease had become a serious health hazard among female undergraduates. Integrated dormitories was one answer to a problem which had other solutions. But in 1963 that belonged to the future. *Playboy* was then averaging fifty applications a week from young women whose aspiration was to appear on its gatefold in the altogether and who, in the judgment of the editors, were qualified to do so, yet even *Playboy* had to trim its sails somewhat to public opinion; for example, it did not yet dare show its Playmates' pubic hair. (It did, however, create an uproar in 1963 with a topless photo of a model who was an almost perfect double for the nation's First Lady.) Hard-core pornography was neither chic nor legal; in November 1963 a three-judge Manhattan court ruled that *Fanny Hill* was obscene and therefore forbidden. "While it is true that the book is well-written, such fact does not condone its indecency," the court found. "Filth, even if wrapped in the finest packaging, is still filth." It is startling to reflect that Linda Lovelace, who would rocket to fame ten years later as the superstar of *Deep Throat*, was then a twelve-year-old girl sucking lollipops in Bryan, Texas.

Among the names not in the news were Gloria Steinem, Kate Millet, Germaine Greer, and Bobby Riggs, then an executive for the American Photograph Corporation. Betty Friedan's *The Feminine Mystique* had just been published, but Women's Lib was, so to speak, still in the uterus. "Nobody," reported that November 22 issue of *Time*, "is more noisily dissatisfied these days than that symbol of stability—the fortyish housewife with teen-age children and a reasonably successful husband," but by the audiometers of the early 1970s the noise was almost imperceptible. The Seven College Conference, which had set up vocational workshops for college women "who are now ready for activity outside the home," had found just fifty such women. None described males as porcine. The vocations were largely limited to education, library science, social work, and—this was regarded as a breakthrough—public relations. Anne Cronin, director of the conference, fielded questions about what men might think with the defensiveness bluestockings had shown since the fall of the Claflin sisters. "In only one or two cases," she told a newspaperman, "have husbands gotten stuffy about their wives' going back into careers. For the most part, they're serious and understanding. We're not breaking up any homes that wouldn't break up anyway."

The fashions of the gentle sex were neither bold nor forward. There were no pantsuits, not even for toiling airline stewardesses. Styles were set by Jacqueline Kennedy—the pillbox hat, the shoes with very pointed toes and very slender heels, the hair length just below the ears and softly curled or bouffant. Skirts were a little below the knee, and the waistless sheath was popular. It was all very feminine. Male supremacy was riding high. No protests followed the showing, as a late movie, of Cary Grant and Myrna Loy in *Mr. Blandings Builds His Dream House*—nobody wondered what *Mrs.* Blandings might want in *her* dream house—and the author of a magazine profile of Dorothy Kilgallen, describing her race around the world as a journalistic stunt in 1936, was allowed to say: "Just like a woman, Dorothy came in late." In the summer of 1963 Ian Fleming's *The Spy Who Loved Me* appeared in paperback with this choice passage:

> All women love semi-rape. They love to be taken. It was his sweet brutality against my bruised body that had made his act of love so piercingly wonderful. That and the coinciding of nerves completely relaxed after the removal of tension and danger, the warmth of gratitude, and a woman's natural feelings for her hero. I had no regrets and no shame. . . . all my life I would be grateful to him, for everything. And I would remember him forever as my image of a man.

The *New York Times Magazine* carried a report on the campus mood that third week of November 1963. In it, undergraduate editors generally found their fellow students to be detached, determined to succeed, and concerned less with issues than with security and their personal lives. In their hours of relaxation Tarzan movies were the current thing. The University of Chicago was trying to revive football. Two Cornell fraternity teams had just played a thirty-hour touch football game; the final score was 664-538. LSU coeds had staged a "drawers raid" on a men's fraternity—all college residences were male or female, of course. Berkeley students, ever in the sexual vanguard, had asked the dispensary there to dispense contraceptives. They weren't militant about it, however; the demand was negotiable and was in fact ignored.

Camelot had ended its Broadway run in January 1963. *Tom Jones* was awarded the Academy Award as the best picture of the year. Sidney Poitier was voted the best actor for his performance in *Lilies of the Field;* Patricia Neal for hers in *Hud.* Films drawing big audiences in November 1963 were *Mary, Mary* and *It's a Mad, Mad, Mad, Mad World.* Popular television shows were *Dr. Kildare, Andy Griffith, My Three Sons, Perry Mason, Hazel, Lucy, The Beverly Hillbillies,* and *Twilight Zone.* NBC's Monday movie scheduled for November 25—it would not be shown—was *Singing in the Rain.*

That year was the high point of the Ajax White Knight and White Tornado ("Cleans like a white tornado!") commercials, according to Harry McMahan of *Advertising Age.* Piel's Beer was presenting the Return of Bert and Harry. Maxwell House Instant Coffee offered a Cup and a Half. The Chevrolet commercial had a car riding on the water of a Venice canal, and Hertz commercials were dropping people into convertibles. Songs which were popular were "Go Away Little Girl," "Dominique," "If I Had a Hammer," "Puff the Magic Dragon," and "Blowing in the Wind."

Best-selling fiction included Mary McCarthy's *The Group,* Morris West's *The Shoes of the Fisherman,* James Michener's *Caravans,* and Helen MacInnes's *The Venetian Affair.* Best-selling nonfiction included James Baldwin's *The Fire Next Time,* Rachel Carson's *Silent Spring,* from which the ecology movement may be said to date, and two books which would be affected by the events of the coming weekend, Jessica Mitford's *The American Way of Death* and Victor Lasky's *J.F.K.: The Man and the Myth.* The first of these acquired historical significance because Robert Kennedy, who had read it, was guided by it in choosing a coffin for his brother's funeral. The Lasky book, which led the nonfiction best-seller lists, was a hatchet job and it would be withdrawn from the bookstores by its publisher.

In sports, Texas was ranked college football's number one. Darrell Royal's marvel that season was a shoeless field-goal kicker named Tony Crosby. The weekend before President Kennedy flew to Dallas, Crosby booted one 42 yards to beat TCU. Among the pros, Jimmy Brown of the Cleveland Browns was at the height of his remarkable powers. The New York Giants and the Chicago Bears were headed for a collision at the end of the National Football League season; Chicago would win the championship 14 to 10. In the American Football League finale, the San Diego Chargers would take the Boston Patriots 51 to 10. There was no superbowl. In hockey the big noise was Gordie Howe of the Detroit Red Wings. Having played 1,132 games in which he had lost twelve teeth and sustained wounds requiring 300 stitches, Gordie scored his 545th goal against the Montreal Canadiens in November 1963; it was a record. In basketball Bob Cousy of the Boston Celtics had hung up his jockstrap at the end of the 1962 season. As a consequence the Celts had been expected to be pushovers, but when Kennedy left the White House for the last time the 1963 season was two months old and the Celtics had lost only one game—by one point. Center Bill Russell was the big (six feet ten inches) reason.

Among the places not in the news that year were Woodstock, Watts, East Village, Grant Park, Wounded Knee, People's Park, My Lai, Khe Sanh, Kent State, Biafra, Lincoln Park, Bangladesh, Attica, the Ho Chi Minh Trail, Chappaquiddick, Bimini, Botswana, Qatar, and Watergate, though the Watergate office-and-apartment complex was under construction beside the State Department in Washington; President Kennedy's funeral procession would pass it. Haight-Ashbury was a drab working-class district in San Francisco. No one living in the Haight, as it would later be known, was then familiar with the hippy terms acid-zap, freak out, superstar, mind-blowing, bummer, joints, munchies, turn on, tune in, rip off, drop out, commune, horse, crash pad, steam, zonked, love-in, be-in, share-in, flower power, trash, Panhandle Park, acid-American Dayglo art, role-playing, bunch-punching, past-blasting, guerrilla theater, psychedelic Satanism, and Christ vibes.

The *New York Times* carried a dispatch from its London bureau about "a group of four male pop singers now highly popular in Great Britain and the cause of numerous teen-age riots." They were the Beatles. In November 1963 they were on their way to the United States, preceded by recordings of their first three hits: "She Loves You," "Wanna Hold Your Hand," and "Standing There."

The Vietnamese generals who had staged the Saigon coup, David Halberstam reported, wanted to see General Harkins replaced, but the Pentagon expressed confidence that Harkins would fulfill his promises to beat the Viet Cong. Any suspicion that the United States might not be able to find a military solution in Vietnam was challenged by Deputy Secretary of Defense Roswell Gilpatric in an address to the Business Council in Hot Springs, Virginia. The U.S. had such lethal power, Gilpatric said, that defiance of it would be an act of self-destruction.

Nicole Alphand, the wife of the French ambassador, was on the cover of the November 22 *Time*. Jimmy Hoffa was being indicted. Charles de Gaulle was vetoing Britain's entrance into the Common Market. Governor Ross Barnett was endorsing the findings of a grand jury which blamed the federal government for the recent disorders that had accompanied the admission of James Meredith to the state university in Oxford. Richard Burton and Elizabeth Taylor, having fallen in love during the filming of *Cleopatra,* were divesting themselves of their spouses and planning an early wedding. The Mona Lisa was in the United States, heavily chaperoned.

In 1963 there were 189,242,000 Americans (in 1973 there would be 209,000,000), of whom 70,000,000 were employed (1973: 80,627,000). Five percent were unemployed. The population center of the United States lay four miles east of Salem, Illinois, having moved fifty-seven miles to the west in the 1950s, the greatest westward drift since the 1880s. World War II was no longer the paramount experience of most Americans. Because of the huge number of war babies, the median age was 29.5.

A startling figure came from organized labor: between 1960 and 1962 unions had lost about a half-million members. The percentage of workmen belonging to them had dropped from 24.4 percent in 1955 to 22.2 percent in 1962, and Murray Kempton, no enemy of unions, was talking about the "twilight" of the labor movement.

One reason for this was the passage of time. Fewer and fewer workers could remember the heroic strikes of the 1930s. At the same time, the character of the work force was changing. In the years since V-J Day the number of blue-collar workers had decreased by four million while the number of white-collar workers—managers, professionals, salesmen, office workers—had grown by nearly ten million.

Furthermore, the blue-collar of November 1963 would hardly have been recognized as a fellow worker by his oppressed father of the 1930s. In June 1963 the weekly pay of the average production worker for slightly more than forty hours' work passed $100—four times the Depression wage for the same job. About 40 percent of all families now earned more than $7,000 a year. John Brooks pointed out that the word "proletarian" had virtually disappeared from the language. "People think that prices are going up," Caroline Bird wrote, "but it is their own standard of living that is rising."

The best place to measure the long-range impact of boom was in the classroom. In his comprehensive study of economic development, Edward F. Denison put education at the very top of factors contributing to economic expansion. Between the Crash in 1929 and the end of the Kennedy Presidency, America's investment in education increased tenfold, to 39 billion dollars a year.

The sociological implications of this can hardly be exaggerated. In 1900 only 4 percent of Americans of college age were enrolled in a college or university. In 1957 the figure was 32 percent; when Kennedy took office it was 40 percent, and when he died it was 50 percent. Andrew Hacker calculated that between 60 and 70 percent of all Americans now belonged to the middle class. It was, in fact, swiftly becoming the only class, the values of which were those which had once belonged to a small, highly educated upper middle class.

"The American economy has become so big," a European diplomat said, "that it is beyond the imagination to comprehend." U.S. editorial writers marveled at West Germany's *Wirtschaftswunder*, but a far greater economic miracle had been taking place at home. A few figures suggest its scope. Approximately 90,000 Americans were now millionaires—as against 27,000 in the early 1950s—and each year now the figure grew by 5,000. Since World War II American investments abroad had leaped from 12 billion dollars to 80 billion. The annual sales of a single corporation, General Motors, were 17 billion dollars, almost equal to a third of the Bundesrepublik's Gross National Product. The *increase* alone of the U.S. Gross National Product in the first four years of the 1960s would be greater than the *entire* GNP of Germany in one year, 1964—122 billion dollars to 100 billion. The value of New York Stock Exchange investments had grown from 46 billion dollars to 411 billion since the war; Wall Street's public relations men spoke glowingly of a "people's capitalism," and with considerable justification—the stocks listed on the Big Board were held by some twenty million Americans.

Social prophets of the time regarded this as an unmixed blessing. Some, like John Kenneth Galbraith, thought that profits should be distributed differently, but the assumption that affluence was benign was virtually unchallenged. Lenny Bruce was just an obscene comic one jump ahead of the law in 1963; Ralph Nader was an obscure lecturer in history and government at the University of Hartford. The New Left notion that the country was threatened not by international Communism but by technology and the sheer magnitude of American institutions—that the immensity of U.S. corporations and the Washington bureaucracy was mere obesity—lay quiet in the womb of time. The faith of liberals in big government was still strong.

"Change is the biggest story in the world today," James Reston said at Columbia University in 1963. Nowhere was this more evident than in the growing mobility of American society. The great internal migration of the early 1940s had continued in the postwar years, fueled by the conclusion of southern blacks that a better life awaited them in the northern cities and by technological innovation. American agriculture in 1963 produced 60 percent more food than in 1940, while the number of hours needed to do the nation's farming dropped from twenty million to nine million. As a consequence, by 1963 the number of Americans living in urban and suburban communities had reached 75 percent. The "farm bloc" no longer struck fear in the hearts of congressmen. The Grange had lost its political potency.

Even the vehicles of change were changing. The railroad depot was becoming one of the loneliest places in metropolitan America; for every passenger mile crossed on trains three were crossed on airplanes. (In 1973 the ratio would be one to thirteen.) Ninety percent of local transport was by auto; altogether, car traffic amounted to nearly 800 billion vehicle miles in 1963. The U.S. Department of Commerce reckoned that there were now 17,000 automobile graveyards in the United States, and with the completion of President Eisenhower's nonstop, limited-access, high-speed interstate highway system, the great American traffic jam was beginning to sprawl across state lines.

Across the street from the flyblown train depots the lights in the old mansard-roofed city hotels were darkening. Over 4,000 of them had shut down completely since V-J Day. The travelers who bypassed them were staying instead at motels, which had been evolving from shabby prewar "tourist cabins" into lush pavilions offering all the traditional services of hotels and a few new ones. Black-and-white television had become standard equipment in all but the grubbiest motels (color TV was still a novelty). There were now 56.4 million television sets in the United States. That fact, combined with the discovery of 1960 census takers that only 8.5 percent of the population lacked radios, meant that a communications system of unprecedented magnitude was ready to report any news flash of national importance. In the early afternoon of November 22 the source for all information would be two wire service reporters clutching commandeered telephones at Dallas's Parkland Memorial Hospital. An investigation conducted the following winter by the National Opinion Research Center of the University of Chicago found that by 1 P.M. Dallas time, a half-hour after the shooting, 68 percent of all adults in the United States—over 75 million people—knew about it. Before the end of the afternoon 99.8 percent knew. Even those without television or radio had ready access to those with it.

On September 2, 1963, the CBS *Evening News* increased its nightly news show to thirty minutes and NBC followed its example on September 9, developments which were to have the most profound implications for the Vietnam War; to fill the extra time, networks would run footage showing, among other things, American soldiers lopping off Viet Cong ears. In November 1963 it had not come to that. There weren't even any television commentators in Saigon then. That year just seventeen Americans were killed in Vietnam and 218 were wounded. The most interesting story from Saigon in the third week of November 1963 was a report on Colt's new M-16 rifle. It was smaller and lighter than the M-14. An Army spokesman explained it was one of the reasons anti-Communist forces were wiping out the Viet Cong so effortlessly in guerrilla warfare.

Polls in foreign countries, tabulated by the United States Information Agency, showed U.S. prestige to be very high in 1963. Other stories from abroad were a report from Katanga, which was ending its two-year secession from the Congo, and an appraisal of Sir Alec Douglas-Home's new Tory government in London. It was shaky; the country was still in a state of shock over Lord Denning's report on the Profumo scandal, starring Christine Keeler, that year's most eminent British prostitute.

At home the Dow Jones industrial average hovered around 732. A Roman Catholic prelate excommunicated New Orleans segregationists who refused to bow to the church's endorsement of integration. None of them had heard of the Fathers Berrigan. Other names not in the news included Daniel Ellsberg, Clifford Irving, William Calley, Jimi Hendrix, James Earl Ray, Jeb Stuart Magruder, Angela Davis, Andy Warhol, Arthur Bremer, Vida Blue, Archie Bunker, Myra Breckenridge, and Spiro T. Agnew, who was then in the second year of a four-year term as a local official in Baltimore County.

No one had heard of Jesus freaks, the *Whole Earth Catalog, Crawdaddy, Screw, Money,* hotpants, waterbeds, *Sesame Street, Love Story,* the Black Liberation Army, or Gay Lib.

The November 1963 issue of the *Reader's Digest* anticipated the future with an article reprinted from *Good Housekeeping:* "Sleeping Pills and Pep Pills—Handle with Extreme Caution!" In the November 24, 1963, *New York Times Magazine,* which was fated to be one of its least read issues, Mary Anne Guitar analyzed some new expressions in subteen slang: "rat fink," "triple rat fink," a "real blast" (party), "fake out," "tough toenails," "the straight skinnies," "Jeez-o-man," "hung up," "hairy," "wuzza-wuzza," and "gasser." Of the preteens, who would become the college generation of 1973, Miss Guitar said that their coinages were no worse, and sometimes more imaginative, than their elders': "According to reliable reports, 'terrific' is the word on the New Frontier."

Among the living, in addition to President Kennedy, were Attorney General Robert F. Kennedy, Martin Luther King, Mary Jo Kopechne, Fred Hampton, Malcolm X, George Lincoln Rockwell, and 45,865 young American men who would die violently in Vietnam over the next nine years.

On November 12, 1963, Mrs. John F. Kennedy played hostess to two thousand underprivileged children on the White House lawn. It was her first official appearance since the death of Patrick the previous August, and while she supervised the distribution of two hundred gallons of cocoa and ten thousand sugar cookies among her guests, a detachment of Scotland's Black Watch Regiment strutted and skirled for them. Hearing the tunes and liking them, the President came out of his oval office to watch the performance. Ten days later she would remember his pleasure and ask them to play again, at his funeral.

Nearly every day now impressions were being imprinted on her memory, to be recalled, brooded over, relived, savored, or regretted after Dallas. The day before the Black Watch appearance for the children, the President took young John, not quite three, to Veterans Day ceremonies at Arlington National Cemetery. To the indignation of some, who thought the occasion should be solemn, the little boy was allowed to toddle into the procession and disrupt it. His father was delighted, and while he beamed down at the child, cameramen put the scene on celluloid. There were those who thought that Kennedy had brought the boy along with that in mind. *Look* was coming out with an exclusive spread of John Jr. pictures; it would have been like the President to stage something for photographers who would feel left out by it.

The admiring spectators at Arlington included Major General Philip C. Wehle, commanding officer of the military district in Washington. Twelve days later he would look down on Kennedy's body on the autopsy table at Bethesda Naval Hospital and recall A. E. Housman's lines "To an Athlete Dying Young":

Today, the road all runners come,
Shoulder-high we bring you home
And set you at your threshold down,
Townsman of a stiller town. . . .

Mrs. Kennedy had many recent recollections which would put the tragedy in context; General Wehle had one. Most Americans hadn't any. To them the blow that fell in Dallas came out of nowhere. They didn't even know that the President was in Texas. His visit was only of local interest there; he had come down to make peace between two feuding Democrats, Senator Ralph Yarborough, the liberal, and Governor John B. Connally Jr., the deviate. Non-Texans were unaware of the trip until the first incredible bulletin reached them with the news that the President had been gunned down by a sniper while riding in a downtown motorcade.

Afterward Americans, giving a shape to their grief, reconstructed the events there. They came to know the grid of downtown Dallas streets; the location of the Texas School Book Depository, from which the shots had come, and Parkland Memorial Hospital, to which the President and Governor Connally, who had also been wounded, had been rushed; and the identity of each figure in the tragedy and the part each had played. In time the country forgot its terrible ignorance in the first hours after the assassination, and how they had learned about it.

Merriman Smith of UPI had been riding in the press pool car, four cars behind the presidential limousine in the motorcade. Moments after the sound of the gunfire, at 1:30 P.M. Washington time, he dictated the first bulletin to his local bureau over the pool car's radiophone: "Three shots were fired at President Kennedy's motorcade in downtown Dallas." That went out on UPI printers at 1:34, two minutes before the presidential car reached the hospital. At 1:36 Don Gardiner of the ABC radio network cut into local programs with it. At 1:40 CBS-TV interrupted *As the World Turns,* a soap opera; viewers beheld a distraught Walter Cronkite relaying Smith's report of the three shots and adding, "The first reports say that the President was 'seriously wounded.'" At 1:45 NBC-TV scuttled another soap opera, *Bachelor Father,* to switch to Chet Huntley. That put the three networks on the air with the news, and they would remain there, with no interruptions for commercials, for three days and three nights, until the President had been buried in Arlington National Cemetery.

Some people first heard about the shooting from those early broadcasts and telecasts. One watcher in Fort Worth was Marguerite Oswald, the assassin's mother; she was tuned to WFAA-TV. In Irving, a Dallas suburb, her daughter-in-law Marina was another viewer. Elizabeth Pozen, the wife of a government official, was listening to WGMS over her car radio in Washington. One of her passengers was Caroline Kennedy, who was going to spend the night with a Pozen child, and when Mrs. Pozen heard the announcer say ". . . shot in the head and his wife Jackie . . ." she instantly switched it off. But most people did not learn what had happened that directly. The news reached them third or fourth hand, from a passing stranger, or a telephone call, or a public address system, or a waiter in a restaurant—often from sources which were so unlikely that a common reaction was utter disbelief. To make sure that it was false, they gathered around transistor radios, car radios, and television sets in bars—whatever was available—and there they learned that it was true after all.

(Some of the reports were inaccurate or misleading, however. At 2:18 Washington time the Associated Press circulated an unconfirmed report that Lyndon Johnson had been "wounded slightly," and at 3:14 Washington time AP teletypes chattered that "A Secret Service agent and a Dallas policeman were shot and killed today some distance from the area where President Kennedy was assassinated." This seemed to support theories of an elaborate plot. It wasn't corrected until 4:33 P.M.)

At 2 P.M. Washington time Kennedy was pronounced dead. The announcement was delayed until Lyndon Johnson could get away from the hospital. In that first hour it was wisely assumed that the gunman had been part of a larger conspiracy. The new President left for the airport at 2:26 P.M. Six minutes later UPI quoted Father Oscar Huber, the Dallas priest who had performed the last rites, as saying, "He's dead, all right." Confirmation by the President's acting press secretary followed, and at 2:35 Washington time—an hour earlier in Dallas—UPI bells chimed on teletype machines around the world:

FLASH

PRESIDENT KENNEDY DEAD

JT135PCS

Meantime attention had shifted to another part of Dallas. Lee Harvey Oswald, having left his rifle in his sniper's nest on the sixth floor of the book depository, had caught a bus outside, ridden in it for seven blocks, and then switched to a taxi. He stopped at his rooming house for a pistol. At 2:15 he committed his second murder in less than a hour, gunning down J. D. Tippit, a Dallas policeman who tried to question him. Oswald was seized thirty-five minutes later in a nearby movie theater. The homicide squad then learned that its new prisoner worked as a stockman in the book depository and was, in fact, the only depository employee missing at the building. The net of circumstantial evidence began to build.

At 3:38 P.M. Lyndon Johnson took the presidential oath of office on *Air Force One* with a stunned and bloodstained Jacqueline Kennedy standing beside him. Nine minutes later the plane took off for Washington's Andrews Field. The flight took less than two and a half hours. Johnson made his first televised statement as President at Andrews Field and was then taken by helicopter to the White House. The Kennedy party followed the coffin to Bethesda and the autopsy, which continued through most of the night. It was 4:34 A.M. when the casket, now covered by an American flag, was carried into the White House and placed upon the catafalque in the East Room. Mrs. Kennedy knelt beside it and buried her face in the flag's field of stars.

The next three days passed in a blur. Saturday was accompanied by drenching rains and high winds in the capital. The groggy country would later remember it as a gap between days, between the shock of Friday's assassination and the murder of the assassin on Sunday. The University of Chicago study indicated that the average adult spent ten hours in front of his television set on Saturday, the weekend's peak, but the watchers didn't learn much. The body remained in the East Room; Kennedy's family, his friends, and senior members of the government called to pay their respects there. On Sunday the coffin was carried up Pennsylvania Avenue on a horse-drawn caisson led by a riderless horse with reversed boots in the stirrups, the symbol of a fallen chieftain. At the same time word of a new, unbelievable outrage came from Dallas. Lee Harvey Oswald, in the process of being transferred to another jail, was mortally wounded by a Dallas night club owner named Jack Ruby. The killing occurred in the presence of seventy uniformed Dallas policemen. Because NBC was televising the transfer, it was also television's first live murder. The President's widow was told about it when she returned to the White House. She called it "one more awful."

On Monday the coffin was taken on the caisson to St. Matthew's Cathedral for a funeral mass and thence to Arlington. Delegations from ninety-two nations, led by Charles de Gaulle, had come to participate in the funeral. Afterward they attended two receptions, one at the State Department and another, much smaller, at the White House; Mrs. Kennedy received them there. That was the end of it, though in a sense that weekend never ended; years later men would still be trying to fathom its meaning. It had been the greatest simultaneous experience in the history of this or any other people. Long afterward Americans would tell one another how they had first heard the news from Dallas, how they felt about the eternal flame Mrs. Kennedy had requested for the grave, and young John's saluting of his father's coffin, and the rest of it. David Brinkley concluded that the assassination was beyond understanding: "The events of those days don't fit, you can't place them anywhere, they don't go in the intellectual luggage of our time. It was too big, too sudden, too overwhelming, and it meant too much. It has to be separate and apart."

Nevertheless, people couldn't stop attempting to incorporate it into their lives. The most obvious approach was to name something after the President. Cape Canaveral was rechristened Cape Kennedy. Idlewild International Airport was renamed. The National Cultural Center was changed to the John F. Kennedy Center for the Performing Arts. The Treasury began minting fifty million Kennedy half-dollars—and couldn't keep them in circulation because they were being hoarded as souvenirs. In every part of the country committees and councils were voting to honor the President by altering local maps. Presently Jacqueline Kennedy was wondering whether she would be driving "down a Kennedy parkway to a Kennedy airport to visit a Kennedy school." The impulse reached abroad. Canada had its Mount Kennedy—the first man to climb it was Robert Kennedy—and the climax was reached when England set aside three acres of the historic meadow at Runnymede, where the Magna Carta was signed, as a Kennedy shrine. In May 1965 Queen Elizabeth presided at the ceremony, dedicating the tract to the President "whom in death my people still mourn and whom in life they loved." Mrs. Kennedy replied that it was "the deepest comfort to me to know that you share with me thoughts that lie too deep for tears."

The hundreds of thousands of letters which Americans sent to Mrs. Kennedy then were often touching precisely because they were emotive and unashamedly demonstrative. To David Bell the fallen President was "a warrior-king"; to Natalie Hemingway "a dear godfather"; and John Steinbeck wrote the widow of "this man who was the best of his people" and who "by his life, and his death, gave back the best of them for their own."

Buried in the bales of envelopes was another memorable letter which was found and answered long afterward:

Richard M. Nixon
810 Fifth Avenue
New York, N.Y. 10021

November 23

Dear Jackie,

In this tragic hour Pat and I want you to know that our thoughts and prayers are with you.

While the hand of fate made Jack and me political opponents I always cherished the fact that we were personal friends from the time we came to the Congress together in 1947. That friendship evidenced itself in many ways including the invitation we received to attend your wedding.

Nothing I could say now could add to the splendid tributes which have come from throughout the world to him.

But I want you to know that the nation will also be forever grateful for your service as First Lady. You brought to the White House charm, beauty and elegance as the official hostess for America, and the mistique [*sic*] of the young in heart which was uniquely yours made an indelible impression on the American consciousness.

If in the days ahead we could be helpful in any way we shall be honored to be at your command.

Sincerely,
DICK NIXON

Montage: JFK / LBJ

How many roads must a man walk down
Before they can call him a man
How many seas must a white dove sail
Before she sleeps in the sand
How many times must a cannonball fly
Before they're forever banned
The answer my friend is blowin' in the wind
The answer is blowin' in the wind

There was only one catch and that was Catch-22, which specified that a concern for one's own safety in the face of dangers that were real and immediate was the process of a rational mind. . . . Orr would be crazy to fly more missions and sane if he didn't, but if he was sane he had to fly them. If he flew them he was crazy and didn't have to; but if he didn't want to he was sane and had to. Yossarian was moved very deeply by the absolute simplicity of this clause of Catch-22 and let out a respectful whistle.

"That's some catch, that Catch-22," he observed.

"It's the best there is," Doc Daneeka agreed.

DISORDERS IN CANAL ZONE CAUSE U.S.-PANAMA DIPLOMATIC BREAK

TFX DEFENDED BY MCNAMARA

WINSTON TASTES GOOD *LIKE* A CIGARETTE SHOULD

—— **Pall Mall** ——

Best actor of 1963: Sidney Poitier in *Lilies of the Field* — **What do you want: good grammar or good taste?**

Best actress of 1963: Patricia Neal in *Hud*

Tom Jones *The Great Escape* *How the West Was Won* *The Leopard*
Cleopatra *The L-Shaped Room*

CASTRO'S DEFECTING SISTER AIDED CIA

MOURN POPE JOHN

Blacks have to fashion a world where they can live with dignity and restraint. I am not interested in being a murderer, but then I am not interested in being a dier, either. I am not going to kill you, but I am not going to let you kill me, said LeRoi Jones

BEST SELLERS: Nonfiction
The Warren Commission Report on the Assassination of President Kennedy
The Fire Next Time by James Baldwin
The American Way of Death by Jessica Mitford
Silent Spring by Rachel Carson
The Kennedy Wit edited by Dill Adler

SCHAEFER the one beer to have *when you're having more than one*

SEVEN STEEL COMPANIES INDICTED FOR PRICE FIXING

LBJ: U.S. WILL DESTROY 480 B-47s IF RUSSIANS WILL GUT 480 TU-16s

HOOVER DEAD AT 90

— **AJAX** — **MACARTHUR DEAD AT 84**

fruiti-juici, fruiti-juici, say, pal, how 'bout a nice HAWAIIAN PUNCH!

HOOTENANNY!

SUB THRESHER LOST WITH 129 ABOARD

Gone was the glow of blue velvet
But in my heart there'll always be
Precious and warm a memory
through the years
And I still can see blue velvet through my tears

BEST SELLERS: Fiction
The Shoes of the Fisherman by Morris West
The Group by Mary McCarthy
The Venetian Affair by Helen MacInnes
The Spy Who Came In from the Cold by John le Carre
Herzog by Saul Bellow

Big John
GO-GO-GOODYEAR
Big Bad John

We demand that no more American youth be sent to fight in a war that is helping neither them nor the Vietnamese people. We have learned lessons from Nazi Germany, and will not go along with the aggressive war-making policies of any government even if it happens to be our own

EXILES BOMB CUBAN REFINERY

LINK PHILBY TO MACLEAN, BURGESS

Dr. Strangelove ***U.S. MOSCOW EMBASSY BUGGED***

Thirty

THE LONG ARM

On an August afternoon in 1964 Dwight Eisenhower described to this writer Lyndon Johnson as he saw him in the Executive Office Building that rainy Saturday, the day after the assassination:

"I'd known him for a long time. He was, as he always is, nervous —walking around and telephoning everyone. . . . I would mention someone in the conversation and he would snatch up the receiver and call the person. He asked my advice about many matters, including the tax cut. I told him that he had to show what he was going to do with his own budget. We also discussed foreign affairs. As far as I could see at that time, Lyndon Johnson's only intention was to find out what was going on and carry policy through. He suggested nothing new or different. He wanted to talk about Laos, Cuba, and so forth. He did seem to be less informed about foreign policy than about domestic policy."

"Lyndon," said the new President's wife, "acts as if there is never going to be a tomorrow." He himself defined his philosophy of leadership with his favorite Biblical quotation, from Isaiah 1:18: "Come now, and let us reason together, saith the Lord," but he confessed that he liked to "show a little garter" while doing it, and in practice he persuaded other men to join what he called his "consensus" less by reasoning with them than by imploring, bullying, and begging them, and he was not above outright extortion. As Senate majority leader he had become one of the greatest manipulators in the history of Capitol Hill; his arm-twisting had been highly regarded there. One of his problems as President was that he never understood that the same wheeler-dealer reputation was a handicap in the White House. Eric Goldman called him "a Machiavelli in a Stetson." The public might endorse his legislative goals, but his manner of reaching them was another matter. The pollster Samuel Lubell found that many Americans planning to vote for Johnson in 1964 were nevertheless suspicious of him. They had a feeling: he was a wheeler-dealer; you had to watch his hands; he was a master politician, useful at times, no doubt, but not entirely trustworthy. His admirers, and he had many of them, protested that this was unjust. While there was much to be said for this, the skepticism was not entirely unjustified. There is no blinking the fact that until early 1966 he deliberately misled the country about the extent of the American commitment in Vietnam, or that three of his closest associates—Bobby Baker, Walter Jenkins, and Abe Fortas—were involved in scandals during his administration.

Yet there was nothing dishonorable about Johnson himself, and nothing petty. At times in that first year he seemed to be everywhere at once, turning out the White House lights and cutting Kennedy's budget to display economy with garter; declaring war on poverty, lobbying personally for Medicare, conferring with the chiefs of state of six American allies ("my prime ministers," he explained to one journalist), settling the U.S.-Cambodian dispute (if only temporarily), offering to destroy 480 B-47 bombers if the Russians would demolish the same number of TU-16s, arranging a U.S.-USSR reduction in the supply of atomic materials, touring Appalachia, persuading the Republican presidential nominee to join him in a moratorium on the race issue during the 1964 campaign, intervening with armed force in the Dominican Republic, and, in a speech on October 31, 1964, envisioning "the Great Society." Everything about the man was gargantuan. As he stepped down from an address to a congressional joint session, a senator congratulated him. "Yes," said Johnson, "I got applause eighty times." The senator checked the record, which confirmed the President; he had been counting the house as he spoke.

In both the oval office and in his bedroom three television sets stood side by side, permitting him to watch commentators on CBS, NBC and ABC at the same time. His telephone console had forty-two buttons; he could put that many callers on hold and deal with them in turn or talk to all of them at once. To sign three bills he used 169 pens, a record. He liked to drive fast. In Texas he took four women reporters for a hair-raising ride, going ninety miles an hour while describing in graphic detail the sex life of a bull. One of his passengers looked at the speedometer and gasped; the President whipped off his five-gallon hat and covered the dashboard with it. His appeals to patriotism were shameless; asked what had happened during a jawbone session about a railroad strike, a labor leader said, "Lyndon has a flag in the corner of his office. He picked it up and ran around the room with it." He spoke of "my army," "my government," and "my taxes." To make certain that no one forgot who he was, he had the presidential seal emblazoned on his cuff links, his boots, his twill ranch jackets, even on plastic drinking cups. He ordered a 44-foot portrait of himself for the Democratic national convention in 1964, and he scheduled the convention for the week of his birthday, August 27, so that the party faithful could present him with the biggest cake of all time. He wanted to roll up the greatest landslide in the history of American politics that November, and he pulled out all the stops. Entering a new city at night, he would cruise through its neighborhoods shouting into a bullhorn, "Howdy, folks! Come to the meetin'! Come to the speakin'!" Jack Gould of the *New York Times* called him "the Y. A. Tittle of handshakers." Once in Los Angeles a pickpocket reaching into a pocket found his hand grasped by that of the President of the United States.

That year the White House press corps entertained themselves by drawing up a list of what could be the shortest books ever written. The top three were *Italian War Heroes*, the *Polish Who's Who*, and *Mistakes I Made*, by Lyndon Baines Johnson. Many of those who knew the President best believed that he never searched his own soul because he never felt secure enough to do it. His problem certainly wasn't a lack of intelligence. Eric Goldman, a Princeton professor who became a Johnson aide, wrote: "After years of meeting first-rate minds in and out of universities, I am sure I have never met a more intelligent person than Lyndon Johnson—intelligent in terms of sheer IQ's, a clear, swift, penetrating mind, with an abundance of its own type of imagination and subtleties." The difficulty appeared to be rooted in the realization that his youth had been culturally deprived. The high school he attended hadn't even been accredited by the easygoing standards of its region.

In a revealing outburst he once said to Hugh Sidey of *Time*, "I don't believe that I'll ever get credit for anything I do in foreign affairs, no matter how successful it is, because I didn't go to Harvard." That was absurd, though his suspicion of intellectuals was not. Their contempt for him—there is no other word for it—was a shocking phenomenon of the 1960s. They jeered at him for pulling the ears of his beagles, as though that mattered. Buttons worn on campuses read, "King Lyndon the First," "Sterilize LBJ: No More Ugly Children," "Hitler Is Alive—in the White House," and—most unforgivable of all—"Lee Harvey Oswald, Where Are You Now That We Need You?" They applauded *MacBird,* which in depicting him as an assassin was in far worse taste than any lapse of his, and they justified their conduct as an expression of mourning for Kennedy—unwilling or unable to realize that Kennedy had chosen Johnson as his Vice President precisely because he was so able. Theodore White noted that "Political jokes were resurrected from as far back as the days of Herbert Hoover and pinned on Johnson; bedroom jokes of the President's life with Lady Bird were of a pornography to match those about Franklin Roosevelt's life with Eleanor." The Secret Service reported that crank letters attacking the President jumped from a hundred a month to over a thousand.

Johnson's speaking manner did not help. He suppressed his natural warmth and earthiness and tried to appear solemn and humble instead. What came through on the TV tube was unction and sanctimony. Instinctively people realized that whatever the real Lyndon Johnson was like, this one was a fake. The feeling that he was a mountebank was heightened by his inability to cast aside the extravagant style of the southern politician, so alien to a nation which had become accustomed to Kennedy understatement. Johnson was derisively christened "Uncle Cornpone," and to some extent he deserved it. Addressing the nation over television after settling the railroad strike, he read a letter he had received from a seven-year-old child in Park Forest, Illinois, named Cathy May Baker. "My grandmother lives in New York," Cathy had written. "She is coming to see me make my first Holy Communion. Please keep the railroads running so that she can come to see me." The President said, "So Cathy's grandmother can now go to see her." As a senator he had been able to get away with this sort of thing, but no more; within twenty-four hours the country learned that the letter was ten days old. Cathy's grandmother had visited her, witnessed the Communion, and returned to New York. Johnson never learned to abandon such stratagems. Later, when the issue was Vietnam, his habitual stretching of the truth would be much more damaging.

Liz Carpenter, one of his devoted Texans, wrote: "When I think of Lyndon Johnson, I always seem to see a Long Arm—reaching out to pick up a telephone, to grab a sheaf of papers, to shake hands, to embrace, to comfort, to persuade, sometimes even to shove —but always to include, yes, always to include." But not everybody. Johnson excluded Robert F. Kennedy. They brought out the worst in each other. It was the strong, irrational dislike of two proud and sensitive men, and it had been evident long before the tragedy in Dallas. Robert Kennedy had opposed his brother's choice of Johnson in Los Angeles, and Johnson at times seemed to oppose the younger Kennedy's very existence. Johnsonians could be very bitter about their predecessors. Liz Carpenter wished her President had been given "some public words of encouragement from the bereaved family after the assassination . . . He never mentioned it, but being a woman and a partisan, I was conscious of the silence . . . the Kennedys looked at the living and wished for the dead and made no move to comfort the country."

Undoubtedly grief for the slain President made Johnson's task harder, but it was not confined to the Kennedy family. Shortly after the assassination Congressman Clarence Cannon of Missouri predicted that "Everything will be Kennedy for a while. Then people will forget." But they did not forget. Magazines issued JFK memorial editions which were quickly sold out. The demand for Kennedy books grew ever more insatiable. Collectors of Americana discovered that holographic Kennedy letters were as valuable as Lincoln letters. An autographed copy of *Profiles in Courage* brought $375. To point up the Kennedy-Johnson transition, the presidential staff took to distributing pictures of both Presidents during Johnsonian trips, but the practice was soon discontinued; for every Johnson picture the public took ten of Kennedy. The Secret Service raged when the new chief executive rebuked an agent for wearing a Kennedy PT boat tie clip, but Johnson's resentment was understandable. He was being shadowed by a ghost.

It must have sometimes seemed to him that he was encountering Kennedys whichever way he turned. He sent Bob and Ethel Kennedy off on a tour of the Far East and the tour was on every front page. Ted Kennedy was hurt in a plane crash and the accident obscured Johnson's announcement that U.S. military might was greater than the combined strength of all the armies and navies in the history of the world. Above all there was Jacqueline Kennedy, whose most trivial remark or appearance could eclipse a statement by the President. Gallup reported that the First Lady, in a break with tradition, was only the second most admired woman in the United States; her predecessor was still first. In July 1964 Mrs. Kennedy moved to New York, and there was hope in the White House that the country's idolatry of her might diminish. It didn't; the mere fact that she continued to prefer bouffant hairdos to hats was enough to do to the women's hat industry what her husband had done to the men's.

Francis B. Sayre, dean of the Episcopalian Washington Cathedral and a Kennedy friend, rose in the pulpit to call Johnson "a man whose public house is splendid in its every appearance but whose private lack of ethic most inevitably introduces termites at the very foundation." The *Washington Star* commented that Sayre's "harsh pronouncement, we suspect, sums up the real mood of a great part of the electorate." Even harder for the President to bear were the vicious rumors that he was implicated in his predecessor's death. A commission headed by Chief Justice Earl Warren found that Kennedy had been murdered by Lee Harvey Oswald, who had acted alone, and the Kennedy family did everything possible to encourage acceptance of the commission's findings, but irresponsible attacks on the Warren Report continued throughout Johnson's years in the White House, sometimes in respectable society. The *New York World Journal Tribune* commented that "Out of respect for the memory of a martyred President, we think it is time to ask the ghouls, the buck-chasers, the sensation-mongers and the character assassins to desist—to shut up until or unless they can put up, as so far they have so notoriously failed to do." It was wasted ink; assaults on the report continued, and reached a high-water mark when the British Broadcasting Company paid a discredited critic $40,000, a record price, for a two-hour film which proved nothing.

The "Bobby problem," as it was called in the White House, became a major headache for Johnson. The new President had been in office less than six months when Washington became aware that the previous President's brother was building a government-in-exile. Comprised of New Frontiersmen who had left the government, the Kennedy people met at Jacqueline Kennedy's Georgetown residence that spring and, after she left Washington, at the attorney general's home, Hickory Hill. They were united in hostility to Johnson. None of them believed that he had been responsible for the tragedy in Dallas, of course, but they did feel that the younger Kennedy had a right to become Johnson's Vice President. They had lost touch with reality. There was never any possibility that the two men might run on the same ticket. In one of his milder comments on Bob Kennedy, President Johnson said, "That upstart's come too far and too fast. He skipped the grades where you learn the rules of life. He never liked me, and that's nothing compared to what I think of him." Johnson people called Bob a former McCarthyite and a "liberal fascist"; they said he was "Rover Boy, without birth control," and that he supported "God and country—in that order, after the Kennedys."

At 1 P.M. on Wednesday, July 29, 1964, the President summoned Attorney General Kennedy to the oval office and told him that he would not be his running mate. Johnson said that he approved of the young Kennedy's ambition and thought it would be fine if Bob ran the country some day. But not yet. He offered him his choice of any other post in the government and asked him if he would run Johnson's coming presidential campaign, as he had his brother's. Bob declined. The manner of announcing the end of Kennedy's vice-presidential ambitions this year was left undecided. Kennedy left believing that the meeting had been confidential. Evidently Johnson didn't think so, for he invited three Washington correspondents to lunch the next day and told them about it. That was bad enough; what was worse was that he couldn't resist using his considerable talents as a mimic to show them how Kennedy had taken it. Bob hadn't said a word at first when he had been told, the President said. He had just gulped. Johnson showed how he had gulped. When the story reached Kennedy he was furious. He confronted the President and accused him of a breach of confidence. Johnson said he hadn't told anyone about the meeting, and when Bob bluntly called him a liar he said, well, maybe there was some conversation he had forgotten; he would have to check his records and his calendar.

The President wanted Kennedy to announce that he wouldn't be on the ticket. Bob wouldn't do it. That left Johnson with a dilemma. He didn't want to offend the national Kennedy following. On the other hand, he felt he couldn't risk leaving the question open; the delegates to the coming Democratic national convention in Atlantic

City were Kennedy people, quite capable of choosing Bob themselves. His solution was bizarre and typically Johnsonian. On July 30 he announced: "With reference to the selection of the candidate for Vice President on the Democratic ticket I have reached the conclusion that it would be inadvisable for me to recommend to the convention any member of my Cabinet or any of those who meet regularly with the Cabinet." He gave no reason. It didn't make sense. In a stroke he had doomed the vice-presidential ambitions not only of Robert Kennedy but also of McNamara, Stevenson, Shriver, Rusk, and Orville Freeman. Johnson said, "Now that damn albatross is off my neck." Bob said, "I'm sorry I took so many nice fellows over the side with me."

In *The Making of the President 1964* Theodore H. White wrote of a historic encounter that summer: "The deft response of American planes to the jabbing of North Vietnam's torpedo boats in the Gulf of Tonkin had been carried off with the nicest balance between boldness and precision." So it seemed then. Later, when disenchantment with the Vietnam War was metastasizing through the country, the events in Tonkin Gulf turned out to be shadowy, imprecise, and, most disturbing, a consequence of deliberate American provocation.

The key to understanding what happened in those waters off North Vietnam during the first week of August 1964 is a U.S. plan for clandestine operations against the Communist forces there whose code designation was 34A. White had never heard of 34A; neither had the American people; neither had Congress, which on the strength of events for which it was responsible was asked to commit, and did commit, the country to a disastrous escalation of the Asian war. To some extent the Gulf of Tonkin incidents may have been misinterpreted and distorted by chance, but those errors would have been inconsequential if men in Washington had not been playing a deeper game. The chief intriguer was President Johnson. He in turn may have been deceived and manipulated by high officers in the Pentagon. All that can be said with certainty is that Congress was maneuvered into supporting hostilities.

Plan 34A was conceived in December 1963, the month after the assassination of President Kennedy. Secretary of Defense McNamara, in Saigon on one of his many inspection trips, liked what he heard of the scheme for stealthy actions against the North Vietnamese. He put General Krulak in charge of it. Back in Washington he described it to President Johnson, who was equally enthusiastic. In execution 34A proved disappointing, however. The attacks by South Vietnamese guerrillas, parachutists, and frogmen were well organized, but the population in North Vietnam liked the Hanoi regime; the saboteurs were betrayed every time. General Harkins and McGeorge Bundy, who were masterminding 34A, switched to commando raids on Communist shore installations by South Vietnamese torpedo boats. Hanoi regarded these as more an annoyance than a threat, but radio intercepts revealed a growing demand for retribution among Communist naval officers commanding the raided North Vietnamese bases.

On Thursday, July 30, 1964, the day that Johnson eliminated Attorney General Kennedy and the rest of his cabinet from the Vice Presidency, a flotilla of South Vietnamese PT boats sailed from Da Nang on a 34A errand. The U.S.S. *Maddox*, an American destroyer, was headed for the same waters; its task was to goad the shore installations into using their radar and then to plot the radar—the naval equivalent of spotting enemy artillery positions so that they can be destroyed by counterbattery fire. On August 1 the destroyer passed the PTs coming the other way; they had just completed their torpedo attack and were returning home. The destroyer entered the combat zone and began its task of provoking radar operators on the coast. North Vietnamese officers there assumed that the *Maddox* and the PT boats were part of the same mission. This assumption was clear to Americans who were monitoring radio messages from three North Vietnamese torpedo boats sent out to investigate the destroyer, and their report to that effect was sent back to the Pentagon. There it was filed in the back of a deep drawer without comment. In its report to the White House the Pentagon merely said that the three Communist PT boats had attacked the *Maddox*, which had responded by sinking one of them.

In the laundered version which was given to the public, the destroyer was said to have been thirty miles from the coast, peacefully sailing through international waters. There was no mention of its assignment, and nothing at all about the South Vietnamese boats. President Johnson ordered the *Maddox* to continue its activities, and a second destroyer, the *C. Turner Joy*, was told to join it. Thus the stage was set for a second Tonkin Gulf incident. The night of August 4, one sailor said later, was "darker than the hubs of hell."

Captain John Herrick, the commander of the destroyer patrol, radioed back that it was clear from interceptions of the North Vietnamese radio that they continued to believe that the American vessels were part of a 34A attack. Like its predecessor, this message was suppressed in the Pentagon. The public was told that American vessels had been the target of a second act of unprovoked aggression, this time when they were sixty-five miles from the coast.

Considering the gravity of the actions based upon it, the evidence in this second episode was surprisingly thin. The Senate Foreign Relations Committee did not hear the full story until three and a half years later. To their astonishment, the senators then learned that there may have been no encounter at all. Blips had appeared on the *Turner Joy*'s radar screen; the destroyer had opened fire. The *Maddox* did, too, although its radar screen was clear. Both ships took evasive action. The captain of the *Maddox* noticed that his signalmen reported torpedoes each time the destroyer turned sharply. After three hours of this Herrick radioed back: "Review of action makes recorded contacts and torpedoes fired appear doubtful. Freak weather effects and overeager sonar man may have accounted for many reports. No actual visual sightings by *Maddox*. Suggest complete evaluation before further action." There were certainly North Vietnamese torpedo boats in the vicinity—destroyer gunfire and carrier-based aircraft sank two of them—but the American vessels were undamaged, and there was a very real doubt over which side had fired the first shot. Fourteen hours after the first reported contact the Pentagon was still asking the destroyers for the names of witnesses, their reliability, and the size, type, and number of attacking North Vietnamese forces.

Lyndon Johnson hadn't waited. On his orders American warplanes were already taking off from the carriers *Ticonderoga* and *Constellation*; their targets were four North Vietnamese torpedo boat bases and an oil depot. The next morning the country learned that thirty-five North Vietnamese boats and 90 percent of the depot had been damaged or destroyed. Johnson appeared on television to report that "aggression by terror against the peaceful villages of South Vietnam has now been joined by open aggression on the high seas against the United States of America." The response, he said, was "limited and fitting. We Americans know, although others appear to forget, the risks of spreading conflict. We seek no wider war."

Possibly his reaction to these brief clashes between small vessels would have been different if he had been facing another opponent in that election year. Three weeks earlier the Republicans had nominated Barry Goldwater in the San Francisco Cow Palace, and was accusing the administration of "timidity before Communism." He brought his admirers to their feet, roaring, with the charge that "the Good Lord raised up this mighty republic to be a home for the brave . . . not to cringe before the bullying of Communism . . . Failures cement the wall of shame in Berlin. Failures blot the sands of shame at the Bay of Pigs. Failures mark the slow death of freedom in Laos. Failures infest the jungles of Vietnam."

By exploiting the events in Tonkin Gulf, Johnson could break the back of that Goldwater issue. All he needed to do was to wrap himself in the flag and ask Congress to give him a free hand to deal with the North Vietnamese pirates. To this end he called the congressional leaders to the White House and asked them for a resolution authorizing him to deal decisively with such challenges. What he wanted, he said, was a joint resolution similar to the ones Congress had given Eisenhower to oppose Communist threats in Formosa in 1955 and the Middle East in 1957. Bill Bundy had already drafted a version for him. The President asked Senator Fulbright, chairman of the Foreign Relations Committee and an old Johnson friend, to be the resolution's floor manager. To his subsequent sorrow, Fulbright agreed.

The cold war was still frigid in 1964; few men on the Hill were ready to urge a soft answer to Communist wrath. But there was one: Wayne Morse of Oregon. On the night after the second Tonkin Gulf incident Morse had a call from someone in the Pentagon. The caller had heard that the senator was going to fight the President's resolution. He suggested that the senator ask two questions. First, he should insist upon seeing the *Maddox*'s log; it would show that the destroyer had been much closer to the shore than civilians realized. Second, he should demand to know the ship's mission; it had been far from innocent.

The next morning Morse studied the wording of the resolution and concluded that it was unconstitutional. Only Congress could declare war, he pointed out to Fulbright. This measure would give blanket approval to the waging of war by the chief executive with no war declaration. Fulbright reminded him of the Formosa and

Middle East resolutions. Morse said they had been unconstitutional, too, but they had been more justifiable than this one. The crises which inspired them had been subject to quick solutions. Not so this one; the struggle in Vietnam seemed interminable, and this open-ended license would allow the President to intervene any time he saw fit. The wording was far too general, Morse said. He implored Fulbright to hold hearings. Impossible, said Fulbright; this was an emergency. Morse denied it, and he was right; but Fulbright had decided to ask for instant passage, making the issue one of senatorial patriotism. That isolated Morse and Ernest Gruening of Alaska, the only colleague to side with him. The measure passed the House 414 to 0, after just forty minutes of discussion. The Senate took longer—eight hours of debate—but that, as one observer later commented, was "less time than the Senate usually took to amend a fisheries bill."

There were few critical comments at the time. The move was seen as a logical extension of a line of thought reaching back to the decision, after Munich, never again to appease aggressors, relying instead on collective security. If we and SEATO's other signatories came to South Vietnam's rescue now, the reasoning went, they would help us if California found itself threatened by Ho Chi Minh, or by Ho and Mao. Dean Rusk flatly stated that to do less would put the United States in "mortal danger." Later there were hoots at this, but there was no derision at the time. The Rusk position was that of practically all public men in both parties; among the senators who voted for the resolution were Eugene McCarthy, George McGovern, Birch Bayh, Albert Gore, Jacob K. Javits, John Sherman Cooper, Frank Carlson, George D. Aiken, and Frank Church. The *New York Times* commented: "The nation's united confidence in the Chief Executive is vital." The *Washington Post* said: "President Johnson has earned the gratitude of the free world." Lou Harris reported that whereas 58 percent of the nation had been critical of Johnson's handling of the war in July, 72 percent now approved. Harris wrote: "In a single stroke Mr. Johnson has turned his greatest political vulnerability in foreign policy into one of his strongest assets." Even Walter Lippmann approved, believing that the President was telling the country that bombing would be the outer limit of American involvement in Vietnam, that he would never send troops. The friends of the administration, which in 1964 meant most of the nation, were jubilant. It was much later that Morse's prophetic words were recalled:

> I believe that history will record that we have made a great mistake in subverting and circumventing the Constitution of the United States . . . by means of this resolution. As I argued earlier today at great length, we are in effect giving the President . . . warmaking powers in the absence of a declaration of war. I believe that to be a historic mistake.

Johnson signed the document the day it was passed, August 7. Eight months later he told a group of visitors with a grin, "For all I know our Navy was shooting at whales out there."

In the summer of 1963 Eliot Janeway, the syndicated economic columnist, speculated about what might happen if black and white workmen found themselves competing for the same jobs. He suggested that the white workers might become resentful of the civil rights movement, and he gave the reaction a name: "backlash." During the winter after Dallas "backlash" acquired a political meaning. Specifically, it was applied to racist support for the presidential primary campaigns of Governor George C. Wallace of Alabama. After displays of strength in Indiana (where he won 30 percent of the vote on May 5) and in Maryland (43 percent on May 19), Wallace's national following dwindled. His popularity seemed to suffer from the dignified demeanor of most blacks, who were still turning their cheek to injustice. In July Wallace quit the race. Yet even as he withdrew, blacks in New York were making history by declining to turn a cheek. As a consequence, headlines began conveying news which was bound to stimulate backlash.

On July 16, the day the Republican presidential candidate accepted his party's nomination in San Francisco, a Manhattan janitor was hosing the sidewalk outside a building of luxury apartments at 215 East Seventy-sixth Street, near the edge of Harlem. Noticing three Negro youths lounging across the street, he impulsively turned the hose on them. That was unwise. To the boys the hose was reminiscent of Bull Connor and Birmingham. Infuriated, they attacked the janitor, holding trash can lids as shields and hurling missiles. A bottle hit him; he fled. One of the boys, James Powell, fifteen, went after him with a knife. At this point an off-duty police lieutenant, Thomas R. Gilligan, arrived on the scene. Gilligan drew his pistol and ordered Powell to drop the knife. Instead the boy lunged at the lieutenant, slashing his right forearm. Gilligan discharged one warning shot and then fired for keeps, killing him instantly.

Young Powell's death aroused all Harlem. For three days the Negroes' rage smoldered. On the third evening, a Saturday, CORE held a protest rally on West 123rd Street. Goaded by an impassioned speaker, a black mob marched to the nearby 29th Precinct station and demanded Gilligan's immediate suspension. When it wasn't forthcoming they rioted, throwing bottles and debris at the policemen. The riot spread and continued for five nights. Dying down there, it then broke out in the Bedford-Stuyvesant section of Brooklyn, and when the violence subsided in Brooklyn it erupted in Rochester, New York, three hundred miles away. On Sunday, August 2, Jersey City blew. Paterson and Elizabeth were next, then Dixmoor, a Chicago suburb, and finally Philadelphia. Hundreds had been injured, and nearly a thousand arrested. A thousand stores were damaged; losses were placed at several million dollars.

The FBI declared that there was no pattern to the riots, that they were "a senseless attack on all constituted authority, without purpose or objective." The report continued: "While in the cities racial tensions were a contributing factor, none of the . . . occurrences was a 'race riot' in the accepted meaning of the phrase." Essentially chaotic, the disorders were nevertheless far from lacking form and significance. Until 1964 whites had always been the aggressors in major American interracial disturbances, of which there had been thirty-three since the turn of the century. Now the situation was reversed; the initiative had passed to the blacks. The race riots of the 1960s shared other characteristics. They came in the summer, in ghettos marked by an absence of contact between the slum population and those who made the key decisions concerning it, and they were sparked by hostility between the Negroes and white policemen.

"Watch out," said Negro Congressman Adam Clayton Powell, often a shrewder man than his critics, black or white, knew. The "black revolution," as he called it, would, he said, have two phases. The first was southern and concerned with "middle-class matters": sitting on buses and at lunch counters, using public toilets, going to the same schools as whites—issues of status. The second phase was northern. It was just beginning, and it was going to be very different, he said. Powell called it "proletarian," and he predicted that it would be "rough." Northern Negroes had always had the rights their counterparts in the South sought. Their concern was what Powell called the "gut issue of who gets the money." They were in a mutinous mood, and they were not moved by Martin Luther King's appeals for nonviolence. Their war cry was: "Burn, baby, burn!"

Although no one knew it at the time, 1964 marked the beginning of a cycle which would devastate the northern cities within three years. In addition to the tumult in New York there were scattered disorders that summer in New Jersey, Philadelphia, Chicago, and St. Augustine, Florida. Race was becoming the country's overriding domestic issue. In northern schools it was the year of the boycott; black parents in New York and Cleveland, dissatisfied with the treatment of their children, kept them at home. Malcolm X formed the Black Nationalist Party in 1964. The consciences of the North had at last been aroused by the injustices in the South. That spring Mrs. Malcolm Peabody, the seventy-two-year-old mother of the governor of Massachusetts, was arrested for participating in the St. Augustine protests, and the declaration of a mistrial in the Medgar Evers murder case, which only a few years earlier would have been accepted passively by Negroes, stimulated recruitment for the most important civil rights program of the year, the Mississippi "Freedom Summer" of 1964.

The immediate importance of the events in Mississippi lay in their impact on the ghettoed blacks in the North. Until 1940, some 75 percent of American Negroes had lived in the South. The long emigration of southern Negroes northward and the coming of age of the children born in their new homes had created a new, militant generation of blacks. Washington, D.C., and Newark now had Negro majorities, and Cleveland, Baltimore, St. Louis, and Detroit were more than one-third Negro. The black birth rate—approximately 40 percent higher than that of whites—had replaced immigration as the U.S. population's expansional factor. The urban slums of the North were swarming with black youths. More than half the country's Negroes were now below the age of twenty-two, and great masses of them lacked parental supervision. Fully 30 percent of the black families in big cities were headed by women who lacked husbands; in New York City alone there were 100,000 illegitimate Negro children in 1964. The revolution in communications meant that TV news programs provided this volatile audience with vivid reports of civil rights developments in the South. "Amid all the sad statistics poured forth about the ghettoes," the *Economist* of London reminded its European readers, "it is worth remembering that . . . some 88 per cent of black American families have television sets."

The Freedom Summer was sponsored by the Council of Federated Organizations (CFO), principally SNCC and CORE. None of the participants expected a graceful reception from white Mississippians. Memories of James Meredith and Medgar Evers were still fresh, and the red-necks and wool-hats of the South were known to be resentful over the Civil Rights Act of 1964. Introduced by John Kennedy and shepherded through Congress by Lyndon Johnson, it extended the bans against discrimination into many new areas. CFO cast its recruiting nets on the campuses of northern colleges and universities, chiefly among white students whose consciences were troubled by injustices to Negroes. A thousand of them volunteered to participate in a drive to register as many voters as possible among Mississippi's 900,000 blacks. They were trained in Oxford, Ohio. On June 19 the first group of 200 left for the South, and on June 21 they reached Jackson.

Almost immediately—it was the following day—three of them were reported missing. They were Michael H. Schwerner, twenty-four, of Brooklyn; Andrew Goodman, twenty, of New York, and James E. Chaney, twenty-one, of Meridian, Mississippi. Schwerner and Goodman were white; Chaney was black. The three were traveling in a 1964 Ford station wagon, and they had been arrested for speeding in Neshoba County, in east central Mississippi. Sheriff Lawrence Rainey and his deputy, Cecil Price, said the youths had disappeared after paying a fine in Philadelphia, the county seat. The station wagon was found the next day fifteen miles northeast of Philadelphia. It had been burned.

The FBI, local law officers, and Navy men stationed in Mississippi conducted a massive search for the missing youths. Rivers and creeks were dragged; helicopters and a photoreconnaissance jet hovered overhead. At the request of the President, Allen Dulles flew down to confer with Governor Paul B. Johnson Jr. A considerable part of the state's white population believed that the three were in Cuba or, as one report had it, in a Chicago bar, drinking beer and laughing at the baffled lawmen looking for them. The prevailing opinion in white Mississippi was that the searchers had no expectation of finding the youths. They were there, the story went, to win Negro votes for President Johnson in the North.

Meanwhile the rest of the CFO volunteers were encountering

other difficulties. In the Mississippi Delta their meetings with local blacks were bombed by the KAF—the Klan Air Force: private planes which soared overhead and dropped satchels of explosives. After several Negro homes had been demolished in McComb, in southwestern Mississippi, several white men were arrested; with them the arresting officers found four high-powered rifles, several carbines and pistols, fifteen dynamite bombs, a five-gallon can of explosive powder, a case of hand grenades, and several thousand rounds of ammunition.

CFO volunteers who distributed handbills in Belzoni, Mississippi, were arrested, charged with "criminal syndicalism," and held in the town jail. A dynamite charge tore out a wall in the home of the mayor of Natchez, who had promised blacks equal protection under the law. A circuit judge denounced men who burned churches, and a cross was burned on his lawn. As the summer waned the leaders of the Freedom Summer movement drew up a list of their casualties. Eighty of the volunteers had been beaten. Three had been wounded by gunfire in thirty-five shootings. Over a thousand had been arrested. Thirty-seven Negro churches and thirty-one homes had been burned or bombed. In addition there were several unsolved murders of blacks which were believed to be attributable to hostility toward the civil rights movement.

Robert Kennedy told the NAACP that the federal government could not undertake preventive police action in the state; it was impractical and probably unconstitutional. J. Edgar Hoover went further. Arriving in Jackson, he deplored what he called an "overemphasis" on civil rights and said his men "most certainly" would not provide the volunteers with protection. At the suggestion of Allen Dulles, however, the President sent more FBI agents to the state. Lights burned all night on the top two floors of a new office building in Jackson, the bureau's Mississippi headquarters. Governor Johnson appealed for public assistance in the search for the three missing civil rights workers. Predictably, that call was unheeded, but the FBI's offer of nearly $30,000 in reward money brought information from two informers. With it, agents rented excavation equipment and dug into a newly erected earthen dam on a farm some six miles southwest of Philadelphia. They found the bodies of the missing three near the base of the 25-foot-high red clay dam and at the center of its 250-foot length. They had been shot to death, and Chaney, the black, had been beaten savagely before being murdered.

On December 4 the FBI arrested twenty-one Neshoba County men, including Sheriff Rainey and Deputy Price. Price was accused of arresting the three youths and turning them over to a lynch mob, which he then joined. Most of the men were Klansmen, and one was the local Klan leader. Civil rights leaders doubted that any of them would be convicted, and for a while it certainly seemed unlikely. Governor Johnson and Mississippi Attorney General Joe Patterson announced that the state would not prefer charges; in their opinion the evidence was inadequate. A federal grand jury in Meridian, Mississippi, did hand down indictments against eighteen of the men, charging them with violating an obscure 1870 statute by conspiring to violate the constitutional rights of the slain men, but the U.S. District Judge was W. Harold Cox, who had helped delay due process in the James Meredith case. On one recent occasion Cox had compared black voter applicants to chimpanzees. He was not expected to give the defendants any trouble.

In the beginning he didn't. In February 1965 he dismissed the felony indictments against the accused, reducing the charges to misdemeanors. For a time it even appeared that the sheriff, his deputy, and a Philadelphia justice of the peace might be awarded damages against the government by a local jury. To reporters it seemed that the defendants were widely regarded as heroes. Confederate flags were displayed outside the federal building; one huge one was run up each morning at the barbershop directly across the street. Television and wire service cameramen were mauled by resentful bystanders. Although the U.S. Supreme Court reversed Judge Cox, ruling that the accused men must stand trial on the conspiracy charges brought by the Justice Department, most observers believed that the case was as good as dead. Certainly the accused thought so. Freed on bond during the trial, they were plainly enjoying their local fame. A battery of twelve defense lawyers called 114 witnesses, most of them to provide alibis or to attest to good character. One lawyer called the informers "traitors." The jury of seven women and five men was all white; eighteen Negro veniremen had been eliminated by defense challenges.

John Doar, prosecuting for the Justice Department, called forty-one witnesses. They revealed that the murders had been no crime of passion. Schwerner, who had preceded the main body of CFO volunteers, had been marked for death by the Klan nine days before he was killed for having eaten and slept in the homes of Negroes. He and his two companions had been seized after a wild chase and taken to a lonely dirt road. One of the klansmen had spun Schwerner around and asked him, "Are you that nigger lover?" Schwerner had replied, "Sir, I know how you feel." Those had been his last words. Goodman, too, had been swiftly murdered. One Klansman had been disappointed because the two white volunteers had been put to death before he could fire. He had shot Chaney, saying, "At least I killed me a nigger."

One day after retiring to consider the evidence the jury reported that it was hopelessly deadlocked. Judge Cox refused to accept the stalemate. Instead he issued new instructions, among them the so-called "dynamite charge" which had been upheld by the Supreme Court in 1898 as a way to jolt a deadlocked jury into a decision. Under it jurors in the minority were urged to "carefully examine and reconsider" their opinions, weighing the feelings of the majority. The judge also told them that he would approve a mixed verdict. During a recess at this point Deputy Price and another defendant, Wayne Roberts, a salesman of automobile trailers, blundered. They told spectators in the federal building corridors that they were going to fix the judge. Roberts was heard to say, "Judge Cox gave the jury the dynamite charge. Well, we have some dynamite for him ourselves." Word of this reached the judge. Ordering them to the bench, he said, "If you think you can intimidate this court, you are sadly mistaken. I'm not going to let any wild man loose on any civilized society." With that, he ordered them locked up and denied them bail. On October 20 the jury found seven of the men, including Price and Roberts, guilty. Sheriff Rainey and seven others were acquitted. Over three years had passed since the crime, but the Justice Department was jubilant. The verdict had made history; for the first time, a federal jury of white Mississippians had convicted white defendants in a civil rights case. On December 29 Judge Cox sentenced the seven to jail terms ranging from three years to ten—the maximum.

It was the year of Goldwater. In seven consecutive national conventions of the past, beginning with the nomination of Landon in 1936, Republican conservatives had suppressed their yearning for a presidential candidate from their own ranks. This time they did not suppress it. This time they turned to Au + H_2O = 1964. They wanted A Choice, Not an Echo, as their placards proclaimed, and on July 15 they nominated Barry Morris Goldwater, Arizona's senior senator and a denizen of deep right field.

The fact is that the party felt desperate. George Gallup had discovered that during the past quarter-century the GOP had lost a third of its members; the number of Americans who regarded themselves as Republicans had diminished 13 percent, while the number of Democrats had increased 11 percent. Goldwater and his people had an explanation for this. The GOP, their argument went, had been choosing "me too" candidates—moderate Republicans who merely repeated Democratic promises. Their conclusion was that because the Democrats were originals and the Republican moderates mere carbon copies, the GOP had been repeatedly defeated, voters tending to prefer the real thing.

Here the skating reached thin ice. Polls indicated that a majority of the electorate favored the middle of the road. The Republican right-wingers denied it. They were convinced that out in the country there was a hidden conservative majority. It was, they insisted, the key fact in American politics. Lacking a home, these disgruntled conservatives had scorned both parties. On election days they went fishing or stayed home. To them the result was a matter of no consequence; either way they were going to be stuck with liberals, leftists, socialists, "collectivists," "bleeding hearts." Nominate a genuine conservative, said the Goldwater ideologues, and this hidden majority would come swarming into the streets and elect a real American.

Although President Kennedy had been convinced that Barry Goldwater would be the Republican nominee in 1964, Goldwater himself wasn't so sure, and other GOP leaders were slow in taking him seriously. The struggle over who would become the standard-bearer turned into an odd one. The Arizonan had announced his candidacy from his sun-drenched Scottsdale, Arizona, patio on January 3. The next Republican to throw a hat in the ring had been a woman, Margaret Chase Smith. The first primary, in New Hampshire, was won with write-in votes by a man who hadn't announced at all, Henry Cabot Lodge. Nelson Rockefeller then divulged that he was available; next William Scranton of Pennsylvania said *he* was.

Until the last of the big primaries, in California on June 2, almost everyone seemed to believe that someone would take it away from Goldwater. The likeliest one was Rockefeller. Then, on May 30, a Saturday, the second Mrs. Rockefeller gave birth to Nelson A. Rockefeller Jr.—thereby reminding California Republicans of the New York governor's recent divorce. Overnight he lost seven percentage points in the Lou Harris poll. On Tuesday Goldwater received 51 percent of the primary vote and Rockefeller 49 percent. At the convention the Arizonan's well-organized legions then deflected all opposition and took the prize with an overwhelming 883 delegate votes on the first ballot. Thereupon the nominee deepened the division in the party by giving the moderates the rough side of his tongue in a memorable passage: "Extremism in the defense of liberty is no vice! And . . . moderation in the pursuit of justice is no virtue!"

Barry Goldwater was fifty-five years old, a man of absolute integrity, and one of the most charming politicians ever to run for the Presidency. Handsome, leonine, silver-haired, with the black horn-rimmed spectacles which were his trademark, he had become one of the most celebrated public men in the nation and certainly the best-known conservative. Goldwater represented a love for the best of the past and defiance toward the worst of the present. In his crisp, low southwestern drawl he reminded the country of American maxims and ethical certitudes which had lost their validity but not their fascination. It was his special talent that he could make them seem both plausible and relevant.

Away from the Senate he was a mishmash of anachronisms. For all his summoning of the legends of the past, he was a major general in the Air Force reserve, a hot jet pilot, and a tremendous admirer of sophisticated technology. (In San Francisco he buckled himself into the cockpit of his private jet and zoomed back and forth over the Cow Palace while his name was being placed in nomination.) He was an expert radio ham; he maintained expensive sending and receiving sets in his suburban Phoenix home and his Washington apartment, and he brought a third to the San Francisco convention. He was also a superb photographer; a volume of his desert studies had been issued. Perhaps his most significant acquisition was the twenty-five-foot flagpole at his Arizona home. It was equipped with a photoelectric device which automatically raised the colors when the dawn light reached it and lowered them as twilight deepened, thereby assuring a display of patriotism even when no one was home.

"Viva olé! Viva olé!" chanted his faithful followers. They were passionate, they were exuberant, and sometimes they were frightening. One unforgettable moment came in the Cow Palace when Nelson Rockefeller took the rostrum to urge the adoption of minority resolutions which had been drafted by the platform committee. The galleries, packed with Goldwaterites, booed him and shouted, "We want Barry!" Some men would be daunted by this, but Rockefeller relished it. "This is still a free country, ladies and gentlemen," he taunted, and as their fury mounted and they roared with rage, he described some of the tactics which had been used against him in the California primary: "These things have no place in America, but I can personally testify to their existence, and so can countless others who have also experienced midnight and early morning telephone calls, unsigned threatening letters, smear and hate literature, strong-arm and goon tactics, bomb threats and bombings, infiltration and take-over of established political organizations by Communist and Nazi methods."

By this time there were people in the galleries who were all but lying on the floor and drumming their heels. Chairman Thruston B. Morton vainly gaveled for order while the Goldwater delegates on the floor—aware that this demonstration of ferocity was hurting their man in the eyes of the television audience—pleaded for quiet. The storm of abuse continued unabated, and Rockefeller, grinning, delivered another thrust: "Some of you don't like to hear it, ladies and gentlemen, but it's the truth."

It was part of the truth. Goldwater and his managers permitted no little old ladies in tennis shoes in their organization. Indeed, one of the weaknesses of their campaign was that it was too disciplined, too lacking in spontaneity. After the convention the senator sent two of his very straight young men, Dean Burch and John Grenier, to take over the Republican National Committee, Burch as chairman and Grenier as executive director. They spent five full weeks putting it in order—five weeks when they should have been campaigning. The day after the election in November Goldwater's finance chairman elatedly announced that his books were in the black.

A shrewder politician would have used his acceptance speech to woo the losers. He might even have visited the vanquished, as Eisenhower had done with Taft in 1952. But Goldwater had been angered by dirty tricks, too, and for all his generosity of spirit he wasn't a healer. In mid-August, much too late, he sat down in Hershey, Pennsylvania, with the party's elders—Rockefeller, Eisenhower, Nixon, Scranton, and George Romney—in an effort to bind up wounds and plan a master election strategy. It was a wasted day. They lacked a conciliatory spirit, and none had any useful campaign ideas. Mostly they complained. It was after this meeting, and in part as a consequence of it, that Republicans running for other offices began avoiding the presidential standard-bearer, even declining to share the same platform with him.

IN YOUR HEART YOU KNOW HE'S RIGHT, read the Goldwater billboards, pins, and bumper stickers. There was some truth to it. In his three books and eight hundred newspaper columns he had tackled many sacred cows which deserved it. Over the past half-century the federal bureaucracy had grown to something in the order of fifty or sixty times its original size. Its officials were often arrogant and overbearing, and some of the practices that the government either employed itself or encouraged in others had plainly outlived their usefulness—among them labor featherbedding, depletion allowances, farm price supports, and subsidies to peanut growers. Senator Goldwater was trenchant on the subject of these, and here millions of Americans knew in their hearts—or at any rate believed—that he was right.

The difficulty was that he had said, done, and written so many other things, some of them bizarre. He had offered to sell TVA for a dollar. He had said that he wished it were possible to saw off the eastern seaboard and let it float out to sea. He had depicted all of America's great cities as sin-steeped Babylons. At various times he had advocated the elimination of rural electrification, the replacement of the National Labor Relations Board, and a new U.S. Supreme Court. Here Americans knew in their hearts that he was wrong.

His opponent was one of the most masterful politicians in the history of the country; as a result, the flaws in Goldwater's armor were deftly exposed, over and over, so that he was put on the defensive and remained there. Atomic warfare was a particularly devastating issue. Speaking in Hartford on October 24, 1963, Goldwater had said that he believed the size of the American military presence could be reduced by as much as a third if NATO "commanders" were authorized to use tactical nuclear weapons in a crisis. That put the Bomb in the campaign, and it remained there to the end.

As exploited by Rockefeller in New Hampshire's January campaign, it was a legitimate campaign issue. The Democrats probably went too far in what became known as their "Daisy Girl" television spot, first shown on September 7. NBC's Monday Night at the Movies that evening, *David and Bathsheba,* starring Gregory Peck and Susan Hayward, was interrupted for an idyllic picture of a child pulling the petals off a daisy and counting them; as she did, the picture dissolved into a mushroom cloud. The Republicans were understandably incensed. Yet Goldwater had failed and continued to fail to clarify his Hartford remarks. At the very least his manner of referring to nuclear weapons was disturbing. A candidate for the Presidency of the United States ought not to speak of "lobbing one into the men's room at the Kremlin." On one occasion when Goldwater was supposed to be exorcising the shadow of the Bomb, Charles Mohr of the *New York Times* counted almost thirty such phrases as "push the button," "atomic holocaust," and "nuclear annihilation." That was not the way to reassure the people. IN YOUR HEART, the Democrats said in a wicked thrust, YOU KNOW HE MIGHT.

Another issue digging graves for Republican hopes was social security. Here the trouble had begun on January 6 in New Hampshire. In reply to a question, Goldwater said that he favored improving social security by making contributions voluntary. The next day's Concord, New Hampshire, *Monitor* carried the head, GOLDWATER SETS GOALS: END SOCIAL SECURITY. The senator protested, but plainly that would be the consequence of voluntary participation; payments to retired workers must come from young workers, who are no more eager than anyone else to pay taxes if they can get out of it. In the Democrats' TV spot on this, two hands tore up a social security card. Since social security affects a hundred million Americans, it would have been hard to find a theme of greater interest.

Goldwater had other problems; he had voted against the nuclear test ban treaty and—the previous June—the Kennedy-Johnson civil rights bill. The consequences of his record became clearer and clearer as one conservative newspaper after another endorsed Johnson, and ultimately even the Republican candidate could see it. Poll figures had never been so lopsided; Gallup had Johnson over

Goldwater 65 to 29 percent. After the election the Arizonan remarked that he should have realized that it was all over in San Francisco, before the campaigning had even begun. As it was, he said, he knew in August that it was hopeless. That had the ring of hindsight. As late as October he was giving lip service, at least, to confidence in victory. Whatever his expectations, though, he never tried to improve his chances with low blows. He admonished audiences that hissed Johnson ("Don't boo the office of the Presidency"). When F. Clifton White, one of his advisers, produced a documentary film called *Choice*, exploiting the ghetto riots with shocking scenes of marauding Negroes, Goldwater called it racist and suppressed it. And he refused to capitalize on, or even to discuss, reports of an impending scandal in the Johnson campaign—the arrest of the President's chief aide on a charge of committing sodomy in a public toilet.

The aide was Walter Jenkins, who, exhausted by overwork, had yielded to temptations he might otherwise have suppressed. Jenkins had left the White House for a few hours on October 7 to attend a cocktail party celebrating the occupancy of new offices by *Newsweek*'s Washington bureau. After several drinks he left and walked two blocks to the Washington YMCA. The basement men's room was known to him as a trysting place for homosexuals. Unfortunately the Washington police knew it, too, and at about 7:30 P.M. Jenkins and an elderly army veteran were arrested by an officer who had been watching them through a peephole. They were taken to a police station, where it was discovered that five years earlier Jenkins had been arrested on the same charge. Newspapermen were reluctant to make this public, but they had no choice once Dean Burch called attention to "a report sweeping Washington that the White House is desperately trying to suppress a major news story affecting the national security"—an early instance of incautious use of this phrase by the Republican right. Once the report was public, Jenkins entered a hospital with a diagnosis of "extreme fatigue." Burch and many of Goldwater's other advisers begged him to avail himself of this opportunity to hammer away at what they called a shocking example of immorality on the highest level of the administration. He declined.

Johnson anxiously commissioned an Oliver Quayle survey to find out how many votes the disaster would cost. None to speak of, was Quayle's surprising conclusion, and the sad incident swiftly faded from public memory. Goldwater's compassion was only part of the explanation for this. Another part was that just as people had begun talking about Jenkins they were rocked by three startling developments in foreign affairs. Within forty-eight hours on October 15–16, Khrushchev was stripped of power and deposed, Communist China announced that it had exploded its first atomic bomb, and Sir Alec Douglas-Home's Conservative government fell. The White House press corps talked of Johnsonian luck. He was having a lot of it; when Lady Bird Johnson headed south with a group of southern administration wives on a sixteen-car train christened "The Lady Bird Special," they were met by hecklers—the one reception sure to win sympathy, and votes, elsewhere.

Johnson met the Lady Bird Special in New Orleans, where he then delivered his finest speech of the campaign. It was risky—a fiery appeal for civil rights, delivered against the advice of Senator Russell Long—and that alone would have made it memorable. The last line, however, made it unforgettable. After appealing for an end to bigotry he said that he was going to enforce and observe the Civil Rights Act of 1964 ("I'm not going to let them build up the hate and try to buy my people by appealing to their prejudice"), and then he told how, when Sam Rayburn first went to Congress, he had had a long talk with an ailing southern senator who said he wished he felt well enough to take one more trip home. "I would like to go back down there and make them one more Democratic speech," Johnson quoted the senator as saying. "I just feel I've got one more in me. Poor old state, they haven't heard a real Democratic speech in thirty years. All they ever hear at election time is *nigra, nigra, nigra.*" The audience gasped, recovered, and gave him a five-minute standing ovation.

The record of other LBJ campaign highlights does not always read so well. This is particularly true in regard to Vietnam. Accusing Goldwater of loose talk and loose thinking about nuclear weapons was powerful political medicine. The Democrats couldn't resist ever stronger doses of it. The "Daisy Girl" TV spot was followed by another on September 17 which was so outrageous that it was run but once; it showed a lovely child eating an ice cream cone while a voice told of strontium 90 poisoning the air and reminded viewers that Goldwater had voted against the test ban treaty. The senator's suggestion that atomic bombs might be used to "defoliate" the Ho Chi Minh Trail was cited as an example of his irresponsibility and militarism. But this was a dangerous topic for Johnson. It reminded voters that Americans were in a hot war in Vietnam and that Goldwater hadn't put them there. To keep the momentum of the peace issue, therefore, the President made certain pledges to the country which would not be forgotten.

In Eufaula, Oklahoma, on September 25 he said: "We don't want our American boys to do the fighting for Asian boys. We don't want to get involved . . . and get tied down in a land war in Asia."

Then in Manchester, New Hampshire, on September 28: "I have not thought we were ready for American boys to do the fighting for Asian boys. What I have been trying to do, with the situation that I found, was to get the boys in Vietnam to do their own fighting with our advice and with our equipment. . . . Now we have lost 190 American lives. . . . I often wake up in the night and think about how many I could lose if I made a misstep. . . . It is not any problem to start a war. . . . I know some folks who think I could start one mighty easy. But it is a pretty difficult problem for us to prevent one, and that is what we are trying to do."

In Akron, Ohio, on October 21: ". . . we are not about to send American boys nine or ten thousand miles away from home to do what Asian boys ought to be doing for themselves."

And in Pittsburgh on October 27: "There can be and will be, as long as I am President, peace for all Americans."

In a bitter joke a year later a girl said, "I was told if I voted for Goldwater we would be at war in six months. I did—and we were." Surely a voter whose sole motive was the preservation of peace, and who carefully followed accounts of speeches in the newspapers, would have voted for Johnson and against Goldwater in November 1964. Later he would feel betrayed, as many did. In El Paso during the campaign the President said, "I pledge you here today I will go to any remote corner of the world to meet anyone, any time, to promote freedom and peace," but the fact was that as long as he believed that American forces could impose a military solution on the Communists he rejected all gestures, including some promising ones, from the Viet Cong and the North Vietnamese. The issue during the campaign had seemed clear-cut. Goldwater recommended the dispatch of U.S. soldiers and aircraft to the support of South Vietnam, and Johnson accused him of reckless warmongering. The President appeared to be sincere. Yet it is difficult to think of any military proposal by Goldwater which Johnson had not taken, despite his vows to the contrary, by the following summer.

On November 3 Lyndon Johnson won election to a full term in the White House. He and Hubert Humphrey carried forty-four states and the District of Columbia, with an aggregate of 486 electoral votes. Goldwater and Congressman William E. Miller took Arizona, Mississippi, Alabama, South Carolina, Louisiana, and Georgia, with 52 electoral votes. The Democrats also swept the congressional races. They won 28 of the 35 senatorial seats, giving them 68 to the Republicans' 32, and picked up 41 House seats. They now dominated the House by better than a two-thirds majority, 295 to 140. The Republicans did make a net gain of one statehouse, but they still had only 17 governors to 33 for the Democrats.

GOLDWATER FOR HALLOWEEN jeered one campaign bumper sticker that had been popular in Washington. Not all the cars displaying it had been owned by Democrats. On election day this writer lunched with Earl Warren in his chambers. The most vivid memory of that occasion was the vehemence with which the Chief Justice expressed the hope that Goldwater would be beaten soundly. Like many another GOP moderate, Warren wanted to see a total rout of the Goldwater conservatives. When disaster befell them the Republicans confirmed a theory of long standing, that their feuds are far more savage than those among Democrats. The conservatives had not only lost an election; in many cases they found themselves being cut dead by members of their own party.

Perhaps Richard Nixon best expressed the frustration and confusion among Republican regulars. Two days after the election he excoriated Nelson Rockefeller, charging that Rockefeller's refusal to help the Goldwater campaign had cost it votes. He called the New York governor a "divider." By the following Tuesday Nixon was having second thoughts. He urged his fellow Republicans to reject "right-wing extremism" while finding a place for all "responsible viewpoints," from liberal to conservative. Yet Nixon's observations were no longer compelling, even among his fellow Republicans. Unlike Rockefeller, he had campaigned tirelessly for the ticket, and apparently it had been a wasted effort. He had collected a lot of IOUs, but it was highly unlikely that they would ever prove valuable.

These were quiet years for Nixon, and in many ways they were good ones. He was making a lot of money. He had time to read and reflect. Except when he was speaking he saw as much of his family as fathers in private life. On the Sunday of that week that the campaign opened, Checkers, the little black and white cocker spaniel that he had turned into a political asset in 1952, died at the age of twelve, and he was there to comfort his daughters. (In October, while he was campaigning in Iowa, he was given another cocker and urged to call it Checkers II, but he gave it away; there was only one Checkers.) Eight weeks after the election his daughter Tricia led the parade at the International Debutante Ball in New York. He escorted her. Next day, the last day but one in 1964, he put a headstone over the grave of Checkers. To many it seemed symbolic.

Until November 1964 Lyndon Johnson had presided in the shadow of President Kennedy, but now he had been elected President in his own right. The hold of the Kennedy legend on the American imagination was still powerful—two of the most charismatic men on Capitol Hill were Robert Kennedy, the new senator from New York, as he now was, and Senator Edward M. Kennedy of Massachusetts, who had been swept back into office by over 900,000 votes—but Johnson was now number one, and the city began to reflect it. Among the songs heard most frequently in bars were "The Eyes of Texas" and "The Yellow Rose of Texas." Middle-aged men wearing cowboy boots and five-gallon hats with their business suits milled around in the lobby of the Washington Hotel on Fifteenth Street, beside the Treasury Building. Washington began to remind visitors of a frontier town, but then, so did the country; the wide-open, anything-goes 1960s were under way.

In 1964 Rudi Gernreich, the California designer, introduced the topless bathing suit, which led to all sorts of things. On a certain level of night club entertainment "topless" women employees became a feature attraction and then a commonplace; in the tawdry Washington cabarets down by the National Archives, as in other American metropolises, waitresses strode about with naked breasts swinging. Next Mary Quant created the miniskirt in London. Girls and many women wore skirts which shrank inch by tantalizing inch as the decade grew older, until, when the microskirt arrived, they had ceased to be tantalizing; all but the most handsome legs had lost their appeal.

Nudity was becoming fashionable in the theater, and as the mid-1960s wore on, seminudity became chic in society. Transparent, or "see-through" dresses were the new thing. Yves Saint Laurent brought out gauze shifts with coy sequins guarding the nipples and the crotch. In Italy the couturier Forquet created a South Seas skirt slung precariously on the hips; for a blouse he substituted a string of beads. Timid women wore either a flesh-colored something called a body stocking underneath, or "fun-derwear"—flashy, gay-colored undergarments to be glimpsed through gauze—but the more daring (and better-endowed) flaunted the works. Naked midriffs reached higher and lower. When the Smithsonian Institution acquired some of the more fantastic new gowns, Republican Congressman H. R. Gross of Iowa rose in the House to protest.

Both sexes in the rising generation insisted upon their right to say whatever they thought "relevant," relevance, like commitment, being one of the new things. Berkeley witnessed the rise of the Free Speech Movement, or the FSM, as it was known in California. That in turn led to the first great student-administration confrontation of the 1960s. The FSM, a coalition formed in the late summer of 1964 by undergraduates, graduate students, and junior faculty, ran the gamut ideologically from Goldwaterism to Maoism. All were united against a university prohibition of on-campus solicitation for political or civil rights demonstrations to be mounted off campus. Mobilizing under the leadership of Mario Savio, a twenty-two-year-old philosophy major from New York, the FSM reached the remarkable conclusion that the university's board of regents was trying to convert the campus into a concentration camp. The purpose of the conspiracy, as they saw it, was to make Berkeley a vast trade school turning out white-collar technicians useful to the establishment—industry, banks, publishing houses, the military, conservative labor unions. Savio cried, "The time has come to put our bodies on the machine and stop it!"

On September 14, 1964, a week before the opening of fall classes, the disorders began, and neither Berkeley nor any other American university would ever be the same. Those who called the FSM Communistic missed the point. It was anarchic, and it scorned all dialectic. A research fellow who approved of the movement explained, "All the old labels are out; if there were any orthodox Communists here, they would be a moderating influence." The movement's contempt for rationalism was at times ludicrous. When police dragged Savio and eight hundred of his followers out of Sproul Hall, the epicenter of the revolt, he cried, "This is wonderful! We'll bring the university to our terms!"

One lazy day the following March a barefoot, long-haired youth paraded through the main gate of the Berkeley campus holding aloft a placard emblazoned in blue with a single four-letter word. He wasn't a student. His name was John J. Thompson, and he was an unpublished poet, a member of Berkeley's so-called "hidden community"—unknown writers and political militants who would be blamed for much of the unrest there later in the decade. The following day a dozen other youths appeared carrying signs with similar messages; one shouted his cherished word into a campus microphone; another read a passage from *Lady Chatterley's Lover* aloud to an arresting officer. No one in the movement went bail for him and his friends. The campus newspaper deprecated this "filthy speech movement." To use another phrase which was entering the language, they suspected the odd crusaders of putting them on.

Yet both their demonstrations and the new uses of taboo words appear to have been aspects of a general revolt against constraints which characterized the 1960s. Thompson and his friends may have been pulling the FSM's leg, but many serious writers were in earnest about their right to use language which until now had been proscribed. They believed that the Supreme Court agreed with them (they were right), and in the long run their impact on society may prove to be more lasting than Savio's civil disobedience. Appearing in print, locker room language was next heard on the stage—for example, in *Who's Afraid of Virginia Woolf?*, which after 664 performances on Broadway became a film in 1966—and then in mixed company, among the sophisticated at first, swiftly followed by the young. In what had once been called polite society one heard, frequently from the loveliest lips, short Anglo-Saxon words formerly limited to unmixed company. The effect on the inhibited older generation was often electrifying.

Like the Pill and the new nudity, this reflected an evolving life-style and a new morality. To many in the older generation it seemed to be no morality at all, and they came to identify it with excessive hair and communes. But the forbidden fruit was just as tasty on the palate of Goldwater's admirers in the Young Americans for Freedom. YAF members never marched in antiwar demonstrations or read *Ramparts*, but when the lights went out they were as active as the most erotic hippy. One survey of casual adulterers found that a majority were short-haired and politically conservative. A Los Angeles entrepreneur who dealt with a community of conservative hedonists told a reporter, "This is the America you don't hear about. It's clean-cut people who don't wear sandals and beards—guys and girls living very normal lives. It's almost blasphemous how American it is."

Colleges had long provided grounds suitable for pairing off, but until the mid-1960s finding a member of the opposite sex off campus who was attractive, agreeable, and prurient had been time-consuming and rather expensive. Now that, too, was changing. Two years before the Johnson-Goldwater race, Grossinger's Hotel in the Catskills held its first weekend for singles only. It was the beginning, though no one knew it then, of another movement. In 1964 a lonesome ensign named Michael G. O'Harro, stationed in Arlington, Virginia, established the beginning of a fortune and a way of life by throwing a party for other young unmarried people—officers, professional men, airline stewardesses, teachers, models, secretaries, and career girls. Three years later O'Harro was back in civilian life and president of an organization called the Junior Officers and Professional Association, with thirty thousand members, twelve local chapters, and a staff of fifty. By then it was possible to vacation at resorts for singles only, take Bahaman cruises or European tours in groups which accepted only bachelors and unmarried girls, and read such singles-only magazines as O'Harro's JOPA *Niteletter*. And O'Harro had competitors. In San Francisco the lonely could meet at Paoli's; Chicago had The Store, Dallas the TGIF (Thank God It's Friday), and Manhattan Mr. Laff's and Friday's.

The logical consequence of all this was the construction of apartment complexes in which the unmarried could rent apartments and visit one another at all hours, and that was what happened. In part it was a reflection of the balkanizing of generations—the tendency of people in one age group to go off by themselves, thus engendering misunderstandings and what would soon be known as "gaps." The first to do it were the elderly, not the young. The earliest "retirement town" was built by Del Webb in Arizona in 1960. Like O'Harro's enterprise it was a tremendous success, inspiring imitators and, in 1965, the first singles community, the South Bay Club in the Los Angeles suburb of Torrance. South Bay's 248 apartments were all rented while it was still going up. Ultimately the firm built thirteen such complexes, including one in Phoenix, with eight thousand tenants who could play bridge, engage in round-table discussions, attend barbecues, stage masked balls, participate in wine tastings, and cohabit without encountering anyone else's husband or wife.

Understandably, a popular topic in the singles-only round-table discussions was birth control. Another was wedlock, often put as a proposition: "Marriage—Is It Defensible?" Matrimony was only one of many social institutions which were under attack in the mid-Sixties. Nothing was sacred any more; during Holy Week in 1966 *Time* asked on its cover, "Is God Dead?" thereby generating an intense theological debate and one memorable bumper sticker: GOD IS ALIVE AND HIDING IN ARGENTINA. People who read *Time*—or anything else—were belittled as old-fashioned and "linear" in Marshall McLuhan's *The Gutenberg Galaxy: The Making of Typographic Man* (1962) and *Understanding Media: The Extensions of Man* (1964).

The iconoclasm of the mid-Sixties did not always pay. Ralph Ginzburg published *Eros* in 1962; the post office ruled that it was smut and he was sentenced to five years in prison. In 1964 he brought out *Fact;* it contained material about Barry Goldwater which was not factual, and when Goldwater sued he was awarded $75,000. In 1967 Ginzburg issued *Avant-Garde;* it flopped. Another loser, though no one would have guessed it in the beginning, was Cassius Clay. After winning the world's championship by knocking out Sonny Liston in one minute flat, the fastest kayo in heavyweight title history, Clay confused fight fans by becoming a Black Muslim, changing his name to Muhammad Ali, refusing induction into the Army on grounds of conscience, and then, like Ginzburg, going to jail.

But anyone could stumble in this hazardous time. The Strategic Air Command, which as the guardian of the U.S. nuclear striking capacity was supposed to be discreet, scared the country, not to mention Europe, when one of its B-52s collided with a jet tanker and dumped four hydrogen bombs in Spanish waters. Norman Mailer was reputed to know something about the writing of fiction, yet in 1965 *An American Dream,* his first novel in ten years, was mercilessly panned by critics. Lyndon Johnson was said to be determined to suppress vulgarian tendencies in order to achieve presidential dignity, but after undergoing an operation he yanked out his shirt so news cameramen could photograph the scar. James Pike, Episcopal bishop of California, resigned when accused of heresy, took up spiritualism, wrote a book about it called *The Other Side,* got lost in the Judean desert, and was found dead in a kneeling position. Betty Grable and Harry James, after twenty-two years of being regarded as the happiest couple in Beverly Hills, were divorced in Las Vegas.

Nothing, it appeared, was as it seemed. In a gubernatorial election Alabamans voted "for Lurleen" to "let George do it." Black militants blamed black lawlessness on tension between the races, but in 1964 the toughest enforcers of the law in the Crown Heights area of Brooklyn were the Maccabees, an organization of middle-class Negro vigilantes. The belief that Americans go to college to make more money took its lumps when the *Wall Street Journal* complained that few Ivy League graduates were going into business; instead they were taking jobs in churches, labor unions, the Peace Corps, and civil rights organizations. Even the cold war wasn't what it had been. In 1966 the United States and the Soviet Union introduced direct air service between Moscow and New York with one round trip each week by Pan American and Soviet Aeroflot.

In 1964 *Dr. Strangelove* faded from the marquees, to be supplanted, in 1965, by *Dr. Zhivago,* which inspired fashion fads for huge fur hats, thigh-high boots, and coat hems that swept the ground. The skateboard became the successor to the hula hoop in 1965, when its manufacturers grossed a hundred million dollars; a skateboard meet at Anaheim, California, was televised by the three networks, and the circulation of the *Skateboard Quarterly* reached fifty thousand. Then the dippy boards faded as the next toy sensation, the super ball, bounced into view. Bicycles returned to what would be a more lasting popularity that same year, when six million were sold and the Long Island Railroad installed bike racks for commuters.

An Associated Press writer observed of 1965 that "the more things were out, the more they were in." There were demands for, among other unlikely articles, tasseled lamps, and sailor suits. Bell-bottoms came on strong. Peter Max, a twenty-five-year-old commercial artist, had a vision of "a huge monumental wave of youth—the youth revolution coming," and in anticipation of it he created psychedelic art. Within five years his designs on decals, posters, scarves, etc., would provide him with an annual income of two million dollars. Pop art masterpieces included a woman's girdle with an enormous eye painted on the back. "Camp" entered the language and was applied to such artifacts as feather boas, antimacassars, bubble gum cards, Shirley Temple photographs, and souvenirs of Atlantic City. Humphrey Bogart and Jean Harlow films enjoyed revivals, and for a while girls again tried to look like Harlow. Big films included *Lord Jim, The Agony and the Ecstasy,* and two broad farces: *Cat Ballou* and *What's New, Pussycat?*

Lou Harris reported a "growing disenchantment with television on the part of the affluent, better-educated section of the adult American public." All three networks appeared to be searching for the lowest common denominator in popular taste, and they were virtually tied in the Nielsen ratings. ("It was inevitable," observed the *New Yorker*. "It shines with the clarity of a mathematical law.") The debasement of network programming was particularly painful at CBS, which in the great days of Edward R. Murrow had appealed to intelligent viewers. Now, under James T. Aubrey Jr., CBS offered mystery dramas, rural comedies, and peepshow sex.

Adlai Stevenson and Winston Churchill died in 1965. J. Edgar Hoover was still alive and running the FBI, but he was becoming senescent. FBI figures indicated that the national crime rate was rising 11 percent a year, and the President's Commission on Law Enforcement and Administration of Justice concluded that possibly three times as much crime was committed as was reported. Social protest was a growing category for law infractions. The anti-Vietnam teach-ins, which began with a twelve-hour all-night seminar at the University of Michigan on March 24, 1965, were perfectly legal, but that was not always true of the nude-ins, lie-ins, and love-ins which followed. Leaders of the Brooklyn chapter of CORE threatened to spoil the opening day of the New York World's Fair on April 22, 1964, with a stall-in—snarling traffic by allowing thousands of cars to run out of gas in the middle of it. They succeeded in cutting the opening day crowd from about 250,000 to 92,646. Nearly three hundred were arrested, including James Farmer, national director of CORE.

The level of violence in the country continued to appall. In the summer of 1966 an itinerant worker named Richard Speck murdered eight student nurses in Chicago. Two weeks later Charles Whitman, an honor student at the University of Texas, climbed to the top of the university's twenty-seven-story tower in Austin and opened fire on passersby below, killing fourteen and wounding thirty, and three months after that an eighteen-year-old student entered the Rose-Mar College of Beauty in Mesa, Arizona, with a pistol and killed four women and a child. He told police he had been inspired by the Chicago and Austin killings. Like Speck and Whitman, he said, he wanted "to get known."

Two legislators from opposite ends of the ideological spectrum were in trouble. Adam Clayton Powell had called a Harlem widow "a bag woman for the police department"; she had been awarded damages, but he ignored the verdict and avoided New York. Senator Tom Dodd of Connecticut was censured by his colleagues for misuse of campaign funds and selling influence to an agent for West German business interests. A New York undercover policeman infiltrated a conspiracy to blow up the Statue of Liberty, the Liberty Bell, and the Washington Monument; the causes of the various plotters ranged from Quebec independence and admiration for Fidel Castro to Negro rights and support of North Vietnam. In New York a Vacation Exchange served as a contact for homeowners who wanted to swap houses during holidays, and from a small city in eastern Massachusetts came the first word of young married couples who swapped spouses. A travel agency advertised a judo tour of Japan: two sweaty weeks for $1,396. President Sarah Gibson Blanding of Vassar told her 1,450 girls that she expected them either to abstain from sexual intercourse or leave the campus. Jack Valenti told an audience of advertising men that "I sleep each night a little better, a little more confidently because Lyndon Johnson is my President."

The Dallas trial of Jack Ruby opened on February 17, 1964, and ended March 14 with a guilty verdict. His lawyer, Melvin Belli, screamed: "This was a kangaroo court, a railroad court, and everyone knew it." Ruby would die of cancer in jail on January 3, 1967. Senator J. William Fulbright delivered a major speech on foreign policy, warning that unless the United States "cut loose from established myths" he would break with the administration. Pope Paul VI spent an October day in New York and addressed the United Nations. Hubert Humphrey, the new Vice President, seemed determined to demonstrate superloyalty to Johnson; echoing an Avis car rental ad, he said, "I'm number two and I have to try harder." Some observers wondered whether the winning Democratic ticket was developing a sadomasochistic relationship. The President almost seemed to enjoy humiliating his Vice President. "Boys, I just reminded Hubert I've got his balls in my pocket," he told reporters.

In 1966 *The Sound of Music* became one of the greatest hits in movie history. People went around saying, "You better believe it." Televison was now almost 100 percent color during prime time. The two pro football leagues merged. *The Valley of the Dolls* and *How to Avoid Probate* were best-sellers. *Cabaret* and *Mame* were big on Broadway. David Merrick put $500,000 into *Breakfast at Tiffany's;* it failed. A clothing firm marketed disposable paper dresses which came in cans, cost a dollar or two, and were discarded when dirty. New male cosmetics included false eyelashes—called "Executive Eyelash"—and an after-shave powder puff—"Brass Knuckles." The summer of 1966 was spoiled for a lot of travelers by the longest and costliest airline strike ever; five major airlines were grounded for forty-three days. That fall the Dodgers lost four in a row—the World Series—to Baltimore. A wacky bumper sticker in California announced: MARY POPPINS IS A JUNKIE.

Labor troubles left New Yorkers without newspapers for 279 days in the mid-Sixties. The *World-Telegram, Journal-American,* and *Herald Tribune* merged into one paper, the *World Journal Tribune* —it was called the *Wijit*—which failed after nine months. After 190 years, superstition finally killed the two-dollar bill; the Treasury Department stopped printing the bills on August 10, 1966, citing "a lack of public demand."

The fall elections of 1966 marked a political turning point. Resentment against ghetto riots and civil rights demonstrations had finally coalesced, making white backlash a potent political force for the first time. Combined with inflation, high interest rates, a scarcity of mortgage money, and the rising cost of living, backlash provided Republican candidates with a powerful springboard. George Romney and Nelson Rockefeller were re-elected with huge majorities. Among the new Republican faces in the Senate were Howard Baker Jr. of Tennessee, Edward W. Brooke of Massachusetts, Mark Hatfield of Oregon, and Charles H. Percy of Illinois; new Republican governors included Ronald Reagan of California and Spiro T. Agnew of Maryland. Altogether the Republicans picked up three seats in the Senate, eight new governors, and 47 seats in the House of Representatives, more than they had lost in 1964.

But by then Johnson had lost interest in legislation. Increasingly, he had become preoccupied with the Vietnam War, believing that its outcome would determine his place in history. Nearly every night at 3 A.M., according to his brother, Sam Ealy Johnson Jr., he would "crawl out of bed, wearily slip on his robe and slippers, then go down to the Situation Room in the basement of the White House to get the latest reports coming in from Saigon."

He was increasingly isolated. Robert A. McNamara, Secretary of Defense in this administration as he had been in Kennedy's, was losing confidence in the ability of bombing to bring the enemy to his knees. McNamara was now engrossed in a fantastic scheme for building an electronic barrier across the waist of Vietnam to stop infiltration from the North. When he abandoned that, his faith in military technology would collapse. Soon the chief White House consultant on Vietnam would be Walt Rostow, whose relation to the embattled and lonely war President, said another aide, was "like Rasputin to a tsar under siege." The conservative 90th Congress would join Rostow in goading Johnson on, passing huge military appropriation bills, encouraging him to sink ever deeper in the Vietnamese mire.

By then it all seemed inevitable. Yet it hadn't been. After his rout of Goldwater, Johnson's consensus had been genuine. The nation had been behind him. His goals had been the country's goals. It had been a time of great hope for him and for the American people, and few gauged correctly the threat from "a raggedy-ass little fourth-rate country," as Johnson once called Vietnam. One member of the First Family was worried, though. "I just hope," Mrs. Johnson had said in the middle of 1965, "that foreign problems do not keep on mounting. They do not represent Lyndon's kind of Presidency."

Thirty-one

A DREAM OF GREATNESS—AND DISENCHANTMENT

President Kennedy had devoted his inaugural address to foreign affairs; President Johnson's four-thousand-word inaugural—which was delivered so slowly and deliberately that one observer said it sounded as though the President were dictating to a stonemason—almost ignored events abroad. The same was true of his second State of the Union message; Vietnam was covered in exactly 131 words. Considering what was to come, the emphasis on economy was odd. ("Last year we saved almost 35 hundred million dollars by eliminating waste in the national government. [Applause.] And I intend to do better this year. [Louder Applause.]") Johnson said that he wanted to be remembered as "the education President and the health President." He intended to complete the unfinished business of the New Deal and the Fair Deal.

He was also going to keep faith with Kennedy. From the New Frontier he had inherited four big bills: civil rights, a proposed tax cut, Medicare, and federal aid to education. Priority went to the first two, but he shepherded all of them through Congress. The battle for Medicare was a spectacular confrontation between a President who was a master parliamentarian and the mighty American Medical Association lobby. In 1945 President Truman had appeared personally before a joint session of Congress to ask for a comprehensive medical insurance program; the AMA had beaten him soundly, and he had taken it hard. This time, five presidential administrations and sixteen congressional sessions later, the AMA doctors came forward with something called Bettercare, which was to be voluntary, handled by the private insurance industry—and wholly inadequate, for the number of Americans over sixty-five had more than doubled since the Truman years.

To battle Johnson the AMA employed twenty-three full-time lobbyists and spent $5,000 a day. The President countered with personal telephone calls and invitations to the White House. He twisted arms and he twisted hearts. On July 30, 1965, just 204 days after Johnson had asked for Medicare, he signed the bill in Independence with eighty-one-year-old Harry Truman beaming alongside. On July 1, 1966, Medicare eligibility came to 160,000 elderly hospital patients in the United States. A New Jersey embroidery worker named Eugene Schneider, sixty-five, entered Polyclinic Hospital in New York at 12:01 that Friday, and treatment for his eye was paid for by the Social Security Administration, making him and Mrs. Robert Avery of Napierville, Illinois, the first Medicare patients. An Associated Press survey indicated that the program had increased hospital occupancy by 3 percent—about 100,000 new patients a week.

Five days after his call for Medicare Johnson had sent Congress another historic message, "Toward Full Education Opportunity," asking a billion dollars for public and parochial schools. Providing federal money for Catholic education was a profound break with the past and a guarantee of searing debate in the House. But Johnson knew that of the forty million American children in school, about six million were in overcrowded parochial schools—schools which would have to be replaced with public money if the church abandoned them. Moreover, excluding them had alienated Catholic legislators on the Hill, who had retaliated by voting against federal funds for public schools. Johnson had decided to include all, and he let it be known that he wanted no amendments, no changing of so much as a comma. All things were possible for him in the 89th Congress—the "Xerox Congress," Goldwater was beginning to call it—and the measure went through both houses of Congress in eighty-seven days. Designating it "the most important bill I will ever sign," the President staged this signing ceremony in the one-room Texas schoolhouse he had attended as a child, with his teacher, now seventy-two and retired, beside him.

A voting rights bill was next, a response to the ever more insistent civil rights movement. The measure was ready for his signature August 6. By now a blizzard of Great Society legislation was sweeping through Congress—over forty bills for education alone, including 2.4 billion dollars for college aid, more education legislation than in all American history until then. There were Johnsonian programs to fight heart disease, strokes, cancer, water pollution, air pollution, roadside billboards, and auto junkyards. Congress established a Department of Housing and Urban Development, a National Foundation for the Arts and the Humanities, and an Administration on Aging. A High-Speed Ground Transportation Act opened the way to a study of mass transit problems. The immigration service was reformed. A big excise tax cut—4.7 billion dollars—was approved. Farm legislation and a Public Works and Economic Development Act gave the federal government a strong role in dealing with the changing face of the land for the first time since the 1930s.

Over 900 million dollars was set aside to deal with America's oldest rural slum, Appalachia. Under the ebullient leadership of Sargent Shriver, who had been the first director of the Peace Corps, the new Office of Economic Opportunity declared war on poverty. OEO programs included Job Opportunities in the Business Sector (JOBS), to provide special help in job placement for the hard-core unemployed; Head Start, for preschool children from poor families, which brightened the future for 1,300,000 of them in its first year; Volunteers in Service to America (VISTA), in effect a domestic peace corps; the Neighborhood Youth Corps, providing a half-million part-time jobs for teen-agers; Upward Bound, enrolling pre-college youths in campus programs; the Community Action Program (CAP), coordinating local health, housing, and employment programs and offering the poor free legal advice; Foster Grandparents, to work with children without homes; and agencies to work with Indians, migrants, and seasonal workers.

Critics christened the Washington office building in which the OEO leased seven floors "The Poverty Palace." Republican Congressman Albert Quie of Minnesota said the OEO undertaking "could become not just a national disgrace but a national catastrophe." Richard Nixon said, "The war on poverty has been first in promises, first in politics, first in press releases—and last in performances." And even Shriver conceded that administration of the most successful of the OEO programs, Head Start, was marred in one state (Mississippi) by nepotism, conflict of interest, misuse of government automobiles, and payments to people who weren't even in the state.

But time would be kind to the OEO, as it was to Roosevelt's WPA. In five years the war on poverty programs would play a key role in lifting thirteen million people out of pauperism. Another part was played by Johnsonian prosperity. The Great Society appeared to be on its way, and Americans seemed appreciative; at the end of Johnson's second year in office the public opinion surveys reported that no other President in their thirty years of polling had received such strong, consistent support throughout the country.

His landslide triumph over Goldwater would have tempted another President to ride roughshod over Congress. Not Johnson; he remembered vividly how Roosevelt, after his great victory in 1936, had been humbled by the defeat of his plan to reorganize the Supreme Court. "I've watched the Congress from either the inside or the outside, man and boy, for more than forty years," he said in the aftermath of the 1964 election, "and I've never seen a Congress that didn't eventually take the measure of the President it was dealing with." Rather than aim for a spectacular Hundred Days, he said, he would send each bill to the Hill only when the legislators were ready for it. He explained: "It's like a bottle of bourbon. If you take a glass at a time, it's fine. But if you drink the whole bottle in one evening, you have troubles. I plan to take a sip at a time and enjoy myself."

The final result was stunning. When the first session of the 89th Congress rose on October 23, it had approved 89 major administration bills and rejected just two: home rule for the District of Columbia and repeal of Section 14(b) of the Taft-Hartley Act, permitting states to ban union shop contracts—and it had been by no means clear on the Hill that the President really wanted the Taft-Hartley change. He was entitled to rest on his laurels. He didn't do it. Ever dissatisfied, he kept casting about for new ways to dominate the news and convert his critics.

One of the oddest was a summit meeting with Soviet Premier Alexei N. Kosygin in Hollybush, the turreted stone home of the president of Glassboro State College in New Jersey. Glassboro was chosen because it was exactly halfway between Washington and U.N. headquarters in New York, where Kosygin was staying; neither leader would call on the other; the little campus was a compromise. The two leaders had no agenda—had, indeed, nothing specific to talk about. Afterward Johnson said, "It helps to try to reason together. That is why we went to Hollybush. Reasoning together was the spirit of Hollybush." There was little else to say, other than that "the exchange of views once more revealed profound differences between the United States and the Soviet Union." The President's popularity rating soared just the same. The very fact that the two men, with nuclear arsenals at their disposal, had talked together seemed to reassure people.

Yet there were many who were not reassured, who regarded Johnson with scorn and often with contempt. LBJ-haters continued to be found in large numbers among the creative communities in large cities and on university faculties. Visiting the United States in 1965, the British journalist Henry Fairlie wrote: "I have found nothing more strange or unattractive than the way in which American intellectuals take pleasure in reviling President Johnson." Fairlie noted that the strictures were "personal" and reflected a "fastidious disdain for the man. . . . He is a slob, one of them said to me. . . . Others say much of the same, if less briefly."

Dwight Macdonald, one of the most caustic of them, wrote of "tasteless, crude" Lyndon Johnson and minted a word, "midcult," to mock the President's middlebrow taste. Macdonald and others like him ridiculed Mrs. Johnson because her favorite television program was *Gunsmoke*. They despised LBJ for enjoying the New Christy Minstrels, telling photographers to "Use my left profile," disliking Peter Hurd's portrait of him, having a daughter who changed her name from Lucy to Luci, and calling the work of serious artists "artsy." Their discontent spread to the much larger number of Americans who were vaguely offended by Johnson's mountebank manner. Millions of others were susceptible because they had loved John Kennedy, grieved for him still, and irrationally felt that Johnson was a usurper. To all these, eventually, were added the vast mass of Americans who felt troubled or even threatened by the escalating violence in the Negro slums in large cities and the growing turmoil on campuses. Johnson's insistence that he was in charge made him an inviting target, and they let fly at him.

At the end of his unprecedented string of legislative successes on the Hill in 1965 he entered Bethesda Naval Hospital for the removal of a stone-obstructed gallbladder. Convalescing, he brooded about the newspapers, which had been baiting him, and his taunters, "those people out there." In exasperation he blurted out, "What do they want—what *really* do they want? I'm giving them boom times and more good legislation than anybody else did, and what do they do—attack and sneer! Could FDR do better? Could anybody do better? What *do* they want?"

Senator Eugene McCarthy, whose role in the collapse of Johnson's consensus would become crucial, found half of the solution to the riddle when he suggested that Johnson was a kind of anachronistic President, providing New Deal remedies—social welfare legislation—for a nation whose dilemmas were very different. It was arguable, for example, that affluence, not poverty, was the great domestic challenge of the 1960s. McCarthy said that the President completely misjudged the temper of the liberal intellectuals: "he keeps going to them with the list of bills he's passed—the laundry list—and he doesn't know that they aren't interested any more."

Johnson raged, "Don't they know I'm the only President they've got?" Sometimes he would add, "Don't they know there's a war on?"

They knew. That was the other half of the answer to the riddle.

After the Gulf of Tonkin incidents there was a lull in American activity in Vietnam until November 1, 1964, when five U.S. military advisers were killed and 76 wounded in a Viet Cong mortar attack on an air base at Bienhoa, twenty miles north of Saigon. On Christmas Eve the guerrillas struck again, planting a bomb at the Brink's Hotel in Saigon. American casualties there were two dead and 58 wounded, and Lyndon Johnson's patriotic instincts were aroused. He strode around the White House saying that he wasn't going to let them kill our boys out there, that they were firing on the flag, that he'd show them he wasn't any "Chamberlain umbrella man." Plainly the North Vietnamese were guilty of aggression. ("Aggression is when one country won't let another one alone. Everybody knows when that is happening.") But depending on the United Nations to act would be a mistake. ("It couldn't pour piss out of a boot if the instructions were printed on the heel.") He wasn't going to go down in history as the President who lost Vietnam. The United States had the power to teach these little-biddy, raggedy-ass Communists a lesson. The Tonkin resolution gave him the authority to use it, and if the Viet Cong didn't back off he would do just that.

The difficulty was in deciding which approach to take. This new enemy, being unconventional, resisted conventional military solutions. The mighty American martial establishment wasn't equipped to deal with their hit-and-run tactics. President Kennedy had sent to Vietnam a 400-man Special Forces group, experts in antiguerrilla warfare, but the Joint Chiefs were unenthusiastic about these husky elitists. At one time, of over a hundred American generals in MACV, not one had gone through counterinsurgency training at Fort Bragg, North Carolina. And of all of them, none was more of a traditional soldier than MACV's new commander, William Childs Westmoreland.

What the Chiefs wanted was heavy bombing of North Vietnam. That would bring the enemy to his knees, they told the White House, and it would also bring him to the negotiating table. Clearly the bombing mystique had a powerful hold on the Johnson administration. Why this was so is less obvious. Two influential Democrats, George Ball and John Kenneth Galbraith, had participated in the U.S. Strategic Bombing Survey after World War II. That study had found that Allied bombing had not only failed to cripple German war production; it had strengthened the morale of the German people. And Germany was highly industrialized. If the Air Force had failed there, certainly its chances against the economy of a backward Asian country were at best doubtful.

Not all of Johnson's advisers had faith in the bombardiers. Ball and Galbraith didn't, and they were far from being alone. Early in 1964 the State Department's Policy Planning Council had conducted an exhaustive survey of the bombing question. The conclusion was that bombing North Vietnam would be ineffective, that it wasn't even likely to boost spirits in South Vietnam. Pier de Silva, John Richardson's successor as CIA station chief in Saigon, thought bombs would be useless; so did Westmoreland. As West Point graduates, both men knew that if you brought in planes you would need troops to protect the landing fields—that the decision to bomb would therefore bring the United States in all the way. Early in 1965, CIA analysts in Saigon completed two lengthy new reports on the same issue. The gist of them was that unleashing the bombers would be worse than futile; there was a strong probability that it would boomerang by touching off a massive infiltration of North Vietnamese troops down the Ho Chi Minh Trail.

That should have given the White House pause. At the very least the President ought to have listened intently to the counsels of caution. But something mysterious was happening to the doves, as opponents of escalation were beginning to be known. There were fewer and fewer of them in the halls of power. In October of 1964, when George Ball at State submitted his first memorandum protesting further American involvement in the war, he had plenty of company. Then, one by one, his allies were transferred or eased out of key positions. Roger Hilsman, Averell Harriman, Michael Forrestal, Paul Kattenburg, William Trueheart—all were gone by the time of Johnson's inaugural. Ball stood alone. Maxwell Taylor, who had agreed with Ball about bombing, was still an insider, but Taylor had changed his mind. He now wanted a green light for the Air Force. He thought the U.S. troop level in Vietnam could be controlled and need never rise above 100,000.

Now only one major White House special assistant was still uncommitted. He was McGeorge Bundy, the President's national security adviser. On January 27, 1965, Bundy proposed that he visit Vietnam as the President's eyes and ears. McNamara concurred, and Johnson's security aide flew to Asia in the first week of February. It was a fateful trip. Bundy was brilliant and experienced, but he had never served in the field. All he knew of war was in memos and reports or on celluloid. The grime and the stench of combat were new to him, and when he encountered them he suffered a physical revulsion. Above all—and this would be decisive—he could not stand the sight of blood.

On the evening of February 5, while Bundy was being feted in Saigon, Spec. 5c Jesse A. Pyle of Marina, California, was taking up sentry duty in a foxhole outside a U.S. stronghold at Pleiku, a mountain town in Vietnam's central highlands. He was still there at 2 A.M. when he saw shadowy figures in black pajamas moving toward him through underbrush. Pyle opened fire; the Viet Cong guerrillas replied with a storm of grenades; Americans in their nearby barracks awoke and joined the fight. The Battle of Pleiku lasted fifteen furious minutes. At the end of it the guerrillas had demolished or damaged sixteen helicopters and six aircraft. Eight U.S. soldiers, Pyle among them, were dead. Another 126 were wounded.

At 2:38 P.M. in Washington, the first account of Pleiku reached the President. After a four-hour National Security Council meeting he ordered Navy jet fighter-bombers from three carriers to attack a Viet Cong staging area at Donghoi, forty miles north of the 17th Parallel. Whether or not the American combat role would grow, he announced, was a decision which "lies with the North Vietnamese aggressors." McNamara said, "I think it's quite clear that this was a test of will." But the most unexpected result of Pleiku was its impact on the President's national security adviser, who, being on the spot, visited the wounded and came away deeply moved. He flew home a hawk. "Well, they made a believer out of you, didn't they?" the President said to him. "A little fire will do that."

Ball was still opposed to the bombing. Vice President Hubert Humphrey was also against it, and he expressed himself so forcefully that Johnson, who now regarded such doubts as unmanly, excluded him from National Security Council meetings. The United States had entered the critical period of decision. McNamara later remarked that all the U.S. errors in Vietnam—and he conceded that there had been many—were committed by the late spring of 1965; after that, he said, there was no way out. In Washington it seemed that the Viet Cong was bent upon provoking the U.S. into massive intervention. Less than three days after Pleiku, black-pajamaed guerrillas blew up the Viet Cuong Hotel, a barracks for American soldiers in the Annamese port of Quinhon; 23 enlisted men were killed and 21 injured. Johnson, infuriated, gave orders for a three-hour bombing of Chanh Hoa and Chap Lee, military depots in North Vietnam.

On February 11 the Viet Cong hit Quinhon again. This time LBJ stayed his hand for forty-eight hours. When he did move, however, it was to take a long step down the road of escalation. Henceforth American reprisals from the air were not to be on a one-for-one, tit-for-tat basis. Instead Johnson ordered a sustained bombing campaign against the North, to be mounted without regard for provocation. Its code name was to be Operation Rolling Thunder. The justification for it was set forth in a sixty-four-page white paper, *Aggression from the North,* which, the State Department said, established "beyond question that North Viet Nam is carrying out a carefully conceived plan of aggression against the South." To defend Da Nang air base, fifty miles southeast of Hue, from which Rolling Thunder would be launched, General Westmoreland asked for two Marine Corps battalions. These 3,500 marines were the first U.S. ground troops to be committed to the war. On March 8 they splashed ashore under overcast skies at Nam O Beach, three miles from Da Nang. Awaiting them were ten smiling Vietnamese girls with flowers.

Elsewhere the landing was more controversial. In Moscow two thousand demonstrators hurled rocks and bricks at the American embassy; two western foreign correspondents were roughed up there. In the United States the teach-ins spread and reached a climax in Washington, where Bundy agreed to debate his critics on a program which would be broadcast to over a hundred campuses. (At the last minute he had to withdraw; the President needed him to deal with another foreign crisis in the Dominican Republic.) The administration sent a "truth team" to visit universities and reply to the charges of faculty doves. Dean Rusk caustically told the American Society of International Law, "I sometimes wonder at the gullibility of educated men and the stubborn disregard of plain facts by men who are supposed to be helping our young to learn—especially to learn how to think."

But the more the critics of the war learned about its South Vietnamese ally the stronger their reservations became. Half of U.S. aid, they learned, was going into the Saigon black market. Vietnamese youths from opulent families were buying their way out of the draft. The desertion rate in the South Vietnamese army was 15 percent. And the politicians in Saigon seemed to have a genius for bad timing. It seemed that at every critical moment in the conflict whatever government was in power would be overthrown by a new regime. Johnson, angered, told his staff that he wanted "no more of this coup shit," but he got it just the same. On February 21, 1965, Lieutenant General Nguyen Khanh was ousted and succeeded by Phan Huy Quat, a physician. (The secretary general of the junta behind Quat was Major General Nguyen Van Thieu, from this point forward a man to watch.) The Quat administration lasted exactly 111 days. When it toppled (the ninth change of government since Diem's assassination) the new prime minister was the colorful chief of the Vietnamese air force, Nguyen Cao Ky, and Thieu was deputy prime minister.

Each new sign of instability in Saigon increased the ranks of the doves, who were rapidly replacing the Republicans as Lyndon Johnson's most effective political opposition. Former Secretary of the Army Cyrus Vance said misgivings about the war were "threatening to tear the United States apart," and in the Senate Frank Church of Idaho, one of the first senatorial doves, warned: "There are limits to what we can do in helping any government surmount a Communist uprising. If the people themselves will not support the government in power, we cannot save it . . . The Saigon government is losing its war, not for lack of equipment, but for lack of any internal cohesion."

That was not yet a popular position, however. When Johnson asked for a 700-billion-dollar supplemental appropriation to finance the escalation, the House approved, 408 to 7, in twenty-four hours, and the Senate followed suit, 88 to 3, in another twenty-four hours. In the popular press a certain stigma was attached to disapproval of American participation in the war. When Majority Leader Mike Mansfield gloomily told the Senate that it might go on "for four, five, or ten years," an Associated Press writer called this an "extreme view." (It was to be eight years.) In its annual review of that year's news the AP, ordinarily the most impartial of institutions, also reported that opponents of the war were giving aid and comfort to enemies of the United States. And when Senator Fulbright held Vietnam hearings in April, providing a forum for such distinguished critics of administration policy as George Kennan and General James Gavin, twenty-four NBC-TV stations refused to carry their network's coverage of them, while CBS-TV blacked them out entirely.

The war was becoming steadily hotter for the Americans in Vietnam. On March 30 a Vietnamese driver parked a black Citroën in front of the U.S. embassy in Saigon and roared off on a companion's motorcycle. In the car were 250 pounds of explosive, which went off at 10:55 A.M., tearing a hole in the side of the building and killing seventeen embassy employees. The next day U.S. planes bombed six North Vietnamese radar installations. It was their fifteenth raid across the border between the two Vietnams since Pleiku. The Viet Cong countered with more explosives. A bicycle loaded with nitroglycerin was parked one evening on the bank of the Saigon River beside My Canh, a floating restaurant popular with foreigners. When it went off forty-four people, twelve Americans among them, were killed. Still the U.S. troop buildup went on. At the beginning of the year there had been some 25,000 American servicemen in the country; by the end of spring the number had tripled.

On June 9 the White House announced that General Westmoreland had been authorized to send U.S. soldiers and marines into battle "when other effective reserves are not available and when in his judgment the general military situation urgently requires it." Four days later Westmoreland decided that circumstances at Dong

Xoai, a district capital sixty miles north of Saigon, justified American intervention. After a clash in the night, 1,200 paratroopers of the U.S. 173rd Airborne joined 1,600 Vietnamese and Australians in aggressive pursuit of the guerrillas. Westmoreland called this a "search and destroy" mission, a phrase which would be used henceforth to describe the strategy, which evolved in these months, of seeking out and then wiping out Viet Cong bands. It was to be a costly and often frustrating process. The Dong Xoai melee was characteristic of the war; after the smoke had cleared it was impossible to say which side had come off best. All the commander of the 173rd could be sure of was that he had lost nineteen men. The casualty lists swiftly lengthened, for the Viet Cong were in the second month of their spring offensive. Long afterward Westmoreland would describe this as the time that the enemy won the war. No one knew it at the time, however. That same month Westmoreland asked Washington for forty-four fresh battalions and authority to use them as he saw fit, and he could not guarantee that even that would do the job.

It was in this period that Lyndon Johnson's deviousness and secretiveness began to shrivel public trust in him. Referring to it on May 23, a copyeditor on the *New York Herald Tribune* put the phrase "credibility gap" over a story by David Wise, the newspaper's White House correspondent. Then Murray Marder of the *Washington Post*, in an article analyzing the feeling, widespread in Washington, that the President was sometimes careless with the truth, wrote: "The problem could be called a credibility gap." Johnson's glittering peace promises in the 1964 campaign were being recalled and contrasted with his new martial stance. Marder noted a "growing doubt and cynicism concerning administration pronouncements in Washington." Reporters were particularly susceptible to it. Because the President had denounced Senator Goldwater for proposing the very policies he himself was now adopting, the press was becoming skeptical of new olive branches being extended by the White House.

Speaking at Johns Hopkins University on April 7, the President declared that the United States was ready for "unconditional discussions" leading toward a negotiated peace. The address was carried around the world by the U.S. Information Agency, and many of its details sounded new and exciting. He proposed that the nations of Southeast Asia, including North Vietnam, join in a crash

Marshall Plan, and he said, "For our part, I will ask Congress to join in a billion-dollar American investment in this effort as soon as it is under way." U.S. farm surpluses would be sent to hungry Asians. He would "shortly name a special team of outstanding, patriotic, distinguished Americans" to guide the United States in all this. An end to the Vietnam War would, of course, be "necessary for final success. But we cannot and must not wait for peace to begin this job." It was all very sensible. It made Asia sound like central Texas.

David Wise's suspicious article was written in the aftermath of this speech, when many flaws in the President's proposition had become apparent. His proposal for truce discussions did have a condition, after all; he ruled out participation by the Viet Cong, which guaranteed Hanoi's rejection of it. Nothing more was heard about the billion-dollar commitment by the United States or the offer of U.S. surplus crops, and the panel of distinguished Americans was never chosen. Within a month what had appeared to be an imaginative approach to the problems of Southeast Asia had taken on the aspect of a publicity stunt. Not only had the President failed to follow through on any part of it; he was showing his real Asian policy in ever more vigorous prosecution of what was fast becoming a major American war.

The first six weeks of Rolling Thunder had been a total failure. Bombing hadn't brought the enemy to his knees, to the negotiating table, or even to what the Johnson administration conceived to be his senses. The Viet Cong were as disrespectful of the American flag as ever. The President decided to raise the ante again. In the third week of April he flew to Honolulu for a two-day conference with Ky and Thieu. Afterward McNamara announced that U.S. aid to Saigon in 1965 would jump from 207 million dollars to 330 million. Another 40,000 American soldiers—"grunts," as they had begun calling themselves—were ordered to Vietnam. Senator Gruening asked Johnson how long winning the war would take, and the President's answer was six months. Hanoi wouldn't be able to stand the bombing longer than that, he said; the Viet Cong would be begging MACV for terms before Christmas.

George Ball was deeply troubled. Intelligence, he knew, pointed toward a very different conclusion. John McCone reported that the CIA concluded the bombs were neither crippling Hanoi nor frightening it. Instead the raids were strengthening the hand of the hard-liners there. One North Vietnamese regiment had already been identified in South Vietnam, and a second was forming at the border. McCone told the National Security Council that a higher American troop level would be met by increased infiltration from the North; the U.S. troop transports on their way to Saigon would be neutralized before the grunts could even be landed. The Pentagon replied that the Air Force was preparing to commit its eight-engine B-52s, designed for nuclear weapons, and that nobody could stand up to B-52s, Phantoms, and F-111s.

But the air war was no longer the only event, nor even the main event, for the Americans in Vietnam. The U.S. military role there was subtly changing. The objective of the American troops was not limited to the protection of airfields now. The grunts were going to intimidate the guerrillas, persuading them that Uncle Sam meant business. Americans at home were unaware of the shift. Afterward James Reston would comment that the President had escalated the war by stealth. Under Johnson, David Halberstam would write years later, the decision makers in Washington "inched their way across the Rubicon without even admitting it" while the task of their press officers became "to misinform the public rather than inform it."

The next quantum jump in Washington's MACV commitment came in July. McNamara returned from his sixth fact-finding tour of Vietnam to report "deterioration" and recommend pledges of more men and more money. Johnson summoned his generals and advisers to Camp David for the weekend of July 17 to find a consensus, though the word, as he used it, had lost its original meaning; for him it had come to mean a ritual of agreement with a decision he had already made—to raise the number of U.S. troops in Vietnam by 50,000. The Joint Chiefs concurred reluctantly. They had hoped for much more; their greatest fear was involvement in partial war. Some of the men at Camp David refused to go along. "Whatever we do," Clark Clifford said prophetically of the Communists, "they will match it." Mike Mansfield also objected, telling the President that he was opposed to sending any more troops, that he thought the war would divide the country. The others approved of the President's judgment; the domino theory, mutual security, containment, and the lesson of Munich still outweighed their misgivings.

After locking up the decision Johnson became furtive. He wanted no further debate. McNamara proposed a reserve call-up of 235,000 men. Instead the President doubled draft calls administratively, raising them from 17,000 to 35,000 a month, on the ground that it would attract less notice than a call-up. He also decided against asking Congress for more money. The new costs could be hidden in the Defense Department's huge budget. He said he didn't want to scare anyone, and for a time he considered making public only part of the increase in troops for Vietnam. Douglas Kiker of the *Herald Tribune* asked him about reports of the expansion. Rumors, Johnson assured him, nothing but rumors; he was just filling out a few units, and accounts predicting that U.S. troops in Vietnam would pursue the Viet Cong aggressively were also untrue. On July 28 he changed his mind and announced the full figure, together with the new, forceful nature of MACV's mission, thereby alienating Kiker and widening the credibility gap. "We did not choose to be the guardians at the gate," the President told an estimated 28 million Americans on noonday television, "but there is no one else."

Distrust was one evil crop he sowed that summer; another was eventual misunderstandings among those he was herding into consensus. The Joint Chiefs thought he was keeping the figures low until he could persuade the civilians that he must go higher; they were counting on an eventual force of a million men. Westmoreland, watching Hanoi reinforce at a faster rate than anyone dreamed possible and sending Washington reports of it, planned on between 640,000 and 648,000 Americans ultimately under his command, confident that when he needed them they would be there. His staff had a contingency plan under which the MACV force level could reach 750,000, a figure which it thought was both sensible and justifiable. But the assumption of the Secretary of Defense was the strangest of all. Years afterward it would still be comprehensible only to those who understood Robert McNamara's very orderly mind and his belief that disorderly events could be made to conform to it. McNamara arbitrarily decided in 1965 that the war would be over by June 30, 1967, the end of that fiscal year. It would be a perfect time for him, making his budget come out even, and he clung to it even after Westmoreland told him that it was impossible.

In one respect, however, McNamara and the Pentagon were more realistic than the White House. The Joint Chiefs urged the President to raise taxes. Their reasoning had nothing to do with economics. They wanted to see the country on a total war footing, and their textbook solution to civilian apathy was higher taxes. As it happened, the economists in the administration wholeheartedly agreed with them. Gardner Ackley, the Michigan professor who headed Johnson's Council of Economic Advisers, told the President that the administration could not have three things—prosecution of the war, continuance of his Great Society programs, and the absence of inflation—unless taxes were raised.

But this was the period in which Johnson was passing huge amounts of social legislation through Congress. If the true cost of the war were known, he feared, that process would come to a shuddering stop. "I don't know much about economics," he said to those around him, a confession that some of them later thought should be engraved on his tomb, "but I do know the Congress. And I can get the Great Society through right now—this is a golden time. We've got a good Congress and I'm the right President and I can do it. But if I talk about the cost of the war, the Great Society won't go through and the tax bill won't go through. Old Wilbur Mills will sit down there and he'll thank me kindly and send me back my Great Society, and then he'll tell me that they'll be glad to spend whatever we need for the war."

At this point he made the ultimate blunder. He fooled himself. Everything would come out all right, he reckoned, if victory could be bought cheap. Maybe that would happen; maybe Hanoi and the Viet Cong guerrillas would collapse. In that event, the estimates from the Pentagon would be overestimates. The wish became father to the thought, and when Ackley and his colleagues became insistent about the need for a 3 to 4 percent tax increase, the President responded by staging an extraordinary charade. Key Congressmen and leaders of the business community were invited to the White House and asked for their opinion about higher taxes. They in turn inquired about the cost of the war. He gave them phony figures. Thereupon they rejected the idea of a tax increase. Johnson then told the Council of Economic Advisers that a tax hike was impossible; he couldn't get it through Congress. Later Edwin Dale Jr., economic correspondent of the *New York Times*, called this the most single irresponsible presidential act in his fifteen years of covering Washington.

Johnson's decision against a tax raise, made in early 1966, was a stupendous blow to fiscal sanity. The federal deficit that year was 9.8 billion dollars. Even deeper vats of red ink lay ahead, for by then the war was costing between two and three billion dollars a month. The estimate the White House was putting out was 800 million dollars, and when Ralph Lazarus of the Business Council said the government's figure was much too low, he received an indignant call from Abe Fortas, who told him that his calculations were wrong and were upsetting the President. Actually Lazarus was right on target. The war cost 27 billion dollars that year, and the deficit was a catastrophic 23 billion dollars. Johnson's legerdemain had brought the beginnings of runaway inflation.

Of all the war's aspects, perhaps the most incomprehensible was the lack of real planning. David Halberstam would later find that "the principals never defined either the mission or the number of troops. It seems incredible in retrospect, but it is true. There was never a clear figure and clear demonstration of what the strategy would be." All that was apparent in 1965 was that the numbers were going ever higher. U.S. soldiers were pouring into Vietnam in August, and by September it was obvious that the troop level was going to top 200,000.

Checking reports of a battle near Saigon, Peter Arnett of the Associated Press drove out of the capital to find clouds of smoke in three colors, South Vietnamese troops in action—and no enemy. He was told that the soldiers were making a color movie for the United States Information Service, "to show how things really are here." Arguments over how things really were there were going full blast on all fronts, including the home front. Lyndon Johnson talked at times as though he were responding to a personal challenge from Ho Chi Minh, the two of them striding toward one another in a *High Noon* confrontation. Terrorist bombings seemed closer to the truth in Saigon, where the list of atrocities lengthened; at dawn on December 4 another truck loaded with 250 pounds of explosives went off, this time outside the Metropole, a hotel for American servicemen; eight were killed and 137 wounded.

Westmoreland's spokesmen often sounded preoccupied with the daily "body count," a singularly insensate phrase which was used to describe Viet Cong casualties. To correspondent Neil Sheehan the war was typified by the enormous casualties among innocent civilians resulting from indiscriminate shelling and bombing. Sheehan asked Westmoreland if it didn't bother him, and the general replied, "Yes, but it does deprive the enemy of the population, doesn't it?"

In 1965 Americans demonstrating against the war were still a relative oddity in most of the country. Few people wished to be counted in favor of immediate, unconditional U.S. withdrawal from Indochina. Even college faculties, one of the most dovish groups in the country, were to be evenly divided as late as 1967 on the issue. Nevertheless, the vigor of the peace movement was already phenomenal. On the weekend of October 15–16 a crowd estimated at 14,000 paraded down Manhattan's Fifth Avenue. Simultaneously another 10,000 marched on the Oakland Army Base—they were turned back at the city line by police—and 2,000 demonstrated in Berkeley. Elsewhere during this "weekend of protest," as it was heralded, fifty students from the University of Wisconsin tried to arrest the commanding officer at Truax Air Force Base as a "war criminal," and protesters staged a "lie-in" at a draft board office in Ann Arbor.

The Fifth Avenue Vietnam Peace Parade Committee declared:

> We demand that no more American youth be sent to fight in a war that is helping neither them nor the Vietnamese people. We have learned lessons from Nazi Germany, and will not go along with the aggressive war-making policies of any government, even if it happens to be our own.

That was reasonable, but elsewhere the rhetoric of the demonstrators, like the war itself, was becoming hateful. It was in Washington the Saturday after Thanksgiving that 20,000 of them first chanted, "Hey! Hey! LBJ! How many kids did you kill today?" Members of the May 2nd Movement (M2M), named for May 2, 1964, when they first took to the streets to protest American involvement in the war, trooped around the White House carrying Viet Cong flags and advertised "bleed-ins" at which blood was collected for North Vietnamese soldiers. In Berkeley the Free Speech Movement had been succeeded by the Vietnam Day Committee, which twice tried to halt troop trains by occupying cars and sitting on the tracks.

On October 15, 1965, a new feature was introduced in demonstrations when David J. Miller, a twenty-two-year-old volunteer in a relief program, mounted a sound truck in New York, announced, "Instead of the speech I prepared I'll let this action speak for itself" —and held a match to his draft card. Miller was arrested a few weeks later, but burning Selective Service cards enjoyed a brief vogue, despite congressional action on August 31 making it a federal offense punishable by a $10,000 fine or five years in jail. Acts of self-immolation continued to be the ultimate protest; a Quaker outside the Pentagon and a Catholic relief worker outside the United Nations turned themselves into human torches.

Counterpickets from the American Nazi Party carried jerricans and placards reading, "Free Gas for Peace Creeps." As usual, nobody wanted any part of them. The tone of most antiprotest protests was relatively mild. A girl in New York carried a sign reading, "I Wish I Had a Draft Card." Earnest demonstrations were organized by the Young Americans for Freedom, the American Legion, and the Veterans of Foreign Wars. "Bomb Hanoi" was the most belligerent sentiment on signs of most of them. Placards at a typical march in Florida read, "We Love America," "Love Our Country," "My Country—Right or Wrong," "Will We Let Them Bury U.S.?" and "No Glory Like Old Glory." Bob Hope told one audience that "If we ever let the Communists win this war, we are in great danger of fighting for the rest of our lives and losing a million kids." That was an extravagant statement, but it was hardly in the same category with accusing the President of murdering children.

The gravest charges lodged by those favoring the war were suggestions that the other side was disloyal. "We won't creep around in the dark with candles like these traitors do," said the police chief of Charlestown, West Virginia. "We'll march at high noon and let free people fall right in and march behind us." Some newspaper accounts of peace vigils in 1965 were inclined to hint broadly at Communist participation, and the FBI, which like Hope was shedding its nonpartisan reputation, virtually credited all such protests to the Kremlin. A government report said: "Control of the anti-Viet Nam movement has clearly passed from the hands of the moderate elements who may have controlled it at one time into the hands of the Communists and extremist elements who are openly sympathetic to the Viet Cong and openly hostile to the United States."

In fact the reverse was true. Despite the inflammatory language and provocative behavior of individual antiwar militants, each demonstration tended to be more respectable than the last. Middle-class conservative housewives and even servicemen in uniform were joining the movement. So, increasingly, were celebrities who felt a pull opposite to Bob Hope's. When stop-the-bombing marchers formed under cloudless skies in Washington on November 27, their number included, in addition to Norman Thomas and James Farmer, such strangers to political action as Dr. Benjamin Spock, cartoonist Jules

Feiffer, novelist Saul Bellow, sculptor Alexander Calder, and author Michael Harrington.

That autumn dispatches from Vietnam reported that famous American military units were being mauled in Vietnam. It was the 101st Airborne Brigade at An Khe in September, the Green Berets at Plei Me in October, and, in November, the 1st Cavalry Division in the Ia Drang Valley. The encounter at Ia Drang, a week before the stop-the-bombing march in Washington, was of special significance; like the Viet Cong offensive the previous spring and the Tet offensive of early 1968, it was a turning point in the war. Troopers of the 1st Cav, pursuing enemy detachments in the aftermath of the Plei Me engagement, met stiff resistance in the valley, near Chu-pong Mountain, seven miles from the Cambodian border and two hundred miles north of Saigon in Vietnam's central highlands. This time the Americans faced not Viet Cong guerrillas, but the North Vietnamese 66th Regiment.

The 66th, an elite unit of the North Vietnamese army, faced a severe test. The 1st Cav was something new in military history, a heliborne division, equipped to take maximum advantage of superior American firepower. The tactics of the Communists, who knew all about the battlefield weapons designed by inventive Americans, called for grappling with the grunts at the closest range, hand to hand if possible, but at most within thirty-four yards, thus nullifying U.S. artillery and tactical air support.

The implications of the Ia Drang fighting were bound to be great. At the time of the Camp David conference in July there had been just two North Vietnamese regiments in the South. Now MACV had confirmed the presence of six regiments from the North, with two more probable and another possible. Others were on their way; General Vo Nguyen Giap, Ho Chi Minh's commander, was continuing to break up his battalions into companies and platoons and send them down the trail faster than the Americans could bring in transports.

Both sides rushed reinforcements into the valley, and although a 1st Cav battalion, flown in, was ambushed and badly chewed up, when it was all over Westmoreland and his deputy, General William Depuy, claimed a victory. The figures seemed to support them; the enemy, attacking in waves like the World War II Japanese and yelling in English, "Kill GI!," had lost 1,200 to the Americans' 200.

But other observers, among them John Paul Vann, who had returned to Vietnam as a civilian, had reached a very different conclusion. The Communists were prepared to accept such losses indefinitely. ("It is," one Viet Cong soldier wrote in his diary, "the duty of my generation to die for our country.") But the U.S. toll in Ia Drang, although much smaller, was a record for Westmoreland's troops; it put American casualties in the war at 1,335 dead and 6,131 wounded. While MACV believed that Westmoreland had found the strategic key to triumph and was eagerly planning more Ia Drangs, Giap took the Vann view. The North Vietnamese general was convinced, and events were to confirm him, that the American people would not accept such casualties in an open-ended commitment. Giap regarded the new phase of the war as a contest between his manpower and Westmoreland's technology, with U.S. public opinion as the referee.

In December McNamara urged a bombing pause on Johnson. Objections came from Rusk, now one of the toughest of the hawks, but the President grounded the B-52s and sent out diplomatic scouts to key world capitals, spreading the word that Washington was ready for peace. Two Italian professors arrived in Hanoi to sound out Ho. At first negotiations seemed possible, but just as word reached Rusk that the Communists were in a conciliatory mood, Hanoi denounced the whole thing as "sheer, groundless fabrication." The Americans were taken aback. After Ia Drang, they thought, it should be obvious to Ho that he faced defeat. The marines were reminded of the tagline of an old Corps joke: "There's always some son-of-a-bitch who doesn't get the word."

In appealing to a joint session of Congress for the voting Rights Act of 1965, Lyndon Johnson concluded his speech with a phrase which had become hallowed by the blood and tears of a new generation of black Americans marching for justice. He said that their cause "must be our cause too. Because it's not just Negroes, but really it's all of us who must overcome the crippling legacy of bigotry and injustice. *And we shall overcome.*"

That was fine liberal eloquence, but at times during the year it appeared to be a doubtful prediction. The eleventh anniversary of the Supreme Court's ruling in Brown v. Board of Education passed on May 17, and racism seemed stronger than ever. C. Vann Woodward, Sterling Professor of History at Yale, said, "Negroes now have less contact with whites in schools than they did a generation ago." Between the middle of 1964 and the middle of 1965 the Ku Klux Klan made its greatest membership gains ever, including the Reconstruction era. In October of 1965 a Birmingham black reportedly bled to death because a white ambulance driver refused to take him to a hospital. An Alabama businessman, speaking of civil rights pickets, casually remarked to a *New York Times* correspondent, "The niggers are going to be in trouble around here when this is all over." The racial climate was not much better in the northern cities; speaking in Marquette Park, on Chicago's South Side, Martin Luther King Jr. said, "I have never seen such hate, not in Mississippi or Alabama, as I see here in Chicago." The attitude of millions of whites seemed symbolized in a lapel pin worn by Dallas County Sheriff James G. Clark Jr. in Selma. It simply read, "Never." Never, it appeared, would men like Clark, in the North as well as the South, accept Negroes as equals.

Confronted by this prejudice, the black mood continued to change. There was a splintering into various camps, many hostile to one another. The assassination of Malcolm X by fellow blacks in upper Manhattan's Audubon Ballroom on February 21, 1965, just as he had reached the threshold of leadership, reflected the depth of the division among the black militants. A sign of Negro despair was the upsurge in groups advocating "repatriation"—a "return to the African homeland." The Deacons for Defense were formed in some fifty Black Belt communities to combat the KKK. Others followed the preaching of Le Roi Jones, who told them that "The majority of American white men are evil"; and of James Forman, who issued a Black Manifesto demanding that white churches and synagogues (the very white institutions, ironically, which had been most ardent in support of the civil rights movement) pay Negroes 500 million dollars in "reparations."

The Muslims became the most famous of the groups advocating separatism, and in Oakland the first tiny pack of Black Panthers emerged in 1966. Daniel Patrick Moynihan came forward in November 1965 with the Moynihan Report, a closely reasoned document which argued that realistic approaches to internal problems in the Negro community must first deal with the worst legacies of slavery: Negro welfare dependency, a divorce rate 40 percent higher than that of whites, and the appalling rate of illegitimacy, one black birth in four being out of wedlock. Moynihan's facts were undisputed, but such was the Negro agony that year, and so shattering the impact of events on Negro pride, that blacks could not face them. Their leaders therefore branded the report racist propaganda and denounced its author as a "fascist."

C. Vann Woodward wrote in 1965 that "insofar as federal laws are capable of coping" with segregation and prejudice, "Congress has just about fulfilled its role." The capstone of such legislation was the voting act of that year. In January Martin Luther King called a press conference to point out that three million of the five million blacks in the South old enough to vote were not registered, and to announce that he was launching an all-out registration drive. It would open in Selma, Alabama, where 325 of 15,000 potential black voters were registered, as against 9,300 of 14,000 whites. Typically, Dr. King led the first group of Negroes ever to stay at Selma's Hotel Albert, previously all-white, and typically he was punched and kicked by a white segregationist while signing the hotel register. His assailant was fined one hundred dollars and sentenced to sixty days in jail, which King thought was a good start toward respect for the law, but then the drive stalled. The blunt truth was that most of Selma's Negroes were indifferent to the right to vote. Something dramatic was needed to arouse them. It was provided—again, this was characteristic—by rural whites who murdered a black would-be voter in nearby Perry County. Local civil rights leaders counted on that, on Sheriff Jim Clark's short temper, and on Governor Wallace's showboating to revive their campaign.

They declared that on March 7 they would stage a protest march. Negro and white sympathizers would hike from Selma to Montgomery, fifty-four miles away, moving straight down the middle of route 80, the Jefferson Davis Highway. Wallace promptly banned the demonstration as a menace to commerce and public safety and sent a hundred state troopers to reinforce Sheriff Clark, who gave a sign of his allegiance to the past by rounding up a mounted posse. On March 7—which would enter Alabama history and folklore as "Black Sunday"—six hundred Negroes and a few white partisans of their cause defiantly marched from the Brown's Chapel African Methodist Episcopal Church to the Edmund Pettus Bridge, spanning the Alabama River. There they ran into Clark's horsemen and troopers wearing gas masks. When they ignored a two-minute warning to disperse, possemen waded into them swinging billy clubs and wet bullwhips. Yellow clouds of tear gas belched from the ranks of the troopers. Routed, the blacks stumbled and crawled back to the church. Accompanying them were television cameramen, whose footage guaranteed that Selma would become overnight a symbol of oppression.

Dr. King had been preaching in Atlanta on Black Sunday. Dropping everything, he flew to Selma, announced that he would lead a second march on Tuesday, and called on clergymen of both races to join him. Over three hundred white ministers, priests, and rabbis responded. Sympathy demonstrations were held in all the great cities of the North. Black activists staged sit-ins at the Department of Justice and the White House, and President Johnson issued a statement blaming Alabama officials for "the brutality with which a number of Negro citizens were treated." He sent John Doar and former Governor LeRoy Collins of Florida to Selma, and they succeeded in arranging a token march, back and forth across the bridge. Sheriff Clark and Dr. King agreed with many misgivings, which in King's case were justified. Militant black youths from SNCC accused him of Uncle Tomism. Coming off the bridge, they mocked him by singing the civil rights song "Ain't Gonna Let Nobody Turn Me Around."

King was turned around that same evening by the first of three murders arising from the Selma crisis, all of whites who sympathized with the civil rights movement. The Reverend James J. Reeb, a Boston Unitarian, was set upon by red-neck hoodlums as he left a Negro restaurant and beaten to death. James Forman of SNCC and five hundred of his followers then threatened to mutiny if Dr. King didn't take a bolder line. An angry crowd of fifteen hundred blacks held a rally in Montgomery's Beulah Baptist Church. King had encouraging news for them. A federal judge, Frank M. Johnson Jr. of Montgomery, had agreed to allow the march from Selma to Montgomery; although such a procession "reaches to the outer limits of what is constitutionally allowed," he had ruled, the mistreatment of the demonstrators had obviously surpassed "the outer limits of what is constitutionally permissible."

Governor Wallace, addressing a televised joint session of the Alabama legislature, condemned the imminent march as comparable to Communist "street warfare" that "ripped Cuba apart, that destroyed Diem in Vietnam, that raped China—that has torn civilization and established institutions of this world into bloody shreds." The state couldn't afford to protect all these outside agitators, he said, and he telegraphed the White House, calling upon the federal government to enforce the decision of the federal judge. That was exactly what Lyndon Johnson had been hoping he would do. The President now had an official request from Wallace to protect the demonstrators, and he complied by sending 1,863 federalized National Guardsmen, 250 U.S. marshals and FBI agents, two regular Army MP battalions, demolition experts to search the road and bridges ahead of those making the hike, and helicopters to hover overhead. In addition, the hikers were provided with huge tents for overnight stops, a 600-gallon water truck, latrine trucks, ambulances, trucks for rubbish, and scout cars to set up campsites in advance. Johnson was showing a little garter.

The march itself was a triumph. Veterans of the movement had become astute at providing TV cameramen with colorful material. Leading the procession were Dr. King, Ralph Bunche, a pretty coed, a sharecropper in overalls, a rabbi, a priest, a nun, and a one-legged marcher on crutches. (The white Alabamans along the way, hopelessly ignorant of how to cultivate a good image, made obscene gestures at the nun and guffawed while chanting, as a cadence for the man with one leg, "Left, left, left.") Although the Alabama legislature indignantly—and unanimously—fulminated against "the evidence of much fornication at the marchers' camps," behavior along the route was peaceful and orderly, a remarkable achievement in light of the number of people involved. Leaving Selma on March 21 there had been 3,200 in the procession; arriving in Montgomery four days later there were 25,000. Dr. King spoke to them on the grounds of the statehouse, which a century ago had been the capital of the Confederacy. He ended by crying four times, "Glory hallelujah!" They disbanded and heavy traffic carried them back on route 80 to Selma. A sullen clump of Ku Klux Klansmen watched them go. As the stream of cars thinned the Klansmen moved in for the second murder.

The victim was Viola Gregg Liuzzo, a red-haired Detroit housewife and the mother of five. Mrs. Liuzzo had told her husband, an agent for the Teamsters Union, "This is something I must do," and after the victorious rally on the statehouse lawn she volunteered to ferry Alabama marchers to their homes. On her last trip she was singing "We Shall Overcome" with her only passenger, a nineteen-year-old Negro barber, when a car full of Klansmen drew alongside on a lonely stretch of road. One of the white hoodlums, an auto mechanic, fired a 38-caliber pistol at her head. She collapsed with blood spurting from her temple; the car careened into a ditch; the terrified young barber hitchhiked into Selma for police help.

The third killing was of an Episcopalian seminarian from New Hampshire who was gunned down in a grocery. The killer, a part-time deputy sheriff, pleaded self-defense and was found innocent by a jury of twelve white Alabama men, though no weapon had been found on the seminarian and witnesses said there had been none. In the death of the Reverend Mr. Reeb, three men were charged a few hours after he had been battered to death. They, too, were acquitted; their jury deliberated just ninety-five minutes. The trial of Mrs. Liuzzo's murderers was the most interesting of the three. One of the Klansmen in the death car had in fact been an undercover man for the FBI; he identified each of his companions, their weapons, and what they had done and said. They were defended in their first trial by Matt H. Murphy Jr., a third-generation Klansman. Murphy's summation was one-hundred-proof racism: "When white people join up with them [blacks], they become white niggers. . . . God didn't intend for us to mix with the black race, I don't care what Lyndon Baines Johnson says." The FBI man, Murphy said, was a violator of his Klan oath, "as treacherous as a rattlesnake . . . purporting himself to be a white man and worse than a white nigger." That jury was hung (10 to 2 for conviction of manslaughter), but Murphy had made his last bow; he was killed in an auto accident during the interval before a second trial. A biased judge presided at those proceedings, which ended in an acquittal, but then the federal government stepped in and tried the Klansmen for violating Mrs. Liuzzo's civil rights. That curious law, which had been the downfall of the Klan killers in Mississippi's Freedom Summer and of the slayers of a Negro Army officer in Georgia, worked once more here with another jury of twelve southern men, and the judge sentenced the defendants to ten years, the maximum.

Selma inspired the voting rights act—Johnson said as much in asking Congress for it on March 15—and the country credited it to Dr. King. It proved to be the peak of his reputation. The events of the previous year in Mississippi having created the first serious doubts about nonviolence, the Alabama murders confirmed the suspicions of the new generation of black activists. These skeptics left Selma convinced that King had nothing more to teach them. The vast majority of the Negro people disagreed; in a subsequent CBS public opinion poll where anonymity was preserved, only 4 percent said they would give active support to Stokely Carmichael, 2 percent to the more militant H. Rap Brown, and 1 percent to Ron Karenga, the most militant of the three, while 40 percent backed the ideals of Dr. King. Nevertheless, the activists had correctly gauged a change in mood. The majority yearned for peace—a majority has always wanted it—but the country was entering a new period, and one of its most striking qualities would be an affinity for violence. In retrospect the death of President Kennedy and the murder of his assassin now seemed to have been omens. Once more a gear had shifted somewhere in the universe. Search and destroy, emerging in Vietnam during the same months in 1965, was one expression of the emerging mood, the Selma murders were another; still others would crowd upon one another in the succeeding months and years as Negro rage and frustration which had been repressed for a century now erupted.

The new inner city temper emerged in Los Angeles on Wednesday, August 11, 1965, in a shabby Negro district of low, faded stucco houses, suggestive of certain poor areas in Puerto Rico, which lay under the approaches to Los Angeles International Airport. Trash never seemed to be properly collected there. There was litter everywhere—broken glass, rusty cans, rotting chicken bones, empty Tokay bottles—and the quality of life was further diminished by the typical white policeman, also known locally as The Man, who had a way of stopping black citizens and demanding, "Let's see your I.D."

That August evening Lee Minikus, an officer of the California Highway Patrol, wanted a look at the I.D. of a young Negro named Marquette Frye; he intended to take him in on suspicion of drunken driving. A knot of people, gathering around, kidded both Minikus and his suspect. It all seemed low-key and harmless, but beneath the surface tension was building. Los Angeles was in the fourth day of a brutal heat wave. People were outdoors, ready to assemble quickly at the promise of excitement. The arrest was taking place at the corner of Avalon Boulevard and Imperial Highway, a busy L.A. intersection through which passed a constant stream of white drivers, often behind the wheels of expensive cars. Most inauspicious of all was the neighborhood. It was 98 percent black, with a population density of 27.3 people per acre (the figure was 7.4 for Los Angeles County as a whole). Negro immigrants had been arriving here in massive numbers since the early 1940s, when an average of 2,000 each month came to work in war industries. Now 420,000 of the 2,731,000 inhabitants of the city were black. Yet in this ghetto there were just five blacks on the 205-man police force. And every month in 1965 another 1,000 Negroes poured into these swarming warrens, often looking for jobs that no longer existed. The temptations of drugs and alcohol awaited their children, and when the children went wrong The Man came after them. These snares, not the inhabitants, were the real transgressors in this district, a region known locally as Watts.

At 7:45 P.M. that Wednesday, California Highway Patrolman Minikus took the Frye youth into custody. Almost immediately he was in trouble. Among those attracted by the winking red light of his squad car was the prisoner's mother. At first she rebuked her son. Then she turned on the police officer. As her manner became distraught and the murmurs of the spectators less good-humored, Minikus nervously radioed for reinforcements. Then he made two mistakes. He attempted to force Frye into the squad car and he turned his back on Frye's mother. She jumped on it. As other officers arrived they pried her loose, and when the crowd began to mutter indignantly they held it at bay with shotguns. Minikus got away with his man, but the price had been exorbitant. Already the use of force was beginning to inspire distorted accounts of what had happened, and with each passing hour the stories grew taller. Two versions were widespread. One had it that a cop had struck a pregnant woman in the belly with his club. In the other, a cop had pushed a woman against the patrol car and tried to choke her. Aroused, the crowd pelted policemen with stones and bottles. By 10 P.M. the spectators had been transformed into a mob which set upon passersby, overturned cars, and smashed shop display windows. The familiar stages of riot escalation now appeared. Police sealed off eight blocks at 11 P.M. Two hours later the rioters burst free and roved Watts, two thousand strong, waylaying strangers, breaking everything fragile, and looting the stores.

At 3 A.M. the level of violence fell—rioters must sleep, too—and police patrols imposed a semblance of order in the ghetto. In the morning shop managers called their insurance companies, clerks cleaned up the mess, and those who knew nothing about riots assumed this one was over. Their disillusionment began at 7:45 P.M. that Thursday, just twenty-four hours after the arrest of young Frye. At first it was all a repetition of Wednesday evening: youths pouncing on passing autos, pelting cops with bricks, breaking windows. The change came at 4 A.M. At that hour the day before, a peace of exhaustion had fallen over the ghetto. This time a second shift of rioters spilled into the streets. These men were older and more vicious. They were also armed. Dick Gregory toured Watts with a bullhorn, begging for order, and was shot in the leg. The ghetto violence was approaching the force of an insurrection, but the authorities didn't realize it yet; a flying wedge of policemen cleared Watts's darkened streets and then announced that the situation was under control.

The truth was revealed to them at 10 A.M., when two white salesmen were attacked in the first incident of daytime violence. At 11 A.M. a policeman wounded a black looter. Governor Edmund Brown, on vacation in Greece, read reports of the growing disorders and hurried home; his lieutenant governor granted a request from the L.A. police chief for National Guard troops. The first contingent of Guardsmen reached Watts Friday afternoon. Even as they were being briefed in an elementary school the version they heard was being outdated by new developments in the ghetto. More than 5,000 rioters now roamed a 150-block area, firing buildings with Molotov cocktails and ambushing firemen who answered the alarms. Watts claimed its first fatality, a sheriff's deputy mortally wounded in the stomach, at 9:40 P.M. Three other deaths quickly followed. National Guard soldiers entering the district with fixed bayonets saw looters, their way illumined by a hundred major fires, carrying guns, appliances, liquor, jewelry—everything of value—from the shops of the ghetto. Crudely lettered signs outside some stores read "Black Brother," "Soul Brother," "Negro Owned," and "Owned by a Brother." Some had been robbed anyway. One gang was trying to burn Oak Park Community Hospital, which was crowded with Negroes hurt in the disorders. Robert Richardson, a black *Los Angeles Times* reporter, wrote: "The rioters were burning their city now, as the insane sometimes mutilate themselves."

On Saturday snipers on rooftops began picking off soldiers and policemen. Firemen were issued bulletproof vests. The Guard force grew to 10,000 men, then to 14,000; a curfew was imposed on 40 square miles Saturday and on 46 square miles Sunday. Intermittent shoot-outs continued until the early hours of Wednesday, August 18, when officers seized 35 blacks after a gunfight at a Black Muslim mosque. That was the end of it. During the six days of madness 34 had been killed, 898 hurt, and over 4,000 arrested. Losses were put at 45 million dollars.

The Watts devastation was called the worst race riot since Detroit in 1943, but it was really in a class by itself. While the death toll was the same, the damage in Detroit had been less than a million dollars. There was trouble elsewhere, too. Coincident with Watts, the West Side of Chicago ran amok when a fire truck, answering an alarm in West Garfield Park on August 12, struck and killed a black woman. Negroes fought cops and 2,000 Guardsmen for two nights, looting and hurling bottles at whites. Over 100 were arrested and 67 hurt. And in Springfield, Massachusetts, far from the ghettos of the great cities, the arrest of eighteen blacks outside a nightclub gave rise to accusations of brutality against seven cops; Molotov cocktail bombings of stores owned by whites then led to mass arrests and, once more, the calling of the National Guard. A protest march by 4,000 Springfield Negroes ended at City Hall, where George Wiley, assistant national director of CORE, told them that "the civil rights struggle in the North" would be "longer, bloodier, and more bitter" than it had been in the South.

It was characteristic of the 1960s that each outbreak of violence was followed by the appointment of a commission to study it. Governor Brown picked a panel of eminent citizens led by John A. McCone to look into Watts. Their findings were published under the title *Violence in the City: An End or a Beginning?* By then everyone knew that Watts was only a beginning, but the searches for remedies followed various paths. The McCone Report came down hard on the need for law and order. Black militants protested that objection to laws oppressing Negroes was what Watts had been all about. Bayard Rustin called it "the first major rebellion of Negroes against their own masochism." Theodore H. White thought that television and radio reporting shared some of the responsibility. White charged that it had gone "beyond reporting and become a factor in itself," and he asked, "Can electronic reporting be curbed in the higher interest of domestic tranquillity?" Martin Luther King, touring the smoking ruins of Watts, received a mixed welcome. He was growing accustomed to this. The torch had been passed to the new generation of black leaders, and it had become a real torch.

If the summer of racial disorders had been hot in 1965, it had also been short. Until Watts burst into flame that second week in August there had been hope that the country might make it that year without a major riot. The next year was a different story. Again Los Angeles sounded the tocsin, but this time it was in March that a gang of Negro students stoned the auto of a white teacher there, attacked other whites, and turned to looting. Angeleno policemen had learned a lot the year before; this new threat was suppressed overnight with only two deaths. Yet if L.A. escaped with fewer scars, the rest of the nation did not. It almost seemed as though every large black community in the United States was in rebellion against society. In Washington, D.C., Negroes rose in April. By May three California cities were embattled. Cleveland erupted in late June, and Omaha, Des Moines, and Chicago two weeks after that. Next came Cleveland, and then in swift succession Brooklyn, Baltimore, Perth Amboy, Providence, Minneapolis, Milwaukee, Detroit, Dayton, Atlanta, San Francisco, and St. Louis; Pompano Beach, Florida; Cordele, Georgia; Cicero, Illinois; and Lansing, Muskegon, Benton Harbor, and Jackson, Michigan. By the end of the summer the toll was seven dead, over 400 hurt, some 3,000 arrested, and more than five million dollars lost to vandals, looters, and arsonists. By the end of 1966, America had been scarred by forty-three race riots that year.

In Cicero a Negro march for open housing ran into a counter-demonstration by hostile whites, who repeatedly tried to lunge past police to harm the blacks. Twelve were hurt; six officers were hit by missiles; 32 of the whites were arrested. Cicero was of special interest because it demonstrated that policemen, far from starting riots, often held together a fragile peace; when Negroes went after them it was often because the cops represented authority and were the only whites in sight. In working-class communities whites often matched, and more than matched, the black rage. The tension between the races was felt on both sides. It was in 1966 that backlash came into its own.

Originally the open housing demonstration had been in Cicero's Marquette Park and led by Martin Luther King. He called it off when a rock hit him and knocked him to his knees. Robert Lucas, Chicago chairman of CORE, defiantly sponsored the new march, explaining that "CORE wants to keep the pressure on." Lucas was one of the new militants, and 1966 was turning into their year, too. Floyd McKissick replaced the more moderate James Farmer as head of CORE and Stokely Carmichael succeeded John Lewis as chairman of SNCC. The development was not as auspicious for the movement as they thought. Carmichael had been in office just a month when an event that none of the civil rights leaders had taken seriously showed the extent of the divisions in their ranks.

On June 5 James H. Meredith announced that he was leaving Memphis to hike 225 miles to Mississippi's state capitol in Jackson. His motive was to prove that American Negroes were unafraid. The McKissicks and Carmichaels thought the idea impractical and visionary—"the silliest idea I ever heard of," one movement leader called it—and they decided to ignore him. Meredith was undaunted. Still guided by a feeling of "divine responsibility," as he had called it in *Three Years in Mississippi*, his account of his ordeal on the Ole Miss campus, he believed that destiny awaited him in his native state, and he was correct, destiny in this case being represented by a middle-aged, unemployed white Mississippian named Aubrey James Norvell. At 4:15 P.M. on the second day of the journey, Meredith and a convoy of FBI agents were striding along U.S. 51 just south of Hernando, Mississippi, when Norvell rose out of the bushes beside the road. "James Meredith!" he yelled. "James Meredith! I only want Meredith!" He fired three shotgun blasts. Doctors in a Memphis hospital found Meredith peppered with birdshot.

None of the wounds was serious. Norvell's real damage had been done to the notion that Meredith's walk needn't be taken seriously. The bursts of gunfire had turned it into a crusade, and everyone in the movement wanted to be part of it. Dick Gregory flew to Memphis to retrace Meredith's steps, and McKissick, Carmichael, and Martin Luther King headed south on foot from the stretch of pavement where Meredith had fallen. Dr. King, borrowing two thousand dollars to launch what he called the Meredith March for Freedom, ordered his Southern Christian Leadership Conference to mobilize resources for another Selma.

It wasn't possible. Selma had been an achievement of united Negro leadership advocating nonviolence. Now King's critics, and particularly those in SNCC, were out in the open. The day after Norvell's ambush Carmichael told a Memphis rally, "The Negro is going to take what he deserves from the white man." King deplored such demagoguery; Roy Whitney of the NAACP and Whitney M. Young Jr. of the Urban League agreed. But the rhetoric of the young militants became more bellicose. In Philadelphia, Mississippi, where in the Freedom Summer of 1964 death had come to three members of the movement—two of them white—a white Mississippian was wounded by gunfire in the dark, and Ralph Featherstone of SNCC, far from regretting the incident, exulted that blacks were no longer meek, that "their reaction is shot for shot." Carmichael spoke up for the Black Panther political party. In Yazoo City young Negroes chanted, "Hey! Hey! Whattaya know! White folks must go —must go!" and that night in the Yazoo City fairgrounds Willie Ricks, a twenty-three-year-old member of SNCC known as "the Reverend" because of his evangelical style, mounted a flatbed truck and delivered a sermon of hate that made older Negro leaders shudder. He spoke of the blood of whites flowing and repeatedly described his goal in two explosive words: "Black power!"

In Greenwood, forty-five miles away, Carmichael was emerging from seven hours in jail. In a way his plight was a consequence of his militancy. White liberals, dismayed by it, were being far less generous with contributions than they had been at the time of Selma. Food and shelter were a problem, and Carmichael had been arrested while trying to erect tents on a Negro school playground. He heard about Ricks's speech just as he himself was climbing another flatbed truck to address a Greenwood rally. Using the repetition and question-and-response techniques which civil rights leaders had adopted so successfully from Negro preachers, he reminded his audience that he had been apprehended by police in a Negro schoolyard. "Everybody owns our neighborhoods except us. . . . Now we're going to get something and we're going to get some representing. We ain't going to worry about whether it's white—maybe black. Don't be ashamed. We . . . want . . . black . . . power!"

They shouted, "That's right!" and he took up the theme: "We . . . want . . . black power! We . . . want . . . black . . . power! We want black power! We want black power! That's right—that's what we want. . . . Now, from now on, when they ask you what you want, you know what to tell them. What do you want?"

"Black power!"

"What do you want?"

"Black power!"

"What do you want? Say it again!"

"Black power!"

What did it mean? Roy Wilkins had no doubts: "The term 'black power' means anti-white power . . . It has to mean going it alone. It has to mean separatism. We of the NAACP will have none of this." Wilkins called the phrase "the father of hatred and the mother of violence." Martin Luther King said much the same thing at first, though later, seeing that the coalition of civil rights groups was coming apart over the issue, he hedged, interpreting it as "an appeal to racial pride, an appeal to the Negro not to be ashamed of being black, and the transfer of the powerlessness of the Negro into positive, constructive power." McKissick saw it as an appeal to joint action: "Unless we can get around to unifying black power, we're going to be in bad shape." But Charles Evers, brother of the martyred Medgar Evers and the ranking NAACP worker in Mississippi, warned that "If we are marching these roads for black supremacy, we are doomed," and A. Philip Randolph, deploring the war cry as "a menace to racial peace and prosperity" said that "No Negro who is fighting for civil rights can support black power, which is opposed to civil rights and integration."

A nationwide *New York Times* survey reported that the dissension among civil rights leaders in Mississippi was reducing public support for the movement. An opinion poll found that 77 percent of whites felt the black power creed was hurting the black cause. James Meredith agreed. "There seems to be a good bit of show going on down there," he said in New York, where he was convalescing. Fully recovered, he rejoined the march and was embraced by King and the others. Nevertheless his doubts remained. "I think something is wrong," he said, and he spoke of "some shenanigans going on that I don't like."

An open break between the old leaders and the new was inevitable. It came at Canton, near the end of the Meredith March, on June 23, after police had refused to let them pitch their tents on another school playground. Refusing to disperse, twenty-five hundred blacks stood their ground. Carmichael cried, "The time for running has come to an end." It hadn't really—when the police charged with nightsticks and tear gas the people scattered—but when King turned down a proposal that they try to put up the tents anyway, the SNCC leadership deserted him. One of them said, "What we do from now on we will do on our own." Then they proposed that the NAACP be excluded from the climactic rally in Jackson on the ground that its support of the march had been tepid. King and an organization of volunteer doctors and nurses, who had provided medical attention during the journey, opposed the resolution, but SNCC, CORE, and two other groups representing young blacks gave it a majority. Charles Evers said, "It's all right. I'll be here when they're all gone." He observed caustically that marches did nothing to register black voters. When the procession reached the statehouse grounds in Jackson, with a band playing "When the Saints Go Marching In," veterans of other civil rights demonstrations noted that the whites who had marched with King in other years were not there.

That did not end the liberal commitment to justice for blacks, of course. Nor did it block programs for Negro progress which were already under way. That same month a six-month boycott of white businesses in Fayette, Mississippi, ended with the hiring of black clerks in Fayette stores, the closing of filling station toilets for colored people, and the swearing in of black policemen and deputy sheriffs. Julian Bond, having been elected to the Georgia legislature three times in twelve months, was finally seated by order of the U.S. Supreme Court. In Selma Sheriff Jim Clark quietly removed his "Never" button as his job went on the ballot. It didn't save him; when Negro voters, registered under the voting act he had opposed, went to the polls, he lost.

Once it had been enough for all blacks that a few blacks made it. The entire race had been proud of the few. No more; typically, Carmichael quoted a Negro woman as saying that September, "The food that Ralph Bunche eats doesn't fill my stomach." The tool and die maker and the three-dollar-a-day cotton picker wanted their share, too. It was human and it was natural, but the militants' way of going about it was hopelessly unrealistic. Negroes constituted only 11 percent of the U.S. population. The talk of black revolution —and there was a lot of it in 1966—was senseless, and SNCC's demand that blacks reject integration was absurd.

Philip Randolph, appalled by the violent confrontations between slum blacks and policemen, suggested in September that "the time has come when the street marches and demonstrations have about run their course." He proposed a new approach, "a shift from the streets to the conference table." In October he, Wilkins, Young,

Rustin, and three other veterans of the civil rights struggle signed a statement repudiating violence, rioting, and demagoguery, and concluding: "We not only welcome, we urge the full cooperation of white Americans." Martin Luther King, while approving in principle, declined to sign on the ground that he did not want to give the impression that he thought the spokesmen for black power were "conclusively and irrevocably committed to error."

For a time Carmichael took a conciliatory line, redefining black power as "black people coming together to form a political force and either electing representatives or forcing their representatives to speak their needs. . . . saying, 'Look, buddy, we're not laying a vote on you unless you lay so many schools, hospitals, playgrounds and jobs on us.'" It didn't last. Soon he was telling audiences that "If we don't get justice we're going to tear this country apart," and calling on Negroes to "fight for liberation by any means necessary." In Prattville, Alabama, he said, "We came here to tear this town up and we're going to tear it up." He called President Johnson a "hunky," a "buffoon," and a "liar." Increasingly he identified himself with the Panthers, whose "Power to the People" slogan meant power to black people and no one else. Then, like Danton being succeeded by Robespierre, Carmichael was replaced as SNCC's chairman by an even more violent racist, H. Rap Brown. When much of downtown Cincinnati went up in flames during five terrible days and nights of Molotov cocktails, Brown told reporters that there would be no peace "until the honky cops get out." Then he said: "SNCC has declared war."

The backlash vote in the 1966 elections was one response to the call for black power. Another was a shift in position by such sensitive politicians as Senator Everett Dirksen. Dirksen had supported civil rights legislation in 1964 and 1965 as "an idea whose time has come," but he scorned the 1966 bill, with Title IV, the "open housing" clause, as "a package of mischief," and that killed it. Curiously, it was a British periodical, the *Economist* of London, which took the most critical view of the new militants. "Many of these 'leaders' are of a lurid fascist type," said the *Economist*. It derided "liberal intellectuals" who "insultingly tell one another that the general anti-white mood among black Americans is similar to the anti-German mood among the French in 1943," observed that "robberies and assaults on white women" were being interpreted by some activists as "almost a noble act of black revolution," and predicted that "a temporary and rather extraordinary toleration by the American people of flamboyant violence is almost certainly about to turn to a harsh white intolerance of it."

Meantime the black racists were flourishing. The Panthers were acquiring what Tom Wolfe pungently called "radical chic" among some affluent urban liberals, and criminals whose notoriety would once have been limited to the police blotter were being seriously discussed as observers with fresh insight into the human dilemma. All were creatures of the ghettos, and the rise of some could be traced directly to the recent riots. Ron Karenga came from the depths of Watts; although he denied that members of US, his black nationalist organization, had engaged in riot activity, four of them had been so charged. Karenga's celebrity was a consequence of the Watts upheaval. The full bill for that convulsion, it was becoming clear, was incalculable. Some of the highest costs would be hidden for years. One item in the legacy of violence was a snub-nosed, eight-shot 22-caliber Iver-Johnson revolver, model 55SA, bought for protection by a frightened Angeleno for $31.95 late in August 1965 in the wake of the disorders. Later he gave it to his daughter, who passed it on to a Pasadena neighbor, who sold it to an employee in Nash's Department Store named Munir "Joe" Sirhan. Eventually Joe turned it over to his kid brother, Sirhan Bishara "Sol" Sirhan, who used it to assassinate Robert F. Kennedy in Los Angeles three years after Watts.

In the twelve-year cycle of the Vietnamese calendar, the Year of the Snake, 1965, gave way to the Year of the Horse, 1966, which in turn was followed by the Year of the Goat, 1967. The Horse was supposed to be lucky, second only to the Year of the Dragon in auspiciousness, but almost half of America's total Vietnam dead by the end of the first ten weeks of 1966—2,559 men—had fallen to Communist guns and bombs in those ten weeks, and that, it turned out, was only the beginning. That year's toll was 4,800 U.S. soldiers killed in action. In May of the following year the total of U.S. dead passed 10,000, and as the war grew older, it grew bloodier. Average weekly losses in the Year of the Goat ran 33 percent higher than in the Year of the Horse. More men died in 1967 than in all the war's previous years. And during that same period there were 53,000 civilian deaths, a matter of increasing concern to the war critics at home.

The toll didn't deter the Pentagon from proposing an ever more vigorous, aggressive policy. The Joint Chiefs kept pressing McNamara to recommend to the President the bombing of petroleum, oil, and lubricant supplies (POL raids, they were called) in North Vietnam. Admiral U. S. Grant Sharp of CINCPAC predicted that this would "bring the enemy to the conference table or cause the insurgency to wither." McNamara finally agreed in March 1966, though the CIA prophesied that POL strikes would not halt infiltration of men and supplies. The CIA was right; despite heavy losses in combat, the number of North Vietnamese soldiers coming down the 1,000-mile Ho Chi Minh Trail grew from 1,500 a month to 3,500 and then to 4,000. By the end of the year Giap was sending an average of 8,800 men a month to the South. Soon the annual replacement rate would be 100,000 men.

Defense Department study groups advised McNamara that despite the bombing the flow of guerrillas southward was "undiminished" and that the raids "had no measurable direct effect" on Hanoi's capacity to make war below the 17th Parallel. The secretary flew over to see for himself; it was his eighth on-the-spot inspection. Returning, he told the President that "pacification has if anything gone backward," and that the air war had not "either significantly affected infiltration or cracked the morale of Hanoi." He recommended a reappraisal of the bombing campaign. The Joint Chiefs strenuously objected to any suggestion of a cutback in the raids. In a memorandum to the President they contended that the military situation had "improved substantially over the past year" and called bombing "a trump card." General Westmoreland, flying home to address a joint session of Congress, reported: "I have never been more encouraged in my four years in Vietnam. . . . We have reached an important point when the end begins to come in view."

McNamara was not encouraged. By now he had seen too many optimistic forecasts go glimmering. In Saigon he had spent a gloomy session with one of his men there who told him that the official cheerfulness was false, that there was no light at the end of the tunnel; the informant was Daniel Ellsberg. In fact Westmoreland was in Washington not to report victories but to ask for more troops. He had ended 1966 with 375,000. By April of 1967 he had 480,000, more than in the Korean War at its peak. He wanted 680,000 men by June 1968, or at the very least 565,000. With the higher figure, he told Johnson, he could end the war in two years; with the smaller figure it would take three years. The President noted unhappily that the Communist force in the South was at a record high. He asked the general, "When we add divisions, can't the enemy add divisions? If so, where does it all end?" Westmoreland said that if Giap's infiltration rate went much higher his supply problems would become difficult. Anyhow, the grunts were killing North Vietnamese quicker than they could be replaced. Johnson asked what would happen if Giap asked for Chinese volunteers. The general replied, "That's a good question."

Already American involvement in the Vietnam War had lasted longer than World War II or the Korean War. The conflict seemed more than ever a struggle between whites and Asians. MACV christened the battles with colorful names which became reminders of agony in the jungle and growing bitterness among an increasingly divided people at home. There was operation Attleboro, and Leatherneck Square, and operations Masher, Double Eagle, and White Wing. Then Dak To, Hill 881 North, Loc Ninh, and operations Crazy Horse, Hawthorne, and Hastings—Hastings, the costliest engagement since Ia Drang. And then Hill 881 South, Khe Sanh, the three red hills of Con Thien, and Ashu. The Iron Triangle, a three-cornered region of abandoned rubber plantations and rain forest between the Saigon River and Route 13 twenty miles north of Saigon, had been a Communist stronghold for twenty years. Operation Cedar Falls in January 1967, an attack on the Triangle by 30,000 grunts, was the largest American drive of the war till then. But operation Junction City, a month later, was even bigger: 45,000 American troops thrusting into Zone C near the Cambodian border to wipe out a Viet Cong base. They did it—and then had to let the enemy reclaim it, because ARVN (Army of the Republic of Vietnam) forces couldn't hold it, even as garrison troops.

Congress, meantime, was making dissent from Johnson's war policies respectable. By later standards the protests were muffled; addressing Hanoi, sixteen senators who opposed the administration's conduct of the war warned that there were limits to their dissent, that they were "steadfastly opposed to any unilateral withdrawal of American troops." Yet the Hill was growing restive. At the request of the President, five senators led by Mike Mansfield spent thirty-five days in Vietnam. When they issued their report Johnson was dismayed; they had found that a year of U.S. campaigning had not altered the progress of the war and that America was becoming trapped in an "open-ended" conflict: "how open is dependent upon the extent to which North Viet Nam and its supporters are willing and able to meet increased force by increased force." Senator Robert F. Kennedy charged that the administration had "switched" from the policy of his brother, so that now, "We're killing innocent people . . . because [the Communists] are 12,000 miles away and they might get 11,000 miles away."

That was the highest level of protest. Senatorial doves might object to Johnson's course in Indochina, but they voted him funds to continue on it, and their language was polite. Fulbright, the most outspoken of them, was never uncivil; when Westmoreland told a New York audience that he was "dismayed . . . by recent unpatriotic acts here at home" and accused the perpetrators of giving aid and comfort to the enemy, Fulbright merely replied that Westmoreland's visit had been planned by the administration "to pave the way for escalation," which was of course true. One step down was Martin Luther King, who called the United States "the greatest purveyor of violence in the world today," and compared American experiments with new weapons in Vietnam, where they were killing peasants, to Nazi tests of "new medicine and new tortures in the concentration camps of Europe." Eartha Kitt used much the same rhetoric in attacking the war at a White House luncheon given by Lady Bird. So did Dr. Spock in telling peace demonstrators that "Lyndon Johnson is the enemy"; so did folk singer Pete Seeger, censored by CBS for a number called "Waist Deep in the Big Muddy," which dealt contemptuously with the President's war policy ("And the old fool says, 'Push on'"), and Captain Howard Brett Levy, a Brooklyn physician who refused to train medical corpsmen assigned to the Army's Special Forces—Green Berets—on the ground that under the Nüremberg Doctrine he would thereby become an accessory to war crimes. One of the charges against Dr. Levy at his court-martial in June 1967 was that he had called the war a "diabolical evil." He was found guilty, sentenced to three years in prison, and led off in handcuffs.

Colleges and universities continued to be the centers of heavier protest. Job recruiters for the CIA, the Dow Chemical Company—manufacturers of napalm, the incendiary jelly—and the armed forces were treated roughly and sometimes ejected from campuses. The revelation on St. Valentine's Day 1967 that $200,000 a year in CIA funds had been subsidizing the National Student Association (NSA), which represented student governments on over three hundred campuses, was enough to cripple the NSA. Students provided the leadership for "Stop-the-Draft Week" in October 1967, including a march to the steps of the Pentagon by more than fifty thousand demonstrators, and they were responsible for imaginative and sometimes shocking protests against the draft—pasting eight draft cards on the door of the American embassy in London, battling Oakland police for five days while attempting to block buses carrying draftees from an induction center to military bases, and seizing and holding the administration building at the University of Chicago for three days to dramatize opposition to the war.

It was not all selfless idealism. College students were of the age most vulnerable to conscription, and as monthly draft calls in 1966 were boosted nearly tenfold over the 1965 average of five thousand, blanket deferments for students became rarer. Resistance to the draft was being expressed openly on posters, buttons, and bumper stickers. The theme of a 1967 hit tune, Arlo Guthrie's "Alice's Restaurant," was draft evasion, and virtually every undergraduate dormitory had a collection of leaflets providing tips on how to get rejected at Selective Service physical examinations. ("Arrive high. If you want to go about the addiction scene in a really big way, use a common pin on your arm for a few weeks in advance.") General Hershey struck back by sending a directive to the country's 4,088 draft boards instructing them to reclassify the protesters 1-A. Congressmen objected that Hershey was exceeding his authority, and the American Civil Liberties Union charged that using the draft to punish dissidents was "outrageous," but Hershey wouldn't back away. One consequence was that the flow of draft evaders to Canada grew until there were some ten thousand young American expatriates there, making new homes with the help of such groups as the Students Union for Peace Action in Toronto.

As the polarization of the country grew, the hawks became more hawkish. In response to back-to-back antiwar speeches by Morse of Oregon ("The United States is leading mankind into World War III out of which will come no victory") and Gruening of Alaska (who called a new war appropriation bill "a blank check for unlimited escalation"), Russell B. Long of Louisiana wrapped himself in the flag in attacking those who "encourage the Communists to prolong the war." Long said, "I swell with pride when I see Old Glory flying from the Capitol . . . My prayer is that there may never be a white flag of surrender up there." Everett Dirksen predicted that if Vietnam fell, "the whole Pacific coastline" of the United States would be "exposed." Manhattan hawks staged Operation Gratitude, a two-day vigil at Battery Park. At the same time, motorists who believed in the war were asked to drive with lights on—and suddenly every highway offered a vivid demonstration of how badly divided the people were.

Lyndon Johnson characteristically said one thing while believing the exact opposite. "No American, young or old, must ever be denied the right to dissent," he declared in June 1966, putting on his white hat. "No minority must be muzzled. Opinion and protest are the life breath of democracy—even when it blows heavy." His deeper feeling was that those who quarreled with his conduct of the war were un-American, and that it was his duty to battle them with any weapon that came to hand. Presidential publicity was effective, and at various times he conferred with Asian allies at Guam, Honolulu, Manila, and Melbourne, staging the trips to coincide with antiwar events he wanted to drive off the front page. It didn't always work. In Australia he discovered that American students weren't the only ones capable of mounting antiwar demonstrations; Melbourne hecklers tossed two plastic balloons filled with paint at his limousine, smearing it red and green, the Viet Cong colors.

His true feelings about opponents of the war boiled over on May 17, 1966, at a Democratic fund-raising dinner in Chicago, when he upbraided "Nervous Nellies" who "will turn on their leaders and on their country and on our own fighting men." By the end of that summer he was avoiding the phrase "Great Society." He had come to prefer the company of political conservatives to that of "knee-jerk liberals" who were such "trouble-makers that they force politicians to the right." In the privacy of the White House he would flatly state that Americans in the antiwar movement were disloyal, that "the Russians" were "behind the whole thing." The FBI and the CIA, he confided to his staff, were keeping him posted on what was "really going on." The doves in the Senate were in touch with Soviet agents, he said; they lunched with them, attended parties at the Russian embassy, and encouraged the children of their aides to date Soviet diplomats in Washington and at the U.N. He asserted, "The Russians think up things for the Senators to say. I often know before they do what their speeches are going to say." In June 1966 the parents of one of the winners of a Presidential Scholarship, a gifted seventeen-year-old girl, turned out to be critics of the war. Word went out to the staff that the girl was to be deprived of her medal. Eric Goldman protested and the order was rescinded, but Goldman was told that before Presidential Scholars were nominated in the future, they and their families would be subjected to FBI checks.

Hawks, following Johnson's example, saw the stain of disloyalty spreading. In 1966 CBS-TV showed marines in the "Zippo squads"—as they called themselves—setting fire to peasant huts, and the Pentagon virtually accused the commentators of treason. When McNamara opposed the bombing of Hanoi in a Montreal speech, noting that the weekly bomb tonnage dropped on North Vietnam already exceeded that of all the bombings of Germany in World War II, he too came under suspicion. He resigned in November 1967, joining Mac Bundy, George Ball, Jack Valenti, George Reedy, Richard Goodwin, and Horace Busby in the exodus of trusted Johnsonian advisers from Washington. The departure of Bill Moyers hurt the President most, but it was Johnson's equivocations which had made Moyers's role as press secretary untenable. Reston wrote of him that he had been wounded at Credibility Gap, and Moyers himself said that the gap had become so bad that "we can't even believe our own leaks." The President, stung by his resignation, accused Moyers of ingratiating himself with the Kennedys and exploiting the White House, using it to better himself at the expense of the administration. He read the clippings, LBJ stormed, and he wasn't stupid; he saw what had been happening; the press secretary had been getting a good press for himself while Johnson's grew worse and worse.

He was right about his public image. By 1967 it was terrible. The Secret Service disclosed that the number of people arrested for threatening the life of the chief executive had increased by over 500 percent since Dallas. The number of people holding Lyndon Johnson responsible for the death of John Kennedy was growing. By May 1967 there were, *Esquire* estimated, some sixty different versions of the Dallas tragedy on sale. Early that year District Attorney Jim Garrison of New Orleans told the press, "My staff and I solved the assassination weeks ago." Subsequent events made it plain that Garrison belonged in a padded cell, not a courtroom, but a Harris poll that May indicated that the number of Americans who doubted the Warren Report had jumped from 44 percent to 66. Many believed Garrison "had something"; others simply came to distrust everything about President Johnson, including the way he entered the White House.

His popularity dropped until in March 1968 Gallup's figures indicated that only 36 percent of the country approved of his conduct of the Presidency. Like Richard Nixon five years later, Johnson responded by withdrawing into a self-imposed isolation. During his campaign against Goldwater three years earlier he had alarmed the Secret Service by his way of wading joyously into seas of humanity. Now his public appearances were confined to reliable audiences —meetings of business executives or service families on military bases, where he could trust his listeners to be respectful. The White House became embattled. Getting past the gates became much more difficult; credentials had to be just so, and dispatch cases were rigorously searched. The President's staff urged him to get out among the people. Even if crowds were hostile the nation would sympathize and admire his courage. Anything would be an improvement on this seclusion. The Secret Service objected. Given the country's ugly mood, they felt that appearances before unscreened groups would be risky, and this time Johnson obeyed them.

More and more he kept watch on his staff and cabinet, alert for further defections. Those who wanted to stay, or who needed his approval for advancement now and his endorsement for future positions, felt they had to display excessive zeal and unquestioning devotion to him. Hubert Humphrey became a superhawk. Larry O'Brien drafted the dead in support of the war, telling an audience in Lexington, Virginia, that if General George C. Marshall were alive he would "no doubt" back Johnson's Vietnam policy in every particular. Nick Katzenbach, appointed attorney general, held in testimony before the Senate Foreign Relations Committee on August 17, 1967, that Congress had authorized the President "to use the armed forces of the United States in whatever way necessary" when it passed the Tonkin Gulf resolution three years earlier, and that this was indeed sufficient warrant for any military commitment the President might make in Indochina, including the bombing of targets close to the Chinese border. This exchange followed:

SENATOR FULBRIGHT: You think it is outmoded to declare war?

MR. KATZENBACH: In this kind of context I think the expression of declaring a war is one that has become outmoded in the international arena.

It was enough, Katzenbach said, that the Senate had approved of American participation in regional defense treaties, in this case

SEATO. He intimated that a President could do whatever he liked with U.S. military power without consulting Congress. At that point a member of the committee rose and strode angrily out of the room muttering, "There is only one thing to do—take it to the country." The senator was Eugene McCarthy of Minnesota.

It was in May 1967, the third and ugliest year of black violence, that Stokely Carmichael resigned as chairman of the misnamed Student Nonviolent Coordinating Committee and flew off to tour Cuba and North Vietnam. "You'll be happy to have me back," he said, referring to his successor, H. Rap Brown, as "a bad man." The rise of Brown was a triumph for militants bent on the rejection of integration and the alienation of white liberals. "If you give me a gun I might just shoot Lady Bird," he said on July 26, and he told Detroit blacks, "The honky is your enemy."

Whites were barred from a national conference on black power in Newark the weekend of July 20–23. The delegates took their theme from Malcolm X: "The day of nonviolent resistance is over." Among the measures they endorsed were resolutions calling for the formation of a "black militia," for "a national dialogue on the desirability of partitioning the United States into two separate nations, one white and one black," and for recognition of "the right of black people to revolt when they deem it necessary and in their interests." Integration was dead, the nearly one thousand delegates declared; absolute segregation of the races was the new goal.

The August 14 issue of Brown's SNCC *Newsletter* denounced Zionism, attacked American Jews, and accused Israel of crushing Arabs "through terror, force, and massacre." That drove from SNCC membership such liberals as Harry Golden and Theodore Bikel and drew the fire of the Anti-Defamation League of B'nai B'rith. The militants were undaunted. To be sure white sympathizers got the message that they were unwelcome, CORE dropped "multiracial" from the constitutional description of its membership. Speaking for CORE, Floyd McKissick issued a Black Manifesto declaring that sit-ins, boycotts, and peaceful demonstrations belonged to the past. "The tactics and philosophy of the civil rights era can take us no further along the road to total equality," he said. "New methods must be found; a new era must begin." The long, hot summers of rioting, he suggested, might be remembered in the future as "the beginning of the black revolution."

Some honkies seemed to take an almost masochistic pleasure in their mortification. Perhaps the most vivid example was the National Conference for New Politics (NCNP), held in Chicago over Labor Day weekend in 1967. The conference was attended by three thousand delegates representing over two hundred groups with varied goals, among them an end to the Vietnam War, better treatment of the poor, and equity for black Americans. The number of votes represented by each delegate was determined by the number of active members in his organization back home. Women Strike for Peace, for example, had 1,000 votes; the Camden Citizens for Peace in Vietnam 31 votes. Negro groups had 5,000 votes. They wanted more. "Black people can't be a plank in someone else's platform," said McKissick. "They must be the platform itself." Forming a Black Caucus, the Negro delegates issued an ultimatum of thirteen points. Among them were a demand for 50 percent black representation on all committees, censure of the "imperial Zionist war," and approval of all measures passed by the Newark conference. They demanded that all this be accepted without change by 1 P.M. that Saturday. An editor of *Ramparts* suggested a modification of the language but withdrew it when a member of the Black Caucus shouted at him, "What right has a white man got amending the black man's resolution?"

After an elderly white woman explained that this was merely a test of the NCNP's "social barometer," the thirteen-point program was accepted by a three-to-one vote. The delegates then gave themselves a standing ovation. Then they received a jolt. The Black Caucus was still dissatisfied. The caucus groups wanted not the 5,000 votes they had been allocated but 28,498 votes—absolute control of the convention. Negro speakers explained from the podium that it was all a matter of trust; whites had to prove that they trusted blacks by adopting the proposal. "An extraordinary development took place," one of the white delegates said afterward. "The walls of the Palmer House began to drip with guilt." Adoption passed, two to one. Thereafter the fate of each resolution before the convention was determined by a young Negro in the front row of the Black Caucus holding a large pink card that represented 28,498 votes. In fact, not much was accomplished. A sizable number of whites had come hoping to nominate a presidential ticket, Martin Luther King for President and Dr. Spock for Vice President. It died stillborn: the Black Caucus regarded Dr. King as a black honky, and Dr. Spock, in his old-fashioned way, still used the word Negro.

Despite Brown-McKissick rhetoric, the flow of blacks into the middle class was increasing. Census figures would later show that the number of Negro families with annual incomes over $10,000 increased from 11 to 28 percent during the 1960s. The way was opening up spectacularly for talented blacks. In 1965 Benjamin O. Davis Jr. became a lieutenant general in the Army. Secretary of Housing and Urban Development Robert C. Weaver, U.S. Senator Edward W. Brooke, Bishop Robert Perry of the Catholic Church, and Judge Constance Baker Motley of the federal bench all reached their eminent offices in 1966. A survey by two private organizations revealed that 1,469 Negroes held public office. Thurgood Marshall was appointed to the Supreme Court in 1967; Air Force Major Robert H. Lawrence became the first Negro astronaut on June 30 (he was killed in December when his plane crashed on a training flight); Elizabeth D. Koontz was elected president of the National Education Association; Dean Rusk's daughter married a black, Guy Gibson Smith; Cleveland and Gary acquired Negro mayors, and Walter E. Washington was named commissioner of the District of Columbia. The very excesses of the black militants seemed to ease the way for some Negro moderates; James Meredith repeated his Mississippi march in 1967, and the only whites to interrupt him asked for his autograph or snapped his picture.

But backlash continued to deliver stinging blows elsewhere. In Boston Louise Day Hicks, a forty-four-year-old grandmother, became a popular figure, and later a congresswoman, on the strength of her stand against remedies for racial imbalance in schools. A black youth was murdered in Detroit's Algiers Motel while under police interrogation; the officer who shot him pleaded self-defense and was acquitted by an all-white jury, showing that such cases were not confined to the Deep South. Adam Clayton Powell was denied his seat in Congress. There was no doubt about his misconduct, but Thomas Dodd, it was noted, was merely censured by the Senate. Father James E. Groppi failed in his campaign for "open" (integrated) housing in Milwaukee. Lester Maddox was sworn in as governor of Georgia, and the winner of Mississippi's gubernatorial race was another racist, John Bell Williams.

But these developments were overshadowed by that summer's havoc in the metropolitan ghettos, bringing to a climax the Negro revolt which had begun two years earlier in Watts. In its fury and the desolation it left behind it was like a war, and indeed there were those who believed that it was a mirror image of the Vietnam violence which could be seen on the television screens in every living room now during the dinner hour. "The government is contradictory," said John Lewis, Carmichael's predecessor as chairman of SNCC, "telling oppressed black men not to be violent in the streets while it carries out the terrible slaughter in Vietnam and finances it with money it should be spending to get things right at home."

That year the first torches were lit on April 8. Nashville police ejected a Negro from a restaurant at Fisk University that evening. Two days of chaos followed, and during the next month Cleveland, Washington, Louisville, Montgomery, and Omaha exploded. May arrived, and June, and Molotov cocktails, looters' clubs, and snipers' rifles appeared with increasing frequency. Major cities hit were New York, Minneapolis, Tampa, Atlanta, Birmingham, Cincinnati, San Francisco, Buffalo, Dayton and Wichita. Then came the first weekend in July and the first real ghetto catastrophe of 1967.

It began according to the now established ritual, with policemen. Late that Friday afternoon squad cars were summoned to the Grove Hall welfare office in Roxbury, a black district in southeast Boston. An organization of women on relief was demonstrating against welfare policy. They wanted more money, and they wanted to be treated with greater civility. It was past closing time, but the women wouldn't leave, and they had locked arms at the doors to prevent the employees from leaving. The cops entered through the windows. A crowd of Negroes gathered. Bottles and stones were thrown. More police arrived with helmets and riot sticks. They charged the mob, as it now was, in a flying wedge. That broke it up, which turned out to be a mistake. Forming small bands, the Negroes roamed Roxbury smashing glass, looting, putting buildings to the torch, and clouting whites. Before dawn a thousand policemen were battling a thousand blacks, and by Sunday evening, when the riot was spent, seventy people had been injured and fifteen blocks of Blue Hill Avenue, a main artery between downtown Boston and the suburbs, were a vast junkyard.

The week after Roxbury was peaceful but tense; nothing in the past two summers encouraged complacency. Urbanists were watching Newark, New Jersey, with particular vigilance. Even in peaceful times Newark would have been considered volatile. In seeking Model Cities grants its administration had frankly described it as "a basic training camp for the poor." Crowded and slummy, its very air was polluted with offensive odors from its many factories. Newark had the country's highest rate of venereal disease, the most crime, and the greatest percentage of condemned housing. Over the past century it had been successively inhabited by Protestants, Irish, Italians, and Jews, and by this time it was second only to Washington as a major city with a black majority. In 1960 Newark's population had been 62 percent white. Now it was 52 percent black and 10 percent Puerto Rican. Most of the 208,000 blacks lived in the shabby Central Ward. The unemployment figure there was twice the national figure, and the black rate of joblessness was twice the city's. In Washington the people at the new Department of Housing and Urban Development whose job it was to watch such things had long been worried about Newark. They thought the city awaited only a police incident to erupt. It came on Wednesday, July 12.

At 9:45 P.M. a black cab driver, arrested for a traffic violation, was brought into the 4th Precinct station in the Central Ward. He argued heatedly with two police officers and exchanged blows with them. Word spread outside that the cabby had been beaten to death. The customary spectators gathered, but nothing much happened there; after they had left officers reported downtown that they had been nothing more than "a bunch of roving kids" anyway. At dusk the next day another crowd assembled, carrying signs but apparently in good humor. Then the first bottle was thrown, and the first brick. The policemen broke up the throng with nightsticks. In twos and threes the Negroes disbanded—and began looting stores. By 11 P.M. plundering was proceeding on a massive scale, snipers were firing from roofs, and fires were blazing high. Newark's 1,400 police couldn't handle it. By daybreak, when 2,600 National Guardsmen and 300 state police arrived, the sun shone down on what Governor Richard J. Hughes called "a city in open rebellion." Almost half of Newark's twenty-four square miles was in the hands of the rioters, and order was not restored until Monday, July 17. By then twenty-seven were dead. The loss was put at ten million dollars. It was the worst disorder since Watts.

Detroit blew the following Sunday after a police raid on a Twelfth Street black nightclub which was selling liquor after 2 A.M., the legal closing time. The crowd milled around, the rumors of brutality spread—this time it was said that a boy wearing handcuffs had been kicked down a stairway—and the crowd, scattered by police, wandered away in small groups and began looting. In some ways this outburst was unusual. Unlike Newark, Detroit had not been regarded as a potential trouble spot. The mayor, elected with Negro support, had introduced measures which, together with the booming automobile business, had helped create a large black middle class. That, in fact, was part of the trouble. The rioters, who had not made it, were as resentful of middle-class Negroes as of whites. Another difference was that looting was integrated in Detroit; blacks and whites ransacked stores side by side. The extent of the arson was almost unbelievable—1,600 fire alarms in eleven days. But the most remarkable aspect of the Detroit riot was its size. Henry Ford called it "the greatest internal violence since the Civil War." The death toll was forty-three. Over seven thousand were arrested. Eighteen blocks of Twelfth Street and three miles of Grand River Avenue were burned to the ground. Aerial photographs of the city resembled Berlin in 1945. Five thousand people were without shelter. And many were insanely jubilant. "Those buildings going up was a pretty sight," said one of the Detroit rioters. "I sat right here and watched them go. And there wasn't nothing them honkies could do but sweat to put it out." He was speaking, of course, of Negro homes.

President Johnson appointed a commission headed by Governor Otto Kerner of Illinois to study outbreaks and find a way to prevent more of them. Hearings were scheduled by the Senate's Subcommittee on Investigations and the House Committee on Un-American Activities—which was under the impression that subversives were responsible for the disorders. And still that summer's rage in the ghettos was unspent. Altogether rioters struck 114 cities in 32 states. The complete toll would never be known, but there were at the very least 88 deaths, more than 4,000 other casualties, and 12,000 arrests. Among the grimmest upheavals were those in Wilmington, Toledo, South Bend, Grand Rapids, Pontiac, Milwaukee, New Haven, Providence, Saginaw, Flint, Portland (Oregon), and Cambridge (Maryland).

The Cambridge uprising was of particular interest. It was one of the few episodes which justified the Un-American Activities Committee's suspicions, and it had an unforeseen impact on national politics. Backlash had been a major factor in Maryland's 1966 gubernatorial campaign; when a racist candidate won the Democratic primary, black voters had backed the Republican nominee, Spiro T.

Agnew, a moderate. Agnew's feelings about law and order were stronger than his views on race, however, and he was outraged when Rap Brown, an outside agitator if there ever was one, told a rally of Eastern Shore Negroes that "It's time for Cambridge to explode." Brown called a Negro school a firetrap which "should have burned down long ago." He urged them to "Get yourself some guns," said that the riots were a "dress rehearsal for revolution," and added that "Violence is as American as cherry pie."

Thereupon Cambridge exploded, the school was burned, and Agnew issued a warrant for Brown's arrest on charges of inciting to riot and arson. "Such a person," said the governor, "cannot be permitted to come into a state with the intention to destroy and then sneak away, leaving these poor people with the results of his evil scheme." Brown was arrested in Alexandria, Virginia, two days later. Afterward he faced other charges for carrying firearms across a state line while under indictment. Meanwhile Governor Agnew's resolute handling of the incident had attracted the attention of the Republican party's national leadership, winning him the admiration of, among others, Richard M. Nixon.

Montage: The Johnson Years

REAGAN FIRES CLARK KERR AS BERKELEY CHANCELLOR: SCORES "PERMISSIVENESS"

U.S. POPULATION SEEN SURPASSING 200 MILLION MARK

Get your head together

APATHY

GOD IS DEAD

U.S., U.S.S.R. CATAPULT VENUS PROBES

KEEP THE FAITH BABY

"LSD is Western yoga," Dr. Leary explained. "The aim of all Eastern religion, like the aim of LSD, is basically to get high; that is, to expand your consciousness and find ecstasy and revelation within."

off the pigs

WE LOVE YOU AND ARE WORRIED,

PLEASE CALL COLLECT,

NO PUNISHMENT

Hare Krishna, Hare Krishna
Krishna Krishna, Hare Hare
Hare Rama, Hare Rama
Rama Rama, Hare Hare

COMPUTER, SET TO SELECT IDEAL MATES, PICKS BROTHER, SISTER

SPEED KILLS

First you get a really strong sex urge. You get a fantastic rush — a feeling that you're speeded up, you think you can do anything. It opens up little doors to the channels in your mind so you actually believe you can do anything. After a while it induces acute paranoia.

Say it loud — I'm black and I'm proud

Bangs manes bouffants beehives Beatle caps butter faces brush-on lashes decal eyes puffy sweaters French thrust bras flailing leather blue jeans stretch pants stretch jeans honeydew bottoms eclair shanks elf boots ballerinas Knight slippers, hundreds of them, these flaming little buds, bobbing and screaming, rocketing around inside the Academy of Music Theater underneath that vast old mouldering cherub dome up there — aren't they supermarvelous!

"There's no room for deathless prose in the novel," Miss Susann said.

3 ASTRONAUTS DIE; LAST PRAYERS TOLD

JACKIE VISITS CAMBODIA, LAUDS ORIENTAL CHARM

WARNING: YOUR LOCAL POLICE ARE ARMED AND DANGEROUS

IN COLD BLOOD: The show-place farm of Herbert Clutter, set in the peaceful, prosperous, picture-book country west of Garden City, Kans. (pop. 11,000), seemed the nation's least likely setting for cold-blooded, methodical murder.

LBJ, BIRD SET FOR LUCI VOWS

DE GAULLE: "VIVE LE QUEBEC LIBRE"

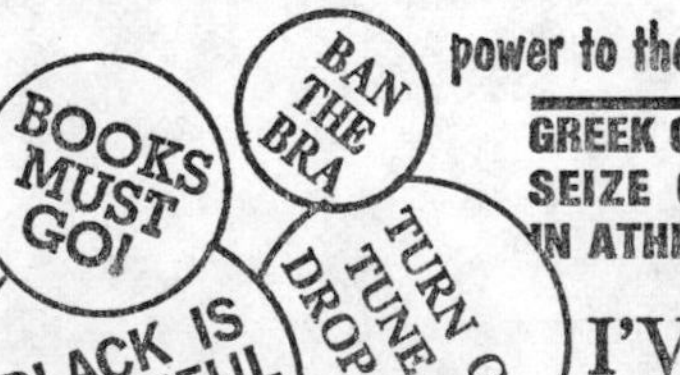

power to the people

GREEK COLONELS SEIZE CONTROL IN ATHENS COUP

The new 100-mm. cigarette, six-tenths of an inch longer than the traditional king-sized ones, had jumped from 2 percent of the market at the beginning of 1967 to 15 percent at the year's close — about $1 billion worth

I'VE GONE TO POT

BLACK POWER

Good grief, Charlie Brown

Thirty-two

UP AGAINST THE WALL

In *The New Industrial State*, published in 1967, John Kenneth Galbraith noted "an interesting and widely remarked phenomenon of recent years," an "ill-defined discontent, especially among students and intellectuals, with the accepted and approved modalities of social thought." These, wrote Galbraith, "whether espoused by professed liberals or conservatives, are held to be the views of 'The Establishment.'"

Actually, by then, blacks, radicals, feminists, and just about everybody else who felt systematically cheated by organized society had taken to calling it and all its works the "establishment." Often the word was used so loosely as to render it meaningless—shoplifting was called a blow to the establishment; the establishment was blamed for poor television programming—but some applications of it indicated a profound instinct for the workings of the system. This was never truer than on the memorable night of Tuesday, November 9, 1965, when antiestablishmentarians felt vindicated, and others dismayed, by the extraordinary failure of one of society's essential services: electrical power.

The sun set over the eastern United States at 4:44 P.M. that afternoon, and the demand for electricity then began building toward its daily peak. Light switches were flipped on in homes and offices. Neon signs lit up. In places of business elevators came into maximum use as workers departed. Subways put on extra trains for commuters, farmers in the country beyond the skyline hitched cows to milking machines, and lighthouses commenced to flash. Children raced in from play and turned on TV sets, while their mothers started supper. The day being autumnal and the temperature 46, thermostats triggered millions of furnaces into operation. Greenhouse heating systems became more active, and reptile houses in zoos were provided with that extra margin of heat without which their vipers and crocodiles would perish. In bars, ice machines began hatching cubes for office workers pausing for that daily drink before setting out for home. On parkways and highways electrically powered gasoline pumps filled the tanks of homeward-bound cars.

All this was a matter of routine to Edward J. Nellis, a slender, balding man of sixty-two and a forty-one-year veteran employee of the Consolidated Edison Company of New York. Nellis was seated in the controller's chair of Con Ed's Energy Control Center at 128 West End Avenue, Manhattan, near Sixty-fifth Street. The center, the hub of the company's electronic universe, is a high-ceilinged, antiseptic, rather Orwellian room whose dials and switches, bathed in brilliant fluorescent light, were all visible to Nellis. By vigilantly scanning them, he could be sure that Con Ed was fulfilling its role not only here in the metropolis, but also as chief member of the Ontario, New York, and New England electric power pool, an area of 80,000 square miles inhabited by 30 million people. At any rate, that was the theory. It entered the realm of intense controversy at about 5:16 P.M., when Nellis, starting from his chair, saw that the needles on all the dials had begun to oscillate wildly.

At the time neither he nor anyone else knew what was happening, though Con Ed's senior engineers had often discussed the possibility of a massive electric failure. They predicted—correctly—what they called a "cascade effect," in which an enormous, unexpected demand for power by one member of the pool would suck up the electricity of all the others. If that occurred, every generator in the pool, also known as the Northeast Power Grid, would automatically shut off to avoid damaging the equipment. All 80,000 square miles would be plunged into instant darkness.

The swinging needles at 128 West End Avenue were the consequence of such a cascade. The trouble lay 315 miles north of Manhattan and four miles west of Niagara Falls, in a Canadian hydrogenerating installation called the Sir Adam Beck Station No. 2. A relay—a device no larger than a breadbox—had been set for 1963 requirements and never readjusted, though power loads had been expanding steadily ever since. At 5 P.M. that afternoon electricity for Toronto was flowing north over six of the Adam Beck plant's lines. At 5:16:11, instruments showed later, the load increased slightly—just enough to trip the incorrectly set relay. That in turn set a circuit breaker in motion, putting one of the six lines out of action. Its load was instantly picked up by the other five, but they couldn't handle it. Overloaded, they were then cut off by their own relays. Two disasters followed almost simultaneously. About 1.6 million kilowatts of energy, destined for Toronto but unable to get through the invalided Adam Beck station, surged southward on the grid's great electric superhighway into upper New York State and New England, knocking out generating plants as it went. That created a power vacuum. The areas stricken by it demanded current from Manhattan—more than Manhattan had. The second calamity swiftly followed. Protective devices were activated all over the Northeast Power Grid. The cascade, or "falling domino" effect as some called it, was taking areas out of the pool automatically. It was complete at 5:38 P.M., when Vermont and southern New Hampshire joined the states to the south. Except for hospitals and other institutions, with their own generators, scarcely a light shone between Niagara and the Hudson. The great blackout had begun.

New York City went out at 5:27 P.M. Nellis had just decided to push the eight buttons which would have cut the metropolis free of the grid, but he was too late. It was a forgivable error: one of the few things unchanged about the consumption of electricity since Thomas Edison invented the first practical incandescent lamp in 1879 is that it still travels at the speed of light. But the consequences were stupefying. Except for Staten Island and one small Brooklyn neighborhood, the power was gone—all of it: illumination, appliances, subways; the works. In unaffected Montclair, New Jersey, a woman looking out her picture window had been admiring the fairylike spectacle of Manhattan alight. She called her teen-age son to share it with him, and when she turned back to the window the city had disappeared. Above Kennedy International Airport, Captain Ron George of Air Canada was entering his glide pattern. He looked down at the runway, glanced at his instruments, glanced back—and saw only Stygian blackness. The airport, too, had vanished.

Reactions in those first moments of the blackout varied, and to a certain extent they reflected individual fears. "The Chinese," thought a woman on Manhattan's East Side. "An attack from outer space!" cried a small boy in an apartment twenty stories above the East River. Two newspaper reporters were struck by the same thought

—that the antiwar movement had scored a real coup. Others were too preoccupied with unexpected crises to wonder who was responsible. In hospitals awaiting the ninety-second shift to emergency power, surgeons were continuing to operate by flashlight. The management of Schrafft's was worrying about $200,000 worth of ice cream. (It all melted.) Governor Rockefeller was climbing fifteen stories of stairs to his apartment. Over 800,000 people were trapped underground in the subways. Sixty of them would spend a harrowing night in an Astoria line BMT train in the Sixtieth Street tunnel under the East River. Far above them, on the Williamsburg Bridge over the river, 1,700 commuters were stranded on four trains. After five hours they would be led to safety.

In department stores, floorwalkers either led their customers out by flashlight or put them to bed in the home furnishing departments. Farmers reacquired the skill of milking cows by hand. Children, deprived of television, were learning to play on their own. Zoo keepers kept mammals alive with blankets and warmed their reptile houses with portable propane gas heaters. Not much could be done for motorists in need of fuel from the electrically operated gas pumps or housewives with cold electric stoves, however. Many who were suddenly idle were calling friends or relatives. The phones were working, and there was an 800 percent increase in local calls that evening. Others were doing other things. Nine months later to the day, all hospitals reported a sharp increase in births.

Thanks to transistors, radio broadcasts were getting through, but they cannot be said to have been much help to their bewildered audience. Breathless commentators spoke of "Canada in darkness . . . Cause unknown . . . worst power failure in the history of the world . . . President Johnson has summoned his emergency planning board . . . immediate investigation . . . sabotage feared." There were hints at war and nuclear holocaust until the Strategic Air Command in Colorado Springs reported "Condition Green," meaning normal. There were some local disturbances—looting in Springfield, Massachusetts, and a major riot at the Massachusetts state prison in Walpole—and a few tragic accidents. The body of one man was found at the bottom of a New York hotel elevator shaft, a burned-out candle in his hand.

In the early hours of that evening, virtually the only light in the grid was provided by candles, flashlights, automobile lights, and a full moon. Then the lights began returning, one area at a time. Vermont and southern New Hampshire came back after blackouts of thirty minutes to two hours. Connecticut had gone black at 5:30 and was slow to recover, but by 11:30 all but twelve of its towns were alight. Greater New York was the slowest of all. Brooklyn was back by 2 A.M. Wednesday, and thousands of sleepers there learned of it in a manner which would be repeated elsewhere; they had turned in leaving wall and lamp switches on, and were awakened when their bedrooms were suddenly flooded with light. Power returned to Queens at 4:20 A.M., to Manhattan and Westchester by 6:58 A.M., and to the Bronx at 7 A.M. Here and there stubborn pockets resisted the restoration of power. Pelham Manor in exclusive Westchester County didn't rejoin the grid until early Thursday. One Pelham Manor woman said afterward that she "burned a lot of candles," "kept the fireplace going," and "kept thinking about how people must have lived in Pelham Manor in the primitive days when there was no electricity."

The following Monday, November 15, 1965, six days after the power had failed, electrical engineers traced the blackout to the Beck plant. The Canadians were embarrassed; they had been insisting that the fault couldn't have been on their side of the border. American utilities spokesmen felt this proved that they had been blameless. But most of the public did not discriminate. They blamed the whole lot, Canadians and Americans alike. At the same time, the tales of their adventures during the blackout were improving in the telling. Eventually many forgot their anxieties at the time and were rejoicing in memories of the freedom from routine. Said a team of *New York Times* reporters:

> In every man there is a corner of rebellion against the machine. We were all delighted at the rediscovery of things that were not plugged into walls—things that were almost forgotten by us—most of all, the wonderful, wonderful candle. What a moment of triumph to know that the huge computers we really did not like and that we suspected really did not like us were lying massively idle and useless, but the old pencil sharpener still worked.

It was all illusion, as the *Times* men conceded. In the end all were "recaptured and brought back submissively to the prison farm of modern technology." The candle and the pencil sharpener were all very well for a hiatus of a few hours, but they would not have seemed wonderful much longer. They could not have transported commuters, or warmed homes, or provided light for reading, or provided any one of the countless services and necessities for which men had come to rely upon technology. The way of life in Pelham Manor in the primitive days when there was no electricity would have come as a savage shock to them. Many would have been unable to survive it. Some thought of what the *Times* writers called "the plugged-in society" as a prison farm, and some had worse names for it, but not many were so vehement about the huge computers that they were prepared to scrap them. There were, however, a few.

Taking their name from a half-witted Leicestershire worker who had attacked a machine a generation earlier, British handcraftsmen thrown out of work by the industrial revolution declared war on shearing frames and power looms in 1811. From a mythical retreat in Sherwood Forest they issued a nonnegotiable demand:

> We will never lay down Arms [till] The House of Commons passes an Act to put down all Machinery hurtful to Commonality, and repeal that to hang Frame Breakers. . . . We petition no more—that won't do—fighting must.
>
> Signed by the General of the Army of Redressers
>
> NED LUDD Clerk

Soreheads standing in the way of laborsaving devices have been known as Luddites ever since, and critics of America's increasingly technocratic society during the Johnson years were frequently accused of Luddism. In instances of rioting students this was sometimes justified. Professors' notes were destroyed, equipment was damaged, and a sign plastered on one Cambridge computer accused it of drawing high wages and fringe benefits at the expense of American workmen. That was as absurd as Ned at his most futile, but the case against technocracy was not entirely preposterous. Intelligent men and women were tired of receiving punch-card mail, riding on push-button elevators, standing in check-out lines, reading about a war being judged by body counts, listening to recorded voices over telephones, and being treated during political campaigns as pollster percentages. As Nicholas von Hoffman pointed out, the demonstrating students were rebellious at being "admitted, tested, and flunked by computers." There was something chilling about Human Inventory, Inc., the Los Angeles matchmaking service which had 6,000 clients and was headed by a former executive in an aerospace company. Everyone had his computer horror stories, and some were choice. An Albany hospital sent a woman a bill for "ritual circumcision." And in 1966 Mayor John F. Collins of Boston was favored to win reelection until, three days before the primary, the city computer, all by itself, prepared, addressed, and mailed 30,000 delinquent sewer tax bills. The mayor was defeated.

Erich Fromm warned: "A specter is stalking in our midst. . . . It is a new specter: a completely mechanized society . . . directed by computers; and in this social process, man himself is being transformed into a part of the total machine." Millions of Americans by the late 1960s were carrying as many as twenty multiple numbers in their wallets, some indicating their various identities, some necessary for daily business, and all tending to reduce them to random particles—zip codes, area codes, blood types, drivers' licenses, automobile licenses, social security numbers, army serial numbers, and numbers of charge accounts, checking accounts, book club memberships, insurance policies, passports, birth and marriage certificates, mortgages, and Veterans Administration claims. The author of *The Beast of Business* recommended playing "computer-card roulette" by closing holes with tape, cutting new holes with a razor blade, and exposing the code number to an electromagnet. When a California janitor received a $5,000 check for two weeks' work, everyone cheered except the aeroelasticity investigators, inertial systems engineers, superconductivity research specialists, and digital circuit design specialists—those, in short, whose great age this was.

John Mauchly, the builder of the first U.S. commercial computers, had predicted that "only four or five giant firms will be able to employ these machines usefully." He underestimated his prodigies. There were 1,000 computers in the United States in 1955. In 1960 government engineers suggested that 15,000 might be in use within five years. The time arrived and 25,000 were in use. By 1967 there were 40,000—some 2,000 for the federal government alone.

All this was disquieting to American humanists. Liberals in politics, they had become more and more traditional in their social attitudes. In the late 1940s they had been alarmed by *Nineteen Eighty-Four*. During the Eisenhower years a genteel shabbiness had acquired a certain cachet among them, for they were especially disturbed by the thing-oriented culture that had ridden in on the wave of technological advances. It appeared to them that the nation was becoming enslaved by manipulators of consumer appetites. Among the figures disgorged by the pullulating computers were analyses of what manipulation of the public was doing to consumer debt. Between 1956 and 1967 it increased 133 percent, to 99.1 billion dollars. Motor car paper alone was up 117 percent, to 31.2 billion dollars. It looked as though Will Rogers had been right; the country was going to the poorhouse in an automobile.

Autos would have been bad enough—thoughtful Americans were just beginning to learn what Detroit was doing to their environment—but the dismay of intellectuals over what was coming to be regarded as the blight of mass opulence went far beyond that. The voracity of the national vending machine seemed insatiable. Disposable personal income had almost doubled since the Eisenhower years, but the faith, so strong in the 1930s, that men would spend wisely if they just had the money, was in shreds. Then Edmund Wilson had written scornfully of "foods that do not nourish, disinfectants that do not disinfect," of "cosmetics that poison the face, lubricants that corrode your car," and "insecticides that kill your trees." But it was precisely these brands which were flourishing in the booming 1960s. At least in the Depression you hadn't been compelled to look at them in your own living room. Television commercials now spewed them forth in all their vulgarity—and in nauseous color to boot—until one wondered what the country was going to do with all the junk. An inspired Mobil commercial provided the answer during the 1969 American League baseball playoffs. With each $3 purchase it offered customers a plastic bag which would hold "22 pounds, four cubic feet" of trash. "You'll be glad you threw it away," said the commercial, and it was true.

Televised sport was a grievance in itself. It turned millions of men who ought to have been active outdoors—for their own health, if nothing else—into beer-drinking, flatulent spectators watching young athletes romp joyously in gilded playpens. The gaudiest pen of all was Houston's 32-million-dollar, air-conditioned Astrodome, with its 46,000 upholstered seats, 30,000-car parking lot, and a steel dome which eliminated the need to issue rain checks. So intent were the superstadium's designers upon making it playable in fog, rain, or darkness that they overlooked one possibility: the sun might shine. When that happened, they discovered to their horror, outfielders lost fly balls in the dazzling dome. Early games were played only on cloudy days, and even so the outfielders had to wear batting helmets. Then the skylights were painted gray—meaning that all games there would require lights, whatever the weather.

To skeptics of the new prosperity the Astrodome was a shrine of tastelessness and overconsumption. Its 53 private boxes, available for five-year leases, rented for $15,000 to $34,000 a season. Private clubrooms, for those bored with the game below, were outfitted with bars and TV and provided by decorators with such themes as "Tahitian Holiday," or "The French Hunt." Over fifty different uniforms were designed for Astrodome workers, depending on their tasks (ground crewmen wore space suits), and each was sent to school for three weeks to learn how to project the proper Astrodome image. The greatest spectacle in the stadium was a home run by the home team Astros. Fans never forgot it, and some visiting pitchers never recovered from it. The electric scoreboard went berserk. Rockets were launched and bombs exploded. Electric cattle wearing the American and Texas flags on their horns bucked wildly. Electric cowboys fired electronic bullets at them. An orchestra crashed through "The Eyes of Texas."

"When in doubt," went an advertising slogan that year, "buy the proven product." But the skeptics had no doubts. They recoiled from all mass merchandise. To them the marketplace was evil. The economic lessons they had learned in their youth had lost all relevance. "The essential mass problem had shifted," Eric Goldman wrote. It was "less food, housing and clothing than how to live with a weirdly uneasy affluence." Goldman described "a maldistribution no longer accepted by a significant section of the population." Certainly that section was highly articulate. Its polemics against maldistribution could be found in any bookstore. A common theme in them was that mass culture led to the garrison-prison state.

Some perceptive authors pointed out to intellectuals that they were not always logical. William H. Whyte Jr. remarked that it was "a retrograde point of view" which failed to recognize that a growth of Babbittry was "a consequence of making the benefits of our civilization available to more people." Caroline Bird noted that "People who are usually compassionate sometimes fail to see how the full employment of the 1960s is responsible for what they experience as a general decline in morals, competence, courtesy, energy, and discipline." John Kenneth Galbraith reminded liberal humanists that they could not pick and choose among technological advances. If they wanted some of them, they would have to put up with the rest. Nor could they accept the wonders of applied science and reject the special relationship between the state and industry which had made it possible: "It is open to every freeborn man to dislike this accommodation. But he must direct his attack to the cause. He must not ask that jet aircraft, nuclear power plants or even the modern automobile in its modern volume be produced by firms that are subject to unfixed prices and unmanaged demand. He must ask that they not be produced." Galbraith remained an eloquent advocate of a higher quality of life, but he told fellow critics that before dismissing the digital society entirely they should reflect that it has brought them much that they enjoy and take for granted; for example, "in the absence of automatic transmission of [telephone] calls, it would require approximately the entire female working force of the country to handle current traffic."

That was in 1967. Galbraith did not anticipate that within four years his assumption that all operators should be female would become fighting words. Yesterday's truism had become today's heresy. This, perhaps, was the overriding fact about the impact of science and technology on the United States. Its changes were convulsive, overwhelming. That was one reason for the jarring aspect of American life in the 1960s. Occupational skills became obsolete so rapidly that career planning was difficult and sometimes impossible for the young. In 1967, for example, the chemical industry calculated that half its business came from the sale of products which hadn't even existed ten years earlier. One of these, the contraceptive pill, played a crucial role in the dramatic revision of American female expectations. At the same time, life expectancy for white females was approaching 80 years (as against 75 years for white males). Science and technology was steadily altering the shape of the future. In 1968 Herman Kahn and the Hudson Institute issued a thousand-page study of what American life would be like in the year 2000. Their prediction was that by then the annual per capita income of Americans would be $7,500 a year. Seven-hour days and four-day weeks would be typical, the institute reported; so would thirteen-week annual vacations. With enjoyment replacing achievement as the goal of men and women, it appeared that the very reason for existence, and even existence itself, would be altered in ways which were now inconceivable.

But anticipating the future was not necessary to grasp what the technological revolution had already done to the United States. A glance backward could be breathtaking. In the early 1930s, when the now gray and balding swing generation was just approaching its teens, the largest category of Americans untouched by progress was the farm bloc—over 30 million people. In those days they lacked knowledge of even the fundamentals of conservation, which was one of the reasons for the devastating dust storms. Without rural electrification, farmers read by lamplight. Without electric power the typical farm wife had to carry as much as 28 tons of water each year from the pump or spring. Her butter churn was operated by hand. She did her laundry in a zinc tub and preserved meat in a brine barrel. Her husband's chores were even more backbreaking. After the morning milking he had two hours' work with the horses before he could set about whatever he had planned for the day. Horses and mules were his major source of locomotion—there were over 20 million of them in the country—and when he went to town he drove over dirt roads. Later his life would be sentimentalized by those who had no idea what it had really been like. Some of the most arrant nonsense would be written about the farm kitchen, when in fact, as Clyde Brion Davis pointed out in *The Age of Indiscretion,* "most of the cooking was frying—and not even in deep fat. The traditional American farmer . . . was scrawny-necked, flat-chested and potbellied from flatulent indigestion."

If the farmer's son was still living on the land a generation later, his world was entirely different. Trees planted by the CCC held the soil firm; strip cropping and contour plowing made for greater yields and sturdier crops. Fifteen billion dollars in farm machinery had ended the tyranny of sweat and drudgery, and the 65 million acres once set aside for raising animal fodder were now used for produce. The development of hybrid corn had increased the nation's corn harvest 20 percent without boosting the acreage needed. Driven to abandon cotton by the boll weevil threat of the 1930s, southern farmers had learned to plant other crops—and had tripled their income. The new farmer in the new rural prosperity drove to market on macadam. And his wife, in a kitchen glittering with appliances, the brine barrel having been replaced by a commodious freezer, fed her family properly. Afternoons she had time to run into town herself. She went to the hairdresser regularly and wore the same synthetic fabrics as her city sisters instead of the gingham dresses and cotton stockings of her mother.

City toil had been transformed, too. The proletariat was disappearing. It was Norbert Wiener who had observed, in *Cybernetics;*

or, Control and Communication in the Animal and the Machine (1948), that "There is no rate of pay which is low enough to compete with the work of a steam shovel and an excavator." Already in the first half of the twentieth century automation had cut the number of common laborers from 11 million to 6 million. Over the next thirteen years the country's work force grew by ten million—to 70.6 million—but the number of laborers continued to dwindle. Blue-collar workers were a shrinking minority. During the Eisenhower years the automobile industry's production force dropped by 172,000 while it turned out a half-million more cars each year. The stature of the once mighty trade unions diminished; machines can't strike. Labor leaders became conservative, suspicious of progress, and in some cases allies of their old foes, the corporations. Meanwhile, less need for male muscle was opening vast areas of employment to the women now entering the labor force, and the trend grew as the objectives of work changed. Instead of making goods, workers were joining the expanding service, amusement, and leisure industries. In the "new mass-consumption society," George E. Mowry wrote, "the old equation of man confronting materials and making something new of them had been changed to man confronting man and persuading him to act."

One masculine stronghold did not change. That was the executive suite. The Hudson Institute held out no hope that business executives might look forward to working less and loafing more in the year 2000. They could not be spared; too much depended upon them. This was a switch from the Roosevelt years. Executive illustriousness had been predicted in James Burnham's widely reviewed book of 1941, *The Managerial Revolution*, but Depression folklore had generally held bosses in contempt, and Depression novelists and dramatists had depicted them as knaves and fools. (Moviegoers may recall the character actor who portrayed this stock role most successfully. He was Edward Arnold.) Yet by the 1960s they were high in the saddle. To be sure, they had little in common with the piratical entrepreneurs of the past. "The Tycoon," said *Fortune*, "is dead." *Time* described the new businessmen as "the professional managers, the engineer-trained technicians" who "took over industrial societies so huge that the average owner"—stockholder—"seldom exercised more than theoretical control." Typically, they ruled not individually and by fiat but by committee, pooling information and expertise in what were variously called executive groups, task forces, assault groups, or, in the modish egalitarian spirit, "working parties." In *The New Industrial State* John Kenneth Galbraith called those who thus shared power the technostructure.

Bright, well-educated, and highly motivated, the men of the technostructure suffered, ironically, in one area to which they gave great attention: public relations. The problem here was refractory and institutional. American industry had always deceived itself and others about its true nature. Professing faith in Herbert Spencer went with the job, like the key to the executive washroom and membership in the Republican party. Executives insisted upon the viability of the profit motive, even though their own careers frequently gave it the lie; they continued to drive themselves although taxes took huge bites of their salaries. The name of John Maynard Keynes was ritualistically hissed even as they defected from Barry Goldwater, who not only criticized Keynes but actually meant it. They encouraged stockholders to think possessively about their corporation, yet the influence of corporate investors, always minimal, had declined even further by the 1960s, and anyone attending their annual meetings could quickly perceive that the decisions made by individuals there depended upon the information which the technostructure chose to provide them.

This masquerade had been noted by economists. Usually the duplicity had been dismissed as harmless. After all, political ethics were honored more often in the breach. The technostructural deceit was graver than it seemed, however. As the Johnson administration grew older with no resolution of the Vietnam conflict, American businessmen were astonished to find that demonstrators were turning on them and accusing them of committing monstrous crimes with products like napalm. They couldn't understand it; didn't these angry people know that management and government were natural antagonists, not co-conspirators? They believed that and thought it should be obvious to everyone. But of course it was untrue. The truth was that by the late 1960s the military-industrial complex which had alarmed Eisenhower at the opening of the decade had continued to grow until the United States had—there is no other name for it—a planned economy.

In 1967 Jean-Jacques Servan-Schreiber startled U.S. readers with such blunt assertions as "Federal agencies have been collaborating with American corporations in developing advanced technology ever since the end of the war," and "In the United States nearly every major industry gets a substantial amount of federal assistance." It scarcely seemed credible. Roosevelt's heirs were still entrenched in Washington, scorning the economic royalists and the moneychangers; presidents of the National Association of Manufacturers condemned Washington paternalism; speakers at the U.S. Chamber of Commerce continued to explain that the government, since it never *made* anything, was essentially parasitic, and that the key to all economic progress was the businessman who was prepared to risk his capital in hope of gain.

This was perhaps true of the child's lemonade stand then being acclaimed in full-page ads extolling free enterprise—though where the child would be without paternal subsidies was unexplained—but it had lost all applicability for the five hundred giant corporations which, by the 1960s, accounted for two-thirds of the nation's industrial production. Where was the risk for the Rand Corporation, whose total budget was underwritten by the U.S. Air Force? What gamble did IBM run when it invested five billion dollars in the perfection of integrated circuits for its third generation of computers, knowing that the Pentagon stood behind every dollar? How could ITT's work on miniaturized electronic devices be called speculation when NASA knew that a manned flight to the moon would be impossible without them? As technology became more sophisticated and the lead time required for new developments lengthened, firms which were asked to break new ground demanded long-term contracts. Industrial executives and government bureaucrats, sharing the same goals, drew up budgets and reached decisions together. If the finished products were useful in marketable wares, there was nothing to stop the executives from cleaning up. Often they did. Integrated circuits—microcircuits which eliminate a chain of linked electronic parts: transistors, resistors, condensers, and tubes—are an example. Huge space rockets could not get off the pad without them. They made Polaris missiles and the swing-wing F-111 fighter possible. Boeing SSTs required them. So did the European Concorde prototype; governments in Europe had not been so cooperative, and when the manufacturers there needed the microcircuits, they had to deal with the only three firms making them, all American: Fairchild, Texas Instruments, and Motorola. The devices, they found, were expensive.

It would be wrong to suggest that the American taxpayer had been swindled in this process. The government was committed to space travel; the electronic computer had become indispensable to the machinery of national strategy; improved methods of transport were in the public interest; national prestige benefited. Indeed, Servan-Schreiber was lost in admiration for the ingenious Yankees: "Behind most of their recent innovations is a huge reservoir of federal funds that have financed the most profitable investment any people ever made for itself." The byproducts of space research alone included tremendous and invaluable gains in understanding refractory metals and equipment for working in vacuums. Through federal guarantees of large outlays of capital, the Pentagon, NASA, the AEC and the Federal Aviation Administration made possible the creation of marvels which would otherwise have waited a generation. Between the invention of photography and the manufacture of cameras, 112 years passed, from 1727 to 1839. The gap was 56 years for the telephone and 35 for radio. By paying for technical development and assuring a market for the end result, Washington had cut the lag to six years for the atomic bomb, five years for the transistor, and three years for the integrated circuit. There is a case to be made against the process, but it is a case against progress. That many Americans would find it persuasive is doubtful.

What was not possible, however, was to argue that industry had maintained its sovereignty—that it remained free to oppose decisions made in Washington. With the administration spending 15 billion dollars a year on research and development, as against 6 billion from business and private agencies, the presumption of domination by the government was inescapable. In 1929 federal, state, and municipal governments accounted for about 8 percent of all economic activity in the United States. By the 1960s the figure was between 20 and 25 percent, far exceeding that in India, a socialist country. The National Science Foundation reckoned that federal funds were paying for 90 percent of research in aviation and space travel, 65 percent in electrical and electronic devices, 42 percent in scientific instruments, 31 percent in machinery, 28 percent in metal alloys, 24 percent in automobiles, and 20 percent in chemicals. Washington was in a position to hold the very survival of great corporations as a hostage. It never came to that, no one was that crude, the matter was never discussed. Nevertheless, big industry had surrendered a large measure of autonomy.

In another time this circumstance would have concerned few Americans and aroused even fewer. Johnsonian prosperity was being enjoyed on all levels of society. Except in times of great distress the United States has rarely been troubled by protesters swarming in the streets and damning the government. Most people have a stake in the system; radical movements have been historically frustrated in their search for American recruits. But the Johnson years were witnessing another significant innovation. Since the war the nation had acquired an enormous student population. At the time of Pearl Harbor about 15 percent of Americans of college age were so enrolled. By the fall of 1965, 40 percent were—over five million youths between eighteen and twenty-one. Within four years the figure would be 6.7 million. Nearly a half-million bachelor degrees were now being awarded each year. More than 30 billion dollars was being spent annually on formal education. Going to class had, in fact, become the largest industry in the United States, making students the country's biggest single interest group.

In the rest of the population this was a source of pride—education had become almost a secular religion, the proposed cure for all social ills—but undergraduates were becoming discontented and restless. Their futures were clouded by the Vietnam War, which grew more hideous and frustrating every day. Their dissatisfaction with the prosecution of the conflict was encouraged by thousands of the nation's 150,000 tenure professors—men shielded from external discipline, who could be removed from their chairs only by death or personal scandal. Finally, many students were troubled by the realization that much of society's enthusiasm for higher education stemmed from its market value. Just as other federal programs enhanced technology by creating microcircuits, so the huge grants to education served to train future technicians, executives, and customers. Undergraduates found that after acquiring a healthy skepticism, a university's greatest gift to them, they were expected to stifle it and become cogs in industrial and governmental bureaucracies. Millions of parents saw nothing wrong with that. Many of the children were beginning to take another view, however. They said to one another: "They are snowing us. They are burying us. We cannot put up with it any more. We're going to overthrow it."

American technology has always been an American strength, a source of wonder and, sometimes, of anxiety. In 1853 a periodical called the *United States Review* had predicted that within fifty years "machinery will perform all work—automata will direct them," leaving people free "to make love, study and be happy." But as the campuses of the 1960s trembled on the verge of upheaval, John Kenneth Galbraith was less sanguine. He sensed a "danger that our educational system will be too strongly in the service of economic goals."

In some way the great student upheavals of the 1960s were even more significant than they seemed at the time. Like the revolutionary fever that swept western Europe in 1848, they may never be fully understood. They cut across national orders and cultural barriers that had long intimidated older generations. Neither oceans nor even the Iron Curtain checked them; as Columbia exploded and Berkeley seethed, campuses erupted in England, Italy, Germany, Holland, Sweden, Spain, Belgium, Japan, Formosa, Poland, Hungary, Yugoslavia, and Czechoslovakia. Americans were preoccupied with the disorders at home, but in at least two foreign capitals, Prague and Warsaw, the damage was more extensive than anything in the United States.

Doubtless part of the explanation for the chain reaction lies in the speed and sophistication of modern communications. The sense of world community was real and growing. Each of the emerging continents was to some degree aware of what was happening on other continents. "Establishment," in its new sense, had been translated into the language of every industrial nation. Student activists, as the riots would demonstrate, hadn't much use for it. This feeling was global. The antipathy was just as strong in Asia or eastern Europe as beneath the elms of Old Wabash.

Nevertheless, the American role was special. The turmoil began in the United States, the world's most affluent nation and the one with the most strongly defined youth subculture. Undergraduates abroad were very conscious of events on American campuses ("What is happening at Columbia?" Sorbonne demonstrators eagerly asked American foreign correspondents in 1968), while U.S. students were largely indifferent to the frenzies overseas. In America, moreover, it was possible to trace the powerful currents which were stirring youth. As Tocqueville noted, Americans have always taken a distinctive, almost Rousseauistic view of youth, and they have turned naturally to education as the solution to every problem, public and private.

But now youth itself had become a problem, and a major one at that. A great source of anxiety was the new political militance. A conservative educator declared that the campuses were harboring "a loose alliance of Maoists, Trotskyites, Stalinists, Cheists, anarchists, utopians, and nihilists." Spiro Agnew made several memorable remarks on the subject. In St. Louis he called student demonstrators "malcontents, radicals, incendiaries, and civil and uncivil disobedients" and said, "I would swap the whole damn zoo for a single platoon of the kind of Americans I saw in Vietnam." On another occasion he described the universities as "circus tents or psychiatric centers for over-privileged, under-disciplined, irresponsible children of well-to-do blasé permissivists."

Parents denied that they were blasé or permissive, and those who disapproved of the demonstrations said they were the work of a minority. Gallup reported that 72 percent of all students had not participated in any of them; a *Fortune* poll concluded that just 12.5 percent of undergraduates held "revolutionary" or "radically dissident" views; SDS recruited just 7 percent. But Groucho Marx spoke for millions of older Americans when he remarked, "it's no good saying that the ones you read about are a minority. They're not a minority if they're all yours and you have to wait for the car to get home to know your daughter hasn't got pregnancy or leprosy."

The figures were deceptive anyhow. Extremists always attract a minority. A minority of northerners were abolitionists in 1861; probably a minority of colonists really wanted independence in 1776. Sympathies, not commitments, are the best indicator of a group's temper, and here the student pattern tells a different story. Gallup found that 81 percent of undergraduates were dissatisfied with college and university administrations. Another poll reported that more than 50 percent expressed major reservations about American foreign and domestic policies.

"The fear of being labeled radical, leftist, or subversive," Harvey Swados observed of academe in the early 1960s, "seems to have all but disappeared." Many, indeed, welcomed it. The undergraduates arriving on campus were often children of the middle-class liberals who had been most outraged—and in some instances had suffered most—during the McCarthy years. Their sons and daughters were determined not to be intimidated or repressed. They joined chapters of such organizations as SDS, Joan Baez's School for Nonviolence, the W. E. B. Du Bois Clubs, and the Young Socialist Alliance. They were in dead earnest but politically inept. Before the decade ended, the tactics of their New Left would offend virtually all potential allies, including their parents—which, some thought, might have been the point.

Yet in some areas they were highly skilled. Their demonstrations were often staged for TV news cameramen with a sense of what was good theater. The picketing in support of the Mississippi Freedom Party at the 1964 Democratic national convention was one example; the October 1967 march on the Pentagon was another. It is equally true that they frequently appeared to be shocking the country for the sake of shock. In 1965 SDS repealed its ban on admitting Communists and Birchers to membership. The New Leftists proclaimed that their sacred trinity consisted of Marx, Mao, and Herbert Marcuse, and they enthusiastically embraced Marcuse's "discriminating tolerance"; *i.e.*, the suppression of points of view which the New Leftists regarded as unsound or dangerous. Their campaigns against ROTC, the draft, and napalm were logical, and walking out on commencement ceremonies was valid protest, but when they advocated dynamiting public buildings, even Marcuse demurred. Some SDS leaders all but salivated over violence. Of the Sharon Tate murders SDS's Bernadine Dohrn said: "Dig it, first they killed those pigs, then they ate dinner in the same room with them, then they even shoved a fork into a victim's stomach! Wild!"

The New Leftists' view of society was essentially conspirational. They saw it as dominated by an establishment which was itself manipulated by a "power elite" of industrialists, military leaders, and corporate giants. They talked darkly of revolution, yet a real revolution starts with strengthening the power of the state—which they were dead set against. Like all movements, theirs had a glossary of special terms: "dialogue," "creative tension," "nonnegotiable demands," and "nonviolent" among others. But their meanings were often obscure. Nonnegotiable demands could be negotiated, for example, and throwing rocks and bottles at policemen was deemed nonviolent.

The alienation of the young militants, expressing itself in disdain for conventional careers, clothing, and politics, had begun at Berkeley in 1964. The next spring, when that campus began to tremble again, President Kerr said, "The university and the Berkeley campus really couldn't face another such confrontation." In fact four more years of turmoil lay ahead. Berkeley was to be but one of many disturbed campuses. In 1965 Berkeley fallout first rocked the University of Kansas when 114 students were arrested there for staging a sit-in at the chancellor's office to protest fraternity and sorority discrimination. Then, within a few days, colleges and universities were embattled from coast to coast.

Yale undergraduates demonstrated after a popular philosophy instructor had been denied tenure. After an anti-ROTC rally at San Francisco State, five were hospitalized. At Fairfield University, a Jesuit school in Connecticut, students broke into a locked stack to put forbidden books on open shelves. Brooklyn College undergraduates booed their president off a platform. At St. John's in New York, the nation's biggest Catholic college, students demanded an end to censorship of their publications. Michigan students demonstrated against higher movie prices, and three deans resigned at Stanford over reading erotic poetry in the classroom. At Fairleigh Dickinson in New Jersey students picketed as "an expression of general student discontent." The uproar continued through 1966 and 1967, with major riots at San Jose State College, Wisconsin, Iowa, Cornell, Long Beach State College, and, once again, San Francisco State. And all this was merely a buildup for the cataclysmic year of 1968. "Yesterday's ivory tower," said the president of Hunter College, "has become today's foxhole."

For all their ardor, the militant undergraduates achieved little. Students are by definition transients; once they are graduated new students arrive, and there is no guarantee that the newcomers may not take a different line—as in fact those in this movement did. SDS, inherently unstable, split into two groups at the end of the decade: Revolutionary Youth Movement I, also known as the Weathermen, and Revolutionary Youth Movement II, which condemned the Weathermen as "adventuristic." The students had other difficulties. One of their basic premises was absurd. "The fantasy," wrote Benjamin DeMott, lay "in the notion that if you're upset about Vietnam, racism, poverty, or the general quality of life, the bridge to blow is college."

A second handicap was the students' exaggerated sense of their own power. In 1966 they confidently challenged the gubernatorial campaign of Ronald Reagan. To their amazement, he won by a margin of almost a million votes. That same day the Republicans gained fifty congressional seats. "One of the most obvious casualties of the 1966 elections," Hunter S. Thompson noted, "was the New

Left's illusion of its own leverage. The radical-hippy alliance had been counting on the voters to repudiate the 'right-wing, war-monger' elements in Congress, but instead it was the 'liberal' Democrats who got stomped." Furthermore, analysts concluded that in California the New Left had actually boosted Reagan's vote by opposing him. Having found a popular issue, Reagan then capitalized on it, forcing Kerr's resignation on the ground that he had been too lenient with student dissidents and appointing Professor Samuel I. Hayakawa, a hard-liner, as president of San Francisco State.

Hostile reactions to politicized students were not confined to California. One Midwest legislature slashed over 38 million dollars from its state university's budget and raised tuition fees. Bills intended to stifle student dissent were introduced in most other legislatures, and eight of them were passed. "Americans," Oregon's Governor Tom McCall said of the demonstrators, were "fed up to their eardrums and eyeballs." Lou Harris reported that 62 percent of students' parents believed that it was more important for colleges to maintain discipline than to encourage intellectual curiosity. "Reduced to its simplest terms," *Life* commented, "the generations disagree on the most fundamental question of all: What is education for?"

Of course, they clashed over other issues, too. The demonstrations were one of the most visible manifestations of youth's subculture in the 1960s, but there was more to their subculture than that. Throughout the decade publicists wrote of "revolutions" in, among others, communications, sex, and drugs. Youth was active in all of them and was partly formed by them, if only because it had concluded that the election returns were what Hunter Thompson called "brutal confirmation of the futility of fighting the Establishment on its own terms." The generation gap had arrived, and it was an abyss.

"Don't trust anyone over thirty!" said the banners and buttons displayed by the most arrogant, and it was cruel; so many Americans over thirty wanted to be young again, to share the fads and enthusiasms of youth. They slipped discs dancing the Watusi and the Swim and the Cottage Cheese, hopped about chasing Frisbees, endangered their lives riding motorcycles, laughed at *The Graduate* and even played with Super Balls. The Beatles having introduced long hair, the kids picked it up, and presently the middle-aged were imitating that, too. Both sexes wore wigs to make them look younger. Often the hippies set fashions for adults. "I watch what the kids are putting together for themselves," said Rudi Gernreich. "I formalize it, give it something of my own, perhaps, and that is fashion." Older Americans caught the discotheque bug and asked children where the action was; young wiseacres told them the Vincent Van Gogh-Gogh and the Long, Long Ago-go. Women went to plastic surgeons for eyelid lifts ($350), nose jobs ($500), rhytidectomies—face lifts—($600), face peelings ($500), dermabrasions—removing acne scars—($275), bosom implants ($165), belly lifts ($500) and thigh lifts ($650). "Being young was *right,*" *Life* observed in a special issue on the 1960s; "as everybody once wanted to be rich, now everybody wanted to be, or seem to be, young. Fashion, films, books, music, even politics leaned toward youth."

Early in the decade half the U.S. population was under thirty. Then half was under twenty-seven, and then it was half under twenty-five, with 40 percent seventeen years old or younger and those under eighteen increasing four times as fast as the rest of the population. Even so, there were many who took a saturnine view of what one called youth's "vinyl-mini-inflatable Disneyland of pop culture." Defenders of the young reminded them that Socrates had written: "Our youth now loves luxury. They have bad manners, contempt for authority, disrespect for their elders. Children nowadays are tyrants." The implication was that since the Greeks were vexed by kids that long ago, today's worriers were making an issue over nothing. Grace and Fred M. Hechinger countered that real questions should be, "What happened to Greece? Or to Rome? Or to any civilization once it substituted self-indulgence for self-discipline?"

At times in the 1960s it almost seemed that America was becoming a filiarchy. Adolescence, wrote the Hechingers, had "evolved into a cult, to be prolonged, enjoyed, and commercially catered to as never before." In the new suburbs, especially, the young appeared to have been reared on a philosophy of instant gratification. Agnew, Billy Graham, and Al Capp distorted the issue, but it did exist and was debatable. "Self-expression" and "child-centered" were part of the permissive jargon; in the schools the trend frequently led to a system of "elective" subjects for pupils too young to know what they were electing. The teacher was to be regarded as a pal, not a superior being. Elementary school teachers were required to work with limited vocabularies, sometimes twenty words or less repeated endlessly. (The result was summed up in the deathless line attributed to a teacher who rammed a tree with her car: "Look look look, oh oh oh, damn damn damn.")

Children told that they were equal to their parents in every way believed that decisions in the home should be put to a vote. This was called "democratic living." Often it meant chaotic living. Writing in *Daedalus,* David Riesman noted the effect on a stranger: "As in the home of a poor peasant which is shared with goats, chickens, and other livestock, guests here may face the hazard of children who are treated as pets and who are not put away with a babysitter when company comes."

Henry A. Murray, another Harvard contributor to *Daedalus,* pointed to one unexpected consequence. Most teen-age aggregates, he observed, were "bound together by an anti-authoritarian, anti-father compact." It was a strong man who could command respect in his own house. Society seemed to be conspiring against him. One of the greatest offenders was television. TV fathers were pitiful weaklings. *Make Room for Daddy*'s ineffectual daddy let his wife dominate him simply because she talked the loudest. Uncle Bentley in *Bachelor Father* was systematically humiliated by his niece and his servant, and Mr. Anderson, the antihero of a series sardonically called *Father Knows Best,* invariably responded to the strange antics of his children by saying, "Let's keep out of it and see what happens."

Advertisers were wary of offending youth; the nation's teen-agers were spending 25 billion dollars a year. It was ironic that student militants should take so vigorous a stand against materialism; their own generation was the most possession-conscious in history. In *The Lonely Crowd* Riesman wrote that in America "children begin their training as consumers at an increasingly young age," that "middle-class children have allowances of their own at four or five," and that the allowances "are expected to be spent, whereas in the earlier era they were often used as cudgels of thrift."

Advertisers courting them addressed teen-agers as "the Now Generation," the "New People," the "Pepsi Generation," and the "Go Anywhere, Do Anything Generation." John Brooks pointed out that they were the most conspicuous beneficiaries of Johnsonian prosperity: "American youth, like everybody else but more spectacularly, was getting rich. A combination of burgeoning national wealth and the settled national habit of indulging the young was putting unprecedented sums of cash in their hands." Keeping them solvent wasn't always easy. In 1964 the Harvard class of '39, hardly indigents, reported that providing their children with money was the chief paternal problem for 78 percent of them. Only 6 percent said that instilling moral values in them was as hard. And they weren't all that moral. For $12.50 a boy could buy a girl a "Going Steady" ring which looked just like a wedding band; certainly no motel manager could tell the difference. If they felt guilty next day, in some places they could pray for forgiveness at teen-age churches. The Emmanuel Hospital in Portland, Oregon, even had a teen-age wing. It was described by Frank J. Taylor in a *Saturday Evening Post* article, "How to Have Fun in the Hospital." Patients enjoyed "unlimited snacks, jam sessions, and wheel-chair drag races." Priggish nutritionists kept their distance; the teen-agers were allowed to "eat hot dogs and hamburgers day after day for lunch and supper."

Literature for the young included *How to Be a Successful Teenager*, by one William C. Menninger. In a chapter on "How to Live with Parents" Menninger described techniques of handling mothers and fathers who tried to dictate to them: "One of the best ways to maintain family peace and insure cooperation is by holding family councils periodically about important matters." There were plenty of other sources of advice for youth. The *Chicago Daily News* carried a column of adolescent gossip called "Keen Teens"; the *Ladies' Home Journal* a department, "Profile of Youth." Pulps for adolescents included *Confidential Teen Romances, Teen Times, Hollywood Teenager, 16 Magazine, Teen World, Teen Parade, Modern Teen,* and *Teen Screen.* Among their magazines were *Ingenue, Calling All Girls,* and *Seventeen,* which observed its seventeenth year of publication in 1961 with a breathless editorial, "It's Our Birthday"—"*Seventeen* is 17 . . . Isn't Everybody?"

I Was a Teen-Age Frankenstein was one of the more memorable films produced for the adolescent trade. The editor of *Teen Magazine,* Charles Laufer, said that "the music market for the first time in history is completely dominated by the young set." They were the most musical generation ever, and their taste, at its best, was very good; the swing generation could hardly improve on the Beatles, Joan Baez, Bob Dylan, and forty-four-year-old B. B. King, whom the youth of the 1960s discovered after he had been ignored by his contemporaries for twenty-one years. Unfortunately the youngsters had other idols who belonged aesthetically with Andy

Warhol's Brillo boxes and Campbell soup cans, among them the ruttish Presley. Presley's voice and appearance were at least his own. That wasn't true of most rock stars. To a striking degree they were all alike—short youths, running to fat, who were prepared for public consumption by strenuous dieting, nose surgery, contact lenses, and luxurious hair styles. And they couldn't sing. Most couldn't even have made themselves heard in the back of a theater. Their voices were amplified in echo chambers and then created on tape, a snippet here and a snippet there, destroying false notes. When they appeared in public, they would mouth the words while the records were being played over the loudspeakers. Wiggling their hips and snapping their fingers, their features always fixed in a sullen expression, they would desecrate good songs: "I loved, I loved, I loved yuh, once in si-ilence," or "The rain, yeah! stays mainly in the puh-lain."

"What I mean to kids," said Janis Joplin, shortly before she killed herself with whiskey and drugs, "is they can be themselves and win." John Lennon of the Beatles said, "We're more popular than Jesus now." Their listeners may have tuned such things out. They were, after all, accustomed to meaningless words—"Learn to forget," said a writer in *Crawdaddy;* it was one of the wiser apostrophes directed to that rock magazine's readers. Purdue polled two thousand teen-agers on the gravest problem facing American youth. A third of them said acne.

Policemen would have disagreed. Over the previous ten years arrests of the young had jumped 86 percent. "Teen-Agers on the Rampage," proclaimed a *Time* head after a single week which had seen violence "among high schools from California to Maine." Professor Ruth Shonle Cavan published the first sociology textbook to deal with upper- and middle-class delinquency, including what she called "alcohol-automobile-sex behavior." Felonies were almost commonplace in some neighborhoods which had once been serene. The FBI reported that Americans aged eighteen or younger accounted for almost half of all arrests for murder, rape, robbery, aggravated assault, burglary, and auto theft—and in the suburbs it was more than half. Beginning in 1960 suburbs began setting up teen-age codes of conduct, but they had no legal status, compliance was voluntary, and their chief value was evidence that parental authority was bankrupt. "Mit dose kids society is nix," said the cop of the Katzenjammer kids, and it often was. Gallup found a startling difference between the values of parents and those of their children. Three out of four youngsters said they knew that cheating on examinations was common. It didn't bother them, Gallup reported.

The first evidence of widespread teen-age drug parties in the paneled rumpus rooms of the affluent was turned up in 1960 by the Westchester County vice squad. After the shock had passed parents said that at least it wasn't liquor. Then police on Santa Catalina Island, the southern California resort, announced that drunkenness had become common among thirteen- and fourteen-year-old children in wealthy families, and in the future they would charge the parents $2.50 an hour to babysit teen-age drunks till parents came to take them home. Nationally the number of adolescents who drank regularly was put at between 50 and 66 percent. In Yonkers, New York, where it was 58 percent among high school juniors and seniors, 64 percent said they drove the family car while doing it. Parents in Rose Valley, a Philadelphia suburb, allowed children to bring their own bottles to parties. Their fathers did the bartending. One wondered what Clarence Day's father would have thought.

Among the recurring news stories of the 1960s—the ghetto disorders, the annual anniversary of Dallas, the war moratoriums—were accounts of rioting at the Newport Jazz Festival and at Fort Lauderdale, the watering places of the young. Yet the extent of teen-agers' drinking ought not to have been surprising. In a sense they were expressing their social role. Opulence, the lack of genuine responsibility, and a position outside the unemployment pool gave them all the attributes of a leisure class.

In their ennui or their cups, youths of the 1960s frequently turned destructive. A brief item from Hannibal, Missouri, gave melancholy evidence of the revision of a cherished American myth. At the foot of Hannibal's Cardiff Hill stands a famous statue of Tom Sawyer and Huckleberry Finn, barefoot and carrying fishing poles; a plaque explains that this is the neighborhood where Tom and Huck "played and roamed at will." But any boys who attempted to emulate them after dark in the late 1960s would have risked arrest. Because of the rise in adolescent vandalism, loitering by the young on Cardiff Hill—and indeed anywhere in Hannibal—was forbidden after 10 P.M.

It was a harsh but necessary law; the vandalism was a real problem, in Missouri and elsewhere. During one week in February 1968 thirty New Haven high school students were arrested in the wake of china-smashing cafeteria riots, five hundred boys in the Chicago suburb of Maywood battled police at a rally protesting the selection of a homecoming queen, and nearly three thousand students at Chicago's Dunbar High left classes to pelt rocks at cars. In a typical suburban incident, an Alexandria, Virginia, gang, the children of government officials, did between $7,000 and $8,000 in damage by smashing automobile windshields with baseball bats. When arrested, they said they had done it "for fun." Another widespread expression of violence was party crashing. For a time there was a rash of such incidents each weekend in Westchester, Fairfield, Rockland, and Bucks counties—the exclusive suburbs ringing New York. Characteristically, six or eight uninvited youths would arrive at the height of a party, break open the parents' liquor cabinet, and destroy glassware and furniture.

Sometimes invited guests were worse. They would rival one another in seeing how much they could damage their host's home. One memorable debutante party celebrated the coming out of blonde Fernanda Wanamaker at her stepparent's thirty-room mansion in Southampton, Long Island. Over eight hundred children of what *Vogue* was then calling "the beautiful people" were invited. After the band had left, a hundred and twenty-seven of them wrecked the mansion, smashing windows, tearing down curtains, swinging on chandeliers, ripping out phones, breaking lamps, carting off appliances and throwing most of the furniture on the beach. The cost of the mischief was estimated to be somewhere between $3,000 and $10,000.

Affluent youths were often the worst offenders, but disorders could break anywhere. On one Independence Day five hundred drunken youths in Arnolds Park, Iowa, hurled rocks, beer bottles, and pieces of concrete at policemen; the tumult was set off when one of them yelled at the police chief, "Hey, punk, we're going to take over this place." In Chicago a free rock concert series—arranged by municipal officials to build camaraderie with youth—had to be canceled. At the first performance the audience rose up swinging tire chains and clubs; 135 were injured, including 65 policemen.

North Dakota University was one of the quietest, best-behaved campuses in the country until the *Student*, its undergraduate newspaper, proposed a weekend of fun in the nearby town of Zap. Zap's Mayor Norman Fuchs, delighted, wrote to all neighboring colleges promising "Zap-Burgers with special seasoning" and lots of "good, clean, beer-busting, food-munching, tear-jerking, rib-tickling fun." He acquired a sweatshirt with the legend "Zap, N.D. or Bust" and announced that the occasion would be called a "Zap-In." There was talk of Zap becoming the Fort Lauderdale of the North. The mayor could scarcely have understood the implications of all that. His town had a population of three hundred. By the evening of Friday, May 9, 1969, nearly a thousand students, 90 percent of them male, had arrived in Zap from five states. The town's three taverns were packed. When the thermometer dropped below freezing the students started a bonfire in the street, ripping out tables and booths from the taverns for firewood. Then they began breaking into stores and houses. Fistfights followed. A fire truck arrived; they seized it and dismantled it. Before five hundred National Guardsmen could arrive, the visitors had done $10,000 worth of damage.

The Fort Lauderdale of the South was never confronted with precisely that problem, freezing temperatures never having been recorded there in May. But Florida was afflicted with youthful firebugs that year just the same. Over a fifteen-month period an incredible number of unexplained fires (120) broke out on the University of Florida campus in Gainesville. Fire marshals thought it possible that the entire campus might be razed. The crisis was resolved when residents in Hume Hall confessed they had done it. Students in the east and west wings had been competing to see which could attract the most fire trucks. What made the incident particularly striking was a circumstance which would have been unthinkable in earlier generations. Hume Hall was a girls' dormitory.

Men's rooms in genteel establishments had long displayed a sign over urinals: PLEASE ARRANGE CLOTHING BEFORE LEAVING WASHROOM. Well-brought-up boys didn't need to be reminded; they had been taught never to fasten the flies of their trousers in public. They were therefore startled when Françoise Dorleac, in the 1966 film *Where the Spies Are,* emerged from a dressing room, reached for her crotch, and casually zipped up her slacks in the presence of her costar, David Niven. It was one of those moments which served as reminders that the delicate balance between the sexes had been altered, probably forever. Women were moving into jobs which had always been considered masculine: telephone linemen, mining engineers, ditch diggers, truck drivers, Secret Service agents. More of them were sharing men's vices, too: public drunkenness, juvenile delinquency, and assault and battery. Women's Liberation leader Ti-Grace Atkinson called marriage "slavery," "legalized rape," and "unpaid labor," and disapproved of love between the sexes as "tied up with a sense of dependency." The Women's Lib movement was not confined to the United States; in 1970 Bernadette Devlin was designated Ireland's Man of the Year by her admirers, and 1,162 pregnant Norwegian women sailors, who had conceived while on the high seas, claimed and were granted compensation from their government. But it was in America that women took to the streets at the end of the 1960s in massive rallies: 3,000 in Chicago, 2,000 in Indianapolis, 2,000 in Boston, and 50,000 in Manhattan, striding down Fifth Avenue with their breasts, unencumbered by brassieres, swaying visibly.

The disappearance of bras among members of the movement was but one of many changes in fashion. When Mia Farrow cropped her hair girls flocked to hairdressers so they, too, could look like boys. They crowded Army-Navy stores buying pea jackets, petty officer shirts, and bell-bottom trousers. Square-toed, low, heavy shoes became popular among them, and so many coeds were using after-shave lotion as perfume that the business journal *Forbes* protested that the sexes were beginning to smell alike. In 1966 Twiggy, the Cockney model, weighed in at ninety-one pounds, and women dieted to look like her, angularity being considered antifeminine. The idea was to look tough. Shiny plastic came into vogue, and hard, metallic fabrics. Pantsuits appeared—not cute slacks but mannish, tailored slacks. The zippers or buttons were no longer on the side; they went straight down the front, like Françoise Dorleac's, and some girls reportedly made them to go all the way through and up the back, so they could stand at urinals. Barbara Tuchman protested that too many women were beginning to look like Lolitas or liontamers. A Woman's Lib leader called her an Aunt Tom.

At the very top of the movement there was some female homosexuality and bisexuality; Kate Millett said she sometimes slept with women, and Joan Baez acknowledged that she had once had a lesbian affair. There was considerable resentment in the movement over being considered "sex objects"; girls objected to being whistled at and featured in fetching ads designed to appeal to males. Most girls in the movement preferred boys, however; Gloria Steinem, a heterosexual Lib leader, said, "Men think that once women become liberated, it will mean no more sex for men. But what men don't realize is that if women are liberated, there will be more sex and better." Betty Friedan attested to "the mounting sex-hunger of American women," and David Riesman noted that "millions of women" had become "knowing consumers of sex" and "pioneers, with men, on the frontier of sex." Elderly Americans, who had called aggressive women "bold" or "forward," couldn't grasp what was happening. Attending his granddaughter's commencement in 1967, General Eisenhower told miniskirted girls: "Ankles are nearly always neat and good-looking but knees are nearly always not." The girls, of course, knew that what interested boys was higher up.

Certainly more girls were on the prowl, often roaming the streets in pairs or appearing at weekends, available, on college campuses. Bachelors dropping in for a drink at Chicago's dating bars in the Rush Street district—The Jail, The Store, The Spirit of '76—would be propositioned by girls who offered to "ball" them and tried to arouse them with a new gesture—the feminine hand, slipped between the man's thighs, squeezing him there. Over a third of the coeds at a New York university admitted to one-night affairs with total strangers. Nationally, during the 1960s, the number of girls reporting premarital intercourse in surveys more than doubled; in a five-year period it rose 65 percent. European surveyors found that twice as many boys as girls there volunteered to describe their sexual experiences; in the United States it was the other way around. The number of coeds reporting the petting of male genitals soared. High school girls tried to achieve a licentious air. To that end, *Seventeen* discovered, the number of its subscribers using mascara had jumped from one in five during the late 1940s to nine in ten. Rudi Gernreich said that twenty years earlier girls tried to look sweet and innocent; now, "before they are seventeen years old they cultivate a wild, consciously sexy look." Demure women all but vanished. Obscene language no longer shocked them; they used it themselves. If they wanted coitus they said so. In the film *All the Loving Couples,* a jaded wife waiting to be swapped said thickly, "When do we get laid?"

Presently she was in the throes of sexual intercourse, on camera, with another woman's husband. The movies, once straitlaced, were exploring all the visual possibilities of the sex act. Under the leadership of Jack Valenti, who left the White House to become president of the Motion Picture Association of America, Hollywood adopted a rating system for films in 1968. Those in the G category would be family movies; the others would be M (suggested for mature audiences), R (restricted to persons sixteen or older unless accompanied by a parent or guardian), or X (no one under sixteen admitted under any circumstances).

In the late 1960s each season's X movies went farther than the last. Even the movie ads in newspapers become something to put out of reach of children. *I Am Curious (Yellow)* was thought shocking when it appeared, showing nudity and coitus, but new productions rapidly made it obsolescent. Ads for *The Minx* said it "makes Curious Yellow look pale," and it did. Then *The Fox* depicted lesbians kissing passionately and a naked woman masturbating in front of a full-length mirror. A beast had intercourse with a woman in *Rosemary's Baby. Bob and Carol and Ted and Alice* was a comedy about wife swapping. *Blow-Up* provided a glimpse of a girl's pubic hair; it was thought daring at the time, but presently ingenious close-ups showed the genitals in intercourse from unusual angles—some from the bottom—and actresses masturbating actors to climax. The ultimate, or so it seemed at the time, was *Deep Throat,* a tremendous hit about cunnilingus and fellatio. At the conclusion of it the heroine took a man down to the hilt of his phallus, displaying a talent which the *New Yorker* compared to that of a sword swallower. The action was photographed at a range of a few feet, and when the man reached orgasm, so did the girl. Technicolor revealed her full body flush.

Dallas District Attorney Henry Wade said: "I wouldn't be too surprised to see a sex circus in the Cotton Bowl." On Manhattan's Forty-second Street, in the block between Seventh and Eighth avenues, a policeman said: "If a little old lady wants to buy the *Times,* she has to climb over three rows of *Screw* to get it." *Screw, Suck, Desire, Gay,* and *Coq*—all the smut magazines competed for circulation by trying to show more flesh of models in lewder poses than the others. In Miami, Bunny Dania, one of the more experienced models, said that when she began posing photographers would show nudes playing volleyball or swimming. "Now," she said, "you've got to have wife swapping and sadism and girls making out with girls. It's moved indoors."

On stage a performer named Jim Morrison described his latest sexual adventure; it had occurred five minutes before curtain time. *Oh! Calcutta!* was billed as "elegant erotica"; its sketches ranged in theme from wife swapping to rape. *Che!* provided a hundred minutes of faked sex acts. Those who preferred the real thing could find it in New York's "Mine-Cini Theater," or in San Francisco taverns where a boy and girl would strip, climb on the bar, and there engage in what was drolly called the act of love. Some spectacles shocked the most hardened observers. A reporter told of going backstage in one Manhattan show and seeing chorus girls, naked, shooting heroin into the backs of their knees while their illegitimate toddlers watched.

Sex became an issue in strange places. After searching his conscience for five years on contraception, Pope Paul rejected it in a 7,500-word encyclical entitled *Humanae Vitae* (*Of Human Life*) on July 29, 1969. Millions of American Catholics were furious. A study by the Urban Life Institute of the University of San Francisco, a Jesuit school, disclosed that 70 percent of them approved of birth control. The vast majority of young priests agreed (though over 90 percent of the older priests did not). In Washington several rebellious priests staged a sit-in, and a hundred and forty-two others sent a letter of protest to the head of their archdiocese, Patrick Cardinal O'Boyle. When the cardinal began a sermon on obedience in St. Matthew's Cathedral, two hundred members of the congregation rose from their pews and stalked out. Seven Buffalo priests were dismissed from a seminary for mutinous remarks. Still the revolt spread. The following year the former auxiliary bishop of the St. Paul-Minneapolis archdiocese married a New York divorcée. Soon stories about priests marrying—often to nuns who had leaped over the wall—lost their novelty.

A lot of carnal knowledge was being acquired in laboratories, observed by scientists in white coats holding stopwatches and other things. The most famous of them were Dr. William H. Masters and Virginia E. Johnson, who eventually married one another. Their findings at the Reproductive Biology Research Foundation in St. Louis were invaluable, but fastidious critics were appalled by the measuring and photographing of copulation; it smacked to them of charcoal filters and flip-top boxes. The most remarkable piece of Masters-Johnson equipment was an electrically powered plastic penis with a tiny camera inside and cold light illumination to allow observation and recording of what was happening inside the vagina. The size of this artificial phallus could be adjusted, and the woman using it could regulate the depth and speed of the thrust. Inevitably it inspired several novels. The best of them was Robert Kyle's *Venus*

Examined (1968). At the end of it a disillusioned heroine returns to the sex laboratory, demolishes the plastic phallus, and is electrocuted.

All this was a great strain for the young. Previous generations had been protected from early sexual entanglements by social custom, the fear of disgrace, and the possibility of venereal disease or pregnancy—a catastrophe for the girl. Now mores had changed spectacularly; society took a tolerant view of premarital affairs. Venereal infection had vanished. (Late in the decade it would reappear as a nationwide epidemic, a consequence of the new promiscuity.) "If it feels good, I'll do it," read a pin popular among college students. Intercourse felt good, and they did it a lot, protected by the Pill, or diaphragms, and various intrauterine devices, loops and coils.

Late in the decade, when abortions became easier to obtain, girls felt even safer. But improved contraceptives were not responsible for the increase in pushovers. It preceded them. Illegitimate births doubled between 1940 and 1960, and 40 percent of the mothers were in their teens. The Hechingers found that in some sophisticated communities a girl was expected to begin sexual intercourse with her steady boyfriend on her sixteenth birthday; if she refrained, she lost status. Pregnancy was so common in an Oakland high school that girls were allowed to attend classes until their confinement. A New York hospital on the privileged East Side reported that the number of unwed mothers jumped 271 percent in six years, and the *New York Times* quoted Dr. Margaret L. McCormack as saying that pregnancy, "once a college problem, is now a high school and junior high school problem." One New York junior high, she said, had 240 pregnancies in one year. The Pill came into widespread use during the winter of 1961–62, and by 1967 the illegitimacy rate among schoolgirls was on the decline. But no one suggested that coitus had lost its popularity.

The sex-drenched state of American culture was undoubtedly responsible for much of the increase in premarital and extramarital intercourse. Sexiness was everywhere—on paperback book racks, television, in ads, magazines, popular songs, plays, musicals, and everyday conversation. Betty Friedan cited a psychological study which found that references to sex in mass media increased by over 250 percent in the 1960s. The *New York Times Book Review* noted the popularity of books about "love" affairs between animals and human beings. Complaints to the U.S. Post Office about smut doubled within six years, to 130,000 in 1965.

"Be Prepared!" proclaimed a poster showing an enormously pregnant girl, smiling broadly, in a Girl Scout uniform. The Scouts asked for damages; the court threw out the case. "Use Contraceptives: Take the Worry Out of Being Close," said a Planned Parenthood ad. The New York Hilton, Manhattan's largest hotel, was renting rooms by the hour. Frustrated persons (or couples) took out ads in the personal column of the *Saturday Review*, or in underground newspapers, soliciting new partners. Everybody knew about key parties for swapping couples; the men threw their house keys on a table and the wives picked them up at random, each then going to bed with the owner of whatever key she had.

Nicholas von Hoffman described a game, manufactured by the Diplomat Sales Company of Los Angeles, which provided "a safe, nicely structured way for two or three couples to end an evening naked, drunk, out of their minds, and lascivious as hell." Called Bumps and Grinds, it was played by the light of one candle (which was included). Players moved around a board like the one used in Monopoly, drawing "Tomcat" and "Pussycat" cards. These advised them to "Take one drink," or "Strip one article of clothing," and so on. The game was rigged for the girls to wind up nude and drunk first. Subsequent moves decided who was going to stagger to the bedroom with whom.

If wife swapping was permissible for the middle-aged, youths argued, what was wrong with wife testing for them? Some communities, troubled by the question and aware of the temptations which prompted it, tried to ward off the great landslide of sex with local regulations. For a while wearers of bikinis on some public beaches were required to have two inches of cloth on each hip. Then President Kennedy's widow was photographed in a three-ring bikini, and the regulations collapsed. Thus clad, or unclad, the young could caress 95 percent of each other's bodies with suntan lotion in public. And as they thus excited one another, transistor radios alongside broadcast suggestive lyrics: "This girl is a woman now/ She knows what it's all about," or "If somebody loves you, it's no good unless she loves you/ All the way," or:

Don't you know the facts of life,
You've got a lot to learn;

I'd like to teach you all,
And get your love in return.

"There is," said a University of Michigan coed, "nobody saying 'No.'" So many were saying yes that it was a wonder one-third of female college undergraduates remained virgins. In some instances, parents actually regarded the absence of coital experience as troubling. All things being equal, they would have preferred that their daughters remained maidens. But in this generation everything else was unequal. A teen-age girl who lacked a normal interest in sex could be in the toils of another new snare for the young. She was possibly—and in some communities probably—a user of heavy drugs.

Early developments in mid-century chemotherapy were benign. The sulfa drugs had arrived in the late 1930s. Then came penicillin (1943), streptomycin (1945), cortisone (1946), ACTH (1949), terramycin and aureomycin (1950), the Salk vaccine (1955), the Sabin vaccine (1960), and the tranquilizers, led by Miltown and Librium, which cut the length of the average mental hospital stay in half. All these were called "miracle drugs" when they first appeared. Because of them, diseases which had afflicted men since the dawn of history were tamed and, in some cases, eliminated. In 1959 over 579 *tons* of tranquilizers were prescribed, which gives some idea of the need they met. As recently as the early 1950s polio terrorized parents during the summer months; 57,000 cases were reported in 1952. Now that was merely a memory.

The first inkling that the drug revolution had a dark side came in 1962, when eight thousand European women who had been taking a new tranquilizer called Thalidomide gave birth to limbless babies. Thanks to Dr. Frances O. Kelsey of the Food and Drug Administration, Thalidomide had not been licensed for general use in the United States. Nevertheless, a few Thalidomide-deformed babies had been born to expectant mothers who had been taking the blue tablets on an investigative basis. If a drug could do that, anything was possible. And the amount of medication in American medicine cabinets was unprecedented. Doctors were now writing nearly two billion dollars' worth of prescriptions each year for pills which included new barbiturates and amphetamines, hypnotics, and antidepressants. In addition, an enormous black market was flourishing. Of the eight billion amphetamines, or pep pills, manufactured each year, about four billion were being sold illegally. Laymen might call the pep pills and barbiturates "soft" drugs and heroin, morphine, and cocaine "hard," but pharmacologists knew it should be the other way around; the older drugs calmed addicts, but the new ones created dangerous, unpredictable moods. Some became part of the culture, familiar enough to have popular nicknames. Among them were "bluejays" (sodium amytal), "redbirds" (seconal), "yellow jackets" (nembutal), and "goofballs" (barbiturates laced with benzedrine).

The most widely discussed of the new compounds was d-lysergic acid diethylamide—LSD. First isolated in 1938 by Dr. Albert Hofmann in the Sandoz Research Laboratories in Basle, Switzerland, it lay around his lab for five years, unappreciated, its properties awaiting discovery. That occurred on April 16, 1943. Absorbing some LSD through the skin of his fingers, Hofmann began hallucinating. His scientific curiosity aroused, he then deliberately took 250 micrograms of it—an amount about the size of a grain of salt. In his diary he explained the effect: "With closed eyes, multihued, metamorphizing, fantastic images overwhelmed me . . . Sounds were transposed into visual sensations so that from each tone or noise a comparable colored picture was evoked, changing in form and color kaleidoscopically." In short, he had taken a trip.

Dr. Humphrey Osmond of the New Jersey Neuropsychiatric Institute neologized a new name for LSD. He called it a psychedelic and said it meant mind-expanding. At the start of the 1960s, the colorless, odorless, tasteless drug was still unknown to the public. Then two Harvard psychologists, Timothy Leary and Richard Alpert, began experimenting with colleagues, writers, artists, clergymen, and volunteer prisoners. Leary and Alpert were dismissed from Harvard in 1963, but by then LSD had achieved its reputation. Taking a trip, or turning on, had come to convey status on campuses. Alarmed, the FDA warned college presidents that taking it was an "insidious and dangerous activity." Sandoz Laboratories stopped making it. Laws barring it in any form were passed in Michigan, New Jersey, Nevada, and California. None of that made any difference; the use of it continued to spread.

LSD became a household word in 1966. Even recluses knew what was meant by tripping, freaking out, and blowing one's mind. Priests and pastors held a conference on the religious aspects of LSD. In discotheques—and also in art galleries and museums—films, slides, and flashing colored lights suggested the impact of an LSD experience. Chilling stories, some of them apocryphal, were told to scare those who were tempted to take a trip. A youth high on LSD was said to have taken a swan dive into the front of a truck moving at 70 mph. Teen-agers under its influence reportedly lay in a field staring at the sun until they were permanently blinded. That was exposed as a lie, but the Associated Press verified the case of a young man who turned himself in to police saying he had been flying on LSD for three days and asking "Did I kill my wife? Did I rape anyone?" and was then charged with the murder of his mother-in-law.

Users described feeling depressed, even homicidal, and told how they had turned themselves into ravens, or Jesus Christ, or tiny people six inches tall. Distraught parents told what had happened to their children: "My boy is on drugs. He went to St. Louis because it's the astrological center of the universe. He has met Hitler and Lincoln." And "Our son came home for Christmas. He looked awful. He rode his little sister's bicycle barefoot through the snow. The neighbors took their children in. People are afraid of him."

But the users of LSD—they called it acid—described their trips as ecstatic. "Who needs jazz, or even beer," wrote a contributor to the *New York Times Magazine*, "when you can sit down on a public curbstone, drop a pill in your mouth, and hear fantastic music for hours at a time in your own head? A cap of good acid costs $5, and for that you can hear the Universal Symphony, with God singing solo and the Holy Ghost on drums."

The Beatles sang "Yellow Submarine," which was a euphemism for a freakout, and another song freighted with LSD meaning, "Strawberry Field." Elementary school children dismayed their mothers by coming home chanting, to the tune of "Frère Jacques":

Marijuana, marijuana,
LSD, LSD,
College kids are making it, high
  school kids are taking it,
Why can't we? Why can't we?

At times it seemed that an entire generation was turning on to drugs. In fact, the hippy movement, or counterculture, which sprang from the self-medication and narcotics, was at first smaller than it appeared to be. It was really an extension of the beat generation of the 1950s. In the early 1960s the beatniks moved into San Francisco's Haight-Ashbury district. A musical combo called the Jefferson Airplane was then playing the first acid rock in an obscure night spot called the Matrix. Their group and the Grateful Dead were being entertained by Ken Kesey and his band of Merry Pranksters at La Honda, Kesey's forest home fifty miles south of San Francisco. It was at La Honda that Kesey and the Pranksters served their guests Kool-Aid spiked with LSD, and there that he wrote *One Flew Over the Cuckoo's Nest* (1962) and *Sometimes a Great Notion* (1964).

Listening to the driving, drowning acid rock, the Pranksters experimented with light and color, wore spectacular clothes, and evolved a life-style which would later become familiar in virtually every American community and in many abroad. It wasn't popular then. The dances at which the Airplane and the Dead played were thinly attended. Most customers still preferred the Charlie Parker brand of jazz. The new musicians painted posters depicting the visual impact of an LSD trip. Few admired them. At first they gave away these early examples of psychedelic art, then they sold them for a dollar each. A *Ramparts* editor said the printing was "36-point illegible," but by 1967 some of the originals would be selling in the best San Francisco art galleries for $2,000.

By then a reporter for the *San Francisco Chronicle* had christened the new bohemians "hippies," and the movement had become first a national and then an international phenomenon. Hippy communes were flourishing in New York, Boston, Chicago, Los Angeles, and Atlanta, and hippy enclaves had been established in Mexico, Canada, London, Rome, Tokyo—even in Laos. By then many charter members of the movement had quit, disgusted by the exhibitionists who were giving colorful interviews to newspapermen and television commentators. "The best year to be a hippy was 1965," said Hunter S. Thompson, the Ernie Pyle of the movement, "but then there was not much to write about, because not much was happening in public and most of what was happening in private was illegal. The real year of the hippie was 1966, despite the lack of publicity, which in 1967 gave way to a nationwide avalanche."

Fortunes were made in the 1967 "Summer of Love" from the sale of DMT, mescaline, methedrine, LSD, and the even more popular —and safer—marijuana to the disillusioned children of the middle and upper middle class who flocked to hippy communes, leaving what they regarded as a stifling straight life to Do Their Thing. Pot, boo, maryjane, grass, or Mary Warner—the various names under which marijuana was known to them—sold in Mexico for $35 a kilogram (2.2 pounds). Smuggled into the United States, a kilo brought $150 to $200. Meted out in 34-ounce bags, it went for as much as $25 an ounce, or $850 the kilo. Joints—marijuana cigarettes—sold on the street for a dollar each. The heroin racket was even more lucrative. Undercover chemists made $700 for every kilo of morphine converted to heroin in Marseilles. Manhattan entrepreneurs paid $10,000 for it and sold it on the street in plastic bags, each containing just 5 percent heroin cut with sugar or quinine powder. In that form the original 2.2 pounds earned $20,000. And the market was expanding rapidly. The Federal Bureau of Narcotics estimated that 68,000 Americans became addicted in a single year.

In literally scores of cities there were share-ins, be-ins, and love-ins. As in the case of the beatniks ten years earlier, San Francisco was the focal point of the movement. The San Francisco *Oracle*, the leading underground newspaper, was published there, and there the original band of Diggers—named for a seventeenth-century English brotherhood that raised food for the poor on land which had been uncultivated—became beggars in order to feed indigent hippies. The distribution was in what was called Panhandle Park; it was known as the Politics of Free.

The issue of how many youths participated in the counterculture depends entirely on definitions. If smokers of marijuana are counted, the number is enormous. Dr. Henry Brill, chairman of the American Medical Association's committee on drug dependence, estimated that the number of Americans who tried pot went from a few hundred thousand in the early 1960s to eight million at the end of the decade, most of them in their teens. That was by far the most conservative of the estimates; the U.S. Public Health Service put the figure at 20 million. A *Playboy* survey reported that 47 percent of the nation's college students admitted smoking marijuana, though only 13 percent said they used it frequently. Members of families with high incomes smoked it most often. Just 2 percent acknowledged injecting methedrine, or speed—liquid amphetamines—directly into their veins, and a mere 1 percent were addicted to other narcotics.

The great year of the hippy may be said to have begun on Easter Sunday, March 26, 1967, when ten thousand boys and girls assembled in New York Central Park's Sheep Meadow to honor love. They flew kites, tossed Frisbees, joined hands in "love circles," painted designs on each other's faces, and chanted: "Banana! Banana!" after a current hoax, that banana scrapings had psychedelic properties. On the other side of the country that Sunday fifteen thousand youths in San Francisco cheered Dr. Leary's Pied Piper spiel: "Turn on to the scene; tune in to what's happening; and drop out—of high school, college, grade school . . . follow me, the hard way."

What came next was a nightmare for tens of thousands of mothers and fathers. With the memories of their Depression childhoods still vivid, the parents of the late 1960s could not grasp that the country had become so prosperous it could afford to support tramps, or that their own children would want to be among the tramps. "The kids looked like bums, often acted like bums," the Associated Press reported, "but they were no ordinary bums. Most had spent their lives in middle-class surroundings, finishing high school, often graduating from college—the American dream." Now their photographs, forwarded by their parents and accompanied by pathetic messages pleading for news of their whereabouts, were hung on bulletin boards in police stations. The pictures weren't much help. Taken when the youngsters were straight, they bore little relation to their new life-style.

The police did what they could. The Salvation Army opened a coffee house in East Village called The Answer, where flower children in their early teens were urged to return home. Runaways in Haight-Ashbury were sheltered at church-sponsored Huckleberry's while mothers and fathers were contacted. A physician opened a free clinic for hippies in San Francisco. Almost immediately he was overwhelmed by pregnancies, cases of venereal disease, and hepatitis caused by dirty syringes. Virtually every hippy in Hashbury had a cold or the flu. Many had tried sleeping in Golden Gate Park, unaware that a hidden sprinkling system automatically started up at dawn.

The greatest health hazard, of course, was the drugs. The hippies had no way of knowing what they were buying; Dr. Louis Lasagna found that many were getting veterinary anesthetics or even plain urine. In that summer many were experimenting with STP, a new compound named for a gasoline additive used in the Hell's Angels motorcycles. Between 5,000 and 10,000 STP capsules were given away. The flower children, liking it, christened it "the caviar of psychedelics." Doctors discovered that it was extremely dangerous;

when taken in combination with chlorpromazine, an LSD antidote, STP could prove fatal. The "speed freaks" or "meth monsters," as other hippies called them, were taking methedrine; when high, they were capable of almost anything. Meantime, in Buffalo, Dr. Maimon M. Cohen announced that preliminary findings in an investigation of LSD and chlorpromazine indicated that mixed together the two could result in chromosome damage, spontaneous abortions, or deformed infants.

That summer tourist buses were routed through Haight-Ashbury to provide a glimpse of the strange scene there. (Sometimes a hippy would run alongside the bus, holding up a mirror.) There, and in East Village, part-time flower children, or "plastics," as they were known—straights who were in effect slumming—were spending their weekends as hippies, returning to their jobs on Monday morning conservatively dressed and well groomed. The attitude of the New Left toward the flower children was equally ambivalent. In the beginning, when Leary succeeded Mario Savio as youth's demigod, New Left writers praised the hippies for their candor and spontaneity. After the Reagan landslide the situation changed. Many disillusioned militants tossed in the sponge, abandoned hope, and chose instead to stay stoned for days at a time. Flower power, they said, was nonpolitical. Stung, New Leftists retorted that the hippies lacked "stability" and "energy," that they were "intellectually flabby," and that they were really "nihilists" whose idea of love was "so generalized and impersonal as to be meaningless." Of course, the hippies replied; that was their thing, and they were going to do it, and up yours.

The immediate threat to the flower children was not from parents, policemen, tourists, or New Leftists. It came from lower-class ethnic groups into whose neighborhoods they had moved. Haight-Ashbury was a working-class district; New York's East Village was inhabited by Italians, Negroes, Poles, Jews, Puerto Ricans, and Ukrainians, all of them trying to climb into the lower middle class. The spectacle of idle youth scorning the class status to which the ghetto inhabitants aspired for their own children infuriated them. The AP quoted a twenty-year-old porter who had just been laid off: "These cats want to drop out. How do you think that makes a guy feel who is just trying to get in?"

"We hippies love people," a flute player protested; "we certainly aren't bigoted." The ethnics, he said wonderingly, thought of his neighborhood as "their turf." They did indeed. A black grumbled that the flower children had "taken over" Tompkins Square Park. The park had belonged to him and his; they didn't have much, but that, at least, had been theirs, and now these maddening, uninvited kids insisted on sharing it. The inevitable happened. Violence, always a menace in ghettos, erupted against the defenseless hippies. On Memorial Day of that year ethnic boys attacked a twenty-nine-year-old flower girl in Tompkins Square and stripped her naked. In Central Park a fifteen-year-old and her seventeen-year-old lover (characteristically she did not know his name; to her he was simply "The Poet") were attacked by blacks; she was raped and he was beaten insensible. In California a seller of drugs was murdered and his right forearm hacked off. A few days later another peddler was killed, stuffed into a sleeping bag, and left hanging from a cliff.

Clearly something ghastly was happening to that summer. Exploiters and predators were also stalking the young. In *The Family* Ed Sanders compared the flower movement to "a valley of plump rabbits surrounded by wounded coyotes." He wrote: "One almost had to live there to understand the frenzy that engulfed the Haight-Ashbury district of San Francisco in the spring and summer of 1967. The word was out all over America to come to San Francisco for love and flowers." But more awaited them in Hashbury than that. "The Haight attracted vicious criminals who grew long hair. Bikers tried to take over the LSD market with crude sadistic tactics. Bad dope was sold by acne-faced methedrine punks. Satanist and satanist-rapist death-freaks flooded the whirling crash pads. People began getting ripped off in the parks. There was racial trouble." In the midst of it, haunting Grateful Dead concerts in the Avalon Ballroom, was a bearded little psychotic who liked to curl up in a fetal position right on the dance floor, and whose secret ambitions were to persuade girls to perform fellatio with dogs and gouge out the eyes of a beautiful actress and smear them on walls. Later he would be well remembered in Hashbury. His name was Charles Manson.

Hippiedom would survive in one form or another, as beatism had —the bohemian strain runs wide and deep in America—but the movement as it had been known that year was doomed. All that was lacking was a final curtain. That came on the night of Saturday, October 8, 1967. A generation earlier, on June 8, 1931, the death of a New York girl bearing the singularly poetic name of Starr Faithfull had symbolized the magic and the depravity of an era then ending; John O'Hara had based *Butterfield 8* on it. Now the squalid Manhattan murder of another genteel girl ended the hippy summer of 1967. Her name was Linda Rae Fitzpatrick. She was eighteen, a blonde, the daughter of a wealthy spice and tea importer. Her home of record was her parents' mansion in Greenwich, Connecticut, but on Sunday, October 9, her naked corpse was found in a boiler room of a brownstone tenement at 169 Avenue B on the Lower East Side.

It was not a good address. Flanked by a flyblown junk shop and a dingy bar and grill, the boiler room reeked of dog excrement and rotting garbage. One naked light bulb shone down on peeling paint, decaying plaster, whitewashed bricks crawling with cockroaches, and a filthy mattress. Linda had come to this noisome trysting place with a tattooed drifter named James "Groovy" Hutchinson. As detectives and the police surgeon put the story together, she had stripped and sprawled on the mattress. At that point Linda and Groovy had discovered that they were not alone. This room was often used as an exchange point for the sale of drugs, and four speed-freaks, all of them flying, decided to share Groovy's girl with him. She refused. When Groovy tried to defend her, his face was bashed in with a brick. After Linda had been raped four times, her face was smashed, too. The bodies had been left face up; her black lace pants were found in a corner.

Three Negro men were swiftly arrested, but the public was more interested in the girl than in her victimizers. Linda had apparently led two lives. In Greenwich she had been the sheltered, well-bred child of an upper-class home. Like her parents she had been an Episcopalian; her favorite relaxation had been riding on the red-leafed bridle paths of the exclusive Round Hill Stables. The previous August, her father recalled, he had expressed his abhorrence of hippies, and her comments had been "much like mine." Her mother recalled that "Linda was never terribly boy crazy. She was very shy." Over Labor Day weekend she had told her mother that she didn't want to return to Oldfields, her expensive boarding school in Maryland. Instead she wanted to live in New York and paint. "After all," her mother said afterward, "Linda's whole life was art. She had a burning desire to be something in the art world." Her parents agreed to her plan when she told them she had a room in a respectable Greenwich Village hotel. Her roommate, she said, was a twenty-two-year-old receptionist of a good family called Paula Bush.

"*Paula* Bush?" said the desk clerk. "Sure, I remember Linda, but there wasn't no Paula Bush. It was *Paul* Bush." In East Village she had consorted with many men, her family learned, and she had used money sent from Greenwich to buy drugs for them and herself. Late in September she thought she was pregnant, and she had confided to another girl that she was worried about the effect of LSD on the baby. Saturday evening, three hours before she died, she had told a friend that she had just shot some speed and was riding high. The cruelest part of the sequel for her parents was the discovery that her East Village acquaintances were indifferent to her death. One hippy girl said that though they mourned Groovy, "The chick wasn't anything to us."

In San Francisco's Golden Gate Park that same week hippies burned a gray coffin labeled "Summer of Love." In it were orange peels, peacock feathers, charms, flags, crucifixes, and a marijuana-flavored cookie. The ceremony was called "The Death of Hip." After the mourners had watched the fire while singing "God Bless America" and "Hare Krishna," they shouted, "Hippies are dead! Now the free men will come through!" Violence had crippled the movement, and so had commercialism. Tourists were crowding craft shops in both the Haight and East Village. Hippies hungering for money were acting in *Indian Givers,* a full-length psychedelic western, in which the sheriff was being played by, of all people, Dr. Timothy Leary. Ron Thelin, proprietor of San Francisco's Psychedelic Shop, said dolefully, "The spirit is gone"; then he went out of business, and Roger Ricco, a veteran member of The Group Image, said, "It isn't the same any more. Where have all the flowers gone?"

Portrait of an American

KARL HESS III

EITHER/OR.

As Karl Hess saw it, every serious man was obliged to take an unyielding stand at one extreme or the other.

Either he was a Minuteman or a Weatherman, a hard-core,

better-dead-than-Red ultraconservative or a New Left militant, a Klansman or a Black Panther, an anti-Semite or a gunman of the Symbionese Liberation Army. If you didn't want the SAC to lob one into the men's room at the Kremlin, you must advocate blowing up the Pan Am Building. There was no middle ground, just one faith and one enemy of the faith, one way to save the world and one way to destroy it. Society was not marvelously complex; it was magnificently simple. One must merely choose between absolutes, between the black and the white, the good and the evil.

In 1954, as a sleek, well-paid spokesman of the ultraconservative right, he wrote in *The American Mercury:*

> It would not be America really if it did not produce men who suddenly tire of palaver and reach for the rifle on the wall, to use themselves or to hand to the underdog who needs it.

In 1970, as a bearded, ragged oracle of the SDS and the Black Panthers, he proudly displayed an announcement of his appearance on the University of Texas campus:

> Union Speakers Comm. (the people who brought you Abbie Hoffman) present: Karl Hess, farout freak, militant, commie, anarchist, pervert!!! Currently assoc. editor of *Ramparts.*

He never saw that the two poles were really one. Superficially it seemed that he had swung from one to the other. In fact he had not budged an inch. He ended where he had begun—at the farthest possible distance from the political center.

Born on a great Philippines estate in 1923, he was molded not by his father, a flamboyant millionaire, but by his mother, a former Washington, D.C., working girl. When strong-minded Thelma Hess discovered that her husband was a philanderer, she left him, returned to Washington with young Karl, and went to work as a switchboard operator rather than accept alimony. She made a rule: before her little son could have a toy, he must read a book. Entering kindergarten, he had finished H. G. Wells's *Outline of History.*

By the time he reached adolescence the husky young Hess had read more than his teachers, and they bored him. To him education was an organized bureaucracy. Already, at fourteen, he had identified the system as his enemy. He fought it by enrolling in two high schools, filing the transfer papers of each at the other. Lying about his age—he looked older than his years—Hess got a job at the Mutual radio network. He was writing news programs when he borrowed his boss's car one day. A policeman gave him a ticket, his true age was discovered, and he was fired. The system had won. It always would, but he would never quit struggling.

Next, as a copyboy on the *Alexandria Gazette*, he became fascinated with politics; that, too, would be a lifelong obsession. The Democrats repelled him. He became a right-wing Republican because the ultraconservatives championed individual liberty. Whatever the merit of his views, there was no questioning his ability. By his twentieth birthday he was a rising star on the *Washington Daily News*. Then the editor phoned him at home to say that FDR had died and he was assigned to the story. Hess replied that Roosevelt's obituary wasn't worth getting out of bed; he was fired.

He became news editor of *Aviation Week*, author of a children's book on natural science, editor of *Fisherman Magazine*, and, between 1950 and 1955, press editor at *Newsweek*. Had he been able to shuck his ideological yoke, he might have had a distinguished journalistic career. As it was, he became increasingly preoccupied with right-wing doctrine, writing an anti-Communist column for the conservative weekly *Pathfinder*, editing *Counter-Attack* and H. L. Hunt's *Facts Forum*, and founding the *National Review* with, among others, William F. Buckley Jr. At the same time he was contributing regularly to the *American Mercury*. In its pages he denounced Robert Oppenheimer, the United Nations, and critics of the National Rifle Association, in which he held a lifetime membership. ("If everybody in Latin America had a pistol, they would have democracy.") The National Guard, he declared, was the country's greatest protection against federal dictatorship. He believed in order, deference to military rank, and the "discipline that comes from respect of an obedience to authority."

By 1960 Hess's lyrical praise of rugged individualism had brought him a sinecure as assistant to the president of Ohio's vast Champion Paper and Fibre Company. He lived in an expensive suburban home with a wife, two children, and seventeen custom-made suits. His job at Champion was to discourage aggressive union organizers and instill loyalty to the company in employees. From time to time the firm loaned him to right-wing think tanks. He compiled *The Conservative Papers* for Congressman Melvin Laird. In 1960 he wrote policy papers for Richard Nixon, and in 1964, as Barry Goldwater's chief adviser, he dashed off the speech in which the senator accepted his party's nomination. Goldwater, he said, offered "a choice, not an echo."

Then something snapped. Lyndon Johnson not only won the election; he won it with contributions from the very big businessmen who had been Hess's heroes. Hess discovered that the backer of one of his right-wing publications had been enriched by federal agricultural subsidies. Most traumatic of all, the magnitude of the Goldwater defeat had made Hess a pariah in GOP circles. By custom, men who have served ably in a losing campaign may expect a job in the service of other members of the party who are still in office. On Capitol Hill he went from door to door, hoping for a place on some Republican payroll. He found none. No one wanted him in any capacity. By the following spring he was broke and desperate, ready to settle for a place as a Capitol elevator operator. Even that was closed to him. He wound up welding bulldozers on the night shift in a Washington machine shop.

That was the year of Johnson's first big Vietnam build-up. Hess was appalled by it. This was the system run amok. He perceived his error, and concluded that "my enemy was not a particular state—not Cuba or North Vietnam, for example—but the state itself." As he saw it, the anti-Commuist zeal of ultraconservatives had led them into a tragic error. They had trusted federal power, and had reaped the triumph of bureaucracy. His new heroes were the Panthers, who called for power to the people, and the Weathermen: "The SDS is raising essential political questions, and the police are beating them down for it." He began to read anarchist literature and to recommend resistance to authority—flouting of the law, draft resistance, hiding of political prisoners, refusing to move if the government condemns your house.

Slowly his life-style changed. He left his wife and grew a beard. The custom-made suits were left in the closet; he now wore a Castro cap, tennis shoes without socks, a tattered field jacket, and faded green denims. Because he refused to pay his taxes, he wasn't allowed to own property. He lived on the Anacostia River, in a houseboat belonging to a girlfriend. To a reporter he said, "I splice lines, paint the deck, and plot against the state." His plotting was limited to lecturing on campuses, exhorting Panther rallies, and writing for *Ramparts* and *Hard Times*, but the FBI was watching him carefully.

His old friends, who were now running the government under Nixon, were dumbfounded. In the corridors of power they whispered stories about him. He was poaching on federal property. He had competed in a motorcycle race and broken a leg. He was seen in the company of known felons, trotting around the District with a knapsack on his back. He had advocated the expropriation of all public and corporate wealth, was carrying an IWW membership card, had been arrested in an antiwar riot, had been gassed in a march on Fort Dix, had spoken at a radical rally from a stage dominated by an enormous black flag, had won a *Playboy* award for the best nonfiction article of the year—a paean to libertarianism.

Aboard the houseboat *Tranquil* the soft-voiced, beefily handsome Hess continued to scheme away. Mounted on the fore bulkhead was his beloved rifle, representing his everlasting belief in the right of a man to protect himself from the bureaucrats who would enslave him. Papers surrounded him: drafts of speeches, notes for an autobiography, pamphlets, the manuscript of a book on the wickedness of the capitalist state. He lamented as "tragic, very tragic" the fact "that Goldwater has now taken his stand on the side of established authority." He had heard that the senator refused to talk about him, but he understood that. "I wouldn't be surprised," he said reflectively, "if Barry thinks I'm crazy."

Thirty-three

THE YEAR EVERYTHING WENT WRONG

IT WAS THE YEAR of the Hong Kong flu and *Hair*. The hundred-and-twenty-one-year-old Pennsylvania Railroad and the hundred-and-fourteen-year-old New York Central merged, and service was twice as bad. First-class postage went from five cents an ounce to six. Helen Keller, Edna Ferber, and John Steinbeck died. Mia Farrow divorced Frank Sinatra. The American ambassador to Guatemala was assassinated.

In Washington the Willard Hotel, where at least seven Presidents, beginning with Franklin Pierce, had been guests at one time or another, went bankrupt. Red China, as it was still called then, exploded its seventh atom bomb, France its first hydrogen bomb. Hitler's bones turned up in Russia. A U.S. Strategic Air Command B-52 crashed in Greenland, near Thule, spilling wreckage contaminated with plutonium-235 over miles of ice, the thirteenth such accident. Biafra starved.

Some things went right. Barbra Streisand was marvelous in *Funny Girl.* Julie Nixon married David Eisenhower. Network censors cut Pete Seeger singing an antiwar song from a Smothers Brothers show, but six months later they changed their minds and let him do it. It was a big year for human transplants, although only one patient in four lived more than six months. The *Washington Daily News* reported that one out of every eight Americans was getting social security benefits. Tiny Tim tiptoed into the limelight. The American Civil Liberties Union decided to support draft evaders.

Laugh-In provided some lively graffiti: "Little Orphan Annie—call the eye bank," "This is your slum—keep it clean," "Forest fires prevent bears," and "George Wallace—your sheets are ready." Publishers issued John Updike's *Couples*, Charles Portis's *True Grit*, and Peter De Vries's *The Cat's Pajamas and Witch's Milk*. It was also the year of Allen Drury's *Preserve and Protect*. "When," asked *Time*, "will Drury cease and desist?"

The general thrust of events was suggested by the disclosure that the Defense Department budget this year would be 72 billion dollars, a record and a depressing one. (Roosevelt's *entire* annual budget, when he was accused of sending the country into the poorhouse, had been 8.8 billion dollars.) New Jersey Congressman Charles S. Joelson, told that the gun control bill had been watered down and that he would have to live with the new version, replied that "tens of thousands of Americans can die with it." The great American traffic jam became denser with the announcement, by the U.S. Bureau of the Census and Public Roads Administration, that 99.9 million automobiles were now registered in the United States, that 78.6 percent of all families owned at least one car, and that every fourth family owned two or more. If a man was younger than twenty-one the chances were that he had sideburns and wore bellbottoms. The young expressed approval of something by calling it "tough" or saying it had "soul" or was "out of sight," and if you didn't agree you were either straight or sick.

That year Dancer's Image won the Kentucky Derby, was disqualified on charges that he had been drugged, and then, to confuse everyone, was designated the official winner—while losing the purse to the runner-up.

In West Virginia the Consolidated Coal Company's No. 9 mine blew, entombing seventy-eight men. The U.S. submarine *Scorpion* was lost with ninety-nine men, which would have been the greatest naval disaster of the year had it not been overshadowed by the spectacular fate of another U.S. ship in the waters off North Korea.

The U.S.S. *Pueblo* was labeled a "technical research ship" by the Pentagon, but she was really an electronic snoop, bristling with antennas and complicated radar gear which enabled her to cruise slowly through the Sea of Japan, taking readings of what was happening to North Korean electronic devices on land. This was perfectly legal, provided she stayed twelve miles out. The North

Koreans knew all about her. During the first two weeks of her first mission in 1968 they had tried to distract her with patrol boats and, overhead, low-flying MIGs. Her crew was therefore not surprised when, on January 23, a fleet of PTs sailed out and began circling her. Then one of the small boats signaled: "Heave to or I will open fire on you." That was new. Commander Lloyd M. Bucher, the *Pueblo*'s captain, replied, "I am in international waters." The PT said: "Follow in my wake." Bucher ignored that until another boat began backing toward him. Seeing that its fenders were rigged with rope mats and rubber tubes to cushion a collision, Bucher radioed his base in Japan: "These fellows are serious." Before the boarding party could arrive, he ordered his men to destroy as much of his intelligence ship's secret equipment as they could, shredding codes and wrecking the gear with sledgehammers, axes, and hand grenades.

The news that a U.S. Navy vessel had been captured—the first since the British seized the U.S.S. *Chesapeake* in 1807—stunned the United States. Dean Rusk said it was "a matter of the utmost gravity" and an "act of war." Republican Senator Wallace F. Bennett of Utah demanded that American ships storm Wonsan harbor, recapture the *Pueblo*, and free her crew. Democratic Senator Thomas J. Dodd wanted the Navy to seize all ships flying the North Korean flag "wherever they may be found on the high seas." Most of Washington took the advice of Rusk to remain calm, however. North Dakota's Karl Mundt, no appeaser, pointed out that "We have enough war worries on our hands without looking for another one." Others on the Hill said that belligerence would merely doom the *Pueblo*'s crew. Two appeals to Russia, asking the Soviet Union to act as mediator, were rejected. Arthur Goldberg, the former Supreme Court justice who was now U.S. ambassador to the United Nations, tried to get the U.N. Security Council to review the incident. He failed.

In the end the case was taken up by American and North Korean negotiators in the tin-roofed Panmunjom shed where the armistice between their armies had been negotiated fifteen years ago. Meanwhile the North Korean Central News Agency was broadcasting what was called a confession by Commander Bucher, saying that he had committed a "criminal act" and "an act of sheer aggression" for which he had "no excuse whatever." An open letter from the commander and his crew said that they were being "provided with all the necessities of life," but the letter was stilted, almost in pidgin English, and therefore not reassuring. In the United States bumper stickers appeared reading, "Remember the *Pueblo*," as though it were possible to forget.

Exactly one week after the seizure of the *Pueblo*, the North Vietnamese launched their most spectacular offensive of the war three thousand miles to the south. General Westmoreland was expecting it, and he thought he knew where it would come: at the big U.S. Marine Corps base at Khe Sanh. Khe Sanh was in many ways like Dienbienphu, the bottom of a red clay, shell-pocked bowl of hills athwart the Communist enemy's chief infiltration route to the south. "This is the cork," an American major explained to reporters. "If they can get past us, they can tear up the countryside way over to the coast."

The bowl was in fact an enemy objective, and was invested by 20,000 North Vietnamese troops. It was to remain under siege for seventy-six days before Operation Pegasus, a force of 30,000 American troops, could break the siege. But Khe Sanh wasn't the chief target of General Nguyen Vo Giap. Giap planned instead to attack almost every population center of any size in South Vietnam.

Tet, the lunar New Year, was observed with a kind of fatalistic gaiety in South Vietnam's cities on the evening of Tuesday, January 30. The next day would be the first of the Year of the Monkey, the most inauspicious of them all. It was going to be worse than they dreamed. Evidence of that was around them, had they known how and where to look. One sign was the large number of husky young strangers arriving in the towns by sampan, scooter, and bicycle. Another was the incredible number of funerals, celebrated with the traditional gongs, flutes, firecrackers, and coffins—coffins packed, it would later be learned, with things other than corpses. Shortly after midnight, when those who had celebrated Tet were fast asleep, the strangers—all members of elite Viet Cong units—assembled and assaulted key points in the capital and a hundred other cities from one end of the country to another: police stations, military bases, government buildings, radio and power stations, and foreign embassies, including that of the United States, which had just been rebuilt after the last terrorist raid at a cost of two and a half million dollars.

Altogether some 60,000 Viet Cong were being committed to the

Tet attack. After twenty-five days of the offensive they controlled large areas of the countryside, including most of the Mekong Delta. Inch by inch American and South Vietnamese troops drove them from the large population centers. The biggest battle was for the ancient imperial city of Hue, where 70 percent of the homes were in ruins. It was of Ben Tre, after air and artillery strikes there had routed the Communists, that an American officer made the memorable comment: "It became necessary to destroy the town to save it." After counting enemy bodies and finding that there were many more of them than of Americans and South Vietnamese, U.S. commanders triumphantly announced that they had won. President Johnson told a press conference that in military terms the Viet Cong drive had been "a complete failure." On television Secretary McNamara said, "It is quite clear that the military objective . . . has not been achieved."

"If this is failure," said Senator George D. Aiken of Vermont, "I hope the Viet Cong never have a major success." Robert F. Kennedy of New York warned against "the delusion" that the Tet campaign constituted "some sort of victory," and Eugene McCarthy of Minnesota said that "if capturing a section of the American embassy and several large cities constitutes complete failure, I suppose by this logic that if the Viet Cong captured the entire country, the administration would be claiming their total collapse." Another senator probably spoke for the largest number of Americans when he asked in bewilderment, "What happened? I thought we were supposed to be winning this war." Certainly that was what the country had been told. Only two months ago General Westmoreland had reported that he could see light at the end of the tunnel. And now this.

As David Halberstam later pointed out, the real casualties of the Tet offensive were "the credibility of the American strategy of attrition" and "the credibility of the man who was by now Johnson's most important political ally"—Westmoreland. If Westmoreland was no longer believable on the war, neither was Johnson. His administration began to come unstuck. John Gardner resigned as Secretary of Health, Education, and Welfare. Goldberg quit the U.N. McNamara left the Pentagon and was replaced by Clark Clifford.

By April 19, 1968, the American force level in Vietnam had risen to 549,000 troops. U.S. combat deaths reached 22,951, and on Sunday, June 23, the war became the longest in American history, surpassing the War of Independence. Both of President Johnson's sons-in-law were there, which in another time would have elicited sympathy for him. But bitterness over the war was too intense now. Draft evaders and Army deserters were forming colonies in Canada and Sweden. Then, as summer and the national conventions of 1968 approached, two events swelled the ranks of the protesters: General Westmoreland asked for 206,000 more men and his headquarters announced that "the Khe Sanh base in Quang Tri province is being inactivated." So much for the cork. All those Marine Corps casualties, all that bravery, and now the general didn't even want it.

On April 10 the White House announced a change in command for U.S. troops in Vietnam. On June 30 the new chief would be a West Point classmate of Westmoreland's, General Creighton Abrams. ("A tough, plain-speaking New Englander," *Time* called him, ". . . who could inspire aggressiveness in a begonia.") What was needed was a man who could preside over an orderly withdrawal, for it was increasingly evident that it would come to that sooner or later. For a time there was hope that it might be soon. In May Hanoi proposed peace talks in Paris. They were scheduled to begin May 10 in the old Hotel Majestic, with Averell Harriman facing Xuan Thuy, who had retired as Ho Chi Minh's foreign minister three years earlier.

But nothing had changed. Six weeks of tortuous diplomacy were required before delegations could be brought into the same room, and then they quarreled about the shape of the table. Meantime enemy attacks had made May the bloodiest month of the war, with 2,000 Americans killed. President Johnson told American Legion and VFW conventions that there could be no truce until the Viet Cong showed some "restraint." Harriman advised him that that seemed unlikely. Clark Clifford toured Vietnam and reported that the Communists were "refitting, regrouping, and rearming" for another blitz. General Abrams studied Westmoreland's plans for a new campaign. They bore the code name Operation Complete Victory.

Angered by Nick Katzenbach's brusque claim that the Tonkin Gulf resolution was sufficient authority for waging war in Vietnam, Senator Eugene McCarthy was further aroused, in October 1967, by Dean Rusk's remark that the real threat to American security was "a billion Chinese." Afterward McCarthy said, "At this point,

I thought I would call a halt." Urged by Allard K. Lowenstein, the leader of an antiwar campaign in search of a candidate, the Minnesota senator filed for the New Hampshire presidential primary. The polls predicted he would get at most 20 percent of the Democratic vote, but two factors increased his chances: the Tet offensive and the support of thousands of college student workers who shaved, scrubbed, and dressed to be "clean for Gene."

On March 12, the day of the primary, McCarthy electrified the country by polling 42 percent of the vote to Johnson's 48 percent. If Republican crossovers were counted, he almost defeated the President, with 28,791 to Johnson's 29,201. Suddenly LBJ looked beatable. The most important immediate consequence of the vote was its impact on Robert F. Kennedy. Kennedy hadn't entered the primary, and as recently as January 20 he had said, "I would not oppose Lyndon Johnson under any foreseeable circumstances." He had explained then that he hesitated because his campaign would divide the party "in a very damaging way." Now he declared that he was "reassessing" his position, and on the Saturday after the New Hampshire primary he elated his admirers—and infuriated McCarthy's—by declaring: "I am announcing today my candidacy for the Presidency of the United States."

The next big primary was in Wisconsin, and the news from there was bad for Johnson. His organization was disintegrating; even the sons and daughters of loyal Democratic politicians there were stumping for McCarthy. Kennedy wasn't entered there, but each day's newspaper brought fresh evidence of his growing strength. Theodore Sorensen, Kenneth O'Donnell, and Arthur Schlesinger had joined his team, and Lawrence F. O'Brien had resigned as postmaster general to manage it. With that as background, President Johnson went on television March 31. He had ordered a reduction in the bombing of Vietnam, he said, and he spoke of the strife in thc country, with "all of its ugly consequences." The nation needed unity, he said. Then:

"I have concluded that I should not permit the Presidency to become involved in the partisan divisions that are developing in this political year . . . I do not believe that I should devote an hour or a day of my time to any personal partisan causes . . . Accordingly, I shall not seek, and I will not accept, the nomination of my party for another term as your President."

Once the impact of Johnson's withdrawal had worn off, it became clear that the contest for the Democratic nomination was going to be a three-way race between McCarthy, Kennedy, and, once he was ready to declare, Vice President Humphrey. Of the three, only McCarthy was on the Wisconsin ballot; he had been running against Johnson there. It was too late to take the President's name off the ballot; McCarthy took 57.6 percent of the Democratic primary vote while Nixon, whose most serious opponents had been George Romney and Nelson Rockefeller, polled 81.3 percent of the Republican vote.

Humphrey announced his candidacy on April 27. Except for Oregon, in which McCarthy won narrowly, the rest of the primaries were all Kennedy. His strongest stands were against the war and for the poor and underprivileged. The leaders of the black movement were his natural allies. This was especially true of Martin Luther King, who had reached the conclusion that Vietnam was the largest serious obstacle to progress for his people; Negroes provided more than their share of combat troops, and money which should have been spent in the ghettos was going into the war. King said: "No one can pretend that the existence of the war is not profoundly affecting the destiny of civil rights progress."

In April 1968 King was in Memphis, supporting a two-month-old strike by 1,300 garbage men, most of them black. Newspapers had taunted him for staying at a plush Holiday Inn, paying $29 a night there, so he moved to a $13-a-night room in the Negro-owned Lorraine Motel. Before dinner on April 4 he was leaning on the second-floor iron railing outside room number 306 talking to fellow workers below. In a nondescript rooming house across the street a sniper crouched with a scope-sighted 30.06 Remington pump rifle. He fired one shot. It penetrated King's neck and exploded against his jaw, cutting his spinal column. He fell away from the rail and against the motel's wall, his hands rigid, reaching for his head.

Martin Luther King had been the greatest prophet of nonviolence since Gandhi, and it was the final irony of his life that the end of it should touch off the worst outburst of arson, looting, and criminal activity in the nation's history. In all, 168 cities and towns were stricken. Washington was the worst hit. An incredible 711 fires were set there. "Get your gun," Stokely Carmichael told blacks, and many did. There were ten deaths in the capital alone, one of them a white man who was dragged from his car and stabbed. President Johnson ordered the flag at half-mast on all federal buildings, the first time this had been done for a Negro, but the terror continued. Buildings within a few blocks of the White House were put to the torch. Nationwide, 2,600 fires were set, 2,600 people were arrested and 21,270 injured. To restore order 55,000 soldiers were required—ten times the number of marines defending Khe Sanh.

Accompanied by the music of spirituals and the tolling of church bells, Martin Luther King's coffin was transported to the grave on an old farm cart drawn by two mules. An estimated 120 million Americans watched the funeral march on television. There were between 50,000 and 100,000 marchers, including most of the nation's leaders, among them Robert Kennedy, Eugene McCarthy, Nelson Rockefeller, and Hubert Humphrey. Governor Lester Maddox of Georgia did not attend, although the funeral was in his state. Maddox refused to close the schools and protested lowering the flag to half-staff. But the man he refused to honor could never again be hurt by bigotry. The words of his epitaph, hewn in his tomb of Georgia marble, were from an old slave hymn; he had used them to close his oration at the Washington march five years before:

Free at last, free at last;
Thank God Almighty, I'm free at last.

John Willard, the name the sniper had used in renting the room from which he fired the shot, was an alias for Eric Starvo Galt, which also turned out to be an alias. Witnesses at the scene of the assassination had seen him race off in a white Mustang bearing Alabama license plates and Mexican tourist stickers. The car was found abandoned in Atlanta, Georgia. The FBI learned that he had bought it for $2,000—cash—using the Galt name. A fugitive now, sought by police around the world, he fled to Toronto. There he adopted a new alias, Ramon George Sneyd, and acquired a Canadian passport by the only procedure necessary—swearing that was his name. Buying a $345 excursion ticket to Europe, he spent two days in Portugal before flying to London. There he vanished, no doubt he thought for good.

But he had made one irrevocable error. His fingerprints had been found in the Memphis rooming house. After a fifteen-day search in the 53,000 prints of wanted men in the Department of Justice, the FBI identified him as James Earl Ray. He had a long record of convictions for forgery, car theft, and armed robbery. In April

1967 Ray had escaped from the Missouri state penitentiary. Now Canadian Mounties picked up his trail from the FBI, and customs officials throughout Europe were alerted to be on the lookout for Ramon G. Sneyd. On June 8 he was picked up at London's Heathrow Airport. Extradited and handcuffed, he was flown back wearing a bulletproof vest, his legs encased in armored trousers; no one wanted another Oswald. He was transported to the Memphis jail in a six-and-a-half-ton truck. Heavy steel plates blocked his cell window. He pleaded guilty and was sentenced to ninety-nine years. The source of his money was never discovered.

Almost two months to the day after Martin Luther King was struck down, and the same week that Ray was arrested, another act of mindless violence cut down the front runner for the Democratic presidential nomination. "An assassin never changed the course of history," Robert Kennedy had said after his brother's death in Dallas, but it wasn't true; that one had, and now his did, too. He had beaten Eugene McCarthy in the Indiana primary, 42 percent to 27, and in Nebraska 51 to 31. On this day, Tuesday, June 4, 1968, he had defeated both Hubert Humphrey—in Humphrey's native state, South Dakota—and McCarthy in the biggest of all the primaries, California.

Kennedy had spent that morning on a beach near Los Angeles with six of his ten children and his wife Ethel, who was pregnant with their eleventh. He followed election reports in suite 512 of the city's Ambassador Hotel. At midnight he took the elevator down to his headquarters in the hotel's Embassy Room and spoke briefly to the elated volunteers there. At the end he said: "So my thanks to all of you and it's on to Chicago, and let's win there." Friends and members of his immediate entourage mimicked his accent, saying: "And it's on to The Factory," that being the name of the popular discotheque where they were going to celebrate with him. But first he had to say a few words in the press room. The crowd was so dense between the rostrum and the Embassy Room's entrance that one member of the party suggested that they leave by a back passageway. Bill Barry, the former FBI agent who was Kennedy's bodyguard, objected. He didn't like the idea. But the senator said, "It's all right," and they stepped into a hot, smelly corridor. Kennedy paused there to shake hands with a seventeen-year-old busboy, Jesus Perez, and answer a question about Humphrey: "It just goes back to the struggle for it—"

He never finished. A Pasadena reporter saw an arm and a gun come out of a knot of spectators. The assassin propped his right elbow on a serving counter and fired at Kennedy, just four feet away. He pumped off all eight shots in the snub-nosed Iver-Johnson revolver before Rafer Johnson, an Olympic champion and a Kennedy friend, could knock the pistol out of his hand. Six men lay bleeding on the floor of the hall, five with slight injuries. The sixth, Kennedy, was wounded mortally. One of the two bullets which had hit him was relatively harmless, but the other had pierced his skull and entered his brain. Ethel knelt beside him. Bobby asked for water. Then he asked, "Is everybody safe?" The busboy gave him a crucifix. Bobby's fingers held the beads, and Ethel prayed, and Roosevelt Grier, the three-hundred-pound Los Angeles Rams' lineman, held the slight, dark assassin in a bear hug.

"Why did you do it?" one member of the party yelled. The killer screamed, "I can explain! Let me explain!" Jesse Unruh, leader of California Democrats, shouted at him, "Why him? Why him?" The gunman answered: "I did it for my country." That seemed preposterous. Then the truth began to emerge. In his psychotic way he really believed he was being patriotic. To everyone else in Los Angeles this had been the day of the California primary, but to Kennedy's murderer it was the first anniversary of the Israeli-Arab six-day war. His name was Sirhan Bishara Sirhan, he was a native of Jordan, and he hated Israel, which Kennedy admired. On the surface that appeared to be the only motive the swarthy little Arab had.

The dying Kennedy was first taken to the Central Receiving Hospital and then to the larger Good Samaritan Hospital. Kept alive by adrenalin injections and by cardiac massage, he underwent surgery almost at once. But it was hopeless. At 1:44, after a few flutterings of life, he died. Lyndon Johnson denounced the country's "insane traffic" in guns. Then he sent a presidential jet to bring the body home, and once more the Kennedys and their friends flew eastward with a coffin in a Boeing 707. The United Nations lowered its flag to half-mast, an unprecedented tribute to one who had never been a chief of state. When the plane arrived in New York ten thousand people had already lined up outside St. Patrick's Cathedral to say goodbye. Candles were placed at each corner of the catafalque, and friends took turns standing vigil. Ted Kennedy, the surviving Kennedy brother, acted as paterfamilias, delivering the eulogy in a trembling voice.

Richard Cardinal Cushing presided. Andy Williams sang "The Battle Hymn of the Republic"; the choir, the Hallelujah Chorus. Then the motorcade proceeded to Pennsylvania Station, where a special train waited, drawn by two black engines. Its destination was Washington, but the crowds standing by the tracks along the way were so great that the trip took eight hours. By then it was night in the capital. With only streetlamps as illumination, the cavalcade wound past the city's huge dark government buildings and across the Potomac, to Arlington. There Bob's grave waited, a dark scar beneath a magnolia tree a few feet from his brother's tombstone. After a brief, simple service there the flag was folded in a triangle and presented to Ethel. The band played:

America! America!
God shed his grace on thee!
And crown thy good with brotherhood,
From sea to shining sea!

Between January 1 and June 15 of 1968 there were 221 major demonstrations, involving nearly 39,000 students, on 101 American campuses. Buildings were dynamited, college presidents and deans were roughed up, obscenities were painted on walls and shouted at policemen, sometimes by well-bred daughters of good families at the ivied Seven Sister colleges for women. Among the institutions of higher learning disrupted by student violence during those months were Temple in Philadelphia, the State University of New York in Buffalo, Oberlin, Princeton, Duke, Chicago's Roosevelt University, Southern Illinois University, Boston University, Marquette, Tufts, Stanford, Colgate, Howard, the University of Oregon, Northwestern, Ohio State, Barnard, Mills College, the University of Connecticut, Trinity, Tuskegee, the University of Chicago, Bowie State in Maryland, UCLA, the University of Miami—

And, of course, Columbia.

Until the third week after the assassination of Martin Luther King the newsiest event on the Morningside Heights campus was its reversal of a decision, made the year before, to accept a gift of royalties from the leasing of a new cigarette filter invented by Robert Strickman, an industrial chemist. That had brought much unwelcome publicity, but the Columbia uprising of April 1968 was much worse. It was the biggest campus confrontation since the Berkeley turmoil four years earlier, and in a way it was more significant, for it marked the emergence of the Students for a Democratic Society. Until then SDS was known to the public as merely one more campus political student organization. After eight years it had 5,500 members, chapters at 200 colleges, and a characteristic student distaste for centralization. In the mid-1960s SDS had become committed to militancy, however. Its leaders were avowed enemies of oppression, racism, and imperialism, all three of them as defined by SDS. It held that American universities had become corrupted by them, and that Columbia was especially wicked.

A college marching song popular among undergraduates on Morningside Heights in merrier days went:

Who owns New York?
Who owns New York?
Why, we own New York!
Why, we own New York!
Who?
C-O-L-U-M-B-I-A!

The SDS reminded fellow students that in fact the university did own 230 million dollars' worth of real estate in Manhattan, including the land under Rockefeller Center, and that much of it was occupied by deteriorating Harlem tenements nearby, making Columbia, in effect, a big slumlord. Six years earlier the university had unwittingly provided the fuel for an eventual explosion by leasing from the city an additional 2.1 acres of nearby Morningside Heights Park's thirty acres. The idea was to build a magnificent 11.6-million-dollar gymnasium there. Negroes living in the adjacent, bottle-strewn Harlem slum would be welcome to enjoy a free gym and swimming pool on the ground floor; the university's department of physical education would use the upper floors. Since the neighborhood was at present infested with prostitutes and drug addicts, with one of the highest crime rates in the city, Columbia's trustees assumed that every resident with a spark of civic pride would embrace the project. They were wrong.

Protesting tenants called the plan "a land grab," and "a desecration of a public park." At that point the university's administration blundered. An architect's conception of the gym was published showing an elaborate, expensive entrance facing the campus and a small, plain door facing Harlem. Leaders of the community group denounced the "separate but unequal facilities," the chairman of the Harlem CORE angrily charged that "This community is being raped," and one hundred and fifty demonstrators shouting "Gym Crow must go!" marched to the gymnasium site and tore down a section of fence. White participants included Mark Rudd, the chairman of Columbia's SDS, and as many followers as he had been able to muster.

Rudd was the kind of New Leftist that J. Edgar Hoover dreamed about. Hoover had just described the SDS as "a militant youth group which receives support from the Communist Party, and which in turn supports Communist objectives and tactics." Columbia students said sarcastically, "The Communists can't take over SDS—they can't find it." It did in fact have few members there. However, their penchant for outrageous words and for outrages themselves gave them, in a phrase of the time, a high profile. Rudd was particularly noisy. On the day that the balloon went up over Morningside Heights he had just returned from a three-week visit to Castro's Cuba. As if to confirm Hoover, he praised it as an "extremely humanistic society."

His opposite number was Columbia's president, sixty-four-year-old Grayson Kirk, aloof, frosty, and a poor administrator. Later a commission headed by Archibald Cox would conclude that under Kirk the administration conveyed "an attitude of authoritarianism and invited mistrust." Kirk had been unresponsive earlier in April when SDS collected 1,500 signatures to a petition demanding that Columbia withdraw from the Institute for Defense Analysis (IDA), an organization of researchers working for the Pentagon on twelve campuses. SDS charged that IDA projects were "aimed at the oppression of the people in Vietnam" and included "riot equipment to commit mass genocide against black people" in the United States.

Leaving the downed fence at the putative gym site that Tuesday, Rudd and his band marched on ivy-covered Hamilton Hall, the headquarters of Columbia College. There, to their surprise, they were met by a conciliatory acting dean, who said that although he had "no intention of meeting any demands under a situation such as this," both the gym and IDA membership were negotiable issues. SDS wasn't interested in that now. Having tasted victory, the insurgents retained momentum by imprisoning the acting dean and two other officials for twenty-six hours. The siege of Columbia had begun.

During the first night the white students discovered something else: black power. The sixty Negro students among them demanded that the whites leave. SDS, they said, wasn't militant enough for them. One version had it that the blacks were carrying guns and planned a shoot-out with policemen. Their white soul brothers didn't think the gym was as bad as that. Some of them felt hurt. "Why should they run this thing?" one of them asked. "There's enough division and polarization in this country as it is." In any event, at 6 A.M. on the second day, Wednesday, April 24, Rudd announced that the whites weren't wanted in Hamilton Hall. Leaving it to the blacks, he and his honkies took over Low Library, where they put up a notice: "Liberated Area. Be Free to Join Us." President Kirk's office was in the library. They broke into it and ransacked it, photographing letters and documents, throwing others away, smoking his cigars, and drinking his sherry. And they had just begun. To reporters they said that they believed they were right in disrupting the university. They cited principles established at the Nuremberg trials of Nazi war criminals. Columbia's administration under Kirk, they said, was as bad as the Nazis.

There were seven hundred of them now. On Thursday a hundred seized Fayerweather Hall, the social science building. Another hundred took over Avery Hall, the architecture center, and on Friday a fifth hall was invaded. Over the balcony of that one they hung a banner: "Rudd Hall, Liberated Zone No. 5." They set up a command post and mimeographed proclamations. One demanded amnesty for all of them, but Kirk refused, saying that failure to take disciplinary action would "destroy the whole fabric of the university community." For a while it looked as though another group of students, the athletes, would evict the rebels. ("If this is a barbarian society," a wrestler said, "then it's survival of the fittest—and we're the fittest.") Kirk wanted no more violence, and he restrained them. He also made a concession: all work on the gymnasium was suspended. Not enough, the demonstrators shouted from the halls; they demanded secession from IDA and a lot of other things they had just thought up. Runners brought them food, blankets, and jars of vaseline. They wanted the vaseline because they had heard that it was protection from Mace. They expected Mace, fired by police.

They were right about the police coming. When the first detachment arrived on Morningside Heights, thirty members of Columbia's junior faculty barred the entrance to Low Hall. It was a deadlock. But then the university's trustees voted "to affirmatively direct" Kirk "to maintain the ultimate disciplinary power over the conduct of students." Thereupon he made what he later called "the most painful" decision of his life, to clear the buildings with force, if necessary—a thousand policemen in flying wedges. Hamilton Hall came first. The Negro students were docile. Black lawyers were there to represent them, and black police officers supervised the operation. After the Negroes left quietly, the building was found to be tidy.

The buildings occupied by whites were another matter. Whatever the provocation, the cops there clubbed, kicked, and punched the students, hurling them down concrete stairways. The police had assured spectators—there were several thousand of them—that they would be safe if they remained behind police barricades, but when it became clear that the spectators were prostudent, they, too, were charged and beaten. All in all, 698 were arrested. Rudd and 72 other students were suspended for a year. Cox was asked to investigate the disorders. After twenty-one days of testimony from seventy-nine witnesses, he and four colleagues issued a 222-page report which was highly critical of both the university administration and the police. While holding no brief for the student ringleaders, the report found that their behavior "was in no way commensurate with the [police] brutality," which had "caused violence on a harrowing scale." Kirk and his staff had "regularly put the students at the bottom" of their priorities, the commission found, concluding that the gym and the IDA issue had in fact been mere surface manifestations of deep student dissatisfaction with the Vietnam War and racism in the United States.

According to a *New York Times* survey, the militant whites in campus riots at Columbia and elsewhere typically came from well-to-do homes in suburbia, had parents who were politically liberal, were students in the humanities rather than the sciences, were brilliant in class, and were predominantly Jewish. An example was Ted Gold, twenty-one, with Rudd a leader in the Columbia uprising and an SDS chairman. Gold said to reporters: "We are working, not just for a revolutionary Columbia, but for a revolutionary America."

At some point in the 1960s a man who had never run a stop sign did it. He was careful, nothing was coming; it was a silly statute, he reasoned; only robots obeyed it. He ran another; in a month he was doing it without qualms, and in another month he was running red lights if they turned red just as he was approaching an intersection. Though he overlooked the connection, he was annoyed because the attendant at his favorite filling station no longer checked his oil and cleaned his windshield unless asked. He switched filling stations; it was the same there. At about the same time a door in his new car developed a hideous rattle; he dismantled it and found that some anonymous worker on a Detroit assembly line had left a Coke bottle in it.

These were little things, but there were others. One morning you found a notice in your milk box. No more milk; the company had stopped deliveries; you had to go to the store. The postal system was a disgrace. Everybody had his horror story about the mails. Waitresses brought you somebody else's order. Cab drivers couldn't find your destination. Your evening paper wasn't delivered. The druggist filled the wrong prescription. The new washer-dryer was a lemon. Deliverymen double-parked and wouldn't move. By the end of the Johnson years it was a national joke. People displayed little signs:

PLAN AHEAD

The building industry was disgraceful; you were lucky if the job was done six months after the date promised. Airliners were late taking off; because they didn't reach your destination on time you had to wait, stacked over it, and when you did land you discovered that your baggage had gone on to another airport. This was so common that frequent travelers bought luggage expressly designed to fit under their seats. Bus and train timetables were fictive. Nearly everyone was dunned at one time or another for bills that were already paid. Nothing, it seemed, functioned any more. From the plumbing and the television to the F-111 swing-wing jet, all was snafu. A New York woman, billed for transatlantic telephone calls she hadn't made, picked up her phone to protest and heard violins playing; a Muzak line had crossed hers. Rex Reed, the writer, tried to use a credit card and was arrested on the ground that Rex Reed was dead. *Time* reported a man who had emptied a pistol firing at a vending machine.

Repairmen and salesclerks were as bad, or worse. The fault was difficult to pin down, but it was everywhere. People didn't seem to care whether things worked any more. The discipline that knits a society together was weakening and at some points giving way altogether. John Kenneth Galbraith attributed it to prosperity. Richard Nixon blamed it on permissiveness.

Jean-Jacques Servan-Schreiber likened the student demonstrators to General Giap in Vietnam, finding them different expressions of the same phenomenon. Clearly the war had something to do with it. Young men from the upper stratum of American society were evading the draft without guilt, encouraged by their parents and often with letters from physicians who lied about their health, also without guilt. Millions sympathized with the draft evaders and deserters making new lives in Toronto and Stockholm. Because the first four to arrive in Sweden had jumped ship from the aircraft *Intrepid,* they were known as the "Intrepid Four." No one there thought the name ambiguous. One member of the colony, a nineteen-year-old South Carolinian, said: "We fall into two categories. There are those who are convinced the United States will blow up the world. There are others who think the United States can be saved before this catastrophe happens."

The war was only part of it. Not since Prohibition had so many people, concluding that some laws were senseless, proceeded to break them. Marijuana was an example. Unlike other drugs it was not habit-forming, unlike tobacco it was not harmful to the user, and unlike alcohol it was not dangerous to society. To the young it was often a matter of status; youths of the better families were known to be smoking it. For a time in 1969 police made a habit of "busting"—another new word—the sons and daughters of the famous.

Looters in the summer riots weren't arrested; you could see them helping themselves on the television news programs; policemen watched them and did nothing. "It seems to me," said Kenneth Clark, the Negro psychologist, "a high-policy decision was made to trade goods and appliances for human lives." Certainly it appeared that an arrest was determined by the identity of the person and place as much as by the act. In mid-May Ralph Abernathy, Martin Luther King's successor, set up a "Resurrection City," which King had planned, on the hallowed ground between the Lincoln Memorial and the Washington Monument. He led a thousand poor people on it, and the government not only failed to take any of them into custody; it gave them portable latrines, phone booths, power lines, showers, and even a zip number: 20013. Late in June, Alvin Johnson, the camp's chief security officer, resigned in anger, saying, "There are rapes, robberies, and cuttings every day, and there is nothing we can do about it." The National Capital Parks Police remained aloof.

In a previous generation Calvin Coolidge had won national recognition, and ultimately the Presidency, by breaking the Boston police strike of 1919. He said that there was "no right to strike against the public safety by anybody, anywhere, any time." In 1937 Franklin Roosevelt had called a strike by civil servants "unthinkable and intolerable." Since then the principle had been embodied in the Taft-Hartley Act and, in the states, by such laws as New York's Condon-Wadlin Act. Nevertheless, on January 1, 1966, Mike Quill led his Transport Workers Union in a strike that paralyzed downtown Manhattan by depriving the city, in effect, of 165 miles of subways and 530 miles of bus routes. When Quill was served with a court order to lead them back, he tore it up in front of television cameras. The city was forced to accept mediation and compromise with him.

Walkouts against the public interest in 1968 included that of the Memphis sanitation workers which Martin Luther King endorsed in his final hours. Another that same year left New York littered with a hundred thousand tons of reeking garbage on the streets before Governor Rockefeller capitulated and granted the garbage workers a $425 pay raise which Mayor Lindsay had rejected earlier. Next, New York policemen picketed City Hall, shouting "Blue power!" They reported "sick" with imaginary ills or watched languidly while drivers left their cars parked at bus stops and in other no-parking zones. The head of the firemen's union bargained by telling his men to ignore such routine tasks as inspecting buildings and fire hydrants. On three separate occasions in the autumn of 1968 a majority of New York's 58,000 teachers walked out. Then air traffic controllers, alarmed at the dense stack-ups overhead, conspired in a deliberate slowdown.

The climax to defiance of public service came at the end of the decade, when over 200,000 of the country's 750,000 postmen decided to stop delivering the mail for pay that started at $6,176 a year and reached $8,442 after twenty-one years. Despite the urging of their leaders, who reminded them that federal law threatened them with a $1,000 fine, a year in prison, the loss of pensions, and blacklisting from other government jobs, the 6,700 members of the Manhattan-Bronx local of the AFL-CIO National Association of Letter Carriers voted to walk out. Soon they were joined by the rest of greater New York's mailmen. The strike spread to Akron, Buffalo, Cleveland, Chicago, Denver, St. Paul, and San Francisco.

It was the first walkout in the history of the U.S. Postal Service, and it was devastating. On an average day New York's post office moves about 25 million letters and packages; the national average is 270 million. Many firms had to suspend operations. New York banks couldn't receive their daily average of 300 million dollars in deposits, 400,000 welfare clients couldn't get their checks, and brokerage firms had to hire armored trucks to move securities on Wall Street. On the sixth day the National Guard began handling the New York mail, and on the eighth day the mailmen resumed their appointed rounds. Like other civil servants who had struck, they profited from their illegal walkout. Congress voted them an 8 percent raise, retroactive to the month before, and established an independent U.S. Postal Service which, among other things, was meant to be more attentive to their grievances.

Among the things that went wrong in 1968 was the choosing of a new Supreme Court Chief Justice. Earl Warren still felt vigorous, but he decided to retire because of his age; he had turned seventy-seven on March 19. On the morning of June 19 he telephoned President Johnson and told him. It was a historic moment. No Court had played a greater role in determining the direction of its time. Under Warren's leadership, the Court had led the way on school desegregation, school prayers, the rights of Communists, pornography, the arrest and conviction of defendants, and the "one man, one vote" ruling ordering legislative reapportionment. Warren had presided over fifteen Court terms. And now Lyndon Johnson, who wanted to do everything as President, could choose a new chief judge. He named Associate Justice Abe Fortas and picked Texas Congressman Homer Thornberry to take Fortas's place.

Both men were old friends of the President. Fortas was as close to the President as any man; the President had put him on the Court three years earlier. Johnson, being Johnson, had to make the new selections complicated. He would not accept Warren's resignation until the Senate had confirmed his choice of Fortas. Then, with Fortas securely in office, Thornberry could move into his old spot.

But the Republicans, believing that they would capture the White House in November, were mulish. They called Fortas and Thornberry "lame duck" nominations and tarred Fortas as a "crony" of the President.

Senator Robert P. Griffin of Michigan emerged as the leader of seventeen hostile Republicans. In the beginning it seemed a lost cause. Everett Dirksen of Illinois, the minority leader in the Senate, called the "cronyism" and "lame duck" arguments "frivolous." "You do not go out looking for an enemy to put him on the Court," he said, and he remarked that Presidents Lincoln, Truman, and Kennedy had appointed friends. Rebuking Griffin, Dirksen said, "It's about time we be a little more circumspect about the kind of language we use." Even when the Senate Judiciary Committee decided to hold hearings—the first time for any nominee to the post of Chief Justice—Fortas seemed safe. The opening witness, Attorney General Ramsey Clark, pointed out that there was ample precedent for the President to keep Warren on the Court until Fortas's confirmation; many lesser federal judges were chosen while their predecessors remained in office.

The problem now was Fortas himself. He spent four terrible days being grilled. Under the Constitution he could not discuss his decisions while on the stand; that would be an outright violation of the principle of separation of powers. Nevertheless, opposition senators spent much of the time reading aloud liberal decisions in which he had participated. Then they questioned him about certain aspects of his conduct as an associate justice. That too was a matter of the separation of powers, but here it hurt him. As a member of the Court he was supposed to remain aloof from the executive department, and he hadn't been. He acknowledged that he had participated in White House meetings about the war and the ghetto riots, and that he had phoned Ralph Lazarus, the Columbus department store tycoon, to give him a tongue-lashing because of Lazarus's statement that Vietnam was affecting the economy.* Fortas protested that there was ample precedent for justices advising Presidents, but here, as always with Johnson, there was the nagging feeling that something shady was going on. One straw was needed to break the camel's back now, and it came when the committee learned that Fortas had accepted $15,000 as the fee for teaching a series of sum-

* See above, pages 1290–1291.

mer groups, the money coming from businessmen who might figure in cases coming before the Court.

The judiciary committee approved the appointment 17 to 6, but the Republican and southern senators staged a filibuster. A two-thirds vote of the Senate was required to end it, and at that point Dirksen pulled the rug from under Fortas. He would not support the move to stop the filibuster, he said, and he wasn't even sure he would vote for the nomination; a Court ruling overturning the death penalty for the killing of a Chicago policeman angered him. The vote on cloture was 45 yes and 43 no, far short of the two-thirds needed. Fortas asked Johnson to withdraw the nomination. The President agreed "with deep regret" and said he would make no appointment at all. The following May *Life* revealed that Fortas had accepted another, $20,000 fee from the family foundation of Louis Wolfsen, whose conviction for stock manipulation had come before the Court. Although he had returned the money, Washington was shocked, and when still other revelations loomed, he resigned. With Fortas and Goldberg gone, and with a Republican in the White House, clearly the future Court would be less liberal.

Americans have a way of anointing and consecrating their heroes, putting them on pedestals that are impossibly high, and then knocking them off. In the autumn of 1968 it was the turn of a heroine: Jacqueline Bouvier Kennedy, who wanted neither the adoration of the past nor the calumny of the present, but merely privacy. She was a woman of beauty and charm. For one terrible weekend in its history the United States needed a presidential widow with those gifts and something else: a histrionic talent. Eleanor Roosevelt was a greater First Lady, but she could not have done that. Jackie Kennedy had given the country's grief dignity and nobility. No woman could have improved on it. But afterward she needed to be alone, and as long as she remained a widow that seemed to be impossible. In Washington tourist buses paused outside her home, and when she moved to New York cabbies recognized her and honked.

To avoid gossip she went out only with happily married public men. Arthur Schlesinger Jr., Robert S. McNamara, and Leonard Bernstein were familiar escorts. Lord Harlech, who as David Ormsby-Gore had been the British ambassador to the United States during the Kennedy years, was now a widower. The press suggested him as a new husband. Movie magazines proposed an elderly Greek shipping magnate, and the fans laughed.

They stopped laughing on October 17, 1968, when Jackie's mother announced: "My daughter, Mrs. John F. Kennedy, is planning to marry Mr. Aristotle Onassis"—the elderly shipping magnate. The son of a Smyrna tobacco merchant, Onassis had acquired a fortune which was estimated at 500 million dollars. Among other things he owned 100 ships, Olympic Airways, several corporations, a 325-foot yacht, the *Christina,* and the Greek island Skorpios. Those who believed the report—who weren't convinced that either the bride's mother was out of her mind or the announcement was a monstrous practical joke—speculated over what to give the couple. The New York Stock Exchange, the Taj Mahal, the *Queen Elizabeth II,* and the De Beers diamond mines were among the suggestions.

JACKIE, HOW COULD YOU? asked the headline in the *Stockholm Expressen.* Onassis was two inches shorter and could have been her father—he was either twenty-three or twenty-nine years older, depending on which birth date you accepted. Onassis was divorced, which meant that Jackie could not hope for the church's blessing. Worst of all was the groom's total lack of a social conscience, the very heart of the Kennedy creed. He once said that his idea of the perfect home would be in a country without taxes. The taxes he did owe were outstanding in several different nations, including the United States. "She's gone from Prince Charming to Caliban," one former Kennedy appointee commented. Bob Hope said, "Nixon has a Greek running mate, and now everyone wants one." It was widely remarked that she wouldn't have done it if Bobby were alive.

The marriage was celebrated on October 20 in a tiny Chapel of the Little Virgin on Skorpios. Tulips had been airlifted from Holland by the tycoon's private jet fleet. The bride wore a lace Valentino original. Her two children were pages. The groom's children were witnesses. The Greek Orthodox ceremony took forty-five minutes; then the couple took communion from one chalice and were crowned with garlands of lemon blossoms, a sign of fertility and purity. After kissing the New Testament they circled the altar in a ritualistic dance. Afterward there was a reception on the white-hulled yacht. The Greek navy and Onassis's own patrol boats kept reporters off the island. His present to her was a ring with a huge ruby surrounded by big diamonds, with matching earrings—a gift worth 1.2 million dollars.

That was only the beginning. According to the veteran journalist Fred Sparks, the pair spent about twenty million dollars their first year together, and their expenditures then continued at the rate of about $384,000 a week. Onassis had given his new wife five million dollars in jewelry alone. And since he was making about fifty million dollars a year, he wasn't even dipping into capital. Keeping out of the newspapers was another matter. Mrs. Kennedy, as she still was, had agreed to hold one press conference on the eve of the wedding. She said then, "We wish our wedding to be a private moment in the little chapel among the cypresses of Skorpios, with only members of the family and their little children. Understand that even though people may be well known, they still hold in their hearts the emotion of a simple person for the moments that are the most important we know on earth—birth, marriage, and death."

Nevertheless, reporters stalked them. They were news and had to be covered. Photographers were worse. One, an Italian, managed, with telephoto lenses, to get a picture of her sunbathing in the nude. But the greatest blow to her new role came not from the secular press but from the Vatican's *L'Osservatore della Domenica.* Branding her "a public sinner," it reported that she would be denied church rites. In Boston Cardinal Cushing protested that "Only God knows" who sins and who doesn't; he pleaded for "love, mutual respect and esteem." Nevertheless, the canon lawyers in the Vatican held fast. In sharing Onassis's bed, they ruled, the wife of America's first Catholic President was profane in the eyes of God.

Richard Nixon's second presidential campaign had begun the previous February in Nashua, New Hampshire, when he registered at a Howard Johnson motel as Mr. Benjamin Chapman. Shortly thereafter pseudonyms became impossible, for his picture was back on front pages, and when he received 79 percent of the vote in the New Hampshire primary, he became the Republican front runner. Thereafter his campaign was one string of triumphs. George Romney was beaten early, after he had said he had been "brainwashed" into supporting the Vietnam War. Nelson Rockefeller dropped out, then came back after Johnson declared that he wouldn't run again, but the only effect of Rockefeller's in-out-in candidacy was to alienate an early supporter of his, Governor Spiro Agnew of Maryland.

Until Nixon chose him to share the ticket, Agnew was unknown outside his state. His name, as he conceded, was "not a household word." A few hours after his name went before the convention a reporter stopped pedestrians in downtown Atlanta and said, "I'm going to mention two words to you. You tell me what they mean. The words are Spiro Agnew." One Atlantan replied, "It's some kind of disease." Another said, "It's some kind of egg," and a third, a little closer to the mark, said, "He's a Greek that owns that shipbuilding firm."

Agnew's credentials, said *Time*, "are not convincing." But they had impressed Nixon. He wanted a running mate who would take the low road and thus serve the purpose he had served for Eisenhower. It was hard to assess Agnew's impact on the electorate, because his opposite number in the campaign turned out to be not the Democratic vice-presidential nominee, Senator Edmund Muskie of Maine, but a third-party candidate, Governor George Wallace of Alabama. Agnew denounced "phony intellectuals who don't understand what we mean by hard work and patriotism"; Wallace attacked "pointy-headed" newspapermen, "scummy anarchists" and "pseudo-intellectuals." Wallace said that if policemen "could run this country for about two years, they'd straighten it out." At the same time, Agnew was saying in Detroit, "If you've seen one ghetto area, you've seen them all." Agnew called a Nisei reporter a "fat Jap" and called Poles "Polacks." His manner was so graceless that a picket greeted him with a placard reading: APOLOGIZE NOW, SPIRO. IT WILL SAVE TIME LATER. Other pickets met Wallace with: IF YOU LIKED HITLER, YOU'LL LOVE WALLACE and WALLACE IS ROSEMARY'S BABY.

One reason the also-rans were so newsy in the early weeks of the campaign was the dreariness of the Republican convention, which came first. "Richard M. Nixon rode to victory," the Associated Press commented, "in a tedious ritual at Miami Beach." Theodore H. White wrote, "Boredom lay on the convention like a mattress." Glee clubs sang. Bands played. John Wayne gave an inspirational reading on "Why I am proud to be an American." Other celebrities supporting Nixon were equally dreary: Art Linkletter, Connie Francis, Pat Boone, Lawrence Welk. The arid speeches of the politicians seemed to go on forever. The only interesting moments came on the periphery of the convention. Senator Edward W. Brooke was reportedly barred from a reception because he was a Negro. Miami blacks rioted; the television commentators said that seventy policemen with shotguns entered the riot area, and the news later was that four Negroes had died. Nixon scribbled away a speech on the yellow legal-length pads which he soon would make famous. In it he called for a return to America's "lift of a driving dream."

The AP reported that the Republicans' security precautions were "the tightest in the memory of convention goers." The second Kennedy assassination had scared the Secret Service, which Johnson at that time had made responsible for the protection of all serious candidates. Agents in helicopters hovered over the convention city. Other agents with rifles and binoculars scanned the crowd from rooftops. A thirty-man riot squad was held in reserve, and the 1,333 delegates had to submit all packages and purses to inspection each time they entered the convention. Some Democrats said it was overdone. Two weeks later their own delegates assembled in Chicago.

The violence that lay ahead in Chicago was not inevitable, but all the ingredients were there. The Committee to End the War in Vietnam, an umbrella organization coordinating over eighty peace groups under David Dellinger, came to jeer at the Chicago police. Hippies, Yippies, peace pickets, McCarthy workers, disillusioned liberals—altogether, they predicted there would be 100,000 of them, and they would march on the convention in the International Amphitheater. Mayor Richard J. Daley took them seriously. He turned Chicago into an armed camp. Manholes around the amphitheater were sealed with tar. A chain link fence seven feet high, with barbed wire on top of it, was thrown around the hall. The city's 11,500 policemen were put on twelve-hour shifts, 5,500 National Guardsmen were alerted, and 7,500 troops of the U.S. Army, airlifted from Fort Hood in Texas on White House orders, were ordered to stand by. Despite the extravagant forecasts, only about 10,000 to 12,000 demonstrators came to confront them.

In the convention, the reason for all this, Humphrey was nominated on the first ballot; McCarthy and George McGovern of South Dakota lagged far behind him. The only real contest was over how the peace issue should be handled in the party platform. The administration plank, the more hawkish of the two, won with 1,567¾ to 1,041¼ for the dovish substitute plank. The figures reflected the depth of the division in the party on the war. Four years earlier Lyndon Johnson had been nominated by acclamation and had won in a landslide. The Chicago convention had been scheduled for the week of his sixtieth birthday, which came that Tuesday. Now he couldn't even come. The Secret Service advised him that it was too risky.

"Stop the war!" shouted the youths in the galleries. (The next day, in a ludicrous change, municipal employees took all the seats and waved banners reading WE LOVE DALEY.) But the most dramatic moment of the week was an outside echo of events inside the hall. Delegates were watching what was happening downtown on television screens, and Senator Abe Ribicoff, looking down from the rostrum on the Illinois delegation fifteen feet in front of him, condemned "Gestapo tactics in the streets of Chicago." Daley and his aides were on their feet, shaking fists and yelling obscenities at him —lip-readers watching television could identify the oaths—and Ribicoff said calmly, "How hard it is to accept the truth."

The full truth about what was happening was complicated. If the policemen had matched the courage and discipline of the U.S. marshals on the Ole Miss campus, their record would have been clean. At the same time, it is fair to point out that some of them were provoked. Afterward they displayed over a hundred weapons they had taken from those they arrested: switchblade knives, studded golf balls, clubs with nails embedded in them, bats with razor blades in the ends, chunks of concrete, and plain rocks.

The sequence of events which eventually erupted beneath the very hotel windows of the major candidates had begun on August 3, the Thursday before the convention, when the Youth International Party—the Yippies—arrived in Chicago with Pigasus, the 125-pound hog they announced they were going to nominate for President. Conspicuous in their beads, sandals, and beards, the Yippies and hippies settled down in Chicago's 1,185-acre Lincoln Park on the North Side. Over the weekend they played guitars, read poetry, and gave speeches. At 11 P.M. Saturday, curfew time, a dozen were arrested. None resisted. Sunday there were 2,000 of them. At 5 P.M. they asked police for permission to take a truck into the park and use it as a bandstand. The cops refused. They then arrested the Yippy leader Jerry Rubin. The crowd, incensed, chanted, "Hell, no, we won't go," "Oink, Oink!" and "Ho-Ho-Ho Chi Minh." Tom Hayden of the New Left explained to the officers that this last meant nothing; it was an international student chant which began in Germany. They ignored him. At curfew time they charged through the park swinging nightsticks. They did the same Monday night, except that this time they were tougher. The evicted demonstrators raced away through the North Side traffic.

On Tuesday seventy priests and ministers erected a ten-foot cross. The demonstrators sang, "We Shall Overcome" and "The Battle Hymn of the Republic." That evening three hundred policemen charged them with tear gas. Choking youths threw stones and bottles, shouting, "Shoot me, pig!" and "Hit me, pig!" The climax came on Wednesday. Demonstration leaders had announced that the protesters would march from the Grant Park band shell to the amphitheater as a show of the solidarity of their opposition to the war. "This is a nonviolent march," Dellinger told an audience of eight thousand. "If you feel you can't respond nonviolently, please leave us." Many did. Nevertheless a Chicago official said, "There will be no march today."

And there wasn't. Instead there was what an investigatory commission later called a "police riot." Policemen with bullhorns shouted, "This is a final warning. Move out now." The crowd did, to a narrow strip of Grant Park across Michigan Avenue from the Conrad Hilton. As they moved they mocked the police with "Oink! Oink!" "Sieg Heil!" and other rude chants. At the intersection of Michigan and Balboa avenues a double line of cops awaited them. The scene was brightly illuminated by TV lights on trucks and the eaves of the Conrad Hilton Hotel, headquarters for the three candidates. As the crowd tensed and then surged back and forth taunting the officers, daring them to attack, the police swooped down on them in two flying wedges, nightsticks swinging, dragging individual demonstrators toward waiting wagons. Hundreds of girls in the throng screamed. The mayhem continued for eighteen mad minutes. What was happening, in a very real sense, was a battle between the upper middle and lower middle class. A journalist said, "Those are our children in the streets, and the policemen are attacking them." But of course the policemen had parents, too.

Apart from the major encounters there were skirmishes all week between patrolmen and demonstrators, and some between patrolmen and nondemonstrators. On Monday evening alone twenty-one newspapermen were hurt. At various times spectators, clergymen, and at least one cripple were clubbed. Hugh Hefner, the publisher of *Playboy*, was walloped, and Mrs. Anne Kerr, a British Labourite, was Maced outside the Conrad Hilton and thrown into a cell. Hotel guests in the lobby were also beaten and jailed. The hotel's air-conditioning shafts sucked up tear gas and wafted it into suite 2525A, where Hubert Humphrey was watching himself being nominated on television. On Friday policemen said they were being pelted by objects from windows above—sardines, herrings, beer cans, ashtrays, cocktail glasses, and ice cubes. They thought—they couldn't tell—that the missiles were coming from the fifteenth floor, corner suite 1505A and 1506A: McCarthy's command post. Without writ or warrant, they ran into the hotel, took elevators up, and clouted the occupants of the suite.

Bloodshed might have been averted in Chicago if Mayor Daley had consented when the demonstrators asked permission to sleep in the meadows and glens of Lincoln Park. Then the policemen could have guarded the fringes of the park until the protesters got bored and left. As it was, by enforcing the curfew the mayor made confrontation inevitable, and under the worst possible circumstances. "The whole world is watching," the youths had chanted at Michigan and Balboa. The world wasn't, but most of the country was—an estimated 89 million, including, at Key Biscayne, an elated Richard Nixon.

In Chicago, Theodore H. White had written in his notes at 8:05 P.M. Wednesday, "The Democrats are finished." Certainly it looked like it, and when Humphrey's campaign began with a sickening lurch his admirers despaired. Among his major handicaps were the alienation of Democrats whose hearts had been captured by McCarthy and who now wore blank campaign pins, lack of money, an inefficient organization, and his inability to free himself from the toils of Lyndon Johnson. Johnson wasn't helping. His attitude toward Humphrey was scornful. He seemed to regard him as contemptible. Asked to comment on him, Johnson said curtly, "He cries too much."

In those early autumn weeks he had something to cry over. Inadequately prepared, Humphrey swung through New Jersey, Delaware, Michigan, Louisiana, Texas, Pennsylvania, Colorado, and California, speaking as often as nine times a day, a sign of his energy—and the lack of judgment on the part of his staff. Advance men served him poorly; crowds were small and tepid. In Philadelphia, Joey Bishop, a local boy accompanying Humphrey, got more applause than Humphrey. There were hecklers at virtually every stop. In Boston an antiwar crowd booed Humphrey and Edward Kennedy off a platform. Humphrey, said one of his workers, "went to Chicago with one albatross," meaning Lyndon Johnson, "and came out with two," meaning Johnson and Daley.

His treasury was all but empty. His rhetoric, which could soar, was laced with bromides. At one point he actually said, "Government of the people, by the people, and for the people is as American as apple pie." Johnson seemed to be sabotaging him; when in September Humphrey said that the withdrawal of U.S. troops could begin at the end of the year, the President said that "no man can predict" when departure might start. Not counting Wallace votes, in August Gallup had Nixon leading by 16 points, and Harris put Nixon's margin at 40 to 31. Even Humphrey was discouraged. He said, "I have pursued impossible dreams before and maybe I am now."

Nixon's campaign was all the other way. He had plenty of money and exultant optimism. His schedule harmonized with deadlines of the network news programs, even allowing them plenty of time to develop their film. He dodged challenges to debate, and Republican senators filibustered a measure to allow public service TV debates without Wallace. He appealed to the "forgotten American"—the man who paid his taxes, didn't riot or break the law, went to church and raised his children to be "good Americans" who would wear the country's uniform with pride as "watchmen on the walls of freedom around the world."

Joe McGinniss described the advertising techniques used by the Nixon people in *The Selling of the President 1968*. One writer observed that to Nixon politics were "products . . . to be sold the public—this one today, that one tomorrow, depending on the discounts and the state of the market." Frank Shakespeare Jr., a Nixon aide, was tremendously excited by the Russian repulsion of Czechoslovakia. "What a break!" McGinniss quoted him as saying. "This Czech thing is perfect! It puts the soft-liners in a hell of a box!"

Nixon said he had a plan to end the war; he couldn't divulge it now because it might disturb the peace talks going on in Paris. He promised to restore law and order by appointing a new attorney general, and he attacked the Supreme Court for being "patently guilty" of freeing defendants on technicalities. He favored approval of the nuclear nonproliferation treaty, but not now, because of Soviet treatment of the Czechs. Business would improve, he said, because he would give businessmen tax credits and other incentives which would create jobs and reduce the number of people on welfare. America, he said, became great, "not because of what government did for the people but because of what people did for themselves."

In October Humphrey began to gain.

He had put Chicago behind him, and as he forgot it, so did his audiences. He dismissed his mockers as "damned fools," introduced the clown, Emmett Kelly, as "Nixon's economic adviser," and accused Nixon of dodging issues. He backed the Supreme Court and the nonproliferation treaty. Union audiences were reminded of what Democratic administrations had done for them. Nixon was "Richard the chicken-hearted"; Wallace and General Curtis LeMay, his running mate, were the "bombsy twins." Humphrey developed a technique of naming the Democratic presidential champions—Roosevelt, Truman, Stevenson, Kennedy—and then, just as the applause started to build, slipping in the name of Lyndon Johnson. Meanwhile his running mate was savaging Agnew. Muskie would say, "Mr. Agnew tells us that we lack a sense of humor," and add dryly: "I think he is doing his best to restore it."

Salt Lake City was a pivot. When Humphrey declared there that he would stop the bombing in Vietnam as "an acceptable risk for peace," the tide started to turn. On October 21 Gallup reported that Humphrey had cut Nixon's lead in half. Fading memories of Chicago was part of it. The habit of voting Democratic for a generation was another part. That June Gallup had found that 46 percent of the people considered themselves Democratic, 27 percent said they were independents, and 27 percent Republicans. (In 1940 it had been 42, 20, and 38 percent, and in 1950 45, 22, and 33.) Liberals who had yearned for Robert Kennedy or McCarthy awoke to the fact that the choice was between Humphrey and Nixon, their bogey for the past twenty years. McCarthy himself, who had been pouting on the Riviera, announced his support of the Democratic ticket five days before the election. Finally there was the difference between the demeanor of the two candidates. Humphrey was at the top of his form; Nixon had begun to sound uncannily like Thomas E. Dewey.

On the afternoon before the election Gallup had 42 percent for Nixon, 40 for Humphrey, 14 percent for Wallace, with 4 percent undecided. Since September Humphrey had gained 12 percent to Nixon's 1 percent, both at the expense of the fading Wallace. That same Monday Harris had Humphrey in the lead with 43 percent over Nixon's 40 percent; Wallace had 14 percent and 4 percent were undecided.

Tuesday night was a spellbinder. Nixon had asked the electorate for a "mandate to govern." What he got was a surge of Humphrey votes which, in the opinion of many analysts, would have won the election if the campaign had lasted another day or two—as it would have, the Democrats reflected grimly, if they hadn't postponed their convention so that it would coincide with the week of Lyndon Johnson's birthday. The figures flashing on the networks' electric scoreboards showed the lead changing hands several times. It seemed at one point that the two leaders were, as the Associated Press put it, "trading state for state." Shortly after midnight Humphrey was leading by 33,000 votes. At dawn it appeared that although he couldn't win in the electoral college, he might win in the popular vote, and there was a distinct possibility that he could thwart a Nixon majority in electoral votes, throwing the election into the House of Representatives, where the Democrats had a majority.

The final electoral results were Nixon 301, Humphrey 191, and Wallace 45. The popular vote was 31,770,222 for Nixon (43.4 percent), 31,267,744 for Humphrey (42.7 percent), and 9,897,141 for Wallace (13.5 percent). The distance between the two leaders was less than .7 of one percentage point. Moreover, the Democrats had retained control of Congress. Nixon would be the first President in one hundred and twenty years to begin his administration with the opposition ruling both Houses on the Hill.

Campaigning in Ohio, Nixon had seen a thirteen-year-old schoolgirl holding a sign which read: "Bring Us Together." That, he said in his moment of triumph, had "touched me most." Did he mean it? With this complex man one could never be sure. "Watch what we do, not what we say," John Mitchell, his attorney-general designate, told a group of thirty southern black leaders. Later, during the Watergate scandals, James Reston would write of Nixon that "There is scarcely a noble principle in the American Constitution that he hasn't defended in theory or defied in practice." But in the pause after his election his credit was strong. Most Americans wanted to believe him, to persuade themselves that he knew how to leave the swamps of the 1960s for higher ground. He had promised to extricate the troops from Vietnam. Since 1961 there had been 24,291 American deaths in the war; it was an immense relief to know that soon the dying would end. The country needed a rest. Now partisan politics could be shelved.

From his windows on the thirty-ninth floor of Manhattan's Pierre Hotel, the President-elect could look out across the wooded sweep of Central Park and see America twinkling in the distance. Not since the pit of the Depression had the country been so torn. Between those whose bumper stickers said LOVE IT OR LEAVE IT and those who said CHANGE IT OR LOSE IT yawned a chasm so broad that no reconciliation was possible now; finding common ground would have to wait until outstanding issues had been resolved, the war being the first of them. In the matter of social questions as liberal a commentator as Eric Sevareid found himself drifting to the right. He looked at the long list of crimes for which Black Panthers had been convicted and was appalled. He watched on television as a Baltimore girl, the mother of seven illegitimate children, furiously blamed society for her plight, and shook his head; he watched black women hurrying to reach home before sunset and said: "I just don't believe that 'law and order' are code words, except for a few. This issue is survival itself."

To those on the left side of the divide, the aroused young ideologues, nothing seemed to be sacred: not the American flag, God, motherhood, knowledge, honor, modesty, chastity, or simple honesty. In 1968 insurance actuaries reportedly discovered that the group in society which failed most often to repay its debts was the young collegians who owed tuition loans; a college president wrote to one defaulter who had just graduated, and back came a photograph of the new alumnus naked and in a cave. It was almost possible to believe that for some middle-class youths the Boy Scout pledge which their fathers had recited had become inverted: they strove to be untrustworthy, disloyal, unhelpful, hostile, discourteous, unkind, disobedient, cheerless, wasteful, craven, dirty, and irreverent.

The campuses of venerable institutions of learning had often become disagreeable and even dangerous places. The one at Wesleyan, a little ivy college in Connecticut, had to be floodlit at night; crossing it was unsafe; there had been an epidemic of muggings there. Universities were confronted with a new disciplinary problem: how to cope with the undergraduate who was putting himself through college by peddling dope to fellow students who had become drug addicts. Crime became commonplace in peculiar places. One respected physician in New England entertained dinner party guests by telling how he and his wife had started shoplifting as children, still did it, and in fact had stolen the centerpiece on the table only three days ago. An assistant dean explained in great detail the information he had given, to a recent undergraduate drafted into the tank corps, on the best way to sabotage a tank. And a July 1967 issue of the *New York Review of Books* carried on its front page a large drawing showing how to make a Molotov cocktail, with a rag soaked in gasoline as the stopper, a fuse of clothesline rope, and instructions to use as fuel a mixture two-thirds gas and one-third soap powder and dirt.

The election of Richard Nixon to the Presidency was a reaction against all this, and a healthy one. The nation wanted no more visionaries for the present. What was needed was a genuine conservative administration, another Eisenhower era. Such a government would resist temptations to cut taxes and try, insofar as possible, to balance the budget, assuring a sound dollar and no inflation. Hostilities in Indochina would be ended as soon as possible, and all foreign policies would be evaluated solely in terms of the national interest of the United States. At home the role of the federal government would be sharply limited and congressional prerogatives restored, and ties would be strengthened between the generations, the races, the wealthy and the impoverished, the different regions in the country, and the religious faiths.

Nowhere was America's exhaustion in 1968 more evident than in the ghettos, which were calmer that year than anyone had prophesied. "We will have a bad summer," Lyndon Johnson had said in the spring. "We will have several bad summers before the deficiencies are erased." Nixon foresaw "war in the streets." The Justice Department had become so sophisticated on the subject of inner city disorders that it had established standards for a major riot. It had to be violent, had to have more than 300 participants, had to last at least twelve hours or more, and had to include gunfire, looting, arson, and vandalism. (A mere "serious disturbance" involved 150 people for three hours.) The Army had trained 15,000 men in seven task forces to cope with civil uprisings, and black leaders predicted that by spring they would be needed, that the biggest eruption ever lay ahead.

Certainly the leaders were setting an example. They taught courses in guerrilla warfare and house-to-house fighting. CORE joined SNCC and Martin Luther King's SCLC in a militant shift to the left, advocating compulsive separation of the races. Eldridge Cleaver's *Soul on Ice,* a best seller of 1968, described Cleaver as a "full-time revolutionary in the struggle for black liberation in America." James Baldwin called the United States the "Fourth Reich," and the disciples of Malcolm X observed the third anniversary of his death with a lack of restraint beyond anything he had advocated. Even black celebrities were taking a hard line. Black sprinters Tommie Smith and John Carlos obscured the glory of American victories at the Olympic games in Mexico City by bowing their heads during the playing of "The Star-Spangled Banner" in honor of their victories and raising black-gloved clenched fists in a defiant gesture. When Cleveland blew in July, the general reaction was here-we-go-again. A tow truck, called to the scene of an accident, was fired upon by snipers. Policemen called to the scene became targets of the riflemen. Within thirty minutes three officers and four blacks were dead, and eight policemen were wounded. The National Guard was summoned, and losses from looting and burning were put at 1.5 million dollars. In the brick canyons of other ghettos police braced themselves for what seemed inevitable.

It didn't come. There were half as many riots as expected and none of the other big cities experienced the havoc of the past three years. "In terms of racial conflict," the AP reported, "it was the coolest summer in five years." There were just nineteen deaths, shocking by pre-Watts standards but nothing like the eighty-seven of the year before. One reason was that the most inflammatory of the inciters weren't in the streets any more. They were in jail, or fugitives. H. Rap Brown had been put away. Cleaver disappeared in late November when his parole was revoked. Huey P. Newton was tried in Oakland for killing a policeman; a jury with a black foreman found him guilty. "If Huey goes, the sky's the limit," said his black-jacketed followers, threatening to terrorize all whites, but when he was sent away for two to fifteen years for manslaughter, nothing happened.

Another reason for the comparative tranquillity was that blacks had realized they themselves were the chief victims of the riots. *Their* stores were looted, *their* cars were destroyed, *their* homes burned, and *their* children endangered. Dr. Hiawatha Harris, a

Watts psychiatrist, said that "the rioting phase, where we burn down businesses in our own areas, is over. The whole movement is in another direction—toward implementing black power and finding our dignity as a people." Measured by education, wages, public service —"by every traditional index of progress," Theodore H. White wrote —American blacks were already moving forward. The change was evident in little ways. The television screen was one. Integration had become a reality there. Almost every serial had a black player now. The neurosurgeon in Peyton Place was a Negro—and one black, "Julia," was a heroine.

A new and more effective way to protest was put forward in Chicago by a Negro minister, Jesse Jackson, who forced white businessmen to hire blacks by telling his congregation to boycott their products. A & P made jobs for 970; Jewel Tea for 661. Operation Breadbasket, as Jackson called it, also persuaded businessmen to open accounts in two Negro banks, increasing their deposits from five million dollars to twenty-two million. Blacks had economic muscle to flex now. The Bureau of the Census later found that the number of Negro families making more than ten thousand dollars a year had risen in the 1960s from 11 percent to 28 percent. They were finally beginning to move into the middle class.

Montage: The Late Sixties

SOMETHING BEAUTIFUL, MAN, LIKE IT BLOWS YOUR MIND

INTERSTATE HIGHWAY SURFACED — MILEAGE PASSES 42,500 MARK —

HONOR U.S. HERO

Among the honors conferred upon General Westmoreland during his brief visit home were the USO Distinguished Service Award, a citation from the South Carolina Legislature, an honorary degree from the University of Buffalo, and the Boy Scout Silver Buffalo Award

for EXPERT white collar girls . . . get the Kelly Girl habit

The U.S. birth rate dropped to 17.9 births, the lowest on record, breaking a mark of 18.9 set in the Depression years of 1933 and 1938

Our motto comes from the novelist Hermann Hesse: "We are in a magic theatre, a world of pictures not reality/ Tonight at the magic theater for madmen only/the price of admission is your mind."

Our battalion managed to retake the town by daybreak. When we moved in only one person was left alive in the place: a small boy who was badly wounded

Take it off, take it all off

NIXON'S THE ONE

U.S. TELSTAR RELAYS TV PIX ACROSS ATLANTIC

This is the dawning of the Age of Aquarius,
The Age of Aquarius

Picture yourself in a boat on a river
With tangerine trees and marmalade skies
Somebody calls you, you answer quite slowly
A girl with kaleidoscopic eyes
Cellophane flowers of yellow and green

"I'm for anything that gets you through the night — booze or religion," Mr. Sinatra said.

A boo-boo

How does it feel, how does it feel
To be without a home
Like a complete unknown
Like a rolling stone?

frug

No strain

SUPPORT OUR BOYS IN VIETNAM

No problem

GOD IS
LOVE IS
I AM

psychedelic, adj. Of, pertaining to, or generating hallucinations, distortions of perceptions, and, occasionally, states resembling psychosis.

What the world needs now
Is love sweet love

People try to put us down
Just because we get around
Things they do look awful cold
Hope I die before I get old

COURT, 8-1, OKAYS STOP, FRISK

WOW! DIG ALL THE BEAUTIFUL FREAKS!

No sweat

Had any lately?

Put silver wings on my son's chest
Make him one of America's best
He'll be a man they'll test one day—
Have him win the green beret

I went up there, I said, "Shrink, I wanna kill. I wanna kill! I wanna see blood and gore and guts and veins in my teeth! Eat dead, burnt bodies! I mean kill, kill!" And I started jumpin' up and down yellin' "KILL! KILL!" . . . and the sergeant came over, pinned a medal on me.

MAKE LOVE NOT WAR

YOU FIGHT AND DIE BUT CAN'T DRINK AT 18

DON'T TRUST ANYONE OVER 30

GIVE A DAMN

Poor People's Campaign 1968

WE SHALL OVER KILL

Student Power

POWs never have a nice day

No way

HIPPY POWER

DROP IT

STONED

Have a nice day

monkey

PEACE

GOD IS ON A TRIP

Would you believe fifty?

V

NIXON, AFTER ALL

1969–1972

Thirty-four

THE RISE OF THE SILENT MAJORITY

RICHARD NIXON'S HEROES included a Democratic President, Woodrow Wilson, and upon learning that President-elect Wilson had announced all his cabinet choices at once in 1913, the President-elect of 1968 decided to do the same thing, on television. The ceremony was held in the Palladium Room of Washington's Shoreham Hotel on December 11, 1968. Nixon asked that each secretary-designate be accompanied by his wife; loyal helpmates, he explained, deserved to share in reflected glory—a condescension which was branded sexist by infuriated feminists. The wives of the new cabinet members seemed to enjoy the occasion, but the national audience was another matter. For viewers the thirty-minute production was flat one critic rudely called it "a political *What's My Line?*"—and many noted that the star kept repeating himself. Each of the twelve secretaries-designate was identified by Nixon as a man who understood not only his specialty but psychology as well. This was called an "extra dimension," a phrase which the President-elect used no fewer than ten times.

In fact, the incoming cabinet was conspicuous for its lack of dimension. Its members were all affluent, white, male, middle-class, and Republican, and seven of them lived west of the Alleghenies, territory which had been the chief source of Republican votes. Nearly all were businessmen, with three—Walter Hickel (Interior), Winton Blount (postmaster general), and John Volpe (Transportation)—from the construction industry. The lack of breadth was not altogether Nixon's fault. He had tried for more diversity. Earlier he had pledged the formation of "a government made up of Republicans, Democrats, and independents," consisting of "the very best men and women I can find in the country, from government, from labor, from all the areas." But the principal areas of Democratic strength had not responded to his overtures. Three blacks, for example, had bluntly turned him down: Whitney Young Jr., Senator Edward Brooke, and Mrs. Ersa Poston, president of the New York Civil Service Commission. So he had wound up with homogeneity instead of a cross section. The Nixon cabinet, a magazine writer commented, "seems to be constructed more of gray fieldstone than glinting steel and glass." But so was its architect. "The men suggest cool competence rather than passion or brilliance," *Time* said. Whatever their shortcomings, no one doubted their integrity.

The presence in the cabinet of such Nixon intimates as William Rogers (State), John Mitchell (Justice), and Robert Finch (HEW) was interpreted as evidence that the new President intended to give it more power than Johnson had; the demise of the kitchen cabinet as a presidential institution was predicted by columnists who did not yet know H. R. Haldeman and John Ehrlichman. To be sure, the President watchers granted, there would be exceptions. As presidential assistant for national security Henry Kissinger was already emerging as a key adviser. Rogers was reported to be reading Kissinger's books. What no one then foresaw was that Nixon's first Secretary of State would be keeping in touch with American foreign policy developments by reading transcripts of Kissinger's press conferences.

Six months after entering the White House the new President received a tremendous psychological boost when NASA's long voyage to the moon, begun eight years earlier on orders from John F. Kennedy, reached its destination. The mission was Apollo 11. It was the capstone of an extraordinary effort—20,000 contractors and 300,000 workers had contributed to it—and while men could argue endlessly over whether it had been worth the cost, its success was undeniably an American triumph. In a proclamation Richard Nixon noted that while exploration had been "a lonely enterprise" in the past, "today the miracles of space travel are matched by miracles of space communication; even across the vast lunar distance, television brings the moment of discovery into our homes and makes us all participants." By "all" he meant more than Americans. The lunar landing was witnessed by the largest television audience ever, some 528 million people.

The possibility of failure was small. U.S. space science had come a long way since its first failures twelve years earlier. Between 1961 and 1966 the sixteen manned flights of the Mercury and Gemini series had demonstrated that man could live and function in space, and the Ranger, Lunar Orbiter, and Surveyor programs had sent back proof that the surface of the moon was safe for astronauts. There had been one dreadful setback. In January 1967 Apollo 1 had exploded on its pad, killing the three-man crew. After twenty-one months of delays manned Apollo command modules had gone up, however, and in late 1968 and early 1969 NASA had followed a rigid schedule, sending up an Apollo every two and a half months in hopes of meeting the Kennedy deadline of May 1961: to land a man on the moon and return him safely to earth "before this decade is out."

Apollo 11, with its 36-story-high Saturn 5 rocket, was fired at Cape Kennedy's launch complex 39A at 9:32 on the morning of July 16, 1969. Aboard were Neil A. Armstrong, the civilian commander, and two Air Force officers, Col. Edwin E. "Buzz" Aldrin Jr. and Lieutenant Colonel Michael Collins. The Saturn's third stage put them into an orbit at a height of 118 miles. After a two-and-a-half-hour check of all instruments systems, they refired the third stage. This gave them a velocity of 24,245 mph, sufficient to throw them beyond the earth's atmosphere and on their way to the moon, a quarter-million miles away.

At a distance of 50,000 miles from the earth Collins maneuvered the command vessel, which had been christened the *Columbia,* until it was nose to nose with the fragile lunar module, called the *Eagle* or simply the LM. Once the *Columbia* and the *Eagle* were hooked together, the Saturn's third stage was jettisoned. On Thursday, the second day of the trip, the men switched on *Columbia*'s engine just long enough to put them in a trajectory which would pass within 69 miles of the back side of the moon on Saturday. Friday afternoon, Cape Kennedy time, Armstrong and Aldrin crept through a tunnel connecting the two vessels and into the *Eagle*, and at the end of that day the astronauts entered the moon's field of gravity. They were now within 44,000 miles of it, and picking up speed.

Saturday afternoon they slowed to 3,736 mph and went into orbit around the moon. Mission Control, their radio link with NASA's

Manned Spacecraft Center in Houston, awoke them at 7:02 A.M. on Sunday, July 20, which was to be the day of the landing. In the *Eagle* Armstrong and Aldrin extended the four landing legs of the ungainly lunar module. "You're 'go' for undocking," Mission Control told them. Now the LM and the *Columbia* separated, and Armstrong said, "The *Eagle* has wings!" At 3:08 P.M. he fired the spacecraft's engine, and down they went, toward the moon's Sea of Tranquillity.

At a distance of 9.8 miles from the surface of the moon they went into a low orbit, sailing over an awesome lunar scape of mountains and craters. At this point a Houston computer started flashing warning lights on their instruments. Rather than turn back this close to their goal, they went forward on instructions from a young guidance officer in Houston, with Armstrong at the controls and Buzz Aldrin calling out speed and altitude readings from the instruments. They had a bad moment during their final descent. The *Eagle* was less than 500 feet from the moon when Armstrong realized that they were about to land in the large, forbidding West Crater, so called because it was four miles west of their target. He flew beyond it, but this unexpected extension of the journey meant that he was rapidly running out of fuel; he had to decide immediately whether to turn about there or risk crashing. In that instant two lights on the panel in front of him glowed. They read LUNAR CONTACT. The *Eagle* had made it.

"Houston, Tranquillity Base here," he said. "The *Eagle* has landed." It was 4:17:42 P.M. Eastern Daylight Time, Sunday, July 20, 1969.

After three hours of checking instruments, the two astronauts asked Houston if they might omit a scheduled four-hour break and disembark now. "We will support it," Houston answered. They put on their $300,000 space suits and depressurized the LM cabin; then Armstrong, moving backward, began his slow descent of a nine-rung ladder. On the second step he pulled a cord, opening the lens of a TV camera and thus allowing half a billion people to watch him move cautiously down to the stark surface.

His 9½B boot touched it, and he said: "That's one small step for a man, one giant leap for mankind." It was 10:56:20 P.M. He shuffled around. "The surface is fine and powdery," he said. "It adheres in fine layers, like powdered charcoal, to the soles and sides of my boots. I only go in a fraction of an inch, maybe an eighth of an inch, but I can see the footprints of my boots and the treads in the fine, sandy particles."

Armstrong put some of the powder in a pocket on the leg of his space suit. Then, nineteen minutes after his debarkation, Aldrin joined him, saying, "Beautiful, beautiful; magnificent desolation." Armstrong drove a stake in the lunar soil and mounted the TV camera on it. The spidery *Eagle* was sixty feet away, and in the middle of the television picture; behind it was the eternal night of outer space. Gravity here was one-sixth G, 16.6 percent of that on earth. Viewers saw the two men bounding about like gazelles and heard Aldrin say, "When I'm about to lose my balance in one direction I find recovery is quite natural and very easy." They planted a three-by-five-foot U.S. flag, the cloth held out from the staff by wires; Aldrin saluted it. They also deposited a container bearing messages from the leaders of seventy-six countries and a stainless-steel plaque reading, "Here men from planet Earth first set foot upon the moon, July, 1969, A.D. We came in peace for all mankind."

Gathering some fifty pounds of rocks for scientific study, they measured the temperature outside their space suits: 234 degrees Fahrenheit in sunlight and 279 degrees below zero in the shade. A strip of foil was set out to collect solar particles, and two instruments were erected, a seismometer to mark lunar disturbances, and a reflector to send readings to telescopes on earth. At midnight they returned to the *Eagle,* and after 21 hours and 37 minutes on the moon they fired their engine and departed. ("You're cleared for takeoff," Mission Control said. "Roger, we're No. 1 on the runway," said Aldrin.) Back in orbit, they rendezvoused with Collins in the *Columbia.* He rehooked the two vessels together. They crawled back through the tunnel to join him, and the *Eagle* was cast loose to float through space and, eventually, to crash on the moon.

At 1:56 A.M. Collins pointed the *Columbia* earthward and fired its engine, freeing the command module from the moon's gravity. The trip home would take sixty hours. That evening, via television, the astronauts sent the world a picture of itself taken at a distance of 175,000 miles. "It's nice to sit here and watch the earth getting larger and larger and the moon smaller and smaller," said Aldrin. Armstrong said, "No matter where you travel, it's nice to get home." On Thursday, moving at a speed of 24,602 mph, they reentered the earth's atmosphere 757 miles over the Pacific. During the crucial part of this phase the spacecraft's shield was scorched by 4,000-

degree heat. Clouds surrounded the command module, and radio contact was lost for three minutes.

Then radar aboard the waiting carrier *Hornet* picked up the descending *Columbia*, which was plunging down 13.8 miles away, beneath three 83-foot orange and white parachutes. The module splashed down in six-foot waves, capsized, and was righted when the three men inside inflated bags on the side. Helicopters from the *Hornet* hovered overhead, guiding the vessel to the spot. President Nixon was waving zoom binoculars on the bridge. The ship's band crashed into "Columbia, the Gem of the Ocean," and all over the United States, and in many foreign cities, church bells rang out, whistles blew, and motorists leaned on their horns.

Richard Nixon's greeting to the Apollo 11 astronauts came at the beginning of a nine-day presidential jet trip around the world. During it he visited six Asian nations: the Philippines, Indonesia, Thailand, South Vietnam, India, and Pakistan. His central purpose there was to drive home his determination to make sure there were no more Vietnams. Stopping overnight in Guam on his way to Manila, he spelled out the Nixon Doctrine for reporters: "Peace in Asia cannot come from the United States. It must come from Asia. The people of Asia, the governments of Asia—they are the ones who must lead the way." In Bangkok he said he wanted to speak plainly: "If domination by the aggressor can destroy the freedom of a nation, too much dependence on a protector can eventually erode its dignity."

That sounded unequivocal, but newspapermen were learning that often when the new President promised to make something perfectly clear, it was about to become opaque. So it was on this Asian swing. Even as he deplored America's overcommitment in Vietnam, he told U.S. troops there that he thought "history will record that this may have been one of America's finest hours," and he also pledged to the Thais: "The United States will stand proudly with Thailand against those who might threaten it from abroad or from within." Telling people what he thought they wanted to hear was an old Nixon weakness; if his hosts weren't elated by his assurances that he would send them some fragments of moon rock, it seemed, he was ready to hint that he might send a few divisions.

There was another explanation. This was a transitional period in his attitude toward Communism. Part of him was still the cold-warrior, ready to pick up any Red challenge, while another part believed that global stability depended on conciliation between Washington on the one hand and Moscow and Peking on the other. In this sense there was such a thing as a new Nixon. His flexibility emerged dramatically toward the end of this trip. He stopped in Bucharest to spend a day with Romanian President Nicolae Ceausescu, and as proof of his friendly feelings he rode through a downpour with the top of his car down. The crowd's response was amazing; people along the way not only cheered vigorously; they also vied with one another to pick up tiny paper American flags which fell to sidewalks, leaving flags of their own country where they lay.

In England Nixon paused for talks with Prime Minister Harold Wilson. This was his second European visit in five months; he had been in office only seventeen days when he had announced a trip to Belgium, Britain, West Germany, Italy, and France—"the blue-chip countries," as he called them. He had always believed that he had a special talent for foreign affairs, and he was certainly making friends among other chiefs of state, even though the most important of them, Wilson, Chancellor Kurt Kiesinger, and President Charles de Gaulle, were not to remain in office long. In that first year the new President was going out of his way to be cordial to a great many people at home and abroad, including some toward whom he had once been very chilly. He flew to Independence to give Harry Truman a grand piano which had once been in the White House and played "The Missouri Waltz" on it—Truman was too polite to tell him he had always hated the song—and he extolled retiring Chief Justice Earl Warren, as "a symbol of fairness, integrity, and dignity."

Even then Nixon kept his distance from the press, but most reporters were generous in their treatment of him. Hugh Sidey of *Life* wrote that the President had "devised a government in his own image—decent, thoughtful, competent, cautious." Although newsmen covering the White House felt that his public appearances were forced and contrived, they had a certain admiration for the pains he took for them, knowing how uncomfortable he was in such situations. They appreciated the diet he carefully followed to avoid appearing jowly, how he tried to stay tanned for television, and the time he spent choosing his wardrobe because he wanted his suits to give the public just the right impression of quiet good taste.

As his presidential image formed, he emerged as a thoughtful, rather lonely man who spent hours hunched over yellow legal tablets in various White House sanctuaries, notably a study off the Lincoln bedroom and a hideaway just across the street in the Executive Office Building. He liked paperwork more than Lyndon Johnson, and people less. The forty-two-button phone was removed from the oval office; Nixon needed only six buttons. He also appeared to be less interested in the news, even news about himself, than Johnson; the teletypes and the television sets of the previous administration were banished to an outer office. His favorite TV programs were Saturday afternoon football games in the autumn and winter, and he nearly always found time to watch them. "I know the job I have is supposed to be the most difficult job in the world," he said, "but it has not yet become for me that great, awesome burden that some have described it."

"Middle America" was a current journalistic phrase, and the new chief executive was its apotheosis. He liked the competitive spirit of Vince Lombardi, the music of Guy Lombardo, the novels of Allen Drury, the piety of Billy Graham, the wit of Bob Hope, and the sales techniques of J. Walter Thompson. Though most of his career had been spent in public service, he had the middle-class distrust of the federal bureaucracy; one of his first acts was to abolish the patronage system for selecting postmasters. (The following year Congress, at his request, established an independent U.S. Postal Service.) As a Middle American he believed in expert advice. The voices he listened to most were those of John Mitchell, Henry Kissinger, John D. Ehrlichman, and H. R. Haldeman. Sidey noted that although the President's programs were a little left of center on paper, "the men he named to high office leaned the other way—and in Washington experience suggested that in the end men would dominate blueprints." Doctrine seemed to mean little to Nixon himself anyway; he had Middle America's penchant for trying various approaches, zigging and zagging from the center, in hope of finding workable solutions. At various times in 1969 he proposed tax reform, tinkered with the ideological balance of the Supreme Court, reduced the troop level in Vietnam, returned Okinawa to Japan, tried to alter the welfare system, outlawed germ warfare, and made various attempts to restrain inflation. In that first year he also displayed Middle American modesty. When his advisers crowded around to congratulate him on his return from his first European journey, he called a halt. "Too soon, too soon," he said. "A year from now we'll know if it was a success."

He was not so modest as a spender. Like thousands of other American executives who had made it, the chief executive was overextending himself to support an elaborate new life-style. He was earning $290,000 a year in salary and expenses. He had a home near the office and a retreat at Camp David, but he mortgaged himself to the hilt just the same. First he bought a pair of brick-and-stucco bungalows on Florida's Biscayne Bay. The cost was put at over $250,000. There the President could spend his leisure hours with an old friend, C. G. "Bebe" Rebozo—a onetime chauffeur and filling station operator who had made a fortune in real estate—aboard Rebozo's elaborate houseboat, the *Cocolobo*. Yet even that wasn't enough for Nixon. While gardeners were still putting in a ten-foot hedge around the Key Biscayne home, the President was in San Clemente, California, buying a $340,000 fourteen-room adobe villa, ordering a $100,000 swimming pool for it, and planning a four-hole golf course on adjacent land, each tee to be marked with a tiny presidential seal.

Although the facts were unknown at the time, Rebozo and another Nixon intimate, aerosol spray valve inventor Robert H. Abplanalp, held mortgages of about $500,000 on the two properties. At the same time, the government was laying out a staggering 10.5 million dollars on the two presidential estates and on houses frequently visited by the Nixons, such as Abplanalp's island in the Bahamas. Much of the money went for such necessities as helipads and military communications, but sums of money running to six figures were spent on landscaping, furniture, and heating systems.

That wasn't the end of it. Indeed, in terms of sheer cost it was only a beginning. Four years later *Fortune* would quote a former official of the Bureau of the Budget as estimating that the expense of President Nixon's household, as of then, had been approximately 100 million dollars. Lyndon Johnson, who was not thrifty, had maintained three Boeing jetliners; when Lady Bird went shopping in New York, she had taken the Eastern Airlines shuttle. All Nixon's relatives, including his sons-in-law, traveled on government planes. At the President's exclusive disposal were five Boeing 707s, eleven Lockheed Jetstars, and sixteen helicopters. He installed an archery range, a swimming pool, and bowling alleys at Camp David; the annual operating costs of the camp went from $147,000 a year under Johnson to $640,000. In addition the chief executive was attended at his various homes by 75 butlers, maids, cooks, and caretakers, 21 gardeners and maintenance workers, 100 Secret Service agents, 300 guards, the crew of the presidential yacht, and the drivers of a fleet of official limousines. Under Richard Nixon the presidential style could only be called lordly.

In his first appearance as President he had appeared in the role of healer. "The greatest honor history can bestow is the title of peacemaker," he had said in his inaugural, and he had made it clear that he was not merely talking about Vietnam. "We find ourselves rich in goods, but ragged in spirit; reaching with magnificent precision for the moon, but falling into raucous discord on earth. . . . We are torn by division, wanting unity. We see around us empty lives, wanting fulfillment. We see tasks that need doing, waiting for hands to do them. To a crisis of the spirit, we need an answer of the spirit. And to find that answer, we need only look within ourselves. . . . We cannot learn from one another until we stop shouting at one another—until we speak quietly enough so that our words can be heard as well as our voices. For its part, government will listen."

It was a shrewd appraisal of the American dilemma, and during his first eight months in the White House Nixon's search for solutions was along those lines. He suppressed his own strong combative instincts, keeping his voice down, his profile low, and his ear to the ground. In seeking advice he cultivated an aura of responsible craftsmanship. He had promised a "small" White House staff in his campaign, and after he won had said that he would run an "open" administration with vigorous counsel from "independent thinkers." As Republicans, he and the members of his administration did not share the Johnsonian conviction that America's troubles could be traced to underprivilege and poverty, but they had their own guiding light. To them the national anguish arose from a loss of faith in religion, the family, the binding force of friendly neighborhood life, and *McGuffey's Reader* patriotism. These were the convictions of small-town America, the great keep of the Republican party. It was hardly their fault that most Americans no longer lived in small towns, or that the attack on the nation's most sacred institutions, from the flag to motherhood, had acquired an irresistible momentum. The furies of the 1960s were not yet spent. The period was still one of violent contention.

Yet some election results in 1969 suggested that backlash was turning the country rightward. Republicans won the Virginia statehouse for the first time in over eighty years and the New Jersey governorship after sixteen Democratic years. Barry Goldwater Jr. was elected to Congress by California's 27th District. Liberal Ralph Yarborough was in trouble in Texas; early the following year he would be toppled in the Democratic primary by a conservative challenger. In Minneapolis an astounding 62 percent of the voters swept Charles S. Stenvig, a previously unknown police detective, into the mayoralty on the strength of Stenvig's advocacy of tough law enforcement in black neighborhoods, and Los Angeles gave Sam Yorty, the closest thing to a racist mayor outside the South, a third term despite an appalling record of absenteeism, drift, strife, and the conviction, on charges of bribery, of three men Yorty had appointed city commissioners.

A trend toward the right did not explain some Nixon difficulties on the Hill. In a truly conservative climate the Pentagon would be sacrosanct, and in 1969 the Defense budget was in peril for the first time in twenty years. Ever since the North Koreans had crossed the 38th Parallel, astronomical annual sums had been appropriated for the military establishment, frequently without even a roll call. The Pentagon outlay had risen from eleven billion dollars to eighty-one billion, but now the generals were confronted by a balky Congress. Frustration over Vietnam was one reason; others included a scandal featuring senior Army noncoms who had been making fortunes through PX kickbacks, dissatisfaction with the excessive costs of Lockheed C-5A transport production, and the discovery that the Army's Chemical Warfare Service was transporting 7,000 tons of nerve and poison gas across the country and dumping it in the Atlantic Ocean. The immediate issue raising congressional hackles, however, was a matter of missilery. The Defense Department wanted to start work on an enormous antiballistic missile (ABM) system which could wind up costing the country as much as a hundred billion dollars.

The ABM was necessary, the Pentagon argued, to deprive the USSR of first-strike power—the ability to cripple U.S. ICBM installations with a single blow and therefore prevent American retaliation. Senate critics led by Edward M. Kennedy replied that the ABM would escalate the arms race, that it would waste money better spent on pollution and in slums, and that its radar and computers were too complicated to work. "History," one technical witness said dryly, "is littered with Maginot Lines." In the end an ABM appropriation passed the Senate by a single vote, but the victory was Pyrrhic. It laid the groundwork for future struggles over Defense programs and sowed seeds of bitterness between Congress and the new administration. Speaking at the Air Force Academy on June 4, President Nixon attacked the forty-nine anti-ABM senators as "new isolationists." Senator Fulbright replied: "The greatest threat to peace and domestic tranquillity is not in Hanoi, Moscow, or Peking but in our colleges and in the ghettos of cities throughout the land."

The split between the President and his adversaries on the Hill widened in two savage battles over Supreme Court nominees. Nixon's choice of Warren E. Burger to succeed Earl Warren as Chief Justice sailed through the Senate, but when he named federal Judge Clement F. Haynsworth Jr. of South Carolina to replace Abe Fortas he touched off a senatorial revolt. The AFL-CIO and the NAACP denounced Haynsworth as antilabor and racist. He might have survived that, but Birch Bayh of Indiana turned up evidence that the judge had ruled in favor of firms in which he held stock. The nomination was rejected 55 to 45, with seventeen Republicans, including Minority Leader Hugh Scott, in the majority. Nixon called the attacks on Haynsworth "brutal, vicious, and . . . unfair." Two months later he announced his second choice, federal Judge G. Harrold Carswell of Florida.

Carswell's chief qualification appeared to be that he wasn't rich and thus, unlike Haynsworth, couldn't be charged with conflict of interest in corporate verdicts. Unfortunately he had other liabilities. A reporter dug out a sentence from a 1948 Carswell speech: "Segregation of the races is proper and the only practical and correct way of life in our states." Confronted with the quotation, the nominee called it "obnoxious and abhorrent," but the NAACP came out against him anyway. Then it was revealed that Carswell had participated actively in a campaign to exclude blacks from a Tallahassee golf club, had insulted civil rights lawyers in his court, and had been often reversed on appeal. This last development inspired a well-meant comment by Senator Roman L. Hruska of Nebraska. He told a television interviewer that "even if he were mediocre, there are a lot of mediocre judges and people and lawyers. Aren't they entitled to a little representation and a little chance? We can't have all Brandeises and Cardozos and Frankfurters and stuff like that. I doubt we can. I doubt we want to."

Later Hruska was asked if he regretted saying it. "Indeed I do," he said, "indeed I do." A GOP floor leader remarked later, "Everywhere I go I hear that word—mediocre. If there was one single thing it was that. You could see the votes deserting in droves." Before Hruska said it, Senator Kennedy had forecast a maximum of 25 votes against Carswell, and Scott had predicted that the most the opposition could muster would be "in the 30s." In fact the ayes were 45 and the nays 51; "the nomination," said the presiding officer, Vice President Agnew, "is not agreed to." Two days later an angry President Nixon told newspapermen that as long as the Democrats controlled the Senate "I cannot successfully nominate to the Supreme Court any federal appellate judge from the South who believes as I do in the strict construction of the Constitution."

This was a far cry from the bring-us-together theme of his inaugural, but it was deliberate. Nixon was abandoning nonpartisanship and was counterattacking. The strategic shift had begun with a televised speech to the nation in response to the first in a series of new antiwar demonstrations which dramatized demands for peace in Vietnam. The President said they were unnecessary because he had "a plan . . . for the complete withdrawal of all United States ground combat forces and their replacement by South Vietnamese forces." He called this "Vietnamization." He said he believed it would succeed and asked for support from "the great silent majority of my fellow Americans." In a thrust at his critics he said: "Let us be united for peace. Let us also be united against defeat. Because let us understand: North Vietnam cannot defeat or humiliate the United States. Only Americans can do that."

Gallup reported that 77 percent of his audience approved of the speech—only 6 percent disapproved it—and Nixon, heartened, decided to send his Vice President into the breach with even more vivid rhetoric. This was to be what Agnew himself called the "politics of polarization," a deliberate effort to isolate the President's critics. He had won Nixon's warm congratulations for assailing the dissidents as "an effete corps of impudent snobs who characterize themselves as intellectuals" and their political supporters as "parasites of passion" and "ideological eunuchs." Because 70 million Americans watched television network news programs, and because the White House was unhappy with TV coverage of the President, Agnew made that his first target.

Speaking in Des Moines on November 13, he took out after "a small group of men, numbering perhaps no more than a dozen anchormen, commentators and executive producers," who "settle upon the twenty minutes or so of film and commentary that is to reach the public." This "unelected elite," he said, was "a tiny and closed fraternity of privileged men . . . enjoying a monopoly sanctioned and licensed by government." He accused it of distorting "our national search for internal peace and stability." A week later he zeroed in on the press, singling out the *New York Times* and the *Washington Post* and deploring "the monopolization of the great public information vehicles and the concentration of more and more power over public opinion in fewer and fewer hands." Both the networks and the newspapers reported a heavy run of mail supporting Agnew and condemning the "eastern liberal establishment." Washington wondered whether Agnew had been speaking for himself or for Nixon. Hubert Humphrey said "Anyone who thinks that the Vice President can take a position independent of the President or his administration simply has no knowledge of politics or government. You are his choice in a political marriage, and he expects your absolute loyalty."

His bombast identified Spiro Agnew as a man of the era, for it was a time of overstatement, of exaggerated gestures and posturing and hyperbole, when everything from eating grapes and lettuce to wearing (or not wearing) a brassiere carried political overtones, and CBS fired the Smothers Brothers, a comedy team, for encouraging guest stars to make flippant remarks about patriotism and the Vietnam War.

A number of courtrooms were preoccupied with political trials. James Earl Ray and Sirhan Sirhan, the assassins of Martin Luther King and Robert F. Kennedy, were being convicted, and in one of the most bizarre actions in American legal history, New Orleans District Attorney Jim Garrison was trying to convince a jury that Clay L. Shaw, a retired Louisiana businessman, had conspired to murder John Kennedy. The key witnesses were a former taxi driver who had vaguely incriminated Shaw while under hypnosis, a drug addict, a paranoid accountant, and a perjurer who ultimately confessed that he had invented his testimony. The trial lasted thirty-four days. The jury voted to acquit Shaw in less than an hour.

Norman Mailer ran for mayor of New York, Dr. Timothy Leary for governor of California. President Nixon appointed Shirley Temple Black, now forty-one, to the U.S. delegation to the United Nations ("because," someone said, "he wanted the world to have a happy ending"). Bernadette Devlin arrived from Ireland to ask New Yorkers for money that would be used for murdering British soldiers. At San Francisco State College, Timothy Peebles, black and nineteen, bungled while trying to set a crude time bomb and blinded himself. SDS Weathermen vowing to "Bring the War Home" rioted in Chicago; sixty were arrested and three shot. Over a five-month period in 1969 Manhattan terrorists bombed the Marine Midland Grace Trust Company, the Armed Forces Induction Center, the Federal Office Building, Macy's, a United Fruit Company pier, and the RCA, Chase Manhattan, and General Motors buildings. On the night of November 13 police arrested three young men and Jane Lauren Alpert, twenty-two, a brilliant Swarthmore student and the daughter of upper-middle-class parents, charging them with conspiring to bomb federal property. Miss Alpert's parents put up a $20,000 bond for her and forfeited it when she vanished.

Environmentalists were angry over the new jumbo jets, taxpayers over teacher strikes, cigarette manufacturers because they had been forbidden to advertise on television after the end of 1970. Honeymooners were irate because the water had been temporarily diverted from Niagara Falls. Believers in flying saucers were indignant at the Air Force, which concluded a two-year investigation of 11,000 reported sightings by declaring that the saucers did not exist. Squeamish theatergoers objected when the 1969 New York Drama Desk Award went to *Peace*, an antiwar play in which the God of War flushed nations down a huge toilet.

To millions of Americans the nation's abrasive new mood appeared to be symbolized when Mel Finkelstein, a *New York Daily News* photographer trying to photograph Jacqueline Kennedy Onassis as she left a Manhattan showing of *I Am Curious (Yellow)*, sprawled on the pavement outside the theater. He said she flipped him over her thigh in a judo maneuver; she said he slipped and fell. Whatever had happened, another cameraman snapped President Kennedy's widow striding away from Finkelstein and the Swedish blue movie. She was wearing a tight black leather miniskirt. In the background a sign advertised WINES AND LIQUORS. Camelot seemed very far away.

It was the roughest year yet on college campuses. Although Gallup found that 72 percent of the country's 6.7 million students had never joined a demonstration, and a *Fortune* poll reported that only 12.8 percent were "revolutionary" or "radically dissident," the minority disrupted or paralyzed institutions in every part of the country. San Francisco State was closed for three weeks. The home of San Mateo Junior College's dean was fire-bombed. A rally of a thousand students and two hundred faculty members forced the resignation of Rice's president, and desperate administrators summoned police to, among others, San Fernando State, Howard, Pennsylvania State, and the University of Massachusetts. At the University of Chicago Bruno Bettelheim said that "many of these kids are very sick—paranoid," and he compared them to German students who had backed Hitler. Their demands continued. Negroes sought more courses in black studies, whites called for an end to ROTC and Dow Chemical recruitment. And all wanted an end to the Vietnam War.

Campus clashes had a way of escalating rapidly, often reaching ugly proportions before authorities—or even some of the participants—clearly understood the issues at stake. At the University of Wisconsin an organization of Negro students, the Black People's Alliance, called a strike. Conservative students of the Young Americans for Freedom decided to cross the blacks' picket lines. Blows were exchanged, and in swift succession the governor called out 1,900 National Guardsmen, bayonets and tear gas were used on the Negroes, over five thousand whites marched on the state capitol to protest this use of force, faculty groups supported the black demands, and the Wisconsin legislature, lashing back, cut the university budget.

Puerto Rican students joined blacks at the City College of New York—CCNY, "the poor man's Harvard"—in locking themselves inside the South Campus and issuing a manifesto demanding that the college's enrollment reflect New York's racial balance, that a black studies program be introduced, and that they control it. Confronted by this threat to academic standards and consequently to the value of their diplomas, the white students mobilized. In the subsequent struggle an auditorium was burned. President Buell Gallagher closed the school twice and then resigned. The faculty senate then approved an almost unbelievable proposal under which 40 percent of the next freshman class would be blacks and Puerto Ricans who would not have to meet the academic requirements of CCNY, which as a consequence could no longer be called the poor man's Harvard.

Harvard itself blew on April 9, when undergraduates invaded University Hall, evicted the deans, and began rifling confidential files. President Nathan Pusey responded by calling on the state police, four hundred of whom fought their way into the building and arrested 197 students. Their classmates—six thousand of them—met in Harvard Stadium and voted to strike in protest. A faculty resolution asked that charges against the 197 be dropped. Pusey agreed, but the judge didn't; he fined them twenty dollars each for criminal trespass and sentenced a twenty-five-year-old graduate student to a year in prison for striking a dean. The university then formally endorsed a faculty resolution calling for agreement to the chief demand of the original group of demonstrators—an end to ROTC at Harvard.

Cornell was no more strife-torn than a dozen other campuses that spring, but a local aspect at Ithaca produced a sequence of photographs which shocked the world. Demanding an autonomous Afro-American college, two hundred and fifty Negro undergraduates took over Willard Straight Hall, the student union, on April 19. When rumors spread inside Willard Straight that a band of whites with guns was on its way, the Negroes acquired weapons themselves. That, said President James A. Perkins, made it "a whole new thing." He capitulated to every black demand, and the Negroes who had seized the building walked out—armed to the teeth, the newspaper pictures showed, with rifles in their hands and bandoliers of ammunition crisscrossed on their chests. The faculty rejected the president's settlement and then reversed itself. The university trustees announced an investigation and Perkins quit.

All this was being watched closely in Washington, where, as might be expected, the Nixon administration's sympathy was with everybody except the rebellious students. HEW Secretary Finch wrote to the head of every institution of higher learning in the country, pointing out that more than a million students were receiving aid which could be terminated if they abused their privileges. Nixon himself spoke out after Reverend Theodore M. Hesburgh, president of Notre Dame, warned his undergraduates that any who resorted to force would be expelled and charged with trespassing. In a "Dear Ted" letter, Nixon wrote Hesburgh, "I want to applaud the forthright stand you have taken," and asked him to forward his opinions on student unrest to Vice President Agnew, who was about to confer with the state governors. Hesburgh advised caution; "even the most far-out students," he observed, "are trying to tell society something that may be worth searching for today." His point was not lost on the governors, who rejected a proposal from Ronald Reagan for a federal inquiry into the student riots.

If Negro activists were busy on the campuses, they were lying low in most inner cities. For the second straight summer the ghettos were relatively quiet. The mood in the ghettos was changing. The turmoil of the mid-1960s had opened new lines of communication with the city halls, and big cities could now field well-trained, well-equipped riot police. The new emphasis among blacks was on political action. With the upsurge in Negro registrations, the election of Negro candidates had become a realistic alternative in many areas to open revolt against society. Howard Lee became the first black mayor of Chapel Hill, North Carolina, in 1969, and Charles Evers won the mayoralty of Fayette, Mississippi, with the slogan: "Don't vote for a black man. Don't vote for a white man. Vote for a good man."

Nixon called the role of the new administration in race relations a "middle course." By any term it was a slowdown in desegregation. The Johnson policy had been to end federal subsidies to schools which failed to integrate. Nixon rejected it, saying, "I do not consider it a victory for integration when the federal government cuts off funds for a school and thereby, for both black and white students in that school, denies them the education they should have." In one of his first press conferences in the White House he conceded that Negroes distrusted him, believing him, despite his earlier record, to be indifferent now to their cause. In his campaign he had made much of promises of help for "black capitalism." Nothing more was heard about it. Instead, in August 1969 Finch proposed a delay in Mississippi school integration.

This was widely regarded as a stratagem to court the South's white voters. It was thwarted late in October when the Supreme Court, in its first major decision since Warren Burger's appointment as Chief Justice, unanimously ruled that "the obligation of every school district is to terminate dual school systems at once and to operate now and hereafter only unitary schools." Nixon responded that he would make every effort to enforce the decree with "full respect for the law."

Although student riots were the work of a minority, American youths in much larger numbers were continuing to assert their separate identity by dressing, speaking, and behaving in ways alien to adult society. Their extraordinarily high visibility was in large part a result of their life-style, which was, and was meant to be, conspicuous and even outrageous. But there were also more of them to be seen. This was the inevitable sequel to the postwar baby boom. In 1960 there had been 27 million Americans between the ages of fourteen and twenty-four. Now there were 40 million of them, accounting for a full 20 percent of the population. Their numbers and their affluence guaranteed that youth's counterculture would grow in magnitude, and that if a sizable proportion of them flocked to any one event, its popularity would be tremendous. Such an event occurred on the weekend of August 15–17, 1969. It was a rock music festival, and it was called Woodstock.

Actually that was a misnomer. Originally the two twenty-four-year-olds who conceived and promoted the festival planned to stage it in the Hudson River village of Woodstock, New York, and it was so advertised. Zoning regulations and local opposition thwarted them there, however, and the event was moved to the six-hundred-acre dairy farm of one Max Yasgur in the Catskill town of Bethel, on White Lake, about seventy miles northwest of New York City. The promoters hoped the kids could find it. They were expecting to draw about 50,000 customers at seven dollars a ticket.

They grossly underestimated the festival's appeal. Max Yasgur's farm was stormed by a multitude of 400,000. Bethel briefly became the third largest city in the state. The surrounding road net was cluttered with abandoned cars, motorcycles, and microbuses decorated with psychedelic drawings. All adjacent exits from the Catskill highway were jammed. Collecting fees from so enormous a throng was impractical, and the promoters had to give up the idea, thereby losing two million dollars. That was one of two things which went wrong at Woodstock. The other was the weather. Two tremendous cloudbursts turned the farm into a swamp. The youths huddled in soggy sleeping bags and under plastic tents and lean-tos fashioned from blankets and pieces of clothing. The lack of normal supplies of food and water, or even of sanitation facilities, should have made Woodstock a disaster.

Instead it was a triumph. Looking out nervously over the huge crowd, one of the first performers said, "If we're going to make it, you had better remember that the guy next to you is your brother." They remembered. A police officer called the audience "the most courteous, considerate, and well-behaved group of kids that I have ever been in contact with in my twenty-four years of police work."

The most helpful hands came from their own ranks. A caravan of Ken Kesey's Merry Pranksters, who had driven all the way from Oregon, doled out a high-protein broth of raisins, oatmeal, and peanuts and set up a hospital tent; a hundred members of the Hog Farm, a Taos, New Mexico, commune, also provided essential services. What really made the event a success, however, was the magnet which had lured so many here: acid rock. The Jefferson Airplane, the Creedence Clearwater Revival, the Family Stone, Jimi Hendrix, Joan Baez, Janis Joplin—these were their folk heroes. They were here in person, and if they could not be seen, they could at least be heard from loudspeakers set atop eighty-foot scaffolds around the stage. And so, despite the rain and constant provocation, the youths in headbands, bell-bottoms, beads, and tie-dyed dungaree shirts made the festival so strong a symbol of generational unity that their future spokesmen would speak of them as the Woodstock Nation.

In an era of rapid change the strengthening of peer group bonds was inevitable. Woodstock was the most spectacular rock festival of 1969, but it was by no means unique. Others that year were held on a ranch near Tentino, Washington, after the state supreme court had overruled objections from the John Birch Society; at Lewisville, Texas ("This crowd is a lot better than Dallas football crowds," a security officer said, while the Lewisville mayor told reporters that the only problem was created by older Texans who came to stare at naked young swimmers in the Garza-Little Elm Reservoir); and at Prairieville, Louisiana, where the attractions included the Grateful Dead, Canned Heat, Country Joe and the Fish, and the Iron Butterfly.

The festival phenomenon was not confined to the United States. It being an American phenomenon, and this being the age of American dominance, the sounds of rock were echoing in western Europe, and particularly in England. HELP BOB DYLAN SINK THE ISLE

OF WIGHT, read banners over that English Channel island. Answering the appeal were 150,000 "oddly dressed people," as a local policeman put it, "of uncertain sex." Dylan himself arrived thirty-six hours after the music began; he wore a white suit, yellow shirt, and green boots. A young female admirer ripped off her clothes, danced nude, and screamed, "I just want to be free." Unlike Woodstock, the Isle of Wight concert wound up heavily in the black.

There was something anomalous here. Fortunes were being made by promoters and entertainers, yet the counterculture which supported them was aggressively antimaterialistic. Unlike swing music, rock was accompanied by an ideological strain. That was one reason many older Americans found it so objectionable. To them, the life-style and the social creed that went with it were unpatriotic, ungodly, immoral, and, if possible, worse. It was possible; their most hideous fears were realized when the ugliest murder of 1969 was committed by a band of hippies run amok. Those offended by the now generation saw it as a vindication of their direst predictions, and the failure of long-haired youth to accept responsibility for it merely deepened their rage.

The victims were actress Sharon Tate, honey blonde and pregnant, and four acquaintances. Their bodies, hideously mutilated and arranged in grotesque positions, were found one August morning in a Los Angeles mansion at 10050 Cielo Drive, overlooking Benedict Canyon. Four months later the killers—who had committed two other murders in the meantime—were found to be members of a commune on the fringe of Death Valley. Their leader was Charles Manson, a thirty-five-year-old ex-convict and, by all accounts, a sexual athlete. The slayers were his protégés: a demented Texas youth and three pretty girls who had been eager to do anything—literally anything—Manson required of them. Their days had been occupied with riding around in dune buggies fashioned from stolen Volkswagens and mounted with machine guns. (Manson had visions of war between the races.) At night they had explored unusual sexual activities—unless, of course, they had been busy stabbing strangers to death.

If Manson and his friends represented the dark side of hippy romanticism, the bright side was youth's social conscience. The best of young America was profoundly disturbed by man's abuse of his fellow man and his surroundings. The ecological issue was the least controversial; the need was obvious—pollution had become unconscionable. Gallup found that 70 percent of Americans put the environmental issue first among the country's domestic problems. Not only the younger generation but organizations on every level of society were awakening to the threat. The United Nations announced plans for a Conference on Human Environment. The President established an Environmental Quality Council. Governors and mayors appointed ecological committees. In Louisville, where a factory with ancient equipment was pouring eleven tons of dirt into the city's air each day, citizens wearing gas masks marched on City Hall bearing a protest petition with 13,000 signatures; the plant then installed new furnaces which cut the daily yield of soot to one hundred pounds.

That helped Louisville, but in the national view it hardly counted. There the dimensions of the problem were overwhelming. Combustion in the U.S. was disgorging 140 million tons of grime into the air every year. The automobiles in Los Angeles alone emitted each day 10,000 tons of carbon monoxide, 2,000 tons of hydrocarbons, and 530 tons of nitrogen oxides. Other pollutants rising into the great sewer in the sky over America were oxides of sulphur, sulphuric acid mists, fly ash, soot, and particles of arsenic, beryllium, cadmium, lead, chromium, and manganese. Annually they accounted for eleven billion dollars in property damage alone. Smog disintegrated nylon stockings, stripped paint from houses, turned other buildings a rusty orange, coated sidewalks with green slime, caused rubber to become brittle and crack, discolored clothing, etched windowpanes, attacked the enamel on teeth, induced pulmonary disease, and otherwise eroded, tarnished, soiled, corroded, and abraded man and his works.

All this had been going on for some time, but it was in 1969 that a combination of events forced the ecological issue into the forefront of the national consciousness. Nuclear power plants on the Hudson and Connecticut rivers on the East Coast, and the Columbia River in the West, were found to be killing fish by the ton with thermal pollution. DDT was also taking its toll of seafood and threatening the bald eagle, emblem of the nation, with extinction. Pedestrians in Manhattan were reported to be breathing air whose level of carbon monoxide was twice the danger level as determined by the federal government. And Everglades National Park in Florida and Sequoia National Park in California were threatened by plans for, respectively, a huge airport and an access road to a ski resort.

Construction of the airport was halted by nineteen groups of aroused conservationists who went to court. The Sierra Club also secured a court order stopping the building of the road by Walt Disney Productions, but the order was only temporary, and in other ways 1969 was a poor environmental year for the Golden State. Nature was partly to blame; three storms, dumping 52 inches of rain, hit the slopes of the San Gabriel Mountains in swift succession. Bridges were washed out and hundreds of homes literally slid down the hills—291 houses in Carpenteria alone, with a population of just 7,200. Life was also edgy along the San Andreas fault, which cuts across one corner of San Francisco and runs twenty miles east of Los Angeles. Tension had been building along the fault since the calamity of 1906; another earthquake was overdue. Californians faced the possibility good-humoredly. Bumper stickers declared, "California Deserves a Fair Shake," and a local best seller in 1969 was *The Last Days of the Late, Great State of California,* a fictional account of a quake. In reality only one tremor of any substance was recorded, on April 28, and its center was in uninhabited desert country.

That, however, was not the full story of the state's experience with geological faults that year. The stresses along another of them, combined with man's folly, provided the nation's ecological horror story of 1969. Late in January an oil drill which had been boring into a high-pressure pool of petroleum and gas 3,486 feet beneath the bottom of the Pacific Ocean was withdrawn for the replacement of a worn bit. Suddenly the well erupted, sending up oil bubbles 200 feet in diameter around the drillers' platform. Meanwhile pressure from the runaway well was being relayed along unmapped fissures in the sand and shale of the sea floor. This was catastrophic; drillers capped the original hole in eleven days, but oil continued to boil forth over a wide area.

Six miles east of the platform lay the immaculate beaches of Santa Barbara, where shore-front property had been selling at as much as $2,000 a foot. In the first week of February the white sands cherished by Santa Barbarans—forty miles of superb waterfront—began turning black. Hundreds of thousands of gallons of gummy crude oil coated yachts and fishing craft with a thick scum which could only be removed by live steam. A *Sports Illustrated* writer reported that petroleum "lay so thick on the water that waves were unformed; they made a squishing sound. . . . The smell of oil followed me up the canyon to our house, a mile from the sea. . . . The tideline was a broad black band that looked from the air like something made on a map by a black crayon."

The most shocking aspect of the disaster was the destruction of marine life. Mussels and rock lobsters died instantly. Porpoises and sea lions disappeared. Pelicans dove straight into the oil and then sank, unable to raise their matted wings, and the beaches were studded with dead sandpipers, cormorants, gulls, grebes, and loons, their eyes horribly swollen and their viscera burned by petroleum. "A very sad-looking mess," said the Audubon Society; another spectator called it "a sickening sight." Residents held protest meetings, picketed government offices with placards demanding BAN THE BLOB, and joined a new ecological group called Get Oil Out (GOO). Damage suits totaling a billion dollars were filed; the cost of the cleanup was put at three million.

More than twelve thousand wires and letters went to Washington. At first the government seemed responsive. The Department of the Interior announced that in the future drills would have to be sheathed in pipe below the depth of 239 feet, which had been the previous requirement. Most important, drilling leases in the Santa Barbara Channel were suspended. Then the petroleum industry began applying pressure. Large sums of money were at stake; the leases, granting the right to drill in nearly one thousand square miles of the Pacific, had been signed a year earlier with a dozen firms which were paying 603 million dollars for the privilege. They wanted the privilege back, and in September the Nixon administration gave it to them—in spite of dire warnings from geologists as to other fissures, and in spite of continuing leaks from the original runaway well.

Youthful participants were conspicuous in all the environmental crusades, carrying petitions in Florida, marching on Louisville City Hall in large numbers, and setting up "laundries" to clean and save the California birds. How deep their convictions ran—to what degree they were merely caught up by the excitement of protest—was, however, another question. In some ways they seemed to be flagrantly inconsistent. Although vehemently opposed to pollution of the environment, for example, they enthusiastically supported by their patronage another form of pollution: the junk food industry.

Fast-food stands, peddling empty calories and little nourishment, had been a feature of the American roadside since the 1920s, but not until the 1960s did they impose a sameness on the landscape outside virtually all American cities by becoming the dominant force in the franchising business. Franchising itself—leasing the rights to a commercial name—was a sign of the times; among its creations were the Holiday Inns, Midas Muffler Shops, Citgo stations, and Howard Johnson's motels. These were conventional and sedate, however, when compared to the quick grill and ice cream shops. The going prices of top franchises in 1969 were $96,000 for a McDonald's ("Over 5 Billion Served") hamburger stand, $37,000 for an A & W stand, $24,500 for a Colonel Sanders ("Finger-Lickin' Good") Kentucky Fried Chicken stand, and from $7,500 to $30,000, depending on the location, for a Dairy Queen ice cream stand. Other emporia of the fatty snack, all of them drawing teen-agers by the millions, were doing business under the signs of Dunkin' Donuts, Bonanza, Hardee's, Burger King, Minnie Pearl's Chicken, Baskin-Robbins, Roy Rogers Roast Beef, and the International House of Pancakes.

If the young approved of these, they might have been expected to sanction another big financial phenomenon of the time, the conglomerates, of which the best known was ITT—the International Telephone and Telegraph Company—under whose banner hotels, car rental agencies, life insurance firms, bakeries, and manufacturers of communications equipment did business. But conglomerate was a dirty word among committed youths; it was associated with government contracts and therefore with the Vietnam War, which was an even greater enemy than pollution. Here passions ran highest, both for antiwar demonstrators and their critics, and here the rising generation was taking the stand for which it would be best remembered.

The word for protest that year was moratorium. The first M-day was scheduled for May 15. Richard Nixon said in advance, "Under no circumstances will I be affected whatever by it," thereby guaranteeing large turnouts to ring church bells, wear black armbands, carry signs and candles, and, above all, to march in thousands of American communities as proof of solidarity against the involvement in Indochina. That Wednesday there were 90,000 protesters on Boston Common, 20,000 in New York, and 22,000 in Washington. Some college campuses reported that half their students were gone. At Whittier College, whose most famous alumnus was in the White House, the wife of the acting president lit a flame which was to burn until the war was over.

November 15 fell on a weekend, and the New Mobe, as it was called, lasted for three days. This time the focus was Washington. Police put the crowd at 250,000; the New Mobe committee said 800,000 participated; there was really no way of reaching an accurate estimate, but certainly nothing like it had ever happened in America before. While the White House was announcing that President Nixon would stay inside, watching a football game on television, the first of 40,000 marchers passed by outside, each bearing a card with the name of an American who had died in Vietnam or the name of a Vietnamese community destroyed by the war. The marchers walked four miles, from Arlington to the Capitol, where the names were placed in huge, flag-draped coffins.

It was orderly. The Army had 9,000 troops in reserve to control unruly demonstrators, but they were not used, and praisers of the crowd's restraint included presidential aide Herbert G. Klein and Republican senators Hugh Scott and John Sherman Cooper. A minority view was expressed by Attorney General John N. Mitchell. Two minor episodes of violence had marred the weekend: an SDS band had attacked the South Vietnamese embassy, and a mob of Yippies had tried to rush the Justice Department building. Both had been turned back by tear gas. Taking note of them, Mitchell said that while "the great majority of participants" in the New Mobe had "obeyed the law," the march had been accompanied "by such extensive physical injury, property damage, and street confrontations that I do not believe that—overall—the gatherings here can be characterized as peaceful."

Spiro Agnew agreed. Washington was not surprised. By now it was clear that whatever other members of the administration might say, the attorney general and the Vice President would be pitiless with Americans who broke the law.

My Lai, which was to become the American Lidice, was a Vietnamese hamlet, too small to be known outside Quang Ngai province on the South China Sea until the hot, humid morning of Saturday, March 16, 1968, when it became an open grave for some 567 old men, women, and children. Even then the name was unfamiliar to most of its attackers, all members of Lieutenant William L. Calley

Jr.'s Americal Division platoon. They called it Pinkville because the area was colored pink on the military maps issued the night before at the platoon leader's briefing.

Calley and his men were members of Task Force Barker, named for Lieutenant Colonel Frank A. Barker Jr., who would die in a helicopter crash three months later, leaving his role in the events of March 16 forever obscure. The question of provocation was also nebulous; it was to be raised at Calley's court-martial. Charlie Company of the division's 11th Infantry Brigade, to which his unit belonged, had been in Vietnam three and a half months. During that time the company had lost almost half of its 190 men to booby traps and sniper fire. At the briefing the lieutenant was told that My Lai was held by the 48th Battalion of the Viet Cong. Captain Ernest Medina, the company commander, later said that he did not know any women and children were there. He told Lieutenant Calley to clean the village out, and Calley passed the word among his men. At daybreak they were helicoptered in, their M-16 automatic rifles loaded and ready.

On landing they found no Viet Cong. Instead there were only defenseless civilians, who, according to Private Paul David Meadlo, were herded by the American soldiers into the center of the hamlet "like a little island." There, where two trails crossed, the lieutenant ordered his men to shoot the inhabitants. Meadlo was one who obeyed—"I poured about four clips"—68 shots—"into them," he said afterward; "I might have killed ten or fifteen of them." Calley stood beside him, pumping automatic fire into the captives at point-blank range. Next the soldiers shoved seven or eight Vietnamese into one of the huts, or "hootches" as the grunts called them, and tossed a hand grenade in after them.

The third phase occurred in an L-shaped drainage ditch, which was to become infamous during the Fort Benning, Georgia, court-martial. There the mass murder took on aspects of an assembly line operation. "There was a variety of people there—men, women, and children," a rifleman testified at Fort Benning. ". . . There was being brought up small groups of people and they were being placed in the ditch and Lieutenant Calley was firing into it." Another witness told how the platoon leader had dealt with a Buddhist priest and a baby. The priest, who was wearing the flowing white robe of his office, held out supplicating hands as though in prayer. He kept repeating, "No Viet, no Viet." Calley, according to the testimony, smashed in the man's mouth with the butt of his M-16, reversed the rifle, "and pulled the trigger in the priest's face. Half his head was blown off." As for the infant, "Lieutenant Calley grabbed it by the arm and threw it into the ditch and fired."

Meanwhile, according to a Houston soldier named Herbert Carter, "We went through the village. We didn't see any VC. People began coming out of their hootches and the guys shot them down and then burned the hootches or burned the hootches and shot the people when they came out. Sometimes they would round up a bunch and shoot them together. It went on like this all day."

Sergeant Michael Bernhardt, whose comrades said he refused to participate, called it "point-blank murder." He said, "Only a few of us refused. I told them the hell with this, I'm not doing it. I didn't think this was a lawful order." Most of the firing had died away before Private Richard Pendleton reached My Lai, "but," he later said, "some guys were still shooting people. . . . There were big groups of bodies lying on the ground, in gullies and in the paddies." Only one American was a casualty—a soldier who had shot himself in the foot rather than take part in the killings.

Among the witnesses were two soldiers whose recollections would later carry special weight. Ronald Haeberle, an Army photographer, recorded the My Lai carnage on film with three cameras. One was official; he turned that in. The other two were his personal property, and he kept them. The second soldier was Warrant Officer Hugh C. Thompson Jr., a helicopter pilot. Thompson saw the L-shaped gully from the air and alerted his commanding officer. "I thought something was wrong out there," he said later, "because I couldn't foresee any way of how the bodies got in the ditch." Thompson returned to the village and rescued sixteen children there. The Army awarded him the Distinguished Flying Cross for "disregarding his own safety."

That was the only sign of official awareness that anything unusual had happened at My Lai. Twelve days later Colonel Barker filed a combat action report describing the attack as "well-planned, well-executed, and successful." In the words of a subsequent congressional report, "it can be reasonably concluded that the My Lai matter was 'covered up' within the Americal Division." Long afterward, when the cover-up had failed, the divisional commander, Major General Samuel Koster—who had gone on to become superintendent of West Point—was reduced in rank, and both he and the assistant divisional commander were censured and deprived of their Distinguished Service Medals. This could hardly have been foreseen then or for some time afterward, however. The first man to do something about My Lai hadn't been there that morning and didn't even hear about it until a month later. He was Ronald Ridenhour, who had been with Charlie Company earlier, in Hawaii; he learned about the massacre from his former comrades. A year later, as a returned veteran, Ridenhour wrote out an account of what had apparently happened and mailed twenty-three copies of it to President Nixon, key congressmen, and officials in the Pentagon and the State Department. He charged that "something rather dark and bloody did indeed occur sometime in March 1968 in a village called 'Pinkville' in the Republic of Vietnam."

That was on March 29, 1969. Within four weeks the Army opened a full-scale inquiry into the slaughter. Evidence was turned over to the provost marshal general on August 4; that same month the Pentagon received copies of photographer Haeberle's slides. On September 5, the day before Calley was scheduled to be discharged, he was accused of killing 109 Vietnamese civilians. Others were charged, including Medina, but only Calley was later found guilty, after a four-month trial which sent a shudder through the nation. Asked about the incident at a news conference when the story first broke, President Nixon said that it "was certainly a massacre," and that "under no circumstances was it justified." He continued: "One of the goals we are fighting for in Vietnam is to keep the people . . . from having imposed upon them a government which has atrocity against civilians as one of its policies."

When Calley was convicted in 1971 of murdering twenty-two Vietnamese and sentenced to life, however, an astonishing change swept the country, and the President's political antennae were quick to pick it up. A majority of Americans seemed to believe that the verdict was undeserved, either because the lieutenant was innocent or because he was being made a scapegoat. The mood, one observer said sardonically, was, "It didn't happen, and besides, they deserved it." Viking Press announced that it had paid $100,000 for Calley's memoirs, and in the first three days after his conviction a record on the Plantation label, "The Battle Hymn of Lieutenant Calley," sold 202,000 copies. After a saccharine voice-over about "a little boy who wanted to grow up and be a soldier and serve his country in whatever way he could," the song began:

My name is William Calley, I'm a soldier of this land,
I've vowed to do my duty and to gain the upper hand,
But they've made me out a villain, they have stamped me with a brand,
As we go marching on.

The White House reported that mail was running a hundred to one against the verdict and sentence. President Nixon ordered Calley released from the Benning stockade and moved to house arrest in his post apartment. Two days later the White House announced that "Yesterday the President made the decision that before any final sentence is carried out in the case of Lieutenant Calley the President will personally review the case and finally decide it." Later Nixon changed his mind, but at the time he seemed to be playing politics with a war crime. Indignant, the lieutenant's prosecutor, Captain Aubrey M. Daniel III, wrote the President that he was "shocked and dismayed at your decision to intervene in these proceedings in the midst of the public clamor."

Five weeks later Secretary of the Navy John H. Chafee announced civilian intervention in the case of another embattled officer—Commander Lloyd M. Bucher of the *Pueblo*, back in the United States with his crew after the North Koreans had released them in exchange for an official American confession of espionage, an apology, and a promise that it would not happen again. Even as he handed it over at Panmunjom, Major General Gilbert H. Woodward said that the admission was false, that he had signed it "to free the crew, and only to free the crew." Still, the statement rankled in the Pentagon, and the Navy recommended a court-martial for Bucher. Chafee vetoed it. The commander and his men, he said, "have suffered enough."

The locust years continued for the military, despite the change in Presidents. Campaigning in 1968, Richard Nixon had said of Bucher's lost ship, "Unless the United States reacts to these slights, you are bound to encourage bigger slights and you are going to have more *Pueblos*. In a new administration I say we've got to stop that kind of action . . . before it gets started." Less than three months after he entered the White House he was confronted by a similar humiliation, and he was as helpless in responding to it as Lyndon Johnson had been. This time the vehicle of mortification was an airborne *Pueblo*, a converted Lockheed Super Constellation which the Navy called an EC121. Unarmed, the EC121 carried thirty-one crewmen and six tons of electronic gear designed to monitor the communications of a potential enemy. On April 15 the North Koreans shot it down, killing all hands. This time there could be no question about the location of the incident. Russian vessels agreed that it had occurred in international waters, between 100 and 120 miles off the coast.

Nixon's first impulse had been to retaliate, but the more he pondered his options, the fewer he had. Short of risking nuclear war, there was little he could do. In the end he could only say, "I have today ordered that these flights be continued. They will be protected. This is not a threat. It is simply a statement of fact."

It was also a statement of frustration, heightened by the year's events in Vietnam. In Paris American negotiators were telling the North Vietnamese that the United States had ruled out hopes for a military solution in Indochina; in Saigon President Thieu was being told that unilateral American withdrawal, or the acceptance of terms amounting to a disguised U.S. defeat, was also unacceptable. What lay between was impotence.

Human kamikazes—Viet Cong with dynamite lashed to their bodies to blow up barbed wire—led attackers on Fire Base Russell, a Marine position just south of the demilitarized zone, and savage fighting erupted around the big U.S. base at Bien Hoa, fifteen miles from Saigon. The most controversial action of the year was the American assault on Apbia Mountain, christened Hamburger Hill by the grunts. Continuing its strategy of the Johnson years, the Army was subjecting the Viet Cong to what the Pentagon called "maximum pressure." Hamburger Hill began as a typical search-and-destroy mission. Nine battalions were set down by helicopters in the A Shau Valley, a corridor for infiltration from Laos. During the subsequent sweep, the 3rd Battalion of the 187th Regiment, 101st Airborne Division, ran into what the divisional commander, Major General Melvin Zais, called "a hornets' nest" of opposition. Pulling back, the battalion dug in and sent a company up to storm the hill.

The attack failed. Two companies then assaulted the crest. They too were thrown back. The next day the whole battalion charged the defenders and was repulsed. Three more battalions were called in. Meanwhile U.S. artillery and aircraft were battering the top of the hill; 2,000 shells and 155 air sorties defoliated the summit. Still the Viet Cong clung to it, sending the American attackers reeling backward each time in a tempest of rifle fire and exploding grenades. Ten successive U.S. charges were routed. On the eighth day 1,000 grunts and 400 South Vietnamese took the hill. General Zais called it "a great victory by a gutty bunch of guys." One week later an Army spokesman announced that Hamburger Hill was being abandoned. He said, "We feel we've gotten everything out of this mountain that we're going to get."

Senators reading the casualty lists—46 Americans had been killed on the slopes of Apbia, and 308 wounded—reacted angrily. Edward M. Kennedy called such assaults "senseless and irresponsible." He asked, "How can we justify sending our boys up against a hill a dozen times or more, until soldiers themselves question the madness of the action?" Some Republicans were also aroused. Aiken of Vermont, the ranking minority member of the Senate Foreign Relations Committee, proposed that the White House "immediately" start "an orderly withdrawal," to turn the war over to "its rightful owners"—the Vietnamese. Scott of Pennsylvania, the GOP whip, urged the withdrawal of "a substantial number" of U.S. soldiers.

Nixon was listening. During his first term he was sensitive to the mood on Capitol Hill. In speeches he remained the irreconcilable cold-warrior, earnestly asserting his belief in a Free Asia, the domino theory, and the rest of it, but his actions were something else. "Vietnam might or might not make us," one of his aides acknowledged, "but there is no question it could break us." The Johnsonian strategy was clearly bankrupt. By March 1969 the number of dead Americans had exceeded the 33,639 killed in Korea. The cost of the war, which continued to top 25 billion dollars a year, continued to generate irresistible inflationary pressure; a 1958 dollar was now worth about seventy-five cents, and economist Milton Friedman was predicting what sounded like a politician's nightmare: an "inflationary recession."

It was now clear that Nixon's most influential foreign policy adviser was not Rogers but Kissinger. Writing in *Foreign Affairs* as a private citizen, Kissinger had proposed two parallel lines of negotiation. Washington and Hanoi, he suggested, might schedule mutual troop withdrawals while the Viet Cong and the South Vietnamese forged a political solution. Now Secretary of Defense Melvin Laird returned from a visit to Saigon with another component of the new President's war policy. Laird believed that the combat efficiency of Thieu's troops could be improved to the point where they might be left on their own. The White House seized on this as a way to implement Vietnamization. Breaking the news to Thieu on Midway, Nixon announced the first cut, of 25,000 men, on June 8.

That same month Clark Clifford proposed in *Foreign Affairs* that the administration "reduce the level of combat" by scheduling the pullout of 100,000 U.S. troops by the end of 1969 and the elimination of "all ground combat forces" by the end of 1970. Clifford wrote: "Nothing we might do could be so beneficial or could so add to the political maturity of South Vietnam as to begin to withdraw our combat troops. Moreover, in my opinion, we cannot realistically expect to achieve anything more through our military force, and the time has come to begin to disengage." Annoyed, Nixon told a national television audience, "I would hope that we could beat Mr. Clifford's timetable, just as I think we've done a little better than he did when he was in charge of our national defense." Aides hastily explained that this was not a commitment, but in September the President announced that he expected to bring home all fighting men "before the end of 1970 or the middle of 1971." A *Life* writer observed at the end of the year, "Politically there did not seem to be much choice. Nixon had to get the U.S. out of Vietnam or face almost certain defeat in the presidential election of 1972."

In Vietnam General Creighton Abrams introduced tactics meant to lower U.S. casualties. Instead of large-scale search-and-destroy missions, tactics on a typical day entailed sending out as many as a thousand patrols of from one hundred to two hundred men each; their orders were to destroy enemy troops and supplies if possible, but to avoid bloodlettings. "Maximum pressure" had been replaced by "protective reaction"; an offensive stance had become defensive. This sounded more impressive in Washington than it really was, however. Two great armies remained in the field, each capable of maiming the other and each led by aggressive commanders. Only forty-six skirmishes were announced in the seven days ending Saturday, July 5, a typical week, but 155 U.S. soldiers were killed. And Abrams's conservative posture did not eliminate the possibility of a big battle, which could flare up at any time.

It happened in late August amid the rolling hills southwest of Da Nang, an area known as the Rice Bowl. A U.S. helicopter crashed there, killing the eight men aboard, and two companies of the 196th Light Infantry Brigade were ordered to recover their bodies. Simultaneously, a thousand North Vietnamese were forming up there to assault the district capital of Hiep Duc. The two forces stumbled into one another and the Communist troops withdrew into a labyrinth of bunkers and trench lines. When the Americans went after them, it was Hamburger Hill all over again. Reinforcements were sucked in until about three thousand Americans and South Vietnamese were pitted against the North Vietnamese Second Division. Both sides battled for possession of a hummock called Hill 102. The struggle ended when grunts of the 196th reached the top—and found it deserted. "It's the old story," a U.S. officer said. "Five days of fighting like hell and on the sixth day they give it to you for nothing." But there was a new story from the Rice Bowl, too, and it was ominous. Company A of the 196th had refused to obey direct orders to descend into the labyrinth and bring back the dead from the wrecked helicopter. Eventually the men did move out, but the specter of mutiny remained, one more dissonant note in the Vietnamese din.

Speaking of crime at home, the President held his hand at neck level and told reporters that the people "have had it up to here." It was in fact a lawless time in the United States; the FBI reported an increase in felonies of 10.6 percent over the previous year. Larceny was up 19 percent, forcible rape 16.8 percent, robbery 12.5 percent, and one offense went right off the chart: skyjacking, the hijacking of airplanes. Between 1950 and 1967 the airlines had reported an average of 2.3 attempted skyjacks a year. In 1969 there were 71, of which 58 went to Cuba—three times as many as the year before. On NBC-TV's *Tonight Show* Johnny Carson said, "There are so many hijackings that one airline changed its slogan to 'Up, up, and olé.'"

The airlines did try a lot of things. Signs in terminals warned that skyjacking was punishable by death, that passengers could be imprisoned just for carrying weapons aboard, and that they could be searched. The public was invited to offer some suggestions. Some memorable ones came in: stewardesses could be trained to seduce skyjackers, passengers should be required to travel naked, trapdoors could be built where the skyjackers would stand, the crew should play the Cuban national anthem over the public address system and then arrest everyone who stood up. Only one innovation worked. Although no U.S. airline scheduled regular flights to Cuba, every pilot flying over the South carried approach maps for Havana's José Martí Airport. With dismal regularity they were billed, through the Swiss government, for Cuban landing fees and incidental expenses.

That year's skyjacking climax came in November, when Captain Donald Cook of TWA's Los Angeles to San Francisco Flight 85 switched on the intercom and said, "There's a man here who wants to go some place, and he's just chartered himself an airplane. Drinks are on the house." The man was a twenty-year-old Marine Corps veteran of Vietnam, Raffaele Minichiello, and he was holding a pistol at the flight engineer's head. Minichiello was cagey about his destination. Cook said later, "Right away I suspected we would be heading south to pick up a few cigars, but that wasn't the way it was." The skyjacker ordered him to fly east.

After refueling at Bangor and Shannon, Ireland, they wound up over Leonardo da Vinci Airport in Rome. It seemed that Minichiello, a native Italian, was homesick. He ordered the control tower to park them in a far corner of the field; then he said he wanted an unarmed policeman as a hostage. Rome's police chief volunteered. The skyjacker made the chief drive him into the country and then released him. Several hours later Minichiello was arrested in a church. "Why did I do it?" he said. "I don't know." His sister said, "I think the war damaged my brother's mind." The Italian public appeared to regard him as a hero—he had, after all, established a skyjacking record: 17 hours in the air and 6,900 miles—but their government took another view. He was sentenced to six years and five months in prison.

Although the somewhat fey Minichiello was a comet in the world of crime, he was not the year's most famous miscreant. That distinction went to a motorist charged merely with leaving the scene of an accident without identifying himself. The misdeed became notorious because the culprit was a U.S. senator bearing a famous name—Edward M. Kennedy—and because the accident had tragic consequences. Until the night of July 18–19, 1969, Ted Kennedy had been the front runner for the next Democratic presidential nomination and a probable winner over Nixon and his minority party. Ted's eulogy at his brother Bob's funeral had moved the nation, and in January he had displayed his family's winning ways by blitzing Russell B. Long of Louisiana, beating him in a party caucus and thereby replacing him as the Senate's Democratic whip. The young Kennedy seemed to be on his way to greatness. Then came Chappaquiddick.

Among the many responsibilities Ted had inherited from his brothers was one for lifting the morale of the family's loyal campaigners. A cookout on July 18 was meant to do that. The hosts were Ted and several friends; their guests were six girls who had worked as volunteer drudges in the "boiler room"—back room—of Robert Kennedy's abortive presidential candidacy the year before. The place was Chappaquiddick Island, which lay just 250 yards off another island, Martha's Vineyard, on Cape Cod's Nantucket Sound.

According to Kennedy's testimony at the inquest six months later, he left the party in his Chrysler at about 11:15 P.M. with one of the girls, Mary Jo Kopechne. Mary Jo was attractive, twenty-eight, and known to her friends as "M.J." The senator said afterward that they were on their way to the two-car ferry which would have carried them back to Martha's Vineyard, where they were registered at different hotels, but the judge at the inquest didn't believe him, and neither did a lot of other people. Mary Jo left her pocketbook at the cookout. She told no one there she was departing, and she didn't ask her roommate for the key to their hotel room. When she and Ted drove off, they left behind ten people (including the Chrysler's chauffeur) who didn't intend to spend the night at the cookout and who, with the departure of the big car, were left with only one small rented auto, obviously inadequate for their return. Finally, and most compellingly, there was the question of the turn Kennedy took.

The blacktop road from the cookout to the ferry was the only surfaced road on Chappaquiddick. Ted left it for a bumpy gravel roadway that led to the beach. He said afterward that this was a mistake. But the turn was a hairpin curving back to the right, and the entrance to it was masked by bushes; you almost had to be looking for it to make it. The senator must have known the difference, the judge insisted; he had been driven over both more than once that day.

The bumpy way Ted and Mary Jo took was called the Dike Road, and a half-mile down it was the Dike Bridge, a narrow, hump-backed wooden structure. This span curved off the dirt road in a 25-degree angle to the left, rising to cross a slim channel in the dike which permitted sea water from the sound, on the right, to flow in and out of Poucha Pond. The bridge was their undoing. Ted didn't make the 25-degree turn. Instead the Chrysler plunged off the right side of the span, rolling as it fell, and hit the bottom of the ten-foot-deep channel wrong side up. At the inquest Kennedy testified that he didn't know he had turned on the wrong road until "the moment I went off the bridge."

> . . . the next thing I recall is the movement of Mary Jo next to me, the struggling, perhaps hitting or kicking me, and I at this time opened my eyes and realized I was upside down, that water was crashing in on me, that it was pitch black. . . . I can remember the last sensation of being completely out of air and inhaling what must have been a half a lung full of water and assuming that I was going to drown and the full realization that no one was going to be looking for us that night until the next morning and that I wasn't going to get out of the car alive, and then somehow I can remember coming up to the last energy of just pushing, pressing, and coming up to the surface.

Carried to the shore by the current, he waded back and dove into the ten feet of water for Mary Jo. He made seven or eight attempts to rescue her, he testified, but toward the end he was so out of breath that he could only hold his head under the water for a few seconds. For fifteen or twenty minutes he lay on the bank, coughing up water. Then, he said, he returned to the cookout, "walking, trotting, jogging, stumbling, as fast as I possibly could." There he told his story to two men, Joseph F. Gargan, a cousin, and Paul F. Markham, a Kennedy campaigner. Gargan and Markham returned to the scene with him and dove for Mary Jo without success. Like him, both men were lawyers, and they told him that this must be reported. He was deeply disturbed, they recalled afterward. He kept saying, "I just can't believe this happened."

At his request they drove him to the ferry slip. The lights of Edgartown, on Martha's Vineyard, lay just across the way. He told them to go back to the cookout but not to tell the girls what had happened. Then, he said, he "suddenly jumped into the water and impulsively swam across." As he crossed the narrow channel "the water got colder, the tide began to draw me out for the second time that evening, I knew I was going to drown." But he made it, rested on the far shore, and walked to the Shiretown Inn, where he was staying.

At the inn his behavior became increasingly incomprehensible. As he himself said later, "My conduct and conversations during the next several hours, to the extent that I can remember them, make no sense to me at all. I regard as indefensible the fact that I did not report the accident to the police immediately." He testified that he "just couldn't gain the strength within me, the moral strength to call Mrs. Kopechne at two o'clock in the morning and tell her that her daughter was dead."

What he did was to change into dry clothes and then complain to the hotel's co-owner that a party in the next room was keeping him awake. In the morning he discussed the weekend's yachting regatta with two couples. Then Gargan and Markham arrived and were aghast to learn that he hadn't reported the crash. He explained at the inquest: "I told them about my own thoughts and feelings as I swam across that channel and how I always willed that Mary Jo still lived." He also said that he wanted to make a telephone call, but apparently the phones in Edgartown wouldn't do; he passed two of them, both outdoors and both public. Taking the ferry back to Chappaquiddick, with Gargan and Markham accompanying him, he used a phone in the ferry-house on the other side. The ferryman asked them if they had heard about the accident. One replied, "We just heard about it." Only then, nearly eleven hours after the wreck, did Ted try to contact the Edgartown police.

Meanwhile the Chrysler had been discovered. At 7 A.M. two young men had crossed the bridge to fish in the surf; returning, they had noticed that the falling tide had exposed the wheel of a car. They had stopped to tell Mrs. Pierre Malm, who lived fifty yards away, and at 8:20 she had phoned Police Chief Dominick J. Arena. Borrowing trunks, the strapping Arena had come, dived down, radioed the automobile license number back for identification, and asked Fireman John Farrar to bring his scuba equipment. It was Farrar who found Mary Jo inside.

Arena's headquarters radioed back that the car was registered to Senator Edward M. Kennedy, and when the chief returned to Edgartown he found the senator waiting for him. Ted said: "I was driving. What do you want me to do? It has to be right." One thing he should do, Arena said, was make a proper report. Ted went into a back room with Markham and wrote one out; it was sketchy; he identified the victim as "one Miss Mary ——, a former secretary of my brother Robert Kennedy," omitting the rest of her name because, he said, he didn't know how to spell it. (Markham didn't, either.) Markham asked the chief to keep the news from the press until Ted could phone Burke Marshall for legal advice. Arena agreed. He waited three hours. Having heard nothing further from Kennedy by then, he gave the newspaper the story and charged Kennedy with leaving the scene of the accident. Of the senator's strange trip that morning to use the Chappaquiddick phone the chief said, "If he had time to take the ferry over and back, he had time to see me."

The medical examiner reported "a positive diagnosis of accidental drowning." Satisfied that there had been no foul play, he released the girl's body without an autopsy, and it was flown to her birthplace in Pennsylvania for burial—a move that brought criticism of the authorities later. In Hyannisport Ted went into seclusion. Seven days later he emerged to plead guilty in Edgartown's century-old courthouse. Judge James A. Boyle gave him the minimum sentence of two months in prison, suspended it, and took away his driver's license. That evening Kennedy went on nationwide television to explain the inexplicable. The speech was not a success. He answered questions which hadn't been asked, maintaining that he had not been "driving under the influence of liquor" and that there was "no truth, no truth whatever," to insinuations of "immoral conduct" by him and Mary Jo. He also seemed to imply that the damage to his career was more momentous than her death when he said that among his preoccupations the night after the accident had been "whether some awful curse actually did hang over all the Kennedys." The talk reminded some people of Nixon's Checkers performance in 1952. Like Nixon, Ted asked his constituents to help him decide whether he should continue in public life. Massachusetts being passionately pro-Kennedy, the response was favorable, and a week later he returned to his senatorial duties.

After the inquest reporters asked him about the judge's opinion that there was "probable cause to believe that Edward M. Kennedy operated his motor vehicle negligently," that "such operation appears to have contributed to the death of Mary Jo Kopechne," and that he found Ted's insistence that he and Mary Jo had been headed for the ferry incredible. Kennedy said: "In my personal view, the inference and the ultimate findings of the judge's report are not justified, and I reject them. . . . At the inquest I truthfully answered all the questions asked of me."

He also said: "I expect to be a candidate for the U.S. Senate in 1972, and I expect to serve out a full six-year term." The White House, taking no chances, was preparing to discredit him with the episode if he changed his mind and ran for President. Within six hours after the recovery of Mary Jo's body, presidential aides had sent a retired New York policeman to Chappaquiddick; according to John Dean, the man "posed as a newspaper reporter and always asked the most embarrassing questions at any press gathering." It was unnecessary. Temporarily, at least, Ted's national following had been diminished. He was no longer a charismatic figure on Capitol Hill. The following year he touched bottom there when Senator Robert C. Byrd of West Virginia challenged his right to continue as party whip. Kennedy had beaten Long 31 to 26. Now he lost to Byrd 31 to 24. Then, in the aftermath of a meeting at the White House, he was subjected to a new humiliation for a Kennedy: commiseration from Richard Nixon.

Portrait of an American

BENJAMIN McLANE SPOCK, M.D.

THE ELDEST OF SIX CHILDREN, born to a mother who wouldn't have a nurse, who wanted to do it all herself, he grew to love the idea of playing parent, feeding the others, even changing their diapers. He came naturally to think of children as very important, and—this from both his parents—was imbued with a New England hair-shirt conscience. Find a stern moral issue, they told him, and fight for it against all odds. He didn't want that. He decided to rebel. For a long time he thought he was going to succeed.

Hamden Hall Country Day School. Andover. Yale. Scroll and Key, and a flash of conventional glory as an oarsman in the 1924 Olympics. Aspiring briefly to becoming an architect, he fell into his parents' puritan mold while spending a summer as a counselor in a camp run by the Newington Crippled Children's Home near Hartford. He watched the orthopedic surgeon working with the children who had polio. Later he said: "I realized how much he was helping them and I decided that I wanted to be a doctor."

Columbia. An internship at New York's Presbyterian Hospital. A residency in pediatrics. Another in psychiatry. Six years of psychoanalytic training. His love for children grew and deepened, and they adored him. "The man with the gentle face and eyes," he was called. In his office toys were everywhere. He built a device for the shy ones—a small flight of steps led through a trap door to the examining table. He wanted them to *want* to be examined, and they did. Years afterward he said: "One of my faults as a pediatrician has always been that I whoop it up too much with the children." But he never really tried to change.

The standard handbook for baby care was Dr. John B. Watson's *Psychological Care of Infant and Child,* published the year after Spock, then a second-year medical student, married Jane Cheney. Watson said: "Never, never kiss your child. Never hold it on your lap. Never rock its carriage."

Young Dr. Spock set himself against all that. While in the Navy during World War II he wrote his *Common Sense Book of Baby and Child Care.* Its opening words set the tone: "You know more than you think you do." Jane typed it from his longhand, and he indexed it himself, from abscess to Zwieback, because, he explained, he knew he would have "a better notion of what words mothers would look for in an index."

Over the next twenty-three years the book sold 22 million copies and was translated into thirty languages. He wrote a column for the *Ladies' Home Journal,* then for *Redbook;* his half-hour television program was seen Sunday afternoons over fifty-two stations of NBC-TV. And all the time Dr. Spock was rising in that most exacting of professions, the teaching of medicine. He taught psychiatry at Minnesota, child psychiatry and development at Pitt, child development in the psychiatry department at Western Reserve in Cleveland. His stand against Watson had made him the champion of indulgence. Troubled by the far swing of the pendulum, he rewrote passages of *Baby and Child Care* in 1956, explaining, "I find that some uncertain parents are interpreting me as an advocate of extreme permissiveness, so in the revisions I'm making in the book, I'm having to emphasize the limits of permissiveness."

Then a deeper challenge stirred Spock's conscience. Raised a conservative Republican, he had been converted to Democratic liberalism by Franklin Roosevelt, and in 1960 he supported John F. Kennedy. But in March 1962, Kennedy resumed nuclear testing. Alarmed, Spock joined the National Committee for a Sane Nuclear Policy (SANE). He campaigned vigorously for Johnson against Goldwater and felt betrayed when, in February 1965, Johnson escalated the Vietnam War. Spock wrote the White House, protesting, and when that proved futile he took to the streets in demonstrations.

"*Excruciatingly* embarrassing," he said of this afterward, "like one of those bad dreams where suddenly you are downtown without any clothes on." Certainly he was unusually conspicuous—six foot four, with a strong craggy face, always wearing a suit with a vest and a watch chain—a grandfatherly figure articulating, with his taut Yankee twang, moral standards which other, younger demonstrators thought hopelessly old-fashioned. But he grew more militant, not less. His critics, and they were many and scathing in these years, ridiculed his concern as a new expression of permissiveness, which they were now presenting as a national bogey. To him the issue was simple decency and justice.

The National Mobilization Committee to End the War in Vietnam. The National Conference for a New Politics. Delivering 992 turned-in draft cards to a coldly furious functionary at the Department of Justice. Submitting to arrest for civil disobedience by crossing a police line at the armed forces induction center on Whitehall Street in Manhattan. Sitting on his long-legged stool at his drafting table, using a ballpoint pen to write—slowly and painfully, as always—"A Call to Resist Illegitimate Authority."

Authority finally struck back to salvage the pride of General Hershey, whose orders to draft antiwar demonstrators had been overruled by the Justice Department. Five antiwar leaders, virtual strangers to one another, were charged with conspiracy to subvert the draft law. They were not accused of committing a crime, just of plotting one. In a word, their offense was dissent. The most outstanding leader, literally towering over the other four, was Benjamin M. Spock, M.D.

The trial was held in Boston's District Court in May and June of

1968. The judge was eighty-five-year-old Francis Ford—rude, vain, and flagrantly partial. The verdict was guilty—"guilty," a juror explained afterward to a reporter, "as charged by the judge." The defendants were sentenced to two years in prison, and two of them, Spock and Chaplain William Sloane Coffin of Yale were fined five thousand dollars each.

Spock said: "There is no shred of legality or constitutionality to this war; it violates the United Nations Charter, the Geneva Accords, and the United States' promise to obey the laws of international conduct. It is totally, abominably illegal. . . . I intend to go on working against the war."

And he did. The U.S. Court of Appeals for the First Circuit threw out the convictions, citing Judge Ford's prejudice. Spock went on, and on. They were still killing his children in the endless night of Vietnam, murdering the generation whose mothers he had counseled, and the sense of duty instilled in his own childhood gave him no rest. Sometimes it almost seemed to him that he could hear the dying crying out across half the world for mercy. Dr. Watson would have turned a deaf ear. ("Never, never kiss your child.") Dr. Spock could not. And slowly, as the nation in its agony turned from the shibboleths of mindless anti-Communism toward the peace of exhaustion, the wisdom of his compassion became clear.

> *Jesus said, Suffer little children, and forbid them not, to come unto me; for of such is the kingdom of heaven.*

But President Nixon called Dr. Spock a bum.

Thirty-five

NATTERING NABOBS

As AMERICA ENTERED the 1970s, the swing generation was in, or about to enter, its fifties, the age at which men begin to discover that the world they have loved is disintegrating. That year the impression carried special force, for there seemed to be an unusual number of reasons for feeling wronged, among them inflation, pollution, crime, the war, the stock market, the generation gap, immorality, riots, cyclamates, traffic, insulting bumper stickers and decals, strikes against the public, racism, and new skyjackings. Nothing worked as it once had. "Not only is there no God," said Woody Allen, "but try getting a plumber on weekends."

Hardly had three weeks of 1970 passed before a U.S. Navy ship set the tone for what was to come by tearing loose from its anchorage in a high wind and ripping a 375-foot hole in the Chesapeake Bay Bridge. To the superstitious it appeared that the new decade was off to an inauspicious start.

Nature appeared to be in a contrary mood elsewhere, too. After two hundred consecutive rainless days, Southern California was ravaged by the worst brush fires in its history, apparently caused by spontaneous combustion, denuding over 500,000 acres—an area nearly as large as Rhode Island. Eleven died in another fire of unexplained origin, in an eighty-five-year-old Minneapolis apartment building. All over the world natural disasters were besetting man; a Venice whirlwind left four dead, a cyclonic tidal wave in East Pakistan left 200,000 dead, and earthquakes in Peru, Turkey, and Iran left tens of thousands dead. Possibly God was angry with people like Woody Allen, who denied Him, or with the irreverent, like the flip college students who wore pins reading: "God Isn't Dead —He Just Doesn't Want to Get Involved."

Certainly religion wasn't the steady rock it had been. Christians who didn't regard God as a bigot were shaken by the new president of the Mormon Church, who said, "There is a reason why one man is born black and with other disadvantages, while another man is born white with great advantages. The Negro evidently is receiving the reward he merits." Episcopalians were agitated over the shelving, after three and a half centuries, of the King James Version of the Holy Bible for a New English Bible. Worst of all, from God's point of view, was the growing power of antichristianity—the worship of strange totems and even of Satan himself.

According to one reliable source, America was supporting 10,000 full-time and 175,000 part-time astrologers. Computers spewed forth ten-dollar horoscopes, a New York hairdresser employed a staff astrologer, a department store sold fifty-dollar annual subscriptions to a Dial-an-Astrologer service, and 300 newspapers with a combined circulation of 30 million carried a regular astrological column. Book clubs offered tarot cards as premiums. At the University of South Carolina 250 students were enrolled in a course on sorcery. Magazine advertisements inquired, "Tired of being on the outside of witchcraft looking in? Get in on the action yourself. Join our Diploma Course in Witchcraft and learn the age-old secrets, including raising power, meditation, prediction, fertility, and initiation rites." Mrs. Sybil Leek, a Houston sorceress who cast spells with a pet jackdaw named Hotfoot Jackson perched on her shoulder, calculated that there were "about eight million initiated witches in the world. I mean real witches, not Hollywood sex orgy, free-for-all types. I personally know of about four hundred regular covens in the United States. It is possible there are thousands of irregular ones."

If heaven was receiving insufficient respect, so were the authorities on earth. After one man had been killed and 105 wounded or injured during a People's Park riot in Berkeley, federal indictments were handed down accusing not the rioters, but ten deputies and two former deputies, who were charged with violating the civil rights of the demonstrators. ("This is the sickest operation any level of government was ever involved in," the sheriff raged.) Black Panthers seemed to be literally getting away with murder; juries or appeals courts threw out homicide charges against them in San Francisco, New Haven, and New York, and in Chicago a special federal grand jury criticized police conduct during the raid in which Panthers Fred Hampton and Mark Clark had been killed. Even the American Indians, who had been at the bottom of the status pyramid since the country was founded, were feeling feisty. The Senate didn't give the country back to them, but a bill did return New Mexico's Blue Lake and 48,000 surrounding acres to the Pueblo tribe.

It was a hard time for U.S. generals, and not just in Vietnam. The Russians arrested two of them on charges of violating Soviet air space. The commanding general of the European Exchange System was stripped of his rank for irregularities by subordinates, and Benjamin O. Davis Jr., who had retired from the Army as a lieutenant general, the highest rank ever held by a black, resigned as director of public safety in Cleveland because, he said, the city's black mayor was providing "support and comfort to the enemies of law enforcement." Anyone wearing a uniform was liable to be subjected to abuse by the tormentors of authority, though it did seem that President Nixon gave the White House police a special handicap. Impressed by the fancy uniforms of Romanian police, the President commissioned Jimmie Muscatello, a Washington tailor, to design new regalia for guards at the Executive Mansion. The result was a $16,000 joke—double-breasted white tunics with gold braid, brass buttons bearing the presidential seal, and black plastic Ruritanian hats. One guard muttered that if he had to wear such livery he wanted a bass drum to go with it. A designer said, "This is not the time for Gilbert and Sullivan at the White House." "You can't please everybody," said Muscatello, who hadn't pleased anybody, not even the President; the tunics stayed in service, but the hats were quietly shelved.

New York gravediggers struck in January. The air traffic controllers went out in April. Grounded passengers were bitter, but they may have been lucky; heavier-than-air transport wasn't at its most reliable in 1970. Air piracy continued, and an Arizonan named A. G. Barkley added a new wrinkle when he entered a TWA cabin with a gun, a razor, and a can of gasoline and announced that he wanted 100 million dollars. He was seized after a gun battle during which the pilot was wounded in the stomach. Boeing's 21-million-dollar jumbo jet, the 747, was off to a slow start, running as much as six hours behind schedule. Even a lunar flight, Apollo 13, broke down some 200,000 miles from home. The three astronauts aboard had to turn back.

Ironically, one of the most successful journeys of 1970 was a 3,200-mile ocean voyage by a papyrus boat, the Ra II, built and sailed by Norwegian explorer Thor Heyerdahl to prove that the ancient Egyptians could have crossed the Atlantic. At least the Ra II reached its destination, Barbados, and while it didn't make money, neither did many commercial carriers, including, most conspicuously, the biggest railroad in the United States. In bankruptcy court with 2.6 billion dollars in debts, the Penn Central was one of many American institutions which were having trouble balancing their books. Another was the motion picture industry; five major Hollywood studios were in the red, with total debts of over 100 million dollars. The great boom of the 1960s seemed to have ended with the decade, and the best evidence was in Wall Street, where the Dow Jones industrial average, which had been within striking distance of 1,000 in December 1968, sank to 631 on May 27.

The gallery at the New York Stock Exchange had been crowded with eager spectators in the years of the Johnson bull market. After the long slide of May 1970 it became a lonelier place. Indeed, the entire city of New York—which its mordant inhabitants now called Fun City—was less popular with tourists. There was the street crime, and there were other perils. On June 1 the city increased its towing fee for illegally parked cars from twenty-five to fifty dollars. That day a Springfield, Massachusetts, mother came to New York and took her children to a film. When she emerged her auto was gone and she owed the city fifty dollars plus a fine. The movie was *The Out-of-Towners,* dealing with the hazards of visiting Manhattan.

While 1970 was a year of doldrums on most California motion picture lots, a director named Russ Meyer finished his twenty-first successful movie that year. He had known from the outset that it would be big box office. None of its predecessors had lost money or grossed less than six figures, and one of them, *Vixen,* filmed for $72,000, had earned over six million. Meyer said: "I don't play games with an audience. In my films you know where you're at in fifteen seconds—the first fifteen seconds." Where you were at was in the middle of what the trade described as "erotica" and others called pornography. Peddling sex had become a big business in the United

States, netting over 500 million dollars a year, and the market seemed insatiable.

The merchandise came in various packages. Main Street theaters showed X-rated films; 1970 hits included *Sexual Freedom in Denmark*, *The Minx* ("Makes *Curious Yellow* look pale"—*New York Daily News*), and Allen Funt's *What Do You Say to a Naked Lady?* ("What *can* you say?" asked its ads. "We say wow"), which was grossing one San Francisco movie house $7,000 a week for round-the-clock showings. Manhattan was supporting two hundred "adult bookstores," and those in the twenty-four-hour-a-day block between Seventh and Eighth avenues displayed their goods like supermarkets, with overhead signs advertising the various departments—heterosexual, homosexual (male), bestiality, flagellation, lesbian, incest, fellatio and cunnilingus. Arcade machines offered skin flicks in color at a quarter a showing. Picture packets contained "Eight revealing poses! $2." Onstage in New York were *Grin and Bare It* with nine nudes in the cast, *The Boys in the Band*, which AP dramatic critic William Glover called "the most unabashed and forthright account of homosexuality yet seen in this era of growing artistic permissiveness," and *Futz*, which dealt with the problems of a yokel who enjoyed coupling with a sow. But the market was much bigger than Broadway. The Arcadian bachelor could resolve his frustrations by sending for obscene LP records; a lonely bachelor girl could purchase a vibrator in a hometown store or a plastic dildo through the mails, and as Professor Morse Peckham of the University of South Carolina observed, in the corner drugstore the public could now "buy for very little money pornographic works which a short time ago were unobtainable for any amount of money."

To Americans over the age of thirty the change was mind-boggling. In their childhoods the word "ass" had been forbidden in mixed company, and the swing generation could remember the uproar over the Hays Office decision to let Clark Gable say "Frankly, my dear, I don't give a damn" in *Gone With the Wind*. Now Jack Valenti approved "horseshit" and "Piss on you" in movies rated for the whole family. Part of the latitude studios now took could be traced to the Supreme Court's 1957 decision, in the case of Roth v. U.S., that to be obscene material must be prurient, offensive to community standards, and "utterly without redeeming social value." Another part of the new license was a byproduct of the new contraceptives, liberalized abortion legislation, and the consequent emancipation of women from the fear of unwanted pregnancy. And much of it, as William Glover had noted, was rooted in the era, in the sexual revolution and the mini-micro-bikini-topless-bottomless mood of the times. Curiosity about sex appeared to be insatiable; Nicholas von Hoffman wrote about a female reporter who, while collecting material for an article about prostitution, went to bed with a strange man for money and reported that the climax was "a moment of stunning pleasure." A mother in Braintree, Massachusetts, came home one afternoon to find her teen-age daughter and a girlfriend in bed naked, experimenting with Sapphic techniques. The word "indiscretion" in its sexual sense all but dropped out of the language, because hardly anybody was discreet any more. A Pennsylvania legislator opposing abortion legislation was unmasked as a hypocrite when a young woman came forward to tell the press that he had been her lover and had paid for her abortion. There had been a time when she would have kept that to herself.

All this was hard on children, who were exposed to it, were more precocious in their dating customs than their parents, and attained puberty at an earlier age. The remedy most often proposed was sex education in the schools. Gallup found that 71 percent of the people approved it, with 55 percent in favor of courses explaining birth control. Among the groups endorsing the teaching of sex were the AMA, the National Education Association, the Sex Education Association, and the Sex Information and Education Council in the United States (SIECUS). Dr. Mary Calderone, executive director of SIECUS, said sex should be taught "not as something you do but as something you are."

SIECUS issued no material; it merely offered professional advice to school systems. That point was obscured by the articulate minority, which was outraged by the very suggestion that reproduction might be discussed in the classroom. "Is the Schoolhouse the Proper Place to Teach Raw Sex?" asked Billy James Hargis's Christian Crusade, firing the opening gun in the ultraright's attack on sex education. The Reverend Billy called SIECUS the "pornographic arm of liberal education," and state boards of education in Oklahoma, California, and Utah rejected sound film strips because they had been approved by SIECUS.

Other organizations in the antisex coalition were the Movement to Restore Decency (MOTOREDE), a Birch front; Parents United for a Responsible Education (PURE), the Mothers Organization for Moral Stability (MOMS), Sanity on Sex (SOS), Parents Opposed to Sex Education (POSE), and Parents Against Unconstitutional Sex Education (PAUSE). "I doubt that one parent in a thousand had heard about sex education a year ago," said a Birch coordinator. "Now they've heard about it, and they don't like what they hear." One group accused the schools of planning to "reveal all the details of intercourse and masturbation to small children"; a school in Parsippany, New Jersey, was called an "academic whorehouse"; a PAUSE leader accused the schools of "undermining what should be taught in the home." An eighth-grade mathematics teacher was jailed for disseminating lewd materials, and a California school superintendent was fired. Ultrarightists also won in Racine, Wisconsin, after charging that sex education was a Communist plot to undermine the morals of the pupils. One of the wilder battles was in San Francisco over an innocuous book titled *A Doctor Talks to Five-to-Eight-Year-Olds*. The ultras there printed a leaflet reproducing an illustration from the book of one toad on another's back. The book explained that it was a mother carrying her baby. The leaflet lost sex education a lot of supporters by changing the caption to "Mating Toads."

At the peak of the controversy sex education was an issue in twenty-seven states. Toward the end of 1970 sanity triumphed and the courses were introduced, to the bewilderment of the children, who wondered what all the fuss had been about. Then, just as superintendents and school boards thought they could divert their professional attention to other matters, their presentation of sex came under attack from an entirely different movement: Women's Lib. Liberated women took it as an article of faith that all except physical differences between males and females were taught, not inherent. They believed that girls were trained to want motherhood and cultivate domestic science, and they regarded the public schools as a major training ground. Demanding that textbooks be revised and teachers reoriented, they joined battle with their adversaries in a struggle which was certain to endure as a major issue of the 1970s.

Millions of Americans had first become aware of the new feminism when Robin Morgan, until then best known as a TV actress in *I Remember Mama*, marched into the 1968 Miss America Pageant pulling a train of blazing brassieres. She was there, she told startled reporters, in her role as founder of the Women's International Terrorist Conspiracy from Hell (WITCH). Feminists paraded through metropolitan shopping districts on August 26, 1970, the fiftieth anniversary of ratification of the Nineteenth Amendment. All that year liberated women were demonstrating that they, like the members of other protest movements, understood the uses of publicity. "Take it off!" one of them yelled at a construction worker, and when she was asked if she meant his hard hat she said, "No, his jockstrap." One June Conlan won a ten-year court fight to become a day laborer digging ditches. Marlene Dixon wrote that "in all classes and groups, the institution functions to a greater or lesser degree to oppress women; the unity of women of different classes hinges upon our understanding of that common oppression." Abby Aldrich Rockefeller, a great-granddaughter of John D., denounced romantic love between men and women as "counterrevolutionary."

"I've had Women's Lib up to here," said Dr. Edgar F. Berman, a physician active in Democratic politics. Democratic Congresswoman Patsy Mink of Hawaii promptly accused Berman of being a sexist with the "basest sort of prejudice against women." As the year wore on, the rhetoric grew more heated. Margaret Mead said, "Women's liberation has to be terribly conscious of the danger of provoking men to kill women. You have quite literally driven them mad." One male spectator at the women's march in New York screamed at them, "All you pigs can't get a man!" while another stood silently by wearing a brassiere. "These chicks," said Hugh Hefner in a memo to his staff, "are our natural enemy. It's time to do battle with them. They are inalterably opposed to the romantic boy-girl society *Playboy* promotes."

Some of the women sounded as frivolous as Hefner. They devoted a great deal of energy to debates over whether they should be known as Mrs., Miss, or Ms.; to attempts to have chairmen called chairpersons, and to attacks on National Airlines for running ads of pretty stewardesses saying, "I'm Doris. Fly me." But the deeper questions they raised were anything but trivial. Over 23 million American women now held full-time jobs; another eight million had part-time jobs. Four of every ten married women were employed, 12 million of them with children at home under eighteen. Superficially this indicated a challenge to male supremacy in the job market, but the nature of the employment and the pay for it still reflected a society in which men, not women, were expected to support families. Men still dominated the most lucrative professions and brought home the bigger slices of bacon. Just 7.6 percent of America's 300,000 doctors, and only 1 percent of the surgeons, were women, while 90 percent of the phone operators and stenographers were female. The average woman was making $3 for every $5 made by a man with the same job. *Life* calculated that a woman needed a B.A. degree to earn as much as a man who left school after the eighth grade. The typical salesman made $8,549; the typical saleswoman $3,461.

By 1970 Women's Lib arguments for equality in employment and education were supported by many men. Demands for free abortions and free day-care centers for children were more controversial, and the masculine population seemed evenly divided on the proposed Twenty-seventh Amendment to the Constitution—the Equal Rights Amendment (ERA), ensuring women complete equality before the law. Yet within two years the Senate would approve ERA and send it to the state legislatures. Under it, women would no longer be required to change their names when they married; they would be given an equal voice in where the family would live; if the husband's job obliged him to move elsewhere, and his wife stayed behind, she would not be liable to a charge of desertion. On the other hand, should a marriage break up, the wife might have to pay alimony. Laws shielding women from danger and physical strain on the job and protecting them from certain sexual outrages would be void. (Rape was an exception.) In addition, women might be drafted and even sent into battle. A pro-ERA contributor to the *Yale Law Journal* argued:

> . . . the effectiveness of the modern soldier is due more to equipment and training than to individual strength. Women are physically as able as men to perform many jobs classified as combat duty, such as piloting an airplane or engaging in naval operations. . . . There is no reason to assume that in a dangerous situation women will not be as serious and well-disciplined as men.

It is doubtful that many housewives wanted to become machine gunners or BAR men, or identified with Elizabeth P. Hoisington, director of the Women's Army Corps, who became America's first female general in June 1970. Nevertheless, millions of American women—especially younger women—had been changed by the movement. There was a new spunkiness about them, a plucky defiance toward those who would manipulate them for selfish ends, and this was illustrated by the disaster which befell the new fashion known to readers of *Women's Wear Daily* as the longuette and to the rest of the country as the midi. Nearly a quarter-century earlier independent women had tried to lead a revolt against the long-skirted New Look, signing manifestos, forming LBK (Little Below the Knee) clubs, and demonstrating against the couturiers.* They had been routed then. Now the modistes were again turning out longer skirts. James Galanos said, "Long is where the direction is," Adele Simpson said, "It's good-bye thigh," and Leo Narducci said, "Women are definitely ready for a fashion change." All were confident that the female herd would grovel and buy their wares.

The first mutinous mutters came from Los Angeles, where one Juli Hutner, president of something called POOFF (Preservation of Our Femininity and Finances), told a reporter: "We're not going to let them pull the wool over our legs as well as our eyes. I know women who'd wear a tin box if Galanos said it was in. I think that's sick. All we ask is a choice." KEEP THE MINI ON THE MARKET and LEGS! LEGS! LEGS! said the placards carried by demonstrating members of Girls Against More Skirt (GAMS). Some of them suggested that the midi was a plot against Women's Lib, that the designers were trying to isolate the feminists by bringing femininity back; others blamed older matrons whose legs weren't sexy any more and who wanted to make nubile girls hide theirs. Gilman Ostrander, a social historian, said the falling stock market was responsible for the midi, and that it was bound to prevail: "The middle-aged, who like long skirts, determine social standards in times of depression or recession. And young people, who like short skirts, determine standards in times of prosperity."

By winter the stock market had gone up, however, and the fashion industry's enthusiasm for the midi had plunged. A *New York Times* survey found that while a few shop owners gallantly professed faith in the longer look ("It's here! Everybody's accepting and loving and buying it!"), most conceded that it had failed wretchedly: "Stores that last fall said they bought lots of midis are now saying they didn't really. What they did buy didn't sell very well. And women's knees are not yet obsolete." To be sure, more skirts covered the knee. But the dress designers had insisted that the midi was a specific length, measuring 44 to 45 inches from shoulder to hem, which put it at mid-calf for most women. The *Times*

* See Vol. I, pages 516–518.

found that only 20 percent of dresses sold at that length, and at the end of the year just 5 percent of the women were wearing them. The other frocks had been returned for shortening or left in the closet.

Bitter retailers said the style had "bombed," or "laid an egg"; one said it "certainly did fashion a disservice and didn't take as a look," and another told a newswoman, "Our customers didn't want it. . . . We were never really able to sell it." The massive attempt to push the calf-length hem did trigger an unintended sartorial shift, however. "The midi," said the *Times,* "virtually killed the dress . . . suddenly there were kickers, gauchos, and pants, pants, pants." Older women bought pantsuits, and their daughters kept their bare knees by donning very short shorts. Bergdorf Goodman called the shorts "cool pants." *Women's Wear Daily,* closer to the mood of the new women, gave them the name that stuck: hotpants.

The streak of violence which had blighted Johnson's administration continued under Nixon, growing, if anything, more lurid. The great metropolitan ghettos continued to be relatively quiet, but the assassin and the pyromaniac now moved with murderous stealth in the black neighborhoods of smaller cities. Six Negroes were shot to death in Augusta, Georgia. A boy was stabbed in an Oklahoma City racial incident. A church which had been used for civil rights meetings in Carthage, Mississippi, was bombed. And there were riots in East Los Angeles, Miami, Houston, Highland Park, Michigan; Michigan City, Indiana; New Bedford, Massachusetts; Asbury Park, New Jersey; South Melbourne, Florida; Aliquippa, Pennsylvania; Oxford, North Carolina; Hot Springs, Arkansas; River Rouge, Michigan; Cairo, Illinois; and three Georgia communities: Perry, Macon, and Athens.

In New York bomb threats were running at a thousand a month. Over a fifteen-month period 368 of the devices had actually exploded in the city, one of them in a second-floor men's room at police headquarters, and Commissioner Howard Leary told a U.S. Senate subcommittee that he could not guarantee the safety of visitors to precinct stations. At times it seemed as though an open season had been declared on American policemen. In 1970 the FBI reported 35,202 assaults on them, almost quadruple the number in 1960, and fifteen officers were killed, most of them by ambushers, in nine months of the year.

The Little Rock police chief said attacks on cops had become "practically a daily occurrence . . . It seemed everyone from school age on up is assaulting police officers." Commissioner Frank L. Rizzo of Philadelphia said, "We are dealing with a group of fanatics—psychopaths," and the director of public safety in Omaha suggested that "the problem being experienced by police departments throughout the nation gives all indications that there is a conspiracy. The timing gives another indication. We are piecing together all the information available and we hope to prove a conspiracy." He didn't do it, and most law enforcement officials thought it wasn't possible—"We look upon the assaults as separate and independent incidents," Leary said—but there was general agreement that at a time when authority was under widespread attack, cops were inevitable targets. As Quinn Tamm of the International Association of Chiefs of Police put it: "Attacks on police are becoming more and more violent as radical groups exhort their members to 'kill the pigs' . . . That blue uniform makes the wearer a highly visible representative of the establishment."

Hostility to the established order was responsible for the bombings. In some instances the bombers boasted about it. After blasts tore into the Manhattan offices of International Business Machines, the General Telephone and Electronics Corporation, and Mobil Oil, a group called Revolutionary Force 9 took credit for them, declaring that the firms were profiteering in Vietnam. In other cases the terrorists, not being skilled in the use of explosives, blew themselves up. Within a month of the IBM, General Telephone, and Mobil eruptions one revolutionist was killed and another gravely injured when their bomb factory fulminated in a tenement on New York's Lower East Side. In Baltimore two black militants, protégés of H. Rap Brown, died after one of their bombs detonated prematurely in their automobile. And on March 6 Greenwich Village was rocked by the most sensational bomb disaster of 1970, killing three young nihilists and involving the names of several wealthy families.

Cathlyn Platt Wilkerson was a recent graduate of Swarthmore; Diana Oughton and Kathy Boudin were Bryn Mawr alumnae; all three were Weatherwomen. Diana was the daughter of an ultraconservative, highly respectable Illinois multimillionaire whose extraordinary family estate had been visited by King Edward VII, then Prince of Wales, a century earlier. Kathy was the niece of I. F. Stone. Her father, Leonard B. Boudin, was a famous lawyer whose clients included Paul Robeson, Judith Coplon, and Julian Bond; later he would defend Daniel Ellsberg. Cathlyn's father owned a chain of radio stations. He and his second wife were on holiday in the Caribbean that month. In his absence Cathlyn was entertaining Diana and Kathy, Ted Gold, who had been active in Columbia's SDS chapter, and another young man—whose identity was to remain a mystery—in the elegant $100,000 Wilkerson town house at 18 West Eleventh Street in Manhattan.

At noon on the day of the catastrophe the sky was clear and sunny over New York, with just a suggestion of approaching spring in the air. No one was in the house next door, which belonged to Dustin Hoffman, the actor, and number 18 appeared to be quiet. Inside, however, the young revolutionaries were busy. Two current Weatherman slogans were "If you don't believe in guns and violence, then you aren't a revolutionary" and "Bring the war home." On Monday one of the boys, dressed as a priest, had driven to New Hampshire to buy two cases of dynamite. Now fifty-seven sticks of TNT were strewn about in a makeshift basement workshop, together with friction tape, roofing nails, clockwork timing mechanisms, doorbell wire, thirty blasting tapes, and lengths of plumbing pipe meant to contain the charges.

Probably no one will ever know exactly what went wrong, but somebody bungled and set the lot off. It may have been Diana; her body was the most mutilated—the head, both hands and a foot were blown off, and the torso was riddled with roofing nails. Gold and the unidentified youth were also dead. The first explosion ripped through the living room wall of Hoffman's house, shattered windows across the street, and rocked a kitchen sixteen doors away. Then the gas mains ignited, touching off two more blasts, and the floors started to collapse.

Inside, stunned and bleeding, were Cathlyn and Kathy, one of them naked and the other partially dressed. Two policemen and a retired fireman—"the girls," John Neary wryly noted in *Life*, "would have called them 'pigs'"—came to their rescue, and a neighbor gave them the use of her shower and loaned them clothing. Then they disappeared. At first firemen thought leaking gas was responsible for the disaster. Then they found the dynamite, the blasting caps, and stacks of SDS pamphlets. Suddenly they wanted to question the survivors. New York authorities learned that Kathy and Cathlyn were out on bail after indictment in Chicago for participating in the

Weathermen's Days of Rage the previous October. When they failed to appear there for trial March 16 the FBI joined the hunt. Their families said the girls had sent word that they were alive but gave no details.

On the other side of the country a weird blend of radical politics and witchcraft was blamed for the worst mass murder in California since the Manson killings. Sheriff's deputies on a routine patrol saw flames in the $250,000 home of Dr. Victor Ohta, an eye surgeon, overlooking Monterey Bay. They called firemen, who went to the Ohta swimming pool in search of water and there found the bodies of the surgeon, his wife, their two sons, and the doctor's secretary. All had been tied up with gaudy scarves and shot in the back of the head. Police found a scribbled message under the windshield wiper of the surgeon's car: "From this day forward anyone . . . who misuses the natural environment or destroys same will suffer the penalty of death. . . . I and my comrades from this day forth will fight until death or freedom against anything or anyone who does not support natural life on this planet. Materialism must die or mankind will stop." The signature was taken from tarot cards: "Knight of Wands, Knight of Cups, Knight of Pentacles, Knight of Swords." The signer, found living in a ramshackle hut a half-mile away, was a bearded youth named John F. Frazier. Frazier's lawyer said that his client had hurt his head in a car accident and had then "changed radically."

That year's most famous black advocate of revolutionary action in California was a dusky twenty-six-year-old beauty, Angela Davis. A daughter of the black middle class, she had been a Birmingham Girl Scout, apparently contented with society until four of her Negro girlfriends were killed in the September 1963 bombing of a church there. At Brandeis University, where she was elected to Phi Beta Kappa, she became an enthusiastic reader of Marx and Herbert Marcuse, and after graduate work at the Sorbonne and in Germany she became Marcuse's student on the San Diego campus of the University of California. There she joined the Black Panthers and the Communist Party. In one speech she told undergraduates that "the government has to be overthrown"; in another she said that "revolution must be tied to dealing with specific problems now, not a lot of rhetoric about revolution, but real, fundamental problems."

She participated in the storming of a campus building in San Diego and was arrested for refusing to leave a police station.

As an assistant professor on the university's Los Angeles campus she was teaching philosophy when, in April 1970, Governor Reagan's Board of Regents voted to fire her, citing a board resolution barring Communists from the faculty. Since both the California and U.S. Supreme Courts had held that Communist membership was insufficient reason to disqualify a professor from teaching in a state university, the board changed the grounds for dismissal to incompetence. A majority of students and UCLA faculty members took Angela's side. Her fellow professors adopted a resolution expressing "our shock, our dismay, our rage" at her removal. They voted to defy the regents by keeping her on the faculty, and the issue was unresolved when a new development put her case in an entirely different light.

As a black militant, Angela had been among those who were agitating for the release of the "Soledad Brothers"—three Negro prisoners, not actually related to one another, who had been charged with killing a white guard at Soledad Prison on January 16. The most interesting of the three was George Jackson, twenty-seven, who was serving five years to life for a 1961 filling station robbery. As the author of *Soledad Brother*, a collection of his prison letters, Jackson would become one of the most famous convicts in the country that fall. Some of the most moving notes in the book were written to Angela, who had first seen him during a hearing in a Salinas courtroom that May. In her own letters to him, and in a diary, she declared that she had "spontaneously" fallen in love with him. She called herself his "lifelong wife" and said she would dedicate her life to freeing him. She added that she didn't care what means she used, a passage which aroused much subsequent interest.

In the first week of August Angela was seen frequently in the company of Jonathan Jackson, George's seventeen-year-old brother. Three guns she owned found their way into Jonathan's possession; so did a twelve-gauge sawed-off shotgun she bought on August 5. That was a Wednesday. On Thursday she and Jonathan were driving around in a small, bright yellow enclosed Ford panel truck he had rented the day before. On Friday the van was parked in a lot outside the San Rafael courthouse, thirteen miles northwest of San Francisco. Minutes later Jonathan, slim and intense, entered a courtroom wearing a raincoat and carrying a small bag.

On the stand at the time was Ruchell Magee, a San Quentin convict who was testifying in the case of James McLain, a fellow prisoner accused of stabbing a guard. Another black inmate, William Christmas, was waiting to be called. Magee, McLain, and Christmas were powerfully built young men, and McLain, who was sitting at the counsel's table, was known at San Quentin as a firebrand, an agitator, and a Panther. Superior Court Judge Harold J. Haley was on the bench. The deputy district attorney was Gary W. Thomas, who was married to the judge's niece. There was a jury, but young Jackson was the only spectator. It was a boring case.

It became much livelier when Jonathan unzipped his bag, drew out one of Angela's revolvers, and slipped a 30-caliber carbine from under his raincoat. "This is it!" he yelled. "I've got an automatic weapon. Everybody freeze!" He ordered the unarmed bailiffs to unlock the handcuffs on McLain, Magee, and Christmas, and handed each of the three unshackled convicts a weapon. He gave the shotgun to McLain, who taped it around the judge's neck so that the muzzle hung a few inches from Haley's chin. The other prisoners tied Thomas and three women jurors together with piano wire. McLain commanded the judge to call the sheriff's office and direct him to give the inmates safe passage out. "I am in the courtroom," Haley said into the telephone on the bench. "There are a number of armed convicts here." McLain grabbed the phone and shouted into it, "You're going to call off your pig dogs. We're going to get out of here. Call them off!"

Herding the hostages before them, the blacks paused before the press room, fifty feet down the hall, but the door was locked. As they continued down the corridor McLain called, "We want the Soledad Brothers released by twelve-thirty today!" In the parking lot they shoved the five hostages into the Ford van. McLain slid behind the wheel; Jonathan gave him the keys; Magee took over the guarding of the judge, and they headed for U.S. 101, about two hundred yards away. Watching them were some hundred law enforcement officers, crouched behind other vehicles and the building. Suddenly a San Quentin guard darted in front of the panel truck and yelled, "Halt!"

The next minute was madness, with gunfire pouring into the panel truck and out from it. At one point the shotgun roared in the back of the van. That was the end for the judge; his jaw and part of his face were blown off. Thomas had a bullet in his spine; he would be paralyzed from the waist down for the rest of his life. One of the jurors was wounded in the arm. Magee had been shot in the chest but was still alive. McLain, Christmas, and Jonathan Jackson were dead.

Three hours later Angela Davis bought an airplane ticket at the San Francisco terminal. Then she vanished.

Under California law, anyone abetting a killer before the act is equally guilty of murder, and a warrant was issued for her arrest. Panther leader Huey P. Newton said he believed that she had been responsible for the courthouse shootings, was proud of her, and hoped others would follow her "courageous example." Charles Garry, a white attorney for the Panthers, cried, "More power to Angela Davis! May she live long in liberty." In fact she remained at large for over two months. On October 13 FBI agents arrested her in Manhattan after she had checked into a Howard Johnson's motel with David Rudolph Poindexter Jr., a wealthy Negro. Poindexter was charged with harboring a fugitive; Angela was extradited and lodged in a San Rafael prison less than five miles from George Jackson's cell in San Quentin.

Nearly a year later, on a hot August day in 1971, Jackson received a visit from his lawyer, Stephen Mitchell Bingham. Bingham was white, a Yale alumnus, and the grandson of Hiram Bingham, who had served Connecticut as governor and U.S. senator. Prison officials later became convinced that the younger Bingham, who had been active in the cause of minority groups, was on a smuggling mission that day. He was carrying two parcels which guards did not search: an expanding brown envelope and a small portable tape recorder. After he completed an hour-long session with Jackson and left, a guard noticed something different about the convict's Afro hairdo. Asked about it, the Negro yanked off a wig and pulled a small automatic pistol from it.

Terror and death followed. On Jackson's orders, twenty-seven prisoners, including the convalescing Ruchell Magee, were released. Then three white guards and two white trusties were murdered; two were shot in the back of the head, and the throats of the others were cut with a dull razor blade. The corpses were piled in a corner of Jackson's cell like bloody rugs. By now San Quentin's sirens were screaming. Still holding the pistol, Jackson bolted out a door and sprinted some seventy-five feet across an open courtyard before sharpshooters in the towers overhead cut him down.

Stephen Bingham was indicted for the murder of the guards and the trusties—the county district attorney said, "There is no way Jackson could have gotten the death gun except during his visit with Bingham"—but he disappeared without a trace, and by the following year authorities were suggesting that he might be dead: that black militants, having used him, may have then killed him. Law enforcement officers were embittered by the deaths of August 21. Negro activists were also outraged. Jackson became a martyr to them. His body was dressed in the Panther uniform—black leather jacket, black beret, and black shirt—and buried beside that of Jonathan. Julian Bond spoke of his "assassination" and of "the expected outcome of his constant attacks on a vicious system which was unable to crush his spirit or his body." California Assemblyman Willie Brown said, "The people in the street are saying this is an execution, that it's ridiculous Jackson could hide a gun in his hair," and Angela Davis wrote of "the loss of an irretrievable love."

Angela's trial in the late spring of 1972 was an international event. Her elegant profile, with the high cheekbones and vast Afro coiffure—she had cut it off while a fugitive, but it had grown back—adorned posters around the world. Militant slogans called her a "political prisoner" and demanded "Free Angela!" The prosecution, protesting that the proceedings had nothing to do with politics or race, that this was a criminal trial, submitted 201 exhibits and testimony from ninety-five witnesses. Three people identified her as Jonathan's companion at a gas station across the street from the courthouse the day before the escape attempt, and others put her with him on each of the three days beforehand.

The defense presented testimony from twelve witnesses (Angela chose not to take the stand) and ridiculed the idea that "a brilliant college professor" could have been implicated in such a harebrained scheme. She and Jonathan hadn't been together as often as some people claimed, her lawyers said. Admittedly she had given him the shotgun, but it had been with the understanding that he would use it only to guard the headquarters of the Soledad Brothers Defense Committee. She had kept the other weapons on a rack in her home for target practice by members of the Che-Lumumba Club. Jonathan had visited her there six days before the courthouse tragedy; probably he had stolen them then.

The attorney presenting the defense summation said that the only evidence against her was "that Angela was closely related to Jonathan Jackson, that her guns were used, that she expressed a desire to free the Soledad Brothers, that Angela expressed love for George Jackson, and that on August 7 Angela made herself unavailable to the authorities." The jury would have fled, too, the lawyer declared, if they had been Negro and had discovered that four guns they owned had been used in the escape attempt at the courthouse: "I say to you, when you look at the situation through the eyes of a black person, you would not wonder why she fled. You would only wonder why she allowed herself to be caught."

After thirteen hours of deliberation the panel found her not guilty. Turning her back on the jurors, Angela left the courtroom to address her admirers outside. A reporter asked her if she thought she had received a fair trial. She said she didn't. "The very fact of an acquittal," she said, "means that there was no fair trial, because a fair trial would have been no trial at all." Setting out on a triumphant tour of the country, she told her supporters: "Starting from this day forward, we must work to free every political prisoner and every oppressed person in this country and the whole world."

Four weeks after the Soledad murder, which had started the chain of events that culminated in Angela's fame, Chicago had witnessed the end of another remarkable trial. It had opened with eight defendants: Yippies Jerry Rubin and Abbie Hoffman; Rennie Davis, David Dellinger, and SDS's Tom Hayden, the three leaders of the National Mobilization Committee which had brought the antiwar demonstrators to Chicago; Bobby Seale of the Panthers; and Lee Weiner and John R. Froines. Before their arrests some of the defendants had scarcely known one another, and in fact the key complaint against them was not the conspiracy count, but the accusation that they had entered Illinois individually to incite a riot—"crossing state lines with a state of mind," said chief counsel William M. Kunstler, while Leonard I. Weinglass, their other attorney, called the statute—which had been passed as a rider to the 1968 Civil Rights Act—"the only federal law where the government can punish someone without the commission of an overt act." They were the first defendants to be indicted under it, though that fact and a great many others were forgotten during the circus into which the proceedings deteriorated.

Kunstler set the tone on the first day of the trial, when he moved for a mistrial because of the way Judge Julius J. Hoffman read the charges to the jury. "Your Honor sounded like Orson Welles reciting the Declaration of Independence," said the lawyer.

"I've never been compared to that great actor, Orson Welles," said the judge, "but I deny the motion."

Altogether, the defense would make more than a score of mistrial motions, and to a great degree the tempestuous character of the proceedings arose from the chasm between Kunstler, Weinglass, and their clients on the one hand, and Judge Hoffman and the state's attorneys on the other. "The trial," wrote Richard Ciccone of the AP Chicago Bureau, "was a collision of generations, ideologies, and life-styles." Judge Hoffman wore a vest; Abbie Hoffman wore love beads and buckskin, and during one uproarious session he and Rubin appeared in judicial robes. Rubin and Hoffman had beards. The defendants and their lawyers grew their hair long, a fact caustically noted by the well-barbered prosecutors, Thomas A. Foran and Richard G. Schultz.

At one point, when Allen Ginsberg was testifying for the defense, the witness showed how he had quieted antiwar Chicago demonstrators in 1968—with a ten-second grunt: "Ah-ooom!" Kunstler protested that the judge was laughing. His Honor denied it. "I just don't understand the language," he said. Ginsberg explained, "It's Sanskrit." The judge said, "That's one I don't know." The transcript shows that there was a great deal the court did not know, but Hoffman did have a clear concept of the decorum which should be observed in his courtroom. During the seventy-four years since his birth in a humble Chicago neighborhood he had come to expect respect from the people who came before him, and neither the Chicago Eight nor their defense staff gave it to him. The first signs of what lay ahead came during a pretrial hearing. Kunstler and Weinglass wanted to ask veniremen how they felt about protest demonstrations, American slums, and the Vietnam War. Judge Hoffman turned them down; he said they couldn't even ask prospective jurors their opinion of hippies and Yippies. The next defense request was for a postponement of the trial until Seale's attorney, Charles Garry, could recover from an operation. Hoffman rejected that, too, and when he followed it by denying Seale's appeal for the right to address the court, telling him that he would have to allow Kunstler to speak for him, he touched off judicial chaos.

"I can only see the judge as a blatant racist," Seale said. The dwarfish judge bounded to his feet. "Did you hear that?" he asked a clerk in disbelief. The Panther leader was cautioned, then and repeatedly afterward, that interruptions would be "dealt with appropriately at some time in the future." Seale retorted, "What can you do to me that hasn't been done to black people for three hundred years?" In the eighth week of the trial the judge started to respond to a series of Seale outbursts: "Look, young man, if you keep this up—" Seale replied: "Look, old man, if you keep denying me my constitutional rights you are being exposed to the world—" Hoffman said: "Mr. Seale, do you want to stop or do you want me to direct the marshal—" Seale said: "I want to argue about this so you can get an understanding of the facts."

His patience exhausted, the judge told the marshal, "Take that defendant into the room there and deal with him as he should be dealt with." After a recess the Panther was carried in gagged and handcuffed to a metal folding chair. Even that didn't silence him. He rattled his fetters against the chair and cried in a muffled voice, "That means I object!" He was moved to a wooden chair and the gag was tightened. At the next session he managed to work free of the gag and shout at the bench: "You fascist dog, you rotten lowlife son-of-a-bitch!" Abbie Hoffman and Rubin jumped up, screaming, and Kunstler asked the court: "Your Honor, when are we going to stop this medieval torture? This is an unholy disgrace to the law . . . I feel so utterly ashamed at this time to be an American lawyer." Judge Hoffman, who had frequently said that he blamed Kunstler and Weinglass for the misconduct of his clients, snapped: "You should be." The following week he ordered the gag removed, and when Seale persisted in his interruptions he sentenced him to four years in prison for contempt. Now those left were christened the Chicago Seven.

They weren't chastened. While Davis was on the stand he accused the judge of being asleep—His Honor warned him that his insolence would be "dealt with appropriately at some time in the future"—and Abbie Hoffman created pandemonium by coming into the courtroom walking on his hands and calling Judge Hoffman a "tyrant," a "Nazi," and "a disgrace to the Jews."

The sharpest exchanges were between the court and the chief defense counsel. The judge explicitly directed Kunstler not to ask in the presence of the jury that Mayor Daley—who had insisted the trial be held despite Justice Department doubts—be declared a hostile witness. The attorney did it anyway, and he almost gave the judge apoplexy by asking Daley point blank whether he had shouted an obscenity at Senator Abraham Ribicoff during the convention. At one point Abbie Hoffman raised his shirt. "Let the record show," the judge said, "that man bared his body in open court." Kunstler said, "Your Honor, I remember when President Johnson showed his stomach scar to a whole nation on television." "Maybe that's why he isn't President any more," His Honor replied. When the lawyer chuckled and was rebuked he said, "Come on, Your Honor, what's the harm in laughter? Sometimes we can't help ourselves." The judge said, "Oh yes, I can see that you can't help yourself."

Toward the end of the trial the court's hostility toward the defendants became flagrant. For two days Hoffman refused to let them use the toilet in the hall; the latrine in the jail, he said, was good enough for them. One day he said they would start a half-hour earlier the following morning. When Kunstler asked the reason he was told, "Because it will be at nine-thirty." The lawyer commented, "That's like a child saying, 'Because, because.'" The judge said, "Let the record show that, in the presence of the jury, Mr. Kunstler compared me to a child." The lawyer was effusive in court, often hilarious or in tears. Sometimes he hugged men, and he kissed Weinglass and one of the witnesses, the Reverend Ralph D. Abernathy. "Let the record show," Judge Hoffman said acidly each time, "that Mr. Kunstler kissed that man." As the end of the trial was to prove, his reasons for these insertions in the transcript were not frivolous.

Defense witnesses included Pete Seeger, William Styron, Judy Collins, Norman Mailer, Julian Bond, Reverend Jesse Jackson, Terry Southern, and Ginsberg, who at Prosecutor Foran's insistence read aloud some of his poems on homosexuality and masturbation, apparently because Foran thought they would offend the ten women jurors. Kunstler and Weinglass argued that Daley and the Chicago police had provoked the violence at the Democratic convention.

Most of the evidence against the Seven came from informers who had mingled with the antiwar demonstrators in Lincoln and Grant parks and had taken everything they heard literally. An undercover policewoman testified that Abbie Hoffman had yelled: "We need a lot of weapons. Get rocks, bricks, stones. Break the bricks in half—they're easier to conceal that way and the girls can carry them." An undercover policeman said the defendants had been determined to create violence as "the first step of the revolution." A Chicago official told the court that Abbie had said to him: "If the city was smart, it would give $100,000 to sponsor our festival. Better yet, give me $100,000 and I'll leave town." The official had construed this as attempted extortion.

After nearly five months of testimony and argument the jury retired and the judge, with obvious relish, began meting out sentences for contempt. It took him two days, with time out for the defendants' screams. As Kunstler heard his clients and his co-counsel being sent away—Weinglass was given two months—he staggered all over the courtroom and collapsed, sobbing, "My life has come to naught at your hands, Judge. Come to mine. Come to mine. Take me next, I don't want to be here any more." The judge took him last. Saying, "No lawyer has ever said the things to me that you said during this trial," he gave him four years and thirteen days in prison.

The jury acquitted all the defendants of conspiracy but convicted Davis, Dellinger, Hayden, Hoffman, and Rubin of crossing state lines to incite a riot. The judge sentenced each of them to five years in prison, fined each $5,000, and assessed them the costs of the prosecution—another $50,000. But the sentences didn't stand. Nearly three years later a U.S. Court of Appeals reversed the convictions. The appellate court found the controversial antiriot statute —the so-called Rap Brown Act—constitutional by a two to one vote but threw out the verdict, citing Judge Hoffman's "antagonistic" behavior and finding that his "deprecatory" attitude toward the defense was "evident in the record from the very beginning."

Indeed, far from vindicating the prosecution, the case of the Chicago Seven became the first of an unparalleled series of judicial disasters for the government. It was followed by the trials of the Harrisburg Seven, the Camden Seventeen, the Seattle Seven, the Kansas City Four, the Evanston Four, the Pentagon Papers case, and the Gainesville Eight. In each of them the defendants were heretics in the eyes of the established order, and in every case the accused were vindicated by a jury, a judge, or an appeals court. Hostility to informers and judicial bias were common threads in the findings. In addition, as Martin Arnold pointed out in the *New York Times*, "despite all evidence to the contrary, people generally believe that the government is competent, and it angers them when the government goes into court with a weak case, often incompetently presented."

The Vietnam War, the real fuel for the riots which had been blamed on the Seven, continued to divide and abrade the country in 1970. At the beginning of the year there had been hope for something better. During the first four months the news from Saigon had been mildly encouraging. U.S. troops under General Abrams were avoiding big battles with the Viet Cong and the North Vietnamese. Nixon was reducing American troops from 543,000 to 340,000, and he assured the country that another 60,000 grunts would be withdrawn by May 1. But an end to the war seemed as remote as ever. In Paris the Communists scorned a five-point Nixon peace proposal, saying, "Our rejection is firm, total, and categorical." David K. E. Bruce, the chief American negotiator, turned down a Communist plan, calling it "old wine in new bottles."

U.S. combat deaths, which had stood at 25,000 during the Chicago protests two years earlier, now passed the 44,000 mark. Barring a breakthrough, Washington let it be known, some 200,000 American soldiers would stay in Vietnam for years. War weariness was becoming increasingly evident in the United States, among the South Vietnamese, and in fighting units. Grunts in the 4th U.S. Division refused to go into battle until they had been persuaded by desperate officers; troops in another division reviled Nixon, shouting obscenities about him when they spotted a war correspondent; soldiers wore peace medals with their dog tags; estimates of marijuana use among U.S. servicemen ran as high as 80 percent, while deaths from overdoses of hard drugs almost tripled. Augmenting all this was an appearance of incompetence at the highest levels of the American military effort. U.S. paratroopers executed a daring raid on a POW camp at Son Tay, twenty-three miles from Hanoi; seventy to a hundred American fliers were believed to be imprisoned there. The raid would have been a success, but intelligence had blundered—all the POWs had been moved. That same week U.S. warplanes pounded North Vietnam for twenty-four hours. The Pentagon first said the sorties were part of a "protective reaction" operation, protecting unarmed American aircraft, then changed its story to acknowledge that supply bases were being attacked. In fact, the shocked nation later learned, the targets of the bombardiers had included hospitals.

Abandonment of the Saigon government was out of the question, the White House declared, because the Communists were said to have a list of three million Vietnamese who would be "dealt with" in a "blood bath." The existence of the list was a matter of some skepticism, and Americans in increasing numbers were ready to desert the regime of General Nguyen Van Thieu anyway. The South Vietnamese seemed unappreciative of their American ally, even hostile toward it. Saigon rioters burned Nixon in effigy, shouting "Down with the Americans" and accusing the United States of prolonging the war. Ominously, Buddhists with kerosene and matches were immolating themselves, as other bonzes had just before the overthrow of Ngo Dinh Diem. David Truong, the son of a South Vietnamese politician, toured the U.S. telling audiences that the grunts and the ARVN troops fighting beside them shared only a mutual hatred of each other.

Meantime the notion that Americans were fighting to defend an Asian democracy was becoming difficult to sustain. David's father ran against Thieu and was clapped in jail, becoming one of over 80,000 political prisoners of the Saigon government. Americans in the field reported the torture of the regime's critics and their convictions by kangaroo courts; the courts continued to sit even after Saigon's supreme court ruled that they were unconstitutional. And Thieu's demands for U.S. wealth appeared to be insatiable. After nearly a decade of unstinting support of Saigon by Washington, he continued to say that he needed more equipment from the United States, more time to train his troops, and a lot more money. Unless he got them, he said, he couldn't take responsibility for the consequences.

The last thing Americans wanted that year was a war in another Southeast Asian country, but that was what the administration gave them. Actually their Air Force had been hammering Communist bases in eastern Cambodia for over a year, though few of them knew it. On orders from the White House, B-52s had conducted 3,630 secret raids on jungle sanctuaries there. The Joint Chiefs had long wanted to send in the infantry. Nixon had demurred at that; he knew that Cambodia's ruler, Prince Norodom Sihanouk, would protest the violation of his country's neutrality. With double bookkeeping and tight security it was possible to suppress information about the B-52 sorties. Once U.S. troops lunged across the frontier that would be impracticable.

On March 18, however, the Cambodian situation was changed dramatically by a coup. Sihanouk, aware that his administration was threatened, was in Russia asking for Soviet help in his effort to get

40,000 Viet Cong and North Vietnamese troops out of his country, when Cambodian General Lon Nol took over the government. Lon Nol was a rightist; he wouldn't denounce a U.S.-ARVN expedition to drive out the Communist intruders. Six weeks after the coup Nixon went on television to tell Americans that an operation to do just that was under way. Its goal was to be the destruction of the Vietnam nerve center, base camps, and underground arsenals above the "Parrot's Beak" northwest of Saigon. "For five years," the President said "neither the United States nor South Vietnam has moved against these sanctuaries because we did not want to violate the territory of a neutral nation." He did not mention the clandestine bombing of Cambodia, which at that time had been in process for fourteen months.

The military value of the invasion of Cambodia was disputed. While it was still being mounted Nixon described it as "an enormous success—far exceeding expectations." Asked about Pentagon claims that the Viet Cong would need six to nine months to recover from it, Thieu said, "I say they will never recover. Cambodia from 1964 to 1969 was a second North Vietnam, a whole rear area." In Saigon, MACV claimed the seizure of 15 million rounds of ammunition, 7,250 tons of food, and 25,000 guns; the death of 11,285 enemy soldiers; and the capture of 2,156. Allied casualties were 1,138 killed and 4,911 wounded.

But now Cambodia had been drawn into the war. The Communist troops which had been squatting in the Parrot's Beak responded to the offensive by driving westward against Lon Nol's army, conquering half the country, threatening its capital, Phnom Penh, and establishing a new, secure supply route in the Mekong valley. Washington was now committed to a new regime which was even less defensible than Thieu's. And some of the expedition's Cambodian goals were unachieved because they had been wholly unrealistic. "American officials," Frances FitzGerald noted in *Fire in the Lake,* "spoke of plans to capture the enemy's command headquarters for the south as if there existed a reverse Pentagon in the jungle complete with Marine guards, generals, and green baize tables." No such command post was found because, of course, there had never been any.

The greatest damage wrought by the Cambodian adventure was its impact on the home front. So great was the public outcry against this new involvement that the Senate, stirring at last to invoke the congressional right to declare war, passed a measure demanding an evacuation of American troops from Cambodia and an end to air support there by July. On campuses the reaction eclipsed all previous protests. By the end of May 415 colleges and universities had been disrupted. It was the first general student strike in the country's history, and it was entirely spontaneous. At the end of the semester 286 schools were still paralyzed, and while 129 others in forty-three states had officially reopened, many classrooms were empty.

On the weekend of May 9–10, more than 100,000 students stormed Washington. The White House was transformed into an armed camp behind a bumper-to-bumper wall of transit buses. The President's first response was contemptuous; talking informally with some Pentagon secretaries, he called the protesters "bums." Then he decided to make a conciliatory gesture. On Friday night of that week he went to the Lincoln Memorial with his valet and Secret Service agents and tried to talk to students sleeping there. "I feel just as deeply as you do about this," he said to them. Trying to find common ground, he launched into a discussion of football and asked one of the students, a Californian, if he enjoyed surfing. "The two Americas," wrote a team of reporters for the London *Sunday Times,* "met and drifted apart in a state of mutual incomprehension."

Equally bewildering for the President was a letter to him from Secretary of the Interior Walter J. Hickel. Hickel had been a conservative businessman, but he was also the father of six sons. He protested that the administration was alienating youth. He was particularly incensed over attacks on the young by Vice President Agnew. Nixon's public response was propitiatory; he assured the secretary that members of the administration would cool their rhetoric. But Hickel had committed a cardinal sin. His letter had appeared in the newspapers before it reached the oval office. On Thanksgiving eve Nixon summoned him to the White House and fired him for lack of "mutual confidence." Within a few hours one of H. R. Haldeman's assistants arrived at the Department of the Interior with a list of men to be purged. Six senior officials were told: "We want your resignation, and we want you out of the building by five o'clock."

If that was tough, the actions on some campuses were rougher. A revolutionist's bomb tore out the sides of the University of Wisconsin's Army Mathematics Research Center, killing a physicist, wounding four, and doing six million dollars' worth of damage.* At predominantly black Jackson State, in Mississippi, an encounter between students and police in front of a dormitory ended tragically when officers opened fire with buckshot, machine gun, rifle and armor-piercing shells, killing two students and wounding nine. A presidential commission headed by former Pennsylvania Governor William W. Scranton called the 28-second fusillade "an unreasonable, unjustified overreaction," but a local grand jury blamed the students, declaring that "when people . . . engage in civil disorders and riots, they must expect to be injured or killed when law enforcement officers are required to reestablish order."

Mississippians weren't the only Americans in that troubled year to feel that students were fair game, and Negroes weren't the only victims. Flag-carrying hardhat Manhattan construction workers who marched into a crowd of antiwar demonstrators that May were enormously popular; when the White House commended them it was interpreted as smart politics. Hostility toward youth cut deep. Older Americans were offended by almost every facet of the youthful subculture: the long hair, the tie-dyed jeans, the loud music, the language, the gestures, the very names of the rock groups—the Cream, the Stones, the Grand Funk Railroad. Most objectionable of all were the heavy drugs. The college students, whom younger teen-agers slavishly aped, put up outrageous psychedelic posters of bleeding colors and distorted images; they spoke casually of getting spaced out, turned on, tuned in, getting it on, getting into it, getting funky or freaky or heavy from narcotics, and they lured adolescents away from parents with rock jamborees which appeared to be, and sometimes were, steeped in sin.

Woodstock had been the high-water mark for the rock bacchanals. According to John Morthland, assistant editor of the weekly *Rolling Stone*, of the forty-eight major festivals slated the following year, only eighteen were held. "The major reason," said Morthland, "is political. The day after a festival is announced, the city council and police come up with some emergency ordinance that makes it impossible to hold it." Authorities taking such steps were acting with the approval—often the entreaties—of residents who had seen

* In November 1973 Karleton Lewis Armstrong, twenty-seven, was convicted of the bombing and sentenced to twenty-three years in prison. His counsel was William Kunstler.

and heard enough of the subculture to know that they didn't want it celebrated in their backyards. They felt vindicated and then some by stories about 1970's most notorious rock gala: the Powder Ridge festival in Middlefield, Connecticut.

Actually Powder Ridge was a nongala; it never went on as scheduled. Promoters had signed up twenty-five bands to play at the three-hundred-acre ski area, but four days before the affair was to begin a citizens' committee convinced a judge that the tiny community didn't have to endure the noise, the pot, the kids in the buff, and the Viet Cong flags. He issued an injunction. That turned the musicians away, but it was too late to stop the audience from gathering; the occasion had been advertised in underground newspapers as far away as Los Angeles, the throng was already on its way, and it arrived, 35,000 strong, on the Friday of that first weekend in August. No entertainment awaited it, no food, no adequate plumbing facilities. Powder Ridge was a disaster waiting to happen, and it happened.

The heat was sweltering, and after pitching their colorful tents the youths divested themselves of clothes. On the first day they swam nude in a small pond beside the ski lodge, but so many of them voided and defecated in it that on Saturday the pond was declared a health hazard. Sanitation was a concern of Dr. William Abruzzi, a bearded, bald physician who was there as a volunteer, but it wasn't his chief worry; that was narcotics. Peddlers roamed through the crowd hawking marijuana, cocaine, heroin ("only a dollar-five-oh for magic magic"), barbiturates, speed, and LSD ("Acid here, the quality goes in before the name goes on"). State police arrested seventy pushers leaving the crowd, one of them with $13,000 in his pocket, but most of them got away. Kids who couldn't afford the hucksters' prices could drink free from vast buckets of "electric water," into which passers-by were asked to drop any drugs they could spare. This ugly stew was blamed by Abruzzi for many of the thousand bad trips he treated, more than the number at Woodstock, where the multitude had been over ten times as large. Every Middlefield resident had tales of what the doped youngsters did. One of the more sensational scenes, attested to by several witnesses, occurred in a small wood near some homes. A boy and a girl, both naked and approaching from different directions, met under the trees. On impulse they suddenly embraced. She dropped to her knees, he mounted her from behind, and after he had achieved his climax they parted—apparently without exchanging a word.

Obviously Powder Ridge had nothing to do with antiwar protest, but to its critics the subculture of the young was all of a piece; any one aspect of it reminded them of the others. The most memorable symbol of college backlash in the days after Nixon's announcement of the Cambodian invasion, the Kent State tragedy, didn't start as a protest. By all accounts the first phases of the disorders there would have occurred anyhow. Unlike Columbia and Berkeley, the university in Kent, Ohio, had no tradition of activism. Football was still big in Kent; after a triumph students would ring the Victory Bell on the Commons. There were proms and bull-and-beer joints in the town. Indeed, the trouble started with a beer bust that muggy Friday night.

Spilling out from a bar, students decided to dance in the street. An angry motorist gunned his engine as if to drive into them. Several young drunks climbed on the car, broke its windows, set fires in trash barrels, and smashed store windows. On orders from Mayor LeRoy Satrom, Kent policemen turned the roisterers out of the taverns. Driving them back toward the campus, they broke up the diehards with tear gas. The next day Kent State's few political militants secured administration approval for a rally that evening. Out of an enrollment of nearly twenty thousand, about eight hundred students came. Shouting "One two three four, we don't want your fucking war!" at faculty members and student marshals, the crowd turned the rally into a demonstration. It got out of hand and disrupted a dance; lighted railroad flares were thrown through the windows of a one-story ROTC building facing the Commons. When firemen appeared, the demonstrators pelted them with rocks and chopped up their hoses with machetes. The building burned to the ground.

Without notifying the university administration, Mayor Satrom appealed for help from the National Guard. Governor James Rhodes responded by sending a five-hundred-man contingent equipped with M-1 rifles, Colt revolvers, and tear gas. Students greeted them by spraying trees with gasoline and setting them afire, but by midnight on Sunday the fires were out and everything seemed to be under control. Meantime Governor Rhodes had arrived on campus. On Tuesday Ohio Republicans were going to vote in a senatorial primary, and Rhodes was one of the candidates. He was trailing badly—in the event he would lose—but he was making a last effort to turn the tide. The situation in Kent seemed exploitable. Calling a press conference, he declared an emergency and said of the students, "We're going to use every weapon of law enforcement to drive them out of Kent . . . They're worse than the Brownshirts, and the Communist element and also the night riders and the vigilantes. They're the worst type of people that we harbor in America."

In fairness to Governor Rhodes, it should be pointed out that he was not the only student-baiter whose words reached the National Guardsmen. Attorney General Mitchell had attacked campus militants as rowdies; so had President Nixon and Vice President Agnew, who had been widely quoted as saying that "The troublemakers among the younger generation are only a bunch of hoodlums who don't deserve to bear the title of American youth." In Kent, Mayor Satrom was making inflammatory remarks, while Brigadier General Robert H. Canterbury of the Guard was virtually inciting to riot. Having sowed the wind, they reaped the whirlwind at noon Monday. Classes were resumed that day and the campus at first appeared to be quiet. Several students rang the Victory Bell at midday and about a thousand gathered for a peaceful demonstration on the Commons while another two thousand watched. Two jeeps appeared. Guardsmen in them shouted through bullhorns: "Evacuate the Commons area. You have no right to assemble." Students raised their middle fingers, flung some stones and yelled: "Pigs off campus! We don't want your war." Brigadier General Canterbury told reporters, "These students are going to have to find out what law and order is all about." Major General Sylvester Del Corso of the Guard, in full view of his troops, picked up several rocks and threw them back at students.

It was now about a quarter past twelve. Two skirmish lines of Guardsmen fired tear gas canisters into the crowd; a few students tossed them back, but they fell short. Other students fled, and a unit of about a hundred troopers chased some of them between two buildings. There the Guardsmen found themselves hemmed in, with a fence in front of them and rock-throwing students on either side. Their plight was not really serious; the rocks didn't come close enough to hit them, and many of the onlookers were laughing. At this point the troopers ran out of tear gas and began retreating up a hill, looking apprehensively over their shoulders. It was a dangerous situation. The Guardsmen were capable of savagery—over the weekend they had bayoneted three students—and their M-1 rifles were loaded with live ammunition. As a presidential commission headed by former Pennsylvania Governor William W. Scranton later put it, "all that stood between the Guardsmen and firing was a flick of a thumb on a safety mechanism and the pull of an index finger on a trigger."

There were suggestions afterward that a group of troopers decided to fire on their tormentors. Photographs show eight or ten of them gathered in what witnesses described as a "huddle." Another curious piece of evidence is a tape of the incident. On it, the fatal thirteen-second salvo is preceded by a single shot. This could have been fired, either as a signal or from fear, by Terence F. Norman, a spurious "freelance photographer" who was really an informer on the FBI payroll. (In addition he may have been in the employ of the university, which also had undercover men.) Norman had a gun, and some spectators say he drew it and fired it, either just before or just after the crucial moment. What is certain is that on reaching the top of the slope at 12:24 P.M. the troopers knelt, aimed at the students, who were hundreds of feet away, too far to harm them, and fired as though on command. (Brigadier General Canterbury, in their midst, managed to be looking the other way.) The fusillade was followed by an awful silence. Into it a girl screamed, "My God, they're killing us!"

Thirteen students had been shot, and four—none of them a militant and one an ROTC cadet—were dead. A stream of blood was gushing from the head of one youth, drenching the textbooks he had been carrying; another boy was holding a cloth against a friend's stomach, trying vainly to stem the bleeding. The troopers made no attempt to help their victims.

In the immediate aftermath none of them were prosecuted for the killings. Although Attorney General Mitchell declared that American education was experiencing the "saddest semester" in its history—"There can be no greater evidence of disorder in society than the sound of gunfire on a college campus," he said—and though an investigation by three hundred FBI agents concluded that the Guardsmen had been in no physical danger, and that they conspired afterward to blame the incident on a threatening mob which never existed, the Justice Department declined even to convene a federal grand jury. Long afterward this was done, but not until March of 1974 were eight indictments handed down.

At the time, an Ohio grand jury exonerated the troopers—and indicted instead twenty-five others, including the president of the student body. Although none of them were convicted, there was a widespread feeling that the victims had got what was coming to them. It was strengthened when President Nixon implied that violent protest had brought violence in return; the incident, he said, "should remind us once again that when dissent turns to violence it invites tragedy." The Scranton Commission said that "61 shots by Guardsmen certainly cannot be justified." Vice President Agnew called their report "pablum for permissiveness," and added that responsibility for what had happened lay with the students, "on the steps of the university administration, and at the door of the faculty lounge." Any other interpretation, he said, would be "scapegoating of the most irresponsible sort."

The campus disorders which greeted Nixon's announcement of the Cambodian adventure formed a key link in the chain of events which led, ultimately, to the burglarizing of the Democratic National Committee's offices in the Watergate complex in Washington two years later. The first link had been a story in the *New York Times* of May 19, 1969, under the byline of William Beecher, who covered the Defense Department for the paper. It began: "American B-52 bombers in recent weeks have raided several Vietcong and North Vietnamese supply dumps in Cambodia for the first time, according to Nixon administration sources, but Cambodia has not made any protest."

Nixon was dismayed. He felt that his worst fears about the irresponsibility of the eastern establishment press had been confirmed, and believed them reconfirmed when the *Times* published technical details of American preparation for the Strategic Arms Limitation Talks (SALT) talks with Russia. Under the Constitution there was little he could do about Beecher and his paper, but he could at least hunt the unknown informants in his administration who were leaking classified information to newspapermen. He consulted Henry Kissinger, who drew up a list of thirteen officials, including five of his own National Security Council aides, who knew about the secret Cambodian bombing. On orders from the President, their telephones were tapped by the FBI; so were the phones of four journalists who had published leaked material: Beecher; Hedrick Smith, the *Times* man at the State Department; Marvin Kalb of CBS; and Henry Brandon of the London *Sunday Times*.

It was the White House's first incursion into the twilight zone of questionable activity, and it was fruitless; Beecher's source was never found.

The President began to entertain misgivings about the efficiency of both Hoover's FBI and Richard Helms's CIA. His doubts deepened after the events of May 1970. Nixon was convinced that the campus outbreaks were the work of foreign instigators, probably Cubans, Egyptians, and eastern Europeans. He asked the CIA to identify them. After an extensive investigation the agency reported that all the agitators were native Americans. The President gave the FBI the same assignment; the bureau brought back the same explanation. Still dissatisfied, the oval office ordered more wiretaps and—something new—house break-ins to search suspected offices and homes. The programs were to be directed by a new domestic security panel consisting of the country's top intelligence men: Hoover, Helms, and the directors of the Defense Intelligence Agency and the National Security Agency. Their marching orders were to be drawn up by a twenty-nine-year-old Hoosier lawyer and presidential speech writer named Tom Charles Huston.

On June 5, 1970, the four intelligence chiefs met in the President's office, were photographed with him, and were told that he wanted them to form a committee supervising national security, with Hoover as chairman. They were to go into action on August 1. Meantime Huston would draft operational plans with the FBI director. During one of their early meetings Hoover tried to dampen the young lawyer's enthusiasm for illegal schemes by explaining the historical development of objective intelligence. Huston replied impatiently, "We're not talking about the dead past; we're talking about the living present." In addition to electronic surveillance and surreptitious entry, his plan envisaged opening mail, recruiting more FBI informers on campuses, and CIA spying on students and other Americans living abroad.

As an attorney, the Indianan was aware that second-story jobs and what he called "mail coverage" were felonies, but he wanted to go ahead anyway. He wrote: "Use of this technique is clearly illegal; it amounts to burglary. It is also highly risky and could result in great embarrassment if exposed. However, it is also the most fruitful tool and can produce the type of intelligence which cannot be obtained in any other fashion." He argued that the advantages "outweigh the risks." Hoover disagreed. In a footnote to the Huston report the director said he didn't want to be chairman of the panel and didn't even want to be a member of it. Huston felt wounded. He sent Haldeman a memorandum in early July commenting on the FBI director's comment: "His objections are generally inconsistent and frivolous—most express concern about possible embarrassment to the intelligence community (i.e., Hoover) from public exposure." On July 23 Nixon signed a "decision memo," drafted by the young lawyer, approving the plan, but when Hoover saw it he protested to Mitchell, who discussed it with the President, who dropped the whole thing. Embittered, Huston resigned that fall and went home to practice law in Indianapolis. His intelligence duties were assigned to a White House newcomer, presidential counsel John Wesley Dean III.

The following spring the *Times* began publishing fresh Pentagon leaks, and Nixon concluded that his administration had become a sieve, that something must be done, that he would have to bypass Hoover. Accordingly, the President established a Special Investigations Unit whose job, as he himself later explained, was to "stop security leaks and to investigate other sensitive security matters."

Unknown to one another then, the men who would make presidential burglary the prelude to the American scandal of the century had been emerging from governmental careers, thus becoming available for new employment. E. Howard Hunt, whose CIA career had been going downhill since the American ambassador in Madrid refused to approve his assignment as deputy station chief there, on the ground that he was an intriguer, had retired at the time of the Kent State tragedy. Four months later James W. McCord Jr. resigned from the CIA, and eight months after that G. Gordon Liddy was fired by the Treasury Department because of an unauthorized speech praising gun ownership at a National Rifle Association rally.

David Young, a thirty-two-year-old lawyer from Kissinger's staff, opened the Special Investigations Unit's headquarters in room 16 in the basement of the Executive Office Building. The *New York Times* carried a brief item reporting that Young and a colleague, Egil Krogh Jr., were doing something about leaks. One of Young's relatives read it and said to him, "Your grandfather would be proud of you, working on leaks at the White House. He was a plumber." David put a sign on the door of his new office: "Mr. Young—Plumber."

The off-year elections of 1970 were waged by the GOP leadership on the basis of a principle laid down by Murray Chotiner, Richard Nixon's first campaign mentor. It was, quite simply, that Americans vote against candidates, not for them. An aspirant for office following Chotiner's precept gave only nominal attention to his own program. Instead he blazed away at the least attractive aspects of his opponent's record, ideas, mannerisms, and private life. If the aspirant couldn't find anything, he invented something. These tactics were what the President's critics had in mind when they spoke of the Old Nixon. The GOP strategy that autumn was to convert all the party's nominees into Old Nixons. It was to be the first hundred-million-dollar congressional election, and the chief Republican firehorse would be the Vice President, or, as presidential adviser Bryce Harlow called him, "Power-pack Agnew."

Certainly the party needed a boost of some sort. The previous November Nixon's approval rating in the Gallup poll had touched 68 percent, but since then it had been eroded by worsening inflation, Cambodia, the Calley case, and rising unemployment. Early in the year Nixon told GOP leaders that they would lose in November if the jobless rate touched 5.5 percent. It went to 5.8 and hit 6 percent before the end of the year. The SALT talks were going well, and in March the nuclear nonproliferation pact was signed, yet neither these nor the administration's plan for revenue sharing generated much interest in the electorate. Its welfare reform plans also lacked appeal. Nixon's vow to preserve "neighborhood schools" without busing was well received in the South, but it angered Negroes in the North, and with the emergence of the black middle class the Negro vote was becoming formidable. By November the country would have thirteen black congressmen, 81 black mayors, 198 black state legislators, and 1,567 local black officeholders.

In the White House the Vice President was regarded as admirably suited to campaign under Chotiner's colors. During his first year in Washington he had been remarkably active at the lectern, delivering seventy-seven major speeches, and his audiences had been large and appreciative. A Gallup poll in 1970 placed him third among America's most respected men, just behind the President and Billy Graham. To be sure, eleven faculty members at the University of Minnesota had appealed to him to stop "driving moderates into the hands of the extremists." Senator George McGovern had called him "a divisive, damaging influence," and Republican Governor Francis

Sargent had announced that he was unwelcome in Massachusetts. But college professors and McGovern were already recognized as the administration's natural enemies, while Sargent's state, with 300,000 students among its inhabitants, had become identified as the most liberal in the union. In any event, Agnew had been among the first members of the administration to spurn the President's inaugural plea to Americans to "stop shouting at one another" ("I intend to be heard over the din," the Vice President had said, "even if it means raising my voice"), and Middle Americans delighted in the choicer passages of Agnewian bombast:

> Some newspapers dispose of their garbage by printing it.
>
> Asking Senator Fulbright's advice on foreign policy is like asking the Boston strangler to massage your neck.
>
> If, in challenging, we polarize the American people, I say it is time for a positive polarization.
>
> Violence rewarded breeds further violence and perpetual violence ultimately produces a brutal counterreaction.
>
> The disease of our times is an artificial and masochistic sophistication—the vague uneasiness that our values are false, that there is something wrong with being patriotic, honest, moral, and hardworking.

Agnew covered 32,000 miles while stumping thirty-two states in the fall of 1970. He set the tone for his campaign in a Palm Springs, California, press conference on September 13, when he called on the electorate to reject the Democrats as "radical liberals." Subsequently he capsulized this as "radic-libs," explaining that the politicians he had in mind could be "depended upon to vote against the interests of law and order and against the interests of a representative society and against the foreign policy of the United States virtually every time." While not endorsing all aspirants in his own party—"I would have to put one Republican senator who seeks election in that group. That's Senator Goodell of New York"—he condemned all opposition nominees: "The Democratic candidates are a team of permissive candidates who have a penchant for indulging the disorderly and fawning upon lawbreakers." His sesquipedalian prose was enlivened by two presidential speech writers, William Safire and Pat Buchanan. With them as phrasemakers, he denounced senatorial doves as "solons of sellout" and "pampered prodigies." All Democratic nominees were lumped together as "nattering nabobs of negativism," "pusillanimous pussyfooters," "vicars of vacillation," "troglodytic leftists," and "hopeless, hysterical hypochondriacs of history" catering to "foolish fads of phony intellectualism." Of his fustian rhetoric he said he liked metaphors and alliteration, "but I don't need gimmicks to get my message across. I am simply stating what America is all about."

Agreeing with him, the President sounded much the same theme while campaigning 17,240 miles in twenty-two states over twenty-three days. In all of them he was on the attack. Like Agnew, he defended no record, described no goals, acclaimed no ideals; that would have violated Chotiner's rule. Instead he stumped against students, narcotics, the SDS, rioters, draft dodgers, flag burners, homosexuals, criminals, promiscuity, and pornography, identifying all of them with the Democrats. The climax came the night before the election, when the Republicans rebroadcast on television one of the President's most strident speeches. The previous Thursday evening in San Jose, California, demonstrators had pelted his limousine with eggs and rocks, tried to smash the windows, and hammered on the doors. "You had to see their faces," an aide who was with him said later; "the hate in those faces—it got to him." *Time* noted that the episode had been "condemned in all responsible and even quasi-responsible quarters." Nevertheless, speaking after it in Phoenix, the President had seemed to blame all his critics for what had happened. He pledged that "No band of violent thugs is going to keep me from going out and speaking with the American people" —the implication was that Democrats were out to stop him—and said of the dissenters, "They're not romantic revolutionaries. They're the same thugs and hoodlums that have always plagued the good people." He concluded: "Our approach, the new approach, demands new and strong laws that will give the peace forces new muscle to deal with the criminal forces in the United States."

The quality of the election eve rebroadcast, like the message it bore, was scratchy, and at times all but incoherent. It lasted fifteen minutes. The next quarter-hour was given over to a paid reply from Senator Edmund Muskie of Maine, speaking for the other party. Muskie was calm, measured—and devastating. Noting that Nixon and Agnew had maligned Democrats and accused them of disloyalty, he said: "That is a lie, and the American people know it is a lie. . . . There are only two kinds of politics . . . the politics of fear and the politics of trust. One says: you are encircled by monstrous dangers. . . . The other says: the world is a baffling and hazardous place, but it can be shaped to the will of men. . . . Thus in voting for the Democratic Party tomorrow you cast your vote for trust . . . for trusting your fellow citizens . . . and most of all for trust in yourself."

Everyone, Muskie pointed out, believes in law and order; the Democrats had voted for the administration's bills to control crime. But what about racial tension, the environment, the economy? And what about national unity? He said: "There are those who seek to turn our common distress to partisan advantages, not by offering better solutions but with empty threat and malicious slander." He called on the voters to repudiate them.

They did. The Democrats gained twelve House seats, widening their margin to 255–180. The Republicans lost eleven governorships. They had led, with 32 statehouses to 18; now they trailed 29–21. The average Democratic candidate ran three percentage points ahead of 1968. Early in the campaign the GOP had entertained hopes of winning eight Senate seats and regaining control there. It had seemed possible, for the Democrats had twice as many Senate seats at stake. After the smoke had cleared, the Republicans had picked up just two of them, and one was of doubtful value; in Connecticut a conservative Democrat, Thomas J. Dodd, had been replaced by a liberal Republican, Lowell P. Weicker Jr.

Trying to put the best possible face on the results, Nixon claimed an "ideological victory," pointing to the defeat of Albert Gore in Tennessee, Joseph Tydings in Maryland, and Charles Goodell in New York, where Conservative party candidate James Buckley had won a three-way race with only 39 percent of the vote. But these gains were offset by the successes of Adlai Stevenson III in Illinois and John V. Tunney in California, and the Texas defeat of George Bush, whom the administration had strongly backed. Most discouraging for the White House were omens for the 1972 election. Apart from Tennessee, the celebrated GOP southern strategy had achieved nothing. Elsewhere Republicans had lost several key legislatures. Special Nixon-Agnew efforts had failed in New Jersey, Wisconsin, North Dakota, Florida, Nevada, and New Mexico, and they had done badly in big states—California, Pennsylvania, Ohio, and Michigan—where the next presidential race would probably be decided.

The president of the liberal Republican Ripon Society summed up the outcome as the GOP's "worst showing since 1964," and said of Nixon's interpretation that "to the degree he claims he has a working ideological majority now, he cannot use Congress as a scapegoat in 1972." The standing joke among Republican governors assembling after the election in Sun Valley, Idaho, was that they should have met in Death Valley. The governor of Indiana, which had given the President his biggest plurality two years earlier, said he was in trouble even there; the governor of New Mexico warned his fellow Republicans that the GOP had "lost the election because the strategy was completely negative." "In November 1970," wrote columnists Rowland Evans and Robert Novak, "the Presidency of Richard Nixon . . . hit bottom." In fact it sank lower. That winter Gallup showed the percentage of Americans who approved of the President dropping from 56 percent to 51 to 50 to 49. In the Harris poll Muskie surged ahead of Nixon by three points, and in subsequent months his margin widened to five points and then to eight points—47 to 39. *Newsweek* raised the possibility that Nixon might be a one-term President.

It was against this background that Nixon and his chief political advisers gathered in Key Biscayne for a postmortem—one of them, reflecting their host's fondness for sports cant, called it "going over the game plan." Mitchell, who was particularly gloomy, said the President had acted as though he had been "running for sheriff." All agreed that they could not afford a repeat performance two years hence. Starting now, Nixon must appear to be aloof from partisan politics, doing his job as President. The new chairman of the Republican National Committee would be Senator Robert Dole of Kansas, a GOP stalwart and a hard-liner.

But that wasn't the most important decision at the meeting. As one who was there put it afterward, "We knew we were in a damn tough fight, and we weren't going to entrust it to a bunch of cautious old hacks down at the committee." Another said later, "The decision was to get politics the hell out of the White House and across the street"—across the street being the steel and glass tower at 1701 Pennsylvania Avenue, a hundred and fifty yards from the White House. There the independent Citizens Committee for the Reelection of the President opened its second-floor offices in March 1971 amid new furniture, fashionable interior decoration, and deep orange pile carpeting. Until John Mitchell resigned from the Justice Department and took it over, it would be run by a protégé of Haldeman's, Jeb Stuart Magruder. Magruder's director of security was to be James W. McCord Jr. His counsel was G. Gordon Liddy. The committee itself was to become known to all, Republicans and Democrats alike, as CREEP.

Early Seventies Montage

IS MOTHER'S MILK FIT FOR HUMAN CONSUMPTION?

AT&T UP 1000% SINCE 1932

Hello darkness, my old friend
I've come to talk with you again
Because a vision softly creeping
Left its seeds while I was sleeping
And the vision that was planted in my brain
Still remains,
Echoing the sound of silence.

You don't need to be a weatherman
To know which way the wind blows

Masters and Johnson estimate that one-half of the marriages in the United States are threatend by sexual dysfunction

Virginia Slims

INSTAMATIC SALES HIT 50,000,000

NIXON PLEDGES SMALL STAFF, OPEN ADMINISTRATION

They Ran Out of Tear Gas

Kent State 1970

Allison Krause, 19
Sandra Lee Scheuer, 20
Jeffrey Glenn Miller, 20
William K. Schroeder, 19

Best Sellers FICTION
Love Story Segal
Islands in the Stream Hemingway
Crystal Cave Stewart
God Is an Englishman Delderfield
The French Lieutenant's Woman Fowles

SILENT MAJORITY

AMERICAN GIs SPREAD CHRISTMAS JOY TO CHILDREN AROUND WORLD

1 IN 8 AMERICANS GET SOCIAL SECURITY CHECKS

That's what it's all about
This has to be the richest country ever

— It can't be all that bad —

IKE DEAD

THE WHITE HOUSE
WASHINGTON

```
TO: The Staff                                  August 17, 1971
From: John Dean
     This memorandum addresses the matter of how we can
maximize the fact of our incumbency in dealing with
persons known to be active in their opposition to our
Administration.  Stated a bit more bluntly -- how we can
use the available federal machinery to screw our
political enemies.
```

moratorium

HOMOSEXUALS MARCH IN NEW YORK

BLACK NATIONALISTS PICK CITY AS TARGET

Is that all there is?
Is that all there is?
If that's not all there is, my friend,
Then let's keep dancing

Letting it all hang out

OUR AMERICAN MADNESS: WHY WE WORK SO HARD AT HAVING FUN

Portnoy's Complaint **(port'-noiz kəm-plānt')** ***n.*** **(after Alexander Portnoy 1933-   ) A disorder in which strongly felt ethical and altruistic impulses are perpetually warring with extreme sexual longings, often of a preverse nature . . . It is believed by Spielvogel that many of the symptoms can be traced to the bonds obtaining in the mother-child relationship.**

SELL 3,000 TOPLESS SWIM SUITS

Effete Snobs for Peace

```
Q: (to witness Atkins) Did there come a time when you killed
     Miss Tate?
A: Yes, I killed her
Q: Describe to the court what happened.
A: Well, I stabbed her, and she fell.  And I stabbed her again.
     I don't know how many times I stabbed her and I don't know
     why I stabbed her . . .
Q: But how can it be right to kill somebody?
A: How can it not be right when it's done with love?
```

— You better believe it —

Best Sellers NONFICTION
The Sensuous Woman "J"
Everything You Always Wanted to Know About Sex Reuben
Inside the Third Reich Speer
Future Shock Toffler
Zelda Milford

Raindrops keep falling on my head
But I'm not complaining
That my eyes will soon be red
Crying's not for me

Sorry about that

How's that for starters?

Ninety percent of all scientists who ever lived are alive now.

Go Naked

Thirty-six

THE DIVIDED STATES OF AMERICA

THAT WINTER NOSTALGIA became big business. Wooden cigar store Indians were bringing as much as $4,000 each; *Superman* comic books issued in 1938, $400. An Italian designer reintroduced the Rita Hayworth look, and his models, showing the shirt dresses and the flaring skirts, strolled to the piped rhythms of swing music. Coeds, reaching even farther back into the past, wore ankle-length turn-of-the-century frocks and steel-rimmed granny glasses. Arrow Shirts were displayed in 1906 layouts; Hertz advertisements featured sepia-toned prints and obsolete Victorian type faces. Hippies wore Mickey Mouse watches. Over three hundred radio stations observed Halloween by rebroadcasting Orson Welles's *War of the Worlds*. One of the most remarkable—and profitable—shows on Broadway was a revival of the 1920s *No, No, Nanette*. In its first week it earned $35,000; tickets went for $25 apiece; "I Want to Be Happy" became a hit again. The choreography was by Busby Berkeley. The star was sixty-year-old Ruby Keeler. When she skipped into her first tap dance to the tune of "Tea for Two," the opening night audience leaped to its feet to give her a roaring ovation.

Among the extraordinary examples of yesterday's appeal was the 1971 reissue of Sears, Roebuck's Catalogue No. 104, for 1897, with new introductions by S. J. Perelman and Richard Rovere. The publishers expected it to be bought only by libraries for reference shelves. Instead it sold 200,000 copies at $14.95. Presently a Nostalgia Book Club opened offices, offering books of old movie ads, collections of pulp magazine stories, and the adventures of Dick Tracy,

Little Orphan Annie, and Buck Rogers. Nancy Drew and Hardy Boys mysteries were selling briskly. The Longines Symphonette Recording Society was reaching millions with albums of 1930s songs and radio broadcasts under such titles as *Remember the Golden Days of Radio, The Great Vocalists of the Big Band Era, Thanks for the Memory, The Years to Remember, Those Memory Years,* and *Theme Songs of the Big Band Era.* The most ambitious project along these lines was a series of Time-Life albums which rerecorded, in stereo sound, the great swing hits of Glenn Miller, Harry James, Artie Shaw, Tommy Dorsey, Les Brown, Woody Herman, Charlie Barnet, Jimmie Lunceford, Claude Thornhill, Lionel Hampton, and, of course, Benny Goodman.

The message was clear: Americans were yearning for the past because they were fed up with the present. Though 1971 was an eventful year, the character of the events was no improvement over 1970. Later inflation would make that of 1971 seem mild, but at the time it seemed outrageous. In February wholesale prices took their sharpest jump in seventeen years. Overall, the cost of living had risen 25 percent in five years. At the same time, FBI figures indicated that serious crimes had increased 176 percent in the 1960s. During the previous year there had been 5.5 million of them in the United States, and whereas one crime in three had been solved in 1960, the rate now was only one in five. Venereal disease had spread dismayingly. The incidence of gonorrhea had attained the proportions of a nationwide epidemic—with no vaccine to prevent infection.

Change continued to alter the country at a startling pace. The figures from the new census, now becoming available, showed among other things that the flight from U.S. farms in the 1960s had reduced the population living on the land by another 40 percent. Rootlessness was up again; six million Americans now lived in trailers. One useful measure of the shifting patterns in urban life was the growth of shopping centers. The first one had been built outside Portland, Maine, in 1959, and over the next decade retail business in the central city there plunged 71 percent. By the second year of the Nixon administration the nation had more than thirteen thousand shopping centers, with more devastating consequences for the stores of downtown America. Another set of figures with ominous implications—which were unappreciated by the Nixon administration—foretold the energy crisis. Since 1945 the consumption of gasoline in the United States had increased fourfold, and the use of electricity sixfold.

It was a rough year for tradition. Rolls-Royce went into receivership. The Army declared that henceforth married WACs and nurses could have babies and remain in uniform. Capitol Hill was rocked when a Weatherman bomb exploded in a men's lavatory just below the Senate chamber. The Roman Catholic Church announced that 1,400 parochial schools had closed their doors in the past five years. *Look* observed National Magazine Week by folding. The Bon Vivant Company, makers of fine soups, collapsed when New Jersey health authorities discovered that what they were selling was botulism; over 1.2 million cans of its vichyssoise had to be destroyed. Radicals won three of four available seats on the Berkeley City Council. The judgment "Thirty dollars or thirty days" was heard for the last time when the Supreme Court ruled that a defendant could not be imprisoned because he was unable to pay a fine.

Campuses were quiet in 1971. The impact of Kent State was obvious. A *Playboy* survey of student opinion found that only 36 percent said, "I would protest now," and even they added, "but not violently." A contributor to the *Daily Californian* wrote: "The level of life in Berkeley has degenerated. The despair of the junkie pervades much of the community. We sit around smoking dope or drinking or thinking of new stereos . . . all too many people are just waiting for life rather than living." John L. Erlich, professor of social work at the University of Michigan, said that "large numbers of students have become discouraged and alienated." Erlich also noted that "larger numbers are still committed to change," however. The chief difference was that activists had stopped demonstrating on campus. The zealots, and there were still a lot of them, were now concentrating on Washington. The cause of their loudest clamor—the war—was drearily the same. If 1970 had been the year of Cambodia in Indochina, 1971 was the year of Laos. In addition it marked an end to any lingering illusions that South Vietnam, under President Nguyen Van Thieu, was on its way to becoming a democracy.

The Gilbert and Sullivan character of South Vietnam's 1971 presidential campaign could be traced to the 1967 election. The Thieu-Ky ticket had won then, but because eleven candidates had been running, the winners had carried only 35 percent of the vote. Thieu hadn't liked that. It still rankled; he felt he had lost face. This time would be different. At his direction the Vietnamese assembly required future nominees who wanted a place on the ballot to secure the signatures of either forty assemblymen or a hundred provincial and municipal councilors (under the second option, each councilor's endorsement must be countersigned by his province chief).

Thieu had two serious challengers: Ky and the popular General Duong Van Minh. Ky and Minh reached a gentleman's agreement: they would stay out of each other's way. Minh also said that he would withdraw if he suspected electoral fraud. Fraud followed; Thieu's supreme court threw out Ky's candidacy on a technicality. Angered, Minh called at the U.S. embassy with proof of other Thieu measures showing that the president was rigging the election, among them written instructions to province chiefs to buy votes, to shift "unfriendly civil servants to other jobs," and to stuff ballot boxes. Minh then quit the race, explaining that he could not "put up with a disgusting farce that strips away all the people's hope of a democratic regime and bars reconciliation of the Vietnamese people."

That left Thieu without opposition, a situation which delighted him but alarmed Washington. After U.S. Ambassador Ellsworth Bunker had protested, the Vietnamese supreme court obligingly reversed itself, ruling that Ky was a valid nominee and that his name could be printed on the ballot. But Ky had pride, too. In addition he suspected that Thieu's orders to the province chiefs had effectively fixed the race. Thereupon *he* withdrew, naming the president as "the principal actor in the farce." The election was held as scheduled, and the principal actor in the farce received 94.3 percent of the vote, the balance representing mutilated ballots. Thieu announced that he was gratified by this "astounding" display of confidence in his leadership, but this was no time for him to be winning Pyrrhic victories. By the end of the year the American troop level there would be down to 158,000, and the ability of his army to stand on its own was in grave doubt.

A South Vietnamese campaign in Laos multiplied the doubts, which was ironic, because it was supposed to do the opposite. To prove the effectiveness of Vietnamization, 16,000 ARVN troops were ordered to cross the demilitarized zone (DMZ), penetrate Laos along route 9, and cut the Ho Chi Minh Trail, that legendary spiderweb of supply paths which by now was fifty miles wide at some points. Few planners in military history had been so careless of secrecy. For weeks in advance confident U.S. officers in Saigon briefed the press on the Hobson's choice which lay ahead for the enemy: the North Vietnamese would either have to abandon their Laotian bases or stand and fight, and if they fought they would be annihilated. To advertise the native character of the drive, a billboard was erected on route 9 two hundred yards from the border of Laos, reading NO U.S. PERSONNEL BEYOND THIS POINT. When reporters pointed out that the operation bore an American code name—Dewey Canyon II—the name was hastily changed to Lam Son 719.

Lam Son 719 was launched on February 8, 1971, to the accompaniment of the continuing drumbeat of publicity. The first reports claimed success. War correspondents knew only that the troops were moving slowly against no apparent opposition. An armored column took two weeks to move eleven miles. Then disaster struck. The enemy attacked with tanks, heavy rockets, massed artillery, and four of North Vietnam's best divisions. In Saigon the deputy U.S. commander, Major General Frederick Weyland, acknowledged that South Vietnam's losses were "worse than Tet." Stalled, the battalion commanders of Thieu's supposedly elite 1st Division asked permission to fall back. They were turned down because, Frances FitzGerald wrote in *Fire in the Lake,* "The American command and the White House had claimed that the ARVN would stay in Laos and occupy the trail until the end of the dry season in May, and the ranking ARVN officers did not dare contradict the Americans."

Infantrymen of the 1st Division panicked, abandoned their positions, blew up their artillery, and desperately hacked their way through jungle to clearings where U.S. helicopters could rescue them. Americans watching televised evening newscasts that week saw terrified ARVN soldiers clinging to the helicopters' skids. Only the intervention of American air power averted total catastrophe. At the end of the forty-five-day campaign the South Vietnamese units had suffered over 50 percent casualties—3,800 killed and 5,200 wounded. Eight battalions were unable to take the field. Traffic on the trail actually increased. When Nixon told the nation in early April, "Tonight I can report that Vietnamization has succeeded," his critics accused him of insulting the country's intelligence.

A response from America's antiwar movement was inevitable. On April 18 the Vietnam Veterans Against the War encamped below Capitol Hill and picketed the Supreme Court. Presidential counsel

Charles W. Colson hurriedly organized the Veterans for a Just Peace, and the Reverend Carl McIntire formed another countergroup, the Patriots for Victory, which called on Nixon to jettison his timid Vietnam policy and "use the sword as God intended." Administration officials accused commentators of exposing their leftist sympathies by failing to give the VJP and the PFV sufficient publicity, but events were moving too fast for both the government and the press. On April 24 a peaceful Washington march was held by some 200,000 protesters. The next week a "People's Lobby" swarmed over the Hill and into draft headquarters, buttonholing congressmen and Selective Service authorities, and the end of the month brought the climax of the capital demonstrations—the arrival of the "Mayday Tribe," which invoked the international distress call on behalf of its avowed objective: "stopping the government."

Just how violent the Tribe's intentions were later became a matter of some controversy. The leaders pointed out that their symbol had been the image of Mohandas Gandhi. It adorned their pamphlets, posters, buttons, and the cover of their tactical manual, which explained the principle of organized civil disobedience. Yet some of their methods were rougher than Gandhi's. Techniques included throwing junk in the street, abandoning autos at key intersections, and lying in front of cars. The Washington police force, which was known as one of the most relaxed in the nation, decided to adopt a strategy of killing the protesters with kindness. It was never given a chance to work. The President sent new instructions from San Clemente. He wanted the government to react more aggressively.

As coordinator of law enforcement tactics he chose Attorney General Mitchell. At the time of the November 1969 demonstrations, Mitchell had told his wife Martha that the peace marchers reminded him of Russian revolutionaries. More recently he had argued before a group of attorneys that the government's right to protect itself must override the right of individuals to privacy. The example he had chosen then was the need, as he saw it, for wiretaps without court orders. The Mayday disorders provided another illustration of the Mitchell approach to law enforcement in a time of political dissent. Under normal procedures, a policeman making an arrest must complete a form, filling in the name of the person charged, the offense, the arresting officer, and the time and place of the alleged infraction. Confronted by an invasion of 12,000 to

15,000 youths, many of them bent upon disrupting Washington traffic, Mitchell decided to cut through what he regarded as red tape.

On the evening of May 1 the vanguard of the Tribe was listening to a rock concert in West Potomac Park, near the Lincoln Memorial, when 750 helmeted officers swinging riot sticks drove them into the streets. Two days later the main battle was joined. Law enforcement officials had been given an overriding mission: keep the traffic flowing. Policemen, National Guardsmen, and regular Army troops broke up large concentrations of demonstrators with tear gas and truncheons. Assault units hovered overhead in military helicopters, ready to pounce. On that first day of the dragnet 7,200 were arrested, many of them peaceful pickets and spectators. It was a record. Altogether 12,614 were taken into custody over a four-day period. The jails wouldn't hold them; the overflow was penned in an open-air stockade at Robert F. Kennedy Memorial Stadium.

There they sang "God Bless America"—derisively—and "We all live in a con-cen-tra-tion camp," to the tune of the Beatles' "Yellow Submarine." Among them was Dr. Spock, shivering in a light raincoat. Abbie Hoffman was arrested in New York and accused of being a Mayday conspirator. He said, "I had about as much to do with the demonstrations in Washington as the Capitol bombing or the earthquake in Los Angeles, which I also expect to be indicted for." He had been picked up after a scuffle, and his nose was injured and taped. He said, "Like, man, that's defacing a national monument."

Congressional doves were appalled by the demonstrations. Tunney of California told reporters that the "foolish and useless" disorders "might well have ruined several months of hard work by the real advocates of peace." As it turned out, the courts rejected the arrests as clear violations of the prisoners' civil rights. The American Civil Liberties Union had anticipated that outcome, but it had been by no means certain at the time. The administration thought the law enforcement officers had performed admirably. Returning from California, Nixon told Republican leaders that he thought the Washington police chief had done "a magnificent job." He said, "John Mitchell and the Department of Justice did a fine job, too. I hope you will all agree to make that point when you leave here." Mitchell said, "I am proud of the Washington city police. I am proud that they stopped a repressive mob from robbing the rights of others." Then he compared the peace demonstrators to Hitler's Nazi brownshirts.

Six weeks after the great Mayday bust the *New York Times* of Sunday, June 13, carried on its first page the dull head: "VIETNAM ARCHIVE: PENTAGON STUDY TRACES 3 DECADES OF GROWING U.S. INVOLVEMENT." The story jumped to six inside pages, where column after column of dense type reprinted U.S. communiqués, recommendations, position papers, cables, and presidential orders, all concerning American activity in Indochina. It was perhaps the most extraordinary leak of classified documents in the history of governments, and it was only a beginning. Subsequent installments, the editors promised, would reveal more.

What the *Times* had acquired was a copy of a massive study commissioned by Robert S. McNamara shortly before his resignation as Secretary of Defense. The Pentagon Papers, as the newspaper called the archive, had been assembled by thirty-five scholars, including analysts from the Rand Corporation think tank, in an office adjoining McNamara's. Altogether there were forty-seven volumes of typescript—4,000 pages of records and 3,000 pages of explication, a total of 2.5 million words. It was all secret, but the secrets were not military. None of it compromised American troops still in Vietnam, and there was nothing from the Nixon years. McNamara had wanted to know how the United States had become entangled in Vietnam's swamps. The papers told how. Some of the documents went back to the Truman administration. They made a lot of officials look inept, foolish, or worse. Among other things the documents revealed that Lyndon Johnson had ordered the drafting of the Tonkin Gulf resolution months before the alleged incident there. Worse, on the very day in 1965 that he had decided to commit American infantry in Vietnam he had told a press conference that he was aware of "no far-reaching strategy that is being suggested or promulgated."

Clark Clifford, McNamara's successor as Secretary of Defense, had never found time to read the study. Henry Kissinger had been one of its researchers, but he hadn't seen the completed project. President Nixon didn't even know of its existence until that fateful Sunday morning that the *Times* began publishing it. Although it affected neither him nor his conduct of the war, he was infuriated. He felt that the ability of a government to keep secrets was vital. The fact that none of his own confidences were involved here was, he thought, beside the point; next time could be different. Furthermore, at a time when he and Kissinger were carefully defining their own Vietnam policy, these documents opened old wounds and raised again the ugly issue of the government's credibility.

On Monday, June 14, the *Times* published its second installment of the papers. Mitchell called the White House and suggested that the administration tackle the newspaper in the courts. Nixon agreed. Mitchell telegraphed the paper, "respectfully" suggesting that it print no more. If the editors went ahead, he warned, they could be convicted under the espionage statute, fined $10,000, and sentenced to ten years in prison. And the government would prosecute; the leak was causing "irreparable injury to the defense interests of the United States." The *Times* ran a front-page account of the attorney general's threat, and published the third installment of the papers alongside it.

That was a wild fortnight in city rooms and courtrooms. A team of government lawyers under Assistant Attorney General Robert Mardian went into federal court in New York on Tuesday, asking for an injunction against the editors. The judge, who had been on the bench exactly five days, scheduled a hearing for Friday and issued a temporary restraining order. The *Times* obediently stopped publication, but on Friday the *Washington Post* began running its own account of the papers. Clearly the *Post*'s editors had access to the same source. Four days later the *Boston Globe* began printing the documents. Meantime the Associated Press had begun sending the *Post* version around the world. Among the papers printing it was the *New York Times*.

Mardian took the *Post* to court, but the federal judge in Washington refused to hand down even a temporary order. The government, he found, could not "impose a prior restraint on publication of essentially historical data." The U.S. Appellate Court voted 2 to 1 to restrain the *Post*. The New York judge refused a permanent injunction against the *Times* but extended his temporary order until appeals courts could rule. Finally, on the following Friday, the two cases—numbers 1873 and 1875—came before the U.S. Supreme Court, which found for the press 6 to 3. Then nine justices handed down no fewer than six opinions. Along with John Harlan, Nixon appointees Burger and Harry A. Blackmun were in the minority.

Mardian had taken the position that the Justice Department was merely attempting to recover stolen papers necessary for national security. The identity of the putative thief was unmentioned then, but the FBI knew. He was Daniel Ellsberg, a summa cum laude graduate of Harvard who had written his doctoral dissertation on the decision making process, worked for Rand, become a McNamara protégé, and helped put the Pentagon Papers together. A hawk at first, he had, like so many others, been transformed by events into a dove. Resigning from Rand because he had become an embarrassment to it, he had become a fellow at the Massachusetts Institute of Technology. He had brooded long over whether to make the papers public. The invasion of Cambodia had finally decided him.

On June 23 Ellsberg, still in hiding, appeared on television at an undisclosed location and identified himself as the source of the documents. The United States, he declared, was to blame for the Vietnam tragedy: "There has never been a year when there would have been a war in Indochina without American money." He said, "I felt as an American citizen, a responsible citizen, I could no longer cooperate in concealing this information from the American people. I took this action on my own initiative, and I am prepared for all the consequences." On June 28 he surrendered to authorities in Boston and was released on $50,000 bail. That same day he was indicted in Los Angeles for stealing government property and violating the Espionage Act. Six months later twelve more criminal charges, including conspiracy, were leveled against him. A former Rand colleague, Anthony J. Russo Jr., was also indicted, together with a Los Angeles advertising woman and a former South Vietnamese ambassador to the United States. Ellsberg said: "I stole nothing and I did not commit espionage. I violated no laws and I have not intended to harm my country."

Surveying the Watergate wreckage in 1973, a team of London *Sunday Times* reporters concluded that "The Pentagon Papers tipped the Nixon administration over the edge." The White House Special Investigations Unit—the Plumbers—acquired the services of two former New York cops, a Runyonesque pair named Jack Caulfield and Tony Ulasewicz. They had been hired by John Ehrlichman two years earlier for political investigations; their assignments, first from Ehrlichman and then from John Dean, had included inquiries into Chappaquiddick, My Lai critics, the drinking habits of anti-Nixon senators, the private life of a Washington columnist, and reports that the brother of an eminent Democrat was a homosexual. In the aftermath of the Pentagon Papers case they received their first assignment as Plumbers.

Anyone who had worked with Ellsberg had a lot of explaining to do in those days, and a man high on everyone's list of possible co-conspirators was Morton B. Halperin, who had directed the assembly of the Pentagon Papers. Halperin had been an Ellsberg friend and later a Kissinger aide. Leaving the government, he had moved to the Brookings Institution, a liberal think tank in Washington. Charles Colson believed that Halperin had been a source of leaks and probably still had classified material. If so, it might be in his Brookings office. Colson sent Ulasewicz on a reconnoitering mission; the ex-cop returned to report that there was no way to burglarize the institution. According to a subsequent account by John Dean, Colson, a hard man to discourage, told Caulfield that "if necessary he should plant a fire-bomb in the building and retrieve the documents during the commotion that would ensue."

That was too much for the New Yorkers. Someone, they felt, should restrain the impulsive Colson. They took the story to Dean, who caught the next plane to San Clemente. He laid the tale before Ehrlichman; Ehrlichman phoned Washington, and no more was said about fire-bombs. It was a costly triumph for Caulfield and Ulasewicz, however. The White House suddenly lost interest in their talents. Jobs which would have come their way in the past now went to the two rising stars in the Plumbers unit: E. Howard Hunt and G. Gordon Liddy. After three months in the cold, Caulfield decided to devise a master plan for political espionage. He hoped to sell it to the Committee for the Reelection of the President. Its code name was Operation Sand Wedge. On November 24 Dean secured an appointment for him with Mitchell. The presentation was not a success. Caulfield had a hunch that someone else was going to get the work, and as he left he knew he was right; sitting in the attorney general's outer office was Gordon Liddy.

During the spring and summer of 1971, when Richard Nixon was secretly having his White House offices wired for sound, his popularity rating in public opinion polls continued to sag. Presidential aides were agonizing over the refractory nature of the Vietnam War, still the most important issue before the country, and debating among themselves how best to reverse the electorate's political mood, so discouragingly expressed in the previous autumn's off-year election. This much was clear to them: they were going to need a lot of money. Fortunately, they were in much better shape than the debt-ridden Democrats. Herbert Kalmbach, the President's personal attorney, had custody of nearly two million dollars in unspent campaign funds from 1968. In January 1971 Kalmbach deposited the first $500,000 of the 1972 war chest in the Newport Beach, California, branch of the Bank of America. It is a matter of some interest that the money was in the form of cashier's checks which he had bought, with cash, in the Security Pacific National Bank branch just across the street. Even then he was taking steps to see that contributions could not be easily traced, because even then he knew that much of the means for the coming campaign would be coming from dubious sources.

Some of those sources emerged during the next few months. The first, in March, was the dairy industry. Early in the month Secretary of Agriculture Clifford Hardin announced that price supports for "manufacturing milk"—used to make cheese and butter—would be $4.66 per hundredweight, unchanged from the year before. The milk manufacturers took steps to reverse the decision. On March 22 they formed a GOP slush fund called the Trust for Agricultural Political Development and put $10,000 in it. The next day sixteen leaders of dairy cooperatives were invited to meet Nixon and Hardin in the oval office. They told the President and the secretary that they wanted a higher federal subsidy. The following day they gave the Nixon war chest another $25,000. The day after that Hardin changed his mind and pegged milk supports at $4.93. The dairy leaders then poured a total of $527,500 into Republican bank accounts.

Another lode was opened a few weeks later. Since the early days of the Nixon administration Harold S. Geneen, president of the International Telephone and Telegraph Corporation (ITT), had been trying to block a Justice Department task force which was working to prevent a merger of ITT and the Hartford Fire Insurance Corporation. Department career lawyers were determined to establish the principle that business competition is illegally crippled by huge sprawling conglomerates like ITT. The government's campaign was being directed by Richard W. McLaren, head of Justice's antitrust division. McLaren was reporting to Deputy Attorney General Kleindienst; Mitchell had supposedly withdrawn from the case because his New York law firm had represented ITT. On April 19, 1971, McLaren and Kleindienst conferred and agreed to carry an appeal to the Supreme Court. Kleindienst telephoned ITT's lawyer to tell him of the decision.

Later that same day Kleindienst received a call from John Ehrlichman, who told him that President Nixon was "directing" Kleindienst to drop the ITT case entirely. The deputy attorney general said that was impossible; he, McLaren, and Solicitor General Erwin Griswold were committed. "Oh?" Ehrlichman said curtly. "We'll see about that." A few minutes later Kleindienst's phone rang again. It was Nixon, who began by saying, "You son of a bitch, don't you understand the English language?" He ordered Kleindienst not to appeal. Disturbed, the deputy attorney general told Mitchell that he would resign rather than capitulate, and he thought McLaren and Griswold would go with him. Shortly thereafter Mitchell told his deputy that he had talked to Nixon and "He says do anything you want on antitrust cases."

The President and the attorney general were being less than candid with Kleindienst. In a subsequent memo to Haldeman, Colson said he was trying to suppress all White House-ITT correspondence because it "would lay this case on the President's doorstep." And Mitchell, for all his talk of having turned the whole thing over to his deputy, had been holding regular meetings with Geneen for the past year. As early as September 1970 Ehrlichman had written to Mitchell criticizing McLaren's attitude and mentioning an "understanding" with Geneen.

Bargaining between the administration and the conglomerate was apparently concluded at a lunch given by the governor of Kentucky at the Kentucky Derby the month after Kleindienst and McLaren thought they had committed the government to a Supreme Court trial. The mediators were Mitchell and Dita Beard, ITT's salty Washington lobbyist. ITT agreed to pay $400,000 and the administration agreed to forget about the antitrust action. In a highly incriminating memorandum dated June 25, 1971, Mrs. Beard told her immediate superior that the only Republicans to know "from whom the 400 thousand commitment had come" were Nixon, Mitchell, Haldeman, and the lieutenant governor of California. She said: "I am convinced that our noble commitment has gone a long way toward our negotiations on the mergers eventually coming out as Hal [Geneen] wants them. Certainly the President has told Mitchell to see that things are worked out fairly. It is still only McLaren's mickeymouse we are suffering. . . . Mitchell is definitely helping us, but it cannot be known."

She ended the memo, "Please destroy this, huh?" It wasn't destroyed, and when it surfaced in a Jack Anderson column the following February 29, ITT's response was to shred all other documents relating to the case and claim that this one had been a forgery. But the Dita Beard note does not stand alone. It is braced by the Ehrlichman correspondence, including a May 5 letter to Mitchell referring to a talk between the President and the attorney general in which they had settled the "agreed-upon ends" in the ITT case. Certain events of that time are also supportive. On May 15 Geneen pledged the $400,000 to the GOP, and at the end of July the Justice Department and the government settled their differences without an appeal to the Supreme Court. ITT was allowed to keep Hartford Fire. "Quite clearly," *Fortune* commented, "Harold S. Geneen has achieved something of a victory."

The key figure in a third deal between the administration and people trying to solve legal problems was Robert L. Vesco, a controversial financier with several ties to the Nixon family. Vesco had given $50,000 to the 1968 Republican campaign through the President's brother, F. Donald Nixon. He was close to the President's other brother, Edward, and beginning in the summer of 1971 he employed the President's nephew Donald as his personal assistant. "He is the one person who has never lied to me, ever," Donald once said of Vesco, a strange statement from a young man with such an eminent relative, and one not many people would make; within two years Vesco would be a fugitive from American justice, living in Costa Rica rather than face Securities and Exchange Commission charges that he had looted Investors Overseas Services, a mutual fund, of 224 million dollars.

Vesco was already in trouble in the early summer of 1971, when, according to the indictment against him, he involved Mitchell and Nixon's Secretary of Commerce, Maurice Stans, in an attempt to buy his way out of the SEC accusations. The understanding was that Vesco would give Stans $250,000 in cash and Mitchell, according to the charges, would "exert his influence on the SEC on behalf of Robert L. Vesco." Edward Nixon later acted as bagman, delivering to Stans $200,000 in a brown attaché case. (The remaining $50,000 came in a second installment.) Mitchell set up meetings between Vesco, the SEC chairman, and the commission's general counsel. The SEC continued to prosecute anyway.

While cash began to accumulate in the GOP war chest, the White House was engaging in various parapolitical activities in 1971, most of them with a view toward the next year's presidential election. One was the compilation of a list of political enemies, which under Colson's guidance expanded to fill a file four inches thick. It included the names of Jack Anderson, James Reston, Jane Fonda, Barbra Streisand, Paul Newman, Gregory Peck, and Carol Channing. The president of the Otis Elevator Company was there—apparently because the Otis elevator in Nixon's San Clemente house didn't work properly—and so was Detroit's black Congressman John Conyers. A notation after Conyers's name read, "Has known weakness for white females." On September 9, 1971, Colson designated twenty names for "go status," but no one on the presidential staff could think of an effective method of attack. Daniel Schorr of CBS ("a real media enemy," Colson called him) was subjected to an FBI check that summer, but the sole consequence was frustration for the White House. Ronald Ziegler put out the explanation that Schorr had been investigated because he was being considered for a government job.

Various Nixon aides—Huston, Dean, Caulfield—tried to talk the Internal Revenue Service into harassing selected taxpayers. All failed, and Commissioner Randolph Thrower resigned for reasons which, he said at the time, were "between me and the President." The White House was driven to the absurd lengths of writing anonymous letters to the IRS hinting at tax evasions by people on Colson's list. It was perhaps an inevitable outgrowth of this malicious foolishness that at some point the conspirators should conclude that someone was conspiring against *them.* The someone, they thought, was J. Edgar Hoover, who kept in his office safe logs of wiretaps he had carried out on White House orders. Robert Mardian persuaded one of Hoover's assistants to steal the logs, and they were locked up in Ehrlichman's safe. Hoover missed them in July 1971. He was enraged.

Men who did not shrink from doing a bag job on the director of the FBI had no qualms about playing rough with Democratic presidential candidates, and it was in these months that what later became famous as Republican "dirty tricks" made their appearance. Mailings critical of Ted Kennedy went out in fake Muskie envelopes; a spurious Muskie aide phoned the Associated Press bureau in Boston with charges that Kennedy was a "divisive influence"; Rowland Evans and Robert Novak were gulled into printing counterfeit Muskie memos which seemed to suggest that he was engaging in questionable activities. On December 1, 1972, Donald H. Segretti gave fifty dollars to the president of the Tampa Young Republicans Club with the understanding that it would be used to discredit the primary campaigns of Senators Muskie and Jackson in Florida. It was the first installment on a project which would eventually lead to Segretti's disbarment, conviction, and imprisonment.

Some tricks were intricate. On the assumption that a third-party Wallace candidacy would hurt Nixon more than any Democratic candidate, various projects were undertaken to sabotage Wallace's American Independent Party. One of the more fantastic of them, masterminded by Mitchell and Jeb Magruder, involved paying the American Nazi Party $10,000 to persuade AIP voters in California to change their registration. The rationale behind this was that if enough voters switched, Wallace's party would have too few registrants to qualify for the ballot. It failed; the AIP actually gained 6,500 members during the period.

Another plot was directed at Ted Kennedy, the most formidable vote getter among President Nixon's possible challengers. Here the reasoning was that since young Kennedy's popularity was a reflection of John Kennedy's charisma, reducing the late President's appeal would hurt Ted. At a press conference on September 16, 1971, Nixon was asked about a recent statement by Senator Henry Jackson to the effect that the Saigon regime would be stronger if it were more democratic. Nixon replied, "If what the senator is suggesting is that the United States should use its leverage now to overthrow Thieu, I would remind all concerned that the way we got into Vietnam was through overthrowing Diem, and the complicity in the murder of Diem, and the way to get out of Vietnam, in my opinion, is not to overthrow Thieu." This was the first time anyone in the government had accused the Kennedy administration of connivance in Diem's death, and it gave Howard Hunt an idea.

Hunt had been poring over the Pentagon Papers. He told Colson that a Kennedy role in the Diem assassination might be assumed "inferentially" from State Department cables of the time. According to Hunt, Colson suggested that he "improve on them"—doctor them. Using a razor blade and a photocopier, Hunt forged two cables.

One, dated three days before the Diem assassination, began: AT HIGHEST-LEVEL MEETING TODAY, DECISION RELUCTANTLY MADE THAT NEITHER YOU NOR HARKINS SHOULD INTERVENE IN BEHALF OF DIEM OR NHU IN EVENT THEY SEEK ASYLUM. Colson referred a *Life* reporter to Hunt, saying of Nixon's accusation, "There's a big story there," but the reporter suspected duplicity and didn't bite.

The failure of this intrigue was Hunt's second disappointment that month. The other, the more bitter of the two, dated back to the previous April. On the tenth anniversary of the Bay of Pigs Hunt had flown to Miami for lunch with a Cuban-American named Bernard L. Barker who had been his principal subordinate then and was now a successful Florida real estate man. It was the opening link in a historic chain of events. The second was Ellsberg's massive leak of the Pentagon Papers. The third began with four men—Nixon, Kissinger, Haldeman, and Ehrlichman—on a helicopter ride between Los Angeles and San Clemente. The four leaders raged over the leak, which the President equated with the Alger Hiss case, and discussed bypassing the FBI with an undercover operation to learn more about it. The decision was made to detach David Young from Kissinger's National Security staff to work full-time with the Plumbers. Young then put the Ellsberg ball in Hunt's court; Hunt put it in Barker's.

But not right away. In the beginning the Plumbers explored what appeared at the time to be an innocent area. Toward the end of July they discovered, from an FBI report which was routinely routed through their office, that for two years Ellsberg had been psychoanalyzed by a Dr. Lewis B. Fielding of Beverly Hills. Two of Hoover's agents had attempted to grill the psychiatrist, but he had demurred, invoking the sanctity of the doctor-patient relationship. Hunt remembered that the CIA had a psychiatric section which drew up analytic profiles of men whose personalities were of special interest to the government. Under the CIA's congressional mandate the subjects were supposed to be foreigners—the most successful had been an analysis of Nikita Khrushchev, prepared just before President Kennedy's Vienna summit with him—but there had been one exception: Captain Lloyd Bucher of the *Pueblo*. Young asked CIA Director Richard Helms to make Ellsberg a second exception. Helms agreed. Early in August the finished profile was forwarded to the CIA.

Nobody there liked it. It wasn't at all what the Plumbers had in mind. The CIA psychiatrists seemed to admire Ellsberg. ("There is no suggestion that the subject [saw] anything treasonous in his act. Rather he seemed to be responding to what he deemed a higher order of patriotism.") On August 11 Young and Egil Krogh sent a minute on the study to Ehrlichman, rejecting it as "very superficial" and underscoring their belief that the CIA could do a better job. They wrote: "We will meet tomorrow with the head psychiatrist, Dr. Bernard Malloy, to impress upon him the detail and depth we expect." They then crossed the line into contemplation of criminal activity. "In this connection," they continued, "*we would recommend* that a covert operation be undertaken to examine all the medical files still held by Ellsberg's psychiatrist covering the two-year period in which he was undergoing analysis." At the bottom of the memorandum were the words "Approve ____ Disapprove ____." After "Approve" Ehrlichman scrawled his initial. He added: "If done under your assurance that it is not traceable."

It was this condition, stipulating that the Plumbers must use undercover operatives with no White House ties, which prompted Hunt to recruit Barker and, through him, two fellow Cubans, Felipe DeDiego and Eugenio R. Martinez. All Hunt told Barker was that he needed him to explore a "national security matter" on authorization from officials "above both the CIA and the FBI." The job, he said, concerned a traitor who was passing information to the Soviet embassy. Except for the fact that the Russians subscribe to the *New York Times,* this was untrue. Later, in prison, Barker found the deception unforgivable. Morality apart (and none of the principals seemed to see any moral issue at the time), Hunt was guilty of incredible carelessness. He failed to tell Barker not to carry in his pocket a telephone number and abbreviated address ("W.H." and "W. House") linking him with Hunt. He didn't even check to be certain that Barker's men were free of government connections. In fact one of them, Martinez, was on the CIA payroll as a Cuban informant.

Meanwhile Hunt and Liddy, his partner in this strange venture, were being outfitted by the CIA—another violation of the provision in the agency's charter forbidding domestic activity. Ehrlichman phoned Marine General Robert E. Cushman Jr., Helms's deputy, asking him to do all in his power to help Hunt, whom he identified as "a bona fide employee, a consultant on security matters." Ehrlichman didn't specify the nature of the mission. During their subsequent meeting Hunt told Cushman that he had been "charged with quite a highly sensitive mission by the White House to visit and elicit information from an individual whose ideology we aren't entirely sure of" and that he needed "flash alias documentation," "pocket litter of some sort," and "some degree of physical disguise, for a one-time op—in and out."

With the approval of Helms, the CIA's technical services division provided Hunt with a social security card and a driving license, both made out to "Edward Joseph Warren." Liddy was given identification in the name of "George Leonard." Hunt was issued a reddish-brown wig and a device, resembling false teeth, to alter the sound of his voice when telephoning. In addition Liddy received a tiny camera hidden in a tobacco pouch. On August 25, 1971, the two Plumbers flew to California on a preliminary reconnaissance mission. They didn't achieve much. After taking a picture of Liddy standing outside Dr. Fielding's office at 450 North Bedford Drive in Beverly Hills, Hunt entered the office, told a cleaning woman that he was a physician, and photographed the room. Both men timed a drive from there to the doctor's home. Then they flew back to Washington, where the plane was met by a CIA messenger who took the films from Hunt and had them developed. At the White House the two Plumbers persuaded their superiors that burglarizing the psychiatrist's office was justifiable. Young brought Ehrlichman up to date and proposed in a new minute that a committee on Capitol Hill be persuaded to look into the leak of the Pentagon Papers: "We have already started on a negative press image of Ellsberg. If the present Liddy/Hunt project is successful, it will be absolutely essential to have an overall game plan developed for its use in conjunction with the congressional investigation."

D-day for the Beverly Hills break-in was September 3, 1971; H-hour was 9 P.M. The operation was staged with all the meticulous attention to detail which had marked Hunt's participation in the Bay of Pigs, and it was just about as successful. Shortly before zero the Cubans checked in at the Beverly Hilton Hotel under assumed names. Two of them donned delivery men's uniforms and took a huge suitcase plastered with labels reading "Rush to Dr. Fielding" to North Bedford Drive. The cleaning woman admitted them and they left the bag with her, unlocking the door as they departed. Liddy was driving around outside, watching for suspicious policemen. Hunt was outside the Fielding home with a walkie-talkie to flash the alarm if the psychiatrist emerged and headed for his office.

At about midnight the Cubans returned to the office, only to discover—an omen of what was to come at the Watergate offices of the Democratic National Committee—that the cleaning woman had relocked the door. Forcing it, they removed a camera and a spotlight from the suitcase. The plan was to photograph Ellsberg's medical history. Unfortunately they couldn't find it. They dumped Dr. Fielding's files on the floor, but there was nothing for them there. All they turned up was an address book with Ellsberg's name in it. They took pictures of that and of the strewn files, to show that they had done their best. After four frustrating hours the team returned to the hotel, where Liddy phoned Washington to tell Krogh that it had been a "clean job"—Dr. Fielding would have disagreed, but Liddy meant only that they hadn't been caught. That was putting the best possible face on it. Back in the capital Hunt had to tell the White House that the mission had been a failure. Ehrlichman, according to his subsequent testimony, said he didn't want them to try again. Ehrlichman had another piece of bad news for Hunt. On instructions from Helms, General Cushman had called to say that while the CIA had been glad to help out, a repetition would be out of the question. The Plumbers were on their own now, and the pressure to produce something to justify their jobs was mounting.

The week after the first second-story job masterminded from the White House a tragic episode pointed up one of the issues deeply dividing Americans during the Nixon years. It lay between the holders of one set of values, who regarded their critics as illiberal and inhumane, and the critics, who scorned the liberals as "permissivists." The incident was the bloodiest prison revolt in the country's history. It occurred in an unlikely setting, amid the white clapboard homes, red barns, and tall silvery silos of western New York's Wyoming County. There, surrounded by dense fields of sweet corn and goldenrod, stood a fifty-five-acre penitentiary compound enclosed by thirty-foot turreted gray concrete walls. Christened after the nearby town, it bore the classical name of the ancient Athenian plain: Attica.

The state called Attica a "correctional facility," but not much correcting was done there. Under the stern administration of Superintendent Vincent Mancusi there was little vocational training and less compassion. Solitary confinement—"the box"—was the penalty for the slightest infraction of the rules, and inmates were systematically beaten in the elevator on the way there. They were allowed one bar of soap and one roll of toilet paper a month. If they worked in the hundred-degree heat of the metal shop, known to them as "the Black Hole of Calcutta," they were paid as little as 25 cents a day. Ugliest of all was the regime's naked racism. Of the 2,254 convicts, 75 percent were black or Puerto Rican, while all 383 guards were white. The keepers openly favored white prisoners, taunted the Negroes, and called their clubs "nigger sticks."

Warden Mancusi's reply to civil libertarians was that he was running a maximum security institution and that Attica's inmates included some of the country's most hardened criminals. It was true. It was also true, and an ill omen, that among them were many of a new convict breed, black militants who regarded themselves as victims of an imperialist society. Attica was, in fact, where other wardens shipped self-styled revolutionists who gave them trouble. Arriving, they smuggled in books by George Jackson and Eldridge Cleaver, held secret rallies when they were supposed to be at sports or in chapel, and circulated inflammatory pamphlets which they wrote in their cells. "If we cannot live as people, we will at least try to die like men," wrote a convict named Charles "Brother Flip" Crowley, and a poem being passed around began:

If we must die—let it not be like hogs,
Hunted and penned in an inglorious spot,
While round us bark the mad and hungry dogs,
Making their mock at our accursed lot.

In July 1971 an organization of militant inmates calling themselves the Attica Liberation Faction sent a proclamation demanding reforms to State Corrections Commissioner Russell G. Oswald. It was a clever move. Oswald had been appointed by Governor Rockefeller because his sweeping improvements in Wisconsin's prison system had been widely acclaimed by penologists, and though he had been in office only six months, he and Mancusi were already at odds on almost every administrative question. After Labor Day Oswald taped a message to the convicts asking for time to make profound changes. Among other things he pledged "meaningful rehabilitative methods, evening vocational programs, better law libraries."

He may have been too late. After the revolt guards found enormous circles drawn around the date September 9 on cell calendars. In July the militants had told Oswald that they felt there was "no need to dramatize our demands," but they changed their minds the following month. The decisive event seems to have been the death of George Jackson in San Quentin on August 21. At breakfast next morning Attica's Negroes protested by fasting. "It was the weirdest thing," a turnkey said afterward. "Nobody picked up a tray or a spoon, and nobody took any food. They just walked through the line and went to their seats and they sat down. They looked straight ahead and nobody made a sound . . . Then we noticed that almost all had some black on them. . . . It scared us because a thing like that takes a lot of organization, a lot of solidarity, and we had no idea they were so well organized."

The evangelical rhetoric of two revolutionists who were later identified as the key leaders, Herbert X. Blyden and "Brother Richard" Clarke, became more strident. Both were New Yorkers and Black Muslims; both had been convicted of armed robbery. Like George Jackson, Blyden was self-taught, a reader of history and philosophy who had been sent to Attica after leading a prison riot in the Tombs, Manhattan's House of Detention. Clarke had been transferred to Attica from a medium security prison whose warden said he had been advocating "the violent overthrow of the institution." His family had noticed that in Attica he was becoming increasingly bitter. Once when his wife was visiting him he said, "Feed the animals, feed the animals. That's what they treat us like here—animals."

On Wednesday, September 8, eighteen days after Jackson had been killed on the other side of the country, an Attica guard was punched by a convict while breaking up a fight in one of the prison exercise yards. That night the two who had been fighting were put in "the box." Other inmates said they were abused as they were dragged away, and a Puerto Rican prisoner threw a tumbler at one of the guards, cutting his face. The riot exploded the following morning. Precisely what touched it off is unclear. According to one account, a work party refused to line up at the rap of keepers' clubs. Another story put the responsibility on guards who, as a reprisal for the previous day's events, arbitrarily canceled the prisoners' exercise period. In a third version, Brother Richard led five convicts who were on their way to breakfast on a rampage, freeing Blyden, who was working in the metal shop, along the way.

However it started, the results were spectacular. Fewer than one hundred guards were on duty. They were overwhelmed, and many were captured. The prison school, the chapel, and the machine shop were put to the torch. While they were being reduced to smoldering debris, raiding parties of inmates raced through the galleries, gates, and catwalks of three of the four rectangular cellblocks —B, C and D. According to a Wyoming County deputy sheriff, they were armed with pipes which they had hidden under loaves of bread on trays in the mess halls. That may be apocryphal; the credibility of Attica's authorities was to be severely damaged before the uprising was over. But even if the inmates lacked weapons at the outset, they soon equipped themselves with them. Using grinding wheels acquired while looting the shops, some of them fashioned spears from scissor blades and broom handles. Others turned out clubs and knives which, when the keepers tried to extinguish the fires, were used to shred the hoses. With tear gas, guards managed to regain control of cellblock C and part of B, but the prisoners retained the rest, locking gates and even welding some of them shut with shop equipment.

Four hours after the revolt had begun, the battlefront hardened along lines which would remain substantially unchanged over the next four days. Cellblock D, the farthest from the administration building and the nearest to the shop, was the rebel stronghold, commanded by Blyden and Clarke. Wearing football helmets or turbans, the rebels—there were 1,280 of them—sprawled under makeshift tents in D yard, and a crude bench at one end of the yard was the epicenter of the revolt. There a rebel secretariat, the People's Central Committee, sat in continuous session, assigning work details, dictating defense measures, and even confining unruly prisoners in a "people's jail." Contacts between the convicts and state authorities were made in negotiating sessions at the table and in an A block corridor, a kind of no-man's-land dubbed the DMZ. A point of special interest was the geographical center of the prison, "Times Square," where catwalks leading to all four cellblocks met. It was held by the rebels. They had wrested it from a twenty-eight-year-old guard, William Quinn, who had battled them with a nightstick and had been overcome only after his skull had been fractured in two places. Some guards swore that they had seen him being brutally thrown from a high catwalk. There was no question that he had been gravely injured. When Clarke saw blood dripping from the unconscious guard's ear he ordered him passed through the DMZ to the authorities. Quinn's condition was a matter of great interest to both sides; if he died, every inmate participating in the uprising could be tried for murder.

Around noon Captain Henry F. Williams of the state police mustered two hundred and fifty troopers with riot equipment and told them: "If somebody on the other side gets killed, well, that's the way it's got to be. You're to take no crap from anybody. Don't lose your weapon and don't lose your buddy." That was tough talk, but it was deprived of much of its force by the fact that precipitate action was likely to lose them thirty-nine buddies—guards being held by the rebels as hostages. The captive keepers had been dressed in convict uniforms, blindfolded, and tied up in D yard. An inmate shouting through a megaphone warned that the hostages would be the first to suffer if the troopers charged, and no one in a position of responsibility, not even Superintendent Mancusi, was eager to call their bluff.

The man with the legal responsibility of dealing with the situation was Commissioner Oswald, who flew in at 2 P.M. Against Mancusi's advice, Oswald decided to enter D yard with Herman Schwartz, a Buffalo law professor trusted by the leaders of the revolt, and confront the rebels in person. He intended to tell them that he could not discuss their complaints until the hostages had been released, an unbreakable rule in penal administration. He did demand their release, but he also listened while Blyden dictated a list of fifteen demands to him. The rebels wanted, among other things, permission to hold political meetings "without intimidation," "religious freedom" for Muslims, an end to mail censorship, the right to communicate with anyone they wished, regular grievance procedures, more recreation and less time in cells, more exercise yards, a full-time physician, a better school, more fruit and less pork, the removal of Warden Mancusi, a committee of outsiders to "oversee" the behavior of the authorities during the revolt, and a federal court injunction against any "physical and mental reprisals" for the inmates' acts during the revolt. To the end of the list Blyden added that some of the convicts, at least, insisted upon "Speedy and safe transportation out of confinement to a nonimperialist country." He said: "We are men. We are not beasts, and do not intend to be beaten or driven. What has happened here is but the sound before the fury of those oppressed."

Oswald's personal courage in entering D yard was considerable. Even as he sat before the secretariat of rebel leaders, some of them were suggesting that he be added to the group of hostages, and though state police sharpshooters atop the prison walls were lining up the inmates around him in their sights, his chances of surviving a real row were negligible. His wisdom in going was another matter. Once he had heard them out and concluded that many of their points were reasonable, the pressure on him to open negotiations was almost irresistible. He yielded to it. As proof of his good faith he agreed to appoint a committee of overseers and to dispatch Schwartz to Federal Judge John T. Curtin, who was at a Vermont judicial conference, in pursuit of the injunction. Oswald did something else which was deeply resented by Mancusi and his staff. He signed a pledge of "No administrative reprisals against prisoners for activities of Sept. 9, 1971." The rebels interpreted this as a guarantee of clemency. The governor's office quickly pointed out that exoneration for criminal acts was out of the question; the commissioner didn't have the power to grant that. But the seeds of misunderstanding had been sown and were bound to bear bitter fruit.

That night Oswald returned to the floodlit prison yard, now further illumined by convicts' campfires. With him he brought a contingent of reporters—a concession to another rebel demand. Much of the time was spent putting together the panel of overseers. The inmates' choices included William Kunstler, Huey P. Newton, Bobby Seale, State Senator John R. Dunne, Tom Wicker of the *New York Times,* who had written sympathetically of George Jackson; Herman Badillo, the first Puerto Rican elected to Congress; and Clarence Jones, Negro publisher of Manhattan's *Amsterdam News.* Later Rockefeller added a number of selections of his own: his secretary, a school superintendent, a retired general, and various legislators and penologists. At one point there were thirty overseers. That was too many to be effective, and the ideological splits among them further weakened the committee.

Schwartz brought back the injunction signed by Judge Curtin. It had been drafted by one of the white prisoners, Jerome S. Rosenberg from Brooklyn, murderer of a policeman, but now the rebels rejected it as inadequate. The overseers were off to a lumbering start. Wicker, Jones, and Julian Tepper of the National Legal Aid and Defenders Association breakfasted with Wyoming County District Attorney Louis James; the best they could wangle from him was a written promise of no "indiscriminate mass prosecutions"—an assurance hardly likely to diminish the fears of the edgy convict secretariat. Another shaky agreement was broken at 4 A.M. Saturday, as the revolt approached the end of its second twenty-four-hour period, when the press pool was barred from the prison. Police hostility toward the reporters had been growing, a grim sign which usually foreshadows actions that policemen do not want outsiders to watch.

Yet Oswald was optimistic that morning. The inmates' demands had grown to thirty, but he had agreed to twenty-eight of them, drawing the line only at complete amnesty, which he now called "nonnegotiable," and the firing of Mancusi. Just as he was expressing confidence that these could be resolved, however, new developments shriveled hopes for a peaceful end to the riot. Quinn died, ending any possibility of leniency for the rebel leaders. Then Bobby Seale arrived. Before entering the prison he told fifty cheering radical demonstrators outside the walls that "If anything happens to those guards, the state and the governor should be charged with murder." Then his entourage passed out copies of a statement from the Panther Central Committee: "The prison guards, called 'hostages,' have actually in reality been placed under arrest by the 1,280 prisoners who are rightly redressing their grievances concerning the harassing, brutal, and inhuman treatment to which they are constantly subjected. . . . A promise of amnesty is the first thing that must be done to start negotiations of the prisoners' . . . demands. This is the only bail the arrested guards can have, from the analysis of the Black Panther party."

Obviously Seale had no interest in a resolution of the crisis. Inside, he told the inmates that they must make their own decisions in dealing with Oswald. In a pathetic display of trust, they begged him for advice. He replied that he could offer them no counsel without the approval of Huey P. Newton. After participating briefly in the overseers' deliberations he left, telling newspapermen that their questions and the armed state troopers were upsetting him. To cap this, Kunstler, in an act of extraordinary irresponsibility, told the rebel secretariat that representatives of "Third World nations are waiting for you across the street." Presumably he meant the fifty demonstrators, but he didn't explain, and the prisoners, now hoping for total victory, lost interest in bargaining with Oswald.

Sunday was a day of mobilization for both sides. Throughout the afternoon trucks arrived to disgorge National Guardsmen, powerful fire hoses, and crates of gas cylinders and gas masks. The overseers issued a statement warning that they were "now convinced that a massacre of prisoners and guards may take place at this institution." Wicker, Jones, Badillo, and Dunne spent over a half an hour on the telephone pleading with Rockefeller to come to Attica, but the governor issued a statement of his own saying that "In view of the fact that the key issue is total amnesty . . . I do not feel that my physical presence on the site can contribute to a peaceful settlement." He and Oswald had already agreed that if the convict leadership did not respond to a final ultimatum, they would have to resort to force. They were not sanguine. Plainly the mood of the prisoners was turning uglier. Gates were being wired to make them electrically hot, trenches were filled with gasoline. Booby traps of peat moss and oil were wired with time charges. Crude rocket catapults were fixed in position; the spears were resharpened. Barricades of metal tables were built along the main catwalk leading from A block to Times Square—a route invading troopers would have to follow. That afternoon rebels paying off old scores stabbed two white convicts to death.

The point of no return was reached early Monday. At 7 A.M. teams of policemen were assigned to specific functions: marksmanship, rescue, barricade demolition, and reserve strength. Two helicopters hovered overhead reporting on the disposition of convict forces and the situation of the hostages. At 8:35 Oswald met Richard Clarke in the DMZ. Brother Richard insisted that the rebels must be assured of "complete, total, unadulterated amnesty" and the dismissal of "that guy Mancusi." He said he wanted another half-hour to confer with other members of the secretariat. Oswald gave it to him. At 9:05 an inmate shouted through a megaphone that all the hostages would be killed by inmate "executioners" if rebel positions were attacked. An Oswald aide called back, "Release the prisoners now. Then the commissioner will meet with you." The convict yelled, "Negative." That was, literally, the last word in the negotiations. Only savagery was left.

Minutes later one of the helicopters radioed that four hostages were "at each corner of Times Square with knives at their throats."

It was a chilling sight: each captive's head was yanked back by the hair, arching his neck; the blades, held by cocked hands, were biting into the flesh. Actually this looked more desperate than it really was. What officials could not know was that they were witnessing a prime example of militant overstatement. The hostages weren't going to die at the rebels' hands. Like the demand for resettlement in "a nonimperialist country" (which had been withdrawn the first time Oswald had raised an eyebrow), the grisly gestures with the homemade daggers were a kind of rhetoric, designed to impress the world and, perhaps, the convicts themselves. There have always been men prepared to die for acts of bravado. Some were about to fall here now, and they were going to take helpless victims with them.

Convinced that the hostages were in grave peril, that they might be massacred anyway—that the danger was imminent and time was of the essence—Oswald said to his aides, "There's no question now—we've got to go in." More than five hundred local law enforcement officers and yellow-clad state troopers were coiled at the doors leading to the catwalks as *Jackpot Two,* a CH-34 helicopter, swooped down on Times Square with a load of tear gas, pepper gas, and mustard gas. The radio dispatcher's voice crackled: "Move in! Move in! The drop has been made! Base to all posts—move in. Launch the offensive!"

Troopers burst through the doors and blasted away at the barricades; marksmen on the gray walls began picking off inmates. Clearing the catwalks of obstacles took ninety minutes. Then the main attack went in. With clouds of turbid gas drifting across Times Square and D yard, it was difficult to see what was going on, and the fact that the hostages were wearing convict uniforms didn't help. Troopers insisted afterward that strong resistance persisted for about two and a half minutes. One said, "They came at us like a banzai charge, waving knives and spears. Those we had to shoot." Another said, "The ones that resisted—throwing spears and Molotov cocktails—were cut down. We caught some men with arms extended to throw weapons. Anybody that resisted was killed."

But some who didn't resist were killed, too. Sporadic firing continued for almost an hour. The New York State Special Commission on Attica (the McKay Commission) later found that the police assault had been "marred by excesses," which included "much unnecessary shooting." Some of the needless violence was attributable to carelessness, possibly even to a contempt for human life. Rockefeller had specifically forbidden prison guards to participate in the assault, but they went in anyhow and were responsible for at least two homicides. Some of the policemen fired shotguns loaded with "oo" buckshot which spread at distances exceeding thirty yards, hitting "unintended targets," the McKay investigators found, and creating "a high risk of injury and death to unresisting inmates and hostages." An attending physician, Dr. Lionel Sifontes of Buffalo, reported afterward that "Many of the ringleaders were approached by guards and shot systematically. Some had their hands in the air surrendering. Some were lying on the ground."

More than 120 men lay wounded or dying. Counting Quinn and the convicts who had been murdered by other prisoners during the uprising, Attica's death toll was 32 inmates and 11 guards or administrative officers—a total of 43. Compounding the confusion in the hours after the recapture of the prison were highly inaccurate reports about how the hostages had died. One Oswald aide said that a guard had been found emasculated, his testicles stuffed in his mouth. Another aide told reporters that "Several of the hostages had their throats slashed." Stories that the guards had been butchered by their captors gained credence from the fact that their bloodstained blindfolds had fallen around their necks. In fact, three surviving guards had suffered throat wounds, but when the medical examiner issued his report the following morning, he found no castrations and no mutilations among the dead. All had been killed from gunfire. And only policemen had carried guns.

Governor Rockefeller said the hostages had "died in the crossfire." Oswald lamely suggested that they "could very well have been used as shields." The rescued hostages vigorously endorsed the police assault, and in Washington President Nixon said that the "painful, excruciating" decision to storm Attica had been the only thing the authorities "could possibly do." The conflict of opinion over what had happened was rapidly becoming ideological. Those who distrusted liberals, penal reforms, "bleeding hearts" and "do-gooders" rejected all criticism of the troopers. They blamed the convicts—in a fierce editorial the *Atlanta Constitution* denounced "the animals of Attica" for trying to impose "kangaroo justice" on the hostages—and many also blamed the overseers. As an exhausted Wicker left Attica a guard at the door hissed at him, "You people will never again be allowed inside this facility under any circumstances."

The other side was also vehement. Newark Mayor Kenneth Gibson called the crushing of the prison revolt "one of the most callous and blatantly repressive acts ever carried out by a supposedly civilized society." Wicker later noted that although sixty inmates had been indicted on some 1,300 counts, not a single law enforcement officer had been charged with anything, despite "evidence of official negligence, official brutality, official indiscipline, official excess—possibly even official murder." After the rebellion had been suppressed, the McKay Commission found there had been "widespread beatings, proddings, kickings." Prisoners had been stripped and forced to run a gauntlet of guards with hickory billy clubs. Wounded guards had been swiftly treated, their families quickly notified. Wounded inmates had been left without medical attention for four hours, their bodies tagged "P1, P2, P3." Four days later the families of some prisoners were still frantically trying to learn whether their sons or husbands were alive or dead. Often Attica wouldn't tell them even that. Those who did hear received curt wires: REGRET TO INFORM YOU THAT YOUR HUSBAND RAYMOND RIVERA NUMBER 29533 HAS DECEASED. THE BODY REPOSES AT THIS INSTITUTION.

"All right we are two nations," John Dos Passos had written bitterly of the chasm between the rich and the starving in Depression America. The rupture was along different lines now, but it cut equally deep. Three years earlier a new occupant of the White House had vowed to "bring us together." He hadn't done it. The people were as far apart as ever, unable to agree on the most elementary issues—justice and mercy, war and peace, right and wrong—and with a new presidential election a year away Americans were beginning to eye anew Richard Nixon's standings in the polls. Here, however, there was a change. As late as early August pollster Albert Sindlinger found that only 27 percent of the voters wanted to see Nixon reelected, but before the month was out his popularity curve paused, leveled out, and slowly rose. The decisive factor was resolute executive action at home and abroad.

The thirty-first world table tennis championships were held in Nagoya, Japan, that April, and the composition of the U.S. team was a tribute to the sport's widespread appeal: a Chrysler personnel supervisor, a Du Pont chemist, an editor of *Sports Illustrated*, a college professor, a black federal employee, an IBM programmer, an immigrant from the Dominican Republic, an employee of a Wall

Street bank, two teen-age girls, two housewives, and two college undergraduates. One of the students, Glenn Cowan of Santa Monica, was the most flamboyant member of the party; he wore tie-dyed purple bell-bottoms and a shirt with a peace symbol, and he kept his shoulder-length hair under control during play with a headband. Possibly because the headband was red, possibly because he was alert and extroverted, Cowan was singled out by players from the People's Republic of China for a historic proposal. How, he was asked, would he and his teammates like to make an all-expenses-paid tour of Red China?

They were delighted—"To quote Chairman Mao," Cowan said after consulting his teammates, "I seem to have struck the spark that started a prairie fire"—and a formal invitation to them from Secretary General Sung Chung of the Chinese table tennis delegation quickly followed. Washington had no objection; just a few weeks earlier the State Department had lifted all restrictions on Americans who wanted to travel in the People's Republic. Everyone concerned, including the ping-pong players, knew that the relationship between the two events was not coincidental. It was generally interpreted as an opening move toward detente, a reflection of the new confidence in Peking since the violent three-year power struggle there, known as the Great Proletarian Cultural Revolution, had ended in the final triumph of Mao and Premier Chou En-lai two years earlier. When seven western newspapermen were granted permission to enter China and cover the tour, it was clear that the world had reached a historic turning point. Obviously the Chinese, like the Russians before them, were using sport for diplomatic purposes. Table tennis acquired a new status overnight. Even President Nixon told his staff that "I was quite a Ping Pong player in my days at law school. I might say I was fairly good at it." Moscow sulked. The Kremlin called Peking's overture to the Americans "unprincipled."

On April 10 the U.S. team crossed from Hong Kong to the border station of Lo Wu via a short, steel-trussed bridge and continued on over another, tin-roofed bridge to the Chinese city of Shumchun. There smiling Communist officials led them to an immaculate cream and blue train. Their first destination was Canton, which since the rupture between Washington and Peking twenty-one years earlier had been rechristened Kwangchow. Along the twenty-three-mile journey there they saw banana groves, lichee trees, rice paddies, and, at strategic intervals, gigantic billboards bearing pictures of Mao. At Canton's new airport they boarded a Soviet-built Ilyushin-18 airliner while loudspeakers blared military marches and quotations from *The Thoughts of Chairman Mao.* An exhortatory sign in the terminal read PEOPLE OF THE WORLD UNITE AND DEFEAT THE U.S. AGGRESSORS AND THEIR RUNNING DOGS. It wasn't meant as an insult to the visitors. Mao's government at that point was drawing a fine line between the American people, whose friendship it wanted, and its government, which Peking Radio continued to excoriate as a conspiracy of "bloodthirsty gangsters."

Even in April Peking's climate retains the bite of winter, but apart from that the capital's reception for the U.S. ping-pong group was all hospitality. Quartered in the elegant Hsinchiao Hotel, they were entertained at banquets and taken on a tour of the nineteenth-century summer palace of the Manchu emperors and the Great Hall of the People. They saw a "revolutionary ballet," *The Red Detachment of Women,* and heard an opera celebrating the victory of Communism over capitalism, *Taking Tiger Mountain by Strategy.* Arriving at Peking's Indoor Stadium for an exhibition match with members of the Chinese team, they were greeted by 18,000 cheering fans and a huge banner reading WELCOME TO THE TABLE TENNIS TEAM FROM THE UNITED STATES. A band struck up the stirring strains of "Sailing the Seas Depends on the Helmsman, Making Revolution Depends on the Thought of Mao Tse-tung." Cowan did the frug.

Chinese tact continued in the table tennis competition. Holding back their first team, which could have crushed the Americans, they sent in second-string players who only won the men's matches 5–3 and the women's 5–4. The hosts called the contests "friendly games." They were not the most striking act of friendship. The following day Chou En-lai met China's ping-pong guests in the red-carpeted reception room of the Great Hall. The members of the United States delegation weren't the only table tennis visitors that week, and since Chinese protocol is rigidly alphabetical, they were preceded by players from Canada, Colombia, England, and Nigeria. But Chou spent most of his time—one and three-quarter hours—with them. He told them, "We have opened a new page in the relations of the Chinese and the American people." To the U.S. newsmen he said that now American correspondents could "come in batches."

That same day, as the Americans left for Hong Kong, President Nixon eased the twenty-year U.S. embargo on trade with China and

Peking resumed telephone contact with Washington and London. There was a lot to talk about; less than two weeks later a presidential commission headed by Henry Cabot Lodge recommended that the People's Republic be admitted to the United Nations provided a way could be found for Nationalist China to retain its seat. Already plans were being laid for a secret visit to Peking by National Security Adviser Henry Kissinger at which the chief topic of conversation would be a state visit by the President himself.

Early in July Kissinger flew to Asia, officially for conferences in Saigon, Thailand, India, and Pakistan. After a ninety minute talk with Pakistani President Agha Muhommad Yahya Khan, Kissinger announced a change in his schedule; he would spend a brief working holiday in the mountain resort of Nathia Gali, thirty-eight miles north of Rawalpindi. The trip wasn't turning out to be particularly newsworthy, and the curiosity of newsmen covering it was unstirred when the Yahya Khan government announced that Kissinger would have to spend an additional day in the resort because of a slight indisposition. He was thought to be suffering from Asian dysentery—"Delhi belly"—and the U.S. embassy encouraged the assumption by putting out word that a doctor had been dispatched to examine him. A correspondent suggested that the presidential adviser would be more comfortable in an air-conditioned Rawalpindi hotel. The embassy spokesman replied that the visitor did not want to embarrass anyone in the capital by his illness.

Actually Kissinger had driven to the Rawalpindi airport with three aides and boarded a Pakistan International Airlines plane for Peking. At noon on July 9 they landed on a deserted field outside the Chinese capital. Driven to a villa on a nearby lake, they lunched and were then joined, at mid-afternoon, by Chou En-lai. Chou and Kissinger conferred late that Friday night, Saturday evening, and Sunday morning. Five pounds heavier because of Chinese hospitality, the presidential adviser—who was still believed to be laid low by a stomach ailment—flew back to Pakistan and rejoined his party after a two-and-a-half day absence. Nothing more was heard from Peking Radio about American officials being gangsters or running dogs. Five days after the Kissinger mission President Nixon flew by helicopter from San Clemente to a Burbank television studio and delivered a four-minute address which astounded the world. He had been invited to visit Red China, he announced, and he was accepting with pleasure. He said: "I have taken this action because of my profound conviction that all nations will gain from a reduction of tensions and a better relationship between the United States and the People's Republic of China." In a reference to Nationalist China the President added that "seeking a new relationship" with Peking would not be "at the expense of our old friends."

It was a promise he could not keep. His plan to seat both Chinas in the United Nations was doomed. Each year the U.N. had come closer to expelling the Taiwan delegation, and this was enough to put it over the top. On October 25 the General Assembly voted Peking in and Chiang Kai-shek's representatives out. American conservatives watching television that day beheld a spectacle of humiliation which would have been unbelievable in the days when Dean Acheson and John Foster Dulles ran U.S. foreign policy; the Algerians and the Albanians embraced, and the Tanzanians danced a jig in the aisles. The reaction in Washington was sharp and angry. Barry Goldwater demanded that the United States quit the U.N. and consign the General Assembly to "some place like Moscow or Peking." Hugh Scott of Pennsylvania spoke contemptuously of "hot-pants principalities" like Tanzania, and presidential press secretary Ronald Ziegler condemned "the shocking demonstration and undisguised glee among some of the delegates following the vote." But these were mere political rituals. The fact was that Chiang's continuing pretensions to great-power status had been doomed from the moment of the first conciliatory gesture toward Glenn Cowan in Nagoya.

One month to the day after his telecast announcing that he would be flying to Peking, Nixon went on the air again with news of another momentous step, this one to rescue the American economy. It badly needed help. The country was sliding into its worst money crisis since the Depression. Then the nation's crippled finances had been further hobbled by Hoover's rigid faith in the economic gospels of Adam Smith and John Stuart Mill. Nixon paid them lip service, but in practice he was anything but inflexible. Hugh Sidey of *Time* observed that the President "clings to what is familiar until the last moment. Then, when the evidence overwhelms him or something happens in his gut, he decides to act, and nothing stands very long in his way. He abandons his philosophy, his promises, his speeches, his friends, his counselors. He marches out of one life into a new world without any apologies or glancing back." At times this could be disconcerting, but in that August of 1971, with the dollar tottering on the brink of disaster, it was heartening.

At the close of World War II the United States had been the wealthiest country in the history of civilization, holding 35 billion of the world's 40-odd billions of monetary gold. The structure of postwar finance had been established the year before at Bretton Woods, New Hampshire, where gold and dollars had been established as the reserves behind the money of every major nation outside the Communist bloc. There wasn't enough gold to support the anticipated flow of foreign trade, so the dollar, the world's strongest money, was made equal to gold. Debts between countries could be paid with either one. America pledged to redeem all available dollars with an ounce of gold for every $35, and other countries expressed the value of their currency in dollars. It worked. Trade prospered. Whenever a country managed to tip the balance of its U.S. trade in its favor—exporting more goods to America than it imported from there—its surplus dollars were used to back new issues of its own money.

Since the United States was rich and the rest of the world was comparatively poor, large sums went overseas to help the needy. It didn't matter; there was so much. Then came the Korean War and the revival of European commerce. By 1961, the end of the Common Market's first year, U.S. gold reserves were down to 17 billion dollars. In 1962 they dropped to 16 billion, in 1963 to 15 billion. At the beginning of the 1970s the reserves stood at 11 billion—almost the bare minimum, since American law required a dollar's worth of gold in Fort Knox for each four dollars in circulation, and the nation's business needed 40 billion in paper and silver. Meantime the balance of trade had become less and less favorable to the United States. In 1960 the country had imported 15 billion dollars' worth of goods and sold 20 billion abroad, leaving a surplus of five billion. By 1970 this margin was down to two billion. In May 1971 it vanished. The nation was trading in the red, and with the Pentagon still hemorrhaging wealth in Vietnam there was no hope of a quick turnaround. Secretary of Commerce Maurice Stans warned that the U.S. faced its first trade deficit since 1893.

That month economists received anxious signals from Germany. The *Wirtschaftswunder* had transformed the Federal Republic into a heavy exporter. Twice during the previous decade the deutsche mark had been revalued upward, altering its value vis-à-vis the dollar and enriching speculators who accumulated reserves of it. Now the pressure was mounting for another revaluation. As a member of the International Monetary Fund established at Bretton Woods, Bonn was obliged to maintain the relationship between the dollar and the mark, buying dollars and selling marks as the mark became more valuable. Because of the unfavorable balance in American trade, speculators had a lot of dollars—or "Eurodollars," as dollars owned abroad were called—to invest. In the first four months of 1971 the stocks of Eurodollars on the continent had taken a frightening jump, from five billion to between 50 and 60 billion, and the German central bank was being flooded with them.

Die Zentralbank bought and bought until Bonn, recognizing early signs of inflation, notified the International Monetary Fund on May 9 that it wouldn't buy any more, Bretton Woods or no Bretton Woods. Instead the Germans proposed to let their currency find its own level under the law of supply and demand. In the idiom of economists they would "float" the mark. It floated up from 25 cents to 27 cents and hung there, relieving the pressure on their central bank and, incidentally, improving the U.S. balance of trade with the Federal Republic, since American goods were now cheaper there. But the respite was brief. Because of what Larry Stuntz of the Associated Press called "that huge pool of Eurodollars sloshing around Europe"—it amounted to the equivalent of all the money circulating in America—speculators were bound to turn elsewhere. They built a fire under the French franc, but Paris, which had been watching the German agony, quickly cut loose from the International Monetary Fund and limited dollar trades. The wildcatters went after the Swiss franc next. Bern followed the example of Paris. It was becoming increasingly hard to unload dollars. Bretton Woods was coming unstuck; *Barron's* was predicting a worldwide panic by fall. Then, early in August, came an authoritative forecast that the U.S. trade deficit for the second quarter would exceed seven billion dollars. This was swiftly followed by a report of the Joint Congressional Economic Committee which declared that the dollar was overvalued, that other currencies should be revalued upward, and that if this wasn't done the United States should stop buying gold. The stock market dove; the Dow Jones industrial average dropped 100 points from its April high. There was virtually no market for Eurodollars now. American tourists in Europe found that the once mighty dollar had become unacceptable currency. World trade was at a standstill; merchants could no longer be sure what their money would buy next week, or even tomorrow.

Americans were getting bad economic news at home, too. Nixon, predicting that 1971 would be a good year and 1972 a bad year, had based his budget on an anticipated Gross National Product of 1,065 billion dollars. It came in at 1,050 billion, and half the gain was inflation. Production was down; unemployment, at 6 percent, was nearing the recession level. At the end of June the administration ended the fiscal year with an appalling 23.2-billion-dollar deficit, just two billion less than Johnson's record-breaking 1968 shortfall and an incredible 24.5 billion below Nixon's expectations. The President had alarmed his conservative supporters by talking in terms of a "full employment balance," a Keynesian concept which holds that a budget is "balanced" if the amount of spending does not exceed the amount which would be collected in taxes if everyone had a job. But even with that yardstick the administration was eight billion in the red. And the future was glum. New labor contracts promised rail workers a hike of 42 percent in 42 months; steelworkers would get 30 percent in three years. Inflation would jump accordingly.

Congress had given the President the Economic Stabilization Act of 1970, authorizing him to "issue such orders as he may deem appropriate to stabilize prices, rents, wages, and salaries." Nixon had opposed the bill. He had been forced to sign it because it set aside basic resources needed for national defense, but he had vowed he would never use it. His plans excluded controls. He didn't even believe in voluntary guidelines or jawboning—using presidential prestige to persuade labor and management to forego wage or price increases.

All this changed in one short weekend at Camp David with his economic advisers. Summoned on twenty-four hours' notice, they drafted an economic message invoking the very powers he rejected, and on Sunday, August 15, he was on television with it. He called the program his New Economic Policy. Among the measures he ordered, or asked Congress for, was a closing of the "gold window"—the United States would no longer exchange dollars for gold. Most imports would be subjected to a 10 percent surtax, designed to make American goods more competitive at home with those from abroad, and in some cases Americans would receive tax breaks if they bought U.S. merchandise. Industry would get tax credit for new investment. The 7 percent excise tax on automobiles would be repealed, an average saving of $200 per car. With few exceptions, all U.S. prices, wages, rents, and dividends would be frozen for ninety days at their present levels. A Cost of Living Council headed by Treasury Secretary John Connally would preside over the freeze.

Nixon had floated the dollar, and the effect was the same as devaluation. In money markets it amounted to 2 percent in the first two weeks. Foreign bankers were understanding; they indicated that they were prepared to revalue their currencies if the U.S. would drop the surcharge. Meanwhile there was little retaliation abroad. The Danes did introduce a surcharge of their own, and the French muttered about imposing one, but there were few threats to build tariff walls against American goods which had suddenly become cheaper. Connally was not a popular man in foreign chancelleries; his insistence that the United States must quickly achieve a 13-billion-dollar swing in its balance of payments provoked protests that so rapid a reversal would destroy the Common Market. But at a September meeting of the International Monetary Fund, financiers from the "Group of Ten" wealthiest nations continued to be sympathetic to the U.S. position. Connally, in turn, hinted that America might reopen the gold window and raise its price—direct devaluation. Subsequent talks in Rome led to an agreement, announced at the Smithsonian Institution in Washington, under which the U.S. surcharge was canceled, the value of other currencies was raised, and the price of gold was provisionally boosted to $38.

On Wall Street the day after Nixon's announcement of the freeze—or Phase One, as it was already being called—the Dow Jones industrial average jumped 32.93 to 888.95 on what was then the busiest day in its history; 31,720,000 shares were traded. In September, the first full month of Phase One, the nation's rise in living costs was held to 2.4 percent and the wholesale price index posted its biggest decline in five years. A few holes were poked in the wage and price ceilings, and inevitably there was a great deal of confusion in some industries, but for the most part the thing worked. Unfortunately it was, by definition, only the first step. On November 13 it would expire. Before then the administration had to find guidelines which provided hope of preserving relative stability while rectifying the injustices which had been frozen into the system.

On October 8 Nixon spoke to the nation again, this time setting up the machinery for Phase Two. The challenge was greater now. Economist Herbert Stein, the chief planner of the new stage, had anticipated the difficulties at the time of the first message. He said, "I knew immediately the problem would not be the freeze, but the unfreeze, the thaw." The goal of this second program was to hold inflation to between 2 and 3 percent a year. Controls would be administered by a seven-man Price Commission and a fifteen-member pay board. There would be no ceiling on profits, the President said, and the success or failure of the plan would depend upon "the voluntary cooperation of the American people."

Fear that both labor and capital might withdraw their representatives from the supervisory panels doomed hopes of keeping inflation below 3 percent. "If the President doesn't want our membership on the Pay Board on our terms, he knows what he can do," Meany told delegates to an AFL-CIO convention in Miami Beach. Nixon boldly flew to the convention hall to reply: "I know exactly what I can do. And I am going to do it." Nevertheless, the board capitulated to Meany in the last week of Phase One, announcing full recognition of deferred wage increases and establishment of 5.5 percent as the annual norm for new raises. Even that line wasn't held; in its first decision under Phase Two the board granted a 15 percent pay boost for coal miners. The price commission was no more effective. It began by approving 7 percent increases in the cost of tinplate manufactured by two steel companies. Within three weeks one-third of the country's 1,500 largest corporations had applied for endorsement of price hikes, and acceptances surpassed rejections by a ratio of 20 to 1.

In December the stock market plunged again. The board continued its conciliatory treatment of labor, but three months later Meany and two other top union leaders pulled out anyway, accusing the majority of bias. The next day Leonard Woodcock of the UAW also quit. That left only one labor member: Frank E. Fitzsimmons, the Teamsters president. Since Nixon's Christmas Week pardon of Jimmy Hoffa, the Teamsters had been in the President's pocket. That clemency had been universally attributed to politics, but few blamed Nixon. Though his standing in the polls had improved somewhat since the lows of summer, it was generally believed that if he was going to be reelected he would need all the help he could get.

Portrait of an American

RALPH NADER

IN THE CONNECTICUT MANUFACTURING CITY of Winsted his Lebanese immigrant father was the local populist, a familiar American type. Customers at Nadra Nader's Highland Sweet Shop, a restaurant and bakery, complained that the proprietor never let them eat in peace. Nadra was always lecturing them about the wrongs, the inequities, the injustices of the system. Like many immigrants, he was a more ardent Democrat than the natives. He went on about the crimes of the Interests and was forever threatening to sue them. In time nearly everyone there tuned him out, with one exception: his youngest son Ralph.

In 1938, at the age of four, Ralph Nader was a tiny spectator when lawyers harangued juries in the local courthouse. At fourteen he became a daily reader of the *Congressional Record.* He won a scholarship to Princeton, where he refused to wear white bucks or other symbols of sartorial conformity and staged a protest against the spraying of campus trees with DDT. He was locked so often in the university library after hours that he was given a key. Characteristically he responded by denouncing the administration for callous disregard of other students' legal rights. In 1955 he was elected to Phi Beta Kappa, graduated magna cum laude, and admitted to Harvard Law School, which he described as a "high-priced tool factory" turning out servants of power.

His reputation as a puritan grew. He foreswore the reading of novels; they were a waste of time. So were movies; he would limit himself to two a year. He scorned plays, tobacco, alcohol, girls, and parties. At Harvard he also quit driving automobiles, but here his motive was different. He had become interested in auto injury cases, and after some research in car technology at nearby MIT he wrote an article for the *Harvard Law Record* entitled "American Cars: Designed for Death."

The problem continued to bother him. Throughout his career he was to be concerned with the protection of the human body—from unsafe natural gas pipelines, food additives, tainted meat, pollution, mining health hazards, herbicides, unwholesome poultry, inadequate nursing homes, and radiation emission from color TVs—but the auto threat was basic. He opened a private law practice in Hartford (which rapidly became a source of free legal advice for the poor) and continued to urge stronger car safety regulations on local governments. Early in 1964 he took his campaign to Washington, where Assistant Secretary of Labor Daniel Patrick Moynihan hired him as a fifty-dollar-a-day consultant to the Labor Department.

Working with Connecticut's Senator Abraham Ribicoff, Nader turned out a two-hundred-page brief calling for auto safety legislation with teeth. A General Motors engineer became the first of his many secret contacts in industry by pointing out the Chevrolet Corvair's tendency to flip over. In November 1965 Nader's first book, *Unsafe at Any Speed: The Designed-in Dangers of the American Automobile,* called the Corvair "one of the nastiest-handling cars ever built" and charged that the industry had taken "four years of the model and 1,124,076 Corvairs before they decided to do something."

Unsafe at Any Speed, which sold 450,000 copies in cloth and paper, brought its author before a Ribicoff committee on February 10, 1966, as an expert witness on hazardous autos. Three weeks later Nader became a national figure when he accused General Motors of harassing him with private detectives, abusive telephone calls, and women who tried to entice him into compromising situations. A GM operative admitted under oath that he had been instructed by his superiors "to get something somewhere on this guy . . . get him out of their hair . . . shut him up." Nader filed suit for 26 million dollars and collected $280,000. Like his book royalties, the money went to the cause; when the National Traffic and Motor Vehicle Safety Act was passed that summer the *Washington Post* declared that "Most of the credit for making possible this important legislation belongs to one man—Ralph Nader . . . a one-man lobby for the public prevailed over the nation's most powerful industry."

Nader set himself up as a watchdog of the National Traffic Safety Agency and then went after the meat packers; the result was the Wholesome Meat Act of 1967. He broadened his attack on exploiters of the consumer to include the Food and Drug Administration, Union Carbide smokestacks, think tanks, unsafe trucks, pulp and paper mills, property taxes, bureaucrats, consumer credit, banks, and supermarkets. One observer said, "Ralph is not a consumer champion. He is just plain against consumption."

Unlike the muckrakers of the Lincoln Steffens era, Nader acquired a conservative constituency. At a time of anarchy and disorder he believed in working within the system. He was a linear thinker, an advocate of law and industrial order. Stockbrokers contributed to his causes. Miss Porter's School sent him volunteer workers. He was acquiring lieutenants now—"Nader's Raiders," a reporter dubbed them—and they were mostly white upper-middle-class graduates of the best schools, with names like Pullman cars: Lowell Dodge, William Harrison Wellford, Reuben B. Robertson III, and William Howard Taft IV. One of them, Edward F. Cox, became a son-in-law of President Nixon.

He installed them in cubbyhole offices in the National Press Building furnished with secondhand desks, chairs bought at rummage sales, apple crate files, and shelves made from planks and bricks. He worked them a hundred hours a week and paid them poverty-level salaries. Royalties from the books they turned out went into his campaigns. They didn't complain; he himself was earning $200,000 a year and spending $5,000.

He lived in an $80-a-month furnished room near Dupont Circle, paid $97 a month office rent, and had no secretary. People gave him briefcases; he turned them into files and traveled instead with his papers in a sheaf of manila envelopes. His black shoes were scuffed, the laces broken and knotted. He wore a gray rumpled suit, frayed white shirts, and narrow ties which had been out of style for years. Standing six feet four inches, with wavy black hair and a youthful face, he was compared by *Newsweek* to a "Jimmy Stewart hero in a Frank Capra movie." His only unusual expense was his telephone bill. It was enormous. He was paying for calls from all his volunteer spies in industry.

Most of his income came from lecture fees. Each week he received fifty invitations to speak; he accepted 150 a year, charging as much as $2,000. He became known as the most long-winded speaker since Walter Reuther, rarely relinquishing the lectern before an hour and forty-five minutes. There was never any flourish at the end. He would simply stop talking and pivot away. College audiences gave him wild ovations, but he never turned back to acknowledge them. If asked to autograph a book he would curtly reply, "No." A friend said, "Ralph is so afraid of being turned into a movie star, of having his private life romanticized, that he has renounced his own private life."

He was an impossible customer. To a waitress he would say when ordering, "Is the ham sliced for each sandwich? Is that genuine or processed cheese? Do *you* eat sugar? You do? Let me tell you something—it's absolutely useless, no food value." To an airline stewardess he said, "The only thing you should be proud to serve on this whole plane is the little bag of nuts. And you should take the salt off the nuts." When Allegheny Airlines had the temerity to bump him from a flight on which he had a confirmed reservation, he filed suit and was awarded $50,000 in punitive damages, half for him and half for the consumer group he had been unable to address because of the missed flight.

Asked by Robert F. Kennedy why he was "doing all this," he answered, "If I were engaged in activities for the prevention of cruelty to animals, nobody would ask me that question." His ultimate goal, he said, was "nothing less than the qualitative reform of the industrial revolution," and he refused to be lured from it by any bait. Nicholas von Hoffman and Gore Vidal proposed him for the Presidency. He said, "I'm not interested in public office. The biggest job in this country is citizen action. Politics follows that."

Yet for all his evangelism, his devotion to the public good, and his monastic life, Nader's impact on society was questionable. At times he seemed to know it. "We always fail," he said once. "The whole thing is limiting the degree of failure." His audiences appeared to regard him as a performer. They applauded him, but it was as though they were applauding an act. Few of them felt compelled to get involved, to follow his example or even his advice. They went right on driving big Detroit cars, eating processed foods, coating themselves with expensive cosmetics and smoking poisonous cigarettes.

In a pensive moment he reflected that "A couple of thousand years ago in Athens, a man could get up in the morning, wander around the city, and inquire into matters affecting his well-being and that of his fellow citizens. No one asked him 'Who are you with?'" Americans of the 1970s did not inquire about him; they knew. Yet they themselves remained uncommitted. The painful fact—excruciating for him—was that however loud their cheers for Ralph Nader, however often they said that they were for him, in this Augustan age of materialism they were not really with him.

Thirty-seven

PRIDE GOETH

THE AGE OF PUBLICITY, as Louis Kronenberger called it, may be said to have begun in the 1920s with flagpole sitting and the ordeal of Floyd Collins, an unlucky youth whose entrapment and eventual death in a Kentucky cave-in was page one news for two weeks in 1925. Ballyhoo became increasingly conspicuous after World War II with the emergence of such exhibitionists as those who took their marriage vows on carnival carrousels, spent their honeymoons in department store windows, bore children under floodlights, and hired halls to celebrate their divorces. "The trouble with us in America," Kronenberger wrote in 1954, "isn't that the poetry of life has turned to prose, but that it has turned to advertising copy." He suggested that next to Marx and Freud, the ideologue with the greatest impact on U.S. lives was Phineas Taylor Barnum.

As American influence spread abroad, so did the Barnum spirit. Among the bizarre stunts overseas which put their perpetrators on front pages in 1972 was a telephoned threat to blow up the luxury liner *Queen Elizabeth II* and the defacing of Michelangelo's *Pietà* in St. Peter's Basilica by an Australian geologist with a twelve-pound hammer, a perverted sense of theater, and the conviction that he was the son of God. They were outrageous, but at least they weren't homicidal, which was more than could be said for many foreign self-promoters. That year was memorable for what might be called the hoopla of death. Murders committed abroad for their publicity value included those of three NATO electronics experts executed by Turkish leftists, twenty-six travelers in Tel

Aviv's Lod Airport by a squad of Japanese terrorists, eleven Israeli athletes at the Munich Olympics by Palestinian Arabs of the Black September ring, and 469 Ulster Catholics and Protestants by Ulster Protestants and Catholics. In addition, Japan's Yasunari Kawabata, the 1968 Nobel Prize winner in literature, took his own life. He thereby followed the example of Yukio Mishima, a young colleague who had protested western influence in his homeland by committing ritualistic hara-kiri in the good old way, eviscerating himself and submitting to decapitation by his best friend.

Americans had no reason to feel smug about this lengthening roll of dishonor overseas. It was Lee Harvey Oswald of Dallas who had first demonstrated to his countrymen in the 1960s that attention must be paid to a daring murderer, and his example had been followed in the United States by, among others, Sirhan Sirhan, of Los Angeles, Charles Whitman of the Austin bell tower, and Robert Benjamin Smith, who had committed mayhem in the Mesa, Arizona, beauty school. In 1972 they were joined by others with similar motivation. Mobster "Crazy Joe" Gallo was gunned down in New York's Little Italy. His sister told reporters, "He changed his image, that's why this happened." When George Jackson's two Soledad colleagues were acquitted in the death of a prison guard, Angela Davis managed to transform it into a public relations triumph; "It's beautiful," she said. The end of *Life* magazine on December 29, closing a big publicity artery, was treated by some politicians as a death in the family. The name of four-star Air Force General John D. Lavelle began appearing on reference books after he had been reprimanded and reduced in rank for unauthorized bombing raids in North Vietnam; his name had been in the papers. Most memorable was Arthur Herman Bremer, who gunned down George Wallace in a Laurel, Maryland, shopping center on the eve of the presidential primary there. On the way to jail Bremer asked officers, "How much do you think I'll get for my memoirs?"

While these malefactions were drearily familiar, some Americans did break new publicity ground that year. Two police cases deserve special recognition because, unlike the Soledad, Gallo, and Wallace incidents, they displayed remarkable imaginative powers on the part of criminals or accusers. The first was the skyjacking of a Southern Airways DC9 jet by pirates who lifted extortion from the realm of the ordinary by threatening to crash the plane into the nuclear research plant at Oak Ridge unless their demands were met.

Though the airliner's tires were shot out by FBI agents, the skyjackers collected two million dollars at the Chattanooga airport and landed in Havana, where, like so many of their predecessors, they were dismayed to find themselves under Cuban arrest and their loot confiscated. The other episode followed a charge by J. Edgar Hoover that peace workers were plotting to kidnap Henry Kissinger and blow up steam pipes beneath Washington, D.C., which carried heat to all federal buildings in the capital. Indicted for conspiracy, six Catholics and a Moslem were tried. The government lost the case, and nine months afterward two of the defendants, Father Philip Berrigan and Sister Elizabeth McAlister, startled their associates at, respectively, the Society of St. Joseph and the Sacred Heart of Mary community, by getting married.

That was thought strange by practitioners of traditional religion, but an even zanier approach to piety was that of the "Jesus people," also known as the "Jesus freaks" or the "street Christians." In reality they represented the latest stage in the youth movement, which had evolved from the beats to the hippies and was searching for a new kick. "Jesus, am I ever high on Jesus!" was one of their rallying cries. Three years earlier Theodore Roszak had declared in *The Making of a Counter Culture* that the movement had clearly defined spiritual aspects. He meant Zen and even odder sects; Christianity was then considered hopelessly square and establishmentarian. Now, however, the cats were wearing crucifixes and Christ T-shirts—"You Have a Lot to Live," read one, echoing a Pepsi-Cola jingle, "And Jesus Has a Lot to Give." They established communes called God's Love, Zion's Inn, and Soul Inn, attended Jesus rock concerts and Christian nightclubs, and made some parents yearn for the days when kids got stoned on old-fashioned marijuana.

As the colleges continued to be almost serene in 1972, peace militants talked about a public relations failure, but administrators of state universities were relieved; taxpayers had been rejecting school bond issues by lopsided votes. President Nixon's press office claimed that he had "scored points" with his constituents by a colorful turn of phrase; he had said he planned to spend more time at Camp David because "I find that up here on top of a mountain, it is easier for me to get on top of the job." On November 14 the New York Stock Exchange achieved a breakthrough in good publicity when the Dow Jones industrial average closed at 1006.16, above 1,000 for the first time in history. (It was, though no one knew it then, a good time to sell.) The public image of Jacqueline Kennedy Onassis shone more brightly, and that of one of her tormentors more dully, after a federal judge in New York ruled that a freelance photographer named Ronald E. Galella had "relentlessly invaded" Mrs. Onassis's privacy. In the future, the court ruled, Galella would be required to stay 50 yards from her, 75 yards from her children, and 100 yards from the family's homes and schools.

These varied events in the Age of Publicity, while noteworthy, were, however, rendered pallid by the accomplishments of two giants of the age. Both were American, both were passionately devoted to advertisements of themselves, and both achieved international recognition in 1972. One was an outlaw, the other merely ill-tempered.

Robert James Fischer, the irascible one, played chess. It is not recorded that he ever did anything else except insult his opponents, fail to make scheduled appearances, alienate his supporters, display greed, break his word, deliver ultimatums, throw temper tantrums, disappear at crucial moments, and become, after a classic tournament with Russia's Boris Spassky in Reykjavik, Iceland, the first U.S. winner of the world chess championship. His countrymen agreed that it couldn't happen to a worse competitor. He stalked off angrily counting a record $156,000 in prize money.

The desperado was named Clifford Irving.

Shortly before Christmas 1971 the publishing firm of McGraw-Hill dispatched a 550-word publicity release of special interest to the New York offices of major editors, newscasters, and wire services. After nearly fourteen years of refusing to be interviewed, photographed, or even seen by members of the press, Howard Hughes, America's reclusive billionaire, had apparently completed, with the help of a collaborator, a 230,000-word account of his life. The clothbound edition of the work would be issued on March 27, 1972, and *Life* would publish three 10,000-word installments from it. "Call this autobiography," the announcement quoted Hughes as saying. "Call it my memoirs. Call it what you please. It is the story of my life in my own words." Also attributed to Hughes in the release were phrases singing the praises of his assistant in the project, Clifford Irving. In the billionaire's putative words, Irving had been picked "because of his sympathy, discernment, discretion and, as I learned, his integrity as a human being."

Hughes's recollections, it seemed, had been taped: "The words in this book—other than some of the questions which provoked them—are my own spoken words." At first editors assumed that the taping sessions had been held in the Bahamas hotel where he had been hiding out for the past year, but the truth seemed to be more dramatic than that; the two men had held over a hundred meetings "in various motel rooms and parked cars throughout the Western Hemisphere."

That was the claim advanced in the publisher's announcement. It would be accepted by the public for a month, and another month would pass before it was withdrawn. In the meantime the story was to become one of the most sensational in the history of the book trade. At one point it drove news of the President's inspection of the Great Wall of China off tabloid front pages. More newspapermen were covering Hughes and Irving than the Vietnam War—nine reporters from the *Los Angeles Times* alone. Thirty postal inspectors were tracking clues in the mails. Paramount reissued *The Carpetbaggers*, a thinly disguised fictional account of Hughes's life. An X-rated film entitled *Helga and Howard* was being shown in Manhattan, Hughes T-shirts were selling well at two dollars apiece, and people were wearing pins which said, "This is a genuine Howard Hughes button."

The genuineness of the autobiography was first questioned in the wake of the December announcement. A spokesman for the Hughes Tool Company denied "the existence of a Hughes autobiography." But the recluse was celebrated for his furtiveness with his closest associates; those who knew him best thought the disclaimer was completely in character, and in fact the editors of the book had expected it. When Managing Editor Ralph Graves of *Life* showed his staff a handwritten letter from Hughes approving serialization of the text, one of them asked, "How do we know the letter's not a forgery?" Graves replied, "It's authentic, all right. We've had it checked by an expert." Albert Leventhal, a McGraw-Hill vice president, told the *New York Times*, "We have gone to considerable efforts to ascertain that this is indeed the Hughes autobiography," and Donald M. Wilson, a *Life* vice president, told another newsman, "Oh, we're absolutely positive. Look, we're dealing with people like McGraw-Hill, and, you know, we're not exactly a movie magazine! This is Time, Inc. and McGraw-Hill talking. We've checked this thing out. We have proof."

To another questioner Wilson said, "We never dealt with the Hughes Tool Company. It doesn't surprise us that they know nothing of this, since Mr. Hughes was totally secretive about the project." The person they had dealt with was Irving, who had been a McGraw-Hill author for twelve years. He had written four unsuccessful novels and, more recently, *Fake!*, an account of Elmyr de Hory, an art forger and Irving's neighbor on the Spanish island of Ibiza. In retrospect it seems that his publishers should have taken a closer look at the author's preoccupation with fraudulence and his story that Hughes insisted upon discussing the matter with no one but him. The truth was that the book was a complete fabrication. Irving had never met Hughes, let alone taped him, and Hughes had never heard of the man who claimed to be his ghost. At first glance McGraw-Hill and *Life* seem to have been inexcusably gullible. But in fact the hoaxer had shown remarkable cunning, and he had also been lucky.

The plot had begun a year earlier with the reproduction in *Newsweek* of an eleven-line handwritten note by Hughes. A month later *Life* published the letter in color. Irving was the son of a cartoonist; he had inherited his father's clever fingers, and he found that with a little practice he could produce whole pages of writing which looked like that of Hughes. The tycoon was in the news that season, and much was being made of his secrecy. Some writers suggested that he might even be dead; no one in the outside world would know. It struck Irving that a book of reminiscences purporting to bear Hughes's imprimatur might go unchallenged by him, especially since he might already be in his grave. He persuaded Richard Suskind, a fellow hack living on the neighboring island of Majorca, to collaborate with him. Later, when the names of both men had become household words, their photographs would be familiar on front pages around the world—Irving, tall and ruggedly handsome, and Suskind, "built," as a friend put it, "like an avalanche with a gargoyle on top." Ultimately their likenesses would represent the ultimate in literary chicanery. In the beginning, however, they appeared to the editors at McGraw-Hill as a writer known for reliability if not talent and his diligent researcher. The editors had no way of knowing that Irving proposed to share the swag with his crony, 75 percent for himself and 25 percent for Suskind. A third member of the conspiracy was Irving's wife Edith, an attractive Swiss painter and the mother of his two children.

Irving played McGraw-Hill with consummate skill, forwarding them apparently genuine letters from Howard Hughes in which the billionaire expressed growing interest in the collaboration. At the appropriate time Hughes's signature appeared on a contract, clause 22 of which specified that "The Publisher agrees that it shall undertake no advertising or promotion or sale of the Work prior to 30 days after acceptance by the Publisher of a complete and satisfactory manuscript for the Work." *Life,* which bought first serial rights for $250,000, also agreed to stay mum. Taking what seemed to be reasonable precautions, the publisher submitted specimens of Hughes's supposed handwriting to an expert, who compared it with samples of the real thing and reported: "The chances that another person could copy this handwriting even in a similar way are less than one in a million." Later another firm of analysts concurred, declaring that it was "impossible, based on our years of experience in the field of questioned handwriting and signatures," that anyone except Howard Hughes could have written the material which had come from Irving.

Most ingenious of all, Irving told his publisher that the eccentric tycoon insisted that checks made out to him bear only his initials: "H. R. Hughes." When the author got them, he turned them over to his wife. Edith, wearing a wig and carrying an altered passport and a stolen identity card, flew to Zurich and opened a Swiss Credit Bank account in the name of "Helga R. Hughes." Into this account, number 320496, she ultimately deposited nearly a million dollars of McGraw-Hill money, which she then withdrew and put in the Swiss Banking Corporation across the street. Meanwhile her husband and Suskind had also been traveling, researching Hughes's life in the New York Public Library, the Library of Congress, Palm Springs, California, the morgues of the *Houston Chronicle* and the *Houston Post,* and—the unkindest cut of all—the files of Time-Life. Their most valuable acquisition was the unpublished manuscript of the memoirs of Hughes's retired chief lieutenant. Irving borrowed it from one of the man's associates and photocopied it. Pooling their information, he and Suskind took turns being "Hughes" and interviewing one another on tape. The tapes were then transcribed, and Irving wrote marginal comments on the resulting thousand-page manuscript in the billionaire's hand. The result seemed so authentic that it fooled men who had known Hughes intimately years earlier.

The conspiracy began to come apart on the afternoon of January 7, 1972, when Hughes, speaking from the Bahamas, held a two-and-a-half-hour press conference over the telephone with seven journalists who had covered him before his withdrawal into seclusion. He branded Irving's book a humbug and, while he was at it, denied reports that his fingernails were six inches long, that he was emaciated, and that his hair hung to his waist. All seven of his listeners agreed that the voice was his. Irving called it a fake, but time was beginning to run out for him. Edith's end of the plot had begun to come to light. A Hughes lawyer had asked his client to fill out a questionnaire, establishing its authenticity with his fingerprints. One of the questions was: "When is the last time you personally endorsed a check for any reason?" Hughes answered in his own hand: "More than ten years ago." The conspirators had assumed that numbered accounts in Swiss banks were inviolate under all circumstances. Not so: in cases of suspected crime details could be revealed, and when the Swiss learned that checks meant for Howard R. Hughes had been cashed by a German-speaking woman calling herself Helga R. Hughes, they knew something was rotten in Zurich. A worldwide search for the mysterious Helga began.

On Thursday, January 20, the day word of this sensational new development reached New York, Irving attended a conference of McGraw-Hill and *Life* executives. Coolly he advanced three possible explanations for it: that he had taped a charlatan pretending to be Hughes, that Hughes had used a "loyal servant" to deposit the checks, and that he, Irving, was a mountebank. Searching the eyes of everyone there, he said in his most sincere voice, "The last of these possibilities I intend to discard, and I hope that you do, too." His presence was superb; they all nodded. Flying back to Ibiza—to the indignation of *Life*, whose editors thought he should stay in New York until the crisis had been resolved—he replied to reporters pointing out the resemblance between Edith and the Swiss descriptions of Helga: "Do you really think I'd involve my family in an enterprise like this?" Back in Manhattan his lawyer, whose suspicions had not yet been aroused, confided to reporters that he thought his client had been duped by a gang of impostors, two of them gifted forgers and the third a six-foot-three beanpole who looked like Howard Hughes.

This was a crucial moment in the conspiracy, and a grasp of it is essential to an understanding of what was happening to Clifford Irving. He had a large part of the money in cash, he had his freedom, and he could have kept both. Other fugitives from justice were living comfortably on Ibiza and Majorca. He, Edith, and Suskind might have remained where they were or flown to any one of several South American countries where their crimes were not extraditable. Expense was no problem; they could have afforded almost anything. The alternative was grim; exposure was now inevitable. Why, then, did Irving fly back to New York and into the trap? The answer, in the opinion of those who were close to him, was that he couldn't resist the publicity. All his life he had craved attention. His books hadn't brought it, but this caper had, and the knowledge that an eager press corps awaited him at Kennedy Airport drew him as though he were helpless. The moth simply could not resist the flame. It is one of the sad little ironies of his story that when he landed there he couldn't answer their questions. He had laryngitis. "Gentlemen, this is a horrible experience," he whispered to them. For once one believes him.

Another irony followed swiftly. Two reporters believed that Irving had been in touch with a former Hughes aide named John Meier. Calling to see him at his lawyer's house, they sent in word: "Just tell Cliff we know all about Meier." Irving had never heard of Meier, but when the message reached him he was stunned. He thought they meant *Meyer*, which sounded the same. The man who had slipped him the unpublished memoirs of Hughes's retired assistant was named Stanley Meyer. If the newsmen had been tipped off to Meyer's role, the plotters were finished, and Irving might as well own up to it. He went out to the district attorney's office, made a partial confession there, and then returned to confront the two waiting newspapermen. "There's something I have to tell you guys," he said, "but it's got to be off the record, O.K.?" Under the circumstances an off-the-record confidence was impossible, but they nodded. He took a deep breath and said, "Well, you may have guessed it and you may not. Helga Hughes is Edith. Edith is Helga."

That should have been the end of it, but it wasn't. Improvising, he said that his wife had been acting at Hughes's direction, and so convincing was the manuscript—and the opinions of the handwriting experts—that the hoax limped along for a few more days. Then two blows demolished it. The manuscript of the retired Hughes assistant's unpublished memoirs surfaced, and the story of Irving's taping sessions with Hughes in various exotic settings was unmasked. He had in fact traveled to those places, sending back picture postcards to McGraw-Hill, but he had made the mistake of mixing pleasure with business. One of his companions had been a willowy blonde scuba diving instructor who had accompanied him to St. Croix in the Virgin Islands; she told the *Chicago Tribune* that she had grown very fond of Irving, whom she had thought was separated from his wife, but that neither of them had encountered Howard Hughes. The second and more damaging of the hoaxer's playmates was a beautiful Danish baroness and entertainer named Nina Van Pallandt. Irving had been indiscreet enough to brag about Nina to a McGraw-Hill editor and reveal her name. Located by postal inspectors, Nina admitted that she had traveled with Irving and said they had, in fact, copulated their way across Mexico. Since Cliff had been constantly at her side, she said, he couldn't possibly have kept any rendezvous with Hughes.

That was the end for Irving. But not for Nina. It is a provocative comment on the value of publicity—*any* publicity—that it was only a beginning for her. For years she had been limping along as an obscure folksinger. Now, suddenly, she was in demand everywhere. She appeared twice on the *David Frost Show*, twice on the *Mike Douglas Show*, twice on the *Dick Cavett Show*, once on the *Today Show*, once on the *Johnny Carson Show*, and on a television special. Manhattan's St. Regis Hotel booked her for three weeks, and she was signed up for appearances in Miami, Dallas, San Juan, and San Francisco. Her manager said the Irving happening was "worth five hit records and an Academy Award." Without doubt she was the most distinguished fornicatrix of 1972.

Howard Hughes was not so fortunate. The uproar had become so great that the Bahaman government began to investigate the fact that his staff lacked work permits and immigration clearance, whereupon he fled to Nicaragua accompanied by six television sets, several crates of Poland water, a document shredder, blood plasma, a refrigerator, a hospital bed, mattresses, office furniture, pots and pans, various boxes of film, several hundred yards of cable, an old electric stove, a heater, and a cheap vinyl couch.

Life was reimbursed by McGraw-Hill, which got most of its money back from the Irvings and Suskind, all three of whom briefly went to prison. But that wasn't the extent of McGraw-Hill's disasters that year. The publisher suffered a long streak of bad luck. After Irving had been led away the publishers had just begun to patch up their image with the success of a book about Indians, *The*

Memoirs of Chief Red Fox, when an awkward truth emerged: *Red Fox* was plagiarized from a work published in 1940. Next the editor of the Irving book was accused of an unethical practice: borrowing money from two other authors, the sum amounting to 10 percent of their advances from the publisher. Then a final touch assured the firm's wretched situation as the laughingstock of the New York communications industry that year. Before the hoax the first floor of the new McGraw-Hill Building on the Avenue of the Americas had been leased to a branch bank. Now the tenant was moving in. Horrified publishing executives saw the gilt lettering going up on the plate-glass windows and realized that there was absolutely nothing they could do about it, because the contracts had long been executed and filed. The signs read: THE IRVING TRUST COMPANY.

On the frosty morning of February 21, 1972, the silver, blue and white fuselage of the *Spirit of '76,* as Nixon called the presidential aircraft, flitted across the muddy ribbon of the Yangtze, headed northward, and entered its glide pattern over Peking. American reporters who had covered China a quarter-century earlier were amazed by the changes in the landscape below: paved roads, irrigation canals, huge collective farms, and trees ("Trees in China!" wrote Theodore H. White) lining the highways. On this historic day the masters of Red China would once more grasp the hands of American leaders in friendship. Anti-Communism would cease to be the dominant note in U.S. foreign policy. It was an occasion for good omens, the eve of George Washington's birthday in the United States and, in Peking, the seventh day of the Year of the Rat, an auspicious time on the Chinese calendar.

The presidential jet touched down at 11:30. A moment of consternation followed. Except for U.S. correspondents and TV technicians, the airport was almost deserted. There were placards, but they had nothing to do with Nixon—LONG LIVE THE CHINESE COMMUNIST PARTY and LONG LIVE THE GREAT SOLIDARITY OF ALL THE WORLD'S PEOPLE. Fewer than four hundred troops were on hand; they were singing a Red Army ballad of the 1930s, "The Three Rules of Discipline and the Eight Points of Attention." America's peripatetic thirty-seventh President had greeted the rulers of Romania, Pakistan, Yugoslavia, Spain, Canada, Brazil, Australia, Japan, India, Ireland, Italy, Germany, Belgium, France, Britain, Austria, and the Vatican. Always there had been crowds. Here there were none.

Dismayed aides wondered what to do if he were left in the lurch. Could they fly home and say it had all been a mistake? At the last moment the inscrutable Chinese became scrutable. Premier Chou En-lai appeared with a handful of officials. Nixon extended his hand, and as millions of Americans watched on television, Chou took it.

The Chinese people were not watching. News of the visitors had been kept from them. The presidential motorcade entered the city on silent streets. All the inhabitants seemed to be elsewhere. But five hours later, when Nixon was still settling down in a two-story buff brick guesthouse, he was unexpectedly summoned to the private study of seventy-eight-year-old Mao, the living legend of the new China. The President and the Chairman chatted for a full hour, accompanied only by Chou and Henry Kissinger. The substance of the conversation remained secret, but obviously there was rapport; at one point the No. 1 International Bandit reached across the tea table and softly held the hand of the No. 1 Imperialist Dog, and next morning a picture of the meeting, with the principals smiling, appeared on the front page of the *People's Daily*. The message was clear: the visit had the Chairman's blessing. Now there was excitement in the streets. When Nixon appeared there, people clapped hands—in unison, to be sure, but that was how things were done here—and Mao designated his fourth wife, the revolutionary firebrand Chiang Ching, to be the President's official hostess.

Each day for five days Nixon and Chou conferred for four hours at a long green table. There was less there than met the eye, as the vague communiqué at the end made clear; it mostly dealt with the need for more friendship among the Chinese and American peoples, and the only real concession came from the President, a promise to withdraw U.S. military forces from Taiwan. But the real significance of the talks is that they were held at all. The President and the First Lady were determined to be amicable. It showed, and was appreciated. Every evening they sat through a three-hour ceremonial banquet in the Great Hall of the People, pluckily grappling their way through eight courses with ivory chopsticks and drinking toasts with *mao tai* while a Chinese orchestra played such tunes as "Billy Boy" and "She'll Be Coming 'Round the Mountain." They watched exhibitions of ping-pong, badminton, and gymnastics, and one evening Chiang Ching took them to a ballet, *The Red Detachment of Women,* which was all about cruel landlords. Nixon, who was trying to reduce the taxes landlords paid in the United States, nevertheless applauded heartily, and next morning his wife gamely continued her inspections of nursing homes, kitchens, agriculture communes and acupuncture clinics, though she was squeamish about needles.

After a visit to Peking's Forbidden City and a walk along the ramparts of the twenty-two-hundred-year-old Great Wall of China, the Nixons left the *Spirit of '76* behind and flew to Hangchow with Chou on a white Ilyushin airliner. There, in the city which Marco Polo had proclaimed as the greatest in the world seven centuries earlier, the President roamed through parks and cruised on historic West Lake with the premier. From Hangchow the presidential party flew on to Shanghai, their last stop, where the communiqué was issued, and then home for a report to the American people.

On the whole his countrymen gave Nixon high marks for his performance, though some thought that at times he had been obsequious. In his Peking speeches he had proposed that the two nations "start a Long March together," and he repeatedly quoted Chairman Mao, saying that "so many deeds cry out to be done, and always urgently," and recommending that his audience "Seize the day, seize the hour." He had also been banal. Shown the elaborately carved sedan chair on which each Ming emperor was carried from the Hall of Supreme Harmony to the red gates of the Forbidden City, the President remarked, "He didn't get much exercise if he was always carried on the chair." Of the Great Wall he said, "A people that can build a wall like this certainly have a great past to be proud of, and a people who have this kind of a past must also have a great future." Then: "As we look at this wall, we do not want walls of any kind between people."

Among the people on the far side of this particular wall were the Russians, and they were uneasy about possible implications of the visit. Tension between Moscow and Peking had been growing since Stalin's death nineteen years earlier. It had reached a peak the previous autumn when Lin Piao, vice chairman of the Chinese Communist Party and Mao's designated successor, had tried to fly to the USSR in a military plane. On orders from Mao and Chou, the craft had been shot down. The Soviets had regarded that as a slur on their hospitality, and now they suspected that the Chinese and the Americans were up to no good. In a Mandarin language broadcast beamed to Mao's subjects, Radio Moscow declared that nothing was "more shameless and hypocritical" than the Shanghai communiqué. China, said the Muscovite commentator, was entering into a "dangerous plot with the ruling circles of the U.S.A."

This was less a sign of anti-Americanism than of the growing friction within the Communist world. The Russians were jealous—unreasonably so, since the Nixons were going to visit them three months later. The prospect of that summit, in turn, had aroused Radio Hanoi, which called it "dark and despicable." Here there was a difference, however. Unlike Peking and Moscow, Hanoi was not interested in detente. On the contrary, the North Vietnamese were prepared to sabotage friendly relations between Washington and the two Communist capitals to the north. They didn't succeed, but they tried hard, and for a time it seemed that they were going to prevail.

News of the Peking talks reached troops of South Vietnam's 3rd Division, just south of the DMZ, over the small Japanese transistor radios then popular among ARVN forces. Not much was happening in that sector, and with the Americans and the Communists sitting down together, Thieu's men had let their guard down. There was another reason for their complacency. Since Nixon's submission of a new eight-point peace plan to the North Vietnamese there seemed to be a real movement toward peace. Thus the 3rd Division didn't feel threatened by the reports of a fresh buildup of Democratic Republic of (North) Vietnam (DRVN) forces across the 17th Parallel. As the sullen gray clouds of the northeast winter monsoon began to clear in March there was a noticeable increase in artillery fire from the north, but the South Vietnamese were unalarmed. They remained in their bunkers and sent out few patrols. Better troops would have been warier, but the 3rd Division was not a crack unit, which was precisely why the DRVN's General Vo Nguyen Giap had marked them as the first target of a new offensive, his biggest drive since Tet four years earlier.

Led by tanks, infantrymen of Giap's 304th Division bounded across the DMZ on March 30 in a savage attack which was the exact opposite of Tet—a power play, a blitz meant to overwhelm Saigon's forces with sophisticated Soviet weapons and the sheer weight of numbers. The assault units quickly captured fifteen border outposts. Over the next five weeks they advanced twenty-two miles in heavy fighting, taking ground which had been successfully and bloodily defended by U.S. Marines. The 3rd Division was virtually destroyed and the provincial capital of Quang Tri was lost. It was, as Defense Secretary Laird called it, a "massive invasion," and it was to be only one of four major North Vietnamese thrusts into South Vietnamese territory.

On April 6, four days after Easter, a DRVN tank column struck from Cambodia, driving ARVN forces from Loc Ninh. In less than a week the attackers had surrounded the provincial capital of An Loc, sixty miles north of Saigon, penning up the entire South Vietnamese 5th Division, which was one of the key units assigned to the defense of Thieu's capital. On April 18 another Red drive routed defenders in the coastal province of Binh Dinh, threatening to cut South Vietnam in half across its narrow waist. Finally, on April 22, four DRVN divisions burst into the Central Highlands, seizing Dak To and virtually encircling the provincial capital of Kontum.

Nixon responded by sending the B-52s north, pounding Hanoi and Haiphong in the first raids there in over three years. Antiwar senators reacted swiftly; Muskie of Maine introduced a resolution calling for an immediate end to all American military activity in North Vietnam. Laird, unmoved, warned Hanoi that the B-52 sorties would continue until all DRVN forces were withdrawn from South Vietnam. He said that the administration regarded the offensive as a "flagrant" violation of the 1954 Geneva accords and that Washington would spare nothing in its determination to turn the invaders back. In reality the White House mood was compounded of as much embarrassment as outrage. For three years the President had been proclaiming the success of Vietnamization, and the dispatches from Saigon strongly suggested that that policy was a failure.

The prospect of humiliation made Nixon a dangerous adversary. On May 8 he took a breathtaking step which he called Operation Linebacker. To cripple the DRVN's war-making capacity he ordered a massive air-sea blockade; the U.S. Navy would mine the waters of Haiphong and other North Vietnamese ports, and U.S. aerial sorties would smash rail lines leading out of southern China. This took him to the brink of confrontation with the very men in Peking and Moscow that he and Kissinger were wooing. He acknowledged the conflict with the Russians. In his televised address he said: "I particularly direct my comments tonight to the Soviet Union. We respect the Soviet Union as a great power. We recognize the right of the Soviet Union to defend its interests when they are threatened. The Soviet Union in turn must recognize our right to defend our interests. . . . Let us and let all great powers help our allies for the purpose of their defense—not for the purpose of launching invasions against their neighbors."

The President's aggressive response to Giap's drive gave new life to the antiwar movement, and the Committee for the Reelection of the President spent thousands of dollars to fake support for it which did not, in fact, exist. So many bogus telegrams were sent that the White House could announce with complete honesty a five-to-one ratio in favor of the move. In addition, a *New York Times* editorial critical of it was answered by a spurious ad headed "The People vs. the *New York Times*," the "People" being Charles Colson and a few aides. That was illegal, and, as it turned out, unnecessary. By the end of that month the North Vietnamese offensive had begun to falter. After laying waste 75 percent of Binh Dinh the DRVN forces there melted away. An Loc and Kontum held out, and a widely heralded Giap attempt to capture Hue never materialized. Abruptly the Hanoi menace seemed diminished. The Communists had committed all but two training divisions to the push, had lost one hundred thousand men, and had won little of strategic value. Their all-or-nothing gamble had failed. Le Duc Tho, a member of North Vietnam's politburo and Hanoi's chief negotiator, sent word to Kissinger that he was ready to reopen the talks in Paris. He still insisted that a cease-fire would be conditional upon Thieu's dismissal, but a genuine suit for peace appeared to be very near.

Moscow had something to do with that. In early May the blockade had made the likelihood of a Nixon-Brezhnev summit seem remote, but the Russians were determined to make the detente work. This became clear when Nikolai S. Patolichev, the Soviet foreign trade minister, called at the White House to exchange a few ideas about world trade. Reporters summoned to the oval office were astonished to find Nixon, Patolichev, and Ambassador Anatoly Dobrynin grinning, laughing, and bantering over how to say "friendship" in the two languages. A correspondent asked the minister whether the President's May 22 visit to Moscow was still on. "We never had any doubts about it," Patolichev replied. "I don't know why you asked." The Russians were simultaneously urging Hanoi to break off hostilities and readying a Kremlin apartment which had once belonged to the czars for occupancy by the President. The North Vietnamese were outraged by the prospect of Soviet and American leaders feasting on caviar and champagne with Giap's dead still warm in their graves, but nothing could stop deals between the world's two dominant powers—which was one of the points the Soviets wanted to make.

Improbable as it seemed to anyone aware of the history of the past two decades, American flags were waving beside the hammer and sickle when the *Spirit of '76,* arriving from Austria, descended over the glittering domes of the Kremlin churches and taxied to a stop beside the waiting figures of the Soviet president, premier, and foreign minister. Brezhnev was not there; like Mao he postponed his reception of Nixon until after the President had unpacked. That evening the Americans were guests of honor at a welcoming banquet in the Grand Kremlin Palace. In the morning the First Lady was off on tours of Soviet schools, Red Square, the famous Moscow subway, and the state-run GUM department store. Her husband's picture was on the front page of *Pravda;* it would be there every day throughout the week of talks. Appearing on the "blue screen," as Russians call their television, Nixon greeted viewers with "*Dobry vecher*" (Good evening), and parted at the end with "*Spasibo i do svidaniya*" (Thank you and goodbye). In between, another voice translated his cordial message, which was rich in the earthy Russian maxims that they cherish.

Unlike the Peking trip, this summit was more than symbolic. The banquets, the toasts, and the ballet performances were lavish, but the real meaning of the visit emerged in conferences beneath the huge gilt chandelier of the Kremlin's St. Vladimir Hall. The White House described the sessions as "frank and businesslike"; Brezhnev, bluff and hearty all week, called them "businesslike and realistic." A routine developed. The two national leaders would reach an agreement, or endorse a Russo-American understanding which might have been negotiated over a period of months or even years. Kissinger and Foreign Minister Andrei Gromyko would settle the details. Then protocol aides would appear with blue and red leather folders, and Nixon and Brezhnev would sign the documents. The two agreed to collaborate in space exploration, achieving a joint docking of a manned spacecraft in 1975. Joint research projects would examine problems of public health, cancer, heart disease, and pollution. Each consented to stop molesting the other's ships on the high seas. Both acknowledged the need to reduce troop strength in central Europe and the necessity for a conference on European security. Most important, they concurred on missile control. The two nations would limit their deployment of ABMs and freeze offensive missiles at current levels for five years.

There were some disappointments. There was no meeting of minds on the Middle East. Nixon wanted the Russians to talk Hanoi into a cease-fire; they wouldn't do it. Brezhnev was eager for a trade pact; the issue had to be referred to a commission for further discussion. The Soviet World War II lend-lease debt of 10.8 billion dollars was unresolved; they offered 300 million, Nixon wanted 800 million, all attempts at a compromise failed. On the other hand, the talks had yielded a dividend, a twelve-point statement of principles to establish rules of diplomacy for great powers, a breakthrough in international law. "We have laid out a road map," said Kissinger. "Will we follow this road? I don't know. It isn't automatic." But unless all signs failed, the implications for the future were vast. The difference between the two great systems of government were now likely to be expressed in treaties, not ideological jehads. Russia, through the coming European security conference, would draw closer to the continent and away from Asia. Trade and technology would continue to draw the two superpowers together, and understandings between them, not the fissioning of a multipolar world, which had been widely predicted, would be the paramount fact of world politics for a long time to come. The cold war was over, ended in large part through the efforts of an American President who had been one of the most resolute of the cold-warriors.

Not the least of its attractions for Nixon was the fact that it had occurred in an election year. In Peking, and then in the Kremlin, he had taken two giant steps toward four more years in the White House. Each passing day now seemed to bring him closer to victory in November. Unfortunately for his place in history, some of those around him weren't satisfied with that. They wanted to be absolutely sure. It was to be his tragedy that they were prepared to go to any lengths to guarantee a second Nixon term. Their attitude was summed up by one of them, Charles Colson, when he posted over his bar the slogan, "If you've got 'em by the balls, their hearts and minds will follow," and said, "For the President I would walk over my grandmother, if necessary." There was a word for the more extreme measures they were taking in pursuit of their goal: criminal. It was about to acquire a synonym: Watergate.

The 1972 campaign had begun to simmer in January, when a Harris poll showed Edmund Muskie running neck and neck with the President in public favor—42 percent for him, 42 percent for Nixon, and 11 percent for George Wallace. The Maine senator was clearly the strongest Democratic candidate; that same month Gallup reported that in a trial free-for-all Muskie emerged with 32 percent, Edward Kennedy with 27, Humphrey with 17, and McGovern with 3. Whoever their opponent, Republicans were preparing to come on strong. Appearing on the *Today Show*, H. R. Haldeman said that critics of the war were "consciously aiding and abetting the enemy," and the White House moved swiftly to exploit suburban indignation over the January decision of Federal Judge Robert R. Merhige Jr., who ordered busing of white schoolchildren in the two counties surrounding Richmond, Virginia, to achieve racial balance in the city's 70-percent-black schools. Judge Merhige would be reversed in June, but by then Muskie's potential adversaries would have rung all the changes on his support of busing.

In Florida Republican zealots were putting the finishing touches on a bogus letter to the Manchester, New Hampshire, *Union Leader* charging that while campaigning in the South Muskie had referred to French Canadians as "Canucks"; this would cripple him in the New Hampshire primary. Other Nixon operatives were taking similar steps to torpedo the senator's campaign, or—in the case of Howard Hunt—planning to burglarize the safe of a Las Vegas editor which was supposed to contain anti-Muskie dirt. At 1701 Pennsylvania Avenue in Washington CREEP was fleshing out its staff. Within a month John Mitchell would resign as attorney general to become in title what he already was in fact: CREEP's director.

Meanwhile the Republican war chest was rapidly being filled while that of the Democrats remained six million dollars in debt. There had always been some truth in the Democratic charge that the GOP was the party of big business. This year there would be no doubt of it. A bill requiring the naming of big donors would become law on April 10. The two chief GOP fund raisers, Secretary of Commerce Maurice Stans and Herbert Kalmbach, the President's personal attorney, were crisscrossing the country in a successful pursuit of contributions from the wealthy before the deadline. As the Nixon men warmed to their task they began to skirt the borders of indiscretion, and sometimes to cross them. Gifts totaling $114,000 were deposited in the Miami bank account of Bernard L. Barker,

Hunt's chief burglar. And although political donations from corporations were illegal even under the old law, the fund raisers solicited them and got them—$100,000 from Ashland Oil, $100,000 from Gulf, $100,000 from Phillips Petroleum, $55,000 from American Airlines, $40,000 from Goodyear, $30,000 from Minnesota Mining and Manufacturing. Ultimately they refused sums of less than $100,000; smaller donations were not worth the trouble. A list of two thousand secret donors was kept in the desk of Rose Mary Woods, the President's secretary, at the White House, where it was known as "Rose Mary's baby."

As the amounts collected mounted into the tens of millions, fertile minds brooded over ways to use them. By far the boldest ideas were the brain-children of Gordon Liddy, and he outlined them at 4 P.M. on January 27, 1972, in the office of the attorney general at the Department of Justice. His audience consisted of Mitchell, Magruder, and John Dean, special counsel to the President. Displaying colored diagrams with such code names as Target and Gemstone, Liddy lectured for a half-hour on a million-dollar operation which included the tapping of Democrats' phones, bludgeoning anti-Nixon demonstrators, and kidnapping antiwar leaders, who would be held in Mexican camps during the Republican national convention, then scheduled to be held in San Diego. One of the more imaginative aspects of the plan called for leasing a yacht and hiring prostitutes during the Democratic convention in Miami Beach. The girls (who would be "the best in the business," Liddy promised) would elicit important information from lusty Democrats and lure them into lewd positions. They would then be photographed by hidden cameras.

It is impossible to say what effect all this had on Liddy's eminent listeners. He himself never talked to federal prosecutors afterward, preferring to remain in jail. Mitchell later told congressional investigators that the submission had been "beyond the pale," Magruder said he was "appalled," and Dean called it "mind-boggling." All that can be said with certainty is that Liddy was invited back the following week for another try, and on the afternoon of February 4 he presented a cheaper, $500,000 version, featuring the clandestine cameras and wiretaps. He passed around eight-by-ten-inch charts describing proposed breaking-and-entering operations at the Fontainebleau Hotel in Miami Beach, McGovern's campaign offices on First Street in southwest Washington, and the Washington headquarters of the Democratic National Committee in the Watergate complex. According to Magruder, the attorney general "didn't feel comfortable" with this rendition either, and Liddy was told to try once again.

The winter wore on, the President flew to China and back, and Liddy still hadn't received a green light for the project. Early in March he and Hunt approached Colson, asking him to intercede with the Republican high command. Phoning Magruder, Colson said, "Gordon Liddy's upset. He's trying to get started on an intelligence operation, and he can't seem to see anybody." He urged Magruder to "get off the stick and get the budget approved for Liddy's plans." The undertaking was now budgeted at $250,000. There were no provisions for assault, abductions, or prostitution, but the proposal to burglarize and bug Democratic and McGovern headquarters remained. On March 30 Magruder flew down to Key Biscayne, where Mitchell was taking a brief holiday in the sun, and laid this final presentation before him. Three men were present—Magruder, Mitchell, and Fred LaRue, a southern Republican strategist—and later each had a different recollection of what transpired. Whatever the precise words used, the plan was accepted, and only Mitchell had the power to do that. Liddy had his green light.

The following week Magruder authorized CREEP's treasurer, Hugh Sloan Jr., to pay out $83,000 to Liddy. Of this, $65,000 was turned over to McCord on April 12; he spent most of it in New York on electronic surveillance equipment. McCord added another man to the assembling Watergate cast on May 1 when he contacted Alfred C. Baldwin III, whose name he had found in the register of the Society of Former Agents of the FBI. All the recruit was told then was that he was wanted as a temporary bodyguard for Martha Mitchell—no plum, as Baldwin realized, but he was assured that if he did a good job it might be "a stepping-stone to a permanent position." Martha didn't think much of her new escort. She later said that he deliberately led her into a hostile demonstration, told all her friends that he was a Democrat, and "walked around in front of everybody in New York barefoot." He was, she said, "the most gauche character I have ever met." But McCord liked Baldwin. He promoted him, moved him into room 419 of Washington's Howard Johnson motel, just across Virginia Avenue from the Watergate, and told him he would be doing some undercover surveillance of radicals in the capital. Returning to the room on the afternoon of Friday, May 26, the former FBI man was surprised to find McCord there, twirling the dials of an elaborate radio receiver. "We're going to put some units over there tonight," McCord said, gesturing across the street, "and you'll be monitoring them." To show how bugs worked, he dismantled the phone in the motel room, inserted a device, and tested it by dialing a local number for a recorded message. If Baldwin handled this job well, he was told, he would be given a similar assignment at the Democratic national convention.

Four days earlier a team of Cuban exiles led by Barker had flown to Washington from Miami and registered at another hotel under assumed names. Now they were moved into the Watergate Hotel. Baldwin's motel room had the advantage of providing a view of Democratic headquarters on the sixth floor of the Watergate complex, but the Cubans' new rooms were closer to the objective. Closer still was the Continental Room of the Watergate Hotel, and it was there, that evening, that Hunt, Liddy, and the Cubans opened the first act of what would turn out to be a classic comedy of errors. With wealthy Republican campaign contributors paying the bill, they ordered $236 in food and wine—almost $30 per man. After the meal everyone left the Continental Room except Hunt and Virgilio Gonzales, Barker's locksmith. These two hid in an adjoining room until waiters had locked up; then Gonzales tried to open a door at the end of the hall which would have let them into a stairwell leading to the sixth floor and the offices of the Democratic National Committee, or, as those familiar with it called it, the DNC. But the latch there was too difficult for Gonzales. So, to their dismay, was the other lock, leading to their escape route through the dining room. Left with no alternative, they settled down for a long and uncomfortable night while their gastric juices gently broke down their share of the banquet.

The others hadn't been idle, but they had been just as ineffectual. Led by Liddy, they had left Virginia Avenue for First Street and McGovern headquarters. The entrance was bathed in light from a nearby street lamp. Opening a dispatch case, Liddy produced a high-powered pellet pistol wrapped in a towel. "Shall I take that out?" he asked, gesturing at the bright light. He was capable of it; a few days earlier he had fired it in a toilet at the staid Hay-Adams Hotel, just across Lafayette Square from the White House. This time McCord discouraged him. The mission had to be aborted anyway. A drunk was loitering in the entrance of the building. He wouldn't leave, and at 5 A.M. they gave up and returned to their beds on Virginia Avenue.

The next evening Hunt took an elevator to the DNC headquarters and walked down through the building, taping door locks open as he went so that McCord and the Cubans could reach their goal from the garage in the Watergate basement. Wearing rubber gloves and carrying walkie-talkies, cameras, and flashlights, the raiding party reached the target area at 1:30 A.M. Two hours later McCord had planted taps in the telephones of Lawrence F. O'Brien's secretary and of R. Spencer Oliver, a party official. Barker, who was under the impression that they were looking for proof that Castro was financing the Democrats, found no evidence of it. In fact, this night was as unproductive as the one before. They were again unable to penetrate McGovern's offices. And the bugs were a disappointment. One didn't work at all, and the other phone, Baldwin discovered, was largely used by secretaries to arrange assignations with married politicians. According to Magruder, Mitchell, after reviewing some two hundred conversations that Baldwin had monitored, said that the information was "worthless," that the money had been wasted, and that he wanted them to try again.

The second and final act of the farce was played out on the night of Saturday, June 17. It began when the Cubans checked into rooms 214 and 314 in the Watergate Hotel and sat down to another banquet. McCord taped the garage door and then crossed to Baldwin's room at Howard Johnson's, where he checked new equipment—soldering irons, batteries, wires, and screwdrivers—which he had purchased earlier in the day. At 12:45 A.M. an important new actor appeared onstage. His name was Frank Wills, and he was a Negro watchman at the Watergate. Discovering the tape, he concluded that it had been left by a maintenance man; removing it, he crossed to Howard Johnson's for a cup of coffee. At about the same time McCord, looking out of Baldwin's window, saw the lights go off in the DNC offices. He phoned Hunt, who was in Watergate room 214 with Liddy, to say that the coast was clear. Patting the radio receiver, McCord said to Baldwin, "Any activity you see across the street, you just get on this unit and let us know." Then he joined the Cubans—Barker, Gonzales, Frank Sturgis, and Eugenio R. Martinez—in the garage. Aghast at finding the door again fastened, they appealed to Gonzales, and this time the locksmith was able to pick the lock open. There was some discussion over whether continuing with the job was an unacceptable risk. They decided to go ahead and mounted steps to the sixth floor, taping latches on the way. At 1:50 A.M. watchman Wills, finishing his coffee, returned to find the garage door taped for the second time. He telephoned the police, and at 1:52 A.M. his call was relayed to Metropolitan Police Car 727, an unmarked cruiser. Inside were three members of the District's "Bum Squad"—plainclothes men wearing T-shirts, windbreakers, and cheap slacks.

It is now 2 A.M., a historic hour. The Bum Squad parks and enters the Watergate, observed by Baldwin, who is standing on the little balcony outside his Howard Johnson's room, enjoying, in his later words, the "beautiful night." Since the three policemen are in informal clothes, he is unalarmed, but when lights begin appearing across the way he quickly radios: "Base headquarters, base one, do you read me?" In room 214 of the Watergate Hotel Hunt replies: "I read you; go on; what have you got?" Baldwin: "The lights went on on the entire eighth floor." Hunt: "We know about that. That is the two o'clock guard check. Let us know if anything else happens." At this point the thrifty Barker, who has been listening to the exchange, turns off his walkie-talkie to save the batteries. Minutes later lights start flickering on and off on the sixth floor, and Baldwin sees two of the plainclothesmen there. One of them is holding a pistol. Baldwin: "Base one, unit one, are our people in suits or are they dressed casually?" Hunt: "Our people are dressed in suits. Why?" Baldwin: "You have some trouble, because there are some individuals out there who are dressed casually and have got their guns out." Hunt—sounding, according to Baldwin, "a bit frantic"—tries to rouse the raiding party, yelling: "Are you reading this? Are you reading this?" Because of the economy-minded Barker, there is no response. It is probably too late anyway. McCord is in the process of dismantling O'Brien's phone when one of the officers sees an arm. He shouts: "Hold it! Stop! Come out!" Baldwin and Hunt hear a walkie-talkie switched on; a hoarse voice whispers into it: "They got us." Then the officers see ten rubber-gloved hands go up. McCord asks: "Are you gentlemen the Metropolitan Police?" The plainclothesmen affirm it, and the Watergate Five are placed under arrest.

Hunt called Howard Johnson's: "Are you still across the street?" Baldwin replied, "Yes I am," and Hunt told him, "Well, we'll be right over." Looking down from his balcony, Baldwin saw Hunt and Liddy emerge. Shortly thereafter Hunt burst into his room. Distraught, he asked, "What is going on, what is going on?" Baldwin said, "Come and see." The street below was swarming with uniformed patrolmen, motorcycles, and police cruisers; McCord, Barker, Gonzales, Sturgis, and Martinez were being led off in handcuffs. Hunt moaned, "I have got to use the bathroom," ran into the toilet, used it, ran out, called a lawyer, and asked Baldwin for McCord's address. They looked about at the electronic litter. Logs of previously intercepted conversations lay around; McCord's wallet and keys were on the bed. "Get all the stuff out of here and get yourself out of here!" Hunt said. "We will be in touch. You will get further instructions." As he dashed for the door Baldwin called after him, "Does this mean I won't be going to Miami?"

The *Washington Post*'s account of the break-in appeared on the front page of its Sunday edition, but few papers gave it that much prominence. The *New York Times* carried thirteen inches inside under the head FIVE CHARGED WITH BURGLARY AT DEMOCRATIC QUARTERS, and most other editors played it down even more. Nevertheless, it was the most interesting story in the papers for certain high officers of the U.S. government and the Republican party, among them H. R. Haldeman, John Ehrlichman, John Mitchell, Maurice Stans, Charles Colson, Gordon Strachan, John Dean, Jeb Magruder, Fred LaRue, and, probably, the President of the United States.

A year later, during the hearings of the Senate Select Committee on Presidential Campaign Activities, chaired by Sam J. Ervin Jr. of North Carolina, Magruder was asked when this glittering array of outlaws decided to cover its tracks, and he answered in a puzzled tone, "I don't think there was ever any discussion that there would not be a cover-up." It was an involuntary reaction, and it began that morning of June 18 in Los Angeles, where several of them were holding meetings on campaign strategy. They were at breakfast in the Beverly Hills Hotel when, at about 8:30 A.M., Magruder took a call in the dining room from Liddy. "Can you get to a secure phone?" Liddy asked. Magruder said he couldn't and asked what was wrong. Liddy said, "There has been a problem." Magruder asked, "What kind of problem?" Liddy told him: "Our security chief has been arrested at the Watergate." "Do you mean Jim McCord?" "Yes." Hanging up, Magruder muttered to LaRue,

"You know, I think last night was the night they were going into the DNC." LaRue told Mitchell, who said, "This is incredible."

Their first response was to protect McCord, then the only one of the five captives known to them. According to Magruder, Mitchell proposed that Liddy approach Richard Kleindienst, the new attorney general, and ask him to spring McCord. Mitchell denied it, but someone at the Beverly Hills Hotel phoned Liddy at 9 A.M. California time—noon in Washington—and told him to do just that. Liddy found Kleindienst at the Burning Tree Country Club and put it to him in the locker room. Kleindienst not only refused to go along; he ordered his visitor to leave the club at once and then called Henry Petersen, who headed the Justice Department's criminal division, and instructed him that under no circumstances would he tolerate special treatment for the Watergate Five.

The FBI had already entered the case, which was beginning to develop unusual aspects. The papers implicating Hunt had been found in Barker's pocket. The prisoners had been carrying $1,300 in $100 bills, and another $3,200 in $100 bills had been discovered in the Cubans' rooms at the Watergate Hotel. Liddy, trying to destroy all evidence of his involvement, had used the shredder at CREEP headquarters to get rid of all documents in his possession, including his $100 bills. Strachan was searching Haldeman's White House files on his instructions and removing everything linking him to the burglars. Magruder phoned an assistant and directed him to take home a Gemstone file because, he said, he was afraid Democrats might raid his office in retaliation. And Howard Hunt was on the lam.

Dean, Colson, and Ehrlichman had held a hurried council of war over what advice they should give to Hunt. According to Dean, Ehrlichman proposed that he be told to leave the country. Dean made the call and then began to worry. Is it, he asked the others, really wise for the White House to give orders of that sort? "Why not?" Ehrlichman replied. "He's not a fugitive from justice." But Colson agreed with Dean, who made a second call canceling the instruction. Hunt decided to flee anyway. He cleaned out his desk, leaving only an empty whiskey bottle and a few Librium tablets. Then he flew to California, where he holed up in the home of a friend until he could no longer resist the pressure to turn himself in. The FBI was on his trail. They had already found Liddy, who had aroused suspicion by refusing to talk to them. Mitchell fired him for that, which seems hypocritical of him, but Liddy understood; he had told Magruder and Dean that he had "goofed," that "I am a good soldier and will never talk," and that "if anyone wants to shoot me on the street I am ready."

Meantime the presidential staff had been agonizing over the fact that disowning Hunt was almost impossible, since he was still on the White House payroll. Dean ordered Hunt's safe in room 552 of the Executive Office Building cleaned out. An aide brought him the contents: a black briefcase or dispatch case and a cardboard box containing, among other things, four walkie-talkies, a tear gas canister, four shoulder harnesses, the forged State Department Vietnam cables from 1963, evidence of his attempt to persuade *Life* that the forgeries were genuine, a folder of the Pentagon Papers, the CIA's Ellsberg profile, and Hunt's reports on Chappaquiddick. Dean looked over this extraordinary accumulation and gasped, "Holy shit!"

In California, meantime, Mitchell had issued a hurried statement trying to explain away McCord, who, he said:

> . . . is the proprietor of a private security agency who was employed by our committee months ago to assist with the installation of our security system. He has, as we understand it, a number of business clients and interests, and we have no knowledge of those relationships. We want to emphasize that this man and the other people involved were not operating either on our behalf or with our consent. I am surprised and dismayed at these reports. There is no place in our campaign or in the electoral process for this type of activity, and we will not permit or condone it.

Among the people who knew that this was a lie was Mitchell's wife. When he returned to Washington on Monday he persuaded her to stay in Los Angeles, where, she said afterward, she was held as a "political prisoner" by Baldwin's successor as her bodyguard. According to her, the guard yanked the phone wires out of the wall when she was telling a UPI reporter that "they don't want me to talk"; then he held her down while another man injected a sedative into her buttocks. There was no way to keep Martha Mitchell quiet, though. Three days later she was calling the reporter again, saying, "I'm not going to stand for all those dirty things that go on." It made a good story, but Martha's credibility was low, and most Americans accepted the official line, which was that the administration had not known anything about those dirty things. Tuesday morning Ronald Ziegler, the former adman who served as Richard Nixon's press secretary, spelled it out. In a scornful mood, he declined even to add to Mitchell's statement. "I am not going to comment from the White House on a third-rate burglary attempt," Ziegler said. "This is something that should not fall into the political process." However, when a handful of *Post* men continued to pursue the story, Ziegler did comment from the White House. He said, "I don't respect the type of journalism, the shabby journalism, that is being practiced by the *Washington Post.*" And Mitchell, referring to the paper's publisher, told one of its reporters, "Katie Graham is going to get her teat caught in a big fat wringer."

In a sense the campaign which followed was the story of Richard Nixon's growing invincibility. Early trial heats had suggested a standoff. Then, as the summer progressed, the President moved ahead until all the polls conceded him about 60 percent of the vote. From then on he was beyond reach. CREEP's tremendous financial advantage—60 million dollars compared to 25 million for the Democrats—had little to do with the outcome. Watergate had even less. He had been elected four years earlier on a tide of protest against the Vietnam War. Ending the hostilities seemed to take him forever, and some 17,000 Americans had been killed there while he was doing it, but by the beginning of 1972 he had reduced the U.S. troop commitment in Vietnam from 549,500 to 139,000, and the Pentagon's weekly casualty list, which had been running at about 300 when he entered the White House, would on September 21, 1972, reach zero and remain near there. Being a political animal, he was quick to exploit this and other opportunities as they arose. In the Florida Democratic primary, for example, George Wallace campaigned on the slogan, "Send them a message," promising that if Floridians voted for him, "President Nixon will do something to halt this busing within thirty days." Wallace knew his Nixon. The President didn't wait thirty days. He demanded a busing moratorium just two days after the returns from there.

The sum of Nixon's skills was a united party led by a nominee who, his past notwithstanding, was now identified as the candidate of peace and detente. His only two rivals for the Republican nomination were Congressman Paul N. McCloskey Jr. of California on the left and John M. Ashbrook of Ohio on the right. They merely served to point up the President's preemption of the GOP center.

McCloskey arrived at the Republican convention—switched to Miami Beach after Dita Beard and ITT had made San Diego too embarrassing—with a single vote, pledged to him by New Mexico's primary law. He expected to have his name placed before the convention, thereby giving critics of Nixon's racial and military policies a chance to be heard, but the Rules Committee limited nominations to candidates controlling the delegations of at least three states. The final vote on the first ballot was: Nixon 1,347, McCloskey 1. The lone New Mexican apologized to the hall.

As a piece of stage management it was awesome. The President had eliminated any possibility of suspense by announcing his intention to keep Agnew on the ticket. Everyone in the party seemed eager to do his bidding. Ronald Reagan chaired the convention, Nelson Rockefeller put Nixon's name in nomination. Knowing the President's passion for order, floor managers limited the demonstration in his behalf to exactly twenty minutes, and to refute claims that the Democrats represented young America, 3,000 conservatively dressed youths were brought to Miami Beach on chartered buses. The boys wore their hair so short that they appeared to belong to another era—which was, of course, the idea.

To be sure, they were not the only young Americans there. Over 5,000 scruffy antiwar militants had camped in the city's Flamingo Park. During the Democratic week they were relatively quiescent, but when the GOP arrived they erupted, and 1,200 were arrested for slashing tires, blocking traffic, smashing store windows, setting bonfires in the streets, and trying to prevent delegates from attending the convention. The Republicans were elated. This, they seemed to be saying to those who objected to their tidy sessions, is what happens when you allow untidiness in politics. During the campaign which followed (in which Nixon hardly participated; he left most of the politicking to surrogates and never mentioned his opponent's name) GOP speakers spoke proudly of their unity and hammered away at the disarray on the other side.

They had a point. Riven in Chicago four years earlier, the Democrats were still absorbed in savage internecine feuds. The new presidential sweepstakes opened all their old wounds and inflicted new ones. At one time or another during the primary months the party's nomination was being sought by Muskie, McGovern, Humphrey, George Wallace, Eugene McCarthy, Fred Harris of Oklahoma, Vance Hartke of Indiana, Henry Jackson of Washington, John Lindsay of New York, Sam Yorty of Los Angeles, Wilbur Mills of Arkansas, Shirley Chisholm of New York, and Edward T. Coll, a young poverty worker from Connecticut who scared the pants off a Democratic National Committeewoman by dangling a rubber rat in front of her during a televised debate. The battle to head the ticket was a melee. Harry Truman, who had called the primaries "just so much eyewash," was vindicated. Like the Republican struggle in 1964, this one routed promising candidates and left the field in the possession of a nominee who would prove hopelessly weak in the general election and whose vulnerability had, in fact, been demonstrated in the very process which had brought him the prize.

Speaking in New Hampshire early in the year of his ill-starred race, Barry Goldwater had sunk a nail in his own coffin by calling, in effect, for the end of social security. On January 13, 1972, eight years later almost to the day, George McGovern told a college audience in Ames, Iowa, that he favored giving every American $1,000 from the federal treasury and limiting inheritances to $500,000 each. The speech didn't attract much attention at the time because McGovern was still a minor figure; in one recognition poll a few months earlier he had scored exactly 2 percent. But later it would return to haunt him, alienating millions who thought the government was too generous already and vast numbers of others who dreamed that one day they would hit the lottery, or something, big.

Part of McGovern's strength lay in the skill with which his organization exploited his obscurity. In New Hampshire, the first test, they successfully established the line that since Muskie was the front runner and from a neighboring state, any showing below 50 percent would be a defeat for him and a McGovern victory. That put the pressure on the Maine senator, who was hurt by the spurious "Canuck" letter and by the *Manchester Union Leader*'s tasteless charge that Mrs. Muskie told dirty jokes. In a televised speech outside the newspaper's office Muskie called its publisher William Loeb a "gutless coward," said "It's fortunate for him he's not on this platform beside me," and wept—perhaps the most expensive tears ever shed by a public man. Even so, Muskie won 46.4 percent of the vote on March 7 as against McGovern's 37 percent. The margin was a sweep, if not a landslide, yet so adroitly had the South Dakotan's aides depicted him as a dark horse that the spotlight was on him.

Florida, the next joust in the primary tournament, had eleven entries. McGovern sensibly said that it was not a state where he "expected to do well," and in fact he did poorly, receiving 6.1 percent of the vote. Wallace was the big winner, surprising everyone, including himself—"We beat the face cards of the Democratic deck," he crowed—and he was trailed by Humphrey, Jackson, and Muskie. The following week Muskie won in Illinois, taking 63 percent to McCarthy's 37 percent. Wisconsin came next. McGovern's troops were superbly organized there, and he led the pack of twelve candidates with 30 percent, followed by Wallace, Humphrey, and Muskie. McGovern won in liberal Massachusetts; Humphrey took Ohio and Indiana; in Nebraska McGovern beat Humphrey by six percentage points; Humphrey walloped Wallace in West Virginia 67 to 33 percent, and North Carolina went to Wallace.

By the middle of May Muskie was out of it and the marathon was settling down to a three-way contest between Wallace, Humphrey, and McGovern. Support for the Alabaman was generally interpreted as a protest vote; he said he would use it to win concessions at the national convention. Then came May 15 in Maryland. Wallace was successively hit by a rock in Frederick, eggs in Hagerstown, popsicles in Salisbury—and six bullets in Laurel. Next day he won both the Maryland and Michigan primaries, but for him, wounded and paralyzed, it was all over. It was, in fact, the end for all the Democratic candidates; without the third-party threat of Wallace siphoning off votes on the right, a Nixon victory was assured. But few realized that at the time, and the winner-take-all California primary on June 6 loomed as a titanic battle between the two survivors. The results were 1,527,392 votes, or 47.1 percent, for McGovern; 1,352,379, or 41.7 percent, for Humphrey. After that plums began toppling into the South Dakotan's lap, and he went to Miami Beach with 1,492.75 delegates—for all practical purposes, the nomination.

What was unappreciated at the time was the impact of the California campaign on McGovern's popularity. Until then no one had cast a harsh light on his program. He was seen as a handsome, decent, plainspoken man who was outraged by the Vietnam War. In three bruising televised debates, Humphrey had destroyed that image, pointing to McGovern's sometimes inconsistent and often quixotic stands on Israel, defense spending, welfare, labor law, unemployment compensation, taxation, and even, in the beginning, on Vietnam. "It was Hubert Humphrey who put McGovern away; no other Democrat could have done it to him like Hubert," pollster

Robert M. Teeter said afterward. "Not only did Hubert give it to him, but it was the first time McGovern got adversary treatment."

The second time was at Miami Beach, when the watching nation saw what had happened to the Democratic party. Four years earlier, on the humid night of August 27, 1968, the Chicago convention had approved by voice vote a Credentials Committee resolution calling for a reform of the process by which convention delegates were chosen. Under the chairmanship of George McGovern, a reform commission had approved by a 10–9 vote a resolution which established a quota for blacks, and then—on a motion from a member who said, "There is no reason why our national convention shouldn't have 50 percent women, 10 to 15 percent young people"—quotas for women and youth. A majority of the commission thought that made sense, but it didn't. The quotas were a denial of the whole principle of representation. Worse, they had the effect of legitimatizing discrimination against all classifications who had no quotas—for example, the elderly, ethnic groups, and organized labor, three traditional sources of the party's strength.

In his keynote address Governor Reubin Askew of Florida declared, "It is impossible to look upon this group without feeling that one has seen the face of America." Certainly he was looking at newcomers to politics. Eight of every ten delegates were attending their first convention; 15 percent were black, 36 percent were women, and 22 percent were under thirty years of age. "Don't pass up any hitchhikers, they might be delegates," said one candidate. There were some hitchhikers—and some others. In their anxiety to assure representation to the underprivileged, the California delegation had included eighty-nine people who were on welfare. McGovern was so determined to offend no minority that he ordered kid-glove treatment of Gay Liberationists, who chanted—on television—"Two-four-six-eight, we don't overpopulate" and "Three-five-seven-nine, lesbians are mighty fine." At the same time an extraordinary number of elected Democrats were being excluded from the floor: 225 of the party's 255 congressmen and the Democratic mayors of Philadelphia, Detroit, Boston, San Francisco, Los Angeles, and Chicago.

Inevitably, the amateurs committed blunders which professionals would have avoided. The few politicians left in the hall were painfully aware of them. "I think we may have lost Illinois tonight," Frank Mankiewicz said glumly when that state's elected delegation was expelled from the convention by McGovern enthusiasts, and on the platform committee Ben Wattenberg sighed, "They just lost Michigan to the Republicans today with their busing plank. No one seemed impressed by the fact that in Macomb County they voted against busing in a referendum last fall by fourteen to one." Hugh Scott chided McGovern as a "triple A" champion who advocated "Acid, amnesty, and abortion." That was unfair, but at one time or another various McGovern supporters did speak well of all three, despite the anguished remonstrations of observers like David Riesman, who pointed out that the floor of a national political convention is not the best place to discuss so sensitive an issue as abortion. The impact of all this on the national television audience cannot be determined with precision, but subsequent events suggest that the number of blacks, women, and youths won over by the requirement that delegations "reasonably" reflect their constituencies by race, sex, and age was overwhelmed by the swarms of voters who were offended by the spectacle in Miami Beach. Of the three groups, only the Negroes went for McGovern in November, and they had been for him long before.

By the time McGovern won the nomination it was probably not worth much. He further devalued it by delivering his acceptance speech at 3 A.M., when most voters were asleep. The first in a series of disasters came less than twelve hours later at a meeting of the Democratic National Committee in the Fontaine Room of the Fontainebleau. McGovern began by announcing that Larry O'Brien had "reached a judgment that he will not stay on as the chairman of the party." That was false—O'Brien was willing to remain—and a number of people there knew it. Mrs. Jean Westwood was chosen as the new chairman. McGovern nominated Pierre Salinger as vice chairman. Charles Evers rose to say that "inasmuch as we are going to try to stay in line with the McGovern rules, I would . . . strongly urge that if we are going to have a female chairman . . . I would like to place in nomination a black man to be co-chairman or vice chairman." He then nominated an unknown Negro—whereupon McGovern said that was fine with him, thus publicly scuttling Salinger.

Unlucky Pierre was betrayed a second time. Later that same day, McGovern asked him to serve as his representative in talks with the North Vietnamese in Paris. Salinger flew to France, the story leaked to UPI, and McGovern issued a statement to the press saying, "Pierre Salinger had no instructions whatsoever from me. He told me he was going to Paris, and he said while he was there he might try to make some determinations of what was going on in the negotiations. But there wasn't the slightest instruction on my part to him." Once again there were people who knew better, among them David Dellinger, who had acted as liaison between McGovern and Hanoi. The nominee challenging Nixon's integrity was himself losing credibility fast.

Then the Eagleton affair exploded. McGovern had just begun a pre-campaign holiday in the Black Hills when reporters learned that Senator Thomas Eagleton of Missouri, his running mate, had twice been hospitalized for psychiatric care, including electroshock therapy. Up to that point the nominee could scarcely be held responsible for that calamity. He hadn't known about Eagleton's medical history at the time he picked him, and when Mankiewicz had asked Eagleton if there were any skeletons in his closet, the reply had been that there were none. The Missourian was at fault there. American ignorance of mental health being what it is, even a mild history of depression disqualifies a politician from running for national office, and the problems of a patient subjected to electroshock treatments are not mild. The obvious solution was to let Eagleton resign gracefully. McGovern didn't do it.

Instead he issued a statement saying that he was "1,000 percent for Tom Eagleton" and had "no intention of dropping him from the ticket." The mimeograph machine in the Black Hills was still warm when the *New York Post,* the *Washington Post,* and the *New York Times*—the most liberal papers in the country—said Eagleton had to go. Matthew Troy, a prominent New York Democrat whose support for McGovern had been unwavering, was quoted as saying, "I have nine kids. I don't want to see them destroyed because some unstable person might become President." Democratic headquarters were deluged with mail, wires, and calls demanding that the vice-presidential nominee quit, and the head of the ticket decided that his support of him wasn't 1,000 percent after all. He agreed to let Mrs. Westwood say on *Meet the Press* that it would be "a noble thing" for the Missourian to withdraw. Then, greeting Eagleton, he told him, "Tom, believe me I had no idea what she was going to say." His running mate replied, "Don't shit me, George." According to Eagleton, "George smirked. Not a smile of faint amusement. Not a frown of slight irritation. A smirk, that's what it was." Eagleton retired from the ticket on July 31, and after five Democrats, including Muskie, had declined to replace him, Sargent Shriver consented. The episode had been one of the most disastrous in the history of presidential politics. McGovern would never recover from it.

From that moment on the Democratic campaign was on the skids. The nominee belatedly courted LBJ, Mayor Daley, organized labor, and the Jewish vote; all were cool. His Washington headquarters disintegrated. Important letters were unanswered. Speaking schedules disappeared. Distinguished Democrats who called with offers to help were insulted by shaggy young volunteers and turned away. At one time—in May—McGovern had been within five percentage points of Nixon. By July, the month of the Democratic convention, he was twenty points behind. After the Eagleton debacle he slipped farther behind. In October, as he furiously rushed back and forth across the country, logging 65,000 miles in the air, he gained slightly. It didn't last. Both Gallup and Harris predicted on election eve that the vote would split 61 percent for Nixon and 39 percent for McGovern. Actually it was 60.7 to 37.5, with splinter candidates getting 1.8.

Nixon had carried forty-nine states; Massachusetts and the District of Columbia went to McGovern. But that was not the full story. The voter turnout was the lowest in twenty-four years. Only 55 percent of the country's registered voters went to the polls; the rest, presumably, rejected *both* candidates. And while the President had forged a historic electoral triumph, his party hadn't done at all well. Democratic congressional candidates had held the GOP to a 12-seat gain in the House—rather than the 41 they needed for control—while gaining two Senate seats, making their margin there 57 to 43, and picking up one statehouse.

McGovern said he was not disheartened. His central issue had been the Vietnam War, and he believed he had done much to end it. In conceding defeat he told his workers, "I want every one of you to remember that if we pushed the day of peace just one day closer, then every minute and every hour and every bone-crushing effort in this campaign was worth the entire effort." That was putting the best possible face on it. Not everyone agreed. Marquis Childs said it had been "one of the most unhappy campaigns in American history." Understandably, Richard Nixon took a different view. Greeting his supporters in Washington's Shoreham Hotel, he said, "I've never known a national election when I could go to bed earlier." As he turned away to retire there, they set up a terrific din, chanting, "*Four more years!*" It was a top-drawer Republican crowd, well-barbered and expensively dressed. The television audience had no way of knowing that some of the most eminent chanters were felons.

In a reference to Watergate, McGovern had described the Nixon administration as "the most corrupt in history," but Gallup had reported in October that barely half the voters had heard of the break-in. Of those, four out of every five did not see it as a reason to vote Democratic. Teeter had found that only 6 percent thought the President was involved. The others tended to blame CREEP—a tribute to the party leadership's wisdom in establishing a reelection headquarters outside the White House. It was an illusion. The big campaign decisions were made at 1600 Pennsylvania Avenue. The men around Nixon continued to be deeply involved in the Watergate cover-up, which, according to subsequent testimony before the Ervin committee, took the following course.

John Dean's immediate problem, once he had seen the contents of Hunt's safe, was how to get rid of it. He took the matter up with Ehrlichman, who suggested he "shred the documents and deep-six the briefcase." Ehrlichman said, "You drive across the river on your way home at night, don't you? Well, when you cross over the bridge, just toss the briefcase in the river." Dean pointed out that it wasn't that simple; too many White House employees, including his own assistant, had seen at least part of what had been in the safe. Ehrlichman's solution was to summon to his office L. Patrick Gray, who had been acting director of the FBI since J. Edgar Hoover's death in May. On June 28, eleven days after the Watergate burglary, Dean gave him the sensitive material there, calling it "political dynamite" which "should never see the light of day." Gray kept it until the end of the year—possibly to blackmail the White House should the President fail to recommend him as permanent director—and then burned it with the Christmas trash, thereby assuring his eventual resignation in disgrace.

That same week the White House made an effort to cloak at least part of the Watergate incident with the mantle of "national security." The President himself was involved in this; later he justified his intervention by saying, "I was advised that there was a possibility of CIA involvement in some way." His concern included the possibility that Hunt's role in the Plumbers might be revealed, exposing other sensitive "national security matters," including, presumably, the burgling of Ellsberg's psychiatrist's office. CIA director Richard Helms and his new deputy, General Vernon Walters, were called to the White House, where Haldeman told him that the DNC break-in was embarrassing Nixon. He said it was "the President's wish" that Walters suggest to Gray that the arrest of five housebreakers "should be sufficient," and that it was not useful to press the investigation any farther, "especially in Mexico"—a reference to the route political contributions had followed in finding their way into Barker's bank account.

At meetings on June 26 and June 28 Dean proposed to Walters that the CIA furnish bail and pay the salaries of the five prisoners. The general said he didn't think that was a good idea, that it might hurt the "apolitical" reputation of the agency. Walters did approach Gray, but not to carry out White House suggestions; instead he warned him that presidential aides were trying to exploit both the agency and the bureau for questionable purposes. Gray already knew this. In addition to his own personal experience he was beginning to feel heat from below; FBI subordinates were telling him that a cover-up had begun and urging him to alert the President. On July 6 he did it with a phone call, cautioning Nixon that "people on your staff are trying to mortally wound you by using the CIA and the FBI and by confusing the question of CIA interest in, or not in, people the FBI wishes to interview." After a pause the President said, "Pat, you just continue to conduct your aggressive and thorough investigation," and hung up.

It was now nearly three weeks since the Watergate arrests, and efforts to conceal the trail of those behind the break-in were in full swing. Gray, having sent up his rocket and seen it sputter into nothing, allowed himself to be duped by Dean. The presidential counsel was permitted to kibitz at FBI interviews with eight White House aides and was given copies of some eighty FBI reports on Watergate. In addition he persuaded Petersen not to call five members of the staff—Colson, Young, Krogh, Strachan, and Dwight Chapin—before the federal grand jury that was looking into Watergate. Instead they testified in a separate room, where jurors could not question them. It was at this time that Kleindienst, Petersen's superior, assured the public that the Justice Department's pursuit of the truth about the break-in was "the most extensive, thorough, and comprehensive investigation since the assassination of President Kennedy."

On August 29 Nixon did some reassuring of his own. He told the country that besides giving all assistance required by the FBI, he had launched his own inquiry: "Within our own staff, under my direction, Counsel to the President, Mr. Dean, has conducted a complete investigation of all leads which might involve any present members of the White House or anybody in the government. I can say categorically that his investigation indicates that no one in the White House staff, no one in this administration, presently employed, was involved in this very bizarre incident." Dean heard this on a newscast and was astonished. He had only been following orders from Haldeman and Ehrlichman. He had conducted no investigation, had written no report, and had not even seen the President. (A year later the White House acknowledged this, saying that Nixon's confidence had been inspired by "assurances" from Ehrlichman.)

In that same statement the President said: "What really hurts in matters of this sort is not the fact that they occur, because overzealous people in campaigns do things that are wrong. What hurts is if you try to cover it up." This, of course, is precisely what was happening. John Mitchell was presiding over cover-up strategy sessions in his office, and, after July 1, when he resigned from CREEP at the importuning of Martha, in his apartment in the Watergate complex. Among those who attended were LaRue, Assistant Attorney General Mardian and Jeb Magruder. At one point Magruder volunteered to take the rap for all of them. This received serious consideration, but in the end it was decided that since he had lacked authority to approve the vast sums Liddy had spent, a guilty plea from him would merely lead to Mitchell and jeopardize Nixon's reelection.

Instead it was decided to make Liddy the cutoff point. Though an eccentric, he was reliable; he wouldn't talk, and they could build a plausible story around him, exaggerating the sums of money given to him for legitimate purposes and saying he had decided on his own to spend it on the burglary. Bart Porter, a Magruder aide, agreed to perjure himself. He would testify that he had given Liddy $100,000 to infiltrate organizations of antiwar radicals. There was one difficulty. Hugh Sloan Jr., CREEP's treasurer, was an honest man. In April he had asked Stans about Liddy's huge budget. ("I don't want to know," Stans answered, "and you don't want to know.") Now, when Magruder told him they were going to alter the figures, saying that Liddy had received only $75,000 or $80,000, Sloan replied, "I have no intention of perjuring myself." Magruder said, "You may have to."

Sloan, under the mistaken impression that he was not the only scrupulous man in the leadership of the reelection campaign, tried to warn several presidential aides that something was terribly wrong at 1701 Pennsylvania Avenue. He went to Chapin first and was advised to take a vacation. Chapin said that "the important thing is that the President must be protected." Then Sloan went to Ehrlichman, recommending that an outsider investigate the committee. "Don't tell me any details," Ehrlichman said, and, like Stans, "I do not want to know." Finally, with FBI agents waiting in his office to question him, Sloan appealed to Mitchell for guidance. The former attorney general said, "When the going gets tough, the tough get going." Sloan got going. He had no choice; Stans told the FBI that he had already resigned.

On September 15 the grand jury indicted Hunt, Liddy, the five men who had been captured in the DNC—and no others. The trail had stopped with them, and the President was greatly relieved. Late that afternoon Dean was summoned to the oval office, where Nixon and Haldeman greeted him warmly. As Dean later testified before the Ervin committee, Nixon said he hoped there would be no trial before the election and that he wanted Dean to keep a list of people giving the administration trouble, because he meant to make life difficult for them after the election. The principal thorn here continued to be the *Washington Post*, which on October 10 reported that the Watergate burglary was part of "a massive campaign of political spying and sabotage . . . directed by officials of the White House and the Committee for the Reelection of the President." The reelection high command reacted swiftly and angrily. Clark MacGregor, Mitchell's successor at CREEP, called the story "vicious and contemptible." Another committee spokesman described it as "a collection of absurdities." To Stans it was "a senseless pack of lies"; to Ron Ziegler, "the shoddiest type of journalism." Their indignation was widely accepted as righteous. The Fourth Estate had fallen sharply in public esteem during the Nixon Presidency. Symbolically, that summer the Supreme Court had ruled 5 to 4—with the administration's four appointees in the majority—that newspapermen could be required to reveal confidences by judges and grand juries. The American Civil Liberties Union declared that "in a relatively short time the press in the United States has moved from what many considered a position of extreme security to one of extreme vulnerability." The men responsible for that were now threatened by vigorous reporting. They responded by stirring the suspicion of "the media" which they themselves had planted in the public mind. Their reward was a short-term success—at the expense of ultimate disgrace.

One plank of the scaffold which awaited them fell into place at 2:27 P.M. on the foggy afternoon of December 8, when United Airlines Flight 553, approaching Chicago's Midway Airport, crashed a mile and a half short of the runway, killing thirty of its forty-five passengers. Among the dead was Mrs. E. Howard Hunt, in whose purse investigators of the accident found $10,000 in cash. A relative said she had been on her way to make a down payment on a Holiday Inn franchise. But where, the authorities wondered, did she get the money? The Hunts had always been strapped. He had wanted badly to buy a partnership in a Washington public relations firm but had been unable to round up the $2,000 required for a down payment. Now his wife's body had been found with a small fortune in $100 notes—just like the Watergate Five.

The money was hush money, and there was a lot more of it. Eleven days after the Watergate arrests the council of war over which Mitchell was presiding had decided, in Dean's words, to raise funds "in exchange for the silence of the men in jail." Herbert Kalmbach was the first to be given the assignment, though apparently he wasn't told the full story. He had arrived the next morning on a night flight from Los Angeles, and after being sketchily briefed by Dean at a rendezvous in Lafayette Park he phoned Stans, who produced $75,100 in campaign funds, all of it in the ubiquitous $100 bills. Over the next two months Kalmbach rounded up between $210,000 and $230,000, of which $154,000 went to Dorothy Hunt. The Californian had qualms over the propriety of this, and on July 26 he went to Ehrlichman with them. "John," he began, "I am looking right into your eyes." He said he wanted to know whether Dean had the authority to give him these instructions, and whether it was right. According to him, Ehrlichman answered, "Herb, John Dean does have the authority, it is proper, and you are to go forward."

At the end of August Kalmbach quit anyway and LaRue became

the new paymaster. Altogether between $423,000 and $548,000 was paid to the Watergate defendants, most of it channeled through Mrs. Hunt. Tony Ulasewicz, who actually delivered the cash, or "the laundry," as he called it, said he came to the conclusion that "something here is not kosher." Not to put too fine a point on it, CREEP was being blackmailed. Shortly after the arrests Hunt had sent Dean a dark message: "The writer has a manuscript of a play to sell." Later, according to McCord, Hunt said that unless his wife's demands were met he would "blow the White House out of the water" and produce "information which could impeach the President." Not only did he want money; he insisted on pledges of presidential clemency. Colson sent him a "general assurance" of this through Hunt's lawyer. In exchange, Hunt agreed to plead guilty and tell the press he knew of no involvement of "higher-ups."

The cover-up strategy seemed to be working. Actually it was about to unravel. The key to the imminent exposure was McCord, who felt a continuing loyalty to his old organization, the CIA, or, as he and other insiders called it, "the company." On June 30, the week presidential aides began trying to involve the agency in the toils of the cover-up, McCord sent Helms an unsigned letter promising to keep him informed and ending: "From time to time I will send along things you may be interested in." It was the first of seven anonymous letters he mailed to the director, and was followed, on December 22, by a warning to an old friend in the agency's security office: "There is tremendous pressure to put the operation off on the company." That same week he wrote John J. Caulfield:

> Dear Jack,
>
> I am sorry to have to tell you this but the White House is bent on having the CIA take the blame for the Watergate. If they continue to pursue this course, every tree in the forest will fall and it will be scorched earth. The whole matter is at the precipice right now. Pass the message that if they want it to blow, they are on exactly the right course. I am sorry that you will get hurt in the fallout.

There was no signature, but none was necessary. Caulfield spread the word that McCord was planning to confess everything, and frantic efforts were made to change his mind—pledges of financial support for his family, executive clemency, rehabilitation and a job when he got out; even what McCord construed as a threat on his life from Caulfield: "You know that if the administration gets its back to the wall, it will have to take steps to defend itself." McCord answered, "I have already thought through the risks and will take them when I'm ready. I have had a good life and my will is made out." Caulfield said, "Everybody is on track but you. You are not following the game plan. Keep silent." But the old spy didn't want any part of this game plan. His mind was made up. In a letter to Judge John J. Sirica, which was read from the bench at the end of the court proceedings, he said that "Others involved in the Watergate operation were not identified during the trial," that "perjury occurred during the trial," and that "there was political pressure applied to the defendants to plead guilty and remain silent." It was a sensational moment, and one of the most fateful in the history of American jurisprudence. With it, the collapse of the Nixon Presidency began.

The President's reelection campaign had been enormously enhanced in its last days by electrifying news from Henry Kissinger: he and Le Duc Tho, Hanoi's chief negotiator, had achieved a breakthrough in their Paris talks. On October 8 the North Vietnamese had dropped their insistence that Thieu be ejected and a coalition government installed in Saigon. Eighteen days later Kissinger told a televised press conference that a final accord could be reached in one more meeting. "Peace," he said, "is at hand."

But it wasn't. On October 23 the White House announced that the signing of the cease-fire agreement was being postponed pending new sessions needed to "clarify" some matters. At least part of the difficulty seemed to lie in Saigon. South Vietnamese Foreign Minister Tran Van Lam attacked the imminent agreement as "unacceptable," and Thieu said it would amount to "a surrender of the South Vietnamese people to the Communists." If necessary, Thieu vowed, his nation would continue the war alone.

When Kissinger tried to reopen certain sensitive topics, Hanoi accused Washington of bad faith and demanded that the settlement be signed as negotiated. The Americans refused, and Le Duc Tho, furious, began advancing counterproposals on such matters as the size of the international truce supervision team and—the most vital subject for the United States—the return of U.S. prisoners of war. Kissinger announced that the other side was raising "one frivolous issue after another," that the team from Hanoi was trying to make substantive alterations "in the guise of linguistic changes."

The President was reported to be angry with both Vietnams; with

Saigon for being mulish and with Hanoi for, as he saw it, going back on its word. On December 14 Kissinger left Paris in despair and Nixon cabled North Vietnam's Premier Pham Van Dong, warning him that unless serious negotiations were resumed within seventy-two hours he would reseed Haiphong harbor with mines and unleash America's aerial might: B-52s, FO4 Phantoms, and Navy fighter-bombers. General Curtis LeMay had once proposed bombing the North back into the Stone Age, and clearly the President had something like that in mind. It was no light threat; his Air Force generals assured him that in two weeks they could saturate the enemy homeland with more tonnage than in virtually all the great raids of World War II. Furthermore, this would be terror bombing on a scale never known before. The B-52 guaranteed that. Pinpoint attacks by them were impossible. Each carried forty tons of bombs in its belly. Flying in "cells" of three, each cell laid its missiles in "boxes" a mile and a half long by a half-mile wide. Until now they had never assailed a city. If they unloaded over Hanoi, massive civilian casualties would be unavoidable.

The seventy-two hours passed, Pham Van Dong did not reply, and Nixon sent the word to U.S. air bases on Guam and in Thailand and carriers in the Gulf of Tonkin: start the blitz. The result was the most savage chapter in the long history of American involvement in Vietnam. Hanoi was pounded around the clock by every type of American aircraft in every kind of weather. Using 100 of the huge green and brown B-52s, U.S. airmen flew over 1,400 sorties in the first week alone. Americans were stunned. Only a few days earlier—until mid-December, in fact—they had been expecting total U.S. disengagement in Indochina, with the prospect that American POWs, some of whom had been in captivity for nearly ten years, might be home for Christmas. Now they were confronted by this bewildering volte-face. And they were offered no presidential explanation. In the past, Nixon, like Johnson before him, had appeared on television to announce new developments in Vietnam. Now he made no attempt at justification. The only White House official to comment was Ziegler, who told reporters that the bombing "will continue until such time as a settlement is arrived at."

The Pentagon briskly ticked off the military targets: truck parks, communications towers, power plants, warehouses, bridges, railways, shipyards, factories, roads, barracks, supply points, landing fields, and antiaircraft and surface-to-air missile (SAM) installations. But most of the objectives were in heavily populated parts of North Vietnam's cities. The Hanoi thermal power plant, for example, was only a thousand yards from the center of the capital. Diplomats and foreign newsmen stationed there sent out descriptions of a stricken city, lacking electricity and often water. Vast neighborhoods were cratered and pocked by explosives. Schools were reduced to smoking sockets in the ground. Torn copybooks lay in the rubble. Parents frantically searched for their children among jagged chunks of shattered concrete.

In the Hanoi suburb of Thai Nguyen almost a thousand civilians were dead or wounded. Coffins were stacked on street corners. The Bach Thai hospital for tuberculars was razed. So was Bach Mai general hospital; doctors carried patients piggyback from the debris. A dispensary was destroyed. One bomb hit a POW camp—incensing Nixon, who reportedly blamed the North Vietnamese for putting prisoners where missiles might fall. The Polish freighter *Josef Conrad* was sunk in Hanoi harbor, killing three of her crew; a Russian and a Chinese ship were mangled. Men in the State Department, which was charged with apologizing for these outrages, were bitter. "The way things are going," one American diplomat said gloomily, "we'll hit the cathedral in Hanoi on Christmas Eve."

In fact Nixon declared a thirty-six-hour truce over Christmas, but the moment it was over the deluge of death resumed. On walls still standing North Vietnamese chalked, "We will avenge our compatriots massacred by the Americans," and "Nixon, you will pay this blood debt." These were gestures of helplessness; the White House was over seven thousand miles away, and soon the last American ground troops would have left Indochina. North Vietnam's only real hostages against the terror were captured U.S. fliers. In the seven years before this blitz B-52s had flown 100,000 sorties and only one had been lost to enemy gunners. Now Hanoi had the strongest antiaircraft defenses in the world, and in these last two weeks of 1972 their fuming muzzles brought down sixteen of the aerial dreadnoughts, each representing fifteen million dollars. More important, ninety-eight crewmen had been captured. The American onslaught over Tonkin had increased the stakes in Paris. There was more pressure on Kissinger as well as on Le Duc Tho.

Other incentives for peace had appeared. Nixon had, not for the last time, misjudged the public's capacity for moral indignation. James Reston called the massive raids "war by tantrum," and Republican Senator William Saxbe of Ohio, who had supported the President's Vietnam policy, now came out against it, saying he was troubled "as an American" and thought most of his countrymen felt "the same way." In Europe the reaction was sharper. London's *Daily Mirror* said, "The American resumption of the bombing of North Vietnam has made the world recoil in revulsion." In Paris *Le Monde* compared the air offensive to the Nazi leveling of Guernica in the Spanish Civil War. Premier Olof Palme of Sweden went farther, equating it with the German extermination of the Jews. That angered the administration, which called the Swedish ambassador to protest, but the feeling in all western chancelleries was almost as strong.

If Washington had underestimated the depth of allied resentment, Hanoi had overestimated the wrath of the Communist world. Comment in Moscow and Peking was perfunctory. Speaking on the fiftieth anniversary of the Soviet Union, Leonid Brezhnev made the mildest of references to the B-52 strikes, and he pointedly sent his children to meet Tricia Nixon Cox and her husband at a U.S. embassy reception there. Both the Russians and the Chinese were urging the North Vietnamese to settle with the Americans. The United States had lost its enthusiasm for opposing "wars of liberation," but the eagerness of the USSR and the People's Republic of China to support them had also diminished. This, perhaps more than the bombing, led Hanoi to send out urgent signals calling for new talks. On December 30 the White House announced a bombing halt and the rescheduling of talks between Kissinger and Le Duc Tho for January 8. It was a sign of the American determination to find a solution that when Thieu sent two South Vietnamese diplomats to Washington with a threat to fight any treaty that did not meet his requirements, Nixon responded by dispatching General Alexander Haig to Saigon with a letter to Thieu telling him, in effect, to shut up.

Soon Kissinger was commuting between Paris and Key Biscayne with a briefcase containing fresh proposals. The break came in late January when the two bargainers met for their twenty-fourth round of talks in forty-two months. Two more days of dickering had been anticipated, but a final understanding was reached in just four hours. The formal end of the war came in the silk-walled conference room of Paris's old Majestic Hotel; simultaneous announcements were broadcast in Washington, Hanoi, and Saigon. (Just working out that process, said Kissinger, had "aged us all by several years.") President Nixon led the nation in prayer, praising the 2.5 million Americans who had served in Vietnam "in one of the most selfless enterprises in the history of nations." He declared that he had achieved "Peace with honor."

But honor had little to do with it. Kissinger appreciated that. In his thoughtful press briefing he observed that "it should be clear by now that no one in the war has had a monopoly of anguish and that no one has had a monopoly of insight." He made no reference to honor, or valor, or glory, or any of the other martial concepts which had become irrelevant to this conflict. "Together with healing the wounds in Indochina," he said, "we can begin to heal the wounds in America." That was the right note to strike, because that was the issue for Americans. After some 46,000 U.S. battle deaths, 300,000 wounded, and the expenditure of 110 billion dollars, they were left, as a direct result of the war, with a grave domestic problem, a spiritual malaise. In the McLuhanesque global village it was not possible to lay waste a distant land without inflicting hideous scars on the United States. Among the casualties had been public esteem for the Presidency, which had led the country into the war; for Congress, which had continued to appropriate vast sums for it; for the courts, which had failed to find it unconstitutional; and for the institution of democracy itself, which, having proved ineffectual in attempting to influence the makers of policy, had degenerated into chaos in the streets. "There has been a sharp decline in respect for authority in the United States as a result of the war," Reston wrote on the occasion of the cease-fire, "a decline in respect not only for the civil authority of government but also for the moral authority of the schools, the universities, the press, the church, and even the family . . . something has happened to American life—something not yet understood or agreed upon, something that is different, important, and probably enduring."

The week of the truce there was an ugly row at Madison Square Garden over whether "The Star-Spangled Banner" should be played before athletic events. At the same time a fresh epidemic of teacher strikes was disrupting classrooms across the country. Neither would have been conceivable during the Depression, the last great trial of the American spirit. The flag had flown over a poorer land then; there had been a great deal of physical suffering in the United States. Teachers had been among the greatest victims of the economic crisis. Often they had been paid in worthless scrip or not at all, and some had shared the little food they had with starving children. But in that tightly disciplined society strikes by them, like disrespect for the national anthem, would have been inconceivable. That does not mean that America was a better country then; plainly it was not. It does mean that it was a different country, inhabited by other people facing challenges wholly unrelated to those of the 1970s.

Perhaps this was what Henry Adams meant when he wrote, in the early years of this century, that the test of twentieth-century Americans would be their capacity for adjustment. Change is a constant theme in the American past. The United States is the only nation in the world to worship it for its own sake, and to regard change and progress as indistinguishable. "We want change. We want progress," Lyndon Johnson said in 1965, "and we aim to get it."

But if that is one aspect of the American national character, there is another, the reverse of the same coin, which reemerged with the end of the Vietnam War. It is the yearning to renounce the present and find restoration in the unconsummated past. "America," John Brooks observed, "has an old habit of regretting a dream just lost, and resolving to capture it next time." The theme is a familiar one in American literature. One thinks of Willa Cather's lost lady and Robert Frost's "The Road Not Taken." Thomas Wolfe wrote: "Remembering speechlessly we seek the great forgotten language, the lost lane-end into heaven, a stone, a leaf, an unfound door. Where? When? O lost, and by the wind grieved, ghost, come back again." So it was that after intervening in foreign conflicts for a third of a century, the people of the United States turned inward once more, seeking comfort in insularity and renewal in isolation. "So we beat on, boats against the current," F. Scott Fitzgerald wrote at the end of his finest novel, "borne back ceaselessly into the past."

Epilogue

ECHOES

SURROUNDED BY HAPPY PERJURERS, Richard Nixon celebrated his second inauguration in a three-day, four-million-dollar extravaganza directed by up-and-coming young Jeb Stuart Magruder. The rhetoric of the January 20 inaugural address, in keeping with the retreat from far-flung world commitments, was less a promise of what the government would do than what it wouldn't. Twelve years earlier another President of the same generation had vowed that "we shall pay any price, bear any burden, meet any hardship, support any friend, oppose any foe, in order to assure the survival and the success of liberty." Now Nixon declared that "the time has passed when America will make every other nation's conflicts our own, or presume to tell the people of other nations how to manage their own affairs." At the same time he prepared to liquidate the domestic programs of liberal administrations with a paraphrase of President Kennedy's most memorable line. Nixon said, "Let each of us ask, not just what will government do for me, but what I can do for myself."

As he paused for effect, a faint sound could be heard from several blocks away. A group of youths was chanting: "Murderer!" "Out now!" "End racism!"

"It's disgusting," a woman from Iowa told a *New York Times* reporter. "Just disgusting. I don't see why we can't do something about these kids." Certainly it was indecorous. Yet counterdemonstrations, like the counterculture, were an expression of the continuing divisions in America, and they had to be endured. There is really no effective way to stifle dissent in an open society; if there were one, Magruder and his employer would have been the first to use it. The chanters—five hundred to a thousand Yippies, SDS militants, and members of the Maoist Progressive Labor Party—were the smallest and rudest band of protesters in the multitude of demonstrators roaming Washington that weekend. With them they carried a loathsome effigy—a ten-foot-long papier-mâché rat with Nixon's face, bearing in its teeth a bloodstained baby doll. That was too much even for the indulgent District police, and they confiscated it. But apart from that group the only really ugly gesture at the inaugural was the lowering of American flags around the Washington Monument and the hoisting of Viet Cong banners in their stead.

The stateliest protest had been held in the Washington Cathedral on Wisconsin Avenue at 9 P.M. the previous evening. After brief remarks by Dean Francis B. Sayre Jr. and former Senator Eugene McCarthy, Leonard Bernstein led a pickup orchestra of local musicians in the gentle, contemplative strains of Haydn's *Mass in Time of War*, with its urgent kettledrums and its final plea, "*Dona nobis pacem*" (Give us peace). In counterpoint, across the city Eugene Ormandy and the Philadelphia Orchestra were saluting the President with Tchaikovsky's bombastic *1812 Overture*. Sixteen of Ormandy's musicians had been excused because they felt it would be demeaning to play before such an audience. Presumably their absence removed any threat to Nixon's life. Even so, the firing of blanks in a cannon, usually the climax of the overture, was omitted at the request of the Secret Service. It was one of the service's less expensive suggestions under that President.

That same evening, critics of Nixon's record in Vietnam delivered to a White House guard a petition setting forth their views. On the sidewalk outside, Father Philip Berrigan performed in a crude skit meant to show how the authorities had mistreated those who had dared to speak out against them. Berrigan pretended to manhandle a woman carrying a peace placard. Lest anyone miss the point of the drama, the priest wore a large sign around his neck reading POLICE. The next day Daniel Ellsberg, who at that time faced possible conviction and sentences totaling 115 years for publishing the Pentagon Papers, addressed a testimonial dinner held by the National Peace Action Coalition. Ellsberg ridiculed the President's inaugural promise of a generation of peace, saying, "He's winding down the war like he's winding down my indictment," and comparing the manufacturers of Vietnam war matériel to the designers of the Nazi death camp at Auschwitz.

Berrigan and Ellsberg were seen by few, but most of the counter-inauguration events were well attended. The Bernstein concert was heard by 3,000 people in the cathedral and another 12,000 to 15,000 who stood in the dank night outside and listened to it over loudspeakers. The petition had been signed by 50,000. And the largest demonstration of all, timed, like the SDS march, to coincide with the President's address on Capitol Hill, drew between 75,000 and 100,000. It began when 2,500 members of the Vietnam Veterans Against the War marched from Arlington National Cemetery to the Washington Monument, continued with the signing of a mock peace treaty there, and ended with an address by New York Congresswoman Bella Abzug, who had been listening to Nixon's speech over a transistor radio and bellowed out her opinion of it.

Some youths in the audience carried obsolete signs reading STOP THE BOMBING. That was ludicrous. The blitz had been stopped three weeks earlier. Other gestures of protest also bordered on the ridiculous. Some of them were wholly unrelated to Vietnam; as Nixon spoke, a tiny biplane, rented by a disgruntled millionaire and closely shepherded by police and Air Force helicopters, trailed a banner which read LEGALIZE GOLD. But there was nothing absurd about the concept of protest. It was far truer to the American spirit than the inaugural address, the cannonless Tchaikovsky overture, and the 1,976 saucily dressed Virginia high school musicians who paraded past the White House, a tribute to Jeb Magruder's vision of what the nation's second centennial would be all about.

In the darkest year of Joe McCarthy a West Virginia college president, testifying in behalf of an embattled liberal, was asked by counsel what America represented to him. He replied that it was "the right to be different." He did not mean merely the eccentric and the whimsically wrong, though there will always be room in the United States for, say, the astrologists, the believers in flying saucers, and the Republican statesmen who bought big Washington houses in 1948 for occupancy during the first Dewey administration. But if liberty is to signify anything substantive, it must also be extended to the last limits of the endurable, shielding under its broad tent the genuinely unpopular champions of causes which the majority regards as reprehensible. Any people can cheer an Eisenhower, a MacArthur, a John Glenn, a Neil Armstrong; it takes generosity of spirit to suffer the Weathermen who hated LBJ, the Birchers who baited JFK, the Liberty Leaguers who heckled FDR.

In the lengthening memories of Americans who were entering their fifties in the Nixon years, the strains on the nation's tolerance had been great. Sometimes it had been too much, and the names of the places where patience was exhausted stain the pages of U.S. history with shame: Attica, Kent State, My Lai, Birmingham, Oxford, the Republic Steel plant in Chicago, the California camps where Americans of Japanese descent were penned up during World War II; and the Bonus Army camp on Anacostia Flats whose destruction was described in the first pages of this book.

Yet they were exceptions. A list of examples of forbearance would be many times longer, and might be regarded as a national roll of libertarian honor. It would include the names of Angela Davis, the Berrigans, Stokely Carmichael, Dr. Spock, the Chicago Seven, Woodstock, Ti-Grace Atkinson, the American Nazis who carried "Free Gas for Peace Creeps" signs, the captain of the *Pueblo,* the Fair Play for Cuba Committee, Edwin Walker, SANE's Linus Pauling, Rosa Parks, the America Firsters, Earl Browder, the Shrine of the Little Flower, William Dudley Pelley, Huey Long, Gerald L. K. Smith, and the emaciated wraiths who greeted the 72nd Congress, on its return to Washington in December 1932, by singing "The International."

Defiers of the popular will, like those who give it voice, deserve remembrance; but so do the silent witnesses who kept the key figures alert and honest and strengthened the country's democratic institutions simply by their presence. In time of crisis they gathered quietly in Lafayette Park, just across Pennsylvania Avenue from the White House; a President had but to look out a window and there they were, reminding him that his employers were watching. They were conspicuously in attendance at the great congressional hearings in which the country's temper was being tested, and often its policy forged, through the past forty years, weighing the Vietnam War, Sherman Adams and Bernard Goldfine, the Bricker Amendment, the Army-McCarthy controversy, the hoodlums exposed by Estes Kefauver, Hiss and Chambers, the five-percenters, Pearl Harbor, Roosevelt's plan for Supreme Court reform, and the part played by Wall Street in the Great Depression. They were the spectators when the Taft bell tower was dedicated, they mourned when Roosevelt and Eisenhower lay in state, and they stood in stricken silence on November 25, 1963, as a caisson bearing the body of John Kennedy clattered across Memorial Bridge toward Arlington and the eternal flame.

There is a school of historians which holds that great events may tell us less about the past than the trivia accumulated by ordinary people—the letters, pressed flowers, prom programs, cherished toys and the like saved by those who loved them and could not bear to throw them away. From time to time construction workers will stumble across such caches, sometimes entombed in old mansions. Occasionally they may find something almost as elaborate as the Westinghouse time capsule which was buried at the New York World's Fair of 1939. Such discoveries always excite curiosity, and the older ones stir speculation over what this or that article meant to people at the time it was put away. With the growing mobility of Americans the accumulation of such troves is rarer, but if members of the swing generation had one—put away, perhaps, in a storeroom the size of Fibber McGee's fabled closet—it might provide insight into what they had been like, what they had endured, what their dreams had been, and which had been realized and which dashed.

Envisaging such a cupboard, we see in front on the top shelf a steel tennis racket, several dieting books, a wide necktie, and a pantsuit broad in the beam. Just behind them are a "Welcome Home POWs" bumper sticker, one for MIAs ("Only Hanoi Knows"), and a peace decal; then a brass-colored PT boat tie clip, and cassette recordings of *Camelot*, Arlo Guthrie's *Alice's Restaurant*, and Carol Channing's *Hello, Dolly*. Behind them, well hidden in a corner beneath a pile of tie-dyed jeans, are well-thumbed copies of *Fanny Hill* and *The Autobiography of a Flea*.

Various items of clothing occupy much of the space on the second shelf: a sheath dress, a gray flannel suit, a man's narrow-brimmed felt hat, several incredibly narrow neckties, a child's coonskin cap, and a straw boater with the legend I LIKE IKE on the hatband. Concealed beneath them is an obsolete item of female apparel: a diaphragm in a white plastic case. Beyond is a curious little silver lapel pin. It resembles the bottom of a man's shoe with a hole in the sole. Nearby are a *My Fair Lady* album, a record of Edith Piaf singing *"Il Pleut,"* a Winky Dink kit, a Mouseketeer cap, and a collapsed Babee-Tenda. Copies of *Fireman Small* and *Peyton Place* lie on top of miscellaneous papers: a pamphlet on how to stop smoking, a Fish House Punch recipe, an *Around the World in Eighty Days* program, a batch of bills from a diaper service, and an envelope containing plans for a home bomb shelter (never opened).

Near the front of the third shelf is a Dior New Look skirt, an Eisenhower jacket which appears to have been worn by a slender man, early nylons, a freshman beanie, a copy of *Tropic of Cancer*, and under it a packet of three Trojans. (They sold for a dollar.) Various certificates: military discharge, marriage license, college diplomas. A ruptured duck pin. An Army divisional patch. Rationing stamps. Navy dog tags, long tarnished. A packet of V-letters. A Nazi helmet; a samurai sword. A Kate Smith Columbia record: "God Bless America." A rhinestone V-for-Victory pin.

The bottom shelf is rather junky. A pair of Thom McAn saddle shoes, very dirty, stand on top of an equally soiled reversible raincoat, beneath which is a sport coat with a belted back. A dead corsage is pressed between two 78 rpm records—"Deep Purple" and "Stardust." Beside them lie campaign pins reading "We Want Willkie" and "FDR." A third pin is shaped like a sunflower. Then: a shabby Philco radio in the form of an arch, a tattered copy of *Gone With the Wind*, a copy of *Ulysses* in which only the last forty pages seem to have been read, Boy and Girl Scout handbooks, and several square Big Little Books. There is a dusty Lionel train transformer, a jump rope, several marbles and one steelie, a splintered hockey stick, a well-oiled first baseman's mitt, a Shirley Temple doll, a sheaf of bubble gum cards, a G-man cap gun. Two Post Toasties box tops. A box of cherry bombs. A Bolo ball attached by elastic to a paddle. A pair of brown corduroy knickers. A hair ribbon. An old stand-up telephone.

Lastly, on the floor of the closet, are a batch of snapshots taken with a box Brownie. There are automobiles in them: a Model A Ford with the windshield down in some, a Chevy sporting a sassy rumble seat in others, and in the older ones, brown with age, a Model T. People are posing by the running boards. It is summer, yet the adults look very formal. The men are wearing stiff collars, the women vast hats and shapeless cotton dresses. But it is the children who seem oddest. Like their parents they are quaintly dressed. There is something else, though. It takes a moment to realize why they look so peculiar. Then you see it. There is an intensity in their expressions. They are leaning slightly forward, as though trying to see into the future. And they are smiling.

Acknowledgments

HARRY SIONS, the editor of this book, died in Philadelphia on March 26, 1974, when the manuscript was in the final stages of preparation for the press. He had completed his final review of the text just a few days earlier. For over seventeen years he was a colleague and a cherished friend; his skill and high intelligence left their mark on every page of this volume, as well as on much of my earlier work.

Don Congdon, my literary agent for a quarter-century, planted the seed for the book by suggesting a study of the American national character. Together with Harry and J. Randall Williams of Little, Brown, he was an unfailing source of encouragement and sound advice. The support of Don and Randy Williams was immense, and is most gratefully acknowledged.

Several other associates and acquaintances were generous with suggestions and insight. I am particularly indebted to Henry Anatole Grunwald, Herman Kahn, Louis Lasagna M.D., Daniel Patrick Moynihan, Arthur M. Schlesinger Jr., and Eric Sevareid. In addition, Harry McMahan of *Advertising Age* was a treasure of information in his special field.

My invaluable assistant, Margaret Kennedy Rider, was loyal, resourceful, and tireless during the long years of research and writing. Epsey Farrell was of great help in her role as researcher, and I am appreciative of the assistance of Ellen G. D'Oench in annotating the manuscript.

No expression of thanks to Wyman Parker, Librarian of Wesleyan

University, and the staff of the university's Olin Library, can really be adequate. For fifteen years they have sheltered me, cheered me, guarded my privacy, and given unstintingly of their considerable technical skills. At a time when their stacks are crammed, all I can give them in return is another book, and an outsize one at that. Moreover, it is imperfect, as all books are. It is true, insofar as diligence and research can establish truth, but it is not the whole truth. No volume, nor even a whole library, can provide that. All an author can offer is a fragment of reality—that, and the hope that it will endure.

CHAPTER NOTES

In these Notes, works are generally cited by the author's name only; for full listings see the Bibliography. If the note is citing an author with more than one work in the Bibliography, a brief title for the work cited is also given in the note. Other forms of citation are:

- Fab Time-Life series *This Fabulous Century* (see entries at Maitland A. Edey and Jerry Korn in the Bibliography)
- NYT *New York Times*
- TA Time Annual *1969: The Year in Review*
- T *Time* magazine
- TC Time-Life series *Time Capsule* (see entry at Maitland A. Edey in the Bibliography)
- W Associated Press series *The World in—* (see listing at Keith Fuller in the Bibliography)
- WA *World Almanac* (cited with the year)
- WM Author's interviews

The words identifying each note are the *end* of the paragraph which the note covers.

PROLOGUE: ROCK BOTTOM
(*pages 1–32*)

1 "Bonus Expeditionary Force": NYT 1/31/32; T 8/15/32; Schlesinger *Crisis* 256; *Baltimore Sun* 7/17/32. *2* off to jail: Fab IV 25. and multiplying misery: *Baltimore Sun* 7/17/32. to the country: *Baltimore Sun* 7/27/32; WM/Herman Kahn 6/5/70; *Washington* 29; Acheson 16–17, 91. *3* on ruling them: Mullett 3–8; "Who's in the Army Now?". elaborate buzzer system: Daniels 181; Gene Smith 12, 48; *Washington* 11. *4* Ike came scurrying: *Saturday Evening Post* 12/20/30; Gene Smith 48; *Washington* 11; NYT 12/25/29, 7/27/41; WM/Herman Kahn; *Foreign Service Journal* February 1955; Eisenhower *Ease* 210; WM/Eisenhower 8/27/64. *5* was rich: *Ease* 219–20; "Who's in the Army Now?"; Rovere *Years* 13; NYT 10/2/43; Mellor 129–30; Farago 105; *Washington* 601. colonies in 1776: T 2/8/32; "Who's in the Army Now?". "an ungraceful angle": "Who's in the Army Now?" *6* trolley car: NYT 9/1/43; WM/Eisenhower; Adams 155. a cottage industry: WM/Herman Kahn; *Washington* xix; Phillips *Blitz* 294–95. "Dat's de propolition": *Washington* xxi, 3, 83, 87; Schlesinger *Upheaval* 428. *7* great god macadam: NYT 5/15/48; Van Camp. *8* D.C., was like: Sylvia Porter "The Vanishing Trains" *Middletown Press* 12/9/69. to American business: NYT 4/29/32, 5/11/32, 4/24/32, 1/17/32; *Washington* 945; "Washington Through the Years"; NYT 2/4/32, 11/9/32; *Washington* 117, 918. *9* scheduled for razing: "Washington Through the Years"; NYT 2/4/32, 11/9/32; *Washington* 117, 918; Shuster 64, 105. exactly what he did: Galbraith *State* 359; *Baltimore Sun* 7/27/32; NYT 7/29/32; Daniels 193. *10* "anywhere in the world": NYT 7/21/32; *Baltimore Sun* 6/5/32, 6/8/32, 6/9/32, 6/10/32, 6/19/32, 6/27/32; T 6/13/32; Gene Smith 136. *11* "their individual cases": NYT 6/19/32; *Ease* 209; Gene Smith 135. about patriotism: NYT 7/29/32; Daniels 192; Gene Smith 152. *12* Chicago's southwest side: NYT 8/17/32, 8/2/32, 7/29/32; T 8/8/32. *13* chief of staff: NYT 7/29/32; *Baltimore Sun* 7/29/32; *Boston Herald* 7/29/32; T 8/8/32; Gene Smith 156. bitterly resented it: Congdon 117; Rovere and Schlesinger 31–33; *Ease* 159, 212. *14* solicitude toward civilians: Gene Smith 159. suit, and all: *Baltimore Sun* 7/29/32; Walter Johnson 3–5; Gene Smith 161. "his mouth again": T 8/8/32. *15* drove him out: Gene Smith 161. *16* his next move: *Ease* 213. disobey a President: Walter Johnson 3–5; *Ease* 213; Fab IV 25–26; *Ease* 213. *17* "feel for them": Fab IV 25–26; T 8/8/32; *Ease* 213; Gene Smith 162. George S. Patton Jr.: Daniels 194; *Crisis* 263; NYT 7/30/32; T 8/8/32; Mellor 103–28. *18* "heroes just now": T 8/8/32. "would surprise me": NYT 7/29/32, 8/4/32; T 8/8/32; Gene Smith 164, 166. "law and order": NYT 7/30/32; Congdon 119; *New Republic* 11/2/32; *Crisis* 263–64. *19* a difficult task: *Baltimore Sun* 7/29/32; "Who's in the Army Now?". "the Bonus marchers?" *Crisis* 261; Daniels 193. *20* "in terrible shape": Gene Smith 169. land in 1932: NYT 7/30/32; Bird 56; *Nation* 8/17/32. *21* "the next station": *Blitz* 40–41; Congdon 102; *Crisis* 251; T 2/6/33; *Blitz* 285; Mowry 75; Walter Johnson 16; WM/Eric Sevareid; Congdon 102, 110. far from home: Sevareid *Dream* 49; *Nation* 8/24/32; Walter Johnson 23; NYT 12/11/32. *22* his old menus: NYT 5/4/32. "real estate company": NYT 9/19/31. *23* "with very pity": *Esquire* June 1960; Bird 24; Wolfe 413–14. "Yes, sir": Goldman *Tragedy* 377; *Time* editors 24; *Tragedy* 274; *Relief for Unemployed Transients* 35–38. *24* venereal infection: Minehan 67–71. and, later, militancy: NYT 3/26/31, 1/20/32; *Upheaval* 428–29; Congdon 171; Bird 130; T 4/10/33, 4/17/33, 12/11/33. day was inevitable: Minehan 18–83. *25* for a quarter: NYT 8/2/41; T 5/12/41. "them at night": Congdon 152; Gene Smith 80; NYT 3/5/29; Gene Smith 206. return of prosperity: Gene Smith 66. *26* such incredible speed: Wolff 198; Gene Smith 97. "both of them": NYT 3/2/32. *27* might be softened: *Years* 78; Walter Johnson 27. people be tabled: Galbraith *Affluent* 15; NYT 1/5/32; Isabel Leighton 277. *28* legislatures, not Congress: Fab IV 25; Leary; Bird 208–209. the building trades: *Crisis* 57; Childs "Main Street"; Sulzberger 27. "make things worse": NYT 1/20/32; *Crisis* 164; *Affluent* 16; Gene Smith 76. *29* would win: Schwartz xiii, xiv; *Affluent* 45; Gene Smith 68. "political log-rolling!": T 5/30/32. "grandiloquent egotists": Mowry 57; *Crisis* 80. *30* "Depression is over": Bird 13. "spare a dime": NYT 12/3/30; Bird 58; *Crisis* 241; T 4/4/32. *31* Business Confidence Week: *Crisis* 177. "worn-out private belongings": Fab IV 76; NYT 1/4/32; Isabel Leighton 222. on American newsstands: *Middletown Press* 7/27/32; headlines T 8/8/32.

I THE CRUELEST YEAR
(*pages 35–82*)

35 could not understand: Gene Smith 103. "protect my children?": NYT 9/6/29; Mowry 68; Gene Smith 81. *36* "to the community": *Commonweal* 9/3/54; Bird 41. overextension of credit: Allen *Change* 144. *37* "got too little": Mowry 64. without historical precedent: Bird 115. *38* jobs was $16.21: Shannon 73; Phillips *Blitz* 32, 34. Howard Johnson, survived: Allen *Since* 132; *Time* editors 63; NYT 3/2/33, 2/6/32; *Theatre Arts* April 1931. *39* "off my pants": *Time* editors 65; Bird 12; T 12/19/32; *Since* 108. *40* a peculiar gait: Bird 226; Schlesinger *Crisis* 167. she could imagine: Bird 227. and an undertaker: Fab IV 46; Bird 40, 116; Shannon 12, 26. *41* dunes of garbage: Shannon 10; Bird 21. an entire family: *Crisis* 167; Bird 36. of their own: *Fortune* September 1932. *42* of two hundred: Gene Smith 174; NYT 1/19/33; Shannon 23. "the Depression, huh?": *Blitz* 34; Fab IV 54; Shannon 23. *43* called starvation wages: Bird 68; Shannon 26. until after sunset: Congdon 36, 45, 47. *44* began to disintegrate: *Crisis* 248; T 3/13/33. and the indigent: Bird 63. game called Eviction: ibid 27. *45* population of 600,000: *American Academy* January 1933. "bill before delivery": Bird 134. excluded from churches: ibid 26. *46* filthy old sheepskin: Schlesinger *Coming* 268; *Blitz* 257. began to disappear: Shannon 93–103 passim. *47* twenty million dollars: ibid 94. thin pocketbooks: ibid 99. "poor people were": NYT 3/8/32. *48* "to our children?": *Crisis* 3; Shannon 53; Fab IV 53. dying of hunger: *Fortune* September 1932; Bird 32. *49* "days of 1932":

Crisis 250; Wolfe 412. might be misunderstood: Bird 19. *50* "mighty vaults": Wolfe 414. "went to hell": *Newsweek* 2/17/33; NYT 2/6/32; Gene Smith 24. *51* "of the lowest": NYT 3/30/32; Congdon 612. couldn't help them: *Crisis* 190; NYT 3/11/32; Daniels 189. "policeman searches you": NYT 6/29/32, 4/14/32; T 10/17/32; *Crisis* 118. *52* taxes in full: *Blitz* 134; Bird 10; NYT 4/26/33; Daniels 183. "ammunition for radicals": NYT 5/12/33, 2/11/32; *New Republic* 5/29/35; T 1/25/32. *53* from trusting investors: T 3/21/32; NYT 3/13/32. "completely shattered": NYT 5/21/33; T 6/19/33; *Time* editors 31. *54* it had become: NYT 6/7/32, 7/29/32; *Crisis* 109; John Brooks *Golconda* 137. he liked it: Mowry 55; NYT 11/8/28; *Crisis* 280. "economic pyramid": NYT 4/8/32. "rich against poor!": NYT 4/14/32; T 4/25/32. *55* "have another Hoover": *Crisis* 175, 280, 288; NYT 7/10/32, 6/11/32; T 7/4/32. "still a Hoover": Rovere *Years* 18; *Crisis* 290. *56* were very direct: NYT 4/27/32, 5/5/32; Gene Smith 116. "here again!" Gene Smith 114. *57* campaign had begun: *Crisis* 309; T 8/8/32. *58* to "brain trust": NYT 7/3/32, 5/23/32; *Since* 78. danger of accidents: T 7/31/33; Fab IV 141. *59* endorse any candidate: *Crisis* 428; Mowry 86. General MacArthur: Gene Smith 178; NYT 11/11/32, 10/16/32. "this extraordinary hour": *Crisis* 434; *Nation* 7/13/32. *60* four years later: T 11/21/32; NYT 9/24/32, 6/17/33; *Crisis* 413, 416. *61* "of lost children": *Crisis* 428. Johnson of California: NYT 9/13/32; Walter Johnson 37. *62* phoned Calvin Coolidge: *Crisis* 194, 199, 204; NYT 11/6/32. would be dead: *Crisis* 201; NYT 10/12/32; T 10/24/32. *63* words had become: Walter Johnson 37; T 11/7/32; NYT 11/8/32; *Crisis* 437. Franklin Delano Ragin: NYT 11/9/32; *Crisis* 218, 437; *Blitz* 73. "do this job": Gene Smith 214. *64* was right: Walter Johnson 45; NYT 11/13/32; Bird 78. "world's in birth": NYT 12/6/32; *Crisis* 448; Shannon 120. *65* "and farmers' republic": NYT 11/8/32; Congdon 148. *66* smashed her face: NYT 1/15/33; *Blitz* 5; *Crisis* 166. "the American system": NYT 3/23/32; Shannon 114; *Coming* 22. *67* "left-wing state": *Crisis* 208; NYT 8/30/32; Bird 116. *68* of Columbia University: *Crisis* 204, 460; NYT 1/26/32, 1/6/32; Schlesinger *Upheaval* 82. "one now": NYT 11/11/32; *Crisis* 266. in Sioux City: Bird 131; *Crisis* 266. *69* "was illegal too": NYT 8/14/32; Daniels 195; Shannon 123, 125. "of other days": NYT 8/22/32; Shannon 121. "eat their gold": *Crisis* 174; *Time* editors 32. *70* about mortgage foreclosures: NYT 8/26/32. press prosecution afterward: *Crisis* 459; T 5/8/33. *71* "than twelve months": T 1/16/33, 2/6/33; NYT 2/12/33; *Crisis* 459. *72* thirty-four years: Bird 4. these. O Pioneers!: ibid 2. *73* before a bath: Gold *1940–41* 7. aluminum juice extractor: T 4/27/42. *74* about hair "coloring": Gold *1940–41* 9, 12. 59 million dollars: *Science* 5/12/33; WM/Louis Lasagna; Bird 133. *75* "Uncle Don": *Blitz* 433. best friend's thoughts: Sevareid *Dream* 4. *76* Lindbergh's *We:* NYT 8/7/27. "destined to encounter": Gold *1940–41* 11. *77* "coal beds" . . . "in a monarchy": Theodore White *1968* 99, 97. *78* clearly visible: T 10/10/32. palms of his hands: NYT 6/16/32; *Since* 16. and cherry bombs: Gold *1940–41* 10. *80* R.N. stewardesses: Bird 2. service improves: Bird 264. "ten years ago": NYT 5/4/37, 11/10/32; T 4/4/32. *81* "my band, son": Bird 30; Gold *1940–41* 48. paper victory: NYT 8/20/32, 9/23/32; Fab V 66. *82* death or even illness: NYT 2/28/32, 8/24/32; T 4/11/32.

II ROOSEVELT!
(*pages 84–111*)

84 the outgoing President: Schlesinger *Crisis* 440; NYT 2/5/53, 7/31/32; Gene Smith 222. *85* "in the future": NYT 11/23/32, 1/8/33; *Crisis* 441. it a holiday: NYT 2/14/33. *86* was "a madman": NYT 2/16/33; *Crisis* 474. had gone under: *Crisis* 466. *87* song for children: Bird 92; NYT 3/2/33, 2/5/33. "could not be greater": *Holiday* February 1960. *88* fog, toward Washington: NYT 3/6/33, 3/2/33. barometer was falling: NYT 3/3/33, 3/2/33. *89* two financial strongholds: NYT 3/3/33. "don't want to": NYT 3/4/33. "must go now": Gene Smith 225. *90* "we can do": NYT 3/3/33, 3/4/33; Fab IV 116. with a cameraman: Schlesinger *Coming* 424; NYT 3/1/33, 3/5/33. *91* "a foreign foe": NYT 3/5/33. *92* tell him so: Walter Johnson 49; Isabel Leighton 275; *Coming* 1. without moneychangers: NYT 3/5/33, 3/6/33; Bird 96. *93* "going any lower": *Holiday* February 1960. they had done: ibid. *94* going into action: NYT 3/10/33. *95* "Are Here Again": NYT 3/9/33; Phillips *Blitz* 120; John Brooks *Golconda* 155. "bit shell-shocked": NYT 3/10/33, 6/17/33; Gunther 139. *96* "Hitler much more"; *Blitz* 106. one vast classroom: *Coming* 555. President's own wife: NYT 3/9/33; *Blitz* 473. *97* "wheels turning around": NYT 3/13/33; *Coming* 557. *98* had won it: *Coming* 530, 574. "is the President": ibid 511; NYT 3/5/33; T 7/31/33. *99* One note ran: Gunther 147; NYT 1/22/61. "President like you": Fab IV 136. "and in itself": ibid; *Coming* 424; T 3/13/33; NYT 3/19/33. "why they left": WM/Herman Kahn. *100* Kleberg's constituents: NYT 5/9/33; Bird 111; *Blitz* 234. "Lord, God Almighty": Acheson 151. them, especially Hiss: WM/Herman Kahn. those of congressmen: NYT 3/7/33, 2/27/33; T 8/21/33. *101* Texas to Canada: NYT 3/25/33; *Coming* 338; Fab IV 130. "the deflationary forces": *Golconda* 154, 155. *102* control for hogs: Isabel Leighton 284; NYT 5/13/33; T 8/21/33. "the United States!": NYT 5/21/33; TC 1930 145. *103* and Ickes achieved: *Coming* 264; NYT 11/8/33. the Florida mainland: NYT 11/9/33; Bird 108. first Nixon administration: NYT 7/12/36, 9/12/36, 5/7/46. *104* anything was possible: NYT 1/22/33. "ax won't work": NYT 6/17/33; Isabel Leighton 291. *105* "authority of government": NYT 6/17/33, 5/8/33; *Coming* 98. "restraint of competition": *Blitz* 218; NYT 11/2/33. *106* it looked real: NYT 8/14/33; T 7/31/33. "on the nose": Walter Johnson 68; T 8/7/33; *Blitz* 48. "back good times": NYT 7/25/33; *Blitz* 220. *107* "American economic life": *Coming* 119, 123; T 11/13/33. *108* had saved capitalism: Fab IV 116; *Blitz* 128. to ask him: T 8/14/33; Schlesinger *Upheaval* 451. *109–111* Eleanor Roosevelt portrait: *Current Biography* 1949, 1963; NYT 11/8/62.

III STIRRINGS
(*pages 112–147*)

112 "am for Johnnie": NYT 10/26/34; Fab IV 100, 109. *113* in her purse: NYT 7/23/34, 2/8/34; Daniels 240. and Clyde Barrow: NYT 7/26/34. *114* he had left: NYT 6/5/34, 6/10/34; Schlesinger *Coming* 294. *115* nascent Liberty League: NYT 9/26/34, 7/3/34; *Coming* 153, 463; John Brooks *Golconda* 198. "virtually terminated": T 4/3/33. concern was espionage: *Coming* 53; NYT 4/6/34. *116* left he could get: Kendrick 136. do the job: NYT 11/7/34. *117* New Year's Day: NYT 5/20/34, 8/30/34, 1/11/34, 8/8/34, 2/23/33. get some rain: NYT 5/29/34. was blowing away: NYT 1/27/37, 9/22/38; *Coming* 70; Brogan 82. *118* threatened with famine: Brogan 81; Walter Johnson 67; Shannon 131. on their floors: NYT 6/21/34; *Coming* 69; Fab IV 60. *119* at 108 degrees: Fab IV 61; NYT 8/13/34; Congdon 289. "off the earth": Phillips *Blitz* 240. *120* of Upton Sinclair: Daniels 247; Sevareid *Dream* 11; NYT 4/14/39; Fab IV 64. a generation later: Schlesinger *Upheaval* 117. the regular Democratic organization: *Upheaval* 111; Daniels 248. "going on before": NYT 9/2/34; *Upheaval* 34. *121 I Got Licked:* NYT 2/24/35; Daniels 248; *Upheaval* 118. New York City: NYT 9/10/36, 11/6/36, 11/8/33. *122* or his effectiveness: NYT 9/17/33; Congdon 195. "support for reaction": NYT 11/18/34; *Upheaval* 176, 182. *123* "be USSA then": NYT 10/29/50; Schulberg 20; Allen *Since* 251. *124* "TAKE IT CLUB": NYT 8/23/34. his own good: NYT 10/25/34. *125* Days of 1935: NYT 10/16/34, 4/1/36, 6/5/35. *126* "perturbed at developments": NYT 1/5/35; *Upheaval* 391, 226. response was a fraud: NYT 4/2/35; *Upheaval* 311. *127* "hand, Mr. Chairman": NYT 8/9/35; Burns *Soldier* 362; *Blitz* 289. cents an hour: NYT 6/20/35. *128* bosses, and Negroes: NYT 5/30/34. "other crime bills": NYT 6/14/34, 7/5/34. *129* the early 1970s: NYT 1/23/35, 1/10/35, 2/5/35, 4/1/35. claim was undisputed: NYT 12/1/35; *Upheaval* 4; Isabel Leighton 242. *130* "let me know": Spivak 6. "toes against eternity": *Upheaval* 20; NYT 12/26/35; T 4/10/33. *131* ground between them: Carlson 58. the political center: NYT 6/9/36, 4/29/34. *132* "the labor problem": Isabel Leighton 241. "we will win": NYT 7/20/35; T 4/10/33; Carlson 57; Isabel Leighton 248. *133* "a holy war": Carlson 58. "unbalanced college professors": Daniels 253. *134* William Howard Taft: NYT 8/18/46. in American politics: NYT 2/1/35. *135* "still weep here": Daniels 204. "of my path": NYT 1/26/32. *136* Avenue in Washington: *Upheaval* 56. "lead the mob": NYT 9/22/35; Daniels 240–43; *Upheaval* 66. *137* his own constituents: Walter Johnson 83–86; Congdon 315. "you want it": *Upheaval* 243–44. "honestly conducted election": Isabel Leighton 357. *138* "has an intellect": NYT 6/26/35; *Upheaval* 249. over the country: NYT 3/8/35. "man a king": *Upheaval* 65. *139* "in knee breeches": NYT 9/29/35. *140* "kill Huey Long": NYT 9/9/35; *Blitz* 302; NYT 9/10/35, 9/15/35; *Upheaval* 340. been dramatically different: *Upheaval* 341. *141* resembling a sermon: NYT 6/17/36. "in the scale": Schlesinger *Thousand* 720. a chain reaction: *Blitz* 296; NYT 7/5/36. *142* a familiar form: *Blitz* 420. *143* King of Swing: Gold *1936–37* 4. in the future: Gold *1940–41* 21. *144* "censorship as possible": Fab IV 180; Mowry 25; *Time* editors 151; T 2/20/33. United States in 1935: Mowry 5. *145* "their Bewildering Offspring": ibid 3. *146* introduced to him: *Blitz* 442. *147* the New Deal: *Time* editors 63; Mowry 112.

IV THE ROOSEVELT REFERENDUM
(*pages 149–178*)

149 to threats overseas: NYT 12/31/33. *150* America was chickenhearted: NYT 7/4/37. aggression in Manchuria: NYT 9/1/35. *151* "is fairly certain": NYT 6/5/34; Gunther 300. was forty-three: NYT 7/27/34; "Who's in the Army Now?" *152* Swarthmore '32; NYT 4/13/35; Schlesinger *Upheaval* 199; Simon 157, 168–69. *153* abolished it: Sevareid *Dream* 59. "right-minded students here": Phillips *Blitz* 477; T 10/3/32. desperately needed cash: NYT 11/9/35. *154* "starving by degrees": Simon 155; *Fortune* June 1936; Simon 155. the university library: Bird 242; Congdon 400. of juvenile distinction: *New Republic* 10/9/35. *155* and roller skates: Gold *1940–41* 21; Fab V 48. suits and white bucks: Gold *1940–41* 4. *156* all Duke dances: Fab IV 241; Gold *1940–41* 21. yet to come: Bird 238. progressive union policies: Fab IV 164; NYT 1/28/32. *157* "return their blows": Schlesinger *Coming* 138, 413. "of his youth": NYT 12/8/35; *Coming* 143. *158* "a quieting influence": Fab IV 164; *Coming* 394. "mines without them": *Coming* 385; NYT 7/17/34; Fab IV 162. *159* "dinkey parlezvous": Bird 149; NYT 2/16/36; *Blitz* 516. "just join up!": NYT 12/8/35. *160* over 400,000: NYT 9/28/34, 11/5/34. time for persuasion: NYT 12/1/34, 3/13/35, 5/17/35. *161* "their goddam heads": Daniels 255; Graham and Gurr 332; *Coming* 396; Bird 152. "of the race": Graham and Gurr 336 ff, 387; NYT 5/22/34; *Coming* 388. *162* underpaid, and sweated: NYT 7/1/34, 2/15/35; *Coming* 406. *163* of Industrial Organizations: Simon 107; NYT 10/20/35, 11/24/35, 12/8/35. "makes us strong!": *Coming* 415. *164* it was illegal: *Upheaval* 448, 451; Mowry 116, 118; NYT 10/30/35. *165* regulate interstate commerce: NYT 5/28/35. issuing a warning: NYT 5/30/35. *166* problems was forbidden: NYT 1/7/36, 5/19/36, 5/26/36; *Upheaval* 488. ceiling over hours: NYT 6/2/36. "of the Court": NYT 10/31/36. *167* one-term President: NYT 12/15/36. from the President; *Upheaval* 633. *168* than half that: Gunther 300; NYT 3/24/35; Daniels 305. OF COUNTRY LEADS: *Upheaval* 571. political assets, luck: ibid 502, 590. *169* the American temper: NYT 1/26/36. died before November: NYT 6/12/36, 6/14/36. paused for breath: NYT 6/11/36. *170* "for to free!": *Blitz* 484. Bell was cracked: Spivak 32; NYT 8/16/36; *Upheaval* 629. for a prayer: NYT 10/16/36. *171* "within the gates": NYT 6/24/36. "you ever saw": Congdon 435; NYT 6/28/36; *Upheaval* 584. *172* in New Orleans: NYT 6/1/36, 11/3/36. was a Communist: NYT 10/16/36. Landon didn't win: *Upheaval* 616. *173* social security number: NYT 10/24/36; *Upheaval* 635. bonfire in him: Congdon 439, 442; NYT 1/1/36. *174* after his departure: NYT 11/1/36; *Upheaval* 639. "campaign manager's prophecies?": WM/DPMoynihan; *Blitz* 488; Bird 181; *Upheaval* 608. out to *Time:* NYT 12/15/36, 11/4/36, 2/19/37; Wish 471; Daniels 275. *175* "known conservative tendencies": *Upheaval* 656. *175–178* Whitney portrait: John Brooks *Once in Golconda* 210–29; T 11/23/36, 3/21/38, 5/9/38, 5/16/38.

V THE CONSERVATIVE PHOENIX
(*pages 179–207*)

180 Dutch East Indies: NYT 6/23/37, 6/8/37. oxygen bomb calorimeter: Congdon 615 and passim. *181* (were Gap-Free): NYT 5/24/37. awaited television: Jack Goodman 279; NYT 3/19/37. kind of year: NYT 1/21/37. *182* "with muffled oars": Schlesinger *Upheaval* 494; Gunther 61; Schlesinger *Thousand* 869. "Chief Justice understood": NYT 1/7/37; *Time* editors 36. *183* the "Court pack": NYT 2/4/37. the same decision: NYT 3/11/37; Phillips *Blitz* 501. *184* "rendezvous with death": *Blitz* 501; NYT 3/10/37, 3/5/37. "the caucus room": *Blitz* 503; Simon 205. in his hand: NYT 3/30/37, 7/7/37, 7/15/37; Congdon 468. *185* was now acceptable: NYT 7/22/37; WA 1937; Congdon 475. including Johnson himself: Goldman *Tragedy* 258. *186* be kept moving: Daniels 285; NYT 3/21/34. "that's the trouble": NYT 3/6/37; Fab IV 164. *187* burst into tears: NYT 12/19/36, 12/29/36; Daniels 266. past the police: NYT 3/25/37. *188* major GM stockholder: NYT 1/1/37; Gunther 147. issuing a statement: Spivak 110; NYT 8/1/37; Gunther 147. SHALL NOT PASS: NYT 2/3/37. *189* "the right thing?": Fab IV 167; Bird 155. outside the plants: *Time* editors 70; Allen *Since* 82; NYT 2/7/37. he was underpaid: Fab IV 170; NYT 4/7/37. *190* "is nothing there": T 5/15/39, 12/2/40. meant to change: NYT 5/16/37; Fab IV 172; Daniels 267. *191* another conversation: NYT 10/27/37; *Since* 292. "Yes, Mr. Fairless": NYT 3/8/37. *192* meet workers' demands: *Blitz* 522–23; Bird 147; NYT 5/28/37. Court, was unmentioned: NYT 5/27/37; Fab

IV 172, 175. *193* "Solidarity Forever": NYT 5/31/37; Isabel Leighton 383 ff. *194* "women doing there?": NYT 6/20/37; Isabel Leighton 386 ff; Fab IV 176. much for them: Isabel Leighton 398; NYT 7/28/37. "intimidate the strikers": NYT 6/16/37; Fab IV 176. *195* except Bethlehem Steel: Isabel Leighton 396. "in our history": NYT 5/27/37. expanding middle class: Walter Johnson 159; NYT 10/29/37. *196* ideals to work: NYT 9/23/37, 2/28/37, 9/25/37. *197* "fifty times more": Bird 183; NYT 9/29/37. of 1929–30: *Since* 305 ff; NYT 10/20/37. was on relief: Mowry 295. *198* days, lay ahead: Galbraith *Affluent* 16; *Thousand* 626; NYT 5/1/38, 4/15/38; *Since* 311. "you would wish": Bird 184. *199* not party lines: *Saturday Evening Post* 9/22/34; Schlesinger *Coming* 483. "Grand!" across it: Daniels 301; *Coming* 569. *200* businessmen, was battening: NYT 12/5/38. "that man's skin": Gunther 56. (Colonel van Rosenfeld): Daniels 300; John Brooks *Golconda* 215. *201* businessmen to Washington: Gunther 50. *202* had syphilis: Simon 111; *Golconda* 216. breathe freely again: NYT 8/15/39. in the fall: *Since* 232. *203* "the New Deal": NYT 7/13/38. could sense it: Mowry 120, 122; *Fortune* January, 1939. for Roosevelt's signature: *Time* editors 37. *204* ugly overture: *Blitz* 507–508. "my own name": NYT 6/25/38. *205* "a commanding position": Burns *Lion* 363, 365. *206* had been committed: NYT 7/9/38, 7/14/38, 7/17/38. New Deal legislation: NYT 7/8/38; *Lion* 363. "a working majority": NYT 9/18/40; *Thousand* 708. *207* "to the forest": *Lion* 366. "President's foreign policy": Childs "They Hate" and "They Still Hate." Empire of Japan: NYT 12/13/37.

VI A SHADOW OF PRIMITIVE TERROR
(*pages 209–253*)

209 convoying anybody: NYT 12/13/37. *210* to declare war: NYT 2/16/32. "remembered the *Maine*": NYT 4/20/38; Fehrenbach 294; Phillips *Blitz* 532. *211* Depression become comprehensible: T 5/29/39; NYT 2/2/37, 7/15/38; *Blitz* 532. doted on Europe: Rovere and Schlesinger 229. *212* "find no one there": NYT 10/6/37; Daniels 295; *Time* editors 292. "less given up": NYT 2/9/37; Daniels 295. Canada were attacked: NYT 12/22/37; *Blitz* 548; Cooke 2; Fehrenbach 294. *213* eight thousand casualties: NYT 7/22/37; Spivak 137; T 3/6/39. *214* United States with impunity: NYT 4/30/37, 1/11/38; Congdon 606. Americans in 1914–18: Daniels 295; NYT 10/9/38. *215* "two-ocean" Navy: NYT 1/29/38. for June 6: NYT 3/22/38, 10/16/38. to the dictators: NYT 10/7/38. *216* a ringside seat: NYT 9/13/37. "you do it?": NYT 5/13/37; *Time* editors 173; *Atlantic* September 1940. said they would try: Kendrick 157 ff. *217* American public opinion: ibid. *218* " 'Heils' ('Hail Victory')": NYT 9/13/38. the Siegfried Line: Congdon 574. *219* the United States: ibid 575. *221* were still preferred: ibid 578. "basely betrayed": NYT 9/21/38. *222* "on its way": ibid. say about it: McCarthy *Hurricane* 3. *223* anything after all: NYT 9/20/38. out to sea: NYT 9/21/38, 9/20/38, 9/22/38. *224* that same night: NYT 9/22/38. *225* house blew away: *Hurricane* 14. only that morning: ibid 3. *226* twenty-nine corpses: NYT 9/23/38. in a nightmare: ibid. *227* was carried away: *Hurricane* 63. "in smoking ruins": ibid 57. U.S. Weather Bureau: ibid 141. *228* of American history: NYT 9/22/38, 9/23/38. "a social power": NYT 9/30/38. "will bring peace": Daniels 303; Fab IV 39. *229* Halloween in 1938: NYT 10/31/38. *230* Sunday prime time: *Blitz* 383; T 11/20/44. *231* everyone agreed: NYT 9/26/38, 10/31/38. *232–236* Quotations from the script are from Cantril. *236* "lot to do": Congdon 589. "Jersey and fire": Cantril 67, 112. *238* time would come: T 4/10/39; NYT 6/29/39. *239* had in mind: Fab IV 112. voice was changing: T 3/13/39; Gold *1940–41* 54. *239–240n* *Harper's* March 1933. *240* him "Mr. Christian": NYT 7/30/39. had ever known: *Time* editors 124. no Grover Whalen: NYT 2/19/39. *241* American society: NYT 2/5/39; Fab IV 268. own food: NYT 5/17/39. *242* fourteen-lane turnpikes: Fab IV 280. "of Hell": NYT 5/15/39. to Hyde Park: NYT 6/11/39. *243* was "half-caste": NYT 6/12/39. tried to retire: T 7/24/39. of bad weather: NYT 9/16/39, 7/6/39; Rovere and Schlesinger 130. *244* "in my belt": NYT 7/19/39. *245* the experimental stage: NYT 5/24/39. *246* "Bullitt, Mr. President" (and next three paragraphs): T 9/11/39; NYT 9/1/39. "Deutschland über Alles": T 9/18/39, 9/25/39. *247* "about salt water": Fehrenbach 29. meant by neutrality: NYT 9/4/39, 9/14/39; T 9/18/39. *248* "willing to answer": NYT 11/3/40. epithet stuck: Fehrenbach 45. *249* however, sleep long: NYT 4/21/39, 5/14/39.

VII THROUGH THE NIGHT WITH A LIGHT FROM ABOVE
(*pages 254–287*)

254 was Viennese: *Saturday Evening Post* 9/7/40. life in ruins: Laurence 32. *255* "that so long?": NYT 11/11/38, 1/29/39. destroy the world: Jungk 71, 75. *256* powerful as TNT: NYT 1/3/39; Laurence 34. *257* on the blackboard: Laurence 35, 44. *258* spread the news: NYT 4/30/39; Laurence 37. ahead of them: Laurence 48. *260* "surrounding territory": Burns *Soldier* 249; Laurence 85. and two glasses: Laurence 83. *261* "requires action": ibid 86. on another ship: ibid, 88. *262* across the Atlantic: NYT 1/20/40; *Scholastic* 10/14/40. by Reynaud himself: NYT 5/15/40, 6/1/40. "liberation of the Old": NYT 6/23/40, 8/23/40. "shall never surrender": NYT 11/16/40. *263* hundred feet below: Fehrenbach 210. "to fight alone": NYT 6/14/40. "wish to live": NYT 12/18/40. *264* "them all dead": NYT 9/8/40. "talk about that": NYT 6/19/40. *265* movements ever since: NYT 7/14/40, 6/5/42, 11/27/42. diamonds, for $5,000: T 7/28/41. United States intervened: ibid. *266* Air Corps colonel: NYT 4/26/41, 4/29/41. *267* the speech "inexcusable": NYT 5/13/42; Fehrenbach 272. "name in Indochina": T 7/8/40; Fehrenbach 84. *268* on their hands: Fehrenbach 59, 101. the American people: NYT 3/1/40. *269* freighters to England: NYT 2/24/42. planes a year: Fab V 22. "the two deals": NYT 6/11/40. *270* board of directors: Fehrenbach 175; NYT 1/21/41. booed Churchill's name: NYT 4/24/41. *Washington Times-Herald:* NYT 9/4/40. *271* Training and Service Bill: NYT 9/17/40, 9/2/40. as U.S. citizens: *American Mercury* April 1940. was Lewis B. Hershey: *Life* 9/30/40; NYT 9/30/40. *272* "have been selected": *Vital Speeches* 9/1/40. Roosevelt was skating: *Life* 8/18/41. "rendered in this": Fehrenbach 267. *273* them Wendell L. Willkie: John Brooks *Leap* 307; T 7/8/40. after the election: T 9/23/40. "the White House!": Daniels 309, 319. *274* the Nazis' choice: Fehrenbach 109; Daniels 317. Superintendent of Sewers: Fab V 23. "any foreign wars": NYT 10/31/40. the White House: Walter Johnson 137. *275 Wall Street Journal:* NYT 11/7/40. the same boat: T 8/26/40. *276* "are at war": T 6/24/40. *278* "to the bone"?: NYT 12/4/40. as lend-lease: Burns *Soldier* 25. it "in kind": NYT 12/18/40; *Soldier* 26. *279* "the United States": *Soldier* 45. to start now: NYT 12/30/40. "devoutly hope not": Fab V 25; *Christian Century* 2/19/41. *280* Duce any more?: T 3/3/41, 3/24/41. the western hemisphere: NYT 12/13/41, 4/11/41. *281* "North Atlantic war": Fehrenbach 227. policy, was inevitable: NYT 6/29/41. *282* "OK FDR": *Soldier* 91. "probably the time": NYT 7/8/41. *283* dangerous Murmansk run: NYT 6/22/41, 6/24/41. (he said wryly): NYT 2/19/41. *284* the Atlantic Charter: T 4/28/41. "no formal document": NYT 8/22/41. *285* that they approved: NYT 9/5/41. "of our nation": NYT 10/18/41; *Soldier* 147. "good *Reuben James?*" NYT 11/1/41. *286* on Japan, too: *Life* 10/7/40. the American Navy: *Soldier* 142. in the theater: *Soldier* 149. *287* December 10, 1941: NYT 12/7/41.

VIII AMERICA ON THE BRINK
(*pages 289–317*)

289 for sheer survival: NYT 7/14/40; *Newsweek* 4/28/41. *290* $832 a year: Burns *Soldier* 53; T 5/12/41, 9/22/41. rheumatic heart disease: T 5/12/41. times a week: *American Journal of Sociology* November 1942; Lifton 199. friend five cents: NYT 1/13/42, 4/15/42, 6/30/42, 9/22/42, 12/11/42. *291* condoms than haircuts: Bird 213; *Fortune* December 1937. *292* on a battlefield: John Brooks *Leap* 30; NYT 5/21/40. cost a quarter: *Leap* 29; NYT 6/13/34. *293* in "illicit relations": Gold *1940–41* 31; *American Magazine* August 1941; *Leap* 28. no longer used: Chapman 28. *294* separate fraternities: NYT 2/23/41. *295* fighting this war: T 10/28/40; *Soldier* 266. "straight to hell": *Fortune* June 1942; *Soldier* 463; Bird 46; T 6/16/41; *Current Biography* 1943. in the North: *Leap* 276; Bird 45; *Time* editors 153; *Soldier* 463. *296* 1960s were born: *Leap* 279. "next Brown Bomber": T 9/29/41; Gold *1940–41* 10. "NAACP-type production": Gold *1941–42* 25, 27. *297* her own people: ibid 27. American Presidents: *Survey* November 1942; *Soldier* 123. *298* in Constitution Hall: *Leap* 275; NYT 2/23/29. outdoor concert possible: NYT 3/31/39. "I can, too": NYT 2/28/39; Congdon 622. *299* the assembly line: NYT 6/26/40; T 1/6/41. and Virginia Woolf: T 1/27/41, 2/10/41, 4/7/41, 4/14/41. "unmolested by authority": *Time* editors 155; *Life* 5/12/41; NYT 5/4/48, 5/9/41; Eisinger 235, 240. *300* December 7, 1941; NYT 7/21/41, 5/3/41. "from behind": Allen *Since* 138. *301* sharp hostesses: T 1/31/44; Gold *1940–41* 21 and passim.

substitute "outlets": *Leap* 238. *302* "on beaches": ibid 10; NYT 9/11/41. demanding private showers: T 4/1/40. "he is mad": T 3/4/40. *303* "and moral views": NYT 3/11/40; T 3/11/40. won round two: T 3/25/40. and "narrow-minded": T 4/8/40. happier about it: WA 1940. *304* the United States: T 4/8/40. *305* urgent, inexplicable request: WA 1941; NYT 10/6/41, 8/12/41, 8/17/41; Daniels 336. cruises to Hawaii: Daniels 336. kill 2,403 Americans: NYT 12/9/41. armed forces—oil: Fehrenbach 297. *306* vehemently anti-Japanese: NYT 12/7/41. Germany and Italy: *Life* 10/7/40; *Soldier* 20. "are no taxicab": T 8/4/41, 9/22/41. *307* neighboring countries: *Soldier* 135–36; Fehrenbach 304. in the Orient: NYT 10/17/41; *Soldier* 146. "at Pearl Harbor": T 11/26/45. *309* know about war?: *Soldier* 78; T 12/10/45. "on Pearl Harbor": T 12/31/45. *310* NOT A DRILL: Daniels 341. *311* bow them out . . . toward the door: *Soldier* 162–63. ATTACK PEARL HARBOR: Sulzberger 144. *312* THE STATE DEPARTMENT: ibid. would be back: NYT 12/18/41; Fab V 71. *313* "fishy to me": Fab V 71. treacherous Orientals: NYT 12/8/41. a Pacific Fleet: Gunther 330. *314* "in Valdosta, Georgia": Daniels 343. "Come anyway" . . . "of peace": Kendrick 239. "On the *ground!*": Fab V 71. *315* "fog of battle": ibid. *316* would dive: ibid. *317* "national interest required": Acheson 37.

IX COUNTERATTACK
(*pages 321–351*)

General source for WWII in the Pacific: William Manchester "Our War in the Pacific" *Holiday* November 1960 pp. 110–11, 152–67. *321* lost a war: NYT 11/29/45. *322* the sky then: T 1/12/42. offensive at once: NYT 1/2/42. coastal waters: NYT 1/2/42, 1/17/42, 1/15/42, 1/20/42, 3/4/42. *323* and San Francisco: NYT 2/3/43, 4/29/42; *Life* 8/10/42; *Time* editors 43; Burns *Soldier* 212. Malaya: NYT 12/15/41. *324* couldn't be turned: NYT 12/8/41, 1/28/42, 1/3/42. "gives a damn": NYT 12/11/41, 3/18/42; T 3/30/42; Rovere and Schlesinger 56. *325* to their fate: NYT 9/27/42, 2/22/42. Abandon Ship: NYT 3/14/42, 3/15/42. the New Hebrides?: NYT 9/30/42. *326* lovely flame trees: NYT 11/2/43. *327* unearthly splendor: *Newsweek* 3/30/42. actually drowned: *Life* 3/22/43; NYT 1/30/43. *328* "come, the better": T 7/9/45. "time to die": NYT 5/7/42. *329* planes and killed him: *Newsweek* 2/1/43; NYT 5/21/43. after he was dead: *Current Biography* 1942; NYT 5/21/43. sealing off China: NYT 2/16/42. *330* "States Marines hiding?": NYT 2/16/42, 2/2/41. and troop movements: NYT 5/6/42, 12/18/42. "men, still unafraid": NYT 1/15/42, 5/6/42. *331* time for Midway: NYT 5/8/42, 6/13/42, 7/15/42, 9/17/42. "Seattle by air": NYT 7/18/42, 9/17/43, 6/5/42; T 6/15/42. *332* patched-up *Yorktown:* NYT 6/5/42; *Life* 11/16/42. sipping rice broth: NYT 6/5/42; T 6/22/42, 6/7/43. *333* hospitalized by October: NYT 8/9/42, 11/22/42; WM/Dr. Louis Lasagna 8/4/70. hundred one night: *Soldier* 284. *334* could win all: Fab V 75; NYT 10/31/42. *335* U-boat challenge: *Soldier* 183. off to combat: NYT 8/11/42, 11/5/43, 8/11/42. *336* "work to do": Fab V 198; T 6/22/42, 2/22/43. as Los Alamos: Jungk 133. *337* "of October 3": T 5/4/42, 6/22/42; NYT 10/4/42. *338* couldn't remember it: Mazo 36. "him to bed": NYT 11/22/42. ready to move: NYT 7/10/42, 9/27/42; T 11/9/42. *339* operation was Torch: Walter Johnson 173. "a cruel initiative": *Scholastic Magazine* 1/11/43; T 11/16/42; NYT 11/9/42; T 11/16/42; *Soldier* 291. "are striking back": *Soldier* 291. *340* through Kasserine Pass: *Saturday Evening Post* 5/29/43; NYT 2/22/43. just 18,500 casualties: *Collier's* 11/9/43. Italians and Sicilians: NYT 5/9/43, 6/12/43. *341* of Axis troops: NYT 8/18/43; *Soldier* 394; NYT 7/26/43; T 9/20/43. "another Dunkerque": NYT 9/16/43, 7/18/43, 7/21/46. toward Naples: NYT 9/11/43. *342* pitiless as ever: NYT 10/2/43, 2/16/44. winters in memory: NYT 2/18/44, 1/19/44. *343* water, and time: NYT 1/3/43. *344* warmth of socks: Mauldin *Front* 36. *345* gasoline called napalm: ibid 93; *Soldier* 344. "deadpan face": NYT 11/21/48; Walter Johnson 156. "a little superfluous": *Front* 32. *346* over to Hitler: NYT 10/2/43. and David Niven: T 6/7/43; NYT 2/21/42. *347* Hopkins's youngest boy: NYT 1/10/42, 11/17/43, 12/25/44, 11/13/44, 4/12/44, 8/19/44, 8/15/44, 2/13/44; John Brooks *Leap* 286. *349* "killed same": *Soldier* 271. *350* to GI prurience: NYT 12/31/43. "einst Lilli Marlene": NYT 10/17/43.

X THE HOME FRONT
(*pages 353–400*)

353 "boy on Bataan": T 3/23/42. *354* the same again: Sevareid *Dream* 215. those of 1929: Burns *Soldier* 460; Jack Goodman 19. "so do comforts": NYT 5/3/45, 4/28/65; Walter Johnson 157; Fab V 148. *355* "in the black": T 3/15/43; Brogan 164. "a hothouse growth": NYT 12/14/60; Allen *Change* 188–90. *356* dismissed as "eggheads": NYT 4/13/38; *Soldier* 461. an overstatement: NYT 3/23/44. *357* "Win-the-War": NYT 12/29/43, 12/8/41. permitted to vote: NYT 12/29/43, 12/8/41. *One World:* NYT 11/4/42; *Soldier* 280; Walter Johnson 165; *Soldier* 337; T 2/7/44, 3/6/44; NYT 2/25/44, 6/16/43, 4/8/43. *358* to the Army: NYT 2/28/43; T 6/26/44. knew, but still: T 4/13/42. *359* "sergeant over there": NYT 2/6/44. (brands as Fleetwoods): T 7/3/44. by 22 percent: T 7/17/44; NYT 2/7/42. *360* on the West Coast: NYT 4/28/44; T 12/21/42; Jack Goodman 50. admirals wanted them: Liddell Hart 384. *361* loss of quality: NYT 2/20/41; *Soldier* 244; *Time* editors 45. of the profits: NYT 8/1/42, 8/24/42; T 8/31/42. *362* and overwhelming them: Sulzberger 418. 44,000,000,000: Fab V 150. *363* country was fighting: NYT 6/20/43; *Soldier* 213 and passim. *364* "the alien Japanese": Walter Johnson 156; NYT 2/1/42, 10/6/53. next three weeks: Fab V 201. "welcome in Kansas": ibid 204. *365* "American or not": ibid 201, 206. it to Washington: NYT 4/23/41. "elder statesman": NYT 11/3/43. *366* "or all persons": NYT 6/19/42, 3/19/42, 2/21/42; Fab V 201. *367* in horse stalls: T 4/6/42; Fab V 204. 1,862 funerals: NYT 11/4/42; Fab V 206. could go hang: *Soldier* 216. *368* were "disloyal": NYT 12/19/44, 12/20/44. more than sing: Fab V 205. *369* "rates were appalling": NYT 10/14/43; Fab V 206. overt outrages subsided: Mauldin *Home* 168. said a word: ibid 170. *370* victory gardens: NYT 1/23/42. *371* asylum and tranquillity: NYT 1/2/42, 2/6/42, 5/1/42, 5/10/42, 5/3/42, 9/7/44, 9/6/42, 10/18/42, 11/22/45, 12/3/45, 11/27/42, 11/1/42; Jack Goodman 467. *372* in Broadway alleys: NYT 7/1/42, 5/2/44, 1/28/45; T 1/15/45. they sold well: NYT 7/23/42, 3/21/42, 9/13/42, 1/21/43, 4/8/43, 10/28/43, 11/21/44. 2/29/44. frustrated women: Jack Goodman 418. *373* pajamas at night: Rovere *Years* 8; Fab V 256. Walter Annenberg's *Seventeen:* Jack Goodman 594. *374* called bobby-soxers: Fab V 27. quietly died: NYT 11/12/44. *375* were at peace: T 8/21/44; Fab V 46–49. "they're nice kids": T 7/5/43. *376* her feet, shrieking: NYT 12/10/43. twenty squad cars: NYT 10/13/44. *377* later, Mia Farrow: NYT 10/31/51, 11/8/51. "*my* lifetime?": Jack Goodman 379. "Sinatra is baffling": *Reader's Digest* January 1945. *378* bobby-soxer rite: NYT 3/6/45; Fab V 47. "like the Paramount": NYT 6/22/45, 6/11/45; Fab V 48. *379* Allies with nothing: Jungk 131; *Soldier* 249. the three tons: Laurence 68–69. *380* might reach 1.07: ibid 70. liquid at it: ibid 76–77. *381* technological problem: ibid 74; NYT 8/7/45. "realistic traditions": *Soldier* 550. *382* "to the project": NYT 11/4/44. *383* whole-souled Communist: NYT 6/16/50, 5/24/50, 6/17/50, 2/4/50. just been formed: NYT 7/18/50; West 217–21. *384* in fact killed: NYT 8/19/50. *385* history greatly altered: NYT 5/25/46. was Klaus Fuchs: Jungk 193; NYT 6/29/46. desert remains obscure: NYT 8/7/45. *386* criminal investigation: NYT 12/7/45. and Winston Churchill: NYT 1/8/43; *Soldier* 316. great battles ahead: *Soldier* 389. *387* "triumphant success": ibid 17, 298, 300, 546. *388* their prewar dreams: ibid 302, 489. "was once white!": ibid 498; NYT 7/27/43. *389* three heart attacks: NYT 10/2/43, 10/8/44; T 4/17/44; *Soldier* 274, 511. "the United States": *Soldier* 453; NYT 7/12/44; Walter Johnson 166. *390* "to the convention": Gunther 360; NYT 7/19/44. would be Truman: NYT 7/19/44, 7/20/44; Phillips *Truman* 37–40. *391* "Senator from Missouri": NYT 7/22/44; T 7/31/44. "about my dog": NYT 11/8/44; *Soldier* 168. *392* value was doubtful: *Soldier* 525. "'the *Chicago Tribune*!'": NYT 10/29/44. *393* "an old man": T 10/23/44, 5/22/44. "they are not true": NYT 10/13/44; T 10/23/44. utterly wretched: NYT 10/22/44. *394* image of vitality: *Soldier* 525. been forever laid: NYT 11/8/44, 11/10/44, 11/12/44; T 11/13/44; Gunther 92. *395* with no scars: *Soldier* 530. seemed so robust: NYT 11/20/44. *396* battery of specialists: T 10/23/44; NYT 4/5/44. a frequent visitor: *Soldier* 448; NYT 4/11/44. *397* "killed himself trying": NYT 4/27/44, 2/25/44; Gunther 340. deliver a speech: *Soldier* 507. *398* "goddamned ghouls": ibid 509. "close to nonsense": ibid 508–509; Acheson 102; Gunther 38. *399* been "a sellout": NYT 2/8/44. his first inaugural: *Soldier* 594.

XI LILACS IN THE DOORYARD
(*pages 402–443*)

402 "was beyond us": NYT 1/23/44, 1/31/44. *403* act of war: NYT 4/17/45, 2/14/44. "the Fifth Army": NYT 5/13/44, 6/5/44. D-Day in Normandy: NYT 6/6/44, 6/7/44. *404* "is mine alone": NYT 6/6/44. "up and consolidated": NYT 7/10/44. *405* stubborn defenders: Burns *Soldier* 475. "O.K. We'll go": NYT 7/11/43; *Soldier* 475. *406* "our united crusade": *Soldier* 475; NYT 6/6/44. sunk off Arromanches: NYT 6/27/44. *407* "men at arms": NYT 7/10/44, 7/19/44, 8/8/44; T 7/3/44. "working for Vichy": NYT 8/26/44, 8/24/44; T 10/16/44. *408* "Fatherland and Führer!": NYT 9/7/44, 9/12/44, 10/21/44; T 10/25/44. "American soldier myself": NYT 12/28/44; T 1/15/45. to celebrate it: NYT 3/9/45, 4/2/45, 4/12/45. *409* U.S.-RUSS JUNCTURE: NYT 4/12/45; *Soldier* 599. Lucy's daughter: *Soldier* 599. *410* "cause for alarm": ibid 595. atom armaments race; Jungk 179. *411* this was done: NYT 8/13/45, 9/28/45, 10/1/66. *412* sharply changed: Speer 227. with the enemy: Jungk 163. uranium research: ibid. "an atom bomb": ibid 164, 166. *413* a textile mill: NYT 9/28/45; Jungk 167. *414* "going to use it": NYT 8/13/45, 9/28/45; Jungk 171. "politics or physics?": Jungk 174. *415* or be annihilated: NYT 11/28/45. "agreed to that": NYT 4/9/46; Jungk 175. *416* began a counteroffensive: NYT 7/23/42. no military significance: NYT 1/3/43, 1/10/43, 1/20/43. *417* range of Rabaul: NYT 7/2/43, 8/29/43. unloaded overhead: NYT 12/28/43. *418* anticipated a Tarawa: NYT 12/4/44. 75 percent casualties: NYT 11/25/43, 2/22/44. *419* approaching Tarawa's: NYT 4/25/44, 5/28/44. were cut off: NYT 6/21/44, 8/11/44. *420* "God protect you": NYT 7/26/44; *Soldier* 489. *421* was to come: NYT 10/20/44. of all time: NYT 10/21/44. *Banzai:* NYT 10/26/44. *422* moments of daylight: NYT 10/28/44. power was finished: NYT 10/26/44. early March, Manila: NYT 12/16/44. *423* Japs on Iwo: NYT 12/25/44. bee in the face: NYT 3/10/45. *424* GIs at leisure: NYT 3/30/45, 4/2/45, 4/13/45. absolutely secure: *Soldier* 599. *425* "laundry to dry": ibid 600; NYT 4/16/45. state documents: Asbell 33. "expert in explosives": NYT 2/13/45. *426* Outer Mongolia: T 2/26/45. "fifteen minutes more": NYT 4/16/45. filling in colors: T 6/4/45. *427* "beautiful woman": Asbell 36. 1:15 P.M.: NYT 4/13/45; *Soldier* 600. on the couch: NYT 4/13/45. *428* anguished snores: Asbell 41. "3:35 o'clock": ibid 44. *429* reach Eleanor Roosevelt: ibid 46. "concert is finished": NYT 4/13/45; *Soldier* 602. Truman at once: NYT 4/13/45; Asbell 53. *430* "was talking about": Truman I 6. "when you can": ibid. "in trouble now": T 4/23/45; Asbell 63. *431* "WARM SPRINGS, GA.": Asbell 78. "man at Warm Springs": ibid 81. *432* with her hands: ibid 84, 91, 99. "So long—out": ibid 93, 150. *433* "most clearly": ibid xi. "lost a friend": ibid 94, 117. *434* "the great man": ibid 94. "the White House": T 4/23/45. *435* "for us all!": NYT 4/13/45; Asbell 87. the man's cheek: Asbell 91. "the next curve": Gunther 144. *435–436* "Hi, Dad" . . . to be vacated: Asbell 105–106. *436* Early drew up: ibid 124. *437* chief improviser: ibid 113. to view it: ibid 128, 134; NYT 4/14/45. *438* clasped hands: Asbell 156. "Lincoln home again": ibid 158, 160. passed overhead: NYT 4/15/45. *439* "be any man's": Asbell 170. President's widow: NYT 4/14/45. *440* Executive Mansion: Asbell 178. sealed forever: NYT 4/15/45; Asbell 183. *441–442* said his son . . . "remember it": *New Yorker* 4/21/45. *443* "Thy servant sleeping": Margaret Truman 90; Asbell 194. "is over": T 4/30/45.

XII A NEW WORLD, UNDER A NEW SUN
(*pages 445–479*)

445 "single moment": Phillips *Truman* 62; Asbell 136. *446* return to obscurity: T 4/23/45; *Truman* 62–63. in history: NYT 11/7/34, 9/15/40. "the President": Asbell 136–37. "for me now": ibid 137. *447* "have ever done": NYT 4/14/45; Asbell 111. *448* "son and bro": NYT 4/13/45; *Truman* 65. *449* "through her teeth": NYT 4/21/45; Margaret Truman 91, 95, 96; *Truman* 62, 144; Asbell 166. "supporter below": T 12/18/50. with greater dignity: ibid. "be game, too": *Truman* 140; T 9/24/45, 9/18/50. *450* "what they meant": *Truman* 63, 71, 169, 79; T 6/4/45; NYT 4/19/45. *451* "the new President": *Truman* 80. "not Henry Wallace": Acheson 104; NYT 7/1/45. "he died?" . . . "it just now": NYT 4/18/45; Asbell 168. *452* of the question: NYT 5/2/45, 5/3/45, 5/5/45, 5/8/45, 5/9/45, 5/10/45; T 5/14/45. *453* larger than Newark: NYT 8/9/45, 7/27/45, 12/16/45. a hand grenade?: Manchester "Our War in the Pacific"; NYT 5/4/45. *454* on Allied losses: NYT 1/28/47; Stimson "The

Decision to Use the Atomic Bomb." *455* been even greater: NYT 6/2/45, 6/8/44; Truman I 332; NYT 6/6/45, 7/23/45. "the gadget": NYT 6/6/45; Burns *Soldier* 459, 251; Jungk 175. "do something different": Jungk 178. *456* "have come in": NYT 12/7/45. *457* "winning the war": Laurence 201. stadium in Chicago: Jungk 192. *458* of a second: Laurence 168–70. as yet undetermined: NYT 8/1/45; *Soldier* 558. *459* same conclusions: NYT 4/26/45; *Truman* 53. "The Fat Man": Jungk 180. *460* greatest war criminals: *Reader's Digest* March 1947; NYT 1/28/47; *Harper's* February 1947; Compton "If the Atomic Bomb Had Not Been Used." no one said much: Jungk 198 and passim. *461* perfecting the mesh: *Current Biography* 1947. *461–462* right microsecond . . . "there be light": NYT 8/7/45; Laurence 10. *462* their window-panes: Laurence 12. *463* blown away: ibid 195. instant peace: Jungk 197, 202. "the Japanese": Truman I 416. *464* "Japanese home islands": ibid 417. "utter destruction": NYT 7/28/45; *Truman* 58. had been passed: *Truman* 59; T 8/13/45. *465* intelligence officer: NYT 8/8/45; Laurence 196, 202–206. *465–466* "of TNT" . . . any of them: Laurence 208–11. *466* "from the Empire": NYT 8/18/45; Laurence 220. "long now, folks": Laurence 221; NYT 11/22/45. *467* "do with it": T 8/13/45, 8/20/45. *468* "I don't": T 10/22/45; NYT 8/9/45; Laurence 225, 228. "devised by man": NYT 7/28/45; *Truman* 68; Laurence 242. *469* turning somersaults: Jungk 211. *470* "such devastation": ibid 213; NYT 11/24/45. of his doing: NYT 8/9/45. *472* countermanded the order: *Harper's* February 1947. formalities of capitulation: NYT 8/15/45; T 8/20/45. *473* followed his example: NYT 8/15/45. "very fragile arch": Morison *Two-Ocean* 572. *474* the United States: NYT 9/2/45. war against Japan: T 7/30/45. *475 General Henry Taylor:* NYT 8/19/45; T 8/27/45. *475–479* Reuther portrait: *Holiday* November and December 1959; NYT 3/28/46, 5/10/70; *Hartford Courant* 5/16/70.

XIII THE FRAYING FLAGS OF TRIUMPH
(*pages 480–509*)

480 in trusting them: NYT 5/13/45; Phillips *Truman* 132, 156. *481* "his own death": NYT 4/23/61, 4/4/61. *482* U.N. General Assembly: NYT 2/20/45. *483* the other leg: NYT 3/17/46; Rovere *McCarthy* 95–98. their way there: NYT 11/6/46; Fab V 221. "Richard M. Nixon": NYT 11/7/46; Mazo 41. *484* "police the world": NYT 7/18/46. *and Child Care:* NYT 9/22/46. from the hills: T 9/9/46. political war chests: NYT 8/15/45. *485* "little fellow there": T 9/3/45; Goldman *Decade* 16. *486* rapid extinction: *Decade* 7; NYT 2/9/40, 9/26/45, 8/14/46; Bird 255; Jungk 341. the black market: *Truman* 101; NYT 8/22/45; *Decade* 251; NYT 1/7/46. *487* "about inflation?" . . . Truman called back: T 9/24/45. postwar inflation: *Decade* 14. *488* in his refrigerator: T 5/6/46; *Decade* 27. "campaign of 1946": NYT 9/6/45; *Truman* 103–104. *489* had ruined them: NYT 1/15/46. "below the belt": NYT 3/11/46. dipped in the polls: NYT 7/26/46; Truman I 487 ff; NYT 1/22/46, 11/10/46. *490* collars than blue: NYT 7/22/44. was intolerable: NYT 9/2/46. *491* of his Presidency: *Commonweal* 2/8/46; T 10/8/45. their heads stubbornly: NYT 1/12/46, 4/26/46; WA 1946. "of the government": T 6/3/46. *492* was deplorable: NYT 5/18/46, 5/24/46. "sons of bitches": *Decade* 23. "do the job!": *Truman* 114 ff. *493* to General Hershey: *U.S. News and World Report* 5/3/46. "has been settled": NYT 5/26/46. *494* "coal with bayonets": *Decade* 25. burned coal: T 6/28/43. *495* and Wagner Acts: NYT 5/22/46; *U.S. News and World Report* 10/11/46. was $3,510,000: NYT 11/22/46, 12/4/46. *496* work at once: NYT 12/6/46. "his balls clank": NYT 12/8/46; *Truman* 124. *497* a heavy blow: NYT 1/8/46. *498* out of uniform: T 6/18/45. stars could, too: NYT 9/18/45, 4/11/51; Acheson 127. point freeze: NYT 7/4/46. *499* TO SPEED SAILINGS: NYT 1/7/46. *500* "wanna go home": NYT 1/12/46. "the nation accepted": NYT 1/10/46. *501* and other instigators: NYT 1/9/46, 1/8/46. "Manila and Le Havre": NYT 9/13/45. departments to himself: NYT 6/16/46. *502* "out of Army": NYT 6/6/46; T 10/22/45; *Newsweek* 1/28/46. "some other country": NYT 11/2/46. *503* in the Ruhr: Acheson 86; Mowry 163. "my way home": NYT 7/10/45; Truman I 334, 337, 411, 412. *504* "not be I": NYT 7/27/45; *Truman* 92, 98. "a great pity": NYT 7/25/46, 11/15/45; Acheson 130, 634. would warn them: Walter Johnson 163. *505* and his President: ibid 226; NYT 9/21/46, 2/14/46. to his speech: NYT 3/6/46, 9/11/46; *Truman* 150. *506* "of his administration": ibid 151; NYT 9/13/46. "my resignation immediately": T 9/23/46. *507* "exactly in line": ibid; Acheson 192. "this subject again": Acheson 191; NYT 9/22/46. *508* "I'm right": Truman I 560. sometime in 1946: *Life* 11/26/45. *509* "Had enough?": NYT 1/11/47; Mazo 47; *Truman* 128; *Decade* 45. "a Republican country": NYT 11/4/48. returned to them: Walter Johnson 228.

XIV LIFE WITH HARRY
(*pages 511–529*)

512 "come to responsibility": Schlesinger *Thousand* 287. *513* bowed your head: NYT 6/11/50; *Business Week* 1/22/49, 2/21/49. as a Red: NYT 12/31/49. teachers looked on: NYT 5/20/56. *514* bipartisan support: NYT 12/23/41; Burns *Soldier* 184, 515; T 2/28/44, 6/28/43, 7/23/45; NYT 5/26/44, 1/22/44, 8/7/45, 12/11/46. "requires it": T 12/10/45; NYT 1/11/45; Eisinger 487. *515* serious uprising: NYT 10/2/45. *516* started to go: NYT 1/3/42. (expensive) New Look: Gold *1940–41* 31; Fab V 248. *517* on the roads: Fab V 251, 253. he didn't know: *Life* 3/1/48. *518* Stalin had become: NYT 1/27/45, 4/24/45, 12/22/45. *519* the absolute limit: Allen *Change* 263; Fab V 221, 260. *520* presidential campaign: NYT 6/23/46, 9/30/47; Kendrick 40. *521* ran one headline: Fab V 210. *522* "after the war?" . . . "most astonishing": O'Neill 3–4. all-time high: O'Neill 4; NYT 10/18/45, 6/17/43, 6/16/45, 4/22/45, 1/1/48, 11/10/46; Fab V 212; WA 1946. *523* game was security: T 6/18/45. *524* was blushing: Friedan 174; Bird 259; Kinsey 194. *525* their enthusiasm: O'Neill 13. Spock had begun: NYT 7/14/46; Gold *1940–41* 31. *526* finding a home: NYT 11/2/47, 6/15/45; Mauldin *Home* 48. "understand our problems": Mauldin *Home* 65; T 12/24/45. *527* "pla-ace to stay": T 1/15/45. well under $10,000: *Newsweek* 10/6/69; O'Neill 38 ff. *528* standard specifications: O'Neill 41; T 7/3/60. *528–529* "think big" . . . much choice: Kimball "Dream Town."

XV A LITTLE TOUCH OF HARRY IN THE NIGHT
(*pages 530–577*)

530 wait until Monday?: NYT 2/23/47; Acheson 217. *531* own silk hat: NYT 2/28/47, 3/2/47, 3/18/47. after September 1945: Acheson 217; Walter Johnson 203, 207; T 12/31/45. *532* no viable alternative: NYT 5/13/45; T 10/1/45. not much else: NYT 7/14/46; T 9/25/44. *533* unprecedented scale: NYT 2/8/47, 3/18/46; Acheson 212; Phillips *Truman* 174. "give the conquered": Goldman *Decade* 33, 34. "it back again": NYT 4/2/47; Rovere and Schlesinger 241. *534* "it at all": NYT 4/17/47; *Decade* 60; T 5/29/50. only as "X": Walter Johnson 208; NYT 7/8/47. under its spell: *Truman* 258, 262. *535* "do the same": ibid 305; Acheson 219. Muehlebach Hotel: NYT 3/13/47, 5/23/47; Mowry 922; *Truman* 171, 176. Kennan's reasoning: NYT 3/14/47; Rovere and Schlesinger 238. *536* "strategic monstrosity": NYT 11/30/47; Lippmann 16–23. strategic nightmare: NYT 10/17/49. *537* few sparks there: Acheson 226. "human beings": NYT 5/9/47; Acheson 227, 229. *538* "in his hand": NYT 6/6/47; George Marshall *European Initiative* 494. could take hold: Walter Johnson 209; *Truman* 184. *539* or foreign bases: NYT 4/14/48, 4/4/48; WA 1952; Mowry 76; *Truman* 192. *540* blockade on Berlin: NYT 2/24/48, 6/25/48. complete rupture: Acheson 260. on either side: ibid 262. *541* be done—yet: NYT 9/11/48; T 9/27/48. French fliers: *Newsweek* 7/12/48; NYT 7/1/48; Clay 381–86. *542* blew it up: ibid; NYT 12/17/48. they were beaten: NYT 4/17/49. grace and generosity: NYT 5/12/49; Walter Johnson 217. *543* their own money: Clay 381–86; NYT 1/25/48. "who owned it": Sevareid *Dream* 392. *544* across the water?: Walter Johnson 221. "colonial empire": NYT 7/16/45, 3/1/50; T 3/12/50. *545* "elsewhere rejected?": Kronenberger 216. *546* "in the night": Acheson 730, 731. could hardly wait: NYT 11/4/48. *547* MacArthur, or Vandenberg: Ross 95. he would lose: *Washington Post* 7/7/48. *548* in the ring: NYT 3/2/48, 3/9/48; Ross 72. General Eisenhower! Ross 11, 64, 66, 75; *Truman* 946; NYT 11/7/46; *Nation* 3/13/48; T 3/13/48. *549* Draft Eisenhower Committee: *N.Y. Herald-Tribune* 7/10/48. to lead them then: ibid; NYT 7/10/48. issues in November: Ross 33. *550* trial run: NYT 4/18/48; Ross 77. problems with Congress?: NYT 9/7/48. like a debacle: *Washington Post* 6/4/48. *551* presidential politics: NYT 6/4/48. "growing entertainment value": Ross 84. *552* "and Czechoslovakia?": ibid 85 ff. "the biggest whistle-stop!": NYT 6/12/48. "what I'm doing!": NYT 6/19/48; T 6/28/48; *Truman* 215. *553* that was something: NYT 7/11/48; Ross 92. this convention year: NYT 9/27/48; John Brooks *Leap* 288. *554* "Federal payrolls": Ross 54. "to dislike him": NYT 1/17/48; Ross 38, 53. their little jokes: NYT 3/29/48; Rovere and Schlesinger 231. *555* "within ourselves": NYT 5/23/48, 6/25/48; *N.Y. World-Telegram* 6/14/48. bargain prices: NYT 9/20/48. *556* run the race: NYT 7/13/48, 7/15/48; Ross 109. to the door: NYT 7/15/48; Ross 116. alone, and waiting: T 7/26/48; NYT 7/15/48. *557* "for real": NYT 7/15/48. fouler than that: ibid; T 7/26/48.

558 "in the world!": T 7/26/48; NYT 7/15/48; Ross 125. "run for office": T 7/26/48. "what they say!": T 7/26/48. *559* "in the stocks!": *Truman* 222; T 7/26/48. "political courage": T 7/26/48. the Democratic South: NYT 7/18/48. to be flourishing: NYT 12/30/47, 9/11/48, 12/31/47; *Truman* 204. *560* "announce his candidacy": NYT 6/13/48; Ross 136. He refused: NYT 8/9/50, 9/11/48; Ross 145, 149. *561* "Christian martyrs": NYT 7/26/48; T 8/2/48, 7/26/48. independent center: NYT 8/30/48, 8/21/48; *Washington Post* 10/22/48. hastened their victories: NYT 11/3/48. *562* "end of it": NYT 7/27/48; Ross 132. judgment of it: NYT 7/28/48. Congress in history: NYT 8/13/48. *563* espionage hearings?: NYT 8/1/48, 8/4/48. always quotable: NYT 9/6/48. *564* "do exactly that": *Truman* 230 ff. "the farmer's back": NYT 9/17/48. *565* have written it: *Truman* 243. wished to say: Ross 180 ff; *Truman* 242. *565–566* "Democratic incumbent" . . . "and irrigation": Ross 182–85. *566* "of the world": NYT 9/21/48. over the country: Ross 206; *Truman* 242. *567* water, and faith: NYT 6/27/48; Ross 203. have a chance: Ross 167; NYT 10/30/48. *568* "that they cherish": Ross 12. would win handily: ibid 196; *Life* 11/1/48, 11/15/48; NYT 10/31/48. *569* "the poorhouse": *Detroit Free Press* 11/3/48. Dewey's inaugural: *Life* 11/15/48. *570* one instance, arrogant: ibid. *571* hedge his bet: NYT 9/10/48. almost hourly: NYT 11/25/48; *N.Y. World-Telegram* 9/24/48; Ross 226. *572* drama outside: Ross 227 ff; Rovere *Years* 48; *Truman* 245 ff. almost instantly: *Life* 11/15/48. *573* DEWEY DEFEATS TRUMAN: NYT 11/15/48. *574* back to sleep: Truman II 220 ff. *575* stared at him: NYT 11/4/48. had some sleep: T 11/8/48. "claims," he said: Ross 227. *576* governor of Illinois: NYT 11/4/48; *Truman* 247. "in American politics": *Truman* 251; Walter Johnson 233. *577* "out of this": NYT 11/6/48, 11/4/48; Ross 230; T 11/15/48. him he shouldn't: NYT 11/23/48; Ross 235.

XVI THE AGE OF SUSPICION
(*pages 579–632*)

579 1648 Pennsylvania Avenue: NYT 4/14/45. *580* Great Society: Phillips *Truman* 163, 164. *581* "of underdeveloped areas": NYT 11/4/64, 1/6/49, 1/21/49; *Truman* 272. was coming from: *Truman* 273. *582* "first proposed it": NYT 6/6/50. on the Hill: NYT 12/1/48, 3/4/49. Secretaries of State: Acheson 249; NYT 1/22/49. *583* suburbia themselves: Whyte 312. *584* amaze the country: NYT 3/14/48. *585* "took up sex": T 9/3/56. *588* "lack of opportunity": Fab V 217; Gold *1940–41* 15. *589* even to society: Eisinger 153; Kronenberger 197. *590* into Bloomington's computers: Guiles 90. solvent of custom: Goldman *Decade* 119. *591* bottle of Hadacol: NYT 1/23/48. *592* "loved in return": Gold *1940–41* 32. "double-breasted suits": ibid. professional athlete: Fab V 221 *593* kill a President: NYT 7/4/46, 11/2/50. lordly spaniel: Fab IV 240. *594* "who like it": Fab V 342. *595* (at the Sorbonne): NYT 9/16/50; Fab V 218. *596* the new decade: NYT 2/5/50. *597* died with it: NYT 4/4/49, 4/25/49, 12/9/49. "but could not": NYT 8/6/49; Acheson 303. *599* "nations having it": Jungk 260; NYT 9/24/49, 3/29/49; *Decade* 100. *601* be heard again: Ross 134. "frittered away": NYT 3/3/48. *602* "down the river": Walter Johnson 214. *603* "I deeply believe": NYT 11/2/46. *604* its Canadian allies: NYT 3/5/46, 2/11/50. *605* for International Peace: NYT 7/30/48, 8/4/48, 8/1/48, 2/11/49, 8/4/48. "bad security risks": NYT 12/5/47. *606* rulings were final: NYT 11/18/49; *Truman* 360. *608* nine years old: NYT 8/19/49. with orthodoxy: NYT 11/9/47. "was sacked anyway": *Truman* 351; NYT 11/18/48. *609* "their reliability": *Truman* 352. *610* the vigilantes: ibid. "question of espionage": ibid 364. plain paper wrappers: NYT 12/10/49. *612* "smoke, there's fire": *Truman* 373. "be all right": NYT 5/20/50, 5/24/50, 7/18/50; West 224. *613* both of them: NYT 6/17/50, 7/18/50, 8/12/50. *615* "Russian code": NYT 8/3/48, 8/1/48. *616* "of the hearings": *New Yorker* 9/4/48. was Alger Hiss: NYT 8/18/48, 11/25/54. *617* him a liar: Acheson 250. heavily lidded eyes: NYT 6/7/49. *618* could prove it: NYT 12/12/48. face to face: NYT 8/4/48. *619* than he knew: Cooke 71. a committee investigator: NYT 8/18/48. *620* "until I return": Cooke 80. *621* anyone named Crosley: NYT 8/26/48. *622* to the Russians: NYT 9/28/48, 11/4/48. he was trapped: NYT 12/7/48, 6/7/49. *623* had the story: NYT 12/11/48, 12/5/48. "expense of Austria": Cooke 92. "the United States": NYT 12/19/48. *624* were chagrined: NYT 12/10/48, 12/16/48. "looks like faltering": Mazo 65–66. *625* on both counts: NYT 11/18/49, 1/22/50, 3/6/49. was a mystery: NYT 12/15/49. *626* it to him: *Truman* 369. had Priscilla Hiss: Cooke 298. he had been: NYT 1/22/50. *627* "with verse 34": NYT 5/13/47, 1/26/50; Acheson 360. "was not easy": ibid 359. *628* "America can do?": NYT 2/13/50, 2/4/50. "do it again": Griffin 28. *628–632* Murrow portrait: *Current Biography* 1953; NYT 4/8/65; *Cue* 2/21/53; Kendrick passim.

XVII INTO THE ABYSS
(*pages 633–674*)

633 "sensible course": Acheson 354. from Hoover: Rovere and Schlesinger 213. *634* "for that purpose": NYT 12/17/49, 2/4/50, 5/24/50; Acheson 355. "chain to Alaska": NYT 3/2/49. January 12, 1950: NYT 1/13/50. *635* the United Nations: Acheson 354; NYT 1/13/50. fend for themselves: NYT 1/13/50. *636* " 'back in there' ": NYT 12/30/49; Acheson 293. "long road back": NYT 1/21/50; Acheson 358. *637* seven years left: NYT 11/6/46, 5/3/57. "recognizes me": *Harper's* August 1950. *638* "shape our policy": NYT 5/4/50. *New Yorker: Harper's* August 1950; Rovere *McCarthy* 128. *639* speak of *traitors:* NYT 2/23/50. "the State Department": *McCarthy* 126. *640* the fugitive list: ibid 127. "curtain of secrecy": NYT 2/20/50; *McCarthy* 130. *641* "not a Communist?": *McCarthy* 132. "in the Department": ibid. *642* "reckless performance": NYT 2/21/50. except McCarthy himself: NYT 2/23/50, 2/26/50. *643* see him discredited: NYT 5/21/50. Levine's *Plain Talk:* NYT 1/27/50, 4/7/50, 5/11/50. *644* "contact you later": *McCarthy* 144. mud-bespattered buckets: ibid 12. "its sleeves rolled": ibid 11. *645* to be told: NYT 4/26/50; Griffith 72. *646* "the State Department": NYT 3/22/50, 3/27/50; *McCarthy* 151, 152. with laughter: NYT 3/27/50, 4/2/50; *McCarthy* 153. *647* "as a Communist": NYT 4/7/50, 4/12/50. all the headlines: NYT 4/2/50, 4/21/50, 4/26/50, 5/2/50. *648* general election: NYT 6/2/50, 6/25/50, 5/3/50, 11/8/50. "the United States": Griffith 73, 100; NYT 4/19/50. *649* "half months ago": *McCarthy* 55. "but Russia's": NYT 6/25/50. *650* "the United States": NYT 1/20/50, 7/6/50. "shine their boots": NYT 3/24/50. *651* around the clock: NYT 8/16/50; Acheson 402. *652* before Monday: NYT 6/25/50; Phillips *Truman* 289. Forest Hills: NYT 1/11/50. "like a cobra": NYT 6/25/50. *653* of their lives: ibid. "Republic of Korea": Acheson 402. White House switchboard: NYT 5/26/50. *654* Success, New York: Acheson 404; NYT 6/26/50. passed 9 to 0: NYT 9/7/50. neutrality impossible: NYT 6/26/50; *Truman* 291. *655* in Indochina: NYT 6/27/50. an earlier Vietnam: NYT 6/29/50, 6/26/50. *656* was unanimous: NYT 6/28/50. "with the subject": NYT 6/29/50. *657* "the Armed Forces": NYT 7/1/50; Acheson 410. in June 1950: NYT 7/6/50. *658* "it amounts to": NYT 6/27/50; *Truman* 302. negative aim: NYT 6/30/50. *659* "battle area": ibid.; *Truman* 302. at once: NYT 7/1/50. for an opinion: ibid; *Truman* 311. *660* the high command: NYT 7/21/50. "want from me?": NYT 7/21/50, 9/1/50. *661* the country's pride: NYT 7/12/50. other U.N. members: NYT 8/1/50. NKPA rear: NYT 9/16/50. *662* a little talk: NYT 10/1/50. "fight communism": NYT 7/31/50. Wake Island: *Truman* 318; NYT 8/29/50. *663* "greatest slaughter": NYT 10/15/50; *Truman* 321. to move north: NYT 10/15/50. *664* "Kim Buck Too?": NYT 10/21/50. history of warfare: NYT 11/10/50. *665* other was doing: NYT 11/24/50, 10/25/50; *Truman* 323. it in Korea: NYT 11/1/50. *666* "Little Big Horn": NYT 11/3/50. had found five: NYT 11/5/50. *667* "of my command": NYT 11/6/50. and power installations: *Truman* 325. *668* Monroe Doctrine: Rovere and Schlesinger 149. "intervention in Korea": *Truman* 322; NYT 10/12/50. *669* "extraordinarily light": NYT 11/10/50, 11/24/50. *670* outcome was different: NYT 12/1/50. help, at Hungnam: NYT 12/7/50. *671* was evacuated: NYT 12/11/50, 12/25/50. "military matters": *Truman* 327. "publicly announced": Acheson 47; NYT 11/29/50. *672* win the war: Acheson 474. *673* "is concurred in": NYT 12/13/50; Rovere and Schlesinger 156; *Truman* 329. *674* along the Yalu: NYT 12/28/50. the U.N. lines: NYT 1/1/50.

XVIII A HOUSE DIVIDED
(*pages 679–732*)

679 "spiritless defeat": NYT 1/4/51; Acheson 489. of the war: NYT 1/24/51, 3/2/51, 3/15/51, 3/31/51. *680* short of treason: Rovere and Schlesinger 245; Walter Johnson 239. balancing the budget: NYT 12/13/50, 12/21/50. the Great Debate: NYT 1/8/51; Mowry 177. *681* Roosevelt's Hundred Days: NYT 1/6/51, 1/9/51, 2/10/51, 1/16/51; WA 1951. "rebuilding of Europe": Truman II 380. *682* to future increases: NYT 12/20/50, 2/2/51; Acheson 494. his doing it: NYT 4/5/51; Walter Johnson 243. *683* "tolls for thee": NYT 11/8/50; Griffith 126. some time ago: NYT 3/3/51; Mazo 141. twelve years later: NYT 4/11/51. *684* STILL SEEN POSSIBLE: NYT 4/11/51; Phillips *Truman* 346; Rovere and Schlesinger 172. *685* "commander in chief": NYT 10/15/50; *U.S. News* 9/1/50; *Truman* 330, 334;

Acheson 518; Truman II 435. Joe Martin: Truman II 442; NYT 4/24/51, 4/6/51. "discussion would be": NYT 4/10/51, 4/6/51; *Truman* 340; Acheson 520. *686* "foregoing message": NYT 4/11/51, 4/9/51; Truman II 448; Acheson 523. *687* Magnuson of Washington: Rovere and Schlesinger 174. daylight in Tokyo: NYT 4/12/51; *Truman* 345. *688* THE PRESIDENTIAL CHAIR: Rovere and Schlesinger 8. might be tried: ibid 8, 12; NYT 4/22/51; *Truman* 345. "God Bless America!": *Truman* 347; NYT 4/14/51, 4/18/51, 4/19/51. *689* "Douglas MacArthur": NYT 4/19/51, 4/20/51. "could not answer": NYT 4/20/51. "duty. Good-bye": NYT 4/20/51. *690* "in my heart": NYT 4/13/51; Rovere and Schlesinger 15; NYT 4/20/51. "just fade away": NYT 4/21/51, 4/20/51; Rovere and Schlesinger 9. *691* Republican national convention: NYT 4/22/51, 6/11/52. village of Panmunjom: NYT 5/19/51, 5/24/51. *692* "one big boom": Goldman *Decade* 181. "lot of money": Michener 49. *693* the United States: NYT 12/25/52. "irreducible minimum": NYT 7/10/51, 10/10/51; Acheson 532, 538. *694* most persuasive: NYT 4/7/49, 2/4/52. "just as stupid": NYT 8/3/47, 2/12/50, 11/5/50, 5/13/51, 8/5/51. *697* increasingly resentful: WA 1952. other people's wars: NYT 1/6/51; Acheson 281. *698* growing much bigger: NYT 8/7/45; Rovere *Years* 244. "Atomic Bombers": Jungk 242. "the hydrogen bomb": *Life* 9/6/54. *699* Super, the better: Jungk 265. leave it to him: ibid 270. "saner than Hitler?": ibid 270 ff. *700* fissionable materials: ibid 274; NYT 9/25/49; Mowry 192. "or super bomb": NYT 1/22/50, 2/4/50, 2/1/50. *701* of a button: NYT 2/5/50, 1/26/64; Jungk 265, 288. *702* it was MANIAC: Jungk 300 ff; NYT 2/28/52. *703* two, and sank: NYT 11/17/52; WA 1952. reporters, "beckons": Fab VI 30; Jungk 305; NYT 8/9/53; *Decade* 137. *704* "militarily acceptable": Jungk 307. came of it: Fab VI 30. *705* "play in, too": Fab VI 25. five days underground: ibid 30, 72. of this one: ibid 1; NYT 8/12/51. *706* themselves in it: John Brooks *Leap* 232; T 3/30/59. *707* "they could picket!": Bird 259; Kluckhohn "Mid-Century"; Schlesinger *Thousand* 740. and stayed there: Fab V 44; O'Neill 19. part of him: NYT 12/9/56; Whyte 147. *708* "on company time": Whyte 74, 81; Riesman 273. largest undergraduate group: Whyte 93. *709* "spot for you": NYT 11/12/52, 7/17/55. *710* what to do: Kronenberger 184. economic security: quoted in Kluckhohn "Evolution." "than he knows": *Decade* 291. *711* on American campuses: Rovere *McCarthy* 9; NYT 12/17/52, 12/21/52, 10/8/54, 6/29/55. *712* torn asunder: Stanley Walker "Book Branding." *713* free enterprise: NYT 10/8/51. "(group-forming) society": *NYT Magazine* 5/25/58; O'Neill 83; Kluckhohn "Evolution." in Dwight, Illinois: T 3/23/70, 3/30/70. *715* his own blood: NYT 3/27/49; Wertham 369. he could get: ibid 365, 377; Fab V 215. *716* larger than radio's: Fab V 215; *Leap* 161; T 5/15/50. *717* "barefoot voice": *Time* editors 176; T 2/27/50. television began: NYT 9/5/51; T 1/16/50. Milton Berle: T 11/20/50. *718* working for pay: Theodore White *1960* 279. toilets in unison: NYT 2/3/54; *Leap* 163; *Decade* 266; Wertham 369. "program or that": Kronenberger 81. *719* Murrow retired: NYT 11/19/51, 7/2/52, 5/12/55. "the . . . the paper": NYT 7/4/41. *720* or documentary film: T 7/23/56. *Break the Bank:* NYT 12/19/52, 6/19/56, 6/29/62. *721* of peeping Toms: T 2/27/56; Kronenberger 24; Tate "The Man of Letters." and Louis Kronenberger: Allen *Change* 272; Kluckhohn "Evolution." *722* went into eclipse: *Time* editors 127; T 1/2/56; *Leap* 168. and used contraceptives: Bird 51. prewar constellations: NYT 10/18/56, 6/28/56, 12/16/55, 10/6/55, 5/21/56, 12/19/57. *723* in the millions: *Leap* 168. a ghost town: NYT 1/10/54. *724* would come later: T 12/24/56; Hechinger and Hechinger 142; NYT 9/5/56. American experience: NYT 12/31/46. *725 Without a Cause:* NYT 12/27/55; Howe "Notes on Popular Culture." regional speech: Goldman *Tragedy* 528; Steinbeck 106. *726* political campaigns: *Leap* 57. *727* crucial shopping moment: T 8/14/44. "off at Westport": NYT 5/26/46. consumer dollar: Fab V 219. motivational research: *Leap* 86; Kendrick 480. *728* among your creditors: *Decade* 302. credit card living: ibid 303. *729* American Gas Association: T 4/27/59. in the USSR also: NYT 4/13/55. Pets in Chicago: NYT 3/10/50, 8/15/51; WA 1950. *730* "name of style": Kronenberger 106. "the money is": WA 1952; Acheson 658; WM/Louis Lasagna; NYT 3/18/55; WA 1952. "get seasick": NYT 11/21/48; WA 1952. *731* a free press: NYT 3/11/52. U.S. had tripled: NYT 11/15/55; T 6/5/50. *732* Hammarskjöld of Sweden: NYT 10/4/51, 12/4/52, 4/8/53.

XIX RIGHT TURN
(*pages 733–784*)

733 nationwide crime: Walter Johnson 247–48. *734* Mayor William O'Dwyer: NYT 3/18/51, 3/13/51. already been developed: NYT 5/8/50. *735* mean treatment: Fab VI 96; NYT 3/15/51. "to walk out": Fab VI 100–101. autumn's World Series: NYT 8/16/52. *"do about it?":*

NYT 3/22/51; Goldman *Decade* 198–99. *736* University of Kentucky: NYT 12/1/51. cheating on examinations: NYT 3/17/53, 1/4/52; Walter Johnson 247–48. *737* five hundred dollars: NYT 4/17/51. *738* a $520 Deepfreeze: NYT 2/6/51; Phillips *Truman* 406. *739* a $9,540 mink coat: NYT 2/3/51, 7/26/51, 2/28/51. "discriminating taste": *Decade* 188. literally wicked: NYT 2/3/51. *740* he hung on: NYT 12/5/51; *Truman* 408–11; NYT 12/5/51, 12/6/51, 12/16/51. appointments secretary: NYT 10/24/51, 7/28/51; *Truman* 409. *741* McGrath and Justice: NYT 7/7/51, 12/23/51, 1/11/52. dismissed McGrath: NYT 2/2/52, 4/4/52, 4/6/52. *742* trying to avert: NYT 4/9/52, 6/3/52. honorable objectives: NYT 12/20/50; Acheson 400. *743* "living American?": NYT 9/24/50; Rovere *McCarthy* 172; Griffith 115–16. "history of man": NYT 6/15/51; *McCarthy* 178–79. between the parties: Acheson 435. *744* " 'done his damnedest' ": Neustadt 96; NYT 4/18/52. Adlai E. Stevenson: NYT 1/24/52; Truman II 490; *Truman* 417. *745* "has any politics": NYT 7/23/52; Adams 13. Eisenhower jacket: Rovere *Years* 13–20. *746* "respect to me": NYT 1/7/52; Kenneth Davis 258. "from Dwight Eisenhower": NYT 1/24/52; *Truman* 415. *747* "was flabbergasted": Truman II 491–92. Democratic nominee: *Years* 342. *748* of that inconceivable: T 1/28/52. "seek the nomination": Kenneth Davis 236; Truman II 492. *749* "seemed thin": NYT 3/30/52; Acheson 632. "Good": NYT 3/31/52; Kenneth Davis 240. "No": Kenneth Davis 240. *750* "beside Alger Hiss": ibid. *750n* misspelled "Stephenson": Mazo 86. "ultimate timidity": NYT 3/31/52. "doesn't inhale": Kenneth Davis 263. he was packing: NYT 3/13/52, 3/20/52. *751* for the nomination: NYT 3/20/52, 4/3/52, 4/2/52, 4/9/52, 4/16/52, 4/23/52; Pusey 16–17. had to say: NYT 6/20/52; *Years* 22. *752* to stamp out: Fab VI 108; *Years* 33. to its hangar: NYT 7/8/52. *753* cattle prod: NYT 7/10/52. a nice point: Mazo 84–86; *Years* 61–62; *Life* 7/19/52. *754* "of another man": NYT 7/11/52; *Years* 27. be turned back: *Years* 27. the national convention: Pusey 15. *755* demanded "fair play": NYT 7/2/52; Walter Johnson 249–50. *756* "that road again!": NYT 7/11/52; Adams 35. *757* Ike had it: NYT 7/7/52, 7/8/52, 7/12/52. "in his administration": NYT 7/12/52. "of the party": Mazo 66–68. *758* on television, too: Adams 34; Mazo 97. *759* chosen their nominee: NYT 11/1/50. friends and admirers: Mazo 100. the White House: *Years* 105. *760* was badly divided: ibid; *Chicago Tribune* 7/13/52. "to his nomination": NYT 4/17/52; Kenneth Davis 264. "should be nominated": NYT 7/21/52; Kenneth Davis 268. *761* "and fair contest": NYT 7/22/52. "for the carnage": Kenneth Davis 269. "be too late": *Years* 342; NYT 7/22/52. "Stevenson of Illinois": NYT 7/23/52. *762* "it embarrass me?" Truman II 496. choice of 1952: NYT 7/26/52. " 'Thy will be done' ": Walter Johnson 260; NYT 7/26/52. "rest of them": Hughes 196. *763* "consequences of each": Kenneth Davis 273–75. "misgovern the people": ibid. and Stevenson friend: NYT 7/27/52, 7/29/52; Kenneth Davis 276–77. "I do not know": Acheson 699–700. proud of it: Kenneth Davis 314; *Decade* 234. *764* "often rather thin": *Years* 36–37. "about his backbone": NYT 9/13/52; Donovan 103. *765* "well concede defeat": *Decade* 222; Walter Johnson 257. next five years: Kronenberger 157. *766* "eggheads are there?": WM/John Alsop 3/23/74. "psychopathic instability": *Decade* 224. of Governor Stevenson: *Truman* 427–28; Walter Johnson 225. *767* his dander up: NYT 9/4/52; *Years* 38; Hughes 493. "his family life": Walter Johnson 259. "discussed them": Hughes 41–43; Pusey 29–32. *768* "few weeks ago": NYT 10/4/52; Pusey 31; Hughes 41–43; Donovan 244; Adams 31–32. *769* state ticket: Griffith 195; *McCarthy* 184. "apply to method": NYT 10/28/52; *McCarthy* 182–83; Pusey 29; NYT 10/4/52. "Stevenson's part": Mazo 66–67; NYT 10/14/52. *770* "was revealed today": *N.Y. Post* 9/18/52. "the beneficiaries": Mazo 118. *771* "to smear me": NYT 9/21/52, 9/19/52; Mazo 117. *772* out of the question: Mazo 116; Nixon 85–87. "hound's tooth?": *Decade* 227. "out all right": Mazo 119–20. *773* seat of power: ibid 120–21. the Ambassador Hotel: Nixon 100. *773–774* "common people" . . . "to be said": Mazo 124; Nixon 108. *774* "television and listen": Mazo 124–25. *775* against the wall: Adams 37; Mazo 126. up the receiver . . . "about politics, too!": Nixon 110; Adams 40–41; Nixon 110–11. *776* "has been questioned": NYT 9/24/52. "everything I own" . . . "is honestly ours": Nixon 115. *777* "to keep it": NYT 9/24/52. *778* "Irish never quit": Nixon 117. "your $75,000 worth": Mazo 132. burst into tears: ibid 131. *779* "beyond expectations": Nixon 118. "dog world, anyhow": Hughes 40. from Dwight Eisenhower: Adams 38–39; Nixon 119. *780* "any time thereafter": NYT 9/25/52. *780n* "genre of weepers": Mazo 136. *781* "Nixon rejoices us": ibid. *782* "ended that night": NYT 10/17/52; Hughes 32–33; NYT 10/25/52; Adams 44. "not much": Adams 44. would be defeated: Kenneth Davis 289–90. *783* went Republican: NYT 11/3/52; 11/5/52. 69.4 percent: Whyte 332. Senate, merely one: *Years* 112–15. *784* said Stevenson: Kenneth Davis 290. "much to laugh": ibid 291. the Secret Service: NYT 11/6/52; Donovan 200–201.

XX WHAT WAS GOOD FOR GENERAL MOTORS
(*pages 786–845*)

786 audience laughed: Fab VI 136. *787* "fallow period": ibid 152; Donovan 202, 203; Davis 320; Acheson 694. sold at $5.95 . . . from her mother: Fab VI 70–71; NYT 4/9/56, 4/23/56; *Life* 6/25/56; T 3/19/56, 6/18/56. *788* as Vitaphone: Fab VI 222, 58; NYT 11/28/52. great as ever: Fab VI 68. *789* frame was plastic: ibid 182–83. sharp, chill wind: NYT 12/6/52; Donovan 17–18. *790* fateful one: NYT 12/6/52; Donovan 17; NYT 11/21/52. "massive retaliation": Donovan 19; NYT 5/13/53; Goldman *Decade* 248–49. *791* "since my return": NYT 12/6/52, 12/10/52; Donovan 19–20. outgoing administrations: Donovan 20; NYT 12/11/52. *792* January 12 and 13: NYT 11/25/52; Adams 5; Hughes 52. Labor Department: NYT 1/17/53; Donovan 105; NYT 9/11/53. do the same: NYT 4/8/53, 4/3/53; Donovan 77; Hughes 77; NYT 2/11/53. *793* "grocery store": Rovere *Years* 111; Donovan 25; NYT 1/24/53; Fab VI 43; Hughes 75–76. "free economy": Hughes 76; NYT 8/28/52; *Decade* 280, 243. *794* times as large: Hughes 67; *Years* 74. "illustrious ruler": Hughes 134; NYT 1/22/53; Mazo 150; NYT 10/1/53; Mazo 251. *795* "East issues settled": Hughes 134–35; Donovan 9; Hughes 76; Adams 99. "except to kids": Donovan 20–21; NYT 1/19/53, 1/25/53, 1/21/53; Donovan 23. senator's fire: Acheson 707; NYT 3/5/53. *796* into history: Phillips *Truman* 431–32; NYT 1/21/53. it every morning: NYT 1/22/53, 1/25/53; Adams 71; Donovan 206. *797* is his reward: NYT 1/22/53. in "deportment": Donovan 69–70; T 1/9/56; Donovan 61. his famous grin: Donovan 3; Hughes 103. *798* "rock the boat": Donovan 200; NYT 2/12/53; Donovan 204–205; Adams 73; *New Republic* 2/18/57. "not to interfere": Donovan 69, 207, 208. *799* "every other individual": Adams 74; NYT 1/22/53; Walter Johnson 321, 319. "Sincerely, DE": Donovan 207, 195; Adams 426. *800* Bernard Baruch: *Years* 315. with Sherman Adams: Donovan 196; Adams 427. *801* "do any harm": NYT 1/3/53; Mowry 329; *Years* 103; Rovere *McCarthy* 188. be reckoned with: NYT 2/8/53, 1/11/53. had to lose: NYT 3/19/53; Griffith 101–102. *802* only seem worse: NYT 3/21/53; Adams 94; Hughes 93; Griffith 202; Donovan 89. "of Mr. Bohlen": Adams 95; NYT 3/26/53. votes to 13: NYT 3/28/53. *803* Joseph R. McCarthy: Adams 95; *McCarthy* 33; Donovan 89; Griffith 204; NYT 3/31/53; *McCarthy* 33–34. half of 1954: NYT 4/26/53, 2/7/53; Walter Johnson 280. "this is done": NYT 6/28/50. *804* applauded vigorously: Hughes 109. IS RESCINDED: Donovan 28. *805* "releashing Chiang": NYT 2/3/53; *Years* 266; Walter Johnson 301. extremely awkward: *Years* 91; Donovan 86–87. *806* and the Russians: Adams 91–92. was deadlocked: Donovan 87. "horse of containment": *McCarthy* 240–41; Donovan 70–71. *807* stricken in Moscow: Schlesinger *Thousand* 187; *Years* 106; NYT 3/6/63. "his death makes": Donovan 41; NYT 3/6/53; Hughes 99–101. "their own toil": Hughes 103–104. *808* "speech about it": ibid. at the end: Hughes 112; NYT 4/17/53; Hughes 110, 105, 112; Adams 97–98. *809* "out to be": Adams 117–18. of the talks: NYT 5/8/52. *810* "with the Communists": Adams 98. a major offensive: Fontaine 66–67; Adams 96; Donovan 122–23. *811* Rhee gave in: Fontaine 67; Adams 101–102; NYT 7/12/53; Donovan 124. "present agreement": *Years* 149. "has been implemented": T 8/10/53. "against Communism": *Years* 145. *812* "Eisenhower's appeasement": Donovan 119, 126. "noticed no change": ibid 125–26. Robert A. Taft: T 10/3/53. *813* further reductions: NYT 1/10/53. strategy followed: Adams 21–22; Donovan 110. counsel despair: NYT 6/5/53. *814* in ill health: T 6/22/53, 8/10/53. "Howard Roberts": NYT 6/14/53. "back in January!": NYT 6/11/53; Adams 25. *815* postponed indefinitely: NYT 7/5/53. "futile battle": NYT 7/27/53. he was dead: NYT 8/1/53. "beyond calculation": NYT 8/1/53. *816* "man, go on": NYT 1/4/53, 8/4/53. "now under discussion": NYT 1/25/54; Donovan 239. *817* "into their business": NYT 8/5/53; Hughes 28–29. "to the ministry": Donovan 85; NYT 3/31/53; Donovan 87. *818* for the demagogue: Hughes 132. "nearly impotent": Walter Johnson 279; *Washington Post* 7/20/53; Donovan 143–44. *819* the House 265-2: Hughes 119–20; NYT 6/2/53; Donovan 133; *Years* 216. *820* late Joseph Stalin: NYT 10/21/53, 10/25/53; Kendrick 36–37; NYT 9/24/53. other Radulovichs: NYT 11/25/53. and the press: NYT 4/16/54; Donovan 287–88. *821* Communists in Asia: NYT 12/19/54; Donovan 285–86, 297–98. "national security": NYT 4/29/53. from the payroll: Donovan 289; NYT 10/24/53; Adams 150, 152; NYT 1/8/54; Mazo 155–56. *822* side down: Donovan 298; NYT 4/29/53. Bricker amendment: Donovan 105, 239; NYT 8/19/53. *823* half-million Americans?: Donovan 238–39; Hughes 144. "for this amendment": NYT 2/18/54, 4/7/53; Hughes 144. *824* "of Almighty God": *Years* 206. listening to him yet: NYT 1/31/54. *825* executive agreements: Donovan 240–41. individual states: Hughes 142–44. *826* "treated that way!":

Adams 410. "forty-eight governments": NYT 7/15/53; Donovan 237. and 42 opposed: NYT 2/26/54, 2/27/54. *827* to resist it: NYT 2/4/54; Donovan 241; Adams 108–109. rejected as unconstitutional: NYT 2/27/54. *828* lost India's friendship: Donovan 309; Hughes 205; Kenneth Davis 343–44; NYT 5/12/53. *829* "embrace this principle": Hughes 147; NYT 7/18/53. "their captivity": Hughes 147–48; Adams 88–89; NYT 7/2/53, 12/1/53. "of this country": Walter Johnson 298; Hughes 285; *Parade* 9/28/69; *N.Y. Herald Tribune* 8/12/58. *830* "enemy attack": Adams 399–400. it would be: ibid. *831* "and then some": NYT 7/7/57; Walter Johnson 309; *Years* 199. "does not happen": NYT 2/11/54. "war may go?" . . . "with large units": Donovan 263. *832* "not look back": NYT 12/31/49, 2/8/50; Acheson 672, 674. *833* Roy 194–95, 172. *834* declare war: Donovan 263. force in Korea: Burns *Soldier* 379. "totalitarian sea": Rostow "The American National Style." *835* and he did: Acheson 677–78. ask for it: NYT 5/16/54; Roy 225, 240; NYT 3/23/54. *836* "resolute today": Jungk 310; NYT 3/30/54. "power in Indochina": *Years* 193. *837* London and Paris: Donovan 259; Adams 122–23. "profound influences": NYT 4/8/54; Adams 120. Congress could act: Roy 271. *838* "such a decision": NYT 4/17/54; Mazo 255–56. was "unlikely": NYT 4/20/54. *839* fire upon himself: NYT 4/17/54. honor of France: T 5/8/72; Roy 340. *840* "may prove inescapable": Kendrick 359. "with a crash": Donovan 267. Cambodia, and Laos: ibid 268. *841* "relations as now": Adams 126–27. "blessing in disguise": Hughes 208. *841–845* Norma Jean Baker portrait: Guiles passim; *Current Biography* 1962; NYT 8/6/62; T 8/17/62.

XXI MR. CHAIRMAN, MR. CHAIRMAN
(pages 847–893)

847 "rolling readjustment": NYT 1/3/54, 2/7/54, 3/2/54, 3/18/54. St. Lawrence Seaway: NYT 5/7/54, 5/8/54. *848* in September: NYT 6/20/53; Donovan 247; NYT 9/1/54. heart disease: NYT 10/8/54, 12/22/54, 7/3/54. called a *hippy:* Fab VI 80. *849* staying in Hollywood: NYT 5/21/54, 4/16/54. *850* telecast March 7, 1955: NYT 10/21/54, 2/26/54; Kendrick 374–75; NYT 7/8/55, 12/26/51, 9/13/54, 11/30/55. morning sickness: NYT 1/16/53; Goldman *Decade* 266. *851* any previous year: Mazo 155. "H-bomb program": NYT 2/7/54; *Decade* 260; NYT 4/13/54; Donovan 294. "except Communists": NYT 6/17/54; Kendrick 41. *852* Hall of Fame: NYT 6/11/54. behind Borden: NYT 6/16/54; Schlesinger *Thousand* 457. *853* he knew it: NYT 7/1/54, 11/11/54; Jungk 317. Joseph R. McCarthy: Donovan 295. refused to take it: Jungk 318. *854* "for the occasion": NYT 4/13/54; Jungk 322, 324. "the devil's work": ibid 324. *854–855* interrogation of Oppenheimer: Jungk 325–26. *855* "interests of security": Donovan 296; Jungk 330. not be overlooked: NYT 7/2/54, 6/30/54. *856* had already formed: Jungk 229–38; NYT 12/3/63, 2/19/67, 6/16/54. flying over India: NYT 2/16/55; Jungk 310; NYT 3/16/54, 4/26/55. *857* everyone on earth: NYT 10/16/55. named Irving Peress: NYT 1/8/55. *858* investigative powers: NYT 2/20/54; Adams 145; NYT 1/31/54. "from him, too": T 3/22/54. *859* Permanent Investigations Subcommittee: ibid; NYT 9/5/52; 1/3/53. "directions please": *Harvard Crimson* 5/7/54. *860* he met McCarthy: T 3/22/54; Rovere *Years* 130. they might go: Rovere *McCarthy* 191. *861* "Cohn Schines best": T 3/22/54; *McCarthy* 200. "issue in 1954": NYT 11/17/53, 11/25/53. " 'of American money' ": NYT 11/25/53. *862* "friendly countries": Donovan 247; NYT 12/2/53. the President: NYT 12/5/53, 12/4/53. *863* Joseph R. McCarthy: *McCarthy* 23; NYT 2/3/54; *Years* 97. McCarthy support: *McCarthy* 22. *864* needed Schine: ibid; NYT 11/5/53. Reber about that: Griffith 245; NYT 3/12/54. Reber-Welch exchange: *McCarthy* 208–209. *865* of the Navy: Straight 30–31. "routine step": ibid 27. *866* "unreasonable about": *McCarthy* 206. "of the Army": Adams 143–45. "to regret it": Donovan 250; Walter Johnson 292; NYT 2/21/54; Straight 200. *867* "will be available": NYT 2/25/54; Straight 61; NYT 2/24/54, 2/25/54. "on his knees": *McCarthy* 31; Griffith 247–48. *868* "known Communists": NYT 3/4/54; Griffith 248–49; NYT 3/5/54. "wreck the Army": NYT 3/5/54, 3/10/54; Griffith 273; NYT 3/11/54, 2/28/54. *869* in the chair: Walter Johnson 292–93; NYT 3/13/54, 3/17/54. "point of order": NYT 4/23/54, 7/11/53. *870* "be so named": Straight 9. "of the Army": Straight 12. *871* "the Communist party": NYT 4/23/54; Straight 235–36. "any place, anywhere": *McCarthy* 221. *872* "to the end": NYT 11/14/54; Straight 84–85. *872–877* Welch-Cohn-Mundt-McCarthy: NYT 6/10/54; Straight 249–53; Transcript of the Hearings 2428–30. *873* "not get the information": ibid 125; NYT 5/5/54; *McCarthy* 216–17. "from a pixie?": NYT 4/28/54. *878* and the CIA: NYT 6/18/54; Transcript 2973–77; NYT 6/19/54. with disfavor: Griffith 264; NYT 11/4/54, 7/20/54. they had won: *Congressional Record* 83rd Congress

2nd Session 6/11/54 8032–33; NYT 7/1/54, 8/1/54. *879* the previous January: *McCarthy* 227; NYT 12/3/54; *McCarthy* 229. "is McCarthywasm": *McCarthy* 231. *880* with a sling: NYT 7/20/54, 11/30/54; *McCarthy* 235–36; NYT 11/18/54. "in the United States": Donovan 280. *881* "of the United States": ibid 277; Adams 164–66; Mazo 152; NYT 9/16/54; Donovan 280–81; Kenneth Davis 300. cheered him accordingly: Walter Johnson 285. exposed as myth: Donovan 274–75. the jitters: NYT 10/12/54; Hughes 75–76. *882* "through with politics": Mazo 138, 152–57; NYT 6/13/54; Mazo 157. "at the polls": NYT 11/5/54; *Years* 230; *Washington Post* 11/4/54. *883* "that goddamned drum": Donovan 282–84. *884* withering "Hardeeharhar": Fab VI 81. *885* bombing or spooking: Hechinger and Hechinger 82; Fab VI 80. *886* "highly emotionalized child": Hechinger and Hechinger 144, 147. "women of means": ibid 148, 154. *887* "her life": ibid 125, 126. "by their families": John Brooks *Leap* 233; Hechinger and Hechinger 126. a billion dollars: *Leap* 233. *888* "the wild frontier!": *Newsweek* 12/27/54; Fab VI 58–59; NYT 6/1/55. *889* carried too far: Hechinger and Hechinger 142–43. of the 1950s: Fab VI 86. "beautiful to feel!": quoted in Fab VI 89. *890* "just your glassy flesh": NYT 3/2/50; quoted in Fab VI 88. *891* "to the wheel": NYT 9/5/57; quoted in Fab VI 89. *892* SMOKE POT: Fab VI 90; *Leap* 237. *893* "everybody goes "Awww!": quoted in Fab VI 84.

XXII WITH ALL DELIBERATE SPEED
(*pages 895–944*)

895–899 American Institute of Public Opinion *The 1954 Pocket Almanac*. *899* "to see me?": Schlesinger *Thousand* 924. *900* in states' rights: NYT 9/9/53, 5/17/54; T 10/12/53, 5/24/54. are inherently unequal: NYT 5/18/54. *902* "just plain nuts": Hughes 241–47, 201. *903* expected of others: Walter Johnson 273; Donovan 159, 154–55. the white South: Walter Johnson 273–74. expanding rapidly: Lerner 78; Donovan 390; Graham and Gurr 389. *904* permanent expulsion: T 2/20/56; John Brooks *Leap* 289; T 3/12/56. closed its file: NYT 9/2/55. *905* "and us white": T 9/10/56. *906* nearly three to one: T 12/10/56, 12/17/56. *907* "machinery had shifted": NYT 12/6/55; T 1/16/56. *908* "to their demands": T 2/6/56. "to hate them": NYT 3/20/56; T 3/5/56. *909* "boycotting the buses": T 2/6/56. "black ape": NYT 3/23/56; T 3/5/56. roared, "No!": T 4/2/56. *910* for civil rights: T 11/26/56. "humility and meekness": T 11/26/56. "That's right": T 12/31/56. *911* "interest demands it": Phillips *Truman* 399. *912* "Chinese civil war": Kenneth Davis 303; Donovan 301. and for all: Adams 131; Donovan 303. *913* "seven-thousand-mile frontier": Donovan 302. Eisenhower's message: NYT 1/25/55. *914* "or anything else": Rovere *Years* 264. offshore islands: Adams 130; Donovan 305; Hughes 166. "of this resolution": Donovan 306. *915* had been removed: NYT 1/30/55; Donovan 307; Kenneth Davis 303. as the Soviets: Walter Johnson 303; *Years* 269–75. in the past: Donovan 75. *916* he said grimly: NYT 6/23/55. "what they're doing": Adams 114, 91. in his briefcase: ibid 177. *917* Parc des Eaux-Vives: *Years* 280; NYT 7/18/55. in helicopters overhead: NYT 7/19/55; *Years* 287. *918* democratic Germany: NYT 7/19/55; Donovan 350. *919* "all our peoples": Donovan 349; NYT 7/22/55; Donovan 344; NYT 7/22/55. just stared: Donovan 344. have proposed it: ibid 345. *920* with MIGs: *Years* 290–91. it didn't melt: Adams 179; Donovan 350. *921* vacation in Denver: NYT 7/25/55; Donovan 352. to Open Skies: NYT 9/25/55; Donovan 359–60. across the hall: NYT 9/25/55; Donovan 360–61; Adams 183. "better come over": Donovan 362–63. *922* President's chances: NYT 9/25/55; Donovan 363; Adams 183. oxygen tent: Adams 154; Donovan 363–65. "to the car": Donovan 366. *923* "My God!": Mazo 189; NYT 9/25/55. into the car: Mazo 190. *924* for some time: Adams 181–82. since the Crash: NYT 9/26/55. chief's absence: Donovan 369; NYT 9/26/55. due until January: *Years* 319–28; Donovan 370–71; Adams 186. *925* "some other guy": Adams 187–88; Donovan 378. accompanied recovery: NYT 10/15/55; Donovan 376; NYT 10/23/55; Donovan 376. *926* "agreeably surprised": NYT 11/12/55, 11/15/55; Donovan 385; Adams 191. to think about: Hughes 174–76; Donovan 397. of this term: NYT 1/9/56; T 1/16/56. "his own appointees": Donovan 393–95; Adams 226. *927* vote for him: Adams 224–26; NYT 2/15/56. "that is, affirmative": T 1/2/56; NYT 3/1/56. *928* hearing aid: T 3/26/56. "in this matter": NYT 3/1/56. "an egghead": T 3/12/56. "Secretary of Agriculture": T 3/19/56. future President: T 1/2/56 (Man of the Year). *929* ribbons of concrete: Chapman 38. six cents to seven: NYT 5/6/56, 7/7/56. year for humor: T 2/27/56. *930* "Aw rutti!": NYT 12/10/56, 8/12/56, 10/18/56, 4/22/56. a million copies: NYT 11/16/56. "through the fence?": T 5/14/56. "the same response": NYT 5/14/56. *931* of American culture: NYT 10/2/58. implications then: NYT 4/21/56, 7/20/56. criminal irresponsibility: NYT 5/5/56,

3/19/56, 4/10/56, 1/13/56, 7/27/56; T 11/12/56. things personally: T 7/2/56. *932* "just plain loaf": *Ladies' Home Journal* October 1960. "came back with": *Redbook* September 1960; NYT 4/22/56, 4/20/56, 8/5/55; T 1/16/56. *933* a million francs: T 1/16/56, 1/23/56. "like the Kellys": NYT 4/5/56, 4/16/56, 4/19/56, 4/20/56; T 4/23/56. *934* IN FEBRUARY: NYT 4/19/56, 4/20/56; T 4/30/56; NYT 8/3/56; T 8/13/56. campaign for reelection: NYT 6/25/56. *935* "Egyptians!": NYT 7/20/56, 7/27/56; T 8/6/56. Eden in 1956: NYT 8/1/56. *936* "quite a combination": TC 1956 106; Hughes 212. "may be necessary": NYT 10/30/56. "honor our pledge": Hughes 214. *937* "the Hungarian people": NYT 11/1/56, 11/4/56; Adams 258–59; NYT 11/6/56; Hughes 220. without outside help: NYT 11/2/56, 11/4/56, 11/3/56. "how *are* you?": NYT 11/7/56. *938* "involved answer": Adams 259. a major issue: NYT 7/18/56. "known and respected": *Years* 368. *939* operating table: NYT 9/25/55, 6/9/56. Walter Reed Hospital: NYT 6/9/56; T 6/18/56. *940* SAY DOCTORS: NYT 6/10/56. him gingerly: Kenneth Davis 327–28. be a catastrophe: NYT 10/12/56; T 11/5/56, 10/29/56; Kenneth Davis 256–57; Mazo 179, 169, 180; NYT 8/14/56. "presidential timber": NYT 7/24/56; Hughes 173. *941* "the Vice President": Mazo 165; NYT 4/27/56, 6/27/56. a major issue: *Thousand* 596; NYT 8/23/56; Kenneth Davis 335. of his "image": McGinniss 27; Kenneth Davis 323. *942* "need to win": NYT 8/12/56; Kenneth Davis 332–35; Hughes 190; NYT 4/22/56; Davis 343. *943* for the challenger: Kenneth Davis 340; NYT 9/6/56. against odds: NYT 10/24/56, 11/6/56. Hoover's in 1928: NYT 11/7/56; Walter Johnson 285–86. "the way I feel": Hughes 224–28. *944* "across the nation": NYT 8/18/56; *Thousand* 8–9; Adams 253; McCarthy *Kennedys* 119; Burns *Kennedy* 190. "for President": McCarthy *Kennedys* 119.

XXIII THE PURSUIT OF HAPPINESS
(*pages 945–961*)

945 as cloudless: NYT 10/5/57. *946* Auto Buy Now: Steinbeck 95; Goldman *Decade* 305; NYT 10/1/58. *It's gone:* NYT 1/2/58; Steinbeck 47. *947* size of Poland's: John Brooks *Leap* 53. "in Detroit": Walter Johnson 263; *Fortune* May 1954. handling their credit: NYT 9/4/57; Galbraith *Affluent* 171–72; Whyte 360. *948* "apparatus of it": Whyte 354–55, 362, 363. "importance of thrift": Bird 259; Whyte 353; Riesman 18; Whyte 19–20. *949* sense of identity: Galbraith *State* 49; Whyte 78, 338. *950* week to spend: Spectorsky 7–8; Whyte 401. *951* "lead the bland": *Affluent* 135, 193–94; Mowry 222; *Affluent* 4–5. community playgrounds: Whyte 350. *952* "policemen, and rats": *Leap* 104–105, 108, 114–15. "well-adjusted": Riesman 16, 26. *953* "and weakness": ibid xviii; Whyte 5. they liked it: *Leap* 138; Whyte 3–4. only natural: Eisinger xiv–xvi; *Leap* 53–54. *954* "fundamental decency": Steinbeck 183; Whyte 321, 319; NYT 12/2/56. her own party: Whyte 316, 368, 389, 315–16. *955* "Man-Trap Set": Spectorsky 191; NYT 11/16/56; Whyte 337; NYT 9/16/55; Friedan 12. "feminist ideology": Friedan 13, 17; Lifton 203. *956* luck elsewhere: Friedan 12; Lifton 202; Friedan 154. *957* considered worse: Packard *Wilderness* 22–23; Walter Johnson 266. coalition faltered: Whyte 332. "his problem?": ibid 389. *958* and resented: Kronenberger 120, 122–23, 223–24. *959* the next generation: Spectorsky 197, 248; Murray "Individuality." *960* "less than ninety": Whyte 428. polled one another: ibid 429. *961* "dreams into reality": *Decade* 307; T 10/21/57; NYT 10/6/57.

XXIV BEEP BEEP
(*pages 963–1000*)

963 "their achievement": NYT 10/1/57; T 10/14/57. *964* "if they did": NYT 10/5/57. ("of the de-emphasis"): Hughes 246; Adams 415. "too late": Adams 416–18; T 11/18/57. *965* "windshield wipers": T 10/21/57; Walter Johnson 313; Hughes 247. "book was home": Goldman *Decade* 313; T 10/21/57; Galbraith *Affluent* xxviii. *966* "be successful": T 10/21/57. source of power: T 11/4/57. *967* coup in itself: T 10/21/57. from outer space: T 10/14/57. *968* the reason why: T 10/14/57. tail-twitching cheerleaders: Rovere *Years* 124. *969* the national income: T 10/14/57; NYT 10/3/57; T 11/18/57. "as we are": T 10/21/57, 11/18/57. *970* of the language: T 10/21/57. or entertain, pupils: ibid; Lynd and Lynd 23. *971* "it the better": T 12/2/57; NYT 11/23/57; T 12/2/57. "or *with* information?": T 11/4/57. *972* survive in space: NYT 10/27/57; T 10/28/57; NYT 11/3/57, 11/14/57. to Columbus: NYT 11/2/57. MOON, IKE: T 11/11/57. *973* would vanish: NYT 10/10/57. a U.S. ICBM: NYT 6/6/57, 8/27/57, 11/29/58. *974* "to the good": Adams 415; Hughes 429. of a solution: Adams 414–15; NYT 12/21/57. *975* "on the moon": Adams 416–18; NYT 11/8/57. "into its interior":

T 10/28/57. *976* U.S. IGY committee: T 3/17/58. *977* starcrossed Edsel: 9/30/54. across the skies: T 10/21/57, 11/18/57. would tell him: NYT 10/10/57. *978* "at this moment": ibid. "err, bollix": T 10/7/57. *979* promises of glory: T 9/26/57. by local police: T 9/16/57. possible demonstrations: NYT 8/31/57. *980* "become a deluge!": T 9/16/57. delay of integration: NYT 9/5/57, 9/16/57, 9/8/57. *981* "at my command": NYT 9/21/57; Adams 345–46. a federal court: NYT 9/15/57; Adams 349–53; T 9/23/57, 9/30/57; NYT 9/25/57. "and judgment": NYT 9/21/57. *982* "got up and bowed": T 9/30/57. *983* phone booth: NYT 9/25/57; T 10/7/57. "do my job": T 10/7/57. to be hostile: ibid. *984* "good judgment": NYT 9/24/57; T 10/7/57. "the Federal Court": Adams 332, 351; NYT 9/24/57; Adams 354. *985* "read it": Adams 354–55; T 10/7/57. "anarchy would result": Adams 355; NYT 9/25/57. *986* Army rule: NYT 9/25/57. *986–987* "Roadblock Alpha" . . . "base of the neck": T 10/7/57. *988* "in America?": NYT 9/27/57; T 10/7/57. government $4,051,000: T 5/19/58. *989* called into service: Adams 356; T 10/7/57. *989n* "of free government": Adams 356. *990* "at random": T 10/14/57, 11/11/57. he retired: T 10/14/57, 5/19/58; NYT 7/31/58. *991* felt shame: NYT 8/2/62, T 10/7/57. *992* ("was working"): NYT 11/10/57; T 11/18/57; *Saturday Review* 11/2/57; T 11/4/57. stood vigil: T 10/4/57; NYT 11/8/57. a major recession: T 11/14/57. *993* was a stroke: T 11/27/57. "wrong with him": Adams 195; T 12/9/57; NYT 11/26/57. "is to it": Adams 196–97. *994* there, he wept: T 12/9/57; NYT 11/27/57; Adams 198. "to be excellent": NYT 11/29/57, 11/30/57. *995* "First ignition!" . . . "explosion occurred": NYT 12/7/57; T 12/16/57. *996* "Custer's last stand": T 12/16/57. *997–1000* Edsel portrait: John Brooks *Edsel;* Cone; Galbraith *Affluent;* Goldman *Decade; Consumer Reports* January and April 1958; *Life* 7/22/57, 8/5/57, 8/21/57; NYT 11/20/56, 8/27/57, 8/29/57, 10/5/57, 10/6/57, 11/28/57, 11/20/59; T 10/21/57, 11/30/59.

XXV THE CRUSADE FALTERS

(*pages 1001–1034*)

1001 ICBM attack: NYT 7/22/59; T 12/7/59; NYT 6/10/59. *1002* called "compacts": T 4/6/59. crew cuts: NYT 1/3/59; TC 1959; NYT 3/3/59; Adams 311; NYT 7/16/58, 11/22/59, 4/10/59. *1003* opened fire: NYT 7/10/59; T 7/20/59. old for her: NYT 5/3/57, 9/6/61, 4/10/59, 10/15/59, 10/8/59, 5/7/59, 3/1/59, 1/15/60, 7/25/61. *1004* the hula hoop: T 9/15/58; NYT 8/11/57. sixty-second birthday: T 12/1/58; NYT 12/7/58. *1005* through East Germany: T 12/1/58. *1006* "intolerable situation": Adams 271. armed forces anywhere: NYT 1/6/57. "this battle": Adams 274. *1007* the warships: ibid 289; NYT 4/26/57. "Eisenhower Doctrine": Adams 289. *1008* Eisenhower consented: NYT 7/15/58, 7/4/58. Lebanese move: T 7/28/58; Adams 291. was expanding: NYT 9/24/58; Adams 293. *1009* in world affairs: NYT 7/16/58; *Time* editors 75. a light cruiser: DeMott 172. *1010* western Europe: Servan-Schreiber 59, 36. "a dear friend": Walter Johnson 266. and Panama City: John Brooks *Leap* 339. *1011* intolerable gloating: *New Republic* 10/27/58. "classless society": Nixon 259. *1012* stayed home: NYT 4/28/58. rocking the boat: Schlesinger *Thousand* 189. *1012–1020* Nixon trip: Mazo 206–46; Nixon 183–228. *1013* "irrational state": NYT 5/9/58; Mazo 233; Nixon 219. *1014* to Nixon's aid: NYT 5/14/58. *1015* was preposterous: Mazo 222. "of this mob": Mazo 225. *1017* Nixon's limousine: NYT 5/14/58. *1018* wobbled toward him: ibid. *1020* against possible attack: ibid. "assistance is requested": ibid. had been friendly: NYT 5/16/58. *1021* he was, too: Nixon 231; T 6/23/58. vicuña story: NYT 1/12/58. tax returns: T 7/14/58; NYT 6/11/58. *1022* "that he had": T 7/7/58. *1024* like Bernard Goldfine?: T 6/30/58. *1025* Washington bureaucracies: Adams 440; T 7/14/58. "as they are": T 6/23/58. *1026* "would be gone": T 6/30/58. "and tirelessly": NYT 6/19/58; Hughes 266–67; Adams 445–46. *1027* should be fired: T 6/30/58. all these years (and following paragraphs): T 7/14/58. *1029* collateral for loans: NYT 7/4/58. "told about it": T 7/14/58. a lot of that: NYT 6/19/58. *1030* White House roster: NYT 6/23/58. *1031* was political: NYT 8/14/58. *1032* "on November 4": NYT 9/10/58; WA 1959 120. lowered upon him: Adams 446–47. *1033* "I can give you": NYT 9/28/58. last cigarette: Adams 447. agreed to go: Hughes 269; Adams 451. "twenty-five states": Nixon 232–33. *1034* "your money": NYT 10/14/58, 10/16/58, 10/17/58, 10/21/58, 10/22/58, 10/23/58. "the White House": NYT 11/6/58, 11/5/58; Nixon 233. "do with Nixon": NYT 11/5/58; Nixon 234; NYT 11/5/58, 11/10/58.

XXVI TATTOO FOR THE GENERAL
(*pages 1036–1085*)

1036 proof of it: Mencken 264. dead ahead: NYT 12/19/58. "be any riots": Fab VII 28. accept contraception: NYT 11/26/59. *1037* "these questions": Kendrick 410; Goldman *Decade* 319; NYT 8/28/58. got their coffee: NYT 10/1/58, 1/3/60. *1038* on restricted beaches: NYT 2/24/60. visible at last: NYT 5/11/60, 6/16/60, 7/19/60, 6/6/60, 7/19/60, 7/26/60, 10/20/60; WA 1962 251. *1039* to do it: NYT 5/14/60; Fab VII 28–29. *1040* facts of life: NYT 5/10/60; WA 1961 168; W 1966 163; NYT 11/26/59. ("Bashful!"): Kendrick 429–30; *Decade* 318; Fab VI 44; NYT 8/29/58; T 10/19/59. "coached or tutored": NYT 11/3/59. *1041* its hearing room: *Decade* 319; NYT 10/15/59. *1042* "intellectual life": Fab VI 44; *Decade* 321–22; NYT 11/3/59. smiled at him: *Decade* 322. *1043* five to one: NYT 11/5/59, 11/6/59. every week: Kendrick 440. *1044* named Truman Capote: NYT 3/11/60; Kendrick 437; *Chicago Daily News* 9/20/58; Nixon 304; NYT 1/5/60, 5/3/60, 11/16/59; T 11/30/59. "matter anyway": T 2/23/59. *1045* "hand of Eisenhower": NYT 4/16/59; Hughes 342. *1046* "will break it": NYT 1/27/59. what it was: T 6/1/59; NYT 5/25/59; T 3/2/59. Soviet officials: WA 1960 108; T 8/3/59; NYT 7/24/59; Hughes 287; NYT 7/24/59. *1047* the "Sokolniki Summit": NYT 7/25/59; Nixon 255–58; T 8/3/59. *1047–1048* "we are stronger" . . . "no free elections": WA 1960 111; Nixon 255–58; T 8/3/59. *1048* Berlin ultimatum: NYT 8/6/59. *1049* in his eyes: NYT 8/26/59, 8/27/59; WA 1960 117; T 9/7/59; NYT 8/8/59. "going splendidly": NYT 9/3/59; T 9/14/59; NYT 9/5/59, 9/8/59. *1050* as their host: NYT 9/16/59. "than his backside": NYT 9/20/59. to a detente: NYT 9/26/59; T 10/5/59. *1051* Soviet Union next year: NYT 9/28/59. them and Khrushchev: T 10/5/59. *1052* "our friends abroad": NYT 11/5/59, 12/4/59. in Casablanca: T 12/14/59, 12/15/59. *1053* 1960, in Paris: NYT 12/23/59, 12/24/59. to join them: T 1/12/59; NYT 8/2/53. *1054* Castro's Trotsky: Schlesinger *Thousand* 220. next to impossible: T 1/12/59, 1/25/59. and they said so: T 1/12/59. *1055* bogeymen everywhere: T 4/27/59; Nixon 351–52; Haynes Johnson 25. to invade Cuba: T 11/9/59, 3/16/59; NYT 2/21/59, 1/22/59; Haynes Johnson 49. "a Communist government": NYT 1/6/59. *1056* suspicions were allayed: Haynes Johnson 30–31, 37. *1057* battle flag: ibid 76. *1058* in the camp: ibid 38. around in slime: ibid 44. *1060* "we will win": ibid 81, 75–76. *1061–1067* general sources: see under Powers in the Bibliography. *1062* Francis Gary Powers: NYT 5/6/60. *1063* "have had any": Adams 455. of his magazine: Hughes 303. *1067* weeks of pandemonium: NYT 5/8/60. *1067–1070* general sources: WA 1961 171; Hughes 300–302; *Decade* 335–38. *1068* complete confession: NYT 5/8/60. flights will continue: NYT 5/10/60. *1069* "planes over here": NYT 5/12/60. is frigid: NYT 5/17/60. *1070* world conciliation: T 5/30/60. no punishment: NYT 5/18/60. before the summit: NYT 5/26/60. "keeping busy?": NYT 5/20/60. *1071* "all of us": Hughes 306. marine helicopter: NYT 6/11/60. eighty-thousand-gun salute: NYT 6/17/60. "all of it": Theodore White *1960* 117; Hughes 310–11. *1072* years in prison: NYT 8/20/60. "us in 1952?": Adams 453. *1072n* was laid off: NYT 2/10/62. *1073* munitions. Then . . . "and will persist": Galbraith *State* 399–400; Adams 325–30; WA 1962 90; NYT 1/18/61. "it is directed": *State* 317–19. *1074* sheriff's, side: NYT 9/27/60; McGinniss 32. *1076* public explanation: Hughes 319, 250; NYT 8/25/60; Nixon 339. margin held steady: NYT 3/10/60. *1077* on and on: NYT 7/14/60. *1078* to Kennedy's 46: NYT 7/27/60. Kennedy 50: NYT 8/27/60. circumstances for him: Nixon 326; NYT 8/30/60. They applauded: NYT 9/8/60, 9/13/60; Sorensen 190–91. *1079* percent undecided: Theodore White *1960* 320. "September 26": Nixon 336; NYT 9/27/60. beard growth: NYT 10/8/60, 10/14/60, 10/22/60. *1080* "fathers, don't we?": NYT 10/13/60, 10/20/60; Nixon 363; *Thousand* 73–74. *1081* reversed the result: Sorensen 209. *1082* "will all support": Nixon 409; Theodore White *1960* 304; Nixon 376–79. Wednesday morning: NYT 12/16/60. "early yet": White *1960* 18. *1084* to be governed: NYT 12/16/60. "in the distance": Nixon 417. *1085* "to all men": Nixon 402.

XXVII A NEW GENERATION OF AMERICANS
(*pages 1089–1131*)

1089 in Cleveland Park: NYT 1/20/61; Schlesinger *Thousand* 1–2. *1090* new administration . . . "our ancient heritage": NYT 1/21/61. "what a day!": Fab VII 37; *Thousand* 5. with greater confidence: Gold *1940–41* 27. *1091* three years earlier: NYT 12/16/60; Manchester

Death 505. and pulling away: Manchester *Portrait* 11–12; NYT 12/18/60; Neustadt 94. typical early days: NYT 1/22/61. *1092* "what you told him": Agronsky 9; NYT 1/22/61; *Portrait* 12–13. rid of it: NYT 2/19/61; WM/Ronald L. Ziegler; Agronsky 9; NYT 12/16/61. *1093* as big as Ike's: NYT 2/26/61; *Portrait* 15. each morning: NYT 2/26/51; *Portrait* 15–16. *1094* cultural coordinator: Halberstam 41; *U.S. News and World Report* 5/1/61; *Thousand* 144; NYT 1/22/61, 6/27/61. Bay of Pigs: NYT 4/21/61; Haynes Johnson 67. *1095* "ill-starred an adventure": Halberstam 66, 69; *Thousand* 292. base was covered: *Thousand* 238; WM/John F. Kennedy October 1961. from the President: Sorensen 296; *Thousand* 239–40. *1096* "the United States?": Sorensen 295–96: NYT 4/21/61. "share their confidence": Sorensen 296; NYT 4/21/61; Haynes Johnson 65; *Thousand* 239, 267. *1097* "little as possible": *Thousand* 249, 259, 246. force were committed: Haynes Johnson 82, 70; NYT 4/17/61. miles away: Haynes Johnson 69, 84. *1098* "the Cubans themselves": *Thousand* 247; NYT 4/13/61; Sorensen 298. fire a rifle: *Thousand* 250; Haynes Johnson 69. chance of winning: NYT 4/21/61. *1099* "would be available": *Thousand* 269, 250; *U.S. News and World Report* 1/7/63; *Thousand* 281; NYT 5/28/61. *1100* on one ship: *Thousand* 270; NYT 4/16/61; Haynes Johnson 94; *U.S. News and World Report* 1/14/63; Haynes Johnson 113. enemy aircraft: Haynes Johnson 77–79; *U.S. News and World Report* 1/14/63. "and rebellion": Haynes Johnson 128–29; *Thousand* 274–75. *1101* by the CIA: Haynes Johnson 95. *1102* "fish is red": NYT 4/26/61; *U.S. News and World Report* 1/14/63; Haynes Johnson 100. and executed: Haynes Johnson 60, 120–22. *1103* "these people there?": ibid 100, 83, 105, 295; *Thousand* 295. *1104* had been lost: Haynes Johnson 103. *1105* back that night: ibid 111, 113. *1106* "air force fields": NYT 4/18/61; *Thousand* 271; Haynes Johnson 92; NYT 4/18/61. "off for Cuba": Haynes Johnson 93. the United States: *Thousand* 291; Haynes Johnson 152. *1107* a thousand wounded: Johnson 136–38. "the main business": ibid 143; *Thousand* 276. *1108* "popular I get": John Kennedy 112; Sorensen 291; *Thousand* 292. "alongside Fidel Castro": *Reader's Digest* November 1964; *Thousand* 285; NYT 4/23/61; *Militant* 5/1/61. *1109* WE NEED YOU: Haynes Johnson 129–30. *1110* Americans were killed: ibid 154–56; *Thousand* 278. WAIT FOR YOU: Haynes Johnson 161, 167. to ransom them: ibid 349; NYT 4/22/61, 12/24/62. "streets of Budapest": Haynes Johnson 174; NYT 4/21/61, 4/19/61. *1111* "nuclear armaments": NYT 4/21/61; *Thousand* 287–88. from the Comintern: NYT 3/2/61. *1112* "of the peril": NYT 4/21/61; Haynes Johnson 175. never forget: *Thousand* 297. *1113* and an interpreter: Halberstam 72; NYT 5/20/61; Fontaine 413. "beginning of the end": NYT 5/8/60, 9/24/60, 9/30/60, 10/13/60. immediate removal: Fontaine 390; NYT 2/14/61. *1114* divided Berlin: NYT 8/31/61; Fontaine 315, 423. intelligence activities: NYT 6/27/48, 5/15/60, 10/23/60. *1115* laugh it off: Fontaine 412–13, 314–15; T 6/9/61; Halberstam 74–75. "Jacqueline Kennedy to Paris": T 6/9/61; NYT 6/3/61. "in my life": *Thousand* 367; Halberstam 76; NYT 6/4/61. *1116* "and blackmailed": NYT 11/15/64. only straitjackets: NYT 6/6/61, 6/11/61; Fontaine 416. "cold winter": Fontaine 416. *1116n* "war over Berlin": Khrushchev 458. *1117* "have to act": Halberstam 76. chauvinistic speeches: WA 1962 113. "it's all over": WA 1962 113; Fontaine 418. Walter Ulbricht: WA 1962 115; NYT 8/6/61. *1118* in East Berlin: T 8/25/61; NYT 8/13/61, 8/16/61; *Thousand* 395. for the "mistake": WA 1962 121; NYT 9/8/61, 9/28/61, 9/2/61; *Thousand* 460–61; Fontaine 425; NYT 10/18/61. *1119* since V-J Day: Fontaine 421–22; NYT 9/19/61. "December 31, 1961": Fontaine 423–25; *Thousand* 400; NYT 10/18/61. *1120* "like the place": *Thousand* 548; Halberstam 76. of real power: NYT 3/19/61. for it—unimportant: NYT 3/1/61. *1121* "White House lawn": NYT 2/24/61; Carpenter 50; Goldman *Tragedy* 388–90; NYT 10/23/61. deeply affected: *Thousand* 396; NYT 8/21/61. *1122* "got out here": NYT 5/10/61; Halberstam 135. "will fly in": NYT 5/13/61; *Life* 10/26/62. *1123* eighteen months: NYT 10/27/72; *Thousand* 322, 539, 541; NYT 5/5/61. *1123n* draftees to Vietnam: WA 1972 88. *1124* not "lose" Indochina: *Thousand* 321; NYT 1/13/51. "your free people": Sorensen 651; *Thousand* 536. "he had inherited": T 1/29/73; Sorensen 652; *Thousand* 537–38. *1125* "matter of time": Theodore White *1968* 16; *Thousand* 542; T 8/4/61. was "essential": Halberstam 173; Sheehan 81. *1126* included troops: Sorensen 650; NYT 5/13/61, 11/10/61; Halberstam 129. "in this period": NYT 3/15/61, 3/16/61, 5/5/61, 5/9/61; Sheehan 80. chance of success: Sheehan 81, 97. *1127* imbued with it: Langer 1271; NYT 10/17/61; *Tragedy* 399; *Thousand* 544. "technological capacity": NYT 1/10/62; *Thousand* 542. political considerations: Sorensen 655. *1128* Viet Cong as heroes: NYT 10/16/61; Sorensen 655; Sheehan 142–43. "to take another": Sorensen 653; *Thousand* 547. *1129* "crazier than hell": Halberstam 177; NYT 11/10/61; Sorensen 655; Halberstam 174. making headway: NYT 2/9/62, 2/14/62; Halberstam 186. *1130* also glowed: NYT 3/27/62; *Current Biography* 1969; Langer 1271; Sheehan 111; NYT 7/25/62. *that* would mean:

Thousand 548–49; Halberstam 203. *1131* (MACV): *Thousand* 549–50; NYT 7/24/62; FitzGerald 165.

XXVIII NOW THE TRUMPET SUMMONED US AGAIN
(*pages 1133–1194*)

1133 hundred years earlier: NYT 5/26/61. *1134* "was always time": O'Donnell and Powers 16–17; Halberstam 286. in the Kremlin: T 4/21/61, 4/28/61. the year before: Sidey 112; NYT 4/12/61. *1135* pre-eminence particularly: Sorensen 524 ff. *1136* "rocket thrust": Sidey 114–15. at 18,000 mph: NYT 4/11/61; Sidey 111–12; NYT 4/12/61. *1137* " 'the Motherland Knows' ": NYT 4/12/61, 4/15/61; T 4/21/61. "of the world": NYT 4/13/61; T 4/21/61. *1138* "Can we leapfrog?": Sidey 129–32; NYT 4/14/61. "nothing more important": NYT 4/14/61; *Newsweek* 7/7/69; Sidey 131. *1139* "Spacetown, U.S.A.": NYT 5/6/61. "safely to earth": NYT 5/26/61; T 6/2/61; Armstrong et al 18. on its way: Sorensen 526. *1140* "taken care of": WA 1963 150; NYT 7/22/61, 8/6/61; WA 1962 128; NYT 2/21/62, 3/4/62; T 3/2/62. "I am go": NYT 2/21/62. *1141* "will you?": T 3/2/62, 2/22/62, 2/21/62. "saw of it": NYT 2/21/62, 2/24/62. *1142* they prayed: NYT 2/22/62. "hot in there": NYT 2/24/62, 2/21/62. *1143* "person ever is": NYT 2/24/62. "needed boost": NYT 2/23/62, 2/27/62, 3/2/62. *1144* into orbit: T 5/12/61; Armstrong et al 17; T 3/12/62. Houston he said: NYT 8/6/61. "peace are there": Sorensen 527–28. freedom riders: NYT 5/5/61. *1145* "the right road": ibid; *Alabama* 221. at the riders: NYT 5/5/61, 5/15/61. *1146* very advanced: NYT 3/6/61. the blacks ask?: Guthman 157; NYT 6/25/60. *1147* "We will move": NYT 5/7/61; Guthman 162. *1148* It did: NYT 5/9/61; Guthman 166–67; NYT 5/14/61; T 5/26/61. *1149* rescued the others: NYT 5/15/61. *1150* was a joke: NYT 5/20/61; Guthman 167; WM/David E. Swift; T 5/26/61. in their credit: NYT 5/16/61. *1151* of the President: NYT 5/20/61, 5/16/61. than Birmingham: NYT 5/21/61, 6/1/61. *1152* heard him say: NYT 5/21/61. "are there now": Guthman 171. "had broken down": NYT 5/21/61; T 6/2/61. *1153* simply proved wrong: NYT 5/21/61. again. Then: NYT 5/22/61. "these people are": Guthman 172–73. *1154* law enforcement officers: NYT 5/22/61. *1155* "survive politically": Schlesinger *Thousand* 936; Guthman 178. succeed Patterson: NYT 11/7/62. in waiting rooms: NYT 5/30/61; *Thousand* 936; NYT 9/23/61; Sorensen 478. *1156* time by then: Angoff and Mencken; NYT 6/25/61. of the century: Guthman 180–81. *1157* of Mississippi: *Thousand* 940; NYT 9/28/62. "of tyranny": NYT 6/26/62, 9/13/62, 9/11/62, 9/14/62. *1158* or make one: NYT 11/4/59. "about a year": Guthman 185. "take a judge?": *Thousand* 941; NYT 9/26/62. *1159* "to believe that": NYT 9/14/62, 9/21/62; Guthman 189. "rights of one": NYT 9/25/62. *1160* "Communists!": NYT 9/26/62. "how it goes?": NYT 10/1/62. "will be there": NYT 9/30/62; *Thousand* 943. *1161* turned back again: NYT 9/28/62; Lord 165–66. point of violence: Guthman 93. *1162* $5,000 a day: NYT 11/16/62. " 'poultry program' ": *Thousand* 944. *1163* broken his word: NYT 10/1/62. in "this afternoon": Lord 196. a campus booth: NYT 10/1/62; Sorensen 287. *1164* "had no choice": NYT 10/1/62, 10/5/62; Lord 209. "uphold that honor": NYT 10/1/62. *1165* "to those fellows": NYT 10/1/62; T 10/12/62; NYT 10/5/62. "trigger-happy" marshals: NYT 10/2/62; T 10/12/62; NYT 10/2/62. *1165n* Guthman 204. *1166* "lives, nigger?": Guthman 203; T 10/12/62; *Thousand* 948. Franklin Roosevelt: NYT 10/2/62, 10/7/62, 1/21/63, 4/12/63, 12/7/62. *1167* "of hate": NYT 6/14/69. "joined chapters": NYT 5/14/61; T 2/16/61. *1168* "muzzle the military": *Thousand* 743; NYT 7/21/61; *Thousand* 1020; *Life* 2/9/62. official proclamation: *Thousand* 1020. "against Communism": *Life* 2/9/62; NYT 10/29/61. *1169* "mental breakdown": DeMott 72, 77. "afternoon comes": *Thousand* 752, 753; NYT 11/17/61, 10/28/61. *1169n* "passersby notice it": NYT 4/4/65. *1170* "the Promised Land": *Thousand* 755. about the President: NYT 9/18/62: *Thousand* 755. *1171* *Air Force One:* Sidey 272–73. do it, too: NYT 1/23/61. *1172* backed down: Sidey 289–90. *1173* didn't believe her: ibid 272; *Thousand* 643; NYT 6/21/62. "is from within": Sorensen 335. Soviet technicians: Abel 6, 929–30. *1174* on the island: NYT 10/11/62. to worry about: Abel 1. *1176* "days ahead": ibid 17. the next morning: ibid 21. calls his brother: ibid 32. *1177* "planning Pearl Harbor": Robert Kennedy 31; Abel 31–42 passim. *1178* are under way: NYT 10/18/62; Abel 43–53 passim. *1179* American tradition: Robert Kennedy 36; *Thousand* 806–807. blockade of Cuba: NYT 11/3/62; Abel 54–68 passim. taken first: NYT 10/20/62. *1180* the stations why: Abel 69–75 passim. weapons in Cuba: Robert Kennedy 48–49. *1181* until Tuesday: NYT 10/23/62. on alert: Abel 76–83 passim. *1182* "flaming crisis": Abel 84–94 passim. "greatest urgency": NYT 10/23/62. six days ago: Robert Kennedy 55. *1183* "Western Hemisphere": NYT 10/23/62. hastily disperses them:

Abel 95–109 passim. *1184* the Security Council: NYT 10/24/62. *1185* "caught the burglars": *Thousand* 817; Abel 123–38 passim. before noon: NYT 10/24/62. ready for war: NYT 10/27/62. is unimportant: NYT 10/25/62, 10/27/62. *1186* "have been impeached": Robert Kennedy 17. "just blinked": ibid 71; Abel 123–38 passim. *1186n* "strain and hurt": Robert Kennedy 69–70. *1187* "of the sites": NYT 10/26/62; Abel 139–51 passim. submit to searches: NYT 10/27/62. *1188* be found: NYT 10/28/62; Abel 152–64 passim. *1189* "very hazardous course": NYT 10/28/62; Robert Kennedy 96–97. committed to Castro: Robert Kennedy 109; NYT 11/3/62. capital be evacuated: Abel 165–79 passim. 40,000 to 50,000: *Thousand* 831. "the Soviet Union": NYT 10/29/62. *1190* "nuclear test ban": Abel 180–86 passim. "go with you": Abel 186; Robert Kennedy 110. *1190–1194* Goldmark portrait: *Current Biography* 1940, 1950; *Newsweek* 1/28/48; T 12/4/50; NYT 12/17/67, 11/27/70, 7/26/71, 8/2/71, 8/3/71.

XXIX DON'T LET IT BE FORGOT
(*pages 1195–1235*)

1195 star role: Fab VII 138; Sorenson 489–90. *1196* ready for him: WA 1963 102; NYT 4/3/63. King's, followed: NYT 4/13/63, 4/14/63, 5/10/63, 4/13/63. *1197* for reinforcements: NYT 5/3/63, 5/8/63, 5/4/63, 5/8/63. base he wished: T 5/24/63; NYT 5/13/63, 5/24/63, 5/19/63. *1198* southern jails: NYT 5/16/63; Sidey 396; NYT 5/16/63, 5/1/63, 5/13/63; Sorensen 489; Schlesinger *Thousand* 964. way of thinking: Guthman 207–208; NYT 1/5/63. *1199* "hands in despair": Guthman 207–10. "risk I take": NYT 5/19/63, 5/22/63, 6/6/63. *1200* on television: NYT 6/10/63. obstruct them: Guthman 215; WA 1963 106, 109–10; Sidey 399–403; *Thousand* 964; Sorensen 493. *1201* "central government": NYT 6/12/63. Wallace walked away: Sidey 401; NYT 6/12/63. "suspected were there": NYT 6/13/63; Guthman 217–18. *1202* "life or law": *Thousand* 965; NYT 6/12/63. "can treat them": NYT 6/12/63; *Thousand* 966. encourage violence: Fab VII 144; Sidey 405; Sorensen 504–505; *Thousand* 969. *1203* HOUSING—NOW!: NYT 8/29/63. Lincoln Memorial . . . "of their character": ibid. *1204* didn't regret it: Sorensen 505. "nonviolent talk": NYT 5/10/63; Fab VII 154; NYT 5/15/63. *"fire next time!"*: Guthman 219–20. *1205* meeting deteriorated: NYT 9/19/63. youth repeated it: Guthman 220–21; *Thousand* 962–63. fire next time: Guthman 221. *1206* the *Honey Fitz:* Sidey 405; NYT 5/30/63. "than I have": NYT 5/14/63. *1207* pay that price: Sidey 416; *Thousand* 978; Halberstam 295. "our own attitude": *Thousand* 891; NYT 6/11/63; Sorensen 733. "since Roosevelt": Sorensen 733. *1208* "beneficial to all": *Thousand* 920. in 1964, either: Sidey 388. to the 88th: *Thousand* 713. *1209* "serves his nation": NYT 6/29/63, 6/6/63; *Thousand* 881; NYT 10/27/63; John Kennedy 817. *1210* he said Texas: NYT 9/4/63, 9/9/63, 10/4–11/63, 10/13/63. "guarded optimism": John Kennedy 11; NYT 1/15/63; *Thousand* 982–86; NYT 4/23/63. *1211* "McNamara says so too": *Thousand* 983. struggle between them: Halberstam 250. a "barbecue show": NYT 5/10/63, 6/11/63; Sorensen 657. *1212* "for all time": NYT 6/16/63, 7/8/63; John Kennedy 459–64. shocking treachery: NYT 6/28/63. *1213* "Binh Xuyen in 1955": Halberstam 261; *Thousand* 989–90; NYT 8/16/63. he tell them?: NYT 8/23/63. "afraid to die": Halberstam 264–65. *1214* "same country?": ibid 266–67; *Thousand* 993. "promptly as possible": Halberstam 283–84; NYT 10/3/63; Goldman *Tragedy* 399. *1215* "people of Vietnam": T 11/8/63; Sorensen 658–59; NYT 9/3/63; Halberstam 272. were reporters: NYT 10/8/63; *Thousand* 966; Halberstam 283; T 11/8/63; NYT 11/1/63; T 10/25/63. *1216* was imminent: NYT 11/3/63, 11/2/63, 11/13/63; T 11/8/63. "fatherland's interests": NYT 11/2/63, 11/3/63. *1217* stabbed repeatedly: NYT 11/2/63; T 12/6/63. but not here: NYT 11/14/63; *Thousand* 997; T 12/6/63; Halberstam 291–93. stable government: NYT 11/3/63. "so could he": NYT 12/3/63; Halberstam 286. *1218* Thursday, November 21: NYT 11/25/63. January 1, 1964: Rose Mary Woods to the author 8/4/64. *1219* effete snobs: NYT 11/20/62; T 11/22/63. (would end publication): NYT 10/16/63; Fab VII 130. "foe of Communism": T 11/22/63. "waning confidence": NYT 5/5/63, 11/16/63. *1220* "been an assassin": NYT 11/16/63. "Spindle, or Mutilate": NYT 9/4/63, 9/4/64; Customer Relations Office, U.S. Post Office, New York City; NYT 7/1/63; Sally Morgan to the author 4/10/63. ("I got screwed"): *Life* 8/23/63; NYT 4/21/63; Greene 115. *1221* in Bryan, Texas: T 6/21/63, 12/6/63, 11/22/63, 1/21/73. *1222* "break up anyway": T 11/22/63, 10/20/63. "of a man": T 10/5/63. in fact ignored: NYT 11/17/63; T 11/22/63. *1223 in the Rain:* NYT 4/14/64. by its publisher: NYT 8/25/63, 5/27/63, 8/9/63, 1/31/63, 8/25/63, 1/31/63, 9/8/63. *1224* (ten inches) reason: NYT 11/18/63, 12/30/63, 11/11/63, 4/25/63; T 11/22/63. and "Standing There": NYT 12/1/63; T 11/15/63; DeMott 78. of self-destruction: NYT 11/3/63. *1225* heavily chaperoned: NYT 11/22/63, 12/7/63, 2/2/63.

the labor movement: John Brooks *Leap* 157–58. nearly ten million: Bird 257. "that is rising": ibid 267. *1226* dollars a year: Servan-Schreiber 83–90. upper middle class: *Leap* 138. million Americans: Theodore White *1964* 365. *1227* political potency: *Leap* 11; NYT 4/16/63; *Leap* 104. across state lines: *Leap* 120–21. *1228* those with it: Manchester *Death* 189–91. in guerrilla warfare: T 9/10/73, 11/22/63. British prostitute: Sidey 390–91; NYT 11/13/63, 6/7/63. *1229* "the New Frontier": *Reader's Digest* November 1963; NYT 11/24/63. at his funeral: NYT 11/14/63; T 11/22/63. *1230* "a stiller town": *Death* 462. *1231* Arlington National Cemetery: ibid 190. *1232* DEAD JT135PCS: NYT 11/23/63; *Death* 221. began to build: NYT 11/23/63. field of stars: *Death* 442. *1233* "one more awful": NYT 11/25/63. "separate and apart": NYT 11/26/63; *Death* 572, 627. *1234* "deep for tears": NYT 11/29/63, 12/25/63, 12/4/63, 12/11/63, 5/5/65. "for their own": NYT 11/30/63; *Death* 642.

XXX THE LONG ARM
(*pages 1237–1274*)

1237 "domestic policy": WM/Dwight D. Eisenhower 8/27/64. *1238* "his administration": Goldman *Tragedy* 20–21, 523; NYT 1/30/67, 10/15/64, 10/3/68. as he spoke: NYT 1/5/65, 11/1/64, 8/20/64. *1239* the United States: NYT 1/21/64; T 1/5/68; NYT 8/28/64; Theodore White *1964* 413. of its region: NYT 2/4/64; *Tragedy* 525. *1240* over a thousand: NYT 1/19/66, 4/28/64; Theodore White *1968* 103–104. *1241* much more damaging: NYT 11/18/67, 4/23/64. "comfort the country": Carpenter 31, 331. *1242* to the men's: NYT 6/20/64, 7/7/64. proved nothing: NYT 9/15/64; *Tragedy* 228–29; NYT 9/25/64. *1243* "after the Kennedys": *Tragedy* 78–79. his calendar: NYT 7/31/64; Theodore White *1964* 315–16, 317. *1244* "side with me": NYT 7/31/64; *Tragedy* 199. American provocation: White *1964* 328; W 1964 152–56. supporting hostilities: NYT 8/8/64, 8/5/64. *1245* one of them: W 1968 46; NYT 8/3/64. *1246* from the coast: NYT 8/2/64, 8/4/64, 8/3/64. North Vietnamese forces: NYT 2/21/68; W 1964 152–56, 1968 46. "no wider war": Halberstam 413–14; *Tragedy* 175; NYT 3/6/64. *1247* "jungles of Vietnam": NYT 7/16/64; WA 1965 41. Fulbright agreed: NYT 8/6/64. *1248* "a fisheries bill": NYT 8/6/64, 8/8/64. *1249* "historic mistake": Fab VII 204; *Tragedy* 181–83; Halberstam 442; NYT 8/7/64; Halberstam 419. stimulate backlash: Theodore White *1964* 281; NYT 5/6/64, 5/20/64, 7/20/64; WA 1965 166. *1250* killing him instantly: White *1964* 266–68; NYT 7/17/64. million dollars: NYT 7/21/64. and white policemen: White *1964* 278; Graham and Gurr 51; *Collier's* 86. *1251* "Burn, baby, burn!": *Tragedy* 172–73. "Freedom Summer" of 1964: NYT 8/3/64, 8/29/64, 8/17/64, 4/3/64. *1252* "television sets": White *1964* 269; John Brooks *Leap* 291–92; *Economist* 5/10/69; White *1964* 277. reached Jackson: NYT 11/8/64; White *1964* 220–22; NYT 6/21/64. had been burned: NYT 6/23/64; W 1964 233–35. in the North: NYT 11/8/64. *1253* rounds of ammunition: NYT 7/9/64. *1254* being murdered: NYT 7/11/64; W 1964 233–35. any trouble: W 1967 210–11; T 10/27/67; NYT 12/5/67, 1/17/65, 2/26/65, 10/29/66, 10/21/67. defense challenges: NYT 2/26/65, 12/14/64; W 1967 220–21. *1255* "me a nigger": W 1967 211. the maximum: NYT 10/21/67; T 10/27/67; NYT 12/30/67. *1256* deep right field: NYT 7/16/64. the real thing: *Leap* 319; White *1964* 458. said *he* was: NYT 1/4/64, 1/28/64, 3/11/64, 1/3/64, 6/7/64. *1257* "is no virtue!": White *1964* 151, 153; NYT 5/31/64, 6/3/64, 7/17/64. *1258* no one was home: White *1964* 252. "Nazi methods": NYT 7/15/64. "it's the truth": ibid. in the black: NYT 7/18/64; White *1964* 377–79. *1259* platform with him: NYT 8/13/64. he was right: *Daedalus* Spring 1958; White *1964* 359. he was wrong: NYT 11/1/63. *1260* to the end: T 11/1/63. KNOW HE MIGHT: White *1964* 384; NYT 9/7/64; White *1964* 387. of greater interest: NYT 10/23/64; White *1964* 361. *1261* public toilet: NYT 6/19/64; White *1964* 385, 375. He declined: T 10/23/64; NYT 10/15/64; WA 1964 175–76. *1262* votes, elsewhere: NYT 10/14/64, 10/16–17/64, 8/15/64; *Tragedy* 359–61. standing ovation: *Tragedy* 245–48. *1263* "war in Asia": NYT 9/26/64. "trying to do": NYT 9/29/64; *Tragedy* 235–37, 412; NYT 10/22/64, 10/28/64. "or themselves": NYT 10/22/64. "all Americans": NYT 10/28/64. *1264* the following summer: *Tragedy* 224, 412–13. for the Democrats: NYT 11/4/64; WA 1964 40; NYT 12/15/64; W 1964 206–10. prove valuable: NYT 11/6/64, 11/11/64. *1265* seemed symbolic: NYT 9/9/64, 10/4/64, 12/30/64, 12/31/64. were under way: NYT 11/4/64, 11/5/64. lost their appeal: W 1966 38; NYT 6/16/64. *1266* House to protest: W 1966 38. "and stop it!": NYT 1/3/65, 2/14/65, 11/21/64; Raskin "Berkeley." *1267* "to our terms!": NYT 12/4/64. putting them on: W 1965 54; NYT 3/11/64. was often electrifying: Fab VII 181. *1268* "American it is": ibid 246. Laff's and Friday's: Ruffner 939; Fab VII 238. *1269* husband or wife: Fab VII 248. *of Man* (1964): T 4/8/66. going to jail: NYT 12/20/63; W 1965 96–97. *1270* in Las

Vegas: WA 1967 93; W 1965 186; Fab VII 172; W 1965 206. Soviet Aeroflot: W 1966 98; Graham and Gurr 187–89; NYT 2/4/65; Bird 235; W 1965 114, 254, 1966 234. for commuters: NYT 1/26/64; Fab VII 109; NYT 12/23/65, 3/3/65; *Life* 5/14/65. *1271 New, Pussycat?:* W 1965 252, 254; Fab VII 177. peepshow sex: Kendrick 509. director of CORE: NYT 7/15/65, 1/24/65; W 1965 24, 1967 47, 120; NYT 4/23/64. *1272* "to get known": NYT 7/17/66; WA 1967 78, 85; NYT 8/2/66; W 1966 232. "is my President": NYT 4/15/63; W 1966 208; NYT 4/28/67; W 1965 107, 264; Fab VII 178. told reporters: NYT 2/18/64, 3/15/64, 1/4/67, 3/26/64, 10/5/65; Carpenter 48; Halberstam 533. *1273* IS A JUNKIE: NYT 11/20/66, 2/4/66; W 1966 239–41; T 3/18/66, 10/10/66. "of public demand": Fab VII 132; NYT 3/22/66; W 1966 164. lost in 1964: W 1966 228–29; NYT 11/9/66; WA 1967 42; NYT 11/10/66; *Tragedy* 334. *1274* "from Saigon": *Tragedy* 498; Fab VII 204–205. the Vietnamese mire: Halberstam 630; NYT 11/28/67, 2/28/66, 4/26/66; *Tragedy* 509; NYT 4/24/66, 9/16/65, 12/15/66, 4/1/66; Halberstam 628. "kind of Presidency": *Tragedy* 378.

XXXI A DREAM OF GREATNESS—AND DISENCHANTMENT
(*pages 1275–1325*)

1275 the Fair Deal: NYT 1/21/61; W 1965 9; Goldman *Tragedy* 281–82; NYT 1/13/66. *1276* Truman years: NYT 9/7/45; Truman II 29. patients a week: *Tragedy* 285 ff; W 1966 136; NYT 7/31/65, 1/2/66. retired, beside him: NYT 1/13/65; *Tragedy* 307; NYT 4/12/65. *1277* since the 1930s: NYT 5/26/65, 7/3/64, 8/11/65, 4/1/65, 12/2/65; W 1965 187; *Tragedy* 332–33. seasonal workers: NYT 3/5/61; *Economist* 5/10/69; W 1966 204–205; NYT 5/19/65. *1278* in the state: W 1966 204–206, 1965 172. throughout the country: Carpenter 15; *Tragedy* 335. "and enjoy myself": NYT 11/5/64; *Tragedy* 259–60. convert his critics: NYT 10/23/65; *Tragedy* 333; W 1965 187; NYT 5/19/65. *1279* to reassure people: NYT 6/26/67; W 1967 118–21; *Life* 6/30/67; T 6/30/67. "if less briefly": *Tragedy* 439. fly at him: ibid 446. *1280* "*do* they want?": W 1965 168; NYT 10/6/65; *Tragedy* 337. "interested any more": NYT 12/1/67; Halberstam 429. "a war on?": *Tragedy* 451. do just that: NYT 11/1/64, 12/25/64. *1281* William Childs Westmoreland: Halberstam 129; NYT 11/17/61, 11/15/64. Ho Chi Minh Trail: Halberstam 355–57, 503, 507–508. *1282* rise above 100,000: NYT 2/26/64, 2/15/65; Halberstam 369–70; NYT 1/8/65. sight of blood: NYT 2/3/65. were wounded: NYT 2/6/65; W 1965 28–30. *1283* "will do that": W 1965 30; Halberstam 521. in North Vietnam: Halberstam 534; Theodore White *1968* 23; NYT 2/11/65. girls with flowers: Halberstam 237; NYT 7/4/65, 2/28/65, 3/9/65. *1284* "how to think": NYT 2/10/65, 5/16/65, 4/24/65. deputy prime minister: Fab VII 205; Halberstam 351; NYT 2/22/65; W 1965 32; NYT 6/31/65. *1285* "internal cohesion": Fab VII 205; W 1965 32; NYT 6/25/65. blacked them out entirely: NYT 5/10–12/65; W 1965 119, 223; Kendrick 16–17. number had tripled: NYT 3/31/65, 4/1/65, 6/26/65, 5/8/65, 6/17/65. *1286* do the job: NYT 6/10/65, 6/14/65; Halberstam 582–83. the White House: *Tragedy* 409; *N.Y. Herald Tribune* 5/23/65; *Washington Post* 12/5/65. *1287* like central Texas: W 1965 119; NYT 4/8/65; *Tragedy* 407–409. terms before Christmas: NYT 4/20–21/65; Halberstam 576–78. *1288* and F-111s: Halberstam 575–79; W 1965 123. "than inform it": Halberstam 584. outweighed their misgivings: NYT 7/21/65; W 1965 123; NYT 7/22/65, 7/29/65; Halberstam 597, 600. *1289* "no one else": Theodore White *1968* 23; NYT 7/24/65; Halberstam 599; NYT 7/29/65; W 1965 118. it was impossible: Halberstam 594, 595, 606, 614. *1290* "for the war": ibid 604–10. *1291* runaway inflation: NYT 5/13/68. to top 200,000: Halberstam 594, 602; NYT 8/4/65; W 1965 26. and 137 wounded: W 1965 240; NYT 12/4/65. "doesn't it?": NYT 10/9/66; Halberstam 550. *1292* in Ann Arbor: *Tragedy* 432, 433; NYT 10/17/65, 10/16/65; WA 1966 87; W 1965 222–23. "be our own": Fab VII 206. on the tracks: W 1965 222–23. *1293* into human torches: NYT 10/16/65, 9/1/65, 11/3/65. murdering children: Fab VII 218–19. "the United States": W 1965 223. *1294* author Michael Harrington: NYT 11/28/65. 66th Regiment: NYT 11/21/65; WA 1966 90–91. bring in transports: Halberstam 612–14. *1295* as the referee: NYT 8/27/66; W 1965 240; NYT 12/4/66; Halberstam 167; WA 1966 91; Halberstam 621; W 1965 238–39. "get the word": NYT 12/3/66; *Tragedy* 322; NYT 3/16/65. *"we shall overcome":* NYT 3/16/65. *1296* Negroes as equals: NYT 8/29/65, 4/20/65; W 1966 168. in "reparations": NYT 2/22/65; W 1965 35–37, 153; *Collier's* 90; W 1969 194. *1297* as a "fascist": Theodore White *1968* 102; NYT 11/25/65. revive their campaign: *Tragedy* 308–11; WA 1966 48, 52; NYT 1/2/65, 3/12/65. *1298* symbol of oppression: NYT 3/7/65, 3/8/65. "Turn Me Around": NYT 3/8/65, 3/9/65. "constitutionally permissible": NYT 3/10/65. *1299* a little garter: *Tragedy* 315; NYT 3/19/65, 3/21/65; W 1965 52–53. the second murder: NYT

3/22/65; *Tragedy* 324; NYT 3/26/65. *1300* police help: NYT 3/26/65. the maximum: NYT 8/21/65, 10/1/65, 3/11/65, 11/30/65; W 1965 196–99; NYT 8/21/65, 12/4/65. *1301* now erupted: WA 1966 57–58; NYT 3/16/65; *Economist* 5/10/69; NYT 5/27/66. "see your I.D.": NYT 6/12/66. *1302* locally as Watts: NYT 8/12/65; W 1965 138. looting the stores: NYT 8/12/65. *1303* under control: NYT 8/11/65, 8/14/65. "mutilate themselves": NYT 8/14/65; W 1965 142. *1304* 45 million dollars: NYT 8/19/65. in the South: *Collier's* 88; W 1965 154–55; NYT 7/20/65. *1305* a real torch: NYT 8/20/65, 12/7/65; *Collier's* 89; Theodore White *1968* 26–27. riots that year: *Collier's* 88–89; Theodore White *1968* 201; NYT 3/16/66; W 1966 166–71. into its own: NYT 10/17/66. *1306* in their ranks: NYT 8/27/66, 8/31/66, 1/4/66. peppered with birdshot: NYT 6/6/66; W 1966 112; NYT 6/7/66. another Selma: NYT 6/7/66, 6/8/66. *1307* "Black power!": W 1964 233–35; NYT 12/5/64. "black . . . power!": NYT 9/10/66. *1308* "Black power!": W 1966 166–67. "rights and integration": NYT 7/3/66. "I don't like": W 1966 116. *1309* were not there: NYT 6/24/66, 6/27/66. polls, he lost: W 1966 124; NYT 12/6/66, 6/1/66. was absurd: Fab VII 155; Graham and Gurr 671. *1310* "committed to error": NYT 9/22/66; W 1966 171; NYT 10/14/66, 10/15/66. "declared war": *Life: The 1960s;* W 1967 106; Theodore White *1968* 201; T 1/5/68; NYT 6/16/67. *1311* "intolerance of it": W 1966 226–29; NYT 10/15/66; *Economist* 5/10/69. years after Watts: NYT 5/27/66; T 6/14/68, 6/21/68; W 1968 119. critics at home: *Collier's* vi; W 1967 34; Sheehan 513. *1312* be 100,000 men: NYT 6/30/66; W 1966 126, 251, 249. "come in view": Sheehan 512; W 1967 248–49; NYT 4/29/67. *1313* "a good question": W 1966 249, 1967 92–94; Halberstam 641; W 1967 91; Halberstam 642. Garrison troops: W 1967 90. *1314* "11,000 miles away": W 1967 94, 1966 32, 1967 251. off in handcuffs: WA 1968 75–76; W 1967 95; Rovere *Muddy* 8, 9; *Collier's* 158; W 1967 132; NYT 6/4/67. *1315* to the war: NYT 12/11/67; W 1967 41–43; Graham and Gurr 515–16; NYT 10/22/67; W 1967 252; Fab VII 212. in Toronto: NYT 11/11/67; W 1967 252. *1316* the people were: W 1966 36; NYT 12/1/66. Viet Cong colors: *Life: The 1960s;* NYT 3/19/67, 10/18/66, 10/23/66, 10/22/66; W 1966 189; *U.S. News and World Report* 10/31/66. *1317* FBI checks: WA 1967 69; NYT 5/18/66; *Tragedy* 499–502. worse and worse: Kendrick 24; NYT 11/28/67, 1/25/67; Halberstam 640; Fab VII 30. the White House: Fab VII 97–98. *1318* obeyed them: NYT 11/7/67; *Tragedy* 511; Halberstam 640. *1319* of Minnesota: *Tragedy* 265; NYT 8/18/67; WA 1968 85. "is your enemy": *Collier's* 196, 422; NYT 5/13/67. the new goal: W 1967 143–44; NYT 7/21/67. "black revolution": NYT 8/16–21/67. *1320* "black man's resolution?": Walter Goodman "Black Power." *1321* the word Negro: ibid. snapped his picture: NYT 6/23/73, 4/17/65, 1/14/66, 1/7/66, 8/25/66, 6/14/67, 7/1/67, 12/9/67, 7/8/67, 9/22/67, 11/8/67, 9/7/67, 6/25/67; W 1966 24, 1970 137. John Bell Williams: NYT 9/27/67, 8/8/67, 1/11/67, 6/24/67, 11/8/67. *1322* "right at home": Good "Odyssey." catastophe of 1967: WA 1968 77; NYT 4/9/67. vast junkyard: NYT 1/3/67. *1323* Wednesday, July 12: W 1967 137–39; Theodore White *1968* 201. since Watts: NYT 7/13/67, 7/14/67, 7/18/67. *1324* of Negro homes: NYT 7/24/67, 8/7/67; Fab VII 148. Cambridge (Maryland): NYT 7/28/67. *1325* "as cherry pie": W 1967 142–43. Richard M. Nixon: NYT 5/23/68.

XXXII UP AGAINST THE WALL
(*pages 1327–1374*)

1327 "of 'The Establishment' ": Galbraith *State* 330–31. electrical power: NYT 11/10/65. *1328* oscillate wildly: Rosenthal and Gelb 17; W 1965 206–13. *1329* blackout had begun: Rosenthal and Gelb 85; W 1965 208–13; NYT 11/16/65. too, had vanished: NYT 11/13/65. *1330* led to safety: *Life* 11/19/65. increase in births: NYT 8/10–12/66. candle in his hand: Rosenthal and Gelb 37. *1331* "no electricity": ibid 66. "sharpener still worked": NYT 11/16/65; Rosenthal and Gelb 12. *1332* NED LUDD Clerk: Graham and Gurr 19. *1333* mayor was defeated: Theodore White *1968* 426–27; *Middletown Press* 10/7/70; NYT 6/11/66, 6/7/67; Fab VII 267. federal government alone: Servan-Schreiber 103, 134. *1334* in an automobile: Galbraith *Affluent* 171–72; Schlesinger *Crisis* 264. it was true: *Affluent* 171–72; Bird 150. *1335* whatever the weather: NYT 7/21/68. "Eyes of Texas": W 1965 78–81. garrison-prison state: Goldman *Tragedy* 257; Arendt 451–59. *1336* "handle current traffic": Whyte 441; Bird 262; *State* 45. now inconceivable: Servan-Schreiber 55–61. *1337* "flatulent indigestion": *Statistical Abstract of the United States 1969* table 891 p. 590; *Time* editors 73. of her mother: *Time* editors 72–73. *1338* "him to act": *State* 243, 247; Mowry 206, 207. *1339* the technostructure: *Time* editors 66; *State* 82. planned economy: NYT 1/21/68. *1340* hope of gain: Servan-Schreiber 81, 141. were expensive: Mowry 200; Servan-Schreiber 134–35. *1341* is doubtful:

Servan-Schreiber 163. of autonomy: John Brooks *Leap* 250; *State* 13, 14; Servan-Schreiber 81–82, 141. *1342* interest group: W 1965 55, 1969 122; Servan-Schreiber 69. "overthrow it": Theodore White *1968* 424; "Democracy Has/Hasn't a Future." *1343* "economic goals": *Leap* 269; *State* 20; *Affluent* 249. the United States: NYT 4/24/68, 7/1/68, 3/9/68. Old Wabash: NYT 6/10/68. *1344* "blasé permissivists": *New Republic* 9/12/70; NYT 10/26/69; W 1970 202. "or leprosy": W 1969 122; Fab VII 59. domestic policies: *New Republic* 9/12/70; NYT 7/24/70; *U.S. News and World Report* 8/3/70. *1345* been the point: *Leap* 327. "stomach! Wild!": NYT 8/25/64, 10/22/67, 3/15/70. deemed nonviolent: Theodore White *1968* 214. *1346* coast to coast: NYT 12/4/64, 3/11/65; W 1965 44–45; NYT 3/9/65. "today's foxhole": NYT 9/2/65, 4/15/65, 3/9/65, 2/21/65, 3/24/65, 2/23/67; Graham and Gurr 516–17; NYT 1/21/67; *Leap* 241. "blow is college": NYT 10/9/69. *1347* San Francisco State: NYT 11/10/66; *Collier's* 79; NYT 1/21/67; W 1967 128; NYT 11/27/68. "education for?": W 1969 125; NYT 3/12/67; W 1969 128. an abyss: *Collier's* 79. *1348* "toward youth": *Life: The 1960s; Hartford Courant* 11/8/69. "for self-discipline?": Hechinger and Hechinger 177. *1349* ("damn damn"): Fab V 28. "company comes": Lifton 80. "see what happens": Murray "Individuality"; *Leap* 145–46. "cudgels of thrift": *Leap* 233; Riesman 100; Packard *Wilderness* 25. *1350* "lunch and supper": *Leap* 233, 145; *Saturday Evening Post* 10/28/61. "Isn't Everybody?": Hechinger and Hechinger 121; Fab V 128; Hechinger and Hechinger 116–17; *Seventeen* September 1961. *1351* "the puh-lain": Hechinger and Hechinger 94, 89–90; *Life: The 1960s;* W 1966 149. said acne: NYT 10/5/70; W 1966 150; NYT 8/5/66, 8/12/66; W 1966 163; Fab VI 148–49, V 28. *1352* Gallup reported: Lifton 111–12; T 2/23/68; Loth 15; Hechinger and Hechinger 165. would have thought: Hechinger and Hechinger 16. leisure class: W 1969 185; NYT 7/7/69. after 10 P.M.: W 1970 128. *1353* and furniture: T 2/23/68; Loth 101–102, 106–107. $3,000 and $10,000: NYT 9/5/63; T 9/13/63. 65 policemen: *Leap* 234; *Hartford Courant* 7/29/70. *1354* worth of damage: W 1969 119. girls' dormitory: *Hartford Courant* 3/13/70. *1355* swaying visibly: NYT 1/27/66; W 1970 192–94; *Wilderness* 353; W 1970 193; *Hartford Courant* 1/27/70; W 1970 190. Aunt Tom: W 1967 258; *Wilderness* 85; NYT 3/29/67; *Life* 2/3/67; *Wilderness* 81; NYT 2/10/66. *1356* higher up: W 1970 193; Friedan 249; Riesman 156; W 1967 134; NYT 6/16/67. "do we get laid?": *Wilderness* 144–45, 60–61. *1357* (under any circumstances): NYT 10/8/68. full body flush: NYT 1/19/68, 11/22/69, 1/14/69, 10/9/69. *1358* toddlers watched: DeMott 53; *Collier's* 131. lost their novelty: W 1968 186–90; NYT 7/30/68, 10/1/68, 9/23/68. *1359* is electrocuted: NYT 4/20/69, 2/12/71; DeMott 112; NYT 2/11/68. loops and coils: *Wilderness* 68; NYT 6/1/70. *1360* in 1965: *Wilderness* 250–51; W 1966 62; NYT 3/18/62, 12/20/63; Fab VII 176. key she had: W 1967 258; T 8/9/68. bedroom with whom: *Middletown Press* 3/6/70. *1361* "love in return": *Wilderness* 60. heavy drugs: ibid 149. merely a memory: NYT 9/26/43; T 6/11/45; NYT 4/13/55, 8/25/60; Phillips *Blitz* 358. *1362* (with benzedrine): NYT 4/12/62; T 8/10/62; NYT 12/13/62; *Newsweek* 8/17/70. taken a trip: W 1966 91. continued to spread: NYT 5/29/63. *1363* his mother-in-law: W 1966 91. "afraid of him": ibid; W 1967 197; NYT 5/14/67. *1364 Great Notion* (1964): *Collier's* 76; NYT 2/4/62, 7/27/64. "nationwide avalanche": *Collier's* 73. *1365* a single year: W 1967 196, 1970 254. Politics of Free: Sanders 39; W 1967 197. other narcotics: Fab VII 84; *Hartford Courant* 8/10/70; W 1967 200. *1366* "the hard way": W 1967 196. up at dawn: ibid 198; NYT 5/5/67. *1367* deformed infants: NYT 6/28/67, 5/5/68. and up yours: NYT 6/8/66; *Collier's* 79. "to get in?": W 1967 201. *1368* from a cliff: NYT 5/31/67. Charles Manson: Sanders 39–40; NYT 8/19/67; Sanders 37–38. *1369* Lower East Side: NYT 10/9/69, 10/10/69. *1369–1370* in a corner . . . "anything to us": W 1967 202; T 10/20/67, 10/13/67; NYT 10/16/67. *1370* "the flowers gone?": T 10/13/67; NYT 10/5/67. *1370–1374* Hess portrait: NYT 9/28/69; Theodore White *1968* 32; Stan Lehr and Louis Rossetto Jr. "The New Right Credo–Libertarianism" *New York Times Magazine* 1/10/71; *Newsweek* 9/29/69; Murray Kempton "Karl Hess: Goldwater Finds His Sorensen" *New Republic* 8/8/64; James Boyd "From Far Right to Far Left–and Farther" *New York Times Magazine* 12/6/70.

XXXIII THE YEAR EVERYTHING WENT WRONG
(*pages 1375–1410*)

1375 was assassinated: T 12/13/68; NYT 12/31/68, 1/10/68, 6/2/68, 4/17/68, 12/21/68, 8/17/68, 1/17/68. Biafra starved: NYT 7/16/68, 8/2/68, 1/23/68, 12/13/68. *1376* "cease and desist?": NYT 9/19/68; Fab VII 176; NYT 9/13/67, 2/15/68, 7/16/68, 7/19/68; T 5/17/68. straight or sick: NYT 9/13/68. the runner-up: NYT 5/5/68, 5/8/68, 12/24/68. off North

Korea: NYT 11/21/68, 5/28/68. *1377* and hand grenades: W 1969 110; NYT 1/24/68. He failed: W 1968 22; NYT 1/25/68. *1378* possible to forget: NYT 1/25/68, 1/27/68. "to the coast": W 1968 84. in South Vietnam: NYT 2/5/68; W 1968 84. million dollars: NYT 1/30/68. *1379* "not been achieved": T 3/1/68; NYT 1/25/68; W 1968 28–35. now this: *Life: The 1960s*. by Clark Clifford: Halberstam 647–48; NYT 4/26/68, 1/19/68. *1380* even want it: W 1968 35, 88; T 4/12/68. three years earlier: T 4/19/68; NYT 4/11/68; T 5/10/68. Complete Victory: W 1968 247–48. *1381* "clean for Gene": Theodore White *1968* 79. "the United States": NYT 3/16/68, 3/17/68. said. Then . . . "as your President": NYT 4/4/68, 4/1/68; T 3/22/68, 4/5/68. *1382* Republican vote: NYT 4/3/68. "civil rights progress": NYT 4/28/68, 5/29/68; W 1967 97. for his head: NYT 4/5/68. *1383* defending Khe Sanh: NYT 4/6/68. "free at last": W 1969 74; NYT 4/10/68. *1384* never discovered: NYT 4/20/68; T 7/26/68, 7/9/68, 3/11/69; WA 1970 913. primaries, California: TC 1968 34; NYT 5/8/68; W 1968 119; NYT 5/15/68, 6/5/68. *1385* "struggle for it–": NYT 6/6/68. a bear hug: TC 1968 34. little Arab had: ibid; W 1968 118, 115; NYT 6/6/68. *1386* trembling voice: NYT 6/5/68, 6/7/68; T 6/14/68; NYT 6/9/68. "to shining sea!": NYT 6/9/68. University of Miami–: W 1968 100. *1387* especially wicked: TC 1968 227–33; NYT 4/24/68; T 5/24/68. They were wrong: W 1968 101–103; TC 1968 227–33. *1388* able to muster: NYT 5/18/68, 5/12/68. "humanistic society": W 1968 101. *1389* as the Nazis: NYT 4/25/68, 4/30/68. *1390* to be tidy: NYT 4/27/68, 4/28/68. the United States: NYT 10/6/68. "revolutionary America": W 1968 101, 1970 58; NYT 3/8/68. *1391* vending machine: T 3/23/70. *1392* "catastrophe happens": Servan-Schreiber xvi; W 1968 53. *1393* remained aloof: T 4/19/68; NYT 5/26/68. compromise with him: NYT 1/4/66; T 2/4/66; W 1966 15–19. deliberate slowdown: T 2/16/68; NYT 2/3/68, 11/2/68; T 11/1/68; NYT 10/20/68, 10/24/68, 9/10/68, 10/15/68, 7/4/68. *1394* and San Francisco: NYT 3/20/70, 3/18/70, 3/20/70. their grievances: NYT 3/27/70, 4/3/70. take Fortas's place: NYT 6/22/68, 6/27/68. *1395* remained in office: NYT 7/17/68. *1396* before the Court: NYT 7/20/68, 9/14/68. be less liberal: NYT 10/3/68; *Life* 5/9/69; W 1968 210–12, 1969 77–79. *1397* the fans laughed: NYT 2/22/68. among the suggestions: NYT 10/18/68. 1.2 million dollars: NYT 10/21/68; W 1968 201. *1398* "marriage, and death": W 1968 201. eyes of God: NYT 11/25/68, 11/7/68, 10/24/68. Agnew of Maryland: NYT 3/14/68, 2/29/68, 3/22/68, 5/1/68. *1399* "shipbuilding firm": NYT 8/9/68; T 8/16/68. IS ROSEMARY'S BABY: T 10/25/68. *1400* "driving dream": W 1968 151; Theodore White *1968* 243; NYT 8/6/68; McGinniss 77; NYT 8/12/68. in Chicago: W 1968 151. confront them: NYT 8/21/68, 8/26/68. *1401* too risky: NYT 8/29/68. "accept the truth": ibid. *1402* North Side traffic: W 1968 161–66. "no march today": NYT 8/24/68. had parents, too: NYT 8/26/68: *New Republic* 9/7/68. *1403* of the suite: Theodore White *1968* 308–309; NYT 8/31/68. elated Richard Nixon: Theodore White *1968* 320. "cries too much": T 9/20/68; *Columbia Journalism Review* Winter 1969. *1404* Johnson and Daley: T 9/20/68. "the world": NYT 9/10/68. "of a box!": McGinniss 31. *1405* Thomas E. Dewey: NYT 10/1/68; WA 1972 19. *1406* Houses on the Hill: NYT 11/6/68, 11/7/68. *1407* could be shelved: T 7/25/69; NYT 8/17/73. "survival itself": *Middletown Press* 1/28/70; WM/Eric Sevareid 6/24/70. *1408* powder and dirt: Theodore White *1968* 196. ever lay ahead: W 1968 181. *1409* seemed inevitable: T 6/21/68; NYT 1/19/68, 10/17/68, 7/24/68. nothing happened: W 1968 181; NYT 5/23/68; T 10/4/68, 9/20/68; NYT 9/28/68. *1410* was a heroine: T 9/13/68; Theodore White *1968* 200; T 5/24/68. into the middle class: T 3/1/68; NYT 6/24/73.

XXXIV THE RISE OF THE SILENT MAJORITY
(*pages 1415–1457*)

1415 ten times: NYT 12/12/68; T 12/20/68. *1416* doubted their integrity: T 12/20/68. *1417* 528 million people: NYT 7/21/69. "decade is out": TA 180–81; NYT 1/28/67. miles away: NYT 7/17/69. picking up speed: W 1969 141–46. *1417–1420* general sources: W 1969 141–52; TA 180–89. *1418* had made it: NYT 7/25/69. July 20, 1969: NYT 7/21/69. *1419* "fine, sandy particles": NYT 7/21/69. "for all mankind": ibid. on the moon: NYT 7/22/69. *1420* on their horns: W 1969 147; NYT 7/25/69. "erode its dignity": NYT 7/23/69, 7/26/69; W 1969 188; TA 11. *1421* where they lay: NYT 8/3/69. "and dignity": NYT 8/4/69, 2/7/69, 3/22/69, 6/24/69. quiet good taste: TA 10. *1422* "have described it": W 1969 189. *1423* "was a success": NYT 2/6/69, 8/7/70; TA 10–11; NYT 11/22/69, 5/15/72. presidential seal: TA 18; NYT 1/19/69, 4/28/69, 6/15/69. heating systems: T 8/20/73, 9/10/73; *Middletown Press* 10/18/73. *1424* "government will listen": NYT 1/21/69. violent contention: TA 11; NYT 6/17/70; *Economist* 5/10/69. *1425* city commissioners: NYT 11/5/69; *Hartford Courant*

5/4/70; NYT 5/28/69. hundred billion dollars: TA 22. *1426* "throughout the land": NYT 2/5/69; W 1969 246–48; Chayes and Wiesner 2; NYT 6/5/69. Carswell of Florida: NYT 6/4/69, 11/22/69, 12/5/69; W 1969 237. *1427* "we want to": NYT 1/22/70, 3/17/70; W 1970 96–99. "the Constitution": NYT 4/9/70. "can do that": NYT 11/4/69; Pater and Pater 244. *1428* his first target: WA 1970 40; NYT 11/14/69. "absolute loyalty": NYT 11/14/69, 11/21/69. Vietnam War: NYT 4/5/69. than an hour: NYT 3/11/69, 4/18/69, 3/1/69. *1429* she vanished: NYT 6/18/69, 8/30/69, 8/23/69, 8/22/69, 8/23/69, 11/11/69, 11/13/69, 12/1/69, 5/15/69. a huge toilet: NYT 3/22/69; TA 134. very far away: *Middetown Press* 10/6/69; NYT 10/6/69. *1430* Vietnam War: WA 1970 907; W 1969 122–28; NYT 3/23/69. university budget: NYT 2/14/25. *1431* poor man's Harvard: NYT 4/23/69, 5/10/69, 6/3/69. ROTC at Harvard: NYT 4/10/69, 4/11/69, 5/12/69. Perkins quit: NYT 6/1/69. *1432* student riots: NYT 2/18/69, 2/28/69. "a good man": NYT 5/7/69; TA 32; NYT 6/5/69. school integration: NYT 8/27/69. *1433* "for the law": TA 12; NYT 10/30/69. called Woodstock: Theodore White *1972* 149. dollars a ticket: *Life: The 1960s;* W 1969 180–85; TA 112–23; NYT 7/17/69. *1434* a disaster: NYT 8/16/69, 8/17/69. "police work": *Life: The 1960s;* NYT 8/18/69. Woodstock Nation: NYT 8/17/69. Iron Butterfly: NYT 8/31/69, 9/1/69. *1435* in the black: W 1969 181. to death: NYT 8/10/69, 12/3/69; Sanders 356. *1436* one hundred pounds: T 1/27/67; W 1969 31–35; TA 112–23; Galbraith *State* 354. *1437* a ski resort: TA 113; NYT 4/28/69, 1/28/69. desert country: NYT 1/16/70; W 1969 125–26, 35; NYT 1/18/70, 4/29/69. a wide area: W 1969 33–34; TA 113–15; NYT 1/31/69. *1438* "black crayon": NYT 2/5/69. at three million: NYT 2/9/69. runaway well: NYT 2/8/69. *1439* House of Pancakes: TA 176. *1440* huge, flag-draped coffins: NYT 11/16/69; W 1969 220–22. "as peaceful": NYT 11/15/69; W 1969 222. *1441* leader's briefing: "The Massacre at Mylai" *Life* 12/5/69; TA 62; W 1969 257, 1971 68–72; NYT 9/7/69. loaded and ready: NYT 1/29/69. *1441–1442* in after them . . . "ditch and fired": W 1971 69–70. *1442* "this all day": W 1969 257. the killings: NYT 11/21/70. "his own safety": NYT 11/19/70, 11/24/70. *1443* "Republic of Vietnam": NYT 5/20/71; T 5/31/71; NYT 9/28/70. "of its policies": NYT 9/7/69. *1444* "go marching on": T 4/12/71; NYT 3/30/71, 4/9/71. "public clamor": NYT 4/4/71. "suffered enough": NYT 12/22/68. *1445* off the coast: NYT 5/7/69. "statement of fact": NYT 5/5/69. storm the hill: W 1969 94–95; TA 220; W 1969 95. *1446* "going to get": W 1969 95. of U.S. soldiers: NYT 5/22/69. "inflationary recession": TA 58. *1447* on June 8: NYT 2/19/70; TA 54. "election of 1972": NYT 6/20/69; W 1969 96; TA 59. at any time: NYT 10/5/69. *1448* Vietnamese din: NYT 8/26/69. " 'up, and olé' ": TA 13; WA 1971 78; TA 36, 37; W 1969 85–87, 240. 1449 to fly east: NYT 11/1/69. in prison: W 1970 231; NYT 11/12/70. *1450* Nantucket Sound: NYT 7/20/69; TA 212; W 1969 26; TA 29; W 1969 249–53; W 1970 74–78. turn Kennedy took: NYT 1/6/70, 4/30/70. *1451* "to the surface": NYT 1/6/70; W 1970 76. *1451–1453* "this happened" . . . "see me": TA 28–29; W 1969 249–53, 1970 75–78. *1453* senatorial duties: NYT 7/26/69. *1454* "asked of me": NYT 4/30/70. from Richard Nixon: NYT 7/22/70. *1454–1457* Spock portrait: *Current Biography* 1956, 1969; *Newsweek* 9/15/69; *Time* 5/31/68; Jessica Mitford *The Trial of Dr. Spock* New York 1969.

XXXV NATTERING NABOBS

(*pages 1458–1497*)

1458 inauspicious start: NYT 1/22/70, 2/23/70; W 1970 13–15. *1459* "Get Involved": NYT 3/8/70, 9/20/70, 11/15/70, 6/1/70, 3/29/70, 3/15/70. Satan himself: NYT 1/19/70, 1/25/70, 3/15/70. "irregular ones": NYT 10/31/69; W 1970 173–75. *1460* the Pueblo tribe; NYT 12/5/69, 12/3/70. quietly shelved: NYT 7/28/70, 1/28/70; W 1970 23. *1461* to turn back: NYT 1/13/70, 3/18/70, 6/5/70, 4/14/70; W 1970 61–68. on May 27: *U.S. News and World Report* 7/27/70; NYT 6/22/70, 5/28/70. visiting Manhattan: NYT 5/19/70; W 1970 122. *1462* seemed insatiable: W 1970 110–13; *Middletown Press* 7/3/70. "amount of money": NYT 2/19/70; W 1970 113; NYT 3/18/70. *1463* that to herself: *Newsweek* 11/12/73; WA 1958 47. "something you are": *Hartford Courant* 6/23/69; W 1970 38. by SIECUS: T 7/25/69. *1464* "Mating Toads": W 1970 39. *1465* as "counterrevolutionary": NYT 8/27/70; W 1970 193; Hargreaves 559; NYT 3/17/70. "*Playboy* promotes": W 1970 191. *1466* saleswoman $3,461: Hargreaves 561–63. "as men": ibid 564–65; NYT 3/23/72. *1467* buy their wares: W 1970 53–54; NYT 6/12/60, 2/26/70. "of prosperity": W 1970 54. *1468* in the closet: NYT 10/25/70, 1/1/71. Macon, and Athens: NYT 5/13/70. of the year: NYT 6/10/70, 6/17/70; W 1970 122. *1469* "of the establishment": W 1970 179. wealthy families: NYT 3/13/70; *Hartford Courant* 3/13/70; NYT 3/12/70; W 1970 58; NYT 3/7/70. *1470* in

Manhattan: NYT 3/9/70; *Hartford Times* 3/14/70; NYT 7/12/72; W 1970 58. contain the charges: NYT 3/7/70; *Life* 3/27/70. to collapse: NYT 3/18/70. *1471* no details: *Life* 3/27/70. "changed radically": NYT 10/21/70, 10/23/70. *1472* police station: T 10/17/69, 6/29/70, 8/31/70, 10/26/70, 1/4/71; W 1970 153–57, 1972 66–67, 118–21. subsequent interest: NYT 9/14/70. *1473* a boring case: NYT 8/8/70. "them off!": T 8/17/70. yelled, "Halt!": ibid. *1474* were dead: *Life* 8/21/70. in San Quentin: NYT 10/14/70. pistol from it: W 1971 168–71; NYT 8/22/71, 8/18/71, 1/6/72; W 1971 168–71. cut him down: NYT 8/22/71. *1475* "irretrievable love": NYT 9/4/71, 8/29/71; W 1971 168–71. *1476* "to be caught": NYT 6/5/72; W 1972 119. "the whole world": NYT 6/5/72. *1476–1480* general source (Chicago Seven): W 1970 34–37. *1477* said the lawyer: NYT 3/21/69. Richard G. Schultz: W 1970 34; NYT 2/7/70. judicial chaos: NYT 12/13/69. *1478* Chicago Seven: NYT 10/30/69, 10/31/69, 11/4/69, 11/6/69. *1479* "can't help yourself": NYT 9/9/73; W 1970 36. *1480* days in prison: NYT 2/16/70; W 1970 34–37. "the very beginning": NYT 2/19/70, 2/21/70; W 1972 225. "incompetently presented": NYT 9/9/73. *1481* "in new bottles": NYT 4/2/70, 7/2/70. included hospitals: W 1970 239; NYT 10/24/70. *1482* of each other: W 1970 239; FitzGerald 448–49. *1483* fourteen months: NYT 5/1/70; Chester et al 24–25. and 4,911 wounded: W 1970 236. never been any: FitzGerald 186. *1484* "mutual incomprehension": NYT 5/10/70, 5/9/70; Chester et al 29. "by five o'clock": NYT 5/7/70, 11/26/70. *1485* "reestablish order": T 11/12/73; NYT 5/16/70, 10/2/70, 7/30/70. *1486* Middlefield, Connecticut: W 1970 161. and it happened: NYT 7/17/70, 7/31/70. *1487* exchanging a word: NYT 8/2/70, 8/3/70. muggy Friday night: T 5/18/70. to the ground: NYT 5/4/70, 5/3/70. *1488* "harbor in America": NYT 5/4/70, 5/7/70. back at students: NYT 9/2/73. *1489* "on a trigger": W 1970 187. "killing us!": NYT 5/15/70. their victims: W 1970 187; NYT 5/5/70. handed down: NYT 5/19/70, 3/30/74. *1490* "irresponsible sort": NYT 10/17/70, 5/5/70; W 1970 190. "any protest": NYT 5/15/69. *1491* Tom Charles Huston: Chester et al 39–40. living abroad: ibid 41. *1492* John Wesley Dean III: W 1973 150. "security matters": NYT 6/29/71, 7/22/73. "Mr. Young—Plumber": Lukas "The Story So Far." *1493* "Power-pack Agnew": Theodore White *1972* 49. black officeholders: ibid 62; NYT 3/6/70. *1494* "and hardworking": W 1970 24, 202. *1495* "all about": NYT 12/14/70. "the United States": T 11/16/70; NYT 10/30/70; Theodore White *1972* 295. *1496* "in yourself": NYT 11/3/70; Theodore White *1972* 76. repudiate them: T 11/16/70. Lowell P. Weicker Jr.: T 11/16/70; NYT 11/5/70, 11/4/70. be decided: Chester et al 11–13; NYT 11/4/70. *1497* one-term President: Theodore White *1972* 59; Chester et al 12–13. a hard-liner: NYT 7/22/73, 1/6/61. alike, as CREEP: NYT 1/6/71; Chester et al 1; Theodore White *1972* 49; Lukas "The Story So Far."

XXXVI THE DIVIDED STATES OF AMERICA
(*pages 1499–1541*)

1499 roaring ovation: NYT 1/21/71. *1500* to prevent infection: NYT 4/4/71, 4/11/71. *1501* electricity sixfold: Theodore White *1972* 155–56, xv. pay a fine: NYT 2/5/71, 3/2/71, 9/18/71, 7/24/71, 3/3/71. becoming a democracy: W 1971 174. *1502* (his province chief): NYT 9/4/67, 6/3/71. "Vietnamese people": NYT 8/20/71, 8/6/71, 8/21/71. in grave doubt: NYT 9/2/71, 8/21/71, 8/23/71, 10/4/71. *1503* "Lam Son 719": Theodore White *1972* 58; W 1971 239–41; FitzGerald 553–55. "the Americans": NYT 2/9/71; FitzGerald 554. country's intelligence: NYT 4/8/71. *1504* "the government": NYT 4/24/71, 4/25/71, 4/27/71; Chester et al 31–34. more aggressively: NYT 4/27/71. *1505* as red tape: NYT 1/15/69; Chester et al 8. Memorial Stadium: W 1971 84–87; NYT 5/3/71, 5/4/71. "national monument": NYT 5/6/71. *1506* Nazi Brownshirts: Chester et al 34; NYT 5/11/71. reveal more: W 1971 182–85; NYT 6/13/71. "or promulgated": NYT 4/28/65. *1507* government's credibility: NYT 6/13/71. alongside it: NYT 6/15/71. *New York Times:* NYT 6/16/71. in the minority: NYT 6/27/71. *1508* finally decided him: ibid. "harm my country": NYT 6/24/71, 6/29/71, 12/31/71. *1509* as Plumbers: Chester et al 52. "that would ensue": NYT 7/5/71; Chester et al 54–55. *1510* dubious sources: NYT 7/11/71. bank accounts: *Nation* 12/20/71; NYT 9/28/71; T 12/17/73. *1511* of the decision: NYT 6/11/69, 3/2/72. "antitrust cases": T 11/12/73. "understanding" with Geneen: Chester et al 147. *1512* "cannot be known": NYT 3/1/72. "of a victory": ibid. 224 million dollars: T 5/21/73, 6/11/73; NYT 11/28/72. *1513* prosecute anyway: NYT 5/23/73. a government job: NYT 2/1/72; Chester et al 85. *1514* and imprisonment: Theodore White *1972* 89. Hunt an idea: NYT 9/17/71; Lukas "The Story So Far." *1515* it in Barker's: NYT 12/16/73. to the CIA: Lukas "The Story So Far." *1516* "not traceable": Chester et al 68. Cuban informant: ibid 70. *1517* "congressional investigation": ibid 69. *1518* for his office: Lukas "The Story So Far." was mounting: ibid. plain: Attica: T 9/27/71; W 1971 160–67; WA 1972 964; NYT 11/18/73, 9/10/71. *1519* clubs "nigger sticks": T 9/27/71. "our accursed lot": ibid. *1520* "so well organized": NYT 9/27/71, 8/22/71; W 1971 161. "like here—animals": NYT 9/17/71; T 9/27/71. *1521* along the way: T 9/20/71. *1522* tried for murder: T 9/27/71. call their bluff: NYT 9/14/71. *1523* "those oppressed": NYT 9/10/71. bitter fruit: T 9/27/71; NYT 9/11/71. the committee: NYT 9/11/71. *1524* "Black Panther party": NYT 7/13/71. *1525* with Oswald: NYT 9/12/71. to death: NYT 9/13/71, 9/14/71. *1526* victims with them: W 1971 165. "the offensive!": NYT 9/14/71; W 1971 160. "was killed": NYT 9/14/71. *1527* "on the ground": NYT 11/18/73. carried guns: NYT 9/14/71. "any circumstances": NYT 9/17/71; W 1971 167. *1528* AT THIS INSTITUTION: NYT 9/17/71; T 9/27/71. home and abroad: T 8/30/71. *1529* of Red China?: NYT 4/1/71; T 4/26/71; W 1971 62–66; WA 1972 950; NYT 4/7/71. Americans "unprincipled": NYT 4/8/71. *1530* "bloodthirsty gangsters": NYT 4/10/71. "come in batches": NYT 4/14/71, 4/15/71. *1531* President himself: NYT 4/14/71. by his illness: T 7/26/71; NYT 7/16/71. *1532* "our old friends": NYT 7/17/71; T 3/6/72; NYT 7/16/71; WA 1972 957. Cowan in Nagoya: NYT 10/27/71; W 1971 204–205; NYT 10/28/71. *1533* was heartening: NYT 8/5/71; T 8/30/71. its own money: W 1971 193. deficit since 1893: T 8/30/71. *1534* flooded with them: W 1971 194. *1535* jump accordingly: ibid 216; NYT 7/29/71. price increases: T 8/30/71. *1536* over the freeze: W 1971 217; NYT 8/15/71. into the system: NYT 8/17/73. *1537* "American people": NYT 10/8/71; WA 1972 964. he could get: NYT 3/23/72, 12/24/71. *1538–1541* Nader portrait: *Current Biography* 1966; T 4/26/71, 7/31/72, 3/14/71, 3/21/71, 10/29/73; *Life* 1/21/72; Charles McCarry *Citizen Nader* New York 1972.

XXXVII PRIDE GOETH
(*pages 1542–1588*)

1542 Phineas Taylor Barnum: Kronenberger 25. *1543* his best friend: T 5/29/72; NYT 5/22/72, 5/31/72, 9/6/72, 4/18/72, 11/36/70, 4/17/72. "my memoirs?": W 1972 71; NYT 4/8/72, 3/28/72, 12/9/72, 5/16/72. *1544* getting married: NYT 11/13/72, 11/14/72; T 6/4/73. old-fashioned marijuana: NYT 3/7/69. *1545* homes and schools: NYT 11/15/72, 7/6/72. "human being": W 1972 102–106; NYT 12/8/71, 1/10/72; Fay et al 3–4. *1546* "Western Hemisphere": Fay et al 2–3. "We have proof": Fay et al 5; NYT 12/9/72, 1/11/72. *1547* also been lucky: NYT 2/12/72. his two children: Fay et al 28. *1548* come from Irving: ibid 72. years earlier: NYT 1/29/72. *1549* Helga began: NYT 1/10/72, 1/22/72. like Howard Hughes: Fay et al 179, 181. *1550* one believes him: NYT 1/27/72. "is Helga": Fay et al 189–90; NYT 1/29/72. *1551* fornicatrix of 1972: *Life* 12/29/72; Fay et al 303. vinyl couch: Fay et al 228; NYT 6/17/72. *1552* TRUST COMPANY: Fay et al 204. Chinese calendar: NYT 2/21/72; Theodore White *1972* viii. *1553* Chou took it: W 1972 76–82; T 3/6/72; NYT 2/22/72. official hostess: NYT 2/22/72. *1554* about needles: ibid. the American people: NYT 2/24/72. "kind between people": ibid. *1555* "of the U.S.A.": W 1972 81–82. four years earlier: W 1972 230–35, 1973 1003; NYT 1/26/72. *1556* of Kontum: NYT 4/7/72, 4/20/72. was a failure: NYT 4/22/72. *1557* "their neighbors": NYT 5/9/72. *1558* wanted to make: NYT 5/12/72, 5/13/72, 5/24/72; T 5/22/72. that they cherish: NYT 5/23/72; T 6/5/72; WA 1972 1010; W 1972 82–83; NYT 5/27/72. *1559* for five years: NYT 5/27/72. of the cold-warriors: W 1972 83. synonym: Watergate: NYT 7/22/73. *1560* support of busing: Theodore White *1972* 75; NYT 1/23/72, 2/8/72, 1/11/72, 6/7/72. CREEP's director: NYT 3/5/72, 7/2/72. *1561* "Rose Mary's baby": NYT 6/11/72. by hidden cameras: NYT 6/15/72; Lukas "The Story So Far." *1562* try once again: Chester et al 136. his green light: NYT 10/23/72. *1563* national convention: Lukas "The Story So Far"; Chester et al 152; NYT 9/17/72. of the banquet: NYT 6/19/72; Lukas "The Story So Far." *1564* on Virginia Avenue: Chester et al 156. to try again: Lukas "The Story So Far." *1565* cheap slacks: NYT 6/18/72. under arrest: ibid; Lukas "The Story So Far." *1566* "going to Miami?": Lukas. of the United States: NYT 6/18/72. *1567* "is incredible": Chester et al 165. on the lam: NYT 7/2/72. *1568* "I am ready": Lukas "The Story So Far." "Holy shit!": Chester et al 176. "or condone it": ibid 168. *1569* "big fat wringer": NYT 9/13/72; Chester et al 202. returns from there: NYT 3/15/72, 3/17/72. *1570* to the hall: NYT 8/7/72, 8/23/72. course, the idea: NYT 8/23/72. the other side: NYT 8/25/72. *1571* him the prize: NYT 1/5/72, 1/11/72, 1/19/72, 2/12/72, 1/26/72, 2/12/72. something, big: Theodore White *1964* 129, *1972* 118–19; NYT 1/14/72. was on him: NYT 3/8/72, 3/14/72. *1572* went to Wallace: NYT 3/15/72, 3/22/72, 4/5/72, 4/26/72, 5/5/72, 5/11/72. the nomination: NYT 5/15/72, 5/16/72, 5/17/72,

6/7/72. *1573* "adversary treatment": NYT 5/29/72, 5/31/72, 6/5/72. party's strength: NYT 8/28/68; Theodore White *1972* 29–30. and Chicago: NYT 7/11/72, 6/3/72; Theodore White *1972* 172. *1574* him long before: Theodore White *1972* 166, 161. scuttling Salinger: NYT 7/13/72, 7/14/72, 7/15/72. *1575* credibility fast: NYT 8/17/72; Theodore White *1972* 214. didn't do it: NYT 7/26/72; W 1972 144; NYT 7/26/72. *1576* recover from it: Theodore White *1972* 203; NYT 7/31/72; White *1972* 205–206; NYT 8/6/72. getting 1.8: NYT 11/8/72. one statehouse: NYT 11/9/72. *1577* were felons: W 1972 203–204. the following course: Chester et al 207; NYT 10/5/72; Theodore White *1972* 327. in disgrace: Chester et al 183–84. *1578* and hung up: ibid 191. *1579* "of President Kennedy": NYT 8/29/72. (from Ehrlichman): NYT 8/30/72. Nixon's reelection: NYT 7/2/72; Lukas "The Story So Far." *1580* "may have to": Chester et al 196. already resigned: ibid 198. *1581* ultimate disgrace: NYT 9/16/72; Lukas "The Story So Far"; NYT 10/11/72, 6/30/72. Watergate Five: NYT 12/10/72; Szulc "The Spy Compulsion." "are to go forward": Chester et al 219. *1582* of "higher-ups": ibid 220. "in the fallout": ibid 225–26. *1583* Presidency began: ibid 229. "is at hand": W 1972 233–35; T 12/25/72, 1/1/73, 1/8/73, 1/15/73, 1/22/73, 2/5/73. the war alone: NYT 10/24/72. *1584* would be unavoidable: NYT 12/14/72. "is arrived at": NYT 12/19/72. *1585* "on Christmas Eve": NYT 12/23/72. Le Duc Tho: NYT 12/25/72; T 8/4/52. *1586* to shut up: NYT 12/31/72. *1587* "Peace with honor": NYT 1/24/72; W 1973 9, 13. "probably enduring": NYT 1/24/73. *1588* "to get it": John Brooks *Leap* 13. "into the past": *Leap* 359; Thomas Wolfe *Look Homeward Angel* (foreword); F. Scott Fitzgerald *The Great Gatsby* (conclusion).

EPILOGUE: ECHOES
(*pages 1589–1594*)

1589 "do for myself": NYT 1/21/73. "End racism!": ibid. *1590* in their stead: NYT 1/20/73, 1/21/73. under that President: NYT 1/20/73. *1591* camp at Auschwitz: NYT 1/21/73. opinion of it: ibid. *1592* heckled FDR: *Baltimore Sun* 12/20/51.

BIBLIOGRAPHY

Aaron, Daniel *Writers on the Left* Harcourt, Brace and World, New York 1961

Abel, Elie *The Missile Crisis* Lippincott, New York and Philadelphia 1966 (Bantam, New York 1966)

Acheson, Dean *Present at the Creation: My Years at the State Department* Norton, New York 1969

Adamic, Louis *My America* Harper, New York 1938

Adams, Sherman *Firsthand Report: The Story of the Eisenhower Administration* Harper, New York 1961

Agronsky, Martin, and others, commentary by *Let Us Begin: The First Hundred Days of the Kennedy Administration* Simon and Schuster, New York 1961

Alabama: A Guide to the Deep South, compiled by workers of the Writers Program of the Works Progress Administration in Alabama; Richard R. Smith, New York 1941

Aldridge, John W. "In the Country of the Young" *Harper's Magazine* October–November 1969

Allen, Frederick Lewis *The Big Change: America Transforms Itself 1900–1950* Harper and Row, New York 1952

—— *Only Yesterday: An Informal History of the Nineteen-Twenties* Harper, New York 1931

—— *Since Yesterday: The Nineteen-Thirties in America, September 3, 1929–September 3, 1939* Harper, New York 1940

Alsop, Stewart "The Lessons of the Cuban Disaster" *Saturday Evening Post* June 24, 1961

American Institute of Public Opinion, ed. *The 1954 Pocket Almanac* Pocket Books, New York 1953

"America's Military Decline: Where We'd Stand in a Fight" *U.S. News and World Report* March 22, 1946

Angoff, Charles, and H. L. Mencken "The Worst American State" *American Mercury* September–November 1931

Appleman, Roy E. *The United States Army in the Korean War: South to the Naktong, North to the Yalu (June–November 1950)* U.S. Government Printing Office, Washington 1961

Arendt, Hannah *The Origins of Totalitarianism* Meridian, New York 1958

Armstrong, Neil, Michael Collins, and Edwin E. Aldrin Jr. *First on the Moon* (written with Gene Farmer and Dora Jane Hamblin) Little, Brown, Boston 1970

Arnold, Thurman "How *Not* to Get Investigated: Ten Commandments for Government Employees" *Harper's Magazine* November 1948

Asbell, Bernard *When F.D.R. Died* Holt, Rinehart and Winston, New York 1961

Asch, Berta, and A. R. Magnus *Farmers on Relief and Rehabilitation* (WPA Research Monograph VIII) U.S. Government Printing Office, Washington 1937

Asch, Nathan *The Road* Norton, New York 1937

Bakal, Carl *The Right to Bear Arms* McGraw-Hill, New York 1966

Barnouw, Erik *A Tower in Babel: A History of Broadcasting in the United States* (Volume I, to 1933) Oxford, New York 1966

—— *The Golden Web: A History of Broadcasting in the United States* (Volume II, 1933–1953) Oxford, New York 1968

Barrett, George "Close-up of the Birchers' 'Founder'" *New York Times Magazine* May 14, 1961

——— "Jim Crow, He's Real Tired" *New York Times Magazine* March 3, 1957

Barrett, William "Dialogue on Anxiety" *Partisan Review* March–April 1947

Barth, Alan *The Loyalty of Free Men* Viking, New York 1951

Bell, Daniel, ed. *The Radical Right: The New American Right* Doubleday, New York 1963 (Anchor, New York 1964)

Bell, Jack *The Johnson Treatment: How Lyndon B. Johnson Took Over the Presidency and Made It His Own* Harper, New York 1965

Bendiner, Robert "Great Expectations, a Quarter of a Century Later" *New York Times Magazine* April 26, 1970

Berger, Peter L. and Brigitte "The Blueing of America" *New Republic* April 3, 1971

Bernstein, Irving *The Lean Years* Houghton Mifflin, Boston 1960

Bird, Caroline *The Invisible Scar* McKay, New York 1966 (Pocket Books, New York 1967)

Bishop, Joseph W Jr. "The Warren Court Is Not Likely to Be Overruled" *New York Times Magazine* September 7, 1969

Bliven, Bruce, "Boulder Dam" *New Republic* December 11, 1935

——— "Sitting Down in Flint" *New Republic* January 27, 1937

Bohr, Niels "On Atoms and Human Knowledge" *Daedalus* Spring 1958

Brecher, Edward M., and Consumer Report Editors *Licit and Illicit Drugs: The Consumers Union Report on Narcotics, Stimulants, Depressants, Inhalants, Hallucinogens, and Marijuana–Including Caffeine, Nicotine, and Alcohol* Little, Brown, Boston 1972

Brogan, D. W. *The American Character* Knopf, New York 1944

Brooks, John *The Fate of the Edsel and Other Business Ventures* Harper and Row, New York 1963

——— *The Great Leap: The Past Twenty-five Years in America* Harper and Row, New York 1966

——— *Once in Golconda: A True Drama of Wall Street 1920–1938* Harper and Row, New York 1969

Brooks, Thomas R. "The New Left Is Showing Its Age" *New York Times Magazine* June 14, 1969

——— "Voice of the New Campus 'Underclass'" *New York Times Magazine* November 7, 1965

Brzezinski, Zbigniew "America in the Technocratic Age" *Encounter* January 1968

Burns, James MacGregor *John Kennedy: A Political Profile* Harcourt, Brace, New York 1960

——— *Roosevelt: The Lion and the Fox* Harcourt, Brace, New York 1956

——— *Roosevelt: The Soldier of Freedom* Harcourt Brace Jovanovich, New York 1970

Butz, Otto "Defense of the Class of '58" *New York Times Magazine* May 25, 1958

Buxton, Frank, and Bill Owen *The Big Broadcast 1920–1950* (A new, revised, and greatly expanded edition of *Radio's Golden Age*) Viking, New York 1972

Byrnes, James F. *Speaking Frankly* Harper, New York 1947

Cantril, Hadley *The Invasion from Mars: A Study in the Psychology of Panic, With the Complete Script of the Famous Orson Welles Broadcast* Princeton University, Princeton 1940

Carlson, Avis D. "Deflating the Schools" *Harper's Magazine* November 1933

Carlson, John Roy *Under Cover: My Four Years in the Nazi Underworld of America* Blakiston, Philadelphia 1943

Carpenter, Liz *Ruffles and Flourishes* Doubleday, New York 1970

Chalmers, Allan K *They Shall Be Free* Doubleday, New York 1951

Chambers, Whittaker *Witness* Random House, New York 1952

Chapman, C. C., and others *Crisis–Transportation* Caterpillar Tractor Company n.d.

Chayefsky, Paddy *Television Plays* Simon and Schuster New York 1955

Chayes, Abram, and Jerome B. Wiesner, eds. *ABM: An Evaluation of the Decision to Deploy an Antiballistic Missile System* Signet, New York 1969

Chester, Lewis, Cal McCrystal, Stephen Aris, and William Shawcross *Watergate: The Full Inside Story* Ballantine, New York 1973

Childs, Marquis "Main Street Twenty Years After" *New Republic* January 18, 1933

——— "They Hate Roosevelt" *Harper's Magazine* May 1936

——— "They Still Hate Roosevelt" *New Republic* September 14, 1938

Clark, George R "Beckerstown, 1932: An American Town Faces the Depression" *Harper's Magazine* October 1932

Clay, Lucius D. *Decision in Germany* Doubleday, New York 1950

Cohen, Morris R. "The Future of American Liberalism" in his *The Faith of a Liberal: Selected Essays* Holt, New York 1946

Cohn, David L. *The Good Old Days: A History of American Morals and Manners As Seen Through the Sears, Roebuck Catalog 1905 to the Present* Simon and Schuster, New York 1950

Collier's 1968 Year Book: Covering the Year 1967 Crowell-Collier, New York 1968

Colton, F. Barrows "The Geography of a Hurricane" *National Geographic Magazine* April 1939

Compton, Karl T. "If the Atomic Bomb Had Not Been Used" *Atlantic Monthly* December 1946

Cone, Fairfax M. *With All Its Faults: A Candid Account of Forty Years in Advertising* Little, Brown, Boston 1969

Congdon, Don, ed. *The Thirties: A Time to Remember* Simon and Schuster, New York 1962

Cooke, Alistair *A Generation on Trial: U.S.A. v. Alger Hiss* Knopf, New York 1950

Cowley, Malcolm "The Flight of the Bonus Army" *New Republic* August 17, 1932

Crane, Burton *A Century of Financial Advertising in the New York Times* New York Times, New York 1957

Daniels, Jonathan *The Time Between the Wars: Armistice to Pearl Harbor* Doubleday, New York 1966

Davis, Forrest *Huey Long: A Biography* Dodge, New York 1935

Davis, Kenneth S. *The Politics of Honor: A Biography of Adlai E. Stevenson* Putnam, New York 1967

"Democracy Has/Hasn't a Future . . . a Present" *New York Times Magazine* May 26, 1968

DeMott, Benjamin *Supergrow: Essays and Reports on Imagination in America* Dutton, New York 1969

Didion, Joan "Just Folks at a School for Nonviolence" *New York Times Magazine* February 27, 1966

Donovan, Robert J. *Eisenhower: The Inside Story* Harper, New York 1956

Dorman, Michael *We Shall Overcome: A Reporter's Eyewitness Account of the Year in Racial Strife and Triumph* Dell, New York 1964

Edey, Maitland A., ed. *This Fabulous Century: Sixty Years of American Life* (Volumes IV, 1930–1940, and V, 1940–1950) Time-Life Books, New York 1969

—— *TIME Capsule: A History of the Year Condensed from the Pages of TIME* (Volumes for 1933, 1941 and 1950, published 1967; for 1932, 1939, 1940, 1942, 1943, 1944, 1945, 1956 and 1959, published 1968, and for 1968, published 1969) Time-Life Books, New York

—— *1969: The Year in Review* Time-Life Books, New York 1970

"The Edsel" *Consumer Reports* January 1958

"The Edsel Story" *Consumer Reports* April 1958

Ehrlich, Paul R. *The Population Bomb* Ballantine, New York 1968

"Eight Scientists Protest Thomas Committee's Methods" *Bulletin of the Atomic Scientists* October 1948

Einstein, Albert, as told to Raymond Swing "Einstein on the Atomic Bomb" *Atlantic Monthly* November 1945

Eisenhower, Dwight D. *At Ease: Stories I Tell to Friends* Doubleday, New York 1967 (Avon, New York 1968)

—— *Crusade in Europe* Doubleday, New York 1948

Eisinger, Chester E., ed. *The 1940s: Profile of a Nation in Crisis* Doubleday Anchor Books, New York 1969

Evans, Rowland Jr., and Robert D. Novak "Nixonomics: How the Game Plan Went Wrong" *Saturday Review* July 1971

Farago, Ladislas *Patton: Ordeal and Triumph* Ivan Obolensky, New York 1963

Faulk, John Henry *Fear on Trial* Simon and Schuster, New York 1964

Fay, Stephen, Lewis Chester, and Magnus Linklater *Hoax: The Inside Story of the Howard Hughes-Clifford Irving Affair* Bantam, New York 1972

Federal Aid for Unemployment Relief: Hearings Before a Subcommittee of the Committee on Manufactures, U.S Senate, 72nd Congress, 1st Session, on S.174 and S.262 U.S. Government Printing Office, Washington 1932

Federal Aid for Unemployment Relief: Hearings Before a Subcommittee of the Committee on Manufactures, U.S Senate, 72nd Congress, 2nd Session, on S.5125 U.S. Government Printing Office, Washington 1932

Federal Cooperation in Unemployment Relief: Hearings Before a Subcommittee of the Committee on Manufactures, U S Senate, 72nd Congress, 1st Session, on S.4592 U.S. Government Printing Office, Washington 1932

Fehrenbach, T.R. *F.D.R.'s Undeclared War* McKay, New York 1967

Ferguson, Otis "The Spirit of Jazz" *New Republic* December 30, 1936

Fischer John "Black Panthers and Their White Hero-Worshippers" *Harper's Magazine* August 1970

FitzGerald, Frances *Fire in the Lake: The Vietnamese and the Americans in Vietnam* Little, Brown, Boston 1972 (Vintage, New York 1973)

Fontaine, André *History of the Cold War: From the Korean War to the Present* Pantheon, New York 1969

Frady, Marshall "Gary, Indiana" *Harper's Magazine* August 1969

Friedan, Betty, *The Feminine Mystique* Norton, New York 1963

Fuller, Keith, project supervisor *The World in 1964: History As We Lived It* Associated Press, New York 1965, and similar volumes for 1965 (published 1966), 1966 (1967), 1967 (1968), 1968 (1969), 1969 (1970), 1970 (1971), 1971 (1972), 1972 (1973), and 1973 (1974)

Galbraith, John Kenneth *The Affluent Society* 2nd ed. Houghton Mifflin, Boston 1969

—— *The New Industrial State* Houghton Mifflin, Boston 1967 (Signet, New York 1968)
Garson, Barbara *MacBird!* Grove, New York 1966
Gellhorn, Walter *Security, Loyalty, and Science* Cornell University, Ithaca 1950
Glass, Remley J. "Gentlemen, the Corn Belt!" *Harper's Magazine* July 1933
Gold, Jay, ed. *The Swing Era (1936–1937: The Movies, Between Vitaphone and Video. 1940–1941: How It Was to Be Young Then. 1941–1942: Swing As a Way of Life)* Time-Life Records, New York 1970
Goldman, Eric F. *The Crucial Decade–and After: America, 1945–1960* Vintage, New York 1960
—— *The Tragedy of Lyndon Johnson*, Knopf, New York 1969
Good, Paul "Odyssey of a Man–and a Movement" *New York Times Magazine* June 25, 1967
Goodman, Jack, ed. *While You Were Gone: A Report on Wartime Life in the United States* Simon and Schuster, New York 1946
Goodman, Paul "The Chance for Popular Culture" *Poetry* June 1949
—— *Growing Up Absurd: Problems of Youth in the Organized Society* Knopf, New York 1956 (Vintage, New York 1960)
Goodman, Walter "The Question of Repression" *Commentary* August 1970
—— "When Black Power Runs the New Left" *New York Times Magazine* September 24, 1967
Goodstone, Tony, ed. *1929 Johnson Smith & Co. Catalogue* Chelsea House, New York 1970
Graham, Hugh Davis, and Ted Robert Gurr *Violence in America: Historical and Comparative Perspectives. A Report to the National Commission on the Causes and Prevention of Violence, June 1969* Signet, New York 1969
"The Great American Roadside" *Fortune* September 1934
"The Great Hurricane and Tidal Wave–Rhode Island: September 21, 1938" Providence Journal Company 1938
Greeley, Andrew N. "Turning Off the People" *New Republic* June 27, 1970
Greene, Gael *Sex and the College Girl* Dial, New York 1964
Greenfield, Jeff "A Member of the First TV Generation Looks Back" *New York Times Magazine* July 4, 1971
Griffith, Robert *The Politics of Fear: Joseph R. McCarthy and the Senate* University Press of Kentucky, Lexington 1970
Grosvenor, Gilbert "Washington Through the Years" *National Geographic Magazine* November 1931
Guiles, Fred Lawrence *Norma Jean: The Life of Marilyn Monroe* McGraw-Hill, New York 1969
Gunther, John *Roosevelt in Retrospect: A Profile in History* Harper, New York 1950 (Pyramid 1962)
Guthman, Edwin *We Band of Brothers* Harper and Row, New York 1971
Halberstam, David *The Best and the Brightest* Random House, New York 1972
Hargreaves, Robert *Superpower: A Portrait of America in the 1970s* St. Martin, New York 1973
Harris, Herbert *American Labor* Yale University, New Haven 1939
Hart, *see* Liddell Hart
Hayek, Friedrich A. *The Road to Serfdom* University of Chicago, Chicago 1944
Hechinger, Grace and Fred M. *Teen-Age Tyranny* Morrow, New York 1962 (Fawcett, New York 1963)
Heffernan, Joseph L. "The Hungry City: A Mayor's Experience with Unemployment" *Atlantic Monthly* May 1932
Heinl, Robert Debs Jr. *Victory at High Tide: The Inchon-Seoul Campaign* Lippincott, Philadelphia and New York 1968
Herbers, John "Communiqué from the Mississippi Front" *New York Times Magazine* November 8, 1964
Hersey, John *Hiroshima* Knopf, New York 1946
Hersh, Seymour M. "My Lai: The First Detailed Account of the Vietnam Massacre" *Harper's Magazine* May 1970
Hicks, Granville "On Leaving the Communist Party" *New Republic* October 4, 1939
Hillman, William *Mr. President: The First Publication from the Personal Diaries, Private Letters, Papers and Revealing Interviews of Harry S. Truman* Farrar, Straus and Young, New York 1952
Hiss, Alger *In the Court of Public Opinion* Knopf, New York 1957
Holmes, Clellon "This Is the Beat Generation" *New York Times Magazine* November 16, 1952
Hook, Sidney "The New Failure of Nerve" *Partisan Review* January–February 1943
Howe, Irving "Notes on Popular Culture" *Politics* Spring 1948
Hughes, Emmet John *The Ordeal of Power: A Political Memoir of the Eisenhower Years* Atheneum, New York 1963
"Hurricane Sweeps Across Northeast, Kills Hundreds" *Life* October 3, 1938

Irving, Clifford, with Richard Suskind *What Really Happened: His Untold Story of the Hughes Affair* Grove, New York 1972
Jackson, George *Soledad Brother: The Prison Letters of George Jackson* Coward-McCann, New York 1970
Jeffries, Ona Griffin *In and Out of the White House: From Washington to the Eisenhowers* Wilfred Funk, New York 1960
Johnson, Haynes, and others *The Bay of Pigs: The Leaders' Story of Brigade 2506* Norton, New York 1964
Johnson, Walter *1600 Pennsylvania Avenue: Presidents and the People Since 1929* Little, Brown, Boston 1963
Jungk, Robert *Brighter Than a Thousand Suns: A Personal History of the Atomic Scientists* Harcourt, Brace and World, New York 1958
Kaplan, Abraham "American Ethics and Public Policy" *Daedalus* Spring 1958
Kateb, George "The Political Thought of Herbert Marcuse" *Commentary* January 1970
Kendrick, Alexander *Prime Time. The Life of Edward R. Murrow* Little, Brown, Boston 1969
Kennan, George F. *American Diplomacy 1900–1950* Mentor, Chicago 1951
——— "America's Administrative Response to Its World Problems" *Daedalus* Spring 1958
——— [X] "The Sources of Soviet Conduct" *Foreign Affairs* July 1947
Kennedy, John F. *Public Messages, Speeches, and Statements of the President, January 1 to November 22, 1963* (in *Public Papers of the Presidents of the United States*) U.S. Government Printing Office, Washington 1964
Kennedy, Robert F. *Thirteen Days: A Memoir of the Cuban Missile Crisis* Norton, New York 1969 (Signet, New York 1969)
Khrushchev, Nikita S. *Khrushchev Remembers* Little, Brown, Boston 1970
Kimball, Penn " 'Dream Town'–Large Economy Size" *New York Times Magazine* December 14, 1952
Kinsey, Alfred C. and others *Sexual Behavior in the Human Male* Saunders, Philadelphia and London 1948
——— *Sexual Behavior in the Human Female* Saunders, Philadelphia and London 1953
Kirk, Russell *The Conservative Mind* Henry Regnery, Chicago 1953
Kluckhohn, Clyde "The Evolution of Contemporary American Values" *Daedalus* Spring 1958
——— "Mid-Century Manners and Morals" in *Twentieth Century Unlimited* (ed. Bruce Bliven) Lippincott, Philadelphia 1950
Korn, Jerry, ed. *This Fabulous Century* Volumes VI (1950–1960) and VII (1960–1970) Time-Life Books, New York 1970
Kronenberger, Louis *Company Manners: A Cultural Inquiry into American Life* Bobbs-Merrill, New York 1954
Langer, William L., ed. *An Encyclopedia of World History* Houghton Mifflin, Boston 1968
Lasagna, Louis, M.D. *The Doctors' Dilemmas* Gollancz, London 1962
Lash, Joseph P. *Eleanor and Franklin: The Story of Their Relationship, Based on Eleanor Roosevelt's Private Papers* Norton, New York 1971
Lasswell, Harold D. "The Universal Peril: Perpetual Crisis and the Garrison-Prison State" in *Perspectives on a Troubled Decade: Science, Philosophy, and Religion 1939–1949* (ed. Lyman Bryson, Louis Finkelstein, and R. M. MacIver) Harper, New York 1950
Lattimore, Owen *Ordeal by Slander* Little, Brown, Boston 1950
Laurence, William L. *Dawn Over Zero: The Story of the Atomic Bomb* Knopf, New York 1946
Lear, Martha "The Second Feminist Wave" *New York Times Magazine* March 10, 1968
Leary, John L. Jr. "If We Had the Dole" *American Magazine* December 1931
Leighton, George R. "And If the Revolution Comes . . . ?" *Harper's Magazine* March 1932
Leighton, Isabel, ed *The Aspirin Age 1919–1941* Simon and Schuster, New York 1949
Lerner, Max *Tocqueville and American Civilization* Harper and Row, New York 1966
Lescohier, Don Divance *Working Conditions* (Volume III of *The History of Labor in the U.S. 1896–1932*) Macmillan, New York 1935
Leuchtenburg, William E., ed. *Franklin D. Roosevelt: A Profile* Hill and Wang, New York 1967
Levine, Mark L., George C. McNamee, and Daniel Greenberg, eds. *The Tales of Hoffman, Edited from the Official Transcript* Bantam, New York 1970
Levinson, Leonard Louis *Wall Street: A Pictorial History* Ziff-Davis, New York 1961
Lewin, Nathan "Kent State Revisited" *New Republic* August 8 and 25, 1973
Liddell Hart, B. H. *History of the Second World War* Putnam, New York 1970
Liebling, A. J. *The Press* Ballantine, New York 1961
——— "The Red Blonde Spy Queen" *New Yorker* August 28, 1948
Life, special double issue, *The 1960s: Decade of Tumult and Change*, vol. 47, no. 13
Lifton, Robert Jay, ed. *The Woman in America* Beacon, Boston 1965
Lilienthal, David E. *This I Do Believe* Harper, New York 1949
Lilly, Doris "Jackie's Fabulous Greek" *Look* June 30, 1970
Lindley, Betty and Ernest K. *A New Deal for Youth: The Story of the National Youth Administration* Viking, New York 1938

Lippmann, Walter *The Cold War: A Study in U.S. Foreign Policy* Harper, New York 1947
Lipset, Seymour Martin, and Earl Raab "The Non-Generation Gap" *Commentary* August 1970
Long-term Economic Growth 1860–1965 (U.S. Department of Commerce, Bureau of the Census) U.S. Government Printing Office, Washington 1966
Lord, Walter *The Past That Would Not Die* Harper and Row, New York 1965
Loth, David *Crime in the Suburbs* Morrow, New York 1967
Love, Gilbert "College Students Are Beating the Depression" *School and Society* June 10, 1933
Lukas, J. Anthony "The Story So Far" *New York Times Magazine* July 22, 1973
—— "The Story Continued" *New York Times Magazine* January 13, 1974
Lynd, Albert *Quackery in the Public Schools* Little, Brown, Boston 1950
Lynd, Robert S. and Helen Merrell *Middletown in Transition: A Study in Cultural Conflicts* Harcourt, Brace and World, New York 1937
MacLeish, Archibald "The Irresponsibles" *Nation* May 18, 1940
Mailer, Norman *Miami and the Siege of Chicago: An Informal History of the Republican and Democratic Conventions of 1968* Signet, New York 1968
—— "The Steps of the Pentagon" *Harper's Magazine* March 1968
Manchester, William "The Great Bank Holiday" *Holiday* February 1960
—— *The Death of a President, November 20–November 25, 1963* Harper and Row, New York 1967
—— "Our War in the Pacific" *Holiday* November 1960
—— *Portrait of a President: John F. Kennedy in Profile* Little, Brown, Boston 1962
Marcuse, Herbert *One-Dimensional Man: Studies in the Ideology of Advanced Industrial Society* Beacon, Boston 1964
Markel, Lester *World in Review* Rand McNally, New York 1972
Marshall, E. Kennerly Jr. "Historical Perspectives in Chemotherapy" in *Advances in Chemotherapy* (Volume I ed. Abraham Goldin and Frank Hawking) Academic Press, New York 1964
—— "The Revolution in Drug Therapy" *Johns Hopkins Magazine* June 1955
Marshall, George C. *European Initiative Essential to Economic Recovery* (Department of State Publication 2882, European Series 25) U.S. Government Printing Office, Washington 1947
Mauldin, Bill *Back Home* William Sloane, New York 1947
—— *Up Front* Holt, New York 1945
Mazo, Earl *Richard Nixon: A Political and Personal Portrait* Harper, New York 1959
McCarry, Charles *Citizen Nader* Saturday Review Press, New York 1972
McCarthy, Joe *Hurricane!* American Heritage Press, New York 1969
—— *The Remarkable Kennedys* Dial, New York 1960
McGinniss, Joe *The Selling of the President 1968* Trident, New York 1969
McLuhan, Marshall *The Gutenberg Galaxy: The Making of Typographic Man* Signet, New York 1962
—— *Understanding Media: The Extensions of Man* McGraw-Hill, New York 1964
McMahan, Harry W. " 'Best of the Year' TV Commercials" *Advertising Age* December 16, 1963
Mellor, William Bancroft *Patton: Fighting Man* Putnam, New York 1946
Mencken, H. L. *Newspaper Days 1899–1906* Knopf, New York 1945
Meryman, Richard "George McGovern Talks" *Life* July 7, 1972
Michael, Paul, ed. *The American Movies Reference Book: The Sound Era* Prentice-Hall, Englewood Cliffs, N.J. 1970
Michener, James A. *America vs. America: The Revolution in Middle-Class Values* Signet, New York 1968
Millis, Walter, ed. *The Forrestal Diaries* Viking, New York 1951
Mills, C. Wright *White Collar: The American Middle Classes* Oxford, New York 1951
Milstein, Tom "A Perspective on the Panthers" *Commentary* September 1970
Minehan, Thomas *Boy and Girl Tramps of America* Farrar and Rinehart, New York 1934
Mitchell, Broadus *Depression Decade: From New Era Through New Deal, 1929–1941* Rinehart, New York 1947
Mitford, Jessica *The Trial of Dr. Spock* Knopf, New York 1969
Modell, John "American Concentration Camps" *Pennsylvania Gazette* February 1974
Moley, Raymond *The First New Deal* Harcourt, Brace and World, New York 1966
Mooney, Booth *The Lyndon Johnson Story* Farrar, Straus, New York 1956
Moorehead, Alan *The Traitors* Scribner, New York 1952
Morison, Samuel Eliot *History of United States Naval Operations in World War II* (15 volumes) Little, Brown, Boston 1947–1962
—— *The Two-Ocean War: A Short History of the United States Navy in the Second World War* Little, Brown, Boston 1963
Morris, Richard B. *Encyclopedia of American History* Harper and Row, New York 1965
Mowry, George E. *The Urban Nation 1920–1960* Hill and Wang, New York 1965
Mullett, Charles F. *The British Empire* Holt, New York 1938

Murray, Henry A. "Individuality: The Meaning and Content of Individuality in Contemporary America" *Daedalus* Spring 1958
Murrow, Edward R. *This Is London* (ed. Elmer Davis) Simon and Schuster, New York 1941
Navasky, Victor S. "Notes on Cult; Or, How to Join the Intellectual Establishment" *New York Times Magazine* March 27, 1966
Neary, John "Bombs Blast a Message of Hate" *Life* March 27, 1970
Nelson, Walter Henry *Small Wonder: The Amazing Story of the Volkswagen* Little, Brown, Boston 1965
"The Neurotic Trillionaire" *Economist* May 10, 1969
Neustadt, Richard E. *Presidential Power: The Politics of Leadership* Wiley, New York 1960
Niebuhr, Reinhold *The Children of Light and the Children of Darkness: A Vindication of Democracy and a Critique of Its Traditional Defense* Scribner, New York 1944
—— "Is There a Revival of Religion?" *New York Times Magazine* November 19, 1950
Nixon, Richard M. *Six Crises* Doubleday, New York 1962
"No One Has Starved" *Fortune* September 1932
Northeast Power Failure November 9 and 10, 1965: A Report to the President by the Federal Power Commission U.S. Government Printing Office, Washington 1965
O'Donnell, Kenneth P. "LBJ and the Kennedys" *Life* August 7, 1970
—— and David F. Powers, with Joseph McCarthy *"Johnny, We Hardly Knew Ye": Memories of John Fitzgerald Kennedy* Little, Brown, Boston 1972
One Hundred Years of Famous Pages from the New York Times, 1851–1951 Simon and Schuster, New York 1951
O'Neill, William L., ed. *American Society Since 1945* Quadrangle, Chicago 1969
Packard, Vance "Resurvey of 'Hidden Persuaders' " *New York Times Magazine* May 11, 1958
—— *The Sexual Wilderness* David McKay, New York 1968
Pater, Alan F. and Jason R. *What They Said in 1969: The Yearbook of Spoken Opinion* Monitor, Beverly Hills, California 1970
Pauling, Linus, and Edward Teller "Fallout and Disarmament" *Daedalus* Spring 1958
Phillips, Cabell *From the Crash to the Blitz* Macmillan, New York 1969
—— *The Truman Presidency: The History of a Triumphant Succession* Macmillan, New York 1966
Pound, Arthur "Bankruptcy Mill" *Atlantic Monthly* February 1932
Powers, Francis Gary "Francis Gary Powers Tells His Story" *New York Times Magazine* April 19, 1970
—— with Curt Gentry *Operation Overflight: The U-2 Spy Pilot Tells His Story for the First Time* Holt, Rinehart, and Winston, New York 1970
Pusey, Merlo J. *Eisenhower, The President* Macmillan, New York 1956
Pyle, Ernie *This Is Your War* Holt, New York 1943
Pynchon, Thomas "A Journey into the Mind of Watts" *New York Times Magazine* June 12, 1966 (Pyramid 1966)
Raskin, A. H. "The Berkeley Affair: Mr. Kerr vs. Mr. Savio & Co." *New York Times Magazine* February 14, 1965
—— "Report on the Communist Party (U.S.A.)" *New York Times Magazine* March 30, 1947
Relief for Unemployed Transients: Hearings Before a Subcommittee of the Committee on Manufactures, U.S. Senate, 72nd Congress, 2nd Session, on S.5121 U.S. Government Printing Office, Washington 1933
Report of the President's Commission on the Assassination of President John F. Kennedy U.S. Government Printing Office, Washington 1964
Report on the International Control of Atomic Energy, A (Prepared for the Secretary of State's Committee on Atomic Energy by a board of consultants) Doubleday, New York 1946
Ridgeway, James "The Cops and the Kids" *New Republic* September 7, 1968
Ridgway, Matthew B. (as told to Harold H. Martin) *Soldier* Harper, New York 1956
Riesman, David, in collaboration with Reuel Denney and Nathan Glazer *The Lonely Crowd: A Study of the Changing American Character* Yale, New Haven 1950
Roosevelt, James, and Sidney Shalett *Affectionately, F.D.R.: A Son's Story of a Lonely Man* Harcourt, Brace, New York 1959
"Roosevelt Wins" *Nation* July 13, 1932
Rosenthal, A. M., and Arthur Gelb, eds. *The Night the Lights Went Out* Signet, New York 1965
Ross, Irwin *The Loneliest Campaign: The Truman Victory of 1948* Signet, New York 1968
Rossiter, Clinton *The American Presidency* Harcourt, Brace, New York 1956 (Mentor, New York 1960)
Rostow, W. W. "The American National Style" *Daedalus* Spring 1958
Rovere, Richard H. *Affairs of State: The Eisenhower Years* Farrar, Straus, and Cudahy, New York 1956
—— *Senator Joe McCarthy* Harcourt, Brace, New York 1959
—— *Waist Deep in the Big Muddy* Little, Brown, Boston 1968

—— and Arthur M. Schlesinger Jr. *The General and the President: And the Future of American Foreign Policy* Farrar, Straus and Young, New York 1951

Roy, Jules *The Battle of Dienbienphu* Harper, New York 1965

Ruffner, Frederick G Jr., ed. *National Organizations of the United States* (Volume I of *Encyclopedia of Organizations*) Gale Research, Detroit 1968

Salisbury, Harrison E *The Shook-Up Generation* Harper, New York 1958

Sanders, Ed *The Family: The Story of Charles Manson's Dune Buggy Attack Battalion* Avon, New York 1972

Scheinfeld, Amram "Kinsey's Study of Female Sexual Behavior" *Cosmopolitan* September 1953

Schlesinger, Arthur M. Jr. *The Coming of the New Deal* Houghton Mifflin, Boston 1958

—— *The Crisis of the Old Order* Houghton Mifflin, Boston 1957

—— *The Politics of Upheaval* Houghton Mifflin, Boston 1960

—— *A Thousand Days: John F. Kennedy in the White House* Houghton Mifflin, Boston 1965

Schrag, Peter "The Forgotten American" *Harper's Magazine* August 1969

—— "Is Main Street Still There?" *Saturday Review* January 17, 1970

Schulberg, Budd *The Disenchanted* Random House, New York 1950

Schwarz, Jordan *1933: Roosevelt's Decision. The United States Leaves the Gold Standard* Chelsea House, New York 1969

Servan-Schreiber, J. J. *The American Challenge* Avon, New York 1969

Sevareid, Eric "The American Dream" *Look* July 9, 1968

—— *Not So Wild a Dream* Knopf, New York 1946

Shannon, David A., ed. *The Great Depression* Prentice-Hall, Englewood Cliffs, N.J. 1960

Shapiro, Nat, ed. *Popular Music: An Annotated Index of American Popular Songs* (Volume I, 1950–1959) Adrian Press, New York 1964

Sheehan, Neil, Hedrick Smith, E. W. Kenworthy, and Fox Butterfield *The Pentagon Papers* Bantam, New York 1971

Sherrill, Robert *Gothic Politics in the Deep South: Stars of the New Confederacy* Ballantine, New York 1968

Shirer, William L. *The Rise and Fall of the Third Reich: A History of Nazi Germany* Simon and Schuster, New York 1960

Shuster, Alvin, ed. *Washington: The New York Times Guide to the Nation's Capital* Robert B. Luce, Washington 1967

Sidey, Hugh *John F Kennedy, President* Atheneum, New York 1963

Silber, Irwin, ed. *Songs America Voted By* Stackpole, Harrisburg, Pennsylvania 1971

Simon, Rita James, ed. *As We Saw the Thirties* University of Illinois, Urbana 1967

Smith, A. Robert, and Eric Sevareid *Washington: Magnificent Capital* Doubleday, New York 1965

Smith, Gene *The Shattered Dream: Herbert Hoover and the Great Depression* Morrow, New York 1970

Smith, John M., and Tim Cankwell, eds. *The World Encyclopedia of the Film* World, New York 1972

Sorensen, Theodore C. *Kennedy* Harper and Row, New York 1965

Soule, George "Are We Going to Have a Revolution?" *Harper's Magazine* August 1932

Sparks, Fred *The $20,000,000 Honeymoon: Jackie and Ari's First Year* Dell, New York 1970

Sparrow, John *After the Assassination: A Positive Appraisal of the Warren Report* Chilmark Press, New York 1967

Spectorsky, A. C. *The Exurbanites* Lippincott, Philadelphia and New York 1955

Speer, Albert *Inside the Third Reich* Macmillan, New York 1970

Spivak, John L. *Shrine of the Silver Dollar* Modern Age, New York 1940

Spock, Benjamin, M.D. *The Common Sense Book of Baby and Child Care* Duell, Sloan and Pearce, New York 1945

Stearns, Marshall *The Story of Jazz* Oxford, New York 1956

Steinbeck, John *Travels with Charley: In Search of America* Viking, New York 1962 (Bantam, New York 1963)

Steiner, Paul *The Stevenson Wit and Wisdom* Pyramid, New York 1965

Stevenson, Adlai *Speeches of Adlai Stevenson* Random House, New York 1952

Stimson, Henry L. "The Decision to Use the Atomic Bomb" *Harper's Magazine* February 1947

Storr, Anthony *Human Aggression* Atheneum, New York 1968

Straight, Michael *Trial by Television* Beacon, Boston 1954

Streit, Peggy "Why They Fight for the P.A.T." *New York Times Magazine* September 20, 1964

Sullivan, Frank *A Pearl in Every Oyster* Little, Brown, Boston 1938

Sulzberger, C. L., ed. *The American Heritage Picture History of World War II* Simon and Schuster, New York 1966

"A Survey of Unemployed Alumni" *School and Society* March 10, 1934

Symes, Lillian "Blunder on the Left: The Revolution and the American Scene" *Harper's Magazine* December 1933

Szulc, Tad "The Spy Compulsion" *New York Times Magazine* June 3, 1973

Tate, Allen "The Man of Letters in the Modern World" *Hudson Review* Autumn 1952

Terkel, Studs *Hard Times: An Oral History of the Great Depression* Pantheon, New York 1970

Tessler, Mark A., and Ronald D. Hedlund "Students Aren't Crazies" *New Republic* September 12, 1970

Thayer, George *The War Business: The International Trade in Armaments* Simon and Schuster, New York 1969

Thompson, Hunter S. "The 'Hashbury' Is the Capital of the Hippies" *New York Times Magazine* May 14, 1967

Time, Editors of *Live Them Again: The Three Decades from Flappers to Flying Saucers, 1923–1953* Simon and Schuster, New York 1953

Tocqueville, Alexis de *Democracy in America* ed. Phillips Bradley (Vol. I) Vintage, New York 1945

Toland, John *But Not in Shame: The Six Months After Pearl Harbor* Random House, New York 1961

Truman, Harry S. *Memoirs,* volumes I (*Year of Decisions,* 1955) and II (*Years of Trial and Hope,* 1956) Doubleday, New York

Truman, Margaret, with Margaret Cousins *Souvenir: Margaret Truman's Own Story* McGraw-Hill, New York 1956

"200,000 Trailers" *Fortune* March 1937

Unemployment in the United States: Hearings Before a Subcommittee of the Committee on Labor, House of Representatives, 72nd Congress, 1st Session, on H.R.206, H.R.6011, H.R.6066 U.S. Government Printing Office, Washington 1932

Van Camp, Sarah "Growing Up in D.C. in Song and Story" (unpublished manuscript)

Vandenberg, Arthur H. *The Private Papers of Senator Vandenberg,* ed. Arthur H. Vandenberg Jr. Houghton Mifflin, Boston 1952

Vanderlip, Frank A. "What About the Banks?" *Saturday Evening Post* November 5, 1932

Villard, Oswald Garrison "An Open Letter to Governor Roosevelt" *Nation* May 11, 1932

—— "Roosevelt and Hoover Militarists Both" *Nation* October 26, 1932

Vorse, Mary Heaton "Rebellion in the Cornbelt: American Farmers Beat Their Plowshares into Swords" *Harper's Magazine* December 1932

Walker, Daniel *Rights in Conflict* Signet, New York 1968

Walker, John and Katherine *The Washington Guidebook* Metro Publishers, Washington 1969

Walker, Stanley " 'Book Branding'—A Case History" *New York Times Magazine* July 12, 1953

Warner, W. Lloyd, and others *Yankee City* Yale University, New Haven 1963

—— and others *Social Class in America: A Manual of Procedure for the Measurement of Social Status* Harper Torchbooks, New York 1960

Washington, City and Capital (Federal Writers' Project, Works Progress Administration, American Guide Series) U.S. Government Printing Office, Washington 1937

"Washington and Its Approaches" *Saturday Evening Post* December 20, 1930

Weaver, Richard M. *Ideas Have Consequences* University of Chicago, Chicago 1948

Webb, John N. *The Migratory-Casual Worker* (WPA Research Monograph VII) U.S. Government Printing Office, Washington 1937

Webbink, Paul "Unemployment in the United States, 1930–1940" *Papers and Proceedings of the American Economic Association* February 1941

Weber, Max *The Protestant Ethic and the Spirit of Capitalism* Scribner, New York 1958

Wecter, Dixon *The Age of the Great Depression* Macmillan, New York 1948

Wertham, Frederic *Seduction of the Innocent* Rinehart, New York 1954

West, Rebecca *The New Meaning of Treason* Viking, New York 1964 (Time-Life Books 1966)

White, Theodore H. *The Making of the President 1960* Atheneum, New York 1961

—— *The Making of the President 1964* Atheneum, New York 1965

—— *The Making of the President 1968* Atheneum, New York 1969

—— *The Making of the President 1972* Atheneum, New York 1973

White, William S. *The Professional: Lyndon B. Johnson* Houghton Mifflin, Boston 1964 (Crest, New York 1964)

Whitehead, Donald F. *The FBI Story: A Report to the People* Random House, New York 1956

White House Historical Association *The White House: An Historic Guide* Washington 1962

Whiteside, Thomas "Corridor of Mirrors: The Television Editorial Process, Chicago" *Columbia Journalism Review* Winter 1968/1969

"Who's in the Army Now?" *Fortune* September 1935

Whyte, William H. Jr. *The Organization Man* Simon and Schuster, New York 1956 (Anchor, New York)

Wiener, Norbert "A Scientist Rebels" *Atlantic Monthly* January 1947

Willkie, Wendell *One World* Simon and Schuster, New York 1943
Wills, Garry *Nixon Agonistes: The Crisis of the Self-Made Man* Houghton Mifflin, Boston 1970 (Signet, New York 1971)
Wilson, Sloan *The Man in the Gray Flannel Suit* Simon and Schuster, New York 1955
Wish, Harvey *Contemporary America* 4th ed. Harper and Row, New York 1966
Wolfe, Thomas *You Can't Go Home Again* Harper, New York 1934
Wolfert, Ira *American Guerrilla in the Philippines* Simon and Schuster, New York 1945
Wolff, Perry Sidney *A Tour of the White House with Mrs. John F. Kennedy* (television program) Doubleday, New York 1962
"Women in Business" *Fortune* September 1935
X [See George F. Kennan]
Yank, Editors of, selected by *The Best from Yank* World, Cleveland 1945
"Youth in College" *Fortune* June 1936
Zeiger, Henry A. *Inquest! Ted Kennedy–Mary Jo Kopechne: Prosecution or Persecution?* Tower, New York 1970

COPYRIGHT ACKNOWLEDGMENTS

The author is grateful to the following publishers, individuals, and companies for permission to reprint excerpts from selected materials as noted below.

Acuff-Rose Publications, Incorporated, for "Tennessee Waltz" by Redd Stewart and Pee Wee King. © Copyright 1948 by Acuff-Rose Publications, Inc. All rights reserved.

Anne-Rachel Music Corporation, for "That Doggie in the Window" by Bob Merrill, copyright 1952 and 1953 by Anne-Rachel Music Corporation; and for "Music Goes 'Round and Around" by Red Hodgson, Edward Farley and Michael Riley, copyright 1935 by Select Music Publications, Inc., copyright renewed 1962 and assigned to Anne-Rachel Music Corporation.

Appleseed Music, Inc., for "Alice's Restaurant" by Arlo Guthrie. © Copyright 1966, 1967, 1969 by Appleseed Music, Inc. All rights reserved.

Belwin Mills Publishing Corp., for "I Can't Give You Anything But Love," by Dorothy Fields and Jimmy McHugh, copyright 1928 by Mills Music, Inc., copyright renewed 1956; and for "Lambeth Walk" by Noel Gay and Douglas Furber, copyright 1937 by Cinephonic Music Co. Ltd., copyright renewed 1965 by Noel Gay Music Co., Inc.

Bennie Benjamin Music, Inc., for words and music from "When the Lights Go On Again (All Over the World)" by Eddie Seiler, Sol Marcus and Bennie Benjamin. Copyright 1942 by Campbell, Loft & Porgie, Inc. Copyright renewed 1969 by Bennie Benjamin and Sol Marcus and assigned to Bennie Benjamin Music, Inc.

Irving Berlin Music Corporation, for the following songs: "I'm Putting All My Eggs in One Basket" by Irving Berlin (page 148), © 1936 Irving Berlin, © renewed 1963 Irving Berlin; "I Left My Heart at the Stage Door Canteen" by Irving Berlin (page 401), © 1942 Irving Berlin, © renewed 1970 Irving Berlin, copyright assigned to Gene Tunney, A. L. Berman and Ralph J. Bunche as trustees, God Bless America Fund; "White Christmas" by Irving Berlin (page 444), © 1940, 1942 Irving Berlin, © renewed 1968, 1969 Irving Berlin; "The Girl That I Marry" by Irving Berlin (page 510), © Irving Berlin, © renewed 1974 Irving Berlin.

Blue Seas and Jac Music, for "Raindrops Keep Fallin' on My Head" by Burt Bacharach and Hal David. © Copyright 1969, 1970 by Blue Seas Music, Inc., Jac Music Co., Inc. and Twentieth Century Music Corp. All rights reserved.

Bourne Co., Music Publishers, for "My Mammy" by Sam Lewis, Joe Young, and Walter Donaldson, © 1920 Bourne Co., New York, N.Y., copyright renewed; and for "Who's Afraid of the Big Bad Wolf" by Frank Churchill and Ann Ronell, © 1933 Bourne Co., New York, N.Y., copyright renewed.

Harold Freedman Brandt & Brandt Dramatic Department Inc., for *Waiting for Lefty* by Clifford Odets. Copyright 1935 by Clifford Odets. Copyright renewed © 1963 by Clifford Odets.

Broadway Music Corporation, for "I'll Be with You in Apple Blossom Time." Words by Neville Fleeson, music by Albert Von Tilzer. Copyright 1920 by Broadway Music Corporation; copyright renewed 1947. Published for the United States by Broadway Music Corporation and by Jerry Vogel Music Co., Inc. International copyright secured. All rights reserved including public performance for profit. All rights outside United States reserved by Broadway Music Corporation and representatives.

Chappell & Co., Inc., for the following songs: "There's a Small Hotel" by Lorenz Hart and Richard Rodgers, copyright © 1936 by Chappell & Co., Inc., copyright renewed; "I've Got Sixpence" by Box/Cox/Hall, copyright © 1941 by Bradbury, Wood Ltd., copyright renewed. Chappell & Co., Inc., publisher; "Juke Box Saturday Night" by Al Stillman and Paul McGrane, copyright © 1942 by Chappell & Co., Inc., copyright renewed; "I'll Be Seeing You" by Irving Kahal and Sammy Fain, copyright © 1938 by Williamson Music, Inc., copyright renewed; "Just You Wait" by Alan Jay Lerner and Frederick Loewe, copyright © 1956 by Alan Jay Lerner and Frederick Loewe.

Cherio Corporation, for "Young At Heart" by Carolyn Leigh and Johnny Richards. © 1954 Cherio Corporation.

City Lights Books, for "America" from *Howl and Other Poems* by Allen Ginsberg. Copyright © 1956, 1959 by Allen Ginsberg.

Coward, McCann & Geoghegan, Inc., for *The White Cliffs* by Alice Duer Miller. Copyright 1940 by Alice Duer Miller; renewed © 1967 by Denning Miller.

Walt Disney Music Company, for "Mickey Mouse March." Words and music by Jimmie Dodd. © 1955 Walt Disney Music Company.

Drake Activities Co., Hallmark Music Co., Inc., Al Hoffman Songs, Inc., and Miller Music Corporation, for "Mairzy Doats" (page 352). Words and music by Milton Drake, Al Hoffman, and Jerry Livingston. Copyright © 1943 Miller Music Corp., N.Y., N.Y. U.S. copyright renewed and assigned to Drake Activities Co., Hallmark Music Co., Inc. and Al Hoffman Songs, Inc. Rights controlled for the world, except United States, its territories and possessions by Miller Music Corp., N.Y., N.Y.

Norma Millay Ellis, for "There Are No Islands, Any More" by Edna St. Vincent Millay, published in the *New York Times,* June 14, 1940. Copyright 1940, © 1968 by Edna St. Vincent Millay.

Redd Evans Music Company, for words and music from "He's 1-A in the Army and He's A-1 in My Heart" by Redd Evans. Copyright 1941 by Redd Evans.

Leo Feist, Inc., for "Chattanooga Choo Choo." Words and music by Mack Gordon and Harry Warren. Copyright © 1941, renewed 1969 Twentieth Century Music Corporation, New York, New York. All rights controlled by Leo Feist, Inc.

Frank Music Corp., for "Hey There" by Richard Adler and Jerry Ross, © 1954 Frank Music Corp.; and for "Standing on the Corner" by Frank Loesser, © 1956 Frank Music Corp.

Glad Music Company, for "Chantilly Lace" by J. P. Richardson. © Copyright 1958 by Glad Music, 314 E. 11th St., Houston, Texas. All rights reserved. International copyright secured.

Golden West Melodies, Inc. for "Just Walking in the Rain" by Johnny Bragg and Robert S. Riley. Copyright 1953 by Golden West Melodies, Inc.

Green Menu Music Factory, Inc., for "Winky Dink and You." Words and music by John Redmond and John Gart. Copyright © 1954 Bark Music Corp. Copyright assigned 1973 to Mitchell Music Corporation.

T. B. Harms Company, for "So in Love" by Cole Porter, © copyright 1948 Cole Porter, sole selling agent T. B. Harms Company, 100 Wilshire Boulevard, Santa Monica, California; and for "A Fine Romance" by Jerome Kern and Dorothy Fields, copyright © 1936 T. B. Harms Company. Copyright renewed T. B. Harms Company, 100 Wilshire Boulevard, Santa Monica, California. International copyright secured. All rights reserved.

Holt, Rinehart and Winston, Inc. and the Society of Authors, London, and Jonathan Cape, Ltd., London, for "To An Athlete Dying Young" from "A Shropshire Lad"–Authorised Edition–from *The Collected Poems of A. E. Housman.* Copyright 1939, 1940, © 1965 by Holt, Rinehart and Winston, Inc. Copyright © 1967, 1968 by Robert E. Symons.

Ludlow Music, Inc., for "Goodnight Irene" (page 675). Words and music by Huddie Ledbetter and John A. Lomax. © copyright 1936 (renewed 1964) and 1950 Ludlow Music, Inc., New York, N.Y.

Maclen Music, Inc., for "Lucy in the Sky with Diamonds" by John Lennon and Paul McCartney. Copyright © 1967 Northern Songs Ltd. All rights for the USA, Canada, Mexico and the Philippines controlled by Maclen Music, Inc. c/o ATV Music Group. All rights reserved.

Edward B. Marks Music Corporation, for "Lilli Marlene." Words and music by Hans Leip, Norbert Schultze, Tommy Connor. © copyright Apollo-Verlag Paul Lincke, Berlin. Sole selling agent in the United States of America and Mexico–Edward B. Marks Music Corporation.

Bill Mauldin, for captions from nine of his cartoons. Captions copyrighted 1944 by United Features Syndicate, Inc.

MCA Music, for "If You Love Me, Really Love Me (Hymne à l'Amour)," English words by Geoffrey Parsons, French words by Edith Piaf, music by Marguerite Monnot, © Copyright 1949, 1953 by France Music Corporation, New York, N.Y., sole selling agent, Duchess Music Corporation, New York, N.Y., for U.S.A. and Canada; and for "Now Is the Hour (Maori Farewell Song)," words and music by Maewa Kaihan, Clement Scott and Dorothy Stewart, © Copyright 1913 by W. H. Paling and Co., Ltd. (Renewed), © Copyright 1946 by Leeds Music Corporation, 445 Park Avenue, New York, N.Y. 10022, by arrangement with Boston

Music Company, Boston, Mass. and W. H. Paling and Co., Ltd., Australia. Both songs all rights reserved.

Miller Music Corporation, New York, New York, for "Happy Bluebirds" by Johnny Gruelle and Will Woodin, copyright © 1930, renewed © 1957 Miller Music Corporation.

Ivan Mogull Music Corporation, for "Nature Boy" by Eden Ahbez. © 1948 by Crestview Music Corp. Sole selling agent: Ivan Mogull Music Corporation.

Morley Music Company, for "Five Minutes More," lyrics by Sammy Cahn, music by Jule Styne, © Copyright 1946 by Morley Music Co., © Copyright renewed and assigned to Morley Music Co.; and for "I'll Walk Alone," lyrics by Sammy Cahn, music by Jule Styne, © Copyright 1944 by Morley Music Co., © Copyright renewed and assigned to Morley Music Co.

Music Music Music Inc., for "Ballad of the Green Berets" by Barry Sadler and Robin Moore. © Copyright 1963, 1964, and 1966 by Music Music Music Inc.

National Broadcasting Company, Inc., for the "Howdy Doody" theme. © Children's Songs, Inc. 1948. Reprinted with the permission of the National Broadcasting Company, Inc.

New Directions Publishing Corporation, for "Marriage" from *The Happy Birthday of Death* by Gregory Corso. Copyright © 1960 by New Directions Publishing Corporation.

Paramount Music Corporation, for "Thanks for the Memory" by Leo Robin and Ralph Rainger. Copyright © 1937 by Paramount Music Corporation. Copyright renewed 1964 by Paramount Music Corporation.

Parker Brothers Games, for a Community Chest card and Park Place title deed card from "Monopoly" ® real estate trading game equipment. © 1935, 1946, 1961 Parker Brothers.

Planetary Music Publishing Corporation, for "The Yellow Rose of Texas" by Don George. Copyright © 1955 Planetary Music Publ. Corp. All rights reserved.

Robbins Music Corporation, New York, New York, for "Goodnight Sweetheart." Words and music by Ray Noble, Jimmy Campbell and Reg Connelly. Copyright © 1931, renewed 1959 Robbins Music Corporation.

Fred Rose Music, Incorporated, for "A White Sport Coat (And a Pink Carnation)" by Marty Robbins, © Copyright 1957 by Fred Rose Music, Inc.; and for "Big Bad John" by Jimmy Dean, © Copyright 1961 by Fred Rose Music, Inc. Both songs all rights reserved.

Shapiro, Bernstein & Co., Inc., for "Beer Barrel Polka" by Lew Brown, Vladimir Timm and Jaromir Vejvota. "Skoda Lasky" copyright 1934 by Jana Hoffmanna, vva., assigned to Shapiro, Bernstein & Co., Inc. Renewed. Copyright 1939 by Shapiro, Bernstein & Co., Inc. Renewed. International Copyright Secured. All rights reserved including public performance for profit.

Shawnee Press, Inc., for the dramatic cantata "The Lonesome Train." Words by Millard Lampell, music by Earl Robinson. © Copyright 1943, Earl Robinson. © Copyright 1945, Sun Music Co., Inc. U.S. Copyrights renewed. Copyrights assigned to Shawnee Press, Inc., Delaware Water Gap, Pa. 18327.

Paul Simon Music, for "The Sound of Silence" by Paul Simon. © 1964 Paul Simon.

Southern Music Publishing Co., Inc., for "Mocking Bird Hill" by Vaughn Horton. Copyright 1949 by Southern Music Publishing Co., Inc.

Time/Life Picture Agency, for the poster "Junk Makes Fighting Weapons" from *Fabulous Century 1940–1950,* published by Time-Life Books.

Venice Music, Inc., for "Tutti Frutti" by Dorothy LaBostrie and Richard Penniman. Copyright 1955, 1956 Venice Music, Inc., Hollywood, California 90069.

Viking Press, Inc., for *Death of a Salesman* by Arthur Miller. Copyright 1949 by Arthur Miller.

Vogue Music, Inc., for "Blue Velvet." Words and music by Bernie Wayne and Lee Morris. Copyright © 1951 Vogue Music, Inc., 100 Wilshire Boulevard, Santa Monica, California 90401. All rights reserved. International Copyright Secured.

Warner Bros. Music, for the following songs: "Miss Otis Regrets" by Cole Porter, © 1934 Harms, Inc. "Bei Mir Bist du Schön" by Sammy Cahn and Saul Chaplin, © 1937 Harms, Inc. Words and music from "They're Either Too Young or Too Old" by Frank Loesser and Arthur Schwartz, © 1943 M. Witmark & Sons. "Happy Days Are Here Again" by Milton Ager and Jack Yellen, © 1929 Advanced Music Corporation. "Brother, Can You Spare a Dime?" by Jay Gorney and E. Y. Harburg, © 1932 Harms, Inc. "Blues in the Night" by Johnny and Harold Arlen, © 1941 Remick Music Corporation. "I'm Just Wild About Harry" by Noble Sissle and Eubie Blake, © 1921 M. Witmark & Sons. All songs copyright renewed, all rights reserved. "Blowin' in the Wind" by Bob Dylan, © 1962 by M. Witmark & Sons. "Like a Rolling Stone" by Bob Dylan, © 1965 M. Witmark & Sons. "My Generation" by James A. Griffin and Mike Z. Gordon, © 1967 Stone Canyon Music. All songs all rights reserved.

United Artists Music Co., Inc., for "Michael." New words and new music arrangement by Dave Fisher. © 1960, 1961 Unart Music Corporation, New York, New York.

Wonderland Music Company, Inc., for "The Ballad of Davy Crockett." Words by Tom Blackburn. Music by George Bruns. © 1954 Wonderland Music Company, Inc.

Yellow Dog Music, Inc., for "Is That All There Is" by Jerry Leiber and Mike Stoller. Copyright © 1966 by Yellow Dog Music, Inc.

INDEX

A,a

A, a /e; eɪ/ *plural* **A's, a's** *n* [C] the first letter of the English alphabet 英语字母表的第一个字母

1 1 **a** /ə; ə; *strong* 强读 e; eɪ/ also 又作 **an** *indefinite article, determiner* **1** used before a noun that names something or someone that has not been mentioned before, or that the person you are talking to does not know about〔用于未曾提及或事先不知道的人或物名称前〕: *Do you have a car?* 你有(小轿)车吗? | *There's a spider in the bath.* 浴缸里有只蜘蛛。—compare 比较 THE **2 a)** used before a noun that is one of a particular group or class of people or things〔用于某个特定群体、阶层的人或事物前〕: *I want to train to be a teacher.* 我想接受培训成为一名老师。**b)** used before someone's family name to show that they belong to that family〔用于某人的姓前表明其属于这个家庭〕: *Only a Peterson would drive a car like that!* 只有彼得森家的人才会那样开车! **3 a)** one 一(个): *a thousand pounds* 一千英镑 | *a dozen eggs* 一打鸡蛋 **b) a lot/a few/a little/a great deal etc** used before certain words that express an amount of something 许多/几个/少许/大量等: *There were a lot of people at the party.* 晚会上有很多人。| *A few weeks from now I'll be in Venice.* 几周以后我会在威尼斯。**4 twice a week/£5 a day etc** two times each week, £5 each day etc; per 每周两次/每天五英镑等: *I get paid once a month.* 我的工资一个月发一次。| *The eggs cost $2 a dozen.* 鸡蛋两美元一打。**5** used before a noun to mean all things of that type〔用于名词前代表一类〕: *A square has four sides.* (=all squares have four sides) 正方形有四条边。**6** used before two nouns that are mentioned together so often that they are thought of as one thing〔用于两个经常被一起提及因此被看做是一个整体的名词前〕: *a cup and saucer* 一副杯碟 | *Does everyone have a knife and fork?* 每个人都有刀叉吗? **7 a)** used before singular nouns, especially words for actions, meaning one example of that action〔用于单数名词,尤其是表示动作的名词前〕: *Take a look at this.* 看看这个。| *It needs a good clean.* 这需要好好清洁一下。**b)** used before the -ing form of verbs when they are used as nouns〔用于动名词之前〕: *a crashing of gears* 齿轮相撞 **c)** used before an UNCOUNTABLE noun when other information about the noun is added by an adjective or phrase〔用于由形容词或短语修饰的不可数名词前〕: *Candidates must have a good knowledge of chemistry.* 候选人必须精通化学。| *a beauty that became legendary* 传奇式的美丽 **8** used before an UNCOUNTABLE noun to mean a type of it 一种〔用于不可数名词前表示种类〕: *a particularly fine Stilton cheese* 一种优质斯第尔顿乳酪 **9** used before the name of a painter or artist etc meaning a particular painting, sculpture etc by that person〔用于画家或艺术家的名字前表示其绘画或雕塑作品〕: *an early Rembrandt* 伦勃朗的一幅早期作品 **10** used before a name to mean having the same qualities as that person or thing〔用于某人或某物的名字前指与其具有同样特性的人或物〕: *She was hailed as a new Marilyn Monroe.* 她被赞为又一个玛丽莲·梦露。**11 a)** used before someone's name when you do not know who they are 某一; 一位〔用于一个你不认识的人名前〕: *There is a Mr Tom Wilkins on the phone for you.* 一个叫汤姆·威尔金斯的人打电话找你。| **a certain** *A certain Lisa Blair wishes to speak to you.* 某位叫莉萨·布莱尔的人想和你说话。**b)** used before names of days, events in the year etc to mean a particular one〔用于日期、事件名称前指某个特定的日子或事件〕: *I can't remember a Christmas like it.* 我想不起有过像这样的圣诞节。**12** used after such, what, rather and (formal) many to emphasize what you are saying〔置于 such、what、rather 和(正式) many 后表示强调〕: *What a day! I was late for work and my car broke down.* 多么糟糕的一天! 我上班迟到了,车也坏了。| *She had spent many a night* (=many nights) *waiting for him to come home.* 多少个晚上她都在等他回家。

A¹ /e; eɪ/ *n* **1** also 又作 **a** [C,U] the sixth note in the musical SCALE¹ (8) of C major or the musical KEY² (4) based on this note A 音〔C 大调音阶中的第六音〕; A 调 **2** [C] the highest mark that a student can get in an examination or for a piece of work A 级, 甲级, 甲等〔表示学业成绩优秀〕: *I got an A in French.* 法语我得了个 A。**3 an A student** *AmE* someone who regularly gets the best marks possible for their work in school or college【美】优等生 **4 from A to B** from one place to another 从一地到另一地: *Hiring a car was the best way to get us from A to B.* 租车是我们从一地到另一地的最好方法。**5 from A to Z** describing, including, or knowing everything about a subject 从头到尾〔表示描述、涵盖或了解一个科目的全部内容〕: *the history of 20th century art from A to Z* 20 世纪艺术通史 **6 A3/A4** standard sizes of paper in the European Union A3/A4 纸〔欧盟纸张标准规格〕 **7** [U] a common type of blood A 型〔一种常见血型〕

A² the written abbreviation of 缩写= AMP

a-¹ /ə; ə/ *prefix* **1** in a particular condition or way 处于某种状况; 以某种方式: *alive* (=living) 活(着)的 | *aloud* 大声地 | *with nerves all atingle* (=tingling) 全身神经都发痛 **2** *old use* in, to, at, or on something【旧】在某物内[边, 上]: *abed* (=in bed) 在床上 | *afar* (=far away) 在远处

a-² /e, æ, ə; eɪ, æ, ə/ *prefix* showing an opposite or the absence of something; not; without 与…相反; 缺乏…; 不; 没有: *amoral* (=not moral) 非道德的 | *atypically* (=not typically) 非[不]典型地

A-1 /ˌe ˋwʌn; ˌeɪ ˈwʌn/ *adj old-fashioned* very good or completely healthy【过时】一流的, 极好的; 完全健康的: *Everything about the resort was A-1.* 这个度假胜地的所有设施都是一流的。

A1, the /ˌe ˋwʌn; ˌeɪ ˈwʌn/ a main British road that goes from London to Edinburgh A1 公路〔英国伦敦到爱丁堡的一条主干道〕

AA /ˌe ˋe; ˌeɪ ˈeɪ/ **1** the written abbreviation of 缩写= ALCOHOLICS ANONYMOUS **2** Automobile Association; a British organization that provides services for people who own cars 汽车协会〔英国为车主提供服务的一个组织〕 **3** [C] Associate of Arts; a two-year college degree in the US 副文学士〔美国大学的一种两年制学位〕

AAA, the¹ /ˌθri ˋez; ˌθriː ˈeɪz◂/ Amateur Athletic Association; a British organization for ATHLETES 业余运动员协会〔英国的一个运动员组织〕

AAA, the² /ˌtrɪpl̩ ˋe; ˌtrɪpəl ˈeɪ◂/ the American Automobile Association; an American organization that provides services for people who own cars 美国汽车协会〔美国为车主提供服务的一个组织〕

aard·vark /ˈɑrdˌvɑrk; ˈɑːdvɑːk/ *n* [C] a large animal from southern Africa that has a very long nose and eats small insects 土豚

Aa·ron /ˈɛrən; ˈeərən/ in the Old Testament of the Bible, a priest who was the brother of Moses 亚伦〔《圣经·旧约》中的一位传道士, 摩西之兄〕

Aaron, Hank /hæŋk; hæŋk/ (1934-) a baseball player famous for hitting more HOME RUNS than Babe Ruth, who had held the record for almost 40 years 艾伦〔(1934-), 棒球运动员, 以本垒打击中次数超过贝布·鲁思保持了近40年的纪录而出名〕

AARP /ˌe e ɑr ˋpi; ˌeɪ eɪ ɑː ˈpiː/ the written abbreviation of 缩写 = the AMERICAN ASSOCIATION OF RETIRED PERSONS

AB /ˌe ˋbi; ˌeɪ ˈbiː/ *n* **1** [U] a common type of blood AB 型〔一种常见血型〕 **2** [C] *AmE* Bachelor of Arts; a university degree in an arts (ART¹ (5)) subject that you get after studying for three or four years【美】文学士

ABA /ˌe bi ˋe; ˌeɪ biː ˈeɪ/ the written abbreviation of 缩写= the AMERICAN BAR ASSOCIATION

a·back /əˋbæk; əˈbæk/ *adv* **be taken aback** to be very surprised or shocked by something 吃了一惊: *For a moment, I was completely taken aback by her request.* 刹那间, 我对她的请求感到十分震惊。

ab·a·cus /ˈæbəkəs; ˈæbəkəs/ *n* [C] a wooden frame with small balls used for counting (COUNT¹ (2)) 算盘

ab·a·lo·ne /ˌæbəˋlonɪ; ˌæbəˈləʊni/ *n* [C,U] a kind of SHELLFISH which is used as food and whose shell contains MOTHER-OF-PEARL 鲍鱼

a·ban·don¹ /əˋbændən; əˈbændən/ *v* [T] **1** to leave someone, especially someone you are responsible for 抛弃, 遗弃〔某人〕: *children abandoned by their parents* 被父母遗弃的孩子 **2** to go away from a place, vehicle etc, permanently, especially because the situation makes it impossible for you to stay 离开, 逃离〔某地方或交通工具等〕: *We had to abandon the car and walk the rest of the way.* 我们只好弃车, 剩下的路走着去。| *Fearing further attacks, most of the population had abandoned the city.* 由于害怕遭受更多的袭击, 大多数市民已逃离该城市。**3** to stop 3

A

doing something because there are too many problems and it is impossible to continue 放弃, 中止: *The game had to be abandoned due to bad weather.* 由于天气不好, 比赛不得不中止。**4** to decide that you no longer believe in a particular idea or principle 放弃〔信仰或原则〕: *They were accused of abandoning their socialist principles.* 他们被指责放弃了社会主义原则。| **abandon hope (of doing sth)** *Imogen had abandoned all hope of ever seeing her brother again.* 伊莫金已经放弃了再次见到哥哥的全部希望。**5 abandon yourself to** *literary* to feel an emotion so strongly that you let it control you completely【文】沉湎于, 放纵〔感情〕**6 abandon ship** to leave a ship because it is sinking〔由于船在下沉而〕弃船(逃生) **—abandonment** *n* [U]

abandon[2] *n* [U] **with gay/wild abandon** in a careless or uncontrolled way without thinking or caring about what you are doing 尽情; 放纵: *The kids hurled pieces of wood on the fire with gay abandon.* 孩子们不管不顾地把木块往火上扔。

a·ban·doned /ə`bændənd; ə'bændənd/ *adj* **1** an abandoned building, car, boat etc has been left completely by the people who owned it and is no longer used 废弃的 **2** someone who is abandoned has been left completely alone by the person who was looking after them 被遗弃的 **3** *literary* behaving in a wild and uncontrolled way【文】无约束的, 无度的, 放荡的

a·base /ə`bes; ə'beɪs/ *v* **abase yourself** to behave in a way that shows you accept that someone has complete power over you 贬低自己, 卑躬屈膝 **—abasement** *n* [U]

a·bashed /ə`bæʃt; ə'bæʃt/ *adj* [not before noun 不用于名词前] embarrassed or ashamed because you have done something wrong or stupid 羞愧的, 窘迫的, 尴尬的: *She looked rather abashed.* 她看起来很羞愧。

a·bate /ə`bet; ə'beɪt/ *v* [I,T] *formal* to become less strong or decrease, or to make something do this【正式】使减少, 使减轻, 使缓解: *We waited for the storm to abate.* 我们等风暴减弱。**—abatement** *n* [U]

ab·at·toir /ˌæbə`twɑr; 'æbətwɑː/ *n* [C] *BrE* a place where animals are killed for their meat; SLAUGHTERHOUSE【英】屠宰场

ab·bess /`æbɪs; 'æbɪ̈s/ *n* [C] a woman who is in charge of a CONVENT (=religious institution for women) 女修道院院长

ab·bey /`æbɪ; 'æbi/ *n* [C] a large church, especially one with buildings next to it where MONKS and NUNS live or used to live 大修道院, 大寺院

ab·bot /`æbət; 'æbət/ *n* [C] a man who is in charge of a MONASTERY (=place where a group of MONKS live) 男修道院院长; 大寺院男住持

Ab·bott and Cos·tel·lo /ˌæbət ənd kɑ`stɛlo; ˌæbət ənd kɒ'steləʊ/ **Bud Abbott** (1896-1974) and **Lou Costello** (1908-59), two popular American COMEDIANS who appeared in many humorous films together in the 1940s and 1950s 阿博特和科斯蒂洛〔即巴德·阿博特(1896-1974)和卢·科斯蒂洛(1908-1959), 他们是广受欢迎的美国喜剧演员, 20世纪40、50年代曾合演过不少喜剧影片〕

abbr. also 又作 **abbrev.** the written abbreviation of 缩写= ABBREVIATION

ab·bre·vi·ate /ə`brivɪˌet; ə'briːvieɪt/ *v* [T] to make a word or expression shorter by missing out letters or using only the first letter of each word 省略, 缩略, 缩写: **be abbreviated to** *'Information technology' is usually abbreviated to 'IT'.* information technology (信息技术) 常被缩略为 IT。**—abbreviated** *adj*

ab·bre·vi·at·ed /ə`brivɪˌetɪd; ə'briːvieɪtɪ̈d/ *adj* made shorter by missing out letters or missing out parts of a story, statement etc 缩写的, 缩略的: *Orders were passed to the commander at the front in an abbreviated form.* 命令以缩略的形式传达给前线指挥员。

ab·bre·vi·a·tion /əˌbrivɪ`eʃən; əˌbriːvi'eɪʃən/ *n* **1** [C] a short form of a word or expression 缩写, 缩略语: *'Dr.' is the written abbreviation of 'Doctor'.* Dr. 是 Doctor (医生/博士) 的缩写形式。**2** [U] the act of abbreviating something 节略, 缩写

ABC[1] /ˌe bi `si; ˌeɪ biː 'siː/ *n* also 又作 **ABCs** *AmE*【美】**1** [singular] the letters of the English alphabet as taught to children〔教儿童的〕英语字母(表) **2 the ABC of** the basic facts about a particular subject 基本知识, 基础知识

ABC[2] *n* [singular,U] American Broadcasting Corporation; one of the national television companies in the US 美国广播公司

ab·di·cate /`æbdəˌket; 'æbdɪkeɪt/ *v* [I,T] **1** to give up the position of being king or queen 放弃〔王位〕, 退〔位〕, 让〔位〕**2 abdicate responsibility** *formal* to refuse to accept responsibility for something any longer【正式】放弃责任 **—abdication** /ˌæbdə`keʃən; ˌæbdɪ̈'keɪʃən/ *n* [C,U]

ab·do·men /æb`domən; 'æbdəmən/ *n* [C] **1** the part of your body between your chest and legs which contains your stomach 腹(部) **2** the end part of an insect's body, joined to the THORAX〔昆虫的〕腹 **—abdominal** /æb`dɑmənl; æb'dɒmɪ̈nəl/ *adj*: *acute abdominal pains* 急性腹痛

ab·duct /əb`dʌkt; əb'dʌkt/ *v* [T] to take someone away by force; KIDNAP 劫持, 绑架; 诱拐: *Police suspect she was abducted late last night.* 警方怀疑她昨天深夜被绑架了。**—abductor** *n* [C] **—abduction** /æb`dʌkʃən; əb'dʌkʃən/ *n* [C,U]

a·bed /ə`bɛd; ə'bed/ *adj* [not before noun 不用于名词前] *old-fashioned* in bed【过时】在床上的

A·bel /`ebḷ; 'eɪbəl/ in the Old Testament of the Bible, the second son of Adam and Eve who was killed by his brother Cain 亚伯〔《圣经·旧约》中亚当和夏娃的次子, 被其兄该隐杀害〕

Ab·e·lard /`æbəˌlɑrd; 'æbəlɑːd/**, Peter** (1079-1142) a French PHILOSOPHER and THEOLOGIAN best remembered for his love for Héloïse, shown in their famous letters to each other 阿贝拉尔〔(1079-1142), 法国哲学家、神学家。他对埃洛伊兹的爱情, 人们记忆至深。他们的往来书信十分著名, 是其爱情的见证〕

Ab·er·deen /ˌæbə`din; ˌæbə'diːn◂/ a port in northeast Scotland. It is the centre of the North Sea oil industry 阿伯丁〔苏格兰东北部港口, 北海石油工业的中心〕

Ab·er·deen·shire /ˌæbə`dinʃə; ˌæbə'diːnʃə/ a county in northern Scotland, with a coast on the North Sea 阿伯丁郡〔苏格兰北部一郡, 位于北海之滨〕

Ab·er·fan /ˌæbə`væn; ˌæbə'væn/ a small town in South Wales where, in 1966, a large pile of waste material from coal MINES fell onto a school and killed 116 children and 28 adults 阿伯梵〔南威尔士一小镇。1966年一大堆废料从煤矿滑落到镇上的一所学校, 造成116名儿童和28名成人死亡〕

a·ber·rant /æb`ɛrənt; 'æbərənt/ *adj formal* not usual or normal【正式】异常的; 脱离常规的: *aberrant behaviour* 异常行为

ab·er·ra·tion /ˌæbə`reʃən; ˌæbə'reɪʃən/ *n* [C,U] an action or event that is different from what usually happens or what someone usually does 偏离; 异常: *a temporary aberration in US foreign policy* 美国外交政策短暂的异常变化 | *a mental aberration* 精神失常

a·bet /ə`bɛt; ə'bet/ *v* **abetted, abetting** [T] to help someone do something wrong or illegal 教唆, 怂恿, 唆使; 伙同〔作案〕— see also 另见 **aid and abet** (AID[2] (2))

a·bey·ance /ə`beəns; ə'beɪəns/ *n* **in abeyance** something such as a custom, rule, or system that is in abeyance is not being used at the present time 搁置; 中止; 暂缓: **fall into abeyance** (=no longer be used) 暂时停用; 暂时中止

ab·hor /əb`hɔr; əb'hɔː/ *v* **abhorred, abhorring** [T not in progressive 不用进行时] *formal* to hate a kind of behaviour or way of thinking, especially because you think it is morally wrong【正式】厌恶, 憎恶: *Some genuinely abhorred slavery, others were simply convinced by the economic arguments against it.* 有些人真正厌恶奴隶制, 而另一些人只是出于经济上的理由才反对奴隶制的。

ab·hor·rence /əb`hɔrəns; əb'hɒrəns/ *n* [U] *formal* a deep feeling of hatred towards something【正式】痛恨

ab·hor·rent /əb`hɔrənt; əb'hɒrənt/ *adj formal* something that is abhorrent is completely unacceptable because it seems morally wrong; REPUGNANT【正式】可恨的, 令人憎恶的: [+to] *The practice of killing animals for food is utterly abhorrent to me.* 我对将动物杀死作为盘中餐的做法非常痛恨。

a·bide /ə`baɪd; ə'baɪd/ *v* **1 can't abide** to dislike something or someone very much because you think they are very annoying 不能容忍 [忍受]: *I can't abide that man – he's so self-satisfied.* 我受不了那个人, 他太自满了。**2** *past tense* also 过去式又作 **abode** /ə`bod; ə'bəʊd/ [I always+adv/prep] *old-fashioned* to live somewhere【过时】居住

abide by sth *phr v* [T] to accept and obey a decision, rule, agreement etc, even though you may not agree with it 遵守〔法律〕; 信守〔协议等〕: *You have to abide by the referee's decision.* 你必须服从裁判的决定。

Abide With Me /·ˌ· `· ·/ a well-known HYMN (=a song of praise to God). In the UK it is always sung before the Cup Final (=an important football game). 《与我同在》〔一首著名赞美诗。英国足协杯决赛开赛前总要唱这首歌〕

a·bid·ing /ə`baɪdɪŋ; ə'baɪdɪŋ/ *adj* an abiding feeling or belief continues for a long time and is not likely to change〔情感或信仰〕永久的, 持久的

a·bil·i·ty /ə`bɪlətɪ; ə'bɪlɪ̈ti/ *n plural* **abilities** [C,U] **1** something that you are able to do, especially because you have a particular mental or physical skill 能力; 技能; 本领: **ability to do sth** *Our ability to think and speak separates us from other mammals.* 思维和说话的能力使我们有别于其他哺乳动物。| **have the ability to do sth** (=be able to do something, espe-

cially something that most people, machines etc cannot do) 有能力做某事〔尤指大部分人、机器等做不了的事〕*These creatures have the ability to withstand very low temperatures.* 这些动物具有忍受极低气温的能力。| **of great/exceptional etc ability** (=very good at something) 特别擅长… *a player of great ability* 非常有才华的运动员 | *No one doubts her abilities as a manager.* 没有人怀疑她当经理的能力。**2** someone's, especially a student's, level of intelligence or skill, especially in school or college work 智能, 智力: *There are children of all abilities in my class.* 我班上的学生智力水平各有不同。| **high/low/average ability** (=having a high, low etc level of intelligence or skill) 高/低/平均智力[技能] | **mixed ability class** (=a class of students with different levels of intelligence) 智力水平有差异的班级 **3 to the best of your ability** to do something as well as you can 竭尽全力

-ability /əˋbɪlətɪ; əˈbɪlɨti/ also 又作 **-ibility** *suffix* makes nouns from adjectives ending in -ABLE and -IBLE〔将以 -able 和 -ible 结尾的形容词转化为名词的后缀〕: *manageability* 可处理(性) | *suitability* 适合(性)

ab·ject /ˋæbdʒɛkt; ˈæbdʒekt/ *adj* **1 abject poverty/misery/failure etc** the state of being extremely poor, unhappy, unsuccessful etc 赤贫/惨痛/惨败等 **2** an abject action or expression shows that you feel very ashamed 自卑的, 卑躬屈膝的: *an abject apology* 低声下气的道歉 —**abjectly** *adv* —**abjection** /æbˋdʒɛkʃən; æbˈdʒekʃən/ *n* [U]

ab·jure /əbˋdʒur; əbˈdʒʊə/ *v* [T] *formal* to state publicly that you will give up a particular belief or way of behaving; RENOUNCE (2)【正式】公开宣布放弃〔某信念、做法〕—**abjuration** /ˌæbdʒuˋreʃən; ˌæbdʒʊˈreɪʃən/ *n* [U]

a·blaze /əˋblez; əˈbleɪz/ *adj* **1 be ablaze** to be burning with a lot of flames, often causing serious damage 熊熊燃烧, 着火: *Within minutes the whole house was ablaze.* 几分钟内, 整座房子就成了一片火海。| **set sth ablaze** (=make something burn a lot) 点燃[放火烧]某物 *A tanker was set ablaze in the gunboat attack.* 油轮遭到炮艇攻击起火了。**2** filled with a lot of bright light or colour 明亮的, 灯火辉煌的: *a passing pleasure-boat, with all its lights ablaze* 一艘驶过的游船, 上面灯火辉煌 | [+with] *Her yard was ablaze with summer flowers.* 她的院子夏季里鲜花五彩缤纷。**3 ablaze with anger/enthusiasm/excitement etc** very angry, excited etc about something 非常生气/热情/激动等 —see also 另见 BLAZE

[1] [1] **a·ble** /ˋebl̩; ˈeɪbəl/ *adj* **1 be able to do sth a)** to have the skill, strength, knowledge etc to do something 有能力做某事, 会做某事: *I've always wanted to be able to speak Japanese.* 我一直希望会讲日语。**b)** to be able to do something because the situation makes it possible for you to do it 可以去做某事: *Despite his enormous workload the President still seems able to find time to go fishing.* 尽管公务繁忙, 总统似乎还能找到时间去钓鱼。| *I haven't been able to read that report yet.* 我到现在还未能看那份报告。—see 见 CAN[1] (USAGE) **2** clever or good at doing something, especially at doing an important job; COMPETENT (1) 熟练的; 胜任的, 称职的: *one of my more able students* 我班上能力比较强的学生之一

-able /əbl̩; əbəl/ also 又作 **-ible** *suffix* [in adjectives 构成形容词] **1** that you can do something to 可以…的: *washable* (=it can be washed) 可洗的 | *unbreakable* (=it cannot be broken) 不会破的, 不易打碎的 | *loveable* (=easy to love) 可爱的 **2** having a particular quality or condition 具有…性质的; 处于…状态的: *knowledgeable* (=knowing a lot) 博学的 | *comfortable* 舒适的 —**-ably, -ibly** [in adverbs 构成副词]: *unbelievably* 令人难以置信地

able-bod·ied /ˌ‥ˋ‥◂/ *adj* physically strong and healthy, especially when compared with someone who is DISABLED 体格健全的, 强壮的: *Every able-bodied man had to fight for his country.* 每一个体格健全的人都必须为祖国而战斗。

able sea·man /ˌ‥ˋ‥/ *n* [C] a low rank in the navy, or someone who has this rank 一等水兵 —see table on page C6 参见 C6 页附录

a·blu·tions /əbˋluʃənz; əˈbluːʃənz/ *n* [plural] *formal or humorous* the things that you do to make yourself clean, such as washing yourself, cleaning your teeth etc【正式或幽默】沐浴; 漱洗

a·bly /ˋeblɪ; ˈeɪbli/ *adv* cleverly, skilfully, or well 能干地; 巧妙地: *ably assisted by her team of researchers* 得到她研究小组人员的大力帮助

ab·ne·ga·tion /ˌæbnɪˋgeʃən; ˌæbnɨˈgeɪʃən/ *n* [U] *formal* the act of not allowing yourself to have or do something that you want【正式】自制, 克己

ab·norm·al /æbˋnɔrml̩; æbˈnɔːməl/ *adj* very different from usual in a way that seems strange, worrying, wrong, or dangerous 不正常的, 反常的; 变态的: *abnormal behaviour* 异常行为 | *an abnormal level of cholesterol* 胆固醇水平异常 | **abnormal for sb to do sth** *My parents thought it was abnormal for a boy to be interested in ballet.* 我父母认为一个男孩子对芭蕾舞感兴趣不正常。

ab·nor·mal·i·ty /ˌæbnɔrˋmælətɪ; ˌæbnɔːˈmælɨti/ *n* [C,U] an abnormal feature or characteristic, especially something that is wrong with part of someone's body〔尤指身体部位〕变异, 变态: *tests that can detect genetic abnormalities in the foetus* 检查胎儿基因异常的试验

ab·nor·mal·ly /æbˋnɔrmlɪ; æbˈnɔːməli/ *adv* **1 abnormally high/low/slow etc** unusually high, low etc, especially in a way that could cause problems 异常地高/低/慢等: *an abnormally high pulse rate* 异常快的脉率 **2** in an unusual and often worrying or dangerous way 异常地〔常指令人担心或危险的行事方式〕

ab·o /ˋæbo; ˈæbəʊ/ *n* [C] *taboo* an offensive word for an Australian ABORIGINE【讳】土佬〔对澳洲土著人的蔑称〕

a·board[1] /əˋbɔrd; əˈbɔːd/ *prep* on or onto a ship, plane, or train 上船[飞机, 火车]; 在船[飞机, 火车]上: **go aboard** *They finally went aboard the plane.* 他们终于登上了飞机。

aboard[2] *adv* **1** on or onto a ship, plane, or train 在船[飞机, 火车]上; 上船[飞机, 火车]: *The plane crashed killing all 200 people aboard.* 飞机失事, 机上 200 人全部遇难。| *The boat swayed as he stepped aboard.* 他上船时, 船晃了起来。**2 All aboard!** *spoken* used to tell passengers of a ship, bus, or train that they must get on because it will leave soon【口】请大家上船[上公共汽车, 上火车]!

a·bode[1] /əˋbod; əˈbəʊd/ *n* [C] *formal or humorous* someone's home【正式或幽默】住所: *Welcome to my humble abode.* 欢迎光临寒舍。| **of no fixed abode** (=having no permanent home) 居无定所

abode[2] the past tense of ABIDE

a·bol·ish /əˋbɑlɪʃ; əˈbɒlɪʃ/ *v* [T] to officially end a law, system etc, especially one that has existed for a long time 废除, 取消: *Slavery was abolished in America in the 19th century.* 美国于 19 世纪废除了奴隶制。—**abolition** /ˌæbəˋlɪʃən; ˌæbəˈlɪʃən/ *n* [U]: *calls for the abolition of the monarchy* 废除君主制的呼声

ab·o·li·tion·ist /ˌæbəˋlɪʃənɪst; ˌæbəˈlɪʃənɨst/ *n* [C] someone who wants to end a system or law 废除主义者

A-bomb /ˋe ˌbɑm; ˈeɪ bɒm/ *n* [C] *old-fashioned* an ATOM BOMB【过时】原子弹

a·bom·i·na·ble /əˋbɑmɪnəbl̩; əˈbɒmɪnəbəl/ *adj* extremely unpleasant or of very bad quality 令人讨厌的, 可恶的; 极差的 —**abominably** *adv*: *Mavis behaved abominably.* 梅维斯表现太差了。

abominable snow·man /ˌ‥‥ ˈ‥/ *n* [C] a large creature like a human that is supposed to live in the Himalayas; a YETI〔据传生活在喜马拉雅山一带的〕雪人

a·bom·i·nate /əˋbɑməˌnet; əˈbɒmɨneɪt/ *v* [T not in progressive 不用进行时] *formal* to hate something very much; ABHOR【正式】憎恨, 厌恶

a·bom·i·na·tion /əˌbɑməˋneʃən; əˌbɒmɨˈneɪʃən/ *n* **1** [C] someone or something that is extremely offensive or unacceptable 令人厌恶的人[事物]: *They considered homosexuality as an abomination.* 他们对同性恋深恶痛绝。**2** [U+of] *formal* great hatred【正式】痛恨

ab·o·rig·i·nal[1] /ˌæbəˋrɪdʒənl̩; ˌæbəˈrɪdʒɨnəl◂/ *adj* **1** *formal* connected with the people or animals that have existed in a place or country from the earliest times; INDIGENOUS【正式】土著的; 土生的 **2** connected with the Australian aborigines 澳洲土著(居民)的

aboriginal[2] *n* [C] an aborigine 土著居民; 土人

ab·o·rig·i·ne /ˌæbəˋrɪdʒənɪ; ˌæbəˈrɪdʒɨni/ *n* [C] a member of the group of people who have lived in Australia from the earliest times (澳洲)土著居民

a·bort /əˋbɔrt; əˈbɔːt/ *v* **1** [T] to stop an activity because it would be difficult or dangerous to continue it 使〔活动〕中止, 夭折: *The shuttle developed a computer problem and the mission had to be aborted.* 航天飞机因电脑出现故障, 飞行任务不得不中止。**2** [T] to deliberately cause a baby to be born too soon so that it cannot live, often because the baby or the mother has medical problems 使〔胎儿〕流产; 堕〔胎〕: *Doctors decided to abort the pregnancy.* 医生决定进行人工流产。**3** [I,T] if a woman aborts or aborts her baby, the baby is born too early and is dead when it is born 流产, 小产

a·bor·tion /əˋbɔrʃən; əˈbɔːʃən/ *n* [C,U] a medical operation in which a baby's development inside a woman is stopped so that it is not born alive 人工流产; 堕胎: **have an abortion** *an*

unmarried mother who had an abortion when she was 16 16岁时做过人工流产的未婚母亲 | *anti-abortion campaigners* 参与反堕胎运动的人

CULTURAL NOTE 文化注释

Although abortion has been legal in the US since 1973 and in the UK since 1967, many people still disagree about whether it should be legal, and about whether it is morally right. Some people are PRO-CHOICE and believe that a woman has the right to choose whether or not to have an abortion. Other people are PRO-LIFE or anti-abortion, and believe that an unborn baby has the right to be born and that abortion is murder. 堕胎1973年在美国合法化, 1967年在英国合法化, 尽管如此, 很多人对堕胎是否应该合法以及是否合乎道德存有异议。一些人赞成堕胎, 认为女性有权选择是否堕胎; 另一些人则反对堕胎, 认为胎儿也有权来到这个世界, 堕胎就是谋杀。— see also 另见 ROE VS. WADE

a·bor·tion·ist /əˋbɔrʃənɪst; əˈbɔːʃənɨst/ *n* [C] someone who does abortions illegally 非法为人堕胎者

a·bor·tive /əˋbɔrtɪv; əˈbɔːtɪv/ *adj* an abortive action is not successful 流产的, 夭折的: *an abortive military coup* 未遂的军事政变 | **abortive attempt/effort** *an abortive attempt to reform local government* 落空了的改革地方政府的计划

a·bound /əˋbaʊnd; əˈbaʊnd/ *v* [I] to exist in very large numbers or quantities 大量存在; 充满: *Rumours abound as to the reasons for his resignation.* 有关他辞职的原因有各种各样的谣传。| *Examples of this abound in her book.* 这样的例子在她书中不胜枚举。

abound with/in sth *phr v* [T] if a place, situation etc abounds with something it contains a very large number or quantity of that thing 盛产, 富于

a·bout[1] /əˋbaʊt; əˈbaʊt/ *prep* **1** on or dealing with a particular subject 关于: *a book about politics* 有关政治的书 | *She said something about leaving town.* 她说到关于离开城镇的事。| **all about** (=all the details of a particular subject) 关于…的全部内容 *Naturally, my mother wanted to know all about it.* 当然, 我母亲想知道事情的全部。**2** in many different directions within a particular place, or in different parts of a place 到处: *We spent the whole afternoon walking about town.* 我们整个下午在城里四处走。| *Books were scattered about the room.* 书本散布在房间里。—see also 另见 ROUND[3] (USAGE) —see picture on page A1 参见 A1 页图 **3** in the nature or character of a person or thing 性格上; 特点上: *There's something really odd about Liza.* 丽莎的为人真有点怪。| *What I like about the movie is the dialogue.* 这部电影, 我喜欢的是其对白。**4 what about/how about** *spoken*【口】**a)** used to ask for news or information about someone or something …怎么样〔用以打听消息〕: *What about Jack? We can't just leave him here.* 杰克怎么办? 我们不能把他丢在这里不管。**b)** used to make a suggestion …怎么样; …好吗〔用以提建议〕: *How about a salad for lunch?* 午饭吃沙拉怎么样? **5** *spoken* used to introduce a subject that you want to talk about【口】〔用来引出一个话题〕有关: *About that car of yours. How much are you selling it for?* 关于你那辆汽车, 你想卖多少钱? | **it's about** *It's about Tommy, doctor. He's been sick again.* 医生, 是有关汤米的, 他又病了。**6 do sth about** to do something to solve a problem or stop a bad situation 想办法做…, 解决…问题: *What can be done about the rising levels of pollution?* 该怎样解决污染加剧问题? **7** if an organization, a job, an activity etc is about something, that is its basic purpose 宗旨是…; 关于: *Basically, the job's all about helping people get the benefits they are entitled to.* 基本上, 这项工作的宗旨是帮助人们得到他们应得的利益。**8 be quick about it** *spoken* used to tell someone to do something quickly【口】快点儿: *Get me a drink and be quick about it.* 给我拿点喝的, 快点儿。**9 while you're about it** *spoken* used to tell someone to do something while they are doing something else because it would be easier to do both at the same time【口】顺便: *Clean up while I'm away and you might as well do the attic while you're about it.* 我不在时, 你彻底清扫一下, 顺便打扫一下阁楼。**10 about your person** *formal* if you hide something about your person, you hide it in your clothes【正式】在身上, 在衣服里: *He had concealed the weapon somewhere about his person.* 他把武器藏在身上某个地方了。**11** *literary* surrounding a person or thing【文】围绕〔某人或某事〕: *Jo sensed fear and jealousy all about her.* 乔能觉察到她既恐惧又妒嫉。

about[2] *adv* **1** more or less a particular number or amount; approximately (APPROXIMATE[1]) 大约, 大概: *I live about 10 miles away.* 我住的地方离这里10英里左右。| **round about** (=used when guessing an exact number or amount) 大概 *We left the restaurant at round about 10.30.* 我们大概是在十点半离开餐厅的。—see graph at 参见 APPROXIMATE[1] 图表 **2** in many different directions within a place or in different parts of a place 到处: *Cushions were scattered about on the chairs.* 好几个垫子散放在几张椅子上。**3** near to you or in the same place as you 在附近, 在…周围: *Is Derrick about? There's a phone call for him.* 德里克在附近吗? 有电话找他。| *Quick! Let's go while there's no-one about.* 快点儿! 我们趁附近没有人赶紧走。**4 there's a lot of sth about/there's not much of sth about** *especially spoken* used to say that something is very common, or that not much of it exists or is available【尤口】某物很普遍/不常见: *I hope she hasn't caught that flu bug. There's a lot of it about at the moment.* 我希望她没感染流感病毒, 目前这种病毒到处都有。**5** *informal* almost【非正式】几乎: *The food's about ready.* 食物就要〔准备〕好了。—see also 另见 **just about** (JUST[1] (8)) **6 that's about it/all** *informal* used to tell someone that you have told them everything you know【非正式】该说的都说了, 这就是全部: *He was a quiet chap, married with kids. That's about it really.* 他话不多, 已婚, 有孩子。大概就是这样。**7** in the opposite direction that you were facing before〔转向〕相反方向: *He quickly turned about.* 他很快转过身。—see also 另见 ROUND[3] (USAGE)

about[3] *adj* **1 be about to do sth** if someone is about to do something or if something is about to happen, they will do it or it will happen very soon 即将[马上]做某事: *Sit down everyone. The film's about to start.* 大家坐下, 电影马上要开始了。**2 not be about to do sth** *informal* used to emphasize that you have no intention of doing something【非正式】不打算做某事: *I've never smoked in my life and I'm not about to start now.* 我从未抽过烟, 现在也不打算抽。—see also 另见 **be up and about** (UP[3] (6))

about-face /ˌ·ˈ·/ *n* [C usually singular 一般用单数] a complete change in the way someone thinks or behaves〔思想、行为的〕大转变: **do an about-face** *The administration seems to have done a complete about-face on gun-control.* 政府对枪支管制〔的态度〕似乎来了个180度大转弯。

about-turn /ˌ·ˈ·/ *n* [C usually singular 一般用单数] *BrE* an about-face【英】大转变

above 在…上方

The picture is above the fireplace/over the fireplace.
画挂在壁炉上方。

The girl jumped over the wall.
那女孩跳过墙。

The man put his hand over the boy's mouth.
那男子用手捂住男孩的嘴。

a·bove[1] /əˋbʌv; əˈbʌv/ *prep* **1** in a higher position than something 在…上方: *Our office is above the hairdresser's.* 我们的办公室在理发店上面。| *Raise your arms above your head.* 把双臂举过头。—see also 另见 OVER[1] —opposite 反义词 BELOW[1] (1) **2** more than a particular number, amount, or level 高于, 超出: *500 feet above sea level* 海拔500英尺 | *Tonight temperatures should be above freezing.* 今晚的温度将会在零度以上。—op-

posite 反义词 BELOW[1] (2) **3** to a greater degree than someone or something else 高于，大于：*The management has always valued hard work above good ideas.* 管理层总是认为努力工作比提好建议重要。| **above and beyond** (=to a much greater degree) 远不止 *bravery above and beyond the call of duty* 超越职责要求的勇敢精神 **4** higher in rank, power, or authority〔权力〕大于；〔地位〕高于：*A captain is above a lieutenant.* 上尉的军衔比中尉高。—opposite 反义词 BELOW[1] (3) **5** louder or having a higher PITCH than other sounds〔声音〕比…高：*You can always hear her voice above everybody else's.* 你总会听到她的嗓门压过其他所有的人。**6 be above (doing) sth** to consider yourself so important that you do not have to do all the things that everyone else has to do 不屑于（做）某事：*She seems to think she's above doing any housework.* 她好像认为做家务有损自己的身份。| *politicians who think they are above the law* 认为自己可以凌驾于法律之上的政客们 **7 above suspicion/reproach/criticism etc** so good that no one can question or criticize you 无可怀疑/责难/批评等 **8 above all (else)** used to emphasize that something is more important than the other things you have already mentioned 尤其是，最重要的是：*Max is fair, hardworking, and above all honest.* 马克斯公正、勤劳，最重要的是诚实。**9 get above yourself** to think you are better or more important than you really are 自高自大，自命不凡 —see also 另见 **over and above** (OVER[1] (13))

2 1 **above**[2] *adv* **1** in a higher place than something else 在上面：*I heard a strange noise coming from the room above.* 我听到楼上房间里传来奇怪的声音。**2** more than a particular number, amount, or level 超过〔某数字、数量或水平〕：*Children aged 10 and above are not allowed in the learner pool.* 10岁及10岁以上的孩子不得在练习池里游泳。**3** higher in rank, power, or authority〔官衔、权势〕在上，以上：*officers of the rank of Major and above* 少校及少校以上军衔的军官 **4** *formal* used in a book, article etc to describe someone or something mentioned earlier in the same piece of writing【正式】上述，上文：*See above.* 见上文。| *Write to the address given above for further information.* 详情请致函上述地址查询。—opposite 反义词 BELOW[2]

USAGE NOTE 用法说明：ABOVE
FORMALITY 正式程度
Above meaning 'mentioned earlier' is only used in technical or official writing. In everyday writing you are more likely to put 表示"上述"意思时，above 只用于专业性的或正式的文体。日常写作中常用：*As I said earlier...* (=*...stated above*) 正如我在前面提到的… | *The facts discussed before...* (=*...discussed above*) 前面讨论的事实… | *Please contact me at the address I have given you* (=*...at the above address*). 请按我给你的地址和我联系。| *from the last few paragraphs* (=*from the above paragraphs*) 从上面的几段中

3 **above**[3] *adj* **1** [only before noun 仅用于名词前] used in a book, article etc to describe someone or something mentioned earlier in the same piece of writing 上述的：*For the above reasons, the management has no choice but to close the factory.* 基于上述原因，资方别无选择，只好关闭工厂。**2 the above** *formal* [singular or plural] the person or thing mentioned before in the same piece of writing【正式】上面提到的人[事]：*The above is the profit before tax.* 上面提到的是税前利润。| *All the above are asked to attend tomorrow's meeting.* 以上各位请全部出席明天的会议。

above board /ˌ·ˈ·◂/ *adj* [not before noun 不用于名词前] honest and legal 光明正大的：**open and above board** *The deal was completely open and above board.* 这笔交易完全是光明正大的。

above-men·tioned /ˌ·ˈ··◂/ *adj* **1** [only before noun 仅用于名词前] *formal* mentioned on a previous page or higher up on the same page【正式】上面的，上述的 **2 the above-mentioned** people whose names have already been mentioned in a book, document etc 上面提到的人 —compare 比较 UNDERMENTIONED

ab·ra·ca·dab·ra /ˌæbrəkəˈdæbrə; ˌæbrəkəˈdæbrə/ *interjection* a word you say when you do a magic trick, which is supposed to make it successful 阿布拉卡达布拉〔魔术表演施行法术时所念的咒语〕

a·brade /əˈbred; əˈbreɪd/ *v* [I,T] *technical* to rub something so hard that the surface becomes damaged【术语】磨损

A·bra·ham /ˈebrəˌhæm; ˈeɪbrəhæm/ in the Old Testament of the Bible, a religious leader who established the Jews as a nation 亚伯拉罕〔《圣经·旧约》中的一位宗教领袖，建立了犹太国〕

a·bra·sion /əˈbreʒən; əˈbreɪʒən/ *n technical*【术语】**1** [C] an area, especially on the surface of your skin, that has been damaged or injured by being rubbed too hard 磨损处，磨伤处：*minor abrasions* 少许磨损 **2** [U] the process of rubbing a surface very hard so that it becomes damaged or disappears 磨损（的过程），磨蚀

a·bra·sive[1] /əˈbresɪv; əˈbreɪsɪv/ *adj* **1** seeming rude or unkind in the way you behave towards people because you say what you think very directly 生硬的；粗鲁的：*a rather abrasive manner* 相当粗鲁的举止 **2** having a rough surface, especially one that can be used to clean other surfaces by rubbing〔尤指可用于擦洗的东西表面〕粗糙的 —**abrasively** *adv*

abrasive[2] *n* [C usually plural 一般用复数] a substance with a rough surface that you use for cleaning other things by rubbing 磨料

abreast 并肩，并排

They cycled three abreast. 他们三个人并排骑车。

a·breast /əˈbrɛst; əˈbrest/ *adv* **1 walk/ride etc abreast** to walk, ride etc next to each other 并肩走/并排骑等：**two/three/four abreast etc** (=with two or more people next to each other) 二/三/四人等并排 **2 keep abreast of** to make sure that you know all the most recent facts or information about a particular subject or situation 了解…的最新情况：*Henry tries to keep abreast of the latest developments in computing.* 亨利设法掌握计算机技术的最新发展。

a·bridged /əˈbrɪdʒd; əˈbrɪdʒd/ *adj* an abridged book, play etc has been made shorter but keeps its basic structure and meaning 删节的，节略的，压缩的 —**abridge** *v* [T] —**abridgement** *n* [C,U]

a·broad /əˈbrɔd; əˈbrɔːd/ *adv* **1** in or to a foreign country 在国外；到国外：*I've never lived abroad before.* 我以前从未在国外生活过。| **go abroad** *She often goes abroad on business.* 她经常出国公干。**2** *formal* if a feeling, piece of news etc is abroad, a lot of people feel it or know about it【正式】广泛流传：*commercial secrets which we did not want to be spread abroad* 我们不想传出去的商业秘密 **3** *old use* outdoors【旧】在户外，室外 2 3

ab·ro·gate /ˈæbrəˌget; ˈæbrəgeɪt/ *v* [T] *formal* to officially end a law, legal agreement, practice etc【正式】取消，废除：*Both governments voted to abrogate the treaty.* 两国政府均投票废除了这项条约。—**abrogation** /ˌæbrəˈgeʃən; ˌæbrəˈgeɪʃən/ *n* [C,U]

a·brupt /əˈbrʌpt; əˈbrʌpt/ *adj* **1** sudden and unexpected 突然的，出其不意的：*an abrupt change of plan* 计划的突然改变 | **abrupt halt** *The bus came to an abrupt halt.* 公共汽车突然停了下来。**2** seeming rude and unfriendly, especially because you do not waste time in friendly conversation; BRUSQUE 唐突的；鲁莽的，莽撞的：*Sorry, I didn't mean to be so abrupt.* 对不起，我不是故意这样无礼的。—**abruptly** *adv* —**abruptness** *n* [U]

ABS /ˌe bi ˈɛs; ˌeɪ biː ˈes/ *n* [U] the abbreviation of 缩写＝ ANTI-LOCK BRAKING SYSTEM

Ab·sa·lom /ˈæbsələm; ˈæbsələm/ in the Old Testament of the Bible, the third son of David, king of Israel 押沙龙〔《圣经·旧约》中以色列国王大卫之第三子〕

ab·scess /ˈæbˌsɛs; ˈæbses/ *n* [C] a painful swollen part of your skin or inside your body that has become infected and is full of a yellowish liquid 脓肿

ab·scond /æbˈskɑnd; əbˈskɒnd/ *v* [I] **1** to suddenly leave the place where you work after having stolen money from it〔携款〕潜逃：[+with] *The chief accountant had absconded with all the money.* 总会计师携带所有的钱款潜逃了。**2** to escape from a place where you are being kept for doing something wrong 逃

走，逃匿: *Several boys have absconded from the detention centre.* 几个男孩子从拘留所逃走了。

A

ab·seil /ˈæbseɪl; ˈæbseɪl/ *v* [I+down] *BrE* to go down a cliff or a rock by sliding down a rope and touching the cliff or rock with your feet【英】〔用绳索〕下降; RAPPEL *AmE*【美】

3 2 **ab·sence** /ˈæbsəns; ˈæbsəns/ *n* **1** [C,U] the fact that someone is not in the place where people expect them to be 不在，缺席: **in/during sb's absence** (=while they are away) 某人不在的时候 *Ms Leighton will be in charge during my absence.* 我不在时，由莱顿女士负责。**2** [U] the lack of something or the fact that it does not exist 缺乏，没有: [+of] *a complete absence of any kind of planning* 毫无计划 | **in the absence of** (=because something is missing or not available) 由于缺乏 *In the absence of any evidence, the police had to let Myers go.* 由于缺乏证据，警察只好把迈尔斯放了。**3 absence makes the heart grow fonder** used to say that being away from someone makes you like them more 人不见，心更念; 久别情更深 —see also 另见 **leave of absence** (LEAVE[2] (3)), **conspicuous by your absence** (CONSPICUOUS (3))

ab·sent[1] /ˈæbsənt; ˈæbsənt/ *adj* **1** not at work, school, a meeting etc, because you are sick or decide not to go 不在的，缺席的: [+from] *students who are regularly absent from school* 经常缺课的学生 **2 absent look/expression etc** a look etc that shows you are not paying attention to or thinking about what is happening 心不在焉的样子/表情等 —see also 另见 ABSENTLY **3** *formal* if something is absent, it is missing or it is not in the place where it is expected to be【正式】缺乏的，不在场的: [+from] *What was absent from the discussion was any kind of direction or purpose.* 这场讨论没有任何方向或目的。

ab·sent[2] /æbˋsɛnt; əbˈsent/ *v* [T] **absent yourself (from)** *formal* to not go to a place or take part in an event where people expect you to be【正式】缺席; 置身于…之外

ab·sen·tee /ˌæbsn̩ˋti; ˌæbsənˈtiː◂/ *n* [C] someone who should be in a place or at an event but is not there 缺席者

absentee bal·lot /ˌ··ˈ··/ *n* [C] *AmE* a process by which people can vote before an election because they will be away during the election【美】缺席投票〔因投票人在选举期间不在而允许其提前投票的程序〕

ab·sen·tee·is·m /ˌæbsn̩ˋtiɪzəm; ˌæbsənˈtiːɪzəm/ *n* [U] regular absence from work or school without a good reason 经常旷工[缺课]

absentee land·lord /ˌ··ˈ··/ *n* [C] someone who lives a long way away from a house or apartment which they rent to other people, and who rarely or never visits it〔住在很远处、很少或从不到访出租房产的〕在外房东，在外业主

absentee vote /ˌ··ˈ·/ *n* [C] *AmE* a vote which you send by post in an election because you cannot be in the place where you usually vote【美】缺席选票〔投票人在选举期间不能到场而通过邮寄方式投的票〕; POSTAL VOTE *BrE*【英】

ab·sen·ti·a /æbˋsɛntɪə; æbˈsentiə/ *n* **in absentia** *formal* when you are not at a court or an official meeting where a decision is made about you【正式】在〔当事人〕缺席的情况下: *They were sentenced in absentia.* 他们在缺席的情况下被判刑。

ab·sent·ly /ˈæbsn̩tlɪ; ˈæbsəntli/ *adv* in a way that shows that you are not paying attention to or thinking about what is happening 心不在焉地: *Laura gazed absently out of the window.* 劳拉出神地注视着窗外。

absent-mind·ed /ˌ··ˈ··◂/ *adj* likely to forget things, especially because you are thinking about something else 心不在焉的，茫然的: *She's getting very absent-minded.* 她变得心神恍惚。—**absent-mindedly** *adv* —**absent-mindedness** *n* [U]

ab·sinth, absinthe /ˈæbsɪnθ; ˈæbsɪnθ/ *n* [U] a bitter green very strong alcoholic drink 苦艾酒

2 3 **ab·so·lute** /ˈæbsəˌlut; ˈæbsəluːt/ *adj* **1** [only before noun 仅用于名词前] *especially spoken* used to emphasize your opinion about something or someone, especially when you think they are very bad, stupid, unsuccessful etc【尤口】纯粹的; 绝对的: **absolute disgrace/disaster/chaos etc** *The house looked an absolute shambles.* 屋子里显得凌乱不堪。| *I think it's an absolute disgrace the way they treat that child.* 我认为他们这样对待那个孩子真是太可耻了。| **an absolute genius/fool/idiot etc** *How did you do that? You're an absolute genius.* 你是怎么做的? 你绝对是个天才。| **absolute nonsense/rubbish** (=used to say that you think that what someone is saying is completely stupid) 一派胡言 **2** absolute silence, freedom, loyalty etc is the state of being completely silent, free etc 完全的; 绝对的: *I have absolute confidence in her.* 我对她绝对有信心。**3** absolute power or authority is complete and unlimited〔权力或权威〕绝对的，无限的: **absolute ruler/monarch** (=a ruler with unlimited power) 专制统治者/君主 **4** definite and not likely to change 确定的; 不会更改的: *I can't give you any absolute guarantees about your safety.* 我不能绝对保证你的安全。**5 in absolute terms** measured by itself, not in comparison with other things 从绝对意义上说: *In absolute terms wages have risen, but not in comparison with the cost of living.* 从绝对意义上说，工资是提高了，但同生活费用相比较就不能这样说了。

ab·so·lute·ly /ˈæbsəˌlutlɪ; ˈæbsəluːtli/ *adv* **1** *especially spoken* completely and in every way【尤口】完全地; 绝对地: [+adj/adv] *He's an absolutely brilliant singer.* 他是个绝对出色的歌唱家。| *You can trust her absolutely!* 你可以完全信任她! | *You look absolutely fantastic in that dress.* 你穿那条裙子简直美极了。| **absolutely no/nothing** (=none or nothing at all) 一点儿没有 *He has absolutely no experience of marketing.* 他毫无销售经验。| *The burglars took absolutely everything.* 窃贼把所有的东西全拿走了。**2 absolutely!** *spoken* used to say that you completely agree with someone【口】正是! 当然!: *Oh yes, absolutely. I think it's a great idea.* 噢，对，我看这绝对是个好主意。**3 absolutely not!** *spoken* used when saying strongly that someone must not do something or when strongly disagreeing with someone【口】绝对不行!: *"Do you let your kids travel alone at night?" "Absolutely not!"* "你让孩子晚上单独外出吗?" "绝对不会!" 1 3

Frequencies of the adverb **absolutely** in spoken and written English 副词 absolutely 在英语口语和书面语中的使用频率

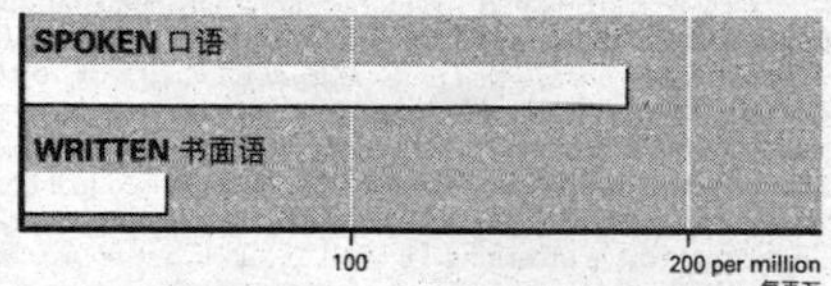

Based on the British National Corpus and the Longman Lancaster Corpus
据英国国家语料库和朗文兰开斯特语料库

This graph shows that the adverb **absolutely** is much more common in spoken English than in written English. This is because it is used to emphasize adjectives like **brilliant**, **stupid**, **fantastic** etc in spoken English. 本图表显示，副词absolutely在英语口语中的使用频率远远高于书面语，因为它在口语中用来强调brilliant, stupid, fantastic 等一类的形容词。

absolute ze·ro /ˌ··ˈ··/ *n* [singular] the lowest temperature that is believed to be possible 绝对零度

ab·so·lu·tion /ˌæbsəˋluʃən; ˌæbsəˈluːʃən/ *n* [U] a process in the Christian religion by which someone is forgiven for the things they have done wrong〔基督教中的〕赦罪; 宽恕

ab·so·lut·is·m /ˈæbsəlutˌɪzəm; ˈæbsəluːtɪzəm/ *n* [U] a political system in which one ruler has complete power and authority 专制主义(制度)，独裁政治

ab·solve /əbˋzɑlv; əbˈzɒlv/ *v* [T] *formal*【正式】**1** to say publicly that someone is not guilty or responsible for something 宣布…无罪; 免除…〔责任等〕: **absolve sb from/of sth** *They were absolved of all responsibility for the accident.* 他们被免于承担这起意外事故的一切责任。**2** [often passive 常用被动态] to forgive someone for something they have done wrong 饶恕

absorb 吸收

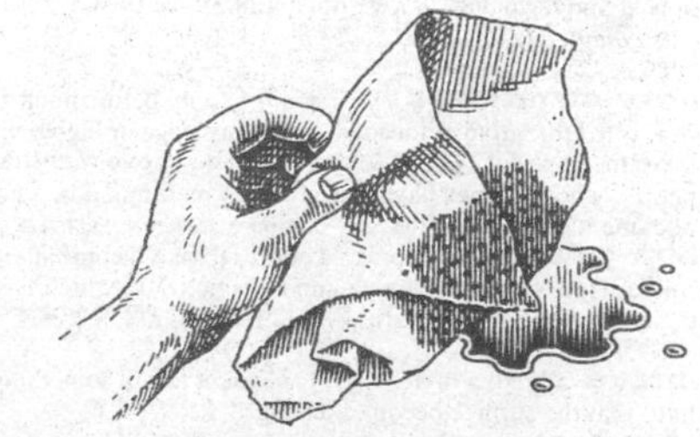

ab·sorb /əbˋsɔrb; əbˈsɔːb/ *v* [T] 3

1 ►LIQUID 液体◄ if something absorbs a liquid, it takes the liquid into itself from the surface or space around it 吸收〔液

体〕: *Plants absorb nutrients from the soil.* 植物从土壤中吸收养分。
2 ▶INFORMATION 信息◀ to read or hear a large amount of new information and understand it 理解, 掌握: *I haven't really had time to absorb everything that he said.* 我还真没有时间弄懂他说的一切。
3 ▶INTEREST 兴趣◀ to interest someone very much 吸引〔某人〕, 使专心: **be absorbed in** *Judith lay on the settee, absorbed in her book.* 朱迪丝躺在沙发椅上专心致志地看书。| **absorb sb's attention** *The video was totally absorbing the children's attention.* 录像完全吸引了孩子们的注意力。
4 ▶BECOME PART OF 成为…的一部分◀ to make a smaller country, company, or group of people become part of your country, company, or group 并入; 吞并: *The US was able to absorb thousands of new immigrants.* 美国能吸收成千上万的新移民。| **be absorbed into** *More and more newspapers are being absorbed into the Murdoch empire.* 越来越多的报纸被并入默多克的新闻帝国。
5 ▶MONEY/TIME ETC 金钱/时间等◀ if something absorbs money, time etc it uses a lot of it 消耗, 花去: *Defence spending absorbs almost 20% of the country's wealth.* 国防开支消耗了这个国家差不多20%的财富。
6 ▶FORCE 力◀ to reduce the effect of a sudden violent movement 消减, 缓冲: *The solid walls absorbed much of the impact of the explosion.* 这些坚固的墙大大减小了爆炸的冲击力。
7 ▶LIGHT/HEAT/ENERGY 光/热/能◀ if a substance or object absorbs light, heat, or energy, it keeps it and does not REFLECT it (=send it back) 吸收: *Black objects absorb heat more.* 黑色的物体吸热多。

ab·sor·bent /əb`sɔrbənt; əb'sɔːbənt/ *adj* able to take in liquids easily 有吸水性的: *absorbent material* 吸水性材料

ab·sorb·ing /əb`sɔrbɪŋ; əb'sɔːbɪŋ/ *adj* enjoyable and interesting and holding your attention for a long time 十分吸引人的, 引人入胜的: *an absorbing documentary about China* 一部引人入胜的关于中国的纪录片

ab·sorp·tion /əb`sɔrpʃən; əb'sɔːpʃən/ *n* [U] **1** [+with/in] the fact of being very interested in something 专注 **2** a process in which a material or object takes in liquid, gas, or heat 吸收 **3** a process in which a country or organization makes a smaller country, organization or group of people become part of itself 合并, 并入

ab·stain /əb`sten; əb'steɪn/ *v* [I] **1** to not vote either for or against something in an election 弃权, 不投票 **2** *formal* to not do something, especially something enjoyable, because you think it is bad for your health or morally wrong【正式】戒除; 回避: [+from] *Pilots must abstain from alcohol for 24 hours before flying.* 飞行员在飞机起飞前24小时必须禁酒。—**abstainer** *n* [C]

ab·ste·mi·ous /əb`stimɪəs; əb'stiːmiəs/ *adj formal or humorous* careful not to have too much food, drink etc【正式或幽默】节俭的; 有节制的, 克制的 —**abstemiously** *adv* —**abstemiousness** *n* [U]

ab·sten·tion /əb`stɛnʃən; əb'stenʃən/ *n* [C,U] a vote in an election which is neither for nor against something or someone 弃权票

ab·sti·nence /`æbstənəns; 'æbstɪnəns/ *n* [U] the practice of not doing something you enjoy, especially not drinking alcohol 禁欲;〔尤指〕戒酒 —**abstinent** *adj*

ab·stract¹ /`æbstrækt; 'æbstrækt/ *adj* **1** based on general ideas or principles rather than specific examples or real events 纯理论上的, 纯概念的: **abstract thought/reasoning** (=thought about complicated ideas rather than about things that are around you) 抽象思维/推理 *a machine that is capable of abstract thought* 能进行抽象思维的机器 **2** existing only as an idea or quality rather than as something real that you can see or touch 抽象的: *Beauty is an abstract concept.* 美是一种抽象的概念。—compare 比较 CONCRETE¹ (2) **3** abstract paintings, designs etc consist of shapes and patterns that do not look like real people or things〔艺术〕抽象派的 —compare 比较 FIGURATIVE (2) —see also 另见 ABSTRACT NOUN

abstract² *n* [C] **1** **in the abstract** considered in a general way rather than being based on specific details and examples 抽象地, 从理论上说: *Talking about bringing up children in the abstract just isn't enough.* 仅仅从理论上谈论培养孩子是不够的。**2** a short written statement of the most important ideas in a speech, article etc 摘要, 梗概 **3** a painting, design etc which contains shapes or images that do not look like real things or people 抽象派作品

ab·stract³ /æb`strækt; əb'strækt/ *v* [T] **1** to use information from a speech, article etc in a shorter piece of writing that contains the most important ideas 作…的摘要, 节录 **2** *formal* to remove something from somewhere or from a place【正式】转移开

ab·stract·ed /æb`stræktɪd; əb'stræktɪd/ *adj* not noticing anything around you because you are thinking carefully about something else 心不在焉的, 出神的 —**abstractedly** *adv*

Abstract Ex·pres·sion·is·m /,.. ·'···/ a style of painting that developed in New York in the late 1940s. It shows shapes and patterns which do not look like real things or people, but are intended to express emotions. It was practised by artists such as Jackson Pollock and Willem de Kooning. 抽象表现派, 抽象表现主义〔20世纪40年代末在纽约兴起的一种绘画风格, 画面表现的不是真人实物而是某种情感, 代表人物有杰克逊·波洛克、威廉·德·库宁等〕

ab·strac·tion /æb`strækʃən; əb'strækʃən/ *n* **1** [C] a general idea about a type of situation, thing, or person, rather than a specific example from real life 抽象概念: *talking in abstractions* 抽象地谈论 **2** [U] a state in which you do not notice what is happening around you because you are thinking carefully about something else 心不在焉, 出神

abstract noun /,.. '·/ *n* [C] a noun that names a feeling, quality, or state rather than an object, animal, or person 抽象名词: *'Hunger' and 'beauty' are abstract nouns.* hunger (饥饿) 和 beauty (美丽) 是抽象名词。

ab·struse /əb`strus; əb'struːs/ *adj formal* difficult to understand in a way that seems unnecessarily complicated【正式】深奥的, 高深的 —**abstrusely** *adv* —**abstruseness** *n* [U]

ab·surd /əb`sɝd; əb'sɜːd/ *adj* completely stupid or unreasonable; RIDICULOUS 荒谬的, 荒唐的, 愚蠢的: *Don't be absurd!* 别那么荒唐! | *It seems quite absurd to expect anyone to drive for 3 hours just for a 20 minute meeting.* 指望一个人开三个小时的车去参加一个20分钟的会议, 看来颇为荒唐。—**absurdity** *n* [C,U]

Absurd, the also 又作 **the Theatre of the Absurd** *n* [singular] a style of play for the theatre that was developed in the 1950s by writers such as Beckett and Ionesco, whose work expresses the belief that human existence has no meaning or purpose. These plays are very different from traditional theatre. The characters do not communicate effectively with each other, and often their words do not make sense. 荒诞派戏剧〔20世纪50年代由剧作家贝克特和尤内斯库等创立的一种戏剧风格。荒诞派戏剧作品表达的思想是, 人类的存在毫无意义或毫无目的。此类戏剧与传统戏剧大相径庭。剧中人物之间难以沟通, 而且台词往往空洞无味〕—**Absurdist** *adj*

ab·surd·ly /əb`sɝdlɪ; əb'sɜːdli/ *adv* **absurdly cheap/difficult/easy etc** so cheap, difficult etc that it seems surprising, unusual, or even funny 出奇地便宜/难/容易等: *Prices on the island seem absurdly low to Western tourists.* 在西方游客看来, 这个岛上的物价便宜得惊人。

Ab·u Dha·bi /,ɑbu `dɑbɪ; ,æbuː 'dɑːbi/ **1** the largest EMIRATE of the United Arab Emirates 阿布扎比〔阿拉伯联合酋长国中最大的酋长国〕**2** the capital city of the United Arab Emirates 阿拉伯联合酋长国首都〕

A·bu·ja /ɑ`budʒɑ; ɑː'buːdʒɑː/ the capital city of Nigeria 阿布贾〔尼日利亚首都〕

a·bun·dance /ə`bʌndəns; ə'bʌndəns/ *n* [singular,U] a large quantity of something 充裕, 丰富: **an abundance of** *an abundance of wavy red hair* 一头浓密的红鬈发 | **in abundance** *Wild flowers grow in abundance on the hillsides.* 山坡上长满了野花。

a·bun·dant /ə`bʌndənt; ə'bʌndənt/ *adj* existing or available in large quantities so that there is more than enough; PLENTIFUL 丰富的, 充裕的: *abundant supplies* 充足的供应

a·bun·dant·ly /ə`bʌndəntlɪ; ə'bʌndəntli/ *adv* **1** in large quantities 大量地: *a force of Marines, abundantly equipped with anti-aircraft guns* 装备大量防空炮的海军陆战队 | *Melons grow abundantly in this region.* 这个地区盛产甜瓜。**2** **abundantly clear** very easy to understand so that anyone should be able to realize it 显而易见: *It's abundantly clear what the outcome will be.* 结果会怎样已非常清楚。| **make sth abundantly clear** (=say something very clearly) 清楚地表达 *Caroline made it abundantly clear that she didn't want Chuck around.* 卡罗琳清楚地表明她不想查克在身边。

a·buse¹ /ə`bjus; ə'bjuːs/ *n* **1** [C,U] the use of something in a way that it should not be used 滥用: [+of] *government officials' abuse of power* 政府官员滥用职权 | **open to abuse** (=able or likely to be used in the wrong way) 易被滥用 *The city's metro system is open to abuse by fare dodgers.* 该市的地铁系统很容 S2 W3

易让逃票者有机可乘。| **alcohol/drug/solvent abuse** (=the practice of drinking too much or taking illegal drugs) 酗酒/药物滥用/溶媒滥用 *The fraud department only deals with the worst abuse.* 反诈骗部门只处理那些最严重的违纪问题。**2** [U] rude or offensive things that someone says to someone else 辱骂，谩骂: *I don't see why I should put up with this kind of abuse from anyone.* 我不明白我为什么要忍受有人这样辱骂我。| **a stream/torrent of abuse** (=a series of rude or angry words) 一连串的粗话[气话] | **shout/scream/hurl abuse at** *The driver leaned out of his window and started hurling abuse at me.* 司机把头探出窗外开始骂我。| **a term of abuse** (=a word or phrase used to insult someone) 骂人话 **3** [U] cruel or violent treatment, often involving forced sexual activity, of someone that you are responsible for or should look after 虐待: *child abuse* 虐待儿童 | *sexual abuse* 性虐待

a·buse[2] /ə`bjuz; ə'bju:z/ *v* [T] **1** to deliberately use something such as power or authority, for the wrong purpose 滥用〔职权〕: *Williams abused his position as Mayor to give jobs to his friends.* 威廉斯滥用自己市长的权力，把许多职务给了朋友。| **abuse sb's trust/confidence etc** (=deceive someone who trusts or depends on you in order to get advantages for yourself) 背信弃义 **2** to treat someone in a cruel and violent way, often sexually, especially someone that you should look after 虐待: *People who were abused as children often turn into child-abusers themselves.* 孩提时代遭受虐待的人往往会变成虐童者。**3** to say rude or offensive things to someone 谩骂，辱骂 **4** to treat something so badly that you start to destroy it 伤害；摧残: *Richards abused his body for years with heroin and cocaine.* 理查兹多年来吸食海洛因和可卡因，身体每况愈下。**5 abuse yourself** to MASTURBATE 手淫

Abu Sim·bel /ˌɑbu `sɪmbl; ˌæbu: 'sɪmbəl/ a village in southern Egypt, famous for its ancient rock TEMPLES (=holy buildings) 阿布·辛拜勒村〔埃及南部一个村落，以古石庙而著称〕

a·bu·sive /ə`bjusɪv; ə'bju:sɪv/ *adj* very rude and using offensive language, especially because you are angry 骂人的，谩骂的: **get/become abusive** *She got quite abusive on the phone.* 她在电话里发了火。—**abusively** *adv* —**abusiveness** *n* [U]

a·but /ə`bʌt; ə'bʌt/ also 又作 **abut on** *v* [T] *technical* if one piece of land or a building abuts another it is next to it or touches one side of it【术语】邻接，毗连

a·bys·mal /ə`bɪzml; ə'bɪzməl/ *adj* very bad; TERRIBLE (3) 极坏的: *the Labour Party's abysmal performance in the last election* 工党在上次选举中非常糟糕的表现 —**abysmally** *adv*: *Educational standards were abysmally low.* 教育水平低极了。

a·byss /ə`bɪs; ə'bɪs/ *n* [C] *literary*【文】**1** a deep empty space, seen from a high point such as a mountain 深渊: *The ocean floor drops away into a dark abyss.* 海底陡然下斜形成黑暗的深渊。**2** a very dangerous or frightening situation 危险[可怕]的局面: *the abyss of a nuclear war* 核战争的深渊 **3** a great difference which separates two people or groups 鸿沟: *the abyss between rich and poor* 贫富之间的天壤之别

Ab·ys·sin·i·a /ˌæbə`sɪnɪə; ˌæbɨ'sɪniə/ the former name for Ethiopia 阿比西尼亚〔埃塞俄比亚的旧称〕

AC **1** the written abbreviation of 缩写= ALTERNATING CURRENT —compare 比较 DC (1) **2** the written abbreviation of 缩写= AIR-CONDITIONING —see also 另见 AC/DC

a/c *BrE*【英】the written abbreviation of 缩写= ACCOUNT[1] (2)

a·ca·cia /ə`keʃə; ə'keɪʃə/ *n* [C] a tree with small yellow or white flowers that grows in warm countries 金合欢属植物〔尤指阿拉伯胶树〕

Acacia Av·e·nue /·,·· '···/ *BrE* the name of an imaginary street that people think of as a typical SUBURBAN street in the UK. It represents a place where ordinary families live in a traditional way. It is used mainly in newspapers.【英】阿卡恰街〔一虚构街名，主要见于报章，被认为是英国典型的市郊街道，居住着普通人家，过着传统的日子〕

ac·a·de·mi·a /ˌækə`dimɪə; ˌækə'di:miə/ *n* [U] the area of activity and work connected with education in colleges and universities 学术界

ac·a·dem·ic[1] /ˌækə`dɛmɪk; ˌækə'demɪk◂/ *adj* **1** [usually before noun 一般用于名词前] connected with education, especially at college or university level 学术的: *She loved the city, with its academic atmosphere.* 她喜欢这城市，喜欢其学术氛围。| *academic books* 学术类书籍 | *a program designed to raise academic standards* 旨在提高学术水平的计划 **2** [usually before noun 一般用于名词前] concerned with studying from books, as opposed to practical work 学术上的；理论上的 **3** something that is academic is not important because it cannot happen or have any effect; THEORETICAL 不合实际的，理论的: **purely academic** *The question of where we go on holiday is purely academic since we don't have any money.* 我们去哪个地方度假这个问题完全不切实际，因为我们根本没有钱。**4** good at studying and getting good results at school or university 学业〔成绩〕优秀的: *He's a popular child, but not very academic.* 他是个受人喜欢的孩子，但学习成绩不太好。—**academically** /-klɪ; -kli/ *adv*

academic[2] *n* [C] a teacher in a college or university 大学教师

a·cad·e·mi·cian /əˌkædə`mɪʃən; əˌkædə'mɪʃən/ *n* [C] a member of an academy 学会会员；院士

academic year /ˌ···· '·/ *n* [C] *especially BrE* the period of the year during which there are school or university classes; school year (SCHOOL[1])【尤英】学年

a·cad·e·my /ə`kædəmɪ; ə'kædəmi/ *n* [C] **1** an important official organization consisting of people interested in the development of literature, art, science etc 研究院；学会: *the American Academy of Arts and Letters* 美国艺术和文学学会 **2** a college where students are taught a particular subject or skill 专科学院: *a military academy* 军事学院 | *the Academy of Music* 音乐学院 **3** a school in Scotland for children between 11 and 16〔苏格兰11到16岁孩子上的〕文法学校

Academy A·ward /·,···· '··/ *n* [C] the formal name for an Oscar 学院奖〔奥斯卡金像奖之正式名称〕

A·ca·di·a /ə`kedɪə; ə'keɪdiə/ an area in North America where French people went to live in the 17th century, consisting of land that now belongs to Maine in the US and to Nova Scotia, New Brunswick, Prince Edward Island, and part of Quebec in Canada. The name Cajun, comes from the word 'Acadian', meaning someone from this place. 阿卡迪亚〔北美一地区，17世纪法国人在此定居，包括今天美国的缅因州、加拿大的新斯科舍省、新不伦瑞克省、爱德华王子岛以及魁北克省的部分地区。Cajun一词来源于Acadian，即阿卡迪亚人〕

a cap·pel·la /ˌɑ kə`pɛlə; ˌæ kæ'pelə/ *adj, adv* sung without any musical instruments 清唱的[地]，无乐器伴奏的[地]

Ac·a·pul·co /ˌɑkə`pulko; ˌækə'pʊlkəʊ/ a city on the west coast of Mexico, known as a popular place for holidays 阿卡普尔科〔墨西哥西海岸一城市，以度假胜地而著称〕

ACAS /`ekæs; 'eɪkæs/ *n* [singular] Advisory Conciliation and Arbitration Service; a British organization that tries to end disagreements about pay, conditions at work etc between the management of a business and its workers 咨询调解仲裁处〔英国一服务机构，旨在协助解决涉及待遇、工作条件等劳资纠纷〕

acc. the written abbreviation of 缩写= ACCOUNT[1]

ac·cede /ək`sid; ək'si:d/ *v*

accede to sth *phr v* [T] *formal*【正式】**1** to agree to a demand, proposal etc, especially after first disagreeing with it〔尤指最初不同意而后来〕同意，答应: *The government would not accede to public pressure.* 政府不会屈从于公众的压力。**2** to achieve a position of power or authority 继任，就职，即位

ac·cel·e·ran·do /ækˌsɛlə`rændo; ækˌselə'rændəʊ/ *adj, adv music* getting gradually faster【音乐】渐快的[地]

ac·cel·e·rate /ək`sɛləˌret; ək'seləreɪt/ *v* **1** [I] if a vehicle or someone who is driving it accelerates, it starts to go faster 加快，加速: *The Ferrari Mondial can accelerate from 0 to 60 mph in 6.3 seconds.* 法拉利蒙迪尔型汽车能在启动后6.3秒内加速到每小时60英里。**2** [I,T] if a process accelerates or if something accelerates it, it happens faster than usual or sooner than you expect (使) 加快；(使) 提前: *measures to accelerate the rate of economic growth* 加快经济增长速度的措施 —opposite 反义词 DECELERATE

ac·cel·e·ra·tion /əkˌsɛlə`reʃən; əkˌselə'reɪʃən/ *n* **1** [U] the rate at which a car or other vehicle can go faster 加速: *The latest model has excellent acceleration.* 最新型号加速性能优越。**2** [singular,U] a process in which something happens more and more quickly 加快 (的过程): *an acceleration in the decline of the coal industry* 煤炭工业加速衰退 **3** [U] *technical* the rate at which the speed of an object increases【术语】加速度

ac·cel·e·ra·tor /ək`sɛləˌretɚ; ək'seləreɪtə/ *n* [C] **1** the part of a vehicle, especially a car, that you press to make it go faster 加速器；油门；GAS PEDAL *AmE*【美】—see picture on page A2 参见A2页图 **2** *technical* a large machine used to make extremely small pieces of matter move at extremely high speeds【术语】粒子加速器

ac·cent[1] /`æksɛnt; 'æksənt/ *n* [C] **1** the way someone pronounces the words of a language, showing which country or which part of a country they come from 口音: *Alex spoke Portuguese with a Brazilian accent.* 亚历克斯讲葡萄牙语带有巴西口音。| **strong/broad accent** *a broad Irish accent* 浓重的爱尔兰口音 —compare 比较 DIALECT **2 the accent is on** if the ac-

cent is on a particular quality, feeling etc, that quality or feeling is emphasized 着眼点在…上，强调: *We put the accent on team work at this club rather than individual skills.* 在这个俱乐部，我们强调团队精神而不是个人技能。**3** the part of a word that you should emphasize when you say it 重音: **[+on]** *In the word 'corset' the accent is on the first syllable.* corset一词的重音在第一个音节上。—see also 另见 STRESS[1] (4) **4** a written mark used above certain letters in some languages to show how to pronounce that letter 重音符号: *an acute accent* 尖音符号

> **CULTURAL NOTE 文化注释**
>
> In both the US and the UK, people have different accents according to the part of the country they come from. In the UK there is a greater variety of accents than in the US, and most British people can recognize which part of the UK someone comes from by their accent. In the US most people would recognize a Southern accent and a New York accent, but would not be able to tell where most other people come from. Accents are also affected by a person's education, and they often show, especially in the UK, the social class that someone belongs to. 英美两国，不同地区的人有着不同的口音。英国的口音差别比美国大，大多数英国人都能从一个人的口音判断出他是哪个地方的人。大多数美国人能辨别出南方口音和纽约口音的人，但其他人来自什么地方则无法辨别。口音也受个人教育的影响，因此经常能体现一个人所属的阶层，在英国尤其如此。
>
> **Accents on radio and television** RP (=Received Pronunciation) is the accent that is traditionally used by MIDDLE-CLASS educated people from the South of England. In the past, almost all the broadcasters, actors etc who featured on the BBC spoke with this accent, and it is sometimes called 'BBC English', but now most types of accent can be heard on radio and television. The standard accent used in US radio and television news broadcasts is based on accents from the Midwest. 广播和电视上的口音：标准发音是英格兰南部受过教育的中产阶级的传统口音，旧时在英国广播公司录制节目的所有播音员、演员等均操此口音，有时称"英国广播公司英语"。但现在，广播和电视上大多数口音均可听到。美国广播和电视新闻播报中的标准口音以中西部口音为基础。— see also 另见 ESTUARY ENGLISH

ac·cent[2] /ˋæksɛnt; əkˈsent/ *v* [T] to emphasize a part of something, especially part of a word in speech 重读

ac·cen·ted /ˋæksɛntɪd; əkˈsentɨd/ *adj* **heavily accented** words or speech that are heavily accented are spoken with a very strong accent 带有浓重口音的

ac·cen·tu·ate /əkˋsɛntʃʊˌet; əkˈsentʃueɪt/ *v* [T] to emphasize something, especially the difference between two conditions or situations 使突出；强调，着重指出 —**accentuation** /əkˌsɛntʃʊˋeʃən; əkˌsentʃuˈeɪʃən/ *n* [C,U]

ac·cept /əkˋsɛpt; əkˈsept/ *v* S1 W1

1 ►GIFT/OFFER/INVITATION 礼物/提议/邀请◄ [I,T] to take something that someone offers you, or to agree to do something that someone asked you to do 接受；同意做〔某事〕: *Please accept this small gift.* 请收下这份小礼物。| *I've decided to accept the job.* 我决定接受这份工作。| *Are you going to accept their invitation?* 你会接受他们的邀请吗？| *We've invited her here to give a talk, and she's accepted.* 我们邀请她到这里演讲，她同意了。| **accept sth from sb** *He is charged with accepting bribes from local companies.* 他被指控接受当地公司贿赂。| **accept a challenge** (=agree to do something difficult) 接受挑战 —see 见 REFUSE[1] (USAGE)

2 ►PLAN/SUGGESTION/ADVICE 计划/建议/忠告◄ [T] to decide to do what someone advises or suggests you should do 采纳: *I wish I'd accepted your advice and kept my money in the bank.* 要是当初我接受了你的建议，把钱存到银行里就好了。

3 ►IDEA/STATEMENT/EXPLANATION 想法/声明/解释◄ [T] to agree that what someone says is right or true 接受，同意: *She managed to persuade the jury to accept her version of events.* 她设法让陪审团接受了她对事件的说法。| **accept that** *I'm willing to accept that some mistakes have been made.* 我愿意承认出了一些差错。

4 ►SITUATION/PROBLEM ETC 情况/问题等◄ [T] to decide that there is nothing you can do to change a difficult and unpleasant situation or fact and continue with your normal life 认可，承认: *There's nothing we can do about it so we'll just have to accept it.* 我们对此没有办法，只好认同。| **accept the fact that** *I found it hard to accept the fact that she's gone.* 我难以接受她已经不在了的事实。

5 ►THINK SB/STH GOOD ENOUGH 认为某人/某物够好◄ [T] to decide that someone has the necessary skill or intelligence for a particular job, course etc or that a piece of work is good enough 认为…符合要求，采用: **accept sb/sth for** *My story's been accepted for the school magazine.* 校刊同意采用我的小说。

6 ►BECOME PART OF 成为…的部分◄ [T] to allow someone to become part of a group, society, or organization and to treat them in the same way as the other members 接纳: *The children gradually began to accept her as one of the family.* 孩子们逐渐接纳她为家中一员。| **accept sb into** *It often takes years for immigrants to be accepted into the host community.* 移民经常需要几年的时间才会被当地社区所接纳。

7 accept blame/responsibility to admit that you were responsible for something bad that happened 接受指责/承担责任: *The ship's owners are refusing to accept any responsibility for the accident.* 船主拒绝对事故承担任何责任。

8 accept sb's apology to say that you are no longer angry with someone after they have said they were sorry about something they have done 接受某人的道歉

9 ►MONEY 钱◄ [T] to allow customers to use a particular kind of money to pay for things 接受〔某种付款方式〕: *We don't accept travelers' checks.* 我们不接受旅行支票。

ac·cep·ta·ble /əkˋsɛptəbḷ; əkˈseptəbəl/ *adj* S3 W3 **1** good enough to be used for a particular purpose or to be considered satisfactory 合意的，令人满意的: *a cheap and acceptable substitute for rubber* 价廉物美的橡胶代用品 | **[+to]** *The dispute was settled in a way that was acceptable to both sides.* 争端以双方都能接受的方式解决了。**2** acceptable behaviour is considered to be morally or socially good enough 〔行为〕可接受的: *Smoking is no longer considered socially acceptable by many people.* 许多人不再认为吸烟是可接受的社会行为。| **acceptable for sb to do sth** *I just don't think it's acceptable for children to interrupt all the time.* 我只是认为，孩子总是打断别人的话是不可接受的。| **acceptable level/amount** (=neither too high nor too low) 可接受的程度/量 *They talk about 'acceptable levels of unemployment'.* 他们谈论关于"可接受的失业水平"。—**acceptably** *adv* —**acceptability** /əkˌsɛptəˋbɪlətɪ; əkˌseptəˈbɪlɨti/ *n* [U]

ac·cept·ance /əkˋsɛptəns; əkˈseptəns/ *n* W3 **1** [U] official agreement to take something that you have been offered 正式接受；认可: **[+of]** *Russia's acceptance of economic aid from Western countries* 俄罗斯对西方国家的经济援助的接受 | **a letter of acceptance** (=a letter you write in which you agree to accept a job, an opportunity to study somewhere etc) 同意书，〔接受工作、学习机会等的〕答复信 **2** [singular,U] the act of agreeing that an idea, statement, explanation etc is right or true 赞同，赞成: **gain/find acceptance** (=become accepted) 被接受 *Feminist ideas have now found widespread acceptance.* 女权主义思想现已被人们广泛接受。**3** [U] the ability to accept an unpleasant situation which cannot be changed, without getting angry or upset about it 承受〔能力〕 **4** [singular,U] the process of allowing someone to become part of a group or a society and of treating them in the same way as the other members 接纳〔过程〕: *Acceptance by their peer group is important to most youngsters.* 被同龄人所接纳，对大多数年轻人来说是很重要的。

ac·cess[1] /ˋæksɛs; ˈækses/ *n* [U] S3 W1 **1** the way by which you can enter a building or reach a place 入口；进入: *Access is by means of a small door on the right.* 可通过右边的小门进入。| **[+to]** *Access to the restrooms is through the foyer.* 去洗手间要穿过门厅。**2** how easy or difficult it is for people to enter a public building or to reach a place 途径: **[+for]** *We're trying to improve access for disabled visitors.* 我们正在设法使残疾访客能更容易进入。| **have easy/good access to** (=be able to reach another place easily) 容易接近 *The house is in a central location with good access to the shops.* 这幢房子在中心地段，离商店比较近。**3** the right to enter a place 进入权；使用权: **have access to** *The public don't have access to the site.* 公众无权进入此地。**4 have access to** to have the right to see official documents, especially secret documents 有权接触〔机密等〕: *Access to the papers is restricted to Defense Department personnel only.* 只有国防部人员才可以接触这些文件。**5** the legal right to see and spend time with your children, a prisoner, an official etc 探视权: *My ex-husband has access to the children once a week.* 我的前夫有权每周探望孩子一次。**6 have access to a phone/a computer etc** to have a telephone, computer etc near you which you can use 附近有电话/电脑等可供使用 **7 gain/get access (to)** to succeed in entering a place or in seeing someone or something 到达〔某地〕；见到〔某人或某物〕: *The police managed to gain access through an upstairs window.* 警察设法通过楼上的一扇窗户进入了屋子。

access² *v* [T] to find information, especially on a computer 访问〔尤指计算机数据〕

ac·ces·si·ble /əkˋsɛsəbl; əkˈsesɨbəl/ *adj* **1** easy to reach or get into 易到达的; 易进入的: *The cove is only accessible by boat.* 这个小海湾只有小船才能进入。—opposite 反义词 INACCESSIBLE **2** easy to obtain or use 易得到的; 易使用的: **easily/readily accessible** *Storing customer details on computer makes them readily accessible.* 把顾客的详细资料储存到电脑里可方便查找。**3** someone who is accessible is easy to meet and talk to, even if they are very important or powerful 易接近的, 随和的, 平易近人的: *I think that you'll find she's very accessible.* 我想你会发现她十分平易近人。**4** easy to understand and enjoy 易懂的: *Buchan succeeds in making a difficult subject accessible to the reader.* 巴肯成功地把一个很难的题目变得为读者易于理解。—**accessibly** *adv* —**accessibility** /əkˌsɛsəˋbɪləti; əkˌsesɨˈbɪlɨti/ *n* [U]

ac·ces·sion /əkˋsɛʃən; əkˈseʃən/ *n formal* 【正式】**1** [U] a process in which someone becomes king, queen, president etc 就职, 即位: **accession to the throne** (=the act of becoming king or queen) 登基 —compare 比较 SUCCESSION **2** [U+to] the act of agreeing to a demand 同意〔要求〕**3** [C,U] an object or work of art that is added to a collection, especially in a MUSEUM〔尤指博物馆的〕新增的藏品

ac·ces·so·ry /əkˋsɛsərɪ; əkˈsesəri/ *n* [C usually plural 一般用复数] **1** something that you add to a machine, tool, car etc so that it can do other things, or in order to make it look attractive 附件, 附属品: *Accessories include a CD player and alloy wheels.* 附件包括CD播放器和合金车轮。**2** [C] something such as a bag, belt, jewellery etc that you wear or carry because it is attractive 装饰物; 小配件〈如手袋、皮带、珠宝等〉: *fashion accessories* 时尚饰品 **3** [C] *law* someone who helps a criminal, especially by helping them hide from the police【法律】同谋, 帮凶, 从犯: **[+to]** *an accessory to murder* 谋杀案的同谋 | **an accessory before/after the fact** (=someone who helps a criminal before or after the crime) 事前/事后从犯

access time /ˈ· · ,·/ *n* [C,U] *technical* the time taken by a computer to find and use a piece of information in its memory【术语】〔电脑的〕存取时间

1 2 **ac·ci·dent** /ˋæksədənt; ˈæksɨdənt/ *n* [C] **1 by accident** in a way that is not planned or intended 偶然, 意外地: *I met her quite by accident.* 我遇见她颇为偶然。**2** a situation in which someone is injured or something is damaged without anyone intending them to be 事故, 意外事件: **have an accident** *Ken's had an accident at work and he's had to go to hospital.* 肯在工作中出了事故, 不得不去医院。| **climbing/skiing/riding etc accident** *Five people have been killed in a climbing accident in Nepal.* 五个人在尼泊尔登山时遇难。**3** a crash involving cars, trains, planes etc 失事; (交通) 事故: **car/automobile/traffic accident** *Her father's been involved in an automobile accident.* 她父亲卷入一起车祸。| **bad/serious/nasty accident** *A serious accident is blocking the southbound side of the M1.* 一起严重的交通事故阻塞了M1高速公路的南向车道。**4** something that happens without anyone planning or intending it 意外: *I'm really sorry about your camera – it was an accident.* 真对不起, 把你的照相机弄坏了 —— 这纯属意外。| **a happy accident** (=a lucky or pleasant event or situation which happens without anyone planning it) 好运气, 侥幸 | **a chapter of accidents** (=a series of unfortunate events that happen without anyone planning them) 一连串意外事故 | **an accident of birth/nature/history etc** (=an event or situation that happens without anyone planning it) 出生/性质/历史等的偶然性 **5 accidents will happen** *spoken* used to comfort someone who feels responsible for something bad that has happened【口】天意注定, 在所难免 **6 have an accident** if a child has an accident, he or she URINATEs by mistake〔小孩〕尿裤子; 尿床

ac·ci·den·tal /ˌæksəˋdɛntl; ˌæksɨˈdentl◂/ *adj* happening without being planned or intended 偶然的, 意外的: *an accidental discharge of toxic waste* 有毒废料的意外泄漏

accidental death /ˌ···· ˈ·/ *n* [U] *law* an expression used by a British court when it has decided that someone's death was caused by an accident【法律】意外死亡〔英国法庭用语〕

ac·ci·den·tal·ly /ˌæksəˋdɛntḷɪ; ˌæksɨˈdentli/ *adv* **1** without intending to 无意地: *I accidentally locked myself out of the house.* 我无意间把自己锁在了门外。**2 accidentally on purpose** *humorous* used to say that someone did something deliberately although they pretend they did not【幽默】明明故意却装出无心的样子; 故意地: *I think John lost his homework accidentally on purpose.* 约翰说他的作业不小心丢了, 我看是故意的。

accident prone /ˈ··· ·/ *adj* tending to get injured or break things easily 易遭遇意外的, 易惹事故的

ac·claim¹ /əˋklem; əˈkleɪm/ *v* [T] **1** to praise someone or something publicly 为…喝彩, 称赞; 推崇: *His last play was acclaimed by the critics as a masterpiece.* 他的最后一部戏剧被评论家赞誉为一部杰作。**2 acclaim sb king/queen/leader etc** *formal* to announce publicly that you accept someone as your king, queen etc【正式】拥戴某人为国王/女王/领袖等

acclaim² *n* [U] praise for a person or their achievements 表扬, 赞赏: **win acclaim** *Gail's artwork has won her international acclaim.* 盖尔的艺术作品为她(自己)赢得了国际声誉。

ac·claimed /əˋklemd; əˈkleɪmd/ *adj* publicly praised by a lot of people 广受欢迎的, 备受推崇的: **highly/widely/universally acclaimed** *Spielberg's highly acclaimed movie, Schindler's List* 斯皮尔伯格备受好评的电影《辛德勒名单》| **critically acclaimed** (=praised by people who are paid to give their opinion on art, music etc) 得到评论家好评的 *a critically acclaimed novel* 得到评论家好评的一部小说

ac·cla·ma·tion /ˌækləˋmeʃən; ˌækləˈmeɪʃən/ *n* [C,U] *formal* a loud expression of approval or welcome【正式】欢呼, 喝彩

ac·cli·ma·tize also 又作 **-ise** *BrE*【英】/əˋklaɪməˌtaɪz; əˈklaɪmətaɪz/ also 又作 **acclimate** /ˋækləˌmet; əˈklaɪmɪt/ *AmE*【美】*v* [I,T] to become used to a new place, situation or type of weather, or to make someone become used to it (使)适应: **get acclimatized** *It usually takes a while to get acclimatized to living in a new place.* 通常需要一段时间才能适应在一个新地方生活。—**acclimatization** /əˌklaɪmətəˋzeʃən; əˌklaɪmətaɪˈzeɪʃən/ *n* [U]

ac·co·lade /ˌækəˋled; ˈækəleɪd/ *n* [C] praise for someone who is greatly admired or a prize given to them for their work 嘉奖, 赞扬: *She received a 'Grammy Award', the highest accolade in the music business.* 她获得了音乐界的最高荣誉"格莱美奖"。

ac·com·mo·date /əˋkɑməˌdet; əˈkɒmədeɪt/ *v* **1** [T] to have or provide enough space for a particular number of people or things 容纳: *The hall can only accommodate 200 people.* 这个大厅只能容纳200人。| *building bigger and bigger highways to accommodate more cars* 修建更宽更广的公路以容纳更多的车辆 **2** [T] to give someone a place to stay, live, or work 为…提供住处[工作场所] **3** [T] to accept someone's opinions and try to do what they want, especially when their opinions or needs are different from yours 迎合; 迁就: *We've made every effort to accommodate your point of view.* 我们已经尽力迁就你们的观点。**4** [I+to, T] *formal* to get used to a new situation or make yourself do this【正式】(使)适应; (使)顺应 **5** [T] *formal* to give someone more time to pay you money that they owe you because they have financial problems【正式】宽限; 通融

ac·com·mo·dat·ing /əˋkɑməˌdetɪŋ; əˈkɒmədeɪtɪŋ/ *adj* helpful and willing to do what someone else wants 随和的, 乐于助人的

ac·com·mo·da·tion /əˌkɑməˋdeʃən; əˌkɒməˈdeɪʃən/ *n* **1** [U] a place for someone to stay, live, or work in 住处; 工作场所: *rented accommodation* 租用的房屋 **2 accommodations** [plural] *AmE formal* the rooms, food, services etc that are provided in a hotel or on a train, boat etc【美, 正式】〔酒店、火车、船等提供的〕住宿膳食服务 **3** [singular,U] *formal* a way of ending an argument which aims to satisfy both sides【正式】和解: **reach an accommodation** *We reached an accommodation between both parties.* 我们双方达成了和解。 2 2

ac·com·pa·ni·ment /əˋkʌmpənɪmənt; əˈkʌmpənimənt/ *n* **1** [C,U] music played at the same time as a song or a tune played on another instrument 伴奏: *She starts by singing 'Amazing Grace' with a simple guitar accompaniment.* 她以吉他伴奏演唱《奇妙的恩典》作开场。**2** [C] something that is provided or used with something else 伴随物; 配料: *White wine makes an excellent accompaniment to fish.* 白葡萄酒是吃鱼时最佳的佐餐酒。**3** [C] *formal* something that happens or exists at the same time as something else【正式】伴随物, 附属物: *The job losses are an inevitable accompaniment of this reorganization.* 职位减少是这次重组的必然产物。**4 to the accompaniment of** while another musical instrument is being played or another sound can be heard 在…伴奏下: *singing to the accompaniment of a piano* 在钢琴伴奏下演唱 | *She left the stage to the accompaniment of loud cheers.* 她在一片欢呼声中离开了舞台。

ac·com·pa·nist /əˋkʌmpənɪst; əˈkʌmpənɨst/ *n* [C] someone who plays a musical instrument while another person sings or plays the main tune 伴奏者

ac·com·pa·ny /ə`kʌmpənɪ; ə'kʌmpəni/ *v* [T] **1** to go somewhere with someone, especially in order to look after them 陪伴，陪同：*Children under 14 must be accompanied by an adult.* 14岁以下儿童必须有成人陪同。**2** to play a musical instrument while someone sings a song or plays the main tune 为…伴奏 **3** [usually singular 一般用单数] to happen or exist at the same time as something else 伴随 **4** if a book, document etc accompanies something, it explains what it is about or how it works 附有，带有，配有：*Please see accompanying booklet for instructions.* 说明请参阅所附的小册子。

ac·com·plice /ə`kɑmplɪs; ə'kʌmpl!s/ *n* [C] a person who helps someone such as a criminal to do something wrong 帮凶，同谋者，共犯

ac·com·plish /ə`kɑmplɪʃ; ə'kʌmplɪʃ/ *v* [T] to succeed in doing something, especially after trying very hard; achieve 完成〔任务等〕，取得〔成功〕：*We have accomplished all we set out to do.* 所有计划要做的事情，我们都已完成。

ac·com·plished /ə`kɑmplɪʃt; ə'kʌmplɪʃt/ *adj* an accomplished writer, painter, singer etc is very skilful 有才华的；有〔艺术〕造诣的

ac·com·plish·ment /ə`kɑmplɪʃmənt; ə'kʌmplɪʃmənt/ *n* **1** [C] something successful or impressive that is achieved after a lot of effort and hard work; achievement 成就，成绩：*This huge increase in growth would be an impressive accomplishment in any economy.* 这么巨大的增长在任何经济体制下，都是了不起的成就。**2** [C] an ability to do something well; skill 才能，才艺：*Playing the piano is one of her many accomplishments.* 弹钢琴是她众多才能中的一种。**3** [U] skill in doing something 技能：*a high level of accomplishment* 高水平技能 **4** [U] the act of finishing or achieving something good 成就；完成，实现

ac·cord[1] /ə`kɔrd; ə'kɔːd/ *n* **1 of your own accord** without being asked or forced to do something 出于自愿，主动地：*It's better that she comes of her own accord.* 她自己主动来更好。**2** [U] *formal* a situation in which two people, ideas, or statements agree with each other【正式】相符合，一致：**be in accord with** *These results are in accord with earlier research.* 这些结果和以前的研究一致。| **in total/perfect accord** *For once the President and myself were in total accord.* 就这一次，总统和我意见完全一致。| **speak with one accord** (=if two or more people speak with one accord they show total agreement with each other by what they say) 完全一致地说；异口同声 **3** [C] a formal agreement between countries or groups 正式协议：*the Helsinki accord on human rights* 赫尔辛基人权协定 **4 with one accord** *formal* if two or more people do something with one accord they do it together【正式】一致地：*With one accord they rushed down to the lake.* 他们一起向湖边冲去。

accord[2] *v formal*【正式】**1** [T] to give someone or something special attention or treatment 给予〔关照〕：**accord sth to** *The Japanese accord a special reverence to trees and rivers.* 日本人特别珍爱树木和河流。**2 accord with** to match or agree with something 符合，一致

ac·cord·ance /ə`kɔrdṇs; ə'kɔːdəns/ *n* **in accordance with** *formal* according to a rule, system etc【正式】按照，依照：*accounts prepared in accordance with the Companies Act 1985* 按照1985年《公司法》准备的账目 | **in accordance with sb's wishes** *He was buried in his home town, in accordance with his wishes.* 根据他生前意愿，他被葬在故乡。

ac·cord·ing as /ə`kɔrdɪŋ əz; ə'kɔːdɪŋ əz/ *conjunction BrE formal* depending on whether【英，正式】根据；取决于

ac·cord·ing·ly /ə`kɔrdɪŋlɪ; ə'kɔːdɪŋli/ *adv* **1** in a way that is suitable for a particular situation or based on what someone has done or said 相应地：*I told them what changes I wanted made and they acted accordingly.* 我告诉他们我希望什么地方需要修改，他们就照我的意见去做。**2** [sentence adverb 句子副词] as a result of something; therefore 因此，从而：*The budget for health care has been cut by 10%. Accordingly, some hospitals may be forced to close.* 保健方面的预算削减了10%。因此，一些医院可能会被迫关闭。

according to /·`··· ·/ **1** as shown by something or said by someone 据…所说［所示］：*According to George, she's a great player.* 据乔治说，她是一个优秀的演员。| *According to our records payment of $56 is now overdue.* 根据我们的记录，有56元的款项逾期未付。**2** in a way that agrees with 随…而定：*We are paid according to how much work we do.* 我们的工资随工作量而定。

ac·cor·di·on[1] /ə`kɔrdɪən; ə'kɔːdiən/ *n* [C] a musical instrument that you pull in and out to produce sounds while pushing buttons on one side to produce different notes 手风琴

> **CULTURAL NOTE 文化注释**
>
> Accordion music is often played in films when the scene is in France, especially Paris, and British people think of the accordion as a typically French musical instrument. In the US people think of the accordion in connection with old-fashioned dance music. 在涉及法国尤其是巴黎的电影场景中，常演奏手风琴音乐，因此英国人认为手风琴主要是一种法国乐器。美国人认为手风琴音乐是一种过时的舞曲。

accordion[2] *adj* [only before noun 仅用于名词前] having many folds like an accordion〔如手风琴般〕可折叠的：*an accordion file* 折叠式文件夹

ac·cost /ə`kɔst; ə'kɒst/ *v* [T] to go towards someone you do not know and speak to them in an unpleasant or threatening way 走上前去跟…唐突地说话，与…搭讪：*On the station she was accosted by a man asking for money.* 在车站，一个男人走到她跟前硬向她要钱。

ac·count[1] /ə`kaunt; ə'kaʊnt/ *n*

1 ►DESCRIPTION 描述◄ [C] **a)** a written or spoken description which gives details of an event 报道，叙述，描写：*There were several different accounts of the story in the newspapers.* 报纸上对此事有不同的说法。| **give an account** *David gave us a vivid account of his trip to Rio.* 戴维向我们生动地讲述了他去里约热内卢旅行的情况。| **blow-by-blow account** (=a description of the details of all an event in the order that they happened) 详细报道 | **eyewitness account** (=a description of events by someone who saw them) 目击者的叙述 *an eyewitness account of the robbery* 目击者对抢劫案的叙述 | **firsthand account** (=a description of events by someone who saw or took part in them) 第一手的叙述 *her fascinating firsthand account of the Chinese Cultural Revolution* 她对亲身经历的中国"文化大革命"令人难以忘怀的叙述 **b)** a detailed scientific description of a process which explains how it happens and what makes it possible 详尽的科学描述：*Chomsky's account of how children learn their first language* 乔姆斯基关于儿童如何学习第一语言的科学描述

2 ►AT A BANK 在银行◄ written abbreviation 缩写为 **a/c** [C] an arrangement that you have with a bank to pay in or take out money 账户：*My salary is paid directly into my bank account.* 我的工资直接存入我的银行账户。| **joint account** (=one that is shared by two people) 共用账户 —see also 另见 BANK ACCOUNT, CHECKING ACCOUNT, CURRENT ACCOUNT, DEPOSIT ACCOUNT, PROFIT AND LOSS ACCOUNT, SAVINGS ACCOUNT

3 take account of sth/take sth into account to consider or include particular facts or details when making a decision or judgment about something 把…考虑在内：*These figures do not take account of changes in the rate of inflation.* 这些数字没有考虑到通货膨胀率的变化。

4 on account of because of something else, especially because of a problem or difficulty 因为，由于：*He can't run very fast on account of his asthma.* 由于患有哮喘，他不能跑得很快。

5 accounts a) [plural] an exact record of the money that a company has received and the money it has spent 账目：*The accounts for last year showed a profit of $2 million.* 去年的账目显示利润为200万美元。**b)** [U] a department in a company that is responsible for keeping these records 会计部：*Eileen works in accounts.* 艾琳在会计部工作。

6 on account if you buy goods on account, you take them away with you and pay for them later 赊账

7 ►WITH A SHOP 与商店◄ [C] an arrangement that you have with a shop which allows you to buy goods and pay for them later; CREDIT ACCOUNT 赊购账：*Can you charge this to my account please?* 你能把这钱记在我的（赊购）账上吗？

8 ►BILL 账单◄ [C] a statement of money that you owe for things you have bought from a shop; bill 账单：**pay/settle your account** (=pay what you owe) 付账/结账 *Accounts must be settled within 30 days.* 30天以内必须结账。

9 ►ARRANGEMENT TO SELL GOODS 售货安排◄ [C] an arrangement to sell goods and services to another company over a period of time〔给予售货安排和服务的〕客户：*Our Sales Manager has secured several big accounts recently.* 我们的销售部经理最近争取到了好几家大客户。

10 by/from all accounts according to what a lot of people say 根据各方面所说：*It's a very exciting film by all accounts.* 人人都说这是一部很精彩的电影。

11 on my/his etc account if you do something on someone's account, you do it because you think they want you to 为了我/他等的缘故：*Please don't leave on my account.* 看在我的情面上，请不要离开。

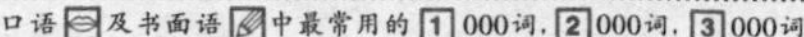

A

12 on your own account by yourself or for yourself 靠自己；为自己：*Carrie decided to do a little research on her own account.* 卡丽决定自己做点研究。
13 on no account/not on any account used when saying that someone must not, for whatever reason, do something 决不：*On no account must you tell him about our plans.* 你决不能把我们的计划告诉他。
14 by your own account according to what you have said, especially when you have admitted doing something wrong 据某人自己所说：*By his own account he was driving too fast.* 他自己也认为开车开得太快。
15 on that account/on this account concerning a particular situation 考虑到那种/这种情况：*There needn't be any more worries on that account.* 考虑到那种情况，就不必担心了。
16 give a good/poor account of yourself to do something or perform very well or very badly 表现好/表现差：*Kevin gave a good account of himself in today's game.* 凯文在今天的比赛中表现出色。
17 bring/call sb to account *formal* to force someone who is responsible for a mistake or a crime to explain publicly why they did it and punish them for it if necessary【正式】责令某人对…作出解释：*The people responsible for the accident have never been brought to account.* 要对这起事故负责任的人至今仍逍遥法外。
18 put/turn sth to good account *formal* to use something for a good purpose【正式】充分利用某物：*Perhaps she could put some of her talents to good account by helping us.* 通过帮助我们，也许她能把自己的某些才能充分发挥出来。
19 of no account/of little account *formal* not important【正式】不重要，无关紧要：*Don't worry about what he said, it's of no account.* 不必担心他说的话，那是无关紧要的。
20 of some account *formal* quite important【正式】相当重要

2 **account²** *v* [T]
account for sth *phr v* [T] **1** to be the reason why something happens 是…的原因：*Recent pressure at work may account for his behavior.* 他的行为也许应归因于他最近的工作压力。**2** to give a satisfactory explanation of why something has happened or why you did something 对…作出〔满意的〕解释：*How do you account for the sudden disappearance of the murder weapon?* 你如何解释凶器突然消失？**3** to make up a particular amount or part of something 占…〔比例〕：*Imports from Japan accounted for 40% of the total.* 进口的日本货占进口总量的40%。**4** to say where all the members of a group of people or things are, especially because you are worried that some of them may be lost 说明…在何处：*Is everyone accounted for?* 是不是所有人都有下落了？**5 there's no accounting for taste** *informal* used when you find it difficult to understand why someone likes something or wants to do something【非正式】人各有所好

ac·coun·ta·ble /əˋkauntəbl; əˈkaʊntəbəl/ *adj* [not before noun 不用于名词前] responsible for the effects of your actions and willing to explain or be criticized for them 负有责任的：[+for] *Managers must be accountable for their decisions.* 经理必须对自己作出的决定负责。| **hold sb accountable for sth** (=consider someone responsible) 认为某人应对某事负责 *Should teachers be held accountable for their students' examination results?* 教师是否应对学生的考试成绩负责？| **accountable to** *The bank was effectively accountable to nobody, and could do whatever it liked.* 这家银行事实上不曾对任何人负责，它想做什么就做什么。—**accountability** /ə͵kauntəˋbɪlətɪ; ə͵kaʊntəˈbɪlɪti/ *n* [U]: *demands for greater police accountability* 要求警察负起更大的责任

ac·coun·tan·cy /əˋkauntənsɪ; əˈkaʊntənsi/ *n* [U] *especially BrE* the profession or work of keeping or checking financial accounts【尤英】会计行业[工作]

3 **ac·coun·tant** /əˋkauntənt; əˈkaʊntənt/ *n* [C] someone whose job is to keep and check financial accounts 会计师；会计员

> **CULTURAL NOTE 文化注释**
> In Britain, people often make jokes about accountants because they are considered to be very boring and dull. 英国人常拿会计开玩笑，因为人们认为他们极其沉闷无聊。

ac·coun·ting /əˋkauntɪŋ; əˈkaʊntɪŋ/ *n* [U] accountancy 会计行业[工作]

ac·cou·tre·ments /əˋkutəmənts; əˈkuːtrəmənts/ also 又作 **accouterments** /əˋkutəmənts; əˈkuːtəmənts/ *AmE*【美】*n* [plural] *formal or humorous* things that you use or carry when doing a particular activity【正式或幽默】装备，配备

Ac·cra /əˋkrɑ; əˈkrɑː/ the capital city of Ghana 阿克拉〔加纳首都〕

ac·cred·i·ta·tion /əˌkrɛdɪˋteʃən; əˌkredɪˈteɪʃən/ *n* [U] official approval for a person or organization 正式认可，授权，委托

ac·cred·it·ed /əˋkrɛdɪtɪd; əˈkredɪtɪd/ *adj* **1** having official approval to do something 得到授权的：*an accredited journalist* 有许可证的记者 **2 be accredited to** if a government official is accredited to another country, they are sent to that country to officially represent their government there〔作为本国政府代表〕被委派往〔他国〕**3** officially accepted as being of a satisfactory standard 经鉴定合格的：*an accredited language school*（经鉴定）合格[认可]的语言学校

ac·cre·tion /əˋkriʃən; əˈkriːʃən/ *n* **1** [C,U] *technical* a layer of a substance which slowly forms on something【术语】增加物；积成物；附着物 **2** [U] *formal* a gradual process by which new things are added and something gradually changes or gets bigger【正式】增加，增大

ac·crue /əˋkru; əˈkruː/ *v* [I,T] *formal*【正式】**1** if advantages accrue to you, you get those advantages over a period of time〔利益、好处等〕产生，形成：*tax benefits that accrue to investors* 给投资者带来的税收利益 **2** if money accrues or is accrued, it gradually increases over a period of time 增加，增多：*The accrued interest will be paid annually.* 累积利息将逐年支付。

acct the written abbreviation for 缩写= ACCOUNT

ac·cu·mu·late /əˋkjumjə͵let; əˈkjuːmjʊleɪt/ *v* **1** [T] to gradually get more and more money, possessions, knowledge etc over a period of time 积累，积聚：*He accumulated a fortune through property speculation.* 他透过房产投机买卖积累了财富。**2** [I] to gradually increase in numbers or amount until there is a large quantity in one place 大量聚积：*Leaves had accumulated around the fallen trunks.* 树叶大量聚积在倒地的树干周围。—**accumulation** /ə͵kjumjəˋleʃən; ə͵kjuːmjʊˈleɪʃən/ *n* [C,U]: *the accumulation of data* 资料的收集

ac·cu·mu·la·tive /əˋkjumjə͵letɪv; əˈkjuːmjʊlətɪv/ *adj* gradually increasing in amount or degree over a period of time; CUMULATIVE 累积的，逐渐增加的 —**accumulatively** *adv*

ac·cu·mu·la·tor /əˋkjumjə͵letə; əˈkjuːmjʊleɪtə/ *n* [C] **1** *technical* a part of a computer that stores numbers【术语】〔计算机的〕累加器 **2** *especially BrE* a kind of BATTERY (1) which can take in new supplies of electricity so that it has enough power to keep working【尤英】蓄电池 **3** a system of betting (BET¹ (1)) on the results of a series of horse races, by which any money you win from a race is bet on the next race 累积赌注

ac·cu·ra·cy /ˋækjərəsɪ; ˈækjʊrəsi/ *n* [U] **1** the ability to do something in an exact way without making a mistake 准确度，精确性 **2** the quality of being correct or true 准确（性）：*I wasn't convinced about the accuracy of the report.* 我并不确信这个报告的准确性。

ac·cu·rate /ˋækjərɪt; ˈækjʊrət/ *adj* **1** accurate information, reports, descriptions etc are correct because all the details are true〔资料、报道、描述等〕准确的：*She was able to give the police an accurate description of her attacker.* 她能把袭击者的情况向警方作出准确的描述。| *a fairly accurate assessment of the situation* 对形势相当准确的评价 **2** an accurate measurement, calculation, record etc has been done in a careful and exact way and is completely correct〔测量、计算、记录等〕精确的，无差错的 **3** a machine that is accurate is able to do something in an exact way without making a mistake〔机器〕精密的：*The cutter is accurate to within 1/2 a millimetre.* 切割器的精密度在½毫米以内。**4** an accurate shot, throw etc succeeds in hitting or reaching the thing that it is intended to hit〔射击、投掷等〕准确的：*a devastatingly accurate shot by the Brazilian captain* 巴西队队长极其精准的一记射门 —**accurately** *adv*: *It's impossible to predict the weather accurately.* 要准确地预报天气是不可能的。 

ac·curs·ed /əˋkɝsɪd; əˈkɜːsɪd/ *adj* **1** [only before noun 仅用于名词前] *formal* very annoying and causing you a lot of trouble【正式】可恶的，可憎的 **2** *old use* someone who is accursed has had a CURSE² (2) put on them【旧】被诅咒的

ac·cu·sa·tion /͵ækjəˋzeʃən; ͵ækjʊˈzeɪʃən/ *n* [C] a statement saying that someone is guilty of a crime or of doing something wrong 控告，告发；指控：*There isn't a word of truth in your accusations.* 你的指控没有一句是事实。| [+of] *accusations of corruption* 对贪污的指控 | **make an accusation against** *Several serious accusations have been made against the former state governor.* 对前任州长提出了几项严重指控。| **face an accusation** (=be accused of something) 面临指控 *The school is facing accusations of racism.* 这所学校面临存在种族主义的指控。| **wild/unfounded accusation** (=one that is completely untrue) 胡乱指控，诬告

A

ac·cu·sa·tive /ə`kjuzətɪv; ə'kju:zətɪv/ *n* [C] *technical* a form of a noun in languages such as Latin or German, which shows that the noun is the DIRECT OBJECT of a verb【术语】〔拉丁文、德文等的〕宾格，受格 —**accusative** *adj*

ac·cu·sa·to·ry /ə`kjuzə͵torɪ; ə'kju:zətəri/ *adj formal* an accusatory remark, look etc from someone shows that they think you have done something wrong【正式】指控的；指责的

3 **ac·cuse** /ə`kjuz; ə'kju:z/ *v* [T] to say that someone is guilty of a crime or of doing something bad 指责；控告：**accuse sb of (doing) sth** *Are you accusing me of lying?* 你是在指责我说谎吗？| *He's accused of murder.* 他被控谋杀。| **stand accused of** (=be officially accused of a serious offence) 正式被指控 *Local officials stand accused of gross mismanagement.* 当地官员被控严重渎职。—**accuser** *n* [C]

ac·cused, the /ə`kjuzd; ə'kju:zd/ *n* [singular or plural] the person or group of people who have been officially accused of a crime or offence in a court of law 被告

ac·cus·ing /ə`kjuzɪŋ; ə'kju:zɪŋ/ *adj* an accusing look from someone shows that they think that you have done something wrong 非难的，谴责的 —**accusingly** *adv*

ac·cus·tom /ə`kʌstəm; ə'kʌstəm/ *v* [T] to make yourself or another person become used to a situation or place 使…习惯于：**accustom yourself to** *It took a while for me to accustom myself to all the new rules and regulations.* 我花了一段时间才逐渐适应了所有新的规章制度。

ac·cus·tomed /ə`kʌstəmd; ə'kʌstəmd/ *adj* **1 be accustomed to (doing) sth** to be used to something 习惯于（做）某事：*He was accustomed to a life of luxury.* 他习惯了奢华的生活。| *I'm not accustomed to getting up so early.* 我不习惯这么早起床。| **get/grow/become accustomed to** *Her eyes quickly became accustomed to the dark.* 她的眼睛很快适应了黑暗。**2** [only before noun 仅用于名词前] *formal* usual【正式】惯常的，通常的：*her accustomed seat at the head of the table* 桌子上首她常坐的位置

AC/DC /͵.. `..; ͵.. '../ *adj slang* sexually attracted to people of both sexes【俚】双性恋的

ace[1] /es; eɪs/ *n* [C] **1** a playing card with a single spot on it, which usually has the highest value in a game〔扑克牌中的〕A牌，幺点牌：*the ace of hearts* 红桃A **2 have an ace up your sleeve** to have a secret advantage which could help you to win or be successful 手中有王牌，有获胜的绝招 **3 hold all the aces** to have all the advantages in a situation so that you are sure to win 占绝对优势 **4 be/come within an ace of** to very nearly succeed in doing something 仅差一点儿：*She came within an ace of getting the job as Export Manager.* 她差一点儿就当上出口部经理。**5** a first shot in tennis or volleyball which is hit so well that your opponent cannot reach the ball and you win the point〔网球或排球〕得分的发球 **6** someone who is extremely skilful at doing something 一流高手，能手：*a World War II flying ace* 第二次世界大战中的王牌飞行员 | *an ace at chess* 下棋高手 **7 ace in the hole** *AmE informal* something that you keep secretly to use when you need it【美，非正式】备用的秘密武器：*That fifty dollars is my ace in the hole.* 那50元是我应急备用的钱。

ace[2] *adj* **1 ace pilot/player/skier etc** someone who is a very skilful pilot, player etc 一流的飞行员/运动员/滑雪者等：*ace footballer Diego Maradona* 一流的足球运动员迭戈·马拉多纳 **2** *BrE slang* very good【英俚】棒极了：*The party was ace.* 晚会棒极了。

ace[3] *v* [T] **1** *AmE informal* to do very well in an examination, a piece of written work etc【美，非正式】考得好，写得好：*I think I aced the History test.* 我觉得我历史考得很好。**2** to hit your first shot in tennis or volleyball so well that your opponent cannot reach the ball〔网球或排球〕发球得分

a·cer·bic /ə`sɝbɪk; ə'sɜ:bɪk/ *adj* criticizing someone or something in a clever but rather cruel way 尖刻的，辛辣的：*acerbic wit* 尖刻挖苦的言辞 —**acerbity** *n* [U]

ac·e·tate /`æsə͵tet; 'æsɨteɪt/ *n* [U] **1** a chemical made from acetic acid 醋酸盐 **2** a smooth artificial cloth used to make clothes 醋酸纤维制品

a·ce·tic ac·id /ə͵sitɪk `æsɪd; ə͵si:tɪk 'æsɨd/ *n* [U] the acid in VINEGAR 醋酸

a·cet·y·lene /ə`sɛtḷ͵in; ə'setɨli:n/ *n* [U] a gas which burns with a bright flame and is used in equipment for cutting and joining pieces of metal 乙炔，电石气 —see also 另见 OXYACETYLENE

ache[1] /ek; eɪk/ *v* [I] **1** if part of your body aches, you feel a continuous, but not very sharp pain there〔隐隐地、持续地〕作痛：*The noise of the traffic made my head ache.* 车辆的噪声使我感到头痛。| *an aching back* 后背疼痛 **2 ache to do sth/for sth** to want to do or have something very much 渴望做某事/拥有某物：*I was aching to tell him the good news.* 我急不可待地想把好消息告诉他。

ache[2] *n* [C] **1** a continuous pain that is not sharp, for example the pain you feel after you have used part of your body too much 疼痛，酸痛：*After three days the ache in his legs had almost gone.* 三天后，他的腿几乎不痛了。| *backache* 后背痛 | **dull ache** (=an annoying ache that is not very painful) 隐隐作痛 *My hand started to hurt with a sort of dull ache.* 我的手开始有些隐隐作痛。| **aches and pains** (=many small pains which you feel at the same time) 浑身疼痛 *Apart from the usual aches and pains, she felt all right.* 除了几处经常性的疼痛以外，她感到身体尚可。**2** a strong feeling of wanting something 渴望 —**achy** *adj*: *My arm feels all achy.* 我的胳膊很痛。

a·chieve /ə`tʃiv; ə'tʃi:v/ *v* **1** [T] to succeed in doing something good or getting the result you wanted, after trying hard for a long time 实现；取得；达到：*Women have yet to achieve full equality in the workplace.* 在工作领域，妇女还没有取得完全平等的地位。| *Britain has achieved the highest rate of economic growth in Europe this year.* 英国今年实现了欧洲最高的经济增长率。| *On the test drive Segrave achieved speeds of over 200 mph.* 在试车时，西格雷夫的车速达到每小时二百多英里。**2** [I] to be successful in a particular kind of job or activity 获得成功：*We want all our students to achieve within their chosen profession.* 我们希望所有的学生在自己选择的专业领域内都能有所成就。—**achievable** *adj* —see 见 OBTAIN (USAGE) 1 1

a·chieve·ment /ə`tʃivmənt; ə'tʃi:vmənt/ *n* **1** [C] something important that you succeed in doing by your own efforts 成绩，成就：*Winning three gold medals is a remarkable achievement.* 赢得三枚金牌是个了不起的成绩。| **no mean achievement/quite an achievement** (=a very impressive achievement) 了不起的成绩 **2** [U] the act of achieving something 实现；完成；达到：*the achievement of economic stability* 经济稳定的实现 | **sense of achievement** (=a feeling of pride when you succeed in doing something difficult) 成就感 *You get a wonderful sense of achievement when you reach the top.* 当你到达最高处时，你会有一种绝妙的成就感。 3 2

a·chiev·er /ə`tʃivɚ; ə'tʃi:və/ *n* [C] someone who is successful because they are determined and work hard 成功人士

A·chil·les /ə`kɪliz; ə'kɪli:z/ in ancient Greek stories, a HERO who was protected by magic so that the only place where he could be hurt was his heel 阿喀琉斯〔古希腊故事中的英雄人物，受魔法保护，唯一的弱点是他的脚踵〕

Achilles' heel /ə͵kɪliz `hil; ə͵kɪli:z 'hi:l/ *n* [C] a weak part of something, especially of someone's character, which is easy for other people to attack 致命的弱点，致命伤：*I think Frank's vanity is his Achilles' heel.* 我认为虚荣心是弗兰克最大的弱点。

Achilles ten·don /ə͵kɪliz `tɛndən; ə͵kɪli:z 'tendən/ *n* [C] the part of your body that connects the muscles in the back of your foot with the muscles of your lower leg 跟腱

a·choo /ə`tʃu; ə'tʃu:/ *n* [C] a word used to represent the sound you make when you SNEEZE 阿嚏〔打喷嚏的声音〕

ac·id[1] /`æsɪd; 'æsɨd/ *n* **1** [C,U] a substance that forms a chemical SALT[1] (4) when combined with an ALKALI. Strong acids can burn holes in material or damage your skin〔化学中的〕酸：*sulphuric acid* 硫酸 **2** [U] *slang* the drug LSD【俚】迷幻药〔麦角酸二乙胺〕 2

acid[2] *adj* **1** having a very sour taste 酸（味）的：*The wine had a very acid taste.* 这种葡萄酒味道很酸。**2 acid remark/comment/tone etc** an acid remark etc uses humour in an unkind way to criticize someone 尖酸刻薄的语言/评论/口吻等 **3 the acid test** a way of finding out whether something is as good as people say it is, whether it works, or whether it is true 决定性试验，严峻的考验：*The acid test will come when the car goes on sale in the US.* 这种汽车在美国出售才是真正的考验来临的时候。**4** *technical* an acid soil does not contain enough LIME[1] (3)【术语】〔土壤〕酸性的 —**acidly** *adv* —**acidity** /ə`sɪdətɪ; ə'sɪdɨti/ *n* [U]

acid house /`.. ͵./ *n* [U] a kind of dance music that is played loudly using electronic instruments 迷幻豪斯音乐〔一种用电子乐器弹奏的快速舞蹈音乐〕

a·cid·ic /ə`sɪdɪk; ə'sɪdɪk/ *adj* **1** very sour 很酸的：*It tastes a bit acidic.* 这东西有点酸。**2** containing acid 含酸的，酸性的

a·cid·i·fy /ə`sɪdəfaɪ; ə'sɪdɨfaɪ/ *v* [I,T] *technical* to become an acid or make something become an acid【术语】(使) 变酸，(使) 酸化

acid rain /͵.. `./ *n* [U] rain that contains harmful acid which can damage the environment and is caused by smoke from factories 酸雨

3 3 **ac·knowl·edge** /ək`nɑlɪdʒ; ək'nɒlɪdʒ/ *v* [T] **1 ▶ADMIT** 承认◀ to admit or accept that something is true or that a situation exists 承认；供认：*a broadcast message acknowledging their responsibility for the bombing* 他们承认对这起爆炸负责任的广播消息 | **acknowledge that** *By November 1914 the government was forced to acknowledge that its policy had failed.* 到1914年11月，政府被迫承认他们的政策失败了。| *It is now generally acknowledged that he was innocent.* 现在大家普遍认为他是无辜的。
2 be acknowledged as to be thought of as being very important or very good by a large number of people 被公认为是…：*Lasalle is widely acknowledged as the world's greatest living authority on Impressionist painting.* 拉萨尔被公认为是当今在世的关于印象派画作的最伟大权威。
3 ▶ACCEPT SB'S AUTHORITY 承认某人的权威◀ to officially accept that a government, court, leader etc has legal or official authority 承认〔政府、法庭、领袖等〕的合法性：*Both defendants refused to acknowledge the authority of the court.* 两名被告都拒绝承认法庭有权审判他们。| **acknowledge sb as** *The people acknowledged Mandela as their leader.* 人民公认曼德拉为他们的领袖。
4 ▶LETTER/MESSAGE ETC 信/口信等◀ to tell someone that you have received their message, letter, package etc 确认〔收悉〕：**acknowledge receipt of** *Please acknowledge receipt of this document by signing the enclosed form.* 请在附表中签收这份文件。
5 ▶SHOW THANKS FOR 表示感谢◀ to publicly announce that you are grateful for the help that someone has given you 〔公开〕表示感谢：*The author wishes to acknowledge the assistance of the Defense Department.* 作者希望对国防部的协助表示感谢。
6 ▶SHOW YOU NOTICE SB 表明注意到某人◀ to show someone that you have seen them or heard what they have said 打招呼，理会：*Tina was so rude, she didn't even acknowledge my presence.* 蒂娜真没礼貌，见到我连个招呼也没打。

ac·knowl·edge·ment, acknowledgment /ək`nɑlɪdʒmənt; ək'nɒlɪdʒmənt/ *n* **1** [C,U] the act of admitting or accepting that something is true 承认：*We have yet to hear any acknowledgement from them that a problem exists.* 我们尚未听到他们承认有问题。**2** [C,U] the act of publicly thanking someone for something they have done 感谢：**in acknowledgement of** *a special award in acknowledgement of all his hard work* 为表彰他的辛勤工作的特别奖 **3** [C,U] a letter written to tell someone that you have received their letter, message etc 收悉通知；回执 **4 acknowledgements** [plural] a short piece of writing at the beginning or end of a book in which the writer thanks all the people who have helped him or her 〔作者的〕致谢

ACLU, the /ˌe si ɛl `ju; ˌeɪ siː el 'juː/ *n* [singular] American Civil Liberties Union; a US organization which gives advice about the Bill of Rights and often represents people in a court of law to make sure their CIVIL RIGHTS are not taken away 美国公民自由联盟，美国民权联盟〔美国一组织，就《人权法案》提供咨询服务，经常代表当事人出庭，以确保他们的公民权不被剥夺〕

ac·me /`ækmɪ; 'ækmi/ *n* **the acme of** *formal* the best and highest level of something【正式】…的顶峰，…的极度：*the acme of perfection* 尽善尽美

ac·ne /`æknɪ; 'ækni/ *n* [U] a skin problem which causes a lot of small raised spots on the face and neck 痤疮，粉刺

ac·o·lyte /`ækəlaɪt; 'ækəlaɪt/ *n* [C] **1** *formal* someone who serves a leader or believes in their ideas【正式】侍者，助手；追随者 **2** someone who helps a priest at a religious ceremony 侍僧，辅祭〔教士的助手〕

a·corn /`ekɔrn; 'eɪkɔːn/ *n* [C] the nut of the OAK tree 橡实

acorn 橡实

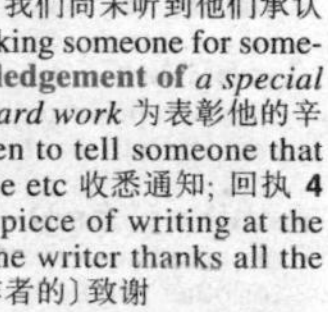

a·cous·tic /ə`kustɪk; ə'kuːstɪk/ *adj* **1** concerned with sound and the way people hear things 声音的；听觉的 **2** an acoustic GUITAR or other musical instrument does not have its sound made louder electronically 原声的，不加电子设备传声的 —**acoustically** /-klɪ; -kli/ *adv*

a·cous·tics /ə`kustɪks; ə'kuːstɪks/ *n* [plural] **1** the qualities of a room, such as its shape and size, which affect the way sound is heard in it 音响效果：*The hall has excellent acoustics.* 礼堂的音响效果很好。**2** the scientific study of sound 声学

ac·quaint /ə`kwent; ə'kweɪnt/ *v* [T] **1 be acquainted (with sb)** to know someone, especially because you have met once or twice before 认识〔某人〕：*I am acquainted with him, but only on a professional basis.* 我认识他，不过只是工作上的接触。| **get/become acquainted** (=start to know someone that you have just met) 相识 *I'll leave you two alone for a while so that you can get better acquainted.* 我让你们两人单独相处一会，你们可以好好认识一下。**2 be acquainted with sth** *formal* to know about something, because you have seen it, read it, used it etc【正式】认识某物；了解某事：*I'm not really acquainted with the southern part of the island.* 我不太了解这个岛南部的情况。| **be fully acquainted with sth** *All our employees are fully acquainted with safety precautions.* 我们所有的雇员都十分熟悉安全措施。**3 acquaint yourself with sth** *formal* to deliberately find out about something【正式】了解某事，查明某事：*She always took the trouble to acquaint herself with the students' interests.* 她总是不辞辛苦地去了解学生们的兴趣。**4 acquaint sb with sth** *formal* to give someone information about something【正式】把某事告诉某人：*My assistant should be able to acquaint you with all the details.* 我的助手会把所有的细节告诉你。

ac·quaint·ance /ə`kwentəns; ə'kweɪntəns/ *n* **1** [C] someone you know, but who is not a close friend 相识的人；泛泛之交 **2 make sb's acquaintance** *formal* to meet someone for the first time【正式】结识某人：*I'm pleased to make your acquaintance.* 我非常高兴结识你。**3 of your acquaintance** *formal* a person of your acquaintance is someone that you know【正式】你认识的〔人〕：*a certain lawyer of my acquaintance* 我所认识的某个律师 **4** [U] *formal* knowledge or experience of a particular subject【正式】所知；了解：**have a passing/nodding acquaintance with** (=have only slight knowledge or experience of something) 对…一知半解 *I must admit I have only a passing acquaintance with his books.* 我必须承认我对他的书只是一知半解。**5 on further/closer acquaintance** *formal* when you start to know someone or something better【正式】进一步了解

ac·quaint·ance·ship /ə`kwentənsʃɪp; ə'kweɪntənsʃɪp/ *n* [U] *formal*【正式】**1** your experience or knowledge of a subject 所知；了解 **2** the fact of knowing someone socially 相识

ac·qui·esce /ˌækwɪ`ɛs; ˌækwi'es/ *v* [I] *formal* to unwillingly agree to do what someone wants, or to let them do what they want, without arguing or complaining【正式】默许，默认；勉强同意：[+in/to] *The book accuses him of silently acquiescing in the Nazis' persecution of the Jews.* 这本书指控他默许纳粹迫害犹太人。

ac·qui·es·cent /ˌækwɪ`ɛsn̩t; ˌækwi'esənt◂/ *adj formal* too ready to agree with someone or do what they want, without arguing or complaining【正式】默认的；顺从的 —**acquiescence** *n* [U] —**acquiescently** *adv*

ac·quire /ə`kwaɪr; ə'kwaɪə/ *v* [T] **1** *formal* to buy or obtain something, especially something expensive or difficult to get【正式】购得，得到〔尤指昂贵的或难以得到的东西〕：*The museum has managed to acquire an important work by Dali.* 博物馆设法弄到了达利的一幅重要作品。**2** to learn or develop knowledge, skills etc by your own efforts, or to become well-known because of your abilities 掌握，获得〔知识、技能等〕：*I look on it as an opportunity to acquire fresh skills.* 我把这当作是一次学习新技能的机会。| *The team has acquired a fearsome reputation.* 这支队伍赢得了令人生畏的名声。**3 acquire a taste for** to begin to like something 慢慢喜欢上：*This beer isn't bad. I'm beginning to acquire a taste for it.* 这啤酒不错。我开始慢慢爱喝了。**4 be an acquired taste** something that people only begin to like after they have tried it a few times 是后来喜欢上的东西 **5** *humorous* to get something by dishonest means【幽默】以不正当的方式获得〔占有〕 2

ac·qui·si·tion /ˌækwə`zɪʃən; ˌækwɪ'zɪʃən/ *n* **1** [U] the act of getting new knowledge, skills etc〔新知识、新技能等的〕习得，得到：*second language acquisition* 第二语言习得 **2** [U] the act of getting land, power, money etc〔土地、权力、钱等的〕获得，得到：*the acquisition of new territory* 新领土的获得 **3** [C] *formal* something that you have bought or obtained, especially a valuable object【正式】获得物〔尤指珍贵物品〕：*The National Gallery's latest acquisition is a painting by Goya.* 国家美术馆最新得到的收藏品是戈雅的一幅绘画作品。 3

ac·quis·i·tive /ə`kwɪzətɪv; ə'kwɪzɪtɪv/ *adj formal* showing too much desire to get new possessions【正式】贪得无厌的

ac·quit /ə`kwɪt; ə'kwɪt/ *v* **acquitted, acquitting 1** [T usually passive 一般用被动态] to give a decision in a court of law that someone is not guilty of a crime 宣判…无罪：*All the defendants were acquitted.* 所有的被告都被宣判无罪。| **acquit sb of sth** *She was acquitted of murder.* 她被宣判谋杀罪不成立。**2 acquit yourself well/honourably** to do something well, especially

something difficult that you do for the first time in front of other people〔尤指首次面对他人〕表现很好 / 表现得体

ac·quit·tal /ə`kwɪtl; ə'kwɪtl/ *n* [C,U] an official statement in a court of law that someone is not guilty 无罪判决,(被)宣判无罪

a·cre /`ekɚ; 'eɪkə/ *n* [C] **1** a unit for measuring area, equal to 4047 square metres 英亩: *They own 200 acres of farmland.* 他们拥有200英亩农田。| *a 200-acre wood* 一片面积为200英亩的树林 —see table on page C3 参见C3页附录 **2 acres of space/room** *BrE informal* a large amount of space【英,非正式】很大面积

a·cre·age /`ekərɪdʒ; 'eɪkərɪdʒ/ *n* [U] the area of a piece of land measured in acres 英亩数; 以英亩计算的面积

ac·rid /`ækrɪd; 'ækrɨd/ *adj* **1** an acrid smell or taste is strong and unpleasant and stings your nose or throat 辛辣的, 刺激性的: *a cloud of acrid smoke* 一团刺鼻的烟雾 **2** *formal* an acrid comment, discussion etc is very critical or angry【正式】刻薄的, 尖酸的

ac·ri·mo·ni·ous /ˌækrə`monɪəs; ˌækrɨ'məʊniəs◂/ *adj formal* an acrimonious meeting, argument etc is full of angry comments because people feel very strongly about something【正式】激烈的, 唇枪舌剑的: *The meeting ended in an acrimonious dispute.* 会议不欢而散。—**acrimoniously** *adv* —**acrimoniousness** *n* [U]

ac·ri·mo·ny /`ækrəˌmonɪ; 'ækrɨməni/ *n* [U] *formal* anger and unpleasantness【正式】尖刻, 刻薄

ac·ro·bat /`ækrəˌbæt; 'ækrəbæt/ *n* [C] someone who entertains people by doing difficult physical actions such as walking on their hands or balancing on a high rope, especially at a CIRCUS (1) 杂技演员

ac·ro·bat·ic /ˌækrə`bætɪk; ˌækrə'bætɪk◂/ *adj* acrobatic movements involve moving your body in a very skilful way, for example by jumping through the air or balancing on a rope 杂技(似)的: *amazing acrobatic feats* 令人称奇的杂技表演 —**acrobatically** /-klɪ; -kli/ *adv*

ac·ro·bat·ics /ˌækrə`bætɪks; ˌækrə'bætɪks/ *n* [plural] acrobatic movements 杂技(表演)

ac·ro·nym /`ækrənɪm; 'ækrənɪm/ *n* [C] a word made up from the first letters of the name of something such as an organization. For example NATO is an acronym for the North Atlantic Treaty Organization. 首字母缩略词〔比如NATO(北约)由North Atlantic Treaty Organization的首字母缩略而成〕

A·crop·o·lis, the /ə`krɑpəlɪs; ə'krɒpəlɪs/ the ancient CITADEL (=a place people can go to if their city is attacked) of Athens, built on a hill in the centre of the city. There are many important ancient Greek buildings on the Acropolis, such as the Parthenon 雅典卫城〔雅典古城堡, 建于市中心的一座山上。卫城有许多重要的古建筑, 如帕台农神庙〕

[S1 W1] **a·cross¹** /ə`krɔs; ə'krɒs/ *prep* **1** going, looking etc from one side of a space, area, or line to the other side 横过, 穿过: *flying across the Atlantic* 飞越大西洋 | *We gazed across the valley.* 我们注视山谷的对面。| *Would you like me to help you across the road?* (=help you to cross it) 要我帮你过马路吗? —see picture on page A1 参见A1页图 **2** reaching or spreading from one side of an area to the other 从一边到另一边: *a deep crack across the ceiling* 天花板上从一端到另一端的深缝 | *the only bridge across the river* 跨越这条河的唯一一座桥 | *Slowly a smile spread across her face.* 慢慢地她的脸上露出了微笑。| *Do you think this shirt is too tight across the shoulders?* 你觉得这衬衫的肩部是不是太紧了? | **right across** *The damn fool has parked right across the entrance to the driveway.* 这傻瓜把车正好停在了车道的入口。**3** on or towards the opposite side of something 在对面; 向对面: *My best friend lives across the road.* 我最好的朋友住在马路对面。| *Jim yelled across the street to his son.* 吉姆向街对面的儿子喊叫。| **just across** *He knew that just across the border lay freedom.* 他知道只要过了边界线就自由了。| **across sth from** *Across the street from where we're standing, you can see the old churchyard.* 从我们现在站的地方往街对面看, 你就会看到旧教堂墓地。**4** in every part of a country, organization etc 在全部…, 在整个…: *a TV series that became popular across five continents* 在五大洲广受欢迎的电视系列片 | **right across** *Teachers are expected to teach a range of subjects right across the curriculum.* 教师应该能讲授整个课程中的多个学科。

[S1 W3] **across²** *adv* **1** from one side of something to the other 从一边到另一边: *There isn't a bridge. We'll have to swim across.* 没有桥, 我们只好游过去。| *We'd got halfway across before Philip realized he'd left his money at home.* 我们都走了一半了, 菲利普才意识到他把钱忘在家里了。**2** if you go, look, shout etc across to someone, you go, look or shout across an area to the place where they are 朝向〔对面〕: *There's Brendan. Why don't you go across and say hello?* 那是布伦丹。你为什么不走过去打个招呼? | *I'm just taking this food across to Sarah. Won't be long.* 我正把这食品拿过去给萨拉。要不了多久。| **across to/at** *The referee looked across at his linesman before awarding the penalty.* 裁判先朝巡边员那边看了一下, 然后判点球。**3 10 feet/10 miles etc across** if something is 10 feet etc across, that is how wide it is 10英尺/10英里宽: *At its widest point the river is 2 km across.* 这条河的最宽处为两公里。**4 across from** opposite something or someone 在…对面: *a woman sitting across from me on the train* 火车上坐在我对面的女人

a·cross-the-board /·ˌ· · '·◂/ *adj* affecting everyone or everything in a situation or organization 全面的, 包括一切的: *an across-the-board pay increase* 全面的加薪 —**across-the-board** *adv*

a·cros·tic /ə`krɔstɪk; ə'krɒstɪk/ *n* [C] a poem or piece of writing in which the first or last letter of each line can be read downwards to spell a word 离合诗〔几行诗句第一个词的首字母或最后一个词的尾字母能组合成词或短语的一种诗体〕

a·cryl·ic /ə`krɪlɪk; ə'krɪlɪk/ *adj* acrylic paints or cloth are made from a chemical substance 丙烯酸的

a·cryl·ics /ə`krɪlɪks; ə'krɪlɪks/ *n* [plural] acrylic paints 丙烯酸涂料

ACT /ˌe si `ti; ˌeɪ siː 'tiː/ *n* [singular] American Conservatory Theater; a REPERTORY theatre (=theatre whose actors perform different plays on different days) in San Francisco, which is also a respected school for training actors 美国演艺学院剧院〔旧金山的一个轮演剧目的剧院, 也是一所演员培训名校〕

[S1 W1] **act¹** /ækt; ækt/ *n* [C]

1 ▶ACTION 行为◀ [C] a particular kind of action 行为, 行动, 动作, 举动: *a criminal act* 犯罪行为 | **act of kindness/revenge/courage etc** *The Bishop condemned the attack as an act of mindless violence.* 主教谴责袭击事件是愚蠢的暴力行为。| *a supreme act of heroism* 高尚的英雄主义行为 | **the sexual act** (=the act of having sex) 性行为

2 be in the act of doing sth to be doing something at a particular moment, especially something that you should not do 正在做某事〔尤指坏事〕: **catch sb in the act (of doing sth)** *The photo shows her in the act of raising her gun to fire.* 照片上她举起枪正要射击。| *The thief was caught in the act.* 小偷作案时当场被捉住。

3 ▶LAW 法律◀ [C] a law that has been officially accepted by Parliament or Congress〔正式通过的〕法令, 法案: *the 1991 Prevention of Terrorism Act* 1991年《防止恐怖主义法案》| *an act of Congress* 国会的一项法令

4 ▶PRETENDING 假装◀ [singular] insincere behaviour in which you pretend to have a particular kind of feeling 装模作样, 装腔作势: *A lot of people think Betty's very kind and caring, but it's all just a big act.* 很多人都认为贝蒂既善良又关心人, 其实那都是故意装出来的。| **put on an act** (=pretend to have a particular feeling) 装模作样, 做戏 *He isn't really ill – he's just putting on an act.* 他并没有真生病, 只不过是在装模作样。

5 get your act together *informal* to do something in a more organized way or use your abilities more effectively【非正式】更有条理些, 加把劲: *She could be an excellent photographer, if only she got her act together a bit more.* 如果她做事能更有条理一点, 她可以成为一名优秀的摄影家。

6 get in on the act *informal* to take part in an activity that someone else has started, especially in order to get a share of the advantages for yourself【非正式】〔为得到好处而〕插手, 参加

7 ▶PLAY 话剧◀ [C] one of the main parts into which a stage play, OPERA etc is divided〔戏剧、歌剧等的〕一幕: *Hamlet eventually kills the king in Act 5.* 在第五幕中, 哈姆雷特终于把国王杀死了。| *Everything is resolved in the final act.* 在最后一幕, 一切都得以解决。

8 ▶PERFORMANCE 演出◀ [C] one of the several short performances in a theatre or CIRCUS (1) show〔戏剧、马戏的〕一段表演; 节目: *They used to do a comedy act together.* 他们过去常常合作表演喜剧。

9 ▶PERFORMER 演员◀ [C] a performer, singer, group of musicians etc 演出者: *top-selling British act 'The Happy Mondays'* 最热门的英国组合"快乐的星期一"

10 act of God an event that is caused by natural forces, such as a storm, flood, or fire, which you cannot prevent or control 天灾, 自然灾害, 不可抗力

11 act of worship an occasion when people pray together and show their respect for God 拜祭; 祈祷

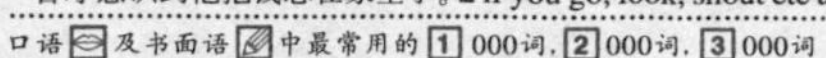
口语及书面语中最常用的 [1] 000词, [2] 000词, [3] 000词

A

12 **balancing/juggling act** the action of doing several different kinds of work at the same time 保持平衡行动〔指同时做几件事或兼顾好几方面的工作〕—see also 另见 **clean up your act** (CLEAN²)

act² *v*

1 ▶**DO SOMETHING** 做某事◀ **a)** [I] to do something to deal with an urgent problem, especially by using your official power or authority〔尤指运用职权或权威〕采取行动: *The UN Security Council must act to end the war in Bosnia.* 联合国安理会必须采取行动结束波斯尼亚的战争。**b)** [I always+adv/prep] to do something in a particular way or for a particular reason 行动, 表现: *The killer claims he was acting in self-defence.* 杀人者声称他那样做是出于自卫。| *I acted more out of compassion than anything else.* 我这样做更多地是出于同情。| **act in good faith** (=do something honestly without intending to deceive anyone) 诚实做事 *The shop manager says they acted in good faith and that they didn't know the camera was damaged.* 商店经理说他们诚实经营, 并不知道照相机是坏的。| **act on (sb's) advice/orders/suggestion etc** (=do what someone has advised, ordered etc) 按照(某人的)忠告/命令/建议等办事 *Acting on a friend's advice, he bought $50,000 of shares in a television company.* 他听了朋友的意见, 买了一家电视公司的五万美元的股票。| **act on information** (=do something because of information you have received) 根据了解到的信息采取行动 *The police were acting on information from a member of the public.* 警察正在根据一位市民提供的消息采取行动。

2 ▶**BEHAVE** 表现◀ [I always+adv/prep] to behave in a particular way 举动; 表现: **act strangely/stupidly/correctly etc** *Henry's been acting very strangely recently.* 亨利近来行为异常。| *The teacher acted perfectly correctly under the circumstances.* 老师在那种情况下这样做完全正确。| **act like/act as if** *If you act like a child, you're going to be treated like a child.* 如果你表现得像个孩子, 人们就会像对待孩子那样对待你。| *He acted as if he'd never seen me before.* 他表现得好像以前从来就没有见过我似的。| **act your age** *spoken* (=used to tell someone to be sensible and stop behaving like a child)【口】别孩子气了 | **act the fool** (=behave in a stupid and annoying way) 做蠢事 *Stop acting the fool, will you!* 别再做蠢事了, 行吗!

3 ▶**HAVE AN EFFECT** 起作用◀ **a)** to have a particular effect or use 起作用: [+as] *The sugar in the fruit acts as a preservative.* 水果中的糖分起着防腐剂的作用。| [+on] *Antibiotics act on the bacteria that cause the disease.* 抗生素对致病细菌发生作用。**b)** to start to have an effect 显效, 生效: *It takes a couple of minutes for the drug to act.* 这种药显效需要几分钟时间。

4 ▶**PRETEND** 假装◀ [I,T] to pretend to have particular feelings, qualities etc 装腔作势: **act innocent/stupid/hurt etc** *She suddenly started acting all upset so that the others would feel sorry for her.* 她突然开始装出伤心的样子以引起其他人的同情。| **act the fool/hero etc** *Whenever they're in public he always acts the loving husband.* 每次他们出现在公共场合, 他总是表现得像个体贴的丈夫。| **act as if/act like** *They were all trying to act as if nothing had happened.* 他们都设法摆出若无其事的样子。

5 ▶**PLAY/FILM ETC** 戏剧/电影等◀ [I,T] to perform in a play or film 演出: *I first started acting when I was 12 years old.* 我12岁时第一次演出。| **act a part/role etc** *Who acted the part of Miss Ceeley?* 谁扮演茜莉小姐这一角色? | **well/badly acted** (=performed well or badly) 演得好/差 *I thought the play was extremely well acted.* 我认为这出戏演得精彩极了。

6 ▶**LAWYER ETC** 律师等◀ **act for sb/act on sb's behalf** to represent someone, especially in a court of law or by doing business for them 代表某人, 代理: *I'm acting on behalf of my client, Mr Harding.* 我代表我的当事人哈丁先生。

7 ▶**DO THE JOB OF** 担任工作◀ **act as** to do a particular job for a short time, for example while the usual person is absent〔暂时性地〕代理〔某人的工作〕: *Mrs Odell is on holiday, and I'm acting as her replacement till she gets back.* 奥德尔夫人在休假, 在她回来以前, 我暂时接替她的工作。| *My brother speaks French – he will act as interpreter.* 我弟弟说法语, 他将充当翻译。—see also 另见 ACTING¹

act sth ↔ **out** *phr v* [T] **1** if a group of people act out an event, they show how it happened by pretending to be the people who were involved in it 演出来 **2** to express your feelings about something through your behaviour or actions, especially when you have been feeling angry or nervous 表现出来: *Teenagers can act out their anxieties in various aggressive ways.* 青少年会以各种好斗的方式宣泄他们的焦虑。

act up *phr v* [I] *informal*【非正式】**1** if children act up, they behave badly 调皮, 捣乱 **2** if a machine or part of your body acts up, it does not work properly 运转不正常, 出毛病: *The photocopier has started acting up again.* 复印机又开始出毛病了。

act·ing¹ /ˈæktɪŋ; ˈæktɪŋ/ *adj* **acting manager/head teacher/director etc** someone who does an important job while the usual person is not there, or until a new person is chosen for the job 代理经理/校长/董事长等

acting² *n* [U] the job or skill of performing in plays, films etc 表演; 演技

ac·tion /ˈækʃən; ˈækʃən/ *n* 

1 ▶**DOING THINGS** 做某事◀ [U] the process of doing in order to deal with a problem or difficult situation 行动, 活动; 动作: *The union is urging strike action.* 工会敦促采取罢工行动。| *We need more action, and less talk!* 我们需要更多的行动, 少一点空谈! | **take action** *The police took firm action to deal with the riots.* 警方采取果断的行动对付骚乱。| **go/spring into action** (=immediately begin doing something with a lot of energy) 采取紧急行动 *As soon as the SOS call was received, the rescue services sprang into action.* 一接到呼救信号, 救援中心立即采取行动。| **course of action** (=a series of actions done in order to deal with something) 一连串的行动 *One possible course of action would be to raise taxes on alcohol and tobacco.* 一连串可能采取的行动是提高酒类和烟草的税率。

2 ▶**SOMETHING DONE** 所做的事◀ [C] something that someone does 行为, 作为: *The child could not be held responsible for his actions.* 不能要求这个小孩对自己的行为负责。| *His prompt action probably saved my life.* 也许是他敏捷的行动救了我的命。

3 **in action** if you see someone or something in action you see them doing the job or activity that they are trained or designed to do 在运转, 在工作, 在活动: *exciting photos of ski jumpers in action* 跳台滑雪者跳下时的精彩照片 | *I'd like to see the new computer system in action.* 我想看看运行中的新计算机系统。

4 **put/call/bring sth into action** to begin to use a plan or idea that you have, and to make it work 使…投入运作, 启动

5 **be out of action** if something or someone is out of action, they are broken or injured, so that they cannot move or work 失灵, 发生故障: *My car's out of action at the moment, so I have to go by bus.* 我的汽车现在出了故障, 所以我只好乘公共汽车去。| **put sth/sb out of action** *The torn ligaments in his knee put him out of action for the rest of the season.* 他膝盖的韧带撕裂使他在余下的赛季里无法参加比赛。

6 ▶**COURT** 法庭◀ [C] the process of taking a case or a claim against someone to a court of law 诉讼: *They began an action to repossess the house.* 他们提起诉讼要求收回这座房子。| **legal/civil/libel etc action** *The European Commission is threatening legal action against Britain and France to protect the environment.* 欧盟委员会威胁说要对英法两国提起诉讼以保护环境。| **bring an action (against)** *They will bring an action against him if he doesn't repay the loan.* 如果他不还贷款, 他们会起诉他。

7 ▶**FIGHTING** 战斗◀ [C,U] fighting or a battle during a war 战斗(行动): *When the action ended there were terrible losses on both sides.* 战斗结束时, 双方都损失惨重。| **in/into action** *The navy was sent into action.* 海军被派去参加战斗。| **killed/wounded/missing in action** *Their son was reported missing in action.* 据报道, 他们的儿子在战斗中失踪。

8 ▶**EXCITING EVENTS** 刺激的事◀ *informal* exciting and important things that are happening【非正式】(令人激动的)事物; (重要的)活动: *I was looking for some action in this hick town.* 我在这小乡镇里寻找一些刺激。| **where (all) the action is** *This is the design studio – where the action is.* 这是设计室——最热闹的地方。

9 ▶**STORY** 故事◀ **the action** the things that happen in a play or book 情节, 故事: *The action of 'Hamlet' takes place in Denmark.*《哈姆雷特》的故事发生在丹麦。

10 ▶**BODY MOVEMENT** 身体动作◀ [C,U] a movement of the body, especially a particular type of movement 动作: *the action of the heart* 心脏的活动 | *the horse's trotting action* 马的小跑

11 ▶**MACHINERY** 机械◀ [singular] the movement of the parts of a clock, gun, piano etc 部件(的活动性能): *The action of this piano is rather stiff.* 这架钢琴的机械部件有些不灵活了。

12 ▶**EFFECT** 作用◀ [U] the way in which something such as a chemical or process has an effect on something else〔化学制品或过程等〕作用: *The rock had been worn away by the action of the falling water.* 石头因落水作用而磨损。

13 **action group/committee/project etc** a group formed to do something specific, especially to change a social or political situation 行动小组/委员会/计划等: *the Child Poverty Action Group* 儿童贫困行动小组

14 a piece of the action *informal* a share of something, such as profits, a business etc【非正式】〔利润、生意等的〕一份

15 actions speak louder than words used to say that you are judged by what you do, rather than by what you say you will do 行动胜于言辞

16 ▶FILMS 电影◀ action! used by film DIRECTORS to tell the actors and other film workers to begin filming 开拍!〔电影导演下令开始拍摄时说的话〕

ac·tio·na·ble /ˈækʃənəbl; ˈækʃənəbəl/ *adj* **1** [not before noun 不用于名词前] if something you say or do is actionable, it is so serious or damaging that a claim could be made against you in a court of law because of it 可控诉的, 可起诉的: *His allegations are actionable in my view.* 我认为对他的指控可以提出起诉。**2** [usually before noun 一般用于名词前] an actionable plan, piece of information etc is one that can be done or used〔计划、信息等〕可行的, 可用的

Action Man /ˈ· · ·/ *n* **1** *trademark* a DOLL (=a child's toy that looks like a small person) dressed as a male soldier and played with usually by boys in the UK【商标】〔英国男孩子常玩的〕玩具兵 —see also 另见 GI JOE **2** *BrE* a man who likes doing sports and activities that are exciting and dangerous【英】喜欢刺激的人, 喜欢冒险的人

action-packed /ˌ· · ˈ·◂/ *adj* an action-packed story or film contains a lot of exciting events 情节错综复杂的; 刺激的

action re·play /ˌ· · ˈ· ·/ *n* [C] *BrE* an important or exciting moment in a sports game on television that is shown again immediately after it happens; INSTANT REPLAY【英】即时重播, 精彩回放〈如电视中体育比赛的精彩瞬间〉

action sta·tions /ˈ· · ˌ· ·/ *interjection* used to order soldiers etc to go to their positions ready for battle 各就各位〔用以对士兵等下命令〕

ac·tiv·ate /ˈæktəˌvet; ˈæktɪ̵veɪt/ *v* [T] **1** to make something, especially an electrical system, start working 起动, 开动, 使活动: *The lock is activated by a magnetic key.* 这个锁用磁性钥匙开。**2** *technical* to make a chemical action or natural process happen【术语】〔化学〕激活, 使活化: *The manufacture of chlorophyll is activated by sunlight.* 叶绿素的制造依靠阳光的照射。**3** *technical* to make something RADIOACTIVE【术语】使产生放射性 —**activation** /ˌæktəˈveʃən; ˌæktɪ̵ˈveɪʃən/ *n* [U]

[2] [2] **ac·tive**[1] /ˈæktɪv; ˈæktɪv/ *adj*

1 ▶DOING THINGS 做事◀ always doing things or ready to do things, especially physical activities 爱运动的; 爱活动的: *We had an active holiday, sailing, swimming and water skiing.* 我们在运动中度过假期, 驾驶帆船、游泳、滑水。| *She may be over 80, but she's still very active!* 她可能已经80多岁了, 但仍然十分喜爱活动!

2 ▶IN AN ORGANIZATION 在组织中◀ involved in an organization, activity etc and always busy doing things to help it 积极的, 活跃的: **active member** *an active member of the local Historical Society* 当地历史学会的积极分子 | **be active in (doing) sth** *He's very active in local politics.* 他积极参加当地的政治活动。| *She's been active in raising money for the new church buildings.* 她积极为兴建新教堂的大楼筹款。

3 active efforts/discussions etc efforts, attempts etc to do something, solve a problem etc, that are made with continuous energy and determination 积极的努力/讨论等: *Active efforts are being made to reach a settlement.* 正在作出积极的努力以达成协议。

4 ▶ELECTRICAL SYSTEM 电力系统◀ *technical* operating in the way it is supposed to【术语】在活动中的, 起作用的: *The alarm becomes active when the switch is turned on.* 一按开关, 警报器就启动了。

5 ▶MILITARY 军事的◀ a) on active service a soldier etc who is on active service is fighting in a war 战时服役 **b) on active duty** *AmE* employed by the army etc, as opposed to being in the reserves (RESERVE[2] (6))【美】服现役

6 ▶VOLCANO 火山◀ likely to explode and pour out fire 活的, 还会爆发的

7 ▶GRAMMAR 语法◀ *technical* if a verb or sentence is active, the person or thing doing the action is the SUBJECT[1] (5). In 'The boy kicked the ball', the verb 'kick' is active.【术语】主动的〈在 The boy kicked the ball 一句中, kick 是主动动词〉—compare 比较 PASSIVE[1] (2)

8 ▶CHEMICAL 化学的◀ *technical* producing a reaction in a substance or with another chemical【术语】活性的 —**actively** *adv*: *The two sides are actively engaged in discussions.* 双方积极参与讨论。

active[2] *n* **the active/the active voice** *technical* the active form of a verb【术语】〔动词的〕主动语态 —compare 比较 PASSIVE[2]

ac·tiv·ist /ˈæktɪvɪst; ˈæktɪ̵vɪ̵st/ *n* [C] someone who works hard to achieve social or political change, especially as an active member of a political organization 积极分子; 活动家: *Greenpeace activists* 绿色和平组织的积极分子 [3]

ac·tiv·i·ty /ækˈtɪvətɪ; ækˈtɪvɪ̵ti/ *n* **1** [U] a situation in which a lot of things are happening or people are doing things, moving around etc 活跃, 热闹: *I missed the noise and activity of the city.* 我怀念这座城市的喧闹和忙碌。| *a huge amount of media activity during the elections* 大选期间频繁的传媒活动 —opposite 反义词 INACTIVITY **2** [C] something that you do for interest or pleasure or because you want to achieve something 活动: *leisure activities* 娱乐活动 | *There'll be plenty of activities laid on for the kids.* 将为孩子们安排许多活动。| *terrorist activities* 恐怖主义活动 [1] [1]

Act of Par·lia·ment /ˌ· · ˈ· · ·/ a law that has been officially accepted by a parliament, especially the British Parliament 议会法案〔议会 (尤指英国议会) 正式接受的法律〕

Act of U·nion, the /ˌ· · ˈ· ·/ **1** the agreement that joined the parliaments of England and Scotland in 1707《联合条例》〔根据该条例, 英格兰和苏格兰议会 1707 年正式合并〕**2** the agreement that ended the Irish parliament in 1800 and made Ireland part of the United Kingdom in 1801《联合条例》〔根据该条例, 爱尔兰1800年解散议会, 1801年加入联合王国〕

ac·tor /ˈæktɚ; ˈæktə/ *n* [C] someone who performs in a play, film, or television programme 演员 [3]

Actors' Stu·di·o /ˈ· · ˌ· · ·/ a school in New York that trains actors, which is famous for teaching Method acting 演员工作室〔纽约的一所演员培训学校, 以传授方法派演技而著名〕

ac·tress /ˈæktrɪs; ˈæktrɪ̵s/ *n* [C] a woman who performs in a play, film, or television programme 女演员

ac·tu·al /ˈæktʃuəl; ˈæktʃuəl/ *adj* [only before noun 仅用于名词前] **1** real, especially as compared with what is believed, expected or intended 实际的, 现实的: *a big difference between the opinion polls and the actual election results* 民意测验和实际选举结果的巨大差异 | *I'm not joking. Those were his actual words.* 我不是开玩笑, 那都是他的原话。| **in actual fact** (=really) 实际上 *In actual fact, there is not much evidence to support these allegations.* 事实上, 没有多少证据支持这些指控。**2 the actual** used to introduce the main part of what you are describing 事实上: *The programme starts at 8.00 but the actual film doesn't start until 8.30.* 节目8点开始, 但实际上电影到8点半才放映。 [1] [2]

ac·tu·al·i·ty /ˌæktʃuˈælətɪ; ˌæktʃuˈælɪ̵ti/ *n* **1** [C usually plural 一般用复数] something that is real; a fact 事实, 真实的情况: *the grim actualities of prison life* 监狱生活的严酷现实 **2** [U] *formal* the state of being real; EXISTENCE (1)【正式】现实 (性) **3 in actuality** *formal* really【正式】真正地

ac·tu·al·ly /ˈæktʃuəlɪ; ˈæktʃuəli/ *adv* **1** [sentence adverb 句子副词] *spoken* used when you are giving an opinion or adding new information to what you have just said【口】实际上, 其实〔用于说明个人观点或补充新的资料〕: *I've known Barbara for years. Since we were babies, actually.* 我认识芭芭拉已多年了, 实际上我们从小就认识。| *I do actually think that things have improved.* 其实我的确认为情况有所好转。| *We had quite a good time, actually.* 事实上, 我们玩得很愉快。| *Well actually you still owe me $200.* 实际上你还欠我 200 元。**2** used when you are telling or asking someone what the real and exact truth of a situation is, as opposed to what people may imagine 实际上, 事实上: *He may look young but he's actually 45.* 他可能看起来年轻, 但实际上已经 45 岁了。| *Disappointed? No, actually I'm rather glad.* 失望? 不, 实际上我相当高兴。| *Unemployment has actually fallen for the past two months.* 近两个月来, 失业人数实际上有所减少。| *Did he actually attack you, or just threaten you?* 他是真的攻击你了, 还是只是威胁你? [1] [1]

Frequencies of the adverb **actually** in spoken and written English 副词 actually 在英语口语和书面语中的使用频率

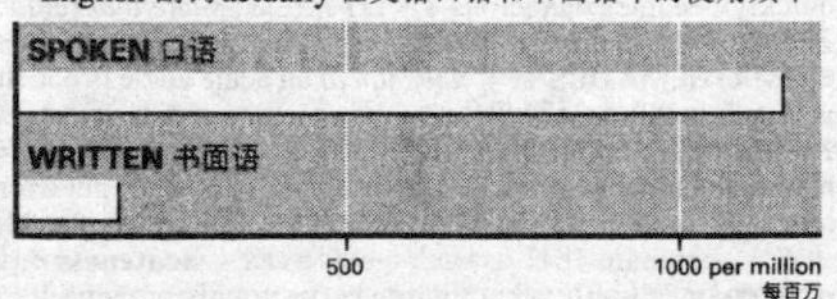

Based on the British National Corpus and the Longman Lancaster Corpus
据英国国家语料库和朗文兰开斯特语料库

This graph shows that the adverb **actually** is much more common in spoken English than in written English. 本图表显示, 副词 actually 在英语口语中的使用频率远远高于书面语。

A

USAGE NOTE 用法说明: ACTUALLY

WORD CHOICE 词语辨析: **actually, currently, at present**

Actually (and **actual**) does not mean 'at the present time' in English. actually (和 actual) 在英语中并不是"现今"的意思。Compare **currently** and **at present** 比较 currently 和 at present: *"Have you ever met Simon?" "I actually met him two years ago."* (=in fact) "你见过西蒙吗?" "事实上我两年前见过他。" | *"Is the company doing well?" "Yes. It's currently doing very well/It's doing very well at present."* "公司现在情况好吧?" "是的。公司目前情况良好。"

In conversation, especially in British English, **actually** can be used to make what you are saying softer, especially if you are correcting someone, disagreeing, or complaining. 在会话中, 特别是英国英语, actually 可使语气更缓和, 尤其是在纠正某人的观点、表示不同意或抱怨时: *"Great! I love French coffee!" "Er, it's German actually."* "太好了! 我喜欢法国咖啡!" "呃, 这其实是德国咖啡。" But it can be used with the opposite effect. 但也可起相反作用: *I didn't ask your opinion, actually.* 实际上, 我并没有问你的意见。

ac·tu·a·ry /ˋæktʃʊˌɛrɪ; ˈæktʃuəri/ *n* [C] someone who advises insurance companies on how much to charge for insurance, after calculating the various risks 保险公司计算师, 精算师

ac·tu·ate /ˋæktʃʊˌet; ˈæktʃueɪt/ *v* [T] **1 be actuated by** *formal* to behave in a particular way because of a feeling or a quality in your character【正式】为…所驱使: *Iago was actuated by malice.* 埃古受到恶念的驱使。**2** *technical* to make a piece of machinery or electrical equipment start to operate【术语】启动, 驱动

Act-Up /ˈ· ·/ an organization in the US and the UK that demands more help and support for people with AIDS "行动起来"组织〔英美一组织, 要求人们给予艾滋病患者更多帮助和支持〕

a·cu·i·ty /əˋkjuətɪ; əˈkjuːɪti/ *n* [U] *formal* the ability to think, see, or hear quickly and clearly【正式】灵敏, 敏锐, 锐利: *mental acuity* 思维敏捷

ac·u·men /əˋkjumən; ˈækjʊmən/ *n* [U] the ability to think quickly and make good judgements 敏锐, 聪明, 机智: **business/political/financial etc acumen** *The firm's success is due to the director's ingenuity and business acumen.* 公司的成功归功于董事的足智多谋和商业头脑。

ac·u·pres·sure /ˋækjʊˌprɛʃɚ; ˈækjʊˌpreʃə/ *n* [U] a method of stopping pain and curing disease by pressing on particular areas of the body 指压 (疗法)

ac·u·punc·ture /ˋækjʊˌpʌŋktʃɚ; ˈækjʊˌpʌŋktʃə/ *n* [U] a method of stopping pain and curing disease by putting special needles into particular parts of the body 针灸, 针刺 (疗法)

a·cute /əˋkjut; əˈkjuːt/ *adj*

1 ▶SITUATION/FEELING ETC 情况/感觉等◀ very serious or severe 严重的: *an acute shortage of water* 严重缺水 | *acute embarrassment* 极其尴尬

2 ▶PAIN 疼痛◀ very severe and sharp 剧烈的

3 acute hearing/acute sense of smell etc an ability to hear or smell things that is very sensitive, so that you are able to notice small differences 灵敏的听觉/嗅觉等

4 ▶INTELLIGENT 聪颖的◀ quick to notice things and able to think clearly and intelligently 敏锐的, 机敏的: **acute understanding/analysis/observations** *Her book is an acute analysis of Middle Eastern history.* 她的书是对中东历史的精辟分析。| **acute observer** *De Tocqueville was an acute observer of American ways.* 德·托克维尔是美国生活方式的敏锐观察家。

5 ▶MEDICAL 医疗的◀ *technical* an acute illness or disease quickly becomes dangerous【术语】急性的: *acute tuberculosis* 急性肺结核 —compare 比较 CHRONIC (1)

6 ▶MATHEMATICS 数学◀ *technical* an acute angle is one that is less than 90°【术语】锐角的 —see picture at 参见 ANGLE[1] 图

7 ▶PRONUNCIATION MARK 发音符号◀ an acute ACCENT (=a mark used to show pronunciation) is the small mark put over a letter, such as é in French 发锐音的, 标有尖音符号 ˊ 的〔如法语 é〕—compare 比较 GRAVE[3], CIRCUMFLEX —**acuteness** *n* [U]

a·cute·ly /əˋkjutlɪ; əˈkjuːtli/ *adv* very strongly or painfully 严重地, 深切地; 痛苦地: *acutely embarrassed* 异常尴尬 | **acutely aware/conscious** *The president is acutely conscious of the need for more doctors and nurses.* 总统敏锐地意识到需要更多的医生和护士。

AD /ˌe ˋdi; ˌeɪ ˈdiː◂/ Anno Domini; used to show that a date is a particular number of years after the birth of Christ 公元: *What will world population be by 2020 AD?* 到公元 2020 年, 世界人口将达到多少? | *in the first century AD* 公元 1 世纪 —compare 比较 BC

ad /æd; æd/ *n* [C] *informal* an advertisement【非正式】广告 —see also 另见 CLASSIFIED AD

ad·age /ˋædɪdʒ; ˈædɪdʒ/ *n* [C] a well-known phrase that says something wise about human experience; PROVERB 格言, 谚语

a·da·gio /əˋdadʒo; əˈdɑːdʒəʊ/ *n* [C] a piece of music to be played or sung slowly 缓慢的音乐, 慢板 —**adagio** *adj, adv*

Ad·am /ˋædəm; ˈædəm/ **1** the first man, according to the Jewish, Christian, and Islamic religions. In the Old Testament of the Bible, Adam lived in the Garden of Eden with Eve, the first woman. 亚当〔犹太教、基督教及伊斯兰教所说的人类的男性始祖。根据《圣经·旧约》, 亚当和人类的女性始祖夏娃一起住在伊甸园〕**2 not know someone from Adam** *informal* to not know someone at all【非正式】根本不认识某人

Adam, Rob·ert /ˋrabɚt; ˈrɒbət/ (1728-92) a Scottish ARCHITECT who designed many famous houses and other buildings, and influenced the development of the NEOCLASSICAL style. He is also famous for designing furniture. 亚当〔(1728-1792), 苏格兰建筑设计师, 设计过不少名宅和建筑, 对新古典主义风格的发展具有一定影响。他也是著名的家具设计师〕

ad·a·mant /ˋædəˌmænt; ˈædəmənt/ *adj formal* determined not to change your opinion, decision, etc【正式】固执的; 坚强不屈的: *We tried to negotiate, but they were adamant.* 我们设法谈判, 但他们很固执。| **adamant that** *Melinda was adamant that she would not travel with us.* 梅琳达坚持不和我们一起旅行。—**adamantly** *adv*

Ad·ams /ˋædəmz; ˈædəmz/, **An·sel** /ˋænsḷ; ˈænsəl/ (1902-84) a US photographer famous for his black-and-white photographs of the countryside in the west of the US 亚当斯〔(1902-1984), 美国摄影师, 以反映美国西部乡村的黑白照片而著称〕

Adams, Ger·ry /ˋdʒɛrɪ; ˈdʒeri/ (1948-) the leader of Sinn Fein, the Irish political party that wants Northern Ireland to unite with the Republic of Ireland 亚当斯〔(1948-), 爱尔兰新芬党领袖。新芬党的目标是实现北爱尔兰和爱尔兰共和国的统一〕

Adams, John (1735-1826) the second President of the US, from 1797 to 1801 亚当斯〔(1735-1826), 1797 年至 1801 年任美国第二任总统〕

Adams, John Quin·cy /dʒan ˋkwɪnsɪ; dʒɒn ˈkwɪnsi/ (1767-1848) the sixth President of the US from 1825 to 1829. He was the son of John Adams, and he is believed to have written the Monroe Doctrine. 亚当斯〔(1767-1848), 1825 至 1829 年任美国第六任总统, 约翰·亚当斯之子。一般认为是他拟定的《门罗宣言》〕

Adams, Sam·u·el /ˋsæmjʊəl; ˈsæmjuəl/ (1722-1803) a US politician and writer who protested against British taxes and law when the UK was still in control of the American colonies (COLONY). He was the main organizer of the Boston Tea Party. 亚当斯〔(1722-1803), 美国政治家、作家。英国统治美洲殖民地期间, 他强烈抗议英国的赋税和法律。他是波士顿倾茶事件的主要组织者〕

Ad·am's ap·ple /ˌ·· ˈ·· ·/ *n* [C] the part at the front of your neck that sticks out slightly and moves when you talk or swallow 喉结, 喉核 —see picture at 参见 HEAD[1] 图

Adam Smith In·sti·tute /ˌ·· ˈ· ·, ···/ a RIGHT-WING British organization that develops ideas about economics and gives advice to businesses and politicians. It is named after Adam Smith, an 18th century Scottish writer on economics. 亚当·斯密学会〔英国一右翼组织。旨在阐述经济学思想, 给商业机构和政治家建言。学会得名于 18 世纪苏格兰经济学作家亚当·斯密〕

a·dapt /əˋdæpt; əˈdæpt/ *v* **1** [I,T] to gradually change your behaviour and attitudes so that you get used to a new situation and can deal with it successfully (使) 适应, (使) 适合: **[+to]** *The children are finding it hard to adapt to their new school.* 孩子们发觉很难适应新学校。| *plants that have adapted themselves to desert conditions* 已适应沙漠环境的植物 **2** [T] to change something so that it can be used in a different way or for a different purpose 改造, 改装: *The car's fuel system was adapted to take unleaded gas.* 汽车的燃油系统经改装可使用无铅汽油。| **[+for]** *The materials can be adapted for use with older children.* 这些材料改一下可给大一点的孩子用。**3 be well adapted to** to be particularly suitable for something 特别适应: *Alpine flowers which are well adapted to the harsh Swiss winters* 特别适应瑞士冬天的严寒气候的高山花卉 **4** [T] to change a book or play so that it can be made into a film, television programme etc 改编 —compare 比较 ADJUST

a·dap·ta·ble /əˋdæptəbḷ; əˈdæptəbəl/ *adj* able to change so as to be suitable or successful in new and different situations 能

适应的, 适应性很强的: *I'm sure she'll cope with the changes very well – she's very adaptable.* 我相信她会很妥善地应付这些变化 —— 她的适应能力很强。| *The American constitution has proved adaptable in changing political conditions.* 事实证明, 美国宪法能适应日益变化的政治形势。—**adaptability** /ə,dæptə`bɪlətɪ; ə,dæptə'bɪlʒti/ *n* [U]

ad·ap·ta·tion /,ædæp`teʃən; ,ædæp'teɪʃən/ *n* **1** [C] a film or play that was first written in a different form, for example as a book 改编 **2** [U] the process by which something changes or is changed so that it can be used in a different way or in different conditions 改造; 适应: *adaptation to the environment* 适应环境

a·dapt·er, adaptor /ə`dæptə; ə'dæptə/ *n* [C] **1** something used to connect two pieces of equipment, especially when they are of different sizes 转接器, 适配器 **2** *BrE* a special type of PLUG[1] (1) that makes it possible to connect more than one piece of equipment to the electricity supply【英】多头插头

ADC /,eɪ di `si; ,eɪ diː 'siː/ the abbreviation of 缩写= AIDE-DE-CAMP

add /æd; æd/ *v*

1 ►PUT WITH 和…放到一起◄ [T] to put something with something else or with a group of other things 添加: **add sth to sth** *Do you want to add your name to the list?* 你想把你的名字加到名单里吗? | *I gave him a rare Swedish stamp to add to his collection.* 我给了他一张珍贵的瑞典邮票, 添加到他的收藏品中。

2 ►COUNTING 计算◄ [I,T] to put two or more numbers together in order to calculate the total 相加, 求和: *Add 6 and 6 to make 12.* 6加6得12。| **add sth to** *Added to what we've already saved, it gives us $550.* 和我们省下的钱加在一起, 一共是550美元。—compare 比较 SUBTRACT —see picture at 参见 MATHEMATICS 图

3 ►INCREASE 增加◄ [I,T] to increase the amount or cost of something by putting something more with it 增加: **add sth to** *The sales tax adds 15% to the price of clothes.* 销售税使服装的价格增加了15%。| [+to] *Conforming to the new regulations will add to the cost of the project.* 遵照新的条例将增加该项目的成本。

4 ►SAY 说◄ [T] to say something more that is related to what has been said already 补充, 继续说: *That's all I have to say. Is there anything you'd like to add, David?* 我要说的就是这些。戴维, 你还有什么要补充的吗? | *"And I don't care what you think," she added defiantly.* "我不在乎你怎么想。"她不服气地补充道。| **add that** *Casey added that everything he had told us was, of course, top-secret.* 凯西补充说, 他告诉我们的话当然全部是绝密的。| **I might add** *spoken* (=used when adding something, especially to complain)【口】而且 *The bus was two hours late, and, I might add, they tried to charge my children the full adult fares.* 公共汽车晚了两小时, 而且, 他们还要我的孩子买全额成人票。

5 ►COOKING 烹饪◄ [T] to mix one food with another while cooking 加入: *Cream the butter and sugar, then add the eggs.* 把黄油和糖搅成糊状, 然后加鸡蛋。

6 ►GIVE A QUALITY 给以某种性质◄ [T] to give a particular quality to an event, place, situation etc 增添: *Fine champagne always adds glamour to an occasion.* 上等的香槟酒总能为一场盛会增加气氛。

7 added to this/if you add to this used to introduce another fact, especially one that makes a situation seem even worse 再考虑到这一点: *If you add to this the young age of the victims, it makes the crime unforgivable.* 如果再考虑到受害者年纪那么轻, 罪行就更加不可饶恕了。

8 add insult to injury to make a situation even more upsetting for someone, when they have already been badly or unfairly treated 既伤害又侮辱; 雪上加霜

9 add fuel to the fire/flames to make a bad situation even worse, especially by making someone more angry 火上加油

add sth ↔ **in** *phr v* [T] to include something with something else 加进, 包括: *By the time we added in the cost of the drinks the bill was over £100.* 我们再加上酒水的开销, 账单超过100英镑。

add sth ↔ **on** *phr v* [T] **1** to make a building larger by building another room 加盖, 加建: *They added on a bedroom at the back.* 他们在后面加盖了一间卧室。**2** to increase the amount or cost of something by putting something more with it 附加, 增加〔…的量或费用〕: *Labor costs could add on a further 25%.* 算上劳动力成本, 费用可能还要增加25%。| [+to] *Service is added on to the bill.* 账单中包含服务费。

add to sth *phr v* [T] to make something such as a feeling or quality stronger and more noticeable 增加, 使更加: *Our explanation seemed only to add to his bewilderment.* 我们的解释似乎只有使他更困惑。| *a certain diffidence which added to his charm* 使他更具魅力的某种谦恭

add up *phr v* **1** [I,T **add** sth ↔ **up**] to calculate the total of several numbers 把…加起来: *Add your scores up and we'll see who won.* 把你的得分加起来, 我们就可以看出谁赢了。**2 not add up** if a set of facts does not add up, it does not provide a reasonable explanation for something 不合情理, 说不通: *He had been arrested for murder, but the evidence just didn't add up.* 他因谋杀罪被捕, 但那些证据并不合理。**3** [I not in progressive 不用进行时] *informal* to increase by small amounts until there is a large total【非正式】积少成多: *There are five of us using the phone so it soon adds up.* 我们五个人用电话, 所以不久就打得很多了。

add up to *phr v* [T not in progressive 不用进行时] to have a particular result 总的来讲; 等于说: *With a meal included in the cost of the ticket, it all adds up to a really good evening's entertainment.* 入场券的费用里还包括一顿饭, 总体来说, 这个晚上的招待真算是不错了。

Ad·dams Fam·i·ly, the /`ædəmz ,fæməlɪ; 'ædəmz ,fæməli/ *trademark* an imaginary family who originally appeared in a US CARTOON STRIP and then in a humorous television programme and in films. They are very interested in death and frightening things, and think that they are normal even though they seem very strange to everyone else【商标】亚当斯家族〔一个虚构的家族。最早出现在美国连环漫画中, 后出现在幽默电视节目和电影中。亚当斯一家人对死亡和恐怖一类东西特别感兴趣。尽管大家都觉得他们看上去十分古怪, 但他们却认为自己很正常〕

ad·ded /`ædɪd; 'ædʒd/ *adj* in addition to what is usual or expected 额外的, 附加的, 增添的: *a breakfast cereal with added vitamins* 添加维生素的早餐麦片 | **added advantage/benefit/precaution etc** (=that makes something better) 额外的优势/益处/预防措施等 *She had a deadbolt fitted as an added precaution.* 她叫人安装了一把门锁作为额外的预防措施。| **added difficulty/problem/complication** (=that makes something worse) 增加的难度/问题/复杂性

ad·den·dum /ə`dɛndəm; ə'dendəm/ *n plural* **addenda** /-də; -də/ [C] *technical* something that is added to the end of a speech or book, usually to give more information【术语】补充; 补遗; 补编; 附录

ad·der /`ædə; 'ædə/ *n* [C] **1** a small poisonous snake living in northern Europe and northern Asia〔北欧和北亚生长的〕蝰蛇 **2** one of several types of snake living in North America〔北美生长的〕乳蛇

ad·dict /`ædɪkt; 'ædɪkt/ *n* [C] **1** someone who is unable to stop taking drugs 吸毒上瘾的人: *treatment centers for addicts* 戒毒中心 | **drug/heroin/morphine etc addict** *Many heroin addicts have contracted AIDS.* 许多有海洛因瘾的人感染了艾滋病。**2** someone who spends too much time doing something they like 对…着迷的人: *a television addict* 电视迷

ad·dic·ted /ə`dɪktɪd; ə'dɪktʒd/ *adj* [not before noun 不用于名词前] **1** unable to stop taking a harmful substance, especially a drug 有瘾的, 上瘾的: [+to] *He is seriously addicted to these tranquillizers.* 他对这些镇静剂已严重上瘾。**2** liking to do or have something so much you do not want to stop 对…痴迷的, 沉迷的: [+to] *kids addicted to computer games* 沉迷于电脑游戏的孩子

ad·dic·tion /ə`dɪkʃən; ə'dɪkʃən/ *n* [C,U] the need to have something regularly because you are addicted to it 成瘾; 癖好: *drug addiction* 毒瘾 | [+to] *a program to deal with addiction to alcohol* 解决酗酒成瘾问题的计划

ad·dic·tive /ə`dɪktɪv; ə'dɪktɪv/ *adj* **1** a drug that is addictive makes you unable to stop taking it 使人成瘾的, 上瘾的: **highly addictive** *Crack is a potent, highly addictive form of cocaine.* 强效可卡因是很易使人上瘾的烈性可卡因。**2** an activity that is addictive is one that you want to keep doing, especially because you enjoy it so much 使人着迷的, 使人沉溺于…的: *I took up skiing a couple of years ago and I find it quite addictive.* 我几年前开始练滑雪, 我发觉这项运动挺令人着迷。

Ad·dis Ab·a·ba /,ædɪs `æbəbə; ,ædʒs 'æbəbə/ the capital city of Ethiopia 亚的斯亚贝巴〔埃塞俄比亚首都〕

Ad·di·son, Joseph /`ædɪsn; 'ædʒsən/ /`dʒozəf; 'dʒəuzɪf/ (1672-1719) an English writer who wrote articles for *The Tatler* and *The Spectator* 艾迪生〔(1672-1719), 英格兰作家,《闲谈者》和《旁观者》杂志撰稿人〕

ad·di·tion /ə`dɪʃən; ə'dɪʃən/ *n* **1 in addition** used when adding another fact to what has already been mentioned 除此之外, 另外: *The hotel itself can accommodate 80 guests and, in addition, there are several self-catering apartments.* 旅馆本身

能容纳80位客人，除此之外，还有几个可供自己做饭的套房。| **in addition to** *He's now running his own research company – that's in addition to his job at the university.* 除了他在大学的工作以外，他现在还经营自己的研究公司。**2** [U] the act of adding something to something else 增添，添加：[+of] *The addition of networking facilities will greatly enhance the system.* 网络设备的增加将会大大增强系统的性能。**3** [C] something that is added to something else, often in order to improve it 增加物，增强物：[+to] *A bottle of wine would make a pleasant addition to the meal.* 一瓶葡萄酒将为这顿饭增色不少。**4** [U] the process of adding numbers or amounts to make a total 加法 —compare 比较 SUBTRACTION **5** [C] *AmE* a room or a part of a building that is added to the main building【美】〔主建筑物的〕扩建部分：*They built a big addition at the back of their house.* 他们在房子后面又加盖了一间很大的房子。

ad·di·tion·al /əˋdɪʃənl; əˈdɪʃənəl/ *adj* more than what was agreed or expected 追加的，附加的，另外的：*An additional charge is made on baggage over the weight allowance.* 行李超重要额外收费。

ad·di·tion·al·ly /əˋdɪʃənlɪ; əˈdɪʃənəli/ *adv* in addition; also 除此之外，也：[sentence adverb 句子副词] *A new contract had been agreed. Additionally, staff were offered a bonus scheme.* 一份新合同已经签订。除此之外，还有一个给员工发奖金的方案。

ad·di·tive /ˋædətɪv; ˈædɪtɪv/ *n* [C] a substance, especially a chemical, that is added to something such as food, to preserve it, give it colour, improve it etc 添加剂，添加物：*Foods sold under this label are guaranteed free from additives.* 贴有这个标签的食品保证不含添加剂。| *lead additives in petrol* 汽油中的铅添加剂

CULTURAL NOTE 文化注释

Laws in the UK and the US allow only additives that are considered safe to be put in foods. In the UK, additives are given an E NUMBER and these are listed on the food's package. In the US, the chemical names are listed on the package. 英美法律只允许被认为是安全的添加剂放入食品中。在英国，每种添加剂有一个电子号码，标在食品包装上。在美国，食品包装上标有添加剂的化学名称。

ad·dle /ˋædl; ˈædl/ *v* [T] to make someone confused and unable to think properly 使混乱，使糊涂：**addle sb's brains** *All that drink has addled his brains!* 全是那些酒使他昏头昏脑！

ad·dled /ˋædld; ˈædld/ *adj* **1** an egg that is addled is no longer good to eat〔蛋〕变质的 **2** confused and unable to think properly 糊涂的，头脑混乱的

add-on /ˈ· ·/ *n* [C] a piece of equipment that can be connected to a computer, such as a MODEM, to make the computer more useful〔电脑的〕附加设备；附件 —compare 比较 PERIPHERAL[2]

ad·dress¹ /əˋdrɛs; əˈdres/ *n* **1** [C] the number of the building and the name of the street and town etc where someone lives or works, especially when written on a letter or package 地址：*I wrote the wrong address on the envelope.* 我在信封上写错了地址。| **change of address** *Please notify us of any change of address.* 地址如有变更，请通知我们。**2** [C] a formal speech made to a group of people who have come especially to listen to it 讲话，演说 **3** [C] a number that shows where a piece of information is stored in a computer's memory〔计算机系统的〕位址，地址 **4 form/style/mode of address** the correct title or name that you use for someone when you are speaking to them 称呼方式/风格/语气

ad·dress² /əˋdrɛs; əˈdres/ *v* [T] **1** to write on an envelope, package etc the name and address of the person you are sending it to 在〔信封、包裹等〕上写姓名和地址：*If you address the letter, I'll mail it for you.* 如果你在信上写上地址，我就替你寄出去。| **address sth to sb** *The letter is addressed to you, not me.* 这封信是写给你的，不是给我的。**2** *formal* to speak directly to someone【正式】向…讲话：*She turned to address the man on her left.* 她转过头对左边的人说话。| **address sth to** *You will have to address your complaints to the Head Office.* 你得向总部投诉。**3 address a meeting/crowd/conference etc** to make a speech to a large group of people 在会上/对人群/在大会上等发表演说：*The meeting was addressed by Senator Howard.* 会上由霍华德参议员作演讲。**4** to use a particular title or name when speaking or writing to someone 称呼：**address sb as** *The president should be addressed as 'Mr President'.* 对总统的称呼应该是"总统先生"。**5** *formal* to discuss, think about, or do something about a particular problem or question, especially with the aim of solving a problem【正式】探讨〔如何处理问题〕：*The article addresses the problems of diseases connected with malnutrition.* 这篇文章主要探讨与营养不良有关的疾病。| **address yourself to** *Marlowe now addressed himself to the task of searching the room.* 马洛现在忙于搜查房间。

ad·dress·ee /ˌædrɛsˋi; ˌædreˈsiː/ *n* [C] the person a letter, package etc is addressed to 收信人，收件人

ad·duce /əˋdus; əˈdjuːs/ *v* [T] *formal* to mention a fact or reason in order to prove, explain, or support what you are claiming is true【正式】举证，引证

-ade /ed; eɪd/ *suffix* [in U nouns 构成不可数名词] a drink made from a particular fruit〔指用某种水果制成的〕饮料，果汁：*orangeade* (=drink made from orange juice) 橙汁

Ad·e·laide /ˋædəˌled; ˈædɪleɪd/ the capital city of the state of South Australia 阿德莱德〔南澳大利亚州首府〕

ad·e·noids /ˋædṇˌɔɪdz; ˈædɪnɔɪdz/ *n* [plural] the small soft pieces of flesh at the back of your throat that sometimes have to be removed because they become swollen 腺样体，增殖体 —**adenoidal** /ˌædṇˋɔɪdl; ˌædɪˈnɔɪdl◂/ *adj*

ad·ept¹ /əˋdɛpt; ˈædept/ *adj* good at doing something that needs care and skill 内行的，熟练的：[+at/in] *Melissa soon became adept at predicting his moods.* 很快梅利莎就善于预测他的情绪。—**adeptly** *adv*

ad·ept² /ˋædɛpt; ˈædept/ *n* [C] someone who is good at doing something 内行，能手

ad·e·quate /ˋædəkwɪt; ˈædɪkwɪt/ *adj* **1** an adequate amount is enough for a particular purpose 适当的，足够的，充分的：*The research cannot be completed without adequate funding.* 没有足够的资金，这项研究就无法完成。| [+for] *Are the parking facilities adequate for fifty cars?* 停车设施能停放得下五十辆车吗？**2** good enough in quality for a particular purpose or activity 可以胜任的：*Without the proper resources the department cannot do an adequate job.* 没有适当的资源，该部门就无法做好工作。| **adequate to do sth** *His explanation did not seem adequate to account for what had happened.* 他的解释似乎不足以说明事情发生的缘由。**3** fairly good but not excellent 差强人意的，过得去的：*Her performance was adequate but lacked originality.* 她的表演还过得去，但缺乏独创性。—**adequately** *adv*: *She wasn't adequately insured.* 她买的保险不够。—**adequacy** *n* [U]

USAGE NOTE 用法说明：ADEQUATE

WORD CHOICE 词语辨析：**adequate, sufficient, enough, good enough, satisfactory, (will) do**

Adequate and **sufficient** are both more formal than **enough**, but all three can be used to talk about quantity. adequate 和 sufficient 比 enough 更正式，但这三个词都可以指数量：*Will you have enough/sufficient/adequate money for the trip?* 你有足够的钱去旅行吗？However, **adequate** often sounds a little negative, suggesting that the amount is only just enough. 然而，adequate 通常带有一点否定含义，表明只是刚好足够：*The water supply here is adequate/sufficient* 这里的供水还足够。

If you want to say that the quality of something is enough, you use **good enough** or **satisfactory**. 如果想表示某物质量好，用 good enough 或 satisfactory：*"I'm afraid your work isn't good enough/satisfactory."* "恐怕你的工作做得不够好/令人满意。" **Satisfactory** is a more formal word. satisfactory 较为正式。

Adequate can be used to talk about both quality and quantity together, especially with uncountable nouns. For example, if you ask: *Is the food adequate?* you might be asking whether there is enough in amount or whether it is good enough. However, with a plural countable noun the quality meaning is more likely. adequate 既可以指质量又可以指数量，尤用于形容不可数名词。例如，如果你问：Is the food adequate? 问的可以是分量足不足，也可以是质量好不好。然而，如果跟可数名词，多指质量：*adequate resources/training/support etc* 足够好的资源/充分的训练/充分的支持等

In spoken English people often use **do** (but not in progressive forms) to talk about something being enough in either of these ways. 在英语口语中，人们经常用 do（不用进行时）来表达"足够"之意：*"Do you have enough money?" "It should do."* (=it should be enough) "你钱够吗？" "应该够。" | *It's not much but it'll have to do.* 不太多，但只好如此了。

ad·here /ədˋhɪr; ədˈhɪə/ *v formal* [I+to] to stick firmly to something【正式】黏附，附着

adhere to sth *phr v* [T] *formal* to continue to behave according to a particular rule, agreement, or belief【正式】坚持; 信守: *adhere to your principles* 坚持原则 | *adhere to the regulations* 遵守规定

ad·her·ence /əd`hɪrəns; əd'hɪərəns/ *n* [U] the act of behaving according to a particular rule or belief, or supporting a particular idea, even in difficult situations 坚持; 信守, 信奉: [+to] *strict adherence to the traditional caste system* 严格遵守传统的种姓制度

ad·her·ent /əd`hɪrənt; əd'hɪərənt/ *n* [C] someone who supports a particular idea, plan, political party etc 信徒; 拥护者; 追随者

ad·he·sion /əd`hiʒən; əd'hiːʒən/ *n* **1** [U] the state of one thing sticking to another 黏附, 黏合, 胶着 **2** [C] *technical* a piece of TISSUE (=flesh) that has grown around a small injury or diseased area【术语】〔身体内组织的〕粘连

ad·he·sive[1] /əd`hisɪv; əd'hiːsɪv/ *n* [C] a substance such as glue that can be used to make two things stick together 胶布; 胶黏剂

adhesive[2] *adj* adhesive material sticks to surfaces 黏着的, 有黏性的: *adhesive tape* 胶布, 胶带

ad hoc /ˌæd `hɑk; ˌæd 'hɒk/ *adj* [usually before noun 一般用于名词前] *Latin* done or arranged only when the situation makes it necessary, and without any previous planning【拉丁】特别〔专门〕安排的: *An ad hoc committee has been set up to deal with the problem.* 成立了一个专门委员会来处理这个问题。| **on an ad hoc basis** *Decisions were made on an ad hoc basis.* 决定是在事先未计划的情况下作出的。—**ad hoc** *adv*

a·dieu /ə`du; ə'djuː/ *n plural* **adieux** /ə`duz; ə'djuːz/ *or* **adieus** [C] *literary* an act of saying goodbye【文】道别; 一路平安: **bid sb adieu** *He bid her a fond adieu.* 他深情地向她道别。—**adieu** *interjection*

ad in·fi·ni·tum /ˌæd ˌɪnfə`naɪtəm; ˌæd ɪnfɪ'naɪtəm/ *adv Latin* continuing or repeated without ever ending【拉丁】无限地, 无止境地

ad·i·os /ˌædɪ`os; ˌædi'əʊs/ *interjection Spanish* goodbye【西】再见

ad·i·pose /`ædəˌpos; 'ædɪpəʊs/ *adj technical* consisting of or containing animal fat【术语】含动物脂肪质的, 脂肪多的: *adipose tissue* 脂肪组织

Ad·i·ron·dacks, the /ˌædɪ`rɑndæks; ˌædɪ'rɒndæks/ also 又作 **the Adirondack Mountains** an area in the north east of New York State, known for its beautiful mountains, forests, and lakes 阿迪朗达克山脉〔纽约州东北部一地区, 以秀丽的山色、森林和湖光著称〕

adj the written abbreviation for 缩写= ADJECTIVE

ad·ja·cent /ə`dʒesn̩t; ə'dʒeɪsənt/ *adj* something that is adjacent to something else, especially a room, building, or area, is next to it 邻近的, 毗连的: [+to] *The fire started in the building adjacent to the library.* 首先起火的是与图书馆毗连的一座建筑物。

ad·jec·ti·val /ˌædʒɪk`taɪvl; ˌædʒɪk'taɪvəl◂/ *adj* **adjectival phrase/clause etc** *technical* a phrase etc that is used as an adjective or that consists of adjectives. For example, 'fully furnished' is an adjectival phrase.【术语】形容词短语/从句等〈例如, fully furnished 就是一个形容词短语〉—**adjectivally** *adv*

ad·jec·tive /`ædʒɪktɪv; 'ædʒɪktɪv/ *n* [C] a word that describes a noun or PRONOUN, such as 'black' in the sentence 'She wore a black hat.' or 'happy' in the sentence 'I'll try to make you happy.' 形容词〔修饰名词或代(名)词〕—compare 比较 ADVERB

ad·join /ə`dʒɔɪn; ə'dʒɔɪn/ *v* [T] if a room, building, or piece of land adjoins another one, it is next to it and joined to it 贴近, 毗邻: *The kitchen adjoins the sitting room.* 厨房紧挨着客厅。—**adjoining** *adj*: *adjoining rooms* 相邻的房间

ad·journ /ə`dʒɝn; ə'dʒɜːn/ *v* **1** [I,T] if a meeting or law court adjourns, or if the person in charge adjourns it, it finishes or stops for a short time (使)〔会议、审讯〕暂停: *The chairman has the power to adjourn the meeting at any time.* 主席有随时暂停会议的权力。| [+for/until] *The trial was adjourned for two weeks.* 审讯延期两个星期。| *Can I suggest we adjourn for lunch now?* 我建议我们现在暂停会议去吃中午饭, 好吗? **2 adjourn to** *humorous* to finish an activity and go somewhere【幽默】转移到…, 移席到: *After the match we adjourned to the pub.* 比赛后我们转移到酒馆。—**adjournment** *n* [C,U]

ad·judge /ə`dʒʌdʒ; ə'dʒʌdʒ/ *v* [T] *formal* to make a judgement about something or someone【正式】宣判, 判决, 裁决: *Any foodstuffs adjudged unacceptable must be disposed of.* 所有被判定为不合格的食品都必须处理掉。

ad·ju·di·cate /ə`dʒudɪˌket; ə'dʒuːdɪkeɪt/ *v* **1** [I,T] to officially decide who is right in an argument between two groups or organizations 裁定, 评定, 评审: [+on/in] *An independent expert was called in to adjudicate.* 邀请了一位与各当事人无关的专家担任评判。| *adjudicate a claim* 裁定要求(的合理性) **2** [I] to be the judge in a competition 担任裁判: *He adjudicated at all the regional music competitions.* 他在所有地方音乐比赛中担任评判。—**adjudicator** *n* [C] —**adjudication** /əˌdʒudɪ`keʃən; əˌdʒuːdɪ'keɪʃən/ *n* [U]

ad·junct /`ædʒʌŋkt; 'ædʒʌŋkt/ *n* [C] **1** [+to] something that is added or joined to something but is not part of it 附件, 附属物 **2** *technical* an ADVERBIAL word or phrase that adds meaning to another part of a sentence, such as 'on Sunday' in 'They arrived on Sunday.'【术语】修饰语, 附加语〈如 They arrived on Sunday 中的 on Sunday〉

ad·jure /ə`dʒur; ə'dʒʊə/ *v* [T] *formal* to try very hard to persuade someone to do something【正式】恳求, 祈求: *Gwendolyn adjured him to be truthful.* 格温德琳恳求他讲出真相。

ad·just /ə`dʒʌst; ə'dʒʌst/ *v* **1** [T] to make small changes to something, especially to its position, in order to improve it, make it more effective etc 调整, 调节: *Check and adjust the brakes regularly.* 定期检查和调节刹车装置。**2** [I,T] to gradually get used to a new situation by making small changes to the way you do things 适应; 使适合: [+to] *Adjusting to the tropical heat was more difficult than they had expected.* 适应热带的炎热气候比他们预料的难。| *They'll soon settle in – kids are very good at adjusting.* 他们很快就会安顿下来, 孩子们很会适应环境。—see also 另见 WELL-ADJUSTED 3

ad·just·a·ble /ə`dʒʌstəbl̩; ə'dʒʌstəbəl/ *adj* something that is adjustable can be changed in shape, size, or position to make it suitable for a particular person or purpose 可调节的, 可校准的: *an adjustable desk lamp* 可调节的台灯

ad·just·ment /ə`dʒʌstmənt; ə'dʒʌstmənt/ *n* [C,U] **1** a small change made to something, such as a machine, a system, or the way something looks 调整, 调节, 校正: **make adjustments** *We've had to make some adjustments to our original calculations.* 我们不得不对我们最初的计算作一些调整。| **slight/minor adjustments** (=small changes) 轻微/细微的调整 **2** a change that someone makes to the way they behave or think〔心态、行为等方面的〕调整: *the adjustments required of someone moving to a foreign country* 移居外国者必须作出的调整

ad·ju·tant /`ædʒətənt; 'ædʒɪtənt/ *n* [C] an army officer responsible for office work〔陆军中的〕副官

ad-lib /æd `lɪb; ˌæd 'lɪb/ *v* **ad-libbed, ad-libbing** [I,T] to say something in a speech, a performance of a play etc without preparing or planning it 即兴表演; 即兴演讲: *She forgot her lines and had to ad-lib the rest of the scene.* 她忘记了台词, 只好即兴表演余下的戏。—**ad-lib** *n* [C] —**ad-lib** /ˌ· `·◂/ *adj, adv*

ad·man /`ædˌmæn; 'ædmæn/ *n plural* **admen** /-ˌmɛn; -men/ [C] *informal* someone who works in advertising【非正式】广告员; 广告制作人

ad·min /`ædmɪn; 'ædmɪn/ *n* [U] *informal especially BrE* ADMINISTRATION (2)【非正式, 尤英】行政部门: *She works in admin.* 她在行政部门工作。

ad·min·is·ter /əd`mɪnəstɚ; əd'mɪnɪstə/ *v* [T] **1** to manage and organize the affairs of a company, government etc 管理, 治理: *the bureaucrats who administer welfare programs* 管理福利计划的官员 | *The Navajo administer their own territory within the United States.* 在美国, 纳瓦霍印第安人管理他们自己的领土。**2** to organize the way a test or punishment is given, or the way laws are used 执行, 实施: *the courts administering justice* 主持正义的法庭 | *The test was administered fairly and impartially.* 考试举办得公平、公正。**3** *formal* to give someone a medicine or drug to take【正式】给予, 用〔药〕

ad·min·is·tra·tion /ədˌmɪnə`streʃən; ədˌmɪnɪ'streɪʃən/ *n* **1** [U] all the activities that are involved in managing and organizing the affairs of a company, institution etc 管理; 经营: *We're looking for someone with experience in administration.* 我们正在寻求一个有管理经验的人。| *They spend too much on administration and not enough on doctors and nurses.* 他们在管理上花费太多, 但对医护人员的资金却投入不足。**2 the administration** the people who manage a company, institution etc 管理者; 经营者; 管理部门, 行政部门: *the college administration* 学院行政部门 **3** [C usually singular 一般用单数] the government of a country at a particular time 政府: *the Kennedy Administration* 肯尼迪政府 | *The problem has been ignored by successive administrations.* 连续几届政府都忽略了这个问题。**4** [U] the act of administering a test, law etc 执行, 施行: *the administration of justice* 司法, 执法 

3 **ad·min·is·tra·tive** /ədˋmɪnəˌstretɪv; ədˈmɪnɨstrətɪv/ *adj* connected with the work of managing or organizing a company, institution etc 行政的; 管理的: *The job is mainly administrative.* 这项工作主要是行政性的。| *administrative duties* 管理职责 —**administratively** *adv*

ad·min·is·tra·tor /ədˋmɪnəˌstretɚ; ədˈmɪnɨstreɪtə/ *n* [C] someone whose job is connected with the management and organization of a company, institution etc 管理人; 行政官员; 主管

ad·mi·ra·ble /ˋædmərəbl; ˈædmərəbəl/ *adj* something that is admirable has many good qualities that you respect and admire 令人钦佩的, 极其出色的: *an admirable achievement* 令人钦佩的成就 —**admirably** *adv*

ad·mi·ral /ˋædmərəl; ˈædmərəl/ *n* [C] a high rank in the British or US navy, or someone who has this rank 海军将官; 海军上将; 舰队司令 —see table on page C6 参见 C6 页附录

Admiral's Cup, the /ˌ‥ ‥ ˈ‥/ an international sailing competition held off the British coast every two years and consisting of four races, including the Fastnet Cup Race 海军上将杯〔在英国沿海两年举行一次的国际帆船比赛, 分四个项目, 其中包括法斯耐特杯赛〕

Ad·mi·ral·ty, the /ˋædmərəltɪ; ˈædmərəlti/ *n* the government department that controls the British navy (英国)海军部

Admiralty Arch /ˌ‥‥ ˈ‥/ a large ARCH (=a structure with a curved top and straight sides) in central London, between the Mall and Trafalgar Square 海军总部拱门〔位于伦敦市中心的林荫道和特拉法尔加广场之间〕

ad·mi·ra·tion /ˌædməˋreʃən; ˌædməˈreɪʃən/ *n* [U] a feeling of admiring something or someone 敬佩, 钦佩, 羡慕: *Daniel gazed at her in admiration.* 丹尼尔用敬佩的目光注视着她。| [+for] *Tippett later developed a deep admiration for Wagner.* 蒂皮特后来对瓦格纳有了深深的敬佩。

3 **ad·mire** /ədˋmaɪr; ədˈmaɪə/ *v* [T not in progressive 不用进行时] **1** to have a very high opinion of someone because of a quality they have or because of something they have done 钦佩, 赞美, 羡慕: *I really admire the way she brings up those kids all on her own.* 我确实佩服她独自一人把那些孩子抚养大。| **admire sb for sth** *Lewis was admired for his work on medieval literature.* 刘易斯因其对中世纪文学的研究而受人仰慕。**2** to look at something and think how beautiful or impressive it is 欣赏, 观赏: *We stopped half way up the hill to admire the view.* 我们上山中途停下来观赏风景。**3 admire sb from afar** to be attracted to someone but without telling them how you feel 暗自仰慕: *Mary was still a good looking woman and Sid had admired her from afar for a long time.* 玛丽风采依旧, 锡德对她仰慕已久。—**admiring** *adj* —**admiringly** *adv*

ad·mir·er /ədˋmaɪrɚ; ədˈmaɪərə/ *n* [C] **1** a man who is attracted to a particular woman 爱慕者〔指爱慕女人的男人〕: *a beautiful woman with many admirers* 有许多爱慕者的漂亮女子 | *a secret admirer* 暗恋者 **2 be an admirer of** to admire someone, especially a famous person, or their work 仰慕…: *The painter Turner was a great admirer of Byron.* 画家特纳是拜伦的忠实崇拜者。

ad·mis·si·ble /ədˋmɪsəbl; ədˈmɪsɨbəl/ *adj* admissible reasons, facts etc are acceptable or allowed, especially in a court of law 可采纳的, 可接受的: *admissible evidence* 可采信的证据 —opposite 反义词 INADMISSIBLE —**admissibility** /ədˌmɪsəˋbɪlətɪ; ədˌmɪsɨˈbɪlɨti/ *n* [U]

3 **ad·mis·sion** /ədˋmɪʃən; ədˈmɪʃən/ *n* **1** [C] a statement in which you admit that something is true or that you have done something wrong 承认; 供认: **admission that** *The Senator's admission that he had lied to Congress shocked many Americans.* 参议员承认他向国会说谎, 令许多美国人深感震惊。| **admission of guilt/failure/defeat etc** *The court may interpret your silence as an admission of guilt.* 法庭也许会将你的缄默作为认罪的表示。| **by/on your own admission** *By his own admission, he is a complete womanizer.* 他自己承认是个好色之徒。**2** [U] permission given to someone to enter or become a member of a school, club, building etc 允许进入[加入]: [+to] *seeking admission to a prestigious university* 设法进入有名望的大学 | **gain admission** *Women gained admission to the club only recently.* 直到最近妇女才获准加入这个俱乐部。**3 admissions** [plural] the process of allowing people to enter a university, institution, hospital etc, or the number of people who can enter 录取 [允许进入] 的过程[人数]: *Doctors are reporting a steep rise in admissions.* 医生报告住院病人的数量在急剧增加。| **admissions policy/procedures/officer etc** *This particular college has a very selective admissions policy.* 这所学院有一个十分严格的录取政策。**4** [U] the cost of entrance to a concert, sports event etc 入场费: *The cost includes free admission to the casinos.* 费用包括赌场免费入场。| *Admission: £3.50.* 入场费: 3.50 英镑。**5** [U] permission to enter a place〔进入某地的〕许可: *No admission after 10pm.* 晚上 10 点以后不准进入。

> **USAGE NOTE 用法说明: ADMISSION**
> WORD CHOICE 词语辨析: **admission, admittance, admissions**
> **Admission** is the usual word. **Admittance** is more formal and only used in the meaning 'permission to go in a building, park etc', usually given by someone in authority. admission是一个常用词。admittance比较正式, 只用于"允许进入建筑物、公园等", 通常需要授权。On a notice you might see告示上可见到: *Private Road: No Admittance.* 私人道路, 禁止进入。
> **Admissions** is the word used by official organizations about the number of people entering a university, school, hospital etc. admissions 用于官方机构, 如大学、学校录取多少人或医院可接纳多少病人住院等: *the admissions officer/policy/procedure* 负责录取工作的官员/录取政策/录取程序 | *We have a lot of emergency admissions.* 我们收了许多急诊病人。

ad·mit /ədˋmɪt; ədˈmɪt/ *v* **admitted, admitting** [T] **1** to accept 2
and agree unwillingly that something is true or that someone 1
else is right 承认, 赞同: *"I was really scared," Jenny admitted.* "我真害怕。"珍妮承认道。| **admit (that)** *You may not like her, but you have to admit that she's good at her job.* 你也许不喜欢她, 但你必须承认她胜任工作。| **I must admit** *spoken* (=when you are admitting something you are embarrassed about)【口】我得承认 *I must admit I didn't actually do anything to help her.* 我必须承认实际上我并没有帮她忙。| **come on, admit it!** *spoken* (=used to try to make someone admit something)【口】快, 承认了吧! *Come on, admit it! You were out with Keith last night?* 快坦白! 你昨晚和基思一起出去了吧? | **freely/openly admit** (=admit without being ashamed) 坦白, 公开承认 *Phillips openly admits to being selfish.* 菲力普斯公开承认自己很自私。**2** also 又作 **admit to** to say that you have done something wrong, especially something criminal; CONFESS (1) 承认〔做错了事, 犯了罪〕: **admit (to) doing sth** *A quarter of all workers admit to taking time off when they are not ill.* 四分之一的工人承认他们没病的时候休过假。| **admit (to) sth** *After questioning he admitted to the murder.* 经过盘问后他承认自己是凶手。**3** to allow someone or something to enter a public place to watch a game, performance etc 允许…进入: **admit sb to/into** *Only ticket-holders will be admitted into the stadium.* 只有持票者才可进入体育场。**4** to allow someone to join an organization, club etc 允许加入, 接纳: **admit sb to/into** *The UK was admitted to the EEC in 1973.* 英国于 1973 年获准加入欧共体。**5 be admitted to hospital** *BrE*【英】**/to the hospital** *AmE*【美】to be taken to a hospital because you are ill 被送进医院: *He was admitted to the hospital Tuesday morning with stomach pains.* 他于星期二上午因胃痛被送进医院。**6 admit defeat** to stop trying to do something because you realise you cannot succeed〔中途〕承认失败, 认输: *Sean kept running, refusing to admit defeat.* 肖恩继续跑, 不甘认输。**7 an admitted alcoholic/atheist etc** someone who has admitted that they are an ALCOHOLIC, etc 自认的酒鬼/无神论者等

admit of sth *phr v* [T] *formal* if a situation admits of a particular explanation, that explanation can be accepted as possible【正式】容许有: *The facts admit of no other explanation.* 事实毋容置疑。

ad·mit·tance /ədˋmɪtn̩s; ədˈmɪtəns/ *n* [U] *formal* permission to enter a place【正式】进入权: **gain admittance** (=get admittance) 获准进入 *Gaining admittance to his private club was no easy matter.* 获准进入他的私人俱乐部不是一件容易事。—compare 比较 ADMISSION (5)

ad·mit·ted·ly /ədˋmɪtɪdlɪ; ədˈmɪtɨdli/ *adv* [sentence adverb 句子副词] used when you are admitting that something is true 诚然, 确实地; 不可否认地: *The technique is painful, admittedly, but it benefits the patient greatly.* 应该承认, 采用这种技术会有点痛, 但对病人十分有益。| *This has led to financial losses, though admittedly on a fairly small scale.* 这已造成了财政损失, 尽管不可否认损失规模比较小。

ad·mix·ture /ædˋmɪkstʃɚ; ədˈmɪkstʃə/ *n* [C+of] *technical* a substance that is added to another substance in a mixture【术语】掺和剂, 混合物, 合剂

ad·mon·ish /ədˋmɑnɪʃ; ədˈmɒnɪʃ/ *v* [T] *formal* to tell or warn someone severely that they have done something wrong【正式】(严正) 警告, 告诫: *The witness was admonished for failing*

to answer the question. 证人因未能回答问题而受到警告。—**admonishment** *n* [C]

ad·mo·ni·tion /ˌædməˋnɪʃən; ˌædməˈnɪʃən/ *n* [C,U] *formal* a warning or expression of disapproval about someone's behaviour【正式】警告, 告诫 —**admonitory** *adj formal*【正式】: *an admonitory glance* 告诫的目光

ad nau·se·am /ˈæd ˋnɔzɪˏæm; ˌæd ˈnɔːziəm/ *adv* if you say or do something ad nauseam, you say or do it so often that it becomes annoying for other people 令人厌烦地: *Look, we've been over this ad nauseam – I think we should move on to the next item.* 看, 这个问题我们都已经说腻了, 我看我们还是进入下一项吧。

a·do /əˋdu; əˈduː/ *n* [U] **without more/further ado** without delaying or wasting any time 不再延误, 不再费时间: *So without further ado, I'll now ask Mr Davis to open the debate.* 不再多说了, 现在我请戴维斯先生宣布辩论开始。

a·do·be /əˋdobɪ; əˈdəʊbi/ *n* **1** [U] earth and STRAW (1) that are made into bricks for building houses 土坯, 泥砖 **2** [C] a house made using adobe 土坯房子

ad·o·les·cence /ˌædḷˋɛsṇs; ˌædəˈlesəns/ *n* [U] the time, usually between the ages of 12 to 18, when a young person is developing into an adult 青春期

ad·o·les·cent /ˌædḷˋɛsṇt; ˌædəˈlesənt◂/ *n* [C] a young person who is developing into an adult 青少年, 青春期的少男少女 —see picture at 参见 CHILD 图

A·do·nis /əˋdonɪs; əˈdəʊnɪ̈s/ **1** in Greek MYTHOLOGY, a beautiful boy whom Aphrodite loved, but who was killed by a BOAR (=a wild pig) while he was hunting 阿多尼斯〔希腊神话中阿佛洛狄忒(爱与美女神)爱恋的美少年, 他在一次狩猎中被野猪咬死〕 **2** an extremely attractive young man 美少年

a·dopt /əˋdɑpt; əˈdɒpt/ *v* [T]

1 ►**CHILD** 孩子◄ to legally make another person's child part of your family so that he or she becomes one of your own children 收养, 领养: *My mother was adopted when she was four.* 我母亲四岁时被人领养。—compare 比较 FOSTER[1] (1)

2 adopt an approach/strategy/policy to start to use a particular method or plan for dealing with something 采用某方法/战略/政策: *The courts have been asked to adopt a more flexible approach to young offenders.* 要求法庭对年轻罪犯采用较灵活的处理方法。

3 ►**STYLE/MANNER** 风格/方式◄ to use a particular style of speaking, writing, or behaving, especially one that you do not usually use 采取, 采用: *"I can't say I blame him," Victor replied, adopting a more conciliatory tone.* "我不是说我要责备他。"维克托回答道, 语气缓和了一些。| *Papers like this tend to adopt a very simple writing style.* 这样的论文往往采用十分朴实的写作风格。

4 ►**ACCEPT A SUGGESTION** 接受建议◄ to formally approve a proposal, especially by voting〔尤指通过表决〕正式批准; 认可; 接受: *They were trying to persuade the UN to adopt an aggressively anti-American resolution.* 他们竭力说服联合国批准一个强烈反美的决议。

5 adopt a name/country to choose it to be your own 选定姓名/国家: *Italy is my adopted country.* 意大利是我选定的国家。

6 ►**ELECTION** 选举◄ *BrE* to officially choose someone to represent a political party in an election【英】提名…为候选人

a·dopt·ed /əˋdɑptɪd; əˈdɒptɪ̈d/ *adj* **1** an adopted child has been legally made part of a family that he or she was not born into 领养的, 过继的: *his adopted son* 他的养子 **2** your adopted country is one that you have chosen to live in permanently〔国家〕被选择居住的

a·dop·tion /əˋdɑpʃən; əˈdɒpʃən/ *n* **1** [C,U] the act or process of adopting a child 收养, 领养 **2** [U] the act of deciding to use a particular plan, method, way of speaking etc 采用, 采纳 **3** [U] *BrE* the choice of a particular person to represent a political party in an election【英】提名某人为候选人

a·dop·tive /əˋdɑptɪv; əˈdɒptɪv/ *adj* an adoptive parent is one who has adopted a child 收养(孩子)的

a·dor·a·ble /əˋdorəbḷ; əˈdɔːrəbəl/ *adj* someone or something that is adorable is so attractive that it fills you with feelings of love 值得爱慕的; 可爱的: *Oh what an adorable little baby!* 啊! 多么可爱的小宝宝!

ad·o·ra·tion /ˌædəˋreʃən; ˌædəˈreɪʃən/ *n* [U] **1** great love and admiration 敬慕, 爱慕: *the look of adoration in his eyes* 他爱慕的眼神 **2** *literary* religious worship【文】宗教崇拜

a·dore /əˋdor; əˈdɔː/ *v* [T not in progressive 不用进行时] **1** to love someone very much and feel very proud of them 敬慕, 爱慕: *Betty adores her grandchildren.* 贝蒂宠爱孙子孙女。**2** *informal* to like something very much【非正式】非常喜欢: *I absolutely adore chocolate.* 我极喜欢巧克力。| *Don't you just adore these cookies?* 你难道不喜欢这些饼干吗?

a·dorn /əˋdɔrn; əˈdɔːn/ *v* [T] *formal* to decorate something【正式】装饰: *church walls adorned with religious paintings* 用宗教绘画作品装饰的教堂墙壁

a·dorn·ment /əˋdɔrnmənt; əˈdɔːnmənt/ *n* **1** [C] something that you use to decorate something 装饰品 **2** [U] the act of adorning something 装饰

a·dren·a·lin /ædˋrɛnḷɪn; əˈdrenəlɪ̈n/ *n* [U] **1** a chemical produced by your body when you are afraid, angry, or excited, which makes your heart beat faster so that you can move quickly 肾上腺素 **2 get the adrenalin going** to make you feel nervously excited and full of energy (使突发性地)紧张[兴奋]起来

A·dri·an IV /ˏedrɪən ðə ˋfɔrθ; ˌeɪdriən ðə ˈfɔːθ/ (1100-1159) the only English pope. He was born in Hertfordshire, England, and his real name was Nicholas Breakspear. He became pope in 1154. 阿德里安四世〔(1100-1159), 历史上唯一英籍教皇。他出生在英格兰赫特福德郡, 真名叫做尼古拉斯·布雷克斯皮尔。1154年成为教皇〕

A·dri·at·ic Sea, the /ˏedrɪˋætɪk si; ˌeɪdriˈætɪk siː/ also 又作 **the Adriatic** the long, narrow sea between Italy and countries such as Slovenia, Croatia, Serbia, and Albania 亚德里亚海〔位于意大利、斯洛文尼亚、克罗地亚、塞尔维亚和阿尔巴尼亚等之间的绵长狭窄海域〕

a·drift /əˋdrɪft; əˈdrɪft/ *adj, adv* **1** a boat that is adrift is not fastened to anything or controlled by anyone 漂浮着(的); 漂流着(的) **2** someone who is adrift is confused about what to do in their life 漫无目标的[地] **3 come adrift** to become separated from something that fastens 散开; 脱落: *Her hair was forever coming adrift from the pins and combs she used to keep it in place.* 她的头发总是从固定头发的发夹或发梳中散开来。

a·droit /əˋdrɔɪt; əˈdrɔɪt/ *adj* clever and skilful, especially in the way you use words and arguments 机敏的, 灵巧的;〔尤指〕口齿伶俐的: *an adroit negotiator* 精明的谈判家 —**adroitly** *adv* —**adroitness** *n* [U]

a·du·ki bean /əˋduki bin; əˈduːki biːn/ *n* [C] a brown and red bean that is used in Chinese and Japanese cooking 赤豆, 小豆 —see picture on page A9 参见 A9 页图

ad·u·la·tion /ˏædʒəˋleʃən; ˌædʒʊˈleɪʃən/ *n* [U] praise and admiration for someone that is more than they really deserve 恭维, 奉承, 谄媚: *basking in the adulation of his fans* 沉浸于他的崇拜者的恭维之中 —**adulatory** /ˋædʒələˏtorɪ; ˌædʒʊˈleɪtəri/ *adj*

ad·ult[1] /ˋædʌlt; ˈædʌlt/ *n* **1** a fully-grown person or animal 发育成熟的人或动物: *Some children find it difficult to talk to adults.* 一些孩子发觉与成年人很难谈得来。**2** someone who is old enough to be considered legally responsible, and can for example vote in elections and get married without their parents' permission〔法律上的〕成年人

adult[2] *adj* **1** [only before noun 仅用于名词前] fully grown or developed 发育成熟的, 成年的: *an adult lion* 成年的狮子 | **adult life** (= the part of your life when you are an adult) 成年的生活 **2** typical of an adult's behaviour or of the things adults do (适合)成年人的; 老成的, 成熟的: *dealing with problems in an adult way* 以老成持重的方式处理问题 **3 adult movie/magazine etc** a film etc that is about sex, shows sexual acts etc 成人电影/杂志等

adult ed·u·ca·tion /ˏ‥ ‥ˈ‥/ *n* [U] education provided for adults outside the formal educational system, usually by means of classes that are held in the evening 成人教育

a·dul·ter·ate /əˋdʌltəˏret; əˈdʌltəreɪt/ *v* [T] to make food or drink less pure by adding another substance of lower quality to it 掺杂; 掺假 —see also 另见 UNADULTERATED —**adulteration** /əˏdʌltəˋreʃən; əˌdʌltəˈreɪʃən/ *n* [U]

a·dul·ter·er /əˋdʌltərɚ; əˈdʌltərə/ *n* [C] *old-fashioned* someone who is married and has sex with someone who is not their wife or husband【过时】奸夫; 淫妇; 通奸者

a·dul·ter·ess /əˋdʌltərɪs; əˈdʌltərɪ̈s/ *n* [C] *old-fashioned* a married woman who has sex with a man who is not her husband【过时】奸妇, 淫妇

a·dul·ter·y /əˋdʌltərɪ; əˈdʌltəri/ *n* [U] sex between someone who is married and someone who is not their wife or husband 通奸, 私通: **commit adultery** *She had committed adultery on several occasions.* 她多次与人私通。—**adulterous** *adj*

CULTURAL NOTE 文化注释

Although it is not a crime to COMMIT adultery in either the US or the UK, many people believe it is morally wrong. Married couples sometimes get a DIVORCE (=end the mar-

> riage officially) because the husband or wife has been UNFAITHFUL (=had sex with someone else). When a married person has a sexual relationship with someone else, people say that he or she is 'having an affair'. 虽然在英美两国通奸不算是犯罪，但很多人仍旧相信这是道德败坏。已婚夫妇有时因一方不忠而离婚。已婚者如果与别人发生性关系，人们就会说这个人"有了外遇"。

ad·ult·hood /ˈædʌlthud; ˈædʌlthʊd/ *n* [U] the time when you are an adult 成年(时期)

ad·um·brate /ædˋʌmbret; ˈædʌmbreɪt/ *v* [T] *formal* to suggest or describe something in an incomplete way【正式】隐约预示，暗示 —**adumbration** /ˌædʌmˋbreʃən; ˌædʌmˈbreɪʃən/ *n* [U]

adv the written abbreviation of 缩写= ADVERB

3 2 **ad·vance**[1] /ədˋvæns; ədˈvɑːns/ *n*

1 in advance before something happens or is expected to happen 预先，提前：*I should warn you in advance, we may be delayed.* 我该预先提醒你，我们也许会被耽搁。| **six months/a year in advance** *Rent is payable three months in advance.* 租金提前三个月支付。| [+of] *Could you distribute copies well in advance of the meeting?* 你能否在会前分发好材料？

2 ►DEVELOPMENT/IMPROVEMENT 发展/改进◄ [C] a change, discovery, or INVENTION that brings progress 进步，进展：*His book argues that there have been major advances for women since 1945.* 他的书认为妇女的状况自从 1945 年以来有了很大的改善。| [+in] *Recent advances in biotechnology have raised moral questions.* 生物技术近期的发展引出了道德问题。

3 ►FORWARD MOVEMENT 向前的移动◄ [C] forward movement or progress 前进：*the army's advance* 部队的推进

4 ►MONEY 金钱◄ [C usually singular 一般用单数] money paid to someone before the usual time 预付款

5 advances [plural] an attempt to start a friendly or sexual relationship with someone 挑逗，勾引：**make advances** *She accused her boss of making advances to her.* 她指控老板对她图谋不轨。

6 ►INCREASE 增加◄ [C] *technical* an increase in the price or value of something【术语】上涨，攀升：*a further big advance in the price of gold* 黄金价格的又一轮暴涨

3 **advance**[2] *v*

1 ►MOVE 运动◄ [I] to move forward, especially in a slow and determined way〔尤指缓慢而坚定地〕前进，推进：**advance on** (=move forward in order to attack) 向…推进 *Troops advanced on the rebel stronghold.* 军队向反叛者的据点推进。| [+across/through/towards] *The army slowly advanced across the frozen tundra.* 部队缓缓地穿越冻土带。

2 ►DEVELOP 发展◄ [I] if something such as technical or scientific knowledge advances, it develops and improves 进展：*Our understanding of human genetics has advanced considerably.* 我们对人类遗传学的理解有了很大进展。

3 advance a plan/idea/proposal etc *formal* to suggest a plan etc so that other people can consider it【正式】提出计划/看法/建议等：*A similar plan was advanced by the British delegation.* 英国代表团提出了一项类似的计划。

4 ►MONEY 金钱◄ [T] to give someone money before they have earned it 预支：**advance sb sth** *Will they advance you some money until you get your first paycheck?* 在你拿到第一次工资以前，他们是否会预支你一些钱？

5 advance a cause/your interests/your career etc to do something that will help you achieve advantage or success 拓展事业/兴趣/职业生涯等

6 ►PRICE 价格◄ [I] *technical* if the price or value of something advances, it increases in amount【术语】〔价格、价值〕上涨：*Oil shares advanced today in heavy trading.* 在今天的大量交易中，石油股价格上涨了。

7 ►CHANGE TIME 改变时间◄ [T] *formal* to change the time when an event should happen to an earlier time or date【正式】提前：*The time of the meeting has been advanced to ten o'clock.* 会议的时间提前到 10 点钟。

8 ►FILM/CLOCK 电影/钟表◄ [T] *formal* if you advance a film, clock etc, you make it go forward【正式】进〔片〕；往前拨〔钟表〕—see also 另见 ADVANCING

advance[3] *adj* **1 advance planning/warning/booking etc** planning etc that is done before an event 预先的计划/警告/订票[订座]等：*We received no advance warning of the storm.* 我们没有收到风暴的预先警报。**2 advance party/team** a group of people who go first to a place where something will happen to prepare for it〔提前到某地为活动做准备的〕先行组

ad·vanced /ədˋvænst; ədˈvɑːnst/ *adj* **1** using the most modern ideas, equipment, and methods 高级的，先进的：*advanced weapon systems* 先进的武器装备 | *high levels of unemployment in the advanced capitalist economies* 发达资本主义经济中的高失业率 —see 见 HIGH[1] (USAGE) **2** studying or dealing with a school subject at a difficult level 高深的，高级的：*advanced learners of English* 高级程度的英语学习者 | *advanced physics* 高等物理(学) **3** having reached a late point in time or development 晚期的：*By this time, the disease was too far advanced to be treated.* 这时，病已发展到晚期，无法医治了。 3

Advanced lev·el /ˌ·ˋ· ˌ··/ *n* [C,U] *formal* A LEVEL【正式】高级程度考试

ad·vance·ment /ədˋvænsmənt; ədˈvɑːnsmənt/ *n* [C,U] *formal* progress or development in your job, level of knowledge etc【正式】进步；进展：*career advancement* 事业进展 | *advancements in science* 科学进步

ad·vanc·ing /ədˋvænsɪŋ; ədˈvɑːnsɪŋ/ *adj* **1** moving forward, especially in order to attack 前进的，向前推进的：*advancing Serbian forces* 向前推进的塞尔维亚部队 **2 advancing years/age** the fact of growing older 年老，年事已高：*Blake had grown much quieter and more serious – another sign of his advancing years.* 布莱克变得越来越少言寡语，越来越严肃 — 这是上了年纪的另一个迹象。

ad·van·tage /ədˋvæntɪdʒ; ədˈvɑːntɪdʒ/ *n* 1 1

1 ►THAT HELPS YOU 有利于你的◄ [C,U] something that helps you to be better or more successful than others 有利条件，优势：[+of] *the advantages of a university education* 受大学教育的优势 | **have an advantage (over)** *For certain types of work wood has advantages over plastic.* 对于某些制品来讲，木头要强于塑料。| **give sb an advantage** *New tax regulations had given them an advantage over their commercial rivals.* 新税收法规使他们比其商业竞争对手更具优势。| **big/great/definite advantage** *Her previous experience gives her a big advantage over the other applicants.* 她以前的经验使她比其他申请者有更多的优势。| **unfair advantage** *Government subsidies give these industries an unfair advantage.* 政府补助金使这些行业有着不公平的优势。| **be to your advantage** (=give you an advantage) 对你有利 | **be at an advantage** (=have an advantage) 占优势 *Candidates with computer skills will be at an advantage.* 具有计算机技能的候选者会有优势。| **gain/seek advantage** (=get or try to get something that will help you against your opponents) 得到/谋求优势 *seeking political advantage by exploiting this sensitive issue* 利用这个敏感的问题谋求政治优势

2 take advantage of sb to treat someone unfairly to get what you want, especially someone who is generous or easily persuaded〔不公正地〕利用某人，占某人的便宜：*Don't lend them the car – they're taking advantage of you!* 不要把车借给他们 — 他们在利用你！

3 take advantage of sth to use a particular situation to do or get what you want〔巧妙地〕利用某物：*I took advantage of the good weather to paint the shed.* 我趁天气好给棚屋刷上油漆。

4 ►STH GOOD 好事物◄ [C,U] a good or useful quality or condition that something has 好处，优点，利益：*one of the many advantages of living in the city* 住在城市的诸多好处之一 | *Is there really any advantage in getting there early?* 早到那儿真的有什么好处吗？| **have the advantage of** *For children of this age, cereals have the advantage of being rich in iron.* 麦片含丰富铁质，对这个年龄的孩子有好处。

5 to good advantage in a way that shows the best features of someone or something 表现出优点地，有利地

6 ►TENNIS 网球◄ **advantage X** used to show that the person named has won the point after DEUCE 某某人占先，某某人领先一分〔终局前平分后先得一分〕：*Advantage Agassi.* 阿加西领先一分。

ad·van·ta·geous /ˌædvənˋtedʒəs; ˌædvənˈteɪdʒəs/ *adj* helpful and likely to make you successful 有利的，有益的：[+to] *terms advantageous to foreign companies* 对外国公司有利的条款 —**advantageously** *adv*

Ad·vent /ˋædvɛnt; ˈædvent/ *n* [singular] the period of four weeks before Christmas in the Christian religion〔基督教的〕降临节〔圣诞节前的四个星期〕

advent *n* **the advent of** the time when something first begins to be widely used …的出现，来临：*the advent of the motor car* 汽车的出现

ad·ven·ti·tious /ˌædvɛnˋtɪʃəs; ˌædvənˈtɪʃəs◂/ *adj formal* happening by chance; unexpected【正式】偶然的 —**adventitiously** *adv*

ad·ven·ture /ədˋvɛntʃɚ; ədˈventʃə/ *n* [C,U] an exciting experience in which dangerous or unusual things happen 冒险(经

历): *a young man looking for adventure* 寻求冒险的青年人 | *Ahab's adventures at sea* 埃哈伯海上历险记

adventure play·ground /ˈ·,··ˈ·/ *n* [C] *BrE* an area of ground for children to play on, with exciting equipment and structures for climbing on【英】历险乐园〔提供富有刺激性的设施及装置供儿童攀爬玩乐的场所〕

ad·ven·tur·er /ədˈvɛntʃərə; ədˈventʃərə/ *n* [C] **1** someone who enjoys adventure 冒险家: *an adventurer traveling the world* 周游世界的冒险家 **2** *old-fashioned* someone who tries to become rich or socially important using dishonest or immoral methods【过时】投机分子; 为求名利不择手段的人

ad·ven·tur·ous /ədˈvɛntʃərəs; ədˈventʃərəs/ *adj* **1** also 又作 **adventuresome** *AmE*【美】eager to go to new places and do exciting or dangerous things 喜欢冒险的, 有冒险精神的: *an adventurous expedition up the Amazon* 向亚马孙河上游的冒险远征 **2** not afraid of taking risks or trying new things 敢作敢为的; 大胆创新的: *Andy isn't a very adventurous cook.* 安迪不是一个大胆创新的厨师。—**adventurously** *adv*

ad·verb /ˈædvɝb; ˈædvɜːb/ *n* [C] a word or group of words that describes or adds to the meaning of a verb, an adjective, another adverb, or a whole sentence, such as 'slowly' in 'He ran slowly.', 'very' in 'It's very hot.', or 'naturally' in 'Naturally, we want you to come.' 副词〈如 He ran slowly 中的 slowly, It's very hot 中的 very, 或 Naturally, we want you to come 中的 naturally〉—compare 比较 ADJECTIVE

ad·ver·bi·al¹ /ədˈvɝbɪəl; ədˈvɜːbiəl/ *adj* used as an adverb 副词的, 状语的: *an adverbial phrase* 副词短语

adverbial² *n* [C] *technical* a word or phrase used as an adverb【术语】状语, 副词语

ad·ver·sa·ri·al /ˌædvəˈsɛrɪəl; ˌædvɜːˈseəriəl◂/ *adj* an adversarial system, especially in politics and the law, is one in which two sides oppose and attack each other 对手的: *the adversarial nature of two-party politics* 两党政治的敌对本质

ad·ver·sa·ry /ˈædvəˌsɛrɪ; ˈædvəsəri/ *n* [C] *formal* a country or person you are fighting or competing against; opponent【正式】对手, 敌手

ad·verse /ədˈvɝs; ˈædvɜːs/ *adj* **1** not favourable 不利的; 反对的; 相反的: *an adverse report* 不利的报道 | *adverse publicity* 起反作用的宣传 **2 adverse conditions/effects etc** conditions etc that make it difficult for something to happen or exist 不利的情况/影响等: *We had to abandon the climb because of adverse weather conditions.* 由于天气不利的影响, 我们不得不放弃这次登山。—**adversely** *adv*

ad·ver·si·ty /ədˈvɝsətɪ; ədˈvɜːsəti/ *n* [U] a situation in which you have a lot of problems that seem to be caused by bad luck 逆境, 不幸, 厄运: *to keep the family together in times of adversity* 处在逆境时让家人团结在一起

ad·vert¹ /ˈædvɝt; ˈædvɜːt/ *n* [C] *BrE* an advertisement【英】广告

ad·vert² /ədˈvɝt; ədˈvɜːt/ *v*

advert to sth *phr v* [T] *formal* to mention something【正式】提及

ad·ver·tise /ˈædvəˌtaɪz; ˈædvətaɪz/ *v* **1** [I,T] to tell people publicly about a product or service in order to persuade them to buy it (为…)做广告(宣传): *Have you tried that new shampoo they've been advertising on TV?* 你试过他们一直在电视上做广告的那种新洗发液吗? **2** [I,T] to make an announcement, for example in a newspaper or on a POSTER, that a job is available, an event is going to happen etc 登广告招聘; 做广告宣传〔某一活动等〕: *a big poster advertising a U2 concert* 一张 U2 音乐会的大型海报 | **[+for]** *I see they're advertising for a new Sales Director.* 我看到他们登广告招聘新的销售部主管。**3** [T] to show or tell something about yourself that it would be better to keep secret 宣扬〔不宜公开的事〕: *Don't advertise the fact that you're looking for another job.* 不要对外宣扬你正在另找工作的事。—**advertiser** *n* [C]

S3 **ad·ver·tise·ment** /ˌædvəˈtaɪzmənt; ədˈvɜːtɪsmənt/ *n* [C] **1** a picture, set of words, a film etc that is used to advertise a product or service〔宣传产品或服务的〕广告: *an advertisement for a free day of skiing in Vermont* 去佛蒙特州免费滑雪一天的广告 **2** a statement in a newspaper that a job is available, an event is going to happen etc〔招聘、活动等的〕广告 **3 be an advertisement for** to show the advantages of something 宣扬…的优点: *He's not a very good advertisement for private education.* 他不是非常理想的私立教育形象代言人。

W3 **ad·ver·tis·ing** /ˈædvəˌtaɪzɪŋ; ˈædvətaɪzɪŋ/ *n* [U] the activity or business of advertising things on television, in newspapers etc 广告(业): *advertising aimed at 18-25 year olds* 针对 18 岁到 25 岁年轻人的广告 | *a career in advertising* 广告业生涯

advertising a·gen·cy /ˈ····ˌ···/ *n* [C] a company that designs and makes advertisements for other companies 广告公司, 广告代理

ad·vice /ədˈvaɪs; ədˈvaɪs/ *n* [U] an opinion you give someone about what they should do 意见; 忠告, 劝告; 建议: **[+on/about]** *There's lots of advice in the book on baby care.* 这本书中有许多婴儿护理方面的建议。| **give advice** *Can you give me some advice about buying a house?* 关于买房子一事, 你能不能给我一点意见? | **legal/medical/professional advice etc** (=advice from someone with special knowledge) 法律/医疗/职业等方面的建议 *If I were you, I'd get some legal advice.* 如果我是你, 我会咨询一些法律方面的建议。| **ask sb's advice** *I want to ask your advice about where to stay in Taipei.* 我想征求你的意见, 到台北住在哪里好。| **follow/take sb's advice** (=do what they advise you) 听从/采纳某人的建议 *I followed my father's advice and sold the car.* 我遵照父亲的建议把车卖了。| *Take my advice and study something practical.* 听我的忠告, 学点实用的东西。| **a word/piece of advice** (=some advice) 一点建议 *Let me give you a piece of advice. Wear a blue or grey suit to the interview.* 让我给你一点建议。穿蓝色或灰色套装去参加面试。| **on sb's advice** (=because they advised you) 根据某人的建议 *On my doctor's advice, I'm taking early retirement.* 根据医生的建议, 我要提前退休。 S1 W1

This graph shows some of the words most commonly used with the noun **advice**. 本图表所示为含有名词 advice 的一些最常用词组。

advice on
give advice
legal/professional/medical advice
ask advice
take advice
advice about
follow advice
a word/piece of advice

2 4 6 8 10 per million 每百万

Based on the British National Corpus and the Longman Lancaster Corpus
据英国国家语料库和朗文兰开斯特语料库

advice col·umn /ˈ·ˌ··ˌ··/ *n* [C] *especially AmE* part of a newspaper or magazine in which someone gives advice to readers about their personal problems【尤美】〔报刊或杂志上的〕咨询栏; AGONY COLUMN *BrE*【英】—**advice columnist** *n* [C]

Ad·vil /ˈædvɪl; ˈædvɪl/ *trademark* a type of medicine to stop pain, made from IBUPROFEN【商标】阿德维尔〔一种止痛药, 主要成分是异丁苯丙酸〕

ad·vi·sa·ble /ədˈvaɪzəbl; ədˈvaɪzəbəl/ *adj* [not before noun 不用于名词前] something that is advisable should be done in order to avoid problems or risks 可取的; 明智的: *For heavy smokers, regular medical checks are advisable.* 抽烟很多的人最好定期进行健康检查。| **it is advisable to do sth** *It is advisable to disconnect the computer before you open it up.* 拆开电脑之前, 最好先切断电源。—**advisability** /ədˌvaɪzəˈbɪlətɪ; ədˌvaɪzəˈbɪləti/ *n* [U]

ad·vise /ədˈvaɪz; ədˈvaɪz/ *v* **1** [I,T] to tell someone what you think they should do, especially when you know more than they do about something 劝告, 忠告; 提供意见: **advise sb to do sth** *Passengers are advised not to leave their bags unattended.* 建议乘客看管好自己的提包。| **advise sb against doing sth** *I'd advise you against saying anything to the press.* 我劝你什么都不要对新闻界讲。| **strongly advise** *You are strongly advised to take out medical insurance when visiting the country.* 极力建议你到该国游览时购买医疗保险。| **advise caution/patience/restraint etc** (=advise people to be careful, patient etc) 建议〔人们〕小心/有耐心/克制等 *The makers advise extreme caution when handling this material.* 制造商建议搬运这种材料时要格外小心。**2** [I,T] to be employed to give advice on a subject about which you have special knowledge or skill (向…)提供〔专业的〕建议[咨询]: **advise on sth** *She's been asked to advise on training the new team.* 她被请求为训练新队伍提供建议。| **advise sb on sth** *He advises us on tax matters.* 他就税收问题向我们提供咨询。**3** [T] *formal* to inform someone about something【正式】通知: **advise sb of sth** *We'll advise you of any changes* S2 W2

in the delivery dates. 发送日期有任何改变，我们都会通知你。| **keep sb advised** (=continue to inform someone) 让某人了解变化的情况 *Keep us advised of the developments.* 请随时告诉我们进展情况。**4 you would be well/ill advised to do sth** used to tell someone that it is wise or unwise to do something 建议你最好做/不做某事…: *You would be well advised to stay in bed and rest.* 你最好卧床休息。

ad·vis·ed·ly /əd`vaɪzɪdlɪ; əd'vaɪzɨdli/ *adv* after careful thought; deliberately 深思熟虑地; 有意地: *He behaved like a dictator, and I use the term advisedly.* 他的所作所为就像个独裁者，我用这个词是经过认真考虑的。

3 3 **ad·vis·er** also 又作 **advisor** *AmE*【美】/əd`vaɪzɚ; əd'vaɪzə/ *n* [C] someone whose job is to give advice because they know a lot about a subject, especially in business, law, or politics 顾问: *an independent financial adviser* 独立金融顾问

ad·vi·so·ry /əd`vaɪzərɪ; əd'vaɪzəri/ *adj* having the purpose of giving advice 提供意见[咨询]的: **advisory committee/body** *the Environmental Protection Advisory Committee* 环境保护顾问委员会 | **advisory role/capacity** *employed in a purely advisory role* 纯粹以顾问身份受聘

ad·vo·ca·cy /`ædvəkəsɪ; 'ædvəkəsi/ *n* [U] public support for a course of action or way of doing things 支持，拥护，提倡

ad·vo·cate[1] /`ædvəket; 'ædvəkeɪt/ *v* [T] to publicly support a particular way of doing things 主张，拥护，鼓吹: *Extremists were openly advocating violence.* 极端主义者公开鼓吹使用暴力。

ad·vo·cate[2] /`ædvəkɪt; 'ædvəkɨt/ *n* [C] **1** someone who publicly supports a particular way of doing things 提倡者，拥护者，鼓吹者: **be an advocate of** *She's a passionate advocate of natural childbirth.* 她竭力主张自然分娩。**2** a lawyer who speaks in a court of law, especially in Scotland〔尤指苏格兰的〕律师 —see also 另见 **play/be the devil's advocate** (DEVIL (4))

adze also 又作 **adz** *AmE*【美】/ædz; ædz/ *n* [C] a sharp tool with the blade at a right angle to the handle, used to shape pieces of wood 手斧，锛子

Ae·ge·an Sea, the /ɪ,dʒiən `si; ɪ,dʒiːən 'siː/ also 又作 **the Aegean** the sea in southeast Europe between Greece and Turkey 爱琴海〔位于欧洲东南部，在希腊和土耳其之间〕

ae·gis /`idʒɪs; 'iːdʒɨs/ *n* **under the aegis of** *formal* with the protection or support of a person or organization【正式】在…的支持[保护]下: *a refugee camp operating under the aegis of the UN* 在联合国保护下的难民营

Ae·ne·as /ɪ`niəs; ɪ'niːəs/ in ancient Greek and Roman stories, a Trojan leader who escaped from Troy after it was captured by the Greeks and went to Carthage, where he met Dido. He later went to Italy where he became the ANCESTOR of the Romans. 埃涅阿斯〔古希腊、古罗马传说中的特洛伊将领。特洛伊被希腊人攻陷后，他逃往迦太基，遇到了狄多。后来，他去了意大利，成为罗马人的祖先〕 —see also 另见 AENEID, The ILIAD, the TROJAN WAR

Ae·ne·id, The /ɪ`niɪd; ɪ'niːɪd/ Virgil's poem about the adventures of Aeneas, a HERO from Greek and Roman MYTHOLOGY《埃涅阿斯纪》〔维吉尔创作的一部史诗，记叙希腊和罗马神话中的英雄埃涅阿斯的冒险经历〕

ae·on also 又作 **eon** *AmE*【美】/`iən; 'iːən/ *n* [C] an extremely long period of time 极长的时期，万古

aer·ate /`eə,ret; 'eəreɪt/ *v* [T] *technical* to put a gas or air into a liquid under pressure【术语】充气于〔…液体〕中 —**aeration** /,eə`reʃən; eə'reɪʃən/ *n* [U]

aer·i·al[1] /`ɛrɪəl; 'eəriəl/ *adj* **1** from a plane 空中的，来自飞机的: *an aerial attack* 空袭 | *aerial photographs* 航拍照片 **2** in or moving through the air 空气中的

aerial[2] *n* [C] a piece of equipment for receiving or sending radio or television signals, usually consisting of a piece of metal or wire〔无线电、电视的〕天线; ANTENNA (2) *AmE*【美】—see picture on page A2 参见 A2 页图

aero- /ɛro; eərəʊ/ *prefix* concerning the air or aircraft 空气(的)；航空(的): *aerodynamics* (=science of movement through air) 空气动力学 | *an aeroengine* 飞机引擎

aer·o·bat·ics /,ɛrə`bætɪks; ,eərə'bætɪks/ *n* [plural] tricks done in a plane that involve making difficult or dangerous movements in the air 特技飞行，航空表演

ae·ro·bic /ɛ`robɪk; eə'rəʊbɪk/ *adj* **1** *technical* using oxygen【术语】需氧的 **2 aerobic exercise** a type of exercise intended to strengthen the heart and lungs 有氧健身运动: *Examples of aerobic exercise are running, cycling, and swimming.* 有氧健身运动的项目有跑步、骑车和游泳。

aer·o·bics /ɛ`robɪks; eə'rəʊbɪks/ *n* [U] a very active type of physical exercise done to music, usually in a class 有氧健身操

aer·o·drome /`ɛrə,drom; 'eərədrəʊm/ *n* [C] *old-fashioned BrE* a place that small planes fly from【过时，英】小型机场

aer·o·dy·nam·ic /,ɛrodaɪ`næmɪk; ,eərəʊdaɪ'næmɪk◂/ *adj* **1** an aerodynamic car, design etc uses the principles of aerodynamics to achieve high speed or low use of petrol 流线型的 **2** *technical* related to or involving aerodynamics【术语】空气动力学的: *aerodynamic efficiency* 空气动力效率 —**aerodynamically** /-klɪ; -kli/ *adv*

aer·o·dy·nam·ics /,ɛrodaɪ`næmɪks; ,eərəʊdaɪ'næmɪks/ *n* [U] **1** the scientific study of how objects move through the air 空气动力学 **2** the qualities needed for something to move through the air, especially smoothly and quickly 空气动力特性

aer·o·gramme /`ɛrə,græm; 'eərəgræm/ *n* [C] a very light letter you send by AIRMAIL 航空邮简[笺]; AIRLETTER *BrE*【英】

aer·o·nau·tics /,ɛrə`nɔtɪks; ,eərə'nɔːtɪks/ *n* [U] the science of designing and flying planes 航空学[术] —**aeronautic** *adj* —**aeronautical** *adj*

aer·o·plane /`ɛrə,plen; 'eərəpleɪn/ *n* [C] *BrE* a flying vehicle with wings and at least one engine; AIRPLANE *AmE*【美】; plane【英】飞机 —see picture at 参见 AIRCRAFT 图

aer·o·sol /`ɛrə,sɑl; 'eərəsɒl/ *n* [U] a small metal container from which a liquid such as paint can be forced at high pressure 小型喷雾器 —see picture at 参见 SPRAY[1] 图

aer·o·space[1] /`ɛro,spes; 'eərəʊspeɪs/ *adj* involving the designing and building of aircraft and space vehicles 航空和航天的: *the aerospace industry* 航空与航天工业

aerospace[2] *n* [U] the industry that designs and builds aircraft and space vehicles 航空与航天工业，宇航工业

Aes·chy·lus /`ɛskələs; 'iːskɨləs/ (?525-?456 BC) an ancient Greek writer who was one of the earliest writers to develop the European style of DRAMA (=plays for the theatre), especially TRAGEDY 埃斯库罗斯〔(公元前?525-前?456)，古希腊作家。他是欧洲舞台剧，尤其是悲剧最早的创始人之一〕

Ae·sop /`isɑp; 'iːsɒp/ (?620-?560 BC) an ancient Greek writer who wrote short stories known as *Aesop's Fables*, which teach moral lessons using characters who are animals. His fables include *The Fox and the Grapes* and *The Tortoise and the Hare.* 伊索〔(公元前?620-前?560)，古希腊作家，《伊索寓言》的作者。书中的角色以动物为主，给人以启迪。代表作有《狐狸与葡萄的故事》和《龟兔赛跑》等〕

aes·thete *especially BrE*【尤英】also 又作 **esthete** *AmE*【美】/`ɛsθit; 'iːsθiːt/ *n* [C] someone who loves and understands beautiful things, such as art and music 审美家

aes·thet·ic *especially BrE*【尤英】also 又作 **esthetic** *AmE*【美】/ɛs`θɛtɪk; iːs'θetɪk/ *adj* **1** connected with beauty and the study of beauty 美学的: *From an esthetic point of view, it's a nice design.* 从美学角度看，这是个很不错的设计。| *a work of great aesthetic appeal* 非常有美学感染力的作品 **2** designed in a beautiful way 有美感的; 有审美能力的: *The building is aesthetic, but not very practical to heat.* 这幢建筑物外型美观，但采暖功能不太好。—**aesthetically** /-klɪ; -kli/ *adv*: *aesthetically pleasing* 给人以美感的

aes·thet·ics *especially BrE*【尤英】also 又作 **esthetics** *AmE*【美】/ɛs`θɛtɪks; iːs'θetɪks/ *n* [U] the study of beauty, especially beauty in art〔尤指艺术方面的〕(审) 美学

ae·ther /`iθɚ; 'iːθə/ *n* [U] an old spelling of ETHER (=the air or sky) 苍穹，苍天〔ether 的旧式拼法〕

ae·ti·ol·o·gy *BrE*【英】, **etiology** *AmE*【美】/,itɪ`ɑlədʒɪ; ,iːti'ɒlədʒi/ *n* [U] the study of what causes disease 病因学; 病原学

a·far /ə`fɑr; ə'fɑː/ *adv* **from afar** *literary* from a long distance away【文】遥远地; 在远处: *I saw him from afar.* 我在远处看到他。

AFC, the *n* [singular] American Football Conference; a group of teams that is part of the NFL 美国橄榄球联合会〔国家橄榄球大联盟的一部分，由许多球队组成〕—see also 另见 NFC

AFDC /,e ɛf di `si; ,eɪ ef diː 'siː/ *n* [singular] Aid to Families with Dependent Children; a US government programme that gives money to poor families, especially single parents 困难家庭补助计划〔美国政府向贫困家庭，尤其是单亲家庭提供补助的一个计划〕

af·fa·ble /`æfəbl̩; 'æfəbəl/ *adj* friendly and easy to talk to 友善的; 和蔼可亲的; 容易交谈的: *an affable guy* 平易近人的人 —**affably** *adv* —**affability** /,æfə`bɪlətɪ; ,æfə'bɪlɨti/ *n* [U]

af·fair /ə`fɛr; ə'feə/ *n* [C]

1 affairs [plural] **a)** public or political events and activities 事情，事务: *world affairs* 世界大事 | *They were accused of interfering in China's internal affairs.* 他们被指责干涉中国的内政。| *the exclusion of women from public affairs* 拒绝妇女参与公共事务 | **foreign affairs** (=political events in other countries) 外交事务 *a foreign affairs correspondent for the CNN* 美国有线新闻网的外事记者 **b)** things connected with your 

personal life, your financial situation etc（个人的）事: *I am not prepared to discuss my financial affairs with the press.* 我不打算向新闻界谈论我的财务问题。—see also 另见 **state of affairs** (STATE[1] (8))
2 ►EVENT 事件◄ an event or set of related events, especially one that is impressive or shocking 事件: *the Watergate affair* 水门事件 | *The dinner was an elegant affair.* 这顿饭很讲究。
3 ►RELATIONSHIP 关系◄ a secret sexual relationship between two people, when at least one of them is married to someone else〔非配偶的〕暧昧关系, 私通: **have an affair (with)** *He had an affair with his boss that lasted six years.* 他和老板的暧昧关系持续了六年。—see also 另见 LOVE AFFAIR
4 ►THING 事物◄ *informal* an object, machine etc of a particular kind【非正式】东西: *The computer was one of those little portable affairs.* 那台电脑是便于携带的那一种。
5 be sb's affair if something is your affair, it only concerns you and you do not want anyone else to get involved in it 是某人自己的事: *What I do in my time is my affair and nobody else's.* 我在自己的时间里做什么是我自己的事, 与别人无关。

[1] [1] **af·fect** /əˋfɛkt; əˈfekt/ *v* [T] **1** to do something that produces an effect or change in someone or something 影响: *How will the tax affect people on low incomes?* 这项税收会如何影响低收入人士? | *a disease that affects the central nervous system* 影响中枢神经系统的疾病 | *emergency relief for the areas affected by the hurricane* 对遭受飓风影响的地区的紧急救助 **2** [usually passive 一般用被动态] to make someone feel strong emotions 使某人产生强烈的感情, 使感动: *We were all deeply affected by the news of her death.* 她去世的消息使我们都深感悲痛。**3** *formal* to pretend to have a particular feeling, way of speaking etc【正式】故作姿态, 假装: *Simon affected boredom to make me think he didn't care.* 西蒙假装厌烦, 让我以为他（对这件事）不在乎。| *to affect a foreign accent* 装外国口音

USAGE NOTE 用法说明: AFFECT
WORD CHOICE 词语辨析: **affect, effect**
Affect is the usual verb and **effect** is the usual noun. affect 通常为动词, 而 effect 通常为名词: *How do you think the changes will affect (v) you?* (NOT 不用 affect on/to/in you) 你认为这些变化会如何影响你? *What effect (n) do you think the changes will have on you?* 你认为这些变化会给你带来什么样的影响? The verb **effect** is fairly formal and is only used in particular meanings, for example, you might **effect** changes or a plan of action (=make them happen). It does not mean the same as **affect**. 动词 effect 相当正式, 只用于表示某种特定的意思, 如造成改变、实施计划等, 和 affect 的意思不一样。

af·fec·ta·tion /ˌæfɛkˋteʃən; ˌæfekˈteɪʃən/ *n* [C,U] behaviour that is not sincere or natural 装模作样, 矫揉造作: *Those beatnik clothes of his are just an affectation.* 他那些"垮掉的一代"式的衣服显得很不自然。
af·fect·ed /əˋfɛktɪd; əˈfektɨd/ *adj* not sincere or natural 做作的, 不自然的: *that stupid affected laugh of hers* 她那愚蠢而又做作的大笑
af·fect·ing /əˋfɛktɪŋ; əˈfektɪŋ/ *adj formal* producing strong emotions of sadness, pity etc【正式】使人感动的: *a deeply affecting story* 感人至深的故事
af·fec·tion /əˋfɛkʃən; əˈfekʃən/ *n* [C,U] a gentle feeling of love and caring 感情; 慈爱; 挚爱: [+for] *Bart felt a great affection for the old man.* 巴特对这位老人有很深的感情。| **show affection** *Their mother never shows them much affection.* 他们的母亲对他们从来没有表现出多少的母爱。
af·fec·tion·ate /əˋfɛkʃənɪt; əˈfekʃənɨt/ *adj* showing in a gentle way that you love someone 亲切的, 有感情的: *an affectionate hug* 亲切的拥抱 | *a very affectionate child* 很有感情的孩子 —**affectionately** *adv*
af·fi·anced /əˋfaɪənst; əˈfaɪənst/ *adj old use* ENGAGED (1)【旧】已订婚的
af·fi·da·vit /ˌæfəˋdevɪt; ˌæfɨˈdeɪvɨt/ *n* [C] *law* a written statement made under OATH (=after promising to tell the truth), for use as proof in a court of law【法律】〔法庭上作证用的书面〕宣誓书, 书面证词
af·fil·i·ate[1] /əˋfɪlɪˌet; əˈfɪlieɪt/ *v* **1 be affiliated with/to** if a group or organization is affiliated to a larger one, it is connected with it or controlled by it 附属于: *a TV station affiliated to CBS* 附属于哥伦比亚广播公司的电视台 **2 affiliate yourself to** to join or become connected with a larger group or organization 加入, 加盟; 并入
af·fil·i·ate[2] /əˋfɪlɪət; əˈfɪliɨt/ *n* [C] a small company, organization etc that is connected with or controlled by a larger one 支会; 分社; 子公司; 附属机构
af·fil·i·a·tion /əˌfɪlɪˋeʃən; əˌfɪliˈeɪʃən/ *n* [C,U] **1** the fact of being involved with or a member of a political or religious organization 联系, 从属关系: *What are her political affiliations?* 她属于什么政治派系? **2** the act of a smaller group or organization joining a larger one 并入, 加盟, 加入
af·fin·i·ty /əˋfɪnətɪ; əˈfɪnɨti/ *n* **1** [singular] a strong feeling that you like and understand someone because you share the same ideas or interests 情投意合; 喜好: [+for/between/with] *I felt an immediate affinity for them.* 我马上就对他们有了好感。**2** [C,U] a close connection between two things because of qualities or features that they share 类同; 密切关系: [+with/between] *There is a remarkable affinity between Christian and Asian concepts of the spirit.* 基督教关于灵魂的概念和亚洲人的看法非常相似。
af·firm /əˋfɝm; əˈfɜːm/ *v* **1** [T] *formal* to state publicly that something is true【正式】断言, 申明, 确认: *The general affirmed rumors of an attack.* 将军证实了袭击的传闻。**2** [T] *formal* to strengthen a feeling, belief, or idea【正式】肯定, 强化〔感觉、信念等〕: *By submitting to male values, they symbolically affirm male superiority.* 通过承认男性价值观, 他们象征性地认同了男子的优越感。**3** [T] *technical* to promise to tell the truth in a court of law, but without mentioning God in the promise【术语】郑重声明,〔不经宣誓而〕承认, 确认 —**affirmation** /ˌæfɚˋmeʃən; ˌæfəˈmeɪʃən/ *n* [C,U]
af·fir·ma·tive /əˋfɝmətɪv; əˈfɜːmətɪv/ *adj* **1 answer/reply in the affirmative** to say 'yes' 肯定地回答 —opposite 反义词 NEGATIVE[1] (3) **2** *formal* a word, sign etc that means 'yes'【正式】〔话或符号〕表示同意的: *an affirmative nod* 点头表示同意 —**affirmatively** *adv*
affirmative ac·tion /ˌ··· ˈ··/ *n* [U] the practice of choosing people for a job or education course who are usually treated unfairly because of their race, sex etc〔鼓励聘用或录取女性、少数族裔等的〕积极行动, 反歧视行动; POSITIVE DISCRIMINATION *BrE*【英】: *an affirmative action employer* 采取积极行动的雇主
af·fix[1] /əˋfɪks; əˈfɪks/ *v* [T+to] *formal* to fasten or stick something to something else【正式】使固定; 粘上, 贴上
af·fix[2] /ˋæfɪks; ˈæfɪks/ *n* [C] *technical* a group of letters added to the beginning or end of a word to change its meaning or use, such as 'untie', 'misunderstand', 'kindness', or 'quickly'【术语】词缀 —compare 比较 PREFIX[1] (1), SUFFIX
af·flict /əˋflɪkt; əˈflɪkt/ *v* [T often passive 常用被动态] *formal* to make someone suffer or experience serious problems【正式】使受痛苦, 折磨: **be afflicted with/by** *a country afflicted by famine* 饱受饥荒困扰的国家
af·flic·tion /əˋflɪkʃən; əˈflɪkʃən/ *n* [C,U] *formal* something, usually a medical condition, that causes pain or unhappiness【正式】痛苦, 苦恼, 折磨: *the afflictions of old age* 老年时的各种苦楚
af·flu·ent /ˋæfluənt; ˈæfluənt/ *adj* having plenty of money, so that you can afford to buy expensive things, live in a nice house etc 富裕的, 富足的: *affluent suburbs with large houses and treelined streets* 房子宽敞、街道绿树成荫的富裕郊区 —**affluence** *n* [U]
af·ford /əˋfɔrd; əˈfɔːd/ *v* [T] **1 can afford a)** to have enough money to buy or pay for something 买得起, 付得起钱: *Only the bigger clubs can afford the enormous fees that these players demand.* 只有较大的俱乐部才能支付得起这些运动员要的高价。| **afford to do sth** *We can't afford to go on vacation this year.* 今年我们没钱去度假。**b)** to have enough time to do something 有足够的时间〔做某事〕: *Helena doesn't feel she can afford any more time away from work.* 海伦娜认为她不能从工作中抽出更多的时间。**c)** to be able to do something without causing serious problems for yourself 承担得起; 有能力做: **afford to do sth** *We simply can't afford to offend such an important customer.* 惹怒这样一位重要客户, 我们可担当不起。**2** *formal* to provide something or allow something to happen【正式】提供, 给予: *The window affords a beautiful view out over the city.* 窗外可以看到城市的美丽景色。—**affordable** *adj* [1] [3]
af·for·es·ta·tion /əˌfɔrəsˋteʃən; əˌfɒrɨˈsteɪʃən/ *n* [U] *technical* the act of planting trees in order to make a forest【术语】植树造林 —opposite 反义词 DEFORESTATION —**afforest** /əˋfɔrɪst; əˈfɒrɨst/ *v* [T]
af·fray /əˋfre; əˈfreɪ/ *n* [C] *law* a noisy fight or quarrel in a public place【法律】在公共场所打架[滋事]
af·fri·cate /ˋæfrɪkɪt; ˈæfrɪkɨt/ *n* [C] *technical* a CONSONANT sound consisting of a PLOSIVE such as /t/ or /d/ that is imme-

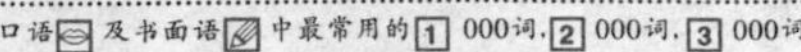

diately followed by a FRICATIVE pronounced in the same part of the mouth, such as /ʃ/ or /ʒ/. The word 'church', for example, contains the affricate /tʃ/.【术语】破擦音〔爆破音如 /t/ 或 /d/ 和摩擦音如 /ʃ/ 或 /ʒ/ 的组合，例如 church 这个词含有破擦音 /tʃ/〕

af·front¹ /əˋfrʌnt; əˈfrʌnt/ *v* [T usually passive 一般用被动态] to offend or insult someone, especially by not showing respect 当众侮辱; 冒犯

affront² *n* [C usually singular 一般用单数] a remark or action that offends or insults someone 侮辱; 冒犯的言行: [+to] *an affront to his pride* 对他自尊心的公然伤害

Af·ghan /ˈæfgæn; ˈæfgæn/ *n* [C] **1** someone who comes from Afghanistan 阿富汗人 **2** a warm cover for a bed made of wool knitted (KNIT¹ (1)) in colourful patterns 阿富汗毛毯 **3** also 又作 **Afghan hound** a tall thin dog with a pointed nose and very long silky hair 阿富汗猎犬 —**Afghan** *adj* —see picture at 参见 DOG¹ 图

Af·ghan·is·tan /æfˋgænəˌstæn; æfˈgænɪ̥stɑːn/ a country in Asia that is west of Pakistan and east of Iran. Population: 26,800,000 (2001). Capital: Kabul 阿富汗〔亚洲国家，位于巴基斯坦以西，伊朗以东。人口: 26,800,000 (2001)，首都: 喀布尔〕

a·fi·cio·na·do /əˌfɪsjəˋnɑdo; əˌfɪʃəˈnɑːdəʊ/ *n* [C] someone who is very interested in a particular activity or subject and knows a lot about it …迷; 狂热爱好者: *a film aficionado* 电影迷

a·field /əˋfild; əˈfiːld/ *adv* **far afield** far away, especially from home 远离〔家乡等〕; 到[在]远方: *Don't go too far afield or you'll get lost.* 不要走得太远，要不然你会迷路的。

a·fire /əˋfaɪr; əˈfaɪə/ *adj, adv* [not before noun 不用于名词前] *literary*【文】**1** burning 着火 (的)，燃烧着 (的): *The oil tanker was afire.* 油轮起火了。**2** filled with strong emotions or excitement 热情的, 充满激情的: [+with] *afire with patriotism* 充满爱国主义的热情

a·flame /əˋflem; əˈfleɪm/ *adj* [not before noun 不用于名词前] *literary*【文】**1** burning 着火的, 燃烧着的 **2** very bright with colour or light 明亮的: [+with] *trees aflame with autumn leaves* 秋叶火红的树木 **3** filled with strong emotions or excitement 热情洋溢的 —**aflame** *adv*

AFL-CIO /ˌe ɛf ˌɛl si aɪ ˋo; ˌeɪ ef ˌel siː aɪ ˈəʊ/ *n* [singular] the American Federation of Labor and Congress of Industrial Organizations; an association of American TRADE UNIONs, which has a lot of influence in the US 劳联—产联〔全称为美国劳工联合会暨产业联合会，是全美很有影响力的一个工会组织〕

a·float /əˋflot; əˈfləʊt/ *adj* [not before noun 不用于名词前] **1** floating on water 漂浮的: *Help me get the boat afloat.* 帮我把那只小船弄下水。**2** having enough money to operate or stay out of debt 不欠债的; 经济上周转得开的: *The company was just barely afloat.* 这家公司仅仅是勉强不欠债。**3** *literary* on a ship【文】在船上的 —**afloat** *adv*

a·foot /əˋfʊt; əˈfʊt/ *adj* [not before noun 不用于名词前] **1** being planned or happening 酝酿中的; 进行中的: *There were plans afoot for a second attack.* 正在策划再次进攻。**2** *old use* moving, especially walking【旧】行动的;〔尤指〕步行的 —**afoot** *adv*

a·fore·said /əˋforˌsɛd; əˈfɔːsed/ also 又作 **a·fore·men·tioned** /əˋforˋmɛnʃənd; əˈfɔːmenʃənd/ *adj* [only before noun 仅用于名词前] *law* mentioned before in an earlier part of a document, article, book etc【法律】上述的, 前述的: *The property belongs to the aforesaid Ms Jones.* 这财产属于前面提到的琼斯女士。—**aforesaid** *n* [singular or plural]: *The aforesaid were present at the meeting.* 上述人员出席了会议。

a·fore·thought /əˋforˌθɔt; əˈfɔːθɔːt/ *adj* —see 见 **with malice aforethought** (MALICE (2))

a·foul /əˋfaʊl; əˈfaʊl/ *adv* **run/fall afoul of** *formal especially AmE* to cause problems by doing something that is against the rules or that goes against people's beliefs【正式, 尤美】和…发生冲突; 和…抵触: *run afoul of the school authorities* 同校方发生冲突

a·fraid /əˋfred; əˈfreɪd/ *adj* [not before noun 不用于名词前] **1 I'm afraid** *spoken* used to politely tell someone something that may annoy them, upset them or disappoint them【口】恐怕: *That's the most we can offer you, I'm afraid.* 恐怕这是我们能提供的最高价。| [+(that)] *I'm afraid you've been given the wrong address.* 恐怕给你的地址不对。| *Excuse me, but I'm afraid this is a non-smoking area.* 对不起，这里不允许吸烟。| **I'm afraid so** (=yes) 恐怕是的 *"Is she really very ill?" "I'm afraid so."* "她真的病得很厉害吗?" "恐怕是的。" | **I'm afraid not** (=no) 恐怕不是 *No, I'm afraid not, but we do have some tickets for tomorrow.* 对不起，恐怕没有了，但我们还有一些明天的票。**2** unwilling to do something because you are worried about what will happen if you do it 不敢 [害怕]〔做某事〕的: [+of] *I didn't tell her because I was afraid of upsetting her.* 我没有把事情告诉她，因为怕她不高兴。| [+(that)] *I didn't say anything because I was afraid the other kids would laugh at me.* 我什么都没说，因为我怕其他孩子嘲笑我。**3** very frightened or worried about something 害怕的, 恐惧的, 担心的: *The poor little thing looked so afraid.* 可怜的小家伙看来很害怕。| **be afraid** *I could see in his eyes that he was afraid.* 从他的眼神里，我能看出他感到害怕。| [+of] *Don't be afraid of the dog – he's quite harmless.* 不要怕这只狗，它不咬人。| **afraid to do sth** *Don't be afraid to ask for help.* 不要怕求人帮忙。| **be afraid of doing sth** *Luke is afraid of going to bed in the dark.* 卢克害怕摸黑去睡觉。| **be afraid for** *They've been laying people off, and Charlie is afraid for his job.* 他们一直在裁员，所以查利很担心自己的工作。**4 afraid of your own shadow** easily frightened or always nervous 胆小怕事; 疑神疑鬼, 草木皆兵

This graph shows how common different grammar patterns of the adjective **afraid** are. 本图表所示为形容词 afraid 构成的不同语法模式的使用频率。

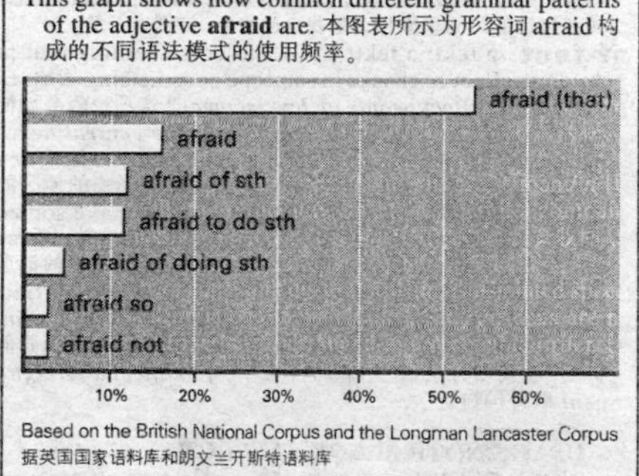

Based on the British National Corpus and the Longman Lancaster Corpus 据英国国家语料库和朗文兰开斯特语料库

a·fresh /əˋfrɛʃ; əˈfreʃ/ *adv formal* if you do something afresh, you do it again from the beginning【正式】再, 重新: **start afresh** *He moved to America to start his life afresh.* 他移居美国开始新生活。

Af·ric·a /ˈæfrɪkə; ˈæfrɪkə/ a CONTINENT (=one of the seven main areas of land on the Earth) that is south of the Mediterranean Sea, and west of Asia and the Indian Ocean 非洲〔七大洲之一，位于地中海以南，亚洲、印度洋以西〕

Af·ri·can¹ /ˈæfrɪkən; ˈæfrɪkən/ *adj* from or connected with Africa 非洲的; 非洲人的

African² *n* [C] someone from Africa 非洲人

African A·mer·i·can /ˌ… ˈ…/ *n* [C] *AmE* an American whose family originally came from Africa, especially as slaves【美】〔尤指祖先曾为黑奴的〕非洲裔美国人, 美国黑人 —see 见 NEGRO (USAGE)

African Na·tion·al Con·gress, the /ˌ… ˌ… ˈ…/ *n* [singular] the ANC

Af·ri·kaans /ˌæfrɪˋkɑns; ˌæfrɪˈkɑːns/ *n* [U] a language of South Africa that is similar to Dutch 南非荷兰语

Af·ri·ka·ner /ˌæfrɪˋkɑnɚ; ˌæfrɪˈkɑːnə/ *n* [C] a South African whose family came from the Dutch people who settled there in the 1600s 南非白人〔母语为南非荷兰语的南非人，尤指17世纪荷兰移民的后裔〕

Af·ro /ˈæfro; ˈæfrəʊ/ *n* [C] a hair style popular with black people in the 1970s in which the hair is cut into a round shape 非洲式 (蓬松) 发型, 埃弗罗发式〔20世纪70年代在黑人中流行的呈圆形的蓬松发型〕

Afro- /æfro; æfrəʊ/ *prefix* **1** of Africa; African 非洲的: *an Afro-American* (=a black American person) 美国黑人, 非洲裔美国人 **2** African and 非洲及…的: *Afro-Asian* (=of both Africa and Asia) 亚非的

aft /æft; ɑːft/ *adj, adv technical* in or towards the back part of a boat【术语】在船尾 (的); 向船尾 (的) —opposite 反义词 FORE²

after- /æftɚ; ɑːftə/ *prefix* coming or happening afterwards 在…以后 (的): *aftercare* (=care given afterwards) 病后的调养 | *after-sales service* 售后服务

af·ter¹ /ˈæftɚ; ˈɑːftə/ *prep* **1** when a particular time or event has happened or is finished 在…后: *After the war many soldiers stayed in France.* 战后, 许多士兵留在法国。| *I go swimming every day after work.* 每天下班后，我都去游泳。| *It's on after the 9 o'clock news.* 在 9 点钟新闻以后播出。| *Do you believe in life after death?* 你相信死后会有来世吗? | **2 days/3 weeks etc after sth** *A few months after his birth we discov-* 

ered that our son was deaf. 儿子出生几个月后，我们发现他耳聋。| **the day/week/year after sth** *We will leave the day after tomorrow.* 我们后天离开。| **soon/not long/shortly after sth** *Not long after the wedding his wife got ill.* 结婚不久，他的妻子就病了。| **straight after sth** (=immediately after) 在某事之后立即 *Come home straight after the performance.* 演出结束后马上就回家。| **come after sth** (=happen after something) 发生在…之后 *The first bomb attack came after midnight.* 第一次轰炸袭击是在午夜之后。—see 见 SINCE[3] (USAGE) **2** following someone or something else in a list, series, piece of writing, line of people etc 排在…之后: *Whose name is after yours on the roll?* 在点名册上，谁的名字排在你的后面? | *The date should be written after the address.* 日期应写在地址之后。—see picture on page A1 参见 A1 页图 **3** when a particular amount of time has passed〔一段时间〕以后: *After 10 minutes remove the cake from the oven.* 十分钟以后，把蛋糕从烤炉中取出。| *After a while things started to improve.* 过了一段时间，情况开始好转。| *After months of argument they decided to divorce.* 几个月的争吵之后，他们决定离婚。**4** *AmE* used when telling the time to say how many minutes it is after the hour【美】〔几点〕过〔几分〕: *The movie starts at a quarter after seven.* 电影 7 点一刻开始放映。**5 day after day/year after year etc** continuously for a very long time 日复一日/年复一年等: *He's worked in that hell-hole week after week, year after year, since he was 18.* 18 岁开始，他就一直在那地狱般的地方工作，日复一日，年复一年。**6** when someone has left a place, has finished doing something etc 在〔离开某地或做完某事〕后: *Remember to close the door after you.* 请记住随手关门。| *I spend all day cleaning up after the kids.* 我整天跟在孩子后面收拾。**7 go/run/chase etc after sb** to follow someone in order to catch them 追赶某人: *Go after him and apologize.* 追上去向他道歉。**8** because of something or as a result of something 由于; 既然: *I'm not surprised he walked out, after the way she treated him.* 她那样对待他，所以我对他的出走并不感到惊奇。| *After your letter, I didn't think I'd ever see you again.* 由于你的这封信，我想我再也不会见你了。**9** in spite of something 尽管，虽然: *After all my hard work she still says it isn't neat enough.* 尽管我下了很大功夫，她还是说不够整洁。**10 call/shout/gaze etc after sb** to speak to or look towards someone as they move away from you 某人走开时叫/喊/凝视: *"You have a nice day, now!" she called after us.* "祝你们过得愉快!" 我们走时她说。**11 be after sb/sth a)** to be looking for someone or something 寻找某人/某物: *Police are after a short man with a tattoo on his cheek.* 警察正在追捕一个脸上有刺青的矮个子男人。| *"Were you after anything in particular?" "No, we're just looking."* "有什么特别想要的吗?" "不，我们只是随便看看。" **b)** *informal* to want to have something that belongs to someone else【非正式】想占有某物: *I think Chris is after my job.* 我想克里斯想要抢我的饭碗。**12 one after another/one after the other** if a series of events, actions etc happen one after another, each one happens soon after the previous one 一个接一个: *Ever since we moved into this house it's been one problem after another.* 自从我们搬进这房子，问题就接连出现了。**13 after all a)** used to say that something is true or is a fact, in spite of another fact or situation 终究: *He wrote to say they couldn't give me a job after all.* 他写信说他们终究还是不能给我一份工作。**b)** used to say that something should be remembered or considered, because it helps to explain why something else is true or is a fact 毕竟: *I don't know why you're so concerned, it isn't your problem after all.* 我不明白你为什么这样担心，这毕竟不是你的问题。**14** used when listing or naming things, to mean that you have not included a particular thing because that is the first or best one 仅次于: *After dancing, going to the movies is my favorite weekend activity.* 除了跳舞，看电影是我最喜欢的周末活动。**15** *especially BrE* given the same name as someone else, especially an older member of your family【尤英】以…命名: *His name is Alessandro, after his grandfather.* 他的名字叫亚历山德罗，是以他祖父的名字命名的。**16** *formal* in the same style as a particular painter, musician etc【正式】具有…风格的，模仿…: *a painting after Rembrandt* 模仿伦勃朗风格的绘画作品 **17 after you** *spoken*【口】**a)** used to say politely that someone else can use or do something before you do 你先请: *"Do you need the copier?" "After you."* "你要用复印机吗?" "你先用吧。" **b) after you with** used to ask someone if you can have or use something after they have finished 在〔某人〕之后〔用某物〕: *After you with that knife, please.* 请你用完刀子后给我。—see also 另见 **a man/woman after my own heart** (HEART (15)), **take after** (TAKE[1])

USAGE NOTE 用法说明: AFTER

WORD CHOICE 词语辨析: **after (prep), in, after (adv), afterwards, later**

You use **after** (*prep*) to talk about something that happens at the end of a period of time that is different from something that happens within that period. 介词 after 用以表示在某段时间以后而不是该段时间内发生的事情: *After a few days I felt much better* (=not until a few days had passed). 几天以后，我感到好多了。You use **in** to talk about something that will happen before a period of time has finished. in 表示某一段时间结束之前将会发生的事: *You'll feel better in a few days* (=by the time a few days has passed). 过几天你会感到好一些。

After (*prep*) is more often used to talk about events in the past, and **in** about the future. 介词 after 常用于指过去，而 in 则指将来: *She left after an hour* (=after an hour had passed). 她在一小时后离开了。| *She'll be leaving in an hour* (=after an hour has passed). 她将在一小时以后离开。

After (*adv*) with the meaning 'afterwards' usually follows another time adverb. 副词 after 在表示"后来"的意义时常跟在另一个时间副词之后: *We arrived just/soon/shortly after.* 我们随后不久就到了。With words that show a length of time, **afterwards** or **later** is more usual. 在与表示一段时间的词连用时，多用 afterwards 和 later: *She arrived three days afterwards/later* (NOT usually 一般不用 *three days after*, though you could say 但是可以用 *after that*). 她于三天之后到达。

If you want to use a word with this meaning on its own, you would usually use **afterwards**. 如果想用一个单词表示"随后"之意，通常用 afterwards: *We went swimming and walked home afterwards.* 我们去游泳，然后步行回家。However, in informal British spoken English people sometimes say **after**. 然而，在非正式的英国口语中，有时也用 after: *We went swimming and walked home after.* 我们去游泳，然后步行回家。You would not usually begin a sentence with **after**, though. 但 after 一般不用于句首: *Afterwards/After that, we left* (NOT 不用 *After, we left*). 后来，我们就离开了。

after[2] *conjunction* when a particular time or event has happened or is finished 在…以后: *After you'd called the police, what did you do?* 报警之后，你做了些什么? | *He changed his name after he left Germany.* 他离开德国以后把名字改了。| **two days/three weeks etc after** *Ten years after I bought the painting I discovered it was fake.* 我买了这幅画十年以后，才发现它是赝品。| **shortly/soon/not long after** *Shortly after the eggs have hatched, the mother goes off in search of food.* 鸡蛋刚刚孵化完，鸡妈妈就去找食物了。 S1 W1

after[3] *adv* after something that has already been mentioned; afterwards 然后，随后: *What are you doing after? Do you want to go for a drink?* 然后你要干什么? 想不想去喝点东西? | **come after** (=happen after something else has happened) 在…后又发生 *Having lost the final pages, we can only guess at what might come after.* 最后几页没有了，我们只能猜想后来会怎么样。| **the day/the year etc after** *Once you've purchased the washing machine we guarantee it for up to 5 years after.* 自你购买洗衣机之日起，我们会保用达五年。| **shortly/soon/not long after** *Not long after, I heard that Mike had been killed in the war.* 没过多久，我听说迈克阵亡了。

after[4] *adj* **1 in after years** *literary* in the years after the time that has been mentioned【文】在以后的几年里 **2** *technical* in the back part of a boat or an aircraft【术语】〔船、飞机〕后部的: *the after deck* 后甲板

af·ter·birth /ˈæftɚˌbɝθ; ˈɑːftəbɜːθ/ *n* [U] the substance that comes out of female humans or animals just after they have had a baby 胞衣，胎盘和胎膜

af·ter·care /ˈæftɚˌkɛr; ˈɑːftəkeə/ *n* [U] *BrE* care or treatment given to someone after they have been in hospital【英】〔病人出院后的〕病后调养

after-ef·fect /ˈ· · ˌ·/ *n* [C usually plural 一般用复数] an unpleasant effect that remains for a long time after the condition or event that caused it 后效; 后作用; 副作用; 后遗效应: *the after-effects of his illness* 他这种病的后遗症

af·ter·glow /ˈæftɚˌglo; ˈɑːftəgləʊ/ *n* [C usually singular 一般用单数] **1** a pleasant feeling that remains after a happy experience〔欢乐后的〕余味，事后愉快的回忆; 余韵: *the afterglow of the party* 对晚会的愉快回忆 **2** the light that remains in the western sky after the sun goes down 晚霞，余晖

af·ter·life /ˈæftɚˌlaɪf; ˈɑːftəlaɪf/ *n* [singular] the life that some people believe people have after death 阴世; 灵界

af·ter·math /ˈæftɚˌmæθ; ˈɑːftəmæθ/ *n* [singular] the period of time after something such as a war, storm, or accident when people are still dealing with the results 后果, 余殃, 余波: *the danger of disease in the aftermath of the earthquake* 地震后引发疫病的危险

af·ter·noon /ˌæftɚˋnun; ˌɑːftəˈnuːn◂/ *n* [C,U] **1** the period of time between midday and sunset or at the end of the day's work 下午, 午后: *We went swimming on Tuesday afternoon.* 星期二下午我们去游泳了。| *Harry went to sleep in the afternoon.* 午后哈里去睡觉了。| *Do you want to go shopping tomorrow afternoon?* 明天下午你想去购物吗? | *tickets for the afternoon performance* 午后演出的票 | **this afternoon** (=today in the afternoon) 今天下午 *Could you babysit for a few hours this afternoon?* 今天下午你能抽出几小时来代我们照看孩子吗? **2 afternoons** *especially AmE* during the afternoon each day【尤美】(每天)下午: *She only works afternoons.* 她只在下午工作。—compare 比较 EVENING

af·ters /ˈæftɚz; ˈɑːftəz/ *n* [plural] *BrE informal* the part of a meal that comes after the main dish; DESSERT【英, 非正式】餐后的甜食

af·ter·shave /ˈæftɚʃev; ˈɑːftəʃeɪv/ *n* [C,U] a liquid with a pleasant smell that a man puts on his face after he shaves (SHAVE[1] (1))〔剃须后用的〕润肤液

af·ter·taste /ˈæftɚˌtest; ˈɑːftəteɪst/ *n* [C usually singular 一般用单数] a taste that stays in your mouth after you have eaten or drunk something〔饮食后口中的〕余味: *The wine leaves a strong aftertaste.* 这种葡萄酒回味悠长。

af·ter·thought /ˈæftɚˌθɔt; ˈɑːftəθɔːt/ *n* [C] **1 as an afterthought** thought of and mentioned after you have finished talking about a particular subject 事后的想法: *He added as an afterthought, "Bring Melanie too."* 他想了想补充道: "把梅拉妮也带来。" **2** something added later, especially something that was not part of the original plan〔尤指原计划所没有的〕后加的东西: *The tiles looked out of place, as if they had been an afterthought.* 这些瓷砖看起来不伦不类, 好像是后加上的。

af·ter·wards /ˈæftɚwɚdz; ˈɑːftəwədz/ *adv* also 又作 **afterward** *AmE*【美】after an event or time that has already been mentioned 随后, 以后, 后来: *The ceremony lasts half an hour and afterward there's a meal.* 仪式持续了半个小时, 然后是进餐时间。| **2 days/3 weeks etc afterwards** *My parents met during the war but didn't marry till five years afterwards.* 我父母在战争期间相识, 但他们五年之后才结婚。—see 见 AFTER[1] (USAGE)

AFTRA /ˈæftrə; ˈæftrə/ *n* [singular] American Federation of Television and Radio Artists; a trade union in the US for actors and actresses who perform on television and radio programmes 美国电视广播艺术家联合会〔美国广播电视演员的一个工会组织〕—compare 比较 EQUITY, SAG

A·ga /ˈɑgə; ˈɑːgə/ *trademark* a type of cooker made of solid iron, which is similar in design to the types of cooker that people used to have in the past.They are popular with middle class people who live in the country.【商标】爱家厨具〔一种用纯铁做成的炊具, 设计类似旧式厨具, 深受生活在乡村的中产阶级喜爱〕

a·gain /əˋgɛn; əˈgen/ *adv* **1** if something happens again, or someone does something again, it happens or they do it one more time 又, 再一次: *Can you say that again? I didn't hear you.* 你能再说一遍吗? 我没听见。| *I'll never go there again.* 我再不会去那儿了。| *I'm sorry, Mr Khan's line is busy. Can you try again later?* 对不起, 卡恩先生的电话占线。你能不能过一会儿再打来? | **once again** (=again, usually for at least the third time) 再次, 再三〔通常三次以上〕*Once again the Allies marched in and pushed back the enemy troops.* 盟军再次进攻, 击退了敌军。| **yet again** (=again, after happening many times before)〔多次以后〕再次 *Can you believe it! He told that story about his teeth yet again.* 你能信吗? 他又一次讲起他的牙齿的事。**2** back to the same state or situation that you were in before 还原, 复原: *His parents stayed and nursed him back to health again.* 他的父母留了下来, 一直护理到他康复。| *It's great to have you home again.* 你又回家了, 真是太好了。**3 all over again** if you do something all over again, you repeat it from the beginning 重新做起, 从头再来: *There's no tape in the machine. We'll have to start the interview all over again.* 机器里没有放磁带, 采访只好从头再来。**4 as much/as many/the same again** the same number or amount added to what there already is 同样再来一遍: *What a fantastic lunch. I could eat the same again.* 好棒的午餐呀! 再有这么多我也能吃得下。| *I thought my job was good until I heard Bernard earns twice as much again.* 要不是听说伯纳德挣的钱是我的两倍, 我还一直以为我的工作不错。**5** used when giving a fact or opinion that either explains something you have just said, or is very different from it 而, 另一方面, 再者: *And again, while the accident was not your fault, the damage must be paid for somehow.* 再者, 虽然事故不是你的过错, 但损失总得赔偿。| **then/there again** *spoken*【口】*Carol's always had nice clothes but then again she earns a lot.* 卡罗尔总有漂亮的衣服穿, 可话又说回来了, 她挣的钱也多。**6 again and again/time and (time) again/over and over again** very often 一再, 屡次: *I've told you again and again, don't play soccer near the windows.* 我再三地告诉你们不要在窗子附近踢足球。**7** *spoken* used when you want someone to repeat information that they have already given you【口】再(说): *What did you say your name was again?* 请再说一遍你叫什么名字? —see also 另见 **now and again** (NOW[1] (6))

a·gainst /əˋgɛnst; əˈgenst/ *prep* **1** opposed to or disagreeing with an idea, belief, proposal etc 反对: *votes for and against the motion* 该项动议的赞成票和反对票 | *It's against my principles to borrow money.* 借钱不符合我的原则。| *Several members spoke against the proposal.* 有几个成员发言反对这个建议。| **be against sth** *I'm against all forms of hunting.* 我反对任何形式的捕猎。| **against sb's wishes** (=when you know someone does not want something to happen) 违背某人的愿望 *They got married against her wishes.* 他们是在她极不情愿的情况下结婚的。| **against sb's will** (=when someone is forced to do something) 违背某人的意志 *She has been kept in the house against her will.* 她被迫关在屋子里。| **against the law** (=illegal) 违法 —see graph at 参见 OPPOSED 图表 **2** fighting or competing with another person, team, country etc 和…交战[竞争, 比赛]: *He was injured in the game against the Cowboys.* 他在与牛仔队的比赛中受了伤。| *We'll be competing against some of the best companies in Europe.* 我们要和欧洲一些一流的公司竞争。| *the fight against terrorism* 反恐怖主义的斗争 **3** in a way that has an unfavourable effect on someone or causes them disadvantage 对〔某人〕不利; 造成劣势: *discrimination against women* 对妇女的歧视 | *Your lack of experience could count against you.* 缺乏经验对你会是个不利因素。| *The planning regulations tend to work against smaller companies.* 计划方面的规章制度一般对小公司不利。**4** touching, hitting, or rubbing another surface 碰, 撞: *The rain drummed against the window.* 雨点打在窗上。| *I like it when the cat rubs its head against my legs.* 我喜欢猫用头在我的腿上蹭来蹭去。| *The car skidded and we could hear the crunch of metal against metal.* 汽车打滑了, 我们能听见金属相碰的嘎吱嘎吱声。**5** next to and touching an upright surface, especially for support 倚着, 靠着: *There was a ladder propped up against the wall.* 一把梯子靠着墙。| *The younger policeman was leaning against the bureau with his arms folded.* 那位较年轻的警官两臂交叉地倚靠在大办公桌旁。—see picture on page A1 参见 A1 页图 **6** in the opposite direction to 逆向: *sailing against the wind* 逆风航行 | *swimming against the current* 逆流游泳 **7** seen or shown with something else behind or as a background 以…为背景; 对照; 衬托: *He caught a glimpse of a man silhouetted against a dimly lit background.* 他瞥见在灯光微弱的背景中有一个男人的侧影。| *knowing what colours look good against your skin* 知道什么颜色能把你的肤色衬得好看 **8** used to describe something in relation to other events that are happening at the same time 在…情况下; 在…背景下: *The reforms were introduced against a background of social unrest.* 改革是在社会动荡的背景下开始的。**9** in comparison with 与…相比: *Only 3% of blacks were registered voters against 97% of the white residents.* 只有3%的黑人为登记选民, 相比之下白人却达到97%。| *She checked the contents of the box against the list.* 她将箱子中的东西和清单相对照。**10** providing protection from harm or damage 防…, 抗…: *insurance against accident and sickness* 意外事故和疾病保险 | *This spray can be used against weevil and other crop pests.* 这种喷雾杀虫剂可用于防治象鼻虫和其他农作物害虫。**11 be/come up against sth** to have to deal with a difficult opponent or problem 必须面对〔难应付的对手或问题〕: *You see, this is what we're up against – the suppliers just aren't reliable.* 你瞧, 这就是我们遇到的难题, 供应商根本不可靠。**12 have sth against sb/sth** to dislike or disapprove of someone or something 不喜欢[不赞成]某人/某事: *It's not that I have anything against babies. I just don't feel very comfortable with them.* 我并不是不喜欢婴儿, 只是觉得跟他们在一起不太舒服。

A·ga Khan, the /ˌɑgə ˋkɑn; ˌɑːgə ˈkɑːn/ (1936-) an Arab leader who is the head of a Muslim group called the Ismailis. He is extremely rich and is famous for owning many RACEHORSES.

阿迦汗〔(1936-)，伊斯兰教伊斯玛仪派领袖。极为富有，以拥有许多赛马而出名〕

Ag·a·mem·non /ˌægəˋmɛmnɑn; ˌægəˈmemnən/ in ancient Greek stories, the king of Mycenae and leader of the Greeks in the Trojan War. When he came home after the war, he was murdered by his wife, Clytemnestra and her lover Aegisthus. 阿迦门农〔古希腊故事中的迈锡尼王，特洛伊战争期间希腊军统帅。战后回到家时，被妻子克吕泰墨斯特拉及其情夫埃癸斯托斯杀害〕—see also 另见 The ILIAD

a·gape /əˋgep; əˈgeɪp/ *adj* with your mouth wide open, especially because you are surprised or shocked〔惊得〕大张着嘴的: *Vince watched, his mouth agape in horror.* 文斯在一旁看着，吓得目瞪口呆。

ag·ate /ˋægɪt; ˈægɪ̣t/ *n* [C] a hard stone with bands of different colours, used in jewellery 玛瑙

-age /ɪdʒ; ɪdʒ/ *suffix* [in nouns 构成名词] **1** the action or result of doing something〔做某事〕的动作或其结果: *Buy a larger size to allow for shrinkage.* (=getting smaller) 由于会缩水，要买大些的。| *several breakages* (=things broken) 几件破损的东西 **2** the cost of doing something〔做某事〕的费用: *Postage is extra.* 邮资另付。**3** a particular state or rank …身份[地位]: *a peerage* (=noble rank) 贵族爵位

1 1 **age**[1] /edʒ; eɪdʒ/ *n*

1 ▶HOW OLD 多大◀ [C,U] the number of years someone has lived or something has existed 年龄; 存在时间: *Francis is the same age as me.* 弗朗西斯和我同龄。| *The boys were six years apart in age.* 男孩们的年龄相差六岁。| *There were dozens of kids there, all different ages.* 那儿有几十个孩子，年龄都不同。| **at the age of** (=when someone is a particular age) 在…年纪时 *Marco won the Grand Prix at the age of 19.* 马尔科19岁就取得了国际汽车大奖赛的胜利。| **4/15 etc years of age** *formal* (=4, 15 etc years old)【正式】4岁/15岁等 *The missing girl is 19 years of age.* 失踪的女孩19岁。| **at age 57/4/18 etc** *AmE* (=when someone is 57 etc years old)【美】57岁/4岁/18岁等时 *Saul entered Yale at age 14.* 索尔14岁考上了耶鲁大学。| **at an early age** (=very young) 很年轻时 *girls who become mothers at a very early age* 年纪很小就做了母亲的女孩 | **act your age** (=behave in a way that is suitable to how old you are) 行为举止与年龄相称 | **sb's age** (=how old someone is) 某人的年龄 *When you get to my age, it's quite difficult getting up stairs.* 当你到了我的年龄，上楼就有点费劲了。| **for his/her age** (=compared with others of the same age) 以他/她的年龄来说 *She's very tall for her age, isn't she?* 以她的年龄来说，她很高，对吧？| **certain age** *Kids get to a certain age and say, right, that's it, and they just go.* 孩子们到了一定年龄，对了，是这样，他们就要离开父母了。

2 ▶LEGAL AGE 法定年龄◀ [U] the age when you are legally old enough to do something 法定年龄: *What's the minimum age for getting a driver's license?* 取得驾驶执照的最小年龄是多少？| **under age** (=too young) 太小，太年轻 *You're not allowed to be drinking, you're under age.* 你年纪太小，不可以喝酒。| **over age** (=too old) 超龄 *Dan's over age, so the army won't accept him.* 丹已经超龄，所以部队不会接收他。

3 ▶PERIOD OF LIFE 人生中的阶段◀ [C,U] one of the particular periods of someone's life 人生的某个阶段: *women of child-bearing age* 育龄妇女 | *Phil's coming up to 13 – rather a difficult age.* 菲尔快13岁了 — 相当麻烦的一个年龄。—see also 另见 OLD AGE, MIDDLE AGE, TEENAGE

4 ▶BEING OLD 老了◀ [U] the state or fact of being old 年老; 时间久: *The newspapers were brown with age.* 时间太久了，报纸都发黄了。| *Age had given his face a sort of crumpled look.* 岁月在他的脸上刻上了皱纹。

5 ▶PERIOD OF HISTORY 历史阶段◀ [C usually singular 一般用单数] a particular period of history 时代，世纪: *the last Ice Age* 最后一次冰河时期 | *We are living in the computer age.* 我们生活在电脑时代。—see also 另见 GOLDEN AGE, **in this day and age** (DAY (29))

6 come of age a) reach the age when you are legally considered to be a responsible adult 到达法定年龄; 成年 **b)** if something comes of age, it reaches a stage of development at which people accept it as being important, valuable etc 到达成熟时期: *It was during this period that the movies really came of age as a creative art form.* 正是在这个时期，电影才真正进入了成熟期，成为一种具有创造性的艺术形式。

7 ages [plural] also 又作 **an age** *informal, especially BrE* a long time【非正式，尤英】长时间: *It'll be ages before we're ready to go.* 我们得要很久以后才能准备好走。| **for ages** *Simon! I haven't seen you for ages!* 西蒙，我已经好久没有见到你了！| **it's (been) ages since** *It's ages since we've played that game.* 我们已经好久没有玩过那种游戏了。| **take ages** *It takes ages to make that recipe.* 按那种烹调方法需要很长时间。

age[2] *v present participle* **ageing** *or* **aging 1** [I,T] to start looking older or to make someone look older, especially because they have suffered a lot（使）变老: *Myra's recent illness has aged her considerably.* 迈拉最近的病使她苍老了很多。**2** [I] to become older 老化，陈旧: *The buildings are ageing, and some are unsafe.* 这些建筑已很陈旧，有些还不安全。**3** [I] to improve and develop in quality and taste, over a period of time 成熟，味道变醇厚: *a wine that has aged well* 陈年老酒

age brack·et /ˈ·, ··/ *n* [C] the people between two particular ages, considered as a group〔介于两个年龄之间的〕年龄段，年龄组: *single people in the 40-50 age bracket* 40至50岁年龄段的独身人士

Age Con·cern /ˈ· ·ˌ·/ a British CHARITY organization that helps old people 老年人慈善会〔英国帮助老年人的一个慈善机构〕

aged[1] /edʒd; eɪdʒd/ *adj* **aged 5/30/25 etc** 5, 30 etc years old 5岁/30岁/25岁等: *The course is open to children aged 12 and over.* 本课程是为12岁及以上的儿童而设。| [+between] *The police are looking for a man aged between 30 and 35.* 警方正在寻找一个年龄介于30到35岁之间的男子。 3

a·ged[2] /ˋedʒɪd; ˈeɪdʒɪ̣d/ *adj* **1** very old 年老的: *my aged parents* 我年迈的父母 **2 the aged** old people 老年人: *plans to help the aged and infirm* 帮助年老体弱者的计划

age dis·crim·i·na·tion /ˈ· ·,··ˈ··/ *n* [U] *AmE* unfair treatment of people because they are old【美】〔对老年人的〕年龄歧视; AGEISM *BrE*【英】

age group /ˈ· ·/ *n* [C] all the people between two particular ages, considered as a group 年龄组，年龄群: *a book written for children in the 12-14 age group* 为12到14岁年龄组的儿童写的书

age·ing[1] *BrE*【英】usually 一般作 **aging** *AmE*【美】/ˋedʒɪŋ; ˈeɪdʒɪŋ/ *adj* [only before noun 仅用于名词前] becoming old, and usually less useful, attractive, suitable etc 变老的; 陈旧的: *aging movie stars* 上了年纪的电影明星 | *an ageing population* 老龄化人口

ageing[2] *BrE*【英】usually 一般作 **aging** *AmE*【美】*n* [U] the process of getting old 老化: *airlines with ageing fleets* 机群老化的航空公司 | *products that claim to halt the ageing process* 宣称能阻止老化的产品

age·is·m also 又作 **agism** /ˋedʒɪzəm; ˈeɪdʒɪzəm/ *n* [U] *BrE* unfair treatment of people because they are old【英】〔对老年人的〕年龄歧视; AGE DISCRIMINATION *AmE*【美】—**ageist** *adj* —**ageist** *n* [C]

age·less /ˋedʒlɪs; ˈeɪdʒləs/ *adj* **1** never looking old or old-fashioned 永不衰老的; 不过时的: *Good clothes should be ageless.* 好衣服应该总不过时。**2** continuing forever 永恒的: *the ageless fascination of the sea* 大海的永恒魅力 —**agelessness** *n* [U]

age lim·it /ˈ· ,··/ *n* [C] the youngest or oldest age at which you are allowed to do something 年龄限制: *The age limit at the new nightclub is 21.* 新夜总会的年龄限制是21岁。

a·gen·cy /ˋedʒənsɪ; ˈeɪdʒənsi/ *n* [C] **1** a business that provides information about other businesses and their products, or that provides a particular service 代办处，代理处，经销处，中介处; 经纪业务: *I got this job through an employment agency.* 我是通过职业介绍所找到这份工作的。—see also 另见 DATING AGENCY, NEWS AGENCY **2** an organization or department, especially within a government, that does a specific job〔尤指政府内的〕局; 部; 处: *a UN agency responsible for helping refugees* 联合国负责帮助难民的机构 **3 by/through the agency of** being done with or as the result of someone's help 由于…的作用; 在〔某人〕的斡旋下 2 1

Agency for In·ter·na·tion·al De·vel·op·ment /,·· ·,···· ·ˈ··/ abbreviation 缩写为 **AID** a US government department that provides money to help poorer countries 国际开发署〔美国一政府部门，向贫困国家提供资金援助〕

a·gen·da /əˋdʒɛndə; əˈdʒendə/ *n* [C] **1** a list of the subjects to be discussed at a meeting〔会议的〕议程: **on the agenda** *the first item on the agenda* 第一项议程 **2 be on the agenda** if something is on the agenda, you are planning to do something about it〔事项的〕待办; 待讨论: **be on top of the agenda/be high on the agenda** (=be very important to do) 最重要的待办事项 *Health care was on top of President Clinton's agenda.* 卫生保健是克林顿总统最急需解决的问题。**3** subjects that everyone has heard of and is talking about 话题，议题: *Environmental issues are racing up the political agenda.* 环境问题正在迅速成为政治议题。—see also 另见 HIDDEN AGENDA 3

a·gent /ˋedʒənt; ˈeɪdʒənt/ *n* [C] 3 2

1 ▶BUSINESS 商业◀ a person or company that represents another person or company in business, in their legal problems

etc 代理人, 代理商; 经纪: *Our agent in Rio deals with all our Brazilian business.* 我们在里约热内卢的业务代表处理我们在巴西的全部业务。| [+for] *We're acting as agents for Mr Watson.* 我们是沃森先生的代理人。—see also 另见 ESTATE AGENT, REAL ESTATE AGENT, LAND AGENT
2 ▶**ARTIST/ACTOR** 艺术家/演员◀ someone who is paid by actors, musicians etc to find work for them 代理人, 经纪人: *My agent has an exciting new script for me to look at.* 我的经纪人有一个精彩的新剧本要我看。
3 ▶**GOVERNMENT AGENT** 政府特工人员◀ someone who works for a government or police department in order to get secret information about another country or organization; SPY 特工人员, 情报员, 间谍: *a Soviet agent in Czechoslovakia* 在捷克斯洛伐克的苏联间谍 —see also 另见 SECRET AGENT, DOUBLE AGENT
4 ▶**CHEMICAL** 化学◀ *technical* a chemical or substance that makes other substances change【术语】作用剂: *Soap is a cleansing agent.* 肥皂是一种清洁剂。
5 ▶**FORCE** 力◀ someone or something that affects or changes a situation 原动力, 动因: **agent for/of change** *Technological advances are the chief agents of change.* 技术进步是变革的主要原动力。

a·gent pro·voc·a·teur /ˌɑʒɑn proˌvɑkəˋtɝ; ˌæʒɒn prɒvɒkəˈtɜː/ *n* [C] *French* someone who is employed to encourage people who are working against a government to do something illegal so that they are caught【法】卧底密探, 坐探

age of con·sent /ˌ· · ˈ·/ *n* [C] the age when someone can legally get married or have a sexual relationship 婚姻合法年龄; (少女对性行为可以自主的) 同意年龄, 合法年龄

Age of En·light·en·ment, the /ˌ· · ˈ· · ·/ also 又作 **the Age of Reason** a period in European history, in the 18th century, when educated people thought that beliefs should depend on reason and scientific proof 启蒙时代 (18 世纪欧洲历史上的一段时期。当时, 受过教育的人都认为, 信仰应以理性和科学实证为依据)

age-old /ˌ· ˈ·◀/ *adj* having existed for a very long time 古老的; 存在已久的: *age-old customs* 古老习俗 | *It's nothing new. It's an age-old problem.* 这不是什么新鲜事。这个问题由来已久。

ag·glom·er·ate /əˋglɑmərɪt; əˈglɒmərɪ̈t/ *n* [singular, U] *technical* a type of rock formed from pieces of material from a VOLCANO that have melted together【术语】(火山爆发后形成的) 集块岩

ag·glom·e·ra·tion /əˌglɑməˋreʃən; əˌglɒməˈreɪʃən/ *n* [C, U] a large collection of things that do not seem to belong together 堆积, 聚集: *an agglomeration of facts* 事实成堆 **—agglomerate** /əˋglɑməˌret; əˈglɒməreɪt/ *v* **—agglomerate** /-rɪt; -rɪ̈t/ *adj*

ag·glu·ti·na·tion /əˌglutṇˋeʃən; əˌgluːtɪ̈ˈneɪʃən/ *n* [U] *technical*【术语】**1** the state of being stuck together 黏结; 凝集; 胶合 **2** the process of making new words by combining two or more words, such as combining 'ship' and 'yard' to make 'shipyard' 黏着法构词 (如 ship 和 yard 合成 shipyard)

ag·gran·dize·ment also 又作 **-isement** *BrE*【英】/əˋgrændɪzmənt; əˈgrændɪ̈zmənt/ *n* [U] a word meaning an increase in power, size, or importance, used especially when you disapprove of this increase 扩大, 提高: *a war fought for national aggrandizement* 为扩张国家势力而发动的战争 | *He did it for his own personal aggrandizement.* 他这样做是为了扩大自己的个人权力。

ag·gra·vate /ˋægrəˌvet; ˈægrəveɪt/ *v* [T] **1** to make a bad situation worse 使…加重, 使…恶化: *Their debt problem was aggravated by a rise in interest rates.* 由于利率上调, 他们的债务问题更加严重。**2** *informal* to make someone angry or annoyed【非正式】惹怒, 激怒: *Stop aggravating the cat!* 不要再惹那只猫了! **—aggravating** *adj* **—aggravatingly** *adv* **—aggravation** /ˌægrəˋveʃən; ˌægrəˈveɪʃən/ *n* [C,U]

ag·gre·gate¹ /ˋægrɪgɪt; ˈægrɪgɪ̈t/ *n* [C] **1** the total after a lot of different parts or figures have been added together 总数, 合计: *Society is not just an aggregate of individuals.* 社会不只是每一个个体的总和。| **on aggregate** *BrE* (=when the points are added together)【英】总分 *Manchester United won 2-1 on aggregate.* 曼联队以 2 比 1 的总分获胜。| **in (the) aggregate** (=as a group or in total) 作为总体 **2** [singular,U] *technical* sand or small stones that are used in making CONCRETE²【术语】粒料, 混凝料

aggregate² *adj* [only before noun 仅用于名词前] *technical* being the total amount of something, especially money【术语】(尤指钱) 总计的: *aggregate income and investment* 总收入和投资

ag·gre·gate³ /ˋægrɪˌget; ˈægrɪgeɪt/ *v* **1** [linking verb 连系动词] to be a particular amount when added together 总计达到, 合计为: **aggregate £100/20 etc** *Sheila's earnings from all sources aggregated £100,000.* 希拉的所有收入总计达十万英镑。**2** [I,T usually passive 一般用被动态] to put things together in a group to form a total; ASSEMBLE 使聚集, 收集: *We made estimates using the aggregated data.* 我们用所收集的数据进行评估。

ag·gres·sion /əˋgrɛʃən; əˈgreʃən/ *n* [U] **1** angry or threatening behaviour or feelings that often result in fighting 攻击性行为; 敌对行为 [心理]: *Television violence can encourage aggression in children.* 电视暴力会助长孩子们的攻击性行为。**2** the act of attacking a country, especially when that country has not attacked first 挑衅; 侵犯; 侵略: *territorial aggression* 领土侵略 | **act of aggression** *an unprovoked act of aggression on a peaceful nation* 对一个和平国家的无故侵犯

ag·gres·sive /əˋgrɛsɪv; əˈgresɪv/ *adj* **1** behaving in an angry, threatening way, as if you want to fight or attack someone 好斗的, 挑衅性的: *The men were drunk, aggressive and looking for a fight.* 那些人喝醉了, 一副挑衅的架势, 想找人打架。**2** someone who is aggressive is very determined to succeed or get what they want 有进取心的, 有冲劲的; 执著的: *A successful businessman has to be aggressive.* 成功的实业家要有股冲劲。**3** an aggressive action or plan is intended to achieve the right result 雄心勃勃的: *an aggressive marketing campaign* 雄心勃勃的营销计划 **—aggressively** *adv* **—aggressiveness** *n* [U] 3

ag·gres·sor /əˋgrɛsɚ; əˈgresə/ *n* [C] a person or country that begins a fight or war with another person or country 挑衅者; 攻击者; 侵略者

ag·grieved /əˋgrivd; əˈgriːvd/ *adj* **1** feeling or showing anger and unhappiness because you think you have been unfairly treated 愤愤不平的; 感到委屈的; 愤恨的: *an aggrieved tone of voice* 委屈的口吻 **2** *law* having suffered as a result of the illegal actions of someone else【法律】受到损害的, 受害方的: **the aggrieved party** (=the person who has suffered) 受害方

ag·gro /ˋægro; ˈægrəʊ/ *n* [U] *BrE informal*【英, 非正式】**1** aggressive behaviour and fighting, especially between young men (尤指年轻人的) 斗殴, 打群架; 纠纷 **2** problems or difficulties that annoy you 烦恼: *We had so much aggro with our insurance claim.* 我们在保险索赔上遇到了很大麻烦。

a·ghast /əˋgæst; əˈgɑːst/ *adj* [not before noun 不用于名词前] feeling or looking shocked by something you have seen or just found out 大为震惊的, 吓呆了的: [+at] *I was aghast at the violence I was witnessing.* 我被眼前的暴力场面吓呆了。

a·gile /ˋædʒəl; ˈædʒaɪl/ *adj* **1** able to move quickly and easily (动作) 敏捷的, 灵活的: *Andy climbed the tree, agile as a monkey.* 安迪像猴子一样敏捷地爬上了树。**2 agile mind** the ability to think very quickly and intelligently 敏捷的思维, 机敏的头脑

A·gin·court /ˋædʒɪnˌkɔrt; ˈædʒɪ̈nkɔːt/ a famous battle in France in 1415, which the English, led by King Henry V, won against the French 阿让库尔战役 (1415 年发生在法国的一场著名战役。英军在国王亨利五世的率领下打败了法军)

ag·ing /ˋedʒɪŋ; ˈeɪdʒɪŋ/ an American spelling of AGEING ageing 的美式拼法

ag·is·m /ˋedʒɪzəm; ˈeɪdʒɪzəm/ an American spelling of AGEISM ageism 的美式拼法

a·gi·tate /ˋædʒəˌtet; ˈædʒɪ̈teɪt/ *v* **1** [I] to argue strongly in public for something you want, especially a political or social change 煽动, 鼓动; 宣传: [+for/against] *unions agitating for higher pay* 工会鼓动要求增加工资 **2** [T] to shake or mix a liquid quickly 搅动; 摇动, 快速混合 (液体) **3** [T] *formal* to make someone feel anxious, upset, and nervous【正式】使 (某人) 焦虑不安

a·gi·ta·ted /ˋædʒəˌtetɪd; ˈædʒɪ̈teɪtɪ̈d/ *adj* so nervous or upset that you are unable to keep still or think calmly 紧张不安的, 焦虑的: *An agitated waiter rushed up to apologize for the delay.* 紧张不安的服务员赶快过去为上菜迟而道歉。| *She got rather agitated.* 她变得颇有点紧张不安。

a·gi·ta·tion /ˌædʒəˋteʃən; ˌædʒɪ̈ˈteɪʃən/ *n* **1** [U] feeling of being so anxious, nervous, or upset that you cannot think calmly 焦虑, 紧张不安: *Perry's agitation was so great he could hardly speak.* 佩里极度焦虑, 几乎说不出话来。**2** [C,U] a public argument or action for social or political change 煽动, 鼓动: [+for/against] *agitation for civil rights* 鼓动争取民权 **3** [U] the act of shaking or mixing a liquid (液体的) 搅动; 摇动, 混合

a·gi·ta·tor /ˋædʒəˌtetɚ; ˈædʒɪ̈teɪtə/ *n* [C] **1** someone who encourages people to work towards changing something in society 鼓动者, 煽动者: *a political agitator* 政治鼓动者 **2** a machine used to shake or mix liquids 搅拌器

a·git·prop /ˋædʒɪt͵prɑp; ˌædʒǐtˈprɒp/ *n* [U] music, literature, or art that tried to persuade people that SOCIALIST ideas were good 宣传鼓动〔指文艺作品〕: *1970s radical agitprop* 20世纪70年代激进的宣传鼓动

a·glow /əˋglo; əˈgləʊ/ *adj* **1** *literary* bright and shining with warmth, light, or colour【文】发(红)光的: *The morning sun set the sky aglow.* 晨曦染红了天空。**2** if someone's face or expression is aglow, they seem happy and excited 容光焕发的,〔兴奋得〕面色发红的: **[+with]** *Linda's face was aglow with happiness.* 琳达脸上洋溢着幸福的表情。

AGM /͵e dʒi ˋɛm; ˌeɪ dʒiː ˈem/ *n* [C] *BrE* annual general meeting; a meeting held once a year by a club, business, or organization, for the members to discuss the previous year's business, elect officials etc【英】年会; ANNUAL MEETING *AmE*【美】

ag·nos·tic /ægˋnɑstɪk; ægˈnɒstɪk/ *n* [C] someone who believes that people cannot know whether God exists or not 不可知论者 —compare 比较 **atheist** (ATHEISM) —**agnostic** *adj* —**agnosticism** /-təˌsɪzəm; -tǐsɪzəm/ *n* [U]

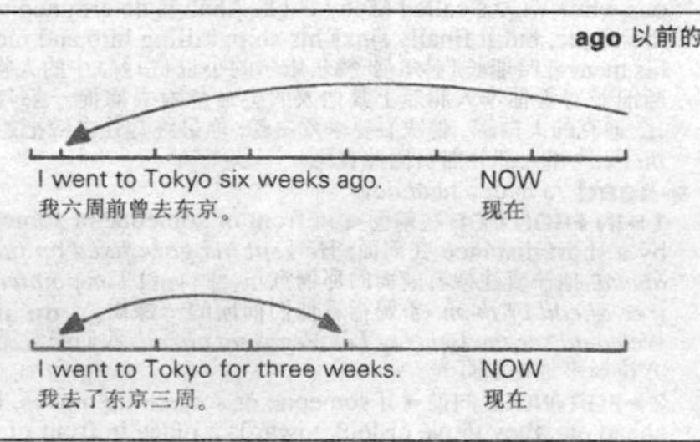

1 1 **a·go** /əˋgo; əˈgəʊ/ *adj* used to show how far back in the past something happened 以往的, 以前的: **5 minutes/an hour/20 years ago** *Michael left the office about half an hour ago.* 迈克尔大约半小时前离开了办公室。| **long ago/a long time ago** *I met Aunt Hetty once, a very long time ago.* 我很久以前见过赫蒂姨妈一次。| **a minute/moment ago** *I had my keys a minute ago, and now I can't find them.* 刚才我的钥匙还在, 现在却找不到了。| **a little/short while ago** *Tom got a letter from him just a little while ago.* 汤姆刚在不久之前收到过他寄来的一封信。| **some time ago** (=a fairly long time ago) 有些时候了 *They moved to a new house some time ago, a couple of years I think.* 他们搬进新居已有些日子了, 我想大概两三年吧。—compare 比较 FOR[1] (8), SINCE

a·gog /əˋgɑg; əˈgɒg/ *adj* [not before noun 不用于名词前] very interested, excited, and surprised, especially at something you are experiencing for the first time 因期待已久而极度兴奋的; 急切的, 渴望的: **(be all) agog (at)** *We were all agog at the sights of New York.* 看到纽约的景色, 我们都兴奋不已。

ag·o·nize also 又作 **-ise** *BrE*【英】/ˋægə͵naɪz; ˈægənaɪz/ *v* [I] to think about a difficult decision very carefully and with a lot of effort 焦虑, 忧愁, 苦恼: **[+over/about]** *There's no point in agonizing over which route to take.* 没有必要为走哪条路线而苦恼。—**agonizing** *n* [U]: *This time there was none of the agonizing and guilt that had accompanied her earlier decision.* 这次没有像以往要她作出决定时的苦恼和内疚。

ag·o·nized also 又作 **-ised** *BrE*【英】/ˋægə͵naɪzd; ˈægənaɪzd/ *adj* expressing very severe pain 痛苦的: *the agonized moans of wounded soldiers* 受伤士兵痛苦的呻吟声

ag·o·niz·ing also 又作 **-ising** *BrE*【英】/ˋægə͵naɪzɪŋ; ˈægənaɪzɪŋ/ *adj* extremely painful or difficult 令人痛苦的, 折磨人的: *agonizing pain* 难忍的疼痛 —**agonizingly** *adv*

ag·o·ny /ˋægənɪ; ˈægəni/ *n* [C,U] **1** very severe pain 极大的痛苦: *the agony of arthritis* 关节炎的剧烈疼痛 | **be in agony** *The poor guy was in agony.* 那可怜的家伙十分痛苦。| **be agony** *spoken*【口】*It was agony having my wisdom teeth out.* 拔掉智齿令我很痛。**2** a very sad, difficult, or unpleasant situation 痛楚, 苦难: *It was agony not knowing if she would live.* 不知道她能不能活下来, 令人感到揪心。—see also 另见 **pile on the agony** (PILE[2]), **prolong the agony** (PROLONG (2))

agony aunt /ˈ··· ˌ·/ *n* [C] *BrE* someone who writes an agony column【英】知心阿姨〔"为您解忧专栏"女撰稿人〕

agony col·umn /ˈ··· ˌ··/ *n* [C] *BrE* a part of a newspaper or magazine in which someone gives advice to readers about their personal problems【英】〔报刊上〕"为您解忧专栏"; ADVICE COLUMN *AmE*【美】

ag·o·ra·pho·bi·a /͵ægərəˋfobɪə; ˌægərəˈfəʊbiə/ *n* [U] *technical* the fear of crowds and open spaces【术语】旷野[广场]恐怖(症) —compare 比较 CLAUSTROPHOBIA

ag·o·ra·pho·bic /͵ægərəˋfobɪk; ˌægərəˈfəʊbɪk◂/ *n* [C] someone who suffers from agoraphobia 旷野[广场]恐怖症患者 —**agoraphobic** *adj*

a·grar·i·an /əˋgrɛrɪən; əˈgreəriən/ *adj* concerning farming or farmers 土地的; 农业的: *an agrarian revolution in 17th century England* 英格兰17世纪的土地革命 | *a split between industrial and agrarian interests* 工业和农业利益的分歧

a·gree /əˋgri; əˈgriː/ *v* 1 1

1 ▶SAME OPINION 同样看法◀ [I,T not in progressive 不用进行时] to have the same opinion about something as someone else 同意, 意见一致: **[+with]** *Mr Larsen seems to think it's too risky and I agree with him.* 拉森先生似乎认为太危险, 我同意他的看法。| **agree** *Teenagers and their parents rarely agree.* 十几岁的孩子跟父母意见很少一致。| **[+that]** *Most scientists agree that global warming is a serious problem.* 大多数科学家都认为全球气候变暖是个严重的问题。| **[+on/about]** *They belong to the same party, but they don't agree on everything.* 他们属于同一个党派, 但并不是在所有事情上都意见一致。| **I quite agree** *BrE spoken* (=I agree completely)【英口】我很同意 *"It's ridiculous." "Yes, I quite agree."* "这很荒谬。""一点没错。" | **I couldn't agree more** *spoken* (=I agree completely)【口】我完全同意 —opposite 反义词 DISAGREE (1) —see 见 REFUSE[1]

2 ▶DECIDE TOGETHER 共同决定◀ [I,T not in progressive 不用进行时] to make a decision with someone after a discussion with them 达成一致; 商定: **agree to do sth** *We agreed to meet up later and talk things over.* 我们同意稍后见面商量一些事情。| **agree that** *It was agreed that Mr. Rollins would sign the contract May 1st.* 约定了罗林斯先生于5月1日在合同上签字。| **[+on]** *They managed to agree on a date for the wedding.* 他们总算商定了婚期。| **[+to]** *We voted to agree to the latest pay offer.* 我们投票赞同最后提出的工资方案。| **agree a price/plan/strategy etc** *We agreed a price and the car was mine.* 我们商定了价格, 车就归我了。| *I think the committee will agree the changes soon.* 我认为委员会将很快就这些改动达成一致意见。

3 ▶SAY YES 给予肯定答复◀ [I,T not in progressive 不用进行时] to say yes to an idea, plan, suggestion etc 赞成, 赞同; 答应: *I suggested we go somewhere for the weekend and she agreed at once.* 我提议我们去某个地方度周末, 她立即表示赞同。| **agree to do sth** *Why don't we agree right now to use recycled paper?* 为什么我们不马上赞同使用再生纸呢?

4 ▶BE THE SAME 同样◀ [I not in progressive 不用进行时] if two pieces of information agree with each other, they are the same 与…一致, 与…符合: **[+with]** *Your story doesn't agree with what the police have told us.* 你的叙述和警察告诉我们的不一样。

5 agree to differ to accept that you do not have the same opinions as someone else and agree not to argue about it 同意各自保留不同意见

agree with *phr v* [T not in passive 不用被动态] **1** to believe that a decision, action, or suggestion is correct or right 赞成, 同意: *I don't agree with any form of terrorism.* 我不赞成任何形式的恐怖主义。**2 not agree with you** if a type of food does not agree with you, it makes you feel ill〔某种食物〕不对胃口, 反胃 **3** if an adjective, verb etc agrees with a word, it matches that word by being plural if the subject is plural etc〔语法上〕呼应, 与…一致

This graph shows how common different grammar patterns of the verb **agree** are in spoken and written English. 本图表所示为动词agree构成的不同语法模式在英语口语和书面语中的使用频率。

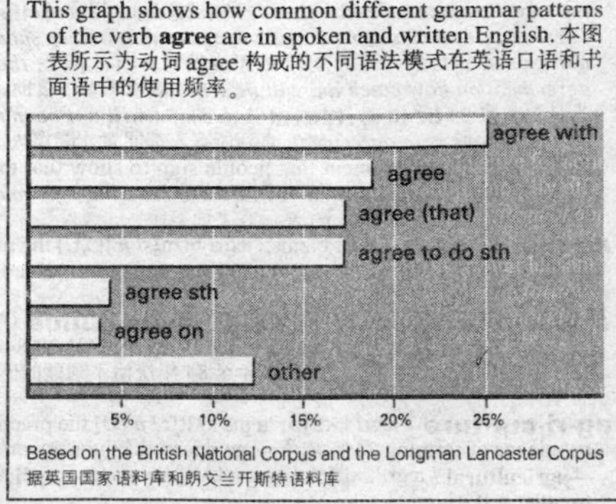

Based on the British National Corpus and the Longman Lancaster Corpus
据英国国家语料库和朗文兰开斯特语料库

A

USAGE NOTE 用法说明: AGREE
GRAMMAR 语法

If you have the same opinion as someone else you **agree with** them. You can also **agree with** (=approve of) their attitude, ideas, plans, rules etc, or an activity or principle that you approve of. 如果表示和某人的观点一致, 用 agree with。agree with 也可以表示同意某人的态度、看法、计划、规则等, 或是赞成一项活动或原则: *Do you agree with corporal punishment?* 你赞成体罚吗?

You **agree** with people **about** or **on** other matters. 在某事上同意某人用 agree about 或 on: *I agree (with you) about Mark/on astrology/about this issue* (NOT 不用 *I agree this issue*). 我同意你关于马克/占星术/这个问题的看法。

If you and others decide on or arrange to do something after discussing it, you **agree on** it. 经过讨论然后达成一致去做某事用 agree on: *We finally agreed on a plan/a date/a solution/a deal.* 最后, 我们就某计划/日期/解决办法/贸易协议达成了一致。More formally you could also say 较正式时也可以说: *We agreed a plan/a date/a solution/a deal.*

If you accept something, especially something that was not your idea and perhaps you do not like, you **agree to** it 接受了别人的看法, 但或许你并不乐意时说 agree to: *She agreed to the plan/the date/the solution/the deal* (NOT 不用 *She agreed the plan etc*). 她接受了这个计划/日期/解决办法/贸易协议。You can also **agree to do** something 你也可以用 agree to do 来表示同意做某事: *They agreed to wait* (NOT 不用 *They accepted to wait*). 他们同意等待。

a·gree·a·ble /ə`griəbl; əˈgriːəbəl/ *adj* **1** pleasant or acceptable 宜人的; 可以接受的: *an agreeable spot for a picnic* 宜人的野餐地点 **2** someone who is agreeable is very nice and is liked by other people〔人〕令人愉快的, 受人喜欢的: *an agreeable young man* 叫人喜欢的年轻人 **3 be agreeable to sth** *formal* to be willing to do something or willing to allow something to be done【正式】欣然同意某事: *Are you sure Branson's agreeable to the idea?* 你肯定布兰森同意这个想法吗?

a·gree·a·bly /ə`griəblı; əˈgriːəbli/ *adv* intended to be pleasant or nice 愉快地: *He smiled agreeably.* 他愉快地笑了。

a·greed /ə`grid; əˈgriːd/ *adj* [only before noun 仅用于名词前] **1** an agreed plan, price, arrangement etc is one that people have discussed and accepted 通过的, 一致同意的: *Reform had not yet been achieved, but it remained the party's agreed priority.* 改革尚未完成, 但它仍是这个党一致同意的首要任务。**2 be agreed** if people are agreed, they have discussed something and agree about what to do 达成一致: **[+on]** *All parties are now agreed on the plan.* 所有党派现在都一致同意这个计划。

S1 W1 **a·gree·ment** /ə`grimənt; əˈgriːmənt/ *n* **1** [C] an arrangement or promise to do something, made by two or more companies, governments, organizations etc 协议, 协定, 合约: *a trade agreement* 贸易协定 | **[+on]** *an agreement on arms reduction* 削减武器协议 | **reach an agreement** *What happens if the warring parties fail to reach an agreement?* 交战双方如果没有达成协议, 将会发生什么事情? | **under an agreement** *Under the agreement, most agricultural prices would be frozen or cut.* 根据协议, 大部分农产品的价格会被冻结或降低。| **have an agreement that** *We had an agreement that Ms Holst would keep me informed of any changes.* 我们有个协议, 如果有任何变化, 霍尔斯特女士都会通知我。**2** [U] a situation in which people have the same opinion as each other 一致(的意见), 相合: **[+that]** *There is agreement among doctors that pregnant women should not smoke.* 医生们一致认为, 孕妇不应吸烟。| **[+on]** *Is there agreement on how much aid will be sent?* 应给予多少援助, 意见是否一致? | **be in agreement** *A decision will not be made until everyone is in agreement.* 直到所有人都同意才能作决定。**3** [C] an official document that people sign to show that they have agreed to something 协议书: *Please read the agreement and sign it.* 请看一下协议书, 然后在上面签字。

ag·ri·busi·ness /`ægrı,bıznıs; ˈægrı,bıznɪs/ *n* [C,U] the production and sale of farm products, or a company involved in this 农业综合经营(公司)

A·gric·o·la /ə`grıkələ; əˈgrıkələ/, **Gnaeus Julius** (AD 37-93) a Roman GENERAL who governed Britain in AD 78-84 阿格里科拉〔(公元 37-93), 公元 78 年至 84 年统治不列颠的罗马将军〕

W2 **ag·ri·cul·ture** /`ægrı,kʌltʃə; ˈægrı,kʌltʃə/ *n* [U] the practice or science of farming 农业; 农学 —compare 比较 HORTICULTURE —**agricultural** /,ægrı`kʌltʃərəl; ,ægrıˈkʌltʃərəl◂/ *adj* —**agriculturalist** *n* [C]

agro- /ægro; ægrəʊ/ *prefix* also 又作 **agri-** /ægrı; ægrı/ concerning farming 农业(的), 与农业有关的: *agrobiology* 农业生物学 | *agribusiness* 农业综合经营

a·ground /ə`graund; əˈgraʊnd/ *adv* **run/go aground** if a ship runs aground, it becomes stuck in a place where the water is not deep enough〔船〕搁浅

a·gue /`egju; ˈeɪgjuː/ *n* [C,U] *old-fashioned* a fever that makes you shake and feel cold【过时】〔疟疾的〕疟状发热, 寒颤

ah /ɑ; ɑː/ *interjection* used to show your surprise, anger, pain, happiness, agreement etc 啊〔表示惊奇、愤怒、痛苦、喜悦、同意等〕: *Ah! There you are!* 啊! 你在这里呀!

a·ha /ɑ`hɑ; ɑːˈhɑː/ *interjection* used to show that you understand or realize something 啊〔表示明白、意识到某事〕: *Aha! So you planned all this, did you?* 啊! 原来这一切都是你事先计划好的, 对吧? —see also 另见 HA[1]

A·hab /`ehæb; ˈeɪhæb/, **Captain** a character in the book *Moby Dick* by Herman Melville. Captain Ahab risks his life and the lives of everyone on his ship by hunting a large dangerous white WHALE called Moby Dick. Ahab is determined to kill the whale, but it finally sinks his ship, killing him and most of his men. 亚哈船长〔赫尔曼·梅尔维尔的小说《白鲸》中的人物。亚哈船长冒着他本人和船上其他人的生命危险去捕捉一条名为莫比·迪克的大白鲸。他决心要杀死白鲸, 但最终却让白鲸把船给撞沉了, 他和大部分船员因此丧生〕

a·head /ə`hɛd; əˈhed/ *adv* 

1 ▶IN FRONT OF 在前面◀ in front of someone or something by a short distance 在前面: *He kept his gaze fixed on the car ahead.* 他一直注视着前面的那辆汽车。| **[+of]** *Tim pointed to a tree ahead of them.* 蒂姆指着他们前面的一棵树。| **up ahead** *We could see the lights of Las Vegas up ahead.* 我们能看见正前方拉斯韦加斯的灯光。

2 ▶FORWARD 向前◀ if someone or something moves, looks ahead etc, they move or look towards a place in front of them 向前: *The ship forged ahead through the thin ice.* 那艘船冲破薄冰全速前进。| **straight ahead** *He's just staring straight ahead in a complete daze.* 他直视前方, 神情一片茫然。

3 ▶BEFORE SB ELSE 在其他人之前◀ arriving, waiting, finishing etc before other people (比…) 更早; (比…) 更靠前: **[+of]** *There were four people ahead of me at the doctor's.* 在诊所里, 有四个人排在我前面。

4 ▶BEFORE AN EVENT 在某事件之前◀ *AmE* before an event happens【美】事前: *You can prepare these salads ahead.* 你可以提前准备这些沙拉。| **ahead of time** *Can you tell me ahead of time if you're coming?* 如果你要来, 能不能事先告诉我?

5 ▶FUTURE 未来◀ in the future 将来, 今后: *Rest now because you have a long journey ahead of you.* 现在休息一下, 因为你接下来还有很长的一段旅程。| **lie ahead** *We should try to predict the type of problems that may lie ahead.* 我们应设法预测一下摆在我们面前的会是何种问题。| **the years/days/months etc ahead** *The decisions you make in the days ahead are going to affect your whole future.* 今后几天你所作的决定会影响你的整个未来。| **plan ahead** (=plan for the future) 提前计划妥当

6 ahead of time/schedule etc earlier than planned or arranged 提前: *We might finish the project ahead of schedule.* 我们也许会比原计划提前完成这个项目。

7 ▶WINNING 获胜◀ winning in a competition or election〔在比赛或选举中〕领先: *Milligan's three-pointer puts them ahead by one.* 米利根的三分球使他们领先一分。

8 go ahead *spoken* used to tell someone they can do something【口】进行吧, 干吧: *"Can I have the sports section?" "Yeah, go ahead, I've read it."* "我可以看看体育版吗?" "当然, 拿去吧, 我已经读过了。"

9 ▶ADVANCED 先进的◀ ideas, achievements etc that are ahead of others, have made more progress or are more developed 先进的; 超越别人的; 胜过: *VEMCO was years ahead of us in their research.* VEMCO 公司在研究方面超前了我们好多年。| **be ahead of its time** (=so new that people do not understand or like it) 走在时代之前 *Her educational theories were way ahead of their time.* 她的教育理论远远超过在他们所处的时代, 是非常超前的。

10 get ahead to make progress and be successful in your job, education etc 取得进步, 获得成功: *Getting ahead at work is the most important thing to her at the moment.* 目前, 对她来说在工作上获得成功是最重要的。

11 go ahead (with sth) to start doing something 着手做, 开始做: *Frank'll be late but we'll go ahead with the meeting anyway.* 弗兰克会晚些时候到, 不过, 我们还是先开会。—see also 另见 GO-AHEAD

12 get/keep ahead (of the game) *AmE informal* to get into or be in a position where you are in control of something, so that it is easier to deal with【美, 非正式】成功; 领先, 超越: *I find it hard to keep ahead of the housework.* 我发觉要做好家务也不容易。

a·hem /m'hm; m'hm; *spelling pronunciation* 根据拼写的读音 ə'hɛm; ə'hem/ *interjection* a sound you make to attract someone's attention when you want to speak to them, warn them etc 啊哼〔用于引起注意、发出警告等〕

-aholic /ə'hɔlɪk; ə'hɒlɪk/ *suffix* [in nouns and adjectives 构成名词和形容词] *informal* someone who cannot stop doing something or using something【非正式】对…痴迷的(人), 沉湎于…的(人): *a workaholic* (=who loves working and cannot stop) 工作狂 | *a chocaholic* (=who loves chocolate) 嗜好巧克力的人

a·hoy /ə'hɔɪ; ə'hɔɪ/ *interjection* used by SAILORS to get someone's attention or greet them 啊嗨〔船员打招呼的喊声〕: **ship ahoy!** (=used to say that a ship is approaching) 啊嗨, 有船!

AI /ˌe 'aɪ; ˌeɪ 'aɪ/ *n* [U] the abbreviation of 缩写= ARTIFICIAL INTELLIGENCE

AID /ˌe aɪ 'di; ˌeɪ aɪ 'diː/ the written abbreviation of 缩写= AGENCY FOR INTERNATIONAL DEVELOPMENT

aid¹ /ed; eɪd/ *n* **1** [U] help, such as money or food, given by an organization to a country or to people who are in a difficult situation 援助, 救助: *Aid is not getting through to the refugees.* 救济品送不到难民手中。| **in aid of** (=in order to help) 用来帮助 *We're collecting money in aid of cancer research.* 我们正筹集资金以资助癌症研究。| **legal aid** (=free legal services) 法律援助 **2** help or advice given to someone who needs it 帮助: **come/go to sb's aid** (=help someone) 帮助某人 *I didn't speak any French, but a nice man came to my aid and told me where to go.* 我不会说法语, 不过一个好心人帮了我的忙, 告诉我怎么走。**3** [C] something such as a machine or tool that helps someone do something 辅助性工具: *A video is a useful aid in the classroom.* 录像在课堂教学中是有用的辅助教具。| **with the aid of** *He was able to prove the existence of the supergun with the aid of a photograph.* 借助于一张照片, 他能证明"超级大炮"的存在。**4 what's this in aid of?** *BrE spoken* used to ask what something is used for or why someone is doing something【英口】这有什么用途? 这样做是什么用意?: *What's this meeting tomorrow in aid of, then?* 那么, 明天的这个会有什么意义? **5** an American spelling of AIDE aide 的美式拼法 —see also 另见 FIRST AID

aid² *v* [T] *formal*【正式】**1** to help someone or something by making their situation or what they are doing easier 帮助, 援助: *an index to aid the reader* 帮助读者的索引 | **aid sb in/with sth** *The local community aided us in our investigation.* 当地社区协助我们调查。—see 见 HELP¹ (USAGE) **2 aid and abet** *law* to help someone do something illegal【法律】协助和教唆, 伙同…作案, 与…同谋

aide also 又作 **aid** *AmE*【美】/ed; eɪd/ *n* [C] someone whose job is to help someone in an important job, especially a politician〔尤指政治家的〕助手, 助理

aide-de-camp /ˌed də 'kæmp; ˌeɪd də 'kɑːmp/ *n plural* **aides-de-camp** (same pronunciation 读音相同) [C] a military officer who helps an officer of a higher rank to do his duties 副官, 随从武官

AIDS /edz; eɪdz/ *n* [U] Acquired Immune Deficiency Syndrome; a very serious disease caused by a VIRUS (1) that stops your body from defending itself against infections 艾滋病, 获得性免疫缺陷综合征

CULTURAL NOTE 文化注释

People who are **HIV positive** have been infected with the VIRUS that causes AIDS, but they do not have **full-blown AIDS** (=they have not developed the disease), and sometimes people are HIV positive for many years without being seriously ill. Because there is still no cure for AIDS, health organizations try to prevent the disease from spreading by advising people about SAFE SEX (=ways of having sex that reduce the risk of getting HIV, especially by using a CONDOM). There are also special organizations that give support and help to people who already have HIV or AIDS. Drugs have helped HIV PATIENTS in Western countries to live longer, but they are not widely available in some poorer countries, for example in Africa. HIV呈阳性的人虽然已感染艾滋病病毒, 但还没有发展成艾滋病。有时, HIV呈阳性的人很多年也不会病情严重恶化。因艾滋病仍无药可医, 卫生组织试图建议人们采取安全的性行为(如使用安全套), 来遏制艾滋病的传播。还有一些专门组织为艾滋病病毒携带者或艾滋病患者提供支持和帮助。西方国家的艾滋病患者借助药物延长寿命, 但在一些较为贫穷的国家, 如非洲各国, 此类药物仍不普及。— see also 另见 TERRENCE HIGGINS TRUST

aid work·er /'· ˌ··/ *n* [C] someone working for an international organization who brings food and other supplies to people in danger from war, famine etc 援助人员, 救援人员: *UN aid workers in former Yugoslavia* 在前南斯拉夫的联合国救援人员

ail /el; eɪl/ *v* **1** [T] *formal* to cause difficulties for someone or something【正式】使痛苦; 使苦恼 **2** [I,T] *old-fashioned* to be ill, or to make someone feel ill or unhappy【过时】(使) 得病; (使) 难受[痛苦]

ai·ling /'elɪŋ; 'eɪlɪŋ/ *adj* **1** an ailing company or ECONOMY¹ (1) is having a lot of problems and is not successful 不景气的, 状况不佳的: *Vice-Chairman John Smith, who transformed GM's ailing European operations in the 80s* 扭转了80年代通用汽车公司在欧洲不景气局面的副主席约翰·史密斯 **2** *formal* ill【正式】生病的: *aged or ailing parents* 年老或有病的父母

ail·ment /'elmənt; 'eɪlmənt/ *n* [C] an illness that is not very serious 疾病, 小病

aim¹ /em; eɪm/ *n* **1** [C] what you are hoping to achieve by a plan, action, or activity 目标, 目的, 意图: **[+of]** *The main aim of the course is to improve students' communication skills.* 这门课程的主要目的是提高学生的沟通技巧。| **with the aim of doing sth** *Research is being done with the specific aim of monitoring customer trends.* 做这个研究的特定目的是了解客户的动向。**2 take aim** to point a gun or weapon at someone or something you want to shoot 瞄准: **[+at]** *Alan took aim at the tiger.* 艾伦瞄准了老虎。**3 sb's aim** someone's ability to hit what they are aiming at when they throw or shoot something 某人击中目标的能力: *Val's aim was very good.* 瓦尔瞄得很准。

aim² *v* **1** [I,T] to choose the place, person etc that you want to hit and carefully point your gun, object etc towards them 瞄准, 对准: *Denver aimed his gun but did not shoot.* 丹佛用枪瞄准了目标, 但没有开枪。| **[+at/for]** *The pitcher aimed at the upper half of the strike zone.* 投手把目标对准击球区的上半区。**2** [I] to try or intend to achieve something 致力于, 打算: **[+at/for]** *It's important that you should have some sort of a goal to aim for.* 有一个为之奋斗的目标是很重要的。| **aim to do sth** *I'm aiming to lose 4kg before the summer holidays.* 我的目标是暑假前减掉4公斤体重。**3 aim sth at sb** to make something in such a way that a particular person or group of people will like it 使某物针对某人: *The program is aimed at a teenage audience.* 这个节目的对象是十几岁的观众。

aim·less /'emlɪs; 'eɪmləs/ *adj* without a clear purpose or reason 无目的[目标]的: *drifting through life in a rather aimless fashion* 过着毫无目标的漂泊生活 —**aimlessly** *adv* —**aimlessness** *n* [U]

ain't /ent; eɪnt/ *spoken* a short form of 'am not', 'is not', 'are not', 'has not', or 'have not', that many people think is incorrect【口】不〔一种不规范的否定缩写形式〕

air¹ /ɛr; eə/ *n*

1 ►GAS 气体◄ [U] the mixture of gases that we breathe and that surrounds the Earth 空气: *air pollution* 空气污染 | *There was a strong smell of burning in the air.* 空气中有一股浓烈的焚烧东西的味道。| **fresh air** (=clean air) 新鲜空气 *Let's go out and get some fresh air.* 让我们出去呼吸些新鲜空气。—see also 另见 **a breath of fresh air** (BREATH (2))

2 ►SPACE ABOVE/BELOW 上/下方的空间◄ the space above the ground or around things 空中, 天空: **through/into etc the air** *He fell 2000 metres through the air without a parachute.* 他在没有开伞的情况下在空中下降了2000米。

3 ►PLANES/FLYING 飞机/飞行◄ a) by air travelling by or using a plane 乘飞机: *It's actually less expensive to go by air to San Francisco.* 乘飞机去圣弗朗西斯科实际上更省钱。**b) air travel/crash/industry etc** involving or connected with planes and flying 乘飞机旅行/飞机失事/航空业等: *the victims of Britain's worst air disaster* 英国最严重空难的死难者

4 ►APPEARANCE 外表◄ if something or someone has an air of confidence, mystery etc, they seem confident, mysterious etc 神态; 样子; 风度; 气氛: *She set about her task with an air of quiet confidence.* 她带着悠然自信的风度开始了自己的工作。

5 it's up in the air *spoken* used to say that something has not been decided yet【口】悬着的, 未定的

6 be on/off (the) air to be broadcasting on the radio or television at the present moment, or to stop broadcasting 正在广播/

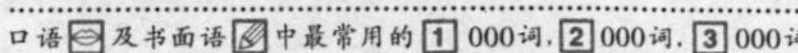

aircraft 飞机

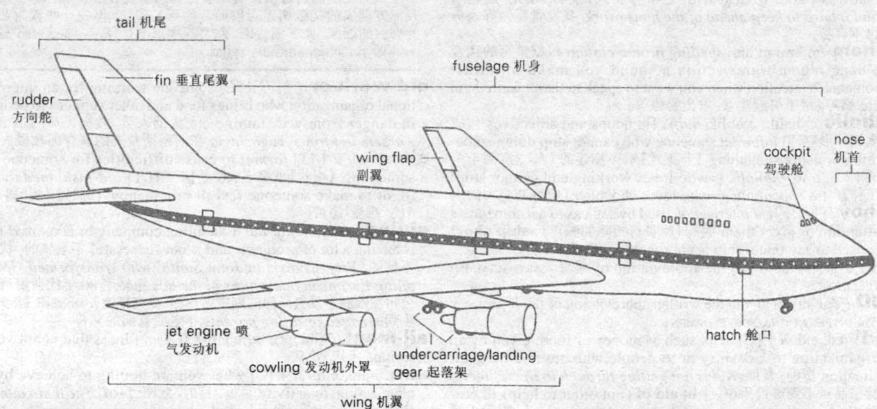

停止广播: *We'll be on air in about 3 minutes.* 大约三分钟后我们开始广播。

7 airs [plural] a way of behaving in which someone tries to make themselves seem more important than they are 装腔作势, 摆架子: **put on airs/give yourself airs** *Trudy is always putting on airs and pretending she's posh.* 特鲁迪总是摆架子, 装高贵。| **airs and graces** *Tristan, with his fancy education and his airs and graces* 摆出受过昂贵的教育、装腔作势的特里斯坦

8 in the air if a particular emotion is in the air, a lot of people seem to feel it at the same time 流传开的: *a sense of excitement in the air* 到处充满了兴奋的气氛

9 ►MUSIC 音乐◄ [C] a name given to a piece of music that means 'tune' 曲调, 旋律 —see also 另见 **hot air** (HOT[1] (29)), ON-AIR, **clear the air** (CLEAR[2] (13)), **disappear/vanish into thin air** (THIN[1] (15)), **walk on air** (WALK[1] (13))

air² *v*

1 ►CLOTHES 衣服◄ [I,T] also 又作 **air sth ↔ out** *AmE*【美】to put a piece of clothing in a place that is warm or has a lot of air, so that it smells clean (把…)晾干: *I've left my sweater on the washing-line to air.* 我已把毛线衫晾在衣绳上。

2 ►ROOM 房间◄ [I,T] also 又作 **air sth ↔ out** *AmE*【美】to let fresh air into a room, especially one that has been closed for a long time (使…)通风

3 ►TV/RADIO 电视/无线电◄ [T] to broadcast a programme on television or radio 广播, 播放

4 air your views/opinions etc to say publicly what you think about something important 发表观点/看法等

5 air your grievances to tell other people about things that you think are unfair 发牢骚, 诉苦 —see also 另见 AIRING

air·bag /ˈɛrˌbæg; ˈeəbæg/ *n* [C] a bag in a car that fills with air to protect the driver or passenger in an accident〔汽车的〕安全气囊

air·base /ˈɛrˌbes; ˈeəbeɪs/ *n* [C] a place where military aircraft begin and end their flights 空军基地

air·bed /ˈɛrˌbɛd; ˈeəbed/ *n* [C] a long rubber or plastic bag that you fill with air and lie on 充气床垫 —see picture at 参见 BED[1] 图

air·borne /ˈɛrˌbɔrn; ˈeəbɔːn/ *adj* **1** a plane that is airborne is in the air 在空中的, 在飞行中的 **2** airborne soldiers are trained to fight in areas that they get to by jumping out of a plane〔士兵〕空降作战的

Air·bus /ˈɛrbʌs; ˈeəbʌs/ *trademark* a group of European companies that builds aircraft which carry a large number of passengers. The aircraft they build are also called Airbus.【商标】空中客车〔一家制造大型客机的欧洲集团公司, 生产的飞机也叫空中客车〕

air chief mar·shal /ˌ· ˈ· ˈ··/ *n* [C] a high rank in the British air force, or someone who has this rank〔英国的〕空军上将 —see table on page C7 参见 C7 页附录

air com·mo·dore /ˌ· ˈ···/ *n* [C] a high rank in the British air force, or someone who has this rank〔英国的〕空军准将 —see table on page C7 参见 C7 页附录

air con·di·tion·ing /ˈ· ·,···/ *n* [C,U] a system that makes the air in buildings, rooms etc colder, or the machine that does this 空(气)调(节)系统 —**air-conditioned** *adj*: *Our offices are fully air-conditioned.* 我们的办公室都装有空调。—**air conditioner** *n* [C]

air·craft /ˈɛrˌkræft; ˈeəkrɑːft/ *n plural* **aircraft** [C] a plane or other vehicle that can fly 飞机; 飞行器, 航空器 —see also 另见 LIGHT AIRCRAFT

aircraft car·ri·er /ˈ·· ,···/ *n* [C] a type of ship that has a large flat surface that planes fly from 航空母舰

air·craft·man /ˈɛrˌkræftmən; ˈeəkrɑːftmən/ *n* [C] a low rank in the British air force, or someone who has this rank〔英国〕空军士兵 —see table on page C7 参见 C7 页附录

air·crew /ˈɛrˌkru; ˈeəkruː/ *n* [C] the pilot and the people who are responsible for flying a plane and looking after the passengers 机组(全体人员), 空勤人员

air·fare /ˈɛrˌfɛr; ˈeəfeə/ *n* [C] the price of a journey by plane 飞机票价

air·field /ˈɛrˌfild; ˈeəfiːld/ *n* [C] a place where planes can fly from, especially one used by military planes〔尤指军用的〕机场

air force /ˈ· ·/ *n* [C] the military organization of a country that uses planes to fight 空军 —compare 比较 ARMY, NAVY

Air Force One /ˌ· · ˈ·/ the name of the plane that the US President uses 空军一号〔美国总统的专用座机〕

air fresh·en·er /ˈ· ,···/ *n* [C,U] a substance used to make the air in a room smell pleasant 空气清新剂

air·gun /ˈɛrˌgʌn; ˈeəgʌn/ *n* [C] *BrE* a gun that uses air pressure to fire a small round bullet【英】气枪; BB GUN *AmE*【美】

air·head /ˈɛrˌhɛd; ˈeəhed/ *n* [C] *slang especially AmE* someone who is stupid【俚, 尤美】傻瓜, 笨蛋

air host·ess /ˈ· ,··/ *n* [C] *BrE* a woman who serves food and drink to passengers on a plane【英】空中小姐, 飞机女服务员

air·i·ly /ˈɛrəlɪ; ˈeərɪ̈li/ *adv* without being serious or concerned 轻松地; 轻率地; 轻浮地: *"I don't really care," he replied airily.* "我不太在意。"他漫不经心地回答。

air·ing /ˈɛrɪŋ; ˈeərɪŋ/ *n* [singular] an occasion when an opinion, idea etc is discussed 公开发表: **give/get an airing** *The question will get a thorough airing at the next meeting.* 这个问题在下次会议上要彻底地公开讨论一下。

airing cup·board /ˈ·· ,··/ *n* [C] *BrE* a warm cupboard in a house where sheets and clean clothes are kept【英】〔烘被单、衣服的〕烘柜

air·lane /ˈɛrˌlen; ˈeəleɪn/ *n* [C] a path through the air that is regularly used by planes 空中航线[航道]

air·less /ˈɛrlɪs; ˈeələs/ *adj* not having enough air or having air that does not move, so that it seems difficult to breathe 空气不足的; 空气不流通的: *The evening was muggy and airless.* 那天晚上天气闷热, 空气不流通。

air·let·ter /ˈɛrˌlɛtɚ; ˈeəˌletə/ *n* [C] *BrE* a very light letter that you can send by AIRMAIL; AEROGRAMME【英】航空信, 航空邮笺

air·lift /ˈɛr,lɪft; ˈeə,lɪft/ *n* [C] an act of taking people or things to an area by plane, when it is difficult or dangerous to use roads〔人员或物资的〕大规模空运；空中补给：*airlifts of food supplies to famine areas* 给闹饥荒地区空运食品 —**airlift** *v* [T]

2 3 **air·line** /ˈɛr,laɪn; ˈeəlaɪn/ *n* [C] a business that runs a regular service to take passengers and goods to different places by plane 航空公司

air·lin·er /ˈɛr,laɪnɚ; ˈeə,laɪnə/ *n* [C] *old-fashioned* a large passenger plane【过时】大型客机，班机

air lock /ˈ· ·/ *n* [C] **1** a small room used for moving between two places that do not have the same air pressure, such as in a space vehicle or a vehicle under water 气压闸舱，密封舱 **2** a BUBBLE[1] (1) in a pipe that stops liquid flowing through it 气泡，气塞，气栓

air·mail /ˈɛr,mel; ˈeəmeɪl/ *n* [U] letters etc that are sent somewhere using a plane, or the system of doing this 航空邮件：*Send the letter by airmail.* 这封信用航空邮寄。

air·man /ˈɛrmən; ˈeəmən/ *n* [C] *plural* **airmen** /-mən; -mən/ a low rank in the US Air Force, or someone who has this rank〔美国〕空军士兵 —see table on page C7 参见 C7 页附录

air·plane /ˈɛr,plen; ˈeəpleɪn/ *n* [C] *especially AmE* a flying vehicle that has one or more engines【尤美】飞机；AEROPLANE *BrE*【英】—see picture at 参见 AIRCRAFT 图

air·pock·et /ˈɛr,pɑkɪt; ˈeə,pɒkɨt/ *n* [C] a current of air that moves downwards and that makes a plane suddenly drop down〔会使飞机突然下降的〕气穴，气阱

2 3 **air·port** /ˈɛr,pɔrt; ˈeəpɔːt/ *n* [C] a place where planes begin and stop flying, that has buildings for passengers to wait in 航空站 [港]，机场

air pump /ˈ· ·/ *n* [C] a piece of equipment used to blow air into something 气泵

air raid /ˈ· ·/ *n* [C] an attack in which a lot of bombs are dropped on a place by planes 空袭

air ri·fle /ˈ· ,· ·/ *n* [C] a type of AIRGUN 气步枪

air·ship /ˈɛr,ʃɪp; ˈeə,ʃɪp/ *n* [C] a large aircraft that has no wings, is filled with gas to make it float, and has an engine 飞船，飞艇

air·sick /ˈɛr,sɪk; ˈeə,sɪk/ *adj* feeling sick because of the movement of a plane 晕机的 —**airsickness** *n* [U]

air·space /ˈɛr,spes; ˈeəspeɪs/ *n* [U] the sky above a particular country, that is thought of as being controlled by that country〔某个国家的〕领空：*The planes had entered Israeli airspace without permission.* 飞机未经允许进入了以色列领空。

air·speed /ˈɛr,spid; ˈeəspiːd/ *n* [singular,U] the speed at which a plane travels 飞行速度，空速

Air·stream /ˈɛr,strim; ˈeə,striːm/ *trademark* a type of silver-coloured TRAILER (=a vehicle which contains beds, a kitchen etc and which is pulled by a car), similar to a bullet in shape. They were first made in the US in the 1930s and continue to be popular and fashionable.【商标】清风房车〔一种银灰色的拖车式活动房，形似子弹。20 世纪 30 年代开始在美国生产，一直流行至今〕

air strike /ˈ· ·/ *n* [C] an attack in which a military aircraft drops bombs or shoots guns at a place 空(中)袭(击)

air·strip /ˈɛr,strɪp; ˈeə,strɪp/ *n* [C] a long narrow piece of land that has been cleared so that planes can fly from it 临时(飞机)跑道，简易机场

air terminal /ˈ· ,· · ·/ *n* [C] **1** a place in a city from where passengers catch buses to the AIRPORT 航空集散站〔旅客乘车往返机场的市内集散处〕 **2** a large building at an AIRPORT where passengers wait to get on planes〔旅客候机的〕航站楼，机场大厦，候机大楼

air·tight /ˈɛrˈtaɪt; ˈeətaɪt/ *adj* not allowing air to get in or out 气封的，密封的：*airtight containers* 密封容器

air time /ˈ· ·/ *n* [U] the amount of time or the number of times that a radio or television station allows a particular song, advertisement etc to be broadcast 播放时段，广播时间：*smaller political parties trying to buy more air time* 设法买到更多广播时间的小政党

air-to-air /,· · ˈ·◂/ *adj* **air-to-air missile** a weapon that one plane shoots at another plane as they are flying 空对空导弹

air traf·fic con·trol·ler /,· ˈ· · · ,· ·/ *n* [C] someone at an airport who gives instructions to pilots by radio 空中交通指挥员 [调度员] —**air traffic control** *n* [U]

air vice-mar·shal /,· ˈ· ·◂/ *n* [C] a high rank in the British Air Force, or someone who has this rank〔英国〕空军少将 —see table on page C7 参见 C7 页附录

air·waves /ˈɛr,wevz; ˈeəweɪvz/ *n* [plural] *old-fashioned*【过时】**the airwaves** radio broadcasts 无线电波；广播：**on the airwaves** (=on the radio) 在广播

air·way /ˈɛr,we; ˈeəweɪ/ *n* [C] **1** *technical* the passage in your throat that you breathe through【术语】〔喉咙的〕气道 **2** an area of the sky that is regularly used by planes 航线：*one of the world's busiest airways* 世界上最繁忙的航线之一

air·wor·thy /ˈɛr,wɝðɪ; ˈeə,wɜːði/ *adj* a plane that is airworthy is safe enough to fly〔飞机〕适于航行的 —**airworthiness** *n* [U]

air·y /ˈɛrɪ; ˈeəri/ *adj* **1** an airy room or building has plenty of fresh air because it is large or has lots of windows 通风的：*an airy first floor restaurant with sea views* 能看到海景、通风良好的一楼餐厅 **2** cheerful and confident, even when you should be serious or concerned about something 快活的，无忧无虑的；漫不经心的：*He dismissed her concerns with an airy wave of the hand.* 他漫不经心地挥一下手，并不理会她的担心。

airy fai·ry /,· · ˈ· ·◂/ *adj BrE* not very clear or practical; VAGUE【英】模糊的；空洞的，不切实际的：*airy fairy ideas* 不切实际的想法

aisle /aɪl; aɪl/ *n* [C] **1** a long passage between rows of seats, shelves, etc in a building or a plane 通道，过道 —see picture at 参见 THEATRE 图 **2** a narrow passage at the side of a church that is separated from the central part by a row of pillars (PILLAR (1))〔教堂两边以一排柱子同中殿隔开的〕侧廊，侧堂，耳堂 **3 go/walk down the aisle** *informal* to get married【非正式】步入教堂，结婚 —see also 另见 **be rolling in the aisles** (ROLL[1] (18))

aitch /etʃ; eɪtʃ/ *n* [C] **1** the letter 'h' written as a word 字母 h **2 drop your aitches** to fail to pronounce the letter 'h' at the beginning of a word 没发词首的 h 音

> **CULTURAL NOTE 文化注释**
>
> In Britain, some people think that people who drop their aitches are from a low social class and are uneducated. 一些英国人认为，不发词首 h 音的人社会地位低，没有受过教育。

a·jar /əˈdʒɑr; əˈdʒɑː/ *adj* [not before noun 不用于名词前] a door that is ajar is slightly open (门)半开着的 —see picture at 参见 OPEN[1] 图

AK /,e ˈk; ,eɪ ˈk/ the written abbreviation of 缩写= ALASKA

ak·a /ˈækə; ˈækə/ the abbreviation of 缩写= 'also known as', used when giving someone's real name together with a different name they are known by 又名，亦称：*John Phillips, aka The Mississippi Mauler* 约翰·菲力普斯，又名"密西西比铁拳"

A·ke·la /ɑˈkelə; ɑːˈkeɪlə/ an adult who leads a group of Cub Scouts in the UK〔英国的〕幼年童子军队长〔由成年人担任〕

a·kim·bo /əˈkɪmbo; əˈkɪmbəʊ/ *adj* **(with) arms akimbo** with your hands on your hips (HIP[1] (1)) so that your elbows point outwards 两手叉腰的：*He stood with arms akimbo, glaring at the intruders.* 他两手叉腰地站着，怒视着闯进来的人。—see picture at 参见 ARM 图

a·kin /əˈkɪn; əˈkɪn/ *adj* **akin to** very similar to something 与…相似的，类似的：*The language is closely akin to Arabic.* 这种语言和阿拉伯语非常相近。

Akron /ˈækrən; ˈækrən/ an industrial city in north east Ohio 阿克伦〔俄亥俄州东北部一工业城市〕

AL /,e ˈɛl; ,eɪ ˈel/ the written abbreviation of 缩写= ALABAMA

-al /əl; əl/ *suffix* also 又作 **-ial 1** [in nouns and adjectives 构成名词和形容词] of or concerning something …的，与…有关的：*coastal waters* (=near the coast) 近海水域 | *political* 政治的 **2** [in nouns 构成名词] the action of doing something …的动作：*her arrival* (=arriving) 她的到达 | *a refusal* 拒绝

à la /ˈɑ lə; ˈæ lə/ *prep* in the style of 按照…的方式，仿照…：*detective stories à la Agatha Christie* 仿照阿加莎·克里斯蒂风格写的侦探小说

Al·a·ba·ma /,æləˈbæmə; ,æləˈbæmə◂/ abbreviation 缩写为 **AL** a state in the southeast of the US, known as the place where the civil rights movement began 亚拉巴马州〔位于美国西南部，以民权运动的发源地而著称〕

al·a·bas·ter /ˈælə,bæstɚ; ˈæləbɑːstə/ *n* [U] a white stone, used for making STATUES or decorative objects 雪花石膏：*an alabaster vase* 雪花石膏(做的)花瓶

à la carte /,ɑ lə ˈkɑrt; ,æ lə ˈkɑːt/ *adj, adv* if food in a restaurant is à la carte, each dish has a separate price 照菜单点菜的 [地]：*an à la carte menu* 点菜单

a·lack /əˈlæk; əˈlæk/ *interjection old use* used to express sorrow【旧】呜呼〔表示哀伤〕

a·lac·ri·ty /əˈlækrətɪ; əˈlækrɨti/ *n* [U] quickness and eagerness 敏捷；欣然：*They accepted our offer with alacrity.* 他们欣然接受了我们的建议。

Aladdin 阿拉丁

A·lad·din /ə`lædın; ə'lædın/ a young male character in a story from The Arabian Nights. Aladdin steals a lamp, which makes a GENIE (=a magical spirit) appear who will give Aladdin anything he asks for. 阿拉丁〔《天方夜谭》一则故事中的青年男子。他偷取了一盏神灯，神灯可让灯神现形，对阿拉丁有求必应〕

Al·a·mein /ˈæləmen; ˈæləmeın/ also 又作 **El Alamein** a place in Egypt where the British army won an important battle against the German army in World War II 阿拉曼〔埃及地名。二战期间，英军在此取得对德军的一场重要胜利〕

Al·a·mo, the /ˈæləmo; ˈæləməʊ/ a MISSION building in San Antonio in Texas, where a famous battle took place in 1836, when the US and Mexico were fighting each other for the control of Texas. The Alamo was defended against 4000 Mexican soldiers by only 180 Americans. 阿拉莫〔位于得克萨斯州圣安东尼奥市的一个传教站。1836年，为争夺得克萨斯的控制权，美国曾与墨西哥在此交战。人数只有180名的美国人以寡敌众，击退了4000名墨西哥士兵的进攻〕

à la mode /ˌɑ lə `mod; ˌæ lə 'məʊd/ *adj, adv* **1** *old-fashioned* according to the latest fashion【过时】时髦的［地］ **2** *AmE* served with ICE CREAM【美】加冰激凌(的): *apple pie à la mode* 加冰激凌的苹果馅饼

Al·a·mo·gor·do /ˌæləmə`gordo; ˌæləmə'gɔːdəʊ/ a town in the US state of New Mexico, near the place where the first NUCLEAR BOMB was exploded in 1945 阿拉莫戈多〔美国新墨西哥州一城镇，1945年在此附近爆炸了第一枚核弹〕

Al-A·non /ˌæl ə`nɑn; ˌæl ə'nɒn/ an international organization that helps people who are related to ALCOHOLICS (=people who cannot stop drinking alcohol) 嗜酒者亲属互助会〔一个帮助嗜酒者亲属的国际性组织〕 —see also 另见 ALCOHOLICS ANONYMOUS

alarms 警报装置

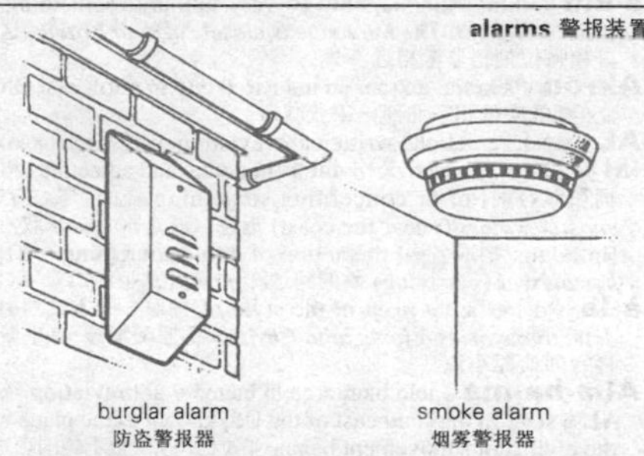

2 **a·larm¹** /ə`lɑrm; ə'lɑːm/ *n* **1** [U] a feeling of fear or anxiety because something dangerous might happen 惊恐，惊慌: *I turned in alarm as the wind blew the door open.* 风把门吹开了，我惊慌地转过身去。 **2** [C] something such as a bell or a light that warns people of danger 警报器: *a fire alarm* 火警装置 | *Something has set the car alarm off.* 什么东西触发了汽车警报器。 **3 sound/raise the alarm** to warn everyone about something bad or dangerous that is already happening 发出警报: **[+about]** *The Red Cross has sounded the alarm about the threat of famine.* 红十字会已发出了饥荒威胁的警报。 **4** an alarm clock 闹钟 —see also 另见 FALSE ALARM

alarm² *v* [T] to make people very worried about a possible danger 使恐慌［不安，焦虑］: *Her high temperature alarmed the doctors.* 她体温很高，使医生感到不安。

alarm clock /·'·· ·/ *n* [C] a clock that will make a noise at a particular time to wake you up 闹钟: *The alarm clock went off at six.* 闹钟6点钟响了。

a·larmed /ə`lɑrmd; ə'lɑːmd/ *adj* **1** frightened and worried 恐慌的，担忧的: *There's no need to look so alarmed!* 不必显得这样恐慌！ | **[+by/at/over]** *Prison authorities have become increasingly alarmed by the number of prisoners trying to escape.* 试图越狱的囚犯的人数之多令监狱方面越来越忧虑。 **2** protected by an alarm system 装有警报系统的

a·larm·ing /ə`lɑrmıŋ; ə'lɑːmıŋ/ *adj* worrying and frightening 令人担忧的，令人恐慌的: *an alarming increase in violent crime* 暴力犯罪案的惊人增长 | **at an alarming rate** (=happening so quickly that it makes people worried) 以惊人的速度 *The rainforest is disappearing at an alarming rate.* 热带雨林正在以惊人的速度消失。 —**alarmingly** *adv*

a·larm·ist /ə`lɑrmıst; ə'lɑːmɪst/ *adj* making people unnecessarily worried about dangers that do not exist 惊慌失措的，大惊小怪的: *an alarmist report on population growth* 危言耸听的人口增长报告 —**alarmist** *n* [C]

a·las¹ /ə'læs; ə'læs/ *adv* [sentence adverb 句子副词] *formal* unfortunately【正式】不幸的是: *There is, alas, no short way to success.* 不幸的是，成功没有捷径。

alas² *interjection old use* used to express sadness, shame, or fear【旧】唉；哎呀〔表示悲伤、羞愧或恐惧〕

A·las·ka /ə'læskə; ə'læskə/ abbreviation 缩写为 **AK** the largest state in the US, northwest of Canada 阿拉斯加州〔美国最大的一个州，位于加拿大的西北面〕 —**Alaskan** *n, adj*

CULTURAL NOTE 文化注释

In the past, people went to Alaska to look for gold, but now it is a popular place for people to go on a CRUISE (=a holiday on a large comfortable boat) to see the WHALES and the ICEBERGS. There is often political CONTROVERSY over whether companies should be allowed to look for oil in certain parts of Alaska's WILDERNESS. 过去人们去阿拉斯加是为了淘金，但现在那里成了人们乘大型游轮观看鲸鱼和冰山的胜地。是否应允许公司去阿拉斯加荒野的某些区域勘探石油，经常引起政治上的争议。

Al·ban /ˈɔlbən; ˈɔːlbən/, **Saint** the first Christian MARTYR in England. He was born in Britain, but served in the Roman army. He became a Christian after helping a priest and was officially killed in 303AD. 圣·奥尔本〔英格兰第一位基督教殉道者。他出生在英国，曾在罗马军中服役。他帮助过一位牧师，后成为基督徒，公元303年遇害〕

Al·ba·ni·a /æl`benıə; æl'beınıə/ a small country in the southeast of Europe next to the Adriatic Sea. Population: 3,500,000 (2001). Capital: Tirana 阿尔巴尼亚〔位于欧洲东南部，濒临亚德里亚海的一个小国。人口：3,500,000(2001)，首都：地拉那〕 —**Albanian** *n, adj*

Al·ba·ny /ˈɔlbənı; ˈɔːlbəni/ the capital city of New York State in the US 奥尔巴尼〔美国纽约州首府〕

al·ba·tross /ˈælbəˌtrɔs; ˈælbətrɒs/ *n* [C] **1** a very large white sea bird 信天翁(鸟) **2 an albatross (around your neck)** something you have done that causes problems for you and prevents you from succeeding 无法摆脱的苦恼；障碍: *His friendship with the gangster, Jimmy Hoffa, had become an albatross around his neck.* 他与匪徒吉米·霍法的交情成了他的包袱。

al·be·it /ɔl`biıt; ɔːl'biːɪt/ *conjunction* even though, used to add information or details that are different from what you have already said 虽然，尽管: *It was a small, albeit very important, mistake.* 这个错误虽小，但很严重。

Al·bert /ˈælbət; ˈælbət/, **Prince** (1819-61) the husband of the British queen Victoria, born in Germany, and also called the "Prince Consort" 艾伯特亲王〔(1891-1861)，英国维多利亚女王的丈夫，亦称"女王夫君"〕

Al·ber·ta /æl'bɝtə; æl'bɜːtə/ a PROVINCE in West Canada 艾伯塔〔加拿大西部一省〕

Albert Dock /ˌ·· ·'·/ a DOCK in Liverpool with popular shops and restaurants that have been built inside its old Victorian Warehouses 艾伯特码头〔位于利物浦，以建于维多利亚时代仓库内的店铺和饭馆而出名〕

Albert Hall, the /ˌ·· '·/ also 又作 **the Royal Albert Hall** a large 19th century building in London where CONCERTS take place (皇家)艾伯特音乐厅〔伦敦一家大型音乐厅，建于19世纪〕

Albert Square /ˌ‥ ˈ‥/ an imaginary place in East London where the characters in the British television programme East Enders live and work 艾伯特广场〔东伦敦一虚构地名。英国电视节目《东伦敦人》中的人物生活和工作的地方〕

al·bi·no /ælˋbaɪno; ælˈbiːnəʊ/ *n* [C] a person or animal with an unusual GENETIC condition, light coloured eyes and very white hair and skin 患白化病的人或动物

Al·bi·on /ælˋbɪən; ælˈbiən/ an ancient name for Britain or England, used especially in poetry 阿尔比恩〔英国或英格兰的古称, 尤用于诗歌〕

[3] **al·bum** /ˋælbəm; ˈælbəm/ *n* [C] **1** a book in which you put photographs, stamps etc〔收集相片、邮票等的〕簿册: *a wedding album* 结婚相册 **2** a record that has about 20 to 25 minutes music on each side 密纹唱片

al·bu·men /ælˋbjumən; ˈælbjʊmɪn/ *n* [U] *technical* the white or colourless part of the inside of an egg【术语】蛋白, 蛋清

Al·bu·quer·que /ˋælbəkɝkɪ; ˈælbəkɜːki/ the largest city in the state of New Mexico, US 阿尔伯克基〔美国新墨西哥州最大城市〕

Al·ca·traz /ˋælkətræz; ˈælkətræz/ a prison on a rocky island in San Francisco Bay, in California. The prison, which was closed in 1963, was famous because it was very difficult to escape from. 阿尔卡特拉斯监狱〔位于加利福尼亚圣弗朗西斯科湾的一座岩岛上, 于1963年关闭, 以难以越狱而著称〕

al·che·my /ˋælkəmɪ; ˈælkəmi/ *n* [U] **1** a science studied in the Middle Ages that involved trying to change ordinary metals into gold 炼金术 **2** *literary* magic【文】魔法, 法术: *By what alchemy did he manage to get elected?* 他用什么魔法当选的? —**alchemist** *n* [C]

Al·cock and Brown /ˌɔlkɑk ənd ˋbraʊn; ˌɔːlkɒk ənd ˈbraʊn/ two British pilots, Sir John William Alcock (1892-1919) and Sir Arthur Whitten Brown (1886-1948), who, in 1919, were the first people to fly an aircraft across the Atlantic without stopping 阿尔科克与布朗〔英国飞行家约翰·威廉·阿尔科克爵士(1892-1919)和阿瑟·惠顿·布朗爵士(1886-1948)。1919年他们成为首次直接飞越大西洋的飞行员〕

[3] **al·co·hol** /ˋælkəˌhɔl; ˈælkəhɒl/ *n* **1** [U] drinks such as beer or wine that contain a substance that can make you drunk 含酒精的饮品, 酒 **2** [C,U] a chemical substance, that can be used for medical or industrial purposes to clean things 酒精, 乙醇

al·co·hol·ic[1] /ˌælkəˋhɔlɪk; ˌælkəˈhɒlɪk◂/ *adj* **1** connected with alcohol or containing alcohol (含)酒精的: *alcoholic beverages* 酒精饮料 **2** caused by drinking alcohol 由酗酒引起的: *an alcoholic stupor* 醉得不省人事 —**alcoholically** /-klɪ; -kli/ *adv*

alcoholic[2] *n* [C] someone who regularly drinks too much alcohol and has difficulty stopping 酗酒者, 嗜酒成瘾者

Alcoholics A·non·y·mous /ˌ‥‥ˈ‥‥/ abbreviation 缩写为 AA an international organization for ALCOHOLICS who want to stop drinking alcohol 匿名嗜酒者互戒协会〔帮助嗜酒者戒酒的一个国际性组织〕

al·co·hol·is·m /ˋælkəhɔlˌɪzəm; ˈælkəhɒlɪzəm/ *n* [U] the medical condition of being an alcoholic 酒精中毒

Al·cott /ˋɔlkɑt; ˈɔːlkət/**, Louisa May** /luˋizə me; luˈiːzə meɪ/ (1832-88) a US writer whose NOVELs for children include *Little Women* and *Good Wives* 奥尔科特〔(1832-1888), 美国作家, 著有儿童小说《小妇人》和《好妻子》〕

al·cove /ˋælkov; ˈælkəʊv/ *n* [C] a place in the wall of a room that is built further back than the rest of the wall 凹室; 壁龛: *The bookcase just fits into the alcove in the living room.* 书橱放在起居室的凹处正合适。

Alde·burgh /ˋɔldbɝo; ˈɔːldbərə/ a town on the coast of Suffolk in eastern England, where there is a music FESTIVAL (=a series of concerts and performances) every summer 奥尔德堡〔英格兰东部萨福克郡沿海一城镇, 每年夏天举办一次音乐节〕

al den·te /æl ˋdɛntɪ; æl ˈdenti/ *adj* food, especially PASTA that is al dente is still firm after it has been cooked〔尤指面食〕烹调得不太烂的, 耐嚼的

al·der·man /ˋɔldɚmən; ˈɔːldəmən/ *n* [C] **1** a member of a town or city council in the US〔美国城镇的〕市参议员 **2** an important member of a town council in Britain in the past〔旧时英国市、镇的〕参事

Al·der·ney /ˋɔldɚnɪ; ˈɔːldəni/ *n* **1** one of the Channel Islands between England and France 奥尔德尼〔英吉利海峡群岛之一〕 **2** a breed of cow kept for milk 奥尔德尼乳牛: *Alderney cattle* 奥尔德尼乳牛

Al·der·shot /ˋɔldɚʃɑt; ˈɔːldəʃɒt/ a town in Hampshire in southern England. It is an important centre for the British army 奥尔德肖特镇〔英格兰南部汉普郡一镇, 英国一军事重镇〕

Al·drin /ˋɔldrɪn; ˈɔːldrɪn/**, Edwin "Buzz"** /ˌɛdwɪn ˋbʌz; ˌedwɪn ˈbʌz/ (1930-) a US ASTRONAUT who became the second man to step on the moon during the Apollo 11 mission of 1969 奥尔德林〔(1930-), 美国宇航员, 1969年乘坐阿波罗11号执行登月计划, 成为人类登上月球的第二人〕

ale /el; eɪl/ *n* [U] **1** a type of beer made from MALT[1] (3) 高酒精度啤酒, 麦芽啤酒 **2** *old-fashioned* beer【过时】啤酒 —see also 另见 LIGHT ALE

al·eck /ˋælɪk; ˈælɪk/ *n* —see 见 SMART ALECK

ale·house /ˋelˌhaʊs; ˈeɪlhaʊs/ *n* [C] *old-fashioned* a place where people drank beer【过时】啤酒馆, 酒馆

a·lert[1] /əˋlɝt; əˈlɜːt/ *adj* **1** always watching and ready to notice anything strange or unusual 警惕的, 警觉的 **2** able to think quickly and clearly 机警的, 机敏的: *Despite her years, she still has a lively and alert mind.* 尽管她年纪很大, 她的思维仍然活跃、敏捷。| *Please remain alert and report any unattended luggage to the authorities.* 请保持警觉, 发现无人看管的行李请向当局报告。**3 be alert to** to realize that you must be careful about something or that something is dangerous 对…保持警惕, 对…警觉: *Tourists need to be alert to the dangers of travelling in the north of the country.* 游客到该国北部旅游必须对可能出现的危险保持警惕。

alert[2] *v* [T] **1** to officially warn someone of something, especially something dangerous, so that they can be ready to deal with it 使…警觉; 向…发出警报: *Alert air traffic control and tell them one engine isn't working.* 向空中交通管制发出警报, 告诉他们一个发动机失灵。| **[+that]** *Police have been alerted that a second prisoner has escaped.* 警方已经接到警报, 又有一个犯人逃走了。**2** to make someone notice something important or dangerous 提醒, 让〔某人〕对…引起重视: **alert sb to sth** *Montessori alerted teachers to the importance of observing children at play.* 蒙台梭利提醒教师们, 注意观察孩子玩耍是很重要的。

alert[3] *n* **1** a warning to be ready for possible danger 警报: *a full-scale flood alert* 最高级别的防洪警报 —see also 另见 RED ALERT **2 be on the alert** to be ready to notice and deal with a situation or problem 保持戒备(状态): *Be on the alert for pickpockets in the crowds.* 人多拥挤时要时刻提防扒手。| **be on full alert** (=completely ready to deal with a dangerous situation) 保持高度戒备状态 *police on full alert against terrorist attacks* 保持高度戒备状态以防范恐怖袭击的警察

A·leu·tian Is·lands /əˋluʃən ˌaɪləndz; əˈluːʃən ˌaɪləndz/ a group of islands off the southwest coast of Alaska 阿留申群岛〔位于阿拉斯加州西南海岸附近〕

A lev·el /ˋe ˌlɛvl; ˈeɪ ˌlevəl/ *n* [C] an examination in a particular subject taken in schools in England and Wales, usually at the age of 18〔英格兰和威尔士中学生通常在18岁参加的某个科目的〕高级程度考试

Al·ex·an·der /ˌælɪgˋzændɚ; ˌælɪgˈzɑːndə/**, Grover Cleveland** /ˋgrovɚ ˋklivlənd; ˈgrəʊvə ˈkliːvlənd/ (1887-1950) a US BASEBALL player and one of the greatest PITCHERs. He played for the Philadelphia Phillies and Chicago Cubs from 1911 to 1930. 亚历山大〔(1887-1950), 美国棒球运动员, 最佳投手之一, 1911年至1930年期间分别在费城费城人队和芝加哥小熊队打球〕

Alexander tech·nique, the /ˌælɪgˋzændɚ tɛkˌnik; ˌælɪgˈzɑːndə tekˌniːk/ *trademark* a system of sitting, standing, and moving, which some believe can help to improve general health【商标】亚历山大健身法〔一套坐、立、行的动作。有人认为, 这套动作有助于身体健康〕

Alexander the Great /ˌ‥ˌ‥ ˈ‥/ (356-323 BC) a king of Macedonia who took control of Greece, Egypt, and most of the countries to the east of the Mediterranean Sea as far as India 亚历山大大帝〔(公元前356-前323), 马其顿国王, 曾征服希腊、埃及以及地中海以东的大部分国家, 远及印度〕

Al·ex·an·dri·a /ˌælɪgˋzændrɪə; ˌælɪgˈzɑːndriə/ a city and port in Egypt on the coast of the Mediterranean Sea 亚历山大港〔埃及一港口城市, 位于地中海沿岸〕

ALF /ˌe ɛl ˋɛf; ˌeɪ el ˈef/ the written abbreviation of 缩写= ANIMAL LIBERATION FRONT

al·fal·fa /ælˋfælfə; ælˈfælfə/ *n* [U] a plant grown especially in the US to feed farm animals 紫花苜蓿

alfalfa sprout /ˈ‥ ˌ/ *n* [C] a young alfalfa plant, eaten raw in SALADs 苜蓿苗(可生食)

Al·fred the Great /ˌælfrɪd ðə ˋgret; ˌælfrɪd ðə ˈgreɪt/ (849-899) king of Wessex (871-899), the southwestern part of England 阿尔弗雷德大帝〔(849-899), 英格兰西南部韦塞克斯王朝国王(871-899)〕

al·fres·co /ælˋfrɛsko; ælˈfreskəʊ/ *adj, adv* in the open air 露天(的), 在户外(的): *an alfresco meal* 野餐 | *We dined alfresco,*

A

on a balcony overlooking the sea. 我们在阳台上吃饭，从那里可以眺望大海。

al·gae /ˋældʒi; ˈældʒiː/ *n* [U] a very simple plant without stems or leaves that grows in or near water 藻类（植物）

Al·garve, the /ælˋgɑrvə; ælˈgɑːv/ an area of southern Portugal, which is a popular place f or holidays 阿尔加维〔葡萄牙南部一地区，著名度假胜地〕

al·ge·bra /ˋældʒəbrə; ˈældʒəbrə/ *n* [U] a type of mathematics that uses letters and other signs to represent numbers and values 代数 —**algebraic** /ˌældʒəˋbre·ɪk; ˌældʒəˈbreɪ-ɪk◂/ *adj* —**algebraically** /-klɪ; -kli/ *adv*

Al·ger /ˋældʒɚ; ˈældʒə/, **Ho·ra·ti·o** /həˋreʃɪo; həˈreɪʃiəʊ/ (1832-99) a US writer, many of whose stories are about poor boys who become rich and successful through hard work and good luck 阿尔杰〔(1832–1899)，美国作家。其小说大多描述穷苦孩子凭借辛劳和好运获得财富和成功的故事〕

Al·ge·ri·a /ælˋdʒɪrɪə; ælˈdʒɪəriə/ a country in northwest Africa on the Mediterranean Sea, between Tunisia and Libya. Population: 31,700,000 (2001). Capital: Algiers. 阿尔及利亚〔非洲西北部国家，位于地中海沿岸，突尼斯和利比亚之间。人口：31,700,000 (2001)，首都：阿尔及尔〕—**Algerian** *n, adj*

Al·giers /ælˋdʒɪrz; ælˈdʒɪəz/ a port on the Mediterranean Sea, which is the capital and largest city of Algeria 阿尔及尔〔地中海沿岸一港口城市，阿尔及利亚首都和最大城市〕

Al·gon·quin Ho·tel, the /ælˌgɑŋkwɪn hoˋtɛl; ælˌgɒŋkwɪn həʊˈtel/ a hotel in New York where many famous and wealthy people have stayed 阿尔贡金酒店〔纽约市一酒店，许多名流富豪在此下榻〕

Al·gon·quin Round Ta·ble, the /ælˌgɑŋkwɪn raʊd ˌtebḷ; ælˌgɒŋkwɪn raʊnd ˈteɪbəl/ a group of writers, including Dorothy Parker, who met in New York's Algonquin Hotel in the 1920s, 30s, and 40s, and exchanged ideas 阿尔贡金圆桌会〔由多萝西·帕克等作家组成的一个文学沙龙。20世纪20年代、30年代和40年代，他们经常聚在纽约市的阿尔贡金酒店交流心得〕

al·go·rith·m /ˋælgəˌrɪðəm; ˈælgərɪðəm/ *n* [C] *technical* a set of instructions for solving a mathematical problem, making a computer program etc that are followed in a fixed order【术语】算法，演算法，计算程序

Al·ham·bra, the /ælˋhæmbrə; ælˈhæmbrə/ a palace built on a hill above Granada in southeast Spain between 1238 and 1358 for Moorish kings, and considered to be Spain's most impressive building in the Moorish style. 艾勒汉卜拉宫〔摩尔人国王的宫殿，位于西班牙东南部格拉纳达的一座小山上，1238至1358年间建成，被认为是西班牙最壮观的摩尔式建筑〕

A·li /ɑˋli; ɑːˈliː/, **Muhammad** /muˋhæməd; mʊˈhæmɪ̈d/ (1942-) a US BOXER who became world heavyweight champion in 1964, and then again in 1974 and 1978, and is one of the greatest boxers ever. He changed his name from Cassius Clay when he became a Muslim in 1964. 阿里〔(1942-)，美国拳击手，1964年、1974年、1978年世界重量级拳击冠军，有史以来最优秀拳击手之一。原名卡修斯·克莱，1964年皈依伊斯兰教后改用现名〕

a·li·as[1] /ˋelɪəs; ˈeɪliəs/ *prep* used when giving someone's real name together with another name they use 又名，化名：*Velma Johnson, alias Annie Jones* 维尔玛·约翰逊，又名安妮·琼斯

alias[2] *n* [C] a false name, usually used by a criminal〔通常指罪犯用的〕假名，化名

Al·i Ba·ba /ˌɑlɪ ˋbɑbɑ; ˌæli ˈbɑːbɑː/ the main character in a story called *Ali Baba and the Forty Thieves*, from *The Arabian Nights*. Ali Baba sees 40 thieves enter a secret CAVE (=a large hole in the side of a cliff or under the ground) by saying the magic words "Open Sesame", which makes a door in the cliff open. He repeats these words, enters the cave, and takes some of the gold that the thieves keep there. 阿里巴巴〔《天方夜谭》故事《阿里巴巴和四十大盗》中的主人公。他看到40个大盗念着"芝麻开门"的魔咒打开山门进入一个暗洞，自己就照着说了，然后进入山洞，拿走大盗存放在那里的一些金子〕

al·i·bi /ˋæləˌbaɪ; ˈælɪ̈baɪ/ *n* [C] **1** someone or something that proves that someone was not in the area where a crime happened and therefore could not have done it（证明）某人不在犯罪现场的证人[证据]：*I've got an alibi for Tuesday night.* 我有星期二晚上不在现场的证据。**2** an excuse for something you have failed to do or done wrong 借口；托辞

Al·ice in Won·der·land /ˌælɪs ɪn ˋwʌndəˌlænd; ˌælɪ̈s ɪn ˈwʌndəlænd/ also 又作 **Alice's Adventures in Wonderland** a book by Lewis Carroll about a girl called Alice who falls down a rabbit hole and arrives in a magical land, where she meets many strange animals and people, and has many strange adventures. People sometimes describe something as being 'Alice-in-Wonderland', when they mean it is the opposite of what is normal or what you expect.《艾丽丝漫游奇境记》〔刘易斯·卡罗尔的一部作品。书中有一个名叫艾丽丝的女孩掉进兔窝而巧遇奇境。她遇到了许多怪人异兽，经历了不少奇遇。"漫游奇境的艾丽丝"有时用来形容一些不合常理或出乎意料的事物〕：*The book is a good introduction to the strange, Alice-in-Wonderland world of theoretical physics.* 这本书非常好，能引领我们走进理论物理学这一奇异、神秘的世界。

Alice Springs /ˌælɪs ˋsprɪŋz; ˌælɪ̈s ˈsprɪŋz/ a town in the Northern Territory of Australia, known as a popular place for tourists 艾丽斯斯普林斯〔澳大利亚北部一旅游城镇〕

A·li·en /ˋelɪən; ˈeɪliən/ (1979) a US horror film about a creature that kills people by living in their bodies《异形》〔(1979)，美国恐怖片，描写一种寄生于人体并致人死亡的外星生物〕

alien[1] *adj* **1** belonging to another country or race; FOREIGN (1) 外国的；异族的：*an alien culture* 异域文化 **2** very different from what you are used to; strange 截然不同的；非常怪异的：[+to] *a way of life that is totally alien to us* 和我们截然不同的生活方式 **3** [only before noun 仅用于名词前] connected with creatures from another world 外星人的：*alien life-forms* 外星球的生命形式

alien[2] *n* [C] **1** *technical* someone who lives or works in your country, but who comes from another country【术语】外侨，侨民：*illegal aliens entering the country* 非法侨民入境 **2** a creature from another world 外星人：*a film about aliens from Mars* 一部关于火星人的电影

a·li·en·ate /ˋelɪənˌet; ˈeɪliəneɪt/ *v* [T] **1** to do something that makes someone unfriendly or unwilling to support you 离间，使疏远[不和]：*The latest tax proposals will alienate many voters.* 最新的税收建议会使很多选民不投我们的票。**2** *law* to give the legal right to a particular piece of land, property etc to someone else【法律】转让，让渡〔土地、财产等〕

a·li·en·a·ted /ˋelɪənetɪd; ˈeɪliəneɪtɪ̈d/ *adj* feeling separated from society or the group of people around you, and often unhappy 被疏远的，疏离于…的：[+from] *the psychological effects of being alienated from normal school life* 远离正常学校生活产生的心理影响

a·li·en·a·tion /ˌelɪənˋeʃən; ˌeɪliəˈneɪʃən/ *n* [U] **1** the feeling of not being part of society or a group 疏离感：*the sense of alienation felt by many black people in our culture* 许多黑人在我们的文化中感受到的疏离感 **2** separation from a person who you used to be friendly with 离间，疏远

a·light[1] /əˋlaɪt; əˈlaɪt/ *adj* [not before noun 不用于名词前] **1** burning 燃烧的：**set sth alight** *Several cars were set alight by rioters.* 好几辆车被暴徒烧着了。**2** someone whose face or eyes are alight is excited and happy 喜悦的 **3** bright with light or colour 亮着的；闪亮的

alight[2] *v* [I] *formal*【正式】**1** if a bird or insect alights on something, it stops flying to stand on something〔鸟、虫等〕飞落，落下 **2** to step out of a vehicle after a journey〔从交通工具上〕下来

a·lign /əˋlaɪn; əˈlaɪn/ *v* [T] **1 align yourself with** to decide to publicly support a political group or country 与…保持一致；与…结盟：*Church leaders have aligned themselves with the opposition.* 教会领袖和反对派达成了一致。| **be aligned with** *a country politically aligned with the West* 政治上与西方结盟的国家 **2** to arrange things so that they form a line or are parallel to each other 使排成一直线

a·lign·ment /əˋlaɪnmənt; əˈlaɪnmənt/ *n* **1** [U] the state of being arranged in a line with or parallel to something 排列成行；排成直线：*the correct alignment of spine and pelvis* 脊柱和骨盆正确的直线排列 **2** [C,U] if countries or groups form an alignment, they support each other 联盟，结盟

a·like[1] /əˋlaɪk; əˈlaɪk/ *adj* [not before noun 不用于名词前] very similar 相同的，相像的：*My mother and I are alike in many ways.* 我和母亲在许多方面很相似。

alike[2] *adv* **1** in a similar way 相似地，相同地：*The twins were dressed alike.* 这对双胞胎穿得一样。**2** equally 同样地，一样地：*I enjoyed being on this course – I learned a lot from teachers and students alike.* 我喜欢上这门课 —— 我从老师和学生身上都学到了很多知识。

al·i·men·ta·ry ca·nal /ˌæləmɛntərɪ kəˋnæl; ˌælɪ̈mentəri kəˈnæl/ *n* [C] the tube in your body that takes food through your body from your mouth to your ANUS 消化道

al·i·mo·ny /ˋæləˌmonɪ; ˈælɪ̈məni/ *n* [U] money that a court orders someone to pay regularly to their former wife or husband after their marriage has ended〔法院判定离婚一方须向另一方定期支付的〕赡养费

a·lit /əˈlɪt; əˈlɪt/ the past tense and past participle of ALIGHT²

[2] [3] **a·live** /əˈlaɪv; əˈlaɪv/ *adj* [not before noun 不用于名词前]
1 ▶NOT DEAD 没有死◀ still living and not dead 活(着)的: *It was a really bad accident – they're lucky to be alive.* 这是一宗十分严重的意外 —— 他们能活着实属幸运。| *None of my grandparents are alive now.* 我的祖父母和外祖父母都已不在世了。| **stay alive** (=continue to live) 活下去 *They managed to stay alive by eating berries and roots.* 他们靠吃浆果和草根设法活了下来。| **keep sb alive** *He's being kept alive on a life-support machine.* 他在靠生命维持机维持生命。
2 ▶CHEERFUL 高兴的◀ active and happy; feel alive 活跃的, 充满活力的: *It was the kind of morning when you wake up and feel really alive.* 这是一个醒来觉得充满活力的早晨。
3 ▶STILL EXISTING 仍存在的◀ continuing to exist 仍然存在的: *Ancient traditions are still very much alive in rural areas.* 不少古老的传统在农村仍然存在。| **keep sth alive** *fighting to keep our academic institutions alive* 为保存我们的学术机构而斗争
4 come alive a) if a situation or event comes alive it becomes interesting and seems real 变得逼真, 变得有生气: *For me the play only came alive in the final act.* 在我看来, 这出戏在最后一幕才真正有点意思。**b)** if someone comes alive they start to be happy and interested in what is happening 活跃起来: *It was as if she came alive when she sat down at the piano.* 她一坐在钢琴旁, 就好像充满了生气。**c)** if a town or city etc comes alive it becomes busy 变得生机勃勃; 变得繁忙: *seaside resorts that come alive in the summer* 夏季变得繁忙的海滨度假胜地
5 bring sth alive to make something interesting 使…变得有生气: *Plays need the sound of human voices to bring them alive.* 戏剧要有对白才有生气。
6 be alive and well a) to be healthy and enjoy life 健康愉快的 **b)** *informal humorous* to be popular and successful【非正式, 幽默】流行, 成功: *The mini skirt is alive and well in Paris this year.* 迷你裙今年在巴黎很流行。
7 be alive and kicking to be very healthy and active 精神饱满; 活跃: *"How's your father nowadays?" "Oh, still alive and kicking."* "你父亲现在怎么样?" "哦, 身体很好呢。"
8 be alive to to realize that something is happening and that it is important 意识到, 注意到: *The company is alive to the threat posed by foreign imports.* 这家公司清楚地意识到进口商品所造成的威胁。
9 be alive with to be full of people, animals, or things that are moving 充满, 到处都是〔活物〕: *a tree trunk alive with ants* 爬满蚂蚁的树干 —see also 另见 **skin sb alive** (SKIN² (3))

al·ka·li /ˈælkəˌlaɪ; ˈælkəlaɪ/ *n* [C,U] a substance that forms a chemical salt when combined with an acid 碱

al·ka·line /ˈælkəˌlaɪn; ˈælkəlaɪn/ *adj* containing an alkali 含碱的, 碱性的

Al·ka-Sel·tzer /ˈælkə ˌsɛltsə; ˌælkə ˈseltsə/ *trademark* a type of medicine that some people take when they have eaten or drunk too much. Alka Seltzer is added to water to make a FIZZY drink.【商标】我可舒适消食片〔一种治疗饮食过度的药品, 泡在开水中饮用, 放入水中时会出现气泡〕

all- /ɔl; ɔːl/ *prefix* **1** consisting or made only of one kind of thing 纯, 全, 单一种类的: *an all-male club* 男性俱乐部 | *an all-wool dress* 纯羊毛连衣裙 **2** for the whole of something 整个的, 全部的: *All-India Railways* 全印度铁路公司 | *an all-night party* (=lasting all night) 通宵晚会 | *an all-night cafe* (=staying open all night) 通宵营业的咖啡馆

[1] [1] **all¹** /ɔl; ɔːl/ *determiner, predeterminer* **1** the complete amount or quantity of; the whole of 全部: *I've got all day tomorrow to do it.* 明天我有一整天做这件事。| *He had worked all his life in the mine.* 他在矿场工作了一辈子。| *Have you done all your homework?* 你所有的作业都做完了吗? | *She didn't say a single word all the way back home.* 回家路上, 她一句话也没说。| **all the time** (=very often, especially in a way that is annoying) 老是, 总是 *It rained all the time we were on holiday!* 我们休假的时候总下雨! **2** every one of 每一个, 所有的: *Someone's taken all my books!* 谁把我的书都拿走了! | *Will all the girls please stand over here.* 女孩子都请站到这边来。| **all kinds of** *The course attracts all kinds of people.* 这门课程吸引了各种各样的人。| *All these questions must be answered.* 所有这些问题都必须回答。| **you all/they all/it all etc** *They all passed the exam.* 他们考试全都及格了。**3** the greatest possible amount of 尽可能的: *With all due respect, I really cannot agree with your last statement.* 尽管我十分尊敬你, 恕我不同意你最后的陈述。**4 of all people/things/places etc** used to show surprise when mentioning a particular person, thing, or place 在所有的人/事/地方之中等唯独…: *Of course you shouldn't have done it – you of all people should know that!* 当然你本不应该做这件事。别人可以不知道, 可你应该知道! **5 all innocence/smiles etc** used to emphasize that someone or something has a particular quality or appearance 一脸无辜的样子/满脸笑容等: *Elsie was all smiles when I saw her again the next morning.* 我第二天早晨再见到艾尔茜的时候, 她一脸笑容。**6 for all...** in spite of a particular fact, quality, or situation 尽管: *For all her rudeness, she's actually quite a kind-hearted old soul.* 尽管粗鲁, 实际上她是个热心肠的老人。**7 go all out/make an all-out effort** to do everything you can to succeed 全力以赴, 竭尽全力: *We're all out to win the cup this year.* 我们今年要全力以赴赢得奖杯。

[1] [1] **all²** *adv* **1** [always+adj/adv/prep] **all alone/new/dark etc** 独自一人/全新/漆黑一片等: *You shouldn't be sitting here by yourself, all alone.* 你不应该一个人孤零零地坐在这儿。| *I'm all confused now!* 我现在全给搞糊涂了! | *The room suddenly went all dark.* 房间里突然一片漆黑。| **all for/all in favour of** (=used to say that you strongly support or agree with something) 完全赞成 *One minute he's all for all Labour policy, the next minute he's knocking it.* 他一会儿完全赞同工党的政策, 一会儿又对其横加指责。**2 one, four, ten all** used when giving the score of a game in which both sides have scored the same〔比分〕一平, 四平, 十平 **3 not all that** *spoken* not very【口】不太: *It doesn't sound all that good, does it?* 这听起来不太好, 是吧? | *I don't think it matters all that much.* 我认为这关系不大。**4 all along** *informal* all the time from the beginning while something was happening【非正式】一直, 自始至终: *I knew all along that this relationship wouldn't last.* 我自始至终都知道这种关系不会长久。| *Maybe this is what they were trying to achieve all along.* 也许这就是他们一直想要实现的目标。**5 all at once a)** happening all together at the same time 同时: *Obviously they can't do everything all at once.* 显然, 他们不能同时做所有的事。**b)** suddenly and unexpectedly 突然, 出其不意地: *All at once, I knew there was something wrong.* 突然间, 我知道出了差错。**6 all over a)** everywhere on an object or surface 遍布表面的: *There were bits of paper all over the floor.* 地板上到处都是碎纸。| *He has cuts all over his legs.* 他的腿上到处是伤口。**b)** everywhere in a place 处处, 到处: *Antique clocks from all over the world are on display.* 来自世界各地的古玩钟表正在展出。| *People came from all over the country.* 人们来自全国各地。| *They're putting up new offices all over the place.* 他们正在各地设立新的办事处。**c)** finished 结束: *I saw my old girlfriend the other day, but that's all over now.* (=our relationship is finished) 前几天, 我见到了我以前的女朋友, 但现在都过去了。**7 that's sb all over** *spoken* that is typical of him or her【口】某人就是这样, 某人是典型…人: *He was late of course, but that's Tim all over!* 当然他又迟到了, 蒂姆就是这样的! **8 all the easier/healthier/more effectively etc** used to emphasize how much easier, etc something is than it would normally have been 更加容易/健康/有效等: *Their success is all the more pleasing when you consider the effort they've made.* 考虑到他们付出的努力, 他们的成功就更令人高兴。| *The job was made all the easier by having the proper tools.* 有了合适的工具, 工作就容易多了。**9 all the same** *spoken* in spite of something that you have just mentioned【口】(虽然…)还是, 仍然: *We realised that the children would have to leave home, but all the same it was difficult when they went.* 我们意识到孩子们必须离开家, 但不管怎么说, 他们真的离开时, 我们还是不太好受。**10 it's all the same to me** used to say that you do not mind what decision is made, that you would be pleased with any choice or that you do not really care 对我无所谓, 没区别: *You can choose what we do, it's all the same to me.* 你可以选择我们做什么, 对我来说都一样。**11 all but** almost completely 几乎, 差不多: *Their screams of excitement all but drowned out the music.* 他们激动的尖叫声几乎淹没了音乐声。**12 all too** much more than is desirable 极; 甚: *All too often it's the mother who gets blamed for her children's behaviour.* 孩子做错了事, 受责备的却往往是母亲。**13 all told** counting or including everyone; all together 总计, 合计: *There were seventeen of us at the meeting, all told.* 我们总共有17人参加会议。**14 it's all up (with)** *informal* used to say that it is impossible for someone to continue doing something, especially when they have been involved in criminal activities【非正式】全完了, 完蛋了 **15 (not) all there** *informal* someone who is not all there cannot think in a clear normal way and seems slightly crazy【非正式】神志(不)正常, 头脑(不)清醒: *I don't think he's quite all there.* 我认为他脑子有些不正常。

all³ *pron* **1** every one or every part of something 每个人; 每样东西; 全部: *I ate the whole packet, all of them!* 我把一整袋全吃了! | *That's all I know about it.* 那是我所知道的全部。| *Not all the children were vaccinated.* 并不是所有的孩子都注射了疫苗。|

I've heard it all before. 这件事我以前全都听过。**2** used to emphasize the most basic or necessary facts or details about a situation 一切，全部：*All you need is a hammer and some nails.* 你需要的不过是一把锤子和一些钉子。| *All I'm asking for is a little respect.* 我要的不过是一点尊重而已。**3 for all sb knows/cares etc a)** used to say that something could happen, especially something very unpleasant or serious, and someone would not know or care about it 某人才不知道/才不在乎呢等：*The old woman could have been lying dead in the house for all her family cared.* 这位老人可能已经死在这幢房子里，可是她家里的人都不在乎。**4 and all a)** the whole thing; including everything or everybody mentioned 全部；包括所有：*They ate the whole fish; bones, tail, head, and all.* 他们把整条鱼都吃掉了，骨头、鱼尾、鱼头等通通吃掉了。**b)** *spoken* an expression meaning as well, used to emphasize what you have just said【口】也，而且〔表示强调〕：*And you can take that smelly coat out of here and all!* 你也可以把那件有味的大衣拿走！| *"Look, it's snowing!" "Oh, it is and all!"* "看，下雪了！""啊，还真下了！" **5 it costs all of 50p/took all of 20 minutes etc** *spoken* used to emphasize or express how large or small an amount actually is【口】足足花了50便士/20分钟等 **6 it was all I could do to...** used to say that you only just succeeded in doing something 我能做的也就是…：*It was all I could do to stop them hitting each other!* 我所能做的也只是阻止他们打架而已！**7 (not) at all** used in questions and negative statements to emphasize what you are saying 无论如何〔都不〕，一点〔都不〕：*They've done nothing at all to try and put the problem right.* 他们根本没有采取任何行动去解决问题。| *They obviously weren't at all happy.* 显然，他们一点儿都不高兴。| *Does he get no pension at all?* 他一点儿养老金也没有拿到吗？| *Do you know anything about it at all?* 这件事难道你一点都不知道吗？| *He's not looking at all well.* (=he looks ill) 他看上去气色很不好。| *"Do you mind if I stay for a bit longer?" "Not at all!"* (=certainly not, please do) "你介不介意我在这儿多留一会？""当然不〔介意〕！" **8 all in all** considering every part of a situation 一般来说，总的说来：*All in all, it's been a pretty bad year for John Major.* 总的说来，对约翰·梅杰来讲这是糟糕的一年。**9 it's all or nothing a)** used to say that unless something is done completely or done in the exact way that you want, something else will happen, especially something unpleasant 要么全部，要么一点儿也没有：*It was all or nothing for Susan; either the company offered her a pay rise or she would leave.* 对苏珊而言，只有两个可能，要么公司给她加薪，要么她离开。**b)** used to say that someone is using all their effort and energy in order to try and do something 竭尽全力 —see also 另见 **all and sundry** (SUNDRY (1)), EACH, EVERY

all⁴ *n* **do/give your all** *literary* to do everything possible to try and achieve something【文】竭尽全力，全力以赴：*The coach expects everyone to give their all in every game.* 教练希望所有队员在每场比赛中都全力以赴。

Al·lah /ˈælə; ˈælə/ *n* the Muslim name for God 真主，安拉〔穆斯林对其所信仰的神的称呼〕

Al·lah·a·bad /ˌæləhəˈbæd; ˌæləhəˈbæd/ a city in north India that is one of the country's oldest and most holy cities 阿拉阿巴德〔印度北部一城市，印度最古老、最神圣的城市之一〕

all-A·mer·i·can /ˌ· ·ˈ···◂/ *adj* **1** having qualities that are considered to be typically American and that American people admire, such as being healthy and working hard 纯粹[典型]美国式的：*an all-American family, cheerful and friendly* 一个典型的美国式家庭，欢乐而温馨 **2** belonging to a group of players who have been chosen as the best in their sport at American universities 全美最佳的〔代表美国大学生最高体育水平〕：*an all-American player out of UCLA* 从美国洛杉矶加州大学选出的全美最佳球员

CULTURAL NOTE 文化注释

Many British people think of an all-American man or woman as being young, healthy, neatly dressed, and quite rich. Many Americans think of an all-American man or woman as white, middle-class, good at sports, and representing traditional values that have been passed down from the past to the present 很多英国人认为，纯粹的美国人年轻、健康、衣着整洁、相当有钱。很多美国人认为，纯粹的美国人是那些来自中产阶级、擅长体育、代表着从过去延续至今的传统价值观的白人：*a clean-living all-American guy* 一位洁身处世的纯粹的美国人

Al·lan-a-Dale /ˌælən ə ˈdel; ˌælən ə ˈdeɪl/ a character who is a member of Robin Hood's group, who is also a musician 阿伦厄戴尔〔罗宾汉旗下的绿林好汉之一，也是一位乐手〕

all-a·round /ˌ· ·ˈ·/ *adj* [only before noun 仅用于名词前] *AmE* good at doing many different things, especially at many different sports【美】〔体育运动〕全能的；ALL-ROUND¹ *BrE*【英】：*an all-around athlete* 全能运动员

al·lay /əˈle; əˈleɪ/ *v* [T] *formal*【正式】**allay fear/concern/suspicion etc** to make someone feel less afraid, worried etc 减轻恐惧/担忧/疑虑等：*His reassurances did little to allay their fears for Robert's safety.* 他的安慰没有起多大作用，他们仍旧十分担心罗伯特的安全。

All Blacks, the /ˌ· ˈ·◂/ the New Zealand international RUGBY union team 全黑橄榄球队〔新西兰国际橄榄球联盟球队〕

all clear, the /ˌ· ˈ·/ *n* **a)** official permission to begin doing something 批准，放行：*We've got the all clear from the board for the new project.* 这个新项目我们已经得到董事会的批准。**b)** a signal such as a loud whistle that tells you that a dangerous situation has ended 解除警报的信号：**give/sound the all clear** *The drone of the bombers faded, and the all clear was sounded.* 轰炸机的轰鸣声逐渐减弱，警报解除的信号响了起来。

all-com·ers /ˌ· ˈ··/ *n* [plural] anyone who wants to take part in a competition whatever their age or experience 所有欲参与竞争的人，所有希望参赛者：*The marathon is open to all-comers.* 马拉松比赛谁都可以报名参加。

al·le·ga·tion /ˌæləˈgeʃən; ˌælɪˈgeɪʃən/ *n* [C] a statement that has not been proved that someone has done something wrong or illegal 指控；宣称：**[+of]** *allegations of fraud* 有欺诈行为的指控 | **allegation that** *allegations that the election had been fixed* 选举结果已经内定的说法

al·lege /əˈlɛdʒ; əˈledʒ/ *v* [T] to say that something is true or that someone has done something wrong even though this has not been proved〔在未证实的情况下〕硬说，宣称，声称；指控：**allege (that)** *It was alleged that policemen had accepted bribes.* 有人声称警察收受了贿赂。| **be alleged to be/do sth** *The new missiles are alleged to be capable of travelling enormous distances.* 据称这种新型导弹可以发射到很远的距离。

al·leged /əˈlɛdʒd; əˈledʒd/ *adj* [only before noun 仅用于名词前] an alleged fact, quality etc is supposed to be true although there is no proof that it actually is 未有证据而被指称的，涉嫌的：*reports of alleged police brutality* 关于警察涉嫌有野蛮行为的报道

al·leg·ed·ly /əˈlɛdʒɪdlɪ; əˈledʒɪ̇dli/ *adv* [sentence adverb 句子副词] used when reporting something that other people say is true, although there is no proof 据说：*He was allegedly caught shop-lifting in his local supermarket.* 据说，他在当地的超级市场行窃时被抓住。

Al·le·ghen·y Moun·tains /ˌæləgenɪ ˈmauntn̩z; ˌælɪ̇geɪni ˈmaʊntɪ̇nz/ also 又作 **the Alleghenies** a range of mountains which go from Virginia to Pennsylvania in the eastern US, and are part of the Appalachians 阿勒格尼山脉〔阿巴拉契亚山脉的一部分，位于美国东部，自弗吉尼亚州绵延至宾夕法尼亚州〕

al·le·giance /əˈlidʒəns; əˈliːdʒəns/ *n* [C,U] loyalty to a leader, country, belief etc〔对领袖、国家、信念等的〕忠诚，效忠：**[+to]** *allegiance to the king* 效忠国王 | **proclaim/pledge allegiance** *I pledge allegiance to the flag of the United States of America.* 我对美国国旗发誓效忠。| **switch allegiance** (=start to support a different person, group etc) 转而投靠，转而拥戴

al·le·go·ry /ˈæləˌgorɪ; ˈælɪ̇gəri/ *n* [C,U] a story, painting etc in which the events and characters represent ideas or teach a moral lesson 寓言，讽喻 **—allegorical** /ˌæləˈgɔrɪkl̩; ˌælɪ̇ˈgɒrɪkəl/ *adj* **—allegorically** *adv*

al·leg·ro /əˈlegro; əˈlegrəʊ/ *n* [C] a piece of music played or sung quickly〔乐曲的〕快板 **—allegro** *adj, adv*

al·le·lu·ia /ˌæləˈlujə; ˌælɪ̇ˈluːjə◂/ *interjection* HALLELUJAH 哈利路亚〔犹太教和基督教对上帝的赞美词〕

all-em·brac·ing /ˌ· ·ˈ··◂/ *adj* including everyone or everything 总括的；包罗万象的：*an all-embracing vision of the cosmos* 宇宙总观

Al·len /ˈælən; ˈælən/, **Woody** /ˈwudɪ; ˈwʊdi/ (1935-) a US film DIRECTOR who also acts in his own humorous films, which are often about people who live in New York City and have problems in their relationships 艾伦〔(1935–)，美国电影导演，也在自己导演的喜剧片中扮演角色。他的作品通常以纽约人的生活和情感问题为题材〕

Al·len·de /ɑˈjɛndɪ; aɪˈendi/, **Sal·va·dor** /ˈsælvəˌdɔr; ˈsælvədɔː/ (1908-73) a SOCIALIST politician who was elected President of Chile in 1970. In 1973 Allende and many of his supporters were killed when the army took control of the government. 阿连德〔(1908-1973)，智利社会主义政治家。1970年当选智利总统。他和他的许多支持者死于1973年的军事政变〕

All-En·gland Club /ˌ·ˈ··, ·/ a club in Wimbledon, London that has grass tennis COURTs, where the famous tennis competition called Wimbledon is played every year. Its official name is the 'All England Lawn Tennis and Croquet Club'. 全英网球俱乐部〔伦敦温布尔登一俱乐部，拥有草地网球场，每年举行著名的温布尔登网球公开赛。正式名称是全英草地网球槌球俱乐部〕

Al·len key /ˋælən ki; ˈælən kiː/ *n* [C] *BrE* a small tool you use to turn an Allen screw (=a type of screw with a hole that has six sides)【英】艾伦螺丝钉扳手，六角螺丝扳手

Allen wrench /ˋælən rɛntʃ; ˈælən rentʃ/ *n* [C] *AmE* an Allen key【美】艾伦螺丝钉扳手，六角螺丝扳手

al·ler·gic /əˋlɝdʒɪk; əˈlɜːdʒɪk/ *adj* **1** having an allergy 过敏的: **be allergic to sth** *I'm allergic to penicillin.* 我对青霉素过敏。**2 allergic reaction/rash** an illness or a red painful area on your skin that some people get because of an allergy 过敏反应；过敏性皮疹 **3 allergic to sth** *informal* always trying to avoid an activity or thing that you do not like【非正式】不喜欢某事，对某事反感: *I think he's allergic to work!* 我看他讨厌工作！

al·ler·gy /ˋælɚdʒɪ; ˈælədʒi/ *n* [C,U] a medical condition in which you become ill or in which your skin becomes red and painful because you have eaten certain foods, touched certain things etc 过敏性反应，过敏症: *Do you suffer from any allergies?* 你对什么过敏吗？| [+to] *an allergy to cat fur* 对猫毛过敏

al·le·vi·ate /əˋliviˌet; əˈliːvieɪt/ *v* [T] to make something less painful or difficult 减轻，缓和〔痛苦或困难〕: *a medicine to alleviate cold symptoms* 减轻伤风症状的药 | *measures to alleviate poverty* 脱贫措施 —**alleviation** /əˌliviˋeʃən; əˌliːviˈeɪʃən/ *n* [U]

al·ley /ˋælɪ; ˈæli/ *n* [C] **1** a narrow street between or behind buildings 小巷，胡同 **2 right up/down sb's alley** *AmE* very suitable for someone【美】正合某人的胃口；非常适合某人: *The job sounds right up your alley.* 这项工作听上去正合你的胃口。—see also 另见 BLIND ALLEY, BOWLING ALLEY

alley cat /ˈ·· ·/ *n* [C] a cat that lives on the streets and does not belong to anyone 流浪猫，野猫

al·ley·way /ˋælɪˌwe; ˈæliweɪ/ *n* [C] an ALLEY (1) 小巷，胡同

all-fired /ˌ·ˈ·◂/ *adv AmE informal* a word meaning completely that you use before describing a quality that you think is extreme【美，非正式】极度，完全: *If he weren't so all-fired sure of himself, I'd like him better.* 如果他不是那么过于自信，我会更喜欢他。

all fours —see 见 **on all fours** (FOUR (4))

all go /ˌ·ˈ·/ *adj* **it's all go** *spoken* used to say that a situation is very busy and full of activity【口】忙碌: *It was all go in the office as the deadline approached.* 由于最后期限日益临近，办公室里一片忙碌。

All Hal·lows' Day /ɔlˋhæloz de; ɔːlˈhæləʊz deɪ/ also 又作 **Allhallows, Allhallowmas** /ɔlˋhæloməs; ɔːlˈhæləʊməs/ *old use* another name for All Saint's Day, November 1st【旧】诸圣日〔11月1日，万圣节的别名〕

3 **al·li·ance** /əˋlaɪəns; əˈlaɪəns/ *n* [C] **1** an arrangement in which two or more countries, groups etc agree to work together in order to try to change or achieve something 联盟，同盟: **[+between]** *the alliance between students and factory workers in the 1960s* 20世纪60年代学生与工人之间的联盟 | **[+with]** *Britain's military alliance with her NATO partners* 英国与其北约伙伴的军事联盟 | **enter into/form an alliance** (=agree to work together) 结盟 *The two countries entered into a defensive alliance.* 两国订立了防御联盟。**2** a group that is formed when two or more countries, groups etc work together 同盟 **3 in alliance (with)** if two groups, countries etc are in alliance, they work together to achieve something or protect one another 与…联盟〔结盟〕: *Relief workers in alliance with local charities are trying to help the famine victims.* 救济人员与当地慈善机构联合起来正在设法帮助那些饥民。**4** *formal* close relationship, especially a marriage, between people【正式】〔家族间的〕亲密关系；〔尤指〕联姻 —see also 另见 **unholy alliance** (UNHOLY (3))

al·lied /ˋælaɪd; ˈælaɪd/ *adj* **1 Allied** belonging to or connected with the countries that fought together against Germany in the First or Second World War, or against Iraq in the Gulf War 结盟的，同盟的〈如在第一、第二次世界大战中共同反对德国，或在海湾战争中共同反对伊拉克的结盟国家〉: *an Allied bombing raid* 联合空袭 | *the Allied forces* 盟军 **2 allied industries/organizations/trades etc** connected with each other because of being similar or dependent on each other; RELATED 相关的工业/组织/贸易等: *Agriculture and allied industries provided the state's main source of revenue.* 农业和相关产业构成了该国收入的主要来源。**3 (be) allied to/with** connected with 与…有关联: *Cultural anthropology is closely allied to the field of social psychology.* 文化人类学与社会心理学领域有着紧密联系。**4** joined by common political, military, or economic aims〔政治、军事或经济〕目标一致的: *their allied effort to convince others of the danger of nuclear power* 他们为使他人认识核能危险而作出的共同努力

Al·lies, the /ˋælaɪz; ˈælaɪz/ *n* [plural] **1** the countries, including Britain, the US, and the USSR etc, that fought together during the Second World War〔第二次世界大战期间的〕同盟国〔包括英、美、苏等〕**2** the countries, including Britain, the US, and France etc that fought together during the First World War〔第一次世界大战期间的〕协约国〔包括英、美、法等〕**3** the countries that fought together against Iraq in the Gulf War in the early 1990s〔20世纪90年代初海湾战争中共同反对伊拉克的〕联合国多国部队

al·li·ga·tor /ˋæləˌgetɚ; ˈæləgeɪtə/ *n* **1** [C] a large animal with a long mouth and sharp teeth that lives in the hot wet parts of the US and China 钝吻鳄 **2** [U] the skin of this animal used as leather 钝吻鳄皮革: *alligator shoes* 鳄鱼皮鞋

all-in /ˌ·ˈ·◂/ *adj* extremely tired 极度疲劳: *You look all-in. Are you o.k.?* 你看起来非常疲劳。你没事吧？

all in *adv* **£5000/$100 all in** if you buy or sell something for a particular price all in, that price includes all services, parts etc 全部在内共5000英镑/100美元

all-in·clu·sive /ˌ·····◂/ *adj* including everything 全部包括的: *an all-inclusive price* 包含全部费用的价格

al·lit·er·a·tion /əˌlɪtəˋreʃən; əˌlɪtəˈreɪʃən/ *n* [U] the use of words that begin with the same sound in order to make a special effect, especially in poetry 头韵(法)〔用起头音相同的几个词来制造一种特别的效果，尤用于诗歌〕

all-night·er /ˌ·ˈ··/ *n* [C] *AmE informal* an occasion when you spend the whole night studying or doing written work in university【美，非正式】〔在大学〕通宵学习

al·lo·cate /ˋæləˌket; ˈæləkeɪt/ *v* [T] to decide officially that a particular amount of money, time etc or something such as a house or job etc should be used for a particular purpose 分配，配给: **allocate sb sth** *The duty officer allocated us a cabin for the night.* 值班军官分配一间小屋给我们过夜。| **allocate sth for sth** *one million dollars allocated for disaster relief* 拨出一百万美元用于救灾 | **allocate sth to** *You need to decide how much time to allocate to each exam question.* 你需要决定每一道试题花多长时间。 2

al·lo·ca·tion /ˌæləˋkeʃən; ˌæləˈkeɪʃən/ *n* **1** [C] the amount or share of something that has been allocated to a person or organization 配给物；配给量，份额 **2** [U] the decision to allocate something 拨给；分配，配给

al·lot /əˋlɑt; əˈlɒt/ *v* **allotted, allotting** [T] to decide officially to give something to someone or use something for a particular purpose 分配；拨出: **allot sth to** *You may find it useful to allot 20 minutes each day to this task.* 你会发现每天拿出20分钟时间做这项工作很有用。| **allot sb sth** *The boys were allotted a room each for studying.* 男孩们每人分到一个房间用于学习。

al·lot·ment /əˋlɑtmənt; əˈlɒtmənt/ *n* **1** [C,U] an amount or share of something such as money or time that is given to someone or something, or the process of doing this 分配物[额]，份额；分配: *The budget allotment for each district is prepared at the provincial headquarters.* 各区的预算份额由各省总部分配。| **[+of]** *the allotment of funds to schools* 拨给学校的资金 **2** [C] a small area of land for growing vegetables that people who live in towns in Britain can rent〔在英国租给城镇居民的〕小块菜地

al·lot·ted /əˋlɑtɪd; əˈlɒtɪd/ *adj* **allotted money/time/resources etc** allotted money etc has been officially given to someone for a particular purpose 分配到的钱/时间/资源等: *The department has spent its allotted budget.* 这个部门已经花完了所分配的预算经费。| **in the allotted time** *I didn't finish the test in the allotted time.* 我没有在规定时间内答完试卷。

all-out /ˌ·ˈ·◂/ *adj* [only before noun 仅用于名词前] an all-out effort or attack involves a lot of energy, determination, or anger 全力以赴的，竭尽全力的: *fears of an all-out war* 对一场恶战的恐惧 —**all out** *adv*: *Canada will have to go all out on the ice if they want to win.* 如果加拿大队想赢，就必须在冰上竭尽全力。

al·low /əˋlaʊ; əˈlaʊ/ *v* [T] **1** to let someone do or have something, or let something happen 允许，容许，准许: **allow sb to do sth** *The committee allowed the oil company to build a refinery on the island.* 该委员会准许该石油公司在岛上建一个炼油厂。| **allow sb sth** *We allow passengers one item of hand luggage each.* 我们允许每位乘客带一件手提行李。| **allow sb in/out/up etc** *I don't allow the cat in the bedroom.* 我不允许猫进入卧室。| **be allowed** (=if something is allowed, it is permitted) 获准 *"Can I smoke?" "I'm sorry, it's not allowed."* "我可以吸烟吗？" "对 1 1

不起, 不可以。" | *Abortions were allowed only for reasons of health.* 只有出于健康原因才允许堕胎。| **allow swimming/smoking/talking etc** *We do not allow eating in the classrooms.* 我们不允许在教室里吃东西。| **be allowed (to do sth)** (=you are permitted to do something) 获准做某事 *I wasn't allowed to stay out after 11 o'clock.* 我不可以在11点以后还不回家。—see graph at 参见 PERMIT[1] 图表 **2** to be sure that you have enough time, money, food etc available for a particular purpose〔为某种目的〕给予〔足够的时间/金钱等〕: *We allowed ourselves plenty of time to get to the airport.* 我们给自己留出了足够的时间去机场。**3** to make it possible for something to happen or for someone to do something, especially something helpful or useful 使有可能: **allow sb to do sth** *A 24-hour ceasefire allowed the two armies to bury their dead.* 24小时的停火协定使交战双方得以埋葬阵亡士兵。| **allow sb sth** *The new seatbelt allows the driver greater freedom of movement.* 这种新式安全带使司机活动更自如。**4** to accept or agree that something is correct or permitted by the rules or the law 认可; 被〔规定或法律〕视为正确[正当]: *The judge allowed the evidence.* 法官认可了这些证据。**5 allow that** *formal* to admit that something is true【正式】承认: *I allow that there may have been a mistake.* 我承认可能有错误。**6 allow me!** *spoken* used as a polite way of offering to help someone do something【口】让我来帮你!: *"Allow me," the waiter said, helping her with her coat.* "让我来帮你。"服务员一边说, 一边帮她拿外衣。

allow for sb/sth *phr v* [T] to consider all the possible facts, problems, costs etc involved in a plan or situation and make sure that you can deal successfully with them 考虑, 顾及: *Allowing for inflation, the cost of the project is $2 million.* 考虑到通货膨胀因素, 这个项目的费用为200万美元。

allow of sth *phr v* [T] *formal* to show that something exists or is possible【正式】容许有…的可能: *The facts allow of only one interpretation.* 这些事实只可能有一种解释。—see graphs at 参见 FORBID, LET, PERMIT[1] 图表

al·low·a·ble /əˈlauəbl; əˈlaʊəbəl/ *adj* **1** acceptable according to the rules 可允许的; 可承认的: *the maximum allowable dosage* 可允许的最大剂量 **2** allowable costs are costs that you do not pay tax on 可扣除的,〔费用〕免税的: *allowable deductions such as alimony and business expenses* 免税的扣除额, 如赡养费和业务开销

S2 W3 **al·low·ance** /əˈlauəns; əˈlaʊəns/ *n* [C] **1** an amount of money that you are given regularly or for a special reason〔定期或出于特殊原因而给予的〕津贴, 补助: *His father gave him an allowance of £1,000 a year.* 他父亲每年给他1000英镑的生活费。| **travel/clothing/housing allowance etc** (=money given officially to spend on travel etc) 旅行/服装/住房等津贴 *Jo's salary includes a monthly clothing allowance.* 乔的薪水里包括每月的服装津贴。**2** an amount of something that it is acceptable or safe 允许量, 限额: *What's your daily calorie allowance?* 你每天的热量摄入量最多是多少? | *The baggage allowance is 75 pounds per person.* 每个人准许带75磅重的行李。**3** an amount of money that you can earn without paying tax on it〔收入的〕免税额: *In 1978 allowances amounted to $7,200 for a family of four.* 1978年, 一个四口之家的收入免税额是7200美元。**4** *especially AmE* a small amount of money that a parent regularly gives to a child【尤美】零用钱; POCKET MONEY (1) *BrE*【英】**5 make allowances** to let someone behave in a way you would not normally approve of, because you know there are special reasons for their behaviour 体谅, 顾及: [+for] *Dad is under a lot of pressure, so we have to make allowances for him.* 爸爸承受着很大的压力, 我们必须体谅他。**6 make (an) allowance for** to consider something when making a decision 考虑到: **make no allowance for** *My brother made no allowance for my shorter legs, and I had to run to keep up.* 我哥哥也不考虑我的腿比较短, 我得跑步才能跟上他。

al·loy[1] /ˈælɔɪ; ˈælɔɪ/ *n* [C,U] a metal that consists of two or more metals mixed together 合金: *Brass is an alloy of copper and zinc.* 黄铜是铜和锌的合金。

al·loy[2] /əˈlɔɪ; əˈlɔɪ/ *v* [T] **1** [+with] *technical* to mix one metal with another【术语】将〔两种金属〕铸成合金 **2** *literary* to lower the value or quality of something by mixing it with something else【文】〔通过掺杂而〕使…降低价值[变坏]

all-pow·er·ful /ˌ·ˈ···◂/ *adj* having complete power or control 有无上权力的, 全能的, 无所不能的: *the all-powerful Senate Foreign Relations Committee* 拥有无上权力的参议院对外关系委员会

all-pur·pose /ˈ·ˌ··/ *adj* [only before noun 仅用于名词前] able to be used in any situation 通用的, 有多种用途的: *an all-purpose cleaner* 万能清洁剂

all right[1] *adj, adv* [not before noun 不用于名词前] *spoken*【口】 S1 W2

1 ▶SATISFACTORY 令人满意的◀ satisfactory or acceptable but not excellent 还算可以(的), 比较满意的[地]: *"What's the food like?" "Well, it's all right I suppose, but the place on Melrose Avenue is better."* "食物味道怎么样?" "嗯, 我认为还可以, 不过麦尔罗斯大街的那家更好。" | *"How's school going, Steve?" "Oh, all right, I guess."* "史蒂夫, 学校情况怎么样?" "噢, 我想还不错。"

2 ▶UNHARMED/WITHOUT PROBLEMS 未受伤害/无问题◀ not hurt, not upset, or not having any problems 安全的[地], 健康的[地], 安然无恙的[地]: *Katie looked really unhappy – I'd better go and make sure she's all right.* 凯蒂看起来很不高兴, 我最好去看看, 确保她没什么事。| **be getting on all right** (=not have any problems or difficulties) 进展顺利, 无麻烦事 *The kids seem to be getting on all right at school.* 孩子们在学校似乎一切都顺利。

3 go all right to happen without any problems 一切顺利, 平安: *Did everything go all right with your test?* 你考试一切都顺利吧?

4 be doing all right to be successful in your job, life etc 一切都不错: *She's doing all right – she's got a job with Microsoft.* 她现在一切顺利, 在微软公司找到了工作。

5 ▶SUITABLE 合适的◀ used when saying whether something is suitable or at a good time 合适的: *I'd really like to see you – would Thursday morning be all right?* 我很想见你 —— 星期四上午行吗?

6 it's all right used to make someone feel less afraid or worried 别怕, 没事: *It's all right, Mommy's here.* 别怕, 妈妈在这儿。

7 it's all right/that's all right a) used as a reply when someone thanks you 别客气: *"Thanks for all your help!" "That's all right – it was nothing really."* "谢谢你的帮助!" "不必客气 —— 这不算什么。" **b)** used to tell someone that you are not angry when they say they are sorry for something 没关系: *"Sorry I'm late." "That's all right."* "对不起, 我迟到了。" "没关系。"

8 is it all right if/would it be all right if used when asking if you can do something〔做某事〕可以吗: *Is it all right if I close the window? It's getting cold in here.* 我可以把窗子关上吗? 这里有点冷。

9 it's/that's all right by me used to agree with someone's suggestion 我认为可以〔指同意某人的建议〕: *"Do you think we could finish early today?" "That's all right by me."* "你认为我们今天能早些完成吗?" "我看可以。"

10 it's all right for you/her etc used to say that someone else does not have the same problems and difficulties that you have 你/她等没有同样问题[困难]: *It's all right for you – you don't have to work with her every day. She's driving me crazy.* 你是没事儿 —— 你不必整天和她在一起工作。她简直逼得我发疯了。

11 ▶CHECK UNDERSTANDING 检查理解程度◀ [sentence adverb 句子副词] used to check that someone has understood what you said, or to show that you have understood 明白(吗): *I'll leave the key with the neighbours, all right?* 我把钥匙放在邻居家里, 明白吗? | *"Connect the positive first and then the negative." "Oh I see, all right."* "先接正极, 然后接负极。" "哦, 我明白了。"

12 ▶GREETINGS 招呼◀ *especially BrE* used when greeting someone and asking about their health, what has happened to them recently etc【尤英】安好, 好吗: *Hi, Stuart – you all right?* 嘿, 斯图尔特 —— 你好吗? | *"How are you John?" "Oh, all right – mustn't grumble!"* "约翰, 你好吗?" "啊, 好的, 还不错。"

13 she's/he's all right *BrE* used when you like someone【英】她/他挺好的: *"She's not bad our boss, is she?" "No, she's all right."* "她是个不错的老板, 对吗?" "对, 她挺好的。"

14 ▶CERTAINLY 当然◀ used to admit that something is true, especially when saying that you also think that something else is not 确实: *Wayne's experienced enough all right, but I don't know if he's right for this particular job.* 韦恩的确有丰富经验, 但我不知道他是否适合这项工作。—see also 另见 **a bit of all right** (BIT[1] (20))

all right[2] *interjection*

1 ▶YES 是◀ **a)** used when agreeing with someone's suggestion or agreeing to do something 好的, 好吧〔用于同意某人的建议或做某事〕: *"Why don't we go to a movie?" "All right. Do you want to stop at Gino's for a pizza first?"* "我们为什么不去看电影呢?" "好吧。你要不要先到季诺餐厅买块比萨饼?" **b)** used when agreeing to do something or to allow something, even though you do not want to 可以〔用于勉强同意或允许某事〕: *"Can I play with my new computer game?" "Oh all right then – so long as you don't make too much noise."* "我可以玩玩新电脑游戏吗?" "可以 —— 只要你不弄出太多的声响。"

2 ►ANNOYED 感到恼了◄ **a)** used when saying that you have heard and understood what someone has said, especially when you are annoyed 得了, 行了〔尤用于不耐烦时〕: *"The train leaves at 5.30." "All right! I'm just coming!"* "火车5点半开。" "知道了! 我就来!" **b)** used when asking what has happened or what someone means, especially in an angry or threatening way 好了〔尤用于愤怒或威吓时〕: *All right, what have you two been doing with that knife?* 好了, 你们俩到底在用那把刀干什么?

3 ►INTRODUCE/CHANGE SUBJECT 介绍/改变话题◄ used to introduce a new subject or activity 好了: *All right, folks, I'd like to introduce our first speaker this evening.* 好了, 各位, 我想介绍一下今晚的第一位演讲者。

all-round[1] /ˌ· ˈ·/ *adj* [only before noun 仅用于名词前] *BrE* good at doing many different things, especially at many different sports【英】才能多方面的, 〔尤指体育〕全能的; ALL-AROUND *AmE*【美】: *an all-round athlete* 全能运动员

all-round[2] /ˌ· ˈ·/ *adv BrE informal* used to say that you are thinking about someone or something generally rather than about particular details【英, 非正式】从各方面来看; 总的说来: *All-round it's not a bad car.* 总的来看, 这辆车不错。

all-round·er /ˌ· ˈ· ·/ *n* [C] *BrE* someone who is good at many different things【英】多才多艺的人; 多面手; 全能运动员

All Saints' Day /ˌ· ˈ· ˌ·/ also 又作 **All Hallows' Day** 1 November, when Christian churches remember all the saints 万圣节〔也叫诸圣日, 11月1日, 基督教教会纪念诸圣的日子〕

all-seat·er sta·di·um /ˌ· · · ˈ· · ·/ *n* [C] *BrE* a stadium where sports are played and there are seats for everyone who is watching【英】全座位体育场

all-sing·ing, all-danc·ing /ˌ· ˈ· ·, ˌ· ˈ· ·/ *adj* [only before noun 仅用于名词前] *BrE humorous* an all-singing, all-dancing machine or system is able to do many different things because it is technically advanced【英, 幽默】〔机器或系统〕无所不能的, 多功能的

All Souls' Day /ˌ· ˈ· ˌ·/ 2 November, when people in Christian churches pray for the souls of those who have died 万灵节〔11月2日, 基督教教会为亡灵祈祷的日子〕—compare 比较 ALL SAINTS' DAY

all·spice /ˈɔlˌspaɪs; ˈɔːlspaɪs/ *n* [U] a powder used in cooking to give food a special taste, made from the fruit of a tropical American tree 多香果粉〔一种用于烹调的香料〕

All-Star /ˌ· ˈ·/ *n* [C] a professional BASEBALL or BASKETBALL player who is one of the best and most popular, and who has been chosen to play in an All-Star team (=a team made up of the best players) 全明星队队员〔经选拔进入全明星队的最佳或最受欢迎的职业棒球或篮球运动员〕

all-star /ˈ· · / *adj* [only before noun 仅用于名词前] including many famous actors or sports players 明星荟萃的: *an all-star cast* 全明星阵容

All-Star break /ˌ· · ˈ·/ in BASEBALL, a period in the middle of the SEASON (=the period in the year when baseball is played) when All-Star games are played 全明星赛时间〔棒球赛季过半时全明星队的比赛时间〕

All-Star game /ˌ· · ˈ·/ a BASEBALL or BASKETBALL game played between teams that are made up of the best and most popular professional players in the sport 全明星对抗赛〔最佳或最受欢迎的职业棒球选手或篮球选手组成的球队之间进行的比赛〕

All's Well that Ends Well /ˌ· ·, · · ˈ· ˌ·/ a humorous play by William Shakespeare about the relationship between the two main characters, Helena and Bertram. People sometimes use the expression 'All's Well that Ends Well' to say that a difficult situation has ended with a good result.《终成眷属》〔莎士比亚的一部幽默喜剧, 描述主人公海伦娜和勃特拉姆的关系。有时, 人们借用All's Well that Ends Well这一说法来表达"苦尽甘来"的意思〕

all-ter·rain bi·cy·cle /ˌ· · · ˈ· · ·/ *n* [C] a MOUNTAIN BIKE 越野自行车, 山地自行车

all-ter·rain ve·hi·cle /ˌ· · · ˈ· · ·/ *n* [C] a motor vehicle with three or four wheels that you can drive on rough ground 适应各种地形的车辆, 越野车

All Things Bright and Beau·ti·ful /ˌ· ·, · · ˈ· · ·/ a HYMN (=a song of praise to God) that used to be commonly taught to children in the UK at school《天下明朗悦目万物》〔英国学校过去常教给孩子诵唱的一首赞美诗〕

All Things Considered /ˌ· ·, · ˈ· ·/ a US news programme broadcast in the evening on National Public Radio stations《无事不想》〔美国全国公共广播电台晚间播放的一档新闻节目〕

all-time /ˈ· ·/ *adj* **1 all-time high/low/best etc** the highest, lowest etc level there has ever been 前所未有[空前]的高/低/好等: *The price of wheat reached an all-time low of 42 cents in 1932.* 1932年小麦的价格降到了前所未有的低价 —— 42美分。 **2 all-time record/classic etc** the best ever known 已知最好的纪录/经典等: *He's one of pro football's all-time great receivers.* 他是职业橄榄球迄今最好的直传球接手之一。

al·lude /əˈlud; əˈluːd/ *v*

allude to sb/sth *phr v* [T] *formal* to mention something or someone indirectly【正式】影射, 暗指: *The character's evil nature is constantly alluded to throughout the play.* 在整出戏中, 该角色的邪恶本性不断地被间接提到。

al·lure[1] /əˈlʊr; əˈljʊə/ *n* [singular,U] a mysterious, exciting, or desirable quality that is very attractive 诱惑, 魅力, 吸引力: *Even in her fifties she had lost none of her seductive allure.* 她虽年逾五十, 魅力却丝毫未减。| *the allure of foreign travel* 出国旅行的诱惑

allure[2] *v* [T] to attract someone, especially because of an exciting or desirable quality 吸引, 诱惑 —**allurement** *n* [C]

al·lur·ing /əˈlʊrɪŋ; əˈljʊərɪŋ/ *adj* attractive or desirable 诱人的, 迷人的, 吸引人的: *a low, alluring voice* 低沉而迷人的嗓音

al·lu·sion /əˈluʒən; əˈluːʒən/ *n* [C,U] something that is said or written that brings attention to a particular subject in a way that is not direct 暗示, 暗指, 间接提到; 典故: [+to] *Eliot's poetry is full of allusions to other works of literature.* 艾略特的诗歌中有许多其他文学作品的典故。—**allusive** /-sɪv; -sɪv/ *adj* —**allusively** *adv*

al·lu·vi·al /əˈluvɪəl; əˈluːviəl/ *adj* made of soil left by rivers, lakes, floods etc 冲积的, 淤积的: *an alluvial plain* 冲积平原

al·lu·vi·um /əˈluvɪəm; əˈluːviəm/ *n* [C,U] *technical* soil left by rivers, lakes, floods etc【术语】冲积层; 冲积土

al·ly[1] /ˈælaɪ; ˈælaɪ/ *n* [C] **1** a country that makes an agreement to help or support another country, especially in a war 同盟国: *a meeting of the European allies* 欧洲诸盟国会议 —see also 另见 ALLIES **2** someone who helps and supports you in difficult situations 盟友, 支持者: *Thatcher and Reagan were close allies.* 撒切尔和里根是亲密的盟友。 W3

al·ly[2] /əˈlaɪ; əˈlaɪ/ *v* [I,T] to join with other people or countries to help and support each other 结盟, 联手: **ally yourself to/with** *They allied themselves to the other western states after the war.* 战后他们与其他西方国家结盟。

al·ma ma·ter /ˈɑlmə ˈmɑtə; ˌælmə ˈmeɪtə/ *n* [singular] **1** the school, college, or university that you used to attend 母校 **2** *AmE* the song of a particular school, college, or university【美】校歌

al·ma·nac /ˈɔlməˌnæk; ˈɔːlmənæk/ *n* [C] **1** a book that gives information about the movements of the sun and moon, the times of the TIDES etc for each day of a particular year 天文年历, 历书 **2** a book that gives information about what happened in a particular subject or activity in a particular year 年鉴: *a football almanac* 足球年鉴

Al·mat·y /ˌɑlməˈti; ˌɑːlməˈtiː/ also 又作 **Alma-Ata** a city in southeast Kazakhstan, the country's capital and largest city, formerly called Vernoye, Verny, or Vernyi 阿拉木图〔哈萨克斯坦东南部一城市, 该国首都和最大城市, 旧称维尔诺叶、维尔内或维尔内尼〕

al·might·y /ɔlˈmaɪtɪ; ɔːlˈmaɪti/ *adj* **1 Almighty God/Father** an expression used to talk about God when you want to emphasize his power 全能的上帝/天父 **2 the Almighty** God〔全能的〕上帝[主] **3 God/Christ Almighty** an expression used when you are angry or upset that some people consider offensive 天啊: *God Almighty, what on earth will they do next?* 天啊, 他们接下来究竟要干什么? **4 almighty din/crash/row** *informal* a very loud noise, argument etc【非正式】巨大的嘈杂声/碰撞声/争吵声: *There was an almighty bang in the garden and the shed went up in flames.* 花园里传来一声巨响, 棚屋化为一片火海。

Al·mo·dóu·var /ælmoˈdovar; ˌælməʊˈdəʊvɑː/, **Ped·ro** /ˈpɛdro; ˈpedrəʊ/ (1951-) a Spanish film DIRECTOR famous for his amusing films about Spanish society. His films are often about people with unusual sexual desires and women with serious emotional problems, and include *Women on the Verge of a Nervous Breakdown* (1988) and *Tie Me Up! Tie Me Down!* (1989). 阿尔莫多瓦〔(1951-), 西班牙导演, 以拍摄反映西班牙社会风情的滑稽影片而出名。他的影片通常描写有着反常性欲的人或有严重情感问题的女性, 如《处于精神崩溃边缘的女性》(1988)和《捆着我! 绑着我!》(1989)〕

al·mond /ˈɑmənd; ˈɑːmənd/ *n* [C] a flat pale nut with a slightly sweet taste, or the tree that produces these nuts 杏仁, 扁桃仁; 杏树, 扁桃树

Almond Joy /ˌ· ˈ·/ *trademark* a type of chocolate bar in the US which is made from COCONUT and ALMONDS【商标】杏仁乐〔美国生产的一种椰肉、杏仁巧克力〕

al·mo·ner /ˈælmənə; ˈɑːmənə/ *n* [C] an official in a British hospital in former times who helped people who were ill with their financial and social problems〔英国旧时帮助病人的〕医院社会工作者

al·most /ˈɔlˌmost; ˈɔːlməʊst/ *adv* very nearly but not completely 几乎，差不多，差一点，将近：*We've almost finished.* 我们差不多干完了。| *We stayed there for almost a week.* 我们在那里逗留了将近一星期。| **almost every** *They sold almost everything.* 他们几乎卖掉了所有的东西。| **almost all** *Almost all the children here speak two languages.* 这儿的孩子差不多都会讲两种语言。| *an almost impossible task* 一项几乎无法完成的任务 | *wines which are almost as expensive as champagne* 同香槟酒差不多一样贵的葡萄酒 | **almost certainly** *The cause is almost certainly a virus.* 几乎可以肯定病因是一种病毒。

USAGE NOTE 用法说明：ALMOST

WORD CHOICE 词语辨析：**almost, nearly, hardly, scarcely, very, extremely**

Both **almost** and **nearly** can be used before words like *all, every,* and *everybody.* almost 和 nearly 都可用于 all，every 和 everybody 等词前：*Almost/nearly all (of) my friends came to the party* (NOT 不用 *Almost of my friends came...* or 或 *Almost my friends came...*). 差不多我所有的朋友都来参加聚会了。

Both can also be used before negative verbs 两个词都可用于否定动词前：*I almost/nearly didn't get up in time.* 我差点没及时起床。However, you do not use **not** with *hardly* or *scarcely.* 但 hardly 和 scarcely 不与 not 连用：*There was scarcely enough time to take a shower.* 几乎没有时间淋浴了。

Almost (NOT **nearly**) can be used before *any* and negative words like *no, nobody, never,* and *nothing.* almost 可用于 any 和否定词 no, nobody, never 和 nothing 之前，但 nearly 不可以：*Almost no one came to the party* (NOT 不用 *Nearly no one...*). 几乎没有人来参加聚会。| *You can find the meaning of almost any word here.* 在这里你几乎可以查到任何单词的意思。However, it is more usual to use **hardly** or **scarcely** with *any, anybody, ever* etc than **almost** with *no, nobody, never* etc: For example, you are more likely to hear 但是 hardly 或 scarcely 与 any, anybody, ever 连用，与 almost 和 no, nobody, never 连用比起来，前者更常用些。例如，你会较多听到人们说：*Hardly anybody came to the party.* 几乎没什么人来参加聚会。而不是：*Almost no one came to the party.*

You can use *not* before **nearly**, but not usually before **almost**. nearly 前可加 not，但 almost 前一般不加 not: *She's not nearly as pretty as her sister* (NOT 不用 *She's not almost as pretty...*). 她不如她姐姐漂亮。

Both **nearly** and **almost** can be used with adjectives that have an extreme meaning. nearly 和 almost 都可与有极端含义的形容词连用：*nearly/almost perfect/frozen/dead/impossible* 几近完美/冻结/死去/不可能。However, they are not usually used with other, less extreme, adjectives. In these cases you are more likely to use **very** or **extremely**. 然而，它们通常不与没有极端含义的形容词连用，在这类情况下，多用 very 和 extremely: *The schools are extremely good there* (NOT 不用 *nearly good*). 那儿的学校特别好。| *The coast was very rocky* (NOT 不用 *almost rocky*). 这儿的海岸岩石极多。**Nearly** is more commonly used in British English, while **almost** is more common in American English. 英国英语里多用 nearly，而美国英语多用 almost。

alms /ɑmz; ɑːmz/ *n* [plural] *old-fashioned* money, food, clothes etc that are given to poor people【过时】施舍物，救济品[金]

alms·house /ˈ· ·/ *n* [C] a place where poor people could live without paying rent in former times 贫民所，救济院

a·loe /ˈælo; ˈæləʊ/ *n* **1** [U] the wood of an Indian tree that smells sweet 沉香木 **2 aloes** [plural] the juices of the leaves of the aloe plant used for making medicine 芦荟(汁)

a·loft /əˈlɔft; əˈlɒft/ *adv formal* high up in the air【正式】在高处，在空中：*a flag flying aloft* 高高飘扬的旗帜

a·lo·ha /əˈloha; əˈləʊhə/ *interjection* used as a greeting or to say goodbye in Hawaii 你好；再见〔表示问候或告别的夏威夷语〕

a·lone[1] /əˈlon; əˈləʊn/ *adj* **1** [not before noun 不用于名词前] without any other people 单独的，独自的：*She lives alone.* 她独居。| **alone together** (=if two people are alone together there is no one else in the place where they are)〔两人〕单独在一起 *Suddenly they found themselves alone together in the room.* 突然，他们发现屋子里只剩他们两个人。**2** without any friends or people who you know 孤独的，无伴的：**all alone** (=completely alone) 孤零零的，独自 *It was scary being all alone in a strange city.* 独自一人身处陌生的城市真令人害怕。**3** [not before noun 不用于名词前] feeling very unhappy and lonely 孤单的，寂寞的：*He felt terribly alone when June left.* 琼走后，他感到非常孤独。**4 you alone know/have/can do sth** used to say that you are the only person who knows or can do something 只有自己知道/有/能做某事：*Julie alone knew the terrible truth.* 只有朱莉一个人知道可怕的事实真相。| *Of all the applicants, she alone had the right qualifications.* 在所有的申请人中，只有她符合条件。**5** used to emphasize that one particular thing is very important or has a great effect in a situation 仅仅…就，只有：*The price alone was enough to put me off the idea.* 单看价格就让我打消了这个念头。**6 be alone in (doing) sth** be the only person to do something 是唯一做某事的人：*You're not alone in feeling upset by all this, believe me.* 相信我，不是只有你一个人因为这一切感到不安。

Frequencies of **alone, on your/her own** and **by yourself** in spoken and written English 在英语口语和书面语中 alone, on your/her own 和 by yourself 的使用频率

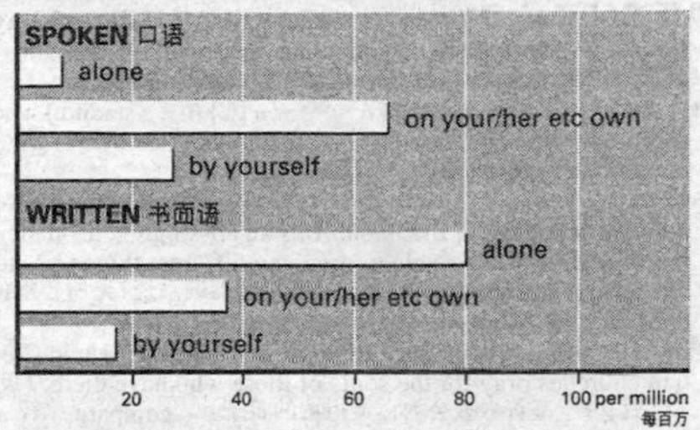

Based on the British National Corpus and the Longman Lancaster Corpus 据英国国家语料库和朗文兰开斯特语料库

In spoken English it is more usual to say **on your own** or **by yourself** rather than **alone**. In written or more formal English **alone** is more common. 英语口语中较常说的是 on your own 或 by yourself，而不是 alone。而在书面语或较正式的英语里则是 alone 更常用。

USAGE NOTE 用法说明：ALONE

WORD CHOICE 词语辨析：**alone, on your own, by yourself, lonely, lonesome, lone, solitary**

If you are **alone**, or less formally, **on your own/by yourself** that just means that no one else is with you, and is neither good nor bad. alone 或不大正式的 on your own/by yourself 都可表示"没别人和你在一起"，既无褒义，也无贬义：*I just wanted to stay at home alone/by myself.* 我只想一个人待在家里。With verbs of action, **on your own** and **by yourself** often suggest that no one is helping you. 与动作动词连用时，on your own 和 by yourself 表示没有人帮忙：*I want to swim alone* (=with no one else there). 我想一个人游泳〔没有旁人在〕。| *I want to swim on my own/by myself* (=either with nobody else there or with other people there but not helping). 我想自己一个人游泳〔意为没有别人在或有别人在也不用帮忙〕。

If you are **lonely** or **lonesome** (*AmE*) you are unhappy because you are alone. lonely 或 lonesome (美) 表示"孤独"和"寂寞"之意：*I feel lonely living away from home.* 离家在外我感到孤独。| *a lonely old man* 孤独的老人。Places etc can be **lonely** or **lonesome** if they make people feel lonely. lonely 或 lonesome 也可用来修饰地点，表示"让人感到寂寞的"：*a lonesome little town on the prairie* 草原上一个人迹罕至的小镇。Things that you do can also be **lonely**. lonely 也可形容事物：*a lonely journey/job/life etc* 孤单的旅程/寂寞的工作/孤寂的生活等。**Lonely** is never an adverb but **alone** often is. lonely 不作副词用，但 alone 常用作副词：*She travelled alone* (NOT 不用 *lonely*). 她独自旅行。

A **lone** or **solitary** person or thing is simply the only one in a place, and therefore might seem a little lonely. lone 或 solitary 修饰人或物表示此人或此物是某个地点唯一的一个，因此会显得寂寞：*a lone figure in the middle of the*

square (=it is the only one there) 广场中心孤零零的一个人影。In spoken English, you are more likely to talk about 英国口语中往往可以这样说: *a figure on its own in the middle of the square* 广场中心孤零零的一个人影。Sometimes **solitary** can suggest that you choose to be alone. 有时 solitary 可指喜欢独处的: *She is a very solitary person.* 她是一个喜欢独处的人。

alone[2] *adv* **1** if you do something difficult alone you do it on your own 单独地, 独自地: *Brian was left to put up the tent alone.* 剩下布赖恩一个人独自搭帐篷。**2 go it alone** to start working or living on your own, especially after working or living with other people 单独行动, 独自干: *After years of working for a big company I decided to go it alone.* 在一家大公司工作多年后, 我决定自己干。**3 leave/let sb alone** to stop annoying or interrupting someone 不打扰某人, 别干涉某人: *Go away and leave me alone, will you?* 走开, 不要烦我, 好吗? **4 leave/let sth alone** to stop touching an object or changing something 不要碰/动某物: *Leave that vase alone or you'll break it!* 不要动那花瓶, 小心打破了! **5 stand alone** if an object or building stands alone it is not near other buildings or objects 孤立, 独处: *I remember my grandparent's house stood alone at the end of the street.* 我记得祖父[母]的房子孤单地伫立在街的尽头。

[1] [1] **a·long**[1] /ə`lɔŋ; ə'lɒŋ/ *adv* **1** if someone or something moves along, they move forward 向前: *I was driving along, thinking about Christmas.* 我一边开车, 一边想着圣诞节。| *He showed me the notes he had made as we went along.* 我们继续下去, 他把他的笔记拿给我看。**2 go/come/be along** to go or come to the place where something is happening, someone is waiting etc 前去/跟来/一起: *We're having a few drinks in the bar – you're welcome to come along.* 我们在酒吧里喝几杯, 欢迎你也一起来。| **be along in a minute** (=arrive soon) 马上到 *There should be another bus along in a minute.* 另一辆公共汽车马上会来。**3 go/come/tag along** to go or come with someone somewhere 一起去/来, 跟随着: *"I'm just out for a walk." "Is it alright if Sharon and I come along too?"* "我想出去走走。" "我和莎伦跟你一起去好吗?" **4 take/bring sb along** to take or bring someone with you somewhere 带某人一起去/来: *Mandy had brought some of her art-school friends along.* 曼迪带了几个她艺校的朋友来。**5 come/go/get along** to improve, develop, or make progress in a particular way 进展, 发展; 进步: **come along fine/nicely/well etc** *"How's she doing after her operation?" "Oh, she's coming along fine."* "她做完手术后怎么样?" "噢, 她情况良好。" | *How are things coming along at work?* 工作进展得如何? **6 along with** together with 与…一起: *Robertson was murdered along with three RUC men near Armagh.* 罗伯逊和三个北爱尔兰皇家警察在阿马附近被杀害。

[1] [1] **along**[2] *prep* **1** if someone or something moves or looks along something, they move or look from one end of it to the other 沿着: *We're driving along Follyfoot Road.* 我们沿着福莱福特路行驶。| *The conductor came hurrying along the corridor.* 列车员沿着通道急匆匆地走过来。| *She glanced anxiously along the line of faces.* 她不安地扫视着这一排面孔。**2** something that is along something else goes down its whole length 沿着…的边缘, 沿着…之傍: *They've put up a fence along Church Lane.* 他们沿着教堂路搭起了篱笆。| *a big crate with some strips of wood along the top* 顶端四周有一些木条的大货箱 | *We found brambles and wild strawberries growing along the disused railway.* 我们发现废弃的铁路两旁长满了黑莓和野草莓。**3** if something is along a passage, wall etc, you can find it at some point there or it has been placed there 在沿…的地方: **just along** (=a short distance from a particular place) 在不远处 *The bathroom is just along the corridor from my room.* 浴室就在离我房间不远的走廊上。| *a waiting room with a bench along one wall* 一边墙边置有长凳的候诊[车]室

[3] **a·long·side** /ə`lɔŋ`saɪd; əˌlɒŋ'saɪd/ *adv, prep* **1** next to or along the side of something 靠着, 沿…一侧: *boats moored alongside each other* 并排停泊在一起的船只 —see picture on page A1 参见 A1 页图 **2** if different types of things, ideas etc are used or exist alongside each other, they are used together or exist at the same time 并存的, 在一起的: *The teacher advised us to use these two course books alongside each other.* 老师建议我们同时用这两本教科书。

a·loof /ə`luf; ə'luːf/ *adj* deliberately staying away from or not talking to other people, especially because you think you are better than they are 冷漠的; 疏远的: **remain/keep/hold yourself aloof** *She preferred to remain distant and aloof.* 她喜欢离群索居。—**aloofly** *adv* —**aloofness** *n* [U]

a·loud /ə`laud; ə'laʊd/ *adv* **1** if you say something aloud you say it in your normal voice 出声地: *Joanne, would you read the poem aloud for us?* 乔安妮, 给我们朗读一下这首诗好吗? **2** in a loud voice 大声地, 高声地: *The pain made him cry aloud.* 他痛得大叫。

al·pac·a /æl`pækə; æl'pækə/ *n* **1** [C] an animal from Peru that looks like a LLAMA 〔秘鲁产的〕羊驼 **2** [U] the cloth made from the wool of an alpaca 羊驼呢绒

al·pha /`ælfə; 'ælfə/ *n* [C usually singular 一般用单数] **1** the first letter of the Greek alphabet 希腊字母表中的第一个字母 **2 the alpha and omega a)** the beginning and the end of something 首尾, 始终 **b)** used to say that something is the best or most important kind of something 最好[最优秀]的东西; 最重要的部分

al·pha·bet /`ælfəˌbɛt; 'ælfəbet/ *n* [C] a set of letters, arranged in a particular order, used in writing language 字母表: *the Cyrillic alphabet* 西里尔字母表

al·pha·bet·i·cal /ˌælfə`bɛtɪkl; ˌælfə'betɪkəl◂/ also 又作 **al·pha·bet·ic** /ˌælfə`bɛtɪk; ˌælfə'betɪk◂/ *adj* relating to the alphabet 字母表的; 按照字母顺序的: **in alphabetical order** *The dictionary is arranged in alphabetical order.* 这本词典是按字母顺序编排的。—**alphabetically** /-klɪ; -kli/ *adv* —see graph at 参见 ORDER[1] 图表

al·pha·nu·mer·ic /ˌælfənu`mɛrɪk; ˌælfənjuː'merɪk◂/ *adj* using letters and numbers 字母数字(混合)的; 文数(式)的: *an alphanumeric code* 字母数字(混合)代码

al·pine /`ælpaɪn; 'ælpaɪn/ *adj* **1** related to the Alps 阿尔卑斯山脉的; 高山的 **2** alpine plants grow near the top of a mountain where trees cannot grow 〔植物〕高山生长的

Alps, the /ælps; ælps/ a range of mountains which go through France, Switzerland, Italy, Germany, and Austria. Many people visit the Alps to ski. 阿尔卑斯山〔横跨法国、瑞士、意大利、德国和奥地利等国的一座山脉, 许多人去阿尔卑斯山滑雪〕

al·read·y /ɔl`rɛdɪ; ɔːl'redi/ *adv* **1** by or before now, or before a particular time 已经〔表示在此之前或某个特定时间之前〕: *The design of the new house is similar to those that have already been built.* 新房子的设计与已建好的那些很类似。| *as I have already mentioned* 正如我已经提到的 **2** used to say that something has been done before and does not need to be done again 已做过: *She asked me to read this chapter, but I've already done it.* 她要我读一下这一章, 但我已经读过了。| *"Do you want a coffee?" "No, I've already got one thanks."* "要来杯咖啡吗?" "不, 谢谢, 我已经有一杯了。" **3** used to say that something has happened too soon or before the expected time 比预期早: *Are you leaving already?* 你这么早就要走吗? | *I've forgotten already!* 我竟然已经忘了! | *Is it 5 o'clock already?* 现在已经5点了吗? **4** used to say that a situation, especially a bad one, now exists and it might get worse, greater, etc 已经〔表示某种情况(尤指不好的情况)已经存在, 而且可能会进一步恶化〕: *The building's already costing us far too much money as it is.* 事实上, 这幢楼已经花费我们太多的钱。—see 见 JUST[1] (USAGE), STILL[1] (USAGE) [1] [1]

al·right /ˌɔl`raɪt; ˌɔːl'raɪt/ *adj, adv* another spelling of ALL RIGHT that many people think is incorrect 〔all right 的另一种拼法, 但许多人认为是错的〕

Al·sa·tian /æl`seʃən; æl'seɪʃən/ *n* [C] *especially BrE* a large dog used especially by police or to guard houses【尤英】阿尔萨斯狼狗, 德国牧羊犬; GERMAN SHEPHERD *especially AmE*【尤美】—see picture at 参见 DOG[1] 图

al·so /`ɔlso; 'ɔːlsəʊ/ *adv* **1** in addition to something else you have mentioned; as well as 而且, 除此之外, 还: *She owns several houses in Leeds and also has business interests in Manchester.* 她不但在利兹拥有几座房产, 在曼彻斯特还持有商业股权。| *I'll take the car because it's a long walk from the station; also the forecast is for rain.* 我会坐汽车, 因为从火车站要走很远的路, 而且天气预报说有雨。| *We can supply samples and there are other laboratories that can be consulted also.* 我们可以提供样品, 并且还有其他实验室可供咨询。| **not only... but also...** *The report has not only attracted much attention but also some sharp criticism.* 报告不仅吸引了很多关注, 也惹来了一些尖锐的批评。**2** used when saying that the same thing is true about another person or thing 也, 同样: *My girlfriend was also called Helen.* 我的女朋友也叫海伦。—see 见 MOREOVER (USAGE) [1] [1]

USAGE NOTE 用法说明: ALSO

WORD CHOICE 词语辨析: also, too, as well, either, neither

When you want to say that something exists or happens in addition to something else, **too** and **as well** are more common than **also** in informal and spoken English. 在非正式

场合或口语中，补充说明某物也存在或某事也发生时，一般用 too 和 as well，而不用 also。In a scientific report you might see 在科学报告中也许可以看到：*The acid also reacts with the coating.* 酸也与涂层产生反应。Or it can be used as part of a more formal request. also 也可用于比较正式的要求：*Could you also type this please?* 你能把这个也打一下吗？In spoken English, **as well** is very common. 在英语口语中，as well 较常用：*Can you come too/as well?* 你也能来吗？| *I was so busy I missed lunch and dinner as well.* 我太忙了，错过午餐又误了晚餐。

If the verb is negative, you use **either**. 如动词是否定形式，用 either: *"I don't like grammar." "I don't like it either."* "我不喜欢语法。""我也不喜欢。" (NOT *I don't like it too* or *I don't also like it*, though *I also don't like it* is possible, but more formal).〔不用 I don't like it too 或 I don't also like it，但可以说 I also don't like it，不过比较正式〕In informal English people usually say **not … either** rather than **neither** 在非正式文体中，人们一般用 not … either 而不用 neither: *She won't come with me or with Grandpa either.* 她既不肯和我一起来，也不肯和爷爷一起来。(If here you said: *She will neither come with me nor with Grandpa,* it would sound very formal and unnatural.)〔如果说：She will neither come with me nor with Grandpa，听起来太正式，不自然。〕

GRAMMAR 语法

Also usually comes after the first auxiliary or modal verb and before the main verb. also 一般用在第一个助动词或情态动词之后、主要动词之前：*The school also has a gymnasium* (NOT usually 一般不用 *The school has also a gymnasium*). 这所学校也有个体育馆。| *He can also sing a little* (NOT usually 一般不用 *… also can*). 他也会唱一点儿。| *Many were bringing up children and also working.* 许多人既要抚养孩子又要工作。

Also usually follows the verb *to be* where it is used alone as a main verb. 动词 to be 单独作为主要动词用时，also 通常跟在其后：*Osaka is also worth a visit.* 大阪也值得一游。**Also** is not usual at the end of a sentence, where **too** and **as well** are common. 句末一般不用 also，而用 too 和 as well。

also-ran /ˈ‥ ·/ *n* [C] someone who has failed to win a competition or election〔比赛或选举的〕失败者，落选者

al·tar /ˈɔltɚ; ˈɔːltə/ *n* [C] **1** a table or raised surface that is the centre of many religious ceremonies, especially in Christianity〔尤指基督教教堂中的〕祭坛，圣台：*the candles on the altar* 圣台上的蜡烛 **2** the part of a church, often at the front, where the priest or minister stands〔神甫或牧师站立的〕讲坛

altar boy /ˈ‥ ·/ *n* [C] a boy who helps a Catholic priest during the church service 祭坛助手

al·tar·piece /ˈɔltɚˌpis; ˈɔːltəpiːs/ *n* [C] a painting or SCULPTURE (2) behind an altar 在祭坛后的绘画或雕刻

al·ter /ˈɔltɚ; ˈɔːltə/ *v* **1** [I,T] to change or make someone or something change 使变化，改变：*Her face hadn't altered much over the years.* 过了这么多年，她的容貌并没有多大改变。| **alter sth** *Nothing can alter the fact that the refugees are our responsibility.* 没有任何事情可以改变我们对难民负有责任这个事实。**2** [T] to make a piece of clothing longer, wider etc 使改动，更改〔把衣服加长、加宽等〕：*You'll have to have the dress altered for the wedding.* 你得请人把裙子改一下，好在婚礼时穿。**3** [T] *AmE* to take away the sexual organs of a male cat or dog【美】阉割〔公猫或公狗〕

al·ter·a·tion /ˌɔltəˈreʃən; ˌɔːltəˈreɪʃən/ *n* [C] a small change that makes someone or something slightly different 变动，改动：*Have you noticed any alteration in the patient's behaviour?* 你注意到病人的行为有什么变化吗？| **to make alterations** *I'm having alterations made to the suit.* 我要请人把我的套装改一下。| **minor alterations** *Your paper is fine except for some minor alterations I've suggested.* 除了我建议的少许改动以外，你的论文写得不错。

al·ter·ca·tion /ˌɔltɚˈkeʃən; ˌɔːltəˈkeɪʃən/ *n* [C,U] *formal* a short but usually noisy argument【正式】争辩，争吵，吵嘴

al·ter e·go /ˈæltɚ ˈigo; ˌæltər ˈiːgəʊ/ *n* [C] **1** another part of your character that is very different from your usual character, or a person in a film, book etc who shows part of the director or writer's character 个性的另一面；化身〔电影和书中反映出导演或作者某些性格特点的人物〕：*Mickey Mouse was Walt Disney's alter ego.* 米老鼠反映了沃尔特·迪斯尼性格的另一面。**2** someone who you trust who thinks about things in the same way as you do 至交，知己，密友

al·ter·nate[1] /ˈɔltɚˌnɪt; ɔːlˈtɜːnɪt/ *adj* [usually before noun 一般用于名词前] **1** two alternate actions, situations, or states happen one after the other in a repeated pattern 轮流的，交替的：*walls painted with alternate strips of yellow and green* 涂有黄绿相间彩条的墙壁 | *alternate rain and sunshine* 时雨时晴 **2** *especially AmE* used instead of the one that was intended to be used; ALTERNATIVE[1] (1)【尤美】可替代的，备用的：*We have to have an alternate plan in case it rains.* 我们必须有一个替代计划，以防下雨。**3** happening or doing something on one of every two days 间隔的：*He works alternate days.* 他隔天工作。| **alternate Mondays/weekends etc** *She visits her parents on alternate weekends.* 她隔个周末去看望父母。

al·ter·nate[2] /ˈɔltɚˌnet; ˈɔːltəneɪt/ *v* [I,T] if two things alternate or you alternate them, they happen one after the other in a repeated pattern（使）轮流，交替：[**+between**] *Her emotions alternated between outrage and sympathy.* 她时而表现出愤怒，时而又流露出同情。| **alternate sth with sth** *We tried to alternate periods of work with sleep.* 我们尽量让工作和睡觉交替进行。—**alternation** /ˌɔltɚˈneʃən; ˌɔːltəˈneɪʃən/ *n* [C,U]

al·ter·nat·ing cur·rent /ˌ‥‥ ˈ‥/ *n* [U] a flow of electricity that regularly changes direction at a very fast rate 交流电 —compare 比较 DIRECT CURRENT

al·ter·na·tive[1] /ɔlˈtɝnətɪv; ɔːlˈtɜːnətɪv/ *adj* **1** [only before noun 仅用于名词前] an alternative idea, plan etc is one that can be used instead of another one 可替代的；另外的；两者择一的：*There doesn't seem to be an alternative option.* 似乎没有另外的选择。**2** [only before noun 仅用于名词前] an alternative system or solution is considered less damaging or more effective than the old one 可取代〔旧有〕的：*alternative sources of energy* 替代能源 —see also 另见 ALTERNATIVE MEDICINE **3** not based on or believing in the established social or moral standards 另类的，非正统的：*an alternative lifestyle* 另类的生活方式 | *alternative theatre* 非正统戏剧 —**alternatively** *adv*: *We could walk or alternatively we could go in Ted's car.* 我们可以走路去，也可以搭特德的车去。

alternative[2] *n* [C] something that you can choose to do or use instead of something else 可供选择的事物：*Check out the alternatives before deciding whether to go to a nearby college.* 在决定是否上一所附近的大学以前，最好查一下有没有其他可以选择的学校。| [**+to**] *a viable alternative to the present system of welfare benefits* 可代替现有福利体制的一个切实可行的方案 | **have no alternative** (=used to say that you feel you must do something) 别无选择 *I had no alternative but to report him to the police.* 除了向警方举报他，我别无选择。| **there's no alternative** *I'm sorry, there's no alternative but to sell the car.* 对不起，我别无选择，只好卖汽车。

alternative medi·cine /ˌ‥‥ ˈ‥/ *n* [U] one of the ways of treating illnesses that is not based on Western scientific methods 替代医学，替代疗法：*Homeopathy is a popular form of alternative medicine.* 顺势疗法是一种流行的替代疗法。

CULTURAL NOTE 文化注释

Alternative medicine Today many people in the UK and US choose to be treated by alternative medicine or complementary medicine. Chinese medicine is also increasingly popular. Most alternative medicine is not available on the National Health Service in the UK, and people have to pay for their treatment. Since the early 1980s alternative medicine has become more and more popular, and although it is not officially accepted by the medical profession, some doctors do accept that such methods can be effective in treating some types of illness. 替代疗法：如今很多英美人选择替代疗法或补充疗法治病。中医也日益流行。在英国，替代疗法大多不属于国民保健制度涵盖的范围，须自行付费。20 世纪80 年代以后，替代疗法日益流行，尽管未被医学界正式承认，仍有一些医生承认替代疗法对某些疾病的确有效。

al·ter·na·tor /ˈɔltɚˌnetɚ; ˈɔːltəneɪtə/ *n* [C] an electric GENERATOR for producing ALTERNATING CURRENT 交流发电机 —see picture at 参见 ENGINE 图

al·though /ɔlˈðo; ɔːlˈðəʊ/ *conj* **1** in spite of the fact that; THOUGH (1) 虽然，尽管：*Although she joined the company only a year ago, she's already been promoted twice.* 虽然她一年前才加入公司，但是已经两次升职。| *Although the car is old it still runs well.* 虽然车很旧，但跑起来仍然不错。**2** but; HOWEVER 但是，然而：*I don't really enjoy sports, although I did watch the game.* 实际上我不太喜欢体育，虽然我的确看过这场比赛。| *I can*

see his point, although, I have to say, I think he's wrong. 我能理解他的观点，但我必须说，我认为他的观点是错误的。

al·ti·me·ter /æl`tɪmətə; 'æltɪ,miːtə/ *n* [C] an instrument used in aircraft that tells you how high you are 高度计[表]

al·ti·tude /`æltə,tud; 'æltɨtjuːd/ *n* **1** [C] the height of an object or place above the sea 海拔，高度：*The plane was flying at an altitude of 30,000 feet.* 这架飞机在三万英尺的高空飞行。**2 high/low altitudes** a high or low level above the sea 海拔高/低的地方：*At high altitudes it is difficult to get enough oxygen.* 在海拔很高的地方很难得到足够的氧气。—compare 比较 ELEVATION (1)

al·to /`ælto; 'æltəʊ/ *n* [C] **1** a woman with a low singing voice 女低音（歌手）**2** [singular] the part of a piece of music that this person sings 中音部

al·to·geth·er¹ /,ɔltə`gɛðə; ,ɔːltə'geðə◂/ *adv* **1** a word meaning completely or thoroughly that is used to emphasize what you are saying 全然，完全〔用于强调所说的内容〕：*It seems to have vanished altogether.* 它似乎完全消失了。| *Eventually they chose an altogether different design.* 最终他们选择了一款截然不同的设计。| *How this is to be achieved is altogether a different matter.* 怎样完成这个目标完全是另一回事。| **not altogether** *I'm not altogether sure if I'd want you as a wife!* 我没有十足把握是否会选你做妻子！| *He did not altogether understand.* 他不完全理解。**2** used to make a final statement about several things you have just said 总的说来，总而言之：*The hotel was nice; the weather was hot; the beaches were beautiful. Altogether I'd say it was a great vacation.* 宾馆很舒适，天气很暖和，海滩很美丽。总的来讲，我得说这个假期很愉快。**3** used when you are stating a total amount 总计：*There were five people altogether.* 总共有五个人。| *How much do I owe you altogether?* 我总共欠你多少钱？

altogether² *n* **in the altogether** *BrE* without any clothes on; NUDE【英】赤身露体

al·tru·is·m /`æltru,ɪzəm; 'æltru-ɪzəm/ *n* [U] the practice of thinking of the needs and desires of other people instead of your own 利他主义，无私 —**altruist** *n* [C]

al·tru·is·tic /,æltru`ɪstɪk; ,æltru'ɪstɪk◂/ *adj* altruistic behaviour shows that you care about others more than you care for yourself 利他主义的，关心他人胜过自己的：*Were his motives completely altruistic?* 他的动机是完全无私的吗？—**altruistically** /-klɪ; -kli/ *adv*

al·um /`æləm; 'æləm/ *n* [C+of] *AmE spoken* a former student of a school, college, university etc【美口】校友

al·u·min·i·um /,æljə`mɪnɪəm; ,æljʊ'mɪniəm◂/ *BrE*【英】**a·lu·min·um** *AmE*【美】/ə`lumɪnəm; ə'luːmɨnəm/ *n* [U] a silver-white metal that is an ELEMENT (=simple substance) and is light and easily made into different shapes 铝

aluminium foil /,····`·/ *n* [U] a very thin sheet of shiny metal that you wrap around food to protect it; TINFOIL〔用于包食物的〕铝箔，锡箔纸

a·lum·na /ə`lʌmnə; ə'lʌmnə/ *n plural* **alumnae** /-ni; -niː/ [C] *formal especially AmE* a woman who is a former student of a school, college, or university【正式，尤美】女校友

a·lum·ni /ə`lʌmnaɪ; ə'lʌmnaɪ/ *n* [plural] *AmE* the former students of a school, college, or university【美】校友：*Berkeley alumni* 伯克利大学的校友 | *the alumni association* 校友会

a·lum·nus /ə`lʌmnəs; ə'lʌmnəs/ *n* [C] *formal especially AmE* a former student of a school, college, or university【正式，尤美】校友

al·ve·o·lar /æl`viələ; ,ælvi'əʊlə◂/ *n* [C] *technical* a CONSONANT sound such as /t/ or /d/ made by putting the end of the tongue at the top of the mouth behind the upper front teeth【术语】齿龈音〈如 t 或 d 等辅音〉—**alveolar** *adj*

al·ways /`ɔlwez; 'ɔːlwɨz/ *adv* **1** all the time, at all times, on every occasion 总是，每次都：*Always lock your bicycle to something secure.* 每次都把脚踏车锁在某个固定物体上。| *Tea is always served at 5 o'clock.* 茶点总是在 5 点钟提供。| *She had always assumed that Gabriel was a girl's name.* 她一直认为加布里埃尔是个女孩名字。| *Anne had always been pretty.* 安妮过去总是漂漂亮亮的。| *He wasn't always a butler.* (=he had other jobs at other times in his life) 他并不一直是当管家的。—see picture at 参见 FREQUENCY 图 **2** for as long as you can remember or for a very long time 一直，长久以来：*I've always wanted to go to Paris.* 我一直都想去巴黎。**3** if you say that you will always do something, you mean that you will do it forever 永远：*I'll always remember that day.* 我会永远记住那一天。| *He said he would love me always.* 他说他会永远爱我。**4** if someone is always doing something, or if something always happens, it happens often, especially in an annoying way 没完没了地，老是：*That wretched car is always breaking down!* 那辆破汽车老是抛锚！| *She's always flirting with him.* 她老是跟他调情。**5 you could always.../there is always...** *spoken* used to make a polite suggestion【口】你随时可以…：*You could always try ringing her again.* 你可以试着随时再给她打个电话。| *If you can't get it locally, there's always mail order.* 如果你在当地买不到，总可以邮购。

USAGE NOTE 用法说明：ALWAYS

GRAMMAR 语法

Always usually comes after the first auxiliary or modal verb and before the main verb. always 通常放在第一个助动词或情态动词之后、主要动词之前：*He always wanted/had a room of his own* (NOT 不用 *He had/wanted always a room of his own*). 他一直想要/有一间属于自己的房间。| *He had always lived there* (*had* is auxiliary here). 他一直住在那儿〔had 在这里是助动词〕。| *You should always be careful walking alone at night* (NOT usually 一般不用 *should be always careful*). 晚上一个人走路你时时都要小心。

Always usually follows the verb *to be* where it is used alone as a main verb. 动词 to be 单独作为主要动词用时，always 通常放在其后：*I am always hungry* (NOT 不用 *I always am hungry*). 我老觉得饿。

SPELLING 拼法

Remember it is **always** 记住其拼法是 always (NOT 不是 *allways* or 或 *all ways*)。

AM /,e`ɛm; ,eɪ 'em◂/ **1** [U] amplitude modulation; a system for broadcasting radio programmes that is not as clear as FM〔广播〕调幅 —see also 另见 FM **2** Assembly Member; a politician who is one of the 60 members of the Welsh Assembly. The Welsh Assembly is the parliament for Wales. 议员〔威尔士政界人士，议会 60 名议员中的一位〕

am¹ /əm; m; *strong* 强读 æm; æm/ *v* the first person singular of the present tense of the verb to BE〔动词 be 的第一人称单数现在时〕

am², AM /`e`ɛm; ,eɪ 'em/ ante meridiem; used when talking about times that are after MIDNIGHT but before MIDDAY 午前，上午：*I start work at 9 am.* 我上午 9 时开始工作。—see also 另见 PM

A.M.A., the /,e ɛm `e; ,eɪ em 'eɪ/ also 又作 **the AMA** the American Medical Association; an organization in the US for doctors and people who do medical research 美国医学会〔美国医生和医学研究者的一个组织〕

a·mal·gam /ə`mælgəm; ə'mælgəm/ *n* **1** [C] *formal* a mixture or combination of different things or substances【正式】混合物：[+of] *Her work is a strange amalgam of different musical styles.* 她的作品是各种音乐风格的奇特混合。**2** [C,U] *technical* a mixture of metals, used to fill holes in teeth【术语】〔补牙用的〕汞合金；汞齐

a·mal·gam·ate /ə`mælgə,met; ə'mælgəmeɪt/ *v* [I+with,T] if two businesses or groups amalgamate, or if one business or group amalgamates with another, they join to form a bigger organization （使）〔公司或集团等〕联合，（使）合并 —**amalgamation** /ə,mælgə`meʃən; ə,mælgə'meɪʃən/ *n* [C,U]

a·man·u·en·sis /ə,mænju`ɛnsɪs; ə,mænju'ensɨs/ *n* [C] *formal* someone whose job is to write down what someone else says or copy what they have written【正式】记录员，誊写员，文书

Amarillo /,æmə`rɪlo; ,æmə'rɪləʊ/ an industrial city in northwest Texas, known for its mineral production and RODEOS 阿马里洛〔得克萨斯州西北部一工业城市，以出产矿物和牛仔竞技表演而闻名〕

a·mass /ə`mæs; ə'mæs/ *v* [T] to gradually collect a large amount of money, knowledge, or information 积聚，积累，大量收集：*For twenty-five years Darwin amassed evidence to support his theories.* 达尔文用了 25 年时间收集大量的证据来支持自己的理论。

am·a·teur¹ /`æmə,tʃʊr; 'æmətə/ *adj* **1** not doing something as your job, but only for pleasure or interest 业余（爱好）的，非职业的：*an amateur golfer* 业余高尔夫球员 | *an amateur orchestra* 业余管弦乐队 **2** amateurish 外行的，生手的

amateur² *n* [C] someone who does an activity for pleasure or interest, not as a job 业余爱好者：*a gifted amateur* 有才华的业余爱好者 —compare 比较 PROFESSIONAL² (1)

amateur dra·mat·ics /,····`··/ *n* [U] *BrE* the activity of producing or acting in plays by people who do it for pleasure and not as a job【英】业余演剧活动；业余戏剧表演

A

CULTURAL NOTE 文化注释

In Britain, most towns have an amateur dramatics group, and because the standard is not always very high, it is sometimes connected with bad over-emotional acting, and many people think of it as being humorous. 英国大部分城镇均有业余演剧团体，因水平往往不是很高，有时人们将其与夸张拙劣的表演联系起来，很多人认为业余表演很滑稽：*When they screamed at each other and he walked out of the meeting, it was like amateur dramatics.* 他们相互叫喊，他离开了会场，那场景就像滑稽的业余表演。

am·a·teur·ish /ˌæməˋtɜɪʃ; ˈæmətərɪʃ/ *adj* not skilfully done or made 不熟练的，外行的：*His paintings are amateurish.* 他的绘画作品还不成熟。—**amateurishly** *adv* —**amateurishness** *n* [U]

am·a·teur·is·m /ˈæməˌtʃurɪzəm; ˈæmətərɪzəm/ *n* [U] the belief that enjoying a sport or other activity is more important than earning money from it 业余爱好主义〔认为享受体育运动或其他活动的乐趣比从中挣钱更为重要〕

am·a·to·ry /ˈæməˌtorɪ; ˈæmətəri/ *adj literary* expressing sexual or romantic love【文】爱情的；色情的

a·maze /əˋmez; əˈmeɪz/ *v* [T] to make someone very surprised 使大为惊奇，使惊愕：*Dave amazed his friends by suddenly getting married.* 戴夫突然间结婚，令朋友们非常吃惊。| *Their loyalty never ceases to amaze me.* 他们的忠诚一直令我惊叹。

a·mazed /əˋmezd; əˈmeɪzd/ *adj* **be amazed** extremely surprised 感到惊奇，惊讶：[+(that)] *I'm amazed you've never heard of Jeremy Bentham.* 你居然从未听说过杰里米·边沁，真让我吃惊。| [+at] *We were amazed at his rapid recovery.* 我们对他这么快就康复感到惊奇。| **amazed to see/hear/find etc** *Visitors are often amazed to discover how little the town has changed.* 旅游者经常会惊奇地发现这个小城几乎没有什么变化。

a·maze·ment /əˋmezmənt; əˈmeɪzmənt/ *n* [U] a feeling of great surprise 吃惊，惊奇：**in amazement** *Ralph gasped in amazement.* 拉尔夫吃惊得倒抽了一口气。| **to my amazement** *To my amazement she came up and shook my hand.* 她竟然走过来和我握手，令我吃了一惊。

2 **a·maz·ing** /əˋmezɪŋ; əˈmeɪzɪŋ/ *adj* **1** extremely good, especially in a surprising and unexpected way 惊人的；了不起的：*He's an amazing player to watch.* 看他比赛那才叫精彩呢。| *an amazing bargain* 令人惊喜的廉价货 **2** so surprising that it is hard to believe 令人惊诧的，让人难以相信的：*amazing stories of strange happenings during Geller's performances* 有关盖勒表演中出现各种怪事的令人称奇的传说 —**amazingly** *adv*: *an amazingly generous offer* 极慷慨的出价

Amazing Grace /·,··ˈ·/ a HYMN (=a song of praise to God) that is popular in the US and in the UK《奇妙的恩典》〔英美流行的一首赞美诗〕

am·a·zon /ˈæməˌzɑn; ˈæməzən/ *n* [C] a tall strong woman 高大而强壮的女人；悍妇 —**amazonian** /ˌæməˋzonɪən; ˌæməˈzəʊnɪən◂/ *adj*

Amazon, the /ˈæməˌzɑn; ˈæməzən/ a river in South America, which goes through Peru and Brazil and is the second longest river in the world 亚马孙河〔位于南美洲，流经秘鲁和巴西，是世界第二大河流〕

Amazon.com /ˈæməzn dɑt kɑm; ˈæməzən dɒt kɒm/ a US WEBSITE that sells books, music, toys etc. You make your order and pay over the Internet, and the books, toys etc are sent to you through the post. Amazon also have websites in other countries such as the UK (amazon.co.uk) and Germany (amazon.de). 亚马逊网上书店〔美国一网站，销售图书、音乐作品和玩具等。买家网上订货、付款，书籍、玩具等通过邮局寄送。亚马逊网上书店在英国、德国等国家也设有网站〕

am·bas·sa·dor /æmˋbæsədɚ; æmˈbæsədə/ *n* [C] an important official who represents his or her government in a foreign country 大使 —**ambassadorial** /æmˌbæsəˋdɔrɪəl; æmˌbæsəˈdɔːriəl/ *adj* —**ambassadorship** /æmˋbæsədɚˌʃɪp; æmˈbæsədəʃɪp/ *n* [C,U]

am·bas·sa·dress /æmˋbæsədrɪs; æmˈbæsədrɪs/ *n* [C] the wife of an ambassador 大使夫人

am·ber /ˈæmbɚ; ˈæmbə/ *n* [U] **1** a yellowish brown colour 琥珀色 **2** a yellowish brown substance used to make jewellery 琥珀 —**amber** *adj*

ambi- /æmbɪ; æmbɪ/ *prefix* both; double 两个，双：*ambidextrous* (=using both hands equally well) 双手都很灵巧的

am·bi·ance /ˈæmbɪəns; ˈæmbiəns/ *n* [singular,U] another spelling of AMBIENCE ambience 的另一种拼法

am·bi·dex·trous /ˌæmbəˋdɛkstrəs; ˌæmbɪˈdekstrəs◂/ *adj* able to use either hand with equal skill 双手都能灵巧运用的

am·bi·ence /ˈæmbɪəns; ˈæmbiəns/ *n* [singular,U] the way a place makes you feel 气氛，情调，环境：*a restaurant with a friendly ambience* 气氛宜人的餐厅

am·bi·ent /ˈæmbɪənt; ˈæmbiənt/ *adj technical*【术语】**ambient temperature/pressure** the temperature etc of the surrounding area 环境温度/压力

ambient music /ˌ···ˈ··/ *n* [U] slow electronic music that you listen to when you want to relax 环境音乐

am·big·u·ous /æmˋbɪgjuəs; æmˈbɪgjuəs/ *adj* **1** having more than one meaning, so that it is not clear which is intended 歧义的；含糊的，不明确的：*an ambiguous sentence* 歧义句 **2** difficult to understand 难以理解的：*His role in the affair is ambiguous.* 他在事件中的角色并不明确。—**ambiguously** *adv* —**ambiguity** /ˌæmbɪˋgjuətɪ; ˌæmbɪˈgjuːɪti/ *n* [C,U]: *Her speech was full of ambiguities and contradictions.* 她的讲话含糊其辞，自相矛盾。

am·bit /ˈæmbɪt; ˈæmbɪt/ *n* [singular] *formal* the range or limit of something【正式】界限，范围：*within the ambit of the law* 在法律允许的范围内

am·bi·tion /æmˋbɪʃən; æmˈbɪʃən/ *n* **1** [U] determination to be successful, rich, powerful etc 抱负，雄心；野心：*Your problem is you have no ambition.* 你的问题在于胸无大志。**2** [C] a strong desire to achieve something 愿望，志向：*My ambition is to become a pilot.* 我的愿望是当一名飞行员。

am·bi·tious /æmˋbɪʃəs; æmˈbɪʃəs/ *adj* **1** determined to be successful, rich, powerful etc 有抱负的，有雄心大志的；野心勃勃的：*an ambitious and hard-working junior manager* 雄心勃勃、工作勤奋的初级（部门）经理 | **be ambitious for sb** (=want them to be very successful) 希望某人成功 *Mothers are often highly ambitious for their children.* 做母亲的往往都希望孩子事业有成。**2** an ambitious plan, idea etc shows a desire to do something good but difficult 雄心勃勃的，需要极大努力或才干才能完成的：*one of the most ambitious engineering projects of modern times* 现代难度最大的工程项目之一 —**ambitiously** *adv* —**ambitiousness** *n* [U]

am·biv·a·lent /æmˋbɪvələnt; æmˈbɪvələnt/ *adj* not sure whether you want or like something or not〔心情〕矛盾的：*Her feelings about getting married are distinctly ambivalent.* 她显然对是否要结婚感到矛盾。—**ambivalence** *n* [U] —**ambivalently** *adv*

am·ble /ˈæmbl; ˈæmbəl/ *v* [I always+adv/prep] to walk in a slow relaxed way 漫步：[+along/across etc] *The old man came out and ambled over for a chat.* 老人出来了，从容地走过去聊天。—**amble** *n* [singular]

Am·bridge /ˈæmbrɪdʒ; ˈæmbrɪdʒ/ an imaginary village in the English countryside where the characters of *The Archers*, a British radio programme, live and work 安布里奇〔虚构的一个英格兰乡村。英国广播节目《阿切尔斯一家》中的人物生活、工作的地方〕

am·bro·si·a /æmˋbroʒə; æmˈbrəʊziə/ *n* [U] food or drink that tastes or smells extremely good 珍馐美味

am·bu·lance /ˈæmbjələns; ˈæmbjələns/ *n* [C] a special vehicle used for taking people who are ill or injured to hospital 救护车 3

am·bu·lance·man /ˈæmbjələnsˌmæn; ˈæmbjələnsmæn/ *n plural* **ambulancemen** /-ˌmɛn; -men/ [C] *BrE* a man whose job is to drive an ambulance or look after the person being taken to hospital【英】救护车男司机；男救护员

am·bu·lance·wom·an /ˈæmbjələnsˌwumən; ˈæmbjələnsˌwumən/ *n plural* **ambulancewomen** /-ˌwɪmɪn; -ˌwɪmɪn/ [C] *BrE* a woman whose job is to drive an ambulance or look after the person being taken to hospital【英】救护车女司机；女救护员

am·bush[1] /ˈæmbuʃ; ˈæmbuʃ/ *n* [C] a sudden attack by people who have been waiting and hiding, or the place where this happens 伏击，埋伏；埋伏地点：**wait/lie in ambush** (=wait to ambush someone) 埋伏着等待袭击某人 *Armed police lay in ambush behind the hedge.* 武装警察埋伏在树篱后面。

ambush[2] *v* [T] to attack someone from a place where you have been hiding 伏击，埋伏突袭

a·me·ba /əˋmibə; əˈmiːbə/ *n* [C] an American spelling of AMOEBA amoeba 的美式拼法

a·me·bic /əˋmibɪk; əˈmiːbɪk/ *adj* an American spelling of AMOEBIC amoebic 的美式拼法

a·me·li·o·rate /əˋmiljəˌret; əˈmiːliəreɪt/ *v* [T] *formal* to make something better【正式】改善，改进：*measures to ameliorate working conditions* 改善工作条件的举措 —**amelioration** /əˌmiljəˋreʃən; əˌmiːliəˈreɪʃən/ *n* [U]

a·men /ˈɑˋmɛn; ɑːˈmen/ *interjection* **1** **Amen** used at the end of a prayer 阿门〔祈祷结束语，意思是"诚心所愿"〕：*Blessed be the Lord, Amen!* 感谢主，阿门！**2** used to show that you agree or approve 同意，赞成：*"I think we can close the meeting now." "Amen to that."* "我认为我们现在可以散会了。""同意。"

a·men·a·ble /əˈminəbl; əˈmiːnəbəl/ *adj* willing to listen or to do something 易接受指导[影响]的，顺从的：[+to] *I'm sure they'll be amenable to rational argument.* 我确信他们是会接受合理意见的。

3 **a·mend** /əˈmɛnd; əˈmend/ *v* [T] to make small changes or improvements to a law or document 修改，修订〔法律或文件〕

a·mend·ment /əˈmɛndmənt; əˈmendmənt/ *n* **1** [C,U] a written change or improvement to a law or document, or the process of doing this 修订，修正：[+to] *an amendment to the resolution* 对决议的修订 | **table an amendment** (=say officially that you want to discuss an amendment) 提交修正案 **2** [C] one of the rights on the list of rights included in the US Constitution 〔美国宪法的〕修正案

a·mends /əˈmɛndz; əˈmendz/ *n* **make amends** to say you are sorry for the harm you have caused and try to make things better 赔不是，道歉；补偿；补救

a·me·ni·ty /əˈmɛnətɪ; əˈmiːnəti/ *n* [C usually plural 一般用复数] something such as a piece of equipment, shop, or park that makes it easier to live somewhere 便利设施；娱乐[消遣]场所：*a town with all the amenities of a larger city* 拥有大城市所有便利设施的小城镇 | **basic amenity** *simple huts with only the most basic amenities* 只具备最简陋设施的小屋

Am·er·a·sian /ˌæməˈreʒən; ˌæməˈreɪʒən◂/ *n* [C] a word meaning someone who has one American parent and one Asian parent 美亚混血儿 —compare 比较 ASIAN-AMERICAN

A·mer·i·ca /əˈmɛrɪkə; əˈmerəkə/ a name commonly used for the US 美国

CULTURAL NOTE 文化注释

Although most English speakers understand that the US is often called America, many people from other countries in North and South America think it is unfair and wrong to use this word to mean only the US. 大多数说英语的人都能理解，美国常被称为America，但很多来自北美和南美其他国家的人认为，该词仅指美国是不公平的，也是错误的。

A·mer·i·can¹ /əˈmɛrɪkən; əˈmerəkən/ *adj* **1** from or connected with the US 美国的：*American forces landed on the island at dawn.* 美国的军队拂晓时在岛上登陆。| *the American writer William Boroughs* 美国作家威廉·伯勒斯 **2** *especially technical* connected with the CONTINENTS of North and South America【尤术语】美洲的：*a species found only in American rivers, especially in Brazil* 一种仅产于美洲尤其是巴西河流的物种

American² *n* [C] someone from the US 美国人

CULTURAL NOTE 文化注释

The population of the US is made up of people of many different races, whose families were originally from many different parts of the world. Many Americans say that they are Irish or Chinese, for example, if their parents or grandparents came from Ireland or China, even if they have never visited that country and cannot speak its language. In writing, people are more likely to say that they are Irish-American or Chinese-American. If someone is asked about their background, they might describe themselves as Irish, Chinese etc if they are in the US. However, if they are in another country and someone asks about their background, they would describe themselves as American. The people who lived in America before Europeans arrived there are called 'Native Americans'. 美国人口由许多不同种族组成，他们的家族从源头上说，来自世界各地。例如，很多美国人的父母或祖父母来自爱尔兰或中国，他们就会说自己是爱尔兰人或华人，即便他们从未去过那里，也不会说那里的语言。书面语中，人们常称自己是爱尔兰裔美国人或华裔美国人。在美国如果某人被问到出身背景，他们可能会说自己是爱尔兰人、华人等。然而出了美国并被问起出身背景时，他们会说自己是美国人。欧洲人到达美洲之前就生活在那里的人叫做"美洲土著居民"。

American A·cad·e·my of Dra·mat·ic Arts, the /ˌ·,···ˌ,····ˌ,··ˈ·/ a school in New York City for training actors, where many famous actors have studied 美国戏剧艺术学院〔位于纽约市，许多著名演员曾在此就读〕

American As·so·ci·a·tion of Re·tired Per·sons, the /ˌ·,···ˌ,····ˌ,·ˈ·/ abbreviation 缩写为 **AARP** an organization in the US for people who are 50 or older, especially people who have stopped working 美国退休人士协会〔美国50岁以上，尤其是退休人士的一个组织〕

American Bar As·so·ci·a·tion, the /ˌ·,···ˈ···,·ˈ/ a large national organization for lawyers in the US 美国律师协会〔美国一全国性大型律师组织〕

American Can·cer So·ci·e·ty, the /ˌ·,···ˈ···,··/ abbreviation 缩写为 **ACS** an organization in the US that provides money for scientists who are studying the causes of cancer and trying to find cures for it. It also gives information to help prevent people getting cancer. 美国癌症协会〔美国一组织，为研究癌症病因和治疗方法的科学家提供资助，同时提供癌症预防信息〕

American Civ·il Lib·er·ties U·nion /ˌ·,···,··ˈ···,··/ *n* [singular] the ACLU

American Civ·il War, the /ˌ·,···,··ˈ·/ a war that was fought in the US between 1861 and 1865 when 11 southern states rebelled (REBEL) against the federal government. The southern states were beaten, and as a result of the war, slaves became free. 美国南北战争〔1861-1865年间美国南部11个州反抗美国联邦政府的一场战争。最终南方诸州战败，奴隶们获得自由〕

American Con·fe·rence, the /ˌ·,···ˈ··/ a group of football teams in the US that play against one another. There is another group of teams called the National Conference, and the best team from that group plays the best team from the American Conference in the Super Bowl, which is the most important game of the year 美国橄榄球联盟〔美国一橄榄球队团体。另一橄榄球队团体叫做国家橄榄球联盟。两个团队中的最佳球队可角逐一年一度最重要的超级碗比赛〕

American Con·ser·va·to·ry Thea·ter, the /ˌ·,···ˈ····,·ˈ/ *n* [singular] the ACT

American Ex·press /ˌ·,···ˈ·/ also 又作 **Amex** *trademark* a US company that has a CREDIT CARD service, exchanges foreign money, and sells traveller's cheques【商标】美国运通公司〔美国一家提供信用卡服务、兑换外币和发行旅行支票的公司〕

American foot·ball /ˌ·,···ˈ·/ *n* [U] *BrE* a game played by two teams of eleven players, who carry, throw, or kick an OVAL (=egg shaped) ball【英】美式橄榄球；FOOTBALL (2) *AmE*【美】—see picture on page A22 参见A22页图

American Goth·ic /ˌ·,···ˈ·/ a painting by the US artist Grant Wood, which shows a very serious-looking farmer holding a PITCHFORK, with his wife standing beside him《美国哥特人》〔美国艺术家格兰特·伍德的作品，画上的一位农夫手持干草叉，表情严肃，旁边站着他的妻子〕

American In·di·an /ˌ·,···ˈ··/ *n* [C] another name for a NATIVE AMERICAN (=someone from one of the first groups of people who lived in America) used especially about people from South America and sometimes considered offensive 美洲印第安人

A·mer·i·can·is·m /əˈmɛrəkənˌɪzəm; əˈmerəkənɪzəm/ *n* [C] a word, phrase, or sound that is typical of the English language as it is used in the US 美国英语，美式英语

A·mer·i·can·ize also 又作 **-ise** *BrE*【英】/əˈmɛrəkənˌaɪz; əˈmerɪkənaɪz/ *v* [T] to make something American in character, for example a way of speaking or writing, or the way something is organized 使美国化 —**Americanization** *n* [U]: *Opponents of the burger bar said they were resisting the Americanization of our culture.* 汉堡包快餐店的竞争对手说他们正抵制我们的文化趋向美国化。

American League, the /ˌ·,···ˈ·/ a group of professional BASEBALL teams in the US which play against each other. Every year, the team that wins in this LEAGUE plays against the winning team of the National League in the World Series. 美国棒球联盟〔美国职业棒球团体。每年的冠军球队与全国棒球联盟的冠军球队参加世界职业棒球锦标赛的角逐〕

American Le·gion, the /ˌ·,···ˈ··/ a national organization for former members of the US armed forces 美国退伍军人协会〔美国全国性的退伍军人组织〕

American Re·vo·lu·tion·a·ry War, the /ˌ·,···,····ˈ·/ also 又作 **the American Revolution; the American War of Independence** *BrE* (1775-83) the war in which people in Britain's colonies (COLONY) in North America became independent and established the United States of America【英】美国革命战争，美国革命，美国独立战争〔(1775-1783)，英国统治的北美殖民地获得独立、建立了美利坚合众国的一场战争〕

American Sa·mo·a /əˌmɛrɪkən səˈmoə; əˌmerəkən səˈməʊə/ a group of islands in the Pacific Ocean, which are a TERRITORY of the US. Population: 54,000 (1995). Capital: Pago Pago. 美属萨摩亚〔太平洋一群岛，属美国领土。人口：54,000 (1995)，首府：帕果帕果〕

A·mer·i·cas, the /əˈmɛrɪkəz; əˈmerəkəz/ North America, Central America, and South America considered together as a group 美洲〔包括北美洲、中美洲和南美洲〕

America's Cup, the /ˌ· ··· ˈ·/ a sailing competition in which teams from the US, Australia, and other nations compete 美洲杯帆船赛〔美、澳等国参加的帆船比赛〕

America the Beau·ti·ful /ˌ· ··· ˈ··/ a PATRIOTIC song which most people in the US learn when they are children《美丽的亚美利加》〔多数美国人在孩提时代学唱的一首爱国歌曲〕

am·e·thyst /ˋæməθɪst; ˈæmɪ̥θɪ̥st/ *n* **1** [C] a valuable purple stone used in jewellery 紫水晶, 紫石英 **2** [U] a light purple colour 紫水晶色, 紫色 **—amethyst** *adj*

Am·ex /ˋæmɛks; ˈæmeks/ *trademark*【商标】the abbreviation of 缩写= AMERICAN EXPRESS

a·mi·a·ble /ˋemɪəbl̩; ˈeɪmiəbəl/ *adj* friendly and likeable 和蔼可亲的, 友好的, 亲切的: *The driver was an amiable young man.* 司机是位和蔼可亲的年轻人。**—amiably** *adv* **—amiability** /ˌemɪəˋbɪlətɪ; ˌeɪmiəˈbɪlɪ̥ti/ *n* [U]

am·i·ca·ble /ˋæmɪkəbl̩; ˈæmɪkəbəl/ *adj* an amicable agreement, relationship etc is one in which people feel friendly towards each other and do not want to quarrel 友好的, 和睦的: *an amicable settlement that was acceptable to both sides* 双方都能接受的友好协议 **—amicably** *adv* **—amicability** /ˌæmɪkəˋbɪlətɪ; ˌæmɪkəˈbɪlɪ̥ti/ *n* [U]

a·mid /əˋmɪd; əˈmɪd/ also 又作 **amidst** *prep* **1** happening while noisy, busy, or confused events are also happening 在…中间, 在…当中: *The dollar has fallen in value amid rumors of weakness in the US economy.* 在美国经济不景气的传言声中, 美元币值下跌了。**2** *especially literary* among or surrounded by【尤文】在…之中; 被…所环绕: *Old gabled houses peeped out from amid the trees.* 树丛中隐约露出一些有山墙的老房子。

a·mid·ships /əˋmɪdˌʃɪps; əˈmɪdˌʃɪps/ *adv* in the middle part of a ship 在船中部

a·midst /əˋmɪdst; əˈmɪdst/ *prep* amid 在…当中, 在…中间

A·min Da·da /ɑˌmɪn ˋdɑdɑ; ɑːˌmiːn ˈdɑːdɑː/, **Id·i** /ˋɪdɪ; ˈɪdi/ (1925-2003) the President of Uganda from 1971 until he was forced to leave the country in 1979. In 1972 he forced 80,000 people of Indian origin to leave Uganda, and many of them came to live in the UK. He was famous for the violent treatment of anyone who opposed him. 阿明·达达〔(1925-2003), 1971 年任乌干达总统, 1979 年被迫流亡国外。1972 年他将80,000名印度人后裔赶出乌干达, 其中不少人移居英国。他以虐待反对者而出名〕

a·mi·no ac·id /əˌmino ˋæsɪd; əˌmiːnəʊ ˈæsɪ̥d/ *n* [C] one of the substances that combine to form PROTEINS 氨基酸

A·mis /ˋemɪs; ˈeɪmɪs/, **Kingsley** /ˋkɪŋzlɪ; ˈkɪŋzli/ (1922-95) a British writer who wrote humorous NOVELs, such as *Lucky Jim* (1954) and *The Old Devils* (1986) 埃米斯〔(1922-1995), 英国作家, 著有幽默小说《幸运的吉姆》(1954)、《老鬼们》(1986) 等〕

A·mish, the /ˋɑmɪʃ; ˈɑːmɪʃ/ a Christian religious group who follow a type of Christianity that has many strict rules about behaviour. For example they must wear old-fashioned clothes and must not use modern inventions such as telephones, cars, or televisions. They have their own land in Pennsylvania and Ohio, where they live separately from other people. 阿曼门诺派〔基督教一派别, 制定有许多严格的行为准则, 例如, 必须穿戴传统服饰, 禁止使用电话、汽车、电视等现代产品; 定居在宾夕法尼亚、俄亥俄一带, 过着与世隔绝的生活〕

a·miss¹ /əˋmɪs; əˈmɪs/ *adv* **1 sth would not come/go amiss** *informal* used to say that something would be suitable or useful in a situation【非正式】某物很合适[有用]: *A cup of tea wouldn't go amiss.* 喝杯茶挺好。**2 take sth amiss** to feel upset or offended about something that someone has said or done 见怪, 对某事生气

amiss² *adj* **be amiss** if something is amiss, there is a problem 有问题: *Elsa continued as if nothing was amiss.* 埃尔莎继续下去, 就好像一切都正常。

am·i·ty /ˋæmətɪ; ˈæmɪ̥ti/ *n* [U] *formal* friendship, especially between countries【正式】〔尤指两国之间的〕友好, 和睦: *a spirit of perfect amity* 精诚合作的精神

Am·man /əˋmɑn; əˈmɑːn/ the capital city of Jordan 阿曼〔约旦首都〕

am·me·ter /ˋæmˌmitɚ; ˈæmitə/ *n* [C] a piece of equipment used to measure the strength of an electric current 安培计, 电流表

am·mo /ˋæmo; ˈæməʊ/ *n* [U] *informal* ammunition【非正式】弹药

am·mo·ni·a /əˋmonɪə; əˈməʊniə/ *n* [U] a poisonous gas or clear liquid with a strong smell 氨, 阿摩尼亚

am·mu·ni·tion /ˌæmjəˋnɪʃən; ˌæmjʊ̥ˈnɪʃən/ *n* [U] **1** bullets, shells (SHELL¹ (2)) etc that are fired from guns 弹药 **2** information that you can use to criticize someone or win an argument against them〔攻击他人的〕炮弹, 证据: *The oil spill was to give environmentalists powerful new ammunition against the oil companies.* 石油泄漏给环境保护主义者提供了新的强有力证据来抨击石油公司。

am·ne·si·a /æmˋniʒə; æmˈniːziə/ *n* [U] the medical condition of not being able to remember anything 记忆丧失, 健忘 (症) **—amnesiac** /-ʒɪæk; -ziæk/ *adj* **—amnesiac** *n* [C]

am·nes·ty /ˋæmnəstɪ; ˈæmnəsti/ *n* [C] **1** an official order by a government that allows political prisoners to go free 赦免, 大赦: *an amnesty for all former terrorists* 对前恐怖分子的大赦 **2** a period of time when you can admit to doing something illegal without being punished 赦免期限〔自首可以免受处罚的期限〕: *an amnesty on illegal handguns* 非法持有枪支的赦免期限

Amnesty In·ter·na·tion·al /ˌ·· ··ˈ···/ an organization that supports HUMAN RIGHTS, especially people's right to express their beliefs without being punished. Its members write to governments to persuade them to set free people who are in prison because of their political or religious beliefs. 大赦国际〔一个维护人权, 尤其是信仰自由的组织, 其成员以书信方式说服各地政府释放因政治或宗教原因而被关押的人士〕

am·ni·o·cen·te·sis /ˌæmnɪosɛnˋtisɪs; ˌæmniəʊsenˈtiːsɪ̥s/ *n* [U] a test to see if an unborn baby has any diseases or other problems, done by taking liquid from the mother's WOMB 羊膜穿刺术〔抽取孕妇子宫羊水以检查胎儿是否患病等的方法〕

a·moe·ba also 又作 **ameba** *AmE*【美】/əˋmibə; əˈmiːbə/ *n plural* **amoebas** or **amoebae** /-bi; -biː/ [C] a very small creature that has only one cell 变形虫, 阿米巴

a·moe·bic also 又作 **amebic** *AmE*【美】/əˋmibɪk; əˈmiːbɪk/ *adj* connected with amoebas 变形虫的, 阿米巴的

a·mok /əˋmʌk; əˈmɒk/ also 又作 **amuck** *adv* **run amok** to suddenly behave in a very violent and uncontrolled way 狂乱, 发狂: *'Gunman runs amok in Shopping Mall'* "持枪歹徒大闹购物中心"

a·mong /əˋmʌŋ; əˈmʌŋ/ also 又作 **a·mongst** /əˋmʌŋst; əˈmʌŋst/ *prep* **1** in the middle of 在…当中, 为…所围绕: *The girl quickly disappeared among the crowd.* 女孩很快消失在人群中。| *I could hear voices coming from somewhere among the bushes.* 我能听到灌木丛中某个地方传来的声音。—see picture on page A1 参见 A1 页图 —see 见 BETWEEN¹ (USAGE) **2 among friends/strangers** with people who are your friends or who you do not know 在朋友/陌生人中间: *Jim relaxed, knowing he was among friends.* 吉姆知道自己是在朋友中间, 就放松多了。**3** through or between 穿过; 在…中间: *We walked among the chestnut woods on the mountain slopes.* 我们在山坡上的板栗树林里穿行。| *She began rummaging among the books on her desk.* 她开始在桌上的书堆中翻找。**4** used to say that something such as a feeling or disease affects many people in a particular group, or that many people in a group have the same opinion 在…群体中: *There is widespread concern among scientists about the long-term consequences of storing nuclear waste underground.* 在地下埋藏核废料的长期后果在科学家中间引起了广泛的关注。| *7,000 job losses among railway workers* 铁路工人中 7000 人失业 **5** used when talking about a particular person or thing in a group of people or things 在… (人员) 中, 是…之一: *She was the eldest among them.* 她是他们当中年纪最大的。| *Innocent civilians were among the casualties.* 死伤者中有无辜平民。| *My grandfather had among his possessions a portrait by Matisse.* 我祖父有一幅马蒂斯画的肖像画。**6 among other** used to say that you are only mentioning one or two people or things out of a much larger group 其中; 包括〔指在众多人或物中只提到一两个〕: **among other things** *At the meeting they discussed, among other things, recent events in Eastern Europe.* 在会议上除了其他议题外, 他们讨论了东欧最近发生的事件。**7** if something is divided or shared among a group of people, each is given a part of it 在…之间分配 **8 talk/quarrel among yourselves** to talk or quarrel with other people 相互谈话/争吵: *Talk among yourselves for a while. I'll be ready soon.* 你们先谈一会儿, 我马上就准备好。

a·mor·al /eˋmɔrəl; eɪˈmɒrəl/ *adj* having no moral standards at all 毫无道德观念的; 没有道德的: *a completely amoral person* 毫无道德观念的人 **—amorality** /ˌeməˋrælətɪ; ˌeɪmɒˈrælɪ̥ti/ *n* [U]

am·o·rous /ˋæmərəs; ˈæmərəs/ *adj* involving or expressing sexual love 求欢的; 色情的: *She resisted his amorous advances.* 她拒绝了他试图跟她发生性关系的种种表示。**—amorously** *adv* **—amorousness** *n* [U]

a·mor·phous /əˋmɔrfəs; əˈmɔːfəs/ *adj formal* having no definite shape or features【正式】无固定形状的, 不定形的: *an amorphous mass of twisted metal* 一堆扭曲变形的金属 **—amorphously** *adv* **—amorphousness** *n* [U]

a·mor·tize also 又作 -ise *BrE*【英】/ˋæmɚ,taɪz; əˈmɔːtaɪz/ *v* [T] *technical* to pay a debt by making regular payments【术语】分期偿还〔债务〕—**amortizable** *adj* —**amortization** /,æmɚtəˋzeʃən; æ,mɔːtaɪˈzeɪʃən/ *n* [C,U]

A·mos and An·dy /,eməs ənd ˋændɪ; ,eɪmɒs ənd ˈændi/ two black characters in old US radio and television programmes, who were played by white actors. People now see these programmes as an example of a white racist view of black people. 阿莫斯和安迪〔美国早期广播、电视节目中的两个黑人人物形象，由白人演员扮演。如今，人们把这些节目看作是白人种族主义者歧视黑人的例证〕

a·mount¹ /əˋmaunt; əˈmaʊnt/ *n* [C,U] **1** a quantity of something such as time, money, or a substance 总数，数量，总额: [+of] *a considerable amount of money* 相当数额的钱 | **a small/large etc amount** *It's best to cook vegetables in a small amount of water.* 烧蔬菜时最好少放些水。**2** the level or degree to which a feeling, quality etc is present〔感情、质量等的〕程度: [+of] *Her case has attracted an enormous amount of public sympathy.* 她的情况得到了无数公众的同情。| **a certain/fair amount of** (=a fairly high level of something) 相当多的 *Dina encountered a fair amount of envy among her colleagues.* 迪娜遭到了不少同事的妒嫉。**3 no amount of sth will do sth** used to say that something has no effect 毫无结果，毫无影响: *No amount of persuasion could make her change her mind.* 怎么劝她也无法让她改变主意。| **any amount of sth** *BrE* (=a lot of)【英】很多 *The school has any amount of resources and equipment.* 这所学校财力雄厚，设备齐全。

USAGE NOTE 用法说明: AMOUNT
GRAMMAR 语法

Amount is usually used with uncountable nouns, and some people think this is the only correct use. amount 一般和不可数名词连用，一些人认为这是唯一正确的用法: *a large amount of money/food/electricity/hard work* 大量的钱/食物/电/艰苦工作 (Note that you do not usually say a **high** or **big** amount 注意一般不用 high 或 big 修饰 amount)。With plural countable nouns it is best to use **number**. 修饰复数可数名词最好用 number: *a large number of mistakes/people* 许多错误/人

However, people often use **amount** with plural countable nouns when what they are talking about is thought of as a group. 但是 amount 也经常和可数名词的复数连用，指整体概念: *We didn't expect such a large amount of people.* 我们没有料到会有这么多人。| *an enormous amount of problems* 一大堆问题

amount² *v*
amount to sth *phr v* [T not in progressive 不用进行时] **1** if figures, sums etc amount to a particular total, they equal that total when they are added together〔数量上〕达到，总计: *Time lost through illness amounted to 1,357 working days.* 因疾病而损失的时间总计达到 1357 个工作日。**2** if an attitude, remark, situation etc amounts to something, it has the same effect 等于，意味着: *The court's decision amounts to a not guilty verdict.* 法庭的裁决等于宣判无罪。**3 not amount to much/anything/a great deal etc** to not seem important, valuable or successful 没多大了不起[价值，成功等]: *Her academic achievements don't amount to much.* 她的学术成果似乎没有多大价值。

a·mour /əˋmur; əˈmʊə/ *n* [C] *literary* a sexual relationship, especially a secret one【文】偷情，不正当的男女关系

am·our prop·re /,æmur ˋprɔprə; ,æmʊə ˈprɒprə/ *n* [U] *literary* the quality of feeling respect for yourself【文】自尊心

amp /æmp; æmp/ *n* [C] **1** also 又作 **ampere** a unit for measuring electric current 安培〔电流单位〕: *a 3 amp fuse* 3 安培的保险丝 **2** *informal* an AMPLIFIER【非正式】放大器，扩音器，扬声器

am·per·age /ˋæmpərɪdʒ; ˈæmpərɪdʒ/ *n* [singular,U] *technical* the strength of an electrical current measured in amps【术语】安培数，电流强度

am·pere /ˋæmpɪr; ˈæmpeə/ *n* [C] an AMP 安培

am·per·sand /ˋæmpɚs,ænd; ˈæmpəsænd/ *n* [C] the sign '&' that means 'and' 表示 and 之符号〔写作 &〕: *Mills & Boon* 米尔斯和布恩〔出版公司名〕

am·phet·a·mine /æmˋfɛtə,min; æmˈfetəmiːn/ *n* [C,U] a drug that gives you a feeling of excitement and a lot of energy 苯丙胺，安非他明〔一种兴奋剂〕

am·phib·i·an /æmˋfɪbɪən; æmˈfɪbiən/ *n* [C] an animal that can live on both land and water 水陆两栖动物

am·phib·i·ous /æmˋfɪbɪəs; æmˈfɪbiəs/ *adj* **1** able to live on both land and water 水陆两栖的 **2 amphibious vehicle** a vehicle that is able to move on land and water 水陆两用车辆 **3 amphibious operation/force/assault** an amphibious operation etc involves ships and land vehicles 水陆两栖行动/部队/攻击

am·phi·thea·tre *especially BrE*【尤英】, **amphitheater** *AmE*【美】/ˋæmfə,θiətɚ; ˈæmfɪ̵,θɪətə/ *n* [C] a large circular building without a roof and with many rows of seats 圆形露天剧场[竞技场]

am·pho·ra /ˋæmfərə; ˈæmfərə/ *n* [C] a tall clay container for oil or wine, used in ancient times〔古代盛油或酒的〕双耳陶罐

am·ple /ˋæmpl; ˈæmpəl/ *adj* **1** more than enough 充足的，充裕的: *There's ample storage space in the new house.* 新房子有充足的贮藏空间。| **ample time/evidence/opportunity etc** *You will have ample opportunity to state your case later.* 以后你会有充分的机会陈述你的案子。**2 ample bosom/figure/torso etc** large in a way that is attractive or pleasant 宽阔的胸膛/丰满的体形/魁梧的身材等 —**amply** *adv*: *Recent US history has amply demonstrated the risks of foreign intervention.* 美国近代历史已经充分证明了外国干预的危险。

am·pli·fi·er /ˋæmplə,faɪɚ; ˈæmplɪ̵faɪə/ *n* [C] a piece of electrical equipment that makes sound louder; AMP (2) 放大器，扩音器，扬声器

am·pli·fy /ˋæmplə,faɪ; ˈæmplɪ̵faɪ/ *v* [T] **1** to make a sound louder, especially musical sound 放大〔声音，尤指音乐声〕: *an amplified guitar* 带有扩音设备的电吉他 **2** *formal* to explain something that you have said by giving more information about it【正式】详述，(进一步) 阐述: *Would you care to amplify that remark?* 请你把意见详述一下好吗？**3** *formal* to emphasize the importance of something【正式】强调〔重要性〕: *Successive reports amplified the case for privatisation.* 一个又一个的报告都强调了私有化的重要性。—**amplification** /æmpləfəˋkeʃən; ,æmplɪ̵fɪ̵ˈkeɪʃən/ *n* [U]

am·pli·tude /ˋæmplə,tud; ˈæmplɪ̵tjuːd/ *n* [U] *technical* the distance between the middle and the top or bottom of a WAVE² (4) such as a SOUND WAVE【术语】振幅；波幅；幅度

am·poule *especially BrE*【尤英】also 又作 **ampule** *AmE*【美】/ˋæmpul; ˈæmpuːl/ *n* [C] a small container for medicine that will be put into someone with a special needle 安瓿〔装注射液的小瓶〕

am·pu·tate /ˋæmpjʊ,tet; ˈæmpjʊ̈teɪt/ *v* [I,T] to cut off someone's arm, leg, finger etc during a medical operation 切除，截肢: *Two of her toes were amputated because of frostbite.* 由于冻伤，她的两个脚趾不得不截掉了。—**amputation** /,æmpjʊˋteʃən; ,æmpjʊ̈ˈteɪʃən/ *n* [C,U]

am·pu·tee /,æmpjʊˋti; ,æmpjʊ̈ˈtiː/ *n* [C] someone who has had an arm or a leg amputated 被截肢者

Am·rit·sar /æmˋrɪtsɚ; æmˈrɪtsə/ a city in the Punjab, in northwest India. It is a holy place for members of the Sikh religion, who visit its famous Golden Temple 阿姆利则〔印度西北部旁遮普邦一城市，被锡克教教徒奉为圣地，参拜的庙宇为著名的金庙〕

Am·ster·dam /ˋæmstɚdæm; ˈæmstədæm/ the capital city of the Netherlands 阿姆斯特丹〔荷兰首都〕

Am·trak /ˋæmtræk; ˈæmtræk/ *trademark* the company which runs passenger trains in the US【商标】美铁公司，(美国) 全国铁路客运公司: *Will you fly or take Amtrak?* 你打算乘飞机还是坐美铁公司的火车？—compare 比较 CONRAIL

a·muck /əˋmʌk; əˈmʌk/ *adv* AMOK 狂乱，发狂

am·u·let /ˋæmjəlɪt; ˈæmjʊ̈lət/ *n* [C] a small piece of jewellery worn to protect against bad luck, disease etc〔随身佩戴的〕护身符，驱邪物

Am·und·sen, Ro·ald /ˋɑmәndsn̩; ˈæməndsən/, /ˋroəld; ˈrəʊəld/ (1872-1928) a Norwegian EXPLORER. He was the first person to sail through the Northwest Passage in 1903-06, and in 1911 he beat Captain Robert Scott in the race to become the first person to reach the South Pole 阿蒙森〔(1872–1928)，挪威极地探险家。1903-1906 年，他乘坐帆船穿越西北航道，开创了人类历史之先河；1911 年在与英国的罗伯特·斯科特上校的竞争中胜出，成为到达南极的第一人〕

a·muse /əˋmjuz; əˈmjuːz/ *v* [T] **1** to make someone laugh or smile 使开心，逗笑: *What amused me most was the thought of Martin in a dress.* 想到马丁穿着连衣裙我就觉得很好笑。**2** to make someone spend time in an enjoyable way without getting bored 给…提供娱乐[消遣]: *Doing jigsaws would amuse Amy for hours on end.* 艾米会连续几个小时津津有味地玩拼图玩具。| **amuse yourself** *The kids amused themselves playing hide-and-seek.* 孩子们玩捉迷藏。

a·mused /əˋmjuzd; əˈmjuːzd/ *adj* **1** someone who is amused by something thinks it is funny so that they smile or laugh 被逗

乐的，感到有意思的：[+at/by] *Clare was highly amused by the little boy's antics.* 克莱尔被小男孩可笑的动作逗得很开心。| *He won't be very amused when he finds out what's happened to his garden.* 等他发现花园里发生的情况时，他就没什么可乐的了。| *James watched the proceedings with an amused grin.* 詹姆斯开心地笑着，注视着事件的过程。**2 keep sb amused** to entertain or interest someone for a long time so that they do not get bored 使某人保持快乐的状态：*If you could just keep them amused while I do the shopping!* 我购物的时候，你要是能哄得他们开开心心的就好了！

a·muse·ment /ə`mjuzmənt; ə'mjuːzmənt/ *n* **1** [U] the feeling you have when you think something is funny 开心，愉悦，乐趣：*Tom's tricks were a source of endless amusement to the other boys.* 汤姆的小戏法给其他孩子带来无尽的乐趣。| **to sb's amusement** (=in a way that makes someone laugh or smile) 令某人发笑 *To everyone's amusement he turned up for work in a straw hat and jeans.* 可笑的是，他戴着草帽，穿着牛仔裤就来上班了。**2 amusements** [plural] special things such as machines or games that are intended to entertain people 娱乐设施；娱乐活动：*The kids can ride on the amusements.* 那些娱乐设施可供孩子们骑在上面。**3** [U] the process of getting or providing pleasure and enjoyment 娱乐

amusement ar·cade /·'·· ·,·/ *n* [C] *BrE* a place where you play games on machines by putting coins into them【英】〔有电子游戏机等娱乐设施的〕游戏厅；游戏机室；VIDEO ARCADE *AmE*【美】

amusement park /·'·· ,·/ *n* [C] a large park with many special machines that you can ride on, such as ROLLER-COASTERs and MERRY-GO-ROUNDs 游乐场

a·mus·ing /ə`mjuzɪŋ; ə'mjuːzɪŋ/ *adj* funny and entertaining 引人发笑的，好笑的，有趣的：*I don't find his jokes at all amusing.* 我不觉得他的笑话有什么好笑。| **highly/vastly amusing** (=very funny) 特别有趣的 *a highly amusing film* 特别有趣的电影 —**amusingly** *adv*

Am·way /`æmwe; 'æmweɪ/ *trademark*【商标】**1** a US company that sells cleaning products, beauty products and kitchen equipment. The products are not sold in stores, but by people who sell them in their free time. 安利公司〔美国一家出售洗涤用品、化妆品、厨具等产品的公司，商品不在商店销售，而是让人们利用业余时间直销〕**2** products made by this company 安利产品：*Jill and Bob sell Amway to earn extra cash.* 吉尔和鲍勃靠销售安利产品赚外快。

S1 W1 **an** /ən; ən; *strong* 强读 æn; æn/ *indefinite article, determiner* [used when the following word begins with a vowel sound 同 a，用于以元音开头的单词前] a 一个，一只，一种等：*an orange* 一个橘子 | *an X-ray* 一次X光检查 | *such an old house* 这样一所旧房子 —see also 另见 A

an- /ən, æn; ən, æn/ *prefix* **1** the form used for A [2] before a vowel sound〔用于以元音开头的词前，相当于a-[2]〕**2** not; without 无，没有：*anarchy* (=without government) 无政府状态 | *anoxia* (=condition caused by lack of oxygen) 缺氧

-an /ən; ən/ *suffix* also 又作 **-ean, -ian** **1** [in adjectives and nouns 构成形容词和名词] someone or something of, from, or connected with a particular thing, place, or person …地方的（人或物）；与…有关的（人或物）：*an American* (=person from America) 美国人 | *the pre-Tolstoyan novel* 托尔斯泰之前的小说 **2** [in nouns 构成名词] someone skilled in or studying a particular subject 精通[研究]…的人：*a historian* (=someone who studies history) 历史学家

-ana /ænə; ɑːnə/ *suffix* [in nouns 构成名词] another form of the suffix -IANA …的汇编；…收藏品〔后缀 -iana 的另一种形式〕：*Americana* 美国史料[文物]

An·a·bap·tist /,ænə`bæptɪst; ,ænə'bæptɪst◂/ a member of a group within the Christian religion that thinks that only people who believe (and therefore not very young children) should be baptized (BAPTIZE) 再洗礼派教徒〔他们认为，只有信教的人（因此不是年幼的孩童）才应接受洗礼〕

an·a·bol·ic ste·roid /,ænəbɑlɪk `stɪrɔɪd; ,ænəbɒlɪk 'stɪərɔɪd/ *n* [C] a drug that makes muscles grow quickly, sometimes used illegally by people in sport 蛋白同化甾类

a·nach·ro·nis·m /ə`nækrə,nɪzəm; ə'nækrənɪzəm/ *n* [C] **1** someone or something that seems to belong to the past, not the present 时代错误；不合时代的人[事物]：*The monarchy is something of an anachronism these days.* 如今君主制是一种不合时代的制度。**2** something in a play, film etc that seems wrong because it is being shown in the wrong period of time〔戏剧、电影等中的〕年代误植 —**anachronistic** /ə,nækrə`nɪstɪk; ə,nækrə'nɪstɪk◂/ *adj* —**anachronistically** /-klɪ; -kli/ *adv*

an·a·con·da /,ænə`kɑndə; ,ænə'kɒndə/ *n* [C] a large South American snake 水蚺〔产于南美的一种大蟒蛇〕

a·nae·mi·a *especially BrE*【尤英】, **anemia** *AmE*【美】/ə`nimɪə; ə'niːmiə/ *n* [U] a medical condition in which there are too few red cells in your blood 贫血症

a·nae·mic *especially BrE*【尤英】, **anemic** *AmE*【美】/ə`nimɪk; ə'niːmɪk/ *adj* **1** suffering from anaemia 贫血的，患贫血症的 **2** seeming weak and uninteresting 没有活力的，无精打采的：*an anaemic performance of King Lear* 有气无力的《李尔王》表演 —**anaemically** /-klɪ; -kli/ *adv*

an·ae·ro·bic /,ænə`robɪk; ,ænə'rəʊbɪk◂/ *adj technical* not needing oxygen in order to live【术语】厌氧的

an·aes·the·si·a *especially BrE*【尤英】, **anesthesia** *AmE*【美】/,ænəs`θiʒə; ,ænɪs'θiːziə/ *n* [U] **1** the use of anaesthetics in medicine 麻醉术 **2** the state of being unable to feel pain 感觉缺失，麻木；麻醉状态

an·aes·thet·ic *especially BrE*【尤英】, **anesthetic** *AmE*【美】/,ænəs`θɛtɪk; ,ænɪs'θetɪk◂/ *n* [C,U] a drug that stops you feeling pain 麻醉剂：**under anaesthetic** (=using an anaesthetic) 在麻醉状态下 *Wisdom teeth are usually removed under anaesthetic.* 拔除智齿通常要施麻醉剂。| **local anaesthetic/general anaesthetic** (=affecting a small part of your body/all of your body) 局部麻醉/全身麻醉

a·naes·the·tist *especially BrE*【尤英】, **anesthetist** *AmE*【美】/ə`nɛsθətɪst; ə'niːsθɪtɪst/ *n* [C] a doctor or nurse who has been specially trained to give people anaesthetics 麻醉师

a·naes·the·tize also 又作 **-ise** *BrE*【英】, **anesthetize** *AmE*【美】/ə`nɛsθə,taɪz; ə'niːsθɪtaɪz/ *v* [T] to give someone an anaesthetic so that they do not feel pain 使麻醉，给…施行麻醉

an·a·gram /`ænə,græm; 'ænəgræm/ *n* [C] a word or phrase that is made by changing the order of the letters in another word or phrase 变位词（组）〔改变某个词或短语的字母顺序后构成的新词或短语〕：*'Silent' is an anagram of 'listen'.* silent 是 listen 的变位词。

An·a·heim /`ænəhaɪm; 'ænəhaɪm/ a city in southern California in the US, which many people go to in order to visit Disneyland 阿纳海姆〔美国加利福尼亚州南部一城市，许多人都去该市的迪斯尼乐园玩〕

a·nal /`enl; 'eɪnl/ *adj* **1** connected with the ANUS 肛门的 **2** showing too much concern with small details, especially in a way that annoys other people 吹毛求疵的：*Don't be so anal.* 不要这么吹毛求疵。

an·al·ge·si·a /,ænæl`dʒiʒə; ,ænəl'dʒiːziə/ *n* [U] *technical* the condition of being unable to feel pain while conscious【术语】痛觉缺失，无痛觉

an·al·ge·sic /,ænæl`dʒizɪk; ,ænəl'dʒiːzɪk◂/ *n* [C] *technical* a drug that reduces pain【术语】止痛剂，镇痛药：*Aspirin is a mild analgesic.* 阿斯匹林是一种温和的镇痛药。—**analgesic** *adj*

a·nal·o·gous /ə`næləgəs; ə'næləgəs/ *adj formal* similar to another situation or thing so that a comparison can be made【正式】相似的，类似的：[+to/with] *Scharf's findings are analogous with our own.* 沙夫的发现和我们的类似。

an·a·logue /`ænl,ɔg; 'ænəlɒg/ *n* [C] **1 analogue clock/watch** a clock or watch that uses moving hands, not changing numbers 指针式时钟/表 **2** *formal* something that is similar to something else in some way【正式】相似物，类似物

analogue com·put·er /,··· ·'··/ *n* [C] a computer that calculates things by measuring changing quantities such as of VOLTAGE rather than using a BINARY system of counting 模拟计算机 —compare 比较 DIGITAL COMPUTER

a·nal·o·gy /ə`nælədʒɪ; ə'nælədʒi/ *n* [C,U] a comparison between two situations, processes etc that seem similar, or the process of making this comparison 类推，类比，比拟：**drawing/draw an analogy** (=make a comparison) 作比较 *analogies between human and animal behaviour* 人和动物行为的比较 | **by analogy (with)** (=using an analogy) 用类比法 *Dr Wood explained the movement of light by analogy with the movement of water.* 伍德博士用水的运动作类比来解释光的运动。

an·a·lyse *BrE*【英】, **analyze** *AmE*【美】/`ænl,aɪz; 'ænəlaɪz/ *v* [T] **1** to examine or think about something carefully, in order to understand it 分析：*A computer analyses the photographs sent by the satellite.* 电脑分析卫星发回的照片。| *analyse the text in detail* 详细分析课文 **2** to examine someone's mental or emotional problems by using analysis (ANALYSIS (3)); PSYCHOANALYSE 对…进行精神分析 W3

a·nal·y·sis /ə`næləsɪs; ə'nælɪsɪs/ *n plural* **analyses** /-,siz; -siːz/ **1** [C,U] a careful examination of something in order to understand it better 分析：*a detailed analysis of the week's news* 一周新闻的详细分析 **2** [C,U] a careful examination of a substance to see what it is made of〔成分〕分析：*Forensic experts are doing analyses of the samples.* 法医专家正在对样本进行分 S3 W1

析。**3** [U] a process in which a doctor makes someone talk about their past experiences, relationships etc in order to help them with mental or emotional problems; PSYCHOANALYSIS 精神分析 **4 in the final/last analysis** used when giving the most basic or important facts about a situation 最终，归根结底: *In the final analysis, profit is the motive.* 归根结底，利润是动力。

an·a·lyst /ˈænlɪst; ˈænəlɪst/ *n* [C] **1** someone who makes a careful examination of events or materials in order to make judgments about them 分析者，化验员: *a food analyst* 食品化验员 **2** a doctor who helps people who have mental or emotional problems by making them talk about their experiences and relationships 精神分析专家，心理（分析）医生 —see also 另见 SYSTEMS ANALYST

an·a·lyt·ic /ˌænlˈɪtɪk; ˌænəlˈɪtɪk◂/ also 又作 **an·a·lyt·i·cal** /-tɪkl; -tɪkəl/ *adj* using methods that help you examine things carefully, especially by separating them into their different parts 分析的，（擅）用分析方法的: *an analytic approach* 分析法

an·a·lyze /ˈænlˌaɪz; ˈænəlaɪz/ *v* [T] the American spelling of ANALYSE analyse 的美式拼法

an·a·paest *BrE*【英】, **anapest** *AmE*【美】/ˈænəˌpɛst; ˈænəpest/ *n* [C] *technical* part of a line of poetry consisting of two short sounds then one long one【术语】〔诗歌的〕抑抑扬格〔前两拍短后一拍长〕—**anapaestic** /ˌænəˈpɛstɪk; ˌænəˈpiːstɪk◂/ *adj*

an·ar·chic /ænˈɑrkɪk; æˈnɑːkɪk/ *adj* lacking any rules or order, or not following the moral rules of society 无政府的；无秩序的，混乱的: *a lawless, anarchic city* 一个没有法律的、失控的城市 | *Orton's anarchic sense of humour* 奥顿不着边际的幽默感

an·ar·chis·m /ˈænəˌkɪzəm; ˈænəkɪzəm/ *n* [U] the political belief that there should be no government and that ordinary people should work together to improve society 无政府主义

an·ar·chist /ˈænəkɪst; ˈænəkɪst/ *n* [C] someone who believes that governments, laws etc are not necessary 无政府主义者 —**anarchistic** /ˌænəˈkɪstɪk; ˌænəˈkɪstɪk◂/ *adj* —**anarchistically** /-klɪ; -kli/ *adv*

an·ar·chy /ˈænəkɪ; ˈænəki/ *n* [U] a situation in which there is no effective government in a country or no order in an organization or situation 无政府状态；混乱状态: *a state of complete anarchy* 完全的无政府状态

a·nath·e·ma /əˈnæθəmə; əˈnæθɪmə/ *n* [singular,U] something that is completely the opposite of what you believe in 令人极其讨厌的事: [+to] *The idea of full-blown majority rule was anathema to many Afrikaners.* 全面的多数裁定原则这一主张令许多南非白人极为反感。

An·a·to·li·a /ˌænəˈtolɪə; ˌænəˈtəʊliə/ the main part of Turkey that is east of the Sea of Marmara 安纳托利亚〔土耳其的主体部分，马尔马拉海以东〕—**Anatolian** *adj*

an·a·tom·i·cal /ˌænəˈtɑmɪkl; ˌænəˈtɒmɪkəl◂/ *adj* connected with the structure of human or animal bodies 解剖（学）的: *an anatomical examination* 解剖检查 —**anatomically** /-klɪ; -kli/ *adv*

a·nat·o·my /əˈnætəmɪ; əˈnætəmi/ *n* **1** [U] the scientific study of the structure of human or animal bodies 解剖（学）**2** [C usually singular 一般用单数] the structure of body, or of a part of a body 〔动、植物的〕解剖构造: *the anatomy of the nervous system* 神经系统的解剖构造 **3** *often humorous* your body【常幽默】身体: *a part of his anatomy that I'd rather not mention* 我不愿提及的他身体的一部分 **4** [C,U] the process of cutting a body into pieces to study its different parts; DISSECTION 解剖 —**anatomist** *n* [C]

ANC, the /ˌe ɛn ˈsi; ˌeɪ en ˈsiː/ the African National Congress; a political group in South Africa that was originally established to fight for political rights for the black population. For many years it was an illegal organization, but it later became the government of South Africa. Its most famous leader is Nelson Mandela. 非洲人国民大会〔南非一政治团体，最初成立的目的是为黑人争取政治权利。长达多年，曾被认为是一个非法组织，后来才组成南非政府。最著名的领袖是纳尔逊·曼德拉〕

-ance /əns; əns/ *suffix*, **-ence** [in nouns 构成名词] the action, state, or quality of doing something or of being something …的动作，…的状态，…的性质: *his sudden appearance* (=he appeared suddenly) 他的突然出现 | *her brilliance* (=she is BRILLIANT) 她的聪颖

an·ces·tor /ˈænsɛstə; ˈænsəstə/ *n* [C] **1** a member of your family who lived a long time ago 祖先，祖宗: *My ancestors were French.* 我的祖先是法国人。**2** the form in which a modern machine, vehicle etc first existed 〔现代机器、车辆等的〕原型: *Babbage's invention was the ancestor of the modern computer.* 巴比奇的发明是现代电脑的原型。—compare 比较 DESCENDANT —**ancestral** /ænˈsɛstrəl; ænˈsestrəl/ *adj*: *the family's ancestral home* 这个家庭的祖居

> **CULTURAL NOTE 文化注释**
> Many people in the US and UK are interested in learning who their ancestors were. They sometimes make a FAMILY TREE showing the names of all the relatives they know from the present and the past. In the past, some people paid professional organizations to help them find out where their family originally came from, but now many people use the Internet to get information about their ancestors. 很多英美人热衷问祖寻根，有时制作家谱，罗列他们所知道的现在和过去所有亲戚的名字。过去，有人聘请专业组织帮助他们找出自己的家族最早来自哪里。但现在，很多人应用互联网获取先辈的信息。

an·ces·try /ˈænsɛstrɪ; ˈænsəstri/ *n* [C usually singular 一般用单数,U] the members of your family who lived a long time ago 祖先；世系: **of French/Scottish etc ancestry** (=having ancestors who were French, Scottish etc) 有法兰西/苏格兰等血统的

an·chor¹ /ˈæŋkə; ˈæŋkə/ *n* [C] **1** a piece of heavy metal that is lowered to the bottom of the sea, lake etc to prevent a ship or boat moving 锚: **weigh anchor** (=lift the anchor so that a ship can start moving) 起锚 | **drop/cast anchor** *We dropped anchor a few yards off-shore.* 我们在离岸几码远的地方抛锚停航。**2** someone or something that provides a feeling of support and safety 可以依靠的人[物]；精神支柱；靠山 **3** *AmE* someone who reads the news on TV and introduces news reports【美】〔电视〕新闻节目主持人; NEWS-READER *BrE*【英】

anchor² *v*
1 ▶**BOAT** 船◀ [I,T] to lower the anchor on a ship or boat to hold it in one place 抛锚，停船: *Three tankers were anchored in the harbor.* 三艘油轮停泊在港湾。
2 ▶**FASTEN** 使固定◀ [T usually passive 一般用被动态] to fasten something firmly so that it cannot move 使稳固，固定: *The panel was firmly anchored by two large bolts.* 嵌板由两个大螺栓牢牢固定着。
3 be anchored in to be strongly connected with a particular system, way of life etc 扎根于〔某种体系、生活方式等〕: *laws anchored in patriarchal society* 植根于父权制社会的法律
4 ▶**SUPPORT** 支持◀ [T] to provide a feeling of support or safety for someone 支持，保护: *Her life was anchored by her religion.* 宗教信仰给她的生活带来了安全感。
5 ▶**TV NEWS** 电视新闻◀ [T] *AmE* to be the person who reads the news and introduces reports on TV【美】主持〔电视新闻节目〕: *Connie Chung anchors the 6 o'clock news.* 康妮·钟主持6点钟的新闻节目。

An·chor·age /ˈæŋkərɪdʒ; ˈæŋkərɪdʒ/ the largest city in Alaska, US, which is a port and a centre of the oil and gas industries 安克雷奇〔美国阿拉斯加州最大港口城市，石油、天然气工业中心〕

an·chor·age /ˈæŋkərɪdʒ; ˈæŋkərɪdʒ/ *n* **1** [C] a place where ships can anchor 泊处，锚地 **2** [C,U] a place where something can be firmly fastened 可固定某物的地方: *Dig deep holes to get good anchorage for your new shrubs.* 坑挖得深一点让新栽的灌木能固定住。

an·cho·rite /ˈæŋkəˌraɪt; ˈæŋkəraɪt/ *n* [C] *literary* someone who lives alone for religious reasons; HERMIT【文】隐士，隐居修道者

an·chor·man /ˈæŋkəˌmæn; ˈæŋkəmæn/ *n plural* **anchormen** /-ˌmɛn; -men/ [C] *AmE* a male anchorperson【美】〔电视新闻〕男主持人

an·chor·per·son /ˈæŋkəˌpɜsn; ˈæŋkəˌpɜːsən/ *n* [C] *AmE* someone who reads the news on TV and introduces reports【美】〔电视新闻〕主持人

an·chor·wom·an /ˈæŋkəˌwʊmən; ˈæŋkəˌwʊmən/ *plural* **anchorwomen** /-ˌwɪmɪn; -ˌwɪmɪn/ *n* [C] *AmE* a female anchorperson【美】〔电视新闻〕女主持人

an·cho·vy /ˈænˌtʃovɪ; ˈæntʃəvi/ *n* [C,U] a very small fish that tastes strongly of salt 鳀鱼

an·cient¹ /ˈenʃənt; ˈeɪnʃənt/ *adj* **1** belonging to a time long ago 古代的: *the ancient civilizations of Asia* 亚洲的古代文明 **2** having existed for a very long time 古老的，年代久远的: *an ancient walled city* 有城墙的古城 **3** *usually humorous* very old【一般幽默】老掉牙的，老的: *That photo makes me look ancient!* 那张照片显得我很老！ W2

ancient² *n* **the ancients** *old use* people who lived long ago, especially the Greeks and Romans【旧】古人〔尤指古希腊及古罗马人〕: *The ancients believed that the sun and moon were planets.* 古人认为太阳和月亮都是行星。

Ancient Mar·i·ner /ˌ·· ˈ···/ the main character in the poem *The Rime of the Ancient Mariner* by Samuel Taylor Coleridge. The Ancient Mariner is an old sailor who shoots and kills an

ALBATROSS (=a very large sea bird). The other sailors think that this will bring them bad luck, and they force him to wear the dead albatross on a rope around his neck so that they will not be punished for his crime. But all the sailors die, and the Ancient Mariner feels guilty and believes he must tell his story to anyone who will listen, to warn them to be kind to all creatures. 老水手〔塞缪尔·泰勒·柯尔律治的叙事长诗《古舟子咏》中的主人公。老水手射死了一只信天翁，船上的其他水手认为，这会给大家带来厄运，于是就逼着老水手把死鸟系在自己的脖子上，以免殃及无辜。后来其他水手果真死了，老水手自感内疚，心想着一定要把这个故事讲给愿意倾听的任何人，告诫他们要善待所有的生灵〕

an·cil·la·ry /ˈænsəˌlɛrɪ; ænˈsɪləri/ *adj* **1 ancillary workers/staff etc** workers who provide additional help and services for the people who do the main work in hospitals, schools etc〔医院、学校等的〕勤杂人员 **2** connected with or supporting something else, but less important than it 相关的；辅助的，附属的，次要的：*Agreement was reached on a number of ancillary matters.* 就一些相关问题达成了一致。

-ancy /ənsɪ; ənsi/ *suffix*, **-ency** [in nouns 构成名词] the state or quality of doing something or of being something …的状态，…的性质：*expectancy* (=state of expecting) 期待，期望 | *hesitancy* 犹豫 | *complacency* (=being COMPLACENT) 自满，自鸣得意

and /ənd; ənd; *strong* 强读 ænd; ænd/ *conj* **1** used to join two words, parts of sentences, etc 和，及，与，又，并〔连接词与词、句子成分间的连词〕：*Do you want a pen and a bit of paper?* 你要笔和纸吗？| *The film starred Jack Lemmon and Shirley MacClaine.* 这出电影由杰克·莱蒙和雪莉·麦克莱恩主演。| *We've dealt with items one, two, and eleven.* 我们已经处理了第一项、第二项和第十一项。| *We'll have to reduce costs and borrow more money.* 我们必须降低费用，再借些钱。| *You need to know what rights you have and how to use them.* 你需要知道你有哪些权利，以及怎样使用这些权利。**2** then; afterwards 然后，其后：*Have your lunch and get a bath.* 先吃午饭，然后去洗澡。| *She picked up the kitten and put it in the box.* 她抱起小猫放进盒子里。| *He knocked on the door and went in.* 他敲敲门走了进去。| **wait and see** *You'll have to wait and see what happens.* 会发生什么事情，你们只好等等看。**3** used to say that something is caused by something else〔用于表示结果〕：*I missed supper and I'm starving!* 我没吃晚饭，所以现在饿极了！| *She took some medicine and was sick.* 她服了些药，觉得想吐。**4** used when adding numbers 加：*Six and four is ten.* 六加四等于十。**5 come and.../go and.../try and... etc** *especially BrE* used instead of 'to'【尤英】〔用于代替 to〕：*Shall we go and have a cup of coffee?* 我们出去喝杯咖啡好吗？| *I'll see if I can try and persuade her to come.* 我看看我能不能设法说服她来。**6** *spoken* used to introduce a statement, comment, question etc【口】〔用于引出一个话题〕：*And now I'd like to introduce our next speaker, Mrs Thompson.* 现在我想介绍下一位发言人汤普森夫人。| *"We're trying to sort out our next holiday." "And where's the favourite place?" "Oh, America."* "我们正在选择下一个度假地。" "哪里最理想？" "啊，美国。" **7** used between repeated words to emphasize what you are saying 越来越…；一连，许多〔用于连接重复的词〕：*More and more people are losing their jobs.* 越来越多的人失业。| *We waited for hours and hours!* 我们一直等了好几个小时！| *That was years and years ago.* 那是多少年以前的事了。| *We ran and ran.* 我们跑了又跑。**8 nice and.../good and...** used to emphasize how nice or good something is 很：*I like my tea nice and hot.* 我很喜欢热茶。**9 a hundred and four/three thousand, five hundred and seventy six etc** used after the word 'hundred' and before the numbers 1 to 99 when saying numbers〔用于 hundred 之后，1 至 99 诸数目之前〕**10 three and three quarters, nineteen and a half etc** used after the whole number and before the FRACTION (2) when saying numbers〔用于整数和分数之间〕：*in about two and a half month's time* 大约两个半月以后 | *five and a quarter percent* 百分之五点二五 **11** used in descriptions of food and drink to mean served with 和，加〔用于描述食物或饮料〕：*Do you want some fish and chips?* 你想要些鱼和薯条吗？| *I'll have a gin and tonic.* 我要一杯加奎宁水的杜松子酒。| **bread and butter** (=bread with butter spread on it) 涂黄油的面包 **2 there are experts and experts/computers and computers etc** used to say that some are much better than others 专家跟专家/电脑跟电脑大不一样 **13 and?** *spoken* used when you want someone to add something to what they have just said【口】那么？还有？：*"I'm sorry." "And?" "And I promise it won't happen again."* "对不起。" "还有呢？" "我保证这样的事再也不会发生了。"

An·dan·te /ænˈdæntɪ; ænˈdænti/ *n* [C] a piece of music played or sung at a speed that is neither very fast nor very slow〔乐曲的〕行板

andante *adj* played or sung at a speed that is neither very fast nor very slow 行板的；徐缓的 —**andante** *adv*

An·der·sen /ˈændəsn; ˈændəsən/, **Hans Chris·tian** /hæns ˈkrɪstʃən; hæns ˈkrɪstʃən/ (1805-75) a Danish writer famous for his many FAIRY TALES which include *The Snow Queen*, *The Little Match Girl*, and *The Ugly Duckling* 安徒生〔(1805-1875)，丹麦著名童话作家，作品有《雪之女王》、《卖火柴的小女孩》、《丑小鸭》等〕

Anderson, E·liz·a·beth Gar·rett /ɪˌlɪzəbəθ ˈgærɪt; ɪˌlɪzəbəθ ˈgærḷt/ (1836-1917) a British woman who became the first woman to be officially accepted as a doctor by the British Medical Association 安德森〔(1836-1917)，英国医学会正式接纳的首位女医生〕

Anderson, Sher·wood /ˈʃɝwʊd; ˈʃɜːwʊd/ (1876-1941) a US writer who wrote *Winesburg, Ohio* (1919), a collection of short stories about the loneliness and dissatisfactions of life in a small town 安德森〔(1876-1941)，美国作家。他创作的短篇小说集《俄亥俄州瓦恩斯堡镇》(1919) 描述孤独和失落的小镇生活〕

An·des, the /ˈændiz; ˈændiːz/ a range of high mountains along the west coast of South America 安第斯山脉〔位于南美洲西海岸的一条山脉〕

an·di·ron /ˈændˌaɪən; ˈændaɪən/ *n* [C] one of a pair of iron objects that holds wood in a FIREPLACE〔壁炉的〕柴架

An·dor·ra /ænˈdɔrə; ænˈdɔːrə/ a very small country in the Pyrenees, on the border between France and Spain, popular as a place for holidays and skiing. Population: 67,600 (2001). Capital: Andorra-la-Vella. 安道尔〔比利牛斯山区一个小国，位于法国和西班牙之间，著名度假与滑雪圣地。人口：67,600 (2001)，首都：安道尔城〕—**Andorran** *n, adj*

-andr- /ændr; ændr/ *prefix technical* concerning males or men【术语】雄性的；男性的；男子的：*androgynous plants* (=plants which are both male and female) 雌雄同株的植物 | *polyandry* (=having more than one husband at the same time) 一妻多夫制

An·drew /ˈændru; ˈændruː/, **Prince** (1960-) the third child of the British queen, Elizabeth II. His official royal title is The Duke of York. 安德鲁王子〔(1960-)，英国女王伊丽莎白二世的第三个孩子，被册封为约克公爵〕

Andrew, Saint (1st century AD) in the Bible, one of Jesus' DISCIPLES. He is the PATRON SAINT of Scotland and St Andrew's Day, 30th November, is celebrated as the Scottish national day. 使徒安德烈〔(公元1世纪)《圣经》中耶稣的门徒之一，苏格兰的主保圣人。11月30日的圣安德烈日是苏格兰的民族节日〕

An·dro·cles and the Li·on /ˌændrəkliz ənd ðə ˈlaɪən; ˌændrəkliːz ənd ðə ˈlaɪən/ an ancient Roman story about a SLAVE called Androcles who escapes from his owner and meets a lion with a THORN (=a sharp pointed part of a plant) in its foot. Androcles removes the thorn. Later he is caught and is made to fight with a lion in the ARENA as punishment for escaping, but the lion is the same one that he helped, and instead of attacking him, it greets him as a friend. 《安德罗克勒思和狮子》〔古罗马故事。故事中，安德罗克勒思从主人家逃出，遇见一头爪上中刺的狮子，就给狮子拔了大刺。后来，他给人抓住，被迫与竞技场的一头狮子搏斗，以此作为对他逃跑的惩罚。然而，与他搏杀的狮子正好是自己救助过的那头狮子，所以狮子非但没有攻击他，反而像朋友一般招呼他〕

an·drog·y·nous /ænˈdrɑdʒənəs; ænˈdrɒdʒɪnəs/ *adj* **1** having both male and female parts 雌雄同体的；雌雄同株的 **2** someone who is androgynous looks both female and male 双性的，兼性的：*Bowie had a kind of androgynous sex appeal.* 鲍伊对男女都有一种吸引力。

an·droid /ˈændrɔɪd; ˈændrɔɪd/ *n* [C] a ROBOT that looks completely human〔似人的〕机器人

An·dy Capp /ˌændɪ ˈkæp; ˌændi ˈkæp/ the main character in a British CARTOON STRIP in newspapers. 安迪·卡普〔英国报纸卡通连环漫画的主要人物〕

CULTURAL NOTE 文化注释

Andy Capp is supposed to be a typical example of a WORKING-CLASS British man who is lazy, enjoys drinking beer in the PUB, and is always annoying his wife. He always has a cigarette in his mouth and wears a CLOTH CAP. Most people now see Andy Capp as a rather old-fashioned character. 安迪·卡普被视为英国劳工阶层的典型：懒惰、喜欢在酒吧喝啤酒、总惹妻子不高兴。他嘴里总叼着香烟，戴顶布帽子。安迪·卡普现在多被看做是较为过时的角色。

an·ec·dot·al /ˌænɪkˋdotl; ˌænɪkˈdəʊtl◂/ *adj* consisting of short stories based on someone's personal experience 轶事的，趣闻的：*Tom gave an anecdotal account of his recent trip to Morocco.* 汤姆叙述了他最近摩洛哥之行的趣闻。| *His findings are based on anecdotal evidence rather than serious research.* 他的发现是基于一些趣闻轶事，而不是认真的研究。

an·ec·dote /ˈænɪkˌdot; ˈænɪkdəʊt/ *n* [C] a short story based on your personal experience〔基于个人经历的〕趣闻，轶事

a·ne·mi·a /əˋnimɪə; əˈniːmiə/ *n* [U] the usual American spelling of ANAEMIA anaemia 的一般美式拼法

a·ne·mic /əˋnimɪk; əˈniːmɪk/ *adj* the usual American spelling of ANAEMIC anaemic 的一般美式拼法

a·nem·o·ne /əˋnɛməˌni; əˈneməni/ *n* [C] a plant with red, white, or blue flowers 银莲花

an·es·the·si·a /ˌænəsˋθiʒə; ˌænɪ̈sˈθiːziə/ *n* [U] the usual American spelling of ANAESTHESIA anaesthesia 的一般美式拼法

an·es·the·si·ol·o·gist /ˌænəsˌθizɪˋɑlədʒɪst; ˌænəsθiːziˈɒlədʒɪ̈st/ *n* [C] *AmE* a doctor who gives ANAESTHETICS to a patient【美】麻醉师

an·es·thet·ic /ˌænəsˋθɛtɪk; ˌænəsˈθetɪk◂/ *n* [C,U] the usual American spelling of ANAESTHETIC anaesthetic 的一般美式拼法

a·nes·the·tist /əˋnɛsθətɪst; əˈniːsθɪ̈tɪ̈st/ *n* [C] the usual American spelling of ANAESTHETIST anaesthetist 的一般美式拼法

a·nes·the·tize /əˋnɛsθəˌtaɪz; əˈniːsθɪ̈taɪz/ *v* [T] the usual American spelling of ANAESTHETISE anaesthetise 的一般美式拼法

a·new /əˋnu; əˈnjuː/ *adv literary*【文】**1 start life anew** to begin a different job, start to live in a different place etc, especially after a difficult period in your life〔尤指困难时期后〕开始新生活：*She resolved to start life anew in Ireland.* 她决心在爱尔兰开始新的生活。**2** if you do something anew, you start doing it again 重新，再

an·gel /ˋendʒəl; ˈeɪndʒəl/ *n* [C] **1** a spirit who lives with God in heaven, often shown as a person dressed in white with wings 天使 **2** someone who is very kind, very good, or very beautiful 仁慈而美丽的人，安琪儿：*That little girl of theirs is an angel.* 他们的小女儿是个小天使。| **be an angel** *spoken* (=used to ask someone to do something for you)【口】行行好，做做好事 *Be an angel and get me my glasses, will you?* 帮帮忙，把我的眼镜拿过来好吗？| **you're an angel** *spoken* (=used to tell someone that you are grateful to them)【口】你真好 *Thanks for mailing those letters, you're an angel.* 谢谢你帮我寄了那些信，你真好。| **sb's no angel** (=used to say that someone behaves very badly) 某人的表现差 *Sam was no angel at school, believe me.* 相信我，萨姆在学校表现很差。**3** a way of speaking to a child or woman you love 乖乖，宝贝儿：*How are you angel?* 你怎么样，宝贝儿？**4** *informal* someone who supports a play, film, music group etc by giving money【非正式】〔尤指戏剧、电影、乐队等的〕赞助人 —see also 另见 GUARDIAN ANGEL

angel dust /ˈ‥ ˌ/ *n* [U] *slang* PCP (=a drug)【俚】天使粉〔一种麻醉致幻剂，即苯环己哌啶〕

Angel Falls /ˌ‥ ˈ/ the highest WATERFALL in the world, which is in southeast Venezuela 安赫尔瀑布〔世界上落差最大的瀑布，位于委内瑞拉东南部〕

an·gel·ic /ænˋdʒɛlɪk; ænˈdʒelɪk/ *adj* **1** looking good, kind, and gentle or behaving in this way 天使般的：*She had an angelic smile, but a dreadful temper.* 她笑起来像个天使，但发起脾气来很可怕。**2** connected with angels 天使的 —**angelically** /-klɪ; -kli/ *adv*

an·gel·i·ca /ænˋdʒɛlɪkə; ænˈdʒelɪkə/ *n* [U] a plant that smells sweet and is used in cooking 白芷〔一种带香味的植物，用于烹调〕

An·gel·i·co /ænˋdʒɛlɪko; ænˈdʒelɪkəʊ/, **Fra** /frɑ; frɑː/ (?1400- 1455) an Italian MONK (=a member of an all-male Christian religious group) and painter, famous for the FRESCO*es* that he painted on church walls 安吉利科〔(?1400-1455)，意大利修士、画家，尤以所画的教堂壁画而著称〕

3 **an·ger**[1] /ˋæŋgɚ; ˈæŋgə/ *n* [U] a strong feeling of wanting to harm, hurt or criticize someone because they have done something unfair, cruel, offensive etc 愤怒，怒火，怒气：*Paul's face was filled with anger and resentment.* 保罗一脸愤怒和不满。| **do sth in anger** (=do it because you have very strong feelings) 生气地做某事 *Her mother hardly ever shouted at her in anger.* 她母亲几乎从来不怒气冲冲地对她喊叫。

anger[2] *v* [T often passive 常用被动态] to make someone angry 使生气，激怒：*What angered me most was his total lack of remorse.* 最使我生气的是他居然一点悔意都没有。

an·gi·na /ænˋdʒaɪnə; ænˈdʒaɪnə/ *n* [U] a medical condition in which you have bad pains in your chest because your heart is weak 心绞痛

angle 角

obtuse angle 钝角

acute angle 锐角

right angle 直角

an·gle[1] /ˋæŋgl; ˈæŋgəl/ *n* [C] **1** the space between two straight lines or surfaces that touch or cross each other, measured in degrees 角：*an angle of 45°* 45 度角 —see also 另见 RIGHT ANGLE **2** a position from which you look at something or photograph it 视角，角度：*This drawing of the monastery was done from an unusual angle.* 这幅画是以独特的视角来描绘寺院的。**3** a way of considering a problem or situation〔看问题的〕角度：*We need to look at the issue from a different angle.* 我们需要从一个不同的角度来看这个问题。**4 at an angle** leaning to one side and not straight or upright 歪着的：*The portrait was hanging at an angle.* 这幅画像挂歪了。**5** the shape formed when two lines or surfaces join〔两条线或两个平面相交的〕夹角，边角：*My head struck the angle of the shelf.* 我的头碰在书架的角上。 3 3

angle[2] *v* [I,T] **1** if you angle something in a particular direction or if it angles in that direction, it is not upright or facing straight ahead（使）按照某一角度转动[移动]：*a mirror angled to reflect light from a window* 为反射窗外的光线而摆成某一角度的镜子 **2** [T] to describe something unfairly by emphasizing some features but not others 带成见地描述，偏向：*a report which was angled in favour of the government* 偏向政府的报告

angle for sth *phr v* [T] to try to get something by making suggestions and remarks instead of asking directly〔以暗示等方法〕猎取，谋取：*She was angling for an invitation to that party.* 她拐弯抹角地想要弄到那个晚会的请柬。

an·gle·poise lamp /ˌæŋglpɔɪz ˋlæmp; ˌæŋgəlpɔɪz ˈlæmp/ *n* [C] *BrE trademark* a type of lamp that can be moved into different positions【英，商标】〔能旋转至不同方位的〕活动（台）灯 —see picture at 参见 LIGHT[1] 图

an·gler /ˋæŋglɚ; ˈæŋglə/ *n* [C] someone who catches fish as a sport 垂钓者 —compare 比较 FISHERMAN

An·gle·sey /ˋæŋglsɪ; ˈæŋgəlsi/ an island off the northwest coast of Wales, which is connected to the rest of Wales by the Menai Bridge 安格尔西岛〔威尔士西北海岸附近一岛屿，经由梅奈大桥与威尔士其他地区相连〕

An·gli·can /ˋæŋglɪkən; ˈæŋglɪkən/ *n* [C] a Christian who is a member of the Church of England 英国圣公会教徒 —**Anglican** *adj* —**Anglicanism** *n* [U]

Anglican Com·mu·nion, the /ˌ‥ ‥ˈ‥/ the group of churches around the world, mostly in English-speaking countries, that are closely related to the practices and beliefs of the Church of England 普世圣公宗，安立甘宗〔以英语国家为主体的世界性教会组织，其礼仪、信仰与英国国教会有着密切的联系〕

an·gli·cis·m /ˋæŋgləˌsɪzəm; ˈæŋglɪ̈sɪzəm/ *n* [C] an English word or expression that is used in another language〔其他语言中的〕英语词语；典型的英国说法

an·gli·cize also 又作 **-ise** *BrE*【英】/ˋæŋgləˌsaɪz; ˈæŋglɪ̈saɪz/ *v* [T] to make something or someone more English 使英语化；使英国化

an·gling /ˋæŋglɪŋ; ˈæŋglɪŋ/ *n* [U] **1** the sport of catching fish 垂钓运动；钓鱼 **2 go angling** to catch fish as a sport 去垂钓 [钓鱼]

Anglo-, anglo- /æŋglo; æŋgləʊ/ *prefix* **1** of England or Britain 英格兰的；英国的：*an anglophile* (=someone who loves Britain) 亲英者，崇英者 **2** English or British and 英格兰 [英国] 和…的：*an Anglo-Scottish family* 英格兰人和苏格兰人组成的家庭 | *an improvement in Anglo-American relations* 英美关系的改善

Anglo-A·mer·i·can[1] /ˌ‥ ˈ‥‥◂/ *adj* between or involving both Britain and the US 英美的：*Anglo-American relations* 英美关系

Anglo-American[2] *n* [C] an American whose family come from Britain 英裔美国人

Anglo-Cath·o·lic /ˌ‥ ˈ‥‥◂/ *n* [C] a Christian who is a member of the part of the Church of England that is similar to the Roman Catholic Church〔与罗马天主教相近的〕英国国教高教会派教徒 —**Anglo-Catholic** *adj* —**Anglo-Catholicism** /ˌ‥ ˈ‥‥/ *n* [U]

Anglo-In·di·an /ˌ‥ ˈ‥‥◂/ *n* [C] **1** someone whose family is partly British and partly Indian 英印混血儿 **2** *old use* a British person who was born or lives in India【旧】出生或居住在印度的英国人 —**Anglo-Indian** *adj*

Anglo-I·rish A·gree·ment /ˌ··,·· ·ˈ··/ an agreement made in 1985 between the governments of the UK and the Republic of Ireland, which gave the Irish the right to take part in discussions about the future of Northern Ireland 英爱协议〔英国政府与爱尔兰共和国政府1985年签署的协议，赋予爱尔兰政府参与讨论北爱尔兰未来的权利〕

an·glo·phile /ˈæŋgloˌfaɪl; ˈæŋgləʊfaɪl/ *n* [C] someone who is not British but likes anything British 亲英者，崇英者 —**anglophilia** /ˌæŋgloˈfɪlɪə; ˌæŋgləʊˈfɪliə/ *n* [U]

an·glo·phobe /ˈæŋgloˌfob; ˈæŋgləʊfəʊb/ *n* [C] someone who dislikes anything British 仇英者 —**anglophobia** /ˌæŋgloˈfobɪə; ˌæŋgləʊˈfəʊbiə/ *n* [U]

an·glo·phone /ˈæŋgloˌfon; ˈæŋgləʊfəʊn/ *adj* anglophone populations or countries have English as one of their languages〔人口或国家〕讲英语的 —**anglophone** *n* [C]

Anglo-Sax·on /ˈæŋglo ˈsæksn̩; ˌæŋgləʊ ˈsæksən◂/ *n* **1** [C] a member of the people who lived in England from about 600 AD 盎格鲁－撒克逊人 **2** [U] the language of the Anglo-Saxons 盎格鲁－撒克逊语 **3** [C] *often humorous* an English person【常幽默】英国人 —**Anglo-Saxon** *adj*

An·go·la /æŋˈgolə; æŋˈgəʊlə/ a country in southwest Africa, north of Namibia and south of the Democratic Republic of Congo. Population: 11,500,000 (2003). Capital: Luanda. 安哥拉〔非洲西南部一国家，位于纳米比亚以北，刚果民主共和国以南。人口：11,500,000（2003），首都：罗安达〕—**Angolan** *n, adj*

an·go·ra /ænˈgorə; æŋˈgɔːrə/ *n* **1** [U] wool or thread made from the fur of an angora goat or rabbit 用安哥拉羊毛[兔毛]制成的织物[毛线] **2** [C] a type of goat, rabbit, or cat with very long soft hair or fur〔一种有柔软长毛的〕安哥拉羊；安哥拉兔；安哥拉猫

an·gos·tur·a /ˌæŋgəsˈturə; ˌæŋgəˈstjʊərə◂/ *n* [U] a slightly bitter liquid used for adding taste to alcoholic drinks〔可增加酒香的〕安哥斯图拉苦味液

an·gry /ˈæŋgrɪ; ˈæŋgri/ *adj* **1** feeling strong emotions which make you want to shout at someone or hurt them because they have behaved in an unfair, cruel, offensive etc way, or because you think that a situation is unfair, unacceptable etc 发怒的，生气的，气愤的：*I was very angry when I heard what happened.* 听到所发生的事情我很气愤。| **angry person/look etc** *an angry letter* 充满愤怒的信 | *There were angry scenes when the police broke up the demonstration.* 警察驱散示威者时出现了愤怒的场面。| **[+with/at]** *She was so angry with him that she threatened to throw him out of the house.* 她很生他的气，威胁说要把他从屋里扔出去。| **[+about/over]** *Parents are justifiably angry about the decision to close the school.* 家长们对于关闭学校的决定表示气愤是情有可原的。| **make sb angry** *It makes me really angry when I hear people talk about 'humane killing'.* 听到人们谈论什么"人道屠宰"时，我真的很气愤。**2 angry with/at yourself** feeling strongly that you wish you had done something or had not done something 生自己的气：*David was angry with himself for letting the others see his true feelings.* 戴维恨自己让别人看出了他的真实感受。**3** *literary* an angry sky or cloud looks dark and stormy【文】黑压压的，雨快来临的 **4** *literary* an angry wound etc is painful and red and looks infected【文】〔伤口〕肿痛发炎的，感染的 —**angrily** *adv*: *"The stupid young fool," he said angrily.* "这个愚蠢的年轻人。"他生气地说。

Angry Young Man /ˌ·· ·ˈ·/ *BrE* a young man who strongly criticizes society and the government. The phrase was first used to describe John Osborne and other British writers in the 1950s.【英】愤怒的青年〔指抨击社会和政府的年轻人，最初用于指称约翰·奥斯本等20世纪50年代的英国作家〕

This graph shows how common different grammar patterns of the adjective **angry** are. 本图表所示为形容词angry构成的不同语法模式的使用频率。

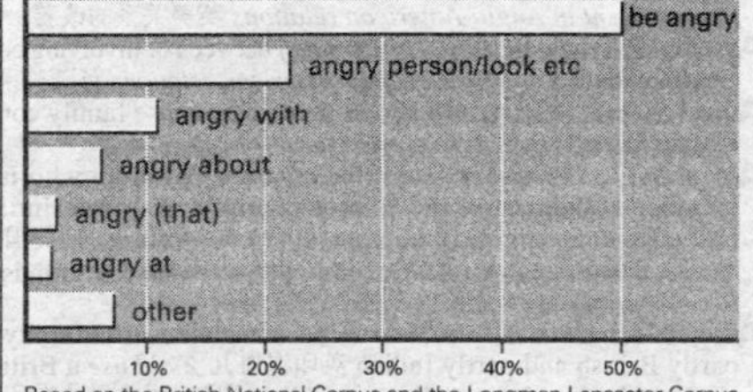

Based on the British National Corpus and the Longman Lancaster Corpus
据英国国家语料库和朗文兰开斯特语料库

angst /æŋst; æŋst/ *n* [U] strong feelings of anxiety and unhappiness because you are worried about your life, your future, or what you should do in a particular situation 焦虑不安，烦恼：*love letters full of angst* 充满焦虑的情书

An·guil·la /æŋˈgwɪlə; æŋˈgwɪlə/ an island in the Caribbean Sea, belonging to the UK. Population: 9,000 (1995). Capital: The Valley. 安圭拉〔加勒比海一岛屿，归属英国。人口：9000（1995），首府：瓦利〕

an·guish /ˈæŋgwɪʃ; ˈæŋgwɪʃ/ *n* [U] mental or physical suffering caused by extreme pain or worry〔精神或身体上的〕极度痛苦：*the anguish of not knowing what had happened to her* 由于不知道她发生了什么事而痛苦不已 —**anguished** *adj*: *anguished cries for help* 痛苦的呼救声

an·gu·lar /ˈæŋgjələ; ˈæŋgjʊlə/ *adj* **1** thin and not having much flesh on your bones 瘦骨嶙峋的：*a tall, angular young man* 又高又瘦的年轻男子 **2** having sharp and definite corners 有尖角的：*an angular room* 有尖角的房间 **3** [only before noun 仅用于名词前] having or forming an angle 有角的，成角的

An·gus /ˈæŋgəs; ˈæŋgəs/ a county in central eastern Scotland, with a coast on the North Sea 安格斯郡〔苏格兰东部中原一郡，濒临北海〕

an·i·mal[1] /ˈænəml; ˈænɪməl/ *n* [C] **1** a living creature such as a dog or cat, that is not an insect, plant, fish, or person 动物，兽类〔指除昆虫、植物、鱼类或人类以外的生物〕：*farm animals* 牲畜，牲口 | **animal welfare/rights etc** *campaigning for animal rights*（保护）动物权利运动 | **animal products/protein/fats etc** (=things that are made or come from animals) 动物产品／蛋白／脂肪等 **2** any living creature that is not a plant, including people 动物〔包括人〕：*Man is a highly intelligent animal.* 人是一种高智慧动物。**3** *informal* someone who behaves in a cruel, violent, or very rude way【非正式】畜牲，凶残野蛮的人：*These football hooligans are just animals.* 这些足球流氓简直是畜牲。**4 a very/completely different animal** *informal* something that is very different from the thing you have mentioned【非正式】非常不同／截然不同的事 **5 a political/social animal etc** *informal* someone who is interested in politics, in meeting other people etc【非正式】善于搞政治／社交等的人

animal[2] *adj* [only before noun 仅用于名词前] **animal urges/instincts etc** human feelings, desires etc that are connected with sex, food, and other basic needs 兽欲／动物本能等

Animal Crack·ers /ˌ··· ˈ··/ *trademark* small sweet BISCUITS shaped like animals, which are sold in a small box, and are popular with children in the US【商标】动物饼干〔一种形似动物的甜饼干，以盒装出售，深受美国儿童喜爱〕

Animal Farm /ˌ··· ˈ·/ a NOVEL by George Orwell which is a SATIRE (=a humorous criticism) on the violent revolution and dictatorial society. In the book, a group of animals take control of a farm so that they can establish a society where they are all equal. The pigs, however, soon become the leaders and say that they are more important, intelligent etc than everyone else, using the phrase "All animals are equal, but some animals are more equal than others."《动物农庄》〔乔治·奥威尔创作的小说，讽刺暴力革命和专制性的社会。小说描写一群动物接管了一个农场，以期建立一个人人平等的社会。然而，猪不久成为领袖人物，声称自己比别的动物更重要、更聪明，美其名曰："动物一律平等，但有些动物比别的动物更加平等。"〕

animal hus·band·ry /ˌ··· ˈ···/ *n* [U] farming that involves keeping animals and producing milk, meat etc 畜牧业

Animal Lib·e·ra·tion Front /ˌ··· ··ˈ·· ˌ·/ abbreviation 缩写为 **ALF** a British organization that protests against using animals in scientific experiments, such as testing drugs or COSMETICS 动物解放阵线〔英国组织，反对使用动物进行药品、化妆品等科学试验〕

animal rights /ˌ··· ˈ·/ *n* [U] the idea that people should treat animals well, and especially not use them in tests to develop medicines or other products 动物权利〔指人们应善待动物，尤其不要把它们用作试验品来研制药物或其他产品〕：**animal rights protestor/campaigner** (=someone who tries to stop cruelty to animals) 动物权利保护者／活动家

an·i·mate[1] /ˈænəmɪt; ˈænɪmɪt/ *adj* living 有生命的，活的：*animate beings* 生物 —opposite 反义词 INANIMATE

an·i·mate[2] /ˈænəˌmet; ˈænɪmeɪt/ *v* [T] to give life or energy to something 赋予…生命；使有生气；激励：*Laughter animated his face for a moment.* 笑使他脸上一时增添了生气。

an·i·ma·ted /ˈænəˌmetɪd; ˈænɪmeɪtɪd/ *adj* **1** showing a lot of interest and energy 生气勃勃的，活跃的，栩栩如生的：*An animated discussion ensued.* 接着进行了一场热烈的讨论。**2 animated cartoon/film/programme** a film made by photograph-

ing a series of pictures, clay models etc 动画片/电影/节目 —**animatedly** *adv*

an·i·ma·tion /ˌænəˋmeʃən; ˌænɪˈmeɪʃən/ *n* [U] **1** the process of making animated films 动画片的制作 **2** liveliness and excitement 兴奋; 生气; 活跃: *They were talking with animation.* 他们谈得兴趣盎然。

an·i·ma·tor /ˋænɪˌmetə; ˈænɪmeɪtə/ *n* [C] someone who makes animated films 动画片制作人

an·i·mis·m /ˋænəˌmɪzəm; ˈænɪmɪzəm/ *n* [U] a religion in which animals and plants are believed to have spirits 泛灵论, 万物有灵论

an·i·mos·i·ty /ˌænəˋmɑsətɪ; ˌænɪˈmɒsɪti/ *n* [C,U] strong dislike or hatred; HOSTILITY 憎恶, 仇恨, 敌意: *There is no personal animosity between the party leaders.* 该党领导人之间并没有个人恩怨。

an·i·mus /ˋænɪməs; ˈænɪməs/ *n* [singluar,U] *formal* a feeling of strong dislike or hatred; HOSTILITY【正式】憎恶, 仇恨, 敌意

an·i·seed /ˋænɪˌsid; ˈænɪsiːd/ *n* [U] the seeds of a plant used in alcoholic drinks and in sweets〔用于酒精饮料和糖果的〕大茴香子

An·ka·ra /ˋæŋkrə; ˈæŋkərə/ the capital city of Turkey 安卡拉〔土耳其首都〕—see also 另见 ISTANBUL

an·kle /ˋæŋkḷ; ˈæŋkəl/ *n* [C] **1** the joint between your foot and your leg 脚踝 —see picture at 参见 FOOT[1] 图 **2 ankle socks/boots** socks or boots that only come up to your ankle〔仅到脚踝的〕短袜/短靴

an·klet /ˋæŋklɪt; ˈæŋklɪt/ *n* [C] a ring or BRACELET worn around your ankle 踝饰, 脚镯

An·na Ka·ren·in·a /ˌænə kəˋrɛnɪnə; ˌænə kəˈrenɪnə/ a book by the Russian writer Leo Tolstoy which many people think is one of the greatest NOVEL*s* ever written. It tells the story of a married woman called Anna Karenina who falls in love with a young army officer.《安娜·卡列尼娜》〔俄国作家列夫·托尔斯泰的作品, 被认为是历史上最伟大的小说之一, 讲述已婚女子安娜·卡列尼娜与一位年轻军官的爱情故事〕

an·nals /ˋænḷz; ˈænlz/ *n* [plural] **1** an official record of events or activities 年鉴, 年报, 编年史: *the Annals of the Zoological Society* 动物学学会年报 **2 in the annals of history/British politics etc** in the whole history of something 在整个历史/英国政治史上: *one of the most disgraceful episodes in the annals of British politics* 英国政治史上最丢脸的事件之一

An·nan /ˋænæn; ˈænæn/, **Ko·fi** /ˋkofɪ; ˈkəʊfi/ (1938-) the Secretary-General of the United Nations from 1997 to 2006. He comes from Ghana, and was formerly responsible for the UN's peacekeeping operations in Bosnia. 安南〔(1938-), 1997年至2006年间始任联合国秘书长, 加纳人, 先前主持过联合国在波斯尼亚的维和行动〕

An·nap·o·lis /əˋnæpəlɪs; əˈnæpəlɪs/ **1** the capital of the state of Maryland in the US. The United States Naval Academy, where navy officers are trained, is in Annapolis. 安纳波利斯〔美国马里兰州首府, 美国海军学院所在地〕 **2** another name for the United States Naval Academy, where officers of the US Navy are given a university education and trained 安纳波利斯〔美国海军学院别称, 美国海军接受大学教育和培训的地方〕: *He graduated from Annapolis in 1993.* 他1993年毕业于安纳波利斯海军学院。

Anne /æn; æn/, **Princess** (1950-) the second child and only daughter of the British queen, Elizabeth II. Her official title is The Princess Royal. 安妮公主〔(1950-), 英国女王伊丽莎白二世的第二个孩子和唯一的女儿, 被册封为大公主〕

Anne, Queen (1665-1714) the queen of Great Britain and Ireland from 1702 to 1714 and the daughter of James II. 安妮女王〔(1665-1714), 大不列颠及北爱尔兰联合王国女王 (1702-1714), 詹姆斯二世之女〕

an·neal /əˋnil; əˈniːl/ *v* [T] to make metal or glass hard by heating it and then slowly letting it get cold 使…退火, 韧炼〔把金属或玻璃加热后缓缓冷却使之坚硬〕

Anne of Cleves /ˌ· ˋ·ˈ/ (1515-1557) a European princess of the DUCHY of Cleves, who became the fourth wife of the English king Henry VIII in 1540. They were divorced after six months. 〔克利夫斯的〕安妮〔(1515-1557), 欧洲克利夫斯公国的一位公主, 1540年成为英国国王亨利八世的第四任妻子, 婚后六个月即离婚〕

Anne of Green Ga·bles /ˌ· · ˋ· ·ˈ/ a children's NOVEL by L. M. Montgomery about a girl called Anne Shirley who is ADOPT*ed* by an older lady and her brother and goes to live on Prince Edward Island in Canada, during the late 1800s《格林·盖布尔斯来的安妮》〔蒙哥马利的一部儿童小说。故事发生在19世纪晚期, 一个名叫安妮·雪莉的小女孩被一位老妇人及其兄弟收养, 后来他们一起移居到加拿大的爱德华王子岛〕

an·nex /əˋnɛks; əˈneks/ *v* [T] to take control of a country or area next to your own, especially by using force〔尤指通过使用武力〕吞并, 兼并, 霸占〔国家或领土〕—**annexation** /ˌænɛksˋeʃən; ˌænekˈseɪʃən/ *n* [C,U]

an·nexe *BrE*【英】, **annex** *especially AmE*【尤美】/ˋænɛks; ˈæneks/ *n* [C] a separate building that has been added to a larger one 附属建筑, 附加建筑

an·ni·hi·late /əˋnaɪəˌlet; əˈnaɪəleɪt/ *v* [T] **1** to destroy something or someone completely 彻底毁灭, 消灭: *stock piles of weapons that could annihilate mankind* 贮藏大量能够摧毁人类的武器 **2** to defeat someone easily and completely in a game, competition, or election〔游戏、比赛或选举中〕彻底战胜: *Tyson annihilated his opponent in the first round.* 泰森在第一个回合就轻取对手。—**annihilation** /əˌnaɪəˋleʃən; əˌnaɪəˈleɪʃən/ *n* [U]

an·ni·ver·sa·ry /ˌænəˋvɝsərɪ; ˌænɪˈvɜːsəri/ *n* [C] a date on which something special or important happened in a previous year 周年纪念(日): *our twentieth wedding anniversary* 我们结婚20周年纪念日

An·no Dom·i·ni /ˋæno ˋdɑməˌnaɪ; ˌænəʊ ˈdɒmɪnaɪ/ *formal* AD【正式】公元

an·no·tate /ˋænəˌtet; ˈænəteɪt/ *v* [T] to add short notes to a book or piece of writing to explain parts of it 给…作注释, 注解: *an annotated edition of 'Othello'*《奥赛罗》的注释本 —**annotation** /ˌænəˋteʃən; ˌænəˈteɪʃən/ *n* [C,U]

an·nounce /əˋnaʊns; əˈnaʊns/ *v* [T] **1** to officially tell people about a decision or something that will happen 宣布, 通告, 公布于众: *They announced their engagement in 'The Times'.* 他们在《泰晤士报》上宣布了订婚的消息。| **announce (that)** *A government spokesman announced that the hostages had been released.* 政府发言人宣布人质已经被释放。**2** to say something in a loud or angry way 大声宣布: **announce (that)** *Winston suddenly announced that he was leaving.* 温斯顿突然宣布他要离开。| **announce a visitor/guest** (=say their name loudly, especially at a special event, so other people will know they have arrived) 通报客人的到来 **3** to give information to people using a LOUDSPEAKER or MICROPHONE, especially at an airport or railway station〔尤指在机场或火车站〕广播: *announcing the arrival of Flight 207 from Minneapolis* 广播报告来自明尼阿波利斯的207次航班到达 **4** to introduce a programme on television or radio〔在电视或电台〕主持〔节目〕 S2 W1

an·nounce·ment /əˋnaʊnsmənt; əˈnaʊnsmənt/ *n* **1** [C] an important or official statement〔重要或正式的〕通告, 宣告, 告示, 声明: **[+about]** *an important announcement about tax increases* 关于增加税收的重要公告 | **announcement that** *We were shocked by the announcement that the mayor was resigning.* 我们对市长要辞职的声明感到震惊。| **make an announcement** *Silence please, Mr Dacre has an announcement to make.* 请安静, 戴克先生有事要宣布。**2** [singular] the act of telling people something important is going to happen 发表, 宣布, 宣告: *the announcement of the general strike* 宣布总罢工 **3** [C] a small advertisement or statement in a newspaper〔报纸上的〕广告, 启事: **birth/wedding/death announcement** *The wedding announcement appeared on the 16th of June.* 结婚启事是6月16日发布的。 S3 W3

an·nounc·er /əˋnaʊnsə; əˈnaʊnsə/ *n* [C] someone who reads news or information on the television or radio〔电视或电台的〕广播员, 播音员, 节目主持人

an·noy /əˋnɔɪ; əˈnɔɪ/ *v* [T] to make someone feel slightly angry and unhappy about something 使烦恼, 烦扰, 打搅: *The way Tina orders us around really annoys me.* 蒂娜把我们差来遣去的做法真使我恼火。| *It annoyed him that the model didn't fit together properly.* 使他懊恼的是这个型号安不上。 S3

an·noy·ance /əˋnɔɪəns; əˈnɔɪəns/ *n* **1** [U] a feeling of slight anger 烦恼, 气恼: *A look of annoyance crossed her face.* 她一脸烦恼。| **to your annoyance** *To his annoyance, he discovered they hadn't waited.* 他发现他们没有等他, 因而感到很气恼。**2** [C] something that makes you slightly angry 令人烦恼的事物: *Alan found the constant noise of the traffic an annoyance.* 不断的汽车噪音让艾伦觉得心烦。

an·noyed /əˋnɔɪd; əˈnɔɪd/ *adj* slightly angry 烦恼 [略感生气] 的: *I'll be annoyed if we don't finish by eight.* 如果我们8点还未完成, 我会很懊恼。| **[+with]** *She was annoyed with Duncan for forgetting to phone.* 邓肯忘了打电话使她气恼。| **[+about/by]** *He was annoyed by her apparent indifference.* 她看起来很冷淡, 这让他很恼火。| **be annoyed that** *Mr Davies was annoyed that the books were missing.* 那些书不见了, 戴维斯先生很懊恼。

an·noy·ing /əˋnɔɪ·ɪŋ; əˈnɔɪ-ɪŋ/ *adj* making you feel slightly angry 令人心烦的: *an annoying habit of interrupting* 打断他人

讲话的令人恼火的习惯 | *The annoying thing is he's usually right.* 令人气恼的是，他通常都是对的。| **it's annoying that** *It's annoying that we didn't know about this before.* 令人恼火的是，我们事先并不知道。—**annoyingly** *adv*: *annoyingly small portions* 量少得让人恼火

an·nu·al[1] /ˋænjuəl; ˈænjuəl/ *adj* **1** happening once a year 一年一度的，每年的: *an annual conference* 年会 **2** based on or calculated over a period of one year 按年度计算的: *Steel output reached an annual figure of one million tons.* 钢的年产量达到100万吨。—**annually** *adv*

annual[2] *n* [C] **1** a plant that lives for one year or season 一年生植物；一季生植物 —compare 比较 BIENNIAL (2), BIANNUAL **2** a book, especially for children, that is produced once a year with the same title but different stories, pictures etc 年刊，年报，年鉴〔尤指儿童年刊〕

annual meet·ing /ˌ··· ˈ··/ *n* [C] a meeting held once a year by a club, business, or organization 年会; AGM *BrE*【英】

an·nu·i·ty /əˋnuətɪ; əˈnjuːɪ̈ti/ *n* [C] a fixed amount of money that is paid each year to someone, usually until they die 年金；(每年的) 养老金

an·nul /əˋnʌl; əˈnʌl/ *v* **annulled, annulling** [T often passive 常用被动态] *technical* to state that a marriage or legal agreement no longer exists【术语】解除〔婚约〕；废止〔契约〕—**annulment** *n* [C,U]

An·nun·ci·a·tion, the /əˌnʌnsɪˋeʃən; əˌnʌnsiˈeɪʃən/ the occasion (celebrated by Christians on 25 March) on which the ANGEL Gabriel appeared and told the Virgin Mary that she would have the baby Jesus 天使传报日，圣母领报节〔基督教在3月25日庆祝的节日，该日天使加百列现身向童贞女马利亚传报她身怀基督〕

an·ode /ˋænod; ˈænəʊd/ *n* [C] *technical* the part of a BATTERY (1) that collects ELECTRONS, often a wire or piece of metal with the sign (+)【术语】正极，阳极〔用"+"号表示〕—compare 比较 CATHODE

an·o·dyne[1] /ˋænəˌdaɪn; ˈænədaɪn/ *adj* expressed in a way that is unlikely to offend anyone 不惹人的，不冒犯他人的: *anodyne topics of conversation* 不冒犯人的话题

anodyne[2] *n* [C] **1** *technical* a medicine that reduces pain【术语】镇痛药 **2** *formal* an activity or thing that comforts people【正式】给人以安慰的事物

a·noint /əˋnɔɪnt; əˈnɔɪnt/ *v* [T] to put oil or water on someone's head or body during a religious ceremony【正式】〔宗教仪式中〕涂油[水]于〔人头或身上〕—**anointment** *n* [C,U]

a·nom·a·lous /əˋnɑmələs; əˈnɒmələs/ *adj* different from what you expected to find 异常的，反常的；不规则的；畸形的: *clearly an anomalous result* 明显反常的结果 —**anomalously** *adv*

a·nom·a·ly /əˋnɑməlɪ; əˈnɒməli/ *n* [C,U] *formal* a strange and unusual feature of a situation or process that often makes it unsatisfactory or unfair, or an example of this【正式】异常现象，反常现象；畸形: *various anomalies in the tax system* 税制上的各种反常现象 | *a genetic anomaly* 遗传变异

a·non[1] /əˋnɑn; əˈnɒn/ *adv literary* soon【文】不久，未几: *See you anon.* 一会儿见。—see also 另见 **ever and anon** (EVER (9))

anon[2] written abbreviation of 缩写= anonymous

an·o·nym·i·ty /ˌænəˋnɪmətɪ; ˌænəˈnɪmɪ̈ti/ *n* [U] **1** the state of not letting your name be known 匿名，不公开姓名: *Every step will be taken to preserve your anonymity.* 将采取各种措施不公开你的姓名。**2** the state of not having any unusual or interesting features 平淡无奇，无个性特征: *the drab anonymity of the city* 城市的单调乏味、平淡无奇 **3** the state of not showing who is involved in something 无署名；作者不明: *the anonymity of a typed envelope* 不具名打印的信封

a·non·y·mous /əˋnɑnəməs; əˈnɒnɪ̈məs/ *adj* **1** unknown by name 无名的，不署名的: *The benefactor wishes to remain anonymous.* 捐助者希望不留姓名。**2** done, sent, or given by someone who does not want their name to be known 匿名的，不知姓名的: *an anonymous donation of £5,000* 一位不具名人士捐赠的5000英镑 | **anonymous phone call/letter etc** (=often unpleasant or containing threats) 匿名电话/信等 **3** without any interesting features or qualities 无特色的: *grey, anonymous housing estates* 灰色的、毫无特色的住宅区 —**anonymously** *adv*

a·noph·e·les /əˋnɑfəˌliz; əˈnɒfɪ̈liːz/ *n* [C] a kind of MOSQUITO, especially the kind that spreads MALARIA 疟蚊

an·o·rak /ˋænəˌræk; ˈænəræk/ *n* [C] *especially BrE* a short coat with a HOOD (1) that keeps out the wind and rain【尤英】带风帽的夹克 [短风雨衣] —see picture at 参见 COAT[1] 图

an·o·rex·i·a /ˌænəˋrɛksɪə; ˌænəˈreksiə◂/ also 又作 **anorexia ner·vo·sa** /-nəˋvosə; nɜːˈvəʊsə/ *n* [U] a mental illness that makes people, especially young women, stop eating 食欲缺乏，厌食(症)

an·o·rex·ic /ˌænəˋrɛksɪk; ˌænəˈreksɪk◂/ *adj* suffering from or connected with anorexia 厌食的 —**anorexic** *n* [C]

an·oth·er /əˋnʌðɚ; əˈnʌðə/ *determiner, pron* **1** used to refer to one more person or thing of the same kind〔同类的〕另一个: *Can you pass me another mug?* 你能再递给我一个大杯吗？| *I'm going to have another beer.* 我要再喝一杯啤酒。| *When you've eaten that, you can have another one.* 吃完那个以后，你还可以再吃一个。| *"I can't find that pencil you've just given me." "Don't worry, here's another."* "我找不到你刚才给我的铅笔。""不要紧，这儿还有一支。" | [+of] *Is this another of your schemes to make money?* 这是你的另一个赚钱方案吗？| **yet another** *He has to go to yet another meeting.* (=he has already been to several) 他还得出席另一个会议。| **from one...to another** *We seem to struggle from one crisis to another.* 我们好像在跟一个又一个危机斗争。| **one after another** (=used to talk about a series of similar things or events) 一个接一个 *Small businesses have been collapsing one after another.* 小型企业纷纷倒闭。**2** a different person or thing or some other kind of person or thing〔不同类的〕另外一个；其他一种: *If that doesn't work, you'll have to find another way of solving the problem.* 如果那个方法不行，你得找另外一种方法去解决问题。| *You can press enter to select this value or type another choice (such as N).* 你可以按输入键选择这个数值，或者输入另一个选项（比如N）。| *We'll talk about that another time.* 那件事我们下次再谈。| **another of** *Another of the speakers suggested abandoning the project altogether.* 另一个发言人建议放弃整个项目。| **...or another** (=used when you cannot be specific about what kind of things or people you mean) …或另一种 *All the kids in this class have learning difficulties of one sort or another.* 这个班上所有的孩子在学习上都有这样那样的困难。| **that is another matter/thing altogether** *You can try it, but whether it will work is another thing altogether.* (=it is likely that it will not work) 你可以试一下，但行不行完全是另一回事。**3** in addition to a particular amount, distance, period of time etc; FURTHER 再一，又〔指数量、距离、时间等〕: *Let the soup simmer for another 10 minutes.* 让汤再炖10分钟。| *I let out another 50 feet of rope.* 我又放出50英尺绳子。| *A room with a sea view will cost another £7.* 窗外有海景的房间另加收七英镑。**4 one another** used after a verb to show that two or more people or things do the same thing to each other〔用于动词之后〕互相: *They seem to love one another very much.* 他们似乎深爱对方。**5 another Chernobyl/another Pele etc** used when talking about a situation or person that reminds you of another famous situation or person, especially because they have extremely good or extremely bad qualities 又一个切尔诺贝利事件/另一个贝利等

An·schluss /ˋɑnʃlus; ˈænʃlʊs/ the name given to the events in which Hitler's Germany took control of Austria in 1938 德奥合并〔指希特勒统治下的德国1938年吞并奥地利的事件〕

ANSI /ˋænsɪ; ˈænsi/ *n* [singular] American National Standards Institute; an organization in the US which sets the standards used for testing the quality and safety of electronic equipment, scientific equipment etc. It has also established a standard set of letters and numbers called the ANSI character set, which is used in computers. 美国国家标准协会〔美国一组织，其职能是制定电子设备、科学仪器等产品的质量与安全性能检测标准。另外，该组织还制定了一套标准字符代码，即"美国国家标准协会字符集"，用于计算机中〕

an·swer[1] /ˋænsɚ; ˈɑːnsə/ *n* 

1 ►REPLY 答复◄ [C,U] something you say when you reply to a question that someone has asked you 回答，答复: *I asked Janine what she thought, but I'm still waiting for her answer.* 我问过雅尼纳怎么想，不过现在仍在等她的答复。| **give (sb) an answer** *You don't have to give them an answer straight away.* 你不必马上就给他们答复。| **the answer is yes/no!** *spoken*【口】*If it's money you're after again, the answer is no!* 如果你想要的又是钱，那么回答是没有！| **in answer to** *In answer to your question, I think you can go.* 我给你问题的回答是，我想你可以走了。

2 ►TEST/COMPETITION ETC 测验/比赛等◄ [C] something that you write or say in reply to a question in a test, exercise, competition etc 答案: *What was the answer to question 4?* 第四题的答案是什么？

3 ►INVITATION/LETTER ETC 请柬/信等◄ [C] a written reply to a letter, invitation, advertisement etc〔信、请柬、广告等的〕回函: *Did you ever get an answer to your letter?* 你收到回信了吗？

4 ►PROBLEM 问题◄ [C] a way of dealing with a problem 解决办法: *There are no easy answers to today's environmental problems.* 当今的环境问题，没有容易的解决办法。| **be the answer to sb's problems/worries etc** *If he could get a job it'd be*

the answer to all his worries. 如果他能找到一份工作，他所有的烦恼就会烟消云散了。

5 not get an answer to not get a reply when you telephone someone or call at their house〔电话〕无应答：*I tried calling him all day but couldn't get an answer.* 我试着给他打了一天电话，但无人应答。

6 sb's answer to someone or something that is considered to be just as good as a more famous person or thing〔与出名之人或物〕极为相似的人[物]：*Britain's answer to the Eiffel Tower* (简直是) 英国的埃菲尔铁塔

S1 W2 **answer**² *v*

1 ►REPLY 答复◄ a) [I,T] to say something to someone as a reply when they have asked you a question, made a suggestion etc 回答，答复：*I had to answer lots of questions about my childhood.* 我必须回答许多关于我童年的问题。| **answer (that)** *When questioned, Hughes answered that he knew nothing about the robbery.* 问到休斯时，他回答说对这宗抢劫案一无所知。| **answer sb** *How much was it? Come on, answer me.* 多少钱？快点告诉我。| *Julie stared at him for a long time before answering.* 朱莉盯着他看了好久才回答。**b)** [T] to deal with someone's question in a satisfactory way 解答：*You still haven't answered my question.* 你还没有解答我的问题。

2 answer criticism/charges/accusations etc to explain why you did something when people are criticizing you 就批评/指控/谴责等作出解释：*How do you answer the criticism that your government has done nothing to help the homeless?* 有人批评你们的政府没有采取任何行动帮助无家可归者，你怎样解释？

3 ►TEST 测试◄ [I,T] to write or say the answer to a question in a test, exercise, competition etc 答（题）：*Answer as many questions as possible in the time provided.* 在规定的时间内尽量多答题。

4 answer the phone/door/a call to pick up the telephone when it rings or go to the door when someone calls 接电话/应门

5 ►LETTER 信◄ [T] to send a reply to a letter, advertisement etc 回信：*Simon got the job by answering an advertisement in the newspaper.* 西蒙通过应征报纸上的一则广告找到了工作。

6 ►DO STH AS A REACTION 作出反应◄ [I,T] to do something as a reaction to criticism or attack 以…行动回应：*The US answered by bombing North Vietnam.* 美国以轰炸北越作为回应。

7 ►DEAL WITH A PROBLEM 处理问题◄ [T] to be a way of dealing with or solving a problem 解决：*"You can borrow my car if you like." "Well, that answers one problem."* "如果你愿意，可以借我的车。""啊，这下解决问题了。"

8 answer a description if someone answers a description, they match that description 与描述的相符合：*A man answering the police's description was seen entering the building.* 有人看到一个和警方描述的相貌特征相符的人进了楼。

9 answer a need to provide something that is needed 满足需要

answer back *phr v* [I,T] to reply in a rude way to someone that you are supposed to obey 回嘴，反驳：**answer sb back** *Don't answer me back young man!* 年轻人，别跟我顶嘴！

answer for sth *phr v* [T] **1** to explain to people in authority why you did something wrong or why something happened, and be punished if necessary 对…负责：*The teachers must answer for their students' disgusting behaviour on the school trip.* 教师应对学生在学校旅行活动期间的不良行为负责。**2 have a lot to answer for** *informal* to be responsible for causing a lot of trouble【非正式】对许多问题负有责任：*That young man's got an awful lot to answer for.* 那个年轻人在许多事情上应承担责任。**3 I can answer for him/her etc** *spoken* used to say that someone will definitely do something【口】我可以担保某人〔一定会做某事〕：*I'm sure John will help us – I can't really answer for the others.* 我确信约翰会帮我们，但别人我真的保证不了。

answer to sb/sth *phr v* [T] **1** to give an explanation to someone, especially about something that you have done wrong 对…负责，作出解释〔尤指错事〕：*Phipps answers to me and me alone.* 菲普斯只对我一个人负责。**2 answer to the name of a)** if a pet answers to a particular name, it comes when you call that name 对（叫…名）有反应：*Their dog answers to the name of Fido.* 他们的狗一听到喊"菲多"这个名字就有反应。**b)** to be called a particular name 名叫，叫做：*George was over six feet tall, but he answered to the name of 'Shorty'.* 乔治身高有六英尺多，但外号却叫"矮子"。

USAGE NOTE 用法说明：ANSWER

WORD CHOICE 词语辨析：**answer, reply, respond, give an answer, get back to**

Answer is the usual verb you use to talk about answering questions. **Reply** is used especially when you mention the actual words that were said. 回答问题一般用 answer，提到回答的原话时往往用 reply：*I was so nervous I couldn't reply/answer.* 我太紧张，没能回答问题。| *"Not in the least," he replied.* "一点也不。"他回答道。

Respond is more formal and less common and often suggests that a criticism is being replied to. respond 较正式，因而不常用，经常暗指对批评作出反应：*So far, the travel agent hasn't responded to our complaint.* 到目前为止，旅行社对我们的投诉尚未作出反应。

If you give someone a piece of information they have asked for, such as a decision you have made, you **give them an answer**. 如果你提供别人想要的信息，比如说你所作的决定，可说 give them an answer：*If we offer you the job, when could you give us an answer?* 如果我们给你这份工作，你什么时候能给我们一个答复？

If you think you can answer someone later but not at once, you say you will **get back to them**. 如果你认为你可以稍后而不是马上答复某人，可说 get back to them：*Sorry, I'll need to think about that and get back to you.* 对不起，我需要考虑一下，然后再答复你。

GRAMMAR 语法

You **answer** (*v*) a question, advertisement etc, not *to/at* it. Normally you **answer** a person too. If you **answer to** someone, they are the person directly responsible for you in an organization, at work etc, and you have to explain to them if anything goes wrong or if you are not doing something properly. 回答问题、应征广告等，用 answer 直接加宾语，不用 to 或 at。通常 answer 的宾语也可以是人。answer to 指在工作单位或某机构中向某人负责，如有问题或者你做错什么事情，就必须对他们作出解释。

You give the **answer** (*n*) **to** a question or criticism, not *of* it. You get an **answer** (*n*) **from** someone, not *of* them. 对问题或批评的回答用介词 to，不用 of。得到某人的答复说 get an answer from，不用 of。

an·swer·a·ble /ˈænsərəbl̩; ˈɑːnsərəbəl/ *adj* **1 be answerable to** to have to explain your actions to someone in authority 须向…说明理由；向…承担责任：*I am answerable to the government for any decisions I make.* 我作出任何决定都要向政府负责。**2** a question that is answerable can be answered 可答复的；可驳斥的

answering ma·chine /ˈ‥ ˌ‥/ also 又作 **answerphone** *BrE*【英】*n* [C] a machine that records your telephone calls when you cannot answer them 录音电话机，电话答录机

ant /ænt; ænt/ *n* [C] **1** a small insect that lives in large groups 蚂蚁 **2 have ants in your pants** *spoken* to be unable to sit or stand still【口】坐立不安

-ant /ənt; ənt/, **-ent** *suffix* [in nouns and adjectives 构成名词和形容词] someone or something that does something 做…的人；用作…的东西；处于…的状态：*a servant* (=someone who serves others) 仆人 | *disinfectant* (=substance for killing germs) 消毒剂，杀菌剂 | *expectant* (=expecting) 期待的 | *pleasant* (=pleasing) 令人愉快的

an·tag·o·nis·m /ænˈtægəˌnɪzəm; ænˈtægənɪzəm/ *n* [U] **1** hatred between people or groups of people〔人或团体之间的〕对抗，敌对：*the great antagonism between Futurists and Cubists* 未来派和立体派之间的强烈对抗 **2** opposition to an idea, plan etc〔对主张、计划等的〕反对，对立：[**+to/towards**] *his obvious antagonism towards the press* 他对新闻界所持的明显对立态度

an·tag·o·nist /ænˈtægəˌnɪst; ænˈtægənɨst/ *n* [C] your opponent in a competition, battle, quarrel etc 对立[对抗]者；对手，敌手 —compare 比较 PROTAGONIST

an·tag·o·nis·tic /ænˌtægəˈnɪstɪk; ənˌtægəˈnɪstɪk◂/ **1** unfriendly; wanting to argue or disagree 对抗的，敌对的：*an antagonistic attitude* 对抗态度 **2** opposed to an idea or group 反对的：[**+to/towards**] *antagonistic to new ideas* 反对新观点 —**antagonistically** /-klɪ; -kli/ *adv*

an·tag·o·nize also 又作 **-ise** *BrE*【英】/ænˈtægəˌnaɪz; ænˈtægənaɪz/ *v* [T] to annoy someone very much by doing something that they do not like 引起…敌对[对抗]：*Do not do anything to antagonize your customers.* 不要做任何得罪顾客的事情。

An·ta·na·na·ri·vo /ˌæntəˌnænəˋrivo; ˌɑːtænɑːəˈriːvəʊ/ the capital city of Madagascar, formerly called Tananarive or Tananarivo 安塔那那利佛〔马达加斯加首都，旧称塔那那利佛〕

An·tarc·tic /æntˋɑrktɪk; ænˈtɑːktɪk/ *n* [singular] the very cold most southern part of the world 南极；南极地区

Ant·arc·tic·a /ænˋtɑrktɪkə; ænˈtɑːktɪkə/ the continent which is the most southern area of land on the Earth and is mostly covered with ice 南极洲〔地球最南端的大陆，几乎全部为冰所覆盖〕— see also 另见 SOUTH POLE

Antarctic Cir·cle /ˌ·,··ˋ··/ *n* [singular] an imaginary line drawn around the world at a certain distance from the most southern point (the South Pole) 南极圈 —compare 比较 ARCTIC CIRCLE —see picture at 参见 EARTH[1] 图

Antarctic O·cean, the /ˌ·,··ˋ··/ the area of sea south of the Antarctic Circle 南极海〔南极圈以南的海域〕

ante- /æntɪ; æntɪ/ *prefix* before 在…以前: *to antedate* (=be earlier than something) 先于，早于 | *antenatal* (=before birth) 出生前的 —compare 比较 ANTI-, POST-, PRE-

an·te[1] /ˋæntɪ; ˈænti/ *n* **up/raise the ante** to increase your demands or try to get more things from a situation, even though this involves more risks 加赌注 —see also 另见 PENNY ANTE

ante[2] *v*

ante up *phr v past tense* **anted** or **anteed, anteing** [I,T **ante up** sth] *AmE* to pay an amount of money, especially in a game of chance【美】付账〔尤指赌资〕

ant·eat·er /ˋæntˌitɚ; ˈæntˌiːtə/ *n* [C] an animal that has a very long nose and eats small insects 食蚁兽

an·te·ced·ent /ˌæntəˋsidnt; ˌæntɪ̤ˈsiːdənt/ *n* [C] **1** *formal* an event, organization, or thing that is similar to the one you have mentioned but existed eariler【正式】先例: *historical antecedents* 历史上的先例 **2** **antecedents** [plural] *formal* the people in your family who lived a long time ago; ANCESTORS【正式】祖先 **3** *technical* a word, phrase, or sentence that is represented by another word, for example a PRONOUN【术语】先行词，前述词 —**antecedent** *adj*

an·te·cham·ber /ˋæntɪˌtʃembɚ; ˈæntɪˌtʃeɪmbə/ *n* [C] a small room connected to a larger room〔连接较大房间的〕前厅，外室

an·te·date /ˋæntɪˌdet; ˈæntɪdeɪt/ *v* [T] *formal* to come from an earlier time in history than something else【正式】比…早，先于，早于: *It antedates the palace at Nineveh.* 这比尼尼微的宫殿还要古老。

an·te·di·lu·vi·an /ˌæntɪdɪˋluvɪən; ˌæntɪdɪ̤ˈluːviən◂/ *adj humorous* very old-fashioned; OUTDATED【幽默】老式的，陈旧的，过时的: *antediluvian ideas about women* 关于女性的陈旧观念

an·te·lope /ˋæntḷˌop; ˈæntɪ̤ləʊp/ *n* [C] an animal with long horns that can run very fast and is very graceful 羚羊

an·te·na·tal /ˌæntɪˋnetḷ; ˌæntɪˈneɪtl◂/ *adj BrE* connected with the medical care given to women who are going to have a baby【英】产前的; PRENATAL *AmE*【美】: *antenatal clinic* 产前诊所 —compare 比较 POSTNATAL

an·ten·na /ænˋtɛnə; ænˈtenə/ *n* [C] **1** *plural* **antennae** /-ni; -niː/ one of two long thin parts on an insect's head, that it uses to feel things 触角；触须 **2** *plural* **antennas** *especially AmE* a wire, ROD (1) etc used for receiving radio and television signals【尤美】天线; AERIAL[2] *BrE*【英】—see picture on page A2 参见A2页图

an·ter·i·or /ænˋtɪrɪɚ; ænˈtɪəriə/ *adj* [no comparative 无比较级] **1** *technical* at or towards the front【术语】(在)前面的；向前的: *anterior vertebrae* 前椎 **2** *formal* happening or existing before something else【正式】较…早的，…之前的，先前的

an·te·room /ˋæntɪˌrum; ˈæntɪrʊm/ *n* [C] a small room that is connected to a larger room, especially where people wait to go into the larger room〔通往较大房间的〕前室；接待室

an·them /ˋænθəm; ˈænθəm/ *n* [C] **1** a formal or religious song 圣歌，赞美诗 —see also 另见 NATIONAL ANTHEM **2** a song that a particular group of people consider to be very important〔某个群体认为非常重要的〕歌曲: *'The Rolling Stones' 'Satisfaction' became an anthem for a generation.* "滚石"乐队的《满足》成了一代人传唱的歌曲。

an·ther /ˋænθɚ; ˈænθə/ *n* [C] *technical* the part of a male flower which contains POLLEN【术语】〔雄蕊的〕花药，花粉囊

ant·hill /ˋæntˌhɪl; ˈæntˌhɪl/ *n* [C] a place where ANTs live 蚁丘，蚁冢

an·thol·o·gy /ænˋθɑlədʒɪ; ænˈθɒlədʒi/ *n* [C] a set of stories, poems, songs etc by different people collected together in one book〔故事、诗、歌曲等的〕选集: *an anthology of American literature* 美国文学选集 —**anthologist** *n* [C]

An·tho·ny /ˋæntənɪ; ˈæntəni/, **Su·san B.** /ˋsuzn̩ bi; ˈsuːzən biː/ (1820-1906) a US woman who tried to help women get the right to vote 安东尼〔(1820-1906)，为妇女力争选举权的一位美国妇女〕

an·thra·cite /ˋænθrəˌsaɪt; ˈænθrəsaɪt/ *n* [U] a very hard type of coal that burns slowly and produces a lot of heat 无烟煤

an·thrax /ˋænθræks; ˈænθræks/ *n* [U] a serious disease of cattle and sheep 炭疽病

anthropo- /ænθrəpə; ænθrəpə/ *prefix technical* like or concerning human beings【术语】人的，人类的: *anthropomorphic* (=having human form or qualities) 被赋予人性的，拟人的

an·thro·poid /ˋænθrəˌpɔɪd; ˈænθrəpɔɪd/ *adj* an anthropoid animal is very like a human〔动物〕似人的，类人的 —**anthropoid** *n* [C]

an·thro·pol·o·gy /ˌænθrəˋpɑlədʒɪ; ˌænθrəˈpɒlədʒi/ *n* [U] the scientific study of people, their societies, CULTUREs etc 人类学 —compare 比较 ETHNOLOGY, SOCIOLOGY —**anthropologist** *n* [C] —**anthropological** /ˌænθrəpəˋlɑdʒɪkl; ˌænθrəpəˈlɒdʒɪkəl◂/ *adj*

an·thro·po·mor·phis·m /ˌænθrəpəˋmɔrfɪzəm; ˌænθrəpəˈmɔːfɪzəm/ *n* [U] **1** the belief that animals or objects have the same feelings and qualities as humans 拟人论，拟人观 **2** *technical* the belief that God can appear in a human or animal form【术语】神与人或动物同形[同性]论 —**anthropomorphic** *adj*

anti- /æntɪ; æntɪ/ *prefix* **1** opposed to; against 反对: *antinuclear* (=opposing the use of atomic weapons and power) 反对使用核武器[核能]的 | *anti-American* 反美的 **2** the opposite of something 相反物，对立面: *anticlimax* (=an unexciting ending instead of the expected CLIMAX[1] (1)) 突降法 | *antimatter* (=material completely opposite in kind to the ordinary material in the universe) 反物质 **3** acting to prevent something 防(止): *antifreeze* (=a liquid added to prevent freezing) 防冻剂 | *antiseptic* (=to stop bacteria) 抗菌的，防腐的 —compare 比较 ANTE-, PRO-

an·ti·air·craft /ˌæntɪˋɛrˌkræft; ˌæntiˈeəkrɑːft/ *adj* [only before noun 仅用于名词前] antiaircraft weapons are used against enemy aircraft 防空的: *antiaircraft missiles* 防空导弹

An·tibes /ɑnˋtib; ɒnˈtiːb/ a city in southeast France on the Mediterranean coast, which is a fashionable place for holidays 昂蒂布〔法国东南部地中海沿岸一城市，时尚度假胜地〕

an·ti·bi·ot·ic /ˌæntɪbaɪˋɑtɪk; ˌæntɪbaɪˈɒtɪk◂/ *n* [C usually plural 一般用复数] a drug that is used to kill BACTERIA and cure infections 抗生素，抗菌素

an·ti·bod·y /ˋæntɪˌbɑdɪ; ˈæntɪˌbɒdi/ *n* [C] a substance produced by your body to fight disease 抗体

An·ti·christ, the /ˋæntɪˌkraɪst; ˈæntiˌkraɪst/ in the Christian religion, a great enemy of Christ who represents the power of evil and is expected to appear just before the end of the world 敌基督〔基督教所称的基督之大敌，代表邪恶势力。一旦出现，世界末日即将来临〕

an·tic·i·pate /ænˋtɪsəˌpet; ænˈtɪsɪ̤peɪt/ *v* [T] **1** to expect that something will happen and be ready for it 预期，预料: *Organisers are anticipating a large crowd at the carnival.* 组织者预计狂欢节人会很多。| **anticipate that** *It is anticipated that next year interest rates will fall.* 人们预计明年的利率会下调。| **anticipate doing sth** *I didn't anticipate having to do the cooking myself!* 我没有预料到要自己做饭！**2** to think about something that is going to happen, especially something pleasant 期待〔尤指好事〕: *Daniel was eagerly anticipating her arrival.* 丹尼尔热切地期待着她的到来。**3** to do something before someone else 先于…之前(做): *Copernicus anticipated in part the discoveries of the 17th and 18th centuries.* 17和18世纪的发现中有一部分哥白尼早已发现。**4** *formal* to use or consider something before you should【正式】预先考虑；提前使用 —**anticipatory** /ænˋtɪsəpəˌtorɪ; ænˌtɪsɪ̤ˈpeɪtəri/ *adj* 3

an·tic·i·pa·tion /ænˌtɪsəˋpeʃən; ænˌtɪsɪ̤ˈpeɪʃən/ *n* [U] the act of expecting something to happen 预期，预料，期望: *They waited, filled with nervous anticipation.* 他们等待着，充满不安和期盼。| **in anticipation of** *The workers have called off their strike in anticipation of a pay offer.* 工人们预料能够得到工钱，便取消了罢工。

an·ti·cler·i·cal /ˌæntɪˋklɛrɪkḷ; ˌæntiˈklerɪkəl◂/ *adj* being opposed to priests having any political power or influence 反对教权的 —**anticlericalism** *n* [U]

an·ti·cli·max /ˌæntɪˋklaɪmæks; ˌæntɪˈklaɪmæks/ *n* [C,U] a situation or event that does not seem exciting because it happens after something that was much better 突降；令人突然泄气之事: *Going back to work after a month travelling in China was bound to be an anticlimax.* 在中国旅行了一个月后再回来工作肯定令人扫兴。

an·ti·clock·wise /ˌæntɪˋklɑkwaɪz; ˌæntɪˈklɒkwaɪz◂/ *adv, adj BrE* moving in the opposite direction to the hands of a clock【英】逆时针方向地[的]; COUNTERCLOCKWISE *AmE*【美】: *Turn the*

lid anticlockwise. 沿逆时针方向转动这个盖子。—opposite 反义词 CLOCKWISE

an·tics /ˈæntɪks; ˈæntɪks/ *n* [plural] behaviour that seems strange, funny, silly, or annoying 古怪而可笑的举动: *The public quickly grew tired of McEnroe's antics on court.* 公众很快对麦肯罗在球场上的可笑举动感到厌倦了。

an·ti·cy·clone /ˌæntɪˈsaɪklon; ˌæntɪˈsaɪkləʊn/ *n* [C] an area of high air pressure that causes calm weather in the place it is moving over 反气旋, 高气压 —see also 另见 CYCLONE

an·ti·de·pres·sant /ˌæntɪdɪˈprɛsənt; ˌæntidɪˈpresənt/ *n* [C, U] a drug used to treat DEPRESSION (=a mental illness that makes people very unhappy) 抗抑郁药

an·ti·dote /ˈæntɪˌdot; ˈæntɪdəʊt/ *n* [C] **1** a substance that stops the effects of a poison 解毒剂: [+to] *There is no known antidote to a bite from this snake.* 尚无解药能治这种蛇咬的伤。**2** something that makes an unpleasant situation better 缓解之物: *laughter, the antidote to stress* 大笑, 舒缓压力的良药

Antietam /ænˈtitəm; ænˈtiːtəm/ also 又作 **the Battle of Antietam** a battle in the American Civil War, in which General Robert E. Lee's army tried to reach Washington but was defeated by Union soldiers 安蒂特姆战役〔美国内战时期的一场战役, 当时罗伯特·E.李将军的军队试图攻入华盛顿, 但被联邦政府军击溃〕

an·ti·freeze /ˌæntɪˈfriz; ˈæntɪfriːz/ *n* [U] a substance that is put in the water in car engines to stop it from freezing 防冻剂, 抗凝剂

an·ti·gen /ˈæntədʒən; ˈæntɪdʒən/ *n* [C] *technical* a substance that makes the body produce antibodies (ANTIBODY)【术语】抗原

An·tig·o·ne /ænˈtɪgənɪ; ænˈtɪgəni/ in ancient Greek stories, a daughter of Oedipus who is told by King Creon that she cannot bury her dead brother. She cannot decide whether she should obey the king or do what she believes to be right. She finally decides to disobey the king, and kills herself before he can punish her. Her story is the subject of the play *Antigone* by Sophocles. 安提戈涅〔古希腊故事中俄狄浦斯的女儿。国王克瑞翁下令不准她掩埋死去的兄弟。是顺从国王的旨意, 还是践行自己的道义观, 她一筹莫展。最终, 她决定违背圣旨, 并且没等到国王治罪就自尽身亡。后来, 该故事成为索福克勒斯的戏剧《安提戈涅》的主题〕

An·ti·gua /ænˈtigə; ænˈtiːgə/ an island in the Caribbean Sea, which is part of the country of Antigua and Barbuda. Population: 65,900 (1996). Capital: St. John's. Antigua and Barbuda includes the islands of Antigua, Barbuda, and Redonda. 安提瓜岛〔加勒比海一岛屿, 归属安提瓜和巴布达(国名)。人口: 65,900 (1996), 该国首都: 圣约翰。安提瓜和巴布达由安提瓜、巴布达、雷东达三个岛屿组成〕 —**Antiguan** *adj, n*

an·ti·her·o /ˌæntɪˈhɪro; ˈæntɪˌhɪərəʊ/ *n* [C] a main character in a book, play, or film who is an ordinary or unpleasant person and lacks the qualities that you expect a hero to have〔书、戏剧或电影中的〕非正统主角;〔缺乏英雄品格的〕反英雄

an·ti·his·ta·mine /ˌæntɪˈhɪstəmin; ˌæntɪˈhɪstəmiːn/ *n* [C,U] a drug that is used to treat an ALLERGY (=an unpleasant reaction to particular foods, substances etc)〔治疗过敏症的〕抗组(织)胺剂

an·ti·knock /ˌæntɪˈnɑk; ˌæntɪˈnɒk/ *n* [U] a chemical substance that is put in petrol to make car engines operate more smoothly〔加于汽油中使汽车运行更顺畅的〕抗震剂, 抗爆剂

anti-lock brak·ing sys·tem /ˌ.. ˈ.. ˌ../ *n* [U] a piece of equipment that makes a vehicle easier to control when you have to stop very suddenly 防抱死刹车装置

an·ti·ma·cas·sar /ˌæntɪməˈkæsɚ; ˌæntɪməˈkæsə/ *n* [C] a piece of decorated cloth that is put on the back of a chair to protect it 椅背套

an·ti·mat·ter /ˈæntɪˌmætɚ; ˈæntiˌmætə/ *n* [U] a form of MATTER (30) (=substance which the things in the universe are made of) consisting of antiparticles〔由反粒子构成的〕反物质

An·ti·och /ˈæntɪˌɑk; ˈæntɪɒk/ a city in southern Turkey, also known as Antakya, which was built in 301 BC and soon became famous for its buildings and trade. In 64 BC it became the eastern capital of the Roman Empire. 安条克〔土耳其东南部一城市, 又名安塔基亚。建于公元前301年, 不久便以建筑和贸易而闻名。公元前64年成为罗马帝国叙利亚省的首府〕

an·ti·par·ti·cle /ˈæntɪˌpɑrtɪk]; ˈæntiˌpɑːtɪkəl/ *n* [C] a very small part of an atom that has the opposite electrical charge to the one usually found in atoms 反粒子

an·ti·pas·to /ˌæntɪˈpɑsto; ˈæntipæstəʊ/ *n* [U] an Italian dish consisting of cold food that you eat before the main part of a meal 意大利式餐前小吃

an·ti·pa·thet·ic /ænˌtɪpəˈθɛtɪk; ˌæntɪpəˈθetɪk◂/ *adj* [+to] *formal* having a very strong feeling of disliking or opposing someone or something【正式】厌恶的, 反感的

an·tip·a·thy /ænˈtɪpəθɪ; ænˈtɪpəθi/ *n* [U+to/towards] *formal* strong dislike or opposition towards someone or something【正式】反感, 厌恶: *a strong personal antipathy towards Nixon* 个人对尼克松的强烈反感

anti-per·son·nel /ˌ.. .. ˈ./ *adj* an anti-personnel weapon is designed to hurt people rather than damage buildings, vehicles etc〔武器〕用于杀人的, 杀伤性的

anti-per·spi·rant /ˌ.. ˈ.. ./ *n* [U] a substance that prevents you sweating (SWEAT[1] (1)) 止汗剂

An·tip·o·des, the /ænˈtɪpəˌdiz; ænˈtɪpədiːz/ *n often humorous* Australia and New Zealand【常幽默】澳大利亚和新西兰 —**Antipodean** /ænˌtɪpəˈdiən; ænˌtɪpəˈdiːən/ *adj*: *antipodean culture* 澳新文化

an·ti·quar·i·an /ˌæntɪˈkwɛrɪən; ˌæntɪˈkweəriən◂/ *adj* [only before noun 仅用于名词前] an antiquarian book shop sells old books 经营古书的; 古文物的; 研究[收藏, 出售]古文物的

an·ti·quat·ed /ˈæntəˌkwetɪd; ˈæntɪkweɪtɪd/ *adj* old-fashioned and not suitable for modern needs or conditions; OUTDATED (1) 过时的, 陈旧的, 老式的: *antiquated laws* 过时的法律

an·tique[1] /ænˈtik; ænˈtiːk/ *adj* **1** antique furniture, jewellery etc is old and often valuable 古时制造的, 古董的: *an antique rosewood desk* 古董红木书桌 **2** *formal* connected with ancient times, especially ancient Rome or Greece【正式】古代的〔尤指古罗马或古希腊的〕

antique[2] *n* [C] a piece of furniture, jewellery etc that was made a very long time ago and is therefore valuable 古董, 古玩, 古物: *The palace is full of priceless antiques.* 宫殿里到处都是无价的古玩。| *an antique dealer* 古玩商

an·tiq·ui·ty /ænˈtɪkwətɪ; ænˈtɪkwɪti/ *n* **1** [U] ancient times 古代: *a tradition that stretches back into antiquity* 可追溯到远古时代的传统 **2** [U] the state of being very old 年代久远: *a building of great antiquity* 很古老的建筑物 **3** [C usually plural 一般用复数] a building or object made in ancient times 古迹, 古物, 古建筑: *a collection of Roman antiquities* 一批古罗马文物

an·tir·rhi·num /ˌæntɪˈraɪnəm; ˌæntɪˈraɪnəm/ *n* [C] a garden plant with white, red, or yellow flowers; a SNAPDRAGON 金鱼草

anti-Se·mite /ˌæntɪ ˈsɛmaɪt; ˌænti ˈsiːmaɪt/ *n* [C] someone who hates Jewish people 反犹太主义者 —**anti-Semitic** /ˌæntɪ səˈmɪtɪk; ˌænti sɪˈmɪtɪk◂/ *adj*

anti-Sem·i·tis·m /ˌæntɪ ˈsɛməˌtɪzəm; ˌæntɪ ˈsemɪtɪzəm/ *n* [U] hatred of Jewish people 反犹太主义

an·ti·sep·tic[1] /ˌæntəˈsɛptɪk; ˌæntɪˈseptɪk◂/ *n* [C] a chemical substance that helps stop a wound becoming infected 抗菌防腐药

antiseptic[2] *adj* **1** helping to prevent infection 抗菌的; 抗感染的: *antiseptic cream* 抗感染药膏 **2** lacking emotion, interest, or excitement 缺乏感情的, 没有情趣的: *dreary antiseptic prose* 乏味、没意思的散文

anti-so·cial /ˌ.. ˈ..◂/ *adj* **1** unwilling to meet people and talk to them, especially in a way that seems unfriendly or rude 不喜欢社交的, 不合群的: *a child who was aggressive and anti-social* 一个好斗又孤僻的孩子 **2** an activity that is anti-social does not give you the chance to meet other people 没有社交机会的, 结交不到人的: *The job's OK, but I have to work very anti-social hours.* 这份工作还可以, 不过我得牺牲社交活动的时间来工作。**3** anti-social behaviour shows a lack of concern for other people 反社会的; 不考虑他人利益的: *Smoking cigarettes in public is increasingly considered anti-social.* 在公共场所吸烟越来越被看作是妨害公众利益的行为。

anti-tank /ˌ.. ˈ.◂/ *adj* an anti-tank weapon is designed to destroy enemy tanks (TANK[1] (3))〔武器〕反坦克的

an·tith·e·sis /ænˈtɪθəsɪs; ænˈtɪθɪsɪs/ *n* [C usually singular 一般用单数] *formal* the exact opposite of something【正式】正相反, 相对; 对立面: *Connie's political views are the complete antithesis of mine.* 康妮的政治观点和我的正相反。

an·ti·thet·i·cal /ˌæntɪˈθɛtɪk]; ˌæntɪˈθetɪkəl/ also 又作 **an·ti·thet·ic** /-ˈθɛtɪk; -ˈθetɪk◂/ *adj formal* exactly opposite to something【正式】正相反的; 对立的: [+to] *completely antithetical to democratic ideals* 和民主理想完全背道而驰的

an·ti·tox·in /ˌæntɪˈtɑksɪn; ˌæntiˈtɒksɪn/ *n* a substance produced by your body or put in a medicine to stop the effects of a poison 抗毒素

anti trust law /ˌ.. ˈ. ˌ./ *n* [C,U] *technical* an American law intended to prevent companies unfairly controlling prices【术语】〔美国〕反托拉斯法; 反垄断法

ant·ler /ˋæntlɚ; ˈæntlə/ *n* [C] one of the two horns of a male DEER 鹿角

An·toi·nette /æntwəˋnɛt; æntwəˋnet/, **Marie** /məˋri; ˈmɑːri/ —see 见 MARIE ANTOINETTE

An·to·ny /ˋæntənɪ; ˈæntəni/, **Mark** (?83-30 BC) an ancient Roman politician and soldier who supported Julius Caesar, and after his death became one of the TRIUMVIRATE of three rulers of the Roman Empire. He fell in love with Cleopatra, and after they were defeated in battle, they both killed themselves. 安东尼〔公元前?83-前30〕,古罗马政治家、军人,尤利乌斯·凯撒的支持者。凯撒死后,安东尼成为罗马帝国的执政三雄之一。他曾与克娄巴特拉相爱,后来战败后双双自杀〕

Antony and Cle·o·pat·ra /ˌ····· ·ˋ··/ a play by William Shakespeare about the relationship between Cleopatra, the queen of Egypt, and the Roman leader Mark Antony《安东尼和克娄巴特拉》〔莎士比亚一剧作,讲述埃及女王克娄巴特拉和罗马统帅安东尼的爱情故事〕

an·to·nym /ˋæntəˌnɪm; ˈæntənɪm/ *n* [C] a word that means the opposite to another word 反义词: *'Good' is the antonym of 'bad'.* good 是 bad 的反义词。—compare 比较 SYNONYM —**antonymous** /ænˋtɑnɪməs; ænˈtɒnɪ̵məs/ *adj*

An·trim /ˋæntrɪm; ˈæntrɪ̵m/ **1** a COUNTY in Northern Ireland 安特里姆郡〔北爱尔兰一郡〕 **2** a town in Northern Ireland 安特里姆〔北爱尔兰一镇〕

Ant·werp /ˋæntwɝp; ˈæntwɜːp/ a city and port in northern Belgium 安特卫普〔比利时北部一港口城市〕

a·nus /ˋenəs; ˈeɪnəs/ *n* [C usually singular 一般用单数] the hole in your body through which solid waste leaves your BOWELs 肛门 —see picture at 参见 DIGESTIVE SYSTEM 图

an·vil /ˋænvɪl; ˈænvɪ̵l/ *n* [C] a heavy iron block on which pieces of metal are shaped using a hammer 铁砧

3 3 **anx·i·e·ty** /æŋˋzaɪətɪ; æŋˈzaɪəti/ *n* **1** [C,U] the feeling of being very worried about something that may happen or may have happened, so that you think about it all the time 焦虑, 不安, 担心: [**+about/over**] *anxiety among staff about job losses* 职员对失业的担心 | *an anxiety attack* 突然间的焦虑 **2** [C] something that makes you worry 使人焦虑的事情: *the anxieties of parenthood* 父母们担心的事 **3** [U] a feeling of wanting to do something very much but being worried that you will not succeed 渴望: **anxiety to do sth** *a natural anxiety to please one's parents* 渴望讨好父母的自然心情

3 3 **anx·ious** /ˋæŋkʃəs; ˈæŋkʃəs/ *adj* **1** very worried about something that may happen or may have happened so that you think about it all the time 焦虑的, 不安的, 担心的: [**+about**] *Helen is anxious about travelling on her own.* 海伦对自己一个人出门旅行感到担心。| *"Feeling scared, Joe?" "No, just a little anxious."* "感到害怕吗, 乔?" "不, 只是有点焦虑。" | **anxious look/expression etc** *an anxious glance at the fuel gauge* 焦虑地看一眼燃油表 | **anxious that** *anxious that it might be cancer* 担心或许是癌症 **2** an anxious time or situation is one in which you feel nervous or worried〔时间或形势〕紧张的, 使人焦虑的: *an anxious couple of weeks waiting for the test results* 等待考试成绩那令人焦急的几周时间 **3** feeling strongly that you want to do something or want something to happen 渴望…的, 急切希望…的: **anxious to do sth** *Peggy is anxious to show that she can cope with extra responsibility.* 佩吉急切地想表明她能承担一些分外的工作。—**anxiously** *adv*: *waiting anxiously by the phone* 在电话旁焦急地等待 —see 见 NERVOUS (USAGE)

1 1 **an·y¹** /ˋɛnɪ; ˈeni/ *determiner, pron* **1** used to refer to each one or all members of a group, saying it does not matter which 任何一个; 无论哪个: *Any child who attempts to escape is beaten.* 凡试图逃走的孩子都要挨揍。| *You can obtain a valuation from any accredited insurance valuer.* 你可以请任何一家官方认可的保险评估公司进行估价。| *Any plan chosen should take these factors into account.* 所有入选方案都必须考虑这些因素。| *before you sign any written agreement* 在你签订任何书面协议以前 | *These tiles are an ideal choice for any bathroom setting.* 这些瓷砖是所有浴室装修的理想选择。| **any of** *before touching the computer or any of its parts* 在触摸电脑或其任何部件之前 | *Do any of you remember?* 你们当中有谁记得吗? | **any other** *Are there any other comments?* 还有其他评论吗? **2** used especially in questions or as part of a negative statement to mean some or even the smallest amount 一点, 一些, 少许: *Few of the students had any knowledge of classical music.* 很少有学生具备古典音乐方面的知识。| *I didn't pay any attention to what he said.* 我一点儿也没注意他说什么。| *She promised not to take any chances.* 她答应不会再冒任何风险。| *He had no friends and didn't deserve any.* 他没有朋友, 也不配有朋友。| **I haven't any idea** (=I do not know at all) 我一点头绪都没有 | **any of** *I don't understand what any of this stuff means.* 我一点儿也不知道这东西是干什么用的。| **any use** *I tried, but it wasn't any use.* (=it was not successful) 我试了, 但一点儿用也没有。| **if any** *I don't suppose there will be more than a dozen left, if any.* (=it is likely that there will be none at all) 我认为即使还有的话也不过十几个。| **in any way** *He was not in any way upset by his wife's decision.* 他丝毫也没有因妻子的决定而感到不高兴。| *If I can help you in any way, let me know.* 如果我在某些方面能帮上你什么忙, 请告诉我。**3** as much as possible; all 尽可能多的, 所有的: *They're going to need any help they can get.* 能得到的帮助他们都需要。**4 in any case/at any rate a)** no matter what may happen; at least 无论如何: *There was nothing else to be done. At any rate, I had learnt something.* 没有什么别的可做了, 但无论如何, 我还是了解到了一些情况。**b)** besides; also 此外, 也, 还: *In any case, he was a rude old man.* 此外, 他还是个粗鲁的老人。**5 just any** used to refer to something that is ordinary and not special 普通的: *You can't wear just any old clothes to that sort of place, you have to dress up.* 去那种场合, 你可不能穿普普通通的旧衣服, 你得穿戴整齐。**6 any old how** in any way 用任何方式: *Just pack them in any old how.* 只要把它们装进去就行。

any² *adv* **1** used especially in negative statements to mean in the least; at all 丝毫, 一点〔尤用于否定句〕: *It can't make it any worse, can it?* 反正没什么坏处, 对吗? | *I'm not any better than you.* 我一点儿也不比你好。| *I can't walk any further.* 我再也走不动了。| *The boy could not stand it any longer.* 那个男孩再也忍受不了了。**2** *AmE spoken* used to mean 'at all' at the end of a sentence【美口】根本〔用于句末〕: *We tried talking to him but that didn't help any.* 我们尽力说服他, 但一点儿用也没有。—compare 比较 EITHER, NEITHER 2

an·y·bod·y /ˋɛnɪˌbɑdɪ; ˈeniˌbɒdi/ *pron* any person or all people; anyone 任何人, 无论谁 1 3

an·y·how /ˋɛnɪˌhaʊ; ˈenihaʊ/ *adv* **1** [sentence adverb 句子副词] *especially spoken* used to say that someone does something or something happens in spite of something else【尤口】无论如何, 不管怎样: *It was felt that the scandal would damage her reputation but the press reported it anyhow.* 大家认为丑闻会败坏她的名声, 但不管怎样, 新闻界还是报道了。**2** in a careless or untidy way 随便地; 杂乱无章地: *The cupboard would hardly close, with all the shoes thrown in anyhow.* 鞋柜乱塞了许多鞋, 几乎关不上了。**3** [sentence adverb 句子副词] *especially spoken* used to add information that limits what has been mentioned before, makes it seem less important etc【尤口】反正, 好歹: *I've never been to a circus, not recently anyhow.* 我没有看过马戏, 反正最近是没看过。**4** [sentence adverb 句子副词] *especially spoken*【尤口】**a)** used when you want to return to the main subject of the conversation 不管怎样〔用于交谈中希望回到主题时〕: *So anyhow, as I was saying, when I arrived Tom was already there.* 不管怎样, 正如我所说, 我到的时候汤姆已经在那儿了。**b)** used when you have not included some details in a story and you are saying what the final result was 结果: *Anyhow, when the doctor came he said there was nothing wrong with me.* 结果, 医生来了却说我什么病也没有。**5** *AmE spoken* used to mean 'anyway' in spoken American English【美口】不管怎样, 反正, 总之: *Martin's not feeling too well but he's going to come over anyhow.* 马丁感到不太舒服, 但他无论如何要来。| *Anyhow the car finally came out of the garage in a worse state than when it went in.* 总之, 汽车最终从修车厂开出来时比进去时的状况还要差。| *Anyhow, what difference does it make what I think?* 然而, 我怎么看又有什么区别呢? | *Why are you calling anyhow?* 你打电话来到底要干什么? —see also 另见 ANYWAY 3

an·y·more /ˌɛnɪˋmɔr; ˌeniˈmɔː/ *adv* **not...anymore** not any longer 不再: *Nick doesn't live here anymore.* 尼克已不住在这里了。| *They used to laugh at Sheila. Not anymore.* 他们过去常嘲笑希拉, 现在不这样了。

an·y·one /ˋɛnɪˌwʌn; ˈeniwʌn/ *pron* **1** any person in a group or in the world, when it is not important to say exactly who 任何人: *Anyone can cook risotto – it's easy!* 谁都会做肉汁烩饭, 这很容易。| *He's cleverer than anyone I know.* 他比我认识的任何人都聪明。| **anyone tall/rich etc** *Anyone stupid enough to believe that deserves everything they get!* 不管谁愚蠢到相信那一点都是咎由自取! | **anyone else** (=a different person) 其他人 *Anyone else would have been too embarrassed, but he walked right up and asked for her autograph.* 换了别人都会感到难为情, 他却偏偏走过去请她签名留念。**2** used in questions and negatives to mean a person 有人, 任何人〔用于疑问句或否定句〕: *Is anyone listening to me?* 有人在听我讲话吗? | *If anyone sees Lisa, ask her to call me.* 如果有谁看见莉莎, 请她打电话给我。| **anyone interesting/rich etc** *Anyone new coming to tonight's* 1 1

meeting? 有哪位是今晚第一次来开会? | **anyone else** (=a different person) 其他人 *Do you know anyone else who wants a ticket?* 你知道还有谁要票吗? —see also 另见 EVERYONE, SOMEONE

an·y·place /ˈɛnɪˌples; ˈenipleɪs/ *adv AmE* anywhere【美】无论何处, 随便哪里: *It's funny, I've never felt anyplace was home before I came to Connecticut.* 说来有趣, 只有我来康涅狄格州以后才觉得是到了家。

Any Ques·tions /ˌ‥ ˈ‥/ a British radio programme in which people ask politicians and other famous people questions about important problems or subjects that are in the news《有问必答》〔英国一广播节目, 听众就新闻中涉及的重要问题或话题向政治家或知名人士提问〕

1 1 **an·y·thing** /ˈɛnɪˌθɪŋ; ˈeniθɪŋ/ *pron* **1** any thing, event, situation etc, when it does not matter exactly which 任何事物, 无论何事: *Anything will do to wedge the door open.* 任何东西都可以, 只要把门楔住让它开着就行了。| *If you believe that, you'll believe anything!* 这样的事你都相信, 那你什么事都会相信了! | *OK, you can borrow the car – anything for a quiet life.* 好吧, 你可以借车, 只要能过上安宁的生活就什么都行。| **anything red/cheap etc** *She'll buy anything reduced in a sale.* 只要是减价的东西, 她什么都买。| **anything else** (=any different thing) 别的什么(东西) *It's got to be Dior – anything else just isn't good enough.* 必须是迪奥的, 别的牌子都不行。**2** used in questions, negatives, and statements expressing possibility to mean 'nothing' or 'something' 任何事物〔用于疑问句或否定句〕: *You can't believe anything she says.* 你不能相信她说的任何话。| *Have you heard anything about the new Garrison Keillor book?* 你有听说过有关加里森·基勒那本新书的事吗? | **anything to say/to do etc** *It was a great health farm but there wasn't really anything to do in the evenings.* 这是一个非常好的健身庄, 只是晚上没有什么事情可做。| **anything new/stupid etc** *We've almost sealed the deal, so don't do anything stupid.* 我们差不多已敲定了这桩交易, 所以不要做任何傻事了。| **anything else** (=any other thing, event etc) 别的东西[事情等] *Would you like anything else to eat?* 你还要吃点儿别的东西吗? **3 anything but clear/happy etc** used to emphasize that someone or something is not clear, happy etc 根本不清楚/不开心等: *The bridge is anything but safe.* 这座桥一点儿也不安全。| *We'd been warned he was a frail, withdrawn man but when I met him he was anything but.* 有人提醒我们他是一个脆弱内向的人, 可当我见到他时, 发现根本不是那样。—see also 另见 SOME

Frequencies of the word **anything** in spoken and written English 单词anything在英语口语和书面语中的使用频率

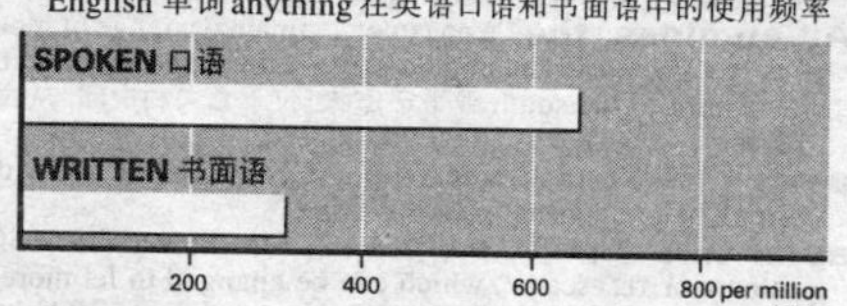

Based on the British National Corpus and the Longman Lancaster Corpus
据英国国家语料库和朗文兰开斯特语料库

This graph shows that the word **anything** is more common in spoken English than in written English. This is because it is used a lot in questions, and is used in some common spoken phrases. 本图表显示单词anything在英语口语中比在书面语中常用, 因为该词经常用于疑问句中, 而且口语中一些常用短语也是由anything构成的。

4 anything like similar in any way to something or someone else 像…, 类似…: *Does she look anything like her mother?* 她长得像她母亲吗? **5 not anything like/near** *spoken* used to emphasize that someone or something is not in a particular condition or state【口】一点也不(像): *We don't have anything like enough money to buy a new car.* 我们根本没有足够的钱买辆新汽车。**6 as easy/fast etc as anything** extremely easy, fast etc 非常容易/快速等: *It was a long lecture and as boring as anything.* 这是一个冗长的讲座, 非常乏味。**7 or anything** or something that is similar 或相似的另一件事物: *Would you like a gin and tonic or anything?* 你要加奎宁水的杜松子酒还是别的什么? **8 for anything** if you will not do something for anything, you will definitely not do it 决不, 怎么也不: *After what happened last time, I wouldn't work for them again for anything.* 自从发生上次的事情以后, 我怎么也不会再为他们工作了。**9 like anything** if you do something like anything, you do it a lot or to a great degree 非常, 极其: *Tom only left last week and I already miss him like anything.* 汤姆上周才离开, 我已经非常想念他。**10**

anything you say used to tell someone you agree with what they suggest when actually you do not 怎么样都行, 好吧〔表示不情愿〕: *"You ought to keep the flat more tidy." "Anything you say."* "你应该让公寓更加整洁。" "好吧。"

an·y·way /ˈɛnɪˌwe; ˈeniweɪ/ *adv* [sentence adverb 句子副词] **1** used to say that someone does something or that something happens in spite of a problem 无论如何, 不管怎样: *He said he didn't know much about computers but that he'd try and help us anyway.* 他说他不太懂电脑, 不过, 他说无论如何也会设法帮助我们。 1 2

Frequencies of the adverb **anyway** in spoken and written English 副词anyway在英语口语和书面语中的使用频率

SPOKEN 口语
WRITTEN 书面语
200 400 600 per million
每百万

Based on the British National Corpus and the Longman Lancaster Corpus
据英国国家语料库和朗文兰开斯特语料库

This graph shows that the adverb **anyway** is much more common in spoken English than in written English. This is because it has some special uses in spoken English. 本图表显示, 副词anyway在口语中比在书面语中要常用得多, 因为它在口语中有一些特殊的用法。

2 used when you are changing the subject of a conversation or returning to a previous subject 对了, 好吧〔用于改变话题或转到前一个话题上〕: *Anyway, what was I saying?* 对了, 我刚才在说什么? **3** used when you want to finish saying something or continue without all the details 总之: *Anyway, I must be going now.* 总之, 我现在得走了。| *Anyway, after three months at the clinic, she'd made a full recovery.* 总之, 在诊所治了三个月, 她完全康复了。**4** used to add some extra information, an opinion or a question to something that you have just said 话又说回来, 反正, 然而: *Sam didn't get the job; but he's not worried because it didn't pay well anyway.* 萨姆没有得到那份工作, 但他并没有担心, 反正报酬也不算高。| *It was nice of you to offer anyway.* 话又说回来, 你主动提出总是件好事。**5** used to find out the real reason for something 究竟, 到底: *So anyway, what were you doing in the park at two in the morning?* 那么, 你凌晨两点在公园里究竟在做什么? | *Why did he visit Alan anyway?* 那他到底为什么去艾伦那里?

an·y·where /ˈɛnɪˌhwɛr; ˈeniweə/ also 又作 **anyplace** *AmE*【美】*adv* **1** in or to any place 无论何处, 随便哪里: *Sit anywhere, there are plenty of seats.* 随便坐吧, 有的是座位。| *Tropical fruit used to be hard to find in Britain but now you can buy it anywhere.* 以前在英国很难看到热带水果, 不过现在到处都能买到。| **[+in]** *Apparently that restaurant does the best curry anywhere in London.* 显然, 那家餐厅做的咖喱食品在伦敦是最好的。| **anywhere else** (=in or to a different place) 别的任何地方 *Anywhere else you'd have to pay airport tax but not when you visit this Pacific island.* 其他任何地方你都得付机场税, 但到这个太平洋岛屿旅游就不用付。**2** used in questions, negatives, and statements expressing possibility to mean 'somewhere' or 'nowhere' 某个地方; 任何地方〔都不〕〔用于表示可能性的疑问句、否定句或陈述句〕: *I can't find it anywhere. Are you sure you left it here?* 我哪里也找不到, 你肯定是放这儿了吗? | *Do they need anywhere to stay for the night?* 他们需要找个地方过夜吗? | *Would you like a ride anywhere?* 你想骑车到什么地方玩玩吗? | **anywhere interesting/cheap etc** *Did you go anywhere exotic on vacation this year?* 你今年假期有没有去什么有异国情调的地方? | **anywhere else** *The photos are great – have you been anywhere else in Mexico?* 这些照片太漂亮了, 你去墨西哥其他地方了吗? **3 not anywhere near a)** used to emphasize that someone or something is not near to another person or thing 老远〔用于强调相隔的距离〕: *What do you mean it was my fault? My car wasn't anywhere near yours.* 你说是我的过错到底是什么意思? 我的车离你的车还老远呢。**b)** used to emphasize that someone or something is not in a particular condition or state 差挺多, 差挺远〔用于强调某人或某物不处于某种状况或状态〕: *The money doesn't come anywhere near compensating for what those people suffered.* 这些钱离补偿那些人的损失还差很远。**4 anywhere between one and ten/anywhere from one to ten etc** used to mean any age, number, amount etc between

A

one and ten when it is difficult to know exactly which age, number etc 从一到十（任何一个），在一到十之间等: *She was one of those women who could be anywhere between forty five and sixty years of age.* 她是那些介乎45到60岁之间的妇女之一。**5 it won't get you anywhere** used to tell someone that they will not be able to change a situation 不会有什么改观，没什么用处: *You can try writing to complain, but I don't think it will get you anywhere.* 你可以试试写投诉信，但我认为没什么用。**6 not getting/going anywhere** not successful or not having plans for the future 没什么成就[发展]: *Terry's a nice enough lad but he's not going anywhere.* 特里是一个很好的小伙子，但没什么发展。—see 见 PLACE[1] (USAGE)

An·zac /ˋænzæk; ˈænzæk/ a soldier from Australia or New Zealand, especially in World War I 澳新军团士兵〔尤指一战期间澳大利亚或新西兰的士兵〕

Anzac Day /ˋ··, ·ˊ/ in Australia and New Zealand, April 25th each year, remembered as the date of the landing at Gallipoli in 1915 澳新军团节，澳新军团日〔4月25日，澳大利亚和新西兰纪念1915年在加利波利半岛登陆的日子〕

AOB /ˌe o ˋbi; ˌeɪ əʊ ˈbiː/ *BrE* the abbreviation of 缩写= 'any other business'; things that have not yet been discussed in the main part of a meeting【英】〔会议主要议题以外的〕任何其他事务

AONB /ˌe o ɛn ˋbi; ˌeɪ əʊ en ˈbiː/ *BrE* Area of Outstanding Natural Beauty; a very beautiful area which is officially protected so that no one is allowed to build on it or change it【英】优美自然风景区〔国家保护的自然风景区，区内禁止任何修建或改造行为〕

a·or·ta /eˋɔrtə; eɪˈɔːtə/ *n* [C] the largest ARTERY (=tube for carrying blood) in the body, taking blood from the heart 主动脉，大动脉

A·o·te·a·ro·a /ˌɑotiəˋroə; ˌɑːəʊtiːəˈrəʊə/ the Maori name for New Zealand〔毛利语〕新西兰

a·pace /əˋpes; əˈpeɪs/ *adv literary* quickly【文】飞快地，急速地: *Multimedia developments continue apace.* 多媒体技术在飞速发展。

a·part /əˋpɑrt; əˈpɑːt/ *adv, adj*

1 ▶DISTANCE 距离◀ if things are apart, they have an amount of space between them 分开，相距，相隔: *Joel stood apart from the group, frowning.* 乔尔皱着眉头，独自站在一边。| **two miles/six feet etc apart** *The two villages are 6 kilometres apart.* 两村之间相距六公里。

2 ▶TIME 时间◀ two hours/six weeks etc apart if things are a particular time apart, they have that much time between them 相隔两小时/六周等: *Our birthdays are exactly a month apart.* 我们俩的生日正好相差一个月。

3 ▶SEPARATE 分开◀ a) if you keep, pull, force etc two things apart, you separate them（把…）分开: *I try to keep my work and private life as far apart as possible.* 我设法把工作和私生活尽可能分开。| *The two boys started fighting so we had to pull them apart.* 两个男孩打起架来，我们不得不把他们拉开。**b)** if you take or pull something apart, or something comes or falls apart, it is separated into many different parts 拆开；散开: *The mechanics took the engine apart.* 机械师把发动机拆开了。| *The chair fell apart in my hands.* 椅子在我手上散了架。

4 ▶SOMEWHERE ELSE 别处◀ in a different place from someone else 与〔某人〕分开在别处: *You never see the twins apart.* 你从未看见这对双胞胎分开过。| *My wife and I are living apart at the moment.* 目前我和妻子分开住。

5 ▶RELATIONSHIP 关系◀ a) be worlds/poles apart if people, beliefs, or ideas are worlds or poles apart, they are completely different from each other 完全不同，截然相反 **b) grow/drift apart** if people or groups grow apart, their relationship slowly ends 逐渐疏远: *Sadly, the family has grown apart since Auntie Barbara died.* 不幸的是，自从芭芭拉姑母去世后，家人之间就慢慢疏远了。

6 ▶CONDITION 情况◀ if something is coming apart or falling apart etc, it is in a very bad condition 破碎(的)，破裂(的): *I must get some new trousers; these are all coming apart.* 我得买些新裤子，这些都破了。| *Well, the relationship's fallen apart, to be honest.* 好吧，说实话，关系已经破裂。

7 joking apart used to say that you want to consider something seriously 说正经的: *Joking apart, we must do something about that hole.* 说正经的，我们确实应采取措施补补那个洞。

8 quite apart from without even considering 撇开…不说，不考虑…: *Quite apart from the cost, there's the question of your health to be considered.* 且不说开销，你的健康问题总应该考虑吧。

9 apart from also 又作 **aside from** *especially AmE*【尤美】**a)** used to introduce one small point which makes a statement not completely true 除了，只是: *This essay's good apart from a couple of spelling mistakes.* 除了有些拼写错误，这篇文章写得不错。**b)** except for 除…以外: *Apart from the occasional visit, what does Alan do for his kids?* 除了偶尔去探望一下，艾伦还为孩子们做了些什么？

a·part·heid /əˋpɑrthet; əˈpɑːtheɪt/ *n* [U] the former South African political and social system in which only white people had full political rights and people of other races, especially black people, were forced to go to separate schools, live in separate areas etc〔旧时南非的〕种族隔离制度

a·part·ment /əˋpɑrtmənt; əˈpɑːtmənt/ *n* [C] **1** *especially AmE* a set of rooms within a large building, usually on one level, where someone lives【尤美】〔一般在同一楼层的〕一套住房，公寓套间; FLAT[2] (1) *BrE*【英】: *How many bedrooms do you have in your new apartment?* 你的新房子有几个卧室？**2** [usually plural 一般用复数] a large room with expensive furniture, decorations etc, used especially by an important person such as a president, prince etc〔大而豪华的〕套间: *the presidential apartments* 总统套间 —see graph at 参见 FLAT[2] 图表

apartment block /ˋ··· ·/ *n* [C] *AmE* a large group of buildings containing many apartments【美】公寓楼群 —see picture on page A4 参见A4页图

apartment build·ing /ˋ··, ·ˊ/ also 又作 **apartment house** /ˋ·· ·/ *n* [C] *AmE* a large building containing many apartments【美】公寓大楼

ap·a·thet·ic /ˌæpəˋθɛtɪk; ˌæpəˈθetɪk◂/ *adj* not excited about something and not caring whether it happens, or not interested in anything and unwilling to make an effort to change and improve things 无兴趣的；无感情的；冷淡的；无动于衷的: *an apathetic electorate* 态度冷淡的选民 —**apathetically** /-klɪ; -kli/ *adv*

ap·a·thy /ˋæpəθɪ; ˈæpəθi/ *n* [U] the feeling of not being interested or not caring, either about a particular thing or about life 漠然，冷淡；无兴趣；无动于衷: *apathy among the public* 公众的冷淡态度

ape[1] /ep; eɪp/ *n* [C] **1** a large monkey without a tail, or with a very short tail, such as a GORILLA or a CHIMPANZEE 猿 **2** an insulting word for a man who behaves in a stupid or annoying way 傻瓜，笨蛋: *Push off you big ape.* 滚开，你这个大笨蛋。**3 go ape** *slang* to suddenly become very angry or excited【俚】突然发怒〔激动〕

ape[2] *v* [T] to copy someone's behaviour, especially in a silly or unkind way〔尤指愚蠢或恶意地〕模仿

Ap·en·nines, the /ˋæpənaɪnz; ˈæpl̩naɪnz/ a range of mountains in a line down the middle of Italy, from the northwest of the country to the south 亚平宁山脉〔位于意大利中部，从西北向南延伸〕

a·per·i·tif /əˌpɛrəˋtif; əˌperl̩ˈtiːf/ *n* [C] an alcoholic drink that is drunk before a meal 饭前酒，开胃酒

ap·er·ture /ˋæpətʃə; ˈæpətʃə/ *n* [C] **1** the hole at the front of a camera or TELESCOPE[1], which can be changed to let more or less light in〔照相机的〕光圈，孔径 **2** *technical* a small hole or space in something which is used for a particular purpose【术语】孔，缝隙: *an inspection aperture* 检查孔

ape·shit /ˋepˌʃɪt; ˈeɪpʃɪt/ *adj* **go apeshit** *slang* to suddenly become very angry or excited【俚】勃然大怒

A·PEX, A·pex /ˋepɛks; ˈeɪpeks/ *adj BrE* Advanced Purchase Excursion; used to describe plane tickets, train tickets etc that are cheaper than the usual price because you buy them several days or weeks before the date when you travel【英】预购优惠的〔提前数日或数周预购机票、火车票等可享受的折价优惠〕: *The Apex fare is just 200.* 预购优惠票价仅200。| *APEX tickets to Edinburgh* 去爱丁堡的预购优惠票

apex *n* [C] **1** *technical* the top or highest part of something【术语】顶点，最高点: *the apex of the triangle* 三角形的顶点 **2** *formal* the most successful part【正式】顶峰: *the apex of his career* 他事业的顶峰

a·phid /ˋefɪd; ˈeɪfɪd/ *n* [C] a type of very small insect that drinks the juices of plants 蚜虫

aph·o·ris·m /ˋæfəˌrɪzəm; ˈæfərɪzəm/ *n* [C] a short wise phrase 格言，警句 —**aphoristic** /ˌæfəˋrɪstɪk; ˌæfəˈrɪstɪk◂/ *adj*

aph·ro·dis·i·ac /ˌæfrəˋdɪzɪˌæk; ˌæfrəˈdɪziæk◂/ *n* [C] a food, drink, or drug that makes you want to have sex 催情剂，春药 —**aphrodisiac** *adj*: *the aphrodisiac properties of the fruit* 这种水果能激发性欲的特性

Aph·ro·di·te /ˌæfrəˋdaɪtɪ; ˌæfrəˈdaɪti/ in Greek MYTHOLOGY, the goddess of love and beauty. In Roman mythology her name is Venus. 阿佛洛狄忒〔希腊神话中的爱与美女神，罗马神话中称维纳斯〕

a·pi·a·ry /ˋepɪ,ɛrɪ; ˈeɪpiəri/ *n* [C] a place where BEEs are kept 养蜂场；蜂房

a·piece /əˋpis; əˈpiːs/ *adv* [only after number or noun 仅用于数词或名词后] costing or having a particular amount each 每个，每人，每件: **ten pence/fifteen dollars etc apiece** *The tomato plants cost 60p apiece.* 番茄苗每株60便士。| **three pages/a ticket etc apiece** (=having three pages etc each) 每个人三页/一张票等 *We shared the gold out equally – three bags apiece.* 我们平分了这些金子，每人三袋。

a·plen·ty /əˋplɛntɪ; əˈplenti/ *adj* [only after noun 仅用于名词后] *old use* in large amounts or numbers, especially more than you need【旧】丰富的，大量的，很多的〔尤指超过需要的〕: *There was food aplenty.* 有很多食物。

a·plomb /əˋplɑm; əˈplɒm/ *n* [U] **with aplomb** in a confident and skilful way, especially when you have to deal with difficult problems or a difficult situation 镇静地，沉着地，泰然自若地: *Ms Sharpe handled their hostile questions with great aplomb.* 夏普女士非常沉着地应付他们挑衅性的问题。

a·poc·a·lypse /əˋpɑkə,lɪps; əˈpɒkəlɪps/ *n* [C] **1 the apocalypse** the destruction and end of the world 世界末日 **2** a dangerous, frightening, and very serious situation causing death, harm, or destruction 大灾难: *3,000 died in the apocalypse of the earthquake.* 有3000人死于这场大地震。

a·poc·a·lyp·tic /ə,pɑkəˋlɪptɪk; ə,pɒkəˈlɪptɪk◂/ *adj* **1** warning people about terrible events that will happen in the future 预言将有大灾难的: *Orwell's apocalyptic vision of the future* 奥威尔对未来的灾难性预言 **2** connected with the final destruction and end of the world 世界末日的

A·poc·ry·pha, the /əˋpɑkrəfə; əˈpɒkrɨfə/ a collection of Jewish writings which form part of the Old Testament in some bibles. They do not appear in the Hebrew bible, or many modern bibles. 外典〔犹太人著作的合集，是某些《圣经》版本《旧约》中的一部分，但并未见于希伯来《圣经》或诸多现代《圣经》版本〕

a·poc·ry·phal /əˋpɑkrəfəl; əˈpɒkrɨfəl/ *adj* an apocryphal story about a famous person or event is well-known but probably not ture 可疑的，杜撰的: *Washington's apocryphal phrase: "Father, I cannot tell a lie."* 传说中华盛顿讲过的一句话："父亲，我不会说谎。"

ap·o·gee /ˋæpə,dʒi; ˈæpədʒiː/ *n* [C] **1** *formal* the most successful part of something【正式】〔权力或成就的〕顶峰: *the apogee of his political career* 他政治生涯的顶峰 **2** *technical* the point where an object travelling through space is farthest from the earth【术语】远地点〔太空中物体运行轨道上离地球最远之点〕

a·po·lit·i·cal /,epəˋlɪtɪkl̩; ,eɪpəˈlɪtɪkəl◂/ *adj* not having any interest in or connection with politics 非政治的；不关心政治的

A·pol·lo /əˋpɑlo; əˈpɒləʊ/ **1** in Greek and Roman MYTHOLOGY, the god of the sun, medicine, poetry, music, and PROPHECY. He is usually shown in pictures and SCULPTUREs as a beautiful young man. 阿波罗〔希腊神话中的太阳、医药、诗歌、音乐、预言之神。在绘画和雕塑作品中常以美男子的形象出现〕 **2** *literary* a very beautiful young man【文】美男子

Apollo Pro·gram /·ˋ·· ,··/ the US government space programme to send people to the moon, which succeeded in 1969 when the Apollo 11 SPACECRAFT landed on the moon 阿波罗计划〔美国政府的载人登月航天计划。1969年阿波罗11号航天器登上月球，计划取得成功〕 —see also 另见 Neil ARMSTRONG

a·pol·o·get·ic /ə,pɑləˋdʒɛtɪk; ə,pɒləˈdʒetɪk◂/ *adj* showing or saying that you are sorry that something has happened, especially because you feel guilty or embarrassed about it 道歉的，抱歉的: *The restaurant manager was very apologetic and said we could have our meal for free.* 餐厅经理深表歉意，并说我们这顿饭可以免费。| *an apologetic letter* 致歉信 —**apologetically** /-klɪ; -kli/ *adv*: *"I know," she said apologetically.* "我知道。"她抱歉地说。

ap·o·lo·gi·a /,æpəˋlodʒɪə; ,æpəˈləʊdʒiə/ *n* [C+for] *formal* a statement in which you defend an idea that you believe in【正式】辩解，辩护

a·pol·o·gist /əˋpɑlədʒɪst; əˈpɒlədʒɨst/ *n* [C] someone who tries to defend and explain an idea or system 辩护者，辩解者: *one of Stalin's western apologists* 斯大林的西方辩解者之一

2 **a·pol·o·gize** also 又作 **-ise** *BrE*【英】/əˋpɑlə,dʒaɪz; əˈpɒlədʒaɪz/ *v* [I] to tell someone that you are sorry that you have done something wrong 道歉，谢罪: *That was an awful thing to say, I think you should apologize.* 那是很难听的话，我想你该道歉。| [+for] *I must apologise for the delay in replying to your letter.* 未能及时复信，我必须向你道歉。| **apologize to** *The US has apologized to Britain for the accident.* 美国已就这次意外事故向英国致歉。| **apologize profusely** (=apologize a lot) 非常抱歉 *She apologized profusely for being late.* 她非常抱歉自己来迟了。

a·pol·o·gy /əˋpɑlədʒɪ; əˈpɒlədʒi/ *n* [C] **1** something that you say or write to show that you are sorry for doing something wrong 道歉，认错: *Your behaviour was outrageous. I demand an apology!* 你的行为太蛮横了，我要求你道歉！| **accept sb's apology** (=forgive them after they have apologized) 接受某人的道歉 *Please accept our sincere apologies.* 请接受我们真诚的道歉。| **owe sb an apology** (=to have done something bad or unfair to someone) 应向某人道歉 *I owe you an apology for what I said last night – I'm really sorry.* 真对不起，我该为昨晚说的话向你道歉。| **make an apology** *The paper was forced to make a grovelling apology.* 报纸被迫作出卑躬的道歉。 **2** *literary* a statement in which you defend something you believe in after it has been criticized by other people【文】辩解，辩护 **3 an apology for** *humorous* a very bad example of something【幽默】权充…的东西；勉强代用的东西: *an apology for a human being* 不像话的人 3

ap·o·plec·tic /,æpəˋplɛktɪk; ,æpəˈplektɪk◂/ *adj* **1** *informal* so angry or excited that your face becomes red【非正式】气得[激动得]脸发红的: *The colonel was apoplectic with rage.* 上校勃然大怒。 **2** connected with apoplexy 中风的

ap·o·plex·y /ˋæpə,plɛksɪ; ˈæpəpleksi/ *n* [U] *old-fashioned* an illness caused by a problem in your brain which can damage your ability to move, feel, or think; STROKE[1] (1)【过时】中风

a·pos·ta·sy /əˋpɑstəsɪ; əˈpɒstəsi/ *n* [U] *formal* the act of changing your beliefs so that you stop supporting a religion, political party etc【正式】叛教；脱党；变节

a·pos·tate /əˋpɑstet; əˈpɒsteɪt/ *n* [C] *formal* someone who has stopped believing in and supporting their old religion or political party【正式】叛教者；脱党者；变节者

a pos·ter·i·o·ri /ˋe pɑs,tɪrɪˋoraɪ; ,eɪ pɒsteriˈɔːraɪ/ *adj Latin formal* using facts or results to form a judgment about what must have happened before【拉丁，正式】由事实或结果推断出原因的，归纳的 —compare 比较 A PRIORI

a·pos·tle /əˋpɑsl̩; əˈpɒsəl/ *n* [C] **1** one of the 12 people chosen by Christ to teach and spread the Christian religion 基督的十二使徒之一，使徒 **2** *formal* someone who believes strongly in a new idea and tries to persuade other people【正式】倡导者，先驱: [+of] *an apostle of revolutionary ideals* 革命理想的先驱

Apostles' Creed, the /·,··ˋ·/ a statement of religious belief in the Christian religion, beginning "I believe in God the Father Almighty ..." 《使徒信经》〔有关基督教信仰的陈述，首句为"我信上帝，全能的父神"〕

ap·o·stol·ic /,æpəsˋtɑlɪk; ,æpəˈstɒlɪk◂/ *adj* **1** connected with the POPE (=leader of the Catholic church) (天主教) 教宗的，教皇的 **2** connected with one of Christ's 12 apostles (基督之) 使徒的

a·pos·tro·phe /əˋpɑstrəfɪ; əˈpɒstrəfi/ *n* [C] **a)** the sign (') used in writing to show that numbers or letters have been left out, as in 'don't' (=do not) and '86 (=1986) 表示省略的撇号 (')〈如 don't 表示 do not，'86 表示 1986〉 **b)** the same sign used before 's' to show that something belongs to someone or something, or is connected with them, as in 'John's book', or 'Charles' mother', or 'Nixon's last year as president' 表示所有格的撇号 (')〈如 John's book, Charles' mother 或 Nixon's last year as president〉 **c)** used before 's' to show the plural of letters and numbers as in 'Your r's look like v's.' 用于 s 前表示字母和数字的复数〈如在 Your r's look like v's.中〉

a·poth·e·ca·ry /əˋpɑθə,kɛrɪ; əˈpɒθɨkəri/ *n* [C] someone who mixed and sold medicines in former times〔旧时的〕药剂师

a·poth·e·o·sis /ə,pɑθɪˋosɪs; ə,pɒθiˈəʊsɨs/ *n plural* **apotheoses** /-siz; -siːz/ [C usually singular 一般用单数] *formal*【正式】 **1** the best and most perfect example of something 典范，最完美的榜样: [+of] *the apotheosis of French 16th century art* 16世纪法国艺术的典范 **2** the state of getting to the highest level of something such as honour, importance etc〔荣誉、重要性等的〕极点，顶峰

ap·pal *BrE*【英】, **appall** *AmE*【美】/əˋpɔl; əˈpɔːl/ *v* [T] to shock someone by being very bad or unpleasant 使惊骇；使充满恐惧: *The whole idea of killing animals for fur appals me.* 杀死动物取其毛皮的想法令我不寒而栗。

Ap·pa·la·chi·a /,æpəˋletʃɪə; ,æpəˈleɪtʃiə/ an area of the Appalachians in the southeast of the US where people have small farms 阿巴拉契亚〔美国东南部阿巴拉契亚山区一地带，当地人拥有小型农场〕

Ap·pa·la·chi·ans, the /,æpəˋletʃɪənz; ,æpəˈleɪtʃiənz/ also 又作 **the Appalachian Mountains** a long range of mountains in northeast America that go southwest from Quebec in Canada

A

to Alabama in the US 阿巴拉契亚山脉〔北美洲东北部一大山系，从加拿大魁北克向西南延伸，直达美国的亚拉巴马州〕

CULTURAL NOTE 文化注释

People who live in Appalachian areas are often poor because the farms are small and there is little other work available. Some people live in mountain areas in small wooden houses that do not have any modern equipment. Bluegrass music started there, and when people think of the Appalachians, they often think of men playing this type of music on the FIDDLE there. 阿巴拉契亚地区的居民一般生活贫困，因为那里的农场很小，其他工作很少。有的山区居民住在小木屋里，没有现代化的设备。蓝草乡村音乐起源于此。提到阿巴拉契亚，人们常会联想到用小提琴演奏这种音乐的男人。

ap·palled /əˈpɔld; əˈpɔːld/ *adj* very shocked by something very bad or unpleasant 对…深感震惊的，惊恐万分的: **[+by/at]** *Rescue workers were appalled at what they saw.* 营救人员对看到的情况深感震惊。

ap·pal·ling /əˈpɔlɪŋ; əˈpɔːlɪŋ/ *adj* **1** so bad or unpleasant that you are shocked 骇人听闻的；令人震惊的；可怕的: *We heard the appalling news about the earthquake.* 听到有关地震的消息我们十分震惊。**2** very bad 极坏的，糟透的: *Morrison's last album was absolutely appalling.* 莫里森的上一张唱片简直糟透了。—**appallingly** *adv: You've behaved appallingly.* 你的表现太差了。| *appallingly bad taste* 极糟糕的味道

ap·pa·loo·sa /ˌæpəˈlusə; ˌæpəˈluːsə/ *n* [C] *AmE* a kind of horse that is pale coloured with dark spots【美】阿帕卢萨马〔一种皮毛色浅、带深色斑点的马〕

ap·par·at·chik /ˌɑpəˈrɑtʃɪk; ˌɑːpəˈrɑːtʃɪk/ *n* [C] an official working for a government or other organization who obeys orders without thinking〔盲从的〕党政工作人员

ap·pa·ra·tus /ˌæpəˈrætəs; ˌæpəˈreɪtəs/ *n plural* **apparatuses** *or* **apparatus** [C,U] **1** tools and machines used especially for scientific, medical, and technical purposes 设备，仪器，装置，器械，用具: *the apparatus shown in the diagram* 图表中显示的器材 | *The astronauts have special breathing apparatus.* 宇航员有特殊的呼吸装置。**2** a system or process for doing something 机制: *the apparatus for settling industrial disputes* 解决劳资纠纷的机制

ap·par·el¹ /əˈpærəl; əˈpærəl/ *n* [U] **1** *formal* clothes, especially clothes worn on a special occasion【正式】〔尤指华丽的〕服装；盛装: *the Queen's ceremonial apparel* 女王的礼服 **2 ladies'/men's/children's apparel** *especially AmE* a word for clothes, often used in shops【尤美】女装/男装/儿童服装〔商店用语〕

apparel² *v* [T+In] *old use* to dress someone, especially in special clothes【旧】为…穿衣〔尤指盛装〕

[2] **ap·par·ent** /əˈpærənt; əˈpærənt/ *adj* **1** easily noticed or understood 显而易见的，明白的: **[+to]** *Her anxiety was apparent to everyone.* 大家都看得出她的焦虑。| **it became apparent that** *It soon became apparent that our opponents were too strong for us.* 很快就看出，我们的对手太强。| **for no apparent reason** (=without a clear reason) 没明确的理由 *Suddenly, for no apparent reason, he walked away.* 他没什么明确的理由就突然走了。**2** seeming to have a particular quality, feeling, or attitude 显得…的，表面上的: *I was shocked by Joe's apparent lack of concern for his child.* 乔对孩子表现出的漠不关心使我很震惊。

[1] [2] **ap·par·ent·ly** /əˈpærəntlɪ; əˈpærəntli/ *adv* **1** [sentence adverb 句子副词] based on what you have heard is true, although you are not completely sure about it 看来，似乎: *Apparently they've run out of tickets for the concert.* 看来，他们卖光了音乐会的票。| *I wasn't there, but apparently it was a good party.* 我当时不在，但据我所知，那聚会搞得不错。**2** according to the way someone looks or a situation appears, although you cannot be sure 显然: *She managed to climb out of the car, apparently unhurt.* 她设法爬出了车外，显然没有受伤。—compare 比较 EVIDENTLY, OBVIOUSLY

ap·pa·ri·tion /ˌæpəˈrɪʃən; ˌæpəˈrɪʃən/ *n* [C] something that you imagine you can see, especially the spirit of a dead person 幽灵，鬼魂: *a ghostly apparition* 鬼魂

[2] [1] **ap·peal¹** /əˈpil; əˈpiːl/ *n* **1** [C] an urgent request for something important such as money or help, especially to help someone in a bad situation 恳求；呼吁: **[+for]** *The United Nations' appeal for a ceasefire has been largely ignored by both sides.* 总的来说，双方对联合国关于停火的呼吁不予理会。| **appeal to sb to do sth** *an appeal to parents to supervise their children* 要家长监护好孩子的呼吁 | **make/launch an appeal** *In 1988 Bob Geldorf launched an urgent appeal for the famine victims.* 1988年，鲍勃·格尔多夫发出了援助饥民的紧急呼吁。**2** [U] a quality that makes you like someone or something, be interested in them, or want them 感染力，吸引力: *Much of Corfu's appeal lies in its lively night life.* 科孚的魅力在于其多姿多彩的夜生活。| **[+for]** *The film has great appeal for young audiences.* 这部电影对年轻观众有很大的吸引力。| **popular/wide appeal** (=liked by many people) 吸引众人的感染力 *CD-ROMs now have wider popular appeal.* 现在越来越多的人喜欢用只读光盘。| **sex appeal** (=the quality of being sexually attractive) 性感 *Marilyn Monroe had amazing sex appeal.* 玛丽莲·梦露非常性感迷人。**3** [C,U] a formal request to a court or to someone in authority asking for a decision to be changed 上诉: **[+to]** *an appeal to the European court of Human Rights* 向欧洲人权法庭提出的上诉 —see also 另见 COURT OF APPEAL

appeal² *v* **1** [I] to make a serious public request for help, money, information etc 恳请，恳求；呼吁: **appeal (to sb) for sth** *The police are appealing to the public for information about the crime.* 警方呼吁公众提供有关这起案件的信息。| *The Bosnian government appealed for help from Western countries.* 波黑政府呼吁西方国家给予帮助。| **appeal to sb to do sth** *She appealed to the kidnappers to release her son.* 她哀求绑架者释放她的儿子。**2 appeal to sb** if someone or something appeals to you, they seem attractive and interesting 吸引某人: *Does the idea of working abroad appeal to you?* 你对出国工作的想法感兴趣吗？| *The magazine is intended to appeal to working women in their 20s and 30s.* 这本杂志的读者对象是二十几岁到三十几岁的职业女性。**3** [I,T] to make a formal request to a court or someone in authority asking for a decision to be changed（提出）上诉: *If you are not satisfied, you can appeal.* 如果你不满意，可以上诉。**4 appeal to sb's better nature/sense of honour/sense of justice etc** to try to persuade someone to do something by reminding them that it is a good, honourable etc thing to do 呼唤某人的良知/荣誉感/正义感等 [3] [3]

Appeal Court /·ˈ· ·/ *n* [singular] the COURT OF APPEAL 上诉法院

ap·peal·ing /əˈpilɪŋ; əˈpiːlɪŋ/ *adj* **1** attractive or interesting 有吸引力的；有趣的: **find sb/sth appealing** *I find the idea of $100,000 dollars a year very appealing.* 我认为每年10万美元很诱人。| *She does look rather appealing in that dress.* 她穿上那件衣服看起来颇有吸引力。**2 appealing look/voice etc** a look etc that shows that someone wants help or sympathy 求助的目光/语气等: *I said I didn't know anything about computers and gave him an appealing look.* 我说我对电脑一无所知，求助地看了他一眼。—**appealingly** *adv*

ap·pear /əˈpɪr; əˈpɪə/ *v* [1] [1]

1 ▶SEEM 似乎◀ [linking verb 连系动词, not in progressive 不用进行时] a word used especially in formal or written English meaning to seem 似乎，好像，看来〔尤用于正式场合或书面语中〕: **appear upset/calm etc** *Roger appeared very upset.* 罗杰看起来很不高兴。| *The city appeared calm after the previous night's fighting.* 经过前一晚的战斗，城市似乎很平静。| **appear to be** *There appeared to be no significant difference between the two groups in the test.* 这两组在测试中似乎没有明显的差异。| **appear to do sth** *The man appeared to have had a heart attack.* 那个人好像心脏病发作了。| **it appears that** *It appears that there has been a change in the plans.* 计划好像作了修改。| **what appears to be** (=something that looks like) 看起来像… *Police have found what appear to be human remains.* 警方已经发现看起来像人的尸体的东西。| **make it appear that** *She put the gun next to the body, to make it appear that the victim had shot himself.* 她把枪放在尸体旁边，使受害者看起来像是自杀的样子。| **so it would appear** (=used to say that it seems likely that something is true, although you are not completely sure) 看起来是这样 *"The boys are completely innocent?" "So it would appear from the press reports."* "这些孩子完全是无辜的？" "从新闻报道看好像是的。"

2 ▶START TO BE SEEN 出现◀ [I] to start to be seen or to suddenly be seen 出现；呈现: *An image appeared on the screen.* 屏幕上出现了一个影像。| *Two faces appeared at our window.* 我们窗前出现了两张面孔。| **[+from]** *The manager hardly ever appeared from his office.* 经理很少走出他的办公室。| **appear out of nowhere** (=suddenly appear in a way that is very surprising) 突然冒出来 *I don't know what caused the marks – they just seemed to appear out of nowhere.* 我不知道这些痕迹是怎么来的 —— 好像是突然从什么地方冒出来似的。| **appear overnight** (=appear very quickly or suddenly) 一夜之间出现 *Software development is a fast-moving business – firms appear*

and disappear virtually overnight. 软件开发是瞬息万变的产业，一夜之间会有许多公司出现，也会有许多公司消失。

3 ▶FILM/TV PROGRAMME ETC 电影/电视节目等◀ [I] to take part in a film, play, concert, television programme etc 参加演出，露面，亮相: [+in/on] *Roseanne Barr has appeared on the show several times.* 罗丝安妮·巴尔已经几次登台演出。| [+at] *Vanessa Redgrave is currently appearing at the Theatre Royal, Drury Lane.* 文莎·雷德格雷夫目前正在德鲁里街的皇家剧院演出。

4 ▶BE WRITTEN/SHOWN 写出/显出◀ [I] to be written or shown on a list, in a book or newspaper, in a document etc 刊登; 发表; 被写进: *Her name appears at the front of the book.* 书的封面上印着她的名字。| *The story appeared in all the national newspapers.* 这篇报道刊登在所有的全国性报纸上。

5 ▶PRODUCT/BOOK 产品/书◀ [I] if a product or book appears, it becomes available to be bought for the first time 初次上市: *When the book finally appeared on the shelves it was a huge success.* 这本书终于上架开售，大获成功。

6 ▶STH NEW/DIFFERENT 新的/不同的事物◀ [I] if something new or surprising appears, it happens or exists for the first time 首次出现，登场: *Several neo-punk bands have recently appeared on the music scene.* 近来在乐坛出现了几支新朋克乐队。

7 ▶LAW COURT 法庭◀ [I] to be present in a court of law for a TRIAL[1] (1) that you are involved in 出庭: *Smith was ordered to appear in court to face charges on the 15th.* 史密斯接到指令在15日出庭面对指控。| **[+on behalf of/for]** *Sir Nicholas Gammon QC appeared on behalf of the defendant.* 王室法律顾问尼古拉斯·甘蒙爵士代表被告出庭。

8 ▶COMMITTEE/INQUIRY 委员会/询问◀ **appear before/in front of sth** to answer questions by members of an official group who are trying to find out about something 到场〔回答问题〕: *The Senator appeared before the Ways and Means Committee.* 这位参议员出席回答众议院岁入委员会的问题。

9 ▶ARRIVE 到达◀ [I] to arrive, especially when people are not expecting you to〔意外地〕到场: *Karen appeared at about 9 o'clock.* 卡伦大约9点到场的。

✍2 **ap·pear·ance** /əˈpɪrəns; əˈpɪərəns/ *n*

1 ▶WAY SB/STH LOOKS 外貌◀ [C,U] the way someone or something looks to other people 外表; 外观: *You mustn't worry about your appearance – you look fine.* 你不用担心自己的外表，你看起来很好。| *They've changed the whole appearance of the building.* 他们改变了建筑物的整个外观。| **judge by appearances** (=judge someone or something by the way they look) 以貌取人 *It's usually best not to judge by appearances.* 最好不要以貌取人。| **have all the appearances of** (=have all the qualities or features that are typical of something) 具备…所有的特征 *The case had all the appearances of a straightforward murder.* 从各方面看，这个案件都像一宗简单的谋杀。| **to/by all appearances** (=based on the way someone or something seems to most people) 从各方面看 *He was, to all appearances, a respectable, successful businessman.* 从各方面看，他是个受人尊敬的成功商人。| **contrary to/against (all) appearances** (=in spite of the way they appear) 跟外表相反 *Contrary to appearances, she's actually quite funny when you get to know her.* 和外表相反，当你了解她以后会发现她实际上很风趣。| **give/create the appearance of** (=seem) 给人以…的印象 *Nigel gives the appearance of being confident, but he isn't really.* 奈杰尔看起来很自信，但实际并非如此。

2 ▶STH NEW 新事物◀ [singular] the point at which something new begins to exist or starts being used 出现，呈现: [+of] *the appearance of the first mammals* 第一批哺乳动物的出现 | *the appearance of buds on the trees* 树上露出了新芽

3 ▶ARRIVAL 到达◀ [C usually singular 一般用单数] the unexpected or sudden arrival of someone or something〔出其不意的〕到来，出现: [+of] *The shouting suddenly stopped with the appearance of Peter's father.* 彼得的父亲一出现，叫喊声突然停止了。

4 ▶PLAY/FILM/CONCERT ETC 戏剧/电影/音乐会等◀ [C] the act of taking part in a film, play, concert etc 登台，表演: **make an appearance** *He made his first appearance on stage in a Broadway review.* 他第一次在百老汇的时事讽刺剧中露面。| *the band's only European appearance this year* 这个乐队今年唯一一次在欧洲的演出

5 keep up appearances to continue to wear good clothes and behave as though you have plenty of money even though you no longer do 维持面子; 装门面

6 for appearances' sake/for the sake of appearances if you do something for appearances' sake, you are trying to make people think you are still happy, successful etc 为了面子关系

7 put in an appearance/make an appearance to go to an event for a short time, because you think you should 露一下面: *At least Marc managed to put in an appearance at the party.* 至少，马克终于想办法在聚会上露了一面。

8 ▶LAW COURT/MEETING 法庭/会议◀ [C] the act of being present at a court of law or official meeting 出庭; 出席: **make an appearance** *He made a brief appearance in court.* 他出庭作了简短的应讯。

ap·pease /əˈpiz; əˈpiːz/ *v* [T] to make someone less angry or stop them from attacking you by giving them what they want 平息; 安抚; 缓解; 姑息

ap·pease·ment /əˈpizmənt; əˈpiːzmənt/ *n* [C,U] the act of trying to persuade someone not to attack you or to make them less angry by giving them what they want 缓和，平息，抚慰: *Chamberlain's policy of appeasement towards Hitler in the 30s* 张伯伦在30年代对希特勒所采取的绥靖政策

ap·pel·late court /əˌpɛlət ˈkɔrt; əˌpelət ˈkɔːt/ *n* [C] a court in which people appeal (APPEAL[1] (3)) against decisions made in other courts of law 上诉法院

ap·pel·la·tion /ˌæpəˈleʃən; ˌæpəˈleɪʃən/ *n* [C] *literary* a name or title【文】名称，称号

ap·pend /əˈpɛnd; əˈpend/ *v* [T+to] *formal* to add something to a piece of writing【正式】附加，增补

ap·pend·age /əˈpɛndɪdʒ; əˈpendɪdʒ/ *n* [C] **1** something that is connected to a larger or more important thing 附加物，附属物 **2** *formal* an arm, leg or other body part【正式】附肢〔指臂、腿或身体其他部位〕

ap·pen·dec·to·my /ˌæpənˈdɛktəmɪ; ˌæpn̩ˈdektəmi/ *n* [C, U] a medical operation in which your APPENDIX (1) is removed 阑尾〔盲肠〕切除术

ap·pen·di·ci·tis /əˌpɛndəˈsaɪtɪs; əˌpendɪ̵ˈsaɪtɪ̵s/ *n* [U] an illness in which your APPENDIX (1) swells and causes pain 阑尾炎，盲肠炎

ap·pen·dix /əˈpɛndɪks; əˈpendɪks/ *n plural* **appendixes** *or* **appendices** /-dɪsiz; -dɪ̵siːz/ [C] **1** a small organ near your BOWEL (2) which has little or no use 阑尾: **have your appendix out** (=have it removed) 切除阑尾 —see picture at 参见 DIGESTIVE SYSTEM 图 **2** a part at the end of a book containing additional information〔书末的〕附录

ap·per·tain /ˌæpɚˈten; ˌæpəˈteɪn/ *v formal*【正式】

appertain to sth *phr v* [T not in passive 不用被动态] to belong to or concern something 属于…; 和…有关联

ap·pe·tite /ˈæpəˌtaɪt; ˈæpɪ̵taɪt/ *n* **1** [U] a desire for food 胃口，食欲: *a healthy appetite* 好胃口 | **lose your appetite** *She has completely lost her appetite since the operation.* 自手术以后，她完全没有食欲。| **have a huge/big/voracious appetite** (=have the ability to eat a lot of food) 胃口好，食欲佳 | **spoil/ruin your appetite** (=eat before a meal and then not want to eat at the meal) 倒胃口，影响食欲 *Don't eat that cake now, you'll spoil your appetite.* 现在不要吃那块蛋糕，会影响食欲的。| **give sb an appetite** (=make them want to eat) 使某人有食欲 *All that walking has given me a big appetite.* 走了那么多路，我胃口好极了。**2** [C] a desire or liking for a particular activity 欲望; 喜爱: [+for] *Paul has no appetite for hard work.* 保罗不喜欢卖力气。| **sexual appetite** *an insatiable sexual appetite* 无法满足的性欲 —see also 另见 **whet sb's appetite (for sth)** (WHET (1))

ap·pe·tiz·er also 又作 **appetiser** *BrE*【英】/ˈæpəˌtaɪzɚ; ˈæpɪ̵taɪzə/ *n* [C] a small dish at the beginning of a meal〔餐前的〕开胃小吃

ap·pe·tiz·ing also 又作 **appetising** *BrE*【英】/ˈæpəˌtaɪzɪŋ; ˈæpɪ̵taɪzɪŋ/ *adj* food that is appetizing smells or looks very good 增进食欲的，开胃的: *an appetizing aroma* 令人垂涎的香味 —**appetizingly** *adv*

Ap·pian Way, the /ˈæpɪən ˌwe; ˈæpiːən ˌweɪ/ the first important Roman Road. It was built in 312BC and runs south from Rome to Brindisi on the Adriatic coast. 阿庇安大道〔古罗马首条要道，建于公元前312年，从罗马向南延伸，直达亚得里亚海沿岸的布林迪西〕

ap·plaud /əˈplɔd; əˈplɔːd/ *v* [I,T] **1** to hit your open hands together to show that you have enjoyed a play, concert, speaker etc; CLAP[1] (1, 2a)（为…）鼓掌 **2** to express strong approval of an idea, plan etc 称赞，赞许: *We applaud the decision to go ahead with the new building.* 我们赞成着手建造新大楼的决定。

ap·plause /əˈplɔz; əˈplɔːz/ *n* [U] the sound of many people hitting their hands together and shouting, to show that they have enjoyed something 鼓掌，掌声: **thunderous applause** (=very loud) 雷鸣般的掌声 | **a round of applause** (=a short period of applause) 一阵掌声 *Let's have a round of applause for our speakers today.* 让我们鼓掌欢迎今天的各位演讲者。

Ap·ple *trademark*【商标】**1** a US computer company whose best-known product is the Macintosh personal computer 苹果电脑公司〔生产著名品牌麦金塔个人电脑的公司〕 **2** a type of computer made by this company. These machines are regarded as being easy to use, and have a different operating system from PCs. They are usually called 'Macs'. 苹果电脑〔以操作简便著称, 操作系统有别于个人电脑, 俗称"麦克"〕

2 3 **apple** /ˋæpḷ; 'æpəl/ *n* [C,U] **1** a hard round fruit that has red, light green, or yellow skin and is white inside 苹果: *apple pie* 苹果馅饼 —see picture on page A8 参见A8页图 **2 be the apple of sb's eye** to be loved very much by someone 是某人心爱的人[掌上明珠]: *Ben was always the apple of his father's eye.* 本一直是父亲疼爱的人。**3 bob/dunk/dip for apples** to play a game in which you must use your teeth to pick up apples floating in water 咬苹果〔指用牙齿叼起浮在水上的苹果的一种游戏〕 —see also 另见 **upset the apple cart** (UPSET[1] (5)), **a rotten apple** (ROTTEN[1] (5))

ap·ple·jack /ˋæpḷ,dʒæk; 'æpəldʒæk/ *n* [U] *AmE* a very strong alcoholic drink made from apples【美】(烈性) 苹果酒, 苹果白兰地

apple pie bed /,‥ ˈ‥ / *n* [C] *BrE* a trick you do to someone's bed in which you fold the sheets in a particular way so that they cannot get into it【英】苹果馅饼式床〔把被单卷起来, 使人无法睡进去的一种恶作剧〕 —see also 另见 SHORT-SHEET

apple-pie or·der /,‥ ‥ˈ‥/ *n* [U] **be in apple-pie order** to be in perfect order or perfectly arranged 整齐, 井然有序: *His tools are always in apple-pie order.* 他的工具总是摆放得整整齐齐。

apple pol·ish·er /ˈ‥ ,‥/ *n* [C] *AmE spoken* someone who tries to gain something, become popular etc by praising or helping someone else without being sincere【美口】马屁精

apple sauce /,‥ ˈ‥/ *n* [U] a food made from crushed cooked apples 苹果酱

Ap·ple·seed /ˋæpḷsid; 'æpəlsi:d/, **John·ny** /ˋdʒɑnɪ; 'dʒɒni/ the NICKNAME of John Chapman (1774-1845), who walked around the eastern US planting apple trees and encouraging other people to plant them 苹果佬〔约翰·查普曼 (1774-1845) 的绰号。他在美国东部地区到处种植苹果树, 也鼓励别人种植〕

ap·pli·ance /əˋplaɪəns; ə'plaɪəns/ *n* [C] a piece of electrical equipment such as a COOKER (1) or WASHING MACHINE, used in people's homes 家用电器; 设备, 工具: *labour-saving domestic appliances* 节省人力的家用电器 —see 见 MACHINE[1] (USAGE)

ap·plic·a·ble /ˋæplɪkəbḷ; ə'plɪkəbəl/ *adj* affecting or connected with a particular person, group, or situation 适合的, 适用的; 生效的: *Please give details about your mortgage, if applicable.* 如适用, 请说明有关你抵押贷款的详细情况。| **[+to]** *Few of these laws are applicable to UK citizens while they are abroad.* 这些法律中几乎没有适用于在国外的英国公民的。—**applicability** /,æplɪkəˋbɪlətɪ; ə,plɪkə'bɪlḷti/ *n* [U]

ap·pli·cant /ˋæpləkənt; 'æplɪkənt/ *n* [C] someone who has formally asked, usually in writing, for a job, university place etc 申请人

1 1 **ap·pli·ca·tion** /,æpləˋkeʃən; ,æplɪ'keɪʃən/ *n*
1 ►WRITTEN REQUEST 书面要求◄ [C,U] a formal, usually written, request for something such as a job, place at university, or permission to do something 申请(书): *Developers have filed a planning application.* 开发商正式提交了开发计划申请书。| **[+for]** *There were more than 300 applications for the six jobs.* 有三百多人申请这六份工作。| **job/membership application** *We received hundreds of job applications.* 我们收到了几百份工作申请。| **application form** (=the paper on which you write your details) 申请表 | **on application (to)** (=when you make an application) (向…) 申请 *Details will be sent on application.* 提出申请后将寄送详细资料。
2 ►PRACTICAL USE 实用◄ [C,U] practical purpose for which a machine, idea etc can be used, or the act of using it for this 用途, 实际应用: *A microcomputer has a wide range of applications for businesses.* 微(型)电脑在商业方面用途很广。| **[+of/to/in]** *the application of this theory to actual economic practice* 这一理论在经济实践中的应用
3 ►PAINT/LIQUID 油漆/液体◄ [C,U] the act of putting something such as paint, liquid, medicine etc onto a surface 涂敷; 敷用: **[+of]** *The application of fertilizer increased the size of the plants.* 施肥使植株生长。
4 ►EFFORT 努力◄ [U] attention or effort over a long period of time 专心, 努力: *Making your new business successful requires luck, patience, and application.* 新的生意要想做好, 你需要运气、耐心和努力。
5 ►COMPUTERS 计算机◄ a piece of SOFTWARE 应用软件: *The top software application last year was Microsoft Office.* 去年最流行的应用软件是微软办公系列。
6 ►RELATION TO STH 与某物的关系◄ [U] the way in which something can affect or be used on something else 适用: **[+to]** *That rule has no application to this case.* 那条规则不适用于这种情况。

ap·plied /əˋplaɪd; ə'plaɪd/ *adj* [usually before noun 一般用于名词前] **applied science/physics/linguistics etc** science etc that has a practical use 应用科学/物理/语言学等 —compare 比较 PURE (10) —opposite 反义词 THEORETICAL (1)

ap·pli·qué /,æplɪˋke; ə'pli:keɪ/ *n* [C,U] the process of sewing decorative pieces of material onto a piece of clothing, or the pieces themselves 缝饰, 补花, 贴花 —**appliqué** *v* [T]

ap·ply /əˋplaɪ; ə'plaɪ/ *v* 1 1
1 ►REQUEST PERMISSION/A JOB 请求准许/求职◄ [I] to make a formal, usually written request for something such as a job, place in university, or permission to do something 申请: **[+to]** *I applied to four universities and was accepted by all of them.* 我向四所大学提出了申请, 都被接受了。| **[+for]** *Fletcher applied for the post of Eliot's secretary.* 弗莱彻申请艾略特的秘书这一职位。
2 ►USE STH 使用某物◄ [T] to use something such as a method, idea, or law in a particular situation, activity, or process 使用, 应用, 运用: *In some cases tribunals fail to apply the law properly.* 在有些案件中, 裁判庭没有正确运用此法律。| **apply sth to** *New technology is being applied to almost every industrial process.* 新技术正被应用到几乎所有工业流程。
3 ►AFFECT STH 影响某事物◄ [I,T not in progressive 不用进行时] to have an effect on or to concern a person, group, or situation 适用于〔某人、某种情况〕; 有效: **[+to]** *The questions on this part of the form only apply to married men.* 表中这部分的问题只适用于已婚男士。| *Many of the restrictions no longer apply.* 许多限制已不再有效。
4 apply yourself to work hard with a lot of attention for a long time 致力于, 专心于: *Stephen would do very well if only he applied himself.* 只要专心致志, 斯蒂芬会做得很好的。
5 ►MAKE STH WORK 使某物起作用◄ [T] to do something in order to make something such as a piece of equipment operate 使…起作用: *apply the brakes* 踩刹车 | *The crystal vibrates when a small electric current is applied to it.* 一点电流就能使水晶振动起来。
6 ►SPREAD PAINT/LIQUID ETC 涂油漆/液体等◄ [T] to put or spread something such as paint, liquid, or medicine onto a surface 涂, 敷: *Apply the cream evenly over the skin.* 将雪花膏均匀地涂在皮肤表面。
7 apply force/pressure to push on something 用力/施压
8 ►USE A WORD 用某词◄ [T] to use a particular word or name to describe something or someone 使用〔某个单词或名称〕: *The term 'mat' can be applied to any small rug.* mat一词可指各种小地毯。

ap·point /əˋpɔɪnt; ə'pɔɪnt/ *v* [T] **1** to choose someone for a position or a job 任命; 委派: *They appointed a new teacher at the school.* 他们给学校委派了一名新老师。| **appoint (sb) as sth** *O'Connell was appointed as Chairman of the Council.* 奥康奈尔被任命为委员会主席。| *The School Board have appointed her Superintendent of the city's schools.* 地方教育委员会任命她为该市所有学校的督学。| **appoint sb to sth** *He's been appointed to the State Supreme Court in California.* 他被派到加利福尼亚州最高法院任职。| **appoint sb to do sth** *She's been appointed to catalog the new books in the library.* 她被派到图书馆为新书登记分类。**2** *formal* to arrange or decide a time or place for something to happen【正式】约定, 指定, 确定〔时间、地点〕: *The committee appointed a day in June for celebrations.* 委员会指定6月的一天进行庆祝。| **the appointed time** (=the time that has been arranged) 约定的时间 *We met him at the appointed time outside the courtroom.* 我们按约定时间在法庭外见到了他。—**appointee** /ə,pɔɪnˋti; ə,pɔɪn'ti:/ *n* [C]: *a presidential appointee* 总统任命的人 —see also 另见 SELF-APPOINTED, WELL-APPOINTED —see 见 HIRE[1] (USAGE) 2 2

ap·point·ment /əˋpɔɪntmənt; ə'pɔɪntmənt/ *n* **1** [C] an arrangement for a meeting at an agreed time and place, for some special purpose 约定, 预约: *a hospital appointment* 看病预约 | *a five o'clock appointment* 5点钟的约会 | **[+with]** *an appointment with the doctor at 10.30* 与医生约定在10点30分看病 | **appointment to do sth** *I have an appointment to see the manager.* 我约好了见经理。| **make an appointment** *Phone his secretary and make an appointment.* 打电话给他的秘书约定时间。| **keep an appointment** (=be present at an appointment as 1 2

arranged) 守约 *If you fail to keep the dentist's appointment you'll have to pay for it.* 如果你和牙医约好时间但到时不去，你得付钱。**2** [C,U] the choosing of someone for a position or job 任命，委任: [+as/to/of] *His appointment as head of department has caused a lot of friction.* 任命他为部门经理引起了很多意见冲突。| **appointments column** *BrE* (=the part of a newspaper where jobs are advertised)【英】〔报纸上的〕招聘广告栏 **3 by appointment** if you do something by appointment, you have to arrange it before you do it 按约定，按事先确定的时间: *The Director sees students by appointment only.* 系主任只按约定的时间见学生。**4** [C] a job or position, usually involving some responsibility 委任的工作[职位]: *He was told he'd got the appointment yesterday morning.* 昨天上午他被告知得到了那个职位。**5 by appointment to the Queen** a phrase that can be used by a business that sells goods or services to the Queen 经女王御准〔可向王室出售商品或提供服务〕

Ap·po·mat·tox /ˌæpə`mætəks; ˌæpəˈmætəks/ a town in Virginia, US, where General Robert E. Lee, the leader of the Confederate army, SURRENDERed to General Ulysses S. Grant, the leader of the Union army, and therefore ended the American Civil War. 阿波马托克斯〔美国弗吉尼亚州一镇。南部联军总司令罗伯特·E.李将军在该地向联邦军总指挥官尤利西斯·S.格兰特将军投降，南北战争以此告终〕

ap·por·tion /ə`pɔrʃən; əˈpɔːʃən/ *v* [T] to decide how something should be shared between various people 分配，分摊: [+among/between] *apportioning available funds among the different schools in the district* 在区内的各所学校分配可用的资金 | **apportion blame/praise etc** (=say who deserves to be blamed or praised) 分清责任/表扬等 *It's not easy to apportion blame when a marriage breaks up.* 婚姻破裂时，很难分清夫妻俩的(过失)责任。—**apportionment** *n* [C,U]

ap·po·site /`æpəzɪt; ˈæpəzɪ̈t/ *adj formal* suitable to what is happening or being discussed【正式】适当的，恰当的，贴切的: *brief but apposite remarks* 简短而恰到好处的言辞 —**appositely** *adv* —**appositeness** *n* [U]

ap·po·si·tion /ˌæpə`zɪʃən; ˌæpəˈzɪʃən/ *n* [U] an arrangement in grammar in which one simple sentence contains two or more noun phrases that are used in the same way and describe the same thing. For example, in the sentence 'The defendant, a woman of thirty, denies kicking the policeman' the two phrases 'the defendant' and 'a woman of thirty' are in apposition. 〔语法〕同位，同格〈如 The defendant, a woman of thirty, denies kicking the policeman (被告，一位三十岁的妇女，否认踢了警察) 一句中，"the defendant"和"a woman of thirty"是同位关系〉

ap·prais·al /ə`prezḷ; əˈpreɪzəl/ *n* [C,U] a statement or opinion judging the worth, value, or condition of something 评价；估计；鉴定: [+of] *What's your appraisal of the situation?* 你对局势如何评价？| *an annual appraisal of employees' work* 对雇员工作的年度评估

ap·praise /ə`prez; əˈpreɪz/ *v* [T] to officially judge how successful, effective, or valuable someone or something is; EVALUATE 评定；鉴定；估价: *A dealer came to appraise the furniture.* 一个商人来对家具作了估价。

ap·pre·cia·ble /ə`priʃəbḷ; əˈpriːʃəbəl/ *adj* large enough to be noticed or considered important 明显的，可觉察到的；值得重视的: *There's no appreciable change in the patient's condition.* 病人状况没有明显改变。—**appreciably** *adv*: *The two plans are not appreciably different.* 这两个计划没有明显区别。

S2 W3 **ap·pre·ci·ate** /ə`priʃɪˌet; əˈpriːʃieɪt/ *v* **1** [T] to understand how good or useful someone or something is 欣赏；赏识；鉴赏: *Her abilities are not fully appreciated by her employer.* 她的才干还没有得到雇主的充分赏识。**2** [T] to be grateful for something that someone has done 感激: *I appreciated his help when we moved.* 我很感激他在我们搬家时给予的帮助。| **I would appreciate it if** (=please do what I ask) 如果你…，我将不胜感激 *I would appreciate it if you would turn the music down.* 如果你把音乐关小一些，我将不胜感激。**3** [T not in progressive 不用进行时] to understand how serious a situation or problem is or what someone's feelings are 完全理解，明白: *I don't think you appreciate the difficulties his absence will cause.* 我认为你不完全了解他的缺席会造成什么样的困难。**4** [I] to gradually become more valuable over a period of time 增值: *Most investments are expected to appreciate at a steady rate.* 人们大多盼望投资会平稳增值。—opposite 反义词 DEPRECIATE (1)

ap·pre·ci·a·tion /əˌpriʃɪ`eʃən; əˌpriːʃiˈeɪʃən/ *n* **1** [U] pleasure you feel when you realize something is good, useful, or well done 欣赏；赏识；鉴赏 **2 show sb your appreciation** to show someone that you are grateful for something they have done 对某人表达感激之情: *To show our appreciation for all your hard work, we'd like to give you a bonus.* 为了对你辛勤工作表示感谢，我们要给你发奖金。**3** [C,U] an understanding of the importance or meaning of something 理解，明白: [+of] *a realistic appreciation of the situation* 对局势实事求是的理解 **4** [singular, U] a rise in value, especially of land or possessions 〔尤指土地或财产的〕增值: *an appreciation of 50% in property values* 资产增值50%

ap·pre·cia·tive /ə`priʃɪˌetɪv; əˈpriːʃətɪv/ *adj* feeling or showing admiration or thanks 有欣赏力的；感激的: *an appreciative audience* 有欣赏能力的观众 | [+of] *The visitors were appreciative of all the kindness they'd received.* 来访者对他们受到的热情接待表示感谢。—**appreciatively** *adv*

ap·pre·hend /ˌæprɪ`hɛnd; ˌæprɪˈhend/ *v* [T] **1** *formal* if a criminal is apprehended, they are found and taken away by the police; ARREST[1] (1)【正式】逮捕，拘押 **2** *old use* to understand something【旧】了解，明白

ap·pre·hen·sion /ˌæprɪ`hɛnʃən; ˌæprɪˈhenʃən/ *n* **1** [C,U] anxiety about the future, especially the worry that you will have to deal with something unpleasant or bad 〔对未来的〕忧虑，担心: *a natural apprehension about being in hospital* 对住院自然会有的忧虑 **2** [U] the act of apprehending someone; ARREST[2] 逮捕，拘押 **3** [U] *old use* understanding【旧】理解: *our apprehension of the nature of God* 我们对上帝神性的理解

ap·pre·hen·sive /ˌæprɪ`hɛnsɪv; ˌæprɪˈhensɪv◂/ *adj* worried or nervous about something that you are going to do, or about the future 〔对将做的事或对未来〕恐惧的；焦虑的: [+about/for] *feeling a little apprehensive about the treatment* 对治疗感到有些恐惧 —**apprehensively** *adv*: *I waited apprehensively for his reply.* 我焦急地等待着他的答复。

ap·pren·tice[1] /ə`prɛntɪs; əˈprentɪ̈s/ *n* [C] someone who agrees to work for an employer for a fixed period of time in order to learn a particular skill or job 学徒，徒弟: *She works in the hairdresser's as an apprentice.* 她在一家美发店当学徒。| *an apprentice electrician* 电工学徒

apprentice[2] *v* [T usually passive 一般用被动态] to make someone an apprentice 使〔某人〕当学徒: **apprentice sb to** *He's apprenticed to a plumber.* 他跟一位管道工当学徒。

ap·pren·tice·ship /ə`prɛntɪsˌʃɪp; əˈprentɪ̈sʃɪp/ *n* [C,U] the job of being an apprentice, or the period of time in which you are an apprentice 学徒身份；学徒年限: *He's serving an apprenticeship as a printer.* 他现在是一名印刷学徒工。| *a five-year apprenticeship* 五年学徒期

CULTURAL NOTE 文化注释

In Britain and the US, the state does not have an official system of apprenticeships. Apprenticeships are usually offered by companies or by skilled workers who need someone to help them and are willing to teach their skill in return for this help. 英美两国没有正式的学徒制度，学徒机会一般是由公司或熟练工人提供的，他们需要帮手，愿意传授技能以期回报。

ap·prise /ə`praɪz; əˈpraɪz/ *v* [T+of] *formal* to inform or tell someone about something【正式】通知；告诉: *I write to apprise you of the latest situation.* 我写信向你通报最新的情况。

ap·proach[1] /ə`protʃ; əˈprəʊtʃ/ *v* S3 W2

1 ►MOVE TOWARDS 向…移动◄ [I,T] to move towards or nearer to someone or something 走近；靠近；接近: *As they approached the wood a rabbit ran out of the trees.* 他们走近树林的时候，一只兔子从树丛里跑了出来。| *The car swerved to avoid an approaching bus.* 小汽车突然转向，躲避一辆开过来的公共汽车。

2 ►ASK 请求◄ [T] to ask someone for something, or ask them to do something, especially when you are not sure they will be interested 接洽，交涉: **approach sb for** *Will you be approaching the bank for a loan?* 你会向银行要求贷款吗？| **approach sb/sth about (doing) sth** *The charity approached several stores about giving food aid.* 慈善机构找了几家商店，请求他们给予食物援助。—see also 另见 APPROACHABLE

3 ►FUTURE EVENT 未来事件◄ [I,T] if an event or a particular time approaches, or you approach it, it is coming nearer and will happen soon 临近: *Our vacation is approaching and we still can't decide where to go.* 我们的假期日益临近，可我们仍定不下来去哪儿。| *He was in his fifties and approaching retirement.* 他五十几岁，快到退休年龄了。

4 ►ALMOST REACH STH 几乎到…◄ [I,T] to almost reach a particular high level or amount, or an extreme condition or state 接近: *temperatures approaching 35°C* 接近35摄氏度的温度 | **nothing/not approaching** (=not at all close in amount) 差得远

Nothing approaching the $200 million was found by the auditors. 审计员查到的数字离两亿美元尚差得很远。 **5 ▶DEAL WITH** 对付◀ [T] to begin to deal with a difficult situation in a particular way or with a particular attitude 对付，处理: *I don't think refusing to negotiate is the right way to approach this problem.* 我认为拒绝谈判不是处理这一问题的正确方法。

S3 W1 **approach²** *n* **1** [C] a method of doing something or dealing with a problem 方法; 步骤: [+to] *a new approach to teaching languages* 教授语言的新方法 **2** [U] movement towards or near to something 靠近; 接近; 临近: *Our approach frightened the birds away.* 我们一靠近，鸟全都受惊飞走了。**3** [C] a road, path etc that leads to a place, and is the main way of reaching it 通路，入口: *The approach to the house was by a minor road.* 进入这幢房子要经过一条小路。**4** [C] a request from someone, asking you to do something for them 要求: **make an approach** *They made approaches to the team to buy one of their players.* 他们与那支球队洽谈要买他们的一个球员。**5 the approach of** the approach of a particular time or event is the fact that it is getting closer …的来临[临近]: *The leaves were turning brown with the approach of autumn.* 随着秋天的临近，树叶变成了褐色。

ap·proa·cha·ble /əˋprotʃəbḷ; əˈprəʊtʃəbəl/ *adj* friendly and easy to talk to 友善的; 易接近的: *The head teacher is very approachable.* 校长非常平易近人。—opposite 反义词 UNAPPROACHABLE

ap·pro·ba·tion /ˌæprəˋbeʃən; ˌæprəˈbeɪʃən/ *n* [U] *formal* official praise or approval【正式】称赞; 认可，批准

S1 W1 **ap·pro·pri·ate¹** /əˋpropri·ɪt; əˈprəʊpri-ɪ̀t/ *adj* correct or suitable for a particular time, situation, or purpose 恰当的; 合适的: *At an appropriate moment I'll offer the visitors some coffee.* 在合适的时候，我会请来访者喝咖啡。| [+for] *Your clothes are hardly appropriate for a job interview.* 你的衣服不太适合求职面试时穿。| [+to] *objectives and strategies which are appropriate to the markets* 适合市场要求的目标和策略 —opposite 反义词 INAPPROPRIATE —**appropriately** *adv*: *Her new job started, appropriately enough, on the first of January.* 她的新工作正好从1月1日开始。—**appropriateness** *n* [U]

ap·pro·pri·ate² /əˋpropriˌet; əˈprəʊprieɪt/ *v* [T] **1** to take something for yourself with no right to do this 挪用; 占用; 盗用: *He is suspected of appropriating government funds.* 他被怀疑挪用政府资金。**2** to take something, especially money, to use for a particular purpose 拨出〔款项〕: **appropriate sth for** *Congress appropriated $5 million for the International Woman's Year.* 国会为"国际妇女年"拨款500万美元。—see also 另见 MISAPPROPRIATE

ap·pro·pri·a·tion /əˌpropriˋeʃən; əˌprəʊpriˈeɪʃən/ *n* [C,U] **1** the process of saving money for a special purpose, or the money that is saved, especially by a business or government 拨款: [+of] *the appropriation of $2 million for the new hospital* 给新医院拨款200万美元 **2** the act of taking control of something without asking permission 擅用; 私占: *the appropriation by the state of all large, profitable businesses* 国家把所有大型赢利企业据为己有

S2 W3 **ap·prov·al** /əˋpruvḷ; əˈpruːvəl/ *n* [U] **1** the fact of believing that someone or something is good or is doing the right things 赞许; 赞成，同意: **win/earn sb's approval** *By doing well at school he hoped to win his parents' approval.* 他在学校表现不错，希望以此得到父母的赞许。| **nod/smile/watch etc in approval** *The audience cheered, yelled and whistled in approval.* 观众发出欢呼声、尖叫声和口哨声表示赞许。—opposite 反义词 DISAPPROVAL **2** the act of officially accepting a plan, decision, or person 批准; 认可: *approval of the plans for the new science lab* 批准建立新科学实验室的方案 | **for approval** *He submitted his credentials to the Medical Faculty for approval.* 他向医学院递交自己的资格证书希望得到认可。| **meet with sb's approval** (=be accepted by someone) 得到某人的批准 *The budget proposals met with the Senate's approval.* 预算提案得到了参议院的批准。| **seal of approval** (=statement that you accept something) 认可，接受 *The IMF has given its seal of approval to the government's economic strategy.* 国际货币基金组织已经认同了该政府的经济策略。**3** official permission to do something 准许，允许，许可: *We need parental approval before allowing students to go on field trips.* 我们需要得到家长的同意才会允许学生去野外考察。**4 on approval** if you buy something on approval, you have the right to return it to the shop if you decide you do not want it〔商品〕包退包换，不满意可退货

S2 W2 **ap·prove** /əˋpruv; əˈpruːv/ *v* **1** [T] to officially accept a plan, proposal etc 批准; 认可: *The Senate approved a plan for federal funding of local housing programs.* 参议院批准了一项关于联邦政府提供地方建房资金的计划。**2** [I] to think that someone or something is good, right, or suitable 赞成，同意: [+of] *Catherine's parents now approve of her marriage.* 凯瑟琳的父母现在同意她结婚。

approved school /·ˈ· ·/ *n* [C,U] a special school in Britain, where children who have done something illegal are sent if they are under 18〔英国的〕少年感化院; 少年(罪)犯教养院

ap·prov·ing /əˋpruvɪŋ; əˈpruːvɪŋ/ *adj* showing support or agreement for something 赞许的; 赞成的: *The professor made no comment about the speech, but gave an approving nod.* 教授对这个演讲未作评论，但点头表示赞许。—**approvingly** *adv*: *She smiled approvingly at the child.* 她对孩子微笑着表示赞许。

approx. the written abbreviation of 缩写= approximately

ap·prox·i·mant /əˋprɑksəmənt; ; əˈprɒksɪ̀mənt/ *n* [C] a consonant sound such as /w/ or /l/ made by air passing between the tongue or lip and another part of the mouth without any closing of the air passage 无擦通音，无摩擦延续音

ap·prox·i·mate¹ /əˋprɑksəmɪt; əˈprɒksɪ̀mɪ̀t/ *adj* an approximate number, amount, or time is a little bit more or less than the exact number, amount etc 大致的，大约的，大概的: *What is the approximate cost of the materials?* 材料的大致费用是多少? —**approximately** *adv*: *The plane will be landing in approximately 20 minutes.* 飞机大约20分钟后着陆。 S3 W3

Frequencies of the adverbs **approximately, about,** and **roughly** in spoken and written English 副词approximately, about 和 roughly 在英语口语和书面语中的使用频率

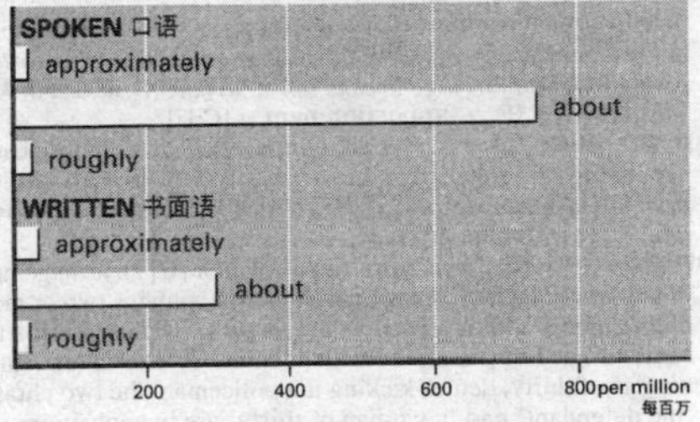

Based on the British National Corpus and the Longman Lancaster Corpus
据英国国家语料库和朗文兰开斯特语料库

All three adverbs are used to mean 'more or less' or 'not exactly'. The graph shows that in this meaning **about** is much more common than **approximately** in both spoken English and written English. **Roughly** is also more common than **approximately** in spoken English. 这三个副词用来表示"大约"、"大概"的意思。本图表显示，表示此义时，about 在口语和书面语中的使用频率都远远高于 approximately。在口语中 roughly 也比 approximately 常用。

ap·prox·i·mate² /əˋprɑksəˌmet; əˈprɒksɪ̀meɪt/ *v* [I, linking verb 连系动词] *formal*【正式】**1** to be close to a particular number 接近: [+to] *Rainfall during the period we were there approximated to the yearly average.* 我们在那里的那段时间降雨量接近年均水平。**2** to be similar to but not exactly the same as something 近似: [+to] *Your story only approximates to the real facts.* 你所说的仅仅是接近事实真相。

ap·prox·i·ma·tion /əˌprɑksəˋmeʃən; əˌprɒksɪ̀ˈmeɪʃən/ *n* [C, U] **1** a number, amount etc that is not exact, but is almost correct 概算，近似值: **rough approximation** (=not exact at all) 估算 *Could you give us a rough approximation of the likely cost?* 你能估算一下成本大概有多少吗? **2** something that is similar to another thing, but not exactly the same 类似物: [+of/to] *It was the nearest approximation to a crisis she had ever experienced.* 这是她所经历过的最近乎于危机的情况。

ap·pur·te·nance /əˋpɝtṇəns; əˈpɜːtɪnəns/ *n* [C usually plural 一般用复数] **1** *formal* things that are an additional and less important part of something larger, for example possessions in a house【正式】附属物，附带物 **2** *technical* an additional right or responsibility connected with owning property【术语】附带权利[责任]

APR /ˌe pi ˋɑr; ˌeɪ piː ˈɑː/ *n* [C usually singular 一般用单数] Annual Percentage Rate; the rate of INTEREST¹ (4) that you must pay when you borrow money 年率，年利率

ap·rès-ski /ˌæpre ˋski; ˌæpreɪ ˈskiː◂/ *n* [singular] activities such as eating and drinking that you take part in after skiing (SKI²) 滑雪后的活动〔如吃喝东西等〕

a·pri·cot /ˈeprɪˌkɑt; ˈeɪprɨkɒt/ *n* **1** [C] a small round fruit that is orange or yellow and has a single large seed 杏 —see picture on page A8 参见A8页图 **2** [U] the colour of this fruit 杏黄色 —see picture on page A5 参见A5页图 —**apricot** *adj*

A·pril /ˈeprəl; ˈeɪprəl/ written abbreviation 缩写为 **Apr** *n* [C,U] the fourth month of the year, between March and May 四月: **on April the sixth/the fifteenth etc** *BrE*【英】/**on April sixth/fifteenth** *AmE*【美】*I arrived on April seventh.* 我于4月7日到达。| **on the sixth/fifteenth etc of April** *My new job starts on the second of April.* 我的新工作从4月2日开始。| **in April** *This office opened in April 1994.* 这个办事处在1994年4月开始运作。| **this/last/next April** *I'm going to Africa next April.* 我明年4月去非洲。

CULTURAL NOTE 文化注释

In the UK and northern US, when people think of April, they think of Easter, spring flowers, LAMBS, and April SHOWERS (=short periods of rain that often happen in April). They also think of April Fools' Day, which is on April 1st. 在英国和美国北部，人们想起4月，则会想起复活节、春天的花朵、羔羊和4月的阵雨，还会想起4月1日的愚人节。

April fool /ˌ‥ ˈ·/ *n* [C] someone who is tricked on April Fools' Day, or the trick that is played on them〔在4月1日〕愚人节时受愚弄的人；在愚人节开的玩笑

April Fools' Day /ˌ‥ ˈ· ˌ·/ also 又作 **All Fools' Day** *old-fashioned*【过时】*n* [singular] April 1st, a day when people play tricks on each other 愚人节

a pri·o·ri /ˌe praɪˈoraɪ; ˌeɪ praɪˈɔːraɪ/ *adj, adv Latin* using previous experiences or facts to decide what the probable result or effect of something will be【拉丁】由因及果的[地]，演绎的[地]: *an a priori statement such as 'It is raining so the streets must be wet.'* "天正在下雨，因此街道肯定是湿的"之类的推理

a·pron /ˈeprən; ˈeɪprən/ *n* [C] **1** a piece of clothing that covers the front part of your clothes and ties around your waist, worn to keep your clothes clean, especially while cooking 围裙 —see picture on page A15 参见A15页图 **2 tied to your mother's/wife's apron strings** too easily controlled by your mother or wife 受母亲/妻子的摆布 **3** also 又作 **apron stage** the part of the stage in a theatre that comes forward towards the people watching 台口〔舞台幕前部分〕 **4** the hard surface in an airport on which planes are turned around, loaded, unloaded etc 停机坪

ap·ro·pos[1] /ˌæprəˈpo; ˌæprəˈpəʊ/ *adv, prep* **apropos of** used to introduce a new subject that is connected with something just mentioned 说到…，关于，就…而言〔用于引入与刚才话题有关的新话题〕: *He had nothing to say apropos of the latest developments.* 至于最新的进展，他没什么要说的。| **apropos of nothing** (=not connected with previous conversation) 突然地，毫无理由地〔改变话题〕*Apropos of nothing, he suddenly asked me if I liked cats!* 他突然没头没尾地问我是否喜欢猫!

apropos[2] *adj* [not before noun 不用于名词前] suitable for a particular situation 适时的，恰当的: *I thought her remarks were very apropos.* 我认为她的话说得很合时宜。

apse /æps; æps/ *n* [C] the curved inside end of a building, especially the east end of a church 半圆室，半圆形殿〔尤指教堂东端的半圆形建筑〕

apt /æpt; æpt/ *adj* **1 apt to do something** having a natural tendency to do something 有做某事倾向的，易于做某事的: *Some of the staff are apt to arrive late on Mondays.* 一些职员星期一常迟到。**2** exactly right for a particular situation or purpose 适当的，恰当的: *an apt and telling remark* 既恰当又能说明问题的话 **3** *formal* quick to learn and understand【正式】敏捷的；聪明的 —**aptness** *n* [U]

ap·ti·tude /ˈæptəˌtud; ˈæptɨtjuːd/ *n* [C,U] natural ability or skill, especially in learning〔尤指学习方面的〕天资，资质: **[+for]** *She has a real aptitude for drawing and painting.* 她在绘画方面的确有天赋。

apt·ly /ˈæptlɪ; ˈæptli/ *adv* **aptly named/described/called etc** named, described etc in a way that seems very suitable 命名/描述/称呼等很恰当: *Lightfoot was aptly named; we never heard him enter.* "轻脚"这个名字起得好，我们从未听到过他进来的声音。

aq·ua·lung /ˈækwəˌlʌŋ; ˈækwəlʌŋ/ *n* [C] a piece of equipment that a swimmer wears on their back under water, that provides air for them to breathe〔潜水者背在背上的〕水肺，水中呼吸器

aq·ua·ma·rine /ˌækwəməˈrin; ˌækwəməˈriːn◂/ *n* **1** [C,U] a greenish blue jewel or the type of stone it comes from 海蓝宝石 **2** [U] a greenish blue colour 蓝绿色，海蓝色 —**aquamarine** *adj* —see picture on page A5 参见A5页图

aq·ua·plane[1] /ˈækwəˌplen; ˈækwəpleɪn/ *n* [C] a thin board that you stand on while you are pulled over the water by a fast boat 滑水板

aquaplane[2] *v* [I] **1** to be pulled over the water on an aquaplane 滑水，站在滑水板上滑行 **2** *BrE* if a car aquaplanes, it slides over a wet road in an uncontrolled way【英】〔汽车〕在积水的路面上失去控制而滑行; HYDROPLANE[2] (1) *AmE*【美】

a·quar·i·um /əˈkwɛrɪəm; əˈkweəriəm/ *n plural* **aquariums** *or* **aquaria** /-rɪə; -riə/ [C] **1** a clear glass or plastic container for fish and other water animals〔玻璃或塑料的〕养鱼缸，水族箱 **2** a building where people go to look at fish and other water animals 水族馆

A·quar·i·us /əˈkwɛrɪəs; əˈkweəriəs/ *n* **1** [singular] the eleventh sign of the ZODIAC, represented by a person pouring water and believed to affect the character and life of people born between January 21 and February 19 宝瓶宫〔黄道第十一宫〕，水瓶座 **2** [C] someone who was born between January 21 and February 19 出生于宝瓶宫[水瓶座]时段〔1月21日至2月19日〕的人

a·quat·ic /əˈkwætɪk; əˈkwætɪk/ *adj* **1** living or growing in water 水栖的；水生的: *an aquatic plant* 水生植物 **2** involving water 水中的，水上的: *aquatic sports* 水上运动 —**aquatically** /-klɪ; -kli/ *adv*

aq·ua·tint /ˈækwəˌtɪnt; ˈækwətɪnt/ *n* [C,U] a method of producing a picture using acid on a sheet of metal, or a picture printed using this method 凹版腐蚀制版法，铜版蚀镂法；用凹版腐蚀法印制成的图画

aq·ue·duct /ˈækwɪˌdʌkt; ˈækwɨdʌkt/ *n* [C] a structure like a bridge, used to carry a water supply across a valley〔跨过山谷的〕输水道，渡槽

a·que·ous /ˈekwɪəs; ˈeɪkwiəs/ *adj technical* containing water or similar to water【术语】水的；似水的；含水的

aq·ui·line /ˈækwəˌlaɪn; ˈækwɨlaɪn/ *adj* **1 aquiline nose** an aquiline nose has a curved shape like the beak of an EAGLE 鹰钩鼻 **2** like an EAGLE 似鹰的

A·qui·nas /əˈkwaɪnəs; əˈkwaɪnəs/, **St Thomas** (1225-74) an Italian THEOLOGIAN (=someone who studies religion and religious beliefs) and PHILOSOPHER whose ideas had an important influence on the Roman Catholic religion 阿奎那〔(1225-1274)，意大利神学家、哲学家。他的思想对罗马天主教产生了重要影响〕

AR /ˌe ˈɑr; ˌeɪ ˈɑː/ the written abbreviation of 缩写= ARKANSAS

-ar /ɚ; ə/ *suffix* **1** [in nouns 构成名词] the form used for -ER in certain words …人〔在某些词中用以代替-er〕: *a beggar* (=person who begs) 乞丐 **2** [in adjectives 构成形容词] of or concerning something 与…有关的: *muscular strength* (=strength of muscles) 肌肉的力量 —see also 另见 -ULAR

Ar·ab /ˈærəb; ˈærəb/ *n* [C] **1** someone whose language is Arabic and whose family have their origin in Arabia or the Middle East 阿拉伯人 **2** also 又作 **Arabian** *AmE*【美】a type of fast graceful horse 阿拉伯马

ar·a·besque /ˌærəˈbɛsk; ˌærəˈbesk/ *n* [C] **1** a position in BALLET 阿拉贝斯克舞姿〔一种芭蕾舞姿〕 **2** a decorative pattern of flowing lines 阿拉伯式花饰

A·ra·bi·a /əˈrebɪə; əˈreɪbiə/ also 又作 **the Arabian Peninsula** the large area of land between the Red Sea and the Gulf which contains Saudi Arabia, Yemen, Oman, Bahrain, Kuwait, Qatar, and the United Arab Emirates 阿拉伯半岛〔位于红海与波斯湾之间的辽阔地域，包括沙特阿拉伯、也门、阿曼、巴林、科威特、卡塔尔和阿拉伯联合酋长国〕

A·ra·bi·an /əˈrebɪən; əˈreɪbiən/ *adj* from or connected with Arabia 阿拉伯的

Arabian Nights, the /ˌ·ˌ‥ ˈ·/ also 又作 **the Thousand and One Nights** a collection of Arabic stories from the 10th century, including *Aladdin*, *Ali Baba*, and *Sinbad*. The stories are told by Scheherazade, a young woman who prevents her cruel husband from killing her by amusing him with a different story every night for a thousand and one nights.《天方夜谭》，《一千零一夜》〔源于公元10世纪的一部阿拉伯故事集，其中包括《阿拉丁》、《阿里巴巴》和《辛巴达》。故事的叙述者山鲁佐德是一位年轻女子。为了免遭残酷的丈夫杀害，她每天晚上给他讲一个有趣的故事，连续讲了一千零一夜〕

Arabian Sea, the /ˌ·‥ ˈ·/ a sea between India and Arabia 阿拉伯海〔印度与阿拉伯半岛之间的海域〕

Ar·a·bic /ˈærəbɪk; ˈærəbɪk/ *n* [U] the language or writing of the Arabs, which is the main language of North Africa, the Middle East, and Arabia 阿拉伯语 —**Arabic** *adj*

A

Ar·a·bic nu·me·ral /ˌ‥ˈ‥/ *n* [C] a sign, such as 1, 2, or 3, used for numbers in the English alphabet and many others 阿拉伯数字 —see also 另见 ROMAN NUMERAL

ar·a·ble /ˈærəbl; ˈærəbəl/ *adj* **1** **arable land/soil** arable land is suitable for growing crops 适于耕作的土地/土壤 **2** concerned with growing crops 与种植有关的

Arab League, the /ˌ‥ˈ/ an organization of Arab countries in North Africa and southwest Asia, which was formed in 1945 阿拉伯(国家)联盟〔北非和亚洲西南部阿拉伯国家的一个组织，成立于1945年〕

Ar·a·fat /ˈærəfæt; ˈærəfæt/, **Yas·ser** /ˈjæsɚ; ˈjæsə/ (1929-2004) a Palestinian politician and leader of the PLO from 1969. He was elected President of the Palestine National Authority in 1996. 阿拉法特〔(1929-2004)，巴勒斯坦政治家，1969年始任巴勒斯坦解放组织领导人，1996年当选巴勒斯坦民族权力机构主席〕

Ar·al Sea, the /ˌærəl ˈsi; ˌærəl ˈsiː/ an inland sea between Kazakhstan and Uzbekistan 咸海〔位于哈萨克斯坦和乌兹别克斯坦之间的一个内陆海〕

Ar·an Is·lands, the /ˈærən ˌaɪləndz; ˈærən ˌaɪləndz/ a group of three small islands off the west coast of the Republic of Ireland 阿伦群岛〔位于爱尔兰共和国西海岸附近，由三个小岛组成〕

Ar·a·rat /ˈærəræt; ˈærəræt/, **Mount** a mountain in eastern Turkey which, according to the Old Testament of the Bible, is where Noah's Ark first reached land after the great flood 亚拉腊山〔位于土耳其东部，据《圣经·旧约》所述，洪水消退后，诺亚方舟首次在此登陆〕

ar·bi·ter /ˈɑrbɪtɚ; ˈɑːbɪtə/ *n* [C] **1** someone whose opinions have a lot of influence on what other people do 权威人士: *an arbiter of taste* 品味鉴赏方面的权威人士 **2** someone or something that settles an argument between two opposing sides 仲裁人；公断人: **be the final arbiter** (=to make the final decision) 是最终的决策者

ar·bi·trage /ˈɑrbətrɑʒ; ˈɑːbɪtrɑːʒ/ *n* [U] *technical* the process of buying something such as a COMMODITY (1) or CURRENCY (1) in one place and selling it in another place at the same time【术语】套利；套汇；套购 —**arbitrageur** /ˌɑbɪtrɑˈʒɝ; ˌɑːbɪtrɑːˈʒɜː/ *n* [C]

ar·bi·tra·ry /ˈɑrbəˌtrɛrɪ; ˈɑːbɪtrəri/ *adj* **1** decided or arranged without any reason or plan, often unfairly 专横的，武断的，霸道的: *Management is weak, morale low and punishment arbitrary.* 管理不力，士气低落，惩罚武断。**2** happening or decided by chance rather than a plan 任意的，随机的: *The figure of 20% is quite arbitrary.* 20%这个数字是相当随机的。—**arbitrariness** *n* [U] —**arbitrarily** /ˈɑrbəˌtrɛrɪlɪ; ˈɑːbɪtrərɪli/ *adv*: *arbitrarily deprived of his duties* 专断地剥夺了他的职责

ar·bi·trate /ˈɑrbəˌtret; ˈɑːbɪtreɪt/ *v* [I,T] to officially judge how an argument between two opposing sides should be settled 仲裁；公断: *A committee will arbitrate between management and unions.* 由一个委员会来仲裁资方和工会的争端。—**arbitrator** *n* [C]

ar·bi·tra·tion /ˌɑrbəˈtreʃən; ˌɑːbɪˈtreɪʃən/ *n* [U] the process of judging officially how an argument should be settled 仲裁；公断: **go to arbitration** (=ask someone to arbitrate) 通过仲裁

Ar·bor Day /ˈɑrbɚ de; ˈɑːbə deɪ/ an unofficial US holiday when people plant trees. Arbor Day is celebrated on different days in different states. 植树节〔美国非官方节日。植树节的日期，各州不一〕

ar·bo·re·al /ɑrˈborɪəl; ɑːˈbɔːriəl/ *adj technical* connected with trees or living in trees【术语】有关树木的；生活在树上的

ar·bo·re·tum /ˌɑrbəˈritəm; ; ˌɑːbəˈriːtəm/ *n* [C] a place where trees are grown for scientific study 〔供科学研究用的〕树木园，植物园

ar·bour *BrE*【英】, **arbor** *AmE*【美】/ˈɑrbɚ; ˈɑːbə/ *n* [C] a shelter in a garden made by making plants grow together on a frame shaped like an ARCH[1] (4)〔花园中长满蔓藤的〕棚架，藤架；凉亭

arc /ɑrk; ɑːk/ *n* [C] **1** a curved shape 弧(状): *the arc of a rainbow* 彩虹的弧状 **2** part of a curved line or a circle 弧线，弧形: *The sun moves across the sky in an arc.* 太阳在天空以弧形运行。—see picture at 参见 CIRCLE[1] 图 **3** a flash of light formed by the flow of electricity between two points 弧光，电弧 —**arc** *v* [T]

ar·cade /ɑrˈked; ɑːˈkeɪd/ *n* [C] **1** a covered passage at the side of a row of buildings with PILLARs and arches (ARCH[1] (1)) supporting it on one side 拱廊 **2** a covered passage between two streets with shops on each side of it 拱廊式街道〔上有盖顶，两边有商店〕 **3** an AMUSEMENT ARCADE 游戏厅；游戏机室 **4** *BrE* also 又作 **shopping arcade** a large building or part of a building where there are many shops【英】室内购物商场

Ar·ca·di·a /ɑrˈkedɪə; ɑːˈkeɪdiə/ *n* [singular] *literary* a place or scene of simple pleasant country life【文】世外桃源，淳朴愉快的田园生活

ar·cane /ɑrˈken; ɑːˈkeɪn/ *adj literary* secret and mysterious【文】秘密的，神秘的: *the arcane mysteries and language of the perfume business* 香水行业的神秘特点和语言

arch- /ɑrtʃ; ɑːtʃ/ *prefix* of the highest class or rank; chief; main 最高等级的；主要的: *an archbishop* (=a chief BISHOP) 大主教 | *our archenemy* (=our main worst enemy) 我们的头号敌人 | *the company's archrivals* (=main competitors) 公司的主要竞争对手

arch 拱门 3

keystone 拱顶石

arch[1] /ɑrtʃ; ɑːtʃ/ *n* [C] **1** a structure with a curved top and straight sides that supports the weight of a bridge or building 拱顶；拱洞 **2** a curved structure above a door, window, or gate 拱门；拱窗 **3** a curved structure of bones in the middle of your foot 足弓 —see picture at 参见 FOOT[1] 图 **4** something with a curved top and straight sides 弓状物；拱形物 —see picture on page A12 参见A12页图

arch[2] *v* [I,T] to form or make something form a curved shape 拱起，(使)成拱形: *Two rows of trees arched over the driveway.* 两排树在车道上方形成拱形。| *She stretched her arms out and arched her back.* 她伸出手臂，拱起了背。

arch[3] *adj* amused because you think you understand something better than other people 戏谑的；调侃的: *an arch tone* 调侃的口吻 —**archly** *adv*: *"I think someone here has a little secret," she said archly.* "我认为这儿某个人有个小秘密。"她狡黠地说。

ar·chae·ol·o·gy *especially BrE*【尤英】, **archeology** *AmE*【美】/ˌɑrkɪˈɑlədʒɪ; ˌɑːkiˈɒlədʒi/ *n* [U] the study of ancient societies by examining what remains of their buildings, graves, tools etc 考古学 —**archaeologist** *n* —**archaeological** /ˌɑrkɪəˈlɑdʒɪkl; ˌɑːkiəˈlɒdʒɪkəl◂/ *adj*: *an archaeological dig* 考古发掘 —**archaeologically** /-klɪ; -kli/ *adv*

ar·cha·ic /ɑrˈke·ɪk; ɑːˈkeɪ-ɪk/ *adj* **1** old and no longer used 不再使用的: *The English used in the letter is an archaic form.* 这封信中使用的英语已过时了。**2** old-fashioned and needing to be replaced 过时的，陈旧的: *The central heating in the building is positively archaic.* 这幢建筑的中央供暖系统已经非常陈旧了。**3** connected to ancient times 古代的

ar·cha·is·m /ˈɑrkɪˌɪzəm; ɑːˈkeɪ-ɪzəm/ *n* [C] an old word or phrase that is no longer used〔不再使用的〕古词，古语

arch·an·gel /ˈɑrkˈendʒəl; ˈɑːkeɪndʒəl/ *n* [C] the chief ANGEL (1) in the Jewish, Christian, and Muslim religions〔犹太教、基督教和伊斯兰教中的〕天使长，大天使

arch·bish·op /ˈɑrtʃˈbɪʃəp; ˌɑːtʃˈbɪʃəp◂/ *n* [C] a priest of the highest rank, who is in charge of all the churches in a particular area 大主教

Archbishop of Can·ter·bu·ry, the /ˌ‥ˈ‥‥/ the priest who is the leader of the Church of England 坎特伯雷大主教〔英国国教会领袖〕

Archbishop of West·min·ster, the /ˌ‥ˈ‥/ the priest who is the leader of the Roman Catholic Church in England and Wales 西敏寺大主教〔英格兰和威尔士罗马天主教会主教长〕

Archbishop of York, the /ˌ‥ˈ/ an important priest in the Church of England, who has the next highest rank to the Archbishop of Canterbury 约克大主教〔地位在英国国教会中仅次于坎特伯雷大主教〕

arch·bish·op·ric /ˌɑrtʃˈbɪʃəprɪk; ˌɑːtʃˈbɪʃəprɪk/ *n* [C] **1** the area governed by an archbishop 大主教的辖区 **2** the rank of archbishop 大主教的职衔

arch·dea·con /ˈɑrtʃˈdikən; ˌɑːtʃˈdiːkən◂/ *n* [C] a priest of a high rank in the Anglican church who works under a bishop〔英国国教的〕副主教

arch·di·o·cese /ˈɑrtʃˈdaɪəˌsɪs; ˌɑːtʃˈdaɪəsɪs/ *n* [C] the area that is governed by an archbishop 大主教辖区

arch·duke /ˈɑrtʃˈdjuk; ˌɑːtʃˈdjuːk◂/ *n* [C] a prince who belonged to the royal family of Austria 大公〔昔日奥地利的皇太子〕

arch·en·e·my /ˈɑrtʃˈɛnəmɪ; ˌɑːtʃˈenəmi/ *n* [C] **1** the main enemy 大敌，天字第一号敌人: *Lex Luthor, Superman's archenemy* 莱克斯·卢瑟，超人的大敌 **2** **the archenemy** *literary* the devil【文】魔王，撒旦

ar·che·ol·o·gy /ˌɑrkɪˋɑlədʒɪ; ˌɑːkiˈɒlədʒi/ *n* [U] the American spelling of ARCHAEOLOGY archaeology的美式拼法

ar·cher /ˋɑrtʃɚ; ˈɑːtʃə/ *n* [C] someone who shoots ARROWS (1) from a BOW³ (1) 射箭运动员；弓箭手

Ar·chers, The /ˋɑrtʃɚz; ˈɑːtʃəz/ a popular British radio programme that started in 1951, and can be heard twice every day. It is about an imaginary family called the Archers, who live on farms in a small village called Ambridge, and their friends and neighbours.《阿切尔斯一家》〔英国一广播节目。1951年开播以来深受欢迎，每天播出两次。该节目讲述阿切尔斯一家人及其朋友和邻居的生活。这个虚构的家庭住在安布里奇村的一个农庄〕

ar·cher·y /ˋɑrtʃərɪ; ˈɑːtʃəri/ *n* [U] the sport of shooting ARROWS (1) from a BOW³ (1) 射箭（运动）

ar·che·type /ˋɑrkəˌtaɪp; ˈɑːkɪtaɪp/ *n* [C] the most typical example of something, because it has all the most important qualities 原型；典型：*Merlin is the archetype of the wise old man.* 墨林是智慧老人的典范。—**archetypal** /ˌɑrkɪˋtaɪpl; ˌɑːkɪˈtaɪpəl◂/ *adj*: *Byron was the archetypal Romantic hero.* 拜伦是典型的浪漫主义英雄。

Ar·chi·me·des /ˌɑrkəˋmidiz; ˌɑːkɪˈmiːdiːz◂/ (?287-212 BC) a Greek MATHEMATICIAN and inventor who discovered Archimedes' Principle 阿基米德〔（公元前?287-前212），希腊数学家、发明家。他发现了阿基米德原理〕

Archimedes' prin·ci·ple /ˌ····ˈ···/ the scientific rule which explains that an object in a liquid is kept up by a force which is equal to the weight of the liquid that the object displaces 阿基米德原理〔一科学定理，即物体在液体中的浮力大小等于该物体排开的液体重量〕

ar·chi·pel·a·go /ˌɑrkəˋpɛləˌgo; ˌɑːkɪˈpeləgəʊ/ *n* [C] a group of small islands and the large area of sea around them 群岛；群岛周围的海域

ar·chi·tect /ˋɑrkəˌtɛkt; ˈɑːkɪtekt/ *n* [C] **1** someone whose job is to design buildings 建筑师，设计师 **2 the architect of sth** the person who originally thought of an important and successful idea …的设计师〔伟大思想的倡导者〕：*Gorbachev was the architect of glasnost.* 戈尔巴乔夫是"公开性"思想的设计师。

ar·chi·tec·ture /ˋɑrkəˌtɛktʃɚ; ˈɑːkɪtektʃə/ *n* **1** [U] the style and design of a building or buildings 建筑风格，建筑式样 **2** [U] the art and practice of planning and designing buildings 建筑学：*He studied architecture at university.* 他在大学里修读建筑学。**3** [U] the structure and design of something 结构：*the architecture of DNA* DNA（脱氧核糖核酸）的结构 **4** [C] *technical* the design of the inside of a computer【术语】计算机的内部设计；架构 —**architectural** /ˌɑrkəˋtɛktʃərəl; ˌɑːkɪˈtektʃərəl◂/ *adj*: *architectural features* 建筑特点 —**architecturally** *adv*: *Architecturally Chengdu is quite different from most of China.* 从建筑学的角度看，成都与中国大多数城市不一样。

ar·chive /ˋɑrkaɪv; ˈɑːkaɪv/ *n* [C] **1 archives** a large number of records that provide information about the history of a country, organization, family etc 档案，案卷 **2** a place where a large number of historical records is stored 档案馆：*the State Archives in Paris* 巴黎的国家档案馆 —**archive** *adj*: *interesting archive material* 有趣的档案资料 —**archival** /ɑrˋkaɪvl; ɑːˈkaɪvəl/ *adj*

ar·chi·vist /ˋɑrkəvɪst; ˈɑːkɪvɪst/ *n* [C] someone who works in an archive 档案保管员

arch·way /ˋɑrtʃˌwe; ˈɑːtʃweɪ/ *n* [C] **1** a passage under an ARCH¹ (1) or arches 拱廊，拱道 **2** an entrance under an arch 拱门：*He was standing in the archway outside the club.* 他站在俱乐部外的拱门内。

-archy /ɚkɪ, ɑrkɪ; əki, ɑːki/ *suffix* [in nouns 构成名词] government; rule 治理；统治：*anarchy* (=no government) 无政府（状态）| *monarchy* (=with one ruler) 君主政体

Arc·tic, the /ˋɑrktɪk; ˈɑːktɪk/ *n* the large area of land surrounding the North Pole 北极；北极地区

arctic *adj* **1** connected with or from the most northern part of the world 北极的 **2** extremely cold 极冷的：*arctic conditions* 极冷的环境

Arctic Cir·cle /ˌ··ˈ··/ *n* [singular] an imaginary line drawn around the world at a certain distance from the most northern point (the North Pole) 北极圈 —compare 比较 ANTARCTIC CIRCLE —see picture at 参见 EARTH¹ 图

Arctic O·cean, the /ˌ··ˈ··/ the ocean that surrounds the North Pole 北冰洋〔北极周围的水体〕

arc weld·ing /ˌ·ˈ··/ *n* [U] a method of joining two pieces of metal together by heating them with a special tool（电）弧焊

-ard /ɚd; əd/ *suffix* [in nouns 构成名词] someone who is usually or always in a particular state 沉湎于…的人：*a drunkard* 酒鬼

Ar·den /ˋɑrdn̩; ˈɑːdn/ an area in Warwickshire, central England, which was formerly a forest. The Forest of Arden is where Shakespeare's play *As You Like It* takes place. 阿登〔英格兰中部沃立克郡一地区，原为一片森林。莎士比亚的戏剧《皆大欢喜》就发生在阿登森林〕

Ar·dennes, the /ɑrˋdɛn; ɑːˈden/ an area of southeast Belgium, North Luxembourg, and northern France, where several important battles happened during World War I and World War II 阿登高地〔包括比利时东南部、卢森堡北部及法国北部的一个地区，两次世界大战期间在此发生过数次重大战役〕

ar·dent /ˋɑrdn̩t; ˈɑːdənt/ *adj* **1** showing strong positive feelings about an activity and determination to succeed at it 热心的；热烈的：*an ardent supporter of free trade* 自由贸易的热心支持者 **2** *literary* showing strong feelings of love【文】显示出炽热爱情的；热情的：*an ardent suitor* 热烈的求婚男子 —**ardently** *adv*

ar·dour *BrE*【英】, **ardor** *AmE*【美】/ˋɑrdɚ; ˈɑːdə/ *n* [U] **1** very strong positive feelings 激情，热诚：*They sang with real ardour.* 他们唱得很有激情。**2** *literary* strong feelings of love【文】炽热的爱情

ar·du·ous /ˋɑrdʒuəs; ˈɑːdjuəs/ *adj* involving a lot of strength and effort 费力的，艰巨的：*an arduous journey through the mountains* 艰难的山区旅行 —**arduously** *adv* —**arduousness** *n* [U]

are¹ /ɚ; ə; *strong* 强读 ɑr; ɑː/ the present tense and plural of 'be' be的现在时复数

are² /ɑr; ɑː/ *n* [C] a unit of area 公亩 —see table on page C3 参见C3页附录

ar·e·a /ˋɛrɪə; ˈeəriə/ *n* [C] **1** a particular part of a country, town etc 地区；区域：*a working-class area of Birmingham* 伯明翰的工人居住区 | *Many areas of Africa have suffered severe drought this year.* 今年，非洲的许多地区都遭遇了严重的旱灾。| **the surrounding area** (=the area around a place) 周围地区 *The police have searched the farm and the surrounding area.* 警察已搜遍了农场及其附近地区。**2** a part of a house, office, garden etc that is used for a particular purpose 场所，地方：*a no-smoking area* 无烟区 | *Come through into the dining area.* 进饭厅来。**3** a particular subject, range of activities, or group of related subjects 领域，范围，方面：[**+of**] *reforms in the key areas of health and education* 卫生及教育关键领域的改革 **4** the amount of space that a flat surface or shape covers 面积：*a formula to calculate the area of a circle* 计算圆面积的公式 | *an area of 2,000 square miles* 2000平方英里的面积 —see 见 **grey area** (GREY¹ (6))

USAGE NOTE 用法说明: AREA

WORD CHOICE 词语辨析: **area, part of the world/the country/town, region, district**

Area is the most general word for a part of the Earth's surface. An **area** can be small or large, and is not usually thought of as a fixed land division. area是指地球表面某一部分最常用的词，它所指的范围可大可小，通常并非固定划分的地方：*the shopping/downtown area of the city* 城市的购物区/商业中心区 | *a rural area of the country* 该国的农村地区 | *the Houston area* 休斯敦地区 Informally you might talk instead about a **part of the world/the country/town**. 非正式场合可以用 part of the world/the country/town 来代替 area: *There's no video shop in our part of town.* 镇上我们这一带没有影音商店。| *New England is a delightful part of the country* (usually 一般 = country area). 新英格兰是一个很有趣的地方。

A **region** is usually large, is usually part of a country,and may or may not be thought of as a fixed land division. region常指较大的地方，一般指国家的一部分，可以是也可以不是固定划分的地区：*the arctic region of Canada* 加拿大的北极地区 | *The southeast is the richest region in England.* 东南部是英格兰最富裕的地区。

A **district** is smaller than a **region**, and is usually an officially fixed area of a country or city. district比region小，通常是一国或一城市中正式固定划分的区域：*the financial district of town* 城市的金融区 | *the central district of Hong Kong* 香港的市中心 | *the Lake District* 湖区

area code /ˈ···ˌ·/ *n* [C] three numbers you use when you want to telephone someone in a different area of the US〔美国电话的〕地区代号［编码］；DIALLING CODE *BrE*【英】

a·re·na /əˋrinə; əˈriːnə/ *n* [C] **1** a building with a large flat central area surrounded by seats, where sports or entertainments take place 表演场地：*The bull was led into the arena.* 公牛被带

进竞技场。**2 the political/public/international etc arena** all the activities and people connected with politics, public life etc 政治/公众/国际等舞台: *Women are entering the political arena in larger numbers.* 越来越多的妇女进入政界。

A·rendt /ˈɛrənt; ˈeərənt/, **Han·nah** /ˈhænə; ˈhænə/ (1906-75) a US political PHILOSOPHER, writer, and teacher, who was born in Germany 阿伦特〔(1906-1975), 美国政治思想家、作家、教师, 生于德国〕

aren't /ɑrnt; ɑːnt/ *v* **a)** the short form of 缩略式= are not: *They aren't here.* 他们不在这儿。**b)** the short form of 缩略式= am not, used in questions〔用于疑问句〕: *I am your friend, aren't I?* 我是你的朋友, 不是吗?

A·res /ˈɑriz; ˈɑːriːz/ in Greek MYTHOLOGY, the god of war. In Roman mythology his name is Mars. 阿瑞斯〔希腊神话中的战神, 罗马神话中称马尔斯〕

a·rête /æˈret; əˈret/ *n* [C] a part of a mountain that consists of a long line of raised rock with steep sides 峻岭, 陡峭的山脊 —see picture on page A12 参见 A12 页图

ar·gent /ˈɑrdʒənt; ˈɑːdʒənt/ *n* [U] *poetic* a silver colour【诗】银色 —**argent** *adj*

Ar·gen·ti·na /ˌɑrdʒənˈtinə; ˌɑːdʒənˈtiːnə/ a large country in the southern part of South America. Population: 37,300,000 (2001). Capital: Buenos Aires. 阿根廷〔南美洲南部一大国。人口: 37,300,000 (2001), 首都: 布宜诺斯艾利斯〕—see also 另见 FALKLANDS WAR

ar·gon /ˈɑrgɑn; ˈɑːgɒn/ *n* [U] a chemically inactive gas that is found in the air and is sometimes used in electric lights 氩

Ar·go·nauts, the /ˈɑrgəˌnɔts; ˈɑːgənɔːts/ in ancient Greek stories, a group of strong, brave men who sailed with Jason in the ship Argo to find the Golden Fleece 阿尔戈英雄〔古希腊传说中同伊阿宋一道驾阿尔戈号船去寻找金羊毛的一群强壮、勇敢的年轻人〕

ar·got /ˈɑrgo; ˈɑːgəʊ/ *n* [C,U] informal expressions used by a particular group of people such as criminals 行话, 隐语, 黑话, 暗语

ar·gu·a·ble /ˈɑrgjuəbl; ˈɑːgjuəbəl/ *adj* not certainly true or correct and therefore easy to doubt 有疑问的, 可争辩的: *Whether or not Webb is the best person for the job is arguable.* 韦布是不是这个职务的最佳人选尚待商榷。| **it is arguable that** (=you can show good reasons why it might be true) 有理由说 *It's arguable that legislation has little effect on young people's behaviour.* 有论据表明, 立法对年轻人的行为没太大影响。—**arguably** *adv*: *Senna was arguably the greatest racing driver of all time.* 塞纳无疑是有史以来最了不起的赛车手。

ar·gue /ˈɑrgju; ˈɑːgjuː/ *v*

1 ▶DISAGREE 不同意◀ [I] to disagree with someone in words, often in an angry way 争论, 争吵: *Did you hear the couple next door arguing last night?* 昨晚你听见隔壁的夫妻在争吵吗? | **[+with]** *I'm not going to argue with you, but I think you're wrong.* 我不想和你争辩, 但是我认为你错了。| **[+about]** *They were arguing about how to spend the money.* 他们就这钱怎么花而争论不休。| **[+over]** (=argue about something, especially about who should have something) 就…争吵 *The family argued bitterly over who should inherit the house.* 这家人就谁应该继承房产激烈地争吵。

2 ▶STATE 表明◀ [I,T] to state, giving clear reasons, that something is true, should be done etc 提出理由: *a well-argued case* 说理充分的案例 | **argue that** *Croft argued that a date should be set for the withdrawal of troops.* 克罗夫特认为应该确定撤军的日期。| **argue for/against** (=argue that something should or should not be done) 据理力争/反对 *You can argue against extending the airport on the grounds of cost.* 你可以以成本太高为理由提出反对扩建机场。| **argue the point** (=discuss something) 讨论 *We could argue this point for hours without reaching any sensible conclusions.* 我们就这一点竟然讨论几个小时而得不出合理的结论。

3 argue sb into/out of sth *especially BrE* to persuade someone to do or not do something【尤英】说服某人做某事/不做某事: *Joyce argued me into buying a new jacket.* 乔伊斯说服我买了一件新夹克衫。

4 ▶SHOW CLEARLY 清楚表明◀ [T] *formal* to show that something clearly exists or is true【正式】显示出, 表明: *The commissioner's statement argues a high level of police involvement.* 长官的陈述表明警方投入了很大警力。

5 argue the toss *BrE informal* to continue to argue about a decision that has been made and cannot be changed【英, 非正式】〔对已决定的事〕唱反调; 挑剔: *How stupid of me to argue the toss with the traffic policeman.* 我真蠢, 和交警去讲理。

ar·gu·ment /ˈɑrgjəmənt; ˈɑːgjʊmənt/ *n* **1** [C] a situation in which two or more people disagree, often angrily 争论, 争辩, 争吵: **[+with]** *an argument with my husband* 跟我丈夫的争吵 | **[+about/over]** *The argument seemed to be about who was going to take the cat to the vet.* 争论似乎是关于由谁带猫去看兽医。| **have an argument** *They were having an argument about the children.* 他们为孩子的事争吵。| **get into an argument** *I got into an argument with the other driver.* 我和另一位司机吵了起来。| **win/lose an argument** *He lost his argument with the doctor.* 他说不过医生。| **heated argument** (=very angry argument) 激烈的争论 **2** [C] a set of reasons that show that something is true or untrue, right or wrong etc 论点, 论据: *Rose's argument is complex and ingenious.* 罗丝的论点全面又富有见地。| **[+for/against]** *a powerful argument against smoking* 反对吸烟的有力论据 | **argument that** *the familiar argument that the costs outweigh the benefits* 得不偿失这一常见的论点 **3** [U] the act of disagreeing or questioning something 异议; 争议: **do sth without (further) argument** *Seamus accepted the suggestion without argument.* 谢默斯完全接受这个建议。| **for the sake of argument** (=in order to discuss all the possibilities) 打个比方, 假定 *Let's say for the sake of argument that you don't take the job, then what?* 假定说你不接受这个工作会怎么样?

ar·gu·men·ta·tive /ˌɑrgjəˈmɛntətɪv; ˌɑːgjʊˈmentətɪv◂/ *adj* someone who is argumentative often argues or likes arguing 好争辩的, 好争吵的: *When he drinks he becomes argumentative.* 他一喝酒, 就爱理论。

Ar·gus /ˈɑrgəs; ˈɑːgəs/ in ancient Greek stories, a creature with many eyes who was used by the goddess Hera as a guard. Newspapers are sometimes called the 'Argus' to give the idea that they are always watching carefully for news. 阿耳戈斯〔古希腊传说中的百眼巨人, 被女神赫拉用作看守。报纸有时被称作"阿耳戈斯", 意思是说他们总是在密切关注新闻线索〕

ar·gy-bar·gy /ˌɑrdʒɪ ˈbɑrdʒɪ; ˌɑːdʒi ˈbɑːdʒi/ *n* [U] *BrE spoken* arguments or quarrelling【英口】争论; 争吵

Ar·gyll and Bute /ɑrˌgaɪl ənd ˈbjut; ɑːˌgaɪl ənd ˈbjuːt/ a COUNTY which includes the islands of Mull, Islay, Jura, and Arran, in central western Scotland, with a coast on the Atlantic Ocean 阿盖尔－比特区〔苏格兰中西部大西洋沿岸一行政区, 包括马尔岛、艾莱岛、朱拉岛和阿伦岛〕

a·ri·a /ˈɑrɪə; ˈɑːriə/ *n* [C] a song that is sung by only one person in an OPERA or ORATORIO 独唱曲; 咏叹调

-arian /ɛrɪən; eəriən/ *suffix* **1** [in nouns 构成名词] someone who is connected with or believes in a particular thing …派[主义]的人: *a vegetarian* (=someone who does not eat meat) 素食主义者 | *a librarian* (=someone who works in a library) 图书馆管理员 —see also 另见 -GENARIAN **2** [in adjectives 构成形容词] for or connected with people of this type 涉及某种人的: *a vegetarian restaurant* 素食餐馆 | *libertarian principles* 自由论者的原则

ar·id /ˈærɪd; ˈærɪ̈d/ *adj* **1** arid land is extremely dry and cannot produce many crops 干燥的, 干旱的; 贫瘠的、不毛的: *Much of Namibia is arid country.* 纳米比亚的大部分地区干旱贫瘠。**2** an arid discussion, period of time etc does not produce anything new 无创见的, 无新意的 —**aridity** /əˈrɪdətɪ; əˈrɪdɪ̈ti/ *adj*

Ar·i·el /ˈɛrɪəl; ˈeəriəl/ a character in the play *The Tempest* by William SHAKESPEARE. Ariel is a spirit with magical powers who works for Prospero 爱丽儿〔莎士比亚戏剧《暴风雨》中的精灵, 掌握魔法, 侍奉普洛斯彼罗〕

Ar·ies /ˈɛriz; ˈeəriːz/ *n* **1** [singular] the first sign of the ZODIAC, represented by a RAM (=male sheep), and believed to affect the character and life of people born between March 21 and April 20 白羊宫〔黄道的第一宫〕, 白羊座 **2** [C] someone who was born between March 21 and April 20 出生于白羊宫时段〔3 月 21 日至 4 月 20 日〕的人

a·right /əˈraɪt; əˈraɪt/ *adv old-fashioned*【过时】**1** correctly 正确地: *if I remember aright* 如果我没有记错的话 **2 set things aright** to settle problems or difficulties 解决问题[困难]

a·rise /əˈraɪz; əˈraɪz/ *v past tense* **arose** /əˈroz; əˈrəʊz/ *past participle* **arisen** /əˈrɪzn; əˈrɪzən/ [I] **1** if a problem or difficult situation arises, it begins to happen 发生: *A crisis has arisen in the Foreign Office.* 外交部发生了危机。**2** if something arises from or out of a situation, event etc, it is caused or started by that situation etc 由…引起: **[+from]** *Can we begin by discussing matters arising from the last meeting?* 我们是不是可以从讨论上次会议出现的问题开始? **3 when the need arises/should the need arise** when or if it is necessary 如果有必要: *Should the need arise for extra staff, we will contact you.* 如果有必要招聘更多的员工, 我们会和你联系。**4** *old-fashioned* to get out of bed, or stand up【过时】起床; 起立; 起来: *Daniel arose at dawn.* 丹尼尔天亮就起床了。**5** if something arises when you are moving towards it, you are gradually able to see it as you move closer 出现, 呈现: *As we sped down the highway, the lights*

of the city arose before us. 我们在公路上疾驰，城市的灯光映入眼帘。**6** *formal* if a group of people arise, they fight for or demand something they want【正式】起来〔表示觉醒〕: *Arise and fight for your rights!* 起来，为自己的权利而战！—see 见 OCCUR (USAGE)

ar·is·toc·ra·cy /ˌærəˋstɑkrəsɪ; ˌærɨˈstɒkrəsi/ *n* **1** [C] the people in the highest social class, who traditionally have a lot of land, money, and power 贵族; 贵族阶级: *dukes, earls, and other members of the aristocracy* 公爵、伯爵及其他贵族成员 | *the new LA rock 'aristocracy'* 洛杉矶摇滚乐的"新贵们" —see also 另见 UPPER CLASS **2** [U] *technical* the system in which a country is governed by the people of the highest social class【术语】贵族政治 —compare 比较 DEMOCRACY

CULTURAL NOTE 文化注释

The UK has an official aristocracy of people who have special titles. There are five different ranks, which are, from highest to lowest: duke, marquis, earl, viscount, and baron. Anyone who has one of these titles is called a PEER. Many people with these titles INHERIT*ed* the title from their father, and they are called HEREDITARY PEER*s*. Others are given the title and are not allowed to pass it on to their children, and they are called LIFE PEER*s*. All life peers are members of the House of Lords. Until 1999, all hereditary peers were members of the House of Lords. Since then, only 92 hereditary peers are allowed to be in the House of Lords, and they are chosen by a vote among all the hereditary peers. 英国有官定的贵族阶层，享有特殊爵位。爵位分五种，从高到低分别是公爵、侯爵、伯爵、子爵和男爵。拥有此等爵位的人叫做贵族。很多人是从父亲那里继承的爵位，称为世袭贵族; 另一些人获授爵位，不可传继给后代，称为终身贵族。终身贵族都是上议院议员。1999年以前，所有世袭贵族都是上议院议员，但此后获准进入上议院的世袭贵族只有92名，他们是由所有世袭贵族投票选出的。

ar·is·to·crat /əˋrɪstəˌkræt; ˈærɨstəkræt/ *n* [C] someone who belongs to the highest social class 贵族(成员)

ar·is·to·crat·ic /əˌrɪstəˋkrætɪk; ˌærɨstəˈkrætɪk◂/ *adj* belonging to or typical of the aristocracy 贵族(似)的: *old, aristocratic families* 老式的贵族家庭 | *an aristocratic manner* 贵族气派

Ar·i·stoph·a·nes /ˌærɪˋstɑfəˌniz; ˌærɨˈstɒfəniːz/ (?457-?385 BC) an ancient Greek writer of humorous plays, who many people consider the greatest writer of Greek COMEDY. His many plays include *The Frogs* and *Lysistrata*. 阿里斯托芬〔(公元前?457-前?385)，古希腊幽默剧作家。许多人认为他是最伟大的希腊喜剧作家。作品颇丰，如《蛙》和《吕西斯忒拉忒》等〕

Ar·is·tot·le /ˋærɪˌstɑtḷ; ˈærɨstɒtl/ (384-322 BC) a Greek PHILOSOPHER and scientist who has had great influence on Western thought. His many works deal with subjects such as science, politics, morality, and literature. 亚里士多德〔(公元前384-前322)，希腊哲学家、科学家，对西方思想产生过重大影响。著作颇丰，涉及科学、政治、道德和文学等诸多学科〕—**Aristotelian** /ˌærɪstəˋtiljən; ˌærɨstɒˈtiːliən/ *adj*

a·rith·me·tic[1] /əˋrɪθməˌtɪk; əˈrɪθmətɪk/ *n* [U] the science of numbers involving adding, multiplying etc 算术 —compare 比较 MATHEMATICS

ar·ith·met·ic[2] /ˌærɪθˋmɛtɪk; ˌærɪθˈmetɪk◂/ also 又作 **ar·ith·met·i·cal** /-tɪkḷ; -tɪkəl/ *adj* involving or related to arithmetic 算术的 —**arithmetically** /-kḷɪ; -kli/ *adv*

arithmetic pro·gres·sion /ˌ···· ·ˈ··/ *n* [C] a set of numbers in order of value in which a particular number is added to each to produce the next (as in 2, 4, 6, 8 ...) 算术级数，等差级数 —compare 比较 GEOMETRIC PROGRESSION

Ar·i·zo·na /ˌærəˋzonə; ˌærɨˈzəʊnə◂/ abbreviation 缩写为 **AZ** a state in the southwest of the US, north of Mexico, known for containing a large area of desert 亚利桑那州〔美国西南部一州，位于墨西哥以北，以广袤的沙漠而著称〕

ark /ɑrk; ɑːk/ *n* [C] **1** a large ship 大船 **2 the Ark** in the Bible, the large boat built by Noah to save his family and the animals from a flood that covered the earth〔《圣经》中的〕诺亚方舟 **3 out of the Ark** *BrE informal* very old or old-fashioned【英，非正式】极陈旧的; 过时的

Ar·kan·sas /ˋɑrkənˌsɔ; ˈɑːkənsɔː/ abbreviation 缩写为 **AR** a state in the south central part of the US, west of the Mississippi River 阿肯色州〔美国中南部一州，位于密西西比河以西〕

Ark of the Cov·e·nant /ˌ· · ·ˈ··/ *n* [singular] a box containing the laws of the Jewish religion that represented to the Jews the presence of God 约柜〔存放犹太教律法的箱子。在犹太人看来，约柜代表上帝的存在〕

Ark·wright /ˋɑrkraɪt; ˈɑːkraɪt/**, Sir Richard** (1732-92) a British factory owner who invented a machine for making cotton into thread, a job that was formerly done by hand. This made him and other factory owners very rich, but it also caused many workers to lose their jobs. 阿克赖特〔(1732-1792)，英国一工厂主。他发明了纺纱机，代替了手工劳动。他和其他工厂主因此而十分富有，但也造成不少工人失业〕—see also 另见 INDUSTRIAL REVOLUTION

Ar·ling·ton Na·tion·al Cem·e·tery /ˌɑrlɪŋtən ˌnæʃənḷ ˋsɛməˌtɛrɪ; ˌɑːlɪŋtən ˌnæʃənəl ˈsemɨtri/ a CEMETERY in Arlington, Virginia, where people who were in the US army, navy, air force, or government are sometimes buried 阿灵顿国家公墓〔弗吉尼亚州阿灵顿一公墓，安葬美国海、陆、空三军的一些军人及一些政府官员〕

arm 手臂; 上肢

arms folded/crossed
两臂交叉

arm in arm
臂挽臂

arms akimbo
两手叉腰

arm[1] /ɑrm; ɑːm/ *n* [C] S1 W1

1 ►BODY 身体◄ one of the two long parts of your body between your shoulders and your hands 手臂; 上肢: *Mom put her arms around me to comfort me.* 母亲搂着我给我安慰。| *Pat appeared carrying a large box under his arm.* 帕特来了，胳膊下面夹着个大盒子。| *a broken arm* 断臂 | **with arms folded/crossed** (=with your arms bent so that they are resting against your body) 两臂交叉 | **take sb by the arm** (=lead someone somewhere by holding their arm) 抓住某人的手臂 *Sid took me by the arm and hurried me out of the room.* 锡德拉着我的胳膊催促我赶快出了房间。| **take sb in your arms** (=gently hold someone with your arms) 拥抱某人 *Gerry took Fiona in his arms and kissed her.* 格里把菲奥娜抱在怀里亲吻。—see picture at 参见 BODY 图

2 ►WEAPONS 武器◄ arms [plural] weapons used for fighting wars 武器装备: *The government is cutting arms expenditure.* 政府正在削减武器开支。| **take up arms (against sb)** (=get weapons and prepare to fight) 拿起武器(对付某人) *Boys as young as 13 are taking up arms to defend the city.* 连13岁的孩子都拿起武器保卫城市。| **lay down your arms** (=put your weapons down and stop fighting) 放下武器(停战) | **under arms** *BrE* (=with weapons and ready to fight)【英】在备战状态中 *All available forces are under arms.* 所有兵种都处于备战状态中。—see also 另见 SMALL ARMS

3 ►FURNITURE 家具◄ the arm of a chair, sofa etc is the part you rest your arms on〔椅子、沙发等的〕靠手臂，扶手

4 ►CLOTHING 衣服◄ the part of a piece of clothing that covers your arm; SLEEVE 袖子

5 arm in arm if you walk arm in arm with someone, you are walking next to them with your arm in theirs 臂挽着臂

6 be up in arms *informal* to be very angry and ready to argue or fight【非正式】(气得)摩拳擦掌，愤怒: *Residents are up in arms about plans for a new road along the beach.* 居民们对在海边建新公路的计划非常愤怒。

7 welcome sb/sth with open arms to show that you are happy to see someone or eager to accept an idea, plan etc 张开双臂欢迎某人／举双手赞成某事: *We welcomed Henry's offer with open arms.* 我们举双手赞成亨利的提议。

8 give your right arm to be willing to do anything to get or do something 愿付出一切: *I'd give my right arm to be 21 again.* 如果我能再回到21岁，我愿付出任何代价。

9 at arm's length if you hold something at arm's length, you hold it away from your body 一臂之距

10 keep sb at arm's length to avoid developing a relationship with someone 疏远某人, 与某人保持一定距离: *Petra keeps all men at arm's length to avoid getting hurt.* 皮特拉跟所有的男人都保持一定距离, 以免自己受到伤害。

11 as long as your arm *informal* a list or written document that is as long as your arm is very long【非正式】〔名单或文字材料〕有胳膊那么长, 冗长

12 ▶PART OF GROUP 团体的一部分◀ a part of a large group that is responsible for a particular type of activity 职能部门; 分支机构: *the political arm of a terrorist organization* 恐怖组织的政治部门

13 ▶OBJECT/MACHINE 物体/机器◀ the arm of an object or piece of machinery is the long thin part that looks or moves like an arm 臂 (状部件): *the arm of a record player* 唱机的唱头臂 —see picture at 参见 GLASS 图

14 ▶DESIGN 设计◀ arms [plural] a set of pictures or patterns, usually painted on a SHIELD, that is used as the special sign of a family, town, university etc; COAT OF ARMS 盾徽, 盾形纹章

15 on your arm *old-fashioned* if a man has a woman on his arm, she is walking beside him holding his arm【过时】挽着你的胳膊走 —see also 另见 **(with) arms akimbo** (AKIMBO), **babe in arms** (BABE (1)), **brothers in arms** (BROTHER[1] (5)), **fold sb/sth in your arms** (FOLD[1] (7)), **twist sb's arm** (TWIST[1] (9))

arm² *v* [T] **1** to provide weapons for yourself, an army, a country etc in order to prepare for a fight or a war 为…提供武器装备, 武装: **arm sb with sth** *We armed ourselves with whatever we could lay our hands on.* 我们用各种能找到的东西武装自己。—see also 另见 ARMED (1), UNARMED **2** to provide all the information, power etc that are needed to deal with a difficult situation or argument 准备好, 装备: *I've armed myself with all the facts I need to prove my point.* 我已准备好充分的事实来证明自己的观点。

ar·ma·da /ɑr`mɑdə; ɑːˈmɑːdə/ *n* [C] a large group of something, usually war ships 大批; 大群〔尤指舰队〕: *a vast armada of foreign visitors* 大批外国游客

Armada, the a collection of armed ships sent by Spain in 1588 to fight against England, which was defeated by the English navy 无敌舰队〔1588年西班牙派遣攻打英国的一支舰队, 后来被英国海军打败〕

ar·ma·dil·lo /ˌɑrmə`dɪlo; ˌɑːməˈdɪləʊ/ *n* [C] a small animal that has a shell made of hard bone-like material, and lives in parts of North and South America 犰狳〔产于美洲的小动物, 身上有骨质硬壳〕

Ar·ma·ged·don /ˌɑrmə`gɛdn̩; ˌɑːməˈgedn/ *n* [singular,U] a terrible battle that will destroy the world 〔会毁灭世界的〕大决战: *a nuclear Armageddon* 核大战

Ar·ma·gnac /ˌɑrmən`jæk; ˈɑːmənjæk/ *trademark* a type of BRANDY (=a strong alcoholic drink) made in southwest France and usually drunk from a small glass after a meal【商标】阿马尼亚克〔产于法国西南部的一种白兰地, 通常饭后倒在小玻璃杯里饮用〕

ar·ma·ment /`ɑrməmənt; ˈɑːməmənt/ *n* **1** [C usually plural 一般用复数] the weapons and military equipment used in an army 军备, 武器: *nuclear armaments* 核武器 **2** [U] the process of preparing an army or country for war by giving it weapons 武装, 备战 (行动) —compare 比较 DISARMAMENT

ar·ma·ture /`ɑrmətʃə; ˈɑːmətʃə/ *n* [C] **1** the part of a GENERATOR, motor etc that turns around to produce electricity, movement etc 〔发电机、电动机等的〕转子, 电枢 **2** a frame that you cover with clay or other soft material to make a model 〔支撑塑像的〕骨架

arm·band /`ɑrmˌbænd; ˈɑːmbænd/ *n* [C] **1** a band of material that you wear around your arm to show that you have an official position, or as a sign of MOURNING 臂章; 袖标;〔服丧时戴的〕臂纱 **2** [usually plural 一般用复数] *BrE* one of two bands of plastic filled with air that you wear around your arms when you cannot swim【英】〔游泳用的充气〕浮臂, 救生臂环

arm·chair¹ /`ɑrmˌtʃɛr; ˈɑːmtʃeə/ *n* [C] a comfortable chair with sides that you can rest your arms on 扶手椅 —see picture at 参见 CHAIR[1] 图

arm·chair² /`ɑrmˌtʃɛr; ˈɑːmtʃeə/ *adj* **armchair traveller/critic etc** someone who talks or reads about being a traveller etc, but does not have any real experience of it 空谈的旅行家/批评者等

S3 W3 **armed** /ɑrmd; ɑːmd/ *adj* **1** carrying weapons, especially a gun 带武器的, 有装备的: *The hostages were kept under armed guard.* 人质由武装卫兵看守。| **[+with]** *The suspect is armed with a shotgun.* 疑犯身上带着猎枪。| **heavily armed** (=with a lot of weapons) 有许多武器装备的 *a heavily armed battleship* 重装甲的战舰 | **armed robbery** (=using guns) 持枪抢劫 | **armed combat** (=fighting with weapons) 枪战 | **armed conflict** (=war) 武装冲突 *This political dispute could lead to armed conflict.* 这一政治争端可能会导致武力冲突。| **armed to the teeth** (=carrying a lot of weapons) 武装到牙齿的; 全副武装的 **2** having something such as knowledge or skills that make it possible for you to do something or deal with something difficult 装备〔足够的知识或技术〕的: **[+with]** *She came to the meeting armed with all the facts and figures to prove us wrong.* 她带着能证明我们错了的所有的事实和数字来参加会议。

armed forc·es /ˌ· ˈ· ·/ *n* **the armed forces** *plural* a country's military organizations, including the army, navy, and airforce 武装力量; 武装部队

Ar·me·ni·a /ɑr`minɪə; ɑːˈmiːniə/ a country in the extreme southwest of Asia, surrounded by Georgia, Azerbaijan, Iran, and Turkey. It used to be a republic of the Soviet Union. Population: 3,300,000 (2001). Capital: Yerevan. 亚美尼亚〔亚洲西南端一国, 位于格鲁吉亚、阿塞拜疆、伊朗和土耳其之间。人口: 3,300,000 (2001), 首都: 埃里温〕—**Armenian** *n, adj*

arm·ful /`ɑrmˌful; ˈɑːmfʊl/ *n* [C] the amount of something that you can hold in one or both arms 〔单臂或双臂的〕一抱 (之量): **[+of]** *an armful of books* 一抱书

arm·hole /`ɑrmˌhol; ˈɑːmhəʊl/ *n* [C] a hole in a shirt, dress, jacket etc that you put your arm through 〔衣服的〕袖孔

ar·mi·stice /`ɑrməstɪs; ˈɑːmɨstɨs/ *n* [C] an agreement to stop fighting, usually for a short time 停战, 休战 (协定) —compare 比较 CEASEFIRE, TRUCE

Armistice Day /ˈ··· ˌ·/ November 11th, celebrated as the ANNIVERSARY of the end of the World War I in 1918 停战纪念日〔即11月11日, 纪念1918年第一次世界大战结束的日子〕—see also 另见 REMEMBRANCE DAY

ar·mour *BrE*【英】, **armor** *AmE*【美】/`ɑrmə; ˈɑːmə/ *n* [U] **1** metal or leather clothing that protects your body, worn by soldiers in battles in former times 〔旧时战士在战斗中穿的〕盔甲: *a knight in shining armour* 穿着闪亮盔甲的骑士 | *suit of armor* 全套盔甲 **2** a strong metal layer that protects military vehicles 装甲: *armour-clad warships* 装甲战舰 **3** a strong layer or shell that protects some plants and animals 〔动植物的〕硬壳, 硬皮 —see also 另见 **a chink in sb's armour** (CHINK[1] (3))

ar·moured *BrE*【英】, **armored** *AmE*【美】/`ɑrməd; ˈɑːməd/ *adj* **1** armoured vehicles have an outside layer made of metal to protect them from attack 装甲的: *armored personnel carriers* 装甲运兵车 **2** an armoured army used armoured vehicles 配备装甲车辆的: *an armoured division* 装甲师

armoured car *BrE*【英】, **armored car** *AmE*【美】/ˌ·· ˈ·/ *n* [C] **1** a car that has special protection from bullets etc, used especially by important people 防弹车 **2** a military vehicle with a strong metal cover and usually a powerful gun 装甲车

ar·mour·er *BrE*【英】, **armorer** *AmE*【美】/`ɑrmərə; ˈɑːmərə/ *n* [C] someone who makes or repairs weapons and ARMOUR 〔制造或修理武器及装甲的〕军械士

armour-plat·ed *BrE*【英】, **armor-plated** *AmE*【美】/ˌ·· ˈ··◂/ *adj* something, especially a vehicle, that is armour-plated has an outer metal layer to protect it 〔尤指车辆〕装甲的 —**armour plating** *n* [U] —**armour plate** *n* [U]

ar·mour·y *BrE*【英】, **armory** *AmE*【美】/`ɑrmərɪ; ˈɑːməri/ *n* [C] a place where weapons are stored 军械库, 武器库

arm·pit /`ɑrmˌpɪt; ˈɑːmˌpɪt/ *n* [C] **1** the hollow place under your arm where it joins your body 腋 (窝) —see picture at 参见 BODY 图 **2** *AmE slang* a very unpleasant or ugly place【美俚】最差的地方, 肮脏的角落: *Butte is the armpit of Montana.* 比尤特是蒙大拿州最差的地方。

arms con·trol /ˈ· ·ˌ·/ *n* [U] the attempts by powerful countries to limit the number and type of war weapons that exist 军备控制

arms race /ˈ· ·/ *n* [C usually singular 一般用单数] the attempt by different countries to produce powerful weapons 军备竞赛: *the nuclear arms race* 核军备竞赛

Arm·strong /`ɑrmstrɑŋ; ˈɑːmstrɒŋ/, **Lou·is** /`luɪ; ˈluːi/ (1900-71) a US JAZZ musician, band leader, and singer, who played the TRUMPET and was also known as 'Satchmo'. He is one of the most important jazz musicians ever. 阿姆斯特朗〔(1900-1971), 美国爵士音乐家、乐队领队、歌手。他演奏小号, 绰号"书包嘴", 被认为是历史上最重要的爵士音乐家之一〕

Armstrong, Neil /nil; niːl/ (1930-) a US ASTRONAUT who was the first man to walk on the moon, in 1969 阿姆斯特朗〔(1930-), 美国宇航员, 1969年成为登上月球的第一人〕

ar·my /ˋɑrmɪ; ˈɑːmi/ *n* **1 the army** the part of a country's military force that is trained to fight on land in a war 陆军: *He joined the army when he was 17.* 他17岁就参军了。| [also+plural verb *BrE* 英] *The army are helping to clear up after the floods.* 洪水过后, 军队在帮助清理灾后现场。| **be in the army** *Both my sons are in the army.* 我的两个儿子都在当兵。**2** [C] a large organized group of people trained to fight on land in a war 武装组织: *The rebel armies have taken control of the radio station.* 叛军已经控制了广播电台。| **raise an army** (=collect and organize an army to fight a battle) 组建军队 **3** [C] a large number of people or animals involved in the same activity 团体; 队伍; 大群: *The village hall is maintained by an army of volunteers.* 村礼堂由一支志愿者队伍维修。—compare 比较 AIRFORCE, NAVY

Arn·hem /ˋɑrnəm; ˈɑːnəm/ a city in the Netherlands where British and allied (ALLY) forces landed in the World War II and where a great many soldiers died 阿纳姆〔荷兰一城市, 二战期间英军和盟军登陆的地方, 大批士兵在此阵亡〕

Ar·nold /ˋɑrnḷd; ˈɑːnəld/, **Ben·e·dict** /ˋbɛnədɪkt; ˈbenɨdɪkt/ (1741-1801) an American military leader, who BETRAY*ed* his country when he changed to support the British during the American Revolutionary War 阿诺德〔(1741-1801), 美军军官。独立战争期间, 他背叛国家, 改变立场, 支持英国〕

Arnold, Mat·thew /ˋmæθju; ˈmæθjuː/ (1822-88) a British writer and poet, famous for his poems such as *Dover Beach* and *The Scholar Gypsy*, as well as for his books and ESSAY*s* discussing literature and society 阿诺德〔(1822-1888), 英国作家、诗人。作品有《多佛滩》、《吉卜赛学者》等诗歌及文学、社会评论, 并以此著名〕

a·ro·ma /əˋromə; əˈrəʊmə/ *n* [C] a strong pleasant smell 芳香, 香气, 香味: *the aroma of toast and fresh coffee* 烤面包片和新鲜咖啡的香味

a·ro·ma·ther·a·py /əˌroməˋθɛrəpɪ; əˌrəʊməˈθerəpi/ *n* [U] a treatment that uses MASSAGE (=rubbing the body) with pleasant smelling natural oils to reduce pain and make you feel well 芳香剂疗法, 香薰疗法 —**aromatherapist** *n* [C]

ar·o·mat·ic /ˌærəˋmætɪk; ˌærəˈmætɪk◂/ *adj* having a strong, pleasant smell 芳香的: *aromatic oils* 芳香油 —**aromatically** /-kḷɪ; -kli/ *adv*

a·rose /əˋroz; əˈrəʊz/ the past tense of ARISE

a·round¹ /əˋraʊnd; əˈraʊnd/ *adv* **1** used to say that something is placed or arranged so that it surrounds something else 四周, (在) 周围: *The winner held up his trophy, with many of the spectators crowded around.* 获胜者高举奖杯, 四周围满了观众。| *a bouquet of a dozen red roses, with a silver ribbon wrapped around* 用银色丝带扎着的一打红玫瑰 | **all around** *The prison was set on an island, with high walls all around.* 监狱设在一个岛上, 四周有高墙。**2** [only after verb 仅用于动词后] used to say that someone or something is moving in a circular movement 旋转; 围绕: *She watched the cogs and wheels going around silently.* 她静静地看着齿轮在旋转。**3 sit/stand/lie etc around** to sit, stand etc without doing anything in particular, especially so that people think you are wasting time 没事闲坐着/站着/躺着等: *There were a few suspicious looking people hanging around outside.* 有几个看起来可疑的人在外面游荡。**4 fool/mess etc around** used to mean that someone is wasting time by doing something stupid or dishonest 无所事事, 混日子; 胡闹: *Stop messing around! I know you've hidden it.* 别胡闹了! 我知道你把它藏起来了。**5** [only after verb 仅用于动词后] in many places or in many different parts of a particular area 到处, 四处: *Don't leave all your papers lying around – anyone could read them.* 不要到处乱放你的文件 —— 谁都能看到。| *When I finished college, I travelled around for a while before I got my first job.* 大学毕业以后, 我找到第一份工作之前到处旅游了一段时间。| *Since it's your first day here, would you like me to show you around?* 这是你到这儿的第一天, 要我带你到处走走吗? **6** if someone is around, they are in the same place as you 附近, 在近处: *He went down to the sports centre but there was no-one around that he knew.* 他去了体育中心, 但周围没有一个他认识的人。| *Why is there never a policeman around when you need one?* 需要警察的时候为什么附近就找不到呢? **7 the best ... around/the most exciting ... around etc** used to say that someone or something is the best, the most exciting thing of this kind 当前最佳的…/最令人激动的…等: *East 17 are one of the most popular groups around.* "East 17" 是当今最受欢迎的演唱组合之一。**8 get around to (doing) sth** to finally do something that you have been intending to do for a long time 找时间做某事; 终于去做某事〔指早就想做的事〕: *I'll get around to the decorating one of these days.* 这几天我要找时间布置一下。**9** facing in the opposite direction 反向: *Slowly he turned the boat around, hoping the patrol would not hear the engines.* 他慢慢将船调过头去, 希望巡逻队不会听到发动机声。**10 have been around** *informal* to have had experience of many different situations, so that you can deal with new situations confidently【非正式】生活经历丰富; 见过世面 **11 2 feet/100 cms etc around** *AmE* having a CIRCUMFERENCE of 2 feet, 100 cms etc【美】周长2英尺/100厘米等 —see also 另见 ROUND², ROUND³ (USAGE)

around² *prep* **1** used to say that something is placed or arranged so that it surrounds something else 环绕, 在…周围: *The whole family were sitting around the dinner table chatting.* 全家人围坐在饭桌旁聊天。| *She had a beautiful woollen shawl wrapped around her shoulders.* 她肩上围着一条漂亮的羊毛披肩。**2** used to say that someone or something is moving in a circular movement 绕着…: *A few wolves were prowling around the deer's carcass.* 几条狼在一只鹿的尸体旁绕圈子。| *There are reports of a light aircraft flying around and around the Sears Tower.* 有报道说一架轻型飞机在希尔斯大厦上空来回盘旋。**3** in many places or parts of a particular area or place 到…四处, 在…各处: *We took a wander around the garden after breakfast.* 早餐后, 我们在花园里到处走走。| *They have branches dotted around the country.* 他们的分支机构遍布全国各地。| **all around** *There were flowers all around the apartment, making it look more homely.* 公寓里到处是鲜花, 更给人一种家的感觉。**4** if someone or something is around a particular place, they are in or near that place 在…附近, 在…近处: *I think he lives somewhere around the centre of town.* 我想他住在市中心附近的某个地方。| *Is there a bank around here?* 这附近有银行吗? **5** if you move or go around something, you move around the side of it instead of going through or over it 绕过…: *If the gate is locked you'll have to go around the side of the house.* 如果大门锁上了, 你们就得从房子侧面绕过去。**6** if something is organized around a particular person or thing, it is organized according to their needs, ideas, beliefs etc 围绕…, 以…为中心; 根据: *Why does everything have to be organised around what Callum wants to do?* 为什么一切都要按照卡勒姆的意愿安排呢? | *Their whole society was built around their belief in their gods.* 他们的整个社会都建立在他们对诸神信仰的基础上。**7 get around** to avoid or solve a particular problem or difficult situation 逃避, 回避; 用计防止: *How do we get around the problem of the new tax laws?* 我们怎样才能避开新税法的问题? **8 around 200/5,000 etc** used when guessing a number, amount etc 200/5000等左右: *There must have been around 40,000 people in the stadium.* 体育场里肯定有四万人左右。| **around about** *Most guests started to make their way home around about 10 o'clock.* 大多数客人在10点钟左右开始回家。—see also 另见 ROUND³

Around the World in Eigh·ty Days /·ˌ· · ˌ· · ˌ· · ˈ· ·/ a book by Jules Verne about an Englishman called Phileas Fogg, who travels around the world in 80 days with his servant Passepartout in order to win a BET《八十天环游地球》〔儒勒·凡尔纳创作的小说。小说中一位名叫斐利斯·福格的英国人及其仆人百事通因跟人打赌而在80天内环游地球〕

a·rous·al /əˋraʊzḷ; əˈraʊzəl/ *n* [U] excitement, especially sexual excitement 唤起;〔尤指性欲的〕激起

a·rouse /əˋraʊz; əˈraʊz/ *v* [T] **1 arouse interest/expectations etc** to make you become interested, expect something etc 引起兴趣/期望等: *Matt's behavior was arousing the interest of the neighbours.* 马特的行为逐渐引起了邻居的兴趣。**2 arouse anger/fear/dislike etc** to make someone feel very angry, afraid etc 激起愤怒/恐惧/讨厌等 **3** to make someone feel sexually excited 激起…的性欲 **4** *formal* to wake someone【正式】唤醒: [+**from**] *Anne had to be aroused from a deep sleep.* 不得不唤醒熟睡中的安妮。

ar·peg·gi·o /ɑrˋpɛdʒɪˌo; ɑːˈpedʒiəʊ/ *n* [C] the notes of a musical CHORD (1) played separately rather than all at once 琶音; 琶音和弦

arr 1 the written abbreviation of 缩写= arranged by (由…) 改编, 改写: *music by Mozart, arr Britten* 莫扎特原曲, 布里顿改编 **2** the written abbreviation of 缩写= arrives or arrival

ar·raign /əˋren; əˈreɪn/ *v* [T] *technical* to make someone come to court to hear what the court says their crime is【术语】提审, 传讯: *arraigned on a charge of murder* 因被控谋杀而被提审 —**arraignment** *n* [C,U]

Ar·ran /ˋærən; ˈærən/ an island in the Firth of Clyde, western Scotland 阿伦岛〔苏格兰西部克莱德地区福斯湾一岛屿〕

ar·range /əˋrendʒ; əˈreɪndʒ/ *v* **1** [I,T] to organize or make plans for something such as a meeting, party, or trip 安排, 筹划: *James is arranging a big surprise party for Helen's birthday.* 詹姆斯正在为海伦张罗一个使她惊喜的生日聚会。| *I'd like to arrange*

a business loan. 我想安排一项商业贷款。| **arrange to do sth** *Have you arranged to meet Mark this weekend?* 你安排了这个周末见马克吗？| **arrange for sb to do sth** *I've arranged for the window cleaner to come on Thursday.* 我已经安排好一个窗户清洁工星期四来。| **arrange sth with sb** *Beth arranged a meeting with the marketing director.* 贝丝安排了和营销总监见面。| **arrange for sth** *The company will arrange for a taxi to meet you at the airport.* 公司将安排一辆出租车去机场接你。| **arrange when/where/how etc** *We still have to arrange how to get home.* 我们还必须安排好怎样回家。| **as arranged** *Matthew arrived at 2 o'clock as arranged.* 马修于两点钟如约而至。**2** [T] to put a group of things or people in a particular order or position 整理，排列，布置：*I've arranged my CDs in alphabetical order.* 我把我的激光唱片按字母顺序排好了。| **arrange sth in pairs/groups etc** *The children were arranged in lines according to height.* 孩子们按身高排成几队。**3** [T] to write or change a piece of music so that it is suitable for particular instruments 改编〔乐曲〕：[+for] *a symphony arranged for the piano* 改编为钢琴演奏曲的交响曲

arranged mar·riage /ˌ·ˈ··/ *n* [C,U] a marriage in which the parents choose a husband or wife for their child 包办婚姻：*Arranged marriages are still common in the Indian community.* 包办婚姻在印度社会仍然很普遍。

ar·range·ment /ə`rendʒmənt; ə'reɪndʒmənt/ *n* **1** [C usually plural 一般用复数] the things that you must organize so that an event, meeting etc can happen 安排，筹划，准备：[+for] *What exactly are the arrangements for the wedding?* 婚礼到底是如何安排的？| **make arrangements** *The local newspaper made arrangements for an interview with Professor Stein.* 当地报纸安排对斯坦教授进行专访。| **seating/travel/sleeping etc arrangements** *I'm not very happy about the sleeping arrangements.* 我对住宿安排不太满意。**2** [C,U] something that has been organized or agreed on; agreement 议定之事，协定：*Our loan is by special arrangement with the bank.* 我们的贷款是经与银行特别协商确定的。| **come to some arrangement** (=make an agreement that is acceptable to everyone) 达成协议 *It would usually cost $500, but I'm sure we can come to some kind of arrangement.* 正常价格是500美元，但我相信我们可以再协商。**3** [C,U] a group of things that have been arranged in an attractive or neat way, or the act of arranging a group of things in this way 整理[布置、排列]好的东西：*a beautiful flower arrangement* 漂亮的插花样式 **4** [C,U] a piece of music that has been written or changed for a particular instrument 改编曲：*an arrangement of an old folk song for chorus* 把一首传唱已久的民歌改编成合唱曲

ar·rant /`ærənt; 'ærənt/ *adj old-fashioned* used to emphasize how bad something is【过时】坏透的，彻头彻尾的，极端的：*arrant nonsense* 一派胡言

ar·ray¹ /ə`re; ə'reɪ/ **1** [C usually singular 一般用单数] a group or collection of things, usually arranged so that you can see them all 排列，陈列：*The museum has a vast array of uniforms and ceremonial robes.* 博物馆展出一系列样式繁多的制服和礼服。**2** [C usually singular 一般用单数] a group of people, especially people who are important or special 队列，一队：*a dazzling array of acting talent* 一群光彩夺目的演艺天才 **3** [C,U] *literary* fine clothes, especially those worn for a special occasion【文】盛装：*The king came aboard with his guests and family in colourful array.* 国王穿着艳丽的盛装与宾客和家人上了船。**4** [C] *technical* a set of numbers or signs, or of computer memory units, arranged in lines across or down【术语】〔数字、符号的〕排列，数列，阵列；数组

array² *v* [T usually passive 一般用被动态] **1** *literary* to arrange something in an attractive way【文】布置，排好 **2** *formal* to put soldiers in position ready for battle【正式】布阵，部署 **3** *literary* to dress in good quality clothes【文】身着盛装，打扮：*She came in arrayed in all her finery.* 她衣着华丽地来了。

ar·rears /ə`rɪrz; ə'rɪəz/ *n* [plural] **1 be in arrears** if someone is in arrears or if their payments are in arrears, they are late in paying something that they should pay regularly, such as rent 拖欠：*Teachers' pay is in arrears and the school says it can't afford to pay.* 教师的工资仍然拖欠着，校方说没钱支付。| **be four weeks/three months etc in arrears** *The rent money is two months in arrears.* 租金拖欠了两个月。| **fall into arrears** (=become late with payments) 拖欠 **2** money that you owe someone because regular payments such as rent have not been paid at the right time 逾期欠款：*We've got 3 months arrears to pay on the video.* 我们买录像机的钱有三个月的欠账未付。**3 be paid in arrears** to be given your wages at the end of the period you have worked …之后付款：*a salary paid monthly in arrears* 每月后行支付的薪金

ar·rest¹ /ə`rɛst; ə'rest/ *v* [T] **1** if the police arrest you, they take you away because they think you have done something illegal 逮捕，拘捕：*Police arrested 26 demonstrators, over half of them women.* 警方逮捕了26名示威者，其中一半以上是妇女。| **arrest sb for sth** *Wayne was arrested for dangerous driving.* 韦恩因危险驾驶被拘留。**2** *formal* to stop something happening or to make it happen more slowly【正式】抑制；阻止：*drugs used to arrest the spread of the disease* 用于控制疾病蔓延的药物 | *arrested development* 受到遏制的发展 **3 arrest your attention** *formal* to make you look or listen to something, because it is interesting or exciting【正式】引起你的注意；吸引你：*Her warning tone arrested my attention.* 她警告的口气引起了我的注意。

arrest² *n* [C,U] the act of taking someone away and guarding them because they may have done something illegal 逮捕：**make an arrest** *The police made several arrests.* 警方逮捕了好几个人。| **be under arrest** (=kept by the police) 被逮捕 *He's under arrest and awaiting trial.* 他被拘留候审。| **place/put sb under arrest** (=arrest someone) 逮捕某人

ar·riv·al /ə`raɪvḷ; ə'raɪvəl/ *n* **1** [U] the act of arriving somewhere 到达，抵达：*the late arrival of the train* 火车误点 | *Joe's sudden arrival spoiled all our plans.* 乔的突然到来破坏了我们所有的计划。| **arrival at/in** *Shortly after our arrival in Turkey Lisa became very ill.* 我们到达土耳其不久，莉萨就病倒了。| **on arrival** (=when you arrive) 到达时 *He was rushed to the hospital but was dead on arrival.* 他被急速送往医院，但到达时已死亡。**2 the arrival of** the time when an important new idea, method, or product is first used or discovered …的到来[出现]：*The arrival of democracy has thrown the economy into chaos.* 民主的出现使经济陷入混乱。**3 new arrival** someone who has just arrived in a particular place to live, work etc 新来的人：*New arrivals in the camp were greeted with suspicion.* 新来到营地的人都受到怀疑。**4** [C] a plane or train that arrives in an airport or station 进站列车；进港飞机 —opposite 反义词 DEPARTURE

ar·rive /ə`raɪv; ə'raɪv/ *v* [I]

1 ▶GET SOMEWHERE 到某处◀ to get to the place you are going to 到达，抵达：*Give me a call to let me know you've arrived safely.* 打个电话给我，告诉我你已平安到达。| **arrive in/at/from** *Elaine should be arriving in the States about now.* 伊莱恩现在该到美国了。

2 ▶BE DELIVERED 送到◀ if something arrives, it is brought or delivered to you 送达：*By the time the letter finally arrived, I'd heard the news.* 信最终送到时我早已知道消息了。

3 ▶EVENT 事件◀ if an event or particular period of time arrives, it happens 发生；降临，来到：*At last the day of the carnival arrived!* 狂欢节的日子终于来到了！

4 ▶STH NEW 新事物◀ if a new idea, method, product etc arrives, it begins to exist or starts being used 出现；启用：*Children don't play outside as much since computer games arrived.* 自从有了电脑游戏，孩子们就不怎么出外玩了。

5 ▶BIRTH 出生◀ to be born 出生：*Sharon's baby arrived just after midnight.* 莎伦的孩子午夜刚过就出生了。

6 arrive at a conclusion/agreement/idea etc to reach an agreement etc after much effort 得出结论/达成协议/有了主意等：*After three weeks of confusion we arrived at the conclusion that there was a security leak.* 经过三个星期的混乱状态，我们得出结论：安全措施有疏漏之处。

7 ▶SUCCESS 成功◀ to achieve success 取得成功：*When he saw his name printed on the door he knew he'd arrived!* 当他看到自己的名字被印在门上，他知道自己成功了。—see 见 REACH¹ (USAGE)

ar·ro·gance /`ærəgəns; 'ærəgəns/ *n* [U] the quality of thinking that you are very important so that you behave rudely 傲慢：*The arrogance of that man – pretending he'd never seen us before!* 瞧那个人多傲慢！装作从来没见过我们的样子！

ar·ro·gant /`ærəgənt; 'ærəgənt/ *adj* so proud of your own abilities or qualities that you behave as if you are much more important than anyone else 傲慢的，趾高气扬的，目中无人的，妄自尊大的：*I found him arrogant and overbearing.* 我发现他妄自尊大，盛气凌人。—**arrogantly** *adv*: *He strutted about the room arrogantly.* 他趾高气扬地在屋子里踱步。

ar·ro·gate /`ærəˌget; 'ærəgeɪt/ *v* **arrogate sth to yourself** *formal* to claim that you have a particular right, position etc without having the legal right to it【正式】霸占；冒称；擅取：*Having seized power he arrogated to himself the right to change the law.* 他攫取大权以后，便僭取了修改法律的权力。

ar·row /`æro; 'ærəʊ/ *n* [C] **1** a weapon like a thin straight stick with a point at one end that you shoot with a BOW³ (1) 箭，矢 **2** a sign in the shape of an arrow, used to show people which direction to go in 箭号，箭头(符号)：*Follow the red arrows to the*

X-ray department. 顺着红箭头指的方向去X光科。—see also 另见 STRAIGHT ARROW

ar·row·head /ˈæroˌhɛd; ˈærəʊhed/ *n* [C] a sharp pointed piece of metal or stone fixed to one end of an arrow 箭镞，箭头

ar·row·root /ˈæroˌrut; ˈærəʊruːt/ *n* [U] flour made from the root of a tropical American plant 葛粉

arse[1] /ɑrs; ɑːs/ *n BrE*【英】**1** [C] an impolite word for the part of your body that you sit on 屁股〔非礼貌用词〕**2** [C] *spoken* an impolite word for a stupid and annoying person; arsehole【口】笨蛋，饭桶〔非礼貌用词〕: *Jake's such an arse, I don't know why she's going out with him!* 我不知道她为何跟杰克这种笨蛋交往! **3 my arse!** *spoken* an impolite way of saying that you do not believe something【口】胡扯!〔非礼貌说法〕: *He says he's got a new car? My arse! He hasn't got any money!* 他说他买了一辆新车? 胡扯! 他根本没有钱! **4 shift/move your arse** *spoken* an impolite way of telling someone to hurry up【口】快点!〔非礼貌用语〕: *Come on! Shift your arse or we'll be late.* 快点! 不然我们就迟到了。**5 be right up sb's arse** *spoken* an impolite way of saying that someone is driving very close to the back of the car in front of them【口】就要撞到前车的尾部〔非礼貌用语〕—see also 另见 ASS, **pain in the arse/ass etc** (PAIN[1] (3)), SMART ARSE

arse[2] *v* [I] *BrE slang*【英俚】**can't/couldn't be arsed** to not do something because you are feeling too lazy 懒得做某事: *I just can't be arsed making my own lasagne this time – I'll buy one instead.* 这次，我不想费事做意大利面条了，我去买一份。

arse about/around *phr v* [I] to waste time 浪费时间; 游手好闲: *He's been arsing about in the garden all day.* 他整天在花园里游荡。

arse·hole /ˈɑrsˌhol; ˈɑːshəʊl/ *n* [C] *BrE*【英】**1** *spoken* an impolite word for a stupid and annoying person【口】傻瓜蛋〔非礼貌用词〕; ASSHOLE *AmE*【美】**2** an impolite word for the ANUS 屁眼，肛门〔非礼貌用词〕

Ar·se·nal /ˈɑrsn̩əl; ˈɑːsənəl/ an English football team from North London 阿森纳队〔英国北伦敦一足球队〕

arsenal *n* [C] **1** a store of weapons 一大批储备的武器: **[+of]** *The police found an arsenal of guns in the terrorist's hideout.* 警察在恐怖分子藏匿的地方发现了一大批枪支。**2** a building where weapons are stored 武器库，军火库

ar·se·nic /ˈɑrsn̩ɪk; ˈɑːsənɪk/ *n* [U] a very poisonous substance sometimes used for killing rats 砷，砒霜

ar·son /ˈɑrsn̩; ˈɑːsən/ *n* [U] the crime of deliberately making something burn, especially a building 纵火(罪)，放火(罪) —**arsonist** *n* [C]

S1 W1 **art**[1] /ɑrt; ɑːt/ *n* **1** [U] the use of painting, drawing, SCULPTURE etc to represent things or express ideas 美术，绘画; 艺术: *an example of Indian art* 印度绘画的典范 | **modern art** *the Museum of Modern Art* 现代美术馆 **2** [U] objects that are produced by art, such as paintings, drawings etc 美术作品; 艺术品: *an art exhibition* 艺术作品展 **3** [U] the skill of drawing or painting 绘画技巧: *He excelled at art at school.* 上学时他擅长绘画。**4 the arts** [plural] art, music, theatre, film, literature etc all considered together 艺术〔指绘画、音乐、戏剧、电影、文学等的统称〕: *more government funding for the arts* 政府对文学艺术投入更多的资金 **5 arts** also 又作 **the arts** [plural] subjects of study that are not scientific, such as history, languages etc 人文学科，文科 —see also 另见 HUMANITIES **6** [C,U] the ability or skill involved in doing or making something 技术; 技巧: **the art of doing something** *Television is ruining the art of conversation.* 电视简直是在糟蹋谈话艺术。| **be quite an art** (=be quite difficult) 需要些技巧，不太容易 *Driving a car through central London is quite an art.* 开车穿过伦敦市中心还真需要点技术。| **have/get sth down to a fine art** (=do something very well) 把某事做得出色[精巧] *I've got the early morning routine down to a fine art.* 我把清晨的例行工作干得很妥当。

art[2] *v* **thou art** *old use* used to mean 'you are' when talking to one person【旧】你是〔you are的古说法〕

art dec·o /ˌɑr ˈdeko; ˌɑː ˈdekəʊ/ *n* [U] a style of art and decoration that uses simple shapes and was popular in Europe and America in the 1920s and 1930s 装饰派艺术(风格)〔20世纪20和30年代流行的一种〕

art di·rec·tor /ˈ· ·ˌ· ·/ *n* [C] someone who organizes the clothes, lights, scenery etc for a film〔电影等的〕美术指导

ar·te·fact, artifact /ˈɑrtɪˌfækt; ˈɑːtɪ̵fækt/ *n* [C] an object such as a tool, weapon etc that was made in the past and is historically important 人工制品〔有史学价值的武器、工具等〕，手工艺品: *an exhibition of ancient Egyptian artefacts* 古埃及器物展览

Ar·te·mis /ˈɑrtəməs; ˈɑːtɪ̵mɪs/ in Greek MYTHOLOGY, the GODDESS of hunting and the moon. In Roman mythology her name is Diana. 阿耳忒弥斯〔古希腊神话中的狩猎和月亮女神，罗马神话中称狄安娜〕

ar·ter·i·al /ɑrˈtɪriəl; ɑːˈtɪəriəl/ *adj* [only before noun 仅用于名词前] **1** involving the arteries 动脉的: *arterial blood* 动脉血 **2 arterial road/railway line etc** a main road, railway line etc 公路/铁路干线等

ar·ter·i·o·scle·ro·sis /ɑrˈtɪrɪˌosklɪˈrosɪs; ɑːˌtɪəriəʊsklɪ̵ˈrəʊsɪ̵s/ *n* [U] a disease in which your arteries become hard, which stops the blood from flowing through them smoothly 动脉硬化(症)

ar·te·ry /ˈɑrtərɪ; ˈɑːtəri/ *n* [C] **1** one of the tubes that carries blood from your heart to the rest of your body 动脉 —compare 比较 VEIN (1) **2** a main road, railway line, river etc 道路干道; 铁路干线; 河的干流

ar·te·si·an well /ɑrˈtiʒən ˈwɛl; ɑːˌtiːziən ˈwel/ *n* [C] a WELL[4] (1) from which the water is forced up out of the ground by natural pressure 自流井，承压井

art·ful /ˈɑrtfəl; ˈɑːtfəl/ *adj* clever at deceiving people 狡猾的，奸诈的: *He's an artful little devil and always gets what he wants.* 他是个狡诈的小家伙，总能得到想要的东西。—**artfully** *adv*: *artfully concealed pockets* 隐藏得很巧妙的衣袋 —**artfulness** *n* [U]

Artful Dodg·er, the /ˌ· ·ˈ· ·/ a character in the book *Oliver Twist* by Charles Dickens. The Artful Dodger is a young PICKPOCKET (=someone who steals things from people's pockets) who belongs to a group of thieves led by Fagin. 逮不住的机灵鬼〔查尔斯·狄更斯《雾都孤儿》中的人物，费金小偷团伙中的小扒手〕

art gal·le·ry /ˈ· ,· · ·/ *n* [C] a building where important paintings are kept and shown to the public 美术馆，艺术画廊

art house /ˈ· ·/ *n* [C] a cinema that shows mainly foreign films or films made by small film companies 艺术影院

ar·thri·tis /ɑrˈθraɪtɪs; ɑːˈθraɪtɪ̵s/ *n* [U] a disease that causes a lot of pain in the joints of your body 关节炎 —**arthritic** /-ˈθrɪtɪk; -ˈθrɪtɪk/ *adj*: *arthritic fingers* 患关节炎的手指

Ar·thur /ˈɑrθɚ; ˈɑːθə/ in old stories, a king of Britain 亚瑟〔传说中的一位不列颠国王〕—**Arthurian** /ɑrˈθʊriən; ɑːˈθjʊəriən/ *adj*

Arthur, Chester Alan (1829-86) a US politician who was a member of the Republican Party and was President of the US from 1881 until 1885 阿瑟〔(1829-1886)，美国政治家、共和党成员，并担任过美国总统(1881-1885)〕

Ar·thu·ri·an Le·gend /ɑrˌθʊrɪən ˈlɛdʒənd; ɑːˌθjʊəriən ˈledʒənd/ old stories about King Arthur, his court at Camelot, the magician Merlin, and the Knights of the Round Table. These stories were first told more than 1000 years ago, and are found in Welsh, English, French, and German literature. 亚瑟王传奇〔亚瑟王及其卡米洛宫廷、术士默林和圆桌骑士的传奇故事。故事相传于一千多年前，见于威尔士、英格兰、法国、德国的文学作品中〕

ar·ti·choke /ˈɑrtɪˌtʃok; ˈɑːtɪ̵tʃəʊk/ *n* [C] **1** also 又作 **globe artichoke** a plant with thick pointed leaves that are eaten as a vegetable 朝鲜蓟，洋蓟 —see picture on page A9 参见A9页图 **2** also 又作 **Jerusalem artichoke** a plant that has a root like a potato that you can eat 菊芋，洋姜 —see picture on page A9 参见A9页图

ar·ti·cle /ˈɑrtɪkl; ˈɑːtɪkəl/ *n* [C] **1** a thing, especially one of a group of things (一件)物品: *Most of our wedding presents were household articles that we really needed.* 我们收到的结婚礼物大都是我们确实需要的家居用品。| **article of clothing/furniture/jewellery etc** *She didn't take much with her, just a few articles of clothing.* 她没带太多东西，只带了几件衣服。**2** a piece of writing about a particular subject in a newspaper, magazine etc 文章，论文，专题: *Have you seen that article in the Star about stress management?* 你看到《星报》上那篇讲述如何应付压力的文章了吗? **3** a part of a law or legal agreement, especially a numbered part 条款: *Article 1 of the constitution guarantees freedom of religion.* 宪法的第一条保障宗教信仰自由。**4** *technical* a word used before a noun to show whether the noun refers to a particular example of something or to a general example of something【术语】冠词: **the definite article** (='the' in English) 定冠词 | **the indefinite article** (='a' or 'an' in English) 不定冠词 **5 articles** *BrE* an agreement by which someone finishes their education, especially as a lawyer, by working for a company【英】见习契约; 师徒合约 **6 an article of faith** something that you feel very strongly about so that it affects how you think or behave 信念，信条 S2 W1

ar·ti·cled /ˈɑrtɪkl̩d; ˈɑːtɪkəld/ *adj* someone who is articled to a company of lawyers, ACCOUNTANTS etc, is employed by that company while they are training to become a lawyer etc 订有见习契约的: *an articled clerk* 订有见习合约的文员

Articles of Con·fed·e·ra·tion, the /ˌ· · · · · · ˈ· ·/ an agreement made in 1781 by the 13 original colonies (COLONY)

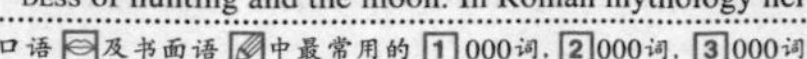
口语 S 及书面语 W 中最常用的 1 000词，2 000词，3 000词

of the US, which established a government for the US, and which was used as the basic law of the country until the Constitution of the United States was written and agreed in 1789《邦联条例》〔1781年美国最初的13个殖民地制定的协定。该条例确定了美国的政府形式, 履行着基本法的职能, 直至1789年制定并通过《美国宪法》〕

ar·tic·u·late¹ /ɑrˋtɪkjəlɪt; ɑːˈtɪkjʊlət/ *adj* **1** able to talk easily, clearly and effectively about things, especially difficult subjects 能清楚表达的; 口齿伶俐的: *bright, articulate 17-year-olds* 聪明且表达能力强的17岁的青年人 —opposite 反义词 INARTICULATE **2** writing or speech that is articulate is very clear and easy to understand even if the subject is difficult 表达清楚的; 发音清晰的 **3** *technical* having joints【术语】有关节的, 分节的: *Grasshoppers are articulate insects.* 蚱蜢是分节昆虫。—**articulately** *adv* —**articulateness** *n* [U]

ar·tic·u·late² /ɑrˋtɪkjəˌlet; ɑːˈtɪkjʊleɪt/ *v* [I] **1** to express what you are thinking or feeling very clearly 清楚地表达: *muddled emotions that I found difficult to articulate* 难以表达清楚的糊涂情感 **2** to speak or pronounce your words clearly and carefully 口齿清楚地讲话[发音]

ar·tic·u·la·ted /ɑrˋtɪkjəˌletɪd; ɑːˈtɪkjʊleɪtɪd/ *adj* having two or more parts that are joined together by a moving joint 铰接式的: **articulated bus/vehicle etc** *It's amazing how easily those articulated lorries turn corners.* 那些铰接式货车转弯非常灵敏, 真令人称奇。

ar·tic·u·la·tion /ɑrˌtɪkjəˋleʃən; ɑːˌtɪkjʊˈleɪʃən/ *n* **1** [U] the production of speech sounds 发音, 咬字: *clear articulation* 清晰的发音 **2** [U] the expression of thoughts or feelings in words〔思想、感情的〕表达: *the articulation of her suffering* 她对所受痛苦的倾诉 **3** [C] *technical* a joint, especially in a plant【术语】关节;〔植物的〕节

ar·ti·fact /ˋɑrtɪˌfækt; ˈɑːtɪfækt/ *n* [C] another spelling of ARTEFACT artefact的另一种拼法

ar·ti·fice /ˋɑrtəfɪs; ˈɑːtɪfɪs/ *n formal*【正式】**1** [U] the use of clever tricks 机智; 诡诈, 窍门: *Her charm was all artifice.* 她的魅力全在于她的机智。**2** [C] a clever trick, especially one used to deceive someone 巧计; 诡计

3 **ar·ti·fi·cial** /ˌɑrtəˋfɪʃəl; ˌɑːtɪˈfɪʃəl◂/ *adj* [usually before noun 一般用于名词前] **1** not made of natural materials or substances 人造的, 人工的: *artificial sweeteners* 人造甜味剂 **2** not real or natural but deliberately made to look real or natural 假的, 仿造的: *an artificial leg* 义肢 **3** artificial behaviour is not natural or sincere because someone is pretending to be something they are not 虚假的, 不真挚的, 矫揉造作的: *an artificial smile* 牵强的微笑 **4** happening because someone has made it happen and not as part of a natural process 人为的: *High import taxes give their goods an artificial advantage in the market.* 高进口税使他们的产品在市场上获得人为的优势。—**artificially** *adv*: *Food prices are being kept artificially low.* 食品价格正被人为地控制在低水平。—**artificiality** /ˌɑrtəˌfɪʃɪˋælətɪ; ˌɑːtɪfɪʃiˈælɪti/ *n* [U]

artificial in·sem·i·na·tion /ˌ····· ··ˈ··/ *n* [U] the process of making a woman or female animal PREGNANT (1) using a piece of equipment, rather than naturally 人工授精

artificial in·tel·li·gence /ˌ····· ·ˈ···/ also 又作 **AI** *n* [U] the study of how to make computers do things that people can do, such as make decisions, see things etc 人工智能

artificial res·pi·ra·tion /ˌ····· ··ˈ··/ *n* [U] a way of making someone breathe again when they have stopped by blowing air into their mouth; MOUTH-TO-MOUTH RESUSCITATION 人工呼吸

ar·til·le·ry /ɑrˋtɪlərɪ; ɑːˈtɪləri/ *n* **1** [U] large guns, especially ones on wheels or fixed in one place, such as on a ship 炮, 大炮 **2 the artillery** the part of the army that uses these weapons 炮兵

ar·ti·san /ˋɑrtəzn̩; ˌɑːtɪˈzæn/ *n* [C] someone who does skilled work with their hands; CRAFTSMAN 工匠, 手艺人

3 2 **art·ist** /ˋɑrtɪst; ˈɑːtɪst/ *n* [C] **1** someone who produces art, especially paintings or drawings 画家, 美术家; 艺术家: *It's not always easy to earn a living as an artist.* 作为画家, 谋生也不是易事。**2** a professional performer, especially in music, dance, or the theatre 艺术家; 艺人: *Many of the artists in the show donated their fee to charity.* 参加演出的许多艺人将演出收入捐给慈善事业。**3** *informal* someone who is extremely good at something【非正式】高手, 技术高超的人: *He's no ordinary baker, the man's an artist.* 他绝不是普通的面包师, 简直是个艺术大师。

ar·tiste /ɑrˋtist; ɑːˈtiːst/ *n* [C] a professional singer, dancer, actor etc who performs in a show 职业演艺人员, 艺人

ar·tis·tic /ɑrˋtɪstɪk; ɑːˈtɪstɪk/ *adj* **1** connected with art or culture 美术的, 艺术的; 美术家的, 艺术家的: *I'm not sure about the artistic merit of much of Dali's work.* 我不太肯定达利大部分作品的艺术价值。**2** showing skill or imagination in any of the arts 富于艺术想象力的, 有艺术才华的: *What a beautiful picture, I never realized you were so artistic.* 多美的画! 我从来没有意识到你这样有艺术才华。**3** an artistic arrangement, design etc looks attractive and has been done with skill and imagination 有艺术技巧的; 有创意的: *food presented in an artistic way* 摆放得很精美的食品 —**artistically** /-klɪ; -kli/ *adv*

art·ist·ry /ˋɑrtɪstrɪ; ˈɑːtɪstri/ *n* [U] skill in a particular artistic activity 创作天资; 艺术才华; 艺术性: *an example of the photographer's artistry* 摄影家艺术才华的范例

art·less /ˋɑrtlɪs; ˈɑːtləs/ *adj* natural, honest, and sincere 天真自然的, 纯朴的; 不造作的: *She chatted away about her life with artless confidence.* 她充满自信, 毫不造作地谈起自己的生活。—**artlessly** *adv* —**artlessness** *n* [U]

art nou·veau /ˋɑr nuˋvo; ˌɑː nuːˈvəʊ/ *n* [U] a style of art that used pictures of plants and flowers, popular in Europe and America at the end of the 19th century 新艺术(派)〔19世纪末流行于欧美的一种装饰艺术风格〕

arts and crafts /ˌ· · ˈ·/ *n* [plural] the arts that involve making things with your hands, such as POTTERY etc 手工艺, 工艺(美术)

Arts Coun·cil, the /ˈ· ˌ··/ an organization in Britain which is supported by the government and provides financial help for many different organizations involved in the theatre, art, music, the cinema etc 艺术总会〔英国政府支持的一个机构, 为戏剧、美术、音乐、电影等事业单位提供资助〕

art·work /ˋɑrtwɝk; ˈɑːtwɜːk/ *n* [U] pictures that are made for a book or magazine, or for another product such as a computer PROGRAM 插图

art·y /ˋɑrtɪ; ˈɑːti/ *BrE*【英】, **art·sy** /ˋɑrtsɪ; ˈɑːtsi/ *AmE*【美】*adj informal* someone who is arty knows a lot about art or does a lot of art【非正式】懂[搞]艺术的: *arty types gathered in a corner at the party* 懂艺术的人聚集在晚会的一角

arty-craft·y /ˌ··ˈ··◂/ *BrE*【英】, **art·sy craft·sy** /ˌɑrtsɪ ˋkræftsɪ; ˌɑːtsi ˈkrɑːftsi◂/ *AmE*【美】*adj* someone who is arty-crafty makes things at home and does all kinds of art, especially in a way that is not very professional 自以为懂艺术的

art·y-fart·y /ˌɑrtɪ ˋfɑrtɪ; ˌɑːti ˈfɑːti◂/ *BrE*【英】, **art·sy-fart·sy** /ˌɑrtsɪ ˋfɑrtsɪ; ˌɑːtsi ˈfɑːtsi◂/ *AmE*【美】*adj informal* someone who is arty-farty tries too hard to show that they are interested in art【非正式】冒充对艺术感兴趣的, 附庸风雅的

Aruba /əˋrubə; əˈruːbə/ an island in the Caribbean Sea, just north of Venezuela. It is a DEPENDENCY of the Netherlands but has its own government. Population: 70,000 (2001). Capital: Oranjestad. 阿鲁巴〔加勒比海一岛屿, 位于委内瑞拉以北, 荷兰属国, 但有独立的政府。人口: 70,000 (2001), 首府: 奥拉涅斯塔德〕

-ary /ɛrɪ; əri/ *suffix* **1** [in adjectives 构成形容词] of or concerning something; that is something …的; 与…有关的: *planetary bodies* (=that are PLANETS) 天体 | *customary* 习惯的 **2** [in nouns 构成名词] someone connected with something 与…有关的人: *the beneficiaries of the will* (=people who get something good from it) 遗嘱的受益人 | *a functionary* (=someone with duties) 小官员 **3** [in nouns 构成名词] a thing or place connected with or containing things of a particular kind 与…有关的东西[场所]: *a library* (=containing books) 图书馆 | *an ovary* (=containing eggs) 卵巢

Ar·y·an /ˋɛrɪən; ˈeəriən/ *n* [C] someone from Northern Europe, especially someone with fair hair and blue eyes 雅利安人,〔尤指金发碧眼的〕北欧人 —**Aryan** *adj*

as¹ /əz; əz; *strong* 强读 æz; æz/ *adv, prep* **1 as old/fat/clever etc as sb/sth** equally old, fat etc as someone or something else 像某人/某物一样老/胖/聪明等: *My brother is not as old as me.* 我弟弟年纪没我大。| *Her ring is twice as big as mine.* 她的戒指有我的两个大。| **as soon as possible** (=as soon as you can) 尽快 | **just as clever/clean/happy etc** *Tina's clever, but her brother is just as clever.* 蒂娜聪明, 她的弟弟同样聪明。—see also 另见 **as good as** (GOOD¹) **2 such as** for example 比如: *a heavy land horse such as a Suffolk* 像萨福克马一样能干重活的马 | *"There are plenty of opportunities for young people." "Oh yeah, such as?"* "年轻人有的是机会。" "是吗, 比方说?" | **such ... as** *The disease attacks such birds as parrots and canaries.* 这种病会侵袭像鹦鹉和金丝雀之类的鸟类。—see also 另见 **no such ... as** (SUCH¹ (6)) **3 as a teacher/mother/actor etc** used when you are describing someone's job or the main purpose of someone or something 作为老师/母亲/演员等: *As parents we are concerned for our children's future.* 作为父母, 我们关注孩子的未来。| *Speaking as your doctor, I would not advise this.* 作为你的医生, 我建议不要这样。| *It's not bad as a first attempt.* 作为第一次尝试, 这样的

结果已经不错了。| *The children all dressed up as animals.* 孩子们都打扮成动物模样。**4 as a result of sth** because of something 作为某事的结果: *Several businesses went under as a result of the recession.* 由于经济衰退, 好几家企业倒闭。**5 be regarded as sth** to be considered to be something 被看作是某物: *'Novecento' is regarded by many as Bertolucci's best film.* 许多人认为《一九○○》是贝托鲁奇最好的电影。—see also 另见 **as one** (ONE[2] (16))

as[2] *conjunction* **1** used in comparisons 像…一样: *I can't run as fast as I used to.* 我跑得不如过去那样快。| *Jim works in the same office as my sister does.* 吉姆和我妹妹在同一个办公室工作。**2** in the particular way or manner mentioned 照…的方法, 正如…: *Do as I say!* 按我说的去做! | *We'd better leave things as they are until the police arrive.* 在警察到来以前, 我们最好保持现场原样。| *As I mentioned in my last letter, I'll be back in Ohio in June.* 正如我上封信提到的, 我将在6月份回到俄亥俄州。| *David, as you know, has not been well lately.* 正如你所知, 戴维近来身体不大好。| **as usual** *Roberta was late as usual.* 罗伯塔和往常一样又迟到了。**3** while or when (正当)…的时候: *I saw Peter as I was getting off the bus.* 我下公共汽车的时候看见了彼得。| *As time passed, things seemed to get worse.* 随着时间的推移, 情况似乎变得更加糟糕了。**4** used to state why a particular situation exists or why someone does something 因为, 由于: *As we're both tired, let's just grab a takeaway.* 我们俩都累了, 来吃点外卖食品吧。| **seeing as** (=since) 因为, 既然 *A cup of tea? I hardly think so, seeing as I'm going out in about two minutes.* 来杯茶? 我想不必了, 你瞧, 我两分钟以后就走。**5** though 尽管, 虽然: *Unlikely as it might seem, I'm tired too.* 尽管看起来不像, 但我的确也累了。| *Try as she might, Sue couldn't get the door open.* 无论休怎样努力, 她就是打不开门。| *As popular as he is, the President hasn't always managed to have his own way.* 尽管总统很受人欢迎, 但他也并非总能按自己的方式办事。**6 so cold/heavy/quick etc as to... or such an idiot/a disaster etc as to...** used to show the reason that makes something happen or not happen 如此冷/重/快等以至于…; 这么个大傻瓜/这么一场灾难等以至于…: *The water was so cold as to make swimming quite impossible.* 水这么冷, 没法游泳。| *How could he have been such an idiot as to trust them in the first place?* 首先, 他怎么这样傻, 竟信任他们呢? **7 so as to do sth** with the purpose of doing something 为了做某事: *The little boy ran off so as not to be caught.* 为了不被抓住, 小男孩跑开了。**8 as for sb/sth** *especially spoken* an expression meaning 'concerning'; used when you are starting to talk about someone or something new that is connected with what you were talking about before【尤口】至于, 就某人/某物而言: *Nick can stay, but as for you, you can get out of my sight.* 尼克可以留下来, 至于你, 最好不要让我看见。**9 as yet** [used in negatives 用于否定句] until and including the present time 到现在为止(尚未): *We've had no word from Colin as yet.* 我们到现在为止也没得到科林的任何消息。**10 as if.../as though... a)** in a way that suggests that something is true or not true 好像: *You look as if you've had a good time.* 你看起来好像玩得挺开心。| *It sounds as though she's been really ill.* 听起来她好像病得很重。| *Mandy felt as if they were all ganging up on her.* 曼迪觉得他们好像在合伙对付她。| **as if to say** *Beckworth shook his head as if to say "don't trust her".* 贝克沃思摇摇头, 好像是要说"别信她"。**b)** used to suggest a possible explanation for something although you do not think that this is the actual explanation 仿佛, 好像: *That news reporter always sounds as if he's drunk.* 那位新闻播音员听上去老像喝醉了酒似的。| *You make it sound as if you have to go without food for days on end!* 你的话听起来好像在说你不得不连续几天不吃东西! **11 it's not as if...** used to say that something is definitely not true, about a situation or someone's behaviour 其实并不: *Why do they never go on holiday? I mean it's not as if they're poor, is it?* 他们为什么从来也不去度假呢? 我的意思是他们并不穷, 对吗? | *I don't know why you're so frightened of her, it's not as if she's got any power over you.* 我不明白你为什么这样怕她, 似乎她并没有摆布你的权力。**12 as if you would/as if you care/as if it matters** used to say that someone would definitely not do something, does not care etc or that something does not matter at all 就好像你会(做)/好像你很在乎/好像事关重大似的: *Margaret told me she'd never speak to me again! As if I cared.* (=I do not care at all) 玛格丽特说她再也不会跟我说话了! 好像我会在乎似的。| *"I reckon Ken's deliberately ignoring us." "As if he would!"* (=he would not ignore us) "我猜肯是故意不理我们的。" "他不会。" **13 as it is a)** according to the situation that actually exists, especially when that situation is different from what you expected or need 事实上, 实际情况是: *They hoped to finish the kitchen by Friday, but as it is they'll probably have to come back next week.* 他们希望星期五把厨房建完, 但事实上, 他们很可能下周还得回来。**b)** already 已经: *Just keep quiet, you're in enough trouble as it is.* 安静点, 你的麻烦已经够多了。**14 as from today/15th December/next June etc** also 又作 **as of today etc** starting from today, 15th December etc and continuing 从即日/12月15日/明年6月等起: *As from today, you are in charge of the office.* 从即日起, 你负责办公室的工作。| *As of now, there will be no more paid overtime.* 从现在起不再有加班费。**15 as against** in comparison with 跟…相比: *Profits this year are $2.5 million as against $4 million last year.* 跟去年的(利润)400万美元相比, 今年的利润是250万美元。**16 as to whether/who/which etc** an expression meaning 'concerning' used when speaking about arguments and decisions 至于是否/谁/哪个等: *Frank was very uncertain as to whether it was the job for him.* 至于这工作是不是适合他, 弗兰克实在拿不准。| *advice as to which suppliers to approach* 关于与哪些供应商接洽的建议 **17 as much as to say** *especially spoken* expressing something in actions rather than words【尤口】等于说: *He shrugged, as much as to say he wasn't interested.* 他耸了耸肩, 等于在说他不感兴趣。**18 as it were** used when describing someone or something in a way that is not quite exact 可以说是: *Jim Radcliffe became our idol as it were, the man we all wanted to be.* 吉姆·拉德克利夫可以说是我们的偶像, 我们都想成为他那样的人。**19 as to** according to a particular standard or principle 根据, 依照: *The fabrics were arranged as to size and colour.* 纺织品按规格和颜色排列。**20 as is/was/does etc** *formal* in the same way as someone or something else is, does etc【正式】…也如此: *Eve's very tall, as was her mother.* 伊芙个子很高, 她妈妈个子也高。| *I voted Labour, as did my wife.* 我投了工党的票, 我妻子也是。—see also 另见 **not ... as such** (SUCH[2] (4)), **as well** (WELL[1] (6)), **as well as** (WELL[1] (5)), **might (just) as well** (MIGHT[1] (8))

asap /ˌe ɛs e ˋpi; ˌeɪ es eɪ ˈpiː/ the abbreviation of 缩写= 'as soon as possible'

as·bes·tos /æsˋbɛstəs; æsˈbestəs/ *n* [U] a grey mineral that does not burn easily, used as a building material or in protective clothing 石棉

as·cend /əˋsɛnd; əˈsend/ *v formal*【正式】**1** [I] to move up through the air 上升, 升高: *He could feel a current of warm air ascending from the street.* 他能感受到一股热流从街上升腾起来。**2** [T] to climb 攀登, 爬: *We were walking on the forest path, ascending a steep slope.* 我们走在森林小路上, 顺着一个陡峭的山坡往上爬。**3** [I,T] to lead up to a higher position 上升, 向上: *The stairs ascended in a graceful curve.* 楼梯呈优美的弧形向上盘旋。**4 ascend the throne** to become king or queen 登上王位, 登基 **5 in ascending order** if a group of things are arranged in ascending order, each thing is higher, or greater in amount, than the one before it 按升序排列 —opposite 反义词 DESCEND

as·cen·dan·cy, ascendency /əˋsɛndənsɪ; əˈsendənsi/ *n* [U] a position of power, influence or control 优势; 支配(地位): [+over/in] *He slowly gained ascendancy in the group.* 他渐渐地控制了这群人。

as·cen·dant[1] /əˋsɛndənt; əˈsendənt/ also 又作 **ascendent** *n* **be in the ascendant** to be or become powerful or popular 有支配力; 占有优势: *During this period the trade union view was in the ascendant.* 这一时期, 工会的观点占了上风。

ascendant[2] also 又作 **ascendent** *adj* **1** becoming more powerful or popular 影响力渐大的; 占优势的 **2** rising 上升的

as·cen·sion /əˋsɛnʃən; əˈsenʃən/ *n* [U] the act of moving up 上升, 升高

Ascension Day /·ˈ·· ·/ a Christian holy day on the Thursday 40 days after Easter, when Christians remember when Christ went up to heaven (the Ascension) 耶稣升天节〔复活节过后40天的星期四〕

as·cent /əˋsɛnt; əˈsent/ *n* **1** [C usually singular 一般用单数] a path or way up to the top of something, for example a mountain 向上的路; 上坡: *a rugged and abrupt ascent* 崎岖陡峭的上坡路 **2** [C usually singular 一般用单数] the act of climbing something or moving upwards 上升, 攀登: *We rested in the valley before beginning the ascent.* 我们开始攀登之前, 在山谷休息了一会儿。**3** [U] the process of becoming more important, powerful, or successful than before 演变, 前进: *the ascent of man to modern civilization* 人类朝着现代文明迈进 —opposite 反义词 DESCENT (1, 2, 4)

as·cer·tain /ˌæsəˋten; ˌæsəˈteɪn/ *v* [I,T] *formal* to find out if a fact that you think is true is really true【正式】弄清, 确定, 查明: *The police were never able to ascertain the true facts.* 警察永远也查不出真相。| [+how/when/why etc] *He could not as-*

A

certain where the clouds ended and the snow-covered rocks began. 他无法确定哪里是云层的边缘，哪里是冰雪覆盖的山岩的起点。—**ascertainable** *adj*

as·cet·ic /əˈsɛtɪk; əˈsetɪk/ *adj* living without any physical pleasures or comforts, especially for religious reasons〔尤指因宗教原因〕苦行的，禁欲的：*the ascetic life of Buddhist monks* 佛教僧人的清苦生活 —**ascetic** *n* [C] —**ascetically** *adv* —**asceticism** *n* [U]

As·cot /ˈæskət; ˈæskɒt/ —see 见 ROYAL ASCOT

ascot *n* [C] *AmE* a wide piece of material worn by men loosely folded around their neck inside their collar; CRAVAT【美】〔男人戴的〕领巾

as·cribe /əˈskraɪb; əˈskraɪb/ *v*

ascribe sth **to** sb/sth *phr v* [T] *formal*【正式】**1** to believe that something happens or exists because of someone or something else 把…归(因)于：*The melody is ascribed to Bach.* 这首曲子被认为是巴赫所作。| *They ascribe the country's difficulties to the last government's policies.* 他们把国家的困境归因于上届政府的政策。**2** to believe something or someone has a particular quality 认为〔某人或某物〕具有…特点：*The Malays ascribe healing properties to this fruit.* 马来人认为这种水果有治病的功效。—**ascribable** *adj* [+to]

ASEAN /ˈæsɪˌæn; ˈæsiˌæn/ *n* [singular] Association of South-East Asian Nations; an association whose aim is to encourage the economic development of southeast Asia. Its members are Indonesia, Malaysia, Thailand, Singapore, Vietnam, Brunei, Laos, Cambodia, Myanmar, and the Philippines. 东盟，东南亚国家联盟〔旨在促进东南亚经济发展的一个组织。成员国有印度尼西亚、马来西亚、泰国、新加坡、越南、文莱、老挝、柬埔寨、缅甸、菲律宾〕

a·sep·tic /əˈsɛptɪk; eɪˈseptɪk/ *adj* a wound that is aseptic is completely clean without any harmful BACTERIA〔伤口〕经消毒的，无菌的

a·sex·u·al /eˈsɛkʃuəl; eɪˈsekʃuəl/ *adj* **1** not having sexual organs or having sex 无性器官的；无性(别)的 **2 a)** not seeming to have any sexual qualities 无性别特征的：*He strikes me as a completely asexual person.* 他给我的印象是个毫无性别特征的人。**b)** not interested in sexual relations 无性欲的，对性不感兴趣的 —**asexually** *adv*: *a plant that reproduces asexually* 无性繁殖的植物

As·gard /ˈæsˌgard; ˈæsgɑːd/ in Norse MYTHOLOGY, the home of the gods and of people who died bravely in battle 阿斯加尔德〔斯堪的纳维亚神话中诸神及英勇牺牲的将士的住所〕—see also 另见 VALHALLA

ASH /æʃ; æʃ/ *n* [singular] Action on Smoking and Health; a British organization that opposes smoking and the TOBACCO industry 吸烟与健康行动组织〔英国一反对吸烟及烟草工业的组织〕

ash *n* [C,U] **1** the soft grey powder that remains after something has been burnt 灰，灰烬：*cigarette ash* 香烟灰 | *The house burnt to ashes.* 那房子烧成了灰烬。**2** a very hard wood, or the tree, common in Britain and North America, that produces this 梣(树)，白蜡树 **3 ashes** [plural] the ash that remains when a dead person's body is burned 骨灰：*We scattered my father's ashes over the lake.* 我们把父亲的骨灰撒入湖中。

3 **a·shamed** /əˈʃemd; əˈʃeɪmd/ *adj* [not before noun 不用于名词前] **1** feeling shame because of something you have done 羞耻的；内疚的；惭愧的：**be ashamed of doing sth** *I was ashamed of having lied to my mother.* 我对向母亲说谎的事感到很内疚。| **be ashamed that** *Barry was ashamed that he had lost his temper.* 巴里因自己发脾气感到很惭愧。| **You ought to be ashamed (of yourself)** *spoken* (=used to tell someone they should feel guilty about something)【口】你应为自己的行为感到羞耻 *You ought to be ashamed of yourself – treating your sister like that!* 你应当为自己那样对待妹妹感到羞愧！**2** feeling uncomfortable or upset, especially because someone does something that embarrasses you 感到不好意思的，难为情的：[+of] *Sherry is at that age when kids are ashamed of their parents.* 谢里正处于因父母而感到难为情的年纪。| **be ashamed to be/do sth** *That kind of behaviour makes me ashamed to be British.* 那种行为使我感到作为一个英国人很惭愧。—see 见 SHAME[1] (USAGE)

ash·can /ˈæʃˌkæn; ˈæʃkæn/ *n* [C] *AmE old-fashioned* a GARBAGE CAN【美，过时】垃圾箱

Ash·croft /ˈæʃkrɔft; ˈæʃkrɒft/, **Dame Peg·gy** /ˈpɛgɪ; ˈpegi/ (1907-91) a popular British actress who appeared in the theatre in many Shakespeare plays, and in films such as *The Thirty-Nine Steps* (1935) and *A Passage to India* (1984) 阿什克罗夫特〔(1907-1991)，颇受观众喜爱的英国女演员。她出演过莎士比亚的许多戏剧，以及《三十九级台阶》(1935)、《印度之行》(1984) 等电影〕

Ashe /æʃ; æʃ/, **Arthur** (1943-93) a US tennis player who, in 1975, was the first black man to win the men's singles competition at Wimbledon 阿什〔(1943-1993)，美国网球运动员。他1975年获温布尔登网球赛男子单打冠军，是获此殊荣的首位黑人选手〕

ash·en /ˈæʃən; ˈæʃən/ *adj* being a pale grey colour like ash 灰色的：*her ashen face* 她面如土色

Ash·es, the /ˈæʃɪz; ˈæʃɪz/ the name given to the competition between the English and Australian CRICKET teams 灰烬杯〔英格兰队与澳大利亚队之间的板球比赛〕

Ashgabat /ˌɑʃgɑˈbɑt; ˌɑːʃgɑːˈbɑːt/ also 又作 **Ashgabad** a city in southwest Turkmenistan, the country's capital and largest city, formerly called Ashkhabad 阿什哈巴德〔土库曼斯坦西南部一城市，该国首都和最大城市，旧称阿什卡哈巴德〕

Ash·mo·le·an Mu·se·um, the /æʃˌmolɪən mjuˈziəm; æʃˌməʊliən mjuːˈziːəm/ also 又作 **the Ashmolean** a famous MUSEUM of ANCIENT history and ARCHAEOLOGY in Oxford, England, which also contains important collections of paintings, jewellery, historical documents etc 阿什莫尔博物馆〔位于英格兰牛津的著名古代史与考古学博物馆。馆藏有重要绘画作品、珠宝、历史文献等〕

a·shore /əˈʃor; əˈʃɔː/ *adv* on or towards the shore of a lake, river, sea, or ocean 在岸上；向岸上：*Brian pulled the boat ashore.* 布赖恩把船拉上岸。

ash·ram /ˈæʃrəm; ˈæʃrəm/ *n* [C] **1** a place where a Hindu holy man lives alone〔印度教高僧的〕静修处 **2** a house where people live together practising the religion of Hinduism〔印度教修行者住的〕修行屋

ash·tray /ˈæʃˌtre; ˈæʃtreɪ/ *n* [C] a small dish where you put used cigarettes 烟灰缸，烟灰碟 —see picture at 参见 TRAY 图 3

Ash Wednes·day /ˌ· ˈ··/ *n* [C,U] the first day of Lent 圣灰星期三〔四旬节的第一日〕

A·sia /ˈeʃə; ˈeɪʃə/ the world's largest CONTINENT (=one of the seven main areas of land), which includes the countries of the Middle East and the countries between the Ural Mountains and the Pacific Ocean, such as India, China, Japan, and part of Russia 亚洲〔世界上面积最大的一个洲，包括中东诸国和乌拉尔山脉与太平洋之间的国家，如印度、中国、日本、俄罗斯的一部分等〕

Asia Mi·nor /ˌ·· ˈ··/ the name for the main part of Turkey east of the Sea of Marmara, which is used especially when talking about the history and ARCHAEOLOGY of this area 小亚细亚〔马尔马拉海以东土耳其的主体部分。人们谈论该地区的历史和考古话题时多用这一术语〕—see also 另见 ANATOLIA

A·sian[1] /ˈeʃən; ˈeɪʃən/ *n* **1** *BrE* someone from Asia, especially India or Pakistan【英】亚洲人〔尤指印度或巴基斯坦人〕**2** *AmE* someone from Asia, especially Japan, China, Korea etc【美】亚洲人〔尤指日本人、中国人、朝鲜人和韩国人等〕

Asian[2] *adj* from Asia or related to Asia 亚洲的；亚洲人的

Asian-A·mer·i·can /ˌ·· ·ˈ···/ *n* [C] an American citizen whose family was originally from Asia 亚裔美国人

a·side[1] /əˈsaɪd; əˈsaɪd/ *adv* **1 move/step aside** to move, step etc to the side 靠一边/站到一边：*I stepped aside just in time, and the car whizzed past.* 我及时退到一边，汽车飞驰而过。**2 put/set/leave sth aside a)** to save part of an amount of money 留存一笔钱：*I've been setting aside a little money each week for our holiday.* 我每周节省一点钱准备用来度假。**b)** to keep something separate or not use it because someone is going to buy or use it later 留出某物，拨出某物：*One of the rooms was set aside for a yoga class.* 留出一个房间上瑜伽课。**c)** to leave something to be considered at another time 把某事放置一边〔以后再考虑〕：*Let's put this question aside for next week.* 我们先把这个问题搁一搁，下周再考虑。**3 brush/sweep sth aside** to treat someone's idea or statement in a way that shows you do not think it is important 不理会/不顾/漠视某事：*Mr. Coleman brushed my suggestion aside and asked for another question.* 科尔曼先生对我的建议不予理会，问了另一个问题。**4 aside from** *especially AmE*【尤美】**a)** except for 除…以外：*Aside from that one little problem, the day was perfect.* 除了那个小问题外，今天过得好极了。**b)** in addition to 此外：*Aside from physical problems, these patients also show a lot of hostility.* 这些病人除了身体方面的问题外，还表现出很多的敌意。**5** used to show that something you have just said is not as important as what you are going to say next 且不谈，且不管：*These problems aside, we think the plan should go ahead.* 这些问题暂不说，我们认为这个计划应马上实施。 3 3

aside[2] *n* [C] **1** words spoken by an actor to the people watching a play, that the other characters in the play do not hear〔戏剧中的〕旁白 **2** a remark made in a low voice that you only intend certain people to hear 私语，小声说的话 **3** a remark or story that is not part of the main subject of a speech 离题的话

As·i·mov /ˈæzəmɑf; ˈæsɪmɒv/, **I·saac** /ˈaɪzək; ˈaɪzək/ (1920-92) a US scientist and writer, born in Russia, and famous for writing SCIENCE FICTION (=stories about life in the future and imaginary developments in science) 阿西莫夫〔(1920-1992)，美国科学家、作家，生于俄罗斯，以科幻小说著称〕

as·i·nine /ˈæsn̩ˌaɪn; ˈæsɪ̣naɪn/ *adj* extremely stupid or silly; RIDICULOUS 极愚蠢的，荒谬的: *What an asinine remark!* 多么愚蠢的话！

ask /æsk; ɑːsk/ *v*

1 ►QUESTION 问题◄ [I,T] to say or write something in order to get an answer, a solution, or information 问，询问，打听，提问: *"What's your name?" she asked.* 她问："你叫什么名字？" | **ask a question** *That kid's always asking awkward questions.* 那孩子总是问一些不好回答的问题。| **ask who/what/where etc** *I was only asking how this could have happened.* 我只是问怎么会发生这样的事情。| **ask sb sth** *She asked an old man the way to the station.* 她向一位老人打听去火车站该怎么走。| **ask sb** *Don't ask him – he won't know anything about it.* 不要问他，他什么也不知道。| **ask if/whether** *Go and ask Pat whether he's coming tonight.* 去问问帕特他今晚是否来。| **ask (sb) about** *Visitors usually ask about the history of the place.* 参观者常常问起这个地方的历史。| **ask around** (=ask in a lot of places or ask a lot of people) 到处打听 *I'm not sure where you can get a good mechanic – you'd better ask around.* 我不清楚到哪儿能找到一个好的修理工，你最好多问问别人。

2 ►FOR HELP ETC 求助等◄ [I,T] to make a request for help, advice, information etc 要求，请求: *If you need anything, you only have to ask.* 你需要什么，只管提出来。| **ask sb to do sth** *Ask John to mail those letters tomorrow.* 请约翰明天把那些信寄出去。| **ask to do sth** *Karen asked to see whoever was in charge.* 卡伦请求见负责人。| **[+for]** *Some people find it difficult to ask for help.* 有些人发觉很难开口求助。| **ask if you can do sth** *Ask your dad if we can borrow his truck.* 问问你爸爸我们可否借他的卡车。—see 见 REQUEST² (USAGE)

3 ►PRICE 价格◄ [T] to want a particular amount of money for something you are selling 索要〔价格〕: **ask $50/£1,000 etc for** *I can't believe he's asking £2,000 for that old car.* 我真不敢相信那辆旧车他居然索价2000英镑。| **ask the earth/a fortune (for)** (=ask far too much money for something) 要价太高，开天价 *They're asking the earth for tickets – we just can't afford it.* 他们简直是开天价，这样的票价我们承受不起。

4 ►INVITE 邀请◄ [T] to invite someone to your home, to go out with you etc 邀请: **ask sb out** (=ask someone, especially someone of the opposite sex, to go to the theatre, a restaurant etc with you) 邀请某人〔特别是异性〕出去〔看电影、吃饭等〕 *Jerry's too scared to ask her out.* 杰里没有勇气邀她出去。| **ask sb in** (=invite someone into your house, office etc) 邀请某人进去 *Don't leave them standing on the doorstep – ask them in!* 别让他们在门口站着——请他们进来！| **ask sb along** (=invite someone to go somewhere with you, especially when you are with a lot of other people) 请某人一起〔去〕 *Get Bill to ask Sheila along.* 让比尔叫希拉一起去。| **ask sb over** (=invite someone to come to your home) 邀请某人去家里

5 be asking for it *spoken* used to say that someone deserves something bad that happens to them【口】自找麻烦，自作自受: *I don't really care he got beat up on – he was asking for it.* 我才不在乎他挨打呢，他自作自受。

6 be asking for trouble to do something that is very likely to have a bad effect or result 自找麻烦: *He thinks anyone who completely trusts anyone else is asking for trouble.* 他认为一个人完全信赖别人是自找麻烦。

7 don't ask me *spoken* used to say you do not know the answer to something【口】别问我〔我不知道〕: *"Where's she gone then?" "Don't ask me!"* "她到底去哪儿了？""别问我！"

8 asking price the price that someone wants to sell something for 索价: *At an asking price of just £250, it's got to be a bargain.* 索价才250英镑，那肯定便宜。

9 ask yourself to try to honestly discover the true reason for something 扪心自问，反思: *The government should ask itself where the responsibility for this mess really lies.* 政府应该深刻反思一下目前的困境责任究竟由谁来负。

10 for the asking if you can have something for the asking, you only have to ask for it and you can have it 只要你提出要求〔你就可以得到它〕

11 I ask you! *spoken* used to express surprise at and disapproval of something stupid that someone has done【口】你瞧瞧！〔表示不赞同、吃惊〕: *She sent her kids to camp dressed all in white. I ask you!* 她竟然让孩子们全穿上白衣服去营地。你瞧瞧！—see 见 REQUEST² (USAGE)

USAGE NOTE 用法说明: ASK

WORD CHOICE 词语辨析: **ask, want to know, inquire, question, interrogate**

Ask is the usual verb for questions. ask 是提问题常用的动词: *"How are you doing?" she asked.* "你近来怎样？"她问道。| *That's a stupid question to ask.* 那个问题问得很愚蠢。Often people use **want to know** when they are talking about what someone else has asked. 谈到别人问什么时常用 want to know: *He wanted to know where I lived/the train times.* 他打听我住在哪儿/火车时刻。

Inquire (or **enquire** *BrE*) has the same meaning but is more formal, and is not followed by a noun or pronoun object. inquire (或 enquire【英】) 与 ask 意思相同，但较为正式，后面不能接名词或代词宾语。At a meeting 在会上: *May I inquire what the committee proposes to do about this?/about the effectiveness of this policy?* (NOT 不用 *...inquire the effectiveness of this policy*) 我可否问一下委员会建议这件事怎么做/这一政策的有效性？

To **question** a person is to ask them a lot of questions, especially officially, and to **interrogate** suggests that someone is being held by force and asked questions that they are unwilling to answer, for example by the police or an enemy. question a person (盘问某人) 是问很多问题，尤指正式的问话，而 interrogate (讯问) 含有强制要求回答他不愿意回答的问题之意，如警察审问或敌方逼问。

GRAMMAR 语法

Remember that you do not follow **ask** with a direct question, unless you are repeating the exact words. 切记，除非是直接引语，否则 ask 后不能直接跟一个问句: *Ask what sort of room he would like* (NOT 不用 *Ask what sort of room would he like*). 问他想要什么样的房间。| *I asked "What sort of room would you like?"* 我问"你想要什么样的房间？"

You **ask** people certain things without using *for* or *about*. 下列情况中，ask 后不用 for 或 about: *I asked him the way/his name/the price/the time/a favour/permission/his advice* (NOT 不用 *asked to him the way*). 我问他路/姓名/价格/时间/求他帮忙/请求他允许/向他咨询。You usually **ask for** or **about** most other things. 以下情况 ask 后加 for 或 about: *Ask one of our guides for directions to Lincoln Center.* 问我们的导游去林肯中心的路线。| *He asked Sharon for a date* (NOT 不用 *He asked a date to Sharon*). 他请莎伦跟他约会。| *Can I ask you about the exam results?* (NOT 不用 *of the exam results*) 我能问你考试成绩吗？

a·skance /əˈskæns; əˈskæns/ *adv* **look askance (at)** to look at or consider something in a way that shows you do not believe it or approve of it〔不高兴地〕侧目，〔以怀疑的目光〕注视，瞟视

a·skew /əˈskju; əˈskjuː/ *adv* not quite straight or in the right position 不正，歪: *Matilda ran towards us with her hat askew.* 玛蒂尔达歪戴着帽子朝我们跑来。

a·slant /əˈslænt; əˈslɑːnt/ *adv* [not before noun 不用于名词前] *formal* not straight up or down, but across at an angle【正式】斜着，歪着 —**aslant** *adj*

a·sleep /əˈslip; əˈsliːp/ *adj* [not before noun 不用于名词前] **1** sleeping 睡着的: *Quiet! The baby is asleep.* 安静点！宝宝在睡觉。| **fast/sound asleep** (=very deeply asleep) 睡得很熟 *You'll be fast asleep by the time we get home.* 我们到家的时候，你早就呼呼大睡了。**2 fall asleep a)** to begin to sleep 入睡: *I always fall asleep watching TV.* 我看电视时总是会睡着。**b)** *literary* used to mean that someone dies when you want to avoid saying this directly【文】长眠 **3** an arm or leg that is asleep has been in one position for too long, so you cannot feel it 发麻，麻木 —see also 另见 **go to sleep** (SLEEP² (3)) **4 half asleep** not paying attention to something because you are tired 半睡眠状态，困倦

A/S level /ˌe ˈɛs ˌlɛvl; ˌeɪ ˈes ˌlevəl/ *n* **1** [U] an examination in British schools, for pupils who have taken GCSE*s* and want to study a wider range of subjects than is possible at A LEVEL〔英国中学的〕高级补充程度会考〔为已通过普通中学教育证书考试的学生而设，让学生可学习多于高级程度所规定的科目〕**2** [C] an examination at this standard in a particular subject 高级补充程度会考的某学科考试

asp /æsp; æsp/ *n* [C] a small poisonous snake from North Africa 角蝰；蝮蛇〔北非的一种小毒蛇〕

as·par·a·gus /əˈspærəgəs; əˈspærəgəs/ *n* [U] a long thin green vegetable with a point at one end 芦笋，石刁柏 —see picture on page A9 参见 A9 页图

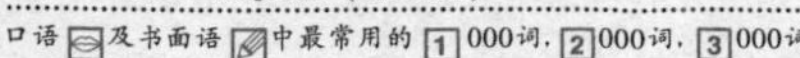
口语 及书面语 中最常用的 1 000词，2 000词，3 000词

ASPCA, the *n* [singular] the American Society for the Prevention of Cruelty to Animals; a charity organization that takes care of animals, especially pets whose owners treated them badly or did not want them, and tries to find new homes for them 美国防止虐待动物协会〔美国慈善机构。职责是保护动物，尤其是被虐待或遗弃的宠物，并努力为其寻找新家〕—compare 比较【英】RSPCA

as·pect /ˈæspɛkt; ˈæspekt/ *n* **1** [C] one part of a situation, idea, plan etc that has many parts 方面: [+of] *Alcoholism affects all aspects of family life.* 酗酒影响家庭生活的各个方面。**2** [C] the direction in which a window, room, front of a building etc faces 朝向，方位: *a south-facing aspect* (方向) 朝南 **3** [C,U] *formal* the appearance of someone or something【正式】面貌，外观，神态: *Her face wore a melancholy aspect.* 她面带忧伤。**4** [C,U] *technical* the form of a verb in grammar that shows whether an action is continuing, or happens always, repeatedly, or once【术语】〔动词的〕体: *'He sings' differs from 'He is singing' in aspect.* He sings 和 He is singing 的体不同。

as·pen /ˈæspən; ˈæspən/ *n* [C] a kind of tree of western North America with leaves that shake in the wind〔北美西部的〕颤杨，大齿杨

as·per·i·ty /æsˋpɛrətɪ; æˈsperɪ̀ti/ *n* [C,U] *formal* a way of speaking or behaving that is rough or severe【正式】〔说话、举止等的〕粗鲁，刻薄: *the asperity of her manner* 她举止的粗鲁

as·per·sion /əˋspɝʒən; əˈspɜːʃən/ *n* **cast aspersions on** *formal* to make an unkind remark or an unfair judgment【正式】诽谤，中伤，诬蔑: *Are you casting aspersions on my wife's character?* 你是不是在诽谤我妻子的人格？

as·phalt /ˈæsfɔlt; ˈæsfælt/ *n* [U] a black sticky substance that becomes hard when it dries, used for making the surface of roads 沥青，柏油 —**asphalt** *v* [T]

as·phyx·i·a /æsˋfɪksɪə; æsˈfɪksiə/ *n* [U] death caused by not being able to breathe 窒息 (而死)

as·phyx·i·ate /æsˋfɪksɪ,et; æsˈfɪksieɪt/ *v* [I,T] *technical* to be unable to breathe air or make someone unable to do so, especially to die or kill someone in this way; SUFFOCATE (1)【术语】(使) 窒息 (而死)；(使) 无法呼吸 —**asphyxiation** /æs,fɪksɪˋeʃən; æs,fɪksiˈeɪʃən/ *n* [U]

as·pic /ˈæspɪk; ˈæspɪk/ *n* [U] a clear brownish JELLY (3) eaten with meat 肉冻

as·pi·dis·tra /,æspɪˋdɪstrə; ,æspɪ̀ˈdɪstrə/ *n* [C] a plant with broad green pointed leaves, often grown in houses 蜘蛛抱蛋〔一种长有宽而尖的绿叶、多摆设于室内的植物〕

as·pi·rant /əˋspaɪrənt; əˈspaɪərənt/ *n* [C+to/for] *formal* someone who hopes to get a position of importance or honour【正式】有志者，有抱负者；〔名誉、地位的〕追求者

as·pi·rate¹ /ˈæspə,ret; ˈæspɪ̀reɪt/ *v* [T] *technical* to make the sound of an 'H' when speaking, or to blow out air when pronouncing some consonants【术语】发字母 H 音，发送气音

as·pi·rate² /ˈæspərɪt; ˈæspɪ̀rɪ̀t/ *n* [C] *technical* the sound of the letter 'H', or the letter itself【术语】(字母) H 音，送气音

as·pi·ra·tion /,æspəˋreʃən; ,æspɪ̀ˈreɪʃən/ *n* **1** [C usually plural 一般用复数,U] a strong desire to have or achieve something 强烈愿望；志向，抱负: *Hannah has always had political aspirations.* 汉纳在政治上一向很有抱负。| [+of] *the aspirations of the working classes* 工人阶级的强烈愿望 **2** [U] the sound of air blowing out that happens when some CONSONANTS are pronounced, such as the /p/ in pin〔某些辅音字母发音的〕送气音〈如 pin 一词中 /p/ 的发音〉

as·pire /əˋspaɪr; əˈspaɪə/ *v* [I] to desire and work towards achieving something important 追求，渴望，有志于: [+to/after] *It was clear that Mrs Thatcher aspired to the leadership of the party.* 显而易见撒切尔夫人立志成为该党的领导人。| **aspire to do sth** *At that time, all serious artists aspired to go to Rome and paint.* 那时，所有认真的画家都渴望去罗马作画。

as·pirin /ˈæspərɪn; ˈæsprɪ̀n/ *n plural* **aspirins** *or* **aspirin** [C, U] a medicine that reduces pain, INFLAMMATION, and fever 阿斯匹林

As·quith /ˈæskwɪθ; ˈæskwɪθ/, **Herbert Henry** (1852-1928) a British Liberal politician and Prime Minister from 1908 to 1916 阿斯奎斯〔(1852-1928)，英国自由党政治家，1908 至 1916年任英国首相〕

ass /æs; æs/ *n* [C]

1 ▶PART OF BODY 身体的部分◀ *especially AmE* an impolite word for the part of your body that you sit on【尤美】屁股，臀部〔非礼貌用语〕: *I tripped and fell flat on my ass.* 我绊倒了，一屁股坐在地上。

2 get your ass in gear also 又作 **move your ass** *spoken* an impolite way of telling someone to hurry【口】赶快，抓紧时间〔非礼貌用语〕: *Get your ass in gear, or you'll miss your plane!* 你他妈的快点，不然你就赶不上飞机了！

3 get off your ass *AmE spoken* an impolite way of telling someone to stop being lazy【美口】别偷懒〔非礼貌用语〕: *If you want to pass this test, you'd better get off your ass and study!* 如果你想考试及格，就要用功学习！

4 kick/whip sb's ass also 又作 **kick (some) ass** *AmE slang* to beat someone easily in a fight, game, or sport【美俚】轻而易举地战胜某人: *Let's get out there and kick some ass.* 让我们一鼓作气，打败他们。

5 be on sb's ass *AmE spoken*【美口】**a)** an impolite way of saying that someone is annoying you by telling you to do things you do not want to do 老逼某人〔做不想做的事；非礼貌说法〕: *My boss is on my ass all the time.* 我的老板老逼着我干活。**b)** an impolite way of saying that someone is driving very close to the back of another car 快撞上前面汽车的屁股了〔非礼貌说法〕

6 get your ass over here *AmE spoken* an impolite way of telling someone to come quickly【美口】快点儿来〔非礼貌说法〕

7 my ass! *AmE spoken* an impolite way of saying that you do not believe something【美口】见鬼！〔表示不相信的非礼貌说法〕: *"He said he ran twenty miles." "Twenty miles my ass!"* "他说他跑了 20 英里。" "20 英里，见他的鬼！"

8 ▶STUPID PERSON 笨人◀ *informal* a stupid, annoying person【非正式】傻瓜，蠢人: **make an ass of yourself** (=do something stupid or embarrassing) 做傻事，出洋相

9 sb doesn't know their ass from their elbow *AmE spoken* an impolite way of saying that someone is stupid【美口】大傻帽儿一个，什么都不知道〔非礼貌说法〕

10 ▶ANIMAL 动物◀ *old use* a DONKEY【旧】驴 —see also 另见 ARSE, **haul ass** (HAUL¹ (6)), **kiss sb's ass** (KISS (6)), **pain in the arse/ass etc** (PAIN¹ (3)), **piece of ass** (PIECE¹ (22)), SMART ARSE

as·sail /əˋsel; əˈseɪl/ *v* [T] **1** [usually passive 一般用被动态] if a thought or feeling assails you, it worries or upsets you 困扰: *Carla was suddenly assailed by doubts.* 卡拉突然为各种疑虑所困扰。**2** to attack someone or something violently 猛烈攻击，打击: **assail sb with sth** *The angry crowd assailed police with stones and bottles.* 愤怒的人群用石头和瓶子袭击警察。

as·sai·lant /əˋselənt; əˈseɪlənt/ *n* [C] *formal* someone who attacks another person【正式】攻击者: *Ms Hervey states that she could not see her assailant's face.* 赫维女士称她没看清袭击她的人的面孔。

As·sam /əˋsæm; əˈsæm/ *n* a type of tea from the Assam state in northeast India 阿萨姆红茶〔产于印度东北部的阿萨姆邦〕

as·sas·sin /əˋsæsɪn; əˈsæsɪ̀n/ *n* [C] someone who murders an important person 暗杀者，刺客: *Kennedy's supposed assassin, Lee Harvey Oswald* 据说是暗杀肯尼迪的人，李·哈维·奥斯瓦德

as·sas·sin·ate /əˋsæsn,et; əˈsæsɪ̀neɪt/ *v* [T] to murder an important person 暗杀，行刺: *a plot to assassinate the President* 刺杀总统的阴谋 —see 见 KILL¹ (USAGE)

as·sas·sin·a·tion /ə,sæsnˋeʃən; ə,sæsɪ̀ˈneɪʃən/ *n* [C,U] the act of assassinating someone 行刺，暗杀: *a terrorist group plotting an assassination* 密谋暗杀的恐怖分子组织 | **assassination attempt** (=a situation in which someone tries but fails to assassinate someone) 行刺的企图 —see also 另见 **character assassination** (CHARACTER (6))

as·sault¹ /əˋsɔlt; əˈsɔːlt/ *n* [C,U] **1** the crime of attacking someone 攻击，袭击 (罪): *increases in violent assaults over the past decade* 近 10 年来暴力袭击事件的增加 | **sexual assault** *three years in prison for sexual assault* 因犯强奸罪被监禁三年 **2** a military attack to take control of a place controlled by the enemy 袭击，攻占: *the platoon's unsuccessful assault on the border positions* 那个排未能攻占边境阵地 **3** an attempt to achieve something difficult, especially using physical force〔尤指靠体力〕攻破 (难关): [+on] *an assault on Mt Everest* (=an attempt to climb it) 攀登珠穆朗玛峰的尝试 **4 assault on** a strong spoken or written criticism of someone else's ideas, plans etc 对…的抨击[攻击]: *the tobacco industry's recent assault on plans to ban cigarettes* 烟草行业最近对禁烟计划的攻击

assault² *v* [T] **1** to attack someone in a violent way 猛袭，攻击，袭击: *Policemen were assaulted by young demonstrators.* 警察遭到年轻示威者的袭击。**2** to strongly criticize someone's ideas, plans etc 抨击，攻击，严厉批评: *The MP was assaulted with a barrage of abuse from angry strikers.* 这位议会议员遭到愤怒的罢工者连珠炮式的辱骂。**3** if a feeling assaults you, it affects you in a way that makes you uncomfortable or upset 使感到难受，困扰: *The noise in the club assaulted our ears.* 俱乐部里的噪音使我们的耳朵感到很不舒服。

assault and bat·ter·y /ˌ· · ˈ· · ·/ *n* [U] *law* the official name for a violent attack and the threats that the attacker makes before it【法律】殴打罪，威胁和暴力行为罪

assault course /ˈ· · ˌ·/ *n* [C] *BrE* an area of land with special equipment to climb, jump over, run through etc that is used for developing physical strength especially by soldiers【英】军事训练场地；OBSTACLE COURSE *AmE*【美】

as·say /əˋse; əˈseɪ/ *v* [T] **1** to test a metal 鉴定，化验，分析〔金属含量〕 **2** *literary* to attempt to do something【文】尝试〔做某事〕: *to assay the impossible* 尝试做不可能成功的事 —**assay** /əˋse; əˈseɪ/ *n* [C]

as·se·gai /ˈæsəˌgaɪ; ˈæsɨ̣gaɪ/ *n* [C] a long thin wooden stick with an iron point, used as a weapon in southern Africa〔非洲南部人用的〕细木柄标枪，长矛

as·sem·blage /əˋsɛmblɪdʒ; əˈsemblɪdʒ/ *n formal*【正式】 **1** [C] a group of people or things that are together〔集合在一起的〕一群人；一批东西 **2** [U] the act of putting parts together in order to make something 组合，装配

as·sem·ble /əˋsɛmbl; əˈsembəl/ *v* **1** [I] if a group of people assemble in one place, they all go there together 集合，聚集: *A large crowd had assembled opposite the American embassy.* 一大群人聚集在美国大使馆对面。 **2** [T] to gather a large number of things or people together in one place 收集；召集: *Over the years we've assembled a huge collection of old books.* 这么多年来，我们收集了大量的旧书。 **3** [T] to put all the parts of something together 组装，装配: *an easy-to-assemble kit* 很容易装配的配套元件

[3][2] **as·sem·bly** /əˋsɛmblɪ; əˈsembli/ *n* **1** [C] a group of people who are elected to make laws for a particular country or area 立法机构；议会: *the New York State Assembly* 纽约州议会 **2** [C+of] a group of people who have gathered together for a particular purpose〔为特定目的〕聚集在一起的人 **3** [C,U] a regular meeting of all the teachers and pupils of a school 全校师生会议，集会 **4** [U] the process of putting parts together in order to make something 组装，装配: *instructions for assembly* 组装说明（书） **5 the right of assembly/freedom of assembly** the right of any group to meet together in order to discuss things 集会的权利/自由

assembly line /ˈ· · · ˌ·/ *n* [C] a system for making things in a factory in which the products move past a line of workers who each make or check one part 装配线，流水作业线

as·sem·bly·man /əˋsɛmblɪmən; əˈsemblimən/ *n* [C] *AmE* a male member of an ASSEMBLY (1)【美】男议员

as·sem·bly·wom·an /əˋsɛmblɪˌwʊmən; əˈsembliˌwʊmən/ *n* [C] *AmE* a female member of an ASSEMBLY (1)【美】女议员

as·sent[1] /əˋsɛnt; əˈsent/ *n* [U] *formal* approval or agreement from someone who has authority【正式】同意，赞成: *a nod of assent* 点头表示赞成 | **the Royal assent** (=act of officially signing a new law by the British King or Queen) 御准〔指英国国王或女王签署新法令〕

assent[2] *v* [I+to] *formal* to agree to a suggestion, idea etc after considering it carefully【正式】〔经审慎考虑后〕同意，赞成

as·sert /əˋsɝt; əˈsɜːt/ *v* [T] **1 assert your rights/independence etc** to state very strongly your right to do or have something 坚持自己的权利/独立等 **2 assert yourself** to behave in a determined way so that people do not make you do things you do not want 坚持自己的想法: *You need to assert yourself more.* 你需要进一步坚持自己的想法。 **3** to state firmly that something is true（坚决）主张；断言: **assert that** *The professor asserted that there was nothing wrong with his theory.* 那位教授坚持认为自己的理论没有错。 **4 assert itself** if an idea or belief asserts itself, it begins to influence something 产生影响: *Milton's influence asserts itself later in his poetry.* 弥尔顿后来对他的诗歌产生了很大的影响。

as·ser·tion /əˋsɝʃən; əˈsɜːʃən/ *n* [C] something that you say or write that you strongly believe 断言，声明，主张: **assertion that** *Wilkinson kept repeating his assertion that he was innocent.* 威尔金森一再声称自己无罪。

as·ser·tive /əˋsɝtɪv; əˈsɜːtɪv/ *adj* behaving in a confident way so that people notice you 果断的，肯定的，自信的 —**assertively** *adv* —**assertiveness** *n* [U]: *assertiveness training* 自信心的训练[培养]

[2][2] **as·sess** /əˋsɛs; əˈses/ *v* [T] **1** to make a judgment about a person or situation after thinking carefully about it 评价，评定: *It's difficult to assess the effects of the new legislation just yet.* 现在还难以评价新法令的效果。 | **assess what/how etc** *We've tried to assess what went wrong.* 我们已试着判断到底哪儿出了毛病。 **2** to calculate the value or cost of something 估价，估计: **assess sth at** *They assessed the value of the house at over $250,000.* 他们估计这所房子值25万美元以上。

as·sess·ment /əˋsɛsmənt; əˈsesmənt/ *n* **1** [C,U] a process in which you make a judgment about a person or situation 评价，估计: *What's your assessment of the situation in Northern Ireland?* 你是怎样评价北爱尔兰的形势的？ **2** [C,U] a calculation about the cost or value of something 核定额: *a tax assessment* 应纳税的核定额 —see also 另见 **continuous assessment** ((CONTINUOUS) (3)) [2][2]

as·ses·sor /əˋsɛsɚ; əˈsesə/ *n* [C] **1** someone who decides how well someone has done in an examination 评分人 **2** someone whose job is to calculate the value of something or the amount of tax someone should pay 估价员；评税员 **3** someone who knows a lot about a subject or activity and who advises a judge or an official committee〔在某种专业知识方面辅助法官或官方委员会工作的〕技术顾问，助理

as·set /ˈæsɛt; ˈæset/ *n* [C] **1** [usually plural 一般用复数] the things that a company owns, that can be sold to pay debts 资产，财产 **2** [usually singular 一般用单数] something or someone that is useful because they help you succeed or deal with problems 有利条件；长处；有用的人: *A sense of humor is a real asset in this business.* 在这行业中，幽默感是一大长处。 | **be an asset to** *I think Rachel would be an asset to the department.* 我认为雷切尔对这个部门来讲是个难得的人才。—compare 比较 LIABILITY —see also 另见 LIQUID ASSETS [2][2]

asset strip·ping /ˈ· · ˌ· ·/ *n* [U] the practice of buying a company cheaply and then selling all the things it owns to make a quick profit 资产倒卖〔低价买进一家公司，再将其全部资产卖出获利〕

as·sev·e·rate /əˋsɛvəˌret; əˈsevəreɪt/ *v* [T+that] to state something very firmly and seriously 郑重声明，断言

ass·hole /ˈæsˌhol; ˈæshəʊl/ *n* [C] **1** an offensive word for someone you think stupid and annoying 蠢货〔冒犯用词〕 **2** an offensive word for the ANUS 屁眼〔冒犯用词〕—see also 另见 ARSEHOLE

as·sid·u·ous /əˋsɪdʒuəs; əˈsɪdjuəs/ *adj formal* very careful to make sure that something is done properly or completely【正式】专心致志的，勤勉的: *an assiduous collector of folk songs* 坚持不懈的民歌收集者 —**assiduously** *adv* —**assiduity** /ˌæsəˋduətɪ; ˌæsɨ̣ˈdjuːɨ̣ti/ *n* [U]

as·sign /əˋsaɪn; əˈsaɪn/ *v* [T] **1** to give someone a particular job or make them responsible for a particular person or thing 分配，分派，指派〔任务〕: **assign sb a job/duty/task** *I've been assigned the job of looking after the new students.* 指派给我的工作是照料新来的学生。 | **assign sb to** *Jan's been assigned to the Asian Affairs Bureau.* 简被派到亚洲事务部。 **2** to decide that something should be done at or during a particular time 订出，确定〔时间或期限〕: *How much time have you assigned for the meeting?* 你给这个会定了多长时间？ **3** *formal* to give money, equipment etc to someone or decide it should be used for a particular purpose【正式】把〔财产、设备等〕转让与: **assign sth to** *The US has already assigned a large part of its foreign aid budget to Rwanda.* 美国已经把对外援助预算中的很大一部分转给了卢旺达。

as·sig·na·tion /ˌæsɪgˋneʃən; ˌæsɪgˈneɪʃən/ *n* [C] a secret meeting, especially with someone you are having a romantic relationship with（秘密）约会；幽会: *a secret assignation at midnight* 午夜的秘密约会

as·sign·ment /əˋsaɪnmənt; əˈsaɪnmənt/ *n* **1** [C] a piece of work that is given to someone as part of their job, or that a student is asked to do〔分配的〕任务；作业: *a history assignment* 历史作业 | **on an assignment** *Joanna's going to Italy on a special assignment for her newspaper.* 乔安娜受委派到意大利去执行报社的一项特殊任务。 **2** [U] the act of giving people particular jobs to do 分配，指派〔任务〕: *the assignment of chores* 分配杂务 [2]

as·sim·i·late /əˋsɪmlˌet; əˈsɪmɨ̣leɪt/ *v* **1** [T] to think about new ideas, information etc so that you feel ready to use them 吸收，理解，掌握: *It will take time to assimilate all these facts.* 充分理解这些事实需要时间。 **2** [I,T] if people assimilate or are assimilated into a country or group, they become part of it and are accepted by other people in it 融入，加入；(使) 同化: [+into] *women being assimilated into the workforce* 加入劳动者行列的妇女 **3** [T] *technical* if you assimilate food, you take it into your mouth and DIGEST[1] (1) it【术语】吸收，消化〔食物〕

as·sim·i·la·tion /əˌsɪmlˋeʃən; əˌsɪmɨ̣ˈleɪʃən/ *n* [U] **1** the process of assimilating or being assimilated 吸收；融合，同化 **2** *technical* the process in which a sound in a word changes because of the effect of another sound next to it, for example the 'p' in 'cupboard'【术语】语音的同化〈如 cupboard 中的 p〉

Assisi —see 见 St FRANCIS OF ASSISI

as·sist¹ /əˋsɪst; əˈsɪst/ *v* **1** [I,T] to help someone to do something, especially by doing all the less important things so that they can spend time doing difficult things 帮助, 协助: **assist (sb) with/in** *I was employed to assist the manager with his duties.* 我受雇协助经理工作。**2** [T] to make it easier for someone to do something 使做…变得更容易: *They had no maps to assist them.* 他们没地图, 很不方便。—see 见 HELP¹ (USAGE)

assist² *n* [C] an action that helps another player on your team to make a point〔体育项目中的〕助攻

as·sist·ance /əˋsɪstəns; əˈsɪstəns/ *n* [U] help or support 帮助, 援助: *financial assistance* 财政援助 | *Can I be of any assistance?* (=can I help you?) 我能帮什么忙吗? | **with the assistance of** *a report drawn up with the assistance of experts* 在专家的协助下起草的报告 | **come to sb's assistance** (=help someone) 帮助某人 *One of her fellow passengers came to her assistance.* 同车的一个乘客过来帮她。—see 见 HELP¹ (USAGE)

as·sis·tant¹ /əˋsɪstənt; əˈsɪstənt/ *adj* **assistant manager/director/cook etc** someone whose job is just below the level of manager, etc 助理经理/主任/厨师等

assistant² *n* [C] **1** someone who helps someone else in their work, especially by doing the less important jobs 助手, 助理, 副手: *a clerical assistant* 文书助理 **2** a SHOP ASSISTANT 商店店员 —see also 另见 PERSONAL ASSISTANT

assistant pro·fes·sor /·,·· ·ˈ··/ *n* [C] the lowest rank of PROFESSOR (2) at an American university〔美国大学的〕助理教授

as·siz·es /əˋsaɪzɪz; əˈsaɪzɨz/ *n* [plural] *old use* a meeting of a court in which a judge who travelled to different towns in Britain dealt with cases【旧】〔英国的〕巡回裁判庭 —**assize** *adj*

assn a written abbreviation of 缩写= ASSOCIATION

assoc a written abbreviation of 缩写= ASSOCIATION

as·so·ci·ate¹ /əˋsoʃɪˌet; əˈsəʊʃieɪt/ *v* **1** **associate sb/sth with** to make a connection in your mind between one thing or person and another 把某人/某事物与…联系起来: *I've never associated you with this place.* 我从未把你和这个地方联系在一起。| *People usually associate Japan with high tech consumer products.* 人们一般把日本和高科技消费品联系在一起。**2** **be associated (with)** to be connected with a particular subject, activity, group etc 与…有关, 与…有瓜葛: *problems associated with cancer treatment* 与治疗癌症有关的问题 | *I wouldn't want to be associated with McKey's project.* 我不想和麦基的项目有任何瓜葛。**3** **associate with sb** to spend time with someone, especially a group who other people disapprove of 与〔他人不赞同的〕人交往[合伙, 结交]: *I don't like these layabouts you're associating with.* 我不喜欢你结交的这些游手好闲的人。

as·so·ci·ate² /əˋsoʃɪɪt; əˈsəʊʃiɨt/ *n* [C] **1** someone who you work or do business with 同事; (生意) 伙伴: *one of his business associates* 他生意上的一个伙伴 **2** someone who has an associate degree 准学位证书持有者

associate³ *adj* **associate member/director/head etc** someone who has some of the same rights or responsibilities as a member etc 非正式会员/副主任/副主管等

associated com·pa·ny /·,····ˈ···/ *n* [C] a company of which 20 to 50 per cent of the shares (SHARE² (5)) are owned by another company 联营公司

associate de·gree /·,··· ·ˈ·/ *n* [C] a degree given after two years of study at a JUNIOR COLLEGE in the US 副学士学位, 准学士学位〔美国两年制初级大学的学位〕

associate pro·fes·sor /·,··· ·ˈ··/ *n* [C] a PROFESSOR (2) at an American university whose job is above the level of ASSISTANT PROFESSOR and below the level of FULL PROFESSOR 副教授 —compare 比较 ASSISTANT PROFESSOR, FULL PROFESSOR

as·so·ci·a·tion /əˌsosɪˋeʃən; əˌsəʊsiˈeɪʃən/ *n* [C] **1** an organization that consists of a group of people who have the same aims, do the same kind of work etc 协会, 社团: *the Association of Master Builders* 建筑师协会 | *an association to help families suffering from alcoholism* 旨在帮助那些遭受酗酒之害家庭的团体 —see also 另见 HOUSING ASSOCIATION **2** a connection with a particular person, organization, group etc 联系, 关系, 关联: *his association with the Green Party* 他与绿党的合作 **3** a feeling or memory that is connected with a particular place, event, word etc 联想: *Scotland has all kinds of happy associations for me.* 苏格兰给我各种各样愉快的联想。**4** **in association with** made or done together with another person, organization etc 与…合伙, 合作: *concerts sponsored by the Arts Council in association with several local businesses* 由艺术委员会和当地几家企业合作承办的音乐会 —see also 另见 FREE ASSOCIATION

Association foot·ball /·,····ˈ·ˈ·/ *n* [U] *BrE formal* FOOTBALL (1)【英, 正式】足球 (运动)

as·so·nance /ˋæsənəns; ˈæsənəns/ *n* [U] *technical* similarity in the vowel sounds of words that are close together in a poem, for example between 'born' and 'warm'【术语】〔声音相似的〕谐音; 〔尤指元音的〕母韵, 半韵, 半谐音〈如 born 和 warm 中的元音〉

as·sort·ed /əˋsɔrtɪd; əˈsɔːtɨd/ *adj* of various different kinds 各种各样的: *assorted sizes* 各种各样的规格 | *assorted cookies* 什锦饼干 —see also 另见 ILL-ASSORTED

as·sort·ment /əˋsɔrtmənt; əˈsɔːtmənt/ *n* [C] a mixture of different things or of various kinds of the same thing 各式各样东西的混合; 什锦: **[+of]** *an odd assortment of knives and forks* 各式各样的刀叉

asst the written abbreviation of 缩写= ASSISTANT

as·suage /əˋswedʒ; əˈsweɪdʒ/ *v* [T] *literary* to make an unpleasant feeling less painful or severe; RELIEVE (1)【文】缓和, 减轻, 平息: *Nothing could assuage his guilt.* 没有任何事能减轻他的负罪感。

as·sume /əˋsum; əˈsjuːm/ *v* [T] **1** to think that something is true, although you have no proof of it 假定, 假设: **assume (that)** *I didn't see your car, so I assumed you'd gone out.* 我没有看见你的汽车, 所以我以为你出去了。| *Assuming that the proposal is accepted, when are we going to get the money?* 假定这个建议被采纳, 我们什么时候能拿到钱? | **we can safely assume** (=used to say that something is certain to happen) 我们可以肯定 *I think we can safely assume that interest rates will go up again soon.* 我认为我们可以肯定利率很快又会上调。| **assume guilt/innocence** (=assume that someone is guilty or not guilty of a crime) 认定〔某人〕有罪/无辜 **2** **assume control/power/responsibilities etc** to start to do a job, especially an important one 开始控制/掌权/承担责任等: *The President assumes his new responsibilities in January.* 总统1月份就任新职。**3** **assume a manner/air/expression etc** *formal* to behave in a way that does not show how you really feel, especially in order to seem more confident, cheerful etc than you are【正式】装出…的态度/样子/表情等: *Andy assumed an air of indifference whenever her name was mentioned.* 每次提到她的名字, 安迪都表现出无所谓的样子。**4** to start to have a particular quality or appearance 呈现出, 出现为: *The problem is beginning to assume massive proportions.* 问题开始显出其严重性。**5** to be based on the idea that something else is correct; PRESUPPOSE 以…为先决条件, 预先假定: **assume (that)** *Your theory assumes that we are willing to pay for services by taxation.* 你的理论以我们愿意通过税收方式支付服务费为前提。

as·sumed /əˋsumd; əˈsjuːmd/ *adj* **under an assumed name** using a false name 用假名: *He registered at the hotel under an assumed name.* 他用假名登记入住酒店。

as·sump·tion /əˋsʌmpʃən; əˈsʌmpʃən/ *n* **1** [C] something that you think is true although you have no proof 假定, 假设: **make an assumption** *A lot of people make the assumption that poverty only exists in the Third World.* 许多人认为贫困仅仅存在于第三世界。| **on the assumption that** *I'm working on the assumption that the money will come through.* 我是在假定能拿到钱的情况下工作。| **underlying assumption** (=a belief that is used to support a statement or idea, even though this belief may not be correct) 潜在的假设 *the underlying assumption that scientific progress is always a good thing* 认为科学进步总是件好事的潜在假设 **2** [U] *formal* the act of starting to have control or power【正式】霸占, 承担, 就任: **[+of]** *the assumption of responsibility* 承担责任, 就职

Assumption, The **1** in the Roman Catholic religion, the Assumption is when the Virgin Mary (=Jesus' mother) went up into heaven, without dying first 圣母升天〔罗马天主教中指圣母灵肉升天, 得到救赎〕 **2** the day (15 August) on which this event is celebrated 圣母升天节〔8月15日〕

as·sur·ance /əˋʃʊrəns; əˈʃʊərəns/ *n* **1** [U] a feeling of calm confidence in your own abilities, especially because you have a lot of experience; SELF-ASSURANCE 自信, 把握: *She spoke in a tone of quiet assurance.* 她以不慌不忙的自信口气说话。**2** [C] a promise that you will definitely do something or that something will definitely happen, especially to make someone less worried 担保, 保证: *Despite my repeated assurances Rob still looked very nervous.* 尽管我再三保证, 罗布看起来还是很紧张。| **assurance that** *I give you my personal assurance that the work will be done very soon.* 我个人向你保证, 这项工作将很快完成。**3** [U] *BrE technical* insurance against events that are certain to happen【英, 术语】(人寿) 保险; INSURANCE (1) *AmE*【美】—see also 另见 LIFE ASSURANCE

as·sure /əˋʃʊr; əˈʃʊə/ *v* [T] **1** to tell someone that something will definitely happen or is definitely true so that they are less

worried 向…保证，使确信，让…放心：**assure sb that** *Mom assured us that everything would be all right.* 妈妈向我们保证一切都不会有问题。| **I (can) assure you** *spoken*【口】*The document is genuine, I can assure you.* 我敢保证，这文件是真的。| **assure sb of sth** *The dealer had assured me of its quality.* 经销商向我保证质量。—see also 另见 **rest assured** (REST² (6)) **2 be assured of** to be able to feel certain that something will happen 有信心，有把握：*The Liberal Democrats are assured of success in the local elections.* 自由民主党人有把握在地方选举中获胜。**3** to make something certain to happen or to be achieved; ENSURE 确保，提供保证：*Excellent reviews have assured the film's success.* 绝佳的评论确保了该影片的成功。—see 见 INSURE (USAGE)

as·sured /əˋʃurd; əˈʃʊəd/ *adj* **1** confident about your own abilities; SELF-ASSURED 自信的：*an assured manner* 自信的态度 **2** certain to happen or to be achieved 确定的，有把握的：*Her political future looks assured.* 她的政治前途看来是有把握的。**3 the assured** *BrE technical* someone whose life has been insured【英，术语】已保寿险的人，受保人

as·sur·ed·ly /əˋʃurɪdlɪ; əˈʃʊərɨdli/ *adv formal* definitely or certainly【正式】肯定地，确定地：*as these three fine examples assuredly demonstrate* 正如这三个很好的例子所示范的

As·taire /əˋstɛr; əˈsteə/**, Fred** /frɛd; fred/ (1899-1987) a US dancer, singer, and actor who appeared in many musical films, often dancing with Ginger Rogers. His most famous film is *Top Hat* (1935). 阿斯泰尔〔(1899-1987)，美国舞蹈家、歌唱家、演员。他曾出演过不少音乐片，常与金杰·罗杰斯合舞。最著名的影片是《大礼帽》(1935)〕

as·te·risk /ˋæstəˌrɪsk; ˈæstərɪsk/ *n* [C] a mark like a star (*), used especially to show something interesting or important 星号 (*) —**asterisk** *v* [T]

As·te·rix /ˋæstərɪks; ˈæstərɪks/ the main character in a CARTOON STRIP set in ancient times. Asterix is a short, humorous French soldier who fights the ANCIENT Romans with his friend Obelix. 阿斯特瑞克斯〔一本以古代为背景的连环漫画中的主要人物。他是个风趣幽默的法国士兵，身材矮小，长着一蓬小胡子，同朋友奥贝里克斯一起与古罗马人作战〕

a·stern /əˋstɝn; əˈstɜːn/ *adv* in or at the back of a ship 在船尾；向船尾

as·te·roid /ˋæstəˌrɔɪd; ˈæstərɔɪd/ *n* [C] one of the many small PLANETs between Mars and Jupiter〔火星与木星之间的〕小行星

asth·ma /ˋæzmə; ˈæsmə/ *n* [U] an illness that causes difficulties in breathing 气喘；哮喘 (病)

asth·mat·ic /æzˋmætɪk; æsˈmætɪk/ *adj* suffering from asthma 患哮喘病的 —**asthmatic** *n* [C] —**asthmatically** /-klɪ; -kli/ *adv*

as·tig·ma·tis·m /əˋstɪgməˌtɪzəm; əˈstɪgmətɪzəm/ *n* [U] difficulty in seeing clearly that is caused by a change in the inner shape of the eye 散光，散视 —**astigmatic** /ˌæstɪgˋmætɪk; ˌæstɪgˈmætɪk◂/ *adj*

a·stir /əˋstɝ; əˈstɜː/ *adj* [not before noun 不用于名词前] *literary*【文】**1** awake and out of bed 起床的 **2** excited about something 激动的，轰动的，骚动的：*The whole village was astir as the visitors arrived.* 客人来到时，全村为之哄动。

as·ton·ish /əˋstɑnɪʃ; əˈstɒnɪʃ/ *v* [T] to surprise someone very much 使〔某人〕吃惊，使〔某人〕惊讶：*Diana astonished her family by winning three competitions in a row.* 黛安娜连续三次获胜，使家人感到惊讶。| **what astonishes someone is** *What astonishes me most is his complete lack of fear.* 最令我吃惊的是，他一点儿也不害怕。

as·ton·ished /əˋstɑnɪʃt; əˈstɒnɪʃt/ *adj* very surprised about something 对…感到吃惊的：*We climbed out of the hole, right in front of two astonished policemen.* 我们爬出洞口，恰好出现在两个警察面前，他们显得很惊讶。| **astonished that** *The man seemed astonished that anyone would want to buy the house.* 这人显得很惊讶，居然有人想买这房子。| **astonished to see/hear/find etc** *We were astonished to find the temple still in its original condition.* 我们惊讶地发现该寺庙仍完好无损。

as·ton·ish·ing /əˋstɑnɪʃɪŋ; əˈstɒnɪʃɪŋ/ *adj* so surprising that it is difficult to believe 令人惊讶的：*an astonishing achievement* 惊人的成就 —**astonishingly** *adv*: *She looked astonishingly beautiful.* 她美得令人称奇。

as·ton·ish·ment /əˋstɑnɪʃmənt; əˈstɒnɪʃmənt/ *n* [U] complete surprise 惊异，惊讶：**in astonishment** *She stared at him in astonishment.* 她吃惊地看着他。| **to your astonishment** *To my astonishment, the keys were in the door.* 令我吃惊的是，钥匙就在门上。

As·ton Mar·tin /ˌæstn̩ ˋmɑrtn̩; ˈæstən ˈmɑːtɨn/ *trademark* a type of fast sports car made by the British company Aston Martin【商标】阿斯顿·马丁跑车〔英国阿斯顿·马丁公司制造的一种运动型跑车〕

As·ton Vil·la /ˌ‥ ˈ‥◂/ the name of a British football club based in Birmingham 阿斯顿维拉〔英国伯明翰一足球俱乐部〕

As·tor /ˋæstɚ; ˈæstə/**, Nan·cy** /ˋnænsɪ; ˈnænsi/ (1879-1964) a British politician, born in the US, who was the first woman to be a member of parliament in the UK 阿斯特〔(1879-1964)，生于美国，英国政治家，英国议会首位女议员〕

as·tound /əˋstaund; əˈstaʊnd/ *v* [T] to make someone very surprised or shocked 使震惊：*The judge's decision astounded everyone.* 法官的判决使大家深感震惊。—**astounded** *adj*: *an astounded look* 吃惊的眼光

as·tound·ing /əˋstaundɪŋ; əˈstaʊndɪŋ/ *adj* so surprising that it is almost impossible to believe 令人震惊的：*house prices shooting up at an astounding rate* 房价以惊人的速度猛涨 —**astoundingly** *adv*: *astoundingly beautiful scenery* 异乎寻常的美景

as·tra·khan /ˌæstrəˋkæn; ˌæstrəˈkæn◂/ *n* [U] black or grey fur used for making coats and hats〔制造衣帽的〕阿斯特拉罕羔羊皮

as·tral /ˋæstrəl; ˈæstrəl/ *adj formal* connected with stars【正式】星的，关于星的：*astral bodies* 星体

a·stray /əˋstre; əˈstreɪ/ *adv* **1 go astray a)** to become lost 迷失，迷路：*One of the documents has gone astray.* 有一份文件不见了。**b)** *humorous* to start behaving in an immoral way【幽默】走入歧途 **2 lead sb astray a)** *often humorous* to encourage someone to do bad or immoral things that they would not normally do【常幽默】把某人引入歧途：*His mother worries that the older boys will lead him astray.* 他母亲担心比他大的孩子会把他带坏。**b)** to make someone believe something that is not true 误导某人：*It's easy to be led astray by the reports in the papers.* 很容易受报纸上的内容误导。

a·stride /əˋstraɪd; əˈstraɪd/ *adv* with one leg on each side of something 跨坐地；跨骑地；跨在…上

as·trin·gent¹ /əˋstrɪndʒənt; əˈstrɪndʒənt/ *adj* **1** *technical* able to make your skin less oily or stop a wound from bleeding【术语】收敛(性)的；止血的：*an astringent lotion* 收敛化妆水 **2** criticizing someone very severely 严厉的，尖刻的：*astringent remarks* 尖刻的言辞 —**astringency** *n* [U]

astringent² *n* [C,U] *technical* a substance used to make your skin less oily or to stop a wound from bleeding【术语】收敛剂；止血药

astro- /æstro; æstrəʊ/ *prefix* concerning the stars, the PLANETs, or space (关于) 星球 [天体，宇宙，太空] 的：*an astronaut* (=someone who travels in space) 宇航员，太空人 | *astrophysics* (=science of the stars) 天体物理学

as·trol·o·ger /əˋstrɑlədʒɚ; əˈstrɒlədʒə/ *n* [C] someone who uses astrology to tell people about their character, life, or future 占星(术)家

as·trol·o·gy /əˋstrɑlədʒɪ; əˈstrɒlədʒi/ *n* [U] the study of the relationship between the movements of the stars and their influence on people and events 占星术 —see also 另见 ZODIAC —**astrological** /ˌæstrəˋlɑdʒɪkl̩; ˌæstrəˈlɒdʒɪkəl◂/ *adj* —**astrologically** /-klɪ; -kli/ *adv*

as·tro·naut /ˋæstrəˌnɔt; ˈæstrənɔːt/ *n* [C] someone who travels and works in a SPACECRAFT 宇航员，太空人

as·tro·nom·i·cal /ˌæstrəˋnɑmɪkl̩; ˌæstrəˈnɒmɪkəl◂/ *adj* **1** astronomical prices, costs etc are extremely high 极巨大的；天文数字的 **2** connected with the study of the stars 星的，天体的，天文(学)的 —**astronomically** /-klɪ; -kli/ *adv*: *astronomically high rents* 巨额租金

as·tron·o·my /əˋstrɑnəmɪ; əˈstrɒnəmi/ *n* [U] the scientific study of the stars 天文学

as·tro·phys·ics /ˌæstroˋfɪzɪks; ˌæstrəʊˈfɪzɪks/ *n* [U] the scientific study of the chemical structure of the stars and the forces that influence them 天体物理学 —**astrophysical** *adj* —**astrophysicist** /-ˋfɪzəsɪst; -ˈfɪzɨsɨst/ *n* [C]

as·tro·turf /ˋæstrotɝf; ˈæstrəʊtɜːf/ *n* [U] *trademark* an artificial surface, like grass, that is used in sports such as football【商标】阿斯特罗人造草皮〔用于体育运动，如足球〕

as·tute /əˋstut; əˈstjuːt/ *adj* able to understand situations or behaviour very well and very quickly, especially so that you can get an advantage for yourself 精明的，敏锐的；狡黠的：*a particularly astute electoral move* 一个特别明智的选举步骤 | *astute investments* 精明的投资 —**astutely** *adv* —**astuteness** *n* [U]

A·sun·ci·ón /əˌsunˋsion; əˌsuːnsiˈəʊn/ also 又作 **Nuestra Señora de La Asunción** a city in southern Paraguay, the country's capital, largest city, and main port, on the River Paraguay 亚松森〔巴拉圭南部一城市，该国首都和最大的城市，巴拉圭河边的主要港口〕

a·sun·der /ə`sʌndə; əˈsʌndə/ *adv* **be torn asunder** *literary* to be broken violently into many pieces【文】破成碎块，散成碎片: *The boat was torn asunder on the rocks.* 船被礁石撞成碎片。

As·wan High Dam /ˌæswɑn haɪ `dæm; ˌæswɑːn haɪ ˈdæm/ a DAM built across the River Nile in southern Egypt. It is one of the largest dams in the world and is used to produce electricity and provide water for farming 阿斯旺高坝〔埃及南部横跨尼罗河的一座大坝，为世界上最大的堤坝之一，用以发电和提供农业用水〕

a·sy·lum /ə`saɪləm; əˈsaɪləm/ *n* **1** [U] protection given to someone by a government because they have escaped from fighting or political trouble in their own country（政治）避难，（政治）庇护 —see also 另见 POLITICAL ASYLUM **2** [C] *old use* a MENTAL HOSPITAL【旧】疯人院，精神病院

a·sym·met·ri·cal /ˌesɪ`mɛtrɪkl; ˌeɪsɪˈmetrɪkəl/ also 又作 **a·sym·met·ric** /-`mɛtrɪk; -ˈmetrɪk◂/ *adj* **1** having two sides that are different in shape 不对称的，不匀称的: *asymmetrical patterns* 不对称图案 **2** *formal* not equal【正式】不相等的 —opposite 反义词 SYMMETRICAL **—asymmetrically** /-klɪ; -kli/ *adv*

a·symp·to·mat·ic /eˌsɪmptə`mætɪk; æˌsɪmptəˈmætɪk/ *adj* if someone or the illness that they have is asymptomatic, there are no signs of the illness 无症状的

As You Like It /ˌ· · ˈ· ·/ a humorous play by William Shakespeare, set in the Forest of Arden, about the adventures and marriages of two couples, Rosalind and Orlando, and Celia and Oliver《皆大欢喜》〔莎士比亚的一部幽默喜剧。该剧以阿登森林为背景，讲述罗萨琳德与奥兰多、西莉娅与奥里弗这两对夫妇的历险和婚姻故事〕

S1 W1 **at** /ət; ət; *strong* 强读 æt; æt/ *prep* **1** used to show a point in space where someone or something is, or where an event is happening 在…〔表示地点〕: *We'll meet at my house.* 我们将在我家见面。| *a huge queue at the bus stop* 公共汽车站的长队 | *They sat down at a corner table.* 他们在角落的桌旁坐下。| **at Jack's/Sue's etc** (=at Jack's house, Sue's house etc) 在杰克/休等的家里 *Pete's round at Mel's.* 皮特在梅尔家附近。| **at the doctor's/the bank/the airport etc** (=at a place you go to for a particular purpose) 在诊所/银行/机场等 *Guess who I met at the dentist's?* 猜猜我在牙科诊所遇到了谁？**2** **at a party/club/funeral etc** at an event while it is taking place 在聚会/俱乐部/葬礼上等: *I met my wife at a disco.* 我在迪斯科舞厅遇见了我的妻子。| *They're all out at the cinema.* 他们都出去看电影了。**3** **at school/work etc** regularly going to school, work etc 上学/上班等: *Is Jessica still at school?* (=does she go to school regularly) 杰西卡还上学吗？**4** **at lunch/dinner etc** eating your lunch, dinner etc 在吃午饭/晚餐等: *I'm sorry, Pam's at lunch just now.* 对不起，帕姆现在在吃午饭。**5** used to show an exact time 在…〔表示确切的时间〕: *The film starts at 8 o'clock.* 电影在8点钟开始。| **at the moment** (=now) 现在，此刻 *We're really busy at the moment.* 我们现在很忙。**6** used to show a particular period of time during which something happens 在…（期间）: *My husband often works at night.* 我丈夫经常在晚上工作。| *We like to go to Midnight Mass at Christmas.* 圣诞节时我们喜欢去做子夜弥撒。**7** used to show the person or thing that an action is directed or aimed at 对着…; 朝…方向: *Protesters threw rotten eggs at the speakers.* 抗议者向演讲者扔臭鸡蛋。| *Jake shot at the deer but missed.* 杰克朝鹿开了一枪，但没打中。| *Look at that!* 看那个！| *Stop shouting at the kids all the time.* 别总是冲着孩子大喊大叫。**8** used to show the thing that caused an action or feeling 对…; 由于…: *The children all laughed at his jokes.* 孩子们听了他说的笑话都大笑起来。| *I'm surprised at you!* 你让我吃惊！| *Dad got really mad at me for scratching the car.* 爸爸对我划坏了汽车感到很生气。**9** used to show the subject or activity that you are considering when making a judgment about someone's ability 在…方面: *Barbara's getting on really well at her new job.* 芭芭拉在新的工作岗位上干得真不错。| *Rosa's a genius at chemistry.* 罗莎在化学方面是个天才。| **good/bad etc at (doing) sth** *Luis was always good at maths.* 路易斯总是很擅长数学。| *Matt's bad at handling people.* 马特不擅长跟人打交道。**10** used to show a continuous state or activity 处于…〔表示情况、状态〕: *two nations at war* 处于交战状态的两国 | *Many children are still at risk from neglect or abuse.* 许多孩子仍处于没人照顾或受虐待的危险中。| *Granny's at peace now.* (=dead) 奶奶已故世了。| **at large** (=if someone or something dangerous is at large they are in a particular area and may harm or kill someone)〔危险人物或野兽〕自由的，逍遥的，未被捕的 *rumours of a black panther at large* 一只黑豹在任意出没的传言 —see picture on page A1 参见A1页图 **11** used to show a price, rate, level, age, speed etc 以…; 在…〔表示价格、比率、水准、年龄、速度等〕: *old books selling at 10 cents each* 以每本十美分（的价格）出售的旧书 | *The house was sold at a price of £250,000.* 房子以25万英镑的价格售出。| *You should have more sense at your age.* 你这个年龄不应该这样不懂事。| *The car was going at about 50 mph.* 汽车以每小时50英里的速度行驶。| *Amanda rode off at a gallop.* 阿曼达匆匆忙忙地骑马走了。**12** **at least/worst/most etc** the least, worst etc thing possible 至少/最糟/至多等: *John has to practise for at least half an hour every day.* 约翰每天至少得练半小时。| *At worst, up to 50% of the population could be affected.* 最坏的情况就是50%的人可能受到影响。| **at the very least/most/worst etc** *That car's worth £250 at the very most.* 那辆汽车充其量也就值250英镑。| **at its/her/their best etc** *The garden is at its best in June.* 花园在6月的景色最美。| *This was Sampras at his most powerful.* 这是处于巅峰期的桑普拉斯。**13** used to show that you are trying to do something but are not succeeding or completing it〔勉强地〕在〔做某事〕: *George was just picking at his food.* 乔治在挑挑拣拣地吃东西。| *Sarah took another sip at her wine.* 莎拉又啜了一小口酒。| *I clutched at the rope but missed.* 我伸手去抓绳子，但没抓着。**14** **at sb's invitation/command** because someone asks or orders you to do something 应某人之邀/据某人之命令: *Rachel attended the dinner at the chairman's command.* 雷切尔在主席的嘱咐下参加了晚宴。**15** **at that** **a)** also or besides 也，还，而且: *It's a new idea, and a good one, at that.* 这是个新主意，还是个好主意哩。**b)** after something happens or as a result of it; then 随即，然后: *Tess called him a liar and at that he stormed out of the room.* 特丝说他是个骗子，他一听便气冲冲地走出了房间。—see also 另见 **leave it at that** (LEAVE[1] (12)) **16** **at a time** at the same time 每次; 同时: *Ben was putting chocolates in his mouth two at a time.* 本每次往嘴里放两块巧克力。**17** **where it's at** *informal* used to describe a place or activity that is very popular, exciting, and fashionable【非正式】流行[精彩，时尚]的场所或活动: *This Hacienda Club is where it's at.* 这种西班牙农场式的俱乐部很流行。—see also 另见 **(not) at all** (ALL[3] (7)) —see picture on page A1 参见A1页图

At·a·turk /`ætətɝk; ˈætətɜːk/, **Ke·mal** /kɛ`mɑl; keˈmɑːl/ (1881-1938) a Turkish politician and army officer who established the modern state of Turkey and became its first President in 1923 阿塔图尔克〔(1881-1938)，土耳其政治家、军官。建立了土耳其共和国，1923年当选第一任总统〕

at·a·vis·tic /ˌætə`vɪstɪk; ˌætəˈvɪstɪk◂/ *adj formal* atavistic feelings are very basic human feelings, that people have felt since humans have existed【正式】返祖的; 原始的

ate /et; eɪt/ the past tense of EAT

-ate /ɪt, et; ət, eɪt/ *suffix* **1** [in adjectives 构成形容词] full of or showing a particular quality 充满…的，有…特点的: *very affectionate* (=showing love) 多情的 **2** [in verbs 构成动词] to make something have a particular quality 使…: *to activate* (=make active) 使活跃，使活动 | *to regulate* (=make regular; control) 使有规律，使合乎规范 **3** [in nouns 构成名词] a group of people with certain duties〔具有某种职责的〕人: *the electorate* (=voters) 选民 | *an inspectorate* 检查员，监察员 **4** [in nouns 构成名词] the job, rank, or degree of a particular type of person 职务，身份，状况: *She was awarded her doctorate.* (=the degree of doctor) 她被授予博士学位。**5** *technical* [in nouns 构成名词] a chemical salt formed from a particular acid【术语】(…酸的）盐: *phosphate* 磷酸盐 **—-ately** /ɪtlɪ; ətli/ [in adverbs 构成副词]: *fortunately* 幸运地; 幸好

a·the·is·m /`eθɪˌɪzəm; ˈeɪθiɪzəm/ *n* [U] the belief that God does not exist 无神论 **—atheist** *n* [C] **—atheistic** /ˌeθɪ`ɪstɪk; ˌeɪθiˈɪstɪk◂/ *adj* **—atheistical** *adj*

A·the·na /ə`θinə; əˈθiːnə/ also 又作 **Athene** /ə`θini, əˈθiːni/ in Greek MYTHOLOGY, the goddess of WISDOM and the arts. In Roman mythology her name is Minerva. 雅典娜〔古希腊神话中智慧与艺术女神，在罗马神话中称密涅瓦〕

Ath·ens /`æθənz; ˈæθənz/ the capital city of Greece. Athens was the most important city of ancient Greece. 雅典〔希腊首都，古希腊最重要的城市〕**—Athenian** /ə`θinjən; əˈθiːniən/ *adj, n*

ath·lete /`æθlit; ˈæθliːt/ *n* [C] someone who is good at or who often does sports 运动员: *a natural athlete* 天生的运动员

athlete's foot /ˌ· ˈ· ˈ·/ *n* [U] a medical condition in which the skin cracks between your toes 脚癣，香港脚

ath·let·ic /æθ`lɛtɪk; æθˈletɪk/ *adj* **1** physically strong and good at sport 强壮的，擅长运动的: *Sven was tall, blonde, and athletic looking.* 斯文个子高，一头金发，看上去像个运动员。**2** connected with athletics 运动的

ath·let·ics /æθ`lɛtɪks; æθˈletɪks/ *n* [U] *BrE* sports such as running and jumping【英】体育，田径（项目）; TRACK AND FIELD *AmE*【美】

-athon /əθɑn; əθən/ *suffix* [in nouns 构成名词] *informal* an event in which a particular thing is done for a very long time, especially to collect money【非正式】〔尤指为筹钱〕持续时间很长的事件, 马拉松式的活动: *a swimathon* 长距离游泳比赛 | *a talkathon* 马拉松式的冗长演说

a·thwart /əˋθwɔrt; əˈθwɔːt/ *prep literary* across【文】横跨过

-ation /eʃən; eɪʃən/ *suffix* [in nouns 构成名词] the act, state, or result of doing something …动作(造成的状态或结果): *an examination of the contents* (=examining them) 对内容的检查 | *the combination of several factors* 几种因素的综合

a·tish·oo /əˋtɪʃu; əˈtɪʃuː/ *spoken* a word used to represent the sound you make when you SNEEZE【口】阿嚏〔打喷嚏的声音〕

-ative /ətɪv; ətɪv/ *suffix* [in adjectives 构成形容词] liking something or tending to do something or show a particular quality 喜欢…的; 有…倾向或特点的: *talkative* (=liking to talk a lot) 喜欢说话的, 多嘴的 | *argumentative* (=enjoying arguments) 喜欢争论的 | *imaginative* (=showing imagination) 富于想象力的

At·lan·ta /ətˋlæntə; ətˈlæntə/ the capital city of the state of Georgia in the US 亚特兰大〔美国佐治亚州首府〕

At·lan·tic, the /ətˋlæntɪk; ətˈlæntɪk/ also 又作 **the Atlantic Ocean** British people sometimes use phrases such as 'across the Atlantic' or 'on the other side of the Atlantic' when they are talking about the US, and Americans use these phrases when they are talking about Western Europe, especially the UK. 大西洋〔英国人有时用"大西洋彼岸"这一说法指称美国, 而美国人则用同一说法指称西欧, 尤其是英国〕: *Scientists from both sides of the Atlantic will meet next month in New York.* 大西洋两岸的科学家下月将在纽约相聚。

Atlantic Cit·y /ˌ·ˌ··ˈ··/ a city in New Jersey, US, on the coast of the Atlantic Ocean, known especially for its CASINOs 大西洋城〔美国新泽西州一城市, 位于大西洋沿岸, 尤以赌场著称〕

Atlantic O·cean, the /ˌ·ˌ··ˈ··/ the ocean between the east coast of North and South America and the west coast of Europe and Africa. The Atlantic Ocean is the world's second largest ocean. 大西洋〔世界第二大洋, 位于南北美洲东岸与欧洲、非洲西岸之间〕

At·lan·tis /ətˋlæntɪs; ətˈlæntɨs/ according to ancient Greek stories, an island continent west of Gibraltar that sank into the Atlantic Ocean after an earthquake 大西岛, 亚特兰蒂斯〔古希腊传说中一岛, 位于直布罗陀海峡以西, 一次地震后沉入大西洋〕

Atlas in Greek MYTHOLOGY, one of the Titans (=the first gods who ruled the universe). After the Titans were defeated by Zeus, Atlas was forced to hold the sky on his shoulders forever. In art, however, Atlas is usually shown holding the world on his shoulders, not the sky. 阿特拉斯〔希腊神话中提坦巨人之一。提坦巨人被宙斯打败后, 阿特拉斯只得双肩扛天, 永无休止。然而, 艺术作品中的他通常是双肩扛地球, 而不是扛着天〕

at·las /ˋætləs; ˈætləs/ *n* [C] a book of maps 地图集, 地图册: *a world atlas* 世界地图册

Atlas Mountains /ˌ·ˈ··ˌ··/ a line of mountains in North Africa that stretches across Morocco, Algeria, and Tunisia 阿特拉斯山脉〔北非一山脉, 横跨摩洛哥、阿尔及利亚和突尼斯〕

ATM /ˌe ti ˋɛm; ˌeɪ tiː ˈem/ *n* [C] *AmE* a machine outside a bank that you use to get money from your account【美】自动柜员机, 自动提款机; CASHPOINT *BrE*【英】

W2 **at·mo·sphere** /ˋætməsˌfɪr; ˈætməsfɪə/ *n* [C,U] **1** **the atmosphere** the mixture of gases that surrounds the Earth 大气(层) **2** the air inside a room〔室内的〕空气: *a smoky atmosphere* 烟雾弥漫的空气 **3** the feeling that an event or place gives you 气氛, 环境: *The atmosphere at home's been depressing since they had that fight.* 自从那次他们打架以来, 家里的气氛日渐压抑。| **atmosphere of crisis/optimism etc** *An atmosphere of optimism dominated the party conference.* 党的会议在乐观的气氛中进行。

at·mo·spher·ic /ˌætməsˋfɛrɪk; ˌætməsˈferɪk◂/ *adj* **1** [only before noun 仅用于名词前] related with the Earth's atmosphere 大气(层)的; 有关大气的: *atmospheric pressure* 气压 **2** beautiful and mysterious 有神秘美感的; 制造气氛的: *atmospheric music* 能制造气氛的音乐

at·mo·spher·ics /ˌætməsˋfɛrɪks; ˌætməsˈferɪks/ *n* [plural] continuous cracking noises that sometimes interrupt radio broadcasts〔无线电的〕大气干扰; 天电

at·oll /ˋætɑl; ˈætɒl/ *n* [C] a CORAL[1] island in the shape of a ring 环状珊瑚岛, 环礁: *an atomic bomb detonated on Bikini Atoll in the Pacific* 一颗原子弹在太平洋的比基尼岛上爆炸

at·om /ˋætəm; ˈætəm/ *n* [C] **1** the smallest part of an ELEMENT (1) that can exist alone or combine with other substances to form MOLECULEs 原子 **2** a very small amount of something 一点儿: *There isn't an atom of truth in it.* 那里面没有丝毫的真实性。

atom bomb /ˈ·· ˌ/ also 又作 **atomic bomb** /ˌ·ˌ·· ˈ/ *n* [C] a NUCLEAR bomb that splits atoms to cause an extremely large explosion 原子弹

a·tom·ic /əˋtɑmɪk; əˈtɒmɪk/ *adj* **1** related to the energy produced by splitting atoms or the weapons that use this energy 原子的; 原子能的; 核能的: *atomic warfare* 核战争 | *an atomic submarine* 核潜艇 **2** connected with the atoms in a substance 原子的; 与原子有关的: *atomic weight* 原子量

atomic en·er·gy /ˌ·ˌ··ˈ···/ *n* [U] NUCLEAR ENERGY 原子能, 核能

at·om·izer /ˋætəmˌaɪzə; ˈætəmaɪzə/ *n* [C] a thing used to make a liquid such as PERFUME[1] (1) come out of a bottle in very small drops like mist 雾化器, 喷雾器: *a perfume atomizer* 喷雾香水瓶 | *a paint atomizer* 喷涂器

a·ton·al /eˋtonl; eɪˈtəʊnl/ *adj* a piece of music that is atonal is not based on a particular KEY[2] (4)〔音乐〕无调的 **—atonally** *adv* **—atonality** /ˌetoˋnælətɪ; ˌeɪtəʊˈnælɨti/ *n* [U]

a·tone /əˋton; əˈtəʊn/ *v* [I] *formal* to do something to show that you are sorry for having done something wrong【正式】赎(罪); 弥补(过失等): **[+for]** *Richard was anxious to atone for his thoughtlessness.* 理查德急切地想弥补自己考虑不周的过失。

a·tone·ment /əˋtonmənt; əˈtəʊnmənt/ *n* [U] *formal* something you do to show that you are sorry for having done something wrong【正式】赔罪, 谢罪; 弥补过失

a·top /əˋtɑp; əˈtɒp/ *prep literary* on top of something【文】在…顶上, 在…上面

-ator /etə; eɪtə/ *suffix* [in nouns 构成名词] someone or something that does something 做…动作的人; 起…作用的事物: *a narrator* (=someone who tells a story) 叙事人 | *a generator* (=machine that produces electricity) 发电机

A to Z /ˌe tə ˋzi; ˌeɪ tə ˈzed/ *n* [C] *trademark* a book with maps that show every street in a British city【商标】〔英国的〕城市指南: *the London A to Z*《伦敦街道图》

at-risk /ˌ·ˈ·◂/ *adj* **at-risk children/patients etc** people who need special care because they are likely to be in danger from violent parents, to become ill etc 需要特别保护的孩子/病人等: **at-risk register** (=an official list of people in this situation) 需特别保护人员名单

at·ri·um /ˋetrɪəm; ˈeɪtriəm/ *n* [C] **1** one of the two spaces in the top of your heart that push blood into the VENTRICLEs 心房 **2** a large high open space in a tall building〔高楼大厦的〕中庭, 天井

a·tro·cious /əˋtroʃəs; əˈtrəʊʃəs/ *adj* extremely bad or showing no ability to do something at all 凶残的; 恶劣的, 糟糕的, 差劲的: *atrocious weather* 恶劣的天气 | *Her singing was atrocious.* 她的演唱很差劲。| *atrocious housing conditions* 恶劣的居住条件 **—atrociously** *adv* **—atrociousness** *n* [U]

a·troc·i·ty /əˋtrɑsətɪ; əˈtrɒsɨti/ *n* [C usually plural 一般用复数, U] an extremely cruel and violent action, especially during a war〔尤指战争中的〕暴行: *one of the worst atrocities of the Vietnam War* 越南战争中最骇人听闻的暴行

at·ro·phy /ˋætrəfɪ; ˈætrəfi/ *v* [I,T] to become weak or make something become weak because of lack of use or lack of blood (使)萎缩, (使)衰退: *therapy to prevent the leg muscles from atrophying* 防止腿部肌肉萎缩的疗法 **—atrophy** *n* [U]

at·tach /əˋtætʃ; əˈtætʃ/ *v* [T] S2 W2

1 ▶**CONNECT** 连接◀ to connect one thing to another 系; 绑; 贴; 固定; 连接; 附上: **attach sth to** *Attach a recent photograph to your application form.* 申请表上请贴一张近照。| **be attached to** *a small battery attached to a little loudspeaker* 装在小喇叭上的一节小电池 | *The web was only attached to the leaf by one thread.* 蜘蛛网只有一根细丝吊在叶子上。

2 ▶**LIKE** 喜欢◀ **be attached to** to like someone or something very much, because you have known them or had them for a long time 喜欢, 依恋: *It's easy to become attached to the children you work with. Too attached, sometimes.* 很容易喜欢上和你相处的孩子们, 有时候会喜欢过头。

3 **attach importance/significance etc** to believe that something is important 重视, 认为…很重要: *People attach too much importance to economic forecasts.* 人们把经济预测看得过于重要。

4 **attach blame** if you attach blame or if blame attaches to someone, they have done something wrong 与…有牵连

5 ▶**FEELING/QUALITY** 感觉/质量◀ **be attached to** if a quality, feeling, idea etc is attached to a person, thing or event, it is connected with them 与…联系起来: *It's easy to let the emotions attached to one situation spill over into others.* 一件事中产生的情绪很容易会加诸于其他事情上。

6 ▶**ORGANIZATION/COMPANY** 组织/公司◀ **be attached to sth** **a)** to work for part of a particular organization, especially

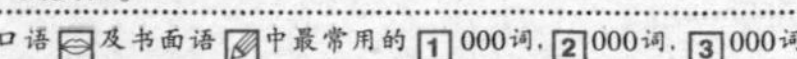

for a short period of time〔尤指短期地〕为…工作: *He was attached to the foreign affairs department of a Japanese newspaper.* 他在一家日本报纸的外事部门工作。**b)** to be part of a bigger organization 附属于…, 属于…的一个分支: *The Food Ministry is attached to the Ministry of Agriculture.* 粮食部隶属于农业部。

at·taché /ˌætəˈʃe; əˈtæʃeɪ/ *n* [C] someone who works in an EMBASSY, and deals with a particular subject〔在大使馆工作并处理某类问题的〕专员, 随员: *a cultural attaché* 文化专员

attaché case /·ˈ·· ·/ *n* [C] a thin case used for carrying business documents 手提公文包

at·tach·ment /əˈtætʃmənt; əˈtætʃmənt/ *n* **1** [C,U] a feeling that you like or love someone or something and that you would be unhappy without them 喜爱, 爱慕, 依恋: **[+to/for]** *I did feel a certain sense of attachment for the strange old guy.* 我的确对这古怪的老人感到有些依恋。**2** [U] belief in and loyalty towards a particular idea 信仰, 忠诚: **[+to/for]** *old people's attachment to traditional customs and ways* 老人们对传统习惯和生活方式的笃信 **3** [C] a part that you can put onto a machine to make it do different things 附件, 附属物, 附加装置: *a versatile food mixer that comes with a range of attachments* 有许多附件的多用途食品搅拌器 **4 on attachment** working for a particular organization, especially for a short period of time 为…短期工作: *He was sent on attachment to their offices in Hong Kong.* 他被派到他们在香港的办事处工作。

2 1 **at·tack¹** /əˈtæk; əˈtæk/ *n*

1 ▶VIOLENCE AGAINST SB 针对某人的暴力行为◀ [C] an act of deliberately using violence against someone 暴力事件, 打斗: **[+on]** *There have been several attacks on foreigners recently.* 最近发生了几次针对外国人的暴力事件。

2 ▶IN A WAR 在战争中◀ [C,U] the act of using weapons against an enemy in a war 进攻, 袭击, 攻击: *The attack began at dawn.* 进攻在拂晓开始。| **[+on]** *a carefully planned attack on Iraqi air bases* 对伊拉克空军基地的一次计划周密的袭击 | **be/come under attack** *Once again we came under attack from enemy fighter planes.* 我们又一次遭到敌人战斗机的攻击。| **launch an attack** (=start an attack) 发动袭击

3 ▶CRITICISM 批评◀ [C,U] a statement that criticizes someone strongly 抨击, 攻击, 非难, 责骂: **[+on]** *recent attacks on the Prime Minister* 最近对首相的抨击 | **be/come under attack** (=be strongly criticized) 遭到猛烈的抨击 *The company came under attack for the firing of 50 employees.* 公司因解雇了50名员工而受到猛烈抨击。| **go on the attack** (=start to criticize someone severely) 严厉批评

4 ▶ACTIONS TO STOP STH 阻止某事的行动◀ [C,U] actions intended to get rid of or stop something such as a system, a set of laws etc〔对体制、法律等的〕抑制, 打击、摒弃: **[+on]** *Mrs Thatcher's attack on the welfare state* 撒切尔夫人对福利国家制度的摒弃

5 ▶ILLNESS 疾病◀ [C] a sudden short period of suffering from an illness, especially an illness that you have often 突然发作: *an attack of asthma* 哮喘发作

6 ▶SPORT 体育◀ [C,U] **a)** an attempt by a group of players to make a GOAL (2) 进攻 **b)** the group of players on a team whose job is to make a GOAL (2) 进攻队员: *the Arsenal attack* 阿森纳队的进攻球员

7 an attack of fear/panic/anxiety etc a short period of time when you feel frightened, worried etc 一阵恐惧/惊慌/焦虑等: *panic attacks* 阵阵惊慌 —see also 另见 HEART ATTACK

2 ? **attack²** *v*

1 ▶ATTACK SOMEONE 攻击某人◀ [I,T] to deliberately use physical violence against someone 袭击, 殴打: *Jim was attacked by a man in the park.* 吉姆在公园里遭到一个男人的袭击。| *dogs trained to attack on command* 经训练一听到命令就攻击的狗 | **attack sb with sth** *She started attacking the burglar with a piece of wood.* 她开始用一块木头猛打进屋行窃的小偷。

2 ▶IN A WAR 在战争中◀ [I,T] to start using guns, bombs etc against an enemy in a war 进攻, 攻击, 袭击: *The village had been attacked by the French airforce.* 这个村子遭到法国空军的袭击。

3 ▶CRITICIZE 批评◀ [T] to criticize someone or something very strongly 抨击, 攻击, 责难: *The senator made a speech attacking Clinton's healthcare program.* 这位参议员发表演说抨击克林顿的卫生保健计划。| **attack sb for sth** *The article attacked the government for its policy on education.* 这篇文章抨击了政府的教育政策。

4 ▶SPORT 体育◀ [I,T] to move forward and try to make a GOAL (2) 进攻: *Brazil began to attack more in the second half of the match.* 巴西队下半场加强了进攻。

5 ▶BEGIN DOING 开始做◀ [T] to begin doing a job or dealing with a problem with determination and eagerness 着手处理, 投入: *She immediately set about attacking the problem.* 她立即着手处理该问题。

6 ▶DISEASE 疾病◀ [T] to damage part of someone's body 给…造成伤害; 侵袭, 侵蚀: *a cruel disease that attacks the central nervous system* 一种破坏中枢神经系统的残酷疾病

at·tain /əˈten; əˈteɪn/ *v* [T] *formal*【正式】**1** to succeed in reaching a particular level or in getting something after trying for a long time 达到, 获得, 赢得: *More women are attaining positions of power in public life.* 越来越多的妇女在公共生活中获得权位。**2** to reach a high level 达到, 涨到: *Share prices attained a high of $3.27.* 每股价格涨到3.27美元之高。—**attainable** *adj*: *This target should be attainable.* 此目标应该能实现。

at·tain·ment /əˈtenmənt; əˈteɪnmənt/ *n formal*【正式】**1** [U] success in getting something or reaching a particular level 获得, 达到, 实现: *the attainment of happiness* 获得幸福 **2** [C] something that you have succeeded in getting or learning, such as a skill 成就, 造诣, 学识, 技能

at·tempt¹ /əˈtɛmpt; əˈtempt/ *n* [C] **1** an act of trying to do something, especially something difficult 努力, 尝试, 企图〔尤指较难的事情〕: **attempt to do sth** *All attempts to control inflation have failed.* 所有控制通货膨胀的尝试都失败了。| **[+at]** *He made one last attempt at the world record.* 他为打破世界纪录作了最后一次努力。| **make no attempt** *The protestors made no attempt to resist arrest.* 抗议者对逮捕未进行抵抗。| **in an attempt to do sth** *In an attempt to diffuse the tension I suggested that we break off for lunch.* 为了消除紧张感, 我建议我们停下来去吃午饭。**2 an attempt on sb's life** an act of trying to kill someone, especially someone famous or important 企图谋杀某人〔尤指名人或重要人物〕 2 1

attempt² *v* [T] to try to do something that is difficult, dangerous, or has never been done before 试图, 尝试, 企图: **attempt to do sth** *Every time I've attempted to convince her, I've failed completely.* 每一次我都试图说服她, 但全然不起作用。| **attempt sth** *Weather conditions prevented them from attempting the jump.* 天气状况使他们无法试跳。 2 2

at·tend /əˈtɛnd; əˈtend/ *v* **1** [I,T] to go to an event such as a meeting or a class 参加, 出席, 到场: *Only 7 people attended the meeting.* 只有七个人参加会议。| *Please let us know if you are unable to attend.* 如你不能出席, 请通知我们。—see 见 JOIN[1] (USAGE) **2** [I,T] to go regularly to a school, church etc 上〔学〕, 去〔教堂〕: *All children between the ages of 5 and 16 must attend school.* 所有5至16岁的孩子必须上学。**3** [T] *formal* to happen or exist at the same time as something【正式】陪伴, 伴随…而至: *the peculiar atmosphere which attends such an event* 笼罩着这事件的古怪气氛 **4** [T] to look after someone, especially because they are ill 看护, 照料 2 2

attend to sb/sth *phr v* [T] **1** to deal with business or personal matters 处理, 料理〔生意或个人事务〕: *I may be late – I have got one or two things to attend to.* 我也许会迟到, 我有一两件事要处理。**2** to help a customer in a shop or a restaurant to buy or order something〔在商店或饭店〕照顾, 接待〔顾客〕—see 见 JOIN[1] (USAGE)

Frequencies of **attend** and **go to** in spoken and written English 在英语口语和书面语中 attend 和 go to 的使用频率

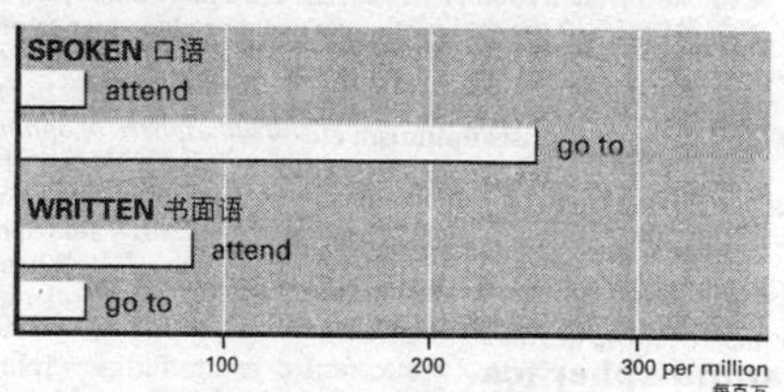

Based on the British National Corpus and the Longman Lancaster Corpus
据英国国家语料库和朗文兰开斯特语料库

Both verbs are used to mean 'be at an event'. The graph shows that in this meaning **go to** is much more common than in spoken English. In written or formal English **attend** is more common.
这两个动词都用于表示"参加"的意思。本图表显示, 口语中用于此义时, go to 的使用频率远远高于 attend。在书面语和正式用语中 attend 则更为常用。

at·tend·ance /əˋtɛndəns; əˈtendəns/ *n* **1** [C] the number of people who attend a game, concert, meeting etc 出席人数，出席者：**high/low attendance** *a low attendance at class of 84's reunion* 84年毕业班校友聚会出席人数很少 **2** [C,U] the number of times that you go to a meeting, class etc that is held regularly 出席（率），到场（次数）：*Many students have a very poor attendance record.* 许多学生的出勤率很低。**3 be in attendance** *formal* to be at a special or important event【正式】出席，参加：*Over 2,000 people were in attendance at yesterday's demonstration.* 有两千多人参加了昨天的示威游行。**4 be in attendance on sb** *formal* to look after someone or serve them【正式】照顾[侍候]某人 —see also 另见 **dance attendance on** (DANCE[2] (5))

at·tend·ant[1] /əˋtɛndənt; əˈtendənt/ *n* [C] **1** someone whose job is to look after or help customers in a public place 服务员：*a car-park attendant* 停车场的服务员 **2** someone who looks after a very important person, such as a king or queen 侍从，随从；卫士

attendant[2] *adj formal*【正式】**1** connected with or caused by something 伴随的，随之而来的，附带的：*nuclear power, with all its attendant risks* 核能及其伴随的危险 **2** going with or being with someone in order to help them 随侍的，负责照料的，服务的，服侍的

at·ten·tion /əˋtɛnʃən; əˈtenʃən/ *n*

1 ▶WATCHING/LISTENING CAREFULLY 仔细看/听◀ a) pay attention to carefully listen to or watch something that is happening, or to be careful about what you are doing 注意，专心，留心：*The teacher got angry with me when I didn't pay attention.* 当我不专心听讲时，老师很生气。| **[+to]** *The TV was on but Di wasn't paying much attention to it.* 电视开着，可是迪没怎么注意看。| **pay no attention to** (=used to tell someone to ignore what someone says because it is not true or not important) 对〔某人的话〕不要在意 *Don't pay any attention to him – he's always saying stupid things.* 别对他太在意，他总是说些蠢话。| **pay little attention to/not pay much attention to** (=behave in a way that shows that you do not think something or someone is very important) 对〔某人或某事〕不太在意 *We heard noises coming from upstairs, but we didn't pay much attention to them.* 我们听到了楼上有动静，但我们没太在意。**b) give sb/sth your attention** to listen to someone or study something carefully, especially so that you can deal with a problem 倾听某人/专注于某事：**give sb your full/undivided attention** *Now he's gone, I can give you my undivided attention.* 现在他已经走了，我可以把全部注意力都放在你身上。

2 ▶INTEREST 兴趣◀ a) [U] the interest that people show in someone or something 兴趣；关心，关注：*She was flattered by all the attention he was giving her.* 他对她很关心，她感到非常高兴。| **give sth attention** *The press has given the story a lot of attention.* 新闻界对这个报道给予很大关注。| **the centre of attention** (=a person who everyone looks at and is interested in) 人们注视的中心（人物）*Some people enjoy being the centre of attention.* 有些人喜欢成为别人关注的对象。| **the focus of attention** (=the situation that people are most concerned about or consider to be most important) 关注的焦点 *The focus of attention has shifted away from domestic issues.* 人们关注的焦点已不再是国内问题。| **hold/keep sb's attention** (=make someone continue to be interested in something) 一直吸引某人的兴趣 *Follett keeps the reader's attention throughout the book.* 福利特的书从头到尾都吸引着读者的兴趣。| **attention span** (=the period of time during which you continue to be interested in something) 注意广度〔能集中于某事的时间〕*Children generally have a short attention span.* 一般说来，孩子们能集中注意力的时间较短。

3 ▶MAKE SB NOTICE 使某人注意到◀ a) attract/catch/get sb's attention to make someone notice you, especially because you want to speak to them or you need their help 吸引/引起/得到某人的注意：*She tried to attract the waiter's attention.* 她设法吸引服务员的注意。**b) attract attention** if someone or something attracts attention, people notice them, especially because they look very interesting or unusual 引人注目：*The band members couldn't go out in the street because they attracted too much attention.* 乐队成员不能到街上去，因为他们太引人注目了。**c) get attention** to make someone notice you and be interested in what you are doing 吸引注意力：*Children are often bad in order to get attention.* 孩子们常常淘气，以吸引别人的注意力。**d) draw attention to** to make people notice and be concerned about something 使人们关注…：*The article was intended to draw attention to the situation in Cambodia.* 这篇文章旨在呼吁人们关注柬埔寨的局势。**e) draw attention away from** to make people stop being concerned about something such as a social problem 转移人们对…的注意力 **f) bring sth to sb's attention** to tell someone, especially someone in authority, about something such as a problem 使某事引起某人注意：*The matter was first brought to my attention earlier this year.* 今年较早时，我第一次注意到这个问题。**g) come to sb's attention** if something such as a problem comes to the attention of someone in authority, they find out about it 吸引某人的注意力，被发现

4 ▶REPAIR/TREATMENT 修理/处理◀ [U] **a)** something you do to repair or clean something, or make it work or be able to be used 维修，保养：*Honda 50cc for sale. Needs some attention.* 本田50cc出售，需要小修。**b)** treatment given to someone who is ill or injured 护理：*medical attention* 医疗护理

5 ▶CARE 关心◀ [C,U] things that you do to help someone which show that you like them 照顾：*Pets need a lot of care and attention.* 宠物需要很多的关心和照顾。

6 ▶SOLDIERS 士兵◀ stand to attention/be at attention to stand up straight in neat lines 站直，立正：**Attention!** (=used when ordering a group of soldiers to stand up straight) 立正！〔军队口令〕

7 ▶SPEECH/ANNOUNCEMENT 演说/通知◀ a) may/could I have your attention? *spoken* used in a formal situation when you want people to listen to you【口】大家请安静一下好吗？〔用于正式场合〕**b) thank you for your attention** *spoken* used at the end of a speech or statement to thank people for listening【口】〔用于演讲结束时〕谢谢大家

8 ▶LETTER 信◀ for the attention of used on the front of an official letter when you want a particular person to read it or deal with it …亲启：*for the attention of the manager* 经理亲启

at·ten·tive /əˋtɛntɪv; əˈtentɪv/ *adj* **1** listening or watching someone carefully because you are interested in them 关注的，注意的，专心的；注意听的：*The professor was pleased to have such an attentive audience.* 听众如此专心听讲让教授非常高兴。**2** making sure someone has everything they need 照顾周到的：**[+to]** *The crew were attentive to the passengers' needs.* 乘务人员很留意乘客的需要。—opposite 反义词 INATTENTIVE —**attentively** *adv*: *He listened attentively and with growing interest.* 他专心地听着，越来越感兴趣。—**attentiveness** *n* [U]

at·ten·u·ate /əˋtɛnju,et; əˈtenjueɪt/ *v* [T] *formal* to make something weaker or have less effect【正式】使变细；使变弱；使效果差；稀释：*an attenuated measles vaccine* 麻疹减毒疫苗 —**attenuation** *n* [U]

at·test /əˋtɛst; əˈtest/ *v* **1** [I,T] to show or prove that something is true 证明，作为（…的）证据：**[+to]** *Luxurious furnishings attested to the wealth of the owner.* 豪华的家具说明主人很有钱。**2** [T] to officially state that you believe something is true, especially in a court of law 作证，证实

at·tes·ta·tion /,ætɛsˋteʃən; ,æteˈsteɪʃən/ *n* [C,U] *formal* a legal statement made by someone in which they say that something is definitely true【正式】证明，证实，证词

at·tic /ˋætɪk; ˈætɪk/ *n* [C] a space or room under the roof of a house often used for storing things 阁楼；顶楼：*She went to college consigning her collection of cuddly toys to the attic.* 她去上大学，把心爱的毛绒玩具都放到了阁楼里。—see picture on page A4 参见A4页图

At·til·a /əˋtɪlə; əˈtɪlə/ also 又作 **Attila the Hun** (?406-453 AD) a king of the Huns (=an ancient people from Asia) who attacked and took control of large parts of the Roman Empire. He is famous for being violent and cruel. 阿提拉〔（公元?406-453），匈奴王。他曾攻占了罗马帝国的大片土地，以暴戾出名〕

at·tire /əˋtaɪr; əˈtaɪə/ *n* [U] *formal* clothes【正式】服装，衣服：*formal evening attire* 晚礼服

at·tired /əˋtaɪrd; əˈtaɪəd/ *adj* [not before noun 不用于名词前] *formal* dressed in a particular way【正式】…穿着的，…打扮的：*more suitably attired for a rave than for school* 打扮得更适合狂欢聚会而不适合上学

at·ti·tude /ˋætə,tud; ˈætɪtjuːd/ *n* **1** [C,U] the opinions and feelings that you usually have about something 态度，心态；感觉：**[+towards]** *Pete's attitude towards women really scares me.* 皮特对待女性的态度真让我害怕。**2** [C,U] the way that you behave towards someone or in a particular situation, especially when this shows how you feel 姿态：*an aggressive attitude* 一副挑衅的架势 | *As soon as they found out I was a doctor their whole attitude changed.* 他们一发现我是医生，整个态度都变了。| **attitude problem** (=behaviour that shows that you do not like to help people or do what you should do) 态度问题 | **have a good/bad attitude** *He has a bad attitude towards his schoolwork.* 他对待功课的态度不端正。**3** [U] *informal* a style of dressing, decorating etc that shows you have the confidence

to do unusual and exciting things without caring what other people think【非正式】我行我素的打扮: **with attitude** *a coat with attitude* 显示自我风格的大衣

At·tlee /ˈætli; ˈætliː/, **Clement** (1883-1967) a British politician in the Labour Party who was Prime Minister from 1945 to 1951. His government established the UK's National Health Service and the modern welfare state. 艾德礼〔(1883-1967),英国工党政治家, 1945至1951年任英国首相。他领导的政府创立了国民保健制度和一个现代福利国家〕

at·tor·ney /əˈtɜnɪ; əˈtɜːni/ *n* [C] *AmE* a lawyer【美】律师 —see 见 LAWYER (USAGE)

2 2 **attorney gen·e·ral** /.,.. ˈ...ˈ.../ *n* [C] the chief lawyer in a state or of the government in the US〔美国联邦或州的〕司法部长; 首席检察官

2 2 **at·tract** /əˈtrækt; əˈtrækt/ *v* [T] **1** to make someone interested in something, or make them want to take part in something 吸引, 引起〔兴趣、关注等〕: **attract sb to sth** *What attracted me most to the job was the chance to travel.* 这份工作最吸引我的是有旅行的机会。| **attract interest/attention etc** *The story has attracted a lot of interest in the media.* 这则报道引起了媒体的广泛关注。**2 be attracted to** to feel that you like someone and want to have a sexual relationship with them 喜爱, 为…所吸引: *I'm not usually attracted to blond men.* 我通常不喜欢金发男人。**3** to make someone like or admire something or feel romantically interested in someone 吸引; 引诱: *I guess it was his eyes that attracted me first.* 我想是他的眼睛先迷住了我。**4** to make someone or something move towards another thing 招引; 吸引: *Leftover food attracts flies.* 剩饭剩菜招引苍蝇。| *low rents designed to attract new businesses to the area* 低租金旨在吸引更多新企业到这地区来

3 **at·trac·tion** /əˈtrækʃən; əˈtrækʃən/ *n* **1** [C,U] a feeling of liking someone, especially in a sexual way 喜爱, 喜欢: *The attraction between them was almost immediate.* 他们几乎是一见钟情。**2** [C] something interesting or enjoyable to see or do 吸引人之物, 有魅力之物, 诱惑物: **tourist attraction** (=a place that many tourists visit) 旅游景点 | **the main attraction** (=the most popular place, person, or activity) 最受欢迎的人; 最吸引人的地方; 最精彩的活动 *The beautiful beaches are the island's main attraction.* 美丽的海滩是这个岛主要的吸引人之处。**3** [C,U] a feature or quality that makes something seem interesting or enjoyable 吸引力, 诱惑力: [+of] *Being your own boss is one of the attractions of owning your own business.* 自己当老板是发展自己事业的魅力之一。**4** [C,U] *technical* a force which makes things move together or stay together【术语】吸引力: *gravitational attraction* 重力, 万有引力

2 2 **at·trac·tive** /əˈtræktɪv; əˈtræktɪv/ *adj* **1** someone who is attractive is good looking, especially in a way that makes you sexually interested in them 有吸引力的, 诱人的: *an attractive young woman* 妩媚动人的年轻女子 | **find sb attractive** *I must admit I've never found him particularly attractive.* 我必须承认我从未发觉他有什么特别迷人的地方。**2** pleasant to look at 好看的, 漂亮的, 美观的: *Kitchen utensils should be attractive as well as functional.* 厨房用具应该既美观又实用。—see 见 BEAUTIFUL (USAGE) **3** having qualities that make you want to accept something or be involved in it 有吸引力的, 引人入胜的: [+to] *a political movement that is very attractive to the younger generation* 对年轻一代很有吸引力的政治运动 | **attractive offer/proposition/package etc** *It's a very attractive offer, and I'll have to give it serious thought.* 这是个非常好的建议, 我会认真考虑一下。—**attractively** *adv* —**attractiveness** *n* [U]

at·trib·u·ta·ble /əˈtrɪbjutəbl; əˈtrɪbjətəbəl/ *adj* [not before noun 不用于名词前] likely to be caused by something 可归因于…的: [+to] *Death was attributable to gunshot wounds.* 死因可能是枪伤。

at·tri·bute[1] /əˈtrɪbjut; əˈtrɪbjuːt/ *v*

attribute sth **to** sb/sth *phr v* [T] **1** to say that a situation or event is caused by something 把…归因于…: *The fall in the number of deaths from heart disease is generally attributed to improvements in diet.* 心脏病死亡人数的下降通常归因于日常饮食的改善。**2** to say that someone was responsible for saying or writing something, painting a famous picture etc 认为…属于…: *a saying usually attributed to Confucius* 一般认为是孔子说的一句名言 **3** to say that someone or something has a particular quality 具有…特性 —**attribution** /ˌætrəˈbjuʃən; ˌætrəˈbjuːʃən/ *n* [U]

at·tri·bute[2] /ˈætrəˌbjut; ˈætrəbjuːt/ *n* [C] a quality or feature, especially one that is considered to be good or useful 特性, 特质, 属性: *What attributes should a good manager possess?* 一名优秀的经理应该具有什么样的特点?

at·trib·u·tive /əˈtrɪbjətɪv; əˈtrɪbjətɪv/ *adj* describing and coming before a noun〔置于名词前〕起修饰作用的, 起定语作用的, 限定的: *In the phrase 'big city', 'big' is an attributive adjective, and in the phrase 'school bus', 'school' is a noun in an attributive position.* 在big city这个词组中, big是起修饰作用的形容词; 而在school bus这个词组中, school是起修饰作用的名词。—**attributively** *adv*

at·tri·tion /əˈtrɪʃən; əˈtrɪʃən/ *n* [U] the process of gradually destroying your enemy or making them weak by attacking them continuously 消耗, 消磨: *a war of attrition* 消耗战

at·tuned /əˈtund; əˈtjuːnd/ *adj* [not before noun 不用于名词前] familiar with the way someone thinks or behaves so that you can react to them in a suitable way 合拍的, 协调的, 适应的: [+to] *British companies still aren't really attuned to the needs of the Japanese market.* 英国公司还没有完全适应日本市场的需求。

At·wood /ˈætwud; ˈætwʊd/, **Margaret** (1939-) a Canadian writer of NOVELs and short stories, known especially for her books about women's lives, such as *Cat's Eye* and *The Handmaid's Tale* 阿特伍德〔(1939-), 加拿大小说家, 尤以创作女性生活题材的小说著名, 如《猫眼》和《女仆的故事》〕

a·typ·i·cal /eˈtɪpɪkl; eɪˈtɪpɪkəl/ *adj* not typical or usual 非典型的, 不同寻常的

au·ber·gine /ˈobəˌʒin; ˈəʊbəʒiːn/ *n* [C,U] *BrE* a large dark purple vegetable【英】紫茄子; EGGPLANT *AmE*【美】—see picture on page A9 参见 A9 页图

au·burn /ˈobən; ˈɔːbən/ *adj* auburn hair is a reddish brown colour 红褐色的, 茶色的 —see picture on page A6 参见 A6 页图

Auck·land /ˈoklənd; ˈɔːklənd/ the largest city of North Island, New Zealand, and an important port 奥克兰〔新西兰北岛最大城市和重要港口〕

auc·tion[1] /ˈokʃən; ˈɔːkʃən/ *n* [C] a public meeting where land, buildings, paintings etc are sold to the person who offers the most money for them 拍卖: **put sth up for auction** (=try to sell something at an auction) 把某物交付拍卖 *The house was put up for auction.* 这所房子被交付拍卖了。| **auction house** (=a company that arranges auctions) 拍卖行

auction[2] *v* [T+off] to sell something at an auction 拍卖

auc·tio·neer /ˌokʃənˈɪr; ˌɔːkʃəˈnɪə/ *n* [C] someone who is in charge of an auction and tells people the prices of the goods 拍卖师

au·da·cious /oˈdeʃəs; ɔːˈdeɪʃəs/ *adj* brave and shocking 大胆的; 愚勇的; 胆大妄为的: *an audacious robbery* 铤而走险的抢劫 —**audaciously** *adv*

au·dac·i·ty /oˈdæsətɪ; ɔːˈdæsəti/ *n* [U] the quality of having enough courage to take risks or say impolite things 鲁莽, 大胆无礼, 放肆: **have the audacity to do sth** *I can't believe he had the audacity to ask me for more money!* 我真不敢相信, 他竟厚颜无耻地还向我要钱!

Au·den /ˈodn; ˈɔːdn/, **W.H.** (1907-73) a British poet who was an important figure in English literature during the 1930s, when he belonged to a group of LEFT-WING writers. He became a US citizen in 1946. 奥登〔(1907-1973), 英国诗人。他是20世纪30年代英国文学界的一位重要人物, 归属于一个左翼作家团体, 1946年成为美国公民〕

au·di·ble /ˈodəbl; ˈɔːdəbəl/ *adj* a sound that is audible is loud enough for you to hear it 听得见的: *an audible sigh of relief* 听得见的舒气声 | **barely audible** (=difficult to hear) 难以听到的 *His voice was barely audible above the roar of the crowd.* 人声嘈杂, 几乎听不见他的说话声。—opposite 反义词 INAUDIBLE —**audibly** *adv* —**audibility** /ˌodəˈbɪlətɪ; ˌɔːdəˈbɪləti/ *n* [U]

au·di·ence /ˈodɪəns; ˈɔːdiəns/ *n* [C] **1** a group of people who watch and listen to someone speaking or performing in public 2 2 听众; 观众: *The audience began clapping and cheering.* 观众开始鼓掌欢呼。**2** the number or kind of people who regularly watch or listen to a particular programme〔某节目的〕固定观众[听众](人数): *The show attracts a regular audience of about 20 million.* 这个节目吸引了大约2000万固定观众收看。| **target audience** (=the kind of people that a programme, advertisement etc is supposed to attract)〔节目、广告等〕针对的观众[听众] **3** a formal meeting with a very important person 谒见, 觐见, 正式拜会: *The princess was granted an audience with the Pope.* 公主获准谒见教皇。

au·di·o /ˈodɪˌo; ˈɔːdiəʊ/ *adj* [only before noun 仅用于名词前] related to recording and broadcasting sound 音频的, 声频的: *an audio signal* 声频信号

au·di·o·tape /ˈodɪoˌtep; ˈɔːdiəʊteɪp/ *n* [C,U] *technical* a long thin band of MAGNETIC material used to record sound【术语】录音磁带

au·di·o·ty·pist /ˈɔdɪoˌtaɪpɪst; ˈɔːdiəʊˌtaɪpɪst/ *n* [C] *BrE* someone whose job is to type letters that have been recorded【英】录音打字员〔听录音打字的人员〕

au·di·o·vis·u·al /ˌɔdɪoˈvɪʒuəl; ˌɔːdiəʊˈvɪʒuəl◂/ *adj* involving the use of recorded pictures and sound 视听的; 视听教学的: *audiovisual equipment* 视听教学设备

au·dit /ˈɔdɪt; ˈɔːdɪt/ *v* [T] **1** to officially examine a company's financial records in order to check that they are correct 查…的账目, 审计, 稽查 **2** *AmE* to attend a university course without having to take any examinations【美】旁听〔大学课程〕**—audit** *n* [C]: *the annual audit* 年度审计

Audit Com·mis·sion /ˌɔdɪt kəˈmɪʃən; ˈɔːdɪt kəˈmɪʃən/ an independent organization in the UK that examines the spending of money by local government councils, and finds ways of reducing their costs 审计署〔英国一独立机构。职责是审查地方委员会的财政支出, 寻求降低支出的途径〕

au·di·tion[1] /ɔˈdɪʃən; ɔːˈdɪʃən/ *n* [C] a short performance by an actor, singer etc that someone judges to decide if they are good enough to act in a play, sing in a concert etc〔面试时〕试听, 试唱, 试演, 试镜: *He failed the audition for the part of the prince.* 他试演王子的角色但失败了。

audition[2] *v* [I,T] to perform in an audition or judge someone in an audition 进行试演 [试唱]; 要求〔某人〕试演 [试唱], 试镜: [+for] *She's auditioning for Ophelia in 'Hamlet'.* 她在试演《哈姆雷特》中的奥菲莉娅一角。| **audition sb (for)** *They auditioned over 2000 people for 'Grease'.* 他们安排了两千多人为音乐剧《油脂》进行试演。

au·di·tor /ˈɔdɪtə; ˈɔːdɪtə/ *n* [C] someone whose job is to officially examine a company's financial records 稽核员, 查账员, 审计员

au·di·to·ri·um /ˌɔdəˈtorɪəm; ˌɔːdɪˈtɔːriəm/ *n* [C] **1** the part of a theatre where people sit when watching a play, concert etc 听众席; 观众席 **2** a large building used for concerts or public meetings 礼堂; 音乐厅

au·di·to·ry /ˈɔdəˌtorɪ; ˈɔːdɪtəri/ *adj* [only before noun 仅用于名词前] *technical* connected with the ability to hear【术语】听觉的

Au·du·bon /ˈɔdəbɑn; ˈɔːdəbɒn/**, John James** (1785-1851) a US NATURALIST (=someone who studies animals and plants) and painter of North American birds 奥杜邦〔(1785-1851), 美国博物学家, 北美禽鸟画家〕

Audubon So·ci·e·ty, the /ˈ···,·ˈ···/ an organization in the US that works to protect wild birds 奥杜邦协会〔美国一野生鸟类保护组织〕

au fait /ˌo ˈfe; əʊ ˈfeɪ/ *adj* **be au fait with** to be familiar with a system or way of doing something 精通; 熟悉: *I'm not really au fait with the computer system yet.* 我还没有真正熟悉这套电脑系统。

Aug the written abbreviation of 缩写= AUGUST

Au·ge·an sta·bles, the /ɔˌdʒiən ˈstebļz; ɔːˌdʒiːən ˈsteɪbəlz/ according to ANCIENT Greek stories, the very dirty buildings where a king named Augeas kept thousands of cattle. Hercules was ordered to clean them, and he did this by changing the direction of a river to make the water flow through the stables. The expression 'to clean the Augean stables' is sometimes used in literature to describe a very difficult unpleasant job. 奥吉亚斯的牛舍〔古希腊传说中, 一位名叫奥吉亚斯的国王饲养了数千头牛, 养牛的地方肮脏不堪。后来赫拉克勒斯奉命清理牛舍, 赫拉克勒斯便引来河水冲洗牛舍。"打扫奥吉亚斯的牛舍"这一表达法有时用于文学作品, 借以形容令人生厌的重活〕

au·ger /ˈɔgə; ˈɔːgə/ *n* [C] a tool used for making a hole in wood or in the ground 螺旋钻, 钻孔机

aught /ɔt; ɔːt/ *pron* **1** *old use* anything【旧】任何事物 **2 for aught I know/care** *old use* used when saying that something may be true but you are not sure or do not care about it【旧】据我所知/我才不管呢

aug·ment /ɔgˈmɛnt; ɔːgˈment/ *v* [T] *formal* to increase the value, amount, effectiveness etc of something【正式】增大; 提高; 加强: *new taxes intended to augment government income* 旨在增加政府收入的新税制

au·gur /ˈɔgə; ˈɔːgə/ *v* [T] **1 augur well** *formal* to be a sign that something will be successful【正式】是好兆头, 主吉: *His unfriendly manner did not augur well for our interview.* 他不友好的举止预示着我们的会面不会有好结果。**2** *literary* to be a sign that a particular thing will happen in the future【文】预卜, 预示, 预言

au·gu·ry /ˈɔgjərɪ; ˈɔːgjəri/ *n* [C] *literary* a sign of what will happen in the future【文】前兆, 预兆, 征兆

Au·gust /ˈɔgəst; ˈɔːgəst/ *written abbreviation* 缩写为 **Aug** *n* [C,U] the eighth month of the year, between July and September 八月: **in August** *The new offices open in August 2003.* 新办事处于2003年8月开始办公。| **last/next August** *I moved here last August.* 我去年8月搬到这里。| **on August 6th** also 又作 **on 6th August** *BrE*【英】*The new store opened on August 6th.* 新商店是8月6日开业的。

> **CULTURAL NOTE 文化注释**
> In the UK and the US, when people think of August, they typically think of summer holidays, no school for children, hot weather, and long days. 英美人想起8月常会想起暑假, 孩子不用去上学, 天气炎热, 白昼变长。

au·gust /ɔˈgʌst; ɔːˈgʌst/ *adj literary* old, famous, and respected【文】威严的, 令人敬畏的, 庄严的

Au·gus·ta /ɔˈgʌstə; ɔːˈgʌstə/ the capital city of the US state of Maine 奥古斯塔〔美国缅因州首府〕

August Bank Hol·i·day /ˌ···ˈ···/ also 又作 **Late Summer Holiday** an official public holiday in Britain on the last Monday in August 八月公共假日〔英国一法定公共假日, 8月的最后一个星期一〕

Au·gus·tine /ˈɔgəstin; ɔːˈgʌstɪn/**, St**[1] also 又作 **St Augustine of Hippo** (354-430 AD) a North African Christian leader, PHILOSOPHER, and writer whose books, such as his *Confessions* and *The City of God*, strongly influenced the development of Christianity 奥古斯丁〔(公元354-430), 北非基督教领袖、思想家、作家。他撰写的《忏悔录》、《论上帝之城》等著作对基督教的发展影响颇大〕

Augustine, St[2] also 又作 **St Augustine of Canterbury** (?-605 AD) an Italian priest who was sent to England by Pope Gregory I to teach the people about Christianity. He became the first Archbishop of Canterbury. 奥古斯丁〔(公元?-605), 意大利牧师。他奉教皇格列高利一世派遣赴英格兰传教, 成为首任坎特伯雷大主教〕

auk /ɔk; ɔːk/ *n* [C] a black and white seabird with short wings 海雀

au lait /o ˈle; əʊ ˈleɪ/ *adj French* with milk【法】加牛奶的: *café au lait* 牛奶咖啡

Auld Lang Syne /ˌɔld læŋ ˈsaɪn; ˌɔːld læŋ ˈzaɪn/ a Scottish song that people sing when they celebrate the beginning of the new year at 12 o'clock (MIDNIGHT) on December 31st《友谊地久天长》〔苏格兰民歌〕

aunt /ænt; ɑːnt/ *n* [C] **1** the sister of your father or mother, or the wife of your father's or mother's brother 姑母; 姨母; 婶婶; 伯母; 舅母: *Aunt Mary* 玛丽姑妈 —see picture at 参见 FAMILY 图 **2** a woman who is a friend of a small child's parents 阿姨, 大妈, 大娘 —see also 另见 AGONY AUNT

Aunt·ie /ˈæntɪ; ˈɑːnti/ a name for the BBC, used humorously to suggest that it is not very exciting or that it treats people who watch or listen to its programmes as children to be educated and protected 大婶〔英国广播公司之谑称, 意在嘲讽其保守严肃的风格, 把受众视为需要教育和呵护的孩童〕

aunt·y, auntie /ˈæntɪ; ˈɑːnti/ *n* [C] *informal* aunt【非正式】阿姨, 大妈, 大娘

au pair /ˌo ˈpɛr; ˌəʊ ˈpeə/ *n* [C] a young woman who stays with a family in a foreign country to learn the language and to look after their children 做换工的姑娘〔住在外国人家里以学习外语并帮助做家务或照看孩子的女留学生〕

au·ra /ˈɔrə; ˈɔːrə/ [C] a quality or feeling that seems to surround or come from a person or a place 气氛, 气息, 韵味: [+of] *Hollywood still has an aura of glamour about it.* 好莱坞的艺术氛围仍然具有魅力。

au·ral /ˈɔrəl; ˈɔːrəl/ *adj* connected with the sense of hearing, or with someone's ability to understand a language 听觉的, 听力的 **—aurally** *adv*

Au·rang·zeb, Aurungzeb /ˈɔrəŋzɛb; ˈɔːrəŋzeb/ (1618-1707) the last Mogul emperor of northern India 奥朗则布〔(1618-1707), 印度北部莫卧儿王朝的末代皇帝〕

au·re·ole /ˈɔrɪˌol; ˈɔːriəʊl/ *n* [C] *literary* a bright circle of light; HALO【文】光环, 光轮; 光晕

au re·voir /ˌo rəˈvwar; ˌəʊ rəˈvwɑː/ *interjection French* goodbye【法】再见, 再会

au·ri·cle /ˈɔrɪkl; ˈɔːrɪkəl/ *n* [C] one of the two spaces inside the top of your heart〔心脏的〕心房, 心耳

Au·ro·ra /əˈrorə; əˈrɔːrə/ in Roman MYTHOLOGY, the goddess of the DAWN (=the beginning of the day when light first appears). In Greek mythology her name is Eos. 奥罗拉〔罗马神话中的曙光女神, 希腊神话中称厄俄斯〕

A

au·ro·ra bo·re·a·lis /ɔˌrɔrə bɔrɪ`ɛlɪs; əˌrɔːrə bɔːriˈeɪlɪs/ *n* [singular] bands of moving light that you can see in the night sky in the far north; the NORTHERN LIGHTS 北极光

Ausch·witz /`aʊʃwɪts; ˈaʊʃwɪts/ the largest and most famous Nazi CONCENTRATION CAMP in World War II, which was in Poland. Over a million people, mostly Jews, died in this camp. 奥斯威辛集中营〔二战期间最大、最臭名昭著的纳粹集中营，位于波兰。死亡人数逾百万，多为犹太人〕

aus·pic·es /`ɔspɪsɪz; ˈɔːspɪsɪz/ *n* [plural] **under the auspices of** *formal* with the help and support of a particular organization【正式】在…的资助下: *a relief project set up under the auspices of the United Nations* 由联合国资助的救济项目

aus·pi·cious /ɔ`spɪʃəs; ɔːˈspɪʃəs/ *adj formal* likely to be successful【正式】吉利的，吉祥的: *It was an auspicious moment for a meeting between the heads of state.* 这正是两国领导人会晤的大好时机。

Aus·sie /`ɔsɪ; ˈɒzi/ *n* [C] *informal* someone from Australia【非正式】澳大利亚人，澳洲人 **—Aussie** *adj*

Aus·ten, Jane /`ɔstɪn; ˈɒstɪn/ (1775-1817) a British writer who wrote in a clever and amusing way about the way of life of English MIDDLE CLASS people of her time. Her NOVELs, which are among the most important works of English literature, include *Pride and Prejudice*, *Sense and Sensibility*, and *Emma*. 奥斯汀〔(1775-1817)，英国作家。她以机智、风趣的笔触描述当时英国中产阶级的生活方式。其小说是英国文学作品中的上乘之作，如《傲慢与偏见》、《理智与情感》和《爱玛》〕

aus·tere /ɔ`stɪr; ɔːˈstɪə/ *adj* **1** plain and simple and without any decoration 朴实的，古朴的: *the austere grandeur of the old church* 简朴庄严的古教堂 **2** someone who is austere is very strict and looks very serious 严肃的 **3** an austere way of life is very simple and has few things to make it comfortable or enjoyable 简朴的，艰苦的，苦修的 **—austerely** *adv*

aus·ter·i·ty /ɔ`stɛrətɪ; ɔːˈsterɪti/ *n* [U] **1** the quality of being austere 朴实，朴素，艰苦 **2** bad economic conditions in which people do not have much money to spend〔经济的〕紧缩，节约: *a time of great austerity after the war* 战后经济紧缩时期

Aus·tin /`ɔstə; ˈɒstɪn/ the capital city of the state of Texas in the US 奥斯丁〔美国得克萨斯州首府〕

Aus·tra·la·sia /ˌɔstrəl`eʒə; ˌɒstrəˈleɪʒə/ the group of islands in the southern Pacific Ocean, including Australia, New Zealand, and Papua New Guinea 澳大拉西亚〔南太平洋一群岛，包括澳大利亚、新西兰和巴布亚新几内亚〕

Aus·tra·la·sian /ˌɔstrəl`eʒən; ˌɒstrəˈleɪʒən◂/ *adj* connected with Australasia 澳大拉西亚的

Aus·tra·li·a /ɔ`streljə; ɒˈstreɪliə/ a large island between the Indian Ocean and the southern Pacific Ocean, which is both a country and a CONTINENT (=one of the seven main areas of land on the earth). Population: 19,300,000 (2001). Capital: Canberra. 澳大利亚，澳洲〔印度洋与南太平洋之间的一个广袤的岛屿，既是一个国家，又是一块大陆。人口: 19,300,000 (2001)，首都: 堪培拉〕

Australia 澳大利亚，澳洲

Australia Day /`·…, ·/ a national holiday in Australia on or near 26 January each year, in memory of when the British first came to Australia in 1788 澳大利亚国庆日〔1月26日前后，以此纪念英国人1788年首次到达澳洲〕

Aus·tra·li·an /ɔ`streljən; ɒˈstreɪliən/ *n* [C] someone from Australia 澳大利亚人，澳洲人 **—Australian** *adj*: *Australian English* 澳大利亚英语

Australian Cap·i·tal Ter·ri·to·ry /·,····,···`····/ an area in southeast Australia that includes the capital city Canberra and Jervis Bay 澳大利亚首都直辖区〔澳大利亚东南部一地区，包括首都堪培拉和杰维斯湾〕

Aus·tri·a /`ɔstrɪə; ˈɒstriə/ a country in central Europe, southeast of Germany and northwest of Hungary. Population: 8,100,000 (2001). Capital: Vienna. 奥地利〔欧洲中部一国家，位于德国东南，匈牙利西北。人口: 8,100,000 (2001)，首都: 维也纳〕

Aus·tri·an /`ɔstrɪən; ˈɒstriən/ *n* [C] someone who is from Austria 奥地利人 **—Austrian** *adj*

Austro- /ɔstro; ɒstrəʊ/ *prefix* **1** Australian and 澳大利亚和…的: *Austro-Malayan* 澳大利亚一马来群岛的 **2** Austrian and 奥地利和…的: *Austro-Hungarian* 奥匈帝国的

au·tar·chy /`ɔtarkɪ; ˈɔːtɑːki/ *n* [U] *formal* a system of government in which one person or group has unlimited power【正式】个人专制，独裁

au·tar·ky /`ɔtarkɪ; ˈɔːtɑːki/ *n technical*【术语】**1** [U] an economic system in which a country produces all the things it needs as opposed to buying them from another country 自给自足〔政策〕**2** [C] a country that has this economic system 实行自给自足政策的国家

au·then·tic /ɔ`θɛntɪk; ɔːˈθentɪk/ *adj* **1** done or made in the traditional or original way 正宗的，原汁原味的: *authentic Chinese food* 正宗的中国食品 **2** a painting, document, book etc that is authentic has been proved to be by a particular person 原作的，真迹的，原创的 **3** based on facts 可靠的，真实的: *an authentic account* 真实可信的说法 **—authentically** /-klɪ, -kli/ *adv*

au·then·tic·ate /ɔ`θɛntɪˌket; ɔːˈθentɪkeɪt/ *v* [T] to prove that something is true or real 证明〔某物〕是真的，鉴定…之真实性: *authenticated reports of human rights violations* 经证实的违反人权情况的报告 **—authentication** /ɔˌθɛntɪ`keʃən; ɔːˌθentɪˈkeɪʃən/ *n* [U]

au·then·tic·i·ty /ˌɔθən`tɪsətɪ; ˌɔːθenˈtɪsɪti/ *n* [U] the quality of being real or true 真实性，确实性，可靠性: *to establish the painting's authenticity* 鉴定这幅绘画作品的真实性

au·thor¹ /`ɔθɚ; ˈɔːθə/ *n* [C] **1** someone who writes books 作者，作家，著作人: *Jeffrey Archer, successful author and politician* 杰弗里·阿彻，成功的作家和政治家 | **the author** (=the person who wrote a particular book)〔某部书的〕作者 *It's clear that the author is a woman.* 显然，这部书的作者是位女性。**2** *formal* the person who starts a plan or idea【正式】〔计划、主张的〕创始人，发起者: *the author of the plan* 这个计划的倡议者 W2

author² *v* [T] to be the writer of a book, report etc 创作，写作

au·thor·ess /`ɔθərɪs; ˈɔːθərɪs/ *n* [C] a woman who writes books 女作家，女作者

au·thor·i·tar·i·an /əˌθarə`tɛrɪən; ɔːˌθɒrɪˈteəriən◂/ *adj* strictly forcing people to obey a set of rules or laws that are often wrong or unfair 独裁的，专制的: *an authoritarian regime* 独裁政权 | *a cruel and authoritarian father* 严酷专断的父亲 **—authoritarian** *n* [C] **—authoritarianism** *n* [U]

au·thor·i·ta·tive /ə`θarəˌtetɪv; ɔːˈθɒrɪtətɪv/ *adj* **1** an authoritative book, account etc is respected because the person who wrote it knows a lot about the subject 权威性的，可信的，可靠的: *Lewis's authoritative account of the history of aviation* 刘易斯对航空工业历史的权威性叙述 **2** behaving or speaking in a confident determined way that makes people respect and obey you 权威的，有威信的，威严的 **—authoritatively** *adv*

au·thor·i·ty /ə`θarətɪ; ɔːˈθɒrɪti/ *n* W1

1 ▶POWER 权力◀ [U] the power you have because of your official position or because people respect your knowledge and experience 权力，权威，威信: *None of us questioned my father's authority.* 对于父亲的权威，我们谁都没有置疑。| **the voice of authority** (=a way of speaking that makes people respect you) 权威的口气 *Witten spoke with the voice of authority.* 威滕以权威的口气说话。

2 the authorities the people or organizations that are in charge of a particular country or area 当局，官方；当权者: *British police are cooperating with the Malaysian authorities.* 英国警方正在和马来西亚当局合作。

3 ▶ORGANIZATION 组织◀ [C] an official organization or a local government department which controls public affairs, provides public services etc 公共事业机构: *the Brewer Transit Authority* 啤酒公司运输部门 | **local authority** *BrE*【英】*You can claim housing benefit from the local authority.* 你可以向地方政府申请领取住房津贴。

4 I have it on good authority used to say that you are sure that something is true because you trust the person who told you about it 我完全相信

5 ►EXPERT 专家◄ [C] someone who knows a lot about a subject and whose knowledge and opinions are greatly respected 权威人士, 大师, 泰斗: [+on] *Professor Erikson is one of the world's leading authorities on tropical disease.* 埃里克森教授在热带疾病方面是世界权威之一。

6 ►PERMISSION 允许◄ [C,U] official permission to do something〔正式的〕许可, 授权: *Whose authority are you acting on?* 是谁授权你这样做的?

au·thor·i·za·tion also 又作 **-isation** *BrE*【英】/ˌɔθərəˋzeʃən; ˌɔːθəraɪˈzeɪʃən/ *n* [C,U] official permission to do something, or the document giving this permission 授权(书), 许可(证): *You need special authorization to park here.* 在此停车要有特别的许可。

au·thor·ize also 又作 **-ise** *BrE*【英】/ˋɔθəˌraɪz; ˈɔːθəraɪz/ *v* [T] to give official or legal permission for something 授权, 批准, 许可, 委任: **authorize sb to do sth** *I'm not authorized to answer your questions.* 我没有得到授权回答你的问题。

authorized cap·i·tal /ˌ···ˈ···/ *n* [U] the largest amount of money a company is allowed to get by selling shares (SHARE[2] (5)) 法定股本, 额定股本〔公司获准发行的最高股份金额〕

Authorized Ver·sion /ˌ···ˈ··/ *n* [singular] the English translation of the Bible made in England in 1611《圣经》钦定本〔1611年英格兰出版的《圣经》英译本〕

au·thor·ship /ˋɔθəˌʃɪp; ˈɔːθəʃɪp/ *n* [U] **1** the fact that you have written a particular book, document etc 原作者; 作者身份, 著作权: *There's no evidence to dispute his claim to authorship.* 没有证据可以对他的著作权要求提出异议。**2** *formal* the profession of writing books【正式】写作职业

au·tis·m /ˋɔtɪzəm; ˈɔːtɪzəm/ *n* [U] a severe mental illness that affects children and prevents them from communicating with other people 孤独症, 自闭症〔尤指儿童因大脑严重障碍而无法与人建立正常的人际关系〕 —**autistic** /ɔˋtɪstɪk; ɔːˈtɪstɪk/ *adj*: *an autistic child* 患孤独症的孩子

au·to /ˋɔto; ˈɔːtəʊ/ *adj AmE old-fashioned* connected with cars【美, 过时】汽车的: *the auto industry* 汽车工业

auto- /ɔtə; ɔːtəʊ/ *prefix* **1** of or by yourself 自己(做)的: *an autobiography* (=book about your own life, written by yourself) 自传 **2** working by itself without human operation 自动的: *an autopump* 自汲唧筒

au·to·bi·og·ra·phy /ˌɔtəbaɪˋɑgrəfɪ; ˌɔːtəbaɪˈɒgrəfi/ *n* **1** [C] the story of your life written by yourself 自传 **2** [U] literature that is concerned with people writing about their own lives 自传体文学 —**autobiographic** /ˌɔtəbaɪəˋgræfɪk; ˌɔːtəbaɪəˈgræfɪk◂/ *adj* —**autobiographical** *adj* —**autobiographically** /-klɪ; -kli/ *adv* —compare 比较 BIOGRAPHY

au·toc·ra·cy /ɔˋtɑkrəsɪ; ɔːˈtɒkrəsi/ *n* **1** [U] a system of government in which one person or group has unlimited power 专制统治, 独裁政体 **2** [C] a country governed in this way 专制[独裁]国家

au·to·crat /ˋɔtəˌkræt; ˈɔːtəkræt/ *n* [C] **1** someone who makes decisions and gives orders to people without asking them for their opinion 独断专行的人 **2** someone who has unlimited power to govern a country 独裁者, 独裁统治者 —**autocratic** /ˌɔtəˋkrætɪk; ˌɔːtəˈkrætɪk◂/ *adj*: *his autocratic control of the White House staff* 他对白宫职员的专断控制 —**autocratically** /-klɪ; -kli/ *adv*

au·to·cross /ˋɔtokrɔs; ˈɔːtəʊkrɒs/ *n* [U] *BrE* a sport in which cars race around a grass field【英】汽车越野赛

au·to·cue /ˋɔtokju; ˈɔːtəʊkjuː/ *n* [C] a machine that shows the words that someone must say while they are being filmed for a television programme〔电视的〕自动提示器, 电子提词器

au·to·graph[1] /ˋɔtəˌgræf; ˈɔːtəgrɑːf/ *n* [C] a famous person's signature that they give to someone who admires them〔名人的〕亲笔签名: *Can I have your autograph?* 我可以要你的签名吗?

autograph[2] *v* [T] if a famous person autographs a book, photo etc, they sign it〔名人〕在…上亲笔签名

auto-im·mune dis·ease /ˌɔtoɪmjun dɪˋziz; ˌɔːtəʊɪmjuːn dɪˈziːz/ *n* [U] a condition in which substances that normally prevent illness in the body, attack and harm parts of it instead 自身免疫病

au·to·mak·er /ˋɔtoˌmekə; ˈɔːtəʊˌmeɪkə/ *n* [C] *AmE* a company that makes cars【美】汽车制造商: *US auto-makers* 美国汽车制造商

au·to·mat /ˋɔtəˌmæt; ˈɔːtəmæt/ *n* [C] *trademark AmE* a restaurant where you put money in machines to get food【商标, 美】自助餐馆〔用自动售货机卖食物的快餐店〕

au·to·mate /ˋɔtəˌmet; ˈɔːtəmeɪt/ *v* [T] to change to a system where jobs are done or goods are produced by machines instead of people 使自动化

au·to·ma·ted /ˋɔtəˌmetɪd; ˈɔːtəmeɪtɪd/ *adj* using machines to do a job or industrial process 自动化的: *a highly automated factory* 高度自动化的工厂

au·to·mat·ic[1] /ˌɔtəˋmætɪk; ˌɔːtəˈmætɪk◂/ *adj* **1** an automatic machine, car etc is designed to be operated in a simple way using only a few controls 自动的, 自动化的: *an automatic rifle* 自动步枪 | *an automatic time switch* 自动定时开关 **2** something that is automatic always happens as a result of something you have done, especially because of a rule or law 必然发生的: *Littering results in an automatic fine of $500.* 乱扔垃圾按规定要罚500美元。**3** done without thinking, especially because you have done the same thing many times before〔尤指习惯性地〕不自觉的, 无意识的, 不假思索的: *It seems difficult to remember at first, but after a while it becomes automatic.* 起初记起来似乎很难, 但是过了一段时间就自然记住了。

automatic[2] *n* [C] **1** a weapon that can fire bullets continuously 自动武器 **2** a car with a system of gears (GEAR[1] (1)) that operate themselves without the driver needing to change them 自动挡汽车〔有自动变速箱的汽车〕

au·to·mat·i·cally /ˌɔtəˋmætɪklɪ; ˌɔːtəˈmætɪkli/ *adv* **1** without thinking about what you are doing 不假思索地, 无意识地: *"Of course," I replied automatically.* "当然了。"我不假思索地回答。**2** as the result of a situation 必然会发生地: *As a student you are automatically entitled to a grant.* 作为一名学生, 你自然有权得到助学金。**3** by the action of a machine, without a person making it work 自动地: *The doors opened automatically as we approached.* 我们走近时, 门自动开了。

automatic pi·lot /ˌ····ˈ··/ *n* [C] a machine that flies a plane by itself without the need for a pilot〔飞机上的〕自动驾驶仪

automatic trans·mis·sion /ˌ····ˈ··/ *n* [U] a system that operates the gears (GEAR[1] (1)) of a car without the driver needing to change them〔汽车的〕自动变速箱

au·to·ma·tion /ˌɔtəˋmeʃən; ˌɔːtəˈmeɪʃən/ *n* [U] the use of machines instead of people to do a job or industrial process 自动化(操作)

au·tom·a·ton /ɔˋtɑməˌtɑn; ɔːˈtɒmətən/ *n* [C] **1** someone who seems to be unable to feel emotions 没有感情的人 **2** a machine, especially one in the shape of a human, that moves without anyone controlling it 自动操作装置, 机器人

au·to·mo·bile /ˋɔtəməˌbil; ˈɔːtəməbiːl/ *n* [C] *AmE* a car【美】汽车: *the automobile industry* 汽车工业

au·ton·o·mous /ɔˋtɑnəməs; ɔːˈtɒnəməs/ *adj* **1** having the power to govern a region, country etc without being controlled by anyone else〔地区、国家等〕自治的, 有自治权的: *an autonomous state* 自治州 **2** *formal* having the ability to work and make decisions by yourself without any help from anyone else【正式】有自立能力的, 自主的 —**autonomously** *adv*

au·ton·o·my /ɔˋtɑnəmɪ; ɔːˈtɒnəmi/ *n* [U] **1** freedom to govern a region, country etc without being controlled by anyone else 自治, 自治权: *a political system that allows a high degree of local autonomy* 允许地方有高度自治权的政治体制 **2** the ability to make your own decisions without being influenced by anyone else 自立能力, 自主能力: *the autonomy of the individual* 每个人的自主能力

au·to·pi·lot /ˋɔtoˌpaɪlət; ˈɔːtəʊˌpaɪlət/ *n* [C] AUTOMATIC PILOT〔飞机上的〕自动驾驶仪

au·top·sy /ˋɔtɑpsɪ; ˈɔːtɒpsi/ *n* [C] *especially AmE* an examination of a dead body to discover the cause of death【尤美】尸体剖检, 验尸; POSTMORTEM *BrE*【英】

au·to·sug·ges·tion /ˌɔtosəˋdʒɛstʃən; ˌɔːtəʊsəˈdʒestʃən/ *n* [U] *technical* the process of making someone believe or feel something, without them realizing that you are doing this【术语】自我暗示(法)

au·tumn /ˋɔtəm; ˈɔːtəm/ also 又作 **fall** *AmE*【美】*n* [C,U] the season between summer and winter, when leaves change colour and the weather becomes slightly colder 秋天, 秋季: *autumn mists* 秋天的雾霭

au·tum·nal /ɔˋtʌmnḷ; ɔːˈtʌmnəl/ *adj* connected with or typical of autumn 秋季的; (似)秋天的: *autumnal colours* 秋天的色调

aux the written abbreviation of 缩写= AUXILIARY, especially of 尤为 AUXILIARY VERB

aux·il·ia·ry[1] /ɔgˋzɪljərɪ; ɔːgˈziljəri/ *adj* **1** auxiliary workers provide additional help for another group of workers, especially nurses or soldiers 辅助的: *an auxiliary nurse* 辅助的护理人员 |

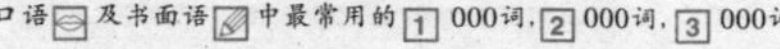
口语及书面语中最常用的 1 000词, 2 000词, 3 000词

auxiliary staff 辅助员工 **2** an auxiliary motor, piece of equipment etc is kept ready to be used if the main one stops working properly 补充的; 备用的: *an auxiliary power supply* 备用的供电设备

auxiliary² *n* [C] **1** a worker who provides additional help for another group of workers, especially nurses or soldiers 辅助人员: *a nursing auxiliary* 护理辅助人员 **2** an auxiliary verb 助动词: *a modal auxiliary* 情态助动词

auxiliary verb /·,··· '·/ *n* [C] a verb that is used with another verb to show its tense, person (PERSON (6)), mood (MOOD (6)) etc. In English the auxiliary verbs are 'be', 'do', and 'have' (as in 'I am running', 'I didn't go', 'they have gone') and all the MODALS. 助动词〔与另一个动词连用表示动词时态、人称及语态的一种动词, 在英语中为 be, do, have 以及所有情态动词〕

AV an abbreviation of 缩写= AUDIO VISUAL

a·vail¹ /ə`vel; ə'veɪl/ *n* **be to no avail/be of no avail** if something you do is to no avail or of no avail, you do not succeed in getting what you want 没结果, 无效果: *We searched the whole area but all to no avail: Robbie had disappeared.* 我们搜遍了整个地方但毫无结果, 罗比失踪了。

avail² *v* **avail yourself of** *formal* to accept an offer or use an opportunity to do something【正式】利用: *He availed himself of this privilege.* 他利用了这项特权。

1 **a·vail·a·ble** /ə`veləbḷ; ə'veɪləbəl/ *adj* **1** something that is available is able to be used or can easily be bought or found 可获得的; 可用的: *Now available in paperback!* 现可以买到平装本了! | *We've already used up all the available space.* 所有可用的空间我们都用上了。| **[+for]** *The university is trying to make more accommodation available for students.* 大学设法为学生提供更多的住处。| **[+to]** *an increase in the number of jobs available to women* 妇女就业机会的增加 | **readily/freely available** (=very easy to obtain by anyone) 容易得到的 *Drugs like crack are freely available.* 强效纯可卡因一类的毒品随处可以得到。| **every available** (=every one that you can get) 每个能找到的 *Every available ambulance was rushed to the scene of the accident.* 所有能找到的救护车都迅速赶往出事地点。**2** [not before noun 不用于名词前] someone who is available is not busy and has enough time to talk to you 有暇的, 可接待客人的: *The president was not available for comment.* 总统没时间对此事发表评论。**3** someone who is available does not have a wife, BOYFRIEND etc, and therefore may want to start a new romantic relationship with someone else 未婚的; 未有伴侣的 **—availability** /ə,velə`bɪlətɪ; ə,veɪlə'bɪlɨti/ *n* [U]: *the availability of affordable housing* 人们买得起的住房供应

av·a·lanche /`ævḷ,æntʃ; 'ævəlɑːnʃ/ *n* [C] **1** a large mass of snow, ice, and rocks that falls down the side of a mountain 雪崩; 山崩: *Two skiers were killed in the avalanche.* 有两名滑雪者在雪崩中丧生。**2** **an avalanche of** a very large number of things such as letters, messages etc that arrive suddenly at the same time〔信件等〕雪片般的, 大量的

Av·a·lon, Avallon /`ævə,lɑn; 'ævəlɒn/ according to old stories about King Arthur, a holy island, which some people believe is near Glastonbury in southwest England, where Arthur was buried. 阿瓦隆岛〔亚瑟王传说中的一个圣岛。有人认为, 该岛在英格兰西南部格拉斯顿伯里附近, 为亚瑟王安息之地〕

av·ant-garde /,ævɑn `gɑrd; ,ævɔːŋ 'gɑːd◂/ *adj* **1** avant-garde music, literature etc is extremely modern and often seems strange or slightly shocking 前卫的, 先锋派的: *an avant-garde play* 先锋派戏剧 **2** **the avant-garde** the group of artists, writers, musicians etc who produce avant-garde books, paintings etc〔画家、作家、音乐家等的〕前卫派: *a member of the avant-garde* 前卫派成员

av·a·rice /`ævərɪs; 'ævərɨs/ *n* [U] *formal* a desire to have a lot of money that is considered to be too strong; GREED【正式】贪得无厌, 贪婪 **—avaricious** /,ævə`rɪʃəs; ,ævə'rɪʃəs◂/ *adj* **—avariciously** *adv*

Ave the written abbreviation of 缩写= AVENUE (1) 大街: *36, Rokesly Ave* 罗克士利大街36号

Ave·bu·ry /`evbɛrɪ; 'eɪvbəri/ a village in Wiltshire, in southern England, where there is a group of ancient standing stones 埃夫伯里〔英格兰南部威尔特郡一村庄, 当地有古代的巨石阵遗址〕

a·venge /ə`vɛndʒ; ə'vendʒ/ *v* [T] *literary* to do something to hurt or punish someone because they have harmed or offended you【文】报…之仇, 为…雪耻: *He wanted to avenge his brother's death.* 他要为弟弟的死复仇。**—avenger** *n* [C]

3 **av·e·nue** /`ævə,nu; 'ævɨnjuː/ *n* [C] **1** **Fifth Avenue/Shaftesbury Avenue etc** used in the names of streets in a town or city 第五大街/莎夫茨伯里大街等 **2** a possible way of achieving something 方法, 途径: *We explored every possible avenue, but couldn't find a solution.* 我们探讨了所有可能的途径, 但没能找到解决办法。**3** *BrE* a road or broad path between two rows of trees, especially one leading to a big house【英】〔通向房子的〕两旁有树的小路: *an avenue of chestnut trees* 两侧有栗子树的小路

a·ver /ə`vɝ; ə'vɜː/ *v* [T] *formal* to say something firmly and strongly because you are sure that it is true【正式】断言; 坚称

av·e·rage¹ /`ævərɪdʒ; 'ævərɪdʒ/ *adj* **1** [only before noun 仅用于名词前] the average amount is the amount you get when you add together several quantities and divide this by the total number of quantities 平均(数)的: *Average earnings in the state are about $1,500 a month.* 这个国家的平均月收入约为1500美元。| *What's the average rainfall for July?* 7月份的平均降雨量为多少? | *an average speed of 200 kph* 平均时速200公里 **2** an average amount or quantity is not unusually big or small 中等的, 适中的: **(of) average height/build/intelligence etc** (=not tall or short, fat or thin etc) 中等个子/身材/智力等 *I'd say he was of average height.* 我会说他是中等身材。**3** having qualities that are typical of most people or things 平常的, 普通的: *The average student spends about two or three hours a night doing homework.* 一般学生每晚要花两三个小时做作业。| *In an average week I drive about 250 miles.* 平常我每周开车250英里。**4** neither very good nor very bad 不好不坏的, 一般的: *There was nothing special about the film – it was just average.* 这部电影没什么特别之处, 很一般。 2 2

average² *n* **1** [C] the amount calculated by adding together several quantities, and then dividing this amount by the total number of quantities 平均数: *The average of 3, 8 and 10 is 7.* 3、8、10的平均数为7。| *House prices have gone up by an average of 2%.* 房价平均上涨了2%。**2** **on average** based on a calculation about how many times something usually happens, how much money someone usually gets, how often people usually do something etc 平均来看: *On average men smoke more cigarettes than women.* 平均来看男子比女子吸烟多。| *Japanese people on average live much longer than Europeans.* 日本人的平均寿命要比欧洲人长得多。**3** [C,U] the usual level or amount for most people or things in a group 平均水平: **above/below average** (=better or worse than average) 高于/低于平均水平 *Susie's school work is well above average.* 苏西的学业成绩远远高于平均水平。| **the national average** *I suppose the national average is about £20,000 per year.* 我假定全国的平均水平是每年两万英镑。—see also 另见 **law of averages** (LAW (11)) 2

average³ *v* [linking verb 连系动词] **1** to usually do something or usually happen a particular number of times, or to usually be a particular size or amount 平均做; 平均是: *I suppose I average about five cups of coffee a day.* 我想我平均每天喝大约五杯咖啡。| *The fish averages about two inches in length.* 这些鱼平均两英寸长。**2** to calculate the average of figures 算出…的平均数

average out *phr v* **1** [T **average** sth ↔ **out**] to calculate the usual number of times that something happens, the usual size of something, or the average amount of a group of figures 算出…的平均数: *I averaged out the total increase at about 10%.* 我算出总增长平均为10%左右。**2** [linking verb 连系动词 **+to/at**] to usually result in a particular number or amount 达到平均量: *The weekly profits average out at about $1,000.* 每周平均利润达到1000美元左右。

a·verse /ə`vɝs; ə'vɜːs/ *adj* **1** **not be averse to** used to say that someone likes to do something sometimes, especially something that is slightly wrong or bad for them 并不反对; 不太讨厌, 并非完全不喜欢: *I don't smoke cigarettes, but I'm not averse to the occasional cigar.* 我不吸烟, 但我不反对偶尔抽一支雪茄。**2** **be averse to** *formal* to be unwilling to do something or to dislike something【正式】不愿意做, 讨厌做

a·ver·sion /ə`vɝʒən; ə'vɜːʃən/ *n* [singular,U] a strong dislike of something or someone 厌恶, 讨厌, 反感: **[+to]** *Despite his aversion to publicity, Arnold was persuaded to talk to the press.* 尽管不喜欢张扬, 阿诺德还是被说服接受报刊采访。| **have an aversion to** *I have an aversion to housework.* 我讨厌做家务。

a·vert /ə`vɝt; ə'vɜːt/ *v* [T] **1** to prevent something unpleasant from happening 防止, 避免: *The tragedy could have been averted if the crew had followed safety procedures.* 如果乘务人员按照安全程序操作, 这场悲剧本来是可以避免的。**2** **avert your eyes/gaze etc** to look away from something that you do not want to see 转移目光: *Lockwood averted his eyes as she undressed.* 洛克伍德在她脱衣时把目光转移开。

Avery /`evərɪ; 'eɪvəri/, **Frederick (Tex)** /`frɛdrɪk; 'fredərɪk/ (1907-80) a US CARTOON film ANIMATOR famous for developing the character Bugs Bunny 艾弗里〔(1907-1980), 美国卡通电影动画大师, 以设计"兔八哥"动画形象而著称〕

a·vi·a·ry /ˋevɪˌɛrɪ; ˈeɪviəri/ *n* [C] a large CAGE where birds are kept 大鸟笼，鸟舍

a·vi·a·tion /ˌeviˋeʃən; ˌeɪviˈeɪʃən/ *n* [U] **1** the science or practice of flying in aircraft 航空，航空学，飞行（术） **2** the industry that makes aircraft 航空工业

a·vi·a·tor /ˋevɪˌetɚ; ˈeɪvieɪtə/ *n* [C] *old-fashioned* a pilot【过时】飞机驾驶员，飞行员

av·id /ˋævɪd; ˈævɪ̣d/ *adj* **avid reader/listener/fan etc** someone who does something, listens to something etc as much as they can 热心的读者/听众/发烧友等: *an avid collector of old jazz records* 爵士乐旧唱片的热心收藏者

Av·ie·more /ˌævɪˋmor; ˌæviˈmɔː/ a town in northern Scotland which is popular for skiing and other winter sports 阿维莫尔〔苏格兰北部一镇，是滑雪等冬季运动胜地〕

av·o·ca·do /ˌævəˋkɑdo; ˌævəˈkɑːdəʊ◂/ also 又作 **avocado pear** /ˌ‥‥ˈ·/ *n* [C] a fruit with a thick green or dark purple skin that is green inside and has a large seed in the middle 鳄梨，牛油果

S2 W1 **a·void** /əˋvɔɪd; əˈvɔɪd/ *v* [T] **1** to do something to prevent something bad from happening 避免，防止: *The other car swerved, trying to avoid a collision.* 另一辆车猛然转弯，以避免撞车。| **avoid doing sth** *This leaflet tells you how to avoid getting ill while travelling.* 这小册子告诉你怎样在旅行期间防止生病。**2** to deliberately stay away from someone or something〔故意〕回避，避开: *Jon was embarrassed and tried to avoid us the next day.* 乔恩很尴尬，第二天设法躲着我们。| *I managed to avoid the worst of the traffic.* 我设法避开了最拥挤的车流。| **avoid sb/sth like the plague** (=stay away from someone or something completely, especially because they are very unpleasant) 像躲避瘟疫一样地避开某人/某物 *I used to aviod that class like the plague.* 我曾经像躲瘟疫一样避开那门课。**3** to deliberately not do something, especially because it is dangerous, unpleasant etc 逃避: *Loopholes are a way of legally avoiding taxes.* 钻税法的空子是合法逃税的一种方法。| **avoid doing sth** *Organic gardeners try to avoid using pesticides.* 实行有机栽培的园丁设法不用杀虫剂。

a·void·ance /əˋvɔɪdn̩s; əˈvɔɪdəns/ *n* [U] the act of avoiding someone or something 回避，避开，避免: [+of] *the avoidance of issues such as domestic violence* 避免家庭暴力事件之类的问题 | **tax avoidance** (=legal ways of not paying tax) 避税 *millions of dollars in lost revenue due to tax avoidance* 因避税而损失了几百万美元的税收

av·oir·du·pois /ˌævɚdəˋpɔɪz; ˌævədəˈpɔɪz/ *n* [U] the system of weighing things that uses the standard measures of the OUNCE (1), POUND[1] (1), and TON (1) 常衡〔以盎司、磅、吨为称量标准的衡制〕—compare 比较 METRIC SYSTEM

A·von /ˋevn̩; ˈeɪvən/ **1** a river in south central England that flows through Stratford-upon-Avon 埃文河〔位于英格兰中南部，流经埃文河畔斯特拉特福〕 **2** a former COUNTY in south-west England 埃文郡〔英格兰西南部先前的一个郡〕

a·vow /əˋvaʊ; əˈvaʊ/ *v* [T] *formal* to say or admit publicly something you believe or promise【正式】承认，公开声明: *He avowed his commitment to Marxist ideals.* 他承认信奉马克思主义理想。—**avowal** *n* [C,U]: *an avowal of love* 公开表示爱慕

a·vowed /əˋvaʊd; əˈvaʊd/ *adj* [only before noun 仅用于名词前] admitted or said publicly 承认的，公开声明的: *an avowed atheist* 公开的无神论者

a·vun·cu·lar /əˋvʌŋkjəlɚ; əˈvʌŋkjʊ̣lə/ *adj* being like an uncle; kind and concerned about someone who is younger 叔伯般的；关心备至的: *an avuncular pat on the shoulder* 像叔伯般地轻拍肩膀 —**avuncularly** *adv*

AWACS /ˋewæks; ˈeɪwæks/ *n* **1** Airborne Warning and Control System; a type of RADAR used by special US military aircraft, which makes it possible for them to find out the position of enemy aircraft and the direction they are travelling in when they are still very far away 机载警报与控制系统〔美国特种军用飞机使用的一种雷达，能测定远处敌机的方位和飞行方向〕 **2** an aircraft that uses this system 空中预警飞机

a·wait /əˋwet; əˈweɪt/ *v* [T] *formal*【正式】**1** to wait for something 等待: *Several men are awaiting trial for robbery.* 几个人因抢劫正在候审。**2** if a situation, event etc awaits you, it is going to happen in the future 将发生在…；期待: *A terrible surprise awaited them at Mr Tumnus' house.* 在图姆纳斯先生家，一件可怕的意外将降临到他们头上。—see 见 WAIT[1] (USAGE)

S3 **a·wake**[1] /əˋwek; əˈweɪk/ *adj* [not before noun 不用于名词前] **1** not sleeping 醒着的: **be awake** *"Are you awake?" Julie whispered from the door.* "你醒了吗?"朱莉在门口轻声问。| *Les shook her awake.* 莱斯把她摇醒。| **wide awake** (=completely awake) 完全醒着，没有睡意 *The baby was wide awake at midnight.* 这个婴儿在半夜还毫无睡意。| **keep sb awake** (=prevent someone from sleeping) 让某人无法入睡 *The noise of the traffic kept me awake.* 交通噪音使我无法入睡。| **stay awake** *One of us ought to stay awake and keep watch.* 我们当中一个人应该醒着值夜。| **lie awake** *I lay awake worrying about my exams.* 我躺在床上睡不着，担心考试的事。**2 be awake to** to understand a situation and its possible effects 注意到，意识到: *The company is awake to the potential of these ideas.* 公司注意到了这些意见的潜在作用。

awake[2] *v past tense* **awoke** /əˋwok; əˈwəʊk/ *past participle* **awoken** /əˋwokən; əˈwəʊken/ [I,T] **1** to wake up, or to make someone wake up（使）醒来，唤醒: *The child awoke and began to cry.* 孩子醒来后就开始哭。**2** if something awakes an emotion or if an emotion awakes, you suddenly begin to feel that emotion 唤起，激发起: *A dull resentment awoke within him.* 他内心突然感到一种隐约的愤恨情绪。

awake sb ↔ **to** sth *phr v* [T] to make someone understand a situation and its possible effects 使领悟，使醒悟；意识到: *Artists finally awoke to the aesthetic possibilities of photography.* 画家终于领悟了摄影的潜在美学价值。

a·wak·en /əˋwekən; əˈweɪkən/ *v formal*【正式】**1** [T] if something awakens an emotion, it makes you suddenly begin to feel that emotion 激发起，唤起: *We need to awaken a new faith in the hearts of non-believers.* 我们需要唤起无信仰者内心的一种新的信念。**2** [I,T] to wake up or to make someone wake up（使）醒来，吵醒: *The noise outside awakened him.* 外面的噪音吵醒了他。

awaken sb ↔ **to** sth *phr v* [T] to make someone understand a situation and its possible effects 使领悟，使醒悟；使意识到: *We must awaken people to the danger to the environment.* 我们必须让人们意识到对环境造成的危害。

a·wak·en·ing /əˋwekənɪŋ; əˈweɪkənɪŋ/ *n* [C] **1** an occasion when you suddenly realize that you understand something or feel something 醒，觉醒，醒悟: *the adolescent's sexual awakening* 青春期的性萌动 | **rude awakening** (=an occasion when you suddenly realize that something is not true or is unpleasant) 猛然觉醒 *Anyone who thinks marriage will be bliss forever is in for a rude awakening.* 认为婚姻会是永远幸福的人都会猛然觉醒。**2** the act of waking from sleep 醒来

a·ward[1] /əˋwɔrd; əˈwɔːd/ *n* [C] **1** something such as a prize or money given to someone to reward them for something they have done 奖，奖赏，奖金，奖品: *Meryl Streep won the best actress award.* 梅丽尔·斯特里普获最佳女演员奖。**2** something, especially money, that is officially given to someone as a payment or judgment 报酬，薪水，工资: *The nurses' pay award was not nearly as much as they had expected.* 护士的工资远没有预想的那么多。 S2 W1

award[2] *v* [T] **1** to officially give someone something such as a prize or money to reward them for something they have done 给予，授予: **be awarded sth** *Einstein was awarded the Nobel Prize for his work in quantum physics.* 爱因斯坦因在量子物理学方面的成就获诺贝尔奖。| **award sb sth** *The university awarded her a scholarship.* 大学给她颁发奖学金。**2** to officially decide that someone should receive a payment or judgment 判给，裁定: **be awarded sth** *After seven years of litigation, he was awarded $750,000 compensation.* 经过七年的诉讼，他终于获得75万美元的赔偿。| **award sb sth** *Management have awarded all factory employees a 5% pay rise.* 资方给所有员工加薪5%。 W3

a·ware /əˋwɛr; əˈweə/ *adj* [not before noun 不用于名词前] **1** if you are aware that something such as a problem or a dangerous situation exists, you realize that it exists 意识到的，明白的，知道的: **aware that** *Were you aware that your son was having difficulties at school?* 你知道你儿子在学校学习有困难吗? | [+of] *Most smokers are perfectly aware of the dangers of smoking.* 大多数吸烟者完全知道吸烟的危害。| **make sb aware of sth** *It's time someone made him aware of the effects of his actions.* 该有人让他意识到他所作所为造成的后果了。| **not that I'm aware of** *spoken*【口】*"Does she have any problems with her marriage?" "Not that I'm aware of."* "她的婚姻出现了问题吗?""据我所知没有。" | **well/acutely aware** (=very aware) 完全/敏锐地知道 *Sara was well aware of Francesca's fear of heights.* 萨拉完全知道弗朗西丝卡有畏高症。**2** if you are aware of something, you notice it, especially because you can see, hear, or smell it 意识到的，注意到的，察觉到的: **aware that** *I gradually became aware that there was someone else in the room.* 我逐渐意识到房间里还有别人在场。| [+of] *He was aware of a faint smell of gas.* 他察觉到隐约有一股煤气味。**3** understanding a lot about what is happening around you and paying S1 W1

A

attention to it, especially because you realize possible dangers and problems 有…意识的: **politically/socially/environmentally etc aware** *Nowadays everyone's much more environmentally aware.* 如今，大家的环境意识强多了。**4 so/as far as I am aware** *spoken* used when you want to emphasize that there may be things that you do not know about a situation【口】就我所知: *So far as I'm aware this is the first time a British rider has won the competition.* 就我所知，这是英国骑师第一次赢得这项竞赛。

3 **a·ware·ness** /əˋwɛrnɪs; əˈweənəs/ *n* [U] **1** knowledge or understanding of a particular subject or situation 意识: *political awareness* 政治意识 | **raise awareness** (=improve people's knowledge) 提高认识 *Health officials have tried to raise awareness about AIDS among teenagers.* 卫生部门官员一直在努力提高青少年对艾滋病的认识。**2** the ability to notice something using your senses 感悟能力: **[+of]** *an artist's awareness of light and color* 画家对光和颜色的感悟能力

a·wash /əˋwɑʃ; əˈwɒʃ/ *adj* [not before noun 不用于名词前] **1** covered with water or another liquid 被〔水或其他液体〕淹没的 **2** containing too many things or people of a particular kind 充斥的, 泛滥的: **[+with]** *TV nowadays is awash with soap operas.* 如今的电视充斥着肥皂剧。

1 1 **a·way**[1] /əˋwe; əˈweɪ/ *adv* **1** to or at a distance from someone or something 离开, 距离…: *Go away!* 走开! | *Dinah was crying as she drove slowly away.* 黛娜哭着慢慢地把车开走了。| **[+from]** *The police tried to keep people away from the accident.* 警察设法阻止人们走近事故现场。| **turn/look away (from sb/sth)** (=turn so that you are not looking at someone or something) 移开视线 **2** if someone is away from school, work or home they are not there 不在〔上班、上学等〕: **[+from]** *You must bring a note from your parents if you've been away from school.* 缺了课必须补交家长的便条。| **away with flu/measles/a cold etc** (=not at school, work etc because you are ill) 由于患了流感/麻疹/感冒等病缺勤 **3 3 miles/5 kilometres etc away** at a distance of 3 miles, 5 kilometres etc from someone or something 离… 3英里/5公里等: *Geneva is about 20 miles away.* 日内瓦离这儿大约20英里远。**4 2 days/3 weeks etc away** if an event is 2 days, 3 weeks etc away, it will happen after 2 days etc have passed 离…还有两天/三周等: *Christmas is only a month away.* 再过一个月就是圣诞节了。| *We live minutes away from the sea.* (=it only takes minutes to get there) 我们住的地方离海边只有几分钟的路。**5** into a safe or enclosed place 放到〔一个安全的地方〕, 放进: *Put your money away, I'm paying.* 把你的钱收起来, 我来付。**6** so as to be gone or used up 消失; 用完: *The music died away.* 音乐声消失了。| *The farm was swept away in the flood.* 农场被洪水冲垮了。| *Ruben gave all his money away to charity.* 鲁宾把所有的钱都送给了慈善机构。| *Support for the Democrats has dropped away.* 支持民主党的人已经减少了。| *The young lovers danced the night away.* (=danced all night) 这对年轻情侣跳舞跳了一整夜。| *Cut away all the dead wood.* 把所有的枯木都砍掉。**7** used to emphasize a continuous action 一直, 继续不断地: *Sue was singing away to herself in the bath.* 休在浴室里一直唱着歌。| *They've been hammering away all day.* 他们整天都在不停地用锤子敲打东西。**8** if a team is playing away, it is playing a game at its opponent's sports field, STADIUM etc 在客场〔比赛〕: *Liverpool are playing away at Everton on Saturday.* 利物浦队星期六在埃弗顿客场进行比赛。**9 away with sb/sth!** *literary* used to tell someone to take someone or something away【文】把某人/某物带走: *Away with the prisoner!* 把囚犯带走! **10 be away** *ScotE* to go or leave a place【苏格兰】走, 离开: *He's just away to the shops.* 他刚走, 去商店了。| *We're away tomorrow.* (=We're leaving tomorrow) 我们明天走。—see also 另见 **far and away** (FAR[1] (9)), **right away** (RIGHT[2] (2))

away[2] *adj* [only before noun 仅用于名词前] an away game or match is played at your opponent's field or sports hall〔比赛〕客场的, 在对方场地进行的 —opposite 反义词 HOME[3] (4)

Away in a Man·ger /ˌ·ˌ· ˈ··/ a popular Christmas CAROL (=a traditional religious song), sung especially by children《马槽歌》〔一首流行圣诞颂歌, 多为孩童吟唱〕

awe[1] /ɔ; ɔː/ *n* [U] **1** a feeling of great respect and admiration for someone or something 敬畏, 畏怯: **with awe/in awe** *Kate gazed at the mountains with awe.* 凯特敬畏地注视着群山。| **fill sb with awe** *The sight of so many jewels in one place filled them with awe.* 看到一个地方有这么多珠宝, 他们大为惊叹。**2 be/stand in awe of sb** to have great respect and admiration for and sometimes a slight fear of someone 对某人非常敬畏: *Because of his reputation as a dancer we were all rather in awe of him.* 他作为一个舞蹈家非常有名望, 所以我们对他非常敬畏。

awe[2] *v* [T usually singular 一般用单数] *formal* if you are awed by someone or something, you feel great respect and admiration for them, and are often slightly afraid of them【正式】使敬畏; 使畏惧: *The girls were awed by the splendor of the cathedral.* 那些女孩对大教堂的壮观景象大为惊叹。—**awed** *adj*: *an awed silence* 出于敬畏的沉默

awe-in·spir·ing /ˈ· ·ˌ··/ *adj* extremely impressive in a way that makes you feel great respect and admiration 令人敬畏的, 令人钦佩的: *a truly awe-inspiring achievement* 真正令人敬佩的成就

awe·some /ˋɔsəm; ˈɔːsəm/ *adj* **1** extremely impressive, serious, or difficult so that you feel great admiration, worry, or fear 令人畏惧的, 可怕的: *an awesome responsibility* 一项令人惊惧的责任 | *the awesome sweep of the scenery* 令人叹为观止的连绵不断的景色 **2** *AmE informal* very good【美, 非正式】很好的, 了不起的: *Their last concert was really awesome.* 他们最后的那场音乐会真不错。—**awesomely** *adv*

awe-strick·en /ˈ· ˌ··/ *adj* = AWESTRUCK

awe·struck /ˋɔˌstrʌk; ˈɔːstrʌk/ *adj* feeling extremely impressed by the importance, difficulty, or seriousness of someone or something 肃然起敬的, 充满敬畏的; 感到惊惧的: *She gazed awestruck at the jewels.* 她充满惊奇地注视着那些珠宝。

aw·ful[1] /ˋɔfl; ˈɔːfəl/ *adj* **1** very bad or unpleasant 糟糕的, 恶劣的, 难受的: *The weather was awful.* 天气很糟糕。| *a really awful book* 十分差劣的书 | *These canned apricots taste awful!* 这些罐头杏真难吃! | *I felt awful about not being able to help.* 我帮不上忙, 心里好难受。**2** [only before noun 仅用于名词前] *spoken* used to emphasize how much or how good, bad etc something is【口】非常的: **an awful lot** (=a very large amount) 非常多的 *I have an awful lot of work to do this week.* 这星期我有一大堆工作要做。| *It made him look an awful fool.* 这使他看起来像个大笨蛋。**3 look/feel awful** to look or feel ill 看上去/感觉像生病: *You look awful – what's wrong with you?* 你看上去脸色不好, 出什么事了? **4** *literary* making you feel great admiration or fear【文】令人敬畏的 —**awfulness** *n* [U] 3

awful[2] *adv* [+adj/adv] *AmE spoken* very【美口】非常: *That kid's awful cute, with her red curls.* 那孩子一头红鬈发, 十分可爱。

aw·ful·ly /ˋɔflɪ; ˈɔːfəli/ *adv spoken* very【口】非常: *It's awfully cold in here. Is the heater on?* 这儿非常冷, 取暖器开了吗?

a·while /əˋhwaɪl; əˈwaɪl/ *adv especially literary* for a short time【尤文】暂时, 片刻

awk·ward /ˋɔkwəd; ˈɔːkwəd/ *adj* **1** making you feel so embarrassed that you are not sure what to do or say 尴尬的, 为难的: *The more she tried to get out of the situation, the more awkward it became.* 她越是想摆脱困境, 情况就越糟。| *an awkward pause* 令人尴尬的短暂沉默 | **make things awkward** (=cause trouble and make a situation very difficult) 使事情变得难办, 使情况变得棘手 *She could make things very awkward if she wanted to.* 如果她想, 她会把事情弄得很难办。**2** not convenient 不方便的: *I'm sorry, have I called at an awkward time?* 对不起, 我的电话打得是否不是时候? **3** moving or behaving in a way that does not seem relaxed or comfortable, especially because you feel nervous or embarrassed 笨拙的, 不灵活的; 别扭的: *I felt a bit awkward on my first day there, but I soon settled in.* 我第一天到那儿感到有点别扭, 但很快就习惯了。| *an awkward wave* 笨拙的挥手动作 | *an awkward teenager* 不灵巧的少年 **4** difficult to use or handle 难用的, 不好操作的: *The camera has a lot of small buttons, which makes it rather awkward to use.* 那照相机有许多小按钮, 用起来不大方便。**5** an awkward person is deliberately unhelpful 难相处的, 不好应付的: **[+about]** *I wish you'd stop being so bloody awkward about everything.* 我希望你不要再处处与人为难。| **an awkward customer** (=someone who is difficult to deal with) 难侍候的顾客 —**awkwardly** *adv*: *"Are you the head tutor ..." she began awkwardly.* "你是校长吗…" 她有些不好意思地问。—**awkwardness** *n* [U] 2

awl /ɔl; ɔːl/ *n* [C] a pointed tool for making holes in leather〔在皮革上钻孔用的〕钻子, 锥子

aw·ning /ˋɔnɪŋ; ˈɔːnɪŋ/ *n* [C] a sheet of material outside a shop, tent etc to keep off the sun or the rain 篷, (帆) 布篷

a·woke /əˋwok; əˈwəʊk/ the past tense of AWAKE

a·wok·en /əˋwokən; əˈwəʊkən/ the past participle of AWAKE

AWOL /ˌe ˌdʌblju o ˋɛl; ˌeɪ ˌdʌbəljuː əʊ ˈel/ *adj* absent without leave; absent from your army group without permission 擅离职守的: **go AWOL** *Two soldiers had gone AWOL the night before.* 前一晚, 有两个士兵擅离职守。

a·wry /əˋraɪ; əˈraɪ/ *adj* **1 go awry** if something goes awry, it does not happen in the way that was planned 出岔子, 走样的, 违背正道的: *My carefully laid plans had already gone awry.* 我精心设计的计划已经出了岔子。**2** not in the correct position 歪的: *He rushed out, hat awry.* 他匆忙出去, 帽子都戴歪了。

aw shucks /ˌɔ ˋʃʌks; ˌɔː ˈʃʌks/ *adj interjection AmE* used in a joking way to show that you feel embarrassed or sad【美】羞怯的，难为情的

axe[1] also 又作 **ax** *AmE*【美】/æks; æks/ *n* [C] **1** a tool with a heavy metal blade on the end of a long handle, used to cut down trees or split pieces of wood 斧头，长柄斧 **2 give sb the axe** *informal* to dismiss someone from their job【非正式】解雇[开除]某人 **3 give sth the axe** *informal* to get rid of something such as a plan, a system, or a service【非正式】砍掉[取消]某事物 **4 have an axe to grind** to do or say something again and again because you want to persuade people to accept your ideas or beliefs 反复说[做]以使人相信: *I have no political axe to grind.* 我翻来覆去地说并非是让人接受我的政治观点。

axe[2] also 又作 **ax** *AmE*【美】*v* [T] *informal*【非正式】**1** to suddenly dismiss someone from their job 突然解雇，突然开除: *plans to axe half the workforce* 裁员一半的计划 **2** to get rid of a plan, system, or service, or reduce the amount of money that is spent on something 砍掉，取消，废止: *Student grants have been axed.* 学生助学金被取消了。

ax·i·om /ˋæksɪəm; ˈæksiəm/ *n* [C] *formal* a rule or principle that is generally considered to be true【正式】公理，规律，原则，原理

ax·i·o·mat·ic /ˌæksɪəˋmætɪk; ˌæksiəˈmætɪk◂/ *adj formal* not needing to be proved because you can easily see that it is true; SELF-EVIDENT【正式】公理的，不需证明的，不言自明的 —**axiomatically** /-klɪ; -kli/ *adv*

ax·is /ˋæksɪs; ˈæksɨs/ *n plural* **axes** /-siz; -siːz/ [C] *technical*【术语】**1** the imaginary line around which a large round object, such as the Earth, turns 轴，轴线: *The Earth rotates on an axis between the North and South Poles.* 地球绕着南北两极之间的地轴自转。—see picture at 参见 EARTH[1] 图 **2** a line drawn across the middle of a regular shape that divides it into two equal parts〔将规则形状平分成相等的两部分的〕中心线 **3** either of the two lines of a GRAPH, by which the positions of points are measured 参考轴线，基准线，坐标轴

Axis, the also 又作 **the Axis powers, the Axis countries** the countries, including Germany, Italy, and Japan, who fought together during World War II against the allies 轴心国〔包括德、意、日等国，二战期间与同盟国作战〕

ax·le /ˋæksl; ˈæksəl/ *n* [C] the bar connecting two wheels on a car or other vehicle 轮轴，车轴 —see picture at 参见 BICYCLE[1] 图

ay·ah /ˋaɪə; ˈaɪə/ *n* [C] *IndE, PakE* a nurse who looks after children【印，巴】保姆，女佣

a·ya·tol·lah /ˌaɪəˋtolə; ˌaɪəˈtɒlə/ *n* [C] a religious leader of the Shiite Muslims, especially a very powerful one 阿亚图拉〔伊斯兰什叶派宗教领袖的尊称〕

Ayatollah Khomeini —see 见 Ayatollah KHOMEINI

aye[1] /aɪ; aɪ/ *adv* **1** used to say yes when voting 是！赞成！对！〔用于表决时〕; **the ayes have it** (=used to say that most people in a meeting have voted in favour of something) 赞成者占多数 —opposite 反义词 NAY **2** *dialect* a word meaning yes, used especially in Scotland【方言】是！对！同意！〔尤用于苏格兰〕 3

aye[2] /e; eɪ/ *adv ScotE old use or poetic* always【苏格兰，旧或诗】永远地，永久地，永恒地

Ayer /ɛr; eə/, **A.J.** (1910-89) a British PHILOSOPHER who wrote *Language, Truth, and Logic* (1936) 艾尔〔(1910-1989)，英国哲学家，著有《语言、真理和逻辑》(1936)〕

Ayers Rock /ˌɛrz ˋrɑk; ˌeəz ˈrɒk/ —see 见 ULURU

Ayr·shire /ˋɛrʃɚ; ˈeəʃə/ **1** a COUNTY in southwest Scotland, now part of Strathclyde region 艾尔郡〔苏格兰西南部一郡，现归属斯特拉斯克莱德地区〕 **2** a brown and white type of cow that is used for producing milk 艾尔夏奶牛〔一种棕白相间的奶牛〕

AZ the written abbreviation of 缩写= ARIZONA

A-Z /ˌe təˋzi; ˌeɪ tə ˈzed/ —see 见 A TO Z

A·zer·bai·jan /ˌɑzəbaɪˋdʒɑn; ˌæzəbaɪˈdʒɑːn/ a country in western Asia, west of the Caspian Sea and north of Iran. Population: 7,700,000 (2001). Capital: Baku. Azerbaijan became independent of the former Soviet Union in 1991. 阿塞拜疆〔亚洲西部一国家，位于里海以西，伊朗以北。人口: 7,700,000 (2001)，首都: 巴库。1991 年脱离前苏联实现独立〕—**Azerbaijani** *n, adj*

A·zores, the /ˋezorz; əˈzɔːz/ a group of islands in the north Atlantic Ocean, west of Portugal, which belong to Portugal 亚速尔群岛〔北大西洋一群岛，位于葡萄牙以西，归属葡萄牙〕

az·ure /ˋæʒɚ; ˈæʒə/ *adj* having a bright blue colour like the sky 天蓝色的，蔚蓝的 —**azure** *n* [U]

B,b

B, b /bi; biː/ *plural* **B's, b's** *n* [C] the second letter of the English alphabet 英语字母表的第二个字母

B *n* **1 a)** the seventh note in the musical SCALE[1] (8) of C major B音〔C大调音阶中的第七个音〕 **b)** the musical KEY[2] (4) based on this note B调 **2** a mark given to a student's work, to show that it is good but not excellent B级, 乙级, 乙等〔表示学业成绩良好〕: *I got a B in History.* 我历史得了个B。—see also 另见 B-MOVIE, B-SIDE

b the written abbreviation of 缩写= born: *Andrew Lanham, b 1885* 安德鲁·拉纳姆, 生于1885年

B & B /ˌbi ənd ˋbi; ˌbiː ənd ˈbiː/ the written abbreviation of 缩写 = BED AND BREAKFAST

B & Q /ˌbi ənd ˋkju; ˌbiː ənd ˈkjuː/ *trademark* a large British DIY store (=shop selling things for decorating or repairing your house and garden). 【商标】百安居〔英国一家大型自助式商店, 主营家庭、花园装修用品〕

B-52 /ˌbi fɪftɪ ˋtu; ˌbiː fɪfti ˈtuː/ a large US military aircraft that is used to drop bombs B-52型轰炸机〔美国军用大型轰炸机〕

BA /ˌbi ˋe; ˌbiː ˈeɪ/ *n* [C] Bachelor of Arts; the title of a first university degree in a subject such as literature, history etc 文学士: *Susan Potter, BA* 苏姗·波特, 文学士 —compare 比较 BSC

baa /bɑ; bɑː/ *v* [I] to make a sound like a sheep 咩〔发出羊叫声〕—**baa** *n* [C]

Baa, Baa, Black Sheep /ˌ·ˈ·ˌ·ˈ/ a NURSERY RHYME (=old song or poem for young children). The rhyme goes: Baa, Baa, Black Sheep, / Have you any wool? / Yes, sir, yes, sir / Three bags full. / One for the master, / One for the dame, / and one for the little boy / who lives down the lane. 《黑绵羊, 咩咩叫》〔一首儿歌, 歌词如下: 黑绵羊, 咩咩叫/请问你, 可有毛?/有有有, 羊答道/满当当, 三大包/赠东家, 送夫人/还有深巷小宝宝〕

Ba·bar /ˋbæbɑr; ˈbɑːbɑː/ the main character in stories for children by Jean de Brunhoff. Babar is an ELEPHANT who is a king. 巴巴尔〔让·德·布吕诺夫创作的儿童故事的主人公。他是一头大象王〕

Bab·bage /ˋbæbɪdʒ; ˈbæbɪdʒ/, **Charles** (1792-1871) a British MATHEMATICIAN who designed a type of calculating machine which modern computers are based on 巴贝奇〔(1792-1871), 英国数学家。他曾设计过一种计算器, 为现代计算机奠定了基础〕

Bab·bitt /ˋbæbɪt; ˈbæbɨt/ a book by Sinclair Lewis about a businessman called George Babbitt who lives in a small US town. People think he is a boring man, because he thinks only about his own business and his position in local society, and he is not interested in other things in life. 《巴比特》〔辛克莱·刘易斯写的一本书。该书讲述美国一小镇商人乔治·巴比特的故事。他在大家的眼里是个没有情趣的人, 只关心自己的生意和在当地社会中的地位, 而对生活中的其他事不感兴趣〕

bab·ble[1] /ˋbæbl; ˈbæbəl/ *v* **1** [I,T] to speak quickly in a way that is difficult to understand or sounds silly 含糊不清地说; 唠唠叨叨: *I have no idea what he was babbling on about.* 我根本不知道他在唠叨些什么。**2** [I] to make a sound like water moving over stones 发出潺潺流水声 —**babbler** *n* [C]

babble[2] *n* [singular] **1** the confused sound of many people talking at the same time 嘈杂的说话声: *the babble of a crowded party* 聚会上人群唧唧喳喳的说话声 **2** a sound like water moving over stones 潺潺声

babe /beb; beɪb/ *n* **1** *literary* a baby 【文】婴儿: **babe in arms** (=one that has to be carried) 怀里的婴儿 **2** a word for an attractive young woman 宝贝儿〔用于称呼年轻貌美的女子〕 **3** a way of speaking to a young woman, often considered offensive 小妞〔对年轻女子的称谓, 通常被认为具有冒犯性〕 **4** a way of speaking to someone you love, especially your wife or husband 亲爱的〔对自己的爱人, 尤指对妻子或丈夫的称呼〕 **5 babe in the woods** *AmE* someone who can be easily deceived 【美】容易上当受骗的人: *He was like a babe in the woods when he first came to New York.* 刚到纽约时, 他经常上当受骗。

ba·bel /ˋbebḷ; ˈbeɪbəl/ *n* [singular,U] the confusing sound of many voices talking together 嘈杂声: *a babel of French and Italian* 有人说法语、有人说意大利语的混杂声

Babe Ruth —see 见 Babe RUTH

Babes in the Wood /ˌ·ˌ·ˌ·ˈ·/ an old story for children about a young brother and sister who are left in the woods by their evil uncle, who wants to get control of their property 《林中弃童》〔一个古老的儿童故事。故事中的一对小兄妹邪恶的叔叔企图霸占他们的财产而将他们遗弃在森林里〕

ba·boon /bæˋbun; bəˈbuːn/ *n* [C] a large monkey that lives in Africa and South Asia 狒狒〔产于非洲和南亚〕

ba·bu, baboo /ˋbɑbu; ˈbɑːbuː/ *n* [C] **1** *IndE old-fashioned* an Indian title of respect 【印, 过时】巴布〔印度人的尊称〕 **2** *BrE* an Indian CLERK or government official of low rank 【英】〔印度人〕书记员

ba·by /ˋbebɪ; ˈbeɪbi/ *n plural* **babies** [C]

1 ▶CHILD 儿童◀ a very young child who has not yet learned to speak or walk 婴儿: *A baby was crying upstairs.* 楼上有婴儿在哭。| *They have a five-year-old boy and a baby girl.* 他们有一个五岁的男孩和一个出生不久的女孩。| **have a baby** (=give birth to a baby) 生孩子 *I think she had the baby in June.* 我认为她是6月份生的孩子。| **be expecting a baby** (=have a baby developing inside your body) 有孕 —see 见 CHILD (USAGE)

2 ▶ANIMAL/PLANT 动物/植物◀ a very young animal or plant 幼兽; 雏鸟; 幼苗: *baby birds* 雏鸟 | *baby carrots* 胡萝卜苗

3 ▶BROTHER/SISTER 兄弟/姐妹◀ a younger child in a family, often the youngest 〔兄弟姐妹中〕年纪最小的一个: *He's the baby of the family.* 他在家里年纪最小。

4 ▶WOMAN 女人◀ *AmE spoken* 【美口】 **a)** a way of speaking to someone that you love 亲爱的〔用于称呼爱人〕: *Mike baby, could you get me a glass of water?* 亲爱的迈克, 你能给我拿杯水来吗? **b)** a way of speaking to a young woman, often considered offensive 小妞〔对年轻女子的称呼, 通常被认为具有冒犯性〕

5 ▶SILLY 傻的◀ someone who is not behaving in a sensible way 幼稚的人: *Don't be such a baby – take your medicine!* 别这么孩子气 —— 吃药吧!

6 ▶RESPONSIBILITY 责任◀ *informal* something special that someone has developed or is responsible for 【非正式】差事, 任务, 分内之事: *Don't ask me about the building contract – that's Robert's baby.* 不要问我关于建筑合同的事 —— 那是罗伯特管的。

baby blues /ˈ·· ·/ *n* [plural] *informal* a feeling of DEPRESSION (1a) that some women suffer from after they have had a baby 【非正式】产后忧郁症: *an attack of the baby blues* 患上产后忧郁症

baby boom·er /ˈ·· ˌ··/ *n* [C] someone born during a period when a lot of babies were born, especially between 1946 and 1964 〔尤指1946年至1964年间〕生育高峰期出生的人

baby car·riage /ˈ·· ˌ··/ *n* [C] *AmE* a thing like a small bed with four wheels, used for taking a baby from one place to another 【美】手推婴儿车, 婴儿推车; PRAM *BrE* 【英】—compare 比较 PUSHCHAIR —see picture at 参见 PRAM 图

Ba·by·cham /ˋbebɪʃæm; ˈbeɪbiʃæm/ *trademark* a type of sweet alcoholic drink with BUBBLES that is sold in the UK. It is a little like CHAMPAGNE but is much less expensive. 【商标】杯杯香〔英国出售的一种甜汽酒, 类似香槟酒, 但价格要便宜得多〕

baby-faced /ˈ·· ·/ *adj* a baby-faced adult has a face like a child 娃娃脸的

Ba·by·gro /ˋbebɪˌgro; ˈbeɪbigrəʊ/ *n* [C] *BrE trademark* a piece of clothing for a baby, that covers their whole body 【英, 商标】〔婴儿穿的〕连身服

ba·by·hood /ˋbebɪˌhud; ˈbeɪbihʊd/ *n* [U] the period of time when you are a baby 婴儿期, 幼儿期

ba·by·ish /ˋbebɪ·ɪʃ; ˈbeɪbi-ɪʃ/ *adj* like a baby or suitable for a baby 婴儿似的, 孩子气的: *The games were a little babyish for nine-year-olds.* 这些游戏对九岁的孩子来说太容易了一点。

Bab·y·lon /ˋbæbɪlən; ˈbæbɨlən/ an ancient Middle Eastern city that was the capital of Babylonia and was famous for its great wealth. People sometimes use the name Babylon to mean a place of pleasure and immoral behaviour. 巴比伦〔中东古城, 巴比伦王国的首都, 以富裕闻名, 有时用来指称奢华淫靡之地〕

baby milk /ˈ·· ·/ *n* [U] *BrE* dried milk mixed with water and fed to babies instead of breast milk 【英】〔用以替代母乳的〕婴儿奶粉; FORMULA (5) *AmE* 【美】

Baby Ruth /ˌ·· ˈ·/ *trademark* a type of chocolate bar in the US which contains PEANUTS, CARAMEL, and NOUGAT 【商标】宝贝露丝巧克力〔美国一种条形巧克力, 内有花生、焦糖及果仁糖〕

ba·by·sit /ˋbebɪˏsɪt; ˈbeɪbisɪt/ *v past tense and past participle* **babysat** /-ˏsæt; -sæt/ *present participle* **babysitting** [I,T] to take care of children while their parents are away for a short time〔临时受雇代外出的父母〕照料(小孩) —**babysitting** *n* [U]: *She earns some extra cash from babysitting.* 她帮人家照看孩子挣些额外收入。| *a babysitting service* 照看孩子的服务

ba·by·sit·ter /ˋbebɪˏsɪtɚ; ˈbeɪbiˌsɪtə/ *n* [C] **1** someone who takes care of children while their parents are away for a short time〔代外出的父母照料小孩的〕临时保姆 **2** *AmE* someone who is paid to look after children while their parents are at work【美】保姆, 靠照看小孩为生的人; CHILDMINDER *BrE*【英】

baby talk /ˈ‥ ˏ/ *n* [U] sounds or words that babies use when they are learning to talk 儿语, 婴儿牙牙学语声

baby tooth /ˈ‥ ˏ/ *n plural* **baby teeth** [C] a tooth from the first set of teeth that young children have 乳牙; MILK TOOTH *BrE*【英】

baby walk·er /ˈ‥ ˏ‥/ *n* [C] a frame on wheels that is used to support a baby while it is learning to walk〔幼儿〕学步车

Ba·call /bəˋkɔl; bəˈkɔːl/, **Lau·ren** /ˋlɔrən; ˈlɔːrən/ (1924-) a US actress who was married to Humphrey Bogart. She appeared with him in the films *To Have and Have Not* and *The Big Sleep*, and in many other films and plays. 白考尔〔(1924-), 美国女演员, 与亨弗莱·博加特结为夫妻。他们一起出演了《有的和没有的》、《沉睡》等许多影片和舞台剧〕

Ba·car·di /bəˋkardɪ; bəˈkɑːdi/ *trademark* a type of white RUM (=strong alcoholic drink), which people often drink with Coca-cola【商标】百家得朗姆酒〔一种白色朗姆酒, 常掺入可口可乐饮用〕

bac·ca·lau·re·ate /ˌbækəˋlɔrɪət; ˌbækəˈlɔːriət/ *n* [C] the last examination you take in French schools and some international schools〔法国和一些国际学校的〕中学毕业考试

bac·ca·rat /ˌbækəˋrɑ; ˈbækərɑː/ *n* [U] a card game usually played for money 巴卡拉纸牌游戏〔一种赌博方式〕

bac·cha·na·li·an /ˌbækəˋnelɪən; ˌbækəˈneɪliən◂/ *adj literary* a bacchanalian party, celebration etc involves alcohol, sex, and uncontrolled behaviour【文】狂饮作乐的: *a bacchanalian orgy* 狂饮作乐的闹宴

Bac·chus /ˋbækəs; ˈbækəs/ in Roman MYTHOLOGY, the god of wine and FERTILITY. In Greek mythology his name is DIONYSUS. 巴克斯〔罗马神话中的酒神与生育之神。希腊神话中称为狄俄尼索斯〕

bac·cy /ˋbækɪ; ˈbæki/ *n* [U] *slang* tobacco【俚】烟草

bach /bætʃ; bætʃ/ *v* **bach it** *AmE old-fashioned* if a man baches it, he lives on his own and looks after himself【美, 过时】〔男子〕过单身生活

Bach /bɑk; bɑːk/, **Jo·hann Se·bas·ti·an** /johɑn səˋbæstɪən; ˈjəʊhæn səˈbæstiən/ (1685-1750) a German musician, one of the most famous and admired European COMPOSERS. He is especially famous for his ORGAN music and his religious CHORAL music (=for musicians and singers), which is typical of the Baroque style. 巴赫〔(1685-1750), 德国音乐家, 最著名、最受推崇的欧洲作曲家之一, 尤其以管风琴曲和代表巴洛克风格的宗教合唱音乐著称〕

Bach·a·rach /ˋbækəræk; ˈbækəræk/, **Burt** /bɝt; bɜːt/ (1929-) a US songwriter whose music is in the EASY LISTENING style and has been recorded by many different singers and musicians. 巴卡拉克〔(1929-), 美国歌曲作家。其音乐节奏舒缓, 为众多歌手和音乐人翻录〕

bach·e·lor /ˋbætʃəlɚ; ˈbætʃələ/ *n* [C] a man who has never been married 未婚男子, 单身汉: **confirmed bachelor** (=a man who intends never to marry) 决定终身不结婚的男子, 决心当一辈子光棍的人 | **eligible bachelor** (=a rich young man who has not yet married) 条件不错的未婚男子

> CULTURAL NOTE 文化注释
>
> If you describe a man as a bachelor, rather than as 'single', you are suggesting that he is someone who may never get married, especially because he does not want the responsibility of being a husband or father. 若某人被称作bachelor而不是single, 那他也许根本不会结婚, 尤其是因为他不想承担做丈夫或父亲的责任。—compare Cultural Note at SPINSTER 比较 SPINSTER 文化注释

bachelor flat /ˈ‥‥ ˏ/ *n* [C] a set of rooms where an unmarried man lives 单身男子公寓

bachelor par·ty /ˈ‥‥ ˏ‥/ *n* [C] *AmE* a party for men only, especially the night before a man's wedding【美】〔尤指在某男子结婚前一晚举行的〕单身汉聚会; STAG NIGHT *BrE*【英】

> CULTURAL NOTE 文化注释
>
> Bachelor parties usually involve a lot of silly uncontrolled behaviour, and everyone drinks a lot of alcohol. In British English, this is called a 'stag party'. 单身汉晚会上每个人都纵情狂饮, 常有失态的蠢事发生, 英国称此为stag party。

bachelor's de·gree /ˈ‥‥ ˏ/ *n* [C] the first level of university degree; BA 学士学位

ba·cil·lus /bəˋsɪləs; bəˈsɪləs/ *n plural* **bacilli** /-laɪ; -laɪ/ [C] *technical* a rod-shaped BACTERIA, of which some types cause diseases【术语】杆菌, 病菌

back¹ /bæk; bæk/ *adv* S1 W1

1 ▶RETURN 回原处◀ in or into the place or position where someone or something was before 回到原处; 恢复原状: *Freddie was supposed to be back at the hotel by six.* 弗雷迪应该在6点钟前回到旅馆。| *Put that book back where you found it!* 把那本书放回原处! | *"We'd better go back," she said regretfully.* "我们最好回去。"她懊悔地说。—see graph at 参见 RETURN¹ 图表

2 ▶AS BEFORE 如前◀ in or into the condition that someone or something was in before 恢复原来的状态: *I just couldn't get back to sleep.* 我再也睡不着了。| *This brings me back to my point about the state of the economy.* 这使我又回到了对经济情况的看法。

3 ▶HOME TOWN 故乡◀ in a place where you or your family lived before 回到〔故乡〕: **[+in/at etc]** *Back in Manitoba we used to skate on the lakes in winter.* 过去在故乡马尼托巴时, 我们常在冬天去湖上滑冰。| *Back home we never did things this way.* 过去在家时, 我们从来不这样做事。

4 ▶NOT FORWARDS 不向前◀ in the direction that you have come from 向后面; 在后面: *George glanced back to see if he was still being followed.* 乔治向身后瞧了一眼, 看看是不是仍有人在跟踪自己。| *He took a few steps back, then took the photo.* 他向后退了几步, 然后拍照。

5 ▶REPLY 回复◀ as a reply or reaction to what someone has done 回复, 回答: *Can you ask Mr Clark to call me back?* 你可以请克拉克先生给我回个电话吗? | *I'll pay you back on Friday.* 我星期五再还钱给你。| *I grinned back at him.* 我也朝他咧嘴笑笑。

6 ▶AGAIN 再◀ once again 再次, 又一次: *Play the tape back for me, will you?* 把磁带再给我放一遍, 好吗? | *Let's go back over these figures just to make sure we're right.* 让我们重新算一下这些数字以确保正确。

7 sit/lie/lean back to sit or lie in a comfortable, relaxed way 舒舒服服地坐/躺/倚着: *Sit back, relax, and enjoy the show!* 坐好, 放松一下, 好好欣赏节目吧!

8 ▶THE PAST 过去◀ in or towards an earlier time 以前, 从前, 过去, 追溯至: **[+in/on]** *Back in the fifties, children respected their elders.* 追溯到50年代, 孩子们都尊敬长辈。| **three years/two months etc back** (=three years ago etc) 三年/两个月等以前 *If I'd known three years back that stocks were going to crash, I'd have sold everything.* 如果我三年前知道股票会暴跌, 我早就全卖掉了。

9 ▶AWAY FROM SB 离开某人◀ away from the person who is speaking 后退〔离开说话人〕: *Stay well back! Let the ambulance through.* 向后退! 让救护车过去。

10 ▶AWAY FROM STH 离开某物◀ away from a surface or area 离开表面: *Pull back the bandage and see if the wound is healing.* 把绷带解下来, 看看伤口是不是在愈合。| *The clouds rolled back and suddenly there was sunlight.* 云层逐渐散开, 阳光突然出现了。

11 back and forth if someone or something goes back and forth, they go in one direction then back to where they started from, and keep repeating this movement 来来回回: *The shuttle bus runs back and forth between the airport and the downtown area.* 班车往返于机场与市中心之间。| *pacing back and forth in the waiting room* 在等候室里来回踱步

12 ▶BOOK 书◀ towards the beginning of a book 往前, 往回: *There's a picture six pages further back.* 书再往回翻六页有一幅图。

13 pay/get sb back (for) to do something unpleasant to someone because they have done something unpleasant to you or someone you care about 回击某人, 还击某人: *I'll pay him back for hurting my sister – just you wait!* 他伤害我妹妹, 我会予以回击的。等着瞧!

14 go back on a promise/agreement etc to do the opposite of what you promised to do 食言/违约等: *You can trust Kate – she'll never go back on her word.* 你可以信任凯特, 她从不食言。

back 背部, 背脊, 后背

John's shirt is on back to front *BrE*【英】/on backwards *AmE*【美】.
约翰的衬衫前后穿反了。

They stood back to back.
她们背靠背站着。

back² *n* [C]

1 ►BODY 身体◄ **a)** the side of a person's or animal's body that is opposite the chest and goes from the neck to the top of the legs〔人或动物的〕背部, 背脊, 后背: *He lifted the bag of golf clubs onto his back.* 他拿起装有高尔夫球棒的袋子背到背上。| *The cat arched its back and hissed.* 那只猫拱起背发出嘘嘘声。| **on your back** (=with your back on the ground) 仰卧 *They lay on their backs and gazed at the sky.* 他们仰躺着凝望天空。| **with your back to** *Stand with your back to the wall and don't move.* 背靠墙站着, 别动。—see picture at 参见 HORSE¹ 图 **b)** the bones that go from your neck to the top of your legs 脊骨: *He broke his back in a motorbike accident.* 在一场摩托车事故中, 他摔断了脊梁。

2 ►PART 部分◄ the part of something that is furthest from the direction in which it moves or faces 后面, 后部: **[+of]** *He kissed her on the back of her head.* 他在她后脑勺上亲了一下。| *I think there's enough room for your stuff in the back of the truck.* 我看卡车后部有足够的地方装你这些东西。| **at the back** *a small shop with an office at the back* 后面有一间办公室的小商店 —see 见 FRONT¹ (USAGE) | **in back (of)** *AmE* (=in or at the back of something)【美】在…后面 *When we go on long journeys by car the kids always ride in back.* 我们开车长途旅行时, 孩子们总是坐在车的后座。| **round the back/out (the) back** *BrE informal* (=behind a house or other building)【英, 非正式】在房屋[建筑物]的后面 *We keep the bikes in a shed out the back.* 我们把自行车放在屋后的车棚里。—opposite 反义词 FRONT¹ (2)

3 ►SURFACE 表面◄ the less important side or surface of something such as a paper or card 较为不重要的一面; 背面, 反面: *Paul scribbled his address on the back of an envelope.* 保罗把他的地址草草地写在信封的背面。| *On the back of the canvas we can see the date: 1645.* 在油画的背面我们可以看到日期: 1645 年。

4 ►CHAIR 椅子◄ the part of a seat that you lean against when you are sitting 椅背, 靠背: **[+of]** *He rested his arm on the back of the sofa.* 他把一只胳膊放在沙发的靠背上。

5 ►BOOK/NEWSPAPER 书/报纸◄ the last pages of a book or newspaper〔书的〕后面;〔报纸的〕最末版: **[+of]** *The index is at the back of the book.* 索引在书的末尾。

6 ►FOOTBALL ETC 足球等◄ one of the defending players on a football or hockey team 后卫

7 at your back a) behind you 在…后面: *They had the wind at their backs as they set off.* 他们出发时顺风。**b)** *literary* supporting you【文】支持: *Caesar marched into Rome with an army at his back.* 凯撒在军队的支持下长驱直入罗马。

8 at/in the back of your mind a thought or feeling that is at the back of your mind is influencing you even though you are not thinking about it 头脑中有…的印象: *At the back of Joe's mind was the feeling that he had seen this place before.* 乔隐约记得以前见过这个地方。

9 back to back a) with the backs towards each other 背靠背: *Stand back to back and we'll see who is taller.* 我们背靠背站着就能看出谁高了。—see also 另见 BACK-TO-BACK **b)** *especially AmE* happening one after the other【尤美】连续地, 一个接一个地: *a marathon basketball tournament with games played back to back* 比赛一场接一场的马拉松式篮球联赛

10 back to front *BrE* in an incorrect position so that what should be the back is at the front; backwards【英】前后倒置: *You've got your sweater on back to front.* 你把毛衣前后穿反了。

11 behind sb's back if you do something behind someone's back, you do it without them knowing 背着某人, 背地里: *She's the kind of person who talks about you behind your back.* 她是那种爱背后讲闲话的人。

12 get/put sb's back up *informal* to annoy someone【非正式】使某人生气, 使某人产生反感, 惹怒某人: *You'll just put people's backs up if you're aggressive all the time.* 如果你总是那样好斗, 你只会把别人惹怒。

13 get off my back *spoken* used to tell someone to stop annoying you or asking you to do things you do not want to do【口】别啰嗦了: *Do me a favour and get off my back!* 劳驾, 别烦我好不好!

14 know sth back to front *BrE*【英】, **know sth backwards** *especially AmE*【尤美】if you know or learn something back to front, you know it very thoroughly 对某事了解得很透彻: *You can't fool her! She knows the regulations back to front!* 你骗不了她! 她对这些规则简直滚瓜烂熟!

15 know somewhere like the back of your hand to know a place extremely well 对某地方了如指掌: *I'll drive, if you want – I know New York like the back of my hand.* 如果你愿意, 我来开车, 我对纽约了如指掌。

16 the back of beyond *informal especially BrE* a very distant place that is difficult to get to【非正式, 尤英】遥远偏僻的地方: *They live on a farm somewhere in the back of beyond.* 他们住在一个非常偏僻的农场。

17 be (flat) on your back to be so ill that you cannot get out of bed 病得不能下床: *He's been flat on his back with flu for three weeks.* 他得了流感, 已卧床三周了。

18 be on sb's back *informal* to be trying to make someone do things they do not want to do【非正式】非让某人做…不可, 硬要某人做…: *Dad's on my back about my homework, so I can't go out tonight.* 爸爸非要我做作业不可, 所以我今晚不能出去。

19 put your back into it *informal* to work extremely hard at something【非正式】全力以赴, 发奋做某事: *If we really put our backs into it, we could finish today.* 如果我们加把劲, 今天能干完。

20 have your back to the wall *informal* to be in a very difficult position with no choice about what to do【非正式】陷入绝境; 被逼得走投无路

21 low-backed/straight-backed/narrow-backed etc with a low, straight, narrow etc back 低背的/直背的/窄背的等: *a high-backed chair* 高背椅

22 turn your back on to refuse to be involved with something 对…不予理睬; 拒绝帮助: *So many of them just turn their backs on their religion when they leave home.* 他们许多人离开家乡后就不再在意原来所信仰的宗教了。

back³ *adj* [only before noun 仅用于名词前] **1** at the back 后面的, 后部的: *a back room* 后屋 | *the back page* 封底 | *a back seat* 后座 —see also 另见 BACK DOOR **2** behind something 在…后面的: *in the backyard* 在后院 **3** from the back 从后面的: *a back view* 从后往前看 | *Go in the back way so you won't be seen.* 从后面的路走不会有人看见你。**4 back street/lane/road etc** a street etc that is away from the main streets 偏僻的街/巷/路等: *a little shop in a back street behind the station* 车站后面街上的小商店 **5 back rent/taxes/pay** money that someone owes from an earlier date 拖欠的租金/税款/工资 **6 back issue/copy/number** an old copy of a magazine or newspaper 过期的报刊杂志: *a pile of back copies of 'Punch' magazine* 一叠旧《笨拙》杂志〔1841 年创刊于伦敦的漫画杂志〕**7** *technical* a back vowel sound is made by raising your tongue at the back of your mouth【术语】〔元音〕舌后的, 舌根的

back⁴ *v*

1 ►MOVE SB 移动某人◄ [I always+adv/prep, T always+ adv/prep] to move backwards, or make someone else move backwards (使)后退, (使)退出: **back towards/across etc** *Stanley backed slowly across the stage.* 斯坦利缓缓地退出舞台。

2 ►MOVE VEHICLE 移动车辆◄ [I,T] to make a car move backwards; REVERSE¹ (2) 后退, 倒退, 倒车: **back (sth) into/out of etc** *If you back your car out of the driveway I can get mine in.* 你把车退出车道, 我的车才能开进去。—see picture on page A3 参见 A3 页图

3 ►SUPPORT 支持◄ [T] to support someone or something, especially with money, power, or influence 支持, 鼓励, 资助: *The bill is backed by environmental lobbyists.* 这个议案得到了环保说客的支持。| *government-backed loans* 政府资助的贷款

4 ▶BACK SURFACE 背面◀ [T usually passive 一般用被动态] to put something on the back surface of a flat piece of material 以…为背衬, 用…装背衬: *Back the photo with strong cardboard.* 用结实的硬纸板作这张照片的背衬。| *a plastic-backed shower curtain* 以塑料作背衬的浴帘

5 ▶BE BEHIND 在后面◀ [T usually passive 一般用被动态] to be at the back of something or behind it 在…的后边: *It was a sunny spot, backed by a wall.* 这是个阳光充足的地方, 后边有一道墙。

6 ▶MUSIC 音乐◀ [T usually passive 一般用被动态] if musicians back a singer or another musician, they play music that makes the main performer sound better 伴奏

7 ▶HORSE/DOG RACE 赛马/赛狗◀ [T] to risk money on whether a horse, dog, team etc wins something 下赌注于: *We backed Eliamana but it finished fourth.* 我们都下注于埃里亚马娜, 但它最后得了个第四。

8 back the wrong horse to support a person, group etc that loses 下错了赌注, 支持了输家

9 ▶WIND 风◀ [I] *technical* if the wind backs, it changes direction, moving around the COMPASS (1) in the direction North-West-South-East【术语】逆时针转, 逆转

back away *phr v* [I] **1** to move backwards, away from something, especially because you are afraid, shocked etc〔尤指因恐惧或震惊而〕躲开; 向后退, 退缩: [**+from**] *The waiter backed away from the table, bowing slightly.* 男服务员从桌旁向后退, 欠身鞠了个躬。**2** to gradually stop taking part in something or supporting something 逐渐退出, 不再支持: *Imperceptibly, the Government has backed away from the plan.* 政府逐渐地不再支持这个计划。

back down *phr v* [I] to accept defeat in an argument, opinion, or claim 放弃〔观点、意见、要求〕; 承认〔错误〕; 认输: *When presented with the evidence, the suspect backed down.* 拿出证据后, 疑犯终于认罪。

back off *phr v* [I] *especially AmE*【尤美】**1** to move backwards, away from something 退后: *Back off, you're crowding me.* 往后退, 别挤我。**2** to stop trying to force someone to do or think something 不再迫使〔某人〕做[考虑]〔某事〕: *I think you should back off for a while and leave Alan to make his own decision.* 我认为你应该暂时不要逼迫艾伦, 让他自己去决定。**3** to gradually stop taking part in something or supporting something 逐渐退出, 不再支持: *Jerry backed off when he realized how much work was involved.* 杰里意识到有多少工作要做之后, 便退出了。

back onto sth *phr v* [T] if a building backs onto something such as a river or field, its back faces it〔建筑物〕背后靠近, 背对着

back out *phr v* [I] to decide not to do something that you had promised to do 不履行〔诺言、合同等〕, 打退堂鼓, 食言, 违约: [**+of**] *They backed out of the contract at the last minute.* 他们在最后时刻退出了合同。

back up *phr v* **1** [T **back** sb/sth ↔ **up**] to say that what someone is saying is true 证实〔某人〕的说法; 支持〔某人〕的说法: *Peggy would back me up if she were here.* 佩姬要是在这儿, 一定会支持我的说法。| *The videotape evidence backed up the manager's story.* 录像带这一证据证实了经理的话。**2** [I,T **back** sth ↔ **up**] to make a copy of the information on a computer PROGRAM or DISK 复制〔计算机程序或磁盘〕 **3** [I,T **back** sth ↔ **up**] to make a car go backwards 倒〔车〕: *Get out of the way – the truck's backing up!* 让开, 卡车在倒车! —see picture on page A3 参见 A3 页图 **4** [I] to move backwards 向后移动: *Back up a bit so that everyone can see.* 往后点儿让大家都能看见。—see also 另见 BACKUP

back·ache /ˈbæk,ek; ˈbækeɪk/ *n* [C,U] a pain in your back 背痛

back·bench /ˌbækˋbɛntʃ; ˌbækˈbentʃ◂/ *n* [C] *BrE* the seats in the British parliament where ordinary MPS (MP (1)) sit【英】后座议员席位: *the backbenches* 后座议员们 —compare 比较 FRONTBENCH

back·bench·er /ˌbækˋbɛntʃɚ; ˌbækˈbentʃə◂/ *n* [C] *BrE* an ordinary British Member of Parliament rather than one of the party leaders【英】后座议员〔不担任政党领袖的普通议员〕: *Angry backbenchers are threatening to vote against the government.* 愤怒的后座议员们威胁要投票反对政府。

back·bit·ing /ˈbæk,baɪtɪŋ; ˈbækbaɪtɪŋ/ *n* [U] unpleasant or cruel talk about someone who is not present 背后说人的坏话: *All this backbiting is destroying company morale.* 所有这些流言飞语都在影响公司的士气。—**backbiter** *n* [C]

back·board /ˈbæk,bɔrd; ˈbækbɔːd/ *n* [C] the board behind the basket in the game of BASKETBALL 篮板 —see picture on page A22 参见 A22 页图

back·bone /ˈbækˋbon; ˈbækbəʊn/ *n* **1** [C] the row of connected bones that go down the middle of your back; SPINE (1) 脊骨, 脊柱 **2 the backbone of** the most important part of an organization, set of ideas etc 骨干; 支柱; 主力, 中坚: *The manufacturing sector forms the backbone of the country's economy.* 制造业是这个国家经济的支柱。**3** [U] moral strength 骨气, 毅力: *The army'll give 'em some backbone!* 部队会锻炼他们的毅力!

back·break·ing /ˈbæk,brekɪŋ; ˈbækbreɪkɪŋ/ *adj* backbreaking work is physically very difficult and makes you very tired〔工作〕累死人的, 非常繁重的

back·chat /ˈbæk,tʃæt; ˈbæktʃæt/ *n* [U] *BrE* a reply to someone who is telling you what to do【英】顶嘴, 回嘴; BACKTALK *AmE*【美】: *None of your backchat, do your homework!* 不要顶嘴, 做你的作业吧!

back·cloth /ˈbæk,klɔθ; ˈbæk-klɒθ/ *n* [C] **1** a painted cloth hung across the back of a stage〔舞台后部的〕背景幕布 **2** the conditions or situation in which something happens〔事件的〕背景: *Against this backcloth of industrial turmoil, violence was always likely.* 在工人骚乱的情况下, 很可能发生暴力事件。

back·comb /ˈbæk,kom; ˈbæk-kəʊm/ *v* [T] *BrE* to comb your hair against the way it grows in order to style it and make it look thicker【英】倒梳(头发)〔使之蓬松〕; TEASE[1] (4) *AmE*【美】

back coun·try /ˈ· ,··/ *n* [U] **1** *especially AustrE* a country area where few people live【尤澳】偏远地区 —compare 比较 BUSH **2** *AmE* an area, especially in the mountains, away from roads and towns【美】偏远山区

back·date /ˈbæk,det; ˌbækˈdeɪt/ *v* [T] to make something have its effect from an earlier date 追溯到, 从〔过去某个日期〕开始生效: **backdate sth from/to** *The pay increase agreed in June will be backdated to January.* 6月份同意增加的工资将从1月份算起。—compare 比较 ANTEDATE, POSTDATE

back door /,·ˈ·/ *n* [C] **1** a door at the back or side of a building 后门, 旁门, 侧门 **2 get in through the back door** to achieve something by having an unfair secret advantage 走后门: *His father works for them so he got in through the back door.* 他父亲给那些人做事, 所以他走了后门。

back·door /ˈbæk,dɔr; ˈbækdɔː/ *adj* [only before noun 仅用于名词前] secret, or not publicly stated as your intention 秘密的, 不公开的: *In what amounts to a backdoor income tax increase, the Chancellor chose to freeze personal tax allowance.* 财政大臣决定冻结个人免税额, 这就等于暗地里提高了个人所得税。

back·drop /ˈbæk,drɑp; ˈbækdrɒp/ *n* [C] **1** *literary* the scenery behind something that you are looking at【文】背景: *the stunning backdrop of the Alps* 极其优美的阿尔卑斯山远景 **2** the conditions or situation in which something happens〔事件的〕背景: *The depression was the backdrop for Steinbeck's greatest works.* 斯坦贝克最著名的作品都是以大萧条时期作为历史背景的。**3** a painted cloth hung across the back of a stage〔舞台后部的〕背景幕布

back·er /ˈbækɚ; ˈbækə/ *n* [C] someone who supports a plan, especially by providing money 支持者, 赞助者, 资助者: *We're still trying to find backers for the housing development scheme.* 我们还在努力为住房开发计划寻找赞助商。

back·fire /ˈbæk,faɪr; ˌbækˈfaɪə/ *v* [I] **1** if a plan or action backfires, it has the opposite effect to the one you intended 发生意外; 产生事与愿违的结果 **2** if a car backfires, it makes a sudden loud noise because the engine is not working correctly〔汽车引擎〕逆火, 回火

back for·ma·tion /ˈ· ·,··/ *n* [C] *technical* a new word formed from an older word, for example 'televise' formed from 'television'【术语】逆构词, 逆成词

back·gam·mon /ˈbæk,gæmən; ˈbækgæmən/ *n* [U] a game for two players, using flat round pieces and DICE[1] (1) on a special board 西洋十五子棋, 西洋双陆棋〔一种供两人玩、以掷骰子决定棋子行进的游戏〕

back·ground /ˈbæk,graʊnd; ˈbækgraʊnd/ *n* **1** [C] someone's family history, education, social class etc 出身, 个人背景: *He's always going on about his working class background.* 他老是埋怨自己出身于工人阶级家庭。| *a background in computer engineering* (有)电脑工程背景 **2** [C,U] the events in the past that explain why something has happened in the way that it has〔事情发生时的〕背景情况: *Without knowing the background to the case, I couldn't possibly comment.* 因为不了解案件的背景情况, 我不可能加以评论。| **background information/details/data etc** *With a bit more background information the report will be fine.* 再加点儿背景资料, 这个报告会很不错。**3** [C] the pattern or colour on top of which something has been drawn, printed etc 背景, 后景; 底色: *red lettering on a white background*

白底红色字母图案 **4 in the background a)** behind the main thing that you are looking at 在不显眼的位置; 在背景中: *In the background of this photo you can see a few of my old college friends.* 在这幅照片的背景中, 你可以看到我的几个大学时的老朋友。**b)** someone who keeps or stays in the background tries not to be noticed 在不被人注意[不显眼]的位置: *A couple of waiters hovered in the background.* 几个服务员在不被人注意的地方来回走动。**c)** a sound that is in the background is present but is not the main thing that you are listening to 隐约的[地]: *In the background I could hear the sound of traffic.* 我隐约能够听到来往的车辆声。**5** [C,U] the sounds that you can hear apart from the main thing that you are listening to 背景声; 杂音: **background noise/music/a lot of background noise** *an irritating background noise of tinny music* 声音不大、令人烦躁的音乐杂声

back·hand /ˈbækˋhænd; ˈbækhænd/ *n* [C usually singular 一般用单数] a hit in tennis and some other games in which the back of your hand is turned in the direction of the hit〔网球等的〕反手击球(技术) —**backhand** *adj* —see picture on page A23 参见 A23 页图

back·hand·ed /ˈbækˋhændɪd; ˌbækˈhændɪ̣d◂/ *adj* **1** a backhanded remark or COMPLIMENT[1] (1) seems to express praise or admiration but in fact means the opposite 间接的, 转弯抹角的, 讽刺挖苦的: *'Brave' can be a backhanded way of saying 'crazy'.* "勇敢"可以是转弯抹角地在说"发疯"。**2** a backhanded shot etc is made with a backhand 反手击球的, 用反手的

back·hand·er /ˈbækˋhændə; ˈbækhændə/ *n* [C] **1** a hit or shot made with the back of your hand 反手一击 **2** *BrE informal* money that you pay illegally and secretly to get something done【英, 非正式】贿赂; 回扣: *Investigators estimate that £35m had been spent on bribes and backhanders.* 调查者估计用于贿赂和回扣的金额达 3500 万英镑。

back·hoe /ˈbækˌho; ˈbækhəʊ/ *n* [C] a large digging machine used for making roads etc〔筑路用的〕大型挖掘机

back·ing /ˈbækɪŋ; ˈbækɪŋ/ *n* **1** [U] support or help, especially with money 支持, 帮助, 资助 **2** [C] material that is used to make the back of an object 衬垫物, 背衬 **3** [C] the music that is played with a singer's voice to make it sound better〔音乐〕伴奏 —**backing** *adj*

back·lash /ˈbækˌlæʃ; ˈbæklæʃ/ *n* [C] a strong but usually delayed reaction against recent events, especially against political or social developments〔对重大事件的〕强烈反应, 反冲: **backlash against** *The 1970s saw the first backlash against the emerging women's movement.* 20 世纪 70 年代, 正在兴起的妇女运动首次遭到强烈抵制。| *The rise in violent crime provoked a backlash against the liberal gun-control laws.* 暴力犯罪的增加引起了对松散的枪支管制法的强烈不满。

back·log /ˈbækˌlɔg; ˈbæklɒg/ *n* [usually singular 一般用单数] a large amount of work, especially that should already have been completed 积压未办之事, 积压的工作: *a backlog of letters* 很多未处理的信

back·pack[1] /ˈbækˌpæk; ˈbækpæk/ *n* [C] *especially AmE* a bag carried on your back, often supported by a light metal frame, used especially by climbers and walkers【尤美】〔尤指登山者或步行者所用的〕背包, 行囊; RUCKSACK *BrE*【英】

backpack[2] *v* [I] *especially AmE* to go walking and camping carrying a BACKPACK[1]【尤美】背着背包徒步旅行; 野外露营: *backpacking along the Appalachian trail* 沿着阿巴拉契亚山路背包徒步旅行 —**backpacker** *n* [C]

back pas·sage /ˌ· ˈ··/ *n* [C] a word meaning ANUS (=the hole where food waste comes out of your body) used to avoid offending people 肛门〔婉词〕

back·ped·al /ˈbækˌpɛdḷ; ˌbækˈpedl/ *v* **backpedalled, backpedalling** *BrE*【英】, **backpedaled, backpedaling** *AmE*【美】[I] **1** to start to change your opinion about something that you had promised 变卦, 改变主意, 出尔反尔: *They are backpedalling on the commitment to cut taxes.* 他们曾经承诺减税, 但现在变卦了。**2** to PEDAL[2] (2) backwards on a bicycle〔骑自行车时〕倒踩脚踏板

back·room boy /ˈbækrum ˌbɔɪ; ˈbækrʊm ˌbɔɪ/ *n* [usually plural 一般用复数] *informal especially BrE* someone such as an engineer or scientist, whose work is important but who does not get much attention or fame【非正式, 尤英】幕后筹划者; 从事秘密研究工作的人员

back seat /ˌ· ˈ·◂/ *n* **1** [C] a seat at the back of a car, behind where the driver sits 汽车后座 **2 back seat driver a)** a passenger in the back of a car who gives unwanted advice to the driver about how to drive 对司机指手画脚、乱指挥其驾驶的后座乘客 **b)** *especially AmE* someone in business or politics who tries to control things that they are not really responsible for【尤美】干涉与自己职责无关事情的人, 多管闲事的人

back·side /ˈbækˋsaɪd; ˈbæksaɪd/ *n informal* the part of your body that you sit on【非正式】屁股, 臀部

back·slap·ping /ˈbækˌslæpɪŋ; ˈbækslæpɪŋ/ *n* [U] noisy cheerful behaviour when people praise each other's achievements more than they deserve〔过分〕喧闹的欢庆〔指相互庆贺成功〕—**backslapper** *n* [C]

back·slash /ˈbækˌslæʃ; ˈbækslæʃ/ *n* [C] a line (\) used in writing to separate words, numbers, or letters 反向斜线符号

back·slide /ˈbækˌslaɪd; ˌbækˈslaɪd/ *v* [I] to start doing the bad things that you used to do, especially after having improved your behaviour 倒退, 退步, 故态复萌: *I haven't had a cigarette for two months, but recently I'm afraid I've begun to backslide.* 我已经两个月没有抽烟了, 但最近又开始抽起来。—**backslider** *n* [C]

back·space /ˈbækˌspes; ˈbækspeɪs/ *n* [usually singular 一般用单数] the part of a TYPEWRITER that you press to move backwards towards the beginning of the line〔打字机的〕退格键

back·spin /ˈbækˌspɪn; ˈbækspɪn/ *n* [U] a turning movement in a ball that has been hit so that the top of the ball turns backwards as the ball travels forwards 倒[回]旋球

back·stage /ˈbækˋstedʒ; ˌbækˈsteɪdʒ◂/ *adv* **1** behind the stage in a theatre, especially in the actors' dressing rooms 在后台〔尤指演员化妆室〕**2** in private, especially within the secret parts of an organization 秘密地, 背地里, 在幕后: *That's the official line, but who knows what really goes on backstage?* 这是官方的路线方针, 但谁知道幕后情况怎么样? —**backstage** *adj*

back·stairs /ˈbækˌstɛrz; ˈbæksteəz/ *adj* [only before noun 仅用于名词前] secret and probably unfair 秘密的, 暗地里的; 中伤的, 不正当的: *backstairs influence* 暗中的影响力

back·street /ˈ· ·/ *adj* backstreet activities are often illegal and done badly 私下的, 偷偷摸摸的: *a backstreet abortion* 非法堕胎

back·stroke /ˈbækˌstrok; ˈbækstrəʊk/ *n* [singular] a way of swimming on your back by moving first one arm then the other backwards while kicking your feet 仰泳, 背泳

back·talk /ˈbækˌtɔk; ˈbæktɔːk/ *n* [U] *AmE* a rude reply to someone who is telling you what to do【美】顶嘴, 回嘴; BACKCHAT *BrE*【英】

back-to-back /ˌ· · ˈ·◂/ *n* [C] *BrE* a house in a row or TERRACE (1) built with its back touching the back of the next row of houses【英】背靠背的房子

back·track /ˈbækˌtræk; ˈbæktræk/ *v* [I] **1** to change your beliefs, statements etc so that they are not as strong as they were earlier 退缩, 取消诺言, 出尔反尔: *Clinton seemed to be backtracking on his policy on Bosnia.* 克林顿在波斯尼亚的政策上似乎有所退缩。**2** to return by the same way that you came 原路返回

back·up /ˈbækˌʌp; ˈbækʌp/ *n* [C,U] **1** something or someone used to provide support and help when it is needed 备用品; 后备人员, 支援人员: *Army units can only operate if they have sufficient backup.* 有足够的后备力量时部队才能作战。**2 backup plan/system/generator** a plan or system that can be used if the main one does not work 备用计划/系统/发电机

back·ward /ˈbækwəd; ˈbækwəd/ *adj* **1** [only before noun 仅用于名词前] made in a direction towards what is behind you 向后的, 后退的: *She went without a backward glance.* 她头也不回地走了。**2** developing slowly and less successfully than most others 落后的; 迟钝的: *some of the more backward countries* 一些更落后的国家 | *a backward child* 迟钝的孩子 —compare 比较 FORWARD[2] —**backwardly** *adv* —**backwardness** *n* [U]

back·wards /ˈbækwədz; ˈbækwədz/ also 又作 **backward** *AmE*【美】*adv* **1** towards the back, the beginning, or the past 向后地, 倒退地; 回顾地: *She pushed me and I fell backwards into the chair.* 她推了我一下, 我倒退回椅子里。| *Can you say the alphabet backwards?* 你能倒背字母表吗? **2** moving or facing the opposite direction to the usual one 背向前地; 倒转地, 逆向地: *He walked backwards away from the King.* 他从国王身边退出。| *You've got your hat on backwards!* 你把帽子前后戴反了! **3** towards a worse state 每况愈下地, 退步地: *The new measures are seen by some as a major step backwards.* 有些人认为新措施是一大倒退。**4 backwards and forwards** first in one direction and then in the opposite direction, usually many times 来回地, 忽前忽后地 **5 bend over/lean over backwards (to do sth)** to try as hard as possible to help or please someone 拼命, 竭尽全力〔帮助或取悦某人〕: *We bent over backwards to help them.* 我们尽了最大努力帮助他们。**6 know sth backwards** *BrE*【英】, **know sth backwards and forwards** *AmE*【美】to know something very well or perfectly 对某事了如指掌, 熟知某事: *All the*

actors know the play backwards and forwards. 所有演员对这个剧本都可以倒背如流。—compare 比较 FORWARD[1]

back·wa·ter /ˈbækˌwɔtə; ˈbækwɔːtə/ *n* **1** a very quiet place not influenced by outside events or new ideas 与世隔绝的地方; 闭塞的地方: *a rural backwater* 一个与世隔绝的村庄 **2** a part of a river away from the main stream, where the water does not move〔河流的〕回水, 死水, 滞水

back·woods /ˈbækˋwudz; ˈbækwudz/ *n* [plural] a distant and undeveloped area away from any towns 边远落后地区

back·woods·man /ˈbækˋwudzmən; ˈbækwudzmən/ *n* [C] **1** someone who lives in the backwoods 边远地区的居民 **2** *BrE* a member of a political party or parliament, especially the House of Lords, who is not very active politically and only sometimes votes, attends meetings etc【英】政治上不很积极的政党成员〔尤指上议院议员只是有时参加会议或投票活动〕

back·yard /ˈbækˋjɑrd; ˌbækˈjɑːd◂/ *n* **1** *BrE* a square flat area behind a house, covered with a hard surface【英】〔铺了硬地面的〕后院 **2** *AmE* an area of land behind a house, usually covered with grass【美】〔常指有草皮的〕后院, 后花园: *The old man grew vegetables in his backyard.* 老人在屋后园子里种了蔬菜。

S3 **ba·con** /ˈbekən; ˈbeɪkən/ *n* [U] **1** salted or smoked meat from the back or sides of a pig, often served in narrow thin pieces〔通常切成薄片的〕咸猪肉, 熏猪肉: **bacon and eggs** (=bacon and eggs cooked in hot fat and served together) 熏猪肉煎蛋 —see also 另见 MEAT **2 bring home the bacon** *informal* to provide enough money to support your family【非正式】挣钱养家 —see also 另见 **save sb's bacon** (SAVE[1])

Bacon, Francis (1909-92) an Irish artist who is famous for painting people and animals in twisted shapes with dark, strong colours 培根〔(1909-1992) 爱尔兰画家。他采用强烈的深色和扭曲的图形描绘人物和动物, 并以此闻名〕

Bacon, Sir Francis (1561-1626) an English politician, PHILOSOPHER, and writer 培根〔(1561-1626), 英国政治家、哲学家、作家〕

bac·te·ri·a /bækˋtɪrɪə; bækˈtɪəriə/ *n* [plural] *singular* **bacterium** very small living things related to plants, some of which cause disease; MICROBES 细菌 — compare 比较 VIRUS (1,2) — **bacterial** *adj*: *a bacterial infection* 细菌感染

bac·te·ri·ol·o·gy /ˌbækˌtɪrɪˋɑlədʒɪ; bækˌtɪəriˈɒlədʒi/ *n* [U] the scientific study of bacteria 细菌学 —**bacteriologist** *n* [C] —**bacteriological** /ˌbækˌtɪrɪəˋlɑdʒɪkl; bækˌtɪəriəˈlɒdʒɪkəl/ *adj*

Bac·tri·an cam·el /ˌbæktrɪən ˋkæml; ˌbæktriən ˈkæməl/ *n* [C] a CAMEL from Asia with two HUMPS[1] (2)〔亚洲的〕双峰骆驼

S1 W1 **bad**[1] /bæd; bæd/ *adj comparative* 比较级 **worse** /wɝs; wɜːs/ *superlative* 最高级 **worst** /wɝst; wɜːst/

1 ▶**HARMFUL** 有害的◀ unpleasant, harmful, or likely to cause problems 不好的, 令人不快的, 糟糕的: *I have some bad news for you.* 我给你带来了坏消息。| *I thought things couldn't possibly get any worse.* 我想事情不可能变得更糟糕。| *It's bad enough being woken by the baby without you keeping me awake as well.* 就算你没有干扰我睡觉, 给那婴孩吵醒我已经够受了。—opposite 反义词 GOOD[1] (2)

2 ▶**LOW QUALITY** 低质量◀ low in quality or below an acceptable standard 差的, 不符合标准的: *The failure of the company was due to bad management.* 该公司因经营不善而破产。| *Your handwriting is so bad I can hardly read it.* 你写的字太差, 我几乎认不出来。| *bad teachers and a lack of funds* 老师水平低且缺乏资金 —opposite 反义词 GOOD[1] (1)

3 ▶**WRONG** 错的◀ morally wrong or evil〔道德品质〕坏的: *He's a bad man – keep away from him.* 他是个坏人, 离他远一点儿。—opposite 反义词 GOOD[1] (16)

4 ▶**SERIOUS** 严重的◀ serious or severe 严重的, 厉害的: *He is recovering from a bad accident.* 经历了一场严重的事故后他正逐渐康复。| *The pain was really bad.* 痛得真厉害。

5 bad time/moment etc a time at which it is very unlucky for something to have happened 不适当的时候: *It's a bad time to have to borrow money, with interest rates so high.* 现在借款真不是时候, 利率这么高。

6 bad for you harmful to you or to your health 对健康有害: *Too much salt can be bad for you.* 食用过多的盐对你身体不好。| *It is bad for a young girl to be on her own so much.* 一个小姑娘要完全靠自己, 身体会吃不消。

7 ▶**FOOD** 食物◀ food that is bad is not safe to eat because it has decayed 已变质的, 腐烂的: *This fish has gone bad.* 这鱼变质了。| *bad apples* 烂苹果

8 bad at maths/tennis/drawing etc having no skill or ability in a particular activity 不擅长数学/网球/绘画等: *I'm really bad at chess.* 我棋下得不好。| *Strategic thinking is what so many companies are bad at.* 许多公司都不善于进行战略思考。

9 bad heart/leg/back etc a heart, leg etc that is injured or does not work correctly 心脏/腿/背等有病[不舒服]: *I haven't been able to do much because of my bad back.* 我因为背伤不能够做太多工作。| *Ouch, that was my bad foot!* 哎唷! 我受了伤的脚!

10 ▶**SWEARING** 诅咒◀ bad language contains swearing or rude words 诅咒的, 污秽的: *all these TV programmes with their violence and bad language* 所有这些充满暴力和污言秽语的电视节目

11 in a bad temper/mood feeling annoyed or angry 脾气/心情不好: *I didn't mean to take my bad temper out on you.* 我不是故意对你发脾气的。

12 ▶**GUILTY** 内疚◀ **feel bad** to feel ashamed or sorry about something 感到遗憾[内疚]: *I felt bad about not being able to come last night.* 我昨天晚上没能来, 非常抱歉。

13 go from bad to worse to become even more unpleasant or difficult 越来越坏, 每况愈下: *The evening went from bad to worse as more and more people left the party.* 随着越来越多的人离开, 晚会变得越来越没意思。

14 be in a bad way *informal especially BrE* to be very ill, unhappy, injured, or in serious trouble【非正式, 尤英】病情严重; 不高兴; 受伤; 处于困境: *She was in a bad way after the funeral.* 葬礼之后, 她非常难受。

15 get a bad name to lose people's respect or trust 名声不好: [**+for**] *The bar had a bad name and was avoided by all the locals.* 这个酒吧名声不好, 当地人都不愿意去。

16 bad egg/lot/sort/type *BrE old-fashioned* someone who is morally bad or cannot be trusted【英, 过时】坏人, 坏蛋, 坏家伙

17 bad penny someone or something that causes trouble and is difficult to avoid 令人讨厌却又难以避开的人[事]: **turn up like a bad penny** (=suddenly appear) 突然出现 *Sure enough, Steve turned up at the party, like a bad penny.* 史蒂夫果然在晚会上出现, 真讨厌。

18 be taken bad *informal especially BrE* to become ill【非正式, 尤英】生病: *He was taken bad in the middle of the night.* 他在半夜里发病了。

19 in bad faith if someone does something in bad faith they are behaving dishonestly and have no intention of keeping a promise 存心不良, 背信弃义: *In order to sue, you have to prove that the company was acting in bad faith.* 要打官司, 你必须证明该公司有欺诈行为。

20 bad news *informal* someone or something that always causes trouble【非正式】讨厌的人[事物]: *Look, just avoid him, I warn you. He's bad news!* 喂, 离他远点儿, 我警告你, 他不是个好东西!

21 bad form *BrE old-fashioned* socially unacceptable behaviour【英, 过时】不礼貌的行为: *It's bad form to argue with the umpire.* 跟裁判员争辩是一种不礼貌的行为。

22 bad blood angry or bitter feeling between people; HOSTILITY 恶感, 敌意, 仇恨: *There's too much bad blood between them.* 他们之间的敌意太深。

Frequencies of the adjective **bad** in spoken and written English 形容词bad在英语口语和书面语中的使用频率

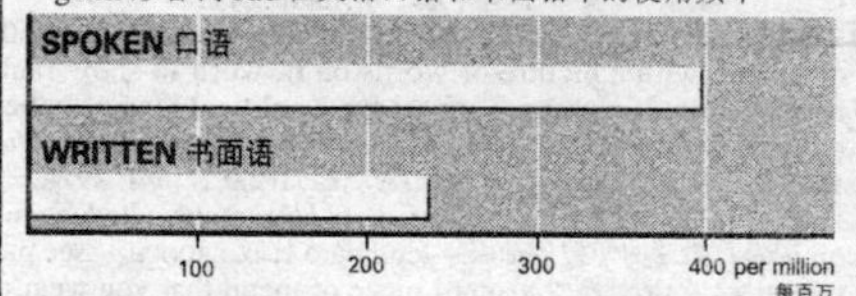

Based on the British National Corpus and the Longman Lancaster Corpus
据英国国家语料库和朗文兰开斯特语料库

This graph shows that the adjective **bad** is much more common in spoken English than in written English. This is because it is used in some common spoken phrases. 本图表显示, 形容词bad在英语口语中的使用频率远远高于书面语, 因为口语中一些常用短语是由 bad 构成的。

bad (*adj*) **SPOKEN PHRASES**
含 bad 的口语短语

23 not bad *especially BrE* used to say that something is good, or better than you expected【尤英】挺不错: *"How are you?" "Oh, not bad."* "你身体怎么样?" "还行。" | *That's not a bad idea.* 那个主意不错。| *"Did you enjoy the course?" "Oh it wasn't too bad."* "你喜欢这门课吗?" "噢, 还可以。"

24 too bad a) used to say that you do not care that something bad happens to someone 咎由自取, 自找的: *"I'm go-*

ing to be late now!" "Too bad, you should have gotten up earlier."“我要迟到了！”“活该，谁叫你那么晚才起床。”**b)** used to say that you are sorry that something bad has happened to someone 太可惜，真遗憾：*It's too bad that you couldn't come to the party last night.* 你昨晚没能来参加聚会，真遗憾。**c)** *BrE old-fashioned* used to say that something is very annoying or unreasonable【英，过时】没道理，很烦人，太不像话：*They can't increase the price like that, it's just too bad!* 他们不能这样乱涨价，太不像话了！
25 bad girl/boy used when a child behaves badly 淘气的女孩／男孩：*Bad girl! Put that glass down!* 淘气丫头！把玻璃杯放下！
26 it's not that bad/it's not as bad as all that used to say that something is not as bad as someone says it is 并不像别人说的那样糟糕：*"Yuk! This cheese is revolting!" "Oh, come on, it's not as bad as all that."*“呸！这干酪都臭了！”“哟，得了，没那么严重！”
27 not too bad/not so bad used to say that something is not as bad as expected 并不像预期的那样糟糕：*The exams weren't so bad after all.* 考试并不像想的那样差。
28 it's bad enough... used to say that you already have one problem, so that you cannot worry about or deal with another one …已经够受的了：*It's bad enough having to bring up three kids on your own without having to worry about money as well!* 就算不需要担心钱的问题，独力抚养三个孩子也已经够受的了！
29 sth can't be bad used to persuade someone that something is good or worth doing 那不错：*You only pay £10 deposit and no interest: that can't be bad, can it?* 你只付10英镑保证金，又不用付利息，那可真不错，对吧？—see also 另见 **make the best of a bad job** (JOB (18)) —**badness** *n* [U]

bad² *n* **1 take the bad with the good** accept not only the good things in life but also the bad things 好坏都忍受；既能享乐，又能吃苦 **2 to the bad** *informal* if you are a particular amount to the bad you are that much poorer or you owe that much【非正式】负债：*Thanks to your mistake, I'm £500 to the bad!* 由于你的过错，我欠下了500英镑的债！**3 go to the bad** *old-fashioned* to begin living in a wrong or immoral way【过时】开始学坏，堕落

bad debt /ˌ· ˈ·/ *n* [C] a debt that is unlikely to be paid 呆账，坏账

bad·die, baddy /ˋbædɪ; ˈbædi/ *n* [C] *BrE informal* someone who is bad, especially in a book or film【英，非正式】〔尤指小说、电影等中的〕坏蛋

bade /bæd; bæd/ the past tense and past participle of BID³

Ba·den-Po·well /ˌbedn̩ ˋpoəl; ˌbeɪdn ˈpəʊəl/, **Lord Rob·ert** /ˋrɑbət; ˈrɒbət/ (1857-1941) a British army officer who is known for starting the SCOUT organizations such as the Scouts and the Guides 巴登-鲍威尔〔(1857-1941)，英国军官，以创建男童子军、女童子军等童子军组织而闻名〕

badge /bædʒ; bædʒ/ *n* [C] **1** *BrE* a small piece of metal, cloth, or plastic with a picture or words on it, worn to show rank, membership of a group, support for a political idea or belief, etc【英】徽章，证章；标记，象征：*They were wearing badges that said 'Nuclear Power – No thanks!'.* 他们佩戴着印有“核能——谢谢，不要了！”字样的徽章。| *a school blazer with a badge sewn on it* 缝着徽章的学校运动服 —compare 比较 BROOCH —see picture at 参见 SIGN¹ 图 **2** a small piece of metal that you wear or carry that shows you have an official position, for example that you are a police officer〔佩戴在身上以显示官职的〕徽章〈如警徽〉**3** a small piece of cloth with a picture on it, given to SCOUTS¹ (1), GUIDES¹ (4) etc to show what skills they have learned〔给童子军等的〕布制徽章：*I got my music badge today.* 今天我得到了音乐徽章。**4 badge of office** an object which shows that you have an official position 职位标识物：*Mayors wear chains around their necks as badges of office.* 市长们脖子上戴着象征职位的链子。

bad·ger¹ /ˋbædʒə; ˈbædʒə/ *n* [C] an animal which has black and white fur, lives in holes in the ground, and is active at night 獾，穴熊

badger² *v* [T] to try to persuade someone by asking them something several times; PESTER 纠缠着要，烦扰：*The children badgered me into taking them to the cinema.* 孩子们缠着我带他们去看电影。| **badger someone to do something** *They kept badgering him to get a home computer.* 他们一直缠着他要买一台家用电脑。

bad guy /ˈ· ·/ *n* [C] *AmE informal* someone who is bad, especially in a book or film【美，非正式】〔尤指小说或电影中的〕坏蛋：*Screen hero Kevin Costner is playing the bad guy for once.* 银幕英雄凯文·科斯特纳这次扮演一个坏蛋。

bad·i·nage /ˌbædn̩ˋɑʒ; ˈbædɪnɑːʒ/ *n* [U] *formal or humorous* playful joking talk【正式或幽默】开玩笑，打趣

bad·lands /ˋbædˌlændz; ˈbædlændz/ *n* [plural] an area of unproductive land in North America with rocks and hills that have been worn into strange shapes by the weather〔尤指北美的〕荒原，怪石嶙峋的不毛之地

Badlands, the /ˋbædˌlændz; ˈbædlændz/ *n* [plural] an area of land in the US, between the southwest of South Dakota and the northwest of Nebraska, where no crops can grow and there are strangely shaped rocks and hills 巴德兰兹〔位于美国南达科他州西南部和内布拉斯加州西北部之间的一个地区。那里五谷不生，怪石嶙峋，丘陵起伏〕

bad·ly /ˋbædlɪ; ˈbædli/ *adv comparative* 比较级 **worse** *superlative* 最高级 **worst 1** in an unsatisfactory or unsuccessful way 坏，差，拙劣地：*The company has been very badly managed.* 这家公司管理不善。| *Pearce played pretty badly in yesterday's semi-final.* 皮尔斯在昨天的半决赛中表现很差。| *badly made furniture* 做工粗糙的家具 | **do badly** (=not be successful) 不成功 *Rob did very badly in the History exam.* 罗伯的历史考得很差。**2** to a great or serious degree 严重地，厉害地，大大地，非常：*He's been limping badly ever since the skiing accident.* 自那次滑雪事故后，他的腿一直跛得很厉害。| *She badly wanted to be chosen for the school hockey team.* 她非常渴望入选学校的曲棍球队。| **badly in need of** (=needing something very much) 急需，非常需要 *He's badly in need of a haircut.* 他急需理发。| **go badly wrong** (=if a situation goes badly wrong it becomes very difficult or serious) 变得十分困难[严重] *Things started to go badly wrong for Eric after he lost his job.* 埃里克失去工作后，生活开始变得很艰难。**3 think badly of** to have a bad opinion of someone or something 对…有看法[有意见]：*I'm sure they won't think badly of you if you tell them you need some time away from work.* 我肯定，如果你告诉他们你需要离开工作岗位一段时间，他们不会对你有什么意见。

badly-off /ˌ·· ˈ·/ *adj comparative* 比较级 **worse-off** *superlative* 最高级 **worst-off** [not before noun 不用于名词前] **1** not having much money; poor 缺钱的，贫穷的：*We're too badly-off to have a holiday.* 我们太穷，没有钱度假。**2 badly-off for** not having enough of something that is needed 不足的，缺乏的：*The school is rather badly-off for equipment.* 学校相当缺乏设备。—opposite 反义词 WELL-OFF

bad·min·ton /ˋbædmɪntən; ˈbædmɪntən/ *n* [U] a game like tennis but played with a SHUTTLECOCK (=small feathered object) instead of a ball 羽毛球（运动）—see picture on page A23 参见A23页图

Badminton Horse Tri·als, the /ˌ··· ˈ· ˌ··/ an important British horse-riding competition held every year at Badminton House in southwest England 巴德明顿马术赛〔英国重要马术比赛，每年在英格兰西南部的巴德明顿赛马场举行〕

bad-mouth /ˈ· ·/ *v* [T] *informal especially AmE* to criticize someone or something【非正式，尤美】说…的坏话，谩骂，批评：*Her former colleagues accused her of bad-mouthing them in public.* 她以前的同事指责她在公开场合说他们的坏话。

bad-off /ˌ· ˈ·◂/ *adj AmE* not having much money; poor【美】缺钱的，贫穷的

bad-tem·pered /ˌ· ˈ··◂/ *adj* easily annoyed or made angry 脾气不好的，急性子的：*He was known as a bad-tempered recluse.* 大家都知道他脾气很坏，不爱与人来往。

Bae·dek·er /ˋbedɪkə; ˈbeɪdɪkə/ *trademark* a type of book providing information for tourists visiting a particular country, originally produced in the 19th century by Karl Baedeker【商标】《贝德克尔旅游指南》〔一种向旅游者提供国别旅游信息的图书，最初由卡尔·贝德克尔于19世纪出版〕：*Can I borrow your Baedeker for France?* 借用一下你的《贝德克尔法国旅游指南》可以吗？| *Look it up in Baedeker.* 请查阅《贝德克尔旅游指南》。

baf·fle¹ /ˋbæfl; ˈbæfəl/ *v* [T] if something baffles someone, they cannot understand or explain it at all 使困惑，难倒：*The question baffled me completely.* 这个问题把我彻底难倒了。—**bafflement** *n* [U] —**baffling** *adj*: *a baffling mystery* 令人不解的谜

baffle² *n* [C] *technical* a board, sheet of metal etc that controls the flow of air, water, or sound into or out of something【术语】〔控制空气、水流或声音进出的〕隔板；折流板；隔音板

BAFTA /ˋbæftə; ˈbæftə/ *n* [C] a prize given each year by the British Academy of Films and Television Arts for the best films, television programmes, actors etc 英国电影电视艺术学院奖〔英

国电影电视艺术学院颁发的年度奖，奖项包括最佳影片奖、最佳电视节目奖、最佳演员奖等）: *Her film won two BAFTAs.* 她的电影获两项英国电影电视艺术学院奖。| *the BAFTA award ceremony* 英国电影电视艺术学院奖颁奖典礼

bags 袋, 包, 囊

duffel bag
〔圆筒状〕旅行袋

satchel
〔皮制的〕小背包, 书包

handbag *BrE*【英】/
purse *AmE*【美】
〔女用〕手提包, 手袋

holdall *BrE*【英】/
carryall *AmE*【美】
大旅行袋

carrier bag *BrE*【英】/
tote bag *AmE*【美】
手提购物袋

backpack
〔登山、远足用的〕背包

toilet bag *BrE*【英】/
shaving bag *AmE*【美】
梳洗用具袋

bag[1] /bæg; bæg/ *n* [C]
1 ▶CONTAINER 容器◀ **a)** a container made of paper, cloth etc, which usually opens at the top 袋, 包, 囊: *a paper bag* 纸袋 | *a sports bag* 运动背包 **b)** a small bag used by a woman to carry her personal possessions; HANDBAG 〔女士的〕手提袋, 手提包: *Don't leave your bag in the office when you go for lunch.* 去吃午饭时, 不要把手袋放在办公室里。**c)** a large bag used to carry your clothes etc when you are travelling 旅行袋: *Just throw your bags in the back of the car.* 把你的行李袋放在车后好了。—see picture at 参见 CONTAINER 图
2 ▶AMOUNT 数量◀ the amount that a bag will hold 一袋的量, 一(满)袋: **[+of]** *two bags of rice per family per month* 每户每月两袋大米
3 ▶WOMAN 妇女◀ *spoken* an insulting word for an unpleasant or unattractive woman【口】丑婆娘; 邋遢女人: *You silly old bag!* 你这愚蠢的丑老太婆!
4 ▶HUNTING 打猎◀ [usually singular 一般用单数] the number of birds or animals that someone catches when they go hunting 〔一次打猎所获的〕捕猎物: *We had a good bag that day.* 那天我们猎获甚丰。
5 ▶A LOT OF 许多◀ **bags of** *spoken especially BrE* a lot of something; plenty【口, 尤英】很多: *She's got bags of money.* 她有的是钱。| *We're not late, we've got bags of time.* 我们没迟到, 还有很多时间。
6 pack your bags *informal* to leave a place where you have been living, usually after an argument【非正式】〔通常在争吵之后〕收拾行李; 走人: *We told her to pack her bags at once.* 我们告诉她立刻收拾行李走人。
7 ▶EYES 眼睛◀ dark circles or loose skin around your eyes, usually because of old age or being tired 眼袋
8 bag of bones *informal* a very thin person or animal【非正式】骨瘦如柴的人[动物]
9 in the bag *informal* certain to be won or achieved【非正式】囊中之物; 十拿九稳, 稳操胜券: *We're sure to win, the match is in the bag.* 我们肯定能赢, 这场比赛已稳操胜券。
10 ▶TROUSERS 裤子◀ **bags** [plural] *BrE old-fashioned* loose-fitting trousers【英, 过时】肥裤子, 宽松的裤子: *Oxford bags* 牛津式的肥裤子
11 ▶INTERESTED 感兴趣的◀ **sb's bag** *informal* something that someone is very interested in or very good at【非正式】某人的爱好; 某人的强项, 某人最擅长之事: *Sorry, computers aren't really my bag.* 对不起, 电脑并不是我的强项。
12 bag and baggage with all your possessions 连同所有财物, 带着全部家当: *They threw her out of the house bag and baggage.* 他们把她连人带东西全都撵出了房子。—see also 另见 BAGS, SLEEPING BAG, **let the cat out of the bag** (CAT (2)), **be left holding the bag** (HOLD[1] (20)), **a mixed bag** (MIXED (6))

bag[2] *v* **bagged, bagging 1** [T] to put materials or objects into bags 把〔东西〕装进袋[包]里 **2** [T] *informal* to kill or catch animals or birds【非正式】猎捕〔兽或鸟〕: *We bagged a rabbit.* 我们抓到了一只兔子。**3** [T] *informal* to manage to get something that a lot of people want【非正式】占有, 抢占, 据为己有[用]: *Try to bag a couple of seats at the front.* 想办法在前边占几个座位。**4** [I] also 又作 **bag out** *informal* to hang loosely, like a bag【非正式】〔像袋子一样〕松散下垂, 鼓胀

bag sth ↔ **up** *phr v* [T] to put small objects or loose substances into bags 把…装入袋中: *We bagged up the money before we closed the shop.* 我们在关上店门之前把钱装进袋子里。

bag·a·telle /ˌbægəˋtɛl; ˌbægəˈtel/ *n* **1** [U] a game played on a board with small balls that must be rolled into holes 九穴桌球游戏 **2** [singular] something that is small and unimportant compared to everything else 小事, 琐事: *It cost about £25, a mere bagatelle for someone as rich as her.* 它价格在25英镑左右, 对她这样有钱的人来说只是区区小数。

bagel 面包圈

ba·gel /ˈbegl; ˈbeɪgəl/ *n* [C] a small ring-shaped type of bread 面包圈

bag·ful /ˈbægful; ˈbægfʊl/ *n plural* **bagfuls** *or* **bagsful** [C] the amount a bag can hold 一袋的量

bag·gage /ˈbægɪdʒ; ˈbægɪdʒ/ *n* **1** [U] *especially AmE* the cases, bags, boxes, etc carried by someone who is travelling; LUGGAGE【尤美】行李: *Check your baggage in at the desk.* 在服务台托运行李。**2** [U] *informal* the beliefs, opinions, and experiences that someone has, which make them think in a particular way【非正式】思想包袱: *Throw away all that emotional baggage and start living!* 扔掉那些感情包袱, 振作起来! **3** [C] *old-fashioned* a rude, unpleasant, annoying woman【过时】惹人讨厌的女人; 蛮妇

baggage car /ˈ‥ ˌ/ *n* [C] *AmE* the part of a train where boxes, bags etc are carried【美】〔火车的〕行李车厢

baggage room /ˈ‥ ˌ/ *n* [C] *AmE* a place, usually in a station, where you can leave your bags and collect them later【美】行李寄存处

Bag·gie /ˈbægɪ; ˈbægi/ *trademark* a type of small clear plastic bag used in the US, especially for carrying food such as SANDWICHES【商标】"袋袋"食品袋〔美国使用的一种透明小塑料袋, 专门用于盛装三明治等食品〕

Bag·gins /ˈbægɪnz; ˈbægɪnz/, **Bil·bo** /ˈbɪlbo; ˈbɪlbəʊ/ an imaginary creature called a Hobbit who is the main character in the book *The Hobbit* by J.R.R. Tolkien 巴金斯〔一个被称作霍比特人的虚构生物, J.R.R.托尔金小说《霍比特人》的主人公〕

bag·gy /ˈbægɪ; ˈbægi/ *adj* baggy clothes hang in loose folds 〔衣服等〕宽松下垂的, 肥大的: *She was wearing jeans and a baggy T-shirt.* 她穿着牛仔裤和又宽又大的T恤。

Bagh·dad /ˈbægdæd; ˌbægˈdæd/ the capital city of Iraq 巴格达〔伊拉克首都〕

bag la·dy /ˈ· ˌ··/ *n* [C] a homeless woman who walks around carrying all her possessions with her 露宿街头、无家可归的女人, 女流浪者

bag·pipes /ˈbægˌpaɪps; ˈbægpaɪps/ *n* [plural] a musical instrument played especially in Scotland in which air stored in a bag is forced out through pipes to produce the sound 〔苏格兰的〕风笛 —**bagpipe** *adj*

bags /bægz; bægz/ *spoken BrE*【口, 英】**Bags I!** used by children to claim something that they want 给我!〔孩子要东西时说的话〕: *Bags I the biggest cake!* 给我最大的蛋糕!

ba·guette /bæˋgɛt; bæˈget/ *n* [C] a long thin LOAF of bread, made especially in France 〔尤指法式〕长棍面包

bah /bɑ; bɑː/ *interjection* used to show disapproval of something 呸!〔表示不赞同或轻蔑〕: *Bah! That's stupid.* 呸! 真蠢!

Ba·ha'i Faith, the /bə,haɪ `feθ; bə,haɪ 'feɪθ/ a religion based on the belief that people should be peaceful and kind, and should accept the fact that other people belong to different races or religions 巴哈伊教〔这一宗教的信仰是，人人应该和睦向善，接受存在不同种族和不同宗教这个事实〕

Ba·ha·mas, the /bə'hɑməz; bə'hɑːməz/ a country consisting of a group of islands in the Atlantic Ocean, southeast of Florida. Population: 298,000 (2001). Capital: Nassau. 巴哈马〔大西洋岛国，位于佛罗里达东南。人口: 298,000 (2001)，首都: 拿骚〕

B

Bah·rain, Bahrein /bɑ`ren; bɑː'reɪn/ a country consisting of a group of islands in the Gulf, near the coast of Saudi Arabia, and known for producing oil. Population: 645,000 (2001). Capital: Manama. 巴林〔海湾地区一国家，由一群岛屿构成，临近沙特阿拉伯海岸，以出产石油闻名。人口: 645,000 (2001)，首都: 麦纳麦〕

Baikal /baɪ`kɑl; baɪ'kɑːl/ also 又作 **Baykal** a lake in Siberia, Russia, which is the oldest and deepest freshwater lake in the world 贝加尔湖〔俄罗斯西伯利亚一湖泊，世界上最古老、最深的淡水湖〕

bail¹ /bel; beɪl/ *n* [U] **1** money left with a court of law to prove that a prisoner will return when their TRIAL¹ (1) starts 保释金: **release sb on bail/grant sb bail** (=let someone out of prison when bail is paid) 交保释金后释放某人/允许保释某人 *She was released on bail of £5,000.* 她在交纳 5000 英镑保释金后获释。| **be on bail** (=be waiting for your trial after bail has been paid) 在保释期间 *While on bail, Marshall committed another assault.* 马歇尔在保释期间又犯了袭击罪。| **stand bail/put up bail** (=pay the bail for someone to be let out) 为某人提供保释金，保释某人 *His father stood bail for him.* 他父亲做他的保释人。**2** one of the two small pieces of wood laid on top of the STUMPS¹ (4) in a game of CRICKET (2) 〔板球〕三柱门上的横木

bail² *v*

bail out *phr v* **1** [T **bail** sb ↔ **out**] to leave a large sum of money with a court so that someone can be let out of prison while waiting for their TRIAL¹ (1) 〔交保释金〕把〔某人〕保释出来: *Clarke's family paid £500 to bail him out.* 克拉克的家人交了 500 英镑保释他出来。**2** [I, T **bail** sth ↔ **out**] also 又作 **bale out** *BrE*【英】to remove water from the bottom of a boat 从〔船底〕舀出水 **3** [T **bail** sb/sth ↔ **out**] to provide money to get someone or something out of financial trouble 〔提供经费〕帮助…摆脱困境: *You can't expect the taxpayer to bail out the car industry indefinitely.* 你不能指望纳税人无限期地帮助汽车工业摆脱困境。**4** [I] *AmE*【美】**a)** to escape from a plane, using a PARACHUTE¹ 跳伞逃脱 **b)** *informal* to leave a place or situation as quickly as you can【非正式】快速逃离，逃脱; **bale out** (BALE²) *BrE*【英】

bai·ley /`beli; 'beɪli/ *n* [C] an open area inside the outer wall of a castle 城堡内之庭院，城堡外庭

Bailey, David (1938-) a British photographer, famous for his photos of fashionable people in the 1960s 贝利〔(1938-)，英国摄影家，20 世纪 60 年代以拍摄时尚人物照著称〕

Bai·ley's /`belɪz; 'beɪliz/ also 又作 **Bailey's Irish Cream** *trademark* a type of sweet alcoholic drink made of Irish WHISKEY mixed with cream【商标】百利甜酒〔爱尔兰威士忌与奶油混合而成的一种甜酒〕

bai·liff /`belɪf; 'beɪlɪf/ *n* [C] **1** *BrE* an official of the legal system who can take people's goods or property when they owe money【英】〔查封财产或货物的〕查封官，执行官: *Last year, all his furniture was seized by bailiffs.* 去年，他所有的家具都被查封官查封了。**2** *AmE* an official of the legal system who watches prisoners and keeps order in a court of law【美】法警，庭吏 **3** *BrE* someone who looks after a farm or land that belongs to someone else【英】农场管理人; 农场主[地主]的管家

bail-out /`· ·/ *n* [C] *informal* financial help given to a person or a company that is in difficulty【非正式】〔紧急财政〕援助: *The directors were hoping for a government bail-out to save the company.* 董事们都希望政府能出资帮助，以解公司燃眉之急。

bain ma·rie /,bæn mə`ri; ,bæn mə'riː/ *n* [C] *French* a pan for cooking things gently usually by cooking them in another pan of water【法】双层蒸锅

Baird /bɛrd; beəd/, **John Lo·gie** /dʒɑn `logɪ; dʒɒn 'ləʊgi/ (1888-1946) a Scottish engineer who invented a television system 贝尔德〔(1888-1946) 苏格兰工程师，发明了电视系统〕

bairn /bɛrn; beən/ *n* [C] *ScotE, N EngE*【苏格兰，英格兰北部】**1** a baby 婴儿 **2** a child 孩子

bait¹ /bet; beɪt/ *n* [singular,U] **1** food used to attract fish, animals, or birds so that you can catch them 饵，诱饵: *Worms make excellent fish bait.* 蚯蚓是极佳的鱼饵。| **take the bait** (=eat it and be caught) 上钩 **2** something used to make someone do something, buy something etc 引诱物，诱饵: **take the bait** (=accept what someone is offering) 接受条件 *The customer takes the bait and that's it, you've got another sale.* 顾客接受了条件，这样一来你又做成了一笔生意。**3 rise to the bait** to become angry when someone is deliberately trying to make you angry 上当发火，中圈套: *Senator O'Brien just smiled, refusing to rise to the bait.* 奥布赖恩参议员只是笑了笑，没有中圈套。

bait² *v* [T] **1** to put bait on a hook to catch fish or in a trap to catch animals 在〔鱼钩或捕兽器〕上装饵 **2** to deliberately try to make someone angry by criticizing them, using rude names etc 故意激怒〔某人〕，使〔某人〕受苦: *The other children took a vicious pleasure in baiting him.* 其他孩子都在恶意取笑他。**3 bear-baiting/badger-baiting etc** the activity of attacking a wild animal with dogs 用狗来攻击熊/獾等〔野兽〕

baize /bez; beɪz/ *n* [U] thick cloth, usually green, used especially to cover tables on which games such as BILLIARDS are played 桌面呢〔多为绿色，尤用来铺于台球等桌面上〕

Ba·ja Cal·i·for·ni·a /,bɑhɑ kælɪ,fɔnɪə; ,bɑːhɑː kælɪ'fɔːniə/ also 又作 **Baja** a PENINSULA (=long thin piece of land) in Mexico that is connected to southern California and goes into the Pacific Ocean. 下加利福尼亚半岛〔墨西哥一半岛，与加利福尼亚南部接壤，另一端伸向太平洋〕

bake /bek; beɪk/ *v* **1** [I,T] to cook something using dry heat, in an OVEN 烘，烤，焙: *I'm baking some bread.* 我在烤些面包。| *baked potatoes* 烤马铃薯 —see picture on page A10 参见 A10 页图 **2** [I,T] to make something become hard by heating it 烘干，烧硬: *In former times, bricks were baked in the sun.* 过去，砖块是放在阳光下晒干的。**3** [I] *informal* to be too hot【非正式】过热: *Open a window it's baking in here!* 开开窗吧，这儿热得像火炉! —see also 另见 HALF-BAKED 3

baked beans /,· '·/ *n* [U] a dish consisting of beans cooked in a sauce made from tomatoes etc〔加番茄酱等的〕烘豆

> **CULTURAL NOTE 文化注释**
>
> Baked beans are a favourite food of many children in Britain. 'Sausage, beans, and chips' is also a typical meal served in a CAFE. Some people like to have beans on toast as a quick simple meal. Baked beans are considered by some people to be JUNK FOOD, eaten by people who are too lazy to cook something better, although other people think that they are good for you. 烘豆是很多英国儿童喜爱的食品。"香肠、烘豆配薯条"也是咖啡馆常供应的菜肴。有人喜欢在烤面包片上放烘豆，以图省事快捷。一些人认为烘豆是垃圾食品，只有不爱做饭的懒人才吃；但也有一些人认为吃烘豆对人有益。
>
> Baked beans are known for causing FLATULENCE and sometimes people make jokes about this. 人们知道，烘豆会引起胃肠胀气，有时候会以此来开玩笑。

Ba·ke·lite /`bekə,laɪt; 'beɪkəlaɪt/ *n* [U] *trademark* a hard plastic used especially in the 1930s and 1940s【商标】〔尤指 20 世纪 30 和 40 年代使用的〕酚醛电木; 酚醛塑料

bak·er /`bekɚ; 'beɪkə/ *n* [C] **1** someone who bakes bread and cakes, especially in order to sell them in a shop 面包师，糕点师 **2 baker's** *especially BrE* a shop that sells bread, cakes etc; bakery【尤英】面包店; 糕点屋

Baker day /`· · ·/ *BrE informal* one of a number of days during the usual school year when teachers receive training and children do not attend school【英，非正式】教师进修日〔指正常学年中教师接受培训，学生无需上学的一段时间中的任何一天〕

baker's doz·en /,· · `· ·/ *n* [singular] *old-fashioned* thirteen of something【过时】一打加一，十三

Baker Street /`· · ·/ a street in London where the DETECTIVE Sherlock Holmes lived in the stories about him by Arthur Conan Doyle 贝克街〔伦敦一街名，亚瑟·柯南·道尔笔下的侦探福尔摩斯居住的地方〕

bak·er·y /`bekərɪ; 'beɪkəri/ also 又作 **baker's** *BrE*【英】/`bekɚz; 'beɪkəz/ *n* [C] a place where bread and cakes are baked, or a shop where they are sold 面包[糕饼]烘房; 面包[糕饼]店

bak·ing pow·der /`· · ,· ·/ *n* [U] a powder used in baking cakes to make them light 发(酵)粉

baking sheet /`· · ·/ *n* [C] a baking tray 烘烤盘

baking so·da /`· · ,· ·/ *n* [U] BICARBONATE OF SODA 小苏打

baking tray /`· · ·/ *n* [C] a flat piece of metal that you bake food on 烤盘 —see picture at 参见 TRAY 图

bak·sheesh /,bæk`ʃiʃ; ,bæk'ʃiːʃ/ *n* [U] money that people in the Middle East give to poor people, to someone who has helped them, or as a BRIBE〔中东地区的〕小费，赏钱; 贿赂; 施舍

Baku /bɑˋku; bɑːˈkuː/ also 又作 **Baky** a city in southeast Azerbaijan, the country's capital and an important port on the west coast of the Caspian Sea 巴库〔阿塞拜疆西南部城市，该国首都和里海西岸重要港口〕

bal·a·cla·va /ˌbæləˋklɑvə; ˌbæləˈklɑːvə◂/ *n* [C] *especially BrE* a warm WOOLLEN hat that covers most of your head and face【尤英】盔式大绒帽〔遮盖住大部分头和面部的羊毛帽〕

bal·a·lai·ka /ˌbæləˋlaɪkə; ˌbæləˈlaɪkə/ *n* [C] a musical instrument with strings on a three-sided box, played especially in Russia 巴拉莱卡琴〔尤指俄国的三角琴〕

balance 平衡

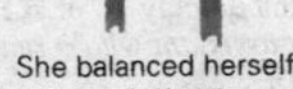

She balanced herself.
她使自己保持平衡。

She lost her balance.
她失去了平衡。

bal·ance¹ /ˋbæləns; ˈbæləns/ *n*

1 ▶STEADY 稳定的◀ [U] a state in which all your weight is evenly spread so that you do not fall 平衡: *You need a good sense of balance to ride a bicycle.* 骑自行车要有良好的平衡感。| **lose your balance** (=be unable to stay steady and not fall) 失去平衡 *I lost my balance and fell on my face.* 我失去平衡，脸着地摔倒了。| **keep your balance** (=manage to stay steady and not fall, especially when this is difficult) 保持平衡

2 ▶EQUALITY 均等◀ [singular] a state in which opposite forces or influences have or are given equal importance 均衡，均势，平衡: **[+between]** *the delicate balance between man and nature* 人与自然之间微妙的平衡 | **[+of]** *a realistic balance of work and relaxation* 劳逸结合，工作与娱乐的实际平衡 | **strike a balance** (=manage to balance opposing forces) 两全其美 *We need to strike a balance between the needs of the community and the rights of the individval.* 我们必须处理好社会需要与个人权利之间的平衡。—opposite 反义词 IMBALANCE

3 on balance if you think something on balance, you think it after considering all the facts 全面考虑之后，权衡利弊，总的说来: *I think on balance I prefer the old system.* 总的说来，我觉得自己更喜欢旧体制。

4 off balance a) unable to stay steady or upright 没站稳的，失去平衡的: *I was still off balance when he hit me again.* 没等我站稳，他又朝我打过来。**b)** surprised or confused 吃惊的，糊涂的: **throw sb off balance** *The abrupt question threw her off balance and she couldn't reply.* 突如其来的问题把她搞糊涂了，她不知道怎样回答。

5 the balance of evidence/probability etc the most likely answer or result produced by opposing information, reasons etc 从各方面的证据/可能性等来看: *The balance of evidence suggests that at least some of the politicians received money.* 从各方面的证据来看，至少有一些政客收了钱。

6 ▶FOR WEIGHING 用于称重量◀ [C] an instrument for weighing things by seeing whether the amounts in two hanging pans are equal 天平，秤

7 ▶BANK 银行◀ [C] the amount of money that you have in your bank account 余数，余额，差额，结余: *Could you tell me what my balance is please?* 你能告知我的户头还有多少余额吗?

8 ▶THE REST 其余的◀ [singular] the amount of something that remains after some has been used or spent 剩余（部分）: **[+of]** *I'd like to take the balance of my vacation in September.* 我想在9月份用完我剩余的假期。

9 ▶OPPOSITE FORCE 相反的力◀ [singular] a force or influence on one side which equals an opposite force or influence 平衡力；制衡作用；抵销因素: *They work well together – her steadiness acts as a balance to his clever but impractical ideas.* 他们合作得很好，她的稳健沉着对他那巧妙却不切实际的想法起到了制衡作用。

10 be/hang in the balance if the future or success of something hangs in the balance, you cannot yet know whether the result will be bad or good 悬而未决: *Meanwhile the fate of the refugees continues to hang in the balance.* 同时，难民的命运仍然悬而未决。

11 tip/swing the balance to influence the result of an event 影响事态的结果: *Your letter of recommendation swung the balance in his favour.* 你的推荐信使情况变得对他有利。

balance² *v*

1 ▶KEEP STEADY 保持稳定◀ [I,T] to get into a steady position, without falling to one side or the other, or to put something into this position（使）平稳，（使）保持平衡: **balance sth on** *She balanced the cup on a huge pile of books.* 她把杯子稳稳地放在一大堆书上。| **[+on]** *He turned around, balancing awkwardly on one foot.* 他转过身去，笨拙地用一只脚站稳。

2 ▶BE EQUAL TO 等于◀ [I,T] to be equal to something else in weight, amount, or importance（使）〔重量、数量、重要性等〕均衡，相抵，相等: *Exports must go down to balance decreased imports.* 必须减少出口以便和下降的进口保持平衡。

3 ▶GO WELL WITH 与…相配◀ [T] to have an opposite effect to something else, so that a good result is achieved 使〔两种相反的效果〕适中: *just enough sugar to balance the acidity of the fruit* 加足够的糖中和一下水果的酸性

4 ▶KEEP STH EQUAL 保持某物均衡◀ [T] to try to give equal importance to two things 平衡好，处理好: *a working mother, balancing home and career* 能处理好家庭和事业两者关系的上班族母亲 | **balance sth with** *She had learned to balance working efficiency with good human relationships.* 她已经学会协调，既要提高工作效率，又要保持良好的人际关系。

5 ▶THINK ABOUT 思考◀ [T] to consider the importance of something in relation to the importance of something else 权衡，斟酌，比较: **balance sth against** *The courts must balance the liberty of the few against the security of the many.* 法庭必须权衡少数人的自由和多数人的安全之间的关系。

6 balance the books/budget to show or make sure that the money that has been spent is equal to the money that is available 使收支平衡

balance beam /ˈ‥, ‥/ *n* [C] a long narrow wooden board on which a GYMNAST performs〔体操〕平衡木

bal·anced /ˋbælənst; ˈbælənst/ *adj* **1** giving equal attention to all sides or opinions; fair 公平的，合理的；均衡的，调和的: *balanced and impartial reporting of the election campaign* 对竞选活动公正而无偏袒的报道 **2** not giving too much importance to one thing; SENSIBLE 不偏不倚的；平和的: *a balanced outlook on life* 平和的生活态度 **3** arranged to include things or people of different kinds in the right amount 均衡的: *a balanced programme of events* 合理的节目安排 | **balanced diet** (=containing the right foods in the right amounts) 均衡饮食

balance of pay·ments /ˌ‥ ‥ ˈ‥/ *n* [singular] the difference between what a country spends in order to buy goods and services abroad, and the money it earns selling goods and services abroad 国际收支差额；国际收支平衡

balance of pow·er, the /ˌ‥ ‥ ˈ‥/ *n* a situation in which political or military strength is shared evenly〔政治或军事的〕力量均势: **hold the balance of power** (=be able to make either side more powerful than the other by supporting them) 举足轻重，掌握决定权 *In a hung parliament the centre parties hold the balance of power.* 在各党派势均力敌的议会里，中间党派的地位举足轻重。

balance of trade /ˌ‥ ‥ ˈ‥/ *n* the difference in value between the goods a country buys from abroad and the goods it sells abroad 贸易差额

balance sheet /ˈ‥ ‥/ *n* [C] a statement of how much money a business has earned and how much money it has paid for goods and services 资产负债表，决算表〔显示收支总差额的报告表〕: *a healthy balance sheet despite the recession* 经济衰退时收支仍然平衡

Bal·an·chine /ˌbælənˋtʃin; ˈbæləntʃiːn/, **George** (1904-83) a US CHOREOGRAPHER (=someone who decides what movements dancers will do to a piece of music) who was born in Russia, and who helped to start the New York City Ballet 巴兰钦〔(1904-1983)，出生于俄罗斯的美国舞蹈编导，曾协助创建纽约芭蕾舞团〕

Balboa /bælˋboə; bælˈbəʊə/, **Vasco Nunez de** (?1475-1519) a Spanish EXPLORER who led the first lasting European town in South America, in Panama, in 1510. In 1513 he crossed the Isthmus of Panama and was the first European to discover the Pacific Ocean, which he then claimed, along with all the coasts it touched, for Spain. 巴尔沃亚〔(?1475-1519)，西班牙探险家，1510年在南美洲的巴拿马建立了欧洲人的第一个永久殖民镇，1513年穿越巴拿马地峡，成为首位发现太平洋的欧洲人，随之宣称太平洋所有海岸归西班牙所有〕

bal·co·ny /ˈbælkənɪ; ˈbælkəni/ *n* [C] **1** a structure you can stand on that sticks out from the upstairs wall of a building 阳台 **2** the seats upstairs at a theatre〔戏院的〕楼座, 楼厅 — see picture at 参见 THEATRE 图

bald /bɔld; bɔːld/ *adj* **1** having little or no hair on your head 秃〔头〕的: *His bald head was badly sunburnt.* 他的秃头被阳光严重灼伤。| **go bald** (=gradually lose your hair) 逐渐秃顶 **2** not having enough of what usually covers something 光秃的, 磨光的, 掉光的: *The car's tires are completely bald.* 这辆汽车的车胎完全磨光了。**3 bald statement/language/truth etc** a statement etc that is correct but gives no additional information to help you understand or accept what is said 不加修饰[直话直说]的声明/语言/道理等 —**baldness** *n* [U]

bald ea·gle /ˌ· ˈ··/ *n* [C] a large North American bird with a white head and neck that is the national bird of the US 白头鹫, 秃鹰〔产于北美, 美国国鸟〕

bal·der·dash /ˈbɔldɚˌdæʃ; ˈbɔːldədæʃ/ *n* [U] *old-fashioned* talk or writing that is silly nonsense【过时】胡言乱语, 废话

bald-faced /ˌ· ˈ·◂/ *adj AmE* making no attempt to hide that you know what you are doing or saying is wrong; BAREFACED【美】厚颜无耻的; 露骨的

bald·ing /ˈbɔldɪŋ; ˈbɔːldɪŋ/ *adj* a balding man is losing the hair on his head 渐渐变秃的: *a spare, already balding man in his mid-thirties* 一位瘦弱的、已开始秃顶的三十五六岁的男人

bald·ly /ˈbɔldlɪ; ˈbɔːldli/ *adv* in a way that is true but makes no attempt to be polite 直言不讳地, 直截了当地, 赤裸裸地: *To put it baldly, stop smoking or you'll be dead in a year.* 坦白说吧, 你如果不戒烟, 最多活一年。

Bald·win /ˈbɔldwɪn; ˈbɔːldwɪn/, **James** (1924-87) a black US writer who wrote NOVELS such as *Go Tell It on the Mountain* and *Another Country* 鲍德温〔(1924-1987), 非裔美国作家, 创作了《向苍天呼吁》、《另一个国家》等作品〕

bale¹ /bel; beɪl/ *n* [C] a large quantity of something such as paper or hay that is tightly tied together especially into a block 大捆, 大包: *a bale of straw* 一大捆稻草

bale² *v* [T] to tie something such as paper or hay into a large block 把〔纸、干草等〕绑成一大捆

bale out *phr v* [I] *BrE*【英】**1** to escape from an aircraft by PARACHUTE¹ 跳伞逃生 **2** to leave a place or situation as quickly as you can 迅速离开; **bail out** (BAIL² (4)) *AmE*【美】

Bal·e·a·ric Is·lands, the /ˌbælɪˈærɪk ˈaɪləndz; ˌbæliærɪk ˈaɪləndz/ also 又作 **the Balearics** /ˌbælɪˈærɪks; ˌbæliˈærɪks/ a group of islands in the western Mediterranean Sea, including Ibiza, Majorca, and Minorca, which belong to Spain 巴利阿里群岛〔位于地中海西部, 属西班牙, 包括伊维萨岛、马略卡岛、梅诺卡岛等〕

bale·ful /ˈbelfəl; ˈbeɪlfəl/ *adj literary* expressing anger, hatred, or a wish to harm someone【文】邪恶的, 恶毒的, 带威胁性的: *a baleful look* 充满恶意的目光 —**balefully** *adv*

Bal·four /ˈbælfɚ; ˈbælfə/, **Arthur James** (1848-1930) a British politician in the Conservative Party, who was Prime Minister from 1902 to 1905 and Foreign Secretary from 1916 to 1919. He was responsible for the **Balfour Declaration**, which supported the idea that a state should be established in Palestine for the Jews. 贝尔福〔(1848-1930), 英国保守党政治家, 1902 年至 1905 年任英国首相, 1916 年至 1919 年任英国外交大臣, 曾起草《贝尔富宣言》, 支持在巴勒斯坦建立一个犹太人国家的主张〕

Ba·li /ˈbɑlɪ; ˈbɑːli/ an island in Indonesia, to the east of Java 巴厘岛〔印度尼西亚一岛屿, 位于爪哇以东〕

balk¹ also 又作 **baulk** *BrE*【英】/bɔk; bɔːk/ *v* **1** [I] to not want to or refuse to do something that is difficult, or frightening 畏缩不前, 犹豫, 打退堂鼓: [I+at] *Perry seemed interested, but balked when he heard the price.* 佩里似乎感兴趣, 但一听价钱就犹豫了。**2** [I+at] if a horse balks at a fence etc, it stops suddenly and refuses to jump or cross it〔马在障碍物前〕突然站住 **3** [T] to stop someone or something from getting what they want 阻止, 妨碍: *eager young men balked by rules and regulations* 为规章制度所限的热情高涨的年轻人 **4** *AmE* to stop, in BASEBALL, in the middle of the action of throwing the ball to the player who is trying to hit it【美】〔棒球投手在投球时〕做假动作, 佯投

balk² also 又作 **baulk** *BrE*【英】*n* [C] a thick rough wooden beam 梁木, 粗木枋

Bal·kans, the /ˈbɔlkənz; ˈbɔːlkənz/ also 又作 **the Balkan States** a large area in southeast Europe which includes Greece, Romania, Bulgaria, Albania, and the former Yugoslavia. It is an area in which there have been many wars and many changes in the borders of the countries. 巴尔干诸国〔欧洲东南部广大区域, 包括希腊、罗马尼亚、保加利亚、阿尔巴尼亚和前南斯拉夫, 是一个战争频发、边界屡变的地区〕

bal·ky /ˈbɔkɪ; ˈbɔːki/ *adj AmE* refusing to do what you are asked or expected to do【美】倔强的, 听不进别人话的: *He's a balky man to have to work with.* 他是个不好共事的人。

ball¹ /bɔl; bɔːl/ *n* [C]

1 ▶TO PLAY WITH 用来玩的◀ a round object that is thrown, kicked, or hit in a game or sport 球: *Bounce that ball to me.* 把球弹给我。| *a tennis ball* 网球

2 ▶ROUND SHAPE 圆形◀ something formed or rolled into a round shape 球状物: *a ball of string* 线团 | *Shape the dough into balls.* 把面团做成球状。

3 the ball of the foot/hand/thumb the rounded part of the foot at the base of the toe, rounded part of the hand at the base of the thumb or fingers 大脚趾根部的肉球/手指根部的圆肉/拇指球 —see also 另见 EYEBALL¹ (1) —see picture at 参见 FOOT¹ 图

4 a fast/good/curved etc ball a ball that is thrown, hit, or kicked fast etc in a game or sport 快球/好球/弧圈球等: *He hit a long ball to right field.* 他向右外场踢了一个长传球。

5 no ball a ball that is thrown too high, low etc towards someone trying to hit it, in the games of CRICKET (2) or ROUNDERS〔板球或圆场棒球的〕投球犯规〔球投得太高或太低〕

6 ▶BASEBALL 棒球◀ *AmE* a ball thrown in BASEBALL that a player is not expected to hit because it is not within the correct area【美】〔棒球运动中投手投出的〕坏球

7 ▶BULLET 子弹◀ a round bullet fired from a type of gun that was used in the past 弹丸, 球形子弹

8 on the ball *informal* thinking or acting quickly【非正式】机警的; 有见识的; 效率高的: *We need an assistant who's really on the ball.* 我们需要一名真正内行的助手。

9 set/start the ball rolling to begin an activity or event or make sure it continues 使事情开始[继续进行]: *Let's start the ball rolling with a few suggestions.* 让我们提几条建议作为开始。

10 the ball is in your court it is your turn to take action or to reply 现在轮到你〔作出反应或采取行动〕: *I've sent him a letter, now the ball's in his court.* 我已经给他发了信, 下面就看他的了。

11 ▶DANCE 跳舞◀ a large formal occasion at which people dance 舞会

12 have a ball *informal* to have a very good time【非正式】玩得很开心: *We had a ball at the party last night.* 昨晚聚会我们玩得很开心。

13 balls [plural] **a)** TESTICLES 睾丸 **b)** *taboo spoken* courage or determination【讳, 口】胆量: *It's not going to be easy. It'll take fight, guts and balls.* 这不容易, 需要斗志、勇气和胆量。**c)** *BrE taboo spoken* something that is stupid or wrong; nonsense【英, 讳, 口】胡说八道: *That's a load of balls!* 那简直是放屁!

14 a ball of fire someone who has a lot of energy and is active and successful 精力充沛, 积极向上的人

15 the whole ball of wax *AmE informal* the whole thing; everything【美, 非正式】一切, 全部, 所有

16 ball-buster/ball-breaker *AmE slang*【美俚】**a)** a problem that is very difficult to deal with 棘手的问题 **b)** an offensive word for a woman who uses her authority over men 对男人发号施令的女人〔冒犯用语〕—see also 另见 BALLS, **not play ball** (PLAY¹ (24))

ball² *v* [T] **1** also 又作 **ball up** to form something into a small round shape so that it takes up less space 把〔某物〕弄成球状 **2** *AmE spoken taboo* to have sex with a woman【美口, 讳】和〔女人〕发生性关系

ball sth ↔ **up** *phr v AmE spoken* to make a situation confused or difficult to deal with【美口】弄糟: *No, we're not going now, Lindsay's managed to ball everything up.* 不, 我们现在不走, 林赛把事情搞得一团糟。—see also 另见 BALLS-UP

bal·lad /ˈbæləd; ˈbæləd/ *n* [C] **1** a short story in the form of a poem 叙事诗歌 **2** a simple song, especially a popular love song 民歌, 歌谣; 流行的情歌

bal·last¹ /ˈbæləst; ˈbæləst/ *n* [U] **1** heavy material that is carried by a ship to make it more steady in the water〔使船只保持平稳的〕压舱物 **2** material such as sand that is carried in a BALLOON¹ (2) and can be thrown out to make it rise〔起稳定气球或操纵高度作用的〕沙囊, 压载物 **3** broken stones that are used as a surface under a road, railway lines etc〔道路、铁路等铺路基用的〕道砟, 石碴

ballast² *v* [T] to fill or supply something with ballast 给〔船〕放压舱物; 给〔气球等〕放沙囊; 为〔铁路〕铺道砟

ball bear·ing /ˌ· ˈ··/ *n* [C] **1** an arrangement of small metal balls moving in a ring around a bar so that the bar can turn more easily 滚珠轴承 **2** one of these metal balls 滚珠

ballboy /ˈ· ·/ *n* [C] a boy who picks up tennis balls for people playing in important tennis matches〔在网球比赛中为球员拾球的〕球童 —see picture at 参见 TENNIS 图

ball·cock /ˈbɔlˌkɑk; ˈbɔːlkɒk/ *n* [C] a hollow floating ball on a stick that opens and closes a hole, to allow water to flow into a container, for example in a TOILET (1) 浮球阀, 浮球栓, 浮球旋塞

bal·le·ri·na /ˌbæləˈrinə; ˌbæləˈriːnə/ *n* [C] a woman who dances in ballets 芭蕾舞女演员

bal·let /ˈbæle; ˈbæleɪ/ *n* **1** [C] a performance in which a special style of dancing and music tell a story without any speaking 芭蕾舞剧; 芭蕾舞曲: *Tchaikovsky wrote several famous ballets.* 柴可夫斯基创作了好几部著名的芭蕾舞曲。**2** [U] this type of dancing 芭蕾舞(艺术) **3** [C] a group of ballet dancers who work together 芭蕾舞团: *the Bolshoi Ballet* (俄国)大剧院芭蕾舞团

ballet danc·er /ˈ· ·ˌ· ·/ *n* [C] someone who dances in ballets 芭蕾舞演员

Ballet Rambert, the —see 见 the RAMBERT DANCE COMPANY

ball game /ˈ· ·/ *n* **1** *AmE* a BASEBALL game【美】棒球比赛 **2** *BrE* any game played with a ball【英】球类比赛 **3 a whole new ball game** a situation that is very different from the one you are used to 完全不同的情况: *I used to be a teacher, so working in an office is a whole new ball game.* 我以前是教师, 因此办公室工作对我是件全新的事物。

ball girl /ˈ· ·/ *n* [C] a girl who picks up tennis balls for people playing in important tennis matches〔在网球比赛中为球员拾球的〕女球童

bal·lis·tic mis·sile /bəˌlɪstɪk ˈmɪsl; bəˌlɪstɪk ˈmɪsaɪl/ *n* [C] a MISSILE (1) that is guided up into the air and then falls freely 弹道导弹

bal·lis·tics /bəˈlɪstɪks; bəˈlɪstɪks/ *n* [U] the scientific study of the movement of objects that are thrown or fired through the air, such as bullets shot from a gun 弹道学, 发射学

bal·loon[1] /bəˈlun; bəˈluːn/ *n* [C] **1** a small brightly coloured rubber bag that can be filled with air and used as a toy or decoration for parties 玩具气球, 装饰性气球 **2** a large bag of strong light cloth filled with gas or heated air so that it can float in the air 热气球: *hot air balloons drifting toward the horizon* 朝着远处地平线飘去的热气球 **3** the circle drawn around the words spoken by the characters in a CARTOON〔卡通漫画中表示人物对白的〕气球状对话框 **4 balloon payment** *AmE* money borrowed that must be paid back in one large sum after several smaller payments have been made【美】〔分期付款中〕最后一笔数目特大的偿付额: *a $10,000 balloon payment due in two years* 最后一笔两年后到期应付的1万美元的分期付款额 **5 go down like a lead balloon** *informal* if a joke, remark etc goes down like a lead balloon, people do not laugh or react as you expected【非正式】〔笑话、讲话等〕未达到预期效果

balloon[2] *v* [I] **1** to get bigger and rounder 膨胀, 鼓起来: [+out/outwards/up] *His cheeks ballooned out as he played his trumpet.* 他吹喇叭时, 两颊都鼓了起来。**2** to become larger in amount 膨胀, 增加: *Mitch's business debts ballooned to $20,000 in just one year.* 只过了一年, 米奇的企业负债就迅速增加到两万美元。

bal·loon·ing /bəˈlunɪŋ; bəˈluːnɪŋ/ *n* [U] the sport of flying in a balloon 乘热气球飞行(运动) —**balloonist** *n* [C]

bal·lot[1] /ˈbælət; ˈbælət/ *n* **1** [C,U] a system of secret voting or an occasion when you vote in this way 无记名投票〔选举或表决〕: *The Club's officers are always chosen by ballot.* 俱乐部的官员一直都是无记名投票选出来的。**2** [C] a piece of paper on which you make a secret vote; BALLOT PAPER〔无记名〕投票用纸, 选票 **3** [C] the number of votes recorded; POLL[1] (3) 投票总数, 投票结果

ballot[2] *v* [I,T] to vote or to decide something by a vote 进行无记名投票; 通过投票选出[决定]: *The chairman is elected by balloting all the shareholders.* 董事长是经全体股东投票选出的。

ballot box /ˈ· · ·/ *n* **1** [C] a box that ballot papers are put in after voting 投票箱 **2 the ballot box** the system or process of voting in an election 投票(法): *The people have expressed their views through the ballot box.* 人们通过投票的方式表达自己的意见。

ballot pa·per /ˈ· ·ˌ· ·/ *n* [C] a piece of paper on which you record your vote 选票

ball park /ˈ· ·/ *n* **1** *especially AmE* a field for playing BASEBALL, with seats for watching the game【尤美】〔有看台的〕棒球场 **2 in the right ball park** *informal* close to the amount, price etc that you want or are thinking about【非正式】大致正确; 差不多: *Their estimate is definitely in the right ball park.* 他们的估计肯定大致是正确的。**3 a ball park figure** a number or amount that is almost but not exactly correct 大致正确的数字: *He said $25,000 but it's just a ball park figure.* 他说是25,000美元, 不过这只是个大致的数目。

ball·play·er /ˈbɔlˌpleə; ˈbɔːlˌpleɪə/ *n* [C] *AmE* someone who plays BASEBALL【美】棒球运动员

ball·point /ˈbɔlˌpɔɪnt; ˈbɔːlpɔɪnt/ also 又作 **ballpoint pen** /ˌ· · ˈ·/ *n* [C] a pen with a ball at the end that rolls thick ink onto the paper 圆珠笔, 原子笔 —see picture at 参见 PEN[1] 图

ball·room /ˈbɔlˌrum; ˈbɔːlrʊm/ *n* [C] a very large room used for dancing on formal occasions 舞厅, 舞场

ballroom danc·ing /ˌ· · ˈ· ·/ *n* [U] a type of dancing that is done with a partner and has different steps for particular types of music, such as the WALTZ[1] (1) 交际舞, 交谊舞〈如华尔兹等〉

balls[1] /bɔlz; bɔːlz/ *interjection taboo* used to show strong disapproval or disappointment【讳】〔表示强烈反对或失望〕胡说八道: *Balls to that! I'm not working Saturday morning!* 胡说!我星期六上午不工作!

balls[2] *v*

balls sth ↔ **up** *phr v BrE taboo slang* to do something very badly or unsuccessfully【英, 讳, 俚】把…弄得一团糟: *He totally ballsed up his exams.* 他考试全考砸了。

balls-up /ˈ· ·/ *n BrE taboo slang* something that has been done very badly or unsuccessfully【英, 讳, 俚】弄得一团糟的事, 烂摊子: *Nigel made a complete balls-up of the arrangements.* 奈杰尔把安排全搞乱了。

ball·sy /ˈbɔlzɪ; ˈbɔːlzi/ *adj AmE spoken* brave and determined【美口】胆识过人的: *He's a ballsy kind of guy.* 他是个胆识过人的家伙。

bal·ly /ˈbælɪ; ˈbæli/ *adj, adv BrE old-fashioned* an expression meaning BLOODY[1] used to avoid offending other people【英, 过时】讨厌的[地], 见鬼的[地]

bal·ly·hoo /ˈbælɪˌhu; ˌbæliˈhuː/ *n* [U] *informal* a situation in which people publicly express a lot of anger, excitement etc【非正式】大吹大擂, 哗众取宠: *After all the promotional ballyhoo, the film flopped.* 尽管搞了大吹大擂的宣传, 这部电影还是不卖座。

balm /bɑm; bɑːm/ *n* [C,U] **1** an oily liquid with a strong, pleasant smell that you rub into your skin, often to reduce pain〔涂抹用的药用〕油, 膏, 止痛膏 **2** *literary* something that gives you comfort【文】安慰(物), 慰藉(物): *Her words were a balm to my shredded nerves.* 她的话对我纷乱的心绪多少是些安慰。

Bal·mor·al /bælˈmɔrəl; bælˈmɒrəl/ a castle in Scotland that the British royal family often use for their summer holidays 巴尔莫勒尔堡〔苏格兰一城堡, 常为英国皇室避暑之用〕

balm·y /ˈbɑmɪ; ˈbɑːmi/ *adj* balmy air, weather etc is warm and pleasant〔空气、天气等〕温和的, 宜人的: *a balmy summer night* 宜人的夏夜

ba·lo·ney /bəˈlonɪ; bəˈləʊni/ *n* [U] *informal*【非正式】**1** something that is silly or not true; nonsense 胡说, 鬼话: *"Don't give me that baloney," he said, winking at Christopher.* 他朝克里斯托弗眨了眨眼说: "别胡说。" **2** *AmE* BOLOGNA【美】博洛尼亚香肠, 大香肠

bal·sa /ˈbɔlsə; ˈbɔːlsə/ *n* [C,U] a tropical American tree or the wood from this tree, which is very light〔美洲热带地区产的〕白塞木树; 白塞木, 轻木

bal·sam /ˈbɔlsəm; ˈbɔːlsəm/ *n* [C,U] BALM, or the tree that produces it 香脂冷杉; 〔上述植物的〕香脂, 香胶

Bal·tic Sea, the /ˌbɔltɪk ˈsi; ˌbɔːltɪk ˈsiː/ also 又作 **the Baltic** a sea that is part of the Atlantic Ocean and is surrounded by Denmark, Sweden, the Baltic States, and Poland 波罗的海〔大西洋的一部分, 沿岸有丹麦、瑞典、波罗的海诸国和波兰〕

Baltic States, the /ˌ· · ˈ·/ Estonia, Latvia, and Lithuania considered together as one group 波罗的海诸国〔爱沙尼亚、拉脱维亚及立陶宛的统称〕

Bal·ti·more /ˈbɔltəmɔr; ˈbɔːltɪmɔː/ a city and sea port on the East Coast of the US, in the state of Maryland 巴尔的摩〔美国东海岸港口城市, 位于马里兰州〕

bal·us·trade /ˌbæləˈstred; ˌbæləˈstreɪd/ *n* [C] a row of upright pieces of stone or wood with a bar along the top, especially around a BALCONY〔尤指阳台周围的〕扶手, 栏杆

Bal·zac /ˈbolzæk; ˈbælzæk/, **Hon·o·ré de** /ˌɑnəˈre də; ˈɒnəreɪ də/ (1799-1850) a French writer who wrote about French society, and is famous for his set of NOVELS called *La Comédie Humaine* 巴尔扎克(1799-1850), 法国作家, 其作品取材于法国社会, 以系列小说《人间喜剧》闻名〕

Bamako /ˌbæməˈko; ˌbɑːmɑːˈkəʊ/ a city in southwest Mali, the country's capital and largest city, on the River Niger 巴马科〔马里西南部城市, 该国首都及最大城市, 位于尼日尔河畔〕

Bam·bi /ˈbæmbɪ; ˈbæmbi/ a CARTOON film by Walt Disney about a young DEER named Bambi《小鹿斑比》〔迪斯尼公司制作的卡通电影, 讲述小鹿斑比的故事〕

bam·boo /bæmˋbu; ˌbæmˈbuː◂/ *n* [C,U] a tall tropical plant with hollow stems that are used for making furniture 竹, 竹子

bam·boo·zle /bæmˋbuzḷ; bæmˈbuːzəl/ *v* [T] *informal* to deceive, trick, or confuse someone【非正式】欺骗, 愚弄, 蒙蔽

3 **ban**[1] /bæn; bæn/ *n* [C] an official order that forbids something from being used or done 禁止, 禁令: *The President supports a global ban on nuclear testing.* 总统支持全球性禁止核试验。—see also 另见 TEST BAN

ban[2] *v* **banned, banning** [T] to say that something must not be done, seen, used etc 禁止, 取缔: *Smoking is banned in the building.* 大楼内禁止吸烟。| **ban sb from doing sth** *Charlie's been banned from driving for a year.* 查利被禁止驾车一年。| **banned book/film/video etc** (=a book etc that is illegal) 禁书/禁止上映的电影/禁播录像等

ba·nal /ˋbenḷ; bəˈnɑːl/ *adj* ordinary and not interesting, because of a lack of new or different ideas 平淡无奇的, 平庸的, 陈腐的: *a banal piece of writing* 平庸之作 —**banality** /bəˈnæləti; bəˈnælḷti/ *n* [C,U]

ba·na·na /bəˋnænə; bəˈnɑːnə/ *n* [C] a long curved tropical fruit with a yellow skin 香蕉 —see picture on page A8 参见A8页图

banana re·pub·lic /·ˌ··ˈ··/ *n* [C] *informal* an insulting word for a small poor country with weak government that depends on financial help from abroad【非正式】香蕉共和国〔侮辱性词语, 指政府软弱, 经济不发达, 需依赖他国财政援助的小国〕

ba·na·nas /bəˋnænəz; bəˈnɑːnəz/ *adj informal*【非正式】**1** crazy or silly 发疯的; 愚蠢的: *People think Mr Allen is bananas because he talks to his plants.* 人们都认为艾伦先生发疯了, 因为他对着他的植物说话。**2 go bananas** become very angry or excited 变得十分气愤[激动]: *Dad will go bananas when he sees this.* 爸爸看到这个会气疯的。

banana skin /·ˈ··ˌ·/ *n* [C] *BrE informal* an embarrassing mistake made by someone in a public position, especially a politician or someone in a government【英, 非正式】引起麻烦〔使人出洋相〕的事件: *This incident could turn into another banana skin for the government.* 这件事可能使政府再次出洋相。

banana split /·ˌ··ˈ·/ *n* [C] a sweet dish with bananas and ICE CREAM 香蕉新地, 香蕉船〔用香蕉和冰淇淋做成的甜点〕

Ban·bu·ry Cross /ˋbænbɛrɪ ˋkrɔs; ˌbænbəri ˈkrɒs/ a stone cross in the small English town of Banbury, near Oxford, which is mentioned in a popular British NURSERY RHYME (=old song or poem for young children) 班伯里十字架〔英格兰牛津附近的小镇班伯里的一座石制十字架, 英国流行的一首童谣中有所提及〕: *Ride a cock horse to Banbury Cross.* 骑着木马去班伯里十字架。

2 2 **band**[1] /bænd; bænd/ *n* [C]

1 ▶**MUSIC** 音乐◀ a group of musicians, especially a group that plays popular music〔尤指演奏流行音乐的〕乐队, 乐团: **jazz/rock/big etc band** (=a band that plays JAZZ etc) 爵士乐队/摇滚乐队/大乐团等 *He plays saxophone in a little-known jazz band.* 他在一个不知名的爵士乐队里吹萨克斯管。| **band leader/singer** (=someone who leads a band, or sings with a band) 乐队领班/主唱

2 ▶**GROUP OF PEOPLE** 人群◀ a group of people formed because of a common belief or purpose 一伙, 一群, 一帮: *a small band of enthusiasts* 一小群热心者

3 ▶**PIECE OF MATERIAL** 材料◀ a flat, narrow piece of material with one end joined to the other to form a circle 系物的带子; 箍带: *papers held together with a rubber band* 用橡皮筋绑在一起的文件 | *a wide silk band* 宽丝带

4 ▶**PATTERN** 图形◀ a thick coloured line 条纹: *There are orange bands around the snake's back.* 这条蛇的背部有橙色条纹。

5 tax/income/age etc band a particular range of tax, income etc in which a group of people belong 税收/收入/年龄等范围: *people within the $20,000 – $30,000 income band* 收入在2万至3万美元这个范围的人

6 ▶**RADIO** 无线电◀ *technical* a range of radio signals【术语】波段, 频带

band[2] *v* [T] to put a band of colour or material on or around something 给…加上条纹边框, 给…镶边

band together *phr v* [I] to unite in order to achieve something 团结起来, 联手: *The two parties banded together to form an alliance.* 两党团结起来结成联盟。

bandage 绷带

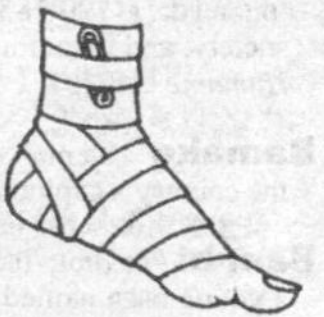

ban·dage[1] /ˋbændɪdʒ; ˈbændɪdʒ/ *n* [C] a narrow piece of cloth that you tie around a wound or around a part of the body that has been injured 绷带

bandage[2] also 又作 **bandage up** *v* [T] to tie or cover a part of the body with a bandage 用绷带包扎: *The nurse bandaged up his sprained ankle.* 护士用绷带包扎他扭伤了的脚踝。

Band Aid /ˈ··/ *trademark* an organization set up by Bob Geldof in 1984 to collect money for people dying of hunger in Ethiopia. This was done by getting many famous popular musicians to make a record together called *Do They Know It's Christmas?*, and by organizing the Live Aid concerts in London and Philadelphia.【商标】义演援助团〔鲍勃·格尔多夫1984年创立的组织, 旨在为埃塞俄比亚饥民筹集资金。该组织曾发动著名流行音乐家制作了名为《他们知道今天是圣诞节吗?》的唱片, 并在伦敦和费城举办了现场募捐音乐会〕

Band-Aid /ˈ··/ *n* [C] *AmE trademark* a piece of thin material that is stuck to the skin to cover cuts and other small wounds【美, 商标】"邦迪"牌创可贴〔一种护创胶布〕; PLASTER[1] (3) *BrE*【英】; ELASTOPLAST *BrE*【英】

ban·dan·na, bandana /bænˋdænə; bænˈdænə/ *n* [C] a large brightly coloured piece of cloth you wear around your head or neck 印花大围巾, 大头巾: *hair tied up in a scarlet bandanna* 扎着鲜红头巾的头发

Ban·da·ra·na·i·ke /ˌbændərəˋnaɪəkə; ˌbændərəˈnaɪḷkə/, **Mrs Sir·i·ma·vo** /sɪrɪˋmɑvo; sɪrɪˈmɑːvəʊ/ (1916-2000) a Sri Lankan politician who became the world's first woman Prime Minister in 1960 班达拉奈克〔(1916-2000), 斯里兰卡政治家, 1960年成为世界上首位女总理〕

Bandar Seri Begawan /ˌbʌndɚ ˌsɛrɪbəˋgɑwən; ˌbʌndə ˌseri bəˈgɑːwən/ a city in northeast Brunei, the country's capital and an important port on the Brunei River, formerly called Brunei Town 斯里巴加湾市〔文莱东北部城市, 该国首都、文莱河重要港口, 旧称文莱镇〕

B and B /ˌbi ənd ˋbi; ˌbiː ənd ˈbiː/ the abbreviation of 缩写= BED AND BREAKFAST: *a small B and B in the Cotswolds* 科茨沃尔德一家提供住宿和早餐的小旅店

band·box /ˋbændˌbɑks; ˈbændbɒks/ *n* [C] a box for keeping hats in〔装帽子的〕圆筒形盒

ban·deau /bænˋdo; ˈbændəʊ/ *n plural* **bandeaux** /-ˋdoz; -dəʊz/ [C] a band of material that you wear around your head to keep your hair in place 束发带

ban·dit /ˋbændɪt; ˈbændḷt/ *n* [C] someone who robs people, especially one of group of people who attack travellers 强盗, 土匪, 歹徒: *Beware of bandits in the mountains.* 当心山里的土匪。—see also 另见 ONE-ARMED BANDIT —**banditry** *n* [U]

band·mas·ter /ˋbændˌmæstɚ; ˈbændˌmɑːstə/ *n* [C] someone who CONDUCTS a military band, BRASS (2) band etc〔军乐队、铜管乐队等的〕乐队指挥

ban·do·lier /ˌbændəˋlɪr; ˌbændəˈlɪə/ *n* [C] a belt that goes over someone's shoulder and is used to carry bullets〔斜挂于肩膀的〕子弹带

bands·man /ˋbændzmən; ˈbændzmən/ *n* [C] a musician who plays in a military band, BRASS (2) band etc〔军乐队、铜管乐队等的〕乐队队员

band·stand /ˋbændˌstænd; ˈbændstænd/ *n* [C] a structure that has a roof but no walls and is used by a band playing music in a park〔有顶盖的〕室外音乐演奏台

band·wa·gon /ˋbændˌwægən; ˈbændˌwægən/ *n* [C] **climb/jump on the bandwagon** to begin to do something that a lot of other people are doing 赶浪头, 顺应潮流, 随大流: *Everyone seems to be jumping on the environmental bandwagon.* 大家似乎都顺应潮流, 开始关注环境问题。

ban·dy[1] /ˋbændɪ; ˈbændi/ *adj* bandy legs curve outwards at the knees 两膝向外曲的, 罗圈腿的 —**bandy-legged** *adj*

bandy[2] *v* **bandy words (with)** *old-fashioned* to quarrel with someone【过时】(与某人)争吵, 斗嘴

bandy sth **about** *phr v* [T] to mention an idea, name, remark etc several times, especially to impress someone 口头传播, 随便散播: *Several different figures have been bandied about – which is correct?* 到处在传的有好几个不同的数字, 究竟哪个是对的?

bane /ben; beɪn/ *n* [singular] something that causes trouble or makes people unhappy 祸根; 灾星: **be the bane of** *Drugs are the bane of the inner cities.* 毒品是城市中心区的祸根。| **the bane of sb's life/existence** (=a cause of continual trouble or unhappiness) 某人一生麻烦[不幸]的缘由 *Ask any laser printer user what the bane of their life is and they'll tell you – replacing the toner.* 问任何一个使用激光打印机的人, 他最不愿意做的事是什么, 他会告诉你——更换碳粉。

bane·ful /ˋbenfəl; ˈbeɪnfəl/ *adj literary* evil or bad【文】邪恶的; 有害的 —**banefully** *adv*

Banff /bænf; bænf/ a town in the Rocky Mountains in Alberta, Canada. It is a popular place for people who ski. 班夫〔加拿大阿尔伯塔省落基山脉一小镇, 是滑雪胜地〕

bang[1] /bæŋ; bæŋ/ *n* **1** [C] a sudden loud noise caused by something such as a gun or an object hitting a hard surface 砰; 啪〔枪声或重物相碰的声音〕: *The front door slammed with a loud bang.* 前门砰的一声关上了。**2** [C] a hard knock or hit against something 猛击, 猛撞; 重打: *That was a nasty bang on the head.* 头撞得可不轻。**3 bangs** [plural] *AmE* hair cut straight across your forehead【美】〔头发的〕前刘海; FRINGE[1] (1) *BrE*【英】—see picture on page A6 参见 A6 页图 **4** [singular] *AmE informal* a strong feeling of pleasure【美, 非正式】快感, 乐趣: *She got a real bang out of seeing the kids in the school play.* 看到孩子们在演学校里排演的戏剧时, 她高兴极了。**5 go off with a bang** to happen in a very successful way 极为成功, 大受欢迎: *The party really went off with a bang!* 聚会真的棒极了!

bang[2] *v*

1 ▶KNOCK/HIT STH 碰到某物◀ [I,T] to hit something hard against something else, making a loud noise 猛敲; 砰然重击: *She banged the phone down.* 她把电话啪的一声放下。| [+on] *They were banging on the door with their fists.* 他们用拳头使劲敲门。

2 ▶CLOSE STH 关上某物◀ [I always+adv/prep, T] to close something violently making a loud noise, or to make something close in this way 很响地使劲关(门): *She banged the door and stomped up the stairs.* 她砰的一声关上门, 噔噔噔上了楼。| **bang shut** *The window banged shut.* 窗户砰的一声关上了。

3 ▶MAKE NOISE 发出响声◀ [I] to make a loud noise or noises 砰砰作响: [+about/around/away] *I could hear the garage door banging in the wind.* 我能听见车库的门被风吹得砰砰作响。

4 ▶HIT STH 碰撞某物◀ [T] to hit a part of your body or something you are carrying against something, especially by accident; BUMP[1] (1)〔意外地〕撞击: *Bobby fell and banged his knee.* 博比摔倒了, 膝盖撞了一下。| *I slipped and banged the guitar against the door.* 我滑了一跤, 吉他撞到了门上。

5 be banging your head against a brick wall *informal* to be wasting your efforts by doing something that does not produce any results【非正式】白费气力, 枉费心机: *Trying to teach that class is like banging your head against a brick wall.* 想要教那个班的学生学点东西完全是白费气力。

6 ▶HAVE SEX 性交◀ [T] *taboo* to have sex with someone【讳】与〔某人〕发生性关系

bang on *phr v* [I] *BrE informal* to talk continuously about something in a boring way【英, 非正式】啰嗦个没完: [+about] *I'm tired of politicians banging on about family values.* 我厌倦了政治家没完没了地谈论家庭的价值观。

bang sth ↔**out** *phr v* [T] *informal*【非正式】**1** to play a tune or song loudly and badly on a piano〔在钢琴上〕使劲乱敲地弹奏〔乐曲、歌曲〕**2** to write something in a hurry, especially on a TYPEWRITER〔尤指在打字机上〕匆忙赶写: *Danielle banged out a few letters, before going home for the day.* 丹妮尔在当天回家前匆忙地写了几封信。

bang sb/sth ↔**up** *phr v* [T] **1** *BrE slang* to put someone in prison【英俚】监禁 **2** *AmE informal* to seriously damage something【美, 非正式】使…严重受损: *a banged-up old Buick* 严重毁坏的旧别克轿车

bang[3] *adv* **1** *informal* directly or exactly【非正式】直接地; 准确地; 正巧, 恰恰: *The train arrived bang on time.* 火车准点到达。**2 bang on** *spoken* exactly correct【口】完全正确: *Yes! Your answer's bang on!* 对! 你的答案完全正确! **3 bang goes** *spoken* used to show that you are unhappy because something you had hoped for will not happen【口】完蛋了, 告吹了: *£750 to repair the car? Bang goes my holiday.* 花 750 英镑修汽车? 那我度假的事就泡汤了。**4** *spoken* in a sudden, violent way【口】突然, 猛然: *He slowed down, and bang! The car behind crashed straight into us!* 他减速后, 后面的车突然直撞向我们!

bang[4] *interjection* used to make a sound like a gun or bomb 砰〔用作模仿枪声或炸弹的声响〕: *"Bang, bang – you're dead," Tommy shouted.* "砰, 砰——打死你了。"汤米喊道。

bang·er /ˈbæŋə; ˈbæŋə/ *n* [C] *BrE informal*【英, 非正式】**1** a SAUSAGE 香肠 **2** an old car in bad condition 破旧的汽车, 老爷车: *Gary's finally scrapped that old banger of his.* 加里终于丢弃了他那辆老爷车。**3** a type of noisy FIREWORK〔声音很响的一种〕爆竹

Bang·kok /ˈbæŋkɑk; bæŋˈkɒk/ the capital city and main port of Thailand 曼谷〔泰国首都、重要港口〕

Ban·gla·desh /ˈbæŋgləˌdɛʃ; ˌbæŋgləˈdeʃ/ a country in South Asia, east of India. Population: 131,270,000 (2001). Capital: Dhaka. 孟加拉国〔南亚国家, 位于印度以东。人口: 131,270,000 (2001), 首都: 达卡〕—**Bangladeshi** *n, adj*

ban·gle /ˈbæŋgl; ˈbæŋgəl/ *n* [C] a solid band of gold, silver etc that you wear loosely around your wrist as jewellery 手镯

Bangui /bɑŋˈgi; bɑːŋˈgiː/ the capital city of the Central African Republic, on the Ubangi River 班吉〔中非共和国首都, 位于乌班吉河沿岸〕

bang-up /ˈ· ·/ *adj AmE informal* very good【美, 非正式】非常好的, 很棒的: *He did a bang-up job fixing the plumbing.* 他把水管修得棒极了。

ban·ish /ˈbænɪʃ; ˈbænɪʃ/ *v* [T] **1** to not allow someone or something to stay in a particular place 驱逐, 赶走; 驱除, 排除: **banish sth from/to** *The children were banished to the backyard.* 孩子们被赶到后院里去了。**2** to send someone away permanently from their country or the area where they live, especially as an official punishment 放逐; 驱逐出境〔尤指作为官方惩罚〕: **banish sb from/to** *Many Soviet dissidents were banished to Siberia.* 许多持不同政见的前苏联人士被流放到西伯利亚。**3 banish sb/sth (from your mind)** to try to stop thinking about something, especially something that worries you 不再想某人/某物 —**banishment** *n* [U]

ban·is·ter /ˈbænɪstə; ˈbænɪstə/ *n* [C] a row of upright sticks with a bar along the top, that stops you from falling over the edge of stairs〔楼梯的〕栏杆, 扶手 —see picture on page A4 参见 A4 页图

ban·jo /ˈbændʒo; ˈbændʒəʊ/ *n* [C] a musical instrument with four or more strings, a long neck and a round body used especially in COUNTRY AND WESTERN music 班卓琴

Banjul /ˈbɑnˌdʒul; ˈbɑːnˌdʒuːl/ the capital city of the Gambia, a port on the Gambia River, formerly called Bathurst 班珠尔〔冈比亚首都、冈比亚河港口, 旧名为巴瑟斯特〕

bank[1] /bæŋk; bæŋk/ *n* [C] S1 W1

1 ▶MONEY 钱◀ a) a business that keeps and lends money and provides other financial services 银行: *The major banks have announced an increase in interest rates.* 几家大银行已宣布提高利率。**b)** a local office of a bank 银行(营业厅): *I have to go to the bank at lunch time.* 午饭时我得去银行。

2 ▶RIVER/LAKE 河/湖◀ land along the side of a river or lake 岸, 堤: *Roger pushed the boat away from the bank.* 罗杰把船从岸边推走。—see 见 SHORE[1] (USAGE)

3 ▶PILE 堆◀ a large pile of earth, sand, snow etc〔土、沙、雪等的〕大堆, 埂, 垄: *There were steep banks of snow at the sides of the road.* 路旁有许多尖形的雪堆。

4 blood/sperm/organ etc bank a place where human blood etc is stored until someone needs it 血库/精子库/器官库等

5 cloud/fog bank etc a large mass of clouds, mist etc 云团/雾团等

6 bank of televisions/elevators/computers etc a large number of machines, television screens etc arranged close together in a row 紧密排成一列的电视/电梯/电脑等

7 ▶GAME 游戏◀ the money in a GAMBLING game that people can win 庄家的赌本 —see also 另见 **break the bank** (BREAK[1] (32))

8 ▶ROAD 路◀ a slope made at a bend in a road or RACETRACK to make it safer for cars to go around〔为使车辆安全拐弯而设于公路或跑道拐弯处的〕内侧斜坡 —see also 另见 BOTTLE BANK, MEMORY BANK

bank[2] *v*

1 ▶MONEY 钱◀ [T] to put or keep money in a bank 把〔钱〕存入银行: *Did you bank that check?* 你把支票存入银行了吗?

2 ▶PARTICULAR BANK 某银行◀ [I] to keep your money in a particular bank 把钱存入某家银行: [+with] *Who do you bank with?* 你把钱存入哪家银行?

3 ▶TURN 转◀ [I] to make a plane, MOTORCYCLE, or car slope to one side when turning〔飞机、摩托车、汽车等转弯时〕倾斜飞行[行驶]: *The plane banked, and circled back toward us.* 飞机倾斜着飞行, 绕圈子朝着我们飞回来。

4 ▶PILE/ROWS 堆/排◀ also 又作 **bank up** *BrE* [T] to arrange something into a pile or into rows【英】把…堆起来[排成行]: *The walls of the space center are banked high with electronic equipment.* 航天中心的墙上排满了电子仪器。

5 ▶CLOUD/MIST 云/雾◀ also 又作 **bank up** [T] to form a mass of cloud, mist etc 聚集成〔云团、雾团等〕: *Banked clouds promised rain.* 云团密布, 预示有雨。

6 ▶FIRE 火◀ also 又作 **bank up** [T] to cover a fire with wood, coal etc to keep it going for a long time 封〔火〕, 压〔火〕: *Josie banked up the fire to last till morning.* 乔西把炉火封好, 这样火可以保持到第二天早晨。

bank on sb/sth *phr v* [T] to depend on something happening or someone doing something 依靠, 指望: **bank on sb doing sth** *We were banking on John being there to show us the way.* 我们指望约翰在那里告诉我们走哪条道。

bank·a·ble /ˈbæŋkəbl; ˈbæŋkəbəl/ *adj informal* a bankable person or quality is likely to help you get money, success etc

【非正式】可靠的，可获利的：*They need a bankable star for the movie.* 他们需要一个富有号召力的明星来为这部电影赚钱。

bank ac·count /ˈ· ·,·/ *n* [C] an arrangement between a bank and a customer that allows the customer to pay in and take out money 银行账户

bank bal·ance /ˈ· ,··/ *n* [singular] the amount of money someone has in their bank account 银行存款；账户余额

B

bank book /ˈ· ·/ *n* [C] a book in which a record is kept of the money you put into and take out of your bank account（银行）存折；PASSBOOK *AmE*【美】

bank card /ˈ· ·/ *n* [C] **1** *AmE* a CREDIT CARD provided by your bank【美】信用卡，银行卡 **2** *BrE* a CHEQUE CARD【英】（银行）支票保付卡，银行支票证

bank draft /ˈ· ·/ also 又作 **banker's draft** *n* [C] a cheque for one bank to another, especially a foreign bank, to pay a certain amount of money to a person or organization〔银行与银行，尤指外国银行之间的〕银行汇票

bank·er /ˈbæŋkə; ˈbæŋkə/ *n* [C] **1** someone who works in a bank in an important position 银行家；经营银行业务者 **2** the player who is in charge of the money in some games〔牌戏或赌博的〕庄家

banker's card /ˈ·· ·/ *n* [C] *BrE* a CHEQUE CARD【英】（银行）支票保付卡，银行支票证

banker's or·der /,·· ˈ··/ *n* [C] *BrE* a STANDING ORDER【英】长期自动转账委托

bank hol·i·day /,· ˈ···/ *n* [C]
1 *BrE* an official holiday when banks and most businesses are closed【英】银行假日；公众假期：*Next Monday is a bank holiday.* 下星期一是银行假日。| *stuck in the bank holiday traffic* 被困在公众假期的交通堵塞之中 | **bank holiday weekend** (=a weekend on which there is a bank holiday on Friday or Monday)〔星期一或星期五〕银行假日的周末，周末银行假日 *Are you going away for the bank holiday weekend?* 周末是银行假日，你要外出吗？

CULTURAL NOTE 文化注释

Bank holiday especially refers to the bank holiday in the Spring (**Spring bank holiday**) and the one in August (**August bank holiday**, also called **Late Summer Holiday**). These two bank holidays are always on a Monday (**Bank Holiday Monday**), and the weekend when they take place is known as a **bank holiday weekend** 银行假日尤指春季的银行假日（春季银行假日）和8月的银行假日（8月银行假日，又称夏末银行假日）。这两个银行假日都在星期一（周一银行假日），银行假日所在的周末称银行假日周末：*There are bound to be traffic jams over the bank holiday weekend as people head for the coast.* 银行假日周末，人们都涌往海滩，必会造成交通堵塞。

2 *AmE* a day during the week when banks are closed by law【美】非周末法定银行休息日；银行停业期

bank·ing /ˈbæŋkɪŋ; ˈbæŋkɪŋ/ *n* [U] the business of a bank 银行业：*the international banking system* 国际银行业体制

bank man·a·ger /ˈ· ,···/ *n* [C] someone who is in charge of a local bank 银行（分行）经理

CULTURAL NOTE 文化注释

The British STEREOTYPE of a bank manager is a boring, old-fashioned MIDDLE-AGED man wearing a suit. 英国银行经理给人留下的典型形象是一个沉闷、老派、着正装的中年男子。

bank note /ˈ· ·/ *n* [C] *especially BrE* a piece of paper money of a particular value that you use to buy things【尤英】钞票，纸币

Bank of A·mer·i·ca /,· · ˈ····/ one of the largest banks in the US 美利坚银行〔美国最大的银行之一〕

Bank of En·gland, the /,· · ˈ··/ the national bank of the UK 英格兰银行〔英国中央银行〕

Bank of Scot·land, the /,· · ˈ··/ one of the main banks in Scotland 苏格兰银行〔苏格兰主要银行之一〕

bank rate /ˈ· ·/ *n* [C] *technical* the rate of INTEREST[1] (4) decided by a country's main bank【术语】〔中央银行所定的〕贴现率

bank·roll¹ /ˈbæŋk,rol; ˈbæŋkrəʊl/ *n* [C] a supply of money 资金，财源

bankroll² *v* [T] *informal* to provide the money that someone needs for a business, a plan etc【非正式】对…融资，为…提供资金；资助：*a software company bankrolled by the Samsung Group* 由三星集团提供资金的软件公司

bank·rupt¹ /ˈbæŋkrʌpt; ˈbæŋkrʌpt/ *adj* **1** unable to pay your debts 资不抵债的；破产的：*Seventeen years of war left the country bankrupt.* 17年的战争使这个国家负债累累。**2 go bankrupt** to be unable to pay your debts and to have to sell your property and goods 破产；倒闭：*The recession has made many small companies go bankrupt.* 经济衰退使许多小企业破产。**3** completely lacking a particular good quality 缺乏〔某种美德〕的；沦丧的：*The opposition attacked the government as morally bankrupt.* 反对党攻击政府道德败坏。

bankrupt² *v* [T] to make a person, business or country bankrupt or very poor 使破产；使极其贫困：*Legal fees almost bankrupted us.* 诉讼费几乎使我们破产。

bankrupt³ *n* [C] someone who has officially said that they cannot pay their debts 破产者

bank·rupt·cy /ˈbæŋkrʌptsɪ; ˈbæŋkrʌptsi/ *n* **1** [C,U] the state of being unable to pay your debts 破产；倒闭：*There has been a sharp increase in bankruptcies in the last two years.* 近两年破产个案急剧增加。**2** [U] a total lack of a particular good quality 缺乏道德：*the moral bankruptcy of this materialistic society* 道德沦丧的实利主义社会

Banks /bæŋks; bæŋks/, **Ernie** /ˈɝnɪ; ˈɜːni/ (1931-) a US BASEBALL player who was the first black member of the Chicago Cubs team 班克斯〔(1931-)，美国棒球运动员，芝加哥小熊队首位黑人球员〕

bank state·ment /ˈ· ,··/ *n* [C] a document sent regularly by a bank to a customer that lists the amounts of money taken out of and paid into their BANK ACCOUNT 银行结单

banned /bænd; bænd/ *adj* not officially allowed to meet or exist 被禁止的；被取缔的：*Leaders of the banned party were arrested last night.* 被取缔党派的领导人昨晚遭到逮捕。

ban·ner¹ /ˈbænə; ˈbænə/ *n* [C] **1** a long piece of cloth on which something is written, often carried between two poles〔通常用两根竿子撑开的〕横幅标语：*Crowds of people carrying banners joined the demonstration.* 成群结队的人打着横幅标语加入了游行示威的队伍。—see picture at 参见 DEMONSTRATION 图 **2** *literary* a flag【文】旗帜 **3** a belief or principle 信仰：*Many of the poor and unemployed rallied to the Communist banner.* 许多穷人和失业者都团结在共产主义的旗帜下。| **under the banner of** (=claiming to support a principle) 在…的旗帜下，在…的名义下，为了…的事业 *The party fought the election under the banner of social justice.* 该党以维护社会正义的名义参加竞选。

banner² *adj AmE* excellent【美】优秀的，极好的：*a banner year for American soccer* 美国足球成绩突出的一年

banner head·line /,·· ˈ··/ *n* [C] words printed in very large letters across the top of the first page of a newspaper〔报纸的〕通栏大标题

Ban·nis·ter /ˈbænɪstə; ˈbænɪ̵stə/, **Sir Roger** (1929-) a British runner who, in 1954, became the first person to run a mile in less than four minutes 班尼斯特〔(1929-)，英国田径运动员，1954年成为四分钟内跑完一英里的第一人〕

ban·nock /ˈbænək; ˈbænək/ *n* [C] *especially ScotE* a flat cake made of OATMEAL or corn【尤苏格兰】燕麦[玉米]薄饼

Ban·nock·burn /ˈbænəkbɝn; ˈbænəkbɜːn/ a village in the central part of Scotland that is known as the place where Robert the Bruce, King of the Scots, defeated the English in a famous battle in 1314 班诺克本〔苏格兰中部地区一村庄。1314年苏格兰国王罗伯特·布鲁斯在此打败了英格兰人。这个村庄因此而出名〕

banns /bænz; bænz/ *n* [plural] a public statement that two people intend to get married, made in a church in Britain〔在英国预先在教堂发布的〕结婚公告

CULTURAL NOTE 文化注释

In Britain, banns are read out in the church in which a couple are getting married on three separate Sundays before a marriage takes place. They include the words, "If any of you know cause or just impediment, why these two persons should not be joined together in holy Matrimony, ye are to declare it". In the US, banns are not usually declared now. 在英国，结婚公告分别于男女双方婚前三个不同的星期日在教堂里宣读。结婚公告包括下列字句："在座诸位若有正当理由认为这两个人不应结合而组成神圣的婚姻，请讲出来。"现在美国很少宣布结婚公告。

ban·quet /ˈbæŋkwɪt; ˈbæŋkwɪ̵t/ *n* [C] a formal dinner for many people on an important occasion 宴会

banqueting hall /ˈ··· ,·/ also 又作 **banquet room** /ˈ·· ·/ *AmE*【美】*n* [C] a large room in which banquets take place 宴会厅

Ban·quo /ˈbæŋkwo; ˈbæŋkwəʊ/ a character in Shakespeare's play *Macbeth*. Macbeth gives secret orders for Banquo to be murdered, but Banquo later returns as a ghost during an important celebration, to remind Macbeth that he is guilty and that his plans will fail. 班柯〔莎士比亚戏剧《麦克白》中的人物。麦克白下密令要人除掉班柯。后来，班柯的鬼魂出现在一次重大庆典上，警告麦克白说，他是有罪的，他的阴谋是不会得逞的〕

ban·shee /ˈbænʃi; bænˈʃiː/ *n* [C] a spirit whose loud cry is believed to be heard when someone is going to die〔传说会大声哭号以预报凶讯的〕报丧女妖

ban·tam /ˈbæntəm; ˈbæntəm/ *n* [C] a type of small chicken 矮脚鸡

ban·tam·weight /ˈbæntəmˌwet; ˈbæntəmweɪt/ *n* [C] a BOXER (1) or WRESTLER who belongs to a group of a particular weight〔拳击、摔跤〕最轻量级选手

ban·ter[1] /ˈbæntɚ; ˈbæntə/ *n* [U] conversation that has a lot of jokes and teasing (TEASE[1] (1)) remarks in it 玩笑，戏谑，妙语：*covering his shyness with a good deal of banter* 用许多逗乐的话掩盖他的腼腆

banter[2] *v* [I] to joke with and TEASE someone 开玩笑，逗乐 —**bantering** *adj* —**banteringly** *adv*

ban·yan /ˈbænjən; ˈbænjən/ *n* [C] an Indian tree with large branches that spread out and form new roots〔印度〕榕树

bap /bæp; bæp/ *n* [C] *BrE* a round soft bread ROLL[2] (2)【英】面包卷

bap·tis·m /ˈbæptɪzəm; ˈbæptɪzəm/ *n* [C,U] **1** a Christian religious ceremony in which someone is touched or covered with water to welcome them into the Christian faith, and sometimes to officially name them〔基督教的〕洗礼，浸礼 **2 baptism of fire** a difficult or painful first experience of something（战）火的洗礼；初次的痛苦经历[考验]：*We went straight into battle the next day. It was a baptism of fire I'll never forget.* 第二天，我们直接走上了战场。这是我永生难忘的一次战火的洗礼。—**baptismal** /bæpˈtɪzml; bæpˈtɪzməl/ *adj*

Bap·tist /ˈbæptɪst; ˈbæptɪst/ *n* [C] a member of a Christian group that believes baptism should only be for people old enough to understand its meaning 浸礼会[浸信会]教友

bap·tize also 又作 **-ise** *BrE*【英】/bæpˈtaɪz; bæpˈtaɪz/ *v* [T] **1** to perform the ceremony of baptism on someone 给…施行洗礼 **2** to accept someone as a member of a particular Christian church by a ceremony of baptism 为…施行洗礼并吸纳入教：*He was baptized a Roman Catholic.* 他受洗礼成为罗马天主教徒。**3** to give a child a name in a baptism ceremony 洗礼时给〔某人〕命名：*She was baptized Sheila Jane.* 她受洗礼时被命名为希拉·简。

S1 W1 **bar[1]** /bɑr; bɑː/ *n* [C]

1 ▶PLACE TO DRINK IN 饮酒场所◀ **a)** a place where alcoholic drinks are served 酒吧 —compare 比较 PUB **b)** *BrE* one of the rooms inside a pub【英】酒吧间：*The public bar was crowded.* 酒吧间里人很多。

2 ▶PLACE TO BUY DRINK 买饮料处◀ a COUNTER[1] (1) where alcoholic drinks are served 出售酒的柜台：*There were no free tables so they stood at the bar.* 因为没有空桌子，他们在酒吧柜台边站着。

3 coffee/snack/salad etc bar a place where a particular kind of food or drink is served 咖啡店/小吃店/沙拉等自助柜台

4 ▶BLOCK OF STH 一块东西◀ a small block of solid material that is longer than it is wide 条，棒，根：*a candy bar* 一块糖 | *a bar of soap* 一块肥皂 —see picture on page A7 参见 A7 页图

5 ▶PIECE OF METAL/WOOD 金属/木头◀ a length of metal or wood put across a door, window etc to keep it shut or to prevent people going in or out〔门、窗等的〕闩；横木；阻碍物：*A lot of houses had bars across the windows.* 许多房屋的窗户上都有铁条。

6 ▶MUSIC 音乐◀ a group of notes and rests (REST[1] (12)), separated from other groups by vertical lines, into which a line of written music is divided〔乐曲中的〕一小节：*She hummed a few bars of the song.* 她哼出了歌曲的几小节。

7 a bar to (doing) sth something that prevents you from achieving something that you want 做某事的障碍：*Bad English is a bar to getting a good job.* 蹩脚的英语对找个好工作来说是个障碍。

8 ▶GROUP OF LAWYERS 律师◀ *law*【法律】**a) the bar** *BrE* the group of people who are BARRISTERS (=lawyers who have the right to speak in a court of law)【英】〔有资格出庭处理诉讼案件的〕大律师 **b)** *AmE* an organization consisting of people who are lawyers【美】律师界，律师业

9 be called to the bar a) *BrE* to become a BARRISTER【英】成为大律师 **b)** *AmE* to become a lawyer【美】成为律师

10 ▶PILE OF SAND/STONES 沙/石堆◀ a long pile of sand or stones under the water at the entrance to a HARBOUR[1]〔港口入口处的〕沙洲；暗礁

11 ▶COLOUR/LIGHT 颜色/光◀ a narrow band of colour or light 线条，条纹，带

12 ▶UNIFORMS 制服◀ a narrow band of metal or cloth worn on a military uniform to show rank〔军服上的〕军阶杠；绶带

13 ▶HEATER 加热器◀ the part of an electric heater that provides heat and has a red light〔电暖气的〕电热线[片]

14 behind bars *informal* in prison【非正式】在狱中

bar[2] *v* **barred, barring** [T] **1** also 又作 **bar up** to shut a door or window using a bar or piece of wood so that people cannot get in or out 闩上，闩住〔门、窗〕**2** [T] to officially prevent someone from entering a place or from doing something 摒除，排挤于…之外；阻止：**bar sb from** *Members voted to bar women from the club.* 会员表决不允许妇女加入该俱乐部。**3** to prevent people from going somewhere by placing something in their way 阻止通行；阻挡，阻拦：*The road ahead was barred by a solid line of policemen.* 前面的道路被警察的密集防线所阻拦。| **bar sb's way** (=prevent someone passing you by standing in front of them) 挡某人的道 *A security guard barred her way.* 警卫拦住了她。

bar[3] *prep* **1** *formal* except【正式】除了…以外：*No work's been done in the office today, bar a little typing.* 除了打点儿字，今天在办公室没做什么工作。**2 bar none** used to emphasize that someone is the best of a particular group 无人可比：*He's the most talented actor in the country, bar none.* 他是该国最有天分的演员，无人可比。—see also 另见 BARRING

barb /bɑrb; bɑːb/ *n* [C] **1** the sharp curved point of a hook, ARROW (1) etc that prevents it from being easily pulled out〔鱼钩、箭头等的〕倒钩，倒刺 **2** a remark that is clever and amusing, but also cruel 带刺的话；讥讽 —see also 另见 BARBED (2)

Bar·ba·dos /bɑrˈbedos; bɑːˈbeɪdɒs/ an island in the Caribbean Sea which is an independent state. Population: 275,000 (2001). Capital: Bridgetown. 巴巴多斯〔加勒比海一独立岛国。人口：275,000 (2001)，首都：布里奇敦〕

bar·bar·i·an /bɑrˈbɛrɪən; bɑːˈbeəriən/ *n* [C] **1** someone from a different tribe or land, who people believe to be wild and not CIVILIZED (1) 野蛮人，未开化的人，粗野的人：*The barbarians conquered Rome.* 野蛮人征服了罗马。**2** someone who does not behave properly, does not show proper respect for education, art etc 大老粗；无教养的人：*educational theories apparently written by barbarians* 显然由未受过良好教育的人写的教育理论

Bar·bar·i·ans, the /bɑrˈbɛrɪənz; bɑːˈbeəriənz/ a Rugby Union team based in Britain, with players from several countries. Teams from other countries which come to Britain often play against the Barbarians. 异族队〔一支英式橄榄球联盟球队，总部设在英国，球员来自好几个国家。访问英国的球队经常与异族队进行比赛〕

bar·bar·ic /bɑrˈbærɪk; bɑːˈbærɪk/ *adj* **1** very cruel and violent; BARBAROUS 野蛮的，凶残的：*a barbaric act of terrorism* 恐怖主义的暴行 **2** like or belonging to a wild or cruel group or society（似）野蛮人的：*barbaric forest tribes* 野蛮的森林部落

bar·bar·is·m /ˈbɑrbəˌrɪzəm; ˈbɑːbərɪzəm/ *n* **1** [U] a state or condition in which people are not educated, behave violently etc 野蛮（的生活方式），未开化（的状态）**2** [U] cruel and violent behaviour 残暴的行为，粗野的举止

bar·bar·i·ty /bɑrˈbærətɪ; bɑːˈbærəti/ *n* [C,U] a very cruel act 残暴；暴行：*The barbarities of the last war must not be repeated.* 上次战争的暴行绝不能重演。

bar·bar·ous /ˈbɑrbərəs; ˈbɑːbərəs/ *adj* **1** shockingly cruel; BARBARIC 非常残忍的，凶残的 **2** wild and not CIVILIZED (1) 野蛮的，无礼的，粗鄙的：*a savage, barbarous people* 凶猛野蛮的民族 —**barbarously** *adv*

barbecue 烧烤野餐

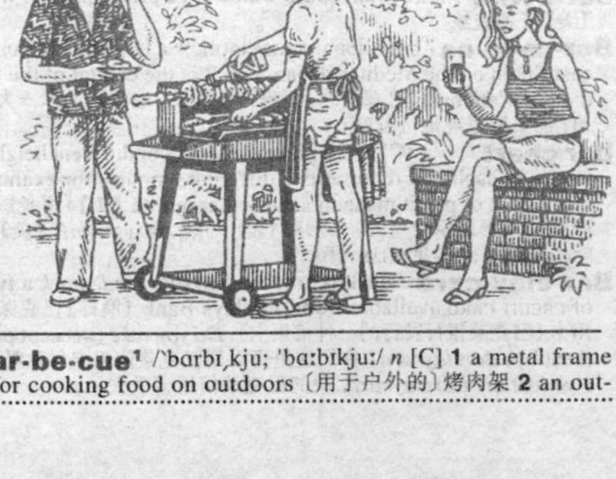

bar·be·cue[1] /ˈbɑrbɪˌkju; ˈbɑːbɪkjuː/ *n* [C] **1** a metal frame for cooking food on outdoors〔用于户外的〕烤肉架 **2** an out-

door party during which food is cooked and eaten outdoors 烧烤野餐: *We had a barbecue on the beach.* 我们在海滩上举行了烧烤野餐。

barbecue² *v* [T] to cook food on a metal frame over a fire outdoors〔用烤肉架〕烧烤〔肉〕: *barbecued chicken*〔用烤肉架烧的〕烤鸡

barbed /bɑrbd; bɑːbd/ *adj* **1** a hook or arrow that has one or more sharp, curved points 有倒钩[倒刺]的, 带刺的 **2** a barbed remark is unkind 尖酸刻薄的: *a barbed comment on his appearance* 对他的外表所作的尖酸刻薄的评论

barbed wire also 又作 **barbwire** /ˌ· ˈ·◂/ *AmE*【美】*n* [U] wire with short, sharp points on it 带刺铁丝: *a high barbed wire fence* 高架带刺铁丝网

bar·bell /ˈbɑrˌbɛl; ˈbɑːbel/ *n* [C] *AmE* a metal bar with weights at each end, which you lift to make you stronger【美】哑铃, 杠铃

bar·ber /ˈbɑrbɚ; ˈbɑːbə/ *n* [C] **1** a man whose job is to cut men's hair and sometimes to SHAVE¹ (1) them〔以男性为服务对象的〕男理发师 **2 barber's** *BrE* a shop where men's hair is cut【英】理发店

Barber, Sam·u·el /ˈsæmjuəl; ˈsæmjuəl/ (1910-81) a US COMPOSER who is famous for his *Adagio for Strings* (1936) 巴伯〔(1910-1981) 美国作曲家, 以其作品《弦乐的柔板》(1936) 而著称〕

Barbera —see 见 HANNA BARBERA

Barber of Se·ville, The /ˌ· · · ˈ· ·/ an OPERA by Rossini, based on a French play by Beaumarchais《塞维利亚的理发师》〔罗西尼根据博马舍的一部法语剧本而创作的歌剧〕

bar·ber·shop /ˈbɑrbɚˌʃɑp; ˈbɑːbəʃɒp/ *n* [U] **1** a style of singing popular songs in four parts in close HARMONY 男声四重唱〔用和声法演唱流行歌曲〕: *a barbershop quartet* 男声四重唱 **2** *AmE* a barber's【美】理发店

barber's pole /ˌ· · ˈ·/ *n* [C] a pole with red and white bands used as a sign outside a barber's shop〔立于理发店外作为招牌的〕旋转标志彩柱

bar·bi·can /ˈbɑrbɪkən; ˈbɑːbɪkən/ *n* [C] a tower for defence at the gate or bridge of a castle 碉堡, 桥头堡, 更楼

Barbican, the /ˈbɑrbɪkən; ˈbɑːbɪkən/ also 又作 **the Barbican Centre** a large group of buildings in central London, which includes two theatres, two cinemas, a concert hall, an ART GALLERY, restaurants, and shops. 巴比肯文化中心〔伦敦市中心一建筑群, 其中有两座剧院、两座电影院、一座音乐厅、一个美术馆、一些餐馆和商店〕: *There's a new Royal Shakespeare Company production of 'A Midsummer Night's Dream' at the Barbican.* 皇家莎士比亚剧团的新作《仲夏夜之梦》在巴比肯上演。

bar·bie /ˈbɑrbɪ; ˈbɑːbi/ *n* [C] *BrE & AustrE informal* a BARBECUE【英和澳, 非正式】〔用于室外的〕烤肉架; 烧烤野餐

Barbie doll /ˈ· · ˌ·/ also 又作 **Barbie** *trademark* a popular type of DOLL in the shape of an attractive young woman, used as a child's toy【商标】芭比娃娃〔大众喜爱的一种玩具娃娃, 形象为迷人的年轻女子〕

bar bil·liards /ˈ·, ·ˈ· ·/ *n* [U] a game played in PUBs in Britain in which players use long sticks to push balls into holes on a table〔英国酒吧内的〕台球, 桌球

bar·bi·tu·rate /ˌbɑrˈbɪtjʊret; bɑːˈbɪtʃʊrɪt/ *n* [C,U] a powerful drug that makes people calm and puts them to sleep 巴比土酸盐〔一种镇静剂、安眠药〕

Bar·bour /ˈbɑrbɚ; ˈbɑːbə/ *trademark* a type of coat made in the UK of a material that wind and rain cannot go through. Barbours are known for being good quality coats, traditionally worn by farmers and other people who live in the country.【商标】巴伯风雨衣〔英国制造的一种外套, 采用防风防雨面料, 以质地优良著称, 是生活在乡村的农民等人的传统服装〕

barb·wire /ˈbɑrbˌwaɪr; ˌbɑːbˈwaɪə◂/ *n* [U] *AmE* BARBED WIRE【美】带刺铁丝

Bar·ce·lo·na /ˌbɑrsɪˈlonə; ˌbɑːsɪ̈ˈləʊnə◂/ a large city in northeast Spain on the Mediterranean Sea. It is the capital of the REGION of Catalonia. 巴塞罗纳〔西班牙东北部、地中海沿岸一大城市, 加泰罗尼亚地区首府〕

bar chart /ˈ· ·/ *n* [C] *BrE* a picture of boxes of different heights, in which each box represents a different amount, for example an amount of profit made in a particular month【英】〔用长短不同的长条形表示数量的〕条形图(表); BAR GRAPH *AmE*【美】—see picture at 参见 CHART¹ 图

Bar·clay·card /ˈbɑrklɪkɑrd; ˈbɑːklikɑːd/ *trademark* a type of CREDIT CARD available from Barclays Bank【商标】巴克莱信用卡〔巴克莱银行发行的一种信用卡〕: *Do you take* (=accept payment by) *Barclaycard?* 你们这里可以用巴克莱信用卡付款吗? | *I've lost my Barclaycard.* 我的巴克莱信用卡丢失了。

Bar·clays Bank /ˌbɑrklɪz ˈbæŋk; ˌbɑːkliz ˈbæŋk/ also 又作 **Barclays** one of the main British banks 巴克莱银行〔英国主要银行之一〕

bar code /ˈ· ·/ *n* [C] a group of thin and thick lines from which a computer reads information about a product that is sold in a shop〔印刷在产品包装上的〕条形码, 条码

bar code 条形码, 条码
0-582-84223-9

bard /bɑrd; bɑːd/ *n* [C] *literary* a poet【文】诗人

Bard of A·von, the /ˌbɑrd əv ˈevən; ˌbɑːd əv ˈeɪvən/ a poetic name for William Shakespeare, based on the name of the River Avon at Stratford, where he was born 埃文河畔诗人〔威廉·莎士比亚的别称, 富有诗意, 因其出生在埃文河畔的斯特拉特福镇而得名〕

Bar·dot /bɑrˈdo; bɑːˈdəʊ/, **Bri·gitte** /brɪˈʒit; brɪˈʒiːt/ (1934-) a French film actress who was famous during the 1950s and 1960s as a SEX SYMBOL (=someone who is famous for being very sexually attractive) 巴多〔(1934-), 法国电影女演员, 20世纪50、60年代作为性感偶像而闻名〕

bare¹ /bɛr; beə/ *adj*

1 ►WITHOUT CLOTHES 未穿衣服◄ not covered by clothes 赤裸的: *Jonathan's bare feet made no sound in the soft sand.* 乔纳森光着脚在松软的沙滩上走, 一点声音都没有。

2 ►LAND/TREES 土地/树木◄ not covered by trees or grass, or not having any leaves 叶子全落的; 光秃秃的: *a bare hillside* 光秃秃的山坡

3 ►ROOMS 房间◄ empty, not covered by anything, or not having any decorations 空的, 无装饰的: *This room looks very bare – you need some pictures on the walls.* 房间显得过于单调 —— 你应该在墙上挂几幅画。

4 the bare facts/truth a statement that tells someone only what they need to know, with no additional details 暴露无遗的事实/赤裸裸的真相: *a journalist who is not content to simply record the bare facts* 不满足于只记录事实真相的记者

5 ►SMALLEST AMOUNT NECESSARY 最少必需量◄ [only before noun 仅用于名词前] the very least amount of something that you need to do something 仅有的, 勉强的, 最低限度的: *He got 40% – a bare pass.* 他得了40分, 刚及格。| **the bare essentials/necessities** *The refugees fled, taking only the bare essentials.* 难民带着仅够维持生活的必需品逃难。| **the bare minimum** (=the smallest amount possible) 最少量 *carrying the bare minimum of equipment* 轻装上阵 | **the barest** (=the smallest or simplest possible) 最少的; 最简单的 *We can provide only the barest outline of the plan.* 我们只能简略地透露计划的要点。

6 the bare bones the most important parts or facts of something without any detail 梗概: *the bare bones of the plan* 计划的梗概

7 lay sth bare a) to uncover something that was previously hidden 显示出某事物, 使某事物暴露: *The excavation laid bare the streets of an ancient city.* 这次发掘挖出了一座古城的街道。**b)** to reveal something that was secret 揭露, 揭发: *The investigation laid bare a million-dollar embezzlement racket.* 这次调查揭露了一宗挪用100万元公款的犯罪勾当。

8 with your bare hands without using a weapon 赤手空拳: *He killed her with his bare hands.* 他仅用一双手就杀死了她。— **bareness** *n*

bare² *v* [T] **1** to let something be seen, by removing something that is covering it 使暴露, 使赤裸, 露出: *The dog bared its teeth.* 狗露出了牙。**2 bare your soul** to reveal your most secret feelings 敞开心扉, 剖白心事, 诉说真情, 披肝沥胆

bare-assed /ˈbɛr ˌæst; ˌbeər ˈæst◂/ *adj AmE slang* having no clothes on【美俚】光屁股的, 赤条条的

bare·back /ˈbɛrˌbæk; ˈbeəbæk/ *adj, adv* on the bare back of a horse, without a SADDLE¹ (1) 无马鞍的[地]: *riding bareback* 骑无鞍马

bare·faced /ˈbɛrˌfest; ˌbeəˈfeɪst◂/ *adj* a barefaced lie, remark etc is clear and makes no attempt not to offend someone 厚颜无耻的; 露骨的; 公然的: *What barefaced cheek – saying that to you!* 多么厚颜无耻 —— 竟然对你说那样的话!

bare·foot /ˈbɛrˌfʊt; ˈbeəfʊt/ also 又作 **barefoot·ed** /ˈbɛrˌfʊtɪd; ˌbeəˈfʊtɪ̈d◂/ *adj, adv* without shoes on your feet 赤脚的[地]: *kids going barefoot all summer* 整个夏天都光着脚的孩子们

bare·hand·ed /ˈbɛrˈhændɪd; ˌbeəˈhændɪ̈d◂/ *adj, adv* having no GLOVEs on, or having no tools or weapons 没有戴手套的[地]; 赤手空拳的[地]: *They fought barehanded.* 他们赤手空拳地搏斗。

bare·head·ed /ˈbɛrˋhɛdɪd; ˌbeəˈhedɪ̣d◂/ *adj, adv* without a hat on your head 光着头的[地], 不戴帽的[地]: *You can't go out bareheaded in this weather!* 这样的天气你出去不能不戴帽子!

bare·leg·ged /ˈbɛrˋlɛgd; ˌbeəˈlegɪ̣d/ *adj, adv* with no clothing on your legs 光着腿的[地], 没穿袜子的[地]

bare·ly /ˈbɛrlɪ; ˈbeəli/ *adv* **1** in a way that almost does not happen, exist etc; just 几乎没有, 仅仅, 勉强地: *Her voice was so low, I could barely hear her.* 她说话的声音很轻, 我几乎听不见。| *We have barely enough money to live on.* 我们的钱只够勉强度日。**2** in a way that is simple, with no decorations or details 贫乏地; 简陋地, 几乎无装饰地: *The room was furnished barely.* 这房间陈设简陋。**3** used to emphasize that something happens immediately after a previous action 刚刚〔表示强调〕: *She'd barely sat down before he started firing questions at her.* 她刚坐下, 他就开始向她提出一连串的问题。

Barents Sea, the /ˌbærənts ˋsi; ˌbærənts ˈsiː/ a sea that is north of Norway and Russia and connected to the Arctic Ocean 巴伦支海〔位于挪威和俄罗斯以北, 连接北冰洋〕

barf /barf; bɑːf/ *v* [I] *AmE informal* to VOMIT[1]【美, 非正式】呕吐 —**barf** *n* [U] —**barfy** *adj*

bar·fly /ˈbar,flaɪ; ˈbɑːflaɪ/ *n* [C] *AmE informal* someone who spends a lot of time in bars【美, 非正式】泡酒吧的人, 酒吧常客 —**barfly** *adj*

bar·gain[1] /ˈbargɪn; ˈbɑːgɪ̣n/ *n* [C] **1** something bought cheaply or for less than its usual price 便宜货, 廉价货: *I might buy a TV, if I can find a bargain in the sales.* 如果我能在大减价中找到便宜货, 我也许会买台电视机。| **be a bargain** *These shoes are a bargain at $22.* 这些鞋每双才22美元, 很便宜。| **bargain holiday/clothes/prices etc** (=a holiday etc that is very cheap) 廉价假期/减价服装/便宜的价钱等 | **bargain hunting** (=looking for things to buy at a cheap price) 到处找廉价货买 *a bargain hunting housewife at the January sales* 在1月份减价促销期间到处找廉价货买的家庭主妇 **2** an agreement, made between two people or groups, to do something in return for something else 协议; 交易: **make a bargain** *We've made a bargain that he'll do the shopping and I'll cook.* 我们已经讲好了, 他去购物我做饭。| **drive a hard bargain** (=succeed in making an agreement that is very much to your advantage) 达成非常有利于自己的协议 *Fischer was determined to drive a hard bargain.* 费希尔决心要达成有利自己的协议。| **keep your side of the bargain** (=do what you promised as part of an agreement) 履行协议 | **strike a bargain** (=reach an agreement) 达成协议 *Management and unions have struck a bargain over wage increases.* 资方和工会就增加工资的问题达成了协议。**3 into the bargain** *especially BrE* in addition to everything else【尤英】此外, 外加, 而且: *He was short, fat, and spotty into the bargain.* 他又矮又胖, 而且一脸粉刺。**4 make the best of a bad bargain** to do the best you can under difficult conditions 困难时尽力而为; 善处逆境, 随遇而安 —**bargainer** *n* [C]: *a wage bargainer* 工资谈判者 —see 见 CHEAP[1] (USAGE)

bargain[2] *v* [I] to discuss the conditions of a sale, agreement etc 讲价钱, 讨价还价; 洽谈〔交易〕条件: **[+for]** *bargaining for better pay* 要求提高薪水

bargain for sth *phr v* also 又作 **bargain on** sth [T usually in negatives 一般用于否定句] to expect that something will happen and make it part of your plans 考虑到, 估计到, 预料到: *We hadn't bargained for such heavy rain, and got really wet.* 我们没料到会下这么大的雨, 结果浑身都湿透了。| **bargain on doing sth** *We can't bargain on finding the right house straight away.* 我们不能指望马上就找到合适的房子。| **more than you bargained for** (=more than you expected) 比预计的…得多 *His wife's angry reaction was more than he bargained for!* 他妻子生气的程度比他预料的要严重!

bargain base·ment /ˌ·· ˈ··/ *n* [C] a part of a large shop, usually in the floor below ground level, where goods are sold at reduced prices〔通常设在大商场地下室的〕廉价商品部

bar·gain·ing /ˈbargɪnɪŋ; ˈbɑːgənɪŋ/ *n* [U] **1** discussion in order to reach agreement about a sale, contract etc 讨价还价; 谈〔交易〕条件: *The 4% pay raise was the result of some hard bargaining.* 经过一番艰苦的讨价还价, 才达成把工资提高4%的协议。**2 bargaining position** the power that a person or group has in a discussion or argument 谈判中所处的地位

barge[1] /bardʒ; bɑːdʒ/ *n* **1** [C] a large low boat with a flat bottom used mainly for carrying heavy goods on a CANAL (1) or river 驳船, 平底载货船 **2** a large rowing boat used for an important ceremony〔用桨划的〕大游船, 画舫〔通常在举行重要仪式时使用〕

barge[2] *v* [I always+adv/prep] to move somewhere in an awkward way, often hitting against things 笨拙地走动; 乱碰乱撞: *She ran around the corner and barged into one of the teachers.* 她跑过拐角处, 和一位老师撞了个满怀。| **barge your way** *He barged his way through the room.* 他跌跌撞撞地穿过房间。

barge in *phr v* [I] to enter or rush in rudely 闯入: *I wish she wouldn't barge in like that.* 我希望她不会那样闯进来。| **[+on]** *Her mother barged in on her and Mike when they were in bed together!* 她和迈克两人正在床上, 这时她母亲闯入了房间!

barge in on *phr v* [T] to interrupt someone rudely 打断〔别人的谈话〕: *Dan's always barging in on other people's conversations.* 丹总是打断别人的谈话。

barg·ee /ˌbarˋdʒi; bɑːˈdʒiː/ *BrE*【英】, **barge·man** /ˈbardʒmən; ˈbɑːdʒmən/ *AmE*【美】*n* [C] someone who drives or works on a barge 驳船船工

barge pole /ˈ· ·/ *n* [C] a long pole used to guide a barge〔驳船用的〕撑篙 —see also 另见 **wouldn't touch sth with a bargepole** (TOUCH[1] (12))

bar graph /ˈ· ·/ *n* [C] an American form of BAR CHART bar chart 的美语形式

bar·hop /ˈbar,hap; ˈbɑːhɒp/ *v* [I] *AmE informal* to visit and drink at several bars, one after another【美, 非正式】串游酒吧〔从一家酒吧喝到另一家酒吧〕; PUB-CRAWL *BrE*【英】

bar·i·tone /ˈbærə,ton; ˈbærɪ̣təʊn/ *n* [C] a male singing voice lower than a TENOR (1) and higher than a BASS[1] (1), or a male singer whose voice is in this range 男中音〔歌手〕

ba·ri·um /ˈbɛrɪəm; ˈbeəriəm/ *n* [U] a soft silvery-white metal 钡

barium meal /ˌ··· ˈ·/ *n* [U] *technical* a chemical substance that you drink before you have an X-RAY[1] (2)【术语】钡餐〔照X光前服用〕

bark[1] /bark; bɑːk/ *v* **1** [I] to make the short, loud sound that dogs and some other animals make〔狗等动物〕吠, 叫: **[+at]** *The dog always barks at strangers.* 这条狗见了陌生人就叫。**2** also 又作 **bark out** [T] to say something quickly in a loud voice 大声嚷, 吼叫: *"Listen up!" the teacher barked.* "听着!"老师吼道。**3 bark up the wrong tree** *informal* to have a wrong idea, especially about how to get a particular result【非正式】打错了主意; 认错了目标: *You're barking up the wrong tree if you think Sam can help you.* 你要是认为萨姆能够帮助你, 那你是找错了对象。**4 bark at the moon** *AmE informal* to worry and complain about something that you cannot change, and that is not very important【美, 非正式】狂犬吠月, 徒劳无功; 杞人忧天 **5** [T] to rub the skin off your knee, elbow etc by falling or knocking against something 擦破〔皮〕: *I stumbled, barking my shins painfully against the step.* 我绊倒在台阶上, 擦破了小腿的皮, 很痛。

bark[2] *n* [C,U] **1** the sharp, loud sound made by a dog 狗叫声 **2** the outer covering of a tree 树皮 **3** a loud sound or voice 响声; 吼叫声: *the bark of the guns* 枪炮声 **4 sb's bark is worse than their bite** used to say that although someone talks in an angry way they would not behave violently 嘴巴凶, 心不狠 **5** *literary* BARQUE【文】三桅[四桅、五桅]帆船

bar·keep·er /ˈbar,kipɚ; ˈbɑːˌkiːpə/ also 又作 **bar·keep** /ˈbar,kip; ˈbɑːkiːp/ *n* [C] *AmE* someone who serves drinks in a bar; BARTENDER【美】酒吧服务员

bark·er /ˈbarkɚ; ˈbɑːkə/ *n* [C] someone who stands outside a place at a CIRCUS (1), FAIR[3] etc shouting to people to come in〔在马戏场、集市等外面〕大声招揽顾客的人

bar·ley /ˈbarlɪ; ˈbɑːli/ *n* [U] a plant that produces a grain used for making food or alcohol 大麦

barley sug·ar /ˈ·· ,··/ *n* [C,U] *BrE* a hard sweet made of boiled sugar【英】麦芽糖

barley wine /ˌ·· ˈ·/ *n* [U] *BrE* a kind of very strong beer【英】大麦酒〔一种烈性啤酒〕

bar·maid /ˈbar,med; ˈbɑːmeɪd/ *n* [C] *BrE* a woman who serves drinks in a bar【英】酒吧女侍应

bar·man /ˈbarmən; ˈbɑːmən/ *n* [C] *BrE* a man who serves drinks in a bar【英】酒吧男侍应; BARTENDER *AmE*【美】

bar mitz·vah /ˌbar ˋmɪtsvə; ˌbɑː ˈmɪtsvə/ *n* [C] **1** the religious ceremony held when a Jewish boy reaches the age of 13 and is considered an adult in his religion〔为年满13周岁的犹太男孩进行的〕受诫礼 **2** a boy for whom this ceremony is held 犹太受诫男孩

barm·y /ˈbarmɪ; ˈbɑːmi/ *adj BrE informal* slightly crazy【英, 非正式】精神有些错乱的; 傻呵呵的

barn /barn; bɑːn/ *n* [C] **1** a large farm building for storing crops, or for keeping animals in 谷仓, 粮秣房, 仓库; 牲口棚 **2** *informal* a large, plain building【非正式】空荡荡的大房子: *a great barn of a house* 一所空荡荡的大房子

bar·na·cle /ˈbarnəkḷ; ˈbɑːnəkəl/ *n* [C] a small sea animal with a hard shell that sticks firmly to rocks and the bottom of boats 藤壶〔附在岩石、船底的甲壳类动物〕

Bar·nard /ˈbɑrnɑrd; ˈbɑːnɑːd/, **Chris·ti·aan** /ˈkrɪstɪən; ˈkrɪstiən/ (1922-2001) a South African doctor who in 1967 performed the first ever heart TRANSPLANT (=an operation to take a heart from someone who has just died and put it into a living person) 巴纳德〔(1922-2001)，南非医生，1967年主刀进行了首例心脏移植手术〕

Bar·nar·do's /bəˋnɑrdoz; bəˈnɑːdəʊz/ a British organization whose aim is to help children who have no parents or to help children whose parents are unable to take care of them 巴纳多斯之家〔英国一组织，旨在帮助孤儿或父母无力抚养的儿童〕

barn dance /ˈ· ·/ *n* [C] **1** a social event at which COUNTRY DANCING is performed 谷仓舞会〔社交集会，会上有乡村舞表演〕 **2** *BrE* a dance performed at this type of event【英】谷仓舞 —compare 比较 SQUARE DANCE

Barnes and No·ble /ˌbɑrnz ənd ˈnobl; ˌbɑːnz ənd ˈnəʊbəl/ *trademark* a US company that sells books【商标】巴诺公司〔美国一图书销售公司〕

bar·ney /ˈbɑrnɪ; ˈbɑːni/ *n* [C usually singular 一般用单数] *BrE informal* a noisy argument【英，非正式】吵吵嚷嚷，大吵大闹

barn·storm /ˈbɑrnˌstɔrm; ˈbɑːnstɔːm/ *v* [I] *AmE* to travel from place to place making short stops to give political speeches, theatre performances, or aircraft flying shows【美】巡回演讲；巡回演出；巡回飞行表演 —**barnstormer** *n* [C] —**barnstorming** *adj*

Bar·num /ˈbɑrnəm; ˈbɑːnəm/, **P.T.** (1810-91) a US businessman who started a CIRCUS called The Greatest Show on Earth, and later the Barnum and Bailey Circus 巴纳姆〔(1810-1891)，美国商人，曾创建了一个名为"人间绝技"的马戏团，后来还创建了巴纳姆和贝利马戏团〕

barn·yard /ˈbɑrnˌjɑrd; ˈbɑːnjɑːd/ *n* [C] **1** a space surrounded by farm buildings; FARMYARD 谷仓场院，农家粮仓旁的院子 **2 barnyard humor** *AmE* humour that is slightly rude【美】粗俗的幽默

ba·rom·e·ter /bəˈrɑmətɚ; bəˈrɒmɪtə/ *n* [C] **1** an instrument for measuring changes in the air pressure and weather or calculating height above sea level 气压计，晴雨表 **2** something that shows or gives an idea of changes that are happening 能显示变化的事物；〔舆论的〕晴雨表；变化的标记：*Infant mortality is a highly sensitive barometer of social conditions.* 婴儿死亡率是反映社会状况的一个非常敏感的晴雨表。—**barometric** /ˌbærəˈmɛtrɪk; ˌbærəˈmetrɪk◂/ *adj* —**barometrically** /-klɪ; -kli/ *adv*

bar·on /ˈbærən; ˈbærən/ *n* [C] **1** a man who is a member of the lowest rank of the British NOBILITY (1) or of a rank of European NOBILITY (1) 男爵〔英国贵族中爵位最低者或欧洲贵族的一个等级〕 **2** a businessman with a lot of power or influence〔工商业〕巨头，大王：*conservative press barons like Beaverbrook* 像比弗布鲁克这样的保守派报业大王 | *Pakistani and Colombian drug barons* 巴基斯坦和哥伦比亚的大毒枭 —see also 另见 ROBBER BARON

bar·on·ess /ˈbærənɪs; ˈbærənɪs/ *n* **1** [C] a woman who is a member of the lowest rank of the British NOBILITY (1)〔英国的〕女男爵 **2** the wife of a baron 男爵夫人

bar·on·et /ˈbærənɪt; ˈbærənɪt/ *n* [C] a British KNIGHT[1] (2) lower in rank than a baron, whose title passes on to his son when he dies 准男爵〔英国最低的世袭爵位，但不是贵族〕

bar·on·et·cy /ˈbærənɪtsɪ; ˈbærənɪtsi/ *n* [C] the rank of a baronet 准男爵爵位

ba·ro·ni·al /bəˈronɪəl; bəˈrəʊniəl/ *adj* **1** a baronial room is very large and richly decorated 富丽堂皇的 **2** belonging to or involving BARONS (1) 男爵的；与男爵有关的

bar·on·y /ˈbærənɪ; ˈbærəni/ *n* [C] the rank of BARON (1) 男爵爵位

ba·roque /bəˈrok; bəˈrɒk/ *adj* **1** belonging to the very decorated style of art, music, buildings etc, that was common in Europe in the 17th century 巴洛克风格的〔17世纪时在欧洲流行的一种华丽的风格，尤见于艺术、音乐及建筑等方面〕：*elaborate baroque facades* 精心建造的具有巴洛克风格的大厦正面 **2** very detailed and complicated 精雕细琢的 —**baroque** *n* [singular]

barque /bɑrk; bɑːk/ *n* [C] a sailing ship with three, four, or five MASTS (=poles that the sails are fixed to) 三桅[四桅、五桅]帆船

bar·rack /ˈbærək; ˈbærək/ *v* [I,T] **1** *BrE* to interrupt someone by shouting, sometimes pretending that you agree with them【英】(对…)起哄；喝倒彩：*The minister was repeatedly barracked during his speech.* 部长在讲话时多次被喝倒彩。**2** *AustrE* to shout to show that you support somone or something【澳】呐喊助威

bar·racks /ˈbærəks; ˈbærəks/ *n* [plural] a group of buildings in which soldiers live 兵营，营房

bar·ra·cu·da /ˌbærəˋkudə; ˌbærəˈkjuːdə/ *n* [C] a large tropical fish that eats flesh 梭子鱼〔大型热带食肉海鱼〕

bar·rage¹ /bəˈrɑʒ; ˈbærɑːʒ/ *n* **1** [C usually singular 一般用单数] the continuous firing of guns, especially large heavy guns, to protect soldiers as they move toward an enemy 掩护炮火：*a barrage of anti-aircraft fire* 高射炮火网 **2** [singular] a lot of questions, comments etc, that are said at the same time or very quickly after each other 连珠炮似的问题[评论等]：[+of] *Despite facing a barrage of criticism, Mr Rees pressed ahead with plans for Theatre Clwyd.* 尽管面对连珠炮似的批评，里斯先生还是加紧推行建造克卢伊德剧院的计划。

bar·rage² /ˈbɑrɪdʒ; ˈbærɑːʒ/ *n* [C] a wall of earth, stones etc built across a river to provide water for farming or to prevent flooding 拦河坝，堰堤

barrage bal·loon /ˈ· · ·ˌ·/ *n* [C] a large bag that floats in the air to prevent enemy planes from flying near the ground〔阻止敌机低飞的〕阻拦气球，阻塞气球

barred /bɑrd; bɑːd/ *adj* **1** a barred window, gate etc has bars across it〔门、窗等〕装有铁栅的，上了闩的 **2** *formal* having bands of different colours【正式】有不同颜色条纹的：*red barred tail feathers* 有红色条纹的尾羽 —see also 另见 BAR

bar·rel¹ /ˈbærəl; ˈbærəl/ *n* [C] **1** a large curved container with a flat top and bottom, made of wood or metal〔中间鼓起的〕桶：*barrels of beer* 几桶啤酒 —see picture at 参见 CONTAINER 图 **2** also 又作 **barrelful** the amount of liquid that a barrel contains, used especially as a measure of oil 一桶之量：*Oil was $30 a barrel.* 石油每桶30美元。**3** the part of a gun that the bullets are fired through 枪[炮]管 —see picture at 参见 GUN[1] 图 **4 have sb over a barrel** to put someone in a situation in which they are forced to accept or do what you want 使某人处于被动[不利]的地位：*The manager had us over a barrel – either we worked on a Saturday or we lost our jobs.* 经理迫使我们作出选择，要么星期六工作，要么失去工作。**5 be a barrel of laughs** [often in negatives 常用于否定句] to be very enjoyable 很好玩：*The meeting wasn't exactly a barrel of laughs.* 那会议其实没什么意思。—see also 另见 PORK BARREL, **scrape (the bottom of) the barrel** (SCRAPE[1] (6)), **lock, stock, and barrel** (LOCK[2] (3)) 3

barrel² *v* **barreled, barreling** [I] *AmE informal* to move very fast, especially in an uncontrolled way【美，非正式】飞奔；高速行驶：*He barreled down the road at 100 miles an hour.* 他以每小时100英里的速度在公路上疾驶。

barrel-chest·ed /ˌ· ·ˈ· ·◂/ *adj* a man who is barrel-chested has round chest that sticks out〔男性〕胸部厚实发达的

barrel or·gan /ˈ· · ˌ· ·/ *n* [C] a musical instrument that you play by turning a handle, used especially in former times 手摇风琴〔尤在旧时使用〕

bar·ren /ˈbærən; ˈbærən/ *adj* **1** land or soil that is barren has no plants growing on it 贫瘠的，荒芜的：*a barren mountainous area* 土地贫瘠的山区 **2** *old use* a woman or a female animal who is barren cannot produce children or baby animals; INFERTILE (2)【旧】〔妇女或雌性动物〕不孕的，不生育的 **3** a tree or plant that is barren does not produce fruit or seeds 不结果实的，不结籽的 **4** *literary* without any useful results【文】无用的；无效果的：*a pointless and barren discussion* 毫无意义、没有任何结果的讨论

bar·rette /bəˈrɛt; bæˈret/ *n* [C] *AmE* a small metal or plastic object used to keep a woman's hair in place【美】〔女用〕发夹；HAIR SLIDE *BrE*【英】

bar·ri·cade¹ /ˈbærəˌked; ˈbærɪkeɪd/ *n* [C] a temporary wall or fence across a road, door etc that prevents people from going through〔临时的〕路障；街垒：*Soldiers fired over the barricades at the rebels.* 士兵们在路障后边朝叛乱分子开火。

barricade² *v* [T] to protect or close something by building a barricade 设路障于；以障碍物阻塞：*Terrorists had barricaded themselves inside the embassy.* 恐怖分子在使馆内筑起工事固守。

Bar·rie /ˈbærɪ; ˈbæri/, **J.M.** (1860-1937) a Scottish writer of plays and NOVELS, famous for his children's story *Peter Pan* 巴里〔(1860-1937)，苏格兰剧作家、小说家，以其创作的儿童剧《彼得·潘》而闻名〕

bar·ri·er /ˈbærɪɚ; ˈbæriə/ *n* [C] **1** a type of fence or gate that prevents people from moving in a particular direction 障碍物；栅栏；关卡：*Crowds burst through the barriers and ran onto the pitch.* 人群冲破栅栏跑进球场。**2** a rule, problem etc that prevents people from doing something, or limits what they can do〔阻止或妨碍人们做事的〕障碍：*an attempt to break down trade barriers* 打破贸易壁垒的尝试 | [+to] *a psychological barrier to success* 阻碍成功的心理障碍 | **language barrier** (=inability 3

to talk to someone because you speak a different language) 语言障碍 **3** a physical object that keeps two areas, people etc apart 屏障: **[+between]** *The mountains form a natural barrier between the two countries.* 群山构成了两国之间的天然屏障。**4 the 10 second/40% etc barrier** a level or amount of 10 seconds, 40% etc, that is seen as a limit which it is difficult to get beyond〔难以超越的〕10秒/40%等难关: *Sprint runners had by then broken the 10 second barrier.* 短跑运动员那时已经突破了10秒大关。—see also 另见 SOUND BARRIER

barrier reef /ˌ· · · ˈ·/ *n* [C] a line of CORAL (=pink stone-like substance) separated from the shore by water 堡礁, 堤礁

bar·ring /ˈbɑrɪŋ; ˈbɑːrɪŋ/ *prep* unless there are 除非, 除了…以外: *Barring any last minute problems, we should finish the job tonight.* 除非最后一分钟出问题, 否则我们今晚应该完成工作。

bar·ri·o /ˈbɑrɪo; ˈbæriəʊ/ *n* [C] *AmE* a part of an American town or city where many poor, Spanish-speaking people live【美】美国城镇中说西班牙语的人集居的贫民区

bar·ris·ter /ˈbærɪstə; ˈbærɪstə/ *n* [C] a lawyer in Britain who can argue cases in the higher law courts〔英国有资格在高等法院出庭的〕讼务律师, 大律师 — compare 比较 SOLICITOR —see 见 LAWYER (USAGE)

bar·row /ˈbæro; ˈbærəʊ/ *n* [C] **1** a small vehicle like a box on wheels, from which fruits, vegetables etc used to be sold〔流动商贩用的二轮或四轮〕手推车 **2** a large pile of earth like a small hill that was put over an important grave in ancient times 古冢, 古墓 **3** a WHEELBARROW 独轮手推车

Barrow, Clyde —see 见 BONNIE AND CLYDE

barrow boy /ˈ· · ·/ *n* [C] *BrE* a man or boy who sells fruit, vegetables etc from a barrow【英】推车售货的男小贩

BART /bɑrt; bɑːt/ *n* Bay Area Rapid Transit; a railway system in the area around the San Francisco Bay, with tracks that go under the ground 湾区捷运系统〔环圣弗朗西斯科海湾地区的地铁系统〕

Bart /bɑrt; bɑːt/ the written abbreviation of 缩写= BARONET

bar·tend·er /ˈbɑrˌtɛndə; ˈbɑːˌtendə/ *n* [C] *AmE* someone who makes, pours, and serves drinks in a bar or restaurant【美】酒吧男侍; 酒保; BARMAN *BrE*【英】

bar·ter¹ /ˈbɑrtə; ˈbɑːtə/ *v* [I,T] to exchange goods, work, or services for other goods or services rather than for money 易货贸易; 物物交换, 以物易物: **barter (with sb) for sth** *I had to barter with the locals for food.* 我只得和当地人换点食物。| **barter sth for sth** *They bartered farm products for machinery.* 他们拿农产品换机器。

barter² *n* [U] **1** a system of exchanging goods and services for other goods and services rather than using money 易货贸易, 以货易货: *an economy based on barter* 以易货贸易为基础的经济 **2** goods or services that are exchanged in this kind of system 易货贸易中的商品[服务]: *Beads were used as barter in the early days of settlement.* 移民初期曾用念珠作为交换物。

Bartók /ˈbɑrtok; ˈbɑːtɒk/, **Béla** (1881-1945) a Hungarian COMPOSER known for using FOLK music in the music he wrote. Two of his best known works are *Concerto for Orchestra* and *The Miraculous Mandarin*. 巴尔托克〔(1881-1945), 匈牙利作曲家。他在音乐作品中运用了民间音乐, 并因此而著称。最著名的两部作品是《乐队协奏曲》和《神奇的官人》〕

Bar·ton /ˈbɑrtn; ˈbɑːtn/, **Cla·ra** /ˈklɛrə; ˈkleərə/ (1821-1912) a US nurse who worked in army camps during the American Civil War and the Franco-Prussian War. She started the American Red Cross in 1881. 巴顿〔(1821-1912), 美国护士, 美国南北战争、普法战争期间曾在军营工作, 1881年创立了美国红十字会〕

Bart's /bɑrts; bɑːts/ an informal name for St Bartholomew's Hospital, which is a very old and famous hospital in London 巴特斯医院〔圣巴塞洛缪医院的非正式称呼, 伦敦一家历史悠久的著名医院〕

Ba·rysh·ni·kov /bəˈrɪʃnɪkɔf; bəˈrɪʃnɪkɒf/, **Mi·khail** /mɪˈkaɪl; mɪˈkaɪl/ (1948-) a Russian BALLET dancer and CHOREOGRAPHER (=someone who decides what movements dancers will do to a piece of music) who left the Soviet Union and came to live in the US 巴里什尼科夫〔(1948-), 俄罗斯芭蕾舞演员、编导, 后来离开前苏联, 定居美国〕

bas·alt /bəˈsɔlt; ˈbæsɔːlt/ *n* [U] a type of dark green-black rock 玄武岩

S1 W1 **base¹** /bes; beɪs/ *v* [T] to establish or use somewhere as the main place for your business or work 把基地设在…, 以…为基地: *a Denver-based law firm* 总部设在丹佛的法律事务所

base sth **on/upon** sth *phr v* [T often passive 常用被动态] to use particular information or facts as a point from which to develop an idea, plan etc 以…为基础, 以…为根据: *The film is based on a novel by Sinclair Lewis.* 该影片是根据辛克莱·刘易斯的小说改编的。

base² *n* S2 W2

1 ▶LOWEST PART 最低的部分◀ [C usually singular 一般用单数] the lowest part of something, or the surface at the bottom of something 底部; 根基; 基础: **[+of]** *There was a chip in the base of the glass.* 玻璃杯底部有个裂口。| *the base of a triangle* 三角形的底边 | *Waves crashed and pounded at the base of the cliff.* 海浪冲击拍打着悬崖的底部。

2 ▶KNOWLEDGE/IDEAS 知识/想法◀ [C] the most important part of something from which new ideas develop〔思想〕基础: *India has a good scientific research base.* 印度有良好的科研基础。| *This provides a good base for the development of new techniques.* 这为新技术的发展提供了良好的基础。

3 ▶COMPANY/ORGANIZATION 公司/组织◀ [C, U] the main place from which a group, company, or organization controls its activities 基地, 根据地, 总部: *Cuba was seen as a base for Communist activity throughout Latin America.* 古巴被视为整个拉丁美洲共产主义活动的基地。| *Report back to base as soon as you see anything.* 发现任何情况立即向总部报告。

4 ▶MILITARY 军事◀ [C] a place where people in a military organization live and work〔军事〕基地: *a naval base* 海军基地

5 ▶PEOPLE/GROUPS 人群◀ [C usually singular 一般用单数] the people, money, groups etc from which a lot of support or power comes〔人、经济等的〕基础, 支柱: *an attempt to strengthen the city's economic base* 加强城市经济基础的努力 | **tax/customer base** (=all the people who pay tax or buy goods in a particular place) 税收/顾客基础 *A reputation for excellent service will expand our customer base.* 优质服务的信誉能扩大我们的顾客基础。| **manufacturing base** (=all the factories, companies etc that produce goods in a country) 生产基础 *The country's manufacturing base has shrunk by 20% during the recession.* 在经济衰退的时候, 该国的制造业基地缩减了20%。—see also 另见 POWER BASE

6 ▶SUBSTANCE/MIXTURE 物质/混合物◀ [singular, U] the main part of a substance to which something else is later added 基础成分, 主要成分: *paint with an oil base* 以油脂为主要成分的颜料

7 ▶BODY/PLANT 身体/植物◀ [C usually singular 一般用单数] the point where part of your body or part of a plant joins with the rest 基部; 连接处: *She had a dull ache at the base of her neck.* 她的脖子根部有点隐隐作痛。

8 ▶SPORT 体育◀ [C] one of the four places that a player must touch in order to get a point in games such as BASEBALL〔棒球等的〕垒

9 be off base *AmE informal* to be completely wrong【美, 非正式】完全错误, 大错特错: *His estimate for painting the kitchen seems way off base.* 他对粉刷厨房的估计似乎差得太远了。

10 ▶CHEMISTRY 化学◀ [C] *technical* a chemical substance that combines with an acid to form a SALT¹ (4)【术语】碱, 盐基

11 ▶NUMBERS 数目◀ [C usually singular 一般用单数] *technical* the number in relation to which a number system or mathematical table is built up【术语】基数

12 touch base (with sb) to telephone someone who you live or work with, or make a short visit, while you are spending time somewhere else〔跟某人〕联系上 —see also 另见 **cover (all) the bases** (COVER¹ (13))

base³ *adj literary* not having good moral principles【文】卑鄙的, 下流的, 无耻的: *base passions* 庸俗的激情 —see also 另见 BASE METAL

base·ball /ˈbesˌbɔl; ˈbeɪsbɔːl/ *n* **1** [U] an outdoor game between two teams of nine players, in which players try to get points by hitting a ball and running around four bases (BASE² (8)) 棒球运动 —see picture on page A22 参见A22页图 **2** [C] the ball used in this game 棒球

CULTURAL NOTE 文化注释

Baseball is one of the most popular sports in the US, and the professional baseball season lasts from April to September. The professional baseball teams are known together as the Major Leagues and they are divided into two groups called the AL (= American League) and the NL (= National League). Both the AL and NL have three DIVISIONS (=groups of teams). These divisions compete with each other during the season, and the winners from each division compete against each other in the POSTSEASON games (=games after the official season ends). The winner of the American League Championship then plays against the winner of the National League Championship

in games called the World Series. Many people in the US watch baseball games on television or listen to them on the radio. Some people are very serious about supporting their favourite teams, but people go to the games as a social event. Because baseball is so popular, people in the US often call it the national PASTIME. 棒球是美国最受欢迎的运动之一，职业棒球的赛季从4月持续到9月。职业棒球队总称大联盟，分为两种，分别叫做美国棒球联盟和全国棒球联盟，两大联盟又各分为三个分组。赛季开始后，各组球队彼此较量，每组胜者又在季后赛中一较高下。接下来，美国棒球联盟锦标赛的胜者挑战全国棒球联盟锦标赛的胜者，两者的比赛叫做世界职业棒球锦标赛。很多美国人在电视上观看或在广播里收听棒球比赛，有些人极为认真地支持自己喜欢的球队。不过，美国人把去现场观看比赛看做一种社交活动。因为棒球如此流行，美国人常把棒球称为全民消遣活动。

baseball cap /ˈ· ·, ·/ *n* [C] a hat that fits closely around your head with a round part that sticks out at the front 棒球帽 —see picture at 参见 CAP[1] 图

base·board /ˈbesˌbɔrd; ˈbeɪsbɔːd/ *n* [C] *AmE* a narrow board fixed to the bottom of indoor walls where they meet the floor【美】〔地板与墙壁相接处的〕踢脚板，壁脚板；SKIRTING BOARD *BrE*【英】

Ba·sel /ˈbɑzl; ˈbɑːzəl/ also 又作 **Basle** the second largest city in northern Switzerland, on the River Rhine 巴塞尔〔瑞士北部第二大城市，位于莱茵河畔〕

base·less /ˈbeslɪs; ˈbeɪsləs/ *adj formal* not based on facts or good reasons【正式】无根据的；无缘无故的：*baseless accusations* 毫无根据的指控

base·line /ˈbesˌlaɪn; ˈbeɪslaɪn/ *n* **1** [C usually singular 一般用单数] *technical* a standard measurement or fact to which other measurements or facts are compared, especially in medicine or science【术语】〔尤指医学或科学中的〕基线，准线 **2** the line at the back of the court in games such as tennis or VOLLEYBALL〔网球场、排球场等的〕底线 —see picture at 参见 TENNIS 图 **3** the area that a player must run in on a BASEBALL field〔棒球场的〕垒线

base·ment /ˈbesmənt; ˈbeɪsmənt/ *n* [C] a room or area that is under the level of the ground 地下室；地库 —see picture on page A4 参见 A4 页图

base met·al /ˌ· ˈ· ·/ *n* [C,U] a metal that is not very valuable, such as iron or lead 普通金属〈如铁、铅等〉—compare 比较 NOBLE[1] (4)

base rate /ˈ· ·/ *n* [C] the standard rate of INTEREST[1] (4) on which a bank bases its charges 基本利率 —compare 比较 PRIME RATE

bas·es /ˈbesiz; ˈbeɪsiːz/ the plural of BASIS

bash[1] /bæʃ; bæʃ/ *v* [I,T] *informal*【非正式】**1** to hit someone or something hard, in a way that causes pain or damage 猛击，猛撞；击碎；打伤：**bash sth on/against** *I bashed my toe against the door.* 我的脚趾头撞到了门上。| [+ **into/against**] *Jay bashed into a table in the dark.* 杰伊在黑暗中撞到了桌子。| **bash down/in/up etc** (=destroy something by hitting it often) 砸破，打碎等 *Police bashed down the door to get in.* 警察破门而入。**2 union/government etc bashing** *BrE* strong criticism of unions, the government etc【英】猛烈抨击工会/政府等 **3** to physically attack a type of person that you do not like 痛打〔某一类人〕：*gay bashing* 痛打同性恋者 —see also 另见 SQUARE-BASHING, **bible basher** (BIBLE (4))

bash away at sth *phr v* [T] *BrE informal* to continue working hard at something【英，非正式】一直努力地做着〔某事〕：*I've been bashing away at this essay for hours.* 这篇文章我已经写了好几个小时了。

bash on sth *phr v* [I,T + **with**] *BrE informal* to continue working in order to finish something【英，非正式】继续努力工作：*Well, better bash on.* 嗯，最好继续努力。

bash[2] *n* [C] **1** *informal* a hard strong hit【非正式】猛击，痛打：*I gave him a bash on the nose.* 我朝他的鼻子猛击了一拳。**2** *informal* a party or celebration【非正式】热闹的聚会；痛快的玩乐，狂欢：*a birthday bash* 生日聚会 **3 have a bash** *BrE spoken* to try to do something, especially when you are not sure that you will succeed【英口】试试看：[+ **at**] *Why not have a bash at windsurfing?* 为什么不尝试一下风帆冲浪？

bash·ful /ˈbæʃfəl; ˈbæʃfəl/ *adj* easily embarrassed in social situations; shy 腼腆的，害羞的，忸怩的：*a bashful smile* 腼腆的一笑 | *Many men are still bashful about discussing their feelings.* 很多男人在谈论自己的感受时还是觉得难为情。—**bashfully** *adv* —**bashfulness** *n* [U]

Ba·sic /ˈbesɪk; ˈbeɪsɪk/ *n* [U] a commonly used computer language〔电脑的〕Basic 程序语言，初学者通用符号指令

basic *adj* **1** forming the main or most necessary part of something 基础的，基本的，根本的：*a meeting to discuss the basic structure of the department* 一个讨论部门基本结构的会议 | *the basic principles of mathematics* 数学的基本原理 **2** at the simplest or least developed level 最简单的，最初级的：*My knowledge of German is pretty basic.* 我所掌握的德语知识是相当初级的。| *The farm lacks even basic equipment.* 这个农场连最基本的设备都没有。**3 basic salary/pay etc** the amount of money that you are paid before any special payments are added 基本工资/底薪等 **4** [only before noun 仅用于名词前] basic desires, rights etc, are ones that everyone has 最基本的，起码的：*Basic human rights are still denied in many countries.* 许多国家的人民连最基本的人权都没有。—see also 另见 BASICS

ba·sic·ally /ˈbesɪklɪ; ˈbeɪsɪkli/ *adv* **1** [sentence adverb 句子副词] *spoken* used when giving the most important reason or fact about something, or a simple explanation of something【口】基本上，本质上，从根本上讲：*Basically, I just don't have enough money.* 基本上，我就是没有足够的钱。| *Well, basically, it's a matter of filling in a few forms.* 其实也就是填几张表的事。**2** in the main or most important ways, without considering additional details or differences 基本地，基本上：*The two structures are basically the same.* 这两种结构基本相同。| *He's basically a nice guy.* 他基本上是个好人。**3** in a very simple way, with only the things that are completely necessary 简单地，初步地：*The office was very basically equipped.* 这办公室的陈设很简陋。

ba·sics /ˈbesɪks; ˈbeɪsɪks/ *n* [plural] the most important and necessary facts about something, from which other possibilities and ideas may develop 基础；基本原则：*Once you know the basics, you can start experimenting with different methods.* 你一旦掌握了基本原则，就可以用各种不同的方法开始试验。| **the basics of** *I learned the basics of first aid on a weekend course.* 我在一个周末班上学会了急救的基本知识。

basic train·ing /ˌ· ˈ· ·/ *n* [U] the period when a new soldier learns military rules and does a lot of exercise〔新兵入伍后的〕基本训练

Ba·sie /ˈbesɪ; ˈbeɪsi/, **Count** (1904-84) a US JAZZ musician who played the piano, and led one of the most famous bands to play SWING (=jazz music of the 1930s and 40s) 巴锡〔(1904-1984)，美国爵士音乐家。他演奏钢琴，是当时最著名的一支摇摆乐乐队的领衔人物〕

bas·il /ˈbæzl; ˈbæzəl/ *n* [U] a sweet-smelling HERB used in cooking 罗勒〔一种带香味，可用于烹调的植物〕

ba·sil·i·ca /bəˋsɪlɪkə; bəˈsɪlɪkə/ *n* [C] a church in the shape of a long room with a round end 长方形廊柱大厅式教堂：*the basilica of St Peter's* 圣彼得大教堂

bas·i·lisk /ˈbæsəˌlɪsk; ˈbæsɪlɪsk/ *n* [C] an imaginary animal like a snake in ancient stories, supposed to be able to kill people by looking at them 蛇怪〔传说中的蛇状怪物，据说其目光能使人丧命〕

ba·sin /ˈbesn̩; ˈbeɪsən/ *n* [C] **1** *BrE* a round container fixed to the wall in a bathroom where you wash your hands and face; SINK[2] (2)【英】洗脸盆 **2** *BrE* a bowl for liquids or food【英】盆；大碗：*Pour the sauce into a basin.* 把调味汁倒入碗中。**3** also 又作 **ba·sin·ful** /ˈbesn̩ful; ˈbeɪsənfʊl/ the amount of liquid that a basin can contain 一盆[一碗]之量：*a basin of hot water* 一盆热水 **4** a bowl-shaped area containing water 水洼；贮水池：*Water splashed in the basin of the fountain.* 喷泉的水池水花四溅。**5** an area of land from which water runs down into a river 流域；盆地；低洼地：*the Amazon basin* 亚马孙河流域 —see also 另见 PUDDING BASIN (1)

Basin Street /ˈ· ·, ·/ a street in New Orleans in the US where JAZZ music originally became popular 贝辛街〔美国新奥尔良市的一条街道，是最早流行爵士乐的地方〕

ba·sis /ˈbesɪs; ˈbeɪsɪs/ *n plural* **bases** /-siz; -siːz/ [C] **1** the facts or ideas from which something can be developed 基础；根据；基本原理：*Their claim had no basis in fact.* 他们的主张并没有任何事实根据。| [+ **for**] *The video will provide a basis for class discussion.* 录像将为课堂讨论提供基本内容。| [+ **of**] *a lecture series that later formed the basis of a new book* 后来成了一本新书的基础的一系列讲座 **2 on the basis of** because of a particular fact or situation 在…的基础上；根据…：*Employers are not allowed to discriminate on the basis of sex.* 雇主不允许有性别歧视。**3 on a daily/weekly etc basis** every day, week etc 按天/周等计算：*All rooms are cleaned on a daily basis.* 所有房间都是每天打扫一次。**4 on a voluntary/part-time etc basis** a system or agreement by which someone or something is VOLUN-

TARY[1] etc 自愿性质/以兼职的形式等: *The machine has been installed on a trial basis.* 这台机器的安装是实验性的。

bask /bæsk; bɑːsk/ *v* [I] **1** to enjoy sitting or lying in the heat of the sun or a fire〔舒适地〕晒太阳; 取暖: [+in] *A lizard was basking in the heat of the afternoon sun.* 一条蜥蜴正在享受下午的阳光浴。**2** to enjoy the approval or attention that you are getting from other people 沉浸在〔别人的赞许中〕: [+in] *She basked in the admiration of her family and friends.* 她沉浸在家人和朋友的赞赏中。—see also 另见 **bask/bathe in sb's reflected glory** (GLORY[1] (4))

Baskervilles —see 见 The HOUND OF THE BASKERVILLES

baskets 篮子; 篓子; 筐子

3 **bas·ket** /ˈbæskɪt; ˈbɑːskɪ̈t/ *n* [C] **1** a container made of thin pieces of plastic, wire, or wood woven together, used to carry things or put things in 篮子; 篓子; 筐子: *a shopping basket* 购物篮 | **clothes/laundry basket** (=for putting dirty clothes in) 洗衣篮 **2** a net with a hole at the bottom hung from a metal ring, through which the ball is thrown in BASKETBALL〔篮球运动的〕篮: **make/shoot a basket** (=get a point in the game) 投篮得分 —see also 另见 **put all your eggs in one basket** (EGG[1] (5)), WASTEPAPER BASKET —see picture on page A22 参见 A22 页图

3 2 **bas·ket·ball** /ˈbæskɪtˌbɔl; ˈbɑːskɪ̈tbɔːl/ *n* [U] a game played indoors between two teams of five players, in which each team tries to win points by throwing a ball through a net, or the ball used in this game 篮球(运动) —see picture on page A22 参见 A22 页图

CULTURAL NOTE 文化注释

Basketball is one of the most popular sports in the US. Many people play and watch basketball games. Most parks have places to play basketball, and people often go there to play in a PICK-UP GAME (=an informal game played by anyone who wants to play when the game is starting). Many people have a basketball net at their homes, as well. Basketball is an important sport in HIGH SCHOOL, and most schools have both girls' and boys' teams that compete against teams from other schools. The best players are RECRUIT*ed* to play on college teams. Many men's college games and some women's college games are shown on television and are watched by large numbers of people. There are professional teams for both women and men: the women's teams play against each other in the WNBA (=Women's National Basketball Association), and the men's teams play in the NBA (=National Basketball Association). 篮球是最受美国人喜爱的运动之一。很多人打篮球，观看篮球比赛。大部分公园都有篮球场，人们常去那里打篮球，随来随玩。很多家庭里还安有篮筐。篮球是高中的重要体育运动，大多数学校均有男队和女队，与其他学校的球队比赛。优秀球员获选进入大学校队。许多大学男队比赛和一些大学女队比赛在电视上播出，观看者甚多。男女均另有职业球队，女队在"全国女子篮球协会"内比赛，男队在"全国篮球协会"内比赛。

basket-case /ˈ· · ·/ *n* [C] *informal* someone who is so nervous or anxious that they cannot deal with simple situations【非正式】遇到点小事就紧张[焦虑]的人

bas·ket·ry /ˈbæskɪtrɪ; ˈbɑːskɪ̈tri/ also 又作 **bas·ket·work** /ˈbæskɪtˌwɜk; ˈbɑːskɪ̈twɜːk/ *n* [U] **1** baskets or other objects made by weaving together thin dried branches 篮筐类〔总称〕 **2** the skill of making baskets 编制篮筐的技艺

Basle /bɑl; bɑːl/ another spelling of BASEL Basel 的另一种拼法

Basque /bæsk; bæsk/ *n* **1** [C] a person from the mountainous area between southern France and northern Spain 巴斯克人〔法国南部与西班牙北部之间山区的居民〕 **2** [U] the language of the Basques 巴斯克语 —**Basque** *adj*: *Basque separatists* (=people who want the Basque area to become a separate state) 巴斯克分离主义者

basque /bæsk; bæsk/ *n* [C] a piece of underwear for a woman that covers her from under her arms to the top of her legs 巴斯克衫〔一种长过腰部的女士紧身内衣〕

bas-re·lief /ˌbɑ rɪˈlif; ˌbɑː rɪˈliːf/ *n* [C,U] *technical* a style of art in which stone or wood is cut so that shapes are raised above the surrounding surface【术语】浅浮雕(作品) —compare 比较 HIGH RELIEF

bass[1] /bes; beɪs/ *n* **1** [C] a man whose singing or speaking voice is very low 男低音(歌手) **2** [singular] the part of a piece of music that this person sings 男低音部 **3** [U] the lower half of the whole range of musical notes〔乐谱的〕低音部 —compare 比较 TREBLE[3] (1) **4** [C] a BASS GUITAR 低音吉他: **on bass** (=playing the bass guitar) 弹低音吉他 *The band features Willie Dixon on bass.* 这个乐队由威利·狄克逊弹低音吉他。**5** [C] a DOUBLE BASS 低音提琴 —**bass** *adj* —**bass** *adv*

bass[2] /bæs; bæs/ *n plural* **bass** *or* **basses** [C] a fish that can be eaten and lives both in rivers and the sea 鲈鱼

bass clef /ˌbes ˈklɛf; ˌbeɪs ˈklef/ *n* [C] a sign (𝄢) at the beginning of a line of written music that shows that the top line of the STAVE[1] (1) is the A below MIDDLE C 低音谱号 —see picture at 参见 MUSIC 图

bas·set /ˈbæsɪt; ˈbæsɪ̈t/ also 又作 **basset hound** /ˈ· · ·/ *n* [C] a dog with short legs and long ears used for hunting 巴吉度猎犬〔一种腿短、耳长的猎犬〕

bass gui·tar /ˌbes gɪˈtɑr; ˌbeɪs gɪˈtɑː/ also 又作 **bass** *n* [C] an electric musical instrument with six strings and a long neck, that plays low notes 低音(电)吉他

bas·si·net /ˌbæsəˈnɛt; ˌbæsɪ̈ˈnet/ *n* [C] *AmE* a small bed that looks like a basket for a young baby【美】(婴儿)摇篮; 〔有篷盖的〕婴儿车

bas·sist /ˈbesɪst; ˈbeɪsɪ̈st/ *n* [C] someone who plays a BASS GUITAR or a DOUBLE BASS 低音吉他手; 低音提琴手

bas·soon /bəˈsun; bəˈsuːn/ *n* [C] a very long wooden musical instrument with a low sound, that is held upright and played by blowing into a thin curved metal pipe 巴松管, 低音管

bas·tard /ˈbæstərd; ˈbɑːstəd/ *n* [C] **1** *slang* an offensive word for someone, especially a man, who you think is unpleasant【俚】讨厌鬼, 臭小子, 坏蛋, 杂种〔冒犯用语〕: *The bastard went and told the police!* 那臭小子去报告了警察! **2** *spoken* an insulting or joking word for a man【口】家伙〔对男子的蔑称或戏称〕: *The poor bastard's been sacked!* 那倒霉的家伙被解雇了! | *You lucky bastard!* 你这家伙真幸运! **3** *BrE spoken* something that causes difficulties or problems【英口】难事, 麻烦事: *This pan is a bastard to clean.* 这锅刷起来真麻烦。**4** *old-fashioned* someone whose parents were not married when they were born【过时】私生子 3

bas·tard·ize also 又作 **-ise** *BrE*【英】/ˈbæstərˌdaɪz; ˈbɑːstədaɪz/ *v* [T] to spoil something by changing its good parts 使变低劣; 使不实: *a bastardized version of the play* 该戏剧粗劣的改编本

bas·tard·y /ˈbæstərdɪ; ˈbɑːstədi/ *n* [U] *old use* the situation of having parents who were not married to each other when you were born【旧】私生子身份

baste /best; beɪst/ *v* [I,T] **1** to pour liquid or melted fat over meat that is cooking〔烹调时〕在(肉上)浇涂油脂 **2** to fasten

cloth with long loose stitches, in order to hold it together so that you can SEW it properly later 用长针脚疏缝，粗缝

Bas·tille, the /bæˈstil; bæˈstiːl/ an old prison in Paris, attacked and destroyed on 14 July 1789 during the French REVOLUTION. This date is now celebrated each year as a French national holiday, **Bastille Day**. 巴士底狱〔巴黎的一座古老监狱，1789年7月14日法国大革命期间被攻破。这个日子现为法国国庆日，即巴士底日〕

B

bas·ti·on /ˈbæstʃən; ˈbæstiən/ *n* [C] **1** something that protects a way of life, principle etc that seems likely to change or disappear 堡垒〔指固守一种生活方式、准则等的事物〕: [+of] *These clubs are the last bastions of male privilege.* 这些俱乐部是男人特权的最后堡垒。**2** a place where a country or army has strong military defences 设防地区，防卫据点: *Pearl Harbor was the principal American bastion in the Pacific.* 珍珠港曾是美国在太平洋的重要军事基地。**3** *technical* a part of a castle wall that sticks out from the rest【术语】棱堡〔城堡和堡垒的突出部分〕

3 **bat¹** /bæt; bæt/ *n* [C]

1 ►ANIMAL 动物◄ a small animal like a mouse that flies around at night 蝙蝠 —see also 另见 FRUIT BAT

2 ►SPORT 体育◄ a) a long wooden stick with a special shape that is used in some sports and games 球棒: *a baseball bat* 棒球棒 **b)** *BrE* a round flat piece of wood with a handle, used to hit a ball in TABLE TENNIS【英】〔乒乓球〕球拍; PADDLE¹ (3) *AmE*【美】

3 be at bat to be the person who is trying to hit the ball in a game of BASEBALL〔棒球比赛中〕轮到击球

4 do sth off your own bat *BrE informal* to do something without being told to do it【英，非正式】主动地，自觉地: *You did all this work off your own bat?* 你是自己主动完成这些工作的吗?

5 do sth right off the bat *AmE informal* to do something immediately【美，非正式】立刻去做: *I asked him to help, and he said yes right off the bat.* 我请他帮忙，他马上就答应了。

6 like a bat out of hell *informal* very fast【非正式】极快地，飞快地: *I drove like a bat out of hell to the hospital.* 我飞快地开车赶往医院。

7 old bat *spoken* an unpleasant old woman【口】丑婆娘，老太婆〔对老妪的冒犯用语〕

8 have bats in the belfry *old-fashioned* to be slightly crazy【过时】有点儿古怪 —see also 另见 **as blind as a bat** (BLIND¹ (1c))

bat² *v* **batted, batting 1** [I,T] to hit the ball with a bat in CRICKET (2) or BASEBALL〔板球、棒球〕用球棒击球 **2 not bat an eye/eyelid** *informal* to not seem to be shocked, surprised, or embarrassed【非正式】连眼都不眨；泰然不动，面不改色: *He didn't bat an eyelid when I said I was leaving.* 我说我要走的时候，他一点也没有表现出在乎的样子。**3 bat your eyes/eyelashes** if a woman bats her eyes, she opens and closes them quickly, especially in order to look attractive to men〔女子〕使眼色〔以吸引男子〕**4 go to bat for** *AmE informal* to help and support someone【美，非正式】支持〔某人〕；为〔某人〕出力: *Andy really went to bat for me when I was accused of stealing that money.* 我被指控偷钱的时候，是安迪出面为我澄清的。**5 bat a thousand** also 又作 **bat a 1000** *AmE informal* to be very successful【美，非正式】很有成就: *She's been batting a thousand ever since she got that new job.* 她得到那份新工作后，表现非常出色。

bat sth ↔ **around** *phr v* [T] *informal* to discuss the good and bad parts of a plan, idea etc【非正式】讨论，商量

bat·boy /ˈbætbɔɪ; ˈbætbɔɪ/ *n* [C] a boy whose job is to look after the equipment of a BASEBALL team 棒球队球童

batch /bætʃ; bætʃ/ *n* [C] **1** a group of people or things that arrive or are dealt with together 一批；一群；一组: *The second batch of student essays was due in.* 第二批学生作文该交上来了。**2** a quantity of food, medicine etc, that is produced or prepared at the same time〔食物、药品等的〕一次生产量[投料量]

batch pro·ces·sing /ˌ·ˈ···/ *n* [U] a type of computer system in which the computer does several jobs one after the other, without needing instructions between each job〔电脑的〕成批处理

bat·ed /ˈbetɪd; ˈbeɪtɪ̣d/ *adj* **with bated breath** feeling very anxious or excited 屏着气〔表示焦急或兴奋〕: *We waited with bated breath for the results of the test to come through.* 我们屏住呼吸，紧张地等待发布考试成绩。

Bath /bæθ; bɑːθ/ a city in southwest England, famous for its old Roman baths and 18th century buildings. 巴斯〔英格兰西南部城市，以古罗马浴场和18世纪建筑而著名〕

2 3 **bath¹** *n plural* **baths**/bæðz, bɑːðz/ [C] **1** *BrE* a large long container that you fill with water and sit in to wash yourself【英】浴缸，澡盆; BATHTUB *especially AmE*【尤美】: **run a bath** (=make water flow into a bath) 往浴缸里放水 **2** an act of washing your body in a bath 洗澡，沐浴: *After a week of camping, I really needed a bath.* 经过一周的露营之后，我真得洗个澡。| **have a bath** *BrE*【英】/**take a bath** *AmE*【美】*Do I have time to take a bath before we go out?* 我洗个澡再出去，来得及吗? | **give sb a bath** (=wash someone in a bath) 给某人洗澡 **3** a container full of liquid in which something is placed for a particular purpose 缸；盆；池: *Plunge the fabric into a bath of black dye.* 把织物投入黑染料缸中。**4 baths a)** *BrE old-fashioned* a public building in which there is a swimming pool【英，过时】〔室内〕公共游泳池 **b)** a public building where people could go in the past to wash themselves 澡堂，公共浴室: *the Roman baths at Cirencester* 赛伦塞斯特的罗马式公共浴室 **5 take a bath** *AmE informal* to lose money, especially in a business deal【美，非正式】赔钱，亏本: *We took a bath in the market over that stock.* 我们买那支股票赔了钱。—see also 另见 BIRDBATH, BUBBLE BATH, HIPBATH, **throw the baby out with the bath water** (THROW¹ (34)), TURKISH BATH

bath² *v BrE*【英】**1** [T] to wash someone in a bath 为〔某人〕洗澡; BATHE¹ (1) *AmE*【美】**2** [I] *old-fashioned* to wash yourself in a bath; BATHE¹ (1)【过时】洗澡

USAGE NOTE 用法说明: BATH

WORD CHOICE 词语辨析: **bathe, bath, have/take a bath, bathtub, have a swim, take/have a dip, swimming bath(s), sunbathe, bathroom**

You **bathe** (*AmE*) or more formally in British English, **bath** to get clean. bathe〔美〕或较为正式的 bath〔英〕是把身体洗干净之义: *He baths/bathes every morning.* 他每天早上都洗澡。However, you are more likely to say that you **have a bath** (*BrE*) or **take a bath** (*AmE*). 但表示洗澡之义，则多用 have a bath〔英〕或者 take a bath〔美〕: *I have/take a bath every day.* 我每天都洗澡。The thing that you **have/take a bath** in is a **bath** (*BrE*) or **bathtub** (*AmE*). 洗澡用的大盆或浴缸叫 bath〔英〕或 bathtub〔美〕。

You **bathe** something gently to make it clean especially for medical reasons. bathe 是指轻轻擦洗，尤指用药水把某种东西浸洗，以进行治疗: *to bathe a cut/your eyes* 洗伤口/眼睛。In British English you say that you **bath** a baby or a sick person, in American English you **bathe** them. 英国英语中说 bath a baby/a sick person (为小孩/病人洗澡)，而美国英语中则用 bathe。

You also **bathe** (*BrE*) when you go swimming, though this meaning is no longer common. bathe〔英〕也有游泳之义，尽管这一意思现已不常用: *to bathe in the sea* (NOT 不用 *take a bath in the sea*) 在海里游泳。You are more likely to use **have a swim** or **take/have a dip** in the sea or a swimming pool. 表示在海中或泳池里游泳更常用的说法是 have a swim 或 take/have a dip。(A slightly old-fashioned word for **swimming pool** in British English is **swimming bath**. 英国英语中略为旧式的用法是把 swimming pool 说成 swimming bath)。You also **sunbathe** in the sun (NOT 不用 *have a sun bath*). sunbathe 是晒日光浴。

Often you say that you are going to the **bathroom** especially in American English, not because you are going to have a bath, but as a polite way of saying that you are going to the toilet. 在美国英语中 go to the bathroom 不是去洗澡之义，而是去厕所的委婉说法。

SPELLING 拼法

Note the spelling of **bathing** and **bathed**. These words can be formed from **bath** with the pronunciation /ˈbɑθɪŋ/bæθt; ˈbɑːθɪŋ/bæθt/. But they can also be formed from **bathe**, with the pronunciation /ˈbeðɪŋ/beðd; ˈbeɪðɪŋ/beɪðd/. 注意 bathing 和 bathed 的拼法。这两个单词可以由 bath 而来，读作 /ˈbɑθɪŋ/bæθt; ˈbɑːθɪŋ/bæθt/，也可以由 bathe 而来，读作 /ˈbeðɪŋ/beðd; ˈbeɪðɪŋ/beɪðd/。

bath chair /ˈ· ·/ *n* [C] a special chair with wheels and a cover, used in the past for moving someone old or sick around〔旧时老人或病人用的〕带篷轮椅 —compare 比较 WHEELCHAIR

bathe¹ /beð; beɪð/ *v* **1** [I,T] *especially AmE* to wash yourself or someone else in a bath【尤美】洗澡；为〔某人〕洗澡; BATH² *BrE*【英】: *I bathed, washed my hair, and got dressed.* 我洗了澡，洗了头，穿好衣服。**2** [I] *BrE old-fashioned* to swim in the sea, a river, or a lake【英，过时】〔去海里、河里、湖里〕游泳: *The children ran off to bathe.* 孩子们跑出去游泳了。**3** [T] to wash or cover part of your body with a liquid, especially as a medical treatment 洗，浸，泡〔尤指用作医疗用途〕: *Bathe the wound in antiseptic.* 用消毒剂洗一下伤口。**4 be bathed in light/moonlight etc** *literary* an area or building that is bathed in light has light shining onto it in a way that makes it look pleasant or

attractive【文】沐浴于阳光/月光等之中: *The castle was bathed in golden autumn sunlight.* 城堡沐浴于金秋的阳光中。**5 be bathed in tears/sweat etc** *literary* to be covered in tears, sweat etc【文】眼泪汪汪/满身大汗等 —see 见 BATH² (USAGE)

bathe² *n* [singular] *BrE old-fashioned* an occasion when you swim in the sea, a river, or a lake【英, 过时】〔在海里、河里或湖里〕游泳: *They went for a bathe.* 他们去游泳了。

bath·er /ˈbeðɚ; ˈbeɪðə/ *n* **1** [C] *BrE old-fashioned* someone who is swimming in the sea, a river, or a lake【英, 过时】〔去海里、河里或湖里的〕游泳者 **2 bathers** [plural] *AustrE* a piece of clothing that you wear for swimming; SWIMSUIT【澳】游泳衣

bath·ing /ˈbeðɪŋ; ˈbeɪðɪŋ/ *n* [U] *BrE old-fashioned* the activity of swimming in the sea, a river, or a lake【英, 过时】〔在海里、河里或湖里〕游泳: *Is the beach safe for bathing?* 这海滩游泳安全吗?

bathing cap /ˈbeðɪŋ ˌkæp; ˈbeɪðɪŋ kæp/ *n* [C] *old-fashioned* a special hat that you wear for swimming【过时】游泳帽

bathing cos·tume /ˈbeðɪŋ ˌkɑstum; ˈbeɪðɪŋ ˌkɒstjuːm/ *n* [C] *BrE old-fashioned* a bathing suit【英, 过时】泳装, 游泳衣

bathing ma·chine /ˈbeðɪŋ məˌʃin; ˈbeɪðɪŋ məˌʃiːn/ *n* [C] a small wooden building on wheels in which people could change their clothes for swimming in the 18th and 19th centuries〔18、19世纪时给游泳者使用的木制带轮的〕更衣车

bathing suit /ˈbeðɪŋ ˌsut; ˈbeɪðɪŋ suːt/ *n* [C] a piece of clothing that you wear for swimming 游泳衣

bathing trunks /ˈbeðɪŋ ˌtrʌŋks; ˈbeɪðɪŋ trʌŋks/ *n* [C] *BrE old-fashioned* a piece of clothing worn by men for swimming【英, 过时】〔男子穿的〕游泳裤

bath mat /ˈ· ·/ *n* [C] a piece of thick cloth that you put on the floor next to the bath 浴室踏脚垫, 地巾

ba·thos /ˈbeθɑs; ˈbeɪθɒs/ *n* [U] a sudden change from a beautiful, moral, or serious subject to one that is ordinary, silly, or not important〔修辞〕突降法〔指由美好、庄重的突然转为平庸可笑的手法〕: *a sentimental poem, trembling on the verge of bathos* 有点矫揉造作的伤感诗

bath·robe /ˈbæθˌrob; ˈbɑːθrəʊb/ *n* [C] a long loose piece of clothing shaped like a coat, that you wear especially before or after having a bath 浴袍, 浴衣 —compare 比较 DRESSING GOWN

S2 W3 **bath·room** /ˈbæθˌrum; ˈbɑːθrʊm/ *n* [C] **1** a room where there is a bath, BASIN (1) etc, and sometimes a toilet 浴室〔一般带有厕所〕 **2** *AmE* a room where there is a toilet【美】卫生间, 厕所: *Can you tell me where the bathroom is?* 你能告诉我卫生间在哪儿吗? | **go to the bathroom** (=use a toilet) 去厕所 *Mommy, I have to go to the bathroom.* 妈妈, 我要上厕所。

bath salts /ˈ· ·/ *n* [plural] a substance that you put in bath water to make it smell nice 浴盐〔使洗澡水带香味〕

bath tow·el /ˈ· ·ˌ·/ *n* [C] a large TOWEL (=piece of material for drying yourself) 浴巾

bath·tub /ˈbæθˌtʌb; ˈbɑːθtʌb/ *n* [C] *especially AmE* a long large container that you fill with water and sit or lie in to wash yourself【尤美】浴缸, 澡盆; BATH¹ (1) *BrE*【英】

bath·y·sphere /ˈbæθɪˌsfɪr; ˈbæθɪsfɪə/ *n* [C] *technical* a strong container used for going deep under the sea, especially to watch plants, animals etc【术语】〔可潜入深海中观察海底生物生活情况的〕探海球, 潜水球

ba·tik /ˈbɑtik; bəˈtiːk/ *n* **1** [U] a way of printing coloured patterns on cloth that involves putting WAX¹ (1) over some parts of the cloth 蜡染法 **2** [C,U] cloth that has been coloured in this way 蜡染布 —see picture on page A16 参见 A16 页图

Bat·man /ˈbætmæn; ˈbætmæn/ *trademark* a popular character in CARTOON STRIPs, films, and television programmes, who wears a black CAPE and a black MASK, and fights criminals【商标】蝙蝠侠〔连环漫画、电影及电视节目中的一个人物, 广受大众欢迎。蝙蝠侠身披黑色斗篷, 头戴黑色面罩, 惩治罪恶之人〕

bat·man *n plural* **batmen** /-mən; -mən/ [C] *technical* an officer's personal servant in the British army【术语】〔英国军官的〕勤务兵

bat·on /bæˈtɑn; ˈbætɒn/ *n* [C] **1** a short thin stick used by a CONDUCTOR (=the leader of a group of musicians) to direct the music〔乐队指挥用的〕指挥棒 **2** a short light stick that is passed from one person to another during a race 接力棒 **3** *especially BrE* a short thick stick used as a weapon by a policeman; TRUNCHEON【尤英】警棍 **4** a short stick that is carried as a sign of a special office or rank 权杖, 官杖 **5** a light metal stick that is spun and thrown into the air by a MAJORETTE〔乐队女指挥所用的〕金属指挥杖

Baton Rouge /ˌbætn̩ ˈruʒ; ˌbætən ˈruːʒ/ the capital city of the US state of Louisiana 巴吞鲁日〔美国路易斯安那州首府〕

bats·man /ˈbætsmən; ˈbætsmən/ *n plural* **batsmen** /-mən; -mən/ [C] the person who is trying to hit the ball in CRICKET (2)〔板球〕击球手

bat·tal·ion /bəˈtæljən; bəˈtæljən/ *n* [C] a large group of soldiers consisting of several companies (COMPANY (9))〔军队的〕营

bat·ten¹ /ˈbætn̩; ˈbætn/ *v* **1 batten down the hatches a)** to prepare yourself for a period of difficulty or trouble 准备面对困境 **b)** to firmly fasten the entrances to the lower part of a ship〔用压条〕封船舱 **2 batten on sb** *especially literary* to live well by using someone else's money, possessions etc【尤文】靠别人养肥自己

batten² *n* [C] a long narrow piece of wood that boards or TILES are fastened to, or that is fixed to other pieces of wood to keep them in place 板条, 压条

Bat·ten·burg /ˈbætn̩bɝg; ˈbætnbɜːg/ a type of cake eaten in the UK, which has a square shape divided into four pink and yellow squares, and is covered with MARZIPAN 巴吞堡〔英国一种蛋糕, 呈四方形, 分为四块, 为粉红和黄色, 上涂一层杏仁糖浆〕

bat·ter¹ /ˈbætɚ; ˈbætə/ *v* [I always+adv/prep, T] to keep hitting something hard, especially in a way that causes damage 捣毁, 打烂; 拍打, 撞击: **[+at/on/against etc]** *The waves battered against the shore.* 波浪拍打着海岸。—**battering** *n* [C,U]

batter² *n* **1** [C,U] a liquid mixture of flour, eggs, milk etc, used in cooking〔面粉、鸡蛋、牛奶等调成的〕面糊: *Fry the fish in batter.* 将蘸上面糊的鱼油炸。**2** [C,U] *AmE* a thick mixture of flour, eggs, milk etc, used for making cakes【美】〔做薄饼用的〕面糊 **3** [C] the person who is trying to hit the ball in BASEBALL〔棒球〕击球手—see picture on page A22 参见 A22 页图

bat·tered /ˈbætɚd; ˈbætəd/ *adj* **1** old and in bad condition 旧的, 破的: *a battered old suitcase* 破旧的衣箱 **2 battered women/children etc** women or children who have been violently treated by their husbands or fathers 遭受虐待的妇女/儿童等: *a shelter for battered wives* 受虐妻子的庇护所

bat·ter·ing ram /ˈ· ··, ·/ *n* [C] a long heavy piece of wood used in wars in the past to break through walls or doors〔古代战争攻城时用于捣毁墙、门的〕破城锤

bat·ter·y /ˈbætərɪ; ˈbætəri/ *n* S2

1 ▶ELECTRICITY 电◀ [C] an object that provides a supply of electricity for something such as a radio or a car 电池: *I need to change the batteries in the flashlight.* 我需要更换手电筒里的电池。| **dead/flat battery** (=a battery that has stopped producing electricity) 废电池 —see picture at 参见 ENGINE 图

2 ▶HENS 母鸡◀ [C] a row of small CAGEs in which chickens are kept to produce large numbers of eggs 层架式鸡笼: *battery hens* 在层架式鸡笼里饲养的母鸡 —compare 比较 FREE-RANGE

3 ▶GUNS 枪炮◀ [C] several large guns used together 炮组, 排炮: *Enemy anti-aircraft batteries immediately responded to the attack.* 敌人的高射炮火对袭击迅速作出反应。

4 recharge your batteries *informal* to rest or relax in order to get back your energy【非正式】休息[放松]以恢复精神体力: *A week in the mountains should recharge my batteries.* 在山里休息一个星期, 我的精神体力应该能恢复过来。

5 a battery of a group of many things of the same kind〔同类事物的〕一排, 一组, 一连串: *Mayer sat at his desk, surrounded by a battery of telephones.* 迈耶坐在桌旁, 被一排电话包围着。

6 ▶CRIME 罪行◀ [U] *law* the crime of hitting someone【法律】殴打罪 —see also 另见 ASSAULT AND BATTERY

Battery Park /ˌ· ·· ˈ·/ a park at the southwestern end of Manhattan next to the Hudson River 巴特利公园〔位于曼哈顿西南端哈得孙河畔的一个公园〕

bat·tle¹ /ˈbætl̩; ˈbætl/ *n* [C] W2

1 ▶BETWEEN ARMIES 军队之间◀ a fight between opposing armies, groups of ships etc, especially one that is part of a larger war〔尤指大型战争中的局部〕战斗, 战役: *the Battle of Trafalgar* 特拉法尔加战役 | **in/into battle** *Her son was killed in battle.* 她儿子在战斗中阵亡。| *sending troops into battle* 派部队参战

2 ▶BETWEEN OPPONENTS 对手之间◀ a situation in which opposing groups or people compete or argue with each other when trying to achieve success or control 较量, 竞争, 争夺: *a long-running legal battle* 旷日持久的法律争讼 | **[+for]** *The president's advisors were engaged in a battle for power.* 总统的顾问在进行一场权力之争。| **[+between]** *a fierce ratings battle between rival TV stations* 相互竞争的电视台之间一场激烈的收视率之战 | **[+with]** *an ongoing battle with my mother about eating properly* 我和母亲有关合理饮食的持续争论

3 ▶ATTEMPT 试图◀ an attempt to solve a difficult problem or change an unpleasant situation 奋斗, 抗争: **[+against]** *The battle against AIDS will continue for years to come.* 和艾滋病的斗争

还要持续很多年。| **fight a losing battle** (=try to achieve something that you cannot achieve) 做毫无希望的事情, 徒劳无功 *I try to get the kids to pick up their clothes, but I'm fighting a losing battle.* 我设法让孩子自己收拾衣服，可是他们不听我的。

4 be half the battle to the most difficult or important part of what you have to do 成功了一半, 胜利大有希望: *If you can get an interview, that's half the battle.* 如果你能得到面试的机会，成功就大有希望了。

5 a battle of wits a disagreement that opposing sides try to win by using their intelligence 智慧的较量: *It became a battle of wits between student and teacher.* 那成了师生间智慧的较量。

6 do battle (with) to argue with someone or fight against someone 与…争论[斗争]: *We had to do battle with the authorities over planning permission for the house.* 关于批准建屋计划的事, 我们必须和当局据理力争。

7 the battle of the sexes the relationship between men and women when it is considered as a fight for power 男女之间权力的竞争

battle² *v* **1** [I,T] to be involved in a struggle or argument when you are trying to achieve something difficult or to deal with something unpleasant or dangerous 与…斗争, 与…搏斗: [+against/with] *She had battled bravely against cancer for many years.* 她勇敢地与癌症抗争了多年。| *I found Maria battling with her maths homework.* 我发现玛丽亚在努力地做数学作业。| [+for] *a pressure group battling for better schools* 为改善学校条件而斗争的压力集团 | **battle to do sth** *Doctors battled to save his life.* 医生们奋力挽救他的生命。| **battle sth** *AmE*【美】*I was already battling a cold.* 我的感冒快挺过去了。**2 battle it out** to keep fighting or opposing each other until one person or team wins 决出胜负: *I left Adrian and Jo battling it out for the trophy.* 我让阿德里安和乔为奖杯一决高低。**3** [I] *literary* to take part in a fight or war【文】参战, 作战

bat·tle·axe *BrE*【英】, **battleax** *AmE*【美】/ˈbætḷ,æks; ˈbætlæks/ *n* [C] **1** *informal* an unpleasant unfriendly woman who tries to control other people【非正式】悍妇 **2** a large AXE (=tool for cutting wood) used as a weapon in the past 战斧

battle cruis·er /ˈ‥ ,‥/ *n* [C] a large fast ship used in war 战列巡洋舰

battle cry /ˈ‥ ·/ *n* [C usually singular 一般用单数] **1** a phrase used to encourage people, especially members of a political organization〔尤指政治组织的〕口号; 呐喊: *'Socialism Now!' was their battle cry.* "现在就实现社会主义!"是他们的口号。**2** a loud shout used in war to encourage your side and frighten the enemy〔战场上的〕呐喊

battle fa·tigue /ˈ‥ ·,·/ *n* [U] a type of mental illness caused by the frightening experiences of war, in which you feel very anxious and upset 战争疲劳症

bat·tle·field /ˈbætḷ,fild; ˈbætlfiːld/ also 又作 **battleground** /ˈbætḷ,graʊnd; ˈbætlgraʊnd/ *n* [C] **1** a place where a battle is being fought or has been fought 战场, 战地 **2** a subject that people disagree or argue a lot about 斗争的主题; 争论的问题: *The housing issue has become a political battleground.* 住房问题已经变成了政治斗争的内容。

bat·tle·ments /ˈbætḷmənts; ˈbætlmənts/ *n* [plural] a low wall around the top of a castle, that has spaces to shoot guns or arrows (ARROW (1)) through〔城堡的〕雉堞; 城垛; 有枪眼的防御墙

Battle of Brit·ain, the /,‥ ·ˈ‥/ the name used for the fights between German and British aircraft in 1940, when British aircraft tried to prevent German aircraft from dropping bombs on British cities 不列颠之战〔指 1940 年的英德空战, 当时英国空军试图阻止德国飞机轰炸英国城市〕

Battle of the Boyne —see 见 the Battle of the BOYNE

Battle of the Bulge, the /,‥ ·ˈ·/ the last main attack by the German army during World War II, when they surrounded the Allies' army in Belgium in 1944 楔入战役〔指 1944 年二战期间德军的最后一次主攻, 当时德军在比利时包围了盟军〕

bat·tle·ship /ˈbætḷ,ʃɪp; ˈbætl,ʃɪp/ *n* [C] the largest kind of ship used in war, with very big guns and heavy ARMOUR (2) 主力舰, 战列舰

bat·ty /ˈbætɪ; ˈbæti/ *adj BrE informal* slightly crazy but not in an unpleasant or frightening way; ECCENTRIC¹ (1)【英, 非正式】有点疯的; 古怪的

bau·ble /ˈbɔbḷ; ˈbɔːbəl/ *n* [C] **1** a cheap piece of jewellery 不值钱的饰物 **2** *BrE* a brightly coloured decoration that looks like a ball and is used to decorate a CHRISTMAS TREE【英】〔装饰圣诞树用的闪亮的〕球形小饰物

baud /bɔd; bɔːd/ *n* [C] *technical* a unit of measurement of the speed at which information is sent to or from a computer, for example through a telephone line【术语】波特〔发报、数据传输速率单位〕

Baudelaire /bodˈlɛr; bəʊdˈleə/, **Charles** (1821-67) a French SYMBOLIST poet, known for *Les Fleurs du Mal* 波德莱尔〔(1821-1867), 法国象征主义诗人, 以诗集《恶之花》闻名〕

Bau·haus /ˈbauhaus; ˈbaʊhaʊs/ a modern style of ARCHITECTURE and design originally taught at the Bauhaus school in Germany in the 1920s and 1930s. Bauhaus buildings are simple and FUNCTIONAL (=designed to be useful rather than beautiful or decorative) 包豪斯学派〔一种现代建筑设计风格, 起源于 20 世纪 20、30 年代德国的包豪斯建筑学校。包豪斯建筑讲求简洁和实用〕—**Bauhaus** *adj*

baulk /bɔk; bɔːk/ a British spelling of BALK balk 的英式拼法

Baum /bɔm; bɔːm/, **L. Frank** (1856-1919) a US writer who wrote the book *The Wonderful Wizard of Oz* 鲍姆〔(1856-1919), 美国作家, 著有《绿野仙踪》〕

baux·ite /ˈbɔksaɪt; ˈbɔːksaɪt/ *n* [U] a soft substance that ALUMINIUM (=a type of metal) is obtained from 铝矾土, 铝土矿

Ba·va·ri·a /bəˈvɛrɪə; bəˈveəriə/ a PROVINCE in southeast Germany whose capital is Munich. Bavaria is called 'Bayern' in German. 巴伐利亚州〔德国东南部一联邦州, 首府慕尼黑。在德语里, 巴伐利亚州称作拜恩州〕

bawd·y /ˈbɔdɪ; ˈbɔːdi/ *adj* bawdy songs, jokes, stories etc are about sex and are funny, enjoyable, and often noisy〔歌曲、笑话、故事等〕淫猥的; 娱人的: *the bawdy 18th century romp, 'Moll Flanders'* 18 世纪的逗乐小说《摩尔·福兰德斯》—**bawdily** *adv* —**bawdiness** *n* [U]

bawdy house /ˈ‥ ·/ *n* [C] *old use* a place where women have sex with men for money【旧】妓院

bawl /bɔl; bɔːl/ *v* **1** [I,T] also 又作 **bawl out** to shout in a loud unpleasant voice 叫嚷, 大喊: *The captain stood at the front, bawling orders.* 队长站在前面, 喊着口令。**2** [I] to cry noisily 大哭, 号哭: *a baby bawling* 婴儿的哭叫

bawl sb ↔ **out** *phr v* [T] *informal especially AmE* to speak angrily to someone because they have done something wrong【非正式, 尤美】痛骂, 大声责备: *Mom bawled me out for the mess in my room.* 妈妈因我的房间太乱而责骂我。

bay¹ /be; beɪ/ *n* [C]

1 ►SEA 海◄ an area of the sea that curves inwards towards the land 湾, 海湾: *I had a view across the bay to white sand and pine trees.* 我能看到海湾那边的白沙和松树。| *Montego Bay*〔牙买加〕蒙特哥贝湾 —see picture on page A12 参见 A12 页图

2 keep/hold sth at bay to prevent something dangerous or unpleasant from happening or from coming too close 使…不能迫近, 遏制: *The growling of dogs held the strangers at bay.* 狗的吠叫使陌生人无法靠近。| *Economic collapse was held at bay by aid from Russia.* 来自俄罗斯的援助使经济不致崩溃。

3 ►AREA 地区◄ an area within a large room that is separated by shelves, walls etc〔建筑物的〕开间, 隔间, 格距: *bays in a library* 图书馆书架间的空处

4 ►VEHICLES 车辆◄ a place where a vehicle can park for a short time〔可供车辆短暂停泊的〕停车间, 停车处: *The bus will depart from bay 3.* 公共汽车将从 3 号停车站开出。| *a loading bay* 装卸场

5 ►TREE 树◄ also 又作 **bay tree** a tree that has leaves which smell sweet and are often used in cooking 月桂树

6 ►HORSE 马◄ a horse that is a reddish brown colour 红棕色的马, 枣红马

bay² *v* [I] **1** if a dog bays, it makes a long high noise, especially when it is chasing something〔猎犬〕不停地吠叫: *the baying of the hounds* 猎犬不停的吠叫声 **2** to make strong demands to get answers to questions or force someone to give you something 穷追: [+for] *a pack of tabloid reporters baying for blood* 一群穷追不舍的小报记者 | *younger men baying at his heels* 紧跟着他的较年轻者

bay³ *adj* a bay horse is a reddish-brown colour〔马〕红棕色的

Bay A·re·a, the /ˈ· ,‥·/ the area of land around the San Francisco Bay in California, including cities such as San Francisco, Oakland, Berkeley, Palo Alto, and San José 圣弗朗西斯科湾地区〔指加利福尼亚圣弗朗西斯科湾沿岸地区, 包括圣弗朗西斯科 (即旧金山)、奥克兰、伯克利、帕洛阿尔托、圣何塞等城市〕

Bay·eux Tap·es·try, the /baɪ,u ˈtæpɪstrɪ; ,baɪɜː ˈtæpɪstri/ a TAPESTRY (=large piece of heavy woven cloth) made in Bayeux, northern France, in the 11th or 12th century, whose pictures tell the story of the Norman Conquest of England in 1066 巴约挂毯〔11、12 世纪法国北部巴约的一种挂毯, 上面的图案描绘的是 1066 年诺曼底人征服英格兰的故事〕

Baykal —see 见 BAIKAL

bay leaf /ˈ· ·/ *n* [C] a sweet-smelling leaf from the bay tree, often used in cooking 月桂树叶〔常用于煮食〕

Bay of Bis·cay, the /ˌbe əv ˈbɪske; ˌbeɪ əv ˈbɪskeɪ/ a large area of sea between the west coast of France and the north coast of Spain 比斯开湾〔法国西海岸与西班牙北海岸之间的一大片海域〕

Bay of Pigs, the /ˌ· · ˈ·/ an area on the south coast of Cuba, which is famous for a military attack that took place in 1961. A group of Cubans living in the US tried to enter Cuba with the aim of ending the government of Fidel Castro. They were trained and supported by the US, but the attack failed. 猪湾〔古巴南海岸的一片海域，因1961年发生的一次军事入侵而闻名。旅居美国的一群古巴人试图进入古巴推翻卡斯特罗政府。他们虽得到了美国的训练和支持，但此次行动仍以失败告终〕

bay·o·net¹ /ˈbeənɪt; ˈbeɪənʒt/ *n* [C] a long blade that is fixed to the end of a RIFLE (=long gun) 〔步枪上的〕刺刀，枪刺

bayonet² *v* [T] to push the point of a bayonet into someone 用刺刀刺

bay·ou /ˈbaɪu; ˈbaɪuː/ *n* [C] a large area of water in the south-east US that moves very slowly and has many water plants 〔美国东南部的〕水流缓慢、水草繁多的小河

Bay·reuth /baɪˈrɔɪt; baɪˈrɔɪt/ a town in southern Germany, known for its regular FESTIVALS of music by Richard Wagner 拜罗伊特〔德国南部小镇，以定期举办瓦格纳音乐节而闻名〕

Bay·watch /ˈbewɑtʃ; ˈbeɪwɒtʃ/ *trademark* a US television programme about a group of LIFEGUARDS (=someone whose job is to save people who get into difficulties when they are swimming in the sea) who work on a beach in California. 【商标】《海岸救险队》〔美国一档电视节目，讲述加利福尼亚海滩救生员的经历〕

bay win·dow /ˌ· ˈ··/ *n* [C] a window that sticks outwards from the wall of a house, usually with glass on three sides 凸窗〔凸出于墙壁之外三面有玻璃的窗户〕

ba·zaar /bəˈzɑr; bəˈzɑː/ *n* [C] **1** a market or group of shops, especially in India or the Middle East 〔尤指印度或中东的〕市场，市集 **2** a sale held to collect money for a good purpose 义卖: *a charity bazaar* 慈善义卖会

ba·zoo·ka /bəˈzukə; bəˈzuːkə/ *n* [C] a long light gun that rests on your shoulder and is used especially for firing at tanks (TANK¹ (3)) 〔扛在肩上发射的反坦克〕火箭筒

BBC /ˌbi bi ˈsi; ˌbiː biː ˈsiː◂/ *n* **1** the British Broadcasting Corporation; the British radio and television company that is paid for by the state 英国广播公司 **2 BBC English** a standard form of English pronunciation used in Britain; RP 〔英国的〕标准发音

BBC World Serv·ice, the /ˌ· · · ˈ· ·/ —see 见 the WORLD SERVICE

BBC World·wide Tel·e·vi·sion /ˌ· · · ˈ· · · ·/ a part of the BBC which broadcasts television programmes, especially news, around the world 英国广播公司国际电视台〔英国广播公司下属的一家面向全球的电视台，尤以新闻节目为主〕

BB gun /ˈbi bi ˌgʌn; ˈbiː biː gʌn/ *n* [C] *AmE* a gun that uses air pressure to force out small round metal balls 【美】气枪; AIRGUN *BrE* 【英】

CULTURAL NOTE 文化注释

In the US, boys often learn how to shoot with a BB gun because it is less dangerous than other types of gun. However, BB guns can kill small animals and birds, and people are sometimes injured by them in accidents. 美国男孩常用气枪练习射击，因为气枪比其他枪支的危险性小。不过，气枪可以打死小动物或鸟类，有时也会意外伤人。

BBQ *n* [C] an abbreviation for 缩写= BARBECUE

BC /ˌbi ˈsi; ˌbiː ˈsiː/ before Christ; used after a date to show that it was before the birth of Christ 公元前: *The Great Pyramid dates from around 2600 BC.* 大金字塔建于公元前2600年左右。—compare 比较 AD

BCCI /ˌbi si si ˈaɪ; ˌbiː siː siː ˈaɪ/ *n* [singular] Bank of Credit and Commerce International; an international bank which failed in 1991 after it was accused of doing business in a dishonest way 国际信贷商业银行〔一家跨国银行，曾被指控不正当经营，1991年倒闭〕

BCE /ˌbi si ˈi; ˌbiː siː ˈiː/ *especially AmE* before common era; used after a date to show that it is before the birth of Christ 【尤美】公元前

be- /bɪ; bɪ/ *prefix* **1** in some verbs, means to treat as a particular thing 视作〔用于动词〕: *Don't belittle him* (=say he is unimportant). 不要小看他。| *He befriended me* (=became my friend). 他成了我的朋友。**2** *literary* in some adjectives, means wearing a particular thing 【文】佩戴，穿戴〔用于部分形容词〕: *a bespectacled boy* (=wearing glasses) 戴眼镜的男孩 **3** *old use* completely; thoroughly 【旧】完全，彻底: *to besmear* (=make very dirty) 把…弄脏，玷污

be¹ /bɪ; bi; *strong* 强读 bi; biː/ *auxiliary verb*  **1** used with a present participle to form the CONTINUOUS (4) tenses of verbs 〔和现在分词构成动词的进行时态〕: **be doing sth** *Don't disturb me while I'm working.* 我工作的时候不要打扰我。| *Gemma was reading when her son called.* 吉玛的儿子打电话来的时候，她正在看书。| *They've been asking a lot of questions.* 他们已经问了许多问题了。| *He's always causing trouble.* 他总是惹麻烦。**2** used with past participles to form the PASSIVE² 〔和过去分词构成被动语态〕: *Smoking is not permitted.* 禁止吸烟。| *I was told about it yesterday.* 我昨天被告知了这件事。| *The house is being painted.* 房子正在刷油漆。| *She has been invited to the party.* 她已被邀参加聚会。| *The flames could be seen several miles away.* 在几英里外都能看到火焰。| *The police should have been informed about this.* 这件事本应向警察报告。**3** used to give an order or to tell someone about a rule 〔表示命令或规则〕: *All guests are to vacate their rooms by 10 am on the day of their departure.* 所有退房的客人必须在离开当日上午10点前腾出房间。| *The children are to be in bed when we get home.* 我们到家后，孩子们就得睡觉。**4** used to show arrangements for the future 〔表示将来的安排〕: *Audrey and Jimmy are to be married in June.* 奥德丽和吉米将在6月结婚。| *We were to have gone away last week but I was ill.* 我们本打算上周走，可是我病了。| *I'll be leaving in about half an hour.* 我大约半个小时后离开。**5** used to show what someone should do or what should happen 〔表示某人应该怎样做或应该发生什么〕: *What am I to tell her* (=what should I tell her?) *when she finds out?* 一旦她发现了，我该怎样对她说呢？| *He is more to be* (=should be more) *pitied than blamed.* 他更应该得到同情而不是责备。**6** used to show what cannot or could not happen 〔表示不能或不会发生什么〕: *We searched everywhere but the ring was nowhere to be found.* 我们找来找去，但哪儿也找不到那只戒指。**7** used to show what had to happen or what did happen 〔表示不得不发生或已发生什么〕: *This discovery was to have a major effect on the treatment of heart disease.* 这个发现对心脏病的治疗产生了重大影响。**8** used in CONDITIONAL¹ (2) sentences that describe a situation that does not or could not exist 〔用于条件句，表示虚拟语气〕: *If I were to do that what would you say?* 如果我做了那件事，你会说什么呢？| *Were we to offer you the job, would you take it?* 如果我们给你这份工作，你会接受吗？**9** *old use* used instead of 'have' to form the PERFECT³ tenses of some verbs 【旧】〔代替 have 构成某些动词的完成时态〕: *Christ is risen* (=has risen) *from the dead.* 基督已从死里复活。

be² *v* **1** [linking verb 连系动词] used to show that someone or something is the same as the subject 〔表示某人或某事与主语相同〕: *It's me.* 是我。| *Lack of money is our biggest problem.* 缺钱是我们最大的问题。| *If I were you, I shouldn't do it.* 如果我是你，我就不会这样做。| **the problem/difficulty etc is doing sth** *The problem is explaining it to her in a tactful way.* 问题是怎样用得体的方法向她解释。| **the problem/difficulty etc is to do sth** *The difficulty is to know what to do for the best.* 困难的是不知道怎样做最好。| **the fact/idea etc is (that)** *The fact is that you know too much.* 事实是你知道得太多了。**2** [I always +adv/prep] used to show position or time 〔表示位置或时间〕: *Where is Simon?* 西蒙在哪儿？| *Jane's upstairs.* 简在楼上。| *The principal's in his office.* 校长在办公室。| *How long has she been here?* 她来这儿有多久了？| *The book is on the table.* 书在桌子上。| *The concert was last night.* 音乐会是在昨晚举行的。| *The party is on Saturday.* 聚会将在星期六举行。**3** [linking verb 连系动词] used to show that someone or something belongs to a group or has a particular quality 〔表示某人或某物属于一个群体或具有某种特征〕: *Snow is white.* 雪是白色的。| *Horses are animals.* 马是动物。| *She wants to be a doctor when she leaves school.* 她毕业后想当医生。| *These shoes are mine.* 这双鞋是我的。| *We were hungry.* 我们饿了。| *I'm not ready.* 我没准备好。| *Be careful!* 小心！| *It's hot today.* 今天很热。| *A knife is for cutting with.* 刀子是用来切东西的。**4** used in short phrases and questions 〔用于短语和疑问句中〕: *It's cold, isn't it?* 天气真冷，是吧？| *He isn't leaving, is he?* 他不是要走，对吧？| *"That's not your coat!" "Yes it is!"* "那不是你的大衣！" "不，是我的！" **5** [linking verb 连系动词] used after 'there' to show that something exists 〔用在 there 之后表示某物的存在〕: *There's a hole in your trousers.* 你的裤子上有个洞。**6 be that as it may** *formal* used to say that even though you accept that something is true it does not change a situation 【正式】即使那

是真的; 尽管如此: *"James has been under a lot of pressure at work recently." "Be that as it may, he ought to spend time with his family."* "詹姆斯最近工作压力很大。" "即使如此, 他也应该找时间陪伴家人。" **7** [I] to exist 存在: *That's just how it is.* 事情的经过就是这样。**8** to remain in the same state or stay calm 维持原来的状态; 保持镇静: *If the baby's sleeping, let her be.* 如果宝宝睡了, 就让她睡吧。**9 let/leave sth be** to let a situation remain as it is without trying to change it 顺其自然: *You just have to let some things be.* 有些事情须顺其自然。**10 the be-all and end all** the most important part of a situation or of someone's life 首要的事情; 最高的目标: *For Jim making money is the be-all and end all of his job.* 对吉姆来讲, 挣钱是他追求的最高目标。

3 2 **beach¹** /bitʃ; biːtʃ/ *n plural* **beaches** [C] an area of sand or small stones next to the sea or a lake 海滩, 沙滩: *It was a hot day, and the beach was already crowded with people.* 天气很热, 海滩上已经挤满了人。—see picture on page A12 参见 A12 页图 —see 见 SHORE¹ (USAGE)

beach² *v* [T] **1** to pull a boat onto the shore away from the water 把〔船〕拖上岸 **2** if a WHALE (=large sea animal) beaches itself or is beached, it swims onto the shore and cannot get back in the water 使〔鲸〕搁浅

beach ball /ˈ· ·/ *n* [C] a large coloured plastic ball filled with air and used for playing games on the beach 沙滩球

Beach Boys, the /ˈ· ·/ a US popular music group formed in 1961. Their songs include *California Girls* and *Good Vibrations.* 沙滩男孩组合〔成立于1961年的美国流行音乐组合, 歌曲包括《加利福尼亚女孩》、《美妙的共鸣》等〕

beach bug·gy /ˈ· ,··/ *n* [C] a vehicle with very large tyres that can be driven on sand 海滩车〔在沙滩上用的装有特大轮胎的机动车〕; DUNE BUGGY *AmE*【美】

beach chair /ˈ· ·/ *n* [C] *AmE* a folding chair with a seat and back made of cloth or plastic, which is used outdoors, especially at the beach; DECKCHAIR【美】〔尤指在海滩上使用的〕帆布躺椅 —see picture at 参见 CHAIR¹ 图

beach·comb·er /ˈbitʃ,komə; ˈbiːtʃ,kəʊmə/ *n* [C] someone who searches beaches for things that might be useful 沙滩拾荒者

beach·head /ˈbitʃ,hɛd; ˈbiːtʃhed/ *n* [C] an area of shore that has been taken from an enemy by force and can be used for landing soldiers on 滩头阵地, 滩头堡: *the Normandy beachheads* 诺曼底滩头阵地

beach·wear /ˈbitʃ,wɛr; ˈbiːtʃweə/ *n* [U] clothes that you wear for swimming, lying on the beach etc 海滩装, 沙滩装

Beach·y Head /,bitʃɪ ˈhɛd; ,biːtʃi hed/ an area of land with very high cliffs on the south coast of England 比奇角〔英格兰南部海岸岩壁高耸的一片区域〕

bea·con /ˈbikən; ˈbiːkən/ *n* [C] **1** a special tower with a bright light, or floating object that sends signals, used to warn boats that they are near the shore 灯塔 **2** a light that is put somewhere to warn or guide people, vehicles, or aircraft 灯标 **3** a radio or RADAR signal used by aircraft or boats to help them find their position and direction 无线电[雷达]信标 **4** *especially literary* a person, idea etc that guides or encourages you【尤文】指路明灯; 指引者; 楷模: *a beacon of hope in a dark world* 黑暗世界里的希望之光 **5** a fire on top of a hill used in former times as a signal〔旧时的〕烽火(台) —see also 另见 BELISHA BEACON

bead /bid; biːd/ *n* [C] **1** one of a set of small, usually round pieces of glass, wood, plastic etc, that you can put on a string and wear as jewellery 珠子; 小珠: *a necklace of amber beads* 琥珀珠子串成的项链 **2** a small drop of liquid such as water or blood〔液体〕小珠, 小滴〈如水珠、血滴等〉: *Beads of sweat stood out on his brow.* 他的额头上渗出了汗珠。**3 draw a bead on** to aim carefully before shooting a weapon〔射击时〕瞄准 —see also 另见 WORRY BEADS

bead·ed /ˈbidɪd; ˈbiːdʒd/ *adj* **1** decorated with beads 带珠子的, 有珠子作装饰的 **2 beaded with sweat/perspiration** with drops of SWEAT (=liquid produced by your body when you are hot) on your skin 汗流浃背, 大汗淋漓

bead·ing /ˈbidɪŋ; ˈbiːdɪŋ/ *n* [U] **1** long thin pieces of wood or stone that are used as a decoration on the edges of walls, furniture etc〔墙壁、家具等的〕串珠状悬饰 **2** a lot of beads sewn close together on clothes, leather etc as decoration〔衣服、皮革等上的〕串珠状装饰物

bea·dle /ˈbidl; ˈbiːdl/ *n* [C] **1** an officer in British churches in former times who helped the priest in various ways, especially by keeping order〔英国旧时教区的〕执事, 牧师助手 **2** an officer in some British universities who helps at special ceremonies〔英国一些大学举行典礼时的〕仪仗官, 礼仪前导官

bead·y /ˈbidɪ; ˈbiːdi/ *adj* **1** beady eyes are small, round, and shiny〔眼睛〕珠子般的; 圆而亮的 **2 have/keep your beady eye(s) on** *humorous* to watch someone or something very carefully【幽默】睁大眼睛仔细地看

bea·gle /ˈbigl; ˈbiːgəl/ *n* [C] a dog with short legs and smooth fur, sometimes used to hunt rabbits 比格尔犬〔短腿软毛的猎兔犬〕

Beagle, HMS the ship on which Charles Darwin travelled to South America, where he studied and collected many different types of plants and animals 比格尔号船〔查尔斯·达尔文曾乘此船去南美考察动植物, 并采集标本〕

beak /bik; biːk/ *n* [C] **1** the hard pointed mouth of a bird 鸟嘴, 喙 **2** *humorous* a large pointed nose【幽默】鹰钩鼻 **3** *BrE old-fashioned* a judge or a male teacher【英, 过时】法官; 男教师

bea·ker /ˈbikə; ˈbiːkə/ *n* [C] **1** *BrE* a drinking cup with straight sides and no handle, usually made of plastic【英】〔直身无柄的〕杯子 **2** a glass cup with straight sides that is used in chemistry for measuring and heating liquids〔实验室用的〕烧杯, 量杯 —see picture at 参见 LABORATORY 图

beam¹ /bim; biːm/ *n* [C]

1 ▶**LIGHT** 光◀ **a)** a shining line of light from the sun, a lamp etc 光束, 光线: *We could see the beams of searchlights scanning the sky.* 我们可以看到探照灯光扫过天空。**b)** a line of light, energy etc that you cannot see 束, 柱: *a laser beam* 激光束 | *The intruder passed through an infrared alarm beam.* 非法闯入者穿过了红外线警报光束。

2 ▶**WOOD/METAL** 木头/金属◀ a long heavy piece of wood or metal used in building houses, bridges etc 梁, 横梁

3 ▶**SMILE** 微笑◀ a wide happy smile 喜色, 笑容: *"Congratulations!" she said, with a beam of delight.* "恭喜你!" 她面带喜色地说。

4 off (the) beam incorrect or mistaken 不正确的, 错误的, 不对头的: *We tried to guess the price but we were way off beam.* 我们猜过价钱, 但我们猜的和实际价钱差得太远了。

5 ▶**SPORT** 体育◀ a long raised wooden bar used in GYMNASTICS, on which you balance and move〔体操〕平衡木

6 ▶**SHIP** 船◀ *technical* the widest part of a ship from side to side【术语】船宽 —see also 另见 **broad in the beam** (BROAD¹ (12))

beam² *v* **1** [I] to smile very happily 笑, 眉开眼笑: *The captain beamed with satisfaction.* 上尉露出了满意的微笑。| *"I got a place!" said Sara, beaming delightedly.* "我被录取了!" 萨拉带着喜悦的微笑说道。**2** [T always + adv/prep] to send a radio or television signal through the air, especially to somewhere very distant 向…发送〔电波〕: *the first ever broadcast beamed across the Atlantic* 首次向大西洋彼岸发出的广播信号 **3** [I,T] to send out a line of light, heat, energy etc 发光; 发热, 发射: *The sun beamed through the clouds.* 阳光穿透了云层。| *X-rays are beamed through the patient's body.* 用X光透视病人的身体。

beam-ends /ˈ· ·/ *n* **be on your beam-ends** *BrE old-fashioned* to have almost no money【英, 过时】经济拮据

Bea·mer, Beemer /ˈbimə; ˈbiːmə/ *especially AmE informal* a name for any car made by BMW【尤美, 非正式】宝马车: *That's his white Beamer convertible over there.* 他的那辆白色宝马敞篷车停在那边。

bean¹ /bin; biːn/ *n* 3

1 ▶**VEGETABLE** 蔬菜◀ **a)** a seed from one of many types of climbing plants, that is often used as food 豆 **b)** a POD (=seed case) from a bean plant that is used as food when the seeds are young 豆荚: *green beans* 青豆荚 —see picture on page A9 参见 A9 页图

2 ▶**PLANT** 植物◀ a plant that produces beans 豆科植物

3 ▶**COFFEE** 咖啡◀ one of many types of seed that is used to make coffee, chocolate etc〔能制成咖啡或巧克力等的〕豆: *coffee beans* 咖啡豆 | *cocoa beans* 可可豆

4 be full of beans *informal* to be very eager and full of energy【非正式】生气勃勃; 精力充沛: *It's the kids' party today and they're full of beans.* 今天是孩子们的聚会, 他们都兴高采烈。

5 not have a bean *informal* to have no money at all【非正式】身无分文: *I can't pay you – I haven't got a bean.* 我不能付钱给你——我一分钱也没有。

6 not know beans (about) *AmE informal* to know nothing at all about a subject【美, 非正式】(对…)一无所知

7 old bean *BrE old-fashioned* used by men when talking to a man they know well【英, 过时】老兄〔用于称呼朋友〕—see also 另见 **spill the beans** (SPILL¹ (3))

bean² *v* [T] *informal* to hit someone on the head with an object【非正式】〔用东西〕打〔某人〕的头部: *I was beaned on the head by a baseball.* 我的头被棒球打了一下。 3

bean·bag /ˈbin,bæg; ˈbiːnbæg/ *n* [C] **1** a very large cloth bag that is filled with pieces of soft plastic and used for sitting on 豆袋坐垫；豆袋椅 **2** a small cloth bag filled with beans, used for throwing and catching in children's games〔儿童投掷游戏用的〕豆袋

bean curd /ˈ· ·/ *n* [C] a soft white food made from SOYBEANS; TOFU 豆腐

bean feast /ˈ· ·/ *n* [C] *BrE informal* a party or celebration【英，非正式】聚会；庆祝会

bea·nie /ˈbinɪ; ˈbiːni/ *n* [C] *AmE* a small round hat that fits close to your head【美】无边小便帽

Bea·no, The /ˈbino; ˈbiːnəʊ/ a popular British COMIC for children《比诺》〔英国流行的儿童连环漫画杂志〕

Bean·town /ˈbintaun; ˈbiːntaʊn/ *AmE informal* a name for the US city of Boston【美，非正式】豆城〔美国波士顿市的别称〕

bean·pole /ˈbin,pol; ˈbiːnpəʊl/ *n* [C] *humorous* a very tall thin person【幽默】〔人〕瘦高个子

bean·sprout /ˈbins,praut; ˈbiːnspraʊt/ *n* [C] the small white stem from a bean seed that is eaten as a vegetable 豆芽 —see picture on page A9 参见A9页图

W1 **bear[1]** /bɛr; beə/ *v past tense* **bore** /bor; bɔː/ *past participle* **borne** /born; bɔːn/ [T]

1 can't bear a) to dislike something or someone so much that they make you very annoyed or impatient 忍受不了：*Oh, I can't bear that man – he really irritates me!* 我真受不了那个人——他真的让我很生气！| *I just can't bear that kind of selfishness.* 我就是无法忍受那种自私。| **can't bear sb doing sth** *He can't bear people smoking while he's eating.* 他忍受不了人们在他吃饭的时候吸烟。**b)** to be so upset about something that you feel unable to accept it or let it happen 接受不了…的事实：*Please don't leave me all alone. I couldn't bear it.* 不要把我一个人留在这儿，我受不了。| **can't bear the thought of** *We just couldn't bear the thought of selling the farm.* 我们就是实在不敢想卖农场的事。| **can't bear to do sth** *Alison couldn't bear to leave and cried all the way to the airport.* 艾利森忍受不了离别之苦，去机场的路上一直在哭。

2 bear in mind (that) to remember a fact or piece of information that is important or could be useful in the future 记住；考虑到：*Bearing in mind that he's only ten, I think he did very well.* 考虑到他只有10岁，我认为他做得非常好。| *I think that's excellent advice to bear in mind.* 我觉得那是个非常好的建议，必须记住。

3 ►BE BRAVE 勇敢◄ to bravely accept or deal with a painful or unpleasant situation 忍受，忍耐，经受住：*She bore the pain with tremendous courage.* 她非常勇敢地忍受了痛苦。| *Listening to their screams was more than we could bear.* 听他们尖叫我们可真受不了。| **grin and bear it** (=accept something unpleasant without complaining) 逆来顺受；苦笑着忍受；默默承受 *It's no good moaning – you'll just have to grin and bear it.* 老是抱怨也没有用——你只能忍下来算了。

4 bear the costs/burden/expense etc *formal* to pay for something【正式】承担费用/负担/开支等：*As usual, the poorest members of society are bearing the burden of tax increases.* 一如既往，社会上最贫穷的人承受着增税的负担。

5 bear responsibility/the blame etc *formal* to be responsible, accept the blame etc for something【正式】承担责任/应受责备等：*In this case, the victim must bear some responsibility for the crime.* 在这起案件中，受害者本人必须承担部分责任。

6 ►SUPPORT 支持◄ to support the weight of something 支撑〔重量〕：*I don't think the table is strong enough to bear your weight.* 我看这桌子承受不住你的重量。| *a load-bearing wall* 承重墙

7 doesn't bear thinking about so unpleasant or shocking that you prefer not to think about it 不堪设想：*The long-term consequences of a nuclear leak don't bear thinking about.* 核泄漏造成的长期后果真是不堪设想。

8 bear a resemblance/relation etc to to be similar to or connected with someone or something else 与…相似/与…有关等：*George doesn't bear much resemblance to his father.* 乔治长得不太像他父亲。| *The things she says bear little relation to what she actually does.* 她说的和她做的不大相符。

9 bear the strain/pressure etc to be strong enough or firm enough to continue despite problems 承受压力等：*She suddenly became a big star, and their marriage was unable to bear the strain.* 她突然间成了大明星，他们的婚姻承受不了这样的压力。

10 bear the brunt of to have to accept the most difficult or damaging part of something 首当其冲：*It's the junior staff who will bear the brunt of the redundancies.* 低级职员将首当其冲被裁员。

11 bear (sb) a grudge to continue to feel annoyed about something that someone did a long time ago 对〔某人〕怀恨在心：*Despite her treatment of him over the years, he bears her no grudges.* 尽管多年来她一直待他不好，他并没有怀恨在心。

12 bear fruit a) if a plan, decision etc bears fruit, it is successful, especially after a long period of time〔尤指计划、决定等长时间之后〕有了成果；成功了：*Our careful investments were finally bearing fruit.* 我们谨慎的投资终于得到了回报。**b)** if a tree bears fruit, it produces fruit〔果树〕结果

13 ►SHOW SIGNS OF 显出…的迹象◄ to show physical or emotional signs of a past experience 显示；具有，带有〔标记或特征〕：*Jim proudly bears the scars of his rugby days.* 吉姆自豪地展示他当橄榄球员时留下的伤疤。

14 not bear examination/inspection etc to not be suitable or good enough to be tested or examined thoroughly 经受不住检查/审查等：*This line of argument doesn't bear much examination.* 这样的论据经不起推敲。

15 bring influence/pressure etc to bear (on) to use your influence or power to get what you want（对…）施加压力；敦促：*The tobacco companies are bringing pressure to bear on the government to stop the advertising ban.* 烟草公司向政府施压，促其取消香烟广告的禁令。

16 bear witness to *formal* to show that something is true or exists【正式】证明，作证：*Her latest film bears witness to her versatility as a director.* 她最近拍的电影证明她是一位多才多艺的导演。

17 bear right/left to turn towards the right or left 向右/左转：*Bear left at the crossroads.* 在十字路口向左转。| *The road bears round to the right.* 这条路过个环岛向右转。

18 ►BABY 婴儿◄ *formal* to give birth to a baby【正式】生育：**bear sb a child/son/daughter** (=have their baby) 为某人生孩子/儿子/女儿 *She bore him three sons.* 她为他生了三个儿子。

19 bear yourself *formal* to walk, stand etc in a particular way, especially when this shows your character【正式】表现；保持某种举止：*Throughout the trial, she bore herself with great dignity.* 在整个审判过程中，她都保持着端庄的举止。

20 ►CARRY 携带◄ *literary* to carry someone or something, especially something important【文】运送；携带；传运：*The emperor was borne along in a sedan chair.* 皇帝是一路坐着轿子来的。| *A messenger arrived, bearing a message from the prince.* 来了一位使者，带来了王子的口信。

21 ►WIND/WATER 风/水◄ *literary* if the wind, sea, or air bears something, it moves it along【文】吹动；传送：*The sound of music was borne along on the wind.* 乐声随风飘送。

22 ►SIGN/MARK 记号/标记◄ *formal* to have or show a sign or mark【正式】带有〔标记〕：*The letter bore no signature.* 这封信上没有署名。

23 ►NAME/TITLE 姓名/头衔◄ *formal* to have a particular name or title【正式】具有，拥有〔名字或头衔〕：*The chest bears the name of Chippendale.* 箱子上有〔英国著名家具公司〕奇彭代尔公司的牌子。

24 bear sb no malice/ill will etc *formal* not to feel angry towards someone【正式】对某人没有恶意/敌意等

Frequencies of the verbs **bear, stand,** and **endure** in spoken and written English 动词bear, stand和endure在英语口语和书面语中的使用频率

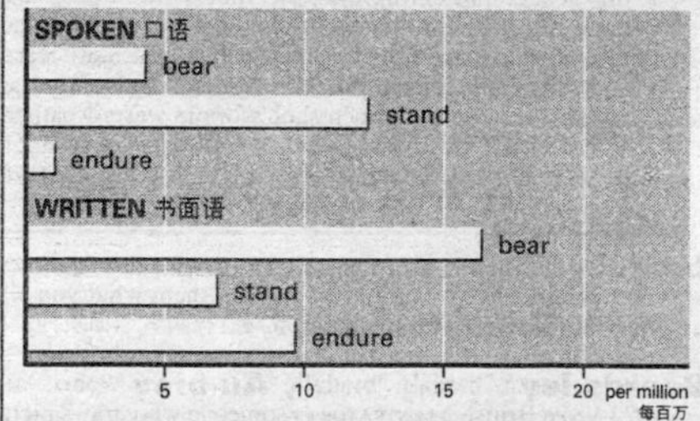

Based on the British National Corpus and the Longman Lancaster Corpus
据英国国家语料库和朗文兰开斯特语料库

All three verbs are used to mean 'accept or deal with an unpleasant situation'. The graph shows that in this meaning **stand** and **bear** are much more common than **endure** in spoken English. In written English, **bear** is the most common and **endure**, a formal word, is fairly common. 这三个动词都用来表示"接受或应付令人不快的局面"。本图表显示，作此意解释时，stand和bear在口语中的使用频率远远高于endure。在书面语中，bear最常用；endure语气正式，也相当常用。

bear down *phr v* **1 bear down on** to move quickly towards someone in a threatening way 向…逼近；冲向：*His aunt bore down on him and insisted he joined them for dinner.* 他的姨妈跑到他身边，坚持要他和他们一起吃饭。| *A powerboat was bearing down on us.* 一艘汽艇向我们逼近。**2** [I] to use all your strength and effort to push or press down on something 使劲推；使劲压下 **3** [T **bear** sb/sth ↔ **down**] *formal* to defeat a person or deal successfully with a difficult situation【正式】压倒；征服；打败

bear on/upon sth *phr v* [T] *formal* to have a connection with something【正式】与…有联系，与…有关

bear sb/sth **out** *phr v* [T] if facts or information bear out a claim, story, opinion etc, they help to prove that it is true 为…作证，证实，支持〔某种说法〕：*Recent evidence bears out the idea that students learn best in small groups.* 最新的证据显示，学生以小组形式学习效果最佳。| *Tell them what really happened. I'll bear you out.* 把真相告诉他们吧，我会为你作证。

bear up *phr v* [I] to show courage or determination during a difficult or unpleasant time 支持住，撑下去；不气馁：*How has he been bearing up since the accident?* 事故发生后，他是怎样挺过来的？

bear with sb/sth *phr v* [T] **1 bear with me** *spoken* used to ask someone politely to wait while you find out information, finish what you are doing etc【口】耐心等待；别着急：*Bear with me a minute, and I'll check if Mr Garrard's in.* 请等一下，让我看看加勒德先生在不在。**2** to be patient or continue to do something difficult or unpleasant 容忍，忍耐：*I tried to bear with her tempers.* 我努力去容忍她的脾气。

bear² *n* [C] **1** a large strong animal with thick fur that eats flesh, fruit, and insects 熊 —see also 另见 TEDDY BEAR, POLAR BEAR **2** *technical* someone who sells shares (SHARE² (5)) or goods when they expect the price to fall【术语】〔股市或期货〕看跌的人：**a bear market** (=when the value of business shares is falling) 熊市 **3** *informal* a big man who is rough or bad-tempered【非正式】粗暴鲁莽的人，脾气暴躁的人 **4 be like a bear with a sore head** *informal* to be rude to people because you are feeling bad-tempered【非正式】脾气暴躁

bear·a·ble /ˈbɛrəbl; ˈbeərəbəl/ *adj* something that is bearable is difficult or unpleasant, but you can deal with it 忍耐得住的，可忍受的，可容忍的：*His friendship was the only thing that made life bearable.* 唯有他的友情能使生活不那么艰难。—**bearably** *adv*

bear claw /ˈ· ·/ *n* [C] *AmE* fruit covered in PASTRY with long cuts made across the top【美】〔顶部带有平行切条的〕熊掌形水果馅饼

beard¹ /bɪrd; bɪəd/ *n* [C] **1** hair that grows around a man's chin 胡须 —compare 比较 MOUSTACHE **2** something similar to a beard, such as hair growing on an animal's chin 须状物〔如动物的胡须〕—**bearded** *adj*

CULTURAL NOTE 文化注释

In the UK, people sometimes use the phrase 'beards and sandals' in a joking way to describe the type of people who are interested in protecting the environment, achieving peace, and eating ORGANIC food (=food produced naturally, without the use of chemicals). It is a STEREOTYPE used to make fun of people such as university teachers who people often think of as having beards and wearing SANDALS (=a light open shoe worn in warm weather). 英国人有时用 beards and sandals 这个短语来戏称热衷环保、维护和平、吃有机食品的人。人们常认为大学教师这类的人爱留胡子、穿凉鞋，因此经常用该短语来取笑他们。

beard² *v* [T] **beard sb in their den** to go and see someone who has influence or authority, and tell them what you want, why you disagree with them etc 敢对有权势者当面责问；太岁头上动土

Beards·ley /ˈbɪrdzlɪ; ˈbɪədzli/, **Au·brey** /ˈɔbrɪ; ˈɔːbri/ (1872-98) a British ILLUSTRATOR (=someone who draws pictures for books) who is famous for his black and white pictures with clear rounded lines 比尔兹利〔(1872-1898) 英国插图画家，以线条清晰浑圆的黑白画著称〕

bear·er /ˈbɛrɚ; ˈbeərə/ *n* [C] **1** *formal* someone whose job is to carry something such as a flag or a STRETCHER (=light bed for a sick person)【正式】持…的人；抬[担、背]着…的人；旗手 **2** someone who brings you information, a letter etc 带信人：*I hate to be the bearer of bad news, but...* 我不愿当一个带来坏消息的人，但是… **3** *law* the bearer of a legal document such as a PASSPORT is the person that it officially belongs to【法律】〔证件的〕持有者 **4** *IndE, PakE* a male servant【印，巴】男仆

bear hug /ˈ· ·/ *n* [C] an action in which you put your arms around someone and hold them very tightly because you like them or are pleased to see them 紧紧的拥抱

bear·ing /ˈbɛrɪŋ; ˈbeərɪŋ/ *n* **1 have some/no etc bearing on** to have some influence, no influence etc on something 对…有/无影响等：*Recent market fluctuations have had a direct bearing on company policy.* 近期市场的波动对公司政策有直接影响。**2 lose your bearings** to become confused about where you are or what you should do next 迷失方向，晕头转向：*I completely lost my bearings in the dark.* 漆黑中我一点儿也辨不清方向。**3 get your bearings** to find out exactly where you are, or feel confident that you know where you are 弄清自己的方位，辨明方向：*Jim'll show you around and help you get your bearings.* 吉姆会带你四处逛逛，帮你熟悉一下这个地方。**4** [singular,U] the way in which you move, stand, or behave, especially when this shows your character 举止，风度 **5** [C] *technical* a direction or angle that is shown by a COMPASS (1)【术语】〔罗盘显示的〕方向，方位；方位角 **6** [C] *technical* part of a machine that turns on another part, or in which a turning part is held【术语】〔机器的〕承座；轴承

bear·ish /ˈbɛrɪʃ; ˈbeərɪʃ/ *adj* **1** rude or bad-tempered 没礼貌的，粗鲁的；暴躁的 **2 a)** a bearish market is one where the prices of shares (SHARE² (5)) are decreasing 行情看跌的 **b)** someone who is bearish expects the price of business shares to go down〔人〕预料股市行情下跌的—**bearishly** *adv*—**bearishness** *n*

bear·skin /ˈbɛrˌskɪn; ˈbeəˌskɪn/ *n* **1** [C,U] the skin of a bear 熊皮 **2** [C] a tall hat made of black fur, worn by some British soldiers for special ceremonies〔一些英国士兵在特殊仪式上戴的〕黑色熊皮高帽

beast /bist; biːst/ *n* [C] **1** *literary* an animal, especially a large or dangerous one【文】〔尤指庞大或危险的〕野兽 **2** *old-fashioned especially spoken* someone who is cruel or unpleasant【过时，尤口】令人讨厌的人，畜生，禽兽：*You filthy beast!* 你这个下流的畜生！**3** *spoken* a job, problem etc that is difficult to deal with【口】难办的事，难题：*Can you undo this jar? It's a real beast to open.* 你能把这瓶子打开吗？它真难开。**4 the beast in sb** the part of someone's character that makes them experience hatred, strong sexual feelings, violence etc 人的兽性：*You bring out the beast in me. Come here!* 你激起了我的野性。过来！

beast·ly /ˈbistlɪ; ˈbiːstli/ *adj old-fashioned especially spoken* very unpleasant; nasty【过时，尤口】令人不快的，讨厌的；恶劣的：*What beastly weather!* 天气真恶劣！—**beastly** *adv*—**beastliness** *n* [U]

beast of bur·den /ˌ· · ˈ··/ *n* [C] *old use* an animal that does heavy work【旧】役畜，力畜

beat¹ /bit; biːt/ *v past tense* **beat** *past participle* **beaten** /ˈbitn; ˈbiːtn/

1 ▶DEFEAT 打败◀ [T] **a)** to get the most points, votes etc in a game, race, or competition 击败，打败，战胜：*Brazil were beaten in the final 2-1.* 巴西队在决赛中以1比2告负。| *I could always beat my brother at chess.* 每次下棋，我都能赢我哥哥。| **beat sb hollow** (=defeat them easily)〔在比赛中〕轻取对方 **b)** to successfully deal with or defeat a problem that you have been struggling with 战胜；克服：*The Administration claims to have beaten inflation.* 政府宣称已成功地遏制了通货膨胀。—see 见 WIN¹ (USAGE)

2 ▶HIT 打◀ [T] to hit someone or something many times with your hand or with a stick〔接连地〕打，击：*In those days children were often beaten at school.* 那些日子，孩子们在学校经常挨打。| *I've been beating the rugs and I'm covered in dust.* 我一直在拍打地毯，所以浑身全是灰尘。| **beat sb to death/beat sb unconscious etc** (=beat them until they die etc) 把某人打死/打昏等 | **beat sb black and blue** (=make marks on their body by beating them hard) 把某人打得青一块紫一块 | **beat the living daylights out of** *informal* (=beat someone very hard)【非正式】痛打，狠揍

3 beat a record/score etc to do better than a record etc that already exists 打破纪录等：*The record set by Kierson in 1984 has yet to be beaten.* 基尔逊在1984年创下的纪录至今无人打破。

4 ▶HIT AGAINST 碰撞◀ [I always+adv/prep] to knock or hit against something continuously〔连续〕撞击，拍打：**beat on/against etc** *Waves beat against the cliffs.* 海浪拍打着悬崖。| *We could hear the rain beating on the roof.* 我们可以听到雨点拍打屋顶的声音。

5 beat sb to it *informal* to get or do something before someone else, especially if you are both trying to do it first【非正式】赶在前面，抢先一步：*I really wanted that car but someone else had beaten me to it.* 我很想要那辆车，但有人抢先一步把它买了。

6 (it) beats me *spoken* used to say that you cannot understand or explain something【口】把我难住了: *"How can these kids afford clothes like that?" "Beats me."* "这些孩子怎么买得起那样的衣服?" "我也搞不清楚。"
7 ▶MIX 混合◀[T] to mix things together with a fork or machine when preparing food 搅拌, 搅打: *Beat the eggs until they are light and fluffy.* 把蛋液打到松软不再黏稠。
8 ▶DRUMS 鼓◀[I,T] if you beat the drums or if drums beat, they make a regular continuous sound 击(鼓), 打(鼓)
9 ▶HEART 心◀[I] when your heart beats, it moves in a regular RHYTHM (1) as it pumps your blood〔心〕跳动: *He's still alive – I can feel his heart beating.* 他还活着, 我能感觉到他的心跳。
10 ▶WINGS 翅膀◀[I,T] if a bird beats its wings or its wings beat, they move up and down quickly and regularly〔鸟〕拍打〔翅膀〕;〔翅膀〕有规律地动
11 you can't beat *spoken* used to say that someone or something is better than anything else【口】什么也比不上: *You can't beat motor racing for excitement and danger.* 什么也比不上赛车那样刺激又惊险。
12 take some beating a) to be difficult to beat 难以战胜: *Schumacher has 42 points, which will take some beating.* 舒马赫得到42分, 要战胜他不容易。**b)** to be better, more enjoyable etc than almost anything else of the same type 是最好的, 是最精彩的: *As a winter sports center, Edmonton takes some beating.* 作为冬季体育运动中心, 埃德蒙顿是最好的。
13 ▶BE BETTER 更好◀[T not in progressive 不用进行式] *spoken* to be much better and more enjoyable than something else【口】好多了, 强多了: *This job sure beats tending bar!* 这工作肯定比当酒吧侍者好多了!
14 beat the rush to do something earlier than normal in order to avoid problems when everyone does it 提前行动〔以避免人多麻烦〕: *Shop now and beat the Christmas rush!* 现在就去购物吧, 避免圣诞节人多拥挤。
15 beat about/around the bush to avoid or delay talking about something embarrassing or unpleasant〔说话〕转弯抹角, 旁敲侧击: *Stop beating about the bush and tell me why you're here.* 不要转弯抹角了, 快告诉我你来干什么。
16 beat the system to find ways of avoiding or breaking the rules of an organization, system etc, in order to achieve what you want 钻制度[规章]等的空子
17 beat it! *spoken* used to tell someone to leave at once because they are annoying you or should not be there【口】走开! 滚开!
18 beat your brains out *AmE informal* to think about something very hard and for a long time【美, 非正式】绞尽脑汁, 苦苦思索
19 beat the rap *AmE informal* to avoid being punished for something you have done【美, 非正式】逃脱惩罚
20 if you can't beat 'em, join 'em *spoken* used when you decide to take part in something although you disapprove of it, because everyone else is doing it and you cannot stop them【口】随大溜〔若阻止不了别人做某事, 那自己也加入一起干〕
21 beat time to make regular movements or sounds to show the speed at which music should be played 打拍子: *a conductor beating time with his baton* 用指挥棒打拍子的乐队指挥
22 can you beat that/it? *spoken* used to show that you are surprised or annoyed by something【口】竟有这等事? 岂有此理? 你听到过[看见过]如此奇怪的人[事]吗?〔表示惊讶或恼火〕: *He's taken the money and gone! Can you beat that?* 他把钱拿走了! 真是岂有此理!
23 beat a path (to sb's door) if people beat a path to your door, they are interested in something you are selling, a service you are providing etc 纷纷前来购买: *They'll be beating a path to your door after this ad.* 他们看过这则广告后, 一定会纷纷前来抢购的。
24 to beat the band *AmE informal* in large amounts or with great force【美, 非正式】大量地; 大力地: *It's raining to beat the band.* 正下着倾盆大雨。
25 beat the heat *AmE informal* to make yourself cooler【美, 非正式】凉快一下: *Let's go swimming to beat the heat.* 我们去游泳吧, 凉快一下。
26 ▶METAL 金属◀[T] to hit metal with a hammer in order to shape it or make it thinner 锤打, (用锤)敲打
27 ▶HUNTING 打猎◀[I,T] to force wild birds and animals out of bushes, long grass etc so that they can be shot for sport 将猎物赶出〔草丛、树丛等〕
28 beat your breast *literary* to show clearly that you are very upset or sorry about something【文】捶胸顿足〔表示愤怒或悲伤〕 —see also 另见 BEATEN, BEATING

beat down *phr v* **1** [I] if the sun beats down, it shines very brightly and the weather is hot〔烈日〕曝晒 **2** [I] if the rain beats down, it is raining very hard〔雨〕下得很大 **3** [T **beat** sb ↔ **down**] to persuade someone to reduce a price 使〔某人〕压低价钱, 杀价: **beat sb down to sth** *He wanted £4,500 for the car but I beat him down to £3,850.* 这辆车他要价4500英镑, 但最后我压到3850英镑。

beat off *phr v* **1** [T **beat** sb/sth ↔ **off**] to prevent someone who is trying to attack you, harm you, or compete against you 击退, 打退, 赶跑: *efforts to beat off our business rivals* 为打败我们的商业对手而作出的努力 | *We managed to beat off the dogs and run away.* 我们设法把狗打跑, 才得以脱身。**2** [I,T **beat** sb ↔ **off**] *AmE taboo slang* to MASTURBATE【美, 讳, 俚】手淫, 自渎

beat out *phr v* **1** [T **beat** sth ↔ **out**] to put out a fire by beating it 扑灭〔火〕 **2** [T **beat** sth **out of** sb] to force someone to tell you something by beating them 拷打逼供: *I had the truth beaten out of me by my father.* 爸爸逼我说出了真相。**3** [T **beat** sth ↔ **out**] if drums beat out a RHYTHM (1) or you beat out a rhythm on the drums, they make a continuous regular sound 用鼓点敲出〔节拍〕 **4** [T **beat** sb ↔ **out**] *AmE* to defeat someone in a competition【美】战胜, 打败: *Roberts beat out Tony Gwynn for the Most Valuable Player Award.* 罗伯茨击败托尼·格温获得最有价值球员奖。

beat up *phr v* **1** [T **beat** sb ↔ **up**] to hurt someone badly by hitting them 痛打, 殴打; 打伤: *They claimed they had been beaten up by the police.* 他们声称曾被警察毒打。**2 beat up on** *AmE* to hit someone and harm them, especially someone younger or weaker than yourself【美】殴打; 欺负〔尤指弱小者〕 **3 beat up on yourself** *AmE informal* to blame yourself too much for something【美, 非正式】太过自责

beat² *n* **1** [C] one of a series of movements or hitting actions〔连续敲打的〕一击, 敲击: *a heartbeat* 心跳 | *the slow beat of the drum* 缓慢的鼓声 **2** [C usually singular 一般用单数] a regular repeated noise 有规律而重复的声音: [+**of**] *the beat of marching feet* 列队行进的脚步声 **3** [singular] the main RHYTHM (1) that a piece of music or a poem has〔音乐或诗歌的〕拍子, 节拍: *Try to follow the beat.* 尽量跟着拍子。**4** [C] one of the notes in a piece of music that sounds stronger than the other notes〔音乐〕强节奏 **5** [singular] the area of a town, city etc that a police officer regularly walks around〔警察的〕巡逻路线 W3

beat³ *adj* [not before noun 不用于名词前] *informal* very tired【非正式】疲惫不堪的: *I'm beat.* 我累极了。| **dead beat** *Come and sit down, you must be dead beat.* 过来坐下, 你一定累坏了。

beat·en /ˈbitn; ˈbiːtn/ *adj* [only before noun 仅用于名词前] **1** beaten metal has been shaped with a hammer to make it thinner〔金属〕锻打的, 锤制而成的 **2** a beaten path, track etc has been made by many people walking the same way〔路等〕被踏成的, 走出来的: *a well beaten path through the forest* 人们在森林中踏出来的路 **3 off the beaten track** a place that is off the beaten track is not well known and is far away from the places that people usually visit〔地方〕不出名的; 人迹罕至的; 偏远的

beat·er /ˈbitə; ˈbiːtə/ *n* [C] **1** an object that is designed to beat something 拍打器; 搅拌器: *an egg beater* 打蛋器 | *a carpet beater* (清理)地毯的掸子 **2** someone who forces wild birds or animals out of bushes, long grass etc so that they can be shot for sport〔把野生动物或鸟赶向猎人枪口的〕猎人助手 **3** *AmE informal* an old car in bad condition【美, 非正式】破旧的汽车, 老爷车

Beat Gen·er·a·tion, the /˙ ·...˙/ the group of young people in the 1950s, including the writers Jack Kerouac and Allen Ginsberg, who refused to accept the values of Western society, and showed this by refusing to work, keeping no material possessions, and wearing their own style of clothes 垮掉的一代〔指20世纪50年代的一群年轻人, 包括杰克·凯鲁亚克和艾伦·金斯堡等作家。他们不愿工作, 不积蓄财物, 身着别具一格的衣服, 以此拒绝接受西方社会的价值观〕

bea·tif·ic /ˌbiəˈtɪfɪk; ˌbiːəˈtɪfɪk◂/ *adj literary* a beatific look, smile etc shows great peace and happiness【文】极乐的; 幸福的; 安息的 —**beatifically** /-kḷɪ; -kli/ *adv*

be·at·i·fy /bɪˈætəˌfaɪ; biˈætɪ̌faɪ/ *v* [T] if the Roman Catholic church beatifies someone who has died, it says officially that they are a holy or special person〔罗马天主教〕为〔死者〕行宣福礼 —**beatification** /bɪˌætəfəˈkeʃən; biˌætɪ̌fɪ̌ˈkeɪʃən/ *n* [U]

beat·ing /ˈbitɪŋ; ˈbiːtɪŋ/ *n* [C] **1** an act of hitting someone many times as a punishment or in a fight 打, 击; 痛打: **give sb a beating** (=beat them) 揍某人一顿 **2 take a beating** to lose very badly in a game or competition 惨败, 败北: *Our team took a real beating on Saturday.* 我队在星期六遭到惨败。—see also 另见 **take some beating** (BEAT¹ (12))

Be·at·i·tudes, the /bɪˋætɪtjudz; biˈætɪ̯tjuːdz/ *n* [plural] in the Bible, a set of eight statements made by Jesus which list the types of people who are 'blessed' (=especially loved by God). Each statement starts with the words "Blessed are...", for example "Blessed are the poor in spirit". 基督八福〔《圣经》中耶稣登山训谕的八福词, 罗列了八种有福之人。每句都有"…有福了"这样的词语, 如"虚心的人有福了。"〕

B

Beat·les, the /ˈbitḷz; ˈbiːtlz/ a British popular music group who made their first record in 1962 and became the most famous and successful group ever. Their records include *Love Me Do, I Want to Hold Your Hand, A Hard Day's Night, Yellow Submarine*, and *Sgt Pepper's Lonely Hearts Club Band*. They had a great influence on the development of popular music. 甲壳虫乐队〔英国一流行音乐组合, 1962年灌制了首张唱片, 成为当时最著名、最成功的一支乐队, 唱片有《请爱我》、《我愿握着你的手》、《忙乱了一天之后的夜晚》、《黄色潜艇》以及《佩珀军士寂寞的心俱乐部乐队》, 对流行音乐的发展产生了重大影响〕

beat·nik /ˈbitnɪk; ˈbiːtnɪk/ *n* [C] one of a group of young people in the late 1950s and early 1960s, who did not accept the values of society and showed this by their clothes and the way they lived 垮掉的一代的人, 〔俗称〕披头族成员〔20世纪50年代末和60年代初出现于美国的反对世俗陈规和传统生活方式的年轻人〕

Bea·ton /ˈbitn̩; ˈbiːtn/, **Sir Ce·cil** /ˈsɛsḷ; ˈsesəl/ (1904-80) a British photographer and designer for fashion, theatre, and film. He is famous for his pictures of famous and wealthy people. 比顿〔(1904-1980), 英国摄影家, 时装、戏剧与电影服装设计师, 以拍摄名流巨富的肖像而著名〕

Bea·trice /ˈbɪətrɪs; ˈbɪətrɪ̯s/ the main female character who guides Dante through Paradise in *The Divine Comedy* 贝雅特里齐〔《神曲》中为但丁指引天堂之路的女子〕

beat-up /ˈ· ·/ *adj informal* a beat-up car, bicycle etc, is old and in bad condition【非正式】破旧的, 破烂的: *a beat-up old Ford Escort* 一辆破旧的福特"护航舰"汽车

beau /bo; bəʊ/ *n plural* **beaux** /boz; bəʊz/ or **beaus** [C] *old-fashioned*【过时】**1** a woman's close friend or lover〔女子的〕密友; 情人 **2** a fashionable, well-dressed man 花花公子, 纨绔子弟; 衣着入时的男子

Beau·jo·lais /ˌboʒəˋle; ˈbəʊʒəleɪ/ *n* [C,U] a type of French red wine 博若莱葡萄酒〔一种法国红葡萄酒〕

Beaujolais nou·veau /bozəˌle nuˋvo; ˌbəʊzəleɪ nuːˈvəʊ/ a type of Beaujolais wine that is drunk almost as soon as it has been made 博若莱新酿葡萄酒〔一种即酿即饮的葡萄酒〕

> **CULTURAL NOTE 文化注释**
> In the UK, there is a competition each year to see who can bring the first bottles from France to England. 英国每年举办一种比赛, 看谁能把新酿造出来的第一批博若莱新酿葡萄酒从法国运到英国。

beau-monde /bo ˋmʌnd; ˌbəʊ ˈmɒnd/ *n* [singular] *French* rich and fashionable people【法】富有而时髦的人

beaut¹ /bjut; bjuːt/ *n* [singular] *AmE & AustrE informal* **a (real) beaut** used to say that something is either very good or very bad【美和澳, 非正式】好事; 丑事: *That last catch was a beaut.* 最后一个接球太棒了[真差劲]。

beaut² *adj AustrE informal* very good【澳, 非正式】棒的, 好的: *"Had a good day?" "It was beaut."* "今天好玩吗?" "棒极了。"

beau·te·ous /ˈbjutɪəs; ˈbjuːtiəs/ *adj poetic* beautiful【诗】美丽的, 优美的: *the beauteous Helen of Troy* 特洛伊城美丽的海伦 —**beauteously** *adv*

beau·ti·cian /bjuˋtɪʃən; bjuːˈtɪʃən/ *n* [C] someone whose job is to give beauty treatments to your skin, hair etc 美容师; 美发师

1 2 **beau·ti·ful** /ˈbjutəfəl; ˈbjuːtɪ̯fəl/ *adj* **1** someone or something that is beautiful is extremely good to look at and gives you a feeling of pleasure 美丽的, 美好的, 优美的: *She was even more beautiful than I had remembered.* 她比我记忆中的更美。| *a beautiful bunch of flowers* 美丽的花束 **2** very good 极好的, 妙极的: *a beautiful experience* 愉快的经历 | *What a beautiful shot!* 多么漂亮的枪法! | *The weather was beautiful.* 天气好极了。—**beautifully** *adv*

> **USAGE NOTE 用法说明: BEAUTIFUL**
> WORD CHOICE 词语辨析: **beautiful, pretty, handsome, good-looking, attractive, sexy**
> **Beautiful** and **pretty** can be used of women, children, and things, but not usually of men, unless you want to suggest that they have female features. beautiful 和 pretty 可以用来形容女子、孩子和事物, 但通常不用来形容男子, 除非这男子带有女人气: *a beautiful girl/house/view* 美丽的女孩/漂亮的房子/优美的景色 | *a pretty child/picture/voice* 漂亮的孩子/精美的图画/美妙的声音。**Beautiful** is the strongest word to describe a very attractive appearance, it suggests that someone has almost perfect good looks. **Pretty** means good-looking in a more ordinary way, but not really beautiful. beautiful 语气最强, 说明某人长得非常漂亮, 几近完美。pretty 表示一般的漂亮, 但不是特别漂亮。
> **Handsome** is not common in spoken English. It is usually used to describe men, especially if they have the strong regular features that men in romantic stories are supposed to have. A **handsome** woman is **good-looking** in a strong, healthy way. handsome 在英语口语中用得不多。它通常用于形容男子, 特别是在浪漫故事中的英俊男子。handsome 也可以用来形容女子, 表示强壮、健美的女性。
> **Good-looking** can be used about men and women, but not usually about things. good-looking 既可形容男子, 也可形容女子, 但通常不用于形容事物: *Gina and Barry are a good-looking couple.* 吉娜和巴里两口子都很好看。
> **Attractive** can be used about men, women, and things. attractive 可以用来形容男子、女子和事物: *an attractive colour/idea/young man* 好看的颜色/好主意/有魅力的年轻男子。
> An **attractive** person may not be very **good-looking** but makes other people sexually interested in them, though not as much as if they are **sexy**. attractive 不一定是长得好看而是很有魅力、很性感, 但语气上不像 sexy 那样强烈。

beau·ti·fy /ˈbjutəˌfaɪ; ˈbjuːtɪ̯faɪ/ *v* [T] to make someone or something beautiful 使美丽, 美化

beau·ty /ˈbjutɪ; ˈbjuːti/ *n*

1 ▶APPEARANCE 外表◀ a) [U] a quality that a place or person has that makes them very attractive to look at 美, 美丽, 漂亮: *Her beauty had faded over the years.* 这么多年过去了, 她的美貌渐渐失色。| *an area of outstanding natural beauty* 景色优美的地方 | **beauty product/tip etc** (=a product etc that is supposed to make you more beautiful) 美容产品/美容小提示等 **b)** [C] *old-fashioned* a woman who is very beautiful【过时】美人: *She was considered a great beauty in her youth.* 她年轻时是个公认的大美人。

2 ▶GOOD QUALITY 优质◀ [U] a quality that something such as a poem, song, emotion etc has, which gives you pleasure or joy 美感: *the beauty of Shakespeare's verse* 莎士比亚诗作之美

3 ▶ADVANTAGE 长处◀ the beauty of a particularly good quality that makes something especially suitable or useful …的优点; …的好处; …的妙处: *The beauty of golf is that you can play it on your own.* 高尔夫球的好处在于可以一个人自己玩。

4 ▶GOOD EXAMPLE 范例◀ [C] *spoken* a very good example of something or an object that is a particularly good, large, or pleasant one of its type【口】很好的样品; 美好的事物: *We had a turkey at Easter – a real beauty it was.* 复活节时我们吃了火鸡, 那真是美味。| *That black eye's a beauty, Justin!* 贾斯廷, 那被打青的眼睛真是够漂亮的!

5 ▶APPROVAL 赞同◀ (you) beauty! *AustrE spoken* used to show that you are very pleased by something【澳口】(你) 太好了! 棒极了!〔表示高兴〕: *Look at this lunch. Beauty!* 看这顿中午饭, 太棒了! | *You beauty! You've made my day.* 你太好了! 你让我太高兴了!

6 beauty is in the eye of the beholder used to say that different people have different opinions about what is beautiful 情人眼里出西施

Beauty and the Beast /ˌ· · · ˈ·/ an old story about a beautiful young girl called Beauty, who is forced to live with a frightening creature called the Beast. The Beast loves her and she gradually begins to care about him too. He continually asks her to marry him, and when she finally agrees, he magically becomes the beautiful prince that he used to be.《美女与野兽》〔一个古老的传说, 讲述一位年轻漂亮姑娘(名叫美女)被迫要与一只可怕的怪物(名叫野兽)一起生活的故事。野兽爱她, 她也渐渐地关心起了野兽。野兽接二连三地向她求婚, 姑娘终于应允, 野兽则奇迹般地恢复了自己以前英俊王子的模样〕

beauty con·test /ˈ· ·, ·ˈ/ *n* [C] a competition in which women are judged on how attractive they look 选美(比赛)

> **CULTURAL NOTE 文化注释**
> Beauty contests became much less popular in the 1980s and 1990s, and many people disapprove of the idea that women should be judged on their appearance. 20世纪80, 90年代, 选美比赛的受关注度大不如前, 很多人不赞成以外貌评判女性。

beauty mark /'‥ ˌ/ *n* [C] *AmE* a small dark mark on a woman's skin【美】美人痣，美人斑；BEAUTY SPOT (2) *BrE*【英】

beauty par·lor /'‥ ˌ‥/ *n* [C] *AmE* a beauty salon【美】美容院

beauty queen /'‥ ˌ/ *n* [C] the winner of a beauty contest 选美皇后〔选美比赛的优胜者〕

beauty sal·on /'‥ ˌ‥/ *n* [C] a place in which you can receive beauty treatments for your skin, hair etc 美容院

beauty shop /'‥ ˌ/ *n* [C] *AmE* a beauty salon【美】美容院

beauty sleep /'‥ ˌ/ *n* [U] *humorous* enough sleep to keep you healthy and looking good【幽默】美容睡眠〔指充分的睡眠有益于美容〕: *I need my beauty sleep.* 我需要睡个美容觉。

beauty spot /'‥ ˌ/ *n* [C] **1** a beautiful place in the countryside 名胜，美景 **2** *BrE* a small dark mark on a woman's skin【英】美人痣，美人斑；BEAUTY MARK *AmE*【美】—see picture on page A6 参见 A6 页图

Beau·voir /bovˋwɑr; 'bəʊvwɑː/, **Si·mone de** /sɪˋmon də; sɪ'məʊn də/ (1908-86) a French writer who had an important influence on the development of FEMINISM. Her most famous book is *The Second Sex*. She was for many years in a relationship with Jean-Paul Sartre. 波伏娃〔(1908-1986)，法国作家，对女性主义的发展产生过重要影响，作品以《第二性》最为著名，曾与让·保罗·萨特相恋多年〕

bea·ver[1] /ˋbivɚ; 'biːvə/ *n* [C] a North American animal that has thick fur, a wide flat tail, and cuts down trees with its teeth 河狸，海狸 —see also 另见 **eager beaver** (EAGER (3))

CULTURAL NOTE 文化注释
People think of beavers as working very hard. 河狸被看做是十分勤劳的动物。

beaver[2] *v*
beaver away *phr v BrE informal* to work very hard, especially at writing or calculating something【英，非正式】卖力地干，努力工作〔尤指写作或计算〕: **[+at]** *He had been beavering away at his homework half the night.* 他整个晚上有一半的时间都在忙着做作业。

Bea·ver·brook /ˋbivɚbrʊk; 'biːvəbrʊk/, **Lord** (1879-1964) a powerful and successful British businessman and politician, who was born in Canada. He owned *The Daily Express* and other newspapers, and also had several important positions in the British government. 比弗布鲁克男爵〔(1879-1964)，英国富商，政治强人，生于加拿大，拥有《每日快报》等几家报纸，曾在英国政府中担任若干要职〕

be·bop /ˋbiˌbɑp; 'biːbɒp/ *n* [U] a type of JAZZ music; BOP[2] (2) 博普爵士乐

be·calmed /bɪˋkɑmd; bɪ'kɑːmd/ *adj literary* a ship or boat that is becalmed cannot move because there is no wind【文】〔舰船〕因无风而静止不动的

be·came /bɪˋkem; bɪ'keɪm/ the past tense of BECOME

S1 W1 **be·cause** /bɪˋkɔz; bɪ'kɒz/ *conjunction* **1** for the reason that 因为: *I do it because I like it.* 我这样做是因为我喜欢。| *She got the job because she was the best candidate.* 她得到了那份工作，因为她是最佳人选。| *"Why can't I go?" "Because you're too young."* "我为什么不能去?""因为你年纪太小了。" **2 because of** as a result of a particular thing or of someone's actions 因为，由于: *He had to retire because of ill health.* 他因为健康状况不佳，所以不得不退休。| *Sandy's very upset and it's all because of you.* (=your fault) 桑迪很生气，这全都怪你。—see 见 OWING (USAGE) **3 just because...** *spoken* used to say that although one thing is true, it does not mean that something else is true【口】仅仅因为: *Just because I'm married doesn't mean that I don't want to see my old friends anymore.* 不能仅仅因为我结婚了就认为我不想再见老朋友。| *David seems to think that just because he's our boss he can talk to us anyway he wants.* 戴维似乎认为就因为他是我们的老板，他爱对我们说什么就可以说什么。

beck /bɛk; bek/ *n* **1** [C] *BrE* a small stream【英】小溪流，山涧 **2 be at sb's beck and call** to always be ready to do what someone wants 听命于某人: *I was tired of being at her beck and call all day long.* 我厌倦了整天受她指使。

Bec·ket /ˋbɛkɪt; 'bekɪt/, **Saint Thomas à** (1118-70) an English priest who became the Archbishop of Canterbury. He had a serious argument with the king, Henry II, and was murdered in Canterbury Cathedral by some of the king's soldiers. 贝克特〔(1118-1170)，英国牧师，曾任坎特伯雷大主教，与国王亨利二世极为不和，在坎特伯雷大教堂被国王的卫兵杀害〕

Beck·ett /ˋbɛkɪt; 'bekɪt/, **Sam·u·el** /ˋsæmjuəl; 'sæmjuəl/ (1906-89) an Irish writer of plays, NOVELs, and poetry who lived in France and is famous for his play *Waiting for Godot* 贝克特〔(1906-1989)，爱尔兰剧作家、小说家和诗人，侨居法国，以其剧本《等待戈多》著称〕

beck·on /ˋbɛkən; 'bekən/ *v* [I,T] **1** to make a signal to someone with your hand or arm, to show that you want them to come towards you〔招手〕示意，召唤: **[+to]** *She beckoned to the child, who came running.* 她用手示意，那孩子就跑过来了。| **beckon sb forward/to/towards etc** *I stood there till she beckoned me across the room.* 我一直站在那儿，直到她示意我走到房间的那一边。**2** if something such as money or happiness beckons, it is so attractive that you have to do something in order to get it 吸引，引诱

be·come /bɪˋkʌm; bɪ'kʌm/ *v past tense* **became** /bɪˋkem; bɪ'keɪm/ *past participle* **become** **1** [linking verb 连系动词] to begin to be something, or to develop in a particular way 成为，变成，变得: *He became King at the age of 17.* 他 17 岁时成为国王。| *After the death of her father she became the richest woman in the world.* 她父亲死后，她成了世界上最富有的女人。| *The weather became warmer.* 天气变得更暖和了。| *We soon became acclimatized to the warmer weather.* 我们很快就适应了较暖和的气候。| *These constant delays are becoming a bit of a bore.* 这种经常性的耽搁成了令人讨厌的事。| *She became increasingly anxious about her husband's strange behaviour.* 她对丈夫的异常行为越来越担忧。| *He withdrew from the competition when it became clear that he stood no chance of winning.* 他知道自己在比赛中没有获胜的希望，便退出了比赛。**2** [T not in progressive 不用进行式] *formal* to suit someone or be suitable for them【正式】适合，适宜；与…相称: *This sort of behaviour hardly becomes a person in your position.* 这种行为与一个有你这样地位的人简直不相称。**3 what has become of...?/whatever will become of...?** used to ask what has happened to someone, especially when you have not seen them for a long time, or what will happen to someone that you are worried about …怎么样了?/…会怎么样?: *Whatever will become of Sam when his wife dies?* 如果萨姆的妻子死了，他会怎么样呢?

USAGE NOTE 用法说明: BECOME

WORD CHOICE 词语辨析: **become, get, turn, go, come**

Become and **get** can be used with most types of adjective to describe changes in people and things. **Become** is more common in writing, and **get** in spoken English, especially where a quick change is involved. become 和 get 两个动词可以和大部分形容词连用，以描述人和事物的变化。become 在书面语中比较常用，而 get 则多用于口语中，特别是指变化非常快: *The sky became/got cloudy.* 天空变得多云了。| *Crime is becoming more widespread.* 违法活动愈来愈普遍。| *It became clear that he was lying.* 他显然在撒谎。| *It gets dark early now.* 现在天黑得早了。| *I'm getting wet standing here.* 站在这儿，我都给淋湿了。| *Your dinner's getting cold.* 你的饭菜都凉了。

When things change colour, **turn** can be used, or less formally **go** (especially if the change does not last long). 说事物改变颜色时可用 turn，非正式情况下也用 go〔尤其当变化不是长久性的〕。Compare 比较: *Jonathan turned/went pale when he heard the news.* 乔纳森听到这个消息时，脸都变白了。| *It's that time of year when the leaves go/turn golden.* 那是一年中树叶变成金黄色的时候。

Go can also be used where someone's mind or body changes for the worse. go 也可用于表示人的精神或身体朝坏的方面变化: *He went crazy/blind/deaf/bald* (but 但说 *He fell sick/ill*). 他疯/瞎/聋/秃了。**Go** is used in a similar meaning with some things. go 也可用于表示某些事物向坏的方面变化: *The meat's gone bad.* 肉变坏了。| *Everything went wrong/haywire.* 所有的事情都一团糟。But in other situations **turn** is used. 但其他情况则用 turn: *The milk's turned/gone sour.* 牛奶变酸了。| *The situation turned nasty.* 局势变得很严峻。

Come is used only in very few expressions where something gets better. come 只用于少数短语中，表示事情向好的方面发展: *It came right in the end.* 结果挺好。| *All my dreams have come true* (NOT 不用 *become/get* here). 我所有的梦想都成了现实。Otherwise people use **become** or **get** again. 除此以外，人们还是用 become 或 get: *He eventually got better.* 他身体最终好了起来。

GRAMMAR 语法

Become is never followed by an infinitive though **come** can be. become 后面不接不定式，但 come 可以: *After a while I came to like Chicago* (NOT 不用 *...became to like...*). 经过一段时间，我逐渐喜欢上了芝加哥。

be·com·ing /bɪˋkʌmɪŋ; bɪˈkʌmɪŋ/ *adj old-fashioned*【过时】**1** clothes that are becoming make you look attractive〔衣服〕合适的, 相配的; 好看的 **2** words or actions that are becoming are suitable for you or for the situation you are in〔说话或行为〕适当的, 适宜的 —**becomingly** *adv*

bec·que·rel /bɛkˋrɛl; ˌbekəˈrel/ *n* [C] *technical* a unit for measuring RADIOACTIVITY (2)【术语】贝克(勒尔)〔放射性强度单位〕

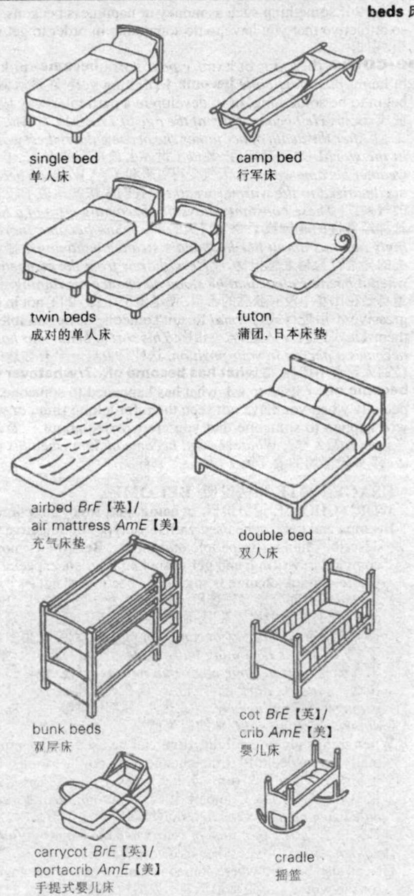

bed¹ /bɛd; bed/ *n*

1 ►SLEEP 睡眠◄ [C,U] a piece of furniture for sleeping on 床: *a spare bed* 备用床 | *a double bed* 双人床 | **in bed** *Simon lay in bed reading for hours.* 西蒙躺在床上看了好几个小时的书。| **go to bed** *In the end, she went to bed without any fuss.* 最后, 她毫无怨言地上床睡觉了。| **make the bed** (=tidy the bed covers) 铺床 | **put sb to bed** *I'll just put the children to bed.* 我马上就让孩子们睡觉。| **get (sb) out of bed** *Sorry for calling so early – I hope I didn't get you out of bed.* 对不起, 这么早给你打电话, 希望没有打扰你休息。| **time for bed** (=time to go to sleep) 到了睡觉的时候 | **take to your bed** *old-fashioned* (=stay in bed because you are ill)【过时】〔因病〕卧床

2 go to bed with *informal* to have sex with someone【非正式】和〔某人〕上床〔发生性关系〕

3 get sb into bed *informal* to persuade someone to have sex with you【非正式】诱使某人发生性关系

4 ►RIVER/LAKE/SEA 河/湖/海◄ [C] the flat ground at the bottom of a river, lake, or sea〔河、湖或海的〕底部: *the sea bed* 海底

5 ►GARDEN 花园◄ [C] an area of a garden, park etc that has been prepared for plants to grow in 苗床; 花圃; 花坛: *rose beds* 玫瑰花坛

6 ►ROCK 岩石◄ [C] a layer of rock 岩层 —see also 另见 BEDROCK (2)

7 ►BASE 基部◄ [singular] a layer of something that forms a base that other things are put on top of 底部; 地基, 基座: [+of] *The hut rests on a bed of concrete.* 小屋盖在水泥地基上。| *prawns on a bed of lettuce* 铺在生菜上面的大虾

8 oyster/coral etc bed an area of the bottom of the sea where there are a lot of OYSTERS etc〔海底的〕牡蛎层/珊瑚层等

9 get out of bed (on) the wrong side *BrE*【英】, **get up on the wrong side of the bed** *AmE*【美】to feel slightly angry or annoyed for no particular reason 不对劲, 心情不好

10 not a bed of roses not a happy, comfortable, or easy situation 不一帆风顺, 不称心如意: *Life isn't always a bed of roses you know.* 要知道, 人生并非总是事事如意的。

11 you've made your bed and you must lie on it used to say that you must accept the bad results of your actions 自作自受, 自食其果

12 be brought to bed (of) *old use* to give birth to a baby【旧】生孩子

bed² *v* [T] **1** *old-fashioned* to have sex with someone【过时】与〔某人〕发生性关系 **2** also 又作 **bed out** to put plants into the ground so that they can grow 栽种于花坛[苗床]里 **3** to fix something firmly onto or into a base 固定在…上; 嵌入; 埋置: *The foundations were bedded in cement.* 地基嵌入水泥之中。

bed down *phr v* **1** [T **bed** sb/sth ↔ **down**] to make a person or animal comfortable for the night 使〔人或牲畜〕安睡 **2** [I] to make yourself comfortable for the night 使自己安睡: *Can I bed down on your sofa?* 我能睡在你的沙发上吗?

bed and board /ˌ· · ˈ·/ *n* [U] food and a place to sleep 膳宿

bed and break·fast /ˌ· · ˈ· ·/ *n* [C, U] a private house or small hotel where you can sleep and have breakfast, or this type of place; B AND B 提供住宿和早餐的私人住家[小旅馆]

be·daub /bɪˋdɔb; bɪˈdɔːb/ *v* [T usually passive 一般用被动态 +with] *formal* to put paint, mud etc onto something in an untidy way【正式】乱涂, 抹; 弄脏

be·daz·zle /bɪˋdæzḷ; bɪˈdæzəl/ *v* [T] to make you think that someone or something is extremely impressive 使眼花缭乱; 使迷醉: *He is bedazzled by the status symbols of these crooks.* 这些代表着社会地位的权杖使他眼花缭乱。

bed bath /ˈ· ·/ *n* [C] a thorough body wash given to someone who cannot leave their bed 为卧病在床的人洗的澡

bed·bug /ˋbɛdˌbʌg; ˈbedbʌg/ *n* [C] an insect that sucks blood and lives in houses, especially in beds 臭虫; 床虱

bed·cham·ber /ˋbɛdˌtʃembɚ; ˈbedˌtʃeɪmbə/ *n* [C] *old-use* a bedroom【旧】卧室

bed·clothes /ˋbɛdˌkloðz; ˈbedkləʊðz/ *n* [plural] the sheets, covers etc that you put on a bed 寝具, 铺盖〔包括被单、床罩等床上用品〕

bed·ding /ˋbɛdɪŋ; ˈbedɪŋ/ *n* [U] **1** sheets, covers etc that you put on a bed 床上用品, 寝具, 铺盖 **2** something soft for animals to sleep on, such as dried grass or STRAW (=dried corn stems)〔供牲畜做窝的干草等〕铺垫物

Bede /bid; biːd/, **the Venerable** (?673-735) an English priest who wrote about early English history. Many people think of him as the first English HISTORIAN. 比德〔(?673-735), 英国牧师, 曾撰写英国早期的历史, 被认为是英国首位历史学家〕

be·deck /bɪˋdɛk; bɪˈdek/ *v* [T usually passive 一般用被动态] *literary* to decorate something such as a building or street by hanging things all over it【文】装饰, 点缀: *a balcony bedecked with hanging baskets* 用吊篮装饰的阳台

be·dev·il /bɪˋdɛvḷ; bɪˈdevəl/ *v* **bedevilled** *BrE*【英】**bedeviled** *AmE*【美】[T usually passive 一般用被动态] *formal* to cause a lot of problems and difficulties for someone or something【正式】搞糟, 搅扰; 使苦恼: *a society bedevilled by racial tensions* 被种族紧张关系搞得一团糟的社会 —**bedevilment** *n* [U]

bed·fel·low /ˋbɛdˌfɛlo; ˈbedˌfeləʊ/ *n* [C] **strange/odd/uneasy etc bedfellows** two or more people, ideas etc that are connected or working together in an unexpected way 奇怪的组合〔指两个或两个以上的人、观点等出人意料地联系在一起〕: *Politics and ecology often make uneasy bedfellows.* 政治和生态经常会奇怪地联系在一起。

Bed·ford·shire /ˋbɛdfɚdʃɚ; ˈbedfədʃə/ a COUNTY in southern England, whose main town is Bedford 贝德福德郡〔英格兰南部一郡, 贝德福德为其主要城镇〕

bed·head /ˋbɛdˌhɛd; ˈbedhed/ *n* [C] the part of a bed that is behind your head when you are sitting up 床头

bed·lam /ˋbɛdləm; ˈbedləm/ *n* [U] a wild noisy place or situation 喧闹嘈杂的地方; 混乱: *The courtroom erupted into bedlam as the judge delivered his verdict.* 法官宣布判决结果时, 法庭里顿时一片哗然。

bed lin·en /ˋ· ˌ··/ *n* [U] the sheets and PILLOWCASES for a bed 被单和枕套

Bed·ou·in /ˋbɛduɪn; ˈbeduɪn/ *n* [C] a member of an Arab tribe that traditionally lives in tents in the desert 贝都因人〔住在沙漠里帐篷中的阿拉伯游牧部落成员〕

bed·pan /ˋbɛdˌpæn; ˈbedpæn/ *n* [C] a low wide container used as a toilet by someone who has to stay in bed〔病人在床上用的〕便盆

bed·post /ˋbɛdˌpost; ˈbedpəʊst/ *n* [C] one of the four main supports at the corners of an old-fashioned bed〔旧式床的〕床柱, 床架杆

be·drag·gled /bɪˋdrægḷd; bɪˈdrægəld/ *adj* looking untidy and dirty, especially because you have been out in the rain〔尤指淋雨后〕湿漉漉的; 又湿又脏的: *She came in wet and bedraggled.* 她又湿又脏地走了进来。

bed·rid·den /ˋbɛdˌrɪdṇ; ˈbedˌrɪdn/ *adj* unable to leave your bed, especially because you are old or ill〔因年老或生病而〕卧床不起的

bed·rock /ˋbɛdˋrɑk; ˈbedrɒk/ *n* [U] **1** the basic ideas and principles of a belief etc 基本事实, 基本原则; 根底, 基础: *Their determination to remain independent was the bedrock on which the war effort rested.* 决心维护独立是他们奋力作战的思想基础。 **2** solid rock in the ground on top of which all the soil rests 基岩, 底岩, 床岩

bed·roll /ˋbɛdˌrol; ˈbedrəʊl/ *n* [C] *AmE* a number of blankets (BLANKET[1] (1)) rolled together and used for sleeping outdoors【美】〔室外睡觉用的〕铺盖卷

S1 W2 **bed·room**[1] /ˋbɛdˌrum; ˈbedrʊm/ *n* [C] **1** a room for sleeping in 卧室: *a hotel with 50 bedrooms* 有50间客房的旅馆 **2 make/have bedroom eyes** to show that you are sexually attracted to someone 挑逗人, 勾引人

bed·room[2] *adj* a bedroom suburb is a place from which people travel to a city to work every day 郊外住宅区的; DORMITORY *BrE*【英】

bed·side /ˋbɛdˌsaɪd; ˈbedsaɪd/ *n* [C] the area around your bed 床侧, 床边: *Relatives have been at his bedside all week, hoping he will regain consciousness.* 亲属们整个星期都围在他的床边, 希望他会恢复知觉。| **bedside lamp/table etc** (=next to your bed) 床头灯/桌等

bedside man·ner /ˌ·· ˋ··/ *n* [singular] a doctor's bedside manner is the way that they talk to the people that they are treating 医生对病人的态度

bed·sit /ˌbɛdˋsɪt; ˌbedˈsɪt/ also 又作 **bed·sit·ter** /-ˋsɪtɚ; -ˈsɪtə/, **bed·sit·ting room** /ˌbɛdˋsɪtɪŋ rum; ˌbedˈsɪtɪŋ rʊm/ *n* [C] *BrE* a rented room used for both living and sleeping in【英】起居室兼卧室的两用房间

bed·sore /ˋbɛdˌsor; ˈbedsɔː/ *n* [C] a sore place on your skin caused by lying in bed for a long time〔长期卧床引起的〕褥疮

bed·spread /ˋbɛdˌsprɛd; ˈbedspred/ *n* [C] a decorative cover for a bed that goes on top of all the other covers 床罩

bed·stead /ˋbɛdˌstɛd; ˈbedsted/ *n* [C] the wooden or metal frame of a bed〔木制或金属制的〕床架

bed·time /ˋbɛdˌtaɪm; ˈbedtaɪm/ *n* [C,U] the time when you usually go to bed 就寝时间: *It's way past your bedtime!* 你该上床睡觉的时间早过了! | *a bedtime story* 哄孩子睡觉时讲的故事

bed wet·ting /ˋ· ˌ··/ *n* [U] the problem that some children have of passing URINE (=liquid from the body) while they are asleep 尿床 —**bed-wetter** *n* [C]

bee /bi; biː/ *n* [C] **1** a black and yellow flying insect with a round body that makes HONEY (1) and can sting you 蜜蜂: *a swarm of bees* 蜂群 —see also 另见 BUMBLEBEE **2 a busy bee** *spoken* someone who enjoys being busy or active【口】忙碌活跃的人 **3 have a bee in your bonnet** *informal* to think something is so important, so necessary etc that you keep mentioning it or thinking about it【非正式】脑海里不断地想着某一件事: *Dad's got a bee in his bonnet about saving electricity.* 爸爸一心想着要省电。**4 think you're the bee's knees** *BrE spoken* used to describe someone who thinks they are very clever, very good at something etc【英口】自以为非常出色: *She thinks she's the bee's knees around here.* 她认为自己是这里最出色的人。**5 working/sewing etc bee** *AmE informal* an occasion when people, usually women, meet in order to do a particular type of work【美, 非正式】〔尤指妇女为某种工作而举行的〕工作会/缝纫会等 —see also 另见 SPELLING BEE, **the birds and the bees** (BIRD (3))

Beeb, the /bib; biːb/ *n spoken* the BBC【口】英国广播公司

beech /bitʃ; biːtʃ/ *n* [C,U] a large tree with smooth grey BARK[2] (2) (=outer covering), or the wood from this tree 山毛榉(木)

Bee·cham /ˋbitʃəm; ˈbiːtʃəm/, **Sir Thomas** (1879-1961) an English CONDUCTOR who established the London Philharmonic Orchestra in 1932 and the Royal Philharmonic Orchestra in 1946 比彻姆〔(1879-1961), 英国指挥家, 1932年创立伦敦爱乐交响乐团, 1946年创立皇家爱乐交响乐团〕

Beecham's pow·ders /ˌ·· ˋ··/ *trademark* a popular type of British medicine for colds or FLU, sold as a powder that you mix with water【商标】比彻姆冲剂〔英国生产的一种感冒或流感冲剂〕

beef[1] /bif; biːf/ *n* **1** [U] the meat from a cow 牛肉: *roast beef* 烤牛肉 **2** [C] *informal* a complaint【非正式】牢骚, 怨言: *OK, so what's the beef this time?* 好了, 这一次又有什么苦要诉? **3 where's the beef?** *spoken especially AmE* used when you think someone's words and promises sound good, but you want to know what they actually plan to do【口, 尤美】葫芦里究竟卖什么药? —see also 另见 BEEF TEA, CORNED BEEF S3

beef[2] *v* [I] *informal* to complain a lot【非正式】老发牢骚, 抱怨: [+about] *They're always beefing about something or other.* 他们总是就这样那样的事发牢骚。

beef sth ↔ **up** *phr v* [T] *informal* to improve something or make it more interesting, more important etc【非正式】加强; 改进; 充实: *a beefed up news story* 一个充实了内容的新闻报道 | *We need to beef the campaign up a bit.* 我们的宣传活动要加把劲儿。

beef·bur·ger /ˋbifˌbɝgɚ; ˈbiːfbɜːgə/ *n* [C] *BrE* a HAMBURGER【英】汉堡包

beef·cake /ˋbifˌkek; ˈbiːfkeɪk/ *n* [C,U] *informal* a strong attractive man with large muscles, or men like this in general【非正式】〔肌肉发达的〕健美男子 —compare 比较 CHEESECAKE

Beef·eat·er /ˋbifˌitɚ; ˈbiːfˌiːtə/ *n* [C] a ceremonial guard at the Tower of London 伦敦塔的仪仗卫兵

beef·steak /ˋbifˌstek; ˈbiːfsteɪk/ *n* [C,U] STEAK (1) 牛排, 牛扒

beef tea /ˌ· ˋ·/ *n* [U] a hot drink made from BEEF[1] (1) that used to be given to people when they were ill〔昔日给病人食用的〕牛肉汤, 牛肉汁

beef·y /ˋbifɪ; ˈbiːfi/ *adj informal* someone who is beefy is big, strong, and often quite fat【非正式】〔人〕大块头的, 强壮的, 肥实的

bee·hive /ˋbiˌhaɪv; ˈbiːhaɪv/ *n* [C] **1** a structure where bees (BEE (1)) are kept for producing HONEY (1) 蜂窝; 蜂箱 **2** a way of arranging a woman's hair in a high pile on the top of her head, which was popular in the 1960s〔20世纪60年代流行的女子〕蜂窝式发型

bee·line /ˋbiˌlaɪn; ˈbiːlaɪn/ *n* **make a beeline for** *informal* to go quickly and directly towards someone or something【非正式】迅速直奔, 径直前往: *Rob always makes a beeline for beautiful women at parties.* 罗布在晚会上总是直奔向漂亮的女士。

Be·el·ze·bub /bɪˋɛlzɪbʌb; biˈelzɪbʌb/ a devil, especially Satan 鬼王别西卜〔魔鬼, 尤指撒旦〕

Beemer /ˋbimɚ; ˈbiːmə/ *n* [C] *informal* a car made by BMW【非正式】宝马车

been /bɪn; biːn/ **1** the past participle of BE **2 have/has been a)** used to say that someone has gone to a place and come back 曾到过〔某地〕: [+to] *I've never been to Japan.* 我从未去过日本。| **have been to do sth** *Have you been to see the Van Gogh exhibition yet?* 你去看过梵高画展了吗? **b)** *BrE* used to say that someone has come to a place and left again【英】来过〔某地〕: *The postman hasn't been yet.* 邮差还没有来过。—see 见 GO[1] (3) **3 been there, done that** *spoken* used to say that you are no longer interested in doing something, because you already have a lot of experience of it【口】由于经历太多而对某事失去兴趣; 腻了

beep[1] /bip; biːp/ *v* **1** [I] if a machine beeps, it makes a short high sound〔机器〕嘟嘟响: *Why does the computer keep beeping?* 为什么电脑不断嘟嘟响? **2** [I,T] if a car horn beeps or you make it beep, it makes a loud noise〔汽车喇叭〕鸣响; 按响

beep[2] *n* [C] **1** a short high sound made by an electronic machine 嘟嘟声: *Leave your message after the beep.* 嘟声过后请留言。**2** the sound of a car horn 汽车的喇叭声音: *Look, there's Jan. Give her a beep.* 看, 那是简, 按喇叭叫她一下。

beep·er /ˋbipɚ; ˈbiːpə/ *n* [C] a small machine that you carry with you, that makes short high electronic sounds to tell you that you must telephone someone; BLEEPER, PAGER 传呼机

beer /bɪr; bɪə/ *n* **1** [U] an alcoholic drink made from MALT[1] (1) and hops (HOP[2] (4)) 啤酒: *a pint of beer* 一品脱啤酒 | *home-brewed beer* 家酿的啤酒 S2 W3

CULTURAL NOTE 文化注释

In the UK, people usually say 'beer' when they are talking about a brown or dark-brown form of the drink, such as BITTER or STOUT. People in the US usually call this darker type of beer ALE or 'dark beer'. The clear pale yellow CARBONATED (= with gas) form of the drink, which is simply called 'beer' in the US and in most other countries, is usually called LAGER in the UK. 英国人所说的beer经常指褐色或烈性深褐色的啤酒，如苦啤酒或烈性黑啤酒。美国人常把这种啤酒叫做麦酒或"黑啤酒"。清亮的淡黄色碳酸啤酒在美国和其他大多数国家都只简单地叫做beer，在英国则称lager（淡啤酒）。

In the UK, if someone says 'do you want a beer' or 'do you fancy a beer', they are asking you if you would like to have either a dark beer or a lager. If you are in a pub and you want a glass of beer or lager, you ask for a 'PINT' or a 'half' (= half a pint). 在英国，如果有人说do you want a beer或do you fancy a beer，是问对方想喝黑啤酒还是淡啤酒。如果是在酒吧点酒，则用pint（品脱）或half（半品脱）。

2 [C] a glass, bottle, or can of beer 一杯[瓶，罐]啤酒: *Do you fancy a beer?* 你想要杯啤酒吗？ **3 not all beer and skittles** *BrE old-fashioned* not just full of pleasure and enjoyment, but involving problems as well【英，过时】并非只是吃喝玩乐 —**beery** *adj*

beer bel·ly /ˈ· ·ˌ/ also 又作 **beer gut** /ˈ· ·/ *n* [C] an unattractive fat stomach caused by drinking too much beer 啤酒肚

beer mat /ˈ· ·/ *n* [C] a small circle of card that you put under a glass, especially in a bar〔尤指酒吧里的〕啤酒杯垫

bees·wax /ˈbizˌwæks; ˈbiːzwæks/ *n* [U] **1** a substance produced by bees (BEE (1)), especially for making furniture polish and CANDLES 蜂蜡〔尤用于制造家具擦光油、蜡烛等〕 **2 none of your beeswax** *AmE spoken* used to tell someone that what they have asked you is private or personal【美口】不关你的事

beet /bit; biːt/ *n* [C,U] **1** also 又作 **sugar beet** a vegetable that sugar is made from 甜菜 **2** *AmE* a plant with a round dark red root that you cook and eat as a vegetable【美】甜菜根; BEETROOT *BrE*【英】 **3 red as a beet** *AmE informal* having a red face, especially because you are embarrassed【美，非正式】〔尤指因尴尬而〕脸红

Beet·ho·ven /ˈbethovən; ˈbeɪthəʊvən/, **Lud·wig van** /ˈludvɪg væn; ˈlʊdvɪg væn/ (1770-1827) a German COMPOSER, one of the best known and most admired ever. His many famous works include *The Fifth Symphony* and *The Emperor Concerto*. 贝多芬〔(1770-1827)，德国作曲家，有史以来最著名、最受崇敬的作曲家之一，曾创作了许多著名作品，其中包括《第五交响曲》和《皇帝协奏曲》〕

Beetle also 又作 **Bug** *informal AmE trademark* a small car made by Volkswagen which has a high, rounded top. It was first produced in the 1930s.【非正式，美，商标】甲壳虫车〔大众汽车公司制造的一种小型轿车，车顶浑圆、较高，最初生产于20世纪30年代〕

bee·tle[1] /ˈbitl; ˈbiːtl/ *n* [C] one of many types of insect with a round hard, usually black, back 甲（壳）虫

beetle[2] *v* [I always+adv/prep] *BrE informal* to go somewhere quickly, especially because you are trying not to be noticed【英，非正式】赶紧离去；悄悄溜掉: *He went beetling off down the corridor.* 他从走廊溜走了。

Bee·ton /ˈbitn̩; ˈbiːtn/, **Mrs** (1836-65) a British woman who wrote a book called *The Book of Household Management*, which was very popular during the 19th and early 20th centuries. The book gives RECIPES (=instructions for cooking particular dishes), and also gives advice about managing a home. 比顿夫人〔(1836-1865)，英国人，著有《家政管理》，19世纪至20世纪初十分畅销，内容为烹饪菜谱介绍和家政管理建议〕

beet·root /ˈbitˌrut; ˈbiːtruːt/ *n* [C,U] **1** *BrE* a plant with a round dark red root that you cook and eat as a vegetable【英】甜菜根; BEET *AmE*【美】—see picture on page A9 参见A9页图 **2 go beetroot** *BrE informal* to become red in the face, especially because you are embarrassed【英，非正式】〔尤指因尴尬而〕脸红

be·fall /bɪˈfɔl; bɪˈfɔːl/ *v past tense* **befell** /-ˈfɛl; -ˈfel/ *past participle* **befallen** /-ˈfɔlən; -ˈfɔːlən/ [T] *formal* if something unpleasant or dangerous befalls you it happens to you【正式】〔不幸的事或灾难〕降临（到）: *We prayed that no harm should befall them.* 我们祈求他们平安无事。

be·fit /bɪˈfɪt; bɪˈfɪt/ *v past tense and past participle* **befitted** [T] *formal* to be proper or suitable for someone【正式】适合，适宜: *The chairman travelled club class, as befitted his status.* 主席乘坐二等舱旅行，这样符合他的身份。—**befitting** *adj* —**befittingly** *adv*

be·fore[1] /bɪˈfɔr; bɪˈfɔː/ *conjunction* **1** earlier than the time when something happens 在…之前: *Say goodbye before you go.* 你临走之前去道个别吧。| *It will be some time before we know the full results.* 再过些时间我们才能知道全部结果。 **2** so that something bad does not happen 以防: *Put that money somewhere safe before it gets stolen.* 把钱放在安全的地方，以防被人偷去。| *That dog ought to be destroyed before it attacks any more children.* 应该把那条狗杀死，以防它再伤害更多的孩子。 **3** used to say that you are willing to suffer or do something unpleasant rather than do something that you do not want to do 宁愿: *He will die before he tells them what they want to know.* 他宁愿死也不愿说出他们想知道的事。 **4 before you know it** *spoken* used to say that something will happen very soon【口】说时迟，那时快；将要: *We'd better set off or it will be dark before we know it.* 天快要黑了，我们得马上出发。 **5** used to warn someone not to laugh at, criticize etc someone or something because they have faults and weaknesses themselves 先不要〔嘲笑或批评别人〕: *Before the chairman starts attacking committee members he ought to remember his own mistakes.* 主席先不要抨击委员会成员，他应该知道自己也有错。 **6** used to warn someone that you will do something unpleasant or harmful to them if they do not do something 要不然；否则: *Get out before I call the police.* 滚出去，要不然我叫警察了。

before[2] *prep* **1** earlier than something〔时间上〕在…以前: *I usually take a shower before having my breakfast.* 我通常在吃早餐前洗个澡。| *The new road should be completed before the end of the year.* 这条新公路将在年底前应该完工。| *He arrived home before me.* 他比我先到家。| *the day before yesterday* (=two days ago) 前天 —see 见 FRONT[1] (USAGE) **2** ahead of someone or something else in a list or order〔名单或次序上〕较…为先；在…之前: *I think you were before me in the queue.* 我认为你排在我的前面。 **3** in the same place, or in front of a person or crowd of people〔方位上〕在…面前: *Italy will face Brazil this afternoon before a crowd of 100,000 spectators.* 今天下午意大利队将在10万名观众面前迎战巴西队。 **4** if something such as a report or evidence is put before a person or group of people they must consider it and make a decision about it〔报告或证据等〕摆在…面前；供…考虑: *The proposal was put before the planning committee.* 该项建议已提交计划委员会审议。 **5** if one quality or person comes before another, it is more important than it〔重要性〕在…之前，比…更重要: *I put my wife and kids before anyone else.* 我把妻子和孩子放在首要地位。| *Quality must come before quantity in my opinion.* 在我看来，质量比数量更重要。 **6** *formal* in front of【正式】在…前面: *The priest stood before the altar.* 那位教士站在圣坛前面。| *The great plain stretched out before them.* 展现在他们面前的是一望无际的平原。 **7** if one place is before another place it is a particular distance in front of that place as you travel towards it 在〔某个地点〕前: *The pub is 100m before the church on the right.* 那家小酒馆在教堂往前100米靠右侧的地方。 **8** *formal* if there is a job or situation before you, you have to do the job or face the situation soon【正式】〔工作、局面〕摆在…面前: *The task of emptying the house lay before us.* 我们面前的任务是把房间里的东西都搬出去。 **9** *formal* if a period of time is before you it is about to start and you can do what you want during it【正式】来临；等着: *We had a glorious summer afternoon before us to do as we pleased.* 我们有一个宜人的夏日午后做自己喜欢的事。 **10** *formal* if you show a particular reaction before someone or something you react in that way【正式】面临: *She trembled before the prospect of meeting him again.* 一想到又要跟他见面，她直打颤。

before[3] *adv* **1** at an earlier time 先前；从前；以前: *Haven't we met before?* 我们以前见过面吧？| *I thought she might take notice of what I said but she just carries on as before.* 我以为她注意到了我的话，可是她表现得还是像以前一样。| **the day/week/month before** *Last week she was in Paris, and the week before she was in Rome.* 上周她在巴黎，前一周她在罗马。| **before long** *I expect the bus will be here before long.* 我估计公共汽车很快就到。| *The kids were playing in the mud and before long they were covered in it.* 孩子们在烂泥地里玩，很快浑身上下都是泥。 **2** *old use* ahead of someone or something else【旧】在…前面: *The king's herald walked before.* 国王的传令官走在前面。

be·fore·hand /bɪˈfɔrˌhænd; bɪˈfɔːhænd/ *adv* before something else has happened or is done 事先，预先，事前: *The police need to be briefed beforehand on how to deal with this sort of situation.* 需要事先告诉警察怎样处理这种情况。| *When you give*

a speech, it's natural to feel nervous beforehand. 你在演讲之前感到紧张是很自然的。

be·friend /bɪˋfrɛnd; bɪˈfrend/ *v* [T] *formal* to behave in a friendly way towards someone, especially someone who is younger or needs help【正式】以朋友态度对待〔尤指对较年轻者或需要帮助者〕: *They befriended me when I first arrived in London as a student.* 我初到伦敦求学时，他们如同朋友一般地照顾我。

be·fud·dled /bɪˋfʌdḷd; bɪˈfʌdəld/ *adj* completely confused 迷惑不解的; 极其糊涂的: *I felt befuddled by all these changes.* 所有这些变化都把我弄糊涂了。

beg /bɛg; beg/ *v*

1 I beg your pardon *spoken*【口】**a)** used to say sorry when you have made a mistake, or said something wrong or embarrassing 请原谅, 对不起: *Oh, I beg your pardon. I thought you meant next Tuesday.* 哟, 对不起, 我还以为你是指下星期二。**b)** used to show that you strongly disagree with something that someone has said, or think it is unacceptable 恕我不敢苟同〔表示不同意某人的观点〕: *"Chicago's an awful place." "I beg your pardon, that's where I'm from!"* "芝加哥是个很糟糕的地方。" "请恕我不敢苟同, 我就是芝加哥人!" **c)** used to ask someone to repeat what they have just said 请再说一遍: *"The meeting's on Wednesday." "I beg your pardon." "I said the meeting's on Wednesday."* "会议星期三开。" "请您再说一遍好吗?" "我说会议星期三开。"

2 ►ASK 要求◄ [I,T] to ask for something in an anxious or urgent way, because you want it very much 请求, 恳求: *She begged and pleaded with them until they finally gave in.* 她一再恳求, 最后他们终于让步了。| **beg (sb) to do sth** *The children begged to come with us.* 孩子们一再恳求和我们一起来。| *I begged Helen to stay but she wouldn't listen.* 我恳求海伦留下来, 可她就是不听。| **beg (sb) for sth** *I'm begging you for help, Greg.* 格雷格, 我恳请你帮忙。| **beg forgiveness/a favour/mercy etc** *Can I beg a favour?* 我可以请你帮个忙吗? | **beg leave to do sth** *formal* (=ask permission to do something)【正式】请求获准做某事

3 ►MONEY/FOOD 金钱/食物◄ [I,T] to ask people to give you food, money etc because you are very poor 乞求施舍, 乞讨: *a begging letter* 乞求信 | **beg from sb** *a ragged child begging from passing shoppers* 向路过的购物者行乞的衣衫褴褛的孩子 | **beg (for) sth** *They were reduced to begging food in the streets.* 他们被迫沦落到在街上乞讨食物。| **beg sth off sb** *spoken*【口】*Can I beg a cigarette off you?* 我能问你要支香烟吗?

4 I beg to differ *spoken formal* to say firmly that you do not agree with something that has been said【口, 正式】恕我不敢苟同: *I must beg to differ on this point.* 在这点上, 恕我不敢苟同。

5 beg the question to discuss something in a way that makes it seem that a fact is definitely true when in fact it may not be 以假定作为论据进行讨论; 回避问题的实质: *This planning proposal begs the question whether we need more sports facilities at all.* 这个建设计划回避了我们是否需要更多体育设施这一实质问题。

6 be going begging *spoken* if something is going begging, it is available for anyone who wants it【口】现成的, 可用的: *There's a bottle of wine going begging if anyone's interested.* 有一瓶葡萄酒在这里, 如果有谁感兴趣的话, 请随便喝。

7 ►DOG 狗◄ [I] if a dog begs, it sits up with its front legs off the ground〔狗〕用后腿站立, 前腿举于胸前

beg off *phr v* [I] to say that you cannot do something that you had agreed to do 恳求免除已经承诺的责任; 请求不做某事: *I'm sorry, but I'm going to have to beg off from the game tonight.* 对不起, 今晚的比赛我请求不去了。

be·get /bɪˋgɛt; bɪˈget/ *v past tense and past participle* **begot** /-ˋgɑt; -ˈgɒt/ *or past tense* **begat** /-ˋgæt; -ˈgæt/ *past participle* **begotten** /-ˋgɑtn̩; -ˈgɒtn/ [T] *formal*【正式】**1** *old use* to become the father of a child【旧】成为…之父 **2** to cause something or make it happen 招致: *Hunger begets crime.* 饥饿招致犯罪。

beg·gar¹ /ˋbɛgɚ; ˈbegə/ *n* [C] **1** someone who lives by asking people for food and money 乞丐: *There's been a huge increase in the number of beggars on London's streets.* 伦敦街头的乞丐人数激增。**2 lucky/lazy/cheeky etc beggar** *BrE spoken* used to describe someone who you think is lucky, lazy etc, in a friendly way【英口】幸运/懒惰/无礼等的家伙: *You lazy little beggar!* 你这懒惰的小家伙! | *"How's Dave?" "The lucky beggar's in the south of France!"* "戴夫好吗?" "这个幸运的家伙正在法国南部!" **3 beggars can't be choosers** used to say that when you have no money, no power to choose etc, you have to accept whatever is available 既然落难, 就不要挑肥拣瘦; 饥不择食

beggar² *v* [T] **1 beggar description/belief etc** *formal* to be impossible to describe, believe etc【正式】无法形容/相信等: *The scenery was so beautiful that it beggared description.* 景色之优美难以用言语来形容。**2** *formal* to make someone very poor【正式】使贫穷: *Drought combined with falling prices to beggar whole communities of farmers.* 干旱加上粮食价格下跌使大批农民陷于贫困。

beg·gar·ly /ˋbɛgɚlɪ; ˈbegəli/ *adj literary* a beggarly amount of money is far too small【文】〔钱〕少得可怜的

beggar-my-neigh·bour /ˌ·· ·ˋ··/ *n* [U] a card game in which the aim is to get all your opponent's cards〔以吃光对手所有牌为胜的〕"吃光"纸牌游戏

Beggar's Op·e·ra, The /ˌ·· ˋ···/ a funny OPERA by John Gay, first produced in 1728. It tells the story of a thief called Macheath, who is sent to Newgate prison, where he meets a woman called Lucy and makes his wife Polly jealous. A modern opera called *The Threepenny Opera*, by Bertolt Brecht, is based on this.《乞丐的歌剧》〔约翰·盖伊创作的一部滑稽歌剧, 首演于1728年。故事情节是, 一个名叫麦克希思的小偷被遣送到纽盖特监狱, 在那里他遇到了一位名叫露西的女子, 这使他的妻子波莉心生嫉妒。现代歌剧《三便士歌剧》是由贝托尔特·布莱希特据此改编而成的〕

beg·gar·y /ˋbɛgərɪ; ˈbegəri/ *n* [U] *formal* the state of being very poor【正式】赤贫: *The failure of their farm reduced them to beggary.* 农场歉收使他们落到一贫如洗的境地。

be·gin /bɪˋgɪn; bɪˈgɪn/ *past tense* **began** /-ˋgæn; -ˈgæn/ *past participle* **begun** /-ˋgʌn; -ˈgʌn/ *v* [I,T] S1 W1

1 ►START DOING/FEELING 开始做/感到◄ to start doing something or start feeling a particular way 开始; 着手: **begin to do sth** *We began to wonder if the train would ever arrive.* 我们开始怀疑火车到底会不会到。| **begin** *I'll begin when you're ready.* 你准备好了我就开始。| **begin sth** *She curled up in bed and began her book.* 她蜷在床上, 开始看书。| **begin doing sth** *I left teaching in 1990 and began working in my present job.* 我1990年离开了教学岗位, 开始做现在的工作。| **begin by doing sth** (=do or say something as the first part of an activity) 从做某事开始 *Can I begin by thanking you all for being here tonight?* 首先让我感谢所有今晚到场的来宾。

2 ►START HAPPENING 开始发生◄ [I,T] if something begins, or you begin something, it starts to happen or exist 开始〔发生或存在〕: *Work on the new bridge will begin next year.* 修筑新桥的工作将于下一年开始。| *It was the coldest winter since records began.* 这是有记录以来最寒冷的冬天。| **[+at]** *The meeting begins at 10.30 am.* 会议在上午10点半开始。| **begin (sth) as** *Roger began his career as a model.* 罗杰的职业生涯从当模特儿开始。

3 to begin with a) *especially spoken* used to introduce the first or most important point that you want to make【尤口】首先: *Well, to begin with, he shouldn't even have been driving my car.* 好吧, 首先他就不应该一直开我的车。**b)** used to say that something was already in a particular condition before something else happened 原来: *I didn't break it! It was like that to begin with.* 不是我弄坏的! 它原来就是那样子。**c)** during the first part of a process or activity 刚开始的时候: *The kids helped me to begin with, but they soon got bored.* 起初孩子们都来帮忙, 但他们很快就厌烦了。—see 见 FIRSTLY (USAGE)

4 ►SPEECH/BOOK 讲话/书◄ [I] if a speech, book, word etc begins with something, it starts with a particular event, activity, letter etc 以…开头: **[+with]** *'Psychosis' begins with a P.* psychosis (精神病) 一词以字母 p 开头。

5 can't begin to understand/imagine etc *spoken* used to emphasize how difficult something is to understand etc【口】根本无法理解/想象等: *I can't begin to imagine how awful it must be to lose your child.* 我简直无法想象你失去了孩子会有多难过。

This graph shows how common different grammar patterns of the verb **begin** are. 本图表所示为动词 begin 构成的不同语法模式的使用频率。

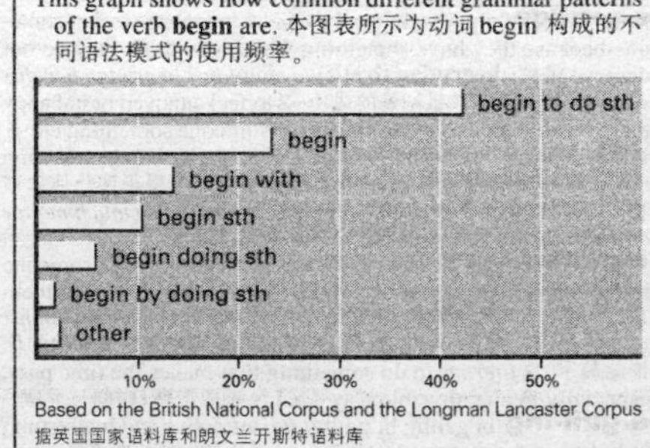

Based on the British National Corpus and the Longman Lancaster Corpus
据英国国家语料库和朗文兰开斯特语料库

Be·gin /ˋbegɪn; ˈbeɪgɪn/, **Me·na·chem** /məˋnɑkɪm; məˈnɑːkɪ̭m/ (1913-92) an Israeli politician and Prime Minister from 1977 to 1983. In 1979 he signed a peace TREATY with President Sadat of Egypt which was known as *The Camp David Agreement*. 贝京〔(1913-1992), 以色列政治家, 1977年至1983年任以色列总理。1979年他与埃及总统萨达特共同签署了一个和平条约, 名为《戴维营协议》〕

be·gin·ner /bɪˋgɪnɚ; bɪˈgɪnə/ *n* [C] **1** someone who has just started to do or learn something 生手; 初学者: *an absolute beginner* 一个不折不扣的初学者 **2 beginner's luck** unusual success that you have when you start something new 新手的好运

be·gin·ning /bɪˋgɪnɪŋ; bɪˈgɪnɪŋ/ *n* [C usually singular 一般用单数] **1** the start or first part of an event, story, period of time etc 开始, 开端, 起点: [+of] *It will be ready at the beginning of next week.* 将在下星期初准备就绪。| *The beginning of the film is very violent.* 这部电影的开头充满暴力镜头。| **in/at/from the beginning** (=at or from the time when a situation, process etc begins) 一开始; 初期 *We pay our rent at the beginning of every month.* 我们每个月的月初交房租。| *I said he would be trouble, right from the beginning.* 从一开始, 我就说他是个麻烦。| **from beginning to end** *The whole trip was a disaster from beginning to end.* 整个旅程从头到尾都是灾难。—see 见 FIRSTLY (USAGE) **2 beginnings** [plural] the early part or early signs of something that later develops and becomes bigger, more important etc 起源; 开端: *the beginnings of the capitalist system* 资本主义制度的起源 | **from small/humble beginnings** *From humble beginnings in Atlanta, it had developed into a multinational corporation.* 该公司从亚特兰大的一间小店起家, 逐渐发展为跨国公司。**3 the beginning of the end** the time when something good starts to end or become less good 〔好的事情〕结束[恶化]的先兆

USAGE NOTE 用法说明: BEGINNING

WORD CHOICE 词语辨析: **at the beginning of, in the beginning**

Something that happens at the very start of an event or period of time happens **at the beginning of** it. at the beginning of 指的是一个事件或一段时间刚刚开始的时候: *At the beginning of the Civil War Fort Sumter was attacked* (NOT 不用 *in the beginning of it*). 南北战争刚开始时, 萨姆特要塞遭到袭击。| *There's a car chase at the beginning* (=at the start of the film). (电影) 一开始有一个追车场面。

If something happens **in the beginning** (not usually with *of*) it happens during a period of time near the start of an event or longer period of time. in the beginning〔一般不与of连用〕指一个事件的前一阶段或初期. *In the beginning the South had some success* (=during the early part of the Civil War). 南北战争初期, 南方取得了一些胜利。| *I was too shy to speak to her in the beginning* (=the first few times I saw her). 起初 (几次见面时) 我太腼腆, 没有和她说话。

SPELLING 拼法

Remember there are two n's in **beginning**. 记住 beginning 中的 n 要双写。

be·gone /bɪˋgɔn; bɪˈgɒn/ *interjection old use* used to tell someone to go away【旧】走开

be·go·ni·a /bɪˋgonɪə; bɪˈgəʊniə/ *n* [C] a plant with yellow, pink, red, or white flowers 秋海棠

be·got /bɪˋgɑt; bɪˈgɒt/ the past tense of BEGET

be·got·ten /bɪˋgɑtn̩; bɪˈgɒtn/ the past participle of BEGET

be·grudge /bɪˋgrʌdʒ; bɪˈgrʌdʒ/ *v* [T] **1** to feel JEALOUS of someone because they have something which you think they do not deserve 嫉妒: **begrudge sb sth** *We shouldn't begrudge her this success.* 我们不应该嫉妒她的成功。**2** to feel annoyed or unhappy that you have to pay something, give someone something etc 吝啬; 舍不得给: **begrudge sb sth** *Surely you don't begrudge him the money for his education?* 想必你不会不舍得花钱让他念书吧? | **begrudge doing sth** *I begrudge spending so much money on train fares.* 我舍不得把这么多钱花在火车票上。

be·guile /bɪˋgaɪl; bɪˈgaɪl/ *v* [T] **1** to persuade or trick someone into doing something, especially by saying nice things to them〔尤指用花言巧语〕欺骗, 哄骗: *Carr beguiled the voters with his good looks and grand talk.* 选民被卡尔那英俊的外表和他的伟论蒙骗了。**2** *literary* to do something that makes the time pass, especially in an enjoyable way【文】轻松地消磨〔时间〕; 消遣

be·guil·ing /bɪˋgaɪlɪŋ; bɪˈgaɪlɪŋ/ *adj* attractive and interesting, but often in a way that deceives you 迷人的; 诱人的: *The prospect of instant riches was too beguiling to ignore.* 瞬间暴富的前景太诱人了, 不能放过。— **beguilingly** *adv*

be·gum /ˋbegəm; ˈbeɪgəm/ *n* [C] *IndE, PakE* a title of respect, used for married Muslim women, especially of high rank【印, 巴】穆斯林贵妇; 夫人〔尤指对地位高的已婚女子的尊称〕

be·gun /bɪˋgʌn; bɪˈgʌn/ the past participle of BEGIN

be·half /bɪˋhæf; bɪˈhɑːf/ *n* **on behalf of** also 又作 **in behalf of** *AmE*【美】**a)** instead of someone, or as their representative 代表: *On behalf of everyone here, may I wish you a very happy retirement.* 我代表在座各位祝你退休愉快。| *The President can't be here today, so I'm going to speak in his behalf.* 总裁今天不能来, 所以我将代表他发言。**b)** because of someone 由于〔某人〕: *Oh, don't go to any trouble on my behalf.* 不要因为我而麻烦你。

Be·han /ˋbiən; ˈbiːən/, **Bren·dan** /ˋbrɛndən; ˈbrendən/ (1923-64) an Irish writer who describes his experience of being in prison because of IRA activities, in his play *The Quare Fellow* and in his novel *Borstal Boy* 贝汉〔(1923-1964), 爱尔兰作家, 在其剧本《怪人》和小说《管教所的少年》中描述了自己因参加爱尔兰共和军活动而身陷囹圄的一段经历〕

be·have /bɪˋhev; bɪˈheɪv/ *v* [I] **1** [always+adv/prep] to do things in a particular way 举动; 表现: *I'm sorry about last night – I behaved like a child.* 对不起, 昨天晚上我表现得太幼稚。**2** also 又作 **behave yourself** to behave in a way that people think is good or correct, by being polite and obeying people, not causing trouble etc 举止规矩有礼; 检点: *Will you children please behave!* 你们这些孩子能不能规矩一点! | *Did Peter behave himself while I was away?* 我不在时, 彼得听话吗? | **well-behaved/badly-behaved** *a badly-behaved class* 不守规矩的班级 —opposite 反义词 MISBEHAVE **3** [I] to do something according to natural laws 循自然规律运行: *Quantum mechanics is the study of the way atoms behave.* 量子力学是研究原子运动的学科。

be·hav·iour *BrE*【英】, **behavior** *AmE*【美】/bɪˋhevjɚ; bɪˈheɪvjə/ *n* [U] **1** the way that someone behaves 举止, 行为: *Can TV violence cause aggressive behavior?* 电视中的暴力会导致攻击性行为吗? | **good/bad behaviour** *The headmaster will not tolerate bad behaviour in class.* 校长不会容忍班上的不规矩行为。| [+towards] *Her father's behaviour towards him was irrational.* 她父亲对待他的态度是不理智的。**2 be on your best behaviour** to behave as well and politely as you can, especially in order to please someone 尽可能好地表现; 尽量行为检点: *I want you both to be on your best behaviour at Grandad's.* 我希望你们俩在爷爷家要尽可能循规蹈矩。**3** the way that an object, animal, substance etc normally behaves 性能; 特点; 活动: *studying the behaviour of the AIDS virus* 研究艾滋病病毒的特性 —**behavioural** *adj*: *behavioural science* 行为科学 —**behaviourally** *adv*

be·hav·iour·is·m *BrE*【英】, **behaviorism** *AmE*【美】/bɪˋhevjərˌɪzəm; bɪˈheɪvjərɪzəm/ *n* [U] *technical* the belief that the scientific study of the mind should be based only on people's behaviour, not on what they say about their thoughts and feelings【术语】行为主义〔认为科学的心理研究应该以研究对象本身表现出的行为为依据, 而不应以人们对自己的思想感情所作的陈述为依据〕—**behaviourist** *n* [C]

be·head /bɪˋhɛd; bɪˈhed/ *v* [T] to cut off someone's head as a punishment 将…斩首, 杀…的头〔尤指作为刑罚〕: *Charles I was beheaded in 1649.* 查理一世于1649年被斩首。

Be·he·moth /bɪˋhimɑθ; bɪ̭ˈhiːmɒθ/ an extremely large, MYTHICAL creature mentioned in the Bible, whose name is now used to describe something very big 比希莫特〔《圣经》中提到的一只神秘的巨兽, 此名现用于描述庞然之物〕

be·he·moth /bɪˋhimɑθ; bɪ̭ˈhiːmɒθ/ *n* [C] *literary* something that is very large【文】庞然大物: *five warships, including two 64,000-ton behemoths* 五艘战舰, 包括两艘六万四千吨的巨舰

be·hest /bɪˋhɛst; bɪˈhest/ *n* [singular] **at the behest of** *formal* because someone has requested or ordered it【正式】在…的要求下, 在…的命令下

be·hind¹ /bɪˋhaɪnd; bɪˈhaɪnd/ *prep* **1** at or towards the back of something 在[向]…后面: *The cat ran out from behind a tree.* 猫从树后跑了出来。| *I got stuck behind a truck all the way to the airport.* 去机场时, 我的车一路上都被堵在一辆卡车的后面。| *Jane shut the door behind her.* 简随手关上身后的门。—see 见 FRONT¹ (USAGE) **2** not as successful or advanced as someone or something else 劣于; 落后于; 低于: *We're three points behind the other team.* 我们落后对方球队三分。| *Mark's always behind the rest of his class in mathematics.* 马克的数学成绩总是不如班上的其他同学。| **behind schedule** (=not arriving or not ready at the right time) 延误; 晚点 *The new building is already three months behind schedule.* 这幢新大厦的工期已经延

误了三个月。**3 what's behind sth** being the secret or hidden reason for something 某事幕后的原因: *I wonder what's behind this sudden change of plan.* 我想知道计划突然改变的真正原因是什么。**4** supporting a person, idea etc 支持: *The workers are very much behind these proposals.* 工人们非常支持这些建议。| **behind sb/sth all the way** (=supporting someone or something totally) 全力支持某人/某事; 作某人/某事后盾 *We're behind you all the way on this one.* 这件事我们自始至终支持你。**5** responsible for a plan, idea etc or for organizing something 对…负责: *The police say that organized groups of children are behind the recent spate of thefts.* 警方说近期连串的偷窃案是由有组织的儿童集团所策划的。| *The Rotary Club is behind the fund-raising for the new hospital.* 扶轮社负责新医院的筹款工作。**6** if an unpleasant experience or situation is behind you it no longer upsets you or affects your life 置于…之后: *Now you can put all these worries behind you.* 现在你可以把这些烦恼全部撇在脑后了。**7** if you have experience behind you, you have learnt valuable skills or got important qualities that can be used 有…的〔经验〕: *Marjorie's got ten years of experience as a social worker behind her.* 玛乔丽已有10年的社会工作经验。**8** if a quality or attitude is behind an appearance you think that it exists in spite of being hidden 〔隐藏〕在…后: *She suspected that a certain cynicism lay behind his cheerful exterior.* 她怀疑他开朗的外表后面隐藏着某种愤世嫉俗的心理。—see also 另见 **behind sb's back** (BACK[2] (11)), **behind bars** (BAR[1] (14))

S2 W3 **behind[2]** *adv* **1** at or towards the back of something 在后面; 向后: *an enormous desk with an old man sitting behind* 后面坐着一位老人的大桌子 | *The house has a huge garden behind.* 房子后面有个大花园。| **close behind/not far behind** *The motorcyclists came first, with the President's car following close behind.* 摩托车队先行开路, 总统专车紧随其后。**2 be/get behind** to be late or slow in doing something 迟; 慢; 落后: *This work should have been finished yesterday; I'm getting terribly behind.* 这项工作本应该昨天完成, 我已经大大地落后了。| **behind with** *We're already three months behind with the rent.* 我们的房租已经拖欠了三个月。**3 stay/remain behind** to stay in a place when other people have left it or gone somewhere else 留下来: *I decided to stay behind and look after the baby.* 我决定留下来照看婴儿。**4 leave sth behind** to leave something in a place where you were before 留下某物; 忘了带某物 **5 fall behind** to be less successful than other people 落后(于他人)

behind[3] *n* [C] *informal* a word meaning BOTTOM[1] (7), sometimes used when you want to avoid saying this directly【非正式】臀部, 屁股

be·hind·hand /bɪˋhaɪndˏhænd; bɪˈhaɪndhænd/ *adv* [+with, in] *formal* late or slow in doing something or paying a debt【正式】迟; 慢; 过期; 拖欠

be·hold /bɪˋhold; bɪˈhəʊld/ *v past tense and past participle* **beheld** /bɪˋhɛld; bɪˈheld/ [T] *literary or old use* to see or to look at something【文或旧】见到, 看, 注视 —see also 另见 LO AND BEHOLD —**beholder** *n* [C]

be·hold·en /bɪˋholdən; bɪˈhəʊldn/ *adj* **feel/be beholden to** to feel that you have a duty to someone because they have done something for you 欠…人情; 对…负有义务: *I hate feeling beholden to anyone.* 我不愿欠任何人的人情。

be·hove /bɪˋhov; bɪˈhəʊv/ *BrE*【英】, **be·hoove** /bɪˋhuv; bɪˈhuːv/ *AmE*【美】*v* **it behoves you to do sth** *formal* you should do something because it is right or necessary or it will help you in some way【正式】某事是应当做的, 做某事是责无旁贷的

Bei·der·becke /ˋbaɪdɚbɛk; ˈbaɪdəbek/, **Bix** /bɪks; bɪks/ (1903-31) an American jazz musician who played the piano and CORNET and was one of the few white musicians to influence the early development of JAZZ 贝德贝克〔(1903-1931), 美国爵士音乐家, 曾演奏钢琴、短号, 是影响早期爵士乐发展的少数白人音乐家之一〕

beige /beʒ; beɪʒ/ *n* [U] a pale dull yellowish brown colour 米黄色; 浅棕色 —**beige** *adj* —see picture on page A5 参见A5页图

Bei·jing /ˌbeˋdʒɪŋ; ˌbeɪˈdʒɪŋ/ the capital city of the People's Republic of China 北京〔中华人民共和国首都〕

be·ing[1] /ˋbiɪŋ; ˈbiːɪŋ/ *v* **1** the present participle of BE **2** used in explanations〔用于解释〕由于: *Being a quiet sort of fellow, I didn't want to get involved.* 作为一个喜欢清静的人, 我不想介入。| *You can't expect them just to ignore it, human nature being what it is.* 从人的本性来说, 你不能期望他们会就此不理此事。**3 being as** *spoken especially BrE* because; as【口, 尤英】因为: *He wasn't that keen to drive, being as he'd had a few drinks.* 他刚喝了点儿酒, 不太想开车。

S2 W3 **being[2]** *n* **1 come into being/be brought into being** to begin to exist 诞生; 出现; 存在: *a society that first came into being in 1912* 于1912年成立的协会 **2** [C] a living thing, especially a person 生物〔尤指人〕: *a human being* 一个人 | *strange beings from outer space* 来自外太空的奇怪生物 **3** [U] *literary* the most important quality or nature of something, especially of a person【文】〔尤指人的〕本质, 本性: **the core/roots/whole of sb's being** *The music seemed to touch the whole of her being.* 看来那支乐曲触动了她整个身心。

Bei·rut /beˋrut; beɪˈruːt/ the capital and largest city of Lebanon 贝鲁特〔黎巴嫩首都和最大城市〕

be·jew·elled *BrE*【英】, **bejeweled** *AmE*【美】/bɪˋdʒuəld; bɪˈdʒuːəld/ *adj* wearing jewels or decorated with jewels 戴珠宝的; 饰以珠宝的: *a bejewelled tiara* 镶有宝石的冠状头饰

Be·kaa Val·ley, the /bɪˌkɑ ˋvælɪ; bɪˌkɑː ˈvæli/ a long valley in Lebanon and Syria, which has been fought for in many wars 贝卡谷〔黎巴嫩和叙利亚之间的一条狭长谷地, 是多次战争的必争之地〕

be·la·bour *BrE*【英】, **belabor** *AmE*【美】/bɪˋlebɚ; bɪˈleɪbə/ *v* [T] **1 belabour the point** to emphasize an idea or fact too strongly, especially by repeating it many times 反复强调; 唠叨 **2** to attack or criticize someone or something severely 严厉抨击 **3** *old use* to beat someone or something hard【旧】痛打; 猛击

Bel·a·rus /ˌbjɛləˋrus; ˌbeləˈruːs/ a country in Eastern Europe, surrounded by Latvia, Lithuania, Russia, Ukraine, and Poland. It used to be part of the Soviet Union. Population: 10,350,000 (2001). Capital: Minsk. 白俄罗斯〔东欧国家, 与拉脱维亚、立陶宛、俄罗斯、乌克兰及波兰接壤, 曾为苏联的一部分。人口: 10,350,000 (2001), 首都: 明斯克〕—**Belarusian** *n, adj*

be·lat·ed /bɪˋletɪd; bɪˈleɪtɪd/ *adj* happening or arriving late 延误的, 迟来的: *belated birthday greetings* 迟到的生日祝福 —**belatedly** *adv*

be·lay /bɪˋle; bɪˈleɪ/ *v* [I,T] *technical* to fix a rope on a ship by winding it under and over in the shape of a figure 8 on a special hook【术语】〔在船上〕将〔绳〕以8字形系于特制的钩上

belch /bɛltʃ; beltʃ/ *v* **1** [I] to let air from your stomach come out noisily through your mouth 打嗝: *He took a mouthful and belched loudly.* 他吃了一口, 接着大声打起嗝来。—see also 另见 BURP (1) **2** [I] to give or send out large amounts of smoke, fire etc 喷出, 冒出〔烟、火等〕: *Blue smoke belched from the car's exhaust pipe.* 汽车的排气管中冒出一股蓝色的烟雾。—**belch** *n* [C]

be·lea·guered /bɪˋligɚd; bɪˈliːgəd/ *adj formal*【正式】**1** having many difficulties, especially because everyone is criticizing you or causing trouble for you 被烦扰的, 被缠住的: *beleaguered parents trying to discipline their children* 为管教孩子而烦恼的父母 **2** surrounded by an army and unable to escape 被围困的

Bel·fast /ˋbɛlfæst; ˌbelˈfɑːst◂/ the capital city of Northern Ireland 贝尔法斯特〔北爱尔兰首府〕

bel·fry /ˋbɛlfrɪ; ˈbelfri/ *n* a tower for a bell, especially on a church〔尤指教堂的〕钟塔, 钟楼 —see also 另见 **have bats in the belfry** (BAT[1] (8))

Bel·gian[1] /ˋbɛldʒən; ˈbeldʒən/ *n* [U] someone from Belgium 比利时人

Belgian[2] *adj* from or connected with Belgium 比利时的

Bel·gium /ˋbɛldʒɪəm; ˌbeldʒəm/ a country in northwest Europe between France and Germany. Population: 10,259,000 (2001). Capital: Brussels. 比利时〔欧洲西北部国家, 位于法国和德国之间。人口: 10,259,000 (2001), 首都: 布鲁塞尔〕

Belgrade /bɛlˋgred; belˈgreɪd/ also 又作 **Beograd** a city in east Serbia, the capital of The Republic of Serbia 贝尔格莱德〔塞尔维亚东部城市, 塞尔维亚共和国首都〕

Bel·gra·no Af·fair, the /bɛlˋgrano əˏfɛɚ; belˈgrɑːnəʊ əˌfeə/ a political argument that followed the British government's order to sink a ship called the General Belgrano, belonging to Argentina's navy, during the Falklands War. The ship was sailing away from the Falkland Islands, not towards them, at the time when it was sunk, and some people criticized the British government's action. 贝尔格拉诺事件〔福克兰群岛战争期间, 英国政府下令击沉阿根廷海军舰艇"贝尔格拉诺将军号"而引起的一场政治争端。当时该舰是驶离而不是驶向福克兰群岛, 因此有人对英国政府的行动提出批评〕

Bel·gra·vi·a /bɛlˋgrevɪə; belˈgreɪviə/ a part of west central London where there are many expensive houses and shops, and many foreign embassies (EMBASSY) 贝尔格莱维亚〔位于伦敦中西部, 有许多豪宅、高档店铺和外国使馆〕

be·lie /bɪˋlaɪ; bɪˈlaɪ/ *v* [T] *formal*【正式】**1** to give someone a false idea about something 使人对…产生错觉; 使人对…误解; 掩饰: *Her pleasant manner belied her true character.* 她讨人喜欢的举止掩盖了她真实的为人。**2** to show that your words, hopes etc are false or mistaken 显示〔言词、希望等〕不真实; 证明…是

虚假的: *Two large tears belied Rosalie's brave words.* 两颗大大的泪珠暴露出罗莎莉并不像她自己所说的那样勇敢。

be·lief /bɪ`lif; bə̇'liːf/ *n* **1** [singular,U] the feeling that something is definitely true or definitely exists 信心; 信念: *religious belief* 宗教信仰 | [+in] *a belief in God* 笃信上帝 | [+that] *a growing belief that war had become inevitable* 越来越相信战争不可避免 | **it is sb's belief that** *It is my belief that racism remains widespread in British society.* 我认为种族主义在英国社会中仍然普遍存在。| **in the belief that** (=because you think something is true) 因为相信 *She started taking money, in the mistaken belief that she would not be discovered.* 她误以为自己不会被察觉，开始偷起钱来。| **contrary to popular belief** (=although most people believe the opposite of this) 和人们一般的认识相反 *Contrary to popular belief, eating carrots does not improve your eyesight.* 和大家普遍的看法相反，吃胡萝卜并不会改善视力。**2** [C] an idea that you believe to be true, especially one that forms part of a system of ideas 信仰; 信条: *political beliefs* 政治信仰 | **hold a belief** (=have a belief) 相信 *Some of them hold very right-wing beliefs.* 他们中的一些人持有很极端的右翼思想。**3** [singular] the feeling that something is good and can be trusted 信任, 信赖: [+in] *If you're selling, you have to have genuine belief in the product.* 如果你卖东西，你必须对这产品真正有信心。| **shake sb's belief in** (=make them doubt what they believe) 动摇某人对…的信心 *The judge's decision shook my belief in the legal system.* 法官的判决动摇了我对法律制度的信心。**4 be beyond belief** to seem too strange or unreasonable to be true 难以置信: *These latest proposals are beyond belief!* 这些最新的提议令人难以置信! —see also 另见 **to the best of your belief** (BEST[3] (4)) —compare 比较 DISBELIEF, UNBELIEF

be·liev·a·ble /bɪ`livəbḷ; bə̇'liːvəbəl/ *adj* something that is believable can be believed because it seems possible, likely, or real 可信的: *What I like about the book is that the characters are all very believable.* 我喜欢这本书的理由是: 书中的人物都很真实可信。—**believably** *adv*

be·lieve /bɪ`liv; bə̇'liːv/ *v* [not in progressive 不用进行式]

1 ►BE SURE STH IS TRUE 确信某事是真的◄ [T] to be sure that something is true or that someone is telling the truth 相信: *You shouldn't believe everything you read.* 你不应该尽信你读到的东西。| **believe (that)** *I can hardly believe he's only 25!* 我很难相信他只有25岁! | **believe sb** *I don't believe her – it can't be true.* 我不相信她的话，那不可能是真的。| **believe sth of sb** *Stealing? I would never have believed it of him!* 偷窃? 我怎么也不相信他会干这种事! | **not believe a word of it** *spoken* (=not believe something at all)【口】压根儿不相信

2 can't/don't believe *spoken* used to say that you are very surprised or shocked by something【口】不信: *It's still raining – I don't believe it!* 还在下雨，我真不能相信! | *I can't believe he's expecting us to work on Sunday as well!* 我简直不能相信，他指望我们星期天也去上班! | *My mum couldn't believe it when I dyed my hair green.* 我妈妈简直不敢相信我把头发染成了绿色。

3 believe it or not *spoken* used when you are going to say something that is true but surprising【口】信不信由你; *Well, believe it or not, they've given me a loan.* 不管你信不信，他们已经给我贷了款。

4 would you believe it! *spoken* used when you are surprised or angry about something【口】你会相信吗?〔表示惊讶或生气〕: *And then he just walked out. Would you believe it!* 接着他便退席了，你能相信吗?

5 believe (you) me *spoken* used to emphasize that something is definitely true【口】相信我: *There'll be trouble when they find out about this, believe you me!* 相信我，这件事如果给他们发现了会很麻烦!

6 you'd better believe it! *spoken* used to emphasize that something is true【口】你该相信!

7 don't you believe it! *spoken* used to emphasize that something is definitely not true【口】千万不要相信!

8 can't believe your eyes/ears *spoken* to be very surprised by something you see or hear【口】不敢相信自己的眼睛/耳朵: *I could hardly believe my eyes when he took a gun out of his pocket.* 他从衣袋里掏出一把枪的时候，我简直不敢相信自己的眼睛。

9 if you believe that, you'll believe anything *spoken* used to say that something is definitely not true, and that anyone who believes it must be stupid【口】谁相信，谁就是傻瓜

10 ►HAVE AN OPINION 持某观点◄ [T] to think that something is true, although you are not completely sure 认为; 料想, 猜想: **believe (that)** *I believe you two have met already.* 我想你们俩已经见过面了。| **believe so/not** (=think that something is true or not) 认为/不认为是这样 *"Have they arrived yet?" "Yes, I believe so."* "他们到了吗?" "我想到了。" | **believe sb to be sth** *The jury believed Beyers to be innocent.* 陪审团认为拜尔斯是无罪的。| **be widely believed** (=a lot of people believe this) 人们普遍认为 *They are widely believed to be planning a takeover bid.* 人们普遍认为他们正计划进行收购。| **have reason to believe (that)** (=have information that makes you believe something) 有理由相信 *We have reason to believe that she knew the victim quite well.* 我们有理由相信她对受害者很熟悉。

11 seeing is believing *usually spoken* used to say that you will only believe that something happens or exists when you actually see it【常口】眼见为实

12 ►RELIGION 宗教◄ [I] to have a strong religious faith 笃信宗教: *She says that those who believe will go to heaven.* 她说信教的人会进天堂。—see also 另见 **make believe** (MAKE[1] (18))

believe in *phr v* [T] **1** to be sure that someone exists 相信…的存在: *Do you believe in God?* 你相信有上帝吗? | *It's amazing how many people believe in ghosts.* 有那么多人相信有鬼魂，真令人吃惊。**2** to support or approve of something because you think it is good or right 相信…的价值: *I don't believe in all these silly diets.* 我不相信这些愚蠢的食谱。| **believe in doing sth** *They believe in letting children make their own mistakes.* 他们相信让孩子自己犯点错对他们有益处。**3** [T **believe in** sb] to be confident that someone can be trusted 信任, 信赖: *The people want a President they can believe in.* 人民想要一个可信赖的总统。| *You've got to believe in yourself, or you'll never succeed.* 你必须相信自己，否则你永远不会成功。

be·liev·er /bɪ`livɚ; bə̇'liːvə/ *n* [C] **1** someone who believes in a particular god, religion, or system of beliefs 宗教信仰者; 信徒 **2 be a (great) believer in** to believe strongly that something is good and brings good results 相信[深信]…的人: *I'm a great believer in co-ed schools.* 我深信男女同校大有益处。

Be·li·sha bea·con /bə,liʃə `bikən; bə,liːʃə 'biːkən/ *n* [C] one of two posts with a round flashing orange light on the top that stand by some road crossings in Britain〔英国的〕行人过道指示灯

be·lit·tle /bɪ`lɪtḷ; bɪ'lɪtl/ *v* [T] *formal* to make someone or something seem small or unimportant【正式】轻视; 贬抑: *He tends to belittle his own efforts.* 他往往轻视自己的努力。

Be·lize /be`liz; bə'liːz/ a country in Central America on the Caribbean Sea, which was a British COLONY until it became independent in 1981. Population: 256,000 (2001). Capital: Belmopan. 伯利兹〔中美洲国家，濒临加勒比海，1981年独立，之前是英国殖民地。人口: 256,000 (2001)，首都: 贝尔莫潘〕

Belize City /ˌ· ·ˈ·/ a seaport on the coast of Belize 伯利兹市〔伯利兹一港市〕

bell /bɛl; bel/ *n* [C] **1** a piece of electrical equipment that makes a ringing sound, used as a signal or to get someone's attention 钟; 铃; 电铃: *The door bell rang but no-one answered it.* 门铃响了，但没有人应答。| *Ring the bell once to make the bus stop.* 按一下铃让公共汽车停下来。—see picture at 参见 BICYCLE[1] 图 **2** [usually singular 一般用单数] the sound of a bell ringing as a signal or a warning 钟声; 铃声: *I didn't hear the bell, did you?* 我没有听到铃声，你呢? | **the bell goes** (=makes a noise) 铃响了 *The bell for the end of school went at 3.30.* 放学铃在3:30响起。**3** a hollow metal object shaped rather like a cup, that makes a ringing sound when it is hit by a piece of metal that hangs down inside it 钟; 响铃: *church bells* 教堂的钟 **4 give sb a bell** *BrE spoken* to telephone someone【英口】给某人打电话: *I must give Vicky a bell later.* 我过一会儿必须给维基打个电话。**5** something in the shape of a bell, hollow and getting wider at the end 钟状物: *the bell of a flower* 钟状的花萼 —see also 另见 DIVING BELL, **ring a bell** (RING[2] (4)), **clear as a bell** (CLEAR[1] (10)), **sound as a bell** (SOUND[3] (5))

> **CULTURAL NOTE 文化注释**
>
> Many of the larger and older Christian churches in both the US and the UK have large bells, which are traditionally rung on Sundays to tell people that a church SERVICE (=religious ceremony) will begin soon. Some churches also ring their bells at weddings or when someone from the church has died. 在英美两国，很多较大较古老的基督教教堂装有大钟，一般在星期日敲响，告诉人们宗教仪式即将开始。一些教堂也会在婚礼时敲钟，或者在教区中有人去世时敲钟。— see also 另见 BIG BEN, LIBERTY BELL

Bell, Al·ex·an·der Gra·ham /,ælɪg`zændɚ `greəm; ,ælɪg'zɑːndə 'greɪəm/ (1847-1922) a Scottish scientist and inventor who lived in the US. He invented the telephone in 1876. 贝尔〔(1847-1922)，侨居美国的苏格兰科学家、发明家，1876年发明了电话〕

Bel·la /ˋbɛlə; ˈbelə/ a British weekly magazine for women, which gives advice about fashion, health, cooking etc《贝拉》〔英国的一份女性周刊，提供时装、保健、烹饪等方面的建议〕

bel·la·don·na /ˌbɛləˋdɑnə; ˌbeləˈdɒnə/ *n* [U] **1** a poisonous plant; DEADLY NIGHTSHADE 颠茄〔一种有毒的植物〕 **2** a substance from this plant, used as a drug〔用作药物的〕颠茄剂

bell-bot·toms /ˈ· ·, ·ˈ·/ *n* [plural] trousers with legs that become wider at the bottom 喇叭裤

bell·boy /ˋbɛlˌbɔɪ; ˈbelbɔɪ/ *n* [C] *BrE* a young man who carries bags, takes messages etc in a hotel【英】〔旅馆中〕做杂役的青年男侍者; BELLHOP *AmE*【美】

belle /bɛl; bel/ *n* [C] *old-fashioned* a beautiful girl or woman【过时】美女，美人，佳丽: **the belle of the ball** (=the most beautiful girl at a dance or party) 舞〔聚〕会之花，舞〔聚〕会上最美的女子

Belle Dame Sans Mer·ci /ˌbɛl ˌdɑm sɑn mɛrˋsi; ˌbel ˌdɑːm sɑːn meəˈsiː/, **La** a famous poem by John Keats in which a KNIGHT meets a beautiful magical woman who says she loves him but then disappears《无情的美人》〔约翰·济慈的一首名诗，诗中的骑士邂逅了一位美丽迷人的女子，她说她爱骑士，可后来却消失了〕

belles-let·tres /ˌbɛl ˋlɛtrə; ˌbel ˈletrə/ *n* [U] *French* literature or writings about literary subjects【法】美文学; 纯文学

bell·hop /ˋbɛlˌhɑp; ˈbelhɒp/ *n* [C] *AmE* a young man who carries bags, takes messages etc in a hotel【美】〔旅馆中〕做杂役的青年男侍者; BELLBOY *BrE*【英】

bel·li·cose /ˋbɛləˌkos; ˈbelɪkəʊs/ *adj literary* always wanting to fight or argue; AGGRESSIVE (1)【文】好战的; 好争吵的; 好斗的 —**bellicosity** *n* [U]

bel·lig·er·ent /bəˋlɪdʒərənt; bɪ̆ˈlɪdʒərənt/ *adj* **1** very unfriendly and unpleasant 敌对的; 好斗的; 好寻衅的: *a belligerent attitude* 敌对的态度 **2** [only before noun 仅用于名词前] *formal* a belligerent country is at war with another country【正式】交战中的 —**belligerence, belligerency** *n* [U]

Bel·li·ni /bɛˋlinɪ; beˈliːni/, **Ja·co·po** /ˋjɑkəpo; ˈjækəpəʊ/ (?1400-?1470) a painter from Venice. He trained his sons Gentile Bellini (?1429-1507) and Giovanni Bellini (?1430-1516), who were also painters. 贝利尼〔(?1400-?1470)，威尼斯画家，他的两个儿子秦梯利·贝利尼(?1429-1507)和乔凡尼·贝利尼(?1430-1516)受过他的训练，也都是画家〕

Bell La·bor·a·to·ries /ˈ· ·, ···/ also 又作 **Bell Labs** /ˈ· ·, ·ˈ·/ a group of laboratories (LABORATORY) in the US where scientists have made many important discoveries and developments in science and technology 贝尔实验室〔美国科学家取得许多重大科技发现和进展的一组实验室〕

bel·low[1] /ˋbɛlo; ˈbeləʊ/ *v* **1** [I,T] to shout loudly, especially in a low voice 咆哮; 以低沉的声音叫喊; 大声喝道: *Tony bellowed instructions from an upstairs window.* 托尼从楼上的窗户那儿大喊该怎么做。**2** [I] to make the deep hollow sound that a BULL[1] (1,2) makes〔公牛般〕吼叫

bellow[2] *n* **1** [C] the deep hollow sound that a BULL[1] (1,2) makes〔公牛的〕吼叫声 **2 bellows** [plural] **a)** an object that you use to blow air into a fire〔送风催火的〕吹风器; 风箱 **b)** part of a musical instrument, such as an ORGAN (2), that uses air to produce sound〔管风琴等的〕风箱

Bellow, Saul /sɔl; sɔːl/ (1915-) a US writer, born in Canada, who won the Nobel Prize for Literature in 1976. His novels include *Humbolt's Gift* and *Herzog*. 贝娄〔(1915-)，美国作家，出生于加拿大，1976年获诺贝尔文学奖，他的小说包括《洪堡的礼物》和《赫尔索格》〕

bell pep·per /ˈ·, ·ˈ·/ *n* [C] *AmE* a hollow red, green, or yellow vegetable【美】灯笼椒; PEPPER[1] (3) *BrE*【英】, CAPSICUM

bell-ring·er /ˈ· ·ˌ·/ *n* [C] someone who rings church bells, usually as part of a team〔教堂的〕敲钟人 —**bell-ringing** *n* [U]

S3 **bel·ly**[1] /ˋbɛlɪ; ˈbeli/ *n* [C]

1 ▶PERSON 人◀ a) your stomach 胃: *a full belly* 吃得饱饱的肚子 **b)** *BrE* the part of your body between your chest and your legs; ABDOMEN (1)【英】肚子，腹部: *She lay on her belly in the long grass.* 她趴在深深的草丛中。

2 ▶ANIMAL 动物◀ the underneath of an animal's body 肚子 —see picture at 参见 HORSE[1] 图

3 ▶OBJECT 物体◀ a curved or rounded part of an object 腹状部分: *the belly of a plane* 飞机的机腹 —see also 另见 POTBELLY

belly[2] *v*

belly out *phr v* [I, T **belly** sth ↔ **out**] to swell or become full, or to make something do this (使)鼓气; (使)胀起: *The sails bellied out in the wind.* 船帆迎风鼓起。

bel·ly·ache[1] /ˋbɛlɪˌek; ˈbeli-eɪk/ *n* [C, U] a pain in your stomach 肚子痛，腹痛

bellyache[2] *v* [I] *informal* to complain a lot, especially about something unimportant【非正式】〔尤指对琐事〕抱怨: **[+about]** *Stop bellyaching about it and get on with the job!* 别再发牢骚了，继续工作吧!

belly but·ton /ˈ· ·, ·ˈ·/ *n* [C] *informal* the small round mark in the middle of your stomach; NAVEL【非正式】肚脐

belly dance /ˈ· · ·/ *n* [C] a dance from the Middle East performed by a woman using movements of her BELLY[1] (1b) and hips (HIP[1] (1)) 肚皮舞〔一种源于中东，由女性运用腹部和臀部动作表演的舞蹈〕—**belly dancer** *n* [C]

belly flop /ˈ· · ·/ *n* [C] a way of jumping into water, in which the front of your body falls flat against the surface of the water 俯跳入水时腹部平拍水面的跳水动作 —**bellyflop** *v* [I]

bel·ly·ful /ˋbɛlɪˌfʊl; ˈbelifʊl/ *n* **have had a bellyful of** *informal* to be annoyed by something because you have heard or experienced too much of it【非正式】已经听[受]够了: *I've had a bellyful of your complaints.* 我已经听够了你的牢骚。

belly-land·ing /ˈ· ·, ·ˈ·/ *n* [C] the act of landing a plane without using special equipment〔飞机不用起落装置〕以机腹着陆

belly laugh /ˈ· · ·/ *n* [C] *informal* a deep loud laugh【非正式】开怀大笑

Bel·mont Stakes, the /ˌbɛlmɑnt ˋsteks; ˌbelmɒnt ˈsteɪks/ a famous race for three-year-old horses that is held every year in New York on the first Saturday of June 贝尔蒙特大奖赛〔每年6月的第一个星期六在纽约举行，由三岁赛马参加的著名赛事〕

be·long /bəˋlɔŋ; bɪˈlɒŋ/ *v* [I] **1** [always+adv/prep] to be in the right place or situation 处在(适当位置)，该在: *Put that chair back where it belongs.* 把椅子放回原处。| *Wild animals like this don't belong in a zoo – they should be allowed to go free.* 这样的野生动物不应该关在动物园里，应该放了它们，给它们自由。**2** to feel happy and comfortable in a place or situation, because you have the same interests and ideas as other people 能适应; 感到自在 S2 W2

belong to *phr v* [T] **1** to be the property of 属于: *The house belonged to my grandfather.* 这座房子原是属于我祖父的。| *Who does this scarf belong to?* 这是谁的头巾? **2** to be a member of a group or organization 是…的成员，属于〔某组织〕: *Do you belong to the tennis club?* 你是网球俱乐部的成员吗? | *They were suspected of belonging to a terrorist organization.* 他们被怀疑是恐怖组织的成员。**3** to be connected with or form part of 与…有关; 是…的一部分: *The film belongs to a rich comic tradition.* 这部电影带着浓厚的喜剧传统。| *He belongs to a different generation.* 他是另一代的人。

be·long·ings /bəˋlɔŋɪŋz; bɪˈlɒŋɪŋz/ *n* [plural] the things that you own, especially those that you can carry with you 所有物; 财产，财物: *Please ensure that you have all your belongings when you leave the train.* 下火车以前，请检查一下自己的物品是否齐全。

Bel·o·rus·sia /ˌbɛloˋrʌʃə; ˌbeləʊˈrʌʃə/ the former name of Belarus 白俄罗斯〔旧称〕

be·lov·ed /bɪˋlʌvɪd; bɪˈlʌvɪ̆d/ *adj literary or humorous*【文或幽默】**1** a beloved place, thing etc is one that you love very much 心爱的，钟爱的，喜爱的: *She returned at last to her beloved country.* 她终于回到了自己热爱的祖国。| *He's always talking about his beloved computer!* 他总是在谈论自己心爱的电脑! | **[+of/by]** *a slogan much beloved of politicians* 深受政治家喜爱的口号 **2 my/her etc beloved** the person that you love most 我/她等心爱的人: *It was a gift from my beloved.* 这是我心爱的人送给我的礼物。—see also 另见 **dearly beloved** (DEARLY (4))

be·low[1] /bəˋlo; bɪˈləʊ/ *prep* **1** in a lower place or position than, or on a lower level than〔地方或位置〕在…的下面; 低于: *I'd like you to trim my hair just below the ears.* 请你把我的头发修剪得刚到耳朵下面。| *Fish were swimming below the surface of the water.* 鱼在水面下游动。—see picture on page A1 参见 A1 页图 —see 见 UNDER[1] (USAGE) **2** less than a particular number, amount, level etc〔数量、水平等〕在…之下: *These families are living below the official poverty line.* 这些家庭生活在官方界定的贫穷线以下。| *Bank charges rose at a level slightly below that of inflation.* 银行收费上涨的水平略低于通货膨胀的水平。| **well/way below** (=very much lower than) 大大低于 *Sales figures for January were well below target.* 1月份的销售数字远远低于原定指标。| **below average** (=not as good as the normal standard) 低于平均水平 *Tom's spelling is well below average.* 汤姆的拼写远远低于平均水平。| **below freezing** (=if the temperature is below freezing it is less than zero degrees) 零度以下 **3** in a lower, less important job than someone else〔职位〕低于: *A captain is below a general.* 上尉的军阶比将军低。 S2 W2

below² *adv* **1** in a lower place or position, or on a lower level 在较低处，在较低的位置: *We looked down from the mountain at the valley below.* 我们从山上俯瞰下面的山谷。| *Jim lives on the fourth floor and Jean-Pierre is on the floor below.* 吉姆住在四楼，让-皮埃尔住在下面的一层。**2** on the lower level of a ship or boat 在船下层: *The Captain told the crew to go below.* 船长叫船员下到舱里去。**3** less than a particular number, age, price etc〔数量、年龄、价格等〕以下，低于: *Children of three and below pay half fare.* 三岁及三岁以下儿童半票。 **4 10°/15°/20° below etc** if a temperature is 10°, 15°, 20° etc below, it is that number of degrees lower than zero 零下10/15/20度等 **5** mentioned or shown lower on the same page or on a later page 在（本页）下文; 在后面一页: *See p.85 below.* 见后面第85页。| *The information below was compiled by our correspondent.* 以下资料是我们的记者收集整理的。**6** in a lower, less important rank or job 在较低级别: *officers of the rank of captain and below* 上尉及上尉以下的军官 **7** *literary* on Earth rather than in Heaven【文】在世上，在人间

Bel·sen /ˈbɛlsn̩; ˈbelsən/ a Nazi CONCENTRATION CAMP in northern Germany during World War II. Thousands of people, especially Jews, were killed in Belsen. 贝尔森集中营〔二战期间纳粹集中营，位于德国北部，成千上万的人被杀害，尤其是犹太人〕

belt¹ /bɛlt; belt/ *n* [C]

1 ►CLOTHES 衣服◄ a band of leather, cloth etc that you wear around your waist 腰带; 带子 —see picture on page A17 参见A17页图

2 ►AREA 地区◄ a large area of land that has particular characteristics〔特定的〕区域，地带: *America's farming belt* 美国农业地区 | *the commuter belt* 乘[驾]车上下班者的居住区 —see also 另见 GREEN BELT

3 ►MACHINE PART 机器部件◄ a circular band of material such as rubber that connects or moves parts of a machine 传动带; 输送带 —see also 另见 CONVEYOR BELT, FAN BELT

4 below the belt *informal* a remark or criticism that is below the belt is unfair or cruel【非正式】不公道的; 不正当的: *That was a bit below the belt, Paul.* 保罗，那样做有点不光明正大。

5 have/get sth under your belt to have achieved something useful or important 获得某物: *You need some work experience under your belt.* 你需要一些工作经验。

6 (at) full belt *spoken* moving as quickly as possible【口】(以）全速地: *Willy was off down the road at full belt.* 威利飞快地开车上路。

7 give sb a belt *spoken* to hit someone hard【口】狠揍某人 —see also 另见 CHASTITY BELT, GARTER BELT, SUSPENDER BELT, **tighten your belt** (TIGHTEN (6))

belt² *v informal*【非正式】**1** [T] to hit someone or something hard 重打，狠揍: *Dan belted the ball at goal.* 丹将球朝球门猛一脚踢去。**2** [I always+adv/prep] *BrE* to travel very fast【英】快速行进: [**+down/along etc**] *We were belting down the motorway at 90 miles per hour.* 我们以每小时90英里的速度在高速公路上疾驶。

belt sth ↔ **out** *phr v* [T] *informal* to sing a song or play an instrument loudly【非正式】引吭高歌; 高声演奏〔乐器〕: *She was belting out old Broadway favourites.* 她在大声地唱着受人喜爱的百老汇老歌。

belt up *phr v* [I] *BrE spoken* used to tell someone rudely to be quiet【英口】住口; 别做声: *Belt up, for Christ's sake!* 看在耶稣的分上，别说话！

Bel·tane /ˈbɛlten; ˈbelteɪn/ an ancient Celtic celebration on May 1st when fires were built (**Beltane fires**) and the cattle brought to them to guard against illness in the coming year 五朔节〔古代凯尔特人在5月1日举行的庆祝活动，人们生火、牵牛，保佑来年不生病〕

belt·ed /ˈbɛltɪd; ˈbeltɨd/ *adj* fastened with a belt 系皮带的，有皮带的: *a tightly belted raincoat* 系紧腰带的雨衣

belt·way /ˈbɛltˌwe; ˈbeltweɪ/ *n* [C] *AmE* a road that goes around a city to keep traffic away from the centre【美】环城公路; RING ROAD *BrE*【英】

be·moan /bɪˈmon; bɪˈməʊn/ *v* [T] to complain or say that you are disappointed about something 抱怨; 叹息; 惋惜: *As usual, they were all bemoaning the lack of decent training facilities.* 跟往常一样，他们都在抱怨没有足够的高质量培训设施。

be·mused /bɪˈmjuzd; bɪˈmjuːzd/ *adj* looking as if you are confused 茫然的; 发呆的; 困惑的: *a bemused expression on his face* 他脸上茫然的神情

ben /bɛn; ben/ *n* [C] *ScotE* mountain; often used as part of a name【苏格兰】山〔常用作名称的一部分〕: *Ben Nevis* 尼维斯山

bench¹ /bɛntʃ; bentʃ/ *n*

1 ►SEAT 座位◄ [C] a long seat for two or more people, used especially outdoors〔尤指户外的〕长凳: *a park bench* 公园里的长凳

2 ►COURT 法庭◄ the bench a) the seat where a judge or MAGISTRATE sits in a court of law 法官席: *Would the prisoner please approach the bench?* 请犯人走近法官席。**b)** the position of being a judge or MAGISTRATE in a court of law 法官: *He was appointed to the bench last year.* 他去年被任命为法官。| **serve/sit on the bench** (=work as a judge or MAGISTRATE) 担任法官

3 ►POLITICS 政治◄ benches [plural] *BrE* the seats in the British parliament where members of a particular party sit【英】议员席: *There were shouts of 'resign!' from the Opposition benches.* 从反对党的议员席传来了"辞职!"的喊声。

4 ►TABLE 桌子◄ [C] a long heavy table used for working on with tools or equipment 长形工作台: *a carpenter's bench* 木工工作台

5 ►SPORT 体育◄ [singular] a seat where members of a sports team sit when they are not playing 候补队员席 —see also 另见 FRONTBENCH, BACKBENCH

bench² *v* [T] *AmE* to remove a sports player from a game for a short time【美】罚〔场上运动员〕出场: *The number three has been benched for aggressive behaviour.* 三号运动员因为攻击性行为被罚离场。

Bench·ley /ˈbɛntʃlɪ; ˈbentʃli/, **Rob·ert Charles** /ˈrɑbət tʃɑrlz; ˈrɒbət tʃɑːlz/ (1889-1945) a humorous US writer and theatre critic who wrote articles for the magazines *Vanity Fair* and *The New Yorker*. He was also an actor and he appeared in many films. 本奇利〔(1889-1945)，美国幽默作家和戏剧评论家，曾为《名利场》和《纽约人》两杂志撰稿。他也是一名演员，出演过许多部电影〕

bench·mark /ˈbɛntʃˌmɑrk; ˈbentʃmɑːk/ *n* [C] **1** something that is used as a standard by which other things can be judged or measured 基准; 规范: *a benchmark for future pay negotiations* 给日后工资谈判作参考的一个尺度 **2** a mark made on a building, post etc that shows its height above sea level, and is used to measure other heights and distances in a SURVEY¹ (3)〔测量用的〕水准（基）点

bend¹ /bɛnd; bend/ *v past tense and past participle* **bent** /bɛnt; bent/

1 ►MOVE YOUR BODY 挪动身体◄ [I always+adv/prep] to move the top half of your body forwards or downwards 俯身; 弯腰: [**+towards/across etc**] *He bent towards me and whispered in my ear.* 他俯下身来对我耳语。| **bend over** (=bend your body at the waist) 弯腰 *She was bending over the basin, washing her hair.* 她弯着腰在脸盆里洗头。| **bend down** (=bend your body at the knees or waist) 弯身 *I bent down to lift the box off the floor.* 我弯下身从地上扛起箱子。

2 ►CURVE 曲线◄ a) [T] to push or press something into a curved shape or fold it at an angle 使弯曲: *Bend your arms and then stretch them upwards.* 两臂弯曲然后向上伸展。| **bend sth back/away etc** *I'll bend the branches back so that you can get through.* 我把树枝向后弯一下，让你过去。**b)** [I] to be in the shape of a curve or to change to this shape 呈弯形; 变弯曲: *The wire bent easily.* 这根金属线容易弯曲。

3 bend the rules to do something that is not normally allowed, but will not cause serious problems, usually in order to help someone else 放宽规则; 通融: *You should really pay today, but we can bend the rules just this once.* 你真的应该今天付款，这次我们就通融一下，下不为例。

4 bend over backwards (to do sth) to try very hard to be helpful 竭尽全力做某事: *I've been bending over backwards to get it done on time for them.* 我已尽了最大努力设法按时为他们完成任务。

5 bend sb's ear *spoken* to talk to someone, especially about something that is worrying you【口】和某人谈心〔尤指谈令人烦恼的事〕

6 on bended knee a) trying very hard to persuade someone to do something 努力劝说; 恳求: *If I go on bended knee to the boss, do you think she'd give me my job back?* 如果我恳求老板，你认为她会重新让我上班吗? **b)** in a kneeling position 跪着

7 bend your mind/efforts/thoughts etc to *formal* to give all your energy or attention to one activity, plan etc【正式】集中全力于…，专心致志于…

bend² *n* [C] **1** a curved part of something, especially a road or river〔尤指道路或河流的〕弯曲处: *The taxi swung around the bend at a terrifying speed.* 出租车在以惊人的速度拐过弯道。| [**+in**] *a sharp bend in the river* 河流中一个急弯 **2** an action in which you bend a part of your body〔身体的〕弯曲（动作）: *We started the session with a few knee bends to warm up.* 我们在上课前先做些活动膝盖的动作来热身。**3 the bends** [plural] a

very painful and serious condition that divers get when they come up from under the sea too quickly 潜涵病，减压病〔潜水员浮出水面过快引致的一种令人非常疼痛的病〕 **4 drive sb round the bend** *spoken especially BrE* to annoy someone【口，尤英】惹恼某人 **5 be/go round the bend** *spoken especially BrE* to be or become crazy【口，尤英】发疯: *You must be round the bend to let her treat you like that.* 你竟然让她那样对待你，你一定是疯了。

ben·der /ˈbɛndɚ; ˈbendə/ *n* [C] *BrE informal*【英，非正式】**1 go on a bender** to drink a lot of alcohol at one time 酗酒，纵酒 **2** an insulting word for a man who is attracted to other men; HOMOSEXUAL 男同性恋者〔侮辱性用语〕

bend·y /ˈbɛndɪ; ˈbendi/ *adj informal*【非正式】**1** easy to bend 易弯曲的: *a bendy rubber doll* 易弯曲的橡胶玩具娃娃 **2** with many curves or angles 弯弯曲曲的: *a bendy road* 一条弯弯曲曲的路

2 **be·neath¹** /bɪˈniθ; bɪˈniːθ/ *prep formal*【正式】**1** in or to a lower position than something, or directly under something 在…之下; 在…正下方; 在…底下: *The dolphins disappeared beneath the waves.* 海豚在波涛下消失了。| *Jo enjoyed feeling the warm sand beneath her feet.* 乔很喜欢踏着脚下温暖的沙子。| **give/buckle/tremble beneath the weight of** (=if something gives, buckles etc beneath the weight of something, it breaks or becomes weaker because it is supporting or carrying a heavy weight) 受…重压而弯曲[变形] *The shelf was buckling beneath the weight of the books piled on it.* 书架在书的重压下变了形。**2** in a lower, less important rank or job than someone else〔等级、职位等〕低于: *She would not speak to people she considered beneath her.* 她不愿跟那些她认为比自己地位低的人讲话。**3** not suitable for someone because of not being good enough 与…不相称: **beneath you** *Vera considered it beneath her even to reply to the insult.* 薇拉认为回应这种侮辱性的言论有损自己的身份。**4** a feeling or attitude that is beneath another feeling or attitude is covered or hidden by it 被…所隐藏[掩盖]: *Dave sensed that something more sinister lay beneath the woman's cheerful exterior.* 戴夫感觉到那个女人开朗的外表下隐藏着某种更阴险的东西。—see picture on page A1 参见 A1 页图

beneath² *adv formal* in or to a lower position【正式】在下面; 朝下: *Madge's skirt was too short and her petticoat was showing beneath.* 马奇的裙子太短，衬裙都露出来了。| *He was standing on the bridge gazing down at the river beneath.* 他站在桥上凝视着下面的河流。

Ben·e·dic·tine /ˌbɛnəˈdɪktɪn; ˌbenəˈdɪktɪn◂/ *n* [C] a member of a Christian religious order of MONKS 本笃会修士 —**Benedictine** *adj*

ben·e·dic·tine /ˌbɛnəˈdɪktɪn; ˌbenəˈdɪktiːn/ *n* [C, U] a strong alcoholic drink; type of LIQUEUR 本尼迪克特甜酒〔最初由本笃会修士酿造的一种烈酒〕

ben·e·dic·tion /ˌbɛnəˈdɪkʃən; ˌbenəˈdɪkʃən/ *n* [C, U] a Christian type of prayer said as a BLESSING (1) 祝福; 祝祷

ben·e·fac·tion /ˌbɛnəˈfækʃən; ˌbenəˈfækʃən/ *n formal*【正式】**1** [U] the act of doing something good, especially by giving money to someone who needs it 善行，施惠; 捐款 **2** [C] money given in this way 慈善捐款

ben·e·fac·tor /ˈbɛnəˌfæktɚ; ˈbenəˌfæktə/ *n* [C] someone who gives money for a good purpose 行善者; 捐助人; 施主: *An anonymous benefactor donated $2 million.* 一位没留姓名的捐助人捐款 200 万美元。

ben·e·fac·tress /ˈbɛnəˌfæktrɪs; ˈbenəfæktrəs/ *n* [C] *old-fashioned* a woman who gives money for a good purpose【过时】女施主; 女性捐助者

ben·e·fice /ˈbɛnəfɪs; ˈbenəfəs/ *n* [C] the pay and position of the priest of a Christian PARISH (1) 圣俸; 圣职

be·nef·i·cent /bəˈnɛfəsn̩t; bɪˈnefəsənt/ *adj formal* doing things to help people; generous【正式】行善的; 仁慈的; 宽厚的 —**beneficence** *n* [U] —**beneficently** *adv*

ben·e·fi·cial /ˌbɛnəˈfɪʃəl; ˌbenəˈfɪʃəl◂/ *adj* producing results that bring advantages 有益的，有利的，有用的: *beneficial effects* 裨益 | **[+to]** *an agreement that will be beneficial to both parties* 对双方都有利的协议 —**beneficially** *adv*

ben·e·fi·cia·ry /ˌbɛnəˈfɪʃɪˌɛrɪ; ˌbenəˈfɪʃəri/ *n* [C] **1** someone who gets advantages from an action or change 受益者，受惠者: *The rich were the main beneficiaries of the tax cuts.* 富人是减税的主要受益者。**2** someone who receives money or property from someone else who has died〔遗嘱中的〕受益人: **[+of]** *He was the chief beneficiary of his father's will.* 他是他父亲遗嘱的主要受益人。

3 1 **ben·e·fit¹** /ˈbɛnəfɪt; ˈbenəfɪt/ *n* **1** [C,U] something that gives you advantages or improves your life in some way 好处，益处，裨益，利益: *an aid program that has brought lasting benefits to the region* 给这一地区带来长远利益的援助计划 | **have the benefit of** *She has had the benefit of a first-class education.* 她因受过一流教育而获益。| **for sb's benefit** (=in order to help someone or to be useful to them) 为了帮助某人; 对某人有益 *All donations are used for the benefit of disabled children.* 所有的捐款都用于残疾儿童的福利。| **reap the benefit** (=use and enjoy the advantages of something you have worked to achieve) 获得益处 | **be of benefit** *formal* (=be useful or helpful in some way)【正式】有益的，有好处的 *The new credit cards will be of great benefit to our customers.* 新信用卡将会为我们的客户带来很多好处。**2** [C,U] *BrE* money provided by the government to people who are sick or unemployed【英】〔政府提供给生病者及失业者的〕救济金，津贴; WELFARE (3) *AmE*【美】: *Are you sure you're getting all the benefits you're entitled to?* 你肯定得到了你有资格领取的所有补助吗? | **housing/child/unemployment etc benefit** *How much unemployment benefit do you get?* 你得到多少失业救济金? | **on benefit** (=receiving benefit) 领救济金 *How long have you been on benefit?* 你领救济金多久了? **3 benefit concert/performance/match** a concert, performance, etc arranged to make money for CHARITY (2) 慈善音乐会/义演/义赛: *a benefit concert for famine relief* 为饥荒灾民筹款的慈善音乐会 **4 give sb the benefit of the doubt** to accept what someone tells you even though you think they may be lying 姑且相信某人 **5** [C usually plural 一般用复数] the money or other advantages that you get from insurance that you have 保险金，保险赔偿: *The benefits include full medical cover when travelling abroad.* 保险赔偿包括你出国时的全额医疗费用。

benefit² *v* **1** [T] to bring advantages to someone or improve their lives in some way 有益于，有利于，对…有好处: *a trade* 2 3
agreement that will greatly benefit the developing world 对发展中国家十分有利的一项贸易协定 **2** [I] to be helped by something 获益，受益，得到好处: *I can see the advantages of this for you, but how will I benefit?* 我能看出这件事对你有益，可是我能得到什么好处呢? | **[+from/by]** *Many thousands have benefited from the new treatment.* 千千万万的人受益于这种新的疗法。

Benefits A·gen·cy, the /ˈ… ˌ…, ˌ…/ a British government organization which pays money to people who are unemployed, old, or ill. 救济社〔给失业者、老人或病人发放补贴的英国政府机构〕

Ben·e·lux /ˈbɛnəlʌks; ˈbenəlʌks/ *n* [singular] the countries of Belgium, the Netherlands, and Luxembourg considered as a group 比利时、荷兰、卢森堡三国; 比荷卢联盟

be·nev·o·lent /bəˈnɛvələnt; bəˈnevələnt/ *adj* kind and generous 仁慈的，仁爱的; 乐善好施的: *A benevolent uncle paid for her to have music lessons.* 一位仁慈的叔叔为她支付了音乐课的费用。| *a benevolent smile* 和蔼的微笑 —**benevolence** *n* [U] —**benevolently** *adv*

Ben·gal /ˌbɛnˈgɔl; ˌbenˈgɔːl◂/ an area of southern Asia that includes Bangladesh and the Indian state of West Bengal. 孟加拉〔南亚一地区，包括孟加拉国和印度的西孟加拉邦〕

Ben·ga·li¹ /bɛnˈgɔlɪ; benˈgɔːli/ *n* **1** [U] the language of Bangladesh or West Bengal 孟加拉语 **2** [C] someone from Bengal 孟加拉人

Bengali² *adj* from or connected with Bengal 孟加拉的

Ben-Gu·ri·on /bɛn ˈgurɪən; ben ˈgʊəriən/, **David** (1886-1973) an Israeli politician who is considered responsible for establishing the independent Jewish nation of Israel. He was also Israel's first Prime Minister. 本-古里安〔(1886-1973)，以色列政治家，一般认为，他创建了独立的犹太人国家以色列。他也是以色列的首任总理〕

Ben Hur /ˌbɛn ˈhɝ; ˌben ˈhɜː/ a NOVEL by Lewis Wallace, whose story takes place during the time of Jesus Christ. The story was made into a famous film in 1959.《宾虚传》〔路易斯·华莱士创作的小说，以耶稣基督时代为背景，1959 年被改编成著名影片〕

Ben·i·dorm /ˈbɛnɪdɔrm; ˈbenɪdɔːm/ a town on the Mediterranean coast of Spain which is a popular place for tourists 贝尼多姆镇〔西班牙地中海沿岸一小镇，游览胜地〕

be·night·ed /bɪˈnaɪtɪd; bɪˈnaɪtəd/ *adj* having no knowledge or understanding 愚昧的，蒙昧无知的 —**benightedly** *adv*

be·nign /bɪˈnaɪn; bɪˈnaɪn/ *adj* **1** kind and gentle 慈祥的; 宽厚亲切的: *He shook his head in benign amusement.* 他亲切且满心欢喜地摇了摇头。**2** a benign TUMOUR (=unnatural growth in the body) is not likely to return after treatment〔肿瘤〕良性的 —compare 比较 MALIGNANT (1) —**benignly** *adv* —**benignity** /bɪˈnɪgnətɪ; bɪˈnɪgnəti/ *n* [U]

Be·nin /bəˈnɪn; beˈniːn/, **the People's Republic of** a country in West Africa, between Togo and Nigeria. Population:

6,591,000 (2001). Capital: Porto Novo. 贝宁人民共和国〔西非国家，位于多哥与尼日利亚之间。人口：6,591,000（2001），首都：波多诺伏〕

Bennett /ˋbɛnɪt; ˈbenɨt/, **Arnold** /ˋɑrnḷd; ˈɑːnəld/ (1867-1931) a British whose NOVELs about the 'Five Towns' describe the lives of ordinary people in the area of the Midlands in the UK, where POTTERY was made. 本涅特〔（1867-1931），英国作家，创作了以"五镇"为题材的小说，描写盛产陶器的英格兰中部地区普通人的生活〕

Bennett, Tony (1925-), a US singer who made several best-selling records in the 1950s and 1960s including *I Left My Heart in San Francisco*. 班尼特〔（1925- ），美国歌手，20世纪50至60年代发行多张畅销唱片，包括《魂系圣弗朗西斯科》〕

Ben Ne·vis /bɛn ˋnɛvɪs; ben ˈnevɨs/ a mountain in Scotland which is 1343 meters high and is the highest mountain in the UK 本尼维斯山〔位于苏格兰，高1343米，英国最高山峰〕

Ben·ny /ˋbɛnɪ; ˈbeni/, **Jack** (1894-1974) a US COMEDIAN who had a very popular radio program and later a popular television program, called *The Jack Benny Show*. He is famous for pretending to always be 39, for playing the VIOLIN badly, and for making jokes about how much he dislikes spending money. 本尼〔（1894-1974），美国喜剧演员，他的广播节目和名为《杰克·本尼秀》的电视节目颇受欢迎，他以老是装扮成39岁的样子、小提琴拉得糟糕、讲述自己多么吝啬的笑话而出名〕

bent[1] /bɛnt; bent/ the past tense and past participle of BEND[1]

bent[2] *adj* **1** something that is bent is no longer flat or straight 弯曲的：*The hinge was bent and the lid wouldn't shut properly.* 合叶弯了，盖子盖不上。**2 bent on** completely determined to do something 下定决心（做）…；专心于…，埋头于…：*He seems bent on success at all costs.* 他好像下定决心不惜任何代价一定要成功。| **bent on doing sth** *She's bent on becoming an actress.* 她一心要成为演员。—see also 另见 HELL-BENT **3** *informal especially BrE* financially dishonest and willing to use your official position unfairly【非正式，尤英】〔经济上〕不老实的，收受贿赂的；贪赃枉法的：*a bent policeman* 贪赃枉法的警察 **4** *BrE slang* an insulting word meaning HOMOSEXUAL【英俚】同性恋的〔侮辱性用语〕**5 bent out of shape** *slang especially AmE* very angry or upset【俚，尤美】非常气愤的；相当不安的

bent[3] *n* [singular] *formal* special natural skill【正式】天赋；特长：*He has an artistic bent.* 他有艺术天赋。

Ben·tham /ˋbɛnθəm; ˈbenθəm/, **Jer·e·my** /ˋdʒɛrəmɪ; ˈdʒerəmi/ (1748-1832) a British PHILOSOPHER who believed that the actions of people and governments should be based on what would bring happiness to the largest number of people 边沁〔（1748-1832），英国哲学家，他认为人民和政府的行为都应立足于为最大多数人谋福祉这一理念〕

Bent·ley /ˋbɛntlɪ; ˈbentli/ *trademark* a type of large, comfortable car, made in Britain, and similar to a Rolls-Royce【商标】宾利轿车〔一款宽敞、舒适的英国小汽车，形似劳斯莱斯轿车〕

Benz /bɛnz; benz/ *AmE* an informal name for a Mercedes-Benz car【美】奔驰汽车〔梅赛德斯-奔驰汽车的非正式名称〕—compare 比较 MERC

Benz, Karl /kɑrl; kɑːl/ (1844-1929) a German engineer who built the first petrol-driven car in 1885. His factory later joined with one started by Gottlieb Daimler, and became the Mercedes-Benz car company. 本茨〔（1844-1929），德国工程师，1885年制造了第一辆以汽油为燃料的汽车。他的工厂后来与戈特利布·戴姆勒的工厂合并，组成梅赛德斯-奔驰汽车公司〕

ben·zene /ˋbɛnzin; ˈbenziːn/ *n* [U] a liquid obtained from coal and used for making plastics 苯〔一种从煤提炼而成的液体，用于制造塑胶〕

ben·zine /ˋbɛnzin; ˈbenziːn/ *n* [U] a liquid obtained from PETROLEUM and used to clean clothes 轻质汽油，轻油精，挥发油〔一种从石油提炼而成的液体，用于清洁衣物〕

Be·o·wulf /ˋbeowʊlf; ˈbeɪəʊwʊlf/ an EPIC (=long poem about gods and great men and women) written in the 8th century in Old English, about a man called Beowulf who kills a powerful frightening creature and becomes a king. 《贝奥武甫》〔公元8世纪用古英语写成的英雄史诗，讲述一个叫贝奥武甫的人杀死一只强大可怕的怪物并当上国王的故事〕

be·queath /bɪˋkwið; bɪˈkwiːð/ *v* [T] **1** to officially arrange for someone to have something that you own after your death 遗赠；遗留：**bequeath sth to sb** *She bequeathed her collection of paintings to the National Gallery.* 她立下遗嘱把自己的藏画赠送给国家美术馆。| **bequeath sb sth** *His father bequeathed him a fortune.* 他父亲留给他一大笔财产。**2** to pass knowledge, customs etc to people who come after you or live after you 把〔知识、风俗等〕传给〔后人〕

be·quest /bɪˋkwɛst; bɪˈkwest/ *n* [C] *formal* money or property which you arrange to give to someone after your death【正式】遗产；遗赠物：*a bequest of $5,000* 5000美元的遗产

be·rate /bɪˋret; bɪˈreɪt/ *v* [T+for] *formal* to speak angrily to someone because they have done something wrong【正式】训斥；严责

be·reaved /bəˋrivd; bɨˈriːvd/ *adj formal*【正式】**1** having lost a close friend or relative because they have recently died〔刚刚〕丧失亲友的：*a bereaved mother* 痛失孩子的母亲 **2 the bereaved** the person or people whose close friend or relative has just died 死者的亲友：*Our sympathies go to the bereaved.* 我们同情死者的亲友。

be·reave·ment /bəˋrivmənt; bɨˈriːvmənt/ *n* [C,U] *formal* the fact or state of having lost a close friend or relative because they have died【正式】丧亲（之痛）；丧友（之痛）；居丧：*depression caused by bereavement or divorce* 痛失亲人或离婚导致的忧伤

be·reft /bɪˋrɛft; bɨˈreft/ *adj formal*【正式】**1 bereft of hope/meaning/life etc** completely without any hope etc 失去希望/意义/生命等：*The party's manifesto is bereft of new ideas.* 这个党的宣言毫无新意。**2** feeling very sad and lonely 伤感的；寂寞的：*He had left, and she felt completely bereft.* 他走了，她深感孤寂。

be·ret /bəˋre; ˈbereɪ/ *n* [C] a round cap with a tight band around the head and a soft loose top part 贝雷帽〔扁圆无檐儿柔软的小帽〕—see picture at 参见 CAP[1] 图

Ber·ge·rac /ˋbɝʒəræk; ˈbɜːʒəræk/, **Cy·ra·no de** /ˋsɪrəno də; ˈsɪrənəʊ də/ (1619-55) a French writer and soldier who fought more than 1000 DUELs (=fights between two people) and was famous for his extremely large nose. His name is also the title of a famous play about his life, written by Edmond Rostand. 贝尔热克拉〔（1619-1655），法国作家、士兵，与人决斗过1000多次，以鼻子超大而出名。他的名字也是一部有关他生平的戏剧名，由艾德蒙·罗斯丹创作〕

Berg·man /ˋbɝgmən; ˈbɜːgmən/, **Ing·mar** /ˋɪŋmɑr; ˈɪŋmɑː/ (1918-2007) a Swedish film maker and one of the most important directors in the history of the cinema. His films, which include *The Seventh Seal* (1956) and *Fanny and Alexander* (1983), often deal with very serious subjects, and with characters who experience a lot of emotional suffering. 伯格曼〔（1918-2007），瑞典电影制片人，被认为是电影史上最重要的导演之一，他的影片包括《第七封印》（1956）和《芳妮和亚历山大》（1983），经常关涉非常严肃的题材，也描写饱受情感之苦的人物〕

Bergman, In·grid /ˋɪŋgrɪd; ˈɪŋgrɪd/ (1915-82) a Swedish actress who became internationally famous. She appeared with Humphrey Bogart in the film *Casablanca*. 褒曼〔（1915-1982），瑞典女演员，国际著名影星，曾与亨弗莱·博加特共同出演《卡萨布兰卡》〕

ber·i·ber·i /ˌbɛrɪˋbɛrɪ; ˌberiˈberi/ *n* [U] a disease of the nerves caused by lack of VITAMIN B 脚气（病）

Be·ring Strait, the /ˌbɪrɪŋ ˋstret; ˌbeərɪŋ ˈstreɪt/ a narrow passage of water between Asia and North America that connects the Bering Sea to the Arctic Ocean 白令海峡〔亚洲和北美洲之间连接白令海和北冰洋的一条狭长水道〕

berk, burk /bɝk; bɜːk/ *n* [C] *BrE spoken slang* a stupid person【英口，俚】傻瓜：*I felt a berk in my jeans when everyone else was in suits.* 别人都穿套装，而我却穿着牛仔裤，感觉像个傻瓜一样。

Berke·ley /ˋbɝklɪ; ˈbɜːkli/ a city on the eastern side of the San Francisco Bay area in California. It is well known for its university. 伯克利市〔加利福尼亚圣弗朗西斯科海湾东岸城市，以加利福尼亚大学伯克利分校著称〕

Berkeley, Busby /ˋbʌzbɪ; ˈbʌzbi/ (1895-1976) a US CHOREOGRAPHER (=someone whose job is to arrange the movements in a dance) who directed the dancing in many films in the 1930s. He is known for his impressive and imaginative style of dances, which were usually performed by groups of young women. 贝克莱〔（1895-1976），美国舞蹈编导，20世纪30年代为许多影片编舞，编导的舞蹈通常由年轻女子舞蹈队表演，风格感人，富有想象力〕

Berke·ley Square /ˌbɑrklɪ ˋskwɛɚ; ˌbɑːkli ˈskweə/ a square in London known in the 17th and 18th centuries as the home of many famous people including Robert Walpole and Clive of India 伯克利广场〔伦敦一广场，以17、18世纪的名人聚集地而闻名，其中有罗伯特·沃波尔和印度的克莱武〕

Berk·shire /ˋbɑkʃɚ; ˈbɑːkʃə/ a COUNTY in the south of England 伯克郡〔英格兰南部一郡〕

Ber·lin /ˌbɝˋlɪn; ˌbɜːˈlin◂/ the capital city of Germany. Berlin was divided into East Berlin and West Berlin after World War

II. It became a united city again when the Berlin Wall was destroyed in 1989. 柏林〔德国首都，二战后被划分为东柏林和西柏林。1989年柏林墙拆除之后，柏林又成为一个统一的城市〕

Berlin, Ir·ving /ˋɝvɪŋ; ˈɜːvɪŋ/ (1888-1989) a US songwriter who wrote many popular songs and successful MUSICALs (=plays or films that use singing and dancing to tell a story). His songs include *Alexander's Ragtime Band* and *White Christmas*. 柏林〔(1888-1989)，美国歌曲作家，写过许多流行歌曲和成功的音乐剧，歌曲有《亚历山大雷格泰姆乐队》和《白色圣诞节》〕

Berlin Wall /, ·· ˈ·/ a wall that divided East and West Berlin, which was built in 1961 and destroyed in 1989. The government of East Germany built the wall in order to prevent people from escaping to West Berlin. 柏林墙〔东、西柏林的分界墙，筑于1961年，1989年被拆除。东德政府修建此墙的目的是防止东德人逃往西柏林〕

Ber·li·oz /ˋbɛrlɪoz; ˈbeəliəʊz/, **Hec·tor** /ˋhɛktɚ; ˈhektə/ (1803-69) a French COMPOSER, whose most famous work is the *Symphonie Fantastique* 伯辽兹〔(1803-1869)，法国作曲家，最著名的作品是《幻想交响曲》〕

Ber·mu·da /bɚˋmjudə; bəˈmjuːdə/ a group of islands in the West Atlantic Ocean which is a popular place for tourists. Bermuda is a British COLONY, but has its own local government. Population: 64,000 (2001). Capital: Hamilton. 百慕大〔位于西大西洋的群岛，著名旅游胜地。虽为英国殖民地，但有自己的地方政府。人口: 64,000 (2001)，首府: 哈密尔顿〕

Bermuda Tri·an·gle, the /·, ·· ˈ···/ an area in the West Atlantic Ocean between Bermuda, Florida, and Puerto Rico. Some people believe that many ships and aircraft have disappeared here without any reason. 百慕大三角区〔位于西大西洋的百慕大、佛罗里达和波多黎各之间的一个区域。据信不少船只和飞机曾在此失踪，但原因不明〕

Bern /bɝn; bɜːn/ also 又作 **Berne** **1** the capital city of Switzerland and of Bern CANTON, on the Aare River. The Swiss government and various international organizations are based there. 伯尔尼〔瑞士首都和伯尔尼州的首府，位于阿勒河河畔，是瑞士政府和各种国际组织的所在地〕 **2** a canton of Switzerland 伯尔尼州〔瑞士的一个州〕—see also 另见 CANTON

Ber·na·dette /ˌbɝnɚˋdɛt; ˌbɜːnəˈdet/, **Saint** also 又作 **St Bernadette of Lourdes** /·, ··· · ˈ·/ (1844-79) a girl who claimed to have seen the Virgin Mary at Lourdes, which made Lourdes a place of pilgrimage, especially for the sick 贝尔娜黛特〔(1844-1879)，一位自称在卢德见过圣母马利亚的女孩，卢德因此成为朝圣之地，对患病的人来说尤其如此〕

Bern·hardt /ˋbɝnhɑrt; ˈbɜːnhɑːt/, **Sa·rah** /ˋsɛrə; ˈseərə/ (1844-1923) a famous French actress. Many people think of her as one of the best actresses ever. 伯因哈特〔(1844-1923)，法国著名女演员，不少人认为她是有史以来最出色的女演员之一〕

Bern·stein /ˋbɝnstaɪn; ˈbɜːnstaɪn/, **Leon·ard** /ˋlɛnɚd; ˈlenəd/ (1918-90) a US musician, famous both as a conductor of classical music and as a writer of popular MUSICALs (=plays or films that use singing and dancing to tell a story), including *West Side Story*. 伯恩斯坦〔(1918-1990)，美国音乐家，既是一位著名的古典音乐指挥家，又是一位知名的通俗音乐剧作曲家，作品包括《西城故事》〕

Ber·ra /ˋbɛrə; berə/, **Yogi** /ˋjogɪ; ˈjəʊgi/ (1925-) a famous US BASEBALL player for the New York Yankees team from 1946 to the 1960s, who was the MVP (=most valuable player) of the American League in 1951, 1954, and 1956. He later became a COACH, and he is famous for saying "It ain't over till it's over". 贝拉〔(1925-)，著名的美国棒球运动员，1946年至60年代效力于纽约扬基队。他是1951、1954及1956年美国棒球联盟最有价值球员，后来成为一名教练。他有一句名言: "比赛没结束永远不算结束。"〕

ber·ry /ˋbɛrɪ; ˈberi/ *n* [C] a small soft fruit with small seeds 浆果，莓 —see picture on page A8 参见 A8 页图

Berry, Chuck (1926-) a US singer, GUITAR player, and songwriter whose music was in the RHYTHM AND BLUES style. His many popular songs include *Johnny B. Goode* and *No Particular Place to Go*, and his style had a big influence on 1960s musicians such as the Rolling Stones. 贝里〔(1926-)，美国歌手、吉他手和歌曲作者，其音乐属于节奏布鲁斯风格，他的流行歌曲包括《J.B.古德》和《无处可去》。他的音乐风格对20世纪60年代的音乐家产生了很大影响，如滚石乐队等〕

ber·serk /bɚˋsɝk; bɜːˈsɜːk/ *adj* **go berserk** to become very angry and violent 狂怒，暴跳如雷

berth¹ /bɝθ; bɜːθ/ *n* [C] **1** a place where a ship can stop and be tied up〔船舶的〕泊位，停泊处 **2** a place for someone to sleep in a ship or on a train; BUNK¹ (1)〔船或火车上的〕卧铺，铺位；舱位 —see also 另见 **give sb/sth a wide berth** (WIDE¹ (7))

berth² *v* [I,T] to bring a ship into a berth or arrive at a berth（使）〔船〕停泊

ber·yl /ˋbɛrəl; ˈberḷ/ *n* [C] a valuable stone that is usually green or yellow 绿柱石，绿玉

be·seech /bɪˋsitʃ; bɪˈsiːtʃ/ *v past tense and past participle* **besought** /bɪˋsɔt; bɪˈsɔːt/ *or* **beseeched** [T] *literary* to eagerly and anxiously ask someone for something【文】恳求，祈求，哀求，央求

be·seem /bɪˋsim; bɪˈsiːm/ *v* [T] *old use* to be suitable or proper for something【旧】适合；与…相称

be·set /bɪˋsɛt; bɪˈset/ *v past tense and past participle* **beset** *present participle* **besetting** [T] *formal*【正式】**1** [usually passive 一般用被动态] to make someone experience serious problems or dangers 困扰；使苦恼: *The business has been beset with financial problems.* 该企业为财务问题所困扰。**2 besetting sin/weakness** *often humorous* a particular bad feature or habit【常幽默】坏习惯，恶习: *Mark's besetting sin is laziness.* 马克最大的恶习是懒惰。

be·side /bɪˋsaɪd; bɪˈsaɪd/ *prep* **1** next to or very close to someone or something 在…旁边，在…近旁: *Wendy came up and sat beside me.* 温迪走过来，坐在我身边。| *We parked the car beside the sports hall.* 我们把车停在体育馆旁边。—see picture on page A1 参见 A1 页图 **2** used to compare two people or things 与…相比: *This year's sales figures don't look very good beside last year's results.* 和去年相比，今年的销售额看来不佳。| *Pat looked big and clumsy beside her younger sister.* 帕特跟她妹妹比起来，个子高，但动作不灵巧。**3 beside yourself** feeling so angry, excited etc that you find it difficult to control yourself〔由于气愤、激动等而〕失去控制；忘形: *He was beside himself with joy when his wife gave birth to their first child.* 妻子生下了第一个孩子时，他欣喜若狂。**4 beside the point** used to say that something that has been mentioned is not directly connected with the main subject or problem that you are talking about 离题，与本题无关: *"How old is she?" "That's beside the point, the question is, can she do the job?"* "她多大了?" "那与本题无关，问题是她能胜任这项工作吗?"

be·sides¹ /bɪˋsaɪdz; bɪˈsaɪdz/ *prep* in addition to a point, statement etc that has just been mentioned 除了…之外: *Will there be anyone else we know at the party besides Will and Janet?* 除了威尔和珍妮特外，聚会上还有我们认识的人吗? | **besides doing sth** *Besides going to French evening classes twice a week she does yoga on Wednesdays.* 她除了每周两次去夜校学法语外，星期三还练瑜伽。

besides² *adv* used when making another point or statement after one that you have already made 而且；还有: *I don't want to go to the cinema; besides I'm feeling too tired.* 我不想去看电影，再说我也太累了。| *My wife and I will be there and four of our friends besides.* 我和妻子会到场，此外还有四位朋友。—see 见 MOREOVER (USAGE)

be·siege /bɪˋsidʒ; bɪˈsiːdʒ/ *v* [T] **1** to surround a city or castle with military force until the people inside let you take control 包围；围攻；围困: *In April 655, Osman's palace in Medina was besieged by rebels.* 公元655年4月，奥斯曼帝国在麦地那的宫殿遭到叛军围攻。**2** [usually passive 一般用被动态] if people, worries, thoughts etc, besiege you, you are surrounded by them〔人、烦恼、想法等〕包围: *Miller was besieged by reporters and press photographers.* 米勒被记者和新闻摄影师团团围住。**3 be besieged with letters/demands/requests etc** to receive a very large number of letters, requests etc 被大量的信件/求助/请求等所困扰

be·smirch /bɪˋsmɝtʃ; bɪˈsmɜːtʃ/ *v* [T] *literary*【文】**besmirch sb's honour/reputation** to spoil the good opinion that people have of someone 败坏[诋毁]某人的名誉

be·som /ˋbizəm; ˈbiːzəm/ *n* [C] a large brush made of sticks tied together around a long handle 长柄扫帚

be·sot·ted /bɪˋsɑtɪd; bɪˈsɒtḷd/ *adj* **be besotted (with)** to love or want someone or something so much that you cannot think or behave sensibly 痴迷(于)；沉醉(于)；(为…)昏了头: *He's completely besotted with her.* 他被她弄得神魂颠倒。

be·sought /bɪˋsɔt; bɪˈsɔːt/ the past tense and past participle of BESEECH

be·speak /bɪˋspik; bɪˈspiːk/ *v past tense* **bespoke** /bɪˋspok; bɪˈspəʊk/ *past participle* **bespoken** /bɪˋspokən; bɪˈspəʊkən/ [T] *literary* to be a sign of something【文】显示，表示: *His easy manner bespoke a knowledge of the world.* 他从容不迫的举止显示出他很通达世故。

be·spec·ta·cled /bɪˋspɛktəkḷd; bɪˈspektəkəld/ *adj* wearing glasses 戴眼镜的

be·spoke /bɪˈspok; bɪˈspəʊk/ *adj BrE old-fashioned* a bespoke suit, coat etc has been specially made to fit one person【英, 过时】〔服装〕定做的

1 1 **best¹** /bɛst; best/ *adj* [superlative of *good* good 的最高级] **1** better than anything else or anyone else in quality, skill, effectiveness etc 最好的: *He was the best teacher in the school.* 他是学校里最好的老师。| *What's the best way to cook this fish?* 这种鱼怎样烹制最好？| *The best thing to do is to stop worrying.* 最好的办法就是别再担心。| **easily the best/by far the best** (=much better than anything else) 绝对是最好的 *I've read all her books but 'Middlemarch' is easily the best.* 她所有的书我都读过, 但《米德尔马奇》绝对是最好的。| **it's best to** *It's best to clean the wall before you paint it.* 油漆之前, 最好先把墙弄干净。**2 best dress/shoes/clothes etc** clothing that you keep for special occasions 最好的穿着/鞋子/衣服等〔留待特殊场合才穿戴〕: *You ought to wear your best shirt.* 你应该穿上你最好的衬衫。**3 best friend** the friend that you know and like better than anyone else 最好的朋友 **4 the next best thing** something that is not exactly what you want but is as similar to it as possible 仅次于最好的: *The next best thing to being with her was to phone and talk.* 能和她在一起最好了, 但打电话和她聊聊也不错。**5 best of all** used to introduce the one fact about a situation that is even better than the other good things 更好的是; 而且: *Yeah, my dad's getting a new car – and best of all, he's going to give me the old one!* 是啊, 我爸爸买了一辆新车。更好的是, 他会把旧车给我！ —see also 另见 **be on your best behaviour** (BEHAVIOUR (2)), **your best bet** (BET² (3)), **the best/better part of** (PART¹ (6))

1 2 **best²** *adv* [superlative of *well* well 的最高级] **1** in a way that is better than any other; most well 最好地: *It works best if you let it warm up first.* 如果先把它预热一下, 用起来就最佳。| *The glacier can best be viewed from above.* 从上面看冰川最美。| *the best-dressed man in Paris* 巴黎穿得最讲究的男人 **2** to the greatest degree; most 最, 极: *You know him best – you should ask him.* 你最熟悉他, 你应该去问他。| *Which did you like best, the music or the dancing?* 你最喜欢的是什么？是音乐还是舞蹈？| *one of our best-loved old cathedrals* 我们最喜爱的旧教堂之一 **3 for reasons best known to herself/himself** used to say that you cannot understand why someone has done something 只有她/他自己才知道的原因: *For reasons best known to herself, she arrived dressed in a gorilla suit!* 出于只有她自己才知道的原因, 她打扮成一只大猩猩到场！**4 as best you can** *spoken* as well as you can, even if this is not very good【口】尽最大努力, 竭力: *I'll translate it as best I can, but my German is very rusty.* 我会尽力把它翻译好, 可是我的德语已很生疏了。**5 had best** *spoken* ought to【口】应该; 最好: *You'd best stay at home till you get over that cold.* 你最好留在家里休息, 直到感冒好了为止。

best³ *n* **1 a)** the best, most helpful, most successful etc situation or results that you can achieve 最佳; 至上; 至善: *We all want the best for our children.* 我们都希望给自己的孩子最好的东西。| *It's the best we can do in the circumstances.* 在这种情况下, 我们所能做到最好的就是这样了。**b)** the person or thing that is better than any other 最好之人; 最佳之物: *She's the best of the new young writers.* 她是新一代年轻作家中最优秀的。**2 do your best** to try as hard as you can to do something 尽力而为; 作出最大努力: *As long as you do your best we'll be happy.* 只要你尽力而为, 我们就满意了。| **do your best to do sth** *We'll do our best to finish it on time.* 我们会尽力按时把它完成。**3 at best** used to emphasize that something is not very good, pleasant, honest, etc even if you consider it in the best possible way 充其量; 至多: *The city was at best an ordinary sort of place.* 这城市充其量只是个普通的地方。| *His answers were at best evasive, at worst very misleading.* 他的回答往好里说是模棱两可, 往坏里说是带有误导性。**4 to the best of your knowledge/belief/ability** used to say that something is as much as you know, believe, or are able to do 就某人所知/所信/能力所及: *I'm sure he'll do the work to the best of his ability.* 我相信他会竭尽全力做好这项工作。**5 the best of both worlds** a situation in which you have the advantages of two different things without any of the disadvantages 两全其美; 各取其长: *They live in a village but it's only an hour from London so they have the best of both worlds.* 他们住在一个村子里, 但离伦敦只有一小时的路程, 所以他们能享受着两者的优点。**6 at your best** performing as well or effectively as you are able to 在最佳状态[巅峰]时: *At her best, she's a really stylish player.* 她处于最佳状态时, 是个很棒的运动员。| *He was never at his best early in the morning.* 在大清早他的状态总不是最佳。**7 make the best of sth/make the best of a bad job** to accept an unsatisfactory situation, and do whatever you can to make it less bad 尽可能善用〔不能令人满意的事物或处境〕; 善处逆境: *We are stuck here so we might as well make the best of it.* 我们反正被困在这儿了, 不如尽量利用这里的条件做些什么。**8 the best of a bad lot** the least bad person or thing in a group of not very good people or things 差中选优 **9 all the best** used to express good wishes to someone for the future 一切顺利！万事如意！: *All the best for the New Year!* 新年万事如意！**10 Sunday best** *old-fashioned* your best clothes, which you only wear on special occasions【过时】盛装 **11 be for the best** *especially spoken* used to say that a particular event may not be as bad as it seems【尤口】也许不是件坏事: *I still don't want him to go but maybe it's for the best.* 我还是不希望他去, 但这也许不是件坏事。**12 at the best of times** if something is not very good, pleasant etc at the best of times, it is usually even worse than this 即使在最好的情况下: *It's not a very exciting town at the best of times.* 即使在最好的时候, 这个小镇也不那么热闹。

best⁴ *v* [T] *old use* to defeat someone【旧】击败, 胜过

best-be·fore date /ˌ· ˈ· ·ˌ ·/ *n* [C] a date on containers of food or drink that shows when they will be too old to eat or drink 最佳食用期, 食品保质期

bes·ti·al /ˈbɛstʃəl; ˈbestiəl/ *adj* inhuman 野蛮的; 兽性的: *Thousands of them had been murdered in the most bestial manner.* 他们当中有成千上万的人被惨无人道地屠杀了。—**bestially** *adv*

bes·ti·al·i·ty /ˌbɛstʃɪˈælətɪ; ˌbestiˈæləti/ *n* [U] **1** sexual relations between a person and an animal 人兽交合, 兽奸 **2** *formal* very cruel behaviour【正式】兽行, 残忍的行为

bes·ti·ar·y /ˈbɛstɪˌɛrɪ; ˈbestiəri/ *n* [C] an old book about strange animals, written in the Middle Ages〔写于中世纪的〕动物寓言集

be·stir /bɪˈstɝ; bɪˈstɜː/ *v* [T] **bestir yourself** *formal* to start to do things, after relaxing or being lazy【正式】发奋, 振作精神

best man /ˌ· ˈ·/ *n* [singular] the man who helps the BRIDEGROOM (=the man getting married) at a wedding ceremony 男傧相, 伴郎

CULTURAL NOTE 文化注释

The best man is usually a friend of the bridegroom, and he is responsible for making sure that the bridegroom arrives at the wedding on time and for giving him the wedding ring during the ceremony. He usually also makes an amusing speech after the ceremony. People sometimes make jokes about the best man losing the wedding ring. 男傧相常为新郎好友, 他负责保证新郎准时来到婚礼现场, 并在举办仪式时递给他婚戒。有时男傧相会在婚礼仪式后发表一段诙谐的讲话。人们有时拿丢失了婚戒的男傧相来开玩笑。— see Feature on page F40 见 F40 页文化特写

be·stow /bɪˈsto; bɪˈstəʊ/ *v* [T] *formal* to give someone something of great value or importance【正式】给予; 赠给; 授予: **bestow sth on/upon** *honours bestowed on him by the Queen* 女王授予他的荣誉

be·stride /bɪˈstraɪd; bɪˈstraɪd/ *v past tense* **bestrode** /bɪˈstrod; bɪˈstrəʊd/ *past participle* **bestridden** /bɪˈstrɪdn; bɪˈstrɪdn/ [T] *literary* to sit or stand on or over something with one leg on each side of it【文】跨坐[立]于…上

best-sel·ler /ˌ· ˈ··/ *n* [C] a very popular book which many people buy 畅销书 —**best-selling** *adj*: *a best-selling author* 畅销书作者

bet¹ /bɛt; bet/ *v past tense and past participle* **bet** *or* **betted**, *present participle* **betting** **1** [I, T] to risk money on the result of a race, game, competition, or other future event 下赌注; 与…打赌: **bet (sb) that** *Sean bet that I wouldn't pass my exam.* 肖恩打赌说我考试不会及格。| **bet (sth) on** *She bet all her money on a horse that came last.* 她把赌注都压在跑在最末的那匹马上。| *No, I don't bet on my own team. It's bad luck.* 不, 我不会在自己的球队上下赌注, 那样会倒霉的。 1

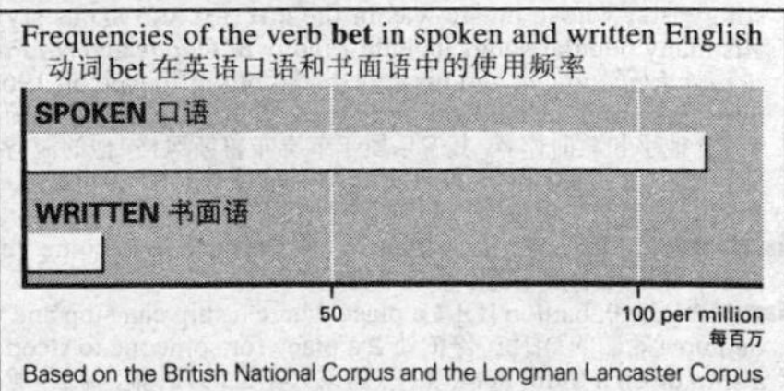

Based on the British National Corpus and the Longman Lancaster Corpus
据英国国家语料库和朗文兰开斯特语料库

This graph shows that the verb **bet** is much more common in spoken English than in written English. This is because it is used in some common spoken phrases. 本图表显示，动词bet在口语中的使用频率远远高于书面语，因为口语中很多常用短语是由bet构成的。

bet (*v*) SPOKEN PHRASES
含 bet 的口语短语

2 I bet a) used to say that you are fairly sure that something is true, something is happening etc, although you cannot prove this 我敢肯定；我敢预言：*I bet Nigel's sitting at home now laughing his head off.* 我敢肯定现在奈杰尔正坐在家里笑个不停。| *I bet it's quite good actually.* 我肯定实际情况会不错。| *I bet you she won't come.* 我有把握对你说她不会来。**b)** used to show that you understand or can imagine the situation that someone has just told you about 我相信；我想得出：*"The strawberries dipped in chocolate were gorgeous." "I bet!"* "草莓蘸巧克力味道好极了。""我想一定不错！" | *"God, I was so angry." "I bet you were."* "天哪，我当时生气极了。""我想你是的。" **c)** used when you are asking someone to guess something 我相信〔用于让某人猜测〕：*I bet you'll never guess who I saw this morning.* 我想你永远也猜不出我今早见到了谁。**d)** used to show that you do not believe what someone has just told you 我才不相信：*"I'm definitely going to give up smoking this time." "Yeah, I bet!"* "这次我肯定会戒烟。""哼！我才不信！" **3 you bet!** used to emphasize that you agree with someone or are keen to do what they suggest 的确！当然！一定！一点不错！：*"Going to the party on Saturday?" "You bet!"* "星期六去参加聚会吗？""当然啦！" **4 you can bet your life/your bottom dollar** used when you are sure that you know what someone will do or what will happen 确信，完全有把握：*You can bet your bottom dollar that relationship will end in tears.* 准没错，这种关系肯定以悲剧收场。

bet[2] *n* [C] **1** an agreement to risk money on the result of a race, game, competition etc 打赌：**have a bet on** *Mom had a bet on the Yankees and won $20.* 妈妈把赌注下在扬基队上，结果赢了20美金。| **place a bet** (=choose a horse, team etc and bet on it) 〔在…上〕下赌注 **2** money that you risk on a bet 赌金，赌注：*I've got a £10 bet on the National.* 我在国家队上下了10英镑的赌注。**3 your best bet** *spoken* used when advising someone of what to do【口】最好的办法：*I think your best bet would be to go back to college and get more qualifications.* 我想你最好的办法是回大学去，取得更多的资历。**4 my bet is (that)** *spoken* used when saying what you expect to happen in the future【口】我认为…：*My bet is that she'll be famous in a few years' time.* 我估计她用不了几年就会出名。**5 a good bet/a safe bet** an action or situation that is likely to be successful or does not involve much risk 极可能成功[稳妥]的做法[情况]：*If you're looking for long-term growth, the government's own saving certificates are a pretty good bet.* 如果你寻求长期增值，政府的储蓄券是最保险的。**6 a safe bet/a sure bet (that)** *spoken* used to say that something seems almost certain【口】几乎不成问题：*I think it's a pretty safe bet that he'll get the job.* 我想他得到这份工作应该不成问题。**7 do sth for a bet** to do something stupid, dangerous etc to win money from someone or to prove that you can do it 为打赌而做某事：*Sandra cut the manager's tie off for a bet!* 桑德拉为了打赌把经理的领带剪掉了！

be·ta /ˋbetə; ˈbiːtə/ *n* **1** [singular] the second letter of the Greek alphabet, β or B 希腊字母表的第二个字母〔即β或B〕 **2** [C] this letter given as a mark for good work by a student〔学生成绩〕乙等，B等

beta-block·er /ˋ‥ˌ‥/ *n* [C] a drug used to help prevent HEART ATTACKS β阻滞药，β受体阻断药〔一种用以预防心脏病的药物〕

be·take /bɪˋtek; bɪˈteɪk/ *v past tense* **betook** /bɪˋtʊk; bɪˈtʊk/ *past participle* **betaken** /bɪˋtekən; bɪˈteɪkən/ **betake yourself to** *literary* to go somewhere【文】前往，赴

be·tel /ˋbitḷ; ˈbiːtl/ *n* [U] a plant whose leaves have a fresh taste, and are chewed (CHEW[1] (2)) by people in Asia 槟榔

betel nut /ˋ‥ ˌ/ *n* [C, U] small pieces of red nut with a bitter taste, that are wrapped in a betel leaf and chewed (CHEW[1] (2)) 槟榔果

bête-noire /ˌbet ˋnwɑr; ˌbet ˈnwɑː/ *n* [singular] *French* the person or thing that you dislike most【法】最令人憎恨[厌恶]的人[事物]

Beth·a·ny /ˋbɛθənɪ; ˈbeθəni/ a village near Jerusalem and the Mount of Olives where several of the important events of the New Testament took place 贝瑟尼〔耶路撒冷和橄榄山附近一村庄，《新约》记载的若干重大事件都发生在此地〕

be·think /bɪˋθɪŋk; bɪˈθɪŋk/ *v past tense and past participle* **bethought** /bɪˋθɔt; bɪˈθɔːt/ **bethink yourself of** *old use* to remember something or think about something【旧】想到；考虑

Beth·le·hem /ˋbɛθlɪˌhɛm; ˈbeθlɪhem/ a town on the West Bank of the River Jordan, near Jerusalem, thought to be where Jesus Christ was born 伯利恒〔耶路撒冷附近，约旦河西岸一城镇，相传为基督耶稣的出生地〕

be·tide /bɪˋtaɪd; bɪˈtaɪd/ *v* **woe betide you** used, especially humorously, to say that someone will be in trouble if they do something 天降祸于某人，某人会倒霉的〔尤为幽默用法〕：*Woe betide anyone who wakes the baby!* 谁要是把婴儿吵醒，他一定会倒霉的！

be·times /bɪˋtaɪmz; bɪˈtaɪmz/ *adv old use* early or soon【旧】早；快

Be·tje·man /ˋbɛtʃɪmən; ˈbetʃəmən/**, Sir John** (1906-84) a British poet who became Poet Laureate (=the poet employed by the Queen to write special poems on important occasions), and who wrote many humorous poems about British society 贝杰曼〔(1906-1984)，英国桂冠诗人，创作了许多以英国社会为题材的幽默诗歌，并因此闻名〕

be·to·ken /bɪˋtokən; bɪˈtəʊkən/ *v* [T] *literary* to be a sign of something【文】预示；显示…的征兆

be·tray /bɪˋtre; bɪˈtreɪ/ *v* [T] **1** to be disloyal to someone who trusts you so that they are harmed or upset 背叛；对…不忠；出卖：**betray sb (to sb)** *What kind of man would betray his own sister to the police?* 什么样的人会向警方出卖自己的妹妹？**2** to be disloyal to your country, for example by giving secret information to its enemies 叛国；泄露〔机密〕：*people who are prepared to betray their country for money* 那些准备为钱财而出卖国家利益的人 **3 betray your beliefs/principles/ideals etc** to stop supporting your old beliefs and principles, especially in order to get power or avoid trouble 背弃自己的信仰/原则/理想等 **4** [not in progressive or passive 不用进行式或被动态] to show feelings that you are trying to hide 暴露出〔真实情感或意图〕：*The tremor in his voice betrayed his nervousness.* 他颤抖的声音暴露出他很紧张。—**betrayer** *n* [C]

be·tray·al /bɪˋtreəl; bɪˈtreɪəl/ *n* [C,U] an act of betraying your country, friends, or someone who trusts you 背叛，出卖；泄露；暴露：*The tax increases are a ruthless betrayal of election pledges.* 增加税收是对选举诺言的无情背叛。

be·troth·al /bɪˋtroðəl; bɪˈtrəʊðəl/ *n* [C] *old use* an agreement that two people will be married; ENGAGEMENT (1)【旧】定亲，订婚

be·trothed /bɪˋtroðd; bɪˈtrəʊðd/ *adj old use*【旧】**1 be betrothed to** to have promised to marry someone 与…订婚，和…定亲 **2 sb's betrothed** the person that someone has agreed to marry 某人的未婚夫[妻] —**betroth** *v* [T]

bet·ter[1] /ˋbɛtɚ; ˈbetə/ *adj* [comparative of *good* good的比较级] **1** more useful, interesting, satisfactory, effective, suitable etc 更好的，较好的：*Your stereo is better than mine.* 你的音响比我的好。| *a better job with a better salary* 一份更好且薪水更高的工作 | *It was one of the better Broadway shows I've seen.* 这是我所看过的百老汇演出中较好的一次。| *There must be a better way to do this.* 一定还有更好的办法来做这件事。| *a better-quality car* 质量更好的汽车 | **much better/far better/a lot better** *It's a much better quality design than the previous model.* 这个设计质量比上一个型号要好得多。**2** [comparative of *well* well的比较级] **a)** more healthy or less ill or painful than before〔健康状况〕好转的：*She is a little better today, the doctor says.* 医生说她今天有些好转。| *I'm feeling much better, thank you.* 我觉得好多了，谢谢你。| **feel better for** (=feel better as a result of) 因…感觉好些 *Go for a walk – you'll feel better for getting some fresh air.* 出去散散步吧，呼吸些新鲜空气你会感觉好一点的。—see 见 IMPROVE **b)** completely well again after an illness 痊愈的，康复的：*When you're better we can see about planning a trip.* 等你病好了，我们可以计划去旅行。**3 get better a)** to improve 改善，变好，进步：*If the weather gets better we could go out for a walk.* 如果天气好转，我们可以外出散散步。| *Her English isn't really getting any better.* 其实她的英语没什么进步。**b)** to recover from an illness or accident 康复，好转：*Are you hungry Sally? I think you must be getting better.* 萨莉，你饿吗？我想你一定是好些了。—see 见 RECOVER **4 have seen better days** *informal* to be in a bad condition【非正式】状态不佳：*The sofa has seen better days but the chairs are still okay.* 沙发已经不行了，但椅子还可以。**5 be no better than**

to be almost as bad as 比…好不了多少: *He's no better than a thief.* 他比小偷好不了多少。**6 better still** used to say that something is even better than the first thing you mentioned〔比第一个提到的事物〕更好: *Go for a walk around the building, or better still around the block.* 围着大楼走走吧，要是能围着街区散步那就更好了。**7 against your better judgment** if you do something against your better judgment, you do it even though you think it may not be sensible 违心地: *Against our better judgment, we allowed her to stay.* 我们违心地允许她留下来。**8 sb's better nature** the part of someone's character that makes them want to be kind and generous, treat people well, etc 人性中善良的一面: *He's become a lot nicer recently. I think she's brought out his better nature.* 最近他变得友好了许多。我想她使他表现出了善良的本性。—see also 另见 **your better half/other half** (HALF² (9)), **best/better part of** (PART¹ (6)) —opposite 反义词 WORSE¹

Frequencies of the word **better** in spoken and written English 单词better在英语口语和书面语中的使用频率

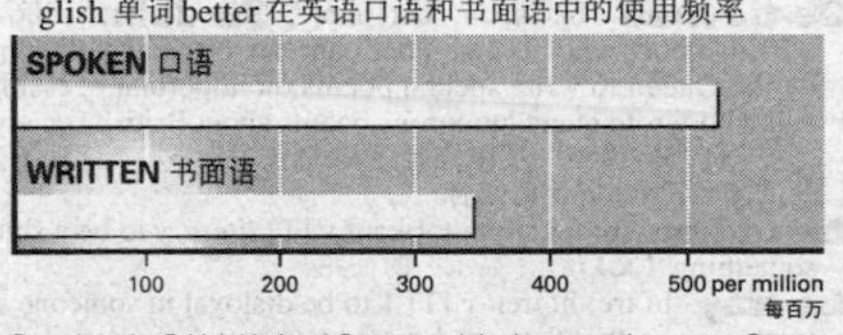

Based on the British National Corpus and the Longman Lancaster Corpus
据英国国家语料库和朗文兰开斯特语料库

This graph shows that the word **better** is more common in spoken English than in written English. This is because it is used in a lot of common spoken phrases. 本图表显示，单词better在口语中的使用频率高于书面语，因为口语中很多常用短语是由better构成的。

better (*adj*) **SPOKEN PHRASES**
含 better 的口语短语

9 sb had better a) used to give advice about what someone should do 某人最好(还是)〔提出建议〕: *She'd better see a doctor if it gets any worse.* 她如果病情加重，最好去看医生。**b)** used to threaten someone 某人最好…〔表示威胁〕: *You'd better keep your mouth shut about this.* 关于这件事你最好闭上嘴。**10 that's better a)** used to praise or encourage someone 这样好一些〔用以赞赏或鼓励某人〕: *Try hitting the ball higher. That's better!* 试着把球打高一点。有进步！**b)** used when trying to comfort someone or make them feel less upset 这就对了〔用以安慰某人〕: *Come on, give me a hug. There, that's better, isn't it?* 来吧，抱我一下。怎么样，这样好一点了，对吧？**11 better** used to say that you or someone else should do something〔建议某人做某事〕最好还是: *Better go and phone her to check she's in.* 最好去给她打个电话，看看她在不在。**12 you'd be better/it would be better to do sth** used to suggest that someone should do one thing rather than another 你最好还是做某事: *It would be better to install a shower rather than a bath.* 安装淋浴器比浴缸更好。**13 better luck next time** used to encourage someone who has done badly in an examination, competition etc 下次还有机会〔用来鼓励在考试、比赛等中的失败者〕 **14 you'd be better off** used when suggesting that someone should do something differently or change their situation 你会更好的: *Believe me, you'd be better off without him, you really would!* 相信我，离开他你会过得更好，肯定会的！**15 what could be better...?/there's nothing better** used to say that something is perfect 还有什么〔比…〕更好的?/没有〔比…〕更好的了: *Three weeks in the sun with nothing to do. What could be better?* 晒三个星期的太阳，什么事情也不用做。还有什么比这更好的？| *There's nothing better than a hot shower in the morning.* 没有什么比早晨洗个热水澡更好的了。**16 is that better?** used to ask someone if they are happier with something after you have changed it 是不是好一些?: *I'll put some more sugar in. There, is that better?* 我再多放些糖。这样好些了吧？**17 it's better than doing sth** used to say that although your situation is not good, it is better than another situation 总比做某事要好: *Maybe I'm not well paid, but it's better than being out of a job.* 也许我的薪酬不高，但总比没工作好。**18 better late than never** used to say that even if something happens late or someone arrives late, this is better than it not happening at all 迟做[到]总比不做[到]好 **19 better the devil you know** used to say that something bad that you know about is better than something bad you know nothing about 再坏的事情，了解总比不了解要好

better² *adv* [comparative of *well* well 的比较级] **1** in a better way 更好地: *He can speak French a lot better than I can.* 他讲法语比我好得多。| *Your bike will run better if you oil it.* 你给自行车上点油就会更好骑。| *The private schools tend to be better equipped.* 私立学校的设施往往较好。**2** to a higher degree; more 更，更加；更多地: *She knows this town better than you do.* 她比你更了解这个城镇。| *I think I like the red one better.* 我想我比较喜欢那个红的。| *Potter is better known for his TV work.* 波特更出名的是他的电视事业。**3 do better** to perform better or reach a higher standard 做得更好: *You'd do better if you practised more.* 你如果多练习，会做得更好。| *We did better than all the other schools.* 我们的成绩比其他学校都好。**4 the sooner the better/the later the better etc** used to emphasize that you would prefer something to happen as soon as possible, as late as possible etc 越快越好/越晚越好等: *School finishes at the end of the week, and the sooner the better as far as I'm concerned.* 周末学校就放假了，在我看来，越早越好。**5 the bigger the better/the faster the better etc** used to emphasize that you want something to be as big as possible, as fast as possible etc 越大越好/越快越好等: *"Do you want me to bring a bottle of wine?" "Sure – the more the better!"* "你要我带一瓶酒吗?""当然，越多越好!" **6 better off** richer than you were before〔比以前〕更富裕. *Today's pensioners are better off than they used to be.* 靠养老金生活的人过得比以前好。| *The average taxpayer will be $80 better off as a result of these changes.* 由于这些变革，纳税者平均将省下80美元。**7 go one better (than)** *informal* to do something more successfully than someone else【非正式】(比…) 做得更好: *That was a good story but I can go one better.* 那个故事不错，不过我可以讲得更好。—compare 比较 WORSE³

better³ *n* **1 the better** used to mean the one that is better when you are comparing two similar people or things 更好的人[事物]: *It's hard to decide which one's the better.* 很难确定哪一个更好。**2 get the better of a)** if your feelings or wishes get the better of you, they make you behave in a way you would not normally behave 胜过，超越: *My curiosity finally got the better of me and I opened the letter.* 最终我还是按捺不住好奇，打开了信。| *I think her nerves got the better of her.* 我想她是太紧张了。**b)** to defeat someone or deal successfully with a problem 战胜〔某人〕；成功地解决〔问题〕 **3 for the better** in a way that improves the situation 有所好转: *a definite change for the better* 明显的好转 | **take a turn for the better** (=improve) 有所改善，好转 *The President's fortunes seem, at last, to have taken a turn for the better.* 总统的命运似乎终于朝好的方向转变了。**4 be all the better for** *especially spoken* to be improved by a particular action, change etc【尤口】那就更好了: *I think it's all the better for that extra ten minutes' cooking.* 我想再煮上10分钟会更好。**5 so much the better** used to say that something would be even better or bring even more advantages 这样更好: *They usually cost about $50, but if you can get one for less, then so much the better.* 它们通常的价格是50美元左右，但如果你能便宜些买下来就更好了。**6 for better or (for) worse** used to say that something must be accepted, whether the results will be good or bad, because it cannot be changed 不管是好是歹: *This type of farming is, for better or worse, rapidly dying out.* 不管是好是坏，这种耕作方式很快就会绝迹。**7 your betters** *old-fashioned* people who are more important than you or deserve more respect【过时】上司；比自己地位高的人 —compare 比较 WORSE² —see also 另见 **elders and betters** (ELDER² (4))

better⁴ *v* [T] **1** to be better than something in quality, amount etc〔在质量、数额等方面〕胜过，超过，优于: *His total of five gold medals is unlikely to be bettered.* 他总共五块金牌的纪录不大可能被超越。**2 better yourself** to improve your position in society by getting a better education or earning more money 提高自己的社会地位 **3** *formal* to improve something【正式】改善，改进: *bettering the lot of the working classes* 改善工人阶级的命运

Better Busi·ness Bu·reau, the /,.. '.. ,../ a US organization for businesses and their customers. When customers believe they have been treated unfairly by a company or have bought a bad product, they often ask the Better Business Bureau for advice. 商业改进局〔美国针对商家和顾客而设立的一个

机构。当顾客认为受到某公司的不公正待遇或购买了劣质产品，通常去该局咨询〕

Better Homes and Gar·dens /ˌ···, ˈ··ˈ··/ a US magazine with lots of pictures of beautiful houses, and articles about how to make your home more beautiful. There is a similar magazine in the UK called *Homes and Gardens*.《住宅与花园美化》〔美国杂志，刊载大量漂亮住宅的照片和有关家庭装饰的文章。英国有一本类似杂志，名为《住宅与花园》〕

bet·ter·ment /ˈbɛtɚmənt; ˈbetəmənt/ *n* [singular] *formal* improvement, especially in someone's social and economic position【正式】改善，提高〔尤指个人的社会和经济地位〕

Bet·ty Boop /ˌbɛtɪ ˈbup; ˌbeti ˈbuːp/ a US CARTOON STRIP character originally drawn in 1930. Betty Boop is an attractive slightly silly young woman with a very short dress, short curled black hair, and large eyes. 贝蒂·布普〔美国连环漫画中的人物，初创于1930年。她是一个十分迷人却有点傻气的年轻女子，身着超短裙，一头黑发短而卷曲，有一双大眼睛〕

Betty Crock·er /ˌbɛtɪ ˈkrɑkɚ; ˌbeti ˈkrɒkə/ a US company that makes mixes, sold in packets, for cakes and other sweet baked foods, and that also sells cookbooks and other related cooking things. 贝蒂妙厨公司〔美国一家包装食品公司，生产用于烤制蛋糕和甜点的混合粉，也销售烹饪书籍和其他烹饪用品〕

Bet·ty Ford Clin·ic, the /ˌbɛtɪ ˌfɔrd ˈklɪnɪk; ˌbeti ˌfɔːrd ˈklɪnɪk/ a hospital in the US where rich and famous people go for treatment to help them stop drinking too much alcohol or taking illegal drugs 贝蒂·福特诊所〔美国一医疗机构，帮助上门求诊的名流巨富戒酒或戒毒〕

S1 W1 **be·tween**[1] /bəˈtwin; bɪˈtwiːn/ *prep* **1** in or into the space or time that separates two things or people 在…之间: *I sat between Sue and Jane at the Christmas party.* 圣诞聚会时，我坐在休和简中间。| *There was a low brick wall between our garden and the field beyond.* 我们花园和外面田地之间有一道矮砖墙。**2** in the time that separates two events 在〔两个事件〕之间: *Are there any public holidays between Christmas and Easter?* 圣诞节和复活节之间有公众假日吗？| *You shouldn't eat between meals.* 你不该在两餐之间吃零食。**3** used to show a range of amounts, numbers, distances etc especially when guessing a particular amount, number etc 在…和…之间〔尤指在某特定数量、数目的范围之内〕: *The project will cost between eight and ten million dollars.* 这项工程的花费在800万到1000万美元之间。**4** used to show a connection between two places 连接…和…: *They're building a new road between Manchester and Sheffield.* 他们正在曼彻斯特和设菲尔德之间建一条新公路。| *a regular air service between London and Paris* 伦敦和巴黎之间的定期航班 **5** used to show the relationship between two situations, things, people etc …与…之间（的关系）: *a long-standing friendship between Bob and Bryan* 鲍勃和布赖恩之间的长久友谊 | *cooperation between the two countries* 两国之间的合作 | *a dispute between management and unions* 资方和工会之间的纠纷 **6** used to show the fact that something is divided or shared among several people, places, or things 在…和…之间〔分享〕: *Tom divided his money between his three children.* 汤姆把钱分给自己的三个孩子。| *Between the four of them they managed to lift her into the ambulance.* 他们四个人一齐动手把她抬上了救护车。| *We collected £17 between us.* 我们共收集到17英镑。| **between doing sth** *Between cooking, writing, and running the farm Elsie was kept very busy.* 埃尔茜既要做饭、写作，又要经营农场，忙得不可开交。**7 in between** at a point in space or time between two places, events etc 介于…之间; 在其间: *In between school and university I did a three-month crash course in Italian.* 在中学毕业后到上大学之前这段时间，我上了三个月的意大利语速成班。| *It's somewhere in between New York and Chicago.* 它在纽约和芝加哥之间的某个地方。**8 between you and me** also 又作 **between ourselves** *spoken* used before telling someone something that you do not want them to tell anyone else【口】你我私下说说，只限于我俩之间: *Between you and me, I think Schmidt's about to resign as chairman.* 这是我俩私下里说的话，我认为施米特即将辞去主席职务。**9 come between you** if something comes between two people, it causes an argument or problems between them 引起纠纷 **10** *especially spoken* used when it is difficult to give an exact description of, or name to something and you therefore have to compare it to two things that are similar to it【尤口】难以界定; 既有些像…，又有些像…: *My job is between a bank-clerk and a messenger boy.* 我的工作既像个银行职员，又像个信差。

S3 **between**[2] *adv* in or into the space that separates two things or people, or in the time that separates two events〔空间或时间〕在其间，当中，中间: *So far I've had temporary jobs with long periods of unemployment between.* 到现在为止我一直在做临时工，其间还有很长一段时间没有工作。| **in between** *She has breakfast and supper but doesn't eat anything in between.* 她只吃早餐和晚餐，两餐之间不吃任何东西。| *a house and stables with a yard in between* 中间隔着院子的房子和马厩

USAGE NOTE 用法说明: BETWEEN

WORD CHOICE 词语辨析: **between, among(st), with, shared by**

Between is usually used to talk about two or a few people or things, thought of separately or one after another. between 通常用于谈及两个或几个独立或相关的人或事物: *the differences between British and American English* 英国英语和美国英语之间的差异 | *the relationship between each member of the family and the other* (NOT 不用 *among*) 家庭成员之间的关系 | *the gaps between the fence posts* 篱笆木桩间的缝隙。In spoken English you will often hear things like 在口语中，你经常会听到这样的用法: *Share this between the twelve of you.*（你们12个人分享。), though some people think only **among** is correct where a group of more than two is involved. 但有些人认为超过两个的应该用 among。

Among(st) is used to talk about a group of three or more people or things together, especially using nouns that name groups. among(st) 用于谈论三个或三个以上的人或事物，尤用于指作为一个整体而言的人或物: *The mountains were hidden among the clouds.* 群山隐没在云中。| *Just talk amongst yourselves for a minute.* 你们互相倾谈一会儿吧。| *Among the books he found one by Salinger* (*between the books* would suggest 暗示 'between two of them'). 在众多的书中，他发现了一本塞林格的作品。

Amongst is more formal than **among**. amongst 比 among 更正式。

Where there is little idea of anything different or separate being involved within a group, you can use **with** after adjectives and verbs or **shared by** with nouns. 如果一群人或事物之间没有什么差异或分不开，可在形容词或动词后接 with，或名词后接 shared by: *This offer was very popular with our customers* (NOT 不用 *between*, though 但可用 *among* is possible) . 这个优惠很受我们的顾客欢迎。| *I always eat with them* (NOT usually 一般不用 *among*). 我常和他们一起吃饭。| *the knowledge shared by the family* 全家人都有的知识 | *an opinion/a view shared by a lot of people* (or 或用 *among*) 许多人都持有的观点

be·twixt /bəˈtwɪkst; bɪˈtwɪkst/ *prep* **1** *poetic or old use* between【诗或旧】在…之间; 在其间 **2 betwixt and between** *old-fashioned* not quite belonging to one group or to another【过时】既不属于这种，也不属于那种; 两者都沾点边儿

Bev·an /ˈbɛvən; ˈbevən/, **A·neu·rin** /əˈnaɪrɪn; əˈnaɪərɪn/ also 又作 **Nye Bevan** (1897-1960) a British politician in the Labour Party, who started the National Health Service when he was Minister of Health from 1945 to 1951. Members of the Labour Party with left-wing opinions used to be called Bevanites. 比万〔(1897-1960)，英国工党政治家，1945-1951年期间任卫生大臣，创立了国民保健制度，并因此闻名。持有左翼观点的工党成员曾一度被称为"比万派"〕

bev·el /ˈbɛvl; ˈbevəl/ *n* [C] *technical*【术语】**1** a sloping edge or surface, usually along the edge of a piece of wood or glass〔常见于木材或玻璃边缘上的〕斜边，斜面 **2** a tool for making this kind of edge or surface 斜角规 **—bevelled** *adj*: *bevelled glass*（边缘）切成斜面的玻璃

bev·elled /ˈbɛvld; ˈbevəld/ *adj* with a sloping edge 成斜角的: *a mirror with bevelled edges* 边缘切成斜面的镜子

bev·er·age /ˈbɛvrɪdʒ; ˈbevərɪdʒ/ *n* [C] *formal* a hot or cold drink【正式】〔热或冷的〕饮料: *alcoholic beverages* 含酒精的饮料

Bev·er·idge Report, the /ˈbɛvərɪdʒ rɪˌport; ˈbevərɪdʒ rɪˌpɔːt/ an important report produced by the British economist William Beveridge in 1942. It introduced the idea of the Welfare State (=the idea that the government should provide free health care, and money for old people and for people who cannot get a job).《贝弗里奇报告》〔英国经济学家威廉·贝弗里奇1942年所做的一份重要报告，首次提出"福利国家"的构想，即政府应为国民提供免费医疗，为老人和失业者提供救济〕

Beverly Hills /ˌbɛvɚlɪ ˈhɪlz; ˌbevəli ˈhɪlz/ an expensive part of Los Angeles, California where many famous film stars live. 贝弗利山〔加利福尼亚洛杉矶一富人区，居住着许多影星〕

bev·y /ˈbɛvɪ; ˈbevi/ *n* [C] a large group of people of the same kind, especially girls or young women 一群人〔尤指少女或年轻

女子〕: [+of] *Tom swaggered in surrounded by a bevy of beauties.* 汤姆在一群美女簇拥下大摇大摆地走了进来。

be·wail /bɪˋwel; bɪˈweɪl/ *v* [T] *literary* to express deep sadness or disappointment about something【文】为…而悲伤[痛惜]; 哀悼

be·ware /bɪˋwɛr; bɪˈweə/ *v* [I,T only in imperative and infinitive 仅用于祈使句及不定式] used to warn someone to be careful because something is dangerous 谨防, 当心, 注意: [+of] *Beware of the dog!* 当心有狗! | *Beware of doing anything to arouse suspicion.* 谨防做出引起别人怀疑的事情。

be·wigged /bɪˋwɪgd; bɪˈwɪgd/ *adj formal* wearing a WIG【正式】戴着假发的

be·wil·der /bɪˋwɪldɚ; bɪˈwɪldə/ *v* [T] to confuse someone 使迷惑; 使昏乱

be·wil·dered /bɪˋwɪldɚd; bɪˈwɪldəd/ *adj* totally confused 困惑的; 不知所措的; 晕头转向的: *Benny looked around, a bewildered expression on his face.* 本尼环顾四周, 脸上带着困惑的表情。

be·wil·der·ing /bɪˋwɪldərɪŋ; bɪˈwɪldərɪŋ/ *adj* confusing, especially because there are too many choices or things happening at the same time 令人困惑的; 令人感到茫无头绪的: *There's a bewildering range of skin care products to choose from.* 可供选择的护肤用品令人目不暇接。

be·wil·der·ment /bɪˋwɪldɚmənt; bɪˈwɪldəmənt/ *n* [U] a feeling of being very confused 困惑; 昏乱

be·witch /bɪˋwɪtʃ; bɪˈwɪtʃ/ *v* [T] **1** to make someone feel so interested or attracted by something that they cannot think clearly 使着迷, 使心醉: *Tim's utterly bewitched by that woman.* 蒂姆完全被那个女人迷住了。| *a bewitching smile* 使人着迷的微笑 **2** to get control over someone by putting a magic SPELL² (1) on them 施魔力于…; 使着魔

S2 W1 **be·yond¹** /bɪˋjɑnd; bɪˈjɒnd/ *prep* **1** on or to the further side of something 在[向]…的那一边; 越过: *Beyond the mountains was the border territory.* 山的那一边是边境地带。—see picture on page A1 参见A1页图 **2** later than a particular time, date etc 迟于; 过了…以后: *The disco went on until beyond midnight.* 迪斯科一直跳到午夜以后。| *The new law extends the ban beyond 1998.* 新的法律将这条禁令延长至1998年后。**3** more or greater than a particular amount, level, or limit 超出〔某个数量、水平或限度〕: *Most people do not choose to work beyond the normal retirement age.* 大多数人过了通常的退休年龄后便不再工作。| *Inflation has now risen beyond the level of 5%.* 通货膨胀已超出了5%的水平。**4** outside the range or limits of someone or something 超出…的范围; 非…可及: *Such tasks are beyond the scope of your average schoolkid.* 这样的任务非你这一般学生的能力可及。| *The light switch was beyond the child's reach.* 那电灯开关孩子是摸不到的。**5 beyond belief/doubt/recognition etc** used to say that you cannot believe something, doubt something etc 难以置信/毫无疑问/认不出来等: *The town centre had changed beyond all recognition.* 镇中心已变得面目全非了。**6 be beyond sb** *especially spoken* to be too difficult for someone【尤口】对某人来说太难: *Algebra was always beyond me.* 代数对我来说一直很难。**7 it is beyond me why/what etc** *spoken* used to say that something seems completely stupid and you cannot understand the reason for it【口】我无法理解: *Why Joan ever married such an idiot in the first place is beyond me.* 首先我不明白琼为什么会和这样一个白痴结婚。**8** used like 'except' in negative sentences 除…以外〔用于否定句〕: *Fred owns nothing beyond the clothes on his back.* 除了身上穿的衣服以外, 弗雷德一无所有。| *I can't tell you anything beyond what you know already.* 除了你已经知道的以外, 我无可奉告。

beyond² *adv* **1** on or to the further side of something 在更远处; 往更远处; 在那边: *They crossed the mountains and headed for the valleys beyond.* 他们越过群山, 到那边的山谷去了。**2** later than a particular time, date etc 迟于某个时间[日期]: *What changes await us in the year 2000 and beyond?* 2000年及那以后会有什么样的变化在等待着我们呢?

beyond³ *n* **the beyond** *literary* whatever comes after this life【文】来世, 再生

be·zique /bəˋzik; bɪˈziːk/ *n* [U] a card game for two or four players, using 64 cards 比齐克牌戏〔二人或四人玩的一种纸牌游戏, 共用64张牌〕

BFI, the /ˌbi ɛf ˋaɪ; ˌbiː ef ˈaɪ/ *n* [singular] the British Film Institute; a British organization which was started in 1933 to encourage people to make films, and which includes the National Film Theatre. 英国电影协会〔创建于1933年, 以促进电影生产。该协会包括国家电影院〕

Bhag·a·vad-Gi·ta, the /ˌbɑgəvɑd ˋgitə; ˌbʌgəvəd ˈgiːtə/ one of the most important holy books of the Hindu religion. 《薄伽梵歌》〔印度教最重要的典籍之一〕

bha·ji, bhajee /ˋbɑdʒi; ˈbɑːdʒiː/ *n* [C] a hot-tasting Indian vegetable cake cooked in BATTER (=a liquid mixture of flour, egg, and milk or water) 印式油饼〔蔬菜外裹以面糊炸成的一种印度食品, 味辛辣〕: *onion bhajis* 印式洋葱油饼

Bhan·gra /ˋbʌŋgrə; ˈbʌŋgrə/ a style of popular music that combines western music with traditional music from India. 彭戈拉音乐〔英国的一种流行音乐风格, 融合西方音乐与印度传统音乐〕

Bho·pal /boˋpɑl; bəʊˈpɑːl/ a city in the north of India, where in 1984 over 2000 people died after poisonous gas escaped from a factory owned by Union Carbide, an American-owned company. 博帕尔〔印度北部城市。1984年, 美国联合碳化物公司在该市的一家工厂发生毒气泄露, 造成2000余人死亡〕

Bhu·tan /buˋtɑn; buːˈtɑːn/ a country in the Himalayas, surrounded by China and India. Population: 2,000,000 (2001). Capital: Thimbu. 不丹〔地处喜马拉雅山的一个国家, 与中国和印度接壤。人口: 2,000,000 (2001), 首都: 廷布〕

Bhut·to /ˋbuto; ˈbuːtəʊ/, **Zul·fi·kar Al·i** /ˋzulfikɑr ˋɑlɪ; ˈzʊlfɪkɑː ˈæli/ (1928-79) a Pakistani politician who was President (1971-73) and then PRIME MINISTER (1973-77) of Pakistan. He was overthrown (OVERTHROW) in a military COUP in 1977 and executed (EXECUTE) in 1979. His daughter Benazir Bhutto was Prime Minister from 1988 to 1990. 布托〔(1928-1979), 巴基斯坦政治家, 先后任巴基斯坦总统(1971-1973)和总理(1973-1977), 1977年在军事政变中被推翻, 1979年被处以极刑。女儿贝娜齐尔·布托于1988至1996年间任巴基斯坦总理〕

bi- /baɪ; baɪ/ *prefix* two; twice; double 双, 两(倍): *bilingual* (=speaking two languages) 双语的 | *to bisect* (=cut in two) 把…二等分 —compare 比较 SEMI- —see also 另见 DI-, TRI-

BIA /ˌbi aɪ ˋe; ˌbiː aɪ ˈeɪ/ the abbreviation of 缩写= THE BUREAU OF INDIAN AFFAIRS

bi·an·nu·al /baɪˋænjuəl; baɪˈænjuəl/ *adj* happening twice each year 一年两次的: *a biannual report* 半年度报告 —compare 比较 ANNUAL¹, BIENNIAL (1)

Biar·ritz /ˌbiˋrɪts; ˌbɪəˈrɪts/ a fashionable holiday town on the coast of southwest France 比亚里茨〔法国西南部沿海一座时尚度假城镇〕

bi·as¹ /ˋbaɪəs; ˈbaɪəs/ *n* **1** [U, singular] a tendency to consider one person, group, idea etc more favourably than others 偏见, 成见; 偏心: *a newspaper with a strong right-wing bias* 有强烈右翼偏见的报纸 | [+against/towards/in favour of] *There was a definite bias against commerce and science in the educational curriculum.* 该教育课程明显歧视商科和理科。**2** [singular] a natural skill or interest in one particular area 专长; 偏爱: *Lydia has a strong artistic bias.* 莉迪娅有很强的艺术天分。**3 on the bias** in a DIAGONAL direction 偏斜地; 成对角地

bias² *v* **biased, biasing** *or* **biassed, biassing** [T] to unfairly influence attitudes, choices, or decisions 使有偏见; 使倾向一方

bias bind·ing /ˌ‥ ˈ‥/ *n* [U] *BrE* cloth in the form of a narrow band, used when sewing edges【英】〔用于缝边的〕斜裁布条

biased, biassed /ˋbaɪəst; ˈbaɪəst/ *adj* unfairly influenced in favour of or against one particular person, opinion etc 有偏见的; 偏袒一方的: *I admit I'm biased, but I think my son's performance was brilliant!* 我承认我有偏见, 但我认为我儿子的表演很出色! | [+against/towards/in favour of] *news reporting that was heavily biased towards the government* 极度偏袒政府的新闻报道

bias tape /ˌ‥ ˈ·/ *n* [U] *AmE* BIAS BINDING【美】〔用于缝边的〕斜裁布条

bib /bɪb; bɪb/ *n* [C] **1** a piece of cloth or plastic tied under a baby's chin to protect its clothes when it is eating〔系于幼儿下巴底下的〕围嘴 **2** the upper part of an APRON (1), DUNGAREES, or overalls (OVERALL³ (2)), above the waist 围裙[工装裤]腰部以上的部分 **3 your best bib and tucker** *humorous* your best clothes【幽默】你最好的衣服

bi·ble, Bible /ˋbaɪbḷ; ˈbaɪbəl/ *n* **1 the Bible** the holy book of the Christian religion, consisting of the OLD TESTAMENT and the NEW TESTAMENT 基督教《圣经》〔包括《旧约全书》和《新约全书》〕 **2** [C] a copy of the Bible 一本《圣经》 **3** [singular] *informal* the most useful and important book on a particular subject【非正式】〔某一专业的〕权威书籍: *It's the anatomy student's bible!* 这是解剖学学生的宝典! **4 bible basher** *BrE*【英】, **bible thumper** *AmE*【美】an insulting expression for someone who tries to spread their own very strong Christian beliefs 基督教的狂热传道者〔侮辱性用法〕

Bible Belt, the /ˈ‥ ·/ an area in the south of the US known for its very religious Christian people, who follow the teachings of the Bible very strictly 圣经地带〔美国南部一地区, 以当地居民笃信基督教, 恪守《圣经》教义而闻名〕

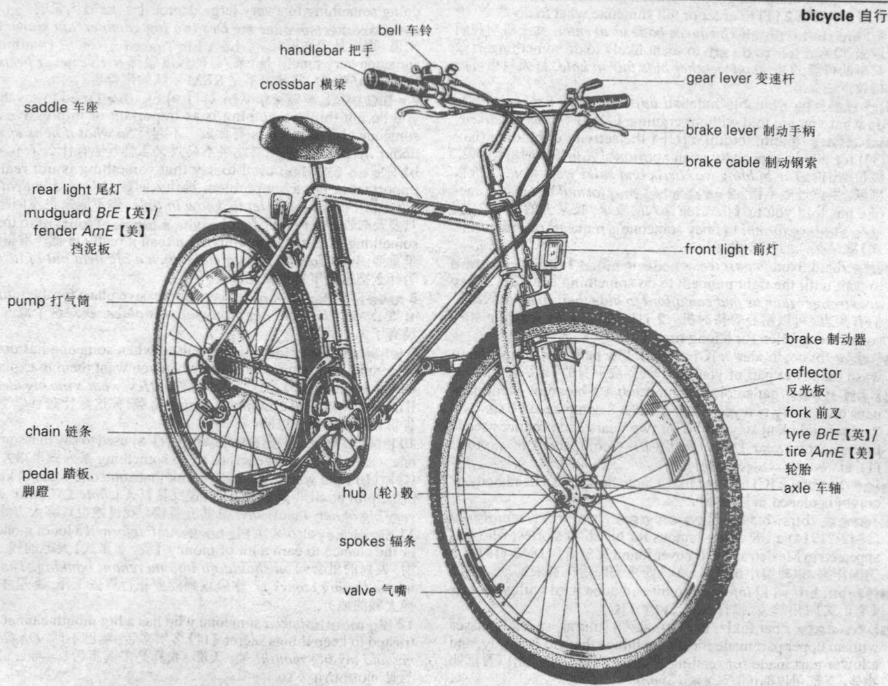

bib·li·cal /ˈbɪblɪkḷ; ˈbɪblɪkəl/ *adj* connected with the Bible《圣经》的; 有关《圣经》的

biblio- /bɪblɪo; bibliəʊ/ *prefix* concerning books 与书籍有关: *a bibliophile* (=someone who likes books) 书籍爱好者

bib·li·og·ra·phy /ˌbɪblɪˈɑgrəfɪ; ˌbɪbliˈɒgrəfi/ *n* [C] **1** a list of all the books and articles used in preparing a piece of writing 参考书目 **2** a list of everything that has been written about a particular subject〔有关某一专题的〕书目; 文献目录 **—bibliographer** *n*

bib·li·o·phile /ˈbɪblɪəˌfaɪl; ˈbɪbliəfaɪl/ *n* [C] *formal* someone who likes books【正式】珍爱书籍者; 藏书家

bib·u·lous /ˈbɪbjələs; ˈbɪbjᵿləs/ *adj humorous or formal* liking to drink too much alcohol【幽默或正式】嗜酒的

Bic /bɪk; bɪk/ *trademark* a type of simple pen that is not expensive; Biro【商标】比克圆珠笔, 拜乐圆珠笔〔一种价格低廉、设计简单的圆珠笔〕

bi·cam·er·al leg·is·la·ture /baɪˌkæmərəl ˈlɛdʒɪsletʃɚ; baɪˌkæmərəl ˈledʒᵻsleɪtʃə/ *n* [C] *technical* a law-making body consisting of two parts, like the Senate and the House of Representatives in the US Congress【术语】两院制的立法机关〈如美国国会的参、众两院〉

bi·car·bon·ate of so·da /baɪˌkɑrbənɪt əv ˈsodə; baɪˌkɑːbənᵻt əv ˈsəʊdə/ also 又作 **bicarbonate**, also 又作 **bi·carb** /ˈbaɪˌkɑrb; ˈbaɪkɑːb/ *informal*【非正式】*n* [U] a chemical substance used especially in baking, and sometimes taken with water as a medicine 小苏打, 碳酸氢钠

bi·cen·te·na·ry /baɪˈsɛntəˌnɛrɪ; ˌbaɪsenˈtiːnəri/ *n* [C] *especially BrE* the day or year exactly 200 years after an important event【尤英】二百周年(纪念): *the bicentenary of Mozart's death* 莫扎特逝世二百周年纪念 **—bicentenary** *adj*

bi·cen·ten·ni·al /ˌbaɪsɛnˈtɛnɪəl; ˌbaɪsenˈteniəl/ *n* [C] *AmE* the day or year exactly 200 years after an important event【美】二百周年(纪念): *the bicentennial of the declaration of independence* 独立宣言发表二百周年纪念 **—bicentennial** *adj*: *bicentennial celebrations* 二百周年庆祝活动

bi·ceps /ˈbaɪsɛps; ˈbaɪseps/ *n plural* **biceps** [C] the large muscle on the front of your upper arm〔上臂前侧的〕二头肌, 肱二头肌 —see picture at 参见 BODY 图

bick·er /ˈbɪkɚ; ˈbɪkə/ *v* [I **+about/over/with**] to argue, especially about something very unimportant〔尤指为琐事〕争吵, 发生口角: *I wish you two would stop bickering.* 我希望你们俩停止争吵。

bi·cy·cle¹ /ˈbaɪsɪkḷ; ˈbaɪsɪkəl/ *n* [C] a two-wheeled vehicle that you ride by pushing its pedals (PEDAL¹ (1)) with your feet; BIKE 自行车, 脚踏车, 单车: *She goes to work on her bicycle.* 她骑自行车上班。| *Can James ride a bicycle yet?* 詹姆斯学会骑自行车了吗?

bicycle² *v* [I always +adv/prep] *formal* to go somewhere by bicycle【正式】骑自行车[脚踏车, 单车]〔去某处〕 **—bicyclist** *n* [C]

bid¹ /bɪd; bɪd/ *n* [C] **1** an offer to pay a particular price for something, especially at an AUCTION¹〔尤指拍卖时的〕出价: [**+for**] *They put in the highest bid for the house.* 他们为这幢房子出了最高价。**2** an offer to do work or provide services for a specific price 投标: [**+for**] *rival bids for the cleaning contract* 对清洁合约的竞争性投标 **3** an attempt to achieve or obtain something〔为争取某物而作出的〕努力: [**+for**] *a bid for power* 权力之争 | **bid to do sth** *a desperate bid to free herself from a loveless marriage* 为摆脱她那段没有爱情的婚姻而作出的不顾一切的努力 **4** a statement of how many points you hope to win in a card game〔玩纸牌者的〕叫牌

bid² *v past tense and past participle* **bid** *present participle* **bidding** **1** [I,T] to offer to pay a particular price for goods, especially in an AUCTION¹〔尤指拍卖时〕出价: **bid (sb) sth for** *She bid £100 for a Victorian chair.* 她为一把维多利亚时代的椅子出价 100 英镑。| *What am I bid for lot 227? Shall we start at $500?* 我该为 227 号拍卖品出多少价呢? 我们从 500 美元开始好吗? **2** [I] to offer to do work or provide services for a specific price, in competition with other offers 投标(竞争): [**+for**] *Three firms bid for the contract on the new buildings.* 有三家公司投标争取承包新楼工程。**3** [I,T] to say how many points you think you will win in a game of cards〔玩纸牌时〕叫牌 **—bidder** *n* [C]

bid³ *v past tense* **bade** /bæd; bæd/ *or* **bid** *past participle* **bidden** /ˈbɪdn̩; ˈbɪdn/ *or* **bid** *present participle* **bidding** *old use or literary*【旧或文】**1** **bid sb good afternoon/good morning etc**

to say good morning, good afternoon etc to someone 祝某人下午好/早安等 **2** [T] to order or tell someone what to do 命令, 吩咐: **bid sb (to) do sth** *The queen bade us to enter.* 女王吩咐我们进去。**3** **bid fair to do sth** to seem likely to do something 有做某事的可能: *The good weather bids fair to hold.* 好天气很可能持续下去。

bid·da·ble /ˈbɪdəbl̩; ˈbɪdəbəl/ *adj especially BrE* willing to do what you are told without arguing【尤英】听话的; 顺从的

bid·ding /ˈbɪdɪŋ; ˈbɪdɪŋ/ *n* [U] **1** the activity of bidding (BID[2] (1)) for goods, especially in an AUCTION[1]〔尤指拍卖时的〕竞买, 喊价, 出价: *The bidding was brisk and sales went well.* 出价很踊跃, 生意进展不错。**2** **at sb's bidding** *formal* because someone has told you to【正式】按某人的要求; 按某人的吩咐 **3** **do sb's bidding** *formal* to obey someone's requests or orders【正式】服从某人的要求[命令]

bide /baɪd; baɪd/ *v past tense* **bode** *or* **bided** **1** **bide your time** to wait until the right moment to do something 等待良机: *They are stronger than us and can afford to bide their time.* 他们比我们有实力, 可以耐心等待时机。**2** [I] *old use* to wait or stay somewhere, often for a long time【旧】等待, 久等

bi·det /bɪˋde; ˈbiːdeɪ/ *n* [C] a small, low bath that you sit on to wash the lower part of your body〔专洗下身的〕坐浴盆

bi·en·ni·al /baɪˋɛnɪəl; baɪˈeniəl/ *adj* **1** a biennial event happens once every two years 两年一次的 —compare 比较 ANNUAL[1] **2** a biennial plant stays alive for two years and produces seeds in the second year〔植物〕两年生的 —compare 比较 ANNUAL[2] (1), BIANNUAL —**biennially** *adv*

bier /bɪr; bɪə/ *n* [C] a frame like a table on which a dead body or COFFIN is placed 棺材架; 停尸架

Bierce /bɪrs; bɪəs/, **Am·brose** /ˋæmbroz; ˈæmbrəʊz/ (1842-?1914) a US writer famous for his short stories, who disappeared in Mexico and was never found 比尔斯〔(1842-?1914), 美国作家, 以短篇小说著名, 在墨西哥失踪后一直未见〕

biff /bɪf; bɪf/ *v* [T] *informal* to hit someone hard with your FIST【非正式】〔用拳头〕狠打, 揍 —**biff** *n* [C]

bi·fo·cals /ˋbaɪˌfokl̩z; baɪˈfəʊkəlz/ *n* [plural] special glasses with an upper part made for seeing things that are far away, and a lower part made for reading 双光眼镜〔镜片上部用以看远处物体, 下部用以阅读〕—**bifocal** *adj*

bi·fur·cate /ˋbaɪfɚˌket; ˈbaɪfəkeɪt/ *v* [I] *formal* if a road, river etc bifurcates, it divides into two separate parts【正式】〔道路、河流等〕分为两支[部分], 分叉 —**bifurcation** /ˌbaɪfɚˋkeʃən; ˌbaɪfəˈkeɪʃən/ *n* [C,U]

big /bɪg; bɪg/ *adj comparative* 比较级 **bigger**, *superlative* 最高级 **biggest**

1 ►**SIZE** 尺寸◄ of more than average size, amount, weight etc 大的; 重的: *a big house* 大房子 | *Your baby's getting big!* 你的宝宝长大了! | *a big increase in prices* 价格的大幅度上涨 | *the biggest hotel in New York* 纽约最大的酒店 | *She had a big grin on her face.* 她咧嘴大笑。| **great big** *spoken* (=extremely big)【口】特大的 *There was this great big spider in the sink.* 洗涤槽里有只特大的蜘蛛。—see 见 WIDE[1] (USAGE)

2 ►**IMPORTANT** 重要的◄ important and serious 重大的, 重要的; 需认真对待的: *a big decision* 重大的决定 | *Buying your own house is a big commitment.* 给自己买房子可是件大事。

3 ►**SUCCESSFUL/POWERFUL** 成功的/强大的◄ *informal* successful or popular especially in business or entertainment【非正式】〔尤指在商业和娱乐业中〕极受欢迎的; 极成功的: *Rap music was really big in the 1980s.* 说唱音乐在20世纪80年代广受欢迎。| *It's becoming quite a big area for tourism.* 这地方逐渐成为旅游胜地。| [+in] *She's very big in the music business.* 她在音乐界很成功。| **make it big** (=become very successful) 取得成功 *After years as a small-time actor, he suddenly made it big in Hollywood.* 他做了多年的配角后, 在好莱坞一举成名。| **the big boys** (=the most powerful and influential people or companies) 极有影响力的人物[公司] *Small firms like ours can't really compete with the big boys.* 像我们这样的小公司真的无法和大公司竞争。—see also 另见 BIG CHEESE, **big name** (NAME[1] (4)), BIG NOISE, **big shot** (SHOT[1] (17)), BIG TIME

4 ►**OLDER** 年长一些的◄ *spoken*【口】**a)** **big sister/brother** your older sister or brother 姐姐/哥哥 **b)** used especially when speaking to children to mean older or more grown-up 年纪大一些的; 长大了的: *Come on, don't cry. You're a big girl now.* 好了, 别哭。你现在是个大女孩了。

5 ►**BAD** 坏的◄ [only before noun 仅用于名词前] *spoken* used to emphasize how bad something is【口】糟的〔表示强调〕: *It's always such a big hassle finding some place to park.* 找个地方停车总是件很麻烦的事。| *I never said that, you big liar!* 我从未说过那样的话, 你这个大骗子!

6 ►**A LOT** 许多◄ [only before noun 仅用于名词前] *informal* doing something to a very large degree【非正式】大量的: **a big eater/drinker/spender etc** *Des is a big gambler you know.* 你知道, 德斯是个大赌徒。| **be a big fan/admirer of** (=admire someone very much) 是〔某人〕的极度崇拜者 *I've never been a big fan of REM.* 我从来不是REM乐队的崇拜者。

7 ►**BIG DEAL** 要事◄ *spoken*【口】**a)** **big deal!** used to say that you do not think something is as important or impressive as someone else thinks it is 有什么了不起!: *So what if he is upset about it? Big deal!* 他对此事不高兴又怎样? 他有什么了不起! **b)** **it's no big deal** used to say that something is not really important or not a big problem 没什么问题: *It's no big deal if you can't come – just let us know in time.* 你不能来也没问题, 只要及时告诉我们就行了。**c)** **make a big deal (out) of** to treat something as if it is more important than it really is 把…看得过于重要: *Why do you have to make such a big deal out of it?* 你为什么把这件事看得如此重要呢?

8 **have big ideas/plans** to have impressive plans for the future 有雄心大志: *I've got big plans for this place.* 我对这个地方已经有了大的计划。

9 **what's the big idea?** *spoken* used when someone has done something annoying, especially when you want them to explain why they did it【口】你这是什么意思?: *Hey, what's the big idea? Who said you could use my computer?* 嘿! 你这是什么意思? 谁告诉你可以用我的电脑?

10 **it is big of sb to do sth** *spoken*【口】**a)** used to say that someone was very kind or generous to do something 某人做事很大度[慷慨] **b)** used when you really think that someone was not kind or helpful at all …真够大方的〔说反话〕: *A whole £5! That was very big of her, I must say!* 总共五英镑! 我说她也真够大方的!

11 **big money** also 又作 **big bucks** *AmE informal* a lot of money, or the chance to earn a lot of money【美, 非正式】大笔的钱; 发财; 发财的机会: *You should go into merchant banking. That's where the big money is.* 你应该到商业银行界去工作, 那里才是挣大钱的地方。

12 **big mouth** *spoken* someone who has a big mouth cannot be trusted to keep things secret【口】多嘴多舌; 嘴巴不严: *Oh God, me and my big mouth!* 噢, 天哪, 我真是多嘴多舌! —see also 另见 BIGMOUTH

13 **be/get too big for your boots** *informal* to be too proud of yourself【非正式】自以为了不起, 自高自大; 摆架子

14 **use/ward/wield the big stick** *informal* to threaten to use your power to get what you want【非正式】挥舞大棒, 执行大棒政策〔用权力相威胁以达到自己的目的〕

15 **big with child** *old use* soon going to have a baby; PREGNANT【旧】快生孩子的; 有身孕的

16 **big enchilada** *humorous AmE* the most important person; the BOSS【幽默, 美】要人; 大亨; 老板 —see also 另见 **think big** (THINK[1] (17)) —**bigness** *n* [U]

USAGE NOTE 用法说明: BIG

WORD CHOICE 词语辨析: **big, large, great**

Big and **large** are both often used to talk about the measurements of things or groups, though **large** is slightly more formal and not so often used of people. 谈事物或群体的大小时, big 和 large 都常用。但 large 较正式, 一般不用于指人: *That shirt doesn't fit me – it's too big/large.* 那件衬衫太大了, 不合我身。| *How big are you round the waist?* 你的腰围有多大? | *a big crowd/company/gap* 一大群人/大公司/大裂缝 | *a large family/city/university* 大家庭/大城市/规模很大的大学。 see also 另见 **fat** WORD CHOICE and 和 **wide** WORD CHOICE.

None of these words are used with uncountable nouns for things you can touch. 这两个词都不与不可数的具体名词连用: *There was a lot of traffic/land/space* (NOT 不用 *big traffic, large land*). 有许多车辆/土地/空间。

Great means famous or important for something good, or, when it is used about ordinary people, just extremely nice. great 意为著名的、重要的, 在指普通人时, 意思是非常好的: *Rembrandt was a great painter.* 伦勃朗是一位伟大的画家。| *Isn't Max a great guy?* 难道马克斯不是个好人吗? —see also 另见 **famous** WORD CHOICE

Great used about the size of things or events is mainly found in literary writing or names and means 'very large and impressive'. great 用于指事物或事件的大小时, 多见于文学作品或名称中, 意为"巨大而令人印象深刻的": *the great city of Samarkand* 大撒马尔罕市 | *A great crowd had gathered.* 聚集了一大群人。| *a great banquet* 盛大的宴会 | *the Great Wall of China* 中国的万里长城 Otherwise

great is used very informally of things just to mean extremely good. 除此以外, great 用于指物时是一个非正式的用法, 意为非常好的: *You look great!* 你看起来精神非常好! | *There's a great view from our hotel room.* 从我们旅馆的房间里能看到非常美丽的景色。| *We had a great time there* (=enjoyable, not necessarily long). 我们在那儿玩得很开心。

You would usually use **great** rather than **big** to describe the size or extent of things you cannot touch. 用于描述抽象事物的大小或程度时, 通常用 great 而不用 big: *She showed great courage/talent/ability.* 她表现出很大的勇气/聪明的才智/强的能力。| *We had great fun.* 我们过得很愉快。| *in great detail* 十分详尽。Where both can be used, **great** is stronger and suggests more importance. 两个词都可以用时, great 比 big 语气更强, 更强调重要性: *It's a big/great pleasure to see you.* 见到你很高兴。| *great/big problem/opportunity/danger* 大问题/好机会/很大的危险。But note that you usually say 但要注意, 一般说: *a big difference/mistake/argument* 很大的差别/大错/大的争论 | *It isn't a big deal* (informal 非正式 = It's not serious or important). 没什么了不起的。

Note that **large** (less often **great** or **big**) is used with these quantity words. 注意 large (较少用 great 或 big) 与下列表示数量的词语连用: *a large amount/scale/number/quantity/extent/proportion/percentage/part/volume/area* 大量/大规模/很多/大量/很大程度/大比例/大百分比/大部分/大体积/大面积。But note only **great** is used in 但下列用法中只用 great: *a great deal* (=a lot) 许多 | *at great length* 很详细地 | *a great height/age* 很高/高龄

big·a·my /ˈbɪgəmɪ; ˈbɪgəmi/ *n* [U] the crime of being married to two people at the same time 重婚(罪) —compare 比较 MONOGAMY, POLYGAMY —**bigamist** *n* [C] —**bigamous** *adj*

Big Ap·ple, the /ˌ· ˈ··/ *informal* a popular name for New York City【非正式】大苹果城〔纽约市的诨名〕: *He went to the Big Apple to make his fortune.* 他上大苹果城发财去了。

Big Bang /ˌ· ˈ·/ the name given to the changes in the system and rules of the London Stock Exchange which came into effect on December 27th, 1986 "大爆炸"改革〔指伦敦证券交易所的交易系统和规则改革, 1986 年 12 月 27 日生效〕: *By October 1987, a year after Big Bang, the inflated City salaries were slipping.* 及至"大爆炸"改革一年之后的 1987 年 10 月, 伦敦市膨胀的薪金一直在回落。

big bang the·o·ry /ˌ· ˈ· ˌ···/ *n* [singular] *technical* the idea that the universe began with a single large explosion (the 'big bang'), and that the pieces are still flying apart【术语】〔关于宇宙起源的〕大爆炸学说 —compare 比较 STEADY STATE THEORY

Big Ben /ˌ· ˈ·/ the large bell in the tower of the Houses of Parliament in London, which rings regularly to tell the time. 大本钟〔伦敦议会大厦塔楼内的大钟, 于整点报时〕

Big Bird /ˌ· ˈ·/ a character in the US children's television show *Sesame Street*, which is a large yellow bird who talks and behaves like a human child. 大鸟〔美国儿童电视节目《芝麻街》中的一个角色, 为一只言行似小孩的黄色大鸟〕

Big Blue /ˌ· ˈ·/ an informal name for the computer company IBM 深蓝〔电脑制造商 IBM 公司的绰号〕

Big Broth·er /ˌ· ˈ··/ **1** a character in the NOVEL *1984* by George Orwell. Big Brother is the leader of the state, and although no one has ever met him there are pictures of him everywhere with the message "Big Brother is watching you". People now use the expression 'Big Brother' to describe any government or organization that has complete power, allows no freedom, and carefully watches what people are doing. "老大哥"〔乔治·奥威尔的小说《一九八四》中的人物。"老大哥"为一国之君, 没有人见过他, 但到处都有他的照片, 上面还写着"老大哥注视着你"的字样。"老大哥"现在用来形容拥有绝对权力、限制公民自由、监督公民所为的任何组织或政府〕: *Increasingly, the state is taking a Big Brother role in this area.* 这个国家在这一地区日益扮演着"老大哥"的角色。**2** a television programme in which ten people are kept in a house without being able to talk to anyone outside the house. Everything they do is filmed. Each week, the people who watch the show vote by telephone to decide who must leave the house. The last person remaining in the house after ten weeks receives a prize of a large amount of money. The programme has been made and shown in several different countries. "老大哥"〔一档电视节目, 十个人被关在一栋房子里, 不能和外面的任何人交谈, 他们的一举一动都被录制下来。每周, 观众通过电话投票决定谁必须先离开那栋房子。十周之后, 留在房子里的最后一个人可获得一大笔奖金。这一节目已在多个国家制作和播放〕

Big Broth·ers /ˌ· ˈ··/ a US organization to help boys, especially boys who have family problems. Each boy has his own Big Brother, who is a man who meets him regularly to give advice, listen to his problems, have fun together etc. "大哥哥"志愿团〔美国一组织, 旨在帮助男孩, 尤其是存在家庭问题的男孩。每个男孩都有自己的"大哥哥"定期同他见面, 给他提供建议, 倾听他的问题, 与他一起玩乐等等〕

big busi·ness /ˌ· ˈ··/ *n* [U] **1** very large companies, considered as a powerful group with a lot of influence 大企业财团 **2** a product or type of activity that people spend a lot of money on 大买卖: *Dieting has become big business.* 节食减肥已经成了一个有利可图的行当。

big cat /ˌ· ˈ·/ *n* [C] *not technical* a large animal of the cat family, such as a lion or tiger【非术语】大型猫科动物〈如狮、虎〉

big cheese /ˌ· ˈ·/ *n* [C] *informal, often humorous* an important and powerful person in an organization【非正式, 常幽默】要人, 大人物

big dipper /ˌ· ˈ··/ *n* [C] **1** a small railway in a FUNFAIR, with steep slopes and sharp curves to give an exciting ride〔游乐场的〕过山车, 云霄飞车 **2 the Big Dipper** *AmE* a group of seven bright stars seen only from northern parts of the world【美】北斗七星; the PLOUGH[1] (3) *BrE*【英】

Big Ea·sy, the /ˌ· ˈ··/ *AmE informal* a name for New Orleans【美, 非正式】忘忧城〔新奥尔良的别称〕: *Slick Mo's Club plays some of the best jazz outside of the Big Easy.* 斯利克·莫俱乐部在忘忧城郊外演奏爵士乐名曲。

Big·foot /ˈbɪgfut; ˈbɪgfʊt/ also 又作 **Sasquatch** an animal like a large hairy human, which some people claim to have seen in the northwest US, but which has never been proved to exist 大脚, 北美野人〔一种大而多毛、酷似人类的动物, 一些人声称在美国西北部见过, 但至今仍无法证实它的存在〕

big game /ˌ· ˈ·/ *n* [U] large wild animals hunted for sport, such as lions and ELEPHANTS 大猎物〈如狮、象〉: *a big game hunter* 猎捕大猎物的人

big·gie /ˈbɪgɪ; ˈbɪgi/ *n* [C] *informal* something very large, important, or successful【非正式】庞然大物; 重要事情; 大热门: *I think their new CD is going to be a biggie.* 我想他们的新唱片会成为大热门。

Biggles 比格尔斯

Big·gles /ˈbɪglz; ˈbɪgəlz/ a character in stories for children by Captain W.E. Johns. Biggles is a military pilot in World War I who is famous for his flying skills and courage. 比格尔斯〔W. E.约翰斯上尉所著儿童故事中的人物。他是一战时期的空军飞行员, 以飞行技巧和勇气著称〕

big gov·ern·ment /ˈ· ˌ···/ *n* [U] *AmE* too much government involvement in people's lives【美】大政府, 政府包办〔指在太多方面干预人们生活的政府〕: *big government welfare policies* 政府全包的福利政策

big gun /ˌ· ˈ·/ *n* [C] *informal* a person or company that has a lot of power and influence【非正式】大人物, 要人; 有影响力的公司: *He's one of the party big guns.* 他是该党的要人之一。

big-head /ˈbɪgˌhɛd; ˈbɪghed/ *n* [C] *informal* someone who thinks they are very important, clever etc【非正式】自高自大的人, 吹牛的人 —**bigheaded** /ˌbɪg ˈhɛdɪd; ˌbɪgˈhedɨd◂/ *adj*

big-heart·ed /ˌ· ˈ··◂/ *adj* very kind and generous 仁慈的; 大度的; 宽宏的 —**big-heartedly** *adv* —**big-heartedness** *n*

big·horn sheep /ˌbɪghɔrn ˈʃip; ˌbɪghɔːn ˈʃiːp/ *n* [C] a wild sheep with long, curved horns that lives in the mountains of western North America〔北美西部山区的〕大角羊

bight /baɪt; baɪt/ *n* [C] **1** a curve in a coast, like a BAY[1] (1) but not as curved 海岸线的弯曲部分, 大湾 **2** a LOOP[1] (1) made in the middle of a rope when tying a knot〔绳子中间的〕绳环, 绳套

Big Is·sue, The /ˌ· ˈ··/ a British magazine which is sold on the streets by people who have nowhere to live. 《畅销》〔由无家可归者沿街兜售的一种英国杂志〕

Big Leagues, the /ˌ· ˈ·/ the Major Leagues (=the teams that play at the highest level of professional BASEBALL) in the US〔代表美国职业棒球最高水准的〕大联盟 —compare 比较 LITTLE LEAGUE

Big Mac /ˌ· ˈ·/ *trademark* a type of large HAMBURGER sold in McDonald's restaurants【商标】巨无霸〔麦当劳快餐店出售的一种汉堡〕

Big Man on Cam·pus /ˌ· · · ˈ··/ *n* [C] *AmE informal* an important and popular male student at a college or university, especially someone who is good at sports【美, 非正式】大学校园里有名气的男学生, 校园名人〔特别是擅长体育者〕

big·mouth /ˋbɪgˌmaʊθ; ˈbɪgmaʊθ/ *n* [C] *informal* someone who cannot be trusted to keep secrets【非正式】多嘴的人, 守不住秘密的人

big name /ˌ· ˈ·/ *n* [C] a famous person or group, especially a musician, actor etc 知名人士[集团]〔尤指音乐家或演员等〕: *Poor attendance at the concert was put down to the lack of big names.* 由于缺少知名音乐家, 这场音乐会的上座率很低。

big noise /ˌ· ˈ·/ *n* [C] *informal* an important and powerful person in an organization【非正式】要人; 有影响力的人

big·ot /ˋbɪgət; ˈbɪgət/ *n* [C] someone who is bigoted 固执己见的人, 思想顽固的人, 执拗的人: *The new sergeant was a bigot, and viewed all black men with suspicion.* 新警官是个有着顽固种族思想的人, 对所有的黑人都持怀疑态度。

big·ot·ed /ˋbɪgətɪd; ˈbɪgətɪd/ *adj* having such strong opinions about race, religion, or politics that you are unwilling to listen to anyone else's opinions〔对种族、宗教或政治〕固执己见的, 顽固不化的: *The decision not to allow disabled athletes to take part was seen as petty and bigoted.* 不让残障运动员参加的决定被认为是狭隘而固执的。

big·ot·ry /ˋbɪgətrɪ; ˈbɪgətri/ *n* [U] bigoted behaviour or beliefs 偏执的行为[信念]: *sensational news stories that just encourage bigotry and intolerance* 只会导致偏执和不容异见的煽情新闻报道

big screen /ˌ· ˈ·/ *n* **the big screen** the cinema, rather than the television or theatre 电影院; 大银幕: *His first big screen part was in a 1957 horror movie, 'The Count'.* 他的第一个银幕角色出现在1957年的恐怖电影《伯爵》中。

big shot /ˈ· ·/ *n* [C] *informal* someone who has a lot of power or influence in a company or an area of business【非正式】要人, 大人物; 有权势之人: *Pete Waterman, the record producer and music-biz big shot* 唱片监制、音乐界大亨皮特·沃特曼

Big Sis·ters /ˌ· ˈ··/ a US organization to help girls, especially girls who have family problems. Each girl has her own Big Sister, who is a woman who meets her regularly to give advice, listen to her problems, have fun together etc. "大姐姐"志愿团〔美国一组织, 旨在帮助女孩, 尤其是存在家庭问题的女孩。每个女孩都有自己的"大姐姐"定期同她见面, 给她提供建议, 倾听她的问题, 与她一起玩乐等等〕

Big Ten, the /ˌ· ˈ·/ also 又作 **the Big 10** a group of ten midwestern US universities who compete with each other in sports. These teams are of very good quality in college sports, and their players often go on to join professional teams. "十强"〔指美国中西部地区在体育方面相互竞争的10所大学, 其运动队竞技水准很高, 队员通常都会加入职业队〕—compare 比较 PAC 10

Big Three, the /ˌ· ˈ·/ *AmE* General Motors, Ford, and Chrysler, which are the three largest American car makers【美】汽车工业三巨头〔指美国的通用、福特和克莱斯勒三大汽车制造商〕: *The Big Three have all announced incentives to boost flagging auto sales.* 汽车工业三巨头都宣布了激励措施, 以改善汽车销售不景气的状况。

big tick·et /ˈ· ·ˈ·/ *adj AmE informal* expensive【美, 非正式】昂贵的: *big ticket items such as cars or refrigerators* 汽车、冰箱等贵重商品

big time /ˈ· ·/ *n* **the big time** the position of being very famous or important, for example in the entertainment business or in politics〔演艺界或政治上的〕头号地位; 最高成就; 第一流水平: *He really made it to the big time when his book was turned into a Hollywood movie.* 他的书被好莱坞拍成电影后, 他真的成了名人。—**big-time** *adj*: *big-time cocaine dealers* 臭名远扬的可卡因贩子

big toe /ˌ· ˈ·/ *n* [C] the largest toe on your foot 大拇趾, 大脚趾头 —see picture at 参见 FOOT[1] 图

big top /ˌ· ˈ·/ *n* [C] the very large tent in which a CIRCUS (1) performance takes place〔马戏团表演用的〕大帐篷

big wheel /ˌ· ˈ·/ *n* [C] *BrE* a machine used in AMUSEMENT PARK*s*, consisting of a very large upright wheel with seats hanging from it, which turns round slowly【英】〔游乐场的〕摩天轮, 大转轮; FERRIS WHEEL *AmE*【美】

big·wig /ˋbɪgˌwɪg; ˈbɪgwɪg/ *n* [C] *informal* an important person【非正式】大人物, 要人

bi·jou /ˋbiʒu; ˈbiːʒuː/ *adj* [only before noun 仅用于名词前] a bijou house or apartment is small and fashionable 小巧雅致的: *a bijou residence in Mayfair* 梅菲尔区小巧雅致的住宅

bike[1] /baɪk; baɪk/ *n* [C] **1** *informal* a bicycle or MOTORCYCLE【非正式】自行车, 脚踏车, 单车; 摩托车 **2 on your bike!** *BrE spoken* used to tell someone rudely to go away【英口】滚开! [S2]

bike[2] *v* [I always+adv/prep] *informal* to ride a bicycle【非正式】骑自行车[脚踏车, 单车]: *She bikes to work every day.* 她每天骑自行车上班。

bik·er /ˋbaɪkɚ; ˈbaɪkə/ *n* [C] someone who rides a MOTORCYCLE, especially as part of a group 摩托车手〔尤指某一组织的成员〕: *A biker's leather jacket says more about him than a thousand words.* 摩托车手穿的皮衣比千言万语更能说明他的身份。

bi·ki·ni /bɪˋkinɪ; bəˈkiːni/ *n* [C] a piece of clothing in two separate parts that women wear for swimming 比基尼式游泳衣, 三点式泳装

Bikini At·oll /bɪˌkinɪ ˋætɑl; bəˌkiːni ˈætɒl/ an island in the Pacific Ocean where the US performed nuclear weapons tests from 1946 until the 1960s 比基尼环礁〔太平洋一岛屿, 1946年至20世纪60年代美国在此进行过核武器试验〕

bikini line /ˌ· ˈ· ·/ *n* [C] the place on a woman's legs where the hair around her sexual organs stops growing 比基尼线〔女性生殖器官的毛发停止生长的地方〕

Bi·ko /ˋbiko; ˈbiːkəʊ/, **Steve** /stiv; stiːv/ (1946-77) a black South African political leader who started the Black Consciousness Movement, an organization that fought against APARTHEID (=the system in which black people had no political rights, and black and white people had to live in different areas). He died while being questioned by the police. 比卡〔(1946-1977), 南非黑人政治领袖, 反对种族隔离制度的"黑人觉醒运动"组织的发起人。他在接受警方审讯时去世〕

bi·la·bi·al /baɪˋlebɪəl; baɪˈleɪbiəl/ *n* [C] *technical* a CONSONANT sound such as /p/ or /b/ that is made using both lips【术语】双唇(辅)音〈如 /p/, /b/〉—see also 另见 LABIAL —**bilabial** *adj*

bi·lat·er·al /baɪˋlætərəl; baɪˈlætərəl/ *adj* **bilateral agreement/arrangement/treaty etc** an agreement etc between two groups or nations 双边协议/约定/条约等 —compare 比较 MULTILATERAL, UNILATERAL —**bilaterally** *adv*

bil·ber·ry /ˋbɪlˌbɛrɪ; ˈbɪlbəri/ *n* [C] a blue-black fruit that grows in Northern Europe or the bush it grows on 欧洲越橘

bile /baɪl; baɪl/ *n* [U] **1** a bitter green brown liquid formed in the LIVER (1), which helps you to DIGEST[1] (1) fats 胆汁 **2** *literary* anger and hatred【文】坏脾气; 乖戾

bilge /bɪldʒ; bɪldʒ/ *n* **1** [C usually plural 一般用复数] the broad bottom part of a ship〔船的〕舱底 **2** [U] *old-fashioned informal* nonsense【过时, 非正式】废话, 胡说

bi·lin·gual /baɪˋlɪŋgwəl; baɪˈlɪŋgwəl/ *adj* **1** written or spoken in two languages 双语的; 包含两种语言的: *a bilingual dictionary* 双语词典 **2** able to speak two languages equally well 会说两种语言的: *Their kids are completely bilingual.* 他们的孩子能流利地说两种语言。—**bilingual** *n* [C] —compare 比较 MONOLINGUAL, MULTILINGUAL

bil·i·ous /ˋbɪljəs; ˈbɪliəs/ *adj* **1** feeling sick〔因胆汁过多而〕感到不适的: *Fatty foods make some people bilious.* 多脂肪的食物会使一些人患上胆汁病。**2** bad-tempered 坏脾气的; 暴躁的 —**biliousness** *n*

bilk /bɪlk; bɪlk/ *v* [T+out of] *informal* to cheat someone, especially by taking their money; SWINDLE[1]【非正式】蒙骗〔尤指骗钱〕

Bil·ko /ˋbɪlko; ˈbɪlkəʊ/, **Sergeant** the main character in a humorous television programme about a US army camp. Bilko is an army officer, played by Phil Silvers, who talks very fast and loves playing cards and finding ways to make money. 比尔科中士〔一部描写美国军营生活的幽默电视剧的主人公。他是一位军官, 说话语速快, 喜欢打牌和想方设法赚钱, 由菲尔·西尔弗斯扮演〕

bill[1] /bɪl; bɪl/ *n* [C] 

1 ▶PAYMENT 付款◀ a) a written list showing how much you have to pay for services you have received, work that has been done etc〔服务费用的〕账单: **[+for]** *The bill for the repairs came to $650.* 修理费用总计650美元。| **pay/settle a bill** *Have you paid the phone bill?* 你付清电话费了吗? **b)** *BrE* a list showing how much you have to pay for food you have eaten in a restaurant【英】〔餐费的〕账单; CHECK[2] (7) *AmE*【美】: *Could we have the bill, please?* 请结账。—see picture on page A15 参见A15页图

2 ▶LAW 法律◀ a written proposal for a new law, which is brought to a parliament so that it can be discussed 议案, 法案: *a*

debate in Congress on the President's new transportation bill 国会对总统的新运输法案进行的辩论

CULTURAL NOTE 文化注释

How a bill becomes a law 议案如何成为法律

Because US law is based on the British legal system, the UK and the US have a similar process for making a bill into a law. 由于美国法制基于英国司法体系，因此英美两国把议案变成法律的程序有类似之处。

In the US A bill is first presented in the Senate or the House of Representatives. This is called the First Reading. A special committee then looks at the details of the bill and can add suggestions and make changes, after which they must vote on it. The committee returns the bill to the House or Senate for the Second Reading, where it is read carefully, discussed, and sometimes changed. The House or Senate reads the bill one more time (this is known as the Third Reading) and then vote on it. If they vote for the bill, the bill is then sent to the other side of Congress to be discussed, possibly changed, and voted on. Once both the Senate and House of Representatives have agreed on the bill, they send it to the President. If the President agrees with the bill, he or she signs it and it becomes a law. If the President does not agree with the bill, he or she can VETO it (=decide not to sign it). The Senate or House of Representatives must then discuss the bill and vote again. If two-thirds of that house votes to support the bill, they can then send the bill to the other house for discussion and a vote. If two-thirds of the other house also votes 'yes', the bill becomes a law, even if the President does not agree with it. 在美国：首先在参议院或众议院提出议案，称为"初读"。然后一个特别委员会核查议案的具体内容，补充建议，作出修正，此后必须对其表决。委员会把议案退回参议院或众议院，开始"二读"，议案经仔细审读和讨论，有时会作修正。参议院或众议院再次审阅议案，称为"三读"，然后对其投票。如果投票通过，议案移交国会的另一院进行讨论，也许还会修改，并再一次投票表决。参众两院一致通过议案，则将议案呈交总统。总统若同意，则会签署议案，使之成为法律。总统不同意则会拒绝签署，参议院或众议院则须继续讨论议案，再次投票。若最初提出议案的参议院或众议院有三分之二代表投票赞成议案，则将议案送交国会另一院供讨论和表决，若另一院也有三分之二的代表投票赞成，即便总统反对，议法案也会成为法律。

In the UK When a new bill is first presented to the House of Commons, this is known as the First Reading. MPs discuss the bill, sometimes adding suggestions and making changes, and then the bill is read again. This is called the Second Reading. Next comes the committee stage, when a committee examines the details of the bill. This is followed by more discussion, called the report stage. The committee returns the bill to the House of Commons for the Third Reading, after which the House of Commons sends the bill to the House of Lords where it is also read and discussed. The House of Lords can add suggestions, but they cannot refuse the bill. Once the bill has been agreed by both sides of Parliament, the King or Queen gives it the ROYAL ASSENT (=approves it) and it officially becomes a law. 在英国：议案初次递交下议院作"初读"，下议院议员讨论议案，有时补充建议，作出修改，然后议案再经审议，称为"二读"。接下来是委员会审议阶段，委员会认真审阅议案具体内容，然后是进一步讨论，叫做"讨论处理阶段"。委员会将议案退回下议院，进行"三读"，此后下议院将议案递交上议院审议。上议院也可补充建议，但不能否决。议会上下两院一致同意，国王或女王御准后，议案正式成为法律。

3 ►MONEY 钱◄ *AmE* a piece of paper money【美】纸币，钞票；NOTE[1] (5) *BrE*【英】: *a five-dollar bill* 一张五美元的钞票

4 fill the bill/fit the bill to be exactly what you need 符合需要；最为合适；管用: *This car fits the bill perfectly. It's cheap and gets good mileage.* 这辆汽车很合适，既便宜又省油。

5 ►CONCERT/SHOW ETC 音乐会/演出等◄ a programme of entertainment at a theatre, concert, cinema etc, with details of who is performing, what is being shown etc 节目单；招贴，海报: **top the bill** (=be the most important performer) 领衔主演 | **a double bill** (=a show in two parts) 双剧目 *a great double bill with two classic horror movies* 两部经典恐怖片同场放映

6 ►ADVERTISEMENT 广告◄ a printed notice advertising an event 广告；招贴；传单

7 give sb/sth a clean bill of health to officially state that someone is in good health or that something is working correctly 给某人/某物开具健康良好证明[合格证明]: *Safety inspectors gave all the rides a clean bill of health.* 安全检查员评定所有的游乐设施都符合安全标准。

8 ►BIRD 鸟◄ a bird's beak 鸟嘴，喙

9 the old bill/the bill *BrE spoken* the police【英口】警察

bill² *v* [T] **1 be billed as** to be advertised or generally described in a particular way 被宣传为: *The election was billed as the make-or-break point for the Liberals.* 这次选举被宣传为自由党人的成败关键。**2 be billed to play/appear etc** if someone is billed to perform somewhere, it has been advertised that they will perform there 海报上宣传某人将演出/出场等: *He was billed to play three successive concerts.* 海报上宣传他将连续演出三场音乐会。**3** to send someone a bill 给…开[送]账单: *Clients will be billed monthly.* 按月给客户开送账单。**4 bill and coo** *literary or humorous* if two lovers are billing and cooing, they are kissing and talking softly【文或幽默】〔情侣间〕接吻和低声地谈情说爱，卿卿我我

Bill·board /ˈbɪlˌbord; ˈbɪlbɔːd/ a US weekly magazine about popular music, that gives the Hot 100 (=a list of the 100 most popular records that week)《告示牌》〔美国的一种流行音乐周刊，每周评出名列前100名的畅销唱片〕

billboard *n* [C] a large sign used for advertising 广告牌[板]; HOARDING (2) *BrE*【英】

bil·let¹ /ˈbɪlɪt; ˈbɪlət/ *n* [C] a private house where soldiers live temporarily 士兵临时营房〔通常为民房〕

billet² *v* [T+on/with] to put soldiers in private house to live there temporarily 给〔士兵〕提供临时住宿

bil·let-doux /ˈbɪle ˋdu; ˌbɪleɪ ˈduː/ *n plural* **billets-doux** /ˌbɪle ˋduz; ˌbɪleɪ ˈduːz/ [C] *French humorous or literary* a love letter【法，幽默或文】情书

bill·fold /ˈbɪlˌfold; ˈbɪlfəʊld/ *n* [C] *AmE* a small flat leather case, used for carrying paper money, credit cards etc in your pocket; WALLET (1)【美】〔装钞票和信用卡等的〕钱包，皮夹子

bill·hook /ˈbɪlˌhʊk; ˈbɪlhʊk/ *n* [C] a tool consisting of a blade with a hooked point and a handle, used for cutting off tree branches etc〔剪枝等用的〕钩镰，钩刀

bil·liards /ˈbɪljɚdz; ˈbɪljədz/ *n* [plural] a game played on a cloth-covered table in which balls are hit with a CUE (=a long stick) against each other and into pockets at the edge of the table 台球，桌球，撞球戏 —compare 比较 POOL[1] (3), SNOOKER[1] —**billiard** *adj* [only before noun 仅用于名词前]: *a billiard table* 台球桌 | *the billiard room* 台球室

bill·ing /ˈbɪlɪŋ; ˈbɪlɪŋ/ *n* **give sb top/star billing** to name a particular performer, actor etc as being the most important person in a show, play etc 在海报上宣传某人领衔主演

Bil·lings·gate /ˈbɪlɪŋzget; ˈbɪlɪŋzgeɪt/ a large fish market in east London. The word 'Billingsgate' was also formerly used to mean swearing and offensive language, because the people who worked in the market were known for this. 比林斯盖特〔伦敦东部一大鱼市。该词以前也指粗俗的骂人话，因为鱼市的工作人员以说粗话出名〕

bil·lion /ˈbɪljən; ˈbɪljən/ *plural* **billion** or **billions** *number* **1** one thousand million 十亿 —see 见 HUNDRED (USAGE) **2** *BrE old use* a million million【英旧】万亿 —**billionth** *determiner, n, pron, adv*

bill of ex·change /ˌ· · ˈ·/ *n* [C] *technical* a signed document ordering someone to pay someone else a particular amount of money【术语】汇票

bill of fare /ˌ· · ˈ·/ *n* [C] *old-fashioned* a list of the food that is served in a restaurant; MENU (1)【过时】〔餐馆的〕菜单

bill of lad·ing /ˌ· · ˈ··/ *n* [C] *technical* a list of the goods being carried, especially on a ship【术语】〔尤指船运〕提（货）单

bill of rights /ˌ· · ˈ·/ *n* [C] a written statement of the most important rights of the citizens of a country 人权法案；权利法案: *One state has proposed the country adopt a bill of rights and replace the Queen as head of state with a president.* 有一个州提议该国采纳一项人权法案，由总统取代女王担任国家元首。

Bill of Rights, the part of the US CONSTITUTION (=the basic laws of the country that cannot easily be changed) which is a list of the rights of US citizens, for example freedom of speech (=the right to say what you want to say, including criticizing the government), and freedom of religion《人权法案》〔美国宪法的一部分，列举了美国公民的权利，如言论自由、宗教信仰自由等〕

bill of sale /ˌ· · ˈ·/ *n* [C] a written document showing that someone has bought something 卖据，卖契

bil·low[1] /ˋbɪlo; ˈbɪləʊ/ *v* [I] **1** also 又作 **billow out** to swell out like a sail〔像帆一样地〕鼓起，扬起：*billowing skirts* 扬起的裙子 **2** *literary* to rise and roll in waves【文】在波涛中翻滚；汹涌奔腾：*smoke billowing upwards* 滚滚上升的浓烟

billow[2] *n* [C usually plural 一般用复数] **1** *literary* a wave, especially a very large one【文】波涛；巨浪 **2** a moving cloud or mass of something such as smoke or cloth 波涛般滚滚而来之物

bil·ly /ˋbɪlɪ; ˈbɪli/ also 又作 **bil·ly·can** /ˋbɪlɪˌkæn; ˈbɪlikæn/ *n* [C] *BrE, AustrE* a tin pot for cooking or boiling water when you are camping【英，澳】〔露营时煮饭烧水用的〕铁皮罐

billy club /ˈ· · ·/ *n* [C] *AmE old-fashioned* a short stick carried by a police officer【美，过时】警棍；TRUNCHEON *BrE*【英】

Billy goat /ˈ· · ·/ *n* [C] *informal* a word for a male goat used especially by or to children【非正式】公山羊〔尤用于儿语〕— compare 比较 NANNY GOAT

billy-o /ˈ· · ·/ *n* **like billy-o** *BrE old-fashioned slang* very fast or with a lot of effort【英，过时，俚】很快地；尽全力；猛烈地：*We ran like billy-o!* 我们拼命地跑。

Billy the Kid /ˌ· · · ˈ·/ (1859-81) a famous criminal in the southwest US who killed many people and stole cattle until he was finally caught and killed 比利小子〔(1859-1881)，美国西南部一个臭名昭著的罪犯。他杀人、偷牛，最终落网并被处决〕

bil·tong /ˋbɪlˌtaŋ; ˈbɪltɒŋ/ *n* [U] *SAfrE* meat dried in the sun【南非】晒干的肉

bim·bo /ˋbɪmbo; ˈbɪmbəʊ/ *n* [C] *informal* an insulting word for an attractive but unintelligent young woman【非正式】〔年轻貌美但头脑简单的〕女人〔侮辱性用语〕：*He picked up some bimbo at the club last night.* 他昨晚在俱乐部勾搭上了一个美艳女郎。

bi·month·ly /baɪˋmʌnθlɪ; baɪˈmʌnθli/ *adj* appearing or happening every two months or twice each month 两月一次的；一月两次的：*bimonthly magazine* 双月刊；半月刊 —**bimonthly** *adv*

bin[1] /bɪn; bɪn/ *n* [C] **1** *BrE* a container for putting waste in【英】垃圾箱，垃圾桶：*Throw it in the bin.* 把它扔到垃圾箱里去。— see picture on page A10 参见 A10 页图 **2** a large container for storing things, such as goods in a shop or substances in a factory 大贮藏箱

bin[2] *v* **binned, binning** [T] *BrE informal* to throw something away【英，非正式】扔掉：*"What should I do with this letter?" "Just bin it!"* "这封信我该怎么处理?" "扔掉就是了!"

bi·na·ry /ˋbaɪnərɪ; ˈbaɪnəri/ *adj technical*【术语】**1 the binary system** a system of counting, used in computers, in which only the numbers 0 and 1 are used〔计算机计数法中的〕二进制 **2** consisting of two parts; double 由两部分组成的；二元的；双重的：*a binary star system* 双星系

bind[1] /baɪnd; baɪnd/ *v past tense and past participle* **bound** /baʊnd; baʊnd/

1 ▶TIE/FASTEN 束/缚◀ [T] *formal or literary*【正式或文】**a)** to tie someone so that they cannot move or escape 捆，绑：*They bound my arms and legs with rope.* 他们用绳子绑住我的双臂和双腿。| **bound and gagged** (=tied up, and with cloth tied around your mouth so you cannot speak) 身体被绑着，嘴被堵住 **b)** also 又作 **bind up** to tie things firmly together with cloth or string〔用布或带子〕束紧；捆扎：*They bound his wounds.* 他们把他的伤口包扎好。

2 ▶UNITE 联合◀ [T] to form a strong emotional or economic connection between two people, countries etc 把…紧紧联系在一起；使关系密切：**bind sth together** *Their shared experiences in war helped to bind the two communities together.* 共同的战争经历使两个团体的关系十分密切。

3 ▶STICK TOGETHER 黏起来◀ [I,T] to stick together in a mass, or to make small pieces of something stick together (使) 黏合；(使) 凝结：*The flour mixture isn't wet enough to bind properly.* 这面粉浆糊水不够，所以不黏。| **bind sth** *The rain will help to bind the soil.* 这场雨有助于使泥土黏合。

4 ▶RESTRICT 限制◀ [T] to reduce someone's freedom of action, for example by giving them a duty or making them promise to do something 约束；使负有义务：*regulations that could bind policy-makers in the future* 能于将来约束决策者的规定 | *The monks are bound by vows of silence.* 僧侣们必须遵守保持缄默的誓言。

5 ▶STITCH 缝◀ [T] to strengthen or decorate something with a border of material 给…加上饰边；给…镶边：*The edges of the blanket were bound with ribbon.* 毯子有丝带饰边。

6 ▶BOOK 书◀ [T] to fasten the pages of a book together and put them in a cover 装订 —see also 另见 BOUND

bind sb over *phr v* [T] *BrE law* to order someone to cause no more trouble by threatening them with legal punishment【英，法律】命令〔某人〕具结[保证]不再闹事：*bound over to keep the peace* 依法具结不得扰乱治安

bind[2] *n* **a bind** *informal* an annoying or difficult situation【非正式】窘境，困境：*It's a real bind having to look after the children.* 要照顾这些孩子真令人为难。

bind·er /ˋbaɪndɚ; ˈbaɪndə/ *n* **1** [C] a removable cover for holding loose sheets of paper, magazines etc 活页封面，活页夹 — see also 另见 RING BINDER **2** [C] a person or machine that fastens the parts of a book together〔书籍〕装订工；装订机 **3** [C,U] a substance that makes things stick together 黏合物 **4** [C] *AmE* an agreement in which you pay something to show that you intend to buy some property【美】〔购买不动产时的〕临时契约

bind·ing[1] /ˋbaɪndɪŋ; ˈbaɪndɪŋ/ *adj* **a binding contract/promise/agreement etc** a promise, agreement etc that must be obeyed 具有约束力[必须履行]的合同/承诺/协议等

binding[2] *n* **1** [C] a book cover〔书籍的〕封面 **2** [U] material sewn or stuck along the edge of a piece of cloth for strength or decoration 镶边；边饰；滚条

bind·weed /ˋbaɪndˌwid; ˈbaɪndwiːd/ *n* [U] a wild plant that winds itself around other plants 旋花属植物；旋花蔓

binge[1] /bɪndʒ; bɪndʒ/ *n* [C] *informal* a short period when you do too much of something, especially drinking alcohol【非正式】狂欢作乐；大吃大喝〔尤指喝酒〕：*a weeklong binge of shopping and theatre-going* 一周的疯狂购物和看戏 | **on a binge** *Ken's gone on a binge with his mates.* 肯和他的伙伴一起饮酒作乐去了。

binge[2] *v* [I] *informal* to eat a lot of food in a short time, especially if you have an EATING DISORDER【非正式】〔尤因患饮食失调症而〕暴食：**[+on]** *Whenever she's depressed she binges on chocolates.* 每当情绪低落时她就猛吃巧克力。

bin·go[1] /ˋbɪŋgo; ˈbɪŋgəʊ/ *n* [U] a game played for money or prizes in which numbers are chosen by chance and called out, and if you have the right numbers on your card you win 宾戈游戏〔一种彩票式游戏，玩者持有一张有数字的牌，如牌上的数字和开叫的号码对上，玩者便胜出〕：*Vera won £20 at bingo.* 薇拉玩宾戈赢了20英镑。

CULTURAL NOTE 文化注释

In Britain, bingo is generally thought of as a game played by WORKING-CLASS women in the evening. In the US, it is usually played by older people and games are often run by the Catholic Church or take place on RESERVATIONS (=land owned by Native Americans). Bingo is illegal in some American states because it is considered to be gambling (GAMBLE). 宾戈游戏在英国被认为是劳动阶层妇女晚间消遣的游戏，在美国则通常是年龄较大的人的游戏，经常由天主教堂组织，或在印第安人居留地举行。在美国的一些州，它被认为是一种赌博，因此是非法的。

bingo[2] *interjection old-fashioned* used when you have just done something successfully and are pleased【过时】瞧，好，妙〔对刚才成功做某事表示的兴奋叫声〕：*Bingo! That's the one I've been looking for.* 太好了！这正是我一直在找的那一个。

bin lin·er /ˈ· ˌ··/ *n* [C] *BrE* a plastic bag used inside a bin (BIN[1] (1)) for holding waste【英】〔置于垃圾箱内的〕塑料垃圾袋

bin·man /ˋbɪnmæn; ˈbɪnmæn/ *n plural* **binmen** /-mɛn; -men/ [C] *BrE* someone who comes to people's houses to collect their waste【英】上门收垃圾的清洁工；GARBAGE COLLECTOR *AmE*【美】

bi·noc·u·lars /bɪˋnɑkjəlɚz; bɪˈnɒkjʊləz/ *n* [plural] a pair of glasses like short telescopes (TELESCOPE[1]), used for looking at distant objects 双筒望远镜

binocular vi·sion /ˌ· ˌ··· ˈ··/ *n* [U] *technical* the ability to FOCUS (=see clearly with) both eyes on one object, which humans, monkeys, and some birds have【术语】〔人、猴及某些鸟类具有的〕双眼视觉

bi·no·mi·al /baɪˋnomɪəl; baɪˈnəʊmiəl/ *n* [C] *technical* a mathematical expression that has two parts connected by the sign + or the sign –, for example 3x+4y or x–7【术语】〔数学〕二项式〈如 3x+4y 或 x–7〉—**binomial** *adj*

bio- /baɪo; baɪəʊ/ *prefix* concerning living things 生物：*biochemistry* (=study of the chemistry of living things) 生物化学

bi·o·chem·is·try /ˌbaɪoˋkɛmɪstrɪ; ˌbaɪəʊˈkemɪstri/ *n* [U] the scientific study of the chemistry of living things 生物化学 — **biochemist** *n* [C] —**biochemical** *adj*

bi·o·de·gra·da·ble /ˌbaɪodɪˋgredəbl; ˌbaɪəʊdɪˈgreɪdəbəl◂/ *adj technical* materials, chemicals etc that are biodegradable are changed naturally by the action of BACTERIA into substances that are not harmful to the environment【术语】微生物可分解的，能进行生物降解的

bi·og·ra·pher /baɪˋɑgrəfɚ; baɪˈɒgrəfə/ *n* [C] someone who writes about someone else's life 传记作者

bi·og·ra·phy /baɪˋɑgrəfɪ; baɪˈɒgrəfi/ *n* **1** [C] an account of a person's life written by someone else〔由他人撰写的〕传记: *Boswell's biography of Dr. Johnson* 博斯韦尔为约翰逊博士写的传记 **2** [U] the part of literature that consists of biographies 传记文学 —compare 比较 AUTOBIOGRAPHY —**biographical** /ˌbaɪəˋgræfɪkl̩; ˌbaɪəˈgræfɪkəl◂/ *adj* —**biographically** /-kl̩ɪ; -kli/ *adv*

bi·o·lo·gi·cal /ˌbaɪəˋlɑdʒɪkl̩; ˌbaɪəˈlɒdʒɪkəl/ *adj* **1** connected with biology 生物学的; 与生物学有关的: *woman's biological function as a bearer of children* 妇女的生育能力 | *the biological sciences* 生物科学 **2 biological father/mother/parent** a child's natural parent, rather than someone who has become its parent through ADOPTION (1) 生父/生母/亲生父[母]

biological clock /ˌ‥‥ˈ·/ *n* [singular] **1** *technical* the time system in plants and animals that controls behaviour such as sleeping and eating; BODY CLOCK【术语】生物钟〔指植物和动物控制某些行为如吃、睡等的一个体系〕 **2** *not technical* the idea that when a woman reaches a certain age, she will soon be too old to have a baby【非术语】受孕生理钟〔指妇女到了一定年龄后不会生育的一种说法〕

biological con·trol /ˌ‥‥ ·ˈ·/ *n* [U] a method of controlling PESTS (=small insects that harm or destroy crops) by using other insects, birds, or animals to kill them 生物控制〔指利用其他昆虫、鸟雀或兽类对害虫进行控制〕

biological war·fare /ˌ‥‥ˈ··/ *n* [U] methods of fighting a war in which BACTERIA are used to poison people, damage crops etc 生物战, 细菌战 —compare 比较 CHEMICAL WARFARE

bi·ol·o·gy /baɪˋɑlədʒɪ; baɪˈɒlədʒi/ *n* [U] **1** the scientific study of living things 生物学: *She has a degree in biology.* 她拥有生物学的学位。 **2** the scientific laws that control the life of a particular type of animal, plant etc〔某种动物或植物的〕生活规律; 生态学: *the biology of bacteria* 细菌的生态学 —**biologist** *n* [C] —**biological** /ˌbaɪəˋlɑdʒɪkl̩; ˌbaɪəˈlɒdʒɪkəl◂/ *adj*: *biological washing powder* (=using special chemicals to wash clothes) 生物洗衣粉 —**biologically** /-kl̩ɪ; -kli/ *adv*

bi·o·mass /ˋbaɪoˌmæs; ˈbaɪəʊmæs/ *n* [U] *technical* plant and animal matter used to provide fuel or energy【术语】〔尤指用作燃料或提供能量的〕生物量

bi·on·ic /baɪˋɑnɪk; baɪˈɒnɪk/ *adj informal* much stronger or faster than a normal person usually because of having electronic arms or legs【非正式】〔由于身体某部分受电子操纵而〕具有超人力量[速度]的

bi·o·phy·sics /ˌbaɪoˋfɪzɪks; ˌbaɪəʊˈfɪzɪks/ *n* [U] the scientific study of matter and natural forces in living things 生物物理学

bi·o·pic /ˋbaɪoˌpɪk; ˈbaɪəʊˌpɪk/ *n* [C] *informal* a film that tells the story of someone's life【非正式】传记影片: *'Great Balls of Fire', the biopic of Jerry Lee Lewis* 一部有关杰里·李·刘易斯生平的电影《大火球》

bi·op·sy /ˋbaɪɑpsɪ; ˈbaɪɒpsi/ *n* [C] the removal of cells, liquid etc from the body of someone who is ill, in order to find out more about their disease and its effects 活组织检查, 活体检视

bi·o·rhyth·ms /ˋbaɪoˌrɪðəmz; ˈbaɪəʊˌrɪðəmz/ *n* [plural] regular changes in the speed at which physical processes happen in your body, which some people believe can affect the way you feel and behave 生物节律〔一种据认为存在于生物体内的周期性的变化现象, 被认为会对情感和行为产生影响〕

bi·o·sphere /ˋbaɪəˌsfɪr; ˈbaɪəsfɪə/ *n* [singular] *technical* the part of the world in which animals, plants etc can live【术语】生物圈〔地球上生命可存在的区域〕

bi·o·tech·nol·o·gy /ˌbaɪotɛkˋnɑlədʒɪ; ˌbaɪəʊtekˈnɒlədʒi/ *n* [U] *technical* the use in science and industry of living things such as cells and BACTERIA, to make drugs or chemicals, destroy waste matter etc【术语】生物技术; 生物工艺学

bi·par·ti·san /baɪˋpɑrtəzn̩; ˌbaɪpɑːtɪ̬ˈzæn/ *adj* consisting of or representing two political parties 由两党组成的; 代表两党的: *Gore proposed a bipartisan committee drawn especially from both houses.* 戈尔提议成立一个由参、众两院议员组成的两党委员会。

bi·par·tite /baɪˋpɑrtaɪt; baɪˈpɑːtaɪt/ *adj* **1** *formal* shared by or agreed on by two different groups【正式】双方同意的; 双方共有的: *a bipartite treaty* 双边条约 **2** *technical* having two parts【术语】有两部分的; 由两部分构成的: *a bipartite leaf* 呈二深裂的叶子 —compare 比较 TRIPARTITE

bi·ped /ˋbaɪpɛd; ˈbaɪped/ *n* [C] *technical* an animal with two legs, including humans【术语】两足动物〔包括人类〕—compare 比较 QUADRUPED —**bipedal** /ˋbaɪpɛdl̩; ˌbaɪˈpedl◂/ *adj*

bi·plane /ˋbaɪˌplen; ˈbaɪpleɪn/ *n* [C] an aircraft with two sets of wings, especially of a type built in the early 20th century 双翼飞机〔尤指20世纪初期有两层机翼的飞机〕—compare 比较 MONOPLANE

birch[1] /bɝtʃ; bɜːtʃ/ *n* **1** [C,U] a tree with smooth BARK (=outer covering) and thin branches, or the wood from this tree 桦树; 桦木 **2 the birch** the practice of hitting people with a stick as a punishment 用桦条笞打的惩罚, 桦木笞 —see also 另见 SILVER BIRCH

> **CULTURAL NOTE 文化注释**
> The birch is still available as a punishment on the Isle of Man, but nowhere else in Britain or the US. Some older people in Britain would like to 'bring back the birch' for football HOOLIGANS and VANDALS. 在马恩岛, 桦木笞仍旧是一种刑罚手段, 但在英国的其他地方或在美国则已不再使用。英国一些年纪较大的人希望"重启桦木笞"来惩治足球流氓和蓄意破坏公物者。

birch[2] *v* [T] to hit someone with a stick as a punishment〔用桦条〕抽打

bird /bɝd; bɜːd/ *n* [C]

1 ▶**BIRD 鸟**◀ a creature with wings and feathers that lays eggs and can usually fly 鸟: *The tree was full of tiny, brightly-coloured birds.* 树上到处都是色彩鲜艳的小鸟。

2 a little bird told me *spoken* used to say that you know something, but you will not say how you found out【口】一个消息灵通的人告诉我: *A little bird told me that you've got engaged.* 有个消息灵通的人告诉我你订婚了。

3 the birds and the bees *humorous* the facts about sex, especially as told to children【幽默】〔尤指对儿童讲述的〕有关两性的基本常识, 性知识

4 birds of a feather *informal* people of the same kind【非正式】同类的人; 志趣相投者

5 give sb the bird a) *AmE informal* to make a very rude sign by putting your middle finger up【美, 非正式】〔竖起中指〕对某人做下流手势 **b)** *BrE* to make rude noises in order to show disapproval of a performer, public speaker etc【英】向〔演员、演讲者等〕发嘘声, 喝倒彩

6 a bird in the hand (is worth two in the bush) used to say that something you already have is worth more than something which is better, but which you cannot be sure of getting 已到手的东西 (总比不一定能到手的东西强)

7 the bird has flown *informal* used to say that the person you are looking for has already left or escaped【非正式】要抓[找]的人跑[走]了

8 be (strictly) for the birds *AmE informal* to be silly, useless, or not practical【美, 非正式】愚蠢的; 毫无用处的; 不实用的

9 ▶**WOMAN 女人**◀ *BrE old-fashioned* a word meaning a young woman which some women think is offensive【英, 过时】年轻女子, 少女, 小妞〔一些女性视此词为冒犯用语〕—see also 另见 DOLLY BIRD

10 ▶**PERSON 人**◀ *old-fashioned* a person of a particular type, especially one who seems strange or unusual【过时】怪人, 古怪[奇特]的家伙: *He's a strange old bird.* 他是个古怪的老头。

11 do bird *BrE slang* to spend a period of time in prison【英俚】蹲监狱 —see also 另见 **eat like a bird** (EAT (1a)), **early bird** (EARLY[1] (10)), **home bird** (HOME[3] (5)), **kill two birds with one stone** (KILL[1] (10))

bird·bath /ˋbɝdˌbæθ; ˈbɜːdbɑːθ/ *n* a stone bowl filled with water for birds to wash in, usually in a garden〔通常在花园里的〕鸟浴池

bird-brained /ˈ· ·/ *adj informal* stupid or thoughtless【非正式】愚蠢的; 欠考虑的

bird dog /ˈ· ·/ *n* [C] *AmE* a dog that is trained to find and bring back birds that have been shot for sport; GUN DOG【美】〔猎鸟时用的〕猎犬

bird·ie[1] /ˋbɝdɪ; ˈbɜːdi/ *n* [C] **1** *spoken* a word meaning a little bird, used especially by or to children【口】小鸟儿〔儿语〕 **2** one STROKE[1] (10) less than PAR (=the usual number of strokes) in a game of GOLF〔高尔夫球中〕比标准杆数少一击入洞, 小鸟球 **3** *AmE* the small object that you hit across the net in a game of BADMINTON【美】羽毛球; SHUTTLECOCK *BrE*【英】 **4 watch the birdie** *old-fashioned* used to tell people that you are going to take a photograph of them【过时】看镜头〔准备按快门时说的一句话〕

birdie[2] *v* [T] to hit the ball into the hole in GOLF with one STROKE[1] (10) less than PAR (=the usual number of strokes)〔高尔夫球中〕以比标准杆数少一击的成绩打入〔洞〕

bird·lime /ˋbɝdˌlaɪm; ˈbɜːdlaɪm/ *n* [U] a sticky substance spread on branches to catch small birds〔涂在树枝上捕小鸟用的〕粘鸟胶

bird of par·a·dise /ˌ· · ˈ· · ·/ *n* [C] a brightly coloured bird from Papua New Guinea 天堂鸟, 极乐鸟〔产自巴布亚新几内亚的一种色彩鲜艳的鸟〕

B

bird of pas·sage /ˌ· · ˈ· ·/ *n* [C] **1** a bird that flies from one area or country to another, according to the seasons 候鸟 **2** *literary* someone who never stays in the same place for long【文】漂泊不定的人

bird of prey /ˌ· · ˈ·/ *n* [C] a bird that kills other birds or small animals for food 猛禽: *The peregrine falcon, a rare bird of prey, is a protected species.* 稀有猛禽游隼是受保护物种。

bird·seed /ˈbɚdˌsid; ˈbɜːdsiːd/ *n* [U] a mixture of seeds for feeding birds〔喂鸟的〕鸟食

bird's-eye view /ˌ· · ˈ·/ *n* [singular] **1** a view of something from high above it 鸟瞰(图),〔自高处俯视的〕全景: *From the plane we had an amazing bird's-eye view of the town.* 从飞机上,我们看到一幅美妙的全城鸟瞰图。**2** a general report or account of something, without many details 概述, 概要

bird·song /ˈbɚdˌsɔŋ; ˈbɜːdsɒŋ/ *n* [U] the musical noises made by birds 悦耳的鸟鸣: *Birdsong and the hum of insects filled the air.* 空中充满了鸟啭和虫鸣。

bird ta·ble /ˈ· ˌ· ·/ *n* [C] *BrE* a high wooden structure in a garden that you put seeds, bread etc on for birds to eat【英】鸟食台〔用来放置鸟食〕

bird·watch·er /ˈ· ˌ· ·/ *n* [C] someone who watches wild birds and tries to recognize different types 野鸟观察者; 野鸟生态研究者 —**birdwatching** *n* [U]

bi·ret·ta /bəˈrɛtə; bɪ̍ˈretə/ *n* [C] a square cap worn by Roman Catholic priests〔天主教神职人员戴的〕法冠, 四角帽

bir·i·a·ni, biryani /ˌbɪrɪˈɑnɪ; ˌbiriˈɑːni/ *n* [C,U] an Indian rice dish with meat, fish, or vegetables and spices (SPICE[1] (1))〔与肉、鱼、蔬菜及香料一起烹制的〕印度烩饭

Bir·ken·stocks /ˈbɚkənstɑks; ˈbɜːkənstɒks/ *trademark* a type of SANDAL (=a shoe that is open at the toes and heel) with a wide, flat bottom, which is designed to be comfortable【商标】勃肯凉鞋〔一种鞋底宽平的皮制凉鞋, 设计舒适〕

Bir·ming·ham /ˈbɚmɪŋəm; ˈbɜːmɪŋəm/ **1** a city in the West Midlands of England, the second largest city in the UK 伯明翰〔位于英格兰中部偏西地区的一座城市, 为英国第二大城市〕**2** a city in Alabama in the US. During the 1960s, there were many protests in Birmingham about the way that black people were treated, as part of the Civil Rights Movement. 伯明翰〔位于美国亚拉巴马州的一座城市。20世纪60年代, 作为民权运动的一部分, 该市举行了多次抗议活动, 抵制对黑人的不公〕

Bir·nam Wood /ˌbɚnəm ˈwʊd; ˌbɜːnəm ˈwʊd/ the wood near **Birnam** in Perthshire, Scotland. In Shakespeare's play *Macbeth*, Macbeth is told that he will only be defeated when Birnam Wood comes to Dunsinane. Later, his enemy's army comes through Birnam Wood and each soldier cuts a large branch to hide himself, so that when the army moves on it looks as if the wood is moving. Macbeth is defeated and killed. 伯纳姆森林〔苏格兰珀斯郡附近的一处森林。在莎士比亚的《麦克白》一剧中, 有人告诉麦克白说, 谁都不会打败他的, 除非伯纳姆森林被移到了邓斯纳恩。后来, 敌军穿越伯纳姆森林时, 每个士兵都用砍下的大树枝把自己隐蔽了起来, 部队行进时就犹如森林在移动, 结果麦克白战败身亡〕

bi·ro /ˈbaɪro; ˈbaɪərəʊ/ *n* [C] *BrE trademark* a pen with a small ball at the end that rolls ink onto paper; BALLPOINT【英, 商标】"伯罗"牌圆珠笔, 原子笔: *Have you got a red biro?* 你有红色的圆珠笔吗? —see picture at 参见 PEN[1] 图

S2 W2 **birth** /bɚθ; bɜːθ/ *n* **1 give birth (to)** if a woman gives birth, she produces a baby from her body 生育, 生孩子: *She gave birth to a fine healthy girl.* 她生了一个健康漂亮的女孩。**2** [C,U] the time when a baby comes out of its mother's body 出生; 分娩: *Congratulations on the birth of your daughter!* 恭喜你生了个女儿! | *Were you present at the birth?* 分娩时你在场吗? | **at birth** *He only weighed three pounds at birth.* 他生下来时只有三磅重。**3** [U] the character, language, social position etc that you have because of the family or country you come from 出身; 血统; 家世, 家系: *of noble birth* 出身高贵 | *She is French by birth.* 她的父母是法国人。**4** [singular] the time when something new starts to exist〔新事物的〕诞生, 出现: *the birth of an idea* 一个想法的萌生 | *the birth of a nation* 一个国家的诞生 **5 the town/country etc of your birth** the town, country etc where you were born 出生地/国等

birth cer·tif·i·cate /ˈ· ·ˌ· · ·/ *n* [C] an official document that shows when and where you were born 出生证明书

birth con·trol /ˈ· ·ˌ·/ *n* [C] the practice of controlling, by various methods, the number of children you have; CONTRACEPTION 节育; 避孕: *a safe method of birth control* 安全的避孕方法

birth·day /ˈbɚθˌde; ˈbɜːθdeɪ/ *n* [C] **1** a day that is an exact number of years after the day when you were born 生日, 诞辰: *a birthday present* 生日礼物 | *It's my 21st birthday next week.* 下星期该到我的21岁生日了。| **happy birthday!** *spoken* (=what you say on someone's birthday)【口】生日快乐!

CULTURAL NOTE 文化注释

Most people in the US and the UK celebrate their birthdays, and their friends and family usually give them presents and **birthday cards** (=a folded piece of card with a picture on the front and a message inside). Young children often have a **birthday party**. Sometimes this party is held in a special place such as an indoor play area, or children are taken to a special event such as swimming or the cinema. Other children have parties at home, and the house is decorated with BALLOONS and children play games such as MUSICAL CHAIRS. In the US, children traditionally eat cake and ICE CREAM at a party, and in the UK they eat JELLY and ice cream. Both children and adults often have a special **birthday cake** with small CANDLES on it. Their friends and family sing them a song called 'Happy Birthday to You', and then the person whose birthday it is blows out all the candles. People often celebrate with a big party for special ages such as 18 and 21, and then 30, 40, 50, 60 etc. 在英国和美国, 大多数人都要过生日, 朋友和家人馈赠礼物和生日贺卡。年幼的孩子通常举行生日聚会, 有时聚会选在市内游乐场等特别地点, 或者大人带孩子去参加特别的活动, 如去游泳、看电影等。其他孩子在家里举行聚会, 用气球装点房间。美国孩子有在聚会上吃蛋糕和冰激凌的传统, 英国孩子则吃果冻和冰激凌。大人和孩子一般都会得到一个特别的生日蛋糕, 上面有小蜡烛。亲友为他们唱《祝你生日快乐》, 然后过生日的人把所有的蜡烛吹灭。人们经常举办大型聚会庆贺特别年龄的生日, 如18岁和21岁, 接下来是30岁、40岁、50岁、60岁等。— see Cultural Note at CELEBRATION, WISH 见 CELEBRATION, WISH 文化注释

2 in your birthday suit *humorous* not wearing any clothes【幽默】光着身子; 赤条条的; 一丝不挂的

Birthday Hon·cours, the /ˈ· · ˌ· ·/ special honours given to a number of British people by the Queen each year on her birthday, as a reward for their achievements or good work 英国女王生日授勋〔英国女王在生日时授予的荣誉称号, 嘉奖成就突出和工作出色的英国公民〕

birth·mark /ˈbɚθˌmɑrk; ˈbɜːθmɑːk/ *n* [C] a permanent red or brown mark on your skin that you have had since you were born 胎记, 胎痣: *Paul had a birthmark on his left cheek.* 保罗左脸颊上有块胎痣。

birth·place /ˈbɚθˌples; ˈbɜːθpleɪs/ *n* [C usually singular 一般用单数] **1** the place where someone was born, especially someone famous〔尤指名人的〕出生地: *Stratford-upon-Avon was Shakespeare's birthplace.* 埃文河畔的斯特拉特福是莎士比亚的出生地。**2** the place where something first started to happen or exist 发源地, 发祥地: *New Orleans is the birthplace of jazz.* 新奥尔良是爵士乐的发源地。

birth·rate /ˈbɚθˌret; ˈbɜːθreɪt/ *n* [C] the number of births for every 100 or every 1000 people in a particular year in a particular place 出生率: *a rapidly rising birthrate* 迅速上升的出生率 —compare 比较 DEATH RATE

birth·right /ˈbɚθˌraɪt; ˈbɜːθraɪt/ *n* [C usually singular 一般用单数] **1** a basic right that you believe you should have because of the family or country you come from 与生俱来的权利: *Freedom of speech is every American's birthright.* 言论自由是每个美国人与生俱来的权利。**2** property, money etc that you believe you should have because it comes from your family 本该继承的(来自家族的)财产: *Charles felt cheated out of his birthright.* 查尔斯觉得本该由他来继承的财产被人骗走了。

Birt·whis·tle /ˈbɚtwɪs]; ˈbɜːtwɪsəl/, **Sir Harrison** (1934-) an English COMPOSER known for his modern music for voices and instruments, including *Tragoedia* and *Ring a Dumb Carillon* 伯特威斯尔〔(1934-), 英国作曲家, 以现代声乐曲和器乐曲闻名, 作品包括《特拉戈蒂亚》和《敲响沉默的排钟》〕

bir·y·a·ni /ˌbɪrɪˈɑnɪ; ˌbiriˈɑːni/ *n* [C,U] another spelling of BIRIANI biriani 的另一种拼法

Biscay, Bay of —see 见 BAY OF BISCAY

bis·cuit /ˈbɪskɪt; ˈbɪskɪ̍t/ *n* **1** [C] *BrE* a thin, flat, dry, usually sweet cake that is usually sold in packages or tins【英】饼干: *chocolate biscuits* 巧克力饼干 | *cheese and biscuits* 奶酪及饼干 —compare 比较 COOKIE (1) **2** [C] *AmE* a type of bread baked in small round pieces【美】烤饼 **3** [U] a light yellowish-brown colour 淡褐色 **4 take the biscuit** *BrE informal* to be the most surprising, annoying etc thing you have ever heard【英, 非正 S3

式】所听到过的最令人惊讶[讨厌等]的事: *His latest excuse really takes the biscuit!* 他最近这个借口真是令人惊讶!

bi·sect /baɪˋsɛkt; baɪˈsekt/ *v* [T] *technical* to divide something, especially a line or angle, into two equal parts【术语】把…一分为二; 把…二等分 —**bisection** /baɪˋsɛkʃən; baɪˈsekʃən/ *n* [U]

bi·sex·u·al[1] /baɪˋsɛkʃuəl; baɪˈsekʃuəl/ *adj* **1** sexually attracted to both men and women 对男女两性都有性欲的 —compare 比较 HETEROSEXUAL, HOMOSEXUAL **2** having qualities or features of both sexes 具有雌雄两性特征的, 雌雄同体的, 两性的: *a bisexual plant* 雌雄同株的植物 —**bisexually** *adv* —**bisexuality** /ˌbaɪˌsɛkʃuˋæləti; ˌbaɪsekʃuˈælɪ̥ti/ *n* [U]

bisexual[2] *n* [C] someone who is sexually attracted to both men and women 对男女两性都有性欲的人, 双性恋者: *a club for bisexuals* 双性恋者俱乐部

Bishkek /ˋbɪʃkɛk; ˈbɪʃkek/ the capital city of Kyrgyzstan, in the Chu River valley, formerly called Frunze and Pishpek 比什凯克〔吉尔吉斯斯坦首都, 位于楚河河谷, 曾被称为伏龙芝和皮什彼克〕

W3 **bish·op** /ˋbɪʃəp; ˈbɪʃəp/ *n* [C] **1** a priest with a high rank in the Christian religion, who is the head of all the churches and priests in a large area〔基督教某些教派管辖大教区的〕主教: *the Bishop of Durham* 达勒姆郡的主教 **2** a piece in the game of CHESS that can be moved any number of squares from one corner towards the opposite corner〔国际象棋的〕象

bish·op·ric /ˋbɪʃəprɪk; ˈbɪʃəprɪk/ *n* [C] **1** the area that a bishop is in charge of; DIOCESE 主教管辖的教区 **2** the position of being a bishop 主教之职位

Bis·marck /ˋbɪzmɑrk; ˈbɪzmɑːk/ the capital city of the US state of North Dakota 俾斯麦市〔美国北达科他州首府〕

Bismarck, Ot·to von /ˋɑto vɑn; ˈɒtəʊ vɒn/ (1815-98) a German politician who was mainly responsible for joining all the separate German states together to form one country, and who then became CHANCELLOR of Germany 俾斯麦〔(1815-1898), 德国政治家, 他的主要功绩是把分散的德意志诸邦国统一为一个国家, 之后担任德意志帝国的第一任总理〕

bis·muth /ˋbɪzməθ; ˈbɪzməθ/ *n* [U] a grey-white metal that is often used in medicine〔金属元素〕铋

bi·son /ˋbaɪsn̩; ˈbaɪsən/ *n plural* **bison** *or* **bisons** [C] an animal like a large cow with long hair, which used to be common in North America; BUFFALO (2) 犎牛〔昔日常见于北美的一种野牛, 肩部长满鬃毛〕: *ancient cave paintings of bison at Lascaux* 拉斯考克斯的古代犎牛洞穴壁画

bisque /bɪsk; bɪsk/ *n* [U] a thick, creamy soup, especially one made from SHELLFISH〔尤指贝类煮成的〕奶油浓汤: *lobster bisque* 龙虾奶油浓汤

Bissau /bɪˋsau; bɪˈsaʊ/ the capital city of Guinea Bissau, a port 比绍〔几内亚比绍共和国首都、港口〕

bis·tro /ˋbistro; ˈbiːstrəʊ/ *n* [C] a small restaurant or bar 小酒吧; 小餐馆

S1 W1 **bit[1]** /bɪt; bɪt/ *n* [C]

1 ▶SLIGHTLY/FAIRLY 略微/相当◀ a bit *informal, especially BrE*【非正式, 尤英】**a)** slightly, but not very; a little 有点儿; 稍微: *Could you turn the radio down a bit, please?* 请把收音机的音量稍微调低一点儿好吗? | *Stay a bit longer – it's still early.* 再待一会儿吧, 还早着呢。| *I think you're a bit young to be watching this.* 我想你年纪还小, 不适合看这个。| **a bit more/less** *Would you like a bit more cake?* 要再来点儿蛋糕吗? | **a bit like** (=a little similar) 有点儿像 *She's a bit like my sister.* 她有点儿像我妹妹。**b)** used when you mean 'very' or 'quite a lot', but you do not want to emphasize it too much 相当〔用于不想过分强调时〕: *It's all a bit depressing, really.* 这真的很令人沮丧。—see graph at 参见 LITTLE 图表

2 ▶AMOUNT 量◀ *informal, especially BrE* a small amount, especially of something that is not a physical object【非正式, 尤英】一点儿; 一些: **[+of]** *Let me give you a bit of advice.* 让我给你一些建议。| *We may need a bit of help.* 我们也许需要一些帮助。| *He still likes to do a bit of gardening.* 他仍然喜欢干些园艺活儿。

3 ▶PIECE 件, 片◀ a small piece of something 一小块; 一小片: **[+of]** *The floor was covered with bits of broken glass.* 地板上全是碎玻璃。| **break/smash/blow sth to bits** *The bridge was blown to bits by the blast.* 那座桥被炸得粉碎。| **fall to bits** *That old table's falling to bits.* 那张旧桌子已经散架了。

4 ▶PART 部分◀ *informal, especially BrE* a part or piece of something larger【非正式, 尤英】部分; 片段; 小块: *You can play on the grass, but keep off the muddy bits.* 你可以在草地上玩, 但要远离泥洼。| **[+of]** *I liked the last bit of the film best.* 我最喜欢这部电影的结尾部分。

5 a good bit/quite a bit *especially BrE* a fairly large amount, or to a fairly large degree【尤英】不少; 颇多: *She knows quite a bit about European history.* 她懂得不少欧洲历史方面的知识。| *She's quite a bit older than me.* 她比我大很多。

6 not a bit *especially BrE* not at all【尤英】一点儿都不: *You're not a bit like your brother, are you?* 你一点儿也不像你弟弟, 对吧? | *I wasn't a bit worried.* 我一点儿也不担心。

7 every bit as just as much as 完全一样; 同样是: *I think she's every bit as pretty as her sister.* 我认为她和她妹妹长得一样漂亮。

8 bit by bit *especially BrE* gradually【尤英】逐渐地, 一点一点地: *It's a slow process, but we're getting there bit by bit.* 这是个缓慢的过程, 但我们正逐步向目标迈进。

9 a bit at a time *especially BrE* in several small parts, not all at the same time【尤英】一次一点儿: *Just do a bit at a time.* 一次就干一点儿。

10 ▶TOOL 工具◀ the sharp part of a tool for cutting or making holes〔工具的〕刀头; 钻头: *a drill bit* 钻头

11 ▶FOR A HORSE 给马用的◀ a metal bar that is put in the mouth of a horse and used for controlling its movements 马嚼子, 马衔 —see picture at 参见 HORSE[1] 图

12 ▶COMPUTER 电脑◀ the smallest unit of information that can be used by a computer 位, 比特, 位元〔电脑使用的最小信息单位〕: *a 16-bit processor* 16位处理器 —compare 比较 BYTE

13 a bit part a very small and unimportant acting job in a play or film 小角色, 配角: *He got a bit part in 'Coronation Street'.* 他在《加冕街》中扮演一个小角色。

14 bits and pieces/bits and bobs *BrE informal* any small things of various kinds【英, 非正式】各种零碎的小东西: *Let me get my bits and pieces together.* 让我把自己的零星杂物收拾好。| *I still had a few bits and bobs of work left to do.* 我还有一些零碎的工作要做。

15 do your bit *BrE informal* to do your share of the work that needs to be done【英, 非正式】尽自己的本分: *I don't mind doing my bit, but I'm not organizing the whole thing on my own.* 我并不介意尽自己的本分, 但整件事情都由我一个人来组织我不干。

16 get the bit between your teeth *BrE* to start doing something in a very determined way, so that you are not likely to stop until it is done【英】执意; 下定决心: *Once she'd got the bit between her teeth, there was no stopping her.* 她一旦下定决心要做某事, 什么也阻挡不了她。

17 take the bit between your teeth *AmE* to make a determined effort to deal with something difficult or unpleasant【美】下定决心处理棘手的事情; 全力以赴: *I just have to take the bit between my teeth and start writing that essay.* 我得狠下决心, 开始写那篇文章。

18 ▶US MONEY 美元◀ a) *AmE old use* $12\frac{1}{2}$ cents【美旧】12.5 美分: *I wouldn't give you two bits for that old book.* 我不会花 25 美分买你的那本旧书。—see also 另见 **two bits** (TWO (7)) **b)** *BrE old use* a small coin【英旧】小硬币: *a three-penny bit* 一枚三便士的硬币

19 ▶YOUNG WOMAN 年轻女子◀ also 又作 **a bit of stuff/fluff/skirt** *spoken* offensive expressions meaning a young woman, especially one who is sexually attractive【口】〔尤指性感的〕年轻女子, 小妞〔冒犯说法〕

20 a bit of all right *BrE informal* used to describe someone you think is sexually attractive【英, 非正式】风骚: *She's a bit of all right.* 她很风骚。

21 a bit on the side *BrE informal often humorous* the girlfriend or boyfriend of someone who is already married or involved in a sexual relationship with someone else【英, 非正式, 常幽默】情妇; 情夫 —see also 另见 **be champing at the bit** (CHAMP[1] (2)), **a bit of rough** (ROUGH[1] (17))

Frequencies of the noun **bit** in spoken and written English
名词bit在英语口语和书面语中的使用频率

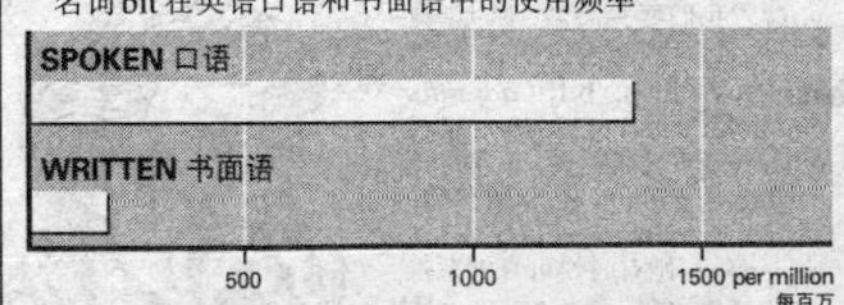

Based on the British National Corpus and the Longman Lancaster Corpus
据英国国家语料库和朗文兰开斯特语料库

This graph shows that the noun **bit** is much more common in spoken English than in written English. This is because **a bit** is more common than **a little** in spoken English, and **bit** is used in a lot of common spoken phrases. 本图表显示, 名词bit在英语

口语中的使用频率远远高于书面语，因为a bit在口语中比a little常用，而且口语中很多常用短语是由 bit 构成的。

bit (*n*) **SPOKEN PHRASES**
含 bit 的口语短语

22 a bit of a problem/surprise/fool etc *BrE* a problem, surprise etc, but not a very big or serious one【英】有点问题/吃惊/愚蠢等：*The party was a bit of a disappointment in the end.* 聚会最后变得有点儿令人失望。| *I had a bit of a shock when I got home.* 我回到家时感到有点儿震惊。| *I'm afraid I'm in a bit of a hurry just now – I'll give you a ring later.* 恐怕我现在有点急事 —— 我过一会儿再给你打电话。

23 with a bit of luck *especially BrE* if things go well and there are no problems【尤英】进展顺利的话：*With a bit of luck we should get it finished tomorrow.* 进展顺利的话，我们明天就能做完。

24 take a bit of doing/fixing etc *BrE* to be difficult to do, fix etc【英】难做/难修理等：*This new system takes a bit of getting used to, doesn't it?* 新体制一时还难以适应，对吧？

25 play the piano a bit/speak French a bit etc *BrE* to be able to play the piano, speak French etc, but not particularly well or often【英】会弹一点儿钢琴/会说一点儿法语等：*I used to act a bit when I was younger.* 我年轻的时候演过一点戏。

26 for a bit/in a bit *BrE* for or after a short period of time【英】一会儿/过一会儿：*Could you mind the baby for a bit?* 你能照顾婴儿一会儿吗？| *I'll see you in a bit then.* 那我们过一会儿见。

27 a bit much *BrE* used to say that something is not fair or reasonable【英】有点儿过分；不公平；不合理：*I thought it was a bit much, asking me to drive him all the way home.* 我认为他要我开车把他一路送到家是有点儿过分。

28 not a bit of it *especially BrE* used to say that something did not happen, even though you expected that it would【尤英】根本就没有〔做某事〕：*He should at least have apologized, but not a bit of it.* 他最起码应该道个歉，但他却毫无表示。

29 the student bit/travelling bit etc the behaviour or experience that is typical of a student, of travelling etc 典型的学生所为/典型的旅游经历等：*Then she gave us the concerned mother bit.* 那时候她给了我们母爱般的关怀。| *He's really gone in for the whole hippy bit.* 其实，他整个就是嬉皮士。

bit² the past tense of BITE¹

bitch¹ /bɪtʃ; bɪtʃ/ *n* [C] **1** a female dog 母狗 **2** *informal* an insulting word for a woman that you dislike or think is unpleasant【非正式】泼妇，臭婆娘，婊子：*She's such a bitch.* 她这个泼妇。| *The silly bitch went and told the police.* 那个蠢婆娘去报告了警察。**3** *AmE spoken* something that causes problems or difficulties【美口】讨厌的事：*I love that silk dress, but it's a bitch to wash.* 我很喜欢那条绸裙子，就是洗起来太麻烦了。—see also 另见 SON OF A BITCH

bitch² *v* [I] *informal*【非正式】**1** to make unpleasant remarks about someone or something 说坏话：**[+about]** *We were all bitching about the boss when she walked in.* 老板走进来的时候，我们正在说她的坏话。**2** to complain continuously 没完没了地发牢骚，埋怨：*Stop bitching!* 别再没完没了地发牢骚！| **[+at]** *AmE*【美】*He kept bitching at me for waking him up.* 他不停地埋怨我把他吵醒了。

bitch-in /ˈbɪtʃən; ˈbɪtʃən/ *adj AmE slang* very good; excellent【美俚】极好的，极棒的：*That's a bitchin car!* 那辆车真棒！| *"We're going to the beach, wanna come?" "Bitchin! Let's go!"* "我们要去海滩，你去吗？" "好极了！我们走吧！"

bite 咬

bitch-y /ˈbɪtʃɪ; ˈbɪtʃi/ *adj informal* unkind and unpleasant about other people【非正式】恶意的，坏心眼儿的：*a bitchy remark* 刻薄的话 | *She can be really bitchy sometimes.* 她有时候可真够恶毒。—**bitchily** *adv* —**bitchiness** *n* [U]

2 **bite¹** /baɪt; baɪt/ *v past tense* **bit** /bɪt; bɪt/ *past participle* **bitten** /ˈbɪtn; ˈbɪtn/

1 ▶WITH YOUR TEETH 用牙◀ [I,T] to cut or crush something with your teeth 咬：*Be careful! My dog bites.* 当心！我的狗咬人。| *Do you bite your fingernails?* 你咬指甲吗？| **[+into/through]** *biting into a juicy apple* 咬一口多汁的苹果 | *They had to bite through the rope to escape.* 他们得把绳子咬断才能逃脱。| **bite sth off** *a man whose arm had been bitten off by an alligator* 被钝吻鳄咬掉一只胳膊的男子

2 ▶INSECT/SNAKE 虫/蛇◀ [I,T] if an insect or snake bites you, it injures you by making a hole in your skin〔昆虫〕叮，蜇；〔蛇〕咬伤：*I was bitten all over by mosquitoes.* 我浑身都被蚊子叮了。

3 ▶FISH 鱼◀ [I] if a fish bites, it takes food from a hook and so gets caught 吞饵，上钩

4 ▶NOT SLIP 不滑◀ [I] to hold firmly to a surface, or rest firmly against it; GRIP² (1) 抓紧；卡紧；咬住：**[+into]** *The ski's edge should bite into the snow.* 滑雪板的边儿应该卡进雪里。

5 ▶HAVE AN EFFECT 有效◀ [I] to have the effect that was intended, especially an unpleasant one 达到预期的效果〔尤指不好的效果〕：*The new tobacco taxes have begun to bite.* 新的烟草税已开始叫人吃不消。

6 bite your tongue to try hard to stop yourself from saying what you really think 强忍住不说：*She was really making me angry, but I bit my tongue.* 她真的让我很生气，但我忍着不作声。

7 bite the dust a) to die, fail, or be defeated 死亡；失败；被击败：*a welfare programme that bit the dust following budget cuts* 削减预算后告吹的福利计划 **b)** to stop working completely 完全不好用；报废：*My old car's finally bitten the dust.* 我的老轿车终于报废了。

8 bite the bullet *informal* to bravely accept something unpleasant【非正式】咬紧牙关忍受痛苦；勇敢地面对：*Decisions have to be taken, and as director you have to bite the bullet.* 必须作出决定，而你作为主任，必须勇敢地面对现实。

9 bite sb's head off *informal* to answer someone or speak to them very angrily, when there is no good reason for doing this【非正式】发火；蛮横粗暴地说话[回答]：*I asked if she needed any help, and she bit my head off!* 我问她是否需要帮忙，她却对我很凶！

10 bite off more than you can chew to try to do more than you are able to do 试图承担力所不及的事

11 he/she won't bite *spoken* used to say that there is no need to be afraid of someone, especially someone in authority【口】不必怕他/她〔尤指权威人士〕：*Well go and ask him – he won't bite!* 去问问他 —— 不用怕他！

12 what's biting you/her etc? *spoken* used to ask why someone is annoyed or upset【口】什么事烦扰着你/她等？愁什么呢？

13 once bitten twice shy used to say that if you have failed or been hurt once, you will be very careful next time 一次吃亏，二次小心；一朝被蛇咬，十年怕井绳

14 bite the hand that feeds you to harm someone who has treated you well or supported you 恩将仇报；以怨报德

15 be bitten by the bug/craze etc to develop a very strong interest in or desire for something 热衷于，迷上：*By then she had been bitten by the travel bug, and could not wait to go again.* 那时候她迷上了旅游，巴不得马上再去一趟。

bite back *phr v* **1** [T **bite** sth ↔ **back**] to stop yourself from saying something or telling someone what you really feel 强忍着不说出来：*She bit back the insult that rose to her lips.* 她强忍着把到嘴边的难听话又咽了回去。**2** [I] to react strongly and angrily when someone criticizes you 回嘴；反唇相讥：*Determined to bite back at car thieves, he wired his Sierra Cosworth to an electric fence.* 他决心要对窃车贼进行反击，于是把他那辆塞拉－考斯沃思汽车用金属线接到电围栏上。

bite into sth *phr v* [T] to cut or press hard against a surface 咬进；陷进；砍入：*The knotted cord bit into my skin.* 那条打结的绳索勒进了我的皮肤。

bite² *n* 3

1 ▶WITH YOUR TEETH 用牙◀ [C] the act of cutting or crushing something with your teeth 咬（的动作）：**give sb a bite** *The cat gave Mike a playful bite.* 猫顽皮地咬了迈克一口。| **have/take a bite of** (=bite a small piece from a larger piece of food) 咬一口 *Can I have a bite of your apple?* 我咬一口你的苹果行吗？

2 ▶WOUND 伤◀ [C] a wound made when an animal or insect bites you 被咬[叮，蜇]的伤口：*My face was covered in mosquito bites!* 蚊子叮得我满脸是伤！

3 a bite (to eat) *spoken* a small meal【口】量少的一餐：*I haven't had a bite to eat all day.* 我从早到晚连一口东西都没有吃。| *Let's grab a bite at the airport.* 我们在机场吃点东西吧。

4 ▶COLD 冷◀ [singular] a feeling of coldness 冷意，寒意：*There's a real bite in the air tonight.* 今晚空气中真的带着一丝寒意。

5 ▶TASTE 味道◀ [U] a pleasantly sharp or bitter taste 辛辣；苦涩：*I like cheese with a bit of bite.* 我喜欢吃带点辣味的干酪。

6 ▶EFFECTIVENESS 效果◀ [U] a special quality in a piece of speech or writing that makes its arguments or criticisms effective and likely to persuade people〔演说或文章的〕犀利; 说服力: *a political satire that lacked bite* 语言并不尖刻的政治讽刺作品

7 ▶FISH 鱼◀ [C] an occasion when a fish takes the food from a hook 吞饵; 上钩: *Sometimes I sit for hours and never get a bite.* 有时我坐上几个钟头也没有一条鱼上钩。

8 **bite-size/bite-sized** the right size to fit into your mouth easily 很小的, 一口大小的: *Cut them into bite-size pieces before serving.* 先切成小块再端上桌。

9 **another bite/a second bite at the cherry** *BrE* a second chance to do something【英】第二次机会

bit·ing /ˈbaɪtɪŋ; ˈbaɪtɪŋ/ *adj* **1** a biting wind is unpleasantly cold 刺骨的: *A biting wind blew down from the hills.* 从山上吹来刺骨的寒风。**2** a biting criticism, remark is cruel or unkind 尖刻的: *biting sarcasm* 尖刻的讽刺 —**bitingly** *adv*

bit·map /ˈbɪtˌmæp; ˈbɪtmæp/ *n* [C] *technical* a computer image consisting of an arrangement of bits (BIT[1] (12))【术语】〔电脑〕位图, 位映像: *bitmap fonts* 位图字体

bit·sy /ˈbɪtsɪ; ˈbɪtsi/ *adj AmE informal* very small【美, 非正式】很小的, 一丁点儿的 —see also 另见 ITSY-BITSY

bit·ten /ˈbɪtn; ˈbɪtn/ the past participle of BITE[1]

bit·ter[1] /ˈbɪtɚ; ˈbɪtə/ *adj*

1 ▶ANGRY/UPSET 生气的/心烦的◀ full of angry, jealous, and unhappy feelings because you think you have been badly treated or that unfair things have happened to you 气愤的; 妒忌的; 郁闷的: *He became bitter and disillusioned as he grew older.* 随着年龄的增长, 他变得越来越愤愤不平, 不再抱任何幻想。| [+about] *They all lost their jobs when the company was taken over, and obviously they're very bitter about it.* 公司被接管后, 他们都失业了, 显然他们对此愤愤不平。

2 ▶CAUSING UNHAPPINESS 造成不愉快◀ [only before noun 仅用于名词前] making you feel very unhappy and upset 痛苦的; 心酸的; 惨痛的; 难以接受的: *Losing the election was a bitter humiliation.* 选举失利是个奇耻大辱。| **a bitter disappointment/blow** *If he failed, it would be a bitter disappointment to his parents.* 如果他失败了, 他的父母将会大失所望。| **from bitter experience** (=because of your own very unpleasant experiences) 有过惨痛的教训 *We had learned from bitter experience not to trust their promises.* 我们有过惨痛的教训, 不再相信他们的承诺。

3 ▶FULL OF HATRED 充满仇恨◀ a bitter argument, attack, struggle etc is one in which people oppose or criticize each other with strong feelings of hate and anger 激烈的; 讽刺的; 充满敌意的; 怨愤的: *bitter opposition to the President's policies* 对总统的政策的激烈反对 | *bitter enemies* 不共戴天之敌

4 ▶TASTE 味道◀ having a strong taste like black coffee without sugar, or very dark chocolate 苦的, 有苦味的: *The medicine tasted bitter and the child spat it out.* 这药太苦, 孩子把它吐了出来。—compare 比较 SWEET[1] (1), SOUR[1] (1)

5 ▶COLD 冷◀ unpleasantly cold 刺骨的, 寒冷的: *a bitter east wind* 寒冷的东风 | **bitter cold** *a bitter cold day in February* 二月里寒冷彻骨的一天 —see 见 COLD[1] (USAGE)

6 **to the bitter end** continuing until the end, in spite of problems or difficulties 坚持到底; 拼到底: *She stayed with him to the bitter end, although it must have been horrible.* 她和他始终待在一起, 尽管这样做肯定很不好受。

7 **a bitter pill (to swallow)** something very unpleasant that you have to accept 不得不接受的现实; 不得不忍受的耻辱: *His failure was a bitter pill to swallow.* 他的失败是个难以吞咽的苦果。—see also 另见 BITTERLY —**bitterness** *n* [U]

bitter[2] *n* **1** [C,U] *BrE* bitter beer of the type drunk in Britain, or a glass of this【英】(一杯) 苦啤酒: *A pint of bitter, please.* 请来一品脱苦啤酒。—compare 比较 MILD **2 bitters** [U] a bitter liquid made from a mixture of plant products and used to add taste to alcoholic drinks〔掺入酒精饮料中的〕苦味配剂

bit·ter·ly /ˈbɪtɚlɪ; ˈbɪtəli/ *adv* **1** in a way that makes you very unhappy, or shows that you are very unhappy 痛苦地; 愤恨地: *The boys complained bitterly about their chores.* 男孩们愤愤不平地抱怨要做家务。| *I was bitterly disappointed.* 我非常失望。| *a decision that she bitterly regretted* 一个令她痛悔不已的决定 **2 bitterly cold** very cold 极其寒冷的

bit·tern /ˈbɪtɚn; ˈbɪtən/ *n* [C] a brown European bird with long legs that lives near water and makes a deep sound 麻鳽〔产于欧洲的褐色长腿水鸟〕

bit·ter·sweet /ˌbɪtɚˈswit; ˌbɪtəˈswiːt◂/ *adj* **1** feelings, memories, or experiences that are bittersweet are happy and sad at the same time 苦乐参半的: *bittersweet memories of childhood* 对童年时代甜蜜而又辛酸的回忆 **2** a taste or smell that is bittersweet is both sweet and bitter at the same time 甜中带苦的

bit·ty /ˈbɪtɪ; ˈbɪti/ *adj BrE informal* having too many small parts that do not seem to be connected to each other【英, 非正式】零碎的, 东拼西凑的, 不连贯的: *I thought the film was rather bitty.* 我认为那部影片有点儿七拼八凑。—**bittiness** *n* [U]

bi·tu·men /bəˈtumən; ˈbɪtʃʊmɪn/ *n* [U] a sticky substance made from petrol products that is used for making the surface of roads 沥青, 柏油 —**bituminous** /bɪˈtjumənəs; bɪˈtjuːmɪnəs/ *adj*

bi·valve /ˈbaɪˌvælv; ˈbaɪvælv/ *n* [C] *technical* any sea animal that has two shells joined together, such as an OYSTER【术语】双壳贝类〈如牡蛎〉

biv·ou·ac[1] /ˈbɪvuˌæk; ˈbɪvu-æk/ *n* a temporary camp built outside without any tents〔无帐篷的〕露营 (地), 野营 (地)

bivouac[2] *v* **bivouacked, bivouacking** [I] to spend the night outside without tents in a temporary camp 露宿: *The climbers bivouacked halfway up the mountain.* 登山者在半山腰上露营过夜。

bi·week·ly /baɪˈwiklɪ; baɪˈwiːkli/ *adj, adv* **1** appearing or happening every two weeks; FORTNIGHTLY 两周一次的[地]: *a biweekly magazine* 双周刊 **2** appearing or happening twice a week; SEMIWEEKLY 一周两次的[地]: *a biweekly television drama* 一周两次播出的电视剧

biz /bɪz; bɪz/ *n* [singular] *informal* a particular type of business, especially one connected with entertainment【非正式】〔尤指与娱乐业有关的〕商业; 生意

bi·zarre /bɪˈzɑr; bɪˈzɑː/ *adj* very unusual or strange 古怪的; 奇异的: *a bizarre coincidence* 奇异的巧合 | *bizarre religious sects* 奇特的宗教派别 —**bizarrely** *adv*

Bizet /biˈze; biːˈzeɪ/, **Georges** (1838-75) a French COMPOSER best known for his OPERAS, which include *Carmen* and *The Pearl Fishers.* 比才〔(1838-1875), 法国作曲家, 以歌剧最为著名, 包括《卡门》和《采珠者》〕

blab /blæb; blæb/ *v* [I] *informal* to tell secret information to someone who is not supposed to know it【非正式】泄露秘密: [+to] *What if they blab to the newspapers?* 如果他们把消息透露给报社该怎么办?

blab·ber /ˈblæbɚ; ˈblæbə/ *v* [I] *informal* to talk in a silly or annoying way, especially for a long time【非正式】瞎说, 胡扯; 喋喋不休: [+on] *I wish she'd stop blabbering on about her boyfriends.* 我真希望她别再没完没了地讲她那些男朋友的事。

blab·ber·mouth /ˈblæbɚˌmaυθ; ˈblæbəmaυθ/ *n* [C] *informal* someone who tells secrets because they always talk too much【非正式】饶舌者; 嘴巴不严的人; 泄露秘密者

black[1] /blæk; blæk/ *adj*

1 ▶COLOUR 颜色◀ having the colour of night or coal 黑色的, 黑的: *a black evening dress* 黑色的晚礼服 | *The mountains looked black against the moon.* 在月光的衬托下, 群山看上去黑乎乎的。| *She has short black hair.* 她留着黑色的短发。—see picture on page A5 参见 A5 页图

2 ▶PEOPLE 人◀ **a)** someone who is black is a member of a dark-skinned race, especially the Negro race 黑人血统的, 黑种的: *Over half the students here are black.* 这里的学生超过一半是黑人。**b)** [only before noun 仅用于名词前] connected with or concerning black people 黑人的, 与黑人有关的: *politics from a black perspective* 黑人的政治见解 | *contemporary black music* 当代黑人音乐 —see 见 NEGRO (USAGE)

3 ▶TEA/COFFEE 茶/咖啡◀ black coffee or tea does not have milk in it 不加奶的: *Two black coffees, please.* 来两杯不加奶的咖啡。—opposite 反义词 WHITE[1] (4)

4 ▶DIRTY 脏的◀ very dirty 黑乎乎的, 脏的: *My hands were black from working on the car.* 我在修车, 手弄得很脏。

5 ▶WITHOUT HOPE 没有希望◀ sad and without much hope for the future; GLOOMY 无希望的; 情况不妙的; 前景暗淡的: *Things were beginning to look pretty black for us.* 看来情况开始对我们有些不妙。| *a feeling of black despair* 感到大失所望 | **a black day** (=when something very sad or upsetting happens) 极糟糕的一天, 极倒霉的一天 *It's been another black day for the motor industry, with announcements of major job losses.* 这天对汽车工业来说又是一个极为糟糕的日子, 许多工厂宣布大规模裁员。

6 ▶ANGRY 生气的◀ full of feelings of anger or hate 怒气冲冲的; 充满仇恨的: *I knew not to irritate him when he was in such a black mood.* 他正在气头上, 我知道不该去惹他。| *Denise gave me a black look.* 丹尼斯恶狠狠地瞪了我一眼。

7 **not be as black as you are painted** not be as bad as people say you are 并不像人们所说的那样坏

8 ▶**EVIL** 罪恶◀ *literary* very bad【文】非常坏的: *black deeds* 恶行 | *a blackhearted villain* 心肠狠毒的恶棍 —see also 另见 BLACKLY —**blackness** *n* [C]

black² *n* 1 [U] the dark colour of night or coal 黑色

CULTURAL NOTE 文化注释

In the US and UK, people traditionally wear black clothes when they go to a funeral, as a sign of sadness. In some old stories and films, especially WESTERNS, the bad character wears black clothes, and the good character wears white clothes. 英美人参加葬礼常着黑色衣服以示悲伤。旧时的一些故事或电影中，尤其在西部片中，坏蛋穿黑色衣服，好人穿白色衣服。

2 [U] black clothes 黑色的衣服: *You look good in black.* 你穿黑色衣服挺好看。3 [C] someone who belongs to a dark-skinned race, especially the Negro race 黑人: *laws that discriminated against blacks* 歧视黑人的法律 —see 见 NEGRO (USAGE) 4 **be in the black** to have money in your bank account〔银行存款〕有盈余，有余额 —opposite 反义词 **be in the red** (RED² (5)) 5 [U] black paint, colour etc 黑色的染料[颜料等]: *Put some more black around your eyes.* 在你的眼圈上再涂些黑色眼影。

black³ *v* [T] 1 *BrE* if a TRADE UNION blacks goods or blacks a company, it refuses to work with them【英】〔指工会〕抵制，杯葛〔货物、公司等〕2 *old-fashioned* to make something black【过时】使变黑，弄黑

black out *v* 1 [I] to lose consciousness; faint 失去知觉; 昏厥: *I completely blacked out after the accident.* 事故发生后，我完全失去了知觉。2 [T **black** sth ↔ **out**] to put a dark mark over something so that it cannot be seen 盖住; 涂黑: *The censors had blacked out several words.* 审查员涂掉了几个词。3 [T **black** sth ↔ **out**] to hide or turn off all the lights in a town or city, especially during war〔尤指战时〕对〔城镇或城市〕实行灯火管制 —see also 另见 BLACKOUT

Black, Conrad /ˈkɑnræd; ˈkɒnræd/ (1940-) a Canadian businessman, whose company owns more than 500 newspapers in various countries, including *The Daily Telegraph* in the UK and *The Chicago Sun Times* in the US 布莱克〔(1940-)，加拿大商人，他的公司拥有不同国家的500余种报纸，包括英国的《每日电讯报》和美国的《芝加哥太阳时报》〕

Black Af·ri·ca /ˌ·ˈ···/ the part of Africa below the Sahara Desert, where most of the people are black 黑非洲〔指撒哈拉沙漠以南的非洲地区，居民以黑人为主〕

black·a·moor /ˈblækəˌmur; ˈblækəmʊə/ *n* [C] *old use* an offensive word for a black person, especially a man【旧】黑人〔冒犯用语，尤指男子〕

black and blue /ˌ· ·ˈ·◂/ *adj* skin that is black and blue has BRUISES (=dark marks) in it as a result of being hit〔皮肤被打得〕青一块紫一块的; 有瘀痕的: *Ron's been skiing. He's black and blue all over!* 罗恩滑雪去了，浑身上下摔得青一块紫一块。

Black and Tans, the /ˌ· ·ˈ·/ a British military force that was active in Ireland from 1918 to 1920, opposing the people who were fighting for independence 黑与棕，爱尔兰王室警吏团〔1918年至1920年活跃在爱尔兰的一支英国军事力量，镇压当地争取独立的民众〕

black and white /ˌ· · ˈ·◂/ *adj* 1 showing pictures or images only in black, white, and grey〔图像或影片〕黑白的: *a black and white photo* 黑白照片 | *an old black and white TV* 一台旧的黑白电视机 2 considering things in a very simple way, as if there are clear differences between good and bad, right and wrong etc 非黑即白的; 绝对化的: *a rather black and white presentation of the situtation* 对形势用简单的非好即坏的观点进行的介绍 | **a black and white decision/issue/question** (=where the difference between two choices is completely clear) 绝对化[黑白分明]的决定/问题 3 **in black and white** in written form, and therefore definite 白纸黑字(写得清清楚楚); 以书面形式: *You'd better get a commitment in black and white first.* 你最好先得到一份书面形式的承诺。| *There it was in black and white – I'd passed the exam!* 白纸黑字写着呢 — 我考试及格了!

black art /ˌ·ˈ·/ *n* [U] also 又作 **the black arts** [plural] BLACK MAGIC 巫术; 魔法

black·ball /ˈblækˌbɔl; ˈblækbɔːl/ *v* [T] to vote against someone, especially so that they cannot join a club or social group 投票反对〔某人〕参加某俱乐部[社会组织]; 排挤

Black Beau·ty /ˌ·ˈ··/ the name of the horse that is the main character in the children's book *Black Beauty* (1877) by Anna Sewell 黑美人〔安娜·休厄尔的儿童读物《黑美人》(1877) 中的主角，为一匹马〕

black belt /ˌ·ˈ·/ *n* [C] 1 a high rank in some types of Eastern self-defence, especially JUDO and KARATE 黑腰带级〔柔道、空手道等的最高等级〕2 someone who has this rank 黑带选手: *Sandy's a blackbelt in judo.* 桑迪是柔道黑带选手。

black·ber·ry /ˈblækˌbɛrɪ; ˈblækbəri/ *n* [C] the black or purple fruit of a type of BRAMBLE 黑莓 —see picture on page A8 参见A8页图

black·ber·ry·ing /ˈblækˌbɛrɪ·ɪŋ; ˈblækbəri-ɪŋ/ *n* [U] **go blackberrying** to go out picking blackberries 去采黑莓

black·bird /ˈblækˌbɜd; ˈblækbɜːd/ *n* [C] a common European and American bird, the male of which is completely black 黑唱鸫，黑鹂〔产于欧洲及美洲，其雄鸟遍体黑色〕

black·board /ˈblækˌbɔrd; ˈblækbɔːd/ *n* [C] a board with a dark smooth surface, used in schools for writing on with CHALK¹ (2) 黑板 —compare 比较 WHITEBOARD

black box /ˌ·ˈ·/ *n* [C] an electronic unit that controls or records information about a machine, especially on an aircraft; FLIGHT RECORDER〔尤指飞机的〕黑匣子，飞行记录器

black com·e·dy /ˌ·ˈ···/ *n* [C,U] a play, story etc that is funny, but also shows the unpleasant side of human life 黑色喜剧

Black Coun·try, the /ˈ·ˌ··/ an industrial area in the West Midlands of England 黑乡〔英格兰中部偏西地区一工业区〕

black·cur·rant /ˌblækˈkɜənt; ˌblækˈkʌrənt◂/ *n* [C] 1 a European plant that grows in gardens and has small blueblack berries (BERRY) 黑醋栗，黑加仑子 2 a berry from this plant 黑醋栗豆，黑加仑子果实: *blackcurrant juice* 黑加仑子汁 —compare 比较 REDCURRANT

Black Death /ˌ·ˈ·/ *n* [singular] the illness that killed large numbers of people in Europe and Asia in the 14th century 黑死病〔14世纪在欧亚蔓延的瘟疫〕—see also 另见 BUBONIC PLAGUE, PLAGUE¹ (2)

black e·con·o·my /ˌ·ˈ····/ *n* [singular] business activity that takes place unofficially, especially in order to avoid tax 地下经济活动，黑市经营〔指为逃避税收而暗中进行的经济活动〕—compare 比较 BLACK MARKET

black·en /ˈblækən; ˈblækən/ *v* 1 [I,T] to become black, or make something black (使)变黑; 把…弄黑: *Smoke had blackened the ceiling of the room.* 烟把房间的天花板熏黑了。2 **blacken sb's name/character/reputation etc** to say unpleasant things about someone in order to make other people have a bad opinion of them 玷污某人的名声/品德/声誉等

Black Eng·lish /ˌ·ˈ··/ *n* [U] the variety of English spoken by some black people in the US 黑人英语〔某些美国黑人讲的英语〕

black eye /ˌ·ˈ·/ *n* [C] darkness of the skin around your eye, because you have been hit〔被打成〕青黑色的眼眶: *Joe came home with a black eye.* 乔带着青黑色的眼眶回家来。

black-eyed bean /ˌ··ˈ·/ *BrE*【英】, **black-eyed pea** *AmE*【美】*n* [C] a small pale bean with a black spot on it 黑眼豆，豇豆

black-eyed Su·san /ˌblæk aɪd ˈsuzn; ˌblæk aɪd ˈsuːzən/ *n* [C] a type of yellow or orange flower that grows in North America〔花朵中心呈黑色的〕金光菊

Black For·est, the /ˌ·ˈ··◂/ an area of southwest Germany where there is a very large forest 黑森林〔德国西南部一处大森林〕

Black Forest Gat·eau /ˌ··ˈ··ˈ·/ *BrE* a cake made with chocolate, cherries (CHERRY), and cream【英】黑森林蛋糕〔一种用巧克力、樱桃和奶油做成的蛋糕〕

black gold /ˌ·ˈ·/ *n* [U] *informal* oil【非正式】石油

black goods /ˈ· ·/ *n* [plural] *BrE* pieces of equipment used in the house that are usually black, such as televisions or HI-FIS【英】黑色家用设备〈如电视、音响等〉—compare 比较 WHITE GOODS

black·guard /ˈblægəd; ˈblægɑːd/ *n* [C] *old use* a man who treats other people very badly; SCOUNDREL【旧】恶棍，流氓，无赖

black·head /ˈblækˌhɛd; ˈblækhed/ *n* [C] a small spot on the skin, with a black centre 黑头粉刺

Black Hills, the /ˌ·ˈ·/ a group of hills in South Dakota in the US, one of which is Mount Rushmore 布莱克丘陵〔位于美国南达科他州的小山群，其中之一是拉什莫尔山〕

black hole /ˌ·ˈ·/ *n* [C] 1 *technical* an area in outer space into which everything near it, including light, is pulled【术语】黑洞 2 *informal* something that seems to keep using up all your money【非正式】无底洞〔指极耗费金钱的事物〕

Black Hole of Cal·cut·ta, the /ˌ··, ··ˈ··/ a small room used as a prison in Calcutta, India. In 1756, 146 British prisoners were put into it, and most of them died in one night.

People sometimes say that a small very crowded room or dark place is "like the Black Hole of Calcutta". 加尔各答黑牢〔印度加尔各答的一座小型监狱。1756年, 146名英国罪犯被囚禁于此, 多数罪犯一夜之间死去。人们有时会把拥挤的小房间或漆黑的地方说成是"像加尔各答黑牢一样"〕

black hu·mour /ˌ· ˈ··/ *n* [U] jokes, funny stories etc that deal with the unpleasant parts of human life 黑色幽默

black ice /ˌ· ˈ·/ *n* [U] an area of ice that is very difficult to see 黑冰: *dangerous driving conditions, with black ice in many areas* 遍地是黑冰的驾驶危险的路面情况

black·ing /ˈblækɪŋ; ˈblækɪŋ/ *n* [U] *old-fashioned* a very thick liquid or polish that is put on objects to make them black【过时】黑色涂料

black·jack /ˈblækˌdʒæk; ˈblækdʒæk/ *n* [U] a card game 二十一点(牌戏)

Black Lace /ˌ· ˈ·/ one of a British series of romantic NOVEL*s*, written mainly for women, which contain a lot of sexual detail《黑色蕾丝》〔英国系列浪漫小说之一, 主要写给女性读者, 含有大量详细的性描写〕—compare 比较 MILLS AND BOON

black lead /ˌblæk ˈlɛd; ˌblæk ˈled/ *n* [U] a soft black substance; GRAPHITE 石墨, 炭精, 黑铅

black·leg /ˈblækˌlɛg; ˈblækleg/ *n* [C] *BrE* someone who continues to work when other workers are on strike (STRIKE[2] (1))【英】罢工期间继续上班的人; 拒不参加罢工者; 工贼

black·list[1] /ˈblækˌlɪst; ˈblækˌlɪst/ *n* [C] a list of people, countries, products etc that are disapproved of, and should therefore be avoided or punished 黑名单: *Friends of the Earth have produced a blacklist of environmentally damaging products.* "地球之友"已经开列了一份破坏环境的产品的黑名单。

blacklist[2] *v* [T] to put a person, country, product etc on a blacklist 将…列入黑名单: *I've been blacklisted by the insurance companies just because of one silly accident!* 仅仅由于一次糊涂的事故, 保险公司已将我列入黑名单!

black lung /ˌ· ˈ·/ *n* [U] *AmE informal* a lung disease caused by breathing in coal dust over a long period of time【美, 非正式】黑肺病, 煤肺病〔因长期吸入煤尘而导致的肺病〕

black·ly /ˈblæklɪ; ˈblækli/ *adv literary* in an angry, threatening, or unpleasant way【文】阴险地; 气冲冲地; 恶狠狠地: *clouds blackly looming* 阴云密布

black mag·ic /ˌ· ˈ··/ *n* [U] magic that is believed to use the power of the Devil for evil purposes 巫术; 魔法 —see also 另见 WHITE MAGIC

black·mail[1] /ˈblækˌmel; ˈblækmeɪl/ *v* [T] to demand money or favours from someone by threatening to tell secrets about them 敲诈; 勒索; 讹诈: **blackmail sb into doing sth** *Don't think you can blackmail me into helping you!* 不要以为你能要挟我来帮你! —**blackmailer** *n* [C]

blackmail[2] *n* [U] **1** the practice of getting money from someone or making them do what you want by threatening to tell secrets about them 敲诈; 勒索; 讹诈 **2** an attempt to make someone do what you want by making threats or by making them feel guilty if they do not 威逼; 恐吓; 挟人就范: *Staff who refused to work on Sundays faced losing their jobs – it was sheer blackmail.* 拒绝星期天上班的员工要面临失业的危险 —— 这纯粹是要挟。| **emotional blackmail** (=by making someone feel guilty) 用感情手段进行的威逼 *She had already tried emotional blackmail to stop him leaving.* 她已经尝试了用感情手段阻止他离开。

black Ma·ri·a /ˌblæk məˈraɪə; ˌblæk məˈraɪə/ *n* [C] *BrE old-fashioned* a vehicle used by the police to move prisoners【英, 过时】囚车

black mar·ket /ˌ· ˈ··◂/ *n* [C] the system by which people illegally buy and sell foreign money, goods that are difficult to obtain etc 黑市(交易): [+in] *There's a thriving black market in vehicle parts.* 汽车零件的黑市交易很兴隆。| **on the black market** *The exchange rate for dollars was much higher on the black market.* 黑市上美元的兑换价高得多。| *black market cigarettes* 黑市香烟 —compare 比较 BLACK ECONOMY

black mar·ket·eer /ˌ· ˌ··ˈ·/ *n* [C] someone who sells things on the black market 黑市商人

Black Mass /ˌ· ˈ·/ *n* [C,U] a ceremony performed by people who pray to the Devil, parts of which are similar to the ceremonies performed by Christians 黑弥撒〔敬拜魔鬼者举行的一种祈祷仪式, 部分礼拜仪式与基督教徒的礼拜仪式相似〕

Black Mon·day /ˌ· ˈ··/ **1** Monday, 19 October 1987, the day on which share prices on the STOCK EXCHANGE suddenly fell by a large amount, and many people lost a lot of money 黑色星期一〔1987年10月19日(星期一), 股票价格暴跌, 许多投资人损失惨重〕 **2** Monday, 28 October 1929, the day on which share prices on the STOCK EXCHANGE suddenly fell by a large amount, leading to the Great Depression of the 1930s 黑色星期一〔1929年10月28日(星期一), 股票价格暴跌, 引发了20世纪30年代的大萧条〕

Black Mus·lim /ˌ· ˈ··/ *n* [C] a member of a group of black people who believe in the religion of Islam and want a separate black society 黑人穆斯林〔指信奉伊斯兰教并要建立独立黑人社会的黑人组织成员〕

black·out /ˈblækˌaut; ˈblækaʊt/ *n* [C] **1** a period of darkness caused by a failure of the electricity supply 停电: *The storm caused a sudden blackout and brought down telephone lines.* 风暴导致突然间停电, 电话线也刮断了。**2** a period during a war when all the lights in a town etc must be turned off〔战时的〕灯火管制 **3** an occasion when you suddenly lose consciousness 突然间的知觉丧失: *You'll have to go to the doctor if you keep getting these blackouts.* 如果你经常突然间失去知觉, 就必须去看医生。**4** a situation in which particular pieces of news or information are not allowed to be reported〔新闻的〕封锁;〔对报道等的〕删除: *A news blackout was imposed during the peace negotiations.* 在和谈期间实施新闻封锁。

Black Pan·thers, the /ˌ· ˈ··/ also 又作 **the Black Panther Party** a group of black people in the US in the 1960s and 1970s, who supported the use of violence to get better treatment for black people 黑豹党〔20世纪60、70年代的一个美国黑人团体, 主张采取暴力手段改善黑人的待遇〕

black pep·per /ˌ· ˈ··/ *n* [U] pepper made from crushed seeds from which the dark outer covering has not been removed 黑胡椒(粉)

Black·pool /ˈblækpul; ˈblækpuːl/ a popular holiday town on the northwest coast of England. Blackpool is famous for its tower (the Blackpool Tower) and ILLUMINATION*s* (=attractive coloured lights). 布莱克浦〔英格兰西北沿海一镇, 为著名度假胜地, 以布莱克浦塔及漂亮灯饰闻名〕

Black Prince /ˌ· ˈ·/, **Edward the** (1330-76) the oldest son of King Edward III of England, who wore black ARMOUR in battle 黑王子〔(1330-1376), 英格兰国王爱德华三世的长子, 作战时身着黑色盔甲〕

black pud·ding /ˌ· ˈ··/ *n* [C,U] *BrE* a kind of thick dark SAUSAGE made from animal blood and fat【英】血肠〔用动物的血和脂肪制成的粗黑香肠〕

> **CULTURAL NOTE 文化注释**
> Black pudding is connected in people's minds with the north of England, where it is popular, especially with WORKING-CLASS people. 血肠常令人联想到英格兰北部, 那里血肠很受欢迎, 在工人阶级中尤其如此。

Black Rod /ˌ· ˈ·/ the title of one of the officials who takes part in the ceremony for opening the British Parliament each year. His job is to go to the House of Commons and tell its members to come to the House of Lords so that they can hear the Queen's speech. 黑杖侍卫〔参加英国议会年度开幕式的礼仪官的头衔, 其职责是召唤下议院议员去上议院聆听女王的演讲〕

Black Sash /ˌ· ˈ·/ an organization of South African women that was started in 1955 to protest against APARTHEID (=the system in which black people had few political rights, and black and white people had to live in different areas) 黑绶带组织〔南非一个反对种族隔离的妇女组织, 创立于1955年〕

Black Sea, the /ˌ· ˈ·/ a large sea that is surrounded by land, and is between Turkey, Bulgaria, Romania, Ukraine, Russia, and Georgia 黑海〔位于土耳其、保加利亚、罗马尼亚、乌克兰、俄罗斯和格鲁吉亚之间的内陆海〕

black sheep /ˌ· ˈ·/ *n* [C usually singular 一般用单数] someone who is regarded by other members of their family or group as a failure or embarrassment 害群之马;〔集体中的〕败类: *She's the black sheep of the family.* 她是个败家子。

Black·shirt /ˈblækˌʃɝt; ˈblækʃɜːt/ *n* [C] a member of a FASCIST organization with a black shirt as part of its uniform〔法西斯组织〕黑衫党党员

black·smith /ˈblækˌsmɪθ; ˈblækˌsmɪθ/ *n* [C] someone who makes and repairs things made of iron, especially HORSESHOE*s* 铁匠, 锻工〔尤指马蹄铁匠〕

black spot /ˈ· ·/ *n* [C] *especially BrE*【尤英】**1** part of a road where accidents often happen 交通事故多发路段, 交通黑点: *an accident black spot* 交通黑点 **2** a place or area where there are more problems than usual 经常出乱子的地区: *the worst unemployment black spots* 失业问题最严重的地区

black·strap mo·las·ses /ˌblækstræp məˈlæsɪz; ˌblækstræp məˈlæsɪz/ *n* [U] *AmE* the darkest, thickest MOLASSES

B

(=thick sweet liquid) produced when sugar is taken from sugar plants【美】赤糖糊

black·thorn /ˈblækˌθɔrn; ˈblækθɔːn/ *n* [C] a European bush that has small white flowers 黑刺李〔一种开白色小花的欧洲灌木〕

black-tie /ˌ· ˈ·◂/ *adj* a black-tie party or social occasion is one at which people wear EVENING DRESS (=special formal clothes)〔社交场合〕穿晚礼服的: *Jan and George are having a party – it's black-tie.* 简和乔治要参加一个必须穿晚礼服的聚会。—compare 比较 WHITE-TIE

black·top /ˈblækˌtɑp; ˈblæktɒp/ *n AmE*【美】**1** [U] a thick black sticky substance that becomes hard as it dries, used to cover roads; BITUMEN 沥青, 柏油 **2** [singular] the surface of a road covered by this substance 铺沥青的路面: *We left the blacktop and drove along a forest road.* 我们离开了柏油路, 沿着一条森林小路行驶。

Black Watch, the /ˌ· ˈ·/ an unofficial name for the Royal Highland Regiment, a large group of soldiers that are part of the British Army and are based in Scotland 黑色警卫〔英国皇家陆军苏格兰高地警卫团的俗称〕

black wa·ter fe·ver /ˌ· ·· ˈ··/ *n* [U] a very severe form of the disease MALARIA 黑尿热〔一种严重疟疾〕

black wid·ow /ˌ· ˈ··/ *n* [C] a very poisonous type of SPIDER that is black with red marks 黑寡妇蜘蛛〔一种毒性极大的蜘蛛〕

blad·der /ˈblædɚ; ˈblædə/ *n* [C] **1** an organ of the body, that is shaped like a bag and contains URINE (=waste liquid from the body) until it is passed out of the body 膀胱 **2** a bag of skin, leather, or rubber, for example inside a football, that can be filled with air or liquid〔可充气或充水的〕囊; 袋 —see also 另见 GALL BLADDER

blade /bled; bleɪd/ *n* [C] **1** the flat cutting part of a tool or weapon 刀刃; 刀锋; 刀片; 刀身: *Keep the blade of your penknife sharp.* 让你的小折刀刀刃保持锋利。| *a packet of razor blades* 一小盒剃刀刀片 —see picture at 参见 TOOL[1] and 及 SWORD 图 **2** the flat wide part of an object that pushes against air or water 桨叶; 螺旋桨叶; 叶片状物: *the blade of an oar* 桨叶 | *a ceiling fan with polished blades* 带有精致叶片的吊扇 **3** a long flat leaf of grass or a similar plant〔狭长而扁平的〕草叶; 叶片: *a blade of grass* 草叶 **4** the metal part on the bottom of an ICE SKATE〔溜冰鞋的〕冰刀 —see also 另见 SHOULDER BLADE

Blade Run·ner /ˈ· ˌ··/ (1982) a US film by the director Ridley Scott, in which a policeman in Los Angeles in the year 2019 has to find and kill a group of intelligent machines that look exactly like people《银翼杀手》〔(1982), 莱德利·斯科特导演的一部美国影片, 讲述 2019 年洛杉矶的一名警察奉命寻找并摧毁一群智慧型机器人的故事〕

blag /blæg; blæg/ *v* [I,T] *BrE slang* to obtain something you want by talking in a clever way【英俚】通过花言巧语得到好处; 巧妙地得到: *He blagged his way in by saying he was a friend of the owner.* 他自称是业主的一位朋友, 从而巧妙地混了进去。

blah[1] /blɑ; blɑː/ *n* [U] **1 blah, blah, blah** *spoken* used when you do not need to complete what you are saying because it is boring or because the person you are talking to already knows it【口】诸如此类的等等: *The answer to question 3, 'which South American country has blah, blah, blah?' is Argentina.* 第三题 "哪个南美洲国家有什么什么?" 的答案是阿根廷。**2** *BrE spoken* remarks or statements that are boring and do not mean much【英口】废话; 乏味的话语: *the usual blah about everyone working harder* 要大家都努力干的陈词滥调

blah[2] *adj AmE spoken*【美口】**1** not having an interesting taste, appearance, character etc 枯燥的; 单调的; 乏味的: *The decor of the house was kind of blah.* 这幢房子布置得有点单调。**2** slightly unwell or unhappy 不舒服的; 不愉快的: *I feel really blah today.* 今天我真的有点不舒服。

Blair /blɛr; bleə/**, Tony** (1953-) a British politician who became leader of the Labour Party in 1994, and Prime Minister in 1997. He won a large victory again in the election in 2001, becoming the first Labour Prime Minister to win two full terms in power, one after the other. 布莱尔〔(1953-), 英国政治家, 1994 年成为工党领袖, 1997 年当选英国首相。2001 年大选再次高票当选, 成为工党第一位连任两届的首相〕

Blake /blek; bleɪk/**, William** (1757-1827) a British poet and artist whose work is an example of Romanticism, and whose best-known poems are in Songs of Innocence and Songs of Experience 布莱克〔(1757-1827), 英国浪漫主义诗人和艺术家, 最著名的诗作是《天真之歌》和《经验之歌》〕

blame[1] /blem; bleɪm/ *v* [T] **1** to say or think that someone or something is responsible for something bad 责怪, 指责; 把…归咎于: *It's not fair to blame me – it's not my fault we lost.* 责怪我是不公平的——我们输了又不是我的错。| **blame sb/sth for** *Mom blamed herself for Danny's problems.* 丹尼出了问题, 妈妈把责任归咎于自己。| *The report blames poor safety standards for the accident.* 报告把事故的起因归咎于没能达到安全标准。| **blame sth on** *Don't go trying to blame it on me!* 别想赖我! | **be to blame** (=be responsible for something bad) 应(为…)承担责任; 该(因…)受到责备 *You're not to blame for what happened.* 发生这种事情不能怪你。**2 don't blame me** *spoken* used when you are advising someone not to do something【口】不要怪我〔用于劝告某人不要做某事〕: *Buy it then, but don't blame me when it breaks down.* 那就买下吧, 可是坏了别怪我。**3 I don't blame you/them etc** *spoken* used to say that you think it was right or reasonable for someone to do what they did【口】我理解某人的做法: *"She's left her husband." "I don't blame her, after the way he treated her."* "她离开她的丈夫了。" "他那样对待她, 也难怪她这样做。" **4 only have yourself to blame** *spoken* used to say that someone's problems are their own fault【口】只能怪你自己: *If he fails his exams, he'll only have himself to blame.* 如果他考试不及格, 那只能怪他自己。**5** to criticize someone or something 批评; 责难: **blame sb/sth for** *The documentary was blamed for its one-sided presentation of the strike.* 人们纷纷批评那部纪录片只片面地反映了这场罢工。

blame[2] *n* [U] responsibility for a mistake or for something bad〔对错误或坏事应负的〕责任: **[+for]** *The government cannot escape blame for the state of the economy.* 对于当前的经济现状, 政府难逃其责。| **get the blame** (=be blamed) 受到责难 *I always get the blame for his mistakes!* 我总是因他的错误而背黑锅! | **take the blame** (=say that something is your fault) 承担责任 *You can't expect Terry to take all the blame.* 你不能指望特里承担全部责任。| **put/lay the blame on** (=say that something is someone else's fault) 把责任推到…身上 *The other driver kept trying to put the blame on me.* 另一个司机竭力把责任往我身上推。

blame·less /ˈblemlɪs; ˈbleɪmləs/ *adj formal* not guilty of anything bad; INNOCENT[1] (1)【正式】无罪的; 无可指责的; 清白的: *I don't think he's entirely blameless.* 我看他并非完全没有过错。| *a blameless life* 清白的一生 —**blamelessly** *adv*

blame·wor·thy /ˈblemˌwɝðɪ; ˈbleɪmˌwɜːði/ *adj formal* deserving blame or disapproval【正式】该受责备的: *blameworthy conduct* 应受谴责的行为

blanch /blæntʃ; blɑːntʃ/ *v* **1** [I] to become pale because you are frightened or shocked〔因害怕或震惊而〕变得(脸色)苍白: *Robin swallowed and blanched. "Oh, God! Pregnant!"* 罗宾咽了一下口水, 脸色苍白地说: "哦, 天哪, 怀孕了!" **2** [T] to put vegetables, fruit, or nuts into boiling water for a short time 用沸水烫〔蔬菜、水果、坚果等〕: *Blanch the peaches and remove the skins.* 把桃子用沸水烫一烫, 然后去皮。**3** [T] to make a plant become pale by keeping it away from light 使〔植物不见阳光而〕变白

blanc·mange /bləˈmɑnʒ; bləˈmɒnʒ/ *n* [C,U] *BrE* a cold sweet food made from CORNFLOUR, milk, and sugar【英】牛奶冻〔用玉米粉、牛奶和糖制成的甜食〕

bland /blænd; blænd/ *adj* **1** without any excitement, strong opinions, or special character 平和的, 温和的; 无动于衷的: *The principal made a few bland comments about the value of education.* 校长对教育的重要性作了一些不痛不痒的论述。| *Their music is pleasant enough, but a little bland.* 他们的音乐很动听, 但缺少激情。**2** food that is bland has very little taste〔食物〕淡而无味的: *a rather bland potato soup* 口味相当淡的马铃薯汤 —**blandly** *adv* —**blandness** *n* [U]

Blan·da /ˈblændə; ˈblændə/**, George** (1927-2010) a US football player who is famous because he played professional football for 26 years and scored more points than any other NFL player. 布兰达〔(1927-2010), 美国著名橄榄球运动员, 职业生涯长达 26 年, 在美国全国橄榄球联盟中得分最多〕

blan·dish·ments /ˈblændɪʃmənts; ˈblændɪʃmənts/ *n* [plural] *formal* praise and nice remarks about someone that are intended to persuade them or influence someone【正式】奉承, 讨好, 甜言蜜语: *She was immune to both their threats and their blandishments.* 她既不怕他们的威逼, 也不为他们的甜言蜜语所动。

blank[1] /blæŋk; blæŋk/ *adj* **1** showing no expression, understanding, or interest 无表情的; 漠然的; 不感兴趣的: *Her eyes were blank and stared right through me.* 她目光呆滞, 直勾勾地望着我。| *a blank look* 毫无表情的眼神 **2** without any writing, print, or recorded sound 无字迹的; 空白的: *Leave the last page blank.* 让最后一页空着。| *a blank cassette* 一盒空白磁带 **3 go blank a)** to be suddenly unable to remember something 脑子突然一片空白, 怎么也想不起来: *When I got into the exam room I*

just panicked and my mind went completely blank. 一进考场，我就慌乱起来，脑子里一片空白。**b)** to stop showing any images, writing etc〔屏幕等〕一片空白：*Suddenly the screen went blank.* 屏幕上突然一片空白。—see also 另见 BLANK VERSE —**blankly** *adv* —**blankness** *n* [U]

blank² *n* [C] **1** an empty space on a piece of paper, where you are supposed to write a word or letter 空白处：*Use this information to fill in the blanks on your form.* 请在表格的空栏处填写这些资料。**2 my mind's a blank** *spoken* used to say that you cannot remember something【口】脑子里一片空白，怎么也想不起来：*I'm trying to think of his name, but my mind's a complete blank.* 我努力在想他的名字，但怎么也想不起来。**3** a CARTRIDGE (=container for a bullet in a gun) that contains an explosive but no bullet〔有火药而无弹头的〕空弹：*Soldiers fired blanks into the crowd.* 士兵向人群发射空弹。—see also 另见 **draw a blank** (DRAW¹ (36)) —**blankness** *n* [U]

blank³ *v* **1** [I] *AmE* to be suddenly unable to remember something【美】突然记不起，脑子突然一片空白：*I blanked in the oral exam.* 考口试时，我脑子一片空白。**2** [T] *BrE spoken* to ignore someone who you would usually greet or speak to【英口】不理睬：*Why did she blank Phil when he came in?* 菲尔进来的时候，她为什么没理人家？

blank sth ↔ **out** *phr v* [T] *informal*【非正式】**1** to cover something so that it cannot be seen 涂掉，删去：*The actual names had been blanked out.* 真实姓名被涂掉了。**2** to completely forget something, especially deliberately〔尤指故意地〕全部忘记：*I tried to blank out everything he had said from my mind.* 我尽量把他的话从脑海中全部抹去。

blank car·tridge /ˌ· ˈ··/ *n* [C] a CARTRIDGE (1) that contains an explosive but no bullet〔有火药而无弹头的〕空弹

blank cheque *BrE*【英】, **blank check** *AmE*【美】/ˌ· ˈ·/ *n* [C] **1** a cheque that has been signed, but has not had the amount written on it〔签过名而未填写金额的〕空白支票 **2 give sb a blank cheque/check** to give someone permission to do whatever they think is necessary in a particular situation 给某人以全权[自由处理权]

blan·ket¹ /ˈblæŋkɪt; ˈblæŋkɨt/ *n* [C] **1** a cover for a bed, usually made of wool 毯子，毛毡 **2** a thick covering or area of something 厚覆盖层：[**+of**] *The valley was covered with a blanket of mist.* 山谷为雾霭所笼罩。—see also 另见 WET BLANKET

blanket² *v* [T usually passive 一般用被动态] to cover something with a thick layer 覆盖；笼罩：[**+in/with**] *All the rooftops were blanketed in snow.* 家家户户的屋顶上都覆盖着积雪。

blanket³ *adj* [only before noun 仅用于名词前] **blanket statement/rule/ban etc** a statement, rule etc that affects everyone or includes all possible cases 全面[适用于所有人]的陈述/规定/禁止等：*a blanket ban on the use of aerosols* 全面禁止使用喷雾器 | *We sent out a blanket mailing to every member of Congress.* 我们给所有的国会议员都寄发了邮件。

blank·e·ty-blank /ˌblæŋkɪtɪ ˈblæŋk; ˌblæŋkɨti ˈblæŋk/ *adj* [only before noun 仅用于名词前] *AmE spoken* used to show annoyance when you want to avoid swearing【美口】该死的：*The blankety-blank key is stuck!* 该死的钥匙卡住了！

blank verse /ˌ· ˈ·/ *n* [U] poetry that has a fixed RHYTHM (1) but does not RHYME² (1) 无韵诗：*Shakespeare's blank verse* 莎士比亚的无韵体诗 —compare 比较 FREE VERSE

blare /blɛr; bleə/ *v* [I,T] to make a very loud unpleasant noise 刺耳地大声鸣响：*Horns blared in the street outside my hotel window.* 我住的旅馆的窗外传来街上的汽车喇叭声。| *blaring sirens* 发出刺耳声音的警报器 | **blare out** *a stereo blaring out rock music* 正在高声播放摇滚乐的立体声音响设备 —**blare** *n* [singular]

blar·ney /ˈblɑrnɪ; ˈblɑːni/ *n* [U] *informal especially BrE* pleasant but untrue things that you say to someone in order to trick or persuade them【非正式，尤英】甜言蜜语；奉承话

Blarney Stone, the /ˈ· · ,·/ a stone in the wall of Blarney Castle in Ireland. People believe that if you kiss it, it will bring you good luck, and the ability to persuade people to do what you want. 布拉尼巧言石〔爱尔兰布拉尼城堡墙上的一块石头，相传亲吻此石将有好运，也会能言善辩，让人信服〕

bla·sé /blɑˈze; ˈblɑːzeɪ/ *adj* not worried or excited about things that most people think are important, impressive etc 漠不关心的；无动于衷的；不感兴趣的；厌倦的：*He's very blasé about money now that he's got that job.* 他得到了那份工作，对钱也就无所谓了。

blas·pheme /blæsˈfim; blæsˈfiːm/ *v* [**I+against**] to speak in a way that insults God or people's religious beliefs, or to use the names of God and holy things when swearing 亵渎〔上帝等〕；辱骂，中伤，口出恶言 —**blasphemer** *n* [C]

blas·phe·my /ˈblæsfɪmɪ; ˈblæsfɨmi/ *n* [C,U] something you say or do that is insulting to God or people's religious beliefs 对上帝的亵渎；亵渎的言辞 —**blasphemous** *adj*: *The book has been widely condemned as blasphemous.* 人们普遍谴责这本书带有亵渎意味。—**blasphemously** *adv*

blast¹ /blæst; blɑːst/ *n*

1 ►AIR/WIND 空气/风◄ [C] a sudden strong movement of wind or air 一阵疾风；一股气流：[**+of**] *A blast of cold air swept through the hut.* 一股寒气冲进了小屋。

2 ►EXPLOSION 爆炸◄ [C] an explosion, or the very strong movement of air that it causes 爆炸；爆炸引起的气浪，冲击波：*Thirty-six people died in the blast.* 有36人在爆炸中丧生。

3 ►NOISE 噪声◄ [C] a sudden very loud noise 突然的巨大声响：*a blast of rock music* 一阵震耳欲聋的摇滚乐 | *The guard gave a blast on his whistle and we were off.* 警卫猛吹了一下哨子，我们就离开了。

4 (at) full blast as strongly, loudly, or fast as possible 全力地；全速地；开足马力：*The radiators were on full blast, but it was still freezing.* 暖气已开到最大，但还是冷得要命。| *a radio going at full blast* 音量开到最大的收音机

5 ►FUN 乐趣◄ [singular] *AmE informal* an enjoyable and exciting experience【美，非正式】欢乐而刺激的经历：*The concert was a blast.* 音乐会很好听。| *We had a blast at the fair.* 我们在游乐场上玩得很开心。

blast² *v*

1 ►EXPLODE 爆炸◄ [I,T] to break a mass of rock into pieces using explosives 爆破〔尤指岩石〕：[**+through**] *We had to blast our way through 50 metres of solid rock.* 我们不得不炸通50米坚固的岩石来开路。| **blast sth through/in** *Slowly they blasted a path through the mountains.* 他们缓慢地在山间炸开一条路。

2 blast! also 又作 **blast her/it etc** *spoken* used when you are very annoyed about something【口】真讨厌！真该死！〔表示厌烦〕：*Oh blast! I've forgotten my key.* 真讨厌！我忘了带钥匙。

3 ►MUSIC 音乐◄ also 又作 **blast out** [I,T] to produce a lot of loud noise, especially music 发出〔许多响亮的声音〕〔尤指音乐〕：*a radio blasting out pop music* 大声播放流行音乐的收音机 | *Dance music blasted from the stereo.* 立体声音响在大声播放舞曲。

4 ►AIR/WATER 空气/水◄ [T] to direct air or water at something with great force 向…喷射〔气或水〕：*Coral can be cleaned by blasting it with a strong jet of water.* 可以用强水流将珊瑚喷洗干净。

5 ►ATTACK 攻击◄ [T] to attack a place or person using bombs or heavy guns 用炸弹[重炮]袭击：*The town was blasted out of existence.* 整个城镇被炸为平地。

6 ►CRITICIZE 批评◄ [T] to criticize something very strongly 抨击，猛烈批评：*The Senator blasted their plans for educational aid.* 这位参议员猛烈抨击他们的教育援助计划。

7 blast sb's hopes to destroy someone's hope of doing something 使某人的希望破灭：*Injury on the team has blasted our hopes of reaching the final.* 队中有球员受伤使我们进军决赛的希望破灭了。

8 ►DESTROY 毁坏◄ [T] *literary* to make something dry up and die, especially because of heat or cold【文】〔以高热或严寒〕使枯萎；摧毁：*Every green thing was blasted by the icy breath of winter.* 冬天的寒气使所有绿色植物都凋谢了。

blast off *phr v* [I] if a SPACECRAFT blasts off, it leaves the ground〔航天器〕离地升空；发射 —see also 另见 BLAST-OFF

blas·ted /ˈblæstɪd; ˈblɑːstɨd/ *adj* [only before noun 仅用于名词前] *spoken* used to express annoyance【口】该死的，讨厌的〔表示厌烦〕：*I wish that blasted baby would stop crying!* 我希望那讨厌的婴孩别再哭了！

blast fur·nace /ˈ· ,··/ *n* [C] a large industrial structure in which iron is separated from the rock that surrounds it〔炼铁的〕高炉，鼓风炉

blast-off /ˈ· ·/ *n* [U] the moment when a SPACECRAFT leaves the ground〔航天器的〕离地升空时刻：*10 seconds to blast-off* 离航天器离地升空还差10秒 —see also 另见 **blast off** (BLAST²)

bla·tant /ˈbletn̩t; ˈbleɪtənt/ *adj* something bad that is blatant is very clear and easy to see, but the person responsible for it does not seem embarrassed or ashamed 公然的；露骨的：*a blatant abuse of power* 公然滥用职权 | *blatant discrimination* 毫不掩饰的歧视 —**blatantly** *adv* —**blatancy** *n* [C]

blath·er /ˈblæðɚ; ˈblæðə/ *v* [**I+about**] to talk for a long time about things that are not important 废话连篇；胡扯 —**blather** *n* [C,U]

blaze¹ /blez; bleɪz/ *v* **1** [I] to burn very brightly and strongly 熊熊燃烧：*The room was warm and cosy, with a fire blazing in the hearth.* 房间温暖而舒适，壁炉里的火在熊熊地燃烧着。**2** [I] to shine with a very bright light 发光，照亮：*The house still blazed*

with lights although it was midnight. 尽管已是午夜，屋子里仍然灯火通明。**3** also 又作 **blaze away** [I] to fire bullets rapidly and continuously 快速而连续地射击: *An enemy plane roared overhead, its guns blazing.* 一架敌机在上空轰鸣，不断地开枪扫射。**4 blaze a trail** to develop important new methods or make important new discoveries 做开路先锋，起先导作用: *The company has blazed a trail in robotic technology.* 这家公司在机器人技术方面开拓了新路。**5 be blazed across/all over** if something is blazed across a newspaper etc, it is written in a way that everyone will notice〔在报刊等上〕以显著位置刊登: *News of their divorce was blazed across all the tabloids.* 小报都在显著位置刊登了他们离婚的消息。—see also 另见 BLAZING

blaze² *n*

1 ►FIRE 火◄ a) [singular] the strong bright flames of a fire 火焰; 烈火: *We soon had a cheerful blaze.* 我们很快燃起了明亮的火焰。**b)** [C] a big dangerous fire 危险的大火: *Wind fanned the blaze, making it impossible for the firefighters to continue.* 风使火势越来越猛，消防队员无法继续灭火。

2 ►LIGHT/COLOUR 光/颜色◄ [singular] very bright light or colour〔光线、色彩等的〕光辉，闪耀; 五彩缤纷: [+of] *a blaze of sunshine* 太阳的光辉 | *The garden is a blaze of colour at this time of year.* 这个时节，花园里花团锦簇，万紫千红。

3 ►GUNS 枪炮◄ [singular] the rapid continuous firing of a gun 急促而连续的射击: [+of] *a blaze of machine gun fire* 一阵机枪的扫射

4 a blaze of anger/hatred/passion etc a sudden show of very strong emotion 突发的怒气/仇恨/激情等: *He was surprised by the sudden blaze of anger in her eyes.* 他对她眼里突然冒出的怒火感到吃惊。

5 in a blaze of glory/publicity etc receiving a lot of praise or public attention 在盛赞/公众瞩目之下等: *Our team finished the season in a blaze of glory, winning the championship with ease.* 我们的球队在一片赞扬声中结束了本季的比赛，轻而易举地取得了冠军。

6 what the blazes/who the blazes etc *spoken old-fashioned* used to emphasize a question when you are annoyed【口，过时】到底在搞什么/究竟是谁等〔用于加强问题的语气，表示厌烦〕: *What the blazes is going on here?* 这里究竟在搞什么鬼？

7 like blazes *old-fashioned* as fast, as much, or as strongly as possible【过时】尽可能地: *We're going to have to work like blazes to get it done on time!* 我们得拼命干，才能按时完成！

8 go to blazes *spoken old-fashioned* used to angrily tell someone to go away【口，过时】滚开

9 ►MARK 记号◄ [C usually singular 一般用单数] a white mark, especially one down the front of a horse's face〔尤指马鼻上的一条〕白斑 —see also 另见 ABLAZE

blaz·er /ˈblezɚ; ˈbleɪzə/ *n* [C] a JACKET (=piece of clothing like a short coat), sometimes with the special sign of a school, club etc on it〔有时带有学校、俱乐部等标记的〕上衣: *a school blazer* 印有校名的外衣

blaz·ing /ˈblezɪŋ; ˈbleɪzɪŋ/ *adj* [only before noun 仅用于名词前] **1** extremely hot 炽热的: *a blazing August afternoon* 一个炎热的八月天的下午 **2** full of strong emotions, especially anger 强烈的〔尤指怒气〕: *He jumped to his feet in a blazing fury.* 他暴跳如雷。| **blazing row** (=very angry argument) 愤怒的争吵

bla·zon¹ /ˈblezn̩; ˈbleɪzən/ *n* [C] a COAT OF ARMS 盾形纹章，盾徽

blazon² *v* [T] **be blazoned on/across etc** to be written or shown on something in a very noticeable way 炫示，(大肆)宣扬

bleach¹ /blitʃ; bliːtʃ/ *n* [U] a chemical used to make things white or to kill GERMS 漂白剂: *I spilled bleach on my blue trousers and ruined them.* 漂白剂溅到我的蓝裤子上，裤子给毁了。

bleach² *v* [T] to make something white, especially by using chemicals or sunlight 使〔颜色〕变淡，使变白; 漂白; 晒白: *bleached blonde hair* 褪色的金发 | *Driftwood lined the shore, bleached by the sun.* 浮木排列在岸边，已晒得退了色。

bleach·ers /ˈblitʃɚz; ˈbliːtʃəz/ *n* [plural] *AmE* seats arranged in rows with no roof covering them, where you sit to watch sport【美】〔体育场的〕露天看台(座位): *We had a good view from the bleachers.* 我们在露天看台上看得很清楚。

bleak /blik; bliːk/ *adj* **1** without anything to make you feel cheerful or hopeful 没有希望的; 令人沮丧的: *bleak news* 令人沮丧的消息 | **a bleak outlook/prospect/future** *With no money and no job, my prospects seemed bleak.* 又没工作又没钱，我的前景似乎很暗淡。**2** cold and without any pleasant or comfortable features 阴冷的; 阴郁的: *a bleak January afternoon* 1月里一个阴冷的下午 | *The landscape was bleak and bare.* 景色一片凄凉。—**bleakly** *adv* —**bleakness** *n* [U]

Bleak House /ˌ· ˈ·/ a NOVEL written by Charles Dickens in 1852-53. It is the story of members of the Jarndyce family who fight each other in a court of law about money and property that belongs to the family.《荒凉山庄》〔查尔斯·狄更斯 1852-1853 年创作的小说，讲述贾恩戴斯一家人在法庭上争夺财产的故事〕

blear·y /ˈblɪrɪ; ˈblɪəri/ also 又作 **bleary-eyed** /ˌ·· ˈ·◂/ *adj* unable to see very clearly, because you are tired or have been crying〔因疲劳或流泪〕视力模糊的; 睡眼惺忪的: *Bleary-eyed, she pulled on her robe and went to the kitchen to make coffee.* 她睡眼惺忪地穿上睡袍去厨房煮咖啡。—**blearily** *adv* —**bleariness** *n* [U]

bleat /blit; bliːt/ *v* [I] **1** to make the sound that a sheep or goat makes〔羊〕咩咩地叫 **2** *informal* to complain in a silly or annoying way【非正式】低声诉苦; 埋怨: *Oh stop bleating!* 别再诉苦了！—**bleat** *n* [C]

bleed /blid; bliːd/ *v past tense and past participle* **bled** /blɛd; bled/

1 ►BLOOD 血◄ a) [I] to lose blood, especially because of an injury〔尤指因受伤〕流血，出血: *Your nose is bleeding.* 你的鼻子流血了。| **bleed profusely** (=bleed a lot) 血流如注 *Marc lay on the ground, bleeding profusely.* 马克躺在地上，鲜血直流。**b)** [T] to take some blood from someone's body in order to treat a disease 给…放血〔以治疗疾病〕

2 ►MONEY 钱◄ [T] to make someone pay an unreasonable amount of money 榨取〔某人〕钱财; 勒索: *She bled him for every last cent.* 她榨尽了他的每一分钱。| **bleed sb dry/white** (=take all their money) 榨干某人的钱财 *developing countries that had been bled dry by massive loan repayments* 需要偿还大量贷款而被榨干钱财的发展中国家

3 my heart bleeds *spoken* used to say that you feel a lot of sympathy for someone, but often in a joking way when you do not think someone deserves any sympathy【口】我的心在流血〔感到悲伤或同情，常用于玩笑〕: *You can't afford a third car? My heart bleeds!* 你买不起第三辆汽车？我真同情你！| [+for] *My heart bleeds for those poor children.* 我为那些可怜的孩子感到悲伤。

4 ►AIR/LIQUID 空气/液体◄ [T] to remove air or liquid from a system in order to make it work properly, for example from a heating system 抽掉〔气体或液体〕: *We need to bleed the radiators.* 我们要把暖气装置中的水放掉。

5 ►COLOUR 颜色◄ [I] to spread from one area of cloth or paper to another 渗开: *Wash it in cold water so the colours don't bleed.* 用冷水洗以防渗色。

bleed·er /ˈblidɚ; ˈbliːdə/ *n* [C] *BrE spoken* a rude word for someone, especially a man, that you dislike【英口】讨厌的家伙〔尤指男子〕

bleed·ing¹ /ˈblidɪŋ; ˈbliːdɪŋ/ *adj* [only before noun 仅用于名词前] *BrE spoken* used to emphasize something when you are angry【英口】该死的，讨厌的〔用于加强语气，表示生气〕: *Get your bleeding hands off my car!* 拿开你那讨厌的手，别碰我的车！

bleeding² *n* [U] the condition of losing blood from your body 流血: *We tied his arm up tightly to stop the bleeding.* 我们把他的胳膊紧紧缠住以止血。

bleeding heart /ˌ·· ˈ·/ also 又作 **bleeding heart lib·e·ral** /ˌ·· ˈ···/ *n* [C] *informal* someone who feels sympathy for poor people or criminals, in a way that you think is not practical or helpful【非正式】心肠过软的人; 假同情者〔指不实际或无助益地同情穷人和罪犯的人〕

bleep¹ /blip; bliːp/ *n* [C] a high electronic sound〔电子仪器发出的〕哔哔声: *The shrill bleep of the telephone woke him up.* 电话刺耳的哔哔声吵醒了他。

bleep² *v* **1** [I] to make a high electronic sound 发出哔哔声: *The computer will bleep when it has completed the search.* 电脑完成搜索时会发出哔哔声。**2** [T] *BrE informal* to let someone know, through their bleeper, that you want them to telephone you【英，非正式】〔用传呼机〕传呼，召唤〔某人〕**3** [T] also 又作 **bleep out** to prevent an offensive word being heard on television or the radio by making a high electronic sound〔电视或收音机中〕用哔哔声盖过〔说话声〕: *All the swear words had been bleeped out.* 所有的粗话都被哔哔声盖过了。

bleep·er /ˈblipɚ; ˈbliːpə/ *n* [C] *BrE* a small machine that you carry with you, that makes short high electronic sounds to tell you that you must telephone someone; BEEPER, PAGER【英】传呼机

blem·ish¹ /ˈblɛmɪʃ; ˈblemɪʃ/ *n* [C] a small mark, especially a mark on someone's skin or on the surface of an object, that spoils its appearance 瑕疵，污点，疤痕

blemish² *v* [T often passive 常用被动态] to spoil the

appearance, beauty, or perfection of something 有损…的完美; 玷污 —see also 另见 UNBLEMISHED —**blemished** *adj*

blench /blɛntʃ; blentʃ/ *v* [I] to make a sudden movement backwards because you are frightened〔因害怕而〕退缩, 退避, 畏缩

blend[1] /blɛnd; blend/ *v* **1** [T] to thoroughly mix together soft or liquid substances to form a single smooth substance 混和, 掺合, 调和: *Blend the sugar, eggs, and flour.* 把糖、鸡蛋和面粉和在一起。**2** [I,T] to combine different features or characteristics in a way that produces an effective or pleasant result, or to become combined in this way 交融; 揉合: *an exciting narrative that blends fact and legend* 融合了事实和传说的精彩叙述 | **[+with/together]** *The aroma of woodsmoke blended with the smell of cooking.* 木头燃烧的香味和烹调的气味混合在一起。**3** [T usually passive 一般用被动态] *technical* to produce tea, tobacco, WHISKY etc by mixing several different types together【术语】〔用不同品种的茶、烟草、威士忌等〕混合调制

blend in *phr v* [I] if something blends in with the things around it, it matches the background very well or suitably 协调; 和谐: **[+with]** *The old house blends in perfectly with the gentle Hampshire countryside.* 这所老房子和宁静的汉普郡乡村十分协调。

blend[2] *n* [C] **1** a product such as tea, tobacco, or WHISKY that is a mixture of several different types 混合物, 混成品 **2** a mixture of different qualities, characteristics, people etc, that combine together well 不同品质[特性, 人]的巧妙组合: *an excellent team, with a nice blend of experience and youthful enthusiasm* 一支既有经验又有年轻人的热忱的优秀队伍

blend·er /ˈblɛndɚ; ˈblendə/ *n* [C] an electric machine that you use to mix liquids and soft foods together〔食品〕搅拌器

Blen·heim Pal·ace /ˌblɛnɪm ˈpælɪs; ˌblenɪ̣m ˈpælɪ̣s/ a very large and beautiful house in Oxfordshire in the UK 布伦海姆宫〔位于英国牛津郡的一座漂亮的大型建筑〕

S3 **bless** /blɛs; bles/ *v past tense and past participle* **blessed** *or* **blest** /blɛst; blest/ [T] **1 be blessed with** to have a special ability, good quality etc 有幸得到; 被赋予: *Fortunately we're both blessed with good health.* 幸运的是我们俩都有健康的身体。| *Nicole had not been blessed with a sense of humour.* 妮科尔天生一点幽默感也没有。**2** to ask God to protect someone or something 祈求上帝祝福[保祐], 求神赐福于: *May God bless you and keep you safe from harm.* 愿上帝保祐你平安无事。**3** to make something holy 使神圣; 视…为圣物; 赞颂: *Then the priest blesses the bread and wine.* 然后牧师将饼和酒圣洁化。**4 bless you!** *spoken*【口】**a)** what you say when someone SNEEZES 长命百岁!〔别人打喷嚏时说〕**b)** *old-fashioned* used to thank someone for doing something for you【过时】谢谢〔某人〕**5 bless him/her etc** *spoken* used to show that you are fond of someone, amused by them, or pleased by something they have done【口】真不错; 干得好〔表示喜欢或满意〕: *"Tim can tie his shoelaces now, Mum." "Can he, bless him!"* "蒂姆会系鞋带了, 妈妈。" "是吗, 他真能干。" | *Bless her little heart.* 这个小宝贝她真行。**6 bless my soul/I'll be blessed!** *spoken old-fashioned* used to express surprise【口, 过时】我的天哪!〔表示吃惊〕

bless·ed /ˈblɛsɪd; ˈblesɪ̣d/ *adj* **1** [only before noun 仅用于名词前] *spoken* used to express annoyance【口】该死的, 倒霉的〔表示烦恼〕: *Now where have I put that blessed book?* 这该死的书我到底放哪儿了? **2** [only before noun 仅用于名词前] very enjoyable or desirable 令人愉快的; 可喜的; 快乐的: *a few moments of blessed silence* 令人惬意的片刻宁静 **3** holy 神圣的; 受上帝祝福的, 有福的: *Blessed are the peacemakers.* 使人和睦的人有福。| *the Blessed Virgin* 圣母马利亚 —**blessedly** *adv* —**blessedness** *n* [U]

bless·ing /ˈblɛsɪŋ; ˈblesɪŋ/ *n*

1 ►STH GOOD/HELPFUL 好的/有助益的事物◄ [C] something that you have or something that happens which is good because it improves your life, helps you in some way, or makes you happy 幸事; 幸运; 福气: *This rain will be a blessing for the farmers.* 对农民来说, 这场雨真是一场甘霖。| **be a (great/real) blessing** *The dishwasher has been a real blessing!* 有洗碗机可真是享福! | **it is a blessing (that)** *It's a blessing no one was badly hurt.* 没有人受重伤, 真是幸运。

2 a mixed blessing a situation that has both good and bad parts 有利亦有弊的事物: *Getting that job was rather a mixed blessing, as it left me very little time to spend with my family.* 得到那份工作有利也有弊, 因为我很少有时间和家人在一起了。

3 blessing in disguise something that seems to be bad or unlucky at first, but which you later realize is good or lucky 表面上带来麻烦或不愉快而实际上使人得福的事; 祸中得福; 坏事变好事

4 count your blessings used to tell someone to remember how lucky they are, especially when they are complaining about something 想想你有多幸运; 不要身在福中不知福

5 ►APPROVAL 赞同◄ [U] someone's approval or encouragement for a plan, activity, idea etc 准许, 同意; 鼓励: **with sb's blessing** *They were determined to marry, with or without their parents' blessing.* 不管父母同意与否, 他们都决心要结婚。| **give your blessing to** *The Defense Department has given its blessing to the disarmament proposals.* 国防部已经批准了裁军的提议。

6 ►FROM GOD 上帝赐予的◄ [C,U] protection and help from God, or words spoken to ask for this〔上帝的〕祝福, 赐福; 保佑; 恩典: *The priest gave the blessing.* 牧师做了祈祷。

bleth·er /ˈblɛðɚ; ˈbleðə/ *v* **[I+on]** *especially ScotE* to talk about things that are not important【尤苏格兰】瞎说一通, 胡扯; 喋喋不休 —**blether** *n* [C,U]

blew /blu; bluː/ *v* the past tense of BLOW[1]

Bligh /blaɪ; blaɪ/, **Captain William** (1754-?1817) an officer in the British navy who was in command of the ship HMS Bounty. Bligh was unpopular because he was a strict leader, so the men on his ship took power from him, and made him leave in a small boat. 布莱〔(1754-?1817), 英国海军军官, "邦蒂"号船长。作为船长, 他十分严厉, 不受人欢迎。结果船员剥夺了他的权力, 逼迫他自己驾驶一条小船离开〕

blight[1] /blaɪt; blaɪt/ *n* [singular] **1** an unhealthy condition of plants in which parts of them dry up and die〔植物〕枯萎病 **2** something that makes people unhappy or that spoils their lives or the environment they live in〔导致烦恼或不幸的〕坏因素; 阴影: *Her guilty secret was a blight on her happiness.* 那使她感到内疚的秘密给她的幸福蒙上了一层阴影。| *the blight of poverty* 贫穷的阴影

blight[2] *v* [T] to spoil or damage something, especially by preventing people from doing what they want to do 使枯萎; 摧残; 使某人遭遇挫折: *a disease which, though not fatal, can blight the lives of its victims* 虽说不会致命、却足以使患者饱受折磨的一场疾病 | *a country blighted by poverty* 一个为贫穷所困扰的国家 —**blighted** *adj*: *blighted hopes* 破灭的希望

blight·er /ˈblaɪtɚ; ˈblaɪtə/ *n* [C] *BrE old-fashioned*【英, 过时】**1** used to talk about someone that you feel sorry for or JEALOUS of 令人同情[妒忌]的家伙: *Poor old blighter.* 可怜的老人。| *You lucky blighter!* 你这走运的家伙! **2** a bad or unpleasant person 令人讨厌的人

Bligh·ty /ˈblaɪtɪ; ˈblaɪti/ *BrE* a name for Britain, which was used especially by British soldiers and other British people working abroad during the 19th and early 20th century【英】英国老家〔英国的别称, 尤为 19 世纪和 20 世纪早期在国外服役的英国士兵和在海外工作的英国人使用〕

bli·mey /ˈblaɪmɪ; ˈblaɪmi/ *interj BrE spoken* used to express surprise【英口】哎呀! 天啊!〔表示惊愕〕: *Blimey, look at that!* 天啊, 你看!

Blimp /blɪmp; blɪmp/ *n* [C] someone, especially an old man, with very old-fashioned political ideas 老顽固, 老保守 —**Blimpish** *adj*

blimp *n* [C] **1** a small AIRSHIP (=type of aircraft without wings) 小型飞艇 **2 Blimp** a COLONEL BLIMP 老顽固, 老保守

blind[1] /blaɪnd; blaɪnd/ *adj* S2 W3

1 ►CAN'T SEE 看不见◄ a) unable to see 瞎的, 盲的, 失明的: *He was nearly blind in one eye.* 他的一只眼睛几近失明。| **go blind** (=become blind) 失明 *In later stages of the disease, sufferers often go blind.* 在此病晚期, 患者常会失明。**b) the blind** [plural] people who are unable to see 盲人: *talking books for the blind* 盲人有声读物 **c) as blind as a bat** *humorous* not able to see well【幽默】什么也看不见: *I'm as blind as a bat without my glasses.* 我不戴眼镜, 就什么也看不见。

2 ►IGNORE 忽视◄ a) be blind to to completely fail to notice or realize something 对…缺乏识别能力的: *They seemed to be blind to the consequences of their decision.* 他们似乎看不到这项决策可能带来的后果。**b) turn a blind eye (to)** to deliberately ignore something that you know should not be happening (对…) 视而不见, (对…) 假装看不见: *The boss sometimes turns a blind eye to smoking in the office.* 老板有时对在办公室吸烟假装看不见。**c) not take a blind bit of notice** *especially spoken* to completely ignore what someone else is doing, especially in a way that is annoying【尤口】对…熟视无睹; 不把…当一回事

3 not make a blind bit of difference *BrE informal* used to emphasize that whatever someone says or does will not change the situation at all【英, 非正式】没有一点儿区别; 于事无补; 无任何作用

4 ►FEELINGS 感觉◄ a) blind faith/loyalty/hate etc strong feelings that you have without thinking about why you have them 盲目的信仰/忠诚/仇恨等: *an unreasoning, blind hatred* 不理智的盲目仇恨 **b) blind panic/rage** strong feelings that are

out of your control 盲目的恐慌/无端的愤怒: *In a moment of blind panic she had pulled the trigger and shot the man dead.* 她在无名的恐惧中扣动了扳机, 将那男子击毙。
5 blind corner/bend/curve a corner on a road that you cannot see beyond when you are driving 看不到的角落/拐弯处
6 the blind leading the blind *often humorous* used to say that people who do not know much about what they are doing are guiding or advising others who know nothing at all【常幽默】盲人给瞎子引路; 瞎指挥
7 ▶AIRCRAFT 飞机◀ blind flying/landing using only instruments to fly an aircraft because you cannot see through cloud, mist etc 只靠仪表操作进行飞行/着陆
8 blind drunk *BrE informal* extremely drunk【英, 非正式】烂醉如泥
9 swear blind to say very firmly that something is definitely true 固执地说; 一口咬定: *Phil swears blind it wasn't him.* 菲尔发誓说那不是他干的。—see also 另见 BLINDLY —**blindness** *n* [U]

blind² *v* [T] **1** to permanently destroy someone's ability to see 使永久失去视力: *He had been blinded in the war.* 他在战争中双目失明。**2** to make it difficult for someone to see for a short time 使目眩: *Opening the door, I was immediately blinded by the glare.* 一开门, 道强光照得我一时什么也看不见。**3** to make someone lose their good sense or judgement and be unable to see the truth about something 使不理解; 使失去判断力: *blinded by emotion* 被情感蒙住了眼睛 | **blind sb to** *He had tremendous charm, which blinded us to his dishonesty.* 他外表很有魅力, 使我们没有看清他的虚伪。**4 blind sb with science** to confuse or trick someone by using complicated language 用专业术语蒙骗某人 —see also 另见 **effing and blinding** (EFF (1))

blinds 窗帘; 百叶窗

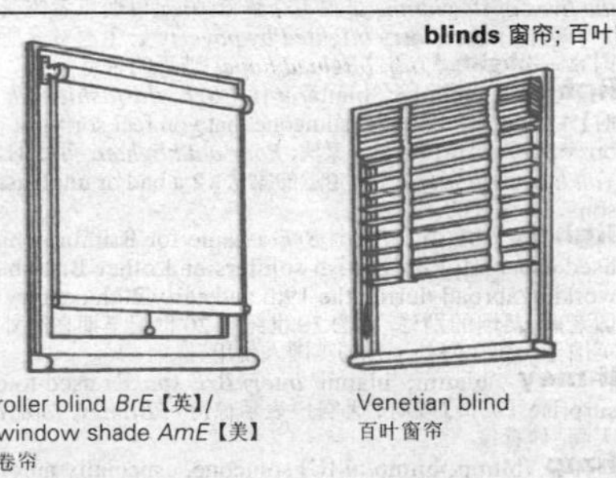

roller blind *BrE*【英】/ window shade *AmE*【美】卷帘

Venetian blind 百叶窗帘

blind³ *n* [C] **1** a covering that can be pulled down over a window; WINDOW SHADE (能上下卷叠的)窗帘; 百叶窗 —see also 另见 ROLLER BLIND, WINDOW SHADE *AmE*【美】, VENETIAN BLIND, SHADE¹ (2b) **2** a trick or excuse to stop someone from discovering the truth 障眼物; 掩饰; 借口: *Her accent was a blind – she isn't really an American.* 她的口音是一种掩饰, 其实她不是美国人。**3** *AmE* a small shelter where you can watch birds or animals without being seen by them【美】(狩猎时窥视猎物的)隐蔽处, 埋伏处; HIDE² (1) *BrE*【英】

blind al·ley /ˌ· ˈ··/ *n* [C] **1** a small narrow street with no way out at one end 死胡同, 死巷 **2** an attempt to achieve something, which does not produce useful results 行不通的方法

blind date /ˌ· ˈ·/ *n* [C] an arranged meeting between a man and woman who have not met each other before 从未晤面的男女间的约会

blind·er /ˈblaɪndə; ˈblaɪndə/ *n* **1** [singular] *BrE informal* an excellent performance, especially in sport【英, 非正式】(尤指体育比赛中)上佳的表现: *He played an absolute blinder!* 他在比赛中的表现真是太棒了! **2 blinders** [plural] *AmE* things fixed beside a horse's eyes to prevent it seeing objects on either side【美】(系于马眼旁使之不能侧视的)马眼罩; BLINKERS *BrE*【英】

blind·fold¹ /ˈblaɪndˌfold; ˈblaɪndfəʊld/ *n* [C] a piece of cloth that covers someone's eyes to prevent them from seeing anything 蒙眼布; 障眼物

blindfold² *v* [T] to cover someone's eyes 蒙住(某人的)眼睛: *Blindfold the prisoner!* 把囚犯的眼睛蒙上!

blindfold³ *adv* also 又作 **blindfolded** /ˈblaɪndˌfoldɪd; ˈblaɪndfəʊldɪd/ **1** with your eyes covered 蒙着眼地 **2 can do sth blindfold** *informal* used to say that it is very easy for you to do something because you have done it so often【非正式】闭上眼都能做某事

blind·ing /ˈblaɪndɪŋ; ˈblaɪndɪŋ/ *adj* **1 blinding light/flash etc** a very bright light that makes you unable to see properly 刺眼的光/闪光等 **2 blinding headache/pain etc** a headache, pain etc that is so strong that it makes you unable to think or behave normally 极其严重的头痛/疼痛等 **3** *BrE spoken* excellent【英口】最佳的, 很棒的: *It's a blinding tape, really funny.* 这录音带棒极了, 真有趣。—**blindingly** *adv*: *blindingly obvious* 极其明显

blind·ly /ˈblaɪndlɪ; ˈblaɪndli/ *adv* **1** not thinking about something or trying to understand it 盲目地: *Don't just blindly accept what you're told.* 不要盲目地相信别人的话。**2** not seeing or noticing what is around you 漫无目标地; 胡乱地: *He felt around blindly for the matches.* 他瞎摸着找火柴。

blind man's buff /ˌ· · ˈ·/ *n* [U] a children's game in which one player whose eyes are covered tries to catch the others 捉迷藏(游戏)

blind-side /ˈblaɪndsaɪd; ˈblaɪndsaɪd/ *v* [T] *AmE informal*【美, 非正式】**1** to hit someone unexpectedly from the side 从侧面偷袭(某人): *blindsided by a bus at the intersection* 在十字路口冷不防被公共汽车撞着 **2** to give someone an unpleasant surprise 给(某人)一个不愉快的意外: *I was blindsided by his suggestion.* 我对他的建议感到很惊讶。

blind spot /ˈ· ·/ *n* [C] **1** something that you are unable or unwilling to understand 不理解的事物; 偏见, 无知: *I have a blind spot where computers are concerned.* 我对电脑一窍不通。**2** the part of the road that you cannot see when you are driving a car (驾车者)看不见的地方; 死角: *The other car was in my blind spot – I just hadn't seen it!* 另一辆车在我视线的死角处——我正巧没看见! **3** the point in your eye where the nerve enters, which is not sensitive to light 盲点(眼神经无光感处)

blink¹ /blɪŋk; blɪŋk/ *v* **1** [I,T] to shut and open your eyes quickly 眨(眼): *I blinked as I came out into the sunlight.* 我走出来到太阳底下时直眨眼睛。**2** [I] if lights blink, they shine unsteadily or go on and off rapidly (灯光)时闪时灭, 闪烁: *The light on your answering machine is blinking.* 你的电话答录机上的指示灯在闪烁。**3 not (even) blink** to not seem at all surprised 丝毫不惊奇: *She didn't even blink when I told her how much it would cost.* 当我告诉她那件东西的价钱时, 她甚至连眼睛都没眨一下。**4 before you could blink** *spoken* extremely quickly【口】没等你眨眼, 很快地

blink² *n* **1 on the blink** *spoken* not working properly【口】失灵, 出毛病: *The radio's on the blink again.* 收音机又出毛病了。**2 the blink of an eye** a very short period of time 一眨眼工夫, 瞬间 **3** [C] the action of quickly shutting and opening your eyes 眨眼

blink·ered /ˈblɪŋkəd; ˈblɪŋkəd/ *adj* **1** having a limited view of a subject or refusing to accept or consider ideas that are new or different 狭隘的, 有偏见的; 保守的: *blinkered and outdated attitudes* 狭隘而又守旧的态度 **2** a horse that is blinkered is wearing blinkers (马)戴眼罩的

blink·ers /ˈblɪŋkəz; ˈblɪŋkəz/ *n* [plural] **1** *BrE* pieces of leather fixed beside a horse's eyes to prevent it seeing objects on either side【英】(系于马眼旁使之不能侧视的)马眼罩; BLINDERS *AmE*【美】**2** *AmE informal* the small lights on a car that you flash on and off to show which direction you are turning【美, 非正式】(汽车上的)转向指示灯; WINKERS *BrE*【英】

blink·ing /ˈblɪŋkɪŋ; ˈblɪŋkɪŋ/ *adj* [only before noun 仅用于名词前] *BrE spoken* used to show that you are annoyed【英口】该死的, 讨厌的[表示厌烦]: *Whose blinking idea was it to come to this awful place?* 谁的鬼主意, 要来这么个破地方?

blip /blɪp; blɪp/ *n* [C] **1** a short high electronic sound or a flashing light on the screen of a piece of electronic equipment (电子仪器发出的)哔哔声; 屏幕上的信号, 光点: *blips on a radar screen* 雷达屏幕上的光点 **2** a short pause or change in a process, or activity, especially when the situation gets worse for a while before it improves again 暂时中断[变化]: *The drop in sales is only a temporary blip.* 销售的下降只是暂时的。

bliss /blɪs; blɪs/ *n* [U] perfect happiness or enjoyment 极乐, 无上幸福, 福佑, 至福: *wedded bliss* 美满婚姻 | *I didn't have to get up till 11 – it was sheer bliss.* 我可以睡到11点, 真幸福啊!

bliss·ful /ˈblɪsfəl; ˈblɪsfəl/ *adj* **1** extremely happy or enjoyable 极其幸福的; 乐而忘忧的: *blissful sunny days* 阳光明媚的日子 **2 blissful ignorance** a situation in which you do not yet know about something unpleasant 对(不幸之事)毫不察觉 —**blissfully** *adv*: *Jean's now married and blissfully happy.* 琼已经结婚了, 生活得美满幸福。

blis·ter¹ /ˈblɪstə; ˈblɪstə/ *n* [C] **1** a swelling on your skin containing clear liquid, caused for example by a burn or continu-

ous rubbing〔皮肤上因烫伤、摩擦而起的〕疱, 水泡: *New shoes always give me blisters.* 新鞋总使我的脚起泡。**2** a swelling on the surface of metal, rubber, painted wood etc〔金属、橡胶或油漆过的木料等表面的〕气泡, 浮泡

blister² *v* [I,T] to develop blisters or make blisters form 起泡; 使起水泡: *The paint will blister in the heat.* 油漆遇高温会起泡。—**blistered** *adj*: *Before long, my hands were blistered from all the digging.* 由于一直在挖, 我的手很快就起了泡。

blis·ter·ing /ˈblɪstərɪŋ; ˈblɪstərɪŋ/ *adj* **1** extremely hot 炎热的, 酷热的: *the blistering heat of the desert* 沙漠中的酷热 **2 blistering attack/criticism etc** very critical remarks expressing anger and disapproval 猛烈的攻击/批评等: *She launched into a blistering attack on her boss.* 她开始猛烈地攻击老板。—**blisteringly** *adv*: *Cover up as the sun can be blisteringly hot.* 遮盖一下吧, 阳光会很酷热。

blithe /blaɪð; blaɪð/ *adj* **1** seeming not to care or worry about the effects of what you do 漫不经心的, 毫不在乎的: *a blithe disregard for the facts* 完全漠视事实 **2** *literary or old use* cheerful and having no worries【文或旧】无忧无虑的, 快乐的 —**blithely** *adv*: *Mollie strolled blithely into the yard.* 莫莉悠闲地蹓跶着进了院子。

blith·er·ing /ˈblɪðərɪŋ; ˈblɪðərɪŋ/ *adj* **blithering idiot** *spoken* someone who has done something very stupid【口】愚蠢的家伙, 傻瓜

blitz /blɪts; blɪts/ *n* [usually singular 一般用单数] **1** a sudden military attack, especially from the air 闪电般的猛烈袭击〔尤指空袭〕; 闪电战 **2 have a blitz on** *informal* to work very hard to completely finish something that needs to be done【非正式】努力地把…办妥: *We'll have to have a blitz on the house before your parents arrive.* 在你父母到来以前, 我们必须把屋子打扫干净。—**blitz** *v* [T]

Blitz, the the time during World War II when German planes dropped many bombs on British cities, especially London 闪电空袭〔二战期间德国对英国城市的空袭, 尤指对伦敦的空袭〕: *Sam had rescued three people from a burning house during the Blitz.* 闪电空袭期间, 萨姆从一幢着火的房子里救出了三人。

blitzed /blɪtst; blɪtst/ *adj especially AmE informal* very tired or very drunk【尤美, 非正式】非常疲劳的; 烂醉如泥的

Blix·en /ˈblɪksn̩; ˈblɪksən/**, Baroness Kar·en** /ˈkærən; ˈkærən/ (1885-1962) a Danish writer who wrote in English using the man's name Isak Dinesen. Her most famous book, *Out of Africa*, describes her life on a coffee farm in Kenya. 布利克森〔(1885-1962), 用英语写作的丹麦作家, 使用男性笔名埃萨克·迪内森。她最著名的小说是《走出非洲》, 讲述她在肯尼亚一家咖啡园的生活〕

bliz·zard /ˈblɪzɚd; ˈblɪzəd/ *n* [C] **1** a severe snow storm 暴风雪: *We got stuck in a blizzard that night.* 那天晚上, 我们被暴风雪所围困。—see picture on page A13 参见 A13 页图 **2** *AmE informal* a sudden large amount of something that you must deal with【美, 非正式】大量〔要处理的事〕: *a blizzard of memos* 一大堆要处理的备忘录

bloat·ed /ˈblotɪd; ˈbləʊtɪ̈d/ *adj* full of liquid, gas, food etc, so that you look or feel much larger than normal 发胀的, 膨胀的; 臃肿的: *They've fished a bloated carcass out of the river.* 他们从河里捞上来一具发胀了的动物尸体。| *I feel really bloated after that meal.* 吃完饭后, 我觉得肚子很胀。

bloa·ter /ˈblotɚ; ˈbləʊtə/ *n* [C] a large fat fish eaten smoked 腌熏鱼

blob /blɑb; blɒb/ *n* **1** a very small round mass of liquid or sticky substance 一滴, 一小团: **[+of]** *a blob of honey* 一滴蜂蜜 —see picture on page A7 参见 A7 页图 **2** something far away that cannot be clearly seen〔远处〕模糊的事物, 一小点: *The church spire was just a distant blob.* 远处的教堂尖塔只能隐约看见。

bloc /blɑk; blɒk/ *n* [usually singular 一般用单数] a large group of people or countries with the same political aims, working together 集团, 阵营: *the former Soviet bloc* 前苏联阵营 —see also 另见 EN BLOC

S2 W2 **block¹** /blɑk; blɒk/ *n* [C]

1 ►SOLID MASS 固体◄ a solid mass of hard material such as wood or stone with straight sides 一大块〔如木、石等通常有直切边的坚硬物体〕: **[+of]** *a block of ice* 一大块冰 —see picture on page A7 参见 A7 页图

2 ►STREET/STREETS 街◄ a) *AmE* the distance along a city street from where one street crosses it to the next【美】街段: *It's three blocks to the store from here.* 这儿到那家商店隔着三条马路。| *She lives down the block.* 她住在街尾。**b)** the four city streets that form a square around an area of buildings 街区: *Let's walk around the block before we go in.* 我们先围着这街区走一圈再进去。

3 ►LARGE BUILDING 大楼◄ a large building divided into separate parts 栋, 座, 幢: *a block of flats* 一栋住宅楼 | *a tower block* 一座高层建筑 | *office blocks* 办公大楼 —see picture on page A4 参见 A4 页图

4 ►QUANTITY OF THINGS 数量◄ a quantity of things considered as a single unit 一组; 一批; 一套; 一叠: **[+of]** *a block of shares in a business* 企业的大宗股票 | *Highlight this block of text.* 突出课文的这一部分。

5 block booking/voting an arrangement that is made for a whole group, to buy something or to vote together 成批订购/集体投票

6 ►UNABLE TO THINK 不能思考◄ [usually singular 一般用单数] the temporary loss of your normal ability to think, learn, write etc〔思考、学习、写作等正常能力的〕暂时丧失, 一时阻塞: **mental/writer's block** *She has a mental block about speaking French.* 她脑子堵塞了, 一句法语也说不出来。

7 ►STOPPING MOVEMENT 阻止行动◄ [usually singular 一般用单数] something in a pipe, road etc that stops things moving through or along it 障碍物, 堵塞物

8 the block a solid block of wood on which someone's head was cut off as a punishment, in former times〔昔时的〕断头台: *He was prepared to go to the block for his beliefs.* 他准备好了为自己的信仰掉脑袋。

9 lay/put your head on the block to risk destroying other people's opinion of you by doing or saying something 冒着败坏自己名声的危险

10 ►SPORT 体育◄ a movement in sport that stops an opponent going forward 阻挡, 拦截 (动作)

11 ►INFORMATION 信息◄ a physical unit of stored information on a MAGNETIC TAPE or DISK 信息组〔指磁带或磁盘上储存信息的物理单位〕

12 ►PRINTING 印刷◄ a piece of wood or metal with words or line drawings cut into it, for printing 印版, 版垫, 衬版, 木印板

13 ►LAND 土地◄ *AustrE, NZE* a large piece of land【澳, 新西兰】一大片土地: *a ten acre block near the city* 城市附近一块 10 英亩的土地 —see also 另见 BLOCK CAPITALS, BUILDING BLOCK, **be a chip off the old block** (CHIP¹ (6)), **I'll knock your block off** (KNOCK¹ (4)), **stumbling block** (STUMBLE (4))

block² *v* [T] **1** also 又作 **block up** to prevent anything moving through a narrow space by placing something across it or in it 阻挡, 堵塞: *Your truck is blocking the road.* 你的卡车堵住了道路。| *My nose is blocked up with this cold.* 由于伤风, 我的鼻子不通气。**2** to stop something happening, developing, or succeeding 阻止, 妨碍, 阻挠: *The Senate blocked publication of the report.* 参议院阻挠这个报告的发表。**3** also 又作 **block off** to be in front of someone so that they cannot see a view, light, the sun etc 挡住〔视线〕: *Can you move? You're blocking my light.* 你挪一下行吗? 你挡住了光。**4 block sb's way** to stand in front of someone, so that they cannot go past 挡住某人的去路: *The teacher stood at the entrance, blocking the children's way.* 老师站在入口处, 挡住了孩子们的路。**5** *technical* to limit the use of a particular country's money【术语】限制使用〔某国货币〕: *a blocked currency* 冻结的货币 S3

block sth ↔ **in/out** *phr v* [T] to make a drawing of something that gives a general idea but is not exact 草拟; 画…的简略图: *I'll just block in the main buildings.* 我仅把主要建筑的草图勾画出来。

block sth ↔ **off** *phr v* [T] to completely close a road or path 封闭, 封锁〔道路〕

block sth ↔ **out 1** to stop light passing 挡〔光〕: *a heavy curtain blocking out the light* 挡光的厚窗帘 **2** [I, T **block** sth ↔ **out**] to stop yourself thinking about something, or remembering it 不去想: *a memory so terrible that she tried to block it out* 她努力不去想的可怕的回忆

block·ade¹ /blɑˈked; blɒˈkeɪd/ *n* [usually singular 一般用单数] the surrounding of an area by soldiers or ships to stop people or supplies leaving or entering〔对某地的〕封锁: *a naval blockade* 海上封锁 | **lift/raise the blockade** (=to end a blockade) 解除封锁 | **impose a blockade** *They've imposed an economic blockade on the country.* 他们对该国实行了经济封锁。

blockade² *v* [T] to put a place under a blockade 封锁: *The ships blockaded the port.* 船只封锁了港口。

block·age /ˈblɑkɪdʒ; ˈblɒkɪdʒ/ *n* **1** [C] something that is stopping movement in a narrow place 堵塞物; 障碍, 阻碍: *a blockage in the pipe* 管子内的堵塞物 **2** [U] the state of being blocked or prevented 被阻塞, 堵塞 (状态)

block and tack·le /ˌ· · ˈ··/ *n* [usually singular 一般用单数] a piece of equipment made with wheels and ropes, used for lifting heavy things〔搬提重物的〕滑车装置, 滑轮组, 绞辘

block·bust·er /ˈblɑkˌbʌstə; ˈblɒkˌbʌstə/ *n* [C] **1** *informal* a book or film that is very good or successful【非正式】轰动一时的电影[书籍]: *the latest blockbuster from Hollywood* 好莱坞最新大片 **2** a very powerful bomb 爆炸力巨大的炸弹

block cap·i·tals /ˌ·ˈ···/ *n* [plural] letters in their large form, eg A, B, C, rather than a, b, c 大写字母: *Complete the form in block capitals.* 用大写字母填写表格。

block·head /ˈblɑkˌhɛd; ˈblɒkhed/ *n* [C] *informal* a very stupid person【非正式】大笨蛋, 大傻瓜: *You silly blockhead!* 你这傻瓜!

block·house /ˈblɑkˌhaʊs; ˈblɒkhaʊs/ *n* [C] a small strong building used as a shelter from enemy guns 碉堡; 掩体

block let·ters /ˌ·ˈ··/ *n* [plural] block capitals 大写字母

block par·ty /ˈ·ˌ··/ *n* [C] *AmE* a party held in the street for all the people living in the area【美】〔为居住在同一街区里所有人举办的〕街头聚会

Bloc Qué·bé·cois /ˌblɑk kebeˈkwɑ; ˌblɒk keɪbeˈkwɑː/ a political party in Canada which wants the PROVINCE of Quebec to be a separate country 魁北克人党〔要求魁北克省独立的一个加拿大政治党派〕

Bloemfontein /ˈblumfɑntɛn; ˈbluːmfɒntein/ a city in South Africa, which is its JUDICIARY centre 布隆方丹〔南非城市, 为该国的司法首都〕

Blofeld, Ernst Stavro the most important enemy of James Bond in the NOVELs by Ian Fleming 布洛菲尔德〔伊恩·弗莱明的系列小说中詹姆斯·邦德最主要的敌人〕

S3 **bloke** /blok; bləʊk/ *n* [C] *BrE informal* a man【英, 非正式】人, 家伙: *The new bloke next door seems a bit weird.* 隔壁新来的那个家伙看起来有点古怪。

blok·ish /ˈblokɪʃ; ˈbləʊkɪʃ/ *adj BrE humorous* if you do blokish things, you behave in a traditionally male way【英, 幽默】男性传统的; 传统上由男人来做的: *playing football, fixing the car and other blokish activities* 踢足球、修汽车及其他男人做的事 —**blokishness** *n* [U]: *amiable blokishness* 和蔼可亲的男性举止

blond /blɑnd; blɒnd/ *adj* **1** another spelling of BLONDE blonde 的另一种拼法 **2** a man who is blond has pale or yellow hair〔男子〕金发的

S3 **blonde¹** /blɑnd; blɒnd/ *adj* **1** blonde hair is pale or yellow in colour〔头发〕金色的, 浅色的 **2** a woman who is blonde has pale or yellow hair〔女子〕金发的, 浅色头发的

S3 **blonde²** *n* [C] *informal* a woman with pale or yellow-coloured hair【非正式】金发女人, 浅色头发的女人: *a beautiful blonde* 金发美女

Blon·die /ˈblɑndɪ; ˈblɒndi/ the main female character in the US CARTOON STRIP which is also called 'Blondie'. 金发女〔美国连环漫画《金发女》的同名女主人公〕

> **CULTURAL NOTE 文化注释**
> Blondie is a kind attractive HOUSEWIFE who is always helping her husband Dagwood whenever he does something wrong. Many people consider Blondie to be an old-fashioned STEREOTYPE of the perfect housewife. 金发女是一位善良迷人的主妇, 她总是在丈夫达格伍德做错事情时帮他解围。很多人认为金发女是旧时完美主妇的典型。

S1 W1 **blood¹** /blʌd; blʌd/ *n*

1 ▶IN YOUR BODY 身体内◀ [U] the red liquid that your heart pumps round your body 血, 血液: *She lost a lot of blood in the accident.* 她在事故中流了很多血。| **give/donate blood** (=have blood taken from you and stored, to be used to treat someone else) 献血, 捐血 | **draw blood** (=make someone bleed) 使〔某人〕出血 *The dog bit her but failed to draw blood.* 狗咬了她, 但没出血。

2 have sb's blood on your hands to have caused someone's death 双手沾满某人的鲜血, 导致某人死亡

3 in cold blood in a cruel and deliberate way 冷血地, 残忍地; 蓄意地: *He murdered the old man in cold blood.* 他残忍地杀害了那位老人。

4 make your blood boil to make you extremely angry 使某人怒火中烧: *The way they treat those people really makes my blood boil.* 他们这样对待那些人真使我非常气愤。

5 make your blood run cold to make you feel extremely frightened 令某人毛骨悚然: *The sudden scream made my blood run cold.* 突然的尖叫声吓得我毛骨悚然。

6 it's like getting blood out of a stone used when you find it difficult to persuade someone to give you or tell you something 犹如想从石头里榨出血来〔指要从某人身上获得某物或探听某事很困难〕

7 blood is thicker than water used to say that family relationships are more important than any other kind 血浓于水; 疏不间亲

8 be after sb's blood to be angry enough to want to hurt or injure someone 恨透了某人; 恨不得咬某人一口

9 sb's blood is up someone is extremely angry and determined to do something about it 动怒, 激动, 冲动: *They tried to stop me, but my blood was up.* 他们设法阻止我, 但我怒不可遏。

10 ▶YOUR FAMILY/GROUP 家庭/团体◀ [U] the family or group to which you belong from the time that you are born 血统, 血缘; 家世, 门第: *There's French blood on his mother's side.* 他母亲有法国血统。

11 be/run in sb's blood if an ability or tendency is in, or runs in, someone's blood, it is natural to them and others in their family 家传的; 天赋的

12 sweat blood to work extremely hard to achieve something 拼命工作: *Beth sweated blood over that article.* 贝丝呕心沥血地写那篇文章。

13 new/fresh blood new members in a group or organization who bring new ideas and energy 新鲜血液, 新增的成员: *It's good to have some new blood in the department.* 系里增添了新成员是件好事。

14 young blood *old-fashioned* a word for a fashionable young man【过时】时尚的年轻人 —see also 另见 **bad blood** (BAD¹ (22)), BLUE-BLOODED, RED BLOOD CELL, WHITE BLOOD CELL, **your own flesh and blood** (FLESH¹ (5))

blood² *v* [T] **1** *BrE* to give someone their first experience of an activity, especially a difficult or unpleasant one【英】使〔某人〕取得初次经验〔尤指在困难或不愉快的活动中〕**2** to give a hunting dog its first taste of blood 使〔猎犬〕初尝血腥味

blood-and-guts /ˌ··ˈ·◂/ *adj AmE informal* full of action or violence【美, 非正式】激烈的, 猛烈的; 充满暴力的: *a blood-and-guts struggle between the two teams* 两队之间的激烈争夺

blood-and-thun·der /ˌ··ˈ··◂/ *adj* [only before noun 仅用于名词前] *BrE* a blood-and-thunder film or story is full of exciting and violent action【英】〔电影、小说等〕充满血腥和暴力场面的

blood bank /ˈ· ·/ *n* [C] a store of human blood to be used in hospital treatment 血库

blood·bath /ˈblʌdˌbæθ; ˈblʌdbɑːθ/ *n* [singular] the violent killing of many people at one time 血洗; 大屠杀

blood broth·er /ˌ·ˈ··/ *n* [C] a man who promises loyalty to another, often in a ceremony in which the men's blood is mixed together 歃血盟誓的兄弟, 结盟的拜把兄弟

blood count /ˈ· ·/ *n* [C] a medical examination of someone's blood to see if it contains the right substances in the right amounts 血球计数, 血细胞计数: *Her blood count is very low.* 她的血细胞计数很低。

blood·cur·dling /ˈblʌdˌkɝdlɪŋ; ˈblʌdˌkɜːdlɪŋ/ *adj* extremely frightening 令人心惊胆战的, 令人毛骨悚然的: *a bloodcurdling shriek* 令人毛骨悚然的尖叫声

blood do·nor /ˈ· ˌ··/ *n* [C] someone who gives their blood to be used in the treatment of other people 献血者, 捐血者

blood feud /ˈ· ·/ *n* [C] a quarrel that lasts for many years between people or families and in which each side murders or injures members of the other side〔家族之间多年的〕宿仇, 血仇

blood group /ˈ· ·/ *n* [C] *BrE* one of the classes into which human blood can be separated, including A, B, AB and O【英】血型〔包括 A 型、B 型、AB 型和 O 型〕; BLOOD TYPE *AmE*【美】

blood heat /ˈ· ·/ *n* [U] the normal temperature of the human body, about 37°C 人体血温〔约 37°C〕

blood·hound /ˈblʌdˌhaʊnd; ˈblʌdhaʊnd/ *n* [C] a large dog with a very good sense of smell, often used for hunting〔嗅觉灵敏, 常用于追踪的〕大警犬, 大猎犬

blood·less /ˈblʌdlɪs; ˈblʌdləs/ *adj* **1** without killing or violence 不流血的; 没有暴力的: *a bloodless coup* 不流血的政变 **2** a bloodless part of your body is very pale 无血色的, 苍白的: *His lips were thin and bloodless.* 他的嘴唇又薄又苍白。**3** lacking in human feeling 无情的, 冷酷的 —compare 比较 BLOODY² —**bloodlessly** *adv* —**bloodlessness** *n* [U]

blood·let·ting /ˈblʌdˌlɛtɪŋ; ˈblʌdˌletɪŋ/ *n* [U] **1** killing people; BLOODSHED 流血, 杀戮: *The violence was a foretaste of the bloodletting to come.* 这次暴力事件预示着一场杀戮将要发生。**2** the medical practice in former times of treating people who were ill by removing some of their blood〔古代医疗的〕放血疗法 **3** the reduction of the number of people working for an organization 人员消耗; 裁员

blood lust /ˈ· ·/ *n* [U] a strong desire to be violent 杀戮欲; 暴力欲

blood mon·ey /ˈ· ,· ·/ *n* [U] **1** money paid for murdering someone 付给（受雇）杀手的酬金 **2** money paid to the family of someone who has been murdered 偿付给被害人亲属的抚恤金

blood or·ange /ˈ· ,· ·/ *n* [C] an orange with red juice〔具深红汁液的〕血橙

blood poi·son·ing /ˈ· ,· · ·/ *n* [U] *technical* a serious medical condition in which an infection spreads from a small area of your body through your blood【术语】血中毒，败血症

blood pres·sure /ˈ· ,· ·/ *n* [U] the force with which blood travels through your body, that can be measured by a doctor 血压: *high blood pressure* 高血压

blood-red /,· ˈ·◂/ *adj* dark red, like blood 血红（色）的: *blood-red lipstick* 血红色的唇膏

blood re·la·tion /ˈ· ·,· ·/ *n* [C] someone related to you by birth rather than by marriage 血缘关系，血亲，骨肉

blood·shed /ˈblʌd,ʃɛd; ˈblʌdʃed/ *n* [U] the killing of people, usually in fighting or war〔常指在搏斗或战争中的〕流血，杀戮，残杀: *taking action to stop the bloodshed* 采取行动阻止流血事件

blood·shot /ˈblʌd,ʃɑt; ˈblʌdʃɒt/ *adj* bloodshot eyes are slightly reddish in colour〔眼睛〕充血的，有血丝的

blood sport /ˈ· ·/ *n* [C] a sport that involves the killing of animals or birds 以猎杀〔鸟兽〕为乐的运动[活动]: *a demonstration against blood sports* 一场抗议捕杀鸟兽的游行

blood·stain /ˈblʌd,sten; ˈblʌdsteɪn/ *n* [C] a mark or spot of blood 血污，血迹 —**bloodstained** *adj*: *a bloodstained handkerchief* 血迹斑斑的手帕

blood·stock /ˈblʌd,stɑk; ˈblʌdstɒk/ *n* [U] horses that have been bred for racing〔用于赛马的〕纯种马: *a bloodstock auction* 纯种马拍卖

blood·stream /ˈblʌd,strim; ˈblʌdstriːm/ *n* [singular] the blood as it flows around your body 循环于体内的血液，血流: *The drug is injected directly into the bloodstream.* 药物直接注射入血液中。

blood·suck·er /ˈblʌd,sʌkɚ; ˈblʌd,sʌkə/ *n* [C] **1** a creature that sucks blood from the body of other animals 吸血的动物；吸血虫 **2** *informal* someone who always uses other people's money or help【非正式】吸血鬼，剥削者

blood·thirst·y /ˈblʌd,θɝstɪ; ˈblʌd,θɜːsti/ *adj* **1** eager to kill and wound, or enjoying seeing killing and violence 嗜杀成性的；耽于暴力的: *ruthless and bloodthirsty warriors* 残暴的斗士 **2** describing or showing violence 涉及暴力的: *The film was too bloodthirsty for me.* 这部电影暴力镜头太多，我不喜欢。—**bloodthirstily** *adv* —**bloodthirstiness** *n* [U]

blood trans·fu·sion /ˈ· ·,· ·/ *n* [C] the process of putting blood into someone's body as a medical treatment 输血

blood type /ˈ· ·/ *n* [C] *AmE* one of the classes into which human blood can be separated, including A, B, AB, and O【美】血型〔包括 A 型、B 型、AB 型和 O 型〕; BLOOD GROUP *BrE*【英】

blood ves·sel /ˈ· ,· ·/ *n* [C] **1** any of the tubes through which blood flows in your body 血管 —see picture at 参见 TEETH 图 **2 burst a blood vessel** to become very angry or upset about something 大动肝火: *My dad nearly burst a blood vessel when I told him I quit college.* 我告诉爸爸我从大学退学时，他气得血管都要炸了。

S3 W3 **blood·y[1]** /ˈblʌdɪ; ˈblʌdi/ *adj, adv spoken especially BrE* used to emphasize what you are saying in a slightly rude way【口，尤英】很，太，十分，非常〔用于以不太礼貌的方式加强语气〕: *It's bloody cold out there!* 外边的天气可真冷！| *It serves you bloody well right.* 你这是活该。| *What a bloody cheek!* 真不要脸！| *Bloody hell!* 该死的！| **not bloody likely** (=definitely not) 绝对不行；休想 *"Are you going to go with him?" "Not bloody likely."* "你要和他一块儿去吗？" "绝对不行。"

bloody[2] *adj* **1** covered in blood or bleeding 流血的；血淋淋的，染满血的 **2** with a lot of killing and injuries 血腥的；伤亡惨重的；残忍的: *a bloody battle* 伤亡惨重的战役 **3 scream/yell bloody murder** *AmE informal* to protest in a loud, very angry way【美，非正式】大声愤怒地抗议: *She was furious – screaming bloody murder at the manager!* 她勃然大怒，对经理人声吼叫！**4 bloody but unbowed** harmed by events but not defeated by them 受到伤害但没有被击垮: *He emerged from the discussions bloody but unbowed.* 讨论终于完结了，他虽受到猛烈抨击，但没有被击垮。**5** *BrE old-fashioned* unpleasant and nasty or unkind【英，过时】讨厌的；恶劣的；不友好的

bloody[3] *v* [T] *formal* to injure someone so that blood comes, or to cover something with blood【正式】使〔某人〕受伤（流血）: *The boy punched Jack and bloodied his nose.* 那个男孩用拳猛击杰克，致使他鼻子流血。

Bloody Mary /,· · ˈ· ·/ an alcoholic drink made from VODKA, TOMATO juice, and SPICES 血玛丽〔一种鸡尾酒，由伏特加、番茄汁和调味品混合调制而成〕—see 见 Queen MARY I

bloody-mind·ed /,· · ˈ· ·◂/ *adj BrE informal* deliberately making things difficult for other people【英，非正式】故意作对的；有意刁难的；顽固的: *Stop being so bloody-minded!* 不要再故意刁难人了！—**bloody-mindedly** *adv* —**bloody-mindedness** *n* [U]

Bloody Sun·day /,· · ˈ· ·/ Sunday, 30th January 1972, when British soldiers in Northern Ireland used force to control a large crowd of people who were protesting against the policy of INTERNMENT (=putting people in prison without a trial if they were believed to be members of the IRA). 13 people were killed when the soldiers fired at the crowd. 血腥星期天〔1972 年 1 月 30 日（星期天），英国士兵在北爱尔兰动用武力镇压抗议政府不经审判即拘禁政策的群众，13 人遭枪杀〕

Bloody Tower /,· · ˈ· ·/ a part of the Tower of London. It became known as the Bloody Tower after two young princes, the NEPHEWS of Richard III, were believed to be murdered there in 1483. 血腥塔〔伦敦塔的一部分，据说有两位年轻王子，也就是理查三世的两个侄子，1483 年在此遭到谋杀，故得其名〕

bloom[1] /blum; bluːm/ *n* **1** [C,U] a flower or flowers 花: *beautiful red blooms* 美丽的红花 | *a mass of bloom on the apple trees* 苹果树上的花团 **2 in (full) bloom** with the flowers fully open〔花朵〕盛开，怒放 **3** [U singular] a covering of fine powder that forms on fruit such as GRAPES or PLUMS〔葡萄或李子等水果表面的一层〕粉霜，粉衣 **4 the bloom of youth/love etc** *literary* the best or happiest time when you are young【文】豆蔻年华；全盛时期

bloom[2] *v* [I] **1** to produce flowers or to open as flowers 开花；〔花〕盛开 **2** to become happy and healthy or successful 精神焕发；兴旺: *Anne has bloomed since she got her new job.* 安妮有了新工作后容光焕发。

Bloom, Le·o·pold /ˈliəpold; ˈliːəpəʊld/ the main character in the NOVEL *Ulysses* by James Joyce 布卢姆〔詹姆斯·乔伊斯的小说《尤利西斯》中的主人公〕

bloom·er /ˈblumɚ; ˈbluːmə/ *n* **1 bloomers** [plural] **a)** *old-fashioned* women's underwear like loose trousers that end at your knees【过时】〔长及膝部的女用〕灯笼内裤 **b)** short loose trousers that end in a tight band at your knees worn by women in Europe and America in the late 19th century〔19 世纪末欧美妇女所穿的长及膝部的〕灯笼裤 **2** [C] *BrE humorous, old-fashioned* an embarrassing mistake in front of other people【英，幽默，过时】〔在大庭广众前犯的〕错误，差错，洋相; BLOOPER (1) *AmE*【美】

bloom·ing /ˈblumɪŋ; ˈbluːmɪŋ/ *adj, adv BrE spoken* used for emphasizing a remark or statement【英口】太，很，非常〔用于加强语气〕: *It's blooming ridiculous!* 这真是太荒唐了！| *Blooming heck! – look at this!* 活见鬼！看看这个！

Blooms·bu·ry /ˈblumzbərɪ; ˈbluːmzbəri/ a busy area in the centre of London which has attractive buildings and SQUARES (=open areas with grass and trees, surrounded on four sides by roads and buildings), where many writers and artists lived in the early part of the 20th century 布卢姆斯伯里〔位于伦敦市中心的一个繁华区，有漂亮的建筑和广场。20 世纪初期这里居住过许多作家、艺术家〕

Bloomsbury Group, the /ˈ· · ·, ·/ a group of artists and writers who lived and met each other regularly in Bloomsbury in the early part of the 20th century. The most famous member of the group was Virginia Woolf. 布卢姆斯伯里社团〔20 世纪初期在布卢姆斯伯里居住并定期聚会的一批艺术家和作家，其中最著名的是弗吉尼亚·吴尔夫〕

Bloomsday /ˈblumz,de; ˈbluːmzdeɪ/ June 16th, celebrated in Dublin as the day in the life of Leopold Bloom which is described in James Joyce's NOVEL *Ulysses*: Bloomsday has turned into a CARNIVAL, attended by thousands of people who know little about James Joyce. 布卢姆日〔即 6 月 16 日，都柏林人庆祝的一个日子，纪念詹姆斯·乔伊斯的小说《尤利西斯》中的人物利奥波德·布卢姆 1904 年 6 月 16 日这一天的经历：布卢姆日已演变成了一个狂欢节。尽管每年都有成千上万的人参与狂欢，但参与者对詹姆斯·乔伊斯却知之甚少〕

bloop·er /ˈblupɚ; ˈbluːpə/ *n* [C] *AmE informal*【美，非正式】**1** an embarrassing mistake made in front of other people〔在大庭广众前犯的〕错误，差错，洋相; BLOOMER (2) *BrE*【英】: *I made a real blooper yesterday.* 昨天我大出洋相。**2** a ball in BASEBALL that is high and slow and easy to catch or hit〔棒球中的〕高吊下旋球

blos·som[1] /ˈblɑsəm; ˈblɒsəm/ *n* [C,U] **1** a flower or all the flowers on a tree or bush〔指树或灌木的〕花，花簇: *orange blossom* 香橙花 **2 in (full) blossom** with the flowers open 鲜花盛开

blossom² *v* [I] **1** if trees blossom, they produce flowers 开花: *a blossoming apple tree* 正在开花的苹果树 **2** also 又作 **blossom out** to become happier, more beautiful, more successful etc 变快乐了；变漂亮了；兴旺：*Pete has really blossomed out in his new school.* 皮特到了新学校真的进步了。

blot¹ /blɑt; blɒt/ *v* **blotted, blotting** [T] **1** to dry a wet surface by pressing soft paper or cloth on it〔用软纸或布等〕吸干 **2 blot your copybook** *informal* to do something that spoils the idea that people have of you【非正式】玷污自己的名声

blot sth ↔ **out** *phr v* [T] to cover or hide something completely 把…遮住，遮盖；涂去；隐藏：*Thick, white smoke completely blotted out the sun.* 浓重的白烟完全遮住了阳光。| *She had blotted out all her memories of the accident.* 她已经抹去了对那场事故的所有记忆。

blot sth ↔ **up** *phr v* [T] to remove liquid from a surface by pressing a soft cloth, paper etc onto it〔用软布或纸张等〕擦干，吸干

blot² *n* [C] **1** a mark or spot that spoils something or makes it dirty 污点，污渍：*ink blots* 墨水渍 **2** a building, structure etc that is ugly and spoils the appearance of a place 破坏了某地方景致的东西〈如楼房等〉: **a blot on the landscape** *That new power station is a real blot on the landscape.* 那座新建的电站真是煞风景。**3** something that spoils the good opinion other people have of you〔尤指名誉的〕污点，瑕疵：*The Colonel's confession is a blot on the army's honor.* 上校的供词玷污了军队的名誉。

blotch /blɑtʃ; blɒtʃ/ *n* [C] a pink or red mark on the skin, or a coloured mark on something〔皮肤上的〕斑，疤；〔衣服等上的〕污渍 —**blotchy** *adj* —**blotched** *adj*

blot·ter /ˈblɑtə; ˈblɒtə/ *n* [C] **1** a large piece of blotting paper kept on the top of a desk 吸墨纸 **2** *AmE* a book in which an official daily record is kept【美】记事本，临时记录簿：*the police blotter* 警察临时记事本

blotting pa·per /ˈ·· ,··/ *n* [U] soft thick paper used for drying wet ink on a page after writing 吸墨纸

blot·to /ˈblɑto; ˈblɒtəʊ/ *adj BrE old-fashioned* drunk【英，过时】烂醉的

blouse /blaus; blaʊz/ *n* [C] a shirt for women 女式宽松短衫，女衬衫：*a silk blouse* 丝质女衬衫

blow¹ /blo; bləʊ/ *v past tense* **blew** /blu; bluː/ *past participle* **blown** /blon; bləʊn/

1 ►WIND MOVING 风移动◄ [I] if the wind or a current of air blows, it moves〔风〕吹，刮：*A cold breeze was blowing.* 寒风在吹。

2 ►WIND MOVING STH 风吹动某物◄ [I usually+adv/prep, T] to move something, or to be moved, by the force of the wind or a current of air 吹动；刮走：*Her hair was blowing in the breeze.* 她的头发在微风中飘扬。| *A sudden draught blew the door shut.* 一阵突如其来的穿堂风把门刮上了。

3 ►AIR FROM YOUR MOUTH 嘴里呼出的空气◄ [I, T] to send out a current of air from your mouth 吹气；喷气：*She blew on her coffee to cool it down.* 她把咖啡吹凉。

4 ►MAKE A NOISE 弄出声响◄ [I,T] to make a sound by passing air through a musical instrument or a horn 吹奏；(使) 鸣响：*The whistle blew for halftime.* 哨子声响起，上半场结束。

5 ►VIOLENCE 暴力◄ [T] to damage or destroy something violently with an explosion or by shooting 炸毁，摧毁：**blow sth away/out/off** *The explosion blew the ship right out of the water.* 爆炸将船掀出水面。

6 ►LOSE MONEY 损失金钱◄ [T] *informal* to spend all your money at one time in a careless way【非正式】乱花，挥霍：*He's blown all his wages on a new stereo.* 他花掉所有的工资买了一台新的立体声音响。

7 ►LOSE AN OPPORTUNITY 失去机会◄ [T] *informal* to lose a good opportunity by making a mistake or by being careless【非正式】失掉，断送：*We've blown our chances of getting that new contract.* 我们失去了得到那份新合同的机会。

8 ►SURPRISE/ANNOYANCE 惊讶/烦恼◄ blow/blow me/blow that etc *BrE spoken* used to show surprise, annoyance, or determination【英口】真没料到；糟糕〔表示惊讶、烦恼或决心〕：*Blow me if she didn't just run off!* 她没有逃走才怪呢！| *Blow it! I forgot to phone Jane.* 糟糕！我忘了给简打电话。

9 ►MAKE A SHAPE 造成某形状◄ [T] to make or shape something by sending out a current of air from your mouth 吹制：**blow a bubble** (=make a ball shape) 吹泡泡 | **blow glass** (=shape glass by blowing into it when it is very hot) 吹制玻璃（器皿）

10 blow sth (up) out of all proportion to make something seem much more serious or important than it is 小题大作；夸大

11 ►LEAVE 离开◄ blow town *AmE slang* to leave a place quickly【美俚】匆忙离开

12 ►ELECTRICITY STOPS 电力中断◄ [I,T] if an electrical FUSE¹ (1) blows, or a piece of electrical equipment blows a FUSE¹ (1), the electricity suddenly stops working because a thin wire has melted〔保险丝〕烧断

13 ►TYRE 轮胎◄ [I,T] if a tyre blows or if a car blows a tyre, it bursts 爆裂；(使) 破裂

14 ►MAKE A SECRET KNOWN 泄密◄ to make known a secret about someone or something 泄露〔秘密〕：*Your coming here has blown the whole operation.* 你来这儿使整个行动泄了密。| **blow sb's cover** (=make known what someone's real job or name is) 泄露某人的真实身份 *It is believed Ames blew the cover of up to twenty agents.* 据信埃姆斯泄露了20个间谍的身份。| **blow the gaff** *BrE slang* (=tell something secret, especially without intending to)【英俚】泄露秘密，告密

15 blow hot and cold *informal* to keep changing your attitude towards someone or something【非正式】(对…) 反复无常，忽冷忽热，摇摆不定：*I can't tell what he wants – he keeps blowing hot and cold.* 我也不知道他要什么，他一直拿不定主意。

16 blow sb a kiss to kiss your hand and then pretend to blow the kiss towards someone 给某人一个飞吻：*She blew him a kiss from across the street.* 她从街对面向他飞吻。

17 blow your mind *informal* to make you feel very surprised and excited by something【非正式】使惊喜，使吃惊：*Meeting her after so many years really blew my mind.* 多年以后再见到她真令我喜出望外。—see also 另见 MIND-BLOWING

18 blow your nose to clean your nose by forcing air through it into a cloth or a piece of soft paper 擤鼻涕

19 blow sth sky-high a) to destroy an idea, plan etc by showing that it cannot be true or effective 粉碎；使破灭：*This new information blows his theory sky-high.* 这个新信息彻底粉碎了他的理论。**b)** to completely destory a building or structure with an explosion 把…炸得粉碎，彻底摧毁

20 blow your top/stack *informal* to become extremely angry quickly or suddenly【非正式】勃然大怒，大发雷霆

21 blow your own trumpet/horn *informal* to praise yourself for your own achievements【非正式】自吹自擂，自夸：*You have to blow your own trumpet sometimes – no one else'll do it for you.* 有时你必须自我吹嘘一下，没有人会代你那样做的。

22 blow the whistle on *informal* to bring something that is wrong to the attention of an authority or the public【非正式】〔向有关当局或公众〕揭发〔错事〕，揭露

23 blow a gasket/fuse *informal* to become very angry and upset【非正式】大怒，暴跳如雷：*Don't tell her that, she'll blow a fuse!* 别告诉她此事，她会大发雷霆的！

blow away *phr v informal, especially AmE*【非正式，尤美】**1** [T **blow** sb ↔ **away**] to kill someone by shooting them with a gun 枪杀：*One move and I'll blow you away!* 动一动我就开枪打死你！**2** [T **blow** sb ↔ **away**] to defeat someone completely, especially in a game〔尤指在比赛中〕彻底战胜〔某人〕：*Nancy blew away the rest of the skaters.* 南希战胜了其他的滑冰运动员。**3** [T **blow** sb ↔ **away**] to completely surprise someone, especially with something they admire〔尤指用某人羡慕的东西〕使人为惊讶

blow down *phr v* [I,T] if the wind blows something down, or if something blows down, the wind makes it fall 吹倒，刮倒：**blow sth ↔ down** *trees blown down in the gale* 被大风刮倒的树木

blow in *phr v* [I] *informal, especially AmE* to arrive unexpectedly【非正式，尤美】突然到来：*Jim blew in about an hour ago – did you see him?* 吉姆大约一小时前突然来了，你见到他了吗？

blow sb/sth **off** *phr v* [T] *AmE slang* to treat someone or something as unimportant【美俚】视〔某人或某事〕不重要；不重视，轻视：*It seems crazy that they blew off Jurassic Park when they were choosing best movies.* 他们真傻，在选择最佳影片时竟然没有瞧上《侏罗纪公园》。

blow out *phr v* **1** [I,T] if you blow a flame or a fire out, or if it blows out, it stops burning 吹灭；熄灭：**blow sth ↔ out** *Blow out all the candles.* 吹灭所有的蜡烛。| *The match blew out before I could light the candles.* 没等我点燃蜡烛，火柴就灭了。**2** [I] if a tyre blows out, it bursts〔车胎〕爆裂 **3** [T] **blow itself out** if a storm blows itself out, it ends〔风暴〕停止：*We sheltered in a barn waiting for the storm to blow itself out.* 我们躲在谷仓里，等风暴停止。**4** [T **blow** sb ↔ **out**] **a)** *AmE spoken* to easily defeat someone【美口】轻而易举地战胜：*We blew them out 28 – zero.* 我们以28比0大胜他们。**b)** *BrE spoken* to disappoint someone by not meeting them or not doing what you have agreed to【英口】失约；失信于〔某人〕：*He blew me out again last night – I've had enough.* 昨晚他又一次失约，我可受够了。

5 [I] if an oil or gas well blows out, oil or gas suddenly escapes 〔油井或气井〕井喷

blow over *phr v* **1** [I,T] if the wind blows something over, or it blows over, the wind makes it fall 刮倒: *Our fence blew over in the storm.* 我们的篱笆被风暴刮倒了。| **blow sth ↔ over** *You could get blown over in a hurricane.* 飓风会把你刮倒。**2** [I] if a storm blows over, it comes to an end 〔暴风雨等〕停止, 平息; 过去 **3** [I] if an argument or unpleasant situation blows over, it no longer seems important or is forgotten 〔重要性〕消失; 被遗忘: *They weren't speaking to each other, but I think it's blown over now.* 他们互相之间不说话, 但我想现在一切都过去了。

blow up 爆炸; 吹气

The car blew up. 汽车爆炸了。

Roald's blowing up a balloon. 罗阿尔德在吹气球。

blow up *phr v* **1** [I,T] to destroy something, or to be destroyed, by an explosion 炸毁; (使) 炸得粉碎: *The plane blew up in midair.* 飞机在半空中爆炸。| **blow sth ↔ up** *Rebels attempted to blow up the bridge.* 叛乱分子企图炸毁桥梁。**2** [T **blow** sth ↔ **up**] to fill something with air or gas 给…充气, 打气: *Stop at the gas station and we'll blow up the tyres.* 在加油站停一下, 我们要给轮胎打气。**3** [T **blow sth ↔ up**] if you blow up a photograph, you make it larger 放大〔照片〕: *How much would it cost to have this photo blown up?* 把这张照片放大要多少钱? **4** [I] if bad weather blows up, it suddenly arrives 〔恶劣天气〕来临: *It looks as though there's a storm blowing up.* 暴风雨好像就要来了。**5** [I] if a situation, argument etc blows up, it suddenly becomes important or dangerous 〔形势、争论等〕变得严峻: *A crisis had blown up over the peace talks.* 和谈出现了危机。**6** [I] to become very angry with someone 大发雷霆: *Jenny's father blew up when she didn't come home last night.* 珍妮昨晚没回家, 她的父亲大为恼火。

3 **blow²** *n* [C]

1 ►HARD HIT 重击◄ a hard hit with the hand, a tool, or a weapon 重击: *a blow on the head* 在头上的一记重击 | *three heavy blows from the hammer* 铁锤的三下重击

2 ►BAD EFFECT 坏效果◄ something that has a bad effect on your confidence or on the possibility of success 〔对信心、成功的可能性等的〕打击: **[+to]** *Her rejection was a serious blow to his pride.* 她的拒绝使他的自尊心受到沉重打击。| **deal a blow** *Withdrawal of government funding dealt a serious blow to the project.* 政府资金的撤出严重打击了这项工程。

3 ►UNHAPPY EVENT 不幸事件◄ an event that makes you very unhappy or shocks you 突然的打击; 不幸: *Her mother's death was a terrible blow.* 她母亲的去世对她是一个可怕的打击。

4 ►BLOWING 吹◄ [C] an action of blowing 〔指动作〕吹: *It took three blows to put out the candles.* 吹了三下才把蜡烛吹灭。

5 come to blows to quarrel seriously and start hitting each other 打起来: *They almost came to blows over the money.* 他们为钱的事差一点儿打起来。

6 soften/cushion the blow to help someone accept something unpleasant or bad 缓和…的打击

7 ►WIND 风◄ [singular] a strong wind or storm 劲风; 风暴 —see also 另见 BODY BLOW, **strike a blow for** (STRIKE¹ (12))

blow-by-blow /ˌ· · ˈ·◂/ *adj* [only before noun 仅用于名词前] a blow-by-blow story, account etc gives all the details of an event as they happened 〔叙述〕极其详尽的: *Jenny bored us all with a blow-by-blow account of her night out.* 珍妮极其详尽地叙述她晚上外出的事, 我们都听烦了。

blow-dry /ˈ· ·/ *v* [T] to dry hair and give it shape by using an electric dryer 〔用吹风机〕吹干〔头发〕; 把〔头发〕吹出发型 —**blow-dry** *n* [C]: *a cut and blow-dry* 剪发并吹风

blow·er /ˈbloə; ˈbləʊə/ *n* [C] **1** a machine that blows out air 吹风机, 鼓风机: *a snow blower for clearing the path* 清扫小径的吹雪机 **2 on the blower** *BrE old-fashioned* on the telephone in order to talk to someone 【英, 过时】打电话: *Get on the blower to him at once.* 马上打电话给他。—see also 另见 GLASSBLOWER

blow-fly /ˈ· ·/ *n* [C] a fly that lays its eggs on meat or wounds 〔产卵于腐肉、创口的〕丽蝇, 绿头苍蝇

blow-hard /ˈ· ·/ *n* [C] *AmE informal* someone who talks about themselves too much 【美, 非正式】自吹自擂者

blow-hole /ˈ· ·/ *n* [C] **1** a hole in the surface of ice to which water animals such as seals (SEAL¹ (1)) come to breathe 〔海豹等动物用来呼吸的结冰水面上的〕冰孔 **2** a hole in the top of the head of a WHALE, DOLPHIN etc through which they breathe 〔鲸鱼、海豚等的〕喷水孔, 鼻孔

blow job /ˈ· ·/ *n* [C] *taboo slang* the practice of touching a man's sexual organs with your lips and tongue to give him sexual pleasure 【讳, 俚】口交

blow-lamp /ˈ· ·/ *n* [C] *BrE* a piece of equipment that produces a small very hot flame, used especially for removing paint 【英】喷灯; BLOWTORCH *AmE* 【美】

blown /blon; bləʊn/ the past participle of BLOW¹

blow-out /ˈbloˌaʊt; ˈbləʊaʊt/ *n* [C] **1** a sudden bursting of a TYRE 轮胎爆裂: *A blow-out at this speed could be really dangerous.* 轮胎在这样的车速下爆裂是很危险的。**2** [usually singular 一般用单数] *informal* a big expensive meal or large social occasion 【非正式】美餐, 盛宴; 大型社交活动 **3** a sudden uncontrolled escape of oil or gas from a well 〔油井或气井的〕井喷 **4** *AmE informal* an easy victory over someone in a game 【美, 非正式】〔比赛中〕轻而易举的胜利

blow·pipe /ˈbloˌpaɪp; ˈbləʊpaɪp/ *n* [C] a tube through which you can blow small stones, poisoned arrows (ARROW (1)) etc, used as a weapon 〔作为武器用的〕吹箭筒, 吹矢枪

blow·torch /ˈbloˌtɔrtʃ; ˈbləʊtɔːtʃ/ *n* [C] *AmE* a piece of equipment that produces a small very hot flame, used especially for removing paint 【美】喷灯; BLOW-LAMP *BrE* 【英】

blow-up /ˈ· ·/ *n* [C] **1** a photograph, or part of a photograph, that has been made larger 放大的照片 **2** [usually singular 一般用单数] a sudden moment of anger 发脾气: *I think they've had a blow-up again.* 我想他们又吵架了。—see also 另见 **blow up** (BLOW¹)

blow·y /ˈbloɪ; ˈbləʊi/ *adj BrE informal* windy 【英, 非正式】刮风的, 风大的

blow·zy, blowsy /ˈblaʊzɪ; ˈblaʊzi/ *adj* a blowzy woman is fat and looks untidy 〔妇女〕体胖而又穿着邋遢的

blub·ber¹ /ˈblʌbə; ˈblʌbə/ *v* **1** also 又作 **blub** [I] to cry noisily, especially in a way that annoys people 号哭: *Stop blubbering, for heaven's sake!* 天哪, 别再哇哇地哭个不停了! **2** also 又作 **blubber out** [T] to say something while crying noisily 边哭边说; 哭诉: *"It's not my fault," she blubbered.* "这不是我的错。" 她哭诉道。

blubber² *n* [U] the fat of sea animals, especially WHALEs 海兽脂肪〔尤指鲸脂〕

bludge /blʌdʒ; blʌdʒ/ *v* [I,T] *AustrE, NZE slang* to get something without working or paying for it 【澳, 新西兰, 俚】(向人) 索取; 不劳而获 —**bludger** *n* [C]

blud·geon¹ /ˈblʌdʒən; ˈblʌdʒən/ *v* [T] **1** [**+into/out of**] to force someone to do something by making threats or arguing with them 强迫, 威胁〔某人做某事〕**2** to hit someone several times with something heavy 用重物接连重击〔某人〕: *bludgeoned to death* 被重击致死

bludgeon² *n* [C] a heavy stick with a thick end, used as a weapon 〔作武器用的〕大头棒

blue¹ /blu; bluː/ *adj* 1 2

1 ►COLOUR 颜色◄ the colour of the clear sky or of the sea on a fine day 蓝色的, 蔚蓝色的, 青色的: *the blue water of the lake* 蔚蓝色的湖水 | *a dark blue raincoat* 深蓝色的雨衣 —see picture on page A5 参见 A5 页图

2 ►SAD 悲伤的◄ [not before noun 不用于名词前] *informal* sad and without hope; DEPRESSED (1a) 【非正式】忧郁的, 沮丧

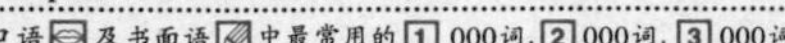

的，悲观的: *That song always makes me feel blue.* 那首歌曲总使我伤感。
3 ▶CONCERNED WITH SEX 与性有关的◀ *informal* concerned with sex in a way that might offend some people【非正式】色情的，淫猥的: *Some of his jokes were a bit blue.* 他的某些笑话有点下流。—see also 另见 BLUE FILM
4 once in a blue moon *informal* hardly ever【非正式】难得有一次，极为罕见: *I only ever see him once in a blue moon.* 我难得见到他。
5 scream/yell blue murder *informal* to shout very loudly in protest against something or because you are in pain【非正式】大声抗议；大声呼救
6 do sth till you're blue in the face *informal* to do something a lot but without achieving what you want【非正式】尽力去做仍无法成功: *You can argue till you're blue in the face, she won't change her mind.* 不管你怎么说，她也不会改变主意的。
7 blue with cold extremely cold 冻得发紫
8 talk a blue streak *AmE informal* to talk a lot without stopping【美，非正式】喋喋不休，说个没完
9 go blue if your skin goes blue, you become blue because you are cold or cannot breathe properly〔因寒冷或不能呼吸而〕脸色发青
10 like blue blazes *AmE informal* extremely【美，非正式】非常，极其: *It hurts like blue blazes!* 疼极了!

blue[2] *n* **1** [C,U] the colour that is blue 蓝色: *the rich greens and blues of the tapestry* 挂毯浓艳的蓝绿色调 | *She nearly always dresses in blue.* 她几乎总穿蓝色衣服。**2 blues** [plural] a slow sad style of music that came from the southern US 布鲁斯音乐〔起源于美国南方的一种缓慢、忧郁的乐曲〕: *a blues singer* 布鲁斯歌手 —see also 另见 RHYTHM AND BLUES **3 the blues** [plural] *informal* feelings of sadness【非正式】忧郁，沮丧: *Don't be surprised if you get the blues for a while after your baby is born.* 如果你在生完孩子后出现暂时的忧郁，你不必感到惊讶。**4 out of the blue** *informal* unexpectedly【非正式】出乎意料地，突如其来地: *a phone call from Jane right out of the blue* 出乎意料地接到了简打来的电话 —see also 另见 **a bolt from/out of the blue** (BOLT[1] (3)) **5 boys in blue** *informal* the police【非正式】警察 **6** [C] **Blue** *BrE* someone who has represented Oxford or Cambridge University at a sport, or the title given to such a person【英】校队选手，"蓝色选手"〔给予曾代表牛津或剑桥大学运动队参赛队员的一种荣誉〕: *a rugger Blue* 橄榄球队的"蓝色选手" **7 the blue** *literary* the sea or the sky【文】海洋；天空

blue[3] *v* [T] *BrE informal* to spend money in a way that is careless or not very responsible【英，非正式】滥用〔钱〕，挥霍: *John blued all his money on drink.* 约翰把他所有的钱都花在酗酒上。

blue ba·by /ˈ· ˌ· ·/ *n* [C] a baby whose skin is slightly blue when it is born because it has a heart problem〔出生时因心脏有先天性缺陷而〕皮肤发青的婴儿

blue·beard /ˈbluˌbɪrd; ˈbluːbɪəd/ *n* [C] a man who marries and kills one wife after another 蓝胡子〔一个连续娶妻杀妻的男人〕

blue·bell /ˈbluˌbɛl; ˈbluːbel/ *n* [C] a small plant with blue flowers that grows in woods 蓝色风铃草

blue·ber·ry /ˈbluˌbɛrɪ; ˈbluːbəri/ *n* [C,U] the small blue fruit of a bushy plant, or the plant itself 蓝莓浆果，紫浆果；乌饭树，蓝莓: *blueberry pie* 蓝莓馅饼 —see picture on page A8 参见 A8 页图

blue·bird /ˈbluˌbɝd; ˈbluːbɜːd/ *n* [C] a small blue bird that lives in North America〔北美的〕蓝色知更鸟，蓝鸫

Blue Birds /ˈ· ˌ·/ an organization in the US for young girls who meet to play games and learn practical skills 蓝鸟少女团〔美国的一个少女组织，其成员会聚在一起玩游戏，学习实用技能〕

blue-blood·ed /ˌ· ˈ··◂/ *adj* belonging to a royal or NOBLE[1] (3) family 贵族血统的，名门出身的: *a blue-blooded French duchess* 有贵族血统的法国女公爵 —**blue-blood** *n* [U]

blue book /ˈ· ·/ *n* [C] **1** *BrE* an official report, usually by a committee, printed by the British Government【英】蓝皮书〔由英国政府印行、通常为某个委员会的官方报告〕**2** *AmE* a book with a blue cover that is used in American colleges for writing answers to examination questions【美】〔美国大学生笔试用的〕蓝色封面的答题册，蓝皮簿

blue·bot·tle /ˈbluˌbɑtl; ˈbluːˌbɒtl/ *n* [C] a large blue fly 青蝇

blue cheese /ˌ· ˈ·/ *n* [C, U] a kind of cheese with blue lines and a strong taste〔带有蓝色霉菌条纹的〕蓝乳酪

blue chip /ˌ· ˈ·◂/ *adj* a blue-chip company or INVESTMENT (1) is profitable and safe〔公司或投资〕稳赚钱的，可靠的，蓝筹〔股〕的: *blue chip stocks and shares* 热门债券和股票 —**blue chip** *n* [C]

blue-col·lar /ˌ· ˈ··◂/ *adj* [only before noun 仅用于名词前] blue-collar workers do hard or dirty work with their hands 蓝领阶级的，体力劳动者的 —compare 比较 PINK-COLLAR, WHITE-COLLAR

Blue Cross /ˌ· ˈ·/ an American medical insurance company 蓝十字会〔美国一家医疗保险公司〕

Blue Dan·ube, The /ˌ· ˈ··/ the title of an extremely popular WALTZ (=a type of music for dancing to), written by Johann Strauss in 1866《蓝色多瑙河》〔小约翰·施特劳斯于 1866 年创作的一首颇受人们喜爱的华尔兹舞曲〕

blue-eyed boy /ˌ· · ˈ·/ *n* [C usually singular 一般用单数] *informal* a man or boy who is liked and approved of by someone in authority【非正式】(男)宠儿: *John was always the blue-eyed boy at school.* 约翰在学校里总是宠儿。

blue film /ˌ· ˈ·/ *n* [C] *BrE informal* a film showing sexual activity; BLUE MOVIE【英，非正式】色情电影

blue·fish /ˈbluˌfɪʃ; ˈbluːfɪʃ/ *n plural* **bluefish** [C] a sea fish that is a bluish colour and is caught for sport and to eat off the North American coast〔北美产的〕青鱼

blue·grass /ˈbluˌgræs; ˈbluːgrɑːs/ *n* [U] **1** a type of music from the southern and western US, played on instruments such as the GUITAR and VIOLIN 蓝草乡村音乐〔美国乡村音乐，起源于南部和西部，通常用吉他或小提琴演奏〕**2** a type of grass found in North America, especially in Kentucky 六月禾〔一种禾本科植物，生长在北美，尤在肯塔基州〕

blue gum /ˈ· ·/ *n* [C] a tall Australian tree that is a type of EUCALYPTUS〔产于澳洲的〕蓝桉树

blue·jay /ˈbluˌdʒe; ˈbluːˌdʒeɪ/ *n* [C] a common large North American bird with blue feathers〔北美产的〕蓝背樫鸟

blue jeans /ˌ· ˈ·/ *n* [plural] *AmE* dark blue trousers made in a heavy material; JEANS【美】牛仔裤

blue law /ˈ· ·/ *n* [C] *AmE* a law to control sexual morals, the drinking of alcohol, working on Sundays etc【美】〔管理性道德、喝酒、星期日工作等的〕清教徒法规，蓝色法规；LICENSING LAWS *BrE*【英】

blue mo·vie /ˌ· ˈ··/ *n* [C] a film showing sexual activity 色情电影

Blue Nile, the /ˌ· ˈ·/ one of the two rivers that form the River Nile. It starts in Ethiopia in East Africa, and flows north to Khartoum in Sudan, where it joins the White Nile. 青尼罗河〔尼罗河的两大源流之一，发源于东非的埃塞俄比亚，向北流向苏丹的喀土穆，与白尼罗河汇合〕

Blue Pe·ter /ˌ· ˈ··/ a children's programme that has been on British television since the late 1950s. It is known for encouraging children to collect money or things for people who are poor or sick, and for showing them how to do and make useful things.《开船旗》〔20 世纪 50 年代末期以来在英国播出的一档儿童电视节目。该节目鼓励儿童为穷人或病人筹集钱物，教他们做有益的事，制作有用的东西〕

blue·print /ˈbluˌprɪnt; ˈbluːˌprɪnt/ *n* [C] **1** a plan for achieving something 计划，设想: *a blueprint for the reform of the tax system* 税制改革计划 **2** a photographic print of a plan for a building, machine etc 蓝图

blue rib·bon /ˌ· ˈ··/ also 又作 **blue riband** *n* [C] *AmE* a small piece of blue material that you give to the first-prize winner of a competition【美】蓝绶带〔颁发给竞赛优胜者作为一等奖标志〕—**blue ribbon** *adj*: *a blue-ribbon recipe* 一流的食谱

Blue Ridge Moun·tains, the /ˌ· · ˈ··/ also 又作 **the Blue Ridge** the part of the Appalachians (=a group of mountains in the eastern US) that goes from southern Pennsylvania to northern Georgia 蓝岭山脉〔阿巴拉契亚山脉的一部分，从宾夕法尼亚州南部延伸至佐治亚州北部〕

blue-rinse /ˌ· ˈ·◂/ *adj BrE*【英】**blue-rinse brigade** *humorous* used to describe older women with traditional RIGHT WING values【幽默】具传统右翼思想的老年妇女，黑发帮 —see also 另见 RINSE[2] (2)

blue-sky /ˈ· ·/ *adj* [only before noun 仅用于名词前] *AmE* blue-sky tests etc are done to test ideas and not for any practical purpose【美】〔测试等〕纯理论的；不切实际的

blue·stock·ing /ˈbluˌstɑkɪŋ; ˈbluːˌstɒkɪŋ/ *n* [C] *BrE old-fashioned* a very well-educated woman【英，过时】有学者气派的女性，才女

bluff[1] /blʌf; blʌf/ *v* [I,T] to pretend that you will do something bad or that you are someone else, especially to get something you want when you are in a difficult or dangerous situation 虚张声势，吓唬；欺骗: *"I'm an accredited British envoy," he bluffed.* "我是官方派来的英国使节。"他吓唬说。| **bluff your way out of/through/past** (=get out of a difficult situation by deceiving someone) 以欺骗手段摆脱困境 *They bluffed their way*

past the prison guard. 他们蒙骗了狱警逃走了。| **bluff it out** (=escape trouble by continuing to deceive someone) 继续蒙骗以脱离困境 | **bluff sb into doing sth** *Rob bluffed the interviewers into believing he'd had lots of experience.* 罗布蒙骗面试考官让他们认为自己很有经验。

bluff² *n* **1** [C,U] an attempt to deceive someone by making them think you will do something when you have no intention of doing it 虚张声势, 吓唬: *Her threat to fire me was little more than a bluff.* 她威胁说要开除我, 但那不过是吓唬人而已。**2 call sb's bluff** to tell someone to do what they threaten because you believe they have no intention of doing it and you want to prove it 促使某人实施其所威胁要做的事; 接受某人挑战 **3** [C] a very steep cliff or slope 峭壁, 悬崖, 陡岸

bluff³ *adj* behaving in a loud, cheerful way, without always considering the way other people feel 率直的, 爽快的, 粗率的: *He tried in his bluff, good-natured way to comfort her.* 他试着用率直而温厚的方式安慰她。—**bluffly** *adv* —**bluffness** *n* [U]

blu·ish /ˋbluɪʃ; ˈbluːɪʃ/ *adj* slightly blue 浅蓝色的; 带青色的: *Her skin had a bluish tinge.* 她的皮肤有点发蓝。

blun·der¹ /ˋblʌndɚ; ˈblʌndə/ *n* [C] a careless or stupid mistake 愚蠢的错误, 疏忽: *A last-minute blunder by the goalkeeper cost them the match.* 守门员最后一分钟的疏忽使他们输掉了这场比赛。

blunder² *v* **1** [I always+adv/prep] to move in an unsteady way, as if you cannot see properly 踉踉跄跄地走, 跌跌撞撞: **blunder around/about/into** *I could hear someone blundering around downstairs.* 我能听到楼下有人在跌跌撞撞地走动。**2** [I] to make a big mistake, especially because you have been careless or stupid 犯愚蠢的错误; 出娄子: *They blundered badly when they appointed him as Chairman.* 他们犯了一个很愚蠢的错误, 就是任命他为主席。—**blunderer** *n* [C]

blun·der·buss /ˋblʌndɚˌbʌs; ˈblʌndəbʌs/ *n* [C] a type of gun used in the past〔老式的〕短程散弹枪

blun·der·ing /ˋblʌndərɪŋ; ˈblʌndərɪŋ/ *adj* [only before noun 仅用于名词前] careless or stupid 粗心的; 愚蠢的: *You blundering idiot! What did you do that for?* 你这个愚蠢的傻瓜! 你为什么要那样做?

blunt¹ /blʌnt; blʌnt/ *adj* **1** not sharp or pointed 钝的, 不锋利的, 不尖的: *All I could find was a blunt pencil.* 我只能找到一支钝铅笔。—opposite 反义词 SHARP¹ (11) —see picture at 参见 SHARP¹ 图 **2** speaking in an honest way even if this upsets people〔说话〕不客气的, 直言不讳的, 耿直的: *Jan was straightforward and blunt as always.* 简总是那样坦率, 直言不讳。—see also 另见 BLUNTLY —**bluntness** *n* [U]

blunt² *v* [T] **1** to make a feeling less strong 减弱: *The bad weather blunted their enthusiasm for camping.* 糟糕的天气减弱了他们去露营的热情。**2** to make the point of a pencil or the edge of a knife less sharp 把〔铅笔尖或刀〕弄钝

Blunt /blʌnt; blʌnt/, **Anthony** /ˋæntənɪ; ˈæntəni/ (1907-83) a British man who was an art historian and director of the Courtauld Institute of Art. In 1979 it was found out that he was a SPY for the Soviet Union when he was a student and during World War II. 布伦特〔(1907-1983), 英国艺术史学家、考陶尔德艺术学院院长。1979年发现, 他在上学和二战期间曾担任过前苏联间谍〕

blunt·ly /ˋblʌntlɪ; ˈblʌntli/ *adv* speaking in a direct, honest way that sometimes upsets people〔说话〕不客气地, 直言不讳地: *"You've drunk too much," she said bluntly.* "你喝得太多了。"她不客气地说。| **to put it bluntly** *spoken*【口】*To put it bluntly, she's not up to the job.* 恕我直言, 她不适合这份工作。

blur¹ /blɝ; blɜː/ *n* [singular] **1** [C] a shape that you cannot see clearly 模糊不清的事物: *Everything's a blur without my glasses.* 不戴眼镜我眼前一片模糊。| *the blur of headlights in the distance* 远处隐隐约约的汽车前灯 **2** an unclear memory of something 模糊的记忆: *The events of that day gradually became a blur in her mind.* 那天发生的事在她的脑海中逐渐变得模糊。

blur² *v* **1** [I,T] to become difficult to see or make something difficult to see, because the edges are not clear (使)模糊, (使)看不清楚: *The ships on the horizon seemed to blur before my eyes.* 远处地平线上的船只看上去似乎模模糊糊的。**2** [I,T] to make the difference between two ideas, subjects etc less clear (使)不明朗, (使)不清楚: *The differences between the two political parties have slowly blurred.* 两党之间的分歧慢慢地已不再明显。—see also 另见 BLURRED —**blurry** *adj*: *a few blurry photos of their holiday together* 几张他们在一起度假时拍的模糊照片

blurb /blɝb; blɜːb/ *n* [C] a short description giving information about a book, new product etc 书的内容提要; 新产品的简介

blurred 模糊的

The words were blurred without his glasses.
他不戴眼镜字就变得模糊了。

blurred /blɝd; blɜːd/ *adj* **1** unclear in shape, or making it difficult to see shapes〔形状〕模糊的: *a blurred photo* 一张模糊的照片 **2** difficult to remember or understand clearly〔记忆〕模糊的; 不太好理解的: *blurred memories* 模糊的记忆

blurt /blɝt; blɜːt/ *v*

blurt sth ↔ **out** *phr v* [T] to say something suddenly and without thinking, usually because you are nervous or excited〔尤指因紧张或激动而〕不假思索地说出, 脱口说出, 说漏嘴: *Peter blurted the news out before we could stop him.* 我们还没来得及阻止, 彼得就脱口说出了那个消息。

blush¹ /blʌʃ; blʌʃ/ *v* [I] **1** to become red in the face, usually because you are embarrassed〔因难为情而〕脸红: *He blushes every time he speaks to her.* 他每次和她说话都脸红。**2** to feel ashamed or embarrassed about something 感到不好意思; 惭愧: **blush to do sth** *I blush to think of the things I did when I was younger.* 想起我年轻时做过的事, 我就感到羞愧难当。**3 the blushing bride** *humorous* a young woman on her wedding day【幽默】含羞的新娘 —**blushingly** *adv*

blush² *n* **1** [C] the red colour on your face that appears when you are embarrassed 脸红, 赧颜: *She felt a blush come to her cheeks when her name was mentioned.* 她的名字被提到时, 她感到一阵脸红。**2 spare my blushes** *old-fashioned* used to say that someone is praising you too much【过时】别让我脸红, 别让我难为情 **3 at first blush** *literary* when first thought of or considered【文】猛一看, 乍看时: *At first blush this discovery would seem to confirm his theory.* 乍一看, 这项发现似乎证实了他的理论。**4** [U] *AmE* blusher【美】胭脂霜[粉]

blush·er /ˋblʌʃɚ; ˈblʌʃə/ *n* [U] cream or powder used for making your cheeks look red or pink 胭脂霜[粉]; blush *AmE*【美】

blus·ter /ˋblʌstɚ; ˈblʌstə/ *v* [I] **1** to speak in a loud, angry way 咆哮, 叫嚷, 叱喝: *He was inclined to bluster when his authority was challenged.* 当他的权威受到挑战时, 他就会声嘶力竭地喊叫。**2** if the wind blusters, it blows violently〔风〕狂吹 —**bluster** *n* [U] —**blustering** *adj*: *blustering wintry weather* 狂风怒吼的寒冷天气

blus·ter·y /ˋblʌstərɪ; ˈblʌstəri/ *adj* blustery weather is very windy〔天气〕恶劣的; 狂风大作的: *a cold and blustery day* 寒风凛冽的一天 —see picture on page A13 参见 A13 页图

Blu-tack /ˋbluˌtæk; ˈbluːtæk/ *trademark* a FLEXIBLE ADHESIVE substance used in the home or office. It is often used to attach POSTERS or decorations to a wall without damaging paint or wallpaper.【商标】蓝丁胶〔一种家用或办公使用的胶粘材料, 通常用于在墙上粘贴海报或饰品, 而不会损坏漆面或墙纸〕

blvd the written abbreviation of 缩写= BOULEVARD

Bly·ton /ˋblaɪtn; ˈblaɪtn/, **E·nid** /ˋinɪd; ˈiːnɪd/ (1897-1978) a British writer of books for children, who invented many characters 布莱顿〔(1897-1978), 英国儿童读物作家, 塑造了不少人物〕

BM /ˌbi ˋɛm; ˌbiː ˈem/ *n* [singular] the abbreviation of 缩写= BRITISH MUSEUM

BMA, the /ˌbi ɛm ˋe; ˌbiː em ˈeɪ/ *n* [singular] the British Medical Association; an organization that represents medical doctors in the UK. There is a similar organization in the US called the A. M.A. 英国医学会〔英国的一个医生组织。美国也有类似的一个组织, 称为美国医学会〕

BMJ, the /ˌbi ɛm ˋdʒe; ˌbiː em ˈdʒeɪ/ *n* [singular] the British Medical Journal; a magazine for doctors, nurses, and others in the medical profession《英国医学杂志》〔一份供医生、护士及医疗行业其他从业人员阅读的杂志〕

B-mov·ie /ˈbi ˌmuvɪ; ˈbiː ˌmuːvi/ *n* [C] a cheaply-made film of low quality〔廉价制作、质量不高的〕二流影片

BMW /ˌbi ɛm ˈdʌbljʊ; ˌbiː em ˈdʌbəljuː/ *trademark* **1** a German company which makes high quality cars and powerful MOTORCYCLES【商标】宝马公司〔德国一家公司, 生产高级轿车和大马力摩托车〕**2** a car made by BMW 宝马汽车

BMX /ˌbi ɛm ˈɛks; ˌbiː em ˈeks/ *trademark* a type of bicycle designed to be ridden over rough ground, with a strong frame and small wide wheels【商标】越野自行车, 小轮车〔针对崎岖地形而设计的一款自行车, 车架结实, 车轮小而宽〕

B'nai B'rith /bəˌne ˈbrɪθ; bəˌneɪ ˈbrɪθ/ an international organization of Jewish people that works to oppose ANTI-SEMITISM (=unfair treatment of Jewish people or violence against them) and that helps Jewish people all over the world 圣约之子会〔犹太人国际性组织, 旨在抵制反犹太主义, 帮助全世界的犹太人〕

BO /ˌbi ˈo; ˌbiː ˈəʊ/ *n* [U] body odour; an unpleasant smell from someone's body caused by sweat 体臭, 狐臭

bo·a /ˈboə; ˈbəʊə/ *n* [C] **1** also 又作 **boa con·strict·or** /ˈ· · ˌ· ·/ a large snake that is not poisonous, but kills animals by crushing them 大蟒蛇 **2** a FEATHER BOA〔一种长蛇形〕女用羽毛围巾

Bo·a·di·ce·a /ˌboədɪˈsiə; ˌbəʊədɪˈsiːə/ —see 见 BOUDICCA

boar /bɔr; bɔː/ *n* [C] **1** a wild pig (公) 野猪 **2** a male pig 公猪

boards 板; 牌子

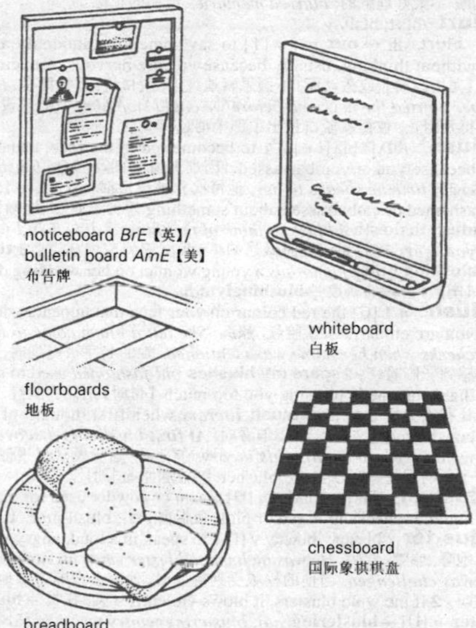

noticeboard *BrE*【英】/ bulletin board *AmE*【美】布告牌

whiteboard 白板

floorboards 地板

chessboard 国际象棋棋盘

breadboard 切面包板

board¹ /bɔrd; bɔːd/ *n*

1 ▶INFORMATION 消息◀ [C] a flat wide piece of wood, plastic etc that shows a particular type of information〔显示资料用的〕硬质板; 布告牌, 公告牌: *I wrote the examples up on the board.* 我把例子写在黑板上。| *Can I put this notice on the board?* 我可以把这个启事贴在布告牌上吗? | *I'll check the departure board for train times.* 我会到布告板处查一下火车的开车时间。—see also 另见 NOTICEBOARD, SCOREBOARD

2 ▶FOR PUTTING THINGS ON 供放东西用◀ [C] a flat piece of wood, plastic, card etc that you use for a particular purpose such as cutting things on, or for playing indoor games〔特殊用途的〕平板: *Cut the bread on the board, not the table!* 把面包放在切板上切, 不要放在桌上切! | *Where's the chessboard?* 棋盘在哪儿? —see also 另见 BREADBOARD, CHOPPING BOARD

3 ▶GROUP OF PEOPLE 人群◀ [C also+plural verb *BrE* 英] a group of people in an organization who make the rules and important decisions 理事会, 委员会, 董事会; 〔官方的〕局, 部: *a board meeting* 委员会会议 | **sit on a board** *He sits on the hospital management board.* 他是医院管理委员会委员。| **board of directors** *There is still only one woman on the board of directors.* 董事会中仍然只有一位女性。

4 ▶FOR BUILDING 用于建筑◀ [C] a long thin flat piece of wood used for making floors, walls, fences etc (长薄) 木板: *We'll have to take the boards up to check the wiring.* 我们必须把地板撬起来检查一下电线。—see also 另见 FLOORBOARD (1)

5 on board on a ship or plane 在船上; 在飞机上: *The ship went down with all its crew on board.* 船和船上的全体船员一起下沉。—compare 比较 ABOARD

6 take sth on board to listen to and accept a suggestion, idea etc 接受〔建议、想法等〕: *The school refused to take any of the parents' criticisms on board.* 学校拒绝接受家长们提出的任何批评。

7 go by the board if a plan goes by the board, it is no longer possible〔计划、安排等〕落空, 失败: *We just don't have the time – so our idea about meeting to discuss it has had to go by the board.* 我们根本没时间, 所以我们本来打算开会讨论一下这件事的想法只好告吹了。

8 across the board if a plan or situation happens across the board, it affects everyone in a particular group, place etc 全面地, 涉及全体地: *We're aiming to increase productivity across the board.* 我们的目标是全面提高生产效率。

9 ▶MEALS 膳食◀ [U] the meals that are provided for you when you pay to stay somewhere 膳食: *I pay $100 a week for room and board.* 我每周付 100 美元膳宿费。| **full/half board** (=all or some meals)〔旅馆等〕供一日三餐的/供部分膳食的

10 ▶THEATRE 剧场◀ the boards [plural] the stage in a theatre 舞台 —see also 另见 **tread the boards** (TREAD¹ (6))

11 ▶SPORT 体育◀ boards [plural] *AmE* the low wooden wall around the area in which you play ICE HOCKEY【美】〔冰球场四周的〕护板

12 college/medical boards *AmE* examinations that you take in the US when you apply to a college or medical school【美】大学/医学院的入学考试 —see also 另见 ABOVE BOARD, DIVING BOARD, DRAWING BOARD, IRONING BOARD, SURFBOARD, **sweep the board** (SWEEP¹ (9))

board² *v* **1** [I,T] *formal* to get on a bus, plane, train etc in order to travel somewhere【正式】登上〔巴士、飞机、火车等交通工具〕: *Passengers are asked to board half an hour before departure time.* 乘客须在起飞 [开车] 前半小时登机 [上车]。**2** [I] if a plane or ship is boarding, passengers are getting onto it 登机; 上船: *Flight N654 for Kathmandu is now boarding at Gate 16.* 飞往加德满都的 N654 号航班现在由 16 号门登机。**3** [I always+adv/prep] to stay in a room in someone's house that you pay for〔在某人家里〕寄宿; 寄膳: *I board with the Nicholsons during the week.* 周一到周五我寄宿在尼科尔森家。**4** [I] to stay at a school at night as well as during the day 在校寄宿: *The students board during the week and go home at weekends.* 学生们平日住在学校里, 周末才回家。

board sth ↔ **out** *phr v* [T] *BrE* to pay money and arrange for an animal to stay somewhere【英】把〔动物〕寄养〔在某处〕: *We'll have to board the cat out while we're away.* 我们外出期间, 得给猫找个地方寄养。

board sth ↔ **up** *phr v* [T] to cover a window or door with wooden boards 用〔木板〕遮住〔堵上〕. *All the windows were boarded up and the place looked totally deserted.* 所有的窗子都被堵上了, 整个地方看起来很荒凉。

board·er /ˈbɔrdɚ; ˈbɔːdə/ *n* [C] **1** a student who stays at a school during the night, as well as during the day 寄宿生, 住校生 **2** someone who pays to live in another person's house with some or all of their meals provided; LODGER〔住在他人家里的〕寄宿者, 寄膳宿者

board game /ˈ· ·/ *n* [C] an indoor game played on a specially designed board made of thick card or wood 棋类游戏

board·ing /ˈbɔrdɪŋ; ˈbɔːdɪŋ/ *n* [U] **1** the act of getting on a ship, plane etc in order to travel somewhere 登机; 上船: *Boarding is now taking place at Gate 38.* 38 号门现在开始登机。**2** narrow pieces of wood that are fixed side by side, usually to cover a broken door or window 并排的木板

boarding card /ˈ·· ·/ *n* an official card that you have to show before you get onto a plane 登机牌, 登机证

boarding house /ˈ·· ·/ *n* [C] a private house where you pay to sleep and eat; GUESTHOUSE 供膳宿的私人住房 —compare 比较 PENSION³

boarding pass /ˈ·· ·/ *n* [C] a boarding card 登机牌, 登机证

boarding school /ˈ·· ·/ *n* [C] a school where students live as well as study 寄宿学校 —compare 比较 DAY SCHOOL

Board of Ed·u·ca·tion /ˌ· · · ˈ· ·/ in the US, a group of people who are elected to make decisions about how schools and colleges are managed, and about how children are educated in a particular county or state 地方教育委员会〔在美国经推选产

生的一组人员，他们决定一县或一州的学校管理事务和少年儿童的教育方式〕

board·room /ˈbɔrd͵rum; ˈbɔːdruːm/ *n* [C] a room where the directors (DIRECTOR (1)) of a company have meetings 董事会会议室

board·walk /ˈbɔrd͵wɔk; ˈbɔːdwɔːk/ *n* [C] *AmE* a raised path made of wood, usually built next to the sea【美】〔常在海滨〕用木板铺成的小道 —compare 比较 PIER (2)

boast[1] /bost; bəʊst/ *v* **1** [I,T] to talk too proudly about your abilities, achievements, or possessions because you want to make other people admire you 夸口，夸耀，吹嘘: *"I can do better than any of them," she boasted.* "我能比他们任何人都做得好。"她夸口说。| [+**about**] *I'm fed up hearing Jan boast about her new job.* 我已听腻了简夸耀她的新工作。| [+**of**] *He enjoyed boasting of his wealth.* 他喜欢夸耀自己的财富。| **boast that** *She was boasting that she could speak six languages fluently.* 她吹嘘说她能流利地讲六种语言。**2** [T] if a place, object, or organization boasts a good feature, it has that good feature〔地方、物体或机构〕拥有〔好的事物或特征〕: *Few teams can boast such a good record in European football.* 在欧洲足坛没有几支队伍拥有这样好的记录。| *The hotel boasts the finest view in Wales.* 这家旅馆拥有威尔士最好的风景。—**boaster** *n* [C]

boast[2] *n* [C] **1** something that you like telling people because you are proud of it 引以为豪的事物: *One of her proudest boasts is that her daughter is a doctor.* 她最值得骄傲的事之一是她的女儿是医生。**2 no idle boast** used to say that something is not a boast but that it is true 绝非吹牛

boast·ful /ˈbost͵fəl; ˈbəʊstfəl/ *adj* talking too proudly about yourself 好自夸的，自吹自擂的: *We all got drunk and became very loud and boastful.* 我们都喝醉了，扯着嗓门自吹自擂起来。—**boastfully** *adv* —**boastfulness** *n* [U]

S1 W2 **boat** /bot; bəʊt/ *n* [C] **1** a vehicle that travels across water 小船，小舟，小艇: *a fishing boat* 渔船 | *a rowing boat* 划艇 | **by boat/in a boat** *We went up the river by boat.* 我们乘小船在河中逆流而上。**2** *informal* a ship, especially one that carries passengers【非正式】轮船〔尤指客轮〕: *We're getting the night boat to Zeebrugge.* 我们乘晚上的船去泽布吕赫。**3 be in the same boat (as)** to be in the same unpleasant situation as someone else 处于相同的倒霉境地；面临同样的危险: *We're all more or less in the same boat, so there's no use complaining.* 我们的处境差不多，所以抱怨也没用。**4 push the boat out** *BrE informal* to spend a lot of money on something, especially on celebrating an event【英，非正式】不惜多花钱庆祝一番: *They really pushed the boat out for their daughter's wedding.* 他们为女儿的婚礼确实花了不少钱。**5 rock the boat** to express a different attitude, opinion, idea etc from what other people are used to, in a way that upsets them 破坏良好［舒适］的现状；扰乱正常秩序: *They rocked the boat by refusing to come to the firm's Christmas lunch.* 他们兴风作浪，拒绝参加公司的圣诞午餐会。—see also 另见 GRAVY BOAT, SAUCE BOAT, **burn your bridges/boats** (BURN[1] (22)), **miss the boat/bus** (MISS[1] (5))

boat·er /ˈbotɚ; ˈbəʊtə/ *n* [C] a hard STRAW (1a) hat with a flat top 平顶硬草帽 —see picture at 参见 HAT 图

CULTURAL NOTE 文化注释

Boaters are often thought of in connection with rich young men at university in Britain in the early part of the 20th century. 平顶硬草帽常让人联想到20世纪初期英国大学里的富有青年。

boat hook /ˈ· ·/ *n* [C] a long pole with an iron hook at the end, used to pull or push a small boat〔一端有钩，用来钩住或推开小船的〕钩篙

boat·house /ˈbot͵haus; ˈbəʊthaʊs/ *n* [C] a building by the side of water that boats are kept in〔水边停放船只的〕船库，棚屋

boat·ing /ˈbotɪŋ; ˈbəʊtɪŋ/ *n* [U] the activity of travelling in a small boat for pleasure 划船；乘游艇: **go boating** *Let's go boating on the lake.* 我们到湖上划船去吧。

boat·man /ˈbotmən; ˈbəʊtmən/ *n* [C] a man who you pay to take you out in a boat or for the use of a boat 出租小船的船主；船夫；桨手

boat peo·ple /ˈ· ͵· ·/ *n* [plural] people who escape from bad conditions in their country in small boats 乘小船出逃的难民，船民

Boat Race, the /ˈ· ·/ a rowing race on the River Thames in Britain, held every year between teams from Oxford University and Cambridge University 划船比赛〔英国牛津大学和剑桥大学一年一度在泰晤士河上举行的一项划船赛事〕

boat·swain /ˈbosn̩; ˈbəʊsən/ *n* [C] an officer on a ship whose job is to organize the work and look after the equipment; BOSUN〔船上的〕水手长；掌帆长

boat train /ˈ· ·/ *n* [C] a train that takes people to or from ships in a port〔与港口船只配合的〕联运火车

Bob /bab; bɒb/ *n* **Bob's your uncle!** *BrE spoken* used to say that something will be easy to do【英口】没问题！放心吧！: *Just copy the disk, and Bob's your uncle!* 复制磁盘吧，没问题的！

bob[1] *v*

1 ►MOVE IN WATER 水中移动◄ [I] to move up and down when floating on the surface of water〔在水面上〕上下快速移动: **bob up and down** *The boat was bobbing up and down on the waves.* 小船在波涛中上下颠簸。

2 ►MOVE SOMEWHERE 移往某处◄ [I always+adv/prep] to move quickly in a particular direction 沿某个方向快速移动: [+**up/down/out etc**] *She bobbed down behind the wall to avoid being seen.* 她快速俯身躲到墙后以免让人看见。

3 bob your head to move your head down quickly as a way of showing respect, greeting someone or agreeing with them 点头〔表示尊敬、问候或赞同〕: *Seymour bobbed his head respectfully and said, "Good evening, Sir."* 西摩恭敬地点点头说："先生，晚上好。"

4 bob (sb) a curtsy to make a quick, small CURTSY to someone 迅速地行半屈膝礼

5 ►HAIR 头发◄ [T] to cut someone's hair so that it is the same length all the way round their head 剪短〔头发〕: *I'm going to get my hair bobbed.* 我要把头发剪短。—see picture at 参见 HAIRSTYLE 图

6 bob for apples to play a game in which you try to pick up apples floating in water, using only your mouth 咬苹果〔指试图用口咬住漂浮在水上的苹果的游戏〕

bob[2] *n* [C] **1** a way of cutting hair so that it is the same length all the way round your head 短齐发（发式）—see picture at 参见 HAIRSTYLE 图 **2** a quick up and down movement of your head, or body, to show respect, agreement, greeting etc 点头；屈膝〔表示尊敬、赞同、问候等〕: *The maid gave a little bob and left the room.* 女仆略微点了点头，然后离开了房间。**3** [plural] *informal* a SHILLING (=coin used in the past in Britain)【非正式】〔旧时的英国硬币〕一先令: *In those days the train fare was three bob.* 那时候火车票要花三先令。—see also 另见 **bits and bobs** (BIT[1] (14))

bob·bin /ˈbabɪn; ˈbɒbɪ̣n/ *n* [C] a small round object that you wind thread onto, especially for a SEWING MACHINE 线轴，绕线筒，管筒 —compare 比较 REEL[1] (1a)

bob·ble[1] /ˈbabl̩; ˈbɒbəl/ *n* [C] *BrE* a small soft ball, usually made of wool, that is used especially for decorating clothes【英】〔用于装饰的〕小羊毛球，小绒球: *Her pullover had bobbles on the front.* 她的套头毛衣前面有几个小绒球。—**bobbly** *adj*: *My sweater's gone all bobbly.* 我的针织套衫都起球了。

bobble[2] *v* [T] *AmE* to drop or hold a ball in an uncontrolled way; FUMBLE (3)【美】漏接〔球〕，失掉〔球〕: *The shortstop bobbled the ball and the runner ran home.* 游击手接球失误，跑垒者跑回本垒。

bobble hat /ˈ·· ·/ *n* [C] *BrE* a WOOLLEN hat with a bobble on the top【英】〔顶上饰有小绒球的〕毛绒帽

bob·by /ˈbabɪ; ˈbɒbi/ *n* [C] *BrE informal old-fashioned* a policeman【英，非正式，过时】警察

bobby pin /ˈ·· ·/ *n* [C] *AmE* a thin piece of metal bent into a narrow U shape that you use to hold your hair in place【美】小发夹; HAIRGRIP *BrE*【英】—see picture at 参见 PIN[1] 图

bobby socks, bobby sox /ˈ·· ·/ *n* [plural] *AmE* girls' short socks that have the tops turned over【美】〔女孩穿的〕短袜

bob·cat /ˈbab͵kæt; ˈbɒbkæt/ *n* [C] a large North American wild cat that has no tail; LYNX 短尾猫〔一种北美野猫〕

bobs /babz; bɒbz/ *n* [plural] —see 见 **bits and bobs** (BIT[1] (14))

bob·sleigh /ˈbab͵sle; ˈbɒbsleɪ/ also 又作 **bobsled** /ˈbab͵slɛd; ˈbɒbsled/ *n* **1** [C] a small vehicle with two long thin metal blades instead of wheels, that is used for racing down a special ice track 雪橇〔一种供比赛用的雪上小型车辆，可在结冰的赛道上高速下滑〕**2** [U] a sports event in which people race against each other in bobsleighs 雪橇比赛: *Sixteen teams took part in the 400m bobsleigh.* 有 16 支队伍参加了 400 米雪橇比赛。—**bobsleigh** *v* [I]

bob·tail /ˈbab͵tel; ˈbɒbteɪl/ *n* [C] **a)** a horse or dog whose tail has been cut short 截短尾巴的马［狗］**b)** a tail that has been cut short 截短了的尾巴 —see also 另见 **ragtag and bobtail** (RAGTAG (2))

bob·white /ˈbabˈhwaɪt; ˈbɒbwaɪt/ *n* [C] a bird from North America, often shot for sport; QUAIL[1] (1) 山齿鹑〔产于北美〕

Boc·cac·ci·o /boˋkatʃɪo; bɒˈkɑːtʃiəʊ/, **Gio·van·ni** /dəuˋvanɪ; dʒəʊˈvɑːni/ (1313-75) an Italian writer whose book of stories called *The Decameron* had an important influence on European literature 薄伽丘〔(1313-1375)，意大利作家，他创作的故事集《十日谈》对欧洲文学具有重要影响〕

boche /bɑʃ; bɒʃ/ *n* **the Boche** an offensive word meaning the Germans or German soldiers, used in Britain during the First and Second World Wars 德国佬，德国鬼子〔第一次世界大战和第二次世界大战时对德国士兵的冒犯用语〕

bod /bɑd; bɒd/ *n* [C] **1** *BrE spoken* a person【英口】人，家伙: *We had to write to some bod at head office to ask for a refund.* 我们只好给总公司的人写封信要求退款。**2** *informal* someone's body【非正式】身体: *Move your bod, will you!* 挪动一下身子，好不好！**3 odd bod** *informal* a strange person【非正式】古怪的人: *He's a bit of an odd bod but very pleasant.* 他有点古怪，但挺友善的。

bode /bod; bəʊd/ *v* **1** the past tense of BIDE **2 bode well/ill (for)** *especially literary* to be a good or bad sign for the future【尤文】预示…的吉／凶: *The results of the opinion poll do not bode well for the Democrats.* 民意调查的结果预示着民主党人的前景并不乐观。

bodge /bɑdʒ; bɒdʒ/ also 又作 **bodge up** *n* [singular] *spoken* a mistake or something that is not as good as it should be【口】差错，失误；比预想的要糟得多的东西: *The builders have made a complete bodge of the kitchen.* 建筑工人把厨房盖得一团糟。—see also 另见 BOTCH —**bodge** *v* [T]

bod·ice /ˋbɑdɪs; ˈbɒdɪ̣s/ *n* [C] **1** the part of a woman's dress above her waist 女服腰以上的部分 **2** a tight-fitting woman's WAISTCOAT worn over a BLOUSE in former times〔旧时的〕女式紧身马甲 **3** *old use* a piece of woman's underwear that covered the upper part of her body; CORSET (1)【旧】紧身女胸衣

bod·i·ly¹ /ˋbɑdlɪ; ˈbɒdɪ̣li/ *adj* [only before noun 仅用于名词前] related to the human body 身体的，肉体的: *Many bodily changes occur during adolescence.* 身体的许多变化都是在青春期发生的。| *bodily sensations* 身体的知觉

bodily² *adv* **1** by moving the whole of your or someone else's body 全身地: *He lifted the child bodily aboard.* 他把孩子一把抱到车上。**2** by moving a large object in one piece 整体地，全部地: *The column was transferred bodily to a new site by the bank of the river.* 那条圆柱被整根转送到河边的一个新地点。

bod·kin /ˋbɑdkɪn; ˈbɒdkɪ̣n/ *n* [C] a long thick needle without a point（钝头）粗长针

Bod·lei·an Li·bra·ry, the /ˌbɑdlɪən ˋlaɪbrɛrɪ; ˌbɒdliən ˈlaɪbrəri/ also 又作 **the Bodleian** the university library of Oxford University, which has many of the country's oldest and most famous books and papers 博德利图书馆〔即牛津大学图书馆，馆藏许多英国最古老、最著名的书籍和文献〕

Bodmin Moor /ˌbɑdmɪn ˋmʊr; ˌbɒdmɪn ˈmʊr/ a MOOR in Cornwall in southwest England, known for its TORS 博德明漠泽〔位于英格兰西南部康沃尔郡的一片漠泽，因突岩而闻名〕

bod·y /ˋbɑdɪ; ˈbɒdi/ *n plural* **bodies** S1 W1

1 ▶SB'S BODY 身体◀ [C] the physical structure of a person or animal〔人或动物的〕身体，躯体: *Many teenagers are self-conscious about their bodies.* 许多青少年对自己的身体感到害羞。| **body heat/temperature/weight etc** *Babies undergo a rapid increase in body weight during the first weeks.* 婴儿的体重在刚刚出生的头几周迅速增加。| **body image** (=the mental picture that you have of your own body) 头脑中自己身体的形象 *negative feelings associated with a changed body image* 由头脑中自己身体形象的改变而引发的负面情绪 | **the body beautiful** (=an idea of the perfect body) 最佳体型 *products designed to help you achieve the body beautiful* 专门设计使人达到最佳体型的产品

2 ▶DEAD BODY 遗体◀ [C] the dead body of a person 尸体: *Neighbours were called in to identify the body.* 邻居们被叫来辨认尸体。

3 ▶GROUP OF PEOPLE 人群◀ [C] a group of people who work together to do a particular job or who are together for a particular purpose 团体，机构，群体: [+of] *Two hundred years ago a body of settlers established themselves on the island.* 二百年前，一群移民来到这个岛上定居。| **governing body** (=a body that controls the work or activities of an organization or group) 管理机构〔部门〕| **student body** (=all the students in a particular school or college) 全体学生 *We have a student body from a wide range of background.* 我们有各种各样背景的学生。| **public body** (=group of people involved in government) 政府公务人员

body 身体

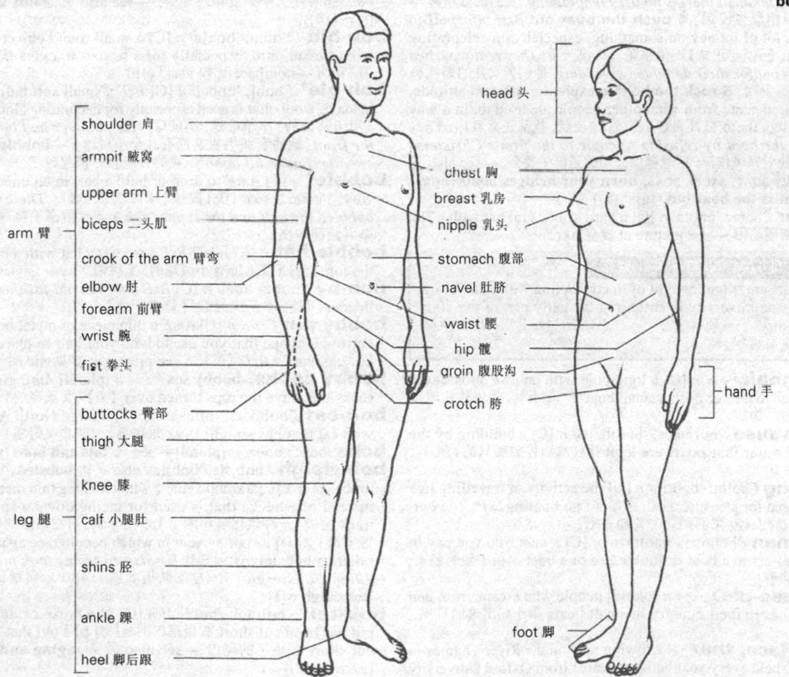

see also pictures at 另见 **head** and 和 **foot** 图

4 **a body of** **a)** a large amount or collection of something 大量的: **body of knowledge/information/literature etc** *Researchers used vast bodies of information to arrive at their findings.* 研究人员利用大量资料取得了研究成果。**b)** the main, central, or most important part of something〔事物的〕主要[最大]部分, 主体: *The bedrooms were connected to the body of the house by a long corridor.* 卧室通过一条长走廊与房屋的主体相连。| *the main body of the report* 报告的主要部分

5 **in a body** if people do something in a body, they do it together in large numbers 全体, 一起: *The demonstrators marched in a body to the main square.* 游行示威者一起朝着主广场走去。

6 ►**CENTRAL PART** 中央部位◄ [C] the central part of a person or animal's body, not including the head, arms, legs or wings〔除头和四肢或翅膀以外的〕躯干部: *Nick has short legs but a long body.* 尼克腿短体长。

7 ►**SEPARATE OBJECT** 分开的物体◄ [C] *technical* an object that is separate from other objects【术语】物体

8 ►**VEHICLE** 车辆◄ [C] the main structure of a vehicle not including the engine, wheels etc 车身: *The body's beginning to rust.* 车身开始生锈。

9 ►**HAIR** 毛发◄ [U] if your hair has body, it is thick and healthy 茂盛, 浓密

10 **over my dead body** *spoken* used to show that you are determined to prevent something from happening【口】除非我死了, 休想: *He'll come to the meeting over my dead body.* 有我在, 他休想来开会。

11 **long/thick etc bodied** having a long, thick etc body 身材细长/粗壮等: *They were thick-bodied men accustomed to hard labour.* 他们身材粗壮, 习惯干重活儿。—see also 另见 ABLE-BODIED

12 **full/medium/light bodied** used to describe how much FLAVOUR (=taste) a wine or beer has, with full bodied wine or beer having the strongest taste〔酒〕味道醇厚/较浓郁/清淡

13 **body and soul** completely 全身心地, 完全地: *She threw herself body and soul into her work.* 她全心全意地投入工作。

14 **keep body and soul together** to continue to exist with only just enough food, money etc 勉强维持生活, 挣钱糊口

15 ►**CLOTHES** 衣服◄ [C] *BrE* a type of tight fitting shirt worn by women that fastens between their legs【英】女式紧身衣; BODY SUIT *AmE*【美】—see picture at 参见 UNDERWEAR 图

16 **body of water** a large area of water such as a lake 水域〈如湖泊〉

USAGE NOTE 用法说明: BODY

WORD CHOICE 词语辨析: **body, figure, build**

A **body** consists of someone's arms, legs, head etc and may be healthy, skinny, dead etc. body包括人的双臂、双腿、头等, 可能是健康、瘦弱或死亡的: *I like to look after my body.* 我要照顾好自己的身体。If you say someone has a *lovely/good/beautiful body* this may suggest you find them sexually attractive. 如果说某人有 a lovely/good/beautiful body (可爱的/好的/健美的身体), 则指这个人很性感。

Your **figure** is the shape of your **body**. **Figure** is usually used about women. figure 指的是人的身材或体型, 多用于女性: *She has a really good figure.* 她的身材真好。| *I won't have a cake, thanks. I'm watching my figure* (=trying not to get fat). 谢谢, 我不吃蛋糕, 我怕发胖。

Build can be used for the size and shape of both men and women. build 既可指男性也可以指女性的胖瘦和体态: *a man/woman of small/heavy/slim build* 体型瘦小/强壮/修长的男子[女子]

body ar·mour /ˈ·· ,··/ *n* [U] clothing worn by the police that protects them against bullets 防弹衣

body bag /ˈ·· ·/ *n* [C] a large bag in which a dead body is removed 运尸袋: *Men will not volunteer to fight once they see the body bags returning.* 人们一旦看到运送回来的运尸袋就不会自告奋勇去打仗了。

body blow /ˈ·· ·/ *n* [C] **1** a serious loss, disappointment, or defeat 严重损失; 大挫折; 大败北: *Hopes of economic recovery were dealt a body blow by this latest announcement.* 最新公布的消息对经济复苏的希望是个沉重打击。**2** a hard hit between your neck and waist during a fight 上半身〔颈与腰之间〕受到的重击

body build·ing /ˈ·· ,··/ *n* [U] an activity in which you do hard physical exercise in order to develop big muscles 健美运动 —**body builder** *n* [C]

body clock /ˈ·· ·/ *n* [C] the system in your body that controls types of behaviour which happen at regular times, such as sleeping or eating; BIOLOGICAL CLOCK 生理时钟, 人体生物钟

body count /ˈ·· ,·/ *n* [C] the number of enemy dead after a period of fighting, or the process of counting their bodies〔敌方〕死亡人数统计; 清点死亡人数

bod·y·guard /ˈbɑdɪˌgɑrd; ˈbɒdigɑːd/ *n* [C] **1** someone whose job is to protect an important person〔重要人物的〕贴身卫士, 保镖, 警卫员: *The Senator arrived, surrounded by personal bodyguards.* 这位参议员在保镖的簇拥下抵达。**2** a group of people who work together to protect an important person 警卫队

body lan·guage /ˈ·· ,··/ *n* [U] changes in your body position and movements that show what you are feeling or thinking 身体语言, 肢体语言: *It was obvious from Luke's body language that he was nervous.* 卢克的动作表明他很紧张。

body o·dour /ˈ·· ,··/ *n* [C] the natural smell of someone's body, especially when this is unpleasant; BO 人体气味; 狐臭, 体臭

body pol·i·tic /ˌ·· ˈ···/ *n* [singular] *formal* all the people in a nation forming a state under the control of a single government【正式】政治实体; 国家;〔被视为一个整体的〕民族

body pop·ping /ˈ·· ,··/ *n* [U] a type of dancing in which the dancer makes short, sudden movements that make them look like a machine or ROBOT (1)〔模仿机器人动作的〕扭身舞, 噗啪舞

body search /ˈ·· ·/ *n* [C] a thorough search for drugs, weapons etc, that might be hidden on someone's body 搜身; 搜身检查: *They did a body search on all the passengers before they boarded the plane.* 他们在乘客登机前逐一进行了安全检查。—**body-search** *v* [T]

body snatch·er /ˈ·· ,··/ *n* [C] someone in the past who dug up dead bodies and sold them to doctors for scientific study〔旧时卖死尸给医生作研究的〕掘墓盗尸者

body spray /ˈ·· ·/ *n* [U] a chemical substance that you put onto your body to make it smell nice 爽身露

body stock·ing /ˈ·· ,··/ *n* [C] a close-fitting piece of clothing that covers the whole of your body 连身[一件式]紧身衣

body suit /ˈ·· ·/ *n* [C] *AmE* a type of tight fitting shirt worn by women that fastens between their legs【美】女紧身衣; BODY (15) *BrE*【英】

bod·y·work /ˈbɑdɪˌwɝk; ˈbɒdiwɜːk/ *n* [U] the metal frame of a vehicle, not including the engine, wheels etc〔汽车的〕车身: *The bodywork's beginning to rust.* 汽车车身开始生锈。

Boe·ing /ˈboɪŋ; ˈbəʊɪŋ/ *trademark* a US company that makes aircraft. Its passenger planes, such as the Boeing 747, are the most common ones used by AIRLINES【商标】波音公司〔美国的一家飞机制造商, 生产的波音747等客机在各航空公司中最为常用〕

Bo·er[1] /bɔr; bɔː/ *n* [C] someone from South Africa whose family came from Holland 布尔人〔荷兰血统的南非白人〕

Boer[2] *adj* connected with the Boers 布尔人的, 与布尔人有关的: *the Boer War* 布尔战争

Boer War, the /ˌ· ˈ·/ also 又作 **the South African War** (1899-1902) a war in South Africa in which the British army successfully fought against two Boer REPUBLICs called the Transvaal and the Orange Free State, and made them part of the British Empire 布尔战争〔(1899-1902), 发生在南非的一场战争。英国在战争中征服了德兰士瓦和奥兰治自由邦这两个布尔人共和国, 并将其纳入大英帝国版图〕

bof·fin /ˈbɑfɪn; ˈbɒfɪ̣n/ *n* [C] *BrE*【英】**1** *old-fashioned* a scientist【过时】科学家, 科技人员 **2** *informal* someone who is very clever but not fashionable【非正式】聪明但不合时尚的人: *He was always a bit of a boffin, even at school.* 他很聪明, 但总是有点不合时尚, 即使在学校时也是如此。

bog[1] /bɑg; bɒg/ *n* **1** [C,U] an area of wet muddy ground that you can sink into 沼泽, 泥塘 —compare 比较 MARSH, SWAMP[1] **2** [C] *BrE slang* a toilet【英俚】厕所

bog[2] *v*

bog sb ↔ **down** *phr v* [T] **1** to become too involved in thinking about or dealing with one particular thing 沉湎于; 被…拖住; 使不可自拔: [+**in**] *Don't let yourself get bogged down in minor details.* 不要陷入这些枝节问题而不能自拔。**2** to become stuck in muddy ground and be unable to move 使陷入泥沼中

bog off *phr v* [I] **bog off!** *BrE spoken slang* used to tell someone rudely to go away【英口, 俚】滚开!: *Just bog off and leave me alone!* 滚开, 别烦我!

Bo·gart /ˈbogɑrt; ˈbəʊgɑːt/, **Hum·phrey** /ˈhʌmfrɪ; ˈhʌmfri/ (1899-1957) a US film actor whose films include *The Maltese Falcon* and *Casablanca* 博加特〔(1899-1957), 美国电影演员, 出演过《马耳他之鹰》和《卡萨布兰卡》〕

bo·gey /ˈbogɪ; ˈbəʊgi/ *n* [C] **1** a problem or difficult situation that makes you feel anxious 使人焦虑的问题[局面]: **lay/put the bogey to rest** (=deal with the problem) 应对困难, 解决问题 *After six successive defeats, Athletico finally laid their bogey to rest*

with a 3-0 win. 连输六场后，竞技队最终摆脱困境，以 3 比 0 的比分获胜。

2 also 又作 **bogy** a piece of MUCUS from inside your nose 鼻涕 **3** also 又作 **bogie, bogy** *technical* an example of taking one shot more than PAR (=the usual number of strokes) to get the ball into the hole in GOLF【术语】〔高尔夫球〕比标准杆数多一击的进球 **4** a bogeyman 鬼怪，怪物

B

bo·gey·man /ˈbogɪˌmæn; ˈbəʊgimæn/ *n* [C] an evil spirit, especially in children's imagination or stories; BOGEY (4)〔孩子想象中的或故事中的〕鬼怪，怪物: *Beware of the bogeyman.* 当心妖怪。

bog·gle /ˈbɑgl; ˈbɒgəl/ *v* **1 the mind/imagination boggles** *informal* if your mind etc boggles when you think of something, it is difficult for you to imagine or accept it【非正式】不敢想；简直不敢相信；听得瞠目结舌: *"Did you know Keith's a father now?" "Good God, no, the mind boggles."* "你知道基思当了父亲吗？" "天啊，不会吧，我简直不敢相信。" | **[+at]** *My mind boggles at the amount of work still to do.* 一想到还有那么多工作要做，我就不敢再想了。**2** [I] to be surprised or shocked by something 吃惊，受惊: **[+at]** *It's a hell of a lot of money, even I boggle at it.* 那是很多很多钱，连我都很吃惊。

bog·gy /ˈbɑgɪ; ˈbɒgi/ *adj* boggy ground is wet and muddy 泥泞的: *There was a boggy patch at the edge of the field.* 在田野的边缘有一块泥泞地。

bo·gie¹ /ˈbogɪ; ˈbəʊgi/ *n* [C] a BOGEY (3)〔高尔夫球〕比标准杆数多一击的进球

bogie² *v* [T] to use one more than PAR (=the usual number of strokes) to get the ball into the hole in GOLF〔高尔夫球〕比标准杆数多一击进球

Bog·nor Re·gis /ˌbɑgnɚ ˈridʒɪs; ˌbɒgnə ˈriːdʒɪs/ also 又作 **Bognor** a town on the south coast of England, popular with tourists 博格诺里吉斯〔英格兰南部沿海的一座城镇，为游客所青睐〕

Bogotà /ˌbogəˈtɑ; ˌbɒgəˈtɑː/ also 又作 **Santa Fé de Bogotá** the capital city of Colombia, in the east Andes mountains 波哥大〔哥伦比亚首都，位于安第斯山脉东部〕

bog roll /ˈ· ·/ *n* [C,U] *BrE slang* TOILET PAPER【英俚】卫生纸，厕纸

bog stan·dard /ˌ· ˈ··◂/ *adj BrE informal* not special or interesting in any way; average【英，非正式】一般的，平常的，普通的

bo·gus /ˈbogəs; ˈbəʊgəs/ *adj* not true or real, although someone is trying to make you think it is 假冒的，伪造的: *bogus insurance claims* 伪造的保险索赔

bo·gy /ˈbogɪ; ˈbəʊgi/ *n* [C] a BOGEY (4) 鬼怪，怪物

Bohème, La —see 见 LA BOHÈME

bo·he·mi·an /boˈhimɪən; bəʊˈhiːmiən/ *adj* living in a very informal or relaxed way and not accepting society's rules of behaviour 不拘于传统的；放荡不羁的: *bohemian cafes frequented by artists, musicians, and actors* 画家、音乐家和演员们经常光顾的新潮咖啡馆 —**bohemian** *n* [C]

Bohr /bor; bɔː/, **Niels Hen·rik Da·vid** /nils ˈhɛnrɪk ˈdævɪd; niːls ˈhenrɪk ˈdɑːvɪd/ (1885-1962) a Danish scientist who made important discoveries in NUCLEAR PHYSICS, especially discoveries about the structure of atoms 玻尔〔(1885-1962)，丹麦科学家，在核子物理领域，尤其在原子结构方面有过重大发现〕

3 **boil¹** /bɔɪl; bɔɪl/ *v* **1** [I,T] when a liquid boils it is hot enough to turn into gas 使达到沸点，煮沸，烧开: *Put the spaghetti into plenty of boiling, salted water.* 把意大利粉放入大量煮沸的盐水中。| **[+at]** *Water boils at 100 degrees centigrade.* 水在 100 摄氏度沸腾。| *We were advised to boil the water before drinking it.* 有人建议我们把水烧开后再喝。**2** [I,T] if something containing liquid boils, the liquid inside it is boiling (使)〔容器里的液体〕沸腾: *The kettle's boiling! Shall I turn it off?* 水壶里的水开了！我把它关了好吗？| **put sth on to boil** (=begin to heat something) 开始把…加热 *I've put the potatoes on to boil.* 我已经把马铃薯加热了。| **boiled dry** (=heated for too long so there is no liquid left) 煮干 **3** [I,T] to cook something in boiling water〔用开水〕煮〔食物〕: *a boiled egg* 煮好的鸡蛋 **4** [T] to wash clothes at a very high temperature〔用高温水〕洗〔衣服〕: *I always boil the cotton sheets.* 我总是用热水洗棉床单。—see also 另见 BOILING POINT, **make your blood boil** (BLOOD¹ (4))

boil away *phr v* if a liquid boils away it disappears because it has been heated too much 煮干；汽化: *Oh no! The soup's almost boiled away.* 啊，不好了！汤几乎要烧干了。

boil down *phr v* **1** [I,T **boil sth ↔ down**] if a food or liquid boils down, it becomes less after cooking 煮稠，浓缩: *Spinach tends to boil down a lot.* 菠菜一煮会缩掉许多。**2** [T] **boil sth down** to make information shorter by not including anything that is not necessary 压缩〔资料等〕: *You can boil this down so that there are just two main categories.* 你可以将其简化为两大类。

boil down to sth *phr v* [T not in progressive 不用进行式] *informal* if a long statement, argument etc boils down to something, that is the main point or cause【非正式】相当于；归结为: *What it boils down to, is that no-one is willing to take on that kind of responsibility.* 归结起来就是没有人愿意承担那样的责任。

boil over *phr v* [I] **1** if a liquid boils over, it rises and flows over the side of the container 沸腾而溢出: *Keep an eye on the milk; don't let it boil over.* 看着牛奶，别让它溢出来。**2** if a situation or an emotion boils over, the people involved stop being calm〔局面或感情〕控制不住: **[+into]** *The argument boiled over into a fight.* 争论演变成了一场打斗。

boil up *phr v* **1** [I] if a situation or emotion boils up, it reaches a dangerous level 发展到危险程度: *She could sense that trouble was boiling up at work.* 她能感受到工作中的麻烦到了危险程度。**2** [T **boil sth ↔ up**] to heat food or a liquid until it begins to boil 把…加热；煮沸: *Boil the fruit up with sugar.* 把水果加糖煮沸。

boil² *n* **1 the boil** the act or state of boiling 煮沸；沸腾: **bring sth to the boil** *Bring the sauce to the boil and simmer for 10 minutes.* 把调味汁煮开，然后用文火煨 10 分钟。| **be coming to the boil** (=almost boiling) 快要开了 | **take sth off the boil** (=stop boiling something by taking it off the heat) 不再煮下去 **2** [C] a painful infected swelling under someone's skin 疖子，疔: *The boy's body is covered in boils.* 这个男孩满身是疮。**3 go off the boil** *BrE* to become less good at something that you are usually very good at【英】生疏了: *Gower has gone off the boil in terms of batting lately.* 高尔最近的击球水平有所下降。

boiled sweet /ˌ· ˈ·/ *n* [C] *BrE* a hard SWEET² (1) that often tastes of fruit【英】〔常带有水果味的〕硬糖；HARD CANDY *AmE*【美】

boil·er /ˈbɔɪlɚ; ˈbɔɪlə/ *n* [C] a container for boiling water that is part of a steam engine, or is used to provide heating in a house 锅炉 3

boiler suit /ˈ· · ·/ *n* [C] *BrE* a piece of loose clothing like trousers and a shirt joined together, that you wear over your clothes to protect them【英】〔衣裤相连的〕工作服

boil·ing /ˈbɔɪlɪŋ; ˈbɔɪlɪŋ/ *adj* **1** very hot 滚热的，酷热的: *Can I open a window? It's boiling in here.* 我可以开一扇窗吗？这儿太热了。| **boiling hot** *It's been boiling hot all Summer.* 炎热的天气持续了整个夏天。—see 见 COLD¹ (USAGE) **2** very angry 非常气愤的: *I was boiling with pent-up rage.* 我怒火中烧。 3

boiling point /ˈ· · ·/ *n* [C] **1** the temperature at which a liquid boils 沸点 **2** the point at which emotions get out of control and a situation stops being calm〔情绪或局面的〕爆发点: **reach boiling point** *Relations between the two countries have almost reached boiling point.* 两国间的紧张关系已经达到白热化的程度。

Boise /ˈbɔɪsɪ; bɔɪsi/ the capital city of the US state of Idaho 博伊西〔美国爱达荷州首府〕

bois·ter·ous /ˈbɔɪstərəs; ˈbɔɪstərəs/ *adj* someone, especially a child, who is boisterous makes a lot of noise and has a lot of energy〔尤指儿童〕喧闹的，活跃的: *a class of boisterous five year olds* 一班爱吵闹的五岁的孩子

bok choy /ˌbɑk ˈtʃɔɪ; ˌbɒk ˈtʃɔɪ/ *n* [U] another spelling of PAK CHOI 白菜〔pak choi 的另一种拼法〕—see picture on page A9 参见 A9 页图

bold /bold; bəʊld/ *adj*

1 ▶PERSON/ACTION 人/行动◀ not afraid of taking risks and making difficult decisions 果敢的；冒险的；无畏的: *a bold leader* 果敢的领导者 | *It's a bold venture starting a business these days.* 如今创办一家企业是敢冒风险之举。

2 ▶MANNER/APPEARANCE 举止/外貌◀ so confident or determined that you sometimes offend people 唐突的，冒失的，鲁莽的，放肆的: **as bold as brass** (=very confident and not showing enough respect) 厚颜无耻 *He came in here, as bold as brass, and asked if he could have his money back.* 他厚颜无耻地来到这儿，问是否可以要回自己的钱。

3 ▶COLOURS/SHAPES 颜色/形状◀ very strong or bright so that you notice them 醒目的，显眼的，轮廓清晰的: *bold geometric shapes* 清晰的几何图形

4 ▶LINES/WRITING 线条/书写◀ written or drawn in a very clear way 粗线条的；粗大醒目的: **a bold hand** (=bold writing) 醒目的粗体字 *Her letter was written in a bold sloping hand.* 她的信是用粗大的斜体字写的。

5 in bold (type) printed in letters that are darker and thicker than ordinary printed letters〔印刷〕用黑体字排印的: *The numbers in this dictionary are in bold type.* 这部词典的数字是用黑体字排印的。

6 make so bold as to do sth *formal* to do something that other people feel is rude or not acceptable【正式】冒昧，胆敢: *One of the staff made so bold as to ask what the director's salary was.* 一个职员冒昧地问主任的工资是多少。

7 if I may be so bold *spoken formal* used when asking someone a question, to show that you hope it will not offend them【口，正式】恕我冒昧地问: *And what, if I may be so bold, is the meaning of this note?* 恕我冒昧地问一句，这个注解是什么意思?

—boldly *adv* **—boldness** *n* [U]

bold·face /ˈboldˌfes; ˈbəʊldfeɪs/ *n* [U] *technical* a way of printing letters that makes them thicker and darker than normal【术语】黑体字，粗体字 **—boldfaced** *adj*

bole /bol; bəʊl/ *n* [C] *literary* the main part of a tree; TRUNK (1)【文】树干

bo·le·ro[1] /bəˈlɛro; bəˈleərəʊ/ *n* [C] a type of Spanish dance, or the music for this dance〔西班牙〕波莱罗舞; 波莱罗舞曲

bol·e·ro[2] /boˈlɛro; ˈbɒlərəʊ/ *n* [C] a short jacket for a woman 女式短上衣

Bo·leyn /bəˈlɪn; bəˈlɪn/, **Anne** (1507-36) the second wife of the English king Henry VIII, who was the mother of Queen Elizabeth I 博林〔(1507-1536)，英国国王亨利八世的第二任妻子，女王伊丽莎白一世的母亲〕

Bol·i·var /ˈbolɪvar; ˈbɒlɪ̵vɑː/, **Simon** (1783-1830) also called the Liberator; a soldier and political leader who, at the time when many parts of South America were ruled by Spain, fought against the Spanish army and won independence for Venezuela, Peru, Bolivia, Colombia, and Ecuador 玻利瓦尔〔(1783-1830)，又称"解放者"，军事家、政治领袖。南美洲许多国家受西班牙统治时期，他率军与西班牙军队作战，为委内瑞拉、秘鲁、玻利维亚、哥伦比亚和厄瓜多尔赢得独立〕

Bo·liv·i·a /bəˈlɪvɪə; bəˈlɪviə/ a country with many mountains in the western part of South America, surrounded by Brazil, Chile, Argentina, Peru, and Paraguay. Population: 8,300,000 (2001). Capital: La Paz. 玻利维亚〔南美洲西部国家，境内多山，与巴西、智利、阿根廷、秘鲁和巴拉圭接壤。人口: 8,300,000 (2001)，首都: 拉巴斯〕 **—Bolivian** *n, adj*

boll /bol; bəʊl/ *n* [C] the part of a cotton plant that contains the seeds〔棉桃的〕圆荚，荚壳

Böll /bol; bəʊl/, **Heinrich** /ˈhaɪnrɪʃ; ˈhaɪnrɪʃ/ (1917-85) a German writer of NOVELS. Among his best-known works are *Group Portrait with Lady* and *The Clown*. He won the Nobel Prize for Literature in 1972. 伯尔〔(1917-1985)，德国小说家，最著名的作品有《一个女士及众生相》和《一个小丑的看法》，1972年获诺贝尔文学奖〕

bol·lard /ˈbalɚd; ˈbɒləd/ *n* [C] **1** *BrE* a short thick post in the street that is used to stop traffic entering an area or to show a JUNCTION more clearly【英】〔街道尽头阻止汽车进入的〕安全柱，矮柱;〔行人安全岛的〕护柱 **2** a thick stone or metal post used for tying ships to when they are in port〔船上或码头上的〕系缆柱

bol·lock /ˈbalək; ˈbɒlək/ *v* [T] *BrE slang* to tell someone angrily that you do not like what they have done【英俚】臭骂: *I'll bollock him for sticking his rubbish in my cupboard.* 他把乱七八糟的东西塞进了我的柜子里，我要好好骂他一顿。

bol·lock·ing /ˈbalәkɪŋ; ˈbɒləkɪŋ/ *n* [C] **give sb a bollocking** *BrE* to tell someone that you are very angry about something they have done【英】斥责[责骂]某人: *I expect I'll get a bollocking from my boss when she finds out.* 我估计老板发现真相后我要挨她一顿臭骂。

bol·locks /ˈbaləks; ˈbɒləks/ *n* [plural] *BrE slang*【英俚】**1** *spoken* used to say rudely that you think something is wrong or stupid【口】胡闹; 废话: *These statistics are total bollocks.* 这些统计数字完全是糊弄人的。| **a load of old bollocks** (=complete nonsense) 一派胡言，胡说八道 *She's just talking a load of old bollocks.* 她简直是一派胡言。**2** *spoken* a word used to emphasize that you are annoyed or angry【口】太糟糕了〔表示厌烦或生气〕: *Oh bollocks! We've missed it.* 真糟糕! 我们没有赶上。**3 bollocks to you/that/it etc** *spoken* used when you refuse to accept or obey something【口】不要想〔表示不接受或不服从〕: *Oh yeah? Well, bollocks to you, mate!* 哦，是吗? 哼，老兄，你休想! **4** the two round male organs that produce SPERM; TESTICLES 睾丸

boll wee·vil /ˌ· ˈ··/ *n* [C] an insect that eats and destroys cotton plants 棉铃象鼻虫

Bol·ly·wood /ˈbalɪwud; ˈbɒliwʊd/ *n* [U] an informal name for the Indian film industry, based on the names 'Hollywood' and 'Bombay', the city where most popular Indian films are made 宝莱坞〔印度电影业的别称，取自"好莱坞"和"孟买"英文单词的合拼，广受欢迎的多数印度影片都是在孟买制作的〕

Bo·lo·gna /bəˈlonjə; bəˈləʊnjə/ the capital city of Emilia-Romagna in north central Italy, built below a group of mountains called the Apennines 博洛尼亚〔意大利中北部艾米利亚－罗马涅区首府，位于亚平宁山麓〕

bo·lo·gna /bəˈlonɪ; bəˈləʊni/ *n* a type of cooked meat often eaten in sandwiches 博洛尼亚香肠，大香肠〔通常夹在三明治里〕

bo·lo·ney /bəˈlonɪ; bəˈləʊni/ *n* [U] another spelling of BALONEY baloney 的另一种拼法

bo·lo tie /ˈbolo ˌtaɪ; ˈbəʊləʊ taɪ/ *n* [C] *AmE* a string worn around your neck that you fasten with a decoration【美】波洛领带〔用饰扣系住的一种细带〕

Bol·she·vik /ˈbolʃəˌvɪk; ˈbɒlʃɪ̵vɪk/ *n* [C] **1** someone who supported the COMMUNIST[1] party at the time of the Russian Revolution in 1917 布尔什维克〔在1917年俄国革命中支持共产党的人〕**2** *old-fashioned* an insulting way of talking about a COMMUNIST[2] or someone who has strong left-wing views【过时】共产党党员; 极左翼分子; 极端激进分子〔为侮辱性词语〕 **—bolshevik** *adj*

bol·shie, bolshy /ˈbolʃɪ; ˈbəʊlʃi/ *adj BrE informal* tending to be angry or annoyed and not to obey people【英，非正式】易怒的; 不服从的; 爱争吵的: *Jack was in one of his bolshie moods again!* 杰克又发牛脾气了! **—bolshiness** *n* [U]

Bol·shoi Bal·let, the /ˌbolʃɔɪ bæˈle; ˌbɒlʃɔɪ ˈbæleɪ/ a famous Russian school and theatre for BALLET, based in Moscow 大剧院芭蕾舞团〔位于莫斯科，是俄罗斯著名的芭蕾舞学校和剧院〕

bol·ster[1] /ˈbolstɚ; ˈbəʊlstə/ *n* [C] a long firm PILLOW[1] (1) that you put under other pillows 长枕垫

bolster[2] also 又作 **bolster up** *v* [T] **1** to help someone to feel better and more positive 增强; 激励: *I did my best to bolster up his confidence.* 我尽力增强他的自信心。**2** to improve something by supporting it〔通过支持〕改进: *a speech designed to bolster her chances at the election* 旨在增加她选举获胜机会的演讲

bolt[1] /bolt; bəʊlt/ *n* [C]

bolt 螺栓; 插销; 弩箭

nut 螺帽 washer 垫圈

bolt 插销

bolt 弩箭

1 ►LOCK 锁◄ a metal bar that you slide across a door or window to fasten it〔门窗的金属〕插销

2 ►SCREW 螺钉◄ a screw with a flat head and no point, for fastening two pieces of metal together 螺栓

3 a bolt from out of the blue news that is sudden and unexpected 晴天霹雳; 飞来横祸: *It was a bolt out of the blue when Alan resigned – completely unexpected.* 艾伦辞职的消息真是晴天霹雳，令人意想不到。

4 bolt of lightning lightning that appears as a white line in the sky 闪电，霹雳 —see also 另见 THUNDERBOLT

5 make a bolt for (it) to suddenly try to escape from somewhere 急忙逃跑，拔腿便跑

6 ►WEAPON 武器◄ a short heavy ARROW (1) that is fired from a CROSSBOW〔短而粗的〕弩箭，矢

7 ►CLOTH 布◄ a large long roll of cloth 一卷，一匹 —see also 另见 **shoot your bolt** (SHOOT[1] (20)), **the nuts and bolts of** (NUT[1] (6))

bolt[2] *v* **1** [I] **a)** to suddenly start to run very fast because you are frightened 奔，窜: *The horse reared up and bolted.* 马用后腿直立起来，跑开了。**b)** to escape from somewhere 逃跑: *Kevin had bolted through the open window.* 凯文从开着的窗子逃走了。**2** also 又作 **bolt down** [T] to eat very quickly 狼吞虎咽: *Don't bolt your food.* 不要狼吞虎咽。**3** to fasten two things together using a BOLT[1] (2) 用螺栓扣住: *We had the safe bolted to the wall.* 我们用螺栓把保险柜固定到墙上。**4** [I,T] to lock a door or window by sliding a bolt across 闩上〔门或窗〕

bolt[3] *adv* **sit/stand bolt upright** to sit or stand with your back very straight 挺直地坐着/站着

bolt·hole /ˈboltˌhol; ˈbəʊlthəʊl/ *n* [C] a place where you can escape to and hide 避难所，藏身处: *a bolthole in the country* 乡下的藏身处

bomb[1] /bam; bɒm/ *n* [C] S2 W3

1 ►WEAPON 武器◄ a weapon made of material that will explode 炸弹; 爆炸装置: *A bomb was planted at the railway station.* 一枚炸弹被放置在火车站内。—see also 另见 ATOM BOMB, HYDROGEN BOMB, LETTER BOMB, NEUTRON BOMB, STINK BOMB, TIME BOMB

2 the bomb used to describe NUCLEAR WEAPONS, and especially the HYDROGEN BOMB 核弹，核武器〔尤指氢弹〕: *a 'ban the bomb' campaign* "禁止核武器"运动

3 cost a bomb *BrE informal* to cost a lot of money【英，非正式】花费很多钱；值很多钱

4 go like a bomb *BrE informal*【英，非正式】**a)** if a car goes like a bomb, it can travel very quickly〔车〕开得飞快 **b)** if a party goes like a bomb, it is very successful〔聚会〕非常成功

5 make a bomb *BrE informal* to get a lot of money by doing something【英，非正式】挣大钱：[**+out of**] *If you could get some of that cheap pottery back to England, you could make a bomb out of it.* 如果你能把那些廉价的陶器带回英国，就能赚大钱。

B

bomb² *v* **1** [T] to attack a place by leaving a bomb there, or by dropping bombs on it from a plane 轰炸，向…投炸弹，炸毁：*The town was heavily bombed in World War II.* 这座城镇在第二次世界大战中遭到猛烈轰炸。**2** [I] *BrE informal* to move or drive very quickly【英，非正式】疾行，飞驶，快速前进：[**+down/along/towards**] *Suddenly a police car came bombing down the high street.* 有一辆警车突然在大街上疾驶而过。**3** [I,T] *AmE informal* to fail a test very badly【美，非正式】〔考试〕不及格，失败：*I bombed my mid-term.* 我的期中考试不及格。**4** [I] *especially AmE* if a play bombs, it is not successful【尤美】〔戏剧〕演砸了，不成功：*His latest play bombed on Broadway.* 他最新的话剧在百老汇演砸了。

bomb sth **↔ out** *phr v* [T] if a building or the people in it are bombed out, the building is completely destroyed 炸毁，炸平：*a bombed out town* 被炸弹夷为平地的城镇

bom·bard /bɑm`bɑrd; bɒm'bɑːd/ *v* [T] **1** to attack a place by firing a lot of guns or throwing bombs continuously at it〔用炮火连续地〕猛炸，轰击：*British ships began bombarding the port of Alexandria.* 英国战舰开始猛轰亚历山大港。**2** to continue asking someone a lot of questions criticizing them, or giving them a lot of information at once 连珠炮似地质问；一下子提供很多信息：*Both leaders were bombarded with questions from the press.* 两位领导人都遭到新闻记者连珠炮似的提问。

bom·bar·dier /ˌbɑmbə`dɪr; ˌbɒmbə'dɪə◂/ *n* [C] **1** the person on a military aircraft responsible for dropping bombs〔飞机上的〕轰炸员，投弹手 **2** a low rank in the Royal Artillery (=part of the British Army)〔英国皇家炮兵〕下士

bom·bard·ment /bɑm`bɑrdmənt; bɒm'bɑːdmənt/ *n* [U] a continuous attack on a place by big guns and bombs 炮轰，轰炸：*Sarajevo is coming under heavy bombardment from Serb forces.* 萨拉热窝正遭到塞族军队的猛烈轰击。| **aerial bombardment** (=attack by planes dropping bombs) 飞机轰炸

bom·bas·tic /bɑm`bæstɪk; bɒm'bæstɪk/ *adj* bombastic language contains long important sounding words that have no real meaning 唱高调的；夸大其辞的：*Pennant's pushy and bombastic manner* 彭南特咄咄逼人又善唱高调的作风 —**bombast** /`bɑmbæst; 'bɒmbæst/ *n* [U]

Bom·bay /ˌbɑm`be; ˌbɒm'beɪ◂/ the largest city in India, on the west coast of the country. It is the capital of Maharashtra state, an important port and industrial centre, and the centre of the Indian film industry. The new name for Bombay is Mumbai. 孟买〔印度最大城市，位于西海岸，马哈拉施特拉邦首府，是印度重要的港口和工业、电影业中心。英文新名为 Mumbai〕

bomb dis·po·sal /'· ·,··/ *n* [U] the job of dealing with bombs that have not exploded, and making them safe 未爆炸弹处理：**a bomb disposal expert/squad/unit etc** *Bomb disposal experts were called in to make the device safe.* 炸弹处理专家奉召到场以确保这个装置的安全。

bombed /bɑmd; bɒmd/ *adj* [not before noun 不用于名词前] *slang* very drunk or affected by illegal drugs【俚】烂醉的；吸了毒的：*I feel like going out and getting completely bombed.* 我想出去喝个不醉不归。

bomb·er /`bɑmə; 'bɒmə/ *n* [C] **1** a plane that carries and drops bombs 轰炸机 **2** someone who puts a bomb somewhere 投弹手；放置炸弹的人

bomber jack·et /'·· ,··/ *n* [C] a short jacket which fits tightly around your waist 紧身短上衣，夹克衫，短夹克

bomb·ing /`bɑmɪŋ; 'bɒmɪŋ/ *n* [C,U] the use of bombs to attack a place 炮轰，轰炸：**wave of bombings** (=series of attacks using bombs) 一连串爆炸 *Hundreds have been killed in the current wave of bombings.* 有好几百人在近日发生的一连串爆炸事件中丧生。

bomb·proof /`bɑm`pruf; 'bɒmpruːf/ *adj* strong enough not to be damaged by a bomb attack 防弹的，避弹的：*a bombproof shelter* 防空洞

bomb scare /'· ·/ *n* [C] a situation where someone telephones and says that there is a bomb in a particular place 炸弹恐吓：*a bomb scare in Central London* 伦敦中心区的炸弹恐吓

bomb·shell /`bɑm,ʃɛl; 'bɒmʃel/ *n* [C] *informal*【非正式】**1** an unexpected and very shocking piece of news 令人震惊的消息；突发意外事件：*His death came as a complete bombshell.* 他的死讯传来，令人深感震惊。**2 drop a bombshell** to suddenly tell someone a shocking piece of news 突然告诉某人一个令人震惊的消息 **3 blonde bombshell** *humorous* an extremely attractive woman with FAIR (=light coloured) hair【幽默】金发美人

bomb shel·ter /'· ,··/ *n* [C] a room or building that is built to protect people from bomb attacks 防空建筑，防空洞

bomb site /'· ·/ *n* [C] a place where a bomb has destroyed several buildings in a town 被炸后的废墟：*They've pulled down so many buildings around here it looks like a bomb site.* 他们把这儿的许多建筑物都推倒了，看起来就像一片被轰炸后的废墟。

bo·na fi·de, bonafide /`bonə `faɪdɪ; ˌbəʊnə 'faɪdi/ *adj* **1** real, true and not intended to deceive someone 真正的；真实的；真诚的：*Only bona fide members are allowed to use the club pool.* 只有真正的会员才允许使用俱乐部的泳池。**2 bona fides** [plural] *BrE* if you check someone's bona fides, you check that they are who they say they are【英】诚意，真诚，善意

bo·nan·za /bə`nænzə; bə'nænzə/ *n* [C] a lucky or successful situation where people can make a lot of money 走鸿运；获利之道；致富之源：*Spielberg's movie ET was a box office bonanza.* 斯皮尔伯格的电影《外星人》票房收入可观。

Bo·na·parte —see 见 NAPOLEON

bon·bon /`bɑn,bɑn; 'bɒnbɒn/ *n* [C] a type of round SWEET² (1) 巧克力夹心软糖，糖果

bonce /bɑns; bɒns/ *n* [C] *slang* your head【俚】头，脑袋

bond¹ /bɑnd; bɒnd/ *n* [C] 3

1 ▶MONEY 钱◀ an official document promising that a government or company will pay back money that it has borrowed, often with INTEREST¹ (4) 债券，证券，公债：*My father put all his money into Canadian Northern Railway bonds.* 我父亲把他所有的钱都投到了加拿大北方铁路的债券上。| *furious trading on the bond market* 债券市场风起云涌的交易

2 ▶UNITE 团结◀ something that unites two or more people or groups, such as love, or a shared interest or idea〔因共同利益或感情而使人联系起来的〕纽带，维系，连结物，关系：[**+between**] *the natural bond between mother and child* 母亲和孩子之间一种自然的紧密关系 | [**+of**] *The two countries are linked by bonds of friendship going back many years.* 两国之间的友好关系可追溯到许多年以前。| [**+with**] *He felt a strong bond with his audience.* 他感到自己和观众有着一种很紧密的联系。

3 bonds [plural] *literary*【文】**a)** something that limits your freedom and prevents you from doing what you want 枷锁，桎梏，限制人自由的东西：[**+of**] *the bonds of slavery* 奴隶制度的枷锁 **b)** chains, ropes etc used for tying up a prisoner 镣铐；绳索：*The prisoners will be freed from their bonds.* 囚犯们将不再戴镣铐。

4 ▶GLUE 胶(水)◀ the way in which two surfaces become fixed to each other using glue 结合，黏合

5 ▶CHEMISTRY 化学◀ *technical* the chemical force that holds atoms together【术语】化学键：*In each methane molecule there are four CH bonds.* 每一个甲烷分子中有四个碳氢键。

6 a written agreement to do something, that makes you legally responsible for doing it 契约，盟约

7 my word is my bond *formal* used to say that you will definitely do what you have promised【正式】我说的话(像契约一样)可靠，我一定会履行诺言

8 in/out of bond *technical* in or out of a BONDED WAREHOUSE【术语】〔进口货物〕存入关栈中以待完税/已完税出关

bond² *v* **1** [I] if two things bond with each other, they become firmly fixed together, especially after they have been joined with glue〔尤指用胶水〕黏合：*It takes less than 10 minutes for the two surfaces to bond.* 两个表面不到10分钟就会黏到一起。**2** [I] to develop a special relationship with someone〔与某人〕培养一种特殊的关系：*the tendency to bond with others of the same sex* 与其他同性的人建立关系的趋势 **3** [T] *technical* to keep goods in a bonded warehouse【术语】〔把货物〕存入关栈 [保税仓库] 中

Bond /bɑnd; bɒnd/, **James** a character in the books by Ian Fleming, and in the films that have been based on these stories. James Bond is a secret AGENT who works for the British government and is sometimes called '007'. 邦德〔伊恩·弗莱明的小说及其电影中的人物，他是一名英国政府的特工，有时被称为"007"〕

bond·age /`bɑndɪdʒ; 'bɒndɪdʒ/ *n* [U] **1** the practice of being tied up for sexual pleasure〔为获得性快感而进行的〕缚住手脚做爱，捆绑起来做爱 **2** *literary* the state of being a slave【文】奴役：*Since the age of 13 he had been in bondage.* 他从13岁起就成了奴隶。**3** the state of having your freedom limited, or being prevented from doing what you want 束缚，限制：*He wanted to*

be free from the bondage of social conventions. 他想摆脱社会习俗的束缚。

bonded ware·house /ˌ‥ ˈ‥/ *n* [C] *technical* an official store for goods that have been brought into a country before tax has been paid on them【术语】〔海关的〕关栈, 保税仓库

bond·hold·er /ˈbɑndˌholdɚ; ˈbɒndˌhəʊldə/ *n* [C] *technical* someone who owns government or industrial bonds (BOND[1] (1))【术语】债券持有人

Bon·di Beach /ˌbɑndaɪ ˈbitʃ; ˌbɒndaɪ ˈbiːtʃ/ a popular beach in Sydney, Australia, where people go SURFING 邦迪海滩〔澳大利亚悉尼的著名海滩, 可以冲浪〕

bond·ing /ˈbɑndɪŋ; ˈbɒndɪŋ/ *n* [U] **1** a process in which a special relationship develops between two or more people 亲密关系的形成: *They're in the bar again doing some male bonding!* 他们一班男士又在酒吧里谈天说地, 联络感情了! **2** *technical* the connection of atoms【术语】〔原子的〕结合

Bond Street /ˈ‥ ‥/ a street in London famous for its expensive shops 邦德街〔伦敦的一条街, 以商品价格昂贵的店铺闻名〕

S2 W2 **bone[1]** /bon; bəʊn/ *n*

1 ►BODY 身体◄ [C] one of the hard parts that together form the frame of a human or animal body 骨头, 骨: *The X-ray showed that the bone was broken in two places.* X光检查显示骨头有两处折断。| **thigh/cheek/jaw etc bone** (=the bone in your thigh etc) 股骨/颧骨/颌骨等 *very prominent cheek bones* 非常突出的颧骨 | **big-boned/fine-boned/small-boned etc** (=with big etc bones) 骨头粗大的/骨架匀称的/骨架小的等 *Grace was a tall, big-boned woman.* 格雷丝是一个高大、粗壮的妇女。| **good/fine bone structure** (=someone with good bone structure has a well-shaped face) 脸形好, 脸部线条优美

2 have a bone to pick with sb *spoken* used to tell someone that you are annoyed with them and want to talk about it【口】对某人不满, 对某人有抱怨

3 the bare bones the simplest and most important details of something 最基本的内容, 梗概: *This is just the bare bones of the plan – it's still in the early stages.* 这只是计划的梗概, 一切还处于初步阶段。

4 make no bones about (doing) sth to not feel nervous or ashamed about doing or saying something 对某事毫无顾忌, 对某事毫不踌躇: *We made no bones about our commitment to Marxism.* 我们毫不犹豫地献身马克思主义。

5 be chilled/frozen to the bone extremely cold 寒冷刺骨

6 a bone of contention something that causes arguments between people 争执的原因: *The question of unpaid overtime became the main bone of contention.* 没有付加班费的问题成了争执的焦点。

7 a bag of bones someone who is much too thin 骨瘦如柴的人

8 bones [plural] *AmE* DICE[1] (1)【美】骰子, 色子

9 close to the bone a remark, statement etc that is close to the bone is close to the truth in a way that may offend someone 苛刻地揭露真相的; 露骨的: *Some of his jokes were a bit close to the bone.* 他的一些笑话有点露骨。

10 cut sth to the bone to reduce costs, services etc as much as possible〔把成本或服务等〕削减到最低程度

11 feel/know it in your bones to be certain that something is true, even though you have no proof and cannot explain why you are certain 从内心里感到; 确信: *That boy's trouble, I can feel it in my bones.* 我从心底里觉得那个男孩会带来麻烦。

12 off the bone meat that is served off the bone has been cut away from the bone〔肉〕脱骨的

13 on the bone meat that is served on the bone is still joined to the bone〔肉〕带骨的 —see also 另见 **as dry as a bone** (DRY[1] (1)), **work your fingers to the bone** (WORK[1] (26))

bone[2] *v* [T] to remove the bones from fish, or meat 剔掉…的骨头, 去掉…的骨

bone up [I] *informal* to study hard for an examination【非正式】〔为考试等〕钻研, 用功: *I'm having to bone up on criminal law for a test next week.* 我在用功温习, 准备下周的刑法测验。

bone chi·na /ˌ‥ ˈ‥◂/ *n* [U] delicate and expensive cups, plates etc that are made partly with crushed bone 骨灰瓷

bone dry /ˌ‥ ˈ◂/ *adj* completely dry 极干的, 干透的: *There had been no rain for months and the land was bone dry.* 几个月没下雨, 地都干透了。

bone·head /ˈbonˌhɛd; ˈbəʊnhed/ *n* [C] *informal* a stupid person【非正式】笨蛋, 傻瓜

bone i·dle /ˌ‥ ˈ‥◂/ *adj* extremely lazy 懒到极点的: *He's not stupid, just bone idle.* 他并不笨, 只是太懒。

bone mar·row /ˈ‥ ˌ‥/ *n* the soft substance in the hollow centre of bones; MARROW (1) 骨髓: *a bone marrow transplant* 骨髓移植

bone meal /ˈ‥ ‥/ *n* [U] a substance used to feed plants that is made of crushed bones〔用作肥料的〕骨粉

bon·er /ˈbonɚ; ˈbəʊnə/ *n* [singular] **1** *AmE taboo* an ERECTION (1)【美讳】〔阴茎〕勃起状态 **2** *AmE informal* a stupid or embarrassing mistake【美, 非正式】愚蠢可笑的错误; 令人尴尬的差错

bone·shak·er /ˈbonˌʃekɚ; ˈbəʊnˌʃeɪkə/ *n* [C] *BrE humorous* an old vehicle that is in very bad condition【英, 幽默】破旧颠簸的车辆

bone-tired /ˌ‥ ˈ‥◂/ *adj* [not before noun 不用于名词前] *AmE informal* extremely tired【美, 非正式】累坏了的: *Dan sat in the rocker by the fire, bone-tired after his journey.* 丹坐在火边的摇椅上, 旅途后累得精疲力竭。

bon·fire /ˈbɑnˌfaɪr; ˈbɒnfaɪə/ *n* [C] a large outdoor fire, either for burning waste, or for a party 篝火, 营火, 火堆: *There was a huge bonfire on Guy Fawkes' night.* 盖依·福克斯之夜点起了盛大的篝火。

bonfire night /ˈ‥ ˌ‥/ *n* [singular] November 5th, when in Britain people light FIREWORKS and burn a GUY[1] (2) on a large outdoor fire; GUY FAWKES' NIGHT 篝火之夜, 营火之夜, 盖依·福克斯之夜〔为纪念1605年盖依·福克斯企图炸毁伦敦议会, 英国于每年11月5日游行, 放烟花并焚烧盖依·福克斯的模拟像〕

bong /bɑŋ; bɒŋ/ *n* **1** [singular] a deep sound made by a large bell 洪亮的钟声 **2** [C] *slang* an object used for smoking CANNABIS in which the smoke goes through water to make it cool【俚】大麻叶烟枪

bon·gos, bongoes /ˈbɑŋgoz; ˈbɒŋgəʊz/ also 又作 **bongo drums** /ˈ‥ ‥/ *n* [plural] a pair of small drums that you play with your hands 小手鼓, 拉丁小鼓

bon·ho·mie /ˌbɑnəˈmi; ˈbɒnəmi/ *n* [U] *French especially literary* a friendly feeling among a group of people【法, 尤文】友好, 和蔼, 性情随和: *The atmosphere of bonhomie was suddenly gone.* 亲切友好的气氛突然消失了。

bonk[1] /bɑŋk; bɒŋk/ *v* [I,T] **1** *BrE slang humorous* to have sex with someone【英俚, 幽默】与…性交 **2** *informal* to hit someone lightly on the head or to hit your head on something by mistake【非正式】敲脑袋, 撞头, 磕, 碰: *He fell, bonking his head against a tree.* 他摔倒了, 头撞到一棵树上。

bonk[2] *n* **1** [singular] *BrE slang humorous* the action of having sex【英俚, 幽默】性交, 性行为: *a quick bonk* 快速交合 **2** [C] *informal* the action of hitting someone lightly on the head, or hitting your head against something【非正式】打脑袋; 撞头 **3** [C] *informal* a sudden short deep sound, for example, when something hits the ground【非正式】〔短促而低沉的〕碰撞声

bon·kers /ˈbɑŋkɚz; ˈbɒŋkəz/ *adj BrE humorous*【英, 幽默】**1** slightly crazy 发疯的: *Fly to Tokyo for one day? You must be bonkers!* 乘飞机去东京一天? 你准是发疯了! **2 drive sb bonkers** to annoy someone 烦扰某人; 使人发疯: *I wish they'd turn that bloody music down – it's driving me bonkers!* 我希望他们把这破音乐关小点儿, 那声音简直要使我发疯了!

bon mot /ˌbɑn ˈmo; ˌbɒn ˈməʊ/ *n* [C] *French* a clever remark【法】隽语, 机智的妙语

Bonn /bɑn; bɒn/ the capital city of the Federal Republic of Germany from 1949 until 1990 波恩〔1949年至1990年德意志联邦共和国首都〕

bon·net /ˈbɑnɪt; ˈbɒnɪt/ *n* [C] **1** *BrE* the metal lid over the front of a car【英】〔汽车的〕发动机盖: *I'll need to check under the bonnet.* 我需要查看一下引擎盖的下面。—see picture on page A2 参见A2页图 **2) a)** a warm hat that a baby wears which ties under its chin〔在颏下系带的〕婴儿帽 **b)** a type of hat that women wore in the past which tied under their chin and often had a wide BRIM[1] (1)〔旧时妇女用的, 在颏下有带子、帽前有宽边的〕包头软帽 —see also 另见 **have a bee in your bonnet** (BEE (3)) —see picture at 参见 HAT 图

Bonney /ˈbɑnɪ; ˈbɑːni/, **William** the real name of Billy the Kid 邦尼〔比利小子的真名〕

Bon·nie and Clyde /ˌbɑnɪ ənd ˈklaɪd; ˌbɒni ənd ˈklaɪd/ two young criminals, Bonnie Parker (a woman) and Clyde Barrow (a man), who stole money from banks and businesses in the US in the 1930s 邦尼和克莱德, 雌雄大盗〔指邦尼·帕克(女)和克莱德·巴罗(男)两名年轻罪犯, 20世纪30年代大肆盗窃美国银行和公司的财物〕

Bon·nie Prince Char·lie /ˌ‥ ˌ‥ ˈ‥/ (1720-88) the popular name of **Charles Edward Stuart**, sometimes also called **the Young Pretender**. He was the grandson of King James II, and believed he had the right to be the British king instead of King George II. He led the second Jacobite Rising against the king in 1745-46, but was defeated at the Battle of Culloden. 英俊的查理王子〔(1720-1788), 查尔斯·爱德华·斯图尔特的别称, 有时也被称为小王位觊觎者。他是国王詹姆斯二世之孙, 认为自

己有权取代国王乔治二世，成为英国国王。1745年至1746年他领导了第二次詹姆斯党人叛乱，但在卡洛登战役中战败〕—see also 另见 James Edward STUART

bon·ny /ˈbɑnɪ; ˈbɒni/ *adj especially ScotE*【尤苏格兰】**1** pretty and healthy 漂亮健康的，健美的：*a bonny baby* 漂亮健康的婴儿 **2** clever or skilful 聪明的；熟练的：*a bonny fighter* 技术高超的拳击手

bon·sai /ˈbɑnsaɪ; ˈbɒnsaɪ/ *n* [C,U] a tree that is grown so that it always stays very small, or the art of growing trees in this way 盆景，盆栽（艺术） **—bonsai** *adj*

bo·nus /ˈbonəs; ˈbəʊnəs/ *n* [C] **1** money added to someone's wages, especially as a reward for good work 奖金；红利；特别津贴：*People who stay more than two years in the job receive a special bonus.* 从事这个工作超过两年者会得到一项特殊津贴。**2** something good that you did not expect in a situation 没有预料到的好事：**added bonus** *It's an added bonus being able to work at home.* 另一个好处是能在家工作。**3 no-claims bonus** a reduction in the cost of your car insurance when you do not make a claim in a particular year 未索赔奖励金〔一种汽车保险优惠〕

bon vi·vant /ˌbɑn viˈvɑnt; ˌbɒn viːˈvɒnt/ also 又作 **bon viveur** /-viˈvɝ; -viːˈvɜː/ *n* [C] *literary French* someone who enjoys good food and wine, and being with people【文，法】讲究饮食和生活的人；享乐主义者

bon voy·age /ˌbɑn vwaɪˈɑʒ; ˌbɒn vwaɪˈɑːʒ/ *interjection French* used to wish someone a good journey【法】一路顺风

bon·y /ˈbonɪ; ˈbəʊni/ *adj* **1** someone or part of their body that is bony is very thin 骨瘦如柴的，瘦得皮包骨的：*Her hand felt cold and bony.* 她的手摸起来又冷又瘦。**2** bony meat or fish contains a lot of small bones〔肉或鱼〕多骨[刺]的 **3** a part of an animal that is bony consists mostly of bone〔动物身体部分〕多骨的

boo¹ /bu; buː/ *v* [I,T] **1** to shout 'boo' to show that you do not like a person, performance, idea etc 发嘘声〔表示反对或反感〕：*Some of the audience started booing.* 一些观众开始发出嘘声。**2 boo sb off (stage)** to shout 'boo' until a performer leaves the stage 喝倒彩；把某人轰下台：*His jokes were so bad he got booed off stage.* 他的笑话很粗俗，被观众喝倒彩轰下了台。

boo² *interjection* **1** *plural* **boos** a noise made by people who do not like a person, performance, idea etc〔表示反对或反感的〕嘘声 **2** a word you shout suddenly to someone as a joke in order to frighten them 哟！〔惊吓别人时发出的声音〕 **3 wouldn't say boo to a goose** an expression used to describe a shy, quiet person 非常羞怯：*Christine wouldn't say boo to a goose.* 克里斯蒂娜非常害羞。

boob¹ /bub; buːb/ *n* [C usually plural 一般用复数] **1** *slang* a woman's breast【俚】〔妇女的〕乳房，奶子 **2** *BrE informal* a silly mistake【英，非正式】愚蠢的错误 **3** *AmE old-fashioned* a stupid or silly person【美，过时】傻瓜，笨蛋

boob² *v* [I] to make a stupid mistake 出错：*I think Jean's boobed again.* 我看琼又犯错了。

boo-boo /ˈ· ·/ *n* [C] *informal* a word meaning a mistake【非正式】错误：*I made a bit of a boo-boo asking her about David!* 我向她打听戴维真的是一个错误！

boob tube /ˈ· ·/ *n* [C] **1** *BrE* a piece of women's clothing made of stretchy material, that covers only her chest【英】（女子）弹力短上衣；TUBE TOP *AmE*【美】**2 the boob tube** *AmE informal* the TELEVISION (1)【美，非正式】电视机：*sitting around watching the boob tube* 围坐在一起看电视

boo·by /ˈbubɪ; ˈbuːbi/ *n* [C] *informal* a silly or stupid person【非正式】傻瓜，蠢材

boo·by hatch /ˈ·· ·/ *n* [singular] *AmE old-fashioned* a mental hospital【美，过时】精神病院

booby prize /ˈ·· ·/ *n* [C] a prize given as a joke to the person who is last in a competition〔指出于善意的玩笑而发给的〕末名奖

booby trap, booby-trap /ˈ·· ·/ *n* [C] **1** a hidden bomb that explodes when you touch something else that is connected to it 伪装地雷[炸弹]，饵雷 **2** a HARMLESS trap that you arrange for someone as a joke〔开玩笑的〕陷阱，机关，恶作剧的把戏：*The booby trap was a bucket of water resting on top of the door.* 恶作剧的把戏是把一桶水放在门顶上。**—booby-trapped** *adj*

boog·er /ˈbugɚ; ˈbʊgə/ *n* [C] *AmE slang*【美俚】**1** used when describing a person or thing 家伙；东西：*You wouldn't want to meet him in a dark alley – he's a mean-looking booger.* 你不会想在黑暗的小巷里见他，他是一个看起来非常卑鄙的家伙。—compare 比较 BUGGER **2** a thick piece of MUCUS from your nose 鼻涕

boo·gey·man /ˈbugɪˌmæn; ˈbuːgimæn/ *n* a BOGEYMAN 鬼怪，怪物

boo·gie¹ /ˈbugɪ; ˈbuːgi/ *v* [I] *informal* to dance, especially to fast popular music【非正式】〔随着快节奏的流行音乐〕跳舞：*Boogie on down!* 使劲跳吧！

boogie² *n* **1** also 又作 **boogie woo·gie** /ˈbugɪ ˈwugɪ; ˌbuːgi ˈwuːgi/ [U] *AmE* a type of music played on the piano with a strong fast RHYTHM (1)【美】布基伍基音乐〔用钢琴演奏的一种节奏强劲的音乐〕**2** [C] *informal* a dance, especially to fast popular music【非正式】〔随着快节奏的流行音乐而跳的〕舞蹈：*Do you fancy going for a boogie on Saturday?* 你喜欢星期六去跳舞吗？

boo·hoo /ˌbu ˈhu; ˌbuː ˈhuː/ *interjection* a word used especially in children's stories to show that someone is crying 呜呜〔尤用于儿童故事中表示哭泣〕

book¹ /buk; bʊk/ *n*

1 ▶PRINTED BOOK 印刷的书◀ [C] a set of printed pages that are fastened together in a cover so that you can read them 书，书籍：*I'm reading a book by Graham Greene.* 我正在读格雷厄姆·格林写的一本书。| *Nothing beats curling up with a good book.* 什么也比不上蜷着身子看一本好书的感觉。

2 ▶BOOK TO WRITE IN 写字的本◀ [C] a set of sheets of paper fastened together in a cover so that you can write on them 本，册，簿：*a note book* 笔记本 | **address/exercise etc book** (=a book for a particular purpose) 地址簿/练习本等

3 ▶SET OF THINGS 成套的东西◀ [C] a set of things such as stamps, matches or tickets, fastened together inside a paper cover 装订成册之物

4 books [plural] **a) ▶ACCOUNTS** 账目◀ written records of the accounts of a business 账目，账簿，会计簿：*Their books show a profit.* 他们的账目本显示有盈利。—see also 另见 **cook the books** (COOK¹ (5)) **b) ▶JOBS** 职业◀ the names of people who use a company's services, or who are sent by a company to work for other people〔顾客或雇员〕名册：**on sb's books** *informal* (=employed by a company or organization)【非正式】受雇于某公司[机构]：*We have over 100 VDU operators on our books at the moment.* 目前，我们在册的视频显示器操作员超过100人。

5 a closed book a subject that you do not understand or know anything about 不理解[一无所知]的学科[主题]；谜：*Chemistry is a closed book to me.* 我对化学一窍不通。

6 one for the books *informal* used to say that something that has happened is unusual or surprising【非正式】新奇[不寻常]的事：*Look! Gaynor's buying the drinks. There's one for the books!* 看！盖纳在买酒。这真是新鲜事！

7 be in sb's good/bad books *informal* used to say that someone is pleased or annoyed with you【非正式】令某人满意/恼火

8 go by the book/do sth by the book to do something exactly according to rules or instructions 照章办事，循规蹈矩：*Tony's the sort of bloke who does everything by the book.* 托尼是那种什么都照章办事的人。

9 in my book *usually spoken* used when giving your opinion【一般口】依我看：*She's all right in my book.* 依我看，她没什么事。

10 ▶PART OF A BOOK 书的部分◀ [C] one of the parts that a very large book such as the Bible is divided into 卷，篇：**[+of]** *the Book of Isaiah*《以赛亚书》

11 bring sb to book *especially BrE* to punish someone for breaking laws or rules, especially when you have been trying to punish them for a long time【尤英】处罚，责罚〔某人〕：*Terry was finally brought to book for fiddling the accounts.* 特里因在账目上做手脚，最终受到了惩罚。—see also 另见 STATUTE BOOK, **take a leaf out of sb's book** (LEAF¹ (2)), **read sb like a book** (READ¹ (13)), **suit sb's book** (SUIT² (5)), **a turn-up for the book(s)** (TURN-UP (2)), **throw the book at** (THROW¹ (27))

book² *v* **1** [I,T] *BrE* to arrange with a hotel, restaurant, theatre etc to go there at a particular time in the future【英】预订，预购，预约：*I've booked a table for two at Mario's tonight.* 今晚我在马里奥饭店预订了两个人的桌位。| *We need to book well in advance for Christmas.* 我们得在圣诞节以前早早预订。| **booked up/fully booked** (=no rooms, tables etc available) 已被订完，订满 *I'm sorry, we're fully booked for the 14th.* 对不起，14日的已全部被预订了。| **booked solid** (=all the tickets etc have been sold)〔票等〕全部售完 *The show's booked solid for months to come.* 未来几个月的演出门票都已售完。**2** [T] to arrange for someone such as a singer to perform on a particular date 预约〔某人〕演出：**booked up/fully booked** (=no time left to do any more performances) 演出时间已排满 *We're booked up right through the summer season.* 我们整个夏季的演出时间都已排满。**3** [T] when a police officer books someone, they write down their name, address etc because they have done something wrong〔尤指警察〕把…记录在案：*Rebecca's been booked*

for speeding. 丽贝卡因超速驾驶被记录在案。**4** [T] *BrE* when a football REFEREE[1] (1) books a player who has broken the rules, they officially write down the player's name in a book【英】〔足球裁判〕记下〔犯规球员〕名字, 记名警告

book in/into *phr v BrE*【英】**1** [I] to arrive at a hotel and say who you are etc〔到达旅馆后〕办理入住登记手续: *I'll call you as soon as I've booked in at my hotel.* 我办完入住登记手续就给你打电话。**2** [T **book** sb **in/into**] to arrange for someone to stay at a hotel 为…预订旅馆房间: *Could you book me in at the Hilton for tonight?* 你能为我在希尔顿酒店预订今晚的房间吗?

book sb **on** sth *phr v* [T] to arrange for someone to travel on a particular plane, train etc 为〔某人〕预订〔飞机票或火车票〕: *She asked her secretary to book her on the next flight to London.* 她请秘书给她预订下一班飞往伦敦的航班。

book·a·ble /ˈbukəbl; ˈbʊkəbəl/ *adj* **1** *BrE* tickets for a concert, performance etc that are bookable can be ordered before it happens【英】可预订的 **2 bookable offence** an offence for which a football player can be punished by having their name written in the referee's (REFEREE[1] (1)) book〔会使足球裁判记名警告的〕犯规

book·bind·ing /ˈbukˌbaɪndɪŋ; ˈbʊkˌbaɪndɪŋ/ *n* [U] the art of fastening the pages of books inside a cover〔书籍的〕装订, 装帧 —**bookbinder** *n* [C]

book·case /ˈbukˌkes; ˈbʊk-keɪs/ *n* [C] a set of shelves for keeping books on 书架, 书柜: *a walnut bookcase* 胡桃木书柜

book club /ˈ· ·/ *n* [C] a club that offers books cheaply to its members〔廉价卖书给会员的〕读书会; 读书俱乐部

book·end /ˈbukˌɛnd; ˈbʊkend/ *n* [C usually plural 一般用复数] one of a pair of objects that you put at the end of a row of books to prevent them from falling over 书挡, 书靠

Book·er Prize, the /ˈbukə ˌpraɪz; ˈbʊkə ˌpraɪz/ *n* [C] an important prize given every year for the best NOVEL in English written by a citizen of the UK or the British Commonwealth 布克奖〔每年颁发给英国公民或英联邦公民的最佳英语小说奖〕: *Booker Prize-winning author Roddy Doyle* 获得布克奖的作家罗迪·多伊尔

book·ie /ˈbukɪ; ˈbʊki/ *n* [C] *BrE informal* a BOOKMAKER【英, 非正式】马票商

[3] **book·ing** /ˈbukɪŋ; ˈbʊkɪŋ/ *n* [C] **1** *BrE* an arrangement to travel by train, use a hotel room etc at a particular time in the future【英】预约, 预订: **make a booking** *Can I make a booking for tonight?* 我可以预订今晚的(票)吗? | *cancel a booking* 取消预订 **2** an arrangement made by a performer to perform at a particular time in the future 演出合同 **3** the act of writing a football player's name in a book as a punishment for breaking the rules〔足球队员〕犯规被记名, 犯规记录

booking of·fice /ˈ·· ,··/ *n* [C] *BrE* a place where you can buy train or bus tickets【英】售票处, 订票处

book·ish /ˈbukɪʃ; ˈbʊkɪʃ/ *adj* **1** someone who is bookish is more interested in reading and studying than in sports or other activities 嗜书的; 好读书的; 喜欢学习的: *Bill was the studious, bookish type.* 比尔是那种勤奋好学的人。**2** based on books rather than on practical experience 按书本行事的, 学究气的

book·keep·ing /ˈbukˌkipɪŋ; ˈbʊkˌkiːpɪŋ/ *n* [U] the job or activity of recording the accounts of an organization 记账, 簿记, 管账

[2] **book·let** /ˈbuklɪt; ˈbʊklɨt/ *n* [C] a very short book that usually contains information 小册子: *free booklet on drug abuse* 关于滥用药物的免费小册子

book·mak·er /ˈbukˌmekə; ˈbʊkˌmeɪkə/ *n* [C] someone whose job is to collect money that people want to risk on the result of a race, competition etc, and who pays them if they guess correctly 马票商, 经营(赛马)赌注登记者

book·mark /ˈbukˌmɑrk; ˈbʊkmɑːk/ *n* [C] a piece of paper, leather etc that shows you the last page you have read in a book 书签

book·mo·bile /ˈbukməˌbil; ˈbʊkməbiːl/ *n* [C] *AmE* a vehicle that contains a library and travels to different places so that people can use it【美】流动图书馆

Book of Com·mon Prayer, The /ˌ· · · ,· · ˈ·/ a book used in Church of England and Episcopal churches, which contains the words spoken by the priest and by the people in church at weekly services and at weddings, funerals etc《英国国教祈祷书》〔英国国教会和美国新教圣公会使用的祈祷书, 载有牧师和信徒在教堂每周的礼拜仪式、婚礼、葬礼等场合诵读的祷文〕

book·plate /ˈbukˌplet; ˈbʊkpleɪt/ *n* [C] a decorated piece of paper with your name on it, that you stick in the front of your books〔贴在书中的〕藏书者标签

book·rest /ˈbukˌrɛst; ˈbʊk-rest/ *n* [C] a metal or wood frame that holds a book upright so that you can read it without holding it in your hands 看书架〔供放置摊开的书用〕

book·sell·er /ˈbukˌsɛlə; ˈbʊkˌselə/ *n* [C] a person or company that sells books 书商

book·shelf /ˈbukˌʃɛlf; ˈbʊkʃelf/ *n plural* **bookshelves** /-ʃɛlvz; -ʃelvz/ [C] a shelf that you keep books on 书架

book·shop /ˈbukˌʃɑp; ˈbʊkʃɒp/ *n* [C] *especially BrE* a shop that sells books【尤英】书店; bookstore *AmE*【美】

book·stall /ˈbukˌstɔl; ˈbʊkstɔːl/ *n* [C] *BrE* a small shop that has an open front and sells books and magazines, often at a station【英】书亭, 书报摊; NEWSSTAND *AmE*【美】

book·store /ˈbukˌstɔr; ˈbʊkstɔː/ *n* [C] *AmE* a shop that sells books【美】书店; bookshop *BrE*【英】

book to·ken /ˈ· ,··/ *n* [C] *BrE* a card that you can exchange for books【英】〔可兑换书刊的〕购书券, 书券: *My aunt always gives me a book token for Christmas.* 我的姨母在圣诞节时总给我购书券。

book va·lue /ˈ· ,··/ *n* [C] the standard value that something such as a car of a particular age, style etc is supposed to have 账面价值, 净值, 实值

book·worm /ˈbukˌwɝm; ˈbʊkwɜːm/ *n* [C] **1** someone who likes reading very much 极爱读书的人, 书虫, 书呆子 **2** an insect that eats books 蠹鱼, 蛀书虫

[3] **boom[1]** /bum; buːm/ *n*

1 ▶**INCREASE IN BUSINESS** 业务增加◀ [singular] a rapid increase of business activity〔生意〕繁荣, 兴旺, 景气: [**+in**] *a sudden boom in the housing market* 房产市场的突然繁荣 | **consumer/investment/property etc boom** *the post-war property boom* 战后的财富增长 | **boom years/times** *These are boom times for voluntary organizations.* 这是志愿机构兴盛的时期。—see also 另见 BOOM TOWN

2 ▶**WHEN STH IS POPULAR** 某事物流行之时◀ [singular] a period when something suddenly becomes very popular or starts happening a lot 流行时期: **jazz/aerobics etc boom** *the jazz boom of the 1950s* 20世纪50年代爵士乐的鼎盛时期

3 ▶**SOUND** 声音◀ [C] a deep loud sound that you can hear for several seconds after it begins, especially the sound of an explosion or a large gun 隆隆声: *the dull boom of the cannons* 隐约传来的大炮轰鸣声 —see also 另见 SONIC BOOM

4 ▶**LONG POLE** 长杆子◀ [C] **a)** a long pole on a boat that is attached to a sail at the bottom 帆的下桁, 帆杆 —see picture at 参见 YACHT 图 **b)** a long pole used as part of a piece of equipment that loads and unloads things〔装卸货物时用的〕吊杆, 起重臂 **c)** a long pole that has a camera or microphone on the end〔一端挂照相机或麦克风的〕活动支架, 吊杆

5 ▶**ON A RIVER** 在河上◀ [C] something that is stretched across a river or a BAY[1] (1) to prevent things floating down or across it〔横拦于河面或海湾以阻止物件漂走的〕挡栅, 水栅

boom[2] *v* **1** also 又作 **boom out a)** [I] to make a loud deep sound 发低沉的声音, 隆隆作响: *Guns boomed in the distance.* 远处大炮隆隆作响。**b)** [T] to say something in a loud deep voice 用洪亮而低沉的声音说: *"Come here, boy," boomed the headteacher.* "过来, 孩子。"校长用洪亮而低沉的声音说。**2** [usually in progressive 一般用进行时] if business, trade, or a particular area is booming, it is very successful〔商业、贸易等〕繁荣;〔城镇等〕兴起; 迅速发展: *The steel industry is booming.* 钢铁工业迅速发展。—**booming** *adj*

boom box /ˈ· ·/ *n* [C] *AmE informal* a GHETTO BLASTER【美, 非正式】手提录音机

boo·me·rang[1] /ˈbuməˌræŋ; ˈbuːməræŋ/ *n* [C] a curved stick from Australia that flies in a circle and comes back to you when you throw it〔出自澳大利亚的抛出后可飞回的〕飞去来镖, 回飞棒, 回力棒

boomerang[2] *v* [I] if a plan boomerangs on someone, it affects them instead of the person who it was intended to affect〔计划〕起反作用, 自作自受, 自食其果

boom town /ˈ· ·/ *n* [C] a town or city that suddenly becomes very successful because there is a lot of new industry〔突然兴旺起来的〕新兴城镇

boon /bun; buːn/ *n* [C usually singular 一般用单数] **1** something that is very useful and makes your life a lot easier 裨益, 恩物, 有用之物: *The new bus service will be a real boon to people in the village.* 新设的公共汽车服务对村民十分有用。**2** *old use* a FAVOUR[1] (1)【旧】恩惠

boon com·pan·ion /ˌ· ·ˈ··/ *n* [C] *literary* a very close friend【文】好友, 挚友

boon·docks /ˈbunˌdɑks; ˈbuːndɒks/ *n* [plural] *AmE informal* a place that is a long way from the nearest town【美, 非正式】偏僻乡村, 荒僻的地方

boon·dog·gle /ˈbun,dagl; ˈbuːn,dɒgl/ *n* [singular] *AmE informal* an officially organized plan or activity that is very complicated and wastes a lot of time, money, and effort【美，非正式】庞大而浪费的计划[活动]

Boone /bun; buːn/, **Daniel** (1734-1820) one of the first white Americans to go to Kentucky, where he started to build a town 布恩〔(1734-1820)，最早进入肯塔基州的美国白人之一，最早在该州兴建了小镇〕

B

boo·nies /ˈbuniz; ˈbuːniz/ *n* [plural] *AmE informal* boondocks【美，非正式】偏僻乡村，荒僻的地方

boor /bʊr; bʊə/ *n* [C] *old-fashioned* a man who behaves in a very rude way【过时】粗鲁[没礼貌]的人〔指男子〕—**boorish** *adj*: *boorish behaviour* 粗鲁的举止 —**boorishly** *adv*

boost¹ /bust; buːst/ *v* [T] **1** to increase something such as production, sales etc because they are not as high as you want them to be 增加；提高；促进：*The advertising campaign is intended to boost sales.* 广告宣传活动旨在增加销售。**2 boost sb's confidence/morale/ego** to make someone feel more confident and less worried 增强某人的自信心/士气/自尊：*He regularly phones to boost her morale.* 他定期打电话鼓励她。**3** to advertise something by discussing or praising it 吹捧；大肆宣传：*a special promotion to boost their new product* 为推销他们的新产品而特别展开的宣传活动 **4** also 又作 **boost up** to help someone reach a higher place by lifting them 向上推起，托一把：*Can you boost me up onto the horse?* 你能帮忙把我托上马吗？

boost² *n* **1** [singular] something that helps someone be more successful and confident, or that helps something increase or improve 激励，鼓舞；增加；改进：[+to] *Last night's victory was a tremendous boost to the team.* 昨晚的胜利对球队是一个巨大的鼓舞。| **give (sb/sth) a boost** *Being chosen to attend the conference gave Matthew a real boost.* 被选去出席会议给马修以很大的激励。| **ego/morale boost** (=an increase in confidence) 自我激励 *He wanted a dizzy blonde as a boost to his ego.* 他想找一个傻乎乎的金发姑娘以增强自己的自信心。**2** [U] an increase in the amount of power available to a ROCKET¹ (1), piece of electrical equipment etc〔火箭、电器等的〕动力增强，助推 **3 give sb a boost (up)** to lift someone so that they can reach a higher place 推起，托某人一把：*If I give you a boost up, could you reach the window?* 如果我托你一把，你够得着窗户吗？

boost·er /ˈbustə; ˈbuːstə/ *n* [C] **1** a small quantity of a drug that increases the effect of one that was given before, so that someone continues to be protected against a disease〔增强药效的〕附加剂量，加强剂 **2** something that helps someone be more successful or to feel more confident 令人鼓舞的事情：**morale booster** *The departmental party was a real morale booster.* 全系聚会对士气是个很大的鼓舞。**3** a ROCKET¹ (1) that is used to provide additional power for a SPACECRAFT to leave the Earth 推进器，助推器：*a giant booster rocket* 巨大的助推火箭 **4** *AmE* someone who gives a lot of support to a person, organization, or an idea【美】拥护者，热心支持者

booster cush·ion /ˈ.. ,../ *BrE*【英】also 又作 **booster seat, booster chair** /ˈ.. ./ *AmE*【美】*n* [C] a special seat for a small child that lets them sit in a higher position in a car or at a table〔小孩子坐的〕垫高座

boot¹ /but; buːt/ *n* [C]

1 ►SHOE 鞋◄ a type of shoe that covers your whole foot and the lower part of your leg 靴子，高腰鞋：*a pair of old army boots* 一双旧军靴

2 ►JOB 职业◄ *informal*【非正式】**a) get the boot** to be forced to leave your job 被开除，被解雇 **b) give sb the boot** to dismiss someone from their job; SACK² (1) 解雇某人：*He was certain they would find out he'd been given the boot.* 他肯定他们会发现他已经被解雇了。

3 ►CAR 汽车◄ *BrE* an enclosed space at the back of a car, used for carrying bags etc【英】〔汽车后部的〕行李厢；TRUNK (2) *AmE*【美】：*At least the boot is of reasonable proportions.* 至少行李箱大小正合适。—see picture on page A2 参见 A2 页图

4 put the boot in *BrE informal*【英，非正式】**a)** to say very unkind things to someone who is already upset 火上浇油：*I know you were angry with him but there was no need to put the boot in like that.* 我知道你对他生气，但也没有必要火上浇油。**b)** to attack someone by kicking them repeatedly, especially when they are on the ground 猛踢〔已倒地的人〕

5 give sth a boot *informal* to give something a quick hard kick【非正式】用脚踢一下某物：*The door wouldn't open so I gave it a boot.* 门打不开，所以我使劲踢了一脚。

6 the boot is on the other foot *BrE* used to say that you now have power over someone who used to have power over you【英】局势逆转；此一时，彼一时

7 to boot used at the end of a list of remarks to emphasize them 并且，加之：*He is dishonest, and a coward to boot.* 他不诚实，而且是个胆小鬼。—see also 另见 **be/get too big for your boots** (BIG (13)), **lick sb's boots** (LICK¹ (7)), **as tough as old boots** (TOUGH¹ (2))

boot² *v* **1** [T] *informal* to kick someone or something hard【非正式】踢：**boot sth/sb in/round/etc** *The goalkeeper booted the ball upfield.* 守门员一脚把球踢到对方半场。**2** [I,T] to make a computer ready to be used by putting in its instructions 进行〔电脑的〕引导启动程序，启动 **3** [T] *AmE* to stop someone from moving their illegally parked vehicle by fixing a piece of equipment to the wheels【美】给〔违规停放的车辆〕加上锁扣；CLAMP¹ (3) *BrE*【英】

boot sb ↔ **out** *phr v* [T] *informal* to force someone to leave a place, job, or organization, especially because they have done something wrong【非正式】赶走；开除：*They were booted out of the pub for fighting.* 他们因为打架被逐出了酒馆。

boot up *phr v* [I,T **boot** sth **up**] to make a computer ready to be used by putting in its instructions; BOOT² (2) 启动〔电脑〕，使〔电脑〕作好使用准备

boot camp /ˈ. ./ *n* [C] a training camp for people who have just joined the US army, Navy, or Marine Corps〔美国海、陆军或海军陆战队的〕新兵训练营

boot·ee, bootie /buˋti; ˈbuːtiː/ *n* [C] a short sock that a baby wears instead of a shoe〔婴儿当鞋穿的〕毛绒袜，毛绒鞋

booth /buθ; buːð/ *n* [C] **1** a small partly enclosed place where one person can do something privately, such as use the telephone or vote〔供一人使用的隔开的〕小间 **2** a tent where you can buy things, play games, or find out information, usually at a market or a FAIR³ (1)〔市场或游乐场上的〕售货棚，摊位，摊档 **3** *especially AmE* a partly enclosed place in a restaurant with a table between two long seats【尤美】〔餐馆内的〕雅座

Booth, John Wilkes /dʒɑn wɪlks; dʒɒn wɪlks/ (1838-65) the man who shot and killed US President Abraham Lincoln 布思〔(1838-1865)，枪杀美国总统亚伯拉罕·林肯的凶手〕

Booth, William (1829-1912) a British religious leader who started the Salvation Army 布思〔英国宗教领袖，曾创立"救世军"〕

boot·lace /ˈbut,les; ˈbuːtleɪs/ *n* [C usually plural 一般用复数] a long piece of string that you use to fasten a boot 鞋带，靴带

boot·leg¹ /ˈbut,lɛg; ˈbuːtleg/ *adj* [only before noun 仅用于名词前] bootleg alcohol or recordings are made and sold illegally 走私的；非法制造及销售的

bootleg² *n* [C] an illegal recording of a music performance 盗版唱片[录音带]：*You could tell from the bad printing that the CD was a bootleg.* 从粗劣的印刷可以看出这张唱片是盗版的。

boots 靴子

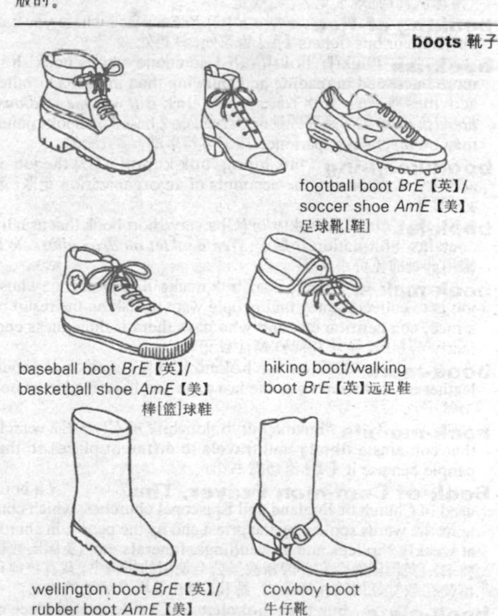

football boot *BrE*【英】/ soccer shoe *AmE*【美】足球靴[鞋]

baseball boot *BrE*【英】/ basketball shoe *AmE*【美】棒[篮]球鞋

hiking boot/walking boot *BrE*【英】远足鞋

wellington boot *BrE*【英】/ rubber boot *AmE*【美】防水橡胶靴

cowboy boot 牛仔靴

boot·leg·ging /ˈbutˌlɛgɪŋ; ˈbuːtlegɪŋ/ *n* [U] illegally making or selling alcohol 非法私酿[销售]酒 —**bootlegger** *n* [C] —**bootleg** *v* [I,T]

boot·lick·ing /ˈbutˌlɪkɪŋ; ˈbuːtˌlɪkɪŋ/ *n* [U] *informal* behaviour that is too friendly to someone in a position of authority, in order to get advantages for yourself【非正式】巴结, 献媚, 拍马屁 —**bootlicker** *n* [C] —**bootlicking** *adj*

boot sale /ˈ· ·/ *n* [C] *BrE* a CAR BOOT SALE【英】旧货出售, 旧物集市

boot·straps /ˈbutˌstræps; ˈbuːtstræps/ *n* [plural] **pull/haul yourself up by your bootstraps** to improve your position and get out of a difficult situation by your own effort, without help from other people 靠自己的努力改善境遇

boot·y /ˈbutɪ; ˈbuːti/ *n* [U] *especially literary* valuable things that a group of people, especially an army that has just won a victory, take away or steal from somewhere【尤文】赃物; 战利品

booze¹ /buz; buːz/ *n* [U] *informal* alcoholic drink【非正式】酒

booze² *v* [I] *informal* to drink alcohol, especially a lot of it【非正式】饮酒; 狂饮: *I expect Jon's out boozing with his mates.* 我估计乔恩出去和朋友一块儿喝酒去了。

booz·er /ˈbuzɚ; ˈbuːzə/ *n* [C] *BrE informal*【英, 非正式】**1** a PUB 小酒馆 **2** someone who often drinks a lot of alcohol 酒徒, 酒鬼, 豪饮者

booze-up /ˈ· ·/ *n* [C] *BrE informal* a party where people drink a lot of alcohol【英, 非正式】狂饮作乐的聚会

booz·y /ˈbuzɪ; ˈbuːzi/ *adj* showing signs of having drunk too much alcohol 酒醉的, 暴饮的: *boozy laughter* 醉酒的笑声 —**boozily** *adv* —**booziness** *n* [U]

bop¹ /bɑp; bɒp/ *v* **bopped, bopping** *informal*【非正式】**1** [T] to hit someone, especially gently 轻打, 轻拍: *I bopped him on the head with my book.* 我用书拍了一下他的头。**2** [I] *BrE* to dance to popular music【英】〔随流行音乐〕起舞

bop² *n* [singular] **1** *BrE informal* a dance【英, 非正式】舞蹈: *It's ages since I had a really good bop.* 我已经好久没有痛快地跳舞了。**2** another word for BEBOP bebop 的另一种说法

Bo Peep /bo ˋpip; bəʊ ˈpiːp/ —see 见 LITTLE BO PEEP

bo·rax /ˈborəks; ˈbɔːræks/ *n* [U] a mineral used for cleaning 硼砂

Bor·deaux /borˋdo; bɔːˈdəʊ/ *n* [C] a wine that comes from the Bordeaux area in France (法国) 波尔多葡萄酒

bor·del·lo /borˋdɛlo; bɔːˈdeləʊ/ *n* [C] *especially literary* a house where men can pay to have sex; BROTHEL【尤文】妓院, 青楼

Bor·den /ˈbordn̩; ˈbɔːdn/, **Liz·zie** /ˈlɪzɪ; ˈlɪzi/ (1860-1927) a US woman who, many people believed, killed her father and his new wife with an AXE in 1892 博登〔(1860-1927), 美国一女子, 有不少人认为, 她 1892 年用斧头砍死了自己的父亲和继母〕

S3 W2 **bor·der¹** /ˈbordɚ; ˈbɔːdə/ *n* [C] **1** the official line that separates two countries, or the area close to this line 国界, 边境, 边界; 边境地区: [+between] *The town lies on the border between the US and Mexico.* 该镇位于美国和墨西哥交界。| [+with] *There has been renewed fighting along the border with Pakistan.* 沿巴基斯坦边境一带又有战事。| **on the border** *Jeumont is a small town on the border between France and Belgium.* 热蒙是法国和比利时交界处的一个小镇。| **cross the border** *The terrorists were stopped trying to cross the Spanish border.* 恐怖分子企图跨越西班牙边界时被拦住了。**2** a band along the edge of something, such as a picture or piece of material 边, 边饰: *writing paper with a black border* 带有黑边的书写纸 **3** a band of soil containing plants at the edge of an area of grass 草地的边缘部分, 〔花园等边缘狭长的〕绿化带: *border plants such as dianthus* 石竹等种在草坪四周的植物

border² *v* [T] **1** to form a border around the edge of something 形成…的边界; 毗邻: *Large trees border the river and the streams.* 毗邻河流和小溪的是大树。| [+on] *The valley is bordered on both sides by high limestone cliffs.* 山谷的两边都是高耸的石灰岩悬崖。**2** if one country borders another country, it is next to it and shares a border with it 与…接壤

border on sth *phr v* [T] to be very close to reaching an extreme feeling or quality 近似, 接近: *excitement bordering on hysteria* 近乎歇斯底里的兴奋

bor·der·land /ˈbordɚˌlænd; ˈbɔːdəlænd/ *n* [C] **1** the land near the border between two countries 边境地带 **2** the borderland between two qualities is an unclear area that contains features of both of them 介乎于两种状况之间的状态; 边缘状态

bor·der·line¹ /ˈbordɚˌlaɪn; ˈbɔːdəlaɪn/ *adj* **borderline case/candidate/decision etc** a situation in which you are not sure whether someone or something is acceptable 难以确定的情况/候选人/决定等: *Borderline candidates will take an oral exam to decide their final result.* 对那些边缘的候选人将进行一次口试决定最终的结果。

borderline² *n* **1** [singular] the point at which one quality, condition, emotion etc ends and another begins 介于两种不同情况之间的不明确界线; 暧昧状况, 含混的情景: *slipping gently over the borderline into sleep* 慢慢地进入睡眠的状态 **2** [C] a border between two countries 分界线, 边界, 国境线

Bor·ders, the /ˈbordɚz; ˈbɔːdəz/ an area in Scotland close to the border with England, known for its low hills 博德斯〔苏格兰临近英格兰边境一地区, 以丘陵著称〕—see 见 SCOTTISH BORDERS

bore¹ /bor; bɔː/ the past tense of BEAR¹

bore² *v* **1** [T] to make someone feel bored, especially by talking too much about something they are not interested in〔尤指以无聊的长话〕使〔人〕厌烦: *I'm sorry I spoke for so long – I hope I didn't bore you.* 对不起, 我说得太久了。我希望没有使你感到厌烦。| **bore sb with** *My father's always boring us with his stories about the war.* 父亲老是讲他在战争中的经历, 我们都厌烦了。| **bore sb to death/tears** (=make them very bored) 使某人烦得要命 **2** [I,T] to make a deep round hole in a hard surface 钻(孔), 开凿, 挖(洞): [+through/into] *To build the tunnel they had to bore through solid rock.* 为了建隧道, 他们必须钻透坚硬的岩石。**3** [+into] if someone's eyes bore into you, they look at you in a way that makes you feel uncomfortable〔令人不安地〕盯住看

bore³ *n* **1** [C] someone who is boring, especially because they talk too much about themselves〔尤指因过多谈论自己而〕令人厌烦的人: *He was something of a bore – going on about his charity work all evening.* 他真烦人, 整个晚上都在讲他的慈善工作。| **soccer/photography etc bore** (=someone who talks too much about photography etc) 一谈起足球/摄影等就没完没了的人 **2** [singular] something that you have to do but do not want to do 令人厌烦的事: *Doing housework is a real bore.* 做家务真是件令人厌烦的事。**3 12-bore/small bore etc** the measurement of the size of the inside of a gun BARREL¹ (3)〔枪炮〕12 毫米口径/小口径等 **4** a borehole 钻孔, 井眼

bored /bord; bɔːd/ *adj* tired and impatient because you do not think something is interesting, or because you have nothing to do 厌烦的, 不感兴趣的: *Children easily get bored.* 孩子们很容易感到厌烦。| [+with] *I'm bored with the same old routine day after day.* 我厌倦了日复一日的例行事务。| **bored stiff/to tears/to death/out of your mind** (=extremely bored) 感到极度厌烦, 烦得要命 *You'd be bored stiff in a job like that.* 做这样的工作你会烦死的。 S3

> **USAGE NOTE 用法说明: BORED**
>
> WORD CHOICE 词语辨析: **bored, boring, interested in, interesting, frightened of, frightening**
>
> With pairs of adjectives like this, the one ending in **-ed** describes the person who has the feeling, the one ending in **-ing** describes whatever gives them that feeling. 在这些成对的形容词当中, 以 -ed 结尾的形容词描写的是人有了这种感受, 而以 -ing 结尾的形容词描写的是使人产生这种感受的人或事物: *I got bored watching TV/talking to Susan.* 我厌倦了看电视/和苏姗谈话。| *TV/Susan was boring.* 电视/苏姗真叫人烦。| *I'm interested in their summer courses* (NOT 不用 *I interested in...* or 或 *I was interesting in/on...* or 或 *I was interested of/on/with/about...*). 我对他们的夏季课程感兴趣。| *Don't be frightened of it – it isn't really frightening.* 不要害怕, 其实并不可怕。
>
> GRAMMAR 语法
>
> You will hear people say they are *bored of* something but many people think only **bored with** is correct. 你会听到有人说 be bored of, 但许多人认为 be bored with 才是正确的: *She's getting really bored with her job.* 她对自己的工作真的厌倦了。

bore·dom /ˈbordəm; ˈbɔːdəm/ *n* [U] the feeling you have when you are bored 厌倦, 厌烦: *the sheer boredom of working in a factory* 在工厂里工作那种真正的乏味

bore·hole /ˈborˌhol; ˈbɔːhəʊl/ *n* [C] a deep hole made using special equipment, especially in order to get water or oil out of the ground 钻孔, 井眼

Bor·ges /ˈborhɛs; ˈbɔːhes/, **Jor·ge Lu·is** /ˈhorhe luˋis; ˈhɔːheɪ luˈiːs/ (1899-1986) an Argentinian poet and writer of short stories. He is famous for his imaginative style of Magic Realism (=a type of literature in which impossible events are described as if they are real). 博尔赫斯〔(1899-1986), 阿根廷诗人、短篇小说家, 以富有想象力的魔幻现实主义风格而闻名〕

Borghese Gallery /bɔr,geze ˋgæləri; bɔː,geɪze ˈgæləri/ a small but important ART GALLERY in Rome which contains works by Raphael, Titian, and Rubens. 博尔盖塞美术馆〔罗马的一个重要的小型美术馆，藏有拉斐尔、提香及鲁本斯的作品〕

Bor·gias, the /ˈbɔrdʒɪəz; ˈbɔːdʒɪəz/ a powerful wealthy Italian family in the 15th and early 16th centuries. **Lucrezia Borgia** (1480-1519) became the Duchess of Ferrara. Her brother Cesare Borgia (1476-1507) was a successful soldier and ruler. 博尔吉亚家族〔15世纪和16世纪早期意大利一个有权势且富有的世族。卢克雷齐娅·博尔吉亚（1480-1519）成为费拉拉公爵夫人，其兄西泽尔·博尔吉亚（1476-1507）是一位卓越的军事家和统治者〕

boring 无趣的，乏味的

The teacher/lecture is boring./The students are bored.
那个老师/那堂课枯燥无味。/学生们不感兴趣。

2 **bor·ing** /ˈbɔrɪŋ; ˈbɔːrɪŋ/ *adj* not interesting in any way 无趣的，无聊的，乏味的，令人生厌的: *Her husband is about the most boring person I've ever met.* 在我所见过的人当中，她的丈夫差不多是最让人厌烦的。| **deadly boring** (=very boring) 极度沉闷 *I always thought maths was deadly boring.* 我一直认为数学枯燥得要命。

born[1] /bɔrn; bɔːn/ a past participle of BEAR[1]

1 2 **born**[2] *adj*

1 be born when a person or animal is born it comes out of its mother's body, or out of an egg 出生，诞生: *Forty lambs were born this spring.* 这个春季有40头羔羊出生。| [+in] *Swift was born in 1667.* 斯威夫特生于1667年。| *I was born in a small southern town in the USA.* 我在美国南部的一个小镇出生。| [+at] *In those days most babies were born at home.* 那时候，大多数婴儿都是在家里出生的。| [+on] *I was born on December 15th 1973.* 我于1973年12月15日出生。| **newly-born** (=recently born) 最近出生的，出生不久的 *a newly-born baby* 新生儿，初生婴儿 | **be born into/to/of** (=be born in a particular situation, type of family etc) 出身为，出生在…的家庭背景 *Frank was born into a wealthy family.* 弗兰克出生于富有家庭。| **be born with** (=have a particular disease, type of character etc since birth) 天生有〔某种疾病、性格等〕 *Jenny was born with a cleft palate.* 珍妮天生腭裂。| **be born blind/deaf/etc** (=be blind, deaf etc when born) 先天失明/失聪等 | **be born lucky/unlucky etc** (=always be lucky, unlucky etc) 生来命好/命苦等 | **Australian/French etc born** (=born in or as a citizen of Australia etc) 在澳大利亚/法国等出生的 *Australian born rock icon Nick Cave* 在澳大利亚出生的摇滚偶像尼克·凯夫

2 be born to do/be sth to be very suitable for a particular job, activity etc 天生适合做〔某项工作、活动等〕

3 born leader/teacher/musician etc someone who has a strong natural ability to lead, teach etc 天生的领袖/教师/音乐家等

4 ►START EXISTING 开始存在◄ [not before noun 不用于名词前] something that is born starts to exist 产生，诞生: *And so the concept of the jet engine was born.* 于是喷气发动机的概念便诞生了。

5 born of/out of existing as a result of something 因为…而形成；是…的产物: *Bill spoke with a cynicism born of bitter experience.* 比尔说话愤世嫉俗是因为他有过痛苦的经历。

6 born and bred born and having grown up in a particular place and having the typical qualities of someone from that place 土生土长: *born and bred in Liverpool* 在利物浦土生土长

7 I wasn't born yesterday *spoken* used to tell someone you think is deceiving you that you are not stupid enough to believe them【口】不要拿我当三岁小孩

8 in all my born days *spoken old-fashioned* used to express surprise at something that you have never heard about or experienced before【口，过时】在我的一生中，有生以来: *Well, I've never heard of such a thing in all my born days!* 我有生以来从未听说过这样的事！

9 there's one born every minute *spoken* used to say that someone has been very stupid or easily deceived【口】随时有人犯傻〔上当〕

10 be born under a lucky/unlucky star to always have good or bad luck in your life 生来就幸运/不幸 — see also 另见 NATURAL-BORN

11 be born with a silver spoon in your mouth to be born into a rich family 生在富贵人家

12 be born on the wrong side of the blanket *humorous* to have parents who were not married when you were born【幽默】父母婚前出生

born-a-gain /ˈ· ·ˌ·/ *adj* **1 born-again Christian** someone who has become an EVANGELICAL Christian after having a religious experience 基督教再生教徒〔指经过悟性体验后接受了基督教福音主义教派的人〕 **2 born-again nonsmoker/vegetarian etc** someone who has recently stopped smoking, eating meat etc, and who wants other people to do the same 开始信奉并鼓吹戒烟/吃素等的人

CULTURAL NOTE 文化注释

Born-again Christians People who become born-again Christians believe that their new faith in Jesus Christ helps them to start a new life. People often think about a typical born-again Christian as someone who has very traditional ideas about family life, sex etc, and who is very eager to persuade other people to join their church. They usually belong to EVANGELICAL churches, and in the US they are known for supporting the MORAL MAJORITY. 基督教再生教徒：基督教再生教徒相信，因为有了对基督的信仰，他们开始了新生。一般认为，典型的基督教再生教徒在家庭生活、性等方面观念非常传统，热衷于说服别人参加这个教派。他们多属福音派教会，在美国以支持争取道德多数运动而闻名。

borne[1] /bɔrn; bɔːn/ the past participle of BEAR[1]

borne[2] *adj* **1 water borne/sea borne/air borne etc** carried by water, the sea, air etc 由水/海洋/空气等传播[携带]的: *water-borne diseases* 由水传播的疾病 **2 be borne in on/upon sb** if a fact is borne in on someone, they realize that it is true 意识到，完全认识到: *Slowly it was borne in on the citizens that the enemy had surrounded the entire town.* 市民渐渐意识到敌人已经把整个城镇包围了。

Bor·ne·o /ˈbɔrnɪo; ˈbɔːnɪəʊ/ the largest island of the Malay Archipelago (=a group of many islands) in southeast Asia. Part of it belongs to Malaysia and part of it to Indonesia, and it also includes the Sultanate of Brunei. Its population is 12,500,000 (1991). 婆罗洲〔东南亚马来群岛最大岛屿，分属马来西亚、印尼，也包括文莱。人口：12,500,000（1991）〕

bo·rough /ˈbɜro; ˈbʌrə/ *n* [C] a town, or part of a large city, that is responsible for managing its own schools, hospitals, roads etc 享有某些自治权的市镇[区]: *The New York borough of Queens* 纽约皇后区 | *Lambeth Borough Council* 兰贝思自治区议会 2

borough coun·cil /ˌ·· ˈ··/ *n* [C] *especially BrE* the organization that controls a borough【尤英】自治区[市]议会

bor·row /ˈbɑro; ˈbɒrəʊ/ *v* [I,T] **1** to use something that belongs to someone else and that you must give back to them later 向别人借，借来，借入: *Can I borrow your pen for a minute?* 我可以借你的笔用一下吗？| **borrow sth from sb** *BrE*【英】 *You are allowed to borrow 6 books from the library at a time.* 你每次可从图书馆借六本书。| **borrow heavily** (=borrow a lot of money) 借巨款 *They borrowed heavily from the bank to start their new business.* 他们向银行贷了巨款来创办新企业。—compare 比较 LEND (1), LOAN[2] (1) —see picture at 参见 LEND 图 **2** to take or copy someone's ideas, words etc and use them in your own work, language etc (擅自)借用，采用；抄袭〔思想、文字等〕: *It is obvious that many ideas in the book have been borrowed.* 显然，这本书里的许多思想都是拾人牙慧的。| [+from] *English borrows words from many languages.* 英语从很多不同的语言中借用了词语。**3 borrow trouble** *AmE informal* to worry about something unnecessarily【美，非正式】自寻烦恼 —see also 另见 **be living on borrowed time** (LIVE[1] (14)) 2 3

USAGE NOTE 用法说明: BORROW

WORD CHOICE 词语辨析: **borrow, lend, loan, hire, rent, get/have the use of, let somebody use**

You **borrow** something **from** another person who is willing to **lend** it **to** you. 从别人那里借是borrow，别人借给你是lend: *I borrowed some money from my sister* (=my sister lent me some money/I was lent some money by my sister). 我向妹妹借了一些钱。〔妹妹借给我一些钱〕 You will hear some native speakers of English saying things like *My sister borrowed me the money,* but this is not considered to be correct. 某些英语国家的人会说 My sister borrowed me the money，但这种说法不对。

In American English **loan** is often like **lend**. 在美国英语中 loan 常同于 lend 的意思: *The current administration has loaned this country a billion dollars.* 现任政府给这个国家贷款十亿美元。In British English **loan** (*v*) is usually used for when someone lends a possession for a long time to a museum etc so that everybody can see it. 在英国英语中loan 通常指某人把藏品长期借给博物馆以便大家能观赏。

If you **borrow** money you have to pay it back later, and you may have to pay for the use of it as well, if you have borrowed it from a bank rather than a friend. If you **borrow** a car/video etc you give it back afterwards but you do not usually pay for the use of it, otherwise you would say **hire** or **rent**. 如果你 borrow (借) 钱，你以后必须归还，如果你从银行借钱，而不是从朋友处借钱，你还需支付利息。如果你borrow (借) 车/录像带等，归还时不必付钱，否则用 hire 或 rent (租)。—see 见 **hire** WORD CHOICE

People do not usually use **borrow** or **lend/loan** for something that cannot be moved such as a room, house, or piece of land. If you pay for using this sort of thing you **hire** or **rent** it, otherwise you **get the use of** it from someone who is willing to **let** you **use** it. 对于房间、房子、土地等不移动的东西，人们通常不说 borrow 或 lend/loan。如果你需付钱，就用 hire 或 rent，否则你可以 get the use of (使用)，因为别人 let (让) 你免费用: *Could you let us use this hall?/ Could we have the use of this hall?* 我们可以借用这个礼堂吗?

bor·row·er /ˈbɑroɚ; ˈbɒrəʊə/ *n* [C] someone who is borrowing money 借款者，借方: *Most borrowers pay 7% interest.* 大多数借款人支付7%的利息。

bor·row·ing /ˈbɑroɪŋ; ˈbɒrəʊɪŋ/ *n* **1** [C] something such as a word, phrase, or idea that has been copied from another language, book etc 借用的词语，外来语；借来的概念: *Names such as Lloyd are Celtic borrowings.* Lloyd 之类的人名都是从凯尔特语中借用的词语。| **[+from]** *His music is full of borrowings from other composers.* 他的音乐中有许多从其他作曲家那里借用的元素。**2** [U] the practice of borrowing money 借钱，贷款: *The banks announced that borrowing had increased.* 银行宣布贷款有所增加。**3 borrowings** the total amount of money that a company or organization owes 欠款总额

borrowing pow·ers /ˈ··· ,··/ *n* [plural] the amount of money that a company is allowed to borrow, according to its own rules〔公司章程所规定的〕举债能力；借款权

bor·stal /ˈbɔrstəl; ˈbɔːstl/ *n* [C,U] *BrE old-fashioned* a special prison for criminals who are not old enough to be in an ordinary prison【英，过时】〔少年罪犯的〕教养院，少年感化院: *Shanie was sent to borstal when she was 14.* 沙妮14岁时被送进少年感化院。

Bosch /bɑʃ; bɒʃ/, **Hie·ron·y·mus** /haɪəˈrɑnɪməs; haɪəˈrɒnɪməs/ (?1460-1516) a Flemish painter famous especially for his religious paintings and his pictures of HELL in his best-known work *The Garden of Earthly Delights* 博斯〔(?1460-1516)，佛兰德斯画家，尤以宗教作品及其最著名的《人间乐园》中对地狱的描绘而闻名〕

bosh /bɑʃ; bɒʃ/ *interjection BrE old-fashioned* a word used when you think that what someone has said is silly or untrue【英，过时】废话，胡说: *"I think Sally has lost weight." "Bosh! She looks fatter than ever."* "我认为萨莉瘦了。" "胡说！她看起来比以前更胖了。" —**bosh** *n* [U]

Bos·ni·a /ˈbɑznɪə; ˈbɒznɪə/ also 又作 **Bosnia-Herzegovina** a country in eastern Europe between Croatia and Serbia. It was formerly a part of Yugoslavia, but it joined with Herzegovina in 1992 to form a new country. Population: 4,400,000 (1993). Capital: Sarajevo. 波斯尼亚〔又名波斯尼亚和黑塞哥维那，东欧国家，位于克罗地亚和塞尔维亚之间，原为南斯拉夫的一部分，1992 年与黑塞哥维那合并为一个新国家。人口: 4,400,000 (1993)，首都: 萨拉热窝〕—**Bosnian** *n, adj*

Bosnian War, the /,··· ˈ·/ (1991-95) a war in Bosnia-Herzegovina, where the three different groups of people living in this area – Serbs, Croats, and Bosnian Muslims – fought each other to gain land 波黑战争〔(1991-1995)，波斯尼亚和黑塞哥维那的塞尔维亚人、克罗地亚人、波斯尼亚穆斯林三个民族之间为争夺土地而引发的一场战争〕

bos·om /ˈbʊzəm; ˈbʊzəm/ *n* **1** [singular] the front part of a woman's chest, or the part of her clothes that covers it〔女人的〕胸部；〔衣服的〕胸襟 **2** [C usually plural 一般用复数] a woman's breast〔女人的〕乳房 **3 the bosom of the family/the Church etc** the situation where you feel safe because you are with people who love and protect you 家庭/教会等的温暖[安全感] **4** [singular] *literary* a word meaning someone's feelings and emotions, used especially when these are bad or unpleasant【文】内心情感: *Drury harboured bitterness and anger in his bosom.* 德鲁里内心深处暗藏着痛苦和仇恨。**5 bosom friend/buddy** a very close friend 密友，知己，心腹之交: *We first met in high school and we've been bosom buddies ever since.* 我们在上中学时认识，从那时起就成为了知心朋友。

bos·om·y /ˈbʊzəmɪ; ˈbʊzəmi/ *adj informal* having large breasts【非正式】胸部隆起的，乳房丰满的

Bos·por·us, the /ˈbɑspərəs; ˈbɒspərəs/ the narrow sea between the European and Asian parts of Turkey, connecting the Black Sea with the Sea of Marmara 博斯普鲁斯海峡〔位于土耳其欧亚两部分之间，连接黑海和马尔马拉海的狭窄海域〕

boss¹ /bɔs; bɒs/ *n* [C] **1** the person who employs you or who is 2 3
in charge of you at work 老板，上司；领班: *I'll have to ask my boss for a day off.* 我要向老板请一天假。| **be your own boss** (=work for yourself rather than being employed by someone else) 自己当老板 **2** *informal* a manager with an important position in a company or other organization【非正式】经理；头头: *Prison bosses launched an investigation into major security lapses.* 监狱的头儿对严重的保安失误展开了调查。| *Bosses got pay increases of 75%, when the workers' pay was cut to £13,000.* 经理们的工资增加了75%，而工人的工资则下降到13,000英镑。**3** the person who is the strongest in a relationship, who controls a situation etc 控制局势的人: *When you first start training a dog it's important to let him see that you're the boss.* 刚开始训练狗时，要让狗知道一切由你作主。| **show sb who's boss** (=make someone realize that you are in control, not them) 让某人知道谁是主子 **4** a round decoration on the surface of something such as the ceiling of an old building 圆形装饰物，饰球〈如旧式建筑物的天花板上的浮凸饰物〉

boss² *v* [T] to tell people to do things, give them orders etc, especially when you have no authority to do it 对…发号施令，指挥〔尤指无权这样做时〕: **boss sb about** *BrE*【英】**/around** *I'm sick of him bossing us around like that. Who does he think he is?* 我已厌倦了他那样对我们发号施令。他以为自己是谁呀?

boss³ *adj slang* very attractive or fashionable【俚】诱人的；时髦的: *That's boss, that new computer game.* 那个新的电脑游戏棒极了。

bos·sa·no·va /,bɑsəˈnovə; ,bɒsəˈnəʊvə/ *n* [C] a dance that comes from Brazil, or the music for this dance〔巴西〕波萨诺伐舞；波萨诺伐舞曲

boss-eyed /,· ˈ·◂/ *adj BrE* having both eyes looking in towards your nose; CROSS-EYED【英】内斜视的，斗鸡眼的，内斜眼的

boss·y /ˈbɔsɪ; ˈbɒsi/ *adj* **1** always telling other people what to do in a way that is annoying 爱发号施令的；专横的: *I like his approach to things – he can show people what to do without being bossy.* 我喜欢他做事的方式，他能告诉别人做什么，却一点也不专横。**2 bossy-boots** *BrE informal* someone who you think tells other people what to do too often【英，非正式】爱发号施令的人: *Don't be such a bossy-boots. Let her decide for herself.* 别老爱指挥别人，让她自己做主吧。—**bossily** *adv* —**bossiness** *n* [U]

Bos·ton /ˈbɑstn; ˈbɒstən/ a city in Massachusetts on the Atlantic coast, the most important city in New England, and one of the oldest cities in the US. Its famous colleges and universities include Harvard and MIT. 波士顿〔大西洋沿岸马萨诸塞州一城市，新英格兰最重要的城市，美国最古老的城市之一。这里的著名高等学府有哈佛大学和麻省理工学院〕

Boston Globe, The /,·· ˈ·/ a US newspaper sold especially in New England《波士顿环球报》〔美国报纸，主要在新英格兰发行〕

Boston Mas·sa·cre, the /,·· ˈ···/ one of the events that started the American Revolutionary War. In 1770 a group of

Boston citizens, who were angry because the British army was in their town, threatened a British soldier. Other soldiers fired their guns into the crowd, killing five people. 波士顿惨案〔引发美国独立战争的事件之一。1770年，一群波士顿市民对英国在当地驻军极为不满，因而对一名英军士兵施威。结果其他士兵向人群开枪，造成五人死亡〕

Boston Pops, the /ˌ.. ˈ./ an ORCHESTRA (=large group of musicians) from Boston, known for its performances and records of well-known pieces of classical music and famous tunes from films and MUSICALS 波士顿通俗交响乐团〔波士顿一交响乐团，以其精彩的演奏和录制的古典音乐，电影、音乐剧曲目而著称〕

Boston Strangler, the /ˌ.. ˈ../ the name newspapers used to describe Albert DeSalvo (1931-73), a man who raped and strangled 13 women aged between 19 and 85 in Boston, US, between June 1962 and January 1964 波士顿扼杀者〔报纸对阿尔伯特·德萨尔沃的称谓，此人于1962年6月至1964年1月期间强奸、扼杀了13名年龄在19岁至85岁的美国波士顿女性〕

Boston Sym·pho·ny Or·ches·tra, the /ˌ.. ˈ... ˈ.../ a US ORCHESTRA (=a large group of musicians) based in Boston, Massachusetts 波士顿交响乐团〔美国马萨诸塞州波士顿市的一家交响乐团〕

Boston Tea Par·ty, the /ˌ.. ˈ. ˌ../ a protest in Boston in 1773 against the British tax on tea, when tea was thrown from British ships into the water. This is often considered to be the event that started the American Revolutionary War. 波士顿倾茶事件〔1773年发生在波士顿的一次反对英国征收茶叶税的抗议活动，英国船只上的茶叶被倾入海中。该事件通常被认为是引发美国独立战争的导火索〕

bo·sun /ˈbosn̩; ˈbəʊsən/ *n* [C] another spelling of BOATSWAIN boatswain 的另一种拼法

Bos·well /ˈbɑzwəl; ˈbɒzwəl/, **James** (1740-95) a Scottish lawyer and writer, famous for his book about the life of Samuel Johnson 鲍斯韦尔〔(1740-1795)，苏格兰律师、作家，以撰写塞缪尔·约翰逊传记而著称〕

Bos·worth Field /ˌbɑzwəθ ˈfild; ˌbɒzwəθ ˈfiːld/ the place where the final battle of the Wars of the Roses was fought in 1485, where Richard III was defeated by Henry Tudor 博斯沃思原野〔1485 年玫瑰战争最后一役的战场，亨利·都铎在此打败理查三世〕

bo·tan·i·cal /bəˈtænɪkl; bəˈtænɪkəl/ *adj* [only before noun 仅用于名词前] connected with plants or the scientific study of plants 植物（学）的 —**botanically** /-klɪ; -kli/ *adv*

botanical gar·den /ˌ.. ˈ... ˈ../ *n* [C] a large public garden where many different types of flowers and plants are grown for scientific study 植物园

bot·a·nist /ˈbɑtn̩ɪst; ˈbɒtən̩ɪst/ *n* [C] someone whose job is to make scientific studies of wild plants 植物学家

bot·a·ny /ˈbɑtn̩ɪ; ˈbɒtəni/ *n* [U] the scientific study of plants 植物学

Botany Bay /ˌ.. ˈ. ˈ./ a place in southeast Australia, close to Sydney, where a narrow part of the sea reaches into the land, which was visited in 1770 by Captain Cook. In the early 19th century, another place in this area was used as a place for sending British criminals as a punishment, and this was also given the name 'Botany Bay'. 植物学湾〔位于澳大利亚东南部，临近悉尼。有一处狭窄的海域探入陆地，是1770年库克船长登陆的地方。19世纪早期，该区域的另一个地方被用作英国犯人的流放地，也取名"植物学湾"〕

botch[1] /bɑtʃ; bɒtʃ/ also 又作 **botch up** *v* [T] *informal* to do something badly, because you have been careless or because you do not have the skill to do it properly【非正式】〔因漫不经心或缺乏技术而〕把…做得拙劣: *The builders really botched up our patio.* 建筑工人把我们的平台做得真拙劣。—**botcher** *n* [C]

botch[2] also 又作 **botch-up** /ˈ. ./ *n* [C] *informal especially BrE* a piece of work, job etc that has been badly or carelessly done【非正式，尤英】拙劣的活儿: **make a botch of** *I've just made an awful botch of my translation.* 我译得一塌糊涂。| **botch job** *That repair was a botch job.* 修理工作干得很差。

both /boθ; bəʊθ/ *predeterminer, determiner, pron* **1** used to talk about two people, things, situations etc together 两者，双方，俩: *Both Helen's parents are doctors.* 海伦的父母都是医生。| *Both sides are keen to reach an agreement.* 双方都很想达成协议。| *"I don't know which book to buy." "Why not buy both of them?"* "我不知道该买哪本书。" "为什么不两本都买?" | *They both started speaking together.* 他们俩开始一起说起来。— compare 比较 EITHER[2] **2 both...and...** used to emphasize that something is true not just of one person, thing, or situation but also of another 不仅…而且…；既…又…: *He's lived in both Britain and America.* 他在英国和美国都生活过。| *She can both speak and write Japanese.* 她不仅会说日语，而且还会写。| *We were treated with both tolerance and compassion.* 他们对待我们既有耐性又有同情心。

both·er[1] /ˈbɑðə; ˈbɒðə/ *v*

1 ▶MAKE AN EFFORT 作出努力◀ [I,T] to make the effort to do something 费心，尽力〔做某事〕，因…操心: [**+about/with**] *BrE*【英】*I'm too busy to bother about fixing it now.* 我太忙，现在没空儿修理。| **(not) bother to do sth** *Unfortunately he didn't bother to check the exact wording of the contract before he signed it.* 遗憾的是，他在签字前没有费心检查一下合同上的确切措辞。| *Nobody listens to me. I don't know why I bother.* 没人听我的。我不知道自己为什么还要费那个劲。| **(not) bother doing something** *I don't know if Sally's coming to the party. I didn't bother asking.* 我不知道萨莉是否会参加聚会，我不想费心去问她。| **don't/didn't/won't etc bother** *"Do you want me to wait for you?" "No, don't bother."* "你想让我等你吗?" "不，你不必了。"

2 ▶WORRY 担心◀ [I,T] to make someone feel slightly worried or upset（使）担心；（使）苦恼: *Being in a crowd really bothers me.* 拥挤在人群里真使我苦恼。| **it bothers sb that** *It really bothered me that he'd forgotten my birthday.* 他把我的生日都忘记了，真让我感到没劲。| **not bother sb** *Mandy hates walking home alone at night but it doesn't bother me.* 曼迪不愿晚上一个人走回家，可我无所谓。

3 ▶ANNOY 使恼怒◀ [I,T] to annoy someone by interrupting them when they are trying to do something 打扰，烦扰: *Danny, stop bothering me while I'm trying to work!* 丹尼，我要工作的时候别再打扰我! | **bother sb about/with sth** *He didn't want to bother her with his financial problems on their honeymoon.* 他不想在蜜月期间因他的经济问题使她扫兴。

4 can't/couldn't be bothered *BrE* used to say that you do not want to do something because you do not have enough energy or interest【英】不想费神[没有心思]去做某事: *I knew I ought to clean the car but I just couldn't be bothered.* 我知道我应该去洗车，但我就是没心思干。| **can't/couldn't be bothered to do sth** *My parents could never be bothered to come and see me in the school play.* 我父母从来不肯来学校看我演话剧。

5 not bothered *especially BrE* if you are not bothered about something, it is not important to you【尤英】无所谓，不在意: *"Which chair do you want?" "I'm not bothered."* "你要哪把椅子?" "我无所谓。" | [**+about**] *He's not really bothered about getting the facts right.* 事实对与否他并不太在意。

6 sorry to bother you *spoken* used as a very polite way of telling someone you want their attention【口】对不起打扰你一下

7 ▶FRIGHTEN 吓唬◀ [T] to upset or frighten someone by repeatedly trying to hurt them, touch them sexually etc 骚扰；恐吓: *Is that man bothering you? Shall I call the police?* 那男人骚扰你了吗? 要不要我报警?

8 hot and bothered angry and worried about something, especially unnecessarily〔尤指不必要地〕心急火燎的: *What are you getting all hot and bothered about? It's not that important.* 你为什么整天心急火燎的? 事情并没有那么重要。

9 not bother yourself/not bother your head to not take time or energy to do something or to think about something, either because it is not important or because it is too difficult 不为…操心[伤脑筋]: [**+with/about**] *Cliff didn't want to bother himself with masses of detail.* 克利夫不想为那些琐事伤脑筋。

10 bother it/them etc *BrE old-fashioned* used to express a sudden feeling of annoyance about something【英，过时】真讨厌〔表示厌烦〕: *Oh bother it! The thread's broken again!* 真讨厌! 线又断了!

bother[2] *n* **1** [U] *especially BrE* trouble or difficulty that has been caused by small problems and that usually only continues for a short time【尤英】麻烦，不便；忧虑；烦恼的事: *It's an old car but it's never caused me any bother.* 那是辆旧车，但从来没有为我带来任何麻烦。| [**+with**] *Joe's been having a bit of bother with his back again recently.* 最近乔的后背又有点不适。| **it's no bother** *spoken* (=used to emphasize that you are happy to help someone and it is not much effort)【口】没关系；不费事 *"Thanks for your help." "It was no bother at all."* "谢谢你帮忙。" "这不算什么。" | **go to the bother (of doing sth)** (=make the effort to do something) 费神去做 *I'm not going to go to the bother of writing again. She never writes back.* 我再也不费神写信了。她从不回信。| **give sb any bother/a lot of bother etc** *Are you sure the station is on your way? I don't want to give you any extra bother.* 你真的顺道路过车站吗? 我不想给你添麻烦。| **save sb/yourself the bother (of doing sth)** *I should have phoned the shop first and saved myself the bother of going there.* 我本应该先给商店打个电话，可以省得我费劲亲自去一趟。**2**

[singular] *BrE* a person or job that is annoying to deal with【英】难对付的事[人]: *Sorry to be such a bother but could you show me how the photocopier works?* 对不起，麻烦你一下，你能示范一下复印机怎样用吗？

bother³ *interjection BrE* used when you are slightly annoyed about something【英】真烦人！真讨厌！〔表示有些恼火〕: *Oh bother! I forgot to phone Jean.* 真糟！我忘了给琼打电话。

both·er·a·tion /ˌbɑðəˈreʃən; ˌbɒðəˈreɪʃən/ *interjection BrE old-fashioned* used when you are slightly annoyed【英，过时】可恶〔表示有些恼火〕: *Botheration. I forgot my glasses.* 可恶，我忘了戴眼镜。

both·er·some /ˈbɑðəsəm; ˈbɒðəsəm/ *adj old-fashioned* slightly annoying【过时】引起麻烦的，讨厌的；令人为难的: *She brushed his hand away like a bothersome fly.* 她像躲令人生厌的苍蝇一样拨开他的手。

Botox¹ /ˈbotɑks; ˈbəʊtɒks/ *trademark* a substance that makes muscles relax, which can be injected into the skin around someone's eyes to make the lines disappear and the skin look younger and more attractive.【商标】肉毒素〔一种使肌肉放松的物质，可注射到眼睛周围的肌肤，达到祛皱功效，使皮肤看起来更年轻、更迷人〕: *Botox injections for wrinkles* 肉毒素除皱注射液

Botox² *v* [T usually passive] *trademark* to use Botox to remove lines on your face【商标】给…注射肉毒素以除去面部皱纹: *Getting Botoxed is pretty simple.* 注射肉毒素美容十分简单。| *He Botoxed his forehead before the next film.* 出演下一部影片前，他给额头上注射了肉毒素。

Bot·swa·na /bɑtsˈwɑnɑ; bɒtˈswɑːnə/ a country in central southern Africa. Population: 1,586,000 (2001). Capital: Gaborone. 博茨瓦纳〔非洲中南部国家。人口：1,586,000（2001），首都：哈博罗内〕

Bot·ti·cel·li /ˌbɑtɪˈtʃɛlɪ; ˌbɒtɪˈtʃeli/, **San·dro** /ˈsaɪndro; ˈsændrəʊ/ (?1444-1510) an Italian painter of the Renaissance 波提切利〔（?1444-1510），意大利文艺复兴时期画家〕

bottles 瓶

wine bottle 酒瓶

beer bottle 啤酒瓶

medicine bottle 药瓶

baby's bottle *BrE*【英】/baby bottle *AmE*【美】婴儿奶瓶

milk bottle 牛奶瓶

hot water bottle 热水袋

S1 W2 **bot·tle¹** /ˈbɑtl; ˈbɒtl/ *n*

1 ►CONTAINER 容器◄ [C] a container with a narrow top for keeping liquids in, usually made of plastic or glass 瓶: *Give the bottle a shake before you open it.* 开瓶前先摇一摇。| [+of] *a bottle of champagne* 一瓶香槟酒

2 ►AMOUNT OF LIQUID 一定量的液体◄ also 又作 **bottleful** [C] the amount of liquid that a bottle contains 一瓶之量: *Between us, we drank three bottles of wine.* 我们俩喝了三瓶酒。

3 ►MILK 牛奶◄ [singular] milk given to babies or young animals in a bottle rather than from their mother's breast〔喂婴儿用的〕瓶装牛奶: *My first baby just wouldn't take a bottle at all.* 我的第一个孩子就是不肯喝瓶装牛奶。

4 ►COURAGE 勇气◄ [U] *BrE informal* courage to do something that is dangerous or unpleasant【英，非正式】勇气，胆量: *I never thought she'd have the bottle to do it!* 我从未想过她会有勇气做这样的事！

5 hit the bottle/take to the bottle to start drinking a lot of alcohol regularly, in order to forget your problems〔为了忘掉烦恼〕开始酗酒

6 be on the bottle to always be drinking a lot of alcohol 爱喝酒，贪杯

7 bring a bottle *BrE*【英】, **bring your own bottle** *AmE*【美】used to describe a party to which you must bring your own alcoholic drink 自带酒水参加聚会

bottle² *v* [T] **1** to put a liquid, especially wine or beer, into a bottle after you have made it 把…装进瓶中: *The wine is bottled at the vineyard.* 这种葡萄酒是在葡萄园里装瓶的。**2** to put vegetables or fruit into special glass containers in order to preserve them 把〔蔬菜或水果〕装瓶保存

bottle out *phr v* [I] *BrE informal* to suddenly decide not to do something because you are frightened【英，非正式】因胆怯而决定不做某事，打退堂鼓: *"Did you tell him?" "No, I bottled out at the last minute."* "你告诉他了吗？""没有，我在最后一分钟退缩了。"

bottle sth ↔ **up** *phr v* [T] to deliberately not allow yourself to show a strong feeling or emotion 抑制〔感情〕；勉强忍住: *It is far better to cry than to bottle up your feelings.* 哭出来比憋在心里要好得多。

bottle bank /ˈ· · ˌ·/ *n* [C] a container in the street that you put empty bottles into, so that the glass can be used again〔大街上〕回收玻璃器皿的空瓶箱

bot·tled /ˈbɑtld; ˈbɒtld/ *adj* **bottled water/beer etc** water, beer etc that is sold in a bottle 瓶装水/啤酒等

bottle-feed /ˈ· · ·/ *v past tense and past participle* **bottle-fed** /-ˌfɛd; -fed/ [T] to feed a baby or young animal with milk from a bottle rather than from their mother's breast 用奶瓶喂 —**bottle-feeding** *n* [U]

bottle green /ˌ· · ˈ·◄/ *n* [U] a very dark green colour 深绿色 —**bottle green** *adj* —see picture on page A5 参见 A5 页图

bot·tle·neck /ˈbɑtlˌnɛk; ˈbɒtlnek/ *n* [C] **1** a place in a road where the traffic cannot pass easily, so that there are a lot of delays 瓶颈路段，狭窄路段，交通阻塞点 **2** a delay in one stage of a process that makes the whole process take longer 障碍；妨碍整个进度的工序: *Having only one person to do the clerical work has caused a real bottleneck.* 只有一个人做文书工作妨碍了整个进度。

bottle o·pen·er /ˈ· · ˌ· · ·/ *n* [C] a small tool used for removing the metal lids from bottles 开瓶器

Bot·tom /ˈbɑtəm; ˈbɒtəm/ a humorous character who is changed into a DONKEY in Shakespeare's play *A Midsummer Night's Dream* 博顿〔莎士比亚的剧作《仲夏夜之梦》中的喜剧人物，剧中的他变成了一头驴〕

S1 W3 **bottom¹** *n*

1 ►LOWEST PART 最底部◄ the lowest part of something 底部，基部；下端，末尾: **the bottom** *From the bottom the skyscraper looked as if it touched the clouds.* 从底下看，那幢摩天大楼好像直插云端。| [+of] *Hold the bottom of the pole and keep it upright.* 托住柱子的末端，使其保持垂直。| **at the bottom** *Go downstairs and wait for me at the bottom.* 下楼去，在底层等我。| **at the bottom of** *Sign your name at the bottom of the page.* 在这页的末尾签上名字。—opposite 反义词 TOP¹ (1)

2 ►SEA/RIVER 海/河◄ the ground under a sea, river etc, or the flat land in a valley 水底；海底；河底: **the bottom** *the sea bottom* 海底 | [+of] *The bottom of the pool is very slippery.* 这个池塘的底部很滑。| **at/on the bottom of sth** *A body was found at the bottom of the canal.* 在运河的底部发现一具尸体。

3 ►LOWEST SIDE 最低面◄ the flat surface on the lowest side of an object〔物体的〕平底: **the bottom** *Take the price tag off the bottom.* 把底下的价格标签拿掉。| [+of] *You have chewing gum stuck to the bottom of your shoe.* 你的鞋底粘上了口香糖。

4 ►CUP/BOX ETC 杯/盒等◄ the lowest inner surface of something such as a cup or container 容器的内底: **the bottom** *Yuk, this cup's got mould in the bottom.* 哗，这个杯子底上都发霉了。| [+of] *The flour is at the bottom of the cupboard.* 面粉在橱柜最下层。

5 ►LOWEST POSITION 最低的位置◄ the lowest position in an organization or company, or on a list etc 最低职位；最后名次: **the bottom** *The team is at the bottom of the league.* 这支球队排在联赛最后一名。| **start at the bottom** *Higgins started at the bottom and worked his way up to managing director.* 希金斯从最基层干起，一级一级地升到了总经理的职位。| **the bottom of the ladder/pile** (=the lowest position in society, an organization etc) 基层；最低职位[职务] —opposite 反义词 TOP¹ (3)

6 the bottom of a road/garden etc *especially BrE* the part of a road, area of land etc that is furthest from where you are【尤

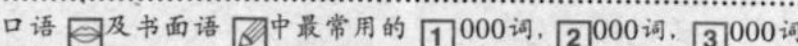

英]路/花园等的尽头: *There's a shop at the bottom of the street.* 街的尽头有家商店。

7 ►BODY 身体◄ [C] the part of your body that you sit on; BUTTOCKS 臀部, 屁股: *I just sat on my bottom and slid down.* 我就坐着滑了下去。

8 ►CLOTHES 衣服◄ [C] also 又作 **bottoms** the part of a set of clothes that you wear on the lower part of your body〔两件一套衣服中的〕裤子: *bikini bottom* 比基尼式内裤 | *pyjama bottoms* 睡裤

9 get to the bottom of to find out the cause of a problem or situation 找出〔某事〕的真相: *I'm going to get to the bottom of this!* 这件事情我要查个水落石出!

10 be at the bottom of to be the basic cause of a problem or situation 是…的根本原因: *I'm sure Carrie's disturbed childhood is at the bottom of her current problems.* 我敢肯定卡丽不幸的童年是她目前问题的根本原因。

11 hit rock bottom/be at rock bottom to reach a very low level, or be in a very bad situation 到最低程度; 处于最糟糕状况: *Morale has hit rock bottom.* 士气到了最低落的程度。| *We bought the house when prices were at rock bottom.* 我们在房价最低时买下了房子。

12 from the bottom of your heart in a very sincere way 从心底里, 由衷地: *Thank you from the bottom of my heart.* 衷心感谢你。

13 big-bottomed/round-bottomed etc having a bottom or base that is big, round etc 底大的/圆底的

14 the bottom dropped out of sb's world used to say that something very bad suddenly happened to someone 厄运突然降临到某人身上, 某人倒大霉

15 the bottom drops out of the market used to say that people stop buying a particular product 出现暴跌的情况

16 bottoms up! *spoken* used to tell someone to enjoy or finish their alcoholic drink【口】干杯!

17 bottom gear the lowest GEAR¹ (1) of a vehicle〔机动车的〕低速挡

18 ►SHIP 船◄ [C] the part of a ship that is below water 船体在水下的部分

19 at bottom the way a person or situation really is, although they may seem different 实际上; 内心里: *She's a good, kind person at bottom.* 她实际上是个热心肠的好人。—compare 比较 TOP¹ —see also 另见 **you can bet your bottom dollar** (BET¹ (4)), **knock the bottom out of** (KNOCK¹ (17)), **from top to bottom** (TOP¹ (19))

1 3 **bottom²** *adj* [only before noun 仅用于名词前] **1** in the lowest place or position 底下的: *The records are kept on the bottom shelf.* 录音带放在底下的架上。| *the bottom right hand corner of the page* 这页的右下角 **2** the least important, successful etc 最无关紧要的; 最差的: *Tim is in the bottom 10% of his class.* 蒂姆排在班上最差的10%中。**3** *especially BrE* in the place furthest away from where you are【尤英】离得最远的: *Most of the sheep were grazing in the bottom field.* 大多数羊在远处的地里吃草。

bottom³ *v*

bottom out *phr v* [I] if a situation, price etc bottoms out, it stops getting worse or lower, usually before improving again〔局面在好转前〕停止恶化;〔价格在回升前〕停止下跌: *The market price of oil got as low as $10 a barrel before it finally bottomed out.* 石油的市场价格降到了每桶10美元的最低点, 然后终于回升。

bottom drawer /ˌ.. ˈ./ *n* [C] *BrE* all the things, especially things that you use in a house, that a woman collects to use when she is married【英】女子结婚前准备的衣物, 嫁妆; HOPE CHEST *AmE*【美】

bot·tom·less /ˈbɑtəmlɪs; ˈbɒtəmləs/ *adj* **1** a sea, hole etc that is bottomless is extremely deep 无底的, 深不可测的, 极深的 **2** seeming to have no end 无尽头的: **a bottomless pit** *a bottomless pit of misery* 痛苦的深渊

bottom line /ˌ.. ˈ./ *n* **the bottom line a)** the profit or the amount of money that a business makes or loses 账本底线,〔账目上〕盈亏一览结算线: *Business today is only interested in the bottom line.* 现今的商家只对账本底线感兴趣。**b)** a situation or fact that exists and that you must accept, even though you may not like it 不得不接受的局面[事实]: *The bottom line is that drinking and driving can kill.* 事实是酒后驾车会出人命。**c)** the lowest amount of money that you are willing to pay or take for something 底价, 最低价: *"What's your bottom line for selling the car?" "I can go down to £450."* "你这辆车的最低售价是多少?" "我能降到450英镑。"

bot·tom·most /ˈbɑtəmˌmost; ˈbɒtəmˌməʊst/ *adj* [only before noun 仅用于名词前] in the lowest, furthest, or deepest position or place 最低的; 最远的; 最深的: *the bottommost reaches of the Amazon* 亚马孙河最深的河段

bottom-up /ˌ.. ˈ./ *adj BrE* a bottom-up plan is one in which you decide on practical details before thinking about general principles【英】〔计划〕从细节到整体的, 从实际出发的, 自下而上的 —opposite 反义词 TOP-DOWN

bot·u·lis·m /ˈbɑtʃəˌlɪzəm; ˈbɒtʃʊlɪzəm/ *n* [U] serious food poisoning caused by BACTERIA in preserved meat and vegetables 肉毒(杆)菌中毒, 腊肠毒菌病

Boudicca 布狄卡

Bou·dic·ca /ˈbudɪkə; ˈbuːdɪkə/ also 又作 **Boadicea** (died AD 60) the Queen of the Iceni people of eastern Britain, who led them in battle against the Romans 布狄卡〔卒于公元60年, 东不列颠爱西尼人的女王, 曾率领爱西尼人与罗马人作战〕

bou·doir /buˈdwɑr; ˈbuːdwɑː/ *n* [C] **1** *old use* a woman's bedroom or private sitting room【旧】〔女子的〕闺房 **2** the bedroom seen as the place where sex happens〔发生性关系的〕寝房: *secrets of the boudoir* 寝房的秘密

bouf·fant /buˈfɑnt; ˈbuːfɒŋ/ *adj* a bouffant hair style is one in which your hair is raised away from your head at the top〔发型〕蓬松的

bou·gain·vil·le·a /ˌbugənˈvɪlɪə; ˌbuːgənˈvɪliə/ *n* [C,U] a plant that has red or purple flowers and grows up walls 九重葛属植物〔一种开红、紫色花的攀缘植物〕

bough /baʊ; baʊ/ *n* [C] a main branch on a tree 粗大的树枝, 主枝

bought /bɔt; bɔːt/ the past tense and past participle of BUY¹

bouil·la·baisse /ˌbujəˈbes; ˌbuːjəˈbes/ *n* [C,U] a strong-tasting soup or STEW¹ (1) made of fish 浓味炖鱼(汤)

bouil·lon /ˈbujɑn; ˈbuːjɒn/ *n* [C,U] a clear soup made by boiling meat and vegetables in water 肉菜清汤

bouillon cube /ˈ.. ./ *n* [C] *AmE* a solid piece of dried meat or vegetables used in soups【美】〔经脱水的〕块状汤料; STOCK CUBE *BrE*【英】

boul·der /ˈboldə; ˈbəʊldə/ *n* [C] a large stone or piece of rock 巨石, 巨砾: *huge boulders choking the stream bed* 堵塞河床的大石块

Boulder Dam /ˌ.. ˈ./ the former name for the Hoover Dam 博尔德水坝〔胡佛水坝的旧称〕

boule·vard /ˈbuləˌvɑrd; ˈbuːlvɑːd/ *n* [C] **1 a)** *BrE* a wide road in a town, usually with trees along the sides【英】林荫大道 **b)** *AmE* a wide road in a town or city【美】宽阔的街道 **2** written abbreviation 缩写为 **Blvd** used as part of the name of a particular road …大道〔街道名称的一部分〕: *Sunset Boulevard* 日落大道

bounce 反弹

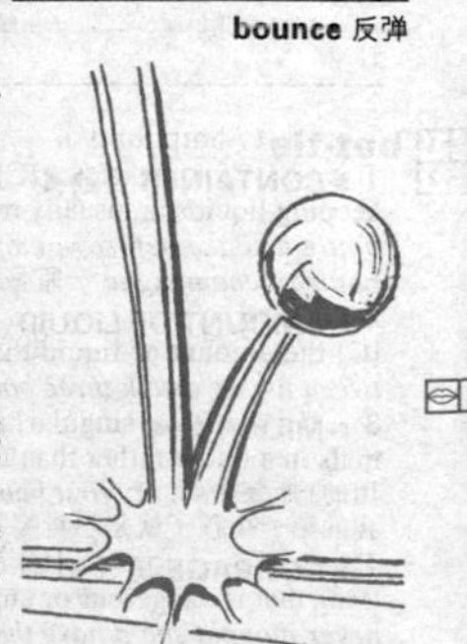

Bou·logne /buˈlon; bʊˈlɔɪn/ a city on the northeast coast of France. It is one of the ports where ships bringing passengers and cars arrive after crossing the English Channel from Dover. 布洛涅〔法国东北沿海一城市, 是从多佛尔穿越英吉利海峡而来的渡轮停泊的港口之一〕

bounce¹ /bauns; baʊns/ *v* 3

1 ►MOVE FROM A SURFACE 从某表面移动◄ [I,T] if a ball or other object bounces, it immediately moves away from a surface it has just hit, or you make it move in this way (使)〔球等〕弹回, (使) 反弹, (使) 跳起: [+off] *The ball bounced off the cross-*

bar and into the net. 球打在球门的横梁上弹进了球门。| **bounce sth on/against etc** *The kids were bouncing stones against the walls.* 孩子们把石头往墙上打。

2 ▶MOVE UP AND DOWN 上下移动◀ [I] to move up and down, especially because you are hitting a surface that is made of rubber, has springs etc 跳上跳下, 蹦蹦跳跳: [+on] *Lyn was bouncing on the trampoline.* 林恩在蹦床上蹦跳。| **bounce up and down** *Stop bouncing up and down on the sofa.* 别再在沙发上跳上跳下了。

3 ▶CHEQUE 支票◀ [I,T] if a cheque bounces or a bank bounces a cheque, the bank will not pay any money because there is not enough money in the account of the person who wrote it〔支票〕被拒付;〔银行〕拒付: *One bounced cheque could spell ruin for a new business.* 一张遭拒付的支票会导致一个新公司的破产。

4 ▶WALK 走◀ [I always+adv/prep] to walk quickly and with a lot of energy 蹦蹦跳跳地走: [+across/along/in etc] *Olivia came bouncing into the room.* 奥利维娅蹦蹦跳跳地走进了房间。

5 ▶WHEN YOU MOVE 移动时◀ [I] if something bounces, it moves quickly up and down as you move 上下晃动: *Her hair bounced when she walked.* 她走路时, 头发上上下下地摆动。

6 bounce ideas off sb to ask someone for their opinion about an idea, a plan etc before you make a decision 征求某人的意见

7 ▶LIGHT/SOUND 光/声◀ [I,T] to REFLECT (1) from a surface 反射: [+off] *radio signals bouncing off the moon* 从月球反射回来的无线电信号

8 bounce sb on your knee to lift a child up and down on your knee 把孩子放在膝上上下颠着

9 be bounced into (doing) sth to be forced to decide something quickly or agree with a particular decision, because you have no time to think about it or you will seem to be wrong if you do not agree 急急忙忙地被迫决定做某事: *Party members claimed that they had been bounced into choosing him as leader.* 党员们声称他们来不及考虑, 被迫选举他为领导人。

bounce back *phr v* [I] to feel better quickly or become successful again after having a lot of problems 恢复元气, 复苏, 重新活跃: *In spite of the difficulties we always managed to bounce back.* 尽管困难重重, 我们总是设法重新振作起来。| *Becker bounced back in the second set.* 贝克尔在第二盘恢复了状态。

bounce² *n* **1** [C] the action of moving up and down on a surface 跳起, 弹回, 反弹: *Try to catch the ball on the second bounce.* 球第二次弹起时就把它接住。**2** [U] the ability to move up and down on a surface, or that surface's ability to make something move up and down 弹性, 弹力: *The ball had completely lost its bounce.* 这球已经完全失去了弹力。**3** [U] a lot of energy 活力, 精力, 朝气: *The dog has a shiny coat and is full of bounce.* 那只狗有着亮闪闪的皮毛, 充满活力。**4** [U] hair that has bounce is in very good condition and goes back to its shape if you press it〔头发的〕弹性

bounc·er /ˈbaunsə; ˈbaʊnsə/ *n* [C] **1** someone whose job is to stand at the door of a club, bar etc and stop unwanted people coming in, or make people leave if they are behaving badly〔夜总会、酒吧等的〕保安人员, 门卫, 保镖 **2** a fast ball in CRICKET (2) that passes or hits the BATSMAN above the chest after it bounces〔板球的〕反弹球〔指反弹后以高过击球手胸部的高度经过或击中击球手的球〕

bounc·ing /ˈbaunsɪŋ; ˈbaʊnsɪŋ/ *adj* **bouncing baby/child** a very healthy baby or young child 健康的婴儿/孩子

bounc·y /ˈbaunsɪ; ˈbaʊnsi/ *adj* **1** a bouncy ball etc quickly moves away from a surface after it has hit it〔球等〕有弹性的; 弹起的 **2** a bouncy surface is made of a substance that makes people move up and down when they are on it〔表面〕有弹性的, 弹力好的: *The bed is nice and bouncy.* 这床弹性很好, 十分舒适。**3** someone who is bouncy is always very happy, confident, and full of energy〔人〕快乐自信的, 精神饱满的, 充满朝气的 **4** hair or material that is bouncy goes back to its shape when you press it〔头发等〕有弹性的 —**bouncily** *adv* —**bounciness** *n* [U]

bound¹ /baund; baʊnd/ the past tense and past participle of BIND¹

S2 W3 **bound²** *adj* [no comparative 无比较级]

1 be bound to to be very likely to do or feel a particular thing 很有可能, 肯定会: *Don't lie to her. She's bound to find out about it.* 别骗她, 她肯定会发现的。| **it is bound to be** (=used to say that something should have been expected) 当然, 早应料到 *"It's hot!" "Well, it was bound to be, I just took it out of the oven."* "真烫!" "当然了, 我刚从烤箱里拿出来。" | **bound to happen** *"Why did Max die, Mom?" "He was an old dog, dear. It was bound to happen one day."* "马科斯为什么死了, 妈妈?" "亲爱的, 这条狗老了, 迟早有这么一天。"

2 ▶DUTY/PROMISE 责任/许诺◀ **a) be bound (by)** if someone is bound by a law, promise, agreement etc, they have to do what it says 负有义务, 有责任受…约束, 理应…: *We are bound by agreements made at the time of the treaty.* 我们受到缔结条约时达成的协议所约束。| **bound (by sth) to do sth** *If he's acting as auditor, he's bound by law to report.* 如果他是审计员, 按法律他有义务报告。| **legally bound** *The two parties are not legally bound until the contract has been signed.* 双方在签订合同以后才有法律义务。**b) be/feel bound to do sth** to feel that you ought to do something 理应做某事, 应该做某事: *John felt bound to tell Katherine about the job, even though he didn't want to work with her.* 约翰感到应该告诉凯瑟琳关于那份工作的事, 尽管他不想和她共事。| **I'm bound to say (that)** *I'm bound to say I think you're taking a huge risk.* 我得说你在冒很大的风险。| **feel duty bound/honour bound to do sth** (=feel very strongly that you have to do or say something, especially because you think it is morally correct) 感到自己有义务做某事

3 ▶CONNECTED/INVOLVED 有联系的/涉及到的◀ **a) be bound up with sth** to be closely connected with a particular problem, situation etc 与某事有密切关系: *Henry's problems are all bound up with his mother's death when he was ten.* 亨利的问题都与他10岁时母亲去世有关。**b) be bound up in sth** to be so involved in a difficult situation etc that you cannot think about anything else 忙于[热衷于, 专心于]某事: *Jim's too bound up in his own worries to be able to help us.* 吉姆太专注于自己的烦恼事, 无法帮助我们。**c) be bound (together) by sth** to share a particular feature or quality 具有同样的特点[性质]: *All the stories are bound by a common theme: jealousy.* 所有这些故事都有一个共同的主题: 妒忌。

4 ▶PLACE/DIRECTION 地方/方向◀ **a) bound for London/college etc** also 又作 **London/college etc bound** travelling towards or going to a particular place 前往伦敦/大学等: *The planes bound for Somalia carry food and medical supplies.* 飞往索马里的飞机装载着食品和医疗用品。| **homeward bound** (=going home) 返家途中 **b) northbound/southbound/eastbound/westbound** travelling in a particular direction 朝北/南/东/西行驶[航行]: *All eastbound trains have been cancelled due to faulty signals.* 由于信号错误, 所有东行的列车都已取消。

5 snow-bound/strike-bound/tradition-bound etc controlled or limited by something, so that you cannot do what you want or what other people want you to 由于大雪/罢工/传统等的限制: *a fog-bound airport* 因大雾而无法正常运作的机场

6 ▶BOOK 书◀ a bound book is covered on the outside with paper, leather etc 用…装订好的, 有封面的: [+in] *a beautiful Bible bound in Moroccan leather* 一部摩洛哥皮面的精美的《圣经》| **leather/velvet etc bound** (=covered in leather, velvet etc) 皮面/天鹅绒面等

7 I'll be bound *old-fashioned* used when you are very sure that what you have just said is true【过时】我确信, 我敢肯定: *He had good reasons for doing that, I'll be bound.* 我确信, 他那样做一定有道理。

8 bound form *technical* a part of a word that is always found in combination with another form, such as 'un' and 'er' in the words 'unknown' and 'speaker'【术语】〔不能独立存在的〕黏附形式〈如unknown和speaker中的un和er〉

bound³ *v* **1** [I always+adv/prep] to run with a lot of energy, because you are happy, excited, or frightened 跳跃着前进, 蹦蹦跳跳地跑: [+up/towards/across etc] *Suddenly a huge dog came bounding towards me.* 一条大狗突然朝我跳过来。**2 be bounded by** if a country or area of land is bounded by something such as a wall, river etc it has the wall etc at its edge 以…为界, 形成…的界限: *a yard bounded by a rusty fence* 被生锈的铁栅栏隔开的院子 | *The US is bounded in the north by Canada and in the south by Mexico.* 美国北面与加拿大接壤, 南面与墨西哥毗邻。

bound⁴ *n*

1 by leaps and bounds/in leaps and bounds *BrE* if someone or something increases, develops etc by leaps and bounds, they increase etc very quickly【英】突飞猛进, 飞速发展: *Julie's reading is improving in leaps and bounds.* 朱莉的阅读能力进步得很快。

2 out of bounds if a place is out of bounds, you are not allowed to go there 不得进入: [+to/for] *Parts of the complex are out of bounds to some personnel.* 这个综合大楼的某些部分禁止一些人员进入。

3 ▶LIMITS 限制◀ **bounds** [plural] **a)** limits or rules that are given by law or exist because of social custom 界限, 极限, 限度, 止境: **stay/keep/remain within bounds** *Richards tried to stay within the bounds set by the financial controller.* 理查德尽

力遵守财务总监作出的规定。| **keep sth within bounds** *Talking is permitted in the classroom as long as it is kept within bounds.* 只要不过分，在教室里谈话是允许的。**b)** *old-fashioned* the edges of a town, city etc【过时】市[镇]的边缘

4 go beyond the bounds of decency/reason/good taste etc to not follow the rules that people normally follow when doing something 超出了得体/理性/雅趣等的限度

5 be within/beyond the bounds of possibility to be possible or impossible 可能/不可能: *Mike's version of events is unlikely, but not beyond the bounds of possibility.* 事情未必如迈克所描述，但也不是不可能的。

6 know no bounds *formal* if someone's honesty, kindness etc knows no bounds, they are extremely honest etc【正式】无止境地，极其地

7 in bounds/out of bounds inside or outside the legal playing area in a sport such as American football or BASKETBALL 界内/出界

8 ▶JUMP 跳◀ [C] a long or high jump made with a lot of energy 跳，跳跃

B

2 3 **bound·a·ry** /ˈbaundərɪ; ˈbaʊndəri/ *n*

1 ▶EDGE 边◀ [C] the official line that marks the edge of a town, country etc 分界线，边界: **[+between]** *the boundary between the US and Canada* 美国和加拿大的分界线 | **draw a boundary** (=decide where one town etc ends and another one starts) 确定分界线 | **boundary line** *the country's boundary line* 国界

2 ▶WALL/FENCE 墙/篱笆◀ [C] something such as a wall or fence that is intended to keep people or things separate 界限，范围: *staying within the boundary of the old city walls.* 留在老城墙的范围以内

3 ▶LIMIT 限制◀ [C usually plural 一般用复数] the highest or most extreme limit that something can reach 限度，界限: **[+of]** *the boundaries of human knowledge* 人类知识的极限

4 ▶BETWEEN FEELINGS/QUALITIES ETC 感情/特质等之间◀ [C] the point at which one feeling, quality etc stops and another starts 分野: **[+of/between]** *People disagree about the boundaries of political parties.* 人们对政党之间的分野观点不一致。

5 push back the boundaries (of) to change the way people think about an idea, belief etc, or greatly increase their knowledge of something 扩展…的领域: *Her new essay really pushes back the boundaries of literary theory.* 她的新论文确实拓展了文学理论的范围。

6 ▶CRICKET 板球◀ [C] the outer limit of the playing area in CRICKET (2), or a shot that sends the balls across this limit for points 球场边界线；击球超过边界线得分

bound·en /ˈbaundən; ˈbaʊndən/ *adj* **your bounden duty** *old-fashioned* something that you should do because it is morally correct【过时】分内的事，应尽的义务

bound·er /ˈbaundɚ; ˈbaʊndə/ *n* [C] *BrE old-fashioned* a disapproving word for a man who has behaved in a way that you think is morally wrong【英，过时】不道德的人: *The man's a bounder.* 那人是个无赖。

bound·less /ˈbaundlɪs; ˈbaʊndləs/ *adj* having no limit or end 无限的，无量的，无穷的: *enthusiasts with boundless energy for their hobby* 对自己的爱好有无穷精力的狂热者 —**boundlessly** *adv* —**boundlessness** *n* [U]

boun·te·ous /ˈbauntɪəs; ˈbaʊntiəs/ *adj literary* very generous【文】慷慨的，大方的

boun·ti·ful /ˈbauntəfəl; ˈbaʊntɪfəl/ *adj literary*【文】**1** if something is bountiful, there is more than enough of it 大量的，充足的: *bountiful harvests* 大丰收 **2** generous 慷慨的: *bountiful God* 宽宏大量的上帝

boun·ty /ˈbauntɪ; ˈbaʊnti/ *n* **1** [C] an amount of money that is given to someone by the government as a reward for doing something, such as catching a criminal〔政府给予的〕奖励金，赏金: *The million-dollar bounty on Noriega's head shows how important it is he is brought to trial.* 悬赏百万美元捉拿诺列加，说明把他绳之以法是多么重要。**2** [U] *literary* the quality of being generous【文】慷慨，好施，仁爱

Bounty, The also 又作 **HMS Bounty** a British naval ship on which there was a famous MUTINY (=when the ordinary sailors take control of a ship by force) in the Pacific Ocean in 1789. The sailors, led by an officer called Fletcher Christian, took power from Captain William Bligh, and made him leave in a small boat. 邦蒂号〔英国海军舰艇，1789年在太平洋上发生著名的哗变，船员在一位名叫弗莱彻·克里斯廷的军官带领下，从船长威廉·布莱手中夺取了指挥权，并迫使船长独自驾一条小船离开〕

bounty hunt·er /ˈ‥ ˌ‥/ *n* [C] someone who catches criminals and brings them to the police in return for a reward 赏金猎人，为获得赏金而搜捕罪犯的人

bou·quet /buˈke; bəʊˈkeɪ/ *n* **1** [C] an arrangement of flowers, especially one that you give to someone 花束 **2** [C,U] the smell of a wine 酒的芳香: *a fruity bouquet* 有水果味的酒香

bour·bon /ˈbɝbən; ˈbʊəbən/ *n* [U] a type of American WHISKEY〔美国产的〕波旁威士忌酒

bour·geois¹ /burˈʒwɑ; ˈbʊəʒwɑː/ *adj* **1** too interested in having a lot of possessions and a high position in society 过分注重名利的，追求物质享受的；市侩的，庸俗的: *the Sixties backlash against bourgeois materialism* 六十年代对过分注重名利的实利主义的强烈反对 **2** belonging to the MIDDLE CLASS 中产阶级的 **3** belonging to or typical of the part of society that is rich, educated, owns land etc, according to MARXISM 资产阶级的 —see also 另见 PETTY BOURGEOIS —compare 比较 PROLETARIAN

bourgeois² *n plural* **bourgeois** [C] **1** someone who is too interested in having a lot of possessions and a high position in society 过分追求物质享受的人，过分看重名利的人 **2** a member of the MIDDLE CLASS 中产阶级的一员 **3** someone who belongs to the part of society which is rich, educated, owns land etc, according to MARXISM 资产阶级的一员 —compare 比较 PROLETARIAT

bour·geoi·sie /ˌburʒwɑˈzi; ˌbʊəʒwɑːˈziː/ *n* **the bourgeoisie** the people in a society who are rich, educated, own land etc, according to MARXISM 资产阶级

Bourne·mouth /ˈbɔrnməθ; ˈbɔːnməθ/ a popular holiday town on the south coast of England 伯恩茅斯〔英格兰南部沿海小镇，为著名度假胜地〕

Bour·sin /burˈsæŋ; buːrˈsæŋ/ *trademark* a type of soft creamy French cheese made with GARLIC and HERBS【商标】波尔斯因奶酪〔一种蒜香和香草风味的法国软质乳酪〕

'bout /baut; baʊt/ *adv, prep spoken* about【口】关于: *"What are you talking 'bout?"* "你在谈什么？"

bout /baut; baʊt/ *n* [C] **1 a bout of flu/nausea/depression etc** a short period of time during which you suffer from an illness 流感/恶心/抑郁等的发作（时期）**2** a short period of time during which you do something a lot, especially something that is bad for you 阵，一回，一场，一番〔尤指做对自己有害的事情〕: *After a near fatal drinking bout, Joe decided to give up alcohol.* 在一次几乎致命的狂饮之后，乔决定戒酒。**3** a BOXING or WRESTLING match 拳击[摔跤]比赛

bou·tique /buˈtik; buːˈtiːk/ *n* [C] a small shop that sells very fashionable clothes or other objects 出售流行服饰的小商店，精品店

bou·ton·ni·ere /butnˈɪr; buːˌtɒniˈeə/ *n* [C] *AmE* a flower that a man wears in the LAPEL of his suit, especially at a wedding【美】别在〔男士西服〕翻领上的花; BUTTONHOLE (2) *BrE*【英】

bo·vine /ˈbovaɪn; ˈbəʊvaɪn/ *adj* **1** *technical* connected with cows【术语】牛的 **2** slow and slightly stupid, like a cow 似牛的；笨拙的；迟钝的，缓慢的: *a bovine expression of contentment* 傻乎乎的满意表情

Bov·ril /ˈbuvrɪl, ˈbɒvrɪl/ *trademark* a type of thick dark-brown substance made from cow's meat, sold in the UK. It is used to make hot drinks or added to food when cooking.【商标】保卫尔牛肉汁〔一种在英国出售的深褐色牛肉制成品，用于制作热饮料或烹饪调味品〕

bov·ver /ˈbɑvɚ; ˈbɒvə/ *n* [U] *BrE old-fashioned slang* violent behaviour, especially by a group of young men【英，过时，俚】〔尤指青少年〕打群架，斗殴；恐吓行为: **bovver boy** (=someone who behaves in a violent way) 小流氓

bow¹ /bau; baʊ/ *v* **1** [I] to bend the top part of your body forward in order to show respect for someone important 鞠躬，躬身行礼: **[+before/to etc]** *He bowed before the king.* 他向国王躬身行礼。**2** [I,T] to bend your body over something, especially in order to see it more closely 探身向前看〔尤指为靠近些看〕: **[+over]** *Professor Teague sat at his desk, bowed over a book.* 蒂格教授坐在桌旁伏身看一本书。| **bow your head** (=bend your neck so that you are looking at the ground) 低头，俯首 | **bow your head in shame** *Phil stood there, his head bowed in shame.* 菲尔站在那儿，羞愧地低下了头。**3 be bowed (under sth)** to be bent because you are carrying something heavy on your back〔被背上重物〕压得躬着身子 **4 bow and scrape** to show too much respect to someone in authority〔对人〕卑躬屈膝，点头哈腰

bow down *phr v* [I] **1** to bend forward from your waist, especially when you are already kneeling, in order to show respect 深度躬身致敬: **[+before/to etc]** *Maria bowed down before the statue.* 玛丽亚在塑像前躬身致敬。**2 bow down to sb** *literary* to let someone give you orders or tell you what to do【文】向某人屈服；屈从于某人

bow out *phr v* [I] **1** to stop taking part in an activity, job etc, especially one that you have been doing for a long time（从…）退出，退场；辞职：**bow out of sth** *Reeves thinks it is time for him to bow out of politics.* 里夫斯认为到了自己从政界退出的时候了。**2** to not do something that you have promised or agreed to do 不守信用，背信弃义

bow to sb/sth *phr v* [T] to finally agree to do something that people want you to, even though you do not want to do it 向…让步，屈服于：*Congress may bow to public pressure and lift the arms embargo.* 国会也许会屈服于公众的压力，解除武器禁运。

bow² /baʊ; baʊ/ *n* **1** [C] the act of bending the top part of your body forward to show respect for someone 鞠躬 **2** also 又作 **bows** the front part of a ship 船头 —compare 比较 STERN² —see picture at 参见 YACHT 图 **3 take a bow** if someone takes a bow, they come on the stage at the end of a performance so that people can APPLAUD them〔表演结束时〕谢幕

bow 蝴蝶结

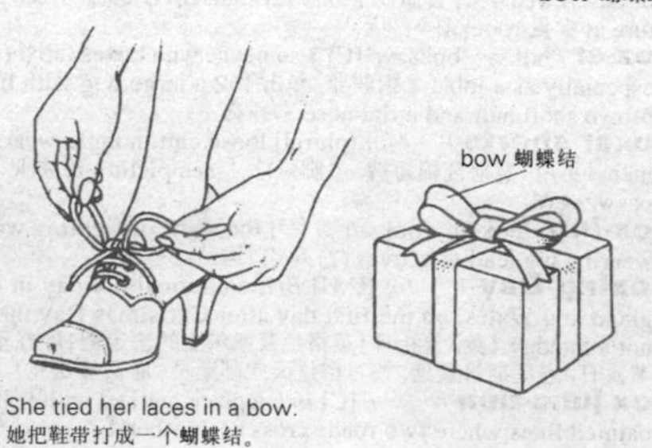

She tied her laces in a bow.
她把鞋带打成一个蝴蝶结。

bow³ /bo; bəʊ/ *n* **1** [C] a weapon used for shooting arrows (ARROW (1)), made of a long thin curved piece of wood 弓 **2** [C] a knot of cloth or string with a curved part on either side, used especially for decoration 蝴蝶结：*Ella wore a big bow in her hair.* 埃拉头上戴着一只大蝴蝶结。**3** [C] a long thin piece of wood with a tight string fastened along it, used to play musical instruments that have strings〔弦乐器的〕弓 **4 bow legs** legs that curve outwards at the knees 弓形腿，罗圈腿 —see also 另见 **have more than one string to your bow** (STRING¹ (8))

bow⁴ /bo; bəʊ/ *v* **1** [I] to bend or curve 弯曲，弯成弓形 **2** [I,T] to play a piece of music on a musical instrument with a BOW³ (3) 用弓拉奏〔乐曲〕

Bow Bells /ˌbo ˈbɛlz; ˌbəʊ ˈbelz/ the church bells of St Mary-le-Bow in London. It is said that a person born within the sound of (=in a place where you can hear) Bow Bells is a true Cockney 勒博排钟〔圣玛丽-勒-博教堂的一组响钟，据说在钟声所及的地方出生的人才是真正的伦敦人〕

bowd·ler·ize also 又作 **-ise** *BrE*【英】/ˈbaudləˌraɪz; ˈbaʊdləraɪz/ *v* [T] to remove the parts of a book, play etc that you think are offensive, and actually ruin it by doing this 删除〔书本、剧本等中〕猥亵鄙俗的字句 —**bowdlerized** *adj*: *a bowdlerized version of 'Antony and Cleopatra'*《安东尼和克娄巴特拉》的删节本

bow·el /ˈbauəl; ˈbaʊəl/ *n* **1 bowels** [plural] the system of tubes inside your body where food is made into solid waste material and through which it passes out of your body; INTESTINE 肠：**move/empty your bowels** (=get rid of solid waste from your body) 排大便 **2** [singular] one part of this system of tubes 肠道：*cancer of the bowel* 肠癌 **3 a bowel movement** *formal* an act of getting rid of solid waste from your body【正式】大解，排便 **4 the bowels of sth** *literary* the lowest or deepest part of something【文】内部，最深处：**the bowels of the earth** (=deep under the ground) 地球内部

bow·er /ˈbauɚ; ˈbaʊə/ *n* [C] *literary*【文】**1** a pleasant place in the shade under a tree, especially in a garden 树荫处：*a rose-scented bower* 有玫瑰香味的树荫 **2** *old use* a woman's bedroom【旧】闺房

Bo·wie /ˈboɪ; ˈbəʊi/**, David** (1947-) an English singer, songwriter, and actor who was extremely successful in the 1970s. His records, such as *The Rise and Fall of Ziggy Stardust and the Spiders from Mars* (1972) influenced many later musicians. 鲍伊〔(1947-)，英国歌手、歌曲作家、演员，20世纪70年代大获成功，他的专辑如《星尘齐格的沉浮与火星蜘蛛》(1972) 等对后来的许多音乐家产生了影响〕

Bowie, James (1790-1836) a US man born in Kentucky who invented the Bowie knife, a large knife with a curved blade. Bowie supported the cause of Texan independence from Mexico, and shared command of the Alamo, where he was killed. 鲍伊〔(1790-1836)，美国人，生于肯塔基州，发明了鲍伊刀（一种弯刃大刀）。鲍伊支持得克萨斯摆脱墨西哥统治的独立事业。他与其他军官一起指挥了阿拉莫之战，最后殉职〕

bow·ing /ˈboɪŋ; ˈbəʊɪŋ/ *n* [U] the skill of using a BOW³ (3) to play a musical instrument 弓法〔用弓拉奏乐器的技巧〕

bowl¹ /bol; bəʊl/ *n* 2 3

1 ►CONTAINER 容器◄ [C] a wide round container that is open at the top, used to hold liquids, flowers etc 碗；钵；盘：*Mix all the ingredients thoroughly in a bowl.* 把所有的配料都放在一个碗里彻底拌和。| [+of] *a bowl of fruit* 一盘水果 | **soup/salad/cereal etc bowl** (=a bowl to eat or serve soup, salad etc from) 汤碗/沙拉碗/麦米碗等

2 ►AMOUNT 数量◄ also 又作 **bowlful** [C] the amount that a bowl will hold 一碗之量：[+of] *a bowl of rice* 一碗米饭

3 ►GAME 游戏◄ a) bowls [plural] *BrE* an outdoor game played on grass in which you try to roll big balls as near as possible to a small ball【英】〔草地〕滚木球戏；LAWN BOWLING *AmE*【美】**b)** [C usually singular 一般用单数] a special game in American football played by the best teams after the normal playing season 美式橄榄球季后赛：*the Rose Bowl* 玫瑰碗赛

4 ►BALL 球◄ [C] *BrE* a ball that you use in the game of bowls【英】〔滚木球戏所用的〕木球

5 ►SHAPE 形状◄ [C] the part of an object such as a spoon, pipe, toilet etc that is shaped like a bowl 碗状物，物体的凹处〈如烟斗的斗、匙子舀物的部分、抽水马桶的桶身等〉

6 ►SPORT 体育◄ [C usually singular 一般用单数] *AmE* a large structure shaped like a bowl, where people go to watch special events; STADIUM【美】环形剧场；椭圆形体育场：*the Hollywood Bowl* 好莱坞环形剧场

bowl² *v* **1** [I,T] to roll a ball along a surface when you are playing the game of bowls〔玩滚木球戏时〕使（球）滚动 **2** [I,T] to throw a ball at the BATSMAN in CRICKET (2)〔玩板球时向击球员〕投（球） **3** also 又作 **bowl out** [T] to make a BATSMAN in CRICKET (2) have to leave the field, by hitting the WICKET (=set of sticks) behind him with a ball〔玩板球时以球击中三柱门〕迫使〔击球员〕出局

bowl along *phr v* [I] to travel or move very quickly and smoothly 平稳而快速地行驶[移动]：*We were really bowling along when suddenly the back wheel fell off.* 我们的汽车正平稳而快速地行驶，突然间后轮掉了。

bowl sb ↔ **out** *phr v* [T] to make a BATSMAN in CRICKET (2) have to leave the field by hitting the WICKET (=set of sticks) behind him with a ball〔玩板球时以球击中三柱门〕迫使〔击球员〕出局

bowl sb/sth ↔ **over** *phr v* [T] **1** to accidentally hit someone so that they fall down, because you are running too quickly 撞倒：*Some kids running past bowled an old lady over.* 一些跑过的孩子把一位老婆婆撞倒了。**2** to surprise, please, or excite someone very much 使大为惊喜：*We were absolutely bowled over by the Parthenon.*〔希腊雅典的〕帕台农神庙使我们倾倒。

bow-legged /ˈboˌlɛgd; ˈbəʊˌlegd/ *adj* having legs that curve outwards at the knees 弓形腿的，罗圈腿的，外弯腿的

bowl·er /ˈbolɚ; ˈbəʊlə/ *n* [C] **1** a player in CRICKET (2) who throws the ball at a BATSMAN〔板球的〕投球手 **2** also 又作 **bowler hat** *especially BrE* a hard round black hat that business men sometimes wear【尤英】〔男用硬圆顶黑色〕常礼帽；DERBY (1) *AmE*【美】—see picture at 参见 HAT 图

> **CULTURAL NOTE 文化注释**
>
> Bowler hats are not often worn now and are thought of as being old-fashioned, but they still appear in humorous drawings and advertisements which show the typical Englishman. 常礼帽现在很少有人戴了，人们认为它已经过时。不过，它还会出现在表现典型英格兰人的幽默画和广告中。

bowl·ing /ˈbolɪŋ; ˈbəʊlɪŋ/ *n* [U] **1** an indoor game in which you roll a large heavy ball along a wooden track in order to knock down a group of PINS (=wooden objects shaped like bottles) 保龄球：**go bowling** (=play this game) 玩保龄球 **2** the act of throwing a ball at the BATSMAN in CRICKET (2)〔玩板球时向击球员〕投球

bowling al·ley /ˈ·· ,·/ *n* [C] a building where you go bowling 保龄球场

bowling ball /ˈ‥ ˌ/ *n* [C] the heavy ball you use in the game of bowling 保龄球

bowling green /ˈ‥ ˌ/ *n* [C] a piece of grass where you play the game of bowls (BOWL[1] (3a)) (草地) 滚木球场

bow·man /ˈbomən; ˈbəʊmən/ *n* [C] *old use* a soldier who shoots arrows (ARROW (1)) with a BOW[3] (1) 【旧】弓箭手

bow·sprit /ˈbauˌsprɪt; ˈbəʊˌsprɪt/ *n* [C] a long pole on the front of a boat that the ropes from the sails are fastened to 船首的斜桅〔系船帆绳索的地方〕

Bow Street /ˈbo strit; ˈbəʊ striːt/ a street in London where there is a police court 博街〔伦敦的一条街, 此处有一治安法庭〕: *He was remanded in custody until 28 June by Bow Street Magistrates.* 他被博街的地方治安法官一直拘留到6月28日。

Bow Street run·ner /ˌ· · ˈ· ·/ *n* [C] a member of the first police force in London, set up in 1748 伦敦警察〔成立于1748年的伦敦第一支警察部队的成员〕

bow tie /ˌbo ˈtaɪ; ˌbəʊ ˈtaɪ/ *n* [C] a short piece of cloth tied in the shape of a bow that men sometimes wear around their neck 蝶形领结 —see picture on page A15 参见A15页图

bow win·dow /ˌbo ˈwɪndo; ˌbəʊ ˈwɪndəʊ/ *n* [C] a window that curves outwards 弓形窗, 圆[凸] 肚窗

bow-wow /ˈbauˈwau; ˌbaʊˈwaʊ/ *interjection* a word used to make the sound a dog makes, used by and to small children〔儿语〕汪汪〔即狗叫声〕

bow-wow /ˈbau ˈwau; ˈbaʊ waʊ/ *n* [C] a word meaning a dog, used by and to small children〔儿语〕狗狗

box[1] /bɑks; bɒks/ *n*

1 ▶CONTAINER 容器◀ [C] a container for putting things in, especially one with four stiff straight sides 盒, 匣, 箱: [+of] *a box of tissues* 一盒纸巾 | *a matchbox* 火柴盒 | **cardboard/wooden box** *You need a filing cabinet, not all these cardboard boxes.* 你需要一个文件柜, 不是这些硬纸板箱。| **toolbox/shoebox etc** (=used for keeping tools etc in) 工具箱/鞋盒等 —see picture at 参见 CONTAINER 图

2 ▶AMOUNT IN A BOX 箱的容量◀ also 又作 **boxful** [C] the amount that a box can hold 一盒[一箱] (之量): [+of] *a box of chocolates* 一盒巧克力

3 ▶SQUARE SHAPE 方形◀ [C] a small square on a page for people to write information in 方框, 方格: *Put an 'X' in the box if you would like to join our mailing list.* 如果你想加入我们的邮寄名单, 请在方框内写上X。

4 ▶IN A THEATRE/COURT 在剧院/法庭中◀ [C] a small area of a theatre or court that is separate from where other people are sitting〔戏院的〕包厢;〔法庭的〕隔间: *the jury box* 陪审团席 —see picture at 参见 THEATRE 图

5 box 25/450 etc an address at a POST OFFICE that people can use instead of their own address; PO BOX 25号/450号等邮政信箱

6 ▶SPORTS FIELD 体育场地◀ [C] a special area of a sports field that is marked by lines and used for a particular purpose〔运动场地用线划定的〕区: *a penalty box* 罚球区

7 ▶WORN DURING SPORTS 运动时穿着的◀ [C] *BrE* a piece of plastic that a man wears over his sex organs to protect them when he is playing a sport, especially CRICKET (2)【英】〔尤指板球运动员的〕下体护身, 护罩

8 ▶DEATH 死亡◀ [C] *informal* a COFFIN【非正式】棺材

9 ▶TREE 树◀ [C,U] a small tree that keeps its leaves in winter and is often planted around the edge of a garden or field, or the wood from this tree 黄杨〔一种冬天不落叶的小树, 常种植在花园四周〕; 黄杨木: *a box hedge* 黄杨篱笆墙

10 give sb a box on the ears *old-fashioned* to hit someone on the side of their head【过时】打某人耳光

11 the box *informal* the television【非正式】电视: *What's on the box tonight?* 今晚有什么电视节目?

12 be out of your box *BrE slang* to be very drunk【英俚】烂醉 —see also 另见 BLACK BOX

box[2] *v* **1** [I,T] to fight someone as a sport by hitting them with your closed hands inside big leather GLOVES (2) (与…) 进行拳击比赛 **2** also 又作 **box up** [T] to put things in boxes 把…装入箱[盒] 内 —see also 另见 BOXED **3** [T] to draw a box around something on a page〔在纸上〕给〔某物〕画框 **4 box sb's ears** *old-fashioned* to hit someone on the side of their head【过时】打耳光

box sb/sth ↔ **in** *phr v* [T] **1** to park so near to another car that it cannot move 紧挨着〔另一辆车〕停车 **2** to surround someone so that they are unable to move freely 封堵: *Steve Cram got boxed in on the final curve.* 史蒂夫·克拉姆在最后一个弯道被人挡住了。**3 feel boxed in a)** to feel that you cannot do what you want to do because a person or situation is limiting you 感觉施展不开, 感到被限制: *Married for only a year, Connie already felt boxed in.* 才结婚一年, 康尼已经感受到了束缚。**b)** to feel that you cannot move freely, because you are in a small space〔被困在狭小的空间内而〕动弹不得

box sth ↔ **off** *phr v* [T] to separate a particular area from a larger one by putting walls around it 把…圈上, 隔开: *We're going to box off that corner to get extra storage space.* 我们要把那个角落隔开以扩大储存空间。

box can·yon /ˈ· ˌ· ·/ *n* [C] *AmE* a deep narrow valley with very straight sides and no way out【美】〔无出口的〕峡谷

box·car /ˈbɑksˌkar; ˈbɒkskɑː/ *n* [C] *AmE* a railway carriage with high sides and a roof, used for carrying goods【美】〔铁路上的〕有盖货车, 棚车

boxed /bɑkst; bɒkst/ *adj* sold in a box or boxes 盒装的: *a boxed set of CDs* 一套盒装的激光唱片

box end wrench /ˌ· · ˈ·/ *n* [C] *AmE* a type of WRENCH[2] (3) with a hollow end that fits over a NUT[1] (2) that is being screwed or unscrewed【美】套筒扳手; RING SPANNER *BrE*【英】—see picture at 参见 TOOL[1] 图

box·er /ˈbɑksɚ; ˈbɒksə/ *n* [C] **1** someone who boxes (BOX[2] (1)), especially as a job〔尤指职业〕拳击手 **2** a large dog with light brown short hair and a flat nose 拳师狗

boxer shorts /ˈ‥ ˌ·/ *n* [plural] loose cotton underwear for men〔男用〕宽松纯棉短裤, 平脚短裤 —see picture at 参见 UNDERWEAR 图

box·ing /ˈbɑksɪŋ; ˈbɒksɪŋ/ *n* [U] the sport of fighting while wearing big leather GLOVES (2) 拳击 (运动)

Boxing Day /ˈ‥ ˌ·/ *n* [C,U] *BrE* a national holiday in England and Wales, on the first day after Christmas Day that is not a Sunday【英】节礼日〔英格兰及威尔士的法定假日, 在圣诞节次日, 遇星期日顺延, 按习俗这天向邮递员、雇员等送礼〕

box junc·tion /ˈ· ˌ· ·/ *n* [C] *BrE* a place marked with yellow painted lines where two roads cross each other【英】路口方形黄线区域

box lunch /ˈ· ˌ·/ *n* [C] *AmE* a lunch that you take to school or work with you in a LUNCHBOX【美】〔尤指带去学校或上班的〕盒装午餐

box num·ber /ˈ· ˌ· ·/ *n* [C] *BrE* an address at the POST OFFICE that people can use instead of their own address【英】(邮政) 信箱号码

box of·fice /ˈ· ˌ· ·/ *n* **1** [C] the place in a theatre, cinema etc where tickets are sold〔戏院、电影院等的〕售票处 **2** [singular] used to describe how successful a film, play, or actor is, by the number of people who pay to see them 票房 (价值): **do well/badly at the box office** (=be very successful or unsuccessful)〔电影〕卖座/不卖座 | **a (big) box office draw** (=a successful actor who many people will pay to see) 有票房号召力的演员

box room /ˈ· ˌ·/ *n* [C] *BrE* a small room in a house where you can store things【英】〔家中的〕储存室, 杂物室

boy[1] /bɔɪ; bɔɪ/ *n* [C] 

1 ▶CHILD 儿童◀ a male child or young man 男孩, 少年: *The boys all wanted to play football.* 这些男孩都想踢球。| **little boy** (=a young male child) 小男孩

2 ▶SON 儿子◀ a son 儿子: *I love my boys, but I'd like to have a girl too.* 我喜欢我的儿子, 但希望再有个女儿。| **little boy** (=a young son) 小儿子 *How old is your little boy?* 你的小儿子多大了?

3 office/paper/delivery etc boy a young man who does a particular job 办公室勤杂员/送报员/送货员等

4 the boys *informal* a group of men who are friends and often go out together【非正式】男性朋友们; 一群男伙伴: *Friday's his night out with the boys.* 星期五晚上是他和一班男性朋友外出的时间。| **one of the boys** (=popular with a group of men) 男伴中的一个

5 ▶ANIMALS 动物◀ a way of addressing a male horse or dog〔对公马或公狗说的〕家伙: *Good boy!* 好家伙!

6 ▶JOB 工作◀ boys *informal*【非正式】**a)** a group of men who do the same job 一群从事同一职业的男人: *Oh no! Wait until the press boys get hold of this story.* 不行! 要等新闻界的朋友采访到这个新闻。**b)** men in the army, navy etc, especially those who are fighting in a war〔尤指在战场上作战的〕士兵, 战友: *our boys on the front lines* 我们在前线的战友们

7 boys will be boys used to say that you should not be surprised when boys behave badly, are noisy etc 男孩子总归是男孩子〔指男孩子生性淘气, 爱吵闹〕

8 city/local/working-class boy *informal* a man of any age considered as being affected by the place and social group that he was born in【非正式】城市/本地/工人家庭出身的男子: *the classic story of a local boy who's made good* 一个本地小

伙子最终成功的经典故事 | *I'm just a country boy.* 我不过是个乡下孩子。

9 old boy/my dear boy *BrE old-fashioned* a friendly way for one man to speak to another man【英, 过时】老兄〔对男性讲话时的招呼用语〕

10 *AmE taboo* an offensive way of addressing a black man【美讳】〔对黑人男性的蔑称〕—see also 另见 BLUE-EYED BOY, **jobs for the boys** (JOB (5)), MAMA'S BOY, MUMMY'S BOY, OLD BOY, WIDE BOY

boy² *interjection spoken especially AmE*【口, 尤美】**1** also 又作 **oh boy** used when you are excited or pleased about something 好家伙〔表示兴奋、欣喜等〕: *Boy, that was a great meal!* 嘿, 那顿饭真不错! **2 oh boy** used when you are slightly annoyed or disappointed about something 哎〔表示烦恼或失望〕: *Oh boy! Bethany's sick again.* 哎! 贝萨妮又病了。

boy·cott¹ /ˈbɔɪˌkɑt; ˈbɔɪkɒt/ *v* [T] to refuse to buy something, use something, or take part in something as a way of protesting 抵制, 排斥, 杯葛; 拒绝参加: *We boycott all products tested on animals.* 我们抵制所有拿动物做试验的产品。

boycott² *n* [C] an act of boycotting something, or the period of time when it is boycotted 抵制行动, 杯葛行动: **[+of/on/against]** *a boycott on South African fruit in the 70s* 20世纪70年代抵制南非水果的活动

boy·friend /ˈbɔɪˌfrɛnd; ˈbɔɪfrend/ *n* [C] a man that you are having a romantic relationship with 〔女子的〕男朋友: *Have you met Jilly's new boyfriend yet?* 你见过吉莉的新男朋友了吗? —see also 另见 GIRLFRIEND

boy·hood /ˈbɔɪhʊd; ˈbɔɪhʊd/ *n* [U] the time of a man's life when he is a boy 男孩的童年, 少年时代: *boyhood memories* 童年的记忆 —see also 另见 GIRLHOOD

boy·ish /ˈbɔɪ-ɪʃ; ˈbɔɪ-ɪʃ/ *adj* **1** a man who is boyish looks or behaves like a boy in a way that is attractive 〔指男人〕男孩似的, 男孩子气的, 天真烂漫的: *boyish good looks* 男孩般的漂亮外貌 **2** a woman or girl who is boyish looks or behaves a little like a boy 〔女人、女孩〕男孩似的, 男孩子气的: *At 45 May still had a trim, boyish figure.* 都45岁了, 梅仍然保持着男孩般匀称的身材。—**boyishly** *adv* —**boyishness** *n* [U]

Boyne /bɔɪn; bɔɪn/, **the Battle of the** a famous battle in 1690 near the River Boyne in Ireland, in which Britain's Protestant King William III defeated the former King James II (a Catholic), and ended the attempts by the Catholic part of the royal family to rule in Britain 博因河战役〔1690年在爱尔兰博因河附近发生的一场著名战役, 信奉新教的英国国王威廉三世打败了信奉天主教的前国王詹姆斯二世, 粉碎了王室天主教成员统治英国的企图〕

Boys' Bri·gade, the /ˈ· ·ˌ·/ an organization which was set up in Britain in 1883 to encourage boys to develop team spirit and responsible behaviour 少年大队〔1883年成立于英国的一个组织, 旨在培养男孩子的团队精神和责任心〕

boy scout /ˌ· ˈ·/ *n* [C] a boy who is a member of an association for boys that teaches them practical skills and develops their characters; SCOUT¹ (1b) 童子军 —see also 另见 GIRL SCOUT, GUIDE

Boys' Own /ˌ· ˈ·◄/ *adj BrE* a phrase used to describe men who are doing brave, exciting things, like a hero in an adventure story. The **Boys' Own Paper** was a boys' magazine sold in the late 19th and early 20th centuries in Britain which contained adventure stories【英】英雄般的〔该短语常用来形容做事勇敢、激动人心的男子, 如同冒险故事中的英雄一般。《男孩专刊》是19世纪末20世纪初在英国销售的一份刊载冒险故事的男孩杂志〕: *He has been called a swashbuckling Boys' Own hero.* 他一直被称作神气活现的英雄。| *His background is the stuff of boys' own papers.* 他的经历充满冒险故事。

boy won·der /ˌ· ˈ··/ *n* [C] a young man who is very successful 年轻有为的男子: *Robson, the boy wonder of the department* 系里的青年奇才罗布森

bo·zo /ˈbozo; ˈbəʊzəʊ/ *n plural* **bozos** [C] *informal* someone who you think is silly or stupid【非正式】笨蛋, 傻瓜: *Who's the bozo in the pyjamas?* 那个穿着睡衣裤的傻瓜是谁?

BPhil /ˌbi ˈfɪl; ˌbiː ˈfɪl/ *n* [C usually singular 一般用单数] Bachelor of Philosophy; a first or second degree that you may get after studying at a British university, but that is not as common as a BACHELOR'S DEGREE 〔英国〕哲学学士

B.P.O.E. *n* [singular] the written abbreviation of 缩写= THE BENEVOLENT AND PROTECTIVE ORDER OF ELKS —see 见 ELKS

BR /ˌbi ˈɑr; ˌbiː ˈɑː/ *n* [singular] British Rail; the organization that controls the British railway system 英国铁路公司

Br 1 the written abbreviation of 缩写= BROTHER **2** the written abbreviation of 缩写= BRITISH

bra /brɑ; brɑː/ *n* [C] a piece of underwear that a woman wears to support her breasts 乳罩, 胸罩 —see picture at 参见 UNDERWEAR 图

CULTURAL NOTE 文化注释

In the 1960s many women who supported the Women's Liberation movement burnt their bras as a protest. 20世纪60年代, 许多支持妇女解放运动的女性烧掉自己的胸罩以示抗议。

brace¹ /bres; breɪs/ *v* **1** [T] to prepare for something unpleasant that is going to happen 准备迎接〔困难〕, 使振作精神: **brace yourself for** *Nancy braced herself for the inevitable arguments.* 南希为这场无可避免的争论作好了准备。| **brace yourself to do** *Jean, you'd better brace yourself to hear bad news.* 琼, 你得作好准备, 有坏消息相告。| **be braced for** *The entire castle was braced for an attack.* 整个城堡都准备好了抵抗袭击。**2** [T] to push part of your body against something solid in order to make yourself more steady 把〔身体〕抵着〔某物, 以保持平衡〕, 使稳住: **brace sth against** *Gina braced her foot against the wall and pulled herself up.* 吉纳用脚抵着墙站了起来。| **brace yourself** *Before he could brace himself she'd shoved him out of the door.* 他还没站稳, 她就把他推出了门。**3** [T] to make something stronger by supporting it 支撑; 加固: *Wait until we've braced the ladder.* 等我们把梯子支撑住再说。**4** [I,T] to make your body or part of your body stiff in order to prepare to do something difficult 〔使身体或身体某部分〕绷紧, 鼓足气力: *Stuart braced his muscles and heaved the fridge aside.* 斯图尔特鼓足力气, 把冰箱推到了一边。

brace² *n*

1 ▶TEETH 牙齿◀ a) brace *BrE*【英】, **braces** *especially AmE*【尤美】a connected set of wires that children sometimes wear on their teeth to make them straight (儿童) 牙齿矫正器 **b)** [C] *BrE* a wire frame that children sometimes have to put over their teeth to make them straight【英】(儿童) 畸齿矫正钢丝架

2 ▶SUPPORT 支持◀ a) [C] something that is used to strengthen, stiffen, or support something 支撑物, 支架: *Cath had to wear a neck brace after the accident.* 事故后, 凯丝只得戴上颈托。**b)** [C usually plural 一般用复数] *AmE* a metal support that someone with weak legs wears to help them walk【美】〔装在腿上帮助腿力弱者行走的〕金属支架; CALLIPERS *BrE*【英】

3 a brace of sth two birds or animals that have been killed for food or sport 〔指鸟兽等猎获物的〕一对, 一双

4 ▶PRINTED SIGN 印刷符号◀ one of a pair of signs { } used to show that information written between them should be considered together 一对大括弧{ }中的一个 —compare 比较 BRACKET¹ (1)

5 braces *BrE* two long pieces of material that stretch over someone's shoulders and fasten to their trousers at the front and the back to stop them falling down【英】〔裤子的〕吊带, 背带; SUSPENDERS *AmE*【美】

brace·let /ˈbreslɪt; ˈbreɪsl̩t/ *n* [C] a band or chain that you wear around your wrist or arm as a decoration 手镯; 臂镯 —compare 比较 BANGLE —see picture at 参见 JEWELLERY 图

brac·ing /ˈbresɪŋ; ˈbreɪsɪŋ/ *adj* bracing air or weather is cold and makes you feel very awake and healthy 〔空气、天气〕令人心神清爽的, 提神的: *a bracing sea breeze* 令人精神爽快的海风

brack·en /ˈbrækən; ˈbrækən/ *n* [U] a plant that often grows in forests and becomes reddish brown in the autumn 蕨; 羊齿植物

brack·et¹ /ˈbrækɪt; ˈbræk̩t/ *n* [C] **1** [usually plural 一般用复数] **a)** *BrE* also 又作 **round bracket** one of the pair of signs ( ) put around words to show that the rest of the writing can be read and understood without these words【英】一对圆括弧( )中的一个; PARENTHESIS *AmE*【美】: **in brackets** *Last year's sales figures are given in brackets.* 去年的销售数字写在括弧中。—see picture at 参见 PUNCTUATION MARK 图 **b)** *AmE*【美】**square bracket** *BrE*【英】a sign like this that is square [ ] 一对方括弧[ ]中的一个 **c) angle bracket** a sign like this that is shaped 〈 〉 一对尖括弧〈 〉中的一个 —compare 比较 BRACE² (4) **2 income/tax/age etc bracket** an income etc that is inside a particular range 收入等级/纳税等级/年龄组别等: *Peter's new job puts him in the highest tax bracket.* 彼得的新工作使他进入了最高的纳税阶层。**3** a piece of metal, wood, or plastic, often in the shape of the letter L, fixed to a wall to support something such as a shelf 〔钉在墙上的〕托架, 托座, 角撑架

bracket² *v* [T] **1** to put brackets around a written word, piece of information etc 把…放在括弧内: *Debit amounts are usually bracketed.* 账簿上的借项数字通常标在括弧内。**2** to consider two or more people or things as being the same type 把…视为同类; 将…相提并论: **[+together/with]** *Women and minors were brack-*

eted together for the legislation. 立法时妇女和未成年人被归为一类。

brack·ish /ˈbrækɪʃ; ˈbrækɪʃ/ *adj* brackish water is not pure because it is slightly salty〔水〕微咸的，略含盐分的

Brack·nell /ˈbræknḷ; ˈbræknəl/, **Lady** a character in Oscar Wilde's play *The Importance of Being Earnest* 布拉克内尔〔奥斯卡·王尔德所著《认真的重要性》一剧中的人物〕

B

brad /bræd; bræd/ *n* [C] *AmE* a small metal object like a button with two metal sticks that are put through several pieces of paper and folded down to hold the papers together【美】圆形纸夹；PAPER FASTENER *BrE*【英】

brad·awl /ˈbrædˌɔl; ˈbrædɔːl/ *n* [C] *especially BrE* a small tool with a sharp point for making holes; AWL【尤英】〔打孔用的〕小锥子，打眼锥

Brad·ford /ˈbrædfɚd; ˈbrædfəd/ an industrial city in the north of England 布雷德福〔位于英格兰北部的一个工业城市〕

Brad·man /ˈbrædmən; ˈbrædmən/, **Sir Don·ald** /ˈdɑnḷd; ˈdɒnəld/ (1908-2001) an Australian CRICKETER, one of the best BATSMEN ever to have played 布雷德曼〔(1908-2001)，澳大利亚板球运动员，有史以来最杰出的击球手之一〕

Brady, Ian —see also 另见 the MOORS MURDERERS

Bra·dy Bunch, The /ˈbredɪ ˌbʌntʃ; ˈbreɪdi ˌbʌntʃ/ a US television programme of the 1960s and 1970s about a large family《布雷迪·邦奇一家》〔20 世纪 60、70 年代美国一档有关一个大家庭的电视节目

> **CULTURAL NOTE 文化注释**
>
> Some people talk about the Brady Bunch as an example of a family that is good and so free from real problems that they could not possibly really exist 有人说布雷迪·邦奇一家是美好家庭的代表，远离现实问题，乃至不可能真的存在：*The family across the street seemed like the Brady Bunch at first, but we soon learned that there were all sorts of tensions underneath.* 街对面的那户人家刚开始好像美满得像是布雷迪·邦奇一家，但很快我们发现表象背后也有各种紧张的关系。

brae /bre; breɪ/ *n* [C] *ScotE* a hill or slope【苏格兰】山坡；斜坡

brag /bræg; bræg/ *v* **bragged, bragging** [I,T] to talk too proudly about what you have done, what you own etc; BOAST[1](1) 自夸，吹嘘："*I came out top in the test,*" *he bragged.* "我考试名列前茅。"他吹嘘道。| [+**about**] *Ben's always bragging about his success with women.* 本总是吹嘘他对女人很有办法。| **brag (that)** *Julia used to brag that her family had a villa in Spain.* 朱莉娅以前老吹嘘她家在西班牙有一所别墅。

brag·ga·do·ci·o /ˌbrægəˋdoʃɪˌo; ˌbrægəˈdəʊʃiəʊ/ *n* [U] *especially literary* proud talk about something that you claim to own, to have done etc【尤文】大吹特吹，自吹自擂

brag·gart /ˈbrægɚt; ˈbrægət/ *n* [C] someone who is always talking too proudly about what they own or have done 自夸者，吹牛者

Brah·ma /ˈbrɑmə; ˈbrɑːmə/ one of the three main gods in the Hindu religion, who is considered to be the god of creation 梵天〔印度教三大神之一，被视为创造之神〕—see also 另见 SIVA, VISHNU

Brah·man /ˈbrɑmən; ˈbrɑːmən/ also 又作 **Brah·min** /ˈbrɑmɪn; ˈbrɑːmḭn/ *n* [C] someone belonging to the highest rank in the HINDU faith 婆罗门〔印度种姓四大等级中的最高等级，即僧侣〕

Brahms /brɑmz; brɑːmz/, **Jo·han·nes** /joˋhænəs; jəʊˈhænəs/ (1833-97) a German writer of music, famous for his symphonies (SYMPHONY) and CONCERTOs 勃拉姆斯〔(1833-1897)，德国作曲家，以交响乐、协奏曲闻名〕

braid[1] /bred; breɪd/ *n* **1** [U] a narrow band of material formed by twisting threads together, used to decorate the edges of clothes〔丝等编成的装饰性〕带子，穗带：*a jacket trimmed with red braid* 边上镶有红色穗带的夹克 **2** [C] *AmE* a length of hair that has been separated into three parts and then woven together【美】发辫，辫子；PLAIT[2] *BrE*【英】：**in braids** *Pippa always wears her hair in braids.* 皮帕总是梳着辫子。—**braided** *adj* —see picture at 参见 HAIRSTYLE 图

braid[2] *v* [T] *especially AmE* to weave or twist together three pieces of hair or cloth to form one length【尤美】把…编成辫子；把…编成辫子；PLAIT[1] *BrE*【英】

braille /brel; breɪl/ *n* [U] a form of printing with raised parts that blind people can read by touching the paper〔盲人用的〕盲文，点字

S2 W2 **brain**[1] /bren; breɪn/ *n*

1 ▶ORGAN 器官◀ [C] the organ inside your head that controls how you think, feel, and move 脑(子)；脑髓：*Messages from the brain are carried by the central nervous system.* 大脑的信息是通过中枢神经系统传递的。

2 ▶INTELLIGENCE 智力◀ [U] also 又作 **brains** *plural* the ability to think clearly and learn quickly 智力，智慧，头脑，脑筋：*If you had any brains you'd know what I meant.* 如果你有点脑子，就会知道我的意思。

3 ▶PERSON 人◀ [C] *informal* someone who is intelligent, with good ideas and useful skills【非正式】极聪明的人，智者：*Some of our best brains are leaving the country to work in the US.* 我们当中一些优秀的人才离开本国到美国工作。—see also 另见 BRAIN DRAIN

4 have sth on the brain *informal* to be always thinking about something【非正式】一直想着某事，牵挂着：*I've got that song on the brain today.* 今天我脑子里一直想着那首歌。

5 be the brains behind sth to be the person who thought of and developed a particular plan, system, or organization, especially a successful one 出谋划策的智囊，主脑

6 brain dead a) in a state where your brain has stopped working properly even though your heart may still be beating 脑死亡 **b)** *informal* stupid and uninteresting, especially because you live a boring life【非正式】不会动脑子的，愚蠢的：*If all she does is watch TV all day, no wonder she's brain dead.* 她整天就知道看电视，难怪她变得呆头呆脑的。

7 pick sb's brains to ask someone a lot of questions about something that they know about 详尽地向某人提问：*I need to pick your brains about this cashflow forecast.* 我需要向你详细问问有关现金流转预测的问题。

8 brain box *BrE informal* a very intelligent person【英，非正式】智商高的人，极聪明的人 —see also 另见 BIRD-BRAINED, HAREBRAINED, **beat your brains out** (BEAT[1] (18)), **rack your brain(s)** (RACK[2] (2))

brain[2] *v* [T] *spoken* to hit someone very hard on the head【口】重击〔某人〕的头部：*I'll brain you if you do that again!* 你再那样做，我就打破你的头！

brain·child /ˈbrenˌtʃaɪld; ˈbreɪntʃaɪld/ *n* [singular] an idea, plan, organization etc that someone has thought of without any help from anyone else 智力产儿，脑力劳动的成果：[+**of**] *The festival was the brainchild of Mayor Reeves.* 举办这个节日是里夫斯市长想出来的好主意。

brain dam·age /ˈ· ˌ··/ *n* [U] damage to someone's brain caused by an accident or illness 脑损伤：*Potts suffered severe brain damage in the crash.* 波茨的大脑在车祸中受到严重损伤。—**brain-damaged** *adj*

brain drain /ˈ· ·/ *n* **the brain drain** a movement of highly skilled or professional people from their own country to a country where they can earn more money 人才流失，人才外流

brain·less /ˈbrenlɪs; ˈbreɪnləs/ *adj* completely stupid 没有头脑的，傻的，愚笨的：*What a brainless thing to do!* 这样做很愚蠢！—**brainlessly** *adv*

brain scan /ˈ· ·/ *n* [C] a process in which detailed photographs of the inside of your brain are taken and examined by a doctor 脑部扫描(检查)

brain·storm /ˈbrenˌstɔrm; ˈbreɪnstɔːm/ *n* **1 have a brainstorm** *BrE informal* to suddenly be unable to think clearly or sensibly【英，非正式】一时糊涂：*I'm sorry, I must have had a brainstorm that afternoon.* 对不起，那天下午我一定是一时糊涂了。**2** [singular] *AmE* a sudden clever idea【美】灵感，突然想到的妙计；BRAINWAVE *BrE*【英】：**have a brainstorm** *Unless you have a brainstorm, I don't see how we're going to get out of this.* 除非你能想出一个妙法，不然我看不出我们如何能摆脱困境。

brain·storm·ing /ˈbrenˌstɔrmɪŋ; ˈbreɪnstɔːmɪŋ/ *n* [U] the act of meeting with a group of people in order to try to develop ideas and think of ways of solving problems 集体解决难题，大家出主意，合力攻关：*a brainstorming session to come up with a slogan for the new shampoo* 为新洗发水想一条广告标语的献策会 —**brainstorm** *v* [I]

brain sur·geon /ˈ· ˌ··/ *n* [C] a doctor who performs operations on people's brains 脑外科医生

brain teas·er /ˈ· ˌ··/ *n* [C] a difficult problem that you enjoy trying to solve〔测试头脑机敏性的〕难题，智力测验游戏

brain·wash /ˈbrenˌwɔʃ; ˈbreɪnwɒʃ/ *v* [T] to make someone believe something that is not true, by using force, confusing them, or continuously repeating it over a long period of time 对…进行洗脑，把某种思想强加于，强行灌输：*Young people are being brainwashed by this religious group.* 这一宗教组织正在对年轻人进行洗脑。| **brainwash sb into doing sth** *Commercials can brainwash consumers into buying things they don't need.* 广告宣传会给消费者洗脑，使他们购买他们并不需要的东西。—**brainwashing** *n* [U]

brain·wave /ˈbren,wev; ˈbreɪnweɪv/ *n* [C] **1** *BrE* a sudden clever idea【英】灵感，突然想到的妙计；BRAINSTORM *AmE*【美】: *I've had a brainwave! Let's go this weekend instead.* 我突然想到了一条妙计，我们改为这个周末去！**2** an electrical force that is produced by the brain and that can be measured 脑电波

brain·y /ˈbrenɪ; ˈbreɪnɪ/ *adj informal* able to learn easily and think quickly; clever【非正式】聪明的，多智的，敏锐的: *He always was the brainy one, except at maths.* 他总是很聪明，只是数学差一些。

braise /brez; breɪz/ *v* [T] to cook meat or vegetables slowly in a small amount of liquid in a closed container 炖，焖，用文火煮 —**braised** *adj*

braising steak /ˈ· ·, ·/ *n* [U] BEEF[1] (1) that needs long slow cooking 供炖[煮]的牛肉

brake[1] /brek; breɪk/ *n* [C] **1** a piece of equipment that makes a vehicle go more slowly or stop, usually operated by pressing on a bar with your foot or hand 刹车，制动器，车闸: *Remember to test your brakes regularly.* 记住定期检查刹车装置。| **put/slam on the brakes** also 又作 **apply the brakes** *formal*【正式】*Moira slammed on the brakes and skidded to a halt.* 莫伊拉猛踩刹车，汽车滑动一下便停住了。—see also 另见 EMERGENCY BRAKE, HANDBRAKE —see picture at 参见 BICYCLE[1] 图 **2 act/serve as a brake on sth** to make something slow or difficult 对某事物起抑制作用，遏制某事物: *Rises in interest rates usually act as a brake on expenditure.* 利率的提高往往会起到抑制消费的作用。**3 put the brakes on sth** to stop something that is happening 阻止某事物: *Well, that pretty much puts the brakes on our plans.* 嗯，这差不多使我们的计划无法实现。

brake[2] *v* [I] to make a vehicle or bicycle go more slowly or stop by using its brake 刹车〔使减速或停住〕: **brake sharply/hard** (=brake quickly) 急刹车 *He braked sharply to avoid the dog.* 为了避开那条狗，他突然急刹车。

brake flu·id /ˈ· ,··/ *n* [U] liquid used in certain kinds of brakes so that the different parts move smoothly 刹车油，制动液

brake light /ˈ· ·/ *n* [C] a light on the back of a vehicle that comes on when you uses the brake〔位于汽车尾部，刹车时即亮起的〕(红色)制动信号灯 —see picture on page A2 参见 A2 页图

brake shoe /ˈ· ,·/ *n* [C] one of the two curved parts that press against the wheel of a vehicle in order to make it go more slowly or stop 闸瓦，制动瓦

bram·ble /ˈbræmbl; ˈbræmbəl/ *n* [C] a wild BLACKBERRY 悬钩子属植物〔尤指野生黑莓〕

bran /bræn; bræn/ *n* [U] the crushed outer skin of wheat or a similar grain that is separated from the rest of the grain when making white flour 麦麸；糠；谷皮

branch[1] /bræntʃ; brɑːntʃ/ *n* [C]

1 ▸ON A TREE 树上◂ a part of a tree that grows outwards from the TRUNK (=stem) and that has leaves, fruit, or smaller branches growing from it 树枝: *a fallen tree branch* 掉下的树枝

2 ▸IN A LOCAL AREA 在当地◂ a shop, office etc in a particular area that is part of a large company 分行；分支机构: *The bank has branches all over the country.* 这家银行在全国各地都有分行。| *a branch office in Boston* 设在波士顿的办事处

3 ▸OF AN ORGANIZATION 某机构的◂ a part of a government or other organization that deals with one particular part of its work〔政府或机构的〕部门: *All branches of government are having to cut costs.* 政府所有部门都要削减开支。

4 ▸OF A SUBJECT 某学科的◂ one part of a large subject of study or knowledge 分科: [+of] *Newton developed a branch of mathematics called calculus.* 牛顿开创了一个数学分支，称为微积分。

5 ▸OF A FAMILY 某家族的◂ a group of members of a family who all have the same grandparents or ANCESTORS〔家族中的〕一支，分支: *the wealthy South American branch of the family* 该家族中一富裕的南美洲分支

6 ▸SMALLER PART 较小的部分◂ a smaller less important part of something that leads away from the larger more important part of it 分支；支线；支流: *a branch of the river Arno* 阿尔诺河的支流

branch[2] *v* [I] to divide into two or more smaller, narrower, or less important parts 分支；分岔: **branch into two** *When you reach Germain Street, the road branches into two.* 到了泽梅因大街，路分岔为两条。

branch off *phr v* [I] **1** if a road, passage, railway etc branches off from another road etc, it separates from it and goes in a different direction 分岔；分支；分道: [+from] *a passage branching off from the main tunnel* 从主隧道岔开的通道 **2** to leave a main road 离开主路[干线]，走入岔道: [+from/into] *We branched off from the main road and turned down a country lane.* 我们离开干道，转入一条乡村小路。**3** to start talking about something different from what you were talking about before 岔开话题: [+into] *Then the conversation branched off into a discussion about movies.* 接着谈话转入对电影的讨论。

branch out *phr v* [I] to do something different from what you usually do 扩大〔兴趣、活动〕范围，开辟新的领域: *Don't be afraid to branch out and try new ideas.* 不要怕另辟蹊径，不妨尝试新的想法。| **branch out into (doing) sth** *Profits were falling until the bookstore branched out into selling CDs and cassettes.* 书店在扩大营业范围兼卖唱片和磁带之前，利润一直在下降。

brand[1] /brænd; brænd/ *n* [C] **1** a type of product made by a particular company 商标，牌子: [+of] *What brand of detergent do you use?* 你用什么牌子的洗涤剂？| **brand leader** (=the brand that sells the most) 主打品牌 | **brand loyalty** (=the tendency to always buy a particular brand) 品牌忠诚度 | **own brand** *BrE*【英】**store brand** *AmE*【美】(=made and sold by a particular store) 自有品牌 **2 brand of humour/politics/religion etc** a particular type of humour, politics etc 某种幽默/政治/宗教等: *a strange, macabre brand of humour* 一种怪异而可怕的幽默 **3** a mark made or burned on an animal's skin that shows who it belongs to〔标明牲畜所属的〕烙印 **4** *literary* a piece of burning wood【文】一块燃烧着的木头 **5** *poetic* a sword【诗】剑

brand[2] *v* [T] **1** to describe someone or something as a very bad type of person or thing, often unfairly 给〔某人〕加上不公的污名: **brand sb as** *You can't brand all football supporters as hooligans.* 你不能给所有的足球迷都加上流氓的恶名。| **brand sb a liar/cheat/whore etc** *In those days, any unmarried mother was branded a whore.* 那时候，任何未婚妈妈都会被加上淫妇的臭名。| **brand sb for life** *Stealing that money has branded Jim for life – no-one will trust him again.* 吉姆终生背上了偷钱的罪名，再没有人信任他。**2** [usually passive 一般用被动态] to make a mark on something, especially by burning, in order to show who it belongs to 给〔某物〕打上烙印〔以标明其主人〕: **brand sth with sth** *Each cow was branded with the ranch's logo.* 每头母牛都烙上了该牧场的标志。

brand·ed /ˈbrændɪd; ˈbrændɪ̣d/ *adj* [only before noun 仅用于名词前] a branded product is made by a well known company and has the company's name on it 有品牌(标志)的

branding i·ron /ˈ· ,··/ *n* [C] a piece of metal that is heated and used for burning marks on cattle or sheep, to show who they belong to〔在牲畜身上烙印用的〕烙铁

bran·dish /ˈbrændɪʃ; ˈbrændɪʃ/ *v* [T+at] to wave something around in a dangerous or threatening way, especially a weapon (威胁性地)挥舞〔尤指武器〕: *A man leapt out brandishing a kitchen knife.* 有一个男人跳了出来，挥舞着一把菜刀。

brand name /ˈ· ,·/ *n* [C] the name given to a product by the company that makes it; TRADE NAME〔某商品的〕商标名称，商品名

brand-new /,· ˈ·◂/ *adj* new and completely unused 全新的，崭新的，未用过的

Bran·do /ˈbrændo; ˈbrændəʊ/, **Mar·lon** /ˈmɑrlən; ˈmɑːlən/ (1924-2004) a US actor who many people think is one of the best actors in the history of the cinema. His films include *The Wild One, On the Waterfront, The Godfather*, and *Apocalypse Now*. 白兰度〔(1924-2004)，美国演员，被认为是电影史上最出色的演员之一，出演过的影片有《野蛮人》、《码头风云》、《教父》和《现代启示录》〕

Brands Hatch /ˌbrændz ˈhætʃ; ˌbrændz ˈhætʃ/ a motor-racing CIRCUIT in Kent, England 布兰兹哈奇环形汽车赛道〔位于英格兰的肯特郡〕

bran·dy /ˈbrændɪ; ˈbrændi/ *n* [C,U] a strong alcoholic drink made from wine, or a glass of this drink (一杯)白兰地(酒)

brandy but·ter /ˈ·· ,··/ *n* [U] a mixture of butter, sugar, and BRANDY, usually eaten with CHRISTMAS PUDDING〔通常和圣诞布丁一起吃的〕白兰地黄油

Bran·son /ˈbrænsn̩; ˈbrænsən/, **Richard** (1950-) a British businessman who started the Virgin companies, which include a record company, an AIRLINE, a financial services company, and a train company 布兰森〔(1950-)，英国企业家，曾创办维珍集团，包括一家唱片公司、一家航空公司、一家金融服务公司和一家铁路运输公司〕

Bran·ston Pick·le /ˌbrænstn̩ ˈpɪkl; ˌbrænstən ˈpɪkəl/ *trademark* a type of CHUTNEY, which is very popular in the UK and is often eaten in SANDWICHEs with cheese.【商标】布兰斯顿酸辣酱〔英国畅销的一种酸辣酱，常与乳酪一起夹在三明治中食用〕

Braque /brɑk; brɑːk/, **Georges** (1882-1963) a French painter who worked with Picasso and was one of those who

started the movement known as CUBISM 布拉克〔(1882-1963)，法国画家，曾与毕加索合作，是立体主义绘画运动的发起人之一〕

brash /bræʃ; bræʃ/ *adj* **1** behaving too confidently and speaking too loudly 无礼的，自以为是的；急躁的，莽撞的：*Brash, noisy journalists were crowding around the ambassador.* 粗鲁吵闹的记者拥挤着围在大使身边。**2** a brash building, place, or object attracts attention by being very colourful, large, exciting etc 醒目的；刺眼的：*The painting was bold, brash and modern.* 这幅画大胆、醒目，而且现代。—**brashly** *adv* —**brashness** *n* [U]

Bra·sil·i·a /brəˋzılıə; brəˈzılıə/ the capital city of Brazil. Brasilia is a new city, which was built in 1960 巴西利亚〔巴西首都，新兴城市，始建于1960年〕

brass /bræs; brɑːs/ *n*

1 ▶METAL 金属◀ [U] a very hard bright yellow metal that is a mixture of COPPER (1) and ZINC 黄铜〔铜锌合金〕: **brass bed/knob/button etc** *an old brass bedstead* 老式铜床架

2 the brass (section) the people in an ORCHESTRA or band who play musical instruments made of brass, such as the TRUMPET[1] (1), horn etc〔管弦乐队等的〕铜管乐器部

3 have the brass *informal* to have the self-confidence and lack of respect to do something that is rude【非正式】厚着脸皮，厚颜无耻：**have the brass to do sth** *I didn't think she'd have the brass to tell him to his face.* 我认为她不会厚着脸皮当面告诉他。

4 ▶DECORATIONS 装饰◀ [C,U] an object made of brass, usually with a design cut into it, or several brass objects 黄铜饰品，黄铜器

5 ▶IN CHURCH 教堂里◀ [C] a picture and writing on brass, placed on the wall or floor of a church in memory of someone who died〔为纪念已故者而嵌在教堂地板上或挂在墙壁上刻有肖像等的〕黄铜纪念牌

6 get down to brass tacks *informal* to start talking about the real business of a meeting【非正式】言归正传，谈实质性问题，谈正事

7 ▶PEOPLE IN TOP JOBS 身居高位者◀ the brass *AmE informal* people who hold the most important positions【美，非正式】要员；TOP BRASS *BrE*【英】

8 it's brass monkeys/brass monkey weather *BrE spoken* used to say that it is very cold【英口】极其寒冷：*It's brass monkeys out there today.* 今天外边特别冷。

9 ▶MONEY 钱◀ [U] *BrE informal* money【英，非正式】钱

10 brass hat *especially BrE slang* a military officer with a high rank【尤英，俚】高级军官 —see also 另见 **as bold as brass** (BOLD (2))

brass band /ˌ· ˈ·/ *n* [C] a band consisting mostly of brass musical instruments such as TRUMPETS, horns etc 铜管乐队

> **CULTURAL NOTE 文化注释**
> When British people think of brass bands, they often think of the industrial towns of the North of England, where brass bands are very popular. In the US, brass bands are popular with older people, and are often part of street processions. 英国人想到铜管乐队，会联想到英格兰北部的工业城镇，那里铜管乐队很受欢迎。铜管乐队在美国受到一些年长的人喜爱，常在街道游行中出现。

brassed off /ˌbræst ˋɔf; ˌbrɑːst ˈɒf/ *adj BrE informal* tired and annoyed【英，非正式】厌倦的，厌烦的：[+**with**] *I'm really brassed off with the way he treats me.* 我真厌倦了他这样对我。

bras·se·rie /ˌbræsəˋrı; ˈbræsəri/ *n* [C] a cheap, informal restaurant usually serving French food〔出售法国食品的〕啤酒店，小餐馆

bras·si·ere /brəˋzır; ˈbræziə/ *n* [C] *formal* a BRA【正式】乳罩，胸罩

brass knuck·les /ˌ· ˈ· ·/ *n* [plural] *AmE* a set of metal rings worn over your KNUCKLES, used as a weapon【美】指节铜套〔一种武器〕；KNUCKLE-DUSTER *BrE*【英】

brass rub·bing /ˈ· ˌ· ·/ *n* [C,U] the act of making a copy of a BRASS (5) in a church by putting a piece of paper over it and rubbing it with a soft pencil, or a picture made in this way〔对黄铜纪念牌上的文字等进行的〕拓印，摹拓

brass·y /ˋbræsı; ˈbrɑːsi/ *adj* **1** yellowish in colour like BRASS (1) 黄铜色的 **2** sounding hard and loud like the sound made by a BRASS (2) musical instrument 声音像铜管乐器的 **3** a woman who is brassy is too loud, confident, or brightly dressed〔妇女〕吵吵嚷嚷的，说话无礼的；打扮艳丽的：*Who's that brassy woman with Les?* 和莱思在一起的泼妇是谁？

brat /bræt; bræt/ *n* [C] *informal* a child, especially a badly behaved one【非正式】小坏蛋，淘气鬼：**spoilt/spoiled brat** *That kid of theirs is a real spoilt brat.* 他们那个孩子真是个宠坏了的淘气鬼。

Bra·ti·sla·va /ˌbrætıˋslɑvə; ˌbrætiˈslɑːvə/ the capital city of Slovakia 布拉迪斯拉发〔斯洛伐克首都〕

Braun /braun; braʊn/, **E·va** /ˋevə; ˈeıvə/ (1910-45) a German Nazi who married Adolf Hitler in 1945 and then killed herself at the same time as he did 布劳恩〔(1910-1945)，德国纳粹分子，1945年与阿道夫·希特勒成婚，后来与他一起自杀〕

bra·va·do /brəˋvado; brəˈvɑːdəʊ/ *n* [U] behaviour that is deliberately intended to show how brave and confident you are 故作勇敢，逞强的行动，虚张声势：*youthful bravado* 年轻人的逞强行为

brave[1] /brev; breıv/ *adj* **1** facing danger, pain, or difficult situations with courage and confidence 勇敢的，无畏的：*a brave cancer victim* 勇敢的癌症患者 | *It was very brave of you to tell her the truth.* 你真勇敢，把事实真相告诉了她。**2** very good 美好的，极好的：*his original brave intentions* 他本来的善意 | **a brave attempt** *Fran didn't win, but it was a brave attempt.* 弗兰没有赢，但这是一次很好的尝试。**3 put on a brave face/front** to pretend that you are happy when you are really very upset 强装欢笑 —**bravely** *adv* 3

brave[2] *v* [T] to deal with a difficult, dangerous, or unpleasant situation 勇敢地面对：*Braving their parents' displeasure, they announced their engagement.* 他们不顾父母的不满，宣布订婚。| **brave the elements** (=go out in bad weather) 在恶劣的天气下外出，顶风冒雨

brave sth ↔ **out** *phr v* [T] to deal bravely with something that is frightening or difficult 勇敢地应对

brave[3] *n* **1** [plural] brave people 勇士：*Today we remember the brave who died in the last war.* 我们今天来纪念那些在上次战争中英勇牺牲的人。**2** [C] a young fighting man from a Native American tribe 印第安部落的青年武士

Brave New World /ˌ· · ˈ·/ a NOVEL written in 1932 by the British writer Aldous Huxley, which imagines an advanced society of the future in which many people seem to have easy and pleasant lives, but in fact no one has any freedom. This phrase, which was first used in Shakespeare's play *The Tempest*, is now used to describe any society like this.《美丽新世界》〔英国作家奥尔德斯·赫胥黎1932年创作的小说，其中虚构了一个先进的未来社会，人们看似过着无忧无虑的幸福生活，但事实上却没有任何自由。该短语最早出现在莎士比亚的戏剧《暴风雨》中，现用来形容诸如此类的社会〕

brav·e·ry /ˋbrevərı; ˈbreıvəri/ *n* [U] actions, behaviour, or an attitude that shows courage and confidence 勇敢的行为[态度]；勇气：*an act of great bravery* 大无畏的行为

bra·vo /ˋbrɑvo; ˈbrɑːvəʊ/ *interjection* used to show your approval when someone, especially a performer, has done something very well 好〔表演精彩时的喝彩声〕：*Bravo! Encore!* 好极了！再来一个！

bra·vu·ra /brəˋvjurə; brəˈvjʊərə/ *n* [U] **1** the act of showing a lot of skill in the way you perform, write, paint etc, especially when you do something very difficult 出色的演出[写作，绘画等] **2** the act of showing great courage 气势磅礴，雄壮

braw /brɔ; brɔː/ *adj ScotE*【苏格兰】**1** a braw woman is beautiful, especially because she is big and strong 漂亮的〔尤指高大、健壮的女人〕**2** braw weather is good〔天气〕晴朗的

brawl[1] /brɔl; brɔːl/ *n* [C] a noisy quarrel or fight among a group of people, especially in a public place〔尤指在公共场所的〕争吵；打(群)架：*a drunken brawl in the street* 街上的酒后殴斗 —**brawler** *n* [C]

brawl[2] *v* [I] to quarrel or fight in a noisy way, especially in a public place〔尤指在公共场所〕打(群)架；争吵

brawn /brɔn; brɔːn/ *n* [U] **1** physical strength, especially when compared with intelligence 体力：*Mina has the brains, I have the brawn.* 明娜有头脑，我有体力。**2** *BrE* meat from a pig's head that has been boiled and pressed in a container and is often served in thin flat pieces【英】〔用猪头肉煮成的〕碎肉冻；HEADCHEESE *AmE*【美】

brawn·y /ˋbrɔnı; ˈbrɔːni/ *adj* very large and strong 强壮的；肌肉发达的：*His brawny arms glistened with sweat.* 他强壮的胳膊上汗水闪闪发光。

bray /bre; breı/ *v* [I] **1** if a DONKEY brays, it makes a loud sound〔驴〕发出叫声 **2** if someone brays, they laugh or talk in a loud, slightly unpleasant way 发出近似驴叫的声音 —**bray** *n* [C] —**braying** *adj*

bra·zen[1] /ˋbrezn̩; ˈbreızən/ *adj* **1** behaving in an immoral way without being embarrassed or ashamed 厚颜无耻的，恬不知耻的：**a brazen hussy** (=a woman who behaves this way, especially sexually) 不知羞耻的荡妇 **2 brazen lie/attitude** a lie or

bad attitude that is shocking because the person responsible is not ashamed of it 无耻的谎言/态度 **3** *literary* having a shiny yellow colour【文】黄铜色的, 金黄色的

brazen² *v*

brazen sth ↔ **out** *phr v* [T] to deal with a situation that is difficult or embarrassing for you by appearing to be confident rather than ashamed〔面对困难或尴尬的处境时〕厚着脸皮干

bra·zen·ly /ˈbreznlɪ; ˈbreɪzənli/ *adv* without showing or feeling any shame 厚颜无耻地: *She brazenly admitted she had spent the night with Greg.* 她厚颜无耻地承认那天晚上她和格雷格在一起。

bra·zi·er /ˈbreʒɚ; ˈbreɪziə/ *n* [C] a metal container that holds a fire and is used to keep people warm in the outside〔供人们取暖的〕火盆

Bra·zil /brəˋzɪl; brəˈzɪl/ the largest country in South America. Population: 174,469,000 (2001). Capital: Brasilia. 巴西〔南美最大国家。人口: 174,469,000 (2001), 首都: 巴西利亚〕

Braz·za·ville /ˈbræzəˌvɪl; ˈbræzəvɪl/ the capital city of the Republic of Congo 布拉柴维尔〔刚果共和国首都〕

W3 **breach¹** /britʃ; briːtʃ/ *n* **1 breach of the law/rules/agreement etc** an action that breaks a law, rule, or agreement between people, groups, or countries 违反[破坏, 不履行]法律/规章/协议等: *a clear breach of the 1994 Trade Agreement* 明显违背1994年的贸易协议 | **be in breach of sth** *We will expel any member found to be in breach of the rules.* 我们将开除任何被发现违反规定的成员。| **breach of contract** *If they fail to deliver the goods, we will sue them for breach of contract.* 如果他们不发货, 我们就控告他们违约。**2 breach of confidence/trust/etiquette etc** an action that breaks the rules of what people consider good or moral behaviour 泄密/失信/违反礼节等: *Bond shook the Queen's hand in a deliberate breach of etiquette.* 邦德和女王握手时故意违反礼节。| *The company regards revealing confidential information as a serious breach of trust.* 公司把泄露机密资料视为严重的背信弃义行为。**3** [C] a serious disagreement between people, groups, or countries with the result that they do not have a good relationship any more〔友好关系的〕破裂, 裂痕: *Britain could not risk a breach with the US over sanctions.* 在制裁问题上, 英国不会冒与美国决裂之险。| **heal the breach** (=make people etc stop disagreeing and be friends again) 修补裂痕, 重归于好 **4 breach of the peace** *BrE law* an action such as fighting that annoys people in a public place【英, 法律】扰乱治安 **5 step into the breach** to help by doing someone else's job or work when they are suddenly unable to do it 代理别人的工作 **6** [C] a hole or broken place in a wall or similar structure, especially one made during a military attack〔尤指被炮火轰开的〕缺口, 破洞: *a breach in the castle wall* 城堡墙上被攻破的缺口 **7 a breach of security/duty etc** the result of someone breaking a system, not doing their duty etc 违反安全原则/失职等: *There had been a major breach of security at the air base.* 在空军基地发生了一宗严重违反安全规则的事故。

breach² *v* [T] **1** to break a hole in a wall or similar structure so that something can pass through 攻破, 在…造成缺口: *The storm had breached the sea wall in two places.* 风暴在海堤上造成两处缺口。**2** to break a law, rule, agreement etc 违背, 违反〔法律、规定、协议等〕: *The committee ruled that Payne was guilty of breaching the rules on sponsorship.* 委员会裁定佩恩违反了赞助规则。

S2 W3 **bread** /brɛd; bred/ *n* [U] **1** a common important food made from flour, water, and YEAST 面包: *Would you like some bread with your soup?* 你喝汤时要吃点面包吗? | **a loaf of bread** (=a large piece of bread that you buy and cut into pieces) 一条面包 | **a slice of bread** (=a thin piece of bread that you cut from a loaf) 一片面包 | **white/brown bread** (=bread baked with white or brown flour) 白/黑面包 **2** *old-fashioned* money【过时】钱 **3 your/sb's bread and butter** *informal* the work that provides you with most of the money that you need in order to live【非正式】某人的生计; 某人的谋生之道: *I don't write just for fun – it's my bread and butter.* 我写作并非只为了乐趣, 它是我的谋生之道。**4 earn your (daily) bread** to earn the money that you need in order to live 谋生, 挣钱糊口 **5 know which side your bread is buttered on** to know who to be nice to in order to get advantages for yourself 知道该奉迎谁以谋求自己的利益 —see also 另见 FRENCH BREAD, SLICED BREAD

bread-and-but·ter /ˌ· · ˈ· ·◂/ *adj* [only before noun 仅用于名词前] **bread-and-butter question/issue** *BrE* a question that is concerned with the most important and basic things【英】生计问题; 最基本的问题: *bread-and-butter political issues such as jobs and housing* 就业和住房等有关民生的政治问题

bread·bas·ket /ˈbrɛdˌbæskɪt; ˈbredˌbɑːskɪt/ *n* **1** [C] a basket for holding or serving bread 面包篮 **2** [singular] the part of a country or other large area that provides most of its food 重要的产粮区, 粮仓: *Zambia could be the breadbasket of Africa.* 赞比亚可能成为非洲重要的产粮区。

bread bin /ˈ· ·/ *n* [C] *BrE* a container for keeping bread in so that it stays fresh【英】〔用来保持面包新鲜的〕面包箱[盒] —see picture on page A10 参见A10页图

bread·board /ˈbrɛdˌbɔrd; ˈbredbɔːd/ *n* [C] a wooden board on which you cut bread 切面包板 —see picture at 参见 BOARD¹ 图

bread·box /ˈ· ·/ *n* [C] *AmE* a BREAD BIN【美】面包箱[盒]

bread·crumbs /ˈbrɛdˌkrʌmz; ˈbredkrʌmz/ *n* [plural] very small pieces of bread left after cutting bread, or deliberately prepared for cooking 面包屑: *Coat the fish with breadcrumbs and fry in a little oil.* 把鱼裹上面包屑, 然后放入少量油里煎。

bread·ed /ˈbrɛdɪd; ˈbredɪd/ *adj* covered in breadcrumbs 沾满面包屑的: *breaded plaice* 沾满面包屑的鲽鱼

bread·fruit /ˈbrɛdˌfrut; ˈbredfruːt/ *n* [C,U] a large tropical fruit that looks like bread 面包果

bread·line /ˈbrɛdˌlaɪn; ˈbredlaɪn/ *n* **1 be/live on the breadline** to be extremely poor 非常穷, 勉强维持生活 **2 be near/below the breadline** to be quite poor or extremely poor, according to official standards 接近/低于最低生活标准线

breadth /brɛdθ; bredθ/ *n* **1** [C,U] the distance from one side of something to the other; width 宽度; 阔度: *What is the breadth of this room?* 这个房间有多宽? | **5 metres/3 feet etc in breadth** *The boat measured eight feet in breadth.* 船的宽度为八英尺。—compare 比较 LENGTH (1), WIDTH (1) **2 breadth of vision/mind/outlook etc** an ability to consider and understand a range of ideas, attitudes, and customs that are very different from your own 眼光广阔/心胸开阔/看法全面等: *a statesman with the breadth of vision of Abraham Lincoln* 像亚伯拉罕·林肯那样有远见卓识的政治家 **3** [U] the fact or quality of including a great variety of people, subjects etc 广博, 渊博; 广度: *a novel of the breadth and magnitude of Tolstoy's 'War and Peace'* 像托尔斯泰的《战争与和平》那样气势恢宏的长篇小说 **4** [C,U] the quality of being very large from one side to the other 幅员辽阔, 广阔: *the breadth of the ocean* 广阔的海洋 —see also 另见 BROAD, HAIR'S BREADTH, **the length and breadth of** (LENGTH (6))

breadth·ways /ˈbrɛdθˌwez; ˈbredθweɪz/ also 又作 **breadth·wise** /-ˌwaɪz; -waɪz/ *adj, adv* with the broad side nearest to the person who is looking at it 横向的[地]; 横着的[地]: *The box should fit in the case breadthways.* 这盒子应该横着放进大箱子。

bread·win·ner /ˈbrɛdˌwɪnɚ; ˈbredˌwɪnə/ *n* [C] the member of a family who earns the money to support the others 挣钱养家的人

S1 W1 **break¹** /brek; breɪk/ *v past tense* **broke** /brok; brəʊk/ *past participle* **broken** /ˈbrokən; ˈbrəʊkən/

1 ►IN PIECES 成片◄ **a)** [T] to make something separate into two or more pieces, for example by hitting it, dropping it, or bending it 使破裂, 打碎; 折断: *The thieves got in by breaking a window.* 窃贼破窗而入。| **break sth in two/in half/into pieces etc** *He broke the roll in two and handed a piece to me.* 他把面包卷掰成两半, 递了一块给我。**b)** [I] to separate into two or more pieces 破裂〔成两部分或更多块〕, 破碎; 断裂: *The frames are made of plastic and they tend to break easily.* 这些框架是塑料制的, 很容易碎裂。

2 ►PART OF YOUR BODY 身体的部分◄ [T] to damage part of your body, especially a bone, and make it split into two or more pieces 骨折, 摔断: *She fell downstairs and broke her hip.* 她摔下了楼, 髋部骨折。

3 ►NOT WORKING 不能再用◄ **a)** [T] to damage something such as a machine so that it cannot work or be used 损坏, 弄坏, 摔坏: *Someone's broken my camera – I can't get it to focus properly.* 不知道是谁摔坏了我的照相机, 我无法调准焦距。| *There's no point in buying him expensive toys, he'll only break them.* 不用给他买贵重的玩具, 他只会把它们弄坏。**b)** [I] if something such as a part of a machine breaks, it stops working〔机器部件等〕失灵, 坏了: *I think the spring's broken.* 我觉得是弹簧断了。

4 ►SURFACE/SKIN 表面/皮肤◄ [I,T] if the surface of something breaks or if you break it, it splits or gets a hole in it 弄破…的表面, 裂开, 破损: *The seal on the jar did not seem to have been broken.* 罐子的密封条似乎没有打开过。

5 ►RULE/LAW ETC 规定/法律等◄ [T] to disobey a rule, law etc 不遵守, 触犯: *Anyone who rides a motorbike without a helmet is breaking the law.* 骑摩托车不戴头盔是违法的。

6 ►PROMISE/AGREEMENT 诺言/协议◄ **break a promise/break an agreement/break your word** to not do what you have promised to do or signed an agreement to do 违背诺言/违反协议/食言: *I felt I had to take her to the film – I didn't want to break my promise.* 我认为必须带她去看电影, 我不想食言。

7 break free/break loose to escape from someone or somewhere by using force 用力挣脱; 逃跑: *I managed to break free by elbowing him in the stomach.* 我用胳膊肘顶他的肚子设法逃脱了。

8 break loose if violent feelings or a violent situation breaks loose, they suddenly start to happen 迸发, 爆发: **all hell broke loose** (=people started behaving in a wild, uncontrolled way) 乱作一团 *The moment the shot rang out all hell broke loose.* 枪响时人们乱作一团。

9 break even to neither make a profit nor lose money 不赔不赚, 不盈不亏, 收支相抵: *Things have been so bad we'll be lucky if we break even.* 情况很糟糕, 如果我们能不赔不赚, 就算幸运了。

10 break a habit to stop wanting to keep doing something, especially something that you should not do 改掉某习惯〔尤指坏习惯〕: *Smoking is a difficult habit to break.* 吸烟是一个难以改掉的习惯。

11 why break the habit of a lifetime? *humorous spoken* used when telling someone that you expect that they will behave in the same way that they have always done, and make the same mistakes【幽默, 口】你不总是这样吗? (为什么要改掉你毕生的习惯呢?): *"I'd better hurry up or I'll be late." "Why break the habit of a lifetime?"* "我得抓紧时间, 不然就迟到了。" "你不总是这样吗?"

12 break sb's heart to make someone very unhappy by ending a relationship with them or by doing something that they do not want you to do 使某人伤心[心碎]: *He's really good looking – I expect he broke all the girls' hearts when he was at school.* 他的确很帅, 我猜想他上学时伤尽了女孩子的心。| *It'll break your father's heart if you tell him you're giving up college.* 如果你告诉你爸爸不上大学了, 他会很伤心。

13 you're breaking my heart/it's breaking my heart *humorous spoken* used when saying jokingly that you are very sad about something, even though you are not【幽默, 口】你/它真让我心痛

14 break your neck *spoken* to hurt yourself very badly, especially by falling onto the ground【口】摔坏, 跌伤〔尤指摔倒在地〕: *The path was really icy and I was lucky I didn't break my neck.* 小路结满了冰, 我很幸运没摔着。

15 I'll break his/her neck *spoken* used when threatening to hurt someone because you are very angry about what they have done【口】我要打扁他/她: *If I get hold of the guy who hit my car I'll break his neck.* 如果我抓到撞我车的那个家伙, 我会打扁他。

16 break the back of to finish the main or worst part of something 完成…的主要的[最艰难的]部分: *The engineers are confident they have broken the back of the problem.* 那些工程师相信他们已经克服了难关。

17 break your back *spoken* to work very hard to try and do something【口】拼死拼活地干; 尽最大的努力: *We've been breaking our backs trying to get the work done on time.* 我们一直在拼命干, 争取如期完成任务。

18 break sb's fall to stop someone from falling straight onto the ground, so that they are not badly hurt 阻止某人摔倒, 使某人免于受伤: *Luckily some trees at the bottom of the cliff broke his fall.* 幸运的是, 悬崖底下的树挡住了他, 使他免于受伤。

19 break a record to do something even faster or even better than the previous best time, amount etc 破纪录: *Christie has broken his own European record in the 100 meters.* 克里斯蒂打破了他自己保持的 100 米欧洲纪录。| **break all records** (=to be much better or much more successful than anything before) 突破以前的纪录 *This year's sales performance is expected to break all records.* 今年的销售成绩有望突破以前的纪录。

20 break for lunch/coffee/dinner etc to stop for a short time in order to have lunch, a drink etc 休息 (一段时间) 吃午饭/喝咖啡/吃晚饭等: *At 12.30 we'll break for lunch, and start again at 2 o'clock.* 12点半, 我们休息吃午饭, 两点钟再开始干。

21 break sb's concentration/flow/train of thought to interrupt someone and stop them from being able to continue thinking or talking about something 分散某人的注意力; 打断某人的谈话/思路: *I never listen to music when I'm working – it breaks my concentration.* 我工作时从不听音乐, 那样会分散我的注意力。

22 ►END A SITUATION 终止某情况◄[T] to stop an unpleasant situation from continuing 结束, 终止, 打破: **break the monotony** *We took turns driving, in order to try and break the monotony.* 我们轮流开车, 以打破旅途的单调。| **break the deadlock/stalemate** (=end a situation in which an agreement or a solution cannot be found) 打破僵局 *a way of ending the deadlock in Bosnia* 打破波斯尼亚僵局的方法

23 break a strike to force workers to end a STRIKE² (1) 迫使〔工人〕结束罢工: *threats to use the army to break the 10-month-old strike* 威胁动用武力结束长达 10 个月的罢工

24 break the silence/calm to end a period of silence or calm by talking or making a noise 打破寂静/平静: *The silence was broken by a burst of machine-gun fire.* 一阵机枪声打破了沉寂。

25 break your silence to start talking about something in public after refusing to do so for a long time 打破沉默: *She has finally broken her silence about the divorce.* 她终于打破沉默, 谈起自己离婚的事。

26 break your links/ties/connection etc to end your connection or relationship with a person, group, organization etc 断绝关系: *The US broke all diplomatic links with North Korea for a 3 month period.* 美国中止了和朝鲜的所有外交联系长达三个月。

27 break sb to completely destroy someone's chances of success or make them feel that they cannot continue 断送了某人的前程, 毁了某人: *the scandal that finally broke him* 最终毁了他的丑闻

28 break sb's spirit/resolve to make someone stop trying to achieve something, or start doing what you want 瓦解某人的士气/决心: *They could not break her spirit.* 他们无法瓦解她的士气。

29 break ranks to behave differently from the other members of a group, who are expecting you to support them 不支持所属的团体: *No one in the party was prepared to break ranks and vote against their leader.* 党内所有的成员都准备团结一致, 全投领导人的票。

30 break the ice a) to make people who have just met each other less nervous and more willing to talk, for example at a party or meeting 打破沉默 [冷场]: *Sharon tried to break the ice by suggesting that we all play a game.* 沙伦想打破沉默, 建议我们玩个游戏。**b)** to do something that shows you want to end an argument, quarrel etc 为结束争端而努力: *Yeltsin offered a ceasefire to the rebels in an attempt to break the ice.* 叶利钦向反叛者提出停火建议, 试图结束争端。

31 it won't break the bank used to say that you can afford to buy something 花得起钱: *It's time we had a holiday, and it won't break the bank.* 我们该去度假了, 出得起这钱。

32 break the bank to win more money in a game of cards than a CASINO or a DEALER (3) is able to pay you 赢了 (庄家) 全部的钱

33 break fresh/new ground to do something completely new that no one has ever done before, or find out new information about a subject 开辟新的领域; 作出新发现: *Researchers claim they are breaking new ground and are getting closer to discovering the causes of the disease.* 研究者声称他们正在作出新的发现, 即将找出这种疾病的诱因。

34 break cover to move out of a place where you have been hiding so that you can be seen 从隐藏处出来: *One of the rhinos broke cover and charged straight at them.* 一头犀牛突然窜出, 直向他们冲来。

35 break camp to pack tents and other equipment and leave the place where you have been camping 开拔, 拔营

36 ►DAY/DAWN 白天/黎明◄[I] if the day or the dawn breaks, light starts to shine in the sky (天) 刚亮, 破晓: *We arrived at Narita just as the dawn was breaking.* 天刚蒙蒙亮, 我们就到达成田机场。

37 ►STORM 暴风雨◄[I] if a storm or the MONSOON breaks, it suddenly begins 来临, 突然出现: *Bonington's team were nearing the summit when the monsoon broke.* 鲍宁顿的小组即将到达顶峰时, 季风突然来临。

38 ►WEATHER 天气◄[I] if the weather breaks, it suddenly changes 突变

39 ►WAVE 波浪◄[I] if a wave breaks, the top part starts to fall down, usually because it is hitting or getting near the shore 落下; 冲击: *waves breaking against the foot of the cliffs* 海浪拍打着峭壁的底部

40 ►VOICE 嗓门◄[I] if a boy's voice breaks, it becomes lower and starts to sound like a man's voice〔男孩发育时的嗓音〕变低变粗, 变声: *I was in the school choir until my voice broke.* 变声前我一直是学校合唱队队员。

41 ►NEWS 新闻◄[I] if news about an important event breaks, it finally becomes known 传开: *The Watergate scandal was about to break.* 水门事件丑闻很快就要被传开。

42 ►CODE 代码◄ [T] to succeed in understanding what the letters or numbers in a secret CODE[1] (4) mean 破解, 破译: *Polish scientists broke the Enigma code shortly before World War II.* 就在第二次世界大战爆发前不久, 波兰科学家破译了"谜"密码。
43 break wind to allow gas to escape from your BOWELS, making a noise and an unpleasant smell; FART[1] (1) 放屁
44 break (sb's) serve to win a game in tennis when your opponent is serving (SERVE[1] (10))〔网球〕破对方发球(局)得分: *Courier broke Sampras' serve in the first game of the third set.* 库里耶在第三盘第一局破了桑普拉斯的发球局。
45 break! used when telling BOXERS or WRESTLERS to stop fighting〔告诉拳击手或摔跤手〕分开!
46 break a leg! *humorous spoken* used to wish someone good luck【幽默, 口】祝你走运!

break away *phr v* [I] **1** to leave a group or political party to form another group, usually because of a disagreement〔从团体或政党中〕脱离出去: **[+from]** *The Nottingham miners broke away from the NUM to form their own union.* 诺丁汉矿工脱离了全国矿工总会, 组成了自己的工会。**2** to move away from someone or something〔从…〕逃脱, 挣脱, 逃离: **[+from]** *They kissed, then she broke away from him and ran to the window.* 他们吻了一下, 然后她从他怀里挣脱, 向窗子跑去。

break down *phr v*
1 ►MACHINE 机器◄ [I] if a large machine, especially a car, breaks down, it stops working 停止运转, 出故障: *The elevators in this building are always breaking down.* 这幢楼里的电梯总出故障。
2 ►FAIL 失败◄ [I] if a discussion, system etc breaks down, it fails because there are problems 失败, 遭受挫折: *Peace talks have broken down over the question of reparations.* 和谈因战后赔款问题而破裂。
3 ►DOOR 门◄ [T **break** sth ↔ **down**] if you break down a door, you hit it so hard that it breaks and falls to the ground 弄坏, 打破
4 ►CHANGE FIXED IDEAS 改变固有想法◄ [T **break** sth ↔ **down**] to change the fixed ideas or feelings that someone or a group of people have so that they agree with yours 改变〔某人固有的观点〕: *It'll be difficult to break down their prejudices about lesbians.* 很难改变他们对女同性恋者的固有偏见。
5 ►CHANGE CHEMICALLY 化学变化◄ [I,T] if a substance breaks down or something breaks it down, it changes as a result of a chemical process (把…) 分解: **break** sth ↔ **down** *Bacteria break down the animal waste to form methane gas.* 细菌把动物粪便分解形成沼气。
6 ►CRY 哭喊◄ [I] to be unable to stop yourself crying, especially in public 感情失去控制, 失声痛哭〔尤指在公共场合〕: *If I go to the funeral, I'll break down.* 要是去参加葬礼, 我会忍不住痛哭。
7 ►BECOME ILL 生病◄ [I] to become mentally or physically ill 精神崩溃; 身体垮掉: *If Tim carries on working like this, he'll break down sooner or later.* 如果蒂姆还继续这样工作, 他迟早会崩溃。
8 ►MAKE STH SIMPLE 使某事物变得简单◄ [T **break** sth ↔ **down**] to separate something such as a job or report into parts, especially so that it is easier to do or understand 把…分类, 把…分成: *a recipe that breaks down the making of creme brulee into simple steps* 把做蛋奶冻分成几个简单步骤的烹饪法 —see also 另见 BREAKDOWN (4)

break for sth *phr v* [T] *AmE* to suddenly run or drive somewhere, especially in order to escape from someone【美】突然跑向, 将车开到(某地)〔尤指想逃跑〕: *Sharkey broke for the exit, but got nabbed.* 夏基跑向出口, 但被抓住了。

break in *phr v* **1** [I] to enter a building by using force, in order to steal something 闯入〔行窃〕: *Someone broke in and took several computers.* 有人闯入屋内, 偷走了几台电脑。—see also 另见 BREAK-IN **2** [T **break** sb/sth ↔ **in**] to make a person or animal get used to a certain way of behaving or working 使习惯于; 驯〔动物〕: *Don't worry about doing the accounts, we'll break you in gently.* 不要担心做会计工作, 我们会让你慢慢熟悉的。**3** [I] to join a conversation by interrupting someone or saying something suddenly 打断, 插嘴: **[+with]** *Dad would occasionally break in with a suggestion.* 爸爸总会不时插话, 提出建议。| **[+on]** *Sorry to break in on you, but your wife is on the line.* 对不起, 打断一下, 你的妻子打电话找你。**4** [T **break** sth ↔ **in**] to make new shoes or boots less stiff and more comfortable, by wearing them 使〔新鞋〕逐渐舒适合脚

break into sth *phr v* [T]
1 ►STEAL 偷窃◄ to enter a building by using force, in order to steal something 闯入〔行窃〕: *Thieves broke into the bank vault by digging a tunnel.* 窃贼挖了一个通道闯入银行金库。
2 break into a run/gallop/trot etc to suddenly start running etc 突然奔跑: *Suzie heard footsteps behind her and broke into a run.* 苏茜听到身后有脚步声拔腿就跑。
3 break into a sweat to start sweating (SWEAT[2] (1)) 开始出汗: *The game was over before I'd even broken into a sweat!* 我还没有出汗, 比赛就结束了!
4 ►NEW BUSINESS ACTIVITY 新的商业活动◄ to become involved in a new activity, especially a business activity 参与〔尤指商业活动〕: *British Airways is trying to break into the American market.* 英国航空公司正设法打入美国市场。
5 ►MONEY 金钱◄ to start to spend money that you did not want to spend (勉强) 动用一部分: *We'll have to break into the £500 your dad gave us.* 我们不得不动用你爸爸给的500英镑。
6 ►INTERRUPT 打断◄ to interrupt an activity by saying or doing something 打扰, 打断: *Sorry to break into your lunch hour, but I must speak to you urgently.* 对不起, 打扰你们吃午饭了, 我有要紧事要说。
7 break into tears/laughter/cheers etc to suddenly start crying, laughing etc 突然大哭/大笑/欢呼起来等

break sb **of** sth *phr v* [T] to make someone stop having a bad habit 使某人改掉〔坏习惯〕: *What can we do to break him of sucking his thumb?* 我们怎样才能使他改掉吮大拇指的习惯?

break off *phr v* **1** [I,T] to suddenly stop doing something, especially talking to someone (使) 突然结束, 中断〔尤指谈话〕: *Fay told her story, breaking off now and then to wipe the tears from her eyes.* 费伊讲述自己的故事, 不时停下来擦擦眼里的泪水。| **break sth ↔ off** *I broke off the conversation and answered the phone.* 我中断了谈话去接电话。**2** [T **break** sth ↔ **off**] to stop a relationship 中止〔关系〕, 断绝: **break off relations/an engagement** *Britain was about to break off diplomatic relations with Libya.* 英国正要和利比亚断绝外交关系。**3** [T] to break a piece from the main part of something (使) 折断: **break sth ↔ off** *I broke off a piece of bread.* 我掰下一块面包。| **break sth off sth** *Why don't you break a branch off the tree and make a walking stick?* 你为什么不折下一根树枝当手杖?

break out *phr v* [I]
1 ►WAR/FIRE ETC 战争/火灾等◄ if something unpleasant such as a fire, war, or disease breaks out, it starts to happen〔不愉快之事〕爆发, 突然发生: *Several scuffles broke out in the crowd.* 人群中发生了几场混战。
2 ►ESCAPE 逃跑◄ to escape from a prison or similar place 逃出: **[+of]** *a plan to break out of jail* 越狱计划 —see also 另见 BREAKOUT
3 ►CHANGE YOUR LIFE 改变生活◄ to change the way you live or behave, especially because you feel bored 改变生活方式: **break out of a routine/rut etc** *I've got to break out of the same old dull routine or I'll go crazy.* 我必须摆脱老套的常规, 不然我会疯的。
4 break out in spots/a rash etc if you break out in spots etc, a lot of red spots appear on your skin 出疹子: *Talcum powder makes me break out in a rash.* 爽身粉使我浑身长满了疹子。
5 break out in a sweat to start sweating (SWEAT[2] (1)) 出汗

break through *phr v* **1** [I,T] to force a way through something 突破; 突围: **break through sth** *At dawn 300 tanks prepared to break through the enemy lines.* 拂晓时, 300辆坦克准备突破敌人的防线。**2** [I,T] if the sun or light breaks through, you can see it through something such as clouds or mist〔太阳或光从云雾中〕透出 **3** [T **break through** sth] to deal successfully with something, especially unreasonable behaviour or bad feelings 克服〔尤指不合理行为或不好的感觉〕: *How could I break through his reserve?* 我该怎样做才能让他开口呢? —see also 另见 BREAKTHROUGH

break up *phr v*
1 ►BREAK INTO PIECES 碎成片◄ [I,T] to break or make something break into many small pieces 打碎; 碎开; 断开: *The stricken tanker began to break up on the rocks.* 油船触礁后开始断裂。| **break sth ↔ up** *Jim started to break the ice up on the frozen lake.* 吉姆开始砸碎湖面上结的冰。
2 ►SEPARATE 分开◄ [T **break** sth ↔ **up**] to separate something into several smaller parts 把…分成几部分: *I want to plant more bushes to break up the garden a bit.* 我想多种一点矮树丛把花园隔成几部分。
3 ►FIGHT 打架◄ [I,T] if a fight etc breaks up or someone breaks it up, the people stop fighting each other 停止; 制止〔斗殴〕: **break** sth ↔ **up** *Three policemen were needed to break up the fight.* 需要三名警察制止这场斗殴。| **break up a demonstration/meeting etc** *The army is on hand to break up any demonstrations against the regime.* 部队随时可以制止反对政权的示威活动。

4 ►MARRIAGE/ORGANIZATION 婚姻/组织◄[I,T] if a marriage, group of people, or organization breaks up, the people in it separate and do not live or work together any more 破裂; 解散, 瓦解: *If a parent dies, the family may break up.* 如果父母中有一人去世, 这个家可能就散了。—see also 另见 BREAKUP (1)

5 ►CROWD 人群◄[I] if a crowd or meeting breaks up, people start to leave 散开, 散场

6 ►SCHOOL 学校◄[I] *BrE* if a school or the students of a school break up, they begin a holiday【英】开始放假: [+for] *When do you break up for Easter?* 你们什么时候开始放复活节假?

7 ►MAKE SB LAUGH 引某人笑◄[T] *AmE* to say or do something that is so funny that people cannot stop laughing【美】使〔人〕捧腹大笑: **break sb up** *Hal really broke me up with that story about the alligator.* 哈尔讲的短吻鳄的故事让我笑破肚皮。

break with sb/sth *phr v* [T] **1** to leave a group of people or an organization, especially because you have had a disagreement with them 与…断绝关系; 与…决裂: **break with sb/sth over sth** *Powell broke with the Conservative Party over Europe.* 由于在欧洲问题上观点不一致, 鲍威尔与保守党断绝了来往。**2** **break with tradition/the past** to stop following old customs and do something in a completely different way 与传统/过去决裂

break² *n*

1 ►A REST 休息◄**a)** [C] a period of time when you stop what you are doing in order to rest, eat etc 小憩, 间歇, 中间休息: **without a break** *Larry had worked all day without a break.* 拉里一整天都在工作, 没有休息。| **tea/coffee/lunch break** *It's time for a coffee break.* 该喝杯咖啡休息一下了。| **have/take a break** *Let's take a ten minute break.* 让我们休息 10 分钟。**b)** [C] a short holiday 短暂的假期: **weekend break** *a travel agent specializing in weekend breaks* 专门办理周末度假的旅行社 | **the Easter/Christmas etc break** (=the public or school holiday at Easter etc) 复活节/圣诞节等假期 **c)** [U] also 又作 **break time** *BrE* the time during the school day when classes stop and teachers and students can rest, eat, play etc【英】课间休息; RECESS¹ (2) *AmE*【美】: *I'll speak to you at break.* 课间休息时我有话对你说。

2 ►A PAUSE IN STH 暂停◄**a)** [C] a period of several weeks or years during which something stops, before continuing again 休假: [+in] *a welcome break in my normal routine* 我正常公事中难得的休假 | **career break** *Demi Moore planned to take a career break to have children.* 黛米·摩尔计划暂停工作生孩子去。**b)** [C] a pause in a conversation or in what someone is saying〔谈话的〕暂停: [+in] *She waited for a break in the conversation.* 她等待谈话暂停。**c)** also 又作 **commercial break** a pause for advertisements during a television or radio programme 广告时间: *Join us again after the break.* 广告之后继续收看我们的节目。

3 ►END/CHANGE 结束/变化◄[singular] an occasion when you end a relationship with a person, organization etc, or change the way that things have always been done in the past 中止关系; 改变生活习惯: [+from] *Medieval thought represents a sharp break from that of the Greeks.* 中世纪思想意味着与古希腊思想的断然决裂。| [+with] *In a break with tradition, they held their wedding at home.* 他们打破传统, 在家举行婚礼。| **a clean break** (=a very clear and definite end to a relationship) 彻底断绝关系 *I don't want a messy divorce, just a quick, clean break.* 我不希望拖泥带水地离婚, 离就快点离, 彻底离。| **make the break** *She's wanted to leave Dave for years, and last week she finally made the break.* 她多年来都想离开戴夫, 上周她终于离开了。

4 ►A SPACE 空隙◄[C] a space between two things or between two parts of something 裂口, 裂缝; 破裂: *The sun shone through a break in the clouds.* 阳光从云层的缝隙中透出来。| **a break in the weather** (=a short period of good weather) 短时间的好天气

5 ►A CHANCE 机会◄[C] *informal* a sudden or unexpected chance to do something, especially be successful in your job【非正式】机会; (好) 运气: **big/lucky break** *My big break came when I was spotted singing in a club by a talent scout.* 我的好运来了, 我在俱乐部唱歌时被一位星探发现。

6 **make a break for sth** to suddenly start running towards something in order to escape from a place 向…方向逃去: *As soon as the guard's back was turned they made a break for the door.* 守卫刚一转过身, 他们就赶快向门口跑去。| **make a break for it** (=try to escape) 企图逃跑

7 ►BROKEN PLACE 破处◄[C] the place where a bone in your body has broken 骨折的地方: *It's a nasty break, the bone has splintered.* 骨折很严重, 骨头已裂成碎片。

8 **give sb/sth a break!** *spoken* used when you want someone to stop talking about something or doing something because it is annoying you【口】住口!; 住手!: *I'm sick of hearing about your problems. Just give it a break.* 你的问题我听厌了, 别说了。

9 **give me a break!** *AmE spoken* used when you do not believe something someone has said【美口】我才不信呢!

10 ►TENNIS 网球◄also 又作 **break of serve** [C] a situation in a game of tennis in which you win a game when your opponent is serving (SERVE¹ (10))〔网球〕破对方发球（局）得胜: **break point** (=the moment when if you win the point, you win a game) 赛点〔比赛中决定胜负的一刻〕

11 ►POINTS 分◄[C] the number of points won by a player when it is their turn to hit the ball in a game such as BILLIARDS or SNOOKER¹〔台球或彩色桌球〕在一次击球机会中连续得分

12 **the break of day** *literary* the time early in the morning when it starts getting light【文】黎明, 拂晓

break·a·ble /ˈbrekəbl; ˈbreɪkəbəl/ *adj* made of a material such as glass or clay that breaks easily 易破碎的

break·age /ˈbrekɪdʒ; ˈbreɪkɪdʒ/ *n* **1** **breakages** [plural] things that have been broken, especially things that belong to someone else that you must pay for 破损物: *a £5 deposit on hiring glasses, in case of breakages* 租眼镜时交五英镑押金以防毁坏 **2** [U] *formal* the act of breaking【正式】破损; 毁坏

break·a·way /ˈbrekəˌwe; ˈbreɪkəweɪ/ *adj* **breakaway group/party/movement** a breakaway group etc has been formed by people who left another group because of a disagreement 另立门户的集团/党/运动: *the breakaway state of Slovenia* 分离出来的斯洛文尼亚 —**breakaway** *n* [C]

break-dance /ˈbrekˌdæns; ˈbreɪkdɑːns/ *v* [I] to do a type of dance involving ACROBATIC movements 跳霹雳舞 —**breakdancing** *n* [U] —**breakdancer** *n* [C]

break·down /ˈbrekˌdaʊn; ˈbreɪkdaʊn/ *n* **1** [C,U] the failure of a system or relationship〔系统〕故障; 损坏;〔关系〕破裂: *Family breakdown can lead to behavioral problems in children.* 家庭破裂会导致孩子的行为出问题。| [+in] *a serious breakdown in relations between the two countries* 两国关系的严重破裂 | [+of] *the gradual breakdown of authority* 权威的逐渐丧失 **2** also 又作 **nervous breakdown** [C] a serious medical condition in which someone becomes mentally ill and is unable to deal with even the simplest situations 精神崩溃: **have/suffer a breakdown** *After the trial Paul had a breakdown.* 审讯后, 保罗崩溃了。**3** [C] an occasion when a car or a piece of machinery breaks and stops working〔汽车或机器〕故障 **4** [C] a written statement explaining the details of something such as a bill or the cost of a plan 分类, 分析: [+of] *Can you prepare a full breakdown of labour costs?* 你能准备一份详细的劳工成本分类清单吗?

breakdown truck /ˈ‥ ˌ‥/ also 又作 **breakdown lor·ry** /ˈ‥ ˌ‥/ *n* [C] *BrE* a vehicle with special equipment used to pull a car that does not work to a place where it can be repaired【英】〔拖走抛锚汽车的〕牵引车, 拖车; TOWTRUCK *AmE*【美】

break·er /ˈbrekə; ˈbreɪkə/ *n* [C] a large wave with a white top that rolls onto the shore〔冲击岸边带有白色浪头的〕碎浪, 浪花

break-e·ven /ˈbrekˈivən; ˌbreɪkˈiːvən◂/ *n* [U] the level of business activity at which a company is making neither a profit nor a loss 不赔不赚; 收支平衡: **breakeven point** *The firm should reach breakeven point after one year.* 一年后这家公司应该达到收支平衡点。—see also 另见 **break even** (BREAK¹ (9))

break·fast /ˈbrɛkfəst; ˈbrekfəst/ *n* [C,U] the meal you have in the morning 早餐: **have sth for breakfast** *We had coffee and toast for breakfast.* 我们早餐喝咖啡, 吃烤面包片。| **working breakfast** (=a breakfast at which you talk about business) 工作早餐 —see also 另见 BED AND BREAKFAST, CONTINENTAL BREAKFAST, **make a dog's breakfast/dinner of sth** (DOG¹ (8)) —**breakfast** *v* [I +on]

CULTURAL NOTE 文化注释

In Britain, people often eat CEREALs such as CORNFLAKES with milk for breakfast. Some people like to have TOAST with MARMALADE or JAM, and they drink a cup of coffee or tea, or a glass of orange juice. Some hotels, cafes, and B AND B's serve a 'full English breakfast', a cooked meal consisting of eggs, BACON, and SAUSAGEs with GRILLed tomatoes or MUSHROOMS and sometimes BAKED BEANS. On cold days, some people like to have PORRIDGE for breakfast. Porridge used to be eaten mostly in Scotland, but it is now popular in all parts of the UK. 英国人早餐一般吃牛奶和玉米片等谷类食品。一些人喜欢吃烤面包片加柑橘酱或果酱, 喝一杯咖啡、茶或橙汁。有的宾馆、咖啡厅和供应早餐的住宿机构提供"全套英式早餐", 包括鸡蛋、熏猪肉、香肠配烤土豆或蘑菇, 有时还有烘豆。天冷的时候, 有的人

喜欢早餐喝麦片粥。以前主要是苏格兰人喝麦片粥，现在麦片粥在英国各地都很流行。

In the US, most people eat cereals such as cornflakes with milk for breakfast and they drink a cup of coffee or a glass of orange juice. Toast, BAGELs, or TOASTed ENGLISH MUFFINs are also popular. In the winter, some people might have hot cereals such as OATMEAL (=porridge) or CREAM OF WHEAT. If someone wants a bigger breakfast, they might have eggs, bacon or sausages and sometimes HASH BROWNS. People in the US also eat eggs, bacon, and sausages with PANCAKEs or WAFFLEs that are covered with butter and MAPLE SYRUP and served on the same plate as the meat and eggs. 大多数美国人早餐吃玉米片等谷类食品和喝牛奶，喝一杯咖啡或橙汁。烤面包片、面包圈和英式焙松饼也很常见。冬天一些人吃热麦片，如麦片粥或"营养麦片"。如果有人想早餐吃得丰富一点，他们会吃鸡蛋、熏猪肉、香肠，有时还有土豆饼。美国人一般吃鸡蛋、熏猪肉、香肠，还有上覆奶油与槭糖浆的烤薄饼或华夫饼干，与肉和蛋盛放在同一个盘子里。

breakfast tel·e·vi·sion /,·· '···/ *n* [U] *BrE* television programmes that are broadcast in the early part of the morning 【英】晨播电视节目

break-in /'· ·/ *n* [C] an act of entering a building illegally and by force, especially in order to steal things〔尤指为盗窃〕非法强行进入，闯入: *Since the break-in we've had all our locks changed.* 自从上次有人非法闯入后，我们换了所有的锁。—see also 另见 **break in** (BREAK[1])

breaking and en·ter·ing /,·· '···/ *n* [U] *law* the crime of entering a building illegally and by force【法律】破门侵入(罪)

break·neck /ˈbrekˌnɛk; ˈbreɪknek/ *adj* **at breakneck speed** extremely and often dangerously fast 以危险的高速〔开车〕

break·out /ˈbrekˌaʊt; ˈbreɪkaʊt/ *n* [C] an escape from a prison, especially one involving a lot of prisoners 逃脱，(结伙)越狱；突围

break·through /ˈbrekˌθru; ˈbreɪkθruː/ *n* [C] an important new discovery in something you are studying, especially one made after trying for a long time 突破；重大进展: **make a breakthrough** *Scientists have made a major breakthrough in the treatment of cancer.* 科学家在癌症治疗上取得了重大突破。

break·up /ˈbrekˌʌp; ˈbreɪkʌp/ *n* [C,U] **1** the act of ending a marriage or relationship〔婚姻或关系的〕破裂: *the consequences of marital breakup on children* 婚姻破裂对孩子的影响 **2** the separation of a group, organization, or country into smaller parts, especially because it has become weaker or there are serious disagreements 分裂；解散；分离；瓦解；崩溃: [+of] *the breakup of the Soviet Union* 苏联的解体

break·wa·ter /ˈbrekˌwɔtɚ; ˈbreɪkˌwɔːtə/ *n* [C] a large strong wall built out into the sea to protect the shore from the force of the waves 防波堤: *forming a natural breakwater against the sea* 形成一道抵御海浪的天然防波堤

breast[1] /brɛst; brest/ *n*

1 ▶PART OF A WOMAN'S BODY 妇女身体的部位◀ [C] one of the two round raised parts of a woman's body that produce milk when she has a baby 乳房: *a woman with a baby at the breast* 正在给婴儿哺乳的妇女 | *breast cancer* 乳腺癌 —see picture at 参见 BODY 图

2 ▶CHEST 胸部◀ [C] the part of your body between your neck and your stomach, especially the upper part of this area 胸部，胸口: *Dick cradled her photograph against his breast.* 迪克把她的照片轻轻贴在胸前。

3 ▶PART OF A BIRD 鸟的部位◀ [C] the front part of a bird's body 胸脯: *a robin with a red breast* 红色胸脯的知更鸟

4 ▶MEAT 肉◀ [U] meat that comes from the front part of the body of a bird such as a chicken 胸脯肉: *turkey breast* 火鸡胸脯肉

5 make a clean breast of it/things to admit that you have done something wrong 和盘托出，完全供认，坦白: *Why not make a clean breast of it and tell them you took the money?* 为什么不和盘托出，告诉他们是你拿的钱?

6 single-breasted/double-breasted a coat, dress etc that is single-breasted etc has one or two rows of buttons down the front〔衣服〕单排扣/双排扣的

7 bare-breasted/small-breasted/red-breasted etc having bare etc breasts 袒胸的/小胸脯的/红色胸脯的等

8 ▶EMOTIONS 感情◀ [C] *literary* where your feelings of sadness, love, anger, fear etc come from【文】胸怀；心情，内心: *a troubled breast* 心烦意乱 —see also 另见 **beat your breast** (BEAT[1] (28))

breast[2] *v* [T] **1** to reach the top of a hill or slope 登上〔山顶〕 **2** to push against something with your chest 以胸部触；挺胸面对

breast·bone /ˈbrɛstˋbon; ˈbrestbəʊn/ *n* [C] a long flat bone in the front of your chest to which the top seven pairs of RIBS[1] (1) are connected 胸骨 —see picture at 参见 SKELETON 图

breastfeed /ˈbrɛstˌfid; ˈbrestfiːd/ *v past tense and past participle* **breastfed** /-ˌfɛd; -fed/ [I,T] to feed a baby with milk from your breast rather than from a bottle 用母乳喂养，哺乳 —compare 比较 SUCKLE, NURSE[2] (6)

breast·plate /ˈbrɛstˌplet; ˈbrestpleɪt/ *n* [C] a leather or metal protective covering worn over the chest by soldiers during battles in former times〔古时士兵打仗时穿的〕护胸甲，胸铠

breast-pock·et /,· '·· / *n* [C] a pocket on the outside of a shirt or JACKET (1), above the breast 胸前口袋

breast·stroke /ˈbrɛstˌstrok; ˈbrest-strəʊk/ *n* [U] a way of swimming in which you push your arms out and then bring them back in a circle towards you while bending your knees towards your body and then kicking out 蛙泳

breath /brɛθ; breθ/ *n* S3 W2

1 ▶AIR YOU BREATHE 呼吸的气◀ **a)** [U] the air that you take in and out of your lungs when you breathe 气息，呼吸: *Paul smelt the cigarette smoke on her breath.* 保罗闻到她的呼吸中带烟草味。| **bad breath** (=breath that smells unpleasant) 口臭 **b)** the process of breathing in and out 呼吸(过程): *Her breath was coming more easily now.* 她的呼吸现在顺畅多了。**c)** [U, singular] the air in your lungs or the act of breathing it in 一口气，(一次)呼吸: *Let your breath out slowly.* 慢慢地呼气。| **take a (big/deep) breath** (=breathe in once)（深深地）吸一口气 *Shaun took a deep breath and dived in.* 肖恩深深地吸了口气，然后跳入水中。| **be out of breath** (=have difficulty breathing because you have just been running, climbing stairs etc) 上气不接下气 | **get your breath back** (=breathe normally again after running or making a lot of effort) 喘过气来 *At the top of the stairs she stopped to get her breath back.* 她到了楼梯顶时停下来喘口气。| **short of breath** (=unable to breath easily, especially because you are unhealthy) 呼吸急促，喘不过气〔尤指不适时〕

2 a breath of fresh air a) something that is new and different in a way you find exciting and enjoyable 一股新风，新的活力: *Osborne's play brought a breath of fresh air to the British theatre.* 奥斯本的戏剧给英国戏剧界带来了生气。**b) take a breath of fresh air** to go outside because it is unpleasantly hot where you are〔去户外〕呼吸新鲜空气

3 hold your breath a) to breathe in and close your mouth to keep the air in your lungs 屏住呼吸: *I just held my breath and prayed I wouldn't sneeze.* 我屏住呼吸，祈求自己不要打喷嚏。**b)** to wait anxiously to see what is going to happen 屏息以待: *We held our breath while Mr Evans read the exam results.* 埃文斯先生宣读考试成绩时，我们都屏息而听。

4 take your breath away to be so beautiful or exciting that you feel as if you nearly stop breathing〔因美丽或激动〕使人目瞪口呆，使大吃一惊: *a view that takes your breath away* 美得让人惊讶的景色

5 under your breath in a quiet voice so that no one can hear you 低声地: *"Son of a bitch," he muttered under his breath.* "畜生。"他低声说。

6 in the same breath a) used to say that someone has said two things at once that are so different from each other they cannot both be true 连着说〔自相矛盾的话〕: *They said that women should have equal pay, and added in the same breath that men need more money.* 他们说妇女应得到同样的报酬，接着又说男人需要更多的钱。**b)** if you mention two people or things in the same breath, you show that you think they are alike 归于同一类，非常相像: *a player who has been mentioned in the same breath as Pete Sampras* 和皮特·桑普拉斯相提并论的运动员

7 with your last/dying breath at the moment when you are dying 临终时: *With his last breath he cursed his captors.* 他临终时诅咒捉拿他的人。

8 a breath of air/wind *literary* a slight movement of air【文】一丝微风: *Scarcely a breath of air disturbed the stillness of the day.* 整天几乎没有一丝风。

9 be the breath of life to sb to be the most important thing in someone's life 某人生命中最重要的东西，不可缺少的东西 —see also 另见 **with bated breath** (BATED), **catch your breath** (CATCH[1] (23)), **draw breath** (DRAW[1] (23)), **gasp for breath** (GASP[1] (2)), **save your breath** (SAVE[1] (15)), **waste your breath** (WASTE[2] (2))

breath·a·lyse *BrE*【英】, **breathalize** *AmE*【美】/ˈbrɛθəˌlaɪz; ˈbreθəlaɪz/ *v* [T] to make someone breathe into a special piece

of equipment in order to see if they have drunk too much alcohol【美】对…作呼气测醉检查

breath·a·lys·er *BrE*【英】, **breathalyzer** *AmE*【美】 /ˈbrɛθəˌlaɪzɚ; ˈbreθəlaɪzə/ *n* [C] *trademark* a piece of equipment used by the police to see if drivers have drunk too much alcohol【商标】呼气测醉器

3 3 **breathe** /brið; briːð/ *v*

1 ▶**AIR** 空气◀ [I,T] to take air into your lungs and send it out again 呼吸: *When you get an asthma attack you can't breathe.* 哮喘病发作时你会喘不过气来。| *People are concerned about the quality of the air they breathe.* 人们关注他们呼吸的空气的质量。| **breathe deeply** (=take in a lot of air) 深深地吸口气

2 ▶**BLOW** 吹◀ [I,T] to blow air or smoke out of your mouth 呼气; 喷出…气味: [**+on**] *Roy breathed on his hands and rubbed them together vigorously.* 罗伊向双手哈了一口气, 然后用力相搓。| **breathe sth over sb** *The fat man opposite was breathing garlic all over me.* 对面那个胖男人冲我呼气, 满是大蒜味。

3 **breathe again/more easily** to relax because something dangerous or frightening has finished 松一口气: *The all-clear was given and we could breathe again.* 解除空袭警报的信号发出了, 我们可以松口气了。

4 **breathe a sigh of relief** to no longer be worried about something that had been worrying or frightening you 轻松地舒了口气

5 **be breathing down sb's neck** to pay very close attention to what someone is doing in a way that makes them feel nervous or annoyed 紧盯某人; 严密监视某人: *How can I concentrate with you breathing down my neck all the time?* 你总是这样盯着我, 我怎么能集中精力?

6 **not breathe a word** to not tell anyone anything at all about something, because it is a secret 不透露风声: *Don't breathe a word, it's supposed to be a surprise.* 不要把这事说出去, 让别人有个惊喜。

7 ▶**WINE** 酒◀ [I] if you let wine breathe, you open the bottle to let the air get to it before you drink it 透气; 散发香味

8 ▶**SAY STH QUIETLY** 轻声说◀ [T] to say something very quietly, almost in a whisper 轻声说话, 低语: *"Wait," he breathed.* "等一下。"他轻声说。

9 **breathe your last** *literary* to die【文】断气, 死

10 **breathe life/excitement/enthusiasm into sth** to change a situation so that people feel more excited or interested 给…注入生命/刺激/热情: *Let's hope Doug can breathe a bit of life into these rather dull people.* 让我们希望道格能给这些沉闷的人们注入新的活力。

11 **breathe fire** to behave and talk very angrily 发火

breathe in *phr v* **1** [I] to take air into your lungs 吸气: *The doctor made me breathe in while he listened to my chest.* 医生听诊我的胸部时要我吸气。**2** [T **breathe** sth ↔ **in**] to breathe air, smoke, a particular kind of smell etc into your lungs 把〔空气、烟雾等〕吸入肺中: *They may be in danger of breathing in asbestos dust.* 他们有吸入石棉尘埃的危险。

breathe out *phr v* **1** [I] to send air out from your lungs 呼气: *Jim breathed out deeply.* 吉姆深深地呼了一口气。**2** [T **breathe** sth ↔ **out**] to send out air, oxygen, a particular kind of smell etc 排出〔某种气体〕: *Green plants breathe out oxygen in sunlight.* 在阳光下, 绿色植物排出氧气。

breath·er /ˈbriðɚ; ˈbriːðə/ *n* **have/take a breather** *informal* to stop what you are doing for a short time in order to rest【非正式】休息一下, 喘一口气 —see also 另见 HEAVY BREATHER

breath·ing /ˈbriðɪŋ; ˈbriːðɪŋ/ *n* [U] the process of breathing air in and out 呼吸: **heavy breathing** (=loud breathing) 沉重的呼吸 *When I picked up the phone all I heard was heavy breathing.* 我拿起电话, 只听到沉重的呼吸声。

breathing space /ˈ· · ·/ *n* [C,U] a short time when you stop doing something difficult, tiring etc, so that you have time to think more clearly about a situation 喘息的时间; 歇息的机会

breath·less /ˈbrɛθlɪs; ˈbreθləs/ *adj* **1** having difficulty breathing, especially because you are very tired, excited, or frightened 气喘吁吁的, 喘不过气来的: *The long climb left Jan feeling breathless.* 长时间的攀登使简感到喘不过气来。**2** unpleasantly hot with no fresh air or wind 使人窒息的, 令人透不过气的: *the breathless heat of a midsummer night in Rome* 罗马仲夏夜令人透不过气的炎热 —**breathlessly** *adv* —**breathlessness** *n* [U]

breath·tak·ing /ˈbrɛθˌtekɪŋ; ˈbreθˌteɪkɪŋ/ *adj* very impressive, exciting, or surprising 使人兴奋的, 激动人心的, 惊险的; 令人惊叹的: *the breathtaking natural beauty of the rain forests* 热带雨林令人惊叹的自然美景 | *a man of quite breathtaking stupidity* 令人惊愕的愚蠢之人 —**breathtakingly** *adv*

breath test /ˈ· ·/ *n* [C] a test in which the police make a car driver breathe into a special bag to see if he has drunk too much alcohol 呼气测醉试验

breath·y /ˈbrɛθɪ; ˈbreθi/ *adj* if someone's voice is breathy, you can hear their breath when they speak〔尤指嗓音〕带有气音的, 带喘息声的

Brecht /brɛkt; brekt/, **Ber·tolt** /ˈbɝtolt; ˈbɜːtəʊlt/ (1898-1956) a German writer of plays and poetry. He is famous for writing plays such as *The Threepenny Opera*, *The Caucasian Chalk Circle*, and *Mother Courage*, which deal with political ideas and are similar in form to ancient Greek plays. 布莱希特〔(1898-1956), 德国剧作家、诗人, 尤以《三分钱歌剧》、《高加索灰阑记》、《大胆妈妈》等剧作闻名。他的戏剧涉及政治观点, 形式同古希腊戏剧类似〕—**Brechtian** *adj*: *a Brechtian style* 布莱希特风格

Brec·on Bea·cons, the /ˌbrɛkən ˈbikənz; ˌbrekən ˈbiːkənz/ a mountainous area and national park between South and Mid Wales 布雷肯比肯斯山国家公园〔位于威尔士南部和中部之间的山区国家公园〕

breech birth /ˈbritʃ ˌbɝθ; ˈbriːtʃ bɜːθ/ also 又作 **breech de·liv·e·ry** /ˈ· ·, · · ·/ *n* [C] a birth in which the lower part of a baby's body comes out of its mother first 臀位分娩

breech·es /ˈbrɪtʃɪz; ˈbrɪtʃɪz/ *n* [plural] short trousers that fasten just below the knees〔长及膝盖的〕束脚短裤; 马裤: *riding breeches* 马裤

breed[1] /brid; briːd/ *v past tense and past participle* **bred** /brɛd; bred/ **1** [I] if animals breed they have babies〔动物〕繁殖, 下崽, 下蛋: *Eagles breed during the cooler months of the year.* 鹰在一年中较凉爽的季节繁殖。**2** [T] to keep animals or plants in order to produce babies or new plants, or in order to develop new or better animals or plants 育种, 饲养繁殖; 培植; 改良〔品种〕: *commercially bred animals* 商业化繁殖的动物 **3** [T] to cause a particular feeling or condition 引起; 酿成, 招致〔一般指不良之事〕: *living conditions that breed violence and despair* 产生暴力与绝望的生活条件 **4** **breed like rabbits** to produce a lot of babies quickly, especially more than you think is desirable 生太多的孩子 —see also 另见 WELL-BRED 3

breed[2] *n* [C] **1** a type of animal or plant, especially one that people have kept to breed, such as cats, dogs, and farm animals〔尤指人工培育的动植物〕品种: *Spaniels are my favourite breed of dog.* 西班牙猎犬是我最喜欢的一种狗。**2** a particular kind of person or type of thing〔人或物的〕某种类型: **a rare/dying breed** *Honest salesmen are a rare breed nowadays.* 如今诚实的推销员已非常难得。| **a new breed of** *the first of a new breed of satellites* 第一颗新型人造卫星

breed·er /ˈbridɚ; ˈbriːdə/ *n* [C] someone who breeds animals or plants as a job 育种者; 饲养者; 繁殖者; 栽培者: *a dog breeder* 育狗人

breed·ing /ˈbridɪŋ; ˈbriːdɪŋ/ *n* [U] **1** the act or process of animals producing babies 生殖, 繁殖: **breeding season** (=the time of the year when an animal has babies) 繁殖季节 **2** the activity of keeping animals or plants in order to produce new or better types 培育, 育种: *the breeding of pedigree dogs* 纯种狗的繁育 | **breeding stock** (=animals you keep to breed from) 种畜 **3** polite social behaviour that someone learns from their family 教养: *The young lieutenant had an air of wealth and good breeding.* 这位年轻中尉具有富有人家受过良好教育的气度。

breeding ground /ˈ· · ·/ *n* [C] **1** a place or situation where something bad or harmful grows and develops〔尤指坏事物的〕滋生地, 温床: [**+for**] *overcrowded slums that are breeding grounds for crime* 过分拥挤的贫民窟是滋生犯罪的温床 **2** a place where animals go in order to breed 繁殖场: *In spring, the birds migrate north to their breeding grounds.* 春天, 鸟儿迁徙到北方的繁殖地。

breeze[1] /briz; briːz/ *n* [C] **1** a gentle wind 微风, 和风: *flowers waving in the breeze* 在微风中摇曳的花朵 —see picture on page A13 参见 A13 页图 **2** **be a breeze** *informal* to be something that is very easy to do【非正式】是不费吹灰之力的事 —see also 另见 **shoot the breeze** (SHOOT[1] (8))

breeze[2] *v* [I always+adv/prep] to walk somewhere in a calm confident way 飘然出现; 信步走进: [**+in/into/out etc**] *She just breezed into my office and said she wanted a job.* 她信步走进我的办公室, 说想找份工作。

breeze through sth *phr v* [T] to finish a piece of work or pass an exam very easily 轻松完成; 轻松通过: *She breezed through the exam.* 她毫不费力地通过了考试。

breeze-block /ˈ· ·/ *n* [C] *BrE* a light brick used in building, made of CEMENT and CINDERS【英】煤渣混凝土空心砖, 煤渣砖; CINDER BLOCK *AmE*【美】

breez·y /ˈbrizɪ; ˈbriːzi/ *adj* **1** a breezy person is cheerful, confident, and relaxed 愉快的; 轻松自信的: *a breezy and relaxed air of confidence* 充满自信的轻松神情 **2** breezy weather is when the wind blows quite strongly〔天气〕有微风的 —**breezily** *adv* —**breeziness** *n* [U]

Bren gun /ˈbrɛn gʌn; ˈbren gʌn/ *n* [C] a light MACHINEGUN 布伦式轻机枪

Brer Rab·bit /ˌbrɛr ˈræbɪt; ˌbreə ˈræbɪ̤t/ the main character in the children's stories by Joel Chandler Harris. Brer Rabbit is a clever rabbit from the South of the US, who always manages to escape from danger or from being caught, usually by running into a BRIER PATCH (=group of bushes with sharp points on their branches). 兔子大哥〔乔尔·钱德勒·哈里斯所著儿童读物中的主人公。它是美国南部的一只机灵的兔子，常奔向荆棘丛中躲避危险或抓捕〕

breth·ren /ˈbrɛðrən; ˈbreðrən/ *n* [plural] *old-fashioned* a way of addressing or talking about the members of an organization or association, especially a religious group【过时】教友（们）; 会友（们）; 弟兄（们）

Breu·ghel —see 见 Pieter BRUEGEL

breve /briv; briːv/ *n* [C] *BrE* a musical note which continues for twice as long as a SEMIBREVE【英】〔乐曲的〕倍全音符，二全音符; DOUBLE WHOLE NOTE *AmE*【美】

bre·vi·a·ry /ˈbrivɪˌɛrɪ; ˈbriːviəri/ *n* [C] a prayer book used in the Roman Catholic church〔罗马天主教神职人员的〕每日祈祷书，简本大日课经

brev·i·ty /ˈbrɛvətɪ; ˈbrevɪ̤ti/ *n* [U] **1** the quality of expressing something in very few words 简洁，简练 **2** shortness of time 短暂，短促: *In the interests of brevity I will summarize my views.* 为简洁起见，我概述一下我的观点。

brew¹ /bru; bruː/ *v* **1** [T] to make beer 酿造〔啤酒〕 **2** [I, T] if tea or coffee brews or you brew it, you pour boiling water over it to make it ready to drink 冲，泡，沏 **3** [I] if something unpleasant is brewing, it will happen soon〔不快之事〕酝酿: *There's trouble brewing at work.* 工作中要有麻烦了。

brew up *phr v* [I] *BrE informal* to make a drink of tea【英，非正式】泡[沏]茶

brew² *n* [C] a drink such as tea or beer 酿造[冲泡]的饮料〈如茶或啤酒〉—see also 另见 HOME BREW

brew·er /ˈbruə; ˈbruːə/ *n* [C] a person or company that makes beer 酿啤酒者; 啤酒公司

Brew·er's /ˈbruəz; ˈbruːəz/ also 又作 **Brewer's Dictionary of Phrase and Fable** a British dictionary of phrases and stories, that first came out in 1870《布氏短语寓言词典》〔英国一本短语和寓言故事词典，首版于1870年〕

brew·er·y /ˈbruərɪ; ˈbruːəri/ *n* [C] a place where beer is made, or a company that makes beer 啤酒厂

Brezh·nev /ˈbrɛʒnɛf; ˈbreʒnef/, **Le·o·nid** /ˈliənɪd; ˈliːənɪd/ (1906-82) the leader of the Soviet Union from 1977 to 1982 勃列日涅夫〔(1906-1982)，1977年至1982年期间的苏联领导人〕

bri·ar, brier /ˈbraɪə; ˈbraɪə/ *n* **1** [C,U] a wild bush with prickly branches 欧石南，荆棘 **2** [C] a tobacco pipe made from a briar 欧石南根烟斗

bribe¹ /braɪb; braɪb/ *v* [T] to pay money to someone to persuade them to help you, especially by doing something dishonest 贿赂，收买: **bribe sb to do sth** *We bribed the doorman to let us in.* 我们贿赂守门人让我们进去。| **bribe sb for sth** *prisoners bribing guards for cigarettes* 贿赂狱警想要香烟的犯人

bribe² *n* [C] an amount of money or something valuable that you give someone to persuade them to help you or to do something dishonest 贿赂〔尤指钱〕: *a New York judge charged with accepting bribes* 一名被指控收受贿赂的纽约法官 —compare 比较 PAYOLA

brib·er·y /ˈbraɪbərɪ; ˈbraɪbəri/ *n* [U] dishonestly giving money to someone in order to persuade them to do something that will help you 行贿; 受贿: *We tried persuasion, bribery and threats, but the guard still wouldn't let us pass.* 我们试着说服警卫，贿赂他，威胁他，他就是不让我们过去。| *He was arrested on suspicion of accepting bribery.* 他因涉嫌受贿而被捕。| **bribery and corruption** (=bribery and dishonest behaviour) 贪污腐化

bric-a-brac /ˈbrɪk ə ˌbræk; ˈbrɪk ə ˌbræk/ *n* [U] small objects that are not worth very much money but are interesting or attractive 小饰品，小摆设

S2 W3 **brick**¹ /brɪk; brɪk/ *n* **1** [C,U] a hard block of baked clay used for building walls, houses etc 砖: *a brick wall* 砖墙 **2** [C] *BrE* a small square block of wood, plastic etc used as a toy【英】积木玩具 **3** [C] *old-fashioned* a good person who you can depend on when you are in trouble【过时】可靠的人，好心人: *Janet's a real brick.* 珍妮特是个真正可信赖的人。**4 you can't make bricks without straw** used to say you cannot do a job if you do not have the necessary materials 巧妇难为无米之炊 —see also 另见 **be banging your head against a brick wall** (BANG² (5)), **drop a brick** (DROP¹ (34)), **come down on sb like a ton of bricks** (TON (5))

brick² *v*

brick sth ↔ **off** *phr v* [T] to separate an area from a larger area by building a wall of bricks 用砖墙隔开: *Some of the rooms had been bricked off.* 有几间房已用墙隔开。

brick sth ↔ **up/in** *phr v* [T] to fill or close a space by building a wall of bricks in it 用砖堵住[围住]: *bricked up windows* 用砖堵住的窗户

Brick Lane /ˌ· ˈ·/ a road in the East End of London, which has a Sunday street market and many Indian restaurants which serve curry dishes. 布里克巷〔伦敦东区一条街，这里有一个周日街市和不少供应咖喱菜品的印度餐馆〕

brick·lay·er /ˈbrɪkˌleə; ˈbrɪkˌleɪə/ *n* [C] someone whose job is to build walls, buildings etc with bricks 泥瓦匠，砌砖工人 —**bricklaying** *n* [U]

brick·work /ˈbrɪkˌwɜk; ˈbrɪkwɜːk/ *n* [U] bricks, or the way they have been used to build a wall, house etc 砌砖工程; 砖建筑物;〔建筑物的〕砖结构: *The brickwork was cracked and in need of repair.* 砖墙出现裂缝，需要修补。

brick·yard /ˈbrɪkˌjɑrd; ˈbrɪkjɑːd/ *n* [C] a place where bricks are made 砖厂; 砖窑

brid·al /ˈbraɪdl; ˈbraɪdl/ *adj* **1** concerning a bride or a wedding 新娘的; 婚礼的: *a bridal car* 结婚花车 **2 the bridal party** the group of people who arrive at the church with the bride 随新娘一起去教堂的人 **3 bridal suite** a special set of rooms in a hotel for a newly married couple〔酒店中的〕新婚套房 **4 bridal shower** *AmE* a party for a woman who is going to be married, given by her friends and family【美】〔朋友和家人〕为即将出嫁的新娘举办的送礼会

bride /braɪd; braɪd/ *n* [C] a woman at the time she gets married or just after she is married 新娘: *You may kiss the bride.* 你可以吻新娘了。

bride·groom /ˈbraɪdˌgrum; ˈbraɪdgruːm/ also 又作 **groom** *n* [C] a man at the time he gets married, or just after he is married 新郎

Brides·head Re·vis·it·ed /ˌbraɪdzhɛd riˈvɪzɪtɪd; ˌbraɪdzhed riːˈvɪzɪ̤tɪ̤d/ a NOVEL by Evelyn Waugh, written in 1945. It is about a rich family who live in a large house in the country, and about upper-class young men at Oxford University in the 1920s.《旧地重游》〔伊夫琳·沃1945年创作的小说。故事写的是住在乡下大宅的一户有钱人家及20世纪20年代牛津大学上流社会的青年〕

brides·maid /ˈbraɪdzˌmed; ˈbraɪdzmeɪd/ *n* [C] a girl or woman, usually unmarried, who helps the bride on her wedding day and is with her at the wedding 女傧相; 伴娘

bride-to-be /ˌ· · ˈ·/ *n* [C] a woman who is going to be married soon 快要当新娘的女子，准新娘: *That's Jonathan's bride-to-be.* 那是乔纳森的准新娘。

bridge¹ /brɪdʒ; brɪdʒ/ *n* [C] S2 W2

1 ▶OVER A RIVER/ROAD ETC 在河/路等的上方◀ a structure built over a river, road etc, that allows people or vehicles to cross from one side to the other 桥，桥梁

2 ▶CONNECTION 连接◀ something that provides a connection between two things; LINK² (1)〔事物之间的〕桥梁，纽带，联系: *The training programme is seen as a bridge between school and work.* 该培训计划被视为学校与工作之间的桥梁。

3 ▶SHIP 船◀ the raised part of a ship from which the officers control it 船桥，舰桥，驾驶台

4 ▶CARD GAME 纸牌戏◀ [U] a card game for four players who play in pairs 桥牌

5 the bridge of your nose the bony upper part of your nose between your eyes 鼻梁

6 ▶PAIR OF GLASSES 眼镜◀ the part of a pair of glasses that rests on the bridge of your nose〔眼镜的〕鼻托，鼻梁架 —see picture at 参见 GLASS¹ 图

7 ▶MUSICAL INSTRUMENT 乐器◀ a small piece of wood under the strings of a VIOLIN or GUITAR, used to keep them in position〔弦乐器的〕弦柱，弦马，琴马

8 ▶FOR TEETH 用于牙齿的◀ a small piece of metal for keeping false teeth in place〔假牙上的〕齿桥 —see also 另见 **build bridges** (BUILD¹ (7)), **burn your bridges** (BURN¹ (22)), **cross that bridge when you come to it** (CROSS¹ (8)), **be (all) water under the bridge** (WATER¹ (7))

bridge² *v* [T] **1** to build or form a bridge over something 在…上架桥: *a fallen tree bridging the stream* 倒下来横跨在小溪上

的树 **2 bridge the gap (between)** to reduce or get rid of the difference between two things 弥合差距: *an attempt at bridging the economic gap between North and South* 旨在弥合南北经济差距的努力

bridge·head /ˈbrɪdʒˌhɛd; ˈbrɪdʒhed/ *n* [C] a strong position far forward in enemy land from which an army can go forward or attack 桥头堡, 桥头阵地

Bridget Jones's Diary /,·· ˈ··ˈ··/ a NOVEL by British writer Helen Fielding. The character Bridget Jones is a British woman in her 30s, who drinks wine, smokes a lot of cigarettes and writes about her troubles in her DIARY.《BJ单身日记》〔英国作家海伦·菲尔丁所著的小说, 主人公布里奇特·琼斯是一位30来岁的英国女士, 她酗酒、抽烟, 经常把自己的烦心事写在日记里〕

Bridge·town /ˈbrɪdʒˌtaʊn; ˈbrɪdʒtaʊn/ the capital city and main port of Barbados, on the southwest coast of the island 布里奇敦〔巴巴多斯首都和主要港口, 位于该岛国的西南沿岸〕

bridging loan /ˈ··, ·/ *n* [C] *BrE* an amount of money lent by a bank to cover the period between buying a new house and selling the old one【英】〔银行提供的短期〕过度性贷款

bri·dle¹ /ˈbraɪdl; ˈbraɪdl/ *v* **1** [T] to put a bridle on a horse 给〔马〕套上笼头 **2** [I,T] to show you are angry about something, especially by making a sudden upward movement of your chin〔对…〕表示愤怒〔尤指猛然昂首〕: *She bridled at his autocratic tone.* 她扬起头对他的专断口气嗤之以鼻。

bridle² *n* [C] a set of leather bands put around a horse's head and used to control its movements 马笼头; 马勒 —see picture at 参见 HORSE¹ 图

bridle path /ˈ·· ·/ also 又作 **bri·dle·way** /ˈbraɪdlˌwe; ˈbraɪdlweɪ/ *n* [C] a path intended for horse-riding, and not suitable for cars〔不能通车的〕骑马专用道

Brie /bri; briː/ *n* [U] a soft French cheese 布里干酪〔法国产的一种软干酪〕

brief¹ /brif; briːf/ *adj*

1 ▶TIME 时间◀ continuing for a short time 短时间的; 短暂的: *a brief visit* 短暂的访问

2 have a brief word to have a short conversation 说几句话: *Could I have a brief word with you, Mr Thomas?* 托马斯先生, 我能和你说几句话吗?

3 be brief to say or write something using only a few words, especially because there is little time 长话短说

4 ▶SPEECH/LETTER 演讲/信◀ using very few words or including few details 简洁的, 简明的: *a brief note of thanks* 简短的感谢信

5 in brief a) in as few words as possible 简而言之; 简单地说: *We should, in brief, invest heavily in digital systems.* 简而言之, 我们应该大量投资于数字系统。 **b)** without any details 粗略地, 梗概地: *a report in brief* 简报

6 someone who is brief does not say very much to someone, often in a rude way 唐突无礼的;〔说话〕草草的: *She was very brief with me when I asked about the contracts.* 当我问她合同的事, 她只草草说了两句。

7 ▶CLOTHES 衣服◀ clothes which are brief are short and cover only a small area of your body 短的, 暴露的: *a very brief bikini* 非常暴露的比基尼泳装

brief² *n* [C] **1** official instructions that explain what someone's job is, what their duties are, how they should behave etc 简短命令, 工作指示: *The architects's brief is to design an extension that is modern but blends with the rest of the building.* 建筑师指示扩建部分建筑物的设计既要现代, 又要与其余的建筑物保持和谐。 **2** a short spoken or written statement giving facts about a law case 案情摘要, 案情简介 **3 briefs** [plural] men's or women's underwear worn on the lower part of the body 贴身短内裤, 三角裤

brief³ *v* [T] to give someone all the necessary information about a situation, so that they are prepared for it 作简单的指示; 为…提供资讯: **brief sb on sth** *The president has been fully briefed on the current situation in Haiti.* 总统已掌握了有关海地当前局势的情况。—compare 比较 DEBRIEF

brief·case /ˈbrifˌkes; ˈbriːfkeɪs/ *n* [C] a case used for carrying papers or documents 公文包, 公事包 —see picture at 参见 SUITCASE 图

Brief En·coun·ter /,· ·ˈ··/ a British film by David Lean made in 1945, from a play by Noel Coward. It is a love story, about a HOUSEWIFE and a doctor, who fall in love but then decide to separate. It is remembered especially for the romantic scenes in a railway station and is known for its realism and artistic filming.《相见恨晚》, 又译《偶遇》〔英国影片, 由大卫·里恩1945年根据诺埃·科沃德的剧本改编制作, 讲述英国一个家庭主妇和一位医生的爱情故事, 他们彼此相爱, 却又决定分手, 给人印象尤为深刻的是火车站的浪漫场景。此片以其现实主义表现手法和拍摄的艺术性著称〕

Brief His·to·ry of Time, A /,·, ··· ˈ·/ a book by Stephen Hawking in which he explains his ideas about how the universe and time began and how they have developed《时间简史》〔斯蒂芬·霍金所著的一本书, 阐述他对宇宙和时间起源与演变的见解〕

CULTURAL NOTE 文化注释

Although *A Brief History of Time* deals with very complicated technical subjects, it sold in very large numbers. But there is a joke that most of the people who bought the book did not read it.《时间简史》讨论的是极为复杂的专业话题, 但销量却极大。不过有个笑话说, 买这本书的人大多并不阅读。

brief·ing /ˈbrifɪŋ; ˈbriːfɪŋ/ *n* [C,U] information or instructions that you get before you have to do something 简要指示; 情况简介; 简报会

brief·ly /ˈbriflɪ; ˈbriːfli/ *adv* **1** for a short time 短暂地, 短时间地: *We stopped off briefly in London on our way to Geneva.* 我们去日内瓦途中, 在伦敦作了短暂停留。 **2** in as few words as possible 概括地, 简洁地, 简要地: *Sonia explained briefly what we were to do.* 索尼娅简要地说明了我们要做的事。| [sentence adverb 句子副词] *Briefly, I think we should accept their offer.* 简而言之, 我认为应该接受他们的建议。

bri·er /ˈbraɪɚ; ˈbraɪə/ *n* [C] a BRIAR 欧石南, 荆棘

brig /brɪg; brɪg/ *n* [C] a ship with two MASTS (=poles) and large square sails 方帆[横帆]双桅船

bri·gade /brɪˈged; brɪˈgeɪd/ *n* [C] **1** a large group of soldiers forming part of an army〔军队的〕旅 **2** an insulting word for a group of people who have the same beliefs 帮, 伙〔侮辱性词语〕: *the antinuclear brigade* 反对使用核能的那一伙人 —see also 另见 FIRE BRIGADE

brig·a·dier /ˌbrɪgəˈdɪr; ˌbrɪgəˈdɪə◂/ *n* [C] a high military rank in the British Army or the person who has this rank 准将 —see table on page C6 参见C6页附录

brigadier-gen·e·ral /,··· ˈ···/ *n* [C] a high army rank or someone holding this rank 准将 —see table on page C6 参见C6页附录

brig·and /ˈbrɪgənd; ˈbrɪgənd/ *n* [C] *literary* a thief, especially one of a group that attacks people in mountains or forests【文】歹徒; 土匪; 强盗; 山贼

brig·an·tine /ˈbrɪgənˌtin; ˈbrɪgəntiːn/ *n* [C] a ship like a BRIG but with fewer sails〔纵横帆〕双桅帆船

bright /braɪt; braɪt/ *adj*

1 ▶LIGHT 光线◀ shining strongly or with plenty of light 光亮的; 闪光的; 发光的: *bright sunlight* 灿烂的阳光 | *bright lights* 灯火通明 | *a new, bright, fully air-conditioned office* 明亮的、全空调的新办事处

2 ▶INTELLIGENT 聪明的◀ intelligent and likely to be successful 聪颖的: *Rosa's a bright child – she should do well at school.* 罗莎是一个聪明的孩子, 在学校里成绩应该不错。| **(have) a bright idea** *We've no money and the last bus has gone. Any bright ideas?* 我们身上没钱了, 最后一班公共汽车也开走了。有什么好主意吗?

3 ▶COLOURS 颜色◀ bright colours are strong and easy to see 鲜艳的, 鲜亮的: *bright red* 鲜红色 | *Wash bright colours separately.* 颜色鲜艳的衣服要分开洗。

4 ▶CHEERFUL 高兴的◀ cheerful or full of life 生气勃勃的; 欢快的; 兴高采烈的: *a bright smile* 灿烂的笑容 | **[+with]** *Her eyes were bright with excitement.* 她十分兴奋, 双眼流露出喜悦的神色。

5 as bright as a button clever and full of life 聪明活泼的

6 not too/very bright a) if your future is not too bright, there is no reason to hope that good things will happen〔前景〕暗淡的: *The future doesn't look too bright for these youngsters on the dole.* 这些靠救济金生活的年轻人前途暗淡。 **b)** *informal* not sensible【非正式】不明智的: *That wasn't very bright, was it?* 那样很不明智, 对吧?

7 look on the bright side to see the good points in something that is bad in other ways 看光明的一面, 抱乐观态度: *Look on the bright side – not having a holiday will mean you save money!* 往好处想, 不去度假还省钱呢!

8 bright and early very early in the morning 大清早: *Max was up bright and early, keen to get started.* 马克斯一大早就起来了, 急着开始工作。

9 bright spark *informal* an intelligent person, often used jokingly about someone who has done something stupid【非正式】

聪明人〔常用作反话〕: *What bright spark forgot to turn the oven off?* 什么人这么聪明，忘了关烤炉？
10 bright and breezy cheerful and confident 快乐而自信的
11 have a bright future/have bright prospects to be likely to be successful in whatever you do as a job 前途光明，前途远大
12 bright-eyed and bushy-tailed *humorous* keen to start doing something, especially because it is new or interesting【幽默】跃跃欲试的
13 the bright lights the interesting exciting life that people are supposed to have in big cities 大城市五光十色的生活: *June went off in search of the bright lights in London.* 琼去伦敦追求大城市五光十色的生活了。
14 bright spot an event or a period of time that is more pleasant when everything else is unpleasant 亮点〔指在其他事情都很糟糕时的一件令人高兴的事或一段快乐的时光〕: *The only bright spot of the weekend was our trip to the theatre.* 这个周末我们唯一高兴的事就是去看戏。—**brightly** *adv*: *The sun shone brightly.* 太阳光芒四射。—**brightness** *n* [U]

bright·en /ˋbraɪtn̩; ˈbraɪtn/ *v* **1** [T] to make something brighter in colour 使…更鲜艳 **2** [I] to become brighter in colour, or to shine with more light 发光; 明亮: *The sky had already begun to brighten.* 天空已开始亮起来。**3** [I,T] to become happier or more excited, or make someone else feel like this (使) 高兴, (使) 兴奋: *His expression brightened when I mentioned the money.* 我一提到钱，他便容光焕发。

brighten sth ↔ **up** *phr v* **1** [T] to make something more attractive or interesting 使更漂亮; 使更有趣: *New curtains would brighten up this room.* 新窗帘会使这个房间变得漂亮些。**2** [I] to start to become happy again 重新高兴起来: *She brightened up as soon as she saw us.* 她一看见我们便高兴起来。**3** [I] to become brighter 变得晴朗: *The weather soon brightened up.* 天气很快就放晴了。

Bright·on /ˋbraɪtn̩; ˈbraɪtn/ a city on the south coast of England, which has been a popular place for holidays since the 18th century. It is famous for the **Brighton Pavilion**, a large building with an unusual ORIENTAL design. 布赖顿〔英格兰南部沿海一城市，18世纪以来一直是著名的度假胜地，以独特的东方风格的大型建筑布赖顿宫闻名〕

brights /braɪts; braɪts/ *n* [plural] *AmE* car HEADLIGHTS when they are on as brightly as possible【美】〔汽车开着的〕车头灯 —see also 另见 HIGH BEAM

brill[1] /brɪl; brɪl/ *adj BrE spoken* very good; BRILLIANT[1] (3)【英口】非常好的; 优秀的

brill[2] *n* [C] a European fish with a thin flat body〔欧洲产的〕菱鲆

bril·liance /ˋbrɪljəns; ˈbrɪljəns/ *n* [U] **1** a very high level of intelligence or skill 才华: *Hendrix's brilliance as a rock guitarist has never been matched.* 作为一个摇滚吉他手，亨德里克斯的才华无人能比。**2** brightness of colour〔颜色〕鲜艳

S3 W3 **bril·liant[1]** /ˋbrɪljənt; ˈbrɪljənt/ *adj* **1** brilliant light or colour is very bright and strong 光亮的, 光辉夺目的, 灿烂的: *The stage was flooded with brilliant light.* 舞台被灯光照得通亮。| *brilliant reds and blues* 色彩缤纷的红蓝色调 **2** extremely good, clever, or skilful 辉煌的; 聪颖的, 才华横溢的: *Cox's performance was brilliant.* 考克斯演技精湛。| **a brilliant idea** *Hugh came up with a brilliant idea for a book.* 休为写一本书想出了绝妙的主意。**3** *BrE* excellent【英】优秀的, 好极的: *"How was your holiday?" "It was brilliant!"* "你假期过得怎么样?" "太棒了!" **4** very successful 极成功的: *a long and brilliant career* 长久而出色的事业 —**brilliantly** *adv*

brilliant[2] *n* [C] *technical* a precious stone cut with a lot of surfaces that shine【术语】多面形钻石 [宝石]

bril·lian·tine /ˋbrɪljən,tin; ˈbrɪljəntiːn/ *n* [U] an oily substance used on men's hair〔男用〕润发油

Bril·lo pad /ˋbrɪlo ˌpæd; ˈbrɪləʊ pæd/ *n* [C] *trademark* a ball of wire filled with soap, used for cleaning pans【商标】洁锅球

brim[1] /brɪm; brɪm/ *n* [C] **1** the bottom part of a hat that sticks out to protect you from sun and rain 帽檐, 帽边 —see picture at 参见 HAT 图 **2 be full to the brim (with)** if a container such as a glass is full to the brim, it is as full as possible 满得要溢出来: *Dave poured whisky till the glass was full to the brim.* 戴夫往杯子里倒了满满的威士忌酒。

brim[2] *v* **brimmed, brimming** [I] to be very full of something 注满, 充盈: [+with] *Andy's eyes brimmed with tears.* 安迪热泪盈眶。| *Eve was brimming with confidence.* 伊夫充满了自信。

brim over *phr v* [I] **1** if a container is brimming over, it is so full of something that this is coming out over its top edge 满到溢出来: [+with] *The barrel was brimming over with water.* 桶里的水满到溢出来了。**2 brim over with confidence/excitement etc** to be very confident, excited etc 充满自信/喜悦之情等

brim·ful, brimfull /ˋbrɪmˋfʊl; ˈbrɪm,fʊl/ *adj* [not before noun 不用于名词前] very full 满到边的; 溢出的; 充满的: [+of/with] *John is brimful of ambition, and ready to fight his way to the top.* 约翰野心勃勃，决心奋斗到最高层。

brim·stone /ˋbrɪm,ston; ˈbrɪmstəʊn/ *n* [U] *old use* SULPHUR【旧】硫磺 —see also 另见 **fire and brimstone** (FIRE[1] (13))

brin·dled /ˋbrɪndl̩d; ˈbrɪndld/ *adj* a brindled cow, cat etc is brown with marks or bands of another colour〔牛、猫等〕褐色底带斑纹的

brine /braɪn; braɪn/ *n* [U] **1** water which contains a lot of salt, used for preserving food 浓盐水: *sardines in brine* 用盐水腌制的沙丁鱼 **2** sea water 海水

bring /brɪŋ; brɪŋ/ *v past tense and past participle* **brought** /brɔt; brɔːt/ [T] **1** to take someone or something to the place you are now, to the place you are going to, or to the place that you have been talking about 带来; 拿来; 领来: *Did you bring anything to drink?* 你带了什么喝的来吗? | *Sheila was at the party and she brought that awful Ronnie with her!* 希拉参加了聚会，还带了那个讨厌的龙尼! | **bring sb sth** *Could you bring me that chair?* 你可以把那把椅子拿给我吗? **2** to cause something such as a problem or reaction 造成, 引起, 导致: *The minister's speech brought an angry reaction from the Teachers' Association.* 部长的讲话激起了教师联合会的愤怒。| *This whole venture has brought nothing but trouble!* 整个的冒险行动带来的只有麻烦! **3 bring with it** if a change, action etc brings with it something such as a problem or advantage, the two things are connected and come together 伴随而来: *Every scientific advance brings with it its own risks.* 每一项科学进展都带有风险。**4** if something such as an event or fact brings people to a place, it makes them go there 促使某人去…: *The discovery of gold brought thousands of prospectors flocking to the Transvaal.* 由于发现了金子，成千上万的淘金者涌向德兰士瓦。**5 bring charges** if the police bring charges against someone, they decide to charge them with a crime 起诉: *There was a six-month investigation, but eventually no charges were brought.* 调查进行了六个月，但最终没有提出起诉。**6 not bring yourself to do sth** if you cannot bring yourself to do something, you cannot make yourself do it 实在不忍心做某事: *She couldn't bring herself to touch it.* 她实在不忍摸一下。**7 bring sth into being** *formal* to make something start to exist【正式】成立, 建立; 产生: *The bureau was brought into being during the Second World War.* 该局是第二次世界大战时成立的。**8 bring sth to the boil** to heat liquid until it starts to boil 把某物烧开[煮开] **9 bring tears to your eyes/bring a lump to your throat** to make you start to feel strong emotions such as pity, sadness, or happiness 使人热泪夺眶而出/使人哽咽: *To see them meet after all this time, it really brings a lump to your throat!* 看到他们久别重逢，真使人难免唏嘘! **10 bring sth to an end/a close/a conclusion etc** to make something finish or stop 结束[停止]某事: *It's time we brought this whole sordid affair to a close.* 我们该结束这整件卑鄙的事情了。**11 bring sth to bear** *formal* to use pressure, influence etc to change a situation【正式】对…施加压力, 敦促: *Unfair pressure has been brought to bear upon the strikers to make them return.* 用不正当的手段对罢工的工人施加了压力迫使他们复工。**12 bring sth to sb's attention/notice** *formal* to tell someone about something【正式】使某人注意某事, 提醒某人注意某事: *Thank you for bringing this mistake to our attention.* 谢谢你提醒我们注意这个错误。**13 what brings you here?** *spoken* used to show that you are surprised to see someone【口】是什么风把你吹来了? **14 bring home the bacon** *informal* to earn the money that your family needs to live【非正式】挣得养家糊口的钱 —see also 另见 **bring sth to a head** (HEAD[1] (45)), **bring sb to heel** (HEEL[1] (9)), **bring sb to their senses** (SENSE[1] (6)), **bring sth home to sb** (HOME[2] (4)), **bring sb/sth to their knees** (KNEE[1] (6))

bring sth ↔ **about** *phr v* [T] to make something happen 引起, 导致, 造成: *Computers have brought about many changes in the workplace.* 电脑给工作场所带来了很多变化。

bring sb/sth **around/round** *phr v* [T] **1 bring the conversation around/round to** to deliberately and gradually introduce a new subject into a conversation 转移话题: *I'll try to bring the conversation around to the subject of money.* 我会试图把话题转到金钱方面。**2** to make someone become conscious again 使…恢复知觉: *We managed to bring her round with some smelling salts.* 我们设法用嗅盐使她恢复了知觉。**3** to manage to persuade someone to do something or to agree with you 说服〔某人〕做〔某事〕; 使同意某种观点: *Give me a day or two and I'll*

S1 W1

B

see if I can bring her around. 给我一两天时间，看我能否使她回心转意。**4** to bring someone or something to someone's house 把某人[某物]带到…：*If I bring it round tomorrow you can check it out.* 如果我明天带来，你可以核对一下。

bring back *phr v* [T] **1** [**bring** sth ↔ **back**] to start to use something such as a law, method, or process that was used in the past 使恢复：*They should bring back the death penalty, that's what I think!* 他们应该恢复死刑，那就是我的想法！| *bringing back the old electric trams* 恢复旧时的有轨电车 **2** [**bring back** sth] to make you remember something 使想起，使忆起：*The smell of new paper always brings back memories of school.* 新纸张的气味总是使我回想起上学时的日子。**3** [**bring** sth ↔ **back**] to take something or someone with you when you come back from somewhere 把…带回来：**bring sb back sth** *Hey, Freddie! Bring me back a few beers would ya!* 嗨，弗雷迪！给我带回几瓶啤酒好吗？| **bring sth back (for sb)** *I brought these back from Kenya for the children.* 这些是我从肯尼亚带回来给孩子们的。**4 it brings us/me back to** used when you want to talk about a particular problem again 这使我们/我再回到〔某问题〕：*This brings us back to the important question of money.* 这使我们又回到钱这一重要问题上。

bring sb/sth ↔ **down** *phr v* [T] **1** to fly an aircraft down to the ground and stop 使〔飞机〕降落：*He brought the Cessna down in a hay-meadow by the river.* 他把赛斯纳小型飞机降落在河边的牧草场上。**2** to move your arm or a weapon, tool etc quickly downwards 放下，使向下：*He brought down the axe with a thud.* 他砰的一声用斧子砍了下去。**3** to shoot at a plane, bird or animal so that it falls to the ground 射下，打落：*A bomber had been brought down by anti-aircraft fire.* 一架轰炸机被防空炮火击落。**4 bring down the government/president etc** to force the government etc to stop ruling 推翻政府/总统等 **5** to knock someone over in a game of football, RUGBY etc〔运动中〕撞倒：*Klinsmann was brought down on the edge of the area.* 克林斯曼在球场边缘被撞倒了。

bring sth ↔ **down on/upon** *phr v* [T] *formal* to make something bad happen to someone, especially yourself【正式】使〔坏事〕发生在…，使…落在〔某人自己〕身上：*His recklessness brought down disaster on the whole family.* 他的鲁莽给全家带来了灾难。

bring sth ↔ **forth** *phr v* [T] *formal* to produce something or make it appear【正式】产生；使出现；生产，生育：*a tragic love affair that brought forth only pain* 只能带来痛苦的爱情悲剧

bring sth ↔ **forward** *phr v* [T] **1** to change an arrangement in the future so that something happens sooner 将…提前：*The meeting's been brought forward to Thursday.* 会议已经提前到星期四举行。**2 bring forward legislation/plans/policies etc** to officially introduce plans etc for people to discuss 提出法案/计划/政策等：*The government has brought forward a plan to tackle urban crime.* 政府提出了一项解决城市犯罪的计划。**3** *technical* to move the total from one set of calculations onto the next page, so that more calculations can be done【术语】把〔账目〕结转〔到次页〕：*The balance brought forward is £21,765.* 结转到次页的余额是21,765英镑。

bring in *phr v* [T] **1** [**bring in** sth] to earn a particular amount or produce a particular amount of profit 盈利；赚钱：*The sale of the house only brought in about £45,000.* 房子只卖了约4.5万英镑。**2** [**bring** sb ↔ **in**] to allow or invite someone to become involved in a discussion, INVESTIGATION etc 使〔某人〕参加：*It all became very serious and the police were brought in.* 事态变得很严重，警察也被叫来了。| *Could I just bring in some members of the audience to get their views?* 我可以邀请一些观众来，听取他们的意见吗？**3 bring in a verdict** when a court or JURY brings in a verdict, it says whether someone is guilty or not 宣判，裁决

bring sb/sth ↔ **off** *phr v* [T] **1** to succeed in doing something very difficult 使成功；圆满完成〔困难的事〕：*Together they brought off a daring diamond robbery.* 他们一起终于做成了一桩大胆的钻石抢劫案。**2** *technical* to help people to leave a ship that is sinking【术语】帮助〔他人〕逃离沉船，救出〔沉船受害者〕

bring sth ↔ **on** *phr v* [T] **1** to make something bad or unpleasant happen 引起，导致；惹来：*a bad cold brought on by going out in the rain* 冒雨外出导致的重感冒 | *Whatever has brought this on? Have I upset you somehow?* 这到底是怎么搞的？我惹你不高兴了吗？**2** to make plants or crops grow faster 加速〔农作物〕生长：*The hot weather has really brought on the roses.* 炎热的天气真的使玫瑰生长得更好。

bring sth **on/upon** sb *phr v* [T] to make something bad happen to someone 引起〔尤指不愉快的事〕；招来，惹来：*You have brought disaster on the whole village!* 你给整个村子带来了灾难！

bring out *phr v* [T] **1** [**bring** sth/sb ↔ **out**] to make something easier to see, taste, notice etc 使…明显；显示出；使…得以发挥：*The oregano really brings out the flavour of the meat.* 牛至叶果然使肉的味道更鲜美。| *Fatherhood seems to have brought out his sense of responsibility.* 当父亲后，他似乎有了责任感。**2 bring out the best/worst in sb** to make someone behave in the best or worst way that they can 把某人最好的方面/最丑陋的一面诱发出来：*Alcohol just brings out the worst in her.* 喝酒把她最丑陋的一面都诱发出来了。**3** [**bring** sth ↔ **out**] to produce a book, record etc to be sold to the public 推出〔书籍、唱片等〕：*The Food Association has brought out a handy guide.* 食品协会推出了一本简易手册。**4** [**bring** sb **out**] to make someone feel more confident, happy, and friendly 使更自信，使不再害羞：*When he went to college it really brought him out.* 上了大学后，他的自信心增强了。**5** [**bring** sb ↔ **out**] *BrE* to make workers stop working and go on strike (STRIKE[2] (1))【英】使罢工：*They are threatening to bring out the power workers next.* 他们威胁说下一步将煽动电力工人罢工。

bring sb **out in** *phr v* [T] *BrE* if something brings you out in spots, a RASH[2] (1) etc, it makes spots etc appear on your skin【英】使长出〔斑点、疹等〕：*Chocolate always brings me out in spots.* 一吃巧克力，我就会长丘疹。

bring sb **round** —see 见 **bring sb around/round**

bring sb **through** (sth) *phr v* [T] to help someone to successfully deal with a very difficult event or period of time 使脱离〔险境〕；使渡过〔难关〕：*It was Churchill, above all, who brought us through the war.* 最重要的是，丘吉尔使我们安全渡过了战争的难关。

bring sb **together** *phr v* [T] to introduce two people to each other or to be the thing that does this 使联合，使携手：*What brought them together was their mutual love of opera.* 是对歌剧的共同爱好使他们两人走到了一起。

bring sb/sth ↔ **up** *phr v* [T] **1** to mention a subject or start to talk about it 提出〔议题〕：*Why did you have to bring up the subject of money?* 你为什么非要提钱这个话题？| *I shall bring up this question at the next meeting.* 我将在下次会议上提出这个问题。—see 见 RAISE[1] (USAGE) **2** [usually passive 一般用被动态] to educate and care for a child until it is grown up 养育，教养〔孩子〕：*He left her to bring up three young children on her own.* 他留下她独自抚养三个年幼的孩子。| **be brought up (as) a Catholic/Muslim etc** *I was brought up a Lutheran.* 我是在路德教的教育下长大的。| **be brought up to do sth** *In my day, children were brought up to respect the law.* 我小时候，孩子们都接受教育要遵守法律。**3** *BrE* to VOMIT[1] something up from your stomach【英】呕吐：*He can't eat anything without bringing it up.* 他吃什么都会吐。**4 bring sb up short/with a start** to make someone suddenly stop talking or doing something 使某人突然停住：*Her question brought me up short.* 她的问题使我突然停住了。**5 bring sb up on a charge of theft/treason etc** to charge someone with a particular crime 指控某人盗窃/叛国等

USAGE NOTE 用法说明: BRING

WORD CHOICE 词语辨析: **bring, take, fetch, carry**

Bring means to take someone or something with you to the place where you are now, to your home, or to the place you have been talking about. bring 表示"带来"，即把某人或某物带到你所在的地方，你的家里，或你所说的地方：*They came to my party and brought me a present.* 他们来参加我的聚会，并给我带来一份礼物。| *When I'm next in San Francisco, bring your new boyfriend to see me.* 我下次到旧金山时，把你新认识的男朋友带来看我。| *Have you brought your camera?* 你把照相机带来了吗？**Bring** is also used in the same way for taking something towards the person being spoken to or talked about. bring 也用于指把某物带给交谈的对象或所谈及的人：*Hold on, I'll bring you a towel.* 稍等一下，我给你拿条毛巾来。| *They brought her everything she needed.* 他们把她需要的东西都带来了。

Take involves moving in the opposite direction to **bring**. take 是"带去"，和 bring 的方向相反：*We went to her party and took her a present.* 我们去参加她的聚会，并带给她一份礼物。| *When I'm in San Francisco I'll take you to Alcatraz.* 我到了旧金山，就带你去阿尔卡特拉斯岛。| *Take your camera when you go out* (NOT usually 这里一般不用 *carry* here). 外出时把照相机带上。| *Can you take me home now?* 你现在能带我回家吗？

Fetch in British English means to go and get something or someone and bring them back. fetch 在英国英语中指去取某物或接某人并将其带回：*Can you fetch Janice from the station?* 你能去车站把贾尼斯接回来吗？**Carry** does not

give any idea as to the direction of movement, but suggests that you are holding something in your arms or with your hands. carry 意为"带"，不含任何方向的意思，而是指用双臂或用双手携带: *Will you carry the baby/the groceries for me?* 你能帮我抱一下孩子/拿一下食品杂货吗?

bringing-up /,‥ˈ‥/ *n* [singular] *AmE* the care and training that parents give their children when they are growing up; UPBRINGING【美】养育，抚养；教养

brink /brɪŋk; brɪŋk/ *n* **1 be on the brink of** to be almost in a new and very different situation 在…的边缘，处在…关头: *Karl is on the brink of a brilliant acting career.* 卡尔即将开始辉煌的演艺生涯。**2 the brink of** *literary* the edge of a very high place such as a cliff【文】〔峭壁等的〕边缘

brink·man·ship /ˈbrɪŋkmənʃɪp; ˈbrɪŋkmənʃɪp/ *BrE*【英】, **brinks·man·ship** /ˈbrɪŋksmən-; ˈbrɪŋksmən-/ *AmE*【美】*n* [U] a method of gaining political advantage by pretending that you are willing to do something very dangerous 边缘政策，冒险政策

brin·y /ˈbraɪnɪ; ˈbraɪni/ *adj* water that is briny contains a lot of salt 盐水的；很咸的

bri·oche /ˈbrioʃ; ˈbriːɒʃ/ *n* [C] a type of sweet bread made with flour, eggs, and butter 黄油蛋糕卷

bri·quette /brɪˈkɛt; brɪˈket/ *n* [C] a block of pressed coal dust, to burn in a fire or BARBEQUE 煤砖，煤饼

Bris·bane /ˈbrɪzbən; ˈbrɪzbən/ a port and the capital city of Queensland state in the east of Australia, the third largest city in the country 布里斯班〔澳大利亚东部昆士兰州首府、港口，该国第三大城市〕

brisk /brɪsk; brɪsk/ *adj* **1** quick and full of energy 轻快的；活泼的；精力充沛的: *a brisk walk* 轻快的步行 **2** quick, practical and showing that you want to get things done quickly 敏捷的，反应快的: *She spoke in a brisk tone.* 她说话语气爽快。**3** trade or business that is brisk is very busy, with a lot of products being sold〔生意〕兴隆的 **4** weather that is brisk is cold and clear〔天气〕清新凉爽的 —**briskly** *adv* —**briskness** *n* [U]

bris·ket /ˈbrɪskɪt; ˈbrɪskɨt/ *n* [U] meat from an animal's chest, especially a cow〔动物，尤指牛的〕胸肉

bris·tle[1] /ˈbrɪsl̩; ˈbrɪsəl/ *n* [C,U] **1** short stiff hair that feels rough 短而硬的毛发；胡碴: *His chin was covered with bristles.* 他满下巴都是胡碴。**2** a short stiff hair, wire etc that forms part of a brush〔制刷子用的〕鬃毛 —see picture at 参见 BRUSH[1] 图

bristle[2] *v* [I] **1** to behave in a way that shows you are very angry or annoyed 显得愤怒: **[+with]** *bristling with rage* 怒发冲冠 | **[+at]** *He bristled at the mere suggestion.* 只要稍微提一下，他就怒不可遏。**2** if an animal's hair bristles, it stands up stiffly because the animal is afraid or angry〔动物因惊慌或愤怒而毛发〕竖立；硬挺

bristle with sth *phr v* [T] to have a lot of something or be full of something 到处都是…；…重重，…丛生: *a battleship bristling with guns* 布满了大炮的战舰

bris·tly /ˈbrɪslɪ; ˈbrɪsli/ *adj* **1** bristly hair is short and stiff〔毛发〕短而硬的 **2** a bristly part of your body has short stiff hairs on it〔身体部位〕长满硬毛的: *a bristly chin* 胡子拉碴的下巴

Bris·tol /ˈbrɪstl̩; ˈbrɪstl/ a city and port in the southwest of England, where the local government for Avon is based 布里斯托尔〔英格兰西南部港口城市，埃文郡地方政府所在地〕

Bristol Chan·nel, the /,‥ˈ‥/ an area of water between South Wales and southwest England which goes from the Atlantic Ocean to the mouth of the Severn River 布里斯托尔海峡〔威尔士南部和英格兰西南部之间的水域，从大西洋延伸至塞文河河口〕

Bristol Cream /,‥ˈ‥/ *trademark* a type of very sweet SHERRY which is made by Harvey's. It is one of the most popular types of sherry in the UK.【商标】布里斯托尔雪利酒，夏薇雪利酒〔由夏薇公司生产的一种甜味雪利酒，是英国最著名的雪利酒之一〕

Brit /brɪt; brɪt/ *n* [C] *informal* someone from Britain【非正式】英国人

Bri·tain /ˈbrɪtn̩; ˈbrɪtn/ Great Britain or the UK 大不列颠，英国

Bri·tan·nia /brɪˈtænjə; brɨˈtænjə/ a female figure representing Britain, formerly shown on some coins. Britannia is usually shown sitting down, wearing a HELMET, and holding a TRIDENT (=an ancient weapon with three points, which looks like a large fork). Next to her feet she has a SHIELD with the design of the British flag on it. There is a popular national song called *Rule Britannia.* 不列颠尼亚〔旧时印在一些硬币上象征英国的女性形象，常以坐姿出现，头戴钢盔，手持三叉戟，脚旁放有一面带有英国国旗图样的盾牌。英国有一首家喻户晓的爱国歌曲，名为《你主沉浮，不列颠尼亚》〕

Britannia 不列颠尼亚

Brit A·wards, the /ˈ‥,‥/ a set of prizes given every year at a public ceremony to the best British popular musicians. There are similar prizes in the US called the Grammy Awards. 全英音乐奖，布里特奖〔一年一度在典礼上颁发给英国最杰出的流行音乐家的系列奖项，美国也有类似的奖项，名为格莱美奖〕

britch·es /ˈbrɪtʃɪz; ˈbrɪtʃɨz/ *n* [plural] *AmE* trousers【美】裤子

Brit·ish /ˈbrɪtɪʃ; ˈbrɪtɪʃ/ *adj* **1** from or connected with Great Britain 不列颠的，英国的: *the British government* 英国政府 **2 the British** people from Britain 英国人

CULTURAL NOTE 文化注释

British people are traditionally considered to be RESERVED (=quiet and unwilling to show their feelings). They also try to 'keep a stiff upper lip' (=try to seem calm when they are really upset or worried). People sometimes say that the British don't like complaining when they receive poor service, for example in a restaurant. Some people now connect Britain with the bad behaviour of English football HOOLIGANS who travel to countries in Europe when their teams are playing there, and with young people who get drunk at holiday RESORTS in countries such as Spain and Greece. 传统看法认为英国人保守、不动声色。人们有时会说，如果饭店等处服务态度不好，英国人并不喜欢抱怨。现在说到英国人，有些人会联想到追随自己支持的球队去欧洲各国的英国足球流氓的恶行，或者联想到在西班牙或希腊等国的度假胜地喝得醉醺醺的英国年轻人。

British A·cad·e·my, the /,‥ˈ‥/ a society that was started in 1901 to encourage the study of language, literature, history, economics etc. Most of its members are university teachers who have done important work in their subjects. There is a similar society for people working in scientific fields, called the Royal Society 英国学会〔成立于1901年的一个协会，旨在推动语言、文学、历史、经济学等领域的研究。成员多为在专业领域里有重要贡献的大学教师。科技工作者也有一个类似协会，名为英国皇家学会〕

British Board of Film Classification, the /,‥,‥ˈ‥,‥/ a special committee in the UK whose job is to watch new films and decide whether children or young people will be allowed to see them. They give each film a certificate, showing which films can be shown to anyone (U), which can be seen by children if an adult goes with them (PG), and which films can only be seen by people over a particular age (12, 15, and 18). There is a similar organization in the US called the Motion Picture Association of America. 英国电影分级委员会〔英国一特别委员会，职责是审查新出影片，决定是否允许儿童或年轻人观看。该委员会给每部影片颁发证书，标明U级的影片，所有人均可观看；PG级影片，由成人陪同的儿童可观看；有的影片仅供特定年龄以上的人群观看（如12、15和18岁）。美国也有一个类似机构，名称为美国电影协会〕

British Broad·cast·ing Cor·po·ra·tion /,‥ˈ‥,‥/ *n* the BBC 英国广播公司

British Co·lum·bi·a /,‥ˈ‥/ abbreviation 缩写为 **BC** a PROVINCE in western Canada, bordering on the Pacific Ocean 不列颠哥伦比亚省〔加拿大西部一省，濒临太平洋〕

British Com·mon·wealth /,‥ˈ‥/ —see 见 COMMONWEALTH

British Coun·cil, the /,‥ˈ‥/ an organization that was set up in 1935 to represent the UK's interests abroad in areas such as education and the arts 英国文化委员会〔成立于1935年，代表英国在教育、艺术等领域海外利益的一个机构〕

British Em·pire, the /,‥ˈ‥/ the group of countries formerly connected with and controlled by Great Britain, which was at its largest at the time of World War I, when it included 25 percent of the world's area 大英帝国，大不列颠帝国〔早先与英国有关联并受其控制的国家，一战时期势力范围最大，占有全世界面积的25%〕

Brit·ish·er /ˈbrɪtɪʃɚ; ˈbrɪtɪʃə/ *n* [C] *AmE* someone from Britain【美】英国人

British Film In·sti·tute, the /,‥ˈ‥,‥/ *n* the BFI 英国电影协会

British Isles /ˌ··ˈ·/ *n* the group of islands that includes Great Britain, Ireland, and the smaller islands around them 不列颠群岛

British Le·gion, the /ˌ··ˈ··/ also 又作 **the Royal British Legion** a British organization which helps people who have been in the armed forces and their families. The British Legion collects money by selling poppies (POPPY) for Remembrance Day. 英国皇家军团〔向退伍军人及其家属提供帮助的一个组织, 在阵亡将士纪念日通过出售人造罂粟花募集钱款〕

British Li·bra·ry, the /ˌ··ˈ···/ the national library of the UK, with centres in London and in Yorkshire, which receives a copy of every book produced in the UK 英国图书馆〔英国国家图书馆, 在伦敦和约克郡设有中心, 收藏英国出版的每一本书籍〕

British Li·ons, the /ˌ··ˈ··/ the Rugby Union team, chosen from players from England, Scotland, Wales, and Ireland to play in international matches 不列颠雄狮队〔一支参加国际比赛的橄榄球联盟队, 队员选自英格兰、苏格兰、威尔士以及爱尔兰〕

British Mu·se·um, the /ˌ··ˌ·ˈ··/ a famous building in London which contains a large and important collection of ancient art, writings, coins, drawings etc 大英博物馆〔伦敦的一幢著名建筑, 馆藏古代艺术、著作、钱币、绘画等大量珍品〕

British O·pen, the /ˌ··ˈ··/ also 又作 **the Open** the most important British GOLF competition, which is held every year in different parts of the UK 英国公开赛〔英国最重要的高尔夫球赛事, 每年在英国不同地区举行〕

British Rail /ˌ··ˈ·/ the national railway system of the UK, which used to be owned by the government 英国铁路网〔英国国家铁路运输系统, 曾为政府所有〕

British Sum·mer Time /ˌ··ˈ···/ *n* [U] the time one hour ahead of Greenwich Mean Time, that is used in Britain from late March to late October 英国夏令时间〔每年从3月底至10月底使用, 比格林尼治标准时间快一小时〕—compare 比较 DAYLIGHT SAVING TIME

British Tel·e·com /ˌ··ˈ···/ abbreviation 缩写为 **BT** the largest company providing telephone services in the UK 英国电信公司〔英国最大的电信服务商〕

Brit·on /ˈbrɪtn; ˈbrɪtn/ *n* [C] *formal* someone from Britain【正式】英国人: *the ancient Britons* 古代英国人

Brit·tan·y /ˈbrɪtənɪ; ˈbrɪtəni/ an area of northwest France with a long coast, between the Bay of Biscay and the English Channel 布列塔尼〔法国西北部一地区, 位于比斯开湾和英吉利海峡之间, 海岸线绵长〕

Brit·ten /ˈbrɪtn; ˈbrɪtn/, **Ben·ja·min** /ˈbɛndʒəmɪn; ˈbendʒəmɪn/ (1913-76) a British musician, COMPOSER, and CONDUCTOR (=someone who directs a group of musicians) who wrote *A Young Person's Guide to the Orchestra* (1945), *A War Requiem* (1962) and the OPERAS *Peter Grimes* (1951) and *Billy Budd* (1951) 布里顿〔(1913-1976), 英国音乐家、作曲家和指挥家, 作品有《青年管弦乐队指南》(1945)、《战争安魂曲》(1962) 及歌剧《彼得·格赖姆斯》(1951)、《比利·巴德》(1951)〕

brit·tle /ˈbrɪtl; ˈbrɪtl/ *adj* **1** hard but easily broken 脆的, 易碎的: *The branches were dry and brittle.* 那些树枝干而易断。**2** a system, relationship etc that is brittle is easily damaged or destroyed 不牢固的: *a very brittle friendship* 很不牢固的友谊 **3** showing no warm feelings 冷淡的: *a brittle laugh* 冷笑

Brix·ton /ˈbrɪkstən; ˈbrɪkstən/ an area of south London which has a large black population 布里克斯顿〔伦敦南部一地区, 黑人人口密集〕

bro /bro; brəʊ/ *n* [C] *spoken*【口】**1** your brother 兄弟; 弟弟; 哥哥 **2** *AmE* a way of greeting a friend【美】兄弟, 哥儿们〔招呼用语〕

broach /brotʃ; brəʊtʃ/ *v* [T] **1 broach the subject/question/matter etc** to mention a subject that may be embarrassing, unpleasant or cause an argument 提及话题/问题/事情等〔尤指尴尬或会引起争论的话题〕: *It's often difficult to broach the subject of sex.* 关于性的话题, 通常不太好开口。**2** to open a bottle or BARREL[1] (1) containing wine, beer etc 开启〔酒瓶、桶等〕

broad[1] /brɔd; brɔːd/ *adj*

1 ▶WIDE 宽的◀ a road, river, or part of someone's body etc that is broad is wide 宽的, 阔的: *We went along a broad carpeted passage.* 我们沿着一条铺着地毯的宽阔走廊走了过去。| *He was six feet tall, with broad shoulders and slender hips.* 他身高六英尺, 宽肩瘦臀。| **6 feet/3 metres etc broad** *The track was three metres broad.* 车道有三米宽。—compare 比较 NARROW

2 ▶INCLUDING A LOT 包括很多◀ including many different kinds of things 广博的; 丰富的; 广泛的: **broad range/spectrum of** *She has a very broad range of interests.* 她兴趣非常广泛。| **broad category/field/area etc** *In general, the paintings fall into two broad categories.* 一般而言, 绘画分为两大类。

3 ▶GENERAL 总的◀ concerning the main ideas or parts of something rather than all the details 粗略的, 概括的, 一般的; 广义的: **broad sense/term/definition etc** *This is education in the broadest sense of the word.* 这是从最广义上说的教育。| **broad consensus/agreement etc** *All the members were in broad agreement.* 所有成员大体上达成了共识。

4 ▶LARGE AREA 大面积◀ covering a large area of land or water 辽阔的, 广大的, 广袤的: *They came to a broad expanse of water.* 他们来到一片广阔的水域。

5 broad grin/smile a big smile which clearly shows that you are happy 开怀大笑: *"A great win," he said with a broad grin.* "一次巨大的胜利。"他大笑着说。

6 in broad daylight if something such as a crime happens in broad daylight, it happens in the daytime when you would expect someone to prevent it 大白天; 光天化日: *The attack happened in broad daylight, in one of the busiest parts of town.* 袭击事件发生在大白天, 是在城镇最繁华的地段。

7 ▶WAY OF SPEAKING 说话方式◀ a broad ACCENT[1] (1) clearly shows where you come from 口音重的: *a broad Scottish accent* 浓重的苏格兰口音

8 broad hint/sarcasm a HINT (=suggestion) etc that is very clear and easy to understand 明白的暗示/讽刺: *dropping broad hints about what she wanted for Christmas* 明白地暗示出她圣诞节想要什么

9 broad humour/wit etc humour etc that is slightly rude 略有些粗俗的幽默/机智等

10 it's as broad as it's long *spoken* used to say that it does not matter which of two things you choose, because neither is clearly better【口】反正都一样; 半斤八两; 不分高低

11 have a broad back to be easily able to deal with hardwork, problems etc 轻松应对困难

12 broad in the beam *informal* having large or fat HIPS【非正式】屁股肥大的

13 a broad church an organisation that contains a wide range of opinions 容纳多种观点的组织: *The Labour Party has to be a broad church.* 工党必须是一个允许多种见解的政党。—see also 另见 BREADTH

broad[2] *n* **1 the Broads** used in the names of some wide parts of rivers in Eastern England〔尤指英格兰东部由河川变宽而成的〕湖沼地区: *the Norfolk Broads* 诺福克郡湖沼地区 **2** [C] *AmE spoken* an offensive way of referring to a woman【美口】女人, 娘儿们〔冒犯性用语〕

broad·band /ˈ·ˌ·/ *n* [U] *technical* a system of sending radio signals which allows several messages to be sent at the same time【术语】〔无线电〕宽[谱]带, 宽波段

broad bean /ˌ·ˈ·/ *n* [C] *BrE* a round pale green bean【英】蚕豆; FAVA BEAN *AmE*【美】—see picture on page A9 参见 A9 页图

broad·brush, broad-brush /ˈbrɔdˌbrʌʃ; ˈbrɔːdbrʌʃ/ *adj* dealing only with the main parts of something, and not with the details 粗略的, 概括的: *a broadbrush strategy for increasing sales* 提高销量的纲要性策略

broad·cast[1] /ˈbrɔdˌkæst; ˈbrɔːdkɑːst/ *n* [C] a programme on the radio or on television〔电台或电视的〕广播节目; 播送节目: *a radio news broadcast* 电台新闻广播 | **live broadcast** (=a programme that you see or hear at the same time as the events are happening) 实况转播

broadcast[2] *v past tense and past participle* **broadcast 1** [I, T] to send out radio or television programmes 广播; 播送: *The interview was broadcast live across Europe.* 这次访问向欧洲各地现场直播。**2** [T] to tell something to a lot of people 使广为传播, 散布: *There was no need to broadcast the fact that he lost his job.* 没有必要大肆宣扬他丢了工作这件事。

broad·cast·er /ˈbrɔdˌkæstɚ; ˈbrɔːdkɑːstə/ *n* [C] someone who speaks on radio or television programmes 播音员: *a well-known journalist and broadcaster* 著名的新闻记者和播音员

broad·cast·ing /ˈbrɔdˌkæstɪŋ; ˈbrɔːdkɑːstɪŋ/ *n* [U] the business of making television and radio programmes〔电视或电台的〕广播工作; 广播事业: *a career in broadcasting* 从事广播事业

Broadcasting House /ˌ··ˈ·/ the central office of the BBC〔英国广播公司〕中央大楼

Broadcasting Stan·dards Coun·cil, the /ˌ···ˌ··ˈ··/ in Britain, a group of people who watch television and listen to radio programmes, and decide whether they contain too much sex or violence or are offensive or unsuitable in any way 英国广播电视节目标准委员会〔审查广播电视节目的一组人员, 确定节目是否含有过多色情或暴力内容或在某些方面含有冒犯性或不适合播出的内容〕

broad·en /ˈbrɔdn; ˈbrɔːdn/ *v* **1** [T] to increase something such as knowledge, experience, or your range of activities 使扩大, 使增加: *Broaden your knowledge of English with this book.* 看这本书来增进你的英语知识。| **broaden your horizons** (=increase your activities and opportunities) 开阔视野 **2** [I,T] to make something broader or to become broader 加宽; (使) 变宽: *The road broadened into an imposing avenue.* 这条路被拓宽成一条壮观的大街。**3 broaden your mind** if an experience broadens your mind, it makes it easier for you to accept other people's beliefs, ways of doing things etc 开阔你的胸襟, 增长你的见识: *Travel broadens the mind.* 旅游使人开阔胸襟。

broaden out *phr v* [I] to gradually become wider 逐渐变宽: *The river broadens out at this point.* 河流在这里开始变宽。

broad gauge /ˈ· ·/ *n* [C] a size of railway track that is wider than the normal size〔铁路的〕宽轨

broad jump /ˈ· ·/ *n* [U] *AmE* a sport in which you try to jump as far as possible; LONG JUMP【美】跳远

broad·loom /ˈbrɔdˌlum; ˈbrɔːdluːm/ *n* [U] *technical* CARPET[1] (1) that is woven in a single wide piece【术语】宽幅地毯

broad·ly /ˈbrɔdlɪ; ˈbrɔːdli/ *adv* **1** in a general way, covering the main facts rather than details 大体上说来, 总体上来讲: *She knows broadly what to expect.* 她大致知道等待她的将会是什么结果。| **broadly speaking** *There are, broadly speaking, four types of champagne.* 香槟酒大致上分为四种。| **broadly similar** *We reached broadly similar conclusions.* 我们得出大致相同的结论。**2 smile/grin broadly** to have a big smile on your face which clearly shows that you are happy or amused 开怀地笑 **3 broadly based** including a range of different things or subjects 多方面的, 全面的: *a broadly based approach to education* 全方位的教育方法

broad·mind·ed, broad-minded /ˈbrɔdˋmaɪndɪd; ˌbrɔːdˈmaɪndɪ̈d◂/ *adj* willing to respect opinions or behaviour that are very different from your own 气量大的, 心胸开阔的, 能容纳不同意见的: *Her parents were broadminded, tolerant and liberal.* 她的父母心胸开阔, 宽容而开明。—opposite 反义词 NARROW-MINDED —compare 比较 SMALL-MINDED —**broadmindedly** *adv* —**broad-mindedness** *n* [U]

Broad·moor /ˈbrɔdmor; ˈbrɔːdmɔː/ a special hospital in the UK for criminals who are very dangerous and mentally ill 布罗德摩尔医院〔英国一家监禁高危精神病犯人的特殊医院〕

Broads, the /brɔdz; brɔːdz/ an area of water leading to the sea in Norfolk, which is a popular place for sailing holidays 布罗兹湖区〔通向诺福克郡海域的一片水域, 为帆船度假胜地〕

broad·sheet /ˈbrɔdˌʃit; ˈbrɔːdʃiːt/ *n* [C] a newspaper printed on large sheets of paper, especially a serious newspaper that people respect〔尤指严肃的〕宽幅报纸 —compare 比较 TABLOID

broad·side[1] /ˈbrɔdˌsaɪd; ˈbrɔːdsaɪd/ *n* [C] **1** a strong criticism of someone or something especially a written one〔尤指书面的〕猛烈抨击: *Can the government survive this latest broadside from its own supporters?* 政府能否顶住其支持者最近的猛烈抨击? **2** an attack in which all the guns on one side of a ship are fired at the same time 舷炮齐射

broadside[2] *AmE*【美】, **broadside on** *BrE*【英】*adv* with the longest side facing something 侧向地: [+**to**] *I brought the boat in broadside to the beach.* 我把船划进来, 侧面对着海滩。

broadside[3] *v* [T] *especially AmE* to crash into the side of another vehicle【尤美】撞上〔另一辆车〕的侧面

broad·sword /ˈbrɔdˌsord; ˈbrɔːdsɔːd/ *n* [C] a heavy sword with a broad flat blade 大砍刀; 阔剑

Broad·way /ˈbrɔdwe; ˈbrɔːdweɪ/ a street in New York City where there are many theatres. Broadway and the area around it is the centre of the city's theatre industry. 百老汇〔纽约市一街道, 有许多剧院, 百老汇一带为纽约市戏剧业中心〕: *The new show will open on Broadway next month.* 那出新戏下月将在百老汇上演。| *a Broadway musical* 百老汇音乐剧

bro·cade /broˋked; brəˈkeɪd/ *n* [U] thick heavy decorative cloth which has a pattern of gold and silver threads 织锦, 锦缎: *brocade curtains* 锦缎窗帘 —**brocaded** *adj*

broc·co·li /ˈbrɑkəlɪ; ˈbrɒkəli/ *n* [U] a green vegetable that has short branch-like stems 花茎甘蓝; 花椰菜, 西兰花 —see picture on page A9 参见 A9 页图

bro·chure /broˋʃur; ˈbrəʊʃə/ *n* [C] a thin book giving information or advertising something 小册子: *a glossy holiday brochure* 印刷精美的度假宣传小册子

brogue /brog; brəʊg/ *n* [C] **1** a thick strong leather shoe with a pattern in the leather 粗革厚底皮鞋; 拷花皮鞋 —see picture at 参见 SHOE[1] 图 **2** [usually singular 一般用单数] an ACCENT (=way of pronouncing words), especially the one used by the Irish or Scottish people〔尤指爱尔兰人或苏格兰人说英语时的〕土腔

broil /brɔɪl; brɔɪl/ *v* [T] *AmE* to cook something under direct heat, or over a flame on a BARBECUE[1] (1)【美】烤; 焙; 炙; GRILL[1] (1) *BrE*【英】: *broiled chicken* 烤鸡

broil·er /ˈbrɔɪlɚ; ˈbrɔɪlə/ *n* [C] **1** *AmE* a special area of a STOVE[1] (1) used for cooking food under direct heat【美】烤架, 烘烤炉; GRILL[2] (1) *BrE*【英】**2** *AmE* a very hot day【美】大热天 **3** a broiler chicken〔适于烧烤的〕嫩鸡

broiler chick·en /ˈ·· ,··/ *n* [C] a chicken that is suitable to be cooked by broiling〔适于烧烤的〕嫩鸡

broil·ing /ˈbrɔɪlɪŋ; ˈbrɔɪlɪŋ/ *adj AmE* broiling weather, sun etc makes you feel extremely hot【美】酷热的, 灼热的: *a day in the broiling sun* 酷热难耐的一天

broke[1] /brok; brəʊk/ the past tense of BREAK[1]

broke[2] *adj* [not before noun 不用于名词前] **1** having no money 破产的, 身无分文的: *I'm fed up with being broke all the time.* 我已受够了一文不名的日子。| **flat broke** *AmE*【美】, **stony broke** *BrE*【英】(=completely broke) 完全破产的, 一文不名的 **2 go broke** if a company or business goes broke, it can no longer operate because it has no money 破产: *A lot of small businesses went broke in the recession.* 经济衰退时, 许多小型企业都破产了。**3 go for broke** *informal* to take big risks trying to achieve something【非正式】孤注一掷: *Why not go for broke and set up your own business?* 你为何不冒个险自己开一家店呢?

bro·ken[1] /ˈbrokən; ˈbrəʊkən/ the past participle of BREAK[1]

broken[2] *adj*

1 ►**PIECE OF EQUIPMENT** 设备◄ not working properly 坏的, 不能使用的: *The vacuum cleaner's broken again.* 吸尘器又坏了。| **get broken** (=become broken) 出毛病, 出故障 *Somehow the heaters got broken.* 不知什么原因, 取暖器坏了。

2 ►**OBJECT** 物体◄ in small pieces because it has been hit, dropped etc 破的; 破碎的; 损坏的; 断裂的: *Mind the broken glass.* 当心碎玻璃。| **get broken** (=become broken) 损坏 *It got broken in the mail.* 这东西在邮寄过程中损坏了。—see picture on page A18 参见 A18 页图

3 ►**BONE** 骨头◄ cracked because you have had an accident 折断的: *a broken leg* 摔断了的腿

4 ►**INTERRUPTED** 断续的◄ interrupted and not continuous 被打断的; 断断续续的: *a broken white line* 白色的虚线 | **broken sleep** (=with interruptions) 时断时续的睡眠 *sixteen nights of broken sleep because of the baby* 由于婴儿闹, 16个夜晚只能断断续续地睡点觉

5 ►**PERSON** 人◄ extremely mentally or physically weak because you have suffered a lot 衰弱的; 沮丧的: *He returned a broken man.* 他回来时很沮丧。

6 broken agreement/promise etc a promise etc in which someone did not do what they promised 未被遵守的协议/承诺等

7 broken English/French etc English, French etc that is spoken very slowly by someone who only knows a little of the language 蹩脚 [不流利] 的英语/法语等

8 broken home a family that no longer lives together because the parents have divorced (DIVORCE[2] (1))〔夫妻离异造成的〕破裂家庭

9 broken marriage a marriage that has ended because the husband and wife do not live together any more 破裂的婚姻

10 a broken heart a feeling of extreme sadness, especially because someone you love has died or left you 破碎的心

broken-heart·ed /ˌ·· ˈ··◂/ *adj* extremely sad, especially because someone you love has died or left you 伤心的, 心碎的: *He dumped her for no apparent reason, and left her broken-hearted.* 他莫名其妙地抛弃了她, 使她伤心欲绝。—**broken-heartedly** *adv*

bro·ker[1] /ˈbrokɚ; ˈbrəʊkə/ *n* [C] someone who buys and sells shares (SHARE[2] (5)) in a company, INSURANCE (1), foreign money etc for other people 经纪人, 掮客; 中间人, 代理商: *an insurance broker* 保险经纪人

broker[2] *v* [T] **broker a deal/settlement/treaty etc** to arrange the details of a deal etc so that everyone can agree to it 就交易/协议/条约等进行调停

bro·ker·age /ˈbrokərɪdʒ; ˈbrəʊkərɪdʒ/ *n* [U] **1** the business of being a broker 经纪业; 掮客业务 **2** the amount of money a broker charges 佣金, 手续费, 经纪费 **3 brokerage house/firm** a company of brokers, or the place where they work 经纪行

brol·ly /ˈbrɑlɪ; ˈbrɒli/ *n* [C] *BrE informal* an UMBRELLA (1)【英, 非正式】雨伞

bro·mide /ˈbromaɪd; ˈbrəʊmaɪd/ *n* **1** [C,U] a chemical compound, sometimes used in medicine to make people feel calm 溴化物; 溴化剂 **2** [C] *formal* a statement which is intended to make someone less angry but which is not effective【正式】老生常谈, 陈词滥调

bronc /braŋk; brɒŋk/ *n* [C] *informal* a BRONCO【非正式】野马

bron·chi·al /ˈbraŋkɪəl; ˈbrɒŋkiəl/ *adj* affecting the bronchial tubes 支气管的: *a bronchial infection* 支气管感染

bronchial tube /ˈ···, ·/ *n* [C usually singular 一般用单数] one of the small tubes that take air into your lungs 支气管 —see picture at 参见 RESPIRATORY 图

bron·chi·tis /branˋkaɪtɪs; brɒŋˈkaɪtɪs/ *n* [C] an illness which affects your bronchial tubes and makes you cough 支气管炎 —**bronchitic** /-ˋkɪtɪk; -ˈkɪtɪk/ *adj*

bron·co /ˈbraŋko; ˈbrɒŋkəʊ/ *n* [C] a wild horse from the western US〔美国西部的〕野马: *a bucking bronco* 跳起的野马

Bron·të /ˈbrantɪ; ˈbrɒnti/ the family name of three sisters from Yorkshire in the north of England, who wrote some of the most famous NOVELs in English. **Charlotte Brontë** (1816-55) wrote *Jane Eyre*, **Emily Brontë** (1818-48) wrote *Wuthering Heights*, and **Anne Brontë** (1820-49) wrote *The Tenant of Wildfell Hall*. 勃朗特〔英格兰北部约克郡三姐妹的姓氏，她们创作的英语小说十分著名，如夏洛蒂·勃朗特(1816-1855)的《简·爱》、艾米丽·勃朗特(1818-1848)的《呼啸山庄》、安妮·勃朗特(1820-1849)的《怀尔德菲尔庄园的佃户》〕

bron·to·sau·rus /ˌbrantəˋsɔrəs; ˌbrɒntəˈsɔːrəs/ *n* [C] a large DINOSAUR with a small head and a long neck 雷龙〔以植物为食的一种恐龙〕

Bronx, the /braŋks; brɒŋks/ a COUNTY, and one of the five BOROUGHs, of New York City 布朗克斯区〔即布朗克斯县，纽约市五个行政区之一〕

Bronx cheer /ˌbraŋks ˋtʃɪr; ˌbrɒŋks ˈtʃɪə/ *n* [C] *AmE* a rude sound you make by putting your tongue between your lips and blowing【美】讥笑声，嘘声；喝倒彩; RASPBERRY (2) *BrE*【英】

bronze¹ /branz; brɒnz/ *n* **1** [U] a hard metal that is made of a mixture of COPPER (1) and TIN¹ (1) 青铜，古铜 **2** [U] the dark red-brown colour of bronze 青铜色，古铜色 **3** [C] a work of art such as a STATUE (=model of a person), made of bronze 青铜器；青铜艺术品 **4** [C] a BRONZE MEDAL 铜(奖)牌

bronze² *adj* **1** made of bronze 青铜制的: *a bronze statuette by Degas*〔法国画家〕德加塑造的小青铜雕像 **2** having the red-brown colour of bronze 青铜色的，古铜色的

Bronze Age /ˈ· ·/ *n* [singular] the time, between about 6,000 and 4,000 years ago, when bronze was used for making tools, weapons etc 青铜器时代〔距今约4000至6000年〕—compare 比较 IRON AGE, STONE AGE

bronzed /branzd; brɒnzd/ *adj* having skin that is attractively brown because you have been in the sun〔皮肤因日晒而呈〕古铜色的

bronze med·al /ˌ· ˈ··/ *n* [C] a MEDAL made of bronze given to the person who comes third in a race or competition 铜牌，铜(奖)章 —**bronze medallist** *n* [C] —see also 另见 GOLD MEDAL, SILVER MEDAL

brooch /brotʃ; brəʊtʃ/ *n* [C] a piece of jewellery that you fasten to your clothes 胸针，饰针; PIN¹ (2) *AmE*【美】—see picture at 参见 PIN¹ 图

brood¹ /brud; bruːd/ *v* [I] **1** to keep thinking for a long time about something that you are worried, angry, or upset about 沉思；忧思；深思: *After the argument Simon sat in his room, brooding.* 争吵之后，西蒙坐在房间里沉思。| **[+over/about/on]** *There's no point brooding over it – she's gone.* 老是想这件事也没用，反正她已经走了。**2** if a bird broods, it sits on its eggs to make the young birds break out 孵卵，抱窝

brood² *n* [C] **1** a family of young birds all born at the same time〔尤指雏鸟的〕一窝 **2** *humorous* a family with a lot of children【幽默】一家的孩子们: *Mary has a whole brood of grandchildren.* 玛丽有一大堆孙子孙女。

brood·er /ˈbrudɚ; ˈbruːdə/ *n* [C] **1** a heated structure for young birds to live in 孵化器 **2** someone who broods a lot 沉思的人

brood·ing /ˈbrudɪŋ; ˈbruːdɪŋ/ *adj* mysterious and threatening 神秘莫测的: *a brooding menacing atmosphere* 神秘而不祥的气氛 —**broodingly** *adv*

brood·y /ˈbrudɪ; ˈbruːdi/ *adj* **1** silent because you are thinking or worrying about something 闷闷不乐的，抑郁的；沉思的: *Damian's been really broody lately.* 达米安近来一直闷闷不乐。**2** *informal* wishing that you had a baby【非正式】想要孩子的: *I get broody when I see baby clothes in shop windows.* 我一看到橱窗里的婴儿服装，就想自己也有个孩子。**3** if a female bird is broody, it wants to lay eggs or to sit on them to make the young birds break out〔雌鸟〕想孵卵的，要抱窝的 —**broodily** *adv* —**broodiness** *n* [U]

brook¹ /brʊk; brʊk/ *n* [C] a small stream 小河，溪流: *a babbling brook* 潺潺的小溪

brook² *v* **not brook sth/brook no sth** *formal* to not allow or accept something【正式】不容忍…: *He would brook no interruptions from subordinates.* 他不容忍下属打断自己。

Brooke /brʊk; brʊk/, **Ru·pert** /ˈrupɚt; ˈruːpət/ (1887-1915) a British poet who was a soldier in World War I. He wrote poems about war and romantic poems about England, including *The Old Vicarage* and *Grantchester*. 布鲁克〔(1887-1915)，英国诗人，一战期间当过兵。他的作品有战争题材的诗歌和英格兰题材的浪漫诗歌，如《牧师旧宅》和《格兰切斯特》〕

Brook·ings In·sti·tu·tion, the /ˈbrʊkɪŋz ɪnstəˌtjuʃən; ˈbrʊkɪŋz ɪnstɪˌtjuːʃən/ a US organization based in Washington, D.C., which examines social and economic problems 布鲁金斯学会〔一个专门研究社会、经济问题的美国机构，总部设在华盛顿哥伦比亚特区〕

Brook·lyn /ˈbrʊklɪn; ˈbrʊklɪn/ an industrial and international port area of New York City, and one of the city's five BOROUGHs 布鲁克林区〔纽约市工业区和国际港口区，该市五个行政区之一〕

Brooklyn Bridge, the /ˌ·· ˈ·/ a bridge connecting Brooklyn with Manhattan 布鲁克林大桥〔连接布鲁克林和曼哈顿的一座桥梁〕

> **CULTURAL NOTE 文化注释**
>
> In the US there is an old joke that IMMIGRANTs arriving in New York City could be sold the Brooklyn Bridge because they did not know the city's well-known buildings or the customs of the people who live there. So 'being sold the Brooklyn Bridge' has come to mean being fooled in a business deal. 美国有个老笑话，说到达纽约的移民因为不知道该市的著名建筑或当地风俗，可能会从别人手里把布鲁克林大桥买下来。因此，being sold the Brooklyn Bridge 后来意指"做生意被骗"。

Brook·side /ˈbrʊksaɪd; ˈbrʊksaɪd/ a popular SOAP OPERA on British television, about a group of people who live in Liverpool《小溪边》〔英国流行电视肥皂剧，讲述生活在利物浦的一群人〕

broom /brum; bruːm/ *n* **1** [C] a large brush with a long handle, used for sweeping floors 扫帚 —see picture at 参见 BRUSH¹ 图 **2** [U] a large bush with small yellow flowers that grows on unused land 金雀花

broom·stick /ˈbrumˌstɪk; ˈbruːmˌstɪk/ *n* [C] a broom with a long handle and small sticks tied at one end that a WITCH (1) is supposed to fly on in children's stories〔童话中女巫骑坐的〕长扫帚柄

Bros the written abbreviation of 缩写= Brothers, used in the names of companies 兄弟公司〔用于公司名称〕: *Jones Bros., tailors* 琼斯兄弟服装公司

broth /brɔθ; brɒθ/ *n* [U] thick soup with meat, rice, or vegetables 肉汤；米汤；菜汤: *chicken broth* 鸡汤 —see also 另见 SCOTCH BROTH

broth·el /ˈbraθəl; ˈbrɒθəl/ *n* [C] a house where men pay to have sex with PROSTITUTEs 妓院

broth·er¹ /ˈbrʌðɚ; ˈbrʌðə/ *n* [C] **1** a male who has the same parents as you (同胞)兄弟；哥；弟: *This is a picture of my brother Andrew.* 这是我弟弟安德鲁的照片。| **elder/older/younger/little etc brother** *My younger brother is a doctor.* 我弟弟是一名医生。—see picture at 参见 FAMILY 图 **2** a male member of a group with the same interests, religion, profession etc as you 弟兄；(男性)同胞；同仁；同行；会友: *Brothers, we must stand together to fight the inequalities of the system!* 弟兄们，我们必须为反对不平等的制度而并肩战斗！**3** *plural* **brothers** or **brethren** a male member of a religious group, especially a MONK〔同教会的男性〕教友，主内兄弟；僧侣；修士: *Brother Justin* 贾斯廷修士 **4** *AmE* a member of a FRATERNITY (=a club of male university students)【美】〔男学生的〕大学生联谊会，兄弟会 **5 brothers in arms** soldiers who have fought together in a war 战友 —see also 另见 BIG BROTHER, BLOOD BROTHER 

brother² *interjection AmE* used to express annoyance or surprise【美】哇！呀！哎！〔表示不耐烦、惊讶〕: *Oh brother! Did he really say that?* 啊！他真那样说的吗？

Brother can you spare a dime /ˌ· · · ·, · ˈ·/ the title of a song written about the Great Depression of the 1930s in the US. In the song, a man who had been rich and respected before the Depression asks people to give him money, as he is now poor.《大哥，给我一毛钱吧》〔歌名。歌词大意是，20世纪30年代美国大萧条之前，有个人很富有且受人尊敬，而今却沦落到了向人讨钱的地步〕

broth·er·hood /ˈbrʌðɚˌhud; ˈbrʌðəhʊd/ *n* **1** [U] a feeling of friendship between people 手足情，同胞之爱: *peace and brotherhood among men* 男人间的亲睦关系 **2** [C] an organiza-

tion or society formed for a particular purpose, especially a religious one〔宗教的〕兄弟会: *the Franciscan brotherhood* 圣方济各兄弟会 **3** [C] *old-fashioned* a union of workers in a particular trade【过时】同业工会 **4** [U] the relationship between brothers 兄弟关系, 手足之情

brother-in-law /ˈ· · · ,·/ *n plural* **brothers-in-law** *or* **brother-in-laws** [C] **1** the brother of your husband or wife 内兄; 内弟; 大伯; 小叔 **2** the husband of your sister 姐夫; 妹夫 **3** the husband of your husband or wife's sister 连襟〔配偶之姐妹的丈夫〕—see picture at 参见 FAMILY 图

broth·er·ly /ˈbrʌðəlɪ; ˈbrʌðəli/ *adj* showing the helpfulness, love, loyalty etc that you would expect a brother to show 情同手足的, 兄弟的, 兄弟般的: *brotherly love* 兄弟之爱 | *He offered me some brotherly advice.* 他给我提了一些兄弟般的劝告。—**brotherliness** *n* [U]

Brothers Grimm /,· · ˈ·/ —see 见 GRIMM

brough·am /ˈbruəm; ˈbruːəm/ *n* [C] a light carriage used in the past which had four wheels and a roof and was pulled by a horse〔古时由一匹马拉的〕四轮箱型马车

brought /brɔt; brɔːt/ the past tense and past participle of BRING

brou·ha·ha /bruˈhɑhɑ; ˈbruːhɑːhɑː/ *n* [U] *old-fashioned* unnecessary noise and activity; COMMOTION【过时】喧闹, 嘈杂; 骚乱

brow /brau; braʊ/ *n* **1** [C] the part of your face above your eyes and below your hair; FOREHEAD 额: **mop/wipe your brow** (=dry your brow with your hand or a piece of cloth when you are hot or nervous) 擦额头(上的汗) | **crease/wrinkle/knit etc your brow** (=tighten the skin on your brow, making lines appear when you are angry or thinking very hard) 紧锁眉头 *"I don't understand," he said, wrinkling his brow.* "我不懂。"他紧锁眉头说。**2** an EYEBROW 眉, 眉毛 **3** **the brow of the hill** *especially BrE* the top part of a slope or hill【尤英】斜坡的上部

brow·beat /ˈbrau,bit; ˈbraʊbiːt/ *v past tense* **browbeat** *past participle* **browbeaten** /-,bitn; -biːtn/ [T+into] to make someone do something by continuously asking them to, especially in an unpleasant threatening way〔声色俱厉地〕威逼, 恫吓: *The witness was being browbeaten under cross-examination.* 证人被盘问时受到威逼。

S2 W2 **brown¹** /braun; braʊn/ *adj* **1** having the colour of earth, wood, or coffee 褐色的; 棕色的: *I'd like a pair of dark brown shoes please.* 我想买一双深棕色的皮鞋。| *brown bread* 黑面包 **2** having skin that has been turned brown by the sun〔皮肤被太阳晒得〕黝黑的: *You're very brown – have you been on vacation?* 你皮肤晒得很黑, 是不是去度假了? | **brown as a berry** (=very brown)〔皮肤〕黝黑的 *She came back as brown as a berry.* 她回来时皮肤晒得黝黑。

brown² *n* [C,U] the colour of earth, wood, or coffee 褐色; 棕色: *the different browns and greens of the landscape* 深浅不同的褐色及绿色的景观 —see picture on page A5 参见 A5 页图

brown³ *v* [I,T] **1** to heat food so that it turns brown or to become brown in this way by being heated (使)〔食品〕烧成褐色: *First brown the meat in a frying pan.* 首先将肉在油锅里炸成褐色。**2** to become brown because of the sun's heat or to make something brown in this way〔太阳〕(使) 变成褐[棕]色: *The children's faces were browned by the sun.* 孩子们的脸被太阳晒得黑黝黝的。**3** **browned off** *BrE informal* annoyed and bored【英, 非正式】厌烦的, 厌倦的

Brown, Capability (1716-83) a British garden designer, who planned many large and famous gardens in castles and large country houses in England 能人布朗〔(1716-1783), 英国园林设计师, 为英格兰的城堡和乡间别墅设计了许多著名花园〕

Brown, Charlie *trademark* a character from the US CARTOON STRIP called *Peanuts* by Charles Schultz. Charlie Brown is a nice boy who is not very confident and is often unlucky. He has a pet dog called Snoopy.【商标】查理·布朗〔查尔斯·舒尔茨创作的美国连环漫画《花生》中的人物, 他是个缺乏自信且常常不走运的乖男孩, 他有只宠物狗, 叫史努比〕

Brown, James (1928-) a US popular musician, singer, and songwriter. Many people consider him one of the greatest soul singers ever. He is sometimes called 'the Godfather of Soul'. 布朗〔(1928-), 美国流行音乐家、歌手和作曲家, 被视为有史以来最伟大的灵歌歌手之一, 有时也被称为"灵乐教父"〕

Brown, John (1800-59) a US ABOLITIONIST (=someone who worked to end slavery) who tried to use violence to end SLAVERY. With followers, he took over a government weapons establishment at Harper's Ferry, Virginia. He was caught and hanged for TREASON. During the American Civil War, a song called *John Brown's Body* became popular in the North. The song is still well known and contains the words: John Brown's body lies amouldering in the grave, /But his soul goes marching on. 布朗〔(1800-1859), 美国废奴主义者, 试图用暴力废除奴隶制。他和他的追随者夺取了政府在弗吉尼亚州哈珀斯费里的军火库, 被俘后以叛国罪被处以绞刑。美国南北战争期间, 北方流行一首名为《约翰·布朗的遗体》的歌曲, 至今仍广为人知, 其中一句是: 约翰·布朗的肉体在墓中腐化, 但英魂却勇往直前〕

Brown, Sir Arthur Whitten —see 见 ALCOCK AND BROWN

brown-bag /ˈ· ·/ *v* [I] *AmE*【美】**1** to bring your LUNCH to work, usually in a small brown paper bag 自带〔牛皮纸袋装的〕午餐上班: *I'm brown-bagging it this week.* 这周我要自己带午餐上班。**2** to bring your own alcohol to a restaurant which does not serve alcohol 自带酒上〔不供应酒的〕餐馆 —**brown-bagging** *n* [U]

brown goods /ˈ· ·/ *n* [plural] *BrE* electrical goods bought to provide entertainment at home, such as televisions and computers【英】棕色商品〔指电视机、电脑等〕—compare 比较 WHITE GOODS

Brown·ie /ˈbraunɪ; ˈbraʊni/ also 又作 **Brownie Guide** /ˈ· · ·/ *n* **1** **the Brownies** the part of the Girl Guides Association that is for younger girls 幼年女童子军 **2** [C] a member of this organization 幼年女童子军成员

brownie *n* [C] **1** a thick flat American chocolate cake 果仁巧克力蛋糕: *fudge brownies* 乳脂果仁巧克力蛋糕 **2** **get/earn brownie points** *informal* if you do something to get brownie points you want people to praise you【非正式】想得到别人的表扬

Brow·ning /ˈbraunɪŋ; ˈbraʊnɪŋ/, **E·liz·a·beth Bar·rett** /ɪˈlɪzəbəθ ˈbærət; ɪˈlɪzəbəθ ˈbærət/ (1806-61) a British poet who married the poet Robert Browning in 1846 布朗宁〔(1806-1861), 英国诗人, 1846 年与诗人罗伯特·布朗宁结婚〕

Browning, Robert (1812-89) a British poet, married to Elizabeth Barrett Browning, whose poems include *The Ring and the Book* and *Home Thoughts from Abroad* 布朗宁〔(1812-1889), 英国诗人, 妻子是诗人伊丽莎白·巴雷特·布朗宁, 诗作有《指环和书》及《海外乡思》〕

brown-nose /ˈ· ·/ *v* [I,T] *informal* to try to make your manager, teacher etc like you by being very nice to them【非正式】拍马屁, 巴结: *You're not going to get that promotion just by brown-nosing!* 你单靠拍马屁是不会升职的! —**brown-nose** *n* [C]

brown out /ˈ· ·/ *n* [C] *AmE* a power failure affecting some but not all the electrical lights in an area【美】部分停电

brown rice /,· ˈ·/ *n* [U] rice which still has its outer layer 糙米

brown·stone /ˈbraun,ston; ˈbraʊnstəʊn/ *n* **1** [U] a type of reddish-brown stone, often used for building〔建筑用的〕褐(砂)石 **2** [C] a house in the US with a front made of this stone, common in New York City 褐(砂)石房屋〔多见于纽约市〕: *office buildings side by side with the more elegant brownstones* 与精致的褐(砂)石房子紧挨着的办公大楼

Brown University an old and respected US university, established in 1764, in Providence, Rhode Island 布朗大学〔美国一所久负盛名的大学, 建于 1764 年, 位于罗得岛州普洛威顿斯〕

Brown v. Board of Ed·u·ca·tion of To·pe·ka also 又作 **Brown vs Board, Brown decision** a US legal case which resulted in a famous decision by the US Supreme Court in 1954. It was decided that black students should be allowed to attend the same schools and universities as white students, and this officially ended SEGREGATION in the US education system. Following this, some children were taken by bus to different schools in order to mix blacks and whites 布朗-托皮卡教育局诉讼案〔美国案例。1954 年美国最高法院裁定, 黑人学生应获准与白人学生在同样的学校和大学读书。此举正式结束了美国教育系统的种族隔离制度, 随后, 一些孩子由公共汽车接送到不同学校, 黑人学生和白人学生一起接受教育〕—see also 另见 PLESSY V. FERGUSON

browse /brauz; braʊz/ *v* [I] **1** to look through the pages of a book, magazine etc without a particular purpose, just reading the most interesting parts 随意翻阅, 浏览〔书刊等〕: [+through] *I was browsing through a newspaper when I spotted your name.* 我在翻阅报纸时突然发现了你的名字。**2** to look at the goods in a shop without wanting to buy any particular thing 浏览商品: *Can I help you, madam, or are you just browsing?* 夫人, 您想买什么, 还是随便看看? **3** [+on] if a goat, DEER etc browses, it eats plants〔牲畜〕吃草 **4** to search computer material 搜索电脑资料, 浏览: *a fast effective browsing tool* 快速高效的浏览工具

Bruce /brus; bruːs/, **Len·ny** /ˈlɛnɪ; ˈleni/ (1926-66) a US COMEDIAN who is remembered for making jokes about subjects such

as sex and race 布鲁斯〔(1926-1966)，美国喜剧演员，人们印象中的他喜欢拿性、种族这类话题开玩笑〕

Bruce, Rob·ert (the) (1274-1329) the King of Scotland from 1307 till his death. Scotland was recognized as independent under him in 1328. 布鲁斯〔(1274-1329)，1307 年起任苏格兰国王，直至去世。在他统治期间，苏格兰的独立于 1328 年得到承认〕

Brue·gel /ˈbrɔɪgəl; ˈbrɔɪgəl/, **Pie·ter** /ˈpitɚ; ˈpitə/ also 又作 **Brueghel** or **Breughel** (?1525-69) a Flemish painter of LANDSCAPES and ordinary people, also called Bruegel the Elder. His sons Pieter (Bruegel the Younger) and Jan were also painters. 勃鲁盖尔〔(?1525-1569)，佛兰德斯画家，擅长风景和普通人物画，又被称为老勃鲁盖尔。他的儿子彼得（即小布鲁盖尔）和扬也都是画家〕

bruise[1] /bruz; bruːz/ *n* [C] **1** a purple or brown mark on your skin that you get because you have fallen, been hit etc 青瘀，伤痕，擦伤 **2** a mark on a piece of fruit that spoils its appearance 〔水果的〕擦痕，碰伤

bruise[2] *v* [I,T] **1** if part of your body bruises or if you bruise it, it gets hit or hurt and a bruise appears（使）碰伤，擦伤，（使）成瘀伤：*She fell off her bike and bruised her knee.* 她从脚踏车上摔下来，擦伤了膝盖。**2** if a piece of fruit bruises or is bruised, it gets a bruise by being hit, dropped etc（使）〔水果〕碰伤，擦伤 —**bruising** *n* [U]: *severe bruising to the face and head* 面部和头部严重擦伤

bruised /bruzd; bruːzd/ *adj* **1 bruised ribs/knee/elbow etc** a part of your body with a bruise on it 挫伤的肋骨/膝盖/胳膊肘等 **2** upset or emotionally harmed by an experience 受伤害的；受挫的

bruis·er /ˈbruzɚ; ˈbruːzə/ *n* [C] *informal* a big strong rough man【非正式】彪形大汉：*Two ugly bruisers barred the door.* 两个丑陋的彪形大汉挡住了门。

bruit /brut; bruːt/ *v*

bruit sth ↔ **abroad** *phr v* [T] *formal* to tell a lot of people about something【正式】传播，散布

Brum /brum; brʌm/ *BrE informal*【英，非正式】the English city of Birmingham 伯明翰〔英国城市〕

Brum·mell /ˈbrʌməl; ˈbrʌməl/, **Beau** /bo; bəʊ/ (1778-1840) an English DANDY (=a man who is very interested in clothes and likes to be very fashionable), who was a friend of George IV before George became king 布鲁梅尔〔(1778-1840)，英国一纨绔子弟，乔治四世即位前的朋友〕

brunch /brʌntʃ; brʌntʃ/ *n* [C,U] a meal eaten in the late morning, as a combination of breakfast and LUNCH 早午餐〔早餐和午餐并为一顿吃〕

Bru·nei /bruˋnaɪ; ˈbruːnaɪ/ a country in the northwest of the island of Borneo in Southeast Asia, which is an independent member of the British Commonwealth. Population: 343,653 (2001). Capital: Bandar Seri Begawan. 文莱〔东南亚婆罗洲西北部国家，英联邦独立成员国。人口：343,653 (2001)，首都：斯里巴加湾市〕

Bru·nel /bruˋnel; bruːˈnel/, **Is·am·bard King·dom** /ˈɪzəmbɑrd ˋkɪŋdəm; ˈɪzəmbɑːd ˈkɪŋdəm/ (1806-59) an English engineer famous for his railway engines, bridges, and iron ships 布律内尔〔(1806-1859)，英国工程师，以设计机车、桥梁和铁船而闻名〕

bru·nette /bruˋnɛt; bruːˈnet/ *n* [C] a woman with dark brown hair 深褐色头发的女子：*a slim brunette* 长着深褐色头发的苗条女子

Brun·hil·de /brunˋhɪldə; brʊnˈhɪldə/ a character in *The Ring of the Nibelungen* who is a princess. She is usually shown as a large strong fair-haired woman in ARMOUR. 布伦希尔特〔《尼伯龙根的指环》中的公主，通常以金发女子的形象出现，高大强壮、身着盔甲〕

brunt /brʌnt; brʌnt/ *n* **bear/take the brunt of sth** to receive the worst part of an attack, criticism etc 受到最严厉的批评[攻击]；首当其冲：*The southern part of the town bore the brunt of the attack.* 城市的南部受到最严重的袭击。

brush[1] /brʌʃ; brʌʃ/ *n*

1 ▶FOR CLEANING 用于清扫◀ [C] an object that you use for cleaning, painting etc, made with a lot of hairs, bristles (BRISTLE[1] (2)), or thin pieces of plastic fixed to a handle 刷子；毛刷；画笔；毛笔：*a hairbrush* 发刷 | *Get a brush and sweep up all that rubbish.* 拿把刷子来，把这些垃圾都清除掉。

2 [singular] a movement which brushes something, to remove dirt, make something smooth, tidy etc〔动作〕刷，梳，擦，拂拭：*I'll just give my hair a quick brush.* 我就很快梳一下头发。

3 ▶TOUCH 接触◀ [singular] a quick light touch, made by

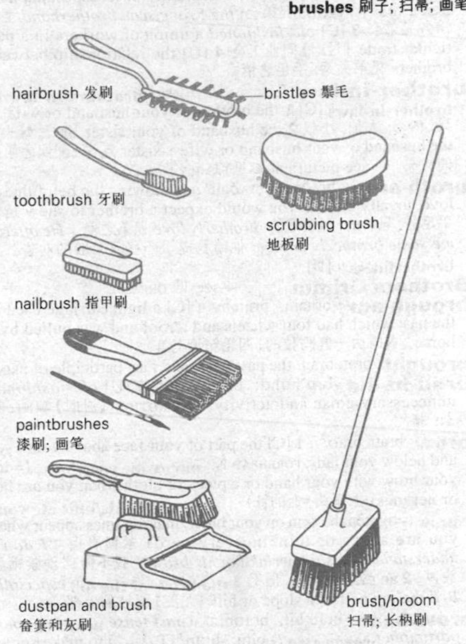

chance when two things or people pass each other 轻触，轻擦：*the brush of her silk dress as she walked past* 她走过时绸衣轻轻擦过

4 ▶BUSHES/TREES 灌木/树◀ [U] **a)** *AmE* small bushes and trees covering an open area of land【美】灌木林，杂树丛 **b)** branches which have broken off bushes and trees 折断的树枝；柴枝

5 a brush with death/a brush with the law etc an occasion when something bad almost happens to you, but you just manage to avoid it 差一点送命/犯法等

6 ▶TAIL 尾巴◀ [C] the tail of a FOX[1] (1) 狐狸尾巴 —see also 另见 **as daft as a brush** (DAFT (1))

brush[2] *v* **1** [T] to clean something or make something smooth and tidy using a brush〔用刷子〕刷，扫，拂拭：*Don't forget to brush your teeth.* 不要忘记刷牙。**2** [T always+adv/prep] to remove something with a brush or with your hand 刷掉；拂去：**brush sth off/away etc** *Brush the crumbs off your jacket, you messy thing.* 把夹克上的面包屑刷掉，你这脏家伙。| *He brushed his hair out of his eyes.* 他把挡住眼睛的头发梳了上去。**3** [I always+adv/prep, T] to touch someone or something lightly by chance when passing them 轻擦而过：[**+against**] *I felt her hair brush against my arm.* 我感到她的头发轻拂着我的胳膊。| **brush sth** *The car brushed the hedges of the narrow lane.* 汽车轻轻擦过小路旁的树篱。**4 brush yourself down** *BrE*【英】, **brush yourself off** *AmE*【美】to tidy yourself, especially after a fall, by using your hands to brush your clothes etc〔用手〕掸掉身上的尘土：*I got up, brushed myself down, and carried on walking.* 我爬起来，掸了掸身上的尘土，继续往前走。

brush sb/sth ↔ **aside** *phr v* [T] to refuse to listen to or consider something 不理会，不顾，漠视：*He simply brushed all my objections aside.* 他根本不顾我的种种反对意见。

brush sth ↔ **down** *phr v* [T] to clean your clothes or an animal thoroughly using a brush〔用刷子〕彻底刷洗

brush sth ↔ **off** *phr v* [T] refuse to listen to someone or their ideas, especially by ignoring them or saying something rude 漠视，充耳不闻：*The President brushed off their pleas for an investigation.* 总统拒绝了他们调查的请求。

brush up (on) sth *phr v* [I] to quickly practise and improve your skills or knowledge 温习，复习：*I must brush up on my French before I go to Paris.* 去巴黎之前，我要好好温习一下法语。

brushed /brʌʃt; brʌʃt/ *adj* [only before noun 仅用于名词前] a brushed cloth has been specially treated to make it feel much softer 拉绒的，起绒的：*brushed cotton* 起绒棉布

brush-off /ˈ· ·/ *n* [singular] a clear sign that you do not want someone's friendship, invitations etc 拒绝，碰钉子：**give sb the brush-off** *I thought Andy liked me, but he gave me the brush-off.* 我以为安迪喜欢我，可是他让我碰了一鼻子灰。

brush·wood /ˋbrʌʃ,wud; ˈbrʌʃwʊd/ *n* [U] small dead branches broken from trees or bushes 折断的小树枝

brush·work /ˋbrʌʃ,wɝk; ˈbrʌʃwɜːk/ *n* [U] the particular way in which someone puts paint on a picture using a brush 画法；绘画风格

brusque /brʌsk; bruːsk/ *adj* using very few words in a way that seems rude but is not intended to be 莽撞的；粗鲁的；唐突的：*He was rather brusque on the phone.* 他在电话上说话有些粗鲁。—**brusquely** *adv*: *"You'd better leave," she said brusquely.* "你最好离开。"她无礼地说。—**brusqueness** *n* [U]

Brus·sels /ˋbrʌslz; ˈbrʌsəlz/ the capital city of Belgium in the centre of the country, from which the business of the European Union and NATO is run 布鲁塞尔〔比利时首都，位于该国中部，是欧盟和北大西洋公约组织总部所在地〕

CULTURAL NOTE 文化注释

In the UK, politicians and newspaper writers who do not like the European Union sometimes use the name Brussels to mean the officials of the European Union, when they are criticizing them for making too many complicated rules about things that they should not be involved in. 不喜欢欧盟的英国政界人士或报刊写手有时用"布鲁塞尔"一词指欧盟官员，批评他们对不该干涉的事物制定了太多复杂的规则。

brus·sels sprout /,brʌslz ˋspraut; ˌbrʌsəlz ˈspraʊt/ *n* [C] a small round green vegetable with many tightly folded leaves 球芽甘蓝（菜），抱子甘蓝；SPROUT[2] (1) —see picture on page A9 参见 A9 页图

bru·tal /ˋbrutl; ˈbruːtl/ *adj* **1** very cruel and violent 无情的，残酷的，野蛮的，凶残的：*a brutal and savage crime* 野蛮残暴的罪行 **2** unkind and not sensitive to people's feelings 不讲情面的，不顾他人感情的：**brutal honesty/frankness etc** *They told us all the details with brutal honesty.* 他们丝毫不讲情面，把所有的细节都告诉了我们。—**brutally** *adv*: *brutally honest* 极其直率的 —**brutality** /bruˋtæləti; bruːˈtælti/ *n* [C,U]: *the brutalities of war* 战争的残酷[野蛮]

bru·tal·ize also 又作 **-ise** *BrE*【英】/ˋbrutl,aɪz; ˈbruːtəlaɪz/ *v* [T usually passive 一般用被动态] **1** to affect someone so badly that they lose their normal human feelings 使残忍；使变无情：*brutalized by their experiences in jail* 因坐过牢而变得无情 **2** to treat someone in a cruel or violent way 虐待：*systematically abused and brutalized* 遭到蓄意辱骂和虐待 —**brutalization** /,brutl̩əˋzeʃən; ˌbruːtəlaɪˈzeɪʃən/ *n* [U]

Bru·te /ˋbrute; ˈbruːteɪ/ **Et tu, Brute?** a phrase from Shakespeare's play *Julius Caesar*, used by Caesar when he realizes that even his good friend Brutus has BETRAY*ed* him and is going to kill him. The phrase goes: "Et tu, Brute?" (and you, Brutus?) 布鲁图，还有你？〔源自莎士比亚戏剧《尤利乌斯·凯撒》。当凯撒意识到连自己的好友布鲁图都背叛了他，并且还要谋害他时，他说道："布鲁图，还有你？"〕

brute[1] /brut; bruːt/ *n* [C] **1** *often humorous* a man who is rough, cruel and not sensitive【常幽默】无人性的家伙〔尤指男人〕：*Don't hit him, you brute!* 别打他，你这个没人性的家伙！**2** *literary* an animal, especially a large or strong one【文】〔尤指大或强壮的〕畜生，动物，兽

brute[2] *adj* **brute force/strength etc** physical strength rather than thought or intelligence 暴力/蛮劲等：*He won, not so much by skill as by brute force.* 他赢了，但不是靠技巧，而是靠蛮劲。

brut·ish /ˋbrutɪʃ; ˈbruːtɪʃ/ *adj* showing no human intelligence or feeling 畜生似的，兽性的，没有人性的 —**brutishly** *adv* —**brutishness** *n* [U]

Bru·tus /ˋbrutəs; ˈbruːtəs/, **Mar·cus** /ˋmarkəs; ˈmɑːkəs/ (? 85-42 BC) a Roman politician who was the chief member of the PLOT to murder Julius Caesar 布鲁图〔(?85-42 BC)，罗马政治家，密谋杀害尤利乌斯·凯撒的主要人物〕

Bry·ant /ˋbraɪənt; ˈbraɪənt/, **Paul "Bear"** (1913-83) a US college football COACH (=teacher) who set a record for winning the most games 布赖恩特〔(1913-1983)，美国大学橄榄球教练，曾创下获胜场数最高纪录〕

Bryl·creem /ˋbrɪlkrim; ˈbrɪlkriːm/ *n* [U] *trademark* a type of oil used on men's hair to make it shiny and smooth【商标】"百利"牌男用发乳

BS /,bi ˋɛs; ˌbiː ˈes/ *n* [U] *AmE informal*【美，非正式】an abbreviation of 缩写= BULLSHIT

BSc /,bi ɛs ˋsi; ˌbiː es ˈsiː/ Bachelor of Science; a first university degree in a science subject 理学士：*Barbara Stone, BSc* 芭芭拉·斯通理学士 —compare 比较 BA

BSE /,bi ɛs ˋi; ˌbiː es ˈiː/ *n* [U] bovine spongiform encephalitis; a deadly brain disease in cows 牛海绵状脑病，疯牛病

BSI, the /,bi ɛs ˋaɪ; ˌbiː es ˈaɪ/ *n* the British Standards Institution; an organization which sets standards for units of measurement, clothes sizes etc, and safety standards for electrical and other goods used in Britain 英国标准协会〔英国的一个机构，负责制定度量衡单位、服装尺寸以及电器和其他产品安全标准〕

B-side /ˋbi saɪd; ˈbiː saɪd/ *n* [C] the less important side of a record 〔唱片的〕B面

BSkyB /,bi skaɪ ˋbi; ˈbiː skaɪ ˈbiː/ *n trademark* British Sky Broadcasting; a company that makes television programmes and broadcasts them in the UK using satellites. It is often referred to as Sky TV【商标】英国天空电视台〔英国一家制作、使用卫星播放电视节目的公司，简称"天空电视"〕

BST /,bi ɛs ˋti; ˌbiː es ˈtiː/ *n* [U] the abbreviation of 缩写= British Summer Time

BT /,bi ˋti; ˌbiː ˈtiː/ *n* the abbreviation of 缩写= BRITISH TELECOM

bub /bʌb; bʌb/ *n* [C] *AmE slang* used to speak to a man, especially when you are angry【美俚】老弟，老兄〔生气时用语〕：*Hey, what do you think you're doing, bub?* 老兄，你这是在干什么？

bub·ble[1] /ˋbʌbl; ˈbʌbəl/ *n* [C] **1** a ball of air in liquid 〔液体中的〕气泡；泡沫：*When water boils, bubbles rise to the surface.* 水开时，水面会起泡泡。| *soap bubbles* 肥皂泡 | **blow bubbles** *She was blowing bubbles in her milk with a straw.* 她把吸管放进牛奶里吹泡泡。**2** a small amount of air trapped in a solid substance 〔固体中的〕气泡：*Examine the glass carefully for bubbles.* 仔细检查一下玻璃，看有没有气泡。**3** also 又作 **speech bubble** *BrE* a circle around the words said by someone in a CARTOON (1)【英】〔卡通画人物对白的〕话框 **4 prick/burst the bubble** to make someone suddenly realize the unpleasant truth about something that seemed wonderful or perfect 使希望或信心破灭：*The relationship was great at first but that bubble soon burst.* 起初关系很好，但很快就吹了。**5 burst sb's bubble** to destroy someone's beliefs or hopes about something 使某人的信心[希望]成为泡影：*Coming second in the contest really burst his bubble.* 在比赛中位居第二使他的希望成为泡影。**6** a large clear plastic tent used to protect a seriously ill person from infection 〔防止病人感染的隔离〕透明圆罩

bubble[2] *v* **1** [I] to produce bubbles 起泡，冒泡；沸腾：*Heat the cheese until it bubbles.* 把乳酪加热到冒泡。| **[+up]** *The cola bubbled up when I unscrewed the lid.* 我打开瓶盖，可乐的泡冒了出来。**2** [I] to make the sound that water makes when it boils 〔水沸腾时〕发出噗噗声：**[+away]** *The water was bubbling away on the stove.* 炉子上的水正发出噗噗的沸腾声。**3** [I] also 又作 **bubble over** to be excited 洋溢，兴奋：**[+with]** *bubbling over with enthusiasm* 充满热情

bubble and squeak /,· · · ˈ·/ *n* [U] a British dish of potatoes and CABBAGE (1) mixed together and cooked in fat 卷心菜煎马铃薯

bubble bath /ˈ· · ·/ *n* **1** [U] a liquid soap that smells pleasant and makes bubbles in your bath water 泡沫液 **2** [C] a bath with this in the water 泡泡浴

bubble gum[1] /ˈ· · ·/ *n* [U] a type of CHEWING GUM that you can blow into a BUBBLE[1] (2) 泡泡糖

bubble gum[2] *adj AmE* connected with children between about seven and thirteen years old【美】七到十三岁儿童的：*a magazine aimed at the bubble gum set* 以七到十三岁儿童为对象的杂志

bubble jet print·er /ˈ· · · ,· ·/ *n* [C] a type of machine for printing from a computer that sprays ink onto the paper 喷墨打印机

bub·bly[1] /ˋbʌblɪ; ˈbʌbli/ *adj* **1** full of BUBBLES 充满泡沫的 **2** someone who is bubbly always seems cheerful, friendly, and eager to do things 活泼的；生龙活虎的，生气勃勃的：*Angie's irresistibly bubbly personality* 安吉十分讨人欢喜的活泼个性

bubbly[2] *n* [U] *informal* CHAMPAGNE【非正式】香槟酒

bu·bon·ic plague /bu,banɪk ˋpleg; bjuːˌbɒnɪk ˈpleɪg/ *n* [U] a very serious disease spread by rats, that killed large numbers of people in the Middle Ages 腺鼠疫 —see also 另见 BLACK DEATH, PLAGUE[1] (2)

buc·ca·neer /,bʌkəˋnɪr; ˌbʌkəˈnɪə/ *n* [C] **1** someone who attacks ships at sea and steals from them; PIRATE[1] (3) 海盗 **2** someone who succeeds, especially in business, by using any method, including cheating 〔尤指生意场上〕不择手段的人

Bu·chan·an /bjuˋkænən; bjuːˈkænən/, **James** (1791-1868) the 15th President of the US (1857-61) 布坎南〔(1791-1868)，美国第十五任总统(1857-1861)〕

Bu·cha·rest /ˌbukəˈrɛst; ˌbuːkəˈrest/ the capital and largest city of Romania 布加勒斯特〔罗马尼亚首都和最大城市〕

1 **buck¹** /bʌk; bʌk/ *n* [C]

1 ▶**MONEY** 钱◀ *AmE, AustrE informal* a dollar【美, 澳, 非正式】元: *He owes me ten bucks.* 他欠我10美元。| **big bucks** (=a lot of money) 许多钱 | **make a fast buck** (=make some money quickly, often dishonestly) 一下子赚得一笔钱〔常指不义之财〕

2 **pass the buck** to try to blame someone else or make them responsible for something that you should deal with 推诿责任: *You were the one who took on this job. Don't try to pass the buck.* 是你接手这项工作的, 别想推诿责任。

3 **the buck stops here** used to say that you are the person who is responsible when no-one else will accept the responsibility 责任到此不能再推

4 ▶**MALE ANIMAL** 雄性动物◀ *plural* **buck** or **bucks** a male DEER, rabbit etc 雄鹿; 雄兔 —compare 比较 DOE

5 **feel/look like a million bucks** *AmE informal* to feel or look very healthy, happy, and beautiful【美, 非正式】感觉精神非常好/看上去很精神

6 **buck naked** *AmE informal* wearing no clothes at all【美, 非正式】赤身裸体的

7 ▶**WELL-DRESSED MAN** 穿戴整齐的男子◀ a well-dressed young man in early 19th-century England〔英国19世纪初的〕纨绔子弟; 花花公子: *a Regency buck* 摄政时期的纨绔子弟

buck² *v*

1 ▶**HORSE** 马◀ [I] if a horse bucks, it kicks its back feet into the air, or jumps with all four feet off the ground 弓背跃起

2 ▶**THROW SB** 摔某人◀ [T] to throw a rider off by jumping in this way〔马〕跳起来把〔骑手〕摔下

3 ▶**CAR** 汽车◀ [I] *AmE* if a car bucks, it moves forward in a way which is not smooth, but stops and starts suddenly【美】〔汽车〕颠簸行驶

4 ▶**OPPOSE** 反对◀ *informal* to oppose something in a direct way; RESIST【非正式】反抗; 抵抗: **[+against/at]** *Initially he bucked against her restraints, but later came to accept them.* 起初, 他反抗她的管束, 但后来逐渐顺从了。| **buck the system** (=avoid the usual rules) 反抗现行制度 *natural rebels, with the guts it takes to buck the system* 天生的反叛者, 有勇气反抗这种制度 | **buck a trend** *The growth of the company has bucked the current recessionary trend in the industry.* 公司的发展顶住了该行业目前衰退的趋势。

buck for sth *phr v* [T] to try very hard to get something, especially a good position at work 努力争取〔尤指好的职位〕: *He's bucking for promotion.* 他在努力争取升职。

buck up *phr v* **1** [I,T **buck** sb **up**] to become more cheerful or make someone more cheerful (使)振作精神, (使)快活起来: *Come on, buck up, things aren't that bad!* 来吧, 不要灰心, 事情没那么糟糕! **2 buck up!** *BrE spoken* used to tell someone to hurry up【英口】加油! 快点!: *Buck up, John! We'll be late.* 约翰, 快点! 我们要迟到了。**3 buck your ideas up** *BrE informal* used to tell someone to try harder to improve their behaviour or attitude【英, 非正式】力图改进; 加紧工作[学习]

Buck, Pearl S. (1892-1973) a US writer who lived for many years in China until 1931 and wrote several NOVELs about that country. She won the Nobel Prize for Literature in 1938. 赛珍珠〔(1892-1973), 美国作家, 旅居中国多年直至1931年, 著有数部取材于中国的小说, 1938年获诺贝尔文学奖〕

buck·a·roo /ˌbʌkəˈru; ˌbʌkəˈruː/ *n* [C] *AmE informal* a word meaning COWBOY (1), used especially when speaking to children【美, 非正式】牛仔〔尤对儿童用语〕

buck·board /ˈbʌkˌbɔrd; ˈbʌkbɔːd/ *n* [C] a light vehicle which has four wheels and is pulled by a horse, used in the US in the 19th century〔尤指美国19世纪单匹马拉的〕四轮平板马车

bucked /bʌkt; bʌkt/ *adj* [not before noun 不用于名词前] *BrE old-fashioned* very pleased【英, 过时】振奋的, 高兴的, 欢欣鼓舞的: **[+at/by]** *We were bucked at the news.* 这消息使我们欢欣鼓舞。

2 **buck·et¹** /ˈbʌkɪt; ˈbʌkɪ̈t/ *n* [C]

1 ▶**CONTAINER** 容器◀ an open container with a handle, used for carrying and holding things, especially earth or water 桶: *a bucket of water* 水桶

2 also 又作 **bucketful** the quantity of liquid that a bucket can hold 一桶之量: **[+of]** *It took four buckets of water to wash the car.* 洗汽车用了四桶水。

3 ▶**PART OF MACHINE** 机器部件◀ a part of a machine shaped like a large bucket and used for moving earth, water etc 铲斗; 勺斗; 戽斗

4 **by the bucket/bucketful** *informal* in large quantities【非正式】一桶一桶地, 大量地: *drinking beer by the bucket* 狂饮啤酒

5 **sweat/weep buckets** *informal* to SWEAT¹ (1) or cry a lot【非正式】大量出汗/嚎啕大哭

6 **in buckets** *informal* if rain comes down in buckets, it is raining very heavily【非正式】〔雨〕倾盆而下 —see also 另见 **kick the bucket** (KICK¹ (12)), **a drop in the bucket** (DROP² (8))

bucket² *v*

bucket down *phr v* [I] *BrE informal* to rain very hard【英, 非正式】〔雨〕倾盆而下: *It's been bucketing down all day.* 倾盆大雨已下了一整天。

bucket shop /ˈ· · ·/ *n* [C] *BrE informal* a business that sells cheap tickets for air travel【英, 非正式】廉价机票分销店

Buck·ing·ham Pa·lace /ˌbʌkɪŋəm ˈpælɪs; ˌbʌkɪŋəm ˈpælɪ̈s/ also 又作 **the Palace** the official home of the British royal family in London. The name of the Palace is sometimes used to mean the officials who are in charge of organizing the Queen's public life. 白金汉宫〔英国王室在伦敦的府邸, 有时被用来指称负责女王公共事务的官员〕: *Buckingham Palace announced today that Her Majesty would be visiting Japan next year.* 白金汉宫今天宣布, 女王陛下将于明年出访日本。

Buck·ing·ham·shire /ˈbʌkɪŋəmʃɚ; ˈbʌkɪŋəmʃə/ a COUNTY in central southern England 白金汉郡〔英格兰中南部一郡〕

buck·le¹ /ˈbʌkl; ˈbʌkəl/ *v* **1** [I,T] to fasten a buckle or be joined together with a buckle 用扣环扣住[扣紧]: *The strap buckles at the side.* 带子是在侧面扣的。| **buckle sth** *buckle a satchel* 扣上书包 | **buckle sth on/up/together** *Lou was buckling on his revolver.* 卢把左轮手枪扣挂在身上。**2** [I,T] to become bent or curved because of heat or pressure, or to make something bend or curve in this way〔因高温、压力等〕(使)弯曲; 扭曲; (使)变形: *The rails buckled under the intense heat of the fire.* 铁轨在火焰的高温作用下变了形。**3** [I] if your knees or legs buckle, they become weak and bend 腿软, 站不直: *I felt a blow and my knees started to buckle.* 我感到挨了一击, 腿一软站不住了。

buckle down *phr v* [I] to start working seriously 开始认真从事; 埋头于: **[+to]** *You'd better buckle down to some revision now.* 你该认真复习了。

buckle up *phr v* [I] *especially AmE* to fasten your SEAT BELT in a car, aircraft etc【尤美】系上安全带

buckle² *n* [C] a metal fastener used for joining the two ends of a belt or STRAP¹, for fastening a shoe, bag etc, or for decoration〔皮带等的〕金属扣环, 扣子; 带扣 —see picture at 参见 FASTENER 图

buck·ler /ˈbʌklɚ; ˈbʌklə/ *n* [C] *especially literary* a small circular SHIELD¹ (1a) with a raised centre【尤文】小圆盾

buck·ram /ˈbʌkrəm; ˈbʌkrəm/ *n* [U] stiff cloth, used in the past for covering books, making the stiff parts of clothes etc 硬粗布〔尤指旧时用来做书的封面或使衣服挺直的粗布〕

Buck's Fizz /ˌbʌks ˈfɪz; ˌbʌks ˈfɪz/ *n* [C,U] a mixture of CHAMPAGNE and orange juice, or a glass of this 香槟橙汁饮料

buck·shee /ˌbʌkˈʃi; ˌbʌkˈʃiː◂/ *adv BrE old-fashioned* without payment; free【英, 过时】免费地 —**buckshee** *adj*

buck·shot /ˈbʌkˌʃɑt; ˈbʌkʃɒt/ *n* [U] a lot of small metal balls that you fire together from a gun〔打猎用的〕霰弹枪子弹

buck·skin /ˈbʌkˌskɪn; ˈbʌkˌskɪn/ *n* [U] strong soft leather made from the skin of a DEER or goat 鹿皮; 硝好的羊皮

buck teeth /ˌ· ˈ·/ *n* [plural] teeth that stick forward out of your mouth 龅牙, 獠牙 —**buck-toothed** /ˌ· ˈ·◂/ *adj*

buck·wheat /ˈbʌkˌhwit; ˈbʌkwiːt/ *n* [U] a type of small grain used as food for chickens, and for making FLOUR 荞麦

bu·col·ic /bjuˈkɑlɪk; bjuːˈkɒlɪk/ *adj literary* connected with the countryside【文】乡村的; 田园生活的: *a church, lovely in its bucolic setting* 坐落在美丽田园中的教堂 —**bucolically** /-klɪ; -kli/ *adv*

Bud /bʌd; bʌd/ *informal* a BUDWEISER (=a type of beer)【非正式】百威啤酒: *Hey, would you like a Bud?* 嘿, 来瓶百威吗?

bud¹ *n* [C] **1** a young tightly rolled up flower or leaf before it opens 芽; 苞; 蓓蕾: *rose buds* 玫瑰花苞 | **in bud** (=having buds

bud 芽; 苞; 蓓蕾

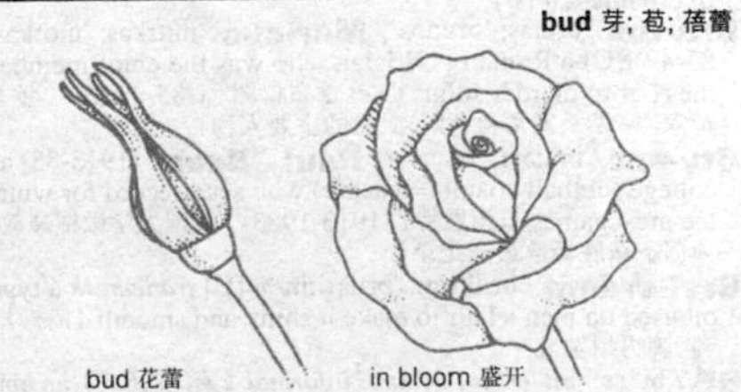

but no flowers yet) 含苞待放 | **come into bud** (=start to produce buds) 长出花蕾 **2** *AmE informal*【美, 非正式】BUDDY 老兄; 喂 —see also 另见 COTTON BUD, TASTE BUD, **nip sth in the bud** (NIP¹ (3))

bud² *v* **budded, budding** [I] to produce buds 发芽, 长出花蕾, 含苞

Bu·da·pest /ˈbudəpɛst; ˌbjuːdəˈpest◂/ the capital and largest city of Hungary, on the River Danube 布达佩斯〔匈牙利首都和最大城市, 位于多瑙河畔〕

Bud·dha /ˈbudə; ˈbʊdə/ **1 the Buddha** (?563-?483 BC) the title given to Gautama Siddhartha, a wealthy man from northern India who gave up all his possessions and family to teach the ideas on which the religion of Buddhism is based 佛陀〔公元前?563-前?483〕, 乔达摩·悉达多的尊称。他是印度北部的一位富人, 放弃所有财产弃家出走, 宣讲佛教教义〕 **2** [C] a STATUE or picture of the Buddha 佛像

Bud·dhis·m /ˈbudɪzəm; ˈbʊdɪzəm/ *n* [U] a religion of east and central Asia, based on the teaching of Gautama Buddha 佛教 —**Buddhist** *n* [C] —**Buddhist** *adj*

bud·ding /ˈbʌdɪŋ; ˈbʌdɪŋ/ *adj* **1 budding singer/actor/writer etc** someone who is just starting to sing, act etc and will probably be successful at it 初露头角的歌手/演员/作家等 **2** [only before noun 仅用于名词前] beginning to develop 开始发展的; 成长中的: *a budding relationship* 开始发展的关系

bud·dy /ˈbʌdɪ; ˈbʌdi/ *n* [C] **1** *informal* a friend【非正式】朋友, 伙伴: *We're good buddies.* 我们是好朋友。**2** *AmE spoken* used to speak to a man you do not know; BUD¹ (2)【美口】老兄; 喂〔用于称呼不认识的男子〕: *Hey, buddy! This your car?* 喂, 老兄! 这是你的车吗? **3** someone who offers to look after and become a friend to a person who has AIDS 艾滋病患者之友〔指自愿照顾并善待艾滋病患者的人〕

buddy-bud·dy /ˈ‥ˌ‥/ *adj AmE informal* very friendly with someone【美, 非正式】十分友好的

buddy sys·tem /ˈ‥ ˌ‥/ *n* [C] *AmE* a system in which two people help each other or keep each other safe【美】〔两人互相照顾的〕结伴制

budge /bʌdʒ; bʌdʒ/ *v* [I,T usually in negatives 一般用于否定句] *informal*【非正式】**1** to move, or move someone or something from one place to another (使) 稍微移动: *Come on – budge. I can't get past.* 嘿, 挪一下, 我过不去。| **budge sth** *The car was stuck in the snow and we couldn't budge it.* 汽车陷在雪地里, 我们怎么也挪不动。| **[+from]** *Will hasn't budged from his room all day.* 威尔整天都没出自己的房间。**2** to make someone change their opinion (使某人) 改变主意: *It's no good, Dad won't budge.* 没有用, 爸爸不会改变主意的。| **not budge an inch** (=not change at all) 寸步不让, 一点也不改变

Budge, Donald (1915-2000) a US tennis player who in 1938 became the first person to win the Wimbledon, US, Australian, and French championships in one year. 布吉〔(1915-2000), 美国网球运动员, 1938 年囊括了温布尔登、美国、澳大利亚和法国网球赛事桂冠, 成为历史上首位大满贯得主〕

bud·ge·ri·gar /ˈbʌdʒərɪˌgɑr; ˈbʌdʒərɪgɑː/ *n* [C] a small brightly-coloured bird that people keep at home as a pet; BUDGIE 虎皮鹦鹉

S1 W2 **bud·get¹** /ˈbʌdʒɪt; ˈbʌdʒɪt/ *n* [C] **1** a plan of how a person or organization will spend the money that is available in a particular period of time, or the money itself 预算: *planning the annual budget* 制定年度预算 | **[+of]** *a welfare program with a budget of $2 billion* 预算为 20 亿美元的福利计划 | **defence/advertising etc budget** (=money available for defence etc) 国防经费/广告费等预算 | **over/under budget** (=having spent more or less than the amount allowed in a budget)〔支出〕高于/低于预算 | **budget deficit** (=a situation in which more money has been spent than is available) 预算赤字 | **balance the budget** (=make sure that only money available is spent) 保持收支平衡 | **be on a tight budget** (=not have much money to spend) 财政紧张, 经济拮据 **2** an official statement that a government makes about how much it intends to spend and what taxes will be necessary 政府预算案

budget² *v* **1** [I] to carefully plan and control how much you spend〔精心地〕制定预算; 按预算来安排开支: *We'll just have to budget more sensibly in the future.* 今后我们必须更合理地安排开支。| **budget for** (=plan how much you need for something) (为…计划) 开支 *We've budgeted for a new car next year.* 我们已计划好了明年买汽车的开支。**2** [I,T] to plan carefully how much of something will be needed 为…作出安排: *She's learned how to budget her time carefully.* 她已经学会了怎样精心安排自己的时间。

budget³ *adj* [only before noun 仅用于名词前] very low in price; cheap 经济的, 特价的, 便宜的: *a budget flight* 低价航班

bud·get·a·ry /ˈbʌdʒɪˌtɛrɪ; ˈbʌdʒɪtəri/ *adj* connected with the way money is spent in a budget 预算的: *budgetary restrictions* 预算限制

bud·gie /ˈbʌdʒɪ; ˈbʌdʒi/ *n* [C] *BrE* a small brightly-coloured bird that people keep at home as a pet; BUDGERIGAR【英】虎皮鹦鹉

Bud·wei·ser /ˈbʌdwaɪzə; ˈbʌdwaɪzə/ also 又作 **Bud** *informal*【非正式】*trademark* a type of US beer【商标】百威啤酒〔一种美国啤酒〕

Bue·nos Ai·res /ˌbwenəs ˈaɪrɪz; ˌbweɪnɒs ˈaɪriz/ the capital city of Argentina, an important international port and one of the largest cities in South America 布宜诺斯艾利斯〔阿根廷首都, 南美洲重要国际港口和最大城市之一〕

buff¹ /bʌf; bʌf/ *n* **1** [C] **film/computer/jazz etc buff** someone who is interested in films, computers etc and knows a lot about them 影迷/电脑迷/爵士乐迷等 **2** [U] a pale yellow-brown colour 浅[暗]黄色, 米色 —see picture on page A5 参见 A5 页图 **3 in the buff** *old-fashioned* having no clothes on; NAKED【过时】赤身裸体的, 一丝不挂的

buff² *v* [T] to make a surface shine by polishing it with a dry cloth〔用软布〕擦亮: *Buff to a shine after waxing.* 打蜡之后用软布擦亮。

Buf·fa·lo /ˈbʌflˌo; ˈbʌfələʊ/ a port at the northeast end of Lake Erie near Niagara Falls in the state of New York, in the US 布法罗〔美国纽约州伊利湖东北岸港口, 位于尼亚加拉瀑布附近〕

buffalo /ˈbʌflˌo; ˈbʌfələʊ/ *n plural* **buffalos, buffaloes,** or **buffalo** [C] **1** an African animal similar to a large cow with long curved horns 水牛 —see also 另见 WATER BUFFALO **2** a BISON〔北美〕野牛

> **CULTURAL NOTE 文化注释**
> In the US in the late 1800s and early 1900s buffaloes were hunted for their skins to make **buffalo robes** and were almost made EXTINCT. The smaller numbers of buffalo made life more difficult for the Native Americans, who ate buffalo meat, and this made the disagreement between Native Americans and white Americans worse. 19 世纪晚期和 20 世纪初期, 美国人猎杀野牛, 获取皮毛, 制作野牛皮长袍, 野牛几乎因此灭绝。野牛数量减少, 使以野牛肉为食的美国原住民生活更加艰难, 他们与白人之间的分歧因此更加扩大了。

Buffalo Bill /ˌ‥ ˈ‥/ (1846-1917) a SCOUT (=a soldier sent out to get information about the enemy) for the US army, who was also a BUFFALO hunter. After leaving the army, he organized the 'Wild West Show', in which he and people such as Annie oakley and Sitting Bull showed their skill at shooting and horse-riding, and tried to give people an idea of what life was like in the American West. Buffalo Bill's real name was William Cody. 野牛比尔〔(1846-1917), 美国陆军侦察兵, 也是一位野牛猎手。他退伍后组织了"西大荒演艺会", 与安妮·奥克莉、印第安酋长"坐牛"一起表演射击和马术, 试图让人们了解美国西部的生活。他的真名叫威廉·科迪〕

buff·er¹ /ˈbʌfə; ˈbʌfə/ *n* [C]

1 ►**PROTECTION** 保护◄ something that protects something else 缓冲物: *The trees act as a buffer against strong winds.* 这些树木起到了缓冲强风的作用。

2 ►**RAILWAY** 铁路◄ one of the two special metal springs on the front or back of a train or at the end of a railway track to take the shock if the train hits something〔铁路车辆或铁轨末端的〕缓冲器

3 buffer zone an area between two armies, which is intended to separate them so that they do not fight〔军事〕缓冲地带

4 buffer state a smaller peaceful country between two larger countries, which makes war between them less likely 缓冲国: *Part of the settlement was to create a Serbian buffer state.* 协议的部分内容是建立塞尔维亚缓冲国。

5 ►**COMPUTER** 电脑◄ a place in a computer's memory for storing information temporarily 缓冲存储器

6 ►**PERSON** 人◄ *BrE old-fashioned* an old man who seems silly【英, 过时】老家伙, 老糊涂: *You stupid old buffer!* 你这老糊涂!

7 ►**FOR POLISHING** 用于擦拭◄ something used to polish a surface〔用于擦亮表面的〕抛光工具: *Where's my nail buffer?* 我的指甲锉在哪里?

8 hit the buffers *informal* an official discussion that hits the buffers does not have a successful result【非正式】受挫

buffer² *v* [T] to reduce the bad effects of something 缓冲, 缓和, 缓解: *buffering the effects of the recession* 缓解经济衰退造成的影响

buf·fet[1] /bəˋfe; ˈbʊfeɪ/ *n* [C] **1** a place in a railway station, bus station etc where you can buy and eat food or drink 快餐部，饮食柜台 **2** a meal of cold food at a party or other occasion, in which people serve themselves at a table and then move away to eat 自助餐: **buffet lunch/supper** *We had a buffet lunch for Hayley's christening.* 我们安排了一顿自助午餐庆祝海利受洗。| **finger buffet** (=with food that you eat with your hands) 可用手拿食物吃的自助餐 **3** *BrE* the part of the train where you can buy food and drink; DINING CAR【英】〔火车上的〕餐车 **4** a piece of furniture in which you keep the things you use to serve and eat a meal 餐具架[柜]

buffet[2] /ˋbʌfɪt; ˈbʌfɪt/ *v* [T usually passive 一般用被动态] **1** if wind, rain, or the sea buffets something, it hits it with a lot of force〔风、雨等〕猛烈袭击: *London was buffeted by storms last night.* 伦敦昨晚遭到暴风雨的袭击。**2** *literary* to treat someone unkindly【文】打击，伤害: *weary of being buffeted by life* 厌倦了生活的打击 —**buffeting** *n* [C]

buffet sb/sth **about** *phr v* [I] to knock or hit something and make it move 撞[击]得〔某人或某物〕使移动

buf·foon /bəˋfun; bəˈfuːn/ *n* [C] *old-fashioned* someone who does silly things that make you laugh【过时】丑角; 粗俗而愚蠢的人 —**buffoonery** *n* [U]

Bug /bʌg; bʌg/ *AmE informal* a BEETLE (=type of small Volkswagen car)【美，非正式】甲壳虫〔大众汽车公司制造的一款小型轿车〕

bug[1] *n* [C] **1** *especially AmE* a small insect, especially one that people think is unpleasant【尤美】小虫子 **2** *informal* an illness that people catch very easily from each other but is not very serious【非正式】小毛病: **pick up a bug** (=get a bug) 得(小)病 | **tummy/stomach bug** (=illness affecting your stomach) 肚子/胃不舒服 **3 the travel/ski/parachuting etc bug** *informal* a sudden strong interest in doing something that usually lasts only a short time【非正式】对旅行/滑雪/跳伞等突然着迷: *bitten by the fitness bug* 对健身着了迷 **4** a small fault in the system of instructions that operates a computer〔电脑程序等的〕故障，毛病 —see also 另见 DEBUG **5** a small piece of electronic equipment for listening secretly to other people's conversations 窃听器

bug[2] *v* **bugged, bugging** [T] **1** *informal* to annoy【非正式】打扰; 激怒; 使厌烦: *It really bugs me when the car behind me drives too close.* 后面的汽车离得太近，真烦人。**2** to put a BUG[1] (5) somewhere secretly in order to listen to conversations 给…装窃听器; 窃听: *Do you think the room is bugged?* 你认为这房间装了窃听器吗?

bug·a·boo /ˋbʌgə͵bu; ˈbʌgəbuː/ *n* [C] *old-fashioned* an imaginary thing or person that children are scared of【过时】吓人的东西; 妖怪

bug·bear /ˋbʌg͵bɛr; ˈbʌgbeə/ *n* [C] something that makes people feel worried or scared 使人烦恼[担心]的东西; 无谓的恐慌: *the old bugbear – racism* 让人不安的老问题——种族主义

bug-eyed /͵bʌgˋaɪd; ͵bʌgˈaɪd◂/ *adj* having eyes that stick out 眼睛瞪大的，眼球突出的

2 **bug·ger**[1] /ˋbʌgɚ; ˈbʌgə/ *n* [C] *spoken especially BrE*【口，尤英】**1** *taboo* someone who is very annoying or unpleasant【讳】坏蛋，可鄙的家伙: *Bill's an obnoxious little bugger.* 比尔是个令人讨厌的小捣蛋鬼。**2** a rude word meaning someone that you pretend to be annoyed with, although you actually like them 家伙，小子〔粗鲁但实际上表示亲昵〕: *What are you doing, you daft bugger?* 你这笨家伙在干什么? **3** a rude word meaning a job or activity that is very difficult 麻烦的事物; 令人头痛的事: *Having to commute so far is a real bugger.* 必须跑这么远的路上下班真是件麻烦事。**4 bugger all** a rude expression meaning nothing, used especially when you are angry 什么也没有〔粗话〕: *There's bugger all we can do about the car now.* 现在我们对这辆车屁办法都没有。| **bugger all help/thanks/work etc** (=none at all) 一点儿也不帮忙/感谢/行不通等 *I got bugger all thanks for driving my boss to the airport.* 我开车送老板到机场，他连句感谢话都没说。**5 play silly buggers** a rude expression meaning to behave in a stupid way that annoys other people 胡闹: *Stop playing silly buggers and get on with your homework!* 别瞎胡闹了，赶快做作业吧! **6** *taboo* a man who regularly has ANAL SEX, especially with other men or boys【讳】鸡奸者

bugger[2] *v* [T] *BrE*【英】**1 bugger (it)!** *spoken* a rude expression used when you are angry because something bad has happened【口】该死; 见鬼: *Bugger it! The car battery is dead.* 活见鬼! 汽车电池没电了。**2 I'll be buggered/bugger me!** *spoken* a rude expression used when you are surprised about something【口】该死的!〔表示非常惊奇〕**3 bugger the ...** *slang* used to say that you do not care about the person or thing you are talking about【俚】管他是谁; 管它怎么样: *Bugger the expense, I'm going to buy it!* 不管多贵，我都要把它买下来! **4 I'll be buggered if...** *slang* used to say angrily that you will not do something【俚】如果…我就该死…: *I'll be buggered if I help them any more.* 如果我再帮他们，我就该死。**5** *taboo or law* to have ANAL sex with someone【讳或法律】与…鸡奸，犯鸡奸罪

bugger about also 又作 **bugger around** *phr v BrE*【英】**1** [I] to behave in a stupid way or waste time 胡闹，瞎折腾: *Stop buggering about and get on with your work.* 别瞎胡闹了，干你的活。**2** [T **bugger** sb **about**] to cause unnecessary problems for someone 给〔某人〕添麻烦，烦扰: *Don't let Peter bugger you about, tell him to leave.* 别让彼得再烦扰你了，叫他离开。

bugger off *phr v* [I often imperative 常用于祈使句] *BrE* an impolite expression meaning to go away, or leave a place, which is very rude when used directly【英】走开，滚开: *Bugger off and leave me alone!* 走开，离我远点! | *Simon's always buggering off home early.* 西蒙总是早早就滚回家了。

bugger sth ↔ **up** *phr v* [T] *BrE* to do something stupid that ruins something or causes trouble【英】损害; 搞糟: *You really buggered up our plans by arriving late.* 你这一迟到，真把我们的计划搞砸了。

bug·gered /ˋbʌgɚd; ˈbʌgəd/ *adj* [not before noun 不用于名词前] **1** *BrE slang* a rude word meaning extremely tired【英俚】精疲力竭的: *That's the last time I work so late. I'm buggered!* 这是我最后一次工作得这么晚，累坏了! **2** *BrE slang* a rude word meaning completely ruined or broken【英俚】损坏的: *The washing machine's buggered.* 洗衣机坏了。**3 I'm buggered** *BrE spoken* used to say that you are very surprised by something or cannot understand it【英口】我很吃惊: *I'm buggered if I know why they didn't come!* 我真奇怪他们为什么没有来!

bug·ger·y /ˋbʌgərɪ; ˈbʌgəri/ *n* [U] *BrE law* ANAL sex【英，法律】鸡奸

bug·gy /ˋbʌgɪ; ˈbʌgi/ *n* [C] **1** *BrE* a light folding chair on wheels that you push small children in【英】折叠式轻便婴儿车; STROLLER *AmE*【美】**2** a light carriage pulled by a horse〔一匹马拉的〕轻型马车 **3** *AmE* a thing like a small bed on wheels, that a baby lies in【美】〔婴儿可躺在里面的〕婴儿车; PRAM *BrE*【英】

bu·gle /ˋbjugl; ˈbjuːgəl/ *n* [C] a musical instrument like a TRUMPET[1] (1) which is used in the army to call soldiers 号角; 军号，喇叭 —**bugler** *n* [C]

Bugs Bun·ny /͵· ˈ··/ a CARTOON rabbit who likes CARROTs and often uses the phrase "What's up, Doc?" 兔八哥〔一只喜欢吃胡萝卜的卡通兔子，经常说: "怎么了，医生?"〕

Bu·ick /ˋbuɪk; ˈbuːɪk/ *trademark* a type of US car made by General Motors【商标】别克〔美国通用汽车公司制造的一款轿车〕

build[1] /bɪld; bɪld/ *v past tense and past participle* **built** /bɪlt; bɪlt/ 1 1

1 ▶MAKE STH 制作某物◀ [I,T] to make something, especially a building or something large 建房; 建筑，建造，盖; 造: *Are they going to build on this land?* 他们要在这块地上建房子吗? | **build sb sth** *Nick said he'd build us a fitted wardrobe.* 尼克说要为我们造一个尺寸合适的大衣柜。

2 ▶MAKE STH DEVELOP 使某物发展◀ [T] to make something develop or form 使发展; 使构成; 创建，建立; 树立; 培养: *Kate's working hard to build a career.* 凯特工作很努力，想开创一番事业。| **build (up) a picture of sb/sth** (=form a clear idea about someone or something) 对某人/某物有清楚的认识 *The police are trying to build up a picture of Haig's daily routine.* 警方在设法弄清黑格的日常活动规律。

3 ▶FEELING 感情◀ [I,T] if a feeling builds or you build it, it increases gradually over a period of time 发展，增进，加剧: *Tension is building between the two countries.* 两国间的紧张关系在加剧。

4 well-built/brick-built etc used for describing how large someone is, what something is made of, or how it was built 体格强壮的/砖结构的等: *a heavily-built man* 体格非常强壮的男人 | *a brick-built house* 砖砌的房子

5 be built of to be made using particular materials 由〔某些材料〕建成: *a cottage built of Cumbrian slate* 用坎布里亚石板造的小屋

6 be built on/around to happen as a result of something 建立在…之上: *The company's success is built on its very popular home computers.* 公司的成功全靠其很畅销的家用电脑。

7 build bridges to try to establish a better relationship between people who do not like each other 沟通〔尤指在对立的人之间〕

build sth ↔ **in** *phr v* [T usually passive 一般用被动态] to make something so that it is a permanent part of a wall, room etc 把…嵌[插，建，装]入

build sth ↔ **into** *phr v* [T] **1** to make something so that it is a permanent part of a wall, room etc 把…嵌[插, 建, 装]入 **2** to make something a permanent part of a system, agreement etc 使成为某物不可分的部分: *A completion date was built into the contract.* 完成日期已订入了合同。—see also 另见 BUILT-IN

build on sth *phr v* **1** [T **build** sth ↔ **on**] to add another room etc to a building in order to have more space 扩建, 增建 **2** [**build on** sth] to use your achievements as a base for further development 以…作为发展的基础: *Now we must build on our success in Italy.* 我们必须把在意大利的成功作为基础。—see also 另见 **be built on** (BUILD[1] (6))

build up *phr v*

1 ►**PRAISE** 赞扬◄[T **build** sb/sth ↔ **up**] to praise someone or something so that other people think they are really good 吹捧, 赞扬, 宣传: *You have to build kids up – make them feel important.* 你必须多表扬孩子, 让他们觉得自己重要。

2 ►**MAKE STRONGER** 使强壮◄[T **build** sb ↔ **up**] to make someone well and strong again, especially after an illness 帮助〔某人〕逐步恢复体力〔尤指病后〕: *Build your mother up with nourishing food.* 让你母亲多吃点营养食品, 使她逐步恢复体力。

3 ►**FEELING** 感情◄[I,T **build** sth ↔ **up**] if a feeling builds up or you build it up, it increases gradually over a period of time 增强; 增加: *Try and build up his confidence a bit.* 设法让他增加对自己的信心。

4 ►**INCREASE GRADUALLY** 逐渐增加◄[I,T **build** sth ↔ **up**] if a substance, force, or activity builds up somewhere or you build it up, it gradually becomes bigger and stronger 逐渐增加; 扩大: *Both sides have built up huge stockpiles of arms.* 双方都已大量增加武器储备。—see also 另见 BUILD-UP (1)

5 build up sb's hopes to unfairly encourage someone to think that they will get what they hope for 〔以不正当的方式〕让某人怀有希望

build up to sth *phr v* [T] to prepare for a particular moment or event 为某个时刻的到来做准备: *I could tell she was building up to some kind of announcement.* 我能看得出她准备向大家宣布点儿事。—see also 另见 BUILD-UP (3)

build[2] *n* [singular,U] the shape and size of someone's body 体格; 体形: *a powerful build* 强壮的体格 —see 见 BODY (USAGE)

W3 **build·er** /ˈbɪldə; ˈbɪldə/ *n* [C] *especially BrE* a person or a company that builds or repairs buildings 【尤英】建筑工人; 建筑商; 建造者

builders' mer·chant /ˈ‥ ˌ‥/ *n* [C] *BrE* a company that stores and sells building materials such as bricks, cement, and sand 【英】建材公司; 建材商

S1 W1 **build·ing** /ˈbɪldɪŋ; ˈbɪldɪŋ/ *n* [C] **1** a structure such as a house, church, or factory, that has a roof and walls 建筑(物): *one of the tallest buildings in the world.* 世界上最高的建筑之一 **2** [U] the process or business of building things 建筑, 建造; 建筑业: *The next major step is the building of a gym.* 下一个重要举措是建一个体育馆。| **building costs/programmes/regulations etc** *Building costs will have to be reduced.* 建筑成本必须降低。

building block /ˈ‥ ‥/ *n* [C] **1** a block of wood or plastic for young children to build things with 积木 **2 building blocks** [plural] the pieces or parts which together make it possible for something big or important to exist 成分, 构成要素: *Amino acids are the fundamental building blocks of protein.* 氨基酸是构成蛋白质的基本成分。

building con·trac·tor /ˈ‥ ‥, ‥/ *n* [C] someone whose job is to organize the building of a house, office, factory etc 建筑承包商

building site /ˈ‥ ‥/ *n* [C] a place where a house, factory etc is being built 建筑工地

building so·ci·e·ty /ˈ‥ ‥, ‥/ *n* [C] *BrE* a type of bank that you pay money into in order to save it and earn interest and that will lend you money to buy a house or apartment 【英】购房[房屋]互助协会〔接受会员存款并付给利息, 会员购房可贷款的商业机构〕; SAVINGS AND LOAN ASSOCIATION *AmE* 【美】

build-up /ˈ‥ ‥/ *n* **1** [U singular] an increase over a period of time 增长; 加强; 集结; 储备: *a heavy build-up of traffic on the motorway* 高速公路上交通流量的急剧增长 **2** [C] a description of someone or something in which you say they are very special or important 〔尤指预先的〕舆论宣传, 吹捧: **give sb a big build-up** *The presenter gave her a big build-up.* 节目主持人事先对她大肆吹捧。**3** [C] the length of time spent preparing an event 准备时间: [**+to**] *the long build-up to the opening of the Channel Tunnel* 海峡隧道开通的漫长准备期 —see also 另见 **build up** (BUILD[1])

built /bɪlt; bɪlt/ the past tense and past participle of BUILD[1]

built-in /ˌ‥ ˈ‥◄/ *adj* forming a part of something that cannot be separated from it 作为固定装置而建造的, 装在结构里的; 固定的; 内在的: *a built-in microphone* 内置的麦克风 —see also 另见 **build in** (BUILD[1])

built-up /ˌ‥ ˈ‥◄/ *adj* a built-up area has a lot of buildings and not many open spaces 布满建筑物的: *speeding in a built-up area* 在一个建筑物密集的地区疾驶

Bu·kow·ski /buˈkaʊski; buːˈkaʊskɪ/, **Charles** (1920-94) a US writer, born in Germany, who wrote several NOVELs, short stories, and collections of poetry. His work often shows both anger and humour. 布科夫斯基〔(1920-1994), 出生于德国的美国作家, 作品有小说、短篇故事和诗集, 既表现愤怒, 又不乏幽默〕

bulb /bʌlb; bʌlb/ *n* [C] **1** the glass part of an electric light, that the light shines from; LIGHT BULB 灯泡: *a 100 watt bulb* 100瓦的灯泡 —see picture at 参见 LIGHT[1] 图 **2** a root shaped like a ball that grows into a flower or plant 〔植物的〕球茎, 鳞茎, 球根: *tulip bulbs* 郁金香球茎

bul·bous /ˈbʌlbəs; ˈbʌlbəs/ *adj* fat and round and unattractive 又圆又胖的: *a bulbous nose* 蒜头鼻子, 圆圆的鼻子

Bul·ga·ri·a /bʌlˈgɛriə; bʌlˈgeərɪə/ a country in southeast Europe next to the Black Sea, between Romania and Turkey. Population: 7,707,000 (2001). Capital: Sofia. 保加利亚〔欧洲东南部国家, 濒临黑海, 与罗马尼亚和土耳其接壤。人口: 7,707,000 (2001), 首都: 索非亚〕—**Bulgarian** *n, adj*

Bulge /bʌldʒ; bʌldʒ/ —see 见 the BATTLE OF THE BULGE

bulge[1] *n* [C] **1** a curved mass on the surface of something, usually caused by something under or inside it 膨胀, 鼓起部: *The wallet made a fat bulge in his pocket.* 钱包把他的口袋撑得鼓鼓的。**2** a sudden temporary increase in the amount or level of something 骤增, 膨胀, 暴涨: *a bulge in the birthrate* 出生率骤增 —**bulgy** *adj*: *bulgy-eyed* 眼睛凸出的

bulge[2] *v* [I] **1** also 又作 **bulge out** to stick out in a rounded shape, especially because something is very full or too tight 鼓起: [**+with**] *His pockets were bulging with candy.* 他的口袋里鼓鼓囊囊塞满了糖块。**2** [**+with**] *informal* to be very full of people or things 【非正式】塞满, 充满

bul·gur /ˈbʌlgɚ; ˈbʌlgə/ *n* [U] a type of wheat which has been dried and broken into pieces 碾碎的干小麦

bu·lim·i·a /bjuˈlɪmiə; bjuːˈlɪmiə/ *n* [U] an illness in which a person cannot stop themselves from eating too much, and then vomits (VOMIT[1]) in order to control their weight 易饥症, 食欲过盛症 —**bulimic** *adj*

bulk[1] /bʌlk; bʌlk/ *n* **1 the bulk (of sth)** the main or largest part of something (某物的) 主要部分; 大半: *the bulk of the workforce* 大部分的劳动力 **2** [C usually singular 一般用单数] a big mass of something 团, 大块 **3** [U] the size of something or someone 体积; 尺寸; 块头: *The dough will rise until it is double in bulk.* 面团发酵后体积能膨胀到原来的两倍。**4 in bulk** if you buy goods in bulk, you buy large amounts each time you buy them 整批的, 大批的

bulk[2] *adj* **1 bulk buying/orders etc** the buying etc of goods in large quantities at one time 大批[大量]购买/订购等 **2** [only before noun 仅用于名词前] bulk goods are sold or moved in large quantities 大批的, 大量的: *bulk flour for commercial bakeries* 为商用面包烘房提供的大量面粉 **3 bulk mail** the posting of large amounts of mail for a smaller cost than usual 大宗邮件寄送

bulk[3] *v* **bulk large** *literary* to be the main or most important part of something 【文】显得重要, 起重大作用

bulk sth ↔ **out** *phr v* [T] to make something look bigger or thicker, by adding something else 使膨胀; 使看起来更厚实[丰满]; 充实: *We can bulk out the report with lots of diagrams.* 我们可以加许多图表使报告更充实。

bulk·head /ˈbʌlkˌhɛd; ˈbʌlkhed/ *n* [C] a wall which divides the structure of a ship or aircraft into separate parts 〔船等的〕舱壁, 隔离壁

bulk·y /ˈbʌlki; ˈbʌlki/ *adj* **1** something that is bulky is bigger than other things of its type and is difficult to carry or store 庞大的, 笨重的, 体积大的; 宽大的: *a bulky parcel* 笨重的包裹 | *a new elastic that is less bulky* 不那么粗的新松紧带 **2** someone who is bulky is big and heavy 又高又胖的 —**bulkiness** *n* [U]

bull[1] /bʊl; bʊl/ *n* [C]

1 ►**MALE COW** 公牛◄ an adult male animal of the cattle family 公牛: *A mean-looking bull was standing in the path.* 小路上站着一头凶恶的公牛。

2 ►**MALE ANIMAL** 雄性动物◄ the male of some other large animals such as the ELEPHANT or WHALE 雄性动物〈如象或鲸等身躯庞大的动物〉

3 **take the bull by the horns** to bravely or confidently deal with a difficult, dangerous, or unpleasant problem 挺身面对困难: *She decided to take the bull by the horns and ask him outright.* 她决定挺身而出，直截了当去问他。

4 ►**NONSENSE** 废话◄ [U] *AmE informal* nonsense or something that is completely untrue【美，非正式】大话；废话，空话: *You never went to Hawaii – that's pure bull.* 纯属吹牛，你从未去过夏威夷。

5 **be like a bull in a china shop** to keep knocking things over, dropping things, breaking things etc 笨手笨脚到处闯祸

6 **like a bull at a gate** if you move somewhere like a bull at a gate, you move there very fast, ignoring everything in your way 猛烈地；凶猛地

7 ►**RELIGION** 宗教◄ an official statement from the POPE 教皇训谕[诏书]

8 ►**CENTRE** 中心◄ the centre of a TARGET[1] (3) that you are shooting at 靶心

9 ►**BUSINESS** 商业◄ someone who buys shares (SHARE[2] (5)) because they expect prices to rise〔股票投机中的〕多头；股市看涨的人 —compare 比较 BEAR[2] (2) —see also 另见 **like a red rag to a bull** (RED[1] (6)), **shoot the bull** (SHOOT[1] (8))

bull² *interjection slang* used to say that you do not believe or agree with what someone has said【俚】废话！胡说！: *Bull! Where did you get that idea?* 废话！你怎么会有那种想法？

Bull, John —see 见 JOHN BULL

bull·dog /ˈbʊlˌdɔg; ˈbʊldɒg/ *n* [C] a powerful dog with a large head, a short neck, and short thick legs 斗牛犬

bulldog clip /ˈ·· ·/ *n BrE* [C] a small metal object that shuts tightly to hold papers together【英】〔夹纸用的〕金属夹

bull·doze /ˈbʊlˌdoz; ˈbʊldəʊz/ *v* [T] **1** to destroy buildings etc with a bulldozer〔用推土机〕推倒 **2** to push objects such as earth and rocks out of the way with a bulldozer〔用推土机〕推平，平整 **3 bulldoze sb into (doing) sth** to force someone to do something that they do not really want to do 强迫某人做某事

bull·doz·er /ˈbʊlˌdozə; ˈbʊldəʊzə/ *n* [C] a powerful vehicle with a broad metal blade, used for moving earth and rocks, destroying buildings etc 推土机

bul·let /ˈbʊlɪt; ˈbʊlɪ̤t/ *n* [C] a small piece of metal that you fire from a gun 枪弹，子弹，弹头: *a bullet through the heart* 穿透心脏的子弹 | **bullet holes/wounds etc** *The door was riddled with bullet holes.* 门上到处是弹孔。—compare 比较 SHELL[1] (2), SHOT[1] (4) —see also 另见 PLASTIC BULLET, **bite the bullet** (BITE[1] (8)) —see picture at 参见 GUN[1] 图

bul·le·tin /ˈbʊlətɪn; ˈbʊlətɪ̤n/ *n* [C] **1** a news report on radio or television〔广播或电视中的〕新闻简报 **2** an official statement that is made to inform people about something important 公告；公报；告示 **3** a letter or printed statement that a group or organization produces to tell people its news〔尤指团体出版的〕小报；会刊

bulletin board /ˈ··· ˌ·/ *n* [C] **1** *AmE* a board on the wall that you put information or pictures on【美】布告牌[栏]; NOTICEBOARD *BrE*【英】: *a windows bulletin board due out next year* 明年到期的窗式布告栏 —see picture on page A14 参见 A14 页图 **2 electronic bulletin board** a place in a computer information system where you can read or leave messages〔电脑的〕电子布告牌

bullet proof /ˈ·· ·/ *adj* something that is bullet proof is designed to stop bullets from going through it 防弹的

bull·fight /ˈbʊlˌfaɪt; ˈbʊlfaɪt/ *n* [C] a type of entertainment popular in Spain, in which a man fights and kills a BULL[1] (1) 斗牛 —**bullfighter** *n* [C] —**bullfighting** *n* [U]

bull·finch /ˈbʊlˌfɪntʃ; ˈbʊlˌfɪntʃ/ *n* [C] a small grey and red European bird 红腹灰雀

bull·frog /ˈbʊlˌfrag; ˈbʊlfrɒg/ *n* [C] a kind of large FROG that makes a loud noise 牛蛙

bull·head·ed /ˌ·ˈ··◂/ *adj* determined to get what you want without really thinking enough about it 愚笨固执的；任性的 —**bull-headedly** *adv* —**bull-headedness** *n* [U]

bull·horn /ˈbʊlˌhɔrn; ˈbʊlhɔːn/ *n* [C] *AmE old-fashioned* a piece of equipment that you hold up to your mouth to make your voice louder【美，过时】手提式扩音器，喇叭筒; MEGAPHONE *BrE*【英】

bul·lion /ˈbʊljən; ˈbʊljən/ *n* [U] bars of gold or silver 金[银]条，金[银]块: *gold bullion* 金条

bul·lish /ˈbʊlɪʃ; ˈbʊlɪʃ/ *adj* **1** [not before noun 不用于名词前] feeling confident about the future〔对未来〕有信心的；乐观的: *very bullish about the company's prospects* 对公司的前景充满信心 **2** *technical* in a business market that is bullish the prices of shares (SHARE[2] (5)) tend or seem likely to rise【术语】股票行情看涨的，做多头的 —**bullishly** *adv* —**bullishness** *n* [U]

bull·necked /ˌbʊlˈnɛkt; ˌbʊlˈnekt◂/ *adj* having a short and very thick neck〔指人〕颈部短粗的

bul·lock /ˈbʊlək; ˈbʊlək/ *n* [C] a young male cow that cannot breed 小阉牛

bull pen /ˈ· ·/ *n* [C] *AmE*【美】**1** the area in a BASEBALL field in which PITCHERs practise throwing〔棒球场中的〕投球练习区 **2** the PITCHERs of a BASEBALL team〔棒球运动中的〕投球手

bull·ring /ˈbʊlˌrɪŋ; ˈbʊlˌrɪŋ/ *n* [C] the place where a BULLFIGHT is held 斗牛场

Bull Run /ˈ· ·/ the place in northeast Virginia in the US where there were two important battles in the American Civil War which the Union forces lost to Confederate forces 布尔河〔美国弗吉尼亚州东北部一地名，美国南北战争期间这里曾发生过两次重大战役，联邦军队败给了南方联军〕

bull ses·sion /ˈ· ˌ··/ *n* [C] *AmE informal* an occasion when a group of people meet to talk in a relaxed and friendly way【美，非正式】闲聊，轻松而友好的交谈: *an all-night bull session* 通宵漫谈

bull's-eye 靶心

target 靶子

The arrow hit the bull's-eye. 箭正中靶心。

bull's-eye /ˈ· ·/ *n* [C] **1** the centre of a TARGET[1] (3) that you try to hit when shooting or in games like darts (DART[2] (2)) 靶心 **2** *BrE* a large hard round sweet【英】大块圆形硬糖

bull·shit¹ /ˈbʊlˌʃɪt; ˈbʊlˌʃɪt/ *n* [U] *informal* a rude word meaning something that is stupid and completely untrue【非正式】瞎扯，胡说八道，废话: *Forget all that bullshit and listen to me!* 别管那些废话，听我说！| **a load of bullshit** *Your so-called plan is a load of bullshit.* 你所谓的计划不过是一堆废话。

bullshit² *v* [I,T] *informal* a rude word meaning that something said is stupid or completely untrue, especially in order to deceive or impress someone【非正式】胡说，瞎吹，乱说: *Don't believe him, he's probably bullshitting.* 别信他的，他可能在乱说。—**bullshitter** *n* [C]

bull ter·ri·er /ˌ· ˈ···/ *n* [C] a strong short-haired dog 短毛㹴〔原产于英国，为斗牛犬和㹴交配所生的杂种犬〕—see also 另见 PIT BULL TERRIER

bul·ly¹ /ˈbʊlɪ; ˈbʊli/ *n* [C] someone who uses their strength or power to frighten or hurt someone who is weaker 恃强凌弱者，以大欺小者；暴徒: *Bullies are often cowards.* 欺负人者常常是懦夫。

bully 欺侮

bully² *v* [T] to threaten to hurt someone or frighten them, especially someone smaller or weaker 欺侮，以大欺小，威逼 —**bullying** *n* [U]: *an attempt to tackle the problem of bullying in schools* 为解决学校里以大欺小的问题所作的尝试

bully off *phr v* [I] to start a game of HOCKEY (1)〔曲棍球〕比赛开始 **—bully-off** *n* [C]

bully[3] *adj* **bully for you/him etc** *spoken* used when you do not think that someone has done anything special but they want you to praise them【口】好极了〔用于表示赞同某人的做法, 但不一定出于真心〕: *Yes. I know you've done all the dishes. Bully for you!* 是的, 我知道你把碗碟都洗了。太好了!

bully beef /ˈ‥ ˌ/ *n* [U] *BrE* CORNED BEEF【英】罐装咸牛肉

bully boy /ˈ‥ ˌ/ *n* [C] *BrE informal* someone who behaves in a violent and threatening way【英, 非正式】恶棍, 暴徒

bul·rush /ˈbʊlˌrʌʃ; ˈbʊlrʌʃ/ *n* [C] a tall plant that looks like grass and grows by water 宽叶香蒲; 灯心草

bul·wark /ˈbʊlwək; ˈbʊlwək/ *n* [C] **1** something that protects you from an unpleasant situation 保障; 堡垒; 保护物: [**+against**] *The Soviet Union was our only bulwark against fascism.* 苏联是保护我们不受法西斯统治的唯一保障。**2 bulwarks** [plural] the sides of a boat or ship above the DECK[1] (1)〔船的〕舷墙 **3** a strong structure like a wall, built for defence 掩体, 壁垒, 堡垒

S3 **bum**[1] /bʌm; bʌm/ *n* [C] *informal*【非正式】**1** *AmE* someone, especially a man, who has no home or job, and who asks people for money【美】流浪乞丐; 无业游民 **2** *BrE* the part of your body that you sit on; BOTTOM[1] (3)【英】屁股 **3 beach/ski etc bum** someone who spends all their time on the beach, skiing (SKI[2]) etc without having a job 沉湎于海滩/滑雪等的人 **4** someone who is very lazy 懒鬼

bum[2] *v* **bummed, bumming** [T] *slang* to ask someone for something such as money, food, or cigarettes【俚】乞讨

bum around *phr v slang*【俚】**1** also 又作 **bum about** [I] to spend time lazily doing nothing 游手好闲, 游荡 **2** [T **bum around** sth] to travel around in an unplanned way living very cheaply 漫游: *a year bumming around Australia* 在澳大利亚漫游一年

bum[3] *adj* [only before noun 仅用于名词前] *slang* bad and useless【俚】蹩脚的, 毫无价值的: *It must be a bum copy. It sounds terrible!* 这肯定是粗劣的复制品, 音质太差劲!

bum bag /ˈ‥ ˌ/ *n* [C] a small bag that you wear around your waist to hold money, keys etc 腰包

bum·ble /ˈbʌmbl̩; ˈbʌmbəl/ *v* [I] **1** also 又作 **bumble on** to speak in a confused way so that no-one can understand you 含糊不清地说: *I really don't know what Karl was bumbling on about.* 我真不知道卡尔在嘟囔些什么。**2** also 又作 **bumble around** to move in an unsteady way 笨拙地行动

bum·ble·bee /ˈbʌmbl̩ˌbi; ˈbʌmbəlbiː/ *n* [C] a large hairy BEE 大黄蜂, 熊蜂

bum·bling /ˈbʌmblɪŋ; ˈbʌmblɪŋ/ *adj* [only before noun 仅用于名词前] behaving in a careless way and making a lot of mistakes 粗心大意的, 常出错的: *bumbling incompetence* 笨手笨脚, 不能胜任

bumf, bumph /bʌmf; bʌmf/ *n* [U] *BrE informal* boring written information that you have to read【英, 非正式】令人乏味的文件; 无大用处的印刷品: *I got a load of bumf from the gas board.* 我从煤气公司得到了一大堆无用的印刷品。

bum·mer /ˈbʌmɚ; ˈbʌmə/ *n* **a bummer** *slang* a situation that is disappointing or annoying【俚】令人失望[烦恼]的情形: *It was a real bummer being ill on holiday.* 在假期生病真扫兴。

S3 **bump**[1] /bʌmp; bʌmp/ *v* **1** [I always+adv/prep, T] to hit or knock against something 猛碰, 撞: [**+against/into etc**] *It was so dark I bumped into a tree.* 天太黑, 我撞到了树上。| **bump sth on/against etc** *I bumped my head on the ledge.* 我的头撞到了壁架上。**2** [I always+adv/prep] to move up and down as you move forward, especially in a vehicle〔车辆〕颠簸而行: [**+along/across etc**] *The bus bumped along the rutted road.* 公共汽车沿着有车辙的路颠簸而行。

bump into sb *phr v* [T] to meet someone that you know when you were not expecting to 巧遇, 邂逅, 碰见: *I bumped into Jean in town this morning.* 今天上午我在城里遇见了琼。

bump sb ↔ **off** *phr v* [T] *informal* to kill someone【非正式】杀死〔某人〕

bump sth ↔ **up** *phr v* [T] *informal* to suddenly increase something by a large amount【非正式】突然大幅度提高, 增加: *In the summer they bump up the prices by ten percent.* 夏天他们突然把价格提高了10%。

bump[2] *n* [C] **1** an area of skin that is raised up because you have hit it on something〔撞击造成的〕肿块: *How did you get that bump over your eye?* 你眼睛上的肿块是怎么回事? **2** a small raised area on a surface 隆起之处: *bumps on the road* 路面隆起之处 **3** *informal* a slight accident in which your car hits something but you are not hurt【非正式】〔汽车〕碰撞: *Jim had a bump in the car.* 吉姆的汽车颠了一下。**4** the sound of something hitting a hard surface 砰然一声; 撞击声: *We heard a bump in the next room.* 我们听到隔壁房间传来砰的一声。| **fall/sit down etc with a bump** *Don sat down with a bump.* 唐扑通一屁股坐了下去。

bump·er[1] /ˈbʌmpɚ; ˈbʌmpə/ *n* [C] **1** *BrE* a bar fixed on the front and back of a car to protect it if it hits anything【英】〔汽车车身前后的〕保险杠; FENDER (1) *AmE*【美】—see picture on page A2 参见A2页图 **2 bumper-to-bumper** bumper-to-bumper traffic is very close together and moving slowly 一辆紧跟一辆

bumper[2] *adj* [only before noun 仅用于名词前] unusually large 特大的; 丰盛的: *a bumper crop*（庄稼）大丰收 | *a bumper edition of a magazine* 特大版的杂志

bumper car /ˈ‥ ˌ/ *n* [C] a small electric car that you drive in a special area at a FUNFAIR and deliberately try to hit other cars 碰碰车

bumper stick·er /ˈ‥ ˌ‥/ *n* [C] a sign on the BUMPER[1] (1) of a car, with a humorous, political, or religious message 贴在汽车保险杠上的小标语〔内容为幽默的、政治性的或宗教性的语句〕

bumph /bʌmf; bʌmf/ *n* [U] another spelling of BUMF bumf 的另一种拼法

bump·kin /ˈbʌmpkɪn; ˈbʌmpkɨn/ *n* [C] *informal* someone from the countryside who is considered to be stupid【非正式】乡巴佬, 土包子

bump·tious /ˈbʌmpʃəs; ˈbʌmpʃəs/ *adj* too proud of your abilities in a way that annoys other people 自吹自擂的, 自高自大的, 自负的 **—bumptiously** *adv* **—bumptiousness** *n* [U]

bump·y /ˈbʌmpɪ; ˈbʌmpi/ *adj* **1** a bumpy surface is flat but has a lot of raised parts so it is difficult to walk or drive on it 高低不平的: *a bumpy lane* 凸凹不平的车道 **2** a bumpy journey by car or plane is uncomfortable because of bad road or weather conditions〔旅程〕颠簸的 **3 have a bumpy ride/time** to have a lot of problems for a long time 走过相当漫长坎坷的道路/度过相当长的困难时期: *Professional soccer has had a bumpy ride in the US.* 职业足球在美国走过了漫长坎坷的道路。—opposite 反义词 SMOOTH[1]

bun /bʌn; bʌn/ *n* [C] **1** *BrE* a small round sweet cake【英】小圆糕点: *a sticky bun* 一个黏乎乎的小圆点心 **2** *especially AmE* a small round type of bread【尤美】小圆面包: *a hamburger bun* 汉堡包 **3** a hairstyle in which a woman with long hair fastens it in a small round shape at the back of her head〔盘在脑后的〕圆发髻 —see picture at 参见 HAIRSTYLE 图 **4 have a bun in the oven** *BrE humorous* to be PREGNANT (=going to have a baby)【英, 幽默】怀孕, 有喜

bunch[1] /bʌntʃ; bʌntʃ/ *n* **1 bunch of flowers/keys/grapes etc** a group of flowers, keys etc that are fastened or held together 一束花/一串钥匙/一串葡萄等 **2** [singular] *informal* a group of people【非正式】〔人〕一群, 一伙: *Our new neighbours are a weired bunch.* 我们的新邻居是一伙很古怪的人。**3 the pick of the bunch** the best among a group of people or things 佼佼者 **4** [singular] *especially AmE* a large number of people or things, or a large amount of something【尤美】大量: [**+of**] *The doctor asked me a bunch of questions.* 医生问了我一连串问题。**5 in bunches** *BrE* if a girl wears her hair in bunches, she ties it together at each side of her head【英】〔把头发分在两边〕扎成两束 **6 thanks a bunch** an expression meaning thank you very much, used jokingly when you are not grateful at all 多谢了〔玩笑说法, 表示毫无感激之意〕 S2

bunch[2] *v* also 又作 **bunch together, bunch up 1** [I] to stay close together in a group 聚成堆[群]: *The children bunched together in groups in the playground.* 孩子们你一群我一伙地聚在操场上。**2** [T] to tighten part of your body 绷紧〔身体的一部分〕: *Sean bunched his fists and strode towards them.* 肖恩握紧拳头, 大步朝他们走去。**3** [T] to hold or tie things together in a bunch 将〔东西〕绑成一束 **4** [I,T] to pull material together tightly in folds (使) 起褶

bun·dle[1] /ˈbʌndl̩; ˈbʌndl/ *n* [C] **1** a group of things such as papers, clothes, or sticks that are fastened or tied together 捆, 把, 扎, 束 **2** [singular] *informal* a lot of money【非正式】一大笔钱: **cost a bundle** *The trip will cost a bundle and we can't pay for it ourselves.* 旅行要花一大笔钱, 我们自己支付不起。| **make a bundle** (=earn or win a lot of money) 赚了大笔钱 **3 be a bundle of nerves** *informal* to be very nervous【非正式】极度紧张 **4 be a bundle of fun/laughs** *informal* an expression meaning a person or situation that is fun or makes you laugh, often used jokingly when they are not fun at all【非正式】出洋相: *You were a bundle of fun last night. What's wrong?* 昨晚你大出洋相, 到底是怎么回事? **5 not go a bundle on sth** *BrE informal* to not like something very much【英, 非正式】不太喜欢某事物:

Jim never drank, and certainly didn't go a bundle on gambling. 吉姆从不喝酒，而且肯定也不太喜欢赌博。

bundle² *v* **1** [T always+adv/prep] to quickly push someone or something somewhere because you are in a hurry or you want to hide them 匆匆打发〔某人〕; 把〔某物〕乱塞: **bundle sb into/through etc** *They bundled Perez into the car, and drove off.* 他们把佩雷斯推上汽车，然后开走了。**2** [I always + adv/prep] to move somewhere quickly in a group 塞进，挤进: [**+into/through etc**] *Six of us bundled into a taxi.* 我们六个人挤进了计程车。

bundle sb **off** *phr v* [T] to send someone somewhere in a hurry 匆匆把〔某人〕送往某地

bundle up *phr v* **1** [T **bundle** sth ↔ **up**] to make a bundle by tying things together 把…扎紧，把…捆上: *Bundle up the newspapers and take them to the skip.* 把这些报纸捆在一起扔进废物桶里。**2** [I,T **bundle** sb **up**] to dress warmly because it is cold (给)〔某人〕穿上暖和的衣服

Bundt cake /ˈbʌnt kek; ˈbʌnt keɪk/ *trademark* a sweet cake shaped like a ring, made in a Bundt pan【商标】邦特烤饼〔用邦特烤盘烘制的环形甜饼〕

> **CULTURAL NOTE 文化注释**
> In the US, a Bundt cake is a typical gift that people take with them when they visit a new neighbour. 在美国，人们拜访新邻居时常送邦特烤饼。

Bundt pan /ˈbʌnt pæn; ˈbʌnt pæn/ *trademark* a type of baking pan shaped like a ring, with high sides and a hole in the middle, used for baking cakes【商标】邦特烤盘〔一种边沿高起、中间留有一孔的环形烤盘，用于烤饼〕: *Pour the batter into a greased Bundt pan.* 将面糊倒入涂过油脂的邦特烤盘。

bung¹ /bʌŋ; bʌŋ/ *n* [C] **1** a round piece of rubber, wood etc used to close the top of a container 塞子 —see picture at 参见 LABORATORY 图 **2** *BrE slang* money given to someone secretly, and usually illegally, to make them do something【英俚】贿赂

bung² *v* [T always+adv/prep] *BrE informal* to put something somewhere quickly and without thinking carefully【英，非正式】投，扔，掷；乱放: **bung sth in/on etc** *Can you bung these clothes in the washing machine?* 你能把这些衣服扔进洗衣机吗？

bung sth ↔ **up** *phr v* [T] **1** to block a hole by putting something in it 阻塞，塞住 **2 be bunged up** *informal* to find it difficult to breathe because you have a COLD【非正式】〔因伤风而鼻子〕不通气

bun·ga·low /ˈbʌŋgəˌlo; ˈbʌŋgələʊ/ *n* [C] **1** *BrE* a house which is all on ground level【英】平房 **2** *AmE* a small house which is often on one level【美】单层小屋 —see picture on page A4 参见 A4 页图

bun·gee cord /ˈbʌndʒɪ ˌkɔrd; ˈbʌndʒi ˌkɔːd/ *n* [C] *AmE* a thick rope that stretches and has hooks on each end【美】〔用于绑紧跳的〕有弹性的绳

bungee jump·ing /ˈbʌndʒɪ ˌdʒʌmpɪŋ; ˈbʌndʒi ˌdʒʌmpɪŋ/ *n* [U] the activity of attaching yourself to something such as a bridge with a bungee cord, then jumping off so you BOUNCE in the air 蹦极〔把自己用一根有弹性的绳系在桥等物体上，然后跳下，再弹回空中的一种运动〕

bung·hole /ˈbʌŋˌhol; ˈbʌŋhəʊl/ *n* [C] a hole for emptying or filling a BARREL¹ (1) 桶孔，桶口

bun·gle /ˈbʌŋgl; ˈbʌŋgəl/ *v* [T] to do something unsuccessfully, because you have made stupid or careless mistakes 做坏，搞糟: *The whole police operation was bungled.* 警方的整个行动给打乱了。—**bungle** *n* [C] —**bungler** *n* [C] —**bungling** *n* [U] —**bungled** *adj*: *a bungled rescue attempt* 一次失败的救援行动

bun·ion /ˈbʌnjən; ˈbʌnjən/ *n* [C] a painful red sore area on the first joint of your big toe 拇趾囊肿，拇囊炎肿

bunk¹ /bʌŋk; bʌŋk/ *n* **1** [C] a narrow bed that is fixed to the wall, for example on a train or ship〔火车、船上的〕卧铺，靠壁床铺，铺位 **2 bunk beds** [plural] two beds that are fixed together, one on top of the other 双层床 —see picture at 参见 BED¹ 图 **3 do a bunk** *BrE informal* to suddenly leave a place without telling anyone【英，非正式】逃走；擅自离开 **4** [U] *informal* nonsense; BUNKUM【非正式】瞎说，废话: *What a load of bunk!* 一大堆废话！

bunk² *v* [I] *informal* also 又作 **bunk down** to lie down to sleep in a particular place【非正式】〔在某处〕睡下: *You can bunk down on the sofa for tonight.* 今晚你可以在沙发上过夜。

bunk off *phr v BrE informal* [I,T **bunk off** sth] to stay away from somewhere such as school or to leave somewhere early without permission【英，非正式】擅自离开；逃走: *I think I'll bunk off classes this afternoon.* 我想今天下午我要逃课。

bun·ker /ˈbʌŋkə; ˈbʌŋkə/ *n* [C] **1** a place where you store coal, especially on a ship or outside a house〔尤指船上或屋外的〕煤仓 **2** a strongly built shelter for soldiers, usually underground 掩体，地堡，掩蔽壕 **3** *BrE* a large hole on a GOLF course, filled with sand【英】〔高尔夫球场的〕沙坑; SANDTRAP *AmE*【美】—see picture on page A23 参见 A23 页图

Bunker Hill, the Battle of /ˌ·· ˈ·/ the first main battle of the American Revolutionary War in Boston, Massachusetts in 1775. Although the British army won the battle, the American COLONISTS killed and wounded more than 1000 British soldiers, and proved that their army was more powerful and effective than the British expected them to be. 邦克山战役〔1775年在马萨诸塞州波士顿打响的美国独立战争首场大战。尽管英国军队获胜，但美洲殖民地人民歼灭并打伤了1000余名英军士兵，从而证明殖民地军队比英国人预料的要强大、善战〕

bunk·house /ˈbʌŋkˌhaus; ˈbʌŋkhaʊs/ *n* [C] a building where workers sleep 工棚；简易工人宿舍

bun·kum /ˈbʌŋkəm; ˈbʌŋkəm/ *n* [U] *informal* nonsense【非正式】废话，胡说八道

bunk-up /ˈ· ·/ *n BrE* [singular] *informal* an act of pushing someone up from below to help them get higher【英，非正式】〔帮助别人攀登时向上的〕一推，一托

bun·ny /ˈbʌnɪ; ˈbʌni/ also 又作 **bunny rab·bit** /ˈ·· ˌ··/ *n* [C] a word for a rabbit, used especially by or to children 兔子〔尤为儿语〕 S3

bun·sen bur·ner /ˌbʌnsn̩ ˈbɝnɚ; ˌbʌnsən ˈbɜːnə/ *n* [C] a piece of equipment that produces a hot gas flame, for scientific EXPERIMENTS 本生灯〔实验室用的一种煤气灯〕—see picture at 参见 LABORATORY 图

bunt /bʌnt; bʌnt/ *v* [I] *AmE* to deliberately hit the ball a short distance in a game of BASEBALL【美】〔棒球比赛中的〕触击，轻打 —**bunt** *n* [C]

Bun·ter /ˈbʌntɚ; ˈbʌntə/**, Billy** the main character in children's stories by Frank Richards about life in an English PUBLIC SCHOOL (=a private school where the students live as well as study) 邦特〔弗兰克·理查德所著有关英国公学生活的儿童读物的主人公〕: *Bunter loves eating and is always getting into trouble.* 邦特爱吃，总是惹麻烦。

bun·ting /ˈbʌntɪŋ; ˈbʌntɪŋ/ *n* [U] small paper or cloth flags on strings, used to decorate buildings and streets on special occasions〔用绳子穿成一长串的〕小彩旗

Buñ·u·el /ˈbunjuɛl; ˈbuːnjuel/**, Lu·is** /luˈis; luːˈiːs/ (1900-83) a Spanish film DIRECTOR famous for his dreamlike images and humorous attacks on the Catholic Church and middle-class moral values. His films include *Le Charme Discrèt De La Bourgeoisie* and *Cet Obscur Objet Du Désir*. 布努埃尔〔(1900-1983)，西班牙电影导演，以其梦幻般的意象及对天主教会和中产阶级道德价值观的幽默抨击而闻名，他导演的影片有《资产阶级审慎的魅力》和《欲望的不可捉摸的对象》〕

Bun·yan /ˈbʌnjən; ˈbʌnjən/**, John** (1628-88) an English PREACHER who wrote *The Pilgrim'S Progress* while he was in prison for his beliefs 班扬〔(1628-1688)，英国传教士，因信仰问题而入狱，期间创作了《天路历程》〕

Paul Bunyan 保罗·班扬

Bunyan, Paul /pɔl; pɔːl/ a GIANT (=an extremely large man) in old American stories. He was a LUMBERJACK (=someone whose job is to cut down trees) from the forests of Canada and the north US, who travelled with a blue ox called Babe. They changed the shape of the land as they walked along, for example by making mountains and also the GRAND CANYON. 班扬

〔美国古老传说中的巨人，牵着名叫娃娃的蓝牛在加拿大和美国北部的森林里伐木。他们所经之处，必改变地貌，如筑起高山，造就大峡谷〕

buoy[1] /bɔɪ; bɔɪ/ *n* [C] an object that floats on the sea to mark a safe or dangerous area 浮标，航标

buoy[2] also 又作 **buoy up** *v* [T] **1** to make someone feel happier or more confident 振奋…的精神；鼓舞: *buoyed by a two goal lead* 为领先两分而振奋 **2** to keep profits, prices etc at a high level 维持〔利润、价格等的高水平〕: *The company's profits were buoyed by a successful publishing venture.* 由于出版风险项目的成功运作，这家公司维持了较高水平的利润。**3** to keep something floating 使浮起

buoy·an·cy /ˋbɔɪənsɪ; ˈbɔɪənsi/ *n* [U] **1** the ability of an object to float〔物体在液体里的〕浮性: *the buoyancy of light wood* 轻质木材的浮性 **2** the power of a liquid to make an object float 浮力: *Salt water has more buoyancy than fresh water.* 盐水的浮力比淡水大。**3** a feeling of cheerfulness and belief that you can deal with problems easily 自信；乐观 **4** the ability of prices, a business etc to quickly get back to a high level after a difficult period〔价格、营业状况等的〕维持力；恢复力；上涨行情；增长趋势

buoy·ant /ˋbɔɪənt; ˈbɔɪənt/ *adj* **1** cheerful and confident 轻松愉快的；自信的: *Phil was in buoyant mood.* 菲尔心情很愉快。**2** buoyant prices etc tend to rise 趋于上升的；上涨的: *a buoyant economy* 欣欣向荣的经济 **3** able to float or keep things floating 有浮力的，易浮起的: *Cork is a very buoyant material.* 软木是一种极易浮起的材料。—**buoyantly** *adv*

bur /bɝ; bɜː/ *n* [C] another spelling of BURR burr的另一种拼法

Bur·ber·ry /ˋbɝbərɪ; ˈbɜːbəri/ *n* [C] *trademark* a kind of RAINCOAT【商标】巴宝莉雨衣

bur·ble /ˋbɝbḷ; ˈbɜːbəl/ *v* **1** [I,T] to talk about something in a confused way that is difficult to understand 嘟嘟囔囔地说；唠叨: *Maggie kept burbling away about how difficult things were.* 玛吉滔滔不绝地说情况太糟。**2** [I] to make a sound like a stream flowing over stones 发出潺潺声；潺潺而流 —**burble** *n* [C]

burbs /bɝbz; bɜːbz/ *n* **the burbs** *AmE informal* the SUBURBS (=areas around a city)【美，非正式】郊区

bur·den[1] /ˋbɝdṇ; ˈbɜːdn/ *n* **1** [C] something difficult or worrying that you are responsible for 重担，负担: **heavy burden** *We're in no position to take on another heavy financial burden.* 我们无法承受又一个沉重的经济负担。**2** [singular] *formal* the main meaning of what someone is saying【正式】要点，要旨，主旨 **3** **the burden of proof** *law* the duty to prove that something is true【法律】举证责任 **4** something that is carried; load 担子；负荷 —see also 另见 BEAST OF BURDEN

burden[2] *v* **1** **be burdened by** to have a lot of problems because of a particular thing 被…所困扰；承受…的负担: *a big company burdened by debt* 债务缠身的大公司 —see also 另见 UNBURDEN **2** **be burdened with** to be carrying something heavy 负载着，背负着: *burdened with grocery bags* 背着沉重的食品袋

bur·den·some /ˋbɝdṇsəm; ˈbɜːdnsəm/ *adj* causing problems or additional work 成为负担的，累赘的；令人烦恼的: *burdensome responsibilities* 繁重的责任

bu·reau /ˋbjʊro; ˈbjʊərəʊ/ *n plural* **bureaux** /-roz; -rəʊz/ *BrE*【英】, **bureaus** *AmE*【美】[C] **1** an office or organization that collects or provides information 提供[收集]消息的办事处[机构]: *an employment bureau* 职业介绍所 **2** *especially AmE* a government department or a part of a government department【尤美】〔政府部门的〕司；局；处；署: *the Federal Bureau of Investigation* 联邦调查局 **3** *BrE* a large desk or writing table【英】大书桌，大写字台 **4** *AmE* a piece of furniture with several drawers, used to keep clothes in; CHEST OF DRAWERS【美】五斗橱，衣柜

bu·reauc·ra·cy /bjʊˋrɑkrəsɪ; bjʊəˈrɒkrəsi/ *n* **1** [U] a complicated official system which is annoying or confusing because it has a lot of rules, processes etc 官僚制度；官僚政治；官僚机构；官僚主义: *plans to eliminate unnecessary bureaucracy* 消除不必要的官僚体制的计划 **2** [C,U] the officials who are employed rather than elected to do the work of a government, business etc 官僚〔指雇用而非选举之政府官员的总称〕；〔工商业的〕高级管理人员

bu·reau·crat /ˋbjʊrəˌkræt; ˈbjʊərəkræt/ *n* [C] someone who works in a bureaucracy and uses official rules very strictly 官僚；官僚主义者；官僚作风的人

bu·reau·crat·ic /ˌbjʊrəˋkrætɪk; ˌbjʊərəˈkrætɪk◂/ *adj* involving a lot of complicated official rules and processes 官僚的；官僚主义的 —**bureaucratically** /-klɪ; -kli/ *adv*

bureau de change /ˌbjʊro de ˋʃɑndʒ; ˌbjʊərəʊ də ˈʃɒndʒ/ *n* [C] *French* an office or shop where you can change foreign money【法】外币兑换所[店]

Bureau of In·di·an Af·fairs, the /.. ˌ... ˌ.., ... ˈ./ abbreviation 缩写为 **BIA** a US government organization which is concerned with the WELFARE and education of Native Americans and with other legal matters concerning RESERVATIONS (=areas set aside for Native Americans to live on) 印第安人事务局〔美国一政府机构，负责处理印第安人的福利、教育事务以及与印第安人居留地有关的法律问题〕

bur·geon /ˋbɝdʒən; ˈbɜːdʒən/ *v* [I] *formal* to grow or develop quickly【正式】急速增长[发展]

bur·geon·ing /ˋbɝdʒənɪŋ; ˈbɜːdʒənɪŋ/ *adj* increasing or developing very quickly 迅速发展的: *a project to improve water supplies to Denver's burgeoning population* 为适应丹佛迅速增加的人口而改善供水的项目

burg·er /ˋbɝgɚ; ˈbɜːgə/ *n* [C] **1** a flat round piece of finely cut BEEF[1] (1), which is cooked and usually eaten in a bread ROLL[2] (2); a HAMBURGER 汉堡包: **cheeseburger** (=a burger with cheese on top of the meat) 乳酪汉堡包 **2** **vegeburger/nutburger** something like a HAMBURGER but made of vegetables, nuts etc 素馅/果仁汉堡包

Bur·gess /ˋbɝdʒɪs; ˈbɜːdʒɪs/, **Guy** (1911-63) a British man who worked for British Intelligence, but was secretly a spy for the former Soviet Union. In 1951 he escaped to the Soviet Union with another British spy, Donald MacLean. 伯吉斯〔(1911-1963)，英国人，为英国情报部门工作，但同时又是前苏联的秘密间谍，1951年同另一位英国间谍唐纳德·麦克林一起逃往苏联〕

burgh /bɝg; ˈbʌrə/ *n* [C] *ScotE* a BOROUGH【苏格兰】享有某些自治权的城镇

bur·gher /ˋbɝgɚ; ˈbɜːgə/ *n* [C] *old use* someone who lives in a particular town【旧】〔自治市的〕市民

bur·glar /ˋbɝglɚ; ˈbɜːglə/ *n* [C] someone who gets into houses, shops etc to steal things 小偷，窃贼 —compare 比较 ROBBER, THIEF —see also 另见 CAT BURGLAR

> **CULTURAL NOTE 文化注释**
> Humorous drawings of burglars show them wearing STRIPED jumpers and carrying a large bag marked SWAG (=things they have stolen). 幽默画里面的窃贼穿着条纹毛衣，手里拎着一个大袋子，上书"赃物"。

burglar a·larm /ˈ.. .ˌ./ *n* [C] a piece of equipment that makes a loud noise when a burglar gets into a building 防盗警报器[铃] —see picture at 参见 ALARM[1] 图

bur·gla·rize /ˋbɝgləˌraɪz; ˈbɜːgləraɪz/ *v* [T] *AmE* to get into a building and steal things from it or from the people inside【美】入室行窃，闯入…行窃; burgle *BrE*【英】

bur·glar·y /ˋbɝglərɪ; ˈbɜːgləri/ *n* [C,U] the crime of getting into a building to steal things 入室盗窃（罪）: *Burglaries in the area have risen by 5%.* 这一地区的入室盗窃案件上升了5%。

bur·gle /ˋbɝgḷ; ˈbɜːgəl/ *v* [T] *BrE* to get into a building and steal things from it or from the people inside【英】闯入…行窃; burglarize *AmE*【美】: *We've been burgled three times!* 我们（家）已经三次被盗！—see 见 STEAL[1] (USAGE)

bur·gun·dy /ˋbɝgəndɪ; ˈbɜːgəndi/ *n* **1** [C,U] red or white wine from the Burgundy area of France〔法国勃艮第地区产的〕葡萄酒 **2** [U] a dark red colour 深（紫）红色 —see picture on page A5 参见A5页图

bur·i·al /ˋbɛrɪəl; ˈberiəl/ *n* [C,U] the act or ceremony of putting a dead body into a grave 埋葬；葬礼

burk /bɝk; bɜːk/ *n* [C] another spelling of BERK berk的另一种拼法

Burke /bɝk; bɜːk/, **Ed·mund** /ˋɛdmənd; ˈedmənd/ (1729-97) a British Whig politician, born in Dublin, Ireland. He wrote many works of political THEORY and was also a great speaker. 伯克〔(1729-1797)，英国辉格党政治家，出生于爱尔兰都柏林，写过不少政治理论著作，也是一位出色的演说家〕

Burke's Peer·age /ˌ. ˈ../ a book that gives details of all the NOBLE families in the UK who have special titles such as 'Duke' or 'Earl'《伯克氏系谱》〔详细介绍英国拥有"公爵"、"伯爵"等贵族头衔家庭的书籍〕

Bur·ki·na Fa·so /burkinə ˋfæso; bʊəˌkiːnə ˈfæsəʊ/ a country in West Africa, to the north of Ghana and the east of Mali, which was formerly called Upper Volta. Population: 12,272,000 (2001). Capital: Ouagadougou. 布基纳法索〔西非国家，南与加纳交界，西与马里接壤，旧称上沃尔特。人口：12,272,000 (2001)，首都：瓦加杜古〕

bur·lap /ˋbɝlæp; ˈbɜːlæp/ *n* [U] *AmE* a type of thick rough cloth【美】〔打包用的〕粗麻布，麻袋布; HESSIAN *BrE*【英】

bur·lesque¹ /bɝˋlɛsk; bɜːˈlesk/ *n* **1** [C,U] speech, acting, or writing in which a serious subject is made to seem silly or an unimportant subject is treated in a serious way 滑稽讽刺的讲话[演出, 文字] **2** *AmE* a performance involving a mixture of comedy and STRIPTEASE, popular in America in the past【美】〔美国旧时的〕滑稽歌舞杂剧〔常包括脱衣舞〕: *a burlesque house* 杂耍表演场

burlesque² *v* [T] to make a serious subject seem silly to amuse people 讽刺, 嘲弄, 使滑稽化

bur·ly /ˋbɝlɪ; ˈbɜːli/ *adj* a burly man is big and strong 壮实的, 魁梧的: *burly rugby players* 壮实的橄榄球球员 —**burliness** *n* [U]

Bur·ma /ˋbɝmə; ˈbɜːmə/ the former name of Myanmar, a country in southeast Asia 缅甸〔旧称, 东南亚国家〕

2 3

burn¹ /bɝn; bɜːn/ *v past and past participle* **burnt** /bɝnt; bɜːnt/ *or* **burned**

① FIRE 火
② CHEMICALS 化学品
③ KILL 杀死
④ PRODUCE POWER/LIGHT 产生力/光
⑤ FEELING/EMOTION 感觉/感情
⑥ MONEY 钱
⑦ CARS 汽车
⑧ OTHER MEANINGS 其他意思

① FIRE 火

1 ►PRODUCE HEAT 产生热◄ [I] to produce heat and flames 燃烧: *Is the fire still burning?* 火还在燃烧吗?

2 ►DESTROY WITH FIRE 烧毁◄ [I,T] to be destroyed by fire or destroy something with fire 焚烧, 烧毁: **burn sth** *I burnt all his old letters.* 我把他的旧信全烧了。

3 burn to the ground/burn to ashes if a building burns to the ground, it is completely destroyed by fire 烧成灰烬

4 burn sth to a crisp/cinder to burn something until it is black, especially by cooking it for too long 将某物烧黑〔尤指烹调时间过长〕—see picture on page A10 参见 A10 页图

5 ►DAMAGE BY FIRE 烧坏◄ [I,T] to damage something or hurt someone with fire or heat, or be hurt or damaged in this way (使) 烧伤 [坏], (使) 烫伤 [坏], (使) 烧焦: *I've burnt my hand.* 我烫伤了手。| *Quick, the toast's burning!* 快! 面包烤焦了! | **burn a hole in** *Be careful you don't burn a hole in the chair with your cigarette.* 小心点, 别让烟头把椅子烧个洞。

② CHEMICALS 化学品

6 [T] to damage or destroy something by a chemical action; CORRODE 腐蚀, 烧毁

③ KILL 杀死

7 be burned to death/burned alive to be killed in a fire 被活活烧死

8 burn sb at the stake to kill someone by tying them to a post on top of a fire 把某人活活烧死在火刑柱上

④ PRODUCE POWER/LIGHT 产生力/光

9 [I,T] if you burn a FUEL, or if it burns, it is used to produce power, heat, light etc 点, 烧: *The central heating boiler burns oil.* 中央供暖锅炉烧油。

10 ►SHINE 发光◄ [I] if a light or lamp burns, it shines or produces light 发光, 照亮: *A light was burning in her window.* 她窗子里亮着灯。

⑤ FEELING/EMOTION 感觉/感情

11 [I,T] to feel unpleasantly hot or make part of your body feel like this 使发烧; 刺痛; 感觉火辣 [灼热, 刺痛]: *I'm afraid the ointment might burn a bit.* 恐怕这种油膏会使皮肤有灼热感。

12 ►BE EMBARRASSED 感到尴尬◄ [I] if your face or cheeks are burning, they feel hot because you are embarrassed or upset 脸发烧[热]

13 be burning with rage/desire etc to feel an emotion very strongly 怒火中烧/产生强烈的欲望等

14 be burning to do sth to want to do something very much 心急如焚地要做某事: *Hannah's burning to tell you her news.* 汉娜心急如焚地要告诉你她的消息。

15 it burns me/her/John etc that *AmE* used to say that something makes someone feel angry or jealous【美】〔某事〕使我/她/约翰等感到气愤[妒忌]: *It really burns me the way they treat us.* 他们那样对待我们, 我很气愤。

16 be/get burned to be emotionally hurt by someone or something 感情受到伤害

⑥ MONEY 钱

17 burn a hole in your pocket if money is burning a hole in your pocket, you want to spend it as soon as you can 急于把钱花掉

18 burn your fingers/get your fingers burned *informal* to suffer the unpleasant results of something that you have done【非正式】自作自受; 自食其果: *George got his fingers badly burned when the travel company collapsed.* 旅行公司倒闭了, 乔治这是自作自受。

19 be/get burned to lose a lot of money, especially in a business deal〔尤指生意上〕赔了很多钱: *A lot of people got burned buying junk bonds.* 很多人因买垃圾债券而损失惨重。

⑦ CARS 汽车

20 ►GO FAST 快速行进◄ [I always+adv/prep] to travel very fast 高速行进: [+**along/through/up etc**] *a sports car burning up the motorway* 一辆在高速公路上疾驶的跑车

21 burn rubber *AmE informal* to start a car moving so quickly that the tyres become very hot and make a loud high noise【美, 非正式】〔因起动太快〕车胎发烫发出响声

⑧ OTHER MEANINGS 其他意思

22 burn your bridges/boats *informal* to do something that you cannot change, that often makes a situation difficult for you【非正式】破釜沉舟, 自绝后路

23 burn the candle at both ends *informal* to work too hard for too long【非正式】过分消耗体力, 起早贪黑地干, 废寝忘食

24 burn the midnight oil *informal* to work or study until late at night【非正式】熬夜工作 [读书], 开夜车

burn away *phr v* [I,T] if something burns away or is burned away, it is destroyed or reduced to something much smaller by fire 烧掉, 烧毁, 烧光

burn down *phr v* **1** [I,T **burn** sth ↔ **down**] if a building burns down or is burned down, it is destroyed by fire〔建筑物〕被烧毁 **2** [I] if a fire burns down, the flames become weaker and it produces less heat 火力减弱, 火头变小 —compare 比较 **burn out** (BURN¹), **burn up** (BURN¹)

burn sth ↔ **off** *phr v* [T] **1** to remove something by burning it 烧掉: *farmers burning off the stubble from the fields* 农民把田里的茬子烧掉 **2 burn off energy/fat/calories etc** to use energy etc by doing physical exercise 消耗能量/脂肪/热量等: *I think I'll go for a walk and burn off a few calories!* 我想散散步, 消耗点儿热量!

burn out *phr v*

1 ►FIRE 火◄ [I,T **burn** sth **out**] if a fire burns out or burns itself out, it stops burning because there is no coal, wood etc left 烧尽, 燃尽

2 be burnt out if something is burnt out, the inside of it is destroyed by fire 被烧空: *The hotel was completely burnt out; only the walls remained.* 旅馆完全烧空, 仅剩四壁。

3 burn yourself out to ruin your health and feel very tired through working too hard, drinking too much alcohol etc〔因工作过累、酗酒等而〕元气大伤, 精力耗尽; 〔身体〕搞垮

4 ►ENGINE 发动机◄ [I,T **burn** sth ↔ **out**] if an engine or electric wire burns out or is burned out, it stops working because it has been damaged by getting too hot 烧坏

5 ►AIRCRAFT 飞机◄ [I] if a ROCKET¹ (1) or JET¹ (1) burns out, it stops operating because all its FUEL has been used 燃油用尽 —see also 另见 BURNOUT (1)

burn up *phr v*

1 ►DESTROY 摧毁◄ [I,T **burn** sth ↔ **up**] if something burns up or is burnt up, it is completely destroyed by fire or great heat 烧毁, 烧尽

2 ▶BURN BRIGHTER 烧得更亮◀ [I] if a fire burns up, it gets stronger and brighter〔火〕旺起来, 烧起来
3 ▶BE HOT 变热◀ [I] *spoken* if someone is burning up, they are very hot【口】〔人〕感到很热
4 ▶MAKE SB ANGRY 使某人生气◀ [T **burn** sb **up**] *informal especially AmE* to make someone angry【非正式, 尤美】使〔某人〕气愤: *The way he treats her really burns me up.* 他那样对待她, 令我十分气愤。
5 **be burned up with anger/jealousy etc** to have your mind full of a strong emotion 怒火中烧/妒火中烧等
6 **burn up energy/fat/calories etc** to use energy etc by doing physical exercise 消耗能量/脂肪/热量等

USAGE NOTE 用法说明: BURN
SPELLING 拼法
In American English the past tense and past participle of the verb is **burned**. 在美国英语中, 该词的过去式和过去分词都是burned: *She burned a hole in my new shirt.* 她把我的新衬衫烧了个洞。In British English **burnt** is used, though **burned** is also used, especially when the action goes on for some time. 在英国英语中, 过去式和过去分词是burnt; 但也用burned, 特别指动作已进行一段时间: *The fire burned brightly.* 火烧得很旺。| *I've burnt my hand.* 我把手烧伤了。| *The house burnt down.* 房子被烧毁了。
In both American and British English, **burnt** is used when the word is used as an adjective. 用作形容词时, 美国英语和英国英语都作burnt: *burnt toast* 烤焦的面包 | *a burnt tree* (=made black by burning) 烧焦的树
This is also true of 以上规则也适用于下列对应词 **spoiled/spoilt, learned/learnt, spilled/spilt, spelled/spelt, smelled/smelt,** and, with a pronunciation difference as well 但有些词的发音不同, **leaned/leant, leaped/leapt, dreamed/dreamt, kneeled/knelt**. e.g. 如 *I learned English for ten years.* 我学过10年英语。| *a spoilt child* 宠坏的孩子

S3 **burn²** *n* [C] **1** an injury or mark caused by fire, heat, or acid〔因火、高温或酸引起的〕灼伤; 烫伤; 伤痕: **severe/minor burns** (=burns that are serious or not serious) 严重/轻度烧伤 **2 the burn** *informal* a painful hot feeling in your muscles when you exercise a lot【非正式】〔大量锻炼使肌肉产生的〕热痛感: *Go for the burn.* 去锻炼一下肌肉, 使其产生热痛感。**3** *especially ScotE* a small stream【尤苏格兰】溪流

Burne-Jones /ˌbɝn ˋdʒonz; ˌbɜːn ˈdʒəʊnz/, **Edward** (1833-98) a British painter who was one of the Pre-Raphaelites 伯恩-琼斯〔(1833-1898), 英国拉斐尔前派画家〕

burn·er /ˋbɝnɚ; ˈbɜːnə/ *n* [C] **1** *AmE* the part of an OVEN or heater that produces heat or a flame【美】燃烧器 [炉]; 炉头, 火眼; GAS RING *BrE*【英】: *a gas burner* 煤气炉头 —see picture at 参见 FONDUE 图 **2 put sth on the back burner** *informal* to delay dealing with something until a later time【非正式】推迟〔做某事〕: *We've had to put the vacation plans on the back burner because of Bob's ill health.* 由于鲍勃身体欠佳, 我们只好推迟度假计划。

Bur·nett /bɚˋnɛt; bɜːˈnet/, **Fran·ces Hodg·son** /ˋfrænsɪs ˋhɑdʒsn; ˈfrɑːnsɪ̆s ˈhɒdʒsən/ (1849-1924) a US writer born in England. She wrote the children's books *Little Lord Fauntleroy* and *The Secret Garden.* 伯内特〔(1849-1924), 出生于英国的美国作家, 她创作的儿童读物有《方特勒罗伊小爵爷》和《秘密花园》〕

burn·ing¹ /ˋbɝnɪŋ; ˈbɜːnɪŋ/ *adj* [only before noun 仅用于名词前] **1** on fire 燃烧着的: *You could see the burning house for miles around.* 你可以在几英里之外看到正在燃烧的房子。**2** feeling very hot 感到发烫的: *burning cheeks* 发烫的双颊 **3 burning ambition/need etc** a very strong need etc 雄心勃勃/急切需要等: **burning ambition** *My burning ambition is to travel around the world.* 我极其渴望环游世界。**4 burning question/issue** a very important and urgent question 亟待解决的问题: *The burning question is, will Rob agree to come?* 当务之急是, 罗布会同意来吗?

burning² *adv* **burning hot** very hot 滚烫的, 酷热的

bur·nish /ˋbɝnɪʃ; ˈbɜːnɪʃ/ *v* [T] to polish metal until it shines 打磨, 抛光擦亮; 使光滑 **—burnished** *adj*: *burnished copper* 磨光的黄铜

bur·nous also 又作 **burnoose** *AmE*【美】/bɚˋnus; bɜːˈnuːs/ *n* [C] a long loose dress or coat worn by Arab men and women〔阿拉伯人穿的〕带包头巾的长袍

burn·out /ˋbɝnˌaʊt; ˈbɜːnaʊt/ *n* [C,U] **1** the time when a ROCKET¹ (1) or JET¹ (1) has finished all of its FUEL and stops operating〔火箭等燃料用尽时的〕熄灭 **2** a state in which you have ruined your health by working too hard〔因拼命工作导致的〕精疲力竭: *teachers suffering from burnout* 精疲力竭的教师们

Burns /bɝnz; bɜːnz/, **George** (1896-1996) a US COMEDIAN and actor who was popular in VAUDEVILLE, on radio, and on television. He was known for always smoking a cigar and for talking to the AUDIENCE (=the people watching). 伯恩斯〔(1896-1996), 美国喜剧演员, 出演的综艺节目、广播电视节目颇受欢迎, 以抽雪茄烟和与观众谈话而闻名〕

Burns, Rob·ert /ˋrɑbɚt; ˈrɒbət/ (1759-96) a Scottish poet who wrote in the Scots DIALECT and is regarded as Scotland's national poet. He wrote about love, country life, and national pride, and his best-known poems include *Tam o'Shanter* and *To a Mouse*. Scottish people all over the world celebrate his birthday on 25 January, **Burns Night**. 彭斯〔(1759-1796), 苏格兰诗人, 他用苏格兰方言写作, 被视为苏格兰民族诗人, 他的诗歌以爱情、乡村生活和民族自豪感为题材, 最著名的诗作有《汤姆·奥桑特》和《致田鼠》。世界各地的苏格兰人于每年1月25日纪念他的诞辰, 即"彭斯之夜"〕

burnt¹ /bɝnt; bɜːnt/ the past tense and past participle of BURN¹

burnt² *adj* **1** damaged or hurt by burning 烧坏的, 烧伤的: *The cake's a little bit burnt, I'm afraid.* 恐怕蛋糕有点烤煳了。**2 burnt offering a)** something that is offered as a gift to a god by being burnt on an ALTAR (1) 燔祭, 供品〔炙熟以祭神之牲畜或果菜〕 **b)** *humorous* food that you accidentally burnt while you were cooking it【幽默】烧焦的食物 S3

burp /bɝp; bɜːp/ *v informal*【非正式】**1** [I] to pass gas noisily from your stomach out through your mouth; BELCH (1) 打嗝 **2** [T] to help a baby to do this, especially by rubbing or gently hitting its back〔按摩或轻拍其背部〕帮助〔婴儿〕打嗝 **—burp** *n* [C]

burr /bɝ; bɜː/ *n* [C] **1** a fairly quiet regular sound like something turning quickly; WHIRR 颤音; 嗡嗡声; 嘎嘎声: *the burr of a sewing machine* 缝纫机的嘎嘎声 **2** a way of pronouncing English with a strong 'r' sound〔发英语r音时颤动小舌的〕粗喉音 **3** also 又作 **bur** the seed container of some plants, covered with PRICKLES¹ (1) that make it stick to things〔某些植物〕带芒刺的种子壳, 刺果, 针球

bur·ri·to /bəˋrito; bəˈriːtəʊ/ *n plural* **burritos** [C] Mexican dish made with a TORTILLA (=flat thin bread) folded around meat or beans with cheese〔包有肉或干酪的〕玉米面饼

bur·ro /ˋbɝo; ˈbʊrəʊ/ *n plural* **burros** [C] *especially AmE* a DONKEY (1), usually a small one【尤美】(小) 毛驴

Bur·roughs /ˋbʌroz; ˈbʌrəʊz/, **Ed·gar Rice** /ˋɛdgɚ raɪs; ˈedgə raɪs/ (1875-1950) a US writer, known for his stories about Tarzan 巴勒斯〔(1875-1950), 美国作家, 以其"人猿泰山"系列故事而闻名〕

Burroughs, William (1914-97) a US writer who wrote about subjects such as drugs, death, and HOMOSEXUALITY. His most famous NOVEL is *The Naked Lunch* (1959). 巴勒斯〔(1914-1997), 美国作家, 作品以毒品、死亡和同性恋为题材, 最著名的小说为《裸体午餐》(1959)〕

bur·row¹ /ˋbɝo; ˈbʌrəʊ/ *v* **1** [I always+adv/prep, T] to make a hole or passage in the ground 掘洞; 钻洞: *burrowing a hole* 挖个洞 | [+into/under etc] *The dog managed to burrow under the fence.* 那只狗设法从篱笆底下钻了过去。**2** [T always+adv/prep] to press your body close to someone or under something because you want to get warm, feel safe etc 偎依, 紧靠: **burrow sth into/under etc** *The baby burrowed her head into my shoulder.* 宝宝把头紧靠在我的肩膀上。**3** [I always+adv/prep] to search for something that is hidden in a container or under other things 寻找, 翻找: [+into/through etc] *Helen burrowed into her pocket for a handkerchief.* 海伦把手伸进口袋里掏手帕。

burrow² *n* [C] a passage in the ground made by a rabbit or FOX¹ (1) as a place to live〔动物, 尤指兔子或狐狸所掘的〕洞穴

bur·sar /ˋbɝsɚ; ˈbɜːsə/ *n* [C] *especially BrE* someone at a school or college who deals with the accounts and office work【尤英】〔大中学校的〕财务[行政]主管

bur·sa·ry /ˋbɝsərɪ; ˈbɜːsəri/ *n* [C] *BrE* an amount of money given to someone so that they can study at a university or college; SCHOLARSHIP【英】〔大学的〕奖学金

burst 胀破

The balloon burst.
气球吹破了。

burst¹ /bɝst; bɜːst/ *v past tense and past participle* **burst**
1 ►BREAK OPEN 裂开◄ [I,T] if something bursts or if you burst it, it breaks open or apart suddenly and violently so that its contents come out（使）破裂；（使）爆裂；（使）胀破；（使）爆炸：*You're going to burst the balloon, if you're not careful.* 你一不小心就会把气球弄爆的。
2 bursting with so full of something that there is no room for any more 充满：*The barracks were bursting with refugees.* 兵营里挤满了难民。
3 ►MOVE SUDDENLY 突然移动◄ [I always+adv/prep] to move somewhere suddenly or quickly, especially into or out of a place 冲，闯，突然出现：[+through/into/in etc] *Don't burst into my bedroom without knocking!* 别不敲门就闯入我的卧室！
4 burst open to suddenly be open 突然开了：*The door burst open to reveal Francis holding a tray.* 门突然开了，可以看到弗朗西丝拿着一个托盘。
5 be bursting to do sth *informal* to want to do something very much【非正式】迫不及待要做某事：*Mona's bursting to tell you the news.* 莫娜迫不及待地要告诉你这个消息。
6 be bursting with pride/confidence/energy etc to be very proud, confident etc 充满自豪／自信／精力等
7 be bursting *informal* to need to go to the toilet very soon【非正式】〔大小便〕憋不住了
8 full to bursting so full that there is no room for any more〔吃得〕太饱：*I can't eat any more, I'm full to bursting!* 我不能再吃了，我已经吃撑了！
9 bursting at the seams so full that nothing else can fit inside 胀满 —see also 另见 **burst sb's bubble** (BUBBLE¹ (5)), **burst the bubble** (BUBBLE¹ (4))

burst in on/upon sb/sth *phr v* [T] to interrupt something at an embarrassing moment 突然闯入，打扰；突然插嘴：*I burst in on the meeting thinking that the room was empty.* 我以为房间里没人，没想到打扰了人家的会议。

burst into sth *phr v* [T] **1** to suddenly begin to make a sound, especially to start singing, crying, or laughing 突然…起来〔尤指哭、笑、唱等〕：*The audience burst into applause.* 观众爆发出一阵掌声。| **burst into song** *Everyone on the bus burst into song as we got closer to home.* 我们快到家时，公共汽车上所有的人都大声唱起来。| **burst into tears** *Benny suddenly burst into tears.* 本尼突然放声大哭。**2 burst into flames** to suddenly start to burn very strongly 突然起火〔尤指火势失去控制〕：*The plane crashed into the hillside and burst into flames.* 飞机撞到山坡上，一下子燃烧起来。

burst out *phr v* **1 burst out laughing/crying etc** to suddenly start to laugh, cry etc 突然大笑／大哭等：*They all burst out laughing at the expression on her face.* 看到她脸上的表情，他们都大笑起来。**2** [T] to suddenly say something forcefully 突然说出：*"I don't believe it!" she burst out angrily.* 她愤愤然脱口而出："我才不信呢！" —see also 另见 OUTBURST (1)

burst² *n* [C] **1** the act of something bursting or the place where it has burst 破裂，爆炸；喷出；裂口：*a burst in the water pipe* 水管上的裂口 **2 a burst of sth a)** a short sudden effort or increase in activity 突然用力，加速：*a burst of speed on the last lap* 最后一圈突然加速 **b)** a short sudden and usually loud sound 突发的响声：*sharp bursts of machine gun fire* 一阵阵刺耳的机关枪声 **c)** a sudden strong feeling or emotion 情感的突然爆发：*bursts of violent temper* 突然大发脾气，勃然大怒

bur·then /ˈbɝðən; ˈbɜːðən/ *n* [C] *literary* a BURDEN【文】重担，负担

bur·ton /ˈbɝtn; ˈbɜːtn/ *n* **gone for a burton** *BrE spoken* lost, broken, or dead【英口】遗失了；损坏了；死了：*This radio's gone for a burton.* 这台收音机不响了。

Burton, Richard (1925-84) a Welsh film and theatre actor, regarded as one of the best of his time. He was married twice to Elizabeth Taylor, and the marriages attracted almost as much attention as his acting. 波顿〔(1925-1984)，威尔士电影和戏剧演员，被认为是当时最出色的演员之一。他与伊丽莎白·泰勒的两度婚姻几乎同他的演技一样引人注目〕

Bu·run·di /bəˈrʌndɪ; bʊˈrʊndi/ a country with many mountains in east central Africa, surrounded by Rwanda, Tanzania, and the Democratic Republic of Congo. Population: 6,224,000 (2001). Capital: Bujumbura. 布隆迪〔中非东部国家，境内多山，与卢旺达、坦桑尼亚和刚果民主共和国接壤。人口：6,224,000 (2001)，首都：布琼布拉〕—**Burundian** *n, adj*

bur·y /ˈbɛrɪ; ˈberi/ *v* [T] 3
1 ►PUT SB IN GRAVE 将某人埋入坟墓◄ to put someone who has died in a grave 埋葬：**bury sb in/at etc** *Gretta wanted to be buried at St Peter's.* 格雷塔希望自己安葬在圣彼得公墓。
2 have buried sb to have had someone you love die 经历亲人的死亡：*Jessie has already buried two husbands.* 杰西先后已有两位丈夫过世。
3 ►PUT STH UNDER EARTH 将某物埋入土中◄ to put something under the earth, often in order to hide it 埋藏
4 ►COVER WITH STH 用某物覆盖◄ [usually passive 一般用被动态] to cover something with other things so that it cannot be found 被…埋住：**bury sth under/beneath etc** *The climbers were buried under a pile of rocks.* 登山者被埋在一堆岩石中。
5 ►FEELING/MEMORY 感觉/记忆◄ to ignore a feeling or memory and pretend that it does not exist 把〔感情〕埋在心里：*a deeply buried memory* 深藏心里的回忆
6 bury your face/head etc (in sth) to press your face etc into something soft, usually to get comfort, to avoid someone, or to be able to smell something 把脸／头等伸到…里去：*Noel turned away, burying his face in the pillow.* 诺埃尔转过身，把头埋在枕头底下。| **bury your face/head in your hands** (=cover your face etc with your hands because you are very upset) 用手捂住脸／头
7 dead and buried completely finished and no longer important 不再重要的：*All the prewar ideas about defence are now dead and buried.* 所有战前防御设想现在都已毫无意义。
8 bury the hatchet/bury your differences to agree to stop arguing about something and become friends again 抛弃前嫌，重归于好
9 ►PUSH STH INTO A SURFACE 将某物嵌入表面◄ to push something, especially something sharp, into something else with a lot of force〔尤指用尖利之物〕用力插入：*The dog buried its teeth in my leg.* 狗使劲咬住我的腿。| **bury itself** (=be pushed, thrown, or shot somewhere and stick there) 把…推[投，扎]进去 *The knife buried itself in the wall a few inches from my head.* 刀扎在墙上离我的头只有几英寸。
10 bury yourself in your work/studies etc to give all your attention to something 埋头工作／学习等：*After the divorce, she buried herself in her work.* 离婚后，她埋头于工作。
11 bury your head in the sand to ignore an unpleasant situation and hope it will stop if you do not think about it 采取鸵鸟政策，闭眼不看现实

Bury My Heart at Wound·ed Knee /,‥ˈ‥, ‥ˈ‥/ a book by Dee Brown which tells the story of the American West in a way that is sympathetic to the Native Americans《魂归伤膝谷》〔迪伊·布朗所著，以同情美洲原住民的口吻讲述发生在美国西部的故事〕

bus¹ /bʌs; bʌs/ *n plural* **buses** also 又作 **busses** *AmE*【美】[C] a large vehicle that people pay to travel on 公共汽车，巴士；大客车：*Hurry up or we'll miss the bus!* 快点，不然我们就赶不上公共汽车了！| **by bus** *I go to work by bus.* 我乘公共汽车上班。| **bus driver/fare etc** *The bus fare is 60p.* 公共汽车车费是60便士。 1 2

bus² *v* **bussed, bussing** also 又作 **bused, busing** *AmE*【美】[T] **1** to take a group of people somewhere in a bus that you HIRE (=pay to use) for the journey 用租用的大客车运送：**bus sb to/into etc** *Children had to be bussed to neighbouring schools.* 得用大客车把孩子们送往附近的学校。**2** *AmE* to take away dirty dishes from the tables in a restaurant【美】收拾〔餐馆饭桌上的脏碗碟〕：**bus tables** *Shelley had a job bussing tables.* 谢利得到一份收拾饭桌的工作。

bus·boy /ˈbʌs,bɔɪ; ˈbʌsbɔɪ/ *n* [C] *AmE* a young man whose job is to help in a restaurant by taking away dirty dishes【美】餐馆勤杂工〔负责收拾脏碗碟的年轻男子〕

bus·by /ˈbʌzbɪ; ˈbʌzbi/ *n* [C] a tall fur hat worn by some British soldiers〔某些英国士兵戴的〕毛皮高顶帽

bush /bʊʃ; bʊʃ/ *n* [C] **1** a low thick plant smaller than a tree and with a lot of thin branches 灌木, 矮树丛: *a rose bush* 玫瑰丛 **2 the bush** wild country that has not been cleared, especially in Australia or Africa〔尤指澳大利亚或非洲的〕未开垦的丛林地 —see also 另见 **beat about the bush** (BEAT[1] (15))

Bush, George Herbert (1924-) the 41st President of the US (1989-93) 布什〔(1924-), 美国第四十一任总统 (1989-1993)〕

Bush, George W. (1946-) the 43rd President of the US (2000-2008). He is the son of the former President George Bush. 布什〔(1946-), 美国第四十三任总统 (2000-2008), 是美国前总统乔治·布什之子〕

bush ba·by /'· ··/ *n* [C] a small African animal that lives in trees and has large eyes and ears, and a long tail〔非洲的〕婴猴, 眼镜猴

bushed /bʊʃt; bʊʃt/ *adj* [not before noun 不用于名词前] *informal* very tired【非正式】筋疲力尽的

bush·el /'bʊʃəl; 'bʊʃəl/ *n* [C] a unit for measuring grain or vegetables equal to 8 gallons or 36.4 litres 蒲式耳〔谷物、蔬菜、水果等的容量单位, 等于 8 加仑或 36.4 升〕—see also 另见 **hide your light under a bushel** (HIDE[1] (7)) —see table on page C5 参见 C5 页附录

Bush House /,· '·/ the building in London from which the BBC World Service broadcasts radio programmes abroad 布什广播大楼〔伦敦的一栋建筑, 英国广播公司国际电台在此向海外播送广播节目〕

bush league /'· ·/ *adj AmE informal* badly done or of such bad quality that it is not acceptable【美, 非正式】做得差的, 干得不好的: *His work is still strictly bush league.* 他的工作还是做得极其差。

bush·man /'bʊʃmən; 'bʊʃmən/ *n* [C] **1 Bushman** a member of a southern African tribe who live in the bush〔非洲〕布须曼人 **2** someone who lives in the Australian BUSH (2)〔生活在澳大利亚的〕丛林人

bush tel·e·graph /,· '···/ *n* [U] *BrE humorous* the way in which people pass important news to each other very quickly【英, 幽默】小道消息: *I'd better warn you, the bush telegraph here works faster than the speed of light.* 我想提醒你, 这里小道消息传播得比光速还快。

bush·whack /'bʊʃˌhwæk; 'bʊʃwæk/ *v AmE*【美】**1** [T] to attack someone suddenly from a hidden place; AMBUSH[2] 伏击, 偷袭 **2** [I,T] to push or cut your way through thick trees or bushes 在丛林中开道, 披荆斩棘 —**bushwhacker** *n* [C]

bush·y /'bʊʃɪ; 'bʊʃi/ *adj* bushy hair or fur grows thickly〔毛发〕浓密的, 多毛的: *a bushy tail* 毛茸茸的尾巴 —**bushiness** *n* [U] —see picture on page A6 参见 A6 页图

busi·ness /'bɪznɪs; 'bɪznɨs/ *n*

① WORK DONE BY COMPANIES 公司业务
② COMPANY 公司
③ SUBJECT 事务
④ STH THAT CONCERNS YOU 与你有关的事
⑤ WORK TO BE DONE 要做的工作
⑥ OTHER MEANINGS 其他意思

① WORK DONE BY COMPANIES 公司业务

1 [U] the activity of buying or selling goods or services that is done by companies 商业, 买卖, 生意, 业务: *Students on the course learn about all aspects of business.* 学这门课程的学生要了解商业各方面的知识。| **in business** *Most of my family are in business.* 我家里大多数人都经商。| **do business with** *We do a lot of business with Italian companies.* 我们与意大利公司有许多业务来往。| **the business community** (=important people who work in business) 商会; 商界 *The policy is backed by the international business community.* 这项政策得到了国际商界的支持。

2 be in business/go into business to be operating as a company or to begin operating as a company 做生意, 经商, 办公司: *Pam's going into business with her sister.* 帕姆要和姐姐一起做生意。

3 go out of business to stop operating as a company 停业, 关门: *Higher interest rates will drive smaller firms out of business.* 高利率会迫使一些小商号倒闭。

4 ▶AMOUNT OF COMPANY WORK 公司业务量◀ [U] the amount of work a company is doing or its value 营业额, 交易量: *We're now doing twice as much business as we did last year.* 我们现在的营业额是去年的两倍。| **business is good/bad/slow etc** *Business is slow during the summer.* 今年夏天生意清淡。| **drum up business** (=increase it) 招揽生意 *Sidney's doing the rounds of the customers, trying to drum up business.* 悉尼在走访顾客, 以招揽生意。

5 ▶NOT PLEASURE 并非乐趣◀ [U] work that you do as part of your job 差事: **on business** *Chris is in London this week, on business.* 克里斯本星期在伦敦出差。| **business trip/lunch/meeting etc** *I try to avoid too many business lunches.* 我尽量避开过多的商务午餐。

6 business is business used to say that profit is the most important thing to consider 公事公办: *Harry may be a friend but business is business, and he's not the best man for the job.* 哈里也许是朋友, 但公事公办, 他不是这项工作的最佳人选。

② COMPANY 公司

7 [C] an organization such as a shop or factory which produces or sells goods or services 商店; 企业; 公司; 事务所; 工厂: *Paul's decided to start his own business.* 保罗决定创办自己的公司。| **run a business** *Mrs Taylor runs an office equipment business.* 泰勒夫人经营着一家办公设备公司。

8 the advertising/printing/shipping etc business work or a job involved with advertising, printing etc 广告业/印刷业/航运业等: *Steve works in the movie business.* 史蒂夫从事电影业。

③ SUBJECT 事务

9 ▶SUBJECT/EVENT 事务/事件◀ [singular] a subject, event, or activity that you have a particular opinion of 事情; 议题; 事务; 业务: *Politics is a serious business.* 政治是一件严肃的事情。| *Tanya found the whole business ridiculous.* 塔尼娅发现整件事情都很荒谬。

10 ▶STH UNCLEAR 不清楚的事物◀ [U] used when you talk about something in general and do not give any details 工作, 事务: *He handles the mail and all that business.* 他负责处理邮件之类的工作。

④ STH THAT CONCERNS YOU 与你有关的事

11 none of your business *spoken* not something that you have a right to know about【口】与你无关: *I know it's none of my business, but what did you decide?* 我知道这不关我的事, 但你是怎样决定的? | *It's none of your business how much I weigh.* 我体重多少不关你的事。

12 mind your own business a) *spoken* used to tell someone that something is private and you do not want them to ask about it or know about it【口】不要多管闲事: *"Where did you go last night?" "Mind your own business!"* "你昨晚去哪儿了?" "别多管闲事!" **b)** to do your normal activities, without showing any interest in what other people are doing 做自己的事〔不关心他人在做什么〕: *I was driving along, minding my own business, when the police pulled me over.* 我在专心开车, 突然警察示意我靠边停下。

13 not your business not something that you are responsible for or that affects you 不关你的事

14 your/sb's business something that affects you but not other people, so other people have no right to know about it 你的/某人的私事: *"Are you going out with Kate tonight?" "That's my business."* "你今晚和凯特一起出去吗?" "那是我的私事。"

15 make it your business to do sth to make a special effort to do something 特意努力做某事, 认为是自己应做的事: *Ruth made it her business to get to know the customers.* 露丝认为了解顾客是自己应做的事。

⑤ WORK TO BE DONE 要做的工作

16 [U] work that must be done in a particular job or period of time 职责, 本分, 任务: *We discussed this week's business.* 我们讨论了本周的任务。| **[+of]** *the routine business of government* 政府的日常事务

17 get down to business to start dealing with an important subject 着手处理重要问题, 认真干起来: *We'd better stop chatting and get down to business.* 我们最好闲话少说, 着手办正事吧。
18 business as usual used to tell you that a shop or business is working normally when you might think it was closed 照常营业
19 any other business subjects to be discussed in a meeting after the main subjects have been dealt with〔会上主要议题讨论之后待议的〕其他问题

⑥ **OTHER MEANINGS 其他意思**
20 be in business *informal* to have all that you need to start doing something【非正式】准备就绪: *Gillian brought the food, Jack the wine and I had some rugs to sit on, so we were in business.* 吉莉恩带来了食品, 杰克带来了酒, 我找了一些坐的垫子, 我们一切准备就绪。
21 mean business *informal* to be determined to do something even if it involves harming someone or making them upset【非正式】当真, 说话算数: *I could tell from the look on his face that he meant business.* 我能从他的表情上看出他是认真的。
22 go about your business to do the things that you normally do 做自己的事, 从事自己的工作: *ordinary people going about their business* 为自己的事奔波的普通人
23 have no business doing sth/have no business to do sth to behave wrongly in doing something 无权做某事, 不应该做某事: *He was very drunk and had no business driving.* 他喝酒太多, 不能开车。
24 like nobody's business *spoken* very well, very much, or very fast【口】很好地; 很多地; 很快地: *Wanda can play the piano like nobody's business.* 万达钢琴弹得很好。
25 not in the business of doing sth not planning to do something, because it is thought to be wrong〔因认为其错误而〕没有做某事的计划[意图]: *This government is not in the business of increasing public spending.* 这届政府没有增加公共支出的打算。
26 (it's) the business *BrE slang* used to say that something is very good or works well【英俚】很好, 工作性能好: *Have you seen David's new car? It's the business.* 你见过戴维的新汽车吗? 真不错。—see also 另见 BIG BUSINESS, **funny business** (FUNNY (3)), **monkey business** (MONKEY[1] (3)), SHOW BUSINESS

business card /ˈ‥ ˌ/ *n* [C] a card that shows the business person's name, position, company, and address〔印有姓名、职务、公司和地址的〕商务名片 —see picture on page A14 参见A14页图
business class /ˈ‥ ˌ/ *n* [U] travelling conditions on an aircraft that are more expensive than TOURIST CLASS but not as expensive as FIRST CLASS (1)〔飞机上的〕二等舱, 商务客位 —compare 比较 ECONOMY CLASS
business end /ˈ‥ ˌ/ *n* **the business end (of sth)** *informal* the end of a tool or weapon that does the work or causes the damage【非正式】〔工具或武器〕起作用的一端, 实用部分: *the business end of a gun* 枪管
business hours /ˈ‥ ˌ/ *n* [plural] the normal hours that shops and offices are open 营业时间; 办公时间
busi·ness·like /ˈbɪznɪsˌlaɪk; ˈbɪzn̩s-laɪk/ *adj* effective and practical in the way that you do things 处事务实的, 有效率的, 讲究实际的: *a businesslike manner* 务实的态度
busi·ness·man /ˈbɪznɪsˌmæn; ˈbɪzn̩smən/ *n plural* **businessmen** /-ˌmən; -mən/ [C] **1** a man who works at a fairly high level in a company 商人; 实业家, 从事工商业的人士 **2 be a good businessman** to know how to deal with money and be successful in business 生财有道
business park /ˈ‥ ˌ/ *n* [C] an area where many companies and businesses have buildings and offices 商业区
business plan /ˈ‥ ˌ/ *n* [C] a document which explains what a company wants to do in the future〔公司〕未来的发展计划
business stud·ies /ˈ‥ ˌ‥/ *n* [plural] a course of study on economic and financial subjects 商业学
business suit /ˈ‥ ˌ/ *n* [C] *AmE* a suit that a man wears during the day, especially in the office【美】〔尤指日常在办公室穿的〕西服, 西装; LOUNGE SUIT *BrE*【英】
busi·ness·wom·an /ˈbɪznɪsˌwʊmən; ˈbɪzn̩sˌwʊmən/ *n plural* **businesswomen** /-ˌwɪmɪn; -ˌwɪmɪn/ [C] **1** a woman who works at a fairly high level in a company 女商人; 女实业家, 从事工商业的女性 **2 be a good businesswoman** to know how to deal with money and be successful in business 生财有道
busk /bʌsk; bʌsk/ *v* [I] *BrE* to play music in a public place in order to earn money【英】街头卖艺 —**busker** *n* [C]

CULTURAL NOTE 文化注释
Busking In the UK, it is quite common to see buskers performing in city centres, hoping that people who pass by will give them money. In London, buskers can be found in the Covent Garden area and in Underground stations. Buskers usually have a box in front of them on the ground where the public can put money if they like the performance. In the UK, buskers have to get a special LICENCE before they are allowed to perform on the streets.
街头卖艺: 英国市中心常可看见卖艺者表演, 希望路人能给他们钱。伦敦的科文特加登区域和地铁里常有卖艺人的身影。卖艺者通常在面前地上放一个盒子, 别人若喜欢他们的表演, 就把钱丢进去。在英国, 卖艺人须获特别执照方可上街卖艺。

bus lane /ˈ‥ ˌ/ *n* [C] a part of a wide road that only buses are allowed to use 公共汽车专用车道
busman's hol·i·day /ˌbʌsmənz ˈhɑləde; ˌbʌsmənz ˈhɒlɪ̆di/ *n* [singular] a holiday spent doing the same work as you do in your job 照常工作的节假日, 有名无实的假日
bus pass /ˈ‥ ˌ/ *n* [C] a special ticket giving cheap or free bus travel〔用于乘搭公共汽车的〕优惠[免费]乘车证
buss /bʌs; bʌs/ *v* [T] *AmE* to kiss someone in a friendly rather than sexual way【美】亲吻〔表示友好〕: *politicians bussing babies* 政治家亲吻幼儿
bus·ser /ˈbʌsɚ; ˈbʌsə/ *n* [C] *AmE* someone who works in a restaurant taking away dirty dishes【美】〔餐馆里收拾脏碗碟的〕勤杂工
bus shel·ter /ˈ‥ ˌ‥/ *n* [C] *especially BrE* a small structure with a roof that keeps people dry while they are waiting for a bus【尤英】公共汽车候车亭
bus sta·tion /ˈ‥ ˌ‥/ *n* [C] a place where buses start and finish their journeys 公共汽车总站
bus stop /ˈ‥ ˌ/ *n* [C] a place at the side of a road, marked with a sign, where buses stop for passengers 公共汽车站
bust[1] /bʌst; bʌst/ *v past tense and past participle* **bust** *BrE*【英】, **busted** *especially AmE*【尤美】[T] *informal*【非正式】
1 ►BREAK 弄破◄ to break something 打烂, 打碎, 弄坏: *I bust my watch this morning.* 今早我把手表摔坏了。| *Tony busted the door down.* 托尼把门砸烂了。
2 ►POLICE 警察◄ *informal*【非正式】**a) bust sb (for sth)** if the police bust someone, they charge them with a crime 指控某人〔犯有某种罪行〕**b)** if the police bust a place, they go into it to look for something illegal 查抄〔住宅〕, 突击搜查〔非法物品〕: *The party was busted by the vice squad.* 警察缉捕队突击搜查该聚会。
3 bust a gut *informal* to try extremely hard to do something【非正式】竭尽全力: *I bust a gut trying to finish that work on time.* 我竭尽全力, 希望如期完成那项工作。
4 ...or bust! *informal* used to say that you will try very hard to go somewhere or do something【非正式】一定要去[做]: *San Francisco or bust!* 我一定要去旧金山!
5 ►MILITARY 军事的◄ *especially AmE* to give someone a lower military rank as a punishment; DEMOTE【尤美】贬降…的军阶; 使降职
6 ►BURST◄ *AmE* to burst【美】使爆裂
bust out *phr v* [I] *informal* to escape from a place, especially prison【非正式】逃跑; 越狱
bust up *phr v informal*【非正式】**1** [I] to argue angrily and stop being lovers, partners, or friends〔关系〕破裂: *They bust up after six years of marriage.* 他们结婚六年后离异了。**2** [T **bust** sth ↔ **up**] to prevent something from continuing 打断, 搞糟: *Angry protesters bust up the meeting.* 愤怒的抗议者打断了会议。**3** [T **bust** sth ↔ **up**] *AmE* to damage or break something【美】损坏, 弄坏: *Hey! Don't bust up my bar!* 喂! 不要砸我的酒吧! —see also 另见 BUST-UP
bust[2] *n* [C] **1** a model of someone's head, shoulders and upper chest, made of stone or metal〔用石头或金属制造的〕半身塑像: [+of] *a bust of Beethoven* 贝多芬的半身塑像 **2** a woman's breasts, or the part of her clothes that covers her breasts〔妇女或其衣服的〕胸部 **3** a measurement around a woman's breast and back 胸围: *Do you have this bra in a bigger bust size?* 你有胸围比这大一号的胸罩吗? **4** *informal* a situation in which the

police go into a place looking for something illegal【非正式】拘捕，搜查，突袭: *major drugs bust* 毒品大搜查

bust³ *adj* [not before noun 不用于名词前] *informal*【非正式】**1 go bust** a business that goes bust cannot continue operating 生意失败，破产，倒闭: *Dad lost his job when the firm went bust.* 公司破产后，爸爸失去了工作。**2** broken 破的，坏的: *The television's bust again.* 电视又坏了。

bus·ter /ˈbʌstɚ; ˈbʌstə/ *n AmE spoken* used to speak to a man who is annoying you or who you do not respect【美口】小子〔对男子的蔑称〕: *You're under arrest, buster!* 小子，你被捕了！

bus·tle¹ /ˈbʌsḷ; ˈbʌsəl/ *v* [I always+adv/prep] to move around quickly, looking very busy 忙乱，忙忙碌碌: **[+about/round etc]** *Madge bustled round the room putting things away.* 玛奇忙着在房间里收拾东西。

bustle² *n* **1** [singular] busy and usually noisy activity 忙碌；熙攘；喧闹: **[+of]** *a continual bustle of people coming and going* 川流不息的来往人群 —see also 另见 **hustle and bustle** (HUSTLE² (1)) **2** [C] a frame worn by women in the past to hold out the back of their skirts〔旧时妇女用来撑裙子的〕裙撑

bus·tling /ˈbʌslɪŋ; ˈbʌsəlɪŋ/ *adj* a bustling place is very busy 繁忙的，热闹的

bust-up /ˈ· ·/ *n* [C] *informal*【非正式】**1** a very bad quarrel or fight 争吵，吵架: *Cathy and I had a real bust-up yesterday.* 我和凯茜昨天实实在在地吵了一架。**2** [C] the end of a relationship〔关系的〕破裂: *the bust-up of their marriage* 他们婚姻的破裂 —see also 另见 **bust up** (BUST¹)

bust·y /ˈbʌstɪ; ˈbʌsti/ *adj informal* a woman who is busty has large breasts【非正式】〔妇女〕乳房大的

S1 W2 **bus·y¹** /ˈbɪzɪ; ˈbɪzi/ *adj*

1 ►WORKING NOW 在工作◄ someone who is busy at a particular time is working and is not available 忙碌的；正在工作的: *She's busy now, can you phone later?* 她现在正忙，你晚些时候打电话来好吗？| **[+with]** *Mr Haynes is busy with a customer at the moment.* 海恩斯先生此时正忙着接待一位顾客。

2 busy doing sth giving something a lot of your time and attention 忙于做某事: *Rachel's busy studying for her exams.* 雷切尔正忙于温习，准备考试。

3 ►TIME 时间◄ a busy period is full of work or other activities 繁忙的: *December is the busiest time of year for shops.* 12月份是商店一年中最繁忙的时期。

4 ►PLACE 地方◄ a busy place is very full of people or vehicles and movement 热闹的，忙碌的: *We live on a very busy road.* 我们住的那条大街很热闹。| *a busy office* 忙碌的办公室

5 ►WORKS HARD 辛苦操劳◄ having very little free time because you always have so much to do 操劳的: *a busy mother of four with a full time job* 既有全职工作，又要照看四个孩子的劳碌母亲

6 keep sb/yourself busy to find plenty of things to do 使某人/自己忙碌: *I kept myself busy to take my mind off smoking.* 我让自己忙于工作，不去想吸烟。

7 ►TELEPHONE 电话◄ *especially AmE* a telephone that is busy, is being used【尤美】〔电话〕占线的; ENGAGED (2) *BrE*【英】: *I'm sorry, the line's busy at the moment, can you try later?* 对不起，电话占线，你过一会儿再打好吗？

8 ►PATTERN 图案◄ a pattern or design that is busy is too full of small details〔图案或设计〕过于繁杂的，琐碎的

9 as busy as a bee very active 忙得不亦乐乎: *The children have been as busy as bees making a collage this afternoon.* 今天下午，孩子们一直在做拼贴画，忙得不亦乐乎。—**busily** *adv*

busy² *v* [T] **busy yourself with** to use your time dealing with something 使自己忙于: *He busied himself with answering letters.* 他忙着回复信件。

bus·y·bod·y /ˈbɪzɪˌbɑdɪ; ˈbɪziˌbɒdi/ *n* [C] someone who is too interested in other people's private activities 好管闲事的人: *You interfering old busybody!* 你这爱管闲事的老家伙！

busy Liz·zie /ˌbɪzɪ ˈlɪzɪ; ˌbɪzi ˈlɪzi/ *n* [C] a small plant with bright flowers 凤仙花

bus·y·work /ˈbɪzɪˌwɝk; ˈbɪziwɜːk/ *n* [U] *AmE* work that seems to be producing a result but is really only keeping someone busy【美】劳而无功的事

S1 W1 **but¹** /bət; bət; *strong* 强读 bʌt; bʌt/ *conjunction* **1** in spite of something, or not as you would expect 但是，然而，尽管如此: *The situation looked desperate but they didn't give up hope.* 形势看来十分危急，但他们并没有放弃希望。| *The car was very cheap but it's been extremely reliable.* 这汽车虽然便宜，但性能很可靠。**2** used to add another statement to one that you have already made, to say that both things are true 但与此同时；另一方面；不过；诚然…但: *These changes will cost quite a lot, but they will save us money in the long run.* 这些改动相当费钱，但从长远的角度看能为我们省钱。| *an expensive but immensely useful book* 一本很贵却大有用处的书 **3** used like however, to explain why something did not happen, why you did not do something etc 只因为，只可惜: *He would have won easily, but he fell and broke his leg.* 他本来胜利在望，可惜跌倒把腿摔断了。| *I'd like to go but I'm too busy.* 我很愿意去，可是实在太忙。**4** used after a negative to emphasize that it is the second part of the sentence that it is true 毋宁说，而是: *They own not one but three houses.* 他们不是拥有一幢，而是三幢房子。| *The purpose of the scheme is not to help the employers but to provide work for young people.* 这个计划的目的不是为了帮助雇主，而是为青年人提供工作机会。| **no choice/alternative etc but to...** *We had no alternative but to fire him.* 我们别无选择，只得解雇他。| **no question/doubt but that...** (=used to say that you are sure that something is true) 毫无疑问 *There's no doubt but that Evans is guilty.* 毫无疑问，埃文斯是有罪的。**5 but for** without 要不是: *But for these interruptions the meeting would have finished half an hour ago.* 要不是几次中断，会议半小时前就开完了。**6 but then (again)** *spoken*【口】**a)** used before a statement that makes what you have just said seem less true, useful, or valuable 然而，不过: *We could ask John to help again, but then I don't want to bother him.* 我们是可以再求约翰帮忙，不过我不想麻烦他。**b)** used before a statement that may seem surprising, to say that it is not really surprising 但另一方面，不过: *Apparently Dinah hasn't been to work all week, but then she always was unreliable, wasn't she?* 黛娜好像一个星期都没来上班，不过，她不总是这样不可靠吗？**7** used to express strong feelings such as anger, surprise etc 嘿，天哪〔用于表示强烈的情感，如愤怒、惊讶等〕: *But that's marvellous news!* 喔，这真是个好消息！**8 you cannot but.../you could not but...** *formal* used to say that you have to do something or cannot stop yourself from doing it【正式】禁不住，情不自禁: *I could not but admire her.* 我不由得对她产生了敬慕之情。**9** used to emphasize a word or statement〔用来加强重复部分的语气〕: *It'll be a great party – everyone, but everyone, is coming.* 这将是一次重大的聚会 —— 每个人，对，每个人都会来。**10** used to change the subject of a conversation 无论如何，反正，好〔用于改变话题〕: *But now to the main question.* 好，现在谈谈主要问题。**11** [usually in negatives 一般用于否定句] *literary* used to emphasize that a statement includes every single person or thing【文】无一例外地: *Not a day goes by but that I think of Geoff.* (=I think of Geoff every day) 我每天都想起杰夫。

USAGE NOTE 用法说明: BUT

WORD CHOICE 词语辨析: **but, however**

But is very frequent in spoken English, where it is often used at the beginning of a sentence. but 经常用于口语，作为句子的开头: *"I read it in a newspaper." "But newspapers aren't always right!"* "我从报上读到的消息。" "但报纸并不总是正确的！"

But is also used in writing, though not usually at the beginning of a sentence. **However** is used especially in more formal writing, often with commas before and after it in the middle of a sentence. but 也用于书面语，但通常不放在句首。however 尤其用在正式文体中，位于句子中间，前后用逗号隔开: *This had been reported in a newspaper. One must remember, however, that newspapers are not always accurate.* 这（消息）在报上已有报道。然而，必须记住，报上的内容也不总是准确的。

GRAMMAR 语法

But or **however** is never used in a main clause beside another clause with **although**. 当从句用 although 时，主句不用 but 或 however: *Although they're very busy, I think they enjoy it.* (NOT 不用 *...but/however I think they enjoy it*) 虽然他们很忙，但我认为他们喜欢这样。You can begin a clause with *but although*, or *however although*. but although 或 however although 可用于引导从句: *I tried doing the accounts, but although I know some maths I found it very difficult* (=and I know some maths but I still found it difficult). 我试着算账，虽然我懂些数学，但仍觉得很难。

but² *prep* **1** apart from; except 除…以外: *What can we do but sit and wait?* 我们除了坐等，还能做些什么呢？| *I could come any day but Thursday.* 除了星期四，我哪天都能来。| **nothing but** (=used when talking about a bad quality or situation to emphasize how bad it is) 完完全全〔强调质量或情况很糟〕*This car's been nothing but trouble.* 这辆车，除了添麻烦，什么用处也没有。| **anything but** (=used to say that a person or situation does not have a good quality) 根本不，一点也不 *Those recep-* S2 W3 

tionists are anything but helpful. 那些接待人员一点也不帮忙。 **2 the last but one/the next but two etc** *especially BrE* the last or next thing or person except for one, two etc【尤英】倒数第二/相隔两个等: *Pauline and Derek live in the next house but one.* (=they live two houses away from us) 保利娜和德里克住的房子和我们隔着一座。

2 3 **but³** *adv* **1** *especially literary* only【尤文】只能, 仅仅, 不过, 至少, 刚刚, 好歹: *You can but try.* 你只能试试看。 **2** *AmE spoken* used to emphasize what you are saying【美口】非常, 极其〔用于加强语气〕: *Go there but fast!* 去吧, 可要快呀! | *They're rich, but I mean rich!* 他们有钱, 我是说很有钱!

but⁴ /bʌt; bʌt/ *n* **no buts (about it)** *spoken* used to say that there is no doubt about something【口】不容置疑, 毫无疑问: *No buts, you are going to school today!* 没什么可以辩解的, 你今天必须上学!

bu·tane /ˈbjuten; ˈbjuːteɪn/ *n* [U] a gas stored in liquid form, used for cooking and heating 丁烷〔用于煮食、取暖的气体〕

butch /bʊtʃ; bʊtʃ/ *adj informal*【非正式】**1** a woman who is butch looks, behaves, or dresses like a man〔女子外表、举止、穿着〕男性化的 **2** a man who is butch seems big and strong, and typically male〔男子〕有男子气的

3 **butch·er¹** /ˈbʊtʃɚ; ˈbʊtʃə/ *n* [C] **1** someone who owns or works in a shop that sells meat 屠宰商; 肉贩 **2 the butcher's** a shop where you can buy meat 肉店, 肉铺 **3** someone who has killed a lot of people cruelly and unnecessarily 刽子手; 屠夫 **4 have/take a butcher's** *BrE slang* to have a look at something【英俚】看一眼

butcher² *v* [T] **1** to kill animals and prepare them to be used as meat 屠宰〔牲口〕 **2** to kill people cruelly or unnecessarily, especially in large numbers 血腥屠杀 **3** *informal* to spoil something by working carelessly【非正式】弄坏, 搞糟: *That hairdresser really butchered my hair!* 理发师把我的头发理坏了!

butch·er·y /ˈbʊtʃərɪ; ˈbʊtʃəri/ *n* [U] **1** cruel and unnecessary killing 残杀, 屠杀: *the butchery of battle* 战场上的血腥屠杀 **2** the preparation of meat for sale 屠宰业

but·ler /ˈbʌtlɚ; ˈbʌtlə/ *n* [C] the main male servant of a house 男管家, 仆役长

CULTURAL NOTE 文化注释

In Britain, the STEREOTYPE of a butler is of a very calm EFFICIENT and polite man who has no sense of humour and never appears to be shocked or surprised by anything. People sometimes make jokes about the fact that, in old British DETECTIVE stories in which someone is murdered, it is often the butler who is found to be the murderer. 在英国, 男管家的典型形象是: 极为镇定、高效、礼貌, 没有幽默感, 不为任何事物大惊小怪。旧时英国侦探小说中, 若有人被谋杀, 凶手常常就是男管家, 人们常以此打趣。

Butler, Rhett /rɛt; ret/ the main male character in the book and film *Gone with the Wind* 白瑞德〔小说和电影《乱世佳人》的男主人公〕

butt¹ /bʌt; bʌt/ *n* [C]

1 be the butt of to be the person or thing that other people often make jokes about 成为…的笑柄: *Paul quickly became the butt of everyone's jokes.* 保罗很快成了大家取笑的对象。

2 ►CIGARETTE 香烟◄ the end of a cigarette after most of it has been smoked 烟蒂, 烟头

3 ►GUN 枪◄ the thick end of the handle of a gun〔工具等〕粗大的一端, 柄: *a rifle butt* 枪托

4 ►CONTAINER 容器◄ a large round container for collecting or storing liquids 大桶: *a rainwater butt* 装雨水的大桶

5 ►ACT OF STRIKING STH 打击某物◄ the act of striking someone with your head 用头顶

6 ►PART OF YOUR BODY 身体部分◄ *AmE informal* the part of your body that you sit on; BUTTOCK【美, 非正式】屁股 —see also 另见 **a pain in the ass/butt** (PAIN¹ (3))

7 get your butt in/out/over *AmE spoken* used to rudely tell someone to go somewhere or do something【美口】别老坐着; 快起来〔粗鲁地告诉某人去某处或做某事〕: *Get your butt out of that bathroom now.* 马上从卫生间里出来。

butt² *v* [I,T] **1** to hit or push against something or someone with your head〔用头〕顶, 撞 **2** if an animal butts someone, it hits them with its horns〔用角〕抵

butt in *phr v* [I] **1** to interrupt a conversation rudely 插嘴: *Stop butting in!* 别再插嘴! **2** *AmE* to become involved in a private situation that does not concern you【美】管闲事: *Things were going real well until you had to butt in!* 在你没参与以前, 情况本来挺好的!

butt out *phr v* [I] *AmE spoken* used to tell someone to stop being involved in something【美口】不要管: *This has got nothing to do with you, so just butt out!* 这件事与你无关, 别瞎管了!

butte /bjut; bjuːt/ *n* [C] *AmE* a hill with steep sides and a flat top【美】〔有平顶和陡坡的〕孤山, 孤峰

but·ter¹ /ˈbʌtɚ; ˈbʌtə/ *n* [U] **1** a solid yellow food made from milk or cream that you spread on bread or use in cooking 黄油, 牛油: *Beat the butter and sugar together.* 把黄油和糖放在一起搅打。 **2 butter wouldn't melt in sb's mouth** used to say that someone seems to be very kind and sincere but is not really 某人装出一副忠厚善良的样子 —**buttery** *adj* 2

butter² *v* [T] to spread butter on something 涂黄油于…: *buttered toast* 抹了黄油的烤面包片

butter sb ↔ **up** *phr v* [T] *informal* to say nice things to someone so that they will do what you want【非正式】奉承, 讨好〔某人〕: *Don't think you can butter me up that easily.* 不要以为你那么容易讨好我。

but·ter·ball /ˈbʌtɚˌbɔl; ˈbʌtəbɔːl/ *n* [C] *AmE informal* someone who is fat, especially a child【美, 非正式】肥胖儿

butter bean /ˈ·· ˌ·/ *n* a large pale yellow bean 利马豆 —see picture on page A9 参见 A9 页图

but·ter·cream /ˈbʌtɚˌkrim; ˈbʌtəkriːm/ *n* [U] a soft mixture of butter and sugar used inside or on top of cakes〔蛋糕表面或里面的〕奶油

but·ter·cup /ˈbʌtɚˌkʌp; ˈbʌtəkʌp/ *n* [C] a small shiny yellow wild flower 毛茛

but·ter·fat /ˈbʌtɚˌfæt; ˈbʌtəfæt/ *n* [U] the natural fat in milk 乳脂

Butterfingers *trademark* a type of chocolate bar in the US which has a hard centre made from PEANUT butter【商标】白脱指〔美国的一种花生酱块夹心巧克力条〕

but·ter·fin·gers /ˈbʌtɚˌfɪŋgɚz; ˈbʌtəˌfɪŋgəz/ *n* [singular] *informal* someone who often drops things they are carrying or trying to catch【非正式】拿不稳东西的人

but·ter·fly /ˈbʌtɚˌflaɪ; ˈbʌtəflaɪ/ *n* [C] **1** a type of insect that has large wings, often with beautiful colours 蝴蝶 **2 have butterflies (in your stomach)** *informal* to feel very nervous before doing something【非正式】〔做某事前〕情绪紧张, 心里发慌: *I always get butterflies before an exam.* 考试前我总是很紧张。 **3 butterfly stroke** a way of swimming by lying on your front and moving your arms together over your head 蝶泳 **4** someone who usually moves on quickly from one activity or person to the next 轻浮易变的人

butterfly 蝴蝶

butterfly nut /ˈ··· ˌ·/ *n* [C] a WING NUT 蝶形螺母

but·ter·milk /ˈbʌtɚˌmɪlk; ˈbʌtəˌmɪlk/ *n* [U] the liquid that remains after butter has been made 脱脂乳, 酪乳

but·ter·scotch /ˈbʌtɚˈskɑtʃ; ˈbʌtəskɒtʃ/ *n* [U] a type of sweet made from butter and sugar boiled together 黄油硬糖, 奶油糖果

butt·hole /ˈbʌtˌhol; ˈbʌthəʊl/ *n* [C] *AmE taboo slang*【美, 讳, 俚】**1** someone's ANUS 屁眼 **2** used to insult someone 笨蛋〔侮辱性用词〕: *You butthole!* 你这傻瓜!

but·tock /ˈbʌtək; ˈbʌtək/ *n* [C usually plural 一般用复数] one of the fleshy parts of your body that you sit on 屁股, 臀部 —see picture at 参见 BODY 图

but·ton¹ /ˈbʌtn̩; ˈbʌtn/ *n* **1** [C] a small round flat object on your shirt, coat etc which you pass through a hole to fasten it 纽扣, 扣子: **do up/undo a button** (=fasten or unfasten a button) 系上/解开扣子 —see picture at 参见 FASTENER 图 **2** [C] a small round object on a machine that you press to make it work 按钮: *Press the pause button.* 按暂停键。—see also 另见 PUSH-BUTTON **3** *AmE* a small metal or plastic BADGE (1,2), often with a message on it【美】〔印有文字的〕金属[塑料]小徽章 **4 button nose/eyes** a nose or eyes that are small and round 小而圆的鼻子/眼睛 **5 on the button** *informal especially AmE* exactly right, or at exactly the right time【非正式, 尤美】非常准确, 准时 —see also 另见 **as bright as a button** (BRIGHT (5)) 2

button² *v* [I,T] also 又作 **button up** **1** to fasten clothes with buttons or to be fastened with buttons 用纽扣扣住, 扣上…的扣子: *I don't like pants that button at the side.* 我不喜欢在侧面系扣的裤子。 | *Sam, make sure Nina buttons up her jacket.* 萨姆, 要确保尼娜把上衣扣好。 **2 button it!** *spoken* used to tell someone impolitely to stop talking【口】住嘴!

button-down /ˈ· · ˌ/ *adj* a button-down shirt or collar has the ends of the collar fastened to the shirt with buttons〔衬衫〕领尖有扣子的 —see picture on page A17 参见 A17 页图

but·ton·hole /ˈbʌtn̩ˌhol; ˈbʌtnhəʊl/ *n* [C] **1** a hole for a button to be put through to fasten a shirt, coat etc 纽孔, 纽扣眼 —see picture on page A17 参见 A17 页图 **2** *BrE* a flower you fasten to your clothes【英】扣在纽孔内或别在衣服上的花; BOUTONNIERE *AmE*【美】

button-through /ˈ· · ˌ/ *adj BrE* a button-through dress or skirt fastens from the top to the bottom with buttons【英】〔衣服〕从上到下都带纽扣的

but·tress¹ /ˈbʌtrɪs; ˈbʌtrəs/ *n* [C] a brick or stone structure built to support a wall 扶壁, 撑墙, 扶垛

buttress² *v* [T] to support a system, idea, argument etc, especially by providing money〔尤指用钱〕支持〔某一体制、主张、论点等〕: *The evidence seemed to buttress their argument.* 证据似乎支持他们的论点。

but·ty /ˈbʌtɪ; ˈbʌti/ *n* [C] *BrE informal* a SANDWICH【英, 非正式】三明治

bux·om /ˈbʌksəm; ˈbʌksəm/ *adj* a woman who is buxom is attractively large and healthy and has big breasts〔女性〕丰满健美的

Frequencies of the verbs **buy, get** and **purchase** in spoken and written English 动词buy, get 和 purchase在英语口语和书面语中的使用频率

Based on the British National Corpus and the Longman Lancaster Corpus 据英国国家语料库和朗文兰开斯特语料库

All three verbs are used to mean 'get something by paying for it'. The graph shows that in this meaning **get** is extremely common in spoken English. However, **get** is informal and is not at all common in written English. **Purchase** is used in formal or business contexts. It is not very common and is used more in written English than in spoken English. 这三个动词都用来表示"付款购得"。本图表显示, 作此意解释时, get 在口语中极其常用, 但 get 语气不正式, 书面语中很少见。purchase 用于正式文体或商业性文体中。这个词不太常用, 在书面语中出现的频率比在口语中高。

S1 W1 **buy¹** /baɪ; baɪ/ *v past tense and past participle* **bought** /bɔt; bɔːt/ **1 a)** [I,T] to get something by paying money for it 买, 购: *Where did you buy that dress?* 那条裙子你在哪儿买的? | **buy sb sth** *Let me buy you a drink.* 我来请你喝杯酒。| **buy sth for** *Sally's buying new curtains for the bedroom.* 萨莉在为卧室买新窗帘。| **buy sth from sb** *I bought this from an old guy in the market.* 这是我在市场上从一个老人那里买到的。| **buy sth for $10/£200 etc** *I bought it for two bucks at a garage sale.* 我在一处宅前旧物出售摊上以两美元买来的。| **buy sth for a song** (=buy something very cheaply) 某物买得便宜极了 —opposite 反义词 SELL¹ (1) **b)** [T] if a sum of money buys something, that is what you can get with it 够买, 能买: *A dollar doesn't buy much these days.* 如今一元买不了什么东西。**2 buy time** to get more time to do something, especially by making excuses 争取时间;〔尤指找借口〕设法拖延: *Tell them we've got problems with the software, it might buy us more time.* 就说我们的软件出了问题, 这样可以争取些时间。**3** [T] *informal* to believe an explanation or reason, especially one that is not very likely to be true【非正式】接受, 相信: *We could say it was an accident, but he'd never buy that.* 我们可以说这是一次意外, 可他怎么也不会相信。**4** [T] *AmE informal* to pay money to someone, especially someone in an official position, in order to persuade them to do something dishonest; BRIBE【美, 非正式】贿赂, 买通: *They say the judge was bought.* 他们说那位法官被买通了。**5 (have) bought it** *informal* to be killed, especially in an accident or war【非正式】〔尤指在意外事故或战争中〕遇难: *Vic bought it somewhere in the desert.* 维克在沙漠中遇难。

buy in sth *phr v* [T] *BrE* to buy something in large quantities【英】大量买进: *We'd better buy in more beer for the party.* 我们最好多买些啤酒聚会时喝。

buy into sth *phr v* [T] **1** to buy part of a business or organization, especially because you want to control it 买进〔企业的股份〕: *Clegg used the money to buy into a printing business.* 克莱格买进了一家印刷厂的股份。**2** *informal* to believe an idea【非正式】相信〔观点〕

buy sb ↔ **off** *phr v* [T] to pay someone money to stop them causing trouble or threatening you; BRIBE¹ 买通〔某人〕, 向〔某人〕行贿; 用钱疏通

buy out *phr v* **1** [T **buy** sb/sth ↔ **out**] to buy someone's shares (SHARE² (5)) of a business that you previously owned together, so that you have complete control 全部收购〔股权、产权〕—see also 另见 BUYOUT **2** [T **buy** sb **out of** sth] to pay money so that someone can leave an organization such as the army before their contract has finished 出钱买回自由〔尤指出钱提前退伍〕

buy up sth ↔ *phr v* [T] to quickly buy as much as you can of something such as land, tickets, food etc〔迅速地〕囤积, 大量买下〔土地、票券、食品等〕: *Much of the land has been bought up by property developers.* 大部分地皮都给房地产开发商买下来了。

buy² *n* **be a good/bad buy** to be worth or to be not worth the price you paid 买得合算/不合算: *The wine is a good buy at £3.49.* 这葡萄酒每瓶3.49英镑, 很合算。—see 见 CHEAP¹ (USAGE)

S3 W3 **buy·er** /ˈbaɪɚ; ˈbaɪə/ *n* [C] **1** someone who buys something expensive such as a house or car 购买者, 买主: *We hope lower house prices will attract more buyers.* 我们希望低廉的房价会吸引更多的买主。—opposite 反义词 SELLER (1) **2** someone whose job is to choose and buy the goods for a shop or company 采购员, 进货员, 买手

buyer's mar·ket /ˌ·· ˈ··/ *n* [singular] a situation in which there is plenty of something available so that buyers have a lot of choice and prices tend to be low 买方市场 —opposite 反义词 SELLER'S MARKET

buy·out /ˈbaɪaut; ˈbaɪaʊt/ *n* [C] a situation in which someone gains control of a company by buying all or most of its shares (SHARE² (5)) 全部买下, 收购全部[大部分]股份 [权]: *a management buyout* 管理层收购

buzz¹ /bʌz; bʌz/ *v*

1 ►MAKE A SOUND 发声◄ [I] to make a continuous sound, like the sound of a BEE 发出嗡嗡声: *The machine made a loud buzzing noise.* 机器发出很大的嗡嗡声。

2 ►MOVE AROUND 四处移动◄ a) [I always+adv/prep] to move around in the air making a continuous sound like a BEE〔蜜蜂等〕嗡嗡地飞: **buzz round/around/about** *A fly buzzed round the room.* 有一只苍蝇在房间里嗡嗡地乱飞。**b)** to move quickly and busily around a place 在〔某个地方〕忙转: **buzz around/round/about** *I spent the day buzzing around town in Dad's car.* 那天我开着爸爸的车在镇上兜了一天。

3 ►EXCITEMENT 激动◄ [I] if a group of people or a place is buzzing, people are making a lot of noise because they are excited 发出一阵兴奋的说话声: **[+with]** *Lineker had the crowd buzzing with excitement.* 莱因克尔使人群发出一阵兴奋的说话声。

4 sb's head/mind is buzzing (with sth) if your head or mind is buzzing with thoughts, ideas etc, you cannot stop thinking about them 某人的头脑中不住地想 (某事)

5 ►EARS 耳朵◄ [I] if your ears or head are buzzing you can hear a continuous low unpleasant sound 耳鸣

6 ►CALL 呼叫◄ [I+for, T] to call someone by pressing a BUZZER 用蜂鸣器召唤〔某人〕: *I'll just buzz my secretary and ask for the file.* 我用蜂鸣器叫秘书送来文件。

7 ►AIRCRAFT 飞机◄ [T] *informal* to fly an aircraft low and fast over buildings, people etc【非正式】低空掠过

buzz off *phr v* [I] *spoken*【口】**1 buzz off!** used to tell someone impolitely to go away 走开! 滚开! **2** to go away 离开, 走开: *I've finished everything, so I'll buzz off now.* 事情我都办完了, 现在我要走了。

buzz² *n* **1** [C] a continuous noise like the sound of a BEE 嗡嗡声, 嗞嗞声 —see picture on page A19 参见 A19 页图 **2** [singular] the sound of people talking a lot in an excited way〔人们〕兴奋的谈笑声: **[+of]** *a buzz of anticipation* 期待的议论声 **3** [singular] *informal* a strong feeling of excitement, pleasure, or success【非正式】兴奋之感; 喜悦心情: **give sb a buzz** *You know Steve, driving fast gives him a real buzz.* 你了解史蒂夫, 开快车使他感到刺激。**4 give sb a buzz** *informal* to telephone someone【非正式】给某人打电话 **5 the buzz** *informal* unofficial news or information that is spread by people telling each other【非正式】小道消息: *The buzz is that Jack is leaving.* 人们都传杰克要离开。

buz·zard /ˈbʌzəd; ˈbʌzəd/ *n* [C] **1** *BrE* a type of large HAWK[1] (1) (=hunting bird)【英】鵟, 鹌鹑 **2** *AmE* a type of large bird that eats dead animals【美】美洲兀鹰

buzz·cut /ˈbʌzˌkʌt; ˈbʌzkʌt/ *n* [C] *AmE* a very short style of cutting hair【美】平头（发型）

buzz·er /ˈbʌzə; ˈbʌzə/ *n* [C] a small electric machine that buzzes (BUZZ[1] (1)) when you press it 蜂鸣器, 蜂音器: *Press the buzzer if you know the answer.* 如果你知道答案, 就按抢答器。

buzz saw /ˈ· ·/ *n* [C] *AmE* a SAW[2] (1) with a round blade that is spun around by a motor; CIRCULAR SAW【美】〔电动〕圆锯

buzz·word /ˈbʌzwɜd; ˈbʌzwɜːd/ *n* [C] a word or phrase from one special area of knowledge that people suddenly think is very important〔重要的〕专门术语, 时髦语: *The 'information superhighway' became a buzzword in the 90s.* "信息高速公路"在20世纪90年代成了时髦语。

by-, bye- /baɪ; baɪ/ *prefix* less important 次要的: *a by-product* (=something made in addition to the main product) 副产品 | *a by-election* (=one held between regular elections) 补（缺）选（举）

by[1] /baɪ; baɪ/ *prep* **1** used especially with a PASSIVE[1] (2) verb to show the person or thing that does something or makes something happen 被, 由〔尤用于被动语态动词之后〕: *I was attacked by a dog.* 一条狗向我扑了过来。| *The building was designed by a famous architect.* 该建筑物是由一位著名建筑师设计的。| *We are all alarmed by the rise in violent crime.* 我们都对暴力犯罪的增加感到震惊。**2** using or doing a particular thing 通过; 用…; 靠…; 乘…: *You can reserve the tickets by phone.* 你可以用电话订票。| *Send it by airmail.* 用航空邮件寄吧。| *I know her by sight.* (=recognize her face) 我能认出她来。| **by doing sth** *She earns her living by selling insurance.* 她以推销保险为生。| **by train/plane/car** *We're travelling to London by train.* 我们乘火车去伦敦。**3** passing through or along a particular place 经过, 沿, 顺, 经由: *They came in by the back door.* 他们从后门进来的。| *It's quicker to go by the country route.* 走乡村那条路会更快。**4** beside or near something 靠近, 在…旁: *She stood by the window looking out over the fields.* 她站在窗边眺望远处的田野。| *Jane went and sat by Patrick.* 简走过去坐在帕特里克身旁。**5** if you move or travel by someone or something, you go past them without stopping 经过…〔的旁边〕: *He walked by without noticing me.* 他走过我身旁而没有注意到我。| *I go by the Vicarage every day on my way to work.* 我每天上班都要经过牧师的住宅。**6** used to show the name of someone who wrote a book, produced a film, wrote a piece of music etc 由…所创作[编著, 导演]: *the 'New World Symphony' by Dvorak* 由德沃夏克创作的《新世界交响曲》**7** not later than a particular time, date etc 不迟于, 在…之前: *The documents need to be ready by next Friday.* 文件最迟需在下星期五准备好。| *I reckon the film should be over by 9.30.* 我估计九点半电影该演完了。**8** according to a particular rule, method, or way of doing things 按照, 依据: *You've got to play by the rules.* 你必须按规则比赛。| *Profits were £6 million, but by their standards this is low.* 利润达到600万英镑, 但按照他们的标准, 这还不算多。**9** used to show the amount or degree of something 数量[程度]达到…: *The price of oil fell by a further $2 a barrel.* 每桶油价又下跌了两美元。| *I was overcharged by £3.* 他们多收了我三英镑。| **by far** (=by a large amount or degree) …得多〔指量和程度〕: *Godard's first film was better by far.* 戈达德的第一部电影要好得多。**10** used to show the part of a piece of equipment or of someone's body that someone takes or holds〔表示承受动作的身体或物体的部分〕: *He took her by the arm and led her across the road.* 他牵着她的手, 领她过了马路。| *She grabbed the hammer by the handle.* 她抓住锤子的柄。**11** used when expressing strong feelings or making serious promises 对…发誓〔表示强烈的情感或庄严的承诺〕: *By God, I'll kill that boy when I see him!* 我对上帝发誓, 我要是看见这小子, 非杀了他不可! **12** used between two numbers that you are multiplying or dividing 用…乘以[除以]…得: *What's 48 divided by 4?* 48除以4等于多少? **13** used when giving the measurements of a room, container etc 乘以, 见方: *a room 15 metres by 23 metres* 一间15米宽23米长的房间 **14** used to show a rate or quantity 以…为单位计: *We're paid by the hour.* 按小时给我们计酬。**15 day by day/bit by bit etc** used to show the way in which something happens 一天一天地/一点一点地等: *Day by day he grew weaker.* 他一天比一天衰弱。**16** used to show the situation or period of time during which you do something or something happens 在…情况下; 在…期间: *You could ruin your eyes reading by torchlight.* 在手电筒光下看书会损害你的眼睛。| **by day/night** *a tour of Paris by night* 夜游巴黎 **17** used to show the connection between one fact or thing and another 就…来说〔表示一个事实与另一个事实间的关系〕: *Colette's French by birth.* 科利特的出生地为法国。| *It's fine by me if you want to go.* 你要去我觉得没有问题。**18** as a result of an action or situation 由于: **by accident** *I saw Maureen quite by accident in the supermarket the other day.* 那天, 我碰巧在超级市场遇见了莫琳。| **by mistake** *I managed to delete an afternoon's work on the computer by mistake.* 由于疏忽, 我竟然把一下午在电脑中做的活儿全删去了。**19** if a woman has children by a particular man, that man is the children's father 与〔某男子〕所生: *Ann's got two children by her previous husband.* 安与前夫生了两个孩子。**20 (all) by yourself** completely alone 单独, 独自: *Dave spent Christmas all by himself.* 戴夫独自一人过圣诞节。

by[2] *adv* **1** if someone or something moves or goes by, they go past〔由旁边〕经过: *As I was standing on the platform the Liverpool train went whizzing by.* 我站在月台上, 开往利物浦的火车飞驰而过。| *Ten years had gone by since I had last seen Marilyn.* 自从我上次见过玛丽莲, 已经过了10年了。| *James walked by without even looking in my direction.* 詹姆斯没有朝我这儿看就走了过去。**2** beside or near someone or something 在附近: *A crowd of people were standing by waiting for an announcement.* 一大群人站在旁边等待消息的发布。**3 put/keep/lay sth by etc** to put something somewhere in order to use it in the future〔将某物〕存放起来, 收着: *Her mother gave her a dinner service to put by for when she got married.* 她母亲给了她一套餐具以备结婚时用。**4 call/stop/go by** to go to someone's house in order to visit them for a short time 短暂访问: *Why don't you stop by for a drink after work?* 下班后为何不过来喝点什么? **5 by and large** *especially spoken* used when talking generally about someone or something【尤口】大体上, 一般地说, 总的说来: *Charities are, by and large, exempt from income tax.* 一般来说, 慈善团体免交所得税。**6 by the by** *spoken* used when mentioning something that may be interesting but is not particularly important【口】顺便说一下: *By the by, Ian said he might call round tonight.* 顺便告诉你, 伊恩说他也许今天晚上会过来。**7 by and by** *especially literary* soon【尤文】不久, 很快

bye- /baɪ; baɪ/ *prefix* another spelling of BY- by-的另一种拼法

bye[1] /baɪ; baɪ/ also 又作 **bye-bye** /ˌ· ˈ·/ *interjection informal* goodbye【非正式】再见, 拜拜: **bye for now** (=used to say that you will see or speak to someone again soon) 一会儿见

bye[2] *n* [C] a situation in a sports competition in which a player or a team does not have an opponent to play against and continues to the next part of the competition 轮空〔指体育比赛中因没有对手而直接进入下一轮比赛〕

bye-byes /ˈ· ·/ *n* **go (to) bye-byes** *BrE* an expression meaning go to sleep, used by or to children【英】去睡觉〔儿语〕

by-e·lec·tion, bye-election /ˈ· ·ˌ· ·/ *n* [C] *especially BrE* a special election to replace a politician who has left parliament or died【尤英】〔英国议会的〕补缺选举

By·el·o·rus·sia /bɪˌɛloˈrʌʃə; biˌeləʊˈrʌʃə/ —see 见 BELARUS

by·gone /ˈbaɪˌgɔn; ˈbaɪgɒn/ *adj* **bygone age/era/days etc** an expression meaning a period of time in the past 过去的时期/年代/岁月等: *The buildings reflect the elegance of a bygone era.* 这些建筑物反映了过去年代的典雅风格。

by·gones /ˈbaɪˌgɔnz; ˈbaɪgɒnz/ *n* **let bygones be bygones** to forget something bad that someone has done to you and forgive them 过去的事就让它过去吧

by·law /ˈbaɪˌlɔ; ˈbaɪlɔː/ *n* **1** [C] a law made by a local government that people in that area must obey（地方）法规 **2** *AmE* a rule made by an organization to control the people who belong to it【美】〔组织、社团的〕章程, 会章

by·line /ˈ· ·/ *n* [C] a line at the beginning of some writing in a newspaper or magazine giving the writer's name〔报刊文章开头的〕作者署名行

by·pass[1] /ˈbaɪˌpæs; ˈbaɪpɑːs/ *n* [C] **1** a road that goes around a town or other busy area rather than through it 旁道, 间道, 小路 **2** *technical* a tube that allows gas or liquid to flow around something rather than through it【术语】旁通管, 分流器, 辅助管 **3 heart bypass/bypass surgery** an operation to direct blood through new VEINS (=blood tubes) outside the heart 心脏搭桥手术, 旁道管手术

bypass[2] *v* [T] **1** to avoid the centre of a city by driving around it 避开; 绕…而行 **2** to avoid obeying a rule, system, or someone in an official position 绕过正常手续或规章: *Francis bypassed the complaints procedure and wrote straight to the director.* 弗朗西斯绕过正常的投诉程序, 直接写信给董事。

by·play /ˈbaɪˌple; ˈbaɪpleɪ/ *n* [U] something that is less important than the main action, especially in a play〔尤指戏剧中的〕穿插动作; 枝节

by-prod·uct /ˈ· ˌ· ·/ *n* [C] **1** something additional that is produced during a natural or industrial process 副产品: *milk by-products such as whey* 如乳清等牛奶的副产品 **2** an unplanned additional result of something that you do 意外收获, 额外收获; 附带的结果 —compare 比较 END PRODUCT

Byrd /bɝd; bɜːd/, **Richard** (1888-1957) a US explorer who was important in the EXPLORATION of and research about Antarctica. He was the first to fly over both the North Pole and the South Pole. 伯德〔(1888-1957), 美国探险家, 是南极洲探险和研究的重要人员, 也是飞越北极和南极的第一人〕

byre /baɪr; baɪə/ *n* [C] *BrE old-fashioned* a farm building in which cattle are kept; COWSHED【英, 过时】牛棚

By·ron /ˈbaɪrən; ˈbaɪərən/, **Lord** (1788-1824) an English writer of ROMANTIC and SATIRICAL poetry, including *Childe Harold's Pilgrimage* and *Don Juan*. He is also famous for his romantic life, which included many love affairs, and for his death of fever in Greece while fighting against the Turks for Greek independence. 拜伦〔(1788-1824), 英国浪漫主义和讽刺诗人, 作品包括《恰尔德·哈罗尔德游记》和《唐璜》。他还以生活浪漫, 有不少风流韵事, 并在抗击土耳其为希腊争取独立期间因高烧死于希腊而知名〕

by·stand·er /ˈbaɪˌstændɚ; ˈbaɪˌstændə/ *n* [C] someone who watches what is happening without taking part; ONLOOKER 旁观者, 局外人, 看热闹的人: **innocent bystander** *Several innocent bystanders were killed by the blast.* 有几个无辜的旁观者在爆炸中丧生。

byte /baɪt; baɪt/ *n* [C] *technical* a unit of computer information equal to eight bits (BIT[1] (12))【术语】字节

by·way /ˈbaɪˌwe; ˈbaɪweɪ/ *n* [C] a small road or path which is not used very much 偏僻小路, 旁道

by·word /ˈbaɪˌwɝd; ˈbaɪwɜːd/ *n* [C] **1 be a byword for** to be so well-known for a particular quality that your name is used to represent that quality 成为…的代名词: *The political system had become a byword for fraud.* 该政治体制成了诈骗的代名词。**2** [singular] a phrase or saying that is very well-known 口头禅; 俗语

by·zan·tine /ˈbɪzənˌtin; baɪˈzæntaɪn/ *adj formal* complicated and difficult to understand【正式】错综复杂的; 弄不明白的: *the byzantine complexity of our tax laws* 我们繁杂难懂的税务法

By·zan·ti·um /bɪˈzænʃɪəm; bɪˈzæntiəm/ an ancient city, centre of the Byzantine Empire. The city was renamed **Constantinople** by Constantine the Great, and is now called **Istanbul**. 拜占庭〔古代城市, 拜占庭帝国的中心。君士坦丁大帝曾将它改名为君士坦丁堡, 现名伊斯坦布尔〕

C,c

C, c /si; siː/ *plural* **C's, c's** *n* [C] **1** the third letter of the English alphabet 英语字母表的第三个字母 **2** the number 100 in the system of ROMAN NUMERALS 罗马数字 100

c 1 the written abbreviation of 缩写= CENTIMETRE(s) 厘米 **2** a written abbreviation of 缩写= CIRCA (=about) 大约, 左右: *born c 1830* 生于 1830 年前后 **3** the written abbreviation of 缩写= CUBIC 立方 **4** the written abbreviation of 缩写= COPYRIGHT when printed inside a small circle 版权, 著作权〔印在小圆圈内〕

C¹ /si; siː/ *n* **1 a)** the first note in the musical SCALE² (8) of C MAJOR¹ (4) C 音〔C 大调音阶中的第一个音〕 **b)** the musical KEY¹ (4) on this note C 音调 **2** a mark given to a student's work to show that it is of average quality C 级, 丙级, 丙等〔表示学业成绩中等〕

C² the written abbreviation of 缩写= CELSIUS 摄氏: *Water boils at 100°C.* 水在 100 摄氏度时沸腾。

C4 /ˌsi ˋfɔr; ˌsiː ˈfɔː/ the written abbreviation of 缩写= CHANNEL 4

C&W /ˌsi ən ˋdʌbəlju; ˌsiː ən ˈdʌbəljuː/ *n* [U] COUNTRY AND WESTERN (=type of music) 乡村和西部音乐

CA /ˌsi ˋe; ˌsiː ˈeɪ/ the written abbreviation of 缩写= CALIFORNIA

ca a written abbreviation of 缩写= CIRCA (=about) 大约, 左右: *dating from ca 1900* 可追溯到 1900 年左右

CAA, the /ˌsi e ˋe; siː eɪ ˈeɪ/ the abbreviation of 缩写= the CIVIL AVIATION AUTHORITY

CAB /ˌsi e ˋbi; ˌsiː eɪ ˈbiː/ the abbreviation of 缩写= the CITIZEN's ADVICE BUREAU

cab /kæb; kæb/ *n* [C] **1** a taxi 出租车, 的士, 计程车: **call (sb) a cab** (=telephone for a taxi) (为某人) 叫一辆出租车 **2** the part of a bus, train or TRUCK¹ (1) in which the driver sits〔公共汽车、火车或卡车的〕司机室, 驾驶室 **3** a carriage pulled by horses that was used like a taxi in former times〔旧时的〕出租马车

ca·bal /kəˋbæl; kəˈbæl/ *n* [C] a small group of people who make secret plans, especially in order to have political power〔尤指为获取政权的〕阴谋小集团

Ca·bal·lé /ˌkæbæˋje; ˌkæbæˈjeɪ/**, Mont·ser·rat** /ˌmɑntsəˋræt; ˌmɒntsəˈræt/ (1933-) a Spanish OPERA singer, who is one of the most important SOPRANOS (=women with high singing voices) of the 20th century 卡芭叶〔(1933-), 西班牙歌剧演唱家, 20 世纪最重要的女高音歌唱家之一〕

cab·a·ret /ˌkæbəˋre; ˈkæbəreɪ/ *n* **1** [C,U] entertainment, usually with music, songs, and dancing, performed in a restaurant or club while the customers eat and drink〔餐厅或夜总会的〕卡巴莱歌舞表演 **2** [C] a restaurant or club where this is performed 卡巴莱〔指有歌舞表演的餐厅或夜总会〕: *the most famous Parisian cabaret, the Moulin Rouge* 最著名的巴黎卡巴莱夜总会——红磨坊

cab·bage /ˋkæbɪdʒ; ˈkæbɪdʒ/ *n* **1** [C,U] a large round vegetable with thick green or purple leaves 卷心菜, 洋白菜, 甘蓝 —see picture on page A9 参见 A9 页图 **2** [C] *BrE informal*【英, 非正式】 **a)** someone who is lazy and shows no interest in anything 对一切都不感兴趣者, 胸无大志者 **b)** someone who cannot think, move, speak etc as a result of brain injury; VEGETABLE (2) 植物人

cab·bie, cabby /ˋkæbɪ; ˈkæbi/ *n* [C] *informal* a taxi driver【非正式】出租车[计程车]司机

> **CULTURAL NOTE 文化注释**
>
> In Britain, cabbies, especially **London cabbies**, are famous for talking a lot to their passengers and expressing strong opinions, especially about politics. 英国, 尤其是伦敦的出租车司机以健谈、思想激进、尤好表达强烈的政治观点而著称。

ca·ber /ˋkebɚ; ˈkeɪbə/ *n* [C] a long heavy wooden pole that is thrown into the air as a test of strength in sports competitions in Scotland〔苏格兰体育竞赛中用于投掷比试的〕长树干, 长木柱: *tossing the caber* 扔木桩, 掷树干

cab·in /ˋkæbɪn; ˈkæbɪn/ *n* [C] **1** a small house, especially one built of wood in an area of forest or mountains〔尤指建于山上或林中的〕小木屋 **2** a small room on a ship in which you live or sleep〔船上生活或睡觉用的〕舱 **3** an area inside a plane where the passengers sit or where the pilot works〔飞机上的〕客舱; 驾驶舱: *the First Class cabin* 飞机头等舱

cabin boy /ˈ· · ˌ·/ *n* [C] a young man who works as a servant on a ship 船舱的男服务员[侍应生]

cabin class /ˈ· · ˌ·/ *n* [U] travelling conditions on a ship that are better than TOURIST CLASS but not as good as FIRST CLASS (1)〔船上的〕二等舱

cabin cruis·er /ˈ· · ˌ· ·/ *n* [C] a large motor boat with one or more cabins for people to sleep in〔有卧舱的〕大游艇

cab·i·net /ˋkæbənɪt; ˈkæbɪnɪt/ *n* [C] **1** [also+plural verb *BrE* 英] the politicians with important positions in a government who meet to make decisions or advise the leader of the government 内阁: *a cabinet meeting* 内阁会议 **2** a piece of furniture with doors and shelves or drawers, used for storing or showing things〔有搁板、拉门或抽屉的〕贮藏柜, 陈列柜: *a drinks cabinet* 酒柜 —see also 另见 FILING CABINET 2 2

> **CULTURAL NOTE 文化注释**
>
> **the Cabinet** In the US and British political systems, most important decisions are made by the President or Prime Minister and his or her cabinet, who have regular meetings. The members of the cabinet are the heads of government departments, such as the country's department of education or department of transport. These people are chosen by the Prime Minister or President. In the UK, most cabinet members are also Members of Parliament, although a few are from the House of Lords. In the US, however, the members of the cabinet are not chosen from Congress, and they are not elected. Instead, the President chooses the people he or she wants to be in the cabinet, and Congress has to approve this choice. 内阁: 在英美两国的政体中, 大多数重要决定出自总统或首相及其内阁。内阁定期举行会议, 内阁成员为政府部门(如教育部、交通部)首脑, 他们由首相或总统选定。英国的大多数内阁成员是下议院议员, 但也有一些成员来自上议院。但在美国, 内阁成员并非选自国会议员, 也非选举产生; 相反, 总统负责组阁, 国会必须认可总统提出的人选。

cabinet-mak·er /ˈ· · · ˌ· ·/ *n* [C] someone whose job is to make good quality wooden furniture 细木工, 家具木工

Cabinet re·shuf·fle /ˌ· · · ˈ· ·/ a change in the members of the British Cabinet, decided by the Prime Minister, in which some members are given different jobs, some members lose their jobs, and new members are brought in 内阁改组〔指英国内阁成员的调整, 由首相决定, 涉及某些内阁成员的职务变动和任免〕

cabin fe·ver /ˈ· · ˌ· ·/ *n* [U] *AmE* a state in which you feel bad-tempered, because you have not been outside for a long time【美】〔长期足不出户而引起的〕幽闭烦躁症

ca·ble¹ /ˋkebḷ; ˈkeɪbəl/ *n* **1** [C] a plastic or rubber tube containing wires that carry telephone messages, electronic signals etc 电缆 **2** [C,U] a thick strong metal rope used on ships, to support bridges etc 缆绳 **3** [U] CABLE TELEVISION 有线电视: *a cable channel* 有线频道 **4** [C] a TELEGRAM 电报 3

cable² *v* [I,T] to send someone a CABLE¹ (4) 发电报: **cable sb sth** *I cabled Mary the good news.* 我发电报把这个好消息告诉了玛丽。

cable car /ˈ· · ˌ·/ *n* [C] **1** a vehicle pulled by a moving CABLE¹ (2), used to take people to the top of mountains 登山缆车 **2** a vehicle used in cities, that is pulled along by a moving CABLE¹ (2)〔城市内的〕索道车

cable car 登山缆车

ca·ble·gram /ˋkebḷˌgræm; ˈkeɪbəlgræm/ *n* [C] a TELEGRAM 电报

cable rail·way /ˈ· · ˌ· ·/ *n* [C] a railway on which vehicles are pulled up steep slopes by a moving CABLE¹ (2)〔登山〕缆车铁路

cable stitch /ˈ· · ˌ·/ *n* [C,U] a knotted pattern of stitches used in KNITTING 缆绳状针织法

cable tel·e·vi·sion /ˌ· · ˈ· · · ·, ˌ· · · ˈ· · ·/ also 又作 **cable TV** /ˌ· · ˈ· ˈ·/ *n* [U] a system of broadcasting television programmes by CABLE¹ (1) 有线电视 —compare 比较 SATELLITE TELEVISION

ca·boo·dle /kə`budl; kə'bu:dl/ *n* **the whole (kit and) caboodle** *informal* everything【非正式】全部: *slash costs by abolishing the whole caboodle: ballot papers, polling booths, even town halls* 大幅降低费用的办法是取消所有的选票、投票站，甚至市政厅

ca·boose /kə`bus; kə'bu:s/ *n* [C] *AmE* the part of a train where the official in charge of its travels, usually at the back【美】守车〔通常在列车末尾，供列车员使用〕; GUARD'S VAN *BrE*【英】

Cab·ot /`kæbət; 'kæbət/, **John** (?1450-98) an Italian sailor and EXPLORER who worked for the English king Henry VII, and who reached the coast of North America in 1497 卡伯特〔(?1450-1498) 意大利航海家、探险家。他曾效力于英王亨利七世，1497年到达北美沿海一带〕

cab rank /'· ·/ *n* [C] *BrE* a place where taxis wait【英】出租车[计程车]候客站，的士站; CABSTAND *AmE*【美】

Ca·bri·ni /kæ`brinɪ; kæ'bri:ni/, **St Fran·ces Xa·vi·er** /`frænsɪs `zevɪr; 'frɑ:nsᵻs 'zeɪviə/ also 又作 **Mother Cabrini** (1850-1917) a Roman Catholic NUN (=a member of a group of religious women), who was born in Italy but who lived in the US, and who built schools, hospitals, and CONVENTS (=buildings where nuns live) in many US cities. She became the first US citizen to be named a SAINT. 卡布里尼〔(1850-1917)，又称卡布里尼修女。她是一位罗马天主教修女，出生于意大利，生活在美国。她在美国不少城市修建了学校、医院和女修道院，是美国第一个被封为圣徒的公民〕

cab·ri·o·let /,kæbrɪə`le; 'kæbriəleɪ/ *n* [C] a car with a roof that can be folded back; CONVERTIBLE² 折篷式汽车

cab·stand /`kæb,stænd; 'kæbstænd/ *n* [C] *AmE* a place where taxis wait for customers【美】出租车[计程车]候客点，的士站; TAXI RANK *BrE*【英】

ca·cao /kə`kɑo; kə'kaʊ/ *n* [C] the seed from which chocolate and COCOA are made 可可豆

cache¹ /kæʃ; kæʃ/ *n* [C] a number of things that have been hidden, or the place where they have been hidden 隐藏物; 隐藏处: *Police found a cache of explosives in a garage in South London.* 警方在伦敦南部发现一个藏有许多炸药的车库。

cache² *v* [T] to hide something in a secret place 隐藏; 贮藏

cach·et /`kæʃe; 'kæʃeɪ/ *n* [U] *formal* if something has cachet, people think it is especially good and desirable【正式】声望;〔高贵的〕身份: *a good college but without the cachet of Harvard or Yale* 一所不错的、但声望不及哈佛或耶鲁的大学

cack-hand·ed /,kæk `hændɪd; ,kæk 'hændᵻd◂/ *adj BrE informal* careless or tending to drop things; CLUMSY (1)【英，非正式】笨手笨脚的

cack·le¹ /`kækl; 'kækəl/ *v* [I] **1** to laugh in a loud unpleasant way, making short high sounds 刺耳地咯咯笑: *Rumplestiltskin rubbed his hands and cackled with delight.* 朗普尔斯蒂尔茨金一边搓着手一边开心地发出咯咯的笑声。 **2** when a chicken cackles, it makes a loud unpleasant sound〔鸡〕咯咯地叫

cackle² *n* **1** [C,U] a short high unpleasant laugh 咯咯刺耳的笑声: *loud cackles of amusement* 因觉得好玩而发出的咯咯大笑 **2** **cut the cackle** *BrE old-fashioned* used to tell someone to stop talking about unimportant things【英，过时】〔用于要求某人〕停止闲扯，别再饶舌了

ca·coph·o·ny /kə`kɑfənɪ; kə'kɒfəni/ *n* [singular] a loud unpleasant mixture of sounds 刺耳嘈杂的声音: *a cacophony of car horns and shouting* 汽车喇叭声与喊叫交织在一起的嘈杂声 —**cacophonous** *adj*

cac·tus /`kæktəs; 'kæktəs/ *n plural* **cacti** /-taɪ; -taɪ/ or **cactuses** [C] a prickly plant that grows in hot dry places〔植物〕仙人掌

CAD /,si e `di, kæd; ,si: eɪ 'di:, kæd/ *n* [U] computer-aided design; the use of COMPUTER GRAPHICS to plan cars, aircraft, buildings etc 电脑辅助设计;〔汽车、飞机、建筑等的〕电脑图形设计

cad /kæd; kæd/ *n* [C] *old-fashioned* a man who cannot be trusted【过时】不可信赖的男人，无赖 —**caddish** *adj*

ca·dav·er /kə`dævɚ; kə'dævə/ *n* [C] *technical* a dead human body【术语】〔人的〕尸体: *He looked like a walking cadaver.* 他看上去枯槁憔悴。

ca·dav·er·ous /kə`dævərəs; kə'dævərəs/ *adj formal* looking extremely pale, thin, and unhealthy【正式】面色灰白的，形容枯槁的: *cadaverous cheeks* 苍白的脸颊

CAD/CAM /`kædkæm; 'kædkæm/ *n* [U] computer-aided design and manufacture; the use of computers to plan and make industrial products 电脑辅助设计和制造; 电脑辅助生产系统

Caddy /`kædɪ; 'kædi/ an informal name for a Cadillac【非正式】卡迪〔卡迪拉克轿车的别称〕

cad·dy¹ *n* [C] **1** also 又作 **caddie** someone who carries the GOLF CLUBS for someone who is playing GOLF〔受雇为打高尔夫球的人背球棒的〕球童 **2** a small box for storing tea 茶叶盒，茶叶罐

caddy², **caddie** *v* [I+for] to carry GOLF CLUBS for someone who is playing GOLF 当〔某人的〕高尔夫球童 —see picture on page A23 参见 A23 页图

ca·dence /`kedn̩s; 'keɪdəns/ *n* [C] **1** the way someone's voice rises and falls, especially when reading out loud〔尤指大声朗读时音调的〕抑扬顿挫 **2** *technical* a set of CHORDS at the end of a line or piece of music【术语】〔乐曲、乐章的一组〕结尾和弦，终止式

ca·den·za /kə`dɛnzə; kə'denzə/ *n* [C] *technical* a difficult part of a CONCERTO in which the performer plays without the ORCHESTRA to show their skill【术语】〔协奏曲中独奏的〕华彩乐段

ca·det /kə`dɛt; kə'det/ *n* [C] **1** someone who is training to be an officer in the army, navy, air force, or police force〔军官学校或警官学校的〕学员 **2** someone who is in a CADET CORPS 军训队员

cadet corps /·'· ·/ *n* [C] an organization that gives simple military training to pupils in some British schools〔英国某些学校中给学生进行军训的〕军训队（组织）

cadge /kædʒ; kædʒ/ *v* [I,T] *BrE informal* to ask someone for food or cigarettes because you do not have any or do not want to pay【英，非正式】乞讨; 索取; MOOCH *AmE*【美】: **cadge sth from/off** *I managed to cadge a lift from Joanna.* 我设法硬是搭了乔安娜的便车。—**cadger** *n* [C]

Cad·il·lac /`kædɪlæk; 'kædɪlæk/ *n* [C] *trademark*【商标】**1** a very expensive and comfortable car made by an American company 卡迪拉克轿车 **2** *AmE informal* something that is regarded as the highest quality example of a particular type of product【美，非正式】精品，一流名牌产品; ROLLS ROYCE *BrE*【英】: *the Cadillac of stereo systems* 立体音响系统中的精品

cad·mi·um /`kædmɪəm; 'kædmiəm/ *n* [U] a type of metal used in batteries (BATTERY (1)) 镉

ca·dre /`kɑdɚ; 'kɑ:də/ *n formal* [C also+plural verb *BrE* 英] a small group of specially trained people in a profession, political party, or military force【正式】骨干队伍: *a cadre of highly trained scientists* 一批受过严格培训的骨干科学家

Caer·nar·fon, **Caernarvon** /kɑr`nɑrvən; kə'nɑ:vən/ a small town in northwest Wales, known for its castle where the British king or queen's oldest son is given the official royal title Prince of Wales 卡那封〔威尔士西北部一小镇。小镇的城堡十分著名，是英国国王或女王的长子被册封为威尔士亲王的地方〕

Cae·sar /`sizɚ; 'si:zə/, **Ju·li·us** /`dʒulɪəs; 'dʒu:liəs/ (100-44 BC) a Roman politician, military leader, and writer, who took control of the government of Rome and changed it from a republic to an empire, making himself the first Roman emperor 凯撒〔(公元前 100-前 44)，罗马政治家、军事领袖、作家。他曾掌握罗马政府的权力，把罗马从共和国变为帝国，从而当上罗马的首位皇帝〕

cae·sar·e·an /sɪ`zɛrɪən; sᵻ'zeriən/ also 又作 **caesarean section** /·,···'··/ *n* [C] an operation in which a woman's body is cut open to take a baby out 剖腹产（手术）; C-SECTION *AmE*【美】

cae·su·ra /sɪ`ʒʊrə; sɪ'zjʊərə/ *n* [C] *technical* a pause in the middle of a line of poetry【术语】〔一行诗中间的〕停顿

café /kæ`fe; 'kæfeɪ/ *n* [C] **1** a small restaurant where you can buy drinks and simple meals 咖啡馆; 小餐馆 **2** a place on a computer NETWORK¹ (4), where people with similar interests discuss things electronically（网络）聊天室: *You can set up a special interest café on e-mail or Internet.* 你不妨设立一个关于电子邮件和互联网的专题聊天室。

caf·e·te·ri·a /,kæfə`tɪrɪə; ,kæfᵻ'tɪəriə/ *n* [C] a restaurant where you choose your own food and carry it to the table, often in a factory, college etc〔工厂、学校等的〕自助餐厅，食堂: *the school cafeteria* 学校食堂

caf·e·tiere /,kæfə`tjɛr; ,kæfə'tjeə/ *n* [C] a special pot for making coffee, with a metal FILTER¹ (1) that you push down〔带有金属滤器的〕咖啡壶

caff /kæf; kæf/ *n* [C] *informal BrE* a café【非正式，英】咖啡馆; 小餐馆

caf·feine /`kæfin; 'kæfi:n/ *n* [U] a substance in tea and coffee that makes you feel more active 咖啡因[碱]

caf·tan /`kæftæn; 'kæftæn/ *n* [C] a long loose piece of clothing like a coat, usually made of silk or cotton and worn in the Middle East〔中东地区人穿的丝质或棉质的〕宽松长袍

cage¹ /kedʒ; keɪdʒ/ *n* [C] a structure made of wires or bars in which birds or animals can be kept 笼子

cage 笼子

cage² *v* **1** [T] to put or keep something in a cage 把…放[关]进笼中: *caged birds* 笼中鸟 **2 feel caged in** to feel uncomfortable and annoyed because you cannot go outside 感觉被束缚, 行动无自由

Cage, John (1912-) an American COMPOSER of very modern music, including *Winter Music* and *Fontana Mix*. 凯奇〔(1912-), 美国先锋派作曲家。创作的作品有《冬日音乐》和《芳塔娜混成曲》〕

cag·ey /ˈkedʒɪ; ˈkeɪdʒi/ *adj informal* unwilling to tell people definitely what your plans, intentions, or opinions are【非正式】〔言谈〕小心谨慎的, 谨言慎行的: **[+about]** *Senator King is being very cagey about whether he'll run for president.* 金参议员对是否参选总统含糊其辞。—**cagily** *adv* —**caginess** *n*

Cag·ney /ˈkægnɪ; ˈkægni/, **James** (1899-1986) a US film actor who appeared as a GANGSTER (=a member of a violent group of criminals) in films such as *The Public Enemy* (1931) and *White Heat* (1949) 贾克内〔(1899-1986), 美国电影演员。他曾在多部影片中扮演歹徒, 如《社会公敌》(1931)和《白热》(1949)〕

ca·goule /kəˈgul; kəˈguːl/ *n* [C] *BrE* a thin coat with a HOOD (=cover for your head) that stops you from getting wet【英】带风帽的薄雨衣

ca·hoots /kəˈhuts; kəˈhuːts/ *n* **be in cahoots (with)** to be working secretly with another person or group, especially in order to do something dishonest 与…合伙; 与…共谋[勾结]: *Perhaps O'Brien was in cahoots with the thieves.* 奥布赖恩可能与小偷有勾结。

CAI, the /ˌsi e ˈaɪ; ˌsiː eɪ ˈaɪ/ *n* [singular] the Confederation of Australian Industry; an Australian organization that helps Australia's industries and businesses to become more successful 澳大利亚工业联合会〔促进澳大利亚工商业发展的一个组织〕

Cain /ken; keɪn/ in the Old Testament of the Bible, Adam and Eve's first son, who killed his younger brother Abel 该隐〔《圣经·旧约》中亚当和夏娃的长子, 他杀死了他的弟弟亚伯〕—see also 另见 **raise Cain** (RAISE¹ (21))

cairn /kɛrn; keən/ *n* [C] a pile of stones, especially at the top of a mountain, to mark a place〔尤指在山顶作为标记的〕石堆, 石标

Cairn·gorms, the /ˈkɛrngɔrmz; ˈkeəngɔːmz/ a group of mountains in Scotland, popular for walking and climbing 凯恩戈姆山脉〔苏格兰一山脉, 以适于漫步、爬山而闻名〕

Cairns /kɛrnz; keənz/ a city and port on the northeast coast of Australia in the state of Queensland 凯恩斯〔澳大利亚东北沿岸一港口城市, 位于昆士兰州境内〕

Cai·ro /ˈkaɪro; ˈkaɪərəʊ/ the capital and largest city of Egypt, a port on the River Nile in the north of the country 开罗〔埃及首都和最大城市, 埃及北部尼罗河港埠〕

cais·son /ˈkesn; ˈkeɪsən/ *n* [C] **1** a large box filled with air, that allows people to work under water〔水下作业用的〕沉箱 **2** a large box for carrying AMMUNITION (1) 弹药箱

ca·jole /kəˈdʒol; kəˈdʒəʊl/ *v* [I,T] to gradually persuade someone to do something by being nice, etc〔用甜言蜜语〕哄骗, 劝诱: **cajole sb into doing sth** *Can't you cajole her into coming?* 难道你不能哄她来吗?

2 3 **cake¹** /kek; keɪk/ *n* **1** [C,U] a soft sweet food made by baking a mixture of flour, fat, sugar and eggs 蛋糕, 糕饼: *a birthday cake* 生日蛋糕 | *Would you like a slice of chocolate cake?* 来块巧克力蛋糕怎么样? —compare 比较 BISCUIT **2 fish cake/rice cake etc** fish, rice etc that has been formed into a flat round shape and then cooked 鱼肉饼/米饼等 **3** [C] a small block of something 块: **[+of]** *a cake of soap* 一块肥皂 **4 be a piece of cake** *spoken* to be very easy【口】很容易做到的事, 轻松愉快的事: *"How do you do that?" "It's a piece of cake! Watch!"* "你怎么做?" "很简单, 看着!" **5 take the cake** *AmE informal* to be worse than anything else you can imagine【美, 非正式】糟糕透顶; **take the biscuit** (BISCUIT (4)) *BrE*【英】: *I've heard some pretty dumb ideas, but that takes the cake!* 我听到许多馊主意, 但那一个是最蠢的! **6 you can't have your cake and eat it** *spoken* used to tell someone that they cannot have the advantage of something without its disadvantages【口】两者不可兼得 **7 a slice of the cake** a part of the money, help etc that is available for everyone to share〔人人都可分享到的财物、帮助等的〕份额 —see also 另见 **sell like hot cakes** (HOT CAKE)

cake² *v* **1 be caked with/in** to be covered with a layer of something thick and hard 厚厚地涂上[沾上]…: *Look at your boots! They're caked with mud.* 看看你的靴子! 沾满了泥巴! **2** [I] if a substance cakes, it forms a thick hard layer when it dries〔干后〕结成硬块

cake·hole /ˈkekˌhol; ˈkeɪk-həʊl/ *n* [C] *BrE spoken* someone's mouth【英口】嘴巴: *Shut your cakehole!* 闭嘴!

cake pan /ˈ· ·/ *n* [C] *AmE* a CAKE TIN (1)【美】蛋糕烤盘

cake tin /ˈ· ·/ *n* [C] *BrE*【英】**1** a metal container in which you bake a cake 蛋糕烤盘 —see picture at 参见 PAN¹ 图 **2** a metal container with a lid, that you keep a cake in 装蛋糕的有盖金属盒

cake·walk /ˈkekˌwɔk; ˈkeɪkwɔːk/ *n* [singular] *AmE informal* a very easy victory【美, 非正式】轻易取得的胜利

cal·a·bash /ˈkæləˌbæʃ; ˈkæləbæʃ/ *n* [C] a large tropical fruit with a shell that can be dried and used as a bowl〔产于热带的〕加拉巴果〔其壳干燥后可作碗用〕, 葫芦

cal·a·brese /ˈkæləbris; ˈkæləbriːs/ *n* [U] a type of BROCCOLI 花茎甘蓝, 西兰花菜, 花椰菜

Cal·ais /kæˈle; ˈkæleɪ/ an industrial city and port on the English Channel in northwest France, used especially by ferries (FERRY) to and from Dover in England 加来〔法国西北部一工业城市和英吉利海峡港埠, 尤为往返英格兰多佛尔的船只停泊之用〕

cal·a·mine lo·tion /ˈkæləˌmaɪn ˈloʃən; ˈkæləmaɪn ˌləʊʃən/ *n* [U] a pink liquid for sore, itchy or sunburnt (SUNBURN) skin 炉甘石药水〔粉红色护肤药水, 可防止皮肤疼痛、瘙痒或日晒后的疼痛〕

ca·lam·i·ty /kəˈlæmətɪ; kəˈlæmɪ̈ti/ *n* [C] a terrible and unexpected event that causes a lot of damage or suffering 灾难, 祸患: *It would be a calamity for the farmers if the crops failed again.* 如果收成再不好, 对农民来说会是很大的灾难。—**calamitous** *adj* —**calamitously** *adv*

cal·ci·fy /ˈkælsəˌfaɪ; ˈkælsɪ̈faɪ/ *v* [I,T] *technical* to become hard, or make something hard, by adding LIME¹ (3)【术语】(使)石灰质化, (使)钙化; (使)硬化

cal·ci·um /ˈkælsɪəm; ˈkælsiəm/ *n* [U] a simple chemical substance in bones, teeth, and CHALK¹ (1) 钙 3

cal·cu·la·ble /ˈkælkjələbḷ; ˈkælkjɪ̈ləbəl/ *adj* something that is calculable can be measured by using numbers 能计算的: *clear and calculable beneficial effects* 清楚而且可以算出来的效益

cal·cu·late /ˈkælkjəˌlet; ˈkælkjɪ̈leɪt/ *v* [T] **1** to find out how much something will cost, how long something will take etc, by using numbers 计算, 核算: *Oil prices are calculated in dollars.* 油价以美元计算。| **calculate how much/how many etc** *I'm trying to calculate how much paint we need.* 我试着算算看我们需要多少涂料。| **calculate (that)** *Sally calculated that she'd have about £100 left.* 萨莉算了一下, 自己还剩下大约100英镑。**2** to guess something using as many facts as you can find 估算, 估计: *It's difficult to calculate what effect all these changes will have on the company.* 很难估计这些变化将会给公司带来什么样的影响。**3 be calculatd to do sth** to be intended to have a particular effect 旨在, 用意在于; 打算; 适于(做)…: *a comment calculated to annoy traditionalists in the party* 旨在惹怒党内传统人士的评论 2 3

calculate on sth *phr v* [T] if you calculate on something you are depending on it for your plans to succeed 指望, 期望: *We're calculating on an early start.* 我们指望早点儿出发。| **calculate on sb/sth doing sth** *Ken hadn't calculated on Polson refusing his offer.* 肯并未料到波尔森会拒绝自己的提议。

cal·cu·lat·ed /ˈkælkjəˌletɪd; ˈkælkjɪ̈leɪtɪ̈d/ *adj* **1** a calculated crime or dishonest action is deliberately and carefully planned 故意的, 蓄意的; 有计划的; 存心欺骗的: *a calculated attempt to deceive the American public* 蓄意欺骗美国公众的企图 **2 take a calculated risk** to do something that involves a risk after thinking carefully about what might happen 冒预料到的风险 —see also 另见 CALCULATE —**calculatedly** *adv*

cal·cu·lat·ing /ˈkælkjəˌletɪŋ; ˈkælkjɪ̈leɪtɪŋ/ *adj* making careful and clever plans to get what you want, without caring about anyone else 有算计的, 工于心计的, 用尽心机(作损人利己之事)的: *a criminal with a cold, calculating mind* 一个冷酷而工于心计的罪犯

cal·cu·la·tion /ˌkælkjəˈleʃən; ˌkælkjɪ̈ˈleɪʃən/ *n* **1** [C,U] a way of using numbers in order to find out an amount, price, or value 计算; 推断; 预测, 估计: *Dee looked at the bill and made some rapid calculations.* 迪伊瞅着账单, 同时进行着速算。**2** [U] careful planning in order to get what you want 盘算, 深思熟虑, 慎重的计划 2

cal·cu·la·tor /ˈkælkjəˌletɚ; ˈkælkjɪ̈leɪtə/ *n* [C] a small electronic machine that can do calculations such as adding and multiplying 计算器[机]: *a solar calculator* (=working using the power of the sun) 太阳能电池计算器[机] 3

cal·cu·lus /ˈkælkjələs; ˈkælkjɪ̈ləs/ *n* [U] the part of mathematics that deals with changing quantities, such as the speed of a falling stone or the slope of a curved line 微积分

Cal·cut·ta /kælˈkʌtə; kælˈkʌtə/ a city and port in East India on the Hooghly River and capital of West Bengal state. The new name for Calcutta is Kolkata. 加尔各答〔印度东部一港口

城市，位于胡格利河畔，为西孟加拉邦首府。现名为 Kolkata〕— see also 另见 the BLACK HOLE OF CALCUTTA

Cal·der /ˈkɔldɚ; ˈkɔːldə/, **Al·ex·an·der** /ˌælɪgˈzændɚ; ˌælɪgˈzɑːndə/ (1898-1976) a US SCULPTOR famous for his large outdoor works of art found in many cities, and for his large MOBILES (=decorations which move when air blows around them) 考尔德〔(1898-1976)，美国雕塑家，以创作的城市户外大型艺术作品和大型活动雕塑著名〕

cal·dron /ˈkɔldrən; ˈkɔːldrən/ *n* [C] the American spelling of CAULDRON cauldron 的美式拼法

Cal·e·do·ni·a /ˌkælɪˈdonɪə; ˌkælɪˈdəʊniə/ an old name for Scotland, used in poetry. Caledonia was originally the Roman name for northern Britain. 喀里多尼亚〔苏格兰旧称，用于诗歌。最初为北不列颠的罗马语名称〕—**Caledonian** *adj*

Caledonian Ca·nal, the /,····· ·ˈ·/ a CANAL (=artificial river) in Scotland which joins the Atlantic Ocean to a line of LOCHs (=lakes), which then connect to the North Sea 喀里多尼亚运河〔苏格兰一运河，将大西洋与一连串湖泊连通，然后与北海相连接〕

cal·en·dar /ˈkæləndɚ; ˈkælɪndə/ *n* [C] **1** pages printed to show the days, weeks, and months of a particular year, that you hang on the wall 日历，月历 **2** *AmE*【美】**a)** a book with separate spaces or pages for each day of the year, on which you write down the things you have to do〔日历〕记事簿；DIARY (2) *BrE*【英】**b)** all the things you plan to do in the next days, months etc 日程表；一览表：*The President's calendar is already very full.* 总统的日程表早已排得满满的。**3** a system for dividing time, that fixes the event from which all years are measured and arranges days into months and years 历法：*the Gregorian calendar* 公历，阳历 **4** all the events in a year that are important for a particular organization or activity〔某个团体或某项活动预定一年内要办的〕大事日程表：*The Derby is a major event in the racing calendar.* 德比马赛在赛马日程表上是一项重要的赛事。

calendar month /,···ˈ·/ *n* [C] **1** one of the twelve months of the year 历月：*Salaries will be paid at the end of the calendar month.* 工资在每个月月底发放。**2** a period of time from a specific date in one month to the same date in the next month〔指某月中的某日至下月中同一日的〕满一个月的时间

calendar year /,···ˈ·/ *n* [C] a period of time from January 1st to December 31st 日历年

calf /kæf; kɑːf/ *n plural* **calves** /kævz; kɑːvz/ [C] **1** the part of the back of your leg between your knee and your ANKLE〔人腿的〕腓，小腿肚 —see picture at 参见 BODY 图 **2** the baby of a cow, or of some other large animals such as the ELEPHANT 小牛，牛犊；〔象等某些大动物的〕仔，幼兽 **3 be in calf** if a cow is in calf, it is going to have a baby〔母牛〕怀孕的 —see also 另见 **kill the fatted calf** (KILL[1] (14))

calf love /ˈ· ·/ *n* [U] PUPPY LOVE 青少年时期的初恋

Cal·gar·y /ˈkælgərɪ; ˈkælgəri/ a city in southern Alberta, Canada, which is next to the Bow and Elbow Rivers and has the most important PETROLEUM industries in the country 卡尔加里〔加拿大艾伯塔省南部一城市，位于鲍河和埃尔博河的汇合处。该市的石油工业在全国举足轻重〕

Cal·i·ban /ˈkælɪbæn; ˈkælɪbæn/ a character in the play *The Tempest* by William Shakespeare. He is an ugly SLAVE owned by Prospero and is only half human, since his mother is a WITCH (=a woman who has magic powers), but his father is a DEVIL (=an evil spirit). 卡利班〔威廉·莎士比亚戏剧《暴风雨》中的人物。他是普洛斯彼罗的奴隶，相貌丑陋。他母亲是个女巫，父亲是个魔鬼，所以他只有一半像人〕

cal·i·ber /ˈkæləbɚ; ˈkælɪbə/ *n* the American spelling of CALIBRE calibre 的美式拼法

cal·i·brate /ˈkæləˌbret; ˈkælɪbreɪt/ *v* [T] *technical* to mark an instrument or tool so that you can use it for measuring【术语】标定，划分，校准〔测量器的〕刻度

cal·i·bra·tion /ˌkælɪˈbreʃən; ˌkælɪˈbreɪʃən/ *n* [U] *technical* a set of marks on an instrument or tool used for measuring【术语】〔测量仪器上的〕刻度

cal·i·bre *BrE*【英】, **caliber** *AmE*【美】/ˈkæləbɚ; ˈkælɪbə/ *n* **1** [U] the level of quality or ability that someone or something has achieved〔人的〕能力，才干；〔事物的〕质量，水准：*We've been lucky in the high calibre of directors we've been able to recruit.* 我们很幸运，能够招聘到高水平的领导人才。**2** [C] *technical*【术语】**a)** the width of the inside of a gun or tube〔枪炮或管子的〕内径，口径 **b)** the width of a bullet〔子弹的〕弹径，直径

cal·i·co /ˈkæləˌko; ˈkælɪkəʊ/ *n* [U] **1** *BrE* heavy cotton cloth that is usually white【英】厚白棉布 **2** *AmE* light cotton cloth with a small printed pattern【美】薄印花棉布 **3 calico cat** *AmE* a cat that has black, white and brown fur【美】〔毛皮黑白棕色相间的〕花斑猫

Cal·i·for·ni·a /ˌkælɪˈfɔrnɪə; ˌkælɪˈfɔːniə/ abbreviation 缩写为 **CA** a state in the southwest of the US, next to the Pacific Ocean, whose main cities include San Francisco and Los Angeles 加利福尼亚〔美国西南部一州。濒临太平洋，主要城市有圣弗朗西斯科和洛杉矶〕

CULTURAL NOTE 文化注释

When British and American people think of California, they often think of beaches, warm sunny weather, and SURFing. The state, especially northern California, is often considered to be more LIBERAL than other states in the US, but it has also elected RIGHT-WING politicians such as Ronald Reagan and Arnold Schwarzenegger as GOVERNOR. In the 1960s, San Francisco was a centre of the HIPPY movement which supported LEFT-WING politics and had RADICAL ideas about changing society. At the University of California, Berkeley, there were many protests against the Vietnam War. California is known as a place where people like to follow the latest fashions in LIFESTYLE, and where people want to stay physically fit and look young. 英美人想到加利福尼亚，常会想到海滩、温暖晴朗的天气和冲浪运动。加利福尼亚，尤其是该州北部常被认为比美国其他各州更为思想开放，但一些右翼政界人士，如罗纳德·里根和阿诺德·施瓦辛格也被选为州长。20世纪60年代，圣弗朗西斯科成为嬉皮士运动的中心。嬉皮士运动支持左翼政治，持激进的观点，试图改良社会。在加利福尼亚大学伯克利分校，曾有很多反对越战的抗议活动。加利福尼亚以人们热衷追逐最新潮流闻名，当地人都想保持体型健美，外表年轻。

California Institute of Technology —see also 另见 CAL TECH

Ca·lig·u·la /kəˈlɪgjulə; kəˈlɪgjʊlə/ (12-41AD) a Roman emperor famous for being extremely violent, cruel, and crazy 加利古拉〔(公元 12-41)，罗马皇帝，以极端野蛮、残暴、疯狂著称〕

cal·i·pers /ˈkælɪpɚz; ˈkælɪpəz/ *n* [plural] the American spelling of CALLIPERS callipers 的美式拼法

ca·liph /ˈkelɪf; ˈkeɪlɪf/ *n* [C] a MUSLIM ruler 哈里发〔伊斯兰教国家的教主和统治者〕

ca·li·phate /ˈkælɪˌfet; ˈkeɪlɪfeɪt/ *n* [C] the country a caliph rules, or the period of time when they rule it 哈里发统治的国家[时期]

cal·is·then·ics /ˌkæləsˈθɛnɪks; ˌkælɪsˈθenɪks/ *n* [plural] the American spelling of CALLISTHENICS callisthenics 的美式拼法

calk /kɔk; kɔːk/ *v* [T] an American spelling of CAULK caulk 的美式拼法

S1 W1

call[1] /kɔl; kɔːl/ *v*

① HAVE/USE A NAME 叫做/称呼
② DESCRIBE SB/STH 描述某人/某事物
③ TELEPHONE 打电话
④ SAY STH LOUDLY 高声说出某事
⑤ TELL/ORDER 告知/命令
⑥ VISIT 拜访
⑦ AGREE 同意
⑧ ARRANGE STH 安排某事
⑨ OTHER MEANINGS 其他意思

① HAVE/USE A NAME 叫做/称呼

1 [T] **be called sth** to have a particular name or title 名称，名叫：*They have a three-year-old son called Matthew.* 他们有个三岁的儿子，名叫马修。| *What was that book called?* 那本书的书名是什么？

2 [T] to use a particular name or title when you speak to

someone 称呼，叫：*My name's Alan, but you can call me Al.* 我的名字是艾伦，但你们可以叫我阿尔。| *Do you want to be called Miss or Ms?* 你愿意被称为小姐还是女士？| **call sb by** *I prefer to be called by my middle name.* 我喜欢别人叫我的中间名。

3 [T] to give someone or something the name they will be known by in the future 为〔某人或某事物〕取名：**call sb/sth sth** *They've decided to call the baby Louise.* 他们决定给宝宝取名为路易丝。

② DESCRIBE SB/STH 描述某人/某事物

4 [T] to use a particular word or phrase to describe someone or something that clearly shows what you think of them 认为…是…，视为：**call sb/sth sth** *Are you calling me a liar?* 你认为我是个说谎者吗？| *You may call it harmless fun, but I call it pornography.* 你可能认为这是毫无恶意的玩笑，但是我却认为它很黄。

5 call yourself sth to claim that you are a particular type of person, although you do nothing to show this is true 自称为…，自我描绘成是…：*He calls himself a Christian, but I've never seen him go to church.* 他称自己是基督徒，但我从未见他去过教堂。

6 call sb names to insult someone by using unpleasant words to describe them 辱骂某人：*The other kids used to call me names.* 别的孩子过去常常辱骂我。—see also 另见 **call a spade a spade** (SPADE (3))

③ TELEPHONE 打电话

7 [I,T] to telephone someone（给某人）打电话：*I tried calling last night but you weren't home.* 昨晚我试着给你打电话，但你不在家。| *He said he'd call me later to make arrangements.* 他说稍后会给我打电话作出安排。—see 见 TELEPHONE¹ (USAGE)

8 [T] to ask someone to come to you by telephoning them 打电话请某人：*I think we should call the doctor.* 我想我们应该打电话请医生来。| *I swear, I'm gonna call the cops!* 我发誓，我会打电话报警！—see graph at 参见 TELEPHONE² 图表 —see also 另见 **call in**

9 call collect *AmE* to make a telephone call that is paid for by the person who receives it【美】打对方付费电话；**reverse the charges** (REVERSE¹ (5)) *BrE*【英】

④ SAY STH LOUDLY 高声说出某事

10 [I,T] to say or shout something loudly so that someone can hear you 喊，叫：*I thought I heard Dad calling me.* 我想我听到爸爸叫我了。| **[+through/down/up]** *"I'm coming!" she called down the stairs.* "我就来！"她朝楼梯下喊道。

11 [T] also 又作 **call out** to read names or numbers in a loud voice in order to get someone's attention 点名：*OK, when I call your name, go and stand in line.* 好！我点到你的名字时，你就过去站到队列中。

⑤ TELL/ORDER 告知/命令

12 [T] to ask or order someone to come to you, either by speaking loudly or sending them a message〔高声或传信〕召唤[命令]〔某人〕来：**call sb into/over** *Later, the boss called Dan into her office.* 后来，老板把丹叫进她的办公室。| **call sb up/down** *AmE*【美】*Marcie got called up to the Principal's office for smoking.* 玛茜因为抽烟被叫到了校长办公室。

13 [T usually passive 一般用被动态] to tell someone that they must come to a law court or official committee 传召〔到法庭等〕：**call sb to do sth** *They were called to give evidence at the trial.* 他们被传召到庭讯中作证。

14 be/feel called to do sth if you are called to do something, you feel that God is telling you to do it 感到〔受上帝〕召唤：*Simon felt called to do missionary work.* 西蒙感到是上帝在召唤自己从事传教工作。

15 call sb/sth to order *formal* to tell people to obey the rules of a formal meeting【正式】命令…遵守议事规程：*I now call this meeting to order.* 现在，我请大家遵守议事规程。

⑥ VISIT 拜访

16 [I] *BrE*【英】also 又作 **call round** to stop at a house or other place for a short time to see someone or do something〔短时间〕拜访〔某人〕，〔短时间〕逗留〔以便做某事〕：*The milkman called while you were out.* 你不在时，送牛奶的人来过。| **call on sb** *We thought we'd call on James on the way home.* 我们觉得，回家的路上应该拜访一下詹姆斯。| **call at sth** *I called at the drycleaner's to collect your suit.* 我去干洗店取了你的衣服。

⑦ AGREE 同意

17 call it £10/2 hours etc *spoken* used to ask someone to agree with a particular suggestion you are making, especially in order to make things simpler【口】就算作 10 英镑/两小时等：*"I owe you £10.20." "Oh, call it £10!"* "我欠你 10 英镑 20 便士。" "喔，就算 10 英镑吧。"

18 call it a draw if two opponents in a game call it a draw, they agree that neither of them has won 打成平局，不分胜负 —see also 另见 **call it quits** (QUITS (2))

⑧ ARRANGE STH 安排某事

19 call a meeting/election/rehearsal etc to arrange for something to happen at a definite time 召集会议/选举/排练等：*We've called an emergency meeting of the governors.* 我们已召集了州长举行紧急会议。

20 call a huddle *AmE informal* to arrange for people to come together to have a meeting【美，非正式】召集会议

⑨ OTHER MEANINGS 其他意思

21 call into question to make people uncertain about whether something is right or true〔使人对某事〕产生疑问：*I feel that my competence is being called into question here.* 我觉得自己的能力在这里受到了怀疑。

22 call it a day *informal* to decide to stop working, especially because you have done enough or you are tired【非正式】今天(的工作)就到此为止：*Come on, let's call it a day and go home.* 好了，今天我们就到此为止，回家吧。

23 call attention to to ask people to pay attention to a particular subject or problem 提请注意：*May I call your attention to item seven on the agenda.* 请大家注意议程上的第七项。

24 ►TRAINS 火车◄ [I+at] if a train calls at a place, it stops there for a short time 短暂停留：*This train will call at all stations to Broxbourne.* 这列开往布罗克斯本的火车沿途所有车站都停。

25 call the tune/shots *informal* to be in a position of authority so that you can give orders and make decisions【非正式】发号施令；操纵

26 call sth to mind a) to remind you of something 使回忆起：*Don't those two call to mind the days when we were courting?* 难道他们俩没让我们回忆起恋爱的日子？**b)** to remember something 想起：*Can you call to mind when you last saw her?* 你记得最后一次见到她是什么时候吗？

27 ►GAMES/SPORTS 游戏/体育◄ [I,T] to guess which side of a coin will land upwards when it is thrown in the air, in order to decide who will play first in a game 抛硬币决定先后次序：*It's your turn to call.* 轮到你来抛硬币了。—see also 另见 SO CALLED, **call sb's bluff** (BLUFF² (2))

call back *phr v* **1** [I,T] to telephone someone again, especially because one of you was not in or was busy〔对方打来电话时因不在或繁忙而事后〕回电话：*No problem, I'll call back later.* 没问题，我过会儿再回电话。| **call sb back** *Can you ask John to call me back when he gets in?* 约翰来后让他给我回电话好吗？**2** [I] *BrE* to return to a place you have been to earlier, especially a house or a shop【英】再来〔尤指某所房子或商店〕：*I'll call back with my car and pick up the painting.* 我会开车再来取这幅画。

call by *phr v* [I] *BrE informal* to stop and visit someone when you are near the place where they live or work【英，非正式】顺路拜访：*I thought I'd call by and see how you were.* 我想我会顺路去看看你怎么样了。

call sb/sth ↔ **down** *phr v* [T] *literary* to pray loudly that something unpleasant will happen to someone or something【文】〔大声〕祈求降祸于…：*calling down the wrath of God* 祈求上帝降怒

call for sb/sth *phr v* [T] **1** to need a particular action, behaviour, quality etc 需要〔某种行动、举止、品质等〕：*Really, Susan, that kind of attitude just isn't called for.* 真的，苏珊，那种态度根本没必要。—see also 另见 UNCALLED-FOR **2** to ask strongly and publicly for money, justice etc in order to change a situation 要求，呼吁：*farmers calling for larger government subsidies* 呼吁政府给予更多补贴的农民 **3** *BrE* to meet someone at their home in order to take them somewhere【英】(去)接〔某人〕：*I'll call for you at 8 o'clock.* 我 8 点钟来接你。**4** *AmE* to say that something is likely to happen, especially when talking about the weather【美】预测〔尤指天气〕：*The forecast calls for more rain.* 天气预报说还会下雨。

call sth ↔ **forth** *phr v* [T] *formal* to make something such as a quality appear so that you can use it; SUMMON【正式】唤起，引起，激起

call in *phr v* [I] **1** to telephone somewhere, especially the place where you work, to tell them where you are, what you are doing etc〔尤指向工作单位〕打电话汇报: **call in sick** (=telephone to say you are too ill to come to work) 打电话请病假 **2** [T **call** sb ↔ **in**] to ask someone to come and see you to help you with a difficult situation 请…来〔帮助〕: *Police have been called in to help find missing Sandra Day, aged 7.* 已经请了警察帮忙寻找失踪的七岁小孩桑德拉·戴。**3 call in a loan/favour** to ask someone to pay back money or to help you with something because you helped them earlier 讨还债款; 要求回报 **4** [I+at/on] *BrE* to visit a person or place while you are on your way somewhere else【英】顺路拜访, 顺路探望: *Could you call in on Mum on your way home?* 你回家时能顺便探望一下妈妈吗?

call sb/sth ↔ **off** *phr v* [T] **1** to order a dog or person to stop attacking someone 叫〔狗或人〕…走开〔以免攻击人〕: *Call off the alsatian – it's frightening my son.* 把狼狗叫走, 它吓着我儿子了。**2** to decide that a planned event will not take place; CANCEL 取消, 撤销〔原计划的活动〕: *There's no rush now – the game's been called off.* 现在不用着急了, 比赛已经取消了。**3 call off a strike/search etc** to decide officially that something should be stopped after it has already started 下令停止罢工/搜寻等: *Rescuers had to call off the search due to worsening weather.* 由于天气恶化, 救援人员决定停止搜寻。

call on/upon sb/sth *phr v* [T] **1** to visit someone for a short time 短暂访问: *Why don't you call on my sister when you're in Brighton?* 你到了布赖顿时何不顺便探望一下我姐姐? **2** to formally ask someone to do something〔正式〕要求〔某人做某事〕: **call on sb to do sth** *The UN has called on both sides to observe the ceasefire.* 联合国已要求双方遵守停火协议。

call out *phr v* **1** [I,T **call** sth ↔ **out**] to say something loudly 大声说出: *Call out the numbers so that we can hear them at the back.* 大声报出那些数字, 让我们在后面坐的人也能听见。**2** [T **call** sb/sth ↔ **out**] **a)** to order an organization to help, especially in a dangerous situation〔尤指在出现某种险情时〕召唤[命令]〔某个组织〕出动: *The National Guard has been called out to help fight fires.* 国民警卫队已奉令帮助灭火。**b)** *BrE* to order workers to go on strike (STRIKE[2] (1))【英】命令〔工人〕罢工

call up *phr v* **1** [I,T] **call** sb ↔ **up** *informal especially AmE* to telephone someone【非正式, 尤美】给〔某人〕打电话 **2** [T **call** sb ↔ **up** *BrE* 英] to officially order someone to join the army, navy, or air force 征召…入伍; DRAFT[2] (2) *AmE*【美】: *I was called up three months after war broke out.* 战争爆发三个月后, 我被征召入伍。**3** [T **call** sb ↔ **up**] to choose someone for a national sports team, especially football 挑选〔某人〕入国家队〔尤指足球队〕: *Hurst was called up for the game against Mexico.* 赫斯特入选国家队, 参加和墨西哥队的比赛。**4** [T **call** sth ↔ **up**] if you call up information on a computer, you make the computer show it to you〔在电脑上〕显示[调出]资讯 **5** [T **call** sb/sth **up**] to make something appear again after it has gone or been forgotten 使回忆起来; 召回: *calling up the spirits of the dead* 召回死者的灵魂

S1 W1 **call²** *n*

1 ►TELEPHONE 电话◄ [C] **a)** an attempt to speak to someone by telephone (一次) 通话; 电话: *Were there any phone calls for me while I was out?* 我不在时有人给我来过电话吗? | **get/receive a call** *I got a call from Jane in Australia last week.* 上周我接到简从澳大利亚打来的电话。| **give sb a call** *I'll give you a call at the weekend.* 周末我会给你打电话。| **make a call** *It's cheaper to make calls after 6pm.* 下午 6 点后打电话便宜些。| **take a call** (=answer a call) 接电话 *I'll take the call in my office.* 我会在办公室里接电话。| **return a call** (=telephone someone who tried to telephone you earlier) 回电话 **b)** a telephone call asking a doctor, the police etc to go somewhere where they are needed 给〔医生、警察等打的〕求助电话: *We're getting calls about a disturbance at a pub in Camden.* 我们接到电话, 说卡姆登一家小酒吧里发生了骚乱。

2 be on call if someone such as a doctor or engineer is on call, they are ready to go and help whenever they are needed as part of their job〔医生、工程师等〕待命的, 随叫随到的: *Don't worry, there's a doctor on call 24 hours a day.* 别担心, 全天 24 小时都有一位医生值班。

3 ►SHOUT/CRY 叫/喊◄ [C] **a)** the sound or cry that a bird or animal makes〔鸟或动物的〕叫声 **b)** a shout or cry that you make to get someone's attention〔引起他人注意的〕呼喊声

4 ►VISIT 拜访◄ [C] a visit, especially for a particular reason〔尤指特殊原因的〕短暂拜访: *Sorry, Doctor Pugh is out on a call at the moment.* 对不起, 皮尤医生现在出诊去了。| **pay/make a call (on)** (=visit someone) 拜访某人 *Why not pay a call on your aunt while you're in Leeds?* 你到了利兹时何不探访一下你姨妈?

5 there isn't much call for used to say that something is not popular or is not needed 没有需求, 不需要: *There isn't much call for black and white televisions these days.* 如今黑白电视机的需求量并不大。

6 there is no call for *spoken* used to tell someone that their behaviour is wrong and unnecessary【口】没有理由, 没必要: *There's no call for swearing – I'm doing my best!* 没必要骂人, 我正竭尽全力!

7 ►REQUEST/ORDER 要求/命令◄ [C] a request or order for someone to do something or go somewhere 号召, 呼吁: *a strike call* 罢工号召 | **call for sb to do sth** *There have been calls for the secretary to resign.* 有人要求部长辞职。

8 ►PLANE 飞机◄ [C] an official message at an airport that a plane for a particular place will soon leave 航班起飞前对旅客的通知: *This is the last call for flight BA872 to Moscow.* 这是飞往莫斯科的 BA872 航班起飞前的最后一次通知。

9 ►DECISION 决定◄ [singular] **a)** the decision made by a REFEREE (=judge) in a sports game〔体育运动比赛中裁判员的〕判决 **b)** *AmE informal* a decision【美, 非正式】决定: **make a call** (=decide) 作决定 | **easy/hard call** (=a difficult or easy decision) 简单/困难的决定 | **it's your call** *spoken* (=it's your decision)【口】这是你自己的决定

10 have first call on a) to have the right to be the first person to use something 具有〔使用某物的〕优先权 **b)** to be the first person that someone will help because you are important to them 处于优先〔受助的〕地位

11 the call of *literary* the power that a place or way of life has to attract someone【文】吸引力, 魅力: *the call of the sea* 大海的魅力

12 the call of nature a need to URINATE (=pass liquid from your body) 要小便 —see also 另见 **be at sb's beck and call** (BECK (2)), PORT OF CALL, ROLL-CALL

Cal·las /ˈkæləs; ˈkæləs/, **Ma·ri·a** /məˋriə; məˈriːə/ (1923-77) a US OPERA singer whose parents were Greek. One of the greatest opera singers of the 20th century, she was famous for her powerful voice and for being able to act as well as sing. 卡拉斯 (1923-1977), 歌剧演唱家, 美籍希腊人。她是 20 世纪最伟大的歌剧演唱家之一, 以嗓音浑厚和演技高超而著称)

call box /ˈ· ·/ *n* [C] **1** *AmE* a public telephone beside a road used to telephone for help【美】路边求救电话 **2** *BrE* a small structure that is partly or completely enclosed, containing a public telephone【英】公用电话亭; PHONE BOOTH *AmE*【美】

call·er /ˈkɔlə; ˈkɔːlə/ *n* [C] **1** someone making a telephone call 打电话者: *An anonymous caller warned the police about the bomb.* 有人打匿名电话警告警方说有炸弹。**2** someone who visits your house 到访者: *If you're not sure who the caller is, ask to see some identification.* 如果你无法确定来访者的身份, 可以要求看看他的证件。

call girl /ˈ· ·/ *n* [C] a PROSTITUTE who makes arrangements to meet men by telephone 电话应召女郎

cal·lig·ra·phy /kəˋlɪgrəfɪ; kəˈlɪgrəfi/ *n* [U] the art of producing beautiful writing using special pens or brushes, or the writing produced this way 书法(艺术); 笔迹 —**calligrapher** *n* [C]

call-in /ˈ· ·/ *n* [C] *AmE* a radio or television programme in which people telephone to give their opinions【美】〔电台或电视台的〕电话热线节目; PHONE-IN *BrE*【英】

call·ing /ˋkɔlɪŋ; ˈkɔːlɪŋ/ *n* [C] **1** a strong desire or feeling of duty to do a particular kind of work, especially religious work; VOCATION (3)〔神的〕感召; 〔从事某种工作的〕强烈冲动; 使命感 **2** *formal* someone's profession or trade【正式】职业, 行业

calling card /ˈ·· ·/ *n* [C] *AmE* a small card with a name and often address printed on it, that people used to give to people they visited; VISITING CARD【美】名片

cal·li·pers *BrE*【英】, **calipers** *AmE*【美】/ˋkæləpəz; ˈkælɪ̵pəz/ *n plural* **1** a tool used for measuring thickness, the distance between two surfaces, or the DIAMETER (=inside width) of something 测径规; 卡钳; 两脚规 **2** *BrE* metal bars that someone wears on their legs to help them walk【英】〔装在双腿上帮助行走的〕金属条; BRACE[2] (2b) *AmE*【美】

cal·lis·then·ics *BrE*【英】, **calisthenics** *AmE*【美】/ˌkæləsˋθɛnɪks; ˌkælɪ̵sˈθenɪks/ *n* [U] a set of physical exercises that are intended to make you thin and healthy 健美(体)操, 健身操

call let·ters /ˈ· ,· ·/ *n* [plural] *AmE* a name made up of letters and numbers used by people operating communication radios to prove who they are【美】〔无线电〕呼号; CALL SIGN *BrE*【英】

call op·tion /ˈ· ,· ·/ *n* [C] *technical* the right to buy a particular number of shares (SHARE² (5)) at a different price within a fixed period of time【术语】〔股票的〕看涨期权, 认购期权, 购买选择权〔指按规定的价格和日期购买一定数量的股票的权利〕

cal·lous /ˈkæləs; ˈkæləs/ *adj* not caring that other people are suffering 无情的, 冷漠的: *We were shocked at the callous disregard for human life.* 对人的生命的无情漠视令我们震惊。| *the callous slaughter of thousands of seals* 数千只海豹的被残杀 —**callously** *adv* —**callousness** *n* [U]

cal·loused /ˈkæləst; ˈkæləst/ *adj* calloused skin is rough and covered in CALLUSes〔皮肤〕硬结的, 起老茧的

C

cal·low /ˈkælo; ˈkæləʊ/ *adj literary* young and without experience; IMMATURE【文】年轻幼稚的, 不成熟的: *a callow youth* 幼稚的年轻人

call sign /ˈ· ·/ *n* [C] *BrE* a name made up of letters and numbers used by people operating communication radios to prove who they are【英】〔电台的〕呼号, 呼叫信号; CALL LETTERS *AmE*【美】

call-up /ˈ· ·/ *n* [C] *BrE* an order to join the army, navy etc【英】〔服兵役的〕征召令; DRAFT¹ (2) *AmE*【美】: *He got his call-up papers in July.* 他在7月收到征召入伍的命令。—see also 另见 **call up** (CALL¹)

cal·lus /ˈkæləs; ˈkæləs/ also 又作 **callosity** /kəˈlɑsətɪ; kəˈlɒsɪ̵ti/ *n* [C] an area of thick hard skin 硬皮, 老茧: *The rowers had calluses on their hands.* 桨手们的手上都长满了老茧。

3 **calm¹** /kɑm; kɑːm/ *adj* **1** quiet and without excitement, nervous activity, or strong feeling 镇静的, 沉着的; 心平气和的: *Richard spoke with calm authority.* 理查德讲话时沉着而威严。| *Keep calm, and try not to panic!* 沉住气, 别惊慌! **2** weather that is calm is not windy〔天气〕无风的 **3** a sea, lake etc that is calm is smooth or has only gentle waves〔海洋、湖泊等〕平静的, 风平浪静的 —**calmly** *adv* —**calmness** *n* [U]

calm² *n* [U] **1** a situation that is quiet and peaceful 平静; 安静; 宁静: *They remained on the terrace after dinner, enjoying the calm of the evening.* 晚餐后他们仍然坐在平台上, 享受着夜晚的宁静。**2 the calm before the storm** a calm peaceful situation before a big argument, problem etc 暴风雨前的平静

calm³ *v* [T] to make someone or something quiet after strong emotion or nervous activity 使平静; 使安静; 使镇定: *Charlie tried to calm the frightened children.* 查利努力安抚受惊吓的孩子们。

calm (sb/sth ↔) **down** *phr v* [I,T] to become quiet after strong emotion or nervous activity, or make someone or something become quiet (使)平静(下来); (使)镇定: *Calm down and tell me what happened.* 冷静点儿, 告诉我发生了什么事。

Cal·or gas /ˈkælɚ gæs; ˈkælə gæs/ *n* [U] *BrE trademark* a type of gas that is sold in metal containers and used where there is no gas supply【英, 商标】液化气

cal·o·rie /ˈkælərɪ; ˈkæləri/ *n* [C] **1** a unit for measuring the amount of ENERGY that food will produce 卡(路里)〔食物的热量单位〕: *An average potato has about 90 calories.* 一个普通的马铃薯含有大约90卡路里。| *a calorie-controlled diet* 控制热量的饮食 | *Burn off the calories with this new exercise bike.* 使用这新买的健身自行车把热量消耗掉。**2** *technical* the amount of heat that is needed to raise the temperature of one gram of water by one degree centigrade【术语】卡路里〔热量单位, 即将一克水的温度提升一摄氏度所需要的热量〕**3 count your calories** to control your weight, especially by calculating the number of calories you eat〔尤指通过计算自己的卡路里摄取量来〕控制体重

cal·o·rif·ic /,kæləˈrɪfɪk; ,kæləˈrɪfɪk◂/ *adj* **1** food that is calorific tends to make you fat〔食物〕含热量的, 使人发胖的 **2** *technical* producing heat【术语】产生热量的

Cal Tech California Institute of Technology; a respected university in Pasadena, California, near Los Angeles. It is known for its high quality teaching and research in science subjects. 加利福尼亚理工学院〔美国一所久负盛名的大学。位于加利福尼亚州的帕萨迪纳, 靠近洛杉矶市。以高水平的理工科教学与研究著称〕

ca·lum·ni·ate /kəˈlʌmnɪ,et; kəˈlʌmni-eɪt/ *v* [T] *formal* to say untrue and unfair things about someone; SLANDER²【正式】诬蔑, 诽谤, 中伤

cal·um·ny /ˈkæləmnɪ; ˈkæləmni/ *n* **1** [C] an untrue and unfair statement about someone intended to give people a bad opinion of them 诬蔑, 诽谤, 诬陷之词 **2** [U] the act of saying things like this 中伤 —see also 另见 SLANDER¹

Cal·va·ry /ˈkælvərɪ; ˈkælvəri/ the Roman name for the place near Jerusalem where, according to the Bible, Jesus Christ died by being crucified (CRUCIFY). Its Aramaic name was Golgotha. 髑髅地〔耶路撒冷附近一地的罗马语名称。据《圣经》记载, 此地为耶稣受难处, 阿拉姆语称各各他〕

calvary *n* [C] a model that represents the death of Jesus Christ 耶稣受难像

calve /kæv; kɑːv/ *v* [I] to give birth to a CALF (=young cow) 生小牛

calves /kævz; kɑːvz/ *n* the plural of CALF

Cal·vin /ˈkælvɪn; ˈkælvɪ̵n/, **John** (1509-64) a French Protestant leader and THEOLOGIAN (=someone who studies religion and religious beliefs), whose ideas strongly influenced the Reformation (=the time when many Christians left the Catholic religion and started the Protestant religion) 加尔文〔(1509-1564), 法国新教领袖、神学家。他的思想对宗教改革运动产生了极大影响〕—see also 另见 CALVINISM

Cal·vin·is·m /ˈkælvɪnɪzəm; ˈkælvɪ̵nɪzəm/ *n* [U] the Christian religious teachings of John Calvin, based on the idea that events on Earth are controlled by God and cannot be changed by humans〔基督教〕加尔文教[主]义〔是其创始人约翰·加尔文的教条, 根据此种思想, 地球上发生的一切都由上帝控制, 人类无法左右〕

Cal·vin·ist /ˈkælvɪnɪst; ˈkælvɪ̵nɪ̵st/ *adj* **1** following the teachings of CALVINISM 加尔文教派的, 追随加尔文主义的 **2** also 又作 **Calvinistic** /,kælvəˈnɪstɪk; ,kælvɪ̵ˈnɪstɪk◂/ having severe moral standards and tending to disapprove of pleasure; PURITANICAL 清教主义的, 道德观念十分严格的 —**Calvinist** *n* [C]

ca·lyp·so /kəˈlɪpso; kəˈlɪpsəʊ/ *n* [C] a West Indian song based on subjects of interest in the news "卡利普索"即兴歌曲〔起源于西印度群岛, 以时事为主题〕

ca·lyx /ˈkelɪks; ˈkeɪlɪks/ *n plural* **calyxes** or **calyces** [C] the green outer part of a flower that protects it before it opens 花萼

cam /kæm; kæm/ *n* [C] a wheel or part of a wheel that is shaped to change circular movement into backwards and forwards movement 凸轮

ca·ma·ra·de·rie /,kɑməˈrɑdərɪ; ,kæməˈrɑːdəri/ *n* [U] friendliness between people who like each other or work together as part of a group 同志[同事]情谊, 友情: *camaraderie of soldiers in the trenches* 士兵们在战壕里建立的情谊

Ca·margue, the /kæˈmɑrg; kæˈmɑːg/ a flat area in southern France at the DELTA of the River Rhône. It is a national park and is famous for its white horses and its large variety of wild animals, especially birds. 卡马尔格〔法国南部罗纳河三角洲一平坦地区。它是法国一个国家公园, 以白马及种类繁多的野生动物, 尤其是鸟类而闻名〕

cam·ber /ˈkæmbɚ; ˈkæmbə/ *n* [C,U] *technical* a slight curve from the centre to the side of a road or other surface that makes water run off to the side【术语】〔道路或其他表面的〕中凸形, 拱势〔中间高两边低的弯度, 以使水向两边流〕

Cam·bo·di·a /kæmˈbodɪə; kæmˈbəʊdiə/ a country in southeast Asia between Thailand and Vietnam. Population: 12,492,000 (2001). Capital: Phnom Penh. Its former name was Kampuchea. 柬埔寨〔东南亚一国家, 位于泰国和越南之间。人口: 12,492,000 (2001), 首都: 金边。该国旧称 Kampuchea〕—**Cambodian** *n, adj*

Cam·bri·an Moun·tains, the /,kæmbrɪən ˈmaʊntn̩z; ,kæmbriən ˈmaʊntɪ̵nz/ a group of mountains that go from north to south through the middle of Wales 坎布里亚山脉〔威尔士中部南北走向的一条山脉〕

cam·bric /ˈkembrɪk; ˈkeɪmbrɪk/ *n* [U] thin white cloth made of LINEN (2) or cotton 细白棉布, 麻纱

Cam·bridge /ˈkembrɪdʒ; ˈkeɪmbrɪdʒ/ **1** a city in eastern England next to the River Cam, which is famous for its old university 剑桥〔英格兰东部一城市。濒临卡姆河, 以历史悠久的剑桥大学而闻名〕**2 Cambridge University** one of the two oldest and most respected universities in the UK, established in the 13th century 剑桥大学〔建于13世纪, 英国历史最悠久、最负盛名的两所大学之一〕: *Several government ministers went to Cambridge* (=were students there). 有好几位政府部长曾在剑桥大学就读。| *a Cambridge graduate* 一位剑桥大学毕业生 —see also 另见 OXFORD **3** a city in East Massachusetts, US, which is next to the Charles River and across from Boston. Harvard University, Radcliffe College, and MIT are all in Cambridge. 坎布里奇〔美国马萨诸塞州东部一城市。濒临查尔斯河, 与波士顿相望。当地有哈佛大学、拉德克利夫学院和麻省理工学院〕

Cambridge Cer·tif·i·cate, the /,· · ˈ· · ·/ an examination in the English language for speakers of other languages, set by the University of Cambridge Local Examinations Syndicate (UCLES) 剑桥英语证书〔剑桥大学地方考试评议会特别委员会针对讲其他语言的人而设置的一种英语语言考试〕

Cam·bridge·shire /ˈkembrɪdʒʃə; ˈkeɪmbrɪdʒʃə/ a COUNTY in eastern England whose main town is Cambridge 剑桥郡〔英格兰东部一郡，首府为剑桥市〕

cam·cor·der /ˈkæm,kɔrdə; ˈkæm,kɔːdə/ *n* [C] a VIDEO camera and recorder in one machine, that you can carry around 手提摄录机

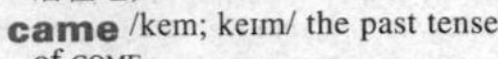

camcorder 手提摄录机

Cam·den /ˈkæmdən; ˈkæmdən/ a BOROUGH in North London which is a fashionable place to live 卡姆登〔伦敦北部一自治区，为时尚人士居住地〕

came /kem; keɪm/ the past tense of COME

cam·el /ˈkæml; ˈkæməl/ *n* [C] a large desert animal with a long neck and either one or two HUMPS (=large raised parts) on its back 骆驼

cam·el·hair /ˈkæmḷhɛr; ˈkæməlheə/ *n* [U] a thick yellowish brown cloth usually used for making coats 驼绒，骆驼呢

ca·mel·li·a /kəˈmiliə; kəˈmiːliə/ *n* [C] a red, pink, or white flower like a rose 山茶（花）

Cam·e·lot /ˈkæməlɑt; ˈkæməlɒt/ according to old stories about King Arthur, the place where Arthur and his knights lived 卡米洛〔古老的亚瑟王传奇中，亚瑟及其骑士的居住之地〕

cam·em·bert /ˈkæməm,bɛr; ˈkæməmbeə/ *n* [C,U] a small round French cheese, that is white outside and yellow inside 卡门贝干酪〔产于法国的外白内黄的小圆形干酪〕

cam·e·o /ˈkæmɪ,o; ˈkæmi-əʊ/ *n plural* **cameos** [C] **1** a short appearance in a film or play by a well-known actor〔由名演员演的〕电影[戏剧]片段: *Denholm Eliot in a cameo role as a butler* 德诺姆·艾略特在一个片段中饰演管家的角色 **2** a small piece of jewellery with a raised figure or shape fixed to a flat surface of a different colour 多彩浮雕宝石 **3** a short piece of writing that gives a clear idea of a person, place, or event〔对人物、地方、事件的〕特写；小品

camera 照相机

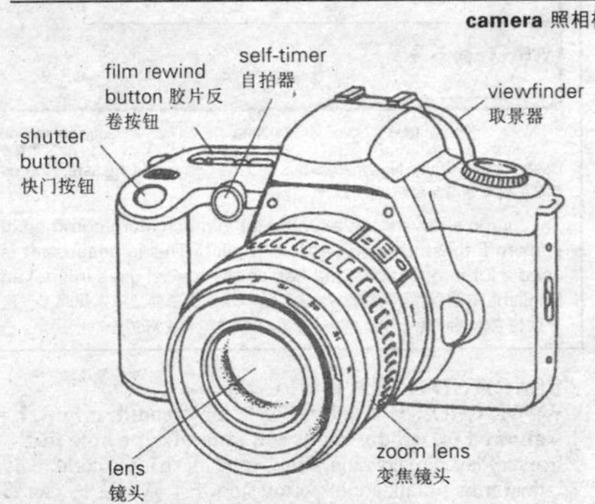

2 3 **cam·e·ra** /ˈkæmərə; ˈkæmərə/ *n* [C] **1** a piece of equipment used to take photographs or moving pictures 照相机；摄影机 **2** the part of the equipment used for making television pictures that changes images into electrical signals（电视）摄像机 **3 in camera** a law case that is held in camera takes place secretly or privately〔诉讼案〕不公开审理地，秘密地，私下地

cam·e·ra·man /ˈkæmərə,mæn; ˈkæmərəmən/ *n* [C] someone who operates a camera for films or television〔电影或电视的〕摄影师

camera-shy /ˈ· · · ,·/ *adj* not liking to have your photograph taken 不喜欢照相的

Cam·e·roon, Cameroun /,kæməˈrun; ,kæməˈruːn/ a country in West Africa, east of Nigeria and next to the Gulf of Guinea. Population: 15,803,000 (2001). Capital: Yaoundé. 喀麦隆〔西非国家，位于尼日利亚以西，濒临几内亚湾。人口：15,803,000 (2001)，首都：雅温得〕—**Cameroonian** *n, adj*

cam·i·knick·ers /ˈkæmɪ,nɪkəz; ˈkæmi,nɪkəz/ *n* [plural] *BrE* a piece of women's underwear that combines CAMISOLE and KNICKERS【英】〔女装〕连裤紧身内衣

cam·i·sole /ˈkæmə,sol; ˈkæmɪsəʊl/ *n* [C] a short piece of women's underwear worn on the top half of the body〔女装〕短内衣，贴身胸衣 —see picture at 参见 UNDERWEAR 图

cam·o·mile, chamomile /ˈkæmə,maɪl; ˈkæməmaɪl/ *n* [C,U] a plant with small white and yellow flowers that are sometimes used to make tea 洋甘菊，春黄菊: *camomile tea* 甘菊茶

cam·ou·flage¹ /ˈkæmə,flɑʒ; ˈkæməflɑːʒ/ *n* **1** the way in which the colour or shape of something makes it difficult to see in the place where it lives 伪装: *The insect's colour provides camouflage from its enemies.* 该昆虫的颜色为其提供了躲避天敌的伪装。**2** a way of hiding something, especially a military object, using branches, paint etc〔尤指军事目标的〕伪装: *anti-aircraft camouflage netting* 防空伪装网 **3** behaviour that is designed to hide something 伪装，掩饰: *Aggression is often a camouflage for insecurity.* 侵略常常是缺乏安全感的掩饰。

camouflage² *v* [T] to hide something by making it look the same as the things around it, or by making it seem like something else〔用伪装〕遮掩，掩饰: *The trucks were well camouflaged with branches.* 卡车都用树枝妥善地遮掩起来。| *symptoms of illness camouflaged by other factors* 被其他因素掩盖的疾病症状

camp¹ /kæmp; kæmp/ *n* **1** [C,U] a place where people stay in temporary shelters, such as tents, usually for a short time 营地: *Let's go back to the camp – it's getting dark.* 我们回营地吧，天快黑了。| **break camp** (=take down a tent or shelter you have been using) 撤营，拔营 **2 prison/labour etc camp** a place where people are kept for a particular reason, when they do not want to be there 战俘营/劳改营等: *a refugee camp* 难民营 —see also 另见 CONCENTRATION CAMP **3** [C,U] a place where young people go to relax and take part in activities, often as members of an organization〔青少年的〕活动营地，度假营地: *scout camp* 童子军营地 | *summer camp* 夏令营 —see also 另见 DAY CAMP, HOLIDAY CAMP **4** [C] a group of people or organizations who have the same ideas or principles, especially in politics〔尤指政治上的〕阵营，派别，集团: *the extreme right-wing camp of the party* 该党的极右翼派别

camp² *v* [I] **1** to set up a tent or shelter and stay there for a short time 扎营，宿营，露营: *We'll camp by the river for the night, and move on tomorrow.* 我们今晚在河边宿营，明天继续前进。| *camping equipment* 露营装备 **2 go camping** to visit an area and stay in a tent 去露营: *We went camping in the mountains last weekend.* 上周末我们到山里露营。

camp out *phr v* [I] **1** to sleep outdoors, usually in a tent〔通常指在帐篷里〕露宿 **2** to stay somewhere where you do not have all the usual things that a house has〔在不具备基本住宿条件的地方〕勉强暂住: *We'll just have to camp out until our furniture arrives.* 在家具运到之前，我们只好对付着住一下了。

camp sth ↔ **up** *phr v* [T] *informal* to deliberately behave in a funny, unnatural way, with too much movement or expression【非正式】做出夸张的举动

camp³ *adj informal*【非正式】**1** a man who is camp moves or speaks in the way that people used to think was typical of HOMOSEXUALS〔男子〕举止言行像同性恋的；娘娘腔的 **2** clothes, decorations etc that are camp are very strange, bright, or unusual〔衣服、装饰等〕稀奇古怪的: *Only you could get away with wearing that outfit – it's so camp!* 只有你才会穿上那套行头——它看上去十分古怪！

cam·paign¹ /kæmˈpen; kæmˈpeɪn/ *n* [C] **1** a series of actions intended to achieve a particular result, especially in politics or business〔尤指政治或商业性的为取得某个结果的〕运动；（宣传）活动: **[+for]** *a campaign for equal rights* 争取平等权利的运动 | **[+against]** *educational campaigns against smoking* 反吸烟的教育运动 | *an advertising campaign* 广告宣传活动 **2** a series of battles, attacks etc intended to achieve a particular result in a war〔军事〕战役

campaign² *v* [I] to lead or take part in a series of actions intended to achieve a particular result 发起[参加]〔旨在获得某种效果的〕运动: **[+for/against]** *a group campaigning against the destruction of the rainforests* 发起反对毁坏雨林运动的团体 —**campaigner** *n* [C]

Campaign for Nu·cle·ar Dis·ar·ma·ment /,· · · · · · · · · · · ·/ *n* [singular] the CND

cam·pa·ni·le /,kæmpəˈnili; ,kæmpəˈniːli/ *n* [C] a high bell tower that is usually separate from any other building〔通常与其他建筑分立的〕钟楼

cam·pa·nol·o·gy /,kæmpəˈnɑlədʒɪ; ,kæmpəˈnɒlədʒi/ *n* [U] the skill of ringing bells 鸣钟术 —**campanologist** *n* [C]

Cam·pa·ri /kæmˈpɑrɪ; kæmˈpɑːri/ *trademark* a bitter red alcoholic drink often drunk before a meal【商标】金巴利开胃酒〔一种常在餐前饮用的红色苦味酒〕

camp bed /,· ˈ·/ *n* [C] *especially BrE* a light, narrow bed that folds flat and is easy to carry【尤英】行军床；折叠床；露营床；COT (2) *AmE*【美】—see picture at 参见 BED¹ 图

Camp Da·vid /ˌ· ˈ··/ the country home of the US President, where the President goes to relax. People remember it especially for the Camp David Agreement, which established peace between Egypt and Israel and was signed at Camp David in 1979. 戴维营〔美国总统的别墅。埃及和以色列 1979 年在此签署了以实现和平为目的的《戴维营协议》，它尤因此事出名〕

camp·er /ˈkæmpɚ; ˈkæmpə/ *n* [C] **1** someone who is staying in a tent or shelter 露营者 **2** *AmE* a sort of room fitted onto or pulled behind a large vehicle that has cooking equipment and beds in it【美】〔食宿用具俱全的〕野营车 **3 happy camper** *spoken* someone who seems to be happy with their situation【口】满足于现状者

Campese, David (1962-), an Australian RUGBY union player who has scored more tries (TRY²) in international games than any other player. 卡普斯〔(1962-)，澳大利亚橄榄球联合会运动员，在国际橄榄球比赛中得分最多〕

camp·fire /ˈkæmpˌfaɪr; ˈkæmpfaɪə/ *n* [C] a fire made outdoors by people who are camping 营火，篝火

Camp Fire /ˈ· ·/ an organization in the US for girls and boys, which teaches them practical skills and helps them develop their character 营火团〔美国一少年组织，该组织给其成员传授实用技能，帮助他们培养品性〕

camp fol·low·er /ˈ·, ˌ···/ *n* [C] **1** someone who supports an organization or a political party, but who is not actually a member of the main group〔党派组织的〕追随者，附和者 **2** someone who was not a soldier but who followed an army from place to place to provide services, especially in the past〔尤指旧时〕随军提供服务的平民

camp·ground /ˈkæmpˌgraʊnd; ˈkæmpgraʊnd/ *n* [C] *AmE* an area where people can camp, that often has a water supply and toilets【美】〔有供水和厕所的〕(野)营地；CAMPSITE *BrE*【英】

cam·phor /ˈkæmfɚ; ˈkæmfə/ *n* [U] a white substance with a strong smell, that is used especially to keep insects away 樟脑

camp rob·ber /ˈ·, ˌ··/ *n* [C] a grey North American bird that does not seem afraid of people and often flies away with food 灰噪鸦〔北美洲一种常叼走食物、不怕人的鸟〕

camp·site /ˈkæmpˌsaɪt; ˈkæmpsaɪt/ *n* [C] **1** *BrE* an area where people can camp, that often has a water supply and toilets【英】〔有供水和厕所的〕(野)营地；CAMPGROUND *AmE*【美】**2** *AmE* a place, usually within a CAMPGROUND, where one person or group can camp【美】〔野营地内可供一人或一群人使用的〕扎营地

camp·stool /ˈkæmpˌstul; ˈkæmpstuːl/ *n* [C] a small folding seat with no back 轻便折凳

cam·pus /ˈkæmpəs; ˈkæmpəs/ *n* **1** the land and buildings of a university or college〔大学或学院的〕校园 **2 big man on campus** *AmE* someone who is well-known for being involved in a lot of student activities, and thinks they are important because of this【美】校园大人物〔指因参与许多学生活动而闻名者〕

cam·shaft /ˈkæmˌʃæft; ˈkæmʃɑːft/ *n* [C] a metal bar that a CAM is fastened to in an engine 凸轮轴

Ca·mus /kæˈmju; kæˈmjuː/, **Al·bert** /ˈælbɛr; ˈælbeə/ (1913-60) a French EXISTENTIALIST writer and PHILOSOPHER who believed that life has no meaning, but that people can still be happy. His most famous NOVELS are *L'Étranger* (1942) and *La Peste* (1948). 加缪〔(1913-1960)，法国存在主义作家、哲学家。他认为，人生毫无意义，但人们仍然可以过得很快乐。最著名的小说为《局外人》(1942) 和《鼠疫》(1948)〕

can¹ /kən; kn; *strong* 强读 kæn; kæn/ *v* [modal verb] **1** to be able to 能，有能力：*He's so tall he can touch the ceiling.* 他那么高，手能碰到天花板。| *This machine can perform two million calculations per second.* 这台机器每秒能够运算 200 万次。| *I can't remember where I put it.* 我不记得把它放在哪里了。| *They have everything that money can buy.* 他们拥有金钱所能买到的一切。| *The police still haven't found her, but they're doing all they can.* 警方还没有找到她，但是正在尽一切努力去做。**2** *spoken* used when asking someone to do something or give you something【口】〔用于拜托、请求〕可以…吗？能…吗？：*Can I have a cigarette please?* 能给我一支香烟吗？| *Can you help me lift this box?* 你能帮我抬起这个箱子吗？**3** *especially spoken* to have permission to do something or to be allowed to do something【尤口】允许，可以：*You can't play football here.* 你们不可以在这里踢足球。| *"Can we go home now please?" "No you can't."* "我们现在可以回家了吗？" "不，不可以。" | *The goalkeeper can't handle the ball outside the penalty area.* (=it is against the rules) 守门员不可以在罚球区外用手触球。**4** to have a particular skill or know how to do a particular activity 懂得，会：*Gabriella can speak French, Russian, and Italian.* 卡布里拉会说法语、俄语和意大利语。| *Can you drive?* 你会开车吗？**5** used to show what is possible or likely 有可能，会：*I am confident that a solution can be found.* 我有信心会找到解决的办法。| *There can be no doubt that he is guilty.* 他有罪，这是毋庸置疑的。| *The word "bank" can have several different meanings.* bank 这个词可有几种不同的意思。| *Can he still be alive after all this time?* 过了这么长的时间，他还可能活着吗？**6** used with verbs connected with the five senses and with verbs connected with thinking〔与表示感官和思维的动词连用〕：*I can hear you easily from here.* 从这里我可以很容易听到你说话。| *You can really taste the garlic in that soup.* 你确实可以尝出汤里的大蒜味儿。| *I can't understand why you're so upset.* 我不明白你为什么如此不安。| *You can imagine how annoyed she was!* 你可以想象出她有多恼怒！**7** [usually in questions and negatives 一般用于疑问句和否定句] used especially when you think there is only one possible answer to a question or one possible thing to do in a particular situation 只能：*Jill's left her husband but can you blame her after the way he treated her?* 吉尔离开了丈夫，但在她丈夫那样对待她之后，你能责怪她吗？| *It's a very kind offer, but I really can't accept it.* 这个提议很好，但我真的不能接受。**8** to have to do something; must 必须，不得不：*If you won't keep quiet you can get out!* 如果你不保持安静，那就只好请你出去了！**9** used especially in expressions of surprise〔尤用于表示惊讶〕究竟…；可能…吗？：*What can it possibly be?* 这究竟是什么呢？| *You can't be serious!* 你不会是认真的吧！| *They can't have arrived already surely!* 他们绝对不可能已经到了！**10** used to show what sometimes happens or how someone sometimes behaves〔用于表示偶尔的可能性〕有时可能会：*It can be quite cold here at night.* 这里夜间有时可能很冷。| *Gerard can be annoying, I know.* 我知道，杰勒德有时会令人相当讨厌的。

Frequencies of the verb **can** in spoken and written English
动词 can 在英语口语和书面语中的使用频率

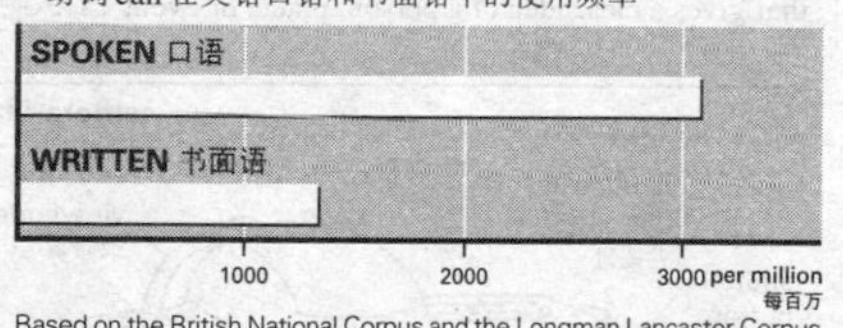

Based on the British National Corpus and the Longman Lancaster Corpus
据英国国家语料库和朗文兰开斯特语料库

This graph shows that the verb **can** is much more common in spoken English than in written English. This is because it is used a lot in questions and has some special uses in spoken English. 本图表显示动词 can 在英语口语中比书面语中常见得多。这是因为它大量使用于疑问句中，而且在英语口语中有某些特别用法。

USAGE NOTE 用法说明：CAN

WORD CHOICE 词语辨析：**can, may, could, might, be allowed to, let, do/would you mind if..., be able to**

In everyday conversation, **can** is used much more commonly than **may** to talk about permission. 在日常会话中，can 要比 may 更常用于表示许可：*You can go now* (=you are allowed to go). 你现在可以走了〔=你被允许离开〕。Some people say that **may** is more correct, however, its use tends to be limited to formal contexts. When talking about permission in the past, people often use **was/were allowed to** or change the sentence and use **let**. 有人说 may 较正确，不过它的用法多局限于正式的语体。当谈论过去的许可时，人们经常使用 was/were allowed to 或者改变句子而使用 let：*He was allowed to leave at ten.* 他获准 10 点钟离开。| *I let him leave at ten* (=I allowed him to go and he did). 我让他 10 点钟离开〔=我允许他离开，然后他也这么做了〕。When you are asking permission, **could** (also **might**, especially in American English) is often used instead of **can**, because it seems less direct and more polite. 当你要求得到许可时，经常用 could〔might 亦可，尤其在美国英语中〕而不用 can，这是因为它似乎不那么直截了当，而且较为礼貌：*Could I borrow your car?* 我可以借用你的汽车吗？**May** is more formal, and is used especially by officials. For example at an airport. may 较为正式，而且尤其常被官员使用。例如在机场时：*May I see your passport, madam?* 夫人，我可以看一下你的护照吗？In everyday English people often say **Do/would you mind if...** or **Is it alright if...** when asking permission. 在日常

英语中要求得到许可时，人们常说 Do/would you mind if… 或 Is it alright if…: *Do you mind if I smoke?* 我抽烟你介意吗？

Can is also used to say that you have the ability to do something. can 还用于表示你具有做某事的能力: *I can swim now* (=I am able to swim). 我现在会游泳了。To talk about something you will have the ability to do in the future, you use **will be able to** 谈论将来有能力做某事时，要用 will be able to: *I'll be able to speak better if I practise more.* 我如果多练习，就会讲得更好。For past ability either **could** or **was/were able to** is used, but sometimes with slightly different meaning. 对于过去的能力，要使用 could 或者 was/were able to，不过有时意义上略有差别。**Could** often suggests more someone's ability that they had for some time (but perhaps did not use). could 较多地用于表示某人在某时期内拥有的能力〔不过也许不一定使用〕: *I could swim when I was eight* (=I knew how to). 我八岁时就会游泳〔=我懂得怎么游〕。| *She couldn't buy a ticket* (=She didn't have enough money). 她无法购票〔=她没有足够的钱〕。**Was/were able to** may suggest more that the situation allowed someone to do something (perhaps with effort). was/were able to 可能较多地用于表示当时的情况允许某人做某事〔也许要付出努力〕: *By arriving at two I was able to swim for an hour* (=The pool was open long enough to allow this). 由于我两点钟到达，得以游了一个小时〔=游泳池开放时间足够长，允许这么做〕。| *I wasn't able to buy a ticket* (=There were none left/I didn't manage to get one). 我没有买到票〔=没有票了/我没能买到〕。**Used to be able to** is used to talk about something that you could do before, but can no longer do now. used to be able to 用于谈论过去能够做到但是现在已无法再做到的事: *He used to be able to run a 100 metres in under 10 seconds, but he's getting a bit old these days.* 他过去能在 10 秒内跑完 100 米，但是如今他有点儿老了。

When you are talking about something that is not certain, you often use **may**, or, with more doubt, **might** or **could**. 谈论不确定的某事时，常用 may，或者有更多疑问时，常用 might 或 could: *The road may/might/could be blocked* (=Perhaps/It is possible the road is blocked). 道路可能被封锁了。| *The road could be blocked* (=It is possible to block the road). 可以把道路封锁起来。For past time **may have/might have/could have** are used 对于过去的时间，则使用 may have/might have/could have: *There may have been an accident* (=Perhaps there was an accident). 可能发生了一些事故。*Might* or *could have* would be more often used here when we now know that there was no accident. 在知道没有发生过事故时，might 或 could have 更为常用。

Can is usually used to ask whether something is possible. can 通常用来询问某事是否可能: *Can this really be true?* (=Is it possible this is true?) 这事会是真的吗？and to say that something is not possible 而且也用来表示某事是不可能的: *That can't be true.* 那不可能是真的。Again **could** shows more doubt (and is commoner in American English) 同样地，could 表示较大的疑问〔而且在美国英语中较常见〕: *Could that really be true?* 那事会是真的吗？

Can is often used with verbs related to the senses and the mind, such as *see, hear, feel, believe.* can 经常和诸如 see, hear, feel, believe 等与感官以及思想有关的动词连用: *Look at this photo – can you see somebody famous in it?* 看看这张照片，你能看到一些名人吗？

GRAMMAR 语法

Remember **can, could, may** and **might** are NEVER used with the *to* infinitive of a verb. 记住，can, could, may 和 might 从不与带 to 的动词不定式连用: *I can help you* (NOT 不用 *I can to help you*). 我可以帮你。

S 2 **can²** /kæn; kæn/ *n* [C] **1** a metal container in which food or drink is preserved without air 罐: *a Coke can* 可乐罐 | **[+of]** *All we've got is a couple of cans of soup.* 我们所拥有的不过是几听罐头汤。—see picture at 参见 CONTAINER 图 **2** a special metal container that keeps the liquid inside it under pressure, releasing it as a SPRAY² (1) when you press the button on the lid〔特制的压力〕喷罐: *a can of hairspray* 一罐喷发胶 **3** *especially AmE* a metal container with a lid that can be removed, used for holding liquid【尤美】有盖金属圆罐[桶]: *Two large cans of paint ought to be enough.* 两大桶油漆应该够了。**4 can of worms** a very complicated situation that causes a lot of problems when you start to deal with it 极为棘手[困难、麻烦]的局面: *I just don't know what to do – every solution I can think of would just open up a whole new can of worms.* 我不知道该怎么办 —— 每个我能想到的解决方案只会开启一个全新的棘手的局面而已。**5 in the can** *informal* a film that is in the can is complete and ready to be shown【非正式】〔影片〕已拍摄好随时可放映的 **6 the can** *slang*【俚】**a)** a prison 监狱 **b)** *AmE* a toilet【美】厕所 —see also 另见 **carry the can** (CARRY¹ (31))

can³ *v* **canned, canning** [T] *especially AmE*【尤美】**1** to preserve food by putting it into a metal container from which all the air is removed 制成罐头 —see also 另见 CANNED (1) **2** *AmE informal* to dismiss someone from a job; SACK² (1)【美，非正式】解雇，开除 **3 can it!** *AmE spoken* used to tell someone to stop talking or making noise【美口】闭嘴！

C

Ca·na /ˈkenə; ˈkeɪnə/ according to the Bible, an ancient town in Galilee where Jesus performed his first MIRACLE, in which he changed water into wine 迦拿〔《圣经》中位于加利利的一座古镇，是耶稣首次行神迹将水变成酒的地方〕

Ca·naan /ˈkenən; ˈkeɪnən/ the name for ancient Palestine which, according to the Bible, God promised to Abraham and his people. Because of this, Canaan is also called the 'Promised Land'. 迦南〔古巴勒斯坦名。据《圣经》记载，上帝把该地应许给亚伯拉罕及其后裔，故也称作"应许之地"〕

Can·a·da /ˈkænədə; ˈkænədə/ a country in North America, north of the US, which is made up of ten PROVINCES. Population: 31,593,000 (2001). Capital: Ottawa. Canada is the second largest country in the world. 加拿大〔北美一国家，为世界第二大国。位于美国以北，由 10 个省组成。人口: 31,593,000 (2001)，首都: 渥太华〕—see also 另见 QUEBEC

Ca·na·di·an ba·con /kəˌnedɪən ˈbekən; kəˌneɪdiən ˈbeɪkən/ *n* [U] *AmE* meat from the back or sides of a pig, served in thin, narrow pieces【美】加拿大式熏猪肉; BACON *BrE*【英】

ca·nal /kəˈnæl; kəˈnæl/ *n* [C] **1** a passage dug out of the ground, either to connect two areas of water so boats can travel between them, or to bring or remove water from somewhere 运河: *the Panama Canal* 巴拿马运河 **2** a passage in the body of a person or animal〔人或动物体内的〕管，道 —see also 另见 ALIMENTARY CANAL

canal boat /·ˈ· ·/ *n* [C] a long narrow boat that is used on a canal 运河船〔行驶于运河上的狭长船只〕

Can·a·let·to /ˌkænḷˈɛto; ˌkænəˈletəʊ/, **An·to·ni·o** /ænˈtonɪo; æˈtəʊniəʊ/ (1697-1768) an Italian painter, famous for his paintings of Venice and of the River Thames in London 卡纳莱托〔(1697-1768)，意大利画家，以描绘威尼斯和伦敦泰晤士河而闻名〕

can·a·lize also 又作 **-ise** *BrE*【英】/ˈkænḷˌaɪz; ˈkænəl-aɪz/ *v* [T] **1** *formal* to direct the actions, energy, etc of a person or group to one particular purpose; CHANNEL² (1)【正式】把…纳入〔某种轨道〕; 把…引向某一目标 **2** to make a river deeper, straighter etc, especially in order to prevent flooding 挖深[修直、加宽]河道 —**canalization** /kəˌnæləˈzeʃən; ˌkænəlaɪˈzeɪʃən/ *n* [U]

can·a·pé /ˈkænəpɪ; ˈkænəpeɪ/ *n* [C] a small piece of bread with cheese, meat, fish, etc on it, served with drinks at a party〔加有乳酪、肉、鱼等的〕小片面包〔通常在聚会上配饮料食用〕

ca·nard /kəˈnɑrd; kæˈnɑːd/ *n* [C] *French* a deliberately false report or piece of news【法】谣传，谎报; 假新闻

ca·nar·y /kəˈnɛrɪ; kəˈneəri/ *n* [C] a small yellow bird that sings and is often kept as a pet 金丝雀

Ca·na·ry Is·lands, the /·ˈ··, ·ˈ·/ also 又作 **the Canaries** a group of islands near northwest Africa which belong to Spain and are popular with tourists 加那利群岛〔位于非洲西北部附近海域，西班牙属地，著名旅游胜地〕

Canary Wharf /·ˌ·· ˈ·/ part of the Docklands area in East London, which includes Canary Wharf Tower, the tallest building in the UK, and many other large office buildings 加那利码头〔伦敦东部码头区的一部分，其中有英国最高建筑加那利码头大厦，以及其他许多办公大楼〕

ca·nas·ta /kəˈnæstə; kəˈnæstə/ *n* [U] a card game in which two sets of cards are used 凯纳斯特纸牌戏〔用两副纸牌一起玩的牌戏〕

Can·ber·ra /ˈkænbərə; ˈkænbərə/ the capital city of Australia 堪培拉〔澳大利亚首都〕

can·can /ˈkænkæn; ˈkænkæn/ *n* [C] a fast dance from France danced by women in a show in which they kick their legs high into the air 康康舞〔由女子表演的、把腿高高踢起的一种法国快节奏舞蹈〕—see picture on the next page 见下页图

cancan 康康舞

2 **can·cel** /ˈkænsl; ˈkænsəl/ *v* **cancelled, cancelling** *BrE*【英】**canceled, canceling** *AmE*【美】[T] **1** to arrange that a planned activity or event will not now happen 取消: *The football game had been cancelled due to rain.* 足球比赛因下雨取消。**2** to end an agreement or arrangement that exists in law 中止〔协议、安排等〕; 废除: *I've cancelled my subscription to the magazine.* 我已停止订阅那本杂志。

cancel sth ↔ **out** *phr v* [T] to have an equal but opposite effect on something, so that a situation does not change 抵销; 中和: *The losses in our overseas division have cancelled out this year's profits.* 我们海外分部的亏损抵销了今年的盈利。

can·cel·la·tion /ˌkænsəˈleʃən; ˌkænsəˈleɪʃən/ *n* [C,U] a decision or statement that a planned or regular activity will not happen 取消, 作废: *The restaurant is fully booked for tonight, but sometimes there are cancellations.* 这家餐厅今天晚上全订满了, 但有时会有取消订桌的。

Can·cer /ˈkænsɚ; ˈkænsə/ *n* **1** [singular] the fourth sign of the ZODIAC represented by a CRAB[1] (1), and believed to affect the character and life of people born between June 22 and July 22 巨蟹座 **2** [C] someone who was born between June 22 and July 22 出生于巨蟹座时段的人〔即在6月22日至7月22日之间出生的人〕

2
2 **cancer** *n* **1** [C,U] a very serious disease in which cells in one part of the body start to grow in a way that is not normal, often causing death 癌(症): *Smoking causes lung cancer.* 吸烟引起肺癌。| *cancer of the jaw* 颚[颌]癌 **2** [C] an activity that is increasing, and causes a lot of harm 弊病, 社会恶习: *Corruption is the cancer of society.* 贪污腐败是社会的毒瘤。—**cancerous** *adj*: *a cancerous growth* 癌性瘤状物

can·de·la·brum /ˌkændḷˈebrəm; ˌkændɨˈlɑːbrəm/ *n* [C] a decorative holder for several candles or lamps〔可插数支蜡烛或灯泡的〕装饰性烛[灯]台

can·did /ˈkændɪd; ˈkændɨd/ *adj* directly truthful, even when the truth may be unpleasant or embarassing 坦诚的, 率直的; 直言不讳的: *The Governor's brutally candid assessment struck a new blow to Mr Major's reputation.* 州长无情的直率评价对梅杰先生的声誉是一个新的打击。—see also 另见 CANDOUR —**candidly** *adv*

can·di·da /ˈkændɪdə; ˈkændɨdə/ *n* [U] *technical* a FUNGUS that causes an infection in the mouth and throat of children or in a woman's VAGINA; THRUSH[1] (2)【术语】念珠菌

can·di·da·cy /ˈkændɪdəsɪ; ˈkændɨdɨsi/ also 又作 **candidature** /ˈkændɪdətʃɚ; ˈkændɨdətʃə/ *especially BrE*【尤英】*n* [C, U] the position of being one of the people who are competing to be elected 候选人资格[身份]

2 **can·di·date** /ˈkændəˌdet; ˈkændɨdɨt/ *n* [C] **1** someone who is being considered for a job or is competing to be elected 候选人; 候补人: [**+for**] *They're interviewing three candidates for the post of sales manager.* 他们正在面试三个应征做销售经理的人选。**2** *especially BrE* someone who is taking an examination【尤英】应考人, 投考者 **3** a person, group, or idea that is suitable for something or likely to get something 极有可能有某结局的人[群体、观点等]: [**+for**] *You smoke, drink, and never get any exercise: you're a prime candidate for a heart attack!* 你又抽烟又喝酒, 可是从不做运动, 最有可能得心脏病!

Can·dide /kɑnˈdid; kɒnˈdiːd/ (1759) a book by the French writer Voltaire which is a SATIRE (=humorous criticism) on the belief that 'everything is for the best in the best of all possible worlds'. Candide is a young man who is taught to be an OPTIMIST, but his experiences show him how bad life is, and he decides that it is best to 'CULTIVATE (=look after) one's own garden'. 《老实人》〔(1759), 法国作家伏尔泰创作的小说, 讽刺“诸事皆完美”的信念。主人公康第德是一名年轻人, 受过乐观主义教育, 但他的亲身经历却表明, 人生难得如意。于是, 他决定最好还是去“打理自家的花园”〕

can·died /ˈkændɪd; ˈkændid/ *adj* [only before noun 仅用于名词前] boiled or baked in sugar as a means of preservation 糖渍的, 蜜饯的: *candied cherries* 蜜饯樱桃

can·dle /ˈkændḷ; ˈkændl/ *n* [C] **1** a round stick of WAX[1] (1) around a WICK (=piece of string) that is burnt to provide light 蜡烛 **2 can't hold a candle to** *informal* to be not as good as someone or something else【非正式】远逊于, 简直不能与…相比: *When it came to giving a good party, no one could hold a candle to the Andersons.* 说到举办一个好的聚会, 谁也比不上安德森夫妇。—see also 另见 **burn the candle at both ends** (BURN[1] (23)) 3

candle 蜡烛

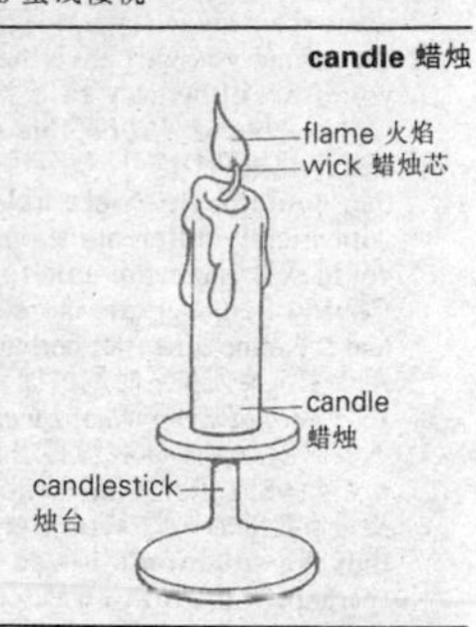

Candle in the Wind /ˈ· · · ˌ·/ a song originally written in 1973 and sung by Elton John. It was recorded again with different words in 1997, in memory of Diana, Princess of Wales, and it sold more copies than any other record ever made. 《风中之烛》〔埃尔顿·约翰初创于1973年并演唱的一首歌曲。1997年为纪念威尔士王妃戴安娜而重新填词录制, 成为有史以来销量最大的唱片〕

can·dle·light /ˈkændḷˌlaɪt; ˈkændl-laɪt/ *n* [U] the light produced when a candle burns 烛光

candle-lit /ˈ· · ·/ *adj* lit by candles 用烛光照明的: *a candle-lit dinner for two* 双人烛光晚餐

Can·dle·mas /ˈkændlmæs; ˈkændlmæs/ a Christian holy day, February 2nd, which celebrates when Jesus Christ was brought to the temple, and the PURIFICATION (=making pure) of his mother Mary 圣母行洁净礼日, 圣烛节〔2月2日的基督教圣日。纪念圣母马利亚把耶稣献给上帝以及前往圣殿行洁净礼之举〕

can·dle·stick /ˈkændḷˌstɪk; ˈkændlˌstɪk/ *n* [C] a specially shaped metal or wooden stick that you put a candle into 烛台 —see picture at 参见 CANDLE 图

can·dle·wick /ˈkændḷˌwɪk; ˈkændlˌwɪk/ *n* [U] **1** also 又作 **candlewicking** thick, soft cotton thread 烛芯 **2** cloth decorated with patterns of raised rows of this thread 烛芯纱〔有凸起花纹的织物〕

can-do /ˌ· ˈ·/ *adj* [only before noun 仅用于名词前] *informal* willing to try anything and expect that it will work【非正式】敢于尝试的: *a can-do attitude towards work* 敢于尝试的工作态度

can·dour *BrE*【英】, **candor** *AmE*【美】/ˈkændɚ; ˈkændə/ *n* [U] sincere HONESTY and truthfulness 诚心诚意, 坦率; 正直: *I appreciate your candour in this matter.* 我很欣赏你在此事中表现出的坦诚。—see also 另见 CANDID

can·dy /ˈkændɪ; ˈkændi/ *n* [C,U] *AmE* sweet food made of sugar or chocolate, or a piece of this【美】糖果, 巧克力糖果; SWEET[2] (1) *BrE*【英】—see graph at 参见 SWEET[2] 图表 3

candy ap·ple /ˈ· ·ˌ· ·/ *n* [C] *AmE* TOFFEE APPLE【美】太妃糖苹果

candy cane /ˈ· · ·/ *n* [C] *AmE* a stick of hard red and white sugar with a curved end【美】棒糖〔红白相间弧形端的条形硬糖〕

can·dy·floss /ˈkændɪˌflɑs; ˈkændiflɒs/ *n* [U] *BrE* sticky threads of pink sugar wound around a stick and eaten as a sweet【英】棉花糖; COTTON CANDY *AmE*【美】

CULTURAL NOTE 文化注释

Candyfloss is connected with CARNIVALS, FAIRS, and AMUSEMENT PARKS. In Britain it is also sold in seaside towns, and people often eat it when they are on holiday. 棉花糖让人联想到狂欢节、集市和游乐场。在英国, 海边城镇也出售棉花糖, 人们常在度假时食用。

can·dy-striped /ˈ· · ˌ·/ *adj* candy-striped cloth has narrow coloured lines on a white background〔布〕白底有彩色条子花纹的

candy strip·er /ˈkændɪ ˌstraɪpɚ; ˈkændi ˌstraɪpə/ *n* [C] *AmE* a young person, usually a girl, who does unpaid work as a nurse's helper in a hospital in order to learn about hospital work【美】医院的实习护士助手

cane[1] /ken; keɪn/ *n* **1** [C] a long thin stick with a curved handle used to help someone walk 手杖, 拐杖 —see also 另见 STICK **2** [U] thin pieces of the stems of plants used for making furniture, baskets etc〔用来制家具、篮子等的〕藤料: *a cane chair* 藤椅 **3** [C] a long, hard, yellow stem of a BAMBOO, used for supporting other plants in the garden〔用来支撑花木的〕竹茎, 竹料 **4** [singular] a long thin stick used especially in former times by teachers to hit children with as a punishment〔旧时老师用来惩罚学生的〕藤条, 藤杖

cane[2] *v* [T] to punish someone, especially a child, by hitting them with a long thin stick 用藤条鞭打〔以示惩罚〕

ca·nine /ˋkenaɪn; ˈkeɪnaɪn/ *adj* being or related to dogs 狗的, 犬科动物的: *a canine welfare organization* 爱狗组织 | *his canine companion, Rex* 他的狗伙伴雷克斯

canine tooth /ˈ· · ·/ *n* [C] one of four sharp pointed teeth in the front of the human mouth; EYE TOOTH〔人的〕犬齿 —see picture at 参见 TEETH 图

can·is·ter /ˋkænɪstɚ; ˈkænəstə/ *n* [C] **1** a round metal case that bursts when thrown or fired from a gun, scattering what is inside 霰弹筒: *Police fired canisters of tear gas into the crowd.* 警察向人群施放催泪弹。**2** a small round container, usually made of metal, for keeping food, liquid etc in〔装食品、液体等的〕金属小圆桶[罐]: *discovered an early copy of 'Napoleon' in an old film canister* 在一个陈旧的电影胶片桶里发现了《拿破仑》的早期拷贝 **3** a round metal container of gas〔圆形金属的〕气体储存罐

can·ker /ˋkæŋkɚ; ˈkæŋkə/ *n* [C,U] **1** an evil influence that spreads quickly and is difficult to destroy 腐败因素; 祸害: *the canker of violence in modern society* 现代社会的暴力恶习 **2** a disease that affects trees or plants〔花木的〕枝枯病, 根瘤病 —**cankerous** *adj* —**cankered** *adj*

can·na·bis /ˋkænəbɪs; ˈkænəbəs/ *n* [U] an illegal drug obtained from HEMP plants and smoked in cigarettes 大麻

canned /kænd; kænd/ *adj* **1** canned food is preserved in a round metal container〔食物〕罐装的; TINNED *BrE*【英】: *canned tomatoes* 罐头西红柿 **2 canned music/laughter etc** music, laughter etc that has been recorded and is used on television or in radio programmes〔在电视或电台节目中使用的〕预录音乐/预录笑声 **3** [never before noun 永不用于名词前] *slang* drunk【俚】喝醉酒的

can·nel·lo·ni /ˌkænəˋlonɪ; ˌkænəˈləʊni/ *n* [U] small tubes of PASTA filled with meat and sometimes cheese, and covered in SAUCE[1]〔塞有肉或干酪并且浇汁的〕粗通心粉

can·ne·ry /ˋkænərɪ; ˈkænəri/ *n* [C] a factory where food is put into cans 罐头食品厂

Cannes /kæn; kæn/ a fashionable expensive town next to the Mediterranean Sea in southern France, which is famous as a holiday centre and because of the Cannes Film Festival, a yearly event when new international films are shown for the first time and are judged 戛纳〔法国南部濒临地中海的一个时尚、高消费小镇。该镇是著名的度假中心, 也因一年一度的戛纳国际电影节著称。电影节上, 新出品的国际影片首次上映参加评奖〕

can·ni·bal /ˋkænəbḷ; ˈkænəbəl/ *n* [C] **1** someone who eats human flesh 食人肉者: *the cannibal killer, Jeffrey Dahmer* 食人杀人狂杰弗里·达默 **2** an animal that eats the flesh of other animals of the same kind 同类相食的动物 —**cannibalism** *n* [U] —**cannibalistic** /ˌkænəbḷˋɪstɪk; ˌkænəbəˈlɪstɪk◂/ *adj*

CULTURAL NOTE 文化注释

In the US and UK, there is an old STEREOTYPE about cannibals that is sometimes used in CARTOONS. They are drawn as men who have a bone through their nose or tied in their hair. They usually wear grass skirts, and are typically shown cooking a MISSIONARY or an EXPLORER in a very big pot. 食人族在英美人眼中有根深蒂固的形象, 有时表现在卡通画中。食人族被画成鼻子上横穿着一根骨头或头发上系有骨头的男人形象, 他们通常穿草裙, 一般在大锅中煮食传教士或探险家。

can·ni·bal·ize also 又作 **-ise** *BrE*【英】/ˋkænəbḷˌaɪz; ˈkænəbəlaɪz/ *v* [T] to take something apart, especially a machine, so that you can use its parts to build something else 拆卸利用, 拆取〔机器零部件〕作为他用

can·non[1] /ˋkænən; ˈkænən/ *n* [C] a large, heavy, powerful gun, usually fixed to two wheels, used in the past〔旧时的双轮〕大炮; 加农炮

cannon[2] *v* [I always+adv/prep] to hit or knock into someone or something, especially while running〔尤指奔跑中〕撞到, 碰到: *She came hurtling round the corner and cannoned straight into me.* 她从拐角处猛冲过来, 和我撞了个满怀。

can·non·ade /ˌkænənˋed; ˌkænəˈneɪd/ *n* [C] a continuous heavy attack by large guns 连续猛烈炮击

can·non·ball /ˋkænənˌbɔl; ˈkænənbɔːl/ *n* [C] a heavy iron ball fired from an old type of large gun〔旧时的球状〕炮弹

cannon fod·der /ˈ· · ,· ·/ *n* [U] *informal* ordinary members of the army, navy etc whose lives are not considered to be very important【非正式】炮灰〔指普通士兵〕

can·not /ˋkænɑt; ˈkænɒt/ *modal verb* **1** a negative form of 'can'. can 的否定形式: *Mrs Armstrong regrets that she cannot accept your kind invitation.* 阿姆斯特朗夫人对无法接受你的邀请感到很遗憾。**2 cannot but** *formal* used to say that you feel you have to do something【正式】不得不, 不能不, 必须: *One cannot but admire her determination.* 人们不能不佩服她的决心。

can·ny /ˋkænɪ; ˈkæni/ *adj* **1** clever, careful, and not easily deceived, especially in business or politics〔尤指在生意或政治方面〕精明的, 机警的, 不易上当的: *a canny political advisor* 精明的政治顾问 **2** *ScotE* nice, good【苏格兰】温和善良的: *a canny lass* 温和善良的少女 —**cannily** *adv*

canoe 独木舟

ca·noe[1] /kəˋnu; kəˈnuː/ *n* [C] a long light boat that is pointed at both ends and which you move along using a PADDLE[1] (1) 独木舟 —see also 另见 **paddle your own canoe** (PADDLE[2] (5))

canoe[2] *v* [I] to travel by canoe 划独木舟, 乘独木舟 —**canoeist** *n* [C]

can·on /ˋkænən; ˈkænən/ *n* [C] **1** a Christian priest who has special duties in a CATHEDRAL〔基督教〕大教堂教士会成员 **2** a piece of music in which a tune is started by one singer or instrument and is copied by each of the others 卡农〔一种复调乐曲〕**3** *formal* a generally accepted rule or standard on which an idea, subject, or way of behaving is based【正式】准则, 标准, 规范: *Her behaviour offends all the canons of good taste.* 她的行为不符合高雅的标准。**4** *formal* a list of books or pieces of music that are officially recognized as being the work of a certain writer【正式】全集, 书目; 真本〔书目〕: *the Shakespearian canon* 莎士比亚著作集 **5** an established law of the Christian church 基督教教规, 基督教教会法

ca·non·i·cal /kəˋnɑnɪkḷ; kəˈnɒnɪkəl/ *adj* **1** according to CANON LAW 按照教规的 **2** *technical* in the simplest mathematical form【术语】〔数学方程式等〕典型的; 标准的

can·on·ize also 又作 **-ise** *BrE*【英】/ˋkænənˌaɪz; ˈkænənaɪz/ *v* [T] to officially state that a dead person is a SAINT (1) 把〔死者〕封为圣人 —**canonization** /ˌkænənaɪˋzeʃən; ˌkænənaɪˈzeɪʃən/ *n* [C,U]

canon law /ˌ· · ˈ·/ *n* [U] the laws of Christian Church 基督教教会法

ca·noo·dle /kəˋnudḷ; kəˈnuːdl/ *v* [I] *BrE old-fashioned* if two people canoodle, they kiss and hold each other in a sexual way【英, 过时】爱抚, 搂抱

can o·pen·er /ˈ· ,· · ·/ *n* [C] *especially AmE* a tool for opening a can of food【尤美】开罐器, 罐头刀; TIN OPENER *BrE*【英】—see picture on page A10 参见 A10 页图

can·o·py /ˋkænəpɪ; ˈkænəpi/ *n* [C] **1** a cover fixed above a bed, seat etc as a decoration or as a shelter〔床或座位上的〕顶罩, 罩篷, 华盖 **2** *literary* something that spreads above you like a roof【文】像天篷的东西: *a canopy of branches* 树枝交织成的天篷 —**canopied** *adj*

canst /kənst; kənst; *strong* 强读 kænst; kænst/ *v* **thou canst** *old use* used to mean 'you can' when talking to one person【旧】〔谈话时用于表示〕你可以, 你能

can't /kænt; kɑːnt/ **1** the short form of 缩略式= cannot: *I can't understand what this means.* 我不懂这是什么意思。| *You can swim, can't you?* 你会游泳, 不是吗? **2** used as the opposite of 'must', to say that something is impossible or unlikely. 不可能, 不太可能〔must 的反义词〕: *They can't have gone out because the light's on.* 他们不可能出去了, 因为灯还亮着。

cant¹ /kænt; kænt/ *n* **1** [U] insincere talk about moral or religious principles by someone who is pretending to be better than they really are〔有关道德或宗教的〕假话, 伪善的话: *a politician's cant about family values* 政客关于家庭价值的虚假言辞 **2** [U] special words used by a particular group of people, especially in order to keep things secret 行话, 隐语, 黑话: *thieves' cant* 小偷的黑话 **3** [C] a sloping surface or angle 斜面; 斜坡; 斜角

cant² *v* [I,T] to lean, or make something lean (使) 倾斜

cantab /ˈkæntæb; ˈkæntæb/ used after the title of a degree from Cambridge University 剑桥大学的〔用于学位名称后〕: *Jane Smith MA (Cantab)* 简·史密斯, 剑桥大学文学硕士

can·ta·loup, cantaloupe /ˈkæntḷ͵op; ˈkæntəluːp/ *n* [C,U] a type of MELON with a hard green skin and sweet orange flesh 罗马甜瓜, 皱皮香瓜 —see picture on page A8 参见 A8 页图

C

can·tan·ker·ous /kænˈtæŋkərəs; kænˈtæŋkərəs/ *adj* bad-tempered and complaining a lot 脾气坏而且爱唠叨的: *a cantankerous old man* 脾气坏而且爱唠叨的老头 —**cantankerously** *adv* —**cantankerousness** *n* [U]

can·ta·ta /kənˈtɑtə; kænˈtɑːtə/ *n* [C] a piece of religious music sung by a CHOIR and single performers 康塔塔, 大合唱〔一种由独唱、重唱和合唱组成的宗教乐曲〕

can·teen /kænˈtin; kænˈtiːn/ *n* [C] **1** a place in a factory, school etc where meals are provided, usually quite cheaply〔工厂或学校等的〕食堂, 餐厅: *lunch in the works' canteen* 在工厂食堂里吃午餐 **2** a small container in which water or other drink is carried by soldiers, travellers etc〔士兵、旅行者携带的〕水壶 **3** *BrE* a set of knives, forks and spoons in a box【英】一盒（全套）刀、叉、汤匙餐具

can·ter¹ /ˈkæntɚ; ˈkæntə/ *v* [I,T] to ride or make a horse run quite fast, but not as fast as possible (使)〔马〕以普通速度跑

canter² *n* **1** [singular] the movement of a horse when it is running fairly fast, but not as fast as possible〔马的〕普通跑步, 中速跑 **2** [C] a ride on a horse at this speed 骑马中速跑 **3** a short or quick journey 短暂旅程: *Paris is now only a canter away due to the Channel Tunnel.* 由于有了海峡隧道, 现在去巴黎只需很短的时间。

Can·ter·bu·ry /ˈkæntɚ͵bɛrɪ; ˈkæntəbəri/ a small city in southeast England which is famous for its 11th century CATHEDRAL, the main church of the Church of England 坎特伯雷〔英格兰东南部一小城市。坐落在坎特伯雷的 11 世纪大教堂是英国国教会主教堂, 该市因此而著名〕

Canterbury Tales, The /͵····ˈ·/ a long poem written by Geoffrey Chaucer in the 14th century, in which PILGRIMS who are travelling to Canterbury tell stories《坎特伯雷故事集》〔杰弗里·乔叟 14 世纪创作的一部长诗。诗中有前往坎特伯雷的朝圣者讲述的故事〕

can·ti·cle /ˈkæntɪkḷ; ˈkæntɪkəl/ *n* [C] a short religious song usually using words from the Bible〔歌词一般取自《圣经》的〕赞美诗, 圣歌

can·ti·le·ver /ˈkæntḷ͵ivɚ; ˈkæntḷiːvə/ *n* [C] a beam that sticks out from an upright post or wall and supports a shelf, the end of a bridge etc 托臂, 悬臂, 悬臂梁, 支架

can·to /ˈkænto; ˈkæntəʊ/ *n plural* **cantos** [C] one of the parts into which a very long poem is divided〔长诗中的〕篇章

Can·ton /͵kænˈtɑn; ͵kænˈtɒn/ a name formerly used for Guangzhou, a large city in southern China 广州〔旧称〕—**Cantonese** *adj*

can·ton *n* [C] one of the areas with limited political powers that make up a country such as Switzerland 小行政区〈如瑞士的州〉

Can·to·nese /͵kæntəˈniz; ͵kæntəˈniːz◂/ *n* [U] a Chinese language spoken in Southern China and Hong Kong 粤语, 广东话

can·ton·ment /kænˈtonmənt; kænˈtuːnmənt/ *n* [C] *technical* a camp for soldiers【术语】军营, 驻地

can·tor /ˈkæntɔr; ˈkæntə/ *n* [C] **1** a man who leads the prayers and songs in a Jewish religious service〔犹太教仪式中的〕带领祈祷和唱诗者 **2** the leader of a CHOIR in a church〔教堂唱诗班的〕领唱者

Ca·nute /kəˈnut; kəˈnjuːt/ (?995-1035) the King of England from 1016 to 1035, who also became King of Denmark and Norway. According to an old story, King Canute once ordered the sea to stop moving towards the land. 克努特〔(?995-1035), 英格兰国王, 1016 年至 1035 年在位, 也是丹麦、挪威国王。据一则古老的传说, 他曾下令让海水停止涨潮〕

can·vas /ˈkænvəs; ˈkænvəs/ *n* **1** [U] strong cloth used to make bags, tents, shoes etc 帆布 **2** [C] a painting done with oil paints, or the piece of cloth it is painted on 油画（布）**3 under canvas** *BrE* in a tent【英】在帐篷内: *We spent the night under canvas.* 我们在帐篷里过夜。

can·vass /ˈkænvəs; ˈkænvəs/ *v* **1** [I,T] to try to get information, support for a political party etc, by going from place to place within an area and talking to people 游说; 拉选票; 征求意见: *The company canvassed 600 people who use their product.* 公司征求了 600 名产品使用者的意见。| *We'll have to canvass the entire area before the referendum.* 在公民投票前我们得在全区拉选票。**2** [T] to talk about a problem, suggestion etc in detail〔详细〕讨论: *The suggestion is being widely canvassed as a possible solution to the dispute.* 这项建议作为解决争端的可行办法, 正受到广泛的讨论。—**canvass** *n* [C] —**canvasser** *n* [C]

can·yon /ˈkænjən; ˈkænjən/ *n* [C] a deep valley with very steep sides of rock that usually has a river running through it〔两边为峭壁, 谷底常有溪流的〕峡谷

cap. also 又作 **caps.** the written abbreviation of 缩写 = capital letter (CAPITAL¹ (3)) 大写字母

caps 帽子

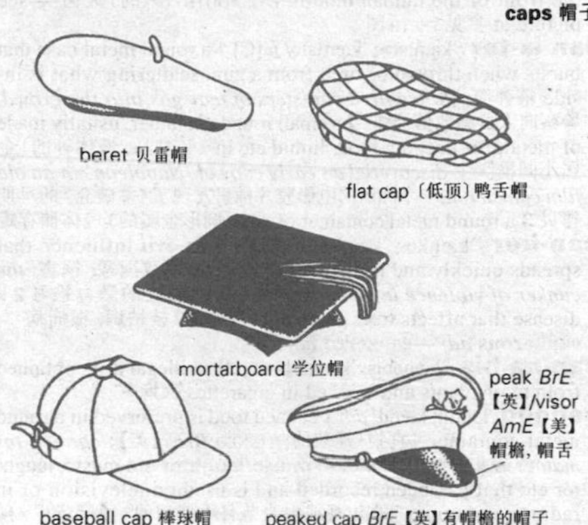

see also picture at 另见 **hat** 图

cap¹ /kæp; kæp/ *n* [C] 3

1 ▶HAT 帽子◀ a) a type of soft flat hat that has a curved part sticking out at the front〔有帽檐的〕帽子 **b)** a covering that fits very closely to your head and is worn for a particular purpose〔紧盖住头部的〕帽子, 便帽: *a swimming cap* 泳帽 | *a shower cap* 浴帽 **c)** a special type of hat that is worn by a particular profession or group of people〔表示职业或所属团体的〕制服帽: *a nurse's cap* 护士帽

2 ▶TOP/COVERING 罩, 盖◀ a protective covering that you put on the end or top of an object〔对物件起保护作用的〕罩, 盖, 套: *Make sure that you put the cap back on that pen.* 务必把笔帽套上。—see also 另见 ICE CAP, TOECAP

3 go cap in hand (to) to ask someone for something, especially money, in a very polite way that makes you seem unimportant 恭敬地请求, 谦卑地要求: *going cap in hand to the bank for a loan* 谦卑地恳求银行贷款

4 if the cap fits *spoken* used to say that someone should regard a remark as criticism of them if they think that the criticism is suitable【口】批评中肯, 恰如其分: *I never said you were a liar, but if the cap fits...* 我从未说过你撒谎, 但如果情况属实…

5 ▶EXPLOSIVE 爆炸物◀ a small paper container with explosive inside it, used especially in toy guns 啪啪纸, 火药纸〔玩具枪中用的纸包火药〕

6 ▶LIMIT 限度◀ an upper limit that is put on the amount of money that can be spent or borrowed in a particular situation〔金额的〕最高限额: *a cap on local council spending* 地方委员会支出的最高限额

7 ▶SEX 性行为◀ a CONTRACEPTIVE made of a round piece of rubber that a woman puts inside her VAGINA〔妇女避孕用的〕子宫帽

8 set your cap at *old-fashioned* if a woman sets her cap at a man, she tries to attract him, especially in order to marry him【过时】〔女子〕向〔男子〕示爱, 追求〔尤指为嫁给某人〕—see also 另见 **a feather in your cap** (FEATHER¹ (2)), **put on your thinking cap** (THINKING¹)

cap² *v* **capped, capping** [T] **1** to say or do something that is better, worse, funnier etc than what someone else has just said or done 胜过, 超越: *She capped my story with an hilarious account of the party.* 她对晚会绘声绘色的描述, 使得我所讲的故

事黯然失色。**2 to cap it all** *spoken* used before describing the worst, funniest etc part at the end of a story or description【口】〔用于故事或描述的结尾〕最有趣[糟糕]的是: *And to cap it all, I found I'd left my purse at home!* 最糟糕的是, 我发现把钱包忘在家里了。**3 be capped with** to have a particular substance on top 为…所覆盖, 为…所笼罩: *snow-capped mountains* 白雪覆盖的群山 | *a graceful tower capped with a gilded dome* 美丽的镀金圆顶塔 **4** *BrE* to choose someone for a national sports team【英】把…选入〔国家队〕: *He's been capped three times for England.* 他三次入选英格兰队 **5** to cover a tooth with a special white substance 给〔牙齿〕上釉 **6** *BrE* to put a limit on the amount of money that can be charged or spent, especially by local government【英】〔尤指地方政府〕对〔收费或开支〕规定上限

CAP, the /ˌsi e ˋpi; ˌsiː eɪ ˈpiː/ the Common Agricultural Policy; a system of laws arranged by the European Union to control the production of food and other farm crops. It set limits on how much farmers can grow, and provided them with financial support. 共同农业政策〔欧盟为控制粮食等农作物产量而指定的一套法规。其目的是限制农民产粮, 给农民提供补贴〕

S3 **ca·pa·bil·i·ty** /ˌkepəˋbɪlətɪ; ˌkeɪpəˈbɪlɨti/ *n* [C] **1** the natural ability, skill, or power that makes you able to do something 能力, 才能: *a child's language capability* 儿童的语言能力 | **capability to do sth** *A willingness and a capability to change are necessary to meet the market's needs.* 愿意并能够作出调整, 这对于满足市场需求是很必要的。| **beyond sb's capabilities** (=too difficult for someone) 超过某人的能力 *I have a good knowledge of French, but simultaneous translation is beyond my capabilities.* 我法语不错, 但是做同声传译却不是我力所能及的。**2** the ability that a country has to take a particular kind of military action〔一国的〕军事能力: *a nuclear weapons capability* 核武力

S2 W2 **ca·pa·ble** /ˋkepəbḷ; ˈkeɪpəbəl/ *adj* **1 capable of (doing) sth** having the skills, power, intelligence etc needed to do something 有能力(做某事): *I don't think Banks is capable of murder.* 我认为班克斯没有能力谋杀。| *The company isn't capable of handling an order that large.* 那家公司没有能力应付那么大的订单。**2** skilled or very good at doing something 熟练的: *a very capable doctor* 一位非常能干的医生 —**capably** *adv*

ca·pa·cious /kəˋpeʃəs; kəˈpeɪʃəs/ *adj formal* able to contain a lot【正式】容量大的: *a capacious suitcase* 大手提箱 —**capaciousness** *n* [U]

ca·pa·ci·tor /kəˋpæsətə·; kəˈpæsɨtə/ *n* [C] a piece of equipment that collects and stores electricity 电容器

S3 W2 **ca·pac·i·ty** /kəˋpæsətɪ; kəˈpæsɨti/ *n* **1** [singular] the amount of space a container, room etc has to hold things or people 容量, 容积; 容纳力: **[+of]** *The fuel tank has a capacity of 12 gallons.* 这个燃料箱的容量为12加仑。| *seating capacity of 500* 500个座位 | **capacity crowd** (=one that fills all the seats in a room, hall etc) 座无虚席 *The orchestra played to a capacity crowd in the Queen Elizabeth Hall.* 管弦乐团在伊丽莎白女王大厅的演奏座无虚席。| **filled to capacity** (=completely full) 挤满; 满座 **2** [C,U] someone's ability to do something 能力, 才能: **[+for]** *a child's capacity for learning* 孩子的学习能力 | *an infinite capacity for love* 无限的爱 | **capacity to do sth** *a capacity to think in an original way* 创造性的思维能力 **3** [singular] *formal* someone's job, position, or duty; ROLE (1)【正式】职位; 地位; 身份; 职责: *Rollins will be working in an advisory capacity on this project.* 罗林斯将以顾问的身份参与此项目。| **do sth in your capacity as** *I attended in my capacity as chairman of the safety committee.* 我是以安全委员会主席的身份参加的。**4** [singular,U] the amount of something that a factory, company, machine etc can produce or deal with〔工厂、公司、机器等的〕产量, 生产力: *Our factories have been working at full capacity all year.* 我们的工厂全年都满负荷生产。

ca·par·i·soned /kəˋpærəsṇd; kəˈpærɨsənd/ *adj* in medieval times a caparisoned horse was one covered in a decorated cloth〔中世纪的马〕配有华丽马衣的

cape /kep; keɪp/ *n* [C] **1** a long loose piece of clothing without SLEEVES that fastens around you neck and hangs from your shoulders 斗篷, 披风, 披肩 **2** a large piece of land surrounded on three sides by water 海角, 岬: *the Cape of Good Hope* 好望角

Cape Ca·nav·er·al /ˌkep kəˋnævərəl; ˌkeɪp kəˈnævərəl/ a CAPE (2) in Florida which is famous for the Kennedy Space Center, where US SPACECRAFT are sent into space. Cape Canaveral was formerly called Cape Kennedy. 卡纳维拉尔角〔佛罗里达州一海角。此地以发射宇宙飞船的肯尼迪航天中心闻名。旧称肯尼迪角〕

Cape Cod /ˌ·ˈ·/ a CAPE (2) in southern Massachusetts in the US which is a popular place for tourists 科德角〔美国马萨诸塞州一海角, 著名旅游胜地〕

Cape Col·oured /ˌ·ˈ··/ also 又作 **Coloured** *n* [C] a South African person of mixed race with black, white, or east Asian origins 开普敦有色人〔黑人、白人或东亚人混血的南非人〕

Cape Hat·te·ras /ˌkep ˋhætərəs; ˌkeɪp ˈhætərəs/ a CAPE (2) in North Carolina in the US, which is a popular place for tourists. It is also well known as a place where there are bad storms that have destroyed many ships. 哈特勒斯角〔美国北卡罗来纳州一海角, 旅游胜地。该地也因暴风雨毁坏众多船只而出名〕

Cape Horn /ˌ·ˈ·/ the extreme end of South America, which is famous for its very bad weather and dangerous ocean currents 合恩角〔南美洲最南端。该地以天气十分恶劣、洋流湍急危险而出名〕

Cape Ken·ne·dy /ˌ·ˈ··/ a former name of Cape Canaveral 肯尼迪角〔卡纳维拉尔角旧称〕

Cape of Good Hope, the /ˌ····ˈ·/ a PENINSULA (=a piece of land surrounded on three sides by water) at the southwestern end of South Africa, where the Atlantic Ocean meets the Indian Ocean 好望角〔南非最西南端一半岛, 大西洋与印度洋汇合处〕

Cape Prov·ince /ˌ·ˈ··/ a PROVINCE in the south of South Africa. Its full name is Cape of Good Hope Province, and it was formerly called Cape Colony. 开普省〔南非南部一省。全称为好望角省, 旧称开普殖民地〕

ca·per¹ /ˋkepə·; ˈkeɪpə/ *v* [I always+adv/prep] to jump about and play in a happy, excited way〔快乐地〕跳跃, 雀跃: *lambs capering in the fields* 在田野里跳跃嬉戏的羔羊

caper² *n* [C] **1** a small dark green part of a flower used in cooking to give a sour taste to food〔用作调味料的〕续随子花芽 **2** *informal* a planned activity, especially an illegal or dangerous one【非正式】欺诈, 违法行为: *If he thinks I'm going along with him on this caper, he's wrong.* 如果他认为我会跟他一块儿去干这种违法的事, 那么他就错了。**3** a short jumping or dancing movement 快速跳跃动作, 快速舞步: **cut a caper** (=dance with little steps or jumps) 雀跃地跳舞[蹦跳]

Cape Town /ˈ··/ a large city in South Africa near the Cape of Good Hope. It is built around Table Mountain, and South Africa's parliament building is there. 开普敦〔南非好望角附近一大城市。该城环绕桌山而建, 为南非议会大厦所在地〕

Cape Verde /ˌkep ˋvɝd; ˌkeɪp ˈvɜːd/ a country that consists of a group of islands in the Atlantic Ocean, west of Senegal. Population: 405,163 (2001). Capital: Praia. 佛得角〔大西洋中一群岛屿组成的国家, 位于塞内加尔以西。人口: 405,163 (2001), 首都: 普拉亚〕

ca·pil·la·ry /ˋkæpḷˌɛrɪ; kəˈpɪləri/ *n* [C] **1** a very small tube as thin as a hair 毛细管 **2** the smallest type of BLOOD VESSEL (=tube carrying blood) in the body 毛细血管

capillary at·trac·tion /ˌ·····ˈ··/ also 又作 **capillary action** /ˌ····ˈ··/ *n* [U] *technical* the force that makes a liquid rise up a narrow tube【术语】毛细管作用, 毛细管引力

S3 W1 **cap·i·tal¹** /ˋkæpətḷ; ˈkæpɨtl/ *n*

1 ►CITY 城市◄ [C] an important town or city where the central government of a country, state etc is 首都; 首府; 省会: *Albany is the capital of New York State.* 奥尔巴尼是纽约州的首府。

2 ►FINANCIAL 金融的◄ [singular,U] money or property, especially when it is used to start a business or to produce more wealth 资本, 资金: *You'll need more capital if you want to open your own business.* 自己创办企业的话需要更多的资金。—see also 另见 WORKING CAPITAL, VENTURE CAPITAL

3 ►LETTER 字母◄ [C] a letter of the alphabet written in its large form as it is, for example at the beginning of someone's name 大写字母 —compare 比较 LOWER CASE

4 ►CENTRE OF ACTIVITY 活动中心◄ [C] a place that is a centre for an industry, business, or other activity〔工商业及其他活动的〕中心: *Hollywood is the capital of the movie industry.* 好莱坞是电影业的中心。

5 make capital out of to use a situation or event to help you get an advantage 利用…, 从…中捞一把[获益]: *The Republicans are sure to make capital out of the closure of the plant.* 共和党人一定会从该厂的倒闭中捞取好处的。

6 ►BUILDING 建筑物◄ the top part of a COLUMN (=a long stone post used in some buildings) 柱头, 柱顶

S3 W3 **capital²** *adj* **1 capital letter** a letter that is written or printed in its large form 大写字母 —compare 比较 LOWER CASE **2 capital offence/crime** an offence etc that is punished by death 可处死刑的罪 **3** *old-fashioned* excellent【过时】极好的: *That's a capital suggestion!* 那建议好极了!

capital as·sets /ˌ···ˈ··/ *n* [plural] *technical* machines, buildings, and other property belonging to a company【术语】固定资产, 资本资产

capital gains /ˌ···ˈ·/ *n* [plural] profits you make by selling your possessions 资本收益〔出售固定资产所得的收益〕

capital gains tax /ˌ···ˈ·ˌ·/ *n* [C] a tax that you pay on profits that you make when you sell your possessions 资本收益税

capital goods /ˈ···ˌ·/ *n* [plural] goods such as machines or buildings that are made for the purpose of producing other goods 资本货物〔指机器等用来制造其他商品的货物〕—compare 比较 CONSUMER GOODS

capital in·ten·sive /ˌ··· ·ˈ··◂/ *adj* a capital intensive business, industry etc needs a lot of money for it to operate properly 资本密集的 —compare 比较 LABOUR-INTENSIVE

cap·i·tal·is·m /ˈkæpətḷˌɪzəm; ˈkæpɪ̵tl-ɪzəm/ *n* [U] a system of production and trade based on property and wealth being owned privately, with only a small amount of industrial activity by the government 资本主义 —compare 比较 COMMUNISM

cap·i·tal·ist[1] /ˈkæpətḷɪst; ˈkæpɪ̵tl-ɪ̵st/ *n* [C] **1** someone who supports capitalism 资本主义者: *the class struggle between workers and capitalists* 工人与资本主义者之间的阶级斗争 **2** someone who owns or controls a lot of money and lends it to businesses, banks etc to produce more wealth 资本家

capitalist[2] also 又作 **cap·i·ta·lis·tic** /ˌkæpɪtḷˈɪstɪk; ˌkæpɪ̵tl-ˈɪstɪk◂/ *adj* using or supporting capitalism 资本主义的: *Marx argued against the capitalist system.* 马克思反驳资本主义制度。| *capitalist societies of the rich West* 西方富国的资本主义社会

cap·i·tal·ize also 又作 **-ise** *BrE*【英】/ˈkæpətḷˌaɪz; ˈkæpɪ̵tl-aɪz/ *v* [T] **1** to write a letter of the alphabet using a CAPITAL[1] (3) letter 把…大写 **2** to supply a business with money so that it can operate 给〔公司〕提供资金 **3** *technical* to calculate the value of a business based on the value of its shares (SHARE[2] (5)) or on the amount of money it makes【术语】〔根据公司的股票价值或其收益〕核定〔公司〕的资本 —**capitalization** /ˌkæpətḷəˈzeʃən; ˌkæpɪ̵tl-aɪˈzeɪʃən/ *n* [U]

capitalize on sth *phr v* [T] to get as much advantage out of a situation, event etc as you can 尽量榨取, 充分利用: *We are well-placed to capitalize on the growth of cable TV.* 我们有条件从有线电视的发展中得到好处。

capital lev·y /ˌ···ˈ··/ *n* [C] *technical* a tax on private or industrial wealth that is paid to the government【术语】资本税

capital pun·ish·ment /ˌ···ˈ···/ *n* [U] punishment by legal killing 死刑, 极刑

CULTURAL NOTE 文化注释

Capital punishment was used in the UK until 1965, and is still used in some states in the US. In the US, people used to be EXECUTE*d* in the ELECTRIC CHAIR, but now they are normally killed by LETHAL INJECTION in which a poison is INJECT*ed* into the body. Politicians still disagree about whether capital punishment should be allowed. Some people believe it is morally wrong to kill a criminal, no matter what they have done. Others believe that capital punishment is morally right if it is used for punishing murderers. In the US, people who do not support the death penalty often protest outside the prison where a criminal is about to be executed. 英国的死刑沿用到1965年, 美国一些州至今仍有死刑。过去美国常在电椅上执行死刑, 但现在一般是将毒药注射入罪犯体内。政界对是否应允许死刑存在仍意见不一。一些人认为处决罪犯不合道义, 无论他做过什么; 另一些人认为, 死刑用于惩戒杀人犯合乎道义。在美国, 反对死刑的人常在罪犯即将被执行死刑的监狱前抗议。

capital trans·fer tax /ˌ···ˈ··ˌ·/ *n* [C,U] *BrE* a tax paid when you receive money, either as a gift or when someone dies【英】资本转移税 —see also 另见 INHERITANCE TAX

cap·i·ta·tion /ˌkæpəˈteʃən; ˌkæpɪ̵ˈteɪʃən/ *n* [C] a tax or payment of the same amount from each person 人头税; 按人收费

Cap·i·tol /ˈkæpətḷ; ˈkæpɪ̵tl/ *n* **1 the Capitol** the building in Washington D.C. where the US Congress meets〔位于华盛顿市的〕美国国会大厦 **2** [C] the building or group of buildings of the central government of one of the 50 states of the US〔美国各州的〕州议会大厦

Capitol Hill /ˌ···ˈ·/ *n* [singular] **1** the US Congress 美国国会 **2** the hill where the Capitol building stands〔美国〕国会山

ca·pit·u·late /kəˈpɪtʃəˌlet; kəˈpɪtʃʊ̈leɪt/ *v* [I] **1** to accept or agree to something that you have been opposing until now 屈服, 不再反对, 停止抵抗: *Helen finally capitulated and let her son have a car.* 海伦最后作出让步, 同意让儿子买一辆车。**2** *formal* to accept defeat by your enemies in a war; SURRENDER[1] (1)【正式】投降 —**capitulation** /kəˌpɪtʃəˈleʃən; kəˌpɪtʃʊ̈ˈleɪʃən/ *n* [C,U]

Cap'n Crunch *trademark* a type of sweet breakfast CEREAL which is popular especially with children in the US【商标】"嘎吱船长"牌早餐甜麦片(尤为美国儿童所喜爱)

ca·pon /ˈkepɑn; ˈkeɪpən/ *n* [C] a male chicken that has had its sex organs removed to make it grow big and fat〔供食用的〕阉鸡

Ca·pone /kəˈpon; kəˈpəʊn/, **Al** /æl; æl/ (1899-1947) one of the most famous US GANGSTER*s* (=criminals who belong to a violent group). From 1925 to 1931 he was the leader of organized crime in Chicago. Because he had a SCAR on his cheek, he was sometimes called 'Scarface'. 卡彭〔(1899-1947), 美国最臭名昭著的匪徒之一。1925至1931年间为芝加哥犯罪集团头目。他脸上有刀疤, 故有时也叫"疤瘢脸"〕

Ca·po·te /kəˈpotɪ; kəˈpəʊti/, **Tru·man** (1924-84) a US writer who wrote the short story *Breakfast at Tiffany's*, which was made into a successful film, and *In Cold Blood* in which he describes a true crime involving two men who murdered a whole family. 卡波特〔(1924-1984), 美国作家。其短篇小说《在蒂芬尼饭店进早餐》被改编成电影并大获成功。创作的《冷血》描述两名男子杀害一家人的真实事件〕

cap·puc·ci·no /ˌkæpəˈtʃino; ˌkæpʊ̈ˈtʃiːnəʊ/ *n* [C,U] Italian coffee made with hot milk and with chocolate powder on top 意大利白咖啡〔一种加热牛奶, 上面撒有巧克力粉的意大利式咖啡〕

Capra /ˈkæprə; ˈkæprə/, **Frank** (1897-1991) a US film DIRECTOR, born in Italy, who made films with a gentle humour and sympathy for ordinary people, such as *Mr. Deeds Goes to Town* (1936), *Mr. Smith Goes to Washington* (1939), and *It's a Wonderful Life* (1946). 卡普拉〔(1897-1991), 美国电影导演, 出生于意大利。他拍摄的影片舒缓而幽默, 对普通人充满同情, 如《第兹先生进城》(1936)、《史密斯先生到华盛顿》(1939) 和《美好的生活》(1946)〕

Ca·pri /kəˈpri; kəˈpriː/ an island near the city of Naples in southern Italy, which is a popular place for tourists 卡普里岛〔意大利南部那不勒斯市附近一岛屿, 旅游胜地〕

ca·price /kəˈpris; kəˈpriːs/ *n* **1** [C,U] a sudden and unreasonable change of mind or behaviour 任性; 反复无常, 多变: *the caprices of a spoilt child* 娇生惯养儿童的任性 **2** [U] the tendency to change your mind suddenly or behave in an unexpected way 反复无常的倾向

ca·pri·cious /kəˈprɪʃəs; kəˈprɪʃəs/ *adj* **1** likely to change your mind suddenly or behave in an unexpected way 反复无常的; 任性的: *as capricious and manipulative as her mother had been* 像她母亲一样任性并有操纵欲 **2** changing quickly and suddenly 善变的: *a capricious wind* 变幻莫测的风 —**capriciously** *adv*

Cap·ri·corn /ˈkæprɪˌkɔrn; ˈkæprɪkɔːn/ *n* **1** [singular] the tenth sign of the ZODIAC represented by a goat and believed to affect the character and life of people born between December 22 and January 19 摩羯宫, 摩羯[山羊]座 **2** [C] someone who was born between December 22 and January 19 生于摩羯[山羊]座时段〔即12月22日至1月19日〕的人

cap·si·cum /ˈkæpsɪkəm; ˈkæpsɪkəm/ *n* [C,U] *technical* a kind of PEPPER (=a green, red, or yellow vegetable)【术语】〔青色、红色、黄色的〕辣椒

cap·size /ˈkæpˌsaɪz; kæpˈsaɪz/ *v* [I,T] if a boat capsizes or if you capsize it, it turns over in the water (使)〔船〕倾覆

cap·stan /ˈkæpstən; ˈkæpstən/ *n* [C] **1** a round machine shaped like a drum, used to wind up a rope that pulls or lifts heavy objects 绞盘, 卷扬机; 起锚机 **2** the round bar that goes round to move the TAPE[1] (12) in a TAPE RECORDER〔录音机的〕主动轮, 旋转轴

cap·sule /ˈkæpsḷ; ˈkæpsjuːl/ *n* [C] **1** a plastic container shaped like a very small tube with medicine inside that you swallow whole〔药物〕胶囊 **2** the part of a SPACECRAFT in which people live and work〔宇宙飞船的〕密封舱〔宇航员生活和居住的地方〕

cap·tain[1] /ˈkæptɪn; ˈkæptɪ̵n/ *n* [C] **1** someone who commands a ship or aircraft 舰长; 船长; 机长: *The Captain and crew welcome you aboard.* 船长和船员们欢迎你登船。**2** a rank in the navy, army or US Air Force or Marines〔陆军〕上尉;〔空军〕(英) 上校, (美) 上尉;〔海军〕上校 —see also 另见 GROUP CAPTAIN —see table on page C6 参见 C6 页附录 **3** someone who leads a team or other group of people 队长, 组长: *Julie's the school tennis captain.* 朱莉是学校网球队队长。**4 captain of industry** someone who owns an important company 工业界巨子[大亨], 实业巨头 3

captain[2] *v* [T] to lead a group or team of people and be their captain 担任…指挥, 率领

Captain Cook —see 见 Captain James COOK

cap·tain·cy /ˈkæptənsɪ; ˈkæptɨnsi/ *n* [C,U] the position of being captain of a team, or the period during which someone is captain 队长职位; 队长任期

Captain Hook /ˌ·· ˈ·/ an evil PIRATE (=someone who sails on the sea, attacking other ships and stealing from them) who has a metal hook in place of one of his hands, and who is the enemy of Peter Pan in the play and book *Peter Pan* by J. M. Barrie 铁钩船长〔J.M.巴里的小说和剧本《彼得·潘》中一只手为金属钩的邪恶海盗。他是彼得·潘的敌人〕

cap·tion /ˈkæpʃən; ˈkæpʃən/ *n* [C] words printed above or below a picture in a book or newspaper or on a television screen to explain what the picture is showing〔图片、报刊文章、电视等的〕题目, 标题; 说明文字

cap·tious /ˈkæpʃəs; ˈkæpʃəs/ *adj literary* always criticizing unimportant things【文】吹毛求疵的

cap·ti·vate /ˈkæptəˌvet; ˈkæptɨveɪt/ *v* [T often passive 常用被动态] to attract someone very much 使着迷; 迷住, 吸引: *I was captivated by his charm and good looks.* 我被他的魅力与帅气迷倒了。

cap·ti·va·ting /ˈkæptəˌvetɪŋ; ˈkæptɨveɪtɪŋ/ *adj* very attractive 极为迷人的: *a captivating smile and beautiful eyes* 迷人的微笑和美丽的双眼

cap·tive¹ /ˈkæptɪv; ˈkæptɪv/ *adj* **1** [only before noun 仅用于名词前] unable to move about freely because of being kept in prison or in a small space 被监禁的, 被关押的: *Captive soldiers passed by in chains.* 被关押的士兵戴着锁链走过。| *captive animals* 关在笼子里的动物 **2 take/hold sb captive** to keep someone as a prisoner 俘虏/关押某人: *The American officers were held captive for three months.* 那些美国军官被关押达三个月之久。**3 captive audience** people who listen or watch someone or something because they have to, not because they are interested 被迫看[听]…的听众[观众]

captive² *n* [C] someone who is kept as a prisoner, especially in a war 战俘, 俘虏, 囚徒

cap·tiv·i·ty /kæpˈtɪvətɪ; kæpˈtɪvɨti/ *n* [U] the state of being kept in a prison, CAGE etc and not allowed to go where you want 被俘(的状态), 拘禁, 囚禁; 束缚: *The hostages were released from captivity.* 人质从囚禁中被释放出来了。| **in captivity** *Many animals do not breed well when kept in captivity.* 许多动物被关入笼中就繁殖得不好。

cap·tor /ˈkæptɚ; ˈkæptə/ *n* [C] someone who is keeping another person prisoner 捉拿者, 捕捉者: *He managed to escape from his captors.* 他设法从捉他的人那里逃了出来。

3 **cap·ture¹** /ˈkæptʃɚ; ˈkæptʃə/ *v* [T]

1 ▶PERSON 人◀ to catch someone in order to make them a prisoner 俘虏, 逮捕: *Government troops have succeeded in capturing the rebel leader.* 政府军成功捕获了叛乱分子的头目。

2 ▶PLACE 地方◀ to get control of a place that previously belonged to an enemy by fighting for it〔用武力从敌人手中〕夺取〔某地〕: *The town of Moulineuf was captured after a siege lasting ten days.* 经过长达10天的围攻, 莫林那辅镇终于被攻陷了。

3 ▶ANIMAL 动物◀ to catch an animal after chasing or following it 捕获

4 ▶BOOK/PAINTING/FILM 书/画/电影◀ to succeed in showing or describing a situation or feeling using words or pictures〔用文字、图片〕记录下: *These photographs capture the essence of working-class life at the turn of the century.* 这些相片记录了世纪之交时工人阶级的生活实况。

5 capture sb's imagination/attention etc to make someone feel very interested and attracted 引起某人想象/吸引某人注意等: *His stories of foreign adventure captured my imagination.* 他所讲的外国历险故事使我心驰神往。

6 capture sb's heart to seem attractive to someone so that they become very fond of you or love you 赢得某人的好感[爱意]

7 ▶BUSINESS/POLITICS 商业/政治◀ to get something that previously belonged to one of your competitors 夺得, 抢占: *Japanese firms have captured over 60% of the electronics market.* 日本公司已经抢占了超过60%的电子市场。

8 ▶COMPUTERS 电脑◀ *technical* to put something in a form that a computer can use【术语】〔电脑〕把…变换成可用于电脑的形式; 记录: *The data is captured by an optical scanner.* 该数据是通过光学扫描器记录下来的。

9 ▶CHESS 国际象棋◀ to remove one of your opponent's PIECES from the board in CHESS〔在国际象棋比赛中〕吃掉〔对方一子〕

capture² *n* **1** [U] the act of catching someone in order to make them a prisoner 捕获, 俘虏: *The two soldiers somehow managed to avoid capture.* 这两名士兵设法逃过了被俘的命运。**2 the capture of Rome/Jerusalem etc** the act of getting control of a place that previously belonged to an enemy 占领罗马/耶路撒冷等

Cap·u·lets and Mon·ta·gues, the /ˌkæpjulɪts ənd ˈmɑntəguz; ˌkæpjɨlɪts ənd ˈmɒntəgjuːz/ two families in the play *Romeo and Juliet* by William Shakespeare. The Capulets are Juliet's family and the Montagues are Romeo's. The two families hate each other, so Romeo and Juliet have to get married secretly. 凯普特莱和蒙太古〔威廉·莎士比亚剧本《罗密欧与朱丽叶》中的两大家族。朱丽叶属凯普特莱家族, 罗密欧属蒙太古家族。两大家族相互仇视, 罗密欧和朱丽叶成婚时只好秘而不宣〕

car /kɑr; kɑː/ *n* [C] **1** a small vehicle with four wheels and an engine, that you use to travel from one place to another 汽车: *I go to work by car.* 我开车去上班。| *Cars were parked on both sides of the road.* 路两边都停着汽车。—see picture on page A2 参见A2页图 **2 sleeping/dining/buffet car** a train carriage used for sleeping etc〔火车〕卧铺车厢/餐车 **3** *AmE* a train carriage【美】〔火车〕车厢 **4** the part of a lift, BALLOON¹ (2), or AIRSHIP in which people or goods are carried〔电梯的〕升降室, 机厢;〔气球、飞艇等的〕吊舱; 座舱; 货舱 1 1

Ca·rac·as /kəˈrɑkəs; kəˈrækəs/ the capital of Venezuela 加拉加斯〔委内瑞拉首都〕

ca·rafe /kəˈræf; kəˈræf/ *n* [C] a glass container with a wide neck, used for serving wine or water at meals 宽颈玻璃瓶, 饮料瓶

car a·larm /ˈ· ·ˌ·/ *n* [C] a special system for protecting cars against thieves that makes a loud noise if anyone touches the car 汽车防盗警报器

car·a·mel /ˈkærəml; ˈkærəməl/ *n* **1** [C] a brown sweet made of sticky boiled sugar〔含有焦糖的〕糖果 **2** [U] burnt sugar used for giving food a special taste and colour〔食品调味或调色用的〕焦糖 —see also 另见 CRÈME CARAMEL —**caramelize** *v* [I,T]

car·a·pace /ˈkærəˌpes; ˈkærəpeɪs/ *n* [C] *technical* a hard shell on the outside of some animals such as CRABS or TORTOISES, that protects them【术语】〔蟹或龟等的〕甲壳

car·at /ˈkærət; ˈkærət/ *n* [C] **1** also 又作 **karat** *AmE*【美】a measurement that shows how pure gold is 开〔黄金的纯度单位〕: *a 22-carat gold chain* 22开的金链 **2** a measurement equal to 200 MILLIGRAMS on the scale of measurement for the weight of jewels 克拉〔宝石重量单位, 相等于200毫克〕

car·a·van /ˈkærəˌvæn; ˈkærəvæn/ *n* [C] **1** *BrE* a vehicle that a car can pull and in which people can live and sleep when they are on holiday【英】〔带有食宿设备的〕旅行拖车; TRAILER (1) *AmE*【美】**2** *BrE* a covered vehicle pulled by a horse in which people such as gipsies (GIPSY) live【英】〔吉卜赛人居住的〕大篷车, 有篷马车; WAGON (1) *AmE*【美】**3** a group of people with animals or vehicles who travel together for protection through dangerous areas such as deserts〔带着牲口、车辆等穿越沙漠等危险地带的〕旅行队

car·a·van·ning /ˈkærəvænɪŋ; ˈkærəvænɪŋ/ *n* [U] *BrE* the practice of having holdays in a caravan【英】乘旅行拖车外出度假: *a caravanning holiday in Cornwall* 乘旅行拖车在康沃尔度假

car·a·van·se·rai /ˌkærəˈvænsəˌraɪ; ˌkærəˈvænsəraɪ/ *n* [C] a hotel with a large open central area, used in the past in Eastern countries by groups of people and animals travelling together〔旧时东方国家里供旅行队过夜且有停车大院子的〕旅店, 客栈

car·a·way /ˈkærəˌwe; ˈkærəweɪ/ *n* [C,U] a plant whose strongtasting seeds are used to give a special taste to food〔其籽有特殊香味, 可用作调味料的〕贳蒿, 葛缕子, 香旱芹

car·bine /ˈkɑrbaɪn; ˈkɑːbaɪn/ *n* [C] a short light RIFLE (=type of gun) 卡宾枪

car·bo·hy·drate /ˌkɑrboˈhaɪdret; ˌkɑːbəʊˈhaɪdreɪt/ *n* **1** [C, U] *technical* one of several food substances such as sugar which consist of oxygen, HYDROGEN and CARBON (1), and which provide your body with heat and energy【术语】碳水化合物, 糖类 **2** [C usually plural 一般用复数] foods such as rice, bread, and potatoes that contain carbohydrates 含碳水化合物的食品〈如米饭、面包、马铃薯等〉

car·bol·ic a·cid /kɑrˈbɑlɪk ˈæsɪd; kɑːˌbɒlɪk ˈæsɨd/ *n* [U] a liquid that kills BACTERIA, used for preventing the spread of disease or infection 石碳酸

carbolic soap /ˌ·· ˈ·/ *n* [U] a strong soap made from coal TAR¹ (1) 石碳酸皂

car bomb /ˈ· ·/ *n* [C] a bomb hidden inside a car 汽车炸弹

car·bon /ˈkɑrbən; ˈkɑːbən/ *n* **1** [U] a simple substance that exists in a pure form as diamonds, GRAPHITE etc or in an impure form as coal, petrol etc 碳 **2** [C,U] CARBON PAPER 复写纸 **3** [C] a CARBON COPY (1) 复写本, 副本

car·bon·at·ed /ˈkarbəˌnetɪd; ˈkɑːbəneɪtɪ̣d/ *adj* carbonated drinks contain small BUBBLES〔饮料〕含二氧化碳的: *carbonated spring water* 有汽矿泉水

carbon black /ˈ·· ·/ *n* [U] a black powder made by partly burning oil, wood etc, used for making rubber〔用于生产橡胶的〕碳黑

carbon cop·y /ˌ·· ˈ··/ *n* [C] **1** a copy, especially of something that has been typed (TYPE[2] (1)), made using CARBON PAPER 复写本, 副本 **2** someone or something that is very similar to another person or thing 极为相似的人[物]: [+of] *The robbery is a carbon copy of one that took place last year.* 这宗抢劫案与去年发生的那宗极为相似。

carbon dat·ing /ˌ·· ˈ··/ *n* [U] a method used to find out the age of very old objects 碳年代测定法

carbon di·ox·ide /ˌ·· ··ˈ··/ *n* [U] the gas produced when animals breathe out, when carbon is burned in air, or when animal or vegetable substances decay 二氧化碳

car·bon·if·er·ous /ˌkarbəˈnɪfərəs; ˌkɑːbəˈnɪfərəs◂/ *adj* producing or containing carbon or coal 碳质的, 产碳的; 含煤的; 碳纪的: *carboniferous rocks* 石碳纪形成的岩石

car·bon·ize also 又作 **-ise** *BrE*【英】/ˈkarbənˌaɪz; ˈkɑːbənaɪz/ *v* [I,T] to change or make something change into CARBON (1) by burning without air (使)碳化, (使)焦化 —**carbonized** *adj*

carbon mo·nox·ide /ˌ·· ·ˈ···/ *n* [U] a poisonous gas produced when CARBON (1), especially petrol, burns in a small amount of air 一氧化碳

carbon pa·per /ˈ·· ˌ··/ *n* [C,U] thin paper with a blue or black substance on one side, that you put between sheets of paper when typing (TYPE[2] (2)) in order to make copies 复写纸

carbon tet·ra·chlo·ride /ˌkarbən tɛtrəˈklɔraɪd; ˌkɑːbən tetrəˈklɔːraɪd/ *n* [U] a colourless liquid used for cleaning dirty marks off clothes 四氯化碳〔用于去除衣服上污迹的一种无色液体〕

car boot sale /ˌ· ˈ· ˌ·/ *n* [C] *BrE* a sale in a CAR PARK or other open space, where people sell things from the back of their cars【英】旧货出售, 旧物集市〔在停车场等地方将旧物放在汽车的行李箱中出售〕

car·bo·run·dum /ˌkarbəˈrʌndəm; ˌkɑːbəˈrʌndəm/ *n* [U] an extremely hard substance made from CARBON (1) and SILICON used for polishing things 金刚砂, 碳化硅

car·boy /ˈkarbɔɪ; ˈkɑːbɔɪ/ *n* [C] a large round bottle used for holding dangerous chemical liquids〔用来装载危险化学溶液的〕圆形大瓶

car·bun·cle /ˈkarbʌŋkl; ˈkɑːbʌŋkəl/ *n* [C] **1** a large painful lump under someone's skin 痈〔生于皮下组织的化脓性炎症〕**2** a red jewel, especially a GARNET (1) 红宝石, 〔尤指〕石榴石

> **CULTURAL NOTE 文化注释**
> In Britain this word is sometimes used to describe a new building in a modern style that spoils the appearance of the older buildings around it (from a speech by Prince Charles in which he described a planned new part of the National Gallery as like a 'monstrous carbuncle' on the face of an old friend). 在英国, 该词有时用来形容破坏原有楼群景观的现代风格新建筑(该词出自查尔斯王子的一篇演说, 他把国家美术馆计划扩建的部分称作老友脸上"难看的痈")。

car·bu·ret·tor *BrE*【英】, **carburetor** *AmE*【美】/ˈkarbəˌretə; ˌkɑːbjʊ̣ˈretə/ *n* [C] a part of a car engine that mixes the air and petrol which burns in the engine to provide power〔汽车发动机的〕汽化器, 化油器 —see picture at 参见 ENGINE 图

car·cass /ˈkarkəs; ˈkɑːkəs/ *n* [C] **1** the body of a dead animal, especially one that is ready to be cut up as meat 动物尸体〔屠宰后用作肉食的牲畜躯体〕**2** **shift/move your carcass!** *spoken* used to tell someone to move from the place where they are sitting or standing【口】挪挪窝儿! 躲开! **3** the decaying outer structure of a building, vehicle, or other object〔建筑物、汽车等的〕残骸, 骨架

car·cin·o·gen /karˈsɪnədʒən; kɑːˈsɪnədʒən/ *n* [C] a substance that can cause CANCER 致癌物(质)

car·cin·o·gen·ic /ˌkarsənəˈdʒɛnɪk; ˌkɑːsɪnəˈdʒenɪk◂/ *adj* likely to cause CANCER 致癌的: *the carcinogenic effects of high-fat diets* 高脂饮食的致癌性

car·ci·no·ma /ˌkarsəˈnomə; ˌkɑːsɪ̣ˈnəʊmə/ *n* [C] *technical* a CANCER【术语】癌

card[1] /kard; kɑːd/ *n*

1 **library/membership/identity etc card** a small piece of plastic or paper that shows that someone belongs to a particular organization, club etc 图书馆/会员/身份等证件: *Employees must show their ID cards at the gate.* 雇员必须在门口出示身份证件。

2 ▶**BIRTHDAY/CHRISTMAS ETC 生日/圣诞等**◀ [C] a piece of thick stiff paper with a picture on the front, that you send to people on special occasions 贺卡: *Did you remember to send Val a birthday card?* 你记得给瓦尔寄生日贺卡了吗?

3 ▶**HOLIDAY 假期**◀ [C] a card with a photograph or picture on one side, that you send to someone when you are on holiday; POSTCARD 明信片: *Don't forget to send us a card from Greece!* 别忘了从希腊给我们寄张明信片!

4 ▶**INFORMATION 资料**◀ [C] a small piece of stiff paper or plastic that shows information about someone or something, especially one that is part of a set used for storing information 档案卡片: *a card index system* 卡片索引系统 | *an expansion card for 386 machines* 386 电脑的扩充卡

5 ▶**STIFF PAPER 卡片纸**◀ [U] *BrE* thick stiff paper【英】厚纸片, (硬)纸板

6 ▶**BANK 银行**◀ [C] a small piece of plastic that you use to pay for goods or to get money from a special machine at a bank 信用卡; 借记卡: *Lost or stolen cards must be reported immediately.* 信用卡丢失或被盗必须马上挂失。—see also 另见 CHARGE CARD, CHEQUE CARD, CREDIT CARD

7 ▶**GAMES 游戏**◀ [C] a small piece of thick stiff paper with numbers and signs or pictures on, that is one of a set of fifty two used to play games such as POKER (1) or BRIDGE[1] (4) 纸牌, 扑克牌: **play cards** (=play a game with cards) 玩牌 | **a pack of cards** (=a complete set of cards) 一副牌

> **CULTURAL NOTE 文化注释**
> The cards used in card games come in two red **suits** – **hearts** and **diamonds**; and two black ones – **clubs** and **spades**. Each **suit** has nine cards numbered two to ten, and also an **ace**, a **king**, a **queen**, and a **jack** or **knave**. To say what a card is, say *the* **king** *of* **hearts** | *the* **jack** *of* **clubs** | *the* **ten** *of* **diamonds** etc. 纸牌游戏中的牌有两组红花色, 分别为红桃和方块, 还有两组黑花色, 为梅花和黑桃。每组牌有从 2 到 10 的 9 张牌, 另有"A"、老"K"、"Q"和"J"。单独一张牌叫做红桃 K、梅花 J、方块 10 等。

8 **cigarette/football/baseball etc card** a small piece of thick stiff paper with a picture on one side that is part of a set which people collect 香烟牌/足球卡/棒球卡等〔可收集成套〕

9 ▶**BUSINESS 商务**◀ [C] a small piece of thick stiff paper that shows your name, job, and the company you work for; BUSINESS CARD; VISITING CARD 名片: *I'll leave my card and you can contact me when it suits you.* 我留下一张名片, 你可以在方便的时候跟我联系。

10 **be on the cards** *BrE*【英】, **be in the cards** *AmE*【美】to seem likely to happen 很可能发生: *Another resignation could be on the cards.* 可能又有人要递交辞呈。

11 **play your cards right** to deal with a situation in the right way so that you are successful in getting what you want 处理得当, 做事精明: *If he plays his cards right Tony might get a promotion.* 如果托尼处事得当的话, 他可能会得到提升。

12 **put/lay your cards on the table** to tell people what your plans and intentions are in a clear, honest way 摊牌, 公开自己的打算[立场]: *I think it's time I put my cards on the table. You see, I'm not really a student.* 我想该说出真相了。其实我根本不是学生。

13 **play/keep your cards close to your chest** to keep your plans, thoughts, or feelings secret〔对自己的计划、想法、感觉等〕秘而不宣, 守口如瓶

14 **hold all the cards** *informal* to have all the advantages in a particular situation so that you can control what happens【非正式】占尽优势, 掌握局势

15 **get/be given your cards** *BrE informal* to have your job taken away from you【英, 非正式】被解雇[免职], 失业

16 **have another card up your sleeve** to have another advantage that you can use to be successful in a particular situation 另有一张王牌, 另有致胜法宝

17 **best/strongest/winning/trump card** something that gives you a big advantage in a particular situation 最厉害的一张王牌, 撒手锏: *The promise of tax cuts proved, as always, to be the Republican Party's trump card.* 一如以往, 许诺减税是共和党的王牌。

18 **sb's card is marked** if someone's card is marked, they have done something that makes people in authority disapprove of them 某人留下了污点, 某人上了黑名单

19 ▶AMUSING/UNUSUAL PERSON 滑稽/与众不同的人◀ [singular] *old-fashioned* an amusing or unusual person【过时】逗人发笑的人, 活宝: *Old Fred's a real card, isn't he!* 老弗雷德真是个活宝, 对吧!

20 [C] the thing inside a computer that the chips (CHIP[1] (4a)) are fixed to, that allows the computer to do specific things〔电脑的〕卡, 插件

21 ▶TOOL 工具◀ [C] *technical* a tool that is similar to a comb and is used for combing, cleaning and preparing wool or cotton for spinning (SPIN[1] (2))【术语】〔梳理送纺前的羊毛、棉花等的〕梳毛[棉]机

22 ▶FOOTBALL 足球◀ [C] a small piece of stiff red or yellow paper, shown to a player who has done something wrong in a game of football 红牌, 黄牌

card[2] *v* [T] **1** to comb, clean, and prepare wool or cotton, before making cloth〔用梳毛机等〕梳理 **2** *AmE* to ask someone to show a card proving that they are old enough to be in a particular place, especially a bar【美】要…出示证件〔尤指在酒吧等场所以检查对方是否够年龄入内〕

car·da·mom /ˈkɑrdəməm; ˈkɑːdəməm/ *n* [C,U] the seeds of an Asian fruit, used to give a special taste to Indian and Middle Eastern food 小豆蔻〔一种亚洲产果实的种子, 用于调味〕

card·board[1] /ˈkɑrdˌbɔrd; ˈkɑːdbɔːd/ *n* [U] a stiff brown material like very thick paper, used especially for making boxes〔尤指可用于制纸箱的〕(硬)纸板, 卡纸: *We covered the hole with a sheet of cardboard.* 我们用一块纸板挡住了洞。

cardboard[2] *adj* **1** made from cardboard 硬纸板制的: *a cardboard box* 硬纸板盒 **2** [only before noun 仅用于名词前] seeming silly and not real 显得愚蠢的; 不真实的: *a romantic novel full of cardboard characters* 充满虚构人物的浪漫小说

cardboard cit·y /ˌ‥ ˈ‥/ *n* [C] an area usually in a large town or city where people who have no home sleep outside using cardboard boxes to try to keep warm〔大城市内露宿者住的〕纸板区, 板房区

cardboard cut-out /ˌ‥ ˈ‥/ *n* [C] **1** a picture drawn on cardboard so that it can stand up on a surface〔画在硬纸板上可竖立的〕图样[形] **2** a person or character in a book, film etc who seems silly or unreal〔作品或电影等中的〕虚构人物, 胡乱编造的角色

card-car·ry·ing /ˈ· ˌ‥/ *adj* **card-carrying member** someone who has paid money to an organization and is a keen member of it 正式成员: *a card-carrying member of the Labour Party* 工党的一名正式党员

card cat·a·log /ˈ· ˌ‥/ *n* [C] *AmE* a box of cards that contain information about something and are arranged in order, for example in a library【美】〔图书馆等内的〕卡片目录, 卡片索引; CARD INDEX *BrE*【英】

card·hold·er /ˈkɑrdˌholdɚ; ˈkɑːdˌhəʊldə/ *n* [C] someone who has a CREDIT CARD〔信用卡的〕持卡人

car·di- /kɑrdɪ; kɑːdi/ *prefix* another form of the prefix CARDIO- 前缀 cardio- 的另一种形式

car·di·ac /ˈkɑrdɪˌæk; ˈkɑːdi-æk/ *adj* [only before noun 仅用于名词前] *technical* connected with the heart【术语】心脏的; 心脏病的: **cardiac arrest/failure** (=when the heart stops working) 心搏停止/心力衰竭

Car·diff /ˈkɑrdɪf; ˈkɑːdɪf/ the capital and main port of Wales 加的夫〔威尔士首府和主要港口〕

car·di·gan /ˈkɑrdɪgən; ˈkɑːdɪgən/ also 又作 **car·die** /ˈkɑrdɪ; ˈkɑːdi/ *BrE informal*【英, 非正式】*n* [C] a knitted JACKET[1] (1) or SWEATER, fastened at the front with buttons〔胸前开扣的〕毛线衣, 〔开襟〕羊毛衫

car·di·nal[1] /ˈkɑrdṇəl; ˈkɑːdənəl/ *n* [C] **1** a priest of high rank in the Roman Catholic Church〔罗马天主教会的〕红衣主教, 枢机主教 **2** a North American bird of which the male is a bright red colour 红衣凤头鸟, 北美红雀〔雄鸟毛色亮红〕 **3** a CARDINAL NUMBER 基数

cardinal[2] *adj* [only before noun 仅用于名词前] very important or basic 最重要的, 主要的; 基本的: *Having clean hands is one of the cardinal rules when preparing food.* 做饭前首先要把手洗干净。| **cardinal error** (=very serious and basic mistake) 重大的失误

cardinal num·ber /ˌ‥ ˈ‥/ *n* [C] a number such as 1, 2 or 3, that shows how many of something there are 基数〈如 1、2、3〉—compare 比较 ORDINAL NUMBER

cardinal point /ˌ‥ ˈ·/ *n* [C] *technical* one of the four main points (north, south, east, or west) on a COMPASS (1)【术语】〔罗盘上的〕基本方位〔指北、南、东、西〕

cardinal sin /ˌ‥ ˈ·/ *n* [C] **1** *informal* something bad or stupid that you must avoid doing【非正式】愚蠢的失误: *the cardinal sin of ignoring public opinion* 无视公众舆论的愚蠢失误 **2** a serious SIN[1] (1) in the Christian religion〔基督教中的〕主罪

cardinal vir·tue /ˌ‥ ˈ‥/ *n* [C] *formal* a moral quality that someone has which people greatly respect or value【正式】大德, 基本德性, 基本道德

card in·dex /ˈ· ˌ‥/ *n* [C] *BrE* a box of cards that contain information about something and are arranged in order, for example in a library【英】〔图书馆等的〕卡片目录, 卡片索引; CARD CATALOG *AmE*【美】

cardio- /kɑrdɪo; kɑːdiəʊ/ *prefix* also 又作 **cardi-** /kɑrdɪ; kɑːdi/ *technical* concerning the heart【术语】(有关)心脏的: *a cardiograph* (=instrument that measures movements of the heart) 心电图仪

car·di·ol·o·gy /ˌkɑrdɪˈɑlədʒɪ; ˌkɑːdiˈɒlədʒi/ *n* [U] the study or science of the heart 心脏病学

card phone /ˈ· ·/ *n* [C] a public telephone in which you must use a special plastic card rather than coins 卡式公用电话

card·sharp /ˈkɑrdˌʃɑrp; ˈkɑːdʃɑːp/ also 又作 **card·sharp·er** /-ˌʃɑrpɚ; -ˌʃɑːpə/ *n* [C] someone who cheats when playing cards in order to make money 靠诈术玩纸牌赢钱的人, 以赌博骗钱的人

card ta·ble /ˈ· ˌ‥/ *n* [C] a small light table that you can fold, used for playing cards 牌桌〔供玩牌用, 桌子可折叠〕

> **CULTURAL NOTE 文化注释**
>
> In the US, children often have to sit at card tables when large families eat a special meal together, for example at Thanksgiving or Christmas, because there is not enough space at the regular table. 在美国, 当一大家人在感恩节或圣诞节等特别日子里聚餐时, 常因普通桌子不够用, 儿童往往只能坐在牌桌上吃。

card vote /ˈ· ·/ *n* [C] *BrE* a way of voting at a TRADE UNION meeting in which your vote represents the votes of all the members of your organization【英】凭卡投票法〔指工会大会上的一种投票方法, 每位代表所投的票的作用相当于他代表的所有人投的票〕

CARE /kɛr; keə/ *n* [singular] Cooperative for American Relief to Everywhere; a US organization that sends special boxes of food, clothing, and medicine called 'CARE packages' to anywhere in the world where they are needed. 美国援外合作署〔美国一组织。合作署向需要援助的世界各地送去装有食物、衣物和药品的特殊盒子, 称"爱心包裹"〕

care[1] /kɛr; keə/ *v* [I,T] S1 W3

1 ▶OBJECTS/EVENTS 物体/事件◀ to feel that something is important, so that you are interested in it, worried about it etc 关心; 在意; 担心: **[+about]** *The only thing he seems to care about is money.* 他好像只在乎钱。| **care who/what/how etc** *Don't you care what happens to them?* 你难道不担心他们出什么事吗? | *I don't care whether we win or lose.* 我不在乎我们是赢还是输。

2 ▶PEOPLE 人们◀ to mind about what happens to someone, because you like or love them 关心, 在乎: *I care about him, and hate to see him hurt like this.* 我关心他, 很不愿意看见他伤成这个样子。| *She felt that nobody cared.* 她觉得无人在乎。

3 who cares? *spoken* used to say that something does not worry or upset you because it is not important【口】有谁在乎呢?: *It's rather old and scruffy, but who cares?* 这东西又旧又破, 但又有谁在意呢?

4 couldn't care less *spoken* used to say rudely that you do not care at all about something【口】不在乎〔粗鲁的说法〕: *I really couldn't care less what you think!* 你怎么想的, 关我什么事!

5 what do I/you/they care? *spoken* used to say that someone does not care at all about something【口】我/你(们)/他们在乎什么呢?〔表示对某事毫不在乎〕: *What do I care? It's your responsibility now!* 这关我什么事呢? 现在是你的责任了!

6 as if I cared! *spoken* used to say that something is not important to you at all【口】我才不在乎呢!: *As if I cared whether he comes with us or not!* 他是否会跟我们一起来我才不在乎呢!

7 for all sb cares *spoken* used to say that something does not matter at all to someone【口】毫不在乎: *We could be starving for all they care!* 我们即使在挨饿, 他们也不在乎。

8 not care to *old-fashioned* not to like to do something【过时】不喜欢做某事: *She doesn't care to spend much time with her relatives.* 她不喜欢花太多时间跟亲戚待在一起。

9 I wouldn't care to *spoken* used to say that you think that something would be an unpleasant experience【口】我不想, 我不愿意: *I wouldn't care to meet him in a dark alley!* 我不想在黑暗的巷子里和他见面!

10 would you care to? *spoken formal* used to ask someone politely whether they want to do something【口，正式】要不要…？…怎么样？〔礼貌说法〕：*Would you care to join us for a drink?* 要不要跟我们一起喝一杯？—see also 另见 CARING

care for sb/sth *phr v* [T] **1** to look after someone who is not able to look after themselves 照顾，照料：*She cared for her father all through his long illness.* 她在父亲长期卧病期间一直照料着他。| *The children are being well cared for.* 孩子们得到了悉心的照料。**2** [usually in negatives and questions 一般用于否定句和疑问句] *formal* to like or want something or someone【正式】喜欢，想要：*Would you care for a drink?* 要喝点什么吗？| *I don't much care for his parents.* 我不太喜欢他的父母。

2 2 **care²** *n*

1 ►LOOKING AFTER SB/STH 照料某人/某物◄ [U] the process of looking after someone or something, especially because they are weak, ill, old etc 照顾，照料，护理：*high standards of medical care* 高水准的医疗服务 | *They shared the care of the children.* 他们共同照顾孩子。| *advice on skin care* 皮肤护理的建议 —see also 另见 DAY CARE CENTER, INTENSIVE CARE

2 ►CAREFULNESS 小心◄ [U] carefulness to avoid damage, mistakes etc 小心，谨慎，注意：*Fragile – handle with care.* 易碎，小心轻放！—see also 另见 **tender loving care** (TENDER¹ (4))

3 take care to be careful 当心，注意：*It's very icy, so take care on the roads.* 路上结冰了，小心。| **take care (that)** *Take care that you don't drop it!* 当心别掉地上！| **take care to do sth** *Take care to keep the power cable away from the blade.* 注意把电线与刀片分开。| **take care with/over sth** *Paul always takes great care over his appearance.* 保罗一向很注意自己的外表。

4 take care of a) to look after someone or something 照看，照料：*Who's taking care of the dog while you're away?* 你不在时谁来照看你的狗？**b)** to deal with all the work, arrangements etc that are necessary for something to happen 处理，对付，注意：*Her secretary always took care of the details.* 细节问题总是由她的秘书来处理。| *Don't worry about your accommodation – it's all taken care of.* 别担心你的住宿问题，一切都解决了。**c)** an expression meaning to pay for something; used when you want to avoid saying this directly〔婉转说法〕承担〔费用〕：*We'll take care of the fees.* 我们将会承担费用。

5 take care! *spoken* used when saying goodbye to family or friends【口】保重！珍重！：*Bye! Take care! See you on Sunday.* 再见，请多保重！周日再见。

6 in care *BrE* a child who is in care is being looked after in a local council home, not by their parents【英】〔地方当局对儿童进行〕收养，监护：**take sb into care** *When he was sent to prison, the children were taken into care.* 他入狱时，孩子们就由收养所照料。

7 ►PROBLEM/WORRY 麻烦/忧虑◄ [C,U] *literary* something that causes problems and makes you anxious or sad【文】恼人之事，烦恼；忧虑：*At last I felt free from my cares.* 我终于摆脱了烦恼。| **not have a care in the world** (=not have any problems or worries) 无忧无虑 | **take the cares of the world on your shoulders** (=worry about other people's problems as well as your own) 忧国忧民

8 care of used when sending letters to someone at someone else's address; c/o 由…转交〔写在信封上，略作 c/o〕

9 driving without due care and attention *BrE law* the crime of driving a car without being careful enough【英，法律】不小心驾驶罪

10 have a care! *spoken old-fashioned* used to tell someone to be more careful【口，过时】小心点！仔细点！〔用于提醒〕

ca·reen /kəˈriːn; kəˈriːn/ *v* [I always+adv/prep] *AmE* to move quickly forwards making sudden sideways movements; LURCH【美】〔车辆等〕歪歪斜斜地疾驶：**[+down/over/along]** *The car careened around the corner and skidded to a halt.* 那辆车左摇右晃地疾驶过街角，打滑着停了下来。

2 2 **ca·reer¹** /kəˈrɪr; kəˈrɪə/ *n* [C] **1** a job or profession that you have been trained for and intend to do for several years 职业，事业：*a career in banking* 从事银行业 | *He realized that his acting career was over.* 他意识到自己的演艺事业已结束。| **career change** (=when you start a completely different job or profession) 改行 | **career structure** (=the opportunities that you have to move upwards in your job or profession) 职业结构〔发展或提升的种种机会〕—see 见 JOB (USAGE) **2 career soldier/teacher etc** someone who intends to be a soldier, teacher etc for most of their life, not just for a particular period of time 职业军人/教师等 **3** the period of time in your life that you spend doing a particular activity 生涯；(一段) 工作经历，履历：*She had not had a very impressive school career up till then.* 在那以前，她在学校里的表现并不怎么样。| *My career as an English teacher didn't last long.* 我的英语教师生涯没持续多久。

career² *v* [I always+adv/prep] to move forwards very fast and often without control〔常指失控地〕猛冲：**[+down/along/towards]** *The truck careered down the hill and into a tree.* 那辆卡车直冲下山，一头撞到一棵树上。

career break /·ˈ· ·/ *n* [C] a short period of time when you do not work in your usual job or profession, for example because you want to look after your children 职业中断〔指在一段时间里暂时不去工作，例如为了照顾孩子〕

career coun·sel·or /·ˈ· ,···/ *n* [C] *AmE* a CAREERS OFFICER【美】就业顾问，就业指导人员

ca·reer·ist /kəˈrɪrɪst; kəˈrɪərɪst/ *n* [C] *especially AmE* someone whose career is more important to them than anything else so that they will do whatever is necessary to be successful【尤美】名利心重的人，一心想飞黄腾达的人；野心家 —**careerist** *adj* —**careerism** *n* [U]

careers of·fic·er /·ˈ· ,···/ also 又作 **careers ad·vis·er** /·ˈ· ·,··/ *n* [C] *BrE* someone whose job is to give people advice about what jobs and professional training might be suitable for them【英】就业顾问，就业指导人员；CAREER COUNSELOR *AmE*【美】

career wom·an /·ˈ· ,··/ *n* [C] a woman whose career is very important to her, so that she may not want to get married or have children 事业型女性：*a fiercely independent career woman* 非常独立的女强人

care·free /ˈkɛr,fri; ˈkeəfriː/ *adj* having no worries or problems 无忧无虑的，无牵挂的：*With the exams over, we felt happy and carefree at last.* 考试结束了，我们感到非常高兴，一身轻松。| *Travel in carefree comfort to your hotel near Paris.* 轻松舒适地旅行到巴黎附近的旅馆入住。

care·ful /ˈkɛrfəl; ˈkeəfəl/ *adj* **1 (be) careful!** *spoken* used to tell someone to think about what they are doing so that they do not have an accident【口】小心点！**2** trying to avoid damaging, harming, or losing something 谨慎的，小心翼翼的：*a careful driver* 谨慎的司机 | **careful to do sth** *I was careful not to say anything about it to the boss.* 我很谨慎，什么也没告诉老板。| **[+with]** *Be careful with that vase – it's very fragile.* 小心那只花瓶，它很易碎。| **careful who/what/how etc** *Be careful how you handle those glasses.* 你搬动那些玻璃杯时要当心。| *I had taught them to be careful crossing the road.* 我教他们过马路时要当心。| **[+about]** *Mara was extremely careful about what she ate.* 玛拉在饮食方面极为谨慎。| **careful (that)** *We were very careful that he didn't find out.* 我们非常小心，因此他并未发觉。**3** paying a lot of attention to detail, so that something is done correctly and thoroughly 细心的；周密的：*After careful consideration, we've decided to accept their offer.* 我们经过周密的考虑之后，决定接受他们的提议。| *a careful study of all aspects of the problem* 对问题全面周密的研究 **4 careful with money** not spending more money than you need to 花钱谨慎 **5 you can't be too careful** *spoken* used to say that you should do everything possible to avoid problems or danger【口】越小心越好 —**carefulness** *n* [U] 1 2

This graph shows how common different grammar patterns of the adjective **careful** are. 本图表所示为形容词careful构成的不同语法模式的使用频率。

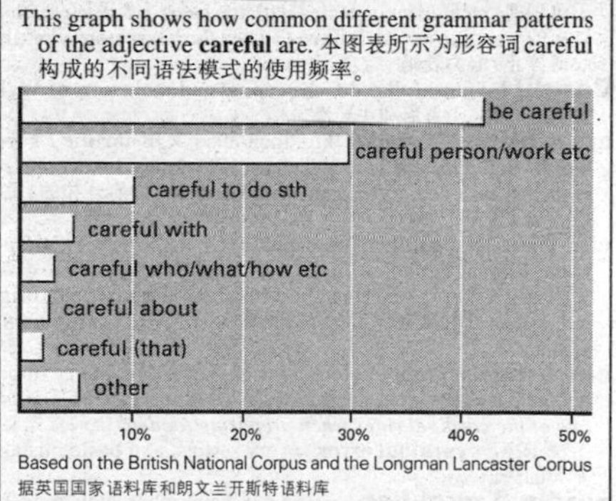

Based on the British National Corpus and the Longman Lancaster Corpus
据英国国家语料库和朗文兰开斯特语料库

care·ful·ly /ˈkɛrfəlɪ; ˈkeəfəli/ *adv* in a careful way 小心地；仔细地：*I carried the bowl carefully in both hands.* 我双手小心翼翼地捧着碗。| **carefully planned/chosen etc** *a carefully planned operation* 精心策划的行动 2 2

care·giv·er /ˈkɛr,gɪvə; ˈkeə,gɪvə/ *n* [C] *AmE* someone who takes care of a child or sick person【美】〔小孩或病人的〕看护者，护理员

care la·bel /ˈ· ,··/ *n* [C] a small piece of cloth in a piece of clothing that tells you how to wash it〔衣服上说明洗涤方法的〕洗涤标签

care·less /ˈkɛrlɪs; ˈkeələs/ *adj* **1** not paying enough attention to what you are doing, so that you make mistakes, damage things etc 不小心的，粗心的；疏忽的：*I had been careless and left the window unlocked.* 我太粗心了，忘记了关窗户。| *a careless student* 粗心大意的学生 **2** done without much effort or attention to detail 草率的，敷衍的：*This is a very careless piece of work – do it again!* 这工作干得太马虎了，重做吧！| *a careless mistake* 疏忽造成的错误 **3** natural and not done with any deliberate effort or attention 漫不经心的，自然的：*He ran a hand through his hair with a careless gesture.* 他漫不经心地用手理了理头发。| *careless charm* 天生[自然流露]的迷人风采 **4 careless of** *formal* deliberately ignoring something【正式】〔故意〕不在乎，不理会：*She turned and, careless of the pain, headed blindly for the door.* 她转过身，忍住痛楚，盲目地朝门口走去。**5** *rare* without problems or worries; CAREFREE【罕】无忧无虑的 —**carelessly** *adv* —**carelessness** *n* [U]

care pack·age /ˈ· ,··/ *n* [C] *AmE* a package of food, sweets etc that is sent to someone living away from home, especially a student at college【美】〔尤指从家里寄给远方在校生的〕爱心包裹

car·er /ˈkɛrɚ; ˈkeərə/ *n* [C] *BrE* someone who stays at home to look after a relative who is old, ill etc【英】〔在家照料年老、生病等的亲人的〕照料者

ca·ress¹ /kəˈrɛs; kəˈres/ *v* [T] **1** to gently touch someone in a way that shows you love them 爱抚，抚摸：*She lovingly caressed the baby's cheek.* 她亲切地抚摸宝宝的脸颊。**2** *poetic* to touch something gently, in a way that seems pleasant or romantic【诗】轻抚，轻拍：*Waves caressed the shore.* 波浪轻轻地拍打着海岸。

caress² *n* [C] a gentle loving touch or kiss 爱抚，抚摸；亲吻

car·et /ˈkærət; ˈkærḷt/ *n* [C] *technical* the mark (ʎ) or (ʌ) used in writing and printing to show where something is to be added【术语】脱字号，补字符号

care·tak·er /ˈkɛr,tekɚ; ˈkeə,teɪkə/ *n* [C] **1** *BrE* someone whose job is to look after a building, especially a school【英】〔尤指学校等建筑物的〕管理员；JANITOR *AmE*【美】**2** someone who looks after a house or land while the person who owns it is not there〔主人不在时照料其房地产的〕看管人 **3** *AmE* someone who looks after other people, especially a teacher, parent, nurse etc【美】照看人，保护人；监护人〔尤指老师、父母、护士等〕

caretaker gov·ern·ment /ˈ···· ,···/ *n* [C] a government that has power only for a short period of time between the end of one government and the start of another〔旧政府已下台、新政府产生前的〕看守政府

care·worn /ˈkɛr,worn; ˈkeəwɔːn/ *adj* looking sad, worried, or anxious 饱经忧患的，因操心而憔悴的：*the careworn face of a mother with hungry children to feed* 有一群饥饿的孩子要喂养的母亲那憔悴的面容

car·fare /ˈkɑrfɛr; ˈkɑːfeə/ *n* [U] *AmE old-fashioned* the amount of money that it costs to travel on a TROLLEY (3) in some cities in the US【美，过时】〔美国一些城市内有轨电车的〕车费

car·go /ˈkɑrgo; ˈkɑːgəʊ/ *n plural* **cargoes** *or* **cargos** [C,U] the goods being carried in a ship, plane, TRUCK¹ (1) etc〔船、飞机、卡车等装载的〕(一批)货物：*We sailed from Jamaica with a cargo of rum.* 我们满载一船朗姆酒从牙买加起航。| *a cargo vessel* 货船

car·hop /ˈkɑr,hɑp; ˈkɑːhɒp/ *n* [C] *AmE old-fashioned*【美，过时】**1** someone who takes care of your car if you are staying a large hotel〔大酒店中为顾客服务的〕看车人 **2** someone who carries food to people's cars at a DRIVE-IN restaurant〔路边汽车餐厅的〕侍者

Car·ib·be·an /,kærəˈbiən; ,kærḷˈbiːən◂/ *adj* from or connected with the islands in the Caribbean Sea 加勒比海(诸岛)的：*Caribbean literature* 加勒比海文学

Caribbean Sea, the /,····ˈ·/ also 又作 **the Caribbean** the sea between Central America, South America, and the Caribbean islands, west of the Atlantic Ocean 加勒比海〔中美洲、南美洲、加勒比诸岛之间的海域，位于大西洋以西〕

car·i·bou /ˈkærə,bu; ˈkærḷbuː/ *n* [C] a North American REINDEER 北美驯鹿

car·i·ca·ture¹ /ˈkærɪkətʃɚ; ˈkærɪkətʃʊə/ *n* **1** [C] a funny drawing of someone that makes some of their features look bigger or more amusing than they really are〔人物〕漫画：*Newspapers often have caricatures of politicians.* 报纸上经常登载政客的漫画。**2** [C] a description of someone that shows only some parts of their character, especially parts that are silly or amusing 讽刺画[文]：*a caricature of a semi-educated village teacher* 对一个半文盲乡村教师的讽刺描写 **3** [U] the skill of making pictures, or writing about people in this way 漫画手法

caricature 漫画

portrait 肖像

caricature 漫画

caricature² *v* [T] to draw or describe someone in a way that makes them seem silly or stupid 把…画成漫画，用漫画表现[讽刺]；使滑稽化：*They are always being caricatured as hardworking bores.* 他们总是被漫画画成勤劳但却令人厌烦的人。

car·i·ca·tur·ist /ˈkærɪkətʃərɪst; ˈkærɪkətʃʊərḷst/ *n* [C] someone who draws or writes caricatures 漫画家

car·ies /ˈkɛrɪz; ˈkeəriz/ *n* [U] *technical* decay in someone's teeth【术语】龋齿：*dental caries* 蛀牙

car·ill·on /ˈkærə,lɑn; ˈkærḷljən/ *n* [C] a set of bells in a tower that are controlled from a piano KEYBOARD¹ (1), or a tune played on these bells〔钟楼上可用键盘弹奏的〕组钟(乐曲)，排钟(乐曲)

car·ing /ˈkɛrɪŋ; ˈkeərɪŋ/ *adj* **1** someone who is caring thinks about what other people need or would like, and tries to help them 关心照顾人的；提供帮助的：*a warm and caring man* 热心助人者 | *a very caring attitude* 非常乐于助人的态度 **2 be past caring** *informal* to not worry about something because you are very tired, upset, or worried about something else【非正式】无暇顾及，〔因沮丧、劳累等而〕无心考虑 **3 caring profession** a job that involves looking after other people 关心照顾人的职业：*Like most of the caring professions, nursing is very badly paid.* 和大多数照顾人的职业一样，护理的报酬很低。

car·jack·ing /ˈkɑr,dʒækɪŋ; ˈkɑː,dʒækɪŋ/ *n* [C,U] the crime of forcing the driver of a car to drive you somewhere or give you their car, by using threats and violence 劫车 —compare 比较 HIJACKING —**carjacker** *n* [C] —**carjack** *v* [T]

Car·lisle /kɑrˈlaɪl; kɑːˈlaɪl/ a city in northwest England, where the local government for Cumbria is based 卡莱尔〔英格兰西北部一城市，坎布里亚郡政府所在地〕

Car·lyle /kɑrˈlaɪl; kɑːˈlaɪl/, **Thom·as** /ˈtɑməs; ˈtɒməs/ (1795-1881) a Scottish writer on political and social subjects, who wrote a famous history of the French Revolution 卡莱尔〔(1795-1881)，苏格兰政治、社会题材作家。他曾写过一部关于法国大革命的著名史书〕

Car·mar·then·shire /kəˈmɑrðənʃɚ; kəˈmɑːðənʃə/ a COUNTY in southwestern Wales 卡马森郡〔威尔士西南部一郡〕

Car·men /ˈkɑrmən; ˈkɑːmen/ an opera written in 1875 by the French COMPOSER Georges Bizet, about a Spanish GYPSY woman called Carmen 卡门〔法国作曲家乔治·比才 1875 年创作的一部歌剧，讲述一位名叫卡门的西班牙吉普赛女子的故事〕

Car·mi·chael /ˈkɑrˈmaɪkḷ; ˈkɑːˈmaɪkəl/, **Stoke·ly** /ˈstoklɪ; ˈstəʊkli/ (1941-98) a former member of the Black Panthers who worked in the 1960s to achieve social and political changes for black people in the US 卡迈克尔〔(1941-1998)，黑豹党前成员，20 世纪 60 年代曾为改变美国黑人的社会、政治地位而努力〕

car·mine /ˈkɑrmɪn; ˈkɑːmḷn/ *n* [U] a deep purplish red colour 紫红色，洋红色，胭脂红 —**carmine** *adj*

Car·na·by Street /ˈkɑrnəbɪ ,strit; ˈkɑːnəbi ,striːt/ a street in London, world famous in the 1960s for its shops selling fashionable clothes for young people卡纳比街〔位于伦敦，20 世纪 60 年代以销售青年时装的众多小店而闻名世界〕

car·nage /ˈkɑrnɪdʒ; ˈkɑːnɪdʒ/ *n* [U] the killing and wounding of lots of people, especially in a war〔尤指战争中的〕大屠杀，残杀：*The battlefield was a scene of terrible carnage.* 战场上是一片可怕的大屠杀景象。

car·nal /ˈkɑrnḷ; ˈkɑːnl/ *adj* a word meaning connected with the body or sex, used especially in religious language 肉体的，性欲的，肉欲的〔尤用于宗教语言〕：*carnal desires* 肉欲 —**carnally** *adv*

car·na·tion /kɑrˈneʃən; kɑːˈneɪʃən/ *n* [C] a white, pink, or red flower that smells sweet and is often worn as a decoration at formal ceremonies 康乃馨

CULTURAL NOTE 文化注释

In England, it is the custom for the men taking part in a wedding and the close members of the two families to wear a single carnation pinned to their jackets or dresses. 按英格兰传统，参加婚礼的男士和双方近亲在上装或礼服上别一朵康乃馨。

car·ne /ˋkarnɪ; 'kɑːni/ *n* [U] —see 见 CHILLI (1)

Car·ne·gie /karˋnegɪ; kɑː'neɪgi/**, An·drew** (1835-1919) a US businessman and PHILANTHROPIST, born in Scotland, who helped to start many public libraries in the US. He also provided most of the money for building Carnegie Hall. 卡内基〔(1835-1919)，美国实业家、慈善家，出生于苏格兰。他在美国捐款兴建了很多图书馆，还为修建卡内基音乐厅提供所需的大部分资金〕

C

Car·ne·gie Hall /,‥ˋ‥/ a large CONCERT HALL in New York City where many famous musicians perform 卡内基音乐厅〔纽约市一大型音乐厅。众多著名音乐家在此演出〕

car·ne·li·an /karˋniljən; kɑː'niːliən/ *n* [C] another spelling of CORNELIAN cornelian 的另一种拼法

car·ney /ˋkarnɪ; 'kɑːni/ *n* [C] *AmE*【美】another spelling of CARNY carny 的另一种拼法

car·ni·val /ˋkarnəvl; 'kɑːn̩vəl/ *n* **1** [C,U] a celebration with dancing, drinking, and a PROCESSION (1) through the streets 狂欢(节)；嘉年华会: *Carnival in Rio* 里约热内卢的嘉年华会 | *the Notting Hill carnival* 诺丁山狂欢节 | *the carnival atmosphere after they won the game* 他们赢得比赛后的狂欢气氛 **2** [C] *AmE* a noisy outdoor event at which you can ride on special machines and play games for prizes【美】游乐场，流动游艺场〔喧闹的户外活动，有机动游戏、摊位游戏等〕; FUNFAIR *BrE*【英】**3** [C] *AmE* an event held at a school in which students play games for prizes【美】〔学校的〕游园会，嘉年华会

car·ni·vore /ˋkarnə,vor; 'kɑːn̩vɔː/ *n* [C] **1** an animal that eats flesh 肉食动物 —compare 比较 HERBIVORE, OMNIVORE **2** *humorous* someone who eats meat【幽默】食荤的人 —compare 比较 VEGETARIAN —**carnivorous** *adj*

car·ny, carney /ˋkarnɪ; 'kɑːni/ *n* [C] *AmE informal* someone who works in a CARNIVAL (2)【美，非正式】流动游艺场的工作〔表演〕人员

car·ob /ˋkærəb; 'kærəb/ *n* [U] the fruit of a Mediterranean tree, that tastes similar to chocolate and is sometimes eaten instead of chocolate〔产于地中海地区的〕角豆树果实〔其味道与巧克力相似〕

car·ol[1] /ˋkærəl; 'kærəl/ also 又作 **Christmas carol** *n* [C] a traditional Christmas song〔圣诞〕颂歌

CULTURAL NOTE 文化注释

At Christmas time, groups of people sing carols, both indoors and outdoors, in places such as shopping centres, railway stations, and public squares. They usually collect money for a good cause, for example homeless people. Sometimes carol singers, especially children, go along the streets from house to house, singing in front of each house and asking for money. In the US carol singers are sometimes invited into people's houses for a drink of COCOA and a biscuit. 圣诞节时人们聚在一起唱颂歌，地点可在室内或户外，如购物中心、火车站、公共广场。他们通常为善事募捐，如帮助无家可归的人。有时唱颂歌的人，尤其是儿童，走街串巷，在每户人家门口演唱募捐。在美国，唱颂歌的人有时会被邀请到家中喝杯可可饮料或吃块饼干。

carol[2] *v* **carolled, carolling** *BrE*【英】**caroled, caroling** *AmE*【美】[I] to sing carols or other songs in a lively way〔欢乐地〕唱圣诞颂歌〔或其他歌曲〕

Car·o·li·nas, the /,kærəˋlaɪnəz; ,kærə'laɪnəz/ the US states of North Carolina and South Carolina〔美国的〕南北卡罗来纳州

ca·rot·id ar·te·ry /kəˋratɪd ,artərɪ; kə'rɒtɪ̣d ,ɑːtəri/ *n* [C] *technical* one of the two arteries (ARTERY (1)) in your neck, that supply blood to your head【术语】颈动脉

ca·rouse /kəˋrauz; kə'raʊz/ *v* [I] *literary* to drink a lot, be noisy, and laugh loudly【文】痛饮，狂饮欢闹 —**carousal** *n* [C,U]

car·ou·sel, carrousel /,kæruˋzɛl; ,kærə'sel/ *n* [C] **1** *AmE* a machine with wooden horses on it that turns round and round, which people can ride on for fun; MERRY-GO-ROUND (1)【美】旋转木马 **2** the circular moving belt that you collect your bags and cases from at an airport〔机场的〕旋转式行李传送带 **3** a circular piece of equipment that you put slides (SLIDE[2] (4)) into for showing on SLIDE PROJECTOR〔幻灯放映机上的〕幻灯片卡盘

carp[1] /karp; kɑːp/ *v* [I usually in progressive 一般用于进行时] to complain about something or criticize someone continually 挑剔，找茬儿，吹毛求疵: *Stop carping!* 别挑剔了！

carp[2] *n plural* **carp** [C] a large fish that lives in lakes, pools, and rivers, which you can eat 鲤鱼

car·pal tun·nel syn·drome /,karpl ˋtʌnl ,sɪndrom; ,kɑːpəl 'tʌnl ,sɪndrəʊm/ *n* [U] *technical* a medical condition in which someone gets a lot of pain and weakness in their wrist【术语】腕管综合征

car park /ˋ· ·/ *n* [C] *BrE*【英】**1** an open area where cars can park 露天停车场; PARKING LOT *AmE*【美】**2** an enclosed building for cars to park in 公共停车房，多层停车场; PARKING GARAGE *AmE*【美】

car·pen·ter /ˋkarpəntɚ; 'kɑːpɪ̣ntə/ *n* [C] someone whose job is making and repairing wooden objects 木匠，木工

car·pen·try /ˋkarpəntrɪ; 'kɑːpɪ̣ntri/ *n* [U] the skill or work of a carpenter 木工手艺；木匠业

car·pet[1] /ˋkarpɪt; 'kɑːpɪ̣t/ *n* **1** [C,U] heavy woven material for covering floors or stairs, or a piece of this material 地毯: *a beautiful Persian carpet* 一张美丽的波斯地毯 | **fitted carpet** (=one that is cut to fit the shape of a room) 固定的地毯 —compare 比较 RUG (1) **2** **carpet of leaves/flowers etc** *literary* a thick layer of leaves etc【文】满地的树叶/花等 —see also 另见 MAGIC CARPET, **sweep sth under the carpet** (SWEEP[1] (13))

carpet[2] *v* [T] **1** [usually in passive 一般用被动态] to cover a floor with carpet 在…上铺地毯: *a carpeted corridor* 铺有地毯的走廊 **2** *informal especially BrE* to blame someone for something they have done; REPRIMAND【非正式，尤英】斥责，责备，责骂 **3** **carpeted with grass/flowers etc** *literary* covered with a thick layer of grass etc【文】覆盖着一层厚厚的草/花等

car·pet·bag /ˋkarpɪt,bæg; 'kɑːpɪtbæg/ *n* [C] a bag used for travelling, usually made of carpet 毯制旅行包

car·pet·bag·ger /ˋkarpɪt,bægɚ; 'kɑːpɪ̣t,bægə/ *n* [C] someone who tries to become active in the political life of another area for their own advantage, especially someone from the North of the US active in the South in the 1860s and 1870s 提包客，外来政客〔尤指19世纪60至70年代间，在美国南方政坛上活跃的北方人〕

carpet bomb /ˋ‥ ,·/ *v* [T] to drop a lot of bombs over a small area to destroy everything in it 对…进行地毯式轰炸

car·pet·ing /ˋkarpɪtɪŋ; 'kɑːpɪ̣tɪŋ/ *n* [U] heavy woven material for making CARPETS 地毯织料

carpet slip·per /ˋ‥ ,‥/ *n* [C] a type of soft shoe that you wear indoors〔室内穿的〕地毯拖鞋

carpet sweep·er /ˋ‥ ,‥/ *n* [C] a simple machine for sweeping CARPETS 地毯清扫器

car pool[1] /ˋ· ·/ *n* [C] **1** a group of car owners who agree to drive everyone in the group to work, school etc on different days so that only one car is used at a time 合伙用车者〔指一群有汽车的人达成协议，轮流用自己的车送大家上班、上学等〕**2** a group of cars owned by a company or other organization that its members can use; MOTOR POOL〔公司等拥有的供其工作人员使用的〕公车队

car pool[2] *v* [I] *AmE* if a group of people car pool, they agree to drive everyone in the group to work, school etc on different days so that only one car is used at a time【美】合伙用车

car·port /ˋkar,port; 'kɑːpɔːt/ *n* [C] a shelter for a car that has a roof and one or two walls, often built against the side of a house〔靠墙搭建的〕敞棚式汽车间，停车棚 —compare 比较 GARAGE[1] (1)

Car·raun·too·hill /,kærənˋtuəl; ,kærən'tuːəl/ the highest mountain in the Republic of Ireland, in the southwest of the country 卡朗图厄尔山〔爱尔兰共和国最高的山，位于该国西南部〕

car·rel /ˋkærəl; 'kærəl/ *n* [C] a small enclosed space with a desk and a light for one person to use in a library〔图书馆内供一个读者使用的带台灯和书桌的〕小单间

Car·re·ras /kæˋrɛrəs; kæ'reərəs/**, Jo·sé** /hoˋze; həʊ'zeɪ/ (1946-) a Spanish OPERA singer with a TENOR voice, who often sings with Luciano Pavarotti and Placido Domingo, two other opera singers 卡雷拉斯〔(1946-)，西班牙男高音歌剧演唱家。他经常与鲁契亚诺·帕瓦罗蒂和普拉西多·多明戈两位歌剧演唱家一起演唱〕

car·riage /ˋkærɪdʒ; 'kærɪdʒ/ *n* **1** [C] a vehicle with wheels that is pulled by a horse, used in former times〔旧时的〕马车 **2** [C] *BrE* one of the connected parts of a train that passengers sit in【英】〔铁路〕客车车厢; CAR (3) *AmE*【美】**3** [U] *formal* the way someone walks and moves their head and body【正式】仪态，姿态，举止 **4** something with wheels that is used to move a heavy object, especially a gun 车架；(有轮) 炮架 **5** [U] *formal espe-*

cially BrE the act of moving goods from one place to another or the cost of moving them【正式, 尤英】运输, 搬运; (货)运费 **6** [C] the movable part of a machine that supports another part〔机器的〕滑架; 溜板; 拖板: *the carriage of a typewriter* 打字机的滑架 —see also 另见 BABY CARRIAGE

carriage clock /ˈ· · ·/ *n* [C] a small clock inside a glass case with a handle on top 旅行钟, 便携式时钟

car·riage·way /ˈkærɪdʒˌwe; ˈkærɪdʒweɪ/ *n* [C] *BrE* the part of a road that a single line of traffic moves along【英】马路; 行车道 —see also 另见 DUAL CARRIAGEWAY

car·ri·er /ˈkærɪɚ; ˈkæriə/ *n* [C] **1** a company that moves goods or passengers from one place to another 运输公司 **2** a military vehicle or ship used to move soldiers, weapons etc〔运送武器、士兵等的〕军车; 运输舰 —see also 另见 AIRCRAFT CARRIER **3** *technical* someone who passes a disease to other people without having it themselves【术语】带菌者, 病媒〔指传播疾病而自身却不受其害者〕**4** a metal frame that is fixed to a bicycle or other vehicle and holds bags etc〔固定在自行车等上的金属〕载物架. **5** a carrier bag 手提购物袋

carrier bag /ˈ· · · ,·/ *n* [C] *BrE* a bag that you are given in a shop, to carry the things you have bought【英】手提购物袋 —see picture at 参见 BAG¹ 图

carrier pi·geon /ˈ· · · ,· ·/ *n* [C] a PIGEON (=type of bird) that has been trained to carry messages 信鸽

car·ri·on /ˈkærɪən; ˈkæriən/ *n* [U] dead flesh that is decaying 腐尸; 腐肉: *Some birds feed on carrion.* 有些鸟类以动物的腐尸为食物。

Car·roll /ˈkærəl; ˈkærəl/, **Lewis** (1832-98) a British writer who wrote two very famous children's stories, *Alice's Adventures in Wonderland* and *Through the Looking Glass*. His real name was Charles Dodgson, and he was also a teacher of mathematics at Oxford University. 卡罗尔〔(1832-1898), 英国作家。他创作了《艾丽丝漫游奇境记》和《镜中世界》两本著名儿童读物。真名查尔斯·道奇森。他还是牛津大学的数学教师〕

car·rot /ˈkærət; ˈkærət/ *n* **1** [C,U] a plant with a long thick orange pointed root that you eat as a vegetable 胡萝卜, 红萝卜 —see picture on page A9 参见 A9 页图 **2** [C] *informal* something that is promised to someone in order to try and persuade them to work harder【非正式】〔为使某人做某事而给予的〕报酬, 好处, 奖品; 许诺: **carrot and stick approach/method etc** (=a way of persuading someone to do something using a mixture of promises and threats) 胡萝卜加大棒[威逼利诱]的方法

car·rot·y /ˈkærətɪ; ˈkærəti/ *adj* hair that is carroty is orange〔头发〕胡萝卜色的, 橘红色的

car·rou·sel /ˌkæruˈzɛl; ˌkærəˈsel/ *n* [C] another spelling of CAROUSEL carousel 的另一种拼法

S1 W1 **car·ry¹** /ˈkærɪ; ˈkæri/ *v* **carried, carrying**

1 ►LIFT AND TAKE 提拿◄ [T] to take something somewhere in your hands or arms, on your back etc 提; 拿; 抱; 带; 扛; 背; 搬: *A porter helped me carry my luggage.* 一位搬运工人帮我搬行李。| *Let me carry that for you.* 让我帮你拿吧。| **carry sth around/out/to etc** *I'm not carrying it around all day!* 我才不会整天到处带着它呢! —see 见 BRING (USAGE)

2 ►VEHICLE/SHIP/PLANE 车/船/飞机◄ [T] to take people or things from one place to another 运送: **carry sth to/down/away etc** *The ship was carrying oil from Kuwait to Japan.* 这艘船把石油从科威特运到日本。| **carry sb/sth** *a coach carrying 44 American tourists* 载有 44 个美国游客的长途客车

3 ►HOW STH IS MOVED 输送方式◄ [T] if a pipe, river, wire etc carries something such as liquid or electricity, the liquid etc flows along it 输送, 传送: **carry sth along/through/across etc** *Pipes carry the water across the desert.* 输水管穿过沙漠把水输送出去。| *Soil from the river banks is carried down towards the sea.* 河水把河两岸的泥土冲向海里。| **carry sth** *Two lines are dedicated to carrying teletext data.* 有两条线路专门用来传送电视文字数据。| **be carried out to sea/downstream etc** (=be taken somewhere by a current of water) 被冲到大海/下游等

4 ►DISEASE 疾病◄ [T] if a person, animal, or insect carries a disease the disease is spread by them 传播〔疾病〕: *Brown rats carried the plague.* 褐色的老鼠传播这种瘟疫。| *Many serious diseases are carried by insects.* 许多严重的疾病都是由昆虫传播的。

5 carry sth in your head/mind to remember information that you need, without writing it down 将某事记在脑海中: *He was required to carry a detailed map of the airport in his head.* 他被要求把那个机场的详细地图记在脑子里。

6 ►HAVE WITH YOU 随身带着◄ [T] to take money, a weapon, or something that you need, with you in your pocket, on your belt, in your bag etc 携带; 佩戴: *I don't usually carry that much cash on me.* 我身上通常不带那么多现金。| **carry a gun/knife etc** *The police here don't carry guns.* 这里的警察不带枪。| **carry arms** (=carry weapons) 携带武器 *a society where men carried arms as a matter of course* 一个把携带武器视为理所当然的社会

7 ►SHOP 商店◄ [T] if a shop carries goods, it has a supply of them for sale 备有〔货物〕供销售: **carry a range/selection** *Selfridges carries a good range of sports equipment.* 塞尔弗里奇商店备有多种运动器材供选购。| *I'm afraid we don't carry that line any more.* 恐怕我们不会再进那种货了。

8 be carrying too much weight/extra pounds etc to weigh too much 超重; 超载, 多载: *He's carrying at least ten kilos too many around.* 他带的东西至少超重了 10 公斤。

9 ►BUILDING 建筑物◄ [T] if a pillar, wall etc carries something, it supports the weight of that thing 支撑, 支持: *These two columns carry the whole roof.* 这两根柱子支撑着整个屋顶。

10 be/get carried away to be so excited, angry, interested etc that you are no longer really in control of what you do or say, or you forget everything else 忘乎所以, 忘形: *Sorry I shouted – I get a little carried away at times!* 对不起, 我不应该吼叫, 我有时有点控制不住。| *We got carried away by the beauty of the music.* 美妙的音乐让我们忘乎所以。

11 carry yourself well/stiffly etc to stand and move in a particular way 举止优雅/僵硬等: *He carried himself upright, like the old soldier he was.* 他站得笔直, 仿佛是一个老兵。

12 ►CHILD 孩子◄ [T] *old-fashioned* if a woman is carrying a child, she is PREGNANT (=going to have a baby)【过时】怀孕

13 ►NEWSPAPER/BROADCAST 报纸/广播◄ [T] if a newspaper or a television or radio broadcast carries a piece of news, an advertisement etc, it prints it or broadcasts it 登载; 广播; 报道: *The trade press carried details of the new laws.* 贸易新闻报道了新法例的详细内容。

14 ►LABEL/WRITING 标签/书写◄ [T] if an object, container etc carries a warning, information etc it is written on it 印有, 写有: *These new perfumes carry an 'exclusive' tag.* 这些新的香水印有"专营"标签。| *a card carrying details of your blood group* 一张写有你血型详情的卡片

15 carry insurance/a guarantee etc to have insurance etc 具有保险/保用期等: *All our products carry a 12 month guarantee.* 我们所有的产品均有一年的保用期。

16 ►HAVE A QUALITY 具有某种特质◄ [T] to have a particular quality such as authority or confidence that makes you believe or not believe someone 具有〔某种特质, 如权威性、信心等〕: *Her manner carried an unmistakable air of authority.* 她的举止具有毋庸置疑的权威性。| **carry conviction** (=to seem very sure about something)〔对某事〕非常确信 *Matthew's voice did not carry much conviction.* 马修的声音听起来并不太坚定。| **carry weight** (=to have some influence over someone) 有影响力 *Her views carry a lot of weight with the committee.* 她的观点对委员会有很大的影响力。

17 ►CRIME 犯罪◄ [T] if a crime carries a particular punishment, that is the usual punishment for the crime 被判处〔某种惩罚〕: *Rape carries the death penalty here.* 强奸在这里要判处死刑。| *a serious crime which carries a long jail sentence* 会被判处长期徒刑的严重罪行

18 carry a (heavy) load/burden to have a lot of work to do or a lot of responsibility for something 承担(大量)工作/重任: *Each team member is expected to carry a fair share of the workload.* 每个组员都应平分工作量。

19 ►USELESS PERSON 无用者◄ [T] if you carry someone who is not doing as much as they should, you manage without the work they should be doing, or the money they should be earning 扶助, 资助, 援助; 供养: *The team simply can't afford to carry anyone.* 队里根本供养不起任何闲人。

20 carry sth too far/to extremes/to excess to do or say too much about something 把某事做[说]得太过分: *Don't you think you're carrying discipline a bit too far? They're only children!* 你不觉得你的惩罚有点太过分了吗? 他们不过是孩子!

21 carry sb to victory/to the top etc to be the reason that a person or group is successful 使某人获胜/成功: *It's that extra enthusiasm that will carry you to the top.* 那份额外的热情会使你成功的。

22 ►PERSUADE 说服◄ [T] if someone carries a group of people, they persuade those people to support them 赢得…的支持: *Her tearful pleas carried the meeting.* 她声泪俱下的请求赢得了与会者的同情。

23 carry the day to persuade a group of people to support you 获得…的支持[赞同]: *His appeal to common sense was what finally carried the day.* 他借着情理最终赢得了大家的支持。

24 as fast as his/her legs could carry him/her as fast as possible 飞快，尽快: *She ran to her mother as fast as her legs could carry her.* 她飞快地跑向母亲。

25 carry all/everything before you *literary* to be completely successful in a struggle against other people【文】获得极大成功，大获全胜

26 ▶VOTE 投票◀ be carried if a suggestion, proposal etc is carried, most of the people at an official meeting vote for it and it is accepted〔建议、提议等〕获得通过: *The amendment to the bill was carried unanimously.* (=everyone agreed to it) 修正法案获得一致通过。| **be carried by 20 votes/50 votes etc** (=20, 50 etc more people voted for something than voted against it) 以20票/50票等的优势获得通过 *The motion to ban the sale of guns was carried by 76 votes.* 禁止出售枪支的动议以76票的优势获得通过。| **declare sth carried** (=to state officially that something has been accepted) 宣布某事获通过 *I declare the resolution carried.* 我宣布该项决议获得通过。

27 ▶SOUND/SMELL 声音/气味◀ [I] if a sound or smell carries to a particular place, it goes as far as that place 传到: *The sounds of laughter carried as far as the lake.* 笑声一直传到湖边。

28 carry one/two/three etc to put a number into the next row to the left when you are adding numbers together〔做加法时将数字〕进一位/二位/三位等: *Nine and three make twelve, put down two and carry one.* 9加3等于12，先写下2，然后进1。

29 ▶BALL 球类◀ [I] if the ball carries a particular distance in GOLF, CRICKET (2) etc, that is how far it travels when it is hit〔高尔夫球、板球等〕能打出（…的距离）

30 carry a torch for sb to be in love with someone who does not love you 对某人钟情[单相思]

31 carry the can (for sb/sth) *BrE informal* to be blamed or punished for something that is someone else's fault as well as your own【英，非正式】(为某人/某事) 独自承担责任[背黑锅]: *Why am I always left to carry the can?* 为什么总让我背黑锅?

32 carry a tune to sing correctly 唱准音调 —see also 另见 CARD-CARRYING, CARRIER, CASH AND CARRY, **fetch and carry** (FETCH (4))

carry sth ↔ **forward** *phr v* [T] **1** to move a total to the next page for adding to other numbers 将〔账目〕转入次页 **2** to make an amount of something such as money or holiday time available for use at a later time 把〔金钱或假期〕结转，结存〔留待日后使用〕

carry sb/sth ↔ **off** *phr v* [T] **1** to do something difficult successfully 成功地完成〔困难的任务、职责等〕: *It's a demanding role, but I'm sure she'll be able to carry it off.* 这是一个富有挑战性的角色，但我深信她能胜任。**2** to win a prize 赢得，获得〔奖品、荣誉等〕: *Jackie carried off most of the awards that evening.* 杰基那天晚上赢得了大部分的奖项。

carry on *phr v* **1** [I,T **carry on** sth] *especially BrE* to continue doing something【尤英】继续做; 坚持: *Don't stop – carry on, everyone!* 大家别停下来，继续干! | **carry on doing sth** *We all carried on singing as if nothing odd was happening.* 我们继续歌唱，就像什么怪事也没发生过一样。| **carry on with sth** *Please carry on with your work.* 请继续干你们的工作吧。| **carry on as normal/as usual/as you are/regardless** *I think we should just carry on as we are for now.* 我想现在我们应该照常进行下去。**2** [I] to continue moving 继续走; 继续行进: *We carried on down the freeway for a while.* 我们沿着高速公路继续行进了一会儿。| *Carry straight on until you get to the traffic lights.* 一直走到红绿灯那里为止。**3** [T **carry on** sth] to continue something that has been started by someone else 继续〔某人未完成的事业、工作等〕; 继承: *He is relying on his son to carry on the family business.* 他指望儿子继承家业。| *When she left I carried on her research.* 她离开后，我便继续进行她那项研究。**4** [T **carry on** sth] to do something for a period of time 继续开展[进行]下去: *Negotiations were being carried on, in spite of the fighting.* 尽管还有战斗，但谈判仍然继续进行。| **carry on a conversation** *They carried on a curious conversation, never looking at each other.* 他们进行了一次奇特的谈话，双方从不看对方一眼。**5** [I] *spoken* to behave in a silly, excited, or anxious way【口】大吵大闹: *Stop carrying on, you two!* 你们俩别吵了! | *Anyone would think they owned the business, the way they carry on!* 看他们大吵大闹的样子，谁都会认为他们是老板! **6** [I] *old-fashioned* to have a sexual relationship with someone, when you should not【过时】与…有不正当性关系: *She's been carrying on with the milkman, I'm certain of it.* 我肯定她跟那个送牛奶的有暧昧关系。

carry sth ↔ **out** *phr v* [T] **1** to do something that needs to be organized and planned 实行，进行; 执行: *They are carrying out urgent repairs.* 他们正在进行抢修。| *A survey is now being carried out nationwide.* 正在进行一次全国性的调查。| *It won't be an easy plan to carry out.* 那并不是一项容易实行的计划。**2 carry out a promise/a threat/an intention/an order etc** to do something that you have said you will do or that someone has asked you to do 履行承诺/实行威胁/实现目的/执行命令等: *We carried out her instructions to the letter.* 我们不折不扣地执行了她的指示。

carry sth ↔ **over** *phr v* [T] **1** if something is carried over into a new set of conditions, it continues to exist when conditions change〔情况变化时〕继续下去: *aspects of the dream which are carried over into wakefulness* 清醒时仍然残存的梦境 **2** to carry something forward 往后延; 积存: *Holiday time can be carried over into next year.* 假期可以积存至明年。

carry through *phr v* [T] **1** [**carry** sth **through**] to complete or finish something successfully, in spite of difficulties 实现，完成: *I'm determined to carry this through.* 我决意完成此事。**2 carry sb through (sth)** to help someone to manage during an illness or a difficult period 帮助〔某人〕度过〔患病、困难等时期〕; 使渡过难关: *Her confidence carried her through.* 信心使她渡过了难关。

carry² *n* [C,U] *technical* the distance a ball or bullet travels after it has been thrown, hit or fired【术语】〔球〕被抛掷的距离; 〔枪的〕射程

car·ry·all /ˈkærɪˌɔl; ˈkæri-ɔːl/ *n* [C] *AmE* a large soft bag or case【美】大手提包，装杂物的大袋子; HOLDALL *BrE*【英】—see picture at 参见 BAG[1] 图

car·ry·cot /ˈkærɪˌkɑt; ˈkærikɒt/ *n* [C] *BrE* a small bed used for carrying a baby【英】手提式婴儿床; PORTACRIB *AmE*【美】—see picture at 参见 BED[1] 图

carrying charge /ˈ··· ˌ·/ *n* [C] *AmE* a charge added to the price of something you have bought by INSTALLMENT PLAN (=paying over several months)【美】〔分期付款购物的〕附加费用

carry-on¹ /ˈ·· ·/ *n* [singular] *BrE spoken* behaviour or a situation that is silly or annoying【英口】愚蠢[令人恼火]的行为[局面]: *What a carry-on!* 真不像话! —see also 另见 **carry on** (CARRY[1])

carry-on² *adj* [only before noun 仅用于名词前] carry-on cases or bags are ones that passengers take onto a plane with them〔行李箱、手提包等〕可随身带着登机的

Carry On film /ˌ··ˈ· ˌ·/ *n* [C] one of a series of very popular humorous British films made especially in the 1960s and 1970s. Many of the actors in one Carry On film also appeared in several others, and most of the jokes are about sex. They have titles such as *Carry on Nurse* (1959) and *Carry on up the Khyber* (1968). 搞笑片〔尤指摄制于20世纪60、70年代的一系列颇受欢迎的英国喜剧片。多数演员较为固定，多数笑话都与性有关。片名都带有"搞笑"二字，如《搞笑护士》(1959)和《在开伯尔山口大搞笑》(1968)〕

carry-out /ˈ·· ·/ *n* [C] *AmE, ScotE* food that you can take away from a restaurant to eat somewhere else, or a restaurant that sells food like this【美，苏格兰】外卖食品; 外卖餐馆; TAKEAWAY *BrE*【英】

carry-o·ver /ˈ·· ˌ··/ *n* [singular] **1** something that affects an existing situation but is the result of a past one 遗留物; 残存物; 剩货: [+**from**] *Grandma is still frugal, a carry-over from the war years.* 外婆仍然保持着战争年代留下来的俭朴作风。**2** an amount of money that has not been used and is available to use later 结转金额: [+**of**] *a carry-over of funds to next year's budget* 结转到下年预算中的资金 —see also 另见 **carry over** (CARRY[1])

car·sick /ˈkɑrˌsɪk; ˈkɑːˌsɪk/ *adj* feeling sick because you are travelling in a car 晕车的 —**carsickness** *n* [U]

Car·son /ˈkɑrsn̩; ˈkɑːsən/, **Kit** (1809-68) a US hunter and soldier who also worked as a guide for John C. Frémont on his journeys in the western part of North America. Carson City in the state of Nevada is named after him. 卡森〔(1809-1868)，美国猎人和军人。他曾是约翰·C.弗里蒙特在北美西部探险的向导。内华达州的卡森城以他的名字命名〕

Carson, Ra·chel /ˈretʃəl; ˈreɪtʃəl/ (1907-64) a US scientist who worked in MARINE BIOLOGY (=the study of the creatures and plants that live in the sea). She wrote several books, including *Silent Spring*, and she was one of the first people to realize that PESTICIDES (=chemicals for protecting crops from insects) were damaging the environment. 卡森〔(1907-1964)，美国海洋生物学家。她著有《寂静的春天》等几部著作，是最先认识到杀虫剂正在破坏环境的科学家之一〕

Carson City /ˌ·· ˈ·/ the capital of the state of Nevada in the US 卡森城〔美国内华达州首府〕

cart[1] /kart; kɑːt/ *n* [C] **1** a vehicle with two or four wheels that is pulled by a horse and used for carrying heavy things〔两轮或四轮的〕马车 —see also 另见 HANDCART **2** *AmE* a large wire basket on wheels that you use in a SUPERMARKET【美】〔超市中的〕手推车; TROLLEY (1) *BrE*【英】**3** *AmE* a small table with wheels, used to move and serve food and drinks【美】〔送食物和饮品的〕手推餐车; TROLLEY (2) *BrE*【英】**4 put the cart before the horse** to do things in the wrong order 本末倒置; 前后颠倒 —see also 另见 **upset the apple cart** (UPSET[1] (5))

cart[2] *v* [T always+adv/prep] **1** *informal* to carry something that is awkward or heavy【非正式】搬运〔笨重物品等〕: *I was really tired after carting all that furniture upstairs.* 我把那些家具搬到楼上后, 真的筋疲力尽了。**2** to carry something in a cart 用车装运: [+**away**] *The corn sacks were carted away.* 装有谷物的袋子被车子运走了。

cart sb **off** *phr v* [T] *informal* to take someone away, especially to prison【非正式】带走, 抓走〔尤指进监狱〕: *The police carted him off this morning.* 今天早上警察把他抓走了。

car tax /ˈ· ·/ *n* [C,U] ROAD TAX 公路税, 通行税

carte blanche /ˌkart ˋblanʃ; ˌkɑːt ˈblɑːnʃ/ *n* [U] complete freedom to do whatever you like in a particular situation, especially to spend money〔尤指开支方面的〕全权, 自由处理权: **give sb carte blanche** *We were given carte blanche to redecorate the hotel.* 我们获授予全权重新装修酒店。

car·tel /ˈkartl̩; kɑːˈtel/ *n* [C] a group of companies who agree to fix prices to limit competition so that they can increase their profits 卡特尔, 同业联盟〔多家公司为限制竞争和增加利润而结成的固定价格联盟〕: *an illegal international oil cartel* 非法的国际石油同业联盟

cart·er /ˈkartɚ; ˈkɑːtə/ *n* [C] *old use* someone whose job is to drive a CART[1] (1)【旧】马车夫, 赶车人

Carter, Jimmy (1924-) the 39th President of the US from 1977 to 1981. Carter helped arrange the peace agreement between Egypt and Israel called the Camp David Agreement 卡特〔(1924-), 美国第三十九任总统(1977-1981)。他曾促成埃及和以色列之间的和平协议, 即《戴维营协议》〕

Car·thage /ˈkarθɪdʒ; ˈkɑːθɪdʒ/ an ancient city on the north coast of Africa, near the modern city of Tunis. Carthage was involved in three wars against the ancient Romans, who eventually destroyed it in 146 BC. 迦太基〔非洲北部沿岸一古城, 位于今突尼斯附近。那里曾进行过三次抗击古罗马人的战争, 最终毁于公元前 146 年〕 —**Carthaginian** /ˌkarθəˈdʒɪnɪən; ˌkɑːθəˈdʒɪniən◂/ *n, adj*

cart·horse /ˈkarthɔrs; ˈkɑːthɔːs/ *n* [C] a large strong horse, often used for pulling heavy loads〔常用于拉重物的〕大马, 役马

Cartier /ˈkartɪˌe; ˈkɑːtieɪ/, **Jacques** (1491-1557) a French EXPLORER who made two important journeys to Canada 卡蒂埃〔(1491-1557), 法国探险家。他曾赴加拿大进行过两次重要的探险〕

car·ti·lage /ˈkartl̩ɪdʒ; ˈkɑːtl̩ɪdʒ/ *n* [C,U] a strong stretchy substance, or piece of this, that is around the joints in a person or animal's body 软骨(组织)

Cart·land /ˈkartlənd; ˈkɑːtlənd/, **Dame Bar·ba·ra** /ˈbarbrə; ˈbɑːbərə/ (1901-2000) a British writer who wrote hundreds of romantic NOVELs in a rather old-fashioned style 卡特兰〔(1901-2000), 英国作家。她创作了数百部旧式的浪漫小说〕

cart·load /ˈkartˌlod; ˈkɑːtləʊd/ *n* [C] the amount that a CART can hold 一货车的装载量: [+**of**] *cartloads of hay* 数车干草

car·tog·ra·phy /karˈtagrəfi; kɑːˈtɒgrəfi/ *n* [U] the skill or practice of making maps 地图制作法; 制图学 —**cartographer** *n* [C]

car·ton /ˈkartn̩; ˈkɑːtn/ *n* [C] **1** a box made of CARDBOARD (=stiff paper) or plastic that contains food or drink 硬纸盒, 厚纸箱; 塑料盒: *a carton of fruit juice* 一盒果汁 | *a milk carton* 牛奶盒 —see picture at 参见 CONTAINER 图 **2** *AmE* a large container with smaller containers of goods inside it【美】〔可内置小容器的〕盒箱, 〔装了一定量商品的〕容器: *a carton of cigarettes* 一条香烟

Carton, Sydney an important character in the book *A Tale of Two Cities* (1859) by Charles Dickens. Carton is a London lawyer who falls in love with Lucie Manette, but Lucie marries Charles Darnay. Darnay is arrested and sentenced to death, but Carton dies by taking Darnay's place. 卡顿〔狄更斯小说《双城记》(1859) 中的一个重要人物。卡顿是伦敦的一名律师, 爱上了露西, 露西却嫁给了达奈。后来, 达奈被捕并判了死刑, 卡顿顶替达奈送了命〕

W3 **car·toon** /karˈtun; kɑːˈtuːn/ *n* [C] **1** a funny drawing in a newspaper, often including humorous remarks about news events (讽刺) 漫画, 幽默画 —compare 比较 COMIC STRIP **2** a short film that is made by photographing a series of drawings 卡通(片), 动画片 **3** a drawing that is used as a model for a painting or other work of art 草图, 底图

car trans·port·er /ˈ· ·,· ·/ *n* [C] a large vehicle on the road or railway, that carries several new cars to a place where they will be sold〔将新车运往销售地的〕车辆运输车[火车]

car·tridge /ˈkartrɪdʒ; ˈkɑːtrɪdʒ/ *n* [C] **1** a metal, CARD-BOARD, or plastic tube containing explosive and a bullet that you use in a gun 弹药筒, 弹壳; 子弹 **2** the small part of a RECORD PLAYER containing the STYLUS (=needle) that takes sound signals from the record〔电唱机上装唱针的〕唱头, 针匣 **3** a container with ink, film, or MAGNETIC TAPE in it, that you put into a pen, camera, or TAPE RECORDER〔钢笔的〕墨水囊, 笔芯; 〔装胶卷的〕暗盒; 〔装卡式录音磁带的〕盒子

cartridge pa·per /ˈ· ·, · ·/ *n* [U] *BrE* thick strong paper used for drawing on【英】〔绘画用的〕厚白纸, 图画纸

cart·track /ˈ· ·/ *n* [C] a narrow road with a rough surface, usually on a farm〔常指农场上路面不平的〕小路, 小径

cart·wheel /ˈkartˌhwil; ˈkɑːt-wiːl/ *n* [C] a movement in which you turn right over by throwing your body sideways onto your hands while bringing your legs over your head 侧手翻, 侧身筋斗 —**cartwheel** *v* [I]

Cart·wright /ˈkartraɪt; ˈkɑːtraɪt/, **Ed·mund** /ˈɛdmənd; ˈedmənd/ (1743-1823) a British engineer who invented machines that were used in factories to make cloth, and that did jobs which were previously done by people 卡特赖特〔(1743-1823), 英国工程师。他曾发明了工业织布机, 代替了手工劳动〕

Ca·ru·so /kəˈruso; kəˈruːsəʊ/, **En·ri·co** /ɛnˈriko; enˈriːkəʊ/ (1873-1921) an Italian OPERA singer who was one of the greatest TENORs of the 20th century 卡鲁索〔(1873-1921), 意大利歌剧演唱家, 20 世纪最伟大的男高音之一〕

carve /karv; kɑːv/ *v* **1** [I,T] to cut a large piece of cooked meat into smaller pieces using a big knife 把〔熟肉〕切成小块; 〔从熟肉上〕割下薄片: *Carve the lamb into slices and arrange in a hot serving dish.* 把羊肉切成片后摆放在一个热的盘子里。—see picture on page A11 参见 A11 页图 **2** [T] to cut shapes out of solid wood or stone 雕, 刻; 把〔木、石等〕雕成〔某物〕: *Michelangelo carved this figure from a single block of marble.* 米开朗基罗用一块大理石雕刻出这个人像。**3** [T] to cut a pattern or letter on the surface of something 刻〔图形或字母〕: **carve sth on/in etc** *Someone had carved their initials on the tree.* 有人将自己姓名的起首字母刻在树上。

carve sth ↔ **out** *phr v* [T] **carve out a career/niche/reputation etc** to become successful and be respected 开创出事业/谋得合适的职位/赢得名声: *She's carved out a very successful career as a photographer.* 她成为了一个非常成功的摄影师。

carve sb/sth ↔ **up** *phr v* [T] **1** if two or more people, governments etc carve something up, they divide it into separate parts and share it between them even though this is wrong 瓜分, 分割: *They ruthlessly carved up Poland.* 他们无情地瓜分了波兰。—see also 另见 CARVE-UP **2** *BrE informal* to drive past another car going in the same direction and then turn in front of it too quickly【英, 非正式】快速超车, 快速切入别人的行车线

carv·er /ˈkarvɚ; ˈkɑːvə/ *n* [C] **1** someone who carves 雕刻师, 雕工; 切肉人 **2** a big knife used for cutting meat; CARVING KNIFE 切肉刀

Carver, George Washington (1860-1943) a US scientist who studied farming and crops, and was one of the first black people in the US to become an important scientist 卡弗〔(1860-1943), 美国农业科学家, 最早的杰出黑人科学家之一〕

car·ver·y /ˈkarvərɪ; ˈkɑːvəri/ *n* [C] *BrE* a restaurant that serves ROAST[3] meat【英】烤肉餐厅

carve-up /ˈ· ·/ *n* [singular] an arrangement between two or more people, governments etc by which they divide something among themselves even though this is wrong 瓜分, 分割

carv·ing /ˈkarvɪŋ; ˈkɑːvɪŋ/ *n* **1** [C] an object or pattern made by cutting a shape in wood or stone for decoration 雕刻物[品]; 雕刻图案 **2** [U] the activity or skill of carving 雕刻工作; 雕刻艺术; 雕刻技巧

carving fork /ˈ· · ·/ *n* [C] a large fork used to hold cooked meat firmly while you are cutting it〔切肉时用来按住肉块的〕大餐叉, 切肉叉

carving knife /ˈ· · ·/ *n* [C] a large knife used for cutting cooked meat〔大的〕切肉刀 —see picture at 参见 KNIFE[1] 图

car wash /ˈ· ·/ *n* [C] a place where there is special equipment for washing cars 洗车处, 洗车场

car·y·at·id /ˌkærɪˈætɪd; ˌkæriˈætɪd/ *n* [C] *technical* a PILLAR (1) in the shape of a female figure【术语】女像柱〔雕成女性形状的建筑物支柱〕

Cas·a·blan·ca /ˌkɑsəˋblæŋkɑ; ˌkæsəˈblæŋkə/ **1** the largest city in Morocco, on the Atlantic coast 卡萨布兰卡〔摩洛哥最大城市，位于大西洋沿岸〕 **2** one of the most popular films in the history of the cinema, made in 1942 with Humphrey Bogart and Ingrid Bergman. *Casablanca* is a romantic story about a man called Rick who has a café in Casablanca, and who helps a husband and wife escape from the Nazis 《卡萨布兰卡》〔电影史上最受欢迎的影片之一。拍摄于 1942 年，由亨弗莱·博加特和英格丽·褒曼主演。影片讲述一个浪漫故事。故事中的里克在卡萨布兰卡经营一家小餐馆，在他的帮助下，一对夫妇逃离了纳粹统治区〕

Cas·a·no·va /ˌkæsəˋnovə; kæsəˈnəʊvə/ *n* [C] a man who has had, or says he has had, a lot of lovers（声称）拥有许多情妇的男子，大情人: *a man with a reputation as a womaniser, a Casanova* 有风流浪子名声的玩弄女性者

Casanova /ˌkæsəˋnovə; ˌkæsəˈnəʊvə/, **Gia·co·mo** /ˋdʒɑkəmo; ˈdʒækəməʊ/ (1725-98) an Italian writer famous for having had many lovers 卡萨诺瓦〔(1725-1798)，意大利作家，因有多个情人而出名〕

cas·bah /ˋkæzbɑ; ˈkæzbɑː/ *n* [C] an ancient Arab city or the market in it 阿拉伯古城，卡斯巴；阿拉伯古城中的市场

cas·cade[1] /kæsˋked; kæˈskeɪd/ *n* [C] **1** a small steep WATERFALL that is one of several together 小瀑布〔大瀑布的分支〕 **2** something that hangs down in large quantities 瀑布状物: **[+of]** *Her hair fell over her shoulders in a cascade of curls.* 她的鬈发瀑布般垂落在肩头。

cascade[2] *v* [I always+adv/prep] to flow, fall or hang down in large quantities 瀑布似地落下；大量倾泻: *Geraniums cascaded over the balcony.* 天竺葵从阳台上垂了下来。| *a cascading stream* 倾泻而下的河流

Cascade Range, the /ˌ·ˈ· ,·/ also 又作 **the Cascades** a group of mountains in the west of the US and Canada, which go from British Columbia in the north down to northern California, where they join with the Sierra Nevada 喀斯喀特山脉〔位于美国和加拿大西部，北起不列颠哥伦比亚省，南至加利福尼亚北部，与内华达山脉相连〕

case[1] /kes; keɪs/ *n*

1 ▶EXAMPLE 例证◀ [C] an example of a particular situation, problem etc 事例，实例: *In some cases, it is necessary to operate.* 在某些情况下，动手术是必要的。| **[+of]** *an extreme case of anorexia* 一个厌食的极端例子 | **case in point** (=a clear example of a situation, problem etc that you are discussing or explaining) 明显的例子 *This latest policy is a case in point.* 这项最新的政策就是一个明证。| **classic case of** (=a typical example of a situation, problem etc) 典型例证 *a classic case of food poisoning* 食物中毒的典型例子

2 ▶SITUATION 情况◀ [C usually singular 一般用单数] a situation that exists, especially as it affects a particular person or group〔尤指影响某人或群体的〕状况，情形；场合: **be the case** *This was found to be the case in many third-world countries.* 在许多第三世界国家里都出现这种情况。| **it is the case (that)** *It is simply not the case that standards have fallen.* 说水准已下降，这根本不符合事实。| **in sb's case** *In Sandra's case, the reasons are less easy to pinpoint.* 就桑德拉的情况来说，较难找出原因。| *I'm not supposed to let anyone in without a card, but I'll make an exception in your case.* 我本来不可以让任何没有证件的人进去的，但就你的情况来说，我就破一回例。| **understate/overstate the case** (=make a situation seem less or more serious than it really is) 把情况淡化/夸大

3 in that case *spoken* used to describe what you will do, or what will happen, as a result of a particular situation or event【口】如果是那样的话: *"I'm afraid I can't come after all." "Well, in that case I'm not going either."* "我恐怕终究来不了。""好吧，如果是那样的话，我也不去了。"

4 in any case *spoken* used to say that a fact or part of a situation stays the same even if other things change【口】不管怎样，无论如何: *We have to go past your house in any case, so we'll take you home.* 不管怎样，我们都要经过你家，所以我们会送你回去。

5 (just) in case *especially spoken*【尤口】**a)** as a way of being safe from something that might happen or might be true 以防万一: *Take an umbrella, in case it rains.* 带把伞吧，以防下雨。| *I'm sure Harry will remember, but why not give him a ring just in case?* 我肯定哈里会记得，但为防万一，为什么不给他打个电话呢？**b)** *AmE* if【美】如果，假使: *In case I'm late, start without me.* 假如我来晚了，你们就先开始吧。

6 it's a case of *spoken* used before describing a situation, especially the one you are now in【口】情况是…: *We don't want to sell the car, but it's a case of having to.* 我们并不想卖掉汽车，但这是没有办法的事。| *It's a case of too many people and not enough jobs.* 情况是人多职位少。

7 in case of used to describe what you should do in a particular situation, especially on official notices 要是…，在…的时候〔尤用于官方告示〕: *In case of fire, break the glass.* 如发生火警，请打碎玻璃。

8 ▶BOX/CONTAINER 箱子/容器◀ [C] **a)** a large box or container in which things can be stored or moved 大箱子，大容器: *a packing case* 包装箱 | *a case of wine* 一箱葡萄酒 **b)** a special box used as a container for holding or protecting something 盒(子)，匣(子)；橱，柜；套，罩；壳: *a jewellery case* 首饰盒 | *The exhibits were all in glass cases.* 展品都放在玻璃罩里。**c)** *BrE* a SUITCASE【英】手提箱: *Shall I take your cases down to the car?* 要我把你的箱子拿到车上吗？—see also 另见 BOOKCASE, BRIEFCASE, PILLOWCASE

9 ▶LAW/CRIME 法律/罪行◀ [C] **a)** a question or problem that will be dealt with by a law court 诉讼案件；官司；个案: *a libel case* 诽谤案 | **win/lose a case** *They lost their case in the High Court, and had to pay damages.* 高等法院判他们输了官司，他们得赔偿损失。**b)** all the reasons that one side in a legal argument can give against the other side〔诉讼中一方的〕理由，论据，证据，申述: *the case for the prosecution* 控方的论据 | **have a case** (=have enough good arguments to go to a law court) 有足够的证据起诉 *The police have a clear case against him.* 警方掌握了不利于他的确凿证据。**c)** an event or set of events that need to be dealt with by the police（犯罪）案件，事件: *investigating a murder case* 调查一宗谋杀案 | **be on the case** (=be in charge of dealing with a particular crime) 负责〔某个〕案件 *Inspector Hacker is on the case.* 哈克督察负责此案。

10 ▶REASON/ARGUMENT 理由/论据◀ [C,U] the facts, arguments, or reasons for doing something, supporting something etc 事实，论据，理由: **[+for/against]** *the case against hanging* 反对绞刑的理由 | *There may be a case for abandoning the scheme altogether.* 或许有理由全盘否决该计划。| **make out a case for** (=provide good reasons for something) 为…提供充分的理由 *I'm sure we can make out a good case for a pay rise.* 我确信我们能够提出增加工资的充分理由。

11 get off my case *spoken* used to tell someone to stop criticizing you or complaining about you【口】别再批评[埋怨]我了: *OK, OK, just get off my case already!* 好了，好了，不要再埋怨我了！

12 be on sb's case *informal* to be criticizing someone continuously【非正式】不停地抱怨[指责]某人: *Dad's always on my case about something or another.* 爸爸老是不停地抱怨我这抱怨我那。

13 ▶PERSON 人◀ [C] someone who is being dealt with by a doctor, a SOCIAL WORKER, the police etc 病人，患者；社会工作者的工作对象；由警方监管的人 —see also 另见 **sad case** (SAD (4)), NUTCASE, BASKET-CASE

14 ▶GRAMMAR 语法◀ [C,U] *technical* the way in which the form of a word changes, showing its relationship to other words in a sentence【术语】格: *case endings* 格词尾 —see also 另见 LOWER CASE, UPPER CASE

case[2] *v* [T] **1 be cased in** to be completely surrounded by a material or substance 被包围: *The reactor will be cased in metal.* 反应器将用金属包起来。**2 case the joint** *slang* to look around a place that you intend to steal from in order to find out information【俚】〔为行窃而〕预先侦察，窥探 —see also 另见 CASING

case·book /ˋkesˌbuk; ˈkeɪsbʊk/ *n* [C] a detailed written record kept by a doctor, SOCIAL WORKER, or police officer of the cases (CASE[1] (13)) they have dealt with 病历；〔社会工作者的〕记录簿；〔警察的〕案件档案

case his·to·ry /ˈ· ,···/ *n* [C] a detailed record of someone's past illnesses, problems etc that a doctor or SOCIAL WORKER studies 病历；〔社会工作者的工作对象的〕个案史

case law /ˈ· ·/ *n* [U] *law* a type of law that is based on decisions judges have made in the past【法律】判例法〔以从前判决的案例为依据的法律〕

case·load /ˋkesˌlod; ˈkeɪsləʊd/ *n* [C] the number of people a doctor, SOCIAL WORKER etc has to deal with〔医生、社会工作者等的〕工作量

case·ment /ˋkesmənt; ˈkeɪsmənt/ *n* [C] a window that opens like a door with HINGES[1] at one side〔像门那样开关的〕门式窗

case stud·y /ˈ· ,··/ *n* [C] a detailed account of the development of a particular person, group, or situation that has been studied over a period of time 个案研究

case work /ˈ· ·/ *n* [U] work that a SOCIAL WORKER does which is concerned with the problems of a particular person or family that needs help 社会（福利）工作，社会辅导工作 —**caseworker** *n* [C]

cash[1] /kæʃ; kæʃ/ *n* [U] **1** money in the form of coins or notes rather than cheques, CREDIT CARD*s* etc 现款，现金: **in cash** *I'm bringing $400 in traveller's cheques and $100 in cash.* 我将带400美元的旅行支票和100美元的现金。—see 见 MONEY (USAGE) | **pay in cash** (=not by cheque etc) 用现金付账 | *Is there any discount if I pay in cash?* 如果我付现金，有折扣吗？| **hard cash** (=notes and coins only) 现金，现款 *In terms of hard cash, we've raised over £200 and in pledges about £8,500.* 我们已筹得超过200英镑现金和大约8500英镑的承诺捐款。**2** *informal* money【非正式】钱: *The company's a bit short of cash right now.* 公司现在现款有点紧。| **be strapped for cash** (=not have enough money) 缺钱 **3 pay cash** to pay immediately using a cheque or cash, but not by adding a debt to your account〔用现金或支票〕付现，当场付款: *Are you paying cash or do you have a trade account?* 你付现款还是有结算账户？| **cash bonus/sale/deposit** (=one in which a direct payment is made) 现金奖励/现金销售/现金存款 **4 cash down** if you pay for something cash down, you pay for it before you receive it 预付 **5 cash on delivery** COD; used to mean that the customer pays the person delivering the goods to them 货到付款 —see also 另见 PETTY CASH

cash[2] *v* [T] **cash a cheque/postal order/draft etc** to exchange a cheque etc for the amount of money it is worth 把支票/邮政汇票/汇票等兑成现金: *Can you cash my traveller's cheques here?* 你们这儿可以把我的旅行支票兑成现金吗？| *Where can I get this cashed?* 我到哪儿能把这（张支票）兑现？—**cashable** *adj*: *cashable at any bank* 可以在任何一家银行兑现的

cash in *phr v* **1** [I] to make a profit from a situation in a way that other people think is wrong or unfair〔靠不正当手段〕赚钱；利用: **[+on]** *He's just cashing in on the fact that his father is a big movie director.* 他不过是利用他父亲是个大导演来赚钱。**2** [T **cash** sth ↔ **in**] to exchange something such as an insurance POLICY (2) for its value in money 把〔保险单等〕兑成现金 **3 cash in your chips** *humorous* to die【幽默】死；完蛋；报销

cash up also 又作 **cash out** *AmE*【美】*phr v* [T] to add up the amount of money received in a shop in a day so that it can be checked〔收银员在打烊后〕结账

cash and car·ry /ˌ· · ˈ··/ *n* [C] a very large shop where customers representing a business or organization can buy large amounts of goods at cheap prices 现款自运商店

cash·book /ˈkæʃˌbuk; ˈkæʃbʊk/ *n* [C] a book in which you keep a record of money received and paid out 现金账簿

cash box /ˈ· ·/ *n* [C] a small metal box with a lock that you keep money in 钱箱，银箱

cash card /ˈ· ·/ *n* [C] a special plastic card used for getting money from a machine outside a bank〔用于自动提款机的〕自动提款卡 —compare 比较 CHEQUE CARD, CREDIT CARD, DEBIT CARD

cash cow /ˈ· ·/ *n* [C] the part of a business you can always depend on to make enough profits 稳赚项目；摇钱树；财源: *seeing the product as a high-yielding cash cow, requiring little investment in the mature stage of its life-cycle* 把那种产品视为一棵巨大的摇钱树，在其成熟期不需要什么投资

cash crop /ˈ· ·/ *n* [C] a crop grown in order to be sold rather than to be used by the people growing it 商品农作物 —compare 比较 SUBSISTENCE CROP

cash desk /ˈ· ·/ *n* [C] the desk in a shop where you pay〔商店的〕收款台，柜台，付款处

cash dis·count /ˌ· ˈ··/ *n* [C] an amount by which a seller reduces a price if the buyer pays immediately or before a particular date 现金折扣〔指因现款购货或在某段时间前付款而给予的优惠折扣〕

cash dis·pens·er /ˈ· ·ˌ··/ *n* [C] *especially BrE* a CASH MACHINE【尤英】自动提款机

ca·shew /ˈkæʃu; ˈkæʃuː/ *n* [C] **1** a small curved nut 腰果 **2** the tropical American tree that produces this〔热带美洲的〕腰果树

cash flow /ˈ· ·/ *n* [singular,U] **1** the movement of money coming into a business as income and going out as wages, materials etc 现金流转: *maintaining a healthy cash flow* 维持良好的现金流转 **2 have cash flow problems** to not have enough money 发生现金周转问题

cash·ier[1] /kæˈʃɪr; kæˈʃɪə/ *n* [C] someone whose job is to receive or pay out money in a shop, bank, hotel etc〔商店、银行、旅馆等的〕柜台出纳[收账]员

cashier[2] *v* [T] to force an officer to leave the army, navy etc because they have done something wrong 罢免；革除〔军官的〕职务

cash-in-hand /ˌ· · ˈ·◂/ *adj* a cash-in-hand payment is made in the form of notes and coins so that there is no record of the payment 用现金支付[结算]的

cash·less /ˈkæʃləs; ˈkæʃləs/ *adj* done or working without using actual money 不用现金的，转账的: *a cashless transaction between two banks* 两家银行间的非现金交易 | *the cashless society* 不用现金的社会

cash ma·chine /ˈ· ·ˌ·/ *n* [C] a machine in or outside a bank from which you can obtain money with a special plastic card 自动柜员机，自动提款机; CASH DISPENSER *especially BrE*【尤英】，ATM *AmE*【美】

cash·mere /ˈkæʃmɪr; ˈkæʃmɪə/ *n* [U] a type of fine soft wool 开士米羊毛；羊绒: *I wish I could afford a cashmere sweater.* 我希望我能买得起一件开士米羊毛衫。

cash·point /ˈkæʃpɔɪnt; ˈkæʃpɔɪnt/ *n* [C] *BrE* a cash machine【英】自动提款机

cash reg·is·ter /ˈ· ˌ···/ *n* [C] a machine used in shops to keep the money in and record the amount of money received from each sale; TILL[2] 现金收入记录机，现金出纳机，收银机

cash-strapped /ˈ· ·/ *adj* not having enough money 缺钱的，财政困难的: *higher school meal prices imposed by a cash-strapped county council* 郡议会因财政困难而导致较高的学校伙食费

cas·ing /ˈkesɪŋ; ˈkeɪsɪŋ/ *n* [C] an outer layer of metal, rubber etc that covers and protects something such as a wire or tyre〔包在电线或轮胎等物体外面起保护作用的〕罩，壳，套；管；外胎

ca·si·no /kəˈsino; kəˈsiːnəʊ/ *n plural* **casinos** [C] a place where people try to win money by playing card games or ROULETTE 赌场: *Doesn't that club have a casino up-stairs?* 那家俱乐部楼上不是有赌场吗？

cask /kæsk; kɑːsk/ *n* [C] a round wooden container used for storing wine or other liquids, or the amount of liquid contained in this〔装酒或其他液体的〕小木桶；一桶之量: *a cask of rum* 一桶朗姆酒

cas·ket /ˈkæskɪt; ˈkɑːskɪt/ *n* [C] **1** a small decorated box in which you keep jewellery and other valuable objects〔装珠宝等贵重物品的〕小盒，小箱 **2** *especially AmE* a COFFIN【尤美】棺材

Cas·pi·an Sea, the /ˌkæspɪən ˈsi; ˌkæspiən ˈsiː/ the largest inland sea in the world, between southeast Europe and Asia. It is surrounded by Russia, Iran, Azerbaijan, Kazakhstan, and Turkmenistan. 里海〔世界上最大的内陆海。位于东南欧和亚洲之间，周边国家有俄罗斯、伊朗、阿塞拜疆、哈萨克斯坦和土库曼斯坦〕

Cas·san·dra /kəˈsændrə; kəˈsændrə/ in ancient Greek stories, the daughter of Priam, King of Troy. The god Apollo gave her the power to see what would happen in the future, but he also made sure that no one would ever believe her. People are sometimes called a 'Cassandra' if they warn that something bad will happen, but no one believes them. 卡桑德拉〔古希腊传说中，特洛伊国王普里阿摩斯的女儿。阿波罗神赋予她预知未来的本领，同时却又让人们不相信她的话。如有人警告他人将发生不幸但却不为人相信，那么就可称其为"卡桑德拉"〕

Cas·satt /kəˈsæt; kəˈsæt/, **Mary** (1845-1926) a US painter who worked mainly in France with the Impressionists 卡萨特〔(1845-1926)，美国画家，曾经主要在法国与印象派画家一起创作〕

cas·sa·va /kəˈsɑvə; kəˈsɑːvə/ *n* [C,U] a tropical plant with thick roots that you can eat, or the flour made from these roots 木薯；木薯淀粉

cas·se·role[1] /ˈkæsəˌrol; ˈkæsərəʊl/ *n* [C] **1** food that is cooked slowly in liquid in a covered dish in the OVEN 炖锅[沙锅]菜肴: *chicken casserole* 沙锅鸡 **2** a deep covered dish used for cooking food in the oven 炖锅，沙锅

casserole[2] *v* [T] to cook food in a casserole 用炖锅[沙锅]烹饪

cas·sette /kəˈsɛt; kəˈset/ *n* [C] **1** a small flat plastic case containing MAGNETIC TAPE, that can be used for playing or recording sound〔录音带的〕卡式盒: *Now available on cassette or CD!* 现有盒式磁带和激光唱片两种产品出售！**2** a closed container with photographic film in it, that can be fitted into a camera〔摄影胶卷的〕暗盒，胶卷盒

cassette play·er /ˈ· ·, ·/ *n* [C] a piece of electrical equipment used for playing cassettes 盒式磁带录音机

cassette re·cord·er /ˈ· ·ˌ·, ·/ *n* [C] a piece of electrical equipment used for recording sound or for playing cassettes on; TAPE RECORDER 盒式磁带录音机

cas·sock /ˈkæsək; ˈkæsək/ *n* [C] a long, usually black, piece of clothing worn by priests〔牧师穿的，多为黑色的〕法衣，长袍

cast[1] /kæst; kɑːst/ *v past tense and past participle* **cast**
1 cast (a) light on/onto a) to provide new information which makes something easier to understand 使〔某事〕更为清楚；阐明；论述: *research findings that cast new light on the origin of*

our universe 为宇宙起源提出新的论点的研究发现 **b)** *literary* to send light onto a surface【文】把光线投在…表面: *The candle cast a flickering light on the wall.* 烛光映在墙上摇曳不定。

2 cast a shadow *literary*【文】**a)** if something casts a shadow over an event, period of time etc, it makes people feel less happy or hopeful because they are worried about it〔在心理上〕投下阴影, 使不快: [+over] *My father's illness cast a shadow over the wedding celebrations.* 我父亲的病使婚礼笼罩着一层阴影。**b)** to make a shadow appear on a surface or area〔在某一表面或区域上〕投下影子: [+on/over/across etc] *The oak tree casts a long shadow across the lawn in the afternoon.* 到了下午, 橡树在草坪上投下长长的树影。

3 ►LOOK 看◄ a) cast a look/glance *literary* to look at someone or something【文】看[瞅]一眼: [+at/towards/around etc] *Sandra waited, casting nervous glances over her shoulder.* 桑德拉等待着, 不时紧张地看看身后。**b) cast an eye over** to check or look at something quickly 迅速地检查[看]: *Could you just cast an eye over these figures before I show them to the bank?* 在我把这些数字交给银行之前, 你能先检查一下吗?

4 cast doubt on to make people feel less certain about something 使怀疑, 使不确信: *Preliminary results from an Anglo-French trial cast doubts on the usefulness of the drug.* 英法两国试用的初步结果使人们对这种药物的疗效有所怀疑。

5 cast a vote also 又作 **cast a ballot** *AmE*【美】to vote in an election 投票: *Barely one in three voters will bother to cast a ballot on February 26th.* 仅有三分之一的选民愿意在2月26日那天去投票。

6 cast a spell on/over a) to use magic words or ceremonies to change someone or something 给…下咒语、用咒语迷惑: *She's a witch! She'll cast a spell on you if she sees you in the wood!* 她是巫婆! 如果她看见你在林子里, 就会对你念魔咒! **b)** to make someone feel very strongly attracted and keep their attention completely 把…迷住, 深深吸引: *Within minutes Sinatra's voice had cast its spell on the audience.* 短短几分钟之内, (美国著名流行歌手) 西纳特拉的歌声就迷倒了所有听众。

7 cast your mind back to try to remember something that happened a long time ago 回想, 回顾, 追忆: [+to] *Cast your mind back to your first day at school.* 回想你第一天上学的情况。

8 cast sth from your mind if you cast worries, fears, doubts etc from your mind, you stop feeling worried, afraid etc 忘却某事〔指烦恼、恐惧、疑惑等〕, 把某事丢到脑后

9 cast aspersions on *formal* to make unfavourable remarks about someone or something【正式】批评; 诋毁, 中伤: *Under the censorship rules, they could not cast aspersions on a foreign power.* 在这种审查制度下, 他们无法对外国强权进行批评。

10 ►METAL 金属◄ [T] to pour liquid metal, plastic etc into a MOULD (=specially shaped container), or to make an object in this way 浇铸, 按模铸造: *a statue of a horse cast in bronze* 青铜浇铸的马塑像

11 ►ACTOR 演员◄ [T] to choose which people will act particular parts in a play, film etc〔为戏剧、电影等〕挑选〔演员〕

12 cast sb as/cast sb in the role of to regard or describe someone as a particular type of person 评价; 描述: *Clarke's trying to cast me in the role of the villain in all of this.* 克拉克在这整件事上都想把我说成是个坏人。

13 ►FISHING 捕鱼◄ [I,T] to throw a fishing line or net into the water 抛 (钓丝); 撒 (网): *There's a trick to casting properly.* 正确地撒网是有诀窍的。

14 ►THROW 抛◄ [T always+adv/prep] *literary* to throw something somewhere【文】投, 抛, 扔, 丢: *Sparks leapt as more wood was cast onto the bonfire.* 往火堆中丢入更多的木头时, 火花不停地四溅。

15 cast sb into prison/into a dungeon/into Hell etc *literary* to force someone to go somewhere unpleasant【文】把…关进监狱/地牢/地狱等: *Memet should, in her opinion, be cast into prison.* 她认为应该把梅米特关入大牢。

16 be cast away to be left alone on a lonely shore or island, as a result of your ship sinking〔因沉船而〕流落荒岛: *If you were cast away on a desert island, what would you miss most?* 如果你因沉船而流落在荒岛上, 你会最想念什么?

17 be cast down *literary* to feel sad and discouraged【文】沮丧, 灰心: *Malcolm too seemed quite cast down.* 马尔科姆似乎也相当沮丧。

18 cast your net wide to consider or try as many things as possible in order to find what you want 想尽方法寻找, 千方百计搜罗: *We'll be casting our net wide to get the right person for the job.* 我们将尽力从各方物色能胜任此项工作的人选。

19 ►CAST ITS SKIN 蜕皮◄ if a snake casts its skin, it gets rid of the top layer〔蛇〕蜕皮

20 cast a shoe if a horse casts a shoe, it loses one of them〔马〕掉一个蹄铁

21 cast a horoscope to calculate the details of someone's HOROSCOPE 用占星术算命

22 cast pearls before swine to offer something that is very valuable or beautiful to someone who does not understand how valuable it is 把好东西送给不识货的人; 明珠暗投; 对牛弹琴 — see also 另见 **the die is cast** (DIE² (3)), **throw in/cast your lot with** (LOT (16))

cast about/around for sth *phr v* [T] to try to think of something to do or say 考虑, 计划: *Having retired early, I am casting about for a way to supplement my income.* 因为退休早, 我正想办法增加收入。

cast sb/sth ↔ aside *phr v* [T] to get rid of someone or something because you no longer like them or they are no longer useful〔因不喜欢或无用而〕把…丢在一旁, 对…置之不理: *When Henry became King, he cast aside all his former friends.* 亨利当上国王后就不理他以前的朋友了。| **cast aside your inhibitions/doubts etc** (=get rid of your feelings of shyness, doubt etc) 消除顾忌/疑惑等

cast off *phr v* **1** [T **cast** sb/sth ↔ **off**] *literary* to get rid of something or someone【文】摆脱, 放弃, 丢掉: *a haven of tranquility where you can cast off the strains and stresses of life* 能让你摆脱生活的紧张和压力的安静地方 **2** [I,T **cast** sth ↔ **off**] to untie the rope that fastens your boat to the shore so that you can sail away〔船只〕解缆起航 **3** [I,T **cast** sth ↔ **off**] to finish a piece of KNITTING by taking the last stitches off the needle in a way that stops them from coming undone〔编织〕收针

cast on *phr v* [I,T **cast** sth ↔ **on**] to start a piece of KNITTING by making the first stitches on the needle〔编织〕起针

cast sb/sth ↔ out *phr v* [T] *literary* to force someone or something to go away【文】把…赶走, 驱逐: *an exorcist who casts out demons* 驱魔法师

cast sth ↔ **up** *phr v* [T] if the sea casts up something, it brings it onto the shore〔海水〕把…冲上岸: *A body had been cast up on the rocks.* 一具尸体被海水冲上了岩石。

cast² *n* [C]

1 ►ACTORS 演员◄ all the people who act in a play or film 演员阵容, 全体演员: *Films like 'Ben Hur' have a cast of thousands.* 像《宾虚传》一类的电影, 演员多达数千人。

2 ►ON YOUR BODY 人体上◄ a hard protective case used around a part of your body to support a broken bone〔固定骨折用的〕石膏: *a plaster cast* 石膏 | *Murray has his leg in a cast.* 默里的腿用石膏固定着。

3 ►FOR SHAPING METAL 浇铸◄ a) a MOULD (=specially shaped container) into which you pour liquid metal, plastic etc in order to make an object of a particular shape 铸模, 模子 **b)** an object made in this way 铸件, 铸造品

4 cast of (sb's) mind/features *formal* the way someone thinks, behaves, or looks【正式】(某人的) 思维方式/特征: *a philosophical cast of mind* 具有哲理的思维方式

5 ►IN FISHING 钓鱼◄ the act of throwing a fishing line 抛钓丝

6 have a cast in your eye *old-fashioned* to have a problem with your eye which forces it to look to the side【过时】〔眼睛〕斜视

7 ►COLOUR 颜色◄ a small amount of a particular colour 色调: *Sage leaves have a silvery cast.* 鼠尾草的叶子是带点银色的。

8 ►EARTH 泥土◄ a small pile of earth thrown out of the ground by WORMS when they make a hole〔蚯蚓钻洞时翻到地面的〕小土堆

cas·ta·nets /ˌkæstəˋnɛts; ˌkæstəˈnets/ *n* [plural] a musical instrument made of two small round pieces of wood or plastic that you knock together in your hand 响板〔一种乐器〕

cast·a·way /ˈkæstəˌwe; ˈkɑːstəweɪ/ *n* [C] someone who is left on a lonely shore or island after their ship has sunk 沉船后漂流到孤岛的人

caste /kæst; kɑːst/ *n* [C,U] **1** one of the fixed and unchangeable social classes into which people are born in India, or the system of having these classes〔印度社会的〕种姓; 种姓制度 **2** a group of people who have the same position in society 社会阶层[等级]: **lose caste** *BrE* (=lose your social position)【英】失去社会地位

cas·tel·lat·ed /ˈkæstəˌletɪd; ˈkæstəleɪtəd/ *adj technical* built to look like a castle【术语】构造似城堡的: *a castellated bell tower* 如城堡似的钟楼

cast·er, castor /ˈkæstɚ; ˈkɑːstə/ *n* [C] **1** a small wheel fixed to the bottom of a piece of furniture so that it can move in any direction〔家具的〕小脚轮, 滚轮 **2** *BrE* a small container with

holes in the top, used to spread sugar, salt etc on food【英】〔顶端有小孔, 用来撒糖、盐等的〕调味瓶; SHAKER (1) *AmE*【美】

caster sug·ar, castor sugar /ˈ‥ ,‥/ *n* [U] *BrE* sugar with very small grains used for cooking【英】细白砂糖

cast·i·gate /ˈkæstəˌget; ˈkæstɪgeɪt/ *v* [T] *formal* to criticize or punish someone severely【正式】严厉责骂, 斥责; 严惩 —**castigation** /ˌkæstəˈgeʃən; ˌkæstɪˈgeɪʃən/ *n* [U]

cast·ing /ˈkæstɪŋ; ˈkɑːstɪŋ/ *n* **1** [U] the process of choosing the actors for a film or play 挑选演员, 分派角色: *a casting director* 负责挑选演员的导演 **2** [C] an object made by pouring liquid metal, plastic etc into a MOULD (=specially shaped container) 铸造品, 铸件 **3 the casting couch** *humorous* a situation in which an actress is persuaded to have sex in return for a part in a film, play etc【幽默】以肉体换角色〔女演员为了获演某个角色而以肉体作为交换条件〕

casting vote /ˈ‥ ,‥/ *n* [C usually singular 一般用单数] the vote of the person in charge of a meeting, which can be used to make a decision when there is an equal number of votes supporting and opposing a proposal〔当赞成和反对票数相等时, 由会议主持人所投的〕决定性一票

cast i·ron /ˌ‥ ˈ‥/ *n* [U] a type of iron that is hard, breaks easily, and is shaped in a MOULD[1] (2) 铸铁; 生铁

cast-i·ron /ˌ‥ˈ‥◂/ *adj* **1 a cast-iron excuse/alibi/guarantee etc** an excuse etc that is very certain and cannot fail 理由充分的借口/无懈可击的辩解/强而有力的保证等 **2** made of cast iron 铸铁制的, 生铁做的: *a cast-iron frying pan* 生铁煎锅 **3** extremely strong or determined 极为强壮的; 坚定不移的: *You need a cast-iron stomach to eat Imran's curry!* 你要吃伊姆兰的咖喱, 就要有个强健的胃!

W3 **cas·tle** /ˈkæsl; ˈkɑːsəl/ *n* [C] **1** a very large strong building, built in the past as a safe place that could be easily defended against attack 城堡, 堡垒: *Warwick Castle* 沃里克城堡 **2** one of the pieces used in a game of CHESS; ROOK[1] (2)〔国际象棋中的〕车 **3 castles in the air** plans or hopes that you have that are unlikely ever to become real; DAYDREAMS 空想, 空中楼阁, 异想天开

cast-off /ˈ‥/ *adj* [only before noun 仅用于名词前] cast off clothes or other goods are not wanted or have been thrown away〔衣物或东西〕被丢弃的, 废弃的

cast-offs /ˈ‥/ *n* [C] clothes that you do not wear any more and give to someone else〔自己不穿而送人的〕旧衣服: *As the youngest of five kids I was always dressed in other people's cast-offs.* 我是五个孩子中年龄最小的一个, 所以总穿别人穿过的旧衣服。

cast·or /ˈkæstə; ˈkɑːstə/ *n* [C] another spelling of CASTER caster 的另一种拼法

Cas·tor and Pol·lux /ˌkæstə ənd ˈpɑləks; ˌkɑːstər ən ˈpɒləks/ in ancient Greek and Roman stories, two brothers who were TWINS (=two children born at the same time), and who had many adventures. The group of stars known as Gemini or the Heavenly Twins is named after them. 卡斯托耳与波鲁克斯〔古希腊、古罗马传说中历经千险的一对孪生兄弟。星象学中的双子座因其而得名〕

castor oil /ˌ‥ ˈ‥◂/ *n* [U] a thick oil made from the seeds of a plant and used in the past as a medicine to make the BOWELS empty〔旧时用作轻泻剂的〕蓖麻油

castor sug·ar /ˈ‥ ,‥/ *n* [U] another spelling of CASTER SUGAR caster sugar 的另一种拼法

cas·trate /ˈkæstret; kæˈstreɪt/ *v* [T] to remove the sexual organs of a male animal or a man 阉割〔雄性动物或男性〕—**castration** /ˌkæsˈtreʃən; kæˈstreɪʃən/ *n* [U]

Castro, the /ˈkæstro; ˈkæstrəʊ/ a fashionable area in San Francisco where many homosexuals live 卡斯特罗〔旧金山一时尚街区。此地居住着许多同性恋者〕

Cas·tro, Fi·del /fiˈdɛl; fiˈdel/ (1927-) a Cuban COMMUNIST leader who led the opposition to the DICTATOR Batista, and forced him to leave the country in 1954. Castro then became Prime Minister of Cuba, and later its President. 卡斯特罗〔(1927-), 古巴共产党领导人。他曾领导人民反对独裁者巴蒂斯塔, 并于1954年迫使他离开古巴。卡斯特罗曾先后担任古巴总理和国家主席〕

cas·u·al /ˈkæʒuəl; ˈkæʒuəl/ *adj*

1 ▶NOT CARING 不在意◀ not caring or seeming not to care about something 漫不经心的, 随随便便的, 不放在心上的: *His casual manner annoyed me.* 他无所谓的态度使我恼怒。| *Karla tried to sound casual, but her excitement was obvious.* 卡拉尽量说得好像漫不经心, 但她的兴奋却是显而易见的。

2 ▶CLOTHES 衣服◀ casual clothes are comfortable clothes that you wear in informal situations 便装的, 非正式场合穿的: *casual shoes* 便鞋

3 casual worker/employment/labour etc a worker, employment etc that a company uses or offers only for a short period of time 临时工/短期工作[职位]等: *They're making do with casual staff.* 他们将就着使用临时工。

4 ▶WITHOUT ATTENTION 不注意◀ without any clear aim or serious interest 漫无目的的, 不认真的, 随便的: *a casual glance at the Times* 随便翻了翻《泰晤士报》| **casual observer** (=someone not looking very carefully) 大意的观察者 *Even to the most casual observer it was obvious she was sick.* 即使是最大意的人也能看出她显然是生病了。

5 ▶NOT PLANNED 非计划的◀ happening by chance without being planned 偶然的, 碰巧的: *a casual meeting* 巧遇 | **casual remark** (=something you say for no particular reason) 随意的言辞

6 casual sex sex that you have without intending to have a serious relationship with the other person 随意的[不负责任的]性关系

7 casual visitor/user etc someone who does not often visit a place, use something etc 偶然来访的客人/不固定的使用者等: *a casual user of the library service* 偶尔去去图书馆的人 —**casually** *adv*: *a casually dressed young man* 穿着随便的年轻人 —**casualness** *n* [U]

cas·u·al·ty /ˈkæʒuəltɪ; ˈkæʒuəlti/ *n* **1** [C] someone who is hurt or killed in an accident or battle〔事故或战斗中的〕伤者; 死者: *First reports of the air crash tell of more than 50 casualties.* 据最初的空难报道, 伤亡人数已超过50人。| **heavy casualties** (=a lot of people hurt or killed) 伤亡惨重 **2 be a casualty of** someone or something that suffers as a result of a particular event or situation 是〔某事件或情况造成的〕受害者[牺牲品]: *The Safer City Project became a major casualty of financial cutbacks.* 城市安全工程成了财政削减下的最大牺牲品。**3 Casualty** [U] *BrE* the part of a hospital that people are taken to when they are hurt in an accident or suddenly become ill【英】急救室, 急症室, 急诊室; EMERGENCY ROOM *AmE*【美】: *Steph works nights in Casualty.* 史蒂夫在急救室上夜班。

cas·u·ist /ˈkæʒuɪst; ˈkæʒuɪst/ *n* [C] *formal* someone who is skilled in casuistry【正式】诡辩家

cas·u·is·try /ˈkæʒuɪstrɪ; ˈkæʒuɪstri/ *n* [U] *formal* the use of clever but often false arguments to answer moral or legal questions【正式】诡辩(术)

ca·sus bel·li /ˈkesəs ˈbɛlaɪ; ˌkɑːsəs ˈbeli/ *n* [C] *Latin* an event or political action which directly causes a war【拉丁】引起战争的事件, 开战的理由

CAT the British Government guide to standards for the Individual Saving Accounts (ISA) introduced in 1999. It stands for reasonable Cost, easy Access, decent Terms. CAT 指南〔英国政府1999年实行的个人储蓄账户标准指南。其中C表示"费用合理", A表示"存取便捷", T表示"条款宽松"〕

cat /kæt; kæt/ *n* [C] S1 W3

1 ▶ANIMAL 动物◀ a) a small animal with four legs that is often kept as a pet or used for catching mice (MOUSE (1)) 猫 **b)** a large animal that is related to this, such as a lion or tiger 猫科动物〈如狮、虎〉

2 let the cat out of the bag to tell a secret, especially without intending to〔尤指无意中〕泄露秘密, 露出马脚

3 put/set the cat among the pigeons to cause trouble by doing or saying something that upsets people, causes arguments etc〔以引人反感的言行〕惹出乱子, 引起轩然大波

4 play cat and mouse with to let someone think they are getting or doing what they want, then prevent them from getting or doing it 把…当作玩物, 愚弄〔某人〕

5 like a cat on hot bricks *BrE*【英】, **like a cat on a hot tin roof** *AmE*【美】so nervous or anxious that you cannot keep still or keep your attention on one thing 像热锅上的蚂蚁, 坐立不安, 心神不定

6 ▶WOMAN 女人◀ *old-fashioned* an insulting word for a woman who you think is unkind or unpleasant【过时】恶毒的女人〔此词具侮辱性〕—see also 另见 CATTY, **raining cats and dogs** (RAIN[2] (4)), **there's not enough room to swing a cat** (ROOM[1] (2))

CULTURAL NOTE 文化注释

People sometimes say that a cat has nine lives, meaning that it always seems to stay alive and unhurt even in dangerous situations. In the UK, some people believe it is good luck for a black cat to walk in front of you. In the US, however, people think this is unlucky. 人们有时说猫有九条命, 意思是说猫即便在危险处境中也能活下来, 毫发无损。一些英国人相信黑猫从自己的面前走过是好兆头, 而在美国, 人们认为是坏兆头。

cat·a·clys·m /ˈkætəˌklɪzəm; ˈkætəklɪzəm/ *n* [C] *literary* a violent and sudden event or change, such as a serious flood or EARTHQUAKE【文】〔突发的〕剧变; 灾难〈如洪水、地震〉**—cataclysmic** /ˌkætəˈklɪzmɪk; ˌkætəˈklɪzmɪk/ *adj*

cat·a·comb /ˈkætəˌkom; ˈkætəkuːm/ *n* [C usually plural 一般用复数] an area of passages and rooms below the ground where dead people are buried 地下墓穴

cat·a·falque /ˈkætəˌfælk; ˈkætəfælk/ *n* [C] a decorated raised structure on which the dead body of an important person is placed before their funeral 灵柩台

Cat·a·lan /ˈkætḷən; ˈkætəlæn/ *n* [U] a language spoken in part of Spain around Barcelona〔西班牙巴塞罗那周边地区使用的〕加泰罗尼亚语

C

cat·a·lep·sy /ˈkætəˌlɛpsɪ; ˈkætəlepsi/ *n* [U] a medical condition in which you cannot control your movements so that your body becomes stiff like a dead body or remains in whatever position it is placed 僵直症, 僵住 **—cataleptic** /ˌkætəˈlɛptɪk; ˌkætəˈleptɪk◂/ *adj*

3 **cat·a·logue¹** also 又作 **catalog** *AmE*【美】/ˈkætḷˌɔg; ˈkætəlɒg/ *n* [C] **1** a book containing pictures and information about goods that you can buy 商品目录, 购物指南: *the Sears catalog* 西尔斯公司商品目录 **2 catalogue of failures/disasters/errors etc** a series of failures, disasters etc that happen one after the other and never seem to stop 一连串的失败/灾难/错误等: *the latest addition to the catalogue of terrorist crimes* 恐怖主义罪行录上的最新补充 **3** a list of all the objects, paintings etc at an EXHIBITION (1) or sale, of all the books in a library etc〔展览会或拍卖会上所有物品、绘画的〕目录, 一览表;〔图书馆的〕目录(册)

catalogue² also 又作 **catalog** *AmE*【美】*v* [T] **1** to put a list of things into a particular order and write it in a catalogue 为…编目录, 把…列入目录中 **2** to give a list of all the events or qualities connected with someone or something 把〔与某人或某物有关的事件或特点〕列出

ca·tal·y·sis /kəˈtæləsɪs; kəˈtælɪ̈sɪ̈s/ *n* [U] the process of making a chemical reaction quicker by adding a catalyst 催化作用, 触媒作用

cat·a·lyst /ˈkætḷɪst; ˈkætl-ɪ̈st/ *n* [C] **1** a substance that makes a chemical reaction happen more quickly without being changed itself 催化剂, 触媒 **2** something or someone that causes an important change or event to happen 导致重大变化的人[事物]; 促进因素: **[+for]** *The police beatings served as a catalyst for the escalation of violence.* 警察打人事件是这场暴力升级的导火线。**—catalytic** /ˌkætḷˈɪtɪk; ˌkætəˈlɪtɪk◂/ *adj*

catalytic con·vert·er /ˌ··· ·ˈ··/ *n* [C] a piece of equipment fitted to the EXHAUST¹ (1) of a car that reduces the amount of poisonous gases sent out into the air when the engine is operating〔安装在汽车排气装置上的〕催化式排气净化器

cat·a·ma·ran /ˌkætəməˈræn; ˌkætəməˈræn/ *n* [C] a sailing boat with two separate HULLS (=the part that goes in the water) 双体船

cat-and-dog /ˌ· · ˈ·/ *adj* [only before noun 仅用于名词前] *BrE informal* a cat-and-dog life is full of quarrels and arguments【英, 非正式】〔生活〕争吵不休的, 充满争吵的, 不和睦的

cat·a·pult¹ /ˈkætəˌpʌlt; ˈkætəpʌlt/ *n* [C] **1** a large weapon used in former times to throw heavy stones, iron balls etc〔古时用的, 能弹射巨石、铁球的〕石弩, 弩炮 **2** *BrE* a small stick in the shape of a Y with a thin band of rubber fastened over its ends, used by children to throw stones【英】〔小孩玩的〕弹弓; SLINGSHOT *AmE*【美】**3** a piece of equipment used to send an aircraft into the air from a ship〔舰上〕飞机起飞的弹射器

catapult² *v* **1** [T always+adv/prep] to push or throw something very hard so that it moves through the air very quickly 把…弹出去, 把…射出去: **catapult sb into/over/out etc** *Sam was catapulted into the air by the force of the blast.* 萨姆被爆炸所产生的冲力抛到空中。**2 catapult sb to fame/stardom etc** to suddenly make someone very famous 使…一举成名: *The movie 'Rebel Without a Cause' catapulted James Dean to stardom.* 电影《无因的反叛》使詹姆斯·迪安一炮走红。

cat·a·ract /ˈkætəˌrækt; ˈkætərækt/ *n* [C] **1** a medical condition of the eye in which the LENS (3) of your eye becomes white instead of clear, so that you cannot see 白内障 **2** *literary* a large WATERFALL【文】大瀑布

ca·tarrh /kəˈtɑr; kəˈtɑː/ *n* [U] an uncomfortable condition in which your nose and throat are almost blocked with thick liquid, for example when you have a cold 卡他,〔鼻、喉等的〕黏膜炎

ca·tas·tro·phe /kəˈtæstrəfɪ; kəˈtæstrəfi/ *n* [C,U] **1** a terrible event in which there is a lot of destruction or many people are injured or die 大灾难; 严重的不幸: *the catastrophe of a world-wide conflict* 一场世界性冲突所造成的大灾难 | *The oil spill threatens an unparalleled ecological catastrophe.* 漏油可能会造成一场前所未有的生态大灾难。**2** an event or situation which is extremely bad for the people involved 麻烦, 困境, 不利的局面: *If the contract is cancelled, it'll be a catastrophe for everyone concerned.* 如果合同取消, 对有关各方都是个大灾难。| *It's a minor catastrophe, isn't it? Plymouth losing?* 只是个小失利, 对吧? 普利茅斯队要输球了吧? **—catastrophic** /ˌkætəsˈtrɑfɪk; ˌkætəˈstrɒfɪk◂/ *adj*: *a catastrophic fall in the price of rice* 大米价格的灾难性下跌 **—catastrophically** /-kḷɪ; -kli/ *adv*

cat·a·ton·ic /ˌkætəˈtɑnɪk; ˌkætəˈtɒnɪk◂/ *adj technical* caused or affected by a condition in which you cannot think, speak, or move any part of your body【术语】(患)僵强症的, (患)强直性昏厥的: *a catatonic trance* 强直性昏厥状态

cat·bird seat /ˈkætbɝd ˌsit; ˈkætbɜːd ˌsiːt/ *n AmE informal*【美, 非正式】**be (sitting) in the catbird seat** to be in a position where you have an advantage 处于有利地位

cat bur·glar /ˈ· ˌ··/ *n* [C] a thief who gets into a building by climbing up walls, pipes etc〔爬墙、攀水管等入屋行窃的〕飞贼

cat·call /ˈkætˌkɔl; ˈkætkɔːl/ *n* [C] a loud whistle or shout expressing dislike or disapproval of a speech or performance〔表示反对或喝倒彩的〕口哨声; 尖叫声: *jeers and catcalls from the audience* 来自观众的嘲笑和嘘声 **—catcall** *v* [I]

catch¹ /kætʃ; kætʃ/ *v past tense and past participle* **caught** 1 1

1 ▸STOP/TRAP SB 抓住某人◂ [T] **a)** to stop someone after you have been chasing them and prevent them from escaping 抓住, 捉住: *"You can't catch me!" she yelled, running away across the field.* "你抓不到我的!"她大声喊道, 一边穿过田野逃跑了。| *If the guerillas catch you, they will kill you.* 要是游击队抓到你, 他们会杀了你。**b)** if the police catch a criminal, they find the criminal and stop him or her from escaping 捕获, 逮住〔罪犯〕: *State police have launched a massive operation to catch the murderer.* 州警方展开了大规模行动搜捕凶手。| *The jewel thieves were never caught.* 偷盗珠宝的窃贼仍然逍遥法外。

2 ▸FIND SB DOING STH 发现某人做某事◂ [T] to find or see someone while they are actually doing something wrong or illegal 撞见, 发现; 当场抓住〔某人正在干坏事〕: **catch sb doing sth** *I caught Howard reading my private letters.* 霍华德在看我的私人信件时让我撞见了。| **catch sb in the act (of)/catch sb red-handed** (=catch someone in the middle of doing something bad) 当场抓住 *a shoplifter caught in the act* 被当场抓住的商店扒手 | *They say Buster was caught red-handed.* 他们说巴斯特被当场捉住。| **catch sb at it** *BrE spoken*【英口】*We know he's been cheating, but we've never caught him at it.* 我们知道他一直在行骗, 不过我们从来没有当场抓到过他。

3 ▸FIND SB UNPREPARED 出其不意◂ catch sb unawares/catch sb off guard/catch sb on the hop *BrE* to do something or happen when someone is not expecting it and not ready to deal with events【英】使某人吃惊/措手不及/猝不及防: *a night attack that caught the enemy unawares* 令敌人措手不及的夜袭 | *Her question caught him off guard.* 她的问题让他猝不及防。| *The dramatic fall in share prices caught even the experts on the hop.* 股票价格暴跌甚至连专家也始料不及。| **be caught napping** *informal* (=not be ready to deal with something unexpected that happens)【非正式】〔对突发事件〕措手不及 | **catch sb with their pants/trousers down** *informal* (=make someone feel embarrassed by arriving or doing something when they are not ready)【非正式】〔出其不意地出现或做某事〕令某人措手不及

4 ▸ANIMAL/FISH 动物/鱼类◂ [T] to trap an animal or fish by using a trap, net, or hook, or by hunting it〔用陷阱、网、钩等〕捕, 捉〔动物或鱼类〕: *It's a useless cat, no good at catching mice.* 这是一只没用的猫, 一点也不会抓老鼠。| *Last time we went fishing I caught a huge trout.* 我们上次去钓鱼时我钓到一条大鳟鱼。| *catching butterflies* 捕捉蝴蝶

5 ▸HOLD 持着◂ a) [I,T] to get hold of and stop an object such as a ball that is moving through the air 接住〔在空中移动的物体〕: *Watch – if you throw the ball, Bouncer can catch it in his mouth.* 注意看, 如果你把球抛出, 邦瑟能用嘴接住。| *"Chuck me over those cigarettes, would you?" "Here you are. Catch!"* "把那些香烟扔给我, 好吗?" "给你。接住!" —see picture on page A22 参见 A22 页图 **b)** [T] to suddenly take hold of someone 突然抓住〔某人〕: *She stumbled forward but Calum caught her in his arms.* 她朝前绊了一下, 但是卡勒姆用双臂抱住了她。| **catch hold of** *Miss Perry caught hold of my sleeve and pulled me back.* 佩里小姐抓住我的袖子, 把我拉了回来。

6 ▸ILLNESS 病◂ [T] to get a disease or illness 患〔病〕, 感染上…: *My sister has mumps. I hope I haven't caught it.* 我妹妹得了流行性腮腺炎。我希望自己没有被传染。| **catch sth from/off** *I think I'm getting the flu – I must have caught it off Gerry.* 我想我得了流感, 一定是从格里那儿传染的。| **catch your death (of**

cold) (=get a very bad cold) 得重感冒 *Don't stand out there in the rain. You'll catch your death.* 别站在外面淋雨，你会得重感冒的。

7 catch a train/plane/bus to get on a train etc in order to travel, or to be in time to get it 赶火车／飞机／公共汽车: *Every morning I catch the 7:15 train to London.* 每天早晨我乘7点15分的列车去伦敦。| *There's a train in now. If you run, you'll just catch it.* 现在有一班火车，你跑步就能赶上。| **have a train etc to catch** *I have to hurry – I have a bus to catch.* 我得赶快，我得赶上搭那辆公共汽车。—see 见 REACH[1] (USAGE)

8 ►BE IN TIME 及时◄ [T] to not be too late to see something, talk to someone etc 及时赶上: *I managed to catch her just as she was leaving.* 我赶在她要离开时见到了她。| **catch the post** *BrE* (=post letters in time for them to be collected that day)【英】赶上收信的时间寄信 —opposite 反义词 MISS[1] (5)

9 ►GET STUCK 被卡住◄ [I,T] if your hand, finger, clothing etc catches or is caught in something, it becomes stuck or fastened there（被）夹住;（被）卡住;（被）钩住: *"What happened to your finger?" "It got caught in the car door."* "你的手指头怎么啦?" "被车门夹了一下。" | *Bobby caught his shirt on a wire fence.* 博比的衬衫被栅栏铁丝钩住了。

10 catch sb's attention/interest/imagination etc if something catches your attention etc, you notice it or feel interested in it 引起某人的注意／兴趣／想象等: *The unusual panelling on the wall caught our attention.* 墙上那不寻常的镶板引起了我们的注意。| *a story that will catch the imagination of every child* 能够激发每个孩子想象力的故事 | **catch sb's eye** (=get sb's attention) 吸引某人的注意 *We need big, bold headlines – something to catch the reader's eye.* 我们需要大字黑体的标题，以便能够引起读者的注意。

11 ►HEAR/UNDERSTAND 听见/理解◄ not catch sth to not hear or not understand what someone says 没听到，没听清; 没听懂: *Could you say that again? I didn't catch the last bit.* 你可以再说一遍吗? 我没听清最后一部分。| *I'm afraid I didn't catch your name.* 我恐怕没听清你的名字。| *Did you catch the announcement?* 你听到那个通知了吗?

12 ►NOTICE 注意◄ [T not in progressive 不用进行时] to see or notice something for a moment〔短暂地〕见到，注意到: **catch sight of/catch a glimpse of** *I suddenly caught sight of her in the crowd.* 我突然在人群中看见了她。| *Fans waited at the airport hoping to catch a glimpse of Gloria Estefan.* 歌迷守候在机场，希望能一睹格洛丽亚·埃斯特芬的风采。| **catch a whiff of** (=notice a smell for a moment)〔短暂地〕闻到〔某种气味〕*Brad caught a whiff of smoke in the air.* 布拉德猛然闻到空气中有一股烟味。

13 ►DESCRIBE WELL 成功描述◄ [T] to show or describe very successfully the character or quality of something, in a picture, a piece of writing etc〔图画、文章等〕成功地描述〔某物的性质或特点〕: *a novel that catches the mood of pre-war Britain* 生动地刻画出战前英国的社会气氛的小说

14 ►BURN 燃烧◄ a) catch fire if something catches fire, it starts to burn accidentally 着火: *Two farm workers died when a barn caught fire.* 谷仓失火，两名农场工人死亡。—see 见 FIRE[1] (USAGE) **b)** [I] if a fire catches it starts to burn 开始燃烧: *For some reason the charcoal isn't catching.* 不知怎的木炭点不着。

15 you won't catch me doing sth *spoken* used to say that you would never do something【口】别指望我会做某事: *You won't catch me ironing all his cotton shirts!* 别指望我会熨烫他所有的棉衬衫!

16 be caught up in to be involved in something unwillingly 被迫卷入〔某事〕: *Children who were caught up in the crime are getting a lot of media attention.* 被胁迫参与犯罪的孩子得到媒体的大量关注。

17 catch yourself doing sth to suddenly realize that you are doing something 突然意识到自己在做某事: *Monica sometimes caught herself envying her students.* 莫妮卡有时会突然意识到自己在嫉妒学生。

18 ►PROBLEM 麻烦◄ [T] to discover a problem and stop it from developing any more 发现〔麻烦并阻止其进一步发展〕: *This kind of cancer can be cured, provided it is caught early enough.* 这种癌症发现得早的话是可以治愈的。

19 ►HIT 击打◄ [T] to hit someone 打〔某人〕: **catch sb on the chin/face etc** *I caught him on the chin with a heavy punch.* 我一记重拳打在他的下巴上。

20 ►SPORT 体育运动◄ a) also 又作 **catch out** [T] to end a player's INNINGS in CRICKET (2) by taking and holding a ball hit off their BAT[1] (2a) before it touches the ground〔板球未着地前〕接住球使〔击球手〕出局 **b)** [I] to be the CATCHER in a game of BASEBALL〔棒球比赛中〕充当接球手

21 ►BE PUNISHED 受惩罚◄ you'll catch it *BrE spoken* used to tell someone that they are going to be in trouble because they have done something wrong【英口】〔因做错事〕你要吃苦头了: *You'll catch it if your mother finds out where you've been.* 如果你妈发现你去过那种地方，你准要挨骂。

22 ►IN A BAD SITUATION 处于困境◄ be caught in/without etc to be in a situation that is difficult, because you cannot easily get out of it or because you do not have what you need〔因为无法克服困难或缺少所需的东西而〕处于困境: *We got caught in a rainstorm on the way here.* 来这里的路上我们遇上了暴风雨。| *an actor caught without a script* 因缺剧本而感到为难的演员

23 catch your breath a) to stop breathing for a moment because something has surprised, frightened or shocked you〔因惊讶、恐惧、震惊而〕屏息 **b)** to pause for a moment after a lot of physical effort in order to breathe normally again 喘口气，缓口气: *Hang on a minute, let me catch my breath!* 稍等一下，让我喘口气!

24 ►SHINE ON 照射◄ [T] if the light catches something or if something catches the light, the light shines on it making it look bright（被光）照射: *The sunlight caught her hair and turned it to gold.* 阳光照在她的头发上，使之变成了金色。

25 ►CONTAINER 容器◄ [T] if a container catches liquid, it is in a position where the liquid falls into it 接住，盛住〔水等液体〕: *Steve! Bring me something to catch the drips under this pipe.* 史蒂夫! 帮我拿个东西过来接住水管的滴水。

26 catch the sun *informal* to become sunburned (SUNBURN) so that your skin is red【非正式】皮肤被晒红: *You've caught the sun on the back of your neck.* 你的脖子背后被晒红了。

catch at sth *phr v* [T] to try to take hold of something 试图抓住: *"You mean there's a real fire?" Heather caught at his arm.* "你是说真的失火了?" 希瑟用力抓住他的手臂。

catch on *phr v* [I] **1** to become popular and fashionable 流行: *It was a popular style in Britain but it never really caught on in America.* 这在英国是个受欢迎的款式，但是在美国却从来没有真正流行起来。**2** to begin to understand or realize something（开始）明白，意识到: **[+to]** *It was a long time before the police caught on to what he was really doing.* 过了好长时间警方才搞清楚他其实在干什么。

catch sb ↔ **out** *phr v* [T] *BrE*【英】**1** to make someone make a mistake, especially in order to prove that they are lying 识破〔错误〕，故意使某人犯错〔尤指为了证明某人撒谎〕: *It's a useful technique for handling people who are trying to catch you out.* 对付那些想让你犯错的人，这可是个很有用的技巧。**2** if an unexpected event catches you out, it puts you in a difficult situation, because you were not ready to deal with it（使）遭遇不测情况: *Didn't they ever tell you they in fact got caught out by the weather?* 难道他们没告诉你他们实际上遇到了坏天气吗?

catch up *phr v* **1** [I,T] to improve so much that you reach the same standard as other people in your class, group etc〔水平〕追上，赶上〔别人〕: *If you miss a lot of lessons, it's very difficult to catch up.* 如果你错过了许多课，就很难赶上了。| **[+with]** *At the moment our technology is more advanced, but other countries are catching up with us.* 目前我们的科技比较先进，不过其他国家正在赶上来。**2** [I, T] to come from behind and reach someone in front by going faster 追上; 超过: **[+with]** *Drive faster, they're catching up with us.* 开快点，他们要赶上我们了。| **catch sb up** *You go on ahead. I'll catch you up later.* 你先走，我稍后就追上你。**3** [I] to do what needs to be done because you have not been able to do it until now 赶做，补做: **[+on]** *I have some work to catch up on.* 我还有一些工作赶着要做。| *a chance to catch up on some sleep* (=after a period without enough sleep) 可以补睡一会儿的机会 | *You have a lot of catching up to do.* 你还有很多事情要补做。

catch up with sb *phr v* [T] **1** to finally find someone who has been doing something illegal and punish them〔终于〕抓住并惩罚〔罪犯〕: *It took six years for the law to catch up with them.* 警察花了六年时间才终于逮住他们。**2** if troubles, duties etc catch up with you, you cannot avoid them any longer〔麻烦、职责等〕缠身

catch²

catch² *n* **1** [C] *informal* a hidden problem or difficulty; SNAG[1](1)【非正式】陷阱，隐患，圈套，诡计: *The rent is only £40 a week – there must be a catch somewhere.* 房租每周只需40镑，这里面一定有些古怪。| **the catch is (that)** *The catch is that you can't enter the competition unless you've spent $100 in the store.* 圈套就在于，你得在该店消费100美元，否则你就进不了比赛。**2** [C] a hook or something similar for fastening a door or lid and keeping it shut 锁钩; 挂钩，吊扣 **3** [C] an act of catching a ball that has been thrown or hit 接球（动作）: *Hey! Nice catch!* 嘿! 多漂

亮的接球！**4** [C] an amount of fish that has been caught〔鱼的〕捕获量: *Local fishermen are reporting record catches.* 当地渔民称捕鱼量创了纪录。**5** [U] a simple game in which two or more people throw a ball to each other 接球游戏: *Let's go outside and play catch.* 我们到外面去玩抛球接球吧。**6 be a good catch** *old-fashioned* if a man is a good catch, he is regarded as a very desirable husband, because he is rich and good-looking【过时】是理想的丈夫〔长得帅气而且富有〕

catch-22 /ˌkætʃ ˌtwɛntɪˈtu; ˌkætʃ twentiˈtuː/ *n* [U] a situation in which you cannot do one thing until you do another thing, but you cannot do that until you have done the first thing, with the result that you can do neither 左右为难, 无法摆脱的困境, 进退维谷: **catch-22 situation** *It's a catch-22 situation – without experience you can't get a job and without a job you can't get experience.* 这是个无法摆脱的困局: 没有经验就找不到工作, 找不到工作你就没有经验。

catch·all[1] /ˈ· ·/ *adj* intended to include all situations or possibilities 无所不包的: **catchall clause/list etc** *a vague catchall clause in an employment contract* 雇用合同里一条模糊的无所不包的条款

catch·all[2] *n* [C] *AmE* a drawer, cupboard etc where you put any small objects【美】放置各种小杂物的抽屉[橱柜等]

catch crop /ˈ· ·/ *n* [C] a vegetable crop that grows quickly, planted between two rows of another crop 间种作物, 填闲作物〔在两行主要作物之间快速生长的蔬菜类农作物〕

catch·er /ˈkætʃɚ; ˈkætʃə/ *n* [C] the player who sits on his heels behind the BATTER[2] (3) in a game of baseball〔棒球运动中的〕接球手 —see picture on page A22 参见 A22 页图

Catcher in the Rye, The /ˌ· · · · ˈ·/ a book by J.D. Salinger about a boy called Holden Caulfield who runs away from school and goes to New York. The book has been especially popular with young people because it describes the problems and experiences of ADOLESCENCE (=the time when a child is developing into an adult).《麦田里的守望者》(J.D. 塞林格所著的一本书, 讲述一个名叫霍尔登·考尔菲尔德的男孩逃学去纽约的故事。该书描述青少年的问题和经历, 因而备受年轻人的青睐〕

catch·ing /ˈkætʃɪŋ; ˈkætʃɪŋ/ *adj* [not before noun 不用于名词前] *informal*【非正式】**1** a disease or illness that is catching is infectious〔疾病〕传染(性)的: *Well, I hope it's not catching.* 嗯, 我希望这种病没有传染性。**2** an emotion or feeling that is catching spreads quickly among people〔情感〕具有感染力的

catch·ment ar·e·a /ˈkætʃmənt ˌɛrɪə; ˈkætʃmənt ˌeəriə/ *n* [C] **1** the area that a school takes its students from, that a hospital takes its patients from etc〔学校〕学生来源的区域;〔医院〕病人集中的地区 **2** the area that a river or lake gets water from〔为河流或湖泊供水的〕集水区, 汇水盆地

catch·pen·ny /ˈ· · ·/ *adj old-fashioned* cheap and of bad quality but made to look attractive【过时】价廉质劣但外表吸引的, 花哨而不值钱的

catch·phrase /ˈkætʃˌfrez; ˈkætʃfreɪz/ *n* [C] a short well-known phrase used regularly by an entertainer or politician, so that people think of that person when they hear it〔演员或政客常用的〕时髦话, 流行的词句

catch·word /ˈkætʃˌwɝd; ˈkætʃwɜːd/ *n* [C] a word or phrase that is easy to remember and is repeated regularly by a political party, newspaper etc; SLOGAN〔政党、报刊等的〕代表性口号, 标语

catch·y /ˈkætʃɪ; ˈkætʃi/ *adj* **catchy song/tune** a song or tune that is pleasant and easy to remember〔歌曲或曲调〕悦耳易记的: *a catchy advertising slogan like 'Go to Work on an Egg'* 朗朗上口的广告标语如"吃个鸡蛋去上班" —**catchily** *adv*

cat·e·chis·m /ˈkætəˌkɪzəm; ˈkætɪ̯ˌkɪzəm/ *n* [singular] a set of questions and answers about the Christian religion that people learn in order to become full members of a church〔基督教的〕教理问答

cat·e·chize also 又作 **-ise** *BrE*【英】/ˈkætəˌkaɪz; ˈkætɪ̯kaɪz/ *v* [T] to teach someone about a religion by using a series of questions and answers 用问答法向〔某人〕传授教义

cat·e·gor·i·cal /ˌkætəˈgɔrɪkl; ˌkætɪ̯ˈgɒrɪkəl◂/ *adj* a categorical statement is a clear statement that something is definitely true 确实的, 明确的: **categorical denial/statement/assurance etc** *Can you give us a categorical assurance that no jobs will be lost?* 你能否明确向我们保证不会出现失业?

cat·e·gor·i·cally /ˌkætəˈgɔrɪklɪ; ˌkætɪ̯ˈgɒrɪkli/ *adv* in such a sure and certain way that there is no doubt 确定无疑地, 断然地, 明确地: **categorically deny/refuse etc** *Forbes has categorically denied his guilt all along.* 福布斯自始至终都断然否认他有任何过错。

cat·e·go·rize also 又作 **-ise** *BrE*【英】/ˈkætəgəˌraɪz; ˈkætɪ̯gəraɪz/ *v* [T] to put people or things into groups according to what type they are, or to say which group they are in; CLASSIFY 对…进行分类; 把…列作: *The population is categorized according to age, sex, and socioeconomic group.* 按年龄、性别和社会经济群体对人口进行分类。| **categorize sth/sb as** *Keene doesn't like to be categorized as a socialist.* 基恩不喜欢人们把他列为社会党党员。—**categorization** /ˌkætəgəraɪˈzeʃən; ˌkætɪ̯gəraɪˈzeɪʃən/ *n* [C,U]

cat·e·go·ry /ˈkætəˌgorɪ; ˈkætɪ̯gəri/ *n* [C] a group of people or things that all have the same particular qualities 类别, 种类, 范畴: **fall into a category** (=belong to a category) 属于某类 *Voters fall into three main categories.* 选民分为三大类。 2 2

ca·ter /ˈketɚ; ˈkeɪtə/ *v* [I,T] to provide and serve food and drinks at a party, meeting etc, usually as a business〔在聚会、会议等上〕(为…) 承包伙食; 承办酒席: **[+for/at]** *Who's catering at your daughter's wedding?* 谁承办你女儿的婚宴? | **cater sth** *AmE*【美】*Shouldn't we get bids for catering the 20th class reunion?* 我们难道不该争取为第 20 届班级聚会提供酒水等服务吗?

cater for sb/sth *phr v* [T] to provide a particular group of people with everything that they need or want 为…提供服务; 满足…的要求: *a holiday company that caters more for the elderly* 一家较多为老年人提供假日活动的公司

cater to sb/sth *phr v* [T] to provide something that a particular type of person wants but that you think is bad, stupid etc 迎合, 投合: *It's the kind of movie that caters to the worst side of human nature.* 这是那种迎合人性阴暗面的电影。

ca·ter·er /ˈketərɚ; ˈkeɪtərə/ *n* [C] a person or company that is paid to provide and serve food and drinks at a party, meeting etc〔聚会、会议等的〕酒席承办者: *What time will the caterers get here?* 饮食承办人什么时候到?

ca·ter·ing /ˈketərɪŋ; ˈkeɪtərɪŋ/ *n* [U] the activity of providing and serving food and drinks at parties for money 承办饮食服务: *Who did the catering?* 谁承办酒席? —see also 另见 SELF-CATERING

cat·er·pil·lar /ˈkætɚˌpɪlɚ; ˈkætəˌpɪlə/ *n* [C] **1** a small creature like a WORM with a lot of legs that feeds on leaves and is the LARVA of a BUTTERFLY or other insect 毛虫〔蝴蝶等昆虫的幼虫〕**2** also 又作 **caterpillar track** a belt made of metal plates that is fastened over the wheels of a heavy vehicle to help it to move over soft ground〔重型车辆的〕履带 **3** also 又作 **caterpillar tractor** a heavy vehicle that is fitted with these belts 履带式拖拉机

cat·er·waul /ˈkætɚˌwɔl; ˈkætəwɔːl/ *v* [I] to make a loud high unpleasant noise like the sound a cat makes 发出〔猫叫似的〕刺耳声 —**caterwaul** *n* [singular]

cat flap /ˈ· ·/ *n* [C] an entrance to the house for your pet cat, consisting of a piece of wood or plastic which hangs down over a hole at the bottom of the door, and which can swing open 供家猫进出房屋的吊门

cat·gut /ˈkætgʌt; ˈkætgʌt/ *n* [U] strong thread made from the INTESTINES of animals and used for the strings of musical instruments〔用来制作琴弦的〕肠线, 肠弦

ca·thar·sis /kəˈθarsɪs; kəˈθɑːsɪ̯s/ *n* [C,U] *formal* a way of dealing with bad or strong feelings and emotions, by expressing or experiencing them through writing, talking, DRAMA etc【正式】〔通过写作、戏剧等〕宣泄情感 —**cathartic** /-tɪk; -tɪk/ *adj*: *It was actually a cathartic experience to write my autobiography.* 写自传确实是我一次宣泄情感的经历。

ca·the·dral /kəˈθidrəl; kəˈθiːdrəl/ *n* [C] a very large church, which is the main church of a particular area under the control of a BISHOP (1) 大教堂,〔主教控制的〕教区总教堂: *Durham cathedral* 德拉姆大教堂 | **cathedral city** (=one with a cathedral) 教区总教堂所在城市

Cath·er /ˈkæðɚ; ˈkæðə/, **Wil·la** /ˈwɪlə; ˈwɪlə/ (1876-1947), a US writer who grew up in Nebraska at the time when Europeans first went to live there. Her books include *O! Pioneers* and *My Antonia*. 凯瑟〔(1876-1947), 美国作家。她在欧洲人最早定居的内布拉斯加长大。其作品有《哦, 拓荒者们》、《我的安东尼亚》等〕

Cath·e·rine of Ar·a·gon /ˌkæθrɪn əv ˈærəgɑn; ˌkæθɪ̯rɪ̯n əv ˈærəgən/ (1485-1536) the first wife of King Henry VIII of England and the mother of Mary I 阿拉贡的凯瑟琳〔(1485-1536), 英格兰国王亨利八世的第一任妻子, 玛丽一世的母亲〕

Catherine the Great /ˌ· · · · ˈ·/ also 又作 **Catherine II** (1729-96) the Empress of Russia from 1762 to 1796. She greatly increased the size of the Russian Empire. 叶卡捷琳娜大帝〔(1729-1796), 俄国女皇, 1762 年至 1796 年在位。她曾极大地扩大了俄国的版图〕

cath·er·ine wheel /ˈkæθərɪn hwil; ˈkæθərɪ̯n wiːl/ *n* [C] a round FIREWORK that spins around 轮转烟火

cath·e·ter /ˈkæθɪtɚ; ˈkæθɪ̣tə/ *n* [C] a thin tube that is put into your body to take away liquids〔置入体内以导出液体的〕导(液)管 —**catheterize** also 又作 **-ise** *BrE*【英】*v* [T]

cath·ode /ˈkæθod; ˈkæθəʊd/ *n* [C] *technical* the negative ELECTRODE from which electric current leaves a piece of equipment like a BATTERY (1)【术语】阴极, 负极—compare 比较 ANODE

cathode ray tube /ˌ.. ˈ. ˌ/ *n* [C] a piece of equipment used in televisions and computers, in which negative ELECTRONS from the cathode produce an image on a screen 阴极射线管, 电子射线管

Cath·o·lic /ˈkæθəlɪk; ˈkæθəlɪk/ *adj* connected with the Roman Catholic Church 与(罗马)天主教有关的: *a Catholic school* 天主教学校 —**Catholic** *n* [C] —**Catholicism** /kəˈθɑləˌsɪzəm; kəˈθɒlɪ̣sɪzəm/ *n* [U]

catholic *adj formal*【正式】**have catholic tastes** to like a wide variety of things 兴趣广泛的 —**catholicity** /ˌkæθəˈlɪsətɪ; ˌkæθəˈlɪsɪ̣ti/ *n* [U]

Cat in the Hat, The /ˌ. . . ˈ. ˌ/ a popular children's book by Dr. Seuss which is written in rhyme and contains drawings《帽中猫》〔索伊斯博士所著的一部流行童话作品。作品以韵体写成, 并配有插图〕

cat·kin /ˈkætkɪn; ˈkætkɪn/ *n* [C] *especially BrE* a soft flower that grows in long thin groups and hangs from the branches of trees such as the WILLOW or BIRCH¹【尤英】〔柳树、桦树等的〕葇荑花序; 杨花; 柳絮

cat lit·ter /ˈ. ˌ../ *n* [U] a substance that people put down in boxes for cats that live indoors, so that they can pass waste from their BOWELS into it 猫砂

cat·nap /ˈkætnæp; ˈkætnæp/ *n* [C] *informal* a very short sleep【非正式】瞌睡, 小睡: *"Where's Grandma?" "She's having a catnap."* "奶奶在哪?" "她正在小睡。" —**catnap** *v* [I]

cat-o'-nine-tails /ˌkæt ə ˈnaɪn ˌtelz; ˌkæt ə ˈnaɪn teɪlz/ *n* [C] a whip made of nine strings with knots on the end, used in the past for punishing people〔旧时用于惩罚人的由九根末尾带结的绳子组成的〕九尾鞭

Cats /kæts; kæts/ a popular MUSICAL (=a play that uses singing and dancing to tell a story) by Andrew Lloyd Webber, which is based on T.S. Eliot's book of poems for children, *Old Possum's Book of Practical Cats.*《猫》〔安德鲁·劳埃德·韦伯根据T.S. 艾略特的儿童诗集《老负鼠讲世上的猫》而创作的一部火爆的音乐剧〕

CAT scan /ˈkæt skæn; ˈkæt skæn/ *n* [C] the image produced by a CAT scanner 电脑化X射线轴向分层造影扫描图

CAT scan·ner /ˈkæt ˌskænɚ; ˈkæt ˌskænə/ *n* [C] an electronic machine used in a hospital to look inside someone's body 电脑化X射线轴向分层造影扫描器

cat's cra·dle /ˌ. ˈ. ./ *n* [U] a game children play with string which they wind around the fingers of both hands to make different patterns〔小孩玩的〕翻绳游戏〔用线绳绕于手指上翻出各种花样的游戏〕

cat's eye /ˈ. ˌ/ *n* [C] one of the line of small flat objects fixed in the middle of the road, that shine when lit by car lights, to guide traffic in the dark〔置于道路中间, 黑暗中可借车灯发光的〕道路反光装置

Cat·skill Moun·tains, the /ˌkætskɪl ˈmaʊntn̩z; ˌkætskɪl ˈmaʊntɪ̣nz/ also 又作 **the Catskills** a group of mountains in the southeast of New York state in the US, part of the Appalachian mountain range 卡茨基尔山脉〔位于美国纽约州东南部, 为阿巴拉契亚山系的一部分〕

cat's paw /ˈ. . ˌ/ *n* [C] *old-fashioned* someone who does unpleasant or dangerous jobs because someone else has ordered them to【过时】奉命做危险或不愉快事情的人, 爪牙, 傀儡

cat suit /ˈ. . ˌ/ *n* [C] a tight piece of women's clothing that covers all of the body and legs in one piece 女式紧身连衣裤

cat·sup /ˈkætsəp; ˈkætsəp/ *n* [U] *AmE*【美】an American spelling of KETCHUP ketchup的美式拼法

cat·te·ry /ˈkætərɪ; ˈkætəri/ *n* [C] *BrE* a place where you can leave cats to be looked after while you are away from home【英】〔临时寄养猫的〕猫屋, 猫窝

cat·tle /ˈkætl̩; ˈkætl/ *n* [plural] cows and BULLS kept on a farm for their meat or milk 牛〔指菜牛或奶牛〕: *herds of cattle* 一群群牛 | **20/100 etc head of cattle** (=20, 100 etc cattle) 20/100 头牛

cattle grid /ˈ. . ˌ/ *BrE*【英】, **cattle guard** *AmE*【美】*n* [C] a set of bars placed over a hole in the road, so that animals cannot go across but cars can 拦畜沟栅〔铺在路中坑洞的若干木棒, 汽车可通过而牲畜则走不过去〕

cat·tle·man /ˈkætl̩mən; ˈkætlmən/ *n* [C] someone who looks after or owns cattle 养牛人, 牧牛工人

cattle mar·ket /ˈ. . ˌ. ./ *n* [C] *BrE*【英】**1** a place where cattle are bought and sold 牛市场 **2** *informal* a disapproving word for a beauty competition or a social event where women are judged only by their sexual attractiveness【非正式】〔只以色相取人的〕选美比赛

cattle truck /ˈ. . ˌ/ *n* [C] *BrE* a vehicle or part of a train that is made to carry cattle【英】运牛的卡车[火车(车厢)]

cat·ty /ˈkætɪ; ˈkæti/ *adj* someone who is catty is unpleasant and often says nasty things about people 爱说恶毒的话的, 坏心眼的, 令人讨厌的: *She's a liar. Does that sound catty, too?* 她是个骗子。这听起来是否也有点刻薄? —**cattily** *adv* —**cattiness** *n* [U]

catty-cor·ner /ˈ. . ., . ˌ/ *adv AmE*【美】KITTY CORNER 成对角线地, 斜线地

Ca·tul·lus /kəˈtʌləs; kəˈtʌləs/, **Gai·us Va·ler·i·us** /ˈgaɪəs vəˈlɪrɪəs; ˈgaɪəs vəˈlɪəriəs/ (?84-?54 BC) an ancient Roman poet, famous especially for his love poems 卡图卢斯〔(?公元前84-?公元前54年), 古罗马诗人, 尤以爱情诗闻名〕

cat·walk /ˈkætˌwɔk; ˈkætwɔːk/ *n* [C] **1** a long raised path that MODELS walk on in a fashion show〔时装模特儿走的〕T型台 **2** a temporary structure for walking on, built around the outside of buildings or between them when they are being built or repaired〔临时的〕步行小道

Cau·ca·sian /kɔˈkeʒən; kɔːˈkeɪziən/ *adj* someone who is Caucasian belongs to the race that has white or pale skin 高加索(人)的, 白种人的 —**Caucasian** *n* [C]

Cau·ca·sus, the /ˈkɔkəsəs; ˈkɔːkəsəs/ an area in the extreme southeast of Europe between the Black Sea and the Caspian Sea, which includes Russia, Georgia, Azerbaijan and Armenia, and contains the Caucasus Mountains 高加索〔欧洲东南端一地区, 位于黑海和里海之间, 包括俄罗斯、格鲁吉亚、阿塞拜疆、亚美尼亚等国以及高加索山脉〕

Caucasus Moun·tains, the a group of mountains in the Caucasus in southeast Europe, which includes Mount Elbruz, the highest mountain in Europe 高加索山脉〔欧洲东南部高加索地区一山脉, 其中包括欧洲最高峰厄尔布鲁士山〕

cau·cus /ˈkɔkəs; ˈkɔːkəs/ *n* [C] a group of people in a political party, who meet to discuss and decide on political plans〔政党的〕决策者, 决策层

cau·dal /ˈkɔdl̩; ˈkɔːdl/ *adj technical* at or related to an animal's tail【术语】〔动物〕尾部的 —**caudally** *adv*

caught /kɔt; kɔːt/ the past tense and past participle of CATCH¹

caul·dron, caldron /ˈkɔldrən; ˈkɔːldrən/ *n* [C] a large round metal pot for boiling liquids over a fire〔煮液体用的〕大锅: *a witch's cauldron* 女巫的大锅 —see picture at 参见 WITCH 图

Caul·field /ˈkɔlfild; ˈkɔːlfiːld/, **Hol·den** /ˈholdn̩; ˈhəʊldən/ the main character in the book *The Catcher in the Rye* by J. D. Salinger. Holden Caulfield has a lot of difficult experiences because he is a TEENAGER. 考尔菲尔德〔J.D. 塞林格小说《麦田里的守望者》中的主人公。少年的他经历了诸多不快的事〕

cau·li·flow·er /ˈkɔləˌflaʊɚ; ˈkɒlɪˌflaʊə/ *n* [C,U] a garden vegetable with green leaves around a large firm white centre 菜花, 花椰菜 —see picture on page A9 参见A9页图

cauliflower cheese /ˌ. . . . ˈ. ˌ/ *n* [U] *BrE* the white part of a cauliflower cooked and eaten with cheese SAUCE【英】乳酪菜花

cauliflower ear /ˌ. . . . ˈ. ˌ/ *n* [C] an ear permanently swollen into a strange shape, especially as a result of an injury〔尤指因受伤而变畸形的〕开花耳朵

caulk, calk /kɔk; kɔːk/ *v* [T] to fill the holes or cracks in something, especially a ship, with an oily or sticky substance that keeps water out〔用防水物料〕填塞〔船等的漏洞或裂缝〕

caus·al /ˈkɔzl̩; ˈkɔːzəl/ *adj* **1 causal relationship/link/connection etc** a relationship etc that exists between two or more events or situations, where one causes the other to happen 因果关系/联系等: *a causal relationship between unemployment and crime* 失业和犯罪之间的因果关系 **2** *technical* a causal CONJUNCTION (3), for example 'because', introduces a statement about the cause of something【术语】表示原因的〔连接词〕—**causally** *adv*

cau·sal·i·ty /kɔˈzælətɪ; kɔːˈzælɪ̣ti/ *n* [U] *formal* the relationship between a cause and the effect that it has【正式】因果关系, 因果性

cau·sa·tion /kɔˈzeʃən; kɔːˈzeɪʃən/ *n* [U] *formal*【正式】**1** the action of causing something to happen or exist 导致; 起因, 惹起 **2** causality 因果关系, 因果性

caus·a·tive /ˈkɔzətɪv; ˈkɔːzətɪv/ *adj formal*【正式】**1** acting as the cause of something 起因的, 成为…的原因的: *causative factors* 起因 **2** *technical* a causative verb expresses an action that causes something to happen or be【术语】〔动词〕使役的 —**causatively** *adv*

cause¹ /kɔz; kɔːz/ *n* S2 W1

1 ►WHAT CAUSES STH 起因◄ [C] a person, event, or thing that makes something happen 原因, 起因: [+of] *What was the*

cause of the accident? 那场事故的起因是什么？| *The doctor had recorded the cause of death as heart failure.* 医生记录了死亡的原因为心脏衰竭。| **root/underlying etc cause** (=the basic cause) 根本/基本原因 *The root cause of the crime problem is poverty.* 贫困是产生犯罪问题的根本原因。| **cause and effect** (=the idea or fact of one thing directly causing another) 因果 —see 见 REASON¹ (USAGE)
2 ►GOOD REASON 恰当理由◄ [U] something that makes it right or fair for you to feel or behave in a particular way 理由, 根据, 缘故: [+for] *There is no cause for alarm.* 没有理由惊慌。| **cause for complaint** (=a reason to complain) 抱怨的理由 *I've got no cause for complaint – I'm doing all right.* 我没有理由抱怨 —— 我一切都好。| **cause for concern** (=a reason to be worried) 担心的理由 *The patient's condition is giving cause for concern.* 病人的状况令人担忧。| **have good cause to** *God knows he's got good cause to be relieved.* 上帝知道他有充分的理由得到解脱。| **with/without good cause** *Many people are worried about the economy, and with good cause.* 许多人正为经济状况担心, 这是有充分的理由的。
3 ►STH YOU SUPPORT 支持的事物◄ **a)** [C] an organization, principle, or aim that a group of people support or fight for 极力维护[支持]的组织[原则、目标]: *How many of them are sympathetic to our cause?* 他们当中有多少人支持我们的事业？| [+of] *her lifelong devotion to the cause of women's rights* 她对女权运动终生不渝的献身 **b) be in/for a good cause** if something you do is for a good cause, it is worth doing because it is intended to help other people, especially through a CHARITY (2) 为了正义的事业,〔尤指〕为慈善: *Well, I don't mind giving if it's for a good cause.* 嗯, 如果是为慈善的话, 我不介意捐赠。
4 make common cause (with) *formal* to join with other people or groups for a particular purpose【正式】〔为某目的〕与…共同合作[齐心合力]: *Faced by an enemy on their territory, the French parties tried to make common cause.* 面对侵犯领土的敌人, 法国各党派都团结起来。
5 ►LAW 法律◄ [C] a case that is brought to a court of law 诉讼案件 —see also 另见 **lost cause** (LOST¹ (13))

cause² *v* [T] to make something happen 导致, 引起, 使发生: *Heavy traffic is causing long delays on the freeway.* 拥挤的交通造成高速公路上的长时间耽误。| **cause sb/sth to do sth** *A dog ran into the road, causing the cyclist to swerve.* 一只狗跑到了道路上, 使得那位骑自行车的人突然转向。| **cause concern/uncertainty/embarrassment etc** (=make people feel worried, unsure, embarrassed etc) 使人感到担忧/不知所措/尴尬等 *The constant changes of policy have caused a great deal of uncertainty in the workforce.* 政策的不断改变使得劳动大军感到疑惑。| **cause sb trouble/problems/inconvenience etc** *Jimmy's behaviour is causing me a lot of problems.* 吉米的所作所为给我带来许多麻烦。| **cause offence** (=offend someone) 冒犯〔某人〕*I'm sorry; I didn't mean to cause offence.* 对不起, 我不是有意冒犯的。

USAGE NOTE 用法说明: CAUSE
GRAMMAR 语法
Something can **cause** death/crime/trouble etc, or **cause** somebody inconvenience/a problem etc. cause 可以表示某事物导致死亡/犯罪/麻烦等, 或为某人带来不便/问题等: *His behaviour caused everyone a lot of worry* (NOT 不用 *caused to everyone...*). 他的行为使大家非常担心。
Something can **cause** someone or something **to** do something. cause 可以用于表示某事物使某人或某物做某事: *The disease caused his face to swell* (NOT *caused that his face swelled*, or *caused his face swell*, though you could say less formally *...made his face swell*). 这种病使他的脸肿起来了〔不用 caused that his face swelled, 或 caused his face swell. 虽然较随便的说法可以是 …made his face swell〕。
SPELLING 拼法
Remember the difference between **cause**, and *because* and *of course*. 记住 cause, because 和 of course 之间的区别。

cause cé·lè·bre /ˌkoz sɛˋlɛbrə; ˌkəʊz seˈlebrə/ *n* [C] *French* an event or legal case that a lot of people become interested in, because it is an exciting subject to discuss or argue about【法】轰动一时的事件; 引起公众关注的诉讼案

cause·way /ˋkoz,we; ˈkɔːzweɪ/ *n* [C] a raised road or path across wet ground or through water〔穿越湿地或水面的〕垫高的堤道, 砌道

caus·tic /ˋkɔstɪk; ˈkɔːstɪk/ *adj* **1** a caustic substance can burn through things by chemical action〔物质〕苛性的; 腐蚀性的 **2** a caustic remark criticizes someone in a way that is unkind but often cleverly humorous〔语言〕尖刻的; 讽刺的 —**caustically** /-klɪ; -kli/ *adv*

caustic so·da /ˌ‥ ˈ‥/ *n* [U] a very strong chemical substance that you can use for some difficult cleaning jobs〔清洁用的〕烧碱; 苛性钠

cau·ter·ize also 又作 **-ise** *BrE*【英】/ˋkɔtə,raɪz; ˈkɔːtəraɪz/ *v* [T] *technical* to burn a wound with hot metal or a chemical to stop the blood or stop it becoming infected【术语】〔用烧灼剂或烙铁〕烙, 烧灼〔伤口以消毒或止血〕

cau·tion¹ /ˋkɔʃən; ˈkɔːʃən/ *n* **1** [U] the quality of being very careful, not taking any risks, and trying to avoid danger 小心, 谨慎, 慎重: **with caution** *We must proceed with caution.* 我们必须谨慎行事。| **great/extreme caution** *the need for extreme caution when handling these animals* 安置这些动物需要极为小心 | **treat sth with caution** (=think carefully about something because it might not be true) 仔细斟酌某事 *Evidence given by convicted criminals should always be treated with caution.* 对已被判刑的罪犯所提供的证据应经常予以仔细审察。**2 word/note of caution** a warning to be careful 警示, 警告〔某人小心〕: *One note of caution, don't let your children try this trick.* 提醒你, 不要让你的孩子尝试这种把戏。**3 throw/fling/cast caution to the winds** to start to take more risks in what you do or say 不顾一切/鲁莽行事: *Throwing all caution to the winds, she swung around to face him.* 她不顾一切地转身面对他。**4** [C] *BrE* a spoken official warning given by someone in authority when you have done something wrong that is not a serious crime【英】〔给犯了轻罪的人的〕正式〔口头〕警告, 训诫: *The judge let him off with a caution.* 法官给他一个训诫就释放了他。**5** [singular] *old-fashioned* an amusing person【过时】滑稽有趣的人

caution² *v* [T] **1** to warn someone that something might be dangerous, difficult etc 警告, 告诫, 提醒: **caution sb about/against** *Geraldine cautioned the boys about talking to strange men.* 杰拉尔丁告诫孩子不要随便和陌生人说话。| **caution (sb) that** *Foreign Office officials were quick to caution that these remarks did not mean there would be a new peace initiative.* 外交部官员迅速告诫说这些评论并不意味着会有新的和平举措。**2** *BrE* to warn someone officially that the next time they do something illegal they will be punished【英】给某人正式警告: **caution sb for/about** *She got cautioned for speeding.* 她因开快车而被警告。

cau·tion·ar·y /ˋkɔʃən,ɛrɪ; ˈkɔːʃənəri/ *adj* giving a warning or advice 警告的, 告诫的: *a cautionary note on the abuse of power* 对滥用职权的警告 | **cautionary tale** (=the story of an event that can be used to warn people) 警世故事 *It's a cautionary tale about how not to buy a computer.* 那是一个关于如何不买电脑的告诫性故事。

cau·tious /ˋkɔʃəs; ˈkɔːʃəs/ *adj* careful to avoid danger or risks 小心的, 谨慎的, 慎重的: *a cautious driver* 一位谨慎的司机 | **cautious about doing sth** *I've always been very cautious about giving my address to strangers.* 我总是很小心, 不轻易把我的地址给陌生人。| **cautious optimism** (=hopes for a good result while being careful not to expect too much) 审慎的乐观 —**cautiously** *adv*: *Sara opened the door cautiously and peeped in.* 莎拉小心翼翼地打开门往里面瞧。—**cautiousness** *n* [U]

cav·al·cade /ˌkævlˋked; ˌkævəlˈkeɪd/ *n* [C] a line of people on horses or in cars or carriages moving along as part of a ceremony〔作为礼仪一部分的〕骑马队; 车队

Cavalier 保王党成员

Cav·a·lier /ˌkævəˋlɪr; ˌkævəˈlɪə◂/ *n* [C] a supporter of the King against parliament in the English Civil War of the 17th century〔英国17世纪内战中的〕保王党成员 —compare 比较 ROUNDHEAD

cavalier *adj* not caring or thinking about other people's feelings 满不在乎的, 随便的, 轻漫的: *The complaints show these companies have been treating the issue in a cavalier way.* 这些投诉说明这些公司在处理这一事件时态度轻率。

cav·al·ry /ˋkævl̩rɪ; ˈkævəlri/ *n* [U] **1** the part of an army that fights on horses, especially in the past〔尤指旧时的〕骑兵(部队) **2** the part of a modern army that uses tanks (TANK¹ (3)) 坦克部队, 装甲兵部队

cav·al·ry·man /ˋkævl̩rɪmən; ˈkævəlrimən/ *n* [C] a soldier who fights on a horse 骑兵

cave¹ /kev; keɪv/ *n* [C] a large natural hole in the side of a cliff or hill, or under the ground 洞穴; 山洞; 岩洞; 窑洞 —see picture on page A12 参见 A12 页图

cave² *v*

cave in *phr v* [I] **1** if the top or sides of something cave in, they fall down or inwards 塌落, 坍塌, 陷下: [+on] *The roof of the tunnel just caved in on us.* 隧道顶坍塌压住了我们。**2** to finally stop opposing something, especially because someone has persuaded or threatened you〔尤指因某人劝说或威胁而〕停止反对; 屈服, 投降: *You don't know, they might cave in straight away and give us what we want.* 你不知道, 他们可能马上就会屈服, 给我们所要求的东西。—**cave-in** *n* [C]

ca·ve·at /ˋkevɪˌæt; ˈkeɪviæt/ *n* [C] *formal* a warning that you must pay attention to something before you make a decision or take a particular action【正式】〔作决定或行动前必须注意的〕警告, 提醒

caveat emp·tor /ˋkevɪˌæt ˋɛmptɔr; ˌkeɪviæt ˈemptɔː/ *n* [U] *Latin* the principle that when goods are sold, the buyer is responsible for checking the quality of the goods【拉丁】〔买主〕购物前验货(原则)

caveman 穴居人

cave·man /ˋkevˌmæn; ˈkeɪvmæn/ *n* [C] **1** someone who lived in a CAVE¹ many thousands of years ago〔史前时代的〕穴居人

CULTURAL NOTE 文化注释

The STEREOTYPE of a caveman is of a man with long hair and beard, wearing an animal's skin round his body, carrying a piece of wood as a weapon, and pulling his wife along behind him by her hair. 穴居人的典型形象是一个留着长发和长须的男子, 身披兽皮, 手持木棍做武器, 拽着妻子的头发一路拖在身后。

2 *informal* a man who behaves rudely or violently【非正式】野蛮人, 举止粗野的人: *He used caveman tactics of rough behaviour towards women.* 他对待妇女极其野蛮无礼。

Cav·en·dish /ˋkævəndɪʃ; ˈkævəndɪʃ/, **Henry** (1731-1810) a British scientist who discovered HYDROGEN and also discovered the chemical COMPOSITION of water (=the different parts it is made from) 卡文迪什〔(1731-1810), 英国科学家。他发现了水的化学成分和氢气〕

cav·ern /ˋkævən; ˈkævən/ *n* [C] a large CAVE¹ 大洞穴

cav·ern·ous /ˋkævənəs; ˈkævənəs/ *adj* a cavernous room, space, or hole is very large and deep〔房间、空间〕像大洞穴的, 大而深的: *a cavernous dining hall* 一个很大的食堂 —**cavernously** *adv*

cav·i·ar, caviare /ˌkævɪˋɑr; ˈkæviɑː/ *n* [U] **1** the preserved eggs of various large fish, eaten as a special very expensive food 鱼子酱 **2 caviar to the general** *BrE literary* something that only a sensitive and educated person can enjoy or understand【英, 文】曲高和寡的事物, 阳春白雪

cav·il /ˋkævl̩; ˈkævəl/ *v* **cavilled, cavilling** *BrE*【英】**caviled, caviling** *AmE*【美】[I+at] *formal* to make unnecessary complaints about someone or something【正式】无端指责, 挑剔, (对…)吹毛求疵

cav·ing /ˋkevɪŋ; ˈkeɪvɪŋ/ *n* [U] the sport of going deep under the ground in CAVES 洞穴探察(体育运动); SPELUNKING *AmE*【美】

cav·i·ty /ˋkævətɪ; ˈkævəti/ *n* [C] **1** *formal* a hole or space inside something【正式】腔, 洞, 窟窿 **2** *technical* a hole in a tooth made by decay【术语】蛀牙洞

cavity wall /ˈ··· ˌ·/ *n* [C] a wall consisting of two walls with a space between them to keep out cold and noise〔防寒或隔音的〕夹层墙, 空心墙

cavity wall in·su·la·tion /ˌ··· ···ˈ··/ *n* [U] a substance put inside a cavity wall to keep heat inside a building 空心墙保暖材料

ca·vort /kəˋvɔrt; kəˈvɔːt/ *v* [I] to jump or dance around noisily in a playful or sexual way 狂舞; 跳跃; 乱跳乱蹦: *Pictures appeared in newspapers of the two of them cavorting on a beach.* 报纸上登出了他们两人在海滩上欢呼雀跃的照片。

caw /kɔ; kɔː/ *n* [C] the loud unpleasant sound made by some types of bird, especially the CROW¹ (1)〔尤指乌鸦等鸟类难听的〕哇哇的叫声 —**caw** *v* [I]

Cax·ton /ˋkækstn̩; ˈkækstən/, **William** (?1422-91) the first person in England to print books. He learned about printing in Germany, where the first books in Europe were printed, then returned to England to start a printing business there. 卡克斯顿〔(?1422-1491), 英格兰印刷业先驱。他曾在欧洲最早印刷书籍的国家 —— 德国学习过印刷术, 之后回到英国创办了一家印刷所〕: *a valuable Caxton Bible* 一本珍贵的卡克斯顿版《圣经》

cay /ki; kiː/ *n* [C] *AmE* a very small low island formed of CORAL¹ or sand【美】珊瑚岛, 沙洲

cay·enne pep·per /ˌkeɪɛnˋpɛpɚ; ˌkeɪen ˈpepə/ *n* [U] the red powder made from a PEPPER¹ (3) that has a very hot taste (红)辣椒粉

cay·man /ˋkemən; ˈkeɪmən/ *n* [C] a South American animal like an ALLIGATOR〔南美的〕短吻鳄

Cay·man Is·lands, the /ˋkemən ˋaɪləndz; ˈkeɪmən ˌaɪləndz/ a group of three islands in the Caribbean Sea, northwest of Jamaica, which are a British DEPENDENCY. Population: 36,000 (2001). Capital: George Town. 开曼群岛〔位于牙买加西北, 加勒比海三个岛屿的总称, 为英国属地。人口: 36,000 (2001), 首府: 乔治敦〕

CB /ˌsi ˋbi; ˌsiː ˈbiː◂/ *n* [U] Citizen's Band; a radio on which people can speak to each other over short distances, especially when they are driving 民用波段〔尤其用于人们驾车时近距离通话的无线电通讯方式〕—**CB-er** *n* [C]

CBC /ˌsi bi ˋsi; ˌsiː biː ˈsiː/ *trademark* Canadian Broadcasting Corporation; a television company that is supported by the Canadian government【商标】加拿大广播公司〔加拿大政府资助的一家电视公司〕

CBE /ˌsi bi ˋi; ˌsiː biː ˈiː/ *n* [C] Commander of the British Empire; an honour given to some British people for things they have done for their country 英帝国大勋章

CBI, the /ˌsi bi ˋaɪ; ˌsiː biː ˈaɪ/ Confederation of British Industry; a British organization that represents employers and managers in British businesses. It provides information about the economic situation, and tries to influence the government to make decisions that will help its members. 英国工业联合会〔英国一组织。该组织代表企业主及经理人员, 提供有关经济形势的信息, 力图影响政府作出有利于其成员的决策〕

CBS /ˌsi bi ˋɛs; ˌsiː biː ˈes/ *trademark* Columbia Broadcasting System; one of the four main national television networks in the US. The other three are ABC, Fox, and NBC【商标】哥伦比亚广播公司〔美国四大全国电视广播网之一。其余三家分别为美国广播公司、福克斯广播公司和全国广播公司〕: *a CBS news reporter* 哥伦比亚广播公司的一名新闻记者

CBSO, the /ˌsi bi ɛs ˋo; ˌsiː biː es ˈəʊ/ the abbreviation of 缩写= the CITY OF BIRMINGHAM SYMPHONY ORCHESTRA

cc 1 carbon copy to; used at the end of a business letter to show that you are sending a copy to someone else 副本交, 抄送呈交: *To Neil Fry, cc. Anthea Baker, Matt Fox* 交: 尼尔·弗赖伊, 副本交: 安西娅·贝克, 马特·福克斯 **2** the abbreviation of 缩写= CUBIC CENTIMETRE 立方厘米: *a 200 cc engine* 200立方厘米的发动机

CCTV¹ the written abbreviation of 缩写= CLOSED CIRCUIT TELEVISION 闭路电视, 有线电视

CULTURAL NOTE 文化注释

CCTV cameras are very common on the streets in towns and cities in the UK, especially in the city centres. In London there are more CCTV cameras than in any other European city. People accept the use of CCTV, even though they may not like being watched, because it makes them feel safer. The police believe it is a good way to stop crime,

and allows them to recognize and catch people who have done something wrong or illegal. However, opponents of CCTV believe that people lose their PRIVACY when they are filmed and that the authorities could use CCTV to control people and not just to prevent crime. 闭路电视在英国城镇尤其是在市中心的街道上十分普遍。伦敦的闭路电视数量为欧洲城市之首。虽然人们可能不喜欢被人监视，但还是接受了闭路电视，因为这让他们感到更安全。警方相信这是防范犯罪的好办法，能让他们辨认和抓捕犯错违法的人。不过，反对使用闭路电视的人认为，镜头之下人们失去了隐私，而且当局不仅会用闭路电视防范犯罪，也会用它来控制民众。

C

CCTV² the written abbreviation of 缩写= China Central Television 中国中央电视台

CD /ˌsi ˋdi; ˌsiː ˈdiː◂/ *n* [C] compact disc; a small circular piece of hard plastic on which high quality recorded sound or large quantities of information can be stored〔电脑的〕光盘，光碟；激光唱片

CD player 激光唱片机

CD player /ˈ· ·/ *n* [C] a piece of equipment used to play COMPACT DISCs 激光唱片机

CD-ROM /ˌsi di ˋrɑm; ˌsiː diː ˈrɒm/ *n* [C,U] compact disc read-only memory; a CD on which large quantities of information can be stored to be used by a computer 只读光盘，只读光碟，光盘只读存储器 —see picture on page A14 参见 A14 页图

CDT /ˌsi di ˋti; ˌsiː diː ˈtiː/ *n* [U] Craft, Design, and Technology; a practical subject studied in British schools 工艺、设计和技术课〔英国学校开设的一门实用学科〕

W3 **cease¹** /sis; siːs/ *v* [I,T] *formal* to stop doing something or stop happening【正式】停止，终止，结束: **cease (doing) sth** *The company ceased trading at 6 pm today.* 这家公司今天下午 6 点就停止交易了。| *It rained all day without ceasing.* 雨不停地下了一整天。| **cease sth** *The committee decided to cease financial support.* 委员会决定终止财政支持。| **cease to do sth** *Most people had already ceased to obey the curfew.* 大多数人早已不再遵守宵禁的命令了。| **cease to exist** *The town which Joyce wrote about has long since ceased to exist.* 乔伊斯所描写的那个小镇早已不复存在了。| **cease fire!** (=used to order soldiers to stop shooting)〔命令士兵〕停止射击！停火！—see also 另见 CEASEFIRE, **wonders will never cease** (WONDER² (6))

cease² *n* **without cease** *formal* without stopping【正式】不停地，持续地

cease-fire /ˋsisˌfaɪr; ˈsiːsfaɪə/ *n* [C] an agreement to stop fighting for a period of time, especially so that a more permanent agreement can be made 停火[停战]协议: *negotiating a ceasefire* 为达成停火协定而谈判 —compare 比较 ARMISTICE, TRUCE

cease·less /ˋsislɪs; ˈsiːsləs/ *adj formal* happening or existing for a long time without changing or stopping【正式】不停的，持续的，不断的: *the ceaseless fight against crime* 对犯罪的不停打击 —**ceaselessly** *adv*

ce·dar /ˋsidɚ; ˈsiːdə/ *n* **1** [C] a large EVERGREEN² tree with leaves shaped like needles 雪松，西洋杉 **2** also 又作 **cedarwood** [U] the hard reddish wood of this tree that smells pleasant 雪松木，杉木

cede /sid; siːd/ *v* [T] *formal* to give something such as an area of land or a right to a country or person, especially when you are forced to【正式】〔尤指被迫〕割让〔领土或主权〕，把…让给 —see also 另见 CESSION

ce·dil·la /sɪˋdɪlə; sɪˈdɪlə/ *n* [C] a mark put under the letter 'c' in French and some other languages, to show that it is an 's' sound instead of a 'k' sound. It is written 'ç'.〔加在法语或其他一些语言的 c 字母下的〕下加符，尾形符〔表示应读成 /s/ 而不是 /k/〕

Cee·fax /ˋsifæks; ˈsiːfæks/ *n* [U] *trademark* an information service that has no sound and is provided on television by the BBC in Britain【商标】〔英国广播公司提供的〕图文电视

cei·lidh /ˋkelɪ; ˈkeɪli/ *n* [C] an evening entertainment with Scottish or Irish singing and dancing 同乐会〔有苏格兰或爱尔兰歌舞的晚间娱乐活动〕

cei·ling /ˋsilɪŋ; ˈsiːlɪŋ/ *n* [C] **1** the inner surface of the top part of a room 天花板，顶棚 —compare 比较 ROOF¹ (2) **2** the largest number or amount of something that is officially allowed 上限，最高限度: *a budget ceiling of $5000* 上限为 5000 美元的预算 | *The government imposed a ceiling on imports of foreign cars.* 政府对进口外国汽车的数量实行了上限规定。**3** *technical* the greatest height an aircraft can fly at or the level of the clouds【术语】最大飞行高度，升限；云幕高度 —see also 另见 **glass ceiling** (GLASS¹ (7)) S3 W3

ce·leb /səˋlɛb; səˈleb/ *n* [C] *informal* a CELEBRITY【非正式】名人，明星

cel·e·brant /ˋsɛləbrənt; ˈseləbrənt/ *n* [C] someone who performs or takes part in a religious ceremony 主持[参加]宗教仪式的人

cel·e·brate /ˋsɛləˌbret; ˈseləbreɪt/ *v* **1** [I,T] to show that an event or occasion is important by doing something special or enjoyable 庆祝: *It's Dad's birthday and we're going out for a meal to celebrate.* 今天是爸爸的生日，我们打算出去吃饭，庆祝一下。| *We've bought champagne to celebrate Jan's promotion.* 我们买了香槟来庆贺简的提升。| **celebrate sth** *My folks are celebrating their 50th anniversary.* 我父母正在庆祝他们的 50 周年纪念。| **celebrate Christmas/Thanksgiving etc** *The Chinese celebrate their New Year in January or February.* 中国人在一月或二月庆祝他们的新年。**2** [T] *formal* to praise someone or something in speech or writing【正式】〔口头或书面〕赞扬，赞美，歌颂: *poems that celebrate the joys of love* 赞美爱情之欢乐的诗歌 **3** to perform a religious ceremony, especially the Christian Mass 主持〔宗教仪式，尤指弥撒〕 W3

cel·e·brat·ed /ˋsɛləbretɪd; ˈseləbreɪtəd/ *adj* famous; talked about a lot 著名的，闻名的: *a celebrated professor* 一位著名的教授 | *a celebrated legal case* 一宗备受关注的法律案件

cel·e·bra·tion /ˌsɛləˋbreʃən; ˌseləˈbreɪʃən/ *n* **1** [C] an occasion or party when you celebrate something 庆祝会，庆祝活动: *I don't feel like getting involved in any New Year's celebrations.* 我不想参加任何新年庆祝活动。**2** [U] the act of celebrating 庆祝: **in celebration of** (=in order to celebrate something) 为…举行庆祝活动 *There'll be a reception in celebration of the Fund's 70th Anniversary.* 为了庆祝基金会成立 70 周年，将会举行一个招待会。 S3

CULTURAL NOTE 文化注释

Special Celebrations People in the US and the UK often celebrate by having parties when they have achieved something important, such as graduating (GRADUATE) from school or university, or getting a new job or home. Many people celebrate important stages in their lives with religious ceremonies such as CHRISTENINGS, BAR MITZVAHS, and weddings. Most people celebrate their birthdays. 特别庆典：英美人取得重大成绩时常举行聚会来庆贺，如从中学或大学毕业，找到新工作或找到新住处时。很多人举行宗教仪式庆祝一生中的重要阶段，如洗礼、成人礼和婚礼。大多数人都要庆祝生日。— see Cultural Note at BIRTHDAY 见 BIRTHDAY 文化注释

People also celebrate their wedding anniversaries (ANNIVERSARY), especially when they have been married for 10, 25, or 50 years. If someone has a party to celebrate a birthday, wedding, anniversary, birth, or graduation, in the UK guests are expected to give them cards and sometimes presents. In the US guests are usually expected to give both presents and cards. In the US there are special parties for women who will soon be married, called bridal SHOWERs and for women who will soon have a baby, called baby showers, when friends give them useful presents for their marriage or new baby. 人们也庆祝自己的结婚周年纪念日，尤其是结婚满 10 年、25 年或 50 年时。在英国，如果某人举行聚会庆贺生日、婚礼、周年纪念、添丁或毕业，客人通常送贺卡，有时送礼物；而在美国，客人则同时送贺卡和礼物。在美国，有为即将结婚的女士举办的特别聚会，名曰"新娘送礼会"，也有为即将生孩子的女士举办的特别聚会，名曰"小宝宝送礼会"，这时朋友们都会送上实用的结婚礼物或新生儿用品。— see Cultural Note at SHOWER 见 SHOWER 文化注释

cel·e·bra·to·ry /ˈsɛləbrətɔrɪ; ˌseləˈbreɪtəri◂/ *adj* [only before noun 仅用于名词前] done in order to celebrate a particular event or occasion 表示庆祝的, 为了庆祝的: *Join us for a celebratory drink in the bar.* 和我们一起去酒吧喝一杯庆祝一下。

ce·leb·ri·ty /səˈlɛbrətɪ; səˈlebrəti/ *n* **1** [C] a famous person, especially someone in the entertainment business〔尤指娱乐界的〕名人, 明星 **2** [U] *formal* the state of being famous; fame【正式】著名; 名誉, 名声

CULTURAL NOTE 文化注释

TABLOID newspapers in the UK often write stories about celebrities and there are many magazines in the UK and the US that have photographs of celebrities on almost every page. The phrase 'the cult of celebrity' is used by people who think that Western society, especially the MEDIA, has become too interested in celebrities. People who appear in reality TV shows such as *Big Brother* become 'famous for being famous', meaning that they become famous for a short time while they are on television, not because they are good actors, musicians etc. 英国小报经常刊发关于名人的文章, 英美很多杂志几乎每页都有名人的照片。有人认为西方社会, 尤其是媒体, 对名人过分关注, 用"名人崇拜"一词来形容这种现象。在《老大哥》等真实电视节目中露面的人"因有名而出名", 也就是说, 他们在电视上露面的短暂时间里成为名人, 而不是因为他们在演艺、音乐等方面出色。

FILM STARS, musicians, models etc who are extremely famous all over the world are called A-list celebrities. People who are not as famous and who would not be recognized by everyone are called C-list (or Z-list) celebrities. 全球范围都极为有名的电影明星、音乐家、模特等被称为A级名人; 不那么有名、不是尽人皆知的名人称为C级(或Z级)名人。

ce·ler·i·ty /səˈlɛrətɪ; səˈlerəti/ *n* [U] *formal* great speed【正式】迅速, 快速

cel·e·ry /ˈsɛlərɪ; ˈseləri/ *n* [U] a vegetable with long pale green stems that you can eat cooked or uncooked 芹菜: *a stick of celery* 一根芹菜 —see picture on page A9 参见A9页图

ce·les·ti·al /səˈlɛstʃəl; səˈlestiəl/ *adj formal*【正式】**1** related to the sky or heaven 天空的, 天上的; 天堂的: **celestial bodies** (=the sun, moon, stars etc) 天体〔太阳、月亮、星星等〕**2** *literary* very beautiful【文】极美的, 异常美丽的

cel·i·bate /ˈsɛləbɪt; ˈseləbət/ *adj* not married and not having sex, especially because of your religious beliefs〔尤指因宗教原因而〕独身的; 禁欲的: *Catholic priests are required to be celibate.* 天主教神父按要求不能结婚。—**celibate** *n* [C] —**celibacy** /-bəsɪ; -bəsi/ *n* [U]: *a vow of celibacy* 奉行独身的誓言

1 **cell** /sɛl; sel/ *n* [C] **1** the smallest part of a living thing that can exist independently 细胞: *cancer cells* 癌细胞 | *red blood cells* 红血球 **2** a small room in a prison, MONASTERY, or CONVENT where someone sleeps 小囚室, 牢房; 〔修道院的〕斗室, 单人房间 **3** a piece of equipment for producing electricity from chemicals, heat, or light 电池: *alkaline battery cells* 碱性电池 **4** a small group of people who are working secretly as part of a larger political organization〔政治组织的〕分部, 秘密活动小组: *a terrorist cell* 恐怖分子小组 **5** a small space that an insect or other small creature has made to live in or use〔蜂巢中单个的〕小蜂窝, 蜂房: *the cells of a honeycomb* 蜂巢的蜂房

cel·lar /ˈsɛlə; ˈselə/ *n* [C] **1** a room under a house or other building, often used for storing things 地窖, 地下贮藏室 **2** a store of wine belonging to a person, restaurant etc〔私人或餐馆的〕酒窖

cel·lar·age /ˈsɛlərɪdʒ; ˈselərɪdʒ/ *n* [U] **1** the charge for storing something in a cellar 地窖贮藏费 **2** the size of a cellar 地窖的面积

cell di·vi·sion /ˈ· ·,··/ *n* [C,U] the process by which plant and animal cells increase their numbers 细胞分裂

cel·list /ˈtʃɛlɪst; ˈtʃeləst/ *n* [C] someone who plays the cello 大提琴演奏者

cel·lo /ˈtʃɛlo; ˈtʃeləʊ/ *n* [C] a large musical instrument shaped like a VIOLIN that you hold between your knees and play by pulling a special stick across wire strings 大提琴

Cel·lo·phane /ˈsɛləˌfen; ˈseləfeɪn/ *n* [U] *trademark* thin transparent material used for wrapping things【商标】〔包装用的〕玻璃纸

cell·phone /ˈsɛlˌfon; ˈselfəʊn/ *n* [C] a cellular phone 手提电话, 移动电话, 手机

cel·lu·lar /ˈsɛljələ; ˈseljələ/ *adj* **1** consisted of or related to the cells of plants or animals 细胞的, 由细胞组成的 **2 cellular blanket/clothes etc** loosely woven covers, clothes etc that keep you warm 有网眼的毯子/外衣等 **3** having a lot of holes; POROUS 多孔的: *cellular rock* 多孔的岩石

cellular phone /ˌ···ˈ·/ *n* [C] a telephone that you can carry around with you, that works from a system that uses a network of radio stations to pass on signals〔利用电台网通讯的〕手提电话, 移动电话, 手机

cel·lu·lite /ˈsɛljulaɪt; ˈseljəlaɪt/ *n* [U] fat that is just below someone's skin and makes it look uneven and unattractive 皮下脂肪团

cel·lu·loid /ˈsɛljəˌlɔɪd; ˈseljəlɔɪd/ *n trademark*【商标】**1 on celluloid** on cinema film 摄在电影胶片上, 在电影里: *Chaplin's comic genius is preserved on celluloid.* 卓别林的喜剧天才在电影里被保存下来。**2** [U] a plastic substance made mainly from CELLULOSE (2) that used to be made into photographic film 赛璐珞〔旧时用以制作摄影胶片的材料〕

cel·lu·lose /ˈsɛljəˌlos; ˈseljələʊs/ *n* [U] **1** the material that the cell walls of plants are made of and that is used to make plastics, paper etc 细胞膜质; 纤维素 **2** also 又作 **cellulose acetate** *technical* a plastic that is used for many industrial purposes, especially making photographic film and explosives【术语】醋酸纤维素〔工业上用于制造摄影胶卷和炸药〕

Cel·si·us /ˈsɛlsɪəs; ˈselsiəs/ abbreviation 缩写为 C *n* [U] a temperature scale in which water freezes at 0° and boils at 100°; CENTIGRADE 摄氏温度: *12° Celsius* 12摄氏度 —**Celsius** *adj*: *a Celsius thermometer* 摄氏温度计

CULTURAL NOTE 文化注释

Celsius and Fahrenheit Most people in the UK use Celsius measurements when talking about the weather, although they often use the word 'Centigrade', which is the older name for this system. Celsius is the officially correct word used by scientists. Weather reports on television and in newspapers in the UK give the temperature in Celsius, and sometimes also in Fahrenheit. In the US people generally use Fahrenheit, and weather reports are always given using Fahrenheit, so in the US, only scientists use Celsius. 华氏温标和摄氏温标: 英国人谈论天气时多用摄氏温标, 虽然他们常用摄氏温标的旧称Centigrade。Celsius是正式的科学用语。英国电视和报纸上播报天气用摄氏温标, 有时也用华氏温标。美国人通用华氏温标, 天气预报总用华氏温标。因此在美国, 只有科学家才使用摄氏温标。

Cel·tic /ˈsɛltɪk; ˈkeltɪk/ *adj* related to the Celts, an ancient European people, or to their languages 凯尔特人的; 凯尔特语的

ce·ment[1] /səˈmɛnt; sɪˈment/ *n* [U] **1** a grey powder made from LIME[1] (3) and clay, that becomes hard when it is mixed with water and allowed to dry, and that is used in building 水泥: *I think he's outside mixing cement and laying bricks.* 我想他正在外面和水泥砌砖。**2** a thick sticky substance that becomes very hard when it dries and is used for filling holes or sticking things together 胶接剂, 接合剂

cement[2] *v* [T] **1** also 又作 **cement over** to cover something with cement 在…上抹水泥 **2** to make a relationship between people or countries firm and strong 加强, 巩固〔关系、友谊〕: *His marriage to Lucy Brett cemented important business ties with her family.* 他和露西·布雷特的婚姻巩固了与她家族的重要商业联系。

cement mix·er /·ˈ· ,··/ *n* [C] a machine with a round drum that turns around, into which you put cement, sand, and water to make CONCRETE; CONCRETE MIXER 水泥[混凝土]搅拌机

cem·e·tery /ˈsɛməˌtɛrɪ; ˈsemətri/ *n* [C] a piece of land, usually not belonging to a church, in which dead people are buried〔通常不属于教会的〕公墓, 墓地 —compare 比较 CHURCHYARD, GRAVEYARD

cen·o·taph /ˈsɛnəˌtæf; ˈsenətɑːf/ *n* [C] a MONUMENT built to remind you of soldiers, sailors etc who were killed in a war and are buried somewhere else〔为葬于别处的阵亡将士立的〕纪念碑

cen·sor[1] /ˈsɛnsə; ˈsensə/ *n* [C] someone whose job is to examine books, films, letters etc and remove anything considered to be offensive, morally harmful, or politically dangerous〔书刊、电影、书信等的〕检查员, 监察员, 审查官

censor[2] *v* [T] to examine books, films, letters etc to remove anything that is considered offensive, morally harmful, or politically dangerous etc 审查〔书刊、电影、信件等〕

cen·so·ri·ous /sɛnˈsɔrɪəs; senˈsɔːriəs/ *adj formal* always looking for mistakes and faults in other people and wanting to criticize them【正式】爱挑剔的, 苛评的, 吹毛求疵的: *She didn't used*

to be so censorious of others' behaviour. 她过去并不是那么挑剔别人的行为的。—**censoriously** *adv* —**censoriousness** *n* [U]

cen·sor·ship /ˈsɛnsɚʃɪp; ˈsensəʃɪp/ *n* [U] the practice or system of censoring something 审查(制度), 检查(体制): *the censorship of television programmes* 电视节目审查制度

cen·sure[1] /ˈsɛnʃɚ; ˈsenʃə/ *n* [U] *formal* the act of expressing strong disapproval and criticism【正式】严厉谴责, 批评: *a vote of censure* 不信任票

censure[2] *v* [T] *formal* to officially criticize someone for something they have done wrong【正式】严厉批评, 正式谴责: *The inspector was officially censured for his handling of the demonstration.* 这名督察因处理这次示威不当而受到官方谴责。

cen·sus /ˈsɛnsəs; ˈsensəs/ *n plural* **censuses** [C] **1** an official process of counting a country's population and finding out about the people 人口普查 **2** an official process of counting something for government planning〔官方进行的〕统计, 调查: *a traffic census* 交通情况调查

cent /sɛnt; sent/ *n* [C] **1** 0.01 of the main unit of currency in some countries, or a coin worth this amount. For example, there are 100 cents in one US dollar. 分; 分币〔一美元或某些十进制货币单位的百分之一〕**2 put in your two cents' worth** *AmE* to give your opinion about something, when other people do not want to hear it【美】〔未获邀请而〕发表意见 —see also 另见 **red cent** (RED[1] (8))

cen·taur /ˈsɛntɔr; ˈsentɔː/ *n* [C] a creature in ancient Greek stories with the head, chest, and arms of a man and the body and legs of a horse〔希腊神话中的〕人头马怪物, 半人半马怪物

cen·te·nar·i·an /ˌsɛntəˈnɛrɪən; ˌsentɪ̈ˈneəriən/ *n* [C] someone who is 100 years old or older 百岁〔或百岁以上〕老人

cen·te·na·ry /ˈsɛntəˌnɛrɪ; senˈtiːnəri/ also 又作 **cen·ten·ni·al** /sɛnˈtɛnɪəl; senˈteniəl/ *AmE*【美】*n* [C] the day or year exactly 100 years after a particular event 一百周年(纪念): *a concert to mark the centenary of the composer's birth* 为该作曲家百年诞辰而举办的音乐会

cen·ter /ˈsɛntɚ; ˈsentə/ *n, v* the American spelling of CENTRE centre 的美式拼法

Center Parcs /ˈsɛntɚ pɑrks; ˈsentə pɑːks/ *trademark* a type of holiday centre providing hotel and tourist services in the UK and in Europe, especially in attractive countryside and forest areas【商标】公园度假中心〔英国和欧洲提供酒店和旅游服务的一类度假中心, 主要位于景色迷人的乡间和森林地区〕

Centers for Dis·ease Con·trol, the /ˌ‥ ‥ ˈ‥ˌ‥ˌ/ abbreviation 缩写为 CDC a US government organization based in Atlanta, Georgia, which works to prevent the spread of infectious diseases, and studies ways to improve people's health 疾病控制中心〔美国一政府机构。总部设在佐治亚州的亚特兰大, 其职能是防止传染病的传播, 研究促进人类健康的新途径〕

centi- /sɛntə; sentɪ̈/ *prefix* also 又作 **cent-** /sɛnt; sent/ **1** 100 一百: *a centipede* (=creature with 100 legs) 蜈蚣[百足虫] **2** 100th part of a unit 百分之一: *a centimetre* (=0.01 metre) 厘米 (=0.01 米) —see table on page C4 参见 C4 页附录

Cen·ti·grade /ˈsɛntəˌgred; ˈsentɪ̈greɪd/ *n* [U] CELSIUS 摄氏度 —**Centigrade** *adj*

cen·ti·gram, **centigramme** /ˈsɛntəˌgræm; ˈsentɪ̈græm/ *n* [C] a unit for measuring weight. There are 100 centigrams in one gram. 厘克〔百分之一克〕—see table on page C3 参见 C3 页附录

cen·time /ˈsɑntim; ˈsɒntiːm/ *n* [C] 0.01 of a FRANC or some other units of money, or a coin worth this amount 生丁〔百分之一法郎〕, 分; 分币

cen·ti·me·tre *BrE*【英】, **centimeter** *AmE*【美】/ˈsɛntəˌmitɚ; ˈsentɪ̈ˌmiːtə/ written abbreviations 缩写为 c and cm *n* [C] a unit for measuring length. There are 100 centimetres in one metre. 厘米〔百分之一米〕—see table on page C3 参见 C3 页附录

cen·ti·pede /ˈsɛntəˌpid; ˈsentɪ̈piːd/ *n* [C] a small creature like a WORM with a lot of very small legs 百足虫, 蜈蚣

cen·tral /ˈsɛntrəl; ˈsentrəl/ *adj* **1** [only before noun, no comparative 仅用于名词前, 无比较级] a central organization, system etc makes decisions or controls the operation of a whole country or large organization 中心的, 中央的: *central planning* 中心计划 | *the central committee of the Chinese Communist Party* 中国共产党中央委员会 | *I'm not advocating central government.* 我不主张建立中央政府。| *All the money is allocated from a central fund.* 所有的资金都是从一个中央基金下拨的。**2** [only before noun, no comparative 仅用于名词前, 无比较级] in the middle of an object or an area 中心的, 中部的, 在中间的: *Central Asia* 中亚 | *The houses face onto a central courtyard.* 这些房子都面向一个中心院子。**3** more important and having more influence than anything else 重要的, 主要的: *Owen played a central role in the negotiations.* 欧文在这次谈判中扮演了重要角色。| [+to] *The inevitability of mass poverty is central to Malthus's argument.* 马尔萨斯的中心论点是人民大众的贫穷是无可避免的。| **of central importance** *Environmental issues are rapidly taking a position of central importance in the political debate.* 环境问题在这次政治辩论中很快成为中心议题。| **central idea/theme/concern etc** *A responsible press was a central theme running through the speech.* 这次演讲的中心主题是出版社的责任感问题。**4** a place that is central is easy to reach because it is near the middle of a town or area 靠近中心区的; 易于到达的: *The house is near Leicester Square, it's very central.* 这房子在莱斯特广场附近, 很好找。—**centrally** *adv*: *Our office is very centrally situated.* 我们的办事处位于市中心。—**centrality** /ˌsɛnˈtrælətɪ; senˈtrælɪ̈ti/ *n* [C]

Central Af·ri·can Re·pub·lic, the /ˌ‥ ˌ‥‥ ‥ˈ‥/ a country in central Africa. Population: 3,577,000 (2001). Capital: Bangui. 中非共和国〔非洲中部一国家。人口: 3,577,000 (2001), 首都: 班吉〕

Central A·mer·i·ca /ˌ‥ ‥ˈ‥/ a narrow piece of land joining North and South America, and consisting of Belize, Guatemala, Honduras, El Salvador, Nicaragua, Costa Rica, and Panama 中美洲〔连接南北美洲的一条狭长地带。这一地带的国家有伯利兹、危地马拉、洪都拉斯、萨尔瓦多、尼加拉瓜、哥斯达黎加和巴拿马〕

central bank /ˌ‥ ˈ‥/ *n* [C] a national bank that does business with the government, and controls the amount of money available and the general system of banks 中央银行

Central Crim·i·nal Court, the /ˌ‥ ˈ‥‥ ˌ/ the official name of the Old Bailey, the most important criminal court in the UK 中央刑事法庭〔英国最主要的刑事法庭"老贝利"的正式名称〕

central gov·ern·ment /ˌ‥ ˈ‥‥/ *n* [C,U] the government of a whole country, as opposed to LOCAL GOVERNMENT 中央政府

central heat·ing /ˌ‥ ˈ‥/ *n* [U] a system of heating buildings in which water or air is heated in one place and then sent around the rest of the building through pipes and RADIATORS or VENTS 中央暖气系统, 集中供热设备

Central In·tel·li·gence A·gen·cy, the /ˌ‥ ‥‥ ‥‥/ *n* [singular] the CIA

cen·tral·is·m /ˈsɛntrəlˌɪzəm; ˈsentrəlɪzəm/ *n* [U] a way of governing a country or controlling an organization in which one central group has power and tells people in other places what to do 中央集权制[主义], 集中制

cen·tral·ize also 又作 **-ise** *BrE*【英】/ˈsɛntrəlˌaɪz; ˈsentrəlaɪz/ *v* [T] to organize the control of a country or organization so that one central group has power and tells people in other places what to do 使…处于中央的控制之下, 实行中央集权制: *an attempt to centralize the economy* 实行中央管理经济的尝试 —compare 比较 DECENTRALIZE —**centralized** *adj*: *centralized planning* 中央统一计划 —**centralization** /ˌsɛntrələˈzeʃən; ˌsentrəlaɪˈzeɪʃən/ *n* [U]

central lock·ing /ˌ‥ ˈ‥/ *n* [U] a system for locking the doors on a car in which all the locks are operated when you turn the key in one lock〔汽车的〕中央锁闭系统

Central Mosque, the /ˌ‥ ˈ/ the main Muslim place of WORSHIP in Britain, in Regents Park, London 中央清真寺〔英国主要的清真寺, 位于伦敦里根特公园内〕

central nerv·ous sys·tem /ˌ‥ ˈ‥ ˌ‥/ *n* [C] the main part of your NERVOUS SYSTEM consisting of your brain and your SPINAL CORD 中枢神经系统

Central Of·fice of In·for·ma·tion /ˌ‥ ‥ ‥‥ˈ‥/ a British government organization that produces books, reports etc giving information about the activities of the various government departments 中央新闻署〔英国一政府机构, 出版书籍, 发布报告, 提供政府各部门的活动信息〕

Central Park /ˌ‥ ˈ/ the main city park in New York City 中央公园〔纽约市主要城市公园〕

central pro·ces·sing u·nit /ˌ‥ ˈ‥‥ ˌ‥/ *n* [C] a CPU〔电脑的〕中央处理器[机]

central res·er·va·tion /ˌ‥ ‥ˈ‥/ *n* [C] *BrE* a narrow piece of ground that separates the two parts of a MOTORWAY【英】〔公路的〕中央分道区; MEDIAN[1] (1) *AmE*【美】—see picture on page A3 参见 A3 页图

cen·tre[1] *BrE*【英】, **center** *AmE*【美】/ˈsɛntɚ; ˈsentə/ *n* **1 ►MIDDLE 中间◄** [C] the middle of a space, area, or object, especially the exact middle〔空间、地域或物体的〕(正)中间, 中心(点): *Draw a line through the centre of the circle.* 画一条线通过那个圆的圆心。| *Tony only likes chocolates with soft centres.* 托尼只爱吃软夹心巧克力。| [+of] *There was an enormous oak table in the centre of the room.* 房间中央有一张巨大的橡木桌子。

2 ▶PLACE/BUILDING 地方/建筑物◀ [C] a place or building which is used for a particular purpose or activity〔供进行某种活动用的〕中心（场所、建筑物等）: *the Fred Hutchinson Cancer Research Centre* 弗雷德·哈钦森癌症研究中心 | *a huge new suburban shopping centre* 位于郊区的新建大型购物中心 | *I'll just get a cab to the conference centre.* 我会坐出租车去会议中心。— see also 另见 GARDEN CENTRE, JOB CENTRE

3 ▶CENTRE OF ACTIVITY 活动中心◀ [C] a place where most of the important things happen that are connected with a particular business or activity〔商业或其他活动的〕中心（地区）: *a major banking centre* 一个主要的银行业中心 | *It's not exactly a cultural centre like Paris.* 这并不完全是像巴黎那样的文化中心。| **[+of]** *The main Control Room is the centre of the communications system.* 主控制室是通讯系统的中心。| *a centre of academic excellence* 学术中心

4 ▶OF A TOWN 城镇的◀ [C] *BrE* the part of a town or city where most of the shops, restaurants, cinemas, theatres etc are【英】〔集中了大部分商店、餐厅、电影院、剧院等的〕城镇的中心; DOWNTOWN *AmE*【美】: **city/town centre** *parking facilities in the town centre* 市中心的停车设施

5 centre of population/urban centre an area where a large number of people live 人口密集地区: *Nuclear installations are built well away from the main centres of population.* 核设施建在远离人口密集的地区。

6 ▶OF ATTENTION/INTEREST 与注意力/兴趣相关的◀ someone or something to which people give a lot of attention〔注意、关注的〕中心: **be the centre of attention** *Betty just loves being the centre of attention.* 贝蒂总是喜欢成为人们关注的焦点。| **be at the centre of a row/dispute/controversy etc** (=be the person or thing most involved in a quarrel etc and therefore getting the most attention) 成为争吵/争论/议论的焦点

7 ▶IN POLITICS 政治上◀ the centre a MODERATE (=middle) position in politics which does not support extreme ideas 中间派[立场], 温和派: *The party's new policies show a swing towards the centre.* 该党的新政策显示出一种倾向中间立场的转变。| **left/right of centre** *As far as I can tell, her political views are slightly left of centre.* 据我所知, 她的政治观点属中间稍稍偏左。

8 ▶IN SPORT 运动◀ [C] a player in games such as football or BASKETBALL who plays in or near the middle of the field or playing area〔足球、篮球等的〕中锋: *the Sonics' six-foot-four-inch centre* 超音速队6英尺4英寸高的中锋

centre² *BrE*【英】, **center** *AmE*【美】 *v* [T] to move something to a position at the centre of something else 集中; 使…处于中心位置: *The title isn't quite centred on the page, is it?* 标题并不在这页的正中间, 是吗?

centre on/upon *phr v* [T] if your attention centres on something or someone, or is centred on them, you pay more attention to them than anything else〔注意力〕集中于…: *The debate centred on the morality of fox hunting.* 这次辩论集中于猎狐行为是否道德的问题上。| **be centred on** *Anyone could see that his interest was centred on Bess.* 谁都能看出, 他的兴趣集中在贝丝身上。

centre around also 又作 **centre round** *BrE*【英】 *phr v* [I,T] if your thoughts, activities etc centre around something or are centred around it, it is the main thing that you are concerned with or interested in 以…为中心, 集中于: *In the 16th century, village life centred around religion.* 16世纪时, 乡村生活是以宗教为中心的。

cen·tre·fold *BrE*【英】, **centerfold** *AmE*【美】 /ˈsɛntɚˌfold; ˈsentəfəʊld/ *n* [C] **1** the two pages that face each other in the middle of a magazine or newspaper〔报纸或杂志的〕中心页跨页版面 **2** a picture covering these two pages, especially one of a young woman with no clothes on 中心跨页的图片〔尤指年轻裸女的图片〕

centre for·ward /ˌ‥ ˈ‥/ *n* [C] an attacking player who plays in the centre of the field in football〔足球的〕中锋

centre of grav·i·ty /ˌ‥ · ˈ‥·/ *n* [singular] the point in any object on which it can balance〔物体的〕重心

cen·tre·piece *BrE*【英】, **centerpiece** *AmE*【美】 /ˈsɛntɚˌpis; ˈsentəpiːs/ *n* [C] **1** a decoration, especially an arrangement of flowers in the middle of a table 置于桌子中央的装饰品〔尤指鲜花〕 **2** [singular] the most important, noticeable or attractive part of something 最重要[最具吸引力]的部分: **[+of]** *The centrepiece of Bevan's policy was the National Health Service.*〔前英国工党领袖〕贝文的政策最核心的一项是国民保健制度。

cen·tri·fu·gal force /sɛnˈtrɪfjʊgl̩ ˈfɔrs; ˌsentrɪˈfjuːgəl◂ ˈfɔːs/ *n* [U] *technical* a force which makes things move away from the centre of something when they are moving around the centre【术语】离心力

cen·tri·fuge /ˈsɛntrəˌfjudʒ; ˈsentrɨfjuːdʒ/ *n* [C] a machine that spins a container around very quickly so that the heavier liquids and any solids are forced to the outer edge or bottom 离心机, 离心分离机

cen·trip·e·tal force /sɛnˌtrɪpətl̩ ˈfɔrs; senˌtrɪpɨtl ˈfɔːs/ *n* [U] *technical* a force which makes things move towards the centre of something【术语】向心力

cen·trist /ˈsɛntrɪst; ˈsentrɨst/ *adj* having political beliefs that are not extreme; MODERATE¹ (2)〔政治上的〕中间派的, 温和派的 —**centrist** *n* [C]

cen·tu·ri·on /sɛnˈturɪən; ˌsenˈtʃʊəriən/ *adj* an army officer of ancient Rome, who was in charge of about 100 soldiers〔古罗马军团的〕百人队队长, 百夫长

cen·tu·ry /ˈsɛntʃərɪ; ˈsentʃəri/ *n* [C] **1** one of the 100-year periods counted forwards or backwards from the year of Christ's birth 世纪, 百年: *twentieth-century art forms such as Cubism* 20世纪的艺术形式, 如立体主义 | *the worst air disaster this century* 本世纪最大的空难 | **at the turn of the century** (=in or around the year 2000) 世纪之交 **2** a period of 100 years 一百年 **3** 100 runs (RUN² (17)) made by one player in the game of CRICKET (2) in one INNINGS〔一名板球运动员在一局所得的〕一百分 S1 W1

CEO /ˌsi i ˈo; ˌsiː iː ˈəʊ/ *n* [C] Chief Executive Officer; the person with the most authority in a large company 行政总裁

ce·phal·ic /səˈfælɪk; sɨˈfælɪk/ *adj technical* connected with or affecting your head【术语】头（部）的; 影响头部的

ce·ram·ics /səˈræmɪks; sɨˈræmɪks/ *n* **1** [U] the art of making pots, bowls, TILES etc, by shaping pieces of clay and baking them until they are hard 陶[瓷]器制法; 陶瓷工艺 **2** [plural] things that are made this way 陶[瓷]器: *an exhibition of ceramics at the crafts museum* 工艺博物馆的陶[瓷]器展览 —**ceramic** *adj*: *ceramic tiles* 瓷砖

Cer·be·rus /ˈsɝbrəs; ˈsɜːbərəs/ in Greek MYTHOLOGY, a dog with three heads who guarded the entrance to Hades (=the place where the spirits of dead people are supposed to live) 刻耳柏洛斯〔希腊神话中把守冥府大门的猛犬, 长有三个头〕

ce·re·al /ˈsɪrɪəl; ˈsɪəriəl/ *n* **1** [C,U] a breakfast food made from grain and usually eaten with milk〔通常与牛奶一起吃、作为早餐的〕谷类食品 **2** [C] a plant grown to produce grain for foods, such as wheat, rice etc 谷类植物, 谷物〈如小麦、稻谷等〉: *cereal crops* 谷类作物 S3

cer·e·bel·lum /ˌsɛrəˈbɛləm; ˌserɨˈbeləm/ *n* [C] *technical* the bottom part of your brain that controls your muscles【术语】小脑

cer·e·bral /səˈribrəl; ˈserɨbrəl/ *adj* **1** *technical* connected with or affecting your brain【术语】脑的, 大脑的; 影响大脑的: *cerebral hemorrhage* 脑出[溢]血 **2** thinking or explaining things in a very complicated way that takes a lot of effort to understand 要运用智力的; 诉诸理性的: *If I'd wanted something cerebral on a Friday night, I'd have stayed at home and read Proust!* 星期五的晚上如果我想要理性点, 我会待在家里读读普鲁斯特的书! | *a cerebral film* 一部引人深思的电影

cerebral pal·sy /ˌ‥· ˈ‥/ *n* [U] a disease caused by damage to the brain before or during birth which results in difficulties of movement and speech 大脑性麻痹, 脑瘫

cer·e·bra·tion /ˌsɛrəˈbreʃən; ˌserɨˈbreɪʃən/ *n* [U] *formal* the process of thinking【正式】大脑活动, 思维, 思考

cer·e·mo·ni·al¹ /ˌsɛrəˈmonɪəl; ˌserɨˈməʊniəl◂/ *adj* used in a ceremony or done as part of a ceremony 礼仪的, 仪式的: *the Mayor's ceremonial duties* 市长的礼仪性职责 | *Native American ceremonial robes* 美洲印第安人的礼袍

ceremonial² *n* [C,U] a special ceremony or the practice of having ceremonies 典礼, 仪式: *an occasion for public ceremonial* 公众仪式场合

cer·e·mo·ni·ous /ˌsɛrəˈmonɪəs; ˌserɨˈməʊniəs◂/ *adj* paying great attention to formal, correct behaviour, as if you were in a ceremony 隆重的; 讲究礼仪的 —**ceremoniously** *adv*: *He ceremoniously burnt the offending documents in the bin.* 他郑重其事地把那些令人讨厌的文件放在垃圾桶里烧了。—**ceremoniousness** *n* [U]

cer·e·mo·ny /ˈsɛrəˌmonɪ; ˈserɨməni/ *n* **1** [C] a formal or traditional set of actions used at an important social or religious event 典礼, 仪式: *the wedding ceremony* 婚礼 | *a graduation ceremony* 毕业典礼 **2** [U] the special actions and formal words traditionally used on particular occasions 礼仪, 礼节: *The queen was crowned with due ceremony.* 女王按照规定的礼仪加冕。**3 without ceremony** in a very informal way, without politeness 随意地; 无礼地: *Without further ceremony, Ed pushed back his chair and went out.* 埃德不再讲什么礼貌, 把椅子往后一推, 走了出去。—see also 另见 **not stand on ceremony** (STAND¹ (45))

ce·rise /sə'riz; sə'ri:z/ *n* [U] bright pinkish red 鲜红色，樱桃红 —**cerise** *adj*

CERN /sɝn; sɜ:n/ Centre Européen de Recherche Nucléaire (European Nuclear Research Centre); a scientific organization based in Geneva, Switzerland that studies PARTICLE physics 欧洲原子能研究中心〔欧洲一粒子物理学研究机构，总部设在瑞士日内瓦〕

cert /sɝt; sɜ:t/ *n* **be a (dead) cert** *BrE informal* to be certain to happen or to succeed【英，非正式】必然发生的，确定的: *So you reckon that this horse is a dead cert to win?* 那么你认为这匹马一定会赢吗？

cert. the written abbreviation of 缩写＝CERTIFICATE

cer·tain[1] /'sɝtn̩; 'sɜ:tn/ *determiner, pronoun* **1** a certain thing, person, place etc is a particular thing, person etc that you are not naming or describing exactly 某，某些，某个: *You can get cheaper fares on certain days of the year.* 在每年的某些日子，你可以买到较为便宜的车票。| *There are certain things I just can't discuss with my mother.* 有些事情我是不能和母亲商量的。| **certain of** *formal* (=several particular people or things in a group)【正式】〔群体中的〕某些〔人或物〕*Certain of the older members objected strongly to the proposal.* 某些年长的成员强烈反对此项建议。**2** some, but not a lot 一些，若干: **a certain amount of** *a certain amount of flexibility* 一定的灵活性 | **to a certain extent/degree** (=in a limited way, but not completely) 在某程度上 *I agree with you to a certain extent but there are other factors to consider.* 在某程度上我同意你的看法，但还有其他一些因素需要考虑。**3 a certain a)** enough of a particular quality to be noticed 稍微的，一些的，一定量的: *There's a certain prestige about going to a private school.* 上私立学校还是有可炫耀之处的。**b)** *formal* used to talk about someone you do not know but whose name you have been told【正式】〔用于谈论不认识但知其名的〕某某，某位: *There's a certain Mrs Myles on the phone for you.* 有位叫迈尔斯太太的人正打电话找你。

This graph shows how common different grammar patterns of the adjective **certain** are. 本图表所示为形容词certain构成的不同语法模式的使用频率。

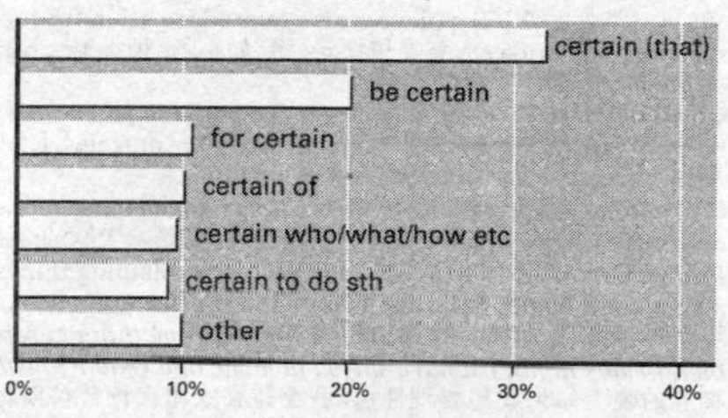

Based on the British National Corpus and the Longman Lancaster Corpus
据英国国家语料库和朗文兰开斯特语料库

certain[2] *adj* **1** [not before noun 不用于名词前] confident and sure, without any doubts 肯定的，确定的，毫无疑问的: *Just so we're absolutely certain, can I check these figures?* 为使我们能绝对确定，我能核查一下这些数字吗？| **certain (that)** *We're certain that by tomorrow, Mr Knowles, you'll have an answer.* 诺尔斯先生，我们肯定你明天就能得到答复。| **certain who/what/how etc** *I'm not certain whether there's a bus service on Sundays.* 我不确定星期天是否也有公共汽车服务。| **[+about/of]** *Now are you certain about that?* 现在你能确定了吗？| *I'm not quite certain of how much is left in that account.* 我不能确定那账户还剩多少钱。**2 know/say for certain** to know something without any doubt 确切知道/肯定地说: *"How much will the repairs cost?" "I couldn't say for certain."* "修理要多少钱？""我说不准。" **3 make certain a)** to do something in order to be sure that something will happen 使确实；确保: **make certain (that)** *Can you draw Harry a map just to make certain he'll find the hotel?* 你能给哈里画张地图以确保他能找到那家旅馆吗？**b)** to check that something is correct or true 核实〔某事〕，把…弄清楚: **[+of]** *I suggest you make certain of your facts before you accuse anybody.* 我建议你在指责别人之前先核实一下你所掌握的事实。**4** if something is certain, it will definitely happen or is definitely true 肯定会发生的，必然的: *a business facing certain bankruptcy* 一家肯定会面临破产的公司 | **it is certain (that)** *It now seems certain that Pam will lose her license.* 现在看来帕姆一定会丢掉执照的。| **certain to do sth** *There's one boy who's certain to succeed!* 有个男孩一定会成功的！| **it is not certain who/what/how etc** *It's not certain where he lived.* (=no one knows definitely) 没有人确切地知道他住哪儿。

cer·tain·ly /'sɝtn̩lɪ; 'sɜ:tnli/ *adv* [sentence adverb 句子副词] **1** without any doubt; of course 的确，一定，毫无疑问，当然: *Certainly we'll consider your suggestion, Alan.* 艾伦，我们当然会考虑你的提议。| *That certainly does change the situation.* 那的确使情况有所变化。| *"Not smoking has made a real difference." "It certainly has."* "不抽烟确实大不相同。""这当然了。" —see OF COURSE (USAGE), SURELY (USAGE)

Frequencies of the adverb **certainly** in spoken and written English 副词certainly在英语口语和书面语中的使用频率

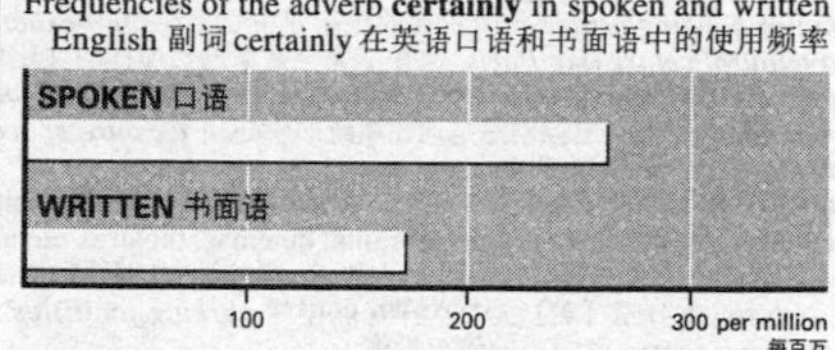

Based on the British National Corpus and the Longman Lancaster Corpus
据英国国家语料库和朗文兰开斯特语料库

This graph shows that the adverb **certainly** is more common in spoken English than in written English. This is because it has some special uses in spoken English. 本图表显示，副词certainly在英语口语中的使用频率远远高于书面语。这是因为它在英语口语中有一些特殊的用法。

certainly (*adv*) **SPOKEN PHRASES**
含 certainly 的口语短语

2 used to agree or give your permission 当然〔用于表示同意或允许〕: *"I'd like a beer, please." "Certainly, sir."* "请给我来杯啤酒。""好的，先生。" | *"Can I come along?" "Certainly."* "我可以一块儿来吗？""当然可以。" **3 certainly not!** used to disagree completely, or to refuse to give permission 当然不！: *"Did you break my camera?" "Certainly not!"* "是你弄坏了我的相机吗？""当然不是！"

cer·tain·ty /'sɝtn̩tɪ; 'sɜ:tnti/ *n* **1** [C] something that is definitely true or that will definitely happen 确定[确实]的事；必然会发生的事: *It's a certainty that prices will go up soon.* 价格不久就会上涨，这是肯定的事。| *Dying's the only certainty in this life.* 死亡是一生中唯一确定的事。**2** [U] the state of being completely certain 确实(性)，确信，确知: *Nowadays there's less certainty about church teachings.* 如今，人们对宗教教义并不是那么深信无疑了。| **with certainty** *You can't say with any certainty where you might be in the future.* 谁也无法肯定自己将来会是什么样的。

cer·ti·fi·ab·le /'sɝtə,faɪəbl; 'sɜ:tɪ̥faɪəbəl/ *adj* **1** *informal* crazy, especially in a way that is dangerous【非正式】〔尤指近乎危险地〕疯狂的: *If you ask me, that man is certifiable.* 要我说，那个人就是疯子。**2** *especially AmE* good enough or correct enough to be officially approved【尤美】〔好或正确得〕可获正式通过的: *a certifiable statement* 可证明的陈述 | *grade A certifiable beef* A级合格牛肉

cer·tif·i·cate /sɚ'tɪfəkɪt; sə'tɪfɪkət/ *n* [C] **1** an official document that states that a fact or facts are true 证明书，证书: **birth/death/marriage certificate** (=giving details of someone's birth, death, or marriage) 出生/死亡/结婚证明书 **2** an official paper stating that you have completed a course of study (毕业)文凭，成绩合格证书

cer·tif·i·cat·ed /sɚ'tɪfə,ketɪd; sə'tɪfɪkeɪtɪ̥d/ *adj especially BrE* having successfully completed a training for a profession【尤英】完成专业培训的，授予证明书的，合格的，取得执照的: *a certificated nurse* 持有证书的合格护士 —**certification** /,sɝtəfə'keʃən; sə,tɪfɪ̥'keɪʃən/ *n* [U]

certified mail /,… '·/ *n* [U] *AmE* a method of sending mail in which the fact that you have sent it is recorded and the person it is sent to must sign their name to prove they have received it【美】挂号邮件; RECORDED DELIVERY *BrE*【英】

certified pub·lic ac·coun·tant /,… ,… '··/ *n* [C] a CPA 执业会计师

cer·ti·fy /'sɝtə,faɪ; 'sɜ:tɪ̥faɪ/ *v* [T] **1** to state that something is correct or true, especially after some kind of test〔尤指经过某种检验〕证明，证实，核证: *You have to get these accounts certified by an auditor.* 这些账目必须由审计师核实。| **certify sb/sth** *Remember that gas boiler we had that was certified dangerous?* 记得我们那台被证实是很危险的燃气锅炉吗？| **cer-**

tify (that) *Sign here to certify that this statement is correct.* 在这儿签名以证实这个声明是正确的。**2** to give an official paper to someone which states that they have completed a course of training for a profession 给〔某人〕颁发（完成专业培训的）合格证书[文凭]: *She was certified as a teacher in 1990.* 她在1990年获教师合格证书。**3** to officially state someone to be mentally ill 正式证明〔某人〕有精神病

cer·ti·tude /ˈsɝtəˌtud; ˈsɜːtɪtjuːd/ *n* [U] *formal* the state of being or feeling certain about something【正式】确信，确定，自信

ce·ru·le·an /səˈruliən; sɪˈruːliən/ *adj technical or literary* deep blue like a clear sky【术语或文】蔚蓝，天蓝色

Cer·van·tes, Mi·guel de /sɝˈvæntiz; sɜːˈvæntiːz/ /mɪˈgwɛl də; mɪˈgwel də/ (1547-1616) a Spanish writer who wrote the NOVEL *Don Quixote*, one of the most important works of European literature 塞万提斯〔(1547-1616)，西班牙作家。他创作的小说《唐吉诃德》是最重要的欧洲文学作品之一〕

cer·vi·cal /ˈsɝvɪkḷ; ˈsɜːvɪkəl/ *adj technical*【术语】**1** related to the neck 颈（部）的: *cervical vertebrae* (=the bones in the back of your neck) 颈椎骨 **2** related to the cervix 子宫颈的: *cervical cancer* 子宫颈癌

cervical smear /ˌ···ˈ·/ *n* [C] *technical* a test for CANCER of a woman's CERVIX【术语】子宫颈涂片检查; PAP SMEAR *AmE*【美】

cer·vix /ˈsɝvɪks; ˈsɜːvɪks/ *n* [C] the narrow passage into a woman's UTERUS 子宫颈

ce·sar·e·an /sɪˈzɛriən; sɪˈzeəriən/ *n* [C] another spelling of CAESAREAN caesarean的另一种拼法

ces·sa·tion /sɛˈseʃən; seˈseɪʃən/ *n* [C,U+of] *formal* a pause or stop【正式】〔暂时的〕休止，停止，中断: *a cessation of hostilities* (=when the fighting stops in a war) 休战

ces·sion /ˈsɛʃən; ˈseʃən/ *n* [C,U] *formal* the act of giving up land, property, or rights, especially to another country after a war, or something that is given up in this way【正式】〔尤指战后一国土地、财产、权利等的〕割让，让与: *John's cession of his kingdom in 1213* 1213年约翰让出了他的王国。—see also 另见 CEDE

cess·pit /ˈsɛsˌpɪt; ˈsesˌpɪt/ *n* [C] **1** also 又作 **cesspool** /ˈsɛsˌpul; ˈsesːpul/ a large hole or container under the ground in which waste from a building, especially from the toilets, is collected 污水坑; 化粪池 **2** a place or situation in which people behave immorally 污秽的场所: *For weeks the affair threatened to be a cesspit of scandal.* 几个星期来，这一事件眼看就要成为丑闻的滋生源。

ce·tac·ean /sɪˈteʃən; sɪˈteɪʃən/ *n* [C] *technical* a MAMMAL (=an animal which feeds its babies on milk) that lives in the sea, such as a WHALE【术语】鲸目动物 —**cetacean** *adj*

Cey·lon /sɪˈlɑn; sɪˈlɒn/ the former name of Sri Lanka. The name 'Ceylon' is still used when talking about tea, which is an important product of Sri Lanka. 锡兰〔斯里兰卡旧称。人们谈论斯里兰卡的重要商品茶叶时仍使用此名称〕: *a cup of Ceylon tea* 一杯锡兰茶

Cézanne, Paul /sɪˈzæn; sɪˈzæn/ /pɔl; pɔːl/ (1839-1906) a French IMPRESSIONIST painter, who helped to develop POST-IMPRESSIONISM and who influenced the development of CUBISM and ABSTRACT art 塞尚〔(1839-1906)，法国印象派画家。他曾对后印象主义的产生发挥过作用，也对立体派和抽象派艺术产生过一定影响〕

cf used in writing to introduce something else that should be compared or considered〔用于文章〕参照; 比较

CFC /ˌsi ɛf ˈsi; ˌsiː ef ˈsiː/ *n* also 又作 **chlorofluorocarbon** a gas used in FRIDGES and AEROSOL cans, now believed to be responsible for damaging the OZONE LAYER 含氯氟烃

CH the abbreviation of 缩写= COMPANION OF HONOUR

Chab·lis /ʃæˈbli; ˈʃæbliː/ *trademark* an expensive type of dry white wine produced in northern Burgundy, France【商标】沙布利〔法国勃艮第北部的一种名贵干白葡萄酒〕

cha-cha /ˈtʃɑ tʃɑ; ˈtʃɑː tʃɑː/ also 又作 **cha-cha-cha** /ˌ··ˈ·/ *n* [C] a dance from South America with small, fast steps 恰恰舞〔源自南美的一种快节奏舞蹈〕

Chad /tʃæd; tʃæd/ a country in north central Africa, between Niger and Sudan. Population: 8,707,000 (2001) Capital: N'djamena. 乍得〔中非北部一国家，位于尼日尔和苏丹之间。人口: 8,707,000 (2001)，首都: 恩贾梅纳〕

chafe /tʃef; tʃeɪf/ *v* **1** [I,T] if a part of your body chafes or if something chafes it, it becomes sore because of something rubbing against it（使）擦伤;（使）擦痛: *Put a soft pad under the saddle to avoid chafing the horse's back.* 在马鞍下放一个软垫子以免擦伤马背。**2** [T] to rub part of your body to make it warm 把〔身上某一部位〕擦热 **3** [I] to be or become impatient or annoyed〔因…而〕恼怒，焦躁，不耐烦: **[+at/under]** *Some hunters are chafing under the new restrictions.* 某些猎人对这些新的限制感到十分恼怒。

chaff¹ /tʃæf; tʃɑːf/ *n* [U] **1** the HUSKs (=outer seed covers) separated from grain before it is used as food 糠; 谷物的外壳 **2** dried grasses and plant stems used for food for farm animals〔作饲料用的〕干草，草料，秣 —see also 另见 **separate the wheat from the chaff** (WHEAT (3))

chaff² *v* [T] *old-fashioned* to make jokes about the person you are talking to, in a friendly way【过时】〔善意地〕戏弄，对〔某人〕开玩笑

chaf·finch /ˈtʃæfɪntʃ; ˈtʃæfɪntʃ/ *n* [C] a common small European bird 苍头燕雀〔欧洲常见的一种小鸟〕

chafing dish /ˈ·· ·/ *n* [C] a container with a HEATER under it, used for cooking food in or for keeping food warm at the table〔在餐桌上烹饪或使食物保温的〕火锅

Cha·gall, Marc /ʃəˈgæl; ʃæˈgæl/ /mɑrk; mɑːk/ (1887-1985) a Russian artist who lived in France and painted in bright colours 夏加尔〔(1887-1985)，旅居法国的俄罗斯画家。其作品色彩鲜艳〕

chag·rin¹ /ʃəˈgrɪn; ˈʃægrɪn/ *n* [U] *formal* annoyance and disappointment because something has not happened the way you hoped【正式】懊恼，失望: **to sb's chagrin** *To the chagrin of the Pentagon, the USSR exploded a nuclear bomb in 1949.* 让五角大楼大为懊恼的是，苏联于1949年引爆了一枚核弹。

chagrin² *v* **be chagrined** *formal* to feel annoyed and disappointed【正式】感到失望，感到懊恼: *Dale was chagrined that she wasn't impressed.* 令戴尔感到失望的是她没有被感动。

chain¹ /tʃen; tʃeɪn/ *n* S3 W2

1 ►JOINED RINGS 连接在一起的环◄ [C,U] a series of rings, usually made of metal, which are joined together in a line and used for fastening things, supporting weights, decoration etc 链子，链条: *Look at the gold chain Tim bought me!* 看，蒂姆买给我的金项链! | *a length of chain* 一段链子 | *a bridge supported on heavy chains* 由粗铁索承受着重量的桥 | *We had to stop and put chains on the tires.* 我们只好停车，在轮胎上加上链条。| **a bicycle chain** (=that makes the wheels turn) 自行车链条 | **chain of office** *BrE* (=a decoration worn by some officials at ceremonies)【英】〔官员在仪式场合佩戴的〕链徽 —see picture at 参见 BICYCLE¹ 图

2 chain of events/circumstances etc [C] a connected series of events etc 一系列[一连串]的事件/情况等: *the chain of events that led to World War I* 引发第一次世界大战的一系列事件 —see also 另见 CHAIN OF COMMAND, FOOD CHAIN

3 ►SHOPS/HOTELS 商店/旅馆◄ [C] a number of shops, hotels, cinemas etc owned or managed by the same company or person 连锁店，连锁集团: **[+of]** *a chain of restaurants* 连锁餐厅 | **hotel/restaurant/retail etc chain** *a major American hotel chain* 美国一家主要的酒店连锁集团

4 ►CONNECTED LINE 连接线◄ [C] people, mountains, islands etc forming a line 连成一行的人[山; 岛屿]: *the largest mountain chain in North America* 北美最大的山脉 | *Everybody link arms to make a chain.* 大家挽臂形成人链。

5 ►PRISONER 囚犯◄ chains [plural] chains fastened to a prisoner's legs and arms, to prevent them from escaping〔锁住囚犯四肢的〕镣铐，锁链: **in chains** *There were a number of men in chains, all sentenced to death.* 有几个人被锁链锁着，他们都被判处了死刑。

6 ►BUYING A HOUSE 购屋◄ [C usually singular 一般用单数] *BrE* a number of people buying houses in a situation where each person must complete the sale of their own house before they can buy the next person's house【英】〔一些人先卖旧屋再买新屋的〕链式购屋法，连环购房链

7 ►MEASURE 度量◄ [C] a measurement of length, used in the past 链〔旧时的长度单位〕—see table on page C4 参见C4页附录

chain² *v* **1** to fasten someone or something to something else, especially in order to prevent them from escaping or being stolen〔尤指为防逃跑或被盗而〕锁在一起，拴住，束缚: **chain sb/sth up** *She wouldn't chain her dog up, and it got killed on the main road.* 她总不把狗拴起来，结果狗在大路上被轧死了。| **chain sb/sth together** *convicts working all chained together* 锁在一起从事劳动的罪犯 | **chain sb/sth to sth** *There's a bicycle chained to the railings out front.* 有一辆自行车拴在前面的栏杆上。**2 be chained to something** to have your freedom restricted because of a responsibility you cannot escape 受到〔责任〕的束缚: *With a sick husband she's chained to the house all day.* 由于丈夫生病，她终日被困在家里。

chain gang /ˈ· ·/ *n* [C] a group of prisoners chained together to work outside their prison 用链子拴在一起服劳役的囚犯

chain let·ter /ˈ· ˌ·· ˌ·/ *n* [C] a letter sent to several people asking them to send a copy of the letter to several more people 连锁信〔寄给数人的信，要求每个收信人复制数份再寄给他人，如此延续下去〕

chain mail /ˈ· ·/ *n* [U] a piece of protective clothing made by joining small metal rings together, worn by soldiers in the past〔旧时军人穿的〕锁子甲，连环甲

chain of com·mand /ˌ· · ·ˈ·/ *n* [C] a system in an organization by which decisions are made and passed from people at the top of the organization to people lower down 指挥系统；指挥链；行政管理系统：*Symonds is third in the chain of command.* 西蒙兹是第三把交椅。

chain re·ac·tion /ˌ· ·ˈ··/ *n* [C] a series of related events or chemical reactions, each of which causes the next 连锁反应；链式反应：*A student playing with chemicals set off a chain reaction in a public toilet and blew it to bits.* 一个学生在公厕里玩化学品，导致一系列连锁反应，把厕所炸成了一片废墟。

chain saw /ˈ· ·/ *n* [C] a tool used for cutting wood, consisting of a circular chain fitted with teeth and driven by a motor 链锯 —compare 比较 CIRCULAR SAW —see picture at 参见 TOOL[1] 图

chain-smoke /ˈ· ·/ *v* [I,T] to smoke cigarettes continuously 一支接一支地抽〔烟〕—**chain-smoker** *n* [C]

chain stitch /ˈ· ·/ *n* [C,U] a way of sewing in which each new stitch is pulled through the last one〔钩针或制绣品的〕链状针法

chain store /ˈ· ·/ *n* [C] one of a group of shops, all of which are owned by one organization; MULTIPLE STORE 连锁店 —see also 另见 CHAIN[1] (3)

chairs 椅子

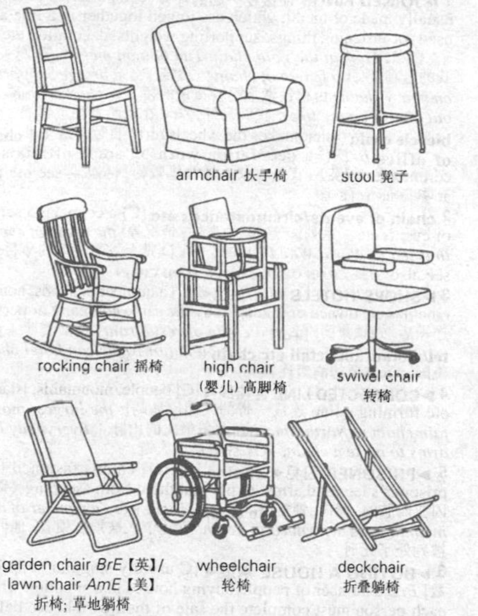

armchair 扶手椅

stool 凳子

rocking chair 摇椅

high chair（婴儿）高脚椅

swivel chair 转椅

garden chair *BrE*【英】/ lawn chair *AmE*【美】折椅；草地躺椅

wheelchair 轮椅

deckchair 折叠躺椅

chair[1] /tʃɛr; tʃeə/ *n* **1** [C] a piece of furniture for one person to sit on, which has a back, a seat, and four legs 椅子：*Grandpa's in his favorite chair by the fireplace.* 祖父坐在火炉边他最喜欢的椅子上。**2** [singular] the position of being in charge of a meeting, or the person who is in charge of it〔会议的〕主持人，主席；主席的席位[职位]：*Address your questions to the chair, please.* 请向主席提出你的问题。| **be in the chair** *Who will be in the chair at tomorrow's meeting?* 谁主持明天的会议？**3** [C] the position of being a professor 大学教授的职位：[**+of**] *a new Chair of Medicine* 一位新任医学教授 **4 the chair** *informal especially AmE* the punishment of death by electric shock given in an ELECTRIC CHAIR【非正式，尤美】电椅死刑

chair[2] *v* [T] to be the CHAIRPERSON of a meeting 担任〔会议〕主席[主持人]：*The commission of inquiry was chaired by a well-known judge.* 调查委员会由一位知名的法官担任主席。

chair-lift /ˈtʃɛrˌlɪft; ˈtʃeəlɪft/ *n* [C] a line of chairs hanging from a moving wire, used for carrying people up and down mountains, especially when they are skiing (SKI[2])〔载运乘客上下山的〕缆车吊椅

chair·man /ˈtʃɛrmən; ˈtʃeəmən/ *n plural* **chairmen** /-mən; -mən/ [C] **1** someone, especially a man, who is in charge of a meeting or directs the work of a committee or organization〔尤指男性的〕主席；〔委员会或组织的〕负责人：*Potts was elected chairman of the education committee.* 波茨当选为教育委员会主席。**2** *BrE* someone who is in charge of a large company or organization【英】〔大组织、大公司的〕董事长；委员长；理事长；总裁：*I think he was the chairman of a big building society before he came here.* 我认为他来这儿之前是一个大型房屋协会的会长。

chair·man·ship /ˈtʃɛrmənˌʃɪp; ˈtʃeəmənʃɪp/ *n* **the chairmanship** the position of being a chairman, or the time when someone has this position 主席职位；主席任期：*A committee was set up under the chairmanship of Edmund Compton.* 成立了一个以埃德蒙·康普顿为主席的委员会。

chair·per·son /ˈtʃɛrˌpɜsn̩; ˈtʃeəˌpɜːsən/ *n plural* **chairpersons** [C] someone who is in charge of a meeting or directs the work of a committee or organization〔主持会议或指导某组织或委员会工作的〕主席；议长；主持人

chair·wom·an /ˈtʃɛrˌwʊmən; ˈtʃeəˌwʊmən/ *n plural* **chairwomen** /-ˌwɪmɪn; -ˌwɪmɪn/ [C] a woman who is a chairperson 女主席；女议长；女主持人

chaise /ʃez; ʃeɪz/ *n* [C] a light carriage pulled by one horse, used in former times〔旧时由一匹马拉的〕轻便马车

chaise longue /ˈʃez ˈlɔŋ; ˌʃeɪz ˈlɒŋ/ *n* [C] *French*【法】**1** a long chair[1] (1) with an arm only at one end, on which you can sit and stretch your legs out〔仅在一端有扶手可坐可躺的〕长椅，躺椅 **2** *AmE* a long chair with a back that can be upright for sitting, or can lie flat for lying down【美】折叠椅，长靠椅

chal·et /ʃæˈle; ˈʃæleɪ/ *n* [C] **1** a house with a steeply sloping roof, common in places with high mountains and snow such as Switzerland〔屋顶陡斜的〕木造农舍，坡顶小木屋〔常见于多山及多雪的地方，如瑞士〕**2** *especially BrE* a small house, especially in a HOLIDAY CAMP【尤英】〔尤指度假营地里的〕小屋

chal·ice /ˈtʃælɪs; ˈtʃælɪ̣s/ *n* [C] a gold or silver decorated cup used for example to hold wine in Christian religious services〔用金或银装饰的〕酒杯〔尤指基督教的圣餐杯〕—see also 另见 **poisoned chalice** (POISON[2] (7))

chalk[1] /tʃɔk; tʃɔːk/ *n* [U] **1** soft white or grey rock formed a long time ago from the shells of small sea animals; LIMESTONE 白垩：*chalk hills* 白垩山地 **2** also 又作 **chalks** [plural] small sticks of this substance, white or coloured, used for writing or drawing 粉笔：*a box of coloured chalks* 一盒彩色粉笔 | *writing in chalk on the blackboard* 黑板上的粉笔字 **3 as different as chalk and cheese** *BrE* completely different from each other【英】截然不同的 —see also 另见 **not by a long chalk** (LONG[1] (16))

chalk[2] *v* [T+**up/on**] to write, mark, or draw something with chalk 用粉笔写[标记，绘画]

chalk sth ↔ **up** *phr v* [T] *informal*【非正式】**1** to succeed in getting something, especially points in a game 赢得〔尤指比分〕；取得：*Seattle chalked up another win last night over Denver.* 西雅图队昨晚又战胜了丹佛队。**2** to record what someone has done, what someone should pay etc 记下〔所做的事、账目等〕：*You can chalk the drinks up to my account.* 你可以把酒钱记到我的账上。**3 chalk it up to experience** to accept a failure or disappointment calmly and regard it as an experience that you can learn something from 平静地接受失败并从中汲取教训

chalk·board /ˈtʃɔkˌbɔrd; ˈtʃɔːkbɔːd/ *n* [C] *AmE* a BLACKBOARD【美】黑板：*Thanks, but the janitor cleans the chalkboard.* 谢谢，但是应该由管理员把黑板擦干净。

chalk·y /ˈtʃɔkɪ; ˈtʃɔːki/ *adj* similar to chalk or containing chalk (像)粉笔的；(像)白垩的：*white chalky soil* 白色的白垩质土壤 | *I can't stand those chalky tasting antacid tablets.* 我受不了那些味如粉笔的抗酸药片。—**chalkiness** *n* [U]

chal·lenge[1] /ˈtʃælɪndʒ; ˈtʃælɪ̣ndʒ/ *n*

1 ▶**STH DIFFICULT** 棘手的事◀ [C,U] something that tests strength, skill, or ability especially in a way that is interesting 挑战，具有挑战性的事物，考验[某人]能力的事物：*I liked the speed and challenge of racing.* 我喜欢赛车的速度和挑战。| **face a challenge** (=be ready to deal with one) 迎接挑战 *The White House has to face yet another foreign policy challenge.* 白宫不得不面临外交政策的又一挑战。| **meet a challenge/rise to a challenge** (=successfully deal with one) 迎接/接受挑战 *a new and vibrant initiative to meet the challenge of the 21st century* 一项迎接21世纪挑战的充满生气的新举措

2 ▶**QUESTIONING OF RIGHTNESS** 对公正性的质疑◀ [C] a refusal to accept that something is right and legal〔对某事的正

确性、合法性等的〕质疑: [+to] *a direct challenge to the Governor's authority* 对总督的权威性提出直接的质疑 | *feminist challenges to the traditional social order* 女权主义对传统社会秩序的质疑

3 ►INVITATION TO COMPETE 挑战◄ a suggestion to someone that they should try to defeat you in a fight, game etc 挑战,〔比赛等的〕提议: *The champions are ready to accept a challenge from any team that is a serious contender.* 冠军队早已准备好接受任何一队有实力的队伍的挑战。

4 ►A DEMAND TO STOP 停止的命令◄ [C] a demand from someone such as a guard to stop and give proof of who you are, and an explanation of what you are doing 喝停盘问

5 ►IN LAW 法律方面◄ [C] *law* a statement made before the beginning of a court case that a JUROR is not acceptable【法律】〔开庭前律师〕反对某人任陪审团成员的声明: *Each lawyer may issue up to six challenges.* 每名律师最多可以提出六次反对某人任陪审员的声明。

S3 W3 **challenge²** *v* [T] **1** to refuse to accept that something is right or legal 质疑〔某事的正确性、合法性等〕, 对…表示怀疑: *What happens if the Finance Committee challenges us on these figures?* 如果财政委员会不相信这些数字, 那我们怎么办? | *political offenders who challenge the authority of our law courts* 怀疑我们法庭的权威性的政治犯 | **challenge sb to do sth** *I challenge Dr Carver to deny his involvement!* 我质问卡弗博士敢不敢否认他与此事有关联! **2** to invite someone to compete or fight against you 向…挑战; 邀请〔某人〕比赛: **challenge sb to sth** *After lunch Carey challenged me to a game of tennis.* 午饭后, 凯里邀我进行了一场网球比赛。—compare 比较 DARE¹ (5) **3** to test the skills or abilities of someone or something; STIMULATE 考验…的技术[能力]; 激发; 激励: *I'm really at my best when I'm challenged.* 接受考验时正是我处于最佳状态的时候。| **challenge sb to do sth** *Every teacher ought to be challenging kids to think about current issues.* 所有老师都应激励学生思考当前的问题。**4** to stop someone and demand proof of who they are, and an explanation of what they are doing 叫住盘问〔某人的身份、意图等〕: *We were challenged by the sentry guarding the gate.* 我们被守门的哨兵拦住查问。**5** *law* to state that a JUROR is not acceptable before a TRIAL¹ (1) begins【法律】〔开审前在选定陪审员时〕对(某候选陪审员)表示反对 —**challenger** *n* [C]

chal·lenged /ˋtʃælɪndʒd; ˈtʃæləndʒd/ *adj* **visually/physically/mentally challenged** *AmE* an expression for describing someone who has difficulty doing things because of blindness etc, used when you want to avoid saying this directly【美】盲人/残疾人士/智障者〔委婉的说法〕

chal·leng·ing /ˋtʃælɪndʒɪŋ; ˈtʃæləndʒɪŋ/ *adj* difficult in an interesting or enjoyable way 具有挑战性的; 需充分发挥能力的: *Teaching young children is a challenging and rewarding job.* 教育儿童是一项具有挑战性和有价值的工作。| *a challenging problem* 一个富有挑战性的难题 —**challengingly** *adv*

W3 **cham·ber** /ˋtʃembɚ; ˈtʃeɪmbə/ *n* **1** [C] an enclosed space, especially in your body or inside a machine〔人体内或某些机器中的〕室; 腔: *a combustion chamber* 燃烧室 | *The heart has four chambers.* 心脏有四个心室。**2** [C] a room used for a special purpose, especially an unpleasant one 作特殊用途的房间〔尤指令人不快者〕: **gas/torture chamber** (=used for killing people by gas or for hurting them) 毒气/用刑室 **3** [C] a large room in a public building used for important meetings 大会议室, 会议厅: *the council chambers* 议事室; 会议室 **4** [C] one of the two parts of a parliament or of the US Congress. For example, in Britain the upper chamber is the House of Lords and the Lower Chamber is the House of Commons〔美国〕参[众]议院; 〔英国〕上[下]议院 **5** [C] *old use* a bedroom or private room【旧】私人房间, 寝室: *the Queen's private chambers* 女王的私人起居室 **6 chambers** [plural] *especially BrE* an office or offices used by BARRISTERS or judges【尤英】〔大律师或法官的〕办公室; 事务所 **7** [C] the place inside a gun where you put the bullet 枪膛, 炮膛 —see picture at 参见 GUN¹ 图

cham·ber·lain /ˋtʃembɚlɪn; ˈtʃeɪmbəlɪn/ *n* [C] an important official who manages things like cooking, cleaning, buying food etc in a king's or NOBLEMAN's court〔国王或贵族的〕管家, 侍从; 宫廷内臣

Chamberlain, Nev·ille /ˋnɛvɪl; ˈnevɪl/ (1869-1940) a British politician in the Conservative Party who was elected Prime Minister in 1937. Many people criticized him for his policy of APPEASEMENT towards Hitler's Germany (=agreeing to their demands). 张伯伦〔(1869-1940), 英国保守党政治家。1937年当选英国首相, 他对纳粹德国采取的"绥靖政策"遭到许多人的批评〕

Chamberlain, Wilt /wɪlt; wɪlt/ (1936-99) a US BASKETBALL player, sometimes called **Wilt the Stilt** because of his height (2.16 metres). He set several records for the number of points he won. 张伯伦〔(1936-1999), 美国篮球运动员。他身高2.16米, 故有时也称"长脚威尔特"。他投篮得分曾创下好几项纪录〕

cham·ber·maid /ˋtʃembɚ,med; ˈtʃeɪmbəmeɪd/ *n* [C] a female servant or worker whose job is to clean and tidy bedrooms, especially in a hotel〔尤指旅馆里的〕女服务员; 打扫房间的女仆

chamber mu·sic /ˈ‥ ,‥/ *n* [C] CLASSICAL music written for a small group of instruments〔古典〕室内乐

chamber of com·merce /,‥ ‥ ˈ‥/ *n* [C] a group of business people in a particular town or area, working together to improve trade〔某地的〕商会

chamber or·ches·tra /ˈ‥ ,‥‥/ *n* [C] a small group of musicians who play CLASSICAL music together〔演奏古典音乐的〕室内乐队

chamber pot /ˈ‥ ·/ *n* [C] a round container for URINE used in a bedroom and kept under the bed in the past 夜壶, 尿壶

cha·me·le·on /kəˋmiliən; kəˈmiːliən/ *n* [C] **1** a LIZARD that can change its colour to match the colours around it 变色龙[蜥蜴] **2** someone who changes their ideas, behaviour etc to fit different situations 善变的人, 见风使舵的人, 改变想法以适应情况的人: *He was a chameleon, able to blend with the customs and people he was living among.* 他是一个适应能力很强的人, 能够融入周围的人和风俗习惯。

cham·ois /ˋʃæmɪ; ˈʃæmwɑː/ *n* **1** [C] a wild animal like a small goat that lives in the mountains of Europe and SW Asia〔生活在欧洲及亚洲西南部山区的〕岩羚羊 **2** also 又作 **chamois leather** /ˈ‥ ,‥/ [C,U] soft leather prepared from the skin of chamois, sheep, or goats and used for cleaning or polishing, or a piece of this leather〔由羚羊、绵羊、山羊等的皮制成的〕软皮革

cham·o·mile /ˋkæmə,maɪl; ˈkæməmaɪl/ *n* [C,U] another spelling of CAMOMILE camomile 的另一种拼法

champ¹ /tʃæmp; tʃæmp/ *v* [I,T] **1** to bite food noisily; CHOMP 大声咀嚼〔食物〕 **2 be champing at the bit** to be unable to wait for something patiently 迫不及待

champ² *n* [C] a CHAMPION¹ (1) 冠军: *The Cowboys are the next World Champs!* 牛仔队是下一个世界冠军!

cham·pagne /ʃæmˋpen; ʃæmˈpeɪn/ *n* [U] a French white wine with a lot of BUBBLES, drunk on special occasions〔法国〕香槟酒

cham·pers /ˋʃæmpɚz; ˈʃæmpəz/ *n* [U] *BrE informal* champagne【英, 非正式】香槟酒

cham·pi·on¹ /ˋtʃæmpɪən; ˈtʃæmpiən/ *n* [C] **1** someone or something that has won a competition, especially in sport〔尤指体育比赛中的〕冠军, 第一名: *the world heavyweight boxing champion* 世界重量级拳击冠军 | **reigning champion** (=the champion at the present time) 现任冠军 **2 champion of** someone who publicly fights for and defends an aim or principle, such as the rights of a group of people〔为某目标或原则如某群人的权利而奋斗的〕斗士: *a champion of women's rights* 女权捍卫者 W2

champion² *v* [T] to publicly fight for and defend an aim or principle, such as the rights of a group of people 公开为〔某目标或原则〕而斗争; 维护: *championing the cause of religious freedom* 维护宗教自由的事业

cham·pi·on·ship /ˋtʃæmpɪən,ʃɪp; ˈtʃæmpiənʃɪp/ *n* **1** [C] also 又作 **championships** [plural] a competition to find which player, team, etc is the best in a particular sport 锦标赛, 冠军赛: *the women's figure skating championships* 女子花样滑冰锦标赛 **2** [C] the position or period of being a champion; TITLE¹ (5) 冠军地位, 冠军称号: *fighting for the world championship* 争夺世界冠军 **3** [U+of] the act of championing something or someone〔对某事或某人的〕支持, 维护 W2

Cham·plain /ʃæmˋplen; ʃɒŋˈplæŋ/, **Lake** a North American lake between New York and Vermont, that goes up to Quebec in Canada 尚普兰湖〔北美洲一湖泊。该湖位于纽约州和佛蒙特州之间, 北抵加拿大魁北克〕

Champlain, Samuel de /sɑmjuˋɛl də; sɑːmjuːˈel də/ (1567-1635) a French EXPLORER and the first governor of French Canada. He explored much of what is now Nova Scotia and established Quebec in 1608. He also was the first European to discover what is now called Lake Champlain. 尚普兰〔(1567-1635), 法国探险家, 法属加拿大首任总督。他的足迹曾遍及新斯科舍省的很多地区, 1608年建立了魁北克城。他是第一个发现尚普兰湖的欧洲人〕

Champs E·ly·sées, the /,ʃɑnz ,eliˋze; ,ʃɒnz eˈliːzeɪ/ an important street in Paris which leads up to the Arc de Triomphe. It is famous for its cafes, where customers sit at tables outside,

and watch people passing by. 香榭丽舍大街〔巴黎一著名街道，通往凯旋门，沿街的咖啡馆十分有名。人们常坐在户外桌边，看行人往来〕

chance[1] /tʃæns; tʃɑːns/ *n*

1 ▶POSSIBILITY 可能性◀ [C,U] how possible or likely it is that something will happen, especially something that you want 机会，可能性: **chance/chances of** *What are her chances of survival?* 她生还的可能性有多大？| **there's a chance (that)** *There's always the chance that something will go wrong.* 总有可能会出现问题。| **a good/fair/slight chance (of)** *The day will be cloudy with a slight chance of some rain later tonight.* 天气将转阴，今晚稍后可能会下雨。| **some/no/little chance** *There seems to be little chance of a ceasefire.* 看来停火的可能性不大。| **chances are** *spoken* (=used to say that something is likely)【口】很可能… *Chances are they'll be out when we call.* 很可能我们去拜访时他们不在。| **a fifty-fifty chance** (=when the chances of something happening or not happening are equal) 50% 的可能性 | **a chance in a million** (=a chance that you are very unlikely to have again) 难得的机会; 少有的机会 *I couldn't pass up going to Japan; it was a chance in a million.* 我不能放弃日本之行，这可是个千载难逢的机会。| **a million to one chance** (=when something is extremely unlikely to happen) 几乎不可能

2 ▶HOW LIKELY TO SUCCEED 成功的机率◀ **a) sb's chances** how likely it is that someone will succeed 某人成功的可能性: *Ryan will be a candidate in next month's elections, but his chances are not good.* 瑞安是下月选举的候选人之一，但他当选的机会不大。| **not fancy/not rate sb's chances** *BrE* (=think someone is unlikely to succeed)【英】认为某人不可能成功 **b) stand/have a chance (of)** if someone or something stands a chance of doing something, it is possible that they will succeed 有希望…: **stand a good chance** (=be likely to succeed) 很可能会成功 *If we did move to London, I'd stand a much better chance of getting a job.* 如果我们真的搬到伦敦，那我找到工作的可能性就会大得多。| **have an outside chance** (=have a slight chance of success) 成功的机会很小 | **have a sporting chance** (=have a fairly good chance of success) 成功的可能性相当大 | **have a fighting chance** (=have a small but real chance of success if a great effort can be made) 需付出极大的努力才有成功的可能 **c) be in with a chance** if a competitor is in with a chance, it is possible that they will win 有成功[获胜]的可能; 可能达到目标: *There're three of us going for promotion, but I figure I'm in with a chance.* 我们有三个人在争取得到提升，但我认为我还是有机会胜出的。

3 by any chance *spoken* used to ask politely whether something is true【口】也许，可能〔用于礼貌地问某事是否属实〕: *Are you Mrs Grant, by any chance?* 你可能就是格兰特太太吧？

4 any chance of... *spoken* used to ask whether you can have something or whether something is possible【口】能…吗〔用于询问是否能拥有某物或某事是否可能〕: *Any chance of a cup of coffee?* 我能要杯咖啡吗？| *Any chance of you coming to the party on Saturday?* 星期六你是否会来参加聚会？

5 no chance!/fat chance! *spoken* used to emphasize that you are sure something could never happen【口】绝对不可能!: *"Maybe your brother would lend you the money?" "Huh, fat chance!"* "也许你哥哥会借钱给你呢?" "哼！绝不可能!"

6 on the off chance if you do something on the off chance, you do it hoping for a particular result, although you know it is not likely 希望〔某事〕发生，对…抱有一线希望: *I didn't really expect her to be at home. I just called on the off chance.* 我并不指望她会在家，我只是打个电话看看。

7 ▶OPPORTUNITY 机会◀ [C] a time or situation which you can use to do something that you want to do 机会，机遇，有利时机: **chance to do sth** *Ralph was waiting for a chance to introduce himself.* 拉尔夫正在等待机会介绍自己。| **[+of]** *our only chance of escape* 我们逃走的唯一机会 | **have/get a chance** *I never get a chance to relax these days.* 我近来一直没机会好好放松一下。| **give sb a chance** *I can explain everything if you'll just give me a chance.* 如果你能给我机会，我会解释这一切。| **take the chance** (=use the opportunity) 把握机会 *You should take the chance to travel while you're still young.* 你应该趁年轻抓紧机会旅游。| **grab the chance/jump at the chance** (=eagerly and quickly use an opportunity) 〔赶紧〕抓住机会 *You're so lucky. If someone invited me over to Florida, I'd jump at the chance.* 你真幸运。如果有人邀请我去佛罗里达的话，我会迫不及待地抓住这个机会。| **miss a chance** (=fail to use the opportunity) 错过机会 *Denise never misses the chance of a free meal.* 丹尼丝从不错过任何吃免费餐的机会。| **a second chance/another chance** (=another chance after you have failed the first time) 第二次机会 *Students will be given further training and a second chance to pass the exam.* 学生们将受到进一步的训练，并获得一次补考的机会。| **last chance** *Friday is your last chance to see the show before it closes.* 星期五是闭幕前你观看那个表演的最后机会。| *You really ought to be punished, but I'll give you one last chance.* (=opportunity to behave well) 你真该受到惩罚，不过我会给你最后一次机会。| **the chance of a lifetime** (=an opportunity you are not likely to get more than once) 千载难逢[一生难得]的机会 | **now's your chance** *spoken* (=used to tell someone to do something immediately because there is a good opportunity)【口】你的机会到了 *Quick! Now's your chance to ask her, before she leaves.* 快点！在她走前可是问她的好机会。| **given half a chance** *spoken* (=if someone were given even a small opportunity)【口】稍有机会 *Rick could do really well, given half a chance.* 如果你给里克一丁点儿机会，他一定能干得很出色的。

8 ▶RISK 冒险◀ **take a chance** to do something that involves risks 冒险: *The rope might break but that's a chance we'll have to take.* 绳子可能会断，但我们只能冒这个险了。| **take chances** *After losing $20,000 on my last business venture, I'm not taking any chances this time.* 上次买卖我损失了 20,000 美元，这次我不会冒任何风险了。| **take a chance on** (=take a chance hoping things will happen in the way you want) 希望事情如愿 *I haven't reserved a table. I'm taking a chance on the restaurant not being full.* 我没预定座位，但愿餐厅不会客满。

9 ▶LUCK 运气◀ [U] the way some things happen without being planned or caused by people 巧合，偶然: *Success is rarely a matter of chance. You have to work at it.* 成功很少靠运气，你得为此而努力。| **by chance** (=without being planned or intended) 偶然地; 碰巧地 *I bumped into her quite by chance in Oxford Street.* 我在牛津大街碰巧遇到她。| **pure/sheer/blind chance** (=nothing except chance) 纯属巧合 *It was pure chance that they ended up working in the same office in the same town.* 真巧，结果他们在同一个小镇的同一个办公室里工作。| **as chance would have it** (=happening in a way that was not expected or intended) 凑巧，碰巧 *As chance would have it, the one time I wanted to see her, she wasn't in.* 真巧，我就这么一次想见她，她却不在。

10 chance would be a fine thing! *spoken* used to mean that the thing you want to happen is very unlikely【口】要有这样的机会就好了!〔用于表示希望发生的事是不可能的〕: *"If he asked me to marry him, I might say yes." "Chance would be a fine thing!"* (=he's unlikely to ask) "如果他向我求婚，我会答应的。" "要能这样就好了!"〔=他不可能会求婚〕—see also 另见 **a game of chance** (GAME[1] (11))

USAGE NOTE 用法说明: CHANCE

WORD CHOICE 词语辨析: **chance, opportunity, occasion**

Both **chance** and **opportunity** can be used for a situation that is suitable for doing something that you want to do. chance 和 opportunity 都可以用来指适于做某事的良机: *I'll have a chance/an opportunity to visit Niagara Falls when I'm in the States.* 我在美国的时候将有机会去看看尼亚加拉大瀑布。You can *get/take/grab/jump at/miss the opportunity/chance* to do something and *give someone the opportunity/chance* to do something. 你可以有/利用/抓住/错失一个机会做某事以及给某人一个机会做某事。

Chance is also used to say it is possible that something might happen. chance 也指某事有可能发生: *There is a chance that I'll see him* (=perhaps I'll see him). 我有可能见到他。

An **occasion** is a moment when something happens, especially when the same thing happens several times. occasion 指某事发生的时刻，尤指同样的事反复发生: *I met her on several occasions* (=several times). 我遇到她好几次了。| *On this occasion I was late* (NOT *In this occasion...* or just *This occasion...*). 这次我迟到了〔不能用 In this occasion…，也不能只用 This occasion…〕。An **occasion** can also be an event. occasion 也可以指事件: *Christmas is a special occasion.* 圣诞节是一个特殊的节日。

In formal English **occasion** (usually [U]) can also mean 'reason'. 在正式英语中，occasion〔通常为不可数名词〕也可指"原因、理由": *The poor service gave them occasion to complain* (=caused them to complain). 糟糕的服务给了他们投诉的理由。

SPELLING 拼法

Remember the two 'p's in **opportunity**. 要记住 opportunity 一词中有两个 p。

chance² *v* **1** *informal* to do something that you know involves a risk【非正式】冒险〔做某事〕: **chance it** *If we creep in quietly, maybe no one will notice. Anyway, let's chance it.* 如果我们悄悄地爬进去，也许没人会注意到。不管怎样，我们就来冒这个险吧。| **chance your luck** *You may lose all your money, but you'll just have to chance your luck like everyone else.* 你可能会输光所有的钱，但你必须像其他人那样试试运气。**2** *literary* to happen in an unexpected and unplanned way【文】偶然[碰巧]发生: **chance to do sth** *She chanced to be passing when I came out of the house.* 我从屋里出来时她恰巧经过。| **it chanced that** *It chanced that we were both working in Paris that year.* 凑巧的是，那一年我们都在巴黎工作。

chance on/upon sb/sth *phr v* [T] to find something or meet someone when you are not expecting to 与…不期而遇，碰上: *Henry chanced upon some valuable coins in the attic.* 亨利无意中在阁楼里发现了一些很珍贵的硬币。

chance³ *adj* [only before noun 仅用于名词前] not planned; ACCIDENTAL 偶然的，意外的: *Their chance meeting brought them back together after seven years apart.* 分别七年后的偶然相遇使他们再次走在一起。

chan·cel /ˈtʃænsḷ; ˈtʃɑːnsəl/ *n* [C] the part of a church where the priests and the CHOIR (=singers) sit〔供牧师和唱诗班坐的〕圣坛

chan·cel·ler·y /ˈtʃænsələrɪ; ˈtʃɑːnsələri/ *n* [C] **1** the building in which a CHANCELLOR has his office 大臣官邸; 总理官署; 大法官的办公处 **2** the officials who work in a CHANCELLOR's office 大臣[大法官等]办公处中的全体官员 **3** the offices of an official representative of a foreign country; CHANCERY 大使馆[领事馆]的办公室

W3 **chan·cel·lor** /ˈtʃænsələ; ˈtʃɑːnsələ/ *n* [C] **1** the Chancellor of the Exchequer〔英国〕财政大臣 **2 a)** the person who officially represents a British university on special occasions〔英国大学的〕名誉校长 **b)** the person in charge of an American university〔美国大学的〕负责人，校长 **3** the chief minister of some countries〔某些国家的〕总理，首相: *Willy Brandt, the former West German Chancellor* 前西德总理威利·勃兰特

Chancellor of the Ex·cheq·uer /ˌ···· ·ˈ··/ *n* [C] the British government minister in charge of taxes and government spending〔英国〕财政大臣

chan·ce·ry /ˈtʃænsərɪ; ˈtʃɑːnsəri/ *n* [singular] **1** *especially BrE* a government office that collects and stores official papers【尤英】档案馆[室]，公文保管处 **2** the part of the British system of law courts which deals with EQUITY (4) 衡平法院〔以正义公平即衡平为总原则，审理不属普通法范围的案件的法院〕**3** the offices of an official representative of a foreign country; CHANCELLERY 外国大使[领事]馆的办公处

chanc·y /ˈtʃænsɪ; ˈtʃɑːnsi/ *adj informal* uncertain or involving a lot of risk【非正式】不确定的; 冒险的: *Acting professionally is a chancy business.* 专业表演是个有风险的行业。—**chanciness** *n* [U]

chan·de·lier /ˌʃændḷˈɪr; ˌʃændəˈlɪə/ *n* [C] a large round structure for holding CANDLEs or lights that hang from the ceiling and is decorated with many small pieces of glass 枝形吊灯

chand·ler /ˈtʃændlə; ˈtʃɑːndlə/ *n* [C] *old use* someone who makes or sells candles【旧】制造[出售]蜡烛者 —see also 另见 SHIP'S CHANDLER

Chandler, Ray·mond /ˈremənd; ˈreɪmənd/ (1888-1959) a US writer of DETECTIVE stories whose most famous character is the private detective Philip Marlowe. His books include *The Big Sleep* and *Farewell, My Lovely*. 钱德勒〔(1888-1959)，美国侦探小说作家。小说中最有名的人物是私家侦探菲利普·米洛。其作品包括《长眠》和《别了，亲爱的》〕

S1 W1 **change¹** /tʃendʒ; tʃeɪmdʒ/ *v*

1 ►BECOME DIFFERENT 变得不同◄ [I,T] to become different 变化，改变: *Susan has changed a lot since I last saw her.* 自从我上次看见苏珊以来，她变了许多。| **changing circumstances/attitudes etc** *Animals must be able to adapt to changing conditions in order to survive.* 为了生存，动物必须能够适应不断变化的环境。| **change out of all recognition** (=change completely) 变得完全认不出 *The town I grew up in has changed out of all recognition.* 我成长生活的小镇已经彻底地变样了。| **change colour** *The leaves are slowly changing colour.* 叶子正在慢慢变色。| **not change your spots** (=never change your character or habits) 本性[习惯]不改

2 ►MAKE STH/SB DIFFERENT 使某物/某人不同◄ [T] to make something or someone different 使变化，改变: *plans to change the voting system* 改变选举制度的计划 | *Having a baby changes your life completely.* 有了孩子会使你的生活彻底改变。

3 ►FROM ONE THING TO ANOTHER 从某物变成另一物◄ [I,T] to stop having or doing one thing and start having or doing something else instead 转变; 转换: **change (from sth) to sth** *We've changed from traditional methods of production to an automated system.* 我们已从传统的生产方式改变为自动化系统。| **change your name/address/job etc** *Emma refused to change her name when she married.* 埃玛结婚后不愿意改姓。| **change jobs/cars etc** (=change from one to another) 换工作/车等 | **change course/direction** (=start to move in a different direction) 改变方向 *Our ship changed course and headed south.* 我们的船改变了航向驶向南方。| **change the subject** (=talk about something else) 换个话题 *I'm sick of politics. Let's change the subject.* 我讨厌政治，咱们换个话题吧。| **change tack** (=try a different method of dealing with a situation) 改变策略 *Perhaps my cold reaction persuaded him to change tack in his dealings with the committee.* 或许是我冷淡的反应令他在和委员会打交道时改变了策略。| **change sides** (=leave one side and join the other one) 改变立场 *Paul decided to change sides halfway through the debate.* 辩论进行到一半的时候保罗决定改变立场。| **change ends** (=to move to opposite ends of a TENNIS COURT or football field during a game)〔网球赛或足球赛中的〕交换场地 *The two teams change ends at half-time.* 下半场开赛时，两队交换了场地。

4 change your mind to change your decision, plan, or opinion about something 改变主意: **[+about]** *If you change your mind about the job, just give me a call.* 如果你对这份工作改变了主意，打电话给我。

5 ►CLOTHES 衣服◄ **a)** [I,T] to take off your clothes and put on different ones 换〔衣服〕: *I'm just going upstairs to change.* 我正要上楼去换衣服。| **[+into/out of]** *Why don't you change into something more comfortable?* 你为什么不换上更舒适的衣服呢? | *It's time you changed your socks.* 你该换双袜子了。| **get changed** (=put on different clothes) 换衣服 **b)** [T] to put fresh clothes on a baby or fresh covers on a bed 给〔婴儿〕换〔衣服〕;〔给床〕换〔床单〕: *I'm just going to change the baby.* 我正要给宝宝换尿布。

6 ►REPLACE STH 取代某事物◄ [T] to put something new in place of something old, damaged, or broken 替换; 更换: *Can you change the light bulb for me?* 你能替我换个灯泡吗? | *changing a tyre* 换轮胎

7 ►EXCHANGE GOODS 换货◄ [T] to exchange something that you have bought, or that a customer has bought from you, especially because there is something wrong with it〔尤指因商品有问题而〕换〔货物〕: *I bought these gloves for my daughter, but they're too large. Can I change them for a smaller size?* 我给女儿买的这副手套太大了，我能换副小一点的吗?

8 ►EXCHANGE MONEY 换钱◄ [T] **a)** to exchange a larger unit of money for smaller units that add up to the same value 换成〔零钱〕: *Can you change a £20 note?* 你能帮我把这20英镑换成零钱吗? **b)** to exchange money from one country for money from another 兑换〔货币〕: **change sth into/for** *I want to change my sterling into dollars.* 我想把英镑换成美元。

9 ►TRAINS/BUSES 火车/公共汽车◄ [I,T] to get out of one train or bus and into another in order to continue your journey 换车，转车: **[+at]** *Passengers for Liverpool should change at Crewe.* 前往利物浦的乘客要在克鲁转车。| **change trains/buses** *You can travel all the way to Paris without having to change trains.* 你可以坐火车直达巴黎，无须转车。| **all change!** *BrE* (=used to tell passengers to get off a train because it does not go any further)【英】全部下车!〔到终点站后叫火车乘客下车时的用语〕

10 change hands if property changes hands, it passes from one owner to another 易手; 易主: *The house has changed hands three times in the last two years.* 在过去的两年中，这房子已转手三次了。

11 change places (with) a) to give someone your place and take their place（和…）换位置: *Would you mind changing places with me so I can sit next to my friend?* 你能和我换一下座位，让我坐在朋友旁边吗? **b)** to take someone else's social position or situation in life instead of yours 交换地位[环境]: *She may be very rich, but I wouldn't want to change places with her.* 她也许很有钱，但我不愿意和她交换位置。

12 change gear to put the engine of a vehicle into a higher or lower GEAR¹ (1) in order to go faster or slower〔汽车的〕换排挡: **change into/out of** *Change into second gear as you approach the corner.* 靠近转弯处时你要换成二挡。| **change up/down** *BrE*【英】*Change down before you get to the hill.* 上坡时你要换成低速挡。

13 change your tune to start expressing a different attitude and reacting in a different way, after something has happened〔某事发生后〕改变论调[态度]: *When I offered him a share of the profits, he soon changed his tune.* 当我提出分给他一些利润时，他立刻改变了态度。

14 ▶WIND 风◀ [I] if the wind changes, it starts to blow in a different direction 改变风向 —see also 另见 **chop and change** (CHOP¹ (5))

change sth ↔ **around** *phr v* [T] to move things into different positions 改变〔物件的〕位置: *When we'd changed the furniture around, the room looked quite different.* 我们把家具改变位置后，房间看上去大不一样了。

change into *phr v* [T] **1** [**change into** sth] to become something different 变成: *When the princess kissed the frog, it changed into a handsome prince.* 公主吻了青蛙之后，它立刻变成了一位英俊的王子。**2** [**change** sth/sb **into** sth] to make something or someone become something different 把…变成…: *You can't change iron into gold.* 你无法使铁变成金。

change² *n*

1 ▶THINGS BECOMING DIFFERENT 事情变得不同◀ [C,U] the process or result of something or someone becoming different 变化，改变，变更: [+in] *a change in the weather* 天气的变化 | *I've noticed a big change in Louise since she got married.* 我发觉路易丝结婚后有了很大的变化。| *changes in the immigration laws* 移民法的修改 | *Many old people find it hard to cope with change.* 许多老年人难以适应变化。| [+of] *a change of temperature* 温度的变化 | **change for the better/worse** (=a change that makes a situation better or worse) 好转/转坏 *When Bill Clinton was elected, we all believed the new administration would be a change for the better.* 比尔·克林顿当选后，我们都相信新政府会有所改善的。| **change of heart** (=change in someone's attitude) 改变态度 *He didn't want kids at first but recently he's had a real change of heart.* 他起初不想要孩子，但最近却改变了主意。

2 ▶FROM ONE THING TO ANOTHER 从一物到另一物◀ [C] the fact of one thing or person being replaced by another 替换: [+of] *a change of government* 政府的更替 | *a change of address* 更改地址 | **change from sth to** *the change from city life to living right out in the countryside* 从城市生活转变成乡村生活 | *The car needs an oil change.* 这辆车需要换油。

3 ▶PLEASANT NEW SITUATION 令人高兴的新状况◀ [singular] a situation or experience that is different from what happened before, and is usually interesting or enjoyable〔有趣或令人愉快的〕转变: [+from] *Roast lamb is a welcome change from the usual junk food.* 老吃垃圾食品，改吃一次烤羊便深受欢迎。| **for a change** *Let's go out to a restaurant for a change.* 我们换换口味上饭馆去吃饭吧！| **it makes a change** *spoken* (=used to say that something is different from usual and better)【口】不同寻常，变好了 *"The train was on time today." "Well, that makes a change."* "火车今天很准时。""哦，真是难得。" | **change of scene/air etc** (=a stay in a different place that is pleasant) 换个〔好〕环境 *How about a week by the sea? The change of air would do you good.* 到海边度假一个礼拜怎么样？换换环境对你有好处。

4 ▶MONEY 钱财◀ [U] **a)** the money that you get back when you have paid for something with more money than it costs 找回的零钱: *I waited for the shopkeeper to hand me my change.* 我等店主找钱。**b)** money in the form of coins 硬币，零钱: **in change** *I have about a dollar in change.* 我有大约一美元的零钱。| **change for £1/$10** (=coins that you give someone in exchange for the same money in a larger unit) 1英镑/10美元的硬币 *Excuse me, have you got change for a pound?* 对不起，你能帮我把一英镑换成零钱吗？| **loose change** *Matt emptied the loose change from his pockets.* 马特把口袋里的零钱都掏了出来。| **small change** (=coins of low value) 零钱，小钱 *When travelling by bus in a strange place, have small change ready.* 在陌生的城市乘搭公共汽车，要准备好零钱。—see 见 MONEY (USAGE)

5 change of clothes/underwear etc an additional set of clothes that you have with you, for example when you are travelling 备换的衣服/内衣等

6 ▶TRAIN/BUS 火车/公共汽车◀ [C] a situation in which you get off one train or bus and get on another in order to continue your journey 换车，转车

7 get no change out of *spoken* to get no useful information or help from someone【口】从〔某人那儿〕得不到有用的资料[帮助]: *I wouldn't bother asking Richard, you'll get no change out of him.* 我不会去问理查德，你从他那儿不会得到任何有用的帮助的。—see also 另见 **ring the changes** (RING² (6))

change·a·ble /ˈtʃendʒəbl; ˈtʃeɪndʒəbəl/ *adj* likely to change or changing often 可变的；易变的；常变化的: *The weather was very changeable.* 这天气变化无常。—**changeably** *adv* —**changeableness** *n* [U] —**changeability** /ˌtʃendʒəˈbɪlətɪ; ˌtʃeɪndʒəˈbɪləti/ *n* [U]

changed /tʃendʒd; tʃeɪndʒd/ *adj* **1 a changed man/woman** someone who has become very different from what they were before as a result of a powerful experience〔由于某种经历后〕有很大改变的: *Since she stopped drinking, she's a changed woman.* 自从戒酒后她整个人都变了。**2 changed circumstances** a change in someone's financial situation 经济状况的改变: *When planning ahead, be aware of the possibility of changed circumstances.* 在为将来作计划时，要注意经济状况变化的可能性。

change·less /ˈtʃendʒlɪs; ˈtʃeɪndʒləs/ *adj literary* never seeming to change【文】不变的，永恒的: *a changeless desert landscape* 毫无变化的沙漠景观 —**changelessly** *adv*

change·ling /ˈtʃendʒlɪŋ; ˈtʃeɪndʒlɪŋ/ *n* [C] *literary* a baby that is said to have been secretly exchanged for another baby by fairies (FAIRY (1))【文】〔传说中〕被〔仙女〕调换的婴儿

change of life /ˌ· · ˈ·/ *n* [singular] the MENOPAUSE 更年期，绝经期

change·o·ver /ˈtʃendʒˌovɚ; ˈtʃeɪndʒˌəʊvə/ *n* [C] a change from one activity, system, or way of working to another〔活动、体制或工作方法的〕改变，转变，变更: *working to ensure that the changeover to the new method is as smooth as possible* 努力确保改用新方法能够顺利进行

change purse /ˈ· ·/ *n* [C] *AmE* a small bag in which coins are kept【美】放零钱的小钱包; PURSE¹ (1) *BrE*【英】—see picture at 参见 PURSE¹ 图

change ring·ing /ˈ· ˌ··/ *n* [U] the art of ringing a set of bells in an order that keeps changing 敲奏组钟的技艺

Changing of the Guard, the /ˌ·· · · ˈ·/ a ceremony that takes place regularly outside Buckingham Palace in London, in which the soldiers who have been guarding the palace are replaced by others〔定时在伦敦白金汉宫外举行的〕英国皇家卫队换岗仪式

changing room /ˈ·· ·/ *n* [C] a room where people change their clothes when they play sports〔运动场等内的〕更衣室; LOCKER ROOM *AmE*【美】

chan·nel¹ /ˈtʃænl; ˈtʃænl/ *n* [C]

1 ▶TELEVISION 电视◀ a television station and all the programmes broadcast by it 频道: *We watched the news on Channel 4.* 我们看了第四频道的新闻节目。| *This is boring – I'm going to switch to another channel.* 这节目太无聊了，我要换台。

2 ▶RADIO 广播◀ a particular range of SOUND WAVES which can be used to send and receive radio messages〔发送和接收无线电信号的〕波道

3 ▶SYSTEM OF INFORMATION 信息系统◀ also 又作 **channels** [plural] a system or method that you use to send or obtain information about a particular subject〔传递或获得资料的〕途径；手段；渠道: *If you go through official channels, your application will take months.* 如果通过正式途径，你的申请要几个月才能批准。

4 ▶FOR WATER 水◀ a passage that water or other liquids flow along 管道；水渠，水沟: *an irrigation channel* 灌溉渠

5 ▶SEA/RIVER 海洋/河流◀ **a)** a passage of water connecting two seas 海峡: **the Channel** (=the English Channel) 英吉利海峡 **b)** the deepest part of a river, HARBOUR¹, or sea passage, especially one that is deep enough to allow ships to sail in 航道

6 ▶IN A SURFACE 在表面◀ a long deep line cut into a surface or a long deep space between two edges; GROOVE¹ (1)〔在表面形成的〕槽，沟: *Slide the plastic door strip into the channel provided.* 把细塑料门条插进槽中。

7 ▶WAY TO EXPRESS YOURSELF 表达方式◀ a way of expressing your thoughts, feelings, or physical energy〔表达思想、感情或发泄精力的〕方式，渠道，途径: *The kids need a channel for all that energy.* 孩子们需要一种途径去发挥他们的精力。

channel² *v* **channelled, channelling** *BrE*【英】**channeled, channeling** *AmE*【美】[T] **1** to control and direct something such as money or energy towards a particular purpose 把〔钱或精力等〕导向〔某一特定目的〕；引导: **channel sth into** *Nancy channels her creativity into her home life.* 南希把她的创造才能用于她的家庭生活中。| **channel sth through** *The famine relief money was channelled through the UN.* 饥荒救济款项是通过联合国分发的。**2** to cut a long deep line in something 在〔某物上〕形成槽: *Water had channelled grooves in the rock.* 水在岩石上形成了一道道深槽。**3** to send water through a passage〔透过管道〕输送〔水等〕: *An efficient irrigation system channels water to the crops.* 有效的灌溉系统把水输送给庄稼。

Channel, the the English Channel 英吉利海峡

Channel 4 /ˌtʃænl ˈfɔr; ˌtʃænl ˈfɔː/ one of the five main television stations in the UK. It broadcasts a wide range of

programmes 第四频道电视台〔英国五大电视台之一, 播出的节目涉猎广泛〕: *a late-night talk show on Channel 4* 第四频道电视台的午夜清谈节目 | *the Channel 4 News* 第四频道电视台新闻

Channel 5 /ˌtʃænl ˋfaɪv; ˌtʃænl ˈfaɪv/ one of the five main television stations in the UK. It broadcasts popular programmes and films. 第五频道电视台〔英国五大电视台之一, 播出大众喜爱的节目和影片〕

channel hop /ˈ· · ·/ *BrE*【英】, **channel surf** *AmE*【美】 *v* [I] to repeatedly change from one television channel to another, only watching a few minutes of any programme 跳频道〔指看电视时不断换频道〕

Channel Is·lands, the /ˈ· · , · ·/ a group of British islands in the English Channel near the coast of France. The main islands are Jersey, Guernsey, Alderney, and Sark. 海峡群岛〔英吉利海峡一群岛, 归属英国, 靠近法国海岸, 主要有泽西岛、根西岛、奥尔德尼岛和萨克岛〕

chan·nel·ling *BrE*【英】, **channeling** *AmE*【美】 /ˈtʃænl-ɪŋ; ˈtʃænl-ɪŋ/ *n* [U] a practice based on the belief that messages can be received from other PLANETS or from dead people 接收外太空信息; 通灵术 —**channeller** *n* [C]

Channel Tun·nel, the /ˌ· · ˈ· ·/ a railway TUNNEL which runs under the English Channel, connecting England and France 英吉利海峡隧道〔位于英吉利海峡底部连接英法两国的铁路隧道〕

chant¹ /tʃænt; tʃɑːnt/ *v* [I,T] **1** to repeat a word or phrase again and again〔有节奏地反复地〕唱, 喊叫: *an angry crowd chanting slogans and waving banners* 反复地喊着口号并挥动着旗帜的愤怒的人群 **2** to sing or say a religious song or prayer in a way that involves singing phrases on one note 吟唱, 背诵〔赞美诗等〕: *a priest chanting the liturgy* 背诵祷文的牧师

chant² *n* [C] **1** words or phrases that are repeated again and again by a group of people 有节奏的一再重复的话语: **take up a chant** *Dave took up the crowd's chant of "More Jobs! More Money!"* 大卫也加入人群中, 不停地喊着"增加职位! 增加工资!" **2** a regularly repeated tune, often with many words sung on one note, especially used for religious prayers 反复唱的曲调〔尤指圣歌〕—see also 另见 GREGORIAN CHANT —**chanter** *n* [C]

chan·try /ˈtʃæntrɪ; ˈtʃɑːntri/ also 又作 **chantry cha·pel** /ˌ· · ˈ· ·/ *n* [C] a small church or part of a church paid for by someone so that priests can pray for them there after they die〔施主为祈求冥福而捐建的〕小教堂

chan·ty also 又作 **chantey** *AmE*【美】 /ˈʃæntɪ; ˈʃænti/ *n* [C] a song sung by sailors as they did their work in former times; SHANTY〔旧时水手唱的〕船歌; 船夫号子

Cha·nu·kah /ˈhɑnəkə; ˈhɑːnʊkə/ *n* HANUKKAH〔纪念古代以色列战功显赫年代的〕献殿节, 光明节

cha·os /ˈkeɑs; ˈkeɪ-ɒs/ *n* [U] **1** a situation in which everything is happening in a confused way and nothing is organized or arranged in order 大混乱; 紊乱; 无秩序状态: **complete/utter/absolute chaos** *There was absolute chaos when the air controllers came out on strike.* 航空调度员罢工时出现了极度混乱的场面。| **in chaos** (=in a state of chaos) 凌乱不堪 *I arrived home to find the house in chaos.* 我回到家中, 发现家里一片凌乱。**2** the state of the universe before there was any order〔天地未形成前〕宇宙的混沌状态

cha·ot·ic /keˋɑtɪk; keɪˈɒtɪk/ *adj* a chaotic situation is one in which everything is happening in a confused way 混乱的, 毫无秩序的: *Traffic conditions tonight are chaotic.* 今晚的交通状况一片混乱。

chap /tʃæp; tʃæp/ *n BrE informal*【英, 非正式】**1** [C] a man, especially a man you know and like〔尤指你认识和喜欢的〕小伙子, 家伙: *a decent sort of chap* 一个正派的小伙子 **2 chaps** [plural] protective leather covers worn over your trousers when riding a horse〔骑马时穿的〕皮套裤

chap·ar·ral /ˌʃæpəˈræl; ˌʃæpəˈræl/ *n* [U] *AmE* land on which small OAK trees grow close together【美】丛林, 茂密的(橡)树林

chap·book /ˈtʃæpˌbʊk; ˈtʃæpbʊk/ *n* [C] *AmE* a small printed book, usually consisting of writings about literature or poetry【美】〔文学或诗歌〕小册子

chap·el¹ /ˈtʃæpl; ˈtʃæpəl/ *n* **1** [C] a small church or a room in a hospital, prison etc in which Christians pray and have religious services〔医院、监狱等中的〕小教堂, 小礼拜堂 **2** [C] a small church or a room or area in a church with its own ALTAR used especially for private prayer and religious services〔教堂内的〕私人祈祷处; 附属小礼拜堂: *a wedding chapel in Las Vegas* 拉斯维加斯的一个婚礼礼拜堂 **3** [C] **a)** a building in England or Wales where Christians who are Nonconformists have religious services〔英格兰或威尔士不属于英国国教的〕教堂 **b)** a Roman Catholic church in Scotland〔苏格兰的〕天主教教堂 **4** [U] the religious services held in a chapel〔小教堂里的〕礼拜仪式: **go to chapel** *Betham goes to chapel every Sunday.* 贝瑟姆每个星期天都去教堂做礼拜。**5** [C] *BrE* the members of a UNION (=workers' organization) in the newspaper or printing industry【英】〔报业或印刷业的〕工会会员

chapel² *adj BrE informal* Nonconformist【英, 非正式】不信奉英国国教的: *He's chapel but his wife is Roman Catholic.* 他不信奉英国国教, 但是他的妻子是天主教徒。

chap·e·rone¹, chaperon /ˈʃæpəˌron; ˈʃæpərəʊn/ *n* [C] **1** an older woman in former times who went out with a young unmarried woman on social occasions and was responsible for her behaviour〔旧时在社交场合陪伴未婚女子并负责监督其行为的〕年长女伴;〔女〕监护人: *I will only allow it if you have Maria as a chaperone.* 除非玛丽亚陪你去, 我才会允许。**2** *AmE* someone, usually a parent or teacher, who attends school dances or visits to help watch the children【美】〔为帮助监护孩子而参加学校舞会或参观的〕家长; 老师

chaperone², chaperon *v* [T] to go out somewhere with a woman as her chaperone 当〔某人〕的年长女伴; 监护; 陪伴

chap·lain /ˈtʃæplɪn; ˈtʃæplɪn/ *n* [C] a priest or other religious minister responsible for the religious needs of a club, the army, a hospital, etc〔社团、军队或医院等的〕牧师: *the prison/school chaplain* 监狱/学校牧师 —see 见 PRIEST (USAGE)

chap·lain·cy /ˈtʃæplɪnsɪ; ˈtʃæplɪnsi/ *n* [C] the position of a chaplain or the place where a chaplain works 牧师的职位; 牧师的办公处

chap·let /ˈtʃæplɪt; ˈtʃæplɪt/ *n* [C] *literary* a band of flowers worn on the head【文】〔戴在头上的〕花冠

Chap·lin /ˈtʃæplɪn; ˈtʃæplɪn/, **Sir Charles (Char·lie)** (1889-1977) a British film actor and DIRECTOR who worked mainly in the US in humorous SILENT FILMS (=films made with no sound) during the 1920s 卓别林〔(1889-1977), 英国电影演员、导演。20世纪20年代, 他主要在美国从事无声喜剧电影工作〕

Chap·pa·quid·dick /ˌtʃæpəˋkwɪdɪk; ˌtʃæpəˈkwɪdɪk/ an island off the coast of the US state of Massachusetts 查帕奎迪克岛〔美国马萨诸塞州沿海一岛屿〕

chapped /tʃæpt; tʃæpt/ *adj* chapped lips or hands are sore, dry, and cracked, especially as a result of cold weather or wind〔尤指因寒冷或风导致唇、手〕干燥的, 皲裂的 —**chap** *v* [T]

chap·ter /ˈtʃæptɚ; ˈtʃæptə/ *n* [C]

1 ►IN A BOOK 书中◄ one of the parts into which a book is divided 章节: *I've only read as far as Chapter 5.* 我只读到了第五章。

2 ►PERIOD 时期◄ a particular period or event in someone's life or in history〔人生或历史的〕一段时期: [+of] *That summer an important chapter of my life came to an end.* 那个夏天, 我一生中一个重要的时期结束了。

3 ►PRIESTS 教士◄ all the priests connected with a CATHEDRAL, or a meeting of these priests 大教堂的所有教士; 大教堂全体教士的会议

4 ►CLUB 俱乐部◄ *especially AmE* the local members of a large organization such as a club【尤美】〔俱乐部的〕地方分会: *the San Fernando Valley chapter of the Sierra Club* 塞拉俱乐部在圣费尔南多山谷的分部

5 give/quote sb chapter and verse to give someone exact details about where to find some information 提供〔资料的〕确实出处

6 a chapter of accidents *BrE* a series of unfortunate events coming one after another【英】一连串的灾祸[意外事件]

Chapter 11 /ˌtʃæptɚ ɪˋlɛvən; ˌtʃæptər ɪˈlevən/ a part of the US BANKRUPTCY laws that allows a company with financial problems to reorganize itself so that it will not be forced to close down〔美国〕《联邦破产法》第11章〔该法规允许财政困难的公司进行重组, 从而避免倒闭〕: *Our competitor has filed for Chapter 11.* 我们的竞争对手已申请破产保护。| *Chapter 11 proceedings*《联邦破产法》第11章重组程序

chap·ter·house /ˈtʃæptɚˌhaus; ˈtʃæptəhaʊs/ *n* [C] a building where the priests connected with a CATHEDRAL meet〔供大教堂教士集会用的〕教士礼堂

char¹ /tʃɑr; tʃɑː/ *v past tense and past participle* **charred, charring 1** [I,T] to burn something so that its outside becomes black (把…)烧焦: *Roast the peppers until the skin begins to char and blister.* 把这些辣椒烤到表皮发黑起泡为止。—see also 另见 CHARRED **2** [I] *BrE old-fashioned* to work as a cleaner in a house, office, public building etc【英, 过时】〔在家庭、办公室、公共建筑等〕当清洁工

char² *n* **1** [C] *BrE old-fashioned* a CHARWOMAN【英, 过时】清洁女工 **2** [U] *BrE old-fashioned* tea【英, 过时】茶: *a cup of char* 一杯茶

char·a·banc /ˈʃærəˌbæŋ; ˈʃærəbæŋ/ *n* [C] *BrE old-fashioned* a large comfortable bus used for pleasure trips【英, 过时】〔大而舒适的〕旅行客车, 大型游览车

char·ac·ter /ˈkærɪktə; ˈkærɨktə/ *n*
1 ▶ALL SB'S QUALITIES 某人所有的品质◀ [C usually singular 一般用单数] the particular combination of qualities that makes someone a particular kind of person〔某人的〕个性, 性格, 气质: *There is a serious side to her character.* 她性格当中也有严肃的一面。| **be in/out of character** (=be typical or untypical of someone's character) 符合/不符合…的个性 *I can't believe she lied to me – it seems so out of character.* 想不到她会对我撒谎, 这不符合她的个性。| **the English/French etc character** *Openness is at the heart of the American character.* 坦诚是美国人性格的核心。—see 见 CHARACTERISTIC[1]
2 ▶QUALITIES OF STH 某物的特征◀ [singular,U] the particular combination of features and qualities that makes a thing or place different from all others〔某物或某地的〕特色, 特点: *the unspoilt character of the coast* 海岸未被破坏的特征 | **[+of]** *In only ten years the whole character of the school has changed.* 仅仅10年间这所学校的所有特点都改变了。| **in character** *Liquids are different in character from both solids and gases.* 液体的特性与固体和气体有所不同。
3 ▶INTERESTING QUALITY 有趣的特点◀ [U] a quality that makes someone or something special and interesting〔使某人或某物特别或有趣的〕特征: *These new houses have very little character.* 这些新房子并没有什么特别之处。
4 ▶MORAL STRENGTH 道德力量◀ [U] a combination of qualities such as courage and loyalty that are admired and regarded as valuable 人格, 好的品质, 品性: *a woman of great character* 一个品格高尚的妇人 | **character building** (=activity aimed at developing these qualities) 品德培养 *outdoor programs that are meant to be character building* 旨在培养优良品格的户外活动计划
5 ▶PERSON 人物◀ [C] **a)** a person in a book, play, film etc〔书、剧本、电影等中的〕人物, 角色: *Hardy's main character is a young milkmaid whose life ends in tragedy.* 哈代笔下的主要人物是一个最终以悲剧收场的年轻挤奶姑娘。**b)** a person of a particular kind, especially a strange or dishonest one 人;〔尤指〕怪人: *a couple of suspicious-looking characters standing outside the house* 站在门外的几个神情可疑的人 **c) be a character** to be an interesting, and unusual person 有趣的人; 不同寻常的人: *Kurt's quite a character – he has so many tales to tell.* 库尔特是个很特别的人, 他有许多不寻常的经历。
6 ▶REPUTATION 声誉◀ [U] *formal* reputation【正式】名誉, 名声, 声誉: *a man of previous good character* 从前拥有良好声誉的人 | **a slur on your character** (=something that harms your character in other people's opinion) 毁坏名誉之事 | **character assassination** (=a cruel and unfair attack on someone's character) 人身攻击, 诽谤
7 ▶LETTER/SIGN 字母/符号◀ [C] a letter, mark, or sign used in writing, printing, or computing〔书写、印刷或电脑的〕字; 字体; 符号: *Chinese characters* 汉字

char·ac·ter·ise /ˈkærɪktəˌraɪz; ˈkærɨktəraɪz/ *v* a British spelling of CHARACTERIZE characterize 的英式拼法

char·ac·ter·is·tic[1] /ˌkærɪktəˈrɪstɪk; ˌkærɨktəˈrɪstɪk◂/ *n* [C usually plural 一般用复数] a quality or feature of something or someone that is typical of them and easy to recognize〔人或物的〕特征, 特性, 特色: *A characteristic of this species is the blue stripe on its back.* 这物种有个特征, 那就是其背部有蓝色的条纹。| *Obstinacy remains one of Gail's less endearing characteristics.* 固执一直是盖尔不太讨人喜欢的一个特点。

characteristic[2] *adj* very typical of a particular thing or of someone's character 典型的; 独特的; 表现〔人或物的〕特性的: *Larry, with characteristic generosity, invited us all back to his house.* 本性慷慨大方的拉里邀请我们所有人回到他家去。| **[+of]** *The flint walls are characteristic of the local architecture.* 燧石墙是当地建筑的一大特色。—**characteristically** /-klɪ; -kli/ *adv*

char·ac·ter·i·za·tion /ˌkærɪktərəˈzeʃən; ˌkærɨktəraɪˈzeɪʃən/ *n* **1** [C,U] the way in which a writer makes a person in a book, film, or play seem like a real person〔书、电影等中的〕人物塑造, 角色刻画: *He writes exciting stories but his characterization is weak.* 他写的故事很有趣, 但人物的塑造却缺乏力度。**2** [U] the way in which the character of a real person or thing is described〔人物性格或事物特征的〕描述, 刻画, 表现: **characterization of sb/sth as** *the characterization of the enemy as 'cruel fanatics'* 敌人被描绘成"残酷的狂热分子"

char·ac·ter·ize also 又作 **-ise** *BrE*【英】/ˈkærɪktəˌraɪz; ˈkærɨktəraɪz/ *v* [T] **1** to be typical of a person, place, or thing〔人、地方或事物〕以…为特征, 以…为典型: *Bright, vibrant colours characterize his paintings.* 他的画以明亮轻快的色彩为特征。**2** to describe the character of someone or something in a particular way; PORTRAY 描述…的特性; 描绘: **characterize sb as sth** *I would characterize Captain Hill as a born leader of men.* 我认为希尔上校是一个天生的领导者。

char·ac·ter·less /ˈkærəktəlɪs; ˈkærɨktələs/ *adj* not having any special or interesting qualities 无特色的; 平凡的: *snack-bars selling mass-produced, characterless food* 出售没有特色的大众食品的小吃店

character ref·e·rence /ˈ···, ···/ *n* [C] REFERENCE (4) 介绍信, 推荐信

cha·rade /ʃəˈred; ʃəˈrɑːd/ *n* **1 charades** [U] a game in which one person acts the meaning of a word or phrase and the others have to guess what it is 手势字谜游戏 **2** [C] a situation in which people pretend that something is true and behave as if it were true, when everyone knows it is not really true 显而易见[容易识破]的伪装: *Their marriage is an empty charade, continued only for the sake of the children.* 他们的婚姻已经形同虚设, 只是为了孩子的缘故才继续维持着。

char·broil /ˈtʃɑrˌbrɔɪl; ˈtʃɑːbrɔɪl/ *v* [T] *AmE* to cook food over a very hot charcoal fire【美】炭烤, 炭炙 —**charbroiled** *adj*

char·coal /ˈtʃɑrˌkol; ˈtʃɑːkəʊl/ *n* [U] a black substance obtained by burning wood, that can be used as FUEL, or sticks of this substance used for drawing 木炭;〔画用〕炭笔: *a sketch drawn in charcoal* 用炭笔画的素描 | *a charcoal grill* 木炭烧烤架

chard /tʃɑrd; tʃɑːd/ *n* [U] a vegetable with large leaves 莙荙菜, 牛皮菜; 瑞士甜菜

Char·don·nay /ˈʃɑrdəne; ˈʃɑːdəneɪ/ **1** a type of GRAPE grown for making wine 霞多丽葡萄〔用于酿酒而种植的一种葡萄〕**2** a type of white wine made from Chardonnay GRAPEs and produced in many countries throughout the world 霞多丽葡萄酒〔用霞多丽葡萄酿造的一种白葡萄酒, 世界许多国家都有生产〕

charge[1] /tʃɑrdʒ; tʃɑːdʒ/ *n*
1 ▶PRICE 价格◀ [C,U] the amount of money you have to pay for goods or services 费用, 价钱: *Gas charges will rise in July.* 7月份煤气价格将上涨。| **[+for]** *When you buy a suit, there is no charge for any alterations.* 买了西服后可以免费修改。| **free of charge** (=at no cost) 免费 *Your order will be delivered free of charge within a ten-mile limit.* 在10英里范围之内, 你将享有免费送货的服务。| **at no extra charge** (=without having to pay more money) 不需额外付费 —see 见 COST[1] (USAGE)
2 ▶CONTROL 控制◀ a) be in charge (of) to be the person who controls or is responsible for a group of people or an activity 负责, 掌管: *Who's in charge around here?* 这儿谁负责? | *the officer in charge of the investigation* 负责调查的长官 —see 见 CONTROL[1] (USAGE) **b) put sb in charge (of)** to give someone complete responsibility over an activity, group of people, organization etc 让…全权负责: *I've been put in charge of the team.* 我被指派负责这个队。**c) take charge (of)** to take control of a situation, organization, or group of people 控制, 掌管〔局面、组织或人〕: *Harry will take charge of the department while I'm away.* 我不在时由哈里负责部门的事务。
3 ▶RESPONSIBILITY/CARE FOR 责任/照料◀ a) be in/under sb's charge if someone or something is in your charge, you are responsible for looking after them 由…照料[照顾]: *The child was in my charge when he ran away.* 他离家出走后, 孩子便由我照顾。| *The files were left in your charge.* 这些文件由你负责处理。**b)** [C] *formal* someone that you are responsible for looking after【正式】被照顾的人: *Sarah bought some chocolate for her three young charges.* 萨拉给自己照顾的三个小孩买了些巧克力。
4 ▶THAT SB IS GUILTY 某人有罪◀ [C] an official statement made by the police saying that someone is guilty of a crime 指控, 控告, 罪名: **[+against]** *The charge against her was arson.* 她被控纵火。| **on a charge** *Young appeared in court on a murder charge.* 扬因被控谋杀罪而出庭。| **charge of burglary/theft/fraud etc** *Owen is facing a charge of armed robbery.* 欧文面临一项持械行劫的控罪。| **bring/press/prefer charges** (=state officially that someone is guilty of a crime) 正式起诉 *As it was his first offence, the store agreed not to press charges.* 由于是初犯, 那家商店同意不起诉他。| **drop the charges** (=decide to stop making charges) 撤销控诉
5 ▶BLAME 责备◀ [C] a written or spoken statement blaming someone for doing something bad or illegal; ALLEGATION〔书面或口头的〕指责, 批评, 责备: *the charge of being an uncaring mother* 被指责为一个漠不关心的母亲 | *a group which earlier rejected the charge that it had put undue pressure on the Prime Minister* 一个早前否认指控说它对首相过分施压的团体 | **counter a charge** (=say that a charge is untrue) 驳斥指控 | **lay/**

leave yourself open to a charge of (=be likely to be blamed for something) 可能遭到非议[指责] *The procedures the doctor followed laid him open to charges of negligence.* 那位医生所采用的程序使他有可能被指责为疏忽。

6 ▶ATTACK 进攻◀ [C] an attack in which soldiers, wild animals etc rush with great force against someone 〔士兵或野生动物等〕猛烈的攻击

7 ▶ELECTRICAL FORCE 电力◀ [U] an electrical force that is put into a piece of electrical equipment such as a BATTERY (1) 电荷; 电量: **on charge** (=taking in a charge of electricity) 在充电 *Leave the battery on charge all night.* 让电池充一晚上的电。

8 ▶EXPLOSIVE 爆炸物◀ [C] an amount of explosive, especially the amount needed to work successfully 〔一定量的〕炸药

9 ▶STRENGTH OF FEELINGS 感情的力量◀ [U] the power of strong feelings 〔感情的〕力量; 感染力: *a novel with a strong emotional charge* 一部具有强烈感染力的小说

10 get a charge out of sth *AmE* to be excited by something and enjoy it very much 【美】从〔某事〕得到快乐[刺激、兴奋]: *I got a real charge out of seeing my niece take her first steps.* 看到侄女踏出第一步, 我高兴极了。

11 ▶AN ORDER TO DO STH 命令◀ [C] *formal* an order to do something 【正式】命令, 指示, 吩咐: **a charge to do sth** *The old servant fulfilled his master's charge to care for the children.* 老仆人按照主人的吩咐照料孩子们。—see also 另见 **reverse the charges** (REVERSE[1] (5))

[1] [2] **charge**[2] *v*

1 ▶MONEY 钱◀ a) [I,T] to ask someone a certain amount of money for something you are selling (向…) 收费; 开价: **charge sb £10/$50 etc (for sth)** *The restaurant charged us £40 for the wine.* 餐厅收我们40英镑的酒水钱。| **[+for]** *We won't charge for delivery if you pay now.* 如果现在付款, 我们将免费送货上门。**b) charge sth to sb's account** to record the cost of something on someone's account, so that they can pay for it later 把某物记在某人的账上: *Charge the room to the company's account.* 把房间费用记在公司的账下。**c)** [T] *AmE* to pay for something with a CREDIT CARD 【美】用信用卡付账: *I charged the shoes on Visa.* 我用威世信用卡付了这鞋子的钱。| **charge it** *"Do you have enough cash for that?" "No, but I can charge it."* "你有足够的现金支付吗?" "不够, 但我可以刷卡。"

2 ▶RUSH/ATTACK 冲击/攻击◀ a) [I,T] to deliberately rush quickly towards someone or something in order to attack them 进攻, 冲锋; 冲向: **[+at/towards/into]** *a three-ton rhino charging towards us* 一头重三吨向我们冲来的犀牛 | **charge sb** *We drew our swords and charged the enemy.* 我们拔剑向敌人冲去。**b)** [I always+ adv/prep] to deliberately run or walk somewhere quickly 快步走向[跑向]: **[+around/through/out etc]** *At playtime, the children charged wildly out of the building.* 一到活动时间, 孩子们便疯狂地跑出门外。

3 ▶WITH A CRIME 有罪◀ [T] to state officially that someone is guilty of a crime 控告; 指控: **be charged with** *The man they arrested last night has been charged with murder.* 昨晚他们逮捕的那人被控犯有谋杀罪。

4 ▶BLAME SB 指责某人◀ [T] *formal* to say publicly that you think someone has done something wrong 【正式】〔公开〕指责, 责备: **charge that** *Labour's Bryan Gould charged that Mr Mellor acted 'improperly'.* 工党的布赖恩·古尔德公开指责梅勒先生的所作所为是"不恰当的"。

5 ▶ELECTRICITY 电◀ [I,T] if a battery charges or if you charge it, it takes in and stores electricity (使) 充电: *If the light comes on, the battery isn't charging.* 如果指示灯亮了, 就表示电池没在充电。

6 ▶ORDER SB 命令某人◀ [T] *formal* to order someone to do something or make them responsible for it 【正式】吩咐, 命令: **be charged with doing sth** *The commission is charged with investigating all the alleged breaches of the rules.* 委员会受命调查所有被指控的违规行为。

7 ▶GUN 枪◀ [T] *old use* to load a gun 【旧】给〔枪〕装子弹

8 ▶GLASS 杯子◀ [T] *formal* to fill a glass 【正式】斟满〔杯〕: *Charge your glasses and drink a toast to the happy couple.* 把酒杯斟满, 为这幸福的一对干杯。

charge·a·ble /ˈtʃɑrdʒəbl; ˈtʃɑːdʒəbəl/ *adj* **1** chargeable costs must be paid 应付费的; 可记在某人账上的: *Living expenses are chargeable to my account.* 生活开支可记在我的账上。**2** chargeable assets or gains have to have tax paid on them 应交税的 **3** a chargeable offence is serious enough for the police to officially state that you are guilty of it 可被指控[控告]的

charge ac·count /ˈ· ·,·/ *n* [C] *AmE* an account you have at a shop that allows you to take goods away with you now and pay later; CREDIT ACCOUNT 【美】〔客户购货用的〕信用[赊欠]账户

charge card /ˈ· ·/ *n* [C] a plastic card that you can use to buy goods in a particular shop and pay for them later 〔可赊购货物的〕记账卡, 签账卡

charged /tʃɑrdʒd; tʃɑːdʒd/ *adj* a charged situation or subject makes people feel very angry, anxious, or excited, and is likely to cause arguments or violence 引起强烈感情的; 〔气氛〕紧张的: **highly charged** *a highly charged press conference* 一个气氛紧张的记者招待会

char·gé d'af·faires /ʃɑrˈʒe dæˈfɛr; ˌʃɑːʒeɪ dæˈfeə/ *n* [C] *French* an official who represents their government during the absence of an AMBASSADOR or in a country where there is no ambassador 【法】代办〔代理大使职务的外交代表〕

charge hand /ˈ· ·/ *n* [C] *BrE* a worker in charge of other workers whose position is below that of a FOREMAN (1) 【英】副领班, 副监工

charge nurse /ˈ· ·/ *n* [C] a nurse in charge of one part of a hospital 护士长; 责任护士

Charge of the Light Bri·gade, the /ˌ· · · ·ˈ· ·/ an unsuccessful attack made by the British CAVALRY (=soldiers riding horses) during the Crimean War. Many British soldiers were killed because they were ordered to ride into a valley which was full of Russian soldiers with heavy guns. Tennyson describes this battle in his poem *The Charge of the Light Brigade* 轻骑旅的冲锋〔克里米亚战争期间英国轻骑兵的一次进攻。许多英军骑兵受命进入一个俄军重炮把守的山谷, 结果送了命, 进攻失败。丁尼生的诗歌《轻骑旅的冲锋》对此有所描述〕

charg·er /ˈtʃɑrdʒɚ; ˈtʃɑːdʒə/ *n* [C] **1** a piece of equipment used to put electricity into a BATTERY (1) 充电器 **2** *literary* a horse that a soldier or KNIGHT rides in battle 【文】战马, 军马

charge sheet /ˈ· ·/ *n* [C] a record kept in a police station of the names of people the police have stated are guilty of a particular crime 〔警察局中的〕案件记录; 被起诉者名簿

Char·ing Cross /ˌtʃærɪŋ ˈkrɑs; ˌtʃærɪŋ ˈkrɒs◂/ one of the main railway stations in London, which has trains going to southern England 查灵·克罗斯火车站〔伦敦主要的火车站之一, 发出的列车开往英格兰南部地区〕

Charing Cross Road /ˌ· · · ˈ·/ a street in central London, famous for its bookshops 查灵·克罗斯街〔伦敦市中心一街道, 以书店出名〕

char·i·ot /ˈtʃærɪət; ˈtʃæriət/ *n* [C] a vehicle with two wheels pulled by a horse, used in ancient times in battles and races 〔古时用于战争或比赛的双轮〕马车; 战车

char·i·o·teer /ˌtʃærɪəˈtɪr; ˌtʃæriəˈtɪə/ *n* [C] the driver of a chariot 马车夫; 双轮战车驾御者

cha·ris·ma /kəˈrɪzmə; kəˈrɪzmə/ *n* [U] a powerful attractive personal quality that has a strong influence over other people and makes them admire you 个人魅力; 超凡气质: *Few Presidents have had the charisma of Kennedy.* 没有几个总统像肯尼迪那样拥有非凡的个人魅力。

char·is·mat·ic /ˌkærɪzˈmætɪk; ˌkærɪ̣zˈmætɪk◂/ *adj* **1** able to attract and influence other people because of a powerful personal quality you have 有吸引力的; 有感召力的; 有魅力的: *Martin Luther King was a very charismatic speaker.* 马丁·路德·金是个很有感召力的演说家。**2 charismatic church/movement** groups of Christians who believe that God can give them special powers, for example the power to cure illness 〔自认为得到神授的特殊能力的〕神授能力基督教派/运动

char·i·ta·ble /ˈtʃærətəbl; ˈtʃærɪ̣təbəl/ *adj* **1** kind and sympathetic in the way you judge people 仁慈的; 宽容的; 具有同情心的: *Let's be charitable and say he didn't know the car was stolen.* 我们宽容点吧, 就当他不知道车已被偷了。—opposite 反义词 UNCHARITABLE **2** concerned with giving help to the poor 慈善的: *a charitable institution* 慈善机构 **—charitably** *adv*

char·i·ty /ˈtʃærətɪ; ˈtʃærɪ̣ti/ *n* **1** [U] money or gifts given to help people who are poor, sick etc 救济(金), 施舍(物): *All the money raised by the concert will go to charity.* 演奏会所得的收入将全部用作善款。| *refugees living on charity* 靠救济过活的难民 **2** [C] an organization that collects money or goods in order to help people who are poor, sick etc 慈善机构, 慈善团体: *Several charities sent aid to the flood victims.* 好几个慈善机构已向水灾灾民给予了援助。| **charity event/walk/concert etc** (=an event organized to collect money for a charity) 为慈善事业筹款的活动/步行/演唱会等 **3** [U] a kind sympathetic attitude you have when judging or criticizing someone 宽容, 宽厚, 宽大: **show charity** *The newspaper stories reporting his suicide showed little charity.* 报纸对他自杀的报道显得很不宽容。**4 charity begins at home** you should help your own family, country etc before you help other people 慈善始于家庭, 施舍先及亲友 [2] [3]

Charity Com·mis·sion, the /ˈ··· ·,·/ a British organization that keeps records of any organization that has been officially recognized as a CHARITY and controls the way that charities are operated 慈善事业委员会〔英国一组织, 保存有正式认可的慈善机构的记录, 同时对其运作实施管理〕

charity shop /ˈ··· ·/ *n* [C] *BrE* a shop that sells things given by people in order to collect money for a charity【英】〔以销售义捐商品来募集善款的〕慈善商店

char·la·dy /ˈtʃɑr,ledɪ; ˈtʃɑː,leɪdi/ *n* [C] *BrE old-fashioned* a CHARWOMAN【英, 过时】〔打扫房子、办公室、大厦的〕清洁女工

char·la·tan /ˈʃɑrlətn; ˈʃɑːlətən/ *n* [C] someone who pretends to have special skills or knowledge 假充内行的骗子: *The man's a complete charlatan, only in it for the money.* 那个人是个彻头彻尾的大骗子, 这么做纯粹为了钱。

Char·le·magne /ˈʃɑrləmen; ˈʃɑːləmeɪn/ (742-814) the King of the Franks, who gained control of most of western Europe in 800 by uniting its Christian countries. The Pope gave him the title of 'Holy Roman Emperor'. Charlemagne had a great influence on European CIVILIZATION by establishing a new legal system and encouraging art, literature, and education. 查理曼〔(742-814), 法兰克国王。公元800年, 他统一了基督教国家, 控制了西欧大部分土地, 被教皇封为"神圣罗马帝国皇帝"。他建立了新的法律体系, 支持艺术、文学和教育, 从而对欧洲文明产生了重大影响〕

Charles /tʃɑrlz; tʃɑːlz/, **Prince** (1948-) the first son of the British queen, Elizabeth II, who is expected to become the next British king. His official royal title is the Prince of Wales. 查尔斯王子〔(1948-), 英国女王伊丽莎白二世的长子, 英国王位的继承人, 王室封号为威尔士亲王〕

Charles I /,tʃɑrlz ðə ˋfɜst; ,tʃɑːlz ðə ˈfɜːst/, **King** (1600-49) the king of England, Scotland, and Ireland from 1625 to 1649. He often disagreed with Parliament and made many unpopular political decisions, and so helped to cause the English Civil War. As a result he was executed in 1649. 查理一世〔(1600-1649), 英格兰、苏格兰及爱尔兰国王。他1625至1649年在位, 常与议会意见相左, 曾作出许多不受欢迎的政治决策, 由此引发英国内战, 结果于1649年被处以极刑〕

Charles II /,tʃɑrlz ðə ˈsɛkənd; ,tʃɑːlz ðə ˈsekənd/, **King** (1630-85) the king of England, Scotland, and Ireland who was the son of Charles I. He officially became king after his father's death in 1649, but he did not return to England to rule until the end of the English Civil War in 1660. He is sometimes called 'the Merry Monarch' 查理二世〔(1630-1685), 英格兰、苏格兰及爱尔兰国王, 查理一世之子。1649年其父死后, 他正式登基, 但直到1660年英国内战结束后才返回英格兰施政。人们有时称他为"风流君主"〕—see also 另见 RESTORATION

Charleston /ˈtʃɑrlstn; ˈtʃɑːlstən/ **1** the capital city of the US state of West Virginia 查尔斯顿〔美国西弗吉尼亚州首府〕**2 the Charleston** a quick dance, popular in the 1920s 查尔斯顿舞〔20世纪20年代流行的一种快步舞〕

char·ley horse /,tʃɑrlɪ ˋhɔrs; ,tʃɑːli ˈhɔːs/ *n* [C singular] *AmE informal* a pain in a large muscle, for example in your leg, caused by the muscle becoming tight; CRAMP[1] (1)【美, 非正式】肌肉痉挛, 抽筋

Char·ley's Aunt /,tʃɑrlɪz ˋænt; ,tʃɑːliz ˈɑːnt/ a popular FARCE (=silly humorous play) by Brandon Thomas (1856-1914) about a man who dresses up as an old lady and pretends to be his friend's aunt《查利的姑妈》〔布兰登·托马斯(1856-1914)创作的一部受人喜爱的闹剧。剧中一名男子装扮成老太太, 冒充他朋友的姑妈〕

char·lie /ˈtʃɑrlɪ; ˈtʃɑːli/ *n* [C] *BrE spoken* a stupid person【英口】笨蛋, 蠢人: **feel a right/proper charlie** (=feel very stupid) 觉得自己很蠢

Charlie Brown /,·· ˈ·/ —see 见 Charlie BROWN

charm[1] /tʃɑrm; tʃɑːm/ *n* **1** [C,U] a pleasant quality someone or something has that makes people like them, feel attracted to them, or be easily influenced by them 魅力, 魔力, 吸引力; 可爱之处: *Dick still has a certain boyish charm.* 迪克仍保有一种稚趣。| *the charms of rural life* 乡村生活的魅力 | **turn on the charm** (=use your charm) 施展魅力 *Wait till Grace turns on the charm, you won't be able to resist.* 等到格雷丝向你展现她的魅力时, 你将会无法抗拒。**2** a piece of magic which involves saying special words; SPELL[2] (1) 魔法; 咒语 **3** a very small object worn on a chain or BRACELET that people think will bring them good luck〔装在手链、手镯上表示吉祥的〕小装饰品; 护身符: *a small gold horseshoe worn as a lucky charm* 作为吉祥物的金铸马蹄形挂坠 **4 work like a charm** to work perfectly or immediately 完全[迅速]地奏效: *I don't know what you sprayed on the roses, but it worked like a charm.* 我不知道你给这些玫瑰喷了什么, 但它非常管用!

charm[2] *v* [T] **1** to attract someone and make them like you, especially so that you can easily influence them 迷住, 吸引: *Collette was charmed by the stranger's elegant manners and rugged good looks.* 科利特被这位陌生人优雅的举止和粗犷而英俊的外表深深吸引住。**2** to gain power over someone or something by using magic 向…施魔法, 用魔法控制 **3 have/lead a charmed life** to be lucky all the time, so that although you are often in dangerous situations nothing ever harms you 总是幸运的, 总能逢凶化吉的 —**charmed** *adj*

charm·er /ˈtʃɑrmɚ; ˈtʃɑːmə/ *n* [C] someone who uses their charm to please or influence people 使人着迷的人: *Even at ten years old, he was a real charmer.* 早在10岁时他就是个讨人喜欢的人。—see also 另见 SNAKE CHARMER

charm·ing /ˈtʃɑrmɪŋ; ˈtʃɑːmɪŋ/ *adj* very pleasing or attractive; nice 迷人的, 有魅力的, 有吸引力的: *What a charming house!* 多漂亮的房子啊! | *Harry can be charming when he wants.* 哈里乐意时非常迷人。—**charmingly** *adv*

charm school /ˈ· ·/ *n* [C] *especially AmE* a school where young women were sometimes sent in the past to learn how to behave politely and gracefully【尤美】〔旧时年轻女子就读的〕礼仪学校

char·nel house /ˈtʃɑrnl ,haus; ˈtʃɑːnl haʊs/ *n* [C] *literary* a place where the bodies and bones of dead people are stored【文】存骸所; 骨灰堂; 停尸间

Cha·ron /ˈkɛrən; ˈkeərən/ in Greek MYTHOLOGY, the FERRYMAN who took the souls of dead people in his boat across the river Styx to Hades 卡隆〔希腊神话故事中载运死者亡灵横渡冥河去阴间的艄工〕

charred /tʃɑrd; tʃɑːd/ *adj* burnt black 乌黑的, 黑色的, 焦黑的: *the charred remains of a corpse* 焦黑的尸骸

charts 图表

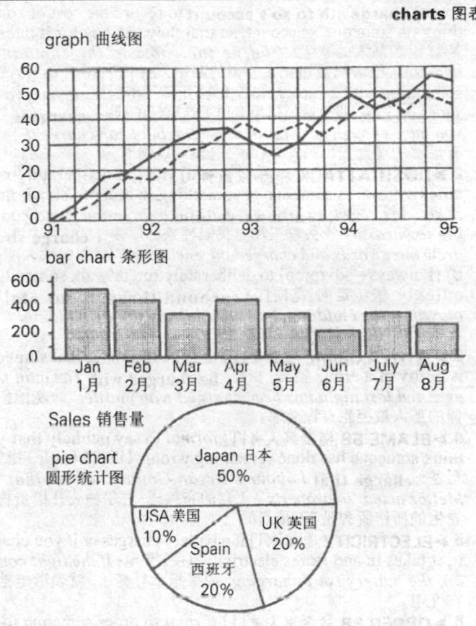

chart[1] /tʃɑrt; tʃɑːt/ *n* [C] **1** information that is clearly arranged in the form of a simple picture, sets of figures, GRAPH etc, or a piece of paper with this information on it 图表, 图: *a flow chart* 流程图 | *a weather chart* 天气图 **2** a detailed map, especially of an area of the sea 地图; 〔尤指〕海图, 航海图 **3 the charts** a list, which comes out weekly, of the most popular records〔流行歌曲每周〕排行榜: **top the charts** *Madonna's song topped the charts for over ten weeks.* 麦当娜的歌曲连续十多周稳居榜首。—see also 另见 BAR CHART, PIE CHART, FLOW CHART

chart[2] *v* [T] **1** to record information about a situation or set of events over a period of time in order to see how it changes or develops 给…制图; 记述: *a study charting the steady progress of women in the 19th century* 记述19世纪妇女稳步发展的一个研究 **2** to make a map of an area of land or sea, or draw lines on a map to show where you have travelled 绘制…的地图[海图]; 把〔途经路线〕绘入地图[海图] —see also 另见 UNCHARTED

3 **char·ter[1]** /ˋtʃɑrtɚ; ˈtʃɑːtə/ *n* **1** [C] a statement of the principles, duties, and purposes of an organization〔组织的〕原则, 章程, 宪章, 宣言: *freedoms embodied in the UN Charter* 联合国宪章所体现的自由 **2** [singular] *BrE informal* a law or official decision that seems to give someone the right to do something most people consider morally wrong【英, 非正式】授予特种权利的法令; 特许状; 特权: *Proposals to cut customs staff amount to little more than a drug-smuggler's charter.* 削减海关人员数量的提议差不多等于给予毒品走私者特权。**3** [C] a signed statement from a government or ruler which allows a town, organization, or university to officially exist and have special rights〔政府或统治者特许城镇、组织或大学存在并享有特权的〕许可证 **4** [U] the practice of paying money to a company to use their boats, aircraft, etc〔船、飞机等的〕包租: *boats available for charter* 可供包租的船

charter[2] *v* [T] **1** to pay for the use of a plane, boat, train etc 包租〔飞机、船、火车等〕: *a chartered plane* 包机 **2** to say officially that a town, organization, or university officially exists and has special rights 特许成立〔城镇、组织或大学〕—see 见 HIRE[1] (1)

chartered ac·coun·tant /ˌ‥ ·ˈ‥/ *n* [C] *BrE* an ACCOUNTANT who has successfully completed special examinations【英】特许会计师; CPA *AmE*【美】

charter flight /ˈ‥ ·/ *n* [C] a low cost journey in a plane on which all the places have been paid for in advance by travel companies for their customers 包机旅行[航班] —compare 比较 **scheduled flight** (SCHEDULE[2])

charter mem·ber /ˌ‥ ˈ‥/ *n* [C] *AmE* an original member of a club or organization【美】〔俱乐部或某组织的〕元老, 创始成员; FOUNDER MEMBER *BrE*【英】

Char·tists, the /ˋtʃɑrtɪsts; ˈtʃɑːtɪsts/ a political group of people that was active in the UK in the 1830s and 1840s. They demanded changes such as giving all men the right to vote and the right to become Members of Parliament. Some of them were sent to prisons in Australia as a punishment. 宪章派〔19 世纪 30、40 年代活跃在英国的一个政治团体。他们要求实行社会变革, 如赋予所有男子选举权和担任议员的权利。其中的一些人最后遭到惩处, 被遣送到了澳大利亚〕

char·treuse /ʃɑrˋtruz; ʃɑːˈtrɜːz/ *n* [U] **1** a strong green or yellow alcoholic drink 沙特勒兹酒, 荨麻酒〔一种呈绿色或黄色的烈性酒〕 **2** a bright green colour 黄绿色

chart-top·ping /ˈ· ˌ‥/ *adj* **chart-topping record/group/hit etc** a record, group etc that has sold the most records in a particular week〔某周内〕高居榜首的唱片/乐队/歌曲等

char·wom·an /ˋtʃɑrˌwʊmən; ˈtʃɑːˌwʊmən/ *n* [C] *BrE old-fashioned* a woman who works as a cleaner, especially in someone's house【英, 过时】〔尤指打扫住宅的〕清洁女工

char·y /ˋtʃɛrɪ; ˈtʃeəri/ *adj* **be chary of doing sth** to be unwilling to risk doing something 小心的, 谨慎的: *Many census authorities have been chary of asking for information on sensitive subjects such as ethnic background.* 许多人口普查机构在问及诸如种族背景等敏感问题时, 都十分谨慎。

Cha·ryb·dis /kəˋrɪbdɪs; kəˈrɪbdɪs/ —see 见 SCYLLA AND CHARYBDIS

3 **chase[1]** /tʃes; tʃeɪs/ *v*

1 ▶FOLLOW 跟随◀ [I,T] to quickly follow someone or something in order to catch them 追逐, 追赶; 追捕: *Outside in the yard, kids were yelling and chasing each other.* 外面院子里, 孩子们叫喊着在互相追逐。| **chase sb along/down/up etc** *The dog spotted a cat and chased it up a nearby tree.* 狗发现了一只猫并把它赶到了附近的一棵树上。| **chase sb away/off** (=chase someone in order to make them leave) 赶走, 驱逐 *Harry chased the boys off with a stick.* 哈里用一根棍子把男孩子们赶了出去。| [+after] *A favorite game was to chase after a passing farm cart and try to grab its tailboard.* 追逐路过的农用车并设法抓住其尾板是人们喜欢的一项游戏。

2 ▶HURRY 赶快◀ [I always+adv/prep] *especially BrE* to rush or hurry somewhere【尤英】急忙赶往: **around/up/down etc** *Mum's been chasing round the shops all day.* 妈妈整天忙于在商场购物。

3 ▶TRY TO GET STH 试图得到某物◀ [I+after, T] to use a lot of time and effort trying to get something such as work or money 努力赢得, 设法获得: *The solicitor's doing everything she can to chase the contract.* 那个律师正尽全力要争取到这份合同。

4 ▶MAN/WOMAN 男人/女人◀ [T] to try hard to make someone notice you and pay attention to you, because you want to have a sexual relationship with them 追求, 求爱: *It was embarrassing – Louise spent the entire party chasing me.* 整个宴会期间路易斯都在追求我, 真是令人尴尬。

5 ▶METAL 金属◀ [T] *technical* to decorate metal with a special tool【术语】镂刻, 雕镂〔金属制品〕: *chased silver* 雕镂银器

6 chase the dragon *slang* to smoke the drug HEROIN【俚】吸食海洛因

chase sb/sth ↔ **up** *phr v* [T] **1** to remind someone to do something they promised to do for you 提醒某人〔实践诺言〕: *I had to chase Dick up to get those reports I asked for last week.* 我得去提醒迪克, 要他去拿我上个星期问他要的那些报告。**2** to try to make something happen or arrive more quickly, because it has been taking too long 加速…的发生进程, 催促: *Can you chase up those photos for me by tomorrow?* 你明天能把这些照片赶洗出来吗?

chase[2] *n* **1** [C] the act of following someone or something quickly in order to catch them 追逐, 追赶; 追捕: *The movie began with a dramatic car chase.* 影片是以一场激烈的汽车追逐开始的。**2 give chase** *literary* to chase someone or something【文】追逐〔某人或某物〕: *The hounds gave chase across the fields.* 猎狗追逐着穿过田野。—see also 另见 PAPER CHASE, WILD-GOOSE CHASE

chas·er /ˋtʃesɚ; ˈtʃeɪsə/ *n* [C] a weaker alcoholic drink which is drunk after a strong one, or a stronger alcoholic drink which is drunk after a weak one 饮烈酒后喝的淡酒; 饮淡酒后喝的烈酒: *a pint of bitter and a whisky chaser* 一品脱苦啤酒后再来点威士忌

chas·m /ˋkæzəm; ˈkæzəm/ *n* **1** [C] a very deep space between two high areas of rock, especially one that is dangerous〔尤指危险的〕裂隙, 深坑, 深渊, 峡谷: *a rope bridge across the chasm* 峡谷上的绳索吊桥 **2** [singular] a big difference between the opinions, experience, ways of life, etc of different groups of people, especially when this means they cannot understand each other〔不同的人在观点、经历、生活方式等方面无法相互理解的〕巨大差距, 分歧: *the chasm between rich and poor* 穷人和富人之间的鸿沟

chas·sis /ˋʃæsɪ; ˈʃæsi/ *n plural* **chassis** /ˋʃæsis; ˈʃæsiːz/ [C] **1** the frame on which the body, engine, wheels etc of a vehicle are built〔汽车的〕底盘; 车架 **2** the landing equipment of a plane〔飞机的〕机架; 起落架

chaste /tʃest; tʃeɪst/ *adj* **1** *old-fashioned* having very high personal moral standards in your sexual behaviour【过时】纯洁的, 贞洁的; 正派的: *Wives are expected to remain chaste, whatever their husbands' behaviour.* 不管丈夫做出了什么行为, 妻子都被要求保持贞节。—compare 比较 CELIBATE —see also 另见 CHASTITY **2** simple and plain in style〔风格〕简单明了的 —**chastely** *adv*

chas·ten /ˋtʃesn̩; ˈtʃeɪsən/ *v* [T usually passive 一般用被动态] to make someone realize that their behaviour is wrong or mistaken 惩戒, 责罚; 磨炼〔某人〕: *Party workers have returned to their home towns, chastened by their overwhelming defeat.* 受到重创后, 这些党的工作者返回了自己的家乡。

chas·tise /tʃæsˋtaɪz; tʃæˈstaɪz/ *v* [T] **1** *formal* to criticize someone severely【正式】严厉谴责, 指责, 责备: *He should be chastised for his insolence.* 他傲慢无礼, 应该受到指责。**2** *old-fashioned* to physically punish someone【过时】体罚 —**chastisement** *n* [C,U]

chas·ti·ty /ˋtʃæstətɪ; ˈtʃæstɪti/ *n* [U] the principle or way of behaving in which you do not behave in a way that is sexually immoral, especially for religious reasons 贞洁, 贞节, 贞操

chastity belt /ˈ‥ˌ ·/ *n* [C] a special belt with a lock, used in former times to prevent women from having sex〔旧时防止妇女私通用的〕贞操带

chat[1] /tʃæt; tʃæt/ *n* [C,U] *especially BrE* an informal friendly conversation【尤英】闲谈, 聊天: *Drop in for a chat if you have an hour to spare this evening.* 如果今晚能抽出一小时的话, 到我家里来聊聊天吧! | **have a chat** *We had a chat about the old days.* 我们聊了聊过去的时光。—see also 另见 BACKCHAT 2

chat[2] **chatted, chatting** *v* [I] *especially BrE* also 又作 **chat away** to talk in a friendly informal way, especially about things that are not important【尤英】闲谈, 聊天: *Danny and Paul chatted away like old friends.* 丹尼和保罗像老朋友似的在聊天。| [+about] *We sat in the café for hours chatting about our experiences.* 我们在咖啡室里坐了几个小时, 大谈各自的经历。| [+with/to] *Helen chatted with most of the guests at the party.* 海伦在晚会上跟大多数客人都攀谈了。

chat sb ↔ **up** *phr v* [T] *BrE* to talk to someone in a way that shows you are sexually attracted to them【英】与…搭讪, 与…调情: *We found Doug in the bar trying to chat up a waitress.* 我们看见道格在酒吧里想要和女侍者搭讪。

chat·eau /ʃæˋto; ˈʃætəʊ/ *n plural* **chateaux** /-toz; -təʊz/ or **chateaus** [C] a castle or large country house in France〔法国的〕城堡; 乡间大别墅; 庄园

chat·e·laine /ˈʃætḷ,en; ˈʃætl-eɪn/ *n* [C] **1** *formal* the female owner, or wife of the owner, of a large country house or castle in France【正式】〔法国的〕乡间别墅[城堡]女主人 **2** a short thin chain fastened to a woman's belt, used in the past for carrying keys〔旧时女子系在腰带上用以悬挂钥匙的〕钥匙链

chat line /ˈ· ·/ *n* [C] *BrE* a telephone service that people call to talk to other people who have called the same service【英】聊天热线〔一种电信服务，打电话到该热线的人互相之间可以进行通话〕

chat show /ˈ· ·/ *n* [C] *BrE* a television or radio show on which people are asked questions and talk about themselves【英】〔电视或电台的〕清谈节目; TALK SHOW *AmE*【美】

chat show host /ˈ· · ,·/ *n BrE* the person who introduces people and asks questions on a chat show【英】访谈节目主持人，清谈节目主持人

Chattanooga /ˌtʃætəˈnugə; ˌtʃætəˈnuːgə/ an industrial city in southeast Tennessee in the US. It was the scene of FIERCE fighting during the American Civil War. 查塔努加〔美国田纳西州东南部一工业城市。美国内战期间此地曾发生过激战〕

chat·tel /ˈtʃætl; ˈtʃætl/ *n* [C] *law old-fashioned* something that belongs to you【法律，过时】动产；私人财产: *In those days women and children were considered chattels.* 在那个时代，妇女和儿童被视为个人财产。—see also 另见 GOODS AND CHATTELS

chat·ter¹ /ˈtʃætɚ; ˈtʃætə/ *v* [I] **1** to talk quickly in a friendly way without stopping, especially about things that are not serious or important 唠叨，喋喋不休: [+to] *You've been chattering to Tom on the phone for ages.* 你在电话上和汤姆唠叨很久了。**2** if birds or monkeys chatter, they make short high sounds〔鸟类或猴子的〕鸣叫；啁啾；吱吱叫 **3** if your teeth are chattering, you are so cold or frightened your teeth are knocking together and you cannot stop them〔因寒冷或恐惧而使牙齿〕打颤；咯咯作响 **4 the chattering classes** *BrE* those people in society who are keen to discuss and have opinions about important or fashionable ideas, subjects, and events【英】整天发表议论的人；爱好评论的人

chatter² *n* [U] **1** a friendly informal conversation about something unimportant 聊天，闲谈；唠叨 **2** a series of short high sounds made by some birds or monkeys〔鸟类或猴子的〕鸣叫声；啾啾叫声；吱吱的叫声 **3** a hard quick repeated sound made by your teeth knocking together or by machines〔牙齿打颤的〕咯咯声；〔机器的〕震颤声: *the chatter of the printer* 打印机发出的吱吱声

chat·ter·box /ˈtʃætɚ,bɑks; ˈtʃætəbɒks/ *n* [C] *informal* someone, especially a child, who talks too much【非正式】喋喋不休的人，话匣子〔尤指小孩〕

Chat·ter·ley /ˈtʃætɚlɪ; ˈtʃætəli/, **Lady** —see 见 LADY CHATTERLEY'S LOVER

chat·ty /ˈtʃætɪ; ˈtʃæti/ *adj especially BrE*【尤英】**1** liking to talk a lot in a friendly way 爱闲聊的，爱说话的，健谈的: *Lorna's normally very quiet, but she was quite chatty yesterday.* 洛娜平时话不多，但昨天却非常健谈。**2** a piece of writing that is chatty has a friendly informal style〔文章〕很随意的，闲谈式的: *a chatty letter* 一封聊天式的信

chat-up line /ˈ· · ,·/ *n* [C] *BrE* something that someone says in order to start a conversation with someone they find sexually attractive【英】挑逗的话，轻佻的话，搭讪的话; LINE¹ (23) *AmE*【美】

Chau·cer /ˈtʃɔsɚ; ˈtʃɔːsə/, **Geof·frey** /ˈdʒɛfrɪ; ˈdʒefri/ (?1340-1400) an English writer who wrote the long poem *The Canterbury Tales*, one of the most important works in English literature. It is about a group of PILGRIMs travelling to Canterbury, who tell each other stories. 乔叟〔(?1340-1400)，英国作家。他的长诗《坎特伯雷故事集》是最重要的英国文学作品之一。诗中有一群朝圣者前往坎特伯雷，他们轮流讲述故事〕

chauf·feur¹ /ˈʃofɚ; ˈʃəʊfə/ *n* [C] someone whose job is to drive a car for someone else〔受雇为他人开车的〕司机

chauffeur² *v* [T] **1** to drive a car for someone as your job 专职为…开汽车 **2** also 又作 **chauffeur around** to drive someone in your car, especially when you do not want to〔尤指非情愿地〕开车载〔某人〕到处去: *I seem to spend most of Saturday chauffeuring the kids around.* 我似乎星期六大都要开车带孩子们到处去转转。

chauf·feuse /ʃoˈfɚz; ʃəʊˈfɜːz/ *n* [C] a woman whose job is to drive a car for someone else〔受雇为他人开车的〕女司机

Chau·tau·qua /ʃəˈtɔkwə; ʃəˈtɔːkwə/ a place in the US state of New York where many people go to enjoy special arts events during the summer, including musical performances and plays 肖托夸〔位于美国纽约州，是人们夏季欣赏音乐、戏剧表演等专项艺术活动的去处〕

chau·vin·is·m /ˈʃovɪn,ɪzəm; ˈʃəʊvḭnɪzəm/ *n* [U] **1** a strong belief that your country is better or more important than any other 盲目的爱国主义，沙文主义，本国至上主义: *cultural chauvinism* 文化沙文主义 **2** the attitude that your own sex is better, more intelligent, or more important than the other sex, especially the male sex 大男[女]子主义，男性[女性]至上主义: **male chauvinism** *The club is a bastion of male chauvinism.* 该俱乐部是捍卫大男子主义的堡垒。

chau·vin·ist /ˈʃovɪnɪst; ˈʃəʊvḭnḭst/ *n* [C] **1** someone, especially a man, who believes that their own sex is better and more important than the other sex 本性别至上主义者〔尤指大男子主义者〕: **male chauvinist (pig)** *My boss is a male chauvinist who thinks no woman could do his job.* 我的老板是个大男子主义者，他认为没有女人能胜任他的工作。**2** someone who believes that their own country is better or more important than any other country 盲目爱国者；沙文主义者 —**chauvinist** *adj*

chau·vi·nis·tic /ˌʃovɪˈnɪstɪk; ˌʃəʊvḭˈnɪstɪk◂/ *adj* **1** having the belief that your own country is better or more important than any other country 盲目爱国的，沙文主义的: *a chauvinistic dislike of all things foreign* 盲目爱国而排斥一切舶来品 **2** having the attitude that your own sex is better or more important than the other sex, especially that men are more important than women 本性别至上主义的〔尤指大男子主义的〕—**chauvinistically** /-klɪ; -kli/ *adv*

Chá·vez /ˈtʃɑvɛz; ˈtʃɑːvez/, **Ce·sar** /seˈzɑr; seɪˈzɑː/ (1927-93) a Mexican-American who was the president of the United Farm Workers of America from 1966 to 1993. He helped poor workers win better wages and protection against the use of harmful chemicals to grow food. 查维斯〔(1927-1993)，墨西哥裔美国人。1966至1993年间，他曾任美国农场工人联合会主席，帮助贫苦工人提高工资，反对使用有害化学品种植作物〕

cheap¹ /tʃip; tʃiːp/ *adj*

1 ▶PRICE 价格◀ not at all expensive, or lower in price than you expected 便宜的，不贵的，廉价的: *You're just not going to find a cheap leather coat* 你是买不到便宜的皮衣的。| *the cheapest TV on the market* 市场上最便宜的电视 | **dirt cheap** (=extremely low in price) 极廉价的，极便宜的 *These CDs are dirt cheap.* 这些激光唱片便宜极了。—see 见 ECONOMIC (USAGE)

2 ▶CHARGING LESS 要价较少的◀ charging a low price 要价低的: *Which store do you suppose is cheaper?* 你认为哪家店的东西较便宜？| *As taxi companies go, they're quite cheap.* 就出租车公司而言，他们算是便宜的。| **cheap and cheerful** *BrE* (=simple and charging a low price, but pleasant)【英】价廉物美的 *a cheap and cheerful bistro, popular with students* 一家很受学生欢迎的，既便宜又舒适的小餐馆

3 ▶BAD QUALITY 劣质的◀ low in price and quality, or not worth much 价廉质劣的；无价值的，不值钱的: *Cheap wine gives me a headache.* 喝了低价劣质的酒，我头会痛。| *You don't think these earrings look too cheap?* 你难道不觉得这副耳环很低俗吗？| **cheap and nasty** *BrE* (=very low in price and quality)【英】低价劣质的 *cheap and nasty T-shirts* 价廉质差的T恤

4 ▶CHEAP TO USE 花费低的◀ not costing much to use or to employ 便宜的，价格低的: *I'll have to have a cheaper car, this one uses too much gas.* 我只能买一辆较便宜的车，这辆车太耗油了。| **cheap labour** *multinational clothing companies exploiting cheap child labour in Bangladesh* 在孟加拉剥削廉价童工的跨国制衣公司

5 ▶NOT DESERVING RESPECT 不值得尊敬◀ showing a lack of honesty, moral principles, or sincere feelings, and therefore difficult to respect 不值得尊敬的，卑鄙的，可耻的: *It makes me feel cheap, but I can't face seeing Mother.* 这让我觉得可耻，但我无法面对教母。| **(just) some cheap sth** *He acts like I'm just some cheap little bimbo.* 他表现得就像我只是个下贱的坏女人。| *This is not some cheap pastime! This is art!* 这不是粗鄙的娱乐消遣！这是艺术！| **cheap thrill** (=excitement that you do not have to work hard for or pay for) 容易得来的[粗鄙的]刺激 *Glue-sniffing is a cheap thrill, and a trend among some schoolchildren.* 吸胶毒简单刺激，在学童中间甚为流行。| **cheap remark/joke etc** (=one that attacks people who cannot defend themselves) 低级的评论/玩笑

6 ▶NOT GENEROUS 不大方的◀ *AmE* not liking to spend money【美】小气的，吝啬的; MEAN² (2) *BrE*【英】: *Frank's so cheap that he reuses Christmas wrapping paper.* 弗兰克真吝啬，他竟使用用过的圣诞礼物包装纸。

7 on the cheap spending less money than is needed to do something properly 没有付足钱的，便宜的，廉价的: *I'm not surprised the roof is leaking – the landlord does everything on the cheap.* 屋顶漏水我一点也不奇怪——房东做什么都贪图便宜。

8 cheap at the price/at any price of such high value, or so good or useful, that the cost is not important 无论价格多么高都值得

9 life is cheap used to say that it is not important if people die 某人的死无足轻重: *Everyone carried a gun or knife during the war, and life was cheap.* 打仗时所有人都持枪带刀的, 生命简直不值钱。—**cheaply** *adv*: *a cheaply furnished room* 一个配置廉价家具的房间 —**cheapness** *n* [U]

USAGE NOTE 用法说明: CHEAP

WORD CHOICE 词语辨析: **cheap, low-priced, inexpensive, not cost a lot, reasonable, good value, a good buy, a bargain, a steal, a snip, low**

Saying that something is **cheap** often suggests it is also bad in quality. 如说某物 cheap, 往往也暗示其质量不高: *Buying cheap shoes is not a good idea in the long run.* 从长远看, 买便宜质劣的鞋是不划算的。| *That necklace looks really cheap and nasty.* 那条项链看起来真是既便宜又难看。**Low-priced** and **inexpensive** do not suggest this, but are not so common in informal spoken English. low-priced 和 inexpensive 则无此含义, 但在非正式口语中不那么常用: *The university needs more low-priced accommodation.* 这所大学需要更多便宜些的住宿设施。In everyday English people often just say that something **doesn't cost a lot/much**. 在日常英语中, 人们说某东西不值钱, 用 doesn't cost a lot/much。

If you want to say that something is good and does not cost as much as it might, you say it is **reasonable, good value**, or **a good buy** 如果你想说一件东西质量好而价格又不高, 你可以说它是 reasonable, good value 或 a good buy: *$200 for a leather jacket seems pretty reasonable to me.* 对我来说, 200 美元买件皮夹克, 不算贵。

If something is **a bargain** it cost very much less than you expected to pay. In informal conversation people often say instead that something is **a steal** (American English) or **a snip** (British English). 如果一件东西是 a bargain, 那就是说它的价格比你预期的要低得多。在非正式谈话中, 人们往往以 a steal〔美国英语〕或 a snip〔英国英语〕代替 a bargain。

The cost of something, a bill, someone's salary etc can be **low** or **reasonable** but not **cheap**. 某物的成本、账单或工资薪水等只能用 low 或 reasonable, 但不能说 cheap。

cheap² *adv* at a low price 便宜地, 廉价地: *Sharon has some really nice furniture she picked up cheap in a sale.* 莎伦在一次大减价时低价买了些很好的家具。| *They're selling linen off cheap in Lewis's.* 刘易斯的店在削价卖掉日用织品。| **sth does not come cheap** (=something is expensive) 某物不便宜 *Houses like that don't come cheap.* 那样的房子是很贵的。| **(be) going cheap** (=selling for a lower price than usual) 降低价格, 廉价出售 *Ask if they've got any flights going cheap.* 去问问他们有没有降价的航班。

cheap·en /ˈtʃipən; ˈtʃiːpən/ *v* **1** [T] to make something or someone seem to have lower moral standards than they had before 降低身份, 贬低: **cheapen yourself by doing sth** *Don't cheapen yourself by accepting their bribe.* 不要因为接受他们的贿赂而降低了自己的身份。**2** [I,T] to become or make something become lower in price or value (使) 减价, (使) 降价: *The dollar's increase in value has cheapened imports.* 美元增值使进口商品便宜了。

cheap·skate /ˈtʃipˌsket; ˈtʃiːpskeɪt/ *n* [C] *informal* someone who does not like spending money and does not care if they behave in an unreasonable way to avoid spending it【非正式】小气鬼, 守财奴, 吝啬鬼: *The cheapskate didn't even offer to pay for the cab.* 这个小气鬼竟然连出租车费都不肯付。

cheat¹ /tʃit; tʃiːt/ *v* **1** [I] to behave in a dishonest way in order to win or to get an advantage, especially in a competition, game, or examination〔尤指在竞赛、游戏或考试中〕欺骗; 作弊: *You're doing it again, you're trying to cheat!* 你又来这一套了, 又想骗人! | **[+at]** *Jack always cheats at cards.* 杰克玩纸牌时总是作弊。| **that's cheating** *Hey, don't look at the next page – that's cheating!* 嘿, 别看下一页 —— 那是作弊! **2** [T] to trick or deceive someone who trusts you 骗取: *Don't just jump to conclusions that you've been deliberately cheated.* 不要这么快就下结论, 说你一直被人故意欺骗。| **cheat sb (out) of sth** *Guy figures he was cheated out of that job by office politics.* 盖伊估计自己是因为办公室的尔虞我诈而丢了那份工作的。**3 feel cheated** to feel that you have been treated wrongly or unfairly and have not got what you deserve 感觉不公平, 被骗: *I feel cheated really. I was meant to go to France and now it's only Leeds.* 我真的感到被骗了, 本来我该去法国的, 结果只去了利兹。**4 cheat death/fate etc** to manage to avoid death etc even though it seemed that you would not be able to 逃避[逃脱]死亡/命运等

cheat on sb *phr v* [T] to be unfaithful to your husband, wife, or sexual partner by secretly having sex with someone else 对〔配偶或性伴侣〕不忠: *I think Winnie's been cheating on me, but I can't prove it.* 我认为温妮一直对我不忠, 但我却无法证实。

cheat² *n* [C] **1** someone who is dishonest and cheats 骗子; 作弊者: *I saw you look at that card, you cheat!* 我看见你偷看了那张牌, 你这个骗子! **2 a cheat** something that is dishonest or unfair 作弊, 欺骗行为; 不公平的事: *That's a cheat! The box is half empty!* 这是个骗局! 这个盒子是半空的!

Chech·nya /ˈtʃɛtʃnjə; ˈtʃetʃnjə/ officially called the Republic of Chechnya. It is situated in the N part of the Caucasus Mountains in Russia. It is one of the districts in the Russian Federation. It borders Georgia in the south. It has an area less than 20,000 km². Population: about 450,000. Capital: Grozny. The people are mostly Muslim. 车臣〔全称车臣共和国, 位于俄罗斯高加索山脉北侧, 为俄联邦主体之一, 南与格鲁吉亚接壤。面积不足 20,000 平方公里, 人口约 450,000。首府: 格罗兹尼。居民大都为穆斯林〕—**Chechen** /ˈtʃɛtʃən; ˈtʃetʃən/ *n, adj*

check¹ /tʃɛk; tʃek/ *v*

1 ►FIND OUT 发现◄ [I,T] to do something in order to find out whether something that you think is correct, true, or safe really is correct, true, or safe 检查, 核对, 查验: *"Are all the windows shut?" "I'll just go and check."* "所有的窗户都关上了吗?" "我去检查一下。" | **check sth** *I'll check my calendar and get back to you.* 我要查查我的日程安排, 然后再答复你。| **[+that]** *They're entitled to check that the will is valid, of course.* 当然, 他们有权去验证那份遗嘱是否有效。| **[+whether/how/who etc]** *Let me just check whether the potatoes are cooked.* 我去看看马铃薯煮好了没有。| **[+for]** *Have these cables been checked for faults?* 有没有对这些电缆进行过故障检查? | **check sth against/with sth** (=compare something with something else to see whether they are the same) 与…相比较 *Upon delivery, the items are checked against the original order.* 送货时, 所有的货物都要对照原订单检查一遍。| **double check** (=look at something twice to be sure about something) 再次检查以确定 *Double check all the spellings, especially of people's names.* 再检查一遍拼写, 尤其是人名的拼写。

2 ►ASK SB 询问某人◄ [I] to ask someone for permission to do something or ask whether something is correct 询问; 征求同意; 核实: *I'm not authorized to give you a refund – I'll have to check first.* 我无权给你退款 —— 我必须先征得同意才行。| **[+that]** *We'd better check that these are the right pills.* 我们最好询问一下, 看看这些药丸是不是对的。| **[+whether/how/who etc]** *Let's stop and check whether this is the right road.* 停一下, 看看是否走对了路线。| **check with sb** *It's wise to check with your doctor before going on a diet.* 在节食之前先咨询一下医生是明智之举。

3 ►NOT DO STH 不做某事◄ [T] to suddenly stop yourself from saying or doing something because you realize it would be better not to 克制〔自己〕; 停止[阻止]〔自己〕做〔某事〕: *Susan quickly turned aside, checking an urge to laugh out loud.* 苏珊很快转过脸去, 努力憋着不笑出声来。| **check yourself** *"You shouldn't have..." he checked himself, trying to stay calm.* "你不应该…"他停下来, 努力保持平静。

4 ►STOP STH 停止某事◄ [T] to stop something bad from getting worse or continuing to happen etc 阻碍, 制止; 抑制: *Speed bumps will be installed to check the neighborhood traffic.* 将在路上安装汽车减速墩以控制附近的交通状况。

5 ►MAKE A MARK 作标记◄ [T] *AmE* to make a mark (√) next to an answer, something on a list etc to show that it is correct or that you have dealt with it【美】给〔答案、清单的项目等〕打勾号; TICK² (2) *BrE*【英】

6 ►BAGS/CASES ETC 袋子/箱子等◄ [T] *AmE* to leave your bags etc at an official place so they can be put on a plane or a train, or to take someone's bags in order to do this【美】托运〔行李〕; 接受托运〔行李〕: *Any luggage over 5 kilos must be checked.* 行李超过五公斤就必须托运。

check in *phr v* **1** [I,T **check** sb **in**] to go to the desk at a hotel or airport and report that you have arrived〔在旅馆〕登记办理入住手续;〔在机场〕办理登机手续: *You need to check in one hour before the flight.* 你必须在飞机起飞前一小时办理登机手续。| **check in at** *Let's check in at the hotel before we get something to eat.* 我们吃东西前先去旅馆办理入住手续吧。—see also 另见 CHECK-IN **2** [T **check** sth ↔ **in**] *AmE* to take a book you have borrowed back to a library【美】〔到图书馆〕归还〔图书〕

check sth ↔ **off** *phr v* [T] to write a mark next to something on a list when you have dealt with it or made sure that it is correct 在〔处理过或核对过的项目后〕打勾: *Check off the names as people arrive.* 人们到达后就在他们的名字旁边打勾。

check out *phr v*

1 ►MAKE SURE 确定◄ **a)** [T **check** sth ↔ **out**] to make sure that something is actually true, correct, or acceptable; INVESTIGATE 调查, 检查, 核实, 查证: *Why don't I check out the bar and see if it's OK?* 我为什么不查看一下门闩, 看看它是否行呢? | **check it out (with)** *Check it out if you don't believe me.* 如果不相信我的话, 你可以去核实一下! **b)** [I] if information checks out, it is proven to be true, correct, or acceptable 证实是对的, 得到证实的, 查证无误的: *If your credit record checks out, they give you a $1000 limit right away.* 如果你的信用记录被证实是可靠的, 他们会立即给你 1000 美元的透支额。

2 ►LOOK AT SB/STH 看某人/物◄ [T **check** sb/sth ↔ **out**] to look at someone or something because they are interesting or attractive 〔因某人或物有趣或吸引人而〕盯着看: *Hey, check this out!* 嘿, 看这个!

3 ►GET INFORMATION 获得资料◄ [T **check** sb ↔ **out**] *informal* to get information about someone, especially to find out if they are suitable for something【非正式】了解…的情况: *It's routine, they check members out before letting them join.* 这是例行公事, 他们对每个入会者都要事先了解一下。

4 ►TEST STH 检测某物◄ [T **check** sth ↔ **out**] to test something to find out if it works, how it works, whether it is suitable for what you want etc 检测〔某物〕: *In here, they stripped down the aircraft and checked them out for airworthiness.* 在这儿, 他们把飞机拆开以检测它是否达到适于飞行的标准。

5 ►HOTEL 旅馆◄ [I] to leave a hotel after paying the bill 办理退房手续, 结账退房: *We checked out at noon.* 我们中午就退房了。

6 ►BOOKS 书籍◄ [T **check** sth ↔ **out**] *AmE* to borrow books from a library【美】〔从图书馆〕借出〔书〕: *The library allows you to check out six books at a time.* 图书馆允许每次借六本书。—see also 另见 CHECKOUT

check sth ↔ **over** *phr v* [T] **1** to look closely at something to make sure it is correct or acceptable 检查; 查看: *Will you check over my essay before I hand it in?* 你能在我交论文之前帮我仔细检查一下吗? **2** to examine someone to make sure they are healthy 体检, 健康检查: *They've checked her over and given her all these tests and she's fine.* 他们对她做了身体检查和所有这些测试, 结果是她很健康。

check up on sb *phr v* [T] to try and make sure that someone is doing what they said they would do or what you want them to do, especially secretly 〔尤指秘密地〕调查, 查核〔某人〕: *Are you trying to check up on me, or what?* 你是在调查我吗, 还是怎么地?

check on sb *phr v* [T] to make sure that someone is safe, has everything they need, etc 检查; 查看〔某人是否安全等〕: *Honey, can you go upstairs and check on the kids?* 亲爱的, 你能上楼看看孩子们的情况吗?

check² *n*

1 ►ON SAFETY/CORRECTNESS/TRUTH ETC 安全/正确/真实等◄ [C] an act of finding out if something is safe, correct, true, or in the condition it should be 〔以确保某物安全、正确、真实等的〕检查; 查核: *the airport's routine security checks* 机场的例行安全检查 | **[+on]** *the need for tighter checks on arms sales* 需要对武器买卖进行更为严格的检查 | **have a check** *Have a check in your bag first and see if it's there.* 先检查一下你的袋子, 看是否在那儿。| **eye/blood pressure/dental etc check** (=done to make sure you are healthy) 眼科/血压/牙齿等的检查 | **carry out a check (on)** *We will carry out a check on options available to you.* 我们将对可供你选择的方案进行检查。| **spot check** (=a quick check of one thing among a group of things, that you do without warning) 抽查, 事先不告知的检查 *Customs officers will do spot checks for drugs and other illegal goods.* 海关人员将进行抽查以检查是否有毒品和其他违禁物品。

2 keep a check (on sb/sth) to watch or listen to something or someone regularly or continuously, in order to control something or gather information 监视; 监听: *Keep a check on your speed.* 要随时检查你的速度。| *Their phones had even been tapped to keep a check on their activities.* 他们的电话甚至被安装了窃听器, 以监视他们的活动。

3 run/do a check to organize an examination of something or someone in order to find out information 进行检查[调查]: **run a check on sb** *Troy's staying late to run some background checks on suspects.* 特洛伊在熬夜调查嫌疑犯的背景。| **do a check for sth** *I'd better do a check for gas leaks.* 我最好检查一下看是否有煤气泄漏。

4 ►A CONTROL ON STH 控制某事◄ something that controls something else and stops it from getting worse, continuing to happen etc 制止(手段), 抑制(手段), 控制: *Higher interest rates will act as a check on public spending.* 高利率会抑制公众消费。| **keep/hold sb/sth in check** (=keep someone or something under control) 控制某人[物] *It was obvious she was barely holding her temper in check.* 很明显, 她几乎不能控制自己的脾气了。

5 ►PATTERN 图案◄ [C,U] a pattern of squares, especially on cloth 〔尤指布料上的〕方格图案: *I don't like checks or stripes, just plain colors.* 我不喜欢方格或条纹, 我喜欢素色的。| **a check shirt/jacket etc** (=made with this cloth) 格子衬衫/夹克等 —see also 另见 CHECKED —see picture on page A16 参见 A16 页图

6 ►FROM YOUR BANK 从银行◄ [C] *AmE* one of a set of printed pieces of paper that you can sign and use instead of money to pay for things【美】支票; CHEQUE *BrE*【英】: **[+for]** *a check for $30* 一张 30 美元的支票 | **by check** *Is it okay to pay by check?* 可用支票支付吗?

7 ►IN A RESTAURANT 在餐馆◄ [C] *AmE, ScotE* a list that you are given in a restaurant showing what you have eaten and how much you must pay; BILL[1] (1b)【美, 苏格兰】账单 —see picture on page A15 参见 A15 页图

8 ►FOR YOUR COAT/BAG 衣物/袋子◄ *AmE*【美】**a) coat check/hat check** a place in a restaurant, theatre etc where you can leave your coat, bag etc to be guarded until you go home 〔餐馆、剧院等的〕衣帽寄存处 **b)** [C] a ticket that you are given so you can claim your things from this place 存放单, 寄存物品的凭证

9 ►MARK 记号◄ [C] *AmE* a mark (√) that you put next to an answer to show that it is correct or next to something on a list to show that you have dealt with it【美】〔表示答案正确或某事项已处理的〕勾号; TICK[1] (1) *BrE*【英】

10 ►CHESS 国际象棋◄ [U] the position of the KING (=most important piece) in CHESS when it can be directly attacked by the opponent's pieces 〔国际象棋中〕被"将军"的局面〔王棋处于被攻击的位置上〕

check·book /ˈtʃɛkˌbʊk; ˈtʃekbʊk/ *n* [C] *AmE* a small book of checks that your bank gives you【美】支票簿; CHEQUEBOOK *BrE*【英】

checked /tʃɛkt; tʃekt/ *adj* checked cloth has a regular pattern of differently coloured squares 有不同颜色方格图案的: *a checked blouse* 格子女衬衫

check·er /ˈtʃɛkɚ; ˈtʃekə/ *n* **1** [C] *AmE* someone who works at the CHECKOUT in a SUPERMARKET【美】〔超市的〕收银员 **2 checkers** [U] a game that two people play with 12 round pieces each, in which the purpose is to take the other player's pieces by jumping over them with your pieces 西洋跳棋; draughts (DRAUGHT[1] (2)) *BrE*【英】— see also 另见 CHINESE CHEQUERS

check·er·board /ˈtʃɛkɚˌbɔrd; ˈtʃekəbɔːd/ *n* [C] *AmE* a board used to play checkers, with 32 white squares and 32 black squares【美】西洋跳棋棋盘〔由 32 个白格和 32 个黑格所构成〕; DRAUGHTBOARD *BrE*【英】

check·ered also 又作 **chequered** *BrE*【英】/ˈtʃɛkɚd; ˈtʃekəd/ *adj* **1** having a pattern made up of squares of two different colours 有方格[格子]图案的: *a checkered tablecloth* 方格桌布 | *checkered tiles in the bathroom* 浴室里的方格瓷砖 **2 have a checkered history/past/career etc** to have had periods of failure as well as successful times in your past 成败参半的历史/过去/事业等: *The company has a pretty checkered history. I'd think carefully before investing.* 这家公司的业绩时好时坏, 投资前我会谨慎考虑。

checkered flag also 又作 **chequered flag** *BrE*【英】/ˌ‥ ˈ‥/ *n* [C] a flag covered with black and white squares that is waved at the beginning and end of a motor race 〔汽车赛开始和结束时用的〕黑白格子旗

check-in /ˈ‥ ·/ *n* **1** [singular] a place where you report your arrival, especially at an airport 〔尤指在机场的〕办理登机手续处[柜台]: *Make sure you're at the check-in by 5:30.* 务必要在 5 点 30 分之前到机场办好登机手续。| **check-in desk** *BrE*【英】, **check-in counter** *AmE*【美】*Go to the check-in desk in zone C.* 去 C 区的办理登机手续柜台。**2** [U] the process of reporting your arrival, especially at an airport 〔尤指到机场〕办理登机手续: *The whole check-in process seems to take forever.* 办理登机手续所花的时间太长了。—see also 另见 **check in** (CHECK[1])

checking ac·count /ˈ‥ ·ˌ·/ *n* [C] *AmE* a bank account that you can take money out of at any time【美】活期存款账户; 支票存款账户; CURRENT ACCOUNT *BrE*【英】—compare 比较 DEPOSIT ACCOUNT

check·list /ˈtʃɛkˌlɪst; ˈtʃekˌlɪst/ *n* [C] a list that helps you by reminding you of the things you need to do for a particular job

or activity〔核对用的〕清单, 检查单: *The guide contains a handy checklist of points to look for when buying a car.* 这本指南载有买车时便于查阅的要点一览表。

check·mate /ˈtʃɛkˌmet; ˈtʃekmeɪt/ *n* [C,U] the position of the KING (=most important piece) in CHESS at the end of the game, when it is being directly attacked and cannot escape〔国际象棋中的〕将军, 将死〔王棋被将死的位置〕

check·out /ˈtʃɛkˌaʊt; ˈtʃek-aʊt/ *n* **1** [C] the place in a SUPERMARKET where you pay for the goods you have collected〔超市的〕付款处, 收银台: *Why can't they have more checkouts open?* 为什么他们不多开几处收银台呢? **2** [C,U] the time by which you must leave a hotel room〔旅店的〕退房时间: *Checkout is at noon.* 退房时间是中午12点之前。—see also 另见 **check out** (CHECK[1])

check·point /ˈtʃɛkˌpɔɪnt; ˈtʃekpɔɪnt/ *n* [C] a place, especially on a border, where an official person examines vehicles or people〔尤指边境的〕关卡; 检查站: *Vehicles were stopped at the checkpoint.* 汽车在检查站被拦住(检查)。

Checkpoint Char·lie /ˌ· · ˈ· ·/ the best-known checkpoint in the Berlin Wall between what was formerly East and West Germany 查利检查站〔原东德与西德之间的柏林墙沿线最著名的关卡〕

check·room /ˈtʃɛkˌrum; ˈtʃek-rʊm/ *n* [C] *AmE* a place in a restaurant, theatre etc where you can leave your coat, bags etc to be guarded【美】〔餐馆、剧院等供存放袋子或衣服等的〕寄存处; 衣帽间; CLOAKROOM (1) *BrE*【英】

check stub /ˈ· ·/ *n* [C] the American spelling of CHEQUE STUB cheque stub 的美式拼法

check-up, check-up /ˈtʃɛkˌʌp; ˈtʃek-ʌp/ *n* [C] a general medical examination that a doctor or DENTIST gives you to make sure you are healthy 体格[健康]检查

ched·dar /ˈtʃɛdɚ; ˈtʃedə/ *n* [U] a hard, smooth, usually yellow or orange cheese 切德干酪, 切德芝士〔一种光滑的硬乳酪, 通常呈黄色或橙色〕

Cheddar Gorge /ˌ· · ˈ·/ a deep valley in the Mendip Hills, southwest England, famous for its caves 切德峡谷〔英格兰西南部门迪普丘陵的一处深谷, 以其岩洞出名〕

3 **cheek[1]** /tʃik; tʃiːk/ *n* **1** [C] the soft round area of flesh on each side of your face below your eye 面颊; 脸蛋儿: *Would you let him kiss you on the cheek?* 你会让他吻你的脸颊吗? | *the smooth pink cheeks of a baby* 婴儿粉嫩光滑的脸蛋儿 —see picture at 参见 HEAD[1] 图 **2** [singular,U] *BrE* disrespectful or rude behaviour, especially towards someone in a position of authority【英】〔尤指对权威〕无礼[放肆]的行为; 厚颜无耻: *I've had enough of that boy's cheek.* 我受够了那男孩的粗鲁无礼。| **have the cheek to do sth** *Billy had the cheek to say it was boring round here, right in front of Nan.* 比利竟当着娜恩的面无礼地说这儿单调乏味。| **have a cheek** *They've got a cheek, charging her for a call when it's her own phone!* 他们真是厚颜无耻, 她用自己的电话竟向她收钱! **3 what a cheek!** *BrE spoken* used to show surprise that someone has behaved rudely or without enough respect【英口】真不要脸! **4 cheek by jowl** if people live or work cheek by jowl they live or work very close together 紧紧靠着, 亲密地在一起: *Families were living cheek by jowl in impossible conditions.* 一个个的家庭挤在恶劣的环境里一起生活。**5 cheek to cheek** if two people dance cheek to cheek, they dance very close to each other in a romantic way 面贴面地〔跳舞〕**6 turn the other cheek** to deliberately avoid reacting in an angry or violent way when someone has hurt or upset you〔对伤害自己的人〕不还手, 不加报复; 抑制住怒气 **7** [C] *informal* one of the two soft fleshy parts of your bottom; BUTTOCK【非正式】屁股 **8 red-cheeked/hollow-cheeked/rosy-cheeked etc** having red, hollow etc cheeks 面色红润/双颊凹陷的等: *He was a merry-faced, ruddy-cheeked little man.* 他个子很小, 一张脸总是红扑扑、笑嘻嘻的。—see also 另见 **tongue in cheek** (TONGUE (3))

cheek[2] *v* [T] *BrE* to speak rudely or disrespectfully to someone, especially to someone older such as your teacher or parents【英】〔尤指对师长〕无礼地说话; SASS *AmE*【美】: *Don't you cheek your mother like that! Go and apologise!* 不要对你母亲如此无礼地说话! 去道歉!

cheek·bone /ˈtʃikˌbon; ˈtʃiːkbəʊn/ *n* [C usually plural 一般用复数] one of the two bones above your cheeks, just below your eyes 颧骨, 颊骨

cheek·y /ˈtʃikɪ; ˈtʃiːki/ *adj BrE*【英】**1** rude or disrespectful, especially towards someone older such as a teacher or parent〔尤指对师长〕厚脸皮的, 不敬的, 放肆的: *Don't be so cheeky!* 别这么无礼! | *The cheeky devil!* 这个无礼的家伙! | **cheeky monkey** *Cheeky monkey! Get your hand out of the biscuit tin.* 你这个厚脸皮的人! 把手从饼干罐中拿开! **2** *approving* disrespectful or not proper, but in a way that is amusing rather than rude【褒】调皮的, 搞笑的: *a scruffy little boy with a cheeky grin* 面露调皮微笑的邋遢小男孩 | *a rather cheeky mini skirt* 太暴露的迷你裙 —**cheekily** *adv* —**cheekiness** *n* [U] —see also 另见 SASSY

cheep /tʃip; tʃiːp/ *v* [I] if a young bird cheeps, it makes a weak, high noise〔雏鸟〕吱吱叫: *baby birds cheeping for food* 嗷嗷待哺的小鸟 —**cheep** *n*

cheer[1] /tʃɪr; tʃɪə/ *n* [C] **1** a shout of happiness, praise, approval, or encouragement 欢呼, 喝彩, 赞美声: **a cheer rises/goes up** *A deafening cheer rose from the crowd as the band walked onto the stage.* 当乐队走上舞台时, 人群中发出了震耳欲聋的欢呼声。| **give a cheer** *Everyone gave a cheer when Gilmore crawled out of the wreck, unhurt.* 当吉尔摩从废墟中毫发无损地爬出来时, 大家都欢呼起来。**2 three cheers for sb!** used to tell a group of people to shout three times as a way of showing support, happiness, thanks etc 给〔某人〕三声欢呼!: *Three cheers for the birthday girl!* 给过生日的女孩三声欢呼! **3** [U] *formal or literary* a feeling of happiness and confidence【正式或文】欢愉, 快活; 乐观: *Christmas cheer* 圣诞节的欢欣 —see also 另见 CHEERS **4** [C] a special CHANT (=kind of poem) that the crowds at a US sports game shout in order to encourage their team to win〔美国体育运动中的〕加油声, 鼓舞声

CULTURAL NOTE 文化注释

Three cheers! People sometimes give 'three cheers' for someone who has achieved something special, in order to show they are happy for them and proud of them. One person shouts, 'Hip hip!', and the rest of the group shout 'Hurray!' This is then repeated two more times. This custom is now rather old-fashioned. 欢呼三次: 人们有时为某人取得特别成绩欢呼三次, 以示为之感到高兴和骄傲。一人高呼: "Hip hip!", 其余人高呼 "Hurray!", 然后重复两次。这一传统现在已相当过时。

cheer[2] *v* **1** [I,T] to shout as a way of showing happiness, praise, approval, or support of someone or something 欢呼, 喝彩: *Everybody cheered when the firemen arrived.* 消防员到达时, 大家都欢呼起来。| **cheer sb** *It says here that thousands packed the city centre to cheer her.* 这儿报道说成千上万的人涌到市中心向她欢呼喝彩。**2** [T usually passive 一般用被动态] to make someone feel more hopeful when they are worried 鼓励; 安慰: *cheering news* 鼓舞人心的消息 | *Kerrie was visibly cheered when we finally saw a light in the distance.* 当我们最终看见远处的灯光时, 克里显然受到鼓舞而振作了起来。

cheer sb/sth ↔ **on** *phr v* [T] to shout encouragement at a person or team to help them do well in a race or competition〔在比赛中〕为…加油; 打气: *They were behind by two touchdowns and she was still cheering them on!* 虽然他们比对方少了两次触地得分, 但她仍在为他们加油!

cheer up *phr v* **1** [I,T] to become less sad, or to make someone feel less sad (使)高兴起来, (使)振作起来: *He'll cheer up if you get him a beer.* 给他杯啤酒, 他的情绪就会好起来。| **cheer** sb ↔ **up** *I'm taking Angie out to cheer her up.* 我要带安吉到外面转转, 让她振作起来。**2 cheer up!** *spoken* used to tell someone not to be so sad【口】振作些! 别发愁啦!: *"Cheer up, Mandy!" "Oh, I'm all right, really."* "别发愁, 曼迪!" "噢, 我很好, 真的没事!" **3 cheering up** the act of trying to make someone feel less sad 鼓舞, 鼓励: **need/want cheering up** *Craig needs cheering up. What should we do?* 要给克雷格打打气, 我们该做些什么呢? | *All I want is a little cheering up.* 我现在需要的只是一些鼓励。

cheer·er /ˈtʃɪrɚ; ˈtʃɪərə/ *n* [C] *AmE* someone who shouts encouragement at a person or team to help them do well in a race or competition【美】拉拉队员: *the loudest cheerer in the grandstand* 在看台上叫得最响的拉拉队员

cheer·ful /ˈtʃɪrfəl; ˈtʃɪəfəl/ *adj* **1** behaving in a way that shows you are happy, for example by smiling or being very friendly 快乐的, 兴高采烈的; 开朗的: *Despite feeling ill, she managed to keep cheerful.* 她尽管身体不舒服, 但仍极力保持精神愉快。| **a cheerful grin/smile/face** (=showing that you are happy) 快活的笑容/微笑/面容 *Nancy gave me a cheerful grin and waved me over.* 南希向我快乐地一笑, 招手示意我过去。**2** something that is cheerful makes you feel happy because it is so bright or pleasant 令人愉快的; 令人振奋的: *I must say I like a cheerful kitchen.* 我得说我喜欢看起来令人愉快的厨房。| *a cheerful letter full of good news* 一封写满好消息的令人振奋的信 **3** tending to be happy most of the time 乐观的: *Basically I'm a cheerful person.* 我基本上是个性格开朗的人。**4** [only before noun 仅用于名词前] a cheerful attitude shows that you are willing to do whatever is necessary in a happy way 愿意的, 乐意的, 欣然的:

cheerful enthusiasm for the job 对工作积极进取的热情 —see also 另见 **cheap and cheerful** (CHEAP[1] (2)) —**cheerfully** *adv*: *"Morning!" she called cheerfully.* "早安！"她高兴地说。—**cheerfulness** *n* [U]

3 **cheer·i·o** /ˈtʃɪrɪ,o; ˌtʃɪəriˈəʊ/ *interjection BrE informal* goodbye【英，非正式】再见

Cheer·i·os /ˌtʃɪrɪˈoz; ˌtʃɪəriˈəʊz/ *trademark* a type of breakfast food, usually eaten with milk. Cheerios are hard circles made mainly of OATS.【商标】奇里奥斯甜麦圈〔一种早餐食品。该食品是以燕麦片为主要原料做成的甜麦圈，通常和牛奶一起食用〕

cheerleaders 拉拉队队员

cheer·lead·er /ˈtʃɪr,lidɚ; ˈtʃɪə,liːdə/ *n* [C] a member of a team of young women who encourage a crowd to cheer at a US sports game by shouting special words and dancing 拉拉队队员: *cheerleaders practicing their routines* 正在进行例行训练的拉拉队

CULTURAL NOTE 文化注释

In the US, every HIGH SCHOOL has a team of cheerleaders (usually girls), chosen for their attractive appearance, confidence, and ability to jump and perform dance-like movements. Professional sports teams also have cheerleaders, who are highly paid and are often highly skilled dancers; the **Dallas Cowboys** (a football team) are famous for their cheerleaders. 在美国，每所高中都有一个拉拉队（通常由女孩组成），挑选队员的标准是漂亮、自信、善于蹦跳和做类似舞蹈的动作。专业运动队也有拉拉队，队员收入丰厚，常为高水平的舞蹈演员。达拉斯牛仔队（一支橄榄球队）以其拉拉队而闻名。

cheer·lead·ing /ˈtʃɪr,lidɪŋ; ˈtʃɪə,liːdɪŋ/ *n* [U] **1** the activity of being a cheerleader 当拉拉队队员: *a cheerleading uniform* 拉拉队的制服 **2** *AmE* the act of loudly supporting an organization, idea etc and not being willing to listen to criticism of it【美】大力支持

cheer·less /ˈtʃɪrlɪs; ˈtʃɪələs/ *adj* cheerless weather, places, or times make you feel sad, bored, or uncomfortable〔天气、地方或时期〕不快乐的；阴郁的；沉闷的；惨淡的: *the dark, cheerless rooms upstairs* 楼上黑暗阴森的房间 | *a grey and cheerless day* 灰暗惨淡的一天 —**cheerlessly** *adv* —**cheerlessness** *n* [U]

cheers /tʃɪrz; tʃɪəz/ *interjection* **1** used when you lift a glass of alcohol before you drink it, in order to say that you hope the people you are drinking with will be happy and have good health 干杯〔用于祝酒〕**2** *BrE informal* thank you【英，非正式】谢谢 **3** *BrE informal* goodbye【英，非正式】再见

cheer·y /ˈtʃɪri; ˈtʃɪəri/ *adj* cheerful, or making you feel happy 欢快的，高兴的；令人愉快的: *a cheery greeting* 愉快的问候 | *Oh, she's fine, as cheery as ever.* 哦，她很好，和往常一样精神饱满。—**cheerily** *adv*

2 3 **cheese** /tʃiz; tʃiːz/ *n* [C,U] **1** a solid food made from milk, which is usually yellow or white in colour, and can be soft or hard 干酪，乳酪，芝士: *half a pound of cheese* 半磅乳酪 | *a cheese sandwich* 乳酪三明治 | *a selection of English cheeses* 精选英格兰乳酪 | **cow's/goat's/sheep's cheese** (=from the milk of a cow etc) 牛奶/山羊奶/绵羊奶制成的干酪 **2 say cheese** used to tell people to smile when you are going to take their photograph 笑一笑〔照相时叫人微笑所说的话〕: *Come on everybody, say cheese!* 来，大家笑一笑！—see also 另见 BIG CHEESE, **as different as chalk and cheese** (CHALK[1] (3))

cheese·board /ˈtʃiz,bɔrd; ˈtʃiːzbɔːd/ *n* [C] **1** a board used to cut cheese on〔切干酪用的〕干酪板 **2** a board used for serving a variety of cheeses 盛干酪的板 —see picture on page A15 参见 A15 页图

cheese·bur·ger /ˈtʃiz,bɝgɚ; ˈtʃiːzbɜːgə/ *n* [C] a HAMBURGER cooked with a piece of cheese on top of the meat 干酪[芝士]汉堡包

cheese·cake /ˈtʃiz,kek; ˈtʃiːzkeɪk/ *n* **1** [C,U] a cake made from a mixture containing soft cheese 乳酪蛋糕 **2** [U] *old-fashioned* photographs of pretty women with few clothes on【过时】显示性感女郎肉体美的照片 —compare 比较 BEEFCAKE

cheese·cloth /ˈtʃiz,klɔθ; ˈtʃiːzklɒθ/ *n* [U] thin cotton cloth used for putting around some kinds of cheeses, and sometimes for making clothes 干酪包布〔一种薄棉布，可包乳酪，也可制衣〕

cheesed off /ˌtʃizd ˈɔf; ˌtʃiːzd ˈɒf/ *adj BrE informal* bored and annoyed with something【英，非正式】感到厌烦的；厌倦的: *You sound cheesed off. What's the matter?* 你听上去很不耐烦，怎么啦？

cheese·par·ing /ˈ· ,··/ *n* [U] *BrE* behaviour that shows you are unwilling to give or spend money【英】花钱斤斤计较；吝啬，小气 —**cheeseparing** *adj*

chee·tah /ˈtʃitə; ˈtʃiːtə/ *n* [C] a member of the cat family that has long legs and black spots on its fur, and can run extremely fast 猎豹

Chee·tos /ˈtʃitoz; ˈtʃiːtəʊz/ *trademark* a popular type of SNACK food sold in bags in the US. Chee-tos are bright orange CRUNCHY fried sticks made from corn, and have a cheese taste.【商标】奇多粟米脆〔美国大众喜欢的一种袋装休闲食品。该食品为松脆的油炸粟米条，呈橘黄色，奶酪味〕

Cheez Whiz /ˈtʃiz ˈhwɪz; ˈtʃiːz ˈwɪz/ *trademark* a type of soft processed cheese that comes in a bottle, which is sold in the US【商标】奇思惠斯干酪〔美国销售的一种瓶装软质干酪〕

chef /ʃɛf; ʃef/ *n* [C] a skilled cook, especially the chief cook in a hotel or restaurant 厨师；〔尤指旅馆或餐馆的〕主厨，厨师长: *a pastry chef* 糕饼师傅 —see picture on page A15 参见 A15 页图

CULTURAL NOTE 文化注释

The STEREOTYPE of a chef is of a man who wears a white coat or APRON and a tall white hat, and who becomes upset or angry easily, especially if his cooking goes wrong. 厨师的典型形象是一个穿白色外套或系围裙、戴白色高帽的男子，暴躁易怒，菜炒坏了时尤其如此。

chef d'oeu·vre /ʃe ˈdœvrə; ˌʃeɪ ˈdɜːvrə/ *n* [C] *French formal* the best piece of work by a painter, writer, etc; MASTERPIECE【法，正式】〔画家、作家等的〕杰作

Ché Gue·va·ra /ˌtʃe gɪˈvɑrə; ˌtʃeɪ gɪˈvɑːrə/ (1926-67) a Marxist military leader, born in Argentina, who developed the method of fighting known as GUERRILLA WARFARE. He helped Fidel Castro gain control of Cuba in 1959. Later he left Cuba and fought in other revolutions, until he was caught by the Bolivian army and killed. 切·格瓦拉（1926-1967），马克思主义军事领导人，生于阿根廷。他发展了游击战术，曾帮助菲德尔·卡斯特罗于1959年夺取古巴政权。之后，他离开古巴，投身于其他革命，最终落入玻利维亚军队手中并遭到杀害〕

Chek·hov /ˈtʃɛkɔf; ˈtʃekɒf/, **An·ton** /ˈæntɑn; ˈæntɒn/ (1860-1904) a Russian writer of plays and short stories. His most famous plays are *The Seagull*, *Uncle Vanya*, and *The Cherry Orchard* 契诃夫〔（1860-1904），俄国剧作家、短篇小说家。最著名的剧本有《海鸥》、《万尼亚舅舅》和《樱桃园》〕—**Chekhovian** /tʃɛˈkovɪən; tʃeˈkəʊviən/ *adj*

Chel·sea /ˈtʃɛlsɪ; ˈtʃelsi/ a fashionable area in the southwest of central London, north of the River Thames 切尔西〔伦敦市中心西南部、泰晤士河北岸一时尚之地〕

Chelsea bun /ˌtʃɛlsɪ ˈbʌn; ˌtʃelsi ˈbʌn/ *n* [C] *BrE* a small, round, sweet cake with dried fruit in it【英】切尔西葡萄干面包

Chelsea Flow·er Show, the /ˌ·· ˈ·· ·/ a large flower show which takes place in London in May every year and is visited by people from all over Britain 切尔西花展〔每年5月在伦敦举行的花卉展览，参观者来自英国各地〕

Chelsea pen·sion·er /ˌ·· ˈ···/ an old person who was once a soldier in the British army and who now lives in a special hospital in Chelsea. Chelsea PENSIONERs wear special red clothes when they go out of the hospital. 切尔西养老者〔住在切尔西一养老院的英国皇家老残军人，他们外出时经常身着特制的红色服装〕

Chel·ten·ham /ˈtʃɛltṇəm; ˈtʃeltənəm/ a town in western England which is famous for its horse racing, its SPA, and its PUBLIC SCHOOLs 切尔滕纳姆〔英格兰西部一镇，以赛马、温泉和公学出名〕

Chel·ten·ham Gold Cup, the /ˌ···ˈ·/ a horse race which is run once a year at Cheltenham, England 切尔滕纳姆金杯赛〔一年一度在英格兰切尔滕纳姆举行的马赛〕

Chel·ten·ham La·dies' Col·lege /ˌ···ˈ··ˌ··/ a PUBLIC SCHOOL for girls in Cheltenham, started in 1853 切尔滕纳姆女子学院〔切尔滕纳姆的一所女子公学, 创建于1853年〕

S3 W3 **chem·i·cal¹** /ˈkɛmɪkl; ˈkemɪkəl/ *n* [C] a substance used in chemistry or produced by chemistry 化学品: *mixing chemicals in a test tube* 把化学物质在试管中混合

W3 **chemical²** *adj* connected with or used in chemistry, or made by a chemical process 化学的; 化学上的; 用化学方法制造的: *the chemical composition of bleach* 漂白剂的化学成分 | *the chemical industry* 化学工业 | *chemical engineering* 化学工程 —**chemically** /-klɪ; -kli/ *adv*: *Chemically, the two substances are very similar.* 在化学性质方面, 这两种物质是很相近的。

chemical re·ac·tion /ˌ····ˈ··/ *n* [C,U] a natural process in which the atoms of chemicals mix and arrange themselves differently to form new substances 化学反应

chemical war·fare /ˌ···ˈ··/ *n* [U] methods of fighting a war using chemical weapons 化学战 —compare 比较 BIOLOGICAL WARFARE

chemical weap·on /ˌ···ˈ··/ *n* [C] a poisonous substance, especially a gas, used as a weapon in war 化学武器〔尤指毒气〕

che·mise /ʃəˈmiz; ʃəˈmiːz/ *n* [C] **1** a piece of women's underwear worn on the top half of her body 〔女式〕宽松内衣 **2** a simple dress that hangs straight from a woman's shoulders 宽松连衣裙

S3 **chem·ist** /ˈkɛmɪst; ˈkemɪ̈st/ *n* [C] **1** a scientist who has a special knowledge in chemistry 化学家 **2** *BrE* someone who is trained to prepare drugs and medicines, who works in a shop 【英】药剂师; DRUGGIST *AmE*【美】—compare 比较 PHARMACIST

S2 **chem·is·try** /ˈkɛmɪstrɪ; ˈkemɪ̈stri/ *n* [U] the science that is concerned with studying the structure of substances and the way that they change 化学 —compare 比较 PHYSICS

chemistry set /ˈ···ˌ·/ *n* [C] a box containing equipment for children to do simple chemistry at home 〔供儿童做简单化学实验用的〕化学箱, 盒装化学实验套件

chem·ist's /ˈkɛmɪsts; ˈkemɪ̈sts/ *n* [C] *BrE* a shop where medicines and TOILETRIES are sold 【英】药店, 药房; DRUGSTORE *AmE*【美】—see also 另见 PHARMACY

chem·o·ther·a·py /ˌkimoˈθɛrəpɪ; ˌkiːməʊˈθerəpi/ *n* [U] the use of drugs to control and try to cure CANCER 〔治疗癌症的〕化学疗法, 化学治疗

che·nille /ʃəˈnil; ʃəˈniːl/ *n* [U] twisted thread with a surface like a soft brush, or cloth made from this and used for decorations, curtains etc 雪尼尔花线; 绳绒线; 绳绒线织物

S2 **cheque** /tʃɛk; tʃek/ *n* [C] *BrE* one of a set of printed pieces of paper that you can sign and use instead of money to pay for things 【英】支票: **[+for]** *a cheque for £200* 一张200英镑的支票 | **write a cheque** *How much should I write the cheque for?* 我该开多少钱的支票? | **by cheque** (=with a cheque) 用支票付 *Can I pay by cheque?* 我能用支票付款吗? | **cash a cheque** (=get cash by writing a cheque) 兑现支票; CHECK *AmE*【美】—see also 另见 DRAFT¹ (3), BLANK CHEQUE, TRAVELLERS CHEQUE

chequebook 支票簿

cheque *BrE*【英】/ check *AmE*【美】支票

chequebook *BrE*【英】/ checkbook *AmE*【美】支票簿

cheque·book /ˈtʃɛkˌbʊk; ˈtʃekbʊk/ *n* [C] *BrE* a small book of cheques that your bank gives you 【英】支票簿; CHECKBOOK *AmE*【美】

chequebook jour·nal·is·m /ˌ··ˈ····/ *n* [U] *BrE* low quality writing in newspapers that pay large amounts of money for details of famous people's private lives 【英】支票新闻; 低级的新闻稿〔指斥巨资获取有关名人私生活详情的拙劣新闻报道〕

cheque card /ˈ··/ also 又作 **cheque guarantee card** /ˌ···ˈ··/ *n* [C] *BrE* a card given to you by your bank that you must show when you write a cheque, which promises that the bank will pay out the money written on the cheque 【英】支票保付卡, 银行支票证 —compare 比较 CASH CARD, CREDIT CARD, DEBIT CARD

chequ·ered /ˈtʃɛkəd; ˈtʃekəd/ *adj* a British spelling of CHECKERED checkered的英式拼法

chequered flag /ˌ··ˈ·/ *n* [C] a British spelling of CHECKERED FLAG checkered flag 的英式拼法

Cheq·uers the official country house of the British Prime Minister, about 30 miles northwest of London 契克斯别墅〔英国首相的乡村官邸, 位于伦敦西北30英里处〕

chequers /ˈtʃɛkəz; ˈtʃekəz/ *n* —see 见 CHINESE CHEQUERS

cheque stub *BrE*【英】, **check stub** *AmE*【美】/ˈ··/ *n* [C] the part of a cheque that is left when you tear it out of a cheque book, used for recording the amount you have spent 支票存根

Cher·bourg /ˈʃɛrburg; ˈʃeəbʊəg/ a city and port in northwest France, one of the ports where ships bringing passengers and cars from the south coast of England arrive after crossing the English Channel 瑟堡〔法国西北部一港口城市, 是英格兰南部沿海的船只横渡英吉利海峡之后停泊的港口之一〕

cher·ish /ˈtʃɛrɪʃ; ˈtʃerɪʃ/ *v* [T usually passive 一般用被动态] **1** to love someone or something very much and take care of them well 珍爱, 珍惜, 钟爱: *his most cherished possession* 他最珍爱的物品 **2** to be very important to someone 视为珍贵[重要]: **cherished hopes/dreams/ideas etc** *one of our cherished hopes, a community centre for the village* 我们心中怀有的一个希望是为村子建一个社区活动中心 | *cherished memories* 珍藏在心底的回忆

Cher·no·byl /tʃɝˈnobḷ; tʃɜːˈnəʊbəl/ a town in Ukraine (formerly part of the Soviet Union) where in 1986 an explosion destroyed large parts of a nuclear power station in the worst accident involving NUCLEAR power 切尔诺贝利〔乌克兰一城镇。1986年这里发生了一起最严重的核能事故, 当地一座核电站大部分设施被炸毁〕

che·root /ʃəˈrut; ʃəˈruːt/ *n* [C] a CIGAR with both ends cut straight 〔两端切平的〕方头雪茄烟

cher·ry /ˈtʃɛrɪ; ˈtʃeri/ *n* **1** [C] a small red or black round fruit with a long thin stem 樱桃: *a bunch of cherries* 一串樱桃 | *cherry tart* 樱桃馅饼 —see picture on page A8 参见A8页图 **2 a)** [C] also 又作 **cherry tree** the tree on which this fruit grows 樱桃树 **b)** [U] the wood of this tree, used for making furniture 樱桃木 **3** a bright red colour 樱桃红, 鲜红 **4 the cherry on the cake/on the top** something additional that you did not expect, that is pleasant to have 意外收获 —see also 另见 **another bite/a second bite at the cherry** (BITE² (9)) S3

cherry bomb /ˈ··ˌ·/ *n* [C] *AmE* a large round red FIRECRACKER (=small loud explosive)【美】樱桃爆竹

cherry bran·dy /ˌ··ˈ··/ *n* [U] a sweet alcoholic drink that tastes of cherries 樱桃白兰地

cherry-pick /ˈtʃɛrɪˌpɪk; ˈtʃeripɪk/ *v* [I,T] to choose exactly the things or people you want, from a group 挑选

cherry to·ma·to /ˈ···ˌ··/ *n plural* **cherry tomatoes** [C] a very small TOMATO 樱桃番茄, 圣女果〔一种很小的番茄〕

cher·ub /ˈtʃɛrəb; ˈtʃerəb/ *n* [C] **1** a picture or figure of a fat, pretty, usually male child with small wings, used as a decoration 小天使〔绘画或雕塑中有翅膀的小男孩〕 **2** *informal* a young pretty child who behaves very well【非正式】漂亮乖巧的儿童 **3** *spoken* used to address a young child in a friendly way【口】宝贝〔对小孩的一种昵称〕: *Come to Mummy, my cherub!* 宝贝, 到妈妈这儿来! **4** *plural* **cherubim** /ˈtʃɛrəbɪm; ˈtʃerʊ̈bɪm/ *biblical* one of the ANGELs that guard the seat where God sits【圣经】〔护卫上帝宝座的〕小天使; 普智天使 —**cherubic** /tʃəˈrubɪk; tʃəˈruːbɪk/ *adj*: *a smile of cherubic innocence* 天使般的纯真笑容

cher·vil /ˈtʃɝvɪl; ˈtʃɜːvɪ̈l/ *n* [U] a strong-smelling garden plant used as a HERB 细叶芹

Ches·a·peake Bay /ˌtʃɛsəpik ˈbe; ˌtʃesəpiːk ˈbeɪ/ a BAY (=area of water connected to the sea) on the US east coast, important for trade and shipping 切萨皮克湾〔位于美国东海岸, 是重要的贸易和海运港口〕

Chesh·ire /ˈtʃɛʃɚ; ˈtʃeʃə/ a COUNTY in northwest England, between Liverpool and North Wales 柴郡〔英格兰西北部一郡, 位于利物浦和威尔士北部之间〕

Cheshire cat, the /ˌ··ˈ·/ a character in *Alice's Adventures in Wonderland* by Lewis Carroll, which disappears very slowly until only its big smile is left. People sometimes say someone is 'grinning like a Cheshire cat' to mean that they have

a big and rather silly smile on their face. 柴郡猫, 笑脸猫〔刘易斯·卡罗尔所著《艾丽丝漫游奇境记》中的一只猫。此猫慢慢消失踪影, 最后只剩下大笑的样子。人们有时会说某人"像柴郡猫一样咧着嘴笑", 意思是说此人满脸堆着憨笑〕

Cheshire cheese /,·· '·/ a hard white British cheese that does not have a strong taste 柴郡干酪

chess /tʃɛs; tʃes/ *n* [U] a game for two players, who move their playing pieces according to fixed rules across a board in an attempt to CHECKMATE (=trap) their opponent's KING (=most important piece) 国际象棋

chess·board /ˈtʃɛsˌbɔrd; ˈtʃesbɔːd/ *n* [C] a square board with 64 black and white squares, each square being next to a square of a different colour, on which chess is played 国际象棋棋盘 —see picture at 参见 BOARD[1] 图

chess·man /ˈtʃɛsmæn; ˈtʃesmæn/ also 又作 **chesspiece** /ˈtʃɛspis; ˈtʃespiːs/ *n plural* **chessmen** /-mɛn; -men/ [C] any of the 16 black or 16 white playing pieces used in the game of chess (国际象棋) 棋子

chest /tʃɛst; tʃest/ *n* [C] **1** the front part of your body between your neck and your stomach 胸部, 胸腔: *a hairy chest* 毛茸茸的胸脯 | *The doctor is going to listen your chest, Cindy.* 辛迪, 医生要听诊你的胸部。—see also 另见 FLAT-CHESTED —see picture at 参见 BODY 图 **2** a large, strong box that you use to store things in or to move your personal possessions from one place to another 箱, 大箱子: *We keep the summer clothes in a chest in the attic.* 我们把夏天穿的衣服放在阁楼上的大箱子里。| *a blanket chest* 毛毯箱 —see also 另见 CHEST OF DRAWERS, HOPE CHEST, MEDICINE CHEST, TEA CHEST, WAR CHEST **3 get something off your chest** to tell someone about something that has been worrying or annoying you for a long time, so that you feel better afterwards 倾吐心中的烦恼

Ches·ter /ˈtʃɛstɚ; ˈtʃestə/ a town in Cheshire in northwest England, where the local government for that county is based. It has many historical buildings, and there is a wall around the old part of the town. 切斯特〔英格兰西北柴郡一镇, 为柴郡地方政府所在地。此地有许多历史性建筑, 旧城区建有城墙〕

ches·ter·field /ˈtʃɛstɚˌfild; ˈtʃestəfiːld/ *n* [C] a soft comfortable SOFA, usually covered with leather 长沙发

chest·nut[1] /ˈtʃɛsnʌt; ˈtʃesnʌt/ *n* **1** [C] a smooth red-brown nut that you can eat 栗子: *roast chestnuts* 炒栗子 | *chestnut stuffing* 栗子馅 **2** also 又作 **chestnut tree** [C] the tree on which this nut grows 栗子树 **3** [U] a reddish brown colour 栗色, 红棕色 **4** [C] a horse that is this colour 红棕色的马, 栗色马 **5 an old chestnut** a joke or story that has been repeated many times 老掉牙的故事[笑话] **6** [C] a HORSE CHESTNUT 七叶树; 七叶树的果实 —see also 另见 WATER CHESTNUT

chestnut[2] *adj* red-brown in colour 栗色的, 红棕色的: *her chestnut hair* 她的红棕色头发

chest of drawers /,·· '·/ *n* a piece of furniture with drawers, used for storing clothes〔有抽屉的〕五斗橱, 衣柜; BUREAU (4) *AmE*【美】

chest·y /ˈtʃɛstɪ; ˈtʃesti/ *adj* **1** *informal especially BrE* having a lot of CATARRH (=thick liquid) in your lungs【非正式, 尤英】患胸部疾病的; 有胸病症状的: *a chesty cough* 发自胸腔的咳嗽 | *He was a bit chesty, so I didn't send him to school.* 他胸部有点不舒服, 所以我没有让他上学。**2** *informal* an impolite word used to describe a woman with large breasts【非正式】〔非礼貌用语, 指女人〕乳房突出的, 大乳房的

chev·a·lier /ˌʃɛvəˈlɪr; ˌʃevəˈlɪə/ *n* [C] *French*【法】**1** a title for someone who has a high rank in a special association in France 骑士: *a Chevalier of the Legion of Honour* 法国勋级会荣誉军团骑士 **2** a member of the lowest rank of the French NOBILITY in the past〔旧时法国〕爵位最低的贵族

che·val mir·ror /ʃəˈvæl ˌmɪrɚ; ʃəˈvæl ˌmɪrə/ *n* [C] a long mirror in a frame which stands upright without being fixed to a wall〔装于直立架上的〕镶框的长镜, 穿衣镜

Chev·i·ot Hills, the /ˌtʃɛvɪət ˈhɪlz; ˌtʃeviət ˈhɪlz/ also 又作 **Cheviots** a range of hills between England and Scotland〔位于英格兰和苏格兰之间的〕切维厄特丘陵

Chev·ro·let /ˌʃɛvrəˈle; ˈʃevrəleɪ/ also 又作 **Chevy** *informal trademark* a type of US car, made by General Motors and especially popular as a family car【非正式, 商标】雪佛兰汽车〔美国通用汽车公司制造的一种汽车, 作为家用车尤其受人欢迎〕

chev·ron /ˈʃɛvrən; ˈʃevrən/ *n* [C] **1** a pattern in a V shape V形图案 **2** a piece of cloth in the shape of a V which a soldier has on their SLEEVE (1) to show their rank〔表示军人等级的〕V形臂章

Chev·y /ˈʃɛvɪ; ˈʃevi/ an informal name for a Chevrolet 雪佛兰汽车〔非正式名称〕

chew[1] /tʃu; tʃuː/ *v* **1** [I,T] to bite food several times before swallowing it 咀嚼; 嚼碎: *This meat's so tough I can hardly chew it!* 这块肉太硬, 我几乎嚼不动! | [+at/on] *a dog chewing on a bone* 在啃着一根骨头的狗 **2** [I,T] to bite something repeatedly in order to taste it or because you are nervous〔因紧张等〕不停地嚼, 咬: *We gave the dog an old shoe to chew on.* 我们扔了一只旧鞋给狗咬。| *Stop chewing your nails – it's disgusting.* 别再咬指甲了, 叫人受不了。**3 chew the cud a)** if a cow or sheep chews the cud, it repeatedly bites food it has brought up from its stomach〔牛、羊等〕反刍 **b)** *informal* to think very carefully before making a decision【非正式】〔在作出决定前〕仔细考虑, 斟酌 **4 chew the fat** *informal* to have a long, friendly conversation【非正式】促膝长谈, 闲聊 —see also 另见 **bite off more than you can chew** (BITE[1] (10))

chew on sth *phr v* [T] **chew on it** *informal* to think about something carefully for a period of time【非正式】仔细考虑, 深思

chew sb **out** *phr v* [T] *AmE, informal* to talk angrily to someone in order to show them that you disapprove of what they have done【美, 非正式】严厉责备〔某人〕: *I know I'm late, you don't have to chew me out!* 我知道我迟到了, 但你没有必要大声责备我呀!

chew sth ↔ **over** *phr v* [T] to think carefully about a question, problem, idea etc. over a period of time 仔细考虑〔问题、意见等〕: *Let me chew it over for a few days, and then I'll let you have my answer.* 让我仔细考虑几天再给你答复。

chew sth ↔ **up** *phr v* [T] to bite something repeatedly with your teeth so that you can make it smaller or softer and swallow it 嚼碎, 咀嚼: *That dog's chewed the carpet up again!* 那条狗又在咬地毯了。

chew[2] *n* [C] **1** the act of biting something repeatedly with the teeth 嚼, 咀嚼 **2** something such as a sweet you chew or special tobacco which you chew but do not swallow 咀嚼物〈如口香糖、烟草〉: *a chew of tobacco* 嚼一嚼烟草

chewing gum /'·· ·/ *n* [U] a type of sweet, that you chew for a long time but do not swallow 口香糖

chew·y /ˈtʃuɪ; ˈtʃuːi/ *adj* food that is chewy has to be chewed a lot before it is soft enough to swallow〔食物〕需多嚼的, 难嚼碎的: *chewy toffees* 难嚼的太妃糖 | *wonderfully chewy chocolate brownies* 耐嚼的美味巧克力蛋糕

Chex /tʃɛks; tʃeks/ *trademark*【商标】**1** a type of breakfast CEREAL sold in the US "切克斯"〔在美国销售的一种早餐谷类食品〕**2 Chex Party Mix** a salty mixture made from Chex, nuts, and PRETZELS, eaten as a SNACK "切克斯"什锦小吃〔由"切克斯"、坚果和椒盐卷饼混合而成的一种咸味小吃〕

Chey·enne /ʃaɪˈæn; ʃaɪˈæn/ *n* **1** the capital city of the US state of Wyoming 夏延〔美国怀俄明州首府〕**2 the Cheyenne** a Native American people that live in the West of the US 夏延族〔美国西部的美洲土著〕**3** [C] a member of the Cheyenne people 夏延人

Chi·an·ti /kɪˈæntɪ; kiˈænti/ *trademark* a type of Italian red wine【商标】基安蒂〔一种意大利红葡萄酒〕

Chi·an·ti·shire /kɪˈæntɪʃɚ; kiˈæntiʃə/ an area of Tuscany, in Italy, where many UPPER-CLASS British people live or go to stay – used humorously 基安蒂郡〔意大利托斯卡纳一地区, 是许多英国上层人士居住或短期逗留的地方。属幽默用法〕: *The Nielsens are off there, too, to Chiantishire, or Tuscany as the Italians like to call it.* 尼尔森一家人也去了基安蒂郡, 也就是意大利人所说的托斯卡纳。

chic /ʃik; ʃiːk/ *adj* very fashionable and expensive and showing good judgment of what is attractive and good style 时髦的; 漂亮的; 雅致的: *a chic black dress* 一条时髦的黑色连衣裙 | *Provençal cuisine has become very chic.* 普罗旺斯式的烹饪大受欢迎。| *a chic restaurant* 一家时髦的餐厅 —**chic** *n* [U]

Chi·ca·go /ʃɪˈkago; ʃɪˈkɑːgəʊ/ the third largest city in the US. It is in the state of Illinois, on the southwest shore of Lake Michigan, and is an important industrial and business centre. Chicago is sometimes called 'the Windy City'. 芝加哥〔美国第三大城市, 位于伊利诺伊州, 密歇根湖西南岸, 是重要的工业和商业中心。芝加哥有时被称作"风城"〕

Chicago Board of Trade, the /·,·· ,· · '·/ an important market in Chicago, US, in which future contracts for the delivery of commodities (COMMODITY) are bought and sold 芝加哥交易所〔美国芝加哥一重要商品期货交易市场〕

Chicago Sym·pho·ny Or·ches·tra, the /·,·· '··· ,···/ abbreviation 缩写为 CSO a US ORCHESTRA (=a large group of musicians) based in Chicago, Illinois 芝加哥交响乐团〔美国伊利诺伊州芝加哥的一个乐团〕

Chicago Trib·une, The /·,·· '··/ a daily newspaper produced in Chicago and also sold in other parts of the US. It is

famous for the high quality of its writing and reporting.《芝加哥论坛报》〔芝加哥出版的一份日报。该报在美国其他地区也有发行，以高品质的稿件和报道著称〕

chi·cane /ʃɪˋken; ʃɪˈkeɪn/ *n* [C] an S shaped bend in a straight road, especially on a track for racing cars〔尤指赛车跑道上的〕S形弯道

chi·ca·ne·ry /ʃɪˋkenərɪ; ʃɪˈkeɪnəri/ *n* [U] *formal* the use of clever plans or actions to deceive people【正式】诡计，欺骗，诈骗: *The legal system got to the truth and settled cases fairly and without chicanery.* 法律部门查清事实真相，公正严明地处理案件。

Chi·ca·no /tʃɪˋkano; tʃɪˈkɑːnəʊ/ *n* [C] *plural* **Chicanos** *AmE* a US citizen who was born in Mexico or whose family came from Mexico【美】墨西哥裔美国人 —**Chicano** *adj*

chi-chi /ˋʃi ʃi; ˈʃiː ʃiː/ *adj informal* stylish or attractive, especially in a way that you think uses too much decoration【非正式】时髦的；吸引人的；过分艳丽的: *a chi-chi nightclub* 富丽堂皇的夜总会

chick /tʃɪk; tʃɪk/ *n* [C] **1** a baby bird 小鸟: *a robin chick* 幼知更鸟 **2** a word meaning a young woman, that some people think is offensive 少女；少妇〔有些人认为此词具冒犯性〕

chick-a-dee /ˋtʃɪk ə ˌdi; ˈtʃɪk ə diː/ *n* [C] a North American bird with a black head 山雀〔一种北美小鸟，头部呈黑色〕

S2 **chick·en¹** /ˋtʃɪkɪn; ˈtʃɪkɪn/ *n*

1 ►BIRD 鸟◄ [C] a common farm bird that is kept for its meat and eggs 鸡: *He keeps chickens on his farm.* 他在农场里养鸡。—see also 另见 HEN, COCK¹ (1), ROOSTER

2 ►MEAT 肉◄ [U] the meat from this bird eaten as food 鸡肉: *roast chicken* 烤鸡 | *fried chicken* 炸鸡 | *chicken soup* 鸡汤

3 ►SB WHO IS NOT BRAVE 懦夫◄ [C] *informal* someone who is not at all brave; COWARD【非正式】胆小鬼，懦夫: *Don't be such a chicken!* 别那么胆小！

4 ►GAME 游戏◄ [U] a game in which children must do something dangerous to show that they are brave〔儿童玩的〕比试胆量的游戏

5 which came first, the chicken or the egg? used to say that it is difficult or impossible to decide which of two things came first or which action is the cause and which is the effect 先有鸡，还是先有蛋?〔表示因果难以区分〕

6 a chicken and egg situation/problem/thing etc a situation in which it is impossible to decide which part caused another and which is the effect of another 因果难以区分的状况/问题/事情等

7 your chickens have come home to roost your bad or dishonest actions in the past have caused the problems that you have now 恶有恶报，自作自受 —see also 另见 **don't count your chickens before they're hatched** (COUNT¹ (8)), SPRING CHICKEN

chicken² *v*

chicken out *phr v* [I] *informal* to decide at the last moment not to do something you said you would do because you are afraid【非正式】〔因害怕而〕临阵退缩: **chicken out of doing sth** *I knew you'd chicken out of telling Dad you want to leave school.* 我知道你最终会不敢告诉爸爸你想退学的事。

chicken³ *adj* [not before noun 不用于名词前] *informal* not brave enough to do something【非正式】没勇气的，胆小的: *Your brother is chicken.* 你哥哥是胆小鬼。

chick·en·feed /ˋtʃɪkɪnˌfid; ˈtʃɪkɪnfiːd/ *n* [U] *informal* an amount of money that is so small that it is almost not worth having【非正式】一笔小数额的钱: *The bank offered to lend us £1,000, but that's chickenfeed compared to what we need.* 银行答应借给我们1000英镑，但这与我们需要的数目相比，简直微不足道。

chicken-fried steak /ˌ‥ˈ ˈ/ *n* [C,U] *AmE* a thin piece of BEEF¹ (1) covered in BREADCRUMBS and cooked in hot fat【美】〔外裹面包屑的〕炸牛排

chicken-heart·ed /ˌ‥ˈ‥◂/ also 又作 **chicken-livered** *adj* not brave; COWARDLY 胆小的，怯懦的

Chicken Lit·tle /ˌ‥ˈ‥/ a story for children in which a chicken called Chicken Little thinks that the sky is falling and persuades many other animal friends that great danger is coming《小小鸡》〔儿童故事，有一只名为"小小鸡"的鸡认为天马上要塌下来，并且还让其他许多动物朋友相信了大难即将来临〕

chick·en·pox /ˋtʃɪkɪnˌpɑks; ˈtʃɪkɪnpɒks/ *n* [U] an infectious illness which causes a slight fever and spots on your skin 水痘

chicken run /ˈ‥ ˌ/ *n* [U] an area surrounded by a fence where you keep chickens〔四周设栏以养鸡的〕鸡栏

chick·en·shit /ˋtʃɪkɪnˌʃɪt; ˈtʃɪkɪnʃɪt/ *n* [C] *AmE informal* a rude word meaning someone who is not at all brave; COWARD【美，非正式】胆小鬼，懦夫〔不礼貌说法〕

chicken wire /ˈ‥ ˌ/ *n* [U] a type of thin wire net used to make fences for chickens〔做鸡栏的〕细铁丝网

chick-pea /ˈ· ˌ/ *n* [C] a large brown PEA which is cooked and eaten; GARBANZO 鹰嘴豆

chick·weed /ˋtʃɪkˌwid; ˈtʃɪkwiːd/ *n* [U] a garden WEED¹ (1) with small white flowers 卷耳；繁缕〔园子里开白色小花的一种杂草〕

chic·le /ˋtʃɪkḷ; ˈtʃɪkəl/ *n* [U] the GUM (=thick juice) of a tropical American tree used in making CHEWING GUM 糖胶树胶〔可制口香糖〕

chic·o·ry /ˋtʃɪkərɪ; ˈtʃɪkəri/ *n* [U] a European plant with blue flowers whose leaves are eaten and whose roots are sometimes used as coffee 菊苣; ENDIVE (2) *AmE*【美】

chide /tʃaɪd; tʃaɪd/ *v past tense* **chided** *or* **chid** /tʃɪd; tʃɪd/ *past participle* **chided, chid** *or* **chidden** /ˋtʃɪdṇ; ˈtʃɪdn/ [I,T] *literary* to speak angrily to someone because you do not approve of something they have done; REBUKE【文】呵斥，指责: *"You naughty children!" she chided.* 她呵斥道:"你们这些淘气鬼！" | **chide sb for sth** *Louise often chided her son for his idleness.* 路易丝常常责骂儿子懒惰。| **chide sb for doing sth** *Mr Jones chided the children for not wearing their coats.* 琼斯先生责怪孩子没有穿大衣。

chief¹ /tʃif; tʃiːf/ *adj* **1** most important; main 最重要的，主要的: *One of the chief causes of crime today is drugs.* 毒品是如今引发犯罪的主要原因之一。| *the prosecution's chief witness* 控方的主要证人 —see also 另见 CHIEFLY **2** highest in rank 最高级的，首席的: *the chief accountant* 首席会计师 | *the chief political correspondent of the Washington Post*《华盛顿邮报》的首席政治记者 **3 chief cook and bottle washer** *humorous* someone in charge of an event, especially someone who must do a lot of small unimportant jobs to make sure it is a success【幽默】事必躬亲的负责人；百管部长；当家: *"Is there any more wine?" "Ask my husband, he's chief cook and bottle washer today!"* "还有酒吗?""去问我丈夫，他今天是百管部长！" S2 W2

chief² *n* [C] W3

1 ►RULER OF TRIBE 部落统治者◄ a ruler of a tribe 部落首领，酋长: *an American Indian tribal chief* 美洲印第安人部落的酋长

2 ►SB IN CHARGE OF AN ORGANIZATION 组织的领导人◄ the most important person in a company or organization 总裁；主管人；领袖；最高领导人: *the chief of Austria's army intelligence* 奥地利军事情报司令 | *Industry chiefs yesterday demanded tough measures against inflation.* 工业巨头们昨天要求采取有力措施对付通货膨胀的问题。

3 the chief *informal* the person in charge of the company or organization you work for【非正式】老板，头儿: *The chief wants to see you right away.* 老板要你立刻去见他。

4 big/great white chief *humorous* the person in charge of a group of people, company, organization etc【幽默】首领；头目；上司

5 too many chiefs and not enough Indians used to say there are too many people saying how something should be done and not enough people doing it 官多兵少；动嘴的多，动手的少

6 ►MAN 人◄ *BrE old-fashioned* used to speak in a friendly way to a man you think is more important than you【英，过时】〔用作表示客气的称呼〕

chief con·stab·le /ˌ·ˈ‥/ *n* [C] a police officer in charge of the police in a large area of Britain【英】〔英国一大地区的〕警察局局长

Chief Ex·ec·u·tive /ˌ·ˈ‥‥/ *n AmE* **the Chief Executive** the President of the US【美】美国总统

chief executive of·fic·er /ˌ·ˈ‥‥ ˌ‥/ *n* [C] the person with the most authority in a large company〔公司的〕行政总裁

chief in·spect·or /ˌ·ˈ‥◂/ *n* [C] a British police officer of middle rank〔英国的〕警察总督察，总巡官

chief jus·tice /ˌ·ˈ‥◂/ *n* [C] the most important judge in a court of law, especially of the US Supreme Court〔尤指美国的〕高等法院院长；首席法官

chief·ly /ˋtʃiflɪ; ˈtʃiːfli/ *adv* mostly but not completely; mainly 大部分地；主要地: *The work consists chiefly of interviewing members of the public.* 这份工作主要是采访公众。| *I lived abroad for years, chiefly in Italy.* 我长年住在国外，主要在意大利。

chief of staff /ˌ·ˈ ˈ/ *n plural* **chiefs of staff** [C] **1** an officer of high rank in the army, navy etc who advises the officer in charge of a particular military group or operation 参谋长 **2** an official of high rank who advises the man in charge of an organization or government〔政府或组织中的〕高级顾问；参事；参谋: *the White House chief of staff* 白宫办公厅主任

Chief Rab·bi /ˌ· ˈ··/ *n* **the Chief Rabbi** the main leader of the JEWISH religion in a country 首席拉比，犹太教会领袖〔一国内的犹太教主要领导人〕

chief su·per·in·ten·dent /ˌ· ····ˈ··◂/ *n* [C] a British police officer of high rank 〔英国警察的〕总警司，警务长

chief·tain /ˈtʃiftɪn; ˈtʃiːftən/ *n* [C] the leader of a tribe or a Scottish CLAN 族长；酋长；〔苏格兰高地氏族的〕宗族长；首领 —**chieftainship** *n* [C,U]

Chief Whip, the /ˌ· ˈ·/ *n* an important member of a British political party whose job is to make sure that members of his party elected to parliament obey party orders 党鞭〔英国政党中的要员，负责确保该党议员遵从党令〕

chif·fon /ʃɪˈfɑn; ˈʃɪfɒn/ *n* [U] a soft thin silk or NYLON material that you can see through 雪纺绸，薄绸：*a pink chiffon ballgown* 粉红色的薄绸礼服

chi·gnon /ˈʃinjɑn; ˈʃiːnjɒn/ *n* [C] *French* a smooth knot of hair that a woman wears at the back of her head【法】〔女人的〕发髻

chi·hua·hua /tʃɪˈwɑwɑ; tʃəˈwɑːwə/ *n* [C] a very small dog from Mexico with smooth hair 奇瓦瓦[吉娃娃]狗〔毛光滑的小狗，产自墨西哥〕

chil·blain /ˈtʃɪlˌblen; ˈtʃɪlbleɪn/ *n* [C] a painful red place on your fingers or toes that is caused by cold and a weak supply of blood〔手指或脚趾上的〕冻疮

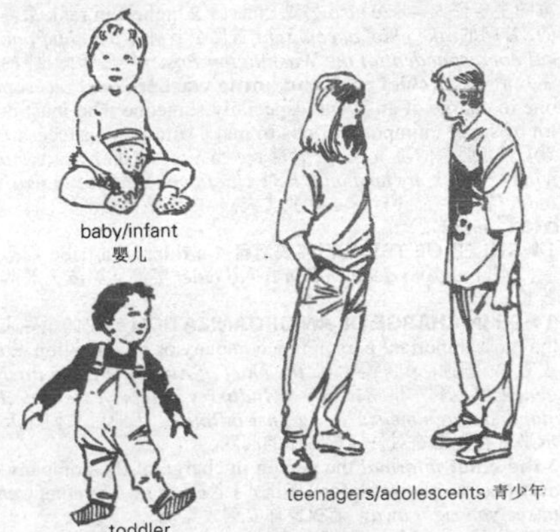

1 1 **child** /tʃaɪld; tʃaɪld/ *n* [C] *plural* **children** /ˈtʃɪldrən; ˈtʃɪldrən/
1 ▶YOUNG PERSON 小孩◀ a young person from the time they are born until they are aged 14 or 15〔14 到 15 岁之前的〕小孩，儿童：*We've always competed, ever since we were children.* 我们总是相互竞争，从小如此。| *Can you sell me a bike suitable for a seven-year-old child?* 你能卖给我一辆适合七岁儿童骑的脚踏车吗？| **as a child** (=when you were a child) 孩提时，儿时 *As a child I remember Grandma singing me to sleep.* 记得我还是个孩子时，外婆总是唱歌哄我入睡。| **a child killer/victim/prostitute etc** (=a child who is a killer etc) 儿童凶手/儿童受害者/雏妓等
2 ▶SON/DAUGHTER 儿女◀ a son or daughter of any age 孩子；儿子；女儿：*How many children did Victoria have?* 维多利亚有几个孩子？| *We'll come if we can find a babysitter for the children.* 如果我们能找到人临时看孩子，我们就会来。| *Is this her first child?* (=is this her first PREGNANCY?) 这是她的第一个孩子吗？| **have a child** (=give birth) 生孩子，分娩 | **an only child** (=someone with no brothers or sisters) 独生子[女]
3 ▶SB INFLUENCED BY AN IDEA 受某想法影响者◀ someone who is very strongly influenced by the ideas and attitudes of a particular person or period of history 深受某人[某时期]影响的人：*Thatcher's children are finding that the world has moved on.* 深受撒切尔的思想影响的人正发觉世界已经向前发展。| [+of] *a real child of the sixties* 真正属于六十年代的人
4 ▶SB WHO IS LIKE A CHILD 孩子气的人◀ someone who is not very experienced in doing something, or who behaves like a child 幼稚的人，行为像孩子的人：*Richard's such a child – he can't even do his own washing and cooking.* 理查德简直像个孩子 —— 他甚至不会洗衣和做饭。
5 children should be seen and not heard an expression meaning that children should be quiet and not talk, used when you disapprove of the way the children are behaving 小孩子应该少说话〔用来叫小孩子安静的一句话〕
6 be with child *old use* to be PREGNANT【旧】怀孕
7 be heavy/great with child *old use* to be nearly ready to give birth【旧】大腹便便即将临盆的 —see also 另见 CHILD'S PLAY

> **USAGE NOTE 用法说明：CHILD**
>
> WORD CHOICE 词语辨析：**child, baby, infant, toddler, teenager, adolescent, youth, young people, kid**
>
> A very young **child** is a **baby** or more formally an **infant** 年纪很小的小孩叫做 baby，较正式的说法是 infant：*Many infants have died in the refugee camps.* 许多婴儿在难民营里夭折。A child who has just learned to walk is a **toddler**. 刚学步的小孩叫做 toddler。
>
> Young people aged 13 to 19 are **teenagers** and a younger teenager may also be called an **adolescent**, but this word is rather formal, and may show a negative attitude. 13-19 岁的青少年叫 teenagers，年龄小些的少年还可叫做 adolescent，但这个词相当正式，而且略带贬义：*a group of giggly adolescent girls* 一群唧唧喳喳的少女
>
> The word **youth** is often used for an older male teenager (15+) in official reports about crimes or bad behaviour. youth 一词常用于正式报告中指犯罪或行为不端的年龄较大〔15 岁以上〕的男性青年：*The police are seeking two youths who raped a teenage girl.* 警方正在搜捕两个强奸了一名少女的男青年。In official names **youth** includes both sexes. 在正式名称中 youth 可指男或女：*a youth club/group/scheme/worker/centre/hostel* 青年俱乐部/青年团体/青年计划/青年工作者/青少年中心/青年旅馆 Often the phrase **young people** is used for this age group in everyday English. 在日常英语中，多用 young people 来指这个年龄组别的青年：*a disco full of young people dancing* 挤满了在跳舞的年轻人的迪斯科舞厅
>
> **Kid** is informal and used both for **child** (up to around 14) kid〔非正式〕可以用来指 child〔大约 14 岁以下〕：*The kids are playing in the yard* 孩子们在院子里玩耍，and for **young people** 也可以用来指 young people：*We met a group of college kids.* 我们遇见了一群年轻的大学生。
>
> GRAMMAR 语法
>
> Remember the plural of **child** is **children**, never *childs* or *childrens*. 记住 child 的复数形式为 children，不是 childs 或 childrens. But in the possessive form you say 但所有格中应为：*this child's education* 这个孩子的教育 | *these children's education* 这些孩子的教育

child·bear·ing /ˈtʃaɪldˌbɛrɪŋ; ˈtʃaɪldˌbeərɪŋ/ *n* [U] **1** the process of giving birth to a baby 怀孩子，分娩，生孩子 **2 child-bearing age** the time in a woman's life when she can have babies 育龄

child ben·e·fit /ˌ· ˈ···/ *n* [U] an amount of money that the British government gives to families with children 儿童津贴〔由英国政府发给家长，直到儿童到某一年龄为止〕

child·birth /ˈtʃaɪldˌbɝθ; ˈtʃaɪldbɜːθ/ *n* [U] the act of having a baby 分娩，生孩子：*His mother died in childbirth.* 他的母亲死于难产。

child·care /ˈtʃaɪldˌkɛr; ˈtʃaɪldkeə/ *n* [U] an arrangement in which someone who is trained to look after children cares for them while the parents are at work 儿童看护，儿童照管：*The company pays £20 a week towards childcare.* 公司每周发 20 英镑儿童看护费。

child·hood /ˈtʃaɪldˌhʊd; ˈtʃaɪldhʊd/ *n* [C,U] the period of time  when you are a child 童年；儿童时代：*I had a happy childhood.* 我有一个快乐的童年。—see also 另见 SECOND CHILDHOOD

child·ish /ˈtʃaɪldɪʃ; ˈtʃaɪldɪʃ/ *adj* **1** related to or typical of a child 孩子的；孩子般的：*a high childish laugh* 孩子般的大笑 **2** behaving in a silly way that makes you seem much younger than you really are 傻气的，孩子气的，幼稚的：*Stop messing around, it's so childish.* 别捣乱，太孩子气了。—compare 比较 CHILDLIKE —**childishly** *adv* —**childishness** *n* [U]

child·less /ˈtʃaɪldlɪs; ˈtʃaɪldləs/ *adj* having no children 无子女的：*a childless couple* 一对没有儿女的夫妻 —**childlessness** *n* [U]

child·like /ˈtʃaɪldˌlaɪk; ˈtʃaɪldlaɪk/ *adj* having qualities that are typical of a child, especially qualities such as INNOCENCE and trust 孩子般的，像孩子似的；天真无邪的：*an expression of childlike innocence* 天真烂漫的表情 —compare 比较 CHILDISH

Child·Line /ˈtʃaɪldlaɪn; ˈtʃaɪldlaɪn/ a British organization that

has a telephone helpline which children can call if they are being badly treated or if they cannot discuss their problems with their family 儿童求助热线〔英国开通帮助热线的一个组织。儿童如受到虐待或者遇到问题不能与家人说时，可拨打此热线〕

child·min·der /ˈtʃaɪldˌmaɪndə; ˈtʃaɪldˌmaɪndə/ *n* [C] *BrE* someone who is paid to look after young children while their parents are at work【英】〔孩子父母外出工作时受雇〕照看孩子的人; BABYSITTER *AmE*【美】—**childminding** *n* [U]

child prod·i·gy /ˌ·ˈ···/ *n* [C] a child who is unusually skilful at doing something such as playing a musical instrument 神童, 天才儿童; 有特殊才能的儿童

child·proof /ˈtʃaɪldˌpruf; ˈtʃaɪldpruːf/ *adj* something that is childproof is designed to prevent a child from opening, damaging, or breaking it 对孩童安全的; 不会被孩童弄坏的; 能防止孩童瞎摸弄的: *a childproof lock* 对儿童安全的锁

chil·dren /ˈtʃɪldrən; ˈtʃɪldrən/ *n* the plural of CHILD

Children in Need /ˌ···ˈ·/ a British CHARITY organization controlled by the BBC, which organizes special television programmes every year to collect money for children who need help in the UK and in other countries "困苦儿童"组织〔英国一慈善机构。此机构由英国广播公司管理，一年一度组织特别电视节目，为英国和其他国家需要帮助的儿童募集资金〕

children's home /ˈ·· ·/ *n* [C] a place in Britain where children live if their own parents cannot look after them〔英国的〕儿童之家，儿童收容所

child's play /ˈ· ·/ *n* [U] something that it is very easy to do 容易的事, 小儿科的事: *Cracking such a simple code was child's play to him.* 破译这么简单的代码对他来说是轻而易举的事。

child sup·port /ˈ· ·ˌ·/ *n* [U] *AmE* money that someone pays regularly to their former wife or husband in order to support their children【美】〔付给前配偶的〕子女抚养费; MAINTENANCE (2) *BrE*【英】

Child Support A·gen·cy, the /ˌ··ˈ·ˌ···/ abbreviation 缩写为 **the CSA** a British government department which deals with child support. It can decide, for example, how much money a father should pay to support his children if he no longer lives with them. 子女抚养事务处〔英国政府一部门，专门处理子女抚养费问题。例如，如果一个父亲不再与其子女一起生活，那么该部门可裁定他应支付的抚养费数额〕

Chil·e /ˈtʃɪli; ˈtʃɪli/ a long narrow South American country between the Pacific Ocean and the Andes mountains. Population: 15,328,000 (2001). Capital: Santiago. 智利〔南美洲一狭长国家，位于太平洋与安第斯山脉之间。人口: 15,328,000 (2001)，首都: 圣地亚哥〕—**Chilean** *n, adj*

chil·i /ˈtʃɪli; ˈtʃɪli/ *n* [C,U] the American spelling of CHILLI chilli 的美式拼法

chill¹ /tʃɪl; tʃɪl/ *v* **1** [I,T] if you chill something such as food or drink or if it chills, it becomes very cold but does not freeze (使) 冷却, (使) 变冷: *Chill the champagne in a bucket of ice.* 把香槟放在冰桶里冷却。| *Serve the melon chilled.* 端上冰镇甜瓜。**2** [T usually passive 一般用被动态] to make someone very cold 使〔某人〕感到很冷: **chilled to the bone/marrow** *Come and sit by the fire, you look chilled to the bone.* 过来坐在火炉边，你看上去冻坏了。**3** [T] *literary* to frighten someone, especially by seeming very cruel or violent【文】〔尤指以残忍和暴力的手段〕使…不寒而栗, 使…寒心: *The look in her eye chilled me.* 她眼中的神情让我不寒而栗。**4** [T] *literary* if you chill someone's hopes or keenness for doing something, you discourage them【文】使失望; 使〔热情〕冷却

chill out *phr v* [I] *especially AmE* to relax completely instead of feeling angry, tired, or nervous【尤美】完全放松, 不紧张: *Chill out, man, I didn't mean to insult you.* 老兄, 放轻松些, 我无意冒犯你。

chill² *n* **1** [singular] a feeling of coldness 寒冷, 寒气: *There's a real chill in the air.* 空气中透着寒意。| **take the chill off** (=heat something slightly) 稍稍加热 *Heat the baby's milk just enough to take the chill off.* 把宝宝的牛奶温一下, 不凉就行。**2** [C] a feeling of fear caused by something that is very unpleasant or cruel 害怕; 心寒: *Her description of the massacre sent a chill through the audience.* 她对大屠杀的描述让观众胆战心惊。| **send a chill down sb's spine** (=make them feel very frightened) 使某人非常恐惧 **3** [C] a mild illness with a fever 小感冒, 轻微发烧: **catch a chill** *It began to snow on the way home and I caught a nasty chill.* 在回家的路上天开始下雪, 我得了重感冒。**4** [singular] a way of behaving or speaking that is very unfriendly 不友好, 冷漠, 冷淡: *There was a marked chill in his voice when he answered.* 他回答时语气明显不友好。

chill³ *adj* unpleasantly cold 寒冷的, 寒气袭人的: *a chill wind* 寒风

chil·ler /ˈtʃɪlə; ˈtʃɪlə/ *n* [C] *informal* a film or book that is intended to frighten you【非正式】恐怖书; 恐怖电影: *the black magic chiller, 'Rosemary's Baby'* 巫术恐怖电影《魔鬼怪婴》

chil·li *BrE*【英】, **chili** *AmE*【美】/ˈtʃɪlɪ; ˈtʃɪli/ *n plural* **chillies, chilies 1** [U] a dish made with beans and usually meat cooked with chillies 辣味牛肉豆子〔一种用牛肉、豆和辣椒做成的菜肴〕: **chilli con carne** (=this dish made with meat) 辣味牛肉豆子 **2** [C] a small, thin type of PEPPER¹ (3) with a very strong, hot taste 辣椒 **3** [U] a hot-tasting red powder made from this PEPPER¹ (3) and used in cooking 辣椒粉

chil·ling /ˈtʃɪlɪŋ; ˈtʃɪlɪŋ/ *adj* something that is chilling makes you feel frightened, especially because it is cruel, violent, or dangerous 令人毛骨悚然的, 令人害怕的: *the chilling sound of wolves howling* 令人毛骨悚然的狼嚎

chilli pow·der /ˈ·· ˌ··/ *n* [U] CHILLI (3) 辣椒粉

chil·lum /ˈtʃɪləm; ˈtʃɪləm/ *n* [C] *slang* a type of pipe used for smoking CANNABIS【俚】吸食大麻用的烟斗

chill·y /ˈtʃɪlɪ; ˈtʃɪli/ *adj* **1** cold enough to make you feel uncomfortable 寒冷的, 严寒的: *The wind's a bit chilly.* 风有点儿冷。**2** unfriendly 冷漠的, 不友好的: *The speech met with a chilly reception.* 这次演讲的反应很冷淡。—see 见 COLD¹ (USAGE)—**chilliness** *n* [singular, U]

chilly bin /ˈ·· ·/ *n* [C] *NZE* a large container used for keeping food or drink cold【新西兰】〔储藏食物或饮料的〕冷藏箱, 冷藏柜

Chil·tern Hun·dreds, the /ˌtʃɪltən ˈhʌndrədz; ˌtʃɪltən ˈhʌndrədz/ the job of representing a particular government area in Buckinghamshire in Britain which no longer exists. Members of Parliament **apply for the Chiltern Hundreds** when they want to stop working before the next general election. 奇尔特恩诸邑执事〔代表英国白金汉郡某一已不复存在的行政区的官职。当议员等不到下次大选就想辞职时，往往就会 apply for the Chiltern Hundreds (提出辞呈)〕

Chilterns, the /ˈtʃɪltənz; ˈtʃɪltənz/ a range of CHALK hills in Eastern England, near London 奇尔特恩丘陵〔英格兰东部一白垩丘陵，位于伦敦附近〕

chi·mae·ra /kaɪˈmɪrə; kaɪˈmɪərə/ *n* [C] another spelling of CHIMERA chimera 的另一种拼法

chime¹ /tʃaɪm; tʃaɪm/ *v* **1** [I,T] if a bell or clock chimes, it makes a ringing sound, especially to tell you what time it is (使) 钟响; 报时: *The grandfather clock chimed six.* 大摆钟敲六点钟了。**2** [I+with] to be the same as something else or to have the same effect 与…协调; 与…一致: *Her views on art chime completely with mine.* 她对艺术的见解和我的完全一样。

chime in *phr v* [I] to say something in a conversation, especially to agree with what someone has just said 插话〔表示赞同〕: *"We'll miss you too," the children chimed in.* 那些孩子插嘴道: "我们也会想念你的。"

chime² *n* [C] **1** a ringing sound made by a bell or clock 钟声; 铃声: *the chime of the doorbell* 门铃声 **2 chimes** [plural] a set of bells or other objects that produce musical sounds〔可敲出音乐的〕一组钟

chi·me·ra, chimaera /kaɪˈmɪrə; kaɪˈmɪərə/ *n* [C] **1** an imaginary creature that breathes fire and has a lion's head, a goat's body, and a snake's tail 喀迈拉〔神话中狮头、羊身、蛇尾的吐火女怪〕**2** something, especially an idea or hope, that is not really possible and can never exist 幻想; 妄想: *trying to present that impossible chimera, 'a balanced view'* 试图提出那种不可能的妄想, 一种"平衡观点"

chi·me·ri·cal /kaɪˈmɛrɪkḷ; kaɪˈmerɪkəl/ *adj literary* imaginary or not really possible【文】幻想的; 不切实际的; 虚幻的

chim·ney /ˈtʃɪmnɪ; ˈtʃɪmni/ *n* [C] **1** a pipe inside a building that goes from a fire to the roof in order to let smoke out 烟囱, 烟筒: *a factory chimney belching smoke* 冒出浓烟的工厂烟囱 —see picture on page A4 参见 A4 页图 **2** a narrow opening in tall rocks or cliffs that you can climb up〔可容人攀登的〕岩石裂缝 **3** the glass cover that is put over the flame in an oil lamp〔煤油灯的〕玻璃灯罩

chimney breast /ˈ·· ·/ *n* [C] *BrE* the part of a wall in a room that encloses a chimney【英】壁炉腔

chimney-piece /ˈ·· ·/ *n* [C] *BrE* a decoration, usually made of brick or stone, built above a FIREPLACE【英】壁炉架; 壁炉台

chimney pot /ˈ·· ·/ *n* [C] a short wide pipe made of baked clay or metal, that is fixed to the top of a CHIMNEY 烟囱管帽

chimney stack /ˈ·· ·/ *n* [C] *BrE*【英】**1** the tall CHIMNEY of a building such as a factory〔工厂等的〕高烟囱; SMOKESTACK *AmE*【美】**2** a group of small chimneys on a roof〔屋顶上多烟道的〕烟囱体, 组合烟囱

chimney sweep /ˈ· · ·/ *n* [C] someone whose job is to clean CHIMNEYS using special long brushes 烟囱清扫工

chim·pan·zee /ˌtʃɪmpænˈzi; ˌtʃɪmpænˈziː/ also 又作 **chimp** /tʃɪmp; tʃɪmp/ *informal*【非正式】*n* [C] an intelligent African animal that is like a monkey without a tail〔非洲产的〕黑猩猩

CULTURAL NOTE 文化注释

In British zoos in the past, chimps were often dressed in clothes, sat at tables, and given food to have a **chimpanzees' tea party** for people to watch, but now this is felt to be cruel. 过去在英国的动物园里，人们常给黑猩猩穿上衣服，让其坐在桌边吃茶点，让人们观看。但现在人们认为这样做不人道。

3 **chin** /tʃɪn; tʃɪn/ *n* [C] **1** the front part of your face below your mouth 颏，下巴: *She sat with her chin in her hands.* 她双手托着下巴坐着。—see picture at 参见 HEAD[1] 图 **2 (keep your) chin up!** *spoken* used to tell someone to make an effort to stay cheerful when they are in a difficult situation【口】不要气馁！不要灰心！: *Chin up! It'll be over soon.* 振作点！很快就会过去的。

Chi·na /ˈtʃaɪnə; ˈtʃaɪnə/ the largest country in eastern Asia. Population: 1,339,000,000 (2010). Capital: Beijing. China's population is the largest of any country in the world. In 1949 it became a socialist state, known as the People's Republic of China (PRC). China is one of the most important economic and industrial powers in the world. 中国〔东亚最大的国家。人口: 1,339,000,000 (2010)，为世界之首; 首都: 北京。中国 1949 年成为社会主义国家，即中华人民共和国。中国是世界上最重要的经济和工业强国之一〕

china *n* [U] **1** a hard white substance produced by baking a type of clay at a high temperature 瓷，瓷料: *china teacups* 瓷茶杯 **2** also 又作 **chinaware** plates, cups etc made of china 瓷制品，瓷器: *We were given a lot of china as wedding presents.* 许多人送瓷器给我们作结婚礼物。

China Sea, the /ˌ· · ˈ·/ the western part of the Pacific Ocean that goes along the coast of China and Vietnam 中国海〔太平洋西部属海，沿岸有中国和越南〕

Chi·na·town /ˈtʃaɪnəˌtaun; ˈtʃaɪnətaʊn/ *n* [C,U] an area in a city where there are Chinese restaurants, shops, and clubs, and where a lot of Chinese people live 中国城，华人区，唐人街

chin·chil·la /tʃɪnˈtʃɪlə; ˌtʃɪnˈtʃɪlə/ *n* **1** [C] a small South American animal bred for its fur〔皮毛具有高价值的〕绒鼠[栗鼠] **2** [U] the pale grey fur of the chinchilla 绒鼠[栗鼠]的毛皮

Chi·nese[1] /tʃaɪˈniz; ˌtʃaɪˈniːz◂/ *n* **1** [U] the language of China 汉语，中文 **2 the Chinese** people from China 中国人 **3** [C] *BrE informal* a meal of Chinese food, or a restaurant that sells Chinese food【英，非正式】中国菜，中餐; 中餐馆

Chinese[2] *adj* from or connected with China 中国的

Chinese che·quers *BrE*【英】, **Chinese checkers** *AmE*【美】/ˌ· · ˈ· ·/ *n* [U] a game in which you move small balls from hole to hole on a board in the shape of a star 中国跳棋，波子棋

Chinese fire drill /ˌ· ˈ· ·/ *n* [singular] *AmE informal* a very confusing situation【美，非正式】混乱的局面

Chinese lan·tern /ˌ· · ˈ· ·/ *n* [C] a small box made of thin paper that you put a light inside as a decoration 纸灯笼

Chinese leaves /ˌ· · ˈ·/ *n* [U] a type of CABBAGE eaten especially in East Asia 白菜，青菜〔尤在东亚地区食用〕—see picture on page A9 参见 A9 页图

Chinese medi·cine /ˌ· · ˈ· · ·/ *n* [U] a kind of medicine that uses HERBS (=dried plants) and ACUPUNCTURE 中国医学，中医

Chinese whis·pers /ˌ· · ˈ· ·/ *n* [U] *BrE* the passing of information from one person to another, and then others, when the information gets slightly changed each time【英】〔以讹传讹或道听途说的〕闲言碎语，传话: *Chinese whispers started about child abuse in Cleveland and developed into a national scandal.* 在克利夫兰发生的虐童事件竟由开始时的闲言碎语演变成了一桩全国性的丑闻。

Chin·gach·gook /tʃɪnˈgɑːtʃguk; tʃɪnˈgɑːtʃgʊk/ a character in several books by James Fenimore Cooper, such as *The Last of the Mohicans*. He is a Native American chief. 钦加其古克〔詹姆斯·费尼莫尔·库珀《最后一个莫希干人》等几本小说中的人物，他是一位美洲土著酋长〕

Chink /tʃɪŋk; tʃɪŋk/ *n* [C] a very offensive word for a Chinese person 中国佬〔对中国人的蔑称〕

chink[1] *n* **1** [C] a small hole in a wall, or between two things that join together, that lets light or air through 裂缝; 裂口; 缝隙: *The sun came through a chink in the curtains.* 阳光从窗帘的缝隙中照了进来。**2** [C] a high ringing sound made by metal or glass objects hitting each other〔金属、玻璃等互相碰击发出的〕叮当声: *the chink of coins* 硬币叮当作响的声音 **3 a chink in sb's armour** a weakness in someone's character, argument etc that you can use to attack them〔性格、论点等的〕漏洞; 弱点

chink[2] *v* [I,T] if glass or metal objects chink or you chink them, they make a high ringing sound when they knock together (使)叮当响: *They chinked their glasses and drank a toast to the couple.* 他们相互碰杯，向那对夫妇敬酒。

chin·less /ˈtʃɪnlɪs; ˈtʃɪnləs/ *adj* **1** having a chin that is small or slopes inwards 没有下巴的，下巴内缩的 **2** *BrE* lacking courage or determination【英】没有勇气的; 犹豫不决的 **3 chinless wonder** a young man from an upper class family who is weak and stupid 无用愚蠢的纨绔子弟

chi·no /ˈtʃino; ˈtʃiːnəʊ/ *n* **1** [U] a strong material made of woven cotton 丝光斜纹布 **2 chinos** [plural] trousers made from this material 丝光斜纹布裤子

chin·strap /ˈtʃɪnˌstræp; ˈtʃɪnstræp/ *n* [C] a band of cloth under your chin to keep a hat or HELMET in place〔系于颏下固定帽子或头盔用的〕颏带

chintz /tʃɪnts; tʃɪnts/ *n* [U] smooth cotton cloth that is printed with flowery patterns and used for making curtains, furniture covers etc〔作窗帘或家具套等用的〕印花棉布: *pink chintz curtains* 粉红色花窗帘

chintz·y /ˈtʃɪntsɪ; ˈtʃɪntsi/ *adj* **1** covered with chintz 印花棉布面子的: *a chintzy sofa* 印花棉布面沙发 **2** *AmE informal* cheap and badly made【美，非正式】廉价劣质的，做工粗糙的: *a chintzy chest of drawers* 做工粗糙的五斗橱 **3** *AmE informal* unwilling to give people things or spend money; STINGY【美，非正式】小家子气的，吝啬的: *We don't need to be chintzy over the Christmas presents this year.* 我们今年买圣诞礼物不需要太小气。

chin up /ˈ· ·/ *n* [C] *AmE* an exercise in which you hang on a bar and pull yourself up until your chin is above the bar; PULL-UP【美】引体向上〔在单杠上做的体能锻炼〕

chin·wag /ˈtʃɪnˌwæg; ˈtʃɪnwæg/ *n* [singular] *informal especially BrE* an informal conversation; CHAT[1]【非正式，尤英】谈天，闲聊 —**chinwag** *v* [I]

chip[1] /tʃɪp; tʃɪp/ *n* [C] 2 3

1 ▸MARK 记号◂ a small hole or mark on a plate, cup etc where a piece has broken off〔物品碰损后留下的〕瑕疵，缺口: **[+in]** *There's a chip in this plate.* 这个盘子有个缺口。

2 ▸PIECE 片，块◂ a small piece of wood, stone, metal etc that has broken off something〔木、石、金属等的〕碎片，碎屑: *Wood chips covered the floor of the workshop.* 车间地板上满是木屑。—see picture on page A7 参见 A7 页图

3 ▸FOOD 食物◂ **a)** *BrE* a long thin piece of potato cooked in oil【英】炸马铃薯[土豆]条; FRENCH FRY *AmE*【美】: *fish and chips* 炸鱼和炸薯条 **b)** *AmE* a thin, flat round piece of potato cooked in very hot oil and eaten cold【美】炸薯片; CRISP[1] *BrE*【英】

4 ▸COMPUTER 电脑◂ **a)** a small piece of SILICON that has a set of complicated electrical connections on it and is used to store and PROCESS[2] (4) information in computers 微型集成电路片，芯片 **b)** the main MICROPROCESSOR of a computer 微处理器

5 have a chip on your shoulder to easily become offended or angry because you think you have been treated unfairly in the past〔因感到委屈而〕好争吵，好生气; 记恨: *He's always had a chip on his shoulder about not going to university.* 他因没能上大学而心怀愤懑。

6 be a chip off the old block *informal* to be very similar to your mother or father in appearance or character【非正式】〔外貌或性格〕酷似父亲[母亲]

7 ▸GAME 游戏◂ a small flat coloured piece of plastic used in GAMBLING to represent a particular amount of money〔用于赌钱的〕筹码

8 ▸SPORT 体育运动◂ a kick in football, RUGBY etc that makes the ball go high into the air for a short distance〔足球、橄榄球等运动中将球踢到空中的短距离的〕撮球

9 when the chips are down *spoken* a serious or difficult situation, especially one in which you realize what is really true or important【口】在重要关头，在紧急时刻: *When the chips are down, you've only got yourself to depend on.* 在紧要关头，你只能靠自已。

10 have had your chips *BrE informal* to be in a situation in which you no longer have any hope of improvement【英，非正式】失势; 完蛋 —see also 另见 BLUE CHIP, **cash in your chips** (CASH[2]), COW CHIP

chip[2] *v* **chipped, chipping 1** [I,T] if something such as a plate chips or if you chip it, a small piece of it breaks off accidentally (使)掉碎片; (使)〔边缘等〕稍有破损，弄缺: *Gary fell and chipped one of his front teeth.* 加里摔了一跤，碰掉一颗门牙。| *These cheap plates chip really easily.* 这些廉价的盘子很容易

碰破。**2** [T] to cut potatoes into thin pieces ready to be cooked in hot oil 将〔马铃薯〕切成小片[条] **3** [T] to hit or kick a ball in football, RUGBY etc so that it goes high into the air for a short distance〔足球、橄榄球等〕撮踢〔球〕

chip sth ↔ **away** *phr v* [T] to remove something, especially something hard that is covering a surface, by hitting it with a tool so that small pieces break off〔用工具将硬覆盖物一点一点地〕清除, 铲掉: *Sandy chipped away the plaster covering the tiles.* 桑迪铲掉了瓷砖上的灰泥。| [+at] *Archaeologists were carefully chipping away at the rock.* 考古学家正仔细地清理那块岩石。

chip away at sth *phr v* [T] to gradually make something less effective or destroy it〔逐步〕削弱; 损害: *The emphasis on testing has chipped away at teachers' autonomy.* 强调测试逐步削弱了老师的自主权。

chip in *phr v* **1** [I] to interrupt a conversation by saying something that adds more detail 插嘴, 插话: *They kept chipping in with facts and figures.* 他们不时地插话, 提供一些事实和数据。**2** [I,T] if each person in a group chips in, they each give a small amount of money so that they can buy something together 共同出钱, 凑钱: *I'd like to chip in if you're getting Mike a birthday present.* 如果你要给迈克买生日礼物的话, 我也想凑一份。

chip sth ↔ **off** *phr v* [T] to remove something by breaking it off in small pieces〔一点一点〕去掉: *Bert chipped the paint off the front door and varnished it.* 伯特将前门上的油漆刮去, 涂上清漆。

chip·board /ˈtʃɪpˌbɔrd; ˈtʃɪpbɔːd/ *n* [U] a type of board made from small pieces of wood pressed together with glue 刨花板; 碎木胶合板

chip·munk /ˈtʃɪpmʌŋk; ˈtʃɪpmʌŋk/ *n* [C] a small American animal similar to a SQUIRREL[1] with black lines on its fur 花鼠, 金花鼠, 花栗鼠〔产于美洲, 背部有黑白花纹〕

chip·o·la·ta /ˌtʃɪpəˈlɑtə; ˌtʃɪpəˈlɑːtə◂/ *n* [C] *BrE* a small thin SAUSAGE【英】奇珀拉特小香肠

chip pan /ˈ· ·/ *n* [C] *BrE* a deep pan with a wire basket inside used for cooking food in hot oil, especially chips (CHIP[1] (3))【英】〔尤指炸薯条用的, 内有滤油网架的〕深平底锅

chipped /tʃɪpt; tʃɪpt/ *adj* a cup, plate etc that is chipped has a small piece broken off the edge of it〔杯子、盘子等〕边缘有缺口的 —see picture on page A18 参见 A18 页图

Chip·pen·dale /ˈtʃɪpəndel; ˈtʃɪpəndeɪl/ Chippendale furniture is made in an 18th century style famous for its graceful shapes and fine decoration, and is named after the English furniture designer Thomas Chippendale (1718-79) 奇彭代尔式(的)〔奇彭代尔式家具按 18 世纪的风格制造, 因外形优美和装饰华丽而著称。此风格得名于英国家具设计师托马斯·奇彭代尔 (1718-1779)〕: *a fine pair of Chippendale chairs* 一对精致的奇彭代尔式椅子

chip·per /ˈtʃɪpɚ; ˈtʃɪpə/ *adj AmE* cheerful and active【美】兴高采烈的; 活泼的; 轻快的; 精力充沛的: *Grandma's over her illness and feeling pretty chipper again.* 奶奶病好了, 又恢复了以前的轻快干练。

chip·pings /ˈtʃɪpɪŋz; ˈtʃɪpɪŋz/ *n* [plural] *BrE* small pieces of stone used when putting new surfaces on roads or railway tracks【英】〔铺路或铁轨用的〕碎石

chip shop /ˈ· ·/ also 又作 **chip·py** /ˈtʃɪpɪ; ˈtʃɪpi/ *informal*【非正式】*n* [C] *BrE* a shop that cooks and sells FISH AND CHIPS and other food【英】〔烹制及出售炸鱼薯条及其他食物的〕薯条店

chi·rop·o·dist /kaɪˈrɑpədɪst; kḭˈrɒpədɪst/ *n* [C] *BrE* someone who is trained to examine and treat foot injuries and diseases【英】足病医生; PODIATRIST *AmE*【美】—**chiropody** *n* [U]

chi·ro·prac·tic /ˌkaɪrəˈpræktɪk; ˈkaɪrəpræktɪk/ *n* [U] a way of treating illness by pressing on and moving the bones in someone's SPINE (1)〔对脊柱的〕指压疗法; 按摩疗法 —**chiropractor** *n* [C]

chirp /tʃɝp; tʃɜːp/ also 又作 **chirrup** *v* [I] **1** if a bird or insect chirps, it makes short high sounds〔鸟或昆虫〕发啁啾声; 吱喳叫, 唧唧叫 **2** to speak in a cheerful, high voice 嘁嘁喳喳地说: *"Yes, all finished," he chirped.* "不错, 全完成了。" 他喜气洋洋地说。—**chirp** *n* [C]

chirp·y /ˈtʃɝpɪ; ˈtʃɜːpi/ *adj BrE informal* cheerful and active【英, 非正式】快活的; 活泼的: *You're very chirpy this morning – have you had some good news?* 你今天上午兴高采烈的, 有什么好消息吗? —**chirpily** *adv* —**chirpiness** *n* [U]

chir·rup /ˈtʃɪrəp; ˈtʃɪrəp/ *v* [I] CHIRP〔鸟或昆虫〕吱喳叫; 嘁嘁喳喳地说

chis·el[1] /ˈtʃɪzḷ; ˈtʃɪzəl/ *n* [C] a metal tool with a sharp edge, used to cut wood or stone 凿子, 凿刀 —see picture at 参见 TOOL[1] 图

chisel[2] *v* **chiselled, chiselling** *BrE*【英】**chiseled, chiseling** *AmE*【美】[T] **1** to use a chisel to cut wood or stone into a particular shape〔用凿子〕凿; 雕; 刻: **chisel sth into/from/in etc** *Martin chiselled a hole in the door for the new lock.* 马丁在门上凿了一个洞以便安装新锁。**2** *old-fashioned* to cheat or deceive someone, by getting more than you deserve【过时】哄骗, 欺骗 —**chiseller** *BrE*【英】**chiseler** *AmE*【美】*n* [C]

Chis·holm /ˈtʃɪzəm; ˈtʃɪzəm/, **Shir·ley** /ˈʃɝlɪ; ˈʃɜːli/ (1924-2005) a US politician who was the first black woman to be elected as a member of Congress in 1969 奇泽姆〔(1924-2005), 美国政治家。1969 年成为首位当选国会议员的黑人女性〕

Chisholm Trail, the /ˈ· ·, ·/ a path used for moving millions of cattle from Texas to Kansas during the 1800s 奇泽姆牛车道〔19 世纪由得克萨斯通往堪萨斯州的一条小道, 经由此处运送了上百万头牛〕

Chi·si·nau the capital and largest city of Moldova, on the Byk River, formerly called Kishinev 基希讷乌〔摩尔多瓦的首都和最大城市, 坐落于贝克河畔, 旧称基什尼奥夫〕

chit /tʃɪt; tʃɪt/ *n* [C] **1** an official note that shows that you are allowed to have something 便条; 字据; 账单; 收条: *Take the chit to the counter and collect your books.* 拿这张便条到柜台取书。**2** *old-fashioned* a young woman who behaves badly and does not respect older people【过时】冒失的女孩[少妇]; 黄毛丫头

chit-chat /ˈ· ·/ *n* [U] *informal* conversation about things that are not very important【非正式】聊天, 闲谈: *boring social chit-chat* 乏味的社交客套话

chit·ter·lings /ˈtʃɪtɚlɪŋz; ˈtʃɪtəlɪŋz/ also 又作 **chit·lings** /ˈtʃɪtlɪŋz; ˈtʃɪtlɪŋz/ **chitlins** /-lɪnz; -lḭnz/ *n* [plural] the INTESTINE of a pig eaten as food, especially in the southern US〔尤在美国南部供食用的〕猪小肠

chit·ty /ˈtʃɪtɪ; ˈtʃɪti/ *n* [C] *BrE informal* a CHIT (1)【英, 非正式】便条; 字据; 收条; 账单

chiv·al·rous /ˈʃɪvḷrəs; ˈʃɪvəlrəs/ *adj* a man who is chivalrous behaves in a polite, kind, generous, and honourable way, especially towards women〔男子〕有骑士风范的; 对〔女士〕彬彬有礼的; 体贴殷勤的: *a chivalrous attitude towards the loser* 对输家的骑士风度 —**chivalrously** *adv*

chiv·al·ry /ˈʃɪvḷrɪ; ˈʃɪvəlri/ *n* [U] **1** behaviour that is honourable, kind, generous, and brave, especially men's behaviour towards women 骑士品质〈如仁慈、慷慨、勇猛、对女士彬彬有礼等〉**2** a system of religious beliefs and honourable behaviour that KNIGHTs in the Middle Ages were expected to follow〔中世纪的〕骑士制度[精神]

chive /tʃaɪv; tʃaɪv/ *n* [C usually plural 一般用复数] a long thin green plant that looks and tastes like an onion, and is used in cooking〔烹调用的〕香葱, 虾夷葱

chiv·vy, chivy /ˈtʃɪvɪ; ˈtʃɪvi/ *v* **chivvied, chivvying** [T] *BrE* to try to make someone do something more quickly, especially in an annoying way【英】催促, 唠叨: **chivvy sb along/up** *Go and see if you can chivvy the kids up a bit.* 去看看你能不能催孩子们快点。

Chlo·e /ˈkloɪ; ˈkləʊi/ —see 见 DAPHNIS AND CHLOE

chlo·ride /ˈkloraɪd; ˈklɔːraɪd/ *n* [C,U] *technical* a chemical compound that is a mixture of chlorine and another substance【术语】氯化物: *sodium chloride* 氯化钠

chlo·ri·nate /ˈklorɪˌnet; ˈklɔːrḭneɪt/ *v* [T] to add chlorine to water to kill BACTERIA〔在水中〕加氯〔消毒〕

chlo·rine /ˈklorin; ˈklɔːriːn/ *n* [U] a greenish-yellow gas that is a chemical ELEMENT (=simple substance) and is often used to keep the water in swimming pools clean 氯, 氯气

chlo·ro·fluo·ro·car·bon /ˌklorofluəroˈkarbən; ˌklɔːrəʊflʊərəʊˈkɑːbən/ *n* [C] *technical* a CFC【术语】含氯氟烃

chlor·o·form /ˈklorəˌfɔrm; ˈklɒrəfɔːm/ *n* [U] a liquid that makes you become unconscious if you breathe it 氯仿, 哥罗仿, 三氯甲烷 —**chloroform** *v* [T]

chlo·ro·phyll /ˈklorəˌfɪl; ˈklɒrəfɪl/ *n* [U] the green-coloured substance in plants 叶绿素

choc /tʃɑk; tʃɒk/ *n* [C] *BrE informal* a CHOCOLATE (2)【英, 非正式】巧克力糖, 朱古力糖

choc·a·hol·ic /ˌtʃɑkəˈhɔlɪk; ˌtʃɒkəˈhɒlɪk/ *n* [C] another spelling of CHOCOHOLIC chocoholic 的另一种拼法

choc·cy /ˈtʃɑkɪ; ˈtʃɒki/ *n* [C] *BrE spoken* a CHOCOLATE (2)【英口】巧克力糖, 朱古力糖

choc-ice /ˈ· ·/ *n* [C] *BrE* a small block of ICE CREAM covered with chocolate【英】巧克力冰激凌, 紫雪糕〔表面裹有一层巧克力的冰砖〕

chock /tʃɑk; tʃɒk/ *n* [C] a block of wood or metal put in front of a wheel, door etc to prevent it from moving〔固定车轮、门等的〕垫木; 塞块; 楔子 —**chock** *v* [T]

chock-a-block /ˌtʃɑk ə ˋblɑk; ˌtʃɒk ə ˈblɒk◂/ *adj* [not before noun 不用于名词前] full of people or things that are very close to each other 挤得满满的: **[+with]** *Disneyland was chock-a-block with people that day.* 迪斯尼乐园那天挤满了人。

chock-full /ˌ· ˈ·◂/ *adj* [not before noun 不用于名词前] *informal* completely full【非正式】装满的, 塞满的: **[+of]** *The bus was chock-full of people.* 公共汽车上挤满了人。

choc·o·hol·ic also 又作 **chocaholic** /ˌtʃɑkəˋhɔlɪk; ˌtʃɒkəˈhɒlɪk/ *n* [C] someone who likes chocolate very much and eats it all the time 嗜吃巧克力的人

2 **choco·late** /ˋtʃɑkəlɪt; ˈtʃɒklɨt/ *n* **1** [U] a sweet brown food eaten for pleasure or used to give foods such as cakes a special sweet taste 巧克力, 朱古力: *a chocolate bar* 一条巧克力 | **chocolate cake/cookie/ice cream etc** (=cake etc that tastes of chocolate) 巧克力味蛋糕/曲奇饼/冰激凌等 | **milk chocolate** (=chocolate made with a lot of milk in it) 牛奶巧克力 | **dark** *AmE*【美】**/plain** *BrE*【英】**chocolate** (=chocolate that does not have much milk in it) 纯巧克力 | **plain** *AmE*【美】**/cooking** *BrE*【英】**chocolate** (=chocolate with no milk in it, used for cooking) 烹调用纯巧克力 | **white chocolate** (=chocolate that is white) 白巧克力 **2** [C] a small sweet that consists of something such as a nut or CARAMEL covered with chocolate 巧克力糖, 朱古力糖: *a box of chocolates* 一盒巧克力糖 **3** [C,U] a hot sweet drink made with milk and chocolate, or a cup of this drink 巧克力饮料; 一杯巧克力饮料

chocolate box /ˈ· · ·/ *adj* [only before noun 仅用于名词前] *BrE informal* very pretty, but in a way that seems false or artificial【英, 非正式】漂亮得有点太假[人工化]的: *a chocolate box village* 图画般的村庄

chocolate chip cook·ie /ˌ· · · ˈ· ·/ *n* [C] a kind of flat COOKIE containing small pieces of chocolate 巧克力碎曲奇

choco·lat·ey /ˋtʃɑkələtɪ; ˈtʃɒklɨti/ *adj* tasting or smelling of chocolate 巧克力味的

1 1 **choice**[1] /tʃɔɪs; tʃɔɪs/ *n*

1 ▶ABILITY TO CHOOSE 选择能力◀ [singular,U] the right to choose or the chance to choose between several things 选择权: *Nowadays both men and women are able to exercise choice as to whom they marry.* 如今, 男女都有选择与谁人结婚的权利。| **[+between]** *a genuinely free choice between candidates* 对候选人真正自由的选择 | **[+of]** *a choice of accommodation* 食宿的选择 | **have a choice** (=be able to choose) 能选择, 有选择的余地 | **give sb a choice** *I'll give you a choice – we can go to the movies or out for a meal.* 我让你来选择——我们可以去看电影, 也可以出去吃饭。| **have no choice** (=be forced to do something because it is the only thing you can do) 没有选择余地 *I had to go back. I was short of money and had no choice.* 我必须回去。我缺钱, 没有别的选择。| **leave sb with no choice** (=be forced to do something because it is the only thing you can do) 使某人别无选择 *He was left with no choice but to resign.* 他别无选择, 只能辞职。

2 ▶ACT OF CHOOSING 选择行为◀ [C] the act of choosing something 选择, 挑选: *The board denied that financial considerations had influenced their choice.* 董事会否认说财政因素影响了他们的选择。| **[+of]** *Alf left the choice of where they would go to Jenny.* 阿尔夫让珍妮决定到哪儿去。| **make a choice** (=choose) 作出选择 *You should find out more before making your final choice.* 你在作最后选择之前, 应该找出更多的资料。

3 ▶RANGE TO CHOOSE FROM 选择范围◀ [singular] the range of people or things that you can choose from 选择范围: *There's a small general store in town, but I don't think there will be much choice.* 镇上有一家小杂货店, 但我想那里的货物品种不会很多。| **[+of]** *There is a choice of dozens of magazines aimed at women readers.* 可供女性读者选择的杂志有几十种。| **have a choice** *In your exam you will have a choice of five questions.* 考试中, 共有五个问题供你选择。

4 ▶THING CHOSEN 选定的东西◀ [C usually singular 一般用单数] the person or thing that someone has chosen 被选中的东西[人], 抉择: *The choices you make now will affect you for many years.* 你现在所作出的抉择将会影响你许多年。| **[+of]** *The choice of Cannes as the venue for the conference was inspired.* 人们想到了于戛纳举行会议的主意。| **first/second etc choice** *Italy was our second choice – all the flights to Greece were booked up.* 去意大利是我们的第二选择, 因为飞往希腊的全部航班都已订购一空了。

5 ▶THING YOU MAY CHOOSE 可以选择的东西◀ [C] one of several things that you can choose 可供选择之物: *The computer will show you several search choices.* 电脑将给你展示好几种搜索办法。

6 of your choice chosen by you without anything limiting what you can choose from 自选的, 随便选择: *Chill and serve with the garnishes of your choice.* 冷却后加一些自己喜欢的装饰菜再端上去。

7 by choice if you do something by choice, you do it because you want to do it and not because you are forced to do it 自己选择的, 自愿的: *The government has claimed that many people are homeless by choice.* 政府声称许多人流离失所是出于自愿的。

8 the drug/treatment/newspaper etc of choice the thing that a certain group of people prefer to use 首选的药/治疗方法/报纸等: *It is the drug of choice for this type of illness.* 这是治疗这种病的首选药。—see also 另见 CHOOSE, HOBSON'S CHOICE

choice[2] *adj* **1** *formal* of a very high quality or standard, used especially of food【正式】〔尤指食物〕上等的, 精选的; 品质优良的: *choice apples* 优质苹果 | *a choice collection of antique books* 一套精选的古书 **2** choice meat, especially BEEF[1] (1), is of a standard that is good but not the best〔尤指牛肉〕中上级的: *choice steak* 中上级牛排 **3 a few choice words/phrases** if you use a few choice words, you say exactly what you mean in an angry way 尖刻的话, 刻薄的话: *He dismissed the objection in a few choice words.* 他用几句尖刻的话驳斥了反对的意见。

choir /kwaɪr; kwaɪə/ *n* [C] **1** a group of people who sing together, especially in a church or school〔学校或教堂等的〕唱诗班; 合唱团 **2** [usually singular 一般用单数] the part of a church in which the choir sits〔教堂中〕唱诗班的席位

choir·boy /ˋkwaɪrˌbɔɪ; ˈkwaɪəbɔɪ/ *n* [C] a young boy who sings in a church choir 唱诗班的男童歌手

choir loft /ˈ· ·/ *n* [C] *AmE* the part of a church, usually at the front, in which the choir sits【美】〔教堂中的〕唱诗班楼座

choir·mas·ter /ˋkwaɪrˌmæstɚ; ˈkwaɪəˌmɑːstə/ *n* [C] *BrE* someone who trains a choir【英】唱诗班的指挥; DIRECTOR (3) *AmE*【美】

choke[1] /tʃok; tʃəʊk/ *v*

1 ▶STOP BREATHING 停止呼吸◀ [I,T] to prevent someone from breathing, or to be prevented from breathing, because your throat is blocked or because there is not enough air (使)窒息, (使)呼吸困难: *The fumes were choking me.* 烟呛得我呼吸困难。| **[+on]** *He choked to death on a fish bone.* 他被一根鱼刺噎死了。

2 ▶INJURE 伤害◀ [T] to prevent someone from breathing and hurt them by putting your hands around their throat and pressing on it 掐住…的脖子: *Stop it – you're choking me!* 住手——你让我透不过气来了!

3 ▶BLOCK 堵塞◀ [I,T] to fill an area or passage so that it is difficult to move through it 阻塞, 塞住, 堵塞: *Weeds choked the canal.* 杂草把水道塞住了。| *The roads were choked with traffic.* 道路被川流不息的车辆堵塞了。

4 ▶VOICE 声音◀ [I,T] if your voice is choked or you choke with laughter or anger, your emotions make your voice sound strange and not very loud 哽咽;〔笑得或气得〕说不出话来: **[+with]** *"She's been raped," he said in a voice choked with emotion.* "她被奸污了。"他悲不自抑地哽咽着说。

5 ▶SAY STH 说出某事◀ [T] also 又作 **choke** sth ↔ **out** to say something one word or phrase at a time in a strange voice, because you are very upset or angry or because you have been laughing 哽住; 一字一顿地说: *"George," he choked out, "is that you, George?"* "乔治,"他一字一顿地说道, "是你吗, 乔治?"

6 ▶SPORTS 体育◀ [I] *AmE informal* to fail at doing something, especially a sport, because there is a lot of pressure on you【美, 非正式】〔因有压力而〕失败, 输: *They choked in the playoffs and lost the series 4 games to 2.* 他们在季后赛中未能发挥水平, 以2:4输了比赛。

7 ▶PLANTS 植物◀ [T] to kill a plant by surrounding it with other plants that take away its light and room to grow 扼杀, 使枯萎: *The thistles choked the corn.* 那些蓟把玉米全压死了。

8 choke a horse *AmE spoken* if something is big enough to choke a horse, it is very big or larger than usual【美口】异常大: *a wad of bills big enough to choke a horse* 一大叠账单

choke sth ↔ **back** *phr v* [T] to control your anger, sadness etc so that you do not show it 抑制, 强忍住: *I stood there trembling and trying to choke back the tears.* 我站在那里, 浑身颤抖, 强忍着泪水。

choke sth ↔ **down** *phr v* [T] **1** to eat something with difficulty, especially because you are ill or upset 咽, 硬吞〔食物〕: *He managed to choke down a sandwich.* 他勉强吞下一份三明治。**2** to choke something back 抑制, 强忍住

choke off *phr v* [T] to prevent someone from doing something or stop something happening 制止, 阻止; 压制: *A higher interest rate will choke off the demand for money.* 高利率会减少货币需求。

choke up *phr v* [I] **be choked up** to be very upset about something 对…紧张; 不知所措: *She and Mark broke up last week, and she's pretty choked up about it.* 她和马克上周闹翻了, 对此她心烦意乱。

choke² *n* **1** [C] a piece of equipment in a vehicle that controls the amount of air going into the engine, and that is used to help the engine start〔汽车引擎的〕阻气门 **2** [U] the controlling of the amount of air going into an engine by using this piece of equipment 用阻气门阻气: *Give it a bit more choke.* 把阻气门开大一点儿。**3** [C] the act or sound of choking 窒息; 噎; 呛[塞]住的声音

choke chain /ˈ· ·/ *n* [C] a chain that is fastened around the neck of a dog to control it〔控制狗的〕狗颈圈

choke·cher·ry /ˈtʃokˌtʃɛrɪ; ˈtʃəʊktʃeri/ *n* [C] a North American tree that produces small sour fruit 北美稠李树

choked /tʃokt; tʃəʊkt/ *adj* [not before noun 不用于名词前] *BrE* upset or angry【英】不安的; 生气的; 心烦意乱的: *I was really choked to hear he'd died.* 听到他的死讯, 我难过得说不出话来。

chok·er /ˈtʃokə; ˈtʃəʊkə/ *n* [C] a piece of jewellery or narrow cloth that fits closely around your neck 短项链; 刚好围住脖子的项圈

chok·y, chokey /ˈtʃokɪ; ˈtʃəʊki/ *n* [U] **in choky** *BrE old-fashioned* in prison【英, 过时】被拘留; 蹲监狱

chol·er /ˈkɑlə; ˈkɒlə/ *n* [U] *literary* bad temper【文】怒气, 暴躁脾气

chol·e·ra /ˈkɑlərə; ˈkɒlərə/ *n* [U] a serious disease of the stomach and BOWELS that is caused by bad water or infected food 霍乱

chol·e·ric /ˈkɑlərɪk; ˈkɒlərɪk/ *adj literary* bad-tempered or angry【文】脾气坏的; 生气的: *an unbalanced choleric individual* 精神错乱、脾气暴躁的人

cho·les·te·rol /kəˈlɛstəˌrol; kəˈlestərɒl/ *n* [U] a chemical substance found in fat, blood, and other cells in your body, which doctors think may cause heart disease 胆固醇

chomp /tʃɑmp; tʃɒmp/ *v* [I+away/on] to bite food noisily 大声地嚼: *chomping away on an apple* 大声嚼着苹果

Chom·sky /ˈtʃɑmskɪ; ˈtʃɒmski/, **No·am** /ˈnoəm; ˈnəʊəm/ (1928-) a US LINGUIST whose many new ideas about language have had a great influence on the study of language. He has also written books about politics, and has often criticized the way the US uses its power. 乔姆斯基〔(1928-), 美国语言学家。关于语言, 他提出了很多新观点, 对语言研究产生了极大影响。他还著有政治著作, 多次批评美国的用权方式〕

choo-choo /ˈtʃu tʃu; ˈtʃuː tʃuː/ *n* [C] *spoken* a word meaning a train, used by or to children【口】〔儿语〕火车

S1 W1 **choose** /tʃuz; tʃuːz/ *v past tense* **chose** /tʃoz; tʃəʊz/ *past participle* **chosen** /ˈtʃozn̩; ˈtʃəʊzən/ [I,T] **1** to decide which one of a number of things, possibilities, people etc that you want because it is the best or most suitable 挑选, 选择; 选取; 选中: **choose sth** *The party has finally chosen a woman as leader.* 这个政党最终选了一位女士当领导。| **choose to do sth** *He chose to learn German rather than French in school.* 他在学校选修德语而非法语。| *Eleanor was chosen to play the role of Juliet.* 埃莉诺被选中扮演朱丽叶的角色。| **choose** *I don't know which one to get. You choose.* 我不知道该要哪个, 你选吧。| **[+between]** *Maria was forced to choose between happiness and duty.* 玛丽亚被迫在幸福与责任之间作出选择。| **choose whether/which/when etc** *You should choose where we eat – I don't mind.* 你来选择到哪儿吃饭吧, 我无所谓。| **choose from** *a story chosen from a collection of fairy tales* 从一部童话故事集选出的一个故事 **2** to decide or prefer to do something or behave in a particular way 情愿; 选定; 决定: *We can, if we choose, take the case to appeal.* 要是我们愿意, 我们可以把案件上诉。| **choose to do sth** *We chose to ignore her rudeness.* 我们决定不理会她的无礼。**3 there is little/nothing to choose between** used when you think that two or more things are equally good and you cannot decide which is better 两者不相上下[同样的好], 难以取舍: *There was little to choose between the two candidates.* 两名候选人不相上下。—see also 另见 CHOICE¹

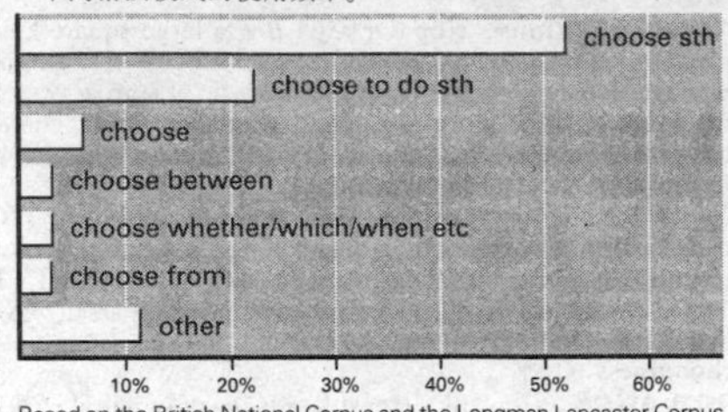
This graph shows how common different grammar patterns of the verb **choose** are. 本图表所示为动词 choose 构成的不同语法模式的使用频率。

Based on the British National Corpus and the Longman Lancaster Corpus
据英国国家语料库和朗文兰开斯特语料库

choos·y, choosey /ˈtʃuzɪ; ˈtʃuːzi/ *adj especially BrE* someone who is choosy will only accept food, clothes, jobs etc that they consider to be very good; PICKY【尤英】爱挑剔的, 过分讲究的: *She didn't much like the job, but she knew she couldn't afford to be choosy.* 她不太喜欢那份工作, 但她知道自己不能太挑剔。

chop¹ /tʃɑp; tʃɒp/ *v* **chopped, chopping**

1 ►CUT STH 切某物◄ [T] also 又作 **chop up** to cut something such as food or wood into smaller pieces 将〔食物、木材等〕切碎; 劈开: *Can you chop some firewood?* 你能劈些木柴吗? | **chop sth into pieces/chunks/segments** *Chop an onion into pieces.* 把洋葱切碎。—see picture on page A11 参见 A11 页图

2 ►REDUCE STH 减少某物◄ [T] to reduce by a large amount the money that can be spent〔大幅度〕削减: *Next year's budget has been chopped by fifty percent.* 明年的财政预算被大幅度削减了百分之五十。

3 ►SWING A TOOL 挥舞工具◄ [I] to swing a heavy tool such as an AXE¹ (1) in order to cut something〔用斧头等〕砍, 劈: **[+away/at]** *Ben's been chopping away at that tree for two hours now.* 本砍那棵树已有两个小时了。

4 ►MAKE A PATH 开路◄ [T] to make a path by cutting down plants 开路, 辟路: *The leader chopped a rough trail through the jungle.* 队长在丛林中开辟出一条崎岖的小路。| **chop your way through** *We chopped our way through the underbrush.* 我们披荆斩棘, 穿过了灌木丛。

5 chop and change *BrE informal* to keep changing your mind【英, 非正式】不停改变主意; 变化无常

6 ►HIT STH 打中某物◄ [T] to hit something by moving your hand downward quickly and suddenly〔用手向下〕砸: *I chopped his wrist and he dropped the knife.* 我猛砸一下他的手腕, 刀从他的手上掉了下来。

chop sth ↔ **down** *phr v* [T] to make a tree or strong plant fall down by cutting it with a sharp tool such as an AXE¹ (1)〔用斧头等利器〕砍倒, 伐倒

chop sth ↔ **off** *phr v* [T] to remove something by cutting it with a sharp tool such as an AXE¹ (1) so that it is no longer connected to something else〔用斧等〕砍掉, 砍断: *Charles I had his head chopped off.* 查理一世被斩首了。

chop² *n* [C]

1 ►MEAT 肉◄ a small flat piece of meat on a bone, usually cut from a sheep or pig〔羊、猪等〕带骨的肉块: *a grilled pork chop* 烤猪排

2 get the chop *BrE informal*【英, 非正式】**a)** to lose your job 被辞退, 被解雇: *Six more salesmen got the chop yesterday.* 昨天又有六名推销员被炒了鱿鱼。**b)** to officially stop something or reduce the amount you are paying for it 被中止; 被削减: *The project got the chop in the last board meeting.* 这个项目在上一次董事会上被取消了。

3 be for the chop *BrE informal* to be very likely to be closed or stopped【英, 非正式】很可能停止[关闭]: *One of the three factories is for the chop.* 三家厂中有一家可能要关掉。

4 ►WITH YOUR HAND 用手◄ a sudden downward movement with your hand 掌劈〔尤用掌侧〕: *a karate chop* 空手道的切击

5 ►WITH A TOOL 用工具◄ the act of hitting something once with a sharp tool such as an AXE¹ (1)〔用斧头等利器〕砍, 劈

6 the chops *informal* the part of your face that includes your mouth and jaw【非正式】颚, 下巴: *I hit him in the chops.* 我打了他的下巴。

chop-chop /ˌ· ˈ·/ *interjection especially BrE* an expression used when you want someone to hurry【尤英】〔用于催促〕快点: *Come on! Chop-chop!* 来吧! 赶快!

Chop·in /ˈʃopæn; ˈʃɒpæn/, **Fréd·é·ric** /ˈfrɛdrɪk; ˈfredərɪk/ (1810-49) a Polish COMPOSER, one of the most admired composers of piano music 肖邦〔(1810-1849), 波兰作曲家, 最受人仰慕的钢琴作曲家之一〕

chop·per /ˈtʃɑpɚ; ˈtʃɒpə/ *n* [C] **1** *BrE* a large square knife used for cutting large pieces of meat【英】大砍刀; 屠刀 **2** *informal* a HELICOPTER【非正式】直升飞机 **3** a type of MOTORCYCLE on which the front wheel is in front of the bars you use to control the vehicle instead of underneath them〔前轮位于车把之前的〕摩托车 **4 choppers** [plural] *slang* teeth【俚】牙齿

chopping board /ˈ· · ·/ also 又作 **chopping block** *n* [C] *especially BrE* a large piece of wood or plastic that you cut meat or vegetables on【尤英】砧板; CUTTING BOARD *AmE*【美】

chop·py /ˈtʃɑpɪ; ˈtʃɒpi/ *adj* choppy water has many small waves and is very rough to sail on〔水面〕浪花起伏的, 波浪滔滔的 —**choppiness** *n* [U]

chop·stick /ˈtʃɑpˌstɪk; ˈtʃɒpstɪk/ *n* [C usually plural 一般用复数] one of the two thin sticks that you use to eat food in many countries in Asia 筷子 —see picture at 参见 STICK² 图

Chop·sticks /ˈtʃɑpstɪks; ˈtʃɒpstɪks/ a simple TUNE that people often play on the piano, especially when they are learning to play the piano or are bored 筷子调〔人们在钢琴上弹奏的一只简单曲调, 尤见于学钢琴时或无聊时弹奏〕

chop su·ey /ˈtʃɑp ˈsuɪ; ˌtʃɒp ˈsuːi/ *n* [U] a Chinese dish made of pieces of vegetables and meat served with rice 炒杂碎〔用肉、蔬菜炒成的中国菜〕

cho·ral /ˈkɔrəl; ˈkɔːrəl/ *adj* [only before noun 仅用于名词前] involving singing by a CHOIR (=group of people) , or intended to be sung by a choir 唱诗班的; 合唱的; 合唱团的: *choral music* 唱诗班音乐 | *a choral concert* 合唱音乐会

cho·rale /koˈrɑl; kɒˈrɑːl/ *n* [C] a piece of music praising God usually sung in a church by a CHOIR (=group of people) 赞美诗, 圣歌: *a Bach chorale* 巴赫谱曲的赞美诗

choral so·ci·e·ty /ˈ· · ·, · · · ·/ *n* [C] *BrE* a group of people who sing together【英】合唱团

chord /kɔrd; kɔːd/ *n* [C] **1** a combination of two or more musical notes played at the same time〔音乐的〕和弦, 和音 **2 strike/touch a chord** to do or say something that people feel is familiar or true 引起〔某人〕内心共鸣; 打动: *His writings struck a chord in the hearts of the rebellious students.* 他的作品在那些反叛学生的心中引起了共鸣。**3** *technical* a straight line joining two points on a curve【术语】〔连接曲线上两点的〕弦 —see picture at 参见 CIRCLE¹ 图

chore /tʃɔr; tʃɔː/ *n* [C] **1** a job that you have to do regularly, especially work that you do to keep a house clean 家庭杂务; 日常零星工作: *household chores* 家庭杂务 **2** something you have to do that is very boring and unpleasant 令人厌烦的工作: *I find motorway driving a chore.* 我觉得在高速公路上驾车是件烦人的事。

chor·e·og·raph /ˈkɔrɪəˌgræf; ˈkɒriəgrɑːf/ *v* [T] to arrange how dancers should move during a performance 设计舞蹈动作, 编舞

chor·e·og·ra·phy /ˌkɔrɪˈɑgrəfɪ; ˌkɒriˈɒgrəfi/ *n* [U] the art of arranging how dancers should move during a performance 编舞(艺术); 舞蹈设计 —**choreographer** *n* [C]

chor·is·ter /ˈkɔrɪstɚ; ˈkɒrɪstə/ *n* [C] a singer in a CHOIR, especially a boy in a school choir that sings in a church 合唱团团员; 〔尤指〕唱诗班的男童歌手

chor·tle /ˈtʃɔrtl̩; ˈtʃɔːtl/ *v* [I] to laugh because you are amused or pleased about something 哈哈笑, 咯咯笑: *Harry chortled with delight.* 哈里高兴地哈哈大笑。—**chortle** *n* [C]

cho·rus¹ /ˈkɔrəs; ˈkɔːrəs/ *n* [C]

1 ▶SONG 歌曲◀ the part of a song that is repeated after each VERSE (=main part in a song) 副歌, 叠句: *Everyone joined in the chorus.* 唱到歌曲的副歌时, 大家也跟着齐唱起来。

2 ▶SINGERS 歌手◀ a large group of people who sing together 合唱团, 歌咏队: *the university chorus* 大学合唱团 —compare 比较 CHOIR (1)

3 ▶MUSIC 音乐◀ a piece of music written to be sung by a large group of people 合唱曲: *the Hallelujah Chorus* 哈利路亚合唱曲

4 ▶GROUP IN MUSICAL PLAY 音乐剧中的歌舞队◀ a group of singers, dancers, or actors who act together in a show but do not have the main parts 歌舞队: *a member of the chorus in the musical '42nd Street'* 音乐剧《第四十二街》歌舞队的成员

5 a chorus of thanks/disapproval/protest etc something expressed by many people at the same time 异口同声的感谢/反对/抗议: [+of] *Peggy's announcement brought a chorus of congratulation.* 佩姬的宣布引来一片祝贺声。

6 in chorus if people say something in chorus, they say the same thing at the same time 一起; 同时; 一致: *"Mom!" the kids cried in chorus.* "妈!"孩子们同时叫了一声。

7 ▶PLAY 戏剧◀ **a)** in ancient Greek plays, the chorus is the group of actors who give explanations or opinions about the play〔古希腊戏剧中〕解释剧情的演员 **b)** in English drama of the early 1600s, the chorus is usually one person who gives explanations or opinions about the play, especially at the beginning or the end〔17世纪早期英国戏剧中开场或终场时〕进行解说者

chorus² *v* [T] if two or more people chorus something, they say it at the same time 同时说, 异口同声地说: *"Good morning," we chorused.* "早安。"我们齐声说道。

chorus girl /ˈ· · ·/ *n* [C] a woman who sings and dances in a group in a play or film〔戏剧或电影中的〕歌舞队女演员

chorus line /ˈ· · ·/ *n* [C] a group of people who sing and dance together, especially while standing in a straight line, in a play or film〔戏剧或电影中的〕歌舞队, 〔尤指〕排成一列的歌舞队

chose /tʃoz; tʃəʊz/ the past tense of CHOOSE

cho·sen /ˈtʃozn̩; ˈtʃəʊzən/ the past participle of CHOOSE —see also 另见 WELL-CHOSEN

chow¹ /tʃaʊ; tʃaʊ/ *n* **1** [U] *slang* food【俚】食物, 食品: *It's chow time!* 该吃饭啦! **2** also 又作 **chow chow** /ˈ· ·/ [C] a dog with long thick fur and a dark-coloured tongue that first came from China 松狮狗〔原产于中国的一种狗, 毛厚, 舌呈蓝黑色〕

chow² *v*

chow down *phr v* [I] *AmE informal* to eat【美, 非正式】吃: *We were chowing down on powdered donuts.* 我们在吃糖粉油炸面圈饼。

chow·der /ˈtʃaʊdɚ; ˈtʃaʊdə/ *n* [U] a thick soup usually made with CLAMs or fish, vegetables, and milk 杂烩海鲜汤, 周打汤

chow·der·head /ˈtʃaʊdɚˌhɛd; ˈtʃaʊdəhed/ *n* [singular] *AmE slang* a stupid person【美俚】傻瓜, 笨蛋

chow mein /ˈtʃaʊ ˈmen; ˌtʃaʊ ˈmeɪn/ *n* [U] a Chinese dish made with meat, vegetables and NOODLEs 炒面

Chré·tien de Troyes /ˌkretjæn də ˈtrwɑ; ˌkreɪtiæn də ˈtrwɑː/ (late 12th century) a French poet who wrote five long poems about King Arthur and his followers, which influenced many other writers 克雷蒂安·德·特罗亚〔(12 世纪晚期) 法国诗人, 曾写过五首有关亚瑟王及其追随者的长诗, 对许多作家产生过影响〕

Christ¹ /kraɪst; kraɪst/ *n* **1** also 又作 **Jesus Christ, Jesus** the man on whose life, death and teaching Christianity is based, believed to be the son of God 基督, 耶稣基督 —see 见 JESUS¹ (USAGE) **2 the Christ** the religious leader who Christians believe saves the world 救世主

Christ² *interjection* used to express annoyance, surprise etc 天哪!〔表示厌烦、吃惊等〕: *Christ! I've left my keys at home.* 天哪! 我把钥匙留在家里了。

chris·ten /ˈkrɪsn̩; ˈkrɪsən/ *v* [T] **1** to be officially given your name at a Christian religious ceremony soon after you are born 为…施洗礼, 〔在洗礼仪式上〕为…命名: **be christened** *She was christened Sarah.* 她在洗礼时给取名为萨拉。**2** to invent a name for someone because it describes them well 给…起绰号[雅号]: *Tony's colleagues christened him Romeo.* 托尼的同事给他起了个绰号叫罗密欧。**3** *BrE informal* to use something for the first time【英, 非正式】首次使用: *We haven't christened the new dinner service yet.* 我们还未用过这套新餐具。

Chris·ten·dom /ˈkrɪsn̩dəm; ˈkrɪsəndəm/ *n* [U] *old-fashioned* all the Christian people or countries in the world【过时】〔全世界所有的〕基督教徒; 基督教国家

chris·ten·ing /ˈkrɪsn̩ɪŋ; ˈkrɪsənɪŋ/ *n* [C,U] a Christian religious ceremony at which someone is officially given their name and becomes a member of a Christian church 洗礼〔给某人施洗礼命名的仪式〕

Chris·tian¹ /ˈkrɪstʃən; ˈkrɪstʃən/ *n* [C] **1** a person who believes in the ideas taught by Jesus Christ or belongs to a Christian church 基督徒 **2** *informal* a good person【非正式】正派的人, 高尚的人, 好人

Christian² *adj* **1** believing the ideas taught by Jesus Christ, or belonging to a Christian church 基督教的; 信奉基督教的; 属基督教教会的: *Christian ministers* 基督教牧师 **2** based on the ideas taught by Jesus Christ 基督教教义的: *Christian doctrine* 基督教教义 **3** also 又作 **christian** behaving in a good, kind way 仁慈的, 慈悲的: *Laughing at his misfortune wasn't a very christian act.* 嘲笑他的不幸是不仁慈的行为。

Christian Aid /ˌ· · ˈ·/ a Christian CHARITY organization that provides money, equipment, advice etc in order to help poorer

countries develop their farming and industry 基督教援助委员会〔基督教一慈善机构，提供资金、设备、建议等帮助贫困国家发展农业和工业〕

Christian Co·a·li·tion, the /,‥ ˈ‥/ a right-wing Christian political group in the US, which tries to influence government decisions, so that laws are based on traditional Christian morals. It is known for opposing ABORTION and equal rights for women and HOMOSEXUALs. 基督教联盟〔美国右翼基督教政治团体，试图影响政府的决策，从而使美国的法律立足于基督教的传统道德观念。该联盟以反对流产、为妇女和同性恋者争取平等权利而著称〕

Christian e·ra /,‥ ˈ‥/ *n* [singular] the period from the birth of Christ to the present 基督纪元; 公元; 西历纪元

Chris·ti·an·i·ty /ˌkrɪstʃɪˋænətɪ; ˌkrɪstiˈænʒti/ *n* [U] the religion based on the life and teachings of Jesus Christ 基督教

Christian name /ˈ‥ ‥/ *n* [C] the name someone is given when they are christened (CHRISTEN (1)), or someone's first name 教名〔洗礼时所取名字〕, 名字; GIVEN NAME *especially AmE*【尤美】: *His Christian name is Michael.* 他的教名是迈克尔。

Christian Sci·ence /,‥ ˈ‥/ *n* [U] a religion started in America in 1866, which includes the belief that illnesses can be cured by faith 基督教科学派〔1866 年于美国创立，主张靠信仰即可治愈疾病的教派〕—**Christian Scientist** *n* [C]

Christian Science Mon·i·tor, The /,‥ ˈ‥, ‥/ a US daily newspaper, owned by the Christian Science religion, which has articles about politics, national and international news, and short stories《基督教科学箴言报》〔由基督教科学派主办的一份美国报纸。该报纸以政治文章、国内外新闻和简要报道而著称〕

Chris·tie /ˋkrɪstɪ; ˈkrɪsti/, **Ag·a·tha** /ˋægəθə; ˈægəθə/ (1890-1976) a British writer who wrote many popular NOVELs about murders and the DETECTIVEs who try to find out who did them. Her most famous characters are Miss Marple and Hercule Poirot, and two of her best-known books are *Murder on the Orient Express* and *Death on the Nile*. 克里斯蒂〔(1890-1976)，英国作家。她创作了大量深受读者喜爱的侦探小说，笔下最出名的人物是马普尔小姐和赫邱尔·波洛。她最著名的两部小说是《东方快车谋杀案》和《尼罗河上的惨案》〕

Chris·tie's /ˋkrɪstɪz; ˈkrɪstiz/ a famous AUCTION house with its main offices in London and New York City, where valuable paintings, old furniture, rare books etc are sold. 克里斯蒂拍卖行〔一家著名拍卖行，在伦敦和纽约设有分行，拍卖名画、古家具、珍本书籍等〕—see 见 SOTHEBY'S

Christ·mas /ˋkrɪsməs; ˈkrɪsməs/ *n* [C,U] **1** also 又作 **Christmas Day** December 25th, the day when Christians celebrate the birth of Christ 圣诞节〔12 月 25 日〕: *Are you going home for Christmas?* 你回家过圣诞节吗? **2** the period before and after this day 圣诞节节期: *It snowed all over Christmas.* 整个圣诞节期间都在下雪。

Christmas cake /ˈ‥ ‥/ *n* [C,U] a special cake eaten in Britain at Christmas〔英国人圣诞节时吃的〕圣诞蛋糕

Christmas card /ˈ‥ ‥/ *n* [C] a card that you send to friends and relatives at Christmas with your good wishes 圣诞（贺）卡

Christmas car·ol /,‥ ˈ‥/ *n* [C] a Christian song sung at Christmas; CAROL[1] 圣诞颂歌

Christmas Carol, A a short NOVEL by Charles Dickens about an unpleasant old man called Scrooge who hates to spend money. On Christmas Eve several ghosts visit him to warn him about what will happen if he does not change. When he wakes up the next morning, he becomes a happy generous person, especially to his worker Bob Cratchit and Cratchit's sick son Tiny Tim.《圣诞颂歌》〔查尔斯·狄更斯所著短篇小说。小说讲述一位讨厌花钱的坏脾气老头斯克鲁奇的故事。圣诞前夕，有几个鬼魂造访他，警告他说，如果他再不改变，就会有不测之事。第二天早晨醒来后，他变成了一个快乐大方的人，对工人鲍勃·克拉基伊特及其患病的儿子小蒂姆尤为慷慨〕

Christmas cook·ie /,‥ ˈ‥/ *n* [C] a COOKIE eaten in the US at Christmas〔美国人圣诞节时吃的〕圣诞小甜饼

Christmas crack·er /,‥ ˈ‥/ *n* [C] a brightly coloured tube of paper containing a small toy that two people pull at Christmas parties 圣诞彩包爆竹〔一种拉开时噼啪作响的彩纸筒，里面装有小玩具〕

Christmas Day /,‥ ˈ‥/ *n* [C,U] December 25th, the day when Christians celebrate the birth of Christ 圣诞节〔12 月 25 日，基督徒庆祝耶稣诞生的日子〕

Christmas din·ner /,‥ ˈ‥/ *n* [C] a special meal eaten on Christmas Day, consisting mainly of TURKEY (2) and vegetables, followed by Christmas pudding 圣诞大餐

CULTURAL NOTE 文化注释

In the US and UK, Christmas dinner typically includes TURKEY with various vegetables and SAUCEs and, in the UK, this is usually followed by CHRISTMAS PUDDING. 在英美两国，圣诞大餐经常包括配有各种蔬菜和调味汁的火鸡。在英国，圣诞大餐后还有圣诞布丁。

Christmas Eve /,‥ ˈ‥/ *n* [C,U] the day before Christmas Day 圣诞前夕, 平安夜, 圣诞夜

Christmas pud·ding /,‥ ˈ‥/ *n* [C] a PUDDING containing a lot of dried fruit eaten at Christmas 圣诞布丁

Christmas stock·ing /,‥ ˈ‥/ *n* [C] a long sock which children leave out on Christmas Eve to be filled with presents 圣诞袜〔小孩子在圣诞夜挂起来盛放礼物的长袜子〕

Christ·mas·sy /ˋkrɪsməsɪ; ˈkrɪsməsi/ *adj informal* typical of or connected with Christmas【非正式】圣诞节的; 与圣诞节有关的: *a nice Christmassy feeling* 一种美妙的过圣诞节的感觉

Christ·mas·time /ˋkrɪsməsˌtaɪm; ˈkrɪsməstaɪm/ *n* [U] the period during Christmas when people celebrate 圣诞节节期

Christmas tree /ˈ‥ ‥/ *n* [C] a FIR tree either real or artificial that you decorate specially for Christmas 圣诞树

Chris·to /ˋkrɪsto; ˈkrɪstəʊ/ (1935-) a US artist, born in Bulgaria, who works with his wife, Jeanne-Claude. He is famous for his large temporary works that change the appearance of the land or of large buildings. 克里斯托〔(1935-)，出生于保加利亚的美国艺术家。他与妻子珍妮-克劳德合作，创作户外大型临时作品，以改变大地或大型建筑的外貌，并因此而闻名〕

Chris·to·pher /ˋkrɪstəfɚ; ˈkrɪstəfə/, **Saint** (?-?250 AD) according to the Christian religion, a man who carried Christ across a river, and who became the PATRON SAINT of travellers 克里斯多弗〔(?-?公元 250)，根据基督教典故，他背负耶稣过河，最后成为旅行者的主保圣人〕

Christopher Rob·in /,‥ ˈ‥/ a character in stories and poems by A. A. Milne. He is a small boy who is a friend of Winnie the Pooh. 克里斯多弗·罗宾〔A. A. 米尔恩创作的故事和诗歌中的一位小男孩，他是小熊维尼的朋友〕

chro·mat·ic /kroˋmætɪk; krəʊˈmætɪk/ *adj* **1** connected with or containing bright colours 彩色的, 颜色鲜艳的 **2** related to the musical scale which consists of SEMITONEs 半音（阶）的: *the chromatic scale* 半音阶

chrome /krom; krəʊm/ *n* [U] a hard ALLOY (=a combination of metals) of chromium and other metals used for covering objects with a shiny protective surface 铬合金

chrome yel·low /, ˈ‥◂/ *n* [U] a very bright yellow colour 铬黄色, 鲜黄色

chro·mi·um /ˋkromɪəm; ˈkrəʊmiəm/ *n* [U] a blue or white metal that is an ELEMENT (=simple substance) and is used for covering objects with a shiny protective surface 铬: *chromium plated* 镀铬的

chro·mo·some /ˋkroməˌsom; ˈkrəʊməsəʊm/ *n* [C] *technical* a part of every living cell that is shaped like a thread which controls the character, shape etc that a plant or animal has【术语】染色体: *x and y chromosomes* x 和 y 染色体

chron- /krɑn; krɒn/ *prefix* another form of the prefix CHRONO- 前缀 chrono- 的另一种形式

chron·ic /ˋkrɑnɪk; ˈkrɒnɪk/ *adj* [usually before noun 一般用于名词前] **1** a chronic disease or illness is one that cannot be cured〔疾病〕慢性的, 长期的: *He's been suffering from chronic arthritis for years now.* 他患慢性关节炎好几年了。**2** a problem or difficulty that you cannot get rid of or that keeps coming back〔问题、困难〕长期的, 反复出现的: *a chronic shortage of language teachers* 语文教师长期不足 | *chronic unemployment* 长期的失业问题 **3 chronic alcoholic/gambler etc** someone who suffers from a particular problem or type of behaviour for a long time and cannot stop 酒鬼/沉迷赌博的人: *Jake was a chronic alcoholic who could not hold down a job.* 杰克酗酒成性, 什么工作也干不长。**4** *BrE informal* extremely bad【英, 非正式】恶劣的; 糟透的: *Don't go to that new restaurant, I've heard the food's chronic.* 不要去那家新餐馆, 听说那儿的食物糟透了。—**chronically** /-klɪ; -kli/ *adv*: *chronically ill* 长期患病的

chron·i·cle[1] /ˋkrɑnɪkl; ˈkrɒnɪkəl/ *n* [C] a written record of a series of events, especially historical events, written in the order in which they happened 编年史, 年代记: **[+of]** *The book provides a detailed chronicle of the events leading up to his death.* 这本书详细记载了导致他死亡的一系列事件。

chronicle[2] *v* [T] to give an account of a series of events in the order in which they happened 将〔一系列事件〕载入编年史中; 记录〔大事〕: *The effect of her parents' separation on her*

childhood is carefully chronicled in the book. 父母分居对她童年造成的影响都详细地记载在这本书中。—**chronicler** *n* [C]

chrono- /krɑno; krɒnəʊ/ also 又作 **chron-** *prefix* concerning time 有关时间的: *a chronometer* (=instrument for measuring time very exactly) 精密计时仪器

chron·o·graph /ˋkrɑnə͵græf; ˈkrɒnəgrɑːf/ *n* [C] a scientific instrument for measuring and recording periods of time 计时仪[器]; 秒表

chron·o·log·i·cal /͵krɑnəˋlɑdʒɪkḷ; ͵krɒnəˈlɒdʒɪkəl◂/ *adj* arranged according to when something happened 按时间先后顺序排列的: **chronological order** *Put the following battles in chronological order.* 将下列战争按时间顺序排列出来。—**chronologically** /-kḷɪ; -kli/ *adv*

chro·nol·o·gy /krəˋnɑlədʒɪ; krəˈnɒlədʒi/ *n* [U] the science of giving times and dates to events 年代学

chro·nom·e·ter /krəˋnɑmətɚ; krəˈnɒmɪ̣tə/ *n* [C] a very exact clock for measuring time, used for scientific purposes 精密计时钟表

chrys·a·lis /ˋkrɪsḷɪs; ˈkrɪsəḷs/ *n* [C] a MOTH or BUTTERFLY at the stage of development when it has a hard outer shell, before being a LARVA and an adult 蝶蛹; 蛾蛹

chry·san·the·mum /krɪsˋænθəməm; krɪˈsænθɪ̣məm/ *n* [C] a garden plant with large brightly coloured flowers 菊(花)

Chrys·ler /ˋkraɪzlɚ; ˈkraɪzlə/ *trademark*【商标】**1** a large US company that makes cars of many different types and sizes. In 1998, Chrysler joined with the German car maker Daimler-Benz to form a new company. 克莱斯勒汽车公司〔美国大型汽车制造商, 生产多种型号的大小汽车。1998 年与德国汽车制造商戴姆勒-奔驰公司合并组成新的公司〕**2** a type of car made by this company 克莱斯勒汽车

chub·by /ˋtʃʌbɪ; ˈtʃʌbi/ *adj* fat in a pleasant healthy-looking way 圆圆胖胖的; 丰满的: *I was chubby even as a baby.* 我还是婴孩时就胖嘟嘟的。| *chubby cheeks* 圆胖的脸颊 —**chubbiness** *n* [U] —see 见 FAT[1] (USAGE)

2 **chuck**[1] /tʃʌk; tʃʌk/ *v* [T] *informal*【非正式】**1** to throw something in a careless or relaxed way〔胡乱或随便地〕扔, 抛: **chuck sth on/out of/into etc** *Tania chucked her bag down on the sofa.* 塔妮娅把袋子胡乱扔在沙发上。| **chuck sb sth** *Chuck me that magazine, would you?* 把那本杂志扔给我好吗? **2 chuck sb** *BrE* to end a romantic relationship with someone【英】甩掉〔某人〕: *Why did Judy chuck him?* 为什么朱迪会甩了他呢? **3 chuck sb under the chin** to gently touch someone under their chin, especially a child 轻抚…的下巴〔尤对小孩〕

chuck sth ↔ **away/out** *phr v* [T] to throw something away 扔掉: *We had to chuck a lot of stuff out when we moved.* 我们搬家时, 不得不扔掉很多杂物。

chuck sb ↔ **out** *phr v* [T] to make someone leave a place, especially because they are behaving badly 迫使〔某人〕离开; 赶走, 撵走: *We got chucked out of the pub last night.* 昨晚我们被撵出酒馆。

chuck sth ↔ **in** *phr v* [T] *BrE* to stop doing something, especially something that is boring or annoying【英】停止; 放弃: *What on earth made him chuck his job in so suddenly?* 究竟是什么原因使他这么突然地辞掉工作呢?

chuck up *phr v* [I,T] *especially BrE slang* to VOMIT[1]【尤英, 俚】呕吐: *I was chucking up all night.* 我吐了一晚上。

chuck[2] *n* **1** [C] part of a machine that holds something so that it does not move〔机器的〕卡盘, 夹盘 **2** *spoken* a word used to address someone in some parts of Northern England【口】嗨〔英格兰北部一些地区称呼的用语〕

chuck·le /ˋtʃʌkḷ; ˈtʃʌkəl/ *v* [I] to laugh quietly 低声轻笑; 暗自笑: *What are you chuckling about?* 你在偷笑什么? —**chuckle** *n* [C]

chuck·le·head /ˋtʃʌkḷ͵hɛd; ˈtʃʌkəlhed/ *n* [C] *AmE informal* a stupid person【美, 非正式】傻瓜, 笨蛋

chuck steak /͵· ˈ·/ *n* [U] meat that comes from just above the shoulder of an animal〔动物的〕颈肉; 牛肩肉排

chuck wag·on /ˈ· ͵··/ *n* [C] *AmE old-fashioned* a vehicle that carries food for a group of people【美, 过时】流动炊事车

chuffed /tʃʌft; tʃʌft/ *adj BrE informal* very pleased or happy【英, 非正式】愉快的, 高兴的: *He's really chuffed about passing the exam.* 他因通过考试而满心欢喜。

chug /tʃʌg; tʃʌg/ *v* **chugged, chugging** [I always+adv/prep] if a car, train etc chugs, it moves slowly making a repeated low sound〔汽车、火车等〕发出嘎嚓声地缓慢前进: [**+along/up/around etc**] *The boat chugged out of the harbour.* 小船突突地驶出港口。—**chug** *n* [C usually singular 一般用单数]

chug-a-lug /ˈ· · ͵·/ *v* [T] *AmE informal* to drink all of something in a glass or bottle without stopping【美, 非正式】一口气喝完: *He chug-a-lugged the entire thing.* 他咕噜咕噜一口气全喝完了。

chum[1] /tʃʌm; tʃʌm/ *n* [C] *old-fashioned* a good friend【过时】好朋友: *Freddie's an old school chum of mine.* 弗雷迪是我的一位老校友。

chum[2]

chum up *phr v* [I] *old-fashioned* to become someone's friend【过时】(与…) 成为朋友: [**+with**] *She soon chummed up with the girl in the next room.* 她不久就与隔壁房间的女孩成了好朋友。

chum·my /ˋtʃʌmɪ; ˈtʃʌmi/ *adj old-fashioned* friendly【过时】友好的 —**chummily** *adv* —**chumminess** *n* [U]

chump /tʃʌmp; tʃʌmp/ *n* [C] *BrE*【英】**1** *old-fashioned* someone who is silly or not very clever【过时】傻瓜, 笨蛋 **2 chump chop/steak** a thick piece of meat with a bone in it 厚肉块/大块牛排 **3 be off your chump** *old-fashioned* to be doing or intend to do something extremely silly【过时】发疯, 发狂

chun·der /ˋtʃʌndɚ; ˈtʃʌndə/ *v* [I] *informal* to VOMIT[1]【非正式】呕吐

chunk /tʃʌŋk; tʃʌŋk/ *n* [C] **1** a large piece of something that does not have an even shape 厚块, 大块: [**+of**] *a chunk of cheese* 一大块乳酪 —see picture on page A7 参见 A7 页图 **2** a large part or amount of something 大量; 大部分: *The rent takes a large chunk out of my monthly salary.* 房租占去我薪水的一大部分。| *It's sad to see another chunk of the old Liverpool gone.* 看到利物浦老城又有很大一部分消失了, 真伤心。

chunk·y /ˋtʃʌŋkɪ; ˈtʃʌŋki/ *adj* **1** thick, solid and heavy 厚重的: *She wore a lot of chunky silver jewellery.* 她戴着很多沉甸甸的银首饰。**2** someone who is chunky has a broad, heavy body〔人〕壮实的

Chun·nel, the /ˋtʃʌnḷ; ˈtʃʌnl/ a name used especially in newspapers for the Channel Tunnel 英吉利海峡隧道〔尤用于报纸〕

church /tʃɝtʃ; tʃɜːtʃ/ *n* **1** [C] a building where Christians go to worship 教堂, 礼拜堂 **2** [U] the religious ceremonies in a church〔教堂的〕礼拜仪式: *Mrs Dobson invited us to dinner after church.* 多布森太太邀请我们做完礼拜后到她家吃饭。**3 the church** the profession of the CLERGY (=priests and other people employed by the church) 牧师 (的职位); 神职人员 **4** [singular, U] the institution of the Christian religion〔基督教〕教会: *separation of church and state* 政教分离 1 1

CULTURAL NOTE 文化注释

In the US and the UK, churches have regular SERVICES on Sundays, and have special services on religious holidays such as Easter and Christmas. Churches are also used for special ceremonies such as weddings, CHRISTENINGS, and funerals, and people who are not Christian are invited to these ceremonies too. 在英国和美国, 教堂每逢周日按常规会举办宗教活动, 复活节或圣诞节等宗教节日也会举办特别的仪式。教堂还用来举办婚礼、洗礼、葬礼等特别仪式, 非基督教徒也受邀参加这些仪式。

church·go·er /ˋtʃɝtʃ͵goɚ; ˈtʃɜːtʃ͵gəʊə/ *n* [C] someone who goes to church regularly 常去教堂做礼拜的人

Chur·chill /ˋtʃɝtʃɪl; ˈtʃɜːtʃɪl/, **Sir Win·ston** /ˋwɪnstṇ; ˈwɪnstən/ (1874-1965) a British politician in the Conservative Party who was Prime Minister during most of World War II and again from 1951 to 1955. Many people remember him as a great leader who made possible Britain's victory in the war. 丘吉尔〔(1874-1965), 英国保守党政治家, 二战期间大部分时间任英国首相, 1951 至 1955 年间再次出任英国首相。作为一位使英国赢得战争的伟人领导人, 他仍为英国许多民众所铭记〕—**Churchillian** /tʃɝˋtʃɪlɪən; tʃɜːˈtʃɪliən/ *adj*: *a stirring Churchillian speech* 丘吉尔的一次令人振奋的演说

church·key /ˋtʃɝtʃ͵ki; ˈtʃɜːtʃkiː/ *n* [C] *AmE informal*【美, 非正式】a BOTTLE OPENER 开瓶器

church·man /ˋtʃɝtʃ͵mən; ˈtʃɜːtʃmən/ *n* [C] *plural* **churchmen** /-mən; -mən/ a priest; CLERGYMAN 牧师; 神职人员

Church of Eng·land, the /͵· · ˈ··◂/ *n* the state church in England, the official leader of which is the Queen or King 英国国教会, 英国圣公会 —**Church of England** also 又作 **C of E** *adj*

Church of Ire·land, the /͵· · ˈ··◂/ an independent Anglican church in the Republic of Ireland and Northern Ireland 爱尔兰圣公会〔爱尔兰和北爱尔兰的基督教圣公会独立教会〕

Church of Je·sus Christ of Lat·ter-day Saints, the /͵· · ͵· · ͵· · ͵· · ˈ·/ the official name of the Mormon church, established in the US by Joseph Smith in 1830 耶稣基督末世圣教徒会〔摩门教会的正式名称, 1830 年由约瑟夫·史密斯在美国创立〕

Church of Scot·land /ˌ· · ˈ· ·◂/ *n* [singular] the state church in Scotland 苏格兰长老会

church school /ˈ· ˌ·/ *n* [C] a school in Britain that is partly controlled by the church〔英国的〕教会学校

church·war·den /ˈtʃɝtʃˈwɔrdn̩; ˌtʃɜːtʃˈwɔːdn/ *n* [C] someone who looks after church property and money〔负责教会财产和财务的〕教会执事

church·yard /tʃɝtʃ jɑrd; ˈtʃɜːtʃjɑːd/ *n* [C] a piece of land around a church where people are buried〔在教堂周围的〕教堂墓地

churl·ish /ˈtʃɝlɪʃ; ˈtʃɜːlɪʃ/ *adj* bad-tempered or impolite 脾气不好的; 无礼的: *It seemed churlish to refuse his invitation.* 不接受他的邀请似乎不太礼貌。—**churl** *n* [C] —**churlishly** *adv* —**churlishness** *n* [U]

churn[1] /tʃɝn; tʃɜːn/ *n* [C] **1** a container used for shaking milk in order to make it into butter〔制造黄油的〕搅乳器 **2** *BrE* a large metal container used to carry milk in【英】〔金属〕奶桶 —see picture at 参见 CONTAINER 图

churn[2] *v* **1** [I] if your stomach churns you feel sick because you are nervous or frightened〔胃因紧张或惊慌而〕剧烈搅动: *My stomach was churning on the day of the exam.* 考试那天我的胃里直翻腾。**2** [T] to make milk by using a churn〔用搅乳器〕搅〔乳〕**3** also 又作 **churn up** [I,T] if water churns or if it is churned, it moves about violently (使)〔水〕剧烈翻腾

churn sth ↔ **out** *phr v* [T] to produce large quantities of something, especially without caring about quality〔不顾质量〕大量生产, 粗制滥造: *The factory churns out thousands of these awful plastic toys every week.* 这家工厂每周生产出成千上万个这类劣质的塑料玩具。

churn up *phr v* **1** [T **churn** sth ↔ **up**] to damage the surface of something, especially by walking on it or driving a vehicle over it〔尤指由于行走或车辆辗压而〕损坏〔某物的表面〕: *The lawn had been churned up by the tractor.* 拖拉机将草坪碾坏了。**2** [T **churn** sb **up**] to make someone upset or angry 使〔人〕紧张[生气]: *The argument had left her feeling all churned up.* 这场争论使她感到非常生气。**3** [I,T] to CHURN[2] (3) (使)〔水〕剧烈翻腾

chute /ʃut; ʃuːt/ *n* [C] **1** a long narrow structure that slopes down, used for sliding things from one place to another or for people to slide down 滑道; 斜槽; 溜槽; 滑梯: *The pool had the added attraction of a water chute.* 那个泳池的又一吸引人之处是有水上滑梯。**2** *informal* a PARACHUTE[1]【非正式】降落伞

Chutes and Lad·ders /ˌ· · ˈ· ·/ *trademark* the name used in the US for the children's game of Snakes and Ladders【商标】"滑道与梯子"棋〔在美国使用的名称, 即儿童游戏"蛇与梯子"棋〕

chut·ney /ˈtʃʌtnɪ; ˈtʃʌtni/ *n* [U] a mixture of fruits, hot-tasting seeds and sugar, that is eaten with meat or cheese 酸辣酱〔水果、辣椒、糖等混合物, 与肉或乳酪一起食用〕: *mango chutney* 芒果酸辣酱

chutz·pah /ˈhutspə; ˈhʊtspə/ *n* [U] *slang* too much confidence, which is often considered to be rude; NERVE[1] (3)【俚】厚脸皮; 放肆, 肆无忌惮: *He wouldn't have the chutzpah to deliver that message.* 他不至于脸皮那么厚去传话儿吧。

CIA /ˌsi aɪ ˈe; ˌsiː aɪ ˈeɪ/ *n* **the CIA** the Central Intelligence Agency; the department of the US government that collects information about other countries, especially secretly〔美国〕中央情报局 —compare 比较 FBI

ciao /tʃau; tʃaʊ/ *interjection informal* used to say goodbye【非正式】再见!

ci·ca·da /sɪˈkedə; sɪ̇ˈkɑːdə/ *n* [C] an insect that lives in hot countries, has large transparent wings, and makes a high singing noise 蝉

cic·a·trice /ˈsɪkətrɪs; ˈsɪkətrɪs/ also 又作 **cic·a·trix** /-trɪks; -trɪks/ *n* [C] *technical* a mark remaining from a wound; SCAR[1] (1)【术语】疤痕; 痂; 伤痕

Ci·ce·ro /ˈsɪsəro; ˈsɪsərəʊ/, **Mar·cus Tul·li·us** /ˈmɑrkəs ˈtʌlɪəs; ˈmɑːkəs ˈtʌliəs/ (106-43 BC) a Roman politician who was a famous ORATOR (=someone who is good at making speeches) and one of the greatest Latin writers 西塞罗〔(公元前106-前43), 罗马政治家、著名演说家, 最伟大的拉丁语作家之一〕

ci·ce·ro·ne /ˌsɪsəˈronɪ; ˌsɪsəˈrəʊni/ *n* [C] *literary* someone who shows tourists interesting places; GUIDE[1] (1a)【文】观光导游

CID /ˌsi aɪ ˈdi; ˌsiː aɪ ˈdiː/ *n* **the CID** the Criminal Investigation Department; the department of the British police that deals with very serious crimes〔英国〕刑事侦缉部

Cid, The /sɪd; sɪd/ —see 见 EL CID

-cide /saɪd; saɪd/ *suffix* [in nouns 构成名词] another form of the suffix -ICIDE 后缀 -icide 的另一种形式: *genocide* (=killing a whole race of people) 种族屠杀 —**-cidal** [in adjectives 构成形容词] —**-cidally** [in adverbs 构成副词]

ci·der /ˈsaɪdɚ; ˈsaɪdə/ *n* [C,U] **1** *BrE* an alcoholic drink made from apples or a glass of this drink【英】(一杯)苹果酒 **2** *AmE* also 又作 **sweet cider** a non-alcoholic drink made from apples or a glass of this drink【美】(一杯)苹果汁 —see also 另见 HARD CIDER *AmE*【美】

Cider with Ro·sie /ˌsaɪdɚ wɪð ˈrozɪ; ˌsaɪdə wɪð ˈrəʊzi/ a NOVEL by Laurie Lee about a boy growing up in a small country village in England during the 1920s and 1930s《同萝西共饮苹果汁》〔劳里·李所著的一部小说, 讲述20世纪20、30年代一个小男孩在英格兰的一个小村庄的成长故事〕

ci·gar /sɪˈgɑr; sɪˈgɑː/ *n* [C] a thing that people smoke made from tobacco leaves that have been rolled into a thick tube shape 雪茄烟

cig·a·rette /ˌsɪgəˈrɛt; ˌsɪgəˈret/ *n* [C] a thin tube of paper filled with finely cut tobacco that people smoke 香烟: *a packet of cigarettes* 一包香烟 S2 W3

cigarette butt /ˌ· · ˈ· ˌ·/ also 又作 **cigarette end** *especially BrE*【尤英】*n* [C] the part of a cigarette that remains when someone has finished smoking it 烟蒂, 烟头

cigarette hol·der /ˌ· · ˈ· ˌ· ·/ *n* [C] a narrow tube for holding a cigarette 香烟烟嘴

cigarette light·er /ˌ· · ˈ· ˌ· ·/ also 又作 **lighter** *n* [C] a small object that produces a flame for lighting cigarettes, CIGARS etc 打火机

cigarette pa·per /ˌ· · ˈ· ˌ· ·/ *n* [C,U] thin paper used to make your own cigarettes 卷烟纸

cig·gy /ˈsɪgɪ; ˈsɪgi/ *n* [C] *BrE spoken* a cigarette【英口】香烟

ci·lan·tro /sɪˈlɑntro; sɪ̇ˈlɑːntrəʊ/ *n* [U] *AmE* the strong-tasting leaves of a small plant, used for giving a special taste to food, especially in Asian and Mexican cooking【美】〔尤用于亚洲和墨西哥菜中调味的〕芫荽叶; CORIANDER *especially BrE*【尤英】

C-in-C /ˌsi ɪn ˈsi; ˌsiː ɪn ˈsiː/ *n* an abbreviation of 缩写= COMMANDER IN CHIEF

cinch[1] /sɪntʃ; sɪntʃ/ *n* [singular] *informal*【非正式】**1** something that is very easy 极容易的事情: *"How was the exam?" "Oh, it was a cinch!"* "考试怎么样?" "噢, 容易得很!" **2** something that will definitely happen 必然发生的事: *It's an absolute cinch that this horse is going to win!* 这匹马肯定会赢!

cinch[2] *v* [T] *AmE*【美】**1** to pull a belt, STRAP[1] etc tightly around something 给…系上带子 **2** to do something so that you can be sure something will happen 确保, 稳保: *They cinched a place in the play-off.* 他们确保了在季后赛中的席位。

cinch[3] *adj AmE* **cinch belt/strap etc** a thin belt etc, made of ELASTIC[1], that you pull so that it is very tight【美】有弹性的带子

Cin·cin·nat·i /ˌsɪnsɪˈnætɪ; ˌsɪnsɪ̇ˈnæti◂/ a city in southwest Ohio in the US, next to the Ohio River. It is an important industrial centre. 辛辛那提〔美国俄亥俄州西南部一城市, 濒临俄亥俄河, 为重要的工业中心〕

cinc·ture /ˈsɪŋktʃɚ; ˈsɪŋktʃə/ *n* [C] *literary* a belt【文】束带, 腰带

cin·der /ˈsɪndɚ; ˈsɪndə/ *n* [C usually plural 一般用复数] a very small piece of burnt wood, coal etc 煤渣; 炭渣; 炉渣: *a cold hearth full of cinders* 满是炉渣的冷却了的炉床 | **burnt to a cinder** (=completely burnt) 烤焦 *The cake was burnt to a cinder.* 蛋糕给烤焦了。

cinder block /ˈ· · ˌ·/ *n* [C] *AmE* a large brick for building made from CEMENT and cinders【美】煤渣砖; BREEZE-BLOCK *BrE*【英】

Cin·de·rel·la /ˌsɪndəˈrɛlə; ˌsɪndəˈrelə/ **1** the main character in a FAIRY TALE called *Cinderella*. Cinderella is a beautiful young woman who is treated like a servant by her cruel STEPMOTHER and STEPSISTERS. When Prince Charming invites all the young women to a BALL (=a large formal party where people dance), Cinderella cannot go because she has only old TORN clothes. Then her fairy godmother appears and magically changes six white mice into horses and a PUMPKIN (=a large, round, yellow vegetable) into a carriage to take her to the ball. She then magically changes Cinderella's old clothes into a beautiful dress and gives her a pair of glass SLIPPERS (=shoes). Cinderella goes to the ball, but her fairy godmother tells her that she must come home before midnight, when the magic will stop working. At the ball the Prince falls in love with her. At midnight she runs away, but she loses one of her glass slippers. The Prince finds the slipper and then makes every unmarried woman in the country try it on. Cinderella puts on the slipper and marries the Prince. 灰姑娘〔童话故事《灰姑娘》中的主人公。她是一位美丽的年轻女子, 被继母和继母的女儿当佣人使唤。一天, 王子邀请所有的年轻女子参加舞会, 灰姑娘却去不成, 因为她只有一身破旧的衣服。接着, 仙姑出现了, 不可思议地把六只白鼠变成了马匹, 把一只南瓜

变成了马车载着她去了舞会。然后，她神奇地把灰姑娘的旧衣服变成美丽的礼服，还给了她一双水晶鞋。灰姑娘去参加舞会了，可仙姑告诉她必须在午夜之前赶回家，因为那时魔力将会消失。舞会上，王子爱上了她。午夜时灰姑娘离开了舞会，不慎丢失了一只水晶鞋。王子找到这只鞋，接着让国内每一位未婚女子都来试穿。灰姑娘穿上正好合脚，就嫁给了王子〕—see also 另见 the UGLY SISTERS **2** a person or thing that has been ignored or treated as less important than other people or things 被忽视或未受到应有重视的人（或物）: [+of] *Their economy was the Cinderella of the industrialized world.* 他们国家的经济是工业发达国家中的"灰姑娘"。—**Cinderella** *adj* [only before noun 仅在名词前]: *Mental health care has been the Cinderella service for too long.* 心理保健工作被忽视得太久了。

C

cinder track /ˈ·· ˌ·/ *n* [C] a race track covered with cinders 煤渣跑道

cine- /sɪnɪ; sɪni/ *prefix BrE* concerning films or the film industry【英】电影（业）的: *a cine-camera* 电影摄影机

cine-cam·e·ra /ˈsɪnɪ ˌkæmərə; ˈsɪni ˌkæmərə/ *n* [C] *BrE* a camera for making moving films, rather than photographs【英】电影摄影机

cine-film /ˈsɪnɪ fɪlm; ˈsɪni fɪlm/ *n* [U] *BrE* film used in a cine-camera【英】电影胶片

3 **cin·e·ma** /ˈsɪnəmə; ˈsɪnȷ̇mə/ *n especially BrE*【尤英】**1** [C] a building in which films are shown 电影院; MOVIE THEATER *AmE*【美】: *What's on at the cinema?* 电影院在上映什么电影？**2** [singular,U] the skill or industry of making films 电影制作; 电影业: *a leading figure in Italian cinema* 意大利电影界数一数二的人物

cin·e·mat·ic /ˌsɪnəˈmætɪk; ˌsɪnȷ̇ˈmætɪk◂/ *adj* connected with films for the cinema 电影的: *a lack of cinematic output* 电影作品的缺乏

cin·e·ma·to·gra·phy /ˌsɪnəməˈtɑgrəfɪ; ˌsɪnȷ̇məˈtɒgrəfi/ *n* [U] *technical* the skill or study of making films【术语】电影摄影术[学]; 电影制片术[学]: *with impressive cinematography by Robert Surtees* 罗伯特·瑟蒂斯高超的摄影术 —**cinematographer** *n* [C]

cin·na·mon¹ /ˈsɪnəmən; ˈsɪnəmən/ *n* [U] a sweet-smelling substance used for giving a special taste to cakes etc 桂皮香料; 肉桂

cinnamon² *adj* having a light yellowish-brown colour 浅黄褐色的, 肉桂色的

Cinque Ports, the /ˈsɪŋk ports; ˈsɪŋk pɔːts/ five sea ports in southeast England (Hastings, Romney, Hythe, Dover, and Sandwich) which, until 1685, had to provide ships for the British king or queen in order to protect the country from attack by sea 五港同盟〔英格兰东南部的五个海港, 即赫斯廷斯、罗姆尼、海斯、多佛尔和桑威奇。1685年以前, 它们必须向英王提供战船, 以保卫该国不受海上攻击〕

ci·pher¹, cypher /ˈsaɪfə; ˈsaɪfə/ *n* [C] **1** a system of secret writing; CODE¹ (4) 密码; 暗号 **2** someone who is not important and has no power or influence 不重要[无影响力]的人: *a mere cypher* 无足轻重的人物 **3** *literary* the number 0; zero【文】〔数字〕零

cipher² *v* [T] to put a message into CODE (=a system of secret writing) 把…译成密码 —compare 比较 DECIPHER

cir·ca /ˈsɝkə; ˈsɜːkə/ *prep formal* used before a date to show that something happened on nearly, but not exactly that date【正式】〔用于日期前〕大约: *manuscripts dating from circa 1100* 可追溯到大约公元1100年的手稿

cir·ca·di·an /sɝˈkedɪən; sɜːˈkeɪdiən/ *adj* [only before noun 仅用于名词前] *technical* connected with a period of 24 hours, used especially when talking about changes in people's bodies【术语】〔尤指体内变化〕昼夜节律的, 生理节奏的, 以24小时为周期的

Cir·ce /ˈsɝsɪ; ˈsɜːsi/ in classical MYTHOLOGY, a woman who did magic and who changed people into pigs, including the friends of Odysseus 喀耳刻〔古典神话中曾把包括奥德修斯的朋友在内的一些人变成猪的女巫〕

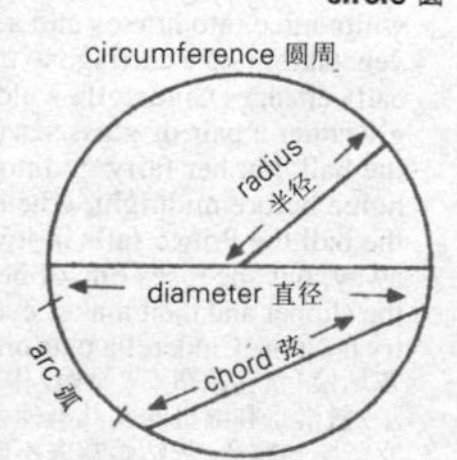

2 2 **cir·cle¹** /ˈsɝkḷ; ˈsɜːkəl/ *n* [C] **1** ▶**SHAPE** 形状◀ a completely round shape, like the letter O 圆（形）: *Draw a circle 10cm in diameter.* 画一个直径10厘米的圆。| *Cut the pastry into circles.* 将油酥面团切成圆状。| **perfect circle** (=exactly round) 完美的圆 —see picture at 参见 SHAPE¹ 图 **2** ▶**GROUP OF PEOPLE/THINGS** 一组人/物◀ a group of people or things forming a round shape 排成一圈的人[物]: *The children stood round in a circle.* 小孩们站成一圈。| *a circle of chairs* 一圈椅子 **3** ▶**SOCIAL GROUP** 社会团体◀ also 又作 **circles** a group of people who know each other 圈子, …界: *a large circle of friends* 交友甚广 | *well-known in fashionable circles* 在时装界很出名 | **move in different circles** (=have different friends, jobs, interests etc) 有不同的活动圈子〔有不同朋友、职业、爱好等〕 **4** **political/literary/scientific etc circles** the people who are involved in politics, literature, science etc 政界/文学界/科学界等: *These ideas have caused an uproar in literary and academic circles.* 这些看法在文学界和学术界引起了轩然大波。 **5** ▶**THEATRE** 剧院◀ *BrE* the upper floor of a theatre, that has seats arranged in curved rows【英】〔有半圆形楼座的〕楼厅包厢; BALCONY (2) *especially AmE*【尤美】—see picture at 参见 THEATRE 图 **6** **go round in circles** to think or argue about something without deciding anything or making progress 绕圈子; 白忙, 瞎忙: *Let's have a break – we're just going round in circles.* 休息一下吧 —— 我们忙了半天也没个头绪。 **7** **come/turn full circle** if a process, argument etc comes full circle, it ends in the same situation in which it began 循环, 兜了一圈回到原位; 周而复始: *By August her feelings had turned full circle.* 到8月份, 她的心情好似兜了一个圈又和原来一样了。—see also 另见 **square the circle** (SQUARE³ (6)), VICIOUS CIRCLE

circle² *v* **1** [T] to draw a circle around something 围绕; 在…上画圈; 圈出: *Circle the correct answer.* 将正确答案圈出来。**2** [I, T] to move around in a circle in the air〔在空中〕盘旋: *The plane circled the airport before landing.* 飞机着陆前在机场上空盘旋了一会儿。

cir·clet /ˈsɝklɪt; ˈsɜːklȷ̇t/ *n* [C] a narrow band of gold, silver, or jewels worn around someone's head or arms〔戴在头上或手臂上的〕环状饰物

cir·cuit /ˈsɝkɪt; ˈsɜːkȷ̇t/ *n* [C] **1** a path that forms a circle around an area, or a journey along this path 环形道路; 环行: *We did a circuit of the old city walls.* 我们绕着旧城墙走了一圈。**2** a track that cars, MOTORBIKES etc race around 赛车道 **3** **the tennis/lecture/cabaret etc circuit** all the places that are usually visited by someone who plays tennis etc 网球运动员/演讲者/歌舞团等巡回表演[比赛等]的地方: *a well-known entertainer on the club circuit* 到各夜总会巡回表演的一位著名演员 **4** the complete circle that an electric current travels 电路, 线路 **5** **do circuits** *BrE informal* to do CIRCUIT TRAINING【英, 非正式】循环训练 —see also 另见 PRINTED CIRCUIT, SHORT CIRCUIT 3

circuit board /ˈ·· ·/ *n* [C] a set of connections between points on a piece of electrical equipment which uses a thin line of metal to CONDUCT (=carry) the electricity; PRINTED CIRCUIT 电路板, 印刷电路

circuit break·er /ˈ·· ˌ··/ *n* [C] a piece of equipment that stops an electric current if it becomes dangerous（电流）断路器

circuit court /ˈ·· ˌ·/ *n* [C] a court of law that happens in a small town when a judge visits from a larger town 巡回法院

cir·cu·i·tous /sɝˈkjuɪtəs; sɜːˈkjuːȷ̇təs/ *adj* **circuitous route/course etc** a way of getting from one place to another that is longer than the most direct way 迂回的路线 —**circuitously** *adv*

cir·cuit·ry /ˈsɝkɪtrɪ; ˈsɜːkȷ̇tri/ *n* [U] a system of electric circuits 电路系统

circuit train·ing /ˈ·· ˌ··/ *n* [U] *BrE* several different exercises done quickly after each other, in order to make you able to do sport better【英】循环训练法

cir·cu·lar¹ /ˈsɝkjələ; ˈsɜːkjȷ̇lə/ *adj* **1** shaped like a circle 圆形的, 环形的: *a circular table* 圆桌 **2** moving around in a circle 循环的; 环行的: *a circular bus route* 环行公共汽车路线 **3** **circular argument/discussion etc** an argument in which you always return to the same statements or ideas that were expressed at the beginning 循环论证/讨论 —**circularity** /ˌsɝkjəˈlærətɪ; ˌsɜːkjȷ̇ˈlærȷ̇ti/ *n* [U]

circular² *n* [C] a printed advertisement, notice etc that is sent to lots of people at the same time〔同时送达很多人的〕印刷品; 通知, 通告

cir·cu·lar·ize also 又作 **-ise** *BrE*【英】/ˈsɝkjələˌraɪz; ˈsɜːkjȷ̇ləraɪz/ *v* [T] to send printed notices or advertisements to a lot of people 给…发通知[传单等]; 传阅〔文件等〕

circular saw /ˌ··· ˈ·/ *n* [C] a round metal blade with small sharp parts around the edge, used for cutting wood 圆锯 —compare 比较 CHAIN SAW

cir·cu·late /ˋsɝkjəˏlet; ˈsɜːkjʊ̈leɪt/ *v* **1** [I,T] to move around within a system, or to make something do this（使）循环: *Blood circulates around the body.* 血液在全身循环。**2** [I] if information, facts, ideas etc circulate, they become known by many people 流传; 传播; 散布 **3** [T] to send goods, information etc to people 发送; 传播: *His agent circulated several copies of the book.* 他的代理人发送了几册书。**4** [I] to move around a group, especially at a party, taking to many different people; MINGLE (2)〔在聚会上〕到处走动, 来回周旋 —**circulatory** /ˋsɝkjələˏtorɪ; ˌsɜːkjʊ̈ˈleɪtəri/ *adj*

cir·cu·la·tion /ˌsɝkjəˋleʃən; ˌsɜːkjʊ̈ˈleɪʃən/ *n* **1** [C,U] the movement of blood around your body 血液循环: *Exercise improves the circulation.* 运动有助于促进血液循环。**2** [U] the exchange of information, money etc from one person to another in a group or society〔资料、货币等的〕流通: **in circulation** *Several thousand of the fake notes are in circulation.* 市面上流通着几千张伪钞。**3** [singular] the average number of copies of a newspaper or magazine that are usually sold each day, week, month etc〔报纸、杂志的〕发行量, 销售量: *Circulation fell when the price was increased to 45p.* 价格涨到45便士后, 发行量便下降了。**4 out of circulation** *informal* not taking part in social activities for a period of time【非正式】不参加社交活动: *Sandy's out of circulation until after her exams.* 桑迪直至考完试后才参加社交活动。**5** [C,U] the movement of liquid, air etc in a system〔液体、空气等的〕流通, 环流

circum- /sɝkəm; sɜːkəm/ *prefix* all the way round something 环绕…: *to circumnavigate the world* (=sail round it) 环游世界 | *to circumvent* (=avoid something by finding a way round) 回避

cir·cum·cise /ˋsɝkəmˏsaɪz; ˈsɜːkəmsaɪz/ *v* [T] **1** to cut off the skin at the end of the PENIS (=male sex organ) 割去〔男性的〕包皮 **2** to cut off the CLITORIS of a female 切除〔女性的〕阴蒂

cir·cum·ci·sion /ˌsɝkəmˋsɪʒən; ˌsɜːkəmˈsɪʒən/ *n* [C,U] the act of circumcising someone, or an occasion when a baby is circumcised as part of a religious ceremony 包皮切除术; 阴蒂切除术; 割礼

cir·cum·fer·ence /sɚˋkʌmfərəns; səˈkʌmfərəns/ *n* **1** [C,U] the distance measured around the outside of a circle 圆周; 周长: *the circumference of the Earth* 地球的周长 | *3 metres in circumference* 周长三米 —see picture at 参见 CIRCLE¹ 图 **2** [singular] the measurement around the outside of any shape; PERIPHERY 周线, 周界;〔任何形状物体的〕周边的长度 —**circumferential** /sɚˌkʌmfəˋrɛnʃəl; səˌkʌmfəˈrenʃəl/ *adj* —see table on page C5 参见 C5 页附录

cir·cum·flex /ˋsɝkəmˏflɛks; ˈsɜːkəmfleks/ *n* [C] a mark placed above a letter in a French word to show its pronunciation, for example, ô〔标在法文元音字母上〕表示音调的符号 —compare 比较 GRAVE³, ACUTE (7)

cir·cum·lo·cu·tion /ˌsɝkəmloˋkjuʃən; ˌsɜːkəmləˈkjuːʃən/ *n* [C,U] *formal* the practice of using too many words to express an idea, instead of saying it directly【正式】婉转曲折的说法, 迂回的说法 —**circumlocutory** /ˌsɝkəmˋlɑkjəˏtorɪ; ˌsɜːkəmˈlɒkjʊ̈təri/ *adj*

cir·cum·nav·i·gate /ˌsɝkəmˋnævəˏget; ˌsɜːkəmˈnævʌ̈geɪt/ *v* [T] to sail completely around the Earth, an island etc 环绕〔地球或岛屿等〕航行 —**circumnavigation** /ˌsɝkəmnævəˋgeʃən; ˌsɜːkəmnævʌ̈ˈgeɪʃən/ *n* [C,U]

cir·cum·scribe /ˌsɝkəmˋskraɪb; ˈsɜːkəmskraɪb/ *v* [T] **1** [often passive 常用被动态] *formal* to limit power, rights, or abilities; RESTRICT【正式】约束, 限制: *All our minds are heavily circumscribed by habit.* 我们的思维深受习惯的制约。**2** *technical* to draw a line around something【术语】在…周围画线: *a circle circumscribed by a square* 正方形中的圆形 —**circumscription** /ˌsɝkəmˋskrɪpʃən; ˌsɜːkəmˈskrɪpʃən/ *n* [U]

cir·cum·spect /ˋsɝkəmˏspɛkt; ˈsɜːkəmspekt/ *adj* **1** thinking carefully about things before doing them; CAUTIOUS 小心的, 谨慎的: *The journalist was circumspect, only tentatively linking the escape with the murder.* 这名记者很谨慎, 只是试探性地将出逃与谋杀联系起来。**2** a circumspect action or answer is done or given only after careful thought〔行动、答案〕深思熟虑的, 考虑周到的 —**circumspectly** *adv* —**circumspection** /ˌsɝkəmˋspɛkʃən; ˌsɜːkəmˈspekʃən/ *n* [U]

S1 W1 **cir·cum·stance** /ˋsɝkəmˏstæns; ˈsɜːkəmstæns/ *n* **1 circumstances** [plural] the conditions that affect a situation, action, event etc 情况, 情形: *The rules can only be waived in exceptional circumstances.* 这些规定只有在特殊情况下才可予以豁免。| **in suspicious circumstances** (=in a way that makes you think something illegal or dishonest has happened) 情形可疑 *He was found dead in suspicious circumstances.* 他被发现死亡, 死因很可疑。| **extenuating circumstances** (=things that have happened which excuse or explain someone's bad behaviour or actions) 情有可原的情况 **2 under/in no circumstances** used to emphasize that something must definitely not happen 决不, 无论如何都不: *Under no circumstances are you to leave the house.* 你无论如何也不能离开这屋子。**3 under/in the circumstances** used to say that a particular situation makes an action, decision etc necessary or acceptable when it would not normally be 在这种情况下, 情形既然如此: *The result was the best that could be expected under the circumstances.* 在这种情况下, 这是我们能期待的最好的结果。**4** [U] the combination of facts, events etc that influence your life, and that you cannot control 无法控制的因素; 环境; 境遇: **force of circumstance** *Force of circumstance compelled us to leave.* 形势所迫, 我们不得不走。| **victim of circumstance** (=someone who is harmed because of the situation they are in, not because they have done anything wrong) 局势的牺牲品, 环境的受害者 **5 live in reduced circumstances** *old-fashioned* to have much less money than you used to have【过时】财政状况不佳, 经济拮据 **6 pomp and circumstance** *literary* grand ceremonial activity, especially on a formal or important occasion【文】盛大隆重的场面

cir·cum·stan·tial /ˌsɝkəmˋstænʃəl; ˌsɜːkəmˈstænʃəl◂/ *adj* **1 circumstantial evidence** *law* facts that make you believe something probably happened, but do not definitely prove that it did【法律】有充分的细节但无法证实的证据, 间接推测的证据 **2 circumstantial account/description etc** *formal* a description etc that includes all the details【正式】详细的叙述/描述 —**circumstantially** *adv*

cir·cum·vent /ˌsɝkəmˋvɛnt; ˌsɜːkəmˈvent/ *v* [T] **1** to avoid a problem or rule that restricts you , especially in a clever or dishonest way〔尤指巧妙地〕回避; 规避: *The company opened an account abroad, in order to circumvent the tax laws.* 该公司在国外开设了一个账户, 以逃避（本国的）税法。**2** *formal* to change the direction in which you are travelling in order to avoid something【正式】〔为避免…而〕改道, 绕过: *We went north in order to circumvent the mountains.* 我们为避开群山, 改向北行进。—**circumvention** /-ˋvɛnʃən; -ˈvenʃən/ *n* [U]

cir·cus /ˋsɝkəs; ˈsɜːkəs/ *n* **1** [C] a group of people and animals who travel around performing skilful tricks as entertainment 马戏团: **circus act** (=a trick performed in a circus) 马戏表演 | **circus ring** (=the round area where tricks are performed) 马戏表演场 **2** [singular] *informal* a meeting, group of people etc that is very noisy and uncontrolled【非正式】乱哄哄的聚会, 热闹的场面: *The first day of school is always such a circus.* 开学第一天总是那么闹哄哄的。**3** [C] in ancient Rome, a place where fights, races etc took place, with seats built in a circle〔古罗马的〕圆形竞技场 **4** [singular] *BrE* used sometimes as the name of a round open area where several streets join together【英】〔数条街道相汇聚的〕圆形广场: *Piccadilly Circus* 皮卡迪利广场

cirque /sɝk; sɜːk/ *n* [C] *technical* a CORRIE【术语】冰围地, 冰斗 —see picture on page A12 参见 A12 页图

cir·rho·sis /sɪˋrosɪs; sʌ̈ˈrəʊsʌ̈s/ *n* [U] a serious disease of the LIVER (1), often caused by drinking too much alcohol 肝硬化〔常由过度饮酒引起〕

Cir·rus /ˋsɪrəs; ˈsɪrəs/ *trademark* a type of service that allows people to get money from their bank account by using any of the cash machines that have a 'Cirrus' sign on it【商标】顺利卡〔一种金融服务, 客户可在带有 Cirrus（顺利卡）标志的任何一台自动提款机提款〕

cirrus *n* [U] a form of cloud that is light and shaped like feathers, high in the sky 卷云 —compare 比较 CUMULUS, NIMBUS (1)

CIS /ˌsi aɪ ˋɛs; ˌsiː aɪ ˈes/ *n* the Commonwealth of Independent States; the name given to a group of states of which the largest is Russia 独立国家联合体, 独联体

cis·sy /ˋsɪsɪ; ˈsɪsi/ *n* [C] *BrE informal* SISSY【英, 非正式】娘娘腔的男子 —**cissy** *adj*

Cis·ter·cian /sɪˋstɝʃən; sʌ̈ˈstɜːʃən/ a MONK (=member of an all-male Christian religious group) belonging to a group that started in France in 1098. The Cistercians follow strict rules, which include little sleep, hard work, and not eating very much. 西多会修士〔属于1098年创建于法国的一个宗教团体, 奉行严格的教规, 包括少睡觉、勤劳和少食〕—**Cistercian** *adj*: *a Cistercian monastery* 一座西多会修道院

cis·tern /ˋsɪstɚn; ˈsɪstən/ *n* [C] a container in which water is stored inside a building〔建筑物内的〕水箱; 贮水槽

cit·a·del /ˋsɪtədl; ˈsɪtədəl/ *n* [C] **1** a strong FORT (=small castle), intended to be somewhere people can go for safety if their city is attacked 城堡; 要塞; 堡垒 **2 the citadel of sth** *literary* a place or situation in which an idea, principle, system etc that you think is important is kept safe; STRONGHOLD【文】保卫…的地方; 有保障的地方: *the last citadel of freedom* 自由的最后堡垒

ci·ta·tion /saɪˋteʃən; saɪˈteɪʃən/ *n* **1** [C] an official statement about someone's character or actions, especially one saying that they have been brave in battle〔尤指对作战英勇者的〕表彰; 嘉奖状: *a citation for bravery* 英勇嘉奖状 **2** [C] a line taken from a book, speech etc; QUOTATION (1) 引文, 引句, 引语 **3** [U] an occasion when someone cites or is cited 引用, 引证

cite /saɪt; saɪt/ *v* [T] **1** to mention something as an example, especially one that supports, proves, or explains an idea or situation 引证, 援引: **cite sth as sth** *Several factors have been cited as the cause of the student unrest.* 好几个因素被引证来说明学生动乱的起因。**2** to give the exact words of something that has been written in order to support an opinion or prove an idea; QUOTE[1] (1) 引用, 引述: *the passage cited above* 上面引用的段落 **3** to call someone to appear before a court of law 传召; 传讯〔到法院〕: *Two managers had been cited for similar infractions.* 两名经理因为类似的违法行为而被传讯。**4** to mention someone by name in a court case 传唤: *Penny was cited in the divorce proceedings.* 彭尼被传唤去办离婚案。**5** *formal* to mention someone because they deserve praise【正式】嘉奖; 表扬, 表彰: **cite sb for sth** *Joe was cited for bravery.* 乔因表现勇敢而受到表彰。

cit·i·fied /ˋsɪtɪˌfaɪd; ˈsɪtɪfaɪd/ *adj* connected with the city or the way people in cities live, especially when this is considered bad 城市的; 城市生活的: *a rural area that has become industrialized and citified* 已被工业化和城市化的农村地区

2 2 **cit·i·zen** /ˋsɪtəzn̩; ˈsɪtɨzən/ *n* [C] **1** someone who lives in a particular town, country, or state and has rights and responsibilities there 市民, 城镇居民: *teaching our children to be good citizens* 教育我们的孩子成为好公民 **2** someone who belongs to a particular country, whether they are living there or not 公民, 国民: *tax advantages for British citizens living and working abroad* 给在国外工作和生活的英国公民的税务优惠 —compare 比较 NATIONAL[2] **3 second-class citizen** someone who feels unimportant because of the way other people treat them 二等公民: *I was made to feel like a second-class citizen as soon as I walked through the door.* 我一进门就感觉自己像二等公民。—see also 另见 SENIOR CITIZEN

Citizen Kane /ˌsɪtizn̩ ˋken; ˌsɪtɨzən ˈkeɪn/ a famous US film made in 1941 by Orson Welles. It tells the story of the life of a very rich businessman who owned several important newspapers. Many people think it is the greatest film ever made. 《公民凯恩》〔奥森·韦尔斯1941年摄制的一部有名的美国电影。故事讲述一位拥有数家重要报纸的富商的生活。许多人认为这是有史以来最优秀的影片〕

cit·i·zen·ry /ˋsɪtəzn̩rɪ; ˈsɪtɨzənri/ *n* [U] all the citizens in a particular place 全体公民[市民]

Citizens Ad·vice Bu·reau, the /ˌ··· ·ˈ· ·ˌ·/ abbreviation 缩写为 **CAB** a British organization supported by the government which gives free advice to ordinary people about legal, financial, and other problems 公民咨询处〔英国政府资助的一个机构, 向公众免费提供法律、理财和其他方面的咨询服务〕

citizen's ar·rest /[illegible]/ *n* [C] the act of taking someone to a police station because you think they have done something wrong 公民(对罪犯)采取的逮捕行动: **make a citizen's arrest** *The stallholder made a citizen's arrest.* 那个摊贩逮捕了罪犯。

Cit·i·zens' Band /ˌ···ˈ◂/ *n* [U] —see 见 CB

cit·i·zen·ship /ˋsɪtəzn̩ˌʃɪp; ˈsɪtɨzənʃɪp/ *n* [U] the legal right of belonging to a particular country 公民权利; 公民身份: **French/US/Brazilian citizenship** *an application for French citizenship* 申请法国国籍[公民资格] | **dual citizenship** (=belonging to two different countries) 双重国籍 *dual citizenship of Canada and the US* 加拿大和美国双重国籍

cit·ric ac·id /ˌsɪtrɪk ˋæsɪd; ˌsɪtrɪk ˈæsɨd/ *n* [U] a weak acid found in some fruits, such as lemons 柠檬酸

cit·ron /ˋsɪtrən; ˈsɪtrən/ *n* [C] a fruit like a LEMON (1) but bigger 香橼, 枸橼

cit·ron·el·la /ˌsɪtrəˋnɛlə; ˌsɪtrəˈnelə/ *n* [U] an oil used for keeping insects away〔驱虫用的〕香茅油

cit·rus /ˋsɪtrəs; ˈsɪtrəs/ also 又作 **citrus tree** /ˈ·· ·/ *n* [C] a type of tree that produces citrus fruits 柑橘属果树 **—citrus, citrous** /ˋsɪtrəs; ˈsɪtrəs/ *adj*

citrus fruit /ˈ·· ·/ *n* [C,U] a fruit with a thick skin such as an orange or LEMON (1) 柑橘属水果〈如橙子、柠檬〉—see picture on page A8 参见A8页图

1 1 **cit·y** /ˋsɪtɪ; ˈsɪti/ *n* **1** [C] a large important town, especially one with a CATHEDRAL〔尤指拥有大教堂的〕城市, 都市: *New York City* 纽约市 | *a capital city* 首府, 首都 | **city dweller** (=someone who lives in a city) 城市居民, 城市人 **2** the people who live in a city 全市居民: *The city has been living in fear since last week's earthquake.* 上周地震后, 全市居民都生活在恐惧中。

City, the also 又作 **the City of London** /ˌ·· ·ˈ·/ *n BrE* an area in central London where there are many large banks and financial organizations, including The Bank of England and The Stock Exchange. The City has an area of about one square mile (about 2.5 square kilometres), and it is sometimes called 'the Square Mile', especially in newspapers. Its name is sometimes used to mean the people who work there and make important financial decisions. There is a similar area in New York City called Wall Street.【英】伦敦商业区, 伦敦城〔伦敦市中心一区域。那里有英格兰银行、证券交易所等许多大型银行和金融机构, 占地约一平方英里(约2.5平方公里), 有时被称为"平方英里城", 尤其多见于报纸。此名称有时指在那里上班并作出重要金融决策的人。纽约市内也有一个类似区域, 称作"华尔街"〕: *The City is optimistic about the outlook for inflation.* 伦敦商业区对通货膨胀的走势持乐观态度。| *a firm of City stockbrokers* 伦敦商业区的一家证券经纪公司 | **city banker/stockbroker etc** (=a banker etc who works in the city) 伦敦城的银行家/证券经纪人等 —see also 另见 INNER CITY

city cen·tre /ˌ·· ˈ··/ *n* [C] *BrE* the main shopping or business area in a city【英】市中心; DOWNTOWN *AmE*【美】

> **CULTURAL NOTE 文化注释**
>
> In the UK and the US, rich people who work in cities have traditionally chosen to live outside the centre of the city in the SUBURB*s*. But in the 1980s and 1990s, people started to move back into the city centres, especially young people with quite a lot of money and no children. As a result, many luxury apartments were built in city centres and house prices greatly increased in these areas. In the UK, this change can be seen especially in London (for example in the Docklands area), Manchester, Birmingham, and Leeds. The DOCK areas and QUAYSIDE*s* of cities such as Liverpool and Bristol have been REDEVELOPE*d*. In the US, the tendency towards city living can be seen in places such as San Francisco and Boston. 英美两国在城市上班的富人习惯住在远离市中心的郊区。但在20世纪80、90年代, 人们开始迁回市中心, 富有而没有子女的年轻人尤其如此。结果, 市中心兴建了很多豪华公寓, 房价暴涨。在英国伦敦(如船坞区)、曼彻斯特、伯明翰和利兹, 这种变化尤其明显。利物浦和布里斯托尔等城市的船坞区和码头沿岸重新得到开发。美国圣弗朗西斯科和波士顿等地也可以看到这种重回市中心居住的潮流。

city desk /ˈ·· ·/ *n* [C] *AmE* a department of a newspaper that deals with local news【美】〔报社的〕本地新闻部

city ed·it·or /ˈ·· ˌ···/ *n* [C] **1** also 又作 **financial editor** *BrE* a JOURNALIST responsible for the financial part of a newspaper【英】负责财经新闻的编辑 **2** *AmE* a JOURNALIST responsible for local news【美】负责本地新闻的编辑

city fa·ther /ˌ·· ˈ··/ *n* [C usually plural 一般用复数] *old use* a member of the group of people who govern a city【旧】市政府官员; 市议员

city hall /ˌ·· ˈ·/ *n* [C,U] *AmE* the local government of a city and the building it uses as its offices【美】市政府(大楼), 市政厅

City of Bir·ming·ham Sym·pho·ny Or·ches·tra, the /ˌ···, ·····, ···/ abbreviation 缩写为 **CBSO** a British ORCHESTRA (=a large group of musicians) based in Birmingham 伯明翰市交响乐团〔英国一交响乐团, 设在伯明翰〕

City of Da·vid, the /ˌ·· ˈ··/ a name for Jerusalem, used in the Bible 大卫城〔指耶路撒冷, 用于《圣经》中〕

city plan·ning /ˌ·· ˈ··/ *n* [U] *AmE* the study of the way cities work, so that roads, houses, services etc can be provided effectively【美】城市规划; TOWN PLANNING *BrE*【英】

city slick·er /ˌ·· ˈ··/ *n* [C] someone who lives and works in a city and has no experience of anything outside it〔对城市以外的情况毫无体验的〕城里人, 城市居民

city-state /ˌ·· ˈ·/ *n* [C] a city, especially in former times, that forms an independent state with the surrounding country area〔尤指旧时的〕城邦: *the city-state of Athens* 雅典城邦

City Technology College /ˌ··ˈ··· ··/ a type of school in Britain that receives some money from business companies and teaches young people useful technical skills 城市技术学院〔英国的一种学校。其运营资金一部分来源于企业, 专门向学生传授实用技能〕

cit·y·wide /ˋsɪtɪˌwaɪd; ˈsɪtiwaɪd/ *adj especially AmE* involving all the areas of a city【尤美】全市范围的: *a citywide campaign to fight racism* 全市范围的反种族主义运动

civ·et /ˋsɪvɪt; ˈsɪvɨt/ *n* **1** [C] also 又作 **civet cat** a small animal like a cat, that lives in Asia and Africa〔产于亚洲和非洲的〕灵

猫, 麝香猫 **2** [U] a strong-smelling liquid from a civet cat, used to make PERFUME 灵猫香〔用作香料〕

civ·ic /ˈsɪvɪk; ˈsɪvɪk/ *adj* [only before noun 仅用于名词前] **1** connected with a town or city 城镇的; 城市的: *the civic authorities* 市政当局 | **civic centre** (=an area in a city where all the public buildings are) 市中心 **2** connected with the people who live in a town or city 市民的, 公民的: *It is your civic duty to vote in the local elections.* 在地区选举中投票是你的公民义务。| **civic pride** (=people's pride in their own city) 市民对自己城市的自豪感

civ·ics /ˈsɪvɪks; ˈsɪvɪks/ *n* [U] *especially AmE* a school subject dealing with the rights and duties of citizens and the way government works【尤美】公民(学)科; 市政学

civ·ies /ˈsɪvɪz; ˈsɪviz/ *n* [plural] CIVVIES 便服〔非军服〕

S2 W2 **civ·il** /ˈsɪvl; ˈsɪvəl/ *adj* **1** [only before noun 仅用于名词前] connected with the people who live in a country 公民的; 民间的: *civil order* 公民秩序 | **civil conflict/disturbance/unrest etc** (=fighting etc between different groups of people living in the same country) 民间冲突/骚动/骚乱等 *the continuing civil conflict in Rwanda* 卢旺达持续不断的民间冲突 | **civil liberty/liberties** (=the freedom that the people in a country have to behave and think as they wish within the law) 公民自由 **2** [only before noun 仅用于名词前] connected with the ordinary people or things in a country rather than the military ones 普通公民的; 平民的; 民用的; 非军事的: *The military and civil authorities are working together to quell the unrest.* 军队和地方当局正联手镇压骚乱。**3** [only before noun 仅用于名词前] involving or dealing with private legal matters, not with criminal ones 民事的: *Many civil cases can be settled out of court.* 许多民事案件都可以在法庭外解决。—see also 另见 CIVIL LAW —compare 比较 CRIMINAL[1] (2) **4** polite in a formal and not a friendly way 客气的; 文明的; 有礼貌的: *Try at least to be civil.* 至少要尽量礼貌一点。

Civil Aviation Au·thor·i·ty, the /ˌ.. ˌ..ˈ... ../ abbreviation 缩写为 **the CAA** a British organization that controls the operation of the air travel industry, especially by making safety rules and directing the traffic of planes in the UK. There is a similar organization in the US called Federal Aviation Administration. 民用航空局〔英国一组织。其职责是制定航空安全规则, 空中交通导航, 对航空运输业的运营进行管制。美国也有一个类似机构, 称为"联邦航空管理局"〕

civil de·fence /ˌ.. .ˈ./ *n* [U] **1** the organization of ordinary rather than military people to help defend their country from military attack 民防 **2** **civil defences** *plural* the things a country does to prepare for a military attack by an enemy 民防工事: *We need to strengthen our civil defences.* 我们需要加强民防工事。

civil dis·o·be·di·ence /ˌ.. ...ˈ.../ *n* [U] action that breaks the law usually taken by a large number of people to protest against something done by the government〔人民针对政府的〕非暴力反抗, 不合作主义

civil en·gi·neer·ing /ˌ.. ..ˈ../ *n* [U] the planning, building, and repair of roads, bridges, large buildings, etc 土木工程 —**civil engineer** *n* [C]

ci·vil·ian /səˈvɪljən; sɪ̥ˈvɪljən/ *n* [C] anyone who is not a member of the army, navy, airforce, or police〔与军人、警察相对的〕平民, 百姓; 文职人员: *the killing of innocent civilians during the bombing campaign* 轰炸中对无辜平民的屠杀 —**civilian** *adj*: *a return to civilian government after years of military rule* 军事统治许多年后恢复文官政府

ci·vil·i·ty /səˈvɪləti; sɪ̥ˈvɪlɪ̥ti/ *n* **1** [U] polite behaviour which most people consider normal 礼貌, 客气, 谦恭: *Please have the civility to knock before you enter next time.* 下次你进来时要有点礼貌 —— 先敲门。**2** **civilities** [plural] *formal* something that you say or do in order to be polite【正式】礼仪; 客套话: *We exchanged civilities when we were neighbours but nothing more.* 我们还是邻居时, 也只是互相客气地打个招呼而已。

civ·i·li·za·tion also 又作 **-isation** *BrE*【英】/ˌsɪvl̩əˈzeɪʃən; ˌsɪvəlaɪˈzeɪʃən/ *n* **1** [C,U] a society that is well organized and developed 文明(社会): *contemporary American civilization* 当代美国文明 | [+of] *the ancient civilizations of Greece and Rome* 希腊和罗马的古代文明 **2** [U] all the societies in the world considered as a whole 文明世界: *The book explores the relationship between religion and civilization.* 本书探索了宗教和文明世界之间的关系。**3** [U] the process in which societies become developed and organized 开化; 教化 **4** [U] *humorous* a place where you feel comfortable or where there is plenty to do【幽默】现代文明生活: *After a week in the mountains all I wanted to do was get back to civilization!* 在山里过了一周后, 我一心只想回到文明生活!

civ·i·lize also 又作 **-ise** *BrE*【英】/ˈsɪvl̩aɪz; ˈsɪvəlaɪz/ *v* [T] *BrE often humorous* to make someone behave in a more sensible or gentle way【英, 常幽默】教化; 使开化, 使文明: *men who need to be domesticated and civilized* 需要驯化和教化的人

civ·i·lized also 又作 **-ised** *BrE*【英】/ˈsɪvl̩aɪzd; ˈsɪvəlaɪzd/ *adj* **1** being well organized and developed socially 开化的, 文明的: *Such things should not be allowed to happen in a civilized society.* 文明社会不容许发生此类事情。**2** pleasant and comfortable 令人愉快的, 舒适宜人的: *"This is very civilized," she said, lying back in the sun with a gin and tonic.* "太舒服了。"她说, 一边躺在阳光下喝着杜松子酒补剂。**3** behaving in a polite sensible way instead of getting angry 心平气和的; 有礼貌的: *Let's try and be civilized about this, shall we?* 我们尽量心平气和地对待这件事, 好吗?

civil law /ˌ.. ˈ./ *n* [U] the area of law deals with the affairs of private citizens rather than with crime 民法, 民事法

civil lib·er·ty /ˌ.. ˈ.../ *n* [U] also 又作 **civil liberties** [plural] the right of all citizens to be free to do whatever they want while respecting the rights of other people 公民自由

civil list /ˈ.. ./ *n* [singular] the sum of money given every year by Parliament to the King or Queen of Britain and to some other people〔英国议会每年批给王室的〕王室费

civil rights /ˌ.. ˈ./ *n* [plural] the rights that every person should have, such as the right to vote or to be treated fairly by the law, whatever their sex, race, or religion 公民权: **civil rights campaigner/movement etc** *50,000 people attended the civil rights demonstration.* 有50,000人参加了民权示威游行。—see also 另见 BILL OF RIGHTS

Civil Rights Act of 1964, the /ˌsɪvl ˌraɪts ækt əv ˌnaɪntin sɪkstɪ ˈfɔr; ˌsɪvəl ˌraɪts ækt əv ˌnaɪntiːn sɪksti ˈfɔː/ a US law which says that businesses must treat people equally whatever their colour or religion, and that they cannot refuse to employ someone because of their colour. This law also says that restaurants and hotels cannot refuse to serve someone because of their colour.《1964年民权法案》〔美国一法律, 规定工商企业应不论肤色或宗教信仰平等待人, 不得以肤色为由拒绝雇用员工。餐厅、旅馆不得以肤色为由拒绝为客人提供服务〕

civil ser·vant /ˌ.. ˈ../ *n* [C] someone employed in the civil service 公务员; 文职人员

> **CULTURAL NOTE 文化注释**
>
> In the UK, the STEREOTYPE of a civil servant is a boring man who wears a dark formal suit. He typically pays too much attention to small unimportant rules in order to seem very official, and people think that he actually does not do much useful work. 英国公务员的典型形象是穿深色正装的乏味男子, 往往过分关注细枝末节的规章, 以使自己显得很有官派。人们认为他实际上没做什么有价值的工作。

civil ser·vice /ˌ.. ˈ../ *n* [singular] the government departments that manage the affairs of the country 政府文职机构, 公职, 行政部门

civil war /ˌ.. ˈ./ *n* [C,U] a war in which opposing groups of people from the same country fight each other in order to gain political control 内战

civ·vies, civies /ˈsɪvɪz; ˈsɪviz/ *n* [plural] *slang* ordinary clothes, as opposed to military uniform, used mainly by people in the army, navy, or airforce【俚】便服〔非军服〕: *sailors on leave wearing their civvies* 穿着便服的休假水兵

civ·vy /ˈsɪvɪ; ˈsɪvi/ *n* [C] *BrE*【英】**1** *slang* a word meaning someone who is not in the army, navy, or airforce, used mainly by people who are or have been in the armed forces【俚】平民〔该词主要为现役或退役军人使用〕**2** **civvy street** *old-fashioned* ordinary life as it is lived outside the army, navy, or airforce【过时】平民生活; 非军人生活

cl the written abbreviation of 缩写= CENTILITRE

clack /klæk; klæk/ *v* **1** [I,T] if you clack something or if it clacks, it makes a continuous short hard sound 发出咔嗒声; 使咔嗒咔嗒地响 **2** [I] *informal* if tongues are clacking, people are talking a lot about something shocking or surprising【非正式】唧唧喳喳谈论, 唠叨: *News of her pregnancy had already set tongues clacking in the neighbourhood.* 她怀孕的消息引起了邻居间唧唧喳喳的议论。—**clack** *n* [singular]

clad /klæd; klæd/ *adj* **1** *literary* wearing a particular kind of clothing【文】穿〔某种特别的〕衣服的: *a model clad in silk and lace* 穿着镶有花边的丝绸服装的模特儿 | **warmly/poorly/scantily clad** (=dressed in a particular way) 穿得暖暖的/衣衫褴褛的/衣着单薄的 **2** **snow-clad/ivy-clad etc** covered in a particular thing 积雪覆盖的/爬满常春藤的等: *an armor-clad ship* 装甲舰[船]

clad·ding /ˈklædɪŋ; ˈklædɪŋ/ *n* [U] a cover of hard material that protects the outside of a building, tank, or engine 覆面〔建筑物外壁、容器或引擎表面的保护层〕

Clai·borne /ˈklebɔrn; ˈkleɪbɔːn/, **Craig** /kreg; kreɪg/ (1920-2000) a US writer of COOKERY books and articles about food in newspapers 克莱本〔(1920-2000)，美国烹饪书籍和报章食品类文章作家〕

claim¹ /klem; kleɪm/ *v* **1** [T] to state that something is true, even though it has not been proved 声称; 断言; 主张: **claim (that)** *Gascoigne claimed he'd been dining with friends at the time of the murder.* 加斯科因声称凶案发生时自己正与朋友进餐。| **claim to be** *She claims to be a descendant of Charles Dickens.* 她宣称自己是查尔斯·狄更斯的后裔。| **claim to have done** *Doctors claimed to have discovered a cure for the disease.* 医生声称已经找到了治疗该病的方法。| **claim responsibility/innocence/credit** (=say officially that you are responsible, innocent etc) 声称有责任/无辜/有功劳 **2** [I,T] to officially demand or receive money from an organization 索赔; 索取: [+on] *You can claim on the insurance if you have an accident while on vacation.* 如果你度假期间出了事可向保险公司索赔。| *The government intends to make legal aid harder to claim.* 政府打算加大法律援助的难度。| **claim benefit/an allowance/damages** (=officially receive money because you do not have a job, are injured etc) 申领救济金/申领补助/要求赔偿金 **3** [T] to state that you have a right to something or to take something that belongs to you 认领; 要求; 索取〔应得的权利或财物〕: *Viscount Lander will claim the title on his father's death.* 兰德子爵在父亲去世后会继承爵位。| *Lost property can be claimed between 10 a.m. and 4 p.m.* 可于上午10点至下午4点认领失物。**4** [T] if a war, accident etc claims lives, people die because of it 夺去, 夺走〔生命〕: *The Kobe earthquake has so far claimed over 3000 lives.* 神户地震已经夺去了三千多人的生命。**5** [T] if something claims someone's attention or time, they have to consider it carefully 值得; 需要〔花时间或精力〕: *The issue of a united Ireland continues to claim our undivided attention.* 爱尔兰统一问题值得我们继续密切关注。

claim² *n* [C]

1 ►MONEY 金钱◄ a) a request for money, especially money that you have a right to 〔根据权利而提出的〕要求, 索款: [+for] *claims for compensation* 要求赔偿 | **make a claim/put in a claim** *They put in a claim on the insurance for the stolen luggage.* 他们在行李被偷后向保险公司提出索赔要求。| **pay claim** (=a request made by workers for more money) 工资要求 | **claim form** (=an official form that you must fill in in order to get money from an organization) 索赔申请表 **b)** the sum of money you request when making such a claim 索赔金额: *The insurance company cannot meet such enormous claims.* 保险公司不能满足如此巨额的索赔。

2 ►STATEMENT 声明◄ a statement that something is true, even though it has not been proved 声称; 断言; 主张: **claim that** *Dino denies claims that he is involved in a drugs ring.* 迪诺否认自己和贩毒集团有关系。| **claim to do/be sth** *the Democratic claim to be the party of women's rights* 民主党声称是妇女权利之党 | **make a claim** *Photographs make a claim to portray reality in a way that paintings never can.* 照片有着绘画永远达不到的真实性。| **make no claim to do something** (=used to say that you do not pretend to be able to do something) 不自称会做某事 *I make no claim to understand the complexities of the situation.* 我不敢断言自己对局势的各种复杂细节都了解。| **dispute a claim** (=say publicly that a statement is not true) 就某种说法提出质疑

3 ►FOR PRAISE/RESPECT ETC 用于表扬/尊敬等◄ something that you say or do, that shows that you deserve to be successful 应得的权利[资格]: [+to] *Judging by last night's performance Ryan must have a claim to a place on the Olympic team.* 从瑞安昨晚的表现来看, 他应该入选奥运队。

4 ►TO OWN OR TAKE SOMETHING 拥有或拿某物◄ a right to have or get something such as land, a title etc that belongs to you 所有权: [+to] *No one can dispute Oliver's claim to the inheritance.* 没有人能对奥利弗的继承权提出质疑。| **have a claim on/to sth** *Surely they have a rightful claim to their father's land.* 的确, 他们对父亲的土地拥有合法的所有权。

5 lay claim to sth to say that you have a right to own something 声称对某物拥有所有权: *Ellen resented the stranger who laid claim to her brother's fortune.* 埃伦对那个自称对她哥哥的财产有继承权的陌生人感到愤恨。

6 stake your claim to say that you have a right to own something, especially when other people also say they have a right to own it 声称对…拥有所有权〔尤指当别人也同时作出相同的声明〕: *If you want some of the furniture, now's the time to stake your claim.* 如果你想要一些家具的话, 现在就该去表明你拥有所有权。

7 claim to fame an expression meaning a reason why someone or something is famous, often used jokingly when mentioning something that is not very important 出名的原因〔常为戏谑说法, 一般指实际上并不怎么重要的东西〕: *My main claim to fame is that I once shook Elvis' hand.* 我之所以出名, 主要是因为我和埃尔维斯握过手。

8 have a claim on sb to have a right to demand someone's time, attention etc 有权得到〔某人的〕注意; 有权占用〔某人的〕时间: *She seems to think she's got an exclusive claim on my time.* 她似乎觉得她有特权占用我的时间。

9 ►LAND 土地◄ something such as a piece of land that contains valuable minerals 要求得到的东西〈如含有矿产的土地〉— see also 另见 **jump a claim** (JUMP¹ (19))

clai·mant /ˈklemənt; ˈkleɪmənt/ *n* [C] **1** someone who claims something, especially money, from the government, a court etc because they think they have a right to it 申请人; 要求者; 索赔人: *The company was ordered to recompense the claimant for damages.* 该公司接到命令要向索赔人作出损失赔偿。**2** someone who makes a claim, for example under a WILL² (2) 继承人; 认领人

clair·voy·ant /klɛrˋvɔɪənt; kleəˈvɔɪənt/ *n* [C] someone who says they can see what will happen in the future 声称能够预见未来的人; 有洞察力的人 —**clairvoyance** *n* [U] —**clairvoyant** *adj*

clam¹ /klæm; klæm/ *n* [C] **1** a SHELLFISH that you can eat, which has a shell in two parts that open and close 蛤; 蛤蜊; 蚬 **2** *AmE informal* someone who does not say what they are thinking or feeling 【美, 非正式】嘴紧的人, 沉默寡言的人 **3 as happy as a clam** *AmE informal* very happy 【美, 非正式】非常高兴; 相当满足

clam² *v*

clam up *phr v* [I] *informal* to suddenly stop talking, especially when you are nervous or shy 【非正式】〔尤指因紧张、害羞而〕拒不开口, 沉默不语: *I just clammed up when her father came in.* 她父亲进来后, 我干脆不说话了。

clam·bake /ˈklæmˌbek; ˈklæmbeɪk/ *n* [C] *AmE* an informal party by the sea where clams are cooked and eaten 【美】海滨烤蛤野餐聚会

clam·ber /ˈklæmbɚ; ˈklæmbə/ *v* [I always+adv/prep] to climb slowly, using your hands and feet 〔手脚并用, 费力地〕攀登, 爬: [+up/over/to etc] *They clambered over the slippery rocks.* 他们爬上了滑溜的岩石。

clam·my /ˈklæmɪ; ˈklæmi/ *adj* feeling wet, cold, and sticky in a way that is unpleasant 冷湿的, 感觉滑腻的, 黏糊糊的: *clammy with sweat* 因为出汗而黏黏的 —**clammily** *adv* —**clamminess** *n* [U]

clam·our¹ *BrE* 【英】, **clamor** *AmE* 【美】 /ˈklæmɚ; ˈklæmə/ *n* [singular,U] **1** a very loud noise, often made by a large group of people or animals 吵闹声, 嘈杂声: *the clamour of factory machinery* 工厂机器的轰鸣声 **2** strong feeling expressed loudly by a large group of people 〔一大批人的〕强烈要求[呼声]: [+for] *the clamour for an all-out strike* 强烈要求全体罢工 —**clamorous** *adj*

clamour² *BrE* 【英】, **clamor** *AmE* 【美】 *v* [I] **1** [always+adv/prep] to demand something loudly 大声疾呼; 强烈要求: [+for] *The audience were on their feet clamouring for more.* 观众站了起来, 高声要求再来一曲。**2** to talk or shout loudly 大声讲话; 大声呼喊: *Children clamoured in the playground.* 孩子们在操场上大声喊叫。

clamp¹ /klæmp; klæmp/ *v* [T] **1** [always+adv/prep] to fasten or hold two things together using a clamp 〔用夹钳〕夹住, 夹紧: **clamp sth together/onto etc** *Clamp the two parts together until the glue dries.* 用夹钳把这两部分夹紧, 直到胶水干了再松开。**2** [always+adv/prep] to put or hold something in a position where it does not move 固定: **clamp sth over/between/around etc** *He clamped a hand over my mouth.* 他用手捂住我的嘴。**3** *BrE* to put a clamp on a car that is illegally parked 【英】〔给非法停放的车辆〕上夹钳; BOOT² (3) *AmE* 【美】

clamp down *phr v* [I] to take firm action to stop a crime or other illegal activity happening 取缔; 压制; 钳制; 镇压: [+on] *The police are really clamping down on drunk drivers.* 警方正在严厉打击酒后驾车行为。

clamp² *n* [C] **1** a piece of equipment for fastening or holding things together 夹子, 夹具, 夹钳 **2** a piece of equipment fastened to the wheel of a car that is parked illegally 〔固定非法停放车辆的〕夹钳, 车轮固定夹; DENVER BOOT *AmE* 【美】

clamp·down /ˈklæmpˌdaun; ˈklæmpdaʊn/ *n* [C usually singular 一般用单数] sudden firm action that is taken to try and reduce crime 严禁; 取缔; 镇压, 压制

clan /klæn; klæn/ *n* [C] **1** a large group of families that often share the same name 宗族, 氏族: *the Campbell clan* 坎佩尔宗族 **2** *humorous* a word meaning a large family, used especially when they are all together on a special occasion【幽默】〔尤指在特殊场合聚在一起的〕大家族; 一大家人: *The whole clan will be here over Christmas.* 我们那一大帮亲戚会来这里过圣诞节。

clan·des·tine /klænˋdɛstɪn; klænˈdestɪn/ *adj* clandestine activities or organizations are secret 秘密的, 暗中从事的: *a clandestine affair* 秘密事务

clang /klæŋ; klæŋ/ *v* [I,T] if a metal object clangs or if you clang it, it makes a loud ringing sound (使) 发出叮当声 **—clang** *n* [singular]

clang·er /ˋklæŋɚ; ˈklæŋə/ *n* **drop a clanger** *BrE informal* to make a careless remark that upsets or embarrasses someone very much【英, 非正式】失言失礼; 犯了明显的错误

clang·our *BrE*【英】, **clangor** *AmE*【美】/ˋklæŋɚ; ˈklæŋə/ *n* [U] the hard ringing sound that is made when metal is hit〔由金属发出的〕铿锵声; 叮当声

clank /klæŋk; klæŋk/ *v* [I,T] if a metal object clanks or if you clank it, it makes a loud heavy sound (使)〔金属〕发出当啷声 **—clank** *n* [C]: *the clank of machinery* 机器的当啷声

clans·man /ˋklænzmən; ˈklænzmən/ *n* [C] a male member of a CLAN 宗族[氏族]的男成员

clans·wom·an /ˋklænzˌwʊmən; ˈklænzˌwʊmən/ *n* [C] a female member of a CLAN 宗族或[氏族]的女成员

clap¹ /klæp; klæp/ *v* **clapped, clapping 1** [I] to hit your hands together loudly and continuously to show that you enjoyed a performance or that you approve of something 拍手, 鼓掌: *The crowd roared with approval and clapped.* 人群发出一片喝彩鼓掌声。—see picture on page A20 参见 A20 页图 **2 clap your hands a)** to hit your hands together loudly and continuously to show that you approve, agree, or have enjoyed something 鼓掌 **b)** to hit your hands together to attract someone's attention or to stop them doing something 拍手〔引起某人的注意或示意某人停止〕: *She clapped her hands and shouted, "Rosie, stop that now!"* 她拍了拍手, 喊道:"罗茜, 停!" **3 clap sb on the back/shoulder etc** to hit someone lightly with your open hand in a friendly way or to show that you are amused 轻拍某人的背部/肩膀等 **4 clap eyes on** *BrE informal* to suddenly see someone or something【英, 非正式】突然看见: *Until this morning I'd never clapped eyes on him.* 今早以前我从来没有见过他。**5 clap your hand on/over etc** to put your hand somewhere quickly and suddenly 突然把手放到: *Babs clapped her hand over her mouth saying, "My God, I think I left the oven on."* 芭布斯突然用手掩住嘴说:"天哪, 我大概没把烤箱关掉。" **6 clap hold of** to take hold of someone or something suddenly 突然抓住: *I clapped hold of him by the shoulder and pushed him out of the front door.* 我猛地一把抓住他的肩膀, 把他推出前门。**7 clap sb in prison/jail/irons** to suddenly put someone in prison or chains 把某人投进监狱 **—clapping** *n* [U]

clap² *n* **1** [singular] a sudden loud sound that you make when you hit your hands together, especially to show that you enjoyed something or that you agree 拍手(声), 鼓掌(声): **give sb a clap** *BrE*【英】*Come on everyone, let's give Tommy a clap.* 来吧各位, 我们都来为汤米鼓掌吧。**2 a clap on the back/shoulder** an act of hitting someone on the back or shoulder to show that you are friendly or amused〔表示友好的〕轻拍背部/肩膀 **3 a clap of thunder** a loud sound made by thunder 雷鸣声 **4 the clap** *slang* GONORRHOEA【俚】淋病

clap·board /ˋklæbɚd; ˈklæpbɔːd/ *n* [C,U] *AmE* a set of boards that cover the outside walls of a building, or one of these boards【美】〔建筑物的〕外墙护墙板, 隔板; WEATHERBOARD (1) *BrE*【英】: *a clapboard house* 装有护墙板的房子

clapped-out /ˌ· ˈ·◂/ *adj BrE informal* a clapped-out car, machine etc is in very bad condition because it is old and has been used a lot【英, 非正式】〔汽车、机器等〕破旧的, 破烂的

clap·per /ˋklæpɚ; ˈklæpə/ *n* [C] **1** the metal thing inside a bell that hits it to make it ring 钟锤; 铃锤 **2** *BrE* a piece of equipment used by farmers that makes a noise to frighten birds away【英】〔农夫用以轰鸟的〕响板 **3 run like the clappers** *BrE informal* to run extremely fast【英, 非正式】飞快地奔跑: *You'll have to run like the clappers if you want to catch that bus.* 你得快跑才能赶上那辆公共汽车。

clap·trap /ˋklæpˌtræp; ˈklæptræp/ *n* [U] *informal* stupid talk【非正式】胡说; 哗众取宠的话

Clare /klɛr; kleə/ a COUNTY in the west of the Republic of Ireland, famous for its mountains and lakes and its wild land on the coast of the Atlantic Ocean 克莱尔郡〔爱尔兰共和国西部一郡, 以境内的山脉、湖泊以及大西洋沿岸的荒野而著称〕

Clare, John (1793-1864) a British poet, who wrote mostly about the English countryside and country life 克莱尔〔(1793-1864), 英国诗人。其作品大多描写英格兰的乡村和田园生活〕

clar·et /ˋklærət; ˈklærət/ *n* [C,U] **1** red wine from the Bordeaux area of France〔法国波尔多地区产的〕红葡萄酒 **2** [U] a dark red colour 暗紫红色 **—claret** *adj*

clar·i·fied but·ter /ˌ··· ˈ··/ *n* [U] butter that has been made clean and pure by heating it〔通过加热而〕提纯的黄油[牛油]

clar·i·fy /ˋklærəˌfaɪ; ˈklærɪfaɪ/ *v* [T] to make something clearer and easier to understand 澄清, 讲清楚, 阐明: *Can you clarify that statement?* 你能把这句话的意思讲清楚一点吗? | **clarify how/what etc** *The report aims to clarify how these conclusions were reached.* 那份报告旨在阐明这些结论是如何得出的。| **clarify your position** (=tell people what you think about a particular subject and what you intend to do about it)〔对某问题〕阐明立场 *Reporters asked the Congressman to clarify his position on welfare reform.* 记者们要求该国会议员阐明他在福利改革问题上的立场。**—clarification** /ˌklærəfəˋkeʃən; ˌklærɪfɪˈkeɪʃən/ *n* [U]

clar·i·net /ˌklærəˋnɛt; ˌklærɪˈnet/ *n* [C] a musical instrument shaped like a long black tube, which you play by blowing into it and pressing keys (KEY² (3)) to change the notes 单簧管, 黑管 **—clarinettist** *n* [C]

clar·i·on call /ˋklærɪən ˌkɔl; ˈklæriən ˌkɔːl/ *n* [C] a strong and direct request for people to do something 强烈的呼唤

clar·i·ty /ˋklærətɪ; ˈklærɪti/ *n* [U] the quality of expressing ideas or thoughts in a clear way 清晰, 清楚; 易懂: *the clarity and precision of his prose* 他的散文思路清晰严谨 | **clarity of vision/purpose** *Churchill's clarity of vision impressed all who knew him.* 丘吉尔的远见卓识给所有认识他的人留下了深刻的印象。

Clark /klɑrk; klɑːk/, **William** (1770-1838) a US EXPLORER 克拉克〔(1770-1838), 美国探险家〕—see also 另见 LEWIS AND CLARK

clash¹ /klæʃ; klæʃ/ *v* **1** [I] if two armies, or groups of people clash, they suddenly start fighting each other (发生) 冲突: *Troops clashed near the border.* 军队在边境附近发生冲突。| [+with] *Police have clashed with demonstrators again today.* 今天警方和示威群众再次发生冲突。**2** [I] if two people or groups of people clash, they argue because their opinions and beliefs are very different〔因意见分歧而〕争论, 争执: [+with] *Democrats clashed with Republicans in a heated debate.* 民主党人和共和党人进行了激烈的争论。**3** [I] if two colours or patterns clash, they look very bad together〔颜色、花样〕不相配, 不协调: [+with] *That purple tie clashes with your red shirt.* 那条紫色领带和你的红衬衫不相配。**4** [I] if two events clash, they happen at the same time in a way that is inconvenient〔两件事情〕撞期: [+with] *Unfortunately, the concert clashed with Ann and Jim's dinner party.* 真可惜, 音乐会与安和吉姆的晚宴撞期了。**5** [I,T] if two pieces of metal clash or if you clash them, they make a loud ringing sound (使) 发出〔金属相碰的〕撞击声: *The cymbals clashed.* 铙钹碰击作响。

clash² *n* [C] **1** a short fight between two armies or groups of people 冲突; 打斗: *border clashes* 边境冲突 **2** an argument between two people or groups of people 争论, 交锋: *a clash of temperament* 脾气不合 | [+between] *angry clashes between Tory and Labour ministers* 保守党和工党部长们的激烈交锋 | **personality clash** (=a situation in which two people do not like each other) 性格上难以相容 **3** a loud sound made by two metal objects being hit together〔金属〕碰撞声: *the clash of swords* 剑的撞击声 **4** a combination of two colours, designs etc that look bad together〔颜色、花样等的〕不相配, 不协调 **5** a situation in which two events happen at the same time in a way that is inconvenient〔时间上的〕冲突, 撞期: *a scheduling clash on TV* 电视节目时间的冲突

clasp¹ /klæsp; klɑːsp/ *n* **1** [C] a small metal object for fastening a bag, belt, piece of jewellery etc 钩; 扣子; 扣环 **2** [singular] a tight hold; GRIP¹ (1) 紧握; 紧抱: *the firm, reassuring clasp of her hand* 她那坚定而使人放心的握手

clasp² *v* [T] **1** to hold someone or something tightly, closing your fingers or arms around them 握紧; 抱紧; 抓住: *A baby monkey clasps its mother's fur tightly.* 小猴子紧紧地抓住母猴的毛。| **clasp sb/sth in your hands/arms** *She clasped the photograph in her hands.* 她将照片紧握在手中。| **clasp sb to your chest/bosom** (=hold someone tightly because you love them or are upset, frightened etc) 抱住; 搂住 **2** to fasten something with a clasp〔用扣环〕扣住; 钩住

clasp knife /ˈ· ·/ *n* [C] a large knife with blades that fold into the handle; JACK-KNIFE¹ (1) 大折刀

1 1 **class¹** /klæs; klɑːs/ *n*

1 ►IN A SOCIETY 社会上◄ a) [C] one of the groups in a society that people can be divided into according to their jobs, income, the kind of family they have etc 阶级, 社会等级: *the professional classes* 专业阶层 | **class differences/distinctions/privileges etc** *Class divisions are as evident in Britain today as ever.* 不论现在或以前阶级划分在英国都同样明显。—see also 另见 LOWER CLASS, MIDDLE CLASS, UPPER CLASS, WORKING CLASS **b)** [U] the system in which people are divided into such groups 社会等级制度: **class system** *The old class system is slowly disappearing.* 旧的社会等级制度正在慢慢消失。

2 ►GROUP OF STUDENTS 学生群◄ [C] a group of pupils or students who are taught together 班, 班级, 年级: *We're in the same class in math.* 我们上数学课是在同一个班的。| [also+plural verb *BrE* 英] *My class are going on an outing to the Lake District.* 我们班要去湖区郊游。

3 ►TEACHING PERIOD 教学时段◄ [C,U] a period of time during which someone teaches a group of people, especially in a school (一节) 课, 上课, 上课时间; LESSON (2) *BrE*【英】: **in class** (=during the class) 上课时 *No talking in class!* 课堂上不许讲话! | **take a class** *BrE* (=teach a class)【英】讲课 | **geography/French/cooking class** (=a period of time during which a particular subject is taught) 地理/法语/烹饪课

4 ►LESSONS 课◄ [C] *AmE* a set of classes you attend in order to study a particular subject【美】(一门) 课程; COURSE¹ (3) *BrE*【英】: *a class in photography at night school* 夜校的摄影课程

5 ►COLLEGE 学院◄ [C] *especially AmE* a group of students who finished studying together in the same year【尤美】同届学生: *I missed a semester and couldn't graduate with my class.* 我落了一学期课, 所以没能和同学一起毕业。| **the class of 1965/1973 etc** *The class of '69 spent almost as much time protesting as learning.* 69年毕业的学生花在抗议和学习上的时间几乎一样多。

6 ►OF ANIMALS/PLANTS ETC 动/植物等的◄ [C] a group of people, animals, or other things that can be considered or studied together because they are similar in some way〔动、植物分类学上的〕纲

7 ►QUALITY 质量◄ [C] a group into which people or things are divided according to their quality〔人或事物的〕等级: *You get a nicer class of people living in this area.* 这个地区居住的人修养较高。| **in a class of its own** (=used to say someone or something is excellent) 极好的, 一流的 *Your mother's cooking is in a class of its own.* 你母亲的烹饪技术一流。| **not in the same class** (=not as good as someone or something) 不及, 不如, 不能与…相比 *He's not in the same class as her at tennis.* 他在网球方面和她是没法比的。—see also 另见 BUSINESS CLASS, CABIN CLASS, CLUB CLASS, ECONOMY CLASS, FIRST CLASS, HIGH-CLASS, LOW-CLASS, SECOND CLASS, THIRD CLASS, TOURIST CLASS

8 ►STYLE 风格◄ [U] *informal* style or skill that you show in the way you do something, that makes people notice and admire you【非正式】〔风格、技巧等的〕优雅, 出众, 令人赞赏: **have/show class** *The team showed real class in this afternoon's match.* 这支队伍在下午的比赛中确实表现出众。| **class player/actress etc** (=very good player, actress, etc) 一流的运动员/女演员等 | **class act** (=used to describe someone who is very skilful, attractive etc) 出类拔萃的人 *The company's very well managed, the class act of the industry.* 这家公司经营得非常好, 在该行业中是数一数二的。

9 ►DEGREE 学位◄ [C] *BrE* one of the three levels into which a university degree is divided according to the quality of the work【英】〔大学学位的〕等级; *a second class degree* 二等[级]学位

class² *v* [T often passive 常用被动态] to consider people, things etc as belonging to a particular group, especially according to an official system 把…归类; 把…看作: **class sb/sth as** *Heroin and cocaine are classed as hard drugs.* 海洛因和可卡因被看作是硬毒品。

class ac·tion /ˌ· ˈ··◂/ *n* [C,U] *AmE* a LAWSUIT arranged by a group of people for themselves and also for others with the same problem【美】集体控告[诉讼]

class-con·scious /ˈ· ˌ··/ *adj* always judging other people according to the social class they belong to 有阶级意识的 —**class-consciousness** *n* [U]

3 **clas·sic¹** /ˈklæsɪk; ˈklæsɪk/ *adj* **1** a classic book, play, film etc is important or special and remains popular for a long time 经典的: *The Coca-Cola bottle is one of the classic designs of the last century.* 可口可乐瓶是上个世纪的经典设计之一。**2** of excellent quality 极优秀的, 第一流的: *Roy scored a classic goal in the 90th minute.* 罗伊在90分钟时踢进了漂亮的一球。**3** a classic style of art or clothing is attractive in a simple traditional way 式样简朴的, 传统式样的: *a classic raincoat* 传统式样的雨衣 **4 a classic example/case etc** a very typical example of something, sometimes in an impressive or humorous way 典型例子/情况等: *Tom made the classic mistake of trying to drive away without releasing the handbrake.* 汤姆犯了一个典型的错误, 没有松开手刹就想开车。

classic² *n* [C] **1** a book, play, or film that is important and has been popular for a long time 名著; 经典作品; 杰作: *'La Grande Illusion' is one of the classics of French cinema.*《大幻影》是法国电影中的经典作品之一。**2** something that is very good and one of the best examples of its kind 典范: *The 1976 semi-final between Borg and Gerulaitis was a classic.* 1976年博格和古库拉提斯间的半决赛堪称典范。**3 classics** [plural] the language, literature, and history of Ancient Rome and Greece 古罗马、古希腊的语言、文学及历史: *Judith studied classics at Oxford.* 朱迪思在牛津读的古典文化课程。**4 that's (a) classic!** *spoken* used when you think something is extremely funny【口】太滑稽了!

clas·si·cal /ˈklæsɪkəl; ˈklæsɪkəl/ *adj* **1** based on or belonging to a traditional style or set of ideas, especially in art or science〔尤指艺术、科学〕经典的; 传统的, 正统的: *classical physics, as opposed to quantum physics* 与量子物理学相对的经典物理学 **2** connected with the language, literature etc of Ancient Greece and Rome 古典的; 古典派的; 与古希腊、罗马有关的: **classical education** (=an education that includes studying Latin and Greek)〔包括希腊文与拉丁文的〕古典教育 3

classical mu·sic /ˌ··· ˈ··/ *n* [U] music that people consider to be serious and that has been popular for a long time 古典音乐

clas·si·cis·m /ˈklæsəˌsɪzəm; ˈklæsɨsɪzəm/ *n* [U] a style of art that is simple, regular, and does not show too much emotion, based on the models of Ancient Greece or Rome 古典主义; 古典风格 —compare 比较 REALISM, ROMANTICISM

clas·si·cist /ˈklæsəsɪst; ˈklæsɨsɨst/ *n* [C] someone who studies classics (CLASSIC² (3)) 古典主义者; 古典学者

Classics Il·lus·tra·ted /ˌ·· ˈ····/ a US series of COMICS (=magazines for children with writing and pictures) which tell well-known stories from literature〔美国的〕文学名著系列漫画

clas·si·fi·ca·tion /ˌklæsəfəˈkeʃən; ˌklæsɨfɨˈkeɪʃən/ *n* **1** [U] a process in which you put something into the group or class it belongs to 归类, 分类, 分级: *the classification of wines according to quality* 把葡萄酒按质分类 **2** [C] a group or class into which something is put 类别, 等级: *job classifications* 工作类别

clas·si·fied /ˈklæsəˌfaɪd; ˈklæsɨfaɪd/ *adj* classified information or documents are ones which the government has ordered to be kept secret〔资料或文件〕保密的, 机密的

classified ad /ˌ··· ˈ·/ also 又作 **classified** *BrE*【英】*n* [C] a small advertisement you put in a newspaper if you want to buy or sell something〔报纸上的〕分类广告; SMALL AD, WANT AD *AmE*【美】

classified di·rec·to·ry /ˌ··· ˈ····/ *n* [C] *BrE* a book that gives a list of the addresses and telephone numbers of companies under the title of their job or business【英】分类电话号码簿

clas·si·fy /ˈklæsəˌfaɪ; ˈklæsɨfaɪ/ *v* [T] **1** to decide what group a plant, animal, book etc belong to according to a system〔依据某系统〕将…分类: **classify sth as** *Is this plant classified as a moss or a lichen?* 这种植物归为苔藓还是地衣? **2** to regard people or things as belonging to a particular type because they have the same physical features, qualities etc 把…归入一类[一个等级] —**classifiable** *adj*

class·is·m /ˈklæsɪzəm; ˈklɑːsɪzəm/ *n* [U] the belief that one social class, especially the one you belong to, is better than another 阶级偏见 —**classist** *adj*

class·less /ˈklæslɪs; ˈklɑːsləs/ *adj* **1** a classless society is one in which people are not divided into different social classes〔社会〕不分阶级[阶层]的 **2** a classless person does not clearly belong to one particular social class 不属于某一特定阶级[阶层]的 —**classlessness** *n* [U]

class·mate /ˈklæsˌmet; ˈklɑːsmeɪt/ *n* [C] a member of the same class in a school, college or, in the US, a university 同班同学

class·room /ˈklæsˌrum; ˈklɑːsrʊm/ *n* [C] a room that you have lessons in at a school or college 教室, 课室 3 3

class strug·gle /ˌ· ˈ··/ *n* [singular,U] the Marxist theory that social reality is a continuing struggle for political and economic power between CAPITALISTS (=the owners of property, factories etc) and the PROLETARIAT (=the workers)〔马克思主义学说中资产阶级与无产阶级的〕阶级斗争

class·work /ˈklæsˌwɝk; ˈklɑːswɜːk/ *n* [U] school work done by students in a class rather than at home 课堂作业 —compare 比较 HOMEWORK (1)

class·y /ˈklæsɪ; ˈklɑːsi/ *adj informal* fashionable and expensive【非正式】昂贵时髦的; 高级的, 上等的: *classy restaurants* 高级餐厅

clat·ter /ˈklætə; ˈklætə/ *v* **1** [I,T] if heavy hard objects clatter, or if you clatter them, they make a loud unpleasant noise（使）发出撞击声: *The tray fell clattering to the ground.* 盘子啪啦一声掉在地上。**2** [I alway+adv/prep] to move quickly and noisily 急速而发出响声地走: **clatter over/down/along etc** *The horse went clattering over the cobbles.* 马咔哒咔哒地走过卵石铺成的街道。 —**clatter** *n* [singular,U]: *the clatter of dishes* 盘碟相碰的当啷声

Clau·di·us /ˈklɔdiəs; ˈklɔːdiəs/ (10 BC-54 AD) the emperor of Rome from AD 41 to 54, who made Britain part of the Roman Empire 克劳狄〔(公元前 10-公元 54)，罗马皇帝，公元 41 至 54 年在位，曾把不列颠纳入罗马帝国的版图〕

S3 W2 **clause** /klɔz; klɔːz/ *n* [C] **1** a part of a written law or legal document covering a particular subject of the whole law or document〔法律等文件中的〕条款，项目: *A confidentiality clause was added to the contract.* 合同中加上了一条保密条款。**2** *technical* a group of words that contains a subject and a verb, but which is usually only part of a sentence【术语】从句，分句，子句 —compare 比较 PHRASE[1] (2)

claus·tro·pho·bi·a /ˌklɔstrəˋfobɪə; ˌklɔːstrəˈfəʊbiə/ *n* [U] a strong fear of being in a small enclosed space or among a crowd of people 幽闭恐惧症 —compare 比较 AGORAPHOBIA

claus·tro·pho·bic /ˌklɔstrəˋfobɪk; ˌklɔːstrəˈfəʊbɪk◂/ *adj* **1** feeling extremely anxious when you are in a small enclosed space 有幽闭恐惧症的: *I get claustrophobic in elevators.* 在电梯里，我有种幽闭恐惧症的感觉。**2** making you feel anxious and uncomfortable as if you are enclosed in a small space〔场所〕导致幽闭恐惧症的: *a claustrophobic atmosphere* 一种能导致幽闭恐惧的气氛

clav·i·chord /ˋklævəˌkɔrd; ˈklævɪ̣kɔːd/ *n* [C] a musical instrument like a piano that was played especially in the past〔尤旧时用的〕击弦古钢琴；翼琴

clav·i·cle /ˋklævəkḷ; ˈklævɪkəl/ *n* [C] *technical* a COLLARBONE【术语】锁骨 —see picture at 参见 SKELETON 图

claw[1] /klɔ; klɔː/ *n* [C] **1** a sharp curved nail on the toe of an animal or bird〔鸟、兽的〕爪: *The cat dug his claws into my leg.* 那只猫用爪子抓我的腿。**2 get your claws into sb a)** if a woman gets her claws into a man, she shows that she is determined to marry him 决心嫁给某人 **b)** to say unpleasant things about someone in order to upset them 攻击某人，中伤某人: *Wait till the papers get their claws into him.* 一直等到报纸攻击他为止。**3** [usually plural 一般用复数] the part of the body of some insects and sea animals that is used for attacking and holding things〔昆虫、虾、蟹等的〕螯，钳 —see picture at 参见 CRAB[1] 图 **4** the curved end of a tool or machine used for pulling nails out of wood and lifting things 拔钉爪，起钉器: *a claw hammer* 拔钉锤

claw[2] *v* [I,T] **1** to tear or pull at something using claws〔用爪〕抓；撕: **[+at]** *The cat keeps clawing at the rug.* 猫不停地用爪子抓地毯。**2** to try very hard to get hold of something 奋力抓住: *Mary clawed at her husband's sleeve, trying to stop him.* 玛丽使劲拽住丈夫的衣袖，想要阻止他。| **claw your way up/along/across etc** (=move somewhere slowly by holding tightly onto things as you move) 慢慢地攀爬

claw sth ↔ **back** *phr v* [T] **1** to get back something that you had lost, by working very hard 夺回，捞回；设法弥补: *Through aggressive advertising, the company managed to claw back its share of the market.* 该公司通过大做广告，成功地夺回了它的那部分市场。**2** *BrE* if a government claws back money that ordinary people have been allowed to keep or get, it gets it back by increasing taxes【英】〔政府用增加税款的手段〕收回〔减免的税款〕

clay /kle; kleɪ/ *n* [U] heavy sticky soil that can be used for making pots, bricks etc 黏土 —see also 另见 **feet of clay** (FOOT[1] (24)) —**clayey** *adj*

Clay, Cas·si·us /ˋkæsɪəs; ˈkæsiəs/ the former name of Muhammad Ali 克莱〔穆罕默德·阿里的原名〕

clay pi·geon shoot·ing /ˌ·ˈ·· ˌ·ˌ··/ *n* [U] *BrE* a sport in which you shoot at pieces of hard clay that are thrown up into the air【英】泥鸽射击运动，飞碟射击〔射击用黏土制成的盘形飞靶〕; SKEET SHOOTING *AmE*【美】

S2 W2 **clean[1]** /klin; kliːn/ *adj*

1 ▶WITHOUT DIRT 无尘的◀ without any dirt or marks 清洁的，干净的: *Are your hands clean?* 你的手干净吗？| *a clean towel* 干净的毛巾 | **sweep/scrub etc sth clean** *Wipe that sink clean when you're done.* 洗完后将水槽擦干净。| **clean and tidy/neat** *Try to keep your room clean and tidy.* 保持房间整洁。| **spotlessly clean** (=very clean) 一尘不染的 *a spotlessly clean kitchen* 一尘不染的厨房

2 ▶HABITS/APPEARANCE 习惯/外表◀ behaving in a way that keeps things clean or having a clean appearance 爱清洁的: *Cats are wonderfully clean creatures.* 猫是极爱干净的动物。

3 ▶AIR/WATER 空气/水◀ containing nothing that is dirty or harmful, such as poisons 纯净的；无病菌的: *Smell that clean air!* 呼吸一下那洁净的空气！

4 ▶FAIR/LEGAL 公平/合法的◀ a) done in a fair or legal way 公平的；不作弊的；合法的: *a clean fight* 公平的打斗 **b)** showing that you have followed the rules or the law 无过失[违法]记录的: *a clean driving licence* 无违规记录的驾驶执照 | *Well, she has a clean record.* (=she is not a criminal) 嗯，她无违法记录。

5 ▶JOKES/HUMOUR 玩笑/幽默◀ not offensive or not dealing with sex 不猥亵的，不下流的；正派的；无挑衅性的: **good, clean fun** *Oh, don't get mad – it was just good, clean fun!* 噢，不要生气，只不过开了个无伤大雅的玩笑！| **keep it clean** (=used to tell someone not to do or say anything morally offensive) 保持清白 | **clean living** (=a way of life in which you do not drink, take drugs, or behave in an immoral way) 清白的生活

6 make a clean breast of it to admit that you have done something wrong so that you no longer feel guilty 全盘托出，坦白供认

7 a clean break a) a quick sudden separation from a person, organization, place etc〔与某人或机构等〕一刀两断，脱离关系；决裂: *Den left the next day, needing to make a clean break.* 因为要彻底脱离关系，丹恩第二天就走了。**b)** a break in a bone or other object that is complete and has not left any small pieces 彻底断裂，折断

8 ▶SMOOTH 平滑的◀ having a smooth or regular edge or surface 表面光滑的；边缘整齐的: *a clean cut* 整齐的切口

9 come clean *informal* to finally tell the truth or admit that you have done something wrong【非正式】最终认错；坦白交代，承认: **[+about]** *It's time you came clean about your affair.* 该承认你做的事了吧。

10 a clean sheet/slate a situation that shows that someone has behaved well or not made any mistakes 过去无过错记录的: *Jed looked forward to starting life again with a clean sheet.* 杰德期望清清白白地重新做人。

11 a clean bill of health a report that says you are healthy or that a machine or building is safe 健康状况良好证明书；机器[建筑物]状况良好证明: *Inspectors gave the factory a clean bill of health.* 检查员证实该工厂状况良好。

12 a clean sweep a) a complete change in a company or organization, made by getting rid of people〔公司或机构的〕大换班；大改变 **b)** a victory in all parts of a game or competition, especially by winning the first three places〔在比赛中〕大获全胜〔尤指获前三名〕: *The 200m race was a clean sweep for France.* 法国运动员包揽了 200 米赛跑的全部奖牌。

13 ▶PAPER 纸◀ a piece of paper that is clean has not yet been used 未用过的，新的

14 a clean copy a piece of writing that contains no mistakes〔文稿〕无错误的

15 ▶WITHOUT WEAPONS/DRUGS 无武器/无毒品◀ [not before noun 不用于名词前] *slang* not having any hidden weapons or illegal drugs【俚】没有私带武器[毒品]的: *They searched him at the airport, but he was clean.* 他们在机场对他进行了搜查，但他身上没有违禁品。

16 ▶NOT HAVING DRUGS 不吸毒的◀ [not before noun 不用于名词前] no longer taking illegal drugs 不再吸毒的: *Dave's been clean for two years now.* 戴夫已经戒毒两年了。

17 ▶POWER/ENERGY 动力/能源◀ producing energy or power without causing POLLUTION 无污染的: **clean energy** (=energy that is produced safely) 无污染能源

18 ▶MOVEMENT 运动◀ a clean movement in sport is skilful and exact〔体育运动〕动作干净利落的

19 as clean as a new pin *BrE*【英】 **as clean as a whistle** very clean 非常清洁的 —see also 另见 CLEANLY, CLEAN-CUT, **keep your nose clean** (NOSE[1] (13)) —**cleanness** *n* [U]

S1 W3 **clean[2]** *v* **1** [I,T] to remove dirt from something by rubbing or washing 把…弄干净，使清洁，清理: *Your shoes need cleaning.* 你的鞋该刷一刷了。—see also 另见 DRY-CLEAN, SPRING-CLEAN **2** [I] to clean a building or other people's houses as your job〔作为工作〕打扫卫生: *Anne comes in to clean twice a week.* 安妮每周来清扫两次。**3** [T] to cut out the inside parts of an animal or bird that you are going to cook 将〔准备食用的动物、家禽等〕开膛取出内脏 **4 clean your plate** to eat all your food〔把食物〕吃完，吃光

clean sb/sth **out** *phr v* [T] **1** [**clean** sth ↔ **out**] to make the inside of a room, house etc clean or tidy 把〔房间、屋子的内部〕打扫干净: *We'd better clean out the attic this week.* 我们本周最好清扫一下阁楼。**2** [**clean** sb/sth ↔ **out**] *informal* to steal everything from a place or all someone's possessions【非正式】把

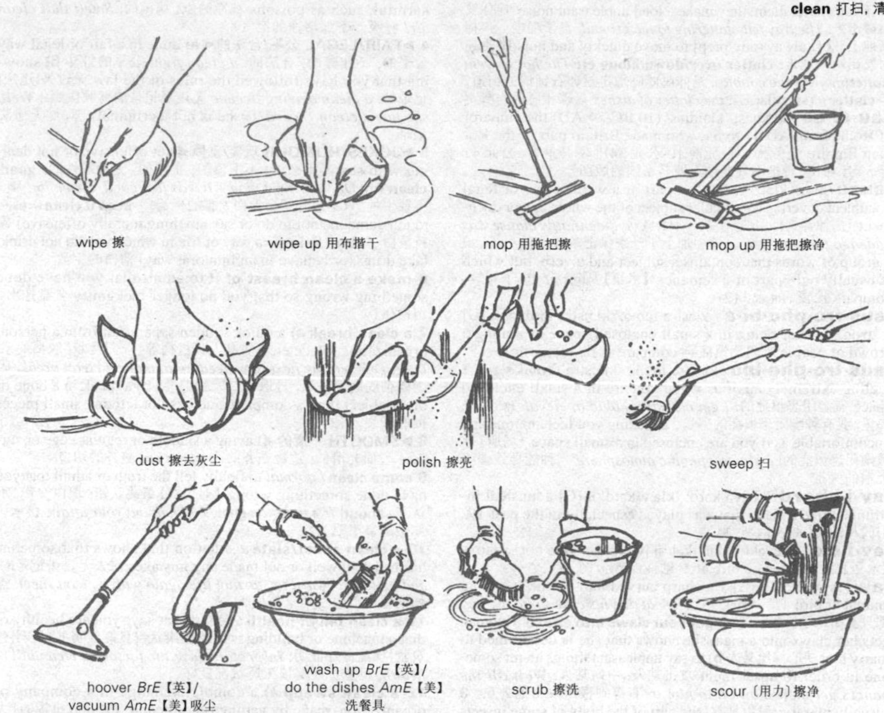

(某处)盗窃一空, 偷光: *Burglars completely cleaned the place out.* 窃贼将所有东西都偷光了。**3** **[clean** sb **out]** *informal* if something expensive cleans someone out, they spend all their money on it so that they have none left【非正式】用[耗]尽…的钱财: *The Paris trip cleaned us out.* 巴黎之旅把我们的钱全用光了。

clean up *phr v* **1** [I,T] to make something completely clean and tidy 打扫干净, 清理: *We spent all Saturday morning cleaning up.* 我们整个星期六上午都在打扫卫生。| *a plan to clean up the bay* 清理海湾的计划 **2** [I,T] to wash yourself after you have got very dirty 把(身体)洗干净: **clean sb/yourself up** *Let me just go clean myself up.* 让我去洗一洗。| **get cleaned up** *Dad's upstairs getting cleaned up.* 爸爸在楼上洗澡。**3** **clean up your act** *informal* to start behaving in a responsible way【非正式】改掉不良行为: *If you don't clean up your act I'll kick you out.* 如果你不改掉坏习惯, 我就让你滚蛋。**4** [I] *informal* to win a lot of money or make a lot of money in a business deal【非正式】赚得[赢得]一大笔钱: *We really cleaned up at the races today!* 今天的赛马确实让我们发了财! **5** [T **clean** sth ↔ **up**] to improve moral standards in a place or organization 肃清, 整顿(秩序、治安): *It's high time British soccer cleaned up its image.* 英国足球该改善一下它的形象了。—see also 另见 CLEAN-UP

clean³ *adv informal* used to emphasize the fact that an action or movement takes place completely and thoroughly【非正式】(行为、动作)完全地; 彻底地: **clean away/through/past** *The robbers got clean away.* 窃贼逃得无影无踪。| *The knife went clean through his finger.* 刀扎透了他的手指。| **clean forget** (=forget completely) 忘得一干二净 *Sorry, I clean forgot your birthday.* 对不起, 我完全忘了你的生日。

clean⁴ *n* [singular] a process in which you clean something 清理, 打扫: *The car needs a good clean.* 车子需要好好地洗一洗。

clean-cut /ˌ·ˈ·◂/ *adj* someone who is clean-cut looks neat and clean 外貌整洁体面的: *clean-cut college boys* 外表整洁体面的男大学生

3 **clean·er** /ˈklinɚ; ˈkliːnə/ *n* [C] **1** someone whose job is to clean other people's houses, offices etc 清洁工人 **2** a machine or substance used for cleaning 清洁器; 清洁剂: *a vacuum cleaner* 真空吸尘器 **3** **the cleaner's** a DRY CLEANER's 洗衣店, 干洗店 **4** **take sb to the cleaner's** *informal*【非正式】**a)** to cheat someone out of all their money or possessions 骗光某人的钱, 使…破产 **b)** to defeat someone completely 彻底打败[击败]: *The Lakers took the Bulls to the cleaner's, winning 96–72.* 湖人队以96-72大胜公牛队。

clean·ing /ˈklinɪŋ; ˈkliːnɪŋ/ *n* [U] a process in which you clean other people's houses, offices etc (为他人的住宅、办公室等作的)清理, 打扫: **the cleaning** *Liz comes on Thursday to do the cleaning.* 莉兹星期四来打扫(房间)。

cleaning lady /ˈ·· ˌ··/ also 又作 **cleaning woman** *n* [C] a woman who cleans offices, houses etc as her job 清洁女工

clean-limbed /ˌ·ˈ·◂/ *adj* tall and active-looking 高大灵活的: *a clean-limbed athlete* 一个高大灵活的运动员

clean·li·ness /ˈklɛnlɪnɪs; ˈklenlinɪ̥s/ *n* [U] the practice of keeping yourself or the things around you clean (保持)清洁; (保持)卫生

clean·ly /ˈklinlɪ; ˈkliːnli/ *adv* quickly and smoothly with just one movement 利落地: *The branch snapped cleanly in two.* 树枝整整齐齐地断成两截。

cleanse /klɛnz; klenz/ *v* [T] **1** to get rid of any dirt from a wound or from your skin 使清洁, 清洗(伤口或皮肤): *Use a piece of gauze to cleanse the cut.* 用一块棉纱清洗伤口。**2** **[+of/from]** *biblical* to make someone no longer guilty for things they have done wrong【圣经】使…免除罪恶, 使…清白, 净化

cleans·er /ˈklɛnzɚ; ˈklenzə/ *n* [C,U] **1** a liquid used for removing dirt or MAKE-UP (1) from your face 洁面乳 **2** a chemical liquid or powder used for cleaning surfaces inside a house, office etc 清洁剂; 去污粉: *cream cleanser for the bathroom* 浴室清洁剂

clean-shav·en /ˌ·ˈ··◂/ *adj* a man who is clean-shaven does not have hair on his face 胡子刮得很干净的 —see picture on page A6 参见A6页图

clean-up /ˈ· ·/ *n* [C usually singular 一般用单数] a process by which you get rid of dirt or waste from a place 清扫; 扫除: *a clean-up program designed to tackle car pollution* 清除汽车污染的计划 | **clean-up campaign/programme/measures** *The mayor launched the clean-up campaign.* 市长发起了清洁运动。

clear¹ /klɪr; klɪə/ *adj*

1 ►EASY TO UNDERSTAND 易懂的◄ expressed in a simple and direct way so that people understand 清楚的，明白的：*clear instructions* 清楚的指示 | *You must never do that again. Is that clear?* 不许你再那样做，明白吗？| **be clear on** *The rules are quite clear on the point.* 在这一点上各项规定都明白易懂。| **clear to sb** *Is all this clear to you?* 你全都明白了吗？| **make sth clear** (=express something strongly) 清楚地阐述 *Taylor's book makes the subject exquisitely clear.* 泰勒的书很清楚地阐释了这一主题。| **make it clear (that)** *Mr Tate made it clear there was to be no compromise.* 泰特先生清楚地说明没有商量的余地。| **make yourself clear** (=express something well) 表达清楚 *To make yourself clear without using facial expressions can be very difficult.* 很难不借助面部表情而清楚地表达自己。| **get sth clear** *Let's get one thing clear; you have my whole-hearted support.* 你要明白一件事，我全力支持你。| **Do I make myself clear?** (=used when you are angry and are telling someone to do or not to do something) 你听明白我的意思了吗？*If I catch you smoking again you're grounded. Do I make myself clear?* 如果再让我发现你抽烟，我就要你好看，我的话你听清楚了吗？| **a clear picture/idea** (=a good understanding) 清晰的理解 | **crystal clear** (=very easy to understand) 很容易理解

2 ►IMPOSSIBLE TO DOUBT 无疑◄ impossible to doubt, question, or be mistaken about 无可置疑的；明白无误的，明确的；明显的：*clear evidence of guilt* 有罪的确凿证据 | *They won by a clear majority.* 他们以明显的多数获胜。| **clear whether/why/how etc** *It is not yet clear whether we will benefit or not.* 我们是否会获益目前还不清楚。| **it is clear that** *It is clear that this situation cannot last much longer.* 很明显这种局势维持不了多久。| **become clear** *It has become increasingly clear that privileges have been abused.* 特权被滥用了，这一点是越来越清楚了。| **a clear case/example of sth** *a clear case of theft* 一宗无可置疑的偷窃案

3 ►CERTAIN 确定◄ **be clear** to feel certain that you know or understand something 确信的；充分了解的：[+about/on] *Are you all clear now about what you have to do?* 大家全都清楚自己要干什么了吗？| **clear whether/what/how etc** *I'm still not really clear how this machine works.* 这台机器该怎样操作，我还不大清楚。

4 ►SUBSTANCE/LIQUID 物质/液体◄ transparent 透明的：*a clear gel* 透明的凝胶

5 ►WATER/AIR 水/空气◄ clean and fresh 清澈的；清新的：*a crystal clear mountain lake* 水晶般清澈的山湖

6 clear sky/day etc without clouds, mist, smoke etc 晴朗的天空/日子等

7 ►EYES 眼睛◄ very pure in colour and without any redness 亮晶晶的，明亮的

8 ►SKIN 皮肤◄ smooth and without any red spots 光洁的

9 ►EASY TO SEE 易见的◄ easy to see 看得清楚的：*The photo was fuzzy, not clear at all.* 照片很模糊，一点都看不清楚。

10 ►EASY TO HEAR 易听见的◄ easy to hear, and therefore easy to understand 听得清的；易懂的：*a clear speaking voice* 口齿清楚 | *The radio reception isn't very clear.* 收音机的接收不太清晰。| **clear as a bell** (=very easy to hear and understand) 像钟声一般清晰洪亮

11 ►AFTER TAX 税后◄ a clear amount of profit, wages etc is what is left after taxes have been paid on it; NET³ (1)〔工资、收入等完税后〕净得的：*I get £200 a week clear.* 我每周的纯收入为 200 英镑。| **a clear $10,000/£400 etc** *It pays a clear $30,000 per year.* 每年净得 30,000 美元。

12 a clear month/two clear weeks/five clear days etc used to say that you have a whole month, two weeks etc to do something without having to do anything else 整整一个月/两个星期/五天〔指该段时间全被用于做某事〕

13 see your way clear (to doing sth) *informal* to have the necessary time or willingness to be able to do something【非正式】认为(做某事)适当；愿意(做某事)：*I was hoping you could see your way clear to lending me $150.* 我希望你会愿意借给我 150 美元。

14 a clear conscience the knowledge that you have done the right thing 问心无愧：*Now I've explained what happened, I can go with a clear conscience.* 我已经将所发生的事情向你解释清楚了，我现在问心无愧。

15 ►NOT BLOCKED 无阻塞的◄ not covered or blocked by anything that stops you from doing or seeing what you want 畅通的；无阻碍的；无遮盖的：*Finally! A clear desk.* 桌子终于整理干净了！| **clear view/look** *From the top floor you get a clear view of the bay.* 从顶层可将海湾一览无遗。

16 ►NOT BUSY 不忙的◄ without any planned activities or events 没事的；不忙的；空闲的：*Next Monday is clear; shall we meet then?* 下周一有空，我们那时见面，怎么样？

17 a clear head the ability to think clearly and quickly 思维敏锐的；头脑清晰的：*I won't drink now – I'll need a clear head to face Susan.* 我不喝(酒)了 —— 我要以清醒的头脑面对苏姗。

18 be clear of to not touch something or to be ahead of someone or something 不挡路的；不妨碍的：*He parked the car clear of the entrance.* 他将车停在不挡进口处的地方。| *United are clear of their nearest rivals.* 联队毫无敌手。

19 as clear as mud *spoken humorous* used to say that something is very difficult to understand【口，幽默】一点都不清楚，极难理解 —see also 另见 ALL CLEAR, CLARITY, CLEARLY, **the coast is clear** (COAST¹ (2)) —**clearness** *n* [U]

clear² *v*

1 ►SURFACE/PLACE 表面/地方◄ [T] to make a surface or place emptier or tidier by removing things that cover it 清除；清理：**clear sth of** *The room had been cleared of all his possessions.* 他房间里的东西都被清理掉了。| **clear a space for** (=move things so that there is room for something else) 为…腾出地方 *Sally cleared a space on her desk for the computer.* 萨莉腾出书桌的一角放电脑。| **clear the table** (=take plates, forks, knives etc off the table after you have eaten) 收拾餐桌

2 ►UNBLOCK 清除障碍◄ [T] to remove something that is blocking something else or causing a problem 清理〔障碍〕；清除〔麻烦〕：*Snowploughs have been out clearing the roads.* 扫雪车一直在清扫路面。| **clear sb/sth from sth** *Police cleared crowds from the area.* 警察把人群从该地区驱走了。

3 ►OF A CRIME/BLAME ETC 关于犯罪/责任的◄ [T usually passive 一般用被动态] to prove that someone is not guilty of something 证明…无罪；洗脱…的嫌疑：*Rawlings was cleared after new evidence was produced.* 提出新的证据后，罗林斯终被证明是无罪的。| **clear sb of (doing) sth** *Maya was cleared of manslaughter.* 马娅已被证明没有犯过失杀人罪。| **clear sb's name** *He fought for years to clear his name.* 他多年来奋力地为自己洗清罪名。

4 ►GIVE/GET PERMISSION 给予/得到许可◄ [T] **a)** to give or get official permission for something to be done 批准；使得到…的许可：*The plans have not yet been cleared by the council.* 这几项计划尚未得到议会的批准。| **clear sth with sb** *I'll have to clear that with my boss first.* 此事我要先取得老板的批准。**b)** to give official permission for a person, ship, or aircraft to enter or leave a country 允许〔入境或出境〕：*The plane took off as soon as it was cleared.* 飞机一得到许可就起飞了。

5 clear sth through customs/clear customs to be allowed to take things through customs (CUSTOM (4)) 允许通过海关，清关

6 ►WEATHER 天气◄ [I] if the weather, sky, mist etc clears, conditions become brighter or easier to see through 变晴朗：*We'll wait till the fog clears.* 我们要等到大雾散去。

7 ►LIQUID 液体◄ [I] if a liquid clears, it becomes more transparent 变清澈

8 ►CHEQUE 支票◄ [I,T] if a cheque clears or if a bank clears it, the money is moved from one bank to another〔经由银行〕结算；兑现

9 clear a debt/loan to get rid of a debt by paying what you owe 还清债务/贷款

10 ►EARN 赚◄ [T] *informal* to earn a particular amount of money after taxes have been paid on it【非正式】净赚：*Diane clears £20,000 a year.* 戴安娜每年净赚 20,000 英镑。

11 clear a fence/hurdle/wall etc to jump over a fence etc without touching it〔不接触地〕越过篱笆/栏架/墙等

12 clear your head/mind to stop worrying or thinking about something or get rid of the effects of drinking too much alcohol 不再想着〔某事〕；保持清醒；放松：*A good walk might clear my head a bit.* 好好散散步也许可让我的头脑清醒一点。

13 clear the air to talk calmly and seriously with someone in order to try to end an argument and feel better 尽释前嫌；消除隔阂[误解]

14 clear the decks to do a lot of work that needs to be done before you can do other things 准备行动：*I'm trying to clear the decks before Christmas.* 我在作过圣诞节的准备。

15 clear your throat to cough in order to be able to speak properly 清嗓子

16 ►FACE/EXPRESSION 面部/表情◄ [I] if your face or expression clears, you stop looking worried or angry 放松；不担心：*Her brow cleared and she smiled.* 她舒展眉头，笑了。

17 ►JOB/DUTY 工作/职责◄ [T] to deal with work that needs to be done 做，干：*Look! I've got all this to clear before the weekend.* 看！周末前我要把这些全干完。

18 ►SKIN 皮肤◄ [I] to no longer have spots 去除斑点, 变得光洁
19 clear the way for to make preparations so that a process can happen 扫清道路, 给…做好准备: *This agreement will clear the way for further talks.* 这个协议将为进一步会谈扫清道路。
20 ►MESSAGE 信息◄ [T] *technical* to discover the meaning of a message in a secret language; DECODE (1)【术语】破译, 破解〔密码〕

clear away *phr v* [I,T] to make a place look tidier by putting things back where they belong 收拾, 整理: *Come on children, time to start clearing away.* 孩子们, 来吧, 该整理整理了。| **clear sth ↔ away** *Let's clear these files away.* 我们来把这些文件收拾好吧。

clear off *phr v* [I] *BrE informal* to leave a place quickly【英, 非正式】迅速离开: *They cleared off when they saw the police coming.* 他们看到警察过来便马上离开了。| **clear off!** *spoken* (=used to tell someone angrily to go away)【口】滚开!

clear out *phr v* **1** [I,T] to make a place tidy by removing unwanted things 清除〔杂物〕; 腾出空间: **clear sth ↔ out** *It's time I cleared those drawers out.* 我该把那些抽屉里的东西清理一下了。**2** [I] to leave a place or building quickly 迅速离开: *I'll give you ten minutes to clear out of here.* 我给你十分钟时间离开这儿。| **clear out!** *spoken* (=used to tell someone angrily to go away)【口】滚开! —see also 另见 CLEAR-OUT

clear up *phr v* **1** [I,T] to make a place look tidier by putting things back where they belong 收拾, 整理; 拾掇: *We'd better start clearing up.* 我们最好开始收拾吧。| **clear sth up** *Come on, Jamie, clear those toys up.* 快点, 杰米, 把那些玩具收拾起来。**2** [T **clear** sth **↔ up**] to find the whole explanation for something that is strange and hard to understand, such as a crime 说明; 解释, 解答: *The Dreyfus case was never completely cleared up.* 德赖弗斯一案一直没能完全弄清楚。**3** [T **clear** sth **↔ up**] to make sure that everyone involved in something understands all the facts and agrees, so that there will be no problems 澄清, 阐明: *There are a couple of points we need to clear up before the meeting begins.* 开会前, 我们还需澄清几点。**4** [I] if the weather clears up, it gets better〔天气〕好转, 转晴 **5** [I] if an illness or infection clears up, it disappears〔疾病或感染〕痊愈, 消失

clear up after sb *phr v* [T] to make somewhere clean and tidy after someone else has made it dirty and untidy 替〔某人〕收拾: *I'm sick of clearing up after you!* 我讨厌替你收拾烂摊子!

clear³ *adv* **1** away from or out of the way 不接触; 不靠近; 远离: *They managed to pull her clear of the wreckage.* 他们设法将她从残骸中拖了出来。**2 keep/stay/steer clear (of)** to avoid someone or something because of possible danger or trouble 避开, 躲开〔以免于危险或麻烦〕: *Steer clear of Marilyn, she's a troublemaker.* 离玛丽莲远点, 她经常招惹麻烦。**3 see clear** *especially AmE* to see something that is a long way away clearly【尤美】清晰地看到〔远景〕: *You can see clear to the mountains today.* 今天你们可以清晰地看到远处的群山。—see also 另见 **loud and clear** (LOUD² (2))

clear⁴ *n* **in the clear a)** not guilty of something 清白, 无罪; *If Middlemass had spoken to Potter at 8:45, Potter was in the clear.* 如果说米德尔马斯跟波特在 8 点 45 分谈过话, 那么波特就是清白的。**b)** no longer having a particular illness or infection 健康, 无疾病

clear·ance /ˈklɪrəns; ˈklɪərəns/ *n* **1** [C,U] the amount of space around one object that is needed to avoid it touching another object 空隙, 余隙; 空间: *The clearance between the bridge and the top of the bus was only ten centimetres.* 桥和公共汽车顶部的距离只有 10 厘米。**2** [U] a process in which official permission is given for a person, ship , or aircraft to leave or enter a country 许可, 批准〔如准予船只或飞机出入境〕: *The pilot requested clearance for an emergency landing.* 飞行员要求准予紧急降落。**3** [C,U] a process by which a cheque goes from one bank to another〔支票的〕交换结算, 兑现 **4** [C,U] the removal of unwanted things from a place 清除, 清理: **slum/land/snow clearance** *a slum clearance project* 贫民窟清拆计划 **5** [U] SECURITY CLEARANCE 安全[保安]审查

clearance sale /ˈ‥ ˌ/ *n* [C] an occasion when goods in a shop are sold cheaply in order to get rid of them 大甩卖, 清仓大贱卖

clear-cut¹ /ˌ‥ ˈ◂/ *adj* **1** definite or easy to understand 明确的; 易懂的: *There's no clear-cut distinction between severe depression and mental illness.* 严重的抑郁症与精神病之间并没有明显的区别。**2** having a definite outer shape 清晰的, 轮廓分明的: *the clear-cut outline of the mountains* 群山清晰的轮廓

clear-cut² *n* [C] *AmE* an area of forest that has been completely cut down【美】砍伐精光的林区

clear-head·ed /ˌ‥ ˈ‥◂/ *adj* thinking clearly 头脑清醒的 —**clear-headedly** *adv* —**clear-headedness** *n* [U]

clear·ing /ˈklɪrɪŋ; ˈklɪərɪŋ/ *n* [C] a small area where there are no trees in the middle of a wood〔树林中的〕小块空地

clearing bank /ˈ‥ ˌ/ *n* [C] one of the banks in Britain that uses a clearing house when dealing with other banks〔英国的〕票据交换银行, 清算银行

clearing house /ˈ‥ ˌ/ *n* [C] a central office that deals with financial affairs of clearing banks 票据交换所

clear·ly /ˈklɪrlɪ; ˈklɪəli/ *adv* **1** [sentence adverb 句子副词] used to show that what you are saying is true and cannot be doubted; OBVIOUSLY 毫无疑问地, 显然地, 明显地: *Clearly, the situation is more complicated than we first thought.* 很明显, 局势要比我们当初预料的复杂。**2** in a way that is easy to see, hear, or understand 清楚地, 明白地: *Please speak clearly.* 请说得清楚点。**3** in a way that is sensible 明智地, 清醒地: *What's wrong with you today? You're not thinking clearly.* 你今天怎么了? 头脑不清醒。

clear-out /ˈ‥ ˌ/ *n* [C usually singular 一般用单数] *BrE* a process in which you get rid of unwanted objects or possessions【英】清除, 清理: **have a clear-out** *I must have a clear-out one of these days.* 我这两天得进行一次大清理。

clear-sight·ed /ˌ‥ ˈ‥◂/ *adj* able to understand a problem or situation well 有眼光的, 有见识的: *a clear sighted analysis* 有见识的分析 —**clear-sightedly** *adv* —**clear-sightedness** *n* [U]

clear·way /ˈklɪrˌwe; ˈklɪəweɪ/ *n* [C] a road in Britain on which vehicles must not stop〔英国的〕禁停路

cleat /klit; kliːt/ *n* [C] **1** a small bar with two short arms around which ropes can be tied, especially on a ship〔尤指船上系绳用的〕羊角; 系索耳 **2** [usually plural 一般用复数] one of a set of pieces of rubber, iron etc fastened to the bottom of a shoe to stop it slipping〔钉在鞋底上的〕防滑条 —see picture at 参见 STUD¹ 图 **3 cleats** [plural] *AmE* a pair of shoes with these pieces【美】防滑鞋 —compare 比较 **spikes** (SPIKE¹ (2))

cleav·age /ˈklivɪdʒ; ˈkliːvɪdʒ/ *n* [C,U] **1** the space between a woman's breasts〔妇女的〕乳沟 **2** *formal* a difference between two people or things that often causes problems or arguments【正式】分裂; 裂痕; 分歧

cleave /kliv; kliːv/ *v* [T] *past tense* **cleaved, clove** /klov; kləʊv/ **cleft** /klɛft; kleft/ *past participle* **cleaved, cloven** /ˈklovən; ˈkləʊvən/ **cleft** *formal*【正式】**1** [I always+adv/prep][T always+adv/prep] to cut something into separate parts using a heavy tool or to be able to be cut in this way 劈开; 割开; 裂开: *The wooden door had been cleft in two.* 木门被劈成了两半。**2** [T] to divide something into two completely separate parts 彻底分开: *Class divisions have cleft the society.* 阶级划分将社会割裂开来。**3 cleave the air/darkness etc** to move quickly through the air etc 迅速地穿过空气/黑暗: *His fist cleft the air.* 他迅速出拳。

cleave to sb/sth *phr v* [T] **1** *formal* to continue to think that a method, belief etc is true or valuable, even when this seems unlikely【正式】忠于; 坚持, 坚守: *John still cleaves to his romantic ideals.* 约翰仍坚持他的浪漫理想。**2** to stick to someone or something or seem to surround them 依恋〔某人〕; 贴住, 粘住〔某物〕

cleav·er /ˈklivɚ; ˈkliːvə/ *n* [C] a heavy knife for cutting up large pieces of meat 剁肉刀, 切肉的大菜刀

clef /klɛf; klef/ *n* [C] a sign at the beginning of a line of written music to show the PITCH¹ (6) of the notes〔置于五线谱一行之首表示高低音的〕谱号: *the treble clef etc* 高音谱号等

cleft¹ /klɛft; kleft/ *n* [C] a natural crack in the surface of rocks or the Earth etc〔地球、岩石等表面的〕裂缝, 裂口: *a deep cleft in his chin* 他下巴上的一条深疤

cleft² *adj* **be in a cleft stick** *BrE* to be in a very awkward situation【英】进退两难, 陷于窘境

cleft³ a past tense and past participle of CLEAVE

cleft pal·ate /ˌ‥ ˈ‥/ *n* [C] a split in the top of someone's mouth that makes it difficult for them to speak clearly 腭裂; 兔唇

clem·a·tis /ˈklɛmətɪs; ˈklemətɪ̣s/ *n* [C,U] a plant with spreading branches and white, yellow, or purple flowers 铁线莲, 女萎〔一种开白、黄或紫色花的攀缘植物〕

Clem·ens /ˈklɛmənz; ˈklemənz/, **Sam·u·el Lang·horne** /ˈsæmjuəl ˈlæŋhɔrn; ˈsæmjʊəl ˈlæŋhɔːn/ the real name of the writer Mark Twain 克莱门斯〔作家马克·吐温的真名〕

clem·ent /ˈklɛmənt; ˈklemənt/ *adj formal*【正式】**1** willing not to punish someone too severely 宽大的, 仁慈的 **2** clemend weather is neither too hot nor too cold; MILD¹ (1)〔气候〕温和的 —opposite 反义词 INCLEMENT —**clemency** *n* [U] —**clemently** *adv*

Clem·en·tine /ˋklɛməntaɪn; 'kleməntaɪn/ a folk song about a girl who DROWNs (=dies from being under water)《克莱门泰因》〔一首讲述溺水身亡的小女孩的民歌〕

clem·en·tine /ˋklɛmən,tin; 'kleməntiːn/ *n* [C] a kind of small, sweet orange 小甜橘 —see picture on page A8 参见 A8 页图

clench /klɛntʃ; klentʃ/ *v* [T] **clench your fists/teeth/jaw etc** to hold your hands, teeth etc together tightly, usually because you feel angry or determined〔因愤怒或下决心而〕握紧拳头/咬紧牙关: *She muttered "Go away" through clenched teeth.* 她咬紧牙说了一句"滚开"。

Cle·o·pat·ra /,kliəˋpætrə; ,kliːə'pætrə◂/ (69-30 BC) a queen of Egypt, famous for her beauty, who became the lover of Julius Caesar and later of Mark Antony 克娄巴特拉〔(公元前 69-前 30 年), 埃及女王, 以美貌出名, 为尤利乌斯·凯撒的情妇, 后为马克·安东尼的情妇〕

Cleopatra's Need·le /,····ˋ··/ one of two ancient Egyptian OBELISKs (=a very tall piece of stone with a pointed end), which were built over 3000 years ago. One is on the Embankment in London, and the other is in Central Park, in New York City. 克娄巴特拉方尖碑〔建于三千多年前的两座古埃及方尖碑之一。一座立于伦敦泰晤士河河堤, 另一座立于纽约市中央公园内〕

clere·sto·ry /ˋklɪr,storɪ; 'klɪəstəri/ *n* [C] *technical* the upper part of the wall of a large church, that has windows in it and rises above the lower roofs【术语】〔大教堂内的〕天窗, 气窗

cler·gy /ˋklɝdʒɪ; 'klɜːdʒi/ *n* **the clergy** [plural] the priests in the Christian church〔基督教的〕神职人员: *the power of the clergy in the Middle Ages* 中世纪教会的权力

cler·gy·man /ˋklɝdʒɪmən; 'klɜːdʒimən/ *n* [C] *plural* **clergymen** /-mən; -mən/ a male priest in the Christian church 神职人员中的一员; 牧师; 教士 —see 见 PRIEST (USAGE)

cler·gy·wom·an /ˋklɝdʒɪ,wumən; 'klɜːdʒi,wumən/ *n* [C] *plural* **clergywomen** /-,wɪmɪn; -,wɪmɪn/ a female priest in the Christian church 女神职人员; 女牧师; 女教士

cler·ic /ˋklɛrɪk; 'klerɪk/ *n* [C] *old-fashioned* a member of the clergy【过时】牧师; 教士; 神职人员

cler·i·cal /ˋklɛrɪkl; 'klerɪkəl/ *adj* **1** connected with office work 文书的, 办事员的: *a clerical error* 笔误 **2** connected with priests 神职人员的; 牧师的; 教士的: *a clerical collar* 牧师领

clerk[1] /klɝk; klɑːk/ *n* [C] **1** someone who keeps records or accounts in an office 办事员; 文员; 簿记员; 职员: *a clerk in a commercial firm* 一家商业公司的文员 **2** an official in charge of the records of a court, town council etc〔法庭、市政厅等负责管理文书的〕文书, 书记员 **3** *AmE* someone who deals with people arriving in a hotel【美】〔旅店的〕接待员: *Leave the keys with the desk clerk.* 把钥匙交给柜台服务员。**4** *AmE old-fashioned* someone who serves people in a shop【美, 过时】〔商店的〕售货员, 店员 **5** *old use* a priest in the Church of England【旧】〔英国国教会的〕牧师

clerk[2] *v* [I] *informal especially AmE* to work as a clerk【非正式, 尤美】当文书[售货员、接待员]

clerk of works /,··ˋ·/ *n* [C] *BrE* someone who is in charge of repairs to the buildings in a particular place【英】〔负责某一建筑物维修工程的〕工程管理员; 现场监工

Cleve·land /ˋklivlənd; 'kliːvlənd/ a city in the US state of Ohio. Some people in the US use Cleveland as an example of a city which is rather boring and not very attractive. 克利夫兰〔美国俄亥俄州一城市。有些美国人说到某个城市没有吸引力甚至乏味无聊时常以克利夫兰为例〕

Cleveland, Grov·er /ˋgrovɚ; 'grəʊvə/ (1837-1908) the twenty-second and twenty-fourth President of the US, from 1885 to 1889, and from 1893 to 1897 克利夫兰〔(1837-1908), 美国第二十二届 (1885-1889) 和第二十四届 (1893-1897) 总统〕

S2 **clev·er** /ˋklɛvɚ; 'klevə/ *adj* **1** *especially BrE* able to learn and understand things quickly; INTELLIGENT【尤英】聪明的, 才思敏捷的: *a clever student* 聪明的学生 | *You tied your shoes up yourself? What a clever girl!* 是自己把鞋系好的吗? 多聪明的小姑娘! **2** able to use your intelligence to get what you want, especially in a slightly dishonest way 耍小聪明的, 滑头的: *a clever lawyer's tricks* 滑头律师所耍的花招 **3** *especially BrE* skilful at doing a particular thing【尤英】灵巧的, 伶俐的: *Bill's very clever with his hands.* 比尔双手很灵巧。| **clever at doing sth** *Deborah's clever at getting people to cooperate.* 德博拉善于让人们合作。**4** designed in an unusual way that is very effective 机敏的; 巧妙的: *What a clever little gadget!* 多么巧妙的小玩意! | *Now that's a clever idea.* 真是好主意! **5** *BrE spoken* used jokingly when someone has done something silly or stupid【英口】真聪明!〔用于开玩笑地表示某人干了一件蠢事〕: *"When I got to the library I found I'd left the books at home." "That was clever!"* "到了图书馆我才发现把书忘在家里了。" "是吗, 真行!" **6 clever clogs/dick** *BrE spoken* used to describe someone who is annoying because they are always right or always think they are right【英口】自以为聪明的人: *All right, clever clogs, we'll do it your way!* 好了, 聪明的家伙, 我们就按你的方式办! **7 be too clever by half** *BrE spoken* to be annoying because you are too confident about your own intelligence or abilities【英口】精明过头的 —**cleverly** *adv* —**cleverness** *n* [U]

cli·ché /kliˋʃe; 'kliːʃeɪ/ *n* [C] an expression that is used too often and has lost most of its meaning 陈词滥调, 老生常谈, 老套: *the old cliché that a chain is only as strong as its weakest link* 常言道, 链条的强度取决于其最薄弱的一环 —**clichéd** *adj*

click /klɪk; klɪk/ *v* **1** [I,T] to make a short hard sound or make something produce this sound (使) 发出咔哒声: *The man opposite kept clicking his ballpoint pen.* 对面的男士一直把圆珠笔弄得咔哒作响。| **click your fingers/tongue** (=make a short hard sound with your fingers or tongue, especially in order to get someone's attention or to express annoyance) 打响指/弹舌头发出啧啧声 | **click your heels** (=knock the heels of your shoes or boots together in a way that soldiers do) 脚后跟咔哒相碰 (立正) | **click shut/click into place** *The bolt clicked into place.* 门闩咔哒一声闩上了。**2** [I] *informal* to suddenly understand or realize something【非正式】突然明白, 恍然大悟: **it clicked (with sb)** *It suddenly clicked. The man at the station must have been her brother.* (我) 突然明白了, 车站上的那个人一定是她哥哥。| *For ages I couldn't do algebra, then one day it clicked.* 很久以来我一直弄不懂代数, 有一天, 我突然顿悟了。**3** [I] *informal* to like someone and share their ideas, opinions etc【非正式】喜欢〔某人〕; 与…有相同兴趣[爱好]: *Petra and I clicked straight away.* 佩特拉和我一拍即合。 S3

click on sth *phr v* [T] to press a button on a computer MOUSE (2) in order to do a computer operation〔使用电脑鼠标〕点击 —**click** *n* [singular]

cli·ent /ˋklaɪənt; 'klaɪənt/ *n* [C] someone who pays for services or advice from a person or organization 客户, 客人, 顾客: *meeting with an important client* 与一位重要的客户会晤 S3 W1

cli·en·tele /,klaɪənˋtɛl; ,kliːɒn'tel/ *n* [singular] all the people who regularly use a shop, restaurant etc〔定期光顾某商店、餐馆等的所有〕顾客, 主顾: *a very select clientele* 一批高级顾客

client state /,··ˋ·◂/ *n* [C] a country that is dependent on the support and protection of a more powerful country〔依赖大国的〕附庸国

cliff /klɪf; klɪf/ *n* [C] a high rock with a very steep side, near the sea〔海边的〕悬崖, 峭壁 —see picture on page A12 参见 A12 页图

cliff·hang·er /ˋklɪf,hæŋɚ; 'klɪf,hæŋə/ *n* [C] a situation or competition that makes you feel very excited or nervous because you have to wait a long time to see how it will end〔直到最后方见分晓的〕竞争, 搏斗; 扣人心弦的比赛: *The election in Russia was a real cliffhanger.* 这次俄罗斯大选是一场真正扣人心弦的竞争。—**cliffhanging** *adj*

Cliff's Notes /,·ˋ·/ **1** a US series of small books that give a short description of the main points of a work of literature, and explain it in simple language《克利夫笔记》丛书〔美国一系列小型丛书, 是以浅显的语言写成的文学作品纲要〕**2** a book in this series (一本)《克利夫笔记》

Clif·ton Sus·pen·sion Bridge /,klɪftn̩ səˋspɛnʃən ,brɪdʒ; ,klɪftən sə'spenʃən ,brɪdʒ/ a very high bridge over the River Avon near Bristol, designed by I.K. Brunel 克利夫顿吊桥〔英国布里斯托尔附近埃文河上的一座高耸的桥梁, 由 I. K. 布鲁内尔设计〕

cli·mac·tic /klaɪˋmæktɪk; klaɪ'mæktɪk/ *adj* a climactic period of time or situation is one in which very important or exciting events happen 高潮的, 形成高潮的: *the hero, dodging bullets in the movie's climactic scene* 在电影的高潮场面中躲闪子弹的主角

cli·mate /ˋklaɪmɪt; 'klaɪmɪt/ *n* [C] **1** a situation that exists at a particular time, especially one which involves people's opinions and attitudes〔某一时期社会上的〕风气; 思潮; 趋势: **social/political/economic climate** *Small businesses are finding it hard to survive in the present economic climate.* 小企业发现在当前的经济形势下很难生存。| **climate of suspicion/hostility/distrust** *a climate of growing racial intolerance* 愈演愈烈的排斥不同种族的风气 **2** the typical weather conditions in a particular area 气候: *Los Angeles' warm, dry climate* 洛杉矶温暖干燥的气候 **3** an area with particular weather conditions 气候带, 地带: *I could not bear living in a tropical climate.* 我不能忍受在热带地区生活。 W3

cli·mat·ic /klaɪˋmætɪk; klaɪ'mætɪk/ *adj* [only before noun 仅用于名词前] connected with the weather in a particular area 气候的: *climatic conditions* 气候情况

cli·max¹ /ˈklaɪmæks; ˈklaɪmæks/ *n* [C usually singular 一般用单数] **1** the most exciting or important part of a story or experience that normally comes near the end 高潮, 顶点: **[+of]** *the climax of an exciting expedition* 一次刺激惊险的远征的高潮 | **reach a climax** *The opera reaches its climax in the third act.* 歌剧在第三幕达到高潮。**2** an ORGASM 性高潮

climax² *v* **1** [I,T] if a situation, process, or story climaxes it reaches its most important or exciting part 达到顶点[高潮]: **[+in]** *Her determination and hard work climaxed in her appointment as chairwoman.* 她的决心和勤奋以被任命为主席而达到了顶点。**2** [I] to have an ORGASM 达到性高潮

climb¹ /klaɪm; klaɪm/ *v*

1 ▶MOVE UP/DOWN 向上/下移动◀ [I always+adv/prep, T] to move up, down, or across something, especially something tall or steep, using your feet and hands〔手脚并用地〕攀登,〔向上或下〕爬: **[+up/down/along etc]** *Some spectators climbed onto the roof to get a better view.* 一些观看者爬到了屋顶上, 以便看得更清楚。| **climb a wall/tree/mountain etc** *The kids are always climbing trees.* 孩子们经常在爬树。

2 ▶WITH DIFFICULTY 艰难地◀ [I always+adv/prep] to move into, out of, or through something slowly and awkwardly 吃力地爬〔进、出〕: **[+through/over/into etc]** *Ian managed to climb through a hole in the hedge.* 伊恩设法从树篱上的一个缺口钻了过去。| **climb into/out of clothes** (=put on or remove clothing slowly) 费力地穿上/脱下衣服

3 ▶SPORT 体育运动◀ [I,T] to climb mountains as a sport 爬山, 登山: *Sir Edmund Hillary was the first man to climb Mount Everest.* 埃德蒙·希拉里爵士是第一个登上珠穆朗玛峰的人。—see also 另见 CLIMBING

4 ▶PATH/SUN/PLANE 小路/太阳/飞机◀ [I] to move gradually to a higher position 徐徐上升; 爬高; 冒起: **[+into/up etc]** *The path climbs high into the hills.* 小路缓缓通向山顶。| *The plane slowly began to climb.* 飞机开始慢慢地往上升。

5 ▶PLANT 植物◀ [I] to grow up a wall or other structure 沿…攀缘而上: *Ivy climbed up the front of the building.* 常春藤沿着建筑物前部攀缘而上。

6 ▶TEMPERATURE/PRICES ETC 温度/价格等◀ [I] to increase in number, amount, or level 上升; 上涨: *The temperature was climbing steadily.* 气温在稳步上升。| **[+to]** *The original estimate of $500 million has now climbed to a staggering $1300 million.* 原先估算的5亿美元现在竟已惊人地涨到13亿美元。

7 ▶IN A LIST 在名单上◀ [I,T] to move higher in a list of teams, records etc as you become more popular or successful 排名升高: **[+to]** *Madonna's new record has climbed to number 2 in the US charts.* 麦当娜的新唱片已跃居美国排行榜第二位。

8 ▶IN YOUR LIFE/PROFESSION 生活中/事业中◀ [I,T] to move to a better position in your social or professional life 提高〔社会地位〕; 晋升: *Steve climbed rapidly in the firm.* 史蒂夫在公司里晋升得很快。| **climb the ladder** (=become more successful) 取得更大成功

9 be climbing the walls *spoken* to become extremely anxious, annoyed, or impatient【口】极度忧虑[烦恼、不耐烦]: *When Colin hadn't arrived home by midnight I was climbing the walls.* 科林半夜了还没回家, 我非常担心。

climb down *phr v* [I] *informal* to admit that you were wrong, especially after being certain that you were right【非正式】认错; 退让, 让步 —**climb-down** *n* [singular]: *a humiliating climb-down* 丢人的屈服

climb² *n* [C usually singular 一般用单数] **1** a process in which you go up towards a place and that usually involves a lot of effort 攀登: *It's quite a climb to the fifth floor!* 爬到五楼, 可不简单! | *a tough climb to the top of the hill* 艰难地爬上山顶 **2** an increase in value or amount 增值; 上升: *After a fairly steady climb, prices stabilized at around $1.65 a litre.* 价格稳步上升后稳定在每升1.65美元左右。**3** an improvement in your professional or social position〔职位或社会地位的〕提高; 晋升 **4** a process in which someone or something gets a higher position in a list because of being popular or successful〔名次的〕攀升: **a climb up the charts/table/league etc** *a sensational climb up the charts for Elton's new album* 埃尔顿那张新专辑的排名大幅度攀升 **5** a steep rock or cliff you climb up 攀登的陡峭悬崖: *You'll need a rope for that climb.* 你需要一根绳索爬上那座峭壁。

climb·er /ˈklaɪmə; ˈklaɪmə/ *n* [C] **1** someone who climbs as a sport 登山运动员 **2** a person or animal that can climb easily 善于攀爬的人[动物]: *Monkeys are good climbers.* 猴子善于攀爬。**3** a plant that grows up a wall or other structure 攀缘植物 —see also 另见 **social climber**

climb·ing /ˈklaɪmɪŋ; ˈklaɪmɪŋ/ *n* [U] the sport of climbing mountains or rocks〔体育运动〕登山: **climbing boots/equipment etc** *Remember to bring climbing boots.* 记得带登山鞋。| **rock/mountain climbing** *Rock climbing can be very dangerous.* 攀岩运动可能会很危险。| **go climbing** (=climb mountains or rocks as a sport) 去登山[攀岩]

climb·ing frame /ˈ‥ ˌ‥/ *n* [C] *BrE* a structure for children to climb on, made from metal bars, wood, or rope【英】〔儿童玩的〕攀爬架; JUNGLE GYM *AmE*【美】

climb·ing i·ron /ˈ‥ ˌ‥/ *n* [C usually plural 一般用复数] a small piece of metal with sharp points that is fastened under boots to make climbing less difficult or dangerous; CRAMPON〔登山靴上的〕铁爪器, 铁钉助爬器

clime /klaɪm; klaɪm/ *n* [C] *poetic* CLIMATE【诗】气候: *They retired to sunnier climes.* 他们退休后到阳光明媚的地方居住。

clinch¹ /klɪntʃ; klɪntʃ/ *v* **1** [T] to succeed in getting or winning something after trying very hard 最终获[赢]得: **clinch the deal/contract** *It was the BM40's superior design that clinched the deal.* 最终达成交易是因为BM40的优良设计。| **clinch the contest/championship/title etc** *Germany scored twice in the last ten minutes to clinch the championship.* 德国队在最后10分钟连进两球, 获得冠军。**2 clinch it** *informal* if an event, situation, process etc clinches it, it makes someone finally decide to do something that they were already thinking of doing【非正式】使〔某人〕最终下决心: *The offer of a company car clinched it and I accepted the job.* 公司提出为我提供专车, 这使我决定接受那份工作。**3** [I] if two people clinch, they hold each other's arms tightly, especially when they are fighting 扭打成一团 **4** [T] to fix a nail firmly by bending the point over 敲弯钉头使钉牢[固定]

clinch² *n* [C] **1** a situation in which two people hold each other's arms tightly, especially when they are fighting〔尤指两人打架时的〕扭抱 **2** a situation in which two people who love each other hold each other tightly; EMBRACE²〔相爱的人之间的〕拥抱

clinch·er /ˈklɪntʃə; ˈklɪntʃə/ *n* [C] *informal* a fact or remark that ends an argument or discussion【非正式】〔结束争论或讨论的〕事实[意见、论点]; 结尾: *The clincher came when police found his fingerprints on the stolen car.* 警方在被偷的汽车上发现了他的指纹, 这就可以下定论了。

cline /klaɪn; klaɪn/ *n* [C] *technical* a series of very small differences in a group of things of the same kind; CONTINUUM【术语】渐变性; 连续体

Cline, Pat·sy /pætsɪ; ˈpætsi/ (1932-63) a US COUNTRY AND WESTERN singer who died in a plane crash 克莱因〔(1932-1963), 美国乡村与西部歌手, 死于飞机失事〕

cling /klɪŋ; klɪŋ/ *v past tense and past participle* **clung** /klʌŋ; klʌŋ/ [I] **1** [always+adv/prep] to hold someone or something tightly, especially because you do not feel safe〔尤指感觉不安全而〕紧紧抓住[抱住]: **[+to/on/at etc]** *I clung onto Duncan for comfort.* 我紧紧抱住邓肯寻求安慰。**2** [always+adv/prep] to stick to someone or something or seem to surround them 缠着; 粘着: **[+to/around etc]** *His wet shirt clung to his body.* 他的湿衬衫紧紧地粘在身上。**3** to stay close to someone all the time because you are too dependent on them or do not feel safe 挨近, 贴近; 依附: *Some children tend to cling on their first day at school.* 有些小孩在上学第一天会有怕生的倾向。

cling to sth *phr v* [T] if you cling to a belief, idea, or feeling, you continue to think that it is true even when this seems extremely unlikely 坚持, 忠于: **cling to the hope that** *We clung to the hope that we might see her again one day.* 我们一直抱着希望终有一天能再见到她。

cling·film /ˈklɪŋfɪlm; ˈklɪŋfɪlm/ *n* [U] *BrE trademark* very thin transparent plastic used to cover food and keep it fresh【英, 商标】保鲜塑料薄膜; PLASTIC WRAP *AmE*【美】

cling·y /ˈklɪŋɪ; ˈklɪŋi/ also 又作 **clinging** /ˈklɪŋɪŋ; ˈklɪŋɪŋ/ *adj* **1** someone who is clingy is too dependent on another person 过于依赖别人的: *a timid, clingy child* 一个胆小且依赖性强的孩子 **2** clingy clothing or material sticks tightly to your body and shows its shape〔衣服或布料〕紧身的

clin·ic /ˈklɪnɪk; ˈklɪnɪk/ *n* [C] **1** a building, often part of a hospital, where people come for special medical treatment or advice 诊所;〔医院的〕门诊部: **dental/family planning/antenatal clinic** *I'll meet you at the family planning clinic.* 在家庭计划中心见。**2** *especially BrE* a period of time during which doctors give treatment or advice to people with particular health problems【尤英】门诊时间: **hold a clinic** *The baby clinic is held on Monday afternoons.* 婴儿门诊在周一下午。**3** a meeting during which a professional person gives advice or help to people〔有专家回答问题的〕座谈会, 咨询会: *an M.P.'s clinic* 下议院议员的座谈会 —compare 比较 SURGERY (3) **4** *AmE* a place where medical treatment is given at a low cost【美】〔医疗费用低廉

的）医务室 **5** *especially AmE* a small hospital in an area far away from large cities which provides medical treatment【尤美】卫生所，诊所〔远离大城市提供医疗服务的小医院〕: *a rural health clinic with ten to fifteen beds* 有十至十五张病床的乡村诊所 **6** *AmE* a group of doctors who work together and share the same offices【美】〔医院的〕科，室; PRACTICE[1] (5) *BrE*【英】**7** an occasion when medical students are taught how to decide what illness a patient has and how to treat it〔医科学生的〕临床实习（课）

3 **clin·i·cal** /ˈklɪnɪk]; ˈklɪnɪkəl/ *adj* **1** [only before noun 仅用于名词前] clinical work, training etc is practical medical work that is done in a hospital or clinic 临床的: *The drug has undergone a number of clinical trials.* 该药已经经过了多次的临床试验。| *clinical medicine* 临床医学 **2** connected with a hospital or clinic 诊所的; 医院的 **3** considering only the facts and not seeming influenced by personal feelings 冷静的; 客观的; 不偏不倚的: *He regarded her suffering with clinical detachment.* 他以一种超然的态度对待她的苦难。**4** a clinical building or room is very plain and clean but not attractive or comfortable 简朴的: *The walls were painted a clinical white.* 墙给漆成朴素的白色。—**clinically** /-kḷɪ; -kli/ *adv*: *clinically tested* 临床试验过的

clinical ther·mom·e·ter /ˌ‥ ·ˈ‥/ *n* [C] a THERMOMETER for measuring the temperature of your body 体温表[计]

clink[1] /klɪŋk; klɪŋk/ *v* [I,T] if two glass or metal objects clink or if you clink them, they make a short ringing sound（使）发出叮当响: **clink glasses** *I clinked glasses with the other guests.* 我和其他客人碰了杯。

clink[2] *n* **1** [singular] the short ringing sound made by metal or glass objects hitting each other〔金属或玻璃物品碰撞发出的〕叮当声: *the clink of glasses* 碰杯声 —see picture on page A19 参见A19页图 **2** *slang* prison【俚】牢房: *They threw him in the clink for two years.* 他们把他投进牢房，关了两年。

clink·er /ˈklɪŋkə; ˈklɪŋkə/ *n* **1** [C,U] the hard material like rocks which is left after coal has been burnt 炉渣，煤渣，烧结块 **2** [singular] *AmE* a bad note in a musical performance【美】奏[唱]错的音: *The singer hit a real clinker.* 那个歌手唱错了音。**3** [singular] *AmE old-fashioned* something or someone that is a total failure【美，过时】彻底失败的东西[人]: *That movie was a total clinker.* 那部电影是一个彻彻底底的失败。

Clin·ton /ˈklɪntən; ˈklɪntən/, **Bill** (1946-) the 42nd President of the US, from 1993 to 2001. Clinton was a popular President for most of his period in office, because the US economy was strong. He is also known for a sex SCANDAL that happened near the end of the time he was president. 克林顿〔(1946-)，美国第四十二任总统，任期从1993至2001年。在任期内的大部分时间，美国经济增长强劲，他因此深得民心。他还因在即将卸任之际发生的性丑闻而出名〕

Clinton, Hil·la·ry Rod·ham /ˈhɪlərɪ ˈrɑdəm; ˈhɪləri ˈrɒdəm/ (1946-) the wife of former President Bill Clinton and formerly the First Lady of the US. In the November 2000 elections she became a New York Senator. In 2009, she became Secretary of State. 希拉里·克林顿〔(1946-)，美国前总统比尔·克林顿之妻，美国前第一夫人。2000年11月当选纽约州参议员，2009年出任国务卿〕

clip[1] /klɪp; klɪp/ *n*

1 ▶FOR FASTENING 使紧固◀ [C] a small metal or plastic object for holding or fastening things together 回形针; 夹子: *Fasten the microphone clip to your shirt front.* 把麦克风夹在衬衫前面。| **hair clip** (=a piece of metal or plastic for keeping hair in the right place) 发夹 —see also 另见 BULLDOG CLIP, PAPERCLIP

2 ▶CUT 剪割◀ [singular] a process in which you make something shorter or tidier by cutting it 修剪: *I'll have to give that hedge a clip.* 我得把树篱修剪一下了。

3 ▶FILM 电影◀ [C] a short part of a film that is shown by itself 剪下的一段电影: *clips from Mel Gibson's new movie* 梅尔·吉布森的新片剪辑

4 a clip round the ear/earhole *BrE informal* a short blow on the side of someone's head【英，非正式】一记耳光

5 ▶GUN 枪◀ [C] a container for bullets which passes them rapidly into the gun so that they can be fired 子弹夹

6 ▶NEWSPAPER 报纸◀ [C] an article that is cut from a newspaper or magazine for a particular reason 剪报

7 $100/50 cents etc a clip *AmE informal* if things cost $100, 50 cents etc a clip, they cost that amount of money each【美，非正式】一次[每个]〔收费〕100美元/50美分

8 at a good/fair etc clip quickly 迅速地: *Traffic was going by at a fair clip.* 往来车辆的速度很快。

9 ▶WOOL 羊毛◀ [C] *AustrE, NZE* the total amount of wool that is taken from a group of sheep at one time【澳，新西兰】一次剪下的羊毛量

clip[2] *v* **clipped, clipping**

1 ▶FASTEN 紧固◀ [I always+adv/prep, T] to fasten something together or to be fastened together using a CLIP[1] (1) 夹住，扣住: **clip sth into/onto/together etc** *The invoices had been carefully clipped together.* 发票已经仔细地夹在一起了。| **[+on/to etc]** *The keys will clip onto your belt.* 钥匙会别在你的皮带上。

2 ▶CUT 剪割◀ [T] to cut small amounts of something in order to make it tidier 修剪; 剪除: *clipping the hedge* 修剪树篱

3 ▶CUT FROM NEWSPAPER 从报上剪下◀ [T always+adv/prep] to cut an article or picture from newspaper, magazine etc〔从报纸、杂志上〕剪下: **clip sth out of/from** *Elsa clipped the article out of the evening paper.* 埃尔莎从晚报上剪下了这篇文章。

4 ▶HIT 打中◀ [T] to hit the surface of something quickly but hard 迅速用力的击打，猛击: *The bullet clipped the car's side mirror.* 子弹猛地击中汽车的侧镜。

5 ▶REDUCE 减少◀ [T] to slightly reduce an amount, quantity etc 减少，减低: *Gunnell clipped a second off the world record.* 冈纳尔将世界纪录缩短了一秒。

6 clip sb's wings to restrict someone's freedom, activities, or power 限制…的自由[行动]; 削弱…的权力: *Getting married has really clipped his wings.* 结婚确实限制了他的自由。

7 clip sb round the ear/earhole *BrE informal* to hit someone quickly on the side of the head【英，非正式】打某人耳光

8 ▶TICKET 票◀ [T] to make a hole in a bus or train ticket to show that it has been used〔于车票上〕打洞

9 clip your words to say words in a quick, short, and not very friendly way 不友好地快速说话

clip·board /ˈklɪpˌbɔrd; ˈklɪpbɔːd/ *n* [C] a small flat board with a clip[1] (1) on top used for holding pieces of paper so that you can write on them 有夹子的书写板

clip-clop /ˌ· ˈ·/ *n* [singular] the sound made by a horse as it walks on a hard surface〔马在硬路面上走发出的〕嘚嘚声 —**clip-clop** *v* [I]

clip joint /ˈ· ·/ *n* [C] *slang* a restaurant or NIGHTCLUB that charges too much for food, drinks etc【俚】索价昂贵的饭店[夜总会]

clip-on /ˈ· ·/ *adj* [only before noun 仅用于名词前] fastened to something with a CLIP[1] (1) 用夹子夹住的: *clip-on earrings* 夹式耳环 —**clip-on** *n* [C] —see picture at 参见 JEWELLERY 图

clipped /klɪpt; klɪpt/ *adj* **1** cut so that it is short and neat 剪短的; 整齐的: *a neatly clipped hedge* 修剪整齐的树篱 **2** a clipped voice is quick and clear but not very friendly 说话急促的

clip·per /ˈklɪpə; ˈklɪpə/ *n* [C] **1 clippers** [plural] a special tool with two blades for cutting small pieces from something 剪（子）: *nail clippers* 指甲剪 **2** a fast sailing ship used in the past〔旧时的〕快速帆船

clip·ping /ˈklɪpɪŋ; ˈklɪpɪŋ/ *n* [C] **1** an article or picture that has been cut out of a newspaper or magazine; CUTTING[1] (2) 剪报 **2** [usually plural 一般用复数] a small piece cut from something bigger 剪下物: *He swept the hedge clippings into a heap.* 他把修剪下来的树篱枝杈扫成一堆。

clique /klik; kliːk/ *n* [C] a small group of people who think they are special and do not let other people join them 派系; 小圈子; 小集团: *A small clique of right-wingers controls local affairs.* 一小撮右翼分子控制了地方事务。

cliqu·ey /ˈklikɪ; ˈkliːki/ also 又作 **cliquish** /ˈklikɪʃ; ˈkliːkɪʃ/ *adj* a cliquey organization, club etc has a lot of cliques or is controlled by them 小集团的，派系的: *That tennis club is too cliquey for my liking.* 那个网球俱乐部太排外，我不喜欢。

clit·o·ris /ˈklɪtərɪs; ˈklɪtərɪ̣s/ *n* [C] a part of a woman's outer sexual organs where she can feel sexual pleasure 阴蒂，阴核

Clive of In·di·a /ˌklaɪv əv ˈɪndɪə; ˌklaɪv əv ˈɪndiə/ (1725-74) a British soldier and government leader, Robert Clive, whose victories over the French and Bengali armies in India helped to establish British rule in India 印度的克莱武〔(1725-1774)，指英国军事家和行政长官罗伯特·克莱武。他在印度曾战胜法军和孟加拉军，确立了英国的殖民统治〕

Cllr *BrE*【英】the written abbreviation of 缩写= COUNCILLOR

cloak[1] /klok; kləʊk/ *n* **1** [C] a warm piece of clothing like a coat without SLEEVES that hangs loosely from your shoulders 斗篷，披风 **2** [singular] an organization, activity, or way of behaving that deliberately protects someone or keeps something secret 伪装; 掩盖物: **[+for]** *The political party is used as a cloak for terrorist activities.* 那个政党只不过是搞恐怖活动的伪装。| **under the cloak of** *prejudice and hypocrisy hiding under the cloak of religion* 在宗教掩饰下的偏见和虚伪

cloak[2] *v* [T usually passive 一般用被动态] **1** to deliberately hide facts, feelings etc so that people do not see or understand them 掩盖，掩饰〔事实、情感等〕: **cloaked in secrecy** *The early*

stages of the talks have been cloaked in secrecy. 初期的会谈一直在秘密中进行。**2 cloaked in darkness/rust/snow etc** *literary* covered in darkness, rust etc【文】在黑暗中/铁锈下/雪下等

cloak-and-dag·ger /ˌ· · ˈ· ◂/ *adj* [usually before noun 一般用于名词前] a cloak-and-dagger situation, activity etc, is very secret and mysterious, often in a way that seems unnecessary 秘密的; 神秘离奇的: *Cloak-and-dagger tactics were used to get the bill through Parliament.* 使用了一些秘密的手段使法案在国会中通过。| **cloak-and-dagger stuff** (=mysterious activities or ways of behaving) 秘密活动, 诡秘的行为 *I'm sick of all this cloak-and-dagger stuff.* 我讨厌所有这些秘密的行动。

cloak·room /ˈklokˌrum; ˈkləʊkrʊm/ *n* [C] **1** a small room where you can leave your coat 衣帽间; 衣帽寄存处; COATROOM *AmE*【美】**2** *BrE* a word meaning a room in a public building where there are toilets, used because you want to avoid saying this directly【英】厕所, 洗手间, 化妆室; REST ROOM *AmE*【美】: *Excuse me, where's the ladies' cloakroom?* 对不起, 女洗手间在什么地方?

clob·ber¹ /ˈklɑbɚ; ˈklɒbə/ *v* [T] *informal*【非正式】**1** to hit someone very hard 狠打, 揍: *I'll clobber you if you say that again.* 如果你再那么说, 我就揍你。**2** to defeat someone very easily in a way that is embarrassing for the team that loses 彻底击败: *The Dallas Cowboys clobbered the Buffalo Bills last night.* 昨晚达拉斯牛仔队大破水牛比尔队。**3** to affect someone or something badly, especially by making them lose money 使…遭受沉重损失: *companies clobbered by foreign competitors* 受到国外竞争者沉重打击的公司 **4** to punish someone severely when they break a law 严惩: *Motorists caught driving without insurance will be clobbered.* 没有保险开摩托车将受到严厉惩罚。

clobber² *n* [U] *informal especially BrE* someone's possessions, especially their clothes【非正式, 尤英】随身带的东西; 衣物: *Don't forget all your clobber if you're staying the night.* 如果在外面过夜, 别忘了带衣服。| **fishing/swimming/football clobber etc** (=clothes and equipment needed for a particular activity) 渔具/泳衣/足球衣物

cloche /kloʃ; klɒʃ/ *n* [C] **1** a hat shaped like a bell, worn by women in the 1920s〔20世纪20年代的〕钟形女帽 **2** a glass or transparent plastic cover put over young plants to protect them during cold weather〔保护幼嫩植物不受严寒侵袭的〕钟形玻璃罩, 透明塑料罩

S2 W3 **clock¹** /klɑk; klɒk/ *n* [C] **1** an instrument in a room or on a public building that shows what time it is (时)钟: *The clock was ticking on the mantelpiece.* 时钟在壁炉台上嘀嗒作响。| **the clock strikes three/half past four etc** *The church clock struck midnight.* 教堂里响起了午夜的钟声。| **the clock says...** (=the clock shows a particular time) 时钟显示〔…点〕| **by the hall/kitchen/church etc clock** (=according to a particular clock) 根据大堂/厨房/教堂的钟 *It's 4:30 by the kitchen clock.* 厨房的钟指明现在是4点30分。| **wind (up) the clock** (=turn a key in a clock so that it keeps working) 上发条 | **set the clock by sth** (=change the time on a clock according to the time on the television, radio etc)〔根据电台、电视等的报时〕调整[校正]时间 | **set the clock for sth** (=turn a screw at the back of a clock so that it will ring at a certain time) 拨好闹钟 *Mary set her clock for 6:30 a.m..* 玛丽把闹钟定在早上6点30分。| **the clock is slow/fast** (=used to show that the clock is showing an earlier or later time than the actual time) 钟慢/快了 *Your clock's ten minutes slow.* 你的钟慢了10分钟。| **clock face** (=the front part of a clock with the numbers on) 钟面 —see also 另见 ALARM CLOCK, CARRIAGE CLOCK, CUCKOO CLOCK, GRANDFATHER CLOCK —compare 比较 WATCH² (1) **2 put the clock(s) back** *especially BrE*【尤英】**set the clock(s) back** *AmE*【美】to change the time shown on the clock to an earlier time, when the time changes officially〔根据官方时间〕将时钟拨慢 **3 put the clock(s) forward** *BrE*【英】**set the clock(s) ahead** *AmE*【美】to change the time shown on the clock to a later time, when the time changes officially〔根据官方时间〕将时钟拨快 **4 put/turn the clock back** to go back to the ideas or methods tried before instead of doing things in a new or modern way 倒退, 开倒车, 倒行逆施: *The new employment bill will put the clock back fifty years.* 新的雇佣法案简直是倒退了五十年。**5 put the clock back/forward** to remember a particular time in the past or imagine a time in the future 让时光倒流/前进: *It put the clock back forty years seeing that old Bette Davis movie.* 看贝特·戴维斯的那部老片使时光倒流了四十年。**6 around the clock/round the clock** *BrE* all day and all night without stopping【英】昼夜, 日以继夜地, 日夜不停地: *Charles has been working round the clock preparing the case.* 查尔斯日以继夜地忙于准备那个案子。**7 against the clock a)** if you work against the clock, you work as quickly as you can because you do not have much time 加快工作, 抢时间: *We're working against the clock to get this proposal finished.* 我们正加紧完成这份建议书。**b)** if you run, swim etc against the clock, you run or swim a particular distance as fast as possible 尽可能快地, 拼命地 **8 watch the clock** to keep looking at the clock to see what time it is because you are bored〔因感到厌烦而〕盯着时钟 **9 live by the clock** to organize your life so that you always do the same things at the same time and are never late〔生活〕有规律, 有条不紊 **10 the twenty-four hour clock** a system for measuring time in which the hours of the day and night have numbers from 0 to 23 二十四小时制时钟 **11 start/stop the clock** to start or stop measuring how much time is left in a game or sport that has a time limit〔在比赛中〕开始/停止计时: *They stopped the clock when Baggio was injured.* 巴乔受伤后暂停计时。**12 the clock a)** an instrument in a vehicle that measures how many miles or kilometres it has travelled〔汽车上的〕行车里程计: *The car had 43,000 miles on the clock.* 里程表上显示这辆车已行驶了43,000英里。**b)** an instrument in a vehicle that measures the speed at which it is travelling 车速表[计] **13 run out the clock/kill the clock** *AmE* if a team runs out the clock at the end of a game, it does not allow the opponents to get the ball so that they cannot earn points【美】〔在比赛末段〕消磨时间不让对方得分 —see also 另见 BIOLOGICAL CLOCK, BODY CLOCK, DANDELION CLOCK, TIME CLOCK

clock² *v* [T] **1** to travel at a particular speed, or to measure the speed at which someone or something is travelling 以…速度行驶; 测出, 记下〔速度〕: *The police clocked him at 95 miles an hour on the freeway.* 警察测出他在公路上行驶的时速为95英里。**2** to record the time taken to travel a certain distance 记录〔所花的〕时间, 为…计时: **clock sb at** *She was clocked at 59 seconds for the first lap.* 她跑第一圈花了59秒。**3 clock this/that!** *BrE spoken* used to tell someone to notice or pay attention to something【英口】注意〔看〕! **4 clock sb one** *BrE informal* to hit someone【英, 非正式】殴打某人, 揍某人: *I clocked him one in the eye.* 我打中他的眼睛。**5 clock a car** *BrE slang* to change the number of miles shown on the CLOCK¹ (12) of a car, in order to sell it for more money【英俚】〔为了使汽车卖更高价而〕更改里程表(数字)

clock in/on *phr v* [I] to record on a special card the time you arrive at or begin work; punch in (PUNCH¹)〔用特制的卡片〕记录上班的时间; 打上班卡: *I clock on at 8:30.* 我8点30分打上班卡。

clock off/out *phr v* [I] to record on a special card the time you stop or leave work; punch out (PUNCH¹)〔用特制的卡片〕记录下班的时间; 打下班卡: *I'm clocking off early today.* 我今天要早点下班。

clock up sth *phr v* [T] to reach a particular number or amount 达到〔某一数量〕: *The Dodgers have clocked up six wins in a row so far this season.* 本赛季到目前为止道奇队已连胜六场。| *I clocked up 90,000 miles in my Ford.* 我的福特车已跑了90,000英里。

clock-ra·di·o /ˌ· ˈ· · ·/ *n* [C] a clock that can be set to turn on a radio in order to wake someone up 收音机闹钟

clock·watch·ing /ˈklɑkˌwɑtʃɪŋ; ˈklɒkˌwɒtʃɪŋ/ *n* [U] the practice of looking often at a clock to see what time it is because you are bored or want to stop working 老是看钟等下班的行为 —**clockwatcher** *n* [C]

clock·wise /ˈklɑkˌwaɪz; ˈklɒkwaɪz/ *adv* in the same direction in which the hands (HAND¹ (40)) of a clock move 顺时针方向地: *Screw the lid on clockwise.* 顺时针方向拧紧盖子。—**clockwise** *adj* —opposite ANTICLOCKWISE *BrE*【英】, COUNTERCLOCKWISE *AmE*【美】

clock·work /ˈklɑkˌwɝk; ˈklɒkwɜːk/ *n* [U] **1** clockwork toys, trains, soldiers etc have machinery inside them to make them move when you turn a key〔玩具上的〕发条装置 **2 go like clockwork** if something you have arranged goes like clockwork, it happens in exactly the way you planned 准确地; 顺利地: *The concert went like clockwork.* 音乐会进行得很顺利。**3 (as) regular as clockwork** very regular 非常准时的; 极有规律的: *Walter came round every Friday, regular as clockwork.* 沃尔特每逢周五便过来, 非常有规律。**4 with clockwork precision/accuracy** in an extremely exact way 极精确地

Clockwork Or·ange, A /ˌ· · ˈ· ·/ a NOVEL written in 1962 by the British writer Anthony Burgess, about a group of young men who live in a future time and behave in a very violent way. It was made into a film by Stanley Kubrick in 1971, but he stopped allowing it to be shown in the UK because he believed that people were copying the violent actions of the actors in the film. 《发条橘》〔英国作家安东尼·伯吉斯1962年创作的一部小

说。小说描写了一群生活在未来、行为暴烈的年轻人。1971 年斯坦利·库布里克将其改编成电影。然而，他认为有些人在模仿影片中的暴力行为，所以终止该片在英国放映〕

clod /klɑd; klɒd/ *n* [C] **1** a lump of mud or earth 土块，泥块 —see picture on page A7 参见 A7 页图 **2** *informal* a stupid person who behaves insensitively【非正式】傻瓜，笨蛋 **—cloddish** *adj*

clod·hop·per /ˈklɑdˌhɑpɚ; ˈklɒdˌhɒpə/ *n* [C] **1** *informal* someone who is awkward and rough【非正式】笨拙的人，粗人 **2 clodhoppers** [plural] *humorous* a pair of heavy strong shoes【幽默】结实笨重的鞋子

clog¹ /klɑg; klɒg/ *v* also 又作 **clog up** [I,T] if something clogs a road, pipe etc, or a road or a pipe clogs, it gradually becomes blocked and no longer works properly 阻塞，塞住；阻碍：*Don't put potato peelings down the drain, they'll clog up the pipe.* 不要把马铃薯皮削在水槽里，会堵塞水管的。| **clog sth with** *The roads were clogged with traffic.* 路上交通阻塞。**—clogged** *adj*: *clogged pores* 堵塞的毛孔

clog² *n* [C usually plural 一般用复数] a shoe made of wood with a leather top that covers the front of your foot but not your heel 木底鞋，木屐 —see also 另见 **clever clogs** (CLEVER (6)) **pop your clogs** (POP¹ (9)) —see picture at 参见 SHOE¹ 图

clois·ter¹ /ˈklɔɪstɚ; ˈklɔɪstə/ *n* [C] **1** [usually plural 一般用复数] a covered passage that surrounds one side of a square garden in a church, MONASTERY etc〔修道院等的〕回廊 **2** a building where MONKS or NUNS live 修道院

cloister² *v* **cloister yourself (away)** to spend a lot of time alone in a room or building, especially because you need to study or work〔尤指因学习或工作而〕使自己与世隔绝

clois·tered /ˈklɔɪstɚd; ˈklɔɪstəd/ *adj* **1** protected from the difficulties and demands of ordinary life 隐居的，隐匿的：*a cloistered existence* 隐居生活 **2** a cloistered building contains cloisters 设有回廊的

clone¹ /klon; kləʊn/ *n* [C] **1** *technical* an animal or plant produced in an ASEXUAL way from a particular cell and looking exactly like this cell【术语】克隆，无性繁殖 **2** *technical* a computer that can use SOFTWARE that was written for a different computer【术语】仿制电脑：*an IBM clone* 仿制 IBM 电脑 **3** *informal* someone or something that seems to be an exact copy of someone or something else【非正式】极为相似的人[物]：*She's a bit of a Madonna clone.* 她和麦当娜就像一个模子里出来的。

clone² *v* [T] to make an exact copy of a plant or animal by taking a cell from it and developing it artificially 使…无性繁殖

clonk /klɑŋk; klɒŋk/ *n* [singular] the sound made when a heavy object falls to the ground or hits another heavy object 咚的响声 **—clonk** *v* [I,T]

clop /klɑp; klɒp/ *v* **clopped, clopping** [I] if a horse clops, its hooves (HOOF¹ (1)) make a loud sound as they touch the ground〔马蹄〕发出嘚嘚声 **—clop** *n* [singular] **—clopping** *n* [singular]

Clo·rox /ˈklɔrɑks; ˈklɔːrɒks/ *trademark* a common type of BLEACH sold in the US【商标】高乐氏〔在美国销售的一种普通漂白产品〕

close¹ /kloz; kləʊz/ *v*

1 ►SHUT 关◄ [I,T] to shut something so that there is no longer a space or hole, or to become shut in this way 关，闭合：*Ann closed her book and stood up.* 安合上书站了起来。| **close a door/window/gate** *Would you mind if I closed the window?* 我可以把窗户关了吗？| **close the curtains/blinds/shutters** *Close the curtains – it's getting dark.* 把窗帘拉上吧，天快黑了。| **close your eyes** *Beth closed her eyes and tried to sleep.* 贝丝合上眼睛想睡觉。—see 见 OPEN² (USAGE)

2 ►NO LONGER EXIST 不再存在◄ also 又作 **close down** [I,T] if a company, shop etc closes or you close it, it stops operating permanently〔永久性〕关闭，停业：*We have reluctantly decided to close the factory.* 我们极不情愿地决定关闭该厂。

3 ►FOR A PERIOD OF TIME 一个时期◄ also 又作 **close up** [I,T] if a shop or building closes or you close it, it stops being open to the public for a period of time; SHUT¹ (5)〔暂时性〕关闭，歇业：*The shops close at six.* 商店 6 点打烊。

4 ►BOOK/SPEECH ETC 书/言语等◄ [I always+adv/prep, T always+adv/prep] if a book, play, speech etc closes or someone closes it, it ends in a particular way 使结束，使停止：**close sth/with/by etc** *The Prime Minister closed his speech by making an appeal for peace.* 首相以呼吁和平的方式结束了演讲。| **[+with/by/when]** *The novel closes when the family are reunited in Prague.* 小说以一家人在布拉格团聚为结尾。| **closing remarks** (=something that you say at the end of an official talk or speech) 闭幕词

5 close an account to stop having an account with a bank 撤销账户

6 ►FINANCIAL/ECONOMIC 金融的/经济的◄ [I always+adv/prep] if business shares (SHARE² (5)) or CURRENCY (1) closes at a particular price, they are worth that amount at the end of a day's trade on the STOCK MARKET〔股市〕以…价格收盘：**[+at/down etc]** *Portland shares closed only 4p down at 112p.* 波特兰股票以 112 点收盘，仅跌了 4 点。

7 close a deal/sale/contract etc to successfully arrange a business deal, sale etc 做成生意/买卖/达成协议等

8 ►OFFER 开价◄ [I] to finish on a particular date 在〔某一日〕结束：*Special offer closes June 3.* 特殊优惠到 6 月 3 日结束。

9 ►DISTANCE/DIFFERENCE 距离/差异◄ [I,T] to make the distance or difference between two things smaller 拉近，减少〔分歧〕：*Society needs to close the gap between rich and poor.* 社会需要缩小贫富差距。| *The other car was closing on us fast.* 另一辆汽车迅速地赶了上来。

10 ►REDUCE ACTIVITIES ETC 减少活动等◄ [T] to make an activity or opportunity no longer available 使…不再存在：*The legislation closes a lot of loopholes in the tax law.* 该项立法填补了税法中的很多漏洞。

11 be closed if a particular subject is closed, you are no longer willing to discuss it 不再谈论某话题：*It was a regrettable incident but I now consider the matter closed.* 这一事件非常令人遗憾，但是我现在不想再谈论它了。

12 ►HOLD STH 抓握某物◄ [I always+adv/prep, T always+adv/prep] if someone's hands, arms etc close around something or they close them around something, they hold it firmly〔手〕抓握；抱紧：**[+around/round/over etc]**: *The baby's tiny hand closed over Ken's finger.* 婴儿的小手紧紧抓住肯的手指。

13 ►WOUND 伤口◄ also 又作 **close up** [I,T] if a wound closes or you close it, it grows back together and becomes healthy, or you sew it together for it to become healthy 合拢，合上：*The surgeon closed the incision neatly.* 外科医生干净利落地缝合了切口。

14 close ranks a) if people close ranks, they join together to protect each other, especially because their group, organization etc is being criticized 团结〔战斗〕 **b)** if soldiers close ranks, they stand closer together〔士兵〕列队靠拢；〔排成〕密集队形

15 close the book(s) on sth to stop working on something, especially a police inquiry, because it is impossible to continue 终止，〔警察〕停止〔盘问〕—see also 另见 CLOSED, CLOSING DATE, CLOSING TIME, **close/shut the door on** (DOOR (16)), **close your eyes to sth** (EYE¹ (39))

close down *phr v* **1** [I,T **close** sth ↔ **down**] if a company, shop etc closes down or is closed down, it stops operating permanently 关闭，停业 **2** [I] *BrE* to stop broadcasting radio or television programmes at the end of the day【英】〔电台、电视台在一天的播送后〕结束播送节目：*BBC 2 closes down at 12:45 tonight.* 今晚英国广播公司第二台于 12 点 45 分停止广播。

close in *phr v* [I] **1** to move closer to someone or something, especially in order to attack them 包围，合拢；靠近：*The snake closed in for the kill.* 蛇凑近准备捕食。| **[+on/around/upon etc]** *The gang closed in on Larry brandishing sticks.* 那帮人挥舞着棍子向拉里围拢过来。**2** if the night, bad weather etc closes in, it becomes darker or gets worse〔天〕变黑；〔天气〕变坏 **3** if the days close in, they become shorter because it is autumn〔白天〕变短

close sth ↔ **off** *phr v* [T] to separate a road, room etc from the area around it so that people cannot go there or use it 隔绝，封锁：*One of the lanes is closed off for repairs.* 一条车道因要维修而被封闭了起来。

close out *phr v* [T] *AmE* if a store closes out a type of goods, they sell all of them cheaply【美】〔商店以低价〕清仓出售，抛售存货：**close sth ↔ out** *We're closing out this line of swimwear.* 我们正在削价销售这种游泳衣。

close up *phr v* **1** [I,T **close** sth ↔ **up**] if a shop or building closes up or is closed up, it stops being open to the public for a period of time〔商店暂时〕停业；歇业；〔建筑物〕关闭；封闭 **2** [I,T] if a group of people close up, they move nearer together 靠近，靠拢：**close up the ranks!** (=used to order soldiers to stand closer together)〔口令〕队伍靠拢！**3** [I,T] if a wound closes up or if something closes it up, it grows together or is sewn together and becomes healthy again〔伤口〕愈合；缝合 **4** [I] to deliberately not show your true emotions or thoughts 掩饰，掩盖〔感情或思想〕：*Every time I ask Jenny about it she just closes up.* 每次我询问珍妮这件事，她只是遮掩搪塞。

close with sb/sth *phr v* [T] *BrE*【英】**1** to agree to do a business deal with someone 同意；与…达成协议：*It was such a good offer that I closed with him on the spot.* 报价非常好，我当场就跟他拍板了。**2** *literary* to begin a fight or battle【文】开始战斗：*The two armies closed with each other around about midday.* 接近中午的时候双方军队开始短兵相接。

close² /klos; kləʊs/ *adj*

① NEAR 靠近的
② LIKELY 可能的
③ CAREFUL 小心的
④ SIMILAR 类似的
⑤ ALMOST LOST/DANGEROUS ETC 几近丢失/危险的等
⑥ FRIENDLY 友好的
⑦ ALMOST CORRECT 几乎正确的
⑧ SPOKEN PHRASES 口语短语
⑨ OTHER MEANINGS 其他意思

① NEAR 靠近的

1 ▶NEAR IN SPACE 空间上靠近的◀ not far 近的: *The shops on Roland Way are the closest.* 罗兰德路上的商店是最近的。| **[+to]** *They chose a spot close to the river for their picnic.* 他们选择了一个离河不远的地方进行野餐。| **in close proximity** *The new housing estate is in close proximity to a nuclear power station.* 新的住宅区靠近核电站。

2 at close range/quarters very near 近距离地: *The victim had been shot at close range.* 被害者是近距离被枪杀的。

3 ▶NEAR IN TIME 时间上靠近的◀ near to something in time〔时间上〕接近的: **[+to]** *Your birthday's close to mine.* 你的生日和我的生日相隔不长。

② LIKELY 可能的

4 ▶LIKELY TO HAPPEN 可能发生的◀ seeming likely to happen or to do something soon 可能的, 接近的: **[+to]** *close to death* 离死亡不远 | **close to doing sth** *The two countries are close to signing a peace agreement.* 两国即将签署和平协议。

③ CAREFUL 小心的

5 a close examination, inspection, observation is one in which you look at something very carefully and thoroughly 彻底而仔细的, 严密的: **take a close look at sth** *Take a closer look at the photo; doesn't it remind you of someone?* 你再仔细地看看那照片, 没有让你想起一个人吗? | **keep a close watch/eye on** (=watch someone or something very carefully) 细心地看 *I'll keep a close eye on the kids; don't worry.* 我会当心看管小孩们的, 不要担心。

6 close confinement/arrest if a prisoner is kept in close confinement or under close arrest, someone guards them carefully to make sure they do not escape 严密囚禁/拘押

④ SIMILAR 类似的

7 if two things are close, they are very similar 酷似的: **[+to]** *There was a look of resentment in her eyes which was close to hatred.* 她眼中有一种近乎敌意的怨恨目光。

8 close to sth if a number or amount is close to another number or amount, it is similar to it〔数量上〕接近某物: *During the recession, the country's growth rate was close to zero.* 萧条时期该国的经济增长率几乎是零。

⑤ ALMOST LOST/DANGEROUS ETC 几近丢失/危险的等

9 ▶COMPETITION/ELECTIONS ETC 比赛/选举等◀ won or lost by a very small amount 几乎平手的, 势均力敌的, 难分高下的: **close game/contest etc** *a close match that could have gone either way* 输赢都有可能的势均力敌的比赛 | **a close second/third etc** (=almost finish a competition in the position ahead of the one you actually get) 与第一/二名相差很近的第二/三名

10 be too close to call if a competition, election, or result is too close to call the two sides have almost exactly the same number of votes, points etc〔比赛、竞选、结果〕势均力敌

11 ▶ALMOST DANGEROUS/EMBARRASSING 几乎危险的/令人尴尬的◀ *spoken* used when you have only just managed to avoid a dangerous or embarrassing situation【口】险些〔造成危险或尴尬局面〕: **that was close** *"Phew, that was close," Frank said as he swerved to avoid the cyclist.* "咳, 真险!"弗兰克侧身躲过自行车手后说道。| **a close call/shave/thing** (=a situation in which something dangerous, embarrassing etc almost happens) 勉强脱险/死里逃生/九死一生

⑥ FRIENDLY 友好的

12 if two people are close, they like or love each other very much 亲近的, 亲密的: *Mom and I are much closer now than we were when I was a teenager.* 我和妈妈现在的关系比起我十几岁时更亲密了。| **[+to]** *I felt closer to Rob that evening than ever before.* 那晚我觉得和罗布比以前更亲近了。| **close friends** *Fiona and I have always been close friends.* 我和菲奥娜一直都是密友。

13 close relation/relative a member of your family such as your brothers, sisters, parents etc 近亲〈如家庭成员〉

14 keep in close contact/touch if two people keep in close contact, they see, talk to, or write to each other regularly 保持密切联系

15 close association/connection/link etc if a relationship, association etc is close, the people in it work or talk together a lot 密切的关系/联系/接触等: *The school encourages close links between teachers and parents.* 学校鼓励老师和家长多接触。| **close cooperation** *What we need now is closer cooperation between the club and supporters.* 我们现在需要的是俱乐部与资助人之间更密切的合作。| **close partners/colleagues** *Dr Henke and I were close colleagues on the research project.* 亨克博士和我曾是该研究项目的亲密同事。

⑦ ALMOST CORRECT 几乎正确的

16 you're close/that's close *spoken* used to tell someone that they have almost guessed or answered something correctly【口】差不多, 你快猜对了: *"Where did you go on holiday this year – Turkey?" "You're close, we went on a 10 day tour to Syria."* "你今年去哪儿度假了? 土耳其吗?" "差不多是那一带。我们去叙利亚旅行了10天。"

17 close, but no cigar *AmE spoken* used when something someone does or says is almost correct or successful【美口】差不多, 但并非完全如此: *It was close, but no cigar for the Dodgers as they lost to the Reds 4-3.* 差不多让你猜中了, 道奇队以3:4败给红人队。

⑧ SPOKEN PHRASES 口语短语

18 the closest thing to/the closest you'll get to something that is very similar to, but not exactly the same as the thing mentioned 最接近…的事物/你所能达到的最接近的事物: *The island was the closest thing to an earthly paradise I can imagine.* 那个岛是我所想到的最像人间仙境的地方。

19 too close for comfort if something that happens is too close for comfort, it frightens you or makes you nervous 使人惊恐[紧张]的: *That car came around the corner just a little too close for comfort.* 那辆车从拐角开出来, 吓了我一跳。

20 close to home a) if something unpleasant happens close to home, you are directly affected by it because you see it in your daily life 发生在身边: *It's one thing seeing violence on the television but when it happens so close to home it's a different matter.* 在电视上看到暴力是一回事, 但是暴力在你身边发生又是另一回事。**b)** if a remark or criticism is close to home, it makes someone feel embarrassed or uncomfortable 令人尴尬[不舒服]的: *Allegations of elitism were too close to home as far as the committee was concerned.* 就该委员会而言, 提出精英主义的说法太令人不悦了。

⑨ OTHER MEANINGS 其他意思

21 ▶WEATHER 天气◀ very warm in a way that is uncomfortable because there seems to be no air 闷热的: *It's very close today.* 今天很闷热。

22 ▶SECRET 秘密◀ [not before noun 不用于名词前] unwill-

ing to tell people your thoughts or feelings; SECRETIVE 遮掩的，守口如瓶的: [+about] *Wanda's always been very close about her past.* 万达对她的过去一直守口如瓶。
23 ►NOT GENEROUS 不大方◄ [not before noun 不用于名词前] not generous; MEAN² (2) 吝啬的: [+with] *You won't get a penny out of him, he's very close with his money.* 你别想从他那儿得到一分钱，他吝啬得很。
24 close shave/haircut a process in which someone's hair is cut very close to the skin on the face or head 剪得很短的胡子／头发
25 close print/stitches etc print etc with little space between the letters, lines etc 密密麻麻的印出的字／针脚等: *I find it difficult to read such close print.* 这样密密麻麻的字，我很难读下去。
26 close work a process or activity which involves looking at or handling things in a very skilful and careful way 精细的工作: *Embroidery is very close work.* 刺绣是个很精细的活儿。
27 close vowel *technical* a close vowel is pronounced with only a small space between the tongue and the top of the mouth【术语】闭元音 —**closeness** *n* [U] —see also 另见 **close to the bone** (BONE¹ (9)), **play your cards close to your chest** (CARD¹ (13))

3 2 **close³** /klos; kləʊs/ *adv* **1** not far away; near 不远，接近地: [+to] *Ships can anchor close to the shore there.* 船可以在离海岸不远处下锚。| **close by** *The Abbots live quite close by.* 阿博特一家住得很近。| **close at hand/close together** (=very near) 近在咫尺／紧挨着 *Three men were standing very close together on the corner.* 三个人紧挨着站在角落里。| **close behind** *James heard footsteps close behind him.* 詹姆斯听到有脚步声紧跟身后。| **get close** *I couldn't get close enough to see what was happening.* 我不能走到近前看究竟发生了什么事。| **stay/keep close** *We must all stay close together.* 我们大家必须留在一块儿。| **hold/draw sb close** (=hold someone against your body because you love them or want to protect them) 搂紧／拉近某人 *He drew her close to him.* 他把她拉到自己身边。**2 close up/close to/up close** from only a short distance away 靠近: *When I saw her close up I realised she wasn't Jane.* 我看到她走近后才意识到她不是简。**3 close on/close to** used when you are guessing a number, age, amount etc or cannot give the exact number etc 几乎，差不多: *The walk took three whole days and covered close on forty miles.* 我们整整走了三天，大约有四十英里。**4 close to sth** to be very similar to something 与某事物极为相似: *When I saw Henry with another woman I felt something close to jealousy.* 当我看到亨利和另一个女人在一起时，我感到颇有些嫉妒。**5 come close to (doing) sth** to almost do something 差点儿(做): *I tell you I was so angry I came close to hitting her.* 我告诉你我很生气，差点儿打了她。| *She came close to tears when she heard the news.* 听到这样的消息，她差点儿掉下眼泪。**6** near to the surface of something 接近表面地，短到齐根地: *An electric razor doesn't really shave as close as a blade.* 电动剃须刀其实没有刀片刮得干净。**7 run sb close** to be almost as successful, skilful etc as someone else 和某人差不多一样成功[熟练等]: *Maxwell runs him close as one of this country's most exciting musicians.* 马克斯韦尔差不多是该国最优秀的音乐家之一。—see also 另见 **sail close to the wind** (SAIL¹ (6))

close⁴ /kloz; kləʊz/ *n* **1** [singular] *formal* the end of an activity or of a period of time【正式】〔活动或一段时间的〕结束，末尾: **the close of** *They returned home tired but happy at the close of the day.* 天黑时他们回到家里，虽然很累，但很高兴。**2 bring sth to a close** end a meeting, lesson etc 结束，停止: *The chairman brought the meeting to a close by thanking everyone for their hard work.* 主席在感谢了每个人的辛劳后，宣布会议结束。**3 come/draw to a close** if a period of time or an activity draws to a close, it ends 结束，终止: *And so, as 2003 draws to a close let's look at some of the major events of the year.* 因此，在2003年即将结束之际，让我们回顾一下本年度发生的一些重大事件。

close⁵ /klos; kləʊs/ *n* **1** [C] *BrE* a word used in street names for a road that has only one way in or out【英】〔用于街道名称〕死巷，死胡同: *They live at 26 Hillside Close.* 他们住在希尔赛德巷26号。**2** the area and buildings surrounding a CATHEDRAL〔大教堂的〕周围地区

close-cropped /ˌklos ˋkrɑpt; ˌkləʊs ˈkrɒpt◂/ *adj* close-cropped grass or hair is cut very short〔草或头发〕剪得很短的

3 **closed** /klozd; kləʊzd/ *adj* **1** shut, especially overnight or for a certain period of time 关闭的: *The shops are closed on Sundays.* 商店星期天关门。| **closed to the public/visitors etc** *The gardens are closed to visitors in winter.* 花园在冬天不对游客开放。**2** restricted to a particular group of people 只限特定人群的: **closed membership** *The golf club has closed membership.* 该高尔夫球俱乐部只限特定的会员参加。**3** not willing to accept ideas or influences from outside 闭关自守的，不受外来影响: **closed society/world/way of life** *Army officers and their families live in a very closed world.* 军官及其家属生活在一个非常封闭的世界里。| **closed mind** (=someone who has a closed mind does not accept new ways of thinking or doing things) 闭塞僵化的思想[头脑] **4 behind closed doors** if official meetings or decisions take place behind closed doors, they take place secretly 不公开地，秘密地 **5 a closed book** a subject or problem that someone knows or understands nothing about 一无所知[毫不理解]的学科[问题]: *Most of mathematics is just a closed book to me.* 我对数学大部分都几乎一窍不通。

closed cir·cuit tel·e·vi·sion /ˌ· ˌ·· ˈ····/ *n* [C,U] a system in which cameras send pictures to television sets that is used in many public buildings to protect them from crime 闭路电视

closed-door /ˌ· ˈ·/ *adj* [only before noun 仅用于名词前] closed-door meetings or talks take place secretly 秘密的

close·down /ˈklozˋdaʊn; ˈkləʊzdaʊn/ *n* **1** [C] a situation in which work in a company, factory etc is stopped, especially permanently〔公司、工厂等〕停工，关闭 **2** [C,U] *BrE* the end of radio or television broadcasts each day【英】〔每天广播或电视节目的〕停止播送

closed sea·son /ˌ· ˈ··/ *n* [C] the American form of CLOSE SEASON close season 的美语形式

closed shop /ˌ· ˈ·◂/ *n* [C] a company, factory etc where all the workers must belong to a particular TRADE UNION 只雇用某一工会会员的企业

close-fist·ed /ˌklos ˋfɪstɪd; ˌkləʊs ˈfɪstɪd◂/ *adj* unwilling to spend money; TIGHT-FISTED 吝啬的，小气的

close-fit·ting /ˌklos ˋfɪtɪŋ; ˌkləʊs ˈfɪtɪŋ◂/ *adj* close-fitting clothes are tight and show the shape of your body〔衣服〕紧身的

close-grained /ˌklos ˋgrend; ˌkləʊs ˈgreɪnd◂/ *adj* close-grained wood has a fine natural pattern〔木头〕纹理细密的

close-knit /ˌklos ˋnɪt; ˌkləʊs ˈnɪt◂/ also 又作 **closely-knit** /ˌ·· ˈ·◂/ *adj* a close-knit group of people have strong friendly relationships with each other 紧密联结在一起的: *a close-knit community* 关系密切的社区

closely /ˋkloslɪ; ˈkləʊsli/ *adv* **1** if you look at or study something closely, you look at it etc hard, trying to notice everything about it 仔细地，严密地: **watch sb closely** *The detective was watching him closely, waiting for a reply.* 侦探紧紧地盯着他，等待答复。**2** if two things are closely connected or related, there is a strong connection between them or they are very much like each other 密切地，紧密地: *These two subjects were closely linked, and it makes sense to consider them together.* 这两个问题密切相关，放在一起考虑是明智的。| **closely resembles** *Their dialect closely resembles that of the northern provinces.* 他们的方言非常接近北部各省的口音。**3** in a way that makes things close together 紧跟地，拥挤地: *a flash of lightning, closely followed by thunder* 一道闪电，紧接着便是雷声 | *We were so closely packed in the elevator, I could hardly move.* 电梯里如此拥挤，我几乎动弹不了。 2 2

close-mouthed /ˌklos ˋmaʊðd; ˌkləʊs ˈmaʊðd◂/ *adj* not willing to say much because you are trying to keep a secret 口紧的

close-out /ˋklozˌaʊt; ˈkləʊzaʊt/ *adj* **closeout sale/price** *AmE* a sale or price that is to get rid of goods cheaply【美】清仓大甩卖／清仓甩卖价: *There's a closeout sale on swimwear at Penney's this week.* 本周彭尼店在清仓甩卖泳衣。—**closeout** *n* [C]

close sea·son /ˋklos ˌsizn̩; ˈkləʊs ˌsiːzən/ *n* [C] *BrE*【英】**1** the period each year when particular animals, birds, or fish cannot legally be killed for sport 禁渔期，禁猎期; CLOSED SEASON *AmE*【美】—opposite 反义词 OPEN SEASON **2** the period during the summer when football teams do not play important games〔夏季足球队不举行重大比赛时的〕足球休赛季节

close-set /ˌklos ˋsɛt; ˌkləʊs ˈset◂/ *adj* close-set eyes are near to each other〔眼睛〕紧靠在一起的: *Lessing's angry, close-set eyes followed him.* 莱辛愤怒得皱起双眉紧紧地盯着他。

clos·et¹ /ˋklɑzɪt; ˈklɒzɪt/ *n* [C] **1 come out of the closet a)** to tell people that you are HOMOSEXUAL after hiding the fact 公开自己的同性恋身份 **b)** to admit you believe something or to discuss something that was previously kept secret 公开承认相信 3

〔某事〕；公开以前保密的事 **2** *especially AmE* a cupboard built into the wall of a room from the floor to the ceiling【尤美】壁橱: *Jean had a closet full of clothes that most teenages would kill for.* 琼有满满一柜子大部分青少年梦寐以求的衣服。—compare 比较 WARDROBE **3** *old use* a small room where people went to study, pray etc alone【旧】密室；祈祷室 —see also 另见 WATER CLOSET, **a skeleton in the closet** (SKELETON (4))

closet² *adj* **closet homosexual/alcoholic etc** someone who is a HOMOSEXUAL, ALCOHOLIC etc but who does not want to admit it 不愿公开承认的同性恋/酗酒者等: *Not all teachers are closet radicals.* 不是所有的老师都不愿意承认自己是激进分子的。

closet³ *v* [T, usually passive 一般用被动态] to shut someone in a room away from other people in order to be alone or to discuss something private 把…关在小房间里；把…引进密室会谈: **closet yourself away** *Bill closeted himself away in his study for hours on end.* 比尔把自己关在书房里一连好几个小时。

close-up /ˈklos ˌʌp; ˈkləʊs ʌp/ *n* [C] a photograph taken from very near 特写照片，近景照: *a close-up of the kitten's face* 小猫的脸部特写 | **in close up** (=from very near) 近镜头特写 *Much of the movie is shot in close-up.* 这部电影不少镜头都是特写。

clos·ing¹ /ˈklozɪŋ; ˈkləʊzɪŋ/ *adj* [only before noun 仅用于名词前] happening or done at the end of a period of time or event 结尾的，结束的: **closing remarks/words/speech/ceremony** *Yeltsin's closing speech was a call for a referendum on land ownership.* 叶利钦在闭幕词中号召就土地所有权问题举行全民投票。| **closing stages/seconds/minutes etc** *The UN was set up during the closing stages of the Second World War.* 联合国是在第二次世界大战将要结束时成立的。

closing² *n* [U] another word for CLOSURE closure 的另一种说法

closing date /ˈ‥ ˌ/ *n* [C] the last date on which it is possible to make a request to do something 限期，截止日期: *Closing date for applications is 6th August.* 申请的截止日期为8月6日。

closing time /ˈ‥ ˌ/ *n* [C,U] the time when a PUB in Britain must stop serving drinks and close〔英国酒吧的〕打烊时间，停止营业时间: *Finish your drinks please – it's well past closing time!* 请快点喝完 —— 已经过了打烊时间很久了！

clo·sure /ˈkloʒɚ; ˈkləʊʒə/ *n* [C,U] **1** a process in which a factory, school, hospital etc permanently stops operating or providing services 关闭，倒闭，停业: *Today the government announced the closure of Bart's Hospital in London.* 今天政府宣布关闭伦敦的巴特医院。**2 closure of a road/bridge etc** a process in which a road, bridge etc is blocked for a short time so that people cannot use it 道路/桥等的封闭

clot¹ /klɑt; klɒt/ **clotted, clotting** *v* [I,T] if blood or milk clots or if something clots it, it becomes thicker and more solid as it dries (使)〔血液或牛奶等〕凝结成块 —see also 另见 CLOTTED CREAM

clot² *n* [C] **1** a thick almost solid mass formed when blood or milk dries〔血液或牛奶等的〕凝块 **2** *BrE informal* a stupid person【英，非正式】笨蛋，呆子: *What did you put the matches in the fridge for, you clot?* 笨蛋，你把火柴放入冰箱里面干吗？

cloth /klɔθ; klɒθ/ *n* **1** [U] material used especially for making clothes 布料: *cotton cloth* 棉布 **2** [C] a piece of cloth used to cover a table; TABLECLOTH 桌布 **3** [C] a piece of cloth used for a particular purpose〔用作某一用途的〕一块布: *She rubbed at the stain with a damp cloth.* 她用湿布擦去了污迹。| **dishcloth/floorcloth etc** *Tim grabbed a dishcloth and mopped up.* 蒂姆抓起抹布，擦了起来。—see picture on page A10 参见A10页图 **4 the cloth** *literary* used to mean priests in the Christian church considered as a group【文】牧师，教士 **5 make sth up out of whole cloth** *AmE informal* if a story, explanation, etc is made up out of whole cloth, it is not true【美，非正式】虚构[编造]某事: *I could tell his excuse was made up out of whole cloth.* 我知道他的借口是编出来的。

cloth cap /ˌ· ˈ·/ *n* [C] *BrE* a soft flat cap with a stiff pointed piece at the front【英】布帽，工作帽

clothe /kloð; kləʊð/ *v* [T usually passive 一般用被动态] *literary*【文】**1** to put clothes on your body 给…穿衣: *Helen was clothed in a simple dress of brown wool.* 海伦穿了一件朴素的棕色毛衫。| **fully/partly/brightly clothed etc** (=dressed in a particular way) 穿得整齐/不整齐/鲜艳的等 *The children lay on the bed, fully clothed and fast asleep.* 孩子们躺在床上，衣服也没脱就熟睡了。**2** to provide clothes for yourself or other people 为…提供衣服: *Volunteers ensure that the children are adequately clothed.* 志愿者保证孩子们有足够的衣服穿。**3 be clothed in** *literary* to be completely covered by something【文】覆盖；笼罩: *an angel clothed in flames* 火焰围绕的天使

clothes 衣服

clothes /kloz; kləʊðz/ *n* [plural] the things that people wear to cover their body or keep warm 衣服，衣物: *I need some new clothes.* 我需要几件新衣服。| **work/school clothes** (=clothes suitable for work or school) 工作服/校服 S2 W2

USAGE NOTE 用法说明: CLOTHES

WORD CHOICE 词语辨析: **clothes, clothing, piece/item of clothing, garment, something to wear, cloth, material, fabric, dress**

Clothes is the usual word for things we wear. clothes 是我们所穿衣服的常用词: *She's got some beautiful clothes* (NOT 不用 *cloths*). 她有几件漂亮衣服。**Clothing** [U] is a more formal word for **clothes** in general. 一般来说，clothing〔不可数〕比 clothes 更正式: *The workers here all have to wear protective clothing* (NOT 不用 *clothings*). 这儿的工人都必须穿防护服。| *a clothes/clothing shop* 服装店。When you are talking about clothes for a particular event, you often say **something to wear**. 如果是特定场合穿的服装，则是 something to wear: *It's Gloria's wedding tomorrow and I haven't got anything to wear* (=I have no suitable clothes). 明天是格洛丽亚的婚礼，我还没有合适的衣服穿。

Clothes is not used with numbers, and in conversation if you want to talk about one **piece/item of clothing** you would usually call it by its name. clothes 不能用数字来形容，如果说 piece/item of clothing 通常要具体说出是什么服装: *I want to buy a new coat* (NOT 不用 *a new cloth/clothing*). 我想买一件新外衣。**Garment** [C] is a rather formal word for a single **piece of clothing**. garment〔可数〕是正式用语，指一件衣服。On a shop notice 商店里有如此告示: *Only three garments may be taken into the fitting room* (NOT 不用 *three clothes*). 只能带三件衣服去试衣间。

Clothes are made from various kinds of **material, fabric** or **cloth** [U], such as woven wool, silk, cotton or acrylic. clothes 是由各种不同的材料 (material)、织物 (fabric) 或布料 (cloth) 制成: *I brought back a lovely piece of cloth from Thailand to make a dress out of.* 我从泰国带了一块很好看的布料回来，准备做一条连衣裙。A **cloth** ([C] with plural **cloths**) is a piece of cloth, used for cleaning surfaces, dishes etc. a cloth (复数 cloths) 指用来擦物体表面、碟子等的布: *Oh dear, I've spilt my beer – have you got a cloth?* 天哪，啤酒溅出来了，你有抹布吗？

A **dress** [C] is a kind of clothing worn by women. dress〔可数〕是指女性所穿的连衣裙: *What a pretty dress she's*

wearing! 她穿的连衣裙多漂亮啊! In certain expressions **dress** [U] is used to mean a particular type of **clothes**. 在某些用语中 dress〔不可数〕是指特种类型的 clothes。*The men were expected to wear casual dress/formal evening dress/national dress/fancy dress for the dinner.* 参加宴会的男士应该穿便装/正式的晚礼服/民族服装/奇装异服。

clothes bas·ket /ˈ· ,··/ *n* [C] *especially BrE* a large basket for clothes that need to be washed, dried, or ironed (IRON[2])【尤英】放〔待洗、待干或待烫〕衣物的篮子

clothes brush /ˈ· ·/ *n* [C] a brush used to remove dirt, dust etc from clothes 衣刷

clothes hang·er /ˈ· ,··/ *n* [C] a HANGER 衣架

clothes·horse /ˈkloz,hɔrs; ˈkləʊðzhɔːs/ *n* [C] **1** *BrE* a frame on which you hang clothes to dry indoors【英】〔室内的〕晾衣架 **2** *AmE informal* someone who thinks too much about clothes and who likes to have many different clothes【美, 非正式】讲究穿着的人

clothes·line /ˈkloz,laɪn; ˈkləʊðzlaɪn/ *n* [C] a rope on which you hang clothes to dry outdoors〔户外的〕晾衣绳; WASHING LINE *BrE*【英】

clothes peg /ˈ· ,·/ *BrE*【英】, **clothespin** /ˈkloz,pɪn; ˈkləʊðz,pɪn/ *AmE*【美】*n* [C] a wooden or plastic object that you use to fasten wet clothes to a clothesline 衣夹 —see picture at 参见 PIN[1] 图

cloth·i·er /ˈkloðɪɚ; ˈkləʊðiə/ *n* [C] *old-fashioned* someone who makes or sells men's clothes or material for clothes【过时】男装裁缝, 男士服装商, 布贩子

cloth·ing /ˈkloðɪŋ; ˈkləʊðɪŋ/ *n* [U] clothes considered as a group, especially the clothes someone is wearing, or a particular type of clothes 衣服, 衣着: *Remember to bring a change of clothing.* 记着带一身换洗衣服。| **clothing manufacturer/industry** *Clothing manufacturers have reported a drop in profits.* 制衣商说利润下降了。| **item/article of clothing** *Bring several warm items of clothing.* 带几件暖和的衣服来。| **waterproof/protective clothing** *Lab workers should wear protective clothing.* 实验室工作人员应穿防护服。

clotted cream /,·· ˈ·/ *n* [U] thick cream made by slowly heating milk and taking the cream from the top 浓缩奶油

clo·ture /ˈklotʃɚ; ˈkləʊtʃə/ *n* [C] *AmE technical* a way of ending an argument over a BILL[1] (2) in the US government and forcing a vote on it【美, 术语】终止辩论提付表决

cloud[1] /klaud; klaʊd/ *n* **1** [C,U] a white or grey mass in the sky that consists of very small drops of water 云: *Dark clouds gathered overhead.* 头顶乌云密布。**2 a cloud of dust/smoke/gas etc** a mass of dust etc in the air 一团尘土/烟雾/气体等 **3** [C] something that makes you feel afraid or worried 阴影, 乌云: [+of] *The clouds of war began to threaten our peaceful life.* 战争的阴云开始威胁到我们平静的生活。| **a cloud on the horizon** (=something that threatens to spoil a happy situation) 麻烦的迹象, 不快 *The only cloud on the horizon was her mother's illness.* 唯一令人担忧的是她母亲病了。| **cast a cloud** (=spoil a happy situation) 破坏高兴的氛围 *The news that several competitors had been taking drugs cast a cloud over the event.* 有几名选手服用药物的消息影响了比赛的气氛。**4 on cloud nine** *informal* very happy about something【非正式】兴奋, 高兴: *Adam was on cloud nine after the birth of his son.* 亚当在儿子出生后欣喜若狂。**5 under a cloud** *informal* if someone is under a cloud, people have a bad opinion of them because they have done something wrong【非正式】遭嫌弃, 受怀疑: *He left the company under a cloud.* 他因不被信任而离开了公司。**6 be/live in cloud-cuckoo-land** to think that a situation is much better than it actually is in a way that makes you seem stupid 生活在理想境界: *If Ben thinks he's getting a pay rise, he's living in cloud-cuckoo-land.* 假如本认为自己会获加薪的话, 那他是想入非非。**7 every cloud has a silver lining** used to say that there is something good even in a situation that seems very sad or difficult 黑暗中总有一线光明 —see also 另见 **have your head in the clouds** (HEAD[1] (11))

cloud[2] *v*

1 ►GLASS 玻璃◄ also 又作 **cloud over/up** [I,T] if a transparent material such as glass clouds or something clouds it, you cannot see through it properly any more (使)变模糊, 使不清晰: *Steam had clouded the windows up.* 水蒸气使窗玻璃变得模糊不清。

2 ►LIQUID 液体◄ also 又作 **cloud up** [I,T] if a liquid clouds or if something clouds it, it becomes less clear (使)变浑浊: *Don't shake the barrel, you'll cloud the beer.* 不要摇晃酒桶, 你会把啤酒摇浑的。

3 ►THOUGHTS/MEMORIES 想法/记忆◄ [T] to make someone less able to think clearly or remember things 搞糊涂: **cloud sb's judgement/memory** *Don't let your personal feelings towards this woman cloud your judgement.* 不要让你对这位妇人的个人感情影响了你的判断力。

4 cloud the issue to make a subject or problem difficult to understand by introducing ideas or information that are not connected with it〔用无关信息〕使问题复杂化: *Bringing in unnecessary details at this stage will only cloud the issue.* 在这个时候加插一些不必要的细节只会使问题复杂化。

5 ►FACE 面部◄ also 又作 **cloud over** [I,T] if someone's expression clouds or if something clouds it, they start to look angry or sad〔脸色〕阴沉, (使)忧郁: *His face clouded when he saw her.* 他看到她时, 脸就沉了下来。

6 ►SPOIL STH 破坏某事物◄ [T] to make something less pleasant than it should have been 冲淡, 毁坏: *Half a billion people vote in a general election clouded by violence and charges of pollrigging.* 在这次因暴力事件和被指控操纵选票而蒙上了阴影的大选中, 有5亿人投了票。

7 ►COVER WITH CLOUD 被云笼罩◄ [T] to cover something with clouds (云)笼罩: *Thick mist clouded the mountaintops.* 浓雾笼罩着山顶。

cloud over *phr v* [I] **1** if the sky clouds over, it becomes dark because it is full of black clouds〔天空〕阴云密布, 乌云翻滚: *The sky's really clouding over; I think we're in for a storm.* 天空布满了乌云, 我看我们将遇到一场暴风雨。**2** [I] if someone's expression clouds over, they start to look angry or sad〔脸色〕阴沉: *Anne's face clouded over as she remembered.* 安妮一想起来脸色就沉了下来。

cloud·bank /ˈklaud,bæŋk; ˈklaʊdbæŋk/ *n* [C] a thick mass of low cloud 低垂浓密的云团

cloud·burst /ˈklaud,bɝst; ˈklaʊdbɜːst/ *n* [C] a sudden storm 骤雨, 大暴雨

cloud·ed /ˈklaudɪd; ˈklaʊdɪ̈d/ *adj* **1** not clear or transparent 模糊不清的; 不透明的: *clouded glass* 不透明的玻璃 **2** a clouded face or expression shows that someone is unhappy or angry 愁容满面的; 面露愠色的

cloud·less /ˈklaudlɪs; ˈklaʊdləs/ *adj* a cloudless sky is clear and bright 晴朗的, 无云的: *sip exotic cocktails under a cloudless sky* 在晴朗的天空下啜饮外国鸡尾酒

cloud·y /ˈklaudɪ; ˈklaʊdi/ *adj* **1** cloudy weather is dark because the sky is full of clouds 多云的, 阴天的: *cloudy with outbreaks of rain* 阴天有阵雨 **2** cloudy liquids are not clear or transparent〔液体〕浑浊的, 不透明的 **3** cloudy thoughts, memories etc are not very clear or exact〔思想、想法、记忆等〕模糊的, 不清晰的

Clou·seau /ˈkluzo; ˈkluːzəʊ/, **In·spec·tor** a humorous character in the Pink Panther films. Clouseau is a French policeman who is always making stupid mistakes and causing accidents, though he does not realize it or intend to. 警官克卢索〔"粉红豹"系列影片中的滑稽角色。他是一名法国警察, 总是犯低级错误, 引发事端, 尽管他本人并没有意识到, 也并非故意〕

clout[1] /klaut; klaʊt/ *n* **1** [U] *informal* the power or authority to influence other people's decisions【非正式】〔影响他人决定的〕力量; 权势: *His job carries a lot of clout.* 他的工作举足轻重。**2** [C] *informal* a hard blow given with the hand【非正式】〔用手〕猛击: *I'll give you a clout round the ear!* 我要让你清醒清醒!

clout[2] *v* [T] *informal* to hit someone hard【非正式】猛击〔某人〕: *Dad clouted me before I had a chance to explain.* 我还没来得及解释, 爸爸就狠狠揍了我一下。

clove[1] /klov; kləʊv/ *n* [C] **1** a SPICE (=something used to give a special taste to food) that has a strong smell, is black, and looks like a pin 丁香; 丁香花苞; 丁香香料 **2 a clove of garlic** one of the parts of a GARLIC root (=a plant similar to an onion) 一瓣大蒜

clove[2] a past tense of CLEAVE

clo·ven /ˈklovən; ˈkləʊvən/ a past participle of CLEAVE

cloven hoof /,·· ˈ·/ *n* [C] a HOOF that is divided into two parts 偶蹄: *Sheep and goats have cloven hooves.* 绵羊和山羊都是偶蹄类动物。

clo·ver /ˈklovɚ; ˈkləʊvə/ *n* [U] **1** a small plant with three leaves on each stem 三叶草, 苜蓿 **2 in clover** *informal* living comfortably because you have plenty of money【非正式】生活舒适而富裕, 养尊处优

clo·ver·leaf /ˈklovɚ,lif; ˈkləʊvəliːf/ *n* [C] **1** the leaf of a clover plant 苜蓿叶, 三叶草的叶子 **2** a network of curved roads which connect two main roads where they cross 苜蓿叶形立体交叉路口

clown¹ /klaʊn; klaʊn/ *n* [C] **1** someone who entertains people in a CIRCUS (1) by dressing in funny clothes, and doing things to make people laugh〔马戏团的〕小丑 **2** someone who often makes jokes or behaves in a funny way 爱开玩笑的人，诙谐的人：*Frankie was a bit of a clown – always up to mischief and practical jokes.* 弗朗妮有点滑稽——总爱弄些恶作剧，开开玩笑。| **class clown** (=someone in a school class who behaves in a funny or silly way)〔在班上常闹笑话的〕课堂小丑 **3** a stupid or annoying person 蠢人；讨厌的人：*I can't understand what she sees in that clown.* 我不理解她在那个蠢货身上看到了什么优点。**4 make a clown of yourself** *informal* to do something stupid or embarrassing【非正式】出洋相

clown 小丑

clown² *v* also 又作 **clown around/about** [I] to behave in a silly or funny way 做蠢事；胡闹：*Stop clowning around, you lot, and get back to your seats!* 别胡闹了，你们这群家伙，都回到座位上去！

clown·ish /ˈklaʊnɪʃ; ˈklaʊnɪʃ/ *adj* silly or stupid 愚蠢的；滑稽的 —**clownishly** *adv* —**clownishness** *n* [U]

cloy /klɔɪ; klɔɪ/ *v* [I] if something sweet or pleasant cloys, it begins to annoy you because there is too much of it〔因过量而〕厌倦，发腻：*Her sweet submissive smile began to cloy after a while.* 不一会儿，她那过于甜蜜柔顺的笑容开始让人厌烦。

cloy·ing /ˈklɔɪ-ɪŋ; ˈklɔɪ-ɪŋ/ *adj* **1** a cloying attitude or quality annoys you because it is too pleasant 令人腻烦的：*cloying sentimentality* 令人生厌的多愁善感 **2** cloying food or smells are sweet and make you feel sick 甜得发腻的：*the cloying stench of cheap perfume* 廉价香水发出的刺鼻香味

cloze test /ˈkloz ˌtɛst; ˈkləʊz test/ *n* [C] a test in which students have to write the correct words into the spaces that have been left empty in a short piece of writing 填空测验

club¹ /klʌb; klʌb/ *n* [C]

1 ►FOR AN ACTIVITY/SPORT 活动/体育的◄ [also+plural verb *BrE* 英] an organization for people who share a particular interest or enjoy similar activities, such as sports or politics 俱乐部：*the Ramblers Club* 漫步者俱乐部 | **rugby/golf/squash club etc** (=a club for people who play a particular sport) 橄榄球/高尔夫球/壁球俱乐部等 | **join a club** *It costs £15 to join the club.* 参加这个俱乐部要交15英镑。| **belong to a club** *She belongs to the local tennis club.* 她是当地网球俱乐部会员。

2 ►PROFESSIONAL SPORT 职业体育运动◄ a professional organization including the players, managers, and owners of a sports team〔职业体育的〕俱乐部：*Tottenham Hotspur Football Club* 托特纳姆热刺足球俱乐部 | [also+plural verb *BrE* 英] *The club have added a new fast bowler to their line-up.* 该俱乐部新吸收了一名板球快投手。| **ball club** *AmE* (=a BASEBALL team)【美】棒球队

3 ►FOR MEN 男人的◄ an organization, usually for men only, where they can relax and enjoy social activities 社交俱乐部

4 ►BUILDING 建筑◄ the building or place where people who belong to an organization meet in order to do activities or play sports 俱乐部会所：*There's a party at the golf club.* 在那家高尔夫球俱乐部有个聚会。

5 book/record club etc an organization which people join in order to buy books, records etc cheaply 读书/唱片等俱乐部〔其会员可以低价购买书籍、唱片等〕

6 ►FOR DANCING/MUSIC 舞蹈/音乐的◄ a place where usually young people go to dance, listen to music, and meet socially 俱乐部；夜总会：*a jazz club* 爵士乐俱乐部 | *Shall we go to a club?* 我们去夜总会怎样？

7 ►FOR HITTING BALL 击球的◄ a special stick used in GOLF to hit the ball; GOLF CLUB (2)〔高尔夫球等的〕球杆，球棒

8 ►WEAPON 武器◄ a thick heavy stick used to hit people or things 大头棒，棍棒

9 ►IN CARD GAMES 纸牌游戏◄ a) a black shape with three leaves printed on cards for games 梅花 **b)** the SUIT (=group of cards) that has this shape printed on them 一手梅花牌：*the ace of clubs* 梅花A

10 in the club *BrE humorous* if a woman is in the club, she is going to have a baby; PREGNANT【英，幽默】怀孕的

11 join the club *BrE*【英】, **welcome to the club** *AmE*【美】used after someone has described a bad situation that they are in, to tell them that you are in the same situation 我们都一样（糟）—see also 另见 COUNTRY CLUB, **fan club** (FAN¹ (1)), YOUTH CLUB

club² *v* **clubbed, clubbing** [T] to hit someone hard with a thick heavy object〔用棍棒〕打：**club sb to death** (=kill someone by hitting them several times with a heavy object) 用棍棒打死某人

club together *phr v* [I] *BrE* to share the cost of something with other people【英】分担费用：*We clubbed together to buy her a present.* 我们凑钱给她买了一份礼物。

Club 18-30 /ˌklʌb ˌetin ˋθɝtɪ; ˈklʌb ˌeɪtiːn ˈθɜːti/ *trademark* a British company that sells low-cost holidays to young people aged between 18 and 30, mainly in places on the Mediterranean coast【商标】18-30俱乐部〔英国一家公司，面向18至30岁的青年提供价格较低的度假服务，主要地点在地中海沿岸〕

club·ba·ble /ˈklʌbəbl̩; ˈklʌbəbəl/ *adj BrE old-fashioned* interesting and good at talking in a friendly and relaxed way with other people【英，过时】合群的；好交际的

club·bing /ˈklʌbɪŋ; ˈklʌbɪŋ/ *n* **go clubbing** *BrE informal* to go regularly to NIGHTCLUBS【英，非正式】定期去夜总会

CULTURAL NOTE 文化注释

Clubbing is a very popular activity in the UK and large cities have many clubs, most of which play dance music. Most clubs have DJs who MIX different records (= play one record after another without a period of time between them, or play two or more records at the same time). Some DJs are more famous than the people who make the records, and the expression 'superstar DJ' is sometimes used to refer to the most popular DJs. 定期去夜总会在英国是一项很流行的活动，大城市有很多夜总会，大多播放舞曲，有混音师。有些混音师比唱片制作人还要有名，最受追捧的混音师有时称为"混音巨星"。

Drugs, especially ECSTASY, are often associated with clubbing, and clubs are known as places where some people take drugs. 夜总会常和毒品尤其是摇头丸联系在一起，成为一些人吸毒的场所。

Some young people also go on holiday to places such as Ibiza in order to go clubbing. 一些年轻人还会去伊维萨岛等地度假，以便光顾那里的夜总会。

club class /ˈ· ·/ *n* [U] the area in a plane where the seats are more expensive than in the normal area, but are not as expensive as FIRST CLASS〔价格介于普通舱和头等舱之间的〕飞机二等舱，商务舱

club foot /ˌ· ˈ·/ *n* **1** [C] a foot that has been badly twisted since birth and that prevents someone from walking properly〔先天性〕畸形足 **2** [U] the medical condition of having a club foot 足畸形 —**club-footed** *adj*

club·house /ˈklʌbˌhaʊs; ˈklʌbhaʊs/ *n* [C] a building used by a club, especially a sports club〔尤指体育〕俱乐部会所（大楼）

Club Med /ˌklʌb ˈmɛd; ˌklʌb ˈmed/ *trademark* a company that sells holidays in many parts of the world, aimed especially at younger people. Its full name is 'Club Méditerranée'. Club Med holidays are based in specially-built villages.【商标】地中海度假村〔一家在世界各地提供度假服务的公司，主要针对年轻人，全称是Club Méditerranée。度假活动安排在专门修建的度假村〕

club sand·wich /ˌ· ˈ· ·/ *n* [C] a large SANDWICH¹ (1) consisting of three pieces of bread with two different kinds of cold food between them 公司三明治，总汇三明治〔通常为三片烤面包，中间夹两层不同的冷食〕

club so·da /ˌ· ˈ· ·/ *n* [C,U] *AmE* a drink consisting of water filled with gas BUBBLES (1)【美】苏打水；SODA WATER *BrE*【英】

cluck¹ /klʌk; klʌk/ *v* **1** [I] if a chicken clucks, it makes a short, low sound〔鸡〕咯咯叫 **2** [I,T] to express sympathy or disapproval by saying something, or by making a short low noise with your tongue〔人用舌〕发啧啧声〔以示同情或反对〕：[**+over/around/about**] *The women stood together clucking over her scandalously short skirt.* 那些女人站成一堆，叽叽呱呱议论着她那有伤风化的短裙。—**clucking** *adj*

cluck² *n* [C usually singular 一般用单数] **1** a low short noise made by hens〔母鸡的〕咯咯声 **2** a sound made with your tongue, used to show disapproval or sympathy〔人用舌发出的〕啧啧声〔常表反对或同情〕：*a disapproving cluck* 表示反对的啧啧声 **3** *especially AmE* a stupid person【尤美】蠢蛋，傻瓜：*You dumb cluck, why'd you tell him?* 你这个笨蛋，你为什么要告诉他？

Clue /klu; kluː/ *trademark* the US name for the game Cluedo【商标】"线索"游戏〔Cluedo 的美国叫法〕

2 **clue¹** *n* [C] **1** an object or piece of information that helps someone solve a crime or mystery 线索, 提示: *He didn't know who had sent the letter, and the envelope provided no clue.* 他不知道谁寄的这封信, 信封上也没有任何线索。| **[+to/about]** *We now have a clue to the time at which the murder took place.* 我们现在对谋杀发生的时间有了一点线索。| **search for clues** *Our search for clues proved fruitless.* 我们没有找到任何线索。**2** a question that you must solve in order to find the answer to a CROSSWORD or PUZZLE² (2)〔纵横填字谜的〕提示语 | **give sb a clue** *I'll give you a clue, Kevin, it's a kind of bird.* 我给你个提示吧, 凯文, 那是一种鸟。**3 not have a clue** *informal*【非正式】**a)** to know nothing at all about the answer to a question or about how to do something 一无所知: *"Do you know how to switch this thing off?" "I'm afraid I haven't got a clue."* "你知道怎么关上这个吗?" "恐怕我对此一无所知。" | **not have a clue where/why etc** *We haven't got a clue where they could have disappeared to.* 他们躲到哪里去了, 我们毫无头绪。**b)** to be very stupid, or very bad at a particular activity 很愚蠢; 很笨拙: *Myra just hits her kids when they start crying; she hasn't got a clue.* 孩子们一哭, 迈拉就打他们。她真蠢。| **[+about]** *No point asking Jill, she hasn't got a clue about maths.* 问吉尔没有用, 她对数学一窍不通。| **not have a clue how/why etc** *Evans hasn't got a clue how to get on with people.* 埃文斯根本不懂如何与人相处。**4** a reason why something happens that you find by studying events, someone's behaviour etc 缘由, 根源: *Childhood experiences may provide a clue as to why some adults develop phobias.* 童年经历可能是一些成年人患恐惧症的原因。

clue² *v*

clue sb ↔ in *phr v* [T] *informal* to give someone information about something【非正式】给〔某人〕提供线索; 告知: *Mark clued me in on how the computer system works.* 马克告诉我电脑系统是如何运行的。

Clue·do /ˈkludo; ˈkluːdəʊ/ *BrE*【英】, **Clue** *AmE*【美】*trademark* a type of board game in which each player becomes a different character, such as Colonel Mustard or Miss Scarlet, in a murder story and tries to discover which character is the murderer, what the murder weapon was, and in which room in the house the murder took place【商标】"线索"游戏〔一种棋盘游戏。每个参与者都在凶杀故事中扮演角色, 如马斯塔德上校、斯卡利特小姐等, 玩法是试图查出凶手、凶器以及发生命案的房间〕

clued-up /ˌ· ˈ·/ *BrE*【英】, **clued-in** *AmE*【美】*adj informal* knowing a lot about something【非正式】所知甚多的: *Ask Margaret, she's pretty clued-up about that sort of thing.* 去问玛格丽特, 她对那种事情知道得很清楚。

clue·less /ˈklulɪs; ˈkluːləs/ *adj informal* having no understanding or knowledge of something【非正式】无线索的, 一无所知的: *He was completely clueless about the rules of the game.* 他对这项游戏的规则一无所知。

clump¹ /klʌmp; klʌmp/ *n* **1** [C] a group of trees, bushes, or other plants growing very close together〔树、灌木或其他植物的〕丛; 簇, 群: **[+of]** *a clump of grass* 草丛 **2** [C] a piece of earth or mud 土块 **3** [singular] the sound of someone walking with heavy steps 沉重的脚步声: *I heard the clump of Ralph's boots going up the stairs.* 我听见拉尔夫上楼时皮靴发出的沉重脚步声。

clump² *v* **1** [I always+adv/prep] to walk with slow noisy steps 以沉重的步子行走: **[+up/down/along etc]** *Grandpa clumped along in his workboots.* 爷爷穿着工作靴, 迈着沉重的步子。**2** [I always+adv/prep, T always+adv/prep] to put something heavy down with a loud noise 把某物重重放下: *She clumped the books down on the desk.* 她把那些书重重地放在书桌上。

clump together *phr v* [I,T] if separate objects clump together, or are clumped together they form a group or solid mass (使) 密集成丛; (使) 凝集成块: *Rinse the rice to prevent the grains clumping together.* 把米淘一下, 以免米粒粘在一起。

clum·sy /ˈklʌmzɪ; ˈklʌmzi/ *adj* **1** moving in an awkward way and tending to break things 笨拙的, 不灵活的: *At 17, she was clumsy, shy and awkward.* 17 岁时, 她做事笨手笨脚, 害羞而局促。| *a clumsy attempt to catch the ball* 试图接球的笨拙动作 | *"Look, you've just knocked that cup over." "Sorry, how clumsy of me."* "看, 你把茶杯碰倒了。" "对不起, 我真是笨手笨脚的。" **2** a clumsy object is not easy to use and is often large and heavy 庞大粗重的 **3** said or done carelessly or in a way that is not delicate and sensitive 粗糙的; 不得体的; 不细心的: *David made a clumsy but well-meaning attempt to comfort us.* 戴维好意想安慰我们, 尽管有些笨拙。| **clumsy excuse/apology** *Becky stammered a clumsy apology.* 贝姬支支吾吾地道了个歉。**—clumsily** *adv* **—clumsiness** *n* [U]

clung /klʌŋ; klʌŋ/ the past tense and past participle of CLING

clunk /klʌŋk; klʌŋk/ *n* [singular] a loud sound made when two solid objects hit each other〔物体相撞发出的〕哐啷的一声 **—clunk** *v* [I,T]

clunk·er /ˈklʌŋkɚ; ˈklʌŋkə/ *n* [C] *AmE informal* an old car or other machine that does not work well【美, 非正式】破旧的汽车[机器]

clunk·y /ˈklʌŋkɪ; ˈklʌŋki/ *adj* clunky shoes are heavy with thick SOLEs (=bottoms)〔鞋〕厚底的

clus·ter¹ /ˈklʌstɚ; ˈklʌstə/ *n* [C] **1** a group of things of the same kind that are very close together 串, 束, 簇; 群, 组: **[+of]** *a cluster of low farm buildings* 一片低矮的农舍 **2** a group of people all in the same place〔聚集在同一地方的〕一群人 **3** *AmE* a small piece of metal pinned to a soldier's uniform to show a high class of honour【美】〔别在军服上代表较高荣誉的〕小金属奖章

cluster² *v* [I always+adv/prep, T always+adv/prep] if a group of people or things cluster somewhere or are clustered somewhere, they form a small group in that place (使) 丛生; 群集: **[+around/together etc]** *A group of children had clustered around the toy shop window.* 一群孩子围在玩具店的橱窗前。

cluster bomb /ˈ·· ,·/ *n* [C] a bomb that sends out smaller bombs when it explodes 榴霰弹, 子母弹, 集束炸弹 **—cluster-bomb** *v* [T]

clutch¹ /klʌtʃ; klʌtʃ/ *v* [I] to hold something or someone tightly, especially because you are frightened, in pain, or do not want to lose something 紧握, 紧抓: *Tom fell to the ground clutching his stomach.* 汤姆跌倒在地, 紧紧捂着肚子。| *A woman clutching a baby stole an elderly woman's purse.* 一个怀抱婴儿的妇女偷了一位老妇的钱包。

clutch at *phr v* **1** [T] to try hard to hold something, especially when you are in a dangerous situation〔尤指危险时〕努力抓住〔某物〕: *Suzie clutched desperately at the muddy river bank.* 苏茜拼命地想抓牢泥泞的河堤。**2 clutch at straws** to try hard to find a sign of hope or a solution, even when these are not likely to exist, in a difficult or dangerous situation〔在困境或险境中〕极力抓住渺茫的生存希望; 急不暇择: *The doctors are really clutching at straws with this new treatment, but they've tried everything else.* 医生们尝试这种新疗法其实是把死马当活马医, 他们已试过其他所有治疗方法了。

clutch² *n* **1** [C] the PEDAL¹ (2) that you press with your foot when driving a vehicle in order to change GEAR¹ (1) | **let in the clutch/let out the clutch** (=put your foot on or take your foot off the clutch) 接合/分离离合器 **2 clutches** *plural* the power, influence, or control that someone has 掌握, 控制, 统治: **in sb's clutches** (=controlled or influenced by someone) 在某人控制之下 *Many state organizations fell into the clutches of the Mafia.* 许多国家机构都落入黑手党的控制之中。**3** [singular] a tight hold that someone has on something 紧握, 紧抓: *I shook myself free of her clutch.* 我从她的紧抱中挣脱出来。**4 a clutch of** a small group of similar things 一小群; 一小簇: **a clutch of eggs/chickens** (=a group of eggs which a hen produces at one time, or the chickens born from these eggs) 一窝蛋/鸡 **5 when it comes to the clutch** *AmE informal* when a difficult situation happens【美, 非正式】有困难的时候: *When it comes to the clutch, you can always count on Tom.* 有困难时, 你都可以找汤姆。

clutch bag /ˈ· ·/ *n* [C] a small bag that women carry in their hand, used especially on formal social occasions 女用无带皮包〔尤用于正式社交场合〕

clut·ter¹ /ˈklʌtɚ; ˈklʌtə/ also 又作 **clutter up** *v* [T] **1** to cover or fill a space or room with too many things, so that it looks very untidy 乱堆, 塞满: *Piles of books and papers cluttered his desk.* 他的书桌堆满了书本和文件。| **be cluttered (up) with** *The front room was cluttered up with ornaments and antique furniture.* 前面的房间堆满了装饰品和古董家具。**2** to fill your mind with unnecessary information 使〔心里〕充满〔不必要的信息〕: *Don't clutter up your mind with useless detail.* 别尽想些无关紧要的细节。**—cluttered** *adj*

clutter² *n* [singular,U] a large number of things that are scattered somewhere in an untidy way 杂乱的东西: *Could you get rid of some of that clutter in your bedroom?* 你能把你卧室那些杂物清理掉一些吗?

Clw·yd /ˈkluɪd; ˈkluːɪd/ a COUNTY in North Wales 克卢伊德郡〔威尔士北部一郡〕

Clyde, the /klaɪd; klaɪd/ a large river which goes through Glasgow 克莱德河〔流经格拉斯哥的一条大河〕

Clyde·side /ˈklaɪdsaɪd; ˈklaɪdsaɪd/ the towns between Glasgow and Greenock on the River Clyde in Scotland, where many famous shipbuilding companies were established in the past 克莱德塞德〔位于苏格兰格拉斯哥和克里诺克附近, 濒临克莱德河, 曾建有许多著名的造船厂〕

Cly·tem·nes·tra /ˌklaɪtəmˋnɛstrə; ˌklaɪtəmˈnestrə/ in ancient Greek stories, the wife of Agamemnon. She murders her husband, and as a result she is killed by her son, Orestes. 克吕泰涅斯特拉〔古希腊神话中阿伽门农之妻。她谋害了丈夫, 最终死于其子俄瑞斯忒斯之手〕

cm the written abbreviation of 缩写= CENTIMETRE

CND /ˌsi ɛn ˋdi; ˌsiː en ˈdiː/ *n* [singular] Campaign for Nuclear Disarmament; a British organization whose aim is to persuade the British government to get rid of its NUCLEAR weapons and close its nuclear military bases 核裁军运动〔英国一组织。其宗旨是说服英国政府销毁核武器, 关闭核军事基地〕

CNN /ˌsi ɛn ˋɛn; ˌsiː en ˈen/ *n* [U] *trademark* Cable News Network; an American organization that broadcasts television news programmes to countries all over the world【商标】〔美国〕有线新闻网

C-note /ˋsi ˌnot; ˈsiː nəʊt/ *n* [C] *AmE slang* a 100 dollar note【美俚】一百美元面值的钞票

CO the abbreviation of 缩写= COLORADO

C.O. /ˌsi ˋo; ˌsiː ˈəʊ◂/ *n* [C] Commanding Officer; an officer who commands a military unit 指挥官

Co. /ko; kəʊ/ **1** the abbreviation of 缩写= COMPANY: *James Smith & Co.* 詹姆斯·史密斯公司 **2 and co** *spoken* used after mentioning a person or thing to mean the other people or things that you consider to belong to their group【口】及其一伙; 以及类似的种种: *I can't say I'm looking forward to seeing Angela and co again.* 我可不想再看见安杰拉那一伙人了。**3** the written abbreviation of 缩写= COUNTY 郡; 县: *Co. Durham* 达勒姆郡

c/o the written abbreviation of 缩写= care of; used especially in addresses when you are sending a letter or parcel to someone who is living in someone else's house etc〔书信用语〕由…转交: *John Hammond, c/o Dowling Music College, Bethesda, Maryland* 烦由马里兰州贝塞斯达道林音乐学院转交约翰·哈蒙德

co /ko; kəʊ/ *prefix* **1** together with 和…一起, 共同: *to coexist* (=exist together or at the same time) 共存 | *coeducation* (=of boys and girls together) 男女合校教育 **2** doing something with someone else as an equal or with less responsibility 和…一起做; 辅助…做, 副: *my co-author* (=someone who wrote the book with me) 我的合著者 | *the co-pilot* (=someone who helps a pilot) 飞机副驾驶员

coach¹ /kotʃ; kəʊtʃ/ *n* [C]

1 ▶IN A SPORT 体育运动中◀ [C] someone who trains a person or team in a sport〔体育〕教练: *a tennis coach* 网球教练 —see 见 TEACH (USAGE)

2 ▶IN A SCHOOL SUBJECT 课程中◀ [C] *especially BrE* someone who gives special instruction to a student in a particular subject, especially so that they can pass an examination【尤英】私人教师, 家庭教师

3 ▶BUS 巴士◀ [C] *BrE* a bus with comfortable seats used for long journeys【英】〔内有舒适座椅的〕长途公共汽车; BUS¹ *AmE*【美】: *We went to Paris by coach.* 我们坐长途公共汽车去巴黎。

4 ▶IN A TRAIN 乘火车◀ [C] *BrE* one of the parts of the train in which the passengers sit【英】旅客车厢; CAR (3) *AmE*【美】

5 ▶PULLED BY HORSES 由马拖拉的◀ [C] a large carriage pulled by horses 公共马车, 四轮大马车

6 ▶A CLASS OF TRAVEL 旅行座位等级◀ [U] *AmE* the cheapest type of seats on a plane or train【美】普通旅客车厢;〔飞机的〕二等舱: *We flew coach out to Atlanta.* 我们坐二等舱飞往亚特兰大。

coach² *v* [I,T] **1** to teach a person or team the skills they need for a sport 当教练, 训练, 培训, 指导: *Nigel coaches a cricket team in his spare time.* 奈杰尔业余时间担任一个板球队的教练。**2** *especially BrE* to give someone special instruction in a particular subject, especially so that they can pass an examination【尤英】为…补习, 辅导: **coach sb in/for** *Chorley had to be coached in most subjects for the first two terms.* 头两个学期, 乔利的大多数科目都得请人补习。**3** to give someone instruction in what they should say or do in a particular situation〔演讲、表演等方面〕予以指导: **coach sb in sth** *The Callaghan girl must be carefully coached in the story she will tell in court.* 必须好好指导一下那个来自卡拉汉的女孩如何在法庭陈述该事件。

coach·buil·der /ˋkotʃˌbɪldɚ; ˈkəʊtʃˌbɪldə/ *n* [C] *BrE* a worker who builds the main outer structure of a car【英】汽车车身制造工

coach·ing /ˋkotʃɪŋ; ˈkəʊtʃɪŋ/ *n* [U] **1** a process in which you teach a person or team the skills they need for a sport 教授, 训练: **tennis/football/rugby coaching etc** *tennis coaching sessions* 网球训练课 **2** a process in which you give a student special instruction in a particular subject〔对学生的〕辅导(工作)

coach·load /ˋkotʃˌlod; ˈkəʊtʃləʊd/ *n* [C] all the people travelling in a COACH¹ (3), especially when it is full〔尤指满座的〕长途公共汽车的全体乘客: *coachloads of football supporters* 一车一车的足球迷

coach·man /ˋkotʃmən; ˈkəʊtʃmən/ *n* [C] someone who drove a COACH¹ (5) pulled by horses in the past〔旧时的〕马车御者, 马车夫

coach sta·tion /ˋ· ˌ··/ *n* [C] *BrE* the place where people begin or end their journeys on buses that travel a long distance【英】长途公共汽车(总)站

coach·work /ˋkotʃˌwɝk; ˈkəʊtʃwɜːk/ *n* [U] *BrE* the main outer structure of a car【英】〔汽车的〕车身

co·ag·u·late /koˋægjəˌlet; kəʊˈægjʊleɪt/ *v* [I,T] if a liquid coagulates or something coagulates it, it becomes thick and almost solid (使)凝结, (使)凝固: *The heat will coagulate the egg mixture.* 热量会使蛋液凝固。—**coagulation** /koˌægjəˋleʃən; kəʊˌægjʊˈleɪʃən/ *n* [U]

coal /kol; kəʊl/ *n* **1** [U] a black mineral which is dug from the earth and burnt to produce heat 煤: *Bring in some coal for the fire.* 往火里加点煤。| *the coal industry* 煤炭工业 **2** [C usually plural 一般用复数] a piece of coal, especially one that is burning〔尤指燃烧着的〕煤块 **3 carry/take coals to Newcastle** *BrE informal* to take something to a place where there is already plenty of it available【英, 非正式】多此一举, 徒劳无功 **4 haul/rake/drag sb over the coals** to speak angrily to someone because they have done something wrong 责备某人, 申斥某人

coal bunk·er /ˋ· ˌ··/ *n* [C] a small building or large container where coal is stored 储煤仓[库, 室]

co·a·lesce /ˌkoəˋlɛs; ˌkəʊəˈles/ *v* [I] *formal* if objects or ideas coalesce, they combine to form one single group【正式】联合, 合并: *These three themes coalesce at the end of the book.* 在本书结尾时, 这三个主题融而为一。—**coalescence** *n* [U]

coal·face /ˋkolˌfes; ˈkəʊlfeɪs/ *n* **1** [C] the part of a coal mine where the coal is cut from the earth〔采煤矿井中的〕采煤工作面 **2 at the coalface** *BrE* actually doing a particular kind of work rather than planning or managing it【英】在实际工作岗位〔而不是计划或管理工作〕: *These new methods will help teachers working at the coalface.* 这些新方法将对老师的实际教学有所助益。

coal·field /ˋkolˌfild; ˈkəʊlfiːld/ *n* [C] an area where there is coal under the ground 煤田

coal gas /ˋ· ·/ *n* [U] gas produced by burning coal, used especially for electricity and heating 煤气 —compare 比较 NATURAL GAS

coal·hole /ˋkolˌhol; ˈkəʊlhəʊl/ *n* [C] *BrE* a small underground room where coal is stored【英】〔地下〕储煤室

coal·house /ˋkolˌhaus; ˈkəʊlhaʊs/ *n* [C] a small building where coal is stored 煤库

Coal·ite /ˋkolaɪt; ˈkəʊlaɪt/ *n* [U] *trademark* a substance similar to coal that does not produce smoke when it is burned【商标】科莱特无烟燃料

co·a·li·tion /ˌkoəˋlɪʃən; ˌkəʊəˈlɪʃən/ *n* **1** [C] a union of two or more political parties that allows them to form a government or fight an election together〔政党之间的〕同盟, 联合: *a three-party coalition* 三党联盟 | **coalition government** (=a government consisting of different political parties) 联合政府 **2** [C] a group of people who join together to achieve a particular purpose, usually a political one〔常为达某种政治目的而组成的〕同盟: *policies designed by a coalition of public officials and local businessmen* 由政府官员及地方商人共同制定的政策 **3** [U] a process in which two or more political parties or groups join together 结合, 联合

coal·man /ˋkolmən; ˈkəʊlmən/ *n* [C] a man who delivers coal to people's houses 运煤工人; 送煤工人

coal mine /ˋ· ·/ also 又作 **coal pit** *n* [C] a mine from which coal is dug 煤矿

coal scut·tle /ˋ· ˌ··/ *n* [C] a specially shaped container with a handle for carrying coal 煤斗, 煤桶

coal tar /ˋ· ·/ *n* [U] a thick black sticky liquid made by heating coal without air, from which many drugs and chemical products are made 煤焦油: *coal tar soap* 煤焦油皂

coarse /kɔrs; kɔːs/ *adj* **1** having a rough surface that feels slightly hard 粗的, 粗糙的: *Hannah's skin was coarse from years of working outdoors.* 由于常年在户外工作, 汉纳的皮肤很粗糙。**2** consisting of threads or parts that are thicker or larger than usual 粗线条构成的; 粗的: *The coarse sand was hot and rough under her feet.* 她脚下的粗沙又烫又扎脚。**3** talking in a rude and offensive way, especially about sex 粗俗的; 猥亵的; 粗鲁的: *coarse jokes* 猥亵的笑话 —**coarsely** *adv* —**coarseness** *n* [U]

coarse fish·ing /,· '·-/ *n* [U] *BrE* the sport of catching fish other than TROUT OR SALMON in rivers and lakes【英】捕捉淡水鱼比赛〔鳟鱼及鲑鱼除外〕

coars·en /ˈkɔrsn; ˈkɔːsən/ *v* [I,T] **1** to become thicker or rougher, or to make something thicker or rougher (使) 变粗, (使) 粗糙: *Hard work had coarsened his hands.* 艰苦的工作使他的手变得粗糙。| *His face swollen and puffy, the features coarsened by over-indulgence.* 因过度放纵, 他的脸变得臃肿肥胖、粗俗难看。**2** to become or to make someone become less polite in the way they talk or behave, especially about sex (使) 变粗鲁, (使) 变粗俗, (使) 变猥亵: *Drinking had coarsened his sexual appetites.* 酗酒使他变得猥亵下流。

S3 W3 **coast¹** /kost; kəʊst/ *n* [C] **1** the area where the land meets the sea 海岸, 海滨; 沿海地区: *We drove along the Pacific coast to Seattle.* 我们驾车沿着太平洋海岸去西雅图。| **on the coast** (=on the land near the sea) 在沿海地区 *I used to live in a small village on the coast of Brittany.* 我过去住在布列塔尼海边的一个小村庄。| **off the coast** (=in the sea near the land) 在近海的 *a small island off the coast of Scotland* 苏格兰近海的一座小岛 | **coast to coast** (=from one coast of a country to the other coast of the same country) 从〔一国〕此岸到彼岸 *They walked coast to coast across England.* 他们徒步穿越了英格兰全境。—see 见 SHORE (USAGE) **2 the coast is clear** *informal* if the coast is clear, it is safe for you to do something without risking being seen or caught【非正式】危险已过: *We raced towards them as soon as the coast was clear.* 危险一过去, 我们立刻奔向他们。

coast² *v* [I] **1** [always+adv/prep] to move in or on a vehicle, especially down a hill, without using any effort or any power from the engine〔尤指乘坐运载工具向下坡〕靠惯性滑行: **[+down/around/along etc]** *Bev coasted downhill on her bicycle.* 贝夫骑着脚踏车靠着惯性滑下山坡。**2** to achieve something without having to try very hard 轻易得到: *Janey's teacher says she's just coasting and could do even better if pushed.* 珍妮的老师说, 她学起来很轻松, 如果加把劲会学得更好。| **[+to/through]** *Polls predict that the party will coast to victory in the next election.* 民意测验预测说, 该政党会在下次选举中轻松胜出。**3** *AmE* to slide down a hill covered in snow on a SLEDGE¹【美】〔乘雪橇〕向下滑: *The kids went coasting all afternoon.* 孩子们整个下午都在乘雪橇滑下山坡。**4** to sail along the coast while staying close to land 沿海航行, 近海航行

coast·al /ˈkostl; ˈkəʊstl/ *adj* [only before noun 仅用于名词前] in the sea or on the land near the coast 近海的, 沿海的, 海岸的: *the coastal waters of Britain* 英国的近海水域

coast·er /ˈkostɚ; ˈkəʊstə/ *n* [C] **1** a small thin object on which you put a glass, or cup, to protect a table from heat or liquids〔杯子等的〕垫子, 托子 **2** a ship that sails from port to port along a coast, but does not go further out to sea 沿海航行的轮船 —see also 另见 ROLLER COASTER

coaster brake /'··· ,/ *n* [C] *AmE* a BRAKE¹ on some types of bicycle that works by moving the pedals (PEDAL¹ (1)) backwards【美】〔脚踏车的〕脚刹车, 倒轮式刹车

coast·guard /ˈkost,gɑrd; ˈkəʊstgɑːd/ *n* **1 the Coastguard** [also+plural verb *BrE* 英] the organization that helps swimmers and ships that are in danger and helps prevent illegal activities such as SMUGGLING 海岸警卫队: *The operation required the cooperation of the Coastguard.* 该行动需要海岸警卫队的合作。**2** [C] a member of this organization 海岸警卫队队员

coast·line /ˈkost,laɪn; ˈkəʊstlaɪn/ *n* [C] the land on the edge of the coast, especially the shape of this land as seen from the air〔尤指从空中鸟瞰的〕海岸线, 海岸地形: *rocky coastline* 多岩石的海岸地貌

S2 W3 **coat¹** /kot; kəʊt/ *n* [C] **1** a piece of clothing that is worn over your clothes to protect them or to keep you warm 大衣, 外套: *The lab assistants wear long white coats.* 那个实验室助手穿着白色的长外套。| **put on/take off your coat** *Billy! Put your coat on, it's cold outside!* 比利, 穿上外套, 外面很冷! **2** *BrE old-fashioned or AmE* a piece of clothing that covers the top part of your body and is worn as part of a suit; JACKET (1)【英, 过时或美】〔常指套装一部分的〕短上衣: *A business suit usually consists of matching pants, coat, and vest.* 一套西服套装通常由配套的裤子、上衣及背心构成。**3** the fur, wool, or hair that covers an animal's body〔动物的〕皮毛: *a dog with a glossy coat* 皮毛光滑的狗 **4** a thin layer of a liquid or other substance that you spread thinly over a surface〔表面的〕覆盖物; 涂层: **[+of]** *He applied a light coat of varnish.* 他上了一层清漆。**5 white-coated/fur-coated/winter-coated etc** wearing a white, fur etc coat 穿着白色/毛皮/冬天穿等的外套 —see also 另见 **cut your coat according to your cloth** (CUT¹ (34)), MORNING COAT

coat² *v* [T] **1** to cover something, especially food, with a thin layer of liquid or another substance 覆盖; 盖; 涂上: *Dust coated the furniture and everything smelled damp.* 家具上沾满了灰尘, 所有的东西闻起来都有股湿湿的味道。| **coat sth with/in** *Herring is good coated in oatmeal and fried.* 油煎涂燕麦片的鲱鱼很好吃。**2 metal-coated/plastic-coated etc** covered with a thin layer of metal etc 金属涂层/塑料涂层等的 **3 sugar-coated a)** covered with sugar 涂了糖的 **b)** making something seem more attractive, desirable etc than it really is 甜言蜜语的, 过于美化的, 言过其实的: *The program depicts a sugar-coated version of family life.* 该节目过于美化家庭生活。

coat check /'· ·/ *n* [C] *AmE* a room in a public building where you can leave your coat while you are in the building; CLOAKROOM【美】衣帽间

coat hang·er /'·,··/ *n* [C] an object that you use to hang up clothes on; HANGER 衣架

coat·ing /ˈkotɪŋ; ˈkəʊtɪŋ/ *n* [C] a thin layer of something that covers a surface 涂层, 外层, 覆盖层: *The tank's metal coating is made from a mixture of copper and zinc.* 油箱的金属涂层是铜和锌的合金。

coat of arms /,· · '·/ *n* [C] *plural* **coats of arms** a set of pictures or patterns painted on a SHIELD¹ (3) and used as the special sign of a family, town, university etc〔用作家族、城镇、大学等标志的〕(盾形) 纹章, 盾徽

coat of arms (盾形) 纹章, 盾徽

coat of mail /,· · '·/ *n* [C] a coat made of metal rings that was worn to protect the top part of a soldier's body in the Middle Ages〔中世纪士兵的〕锁子铠甲

coat rack /'· ·/ *n* [C] a board or pole with hooks on it that you hang coats on〔有挂钩的〕挂衣架 —see picture on page A15 参见 A15 页图

coat·room /ˈkot,rum; ˈkəʊtrʊm/ *n* [C] *AmE* a room in a public building where you may leave your coat, hat etc while you are there; CLOAKROOM (1)【美】衣帽间

coat·stand /ˈkot,stænd; ˈkəʊtstænd/ *n* [C] a tall pole with hooks at the top that you hang coats on 衣帽架

coat·tails /ˈkot,telz; ˈkəʊt-teɪlz/ *n* [plural] **1 (ride/hang) on sb's coattails** if you achieve something on someone's coattails, you achieve it with the help or influence of someone powerful 在…的提携下, 紧跟…之后: *A number of Republican congressmen were elected on Reagan's coattails.* 在里根的提携下, 一些共和党国会议员当选。**2** the cloth at the back of a TAILCOAT that is divided into two pieces〔燕尾服的〕燕尾

coats 大衣, 外套, 短上衣

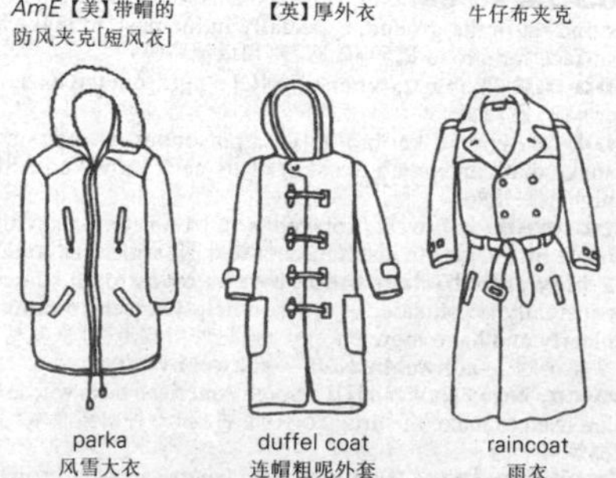

coax /koks; kəʊks/ *v* **1** [I,T] to persuade someone to do something that they do not want to do by talking to them in a kind, gentle, and patient way 劝诱; 哄; 诱导: *"Please, Vic, come with us," Nancy coaxed.* "求你了，维克，跟我们一块儿来吧。"南希哄劝道。| **coax sb into/out of doing (sth)** *We had to coax Alan into going to school.* 我们得哄着艾伦去上学。| **coax sb to do sth** *The bear coaxed its cubs to enter the water.* 那头熊哄着幼熊下水。| **coax sb down/out/back etc** *I managed to coax her round to my point of view.* 我成功地说服她同意我的观点。**2** [T] to make something such as a machine do something by dealing with it in a slow, patient, and careful way 耐心地摆弄〔机器等〕: **coax sth out of/from sth** *He coaxed a fire out of some dry grass and twigs.* 他用一些干草和小树枝小心翼翼地生了堆火。| **coax sth down/round/back etc** *We coaxed the pennies out of the piggybank with the blade of a knife.* 我们用刀片耐心地将硬币从小猪扑满中取出。—**coaxing** *n* [U] —**coaxingly** *adv*

cob /kɑb; kɒb/ *n* [C] **1** a CORNCOB 玉米棒子芯 **2** *BrE* a round LOAF of bread【英】圆头面包 **3** a type of large nut from the HAZEL[1] tree; COBNUT 欧洲榛子 **4** a type of horse that is strong and has short legs 一种壮实的矮脚马 **5** a male SWAN[1] 雄天鹅

co·balt /ˈkobɔlt; ˈkəʊbɔːlt/ *n* [U] **1** a shiny silver-white metal that is a chemical ELEMENT (=simple substance), and that is used to make some metals and to give a blue colour to some substances 钴; 钴类颜料 **2** a bright blue-green colour 钴蓝色: *the parrot's cobalt feathers* 鹦鹉的钴蓝色羽毛 —**cobalt** *adj*

Cobb /kɑb; kɒb/, **Ty** /taɪ; taɪ/ (1886-1961) a US BASEBALL player. He was the first person to score 4000 base hits. 科布〔(1886-1961)，美国棒球运动员。他是首位击出4000次安全打的选手〕

cob·ber /ˈkɑbɚ; ˈkɒbə/ *n* [C] *AustrE, NZE informal* a word meaning a friend, used especially by men talking to other men【澳，新西兰，非正式】哥们，伙伴，朋友〔常用于男性间〕

cob·ble[1] /ˈkɑbḷ; ˈkɒbəl/ *v* [T] **1** *old-fashioned* to repair or make shoes【过时】修〔鞋〕; 制〔鞋〕**2** to put COBBLESTONES on a street 用鹅卵石铺路

cobble sth ↔ **together** *phr v* [T] *informal* to quickly make something that is useful but not perfect【非正式】〔匆忙而草率地〕拼凑: *The diplomats cobbled together an agreement.* 外交官们匆忙达成了一项协议。| *She cobbled together a tent from a few pieces of string and a sheet.* 她用几根细绳和一张床单胡乱搭了一个帐篷。

cobble[2] *n* [C] a cobblestone 鹅卵石，圆石

cob·bled /ˈkɑbḷd; ˈkɒbəld/ *adj* a cobbled street is covered with cobblestones〔街道〕铺鹅卵石的

Cob·bleigh /ˈkɑblɪ; ˈkɒbli/ **old Uncle Tom Cobbleigh and all** a line from an old British song about a large group of people who do things together. The people are all listed by name, and the list ends with the words 'old Uncle Tom Cobbleigh and all'. The phrase is now used to say that every possible person was present or involved in something. "以及科布利老伯"〔英国一首老歌中的歌词。歌词描写一大群人在一起干活的场景。干活的人按姓名逐一排列，最后是科布利老伯。old Uncle Tom Cobbleigh and all 这一短语现用来表示该来的人都来了或参与了某种活动〕

cob·bler /ˈkɑblɚ; ˈkɒblə/ *n* [C] **1** *AmE* cooked fruit covered with a sweet, bread-like mixture【美】酥皮水果馅饼: *peach cobbler* 酥皮桃馅饼 **2** someone who makes and repairs shoes 鞋匠 **3 cobblers** *BrE spoken informal* something that someone says which you think is stupid or untrue【英口，非正式】蠢话; 假话: **a load of (old) cobblers** *I've never heard such a load of old cobblers in my life!* 我这辈子还没听说过那样的蠢话！

cob·ble·stone /ˈkɑbḷˌston; ˈkɒbəlstəʊn/ *n* [C] a small round stone set in the ground, especially in the past, to make a hard surface for a road 鹅卵石，圆石〔用以铺路等〕

cob·nut /ˈkɑbˌnʌt; ˈkɒbnʌt/ *n* [C] a nut from the HAZEL[1] tree; COB (3) 欧洲榛子

co·bra /ˈkobrə; ˈkəʊbrə/ *n* [C] a poisonous African or Asian snake that can spread the skin of its neck to make itself look bigger 眼镜蛇

cob·web /ˈkɑbˌwɛb; ˈkɒbweb/ *n* [C] **1** a net of sticky threads made by a SPIDER to catch insects 蜘蛛网; SPIDERWEB *AmE*【美】**2 blow/brush/clear the cobwebs away** to do something, especially go outside, in order to help yourself to think more clearly and have more energy〔通过外出散步等〕恢复精神，使头脑清醒 —**cobwebbed** *adj* —**cobwebby** *adj*

co·ca /ˈkokə; ˈkəʊkə/ *n* [U] a South American bush whose leaves are used to make the drug COCAINE 古柯〔一种南美灌木，其叶可提炼可卡因〕

Coca-Co·la /ˌ‥ˈ‥/ *n* [C,U] *trademark* a sweet brown non-alcoholic drink【商标】可口可乐

co·caine /koˈken; kəʊˈkeɪn/ *n* [U] a drug, usually in the form of a white powder, that is taken illegally for pleasure or used in some medical situations to prevent pain 可卡因，古柯碱: *Jimmy was high on cocaine.* 吉米吸了可卡因，精神恍惚。—see also 另见 CRACK[2] (10)

coc·cyx /ˈkɑksɪks; ˈkɒksɪks/ *n plural* **coccyxes** *or* **coccyges** /kɑkˈsaɪdʒiz; kɒkˈsaɪdʒiːz/ [C] *technical* the small bone at the bottom of your SPINE (1); TAILBONE【术语】尾骨 —see picture at 参见 SKELETON 图

coch·i·neal /ˌkɑtʃəˈnil; ˌkɒtʃəˈniːl◂/ *n* [U] a red substance used to give food a red colour 胭脂虫红〔用于给食物染上红色的一种物质〕

Co·chise /koˈtʃis; kəʊˈtʃiːs/ (?1815-74) a Native American chief of the Apaches who fought against US soldiers from 1861 to 1872 in order to prevent them taking land from his people 科奇斯〔(?1815-1874)，美洲土著居民阿帕切人的酋长，1861至1872年间与美军进行过抗争，阻止他们掠夺族人的土地〕

coch·le·a /ˈkɑkliə; ˈkɒkliə/ *n plural* **cochleas** *or* **cochleae** /-lɪi; -li-aɪ/ [C] *technical* a part of the inner ear【术语】耳蜗

cock[1] /kɑk; kɒk/ *n*

1 ▶CHICKEN 鸡◀ [C] *especially BrE* an adult male chicken【尤英】公鸡; ROOSTER *AmE*【美】—see also 另见 COCK-A-DOODLE-DOO

2 ▶SEX ORGAN 性器官◀ [C] *taboo* a PENIS【讳】阴茎，鸡巴

3 cock and bull story a story or excuse that is silly and unlikely but is told as if it were true 荒诞无稽的故事; 编造的借口: *She gave me some cock and bull story about the dog eating her homework.* 她对我编了一个荒唐的故事，说狗吃掉了她的家庭作业。

4 ▶CONTROL FLOW 控制流动◀ [C] something that controls the flow of liquid out of a pipe or container; TAP[1] (1) 龙头; 旋塞; 阀门 —see also 另见 BALLCOCK, STOPCOCK

5 ▶MALE BIRD 雄鸟◀ [C] an adult male bird of any kind 雄鸟，雄禽: *a cock robin* 一只雄性知更鸟

6 ▶MAN 男人◀ [C] *BrE old-fashioned* a word used by a man when talking to another man he knows well【英，过时】老兄，伙计〔用于男性之间的称呼〕

7 cock of the walk *old-fashioned* if you describe someone as behaving like the cock of the walk, they are behaving as if they were better or more important than other people【过时】逞威风的头领; 称王称霸的人 —see also 另见 **half cocked** (HALF[1] (11))

cock[2] *v* [T] **1** to lift a part of your body so that it is upright, or hold a part of your body at an angle 竖起，翘起〔身体的一部分〕; 将〔身体的一部分〕转向一边: *Paul cocked his head to one side as he considered my idea.* 保罗侧着头，考虑着我的意见。| *The little dog cocked a leg against the lamppost and urinated.* 那只小狗将一条腿翘在街灯柱上撒尿。**2** to pull back the HAMMER[1] (5) of a gun so that it is ready to be fired 扳起〔枪的〕扳机 **3** to put your hat on at an angle; TILT[1] (1) 歪戴〔帽子〕**4 keep an ear cocked** *informal* to pay close attention because you want to be sure you hear something you expect or think may happen【非正式】竖起耳朵听: *She kept an ear cocked for the sound of Joe's key in the front door.* 她竖起耳朵听着乔转动钥匙开前门的声音。**5 cock a snook** *BrE informal* to show clearly that you do not respect someone or something【英，非正式】嗤之以鼻，不屑一顾: **[+at]** *The artist cocked a snook at the critics by exhibiting an empty frame.* 为表示对评论界的不屑，该艺术家展出了一副空画框。

cock sth ↔ **up** *phr v* [T] *BrE informal* to spoil something such as an arrangement or plans, especially by making a stupid mistake【英，非正式】把〔安排或计划〕搞砸，弄糟: *His secretary really cocked up his travelling schedule and he's furious about it.* 他的秘书确实把他的出差日程弄得一团糟，他对此愤怒不已。—see also 另见 COCK-UP

cock·ade /kɑkˋed; kɒˈkeɪd/ *n* [C] a small piece of cloth used as a decoration on a hat to show rank, membership of a club etc〔显示级别、身份等的〕帽徽，帽上的花结

cock-a-doo·dle-doo /ˌkɑk ə ˌdudḷ ˋdu; ˌkɒk ə ˌduːdl ˈduː/ *n* [C] the loud sound made by an adult male chicken〔公鸡啼叫的〕喔喔声

cock-a-hoop /ˌkɑk ə ˋhup; ˌkɒk ə ˈhuːp/ *adj* [not before noun 不用于名词前] pleased and excited about something, especially something you have done 得意洋洋的，兴高采烈的: **[+at/about]** *Robert's cock-a-hoop about his new job.* 罗伯特对他的新工作颇为得意。

cock-a-leek·ie /ˌkɑk ə ˋlikɪ; ˌkɒk ə ˈliːki/ *n* [U] a type of Scottish soup made with chicken, vegetables, and LEEKS〔苏格兰〕鸡肉韭菜汤

cock·a·ma·mie /ˌkakəˋmemɪ; ˌkɒkəˈmeɪmi◂/ *adj AmE informal* a cockamamie story or excuse is not believable or does not make sense【美, 非正式】荒谬的, 蹩脚的: *What cockamamie idea will he think up next?* 他还会冒出什么荒谬的想法?

cock·a·too /ˌkakəˋtu; ˌkɒkəˈtuː/ *n* [C] an Australian PARROT[1] (1) with a lot of feathers on the top of its head〔澳大利亚〕凤头鹦鹉, 葵花鹦鹉

cock·chaf·er /ˋkakˌtʃefɚ; ˈkɒktʃeɪfə/ *n* [C] a European BEETLE (=a kind of insect) that damages trees and plants 金龟〔产于欧洲的一种害虫〕

cock·crow /ˋkakˌkro; ˈkɒk-krəʊ/ *n* [U] *literary* the time in the early morning when the sun rises; DAWN[1] (1)【文】黎明, 鸡鸣时分

cocked hat /ˌ· ˈ·/ *n* [C] **1 knock/beat sb/sth into a cocked hat** to be a lot better than someone or something else 远远胜过某人/某物: *My mother is such a good cook she knocks everybody else into a cocked hat.* 妈妈的厨艺高超, 无人能及。**2** a hat with the edges turned up on three sides, worn in the past〔旧时〕帽沿上卷的三角帽

cock·e·rel /ˋkakərəl; ˈkɒkərəl/ *n* [C] a young male chicken 小公鸡

cocker span·iel /ˌkakɚ ˋspænjəl; ˌkɒkə ˈspænjəl/ *n* [C] a dog with long ears and long silky fur 可卡犬

cock-eyed /ˌ· ˈ·◂/ *adj informal*【非正式】**1** an idea, situation, plan etc that is cock-eyed is strange and not practical 荒谬的, 不切实际的: *The whole idea is completely cock-eyed.* 这个主意整个儿荒唐透顶。**2** not straight but set at an angle 倾斜的, 歪的: *I think you put that shelf up cock-eyed.* 我觉得你把那个书架放歪了。

cock fight /ˈ· ·/ *n* [C] a sport, illegal in many countries, in which two male chickens are made to fight 斗鸡〔在许多国家为非法活动〕—**cockfighting** *n* [U]

cock·horse /ˋkakhɔrs; ˌkɒkˈhɔːs/ *n* [C] *old use* a HOBBYHORSE【旧】木马, 竹马

cock·le /ˋkakḷ; ˈkɒkəl/ *n* [C] **1** a common European SHELLFISH that is often used for food 鸟蛤 **2 warm the cockles of sb's heart** to make someone feel happy and full of good feelings towards other people 使人由衷地感到高兴: *Seeing her delight in her new baby just warms the cockles of your heart.* 看到她有了小宝宝而幸福的样子, 你会由衷地为她高兴。

cock·le·shell /ˋkakḷˌʃɛl; ˈkɒkəlʃel/ *n* [C] **1** the heart-shaped shell of the cockle 鸟蛤壳 **2** *literary* a small light boat【文】轻舟, 小船

cock·ney /ˋkaknɪ; ˈkɒkni/ *n* **1** [C] someone, especially a WORKING CLASS person, who comes from the eastern area of London 伦敦东区佬〔尤指工人阶层〕**2** [U] a way of speaking English that is typical of someone from this area 伦敦东区土话 —**cockney** *adj*

cock·pit /ˋkakˌpɪt; ˈkɒkˌpɪt/ *n* [C] **1** the area in a plane, small boat, or racing car where the pilot or driver sits〔飞机的〕驾驶舱;〔小船的〕舵手座;〔赛车的〕驾驶座 —see pictures at 参见 AIRCRAFT and 和 YACHT 图 **2** a small, usually enclosed area where COCK FIGHTs took place in former times 斗鸡场

cock·roach /ˋkakˌrotʃ; ˈkɒk-rəʊtʃ/ *n* [C] a large black insect often found in old or dirty houses 蟑螂; ROACH (1) *AmE*【美】

cocks·comb /ˋkaksˌkom; ˈkɒks-kəʊm/ *n* [C] **1** the red flesh that grows from the top of a male chicken's head〔公鸡的〕鸡冠 **2** also 又作 **coxcomb** the cap worn by a JESTER (=someone employed to amuse a king in the past) 小丑[弄臣]戴的帽子

cock·suck·er /ˋkakˌsʌkɚ; ˈkɒkˌsʌkə/ *n* [C] *AmE taboo* an insulting way of talking to a man【美, 讳】狗杂种, 混蛋〔尤指男性〕

cock·sure /ˋkakˋʃʊr; ˌkɒkˈʃʊə/ *adj informal* too confident of your abilities or knowledge, in a way that is annoying to other people【非正式】过于自信的, 自以为是的: *He seemed to be rather cocksure, this young man.* 这个年轻人看来太过自负了。

cock·tail /ˋkakˌtel; ˈkɒkteɪl/ *n* [C] **1** an alcoholic drink made from a mixture of different drinks 鸡尾酒 **2 seafood/prawn/lobster cocktail** a mixture of small pieces of fish, PRAWNs, or LOBSTER, served cold and eaten at the beginning of a meal〔西餐作为第一道进食的〕凉拌海鲜/对虾/龙虾 **3 fruit cocktail** a mixture of small pieces of fruit 什锦水果粒 **4** a mixture of dangerous substances, especially one that you eat or drink〔尤指服用的〕危险品混合物: *a lethal cocktail of pain-killers and amphetamines* 由镇痛剂和苯丙胺混合而成的致命物质 —see also 另见 MOLOTOV COCKTAIL

cocktail dress /ˈ· · ˌ ·/ *n* [C] a formal dress for wearing to parties or other evening social events〔正式场合穿的〕(晚)礼服

cocktail lounge /ˈ· · ·/ *n* [C] a public room in a hotel, restaurant etc, where alcoholic drinks may be bought〔旅馆、餐厅等供应酒类饮料的〕休息室, 酒吧间

cocktail par·ty /ˈ· · ˌ · ·/ *n* [C] a party at which alcoholic drinks are served and for which people usually dress formally 鸡尾酒会

> **CULTURAL NOTE 文化注释**
>
> A cocktail party is thought of as an UPPER-CLASS activity for fashionable people and also as a party that is typically held at a formal public occasion, for example before a PRESS CONFERENCE or at the LAUNCH of a new book. 鸡尾酒会被看成是时髦的上流人士的活动, 一般在正式的公开场合举行, 如新闻发布会前或新书发布会上。

cocktail shak·er /ˈ· · ˌ · ·/ *n* [C] a container in which cocktails are mixed 鸡尾酒调酒器

cocktail stick /ˈ· · ·/ *n* [C] a short pointed stick on which small pieces of food are served 取食签〔用来挑起小块食物〕—see picture at 参见 STICK[2] 图

cocktail wait·ress /ˈ· · ˌ · ·/ *n* [C] *AmE* a woman who serves drinks to people sitting at tables in a BAR[1] (1)【美】酒吧女侍者

cock-up /ˈ· ·/ *n* [C] *BrE spoken* something that has been done very badly, so that it spoils someone's plans or arrangements【英口】混乱, 一团糟: *God, what a cock-up!* 天哪! 这真糟透了!

cock·y /ˋkakɪ; ˈkɒki/ *adj informal* too confident about yourself and your abilities, especially in a way that annoys other people【非正式】骄傲自大的, 趾高气扬的: *He's very clever, but far too cocky.* 他非常聪明, 但是太狂妄自大了。—**cockily** *adv* —**cockiness** *n* [U]

co·coa /ˋkoko; ˈkəʊkəʊ/ *n* [U] **1** also 又作 **cocoa powder** a brown powder made from the crushed cooked seeds of a tropical tree, used to make chocolate and to give a chocolate taste to foods 可可粉 **2** a sweet hot drink made with this powder, sugar, and milk or water 可可饮料〔由可可粉、糖及奶或水制成〕: *a cup of cocoa* 一杯可可

cocoa bean /ˈ· · ·/ *n* [C] the small seed of a tropical tree, that is used to make cocoa 可可豆

cocoa but·ter /ˈ· · ˌ · ·/ *n* [U] a fat obtained from the seeds of a tropical tree, used in making some COSMETICS 可可油〔可制化妆品等〕

co·co·mat /ˋkokəˌmæt; ˈkəʊkəmæt/ *n* [U] *AmE* COCONUT MATTING【美】椰衣垫

co·co·nut /ˋkokənʌt; ˈkəʊkənʌt/ *n* **1** [C] the large brown seed of a tropical tree, which has a hard shell containing white flesh that you can eat and a milky liquid 椰子 —see picture on page A8 参见 A8 页图 **2** [U] the white flesh of this seed, often used in cooking 椰肉: *shredded coconut* 椰丝

coconut mat·ting /ˌ· · · ˈ· ·/ *n* [U] *BrE* a rough material used to cover floors that is made from the outer part of a coconut shell【英】〔用椰壳纤维制成的〕椰衣垫; cocomat *AmE*【美】

coconut milk /ˈ· · · ˌ ·/ *n* [U] the liquid inside a coconut 椰子汁

coconut shy /ˈ· · · ˌ ·/ *n plural* **coconut shies** [C] *BrE* a game in which you try to knock coconuts off posts by throwing balls at them【英】一种以球投落椰子的游戏

co·coon[1] /kəˋkun; kəˈkuːn/ *n* [C] **1** a silk cover that young MOTHs and other insects make to protect themselves while they are growing 茧; 卵袋 **2** something that wraps around you completely, especially to protect you〔用以包裹全身的〕保护性衣物; 防护膜: **[+of]** *The baby peered out of its cocoon of blankets.* 宝宝从裹在身上的毛毯中向外张望。

cocoon[2] *v* [T] to protect or surround someone or something completely, especially so that they feel safe 紧裹; 密封〔以感觉安全〕: **[+in]** *cocooned in a reassuring network of friends and relatives* 处在亲朋好友的层层保护中 —**cocooned** *adj*: *a rich, cocooned existence on the East Side* 东区的富人

Co·co the Clown /ˌkoko ðə ˋklaun; ˌkəʊkəʊ ðə ˈklaʊn/ (1900-74) a Russian-born CLOWN, one of the greatest CIRCUS performers ever 小丑科科〔(1900-1974), 生于俄国的丑角演员, 是有史以来最杰出的马戏表演家之一〕

Coc·teau /ˌkɑkˋto; ˈkɒktəʊ/, **Jean** /ʒɑn; ʒɒn/ (1889-1963) a French writer and film director, who was an important member of the SURREALIST movement. His work includes the films *Orphée* (1950) and *Les Enfants Terribles* (1950), and the play *La Machine Infernale* (1934). 科克托〔(1889-1963), 法国作家、电影导演, 超现实主义运动的重要成员。其作品有影片《奥尔菲》(1950)、《调皮捣蛋的孩子们》(1950)和剧本《爆炸装置》(1934)〕

COD /ˌsi o ˋdi; ˌsiː əʊ ˈdiː/ the abbreviation of 缩写= cash on delivery; a situation in which you pay for goods when they are delivered to you 货到付款

cod /kɑd; kɒd/ *n* **1** [C] a large sea fish that lives in the North Atlantic 鳕鱼 **2** [U] the white flesh of this fish, eaten as food 鳕鱼肉: *Cod and chips twice, please.* 请来双份的鳕鱼和薯条。

co·da /ˋkodə; ˈkəʊdə/ *n* [C] **1** an additional part at the end of a piece of music that is separate from the main part〔乐曲、乐章的〕尾声, 结束乐段 **2** a separate piece of writing at the end of a work of literature or a speech〔文学作品或演说词的〕结尾, 结局

cod·dle /ˋkɑdl̩; ˈkɒdl/ *v* [T] to treat someone in a way that is too kind and gentle and that protects them from pain or difficulty 悉心照料; 溺爱, 娇纵: *Don't coddle the child – he's fine!* 别太惯着孩子, 他没事儿!

code¹ /kod; kəʊd/ *n* [C]

1 ▶BEHAVIOUR 行为◀ a set of rules that tell people how to behave in their life or in certain situations 行为准则; 道德规范: **code of conduct/behaviour** *Fry rejected the accepted code of behaviour and married one of his servants.* 弗赖伊冲破传统的约束, 与他的一个用人结了婚。

2 ▶RULES/LAWS 规章/法律◀ a set of written rules or laws 法典, 法规: *Each state in the US has a different criminal and civil code.* 美国各州都制定了不同的刑法及民法法规。| **dress code** (=rule about what clothes you must wear in a school, business etc) 着装规定

3 code of practice a set of rules that people in a particular business or profession agree to obey 行业规则: *The film industry wants to produce a code of practice for employers.* 电影界希望为雇主们制定一套行规。

4 ▶SECRET MESSAGE 秘密信息◀ a system of words, letters, or signs that you use instead of ordinary words when you are writing something that you want to keep secret 密码; 代码; 代号: **in code** *Send your reports in code.* 用密码将你的报告发送过来。| **break/crack a code** (=manage to understand a secret code) 破译密码

5 ▶SIGNS GIVING INFORMATION 信息符号◀ a set of numbers, letters, or signs that show what something is or give information about it 编码, 编号, 标记: *Most countries have some form of postal code that speeds mail delivery.* 大多数国家都有一套邮政编码以加快邮递速度。—see also 另见 BAR CODE, POSTCODE, ZIP CODE

6 ▶TELEPHONES 电话◀ also 又作 **dialling code, STD code** *BrE* the group of numbers that come before a telephone number when you are calling from a different area【英】长途电话区号; AREA CODE *AmE*【美】: *What's the code for Aberdeen?* 阿伯丁的区号是多少?

7 ▶COMPUTERS 电脑◀ a set of instructions that tell a computer what to do〔电脑的〕编码 —see also 另见 MACHINE CODE, SOURCE CODE

8 ▶SOUNDS/SIGNALS 声音/信号◀ a system of sounds or signals that represent words or letters when they are sent by machine〔电报等发出的〕电码: *a telegraphic code* 一份电码 —see also 另见 MORSE CODE

code² *v* [T] **1** to put a set of numbers, letters, or signs on something to show what it is or give information about it 把…编码[编号]: *Product orders should be coded according to where they will be shipped.* 产品订单必须按照运送地点编号。**2** to put a message in code so that it is secret 把…编成密码 **3 colour code** to mark a group of things with different colours so that you can tell the difference between them 颜色编码 —**coded** *adj*: *a coded message* 用密码编成的信息

co·deine /ˋkodɪˌin; ˈkəʊdiːn/ *n* [U] a drug used to stop pain 可待因〔用以镇痛的药物〕

code name /ˋ· ·/ *n* [C] a name that keeps secret someone's real name or a real plan〔情报人员、计划等的〕代号 —**code name** *v* [T]

co·dex /ˋkodɛks; ˈkəʊdeks/ *n* [C] *plural* **codices** /-dɪsiz; -dʒsiːz/ *technical* an ancient book written by hand【术语】〔古籍的〕手抄本: *a sixth-century codex* 一本公元6世纪的手抄本

cod·fish /ˋkɑdˌfɪʃ; ˈkɒdˌfɪʃ/ *n* [C] a COD 鳕鱼; 鳕鱼肉

cod·ger /ˋkɑdʒɚ; ˈkɒdʒə/ *n* [C] *informal* **old codger** an old man【非正式】老家伙: *He's a charming old codger.* 他是个很有魅力的老头儿。

co·di·fy /ˋkɑdəˌfaɪ; ˈkəʊdʒfaɪ/ *v* [T] to arrange laws, principles, facts etc in a system 将〔法律、条例、事实等〕编集成典; 编纂 —**codification** /ˌkɑdəfəˋkeʃən; ˌkəʊdʒfʒˈkeɪʃən/ *n* [C,U]

cod-liver oil /ˌ· · · ˈ·◂/ *n* [U] a yellow oil from a fish that contains a lot of substances that are important for good health 鱼肝油

cod·piece /ˋkɑdˌpis; ˈkɒdpiːs/ *n* [C] a piece of coloured cloth worn by men in the 15th and 16th centuries to cover the opening in the front of their trousers〔15、16世纪时男裤前面开口处的〕下体盖片, 遮阴布

cods·wal·lop /ˋkɑdzˌwɑləp; ˈkɒdzˌwɒləp/ *n* [U] *BrE spoken*【英口】**a load of codswallop** something that someone says which you think is stupid or untrue 胡说八道, 一派胡言

Co·dy /ˋkodɪ; ˈkəʊdi/, **Wil·liam Fred·e·rick** /ˋwɪljəm ˋfrɛdrɪk; ˈwɪljəm ˈfredərɪk/ the real name of Buffalo Bill 科迪〔野牛比尔的真名〕

co·ed¹ /ˋkoˋɛd; ˌkəʊˈed◂/ *adj* using a system in which students of both sexes are educated together 男女同校的: *The university became coed in 1967.* 这所大学在1967年开始实行男女同校。

coed² *n* [C] *AmE old-fashioned* a woman student at a university【美, 过时】〔大学的〕女生

co·ed·u·ca·tion /ˌkoɛdʒəˋkeʃən; ˌkəʊedjʒˈkeɪʃən/ *n* [U] a system in which students of both sexes are educated together 男女同校(制) —**coeducational** *adj formal*【正式】

co·ef·fi·cient /ˌkoəˋfɪʃənt; ˌkəʊʒˈfɪʃənt/ *n* [C] *technical* the number by which something that varies is multiplied【术语】系数: *In 8pq the coefficient of pq is 8.* 8pq的pq系数为8。

co·e·qual /ˌkoˋikwəl; ˌkəʊˈiːkwəl◂/ *adj formal* if people are coequal, they have the same rank, ability, importance etc【正式】〔级别、能力、重要性等方面〕相等的: *three managers of coequal status* 三个同等级别的经理 —**coequally** *adv*

co·erce /koˋɝs; kəʊˈɜːs/ *v* [T] to force someone to do something they do not want to do by threatening them 强制; 胁迫; 迫使: **coerce sb into doing sth** *The rebels coerced the villagers into hiding them from the army.* 反叛者强迫村民们将他们隐藏起来, 以逃脱军队的搜捕。

co·er·cion /koˋɝʒən; kəʊˈɜːʃən/ *n* [U] the use of threats or orders to make someone do something they do not want to do 强迫; 胁迫, 逼迫: *Soames said he had been under coercion when he confessed.* 索姆斯说自己是迫于压力才不得已招供的。

co·er·cive /koˋɝsɪv; kəʊˈɜːsɪv/ *adj* using threats or orders to make someone do something they do not want to do 强制的; 胁迫的: *coercive measures to reduce absenteeism* 减少旷工现象的高压措施 —**coercively** *adv*

co·e·val /koˋivl; kəʊˈiːvəl/ *adj formal* happening or existing during the same period of time【正式】同时代的; 同年代的: **[+with]** *The development of stone tools was coeval with the appearance of farming settlements.* 石器的发展与农业部落的出现处于同一时期。

co·ex·ist /ˌko ɪgˋzɪst; ˌkəʊɪgˈzɪst/ *v* [I] *formal* to exist at the same time or in the same place, especially peacefully【正式】〔尤指和平地〕共存, 共处: **[+with]** *great wealth coexisting with extreme poverty* 庞大的财富与极度贫困同时存在

co·ex·ist·ence /ˌko ɪgˋzɪstəns; ˌkəʊɪgˈzɪstəns/ *n* [U] *formal*【正式】**1** the state of existing together at the same time or in the same place 共存, 同时存在: *the coexistence of the traditional novel with experimental writing* 传统小说与实验性写作的共存 **2 peaceful coexistence** if two or more countries or people have a peaceful coexistence, they are not fighting one another 和平共处 —**coexistent** *adj*

C of E /ˌsi əv ˋi; ˌsiː əv ˈiː/ *n BrE* an abbreviation for 缩写= Church of England【英】英国国教, 英国圣公会

cof·fee /ˋkɔfi; ˈkɒfi/ *n* [U] **1** a hot, dark brown drink that has a slightly bitter taste 咖啡: *Do you want a cup of coffee?* 你要来杯咖啡吗? | **black coffee** (=coffee with no milk added) 不加牛奶的咖啡, 黑咖啡 | **white coffee** *BrE* (=coffee with milk added)【英】加牛奶的咖啡 **2** [C] *especially BrE* a cup of this drink【尤英】一杯咖啡: *Who wants a coffee?* 谁想要一杯咖啡? **3** a brown powder that you use to make coffee 咖啡(粉): *a pound of coffee* 一磅咖啡 | **instant coffee** (=a powder that you use to make coffee quickly) 速溶咖啡 **4** [U] a light brown colour 咖啡色, 浅褐色 —see picture on page A5 参见 A5 页图 —see also 另见 **wake up and smell the coffee** (WAKE¹)

CULTURAL NOTE 文化注释

Coffee has been a popular drink for over 200 years. In both the UK and the US, many people feel that they have not started the day properly until they have had a cup of coffee in the morning. Coffee is considered a drink for adults. 咖啡成为受人欢迎的饮料已有二百多年, 很多英美人觉得早上喝一杯咖啡一天才算正式开始。咖啡被看成是成人的饮料。

'Black coffee' is coffee without any milk or cream added to it. 'White coffee' is coffee with milk or cream. In the UK, a lot of people drink 'instant coffee' rather than 'fresh

coffee' or 'ground coffee'. Although you can buy instant coffee in the US, it is not very popular. Some people who are careful about what they eat or drink have stopped drinking coffee or drink only DECAFFEINATED coffee because the CAFFEINE in coffee is bad for you. "黑咖啡"指不加牛奶或奶油的咖啡,"白咖啡"指加牛奶或奶油的咖啡。很多英国人喝速溶咖啡,而不是新煮咖啡或现磨咖啡。速溶咖啡在美国虽然也卖,但不太流行。一些注重饮食的人开始不喝咖啡,或只喝去咖啡因的咖啡,因为咖啡中含有的咖啡因对身体有害。

Over the last 20 years, coffee bars have become very popular in both the US and the UK, and most cities have a large number of coffee bars. They serve different sorts of coffee such as CAPPUCCINO (=coffee with FROTHY milk), ESPRESSO (=a small amount of strong black coffee), MOCHA (=coffee, cocoa, milk, and cream) or LATTE (=coffee with hot milk). 过去二十年来,咖啡馆在英美十分盛行,大多数城市里咖啡馆林立,提供各种咖啡,如卡布奇诺、蒸馏咖啡、摩卡咖啡和拿铁咖啡。— see also Cultural Note at TEA 另见 TEA 文化注释

coffee bar /ˈ·· ˌ/ *n* [C] *BrE* a small restaurant that serves coffee and other non-alcoholic drinks, sandwiches (SANDWICH[1] (1)) and cakes etc【英】小型咖啡馆 —compare 比较 COFFEE SHOP

coffee bean /ˈ·· ˌ/ *n* [C] the seed of a tropical tree that is used to make coffee 咖啡豆

coffee break /ˈ·· ˌ/ *n* [C] a short time when you stop working to have a cup of coffee; TEA BREAK〔工作间隙喝咖啡的〕休息时间

cof·fee·cake /ˈkɔfɪˌkek; ˈkɒfikeɪk/ *n* [C,U] **1** *AmE* a sweet heavy cake usually eaten with a cup of coffee【美】咖啡蛋糕〔喝咖啡时吃的一种甜糕点〕**2** *BrE* a cake tasting of coffee【英】咖啡味的糕点

coffee grind·er /ˈ·· ˌ·ˌ/ *n* [C] a small machine that crushes coffee beans 咖啡豆研磨机

coffee house /ˈ·· ˌ/ *n* [C] a restaurant that serves coffee, cakes etc 咖啡馆

coffee ma·chine /ˈ·· ·ˌ·/ *n* [C] a machine that gives you a cup of coffee, tea etc, when you put money in it〔饮料〕自动售卖机

cof·fee·mak·er /ˈkɔfɪˌmekɚ; ˈkɒfiˌmeɪkə/ *n* [C] an electric machine that makes a pot of coffee 煮咖啡器,咖啡壶

coffee mill /ˈ·· ˌ/ *n* [C] a COFFEE GRINDER 咖啡豆研磨机

coffee morn·ing /ˈ·· ˌ·ˌ/ *n* [C] *BrE* a social occasion when a group of people meet to talk and drink coffee, and usually give money to help a church or another organization【英】〔通常为募捐而举行的〕咖啡早茶会

coffee pot /ˈ·· ˌ/ *n* [C] a container from which coffee is served 咖啡壶

coffee shop /ˈ·· ˌ/ *n* [C] **1** *AmE* a restaurant that serves cheap meals【美】小吃部 **2** *BrE* a place in a large shop or a hotel that serves meals and non-alcoholic drinks【英】〔大型商店或旅馆供应餐点、饮料的〕咖啡厅

coffee ta·ble /ˈ·· ˌ·ˌ/ *n* [C] **1** a low table on which you put cups, newspapers etc 茶几,矮茶几,咖啡桌 **2 coffee table book** a large expensive book that usually has a lot of pictures in it and is meant to be looked at rather than read〔装潢精美而内容空洞的〕大开本精装图书[画册]

cof·fer /ˈkɔfɚ; ˈkɒfə/ *n* [C] **1 coffers** the money that an organization, government, etc, has available to spend 资金: *What happened to the money put into the union coffers three years ago?* 三年前注入工会资金的那笔钱哪里去了? **2** a large strong box often decorated with jewels, silver, gold etc, and used to hold valuable or religious objects 珠宝盒,珠宝箱;保险箱 **3** a cofferdam 围堰;潜水箱;沉箱

cof·fer·dam /ˈkɔfɚˌdæm; ˈkɒfədæm/ *n* [C] a large box filled with air that allows people to work under water 围堰,〔用于水下工作的〕潜水箱;沉箱

cof·fin /ˈkɔfɪn; ˈkɒfɪn/ *n* [C] a long box in which a dead person is buried or burnt 棺材,灵柩; CASKET *AmE*【美】—see also 另见 **a nail in sb's/sth's coffin** (NAIL[1] (3))

cog /kɑg; kɒg/ *n* [C] **1** a wheel with small bits sticking out around the edge, that fit together with the bits of another wheel as they turn around in a machine 齿轮 **2** one of the small bits that stick out on a cog 嵌齿;轮齿 **3 a cog in the machine/wheel** someone who is not important or powerful, who only has a small job or part in a large business or organization 无足轻重的人物,小人物

cog 齿轮

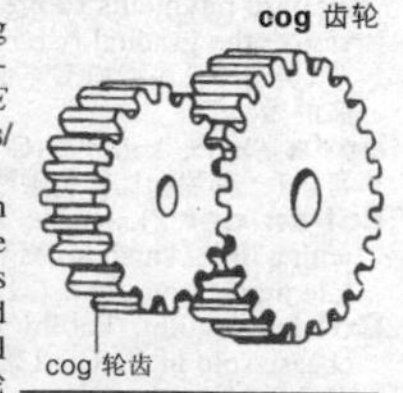

co·gent /ˈkodʒənt; ˈkəʊdʒənt/ *adj formal* something such as an argument that is cogent is reasonable, so that people are persuaded that it is correct【正式】令人信服的,有说服力的: **cogent argument/ reasons/answers etc** *Professor Calder presented a cogent examination of the facts.* 考尔德教授做了一个令人信服的测试,证明了这些事实。—**cogently** *adv* —**cogency** *n*

cog·i·tate /ˈkɑdʒəˌtet; ˈkɒdʒɪteɪt/ *v* [I+about/on] *formal* to think carefully and seriously about something【正式】仔细考虑 —**cogitation** /ˌkɑdʒəˈteʃən; ˌkɒdʒɪˈteɪʃən/ *n* [U]

co·gnac /ˈkonjæk; ˈkɒnjæk/ *n* [C,U] a kind of BRANDY (=strong alcoholic drink) made in France, or a glass of this drink〔法国〕干邑白兰地(酒);一杯干邑白兰地(酒)

cog·nate[1] /ˈkɑgnet; ˈkɒgneɪt/ *adj* cognate words or languages have the same origin〔词语、语言〕同源的

cognate[2] *n* [C] a word in one language that has the same origin as a word in another language 同源词: *The German 'hund' is a cognate of the English 'hound'.* 德语"hund"是英语"hound"的同源词。

cog·ni·tion /kɑgˈnɪʃən; kɒgˈnɪʃən/ *n* [U] **1** *formal* understanding【正式】理解,领悟 **2** *technical* the process by which you see or hear something, recognize it, and understand it【术语】认识,认知: *the regions of the brain that are responsible for memory and cognition* 大脑主管记忆与认知的区域

cog·ni·tive /ˈkɑgnətɪv; ˈkɒgnɪtɪv/ *adj formal or technical* related to the process of knowing, understanding, and learning something【正式或术语】认知的,认知过程的: *cognitive psychology* 认知心理学 —**cognitively** *adv*

cog·ni·zance also 又作 **cognisance** *BrE*【英】/ˈkɑgnəzəns; ˈkɒgnɪzəns/ *n* [U] *formal*【正式】**1** knowledge or understanding of something 知道,认识 **2 take cognizance of** to understand something and consider it when you take action or make a decision 注意到;承认

cog·ni·zant also 又作 **cognisant** *BrE*【英】/ˈkɑgnɪzənt; ˈkɒgnɪzənt/ *adj* [not before noun 不用于名词前] having knowledge or information about something; AWARE 知道的,认识到的,了解的: *Colby was cognizant of these goals, but was unmoved by them.* 科尔比注意到了这些目标,但却不为所动。

cog·no·men /kɑgˈnomən; kɒgˈnəʊmən/ *n* [C] **1** *formal* a name used instead of someone's real name, or a description added to someone's name, for example 'the Great' in 'Alexander the Great'【正式】绰号,外号 **2** *technical* a SURNAME (=last name or family name), especially in ancient Rome【术语】〔尤指古罗马人的〕姓氏

co·gno·scen·ti /ˌkɑnjoˈʃɛnti; ˌkɒnjəʊˈʃentiː/ *n* **the cognoscenti** people who have special knowledge about a particular subject, especially art, literature, or food〔尤指艺术、文学、食品等方面的〕行家,鉴赏家

cog·wheel /ˈkɑgˌhwil; ˈkɒgwiːl/ *n* [C] a COG (1) 齿轮

co·hab·it /ˌkoˈhæbɪt; ˌkəʊˈhæbɪt/ *v* [I] *formal* to live with another person as though you were married【正式】〔男女〕同居 —**cohabitation** /ˌkohæbɪˈteʃən; kəʊˌhæbɪˈteɪʃən/ *n* [U]

Co·han /ˈkoɪn; ˈkəʊɪn/**, George M.** (1878-1942) a US actor, writer, and songwriter, who wrote several musical plays and many well-known songs, including *Give My Regards to Broadway* and *I'm a Yankee Doodle Dandy* 科汉〔(1878-1942),美国演员、作家、歌曲作家。他曾创作了好几部音乐剧和许多著名歌曲,其中包括《代我问候百老汇》和《我是美国花花公子》〕

co·here /koˈhɪr; kəʊˈhɪə/ *v* [I] *formal*【正式】**1** if the ideas or arguments in a piece of writing cohere, they are connected in a clear and reasonable way〔思想、论据等〕连贯,有条理,一致 **2** if two objects cohere, they stick together 黏着,黏合,附着

co·her·ence /koˈhɪrəns; kəʊˈhɪərəns/ also 又作 **co·her·en·cy** /-rənsɪ; -rənsi/ *n* [U] **1** a reasonable connection or relation between ideas, arguments, statements etc 连贯(性),条理(性),一致(性): *An overall theme will help to give your essay coherence.* 围绕一个主旨将使你的文章连贯紧凑。**2** if a group has coherence, its members are connected or united because they share common aims, qualities, or beliefs 凝聚(力): *A common religion ensures the coherence of the tribe.* 共同的宗教信仰确保了该部落的凝聚力。

co·her·ent /koˈhɪrənt; kəʊˈhɪərənt/ *adj* **1** if a piece of writing, set of ideas etc is coherent, it is easy to understand because the information is presented in an orderly and reasonable way 连贯的,有条理的,一致的: *Finally! A textbook that provides a coherent approach to the subject.* 终于有了一本连贯地阐述该主题的课本。**2** if someone is coherent, they are talking in a way

that is clear and easy to understand〔话语等〕条理清楚的, 易于理解的: *My head hurt so much I couldn't give a coherent answer.* 我的头伤得很重, 我回答不清楚。—**coherently** *adv*

co·he·sion /koˋhiʒən; kəʊˈhiːʒən/ *n* [U] **1** if there is cohesion among a group of people, a set of ideas etc, all the parts or members of it are connected or related in a reasonable way to form a whole 团结, 凝聚（力）: *Religious beliefs can provide cohesion in diverse societies.* 宗教信仰能够为多元的社会提供凝聚力。**2** a close relationship, based on grammar or meaning, between two parts of a sentence or a larger piece of writing〔句子、文章等的〕紧凑 —**cohesive** /-hisɪv; -hiːsɪv/ *adj* —**cohesively** *adv* —**cohesiveness** *n* [U]

co·hort /ˋkohɔrt; ˈkəʊhɔːt/ *n* [C] a word meaning a person or group of people who support a particular leader, used especially when you disapprove of them 追随者, 党羽: *Get the Mayor and his crooked cohorts out of City Hall!* 把市长和他那群狡诈的党徒赶出市政厅!

COI /ˌsi o ˋaɪ; ˌsiː əʊ ˈaɪ/ the abbreviation of 缩写= CENTRAL OFFICE OF INFORMATION

coif·fure /kwaˋfjʊr; kwɒˈfjʊə/ *n* [C] *formal* the way someone's hair is arranged; HAIRDO【正式】发型, 发式 —**coiffured** *adj*

coil¹ /kɔɪl; kɔɪl/ *v* [I,T] to wind or twist into a series of rings, or to make something do this; SPIRAL³ (1) （使）卷缠; （使）盘绕: *snakes coiled in the grass* 盘在草丛中的蛇 | **coil sth** *Please coil the cords neatly before you put them away.* 请你把那些细绳卷好后放在一边。—**coiled** *adj*

coil² *n* [C] **1** a continuous series of circular rings into which something such as wire or rope has been wound or twisted （一）卷, （一）圈, （一）匝: **[+of]** *Coils of barbed wire were stretched around the compound.* 院子四周围着一圈圈带倒刺的铁丝。**2** a wire or a metal tube in a continuous circular shape that produces light or heat when electricity is passed through it〔电路的〕线圈; 绕组: *the coil in a light bulb* 灯丝 **3** the part of a car engine that sends electricity to the SPARK PLUGS〔汽车发动机的〕盘管 —see picture at 参见 ENGINE 图 **4** a CONTRACEPTIVE that is a flat curved piece of metal or plastic that is fitted inside a woman's UTERUS; IUD〔子宫〕避孕环

coin¹ /kɔɪn; kɔɪn/ *n* **1** [C] a piece of metal, usually flat and round, that is used as money 硬币 —compare 比较 BILL¹ (3), NOTE¹ (5) **2 toss/flip a coin** to choose or decide something by throwing a coin into the air and guessing which side of it will show when it falls 抛硬币决定〔某事〕: *Let's toss a coin to see who goes first.* 让我们抛硬币决定谁先去。**3 the other side of the coin** a different or opposite way of thinking about something 事情的另一面: *Children should learn to respect the police, but the other side of the coin is that the police should earn that respect.* 孩子们应该学会尊重警察, 但反过来, 警察也必须以行动赢得这种尊敬。**4 two sides of the same coin** two problems or situations that are so closely connected that they are really just two parts of the same thing 同一事情密切相关的两个方面: *You can't cure poverty without also doing something about improving education; they're two sides of the same coin.* 不提高教育水平就无法根治贫困, 它们是密切相关的两个方面。**5** [U] money in the form of metal coins 钱币, 硬币 **6 pay sb back in their own coin** *BrE old-fashioned* to treat someone in the same unpleasant way as they have treated you【英, 过时】以其人之道还治其人之身, 以牙还牙

coin² *v* [T] **1** to invent a new word or expression, especially one that many people start to use 创造, 杜撰〔新字等〕: *The term 'Information Highway' was coined a few years ago.* "信息高速公路"这个术语是几年前造出来的。**2 to coin a phrase** *spoken* used as a joke when you have just said something so familiar and ordinary that it is funny【口】套句老话说, 常言说得好: *"Alone at last," he said, "to coin a phrase!"* 他说:"套句老话, 最后还是独身一人。" **3 coin money/coin it** *BrE spoken* to earn a lot of money very quickly【英口】大发其财, 暴富: *That new restaurant on the corner must be coining it.* 街角那家新开的餐馆一定财源滚滚。**4** to make pieces of money from metal 铸〔币〕

coin·age /ˋkɔɪnɪdʒ; ˈkɔɪnɪdʒ/ *n* **1** [U] the system of money used in a country〔一国的〕货币制度: *Britain did not use decimal coinage until 1971.* 英国直到1971年才使用十进位币制。**2** [C] a word or phrase that has been recently invented 新造的词汇[短语]: *The phrase 'glass ceiling' is a fairly recent coinage.* "玻璃天花板"是最近新出现的一个词。**3** [U] the use of new words or phrases 新词[短语]的使用 **4** [U] the making of coins 铸币, 造币

co·in·cide /ˌkoɪnˋsaɪd; ˌkəʊɪnˈsaɪd/ *v* [I] **1** to happen at the same time as something else, especially by chance; CONCUR (2) 巧合; 同时发生: *Suspects are interviewed in separate rooms to see if their stories coincide.* 嫌疑犯被放在不同房间询问口供, 看看他们的说法是否吻合。| **[+with]** *The Suez crisis happened to coincide with the uprising in Hungary.* 苏伊士运河危机碰巧发生在匈牙利内乱时期。| **be planned/timed/arranged to coincide** *The Queen's visit has been planned to coincide with the school's 200th anniversary.* 女王的访问被安排在该校200周年校庆之际。**2** [not in progressive 不用进行式+**with**] if two people's ideas, opinions etc coincide, they are the same〔想法、观点等〕相符, 一致

co·in·ci·dence /koˋɪnsədəns; kəʊˈɪnsɪdəns/ *n* **1** [C,U] a surprising and unexpected situation in which two things that are connected happen at the same time, in the same place, or to the same people 巧合, 巧事; 同时发生: *What a coincidence! I didn't know you were going to be in Geneva too!* 真是碰巧! 我原本不知道你也要去日内瓦! | **by coincidence** *My mother is called Anna, and by a funny coincidence my wife's mother is also called Anna.* 我妈妈叫安娜, 有趣的是碰巧我丈母娘也叫安娜。| **be sheer/pure coincidence** (=happen completely by chance) 纯属巧合 | **not a coincidence/more than coincidence** (=used when you think something did not happen by chance) 蓄意, 非巧合 *It can't be a coincidence that four jewelry stores were robbed in one night.* 一夜之间四家珠宝店被劫, 这不可能是巧合。**2** [singular] *formal* if there is a coincidence between two ideas, opinions etc, the ideas etc are the same【正式】〔思想、观点等的〕一致, 相符: **[+of]** *a coincidence of opinion among the board members* 董事会成员的共识

co·in·ci·dent /koˋɪnsədənt; kəʊˈɪnsɪdənt/ *adj formal* existing or happening at the same place or time【正式】同时[同地]发生的; 同时[同地]存在的; 巧合的

co·in·ci·den·tal /koˌɪnsəˋdɛntl; kəʊˌɪnsɪˈdentl/ *adj* happening completely by chance without being planned 巧合的, 碰巧的: **purely/completely coincidental** *Any similarity between this film and real events is purely coincidental.* 本片与真实事件如有雷同, 纯属巧合。—**coincidentally** *adv* [sentence adverb 句子副词]: *Coincidentally, two of the men came up with similar improvements concerning pumps.* 非常凑巧, 其中两人对水泵提出了相似的改进意见。

co·in·sur·ance /ˌko·ɪnˋʃʊrəns; ˌkəʊɪnˈʃʊərəns/ *n* [U] *AmE*【美】**1** a type of insurance in which the payment is split between two people, especially between an employer and a worker 共同保险〔尤指雇主与雇员共同承担的保险〕: *health coinsurance* 健康共同保险 **2** insurance that will only pay for part of the value of something 部分保险

co·in·sure /ˌko·ɪnˋʃʊr; ˌkəʊɪnˈʃʊə/ *v* [T] *AmE* to buy or provide insurance in which the payment is split between two people, or insurance that will only pay for part of the value of something【美】购买[提供]共同[部分]保险

Coin·treau /kwanˋtro; ˈkwɒntrəʊ/ *trademark* a type of colourless French LIQUEUR (=a sweet and very strong alcoholic drink), which tastes of oranges【商标】"君度"牌利口酒〔一种法国利口酒, 无色, 带有橙味〕

coir /kɔɪr; kɔɪə/ *n* [U] the rough material that covers the shell of a COCONUT, used for making MATs, ropes etc〔用于制作垫子、绳子等的〕椰子壳的粗纤维

co·i·tus /ˋkoɪtəs; ˈkəʊɪtəs/ *n* [U] *technical* the act of having sex; SEXUAL INTERCOURSE【术语】性交 —**coital** *adj*

coke /kok; kəʊk/ *n* **1 Coke** [C,U] *trademark* the drink COCA-COLA【商标】可口可乐: *Regular fries and a large Coke, please.* 请来一客普通装炸薯条和一大杯可乐。**2** [U] *informal* COCAINE【非正式】可卡因, 古柯碱 **3** [U] a solid black substance produced from coal and burned to provide heat 焦炭, 焦煤

Col. *n* the written abbreviation for 缩写= COLONEL

col¹ /kal; kɒl/ *n* [C] a low point between two high places in a mountain range; PASS² (5) 山口, 山坳

col² the written abbreviation for 缩写= COLUMN

col- /kəl; kəl/ *prefix* the form used for CON- before l 前缀 con- 的一种形式〔用在l前面〕: *to collaborate* (=work together) 合作

COLA /ˋkolə; ˈkəʊlə/ *n* Cost of Living Adjustment; in the US, an increase to people's wages or social security and welfare payments to prevent them being affected by INFLATION (=the gradual rise in the price of goods etc) 生活费用调节〔美国给公民增加工资或社会保障与福利救济金以抵补通货膨胀的做法〕

co·la /ˋkolə; ˈkəʊlə/ *n* [C,U] a brown, sweet, CARBONATED drink 可乐〔一种甜味棕褐色碳酸饮料〕: *a can of cola* 一罐可乐

col·an·der /ˋkʌləndɚ; ˈkʌləndə/ *n* [C] a metal or plastic bowl with a lot of small holes in the bottom and sides, used to separate liquid from food〔过滤或淘洗食物用的〕滤锅, 滤器

Col·by /ˋkolbɪ; ˈkəʊlbi/ *trademark* a type of orange-coloured cheese sold in the US【商标】科尔比干酪〔在美国出售的一种橘黄色干酪〕

Col·ches·ter /ˈkoltʃɛstɚ; ˈkəʊltʃɪstə/ a town in Essex, southeast England. It was the Roman capital of Britain and claims to be the oldest town in the UK. 科尔切斯特〔英格兰东南部埃塞克斯郡一小镇。小镇曾为罗马时期英国的都城，据称是英国最古老的城镇〕

cold¹ /kold; kəʊld/ *adj*

1 ►OBJECTS/SURFACES/LIQUIDS/ROOMS ETC 物体/表面/液体/房间等◄ having a low temperature 温度低的，冷的：*a blast of cold air* 一股冷空气 | *We slept on the cold ground.* 我们睡在冰冷的地上。| **feel cold** *The office always feels so cold first thing on Monday morning.* 星期一早晨，办公室总让人觉得很冷。| **ice/stone/freezing cold** (=very cold) 非常冷，冰冷 *The radiator is stone cold; isn't the heating working?* 暖气管冰凉，是不是暖气停了？| **as cold as ice** (=very cold) 冰冷的 | **go cold** *BrE*【英】/**get cold** (=become cold) 变冷 *My tea's gone cold.* 我的茶已经凉了。| *Come and eat or your dinner will get cold!* 过来吃饭吧，再不吃就凉了！—see picture at 参见 HOT¹ 图

2 ►WEATHER 天气◄ when there is cold weather, the temperature of the air is very low〔天气〕冷的，寒冷的：*It was so cold this morning I had to scrape the ice off my windshield.* 今天早晨太冷了，我不得不把挡风玻璃上的冰刮掉。| **cold winter/evening/January etc** *the coldest winter on record* 有史以来最冷的一个冬天 | **be cold out/outside** *Put on a coat; it's cold out.* 穿上外套，外面很冷。| **get cold** (=become cold) 变冷 *The weather gets colder around the middle of October.* 十月中旬左右，天气开始转凉。| **turn cold** (=become cold or colder, especially suddenly)〔尤指突然〕变冷

3 ►PEOPLE 人们◄ **be/feel/look/get cold** if you are cold, your body is at a low temperature 感到冷：*Could you turn up the heater, I'm cold.* 你能把取暖器打开吗？我很冷。| **be blue with cold** (=be so cold that your skin looks slightly blue) 冻得发紫 | **as cold as ice** (=very cold) 冰凉的 *My feet are as cold as ice.* 我的脚冰凉。

4 ►LACKING FEELING 缺乏情感◄ lacking normal human feelings such as sympathy, pity, humour etc 冷漠的，冷酷的：*a cold, calculated murder* 一宗冷酷的蓄意谋杀（案）| *He's a very cold man, very aloof and arrogant.* 他是个冷漠的人，难于接近，十分傲慢。

5 ►UNFRIENDLY 不友好的◄ unfriendly and behaving as though you do not care much about other people 冷淡的，不友好的，不热情的：*Martin was really cold towards me at the party.* 那次聚会上，马丁对我十分冷淡。

6 ►FOOD EATEN COLD 冷餐食品◄ cold food is cooked but not eaten hot〔食物〕冷的，凉的：*We brought cold chicken and a bottle of wine to the picnic.* 我们带了冷鸡肉和一瓶红酒准备野餐。| *a cold buffet which the guests helped themselves to* 客人自助的冷餐会

7 get/have cold feet *informal* to suddenly feel that you are not brave enough to do something you planned to do【非正式】临阵退缩，胆怯：*You're not getting cold feet about marrying him, are you?* 你不会在要嫁给他时打退堂鼓吧？

8 give sb the cold shoulder *informal* to deliberately ignore someone or be unfriendly to them, especially because they have upset or offended you【非正式】故意冷落某人，冷待某人

9 cold (hard) cash *AmE informal* money in the form of paper money and coins rather than cheques or CREDIT CARDS【美，非正式】现款

10 leave sb cold to not feel interested in or affected by something in any way 未打动某人，未引起…的兴趣：*Opera just leaves me cold – I can't understand why people like it.* 我对歌剧没什么兴趣——我不明白为什么人们喜欢它。

11 cold shower a SHOWER¹ (2) without any hot water 冷水淋浴：**take a cold shower** (=used to tell someone to stop feeling sexually excited) 不要性冲动

12 ►TRAIL/SCENT 痕迹/气味◄ if someone's trail or scent is cold, you cannot find out which way they have gone because it has been a long time since they passed a particular place〔痕迹、气味等〕已变淡的：*We had the dogs after him, but the trail had gone cold.* 我们已经派出猎犬追踪他，但他留下的气味已经很淡了。

13 ►GAME 游戏◄ [never before noun 从不用于名词前] used in a children's game, to say that someone is far away from the hidden object they are trying to find〔儿童游戏中〕远离隐藏物的；远未猜中的：*You're getting colder!* 你猜得越来越离谱了！

14 ►LIGHT/COLOUR 光线/颜色◄ a cold colour or light reminds you of things that are cold〔色、光等〕给人冷淡感的，冷的：*The moon shone with a cold, clear light.* 月亮发出清冷的光。| **in the cold light of day** (=in the morning, when you see things clearly) 在清晨 *In the cold light of day, we wondered whether we'd made the right decision.* 天大亮后，我们怀疑自己作出的决定是否正确。

15 cold steel *literary* a weapon such as a knife or sword【文】〔刀、剑等〕利器 —see also 另见 **in cold blood** (BLOOD¹ (3)), **cold fish** (FISH¹ (8)), **blow hot and cold** (BLOW¹ (15)), **cold comfort** (COMFORT¹ (7)), **pour cold water over/on** (POUR (7)), **a cold sweat** (SWEAT² (3)) —**coldly** *adv* —**coldness** *n* [U]

USAGE NOTE 用法说明：COLD

WORD CHOICE 词语辨析：**cold, cool, hot, warm, chilly, freezing, boiling, baking, heated**

Cold means at a lower temperature than **cool**, often one that is not comfortable. **Cool** often suggests a pleasantly low temperature. cold 的寒冷程度高于cool，常指令人不适的寒冷。cool 则指使人舒服的凉爽感：*I hate cold weather.* 我讨厌冷天气。| *It's lovely and cool in here.* 这儿的天气凉爽宜人。

In the same way, **hot** suggests a higher temperature than **warm**, or a temperature which would not be comfortable for a long period. **Warm** often suggests a pleasantly high temperature. 同样，hot 所指的温度高于 warm，常指令人不舒服的持续高温。warm 则指令人愉悦的暖和感：*The handle is too hot to touch.* 那个手柄热得没法碰。| *I could lie in a warm bath for hours.* 我可以在温水中泡上几个小时。

When talking of **cold** air or weather people often say it is **chilly** or, if it is very cold, **freezing** or **bitterly cold**. Very **hot** weather is **boiling** or **baking**. Cold weather may be called **the cold**. 人们谈论寒冷的空气或天气通常会说 chilly，如果十分寒冷，则用 freezing 或bitterly cold。非常炎热的天气用 boiling 或 baking。冷天气可称为 the cold：*My feet were purple with the cold* (=because of the cold, NOT 不用 *purple because of cold*). 我的脚冻得发紫了。| *I don't like the cold* (NOT 不用 *I don't like cold*). 我不喜欢冷天。

A cold is an illness. a cold 指感冒：*My nose runs when I have a cold* (NOT 不用 *have cold*). 我感冒时流鼻涕。| *I've caught a cold from my husband* (NOT 不用 *caught cold*). 我从丈夫那染的感冒。Compare 比较：*I got cold waiting for the bus without a coat* (=felt cold, not the same as ...*got a cold* = caught the illness). 等公共汽车时，我没有穿外套，觉得很冷。

When talking about people's character or behaviour, **cold** usually means lacking any emotion or friendly feelings. 描述人的性格或行为时，cold 通常指冷漠或不友好：*a cold start* 一个冷淡的开端 | *His manner towards her was very cold.* 他对她的态度极为冷漠。**Cool** can mean less friendly, enthusiastic etc than usual. cool 则指没有平常那么友好或热情：*When Bill arrived, more than an hour later, he got a rather cool reception.* 比尔一个多小时后赶到，受到了冷淡的接待。**Cool** can also mean calm and not getting excited or showing your emotions. cool 亦指冷静的、平静的：*a cool head in a crisis* 危机时刻冷静的头脑。**Warm** often means friendly and welcoming. warm 则指友好的、好客的：*a warm smile* 友好的微笑

Heated arguments, discussions etc are ones in which people disagree and get angry. 用 heated 形容争论、讨论等，指气氛激烈。

cold² *n* **1** [U] **the cold** a very low temperature outside 冷，寒冷：*Don't go out in the cold without your coat!* 外面天气很冷，穿上外套再出去吧！**2** [C] a slight illness that makes it difficult to breathe through your nose and makes your throat hurt 感冒，伤风：*I've got a bad cold.* 我得了重感冒。| **catch a cold** (=become ill) 得感冒 *Keep your feet dry so you don't catch a cold.* 双脚保持干燥，就不会感冒。| **catch your death of cold** (=used to warn someone that they may become very ill if they do not keep themselves warm in cold weather) 得重感冒 —see also 另见 COMMON COLD **3 come in from the cold** to become accepted or recognized, especially by a powerful group of people 被〔团体〕承认[接纳] **4 leave sb out in the cold** *informal* to not include someone in an activity【非正式】把某人排挤在〔集体活动〕之外，不理睬某人：*If you don't start working harder, you'll be left out in the cold when it comes time for promotion.* 如果你不开始努力工作，晋升时就没你的份。

cold³ *adv* **1** *AmE* suddenly and completely【美】完全地，彻底地；突然地，贸然地：*Then Paul stopped cold. "What was that noise?"* 保罗突然停下来问道："那是什么声音？" **2 out cold** unconscious, especially because you have been hit on the head

〔尤指头被击打后〕不清醒地:**knock sb (out) cold** (=hit someone so that they become unconscious) 将某人打晕 **3** without preparation 无准备地: *I can't just get up there and make a speech cold!* 我无法毫无准备就上去演讲!

cold-blood·ed /ˌ·ˈ··◂/ *adj* **1** a cold-blooded animal, such as a snake, has a body temperature that changes with the temperature of the air or ground around it 〔动物〕冷血的〈如蛇〉 —compare 比较 WARM-BLOODED **2 cold-blooded killer/murder/violence etc** a person or their actions that show they feel no pity and do not care if other people suffer 无情的[残酷的]杀手/谋杀犯/暴行等—**cold-bloodedly** *adv*—**cold-bloodedness** *n* [U]

cold call /ˌ·ˈ·/ *n* [C] if someone who is selling something makes a cold call, they telephone someone they have never met and try to sell something 〔无事先接触而打给潜在主顾的〕冷不防电话

C

Cold Com·fort Farm /ˌ···ˈ·/ a humorous NOVEL by Stella Gibbons about a farm in southern England, where the owners and workers are all crazy or very strange《令人难以宽慰的农庄》〔斯特拉·吉本斯创作的一部幽默小说。小说描写英格兰南部一个农庄, 农庄的主人和雇工不是疯狂不已, 就是稀奇古怪〕

cold cream /ˈ··/ *n* [U] a thick, white, sweet-smelling, oily cream used for cleaning your face and making it softer 冷霜, 润肤膏

cold cuts /ˈ··/ *n* [plural] *especially AmE* thinly cut pieces of various types of cold cooked meat【尤美】什锦肉片冷盘

cold-heart·ed /ˌ·ˈ··◂/ *adj* behaving in a way that shows no pity or sympathy 铁石心肠的, 冷酷无情的—**cold-heartedly** *adv* —**cold-heartedness** *n* [U]

Col·ditz /ˈkoldɪts; ˈkəʊldɪts/ a castle in Germany in which prisoners-of-war were kept during World War II. Colditz was famous because it was very difficult to escape from. 科尔迪茨堡〔德国一城堡。二战期间曾用于关押战俘, 以看管十分严密而闻名〕

cold snap /ˈ··/ *n* [C] a sudden short period of extremely cold weather 寒汛(期), 冷汛(期); 乍冷, 骤冷

cold sore /ˈ··/ *n* [C] a painful spot on your lips or inside your mouth that you may get when you are ill with a cold 〔伤风、感冒时出现的〕唇疮疹, 嘴边疮疹

cold spell /ˈ··/ *n* [C] a period of several days or weeks when the weather is much colder than usual 寒潮期

cold stor·age /ˌ·ˈ··/ *n* [U] **1** if you keep something such as food in cold storage, you keep it in a cold place so that it will stay fresh and in good condition 冷藏 **2 put/go/be in cold storage** to not take action on a plan or idea until later in the future 把〔计划或主意〕搁置起来: *We'll have to put the project into cold storage until we can get the funding.* 我们将不得不搁置这项工程, 直到得到所需资金。

cold store /ˈ··/ *n* [C] a very cold room that is kept cold by a machine and used to store food, fur coats etc to keep them fresh or in good condition〔存放食品、动物毛皮等的〕冷藏库

Cold·stream Guards, the /ˌkoldstrɪm ˈgardz; ˌkəʊldstriːm ˈgɑːdz/ a famous REGIMENT (=a large group of soldiers) in the British army, formed in about 1660 科尔德斯特里姆警卫军团〔英国一著名军团, 建于1660年前后〕

cold sweat /ˌ·ˈ·/ *n* [singular] a reaction by your body when you are nervous or afraid, in which you SWEAT[1] (1) but still feel cold 冷汗: *The thought of the trial made him break out in a cold sweat.* 一想到审判, 他就浑身冒冷汗。

cold tur·key /ˌ·ˈ··/ *n* [U] **go cold turkey** to suddenly stop taking a drug you are addicted to and to experience a sort of illness because of it 突然停止服用毒品而感到不舒适: *Marcia went cold turkey off heroin.* 马西娅突然戒了海洛因。

cold war /ˌ·ˈ·◂/ *n* [singular,U] an unfriendly political relationship between two countries who do not actually fight each other 冷战

Cold War, the the political struggle between the US and the Soviet Union, which began after World War II and went on until the 1990s 冷战〔美国和苏联之间的政治斗争。冷战始于二战之后, 终于20世纪90年代〕

Cole /kol; kəʊl/, **Nat King** /næt kɪŋ; næt kɪŋ/ (1917-65) a US singer famous for his soft, smooth voice, and for his recordings of love songs such as *When I Fall in Love*, *Unforgettable*, and *Mona Lisa* 科尔〔(1917-1965), 美国歌手。他以轻柔圆润的嗓音和录制的爱情歌曲《当我坠入爱河》、《难以忘怀》、《蒙娜丽莎》等闻名〕

Cole, Old King —see 见 OLD KING COLE

Co·le·ridge /ˈkolərɪdʒ; ˈkəʊlərɪdʒ/, **Sam·u·el Tay·lor** /ˈsæmjuəl ˈtelɚ; ˈsæmjuəl ˈteɪlə/ (1772-1834) a British poet who wrote *The Rime of the Ancient Mariner* and *Kubla Khan*. He and his friend William Wordsworth were leaders of the Romantic movement in Britain. 科尔律治〔(1772-1834), 英国诗人。创作的作品有《古舟子咏》和《忽必烈汗》。他和他的朋友威廉·华兹华斯是英国浪漫主义运动的领袖〕

cole·slaw /ˈkolˌslɔ; ˈkəʊlslɔː/ *n* [U] a SALAD made with thinly cut raw CABBAGE (1) 凉拌卷心菜丝

Col·ette /koˈlɛt; kɒˈlet/ (1873-1954) a French writer who was famous for her NOVELS *Chéri* and *Gigi* 科莱特〔(1873-1954), 法国作家, 以小说《亲爱的》和《吉吉》而出名〕

co·ley /ˈkolɪ; ˈkəʊli/ *n* [C,U] a large North Atlantic sea fish or the flesh of this fish eaten as food 绿青鳕鱼(肉)

col·ic /ˈkalɪk; ˈkɒlɪk/ *n* [U] if a baby suffers from colic, it has severe pain in its stomach and BOWELS (1) 胃绞痛, 急性腹痛—**colicky** *adj*

Col·i·se·um /ˌkalɪˈsiəm; ˌkɒlɪˈsiːəm/ —see 见 COLOSSEUM

co·li·tis /kəˈlaɪtɪs; kəˈlaɪtɪs/ *n* [U] *technical* an illness in which part of your COLON (2) swells, causing pain【术语】结肠炎

col·lab·o·rate /kəˈlæbəˌret; kəˈlæbəreɪt/ *v* [I] **1** to work together with someone in order to achieve something, especially in science or art〔尤指在科学、艺术等方面〕合作, 协作: [**+on/with**] *He was one of the scientists who collaborated with Oppenheimer on the atomic bomb.* 他是与奥本海默一起从事原子弹研究的科学家之一。| **collaborate to do sth** *The gallery and the university collaborated to mount an exhibition of rare drawings.* 该画廊与那所大学合作举办了一次珍品画展。| **collaborate in doing sth** *Watson and Crick collaborated in discovering the structure of DNA.* 沃森和克里克合作致力于揭示DNA的结构。**2** [**+with**] to be disloyal to your country by helping an enemy army or government that has taken control of your country 通敌, 与〔占领者〕合作

col·lab·o·ra·tion /kəˌlæbəˈreʃən; kəˌlæbəˈreɪʃən/ *n* [U] **1** [**+between/with**] the act of working together with another person or group to achieve something, especially in science or art〔尤指在科学、艺术等方面的〕合作, 协作; **in collaboration with** *The company is building the centre in collaboration with the Institute of Offshore Engineering.* 该公司正与海洋工程学院合建这座中心。**2** [**+with**] help given to an enemy army or government that has taken control of your country〔与敌人或占领者〕勾结, 通敌

col·lab·o·ra·tive /kəˈlæbəretɪv; kəˈlæbərətɪv/ *adj* [only before noun 仅用于名词前] **collaborative effort/work/project etc** involving two or more people working together to achieve something 合力/合作/协作项目等

col·lab·o·rat·or /kəˈlæbəretɚ; kəˈlæbəreɪtə/ *n* [C] **1** someone who helps their country's enemies, for example by giving them information, when the enemy has taken control of their country 通敌者,〔与占领者〕勾结者: *Their job was to identify enemy collaborators.* 他们的工作是找出通敌者。**2** someone who works with other people in order to achieve something, especially in science or art〔尤指在科学、艺术等方面的〕合作者, 协作者: *collaborators on a biography of Dickens* 协作出版狄更斯传记的工作人员

col·lage /kəˈlaʒ; ˈkɒlɑːʒ/ *n* **1** [C] a picture made by sticking other pictures, photographs, cloth etc onto a surface〔把画片、照片、布块等粘贴而成的〕拼贴画 **2** [U] the art of making such pictures 拼贴艺术

col·la·gen /ˈkalədʒən; ˈkɒlədʒən/ *n* [U] a PROTEIN substance, sometimes put into women's face creams 胶原(蛋白)

col·lapse[1] /kəˈlæps; kəˈlæps/ *v* S3

1 ▶STRUCTURE 结构◀ [I] if a building, wall, piece of furniture etc collapses, it suddenly falls down because its structure is weak or because it has been hit with a sudden violent force 倒塌; 塌下: *The roof is in danger of collapsing.* 屋顶有倒塌的危险。| *Uncle Ted's chair collapsed under his weight.* 特德叔叔的椅子承受不了他的重量而垮掉了。

2 ▶FAIL 失败◀ [I] if a system, idea, or organization collapses, it suddenly fails or becomes too weak to continue〔系统、观点、组织等〕突然失败, 垮掉, 崩溃, 瓦解: *The business finally collapsed because of rising debts.* 由于债务增加, 该企业最后垮了。

3 ▶ILLNESS 疾病◀ [I] to suddenly fall down or become unconscious because you are ill〔因病〕突然倒下[昏倒]: *He collapsed with a heart attack while he was dancing.* 他跳舞时心脏病突发而倒下了。

4 ▶SIT 坐◀ to suddenly sit down, especially because you are very tired〔尤指因精疲力竭而〕突然坐倒: *I was so exhausted when I got home, I just collapsed on the sofa.* 我到家时已经筋疲力尽, 一屁股瘫坐在沙发上。

5 ▶MAKE STH SMALLER 使某物变小◀ [I,T] if a piece of furniture or equipment collapses or you collapse it, you can fold it

so that it becomes smaller〔家具、仪器等〕折叠起来; 套缩起来: *The legs on our card table collapse so we can store it in the closet.* 我们的牌桌桌腿可以折叠,我们可以把牌桌放进壁橱中。

6▶MEDICAL 医疗的◀ [I] if a lung or a BLOOD VESSEL collapses, it suddenly becomes flat, so that it no longer has any air or blood in it〔肺或血管〕突然萎陷

collapse² *n*

1▶BUSINESS/SYSTEM/IDEA ETC 业务/系统/想法等◀ [singular,U] a sudden failure in the way something works, so that it cannot continue 突然失败; 突然瓦解: *The country's economic collapse led to political chaos.* 该国的经济崩溃导致了政治动乱。

2▶BUILDING/STRUCTURE/FURNITURE ETC 建筑/结构/家具等◀ [U] the act of suddenly falling down because of a weakness in something's structure or because something has hit it violently 突然倒塌: *the collapse of an apartment building during the earthquake* 地震时一幢公寓倒塌

3▶ILLNESS 疾病◀ [singular] a sudden illness that makes you fall down or become unconscious〔因突发的疾病导致的〕昏倒, 昏迷;〔健康的〕垮掉

4▶MONEY/PRICES ETC 钱/价格等◀ [singular] a sudden decrease in the value of something〔货币、价格等的〕突然贬值, 暴跌: *the collapse of the stock market in 1987* 1987 年股市的暴跌

col·lap·si·ble /kə`læpsəbḷ; kə'læpsɪbəl/ *adj* something collapsible can be folded so that it takes less space 可折叠的; 可套缩的: *a collapsible bicycle* 可折叠式自行车

col·lar¹ /`kɑlɚ; 'kɒlə/ *n* [C]

1▶CLOTHING 衣服◀ a stiff band of material on a shirt, dress, or coat that fits around someone's neck 衣领, 领子 —see picture on page A17 参见 A17 页图

2▶CAT/DOG 猫/狗◀ a narrow band of leather or plastic that is fastened around an animal's neck〔动物脖子上的〕颈圈, 项圈

3 hot under the collar *spoken* angry or excited 生气的, 愤怒的, 激动的: *Calm down! There's no need to get all hot under the collar.* 冷静一下! 没必要这么激动。

4▶COLOURED FUR/FEATHERS 彩色毛皮/羽毛◀ a band of fur, feathers, or skin around an animal's neck that is a different colour from the rest of the fur etc〔动物颈部的〕毛色别于身体其他部分的条纹

5▶WORK ANIMAL 役畜◀ a thick leather ring put over the shoulders of a work animal to help it pull machinery or a vehicle 轭,〔马具等〕颈圈

6▶MACHINE 机器◀ a part of a machine that is shaped like a ring 箍; 垫圈; 束套; 套管

7▶POLICE 警察◀ *slang* if the police make a collar, they catch a criminal【俚】捕获, 逮捕 —see also 另见 BLUE-COLLAR, WHITE-COLLAR, DOG COLLAR

collar² *v* [T] *informal*【非正式】**1** to catch someone and hold them so that they cannot escape 抓住; 逮捕: *The police collared him before he could get out of the country.* 警察在他逃出国之前逮捕了他。**2** to find someone so that you can talk to them 找到〔某人〕谈话: *See if you can collar Tim. I need to know when he'll be ready.* 看你能不能把蒂姆找来谈谈话, 我要知道他什么时候会准备好。

col·lar·bone /`kɑlɚ`bon; 'kɒləbəʊn/ *n* [C] one of the pair of bones that go from the bottom part of your neck to your shoulders 锁骨 —see picture at 参见 SKELETON 图

col·lard greens /`kɑlɚd `grinz; ˌkɒləd 'gri:nz/ *n* a green leafy vegetable cooked and eaten as food 羽衣甘蓝〔可食用〕

collar stud /'‥ ·/ *n* [C] an object like a button, used to fasten old-fashioned collars to shirts 领扣〔把老式的领子扣在衬衣上用〕

col·late /kə`let; kə'leɪt/ *v* [T] **1** to arrange sheets of paper in the correct order before they are in a book etc〔装钉前〕检点〔印张〕, 配〔页〕; 整理〔印张等〕: *a photocopier that collates and staples* 能整理和装订书页的复印机 **2** *formal* to gather information together, examine it carefully, and compare it with other information to find any differences【正式】校对, 核对, 校勘

col·lat·e·ral¹ /kə`lætərəl; kə'lætərəl/ *n* [U] *technical* property or other goods that you promise to give someone if you cannot pay back the money they lent you; SECURITY (4)【术语】担保品, 抵押品: **put sth up as collateral** (=promise it in this way) 将某物作为抵押品

collateral² *adj formal*【正式】**1** connected with something or happening as a result of it, but not as important 附属的, 附带的, 次要的: *A collateral aim of better education is reducing unemployment.* 提高教育水平有一个附带的目标, 即减少失业。**2** collateral relatives are members of your family who are not closely related to you〔亲戚〕旁系的, 非直系的

col·la·tion /kə`leʃən; kə'leɪʃən/ *n formal*【正式】**1** [U] the examination and comparing of information 校对, 校勘 **2** [U] the arranging of sheets of paper in the correct order〔装钉前的〕配页; 整理 **3** [C] *formal* a small, usually cold meal【正式】小吃〔一般指冷食〕

col·league /`kɑlig; 'kɒli:g/ *n* [C] someone you work with, used especially by professional people or managers 同事, 同僚: *a colleague of mine at the bank* 我在银行的一位同事 S3 W2

col·lect¹ /kə`lɛkt; kə'lekt/ *v* S1 W2

1▶BRING TOGETHER 集合一起◀ [T] to get things of the same type from different places and bring them together 收集, 采集; 使集中: *Researchers spent 6 months collecting facts and figures.* 调查人员花了六个月的时间收集事实和数据。| *Could you collect some branches for a fire?* 你可以去收集一些树枝生个火吗?

2▶KEEP OBJECTS 保存物品◀ [T] to get and keep objects because you think they are attractive or interesting 收藏: *The family's been collecting modern art for thirty years.* 这个家庭收藏现代艺术品已经有三十年了。

3▶MONEY 钱◀ a) [T] to ask for or obtain money you are owed or something you have won 收〔账、债或税等〕; 获得; 领取: *He's collected his second gold medal of these Olympics.* 他已经获得了第二枚奥运金牌。**b) collect (money) for sth** to ask people to give you money for a particular purpose 为…筹款[集资]: *We're collecting for Save the Children.* 我们在为"救助儿童会"筹款。

4▶INCREASE IN AMOUNT 增加数量◀ [I,T] if something collects in a place or you collect it there, it gradually increases in amount 聚集, 增加: *Rain collected in pools on the uneven road.* 起伏不平的路上积了一摊摊的雨水。| *solar panels for collecting the sun's heat* 采集太阳热能的太阳能电池板

5▶CROWD 群◀ [I] to come together gradually to form a group of people 聚集: *A crowd was beginning to collect around the scene of the accident.* 人群开始聚集在事故现场。

6▶DUST/DIRT 尘/土◀ [T] to become covered in dust etc 积〔灰等〕: *All the furniture had collected a fine layer of dust.* 所有家具都积了薄薄的一层灰尘。

7▶TAKE SB/STH FROM A PLACE 从某处带走某人/物◀ [T] *especially BrE* to come to a particular place in order to take someone or something away【尤英】领取; 接走: *Martin's gone to collect the children from school.* 马丁已经去学校接孩子们了。

8 collect yourself/collect your thoughts etc to make an effort to remain calm and think clearly and carefully about something 使〔自己〕镇静; 集中〔思想〕: *He paused for a moment to collect himself, then pushed open the door.* 他停了停, 努力让自己镇定, 然后推开那扇门。

collect² /kə`lɛkt; kə'lekt/ *adv AmE*【美】**1 call/phone sb collect** when you telephone someone collect, the person who receives the call pays for it 打受话人付费电话 **2 collect call** a telephone call paid for by the person who receives it 由受话人付费的电话

col·lect³ /`kɑlɛkt; 'kɒlɪkt/ *n* [C] a short prayer in some Christian services〔某些基督教仪式中的〕短祷文

col·lect·a·ble /kə`lɛktəbḷ; kə'lektəbəl/ also 又作 **col·lect·i·ble** /-əbḷ; -ɪbəl/ *adj* something that is collectable is likely to be bought and kept as part of a group of similar things, especially because it might increase in value 可收集的; 适于收藏的: *Art Deco glassware is very collectable right now.* 装饰派艺术玻璃制品现在非常有收藏价值。

col·lect·ed /kə`lɛktɪd; kə'lektɪd/ *adj* **1** in control of yourself and your thoughts, feelings, etc. 镇定的, 泰然自若的 **2 collected works** all of someone's books, poems etc printed in one book or set of books〔某人的作品等〕全集

col·lect·i·ble /kə`lɛktəbḷ; kə'lektbəl/ also 又作 **collectable** *n* [C] an object that you keep as part of a group of similar things 收藏品: *Miss Kelly's house was full of collectibles, displayed on every possible surface.* 凯莉小姐的房子每个能摆东西的地方都摆满了收藏品。

col·lec·tion /kə`lɛkʃən; kə'lekʃən/ *n* S2 W1

1▶SET/GROUP 套/组◀ a) [C] a set of similar things that are kept or brought together because they are attractive or interesting〔一批〕收藏品: *a stamp collection* 一批邮票收藏品 | [+of] *a magnificent collection of prehistoric tools* 一批珍贵的史前工具收藏品 **b)** [C] a group of things that are put together〔一批〕收集的东西: *A collection of empty wine bottles stood on the back porch.*〔房子〕后面的门廊陈列着一批空酒瓶。

2▶MONEY 钱◀ a) [C] the act of asking for money from people for a particular purpose 募捐: **have a collection** *Every Christmas we have a collection and give the money to a charity.* 每个圣诞节我们都会募捐, 将所得的款项捐给慈善机构。| **take (up)**

a collection *We'll be taking up a collection at the end of tonight's service.* 我们在今晚的仪式之后将举行捐款活动。**b)** [U] the act of obtaining money that is owed to you 收账, 收债: *Resistance to the new tax is making collection difficult.* 人们拒绝缴纳新税使征税变得困难。

3 ▶TAKING STH AWAY 拿走某物◀[C,U] the act of taking something from a place, especially when this is done regularly〔尤指定期的〕收取: *Garbage collections are made every Tuesday morning.* 每星期二早上收一次垃圾。

4 ▶BRINGING TOGETHER 集合一起◀[U] the act of bringing together things of the same type from different places to form a group 收集, 采集: *the collection of reliable data* 可靠数据的收集

5 ▶CLOTHES 衣服◀[C] a number of different pieces of clothing designed by someone for a particular time of year 特定季节的时装: *the Paris spring collections* 巴黎春季时装展

6 ▶PEOPLE 人们◀[C usually singular 一般用单数] a group of people, especially people you think are strange or unusual in some way〔尤指奇特的〕一群人: *There was an interesting collection of people at the wedding.* 那次婚礼聚集了一群有趣的人。

7 ▶BOOKS/MUSIC 书/音乐◀[C] several stories, poems, pieces of music etc that are in one book or on one record〔书本、音乐的〕全集; 专辑: *a new collection of Frost's poetry* 新的弗罗斯特诗集

collection box /·'··, ·/ *n* [C] a container with a small opening in the top into which people put money for CHARITY (2) 募捐箱

collection plate /·'··, ·/ *n* [C] a large, almost flat dish in which you put money during some religious services 募捐盘

3 **col·lec·tive[1]** /kə`lɛktɪv; kə'lektɪv/ *adj* [only before noun 仅用于名词前] involving a group, or shared or made by every member of a group 集体的; 共同的; 共有的: **collective decision/responsibility etc** *a collective decision on the part of the management* 管理层的共同决定

collective[2] *n* [C] **1** a group of people who work together to run something such as a business or farm 集体企业[农庄]人员 **2** the business or farm that is run by this group 集体经营的企业[农庄]

collective bar·gain·ing /·,·· '···/ *n* [U] the discussions held between employers and a union in order to reach agreement on wages, working conditions etc〔劳资双方就工资、工作条件等进行的〕集体谈判

collective farm /·,·· '·/ *n* [C] a large farm that is owned by the government and controlled by the farm workers〔由农业工人管理的〕(国营) 集体农庄

col·lec·tive·ly /kə`lɛktɪvlɪ; kə'lektɪvli/ *adv* as a group 集体地, 共同地: *The islands, which are northwest of Australia, are collectively known as Indonesia.* 澳大利亚西北方诸岛屿统称为印度尼西亚。

collective noun /·,·· '·/ *n* [C] *technical* a noun, such as 'committee' or 'family', that is the name of people or things considered as a unit【术语】集合名词

col·lec·tiv·is·m /kə`lɛktɪv,ɪzəm; kə'lektɪvɪzəm/ *n* [U] a political system in which all businesses, farms etc are owned by the government 集体主义 (制度) —**collectivize** *v* [T] —**collectivist** *n*

col·lec·tor /kə`lɛktɚ; kə'lektə/ *n* [C] **1** someone whose job is to collect taxes, tickets, debts etc 收税人; 收票员; 收款人 **2** someone who collects things that are interesting or attractive 收集者; 收藏家: *a coin collector* 钱币收藏家 **3 collector's item** something that a collector would like to have 值得收藏的东西; 可收藏的东西: *Original teddy bears have become real collectors' items.* 第一批泰迪熊已经成为值得收藏的东西。

1 2 **col·lege** /`kɑlɪdʒ; 'kɒlɪdʒ/ *n*

1 ▶ADVANCED EDUCATION 高级教育◀[C,U] **a)** *especially BrE* a school for advanced education, especially in a particular subject or skill【尤英】学院; 技术专科学校: *a teacher training college* 师范学院 —see also 另见 SIXTH FORM COLLEGE **b)** *AmE* a school for advanced education where you can get a BACHELOR'S DEGREE【美】大学,〔大学的〕本科部: *Which colleges have you applied to?* 你申请了哪些大学? | **college campus/class/graduate etc** *Many firms will only hire college graduates.* 许多公司将只雇用本科毕业生。| **go to college** (=attend a college or university) 上大学 —see also 另见 JUNIOR COLLEGE —compare 比较 UNIVERSITY

2 ▶PART OF UNIVERSITY 大学的部分◀[C] one of the groups of teachers and students that form a separate part of some universities, especially in Britain〔尤指在英国附属于大学的〕学院: *Trinity College, Cambridge* 剑桥大学三一学院

3 ▶BUILDINGS 建筑物◀[C] the buildings used by any of these organizations 学院[学校] (的建筑物)

4 ▶STUDENTS AND TEACHERS 师生◀[C also+plural verb *BrE* 英] the students and teachers of one of these organizations 学院的全体师生: *The whole college turned up to the memorial service.* 该学院全体师生都出席了纪念仪式。

5 ▶ORGANIZATION 组织◀[C] a group of people who have special rights and duties within a profession or organization 学会, 协会, 社团: *the Royal College of Nursing* 皇家护理学会 —see also 另见 ELECTORAL COLLEGE

6 ▶SCHOOL 学校◀[C] *BrE* a word used in the name of some large schools, especially PUBLIC SCHOOLS【英】公学, 书院;〔规模大的〕中学

college boards /, ·· '·/ *n* [plural] a set of examinations that students in the US must take in order to enter a college or university〔美〕大学入学考试

col·le·gi·ate /kə`lidʒɪt; kə'li:dʒiət/ *adj* **1** involving or related to a college 大学的; 学院的: *inter-collegiate competition* 大学之间的竞争 **2** organized into colleges 由学院组成的: *a collegiate university* 由学院组成的大学

col·lide /kə`laɪd; kə'laɪd/ *v* [I] **1** to hit something or someone that is moving in a different direction from you 碰撞; 相撞: *Two supertankers collided in the rough seas.* 两艘超级油轮在波涛汹涌的海面上相撞。| **[+with]** *Donna swerved to avoid colliding with a taxi.* 唐娜猛然转变方向, 以免和一辆出租车相撞。**2** to have an argument with a person or group, especially on a particular subject 冲突, 抵触: **[+with]** *The President has again collided with Congress over his budget plans.* 总统在预算计划上又一次与国会发生冲突。

col·lie /`kalɪ; 'kɒli/ *n* [C] a middle sized dog with long hair, kept as a pet or trained to look after sheep 柯利牧羊犬 —see picture at 参见 DOG[1] 图

col·li·er /`kaljɚ; 'kɒliə/ *n* [C] *BrE*【英】**1** *formal* someone whose job is to cut coal in a mine; MINER【正式】煤矿工人 **2** a ship that carries coal 运煤船

col·lie·ry /`kaljərɪ; 'kɒljəri/ *n* [C] *BrE* a COAL MINE and the buildings and machinery connected with it【英】〔包括地面建筑和设备等在内的〕煤矿

Col·lins /`kalɪnz; 'kɒlɪnz/, **Mi·chael[1]** (1890-1922) an Irish politician and military leader who was involved in the fight to make Ireland independent of the UK. He helped to achieve the agreement that established the southern part of Ireland as an independent state, but he was killed by political opponents who wanted independence for the whole of Ireland. 科林斯〔(1890-1922), 爱尔兰政治家、军事首脑。他曾参加过爱尔兰独立战争, 促成了一项使爱尔兰南部实现独立的协议, 最后却遭到希望整个爱尔兰独立的政敌杀害〕

Collins, Michael[2] (1930-) a US ASTRONAUT who was one of the three-man team involved in the first landing on the moon in 1969. Collins stayed in the main SPACECRAFT, Apollo 11, while his companions Neil Armstrong and Edwin 'Buzz' Aldrin landed on the moon. 科林斯〔(1930-), 美国宇航员, 1969 年实现人类首次登月的三位宇航员之一。他在主太空飞船阿波罗 11 号中守候, 其同伴尼尔·阿姆斯特朗和艾德温·奥尔德林登上了月球〕

Collins, Wil·kie /`wɪlkɪ; 'wɪlki/ (1824-89) a British writer who wrote *The Moonstone*, the first DETECTIVE NOVEL in English, and *The Woman in White* 科林斯〔(1824-1889), 英国作家。著有第一部用英语写的侦探小说《月亮宝石》和另一部小说《白衣女人》〕

col·li·sion /kə`lɪʒən; kə'lɪʒən/ *n* [C,U] **1** an accident in which two or more people or vehicles hit each other while moving in different directions 碰撞 (事件): **[+with]** *The school bus was involved in a collision with a truck.* 这辆校车与一辆货车相撞。| **head-on collision** (=between two vehicles moving directly towards each other)〔车辆〕迎头相撞 **2 [+between]** a strong disagreement between two people or groups 冲突, 抵触 **3 be on a collision course a)** to behave in a way that will cause a serious disagreement or even a war 势将发生冲突: *Environmentalists and loggers are on a collision course, with no compromise in sight.* 环保主义者与伐木工人势将发生冲突, 看来没有任何妥协的余地。**b)** to be moving in a direction in which you will hit another person or vehicle 将会发生碰撞

col·lo·cate /`kalo,ket; 'kɒləkeɪt/ *v* [I+with] *technical* when words collocate, they are often used together and sound natural together【术语】〔词语的〕组合, 连用, 搭配 —**collocate** /`kaləkət; 'kɒləkət/ *n* [C]

col·lo·ca·tion /,kalo`keʃən; ,kɒlə'keɪʃən/ *n* [U] *technical* [C,U] the way in which some words are often used together,

or a particular combination of words used in this way【术语】〔词语等习惯上的〕组合, 搭配; 连用: *"Commit a crime" is a typical collocation in English.* commit a crime 是英语中一个典型的搭配。

col·loid /ˈkɑlɔɪd; ˈkɒlɔɪd/ *n* [C] *technical* a mixture of substances in which one substance is completely mixed with another but not DISSOLVED【术语】胶体; 胶质; 胶态 —compare 比较 SUSPENSION (4)

col·lo·qui·al /kəˈlokwɪəl; kəˈləʊkwiəl/ *adj* language or words that are colloquial are used mainly in conversation rather than in writing or formal speech 口语的, 会话的 —**colloquially** *adv*

col·lo·qui·al·is·m /kəˈlokwɪəlˌɪzəm; kəˈləʊkwiəlɪzəm/ *n* [C] an expression or word used mainly in conversation 口语体, 会话体, 口语用词

col·lo·quy /ˈkɑləkwɪ; ˈkɒləkwi/ *n* [C] *formal* a conversation【正式】会话, 谈话 —compare 比较 SOLILOQUY

col·lude /kəˈlud; kəˈluːd/ *v* [I] *formal* to work with someone secretly, especially in order to cheat or deceive other people【正式】共谋, 勾结, 串通: [**+with**] *He was accused of colluding with the occupying forces.* 他被控与占领军勾结。

col·lu·sion /kəˈluʒən; kəˈluːʒən/ *n* [U] *formal or law* a secret agreement that two or more people make in order to do something dishonest【正式或法律】共谋, 勾结, 串通

col·ly·wob·bles /ˈkɑlɪˌwɑblz; ˈkɒliˌwɒbəlz/ *n* **the collywobbles** *BrE informal* an uncomfortable feeling that you get when you are very nervous【英, 非正式】紧张感, 焦虑感

Co·logne /kəˈlon; kəˈləʊn/ a city in northern Germany on the River Rhine. It is a port and an industrial centre. Its German name is Köln. 科隆〔德国北部一城市、港口和工业中心, 濒临莱茵河。德语名为 Köln〕

co·logne *n* [U] a liquid that smells slightly of flowers or plants that you put on your neck or wrists 古龙香水, 科隆香水 —compare 比较 PERFUME[1] (1)

Co·lom·bi·a /kəˈlʌmbɪə; kəˈlɒmbiə/ a country in northern South America, with coasts on both the Pacific Ocean and the Caribbean Sea. Population: 40,349,000 (2001). Capital: Bogotá. 哥伦比亚〔南美洲北部一国家, 濒临太平洋和加勒比海。人口: 40,349,000 (2001), 首都: 波哥大〕—**Colombian** *n, adj*

Co·lom·bo /kəˈlʌmbo; kəˈlʌmbəʊ/ the capital city and main port of Sri Lanka 科伦坡〔斯里兰卡首都和主要港口〕

co·lon /ˈkolən; ˈkəʊlən/ *n* [C] **1** the sign (:) that is used in writing and printing to introduce an explanation, example, QUOTATION (1) etc 冒号 —compare 比较 SEMICOLON —see picture at 参见 PUNCTUATION MARK 图 **2** *technical* the lower part of the BOWELs, in which food is changed into waste matter【术语】结肠 —see picture at 参见 DIGESTIVE SYSTEM 图

colo·nel /ˈkɝnl; ˈkɜːnl/ *n* [C] a high rank in the Army, Marines, or the US Air Force, or someone who has this rank〔陆军、海军陆战队或美国空军的〕上校军衔; 上校 —see table on page C6 参见 C6 页附录

Colonel Blimp /ˌ‥ ˈ‥/ *n* [C] *BrE* an old man with very old-fashioned ideas, who thinks he is important【英】老顽固, 守旧分子

Colonel Bo·gey /ˌkɝnl̩ ˈbogɪ; ˌkɜːnl ˈbəʊgi/ a well-known British military MARCH (=a piece of music with a very regular beat, written for soldiers to march to)《波吉上校》〔一首著名的英国军队进行曲〕

Colonel San·ders /ˌkɝnl̩ ˈsændɚz; ˌkɜːnl ˈsɑːndəz/ the man who developed the RECIPE for making Kentucky Fried Chicken, sold in fast food restaurants which are called KFC. His name is sometimes used to mean the product or the restaurant. 桑德斯上校〔曾研发出快餐店出售的"肯德基炸鸡"配方的人。有时, 人们借用他的名字指称肯德基产品或快餐店〕

co·lo·ni·al[1] /kəˈlonɪəl; kəˈləʊniəl/ *adj* **1** connected with or related to a country that controls and rules other countries 殖民的: *a major colonial power* 一殖民大国 **2** made in a style that was common in the US in the 18th century〔18 世纪美国〕殖民地时期制造的; 仿殖民地时期式样的: *a large colonial house* 一栋殖民时期修建的大宅子 **3** connected with the US when it was under British rule〔指美国独立前〕受英国殖民统治时期的: *an old colonial port on the coast*〔美国〕海岸边英国殖民地统治时期的旧港口 **4** *BrE* behaving in a way that shows you believe you are better than the people in the foreign country where you live【英】殖民主义的: *He still has a colonial mentality.* 他仍然怀有殖民主义的倨傲心理。—see also 另见 COLONY

colonial[2] *n* [C] someone who lives in a COLONY but who is a citizen of the country that rules the colony〔宗主国的〕殖民地居民

CULTURAL NOTE 文化注释

The STEREOTYPE of a colonial is of an UPPER-CLASS older person (if a man, with a MOUSTACHE), who has strong RIGHT-WING opinions. 殖民地居民的典型形象是一位上流社会的长者, 如果是男性, 嘴唇上还留着小胡子, 持强烈的右翼观点。

co·lo·ni·al·is·m /kəˈlonɪəlˌɪzəm; kəˈləʊniəlɪzəm/ *n* [U] the principle or practice in which a powerful country rules a weaker one and establishes its own trade and culture there 殖民主义; 殖民政策 —compare 比较 IMPERIALISM

co·lo·ni·al·ist /kəˈlonɪəlɪst; kəˈləʊniəlɪst/ *n* [C] a supporter of colonialism 殖民主义者—**colonialist** *adj*: *a savage colonialist war* 野蛮的殖民主义战争

col·o·nist /ˈkɑlənɪst; ˈkɒlənɪst/ *n* [C] someone who settles in a new colony 开拓殖民地者; 殖民者: *Dutch colonists in South America* 南美的荷兰殖民者

col·o·nize /ˈkɑləˌnaɪz; ˈkɒlənaɪz/ *v* [T] to establish political control over an area or over another country, and send your citizens there to settle 开拓〔某地〕成殖民地 —**colonization** /ˌkɑlənaɪˈzeʃən; ˌkɒlənaɪˈzeɪʃən/ *n* [U] —**colonizer** *n* [C]

col·on·nade /ˌkɑləˈned; ˌkɒləˈneɪd/ *n* [C] a row of upright stone posts that usually support a roof or row of arches 柱廊—**colonnaded** *adj*

col·o·ny /ˈkɑlənɪ; ˈkɒləni/ *n* [C] **1** a country or area that is under the political control of a more powerful country, usually one that is far away 殖民地: *Algeria was formerly a French colony.* 阿尔及利亚以前是法属殖民地。—see also 另见 CROWN COLONY, DOMINION (3), PROTECTORATE **2** a group of people who live in a colony 移民队, 殖民团 **3** one of the 13 areas of land on the east coast of North America that later became the United States〔美国独立前的〕十三个州之一: *Connecticut was one of the original colonies.* 康涅狄格是美国独立前的最初十三个州之一。**4** a particular group of people or the place where they live 聚集人群; 聚居地[区]: *an artists' colony* 一个艺术家聚居区 | *a leper colony* 一个麻风病患者聚居地 **5** a group of animals or plants of the same type that are living or growing together 群; 群体; 集群; 群落: *Breeding colonies of rare birds were threatened by the oil spill.* 溢出的石油威胁到正在繁衍的珍稀鸟类群体。

col·or /ˈkʌlɚ; ˈkʌlə/ the American spelling of COLOUR colour 的美式拼法

Col·o·ra·do /ˌkɑləˈrædo; ˌkɒləˈrɑːdəʊ◂/ abbreviation 缩写为 CO a state in the western US, mostly in and around the Rocky Mountains. Its capital city is Denver. Colorado is a popular place for both winter and summer holidays. 科罗拉多州〔美国西部一州, 大部分地区位于落基山一带。首府: 丹佛。该州是冬夏皆宜的度假胜地〕

Colorado Riv·er, the /ˌ‥‥ ˈ‥/ a long river in the western US which flows through the Grand Canyon, several US states, and into Mexico 科罗拉多河〔美国西部的一条大河, 流经大峡谷和好几个州, 然后流入墨西哥〕

col·o·ra·tion /ˌkʌləˈreʃən; ˌkʌləˈreɪʃən/ *n* [U] the way something is coloured or the pattern these colours make; COLOURING 着[配]色(法), 染色(法)

col·o·ra·tu·ra /ˌkʌlərəˈturə; ˌkɒlərəˈtʊərə/ *n* **1** [U] a difficult piece of music that is meant to be sung fast〔声乐的〕花腔; 花腔音乐 **2** [C] a woman, especially a SOPRANO, who sings this type of music 花腔女高音歌手

col·or·ize *AmE*【美】, **col·our·ize** also 又作 **-ise** *BrE*【英】/ˈkʌləˌaɪz; ˈkʌləraɪz/ *v* [T] to add colour to an old film that was made in black and white 着彩色于〔黑白影片〕—**colourization** *n* [U]

color line /ˈ‥ ˌ‥/ *n* [singular] *AmE* the set of laws or social customs in some places that prevents people of different races from going to the same places or taking part in the same activities【美】〔种族歧视制度下的〕种族分界线, 肤色障碍; COLOUR BAR *BrE*【英】: *Friendship across the color line was rare then.* 那时超越种族界线的友谊是极为少见的。

co·los·sal /kəˈlɑsl̩; kəˈlɒsəl/ *adj* extremely large 巨大的, 庞大的: *a colossal statue* 巨大的雕像 | *Their secret to success was manufacturing cheap goods on a colossal scale.* 他们成功的秘诀是大量制造廉价商品。—**colossally** *adv*

Col·os·se·um, the /ˌkɑləˈsiəm; ˌkɒləˈsiːəm/ also 又作 **the Coliseum** an AMPHITHEATRE (=large circular theatre without a roof) in Rome which was built during the first century AD and is now one of the most famous ancient Roman buildings. Fights involving GLADIATORs were organized there as a form of

entertainment. 圆形竞技场〔建于公元1世纪，现为最著名的古罗马建筑之一。圆形竞技场是古代角斗士搏斗供人娱乐的场所〕

co·los·sus /kə`lɑsəs; kə'lɒsəs/ *n* [C] someone or something that is very big or very important 巨大的人[物]; 伟人; 极重要的人[物]: *An intellectual colossus like Leonardo comes along only once in a generation.* 像莱奥纳多那样的天才，一代人中也才出一个。

Colossus of Rhodes, the /kə,lɑsəs əv `rodz; kə,lɒsəs əv 'rəʊdz/ an extremely large ancient STATUE of the god Apollo on the Greek island of Rhodes. It was built to guard the entrance to the HARBOUR, and was one of the Seven Wonders of the World. It was destroyed by an EARTHQUAKE in 224 BC. 罗得岛巨人像〔希腊罗得岛上的一座巨型阿波罗神雕像。修建雕像的目的是守护海港入口。它是世界七大奇迹之一，毁于公元前224年的一次地震〕

colour[1] *BrE*【英】, **color** *AmE*【美】/`kʌlɚ; 'kʌlə/ *n*

1 ►A COLOUR 一种颜色◄[C] red, blue, yellow, green, brown, purple etc 色彩, 彩色: *"What colour are your eyes?" "They're brown."* "你的眼睛是什么色的?" "褐色的。" | *My favourite colour is purple.* 我最喜欢紫色。| **light/bright/pastel etc colour** *Children like bright colours.* 孩子们喜欢鲜艳的色彩。| **be an orange/greenish etc colour** *It was kind of an orange-red colour.* 它带点橘红色。—see picture on page A5 参见 A5 页图

2 ►COLOUR IN GENERAL 颜色的通称◄[C,U] the appearance of something, especially something with a lot of different colours 色, 颜色: *Chameleons can change colour to match their surroundings.* 变色龙能够随着环境改变身体的颜色。| *I had always wanted to go to New England to see the fall colours.* (=the colours of the trees) 我一直都想着去新英格兰观看秋日的各种色调。

3 in (full) colour a television programme or film that is in colour contains colours such as red, green, and blue rather than just black and white 〔电视节目或电影〕彩色的

4 ►SB'S RACE 某人的种族◄[C,U] how dark or light someone's skin is, which shows which race they belong to 〔不同人种的〕肤色: *people of all colours* 各色人种 | *discrimination on the basis of color* 对有色人种的歧视 —see also 另见 COLOURED

5 ►SB'S FACE 某人的脸◄[C,U] the general appearance and colour of a person's skin, especially when this shows the state of their health or emotions 脸色; 气色; 血色: *Well, you look better than you did. You've got some colour in your face now.* 不错, 你看起来比以前好多了。现在你脸上已经有些血色了。| **a high colour** (=a red colour in someone's face that shows they are ill) 〔脸部因生病而呈现的〕红晕, 潮红

6 ►SUBSTANCE 物质◄[U] a substance that makes something red, blue, yellow etc 颜料; 染料: *After a few washes, dark clothes begin to lose their colour.* 洗了几次以后, 深色衣服就开始褪色。

7 ►STH INTERESTING 趣事◄[U] interesting and exciting details or qualities that a place or person has 生动, 趣味: *The old market is lively, full of colour and activity.* 那个旧市场热闹非凡, 充满趣味与活力。| **add/give colour to** (=make something more interesting) 使…更生动有趣 *A few illustrations or anecdotes will add colour to your report.* 添加一些例子或趣闻轶事将使你的报告增色。

8 lend/give colour to sth to make something, especially something unusual, appear likely or true 使〔尤指不寻常的事〕显得可信[真实]: *We now have independent evidence that lends colour to the accusation of fraud.* 我们如今有独立的证据, 证明欺诈罪成立。

9 off colour a) not in good health 不健康的: *You look a little off colour today.* 你今天看起来气色有点不太好。**b)** jokes, stories etc that are off-colour are rude and often about sex 粗俗的, 下流的, 龌龊的, 色情的

10 colours [plural] **a)** the colours that are used as a sign to represent a team, school, club etc 〔代表球队、学校、俱乐部等标志的〕标志色: *The national colours of Italy are green, white, and red.* 意大利的国旗颜色是绿、白、红三色。**b)** *especially BrE* a flag, RIBBON, BADGE etc that you wear or carry to show that you belong to or support a team, school etc【尤英】〔表示属于或支持某团队、学校等而佩戴或手持的〕旗帜, 缎带, 徽章

11 show yourself in your true colours to behave in a way that shows what your real character is, especially if you are unpleasant or dishonest 露出真面目

12 see the colour of sb's money *spoken* to have definite proof that someone has enough money to pay for something【口】确信〔某人〕有支付能力: *"A whiskey, please." "Let's see the colour of your money first."* "请来杯威士忌。" "让我们先看看你的钱够不够。"

13 nail your colours to the mast to say clearly what your opinion is on a particular subject 阐明你的观点

colour in *BrE*【英】/**color in** *AmE*【美】着色

colour[2] *BrE*【英】, **color** *AmE*【美】*v* **1** [T] to make something coloured rather than just black, white, or plain 给…着色[染色]: *Do you colour your hair or is it naturally red?* 你是染了发, 还是本来就是红色的? | **colour sth red/blue etc** *Sunset came and coloured the sky a brilliant red.* 日落时分, 天空被染上了一片艳丽的红色。**2** also 又作 **colour in** [I,T] use coloured pencils to put colours inside the lines of a picture 〔用彩笔〕着色, 填色: *As a kid, I used to love colouring in shapes.* 小时候, 我常常喜欢给各种图形填色。**3** [I] when someone colours, their face becomes redder because they are embarrassed 〔因尴尬而〕脸红 **4** [T] **colour sb's judgment/opinions/attitudes etc** to influence the way someone thinks about something, especially so that they become less fair or reasonable 使某人的判断/观点/态度等带有偏见: *Don't you think your opinions are coloured by prejudice?* 你不认为你的观点带有偏见吗? —see also 另见 **colour code** (CODE[2] (3))

colour[3] *BrE*【英】, **color** *AmE*【美】*adj* **colour television/photograph/monitor etc** a television etc that produces or shows pictures in colour rather than in black, white and grey 彩色电视/照片/监视器等 —opposite 反义词 MONOCHROME

colour bar *BrE*【英】, **color bar** *AmE*【美】/'‥ ·/ *n* [C usually singular 一般用单数] a set of laws or social customs that prevent people of different races from going to the same places or taking part in the same activities 〔法律上或社会上对有色人种设置的〕种族分界线, 肤色障碍; COLOR LINE *AmE*【美】

colour-blind *BrE*【英】, **color-blind** *AmE*【美】/'‥ ·/ *adj* **1** unable to see the difference between all or some colours 色盲的 **2** treating people from different races equally and fairly 没有种族成见的: *The law should be colour-blind.* 法律不应存在种族歧视。—**colour-blindness** *n* [U]

colour-co·or·di·nat·ed *BrE*【英】, **color-coordinated** *AmE*【美】/'‥ ·, ‥··/ *adj* clothes, decorations etc that are colour-coordinated have colours which look good together 〔衣服、装饰等〕颜色协调的 —**colour-coordination**/, ‥ ‥·'‥/ *n* [U]

col·oured[1] *BrE*【英】, **colored** *AmE*【美】/`kʌlɚd; 'kʌləd/ *adj* **1** having a colour such as red, blue, yellow etc, rather than being black, white, or plain 有颜色的, 彩色的: *colored glass* 彩色玻璃 | *brightly coloured tropical birds* 色彩斑斓的热带鸟类 **2** an offensive word for someone who belongs to a race of people with dark or black skin 有色人种的〔冒犯用词〕—see 见 NEGRO (USAGE) **3** *SAfrE* someone whose parents or grandparents were both white and black【南非】〔白人与有色人种所生的〕混血儿

coloured[2] *BrE*【英】, **colored** *AmE*【美】*n* [C] an offensive word for someone belonging to a race of people with dark skin 有色人种的人〔尤指肤色深的人种, 带歧视性称呼〕—see 见 NEGRO (USAGE)

col·our·fast *BrE*【英】, **colorfast** *AmE*【美】/`kʌlɚ,fæst; 'kʌləfɑːst/ *adj* cloth that is colourfast will not lose its colour when it is washed 〔衣料〕不褪色的, 不掉色的 —**colourfastness** *n* [U]

col·our·ful *BrE*【英】, **colorful** *AmE*【美】/`kʌlɚfəl; 'kʌləfəl/ *adj* **1** having bright colours or a lot of different colours 富于色彩的, 颜色鲜艳的: *a colourful display of flowers* 一场色彩缤纷的花展 **2** interesting, exciting, and full of variety 有声有色的, 富于刺激性的, 生动有趣的: **colourful career/life/period etc** *Charlie Chaplin had a long and colourful career.* 查理·卓别林的演艺生涯漫长而丰富多彩。| **colourful character/figure** (=someone who is interesting and unusual) 有趣且不寻常的人物 *The old galley cook was the most colourful character on the*

ship. 那个老厨师是整条船上最有趣的人。**3** colourful language, speech etc uses a lot of swearing〔语言、演说等〕大量使用咒骂语的 **—colourfully** *adv*

col·our·ing *BrE*【英】, **coloring** *AmE*【美】/ˈkʌlərɪŋ; ˈkʌlərɪŋ/ *n* **1 food colouring** a substance used to give a particular colour to food 食物色素 **2** [U] the colour of someone's skin, hair, and eyes〔皮肤、头发及眼睛等的〕颜色: *Mandy has her mother's fair colouring.* 曼迪的肤色和她母亲的一样白。**3** [U] the colours of an animal, bird, or plant〔动物、鸟类或植物的〕颜色, 色彩, 色调: *The black and yellow colouring of some insects acts as a warning to predators.* 某些昆虫身上的颜色黄黑交错, 是对天敌的一种警告。

col·our·less *BrE*【英】, **colorless** *AmE*【美】/ˈkʌlələs; ˈkʌlələs/ *adj* **1** having no colour 无色的: *Water is a colorless liquid.* 水是一种无色的液体。**2** not interesting or exciting; DULL[1] (1) 无趣味的; 不刺激的; 不生动的: *Everything about this town seems drab and colourless to me.* 在我看来, 这个镇的所有一切既单调又无趣。**—colourlessly** *adv* **—colourlessness** *n* [U]

colour scheme *BrE*【英】, **color scheme** *AmE*【美】/ˈ‥ ·/ *n* [C] the combination of colours that someone chooses for a room, painting etc〔房间、画作等的〕色彩设计, 色调搭配: *a sophisticated colour scheme* 高水平的色彩设计

colour sup·ple·ment /ˈ‥ ˌ‥·/ *n* [C] *BrE*【英】a magazine printed in colour and given free with a newspaper, especially a Sunday newspaper〔尤指星期日随报附送的〕彩色增刊

Colt /kolt; kəʊlt/ *n* [C] *trademark* a kind of PISTOL【商标】科尔特牌手枪: *a Colt 45* 科尔特45型手枪

colt *n* [C] a young male horse 雄马驹 —compare 比较 FILLY

colt·ish /ˈkoltɪʃ; ˈkəʊltɪʃ/ *adj* a young person or animal that is coltish has a lot of energy but moves in an awkward way 活蹦乱跳的; 活泼的: *her long coltish limbs* 她那修长、有活力的肢体

Col·trane /kɑlˈtren; kɒlˈtreɪn/, **John** (1926-67) a US JAZZ musician who played the SAXOPHONE and had a great influence on the development of modern jazz 科尔特兰〔(1926-1967), 美国爵士音乐家、萨克斯管演奏家, 曾对现代爵士乐的发展产生重大影响〕

Columbia /kəˈlʌmbɪə; kəˈlʌmbiə/ —see 见 DISTRICT OF COLUMBIA

Columbia the capital city of the US state of South Carolina 哥伦比亚〔美国南卡罗来纳州首府〕

Columbia U·ni·ver·si·ty /·ˌ‥ ‥ˈ‥/ a private university in New York City, which is one of the Ivy League colleges. It is especially famous for its school of journalism 哥伦比亚大学〔纽约市一所私立大学, 常春藤联合会成员, 其新闻学院尤为著名〕

Col·um·bine /ˈkɑləmˌbaɪn; ˈkɒləmbaɪn/ a character in old European plays, who is the woman Harlequin loves 科伦比纳〔欧洲古老戏剧中的人物, 为哈乐根所爱的女子〕

columbine *n* [C] a garden plant with delicate leaves and bright flowers that hang down 耧斗菜〔园艺植物〕

Col·um·bus /kəˈlʌmbəs; kəˈlʌmbəs/ the capital city of the US state of Ohio 哥伦布〔美国俄亥俄州首府〕

Columbus, Chris·to·pher /ˈkrɪstəfɚ; ˈkrɪstəfə/ (1451-1506) an Italian sailor and EXPLORER who many people think of as the first European to discover America, in 1492. He arrived in America by accident when he was trying to find a new way to Asia by sailing west from Spain. Most people now think that the first discovery of America by Europeans was about 500 years earlier, by the Norwegian Leif Ericsson 哥伦布〔(1451-1506), 意大利航海家、探险家, 被认为是1492年首位发现美洲大陆的欧洲人。当时, 他试图找到一条由西班牙通往亚洲的新航道, 却偶然间到达了美洲。现在, 多数人认为, 首次发现美洲大陆的欧洲人是挪威的莱弗·埃里克松, 比哥伦布早500来年〕

Columbus Day /·ˈ‥ ˌ·/ a US public holiday held on October 12th to honour Christopher Columbus 哥伦布纪念日〔10月12日, 美国公共假日, 旨在纪念克里斯托弗·哥伦布〕

S2 W2 **col·umn** /ˈkɑləm; ˈkɒləm/ *n* [C] **1** a tall, solid, upright, stone post used to support a building or as a decoration 支柱; 柱, 圆柱: *a graceful Ionic column* 一根典雅的爱奥尼亚式圆柱 **2** a long moving line of people or things〔人或物排成的移动的〕(一) 队, (一) 列; 纵行[列]: *A long, winding column of soldiers marched through the streets.* 一长队士兵沿着街道蜿蜒前进。**3** one of two or more lines of print that go down the page of a newspaper or book and that are separated from each other by a narrow space〔报刊、书籍上的〕栏: *Turn to Page 5, column 2.* 翻到第5页第2栏。**4** a line of numbers or words written under each other that goes down a page〔数字、单词的〕列: *Add up the numbers in each column separately.* 分别将各列数字相加。**5** an article on a particular subject or by a particular writer that appears regularly in a newspaper or magazine〔报纸、杂志的〕专栏 (文章): *a weekly column* 每周专栏 | *She writes the gardening column in the Express.* 她为《快报》撰写园艺专栏。**6** something that has a long, thin shape, like a column 柱状物: **[+of]** *a column of smoke* 一柱轻烟 —see also 另见 FIFTH COLUMN, PERSONAL COLUMN, SPINAL COLUMN

col·umn·ist /ˈkɑləmɪst; ˈkɒləmɪst/ *n* [C] someone who writes articles, especially about a particular subject, that appear regularly in a newspaper or magazine〔报刊、杂志的〕专栏作家

com- /kəm; kəm/ *prefix* the form used for CON- before b, m, or p〔前缀 con- 的一个形式, 用于 b, m 或 p 前〕: *compassion* (=sympathy) 同情

co·ma /ˈkomə; ˈkəʊmə/ *n* [C] a state in which someone remains unconscious for a long time, usually caused by a serious illness or injury〔因重病或重伤而引起的〕昏迷: **be/lie in a coma** *Marina Stefani, 25, has been in a coma for the past four months.* 25岁的玛丽娜·斯蒂芬尼在过去的四个月里一直处于昏迷状态。

co·ma·tose /ˈkoməˌtos; ˈkəʊmətəʊs/ *adj* **1** *technical* in a coma【术语】昏迷的 **2** *informal* so tired that you cannot think properly【非正式】〔因疲倦而〕呆滞的, 麻木的: *Working till you're comatose doesn't help anybody.* 工作得精疲力竭对谁都没好处。

comb[1] /kom; kəʊm/ *n* **1** [C] a flat piece of plastic, metal etc with a row of thin teeth on one side, used for making your hair tidy 梳子 **2** [C] a small flat piece of plastic, metal etc with a row of thin teeth on one side, used for keeping your hair back or for decoration〔将头发固定于脑后或作装饰用的〕梳状饰物, 发插 **3** [singular] a process in which you make your hair tidy or straight using a comb 梳理: *Your hair needs a good comb.* 你的头发需要好好梳理一下。**4** [C] the red piece of flesh that grows on top of a male chicken's head〔公鸡的〕鸡冠, 肉冠 **5** [C] a HONEYCOMB 蜂巢 —see also 另见 FINE-TOOTH COMB

comb[2] *v* [T] **1** to make hair or fur tidy or straight using a comb 梳, 梳理: *Your hair's a mess! Go comb it.* 你的头发乱七八糟的! 去梳一梳。**2** to search a place thoroughly 彻底搜寻, 四处搜查: **comb sth for** *The police combed the woods for the missing boy.* 警察在林子里彻底搜查, 寻找那个失踪的男孩。

comb sb/sth ↔ **out** *phr v* [T] **1** to make hair or fur straight and smooth using a comb 梳理〔头发、毛发等〕: *It took over an hour to comb out all the tangles in Buster's fur.* 将巴斯特的毛发梳理整齐花了一个多小时。**2** *informal* to get rid of unnecessary people from within a group【非正式】裁减〔冗员〕**3 [+from]** to find and collect specific pieces of information from a larger amount of information〔在大量信息中〕搜寻并收集专门信息 **—comb out** *n* [singular]

comb through *phr v* [T] to search through a lot of objects or information in order to find a specific thing or piece of information〔在大量物件或信息中〕仔细搜寻: *Marta combed through a box of old photographs, looking for the baby portrait.* 玛尔塔在一盒旧照片中寻找那张婴儿照。

com·bat[1] /ˈkɑmbæt; ˈkɒmbæt/ *n* **1** [U] organized fighting, especially in a war〔尤指战争中的〕战斗: **active/armed combat** *These troops have very little experience of active combat.* 这些部队没有多少实战经验。| **in combat (with)** *Corporal Gierson was killed in combat.* 吉尔森下士阵亡了。| **combat mission/activity/unit etc** *The women were excluded from the combat units.* 妇女不得参加战斗小组。| **combat plane/jacket/boots** *A combat plane flew overhead.* 一架战斗机从头顶掠过。| **locked in mortal combat** (=fighting until one of the opponents dies) 决一死战, 殊死战斗 **2** [C] a fight or battle 斗争; 格斗: **[+between/against]** *a combat between good and evil* 善恶之争 | **single combat** (=a formal fight between only two people) 一对一的格斗

com·bat[2] /ˈkɑmbæt; ˈkɒmbæt/ *v* **combatted, combatting** *BrE*【英】[T] *formal*【正式】**1** to take action in an organized way in order to oppose something bad or harmful 与…斗争: *a neighborhood watch system to help combat crime* 帮助打击犯罪的邻里警报系统 | *new strategies to combat inflation* 与通货膨胀作斗争的新战略 **2** to fight against an enemy or opponent in order to try and defeat them 与…战斗

com·ba·tant /ˈkɑmbətənt; ˈkɒmbətənt/ *n* [C] someone who fights in a war 战斗人员, 战士

combat fa·tigue /ˈ‥ ·ˌ·/ *n* [U] *technical* BATTLE FATIGUE【术语】战斗疲劳症

com·ba·tive /kəmˈbætɪv; ˈkɒmbətɪv/ *adj* ready and willing to fight or argue 好斗的; 好争论的: *a combative committee member* 一位好斗的委员 **—combatively** *adv* **—combativeness** *n* [U]

com·bi·na·tion /ˌkɑmbəˈneʃən; ˌkɒmbɪˈneɪʃən/ *n* **1** [C,U] two or more different things, qualities, substances etc that are used or put together 结合, 联合; 混合: *a perfect wine and food combination* 美酒佳肴的完美组合 | **[+of]** *A combination of fac-* S3 W2

tors may be responsible for the increase in cancer. 各种因素的综合作用可能导致癌症发病率的上升。| *a screen heroine who is a combination of the modern and the traditional* 一位融合了传统与现代气质的银幕女星 | *A combination of tact and authority was needed to deal with the situation.* 处理这类情况需要机智，也需要加以威慑。| **in combination (with)** *Certain drugs which are safe when taken separately are lethal in combination.* 某些药品在分开服用时是安全的，但在混合服用时则会致命。**2** [C] a number of things chosen from a group and put in a particular order 组合，搭配：*Certain combinations of sounds are not possible in English.* 在英语中，某些音是不可能组合的。| *an unusual combination of colours* 不寻常的色彩搭配 **3** [C] the series of numbers or letters you need to open a combination lock〔密码锁的〕号码组合：*I've forgotten the combination for my bicycle lock!* 我忘记了自行车锁的号码组合了！**4 a winning combination** a mixture of different people or things that work successfully together 成功的搭档；默契的组合 **5** [U] *especially AmE* used before a noun in some phrases to mean that something does more than one job or uses more than one method【尤美】组合物；合并体：*a combination of washer and dryer* 洗衣和脱水两用洗衣机 | *combination chemotherapy* 混和式化学疗法 **6 combinations** [plural] *BrE old-fashioned* a piece of underwear covering the upper part of your body and legs, worn especially in the past; UNION SUIT【英，过时】〔尤指旧时穿的〕连衣裤

combination lock /‥'‥ ˌ/ *n* [C] a lock which can only be opened by using a series of numbers or letters in a particular order 号码[密码]锁，转字锁

com·bine¹ /kəm`baɪn; kəm'baɪn/ *v* **1** [I,T] if you combine two or more different things, ideas, or qualities or if they combine, they begin to exist or work together（使）结合；（使）组合：*I'm looking for a job in which I can combine the different aspects of my experience so far.* 我正在寻找一份能结合应用我的不同经验的工作。| **combine to do sth** *Several factors had combined to harm our friendship.* 几个因素凑在一起，伤害了我们的友谊。| **combine sth with** *The new software package combines power with maximum flexibility.* 这种新的套装软件既功能强大，又极为灵巧。| **combined with** *Heat treatment is most effective if combined with regular physiotherapy.* 热疗若与常规物理疗法结合使用最为有效。| **combined effect/effects** (=the result of two or more different things used or mixed together) 共同作用/效果 *The combined effects of the heat and too much alcohol made Sheila feel nauseous.* 由于气温太高与过量酒精的共同作用，希拉觉得一阵恶心。**2** [I,T] if two or more different substances, liquids etc combine or if you combine them, they mix or join together to produce a new single substance, liquid etc（使）化合，（使）组合，调和：**combine to do sth** *Different amino acids combine to form proteins.* 不同种类的氨基酸组合形成蛋白质。| **combine sth** *Combine all the ingredients in a salad bowl.* 将所有材料放在沙拉碗中调拌。| **combine sth with** *Steel is produced by combining iron with carbon.* 钢是由铁加碳制造而成。**3** [T] to do two very different activities at the same time 同时做〔两件完全不同的事〕：**combine sth with** *You can't combine studying for your exams with a wild social life!* 你不能在备考的同时到处疯玩！| **combine sth and sth** *It's no easy task combining family responsibilities and a full-time job!* 在尽到家庭责任的同时又要从事全职工作，这可不是件容易的事！| **combine business with pleasure** (=work and enjoy yourself at the same time) 既工作又娱乐 **4** [I,T] if two or more groups, organizations etc combine or if you combine them, they join or work together in order to do something（使）联合〔以达成某项目〕；合并：**combine to do sth** *Two of the smaller groups had combined to form one large team.* 这些小群体中有两个已经联合成立了一个较大的派系。| **combine sth** *a report on the advantages of combining small village schools* 一份关于合并小型乡村学校好处的报告

com·bine² /`kɑmbaɪn; 'kɒmbaɪn/ *n* [C] **1** also 又作 **combine harvester** a machine used by farmers to cut grain, separate the seeds from it, and clean it 联合收割机 **2** a group of people or organizations who work together for a particular purpose〔为某一目的而组成的〕联盟，联合（体）：*The factory was sold to a British combine after the war.* 战后该工厂被卖给了一家英国联合企业。

com·bined /kəm`baɪnd; kəm'baɪnd/ *adj* **1** [only before noun 仅用于名词前] done, made, or achieved by several people or groups working together 结合的，联合的，共同的：**combined effort/action/operation** *"Who cooked the dinner?" "Well, it was a combined effort really."* "谁做的这顿饭？""哦，其实是大家一起做的。" | **combined salaries** (=the total amount of money that two or more people earn)〔两人或多人〕共同赚得的钱 **2** having two very different feelings at the same time〔情感〕复杂的，矛盾的：*Ann felt a combined relief and sadness.* 安既舒了口气，又觉得难过。

combining form /‥'‥ ˌ/ *n* [C] *technical* a form of a word that has a meaning but cannot be used alone, and is used with other words to make new ones such as 'Anglo', meaning 'English', in the word 'Anglo-American'【术语】复合词；构词成分〔如"Anglo-American"中的"Anglo"〕

com·bo /`kɑmbo; 'kɒmbəʊ/ *n* [C] *informal*【非正式】**1** a small band that plays JAZZ[1] (1) or dance music〔演奏爵士乐或舞曲的〕小型乐队 **2** *AmE* any combination of different things, especially a meal at a FAST FOOD restaurant【美】〔尤指快餐店的〕杂烩饭；什锦饭：*I'll have the fish combo to go.* 我要带一份鱼烩饭走。

com·bus·ti·ble /kəm`bʌstəbḷ; kəm'bʌstɪ̈bəl/ *adj* able to burn easily 可燃的，易燃的：*Alcohol is highly combustible.* 酒精非常易燃。

com·bus·tion /kəm`bʌstʃən; kəm'bʌstʃən/ *n* [U] **1** the process of burning 燃烧 **2** *technical* chemical activity which uses oxygen to produce light and heat【术语】〔产生高温和光的〕燃烧 **3 combustion chamber** the enclosed space in which combustion happens 燃烧室 —see also 另见 INTERNAL COMBUSTION ENGINE

come¹ /kʌm; kʌm/ *v past tense* came /kem; keɪm/ *past participle* come

① MOVE 移动	⑥ REACH AS FAR AS 直到
② TRAVEL 旅行	⑦ SPOKEN PHRASES 口语短语
③ ARRIVE 到达	⑧ IN AN ORDER/POSITION 处于某个次序/位置
④ REACH A CONDITION/STATE 达到某种条件/状态	⑨ OTHER MEANINGS 其他意思
⑤ HAPPEN/EXIST 发生/存在	⑩ PHRASAL VERBS 短语动词

① MOVE 移动

1 [I] a word meaning to move towards someone, or to visit or arrive at a place, used when the person speaking or the person listening is in that place 来；来到；来临：*Come a little closer.* 走近点儿。| *Sarah's coming later on.* 萨拉一会儿就来。| *I've come about the job you advertised.* 我来应征你招聘的职位。| **[+to/towards/here etc]** *Come here and look at this.* 到这儿来看看这个。| *When are you coming back?* 你什么时候回来？| **come and do sth** *Can I come and see you tomorrow?* 我明天能来看看你吗？| **come to do sth** *A man comes to clean the windows on Fridays.* 每星期五都有人来擦窗户。| **come for sb** (=in order to take them somewhere) 来接某人 *When is Anton coming for you?* 安东什么时候来接你？| **come running/flying/speeding etc** *Jess came flying round the corner and banged straight into me.* 杰斯从拐角处飞跑出来，和我撞个满怀。| **come to dinner/lunch** *What day are your folks coming to dinner?* 你们大家什么时候过来吃顿饭呀？

2 ►MOVE WITH SB 与某人同行◄ [I] to move to a particular place with the person who is speaking 同行，同来：*Can Billy come too?* 比利也能来吗？| **[+with]** *Would you like to come to the concert with me?* 你愿意和我一起去听音乐会吗？| **[+along]** *There's room for one more, if you want to come along.* 如果你想一道来的话，还有一个位置。

② **TRAVEL 旅行**
3 [I] to travel a particular distance or in a particular way to reach the place you are in or talking about〔尤指沿特定的路线〕到达；至：*We rode back the way we had come.* 我们沿着来时的路线骑了回去。| **come by/on/with etc** *Did you come on a coach or by train?* 你是乘长途公共汽车还是火车来的？| **come far/miles/a long way etc** *Some of the birds have come thousands of miles to winter here.* 一些鸟飞了数千英里到这儿来过冬。| *It would be a shame to have come all this way and not see them.* 老远赶来却没有见着他们，太可惜了。

③ **ARRIVE 到达**
4 [I] to arrive or be sent somewhere 来到；被送至〔某处〕：*The phone bill has come at a bad time.* 这张电话费账单来得真不是时候。
5 ▶TIME/EVENT 时间/事件◀ [I] if a time or event comes, it arrives or happens〔时间、事件〕到来；发生：*The moment had come for me to break the news to her.* 是时候让我将这个消息告诉她了。| *Christmas seems to come earlier every year.* 圣诞节似乎一年比一年来得早。| **coming soon** (=used especially in advertisements) 即将〔上演、来货等〕〔尤用于广告〕*Coming soon, to a theater near you!* 即将上演，就在你附近的一家剧院！| **the time is coming/will come** *The time will come when you'll thank me for this.* 你就要为此而感谢我了。

④ **REACH A CONDITION/STATE 达到某种条件/状态**
6 come to sth an expression used in some phrases, meaning to reach a particular state or position 得出某物；达到某种状态[境地]：**come to a decision/the conclusion** *I've come to the conclusion that we've made a mistake.* 我已经得出了结论，那就是我们犯了个错误。| **come to power/trial etc** *When does Alan's case come to court?* 艾伦的案子何时提到法庭受审？| **come to an end/halt/stop etc** *Yes, I saw the van come to a screeching halt right there.* 是的，我看见那辆货车就在那儿嘎的一声停了下来。
7 come open/undone etc to become open etc 松开，解开：*Your shoelace is coming untied.* 你的鞋带松了。| *The bottle came open in my bag!* 我袋子里的那个瓶子开了！—see also 另见 **a dream come true** (DREAM[1] (5))
8 come to do sth to begin to do something, especially to have a particular feeling or opinion about someone or something as a result of time or experience 开始做某事〔尤指随着时间或经历的增长，开始对某人或某物产生特殊感情或特定看法〕：*In time you may come to like it here.* 你最终可能会喜欢这儿的。| *That's the kind of behavior we've come to expect from him.* 那正是我们期待他会表现出来的品行。| *You've come to mean a lot to me.* 你开始对我变得很重要。
9 come into sth to begin to be in a particular state or position 变成，成为；进入〔状态〕：*As we turned the corner, the town came into view.* 我们拐过街角，小镇就出现在眼前。| *The new law comes into effect next month.* 这项新法律下个月开始生效。

⑤ **HAPPEN/EXIST 发生/存在**
10 [I] to happen or appear 发生；出现：*Your chance will come one day.* 你的机会总有一天会出现的。| *No good will come from all this.* 这么做不会有好结果。| **sth comes and goes** *"How's the pain?" "Well, it comes and goes."* "疼得怎么样了？""哦，一阵儿一阵儿地疼。"| **come in twos/threes etc** (=happen two, three etc times, closely together) 接二连三地 *Trouble always comes in threes.* 祸不单行。
11 [I] to exist 存在：**come in different shapes and sizes** *Cats come in many shapes and sizes.* 猫的体形各异，大小也不一样。
12 as nice/as stupid etc as they come extremely nice, stupid etc 极好的/极蠢的等：*Don't get Bill angry – he's as mean as they come.* 别惹比尔生气 —— 他小气得不得了。
13 take it as it comes to accept something exactly as it happens or is given to you, without trying to change it or plan ahead 原样接受；既来之，则安之：*For the moment I'm just taking each day as it comes.* 我现在只是得过且过。
14 the best/worst is yet to come used to say that better or worse things can be expected to happen in the future 最好的/最坏的还在后头
15 come what may whatever happens 无论发生什么：*Come what may, I'll never leave you.* 无论发生什么，我永远也不会离开你。
16 come to pass *literary* to happen after a period of time【文】〔一段时间以后〕发生：*It came to pass that they had a son.* 斗转星移，他们终得一子。

⑥ **REACH AS FAR AS 直到**
17 [I always+adv/prep] to reach a particular place 到达〔某处〕：**come up to/down to etc** *The water is pretty deep – it comes right up to my neck.* 水相当深 —— 直淹到了我的脖子。| *Carrie's hair comes down to her waist.* 卡丽的头发长及腰部。

Frequencies of the verb **come** in spoken and written English
动词 come 在英语口语和书面语中的使用频率

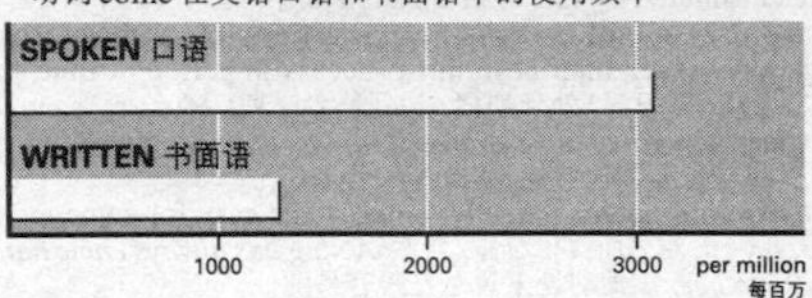

Based on the British National Corpus and the Longman Lancaster Corpus
据英国国家语料库和朗文兰开斯特语料库

This graph shows that the verb **come** is much more common in spoken English than in written English. This is because it is used in a lot of common spoken phrases. 本图表显示动词 come 在英语口语中比在书面英语中较为常用。这是因为很多常用口语短语是由 come 构成的。

⑦ **SPOKEN PHRASES 口语短语**
18 here comes John/Shelia etc used when someone is coming towards you and you want the person you are with to notice them 约翰/谢莉娅等来了：*Look out, here comes the boss!* 小心，老板过来了！
19 how come? used to ask someone why something has happened 怎么会…？：*How come Tyler's still here?* 泰勒怎么还在这儿？
20 come to think of it/come to that used when you want to add something you have just realized or been reminded of 还有…；〔刚好想起〕说起来…：*It was really fun – come to think of it, I should write Jim a thank-you note.* 这可真是有趣 —— 哦，说起来，我应该给吉姆写封感谢信。| *I haven't seen her for weeks – or her parents, come to that.* 我好几个星期没见到她了 —— 哦，也没见到她的父母。
21 come again? used to ask someone to repeat what they have just said 再说一遍好吗？
22 come July/next year/the wedding etc at a particular time in the future 将要到来的七月/明年/婚礼等：*Come Monday, we'll be in our new house.* 下星期一我们将住进新房子。
23 come (now) *old-fashioned* used to comfort or gently encourage someone【过时】〔用于安慰或鼓励〕好了；行了：*Come, Sarah, don't cry.* 好了，萨拉，别哭了。
24 come, come!/come now *old-fashioned* used to tell someone that you do not accept what they are saying or doing【过时】〔表示不赞同〕哦，不；别这样：*Come now, try to be more polite.* 别这样，尽量礼貌点。
25 don't come the innocent/victim etc with me *BrE* used to tell someone not to pretend to you that they are innocent, a victim etc【英】别在我面前装无辜/可怜等：*Don't come the poor struggling artist with me. You're just lazy!* 别在我面前装成个可怜巴巴勉强过活的艺术家。你就是懒！

⑧ **IN AN ORDER/POSITION 处于某个次序/位置**
26 [I always+adv/prep] to be in a particular position or rank in order, importance, or quality〔在级别、顺序、重要性、质量上〕处于：**come before/after** *The singing comes before the Mayor's speech.* 歌曲之后是市长的讲话。| **come first/second etc** *"How was the tournament?" "We came last."* (=we did not win any games) "比赛结果如何？""我们排在最后。"| *My family always comes first.* (=is the most important thing in my life) 我的家庭在我心中总是最重要的。

⑨ **OTHER MEANINGS 其他意思**
27 ▶BE SOLD/AVAILABLE 出售/有供应◀ [I] to be sold, produced, or available 在出售；生产中；有供应：*Yogurt comes in many flavors.* 出售的酸奶有多种口味。| *The camera comes complete with batteries.* 这种相机配有电池。| **come cheap** *Houses like that don't come cheap.* 那些房子不便宜。
28 have come a long way to have made a lot of progress 有长足进步，有极大发展：*Computer technology has come a long way since the 1970's.* 电脑技术自 20 世纪 70 年代以来已取得了极大的进步。
29 come as a surprise/relief/blow etc (to sb) to make some-

one feel surprised, RELIEVED etc 使…惊奇/松一口气/受到打击等: *The news came as a complete shock to him.* 这个消息对他震撼极大。| **it comes as no surprise that** (=used to say that you were expecting something) 意料之中, 未出乎意料 *It comes as no surprise that their marriage is over.* 他们婚姻的结束并不出人意料。

30 come of age a) to reach an age, usually 18 or 21, when you are considered by law to be an adult 成年; 达到法定年龄〔通常为18或21岁〕 **b)** if an artist, style, or organization comes of age, they reach their best, most successful period of time〔艺术、风格、组织等〕处于巅峰, 达到黄金时期: *Mozart's music came of age when the baroque style was at its height.* 在巴罗克艺术风格最盛行的时候, 莫扎特的音乐也达到了巅峰。

31 come easily/naturally (to sb) to be easy for someone to do, say etc 对…而言很容易/自然: *Acting has always come naturally to her.* 表演对她来说总是很容易的。

32 years/weeks/days etc to come used to emphasize that something is still in the future or will continue into the future 未来几年/几周/几天等: *Nuclear waste will remain hazardous for generations to come.* 核废料仍将对未来几代人产生危害。—see also 另见 COMING¹

33 ►SEX 性◄ [I] *slang* to have an ORGASM【俚】达到性高潮

34 come to hand things that come to hand are easy to reach or use, or are easily available 唾手可得: *Just use whatever comes to hand.* 只要抓到什么就用什么。

35 come to mind if someone or something comes to mind, you think of them when you are trying to find a solution to something 进入脑海, 想到, 记起: *We need a new secretary. Does anyone good come to mind?* 我们需要一名新秘书。想到什么好的人选吗?

36 come to life a) to become exciting or seem almost real 恢复生气; 逼真: *When he reads out loud, Papa makes stories come to life.* 爸爸大声朗读故事, 读得活灵活现。**b)** to wake up or begin to grow again 苏醒: *spring buds coming to life* 又开始重新绽放的春芽儿

37 come clean *informal* to admit that you have done something wrong【非正式】认错, 全盘招供: [+about] *I think you should come clean about where you were last night.* 你必须老实交待昨晚去了哪儿。

38 come right out and say sth to speak in a direct, often surprising way 坦言, 直截了当地说〔常指出人意料地〕: *Susie came right out and asked Bert what he thought of her.* 苏茜直截了当地问伯特他对她的看法。

39 not know whether you are coming or going *informal* to feel confused because you are doing too many things, so that nothing is organized【非正式】〔因事情过多而〕不知所措, 毫无头绪

40 come good/right *BrE informal* to end or finish well or correctly【英, 非正式】圆满结束: *Don't worry, it'll all come right in the end.* 别担心, 最终一切都会好起来的。

⑩ PHRASAL VERBS 短语动词

come about *phr v* [I] **1** to happen, especially in a way that seems impossible to control 发生; 产生〔尤指不受控制地〕: **how did it come about that** *How did it come about that humans speak so many different languages?* 人类是怎么会说这么多种语言的? **2** when a ship comes about, it changes direction〔船〕转向, 改变方向

come across *phr v* **1** [T not in passive 不用被动态] to meet, find, or discover someone or something by accident or by chance 偶遇; 偶然发现: *He had never come across a person quite like Sheila.* 他从没遇到过像希拉这样的人。| *I came across some old photos in the attic.* 我在阁楼上偶然翻到一些旧照片。**2** [I] **a)** if an idea comes across to someone, they understand it clearly 被理解: *Your point really came across at the meeting.* 你在会议上的观点确实被大家了解了。**b)** if someone comes across in a particular way, they give other people that feeling or opinion about them 给人的印象是: *He came across as being rather arrogant.* 他给人的印象是相当傲慢。| **come across well/badly** *I don't think I came across very well in the interview.* 我想我在那次面试中表现不太好。| **come across as (being) sth** *Sometimes you come across as being nervous.* 有时你显得很紧张。

come across with sth *phr v* [T] *BrE spoken*【英口】 **come across with the goods** to provide money or information when it is needed 给予所需钱财; 提供所需资料

come after sb *phr v* [T not in passive 不用被动态] to look for someone until you find them so you can hurt them, punish them, or get something from them 查找〔某人〕: *I heard the tax people are coming after him for unpaid VAT.* 我听说税务人员正为他未缴增值税而找他。

come along *phr v* [I] **1 be coming along** *informal* to be developing, or improving, especially in education or health【非正式】〔尤指教育或健康〕进步, 进展: [+with] *How's Martin coming along with his English?* 马丁的英语学得怎么样了? | *Mother's coming along nicely, thank you.* 妈妈恢复得很好, 谢谢你。**2** to appear or arrive at a time you do not expect or cannot know about 出现; 来到; 发生: *Take any job opportunity that comes along.* 抓住任何工作机会。| *A bus should come along any minute now.* 公共汽车随时都可能会来。**3 a)** to follow someone somewhere 跟随: *Do you mind if I come along with you?* 如果我跟你去你会不会介意? **b)** to go somewhere with someone 跟〔某人〕去: *You go on ahead – I'll come along later.* 你先走, 我随后就来。**4 come along!** *especially BrE spoken*【尤英口】 **a)** used to tell someone to hurry up 快点, 赶快: *Come along now, children.* 现在得快点儿啦, 孩子们。**b)** used to encourage someone to try harder 加油, 加把劲: *Come along, surely someone knows the answer.* 尽量想一下, 肯定有人知道答案。

come apart *phr v* [I] **1** to split or fall into pieces without anyone using force 破裂; 崩溃, 垮掉: *The book just came apart in my hands.* 书在我手上就那么散开来了。**2 come apart at the seams** to become unable to deal with a situation, or impossible to be dealt with 无力处置; 无法处理: *It felt as if his whole life was coming apart at the seams.* 看来他的整个人生似乎彻底完了。

come around *phr v* [I] **1** *AmE* to visit someone at home or at the place where they are【美】拜访, 探访: *Mind if I come around after work?* 介不介意我下班后顺便拜访一下? **2** *AmE* to change your opinion so that you now agree with someone【美】回心转意, 改变观点: *It took some persuading, but he finally came around.* 劝服他花了些功夫, 但他最后还是回心转意了。**3** if a regular event comes round, it arrives or happens as usual〔如往常一样〕发生; 降临: *Thanksgiving comes around so quickly, doesn't it?* 这么快又要到感恩节了, 不是吗? **4** *AmE* to become conscious again【美】再度苏醒, 恢复知觉: *It was three weeks before she came around.* 三个星期以后她才苏醒过来。

come at sb/sth *phr v* [T not in passive 不用被动态] **1** to move towards someone in a threatening way 扑向, 向…逼近: *Meg came at me with a knife.* 梅格拿着刀向我冲过来。**2** if pieces of information, images etc come at you, you feel confused because there are a lot of them all at the same time〔大量信息、图像等〕涌向, 涌至 **3** *informal* to consider or deal with a problem【非正式】考虑; 处理〔问题〕: *We need to come at the problem from a different angle.* 我们需要换个角度来考虑这个问题。

come away *phr v* [I] **1** if part of something comes away from something else, it becomes separated when you are using it normally 脱落, 脱离: *I didn't break it! The handle came away in my hand.* 不是我折断的! 这个手柄是自己掉到我手上的。**2** to leave a place 离开〔某地〕: *Come away, Ben. There's going to be trouble.* 离开吧, 班恩, 会有麻烦的。

come back *phr v* [I] **1 it's all coming back to me** *spoken* to say that you are finally beginning to remember something【口】终于记起来 **2** to become fashionable or popular again 再度时髦, 重新流行: [+in] *Miniskirts have come back in this season.* 迷你裙在本季又开始流行了。**3** to reply in a forceful, quick, and often unkind way; RETORT¹ 回嘴, 反驳, 驳斥: [+at] *I don't want anyone coming back at me over this.* 我不希望任何人在这一点上驳斥我。| [+with] *coming back with a nasty retort* 迅速有力地驳斥 —see also 另见 COMEBACK

come before sb *phr v* [T] *formal* to be sent to a person or group in authority in order to be considered or judged【正式】被提交…讨论[处置]: *When you come before the judge, tell the whole truth.* 到法官面前, 你要讲出所有的真相。

come between sb *phr v* [T not in passive 不用被动态] **1** to cause trouble between two or more people 离间, 挑拨: *Why should a little argument come between friends?* 为什么一点小争吵要惹得朋友反目呢? **2** to prevent someone from giving enough attention to something 妨碍〔某人〕做〔某事〕: *I don't let anything come between me and my work.* 我不会让任何事情妨碍我的工作。

come by sth *phr v* [T not in passive 不用被动态] **1** to obtain something that is rare or difficult to find 弄到, 获得: *How on earth did you come by these tickets?* 你到底是怎么弄到这些票的? | **be hard to come by** (=to be difficult to obtain or find) 难于得到; 难以发现 *Jobs are hard to come by these days.* 如今工作很难找。**2** *AmE* to make a short visit to a place on your way to somewhere else【美】顺路拜访, 顺道看望: *I'll come by the*

house and get my stuff later, OK? 我顺便去一下那幢房子，然后再去拿东西，好吗？

come down *phr v* [I]

1 ▶BECOME LOWER 变低◀ **a)** if a price, level etc comes down, it becomes lower〔价格、水平等〕下降，降低: *Wait to buy a house until interest rates come down.* 等利率调低时再去买房子吧。**b)** [+to] to offer or accept a lower price 提出[接受]低价: *Do you think the dealer would come down at all?* 你认为那个商人会降价吗？

2 ▶TRAVEL SOUTH 南行◀ to travel south or away from an important place such as a big city, to the place where the speaker is 南下，〔从大城市〕来到: *Come down for the weekend sometime.* 什么时候来这儿度周末。| [+to] *Are you coming down to Knoxville for Christmas?* 你来诺克斯维尔过圣诞节吗？

3 ▶BUILDING 建筑物◀ if a building comes down, it is destroyed by being pulled down〔建筑〕被拆毁

4 come down in sb's opinion/estimation to do something that makes someone respect you less 在某人心中地位下降: *John really came down in my opinion after that.* 从那以后约翰在我心目中的地位一落千丈。

5 come down in the world to become poorer or less successful than you used to be. 落泊，潦倒；失势

6 come down on the side of also 又作 **come down in favour of** to decide to support someone or something after thinking about a problem for a long time〔深思熟虑之后〕决定支持某人[某事]

7 come (back) down to earth to suddenly have to start dealing with ordinary practical problems after ignoring them for a time 跌回现实，回到现实中: *"Charles!" He stopped day-dreaming and came back down to earth, startled.* "查尔斯！"他从白日梦中惊醒过来回到现实，满脸惊讶。

8 ▶DRUGS 毒品◀ [+off/from] *informal* to stop being affected by a powerful drug such as HEROIN or LSD that you have taken【非正式】〔毒品药性过后〕清醒过来

9 ▶LEAVE UNIVERSITY 离开大学◀ [+from] *BrE* to leave a university, especially Oxford or Cambridge, after completing a period of study【英】〔尤指在牛津或剑桥大学结业后〕离校

come down on sb/sth *phr v* [T not in passive 不用被动态] to punish someone or criticize them severely 严惩；痛斥: **come down on sb for doing sth** *My parents really came down on me for being out so late.* 我父母因为我在外待得太晚，实实在在地教训了我一顿。| **come down hard on** (=punish someone very severely) 非常严厉地惩罚 *We're going to come down hard on car theft.* 我们将严厉打击盗车行为。| **come down like a ton of bricks** (=punish someone extremely severely) 极为严厉地惩罚〔某人〕

come down to sb/sth *phr v* [T not in passive 不用被动态] **1** if a complicated situation or problem comes down to something, it is the single most important point or choice 归结为: **it comes down to** *It all came down to a choice between cutting wages or cutting staff.* 归根到底，就是在减薪或裁员之中作出选择。**2** if a document, object, idea etc comes down to someone, it has survived from a long time ago until the present 落到…手中；传到…手里: *The text which has come down to us is only a fragment of the original.* 那本课本到我们手里的时候已经破烂不全了。

come down with sth *phr v* [T not in passive 不用被动态] *informal* to become ill with something infectious, especially something that is not very serious【非正式】染上〔病〕，患〔小病〕: *I think I'm coming down with a cold.* 我想我得了感冒了。

come for sth/sb *phr v* [T] **1** to arrive to collect someone or something 来接；来拿: *I've come for the carpet I ordered.* 我来取我订购的毛毯。| *Shall I come for you at about six then?* 那么我大概6点来接你好吗？**2** to try to harm someone or take them away where they do not want to go 试图伤害；强行带走: *When the secret police come for you, you'll talk, believe me!* 秘密警察来抓你的时候，你肯定会说的，相信我好了！

come forward *phr v* [I] **1** to offer yourself for a job, election etc 毛遂自荐，自告奋勇，主动争取: [+as] *More women are coming forward as candidates than ever before.* 比起以前，较多的女性主动自荐为候选人。| **come forward to do sth** *We need more volunteers to come forward to help.* 我们需要更多志愿者来帮忙。**2** to offer help to someone in authority who needs it or has asked for it〔向有需要的官方人士〕提供帮助: [+with] *A young girl has come forward with a description of the attacker.* 一位年轻女孩对该袭击者作了一番描述。

come from sb/sth *phr v* [T not in progressive 不用进行式] **1** to have started, been produced or first existed in a particular place, thing or time 始于；产自；来自: *Where do you come from originally?* 你老家是哪儿？| *Milk comes from cows.* 牛奶是从奶牛身上挤出来的。| *The passage she quoted came from Dickens.* 她引用的那段话出自狄更斯的作品。**2 coming from him/her/you etc** *spoken* used to criticize what someone has said because they say one thing and behave in the opposite way【口】可不是这么回事〔用于指责某人言行不一〕: *Pretentious? Me? That's rich, coming from you!* 自命不凡？我？真好笑，你竟说这话！**3 come from doing sth** also 又作 **come of doing sth** to be the result of doing something 是某事的结果: *"I feel sick." "That's what comes from drinking too much."* "我觉得恶心。""那是因为你喝得太多了。"

come in *phr v* [I]

1 ▶ARRIVE 到达◀ to arrive or be received 到达；接到: *As long as money's coming in, I'm happy.* 只要钱到了，我就开心了。| *Reports are coming in of a bad earthquake in Mexico.* 传来了墨西哥发生强烈地震的消息。| *Jenny's train comes in at eight.* 珍妮坐的火车8点到。

2 ▶ENTER 进入◀ to enter a room or house 进入〔房间或屋子〕: *Come in! Take a seat.* 进来！坐下吧。

3 ▶BE INVOLVED 被卷入◀ **a)** to be involved in a plan, deal etc 卷入，参与: *We need financial advice – that's where Kate comes in.* 我们需要财政咨询 —— 那正是用得着凯特的地方。| [+on] *It'll cost you $1000 to come in on the scheme.* 参与该计划将花掉你1000美元。**b)** to interrupt or enter a conversation or discussion 打断[加入]谈话[讨论]: *Excuse me, can I come in here?* 对不起，我能在这儿打断一下吗？

4 ▶BECOME FASHIONABLE 变得时髦◀ to become fashionable or popular to use 流行起来；开始被采用: *When platform shoes came in I thought they looked ridiculous.* 当厚底鞋刚流行时，我觉得那种鞋看起来很可笑。—opposite 反义词 **go out** (GO[1])

5 come in first/second etc to finish first, second etc in a race or competition〔在竞赛中〕得第一名/第二名等: *I came in a long way behind everyone else.* 我远远地落在其他人身后。

6 come in useful/handy to be useful 有用，用得上: *Bring some rope along; it might come in handy.* 带上一些绳子，可能派得上用场。

7 ▶SEA 海◀ when the TIDE (=level of the sea) comes in, it rises〔潮〕涨 —opposite 反义词 **go out** (GO[1]) —see also 另见 **come in from the cold** (COLD[2] (3))

come in for sth *phr v* [T] **come in for criticism/blame/scrutiny** to be criticized, blamed etc for something 挨批评，受责备: *The police came in for a lot of criticism for excess brutality.* 警方因为过度使用暴力而遭到大量批评。

come into sth *phr v* [T, not in passive 不用被动态] **1 come into money/a fortune** to receive money, land etc after someone has died; INHERIT (1) 继承遗产 **2** to be involved in something 卷入〔某事〕: *Mary, a minor character, doesn't come into the story much.* 玛丽是个配角，在故事中没有多少叙述。**3 luck/love/pride etc doesn't come into it!** *spoken* used to say that what someone has just mentioned is completely unimportant【口】没有丝毫运气/爱情/得意等: *"Your brother was very lucky to win." "It was skill – luck didn't come into it."* "你兄弟赢得真有运气。""那是技巧，一点儿也不是运气。" **4 come into fashion** to become a popular thing to wear or do 变得流行，风行: *A-line skirts are coming into fashion again.* A字裙重新流行起来了。**5 come into your own** to become very good, useful, or important in a particular situation〔在某一特殊情况下〕显示出用处[重要性]: *On icy roads like these, a four-wheel drive really comes into its own.* 在这种冰封的路面上，四轮驱动车是再合适不过的了。

come of sth *phr v* [T] to result from something 由于…而产生，是…的结果: *Nothing came of my attempts to find her.* 我试图找到她，但没有任何结果。| *"I'm fat." "That's what comes of not exercising."* "我很胖。""那是由于不运动的结果。"

come off *phr v* **1** [I,T not in passive 不用被动态] to stop being connected to something or stop sticking to something 脱落，掉落，分开: *How did your button come off?* 你的纽扣怎么掉的？| [+onto] *Some wet paint came off onto her hands.* 一些没干的漆沾到她的手上。| **come off sth** *The hook came off the wall when I hung my coat on it.* 我把外套挂到墙上的时候，挂钩掉下来了。**2 come off well/badly etc a)** to happen well, badly etc 进行得很顺利/糟糕等: *Despite the problems, the wedding came off very well.* 尽管有这些问题，婚礼还是进行得非常顺利。**b)** to do something successfully, badly etc 做得成功/失败: *The vice-president came off badly in the TV debate.* 那位副总统在电视辩论中表现糟糕。**3 come off it!** *spoken*【口】**a)**

used to tell someone that you think they are lying, or saying something stupid 别撒谎了, 别说蠢话: *"I can't stand Claire." "Come off it, Joe, you asked her out last week!"* "我真受不了克莱尔。" "别装蒜了, 乔, 你上星期还约她出去呢!" **b)** used to tell someone to stop doing or saying something annoying 别吵了, 别闹了: *Come off it, Dave, that's enough now!* "别闹了, 戴夫, 该闹够了!" **4** [I] to have the intended effect; succeed 达到预期效果; 成功: *Irene tried, but her joke didn't quite come off.* 艾琳试了一下, 但她的玩笑没怎么起到作用。**5 come off heroin/tranquillizers etc** to stop taking a drug that is ADDICTIVE (=makes you want to keep taking it) 戒除海洛因/镇静剂等

come on *phr v*

1 ▶START 开始◀ [I] **a)** if a light or machine comes on, it starts working 〔灯、机器等〕打开; 开动: *A dog started barking and lights came on in the house.* 一只狗开始吠叫, 屋里的灯亮了起来。**b)** if a slight illness comes on, you start to have it 患〔小病〕: *I can feel a headache coming on.* 我觉得头有点疼。**c)** if a television or radio programme comes on, it starts 〔电视或电台节目〕开始, 启播: *What time does the movie come on?* 电影什么时候开演? **d) it comes on to do sth** *BrE spoken* it starts to do something【英口】开始做〔某事〕, 开始发生: *It came on to rain.* 开始下雨了。

2 come on! *spoken*【口】**a)** used to tell someone to hurry up 快点: *Come on, we'll be late!* 快点儿, 我们要迟到了! **b)** also 又作 **come along!** *BrE*【英】used to encourage someone to try harder 加油, 加把劲: *Come on, guys, you can do it!* 加油, 小伙子们, 你们一定会成功! **c)** used to encourage someone to be more cheerful 高兴一点, 乐观一点: *Come on, let's see a smile.* 高兴点, 笑一笑。**d)** used to show someone that you know that what they have just said was not true or right 别逗了; 算了吧, 得了吧: *Oh come on, don't lie to me!* 哦, 得啦, 别对我撒谎! **e)** used to make someone angry enough to want to fight you, or to do something they would not normally do 〔用于挑衅对方〕来呀, 来吧: *Come on, then, hit me! I dare you!* 那就来吧, 打我呀! 谅你也不敢!

3 be coming on to be improving or making progress, especially in education or health 〔尤指在教育或健康方面〕改善, 提高: [+**with**] *How are you coming on with your training?* 你的训练进展得怎么样?

4 ▶DISCOVER 发现◀ [T **come on** sb/sth] to find or discover someone or something by chance 偶然找到, 偶然发现: *Turning the corner, I came on a group of picnickers.* 拐过街角, 我碰上一群野餐的人。

5 come on strong *informal* to make it very clear to someone that you think they are sexually attractive【非正式】献殷勤, 向〔某人〕表示强烈好感

come on to sb/sth *phr v* [T] **1** *spoken* to move forward in a speech or discussion to a new subject【口】〔演讲或讨论中〕转到〔新话题〕: *I'll come on to this question in a few moments.* 待会儿我会谈到这个问题。**2** *informal* if someone comes on to another person, they make it very clear that they are sexually interested in them【非正式】对〔某人〕表示好感, 献殷勤

come out *phr v* [I]

1 ▶BECOME KNOWN 被知道◀ to become publicly known, especially after being hidden 显露, 泄露: *It was several weeks before the truth of the matter came out.* 事实真相几个星期以后才得到披露。

2 ▶BECOME CLEAR 变清楚◀ if a fact comes out when you consider something, it becomes much easier to see than it was before 〔事实〕变得清楚: *The family resemblances come out strongly in the wedding photos.* 从结婚合照上, 可以看出这个家庭的成员明显长得很像。

3 ▶BECOME AVAILABLE 成为有售的◀ if a book, record etc comes out, it becomes publicly available 〔书、唱片等〕出版; 发行: *A second edition will come out next year.* 第二版将在明年出版。

4 ▶BE SAID 被说到◀ if something you say comes out in a particular way, that is how it sounds or how it is understood 〔词语、言语〕说出, 道出: *The words came out in little more than a whisper.* 这些话是悄悄说出的。| **come out all wrong** (=not sound the way you had intended) 与想表达的意思完全不同

5 ▶FINISH IN A PARTICULAR WAY 以特别的方式结束◀ **come out well/badly/ahead etc** to finish an action, process etc in a particular way or with a particular result 结果不错/很糟/很成功等: *If you spend a little more time on your work now, you'll come out ahead in the end.* 如果你现在能在工作上多花一点儿时间, 你最终会成为佼佼者的。| *I can never get cakes to come out right.* 我从来都做不好蛋糕。

6 ▶SAY PUBLICLY 公开说◀ [always+adv/prep] to say publicly that you strongly support or oppose a particular plan, belief etc 公开表示〔赞同或反对的〕观点: [+**for/against etc**] *The board of directors has come out strongly in favour of a merger.* 董事会强烈地公开表示支持一项合并。| **come out and say/state etc sth** *No one will come out and say it, but basically they can't stand her.* 没人会出来说什么, 不过基本上他们都受不了她。

7 ▶DISAPPEAR 消失◀ if colour or a mark comes out, it disappears, especially because it has been washed 〔尤指经过水洗后颜色、污渍〕褪去, 消失: *Ink stains will usually come out if you use a little methanol.* 如果你用一点儿甲醇, 墨水迹通常能洗掉。

8 ▶SUN 太阳◀ if the sun, moon, or stars come out, they appear in the sky 〔太阳、月亮、星辰〕出现, 显现

9 ▶FLOWER 花◀ if a flower comes out, it opens 〔花朵〕开放: *I love it when the snowdrops start to come out.* 我喜欢开始绽放的雪花莲。

10 ▶PHOTOGRAPH 照片◀ if a photograph or a subject of a photograph comes out, it looks the way the photographer wanted it to 〔照片等〕显像, 洗出: *Some of the wedding photos didn't come out* 有些结婚照冲洗不出来。| *That sunset really came out well, didn't it?* 那张日落的照片的确照得很好, 不是吗?

11 ▶HOMOSEXUAL 同性恋的◀ [+**to**] if someone comes out, they say openly that they are HOMOSEXUAL 公开宣布自己为同性恋者

12 ▶WORKER 工作者◀ *BrE* to refuse to work; STRIKE² (1)【英】罢工, 举行罢工: *The teachers are coming out in support of their pay claim.* 教师们正在举行罢工, 以支持他们提出增加工资的要求。

13 ▶GIRL 女孩◀ *old-fashioned* if a young woman comes out, she is formally introduced into UPPER-CLASS society, usually at a dance【过时】〔尤指年轻女子通过舞会〕正式进入上流社交界

come out in sth *phr v* [T not in passive 不用被动态] *BrE*【英】**come out in spots/a rash etc** to become partly covered by marks because you are ill or sensitive to particular foods or drugs 〔因生病或过敏而〕出疹子: *If I eat eggs, I come out in a rash.* 我一吃鸡蛋身上就出疹子。

come out with sth *phr v* [T not in passive 不用被动态] *informal* to say something, especially suddenly or in a way that is not expected【非正式】〔尤指突然地或出乎意料地〕说出, 提出: *Tanya came out with a really stupid remark.* 塔尼娅突然冒出一句蠢话。

come over *phr v* **1** [I] **a)** to visit someone's house or the place where they are 来访, 拜访: *Can I come over and see you on Friday night?* 我可以星期五晚上来拜访你吗? **b)** to make a journey, from another country and travelling east or west, to a place where you are now 〔从别国、远方等〕过来: [+**to/from**] *When did your family first come over to America?* 你的家人第一次来美国是什么时候? **2** [T **come over sb** not in passive 不用被动态] if a strong feeling comes over someone, they suddenly experience it 突然感到: *A wave of sleepiness came over me.* 我突然觉得很困。| **not know what has come over sb** (=be unable to explain someone's strange behaviour) 无法解释某人的古怪行为 *I'm sorry I was so rude – I don't know what came over me!* 对不起, 我不该那么失礼 —— 我不知道自己是怎么了! **3** [I] **a)** if an idea comes over to someone, they understand it clearly 〔观点〕被理解 **b)** if someone comes over in a particular way, they give other people that feeling or opinion about them 表现为; 显得: [+**as**] *I don't think I came over as a confident manager at the interview.* 我觉得我在面试中表现得不像个自信的经理人。**4 come over (all) shy/nervous etc** *informal especially BrE* to become shy, nervous etc【非正式, 尤英】变得害羞/紧张等

come round *BrE*【英】*phr v* [I] **1** to visit someone at home or at the place where they are 顺路来访, 拜访: *Why don't you come round for lunch?* 你为什么不顺道来吃午饭呢? **2** to change your opinion so that you now agree with someone 回心转意; 改变立场[观点]: [+**to**] *I'm sure Bradley will come round to our way of thinking.* 我肯定布拉德利会改变立场, 同意我们的想法的。**3** if a regular event comes round, it arrives or happens as usual 〔如往常〕降临, 发生: *Your birthday's coming round again, isn't it?* 你的生日又快到了, 是不是? **4** to become conscious again 恢复知觉, 苏醒: *Kim was muttering, and seemed to be coming round.* 金正在咕哝着发出声音, 看来要苏醒了。

come through *phr v* **1 a)** [I] if a piece of news, a result etc comes through, it becomes known or heard 〔消息、结果等〕公开; 被知晓: *Listen! There's something coming through on the radio now.* 听! 现在收音机里有什么消息要播送。| *We're still*

waiting for our exam results to come through. 我们仍然在等待考试成绩公布。**b)** if an official document comes through, it arrives〔官方文件〕到达: *Has your giro come through yet?* 你的银行转账到了吗? **2** [T **come through** sth] to continue to live, exist, be strong, or succeed after a difficult or dangerous time 经历…而活着; 安然度过: *We're so relieved that Bill came through the operation all right.* 比尔的手术成功了, 这让我们大大松了口气。| *Amazingly, our house came through the storm without much damage.* 我们的房子在那场暴风雨中没受多大损坏, 这真是奇迹。

come through with sth *phr v* [T] to give people something important, especially when they have been worried that you would not produce it in time 交出; 交付; 提供: *Our representative in Hong Kong finally came through with the figures.* 我们在香港的代表最终提供了数据。

come to *phr v*

1 ►REACH A STATE 达到某种状态◄ [T **come to** sth] **a) it has come to this** *spoken* used to express shock that a situation has become so bad【口】竟糟到这种地步, 竟如此糟糕: *"I want back all the jewellery I gave you." "So, it's come to this, has it, our wonderful marriage?"* "我想要回所有我给你的首饰。" "那么, 我们美满的婚姻已经这么糟了吗?" **b)** to reach a particular state or position, especially a bad one 落到…田地; 至于…地步: *All those years, and in the end it came to nothing.* 那么多年, 最后却落得一事无成。| *If it comes to a fight, you can depend on me!* 如果要打架的话, 你可以放心, 有我呢! **c) what's it all coming to?/what's the world coming to?** *spoken* used to show how shocked or disappointed something has made you feel【口】这是怎么回事? 这有什么意思?〔用于表示震惊或失望〕

2 come to £20/$30 etc to be a total amount of £20, $30 etc 总额为 20 英镑/30 美元等: *That comes to £23.50, madam.* 总共 23.50 英镑, 夫人。

3 [T not in passive 不用被动态] if a thought or idea comes to you, you realize or remember it, especially suddenly〔想法、主张等〕突然被…忆起, 被想起: *The solution came to him in a flash.* 他灵机一动, 想到了解决方法。| *I've forgotten her name, but maybe it'll come to me later.* 我忘了她的名字, 不过以后也许会想起来的。

4 [I] to become conscious again 恢复知觉, 苏醒: *When Jack came to, he was lying in an alley and his wallet was gone.* 杰克醒过来的时候, 他正躺在一个巷子里, 钱包已经不见了。

5 when it comes to *informal*【非正式】**a)** on the subject of 涉及, 谈到: *I can use a computer, but when it comes to repairing them, I know nothing.* 我会使用电脑, 但若谈到修理, 我就一窍不通了。**b)** when you are dealing with something 处理, 处置: *When it comes to relationships, everyone makes mistakes.* 在处理人际关系的时候, 每个人都会犯错误的。

6 have sth coming (to you) *informal* to deserve to be punished or to have something bad happen to you【非正式】(你) 活该遭报应: *"Ron's been expelled from school." "Well, he had it coming."* "罗恩被学校开除了。" "哦, 他活该。" | *I hope you get what's coming to you, you sod!* 你这个卑鄙的家伙, 我希望你会遭报应!

7 come to yourself *old-fashioned informal* to gain control of your emotions again【过时, 非正式】重新控制自己, 恢复自制力

come under sth *phr v* [T not in passive 不用被动态] **1** to be governed, controlled, or influenced by something 受…管辖[支配, 影响]: *Your case comes under the jurisdiction of the county courts.* 你的案子由郡法庭进行审理。| *All doctors come under the same rules of professional conduct.* 所有医生都要遵守同样的职业行为规范。**2 come under attack/fire/scrutiny** to be attacked, shot at etc 被袭击/枪击/监视: *Some members in the party have come under attack from radicals in recent weeks.* 最近几周, 该党的一些成员遭到激进分子攻击。**3** if a piece of information comes under a particular title, subject etc, it can be found there in a book, library etc 可在…之下查到; 列在…下: *'Phobias' – that will come under Psychology in section twelve.* "Phobias (恐惧症)" 这个词可以在第 12 节 "心理学" 下查到。—see also 另见 **come under the hammer** (HAMMER[1] (2))

come up *phr v* [I]

1 ►APPEAR OR HAPPEN 出现或发生◄ **a)** to be mentioned or suggested as something to be considered or given attention 被提到, 被讨论, 被考虑: *A lot of new questions came up at the meeting.* 在此次会议上, 许多新问题被提了出来。| *Your name came up in our conversation once or twice.* 你的名字在我们谈话时被提到一两次。**b) be coming up** if an important event is coming up, it is being arranged and will happen soon 即将开始, 即将到来: *Don't you have a birthday coming up soon?* 你的生日不是快到了吗? **c)** if a legal case comes up, it is dealt with in a court of law 开庭审理: *Your case comes up next week.* 你的案件下周开庭审理。**d)** if a job or position comes up, it becomes available〔工作或职位〕出现空缺: *A vacancy has come up in the accounts department.* 会计部空出了一个职位。

2 ►TRAVEL NORTH 北行◄ to travel north or towards an important place such as a big city 北上, 去大城市: [+to] *Why don't you come up to New York for the weekend?* 你为什么不去纽约度周末呢?

3 ►MOVE NEAR 靠近◄ to move near someone or something, especially by walking〔尤指步行〕走近: [+to/behind etc] *Come up to the front of the room so everyone can see you.* 走到房间前面来, 让大家都能看见你。| *Aagh! Don't come up behind me like that!* 哎哟! 别那样从后面走近我。

4 ►SUN/MOON 太阳/月亮◄ **a)** when the sun or moon comes up, it rises〔太阳或月亮〕升起: *The sun was coming up by the time I finished the essay.* 我完成那篇文章的时候, 太阳已冉冉升起。**b)** when a plant comes up, it begins to be seen above the ground〔植物从地上〕长出, 发芽: *Look, the daffodils are coming up.* 看, 水仙花发芽了。**c)** when food comes up, it rises back from your stomach after being swallowed〔食物〕呕出, 吐出: *I suddenly felt nauseous and then the whole lot came up.* 我突然觉得恶心, 刚吃的东西一股脑儿全吐了出来。

5 ►PROBLEM 问题◄ if a problem or difficulty comes up, it suddenly appears or starts to affect you 突然出现〔问题、困难〕: **sth comes up** *Sorry I can't go with you – something has suddenly come up.* 对不起, 我不能跟你一起去了 —— 我突然有急事。

6 coming (right) up! *spoken* used to say that something, especially food or drink, will be ready very soon【口】〔尤指食品、饮料〕马上就来, 立刻就好: *"Two martinis, please." "Coming up!"* "请来两杯马蒂尼。" "马上就来!"

7 come up in the world to become richer or more successful in society 更富有, 更成功: *She had come up in the world since her days on the flower stall.* 自从她摆了个花摊以来, 她的日子过得越来越优裕了。

8 ►BEGIN AT UNIVERSITY 开始上大学◄ *BrE* to begin studying at a university, especially Oxford or Cambridge【英】〔尤指在牛津或剑桥〕入学, 就读

come up against sth/sb *phr v* [T not in passive 不用被动态] to have to deal with opposition, problems, unfairness etc; ENCOUNTER[1] (1) 得处理[面对]〔反对意见、问题或不公正〕: *You've got no idea of what you're going to come up against.* 你想不到将会面对什么。

come up for sth *phr v* **1** [T] **come up for review/re-examination etc** to have a fixed time in the future when something will be examined, changed etc 定期检查/修改等: *The new regulations come up for review in April.* 这些新规则在 4 月份将予以检讨。

2 come up for re-election/selection to reach the time when people have to vote about whether you should continue in your political position 到重新选举期

come upon sth/sb *phr v* [T not in passive 不用被动态] *literary* to find or discover something or someone by chance【文】〔偶然〕遇见; 发现: *Suddenly I came upon a clearing in the wood.* 我在林中突然发现一片空地。

come up to sth *phr v* [T] to be as good as something else or as an expected standard 比得上; 达到〔标准〕: *This doesn't come up to the standard of your usual work.* 这次你的工作不及你一贯的水准。—see also 另见 **not come/be up to scratch** (SCRATCH[2] (3))

come up with sth *phr v* [T] **1** to think of an idea, plan, reply etc 想出, 提出〔主意、计划、回答等〕: *Is that the best excuse you can come up with?* 那就是你能想出的最好借口吗? | *Someone had better come up with a solution fast.* 最好有人能尽快想出解决办法。**2** to produce a sum of money that is needed 提供〔所需钱款〕: *How am I supposed to come up with $10,000?* 我怎么能拿得出一万美元来?

come² *n* [U] *slang* a man's SEMEN (=the liquid he produces during sex)【俚】精液

come·back /ˈkʌmˌbæk; ˈkʌmbæk/ *n* [C usually singular 一般用单数] **1 make/stage a comeback** if a person, activity, style etc makes a comeback, they become popular again after being unpopular for a long time 东山再起; 复原: *The miniskirt made a comeback in the late 1980s.* 迷你裙在 20 世纪 80 年代末期再度流行。**2** a quick reply that is often clever, funny, and

insulting; RETORT[2] (1)〔机智、幽默或尖刻的〕回答, 反驳: *I couldn't think of a good comeback.* 我想不出什么巧妙的回答。—see also 另见 **come back** (COME[1]) **3** a way of getting payment or a reward for something wrong or unfair that has been done to you 得到补偿[补救]的方法: *Check your contract carefully, or you may have no comeback if something goes wrong.* 仔细检查一下你的合同, 否则如果出了什么差错, 你可能得不到任何补偿。

co·me·di·an /kəˋmidɪən; kəˈmiːdiən/ *n* [C] **1** someone whose job is to tell jokes and make people laugh〔讲笑话或演滑稽戏的〕演员 **2** *old use* someone who plays funny characters in plays or films【旧】喜剧演员; 滑稽演员

co·me·di·enne /kə͵midɪˋɛn; kə͵miːdiˈen/ *n* [C] *old-fashioned* a female comedian【过时】女喜剧演员; 女滑稽演员

come·down /ˋkʌm͵daun; ˈkʌmdaʊn/ *n* [C usually singular 一般用单数] *informal* a situation that is not as good, important, interesting etc as the situation you had previously【非正式】落泊, 潦倒; 失势: *The 'King of Wall Street' is bankrupt! What a comedown!* "华尔街之王"破产了! 真是落泊! —see also 另见 **come down** (COME[1])

com·e·dy /ˋkɑmədɪ; ˈkɒmɪ̵di/ *n* **1** [C,U] a play, film etc that is intended to entertain people and make them laugh 喜剧: *a comedy starring Eddie Murphy* 由〔美国黑人喜剧演员〕埃迪·墨菲主演的一部喜剧 | *Come to Comedy Night at the Albion!* 到阿尔比恩的喜剧之夜去! **2** [U] the quality in something such as a book or play that makes people laugh; HUMOUR[1] (1) 喜剧性, 喜剧成分; 幽默: *Can't you see the comedy of the situation?* 你不觉得这种情况滑稽吗? —see also 另见 BLACK COMEDY, SITUATION COMEDY

Comedy of Er·rors, The /͵· · · ˈ· ·/ a humorous play by Shakespeare about two sets of IDENTICAL TWINS (=two children born to the same mother at the same time, who look exactly the same). There are many confusing and amusing situations because the other characters think that they are dealing with one twin when in fact they are dealing with the other. The phrase 'a comedy of errors' is often used to describe a situation that is so full of mistakes and problems that it seems funny.《错误的喜剧》〔莎士比亚的一部喜剧。该剧讲述两对同卵双胞胎的故事。剧中的人物老是会认错双胞胎, 全戏充满混乱可笑的场景。同名短语常被用来形容一个错误、麻烦百出, 看似滑稽可笑的情景〕

comedy of man·ners /͵· · · ˈ· ·/ *n* [C] a comedy that makes the behaviour of a particular group, especially the UPPER CLASS, seem silly〔讽刺某一群体, 尤其是上流社会的〕风俗喜剧

come-hith·er /͵· ˈ· ·/ *adj old-fashioned* **come-hither look/eyes** a way of looking at someone that shows you think they are sexually attractive【过时】挑逗的眼神/诱惑的目光

come·ly /ˋkʌmlɪ; ˈkʌmli/ *adj literary* a comely woman has an attractive appearance【文】〔女性〕标致的, 秀丽的 —**comeliness** *n* [U]

come-on /ˈ· ·/ *n* [C] **1** *informal* something that a business offers cheaply or free in order to persuade you to buy something【非正式】〔商业的〕促销品; 赠品: *The competition for a free trip is just a come-on.* 争取免费旅行的比赛不过是一种商业促销行为。**2 give sb the come-on** *BrE spoken* to behave in a way that shows someone very clearly that you are sexually interested in them【英口】勾引, 挑逗 —see also 另见 **come on** (COME[1])

com·er /ˋkʌmɚ; ˈkʌmə/ *n* **all comers** *informal* anyone who is interested, especially anyone who wants to take part in a competition【非正式】参加者; 来者: *The contest is open to all comers.* 该项竞赛对所有人开放。—see also 另见 LATECOMER, NEWCOMER

co·mes·ti·bles /kəˋmɛstəbḷz; kəˈmestɪ̵bəlz/ *n* [plural] *formal* food【正式】食物, 食品

com·et /ˋkɑmɪt; ˈkɒmɪ̵t/ *n* [C] an object in space like a bright ball with a long tail that moves around the sun 彗星: *Halley's comet* 哈雷彗星

come·up·pance /kʌmˋʌpəns; kʌmˈʌpəns/ *n* [singular] *informal* a punishment or something bad that happens to you which you really deserve【非正式】应得的惩罚; 报应: **get your comeuppance** *You'll get your comeuppance one day, you'll see!* 瞧着吧, 总有一天你会得到报应的!

com·fort¹ /ˋkʌmfɚt; ˈkʌmfət/ *n* W3

1 ▶EMOTIONAL 情感的◀ [U] a feeling of being more calm, cheerful, or hopeful after you have been worried or unhappy 安慰, 慰藉: *I looked to my family for comfort when things got difficult at work.* 工作中遇到困难时, 我向家人寻求安慰。| **bring/give comfort** *The service is there to give the advice and comfort people need.* 那里的服务在于为人们提供所需的建议及抚慰。| **take/draw/derive comfort from** *Mrs. Oliphant drew great comfort from the familiar hymns.* 奥利芬特夫人从熟悉的圣歌中得到极大的安慰。| **it's no/some/any comfort** *If it's any comfort, we didn't win anything either.* 就算有点安慰, 我们也没有赢得什么。

2 ▶PHYSICAL 身体的◀ [U] a feeling of being physically relaxed and satisfied, so that nothing is hurting you, making you feel too hot or cold etc 舒适感, 满足感: **for comfort** *I usually dress for comfort rather than style.* 我的衣着通常讲究舒适而非追求时尚。| **too cold/hot/high etc for comfort** (=physically unpleasant for a particular reason) 因太冷/热/高等而身体不适 | **in comfort/in the comfort of** *Now you can watch your favorite movies in the comfort of your own home.* 现在你可以舒舒服服地在自己家里看你最喜欢的电影了。| **built/made/designed for comfort** *a new climbing boot designed for comfort and safety* 一种新型舒适安全的登山鞋

3 ▶MONEY/POSSESSIONS 钱/财产◀ [U] a way of living in which you have all the possessions, money etc that you need or want 舒适, 安逸: *I intend to retire in comfort!* 我想在退休后过上安逸的生活!

4 comforts [plural] the things that make your life more pleasant and comfortable, especially things that are not necessary 使生活舒适之物; 奢侈品: **all the comforts of home** *The beach cabin has all the comforts of home.* 那座海滨小屋有一切家用舒适品。| **material comforts** (=money and possessions) 金钱, 财产 | **creature comforts** (=things such as comfortable chairs and warm rooms) 物质享受〈如舒适的椅子、温暖的房间〉 *Alicia was too fond of her creature comforts to go camping.* 艾丽西亚十分喜爱家里的舒适享受, 不想去露营。

5 ▶SB/STH THAT HELPS 有用的人/物◀ [C] someone or something that helps you feel happier or calmer when you have been worried or unhappy 安慰者; 慰藉物: **be a comfort to** *Jerry's been a real comfort to me since Max died.* 马克斯去世后, 杰里成了我真正的安慰。| **comfort eating/shopping etc** (=eating etc that makes you feel better) 让人好受[给人抚慰]的饮食/购物等 | **it's a comfort** *It's a comfort to know there's someone to keep an eye on the kids.* 知道有人照料着那些孩子, 真令人安慰。

6 too close/near etc for comfort something that is too close for comfort makes you feel worried, unhappy, or uncomfortable, because it is dangerous in some way〔因危险而〕使人忧虑[不快, 不适]的事情: *The cars were whizzing past us much too close for comfort.* 一辆辆汽车紧贴着我们身边呼啸而过, 令我们提心吊胆。

7 cold/small comfort a small piece of good news that does not make you feel better about a bad situation 不起作用的安慰: *The promise that I might one day be rehoused was cold comfort.* 对于将来可给我提供新居所的承诺, 并不令人觉得欣慰。—**comfortless** *adj*

comfort² *v* [T] to make someone feel calmer and more hopeful by being kind and sympathetic to them when they are worried or unhappy 安慰, 慰问: *Nothing I could do or say could comfort Diane when her son died.* 黛安娜的儿子死后, 我不论做什么或说什么都无法安慰她。—**comforting** *adj* —**comfortingly** *adv*

com·for·ta·ble /ˋkʌmfɚtəbḷ; ˈkʌmftəbəl/ *adj* S2 W3

1 ▶FEELING PHYSICALLY COMFORTABLE 身体感觉舒适的◀ feeling physically relaxed and satisfied, without feeling any pain or being too hot, cold etc〔人〕舒适的, 舒坦的; 满意的: *I was so comfortable and warm in bed I didn't want to get up.* 床上又舒服又暖和, 我一点都不想起床。| **make yourself comfortable** *Sit down and make yourself comfortable while I put the kettle on.* 请坐, 别客气, 我烧点开水。

2 ▶CLOTHES/FURNITURE/PLACES ETC 衣服/家具/地方等◀ making you feel physically relaxed and satisfied 舒适的; 令人满意的: *Joyce has a comfortable apartment in Portland.* 乔伊丝在波特兰有一所舒适的公寓。| *comfortable shoes* 舒服的鞋 | **comfortable to sit/lie/stand on etc** *Is your chair comfortable to sit on?* 你的椅子坐上去舒服吗?

3 ▶NOT WORRIED 不担忧的◀ if you are comfortable with an idea, person, or activity, you do not feel worried about it 放心的; 欣慰的: *I'm not comfortable with the idea of you having a motorcycle.* 你骑摩托车这主意让我不放心。| **feel comfortable** *an office environment you can feel comfortable in* 令人舒心的办公环境

4 ▶MONEY 钱◀ having enough money to live on without worrying about paying for things 宽裕的, 小康的: *The Austins aren't rich, but they're comfortable.* 奥斯汀一家并不富有, 但他们手头还算宽裕。

5 ▶ILL/INJURED 生病的/受伤的◀ if someone who is ill or injured is comfortable, they are not in too much pain〔患者或伤者〕感觉不太疼痛的

6 ▶RACE/COMPETITION 赛跑/竞赛◀ a number of points or a

distance that will allow you to win easily 轻松获胜的，轻松赢得的: *Cantona scored to give United a comfortable 3-0 lead at half-time.* 坎通纳的进球使得联队在上半场结束时以3比0轻松领先。

7►BELIEF/IDEA/OPINION 信仰/念头/意见◄ a belief etc that you do not think very seriously about and that ignores problems or difficulties〔信仰等〕忽略困难的；不严谨的: *the comfortable middle class belief that everyone who works hard will succeed* 认为每个人只要努力工作就会成功的过于乐观的中产阶级信念 —**comfortably** *adv* —see also 另见 UNCOMFORTABLE

com·fort·er /ˈkʌmfətə; ˈkʌmfətə/ *n* [C] **1** someone who comforts you 安慰者，慰问者 **2** *AmE* a cover for a bed that is filled with a soft warm material such as feathers【美】〔铺床的〕加衬芯床罩; DUVET *BrE*【英】**3** *old use* a warm SCARF【旧】羊毛围巾

com·fy /ˈkʌmfɪ; ˈkʌmfi/ *adj spoken* comfortable【口】舒适的，舒服的: *a comfy chair* 舒适的椅子

com·ic¹ /ˈkɑmɪk; ˈkɒmɪk/ *adj* amusing you and making you want to laugh 滑稽的，好笑的: *a comic performance* 滑稽表演 | **comic writer/actress/performer etc** (=someone who writes or performs things that make you laugh) 喜剧作家/女演员/演出者等 | **comic relief** (=a situation in a serious story that makes you relax a little because it is funny)〔情节严肃的故事中的〕喜剧情节 | **comic verse/song etc** (=a song etc that entertains you and makes you laugh) 滑稽诗/歌曲等 —opposite 反义词 TRAGIC (2)

comic² also 又作 **comic book** /ˈ·· ·/ *AmE*【美】*n* [C] **1** a magazine for children that tells a story using comic strips 连环漫画，连环漫画册 **2** someone whose job is to tell jokes and make people laugh; COMEDIAN 喜剧演员: *a stand-up comic* 一位说单口笑话的喜剧演员

com·i·cal /ˈkɑmɪkl; ˈkɒmɪkəl/ *adj* behaviour or situations that are comical are funny in a strange or unexpected way 滑稽的，荒诞可笑的: *The cat looked so comical with the bow on its head!* 那只猫头上打着个蝴蝶结，看上去太滑稽了！—**comically** /-klɪ; -kli/ *adv*

comic op·e·ra /ˌ·· ˈ···/ *n* [C,U] an OPERA with an amusing story in which the singers speak as well as sing 喜歌剧

Comic Re·lief /ˌ·· ·ˈ·/ a British CHARITY organization which was started by professional COMEDIANS. Once a year they have a special day when they collect money for people who need help in the UK and other countries. 喜剧演员济贫会〔英国一慈善机构，由职业喜剧演员创立。他们一年一度在一个特定的日子为英国和其他国家需要帮助的人筹集资金〕

comic strip /ˈ·· ·/ *n* [C] a series of drawn pictures inside boxes that tell a story 连环漫画 —compare 比较 CARTOON (1)

com·ing¹ /ˈkʌmɪŋ; ˈkʌmɪŋ/ *n* **1 the coming of sth/sb** the time when something new begins, especially something that will cause a lot of changes 某事物/某人的到来[降临]: *With the coming of railways, new markets opened up.* 随着铁路的建成，新市场打开了。**2 comings and goings** *informal* the movements of people as they arrive at and leave places【非正式】来来往往，进进出出: *Mrs Williams next door knows all the comings and goings of everyone in the neighbourhood.* 隔壁的威廉斯夫人清楚地知道每个邻居的进进出出。

coming² *adj* [only before noun 仅用于名词前] *formal* happening soon【正式】即将发生的: *the clouds of the coming storm* 暴风雨前的乌云 —see also 另见 UP-AND-COMING

coming of age /ˌ·· · ˈ·/ *n* [singular] the point in a young person's life, usually the age of 18 or 21, at which their society considers them to be an adult 成年〔通常为18岁或21岁〕

> **CULTURAL NOTE 文化注释**
>
> At 18 British people are allowed to vote in elections, get married without the permission of their parents, and buy and drink alcohol in a PUB. In the US, either the 18th or 21st birthday might be thought of as a coming of age; at 18 people are allowed to vote and get married, but in many states you cannot buy alcohol until you are 21. 英国人年满18岁可参加投票，可以无须父母允许而结婚，可以在酒吧买酒和饮酒。美国人把18岁或21岁生日视为成年的标志。年满18岁的美国人可参加投票和结婚，但在许多州只有到了21岁才可以买酒。

com·ma /ˈkɑmə; ˈkɒmə/ *n* [C] the mark (,) used in writing and printing to show a short pause 逗号 —see also 另见 INVERTED COMMA —see picture at 参见 PUNCTUATION MARK 图

[W2] **com·mand¹** /kəˈmænd; kəˈmɑːnd/ *n*

1►ORDER 命令◄ [C] an order that should be obeyed 命令；指示: *Fire when I give the command.* 我一下命令就开火。

2►CONTROL 控制◄ [U] the control of a group of people or a situation 指挥；管辖；控制: **be in command** *Judge Hathaway was in complete command of the courtroom.* 哈撒韦法官完全控制了法庭的局面。| **have sth under your command** *We suspect that Don Sacco has several gangs under his command.* 我们怀疑唐·萨科手下有几帮匪徒。| **take command** (=begin controlling and making decisions) 掌握，开始控制 *Janet took command of the situation and got everyone out of the building safely.* 珍尼特控制了局势并让所有人安全撤离那栋建筑。| **at sb's command** (=available to be used by someone whenever they want) 服从某人，听从某人吩咐 *Each congressman has a large staff at his command.* 每位国会议员都有一大群下属听从吩咐。| **have command** *Flynn had command of a squadron on the Western Front.* 弗林在西线指挥一支中队。

3►MILITARY 军事的◄ [C also+plural verb *BrE* 英] **a)** a part of an army, navy etc that is controlled separately and has a particular job 部队；兵团: *pilots of the Southern Air Command* 南方空军兵团的飞行员 **b)** a group of officers or officials who give orders 司令部；指挥部: *Are you criticizing the High Command?* 你是在指责最高司令部吗？**c)** the group of soldiers that an officer is in control of〔同一军官统率的〕部队，军队

4 have (a) command of to have a good knowledge of something, especially a subject such as a language 掌握，精通〔尤指语言〕: *Jill has an impressive command of French.* 吉尔精通法语，令人印象深刻。

5►COMPUTER 电脑◄ [C] an instruction to a computer to do something〔电脑的〕指令

6 at your command if you have a particular skill at your command, you are able to use that skill well and easily〔技能等〕娴熟，运用自如: *a carpenter with years of experience at his command* 一位经验老到的木匠

7 be in command of yourself/your faculties to be able to control your emotions and thoughts 控制自己〔指情绪、思想等〕: *Kathleen walked in, tall, slim, confident and in total command of herself.* 凯瑟琳走了进来，她身材修长，满怀自信，神态自如。

command² *v*

1►ORDER 命令◄ [I,T] to tell someone officially to do something, especially if you are a military leader, a king etc〔尤指军官、国王等〕命令，下令: **command sb to do sth** *Captain Picard commanded the crew to report to the main deck.* 皮卡德船长命令全体船员到主甲板上集合。| **command that** *The General commanded that the regiment attack at once.* 将军下令该团立刻发起进攻。

2►LEAD THE MILITARY 率领军队◄ [I,T] to be responsible for giving orders to a group of people in the army, navy etc 统率；指挥〔军队〕: *He commands the 4th Battalion of the Scots Guard.* 他统率苏格兰卫队第四营。

3►DESERVE AND GET 应得并获得◄ [T] to get something such as attention or respect because you are important or popular 赢得；博得〔尊敬、注意等〕: *Dr. Young commands a great deal of respect as a surgeon.* 扬医生是德高望重的外科医生。| *"Supermodels" can command extremely high fees.* "超级模特儿"能够获取巨额报酬。

4►CONTROL 控制◄ [T] to control something 对…有支配权；掌握: *The party which commands a majority of seats in Parliament forms the government.* 由在议会拥有多数席位的党派组成政府。

5►VIEW 景色◄ if a place commands a view, you can see something clearly from it 俯瞰；眺望；清楚地看到: *The Ramses Hilton commands a magnificent view of Cairo.* 在拉姆西斯－希尔顿酒店能尽览开罗的美景。

com·man·dant /ˌkɑmənˈdænt; ˌkɒmənˈdænt/ *n* [C] the chief officer in charge of a military organization 司令官，指挥官: *the commandant of a prison camp* 监狱长

com·man·deer /ˌkɑmənˈdɪr; ˌkɒmənˈdɪə/ *v* [T] to take someone else's property for your own use, especially during the war〔尤指战争时期〕征用，强征〔私人财产〕: *The local hotel was commandeered for the wounded.* 当地的宾馆被征用，以安置伤员。

com·mand·er /kəˈmændə; kəˈmɑːndə/ *n* [C] **1** an officer of any rank who is in charge of a group of soldiers or a particular military activity 指挥官，长官: *the American Commander, General Otis* 美军指挥官奥蒂斯将军 | *our platoon commander* 我们的排长 **2** a high rank in the navy, or someone who holds this rank 海军中校 —see table on page C6 参见C6页附录 **3** a British police officer of high rank 英国高级警官 —see also 另见 WING COMMANDER

commander in chief /ˌ·· · ˈ·/ *n* [C usually singular 一般用单数] someone of high rank who is in control of all the mili-

tary organizations in a country or of a specific military activity 总司令; 最高统帅: *The Queen is Commander in Chief of the British armed forces.* 女王是英国军队的最高统帅。

com·mand·ing /kəˋmændɪŋ; kəˈmɑːndɪŋ/ *adj* **1** having the authority or position that allows you to give orders 指挥的, 统率的: *a commanding officer* 指挥官 | *Japan's commanding economic position* 日本在经济领域的领导地位 **2** making people respect and obey you 令人肃然起敬的; 威严的: *Papa's commanding presence* 爸爸那威严的气度 **3** a commanding view or position is one from which you can clearly see a long way 居高临下的, 视野开阔的 **4** being in a position from which you are likely to win a race or competition easily 遥遥领先的, 胜券在握的: *a commanding lead* 遥遥领先

com·mand·ment /kəˋmændmənt; kəˈmɑːndmənt/ *n* [C] **1** one of the ten rules given by God in the Bible that tell people how they must behave 戒条〔《圣经》所指的十诫之一〕 **2** *literary* a command【文】命令

command mod·ule /·ˈ· ,··/ *n* [C] *technical* the part of a space vehicle from which its activities are controlled【术语】〔航天器中的〕指令舱, 指挥舱

com·man·do /kəˋmændo; kəˈmɑːndəʊ/ *n plural* **commandos** or **commandoes** [C] **1** a soldier or a small group of soldiers who are specially trained to make quick attacks into enemy areas 突击队(员): *a commando raid* 突击队的一次偷袭 **2 the commandoes** a UNIT (1) of the British Royal Marines〔英国皇家海军陆战队的〕小队

command per·form·ance /·,· ·ˈ··/ *n* [C usually singular 一般用单数] a special performance at a theatre that is given at the request of a king, president etc 奉命专场演出; 御前演出

command post /·ˈ· ·/ *n* [C] the place from which military leaders and their officers control activities 指挥部, 司令部

com·mem·o·rate /kəˋmɛmə,ret; kəˈmeməreɪt/ *v* [T] to do something to show that you remember and respect someone important or an important event in the past 庆祝, 为…举行纪念活动: *a parade to commemorate the town's bicentenary* 庆祝该镇建镇 200 周年的游行 —**commemorative** /kəˋmɛmərətɪv; kəˈmemərətɪv/ *adj*: *a commemorative plaque* 纪念牌匾

com·mem·o·ra·tion /kə,mɛməˋreʃən; kə,meməˈreɪʃən/ *n* [U] something that makes you remember and respect someone important or an important event in the past 纪念; 纪念活动: **in commemoration of** *a service in commemoration of those who died in the war* 纪念战争死难者的仪式

com·mence /kəˋmɛns; kəˈmens/ *v* [I,T] *formal* to begin or to start something【正式】开始; 着手: **[+with]** *A trial commences with opening statements.* 审判以宣读开庭词开始。| **commence sth** *Your first evaluation will be six months after you commence employment.* 你工作六个月后, 将接受第一次业务评估。| **commence doing sth** *You may commence reading, Jeremy.* 杰里米, 你可以开始看书了。

Frequencies of **commence**, **start** and **begin** in spoken and written English 英语口语和书面语中 commence, start 和 begin 的使用频率

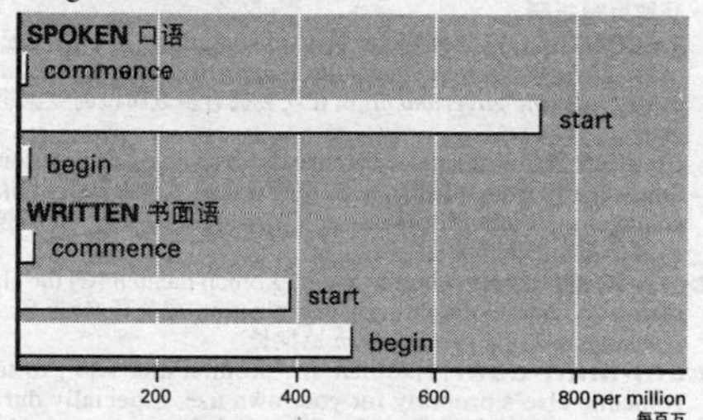

Based on the British National Corpus and the Longman Lancaster Corpus
据英国国家语料库和朗文兰开斯特语料库

This graph shows that in spoken English **start** is the most common of the three verbs. In written English **begin** is the most common. **Commence**, a formal word, is the least common of the three verbs in spoken and written English. 本图表显示, 在英语口语中 start 是三个动词中最常用的。在书面语中 begin 最常用, commence 是一个正式的词。在英语口语和书面语中是三个动词中最不常用的。

com·mence·ment /kəˋmɛnsmənt; kəˈmensmənt/ *n formal*【正式】**1** [C,U] beginning 开始, 开端: **[+of]** *the commencement of the proceedings* 诉讼程序的开始 **2** [C] *AmE* a ceremony at which university, college, or high school students receive their DIPLOMAS; GRADUATION【美】〔大学及高中的〕毕业典礼

com·mend /kəˋmɛnd; kəˈmend/ *v* [T] *formal*【正式】**1** to praise or approve of someone or something, especially publicly〔尤指公开地〕赞扬: **commend sb for sth** *A Chester man was commended for his public-spirited action.* 一位切斯特的男性居民由于热心公益而受到表扬。| **highly commended** *Bartholomew's work has been highly commended.* 巴塞洛缪的作品大受好评。**2** to tell someone that something is good or deserves attention; RECOMMEND 推荐, 推崇: *I commend this bill to the House.* 我向议院提交了这项议案。| **not have much to commend it** (=not be satisfactory) 不令人满意的 *The hotel doesn't have much to commend it.* 这家旅馆实在不能令人满意。**3** *old use* to give someone to someone else to take care of【旧】托…照顾, 把…交托给

com·men·da·ble /kəˋmɛndəbḷ; kəˈmendəbəl/ *adj formal* deserving praise【正式】值得称赞的, 值得表扬的: *a highly commendable effort* 值得高度称赞的努力 | *Baldwin answered with commendable frankness.* 鲍德温回答时所表现的坦诚令人赞许。—**commendably** *adv*

com·men·da·tion /,kɑmənˋdeʃən; ,kɒmənˈdeɪʃən/ *n* [C, U] *formal* an official statement praising someone, especially someone who has been brave or very successful【正式】〔尤指对勇敢或很成功的人所作的正式的〕称赞, 表扬

com·men·su·rate /kəˋmɛnʃərɪt; kəˈmenʃərḷt/ *adj formal* matching something in size, quality, or length of time【正式】〔在尺寸、质量或时间长度上〕与…相当的; 相称的: **[+with]** *a salary commensurate with your experience* 与你的经验相称的工资

com·ment¹ /ˋkɑmɛnt; ˈkɒment/ *n* **1** [C,U] an opinion that you express about someone or something 意见, 评论: *Does anyone have any questions or comments?* 有谁有问题或意见吗? | **make a comment (on/about)** *The police chief made no comment about the bomb attack.* 警察总长对炸弹袭击事件保持缄默。| **be fair comment** *BrE spoken* (=be criticism that is reasonable or deserved)【英口】作出合理的批评; 应得的评论 **2** [U] criticism or discussion of something someone has said or done〔对某人所说或所做事情的〕批评; 议论: *The Prime Minister's speech received much comment in the press.* 新闻界对首相的演说议论纷纷。| **no comment** *spoken* (=used by people in public life when they do not want to answer questions about a subject)【口】无可奉告〔政治家等人不想回答问题时使用〕 **3 be a comment on** to be a sign of the bad quality of something 是〔反映事物不足之处的〕标志, 特征: *The number of adults who cannot read is a comment on the quality of our schools.* 成人文盲的数量是我们学校教育质量差的反映。

comment² *v* [I,T] to express an opinion about someone or something 评论, 发表意见: **[+on]** *People were always commenting on my sister's looks.* 人们总是对我妹妹评头论足。| **comment that** *Some critics have commented that the film is unnecessarily violent.* 一些评论家批评这部电影充斥着不必要的暴力。

com·men·ta·ry /ˋkɑmən,tɛrɪ; ˈkɒməntəri/ *n* **1** [C] a spoken description of an event, given while the event is happening, especially on the television or radio〔尤指在电视或电台上对实况进行的〕解说, 报道: *Stop shouting! I can't hear the baseball commentary.* 别吵啦! 我听不见棒球解说了。| **[+on]** *Do they have a commentary on the parade?* 他们会对这次游行进行实况报道吗? | **running commentary** (=a continuous description of something)〔对某一事件进行的〕连续报道 **2** [C,U] something such as a book or article that explains or discusses a book, poem, idea etc〔对书、诗歌、思想等的〕评说; 注释: *political commentary* 政论 **3 be a sad commentary on** to be a sign of how bad a particular situation is〔情况或局势〕令人沮丧[不容乐观]的表现: *The whole incident was a sad commentary on the state of British football.* 整个事件是英国足球现状不容乐观的表现。

com·men·tate /ˋkɑmən,tet; ˈkɒmənteɪt/ *v* [I+on] to describe an event, such as a sports game on television or radio 为〔体育比赛等〕作解说

com·men·ta·tor /ˋkɑmən,tetɚ; ˈkɒmənteɪtə/ *n* [C] **1** someone who knows a lot about a particular subject, and who writes about it or discusses it on the television or radio 评论员: *political commentators* 政治评论员 **2** someone who describes an event as it is happening on television or radio 实况播音员; 实况解说员: *David Vine, the BBC's commentator on winter sports* 戴维·瓦因 —— 英国广播公司冬季运动的解说员 | *a sports commentator* 体育赛事的解说员

com·merce /ˋkɑmɝs; ˈkɒmɜːs/ *n* [U] **1** the buying and selling of goods and services; TRADE¹ (1) 买卖, 贸易; 商务; 商业:

measures promoting local commerce and industry 促进当地商业和工业发展的措施 **2** *old-fashioned* relationships and communication between people【过时】联系；交流 —see also 另见 CHAMBER OF COMMERCE

com·mer·cial¹ /kə`mɝʃəl; kə'mɜːʃəl/ *adj* **1** related to business and the buying and selling of goods and services 商业的；商务的：*Our top priorities must be profit and commercial growth.* 我们要以利润和贸易增长作为重中之重。**2** related to the ability of a product or business to make a profit〔产品、经营〕能赚钱的，营利的：*Gibbons failed to see the commercial value of his discovery.* 吉本斯没有意识到自己的发现所具有的商业价值。| **a commercial success/failure** *The film was a huge commercial success.* 这部电影的票房收入非常可观。**3** [only before noun 仅用于名词前] a commercial product is one that is produced in large quantities and sold to the public rather than only to other businesses〔产品〕商品化的：*All commercial milk is pasteurized.* 牛奶产品都是经过杀菌的。**4** commercial business or activity produces goods and services in large quantities 大量生产的〈如产品和劳务〉：*a large commercial fish farm* 大型商业养鱼场 **5** more concerned with money than with quality 商业化的〔更重视金钱而忽视质量〕：*I used to like their music but they've become very commercial.* 过去我很喜欢他们的音乐，但他们已经变得纯粹是以赚钱为目的了。**6 commercial radio/TV/channel etc** radio or television broadcasts that are produced by companies that earn money through advertising〔靠广告维持的〕商业电台/电视/频道等

commercial² *n* **1** [C] an advertisement on television or radio〔电视或电台的〕商业广告：*a soap powder commercial* 肥皂粉广告 **2 commercial break** the time when advertisements are shown during a television or radio programme 广告时间〔电视或电台节目中播插广告的时间〕

commercial bank /·,··'·/ *n* [C] *technical* the kind of bank that provides services for customers and businesses and that is used by most ordinary people【术语】商业银行

Commercial Court, the /·'··,·/ a British court of law for cases relating to companies and banks. It decides whether they can move goods to particular places, join with other businesses, get the right to use a particular name, provide different services etc.〔英国〕商事法庭〔审理有关公司和银行案件的法庭，就货物运送、公司合并、名称使用权、变更服务等问题作出裁决〕

com·mer·cial·is·m /kə`mɝʃəlɪ,zəm; kə'mɜːʃəlɪzəm/ *n* [U] the principle or practice of being more concerned with making money from buying and selling goods than you are about their quality 营利主义，利润第一：*the commercialism of modern culture* 现代文化的实利主义

com·mer·cial·ize /kə`mɝʃəl,aɪz; kə'mɜːʃəlaɪz/ also 又作 **-ise** *BrE*【英】*v* [T] **1** [usually passive 一般用被动态] to be more concerned with making money from something than about its quality 使商业化，使成为营利手段：*Christmas has become so commercialized nowadays.* 圣诞节现已变得如此商业化了。**2** to sell something to the public in order to make a profit, especially something that would not usually be sold 使商品化〔尤指通常不销售的东西〕：*commercializing space launches to help pay for more space research* 把太空发射商品化以获取更多的太空研究费用 —**commercialization** /kə,mɝʃələ`zeʃən; kə,mɜːʃəlaɪ'zeɪʃən/ *n* [U]

com·mer·cial·ly /kə`mɝʃəlɪ; kə'mɜːʃəli/ *adv* **1** [sentence adverb 句子副词] considering whether a business or product is making a profit 从商业角度来看：*Commercially, the movie was a flop.* 从商业角度来看，这部电影一败涂地。| **commercially viable** *The project is no longer commercially viable.* 这个项目从商业角度看不再可行。**2** produced or used in large quantities as a business 大量生产[使用]：*commercially farmed land* 大规模开垦的土地 **3** if a new product is commercially available, you can buy it in shops 经营上，营业上

commercial trav·el·ler /·,··'···/ *n* [C] *BrE old-fashioned* someone who travels from place to place selling goods for a company【英，过时】销售代表，推销员

com·mie /`kɑmɪ; 'kɒmi/ *n* [C] *especially AmE* an insulting word for a COMMUNIST【尤美】共党分子〔蔑称〕

com·mis·e·rate /kə`mɪzə,ret; kə'mɪzəreɪt/ *v* [I + with] *formal* to express your sympathy for someone who is unhappy about something【正式】怜悯，同情〔某人的不幸〕

com·mis·e·ra·tion /kə,mɪzə`reʃən; kə,mɪzə'reɪʃən/ *n formal*【正式】**1** [U] a feeling of sympathy for someone when something unpleasant has happened to them 怜悯，同情 **2 commiserations** [plural] used to express sympathy to someone, especially someone who has lost a competition〔尤指对某人在比赛中落败的〕同情：*our commiserations to the losing team* 我们对落败球队的同情

com·mis·sar·i·at /,kɑmə`sɛrɪət; ,kɒmɪ̣'seəriət/ *n* [C] a military department that is responsible for supplying food 军需部〔负责提供食品〕

com·mis·sa·ry /`kɑmə,sɛrɪ; 'kɒmɪ̣səri/ *n* [C] **1** *BrE* an officer in the army who is in charge of food supplies【英】军需官 **2** *AmE* a shop that supplies food and other goods in a military camp【美】军营商店 **3** *AmE* a place where you can eat in a large organization such as a film STUDIO (2), factory etc【美】〔电影制片厂、工厂等的〕餐厅，食堂

com·mis·sion¹ /kə`mɪʃən; kə'mɪʃən/ *n*

1 ▶PEOPLE 人们◀ [C] a group of people who have been given the official job of finding out about something or controlling something 调查团；考察团；委员会：*The Government has set up a commission to suggest improvements to the education system.* 政府已经成立一个委员会，负责提出建议，改善教育体制。

2 ▶MONEY 钱◀ [C,U] an amount of money that is paid to someone according to the value of the goods they have sold 佣金；酬金；回扣：*The dealer takes a 20% commission on the sales he makes.* 这个商人收取销售额的20%作为佣金。| **be on commission** (=be paid according to what you sell) 根据销售额付酬

3 ▶JOB 工作◀ [C] **a)** a request for an artist or musician to make a piece of art or music, for which they are paid 聘请，委托〔艺术家或音乐家，要求他创作一件作品〕：*a commission from the Academy for a new sculpture* 来自学院的委托，要求制作一尊新雕塑 **b)** *formal* a duty or job that you ask someone to do【正式】委派，任命

4 out of commission **a)** not working or not able to be used at the present time 不能工作；暂时失灵：*One of the ship's anchors was out of commission.* 船的一个锚坏了。**b)** *informal* ill or injured【非正式】生病的；受伤的

5 ▶ARMY/NAVY ETC 陆军/海军等◀ [C] an officer's position in the army, navy etc and the authority that is given to them〔军队中的〕军官地位；军官职权

6 ▶CRIME 罪行◀ [U] *formal* the commission of a crime is the act of doing it【正式】犯罪

7 in commission if a military ship is in commission, it is still being used by the navy〔船舰〕仍在服役的

commission² *v* [T] **1** to formally ask someone to write an official report, produce a work of art for you etc 委托〔写正式报告等〕：*We'll be commissioning a report on teenage alcoholism.* 我们将委托别人写青少年酗酒现象的报告。| **commission sb to do sth** *I've been commissioned to write a new play!* 有人托我写一部新剧本！**2 be commissioned** be given an officer's rank in the army, navy etc〔在军队中〕被授予军官军衔

Commission, the an informal name for the European Commission 欧盟委员会〔欧盟委员会的非正式名称〕

com·mis·sion·aire /kə,mɪʃən`ɛr; kə,mɪʃə'neə/ *n* [C] *BrE* someone whose job is to stand at the entrance to a hotel, theatre, or cinema and help people【英】〔旅馆、剧院、电影院的〕看门人；DOORMAN *AmE*【美】

commissioned of·fic·er /·,··'···/ *n* [C] a military officer who has a commission 执勤军官

com·mis·sion·er /kə`mɪʃənɚ; kə'mɪʃənə/ *n* [C] **1** someone who is officially in charge of a government department in some countries〔某些国家政府部门的〕长官：*Commissioner Addo is responsible for Education.* 阿多主管教育工作。**2** the head of the police department in some parts of the US〔美国部分地区的〕警察局长 **3** a member of a COMMISSION¹ (1) 委员 **4 commissioner for oaths** *BrE* a lawyer who may legally be a WITNESS to particular legal documents【英】宣誓公证人〔在法律上能负责见证签署文件的律师〕

Commission for Ra·cial E·qual·i·ty, the /·,···,···'···/ abbreviation 缩写为 **the CRE** a British government organization established in 1976 to make sure that people of all races are treated fairly and equally by employers, schools, etc. 种族平等委员会〔英国一政府机构，成立于1976年。其宗旨是确保不同种族的人都能得到雇主、学校等的公平待遇〕

com·mit /kə`mɪt; kə'mɪt/ *v* **committed, committing** [T]

1 ▶CRIME 罪行◀ to do something wrong or illegal 犯〔错误、罪〕：**commit a crime** *Women commit fewer crimes than men.* 女性比男性的犯罪率低。| **commit murder/rape/adultery etc** *Brady committed a series of brutal murders.* 布雷迪犯下了一系列残忍的谋杀案。| **commit suicide** (=kill yourself deliberately) 自杀

2 ▶SAY THAT SB WILL DO STH 保证某人会做某事◀ to say that someone will definitely do something or must do something 使承担义务，作出保证：**commit sb to sth** *My agent has*

already committed me to an appearance. 我的代理人已保证我会出场。| **commit sb to doing sth** *The contract commits him to playing for the team for the next three years.* 该合约规定以后三年他要为该球队效力。

3 commit yourself to say that you will definitely do something 答应, 承诺: *You don't have to commit yourself at this stage.* 在这个阶段你不必承诺什么。| *We can't commit ourselves to any concrete proposals.* 我们不能允诺支持什么具体的建议。| **commit yourself to doing sth** *Sorry, I've already committed myself to working for Clive.* 对不起, 我已经答应为克莱夫工作了。| **not commit yourself** (=refuse to say whether you will do something) 拒绝允诺 *Roxburgh decided that it would be wiser not to commit himself.* 罗克斯伯格认为不许诺比较明智。

C

4 ►MONEY/TIME 金钱/时间◄ to decide to use money, time, people etc for a particular purpose 拨出…供使用, 调拨: **commit sth to sth** *A large amount of money has been committed to this project.* 已经拨了一大笔钱给这项工程。

5 ►PRISON/HOSPITAL 监狱/医院◄ to order someone to be put in a hospital or prison 把…关进监狱[医院], 监禁: *You're crazy! You ought to be committed!* 你疯了! 你该进精神病院!

6 commit sth to memory to learn something so that you remember it 牢记某事

7 commit sth to paper to write something down 写下某事

S2 W2 **com·mit·ment** /kəˋmɪtmənt; kəˈmɪtmənt/ *n* **1** [C] a promise to do something or to behave in a particular way 承诺: *Jim's afraid of emotional commitments.* 吉姆害怕感情上的承诺。| [+to] *a commitment to equal pay and opportunities* 承诺提供平等的工资和机会 **2** [U] the hard work and loyalty that someone gives to an organization, activity etc〔对某一组织、某项活动等所付出的〕辛劳, 忠诚, 奉献: *I was impressed by the energy and commitment shown by the players.* 我对选手们表现出的活力和奉献的精神印象深刻。| [+to] *Her commitment to work is beyond question.* 她的敬业精神是不容置疑的。**3** [C] something that you have previously arranged to do at a certain time and that prevents you from doing anything else at that time 承诺的事: *She's got several teaching commitments over the summer.* 整个夏天她答应要进行几项教学活动。**4** [C] an amount of money that you have to pay regularly and that prevents you from spending your money on other things 承付款项, 债务: *a heavy mortgage commitment* 一笔数额巨大的抵押贷款债务 **5** [U] *especially AmE* the use of money, time, people etc for a particular purpose【尤美】〔为某种目的, 钱、时间和人力等的〕使用, 花费: *The plan involves commitment of money and staff time.* 这个计划涉及资金的使用和职员工作时间的安排。

com·mit·tal /kəˋmɪtl; kəˈmɪtl/ *n* [C,U] **1** the process in which a court sends someone to a mental hospital or prison 送入精神病院; 收监 **2** *formal* the burying or cremating (CREMATE) of a dead person【正式】下葬; 火化

com·mit·ted /kəˋmɪtɪd; kəˈmɪtɨd/ *adj* willing to work very hard at something 乐于献身的, 尽责的: *a committed group of environmentalists* 一群尽职尽责的环境保护者

S3 W1 **com·mit·tee** /kəˋmɪtɪ; kəˈmɪti/ *n* **1** [C] a group of people chosen to represent a larger group in order to do a particular job, make decisions etc 委员会: *He's on the finance committee.* 他是财政委员会的成员。| [also+plural verb *BrE*【英】] *The committee have decided to raise membership fees for next year.* 该委员会已决定提高明年的会费。**2 welcoming committee** a group of people often sent by a large organization to welcome an important visitor〔由大型组织派出的〕欢迎团

com·mode /kəˋmod; kəˈməʊd/ *n* [C] **1** *BrE* a piece of furniture shaped like a chair that can be used as a TOILET【英】〔座椅式的〕便桶 **2** *AmE dialect* a TOILET【美, 方言】马桶 **3** *old use* a piece of furniture with drawers or shelves【旧】衣柜, 五斗橱

com·mo·di·ous /kəˋmodɪəs; kəˈməʊdiəs/ *adj formal* a house or room that is commodious is very big【正式】〔房子或房间〕宽敞的, 大的 —**commodiously** *adv*

com·mod·i·ty /kəˋmɑdətɪ; kəˈmɒdɨti/ *n* [C] **1** a product that can be sold to make a profit 商品: *agricultural commodities* 农业商品 **2** *formal* a useful quality【正式】有用的性质; 有用的东西: *Time is a precious commodity.* 时间是宝贵的财富。

com·mo·dore /ˋkɑməˌdɔr; ˈkɒmədɔː/ *n* [C] **1** a high rank in the navy, or someone who has this rank 海军准将 —see table on page C6 参见C6页附录 **2** the CAPTAIN in charge of a group of ships that are carrying goods 商船队队长

S1 W1 **com·mon¹** /ˋkɑmən; ˈkɒmən/ *adj*

1 ►A LOT/LARGE AMOUNT 大量◄ existing in large numbers or happening often and in many places 大量的; 常见的, 多发的: *Heart disease is one of the commonest causes of death.* 心脏病是最常见的致死原因之一。| [+among] *Bad dreams are fairly common among children.* 小孩做噩梦是司空见惯的。| **it is common for sth to happen** *It's very common for new fathers to feel jealous of the baby.* 新爸爸常常会妒忌自己的宝宝。| **common belief/assumption/practice etc** *It's a common but false assumption that all mentally ill people are violent.* 有一种普遍但是错误的观点, 认为所有精神病人都很凶暴。

2 ►SAME/SIMILAR 相同的/类似的◄ [usually before noun 一般用于名词前, no comparative 无比较级] common aims, beliefs, ideas etc are shared by several people or groups〔目的、信仰、思想等〕共同的: *They had a satisfying sense of working towards a common goal.* 他们朝同一目标努力的这种意识令人满意。| [+to] *a theme that is common to all her novels* 她全部小说中的共同主题 | **common ground** (=shared opinions, beliefs etc among people who are usually separate)〔一般有分歧的人的观点、信仰等的〕共同基础 *The two parties met to establish some common ground.* 两个党派为达成共识而会面。

3 ►SHARED BY EVERYONE 共有◄ [usually before noun 一般用于名词前, no comparative 无比较级] belonging to or shared by everyone in a society〔社会〕共有的, 公共的: [+to] *These problems are common to all societies.* 这些问题是所有社会共有的。| **the common good** (=the advantage of everyone) 公益 *Do they seriously think they're acting for the common good?* 他们真以为他们从公众利益出发来考虑的吗? | **common knowledge** (=something everyone knows) 众所周知的事 *In a small town everyone's actions are common knowledge.* 在一个小镇上每个人的一举一动都难以逃过大家的眼睛。| **common land** (=owned by the public) 公有土地 | **by common consent** (=agreed by everyone) 一致同意 *Joe was chosen as captain by common consent.* 大家一致通过选举乔为队长。

4 common courtesy/decency a polite way of behaving that you expect from people 通常的礼貌, 礼节: *It's only common courtesy to write and thank them for the present.* 写信感谢他们送礼只是出于通常的礼貌。

5 ►ORDINARY 普通的◄ [only before noun 仅用于名词前, no comparative 无比较级] ordinary and not special in any way 普通的, 平凡的: *The common people will not benefit from these reforms.* 老百姓将不会从这些改革中受益。| *common salt* 食盐 | **the common man** (=ordinary people) 普通人 | **common-or-garden** *BrE slang* (=very common and ordinary)【英俚】很普通, 很一般

6 ►PERSON 人◄ *especially BrE old-fashioned* an offensive word for someone from a low social class【尤英, 过时】粗鄙的, 劣等的〔对下层社会成员的冒犯用语〕: *Stop that! People will think we're common.* 别那样! 别人会以为我们是粗人。| **as common as muck** *BrE* (=extremely common)【英】极其普通的

7 common practice a usual or accepted way of doing things 惯例: *Sending kids away to school was common practice among the upper classes.* 上层阶级家庭将孩子送往寄宿学校是惯例。

8 the common touch the ability of someone in a position of power or authority to talk to and understand ordinary people 平易近人的品质: *He's made it to the top without losing the common touch.* 他虽已晋升高位, 却仍然平易近人。

common² *n* **1 have sth in common (with sb)** to have the same interests, attitudes etc as someone else (与某人) 有相同的兴趣、态度等: *To my surprise, I found I had a lot in common with this stranger.* 令我吃惊的是, 我发现自己和这个陌生人有许多共同点。**2 have sth in common (with sth)** if objects or ideas have something in common, they share the same features (与某事物) 有相同的特点: *Their methods have a lot in common.* 他们的方法有很多相同之处。**3 in common with sb/sth** in the same way as someone or something else 与某人/某物一样: *In common with a lot of other countries, we're in an economic recession.* 同许多别的国家一样, 我国也处在经济萧条时期。**4** [C] a large area of grass in a village that people walk or play sport on〔村庄里〕公用活动草地 **5** *technical* having the same relationship to two or more quantities【术语】与两个以上的量关系相同的: *5 is a common factor of 10 and 20.* 5是10和20的公约数。

Common Ag·ri·cul·tu·ral Pol·i·cy, the /ˌ‥ˈ‥‥ ˌ‥‥/ *n* [singular] the CAP

common cold /ˌ‥ ˈ‥/ *n* [C] a slight illness in which your throat hurts and it is difficult to breathe normally 感冒, 伤风

common de·nom·i·na·tor /ˌ‥ ˈ‥‥‥/ *n* [C] **1** an attitude or quality that all the different members of a group have 共同点〔一组织中不同成员共有的态度或品质〕: *The common denominator in these very different schemes is that they aim to reduce pollution.* 这些计划极为不同, 但它们的共同点是以减少污染为目标。**2** *technical* a number that can be divided exactly by all the DENOMINATORS (=bottom number) in a set of fractions (FRACTION

(2))【术语】公分母 3 **the lowest common denominator** the least attractive, least intelligent people or features in a situation 最无知的人[特点], 最无趣的人[特点]: *trashy TV programs that appeal to the lowest common denominator* 满足低级趣味的低劣电视节目

Common En·trance Ex·am·i·na·tion, the /,·· '·····,··/ an examination in the UK, taken in preparatory schools by children between the ages of 12 and 14, in order to be able to go to a PUBLIC SCHOOL (=expensive private school) 统一入学考试〔英国 12 至 14 岁的学生在预备学校参加的公学升学考试〕

com·mon·er /ˈkɑmənə; ˈkɒmənə/ *n* [C] someone who is not a member of a NOBLE[1] (3) family 平民: *Sarah Ferguson was a commoner before she married the Duke Of York.* 在嫁给约克公爵之前, 萨拉·弗格森是个平民。

common frac·tion /,·· '··/ *n* [C] *AmE* a FRACTION[1] (2) that is shown by a number above and a number below a line, such as ½, rather than as a DECIMAL[2]【美】普通分数, 简分数; VULGAR FRACTION *BrE*【英】

common law[1] /'·· ·/ *adj* [only before noun 仅用于名词前] 1 **common-law marriage/husband/wife** a relationship that is considered to be a marriage because the man and woman have lived together for a long time 事实[同居]婚姻, 事实婚姻的男方/女方〔由于男女长期同居而被认为具有婚姻关系〕 2 according to or related to COMMON LAW[2] 根据习惯法的; 有关普通法的: *common law rules* 习惯法条例

common law[2] /,·· '·/ *n* [U] the law of England that has developed from common customs and the decisions of judges rather than from laws made by Parliament 普通法, 习惯法〔即普遍的习俗和法官的判决发展而来而不是议会制定的英国法律〕

W3 **com·mon·ly** /ˈkɑmənlɪ; ˈkɒmənli/ *adv* usually or by most people 通常, 一般地, 由大多数人〔同意等〕: *commonly agreed principles* 多数人认可的原则 | *Sodium chloride is more commonly known as salt.* 氯化钠一般称为盐。

Common Mar·ket, the /,·· '··◂/ *n old-fashioned* the EUROPEAN UNION【过时】共同市场〔欧盟的前身〕

common noun /,·· '·◂/ *n* [C] *technical* in grammar, a common noun is any noun that is not the name of a particular person, place, or thing【术语】普通名词〔在语法中, 任何不是某人、某地或某物的名词都是普通名词〕: *'Book' and 'sugar' are common nouns.* book 和 sugar 是普通名词。—compare 比较 PROPER NOUN —see also 另见 NOUN

com·mon·place[1] /ˈkɑmən,ples; ˈkɒmənpleɪs/ *adj* happening or existing in many places, and therefore not special or unusual 平常的; 平凡的; 不足为奇的: *Car thefts are commonplace in this part of town.* 在城市的这个地段偷车是家常便饭。

commonplace[2] *n* 1 [C usually singular 一般用单数] something that happens or exists in many places, so that it is not unusual 平常的事, 司空见惯的事: *One-parent families are now a commonplace in our society.* 在我们的社会中, 单亲家庭现在是很平常的。2 **the commonplace** ordinary or boring 一般, 没有特色, 单调乏味: *In my view, his paintings verge on the commonplace.* 我认为他的画几近平庸。

common room /'·· ·/ *n* [C] *BrE* a room in a school or college that a group of teachers or students use when they are not teaching or studying【英】〔中小学或大学的〕师生公共休息室

Com·mons /ˈkɑmənz; ˈkɒmənz/ *n* **the Commons** the larger and more powerful of the two parts of the British parliament, whose members are elected by citizens〔英国议会的〕下议院〔议员由公民选举产生〕: *enough votes to force a bill through the Commons* 能使某议案在下议院强行通过的足够选票 | **in the Commons** (=among the Members of Parliament) 在下议院议员之间 —compare 比较 **the Lords** (LORD (2))

common sense /,·· '·◂/ *n* [U] the ability to behave in a sensible way and make practical decisions 常识: *Use your common sense for once!* 请你也用常理来判断一回吧! —**common-sense** *adj*: *a common-sense approach to the economy* 按常理来处理经济的政策

com·mon·wealth /ˈkɑmən,wɛlθ; ˈkɒmənwelθ/ *n* 1 **the Commonwealth** an organization of about 50 countries that were once part of the British EMPIRE (1) and which are now connected politically and economically 英联邦〔由曾隶属于大英帝国的约 50 个国家组成〕: *the Commonwealth Games* 英联邦运动会 2 [C] *formal* an association of countries with political or economic links【正式】〔由在政治或经济上有联系的国家组成的〕联合体: *In 1991 the USSR became the Commonwealth of Independent States.* 1991 年苏联成为了"独立国家联合体"。

Commonwealth Games, the /,··· '·/ an international sports event in which the member countries of the British Commonwealth compete in various sports. The games take place every four years in one of the competing countries 英联邦运动会〔英联邦成员国进行的国际体育盛会。每四年一次, 在其中一个参赛国举行〕

com·mo·tion /kəˈmoʃən; kəˈməʊʃən/ *n* [singular, U] sudden noisy activity 突然的混乱, 喧闹: *They heard a commotion downstairs.* 他们听见楼下一阵骚动。| **cause a commotion** *The bar was packed, and the winning touchdown caused an immense commotion.* 酒吧里挤满了人, 决胜负的触地得分引起了极大的骚动。

com·mu·nal /ˈkɑmjunḷ; ˈkɒmjʊnəl/ *adj* 1 shared by a group, especially a group of people who live together〔为同一群体所〕共有的, 公共的, 社区的: *a communal bathroom* 一个公用浴室 2 involving people from many different races, religions, or language groups 种族间的; 教派间的: *rising communal tension in India* 印度日趋严重的种族对抗

com·mune[1] /ˈkɑmjun; ˈkɒmjuːn/ *n* [C] 1 a group of people who live together and who share the work and their possessions〔生活在一起、分享财产、分担职责的〕群居团体, 社区 2 a group of people who work as a team, especially on a farm, and give what they produce to the state 公社〔尤指在农场上合作生产的一群人, 他们的产品交与国家〕 3 the smallest division of local government in countries such as France and Belgium〔法国和比利时等国的〕最小的地方行政区

com·mune[2] /kəˈmjun; kəˈmjuːn/ *v* [I] *formal* to share your thoughts and feelings with someone or with nature without using words【正式】与〔某人或大自然〕无言地进行思想感情交流, 沟通; 神交: *communing with nature* 与自然界契合

com·mu·ni·ca·ble /kəˈmjunɪkəbḷ; kəˈmjuːnɪkəbəl/ *adj* 1 a communicable illness is infectious〔疾病〕传染性的 2 able to be communicated 可传达的: *Her ideas were not easily communicable to others.* 她的想法不容易传达给他人。—**communicably** *adv*

com·mu·ni·cant /kəˈmjunɪkənt; kəˈmjuːnɪkənt/ *n* [C] someone who receives COMMUNION (2) regularly in the Christian church〔基督教会中的〕按时领受圣餐者

com·mu·ni·cate /kəˈmjunə,ket; kəˈmjuːnɪkeɪt/ *v* S3 W3

1 ▶**EXPRESS** 表达◀[T] to express your thoughts and feelings clearly, so that other people understand them 表达〔思想、感情〕: *A baby communicates its needs by crying.* 婴儿用哭声来表达需要。| **communicate sth to sb** *Without meaning to, she communicated her anxiety to her child.* 她无意中向孩子流露了她的焦虑。| **communicate itself** *Dissatisfaction with working conditions communicated itself throughout the workforce.* 工人间流露出对工作条件的不满。

2 ▶**EXCHANGE INFORMATION** 交流信息◀[I,T] to exchange information or conversation with other people, using words, signs etc〔用符号等〕与〔他人〕交流信息; 交谈: *He learnt how to use sign language to communicate with deaf customers.* 他学会了用手语与失聪的顾客交谈。

3 ▶**CONTACT** 联系◀[I] *formal* to contact someone, especially by telephone or by writing a letter【正式】〔尤指用电话、书信等〕与他人联系

4 ▶**UNDERSTAND** 理解◀[I] if two people communicate, they can easily understand each other's thoughts and feelings 沟通〔思想、情感〕: [+with] *Parents sometimes find it difficult to communicate with their teenage children.* 孩子长到十几岁, 父母有时会发觉难以与他们交流。

5 ▶**ROOMS** 房间◀[I] if rooms or parts of a building communicate, you can get directly to one from the other〔不同房间或楼房的不同部分〕互通, 相连

6 ▶**DISEASE** 疾病◀[T usually passive 一般用被动态] to pass a disease from one person or animal to another〔疾病〕传染: *research into how the AIDS virus is communicated* 对艾滋病病毒传染途径的研究

com·mu·ni·ca·tion /kə,mjunəˈkeʃən; kə,mjuːnɪˈkeɪʃən/ *n* S2 W1

1 [U] the process by which people exchange information or express their thoughts and feelings 信息交流; 思想感情表达: *Good communication is vital in a large organization.* 在一个庞大组织中良好的沟通是极为重要的。| **means of communication** *Radio was the pilot's only means of communication.* 无线电曾经是飞行员唯一的通讯手段。2 **communications** [plural] **a)** ways of sending information, especially using radio, telephone or computers 各种通讯手段〔尤指无线电、电话或电脑〕: *Modern communications enable more and more people to work from home.* 各种现代通讯手段使越来越多的人能在家里工作。**b)** ways of travelling and sending goods, such as roads, railways etc 交通: [+with] *Paris has good communications with many European cities.* 巴黎与许多欧洲城市之间的交通便捷。3 [C] *formal* a letter, message or telephone call【正式】函件; 信息; 电话通讯:

a communication from the Ministry of Defence 来自国防部的函件 **4 communication skills** ways of expressing yourself well so that other people will understand 沟通技巧: *a week's course in improving communication skills* 提高交流技巧的一周课程 **5 be in communication with** *formal* to talk or write to someone regularly or occasionally【正式】〔定期或偶尔〕与〔某人〕交谈[通信]

communication cord /·,··ˈ·· ·/ *n* [C] *BrE* a chain that a passenger pulls to stop a train in an EMERGENCY (=a sudden dangerous situation)【英】〔在发生紧急情况时, 火车乘客拉动要求停车的〕紧急制动索

communications sat·el·lite /·ˈ··ˈ· ,··/ *n* [C] a piece of equipment in space that travels around the Earth and is used for radio, television, and telephone signals around the world 通讯卫星

com·mu·ni·ca·tive /kəˈmjunəˌketɪv; kəˈmjuːnɪ̵kətɪv/ *adj* **1** able to talk easily to other people 健谈的, 善于言谈的: *It's hard to know what she's thinking; she's not very communicative.* 很难知道她的想法, 她不太爱说话。**2** relating to the ability to communicate, especially in a foreign language 表达能力〔尤指外语〕: *students' communicative skills* 学生们的交流技能

com·mu·nion /kəˈmjunjən; kəˈmjuːnjən/ *n* **1** [U] *formal* a special relationship with someone or something in which you feel that you understand them very well【正式】〔与某人或某物之间的〕情感交融: [**+between/with**] *He sought meaningful communion with another human being.* 他寻求与他人进行有意义的沟通。**2** [U] also 又作 **Holy Communion** the Christian ceremony in which people eat bread and drink wine as signs of Christ's body and blood 圣餐〔一种基督教仪式〕**3** [C] *formal* a group of people or organizations that share the same religious beliefs【正式】教会; 教派, 宗教团体: *He belongs to the Anglican communion.* 他是圣公会的教徒。

com·mu·ni·qué /kəˌmjunəˈke; kəˈmjuːnɪ̵keɪ/ *n* [C] an official report or announcement 公报: *The palace has issued a communiqué denying the paper's allegations.* 王室发表公报否认报纸上的指控。

Com·mu·nis·m /ˈkɑmjuˌnɪzəm; ˈkɒmjɪ̵nɪzəm/ *n* [U] **1** a political system in some countries in which the government controls the production of all food and goods, and which has no different social classes 共产主义制度 **2** the belief in this political system 共产主义的信念

CULTURAL NOTE 文化注释

Most people in the US and the UK think of Communism in relation to the former Soviet Union. The end of Communism in the former Soviet Union in 1991 meant the end of the COLD WAR, a period of bad relations between the US and the Soviet Union, when many people were afraid that there would be a NUCLEAR WAR. In the US during the 1950s and 1960s people were very afraid of Communism and believed that American Communists were not loyal to their country. People who supported Communist ideas were strongly disapproved of, and were called 'Commies', 'Reds', or 'Pinkos'. Senator Joseph McCarthy tried to find and punish American Communists, and many people who were thought to be Communists lost their jobs, and some were sent to prison. 美国和英国的大多数人认为共产主义与前苏联有关。1991 年共产主义在前苏联的终结标志着冷战的结束。冷战期间, 美苏两国关系紧张, 很多人担心会爆发核战。20世纪50、60年代美国人惧怕共产主义, 认为美国共产党员不忠于自己的国家。支持共产主义的人受到诋毁, 被称作 Commies、Reds 或 Pinkos。参议员约瑟夫·麦卡锡搜捕和惩罚美国共产党员, 致使很多被认为是共产党员的人丢掉工作, 有的被投入监狱。

In the UK and Europe, the idea of Communism was not as strongly disapproved of as it was in the US. There were Communist organizations in the UK, and they had an influence on the TRADE UNION movement. 在英国和欧洲其他国家, 共产主义不像在美国过去那样受到强烈诋毁。英国曾有共产主义组织, 对工会运动产生过影响。— see also 另见 HUAC, MCCARTHYISM

Com·mu·nist¹ /ˈkɑmjuˌnɪst; ˈkɒmjɪ̵nɪ̵st/ *adj* connected with Communism 共产主义的: *Communist countries* 共产主义国家 | *a communist leader* 共产主义领袖

Communist² *n* [C] **1** someone who is a member of a political party that supports Communism 共产党员, 共产党人 **2** someone who believes in Communism 共产主义者

communist bloc /,··· ˈ·/ *n* [singular] the group of countries, mostly in Eastern Europe, that had Communist governments and supported the former Soviet Union 共产主义阵营〔指曾经有共产党政府并支持前苏联的国家, 这些国家大都在东欧〕

Communist bloc, the /ˈ··· ,·/ also 又作 **the Eastern bloc** the former Soviet Union and the countries of eastern Europe which had Communist governments and were under Soviet influence, especially between the end of World War II and about 1990 共产主义阵营, 东欧集团国家〔指第二次世界大战结束至 1990 年间的苏联, 以及受其影响的由共产党政府执政的东欧国家〕

Communist Man·i·fes·to, The /,··· ··ˈ··/ a book by Karl Marx and Friedrich Engels, written in 1848, which explains the main ideas of Communism and describes how society would need to change in order to achieve this《共产党宣言》〔卡尔·马克思和弗里德里希·恩格斯 1848 年共同撰写的一本书。该书阐述共产主义的主要思想和实现共产主义所需的社会变革〕

Communist Par·ty /ˈ··· ,··/ *n* a political party based on the principles of Marxism-Leninism, and believing that most economic activity (such as factories, banks, and farming) should be owned or controlled by the government 共产党〔基于马克思列宁主义而建立的政党。该政党认为, 国家的大部分经济活动应由政府掌控〕

CULTURAL NOTE 文化注释

The former Soviet Union and most countries of Eastern Europe were governed by a Communist Party until the beginning of the 1990s. In the US, Communism is regarded as anti-American, and in the UK the Communist Party (which changed its name to the Democratic Left in 1991) has very little political influence. Although the Communist party used to have a lot of political influence in France and Italy, it no longer does. 20 世纪 90 年代初期以前, 苏联和东欧大部分国家由共产党执政。在美国, 共产主义被看做是反美的。在英国, 共产党 (1991 年更名为左翼民主党) 政治影响微乎其微。共产党曾在法国和意大利有很大影响, 但现在情况已经不同。

com·mu·ni·ty /kəˈmjunətɪ; kəˈmjuːnɪ̵ti/ *n*

1 ▶PEOPLE 人们◀ [C, also+plural verb *BrE* 英] *BrE* all the people who live in the same area, town etc【英】〔同住一地区的人所构成的〕社区: *an arts centre built to serve the whole community* 为整个社区服务的艺术中心 | **community affairs/needs/relations etc** *We meet once a month to discuss community problems.* 我们每月开会一次讨论社区问题。| **community spirit** (=the desire to be friendly with and help other people who live in the same community) 社区精神〔指同一社区内友好互助的精神〕

2 ▶PARTICULAR GROUP 特定团体◀ sense of community the feeling that you belong to a group of people because you live in the same area 社区归属感〔居住在同一地的人们所有的一种归属感〕

3 [C] a group of people who share the same nationality or religion or who are similar in another way〔由同国籍、同宗教等构成的〕群体; 社区: *There are many different ethnic communities living in New York.* 纽约有许多不同民族聚居的社区。| *the gay community* 同性恋群体

4 the community society and the people in it 社会; 公众: *The trend is towards reintegrating mentally ill people into the community.* 目前的趋势是将精神病人重新融入社会中。| **the international community** (=all the countries of the world) 国际社会 —see also 另见 EC

5 ▶PLANTS/ANIMALS 植物/动物◀ [C] a group of plants or animals that live in the same environment 群落〔生长或生活在同一环境中的植物或动物群〕: *Communities of otters are slowly returning to several British rivers.* 水獭群落又慢慢地回到几条英国河流里。

community cen·tre *BrE*【英】**community center** *AmE*【美】/·ˈ··· ,··/ *n* [C] a place where people from the same area can go for social events, classes etc 社区活动中心

community chest /·ˈ··· ,·/ *n* [C] *AmE* money that is collected by the people and businesses in an area to help poor people【美】〔救济穷困者的〕社区福利金, 公益金

community col·lege /·ˈ··· ,··/ *n* [C,U] a college in the US that students can go to for two years in order to learn a skill or to prepare for university; JUNIOR COLLEGE 社区学院〔美国两年制学院, 学生学一项技艺或大学预科课程〕

CULTURAL NOTE 文化注释

It costs much less to go to a community college than to go to a university. Many students study there for two years before going to a university to do the final two years of a degree course. Other students who go to a community college do not intend to go to university, and study practical subjects that will help them get a job. Working people also attend community colleges to improve their knowledge and skills. 上社区学院的费用远较一般大学为低。很多学生在社区学院学习两年，然后去一般大学完成最后两年的学位课程。也有一些社区学院的学生不想再去一般大学，只是学习一些有助于他们找到工作的实用科目。在职员工也上社区学院来提高知识和技能。

community prop·er·ty /ˌ···ˈ···/ *n* [U] *law* property such as houses or land, that is considered to be owned by both a husband and wife in US law【法律】夫妻共有财产〔美国法律视为夫妻共有的房屋、土地等财产〕

community ser·vice /ˌ···ˈ··/ *n* [U] **1** work that someone does without being paid to help other people 社区服务〔指为他人提供的无偿服务〕 **2** a punishment given for some crimes, in which the criminal has to do useful work to help people 社区服务〔一种惩罚，由犯人为他人做一些有益的工作〕

com·mu·ta·ble /kəˋmjutəbḷ; kəˈmjuːtəbəl/ *adj* **1** *law* a punishment that is commutable can be made less severe【法律】可减刑的 **2** payments that are commutable can be exchanged for another type of payment〔支付方式〕可以改换的

com·mu·ta·tion /ˌkɑmjuˋteʃən; ˌkɒmjʊˈteɪʃən/ *n* **1** [C,U] a reduction in how severe a punishment is 减刑: *commutation of a death sentence to life* 由死刑改为无期徒刑的减刑 **2** [U] *formal* the act of replacing one method of payment with a different method【正式】〔支付方式的〕替换 **3** [C] *technical* a payment of one type made instead of an equal payment of another type【术语】抵偿（金）

com·mu·ta·tive /kəˋmjutətɪv; kəˈmjuːtətɪv/ *adj technical* a mathematical operation that is commutative can be done in any order【术语】〔数学运算顺序〕交换的，可换的〔指顺序不影响结果〕

com·mute¹ /kəˋmjut; kəˈmjuːt/ *v* **1** [I] to regularly travel a long distance to get to work 经常走很长的路程去上班，通勤: **[+to/from/between]** *Jim commutes from Weehawken to Manhattan every day.* 吉姆每天上下班往来于威霍肯与曼哈顿之间。 **2** [T] to change the punishment given to a criminal to one that is less severe 减刑: **commute a sentence (to)** *The sentence was later commuted to life imprisonment.* 这个判决后来减刑为终身监禁。 **3 commute sth for/into sth** to exchange one thing, especially one kind of payment, for another 把某物改换为另一物〔尤指支付方式〕: *He commuted his pension for a lump sum.* 他把按时分期领取的退休金改为一次领清。

commute² *n* [C usually singular 一般用单数] *especially AmE* the journey to work every day【尤美】每天去上班的路程: *My morning commute takes 45 minutes.* 我早上上班路上要花45分钟。

commuters 每天走很长的路程去上班的人

com·mut·er /kəˋmjutɚ; kəˈmjuːtə/ *n* [C] someone who travels a long distance to work every day 每天走很长的路程去上班的人，通勤者: *a carriage full of home-going commuters* 车厢里挤满了下班回家的人

CULTURAL NOTE 文化注释

In the US, people mainly think of commuters as people who spend a long time driving to work, especially because of TRAFFIC JAMS. In the UK, the STEREOTYPE of a commuter is of a person wearing formal business clothes who sits and reads a newspaper on the train to the office and does not talk to anyone else. 在美国，通勤者主要指因为交通拥堵要开很久车去上班的人。在英国，通勤者的典型形象是一个着正装的男子，坐火车去上班，在车上读报，不同别人交谈。

commuter belt /ˈ···ˌ·/ *n* [C] an area around a large city from which many people travel to work every day 大城市四周的居住地带〔许多人每天从那里出发去工作地点〕

Comoros /ˋkɑməˌroz; ˈkɒmərəʊz/ a country consisting of three islands in the Mozambique Channel between northwest Madagascar and southeast Africa. Population: 596,202 (2001). Capital: Moroni. 科摩罗〔由莫桑比克海峡的三个岛组成的一个国家，位于马达加斯加岛西北方，非洲东南方。人口: 596,202 (2001)，首都: 莫罗尼〕

comp /kɑmp; kɒmp/ *n* [C] **1** *AmE informal* a ticket for a play, sports game etc that is given away free【美，非正式】〔戏剧、体育比赛等的〕招待券，免费券 **2** *BrE spoken* a COMPREHENSIVE SCHOOL【英口】综合中学

com·pact¹ /kəmˋpækt; kəmˈpækt/ *adj* **1** small and easy to carry 小巧便携的: *a compact camera* 小巧的照相机 **2** small but arranged so that everything fits neatly into the space available 小而紧凑的: *The dormitory rooms were compact, with a desk, bed and closet built in.* 宿舍房间虽小却安排紧凑，配有书桌、床和壁橱。 **3** firmly and closely packed together; DENSE (1) 紧密的；密集的: *The bushes grew in a compact mass.* 灌木长成茂密的一片。 **4** small but solid and strong 矮小结实的，壮实的: *a small compact-looking man* 个子矮小、看上去却很结实的男人 **5** expressing things clearly in only a few words 简洁的 **—compactly** *adv* **—compactness** *n* [U]

com·pact² /ˋkɑmpækt; ˈkɒmpækt/ *n* [C] **1** a small flat container with a mirror, containing powder for a woman's face〔内有镜子的〕女式化妆粉盒 **2** *AmE* a small car【美】小型汽车 **3** *formal* an agreement between two or more people, countries etc【正式】〔人与人、国与国之间的〕协定

com·pact³ /kəmˋpækt; kəmˈpækt/ [T] *v* to press something soft or something made of small pieces together, so that it becomes smaller or more solid〔将某柔软或由小块组成的物质〕压紧，压实 **—compacted** *adj*

compact disc /ˌ··ˈ·/ *n* [C] a small circular piece of hard plastic on which music, or large quantities of information can be stored; CD 激光唱片；〔电脑〕光碟，光盘: *The new album is available on vinyl, cassette, or compact disc.* 这张新专辑的塑胶唱片、录音带、激光唱片都可以买到。

compact disc play·er /ˌ··ˈ·ˌ··/ *n* [C] CD PLAYER 激光唱机

com·pan·ion /kəmˋpænjən; kəmˈpænjən/ *n* [C] **1** someone you spend a lot of time with especially someone you are travelling with or a friend 同伴；同行者: *His dog became his closest companion during the last years of his life.* 他的狗成了他晚年最亲密的伴侣。| **constant companion** (=someone you are always with) 形影不离的伙伴 **2** one of a pair of things that go together or can be used together 构成一对的两件物品中的一件: **[+to]** *This book is a companion to the author's first work.* 这本书是作者第一部作品的姊妹篇。| **companion volume/album/statement etc** *Paul Simon has just released a companion album to his Greatest Hits.* 保罗·西蒙刚刚发行了他《最流行的歌曲集》的姊妹集。 **3** someone, especially a woman, who is paid to live or travel with an older person 伴侣〔尤指受雇陪一位老人一起生活或旅行的女子〕 **4** used as part of the title of a book on a particular subject, especially a book that explains something 手册，指南〔用于书名〕 W3

com·pan·io·na·ble /kəmˋpænjənəbḷ; kəmˈpænjənəbəl/ *adj* pleasantly friendly 和善的；友善的: *They sat together in companionable silence.* 他们友好地默默坐在一起。 **—companionably** *adv*

Companion of Hon·our, the /ˌ··· ˈ··/ a special title or honour that is given by the British queen or king to someone who has achieved something very important for the country. A person who received this title can use the letters CH after his or her name. 荣誉勋爵〔英国女王或国王给对国家有重要贡献的人士授予的一种特别荣誉头衔。获得此头衔者可以在其姓名后加上CH〕

com·pan·ion·ship /kəmˋpænjənʃɪp; kəmˈpænjənʃɪp/ *n* [U] a friendly and comfortable relationship with someone 友谊; 友好交往: *When Stan died, it was the companionship I missed.* 斯坦死后，我怀念我们的友情。

com·pan·ion·way /kəmˋpænjənˌwe; kəmˈpænjənweɪ/ *n* [U] the steps going from one DECK (=level) of a ship to another deck 升降口扶梯〔两层船舱之间的梯子〕

com·pa·ny /ˋkʌmpənɪ; ˈkʌmpəni/ *n*

1 ▶BUSINESS 公司◀ [C] an organization that makes or sells goods or services in order to get money 公司: *Craig got a job working for an insurance company.* 克雷格在保险公司找到了一份工作。| [also+plural verb *BrE* 英] *The company are hoping to expand their operations abroad.* 该公司想把业务扩展到国外。| **manage/run a company** *In ten years Geoff went from working in the mail room to running the company.* 在10年之间，杰夫从收发员晋升到管理整家公司。| **set up/start a company** *The company was set up just after the war.* 这家公司是战后不久创建的。| **a company goes bankrupt/bust/out of business** (=stops doing business because it owes so much money) 公司〔由于负债过多而〕破产/倒闭 *Quite a few companies went bankrupt in the late 1980s.* 在20世纪80年代后期有相当数量的公司破产。| **company directors/employees/policy etc** *It's not company policy to exchange goods without a receipt.* 调换货品而不附发票，这不符合公司的规定。—see also 另见 PUBLIC COMPANY

2 ▶OTHER PEOPLE 别人◀ [U] another person, or other people, that you can talk to or who stop you feeling lonely 同伴，朋友: *They obviously enjoy each other's company.* 显然他们两个在一起非常高兴。| **keep sb company** *Rita's husband is away for the week, so I thought I'd go over and keep her company.* 丽塔的丈夫这个星期外出不在家，所以我想我应该去她那儿给她作伴。| **be good company** (=if someone is good company, you enjoy being with them) 好伙伴 | **as company** *Bessie was glad to have the dog as company.* 贝茜很高兴有这只狗为伴。| **in sb's company/in the company of sb** (=with someone) 与某人在一起 *I couldn't help feeling uneasy in the company of such an important man.* 和如此重要的人物在一起，我不由自主地感到不自在。| **in company with sb** (=together with another person or with a group) 和…一起 *He left for New York, in company with the orchestra.* 他与乐队一同前往纽约。

3 ▶GUESTS 客人◀ [U] a guest or guests who are visiting you in your home, or someone who is coming to see you 客人: **have company** *It looks like the Hammills have company – there are three cars in the driveway.* 哈米尔家好像有客人，汽车道上停了三辆汽车。| **expect company** (=be waiting for guests to arrive) 等待客人到来 *We're expecting company this evening.* 今晚我们有客人要来。

4 ▶FRIENDS 朋友◀ [singular, U] the group of people that you are friends with or that you spend time with 同伴，伙伴: **in pleasant/elevated etc company** *She was too shy to mix in such elevated company.* 她太害羞，无法融入这样的上流圈子。| **the company sb keeps** (=the people you spend time with) 某人交往的人 *People do tend to judge you by the company you keep.* 人们往往根据你交往的人来判断你的为人。| **bad company** (=people who do things you disapprove of) 不良的伙伴，损友 *Parents worry that their children are being led into bad company.* 父母担心自己的孩子被引诱去与坏人交往。| **not like the company sb is keeping** (=disapprove of the people someone is friends with) 不喜欢某人的朋友 | **keep company with sb** *old-fashioned* (=spend time with someone)【过时】与某人作伴

5 ▶PERFORMERS 表演者◀ [C] a group of actors, dancers, or singers who work together 剧团，歌舞团体: *Our local theatre gets a lot of touring companies.* 我们本地剧院常有巡回演出团表演。

6 be in good company used to tell someone that important or respected people have done something similar to what they have done, so they should not be ashamed〔用于告诉某人〕有地位的人也做过类似的事〔因此他用不着感到惭愧〕

7 ▶GROUP 人群◀ [U] a group of people who are together in the same place, often for a particular purpose or for social reasons〔为某种目的或社交原因而聚集在一起的〕一群人: *These remarks made the assembled company burst into sudden applause.* 这番话使与会者爆发出热烈掌声。| **in company** (=surrounded by other people, especially at a formal or social occasion) 在大庭广众之中〔尤指在正式或社交场合〕 *Parents need to teach their children how to behave in company.* 父母应当教导孩子怎样在别人面前举止得体。

8 and company *especially spoken* used after a person's name to mean that person and their friends【尤口】〔用于某人的名字之后表示此人〕及其朋友: *"Who's going to the party?" "Jim and company, I guess."* "谁会去参加晚会?" "我想吉姆和他的朋友们会去。"

9 ▶ARMY 军队◀ [C] a group of about 120 soldiers who are usually part of a larger group 连〔约120个士兵组成，常为较大支部队的一部分〕

10 two's company, three's a crowd used to suggest that two people would rather be alone together than have other people with them 两人为伴，三人不欢〔用来表示宁可只有两个人而不要更多的人加入他们〕

11 in company with sth if something happens in company with something else, both things happen at the same time 与另一件事同时发生: *Democracy progressed in company with the emancipation of women.* 民主制度是与妇女解放同时发展的。—see also 另见 **part company** (PART[2] (3)), **present company excepted** (PRESENT[1] (5))

company car /ˌ··· ˈ·/ *n* [C] a car that your employer gives you while you work for them〔公司给雇员使用的〕公车

company law /ˌ··· ˈ·/ *n* [U] the area of law that concerns how businesses operate and what their duties are to each other, to customers, and to governments 公司法

company sec·re·ta·ry /ˌ··· ˈ····/ *n* [C] *BrE* a member of a company who deals with money, legal matters etc【英】公司秘书〔公司里负责财务、法律事务等的职员〕

com·pa·ra·ble /ˋkɑmpərəbl; ˈkɒmpərəbəl/ *adj* **1** similar to something else in size, number, quality etc, so that you can make a comparison〔在大小、数量、质量等方面〕类似的，同类的，相当的: *A comparable car would cost far more abroad.* 一辆同等的汽车在国外的价格高很多。| **[+with/to]** *Is the pay rate comparable to that of other companies?* 这个工资比率可以和别的公司相比吗? | **comparable in size/importance etc** *The planet Pluto is comparable in size to the moon.* 冥王星的大小与月球相当。**2** being equally important, good, bad etc〔重要性、好坏等〕同等的，可相提并论的: *In my view these two artists just aren't comparable.* 我认为这两位艺术家不能相提并论。| **[+with/to]** *His poetry is hardly comparable with Shakespeare's.* 他的诗不能与莎士比亚的诗相提并论。—**comparability** /ˌkɑmpərəˋbɪlətɪ; ˌkɒmpərəˈbɪlɪ̣ti/ *n* [U]

com·pa·ra·bly /ˋkɑmpərəblɪ; ˈkɒmpərəbli/ *adv* in a similar way or to a similar degree 类似地; 在相似程度上: *Earnings have risen comparably in the industrial sector.* 在工业部门利润也以相当的幅度增长。

com·par·a·tive[1] /kəmˋpærətɪv; kəmˈpærətɪv/ *adj* **1 comparative comfort/freedom/wealth etc** comfort, freedom etc that is fairly satisfactory when compared to another state of comfort etc 相对的舒适/自由/财富等: *After a lifetime of poverty, his last few years were spent in comparative comfort.* 他穷了一辈子，晚年相对而言还过得比较舒适。**2 comparative beginner/newcomer/genius etc** someone who is not really a beginner etc, but who seems to be one when compared to other people 相对的初学者/新来者/天才等: *After living here five years, we're still considered comparative newcomers.* 我们在这里生活了五年，可是与别人相比我们仍被视为新来的。**3 comparative study/analysis/literature etc** a study etc that involves comparing something to something else 比较研究/分析/文学等: *a comparative study of different sociological groups* 对不同社会群体的比较研究 **4** the comparative form of an adjective or adverb shows an increase in size, degree etc when it is considered in relation to something else. For example, 'bigger' is the comparative form of 'big', and 'more comfortable' is the comparative form of 'comfortable'. 比较级的〔指形容词、副词的比较级形式〕

comparative[2] *n* **the comparative** the form of an adjective or adverb that shows an increase in size, degree etc when something is considered in relation to something else. For example, 'bigger' is the comparative of 'big', and 'more comfortable' is the comparative of 'comfortable'.〔形容词、副词的〕比较级形式〈如 bigger 是 big 的比较级，more comfortable 是 comfortable 的比较级〉

com·par·a·tive·ly /kəmˋpærətɪvlɪ; kəmˈpærətɪ̣vli/ *adv* as compared to something else or to a previous state 相对地; 比较地: *The children were comparatively well-behaved today.* 今天孩子们比较乖。| **comparatively speaking** *This part of the coast is still unspoiled, comparatively speaking.* 相比而言，这部分海岸尚未受到破坏。

compare[1] /kəmˋpɛr; kəmˈpeə/ *v*

1 ▶SIMILAR/DIFFERENT 类似的/不同的◀ [T] to consider two or more things, people, ideas etc, in order to show how they are similar to or different from each other 比较: *The report com-*

pares the different types of home computer currently available. 这份报告比较了目前可以买到的不同型号的家用电脑。| **compare sth to/with** *There is nothing to compare with a nice cold drink when you get home after work.* 下班回家后，没有什么能比得上喝上一杯美味的冷饮更好。| **compare and contrast** (=an expression used when telling students to write about the similarities and differences in works of literature, or art) 比较对照〔用来要学生论述文学或艺术作品之间的异同〕

2 compared to/with used when considering the size, quality, or amount of something in relation to something similar〔尺寸、质量、数量〕与…相比: *Compared to our small apartment, our uncle's house seemed like a palace.* 跟我们的小公寓房比起来，叔叔的房子就像是宫殿一般。| *Statistics show a 20% reduction in burglary compared with last year.* 统计数字表明，与去年相比，盗窃案下降了20%。

3 ►LIKE/EQUALLY GOOD 像/同样好◄ [T] to say that something or someone is like someone or something else, or that it is equally good, large etc〔表示某物、某人与另一物、另一人〕相像〔或一样好，一样大等〕: **compare sth/sb to** *You can't compare the war in Somalia to the Vietnam War.* 你不能将索马里那场战争比作越南战争。

4 does not compare if something or someone does not compare with something else, it is not as good, large etc 不能相比: *My old car was a real beauty. This one just doesn't compare.* 我从前那辆车真是漂亮，这一辆就差得远了。

5 ►BETTER/WORSE 较好/较糟◄ to be better or worse in some way than someone or something else〔在某方面〕比〔某人/某物〕好[差]: **[+with]** *How does life in Britain compare with life in the States?* 与美国的生活相比，英国的生活如何？| **compare favourably/unfavourably** *The imported fabrics are 30% cheaper and compare very favorably in quality.* 进口布料价格要便宜30%，而且质地不错。

6 compare notes if two people compare notes, they talk about something they have both done, in order to see if they have the same opinions, ideas etc about it〔两人对所做过的事〕交换意见: *The pair got together in Paris to compare notes on current research.* 那两个人在巴黎见面以交换意见，讨论研究的最新情况。

compare[2] *n* **beyond/without compare** *literary* a quality that is beyond compare is the best of its kind【文】无可比拟; 无可匹配: *a beauty and an elegance beyond compare* 无与伦比的美丽与优雅

S3 W2 **com·pa·ri·son** /kəmˋpærəsn; kəmˈpærɨsən/ *n*

1 ►COMPARING 比较◄ [U] the process of comparing two people or things〔两人或两物的〕比较: **[+with]** *Comparison with the director's earlier movies seems inevitable.* 似乎难免要与该导演的早期电影作一比较。| **by comparison** (=compared to someone or something else) 相比之下 *After months of being in a tropical climate, Spain seemed cool by comparison.* 在热带气候里待了几个月后，西班牙相比之下似乎很凉爽。| **for comparison** (=for the purpose of comparing) 为了比较 *He showed us the original text for comparison.* 他让我们看了原文以作比较。| **in comparison with/to** (=compared to someone or something else) 与…相比 *In comparison with the States, the UK is tiny.* 和美国相比较，英国很小。| **invite comparison** (=if an object, idea etc invites comparison with something else, it reminds you of it so that you compare them) 让人想比较〔某物、某想法等使人想到另一物，因而对它们进行比较〕 *Her paintings invite comparison with those of the early Impressionists.* 她的画不由得让人将它们与早期印象派作品相比较。| **on comparison** (=after you have compared two things to see if they are similar or different) 在比较之后 *On comparison, the Escort was the more reliable car.* 经过比较，证明"护航"牌汽车更为可靠。| **stand/bear comparison** (=compare favourably with someone or something) 比得上，不亚于 *Irving's work bears comparison with the best of the modern novelists.* 欧文的作品可与最出色的现代小说作品相媲美。

2 ►JUDGEMENT 判断◄ [C] a statement or examination that considers how similar or different two people, places, things etc are 比较; 比较报告: **[+of]** *a comparison of smog levels in Chicago and Detroit* 对芝加哥和底特律烟雾水平所作的比较 | **[+between]** *a comparison between the two novels* 对这两部小说的比较

3 ►BE LIKE STH 像某物◄ [C] a statement that someone or something is like someone or something else 比拟, 比喻: **[+to]** *The comparison of the mall to a zoo seemed entirely appropriate.* 将购物中心比作动物园好像非常合适。| **make a comparison** (=consider the similarities between two things) 作比较〔显示两者之间的共同点〕 *You can't make a comparison between American and Japanese schools – they're too different.* 美国的学校和日本的学校不能相提并论，它们太不相同了。| **draw a comparison** (=show a similarity between two ideas or things) 作出比较〔显示两者间的一个共同点〕 *It's tempting to draw a comparison between this and the Watergate scandal.* 将这件事和水门丑闻相比: 这个想法实在很有诱惑力。

4 there's no comparison *spoken* used when you think that someone or something is much better than someone or something else【口】不能相比〔用来表示某人或某物比另一人或物好得多〕: *There's just no comparison between the junk he sings now and his earlier songs.* 他现在唱的这些垃圾歌曲不能与他以前的歌相比。

5 ►GRAMMAR 语法◄ [U] a word used in grammar meaning the way an adverb or adjective changes its form to show whether it is COMPARATIVE[1] (4) or SUPERLATIVE[1] (2)〔形容词或副词的〕比较(变化)

com·part·ment /kəmˋpɑrtmənt; kəmˈpɑːtmənt/ *n* [C] **1** one of the separate areas into which a plane, ship, or train is divided〔火车、飞机、轮船上的〕车厢, 舱: *a non-smoking compartment* 无烟车厢 **2** one of the separate parts of something such as a desk or box, where you can keep things〔书桌或盒子的〕分隔间, 隔层: *Put the ice cream back in the freezer compartment.* 将冰淇淋放回冷冻室。—see also 另见 GLOVE COMPARTMENT

com·part·men·tal·ize also 又作 **-ise** *BrE*【英】/ˌkɑmpɑrtˋmɛntḷaɪz; ˌkɒmpɑːtˈmentlaɪz/ *v* [T] to divide things into separate groups, especially according to what type of things they are〔尤指根据事物的种类〕划分, 分类 **—compartmentalized** *adj* **—compartmentalization** /ˌkəmpɑrtˌmɛntḷəˋzeʃən; ˌkɒmpɑːtˌmentl-aɪˈzeɪʃən/ *n* [U]

com·pass /ˋkʌmpəs; ˈkʌmpəs/ *n* **1** [C] an instrument that shows directions 指南针, 罗盘: *a map and compass* 一张地图和一个指南针 | **compass point** (=one of the 32 marks on a compass that shows you the exact direction) 罗盘上的方位刻度 **2** [C] an instrument that you use to draw circles or measure distances on maps 圆规; 两脚规 **3** [U] *formal* the area or range of subjects that someone is responsible for or that is discussed in a book【正式】〔某人负责或书中论述的〕范围: **[+of]** *Within the brief compass of a single page the author covers most of the major points.* 在短短一页的篇幅中，作者涵盖了大部分主要观点。

com·pas·sion /kəmˋpæʃən; kəmˈpæʃən/ *n* [U] a strong feeling of sympathy for someone who is suffering, and a desire to help them 怜悯; 同情: **[+for]** *compassion for the poor and sick* 对穷人和病人的同情 | **feel/show compassion** *"Come have a drink," offered Cook, feeling compassion.* 库克心生同情，说道: "来喝一杯。" | **be filled with compassion** (=feel a lot of compassion) 充满了怜悯

com·pas·sion·ate /kəmˋpæʃənɪt; kəmˈpæʃənɨt/ *adj* feeling sympathy for people who are suffering 有怜悯心的, 表示同情的: *a caring, compassionate man* 满怀关爱怜悯的人 | *a compassionate smile* 同情的微笑 **—compassionately** *adv*

compassionate leave /ˌ·ˌ··· ˈ·/ *n* [U] special permission to have time away from work because one of your relatives has died or is very ill〔由于亲属去世或病重而特许的〕事假

com·pat·i·bil·i·ty /kəmˌpætəˋbɪlətɪ; kəmˌpætɨˈbɪlɨti/ *n* [U] **1** the ability to exist or be used together without causing problems 相容〔能够并存或同时使用而不致产生问题〕 **2** *technical* the ability of one piece of computer equipment to be used with another one, especially when they are made by different companies【术语】〔电脑设备的〕兼容性

com·pat·i·ble[1] /kəmˋpætəbḷ; kəmˈpætɨbəl/ *adj* **1** *technical* compatible machines, methods, ideas etc can exist together or be used together without causing problems【术语】相容的, 兼容的〔机器、方法、想法等能共存或配套使用而不致产生问题〕: *The new software is IBM compatible* (=can be used with IBM computers). 这个新软件与IBM机兼容。| **[+with]** *The project is not compatible with the company's long-term aims.* 这项计划与公司长远目标相违背。**2** two people that are compatible are able to have a good relationship 能和谐相处的

compatible[2] *n* [C] a piece of computer equipment that can be used with another piece, especially one made by a different company〔尤指另一公司制造的〕电脑兼容设备: *IBM compatibles* IBM兼容机

com·pat·ri·ot /kəmˋpetrɪət; kəmˈpætriət/ *n* [C] someone who was born in or is a citizen of the same country as someone else; COUNTRYMAN 同国人, 同胞: *Stich defeated his compatriot Becker in the quarter final.* 斯蒂克在四分之一决赛中击败了他的同胞贝克尔。

com·pel /kəm`pɛl; kəm'pel/ *v* **compelled, compelling** [T] **1** to force someone to do something 强迫; 逼迫: **compel sb to do sth** *reports that children were compelled to participate in bizarre rituals* 关于孩子们被迫参加古怪仪式的报道 | **feel compelled to do sth** (=feel very strongly that you must do something) 强烈感到必须做某事 *Harrison felt compelled to resign because of the allegations in the press.* 由于新闻界的指控，哈里森强烈地感到他必须辞职。**2** *formal* to make people have a particular feeling or attitude【正式】引起〔某种感情或态度〕: *His appearance on stage compelled the audience's attention.* 他在舞台上一亮相就吸引了观众的注意力。—compare 比较 IMPEL

com·pel·ling /kəm`pɛlɪŋ; kəm'pelɪŋ/ *adj* **1** extremely interesting or exciting 令人激动的，极为有趣的: *a compelling personality* 极有吸引力的性格 **2 compelling argument/reason/cases etc** an argument etc that makes you feel it is true or that you must do something about it 令人信服的论点/理由/案例等: *He felt a compelling need to tell someone about his idea.* 他急需把自己的想法告诉别人。—**compellingly** *adv*

com·pen·di·ous /kəm`pɛndɪəs; kəm'pendiəs/ *adj formal* a book that is compendious gives information in a short but complete form【正式】扼要的，简明的 —**compendiously** *adv*

com·pen·di·um /kəm`pɛndɪəm; kəm'pendiəm/ *n plural* **compendiums** *or* **compendia** /-dɪə; -diə/ [C] *formal*【正式】**1** a book that contains a complete collection of facts, drawings etc on a particular subject 手册，大全〔关于某题目的详尽资料、图解等〕: *a cricketing compendium* 板球运动手册 **2** *BrE* a set of different BOARD GAMEs in one box【英】〔装在一个盒子里的〕一套几种棋盘游戏

com·pen·sate /`kampən͵set; 'kɒmpənseɪt/ *v* **1** [I] to replace or balance something good that has been lost or is lacking, by providing or doing something equally good 弥补，补偿: *Because my left eye is so weak, my right eye has to work harder to compensate.* 因为我左眼视力差，右眼就要辛苦点来弥补一下。| **[+for]** *Her intelligence more than compensates for her lack of experience.* 她才智过人，因此虽然经验不足，也游刃有余。**2** [I, T] to pay someone money because they have suffered injury, loss or damage 赔偿，补偿: **compensate sb for sth** *The firm agreed to compensate its workers for their loss of earnings.* 该公司同意补偿工人的收入损失。

3 **com·pen·sa·tion** /͵kampən`seʃən; ͵kɒmpən'seɪʃən/ *n* **1** [U] money that someone pays you because they have harmed or hurt you in some way 补偿费，赔偿金: **[+for]** *compensation for injuries at work* 工伤补偿金 | **in compensation** *The plane was cancelled, and all we got in compensation was a free meal.* 航班取消，我们得到的补偿仅仅是一顿免费餐。| **as compensation** *The workers were given 30 days' pay as compensation.* 工人获得30天的薪金作为补偿。| **pay sb compensation** *The idea is that criminals should pay compensation to their victims.* 这个想法就是罪犯应对受害者作出赔偿。| **seek/claim compensation** (=ask officially for compensation) 正式要求赔偿 | **award/grant compensation** (=pay compensation) 给予补偿 *The court awarded Jamieson £15,000 compensation.* 法院裁定给予贾米森1.5万英镑赔偿。**2** [C,U] something that makes a sad or an unpleasant situation better or happier〔舒缓不佳境遇的〕补偿物，赔偿物: *One of the few compensations of being unemployed was seeing more of the family.* 失业带来的少数好处之一就是能更多地与家人在一起。| **by way of compensation** (=in order to make a situation better) 为了使情况改善 *By way of compensation he offered to take her out for a meal.* 他主动提出请她吃饭，以此作为一种补偿。**3** [C,U] actions, behaviour etc that replace or balance something that is lacking〔行为举止等作为〕弥补，补偿: **[+for]** *Linda's aggressiveness is really just a compensation for her feelings of insecurity.* 琳达的咄咄逼人实际上只是对她缺乏安全感的一种补偿。| **as compensation** *Lip reading can act as compensation for loss of hearing.* 唇读可以弥补听力的丧失。

com·pen·sa·to·ry /kəm`pɛnsə͵torɪ; ͵kɒmpən'seɪtəri◂/ *adj* [usually before noun 一般用于名词前] **1** intended to reduce the harmful effects of something or to make them easier to bear 弥补性质的，补偿性质的 **2** compensatory payments are paid to someone who has been harmed or hurt in some way 赔偿的: *She was awarded a large sum in compensatory damages.* 她得到了一大笔损害赔偿金。

com·pere /`kampɛr; 'kɒmpeə/ *n* [C] *BrE* someone who introduces the people who are performing in a television programme, theatre show etc【英】〔电视节目、舞台表演等的〕节目主持人; EMCEE *AmE*【美】: *He plays a sleazy, no-talent TV compere.* 他扮演一名格调低下而又缺少才华的电视节目主持人。—**compere** *v* [I,T] *BrE*【英】| *UTV's Pamela Ballentine will compere the show.* UTV（综合频道）的帕梅拉·巴伦坦将主持这次的演出。

com·pete /kəm`pit; kəm'piːt/ *v* [I] 3 3

1 ▶PERSON/BUSINESS 人/企业◀ to try to be more successful than another person or organization, especially in business 竞争〔尤指商业方面〕: **[+with]** *They found themselves competing with foreign companies for a share of the market.* 他们发现自己在与外国公司争夺市场份额。| **[+for]** *She and her sister are always competing for attention.* 她和她姐姐[妹妹]老是争着出风头。| **[+against]** *businesses competing against each other* 相互竞争的企业 | **compete to do sth** *Several advertising agencies are competing to get the contract.* 几家广告代理商在竞争，力求得到这份合同。| **can't compete** (=be unable to compete, especially with something bigger or better) 无法竞争〔尤指与比自己强大的对手〕*Small, independent bookstores simply can't compete with the big national chains.* 规模小的个体书店怎么样也竞争不过大型的全国连锁店。

2 ▶IN A COMPETITION 竞赛中◀ to take part in a competition or sporting event 参加比赛: *How many runners will be competing in the marathon?* 有多少赛跑运动员将参加本次马拉松?

3 can't compete with sb/sth to not be as interesting, attractive etc as someone or something else 敌不过某人/某物: *Melinda was plain and knew she couldn't compete with her sister where boys were concerned.* 梅琳达相貌平平，她知道在吸引男孩子这方面自己比不上姐姐[妹妹]。

4 ▶SOUND/SMELL 声音/气味◀ **[I+with]** if a sound or smell competes with another sound or smell, you can hear both equally well 同时听见[闻到]: *The songs of the birds competed with the sound of the church bells.* 鸟鸣声与教堂钟声一同响起。

5 ▶IDEAS/ARGUMENTS 想法/论点◀ if two ideas, arguments, claims etc compete with each other, they cannot both be right 竞争，对抗

com·pe·tence /`kampətəns; 'kɒmpɪtəns/ *n* **1** [U] the ability and skill to do what is needed 称职; 胜任: *No one questioned his competence as a doctor.* 没有人怀疑过他当医生的能力。| *a high level of managerial competence* 高水平的管理才干 **2** [U] *law* the legal power of a court of law to hear and judge something in court【法律】〔法院审判案件的〕权限; 管辖权 **3** [U] a special area of knowledge 知识范围: *It is not within my competence to make such judgements.* 做这种判断不在我知识范围之内。**4** [C] a skill needed to do a particular job〔做某种工作所必须的〕技能: *Typing is considered by most employers to be a basic competence.* 大多数雇主认为打字是一种基本技能。

com·pe·tent /`kampətənt; 'kɒmpɪtənt/ *adj* **1** having enough skill or knowledge to do something to a satisfactory standard 能干的，胜任的: *She's a highly competent linguist.* 她是一位非常有才干的语言学家。| **competent to do sth** *I don't feel competent to give an opinion at the moment.* 我目前还没有足够的把握来发表看法。**2** a piece of work, performance etc that is competent is satisfactory but not especially good 合格的，令人满意的〔但不见得特别好〕: *The workmen did a competent job.* 这些工人活干得不错。**3** [not before noun 不用于名词前] having the legal power to deal with something in a court of law 有权在法庭上处理某事: **be competent to do sth** *This court is not competent to hear your case.* 这个法庭无权审理你的案子。—**competently** *adv*

com·pet·ing /kəm`pitɪŋ; kəm'piːtɪŋ/ *adj* **competing claims/interests/theories etc** competing claims etc are two claims that cannot both be accepted 相互冲突的要求/利益/理论等: *We've got several competing priorities to decide between.* 我们有好几项紧急事情需要决定处理顺序。

com·pe·ti·tion /͵kampə`tɪʃən; ͵kɒmpɪ'tɪʃən/ *n* **1** [U] a situation in which people or organizations compete with each other 竞争: **[+between]** *Sometimes there's a lot of competition between children for their mother's attention.* 为了得到母亲的宠爱，有时孩子们会相互竞争。| **[+for]** *Competition for the job was intense.* 该职位竞争很激烈。| **[+among]** *This price reduction is due to competition among suppliers.* 这次的降价源于供货商之间的竞争。| **be in competition with** (=be competing with) 与…竞争 | **fierce/stiff/intense etc competition** *There is fierce competition between the three leading soap manufacturers.* 三大肥皂制造商之间竞争很激烈。| **in the face of competition** (=in a situation where you are competing) 面对竞争 *In the face of such strong competition, small grocery stores are going out of business.* 面对如此强大的竞争，小杂货店纷纷倒闭。**2** [singular, U] the people or groups that are competing against you, especially in business or in a sport 竞争对手: **the competition** *Going to trade fairs is an ideal opportunity to size up the competition.* 参加贸易商品展览会是估量对手的理想机会。| **no/not much/little etc competition** (=no one who is likely to be better than you) 没有对手，不太多/极少的对手 *Lewis is bound to win* 1 1

the race; there's just no competition. 刘易斯注定要获胜，因为根本没有比他更强的对手。| **a lot of/considerable/fierce etc competition** (=people who are very strong or skilful) 许多强的/相当多强的/强劲的对手 *The team overcame fierce competition for their place in the finals.* 这支球队战胜了强劲的对手，打进决赛。| **foreign competition** (=companies from other countries that you are competing with) 来自外国企业的竞争 **3** [C] an organized event in which people or teams compete against each other, especially using their skill〔尤指运用技能的〕比赛: *United were knocked out of the competition in the first round.* 曼联队在第一轮比赛中就败下阵来。| *a crossword competition* 填字游戏比赛 | **competition to do sth** *a competition to find a designer for the new airport building* 为新机场大楼招聘设计师而举行的竞赛 | **win/lose a competition** *Who won the volleyball competition?* 谁赢了这次排球比赛? | **enter a competition** *Teams from high schools all over the state have entered the competition.* 全州各地中学的运动队都参加了这次比赛。

S2 W3 **com·pet·i·tive** /kəmˋpɛtətɪv; kəmˈpetɪ̈tɪv/ *adj* **1** a competitive situation is one in which people or organizations try very hard to be more successful than others 充满竞争的: *an extremely competitive market* 竞争非常激烈的市场 | **highly/fiercely/intensely competitive** *Advertising is an intensely competitive business.* 广告业是一个竞争激烈的行业。**2** products or prices that are competitive are cheaper than others but still of good quality 具有竞争力的〔指比较便宜而质量不减的商品或价格〕: *The hotel offers a high standard of service at competitive rates.* 这家酒店以优惠的价格提供高标准的服务。**3** someone who is competitive is determined to be more successful than other people 好胜的: *I hate playing tennis with Steve. He's too competitive.* 我讨厌和史蒂夫打网球，他只能赢不能输。**4 competitive edge** a strong desire to win or do well that gives someone an advantage 好胜的锋芒〔因强烈的求胜欲望而占有的优势〕: *The team seems to have lost their competitive edge in recent months.* 在最近几个月里这支球队的锋芒似乎削弱了。—**competitively** *adv*

com·pet·i·tive·ness /kəmˋpɛtətɪvnəs; kəmˈpetɪ̈tɪvnɪ̈s/ *n* [U] **1** the ability of a company or a product to compete with others 竞争力: *New machinery has enhanced the company's productivity and competitiveness.* 新机器提高了公司的生产力，增强了竞争力。**2** the desire to be more successful than other people 好胜，要强: *Her enthusiasm and competitiveness rubbed off on everyone.* 她的热情和好强感染了每一个人。

com·pet·i·tor /kəmˋpɛtətə; kəmˈpetɪ̈tə/ *n* [C] **1** a person, team, company etc that is competing with another 竞争者: *The firm's major competitors are all in France.* 该公司主要的竞争对手都在法国。**2** someone who takes part in a competition 选手，参赛者: *Two of the competitors failed to turn up for the race.* 两名参赛者比赛时没有出场。

com·pi·la·tion /ˌkɑmpɪˋleʃən; ˌkɒmpɪ̈ˈleɪʃən/ *n* **1** [C] a book or list, record etc which is made up of different pieces of information, songs etc 辑，集，集子: **compilation album/cassette** *a compilation album of Christmas music* 圣诞音乐汇编唱片集 **2** [U] the process of making a book, list, record etc from different pieces of information, songs etc 编纂，编辑；汇编: *the compilation of a dictionary* 词典的编纂

com·pile /kəmˋpaɪl; kəmˈpaɪl/ *v* [T] **1** to make a list, record etc using different pieces of information, songs etc 编辑，编纂；编制；汇编: *The document was compiled by the Department of Health.* 这份文件是由卫生部编制的。| **compile sth from/for sth** *These notes were compiled from lectures and seminars.* 这些笔记是由讲座和研讨会记录整理而成的。**2** to put a set of instructions into a computer in a form that you can understand and use 编译〔电脑用语〕

com·pil·er /kəmˋpaɪlə; kəmˈpaɪlə/ *n* [C] **1** someone who collects different pieces of information or facts to be used in a book, report, or list 编辑者，编纂者 **2** a set of instructions in a computer that changes a computer language known to the computer user into the form needed by the computer〔电脑的〕编译程序

com·pla·cen·cy /kəmˋplesn̩sɪ; kəmˈpleɪsənsi/ *n* [U] a feeling of satisfaction with what you have achieved which makes you stop trying to improve or change things 自满，故步自封: *There are no grounds for complacency in today's competitive environment.* 在今天这种充满竞争的环境下，没有理由自满。

com·pla·cent /kəmˋplesn̩t; kəmˈpleɪsənt/ *adj* pleased with what you have achieved so that you stop trying to improve or change things 自满的；得意的: *There's a danger of becoming complacent if you win a few games.* 如果你赢了几场比赛就会有自满的危险。| [+about] *We simply cannot afford to be complacent about the future of our car industry.* 我们没有资格对汽车业的前景沾沾自喜。—**complacently** *adv*

S2 W3 **com·plain** /kəmˋplen; kəmˈpleɪn/ *v* **1** [I,T not in passive 不用被动态] to say that you are annoyed, dissatisfied, or unhappy about something or someone 抱怨；不满，发牢骚: *They've already been given a 10% raise so why are they complaining?* 已经给他们加薪 10%，他们怎么还在抱怨? | *"You never ask my opinion about anything," Rod complained.* 罗德抱怨道："不论什么事，你从来都不问问我的意见。" | [+about] *She often complains about not feeling appreciated at work.* 她因为感到自己在工作上不受赏识而常常抱怨。| **complain (that)** *People complain that they don't get enough information.* 人们抱怨得不到足够的信息。| **complain to sb** *Neighbours complained to the police about the dogs barking.* 邻居因为狗吠扰民向警察投诉。| **complain bitterly** *Employees complained bitterly about working conditions.* 雇员对工作条件极为不满。**2 can't complain** *spoken* used to say that a situation is satisfactory generally in spite of the fact there may be a few problems【口】〔虽然有些问题，但〕〔总体上〕还算满意: *Old age is creeping up, but I can't complain.* 老年悄然而至，但一切还算满意。

complain of sth *phr v* [T] to say that you feel ill or have a pain in a part of your body 诉说有…病痛，诉苦: *Dan's been complaining of severe headaches recently.* 丹最近总是说头疼得厉害。

com·plain·ant /kəmˋplenənt; kəmˈpleɪnənt/ *n* [C] *law* someone who makes a formal complaint in a court of law; PLAINTIFF【法律】原告

S2 W3 **com·plaint** /kəmˋplent; kəmˈpleɪnt/ *n* **1** [C,U] a written or spoken statement in which someone complains about something〔口头或书面的〕投诉: *The sales assistants were trained to deal with customer complaints in a friendly manner.* 售货员都受过培训以礼貌的态度处理顾客的投诉。| [+about] *We have received a number of complaints about your conduct.* 我们收到几宗针对你行为的投诉。| [+against] *All complaints against police officers are carefully investigated.* 针对警察的所有投诉都予以仔细调查。| **complaint that** *We are concerned by complaints that children are being bullied.* 我们关注有关孩子们受到欺侮的投诉。| **make a complaint** (=complain formally to someone) 正式投诉 *If you wish to make a complaint you should see the manager.* 如果你要投诉，应该去找经理。| **have/receive a complaint** *The BBC received a stream of complaints about the programme.* 关于这个节目英国广播公司收到许多投诉。| **file/lodge/submit a complaint** *formal* (=complain officially to someone)【正式】正式〔向某人〕投诉 *"I wish to lodge an official complaint." the woman said.* 那女人说道，"我要提出正式投诉。" | **letter of complaint** *The Council received over 10,000 letters of complaint.* 市议会收到一万多封投诉信件。| **reason/cause/grounds for complaint** *Anyone dismissed because of their race has legitimate grounds for complaint.* 由于种族的原因而被解雇的人都有正当的投诉理由。| **complaints procedure** (=a system for dealing with official complaints) 投诉程序 **2** [C] something that you complain about 投诉的事物: *Our main complaint is the poor standard of service.* 我们投诉的主要是服务质量差。**3** [C] an illness that affects a particular part of your body 疾病: *Mr Riley is suffering from a chest complaint.* 赖利先生患了胸部疾病。| *minor skin complaints* 皮肤上的小毛病

com·plai·sance /kəmˋplezn̩s; kəmˈpleɪzəns/ *n* [U] *formal* willingness to do what pleases other people【正式】迁就，殷勤 —**complaisant** *adj* —**complaisantly** *adv*

Com·pleat An·gler, The /kəmˌplit ˋæŋglə; kəmˌpliːt ˈæŋglə/ a book about FISHING (=the sport of catching fish) written by Izaak Walton in the 17th century《垂钓高手》〔艾萨克·沃尔顿 17 世纪撰写的一部垂钓论著〕

com·plect·ed /kəmˋplɛktɪd; kəmˈplektɪ̈d/ *adj* **fair/dark complected** *AmE* having fair or dark skin【美】皮肤白皙的/黝黑的

com·ple·ment¹ /ˋkɑmpləmənt; ˈkɒmplɪ̈mənt/ *n* [C] **1** someone or something that emphasizes the good qualities of another person or thing 补足物；补充；使完备之物: [+to] *A fine wine is a complement to a good meal.* 美酒佳肴，相得益彰。**2** the number or quantity needed to make a group complete 足数，足额，全数〔指使某物齐全的数目或数量〕: **a full complement (of)** (=all the people or things that form a complete group)〔构成一个完整群体的〕所有的人[物] *Each new cell will carry its full complement of chromosomes.* 每个新的细胞都包含全部数量的染色体。**3** *technical* a word or phrase in grammar that follows a verb and describes the subject of the verb【术语】补语: *In 'John is cold' and 'John became chairman', 'cold' and 'chairman' are*

complements. 在 John is cold 和 John became chairman 中, cold、chairman 是补语。**4** *technical* an angle that together with another angle already mentioned makes 90 degrees【术语】余角 —compare 比较 COMPLIMENT¹

com·ple·ment² /ˋkɑmplə,mɛnt; ˈkɒmpl¦ment/ *v* [T] to show up the good qualities in someone or something, or make them seem more attractive (使)〔优点〕显现; 使更具吸引力: *The white silk of her blouse complements her olive skin perfectly.* 白色的绸衬衫完美地衬托出她橄榄色的皮肤。| *Sally's tact and reserve complemented John's go-getting attitude.* 萨莉的机智与沉稳使约翰勇敢进取的态度更为突出。—compare 比较 COMPLIMENT²

com·ple·men·ta·ry /,kɑmpləˋmɛntərɪ; ,kɒmpl¦ˈmentəri◂/ *adj* **1** making someone or something better or more attractive by emphasizing its good qualities or having qualities that the other person or thing lacks 补充的; 补足的: *The computer and the human mind have different but complementary abilities.* 电脑与人脑各自不同却又互为补充。**2** *technical* two angles that are complementary add up to 90 degrees【术语】余角的; 互为余角的

S2 W1 **com·plete¹** /kəmˋplit; kəmˈpliːt/ *adj* **1** a word used to emphasize that a quality you are describing is as great or extreme as possible 十足的, 完全的: *Their engagement came as a complete surprise to me.* 他们的订婚使我大吃一惊。| *The police were in complete control of the situation.* 警方已完全控制了局势。| **a complete idiot/failure/wimp etc** *I felt a complete fool.* 我觉得自己是个十足的傻子。**2** having all parts, details, facts etc included and with nothing missing 完整的, 全部的, 整个的: *The captain ordered a complete baggage check.* 船长命令对行李进行彻底检查。| *Buy one of those plate severy month until your collection is complete.* 你每月买一只这套碟子, 直到买齐。| *The party didn't seem complete without Clare.* 没有克莱尔这个晚会显得不完整。| **the complete works of** (=a book or books containing every play, story or poem by a particular person) …的作品全集 *the complete works of Shakespeare* 莎士比亚全集 **3** [not before noun 不用于名词前] finished 已完成的; 已结束的: *The work on the new building is nearly complete.* 新楼房的工程已接近完工。**4 complete with** having equipment or features 装备有〔某设备〕, 具有〔某特点〕: *The house comes complete with swimming pool and sauna.* 这栋房子配备有游泳池和桑拿浴设备。**5 the complete footballer/host etc** someone who is good at all parts of an activity 全能的足球员, 周到的晚会主持人等: *Best's vision and ball control made him the complete footballer.* 贝斯开阔的视野和极佳的控球能力使他成为全能的足球运动员。—**completeness** *n* [U]

S2 W1 **complete²** *v* [T] **1** to finish doing something especially when it has taken a long time 结束, 完成〔尤指经历长时间之后〕: *The students have just completed their course.* 学生刚刚完成了他们的课程。| *The building took two years to complete.* 这幢大楼花了两年才建成。**2** to make something whole or perfect by adding what is missing 使完整, 使圆满: *This exercise involves completing sentences.* 这个练习训练填充句子。| *He only needs one more stamp to complete his collection.* 他只差一枚邮票, 就收集全了。| **complete a form/questionnaire** (=give information that is needed) 填表格/填写问卷

com·plet·ed /kəmˋplitɪd; kəmˈpliːt¦d/ *adj* containing all the necessary parts or answers needed to finish something 完整的; 已完成的: *Send your completed form to the following address.* 请将已填好的表格寄往下列地址。

S1 W2 **com·plete·ly** /kəmˋplitlɪ; kəmˈpliːtli/ *adv* in every way; totally 完全地, 全部地, 彻底地: *I completely forgot that it was his birthday yesterday.* 我完全忘了昨天是他的生日。| [+adj/adv] *She was bored with work and wanted to do something completely different.* 她对工作感到厌烦, 想干点截然不同的事。| *I felt completely relaxed.* 我觉得完全放松下来了。

com·ple·tion /kəmˋpliʃən; kəmˈpliːʃən/ *n* [U] **1** the state of being finished 完成, 结束: **near completion** (=almost finished) 接近完成 *The new houses are nearing completion.* 那些新房子即将建成。| **completion date** (=the time by which something must or will be finished) 完成的日期; 完成的限期 *The builders have given us December 22nd as a completion date.* 建筑商将竣工日期定在12月22日。**2** the act of completing or finishing something 完成, 完结: [+of] *The job is subject to your satisfactory completion of the training course.* 你能否得到这份工作取决于你能否圆满完成培训课程。| **on completion** *We paid them on completion of the work.* 他们把工作完成后, 我们付了款。**3** the final point in the sale of a property, such as a house, when the documents have all been signed and all the money paid 销售完成〔指在房屋等财产销售中, 契约等已签订, 钱款都已付清〕

S3 W2 **com·plex¹** /kəmˋplɛks; ˈkɒmpleks/ *adj* **1** consisting of many different parts or processes that are closely connected 复杂的〔指由许多密切联系的部分或过程构成〕: *There is a complex network of roads round the city.* 这座城市周围有一个复杂的道路网络。| *Photosynthesis is a highly complex process.* 光合作用是一个非常复杂的过程。**2** difficult to understand or deal with 难以理解的, 难处理的; 复杂的: *Mental illness is by its nature very complex.* 精神病就其本质来说是十分复杂的。| *a complex problem* 一个复杂的问题 **3** *technical* a complex word or sentence contains a main part and one or more other parts【术语】〔词、句〕复合的

com·plex² /ˋkɑmplɛks; ˈkɒmpleks/ *n* [C] **1** a group of buildings that are close together, or a large building containing smaller buildings that are used for the same purpose 综合楼群〔由众多大楼或一座主楼和诸多辅楼组成〕: *They are building a vast new shopping complex in the town.* 他们正在市区兴建一处巨大的综合性商场。| **leisure/sports/cinema complex** *a 12-screen cinema complex* 拥有12个放映厅的电影院 **2** an emotional problem in which someone is unnecessarily anxious about something or thinks too much about something 情结, 夸大的情绪反应: **have a complex about sth** *She's has some kind of a complex about her nose.* 她对自己的鼻子感到莫名其妙的担心。| **give sb a complex** *You'll give Graham a complex if you keep going on about how fat he is.* 如果你老是对格雷厄姆说他有多胖, 就会惹得他心绪不宁。**3 a complex of roads/regulations etc** a large number of things which are closely connected and difficult to understand 纵横交织的道路网/纷繁芜杂的条例等 —see also 另见 INFERIORITY COMPLEX, OEDIPUS COMPLEX, PERSECUTION COMPLEX

com·plex·ion /kəmˋplɛkʃən; kəmˈplekʃən/ *n* **1** [C] the natural colour or appearance of the skin on your face 面色; 面容: *Drinking lots of water is good for the complexion.* 多喝水对面色有好处。| **a pale/ruddy complexion etc** (=a pale, red face etc) 面色苍白/红润等 **2** [singular] the general character or nature of something 一般性质; 一般特征: **put a (whole) new complexion on** (=change a situation) 使〔某事〕大为改观 *These latest findings have put a whole new complexion on the affair.* 最近的这些发现使这件事大为改观。

com·plex·i·ty /kəmˋplɛksɪtɪ; kəmˈpleks¦ti/ *n* [U] **1** the state of being complicated 复杂性, 错综复杂: *Many claimants are put off by the sheer complexity of insurance company rules.* 许多索赔人往往由于保险公司十分复杂的规章制度而作罢。**2 the complexities of** the problems and difficulties involved in a situation or process〔某局势或过程中〕所牵涉的问题和困难: *the complexities of the tax laws* 税法的错综复杂

com·pli·ance /kəmˋplaɪəns; kəmˈplaɪəns/ *n* [U] *formal*【正式】**1** OBEDIENCE to a rule, agreement, or demand 服从, 听从, 遵守〔规则、协议、要求〕: *Compliance with the law is expected of all citizens.* 所有公民都要遵守法律。| **in compliance with** *In compliance with her wishes, she was buried next to her husband.* 依照她的愿望, 她被葬在丈夫旁边。**2** the tendency to agree too willingly to someone else's wishes or demands 过于顺从, 屈从: *Her compliance with everything we suggested made it difficult to know what she really felt.* 她对我们所有的提议言听计从, 使人难以了解她真正的想法。

com·pli·ant /kəmˋplaɪənt; kəmˈplaɪənt/ *adj* willing to obey, or agree to other people's wishes and demands〔对他人的意愿和要求〕顺从的; 听从的, 服从的: *He soon settled down and became a compliant patient.* 他很快就安静下来, 成了安分的病人。—**compliantly** *adv* —see also 另见 COMPLY

com·pli·cate /ˋkɑmplə,ket; ˈkɒmpl¦keɪt/ *v* [T] **1** to make a problem or situation more difficult 使〔问题或情况〕更复杂, 更麻烦: *The situation is complicated by the fact that I've got to work late on Friday.* 我周五得加班, 这使情况更复杂了。| **to complicate matters/things** *Just to complicate things, the car has broken down!* 汽车抛锚了, 使事情更加麻烦! **2** [usually passive 一般用被动态] to make an illness worse 使〔疾病〕恶化: *a heart condition complicated by pneumonia* 因肺炎而恶化的心脏病

com·pli·cat·ed /ˋkɑmplə,ketɪd; ˈkɒmpl¦keɪt¦d/ *adj* **1** difficult to understand or deal with 难懂的; 难处理的: *They had to begin the complicated task of sorting out his legal affairs.* 他们不得不着手整理他的法律事务, 这是件繁杂的工作。| *a complicated set of instructions* 一组复杂难懂的说明 | **extremely/highly complicated** *a highly complicated situation* 极其复杂的情况 **2** consisting of many closely related or connected parts 结构复杂的: *The human brain is an incredibly complicated organ.* 人脑是一个结构极其复杂的器官。 S2

com·pli·ca·tion /,kɑmpləˋkeʃən; ,kɒmpl¦ˈkeɪʃən/ *n* **1** [C, U] a problem or situation that makes something more difficult

to understand or deal with 使复杂化的问题[情况]: *The fact that the plane was late added a further complication to our journey.* 飞机误点给我们的旅行带来更大麻烦。**2** [C, usually plural 一般用复数] a medical problem or illness that happens while someone is already ill and makes medical treatment more difficult 并发症: *Pneumonia is one of the common complications faced by bed-ridden patients.* 肺炎是卧床病人所面临的常见并发症之一。

complicit /kəm`plɪsət; kəm'plɪsɪ̵t/ *adj* involved in or knowing about a situation, especially one that is morally wrong or dishonest 同谋的, 串通一气的: *They exchanged complicit smiles.* 他们相视而会心微笑。| **complicit in sth** *The careers of the officers complicit in the cover-up were ruined.* 由于参与掩饰真相, 这些军官的前途都毁掉了。

com·plic·i·ty /kəm`plɪsətɪ; kəm'plɪsɪ̵ti/ *n* [U] *formal* a process in which someone is involved in a crime or illegal activity together with other people【正式】共犯, 同谋; 串通: [+in] *Jennings denied complicity in the murder.* 詹宁斯否认自己参与了谋杀案。

com·pli·ment¹ /`kɑmpləmənt; 'kɒmplɪ̵mənt/ *n* [C] **1** a remark that expresses admiration of someone or something 赞美; 恭维(话): *"You have lovely hair", Bob told Emma, who blushed at the compliment.* 鲍勃对埃玛说"你的头发真美", 这句恭维话让爱玛脸都红了。| *Maria's used to receiving compliments on her appearance.* 玛丽亚已经习惯于接受别人对她容貌的赞美。| **pay sb a compliment** (tell someone that they look nice, have done something well, etc) 恭维某人; 赞美某人 | **take sth as a compliment** (=be pleased about what someone has said about you) 这么说我很高兴 *"James described you as a bold, brave feminist." "Oh well, I'll take that as a compliment."* "詹姆斯说你是位大胆无畏的女权主义者。""是吗? 他这么讲我很高兴。" | **shower sb with compliments** (=praise someone very much) 对某人百般恭维 | **return a compliment** (=say something nice to someone after they have said something nice to you) 回敬〔别人的〕称赞 | **fish for compliments** (=try to make someone say something nice about you, usually by asking them a question) 引诱别人来夸奖自己〔一般通过提问〕**2** **pay sb the compliment of doing sth** to do something that shows you trust someone else and have a good opinion of them 对某人做某事表示信任和好感: *They paid me the ultimate compliment of electing me as their representative.* 他们选我为他们的代表, 显示了对我的高度信任。**3** **compliments** *plural* used to express praise, admiration or good wishes 致意; 赞美; 祝贺: **my compliments to the chef** (=used to tell someone that they cook very well) 向厨师致意〔用于称赞人善于烹饪〕*This Stilton and celery soup is delicious; my compliments to the chef!* 这种斯第尔顿干酪和芹菜汤太好吃了, 请向厨师致谢! | **compliments of the season** (=used as a spoken or written greeting at Christmas and New Year) 谨致节日祝贺〔口头或书面祝贺, 用于圣诞节和新年时〕**4 a) with the compliments of.../with our compliments** an expression printed on a small piece of paper used by a company or organization when they send goods or information …向您致意/我们谨向您致意〔公司或其他机构运货或传信时印于小纸条上的用语〕: *With the compliments of J. Nocuold & Son* J.那古尔德父子公司向您致意 **b)** used when a person or company gives you something such as a free ticket, meal etc 问候, 致意〔某人或某公司向你赠送诸如戏票、餐饮时用语〕: *Please accept these tickets with our compliments.* 几张戏票请收下, 顺致问候。**5 a) return the compliment** to do something to help someone after they have helped you 回礼, 答谢: *Thanks for helping me move the furniture; I'll try to return the compliment one day.* 谢谢你帮我搬家具, 我哪一天也会设法答谢。**b)** to say or do something unpleasant to someone after they have behaved badly towards you〔在受到别人无礼对待之后〕回敬〔某人〕: *"Gemma called you a fat liar." "Gee thanks. Remind me to return the compliment."* "姬玛说你满嘴谎话。""嘿, 谢谢。请提醒我回敬她。" **6** **back-handed compliment** *BrE*【英】, **left-handed compliment** *AmE*【美】something that someone says to you which is unpleasant and pleasant at the same time 同时包含贬低及赞美的恭维话: *"A lot of people seem to resent you, but I like you", she said. Talk about a back-handed compliment.* "似乎许多人讨厌你, 但我喜欢你。"她说。此话真可谓褒贬俱备。—compare 比较 COMPLEMENT¹

com·pli·ment² /`kɑmplə,mɛnt; 'kɒmplɪ̵ment/ *v* [T] to say something nice to someone in order to praise them 赞美, 恭维: **compliment sb on sth** *Bob complimented me on my new hairstyle.* 鲍勃称赞我的新发型。—compare 比较 COMPLEMENT²

com·pli·men·ta·ry /,kɑmplə`mɛntərɪ; ,kɒmplɪ̵'mentəri◂/ *adj* **1** expressing admiration, praise or respect 赞美的, 赞扬的; 尊敬的: *Your teacher made some very complimentary remarks about your work.* 你的老师对你的作业大加称赞。| [+about] *Donleavy was highly complimentary about Coleman's work.* 唐利维高度赞扬了科尔曼的工作。**2** given free to people 免费的: *There was a complimentary bottle of champagne in the hotel room.* 宾馆房间内有一瓶免费供应的香槟。| **complimentary ticket/seat etc** *We've got two complimentary tickets for the Barcelona game.* 我们有两张巴塞罗那队比赛的赠票。

compliment slip /'··· ,·/ *n* [C] a small piece of paper with a company's name and address on it, that it sends with goods instead of a proper letter 致意便条〔印有公司名称及地址, 附在向顾客寄送的商品上〕

com·pline /`kɑmplɪn; 'kɒmplɪ̵n/ *n* [U] a Christian church service held late in the evening, especially in the Roman Catholic church〔尤指罗马天主教的〕晚祷 —compare 比较 EVENSONG, VESPERS

com·ply /kəm`plaɪ; kəm'plaɪ/ *v* [I] *formal* to do what you have to do or are asked to do【正式】服从, 遵守: [+with] *Failure to comply with the regulations will result in prosecution.* 不遵守规则将招致起诉。—see also 另见 COMPLIANCE

com·po·nent /kəm`ponənt; kəm'pəʊnənt/ *n* [C] one of several parts that together make up a whole machine or system〔机器或系统的〕零件; 成分; 组成部分: *The repair shop sells electrical components.* 修理店出售电器零件。| *Counselling is an important component of our rehabilitation programme.* 咨询服务是我们康复计划中的重要一环。—compare 比较 CONSTITUENT¹ (2) S3 W2

com·port /kəm`port; kəm'pɔːt/ *v* **comport yourself** *formal* to behave yourself in a particular way【正式】行动, 表现: *He always comported himself in an exemplary manner.* 他的行为举止始终可为人表率。—**comportment** *n* [U]

com·pose /kəm`poz; kəm'pəʊz/ *v* **1** **be composed of** to be formed from a group of substances or parts 由…组成: *Water is composed of hydrogen and oxygen.* 水由氢和氧组成。**2** [T not in progressive 不用进行式] if different things or people compose something else, they combine together to form it 组成, 构成: *the individual letters that compose a word* 组合成词的单个字母 **3** [I,T] to write a piece of music 作曲: *Could you compose a piece for the concert?* 你能为音乐会创作一支曲子吗? **4** **compose a letter/poem/speech etc** to write a letter, poem etc, thinking very carefully about it as you write it 写信/诗/讲稿等: *compose a letter of complaint* 写一封投诉信 **5** **compose your thoughts/features** to make yourself feel or look calm 镇静心情/使外表平静: *He felt he needed a quiet place where he could compose his thoughts.* 他觉得自己需要一个安静的地方以平静思绪。| **compose yourself** (=try hard to become calm after feeling very angry, upset, or excited)〔生气、烦躁、激动后〕极力使自己平静下来 **6** [T] to arrange the parts of a painting, photograph or scene etc in a way that achieves a particular result〔为达到特殊效果而〕为〔绘画、照片场景〕构图: *The photographer will need plenty of time to compose the shot.* 摄影师需要足够的时间来为他这幅照片构图。

com·posed /kəm`pozd; kəm'pəʊzd/ *adj* seeming calm and not upset or angry 看起来平静的, 镇定的: *He appeared very composed despite the stress he was under.* 尽管压力很大, 他看起来仍十分镇定。

com·pos·er /kəm`pozə; kəm'pəʊzə/ *n* [C] someone who writes music 作曲家

com·po·site¹ /kəm`pɑzɪt; 'kɒmpəzɪ̵t/ *adj* [only before noun 仅用于名词前] made up of different parts or materials 由不同成分或材料组成的: *a composite problem* 一道复合题 | *composite molecules* 合成分子

composite² *n* [C] **1** something made up of different parts or materials〔由不同成分或材料组成的〕复合物, 混合物: *Behaviour is a composite of individual and group influences.* 行为是个体与集体共同影响的产物。| *If she wants to be a model, she'll need a composite of good photographs.* 她如果想做模特儿, 就需要一批多种多样的高质量照片。**2** a method used by the police for producing a picture of a possible criminal from descriptions given by a WITNESS or WITNESSES 合成照片〔警方根据证人描述绘制用以识别罪犯的方法〕; IDENTIKIT *BrE*【英】

com·po·si·tion /,kɑmpə`zɪʃən; ,kɒmpə'zɪʃən/ *n* W3
1 ▶MAKING A WHOLE 构成整体◀ [U] the way in which something is made up of different parts, things, members etc 组成, 构成: *There were dramatic changes in the composition of the committee after the election.* 选举之后, 该委员会的构成发生了大变动。| [+of] *He's doing research into the chemical composition of plants.* 他正在研究植物的化学构成。| **in composition** *The suburbs are mainly working class in composition.* 各个郊区的人口主要是劳工阶级。

2 ▶MUSIC/ART ETC 音乐/艺术等◀a) [C] a piece of music or art, or a poem〔音乐、美术、诗歌的〕作品: *She's very fond of Bach's later compositions.* 她十分喜爱巴赫的后期作品。b) [U] the art or process of writing pieces of music, poems etc〔音乐、诗歌等的〕创作; 作曲; 写作

3 ▶PHOTOGRAPH/PICTURE 照片/图画◀[U] the way in which the different parts that make up a photograph or painting are arranged〔照片、绘画等的〕布局: *The composition of these photographs is superb.* 这些照片的布局极为精巧。

4 ▶SCHOOL SUBJECT 学校科目◀[C,U] *old-fashioned* a short piece of writing about a particular subject that is done especially at school【过时】作文〔尤指学生作业〕: *a 400-word composition about Autumn* 一篇以秋天为题的 400 字作文

5 ▶PRINTING 印刷◀[U] *technical* the process of arranging words, pictures etc on a page before they are printed【术语】排字; 排版

com·pos·i·tor /kəmˋpɑzɪtə; kəmˈpɒzɨtə/ *n* [C] someone who arranges letters, pictures etc on a page before they are printed 排字[版]工人

com·pos men·tis /ˋkɑmpəs ˋmɛntɪs; ˌkɒmpəs ˈmentɨs/ *adj* [not before noun 不用于名词前] *often humorous* able to think clearly and be responsible for your actions【常幽默】心智健全的: *It's too early in the morning – I'm not compos mentis!* 大清早的, 我还不太清醒呢!

com·post[1] /ˋkɑmpost; ˈkɒmpɒst/ *n* [U] a mixture of decayed plants, leaves etc used to improve the quality of soil 堆肥, 混合肥料: **compost heap** (=a place in a garden where you pile decayed leaves, plants etc in order to make compost) 堆肥堆

compost[2] *v* [T] **1** to make plants, leaves etc into compost 将〔植物、树叶等〕制成堆肥 **2** to put compost onto soil 给〔土壤〕施堆肥

com·po·sure /kəmˋpoʒə; kəmˈpəʊʒə/ *n* [singular, U] a calm feeling which you have when you feel confident about dealing with a situation 冷静, 镇定: **keep/maintain your composure** (=stay calm) 保持冷静 *They maintained an admirable composure throughout the ordeal.* 他们在那场考验中始终保持着令人佩服的镇静。| **lose your composure** (=get angry or upset) 生气, 慌张烦躁 | **recover/regain your composure** (=become calm after feeling angry or upset)〔心情〕恢复平静

com·pote /ˋkɑmpot; ˈkɒmpɒt/ *n* [C,U] fruit cooked in sugar and water and eaten cold 糖水水果〔用糖和水烹调的水果, 通常冷食〕

com·pound[1] /ˋkɑmpaʊnd; ˈkɒmpaʊnd/ *n* [C] **1** *technical* a substance containing atoms from two or more elements (ELEMENT (1))【术语】化合物: *Sulphur dioxide is a compound of sulphur and oxygen.* 二氧化硫是硫与氧的化合物。**2** a combination of two or more things or qualities that make up a situation 由两件或更多事情, 两种或更多情况结合造成的局势: *social unrest caused by a compound of unemployment and poverty* 失业与贫困并存所导致的社会动荡 **3** an area that contains a group of buildings and is surrounded by a fence or wall〔四周有篱笆或围墙的〕建筑群: *a prison compound* 监狱大院 **4** *technical* a noun or adjective made up of two or more words【术语】复合名词; 复合形容词: *The noun 'flower shop' and the adjective 'self-made' are compounds.* 名词 flower shop 及形容词 self-made 均为复合词。

compound[2] *adj* **1** **compound eye/leaf etc** *technical* a single eye, leaf etc that is made up of two or more parts or substances【术语】复眼/复叶等 **2** **compound noun/adjective** *technical* a noun or adjective that is made up of two or more words【术语】复合名词/复合形容词

com·pound[3] /kəmˋpaʊnd; kəmˈpaʊnd/ *v* [T] **1** to make a difficult situation even worse by adding more problems 使恶化, 加重: **be compounded by** *Our difficulties were compounded by the language barrier.* 我们的困难因语言障碍而加重了。**2** to make something by mixing different parts or substances together 使混合; 使合成; 使化合: *Scientists are able to compound an increasing number of substances to produce new drugs.* 科学家们能够通过合成越来越多的不同物质来制造新药品。**3** *AmE* to pay INTEREST[1] (4) that is calculated on both the sum of money and the INTEREST[1] (4)【美】以复利计算支付〔利息〕: *My bank compounds interest quarterly.* 我的银行按季度以复利计算支付利息。

compound frac·ture /ˌ‥ ˈ‥/ *n* [C] *technical* a broken bone that cuts through someone's skin【术语】哆开骨折, 有创骨折

compound in·terest /ˌ‥ ˈ‥‥/ *n* [U] INTEREST[1] (4) that is calculated on both the sum of money lent or borrowed and on the unpaid INTEREST already earned or charged 复利 —compare 比较 SIMPLE INTEREST

com·pre·hend /ˌkɑmprɪˋhɛnd; ˌkɒmprɪˈhend/ *v* [I,T not in progressive 不用进行式] *formal* to understand something that is complicated or difficult【正式】理解, 领悟〔复杂或困难事物〕: *Even scientists do not comprehend these phenomena.* 即使是科学家也不理解这些现象。| **comprehend how/why/what etc** *I fail to comprehend how this was allowed to happen.* 我不理解怎么会允许这种事发生。| **fully comprehend** (=understand completely) 彻底理解

com·pre·hen·si·ble /ˌkɑmprɪˋhɛnsəbḷ; ˌkɒmprɪˈhensɨbəl/ *adj* easy to understand 易于理解的: *The book offers an easily comprehensible explanation of the subject.* 这本书对这个主题提供了浅显易懂的解释。| [+to] *Such detailed analyses are not comprehensible to the average person.* 如此详细的分析对于一般人来说并不容易懂。—opposite 反义词 INCOMPREHENSIBLE —**comprehensibly** *adv* —**comprehensibility** /ˌkɑmprɪˌhɛnsəˋbɪlətɪ; ˌkɒmprɪhensɨˈbɪlɨti/ *n* [U]

com·pre·hen·sion /ˌkɑmprɪˋhɛnʃən; ˌkɒmprɪˈhenʃən/ *n* **1** [U] the ability to understand something 理解〔力〕: *a reasonable comprehension of the subject* 对这个主题的较深入理解 | **beyond (sb's) comprehension** (=impossible to understand) 不能理解, 无法理解 *How she managed to pass her exam after doing so little work is beyond my comprehension.* 她没有怎么用功就通过了考试, 这让我无法理解。**2** [U] knowledge of what a situation is really like 了解: *Most politicians have no real comprehension of what it is like to be poor.* 大多数政治家对于什么是贫困并无真正的了解。**3** [C,U] an exercise given to students to test how well they understand written or spoken language 阅读[听力]理解测试: **reading/listening comprehension** (=a piece of written or spoken language which tests how well students understand) 阅读/听力理解测试

com·pre·hen·sive /ˌkɑmprɪˋhɛnsɪv; ˌkɒmprɪˈhensɪv◂/ *adj* 3
1 including all the necessary facts, details, or problems that need to be dealt with; thorough 详尽的; 全面的; 彻底的: *There was a comprehensive inspection of the nuclear plant.* 对核工厂进行了一次全面的视察。| **comprehensive study/list/coverage etc** *a comprehensive account of the events leading up to the Second World War* 对导致第二次世界大战的各种事件的详尽叙述 | **comprehensive insurance/cover/policy** (=a type of insurance that pays for damage whether it is caused by you or someone else) 综合保险〔指损失不论是否投保人造成, 都得到补偿〕**2** **comprehensive education/system** a system of education in which pupils of different abilities go to the same school or are taught in the same class 综合教育/体系 —**comprehensively** *adv* —**comprehensiveness** *n* [U]

CULTURAL NOTE 文化注释

The comprehensive system in Britain was started in 1965. Before that, children took an examination called the ELEVEN-PLUS at the age of eleven. If they passed it they went to a GRAMMAR SCHOOL and if they failed it they went to a SECONDARY MODERN school. The comprehensive system was introduced because people felt that it was unfair to separate children into different schools at the age of eleven. Most children in the UK now go to a comprehensive school near where they live, but there are still a small number of grammar schools left. Some parents try to send their children to grammar schools, believing that the standard of education is higher than in comprehensive schools. 英国的综合教育体系始于 1965 年。此前, 儿童在 11 岁时参加中学甄别考试, 通过者入读文法学校, 未通过者入读中等学校。引入综合教育体系, 是因为人们觉得把 11 岁的孩子分入不同学校不公平。大多数英国儿童现在就近入读综合中学, 但仍存有少数文法学校。有的父母相信, 文法学校的教育水平高于综合中学, 因此试图把孩子送到那里。

Since 1994, many comprehensive schools have become specialist schools, and now more than half of all comprehensives are specialist schools. This means that they provide the usual education that all children receive, but also offer very good quality instruction in certain areas, such as sport, PERFORMING ARTS, or the sciences. 1994 年以后, 很多综合中学成为专科中学, 数量现已过半。也就是说, 这些中学提供针对所有孩子的常规教育, 也在体育、表演艺术或科学等一些领域提供质量极高的指导。— see also 另见 PUBLIC SCHOOL

comprehensive school /‥ˈ‥ ˌ/ also 又作 **comprehensive** *n* [C] a state school in Britain for pupils of different abilities over the age of 11〔英国招收年满 11 岁不同资质学生的〕综

合中学: *Kylie goes to the local comprehensive.* 凯莉上的是本地的综合中学。

com·press¹ /kəm`prɛs; kəm'pres/ *v* **1** [I,T] if you compress something it is pressed so that it takes up less space 压紧; 压缩: **compress sth into** *The machine compresses old cars into blocks of scrap metal.* 机器把旧汽车压成一块块的废钢铁。| **compressed air/gas etc** *Compressed gas was escaping through a hole in the cylinder.* 压缩的气体当时正在从汽缸的一个孔中逸出。**2** [T] to write or express something using fewer words 压缩〔文字或话语〕: *Try to compress and simplify your notes so that they are easier to learn.* 尽量压缩并简化你的笔记, 这样学起来比较容易。**3** [T usually passive 一般用被动态] to reduce the amount of time that it takes for something to happen or be done 压缩〔做某事的时间〕: **compress sth into** *What would normally have been a three-year training course had to be compressed into eighteen months.* 在正常情况下, 需要3年的培训课程不得不被压缩到18个月。—**compressible** *adj* —**compression** /-`prɛʃən; -'preʃən/ *n* [U]

com·press² /`kamprɛs; 'kɒmpres/ *n* [C] a small thick piece of material that you put on part of someone's body to stop blood flowing out or to make it less painful〔用以止血、止痛等的〕敷布, 压布: **cold/hot compress** *Apply a cold compress to the injured part of the limb.* 将冷敷布敷在肢体的受伤处。

com·pres·sor /kəm`prɛsɚ; kəm'presə/ *n* [C] a machine or part of a machine that compresses air or gas 压气机; 〔机器中的气体〕压缩器

W3 **com·prise** /kəm`praɪz; kəm'praɪz/ *v* [not in progressive 不用进行式] *formal*【正式】**1** [linking verb 连系动词] to consist of particular parts, groups etc 包括, 由…构成: *The house comprises 2 bedrooms, a kitchen, and a living room.* 这座房子有两间卧室、一间厨房以及一间起居室。| **be comprised of** *The city's population is largely comprised of Asians and Europeans.* 这座城市的人口主要由亚洲人与欧洲人构成。**2** [T] if different people or things comprise something they combine together to form it 构成; 组成: *Women comprise a high proportion of part-time workers.* 兼职人员中妇女占很大一部分。—see also 另见 CONSTITUTE

USAGE NOTE 用法说明: COMPRISE

WORD CHOICE 词语辨析: **make up, consist of, compose, comprise, include, constitute**

Things **consist of** or **are made up of** a series of parts, or more formally **are composed of/comprise** all their parts 事物如果由一系列部分组成, 通常用 consist of 或 are made of; 更正式则用 are composed of/comprise: *New York City comprises Manhattan, Queens, Brooklyn, The Bronx and Staten Island.* 纽约市由曼哈顿、昆斯区、布鲁克林、布朗克斯以及斯塔滕岛组成。| *a street composed mainly of detached houses* (NOT 不用 *composed by/from*) 主要由独立的房屋构成的街道 | *a family made up of six people* 一个由六个人组成的家庭 | *Dinner consisted of a starter, a main course and a dessert* (NOT 不用 *consisted in/on* or 或 *was consisted of*). 这顿晚饭由一道开胃菜、一道主菜和一道甜点组成。

You will sometimes hear native speakers using **comprise** with *of*, but some people think this is incorrect 有时你会听见英美人在 comprise 后面用 of, 但有人认为这种用法不正确: *The company comprised of/is comprised of five divisions.* 这家公司由五个部门组成。

If you only mention some of the parts, you use **include**. 如果仅仅提及一个整体中的某些部分, 则使用 include: *New York City includes Brooklyn and Queens.* 纽约市包括布鲁克林区及皇后区。

All the parts of something together **make up** or more formally **constitute** or (less frequently) **comprise** the whole. 组成某物的所有部分合在一起构成一个整体用 made up, 比较正式时用 constitute 或 comprise〔不十分常用〕: *Manhattan, Queens, Brooklyn, The Bronx and Staten Island constitute/comprise New York City.* 曼哈顿、皇后区、布鲁克林、布朗克斯和斯坦登岛构成纽约市。| *How many people make up a basketball team?* 一支篮球队由多少人组成?

GRAMMAR 语法

These words are not used in progressive tenses in these meanings. 这些词用于上述意思时不能使用进行时态。

com·pro·mise¹ /`kamprə,maɪz; 'kɒmprəmaɪz/ *n* **1** [C,U] an agreement between two people that is achieved by both people accepting less than they wanted at first〔由于双方让步而达成的〕折中; 妥协: *Compromise is an inevitable part of marriage.* 妥协在婚姻生活中是不可避免的。| **reach a compromise** *Talks continue in the hope that the two factions will reach a compromise.* 谈判继续下去, 希望双方能达成妥协。| **make a compromise** *Everybody has to be prepared to make compromises.* 每个人都必须准备作出让步。**2** [C] an idea or thing that is the result of an agreement between two people or groups who want different things 折中办法[协议]: **[+between]** *The treaty represents a political compromise between the two nations.* 这一条约体现了两国间的一次政治妥协。

compromise² *v* **1** [I] to reach an agreement with someone by both of you accepting less than you wanted at first 妥协, 让步: *She was forced to compromise in order to avoid a major argument.* 为了避免一场激烈争论, 她被迫让步。| **[+on]** *We managed to compromise on a price for the car.* 我们终于就汽车的价格达成妥协。| **[+with]** *Can't you boys compromise with each other? Play football this morning and tennis this afternoon.* 你们男孩子难道就不能各让一步吗? 今天早上踢足球, 下午打网球。**2 compromise your principles/beliefs/ideas etc** to do something that is against your principles etc and which therefore seems dishonest or shameful 违背原则/信仰/理想等: *He tried to make money without compromising his moral values.* 他努力在不违背自己道德标准的前提下赚钱。| **compromise yourself** (=do something dishonest or embarrassing that puts you in a difficult position)〔做不光彩的事情而〕使自己处于困境 **3 compromise your chances** to spoil the chances of something good happening 使自己丧失机会: *That kind of behaviour will compromise your chances of promotion.* 那种行为将使你失去晋升的机会。

com·pro·mis·ing /`kamprə,maɪzɪŋ; 'kɒmprəmaɪzɪŋ/ *adj* making it seem or proving that you have done something morally wrong or embarrassing 使处于理亏[难堪]境地的: **compromising situation/position etc** *The magazine had shown him in a compromising position with his political researcher.* 该杂志暴露了他和他的政治研究员一段不光彩的经历。| **compromising letter/photograph/picture etc** *A large number of compromising letters fell into the hands of Tsarist investigators.* 大批可能惹麻烦的信件落在了沙皇调查官员的手中。

comp·trol·ler /kən`trolɚ; kən'trəʊlə/ *n* [C] *formal* an official title for a CONTROLLER (2)【正式】审计员, 审计官

com·pul·sion /kəm`pʌlʃən; kəm'pʌlʃən/ *n* **1** [C] a strong and unreasonable desire that is difficult to control〔难以克制的〕强烈欲望, 冲动: *Constantly washing her hands became a compulsion that needed treatment.* 她不停地洗手, 这已成为一种需要治疗的强烈欲望。| **compulsion to do sth** *I had a sudden compulsion to hit her.* 我突然有种特想揍她的冲动。**2** [singular, U] a force or influence that makes someone do something〔使某人做某事的〕力量; 影响: **compulsion to do sth** *Please note that you are under no compulsion to sign the agreement.* 请注意, 您是否签此协议, 完全自愿。—see also 另见 COMPEL

com·pul·sive /kəm`pʌlsɪv; kəm'pʌlsɪv/ *adj* **1** compulsive behaviour is very difficult to stop or control, and is often a result of or a sign of a mental problem 难以抑制的〔难以抑制的行为往往是精神病的一种症候〕: *Compulsive spending is often a symptom of deep unhappiness.* 肆意地挥霍常常是内心郁闷的一种征象。**2 a compulsive liar/gambler/drinker etc** someone who has such a strong desire to lie etc that they are unable to control it 有强烈说谎/赌博/酗酒等的欲望而无法自制的人 **3** a book, programme etc that is compulsive is so interesting that you cannot stop reading or watching it 吸引人的; 有趣的: **compulsive reading/viewing** (=very interesting to read or watch) 引人入胜的书刊/有趣的电视节目 *'Gardening World' – compulsive viewing for gardeners.*《园艺世界》——园艺爱好者百看不厌的节目。—**compulsively** *adv* —**compulsiveness** *n* [U]

com·pul·so·ry /kəm`pʌlsərɪ; kəm'pʌlsəri/ *adj* something that is compulsory must be done because it is the law or because someone in authority orders you to; OBLIGATORY 规定的; 强迫的; 义务的: *In Britain, education is compulsory between the ages of 5 and 16.* 在英国5岁至16岁是义务教育时期。| *compulsory lay-offs* 强迫解雇 —**compulsorily** *adv* —compare 比较 VOLUNTARY¹ (4)

com·punc·tion /kəm`pʌŋkʃən; kəm'pʌŋkʃən/ *n* [U] *formal* a deep feeling of shame or guilt【正式】羞愧; 内疚; 懊悔

com·pu·ta·tion /,kampjə`teʃən; ,kɒmpjʊ'teɪʃən/ *n* [C,U] *formal* the process of calculating or the result of calculating【正式】计算; 计算的结果

com·pute /kəm`pjut; kəm'pjuːt/ *v* [I,T] *formal* to calculate a result, answer, sum etc【正式】计算〔结果、答案、总数等〕

com·put·er/kəmˋpjutə; kəmˈpjuːtə/ *n* [C] an electronic machine that can store information and do things with it according to a set of instructions called a PROGRAM 电脑，计算机: *the latest computer software* 最新的电脑软件 | *a new computer-controlled heating system* 一套全新的由电脑控制的供暖系统 | *The doctor has all the patient's details on computer.* 医生在电脑中储存了这名病人的全部情况。| **computer system/analysis/applications/networks etc** *We've just had a new computer system installed at work.* 我们刚刚安装了工作用的新的电脑系统。| **computer literacy** (=basic knowledge of and ability to use computers) 基础电脑知识和运用电脑的能力 | **computer literate** (=able to use a computer) 会使用电脑的 —see also 另见 MICROCOMPUTER, MINICOMPUTER, PERSONAL COMPUTER, LAPTOP

computer-aid·ed de·sign/·ˌ··· ·ˈ·/ *n* [U] CAD 电脑辅助设计

computer dat·ing a·gency/·ˌ··ˈ··ˌ···/ *n* [C] a company that uses computers to try to find suitable partners for people by matching their interests etc 电脑婚姻介绍所

computer game/·ˈ··ˌ·/ *n* [C] a game that you play on a computer 电脑游戏

computer graph·ics/·ˌ··ˈ··/ *n* [plural] the pictures and images that you see on a computer screen 电脑图像

com·put·er·ize also 又作 **-ise** *BrE*【英】/kəmˋpjutəˌraɪz; kəmˈpjuːtəraɪz/ *v* [T] to use a computer to control an operation, system etc 用电脑操作: *They have decided to computerize the accounts department.* 他们已经决定让会计部门用电脑操作。| *Our local supermarket now has a fully computerized checkout system.* 我们本地的超级市场现在已经有了一套全电脑化的收费系统。—**computerization**/kəmˌpjutərəˋzeʃən; kəmˌpjuːtəraɪˈzeɪʃən/ *n* [U]

computer mod·el·ling/·ˌ··ˈ···/ *n* [U] the representation of a problem, situation, or real object in a form in which you can see it from all angles on a computer 电脑模型制作，电脑模拟〔指在电脑上以可以从各种角度观察的形式呈现一个问题、局面或实物〕: *computer modelling of the city's traffic flow* 城市交通情况的电脑模拟

computer pro·gram/·ˌ··ˈ··/ *n* [C] a list of instructions that you need to give to a computer in order to make it do a particular thing 电脑程序 —**computer programmer** *n* [C]

computer sci·ence/·ˌ··ˈ··/ *n* [U] the study of computers and what they can do 电脑科学，计算机科学: *a BSc in Computer Science* 计算机科学的理学士

computer vi·rus/·ˌ··ˈ··/ *n* [C] a VIRUS (3) 电脑病毒

com·put·ing/kəmˋpjutɪŋ; kəmˈpjuːtɪŋ/ *n* [U] the use of computers as a job or in business etc 电脑应用: *Have you ever done any computing?* 你以前干过电脑应用的工作吗?

com·rade/ˋkɑmræd; ˈkɒmrɪ̈d/ *n* [C] **1** *formal* a friend, especially someone who shares difficult work or danger【正式】〔尤指共患难的〕朋友: *He misses his comrades from his days in the Army.* 他想念服役时结识的战友。**2** someone who is a fellow member of a union, political party etc at the same time as you are, used especially of people in Communist groups 同志〔指同属一个工会或政党的成员，多为共产党团体中的人使用〕: *Comrades, please support this motion.* 同志们，请支持这项动议。—**comradely** *adj*

comrade in arms/ˌ··· ·ˈ·/ *n* [C] someone who has worked, fought with you or worked with you to achieve particular aims 战友

com·rade·ship/ˋkɑmrædˌʃɪp; ˈkɒmrɪ̈dʃɪp/ *n* [U] *formal* friendship and loyalty among people who work together, fight together etc【正式】〔一同工作、战斗的人们等之间的〕友谊，忠诚，同志情谊: *It was the spirit of comradeship that made victory possible.* 正是同志情谊的精神使胜利成为可能。

Con the written abbreviation of 缩写= CONSERVATIVE or 或 conservative party

con-/kən; kən/ *prefix* together; with 与…一起，与…一道: *a confederation* 联盟 | *to conspire* (=plan together) 合谋

con[1]/kɑn; kɒn/ *v* **conned, conning** [T] *informal*【非正式】**1** to get money from someone by deceiving them 骗钱；诈骗: **con sb out of** *He conned me out of £5!* 他从我这里骗走了五英镑! **2** to persuade someone to do something by deceiving them 诱骗: **con sb into doing sth** *We were conned into signing the contract.* 我们上当了，签了这个合同。

con[2] *n* [C] **1** a method or process of getting money from someone, especially by pretending to be someone else〔尤指假冒身份的〕诈骗: *There are hardly any chocolates in this box at all – what a con!* 这个盒子里没有什么巧克力——真是骗人! —see also 另见 MOD CONS, **the pros and cons** (PRO[1] (3)) **2** *slang* a prisoner【俚】犯人，囚犯

Con·an Doyle/ˌkonən ˋdɔɪl; ˌkəunən ˈdɔɪl/, **Sir Arthur** (1859-1930) a British doctor and writer who is famous for his stories about the DETECTIVE Sherlock Holmes and his friend Dr Watson 柯南道尔〔(1859-1930)，英国医生、作家，以创作的夏洛克·福尔摩斯侦探及其朋友华生医生的故事而闻名〕

con-artist/ˈ·ˌ··/ *n* [C] *informal* someone who tricks or deceives people in order to get money from them【非正式】骗子，行骗者

con·cat·e·na·tion/kənˌkætn̩ˋeʃən; kɒnˌkætɪ̈ˈneɪʃən/ *n* [C, U] *formal* a series of events or things joined together one after another【正式】一连串事件[物品]: *a strange concatenation of events* 一连串怪事

con·cave/ˌkɑnˋkev; ˌkɒnˈkeɪv◂/ *adj* a concave surface is curved inwards in the middle 凹的，凹面的 —opposite 反义词 CONVEX

con·cav·i·ty/kɑnˋkævətɪ; kənˈkævɪ̈ti/ *n formal*【正式】**1** [U] the state of being concave 凹陷 **2** [C] a place or shape that is curved inwards 凹陷处；凹面；凹处

con·ceal/kənˋsil; kənˈsiːl/ *v* [T] *formal*【正式】**1** to hide something carefully 隐匿，隐藏: *Customs officers found the cannabis concealed inside the case.* 海关官员发现了藏在箱子里的大麻。| *The path was concealed by long grass.* 小路被掩盖在深深的草丛中。**2** to hide your real feelings or the truth 隐藏真实感情；隐瞒真相: **conceal sth from sb** *Don't try to conceal anything from me.* 什么事都别想瞒我。—**concealment** *n* [U]

con·cede/kənˋsid; kənˈsiːd/ *v*

1 ▶**ADMIT STH IS TRUE** 承认某事是真的◀ [T] to admit that something is true or correct although you wish it was not true (不得不)承认: *"You could be right I suppose", Sheila conceded.* 希拉承认道:"我想你可能是对的。" | **concede (that)** *I concede that he's a good runner, but I still think I can beat him.* 我承认他是出色的赛跑运动员，可是我仍然相信自己能战胜他。

2 ▶**ADMIT DEFEAT** 认输◀ [I,T] to admit that you are not going to win a battle, argument, or game because you are not strong enough or good enough to win 承认(失败)，认(输): *The army conceded and the enemy claimed victory.* 该军队承认战败，敌人宣称胜利。| **concede defeat** *Matthew kept on arguing, unwilling to concede defeat.* 马修不断地争辩，不愿意认输。

3 concede a goal/point etc to not be able to stop your opponent from getting a goal, point etc during a game 不能阻止对方进球/得分等: *Manchester United were unlucky to concede a goal before half-time.* 在上半场比赛，曼彻斯特联队不幸被对方攻进一球。

4 ▶**GIVE STH AS A RIGHT** 给予权利◀ [T] to give something to someone as a right or PRIVILEGE (1) 给予〔某人权利〕: **concede sth to** *The richer nations will never concede equal status to the poorer countries.* 富裕的国家决不会给穷国同等的地位。

5 ▶**GIVE STH UNWILLINGLY** 不情愿地给予◀ [T] to give something to someone unwillingly after trying to keep it〔在试图保留之后不情愿地〕让予: **concede sth to** *After the First World War Germany conceded a lot of land to her neighbours.* 第一次世界大战之后，德国把许多土地割让给邻国。—see also 另见 CONCESSION

con·ceit/kənˋsit; kənˈsiːt/ *n* **1** [U] an attitude that shows you have too high an opinion of your own abilities or importance; CONCEITEDNESS 自负，自高自大: *The conceit of the woman – it's unbelievable!* 这个自高自大的女人——真是不可思议! **2** [C] *technical* an unusual, cleverly expressed comparison of two very different things, especially in poetry【术语】〔尤指诗歌中〕别出心裁的比喻

con·ceit·ed/kənˋsitɪd; kənˈsiːtɪ̈d/ *adj* behaving in a way that shows you think you are very clever, skilful, beautiful etc 自负的，骄傲自满的，自高自大的: *He's a conceited little so-and-so.* 他是一个自命不凡的小混蛋。—**conceitedly** *adv*: *"I knew that", he said conceitedly.* "那件事情我知道。"他大模大样地说。

con·cei·te·dness/kənˋsitɪdnɪs; kənˈsiːtɪ̈dnɪ̈s/ *n* [U] CONCEIT 自负，自傲

con·cei·va·ble/kənˋsivəbl̩; kənˈsiːvəbəl/ *adj* able to be believed or imagined 可以相信的，可想象的: *He could talk intelligently on almost any conceivable subject.* 几乎什么能想到的话题他都能说得头头是道。| *What conceivable reason could they have for doing such crazy things?* 真想不出来他们有什么理由做这么疯狂的事? | **conceivable (that)** *It is conceivable that the peace mission will succeed.* 有理由相信和谈代表团是会成功的。—opposite 反义词 INCONCEIVABLE —**conceivably** *adv*

con·ceive/kənˋsiv; kənˈsiːv/ *v* **1** [T] to think of a new idea, plan etc and develop it in your mind 构思；设想；想出: *Scientists first conceived the idea of the atomic bomb in the 1930's.* 在20世纪30年代科学家第一次有了原子弹的设想。**2** [T] *formal* to

imagine a particular situation【正式】想象〔某一具体情况〕: **conceive what/why/how etc** *I find it difficult to conceive why the government introduced the policy in the first place.* 先不说别的，首先我很难想象政府为什么要推行这项政策。| **conceive of sth** *I can't conceive of any reason why we can't come.* 我想象不出我们有什么理由不能来。| **conceive of doing sth** *I would never conceive of treating someone the way Helen treats John.* 我不能想象有人会像海伦对待约翰那样对待别人。**3** [I,T] to become PREGNANT 怀孕；受孕: *fertility treatment for women who have difficulty conceiving* 对受孕困难的女性进行治疗

con·cen·trate¹ /ˋkɑnsn̩ˏtret; ˈkɒnsəntreɪt/ *v* **1** [I] to think very carefully about something that you are doing 专注，专心；集中注意力: *Keep the noise down will you – I'm trying to concentrate.* 把声音弄小点，行吗？我正在集中精力。| **[+on]** *She was too distracted to concentrate properly on her book.* 她心烦意乱，根本无法专心读书。**2 be concentrated on/in/around etc** to be present in particularly large numbers or amounts in a particular place 集中于；汇集于: *Italian industry is concentrated mainly in the north of the country.* 意大利的工业主要集中在该国北部。| *The mass of the sphere is concentrated at its center.* 这个球体的质量聚在它的中心。**3** [T] if something concentrates the mind it makes you think very clearly 使…头脑清醒: *Relaxing in a jacuzzi concentrates the mind wonderfully.* 在"极可意"涡流式浴缸中放松，使人精神百倍。**4** [T] to make a liquid stronger by removing some of the water from it 浓缩〔液体〕

concentrate sth ↔ **on** *phr v* [T] to pay particular attention to something, work particularly hard at it etc, and make that the most important thing you are doing 把注意力集中于，全神贯注于: *The discussion concentrated on improving the company's image.* 这次讨论集中于如何改善公司的形象。| **concentrate your attention/efforts/thoughts etc on** *Virgos should concentrate their efforts on work this month.* 处女座出生的人这个月应把注意力集中在工作上面。

concentrate² *n* [C,U] a substance or liquid which has been made stronger by removing the water from it 浓缩物；浓缩液: *orange concentrate* 浓缩橙汁

con·cen·trat·ed /ˋkɑnsn̩ˏtretɪd; ˈkɒnsəntreɪtɪ̈d/ *adj* **1** a concentrated liquid or substance is made stronger by removing water from it 浓缩的: *concentrated hydrochloric acid* 浓盐酸 | *concentrated orange juice* 浓缩橙汁 **2** [only before noun 仅用于名词前] showing determination to do something 全神贯注的；全力以赴的: *He made a concentrated effort to improve his work.* 他集中力量改进自己的工作。

con·cen·tra·tion /ˏkɑnsn̩ˋtreʃən; ˌkɒnsənˈtreɪʃən/ *n* **1** [U] the ability to think about something carefully or for a long time 专心，集中注意力: *Her work as a simultaneous translator requires strong powers of concentration.* 作为同声传译员，她的工作需要高度集中精力。**2** [U] a process in which you put a lot of attention, energy etc into a particular activity 集中注意力，集中精力: **[+on]** *Concentration on strengthening the team's defence is essential.* 集中力量加强球队的防守是必要的。**3** [C,U] a large amount of something in one place or area 在一处大量集中某事物: **[+of]** *There is an increasing concentration of power in central government.* 越来越多的权力集中于中央政府。**4** [C] *technical* the amount of a substance contained in a liquid【术语】〔液体中某物质的〕浓度: *a high concentration of sulphuric acid* 高浓度硫酸

concentration camp /ˏ..ˈ.. ˏ./ *n* [C] a prison where large numbers of ordinary people are kept, especially during a war, and are treated extremely cruelly 集中营

con·cen·tric /kənˋsɛntrɪk; kənˈsentrɪk/ *adj technical* having the same centre【术语】同心的: *concentric circles* 同心圆 —compare 比较 ECCENTRIC¹ (2)

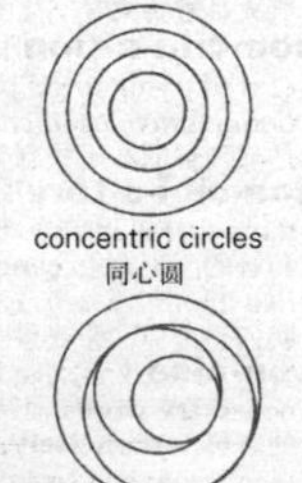
concentric 同心的
concentric circles 同心圆
eccentric circles 不同心圆

con·cept /ˋkɑnsɛpt; ˈkɒnsept/ *n* [C] someone's idea of how something is, or should be done 概念，观念；想法: *a revolutionary concept in industry* 工业上的革命性概念 | **[+of]** *It's difficult to grasp the concept of infinite space.* 要领会无限空间的概念很困难。

con·cep·tion /kənˋsɛpʃən; kənˈsepʃən/ *n* **1** [C,U] a general idea about what something is like, or a general understanding of something 概念；观念，思想；想法: **[+of]** *He's got a really strange conception of friendship.* 他对友谊有一种非常独特的见解。| **have no conception of** *You've no conception of what conditions are like.* 你对情况一无所知。**2** [U] a process in which someone forms a plan or idea 构思，构想，设想: *The conception of the book took five minutes, but writing it took a year.* 这本书的构思花了五分钟，而写出来却花了一整年。**3** [C,U] the process by which male and female sex cells join together in a woman's body and the woman becomes PREGNANT 受孕，怀孕

con·cep·tu·al /kənˋsɛptʃuəl; kənˈseptʃuəl/ *adj formal* based on ideas【正式】概念的: *the conceptual framework of the play* 这部剧的概念框架 —**conceptually** *adv*

conceptual art /ˏ.,... ˈ./ *n* [U] *technical* art in which the main aim of the artist is to show an idea【术语】概念艺术〔以显示概念为目的的艺术〕

con·cep·tu·al·ize also 又作 **-ise** *BrE*【英】/kənˋsɛptʃuəlˏaɪz; kənˈseptʃuəlaɪz/ *v* [I,T] to form an idea 形成概念，使概念化: *two schools of thought that conceptualize things differently* 对事物进行不同诠释的两个思想派别

con·cern¹ /kənˋsɝn; kənˈsɜːn/ *n*

1 ►WORRY 担忧◄ a) [C] something that worries you 担心的事，关切的事: *The main concern is that the health of the employees will be at risk.* 最令人担忧的事是雇员的健康将面临威胁。**b)** [U] a feeling of worry, especially about something such as a social problem, someone's health etc 忧虑；担心: *The recent rise in crime is a matter of considerable public concern.* 近来犯罪增多是民众极为关切的事。| **[+about/over]** *There is growing concern about the effects of pollution on health.* 对于污染影响健康的关注越来越强烈。| **concern for sb** *A government spokesman expressed concern for the lives of the hostages.* 政府发言人对人质的生命安全表示担忧。| **cause concern/be a cause for concern** *The depletion of the ozone layer is causing widespread concern among scientists.* 臭氧层的锐减在科学家之间引起广泛关注。

2 be of concern (to sb) if something is of concern to you, it is important to you and you feel worried about it 令〔某人〕感到担心的；是〔某人〕所关心的: *The rise in unemployment is of great concern to the government.* 失业率的上升是政府关心的一件大事。

3 [C,U] something that is important to you or that involves you 与某人有关的事，对某人重要的事: *His main concern is to be able to provide for his family.* 他主要关心的是能够养活他一家人。

4 ►FEELING FOR SB 对某人的情感◄ [singular, U] a feeling of wanting someone to be happy and healthy 关心；关怀: **[+for]** *parents' loving concern for their children* 父母对子女的关爱

5 sb's concern if something is your concern, you are responsible for it 由某人负责的事: *The money side of the business is your concern.* 企业的财务管理是你的职责。

6 not sb's concern/none of sb's concern if something is not your concern, you are not interested in it and you do not need to worry about it or become involved in it 某人不感兴趣的事；与某人无关的事: *How much money I earn is none of your concern.* 我赚多少钱与你不相干。

7 ►BUSINESS 企业◄ [C] a business or company 企业；公司: *The restaurant is a family concern.* 这家餐馆是一个家庭开办的。| **a going concern** (=a business that is financially successful) 一家生意兴隆的企业

concern² *v* [T] **1** if an activity, situation, rule etc concerns you, it affects you or involves you〔活动、情况、规则等〕对…有影响；与…相关: *The tax changes will concern large corporations rather than small businesses.* 税收上的变化影响到的是大公司而不是小企业。**2** [not in passive 不用被动态] to make someone feel worried or upset 使忧虑，使担心: *The fact that she spends so much time on her own really concerns me.* 她很多时间都是一人独处，这真让我担心。**3** [not in passive 不用被动态] if a story, book, report etc concerns someone or something, it is about them〔故事、书、报告等〕与…有关，关于: *This article concerns a man who was wrongly imprisoned.* 这篇文章写的是一个被冤枉而入狱的人。**4 concern yourself with/about sth** to become involved in something because you are interested in it or because it worries you 关心，担心: *More and more people are concerning themselves with environmental problems.* 越来越多的人关心起环境问题。**5 to whom it may concern** an expression written at the beginning of a formal letter when you do not know the name of the person you want to communicate with 敬启者〔写在正式信函开头的一句套话，用于写信人不知道收信人的姓名时〕—see also 另见 CONCERNED

con·cerned /kənˋsɝnd; kənˈsɜːnd/ *adj*

1 [not before noun 不用于名词前] involved in something or affected by it〔与某事〕有关的，有牵连的: *The affair is greatly regretted by everyone concerned.* 所有相关人士都对此事感到极为遗憾。| *Divorce is very painful, especially when children are*

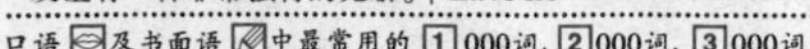

concerned. 离婚是非常痛苦的，如果有孩子的话，尤其痛苦。| [+in] *Everyone concerned in the incident was questioned by the police.* 所有与这个事件有关的人都受到警方盘问。| [+with] *all the people concerned with children's education* 所有关心儿童教育问题的人

2 ▶WORRIED 忧虑◀ worried about something 焦急的，担忧的：*Concerned parents approached the school about the problem.* 焦虑的家长就此问题与校方联系。| [+about] *Ross has never been particularly concerned about what other people think of him.* 罗斯对别人如何看待自己从来不太在意。| [+for] *Rescuers are concerned for the safety of two men trapped in the mine.* 营救队队员对困在矿下的两个人的安全感到担忧。| **concerned that** *He's concerned that he won't get his money back.* 他担心无法拿回自己的钱。—see 见 NERVOUS (USAGE)

3 as far as I'm concerned *spoken* used when giving your opinion about something or saying how it affects you, especially when you do not care what other people think【口】在我看来；就我而言〔用于陈述自己对某事的看法或对自己有何影响，尤指不在乎别人怎么说〕：*As far as I'm concerned the whole idea is crazy.* 在我看来，这一想法十分荒唐。

4 ▶BE IMPORTANT TO 对…是重要的◀ [never before noun 不用于名词前] believing that something is important 关切的，关心的：[+with] *Congressmen seem to be far more concerned with getting elected than with passing legislation.* 看来众议员们关心自己当选远甚于关心立法。| **be concerned to do sth** *We are concerned to sort this out as quickly as possible.* 我们关切的是尽快把这件事处理掉。

5 where/as far as sth is concerned *spoken* used when saying what particular thing you are talking about【口】就…而言〔用来表明你在谈论一件什么样的事情〕：*Where money is concerned, I always try to be very careful.* 凡是涉及钱的地方，我总是尽量小心谨慎。

6 ▶LOVE/CARE 爱/关心◀ caring about someone and whether they are happy and healthy 挂念的：[+for/about] *How can you expect me not to be concerned about my own son?* 你怎么会以为我不挂念我的儿子呢？

7 be concerned with if a book, story etc is concerned with a person, subject etc it is about that subject〔书、故事等〕关于，与…有关：*This story is concerned with a Russian family in the 19th century.* 这个故事写的是 19 世纪的一个俄国家庭。—**concernedly** /kən`sɝndlɪ; kən'sɜːnɪ̆dli/ *adv*

3 **con·cern·ing** /kən`sɝnɪŋ; kən'sɜːnɪŋ/ *prep formal* a word meaning 'about', used to show you are talking or writing about a particular thing or person【正式】关于：*Police are anxious to hear any information concerning his whereabouts.* 警方急于要获悉有关他的下落的任何消息。

3 3 **con·cert** /`kɑnsɝt; 'kɒnsət/ *n* [C] **1** a performance given by musicians 音乐会：*We went to a concert of Vivaldi's 'Four Seasons'.* 我们去听了维瓦尔第的《四季》音乐会。| *a pop concert* 流行歌曲音乐会 **2 in concert (with)** *formal*【正式】**a)** people who do something in concert do it together after having agreed on it 与…一起〔行动〕：*The various governments decided to act in concert over this matter.* 各国政府决定采取一致行动处理这个问题。**b)** playing or singing at a concert〔在音乐会上〕演出：*Michael Jackson in concert at the Palladium* 在帕拉迪姆剧场举行演唱会的迈克尔·杰克逊

con·cert·ed /kən`sɝtɪd; kən'sɜːtɪ̆d/ *adj* **concerted effort/attempt/action etc** a concerted effort etc is done by people working together in a carefully planned and very determined way 一致的努力/尝试/行动等：*a concerted campaign to raise public awareness of environmental issues* 提高公众对环境问题重视程度的联合行动 —**concertedly** *adv*

con·cert·go·er /`kɑnsɝt,goɚ; 'kɒnsət,gəʊə/ *n* [C] someone who often goes to concerts 音乐会的常客

concert hall /'‥ ·/ *n* [C] a large public building where concerts are performed 音乐会堂，音乐厅

con·cer·ti·na[1] /,kɑnsɚ`tinə; ,kɒnsə'tiːnə/ *n* [C] a small musical instrument like an ACCORDION that you hold in your hands and play by pressing in from each side 六角形手风琴

concertina[2] *v past and past participle* **concertinaed** [I] *BrE* if something concertinas, it folds together upon itself【英】折裥状压缩[折叠]：*The bonnet of the car had concertinaed as a result of the crash.* 汽车车盖由于撞击而皱缩。

con·cert·mas·ter /`kɑnsɚt,mæstɚ; 'kɒnsət,mɑːstə/ *n* [C] *AmE* the most important VIOLIN player in an ORCHESTRA【美】〔交响乐团中的〕首席小提琴手

con·cer·to /kən`tʃɛrto; kən'tʃɜːtəʊ/ *n plural* **concertos** [C] a piece of music for one or more SOLO[1] (2) instruments and an ORCHESTRA 协奏曲

con·ces·sion /kən`sɛʃən; kən'seʃən/ *n*

1 ▶STH YOU ALLOW SB 让与某人之物◀ [C] something that you allow someone to have in order to end an argument or a disagreement〔为了结束争端而〕让步：**make a concession** *We will never make any concessions to terrorists.* 我们决不向恐怖分子作出任何让步。—see also 另见 CONCEDE

2 ▶A RIGHT 权利◀ [C] a special right that a particular person or group of people is allowed to have, for example by the government or an employer〔政府或雇主等许可的〕特权；特许权：*tax concessions* 税收优惠 | *Greyhound Inc won the concession of running hotels in Glacier Park.* 灰狗客运有限公司获得了在冰川公园开设旅馆的特权。

3 ▶PRICE REDUCTION 降价◀ [C] *BrE* a reduction in the price of tickets, FARES etc for certain groups of people, for example old people or children【英】〔对特殊群体，如老人、儿童，在票价等费用上的〕价格优惠

4 concessions [plural] *AmE* the things sold at a concession stand【美】营业摊点上出售的商品

5 ▶ACT OF ALLOWING 许可行为◀ [U] *formal* the act of giving or allowing something as a right【正式】容许；许可

6 ▶RIGHT TO SELL STH 销售权◀ [C] *AmE* the right to sell something within the building of a larger business, or the area you are allowed to sell something in【美】〔有权在较大商店内部销售商品的〕货摊，销售点：*a hamburger concession in the mall* 大商场里的汉堡包店

con·ces·sion·aire /kən,sɛʃən`ɛr; kən,seʃə'neə/ *n* [C] *informal* someone who has been given a CONCESSION (2), especially to run a business【非正式】特许权的获得者〔尤指做生意的权利〕

con·ces·sion·ar·y /kən`sɛʃən,ɛrɪ; kən'seʃənəri/ *adj* **1** given as a concession 特许的；让步的；让与的 **2** *BrE* specially reduced in price, for example for old people or children【英】特别〔为老年人或儿童等〕降价的：*Local authorities have the power to set up concessionary fare schemes.* 本地当局有权制定降价乘车方案。

concession stand /·'‥ ,·/ *n* [C] *AmE* a small business that sells food, drinks or SOUVENIRS at sporting events, places that tourists visit and some theatres【美】〔体育比赛场地、旅游景点和某些剧院开设的出售食品、饮料或纪念品的〕营业摊点，小商店

con·ces·sive clause /kən,sɛsɪv `klɔz; kən,sesɪv 'klɔːz/ *n* [C] *technical* a CLAUSE (2), often introduced by 'although,' that introduces a fact or idea that seems to be the opposite of the main fact or idea. For example, the sentence 'Although it's old, it works well.' begins with a concessive clause.【术语】让步从句〔指常以 although 引导的从句。例如在"Although it's old, it works well.（这东西虽然旧了，但仍然很好用。）"中，就以一个让步从句开头〕

conch /kɑntʃ; kɒntʃ/ *n* [C] the large twisted shell of a tropical sea animal that looks like a SNAIL 海螺壳

con·chie /`kɑntʃɪ; 'kɒntʃi/ *n* [C] *BrE old-fashioned informal* an insulting word for a CONSCIENTIOUS OBJECTOR【英，过时，非正式】〔因宗教或道德的原因而〕拒绝服兵役者〔侮辱性词语〕

con·ci·erge /,kɑnsɪ`ɛrʒ; ,kɒnsi'eəʒ/ *n* [C] *French*【法】**1** someone who looks after a building, usually by watching the entrance to see who comes in and goes out, especially in France〔尤指法国的〕看门人，楼房管理员 **2** *especially AmE* someone whose job in a hotel is helping guests, for example by giving them advice about local restaurants etc【尤美】〔旅馆内协助客人的〕服务人员〔如介绍当地餐馆等〕

con·cil·i·ate /kən`sɪlɪ,et; kən'sɪlieɪt/ *v* [T] *formal* to do something to make people more likely to stop arguing, especially by giving them something they want【正式】安抚；调停：*Negotiators were called in to conciliate between the warring factions.* 谈判人员被请来在交战的两派之间进行调解。—**conciliator** *n* [C]

con·cil·i·a·tion /kən,sɪlɪ`eʃən; kən,sɪli'eɪʃən/ *n* [U] the process of trying to get people to agree 说服；调解：*peaceful negotiation attempts at conciliation through compromise* 通过妥协达成和解的和平谈判努力

con·cil·i·a·tory /kən`sɪlɪə,torɪ; kən'sɪliətəri/ *adj* doing something that is intended to make someone stop arguing with you 和解的，调停的：**conciliatory gesture/message/tone etc** *We'd like to offer you free theater tickets as a conciliatory gesture.* 我们想送你几张戏票以示和解。

con·cise /kən`saɪs; kən'saɪs/ *adj* short and clear, with no unnecessary words 简洁的；简明的：*a concise explanation* 简明的解释 —**concisely** *adv* —**conciseness** also 又作 **concision** /kən`sɪʒən; kən'sɪʒən/ *formal n* [U]【正式】

con·clave /`kɑŋklev; 'kɒŋkleɪv/ *n* [C] a private and secret meeting 秘密会议：*A conclave of cardinals was held to elect a new pope.* 红衣主教举行了秘密会议选举一位新教皇。

con·clude /kən`klud; kən'klu:d/ *v* [T] **1** to decide that something is true after considering all the information you have 作出结论，断定: **conclude that** *The enquiry concluded that the accident had been caused by human error.* 调查结论认为这次事故是人为失误造成的。| **conclude from sth that** *Davis concludes from an analysis of traffic accidents that the speed limit should be lowered.* 戴维斯通过对交通事故的分析认定应该降低时速限制。**2** [T] to complete something you have been doing, especially for a long time 完成，结束: **conclude your work/investigation/research etc** *I will be publishing my results only when I have concluded my research.* 我完成了研究才会发表结论。**3** [I always+adv/prep,T] to end something such as a meeting or speech by doing or saying one final thing〔以做某事或讲某话来〕结束〔会议或演说〕: [+with/on/as/by etc] *The session usually concludes with an informal discussion.* 会议通常以一场非正式的讨论作为结束。| **conclude sth** *We were finally able to conclude the meeting and go home.* 最后我们总算结束了会议回家去。| **conclude sth with/by etc** *The service was concluded with a hymn.* 礼拜以唱圣歌结束。**4 conclude an agreement/treaty/contract etc** to finish arranging an agreement etc successfully 达成协议/缔结条约，签订合同等: *After months of negotiations they concluded the sale.* 经过几个月的谈判之后，他们签订了销售合同。

con·clu·ding /kən`kludɪŋ; kən'klu:dɪŋ/ *adj* **concluding sentence/remark/stages etc** the last sentence, stage etc in an event or piece of writing 结束句/语/阶段等: *He makes his position perfectly clear in the concluding paragraph.* 在最后一段他清楚地表明了自己的观点。

con·clu·sion /kən`kluʒən; kən'klu:ʒən/ *n* **1** [C] something you decide after considering all the information you have 结论: *These are the report's main conclusions.* 这些就是这篇报告的主要结论。| [+that] *Becky came to the conclusion that he must have forgotten.* 贝姬得出结论，认为他肯定已经忘记了。| **lead to/point to/support the conclusion (that)** *All the evidence pointed to the conclusion that he was guilty.* 所有证据都表明他是有罪的。| **draw a conclusion** *From these facts we can draw some conclusions about how the pyramids were built.* 从这些事实我们可以得出一些关于金字塔是如何建造的结论。| **jump to conclusions** (=decide that something is true too quickly, without knowing all the facts) 匆忙地下结论，草率下结论 *Don't jump to conclusions – just because they're late doesn't mean they've had an accident!* 别轻易下结论，他们迟到并不意味着他们出事了！**2** [C] the end or final part of something 结尾，末尾: *I found the conclusion of his book very interesting.* 我认为他的书的结尾非常有意思。**3 in conclusion** used in a piece of writing or a speech to show that you are about to finish what you are saying 总而言之〔用于文章或讲话的末尾，表明即将结束〕: *In conclusion, I would like to say how much I have enjoyed myself today.* 最后，我想说我今天很开心。**4** [U] the final arrangement of something such as a business deal 缔结，签订: [+of] *the conclusion of a peace treaty* 和平条约的签订 **5 be a foregone conclusion** to be certain to happen even though it has not yet officially happened 是预料之中的结果: *The outcome of the battle was a foregone conclusion.* 战斗的结果早在预料之中。

con·clu·sive /kən`klusɪv; kən'klu:sɪv/ *adj* something that is conclusive is certainly true, so there is no doubt or uncertainty 令人确信的；毫无疑问的: **conclusive proof/evidence/findings etc** *The investigation failed to provide any conclusive evidence.* 调查未能提供任何令人信服的证据。—opposite 反义词 INCONCLUSIVE —**conclusively** *adv*

con·coct /kən`kakt; kən'kɒkt/ *v* [T] **1** to invent a clever story, excuse, or plan, especially in order to deceive someone 编造；捏造；虚构: *John concocted an elaborate excuse for being late.* 约翰为迟到编了一个巧妙的借口。**2** to make something especially food or drink, by mixing different things, especially things that are not usually combined〔食物、饮料的〕配制，调配，拼凑: *Jean concocted a great meal from the leftovers.* 琼把剩菜剩饭拼凑成一顿美餐。

con·coc·tion /kən`kakʃən; kən'kɒkʃən/ *n* [C] something, especially a drink, made by mixing different things, especially things that are not usually combined〔尤指不常混合的酒的〕配制物，调配物: *She offered him a green concoction with fruit floating in it.* 她给他一杯绿色的调制饮料，上面有水果漂浮。

con·com·i·tant¹ /kən`kamətənt; kən'kɒmɪtənt/ *adj formal* existing or happening together, especially as a result of something【正式】伴随的，并存的: *war with all its concomitant sufferings* 战争及由战争引起的一切苦难—**concomitantly** *adv*

concomitant² *n* [C] *formal* something that often or naturally happens with something else [+of]【正式】伴随物: *Deafness is a frequent concomitant of old age.* 耳聋常随年老而出现。

Concord /`kankərd; 'kɒŋkɔ:d/ the capital city of the US state of New Hampshire 康科德市〔美国新罕布什尔州首府〕

con·cord /`kaŋkərd; 'kɒŋkɔ:d/ *n* [U] **1** *formal* the state of having a friendly relationship, so that you agree on things and live in peace【正式】一致，和谐，协调 **2** *technical* in grammar, concord between words happens when they match correctly, for example when a plural noun has a plural verb following it【术语】〔词与词在语法上的〕搭配的一致〈如复数名词跟随复数名词〉

con·cor·dance /kən`kɔrdn̩s; kən'kɔ:dəns/ *n* **1** [U] the state of being similar to something else or in agreement with it 一致；协调: *the concordance between the proposals* 两项建议间的一致性 **2** [C] *technical* an alphabetical list of all the words used in a book or set of books by one writer, with information about where they can be found and usually about how they are used【术语】〔某作家在某(套)书中所用的全部词语的〕索引: *a Shakespeare concordance* 莎士比亚词语索引 | *computerized concordances* 电脑化词语索引

con·cor·dant /kən`kɔrdn̩t; kən'kɔ:dənt/ *adj formal* being in agreement or having the same regular pattern【正式】一致的；属于同一规格[模式]的

Con·corde /`kaŋkərd; 'kɒŋkɔ:d/ *trademark* a type of passenger aircraft, which can fly at twice the speed of sound and is the fastest in the world. Concorde is a long thin plane with a long pointed front. It was built by British and French designers and engineers working together【商标】协和式飞机〔世界上速度最快的客机，其速度是音速的两倍。机头尖长，机身细长，由英法设计师、工程师合作建造〕: *He liked to travel in style, so he was going on Concorde.* 他喜欢豪华旅游，所以打算乘坐协和式飞机。

con·course /`kaŋkɔrs; 'kɒŋkɔ:s/ *n* [C] **1** a large hall in a building such as an airport or train station where crowds of people can gather〔火车站、飞机场等的〕大厅 **2** a large crowd that has gathered together 聚集的人群: *a large concourse of people* 一大群人

con·crete¹ /`kankrit; 'kɒŋkri:t/ *adj* **1** made of concrete 混凝土的: *a concrete floor* 混凝土地板 **2** clearly based on fact, rather than on beliefs or guesses 有真凭实据的: *concrete information about the identity of the murderer* 关于凶手身份的确切资料 —compare 比较 ABSTRACT¹ (2) **3** definite and specific rather than general 具体的: *Have you got any concrete proposals as to what we should do?* 我们应该做些什么，你有没有具体的建议?—**concretely** *adv*

con·crete² *n* [U] a substance used for building that is made by mixing sand, very small stones, cement, and water 混凝土

con·crete³ *v* [T] to cover something such as a path, wall etc with concrete 用混凝土浇筑[覆盖]〔小路、墙等〕

concrete jun·gle /,.. '../ *n* [C usually singular 一般用单数] an unpleasant area in a city that is full of big ugly buildings and has no open spaces 水泥丛林〔指到处是丑陋的高楼林立，没有开旷空地的城区〕

concrete mix·er /'.. ,../ *n* [C] a CEMENT MIXER 混凝土搅拌机

con·cu·bi·nage /kan`kjubənɪdʒ; kɒn'kju:bɪnɪdʒ/ *n* [U] *formal* the system or practice of living together as man and wife without being married【正式】姘居，同居

con·cu·bine /`kaŋkju,baɪn; 'kɒŋkjʊbaɪn/ *n* [C] a woman who lives with and has sex with a man who already has a wife or wives, but who is socially less important 妾；姨太太

con·cur /kən`kɜ; kən'kɜ:/ *v* **concurred, concurring** [I] *formal*【正式】**1** to agree with someone or have the same opinion as them〔与某人〕意见一致，同意: [+with] *The judge stated that he concurred with the ruling.* 法官表示同意此项裁决。**2** to happen at the same time; COINCIDE (1) 同时发生的事: **concur to do sth** *Everything concurred to produce the desired effect.* 所有的事情都在同一时间发生，产生了预期的效果。

con·cur·rence /kən`kɜəns; kən'kʌrəns/ *n formal*【正式】**1** [U] agreement 同意: [+with] *Jules expressed his concurrence with the suggestion.* 朱尔斯表示同意这个建议。**2** [C] an example of events, actions etc happening at the same time 同时发生的事: [+of] *a strange concurrence of events* 机缘巧合下发生的一系列事件

con·cur·rent /kən`kɜənt; kən'kʌrənt/ *adj* **1** existing or happening at the same time 同时存在或发生的: *He is serving two concurrent prison sentences.* 他在监狱里同时为两项合并判决服刑。**2** *formal* in agreement【正式】同意的，一致的: [+with] *My opinions are concurrent with yours.* 我的观点与你一致。—**concurrently** *adv*: *two prison sentences to run concurrently* 同时生效的两个徒刑的判决

con·cuss /kən`kʌs; kən'kʌs/ *v* [T often passive 常用被动态] if something hits your head and concusses you, it makes you lose consciousness or feel sick for a short time because your brain is temporarily damaged 使脑震荡: *The driver of the car was badly concussed.* 汽车司机给撞成了严重的脑震荡。

con·cus·sion /kən`kʌʃən; kən'kʌʃən/ *n* [U] a small amount of damage to the brain that makes you lose consciousness or feel sick for a short time, usually caused by something hitting your head 脑震荡

con·demn /kən`dɛm; kən'dem/ *v* [T]
1 ▶DISAPPROVE 责备◀ to say very strongly that you do not approve of something or someone, especially because you think it is morally wrong 指责, 谴责: *Politicians were quick to condemn the bombing.* 政治家们很快就对炸弹爆炸事件予以谴责。| **condemn sth/sb as** *The law has been condemned as an attack on personal liberty.* 这项法律被指责为对人身自由的侵犯。| **condemn sb/sth for doing sth** *She knew that society would condemn her for leaving her children.* 她知道会因为遗弃孩子而受到社会的谴责。
2 ▶PUNISH 惩罚◀ to give someone a severe punishment after deciding they are guilty of a crime 给…判罪, 给…判刑: **condemn sb to death** *The prisoner was condemned to death.* 这名犯人被判处死刑。
3 ▶FORCE TO DO STH 强迫做某事◀ if a particular situation condemns someone to something, it forces them to live in an unpleasant way or to do something unpleasant 迫使〔某人〕处于不幸的境地; 迫使〔某人〕做不愿做的事: **condemn sb to sth** *people condemned to a life of poverty* 被迫一辈子受穷的人 | **condemn sb to do sth** *A significant proportion of such children are condemned to fail.* 那些孩子中的很大一部分是注定通不过的。
4 ▶BUILDING 建筑物◀ to state officially that a building is not safe enough to be used 宣告某楼房不适于居住: *an old house that had been condemned* 一幢已被宣布为危房的老房子
5 ▶SHOW GUILT 表明有罪◀ if the way you look or behave condemns you, it shows that you are guilty of something〔某人的神情或举止〕表明…有罪: *His nervousness condemned him.* 他紧张的神情表明他是有罪的。

con·dem·na·tion /ˌkandɛm`neʃən; ˌkɒndəm'neɪʃən/ *n* [C, U] an expression of very strong disapproval of someone or something 责难, 谴责, 责备: **[+of]** *Condemnation of the latest violence came from all political parties.* 所有的政党都对最近发生的暴力事件进行了谴责。

con·dem·na·to·ry /kən`dɛmnəˌtɔrɪ; kən'demnətəri/ *adj* expressing strong disapproval 表示强烈谴责的

con·demned /kən`dɛmd; kən'demd/ *adj* someone who is condemned is going to be punished by being killed 被判死刑的

condemned cell /·,· '·/ *n* [C] *BrE* a room for a prisoner who was going to be punished by death【英】死刑犯的牢房, 死牢

con·den·sa·tion /ˌkandɛn`seʃən; ˌkɒnden'seɪʃən/ *n* **1** [U] small drops of water that are formed when gas changes to liquid〔气体冷凝形成的〕水滴: *There was a lot of condensation on the windows.* 窗户上结了许多水珠。**2** [U] *technical* the process of change from gas to liquid【术语】凝结, 冷凝: *the condensation of steam into water* 蒸汽冷凝成水 **3** [C,U] *formal* the act of making something shorter【正式】缩短, 压缩: *the condensation of his report* 对他所写报告的压缩

con·dense /kən`dɛns; kən'dens/ *v* **1** [I,T] if gas condenses or is condensed, it becomes a liquid as it becomes cooler (使)凝结, (使)冷凝: *Steam condensed on the bathroom mirror.* 蒸汽在浴室的镜子上冷凝成水珠。| **[+into]** *The gaseous metal is cooled and condenses into liquid zinc.* 气态的金属被冷却并冷凝成为液态锌。**2** [T] to make a liquid thicker by removing some of the water 浓缩: *condensed soup* 浓汤 **3** [T] to make something that is spoken or written shorter, by not giving as much detail or using fewer words to give the same information 将〔讲话或文章〕压缩: **condense sth into sth** *This whole chapter could be condensed into a few paragraphs.* 这一整章可以缩写为几个段落。

condensed milk /·,· '·/ *n* [U] a type of thick sweet milk sold in cans 浓缩牛奶, 炼乳 —compare 比较 EVAPORATED MILK

con·dens·er /kən`dɛnsɚ; kən'densə/ *n* [C] **1** a piece of equipment that makes a gas change into liquid 冷凝器 **2** a machine for storing electricity, especially in a car engine 电容器

con·de·scend /ˌkandɪ`sɛnd; ˌkɒndɪ'send/ *v* [I] **1** to behave as if you think you are better or more important than other people〔行为举止〕显示出自以为高人一等: *She'd be a better teacher if she didn't condescend to her students.* 她如果不是傲慢地对待学生的话, 她会是一个好老师。**2** to do something in a way that shows you think it is below your social or professional position 屈尊, 俯就, 降低身份: **condescend to do sth** *The managing director condescended to have lunch with us in the canteen.* 总经理屈尊来到食堂与我们一起吃午饭。—**condescension** /-`sɛnʃən; -'senʃən/ *n* [U]

con·de·scend·ing /ˌkandɪ`sɛndɪŋ; ˌkɒndɪ'sendɪŋ◂/ *adj* behaving as though you think you are better or more important than other people 带着优越感的: *Professor Hutter's manner is extremely condescending.* 赫特教授的态度极为傲慢。—**condescendingly** *adv*

con·di·ment /`kandəmənt; 'kɒndɪmənt/ *n* [C] *formal* a powder or liquid, such as salt or KETCHUP that you use to give special taste to food【正式】〔盐、番茄酱等的〕调味品, 佐料

con·di·tion[1] /kən`dɪʃən; kən'dɪʃən/ *n*
1 ▶STATE 状态◀ [singular] the state that something is in 状况, 状态: **[+in]** *What sort of condition is your new house in?* 你的新房子目前是什么状况? | **[+of]** *The garden was in a condition of total neglect.* 这个花园一片荒芜。| **be in good/bad/perfect/awful etc condition** *The car has been well maintained and is in excellent condition.* 这辆汽车一直保养得很好, 处于极佳状态。| **in that condition** *spoken* (=in a bad state)【口】状态不好 *You can't wear a jacket in that condition!* 这样破的夹克你不能穿!
2 a) conditions [plural] the situation in which people live or work, especially the physical things such as pay or food that affect the quality of their lives〔生活或工作的〕条件: **working/driving/living etc conditions** *Poor working conditions lead to demoralized and unproductive employees.* 工作条件差导致雇员工作积极性不高, 生产率低下。| **under excellent/terrible etc conditions** *The people are living in makeshift tents under the most appalling conditions.* 人们在极其恶劣的条件下住在临时搭建的帐篷里。**b)** the weather at a particular time, especially when you are considering how this will affect you〔某特定时期的〕天气情况〔尤指会对人产生影响时〕: *Police are advising people to stay at home until weather conditions improve.* 警方建议人们待在家里直到天气情况好转。| **freezing/stormy/icy conditions** *Blizzard conditions are making the roads extremely hazardous.* 大风雪天使道路极为危险。**c)** all the things that affect the way something happens〔影响某事发生的〕情况, 条件: *The experiment must be done under laboratory conditions.* 这项试验必须在实验室条件下进行。
3 ▶AGREEMENT/CONTRACT 协议/合同◀ [C] something that is stated in a contract or agreement that must be done 条款, 条件: *Have you read the conditions of employment carefully?* 你有没有仔细阅读关于雇用的条款? | **[+for]** *There were strict conditions for letting us use their information.* 让我们使用他们的资料有严格的条件。| **lay down/impose conditions** (=state what must be done) 规定/强加条件 *The allies laid down several conditions for their continued support.* 各盟国对继续给予支持规定了几项条件。| **meet/satisfy a condition** (=obey what is demanded by a condition) 满足要求, 满足条件 *The bank agreed to extend the loan if certain conditions were met.* 如果某些条件得到了满足, 银行同意延长这项贷款的期限。| **under the conditions of sth** *Under the conditions of the agreement the work must be completed by the end of the month.* 按照协定的条款, 工作必须在月底前完成。| **on condition that/on one condition** (=only if a particular thing happens) 只有在某条件下 *Ron lent me the money on condition that I pay it back next month.* 罗恩把钱借我, 条件是下月归还。
4 ▶STH THAT MUST BE DONE 必做的事◀ [C] something that must happen first before something else can happen 先决条件, 前提: **[+for/of]** *Finance ministers claimed that all the conditions for an economic revival were in place.* 财政部长们声称经济复苏的一切条件都已齐备。
5 ▶AN ILLNESS 疾病◀ [C] an illness or health problem that affects you permanently or for a very long time 长期疾病: *People suffering from this condition should not smoke.* 得这种病的人不应该吸烟。| **a heart/lung etc condition** *She has a serious heart condition.* 她有严重心脏病。
6 ▶STATE OF HEALTH 健康状态◀ [U, singular] a person or animal's state of health〔人或动物的〕健康状况: *The hospital described his condition as 'satisfactory'.* 医院将他的身体情况描述为"令人满意"。| **out of condition** (=unhealthy or unfit) 身体不佳 *The horse is still out of condition after a serious illness.* 生了一场大病后, 这匹马的健康情况依然不佳。| **in no condition to do sth** (=too ill, drunk, or upset to be able to do something)〔因病重、酒醉或生气而〕不能做某事 *After a whole bottle of wine he was in no condition to drive.* 喝下一整瓶酒后, 他不能开车了。

7 on no condition never, in no possible situation 绝对不可: *This equipment should on no condition be used by untrained staff.* 没有受过训练的人员绝对不可以操作这台设备。
8 ►SITUATION OF GROUP 群体状况◄ [singular] the situation or state of a particular group of people 某一群人的状况: *Few people can really appreciate the condition of the poor in our cities.* 很少人能真正体会到我们城市中穷人的状况。

condition² *v* [T] **1** to make a person or an animal think or behave in a certain way by influencing or training them over a period of time〔通过影响或训练〕使习惯于; 使适应: *People are conditioned by the society and age they live in.* 人们受到他们所生活的社会和时代的制约。| **condition sb to do sth** *The animals were conditioned to expect food at the sound of the bell.* 这些动物受过训练, 一听见铃声就知道有食物可吃了。—see also 另见 CONDITIONING **2** *formal* to control or decide the way in which something can happen or exist【正式】控制; 制约: *What I buy is conditioned by the amount I earn.* 我买些什么是由我挣多少钱决定的。**3** to keep hair or skin healthy by putting a special liquid on it〔对头发、皮肤〕保养, 养护: *This shampoo conditions your hair as well as washing it.* 这种香波既可洗发又可护发。—see also 另见 CONDITIONER

con·di·tion·al¹ /kən`dɪʃənḷ; kən'dɪʃənəl/ *adj* **1** if an offer, agreement etc is conditional, it will only be done if something else happens〔帮忙、协议等〕有条件的: **be conditional on/upon** *a conditional acceptance* 有条件的接受 | *His agreement to buy our house was conditional on our leaving all the furniture in it.* 他同意买我们的房子, 条件是要把所有家具留下。—opposite 反义词 UNCONDITIONAL **2** in grammar, a conditional sentence is one that begins with 'if' or 'unless' and expresses something that must be true or happens before something else can be true or happen〔语法上〕条件的〔条件句以 if (如果) 或 unless (除非) 开头〕—**conditionally** *adv*

conditional² *n* [C] a sentence or CLAUSE (2) that is expressed in a conditional form 条件句; 条件子[从]句

conditional dis·charge /·,···`··/ *n* [C usually singular 一般用单数] a judgment made by a court that allows someone who has done something illegal not to be punished as long as they obey rules set by the court 有条件的释放〔指一种法庭裁决, 允许有违法行为的人在遵守法庭规定的情况下不受惩罚〕

con·di·tion·er /kən`dɪʃənɚ; kən'dɪʃənə/ *n* [C,U] **1** a liquid that you put onto your hair after washing it to make it softer 护发素 **2** a liquid that you wash clothes in to make them softer 织物柔软剂, 衣物柔顺剂

con·di·tion·ing /kən`dɪʃənɪŋ; kən'dɪʃənɪŋ/ *n* [U] the process by which people or animals are trained to behave in a particular way when particular things happen 条件作用, 形成条件反射的过程: *Most adults are unaware of the social conditioning they have been subject to since childhood.* 大部分成年人都没有意识到他们自童年以来受社会环境潜移默化的过程。—see also 另见 AIR CONDITIONING

con·do /`kɑndo; 'kɒndəʊ/ *n* [C] *AmE informal* a CONDOMINIUM【美, 非正式】公寓; 公寓楼

con·dole /kən`dol; kən'dəʊl/ *v*
condole with sb *phr v* [T] *formal* to express sympathy for someone's problems【正式】对别人的困难表示同情

con·do·lence /kən`doləns; kən'dəʊləns/ *n* [C usually plural 一般用复数, U] sympathy for someone who has had something bad happen to them, especially when someone has died〔尤指有人去世时〕同情, 悼唁: *a letter of condolence* 悼唁信 | **send/offer your condolences** (=formally express your sympathy when someone has died) 表示哀悼, 致哀 *I'd like to offer my condolences to the victim's parents.* 我谨对受害人的父母表示哀悼。—compare 比较 COMMISERATION

con·dom /`kɑndəm; 'kɒndəm/ *n* [C] a thin rubber bag that a man wears over his PENIS (=sex organ) during sex, to prevent a woman having a baby, or to protect against disease 安全套, 避孕套

con·do·min·i·um /,kɑndə`mɪnɪəm; ,kɒndə'mɪniəm/ *n* [C] **1** *especially AmE* one apartment in a building with several apartments, each of which is owned by the people living in it【尤美】公寓 (楼里的一套住宅) **2** a building containing several of these apartments 公寓楼

con·done /kən`don; kən'dəʊn/ *v* [T] to accept or forgive behaviour that most people think is morally wrong 宽恕, 原谅〔一般人认为不道德的行为〕: *I cannot condone the use of violence under any circumstances.* 我不能原谅在任何情况下使用暴力。

con·dor /`kɑndɚ; 'kɒndɔː/ *n* [C] a very large South American VULTURE (=a bird that eats dead animals) 神鹰, 秃鹰, 兀鹫

con·duce /kən`djus; kən'djuːs/ *v*
conduce to/towards sth *phr v* [T] *formal* to help to produce a particular quality or state【正式】有助于

con·du·cive /kən`djusɪv; kən'djuːsɪv/ *adj* **be conducive to** *formal* if a situation is conducive to something such as work, rest etc, it provides conditions that make it easy for you to work【正式】有助于, 有益于: *With so much noise outside, the room is hardly conducive to work.* 外面这么吵, 在这个房间里简直无法工作。

con·duct¹ /kən`dʌkt; kən'dʌkt/ *v* S3 W2
1 conduct a survey/experiment/inquiry etc to carry out a particular process, especially in order to get information or prove facts〔尤指为获取信息或证实某事时〕进行调查/实验/调查研究等: *The company conducted a survey to find out local reaction to the leisure centre.* 公司进行了一次调查, 研究当地人对休闲中心的反应。
2 ►MUSIC 音乐◄ [I,T] to stand in front of a group of musicians and direct their playing 指挥: *The orchestra is conducted by John Williams.* 这个交响乐团由约翰·威廉斯指挥。
3 ►ELECTRICITY/HEAT 电/热◄ [T] if something conducts electricity or heat, it allows the electricity or heat to travel along or through it 传导: *Plastic and rubber won't conduct electricity, but copper will.* 塑料和橡胶不导电, 但铜是导电的。
4 ►SHOW SB STH 带某人参观◄ [T always+adv/prep] to show someone a building or place by leading them around it 带领某人参观某地: *The guide conducted us round the castle.* 导游陪伴我们游览了城堡。
5 conduct yourself *formal* to behave in a particular way, especially in a situation where people judge you by the way you behave【正式】行为, 表现〔尤指人们借此作出评判〕: *Public figures have a duty to conduct themselves responsibly.* 公众人物必须行为端正负责。

con·duct² /`kɑndʌkt; 'kɒndʌkt/ *n* [U] *formal*【正式】**1** the way someone behaves, especially in public, in their job etc〔社会、职业等的〕行为举止: *The reporter was accused of unprofessional conduct.* 这个记者被指责违反职业操守。**2** the way a business, activity etc is organized〔某项生意、活动的〕组织安排; 管理; 经营: *There was great dissatisfaction with the conduct of the negotiations.* 对谈判的进行情况存在极大的不满。 W3

con·duc·tion /kən`dʌkʃən; kən'dʌkʃən/ *n* [U] the passage of electricity through wires, heat through metal, water through pipes etc〔电、热的〕传导;〔水的〕输送

con·duc·tive /kən`dʌktɪv; kən'dʌktɪv/ *adj technical* able to conduct electricity, heat etc【术语】〔对电、热等〕具有传导性的: *Copper is a very conductive metal.* 铜是一种传导性极强的金属。—**conductivity** /,kɑndʌk`tɪvətɪ; ,kɒndʌk'tɪvḷti/ *n* [U]

con·duc·tor /kən`dʌktɚ; kən'dʌktə/ *n* [C] **1** someone who stands in front of a group of musicians or singers and directs their playing or singing〔乐队、合唱队的〕指挥 **2** someone whose job is to collect payments from passengers on a bus or train〔火车、公共汽车的〕售票员 **3** something that allows electricity or heat to travel along it or through it〔电或热的〕导体: *Wood is a poor conductor of heat.* 木头的导热性能极差。**4** *AmE* someone who is in charge of a train or the workers on a train【美】〔火车的〕列车长

con·duc·tress /kən`dʌktrɪs; kən'dʌktrḷs/ *n* [C] *old-fashioned* a female conductor【过时】〔火车、公共汽车的〕女售票员

con·duit /`kɑndʊɪt; 'kɒndɪt/ *n* [C] **1** a pipe or passage through which water, gas, a set of electric wires etc pass〔水、气、电线等的〕管道, 导管 **2** a connection between two things that allows people to pass ideas, news, money, weapons, drugs etc from one place to another〔传递信息、新闻、金钱、武器、毒品等的〕渠道, 通道: *The countries have been a conduit for the arms supplied to the terrorists.* 这些国家一直是恐怖分子武器供应的通道。

cone¹ /kon; kəʊn/ *n* [C] **1** a solid or hollow shape with a round base, sloping sides, and a point at the top, or something with this shape 圆锥体 **2** an object shaped like a large cone that is put on a road to prevent cars from going somewhere or to warn drivers about something〔公路上阻止车辆通行或向司机发出警示的〕圆锥形路标, 锥筒 **3** the fruit of a PINE¹ (1) or FIR tree 球果; 松球 —see also 另见 CONIFER **4** a piece of thin, cooked cake, shaped like a cone, that you put ICE CREAM (2) in〔装冰激凌的〕圆锥形蛋卷; CORNET (2) *BrE*【英】

cone² *v*
cone sth ↔ **off** *phr v* [T] to close a road or part of a road by putting a row of cones across it or along it 用圆锥形路标封闭〔道路或部分道路〕

co·ney /`konɪ; 'kəʊni/ *n* [C] another spelling of CONY cony 的另一种拼法

Coney Is·land /ˌ‥ˈ‥/ an area of Brooklyn, New York, famous for its amusement park and beach 科尼艾兰〔纽约布鲁克林一区, 以游乐场和海滩闻名〕

con·fab /ˈkɑnfæb; ˈkɒnfæb/ *n* [C] *informal* a conversation that is private and friendly【非正式】友好的私下交谈: *We'll have a quick confab to talk about what he wants.* 我们将简单地谈谈他的需要。

con·fab·u·late /kənˈfæbjəˌlet; kənˈfæbjʊleɪt/ *v* [I] *formal* to talk together【正式】交谈

con·fab·u·la·tion /kənˌfæbjəˈleʃən; kənˌfæbjʊˈleɪʃən/ *n* [C] *formal* a private conversation【正式】私下交谈

con·fec·tion /kənˈfɛkʃən; kənˈfekʃən/ *n* [C] *formal* a beautifully prepared sweet food【正式】制作精美的糖果[甜点心]

con·fec·tion·er /kənˈfɛkʃənɚ; kənˈfekʃənə/ *n* [C] someone who makes or sells sweets, cakes etc〔制作或出售糖果、冰激凌、糕点等的〕甜食商

confectioner's sug·ar /ˈ·‥ ˌ‥/ *n* [U] *AmE* a kind of sugar that is very powdery【美】〔生产糖果用的〕绵糖; ICING SUGAR *BrE*【英】

con·fec·tion·e·ry /kənˈfɛkʃənˌɛrɪ; kənˈfekʃənəri/ *n* **1** [U] sweets, cakes etc 糖果, 糕饼 **2** [C] a shop that sells sweets, cakes etc 糖果糕饼店

con·fed·e·ra·cy /kənˈfɛdərəsɪ; kənˈfedərəsi/ *n* [C] a union of people, parties, or states, especially for political purposes or trade〔尤指为政治或贸易目的的〕联盟, 同盟

Confederacy, the /·ˌ‥ˈ·/ also 又作 **the Confederate States** in the American Civil War, the southern states of the US, which fought the northern states (the Union) and lost 南部邦联〔美国南北战争时期的南部诸州。曾与北部联邦进行战争, 最终失败〕

con·fed·e·rate[1] /kənˈfɛdərɪt; kənˈfedərɪ̵t/ *n* [C] **1** someone who helps someone else do something, especially something secret or illegal 共犯, 同谋, 党羽: *It was important that they didn't think he was John's confederate in the robbery.* 重要的是他们不认为他和约翰同谋抢劫。**2** a member of a confederacy 联盟者, 同盟者, 盟友; 盟国

confederate[2], **Confederate** *adj* belonging to a confederacy or the Confederacy 联盟的;〔美国南北战争时期〕南部邦联的: *The Confederate Army* 南部邦联军队

con·fed·e·rate[3] /kənˈfɛdəˌret; kənˈfedəreɪt/ *v* [I,T] to combine or to combine something in a confederacy (使)联合[结盟]: [+with] *In 1949 Newfoundland was confederated with Canada through a referendum.* 1949年纽芬兰通过全民公决与加拿大结盟。

Confederate flag /kənˌfɛdərɪt ˈflæg; kənˌfedərɪ̵t ˈflæg/ *n* [C] also 又作 **the flag of the Confederacy**, which is still used, especially by people in the South of the US, to show support for the ideas of the Confederacy and for Racism against black people 南部邦联旗〔至今仍在使用, 在美国南方人当中尤为如此, 借以支持南部邦联的思想及歧视黑人的种族主义〕

CULTURAL NOTE 文化注释

The Confederate flag is still often seen today, especially in the South. Some people fly the flag just to show that they are proud to be a Southerner, but other people fly the flag to show that they think that white people are better than black people. 今天, 尤其在美国南部, 南部邦联旗仍可见到。很多人升南部邦联旗, 仅仅表示他们以身为南方人而自豪, 另一些人则借此表明白人要比黑人优秀。

con·fed·e·ra·tion /kənˌfɛdəˈreʃən; kənˌfedəˈreɪʃən/ *n* [C] a confederacy 联盟; 同盟

Confederation of Brit·ish In·dus·try, the /‥ˌ‥ ‥ˌ‥ˈ‥/ *n* [singular] the CBI

con·fer /kənˈfɝ; kənˈfɜː/ *v* **conferred, conferring** *formal*【正式】**1** [I] to discuss something with other people, so that everyone can express their opinions and decide on something 商谈, 商议, 讨论: [+with] *The congresswoman is conferring with her advisors on the matter.* 这位女国会议员正就此事与顾问们商议。**2** **confer a title/degree/honour etc** [T] to officially give someone a title etc, especially as a reward for something they have achieved 授予称号/学位/荣誉等: [+on/upon] *An honorary degree was conferred on him by the University.* 大学授予他一个荣誉学位。—**conferment** *n* [C,U]

con·fe·rence /ˈkɑnfərəns; ˈkɒnfərəns/ *n* [C] **1** a large formal meeting where a lot of people discuss important matters such as business or politics, especially for several days 会议〔指很多人参加讨论重要事宜的大型会议, 尤指历时数天的会议〕: [+on] *a scientific conference on the ozone layer* 讨论臭氧层问题的科学会议 | **hold a conference** (=have a conference) 举行会议 | **attend a conference** (=go to a conference) 出席会议 *Representatives from over 100 countries attended the International Peace Conference in Geneva.* 来自一百多个国家的代表出席了在日内瓦举行的国际和平大会。| **conference centre/table/room** (=a building, table etc used for conferences) 会议中心/桌/室 *The university has a conference centre in the mountains.* 这所大学在山中建有一处会议中心。—see also 另见 PRESS CONFERENCE **2** a private meeting for a few people to have formal discussions 讨论会, 协商会〔少数人参加的正式讨论问题的秘密会议〕: [+with] *After a brief conference with his aides, he left for the airport.* 和他的助手进行简短的讨论后, 他动身去机场。| **have/hold a conference** *Everyone go and rest, and we'll have a conference about our next move later.* 大家都出去休息一下, 过一会儿我们再开会讨论下一步怎么办。| **in conference** *The manager cannot see you now; she's in conference.* 经理现在不能见你, 她正在开会。**3** *AmE* a group of teams that play against each other; LEAGUE[1] (1)【美】〔运动〕联合会: *College football has two main conferences, the Pac Ten and the Big Ten.* 大学美式橄榄球有两大联合会: 太平洋十大学协会和十大学联合会。

conference call /ˈ‥ ˌ·/ *n* [C] a telephone call in which several people in different places can all talk to each other 电话会议

con·fess /kənˈfɛs; kənˈfes/ *v* [I,T] **1** to admit that you have done something wrong or illegal, especially to the police〔尤指向警察〕坦白, 招认, 招供: *After three hours of questioning the suspect broke down and confessed.* 经过三个小时的审问, 嫌疑犯崩溃了, 招认了一切。| **confess to doing sth** *Edwards confessed to being a spy for the KGB.* 爱德华兹承认为克格勃当间谍。| **confess that** *She confessed that she killed her husband.* 她承认是她杀死了自己的丈夫。| **confess to murder/a crime/robbery etc** *Occasionally people confess to crimes they haven't committed just to get attention.* 有时人们会承认自己并未犯的罪行, 只是为了受到注意。**2** to admit something that you feel embarrassed about 承认〔使自己尴尬的事情〕: **confess that** *Marsha confessed that she didn't really know how to work the computer.* 玛莎承认她其实并不会使用电脑。| **confess to doing sth** *He confessed to having a secret admiration for his opponent.* 他承认私底下很钦佩他的对手。| **confess yourself puzzled/baffled etc** *The police have confessed themselves baffled by this strange and savage crime.* 警方已经承认对这一怪异而野蛮的罪行感到无从下手。| **I (must) confess** *spoken* (=used when admitting something you feel slightly embarrassed about)【口】我(必须)承认〔用于承认自己略感尴尬的事〕*I must confess I don't visit my parents as often as I should.* 我必须承认我并没有像我应该做到的那样经常去看我的父母。**3** to tell a priest or God about the wrong things you have done so that you can be forgiven〔向神父或上帝〕忏悔

con·fessed /kənˈfɛst; kənˈfest/ *adj* [only before noun 仅用于名词前] having admitted publicly that you have done something 已公开承认的, 已招供的: *a confessed criminal* 已经招供的罪犯 —see also 另见 SELF-CONFESSED —**confessedly** /-ˈfɛsɪdlɪ; -ˈfesɪ̵dli/ *adv*

con·fes·sion /kənˈfɛʃən; kənˈfeʃən/ *n* **1** [C] a formal statement that you have done something wrong or illegal 供认, 招供: *The police officer wrote down every word of Smith's confession.* 警官记录下史密斯招供时所说的每一个字。| [+of] *a confession of failure* 承认失败 | **make a confession** *At 3 a.m. Higgins broke down and made a full confession.* 在凌晨3点, 希金斯崩溃了并交代了一切。**2** [C,U] a private statement to a priest about the bad things that you have done〔对神父作的〕忏悔, 告解 **3** [C] *formal* a statement of what your religious beliefs are【正式】关于自己宗教信仰的声明: *a confession of faith* 信仰声明

CULTURAL NOTE 文化注释

Many Christians believe that God will forgive their SINS (=the things they have done that are wrong) if they confess them (=admit them to God or to a priest). In the Roman Catholic religion, people go to a priest to confess their sins. They usually begin their confession by saying, "Bless me, father, for I have sinned." The priest then listens to their sins and gives them ABSOLUTION (=complete forgiveness).The priest is never allowed to tell anyone what that person has confessed, even if the person has COMMITTED a crime. 很多基督徒相信, 如果忏悔, 上帝就会饶恕他们的罪过。罗马天主教信徒去神甫那里忏悔, 忏悔的开场白通常是: "保佑我, 神甫, 因为我有罪。"然后神甫听他悔罪, 赦免他。即便此人犯了罪, 神甫也不可将其忏悔泄露给他人。

es·sion·al¹ /kən`fɛʃənl; kən'feʃənəl/ *n* [C] a place in ...rch, usually an enclosed room, where a priest hears people ...e their confessions〔教堂里的〕告解室

...fessional² *adj* confessional speech or writing contains ...vate thoughts or facts that you normally want to keep secret, ...specially private information about things you have done that were wrong 自白的; 忏悔的

con·fes·sor /kən`fɛsɚ; kən'fesə/ *n* [C] the priest who someone regularly makes their confession to 告解神甫〔常听取某人告解的神甫〕

con·fet·ti /kən`fɛtɪ; kən'feti/ *n* [U] small pieces of coloured paper that you throw over a man and woman who have just been married, especially when they come out of church〔婚礼时向新郎新娘抛撒的〕五彩纸屑〔尤在他们步出教堂时〕

con·fi·dant /ˌkɑnfə`dænt; 'kɒnfɪ̈dænt/ *n* [C] someone you tell your secrets to or who you talk to about personal things 知己, 密友, 心腹朋友

con·fi·dante /ˌkɑnfə`dænt; 'kɒnfɪ̈dænt/ *n* [C] a female confidant 女性知己[密友]

con·fide /kən`faɪd; kən'faɪd/ *v* [T] **1** to tell someone you trust about personal things that you do not want other people to know 吐露〔自己的隐私〕: **confide to sb that** *He confided to his friends that he didn't have much hope for his marriage.* 他私下告诉他的朋友说他对自己的婚姻已不抱太大的希望。**2** *formal* to give something you value to someone you trust so they look after it for you【正式】托付: **confide sth to sb** *He confided his money to his brother's safe-keeping.* 他把钱托付给他弟弟保管。

confide in sb *phr v* [T] to tell someone about something very private or secret, especially a personal problem, because you feel you can trust them 向某人吐露个人隐私: *It's important to have someone that you can confide in.* 有个能说心里话的人是很重要的。

2 2 **con·fi·dence** /`kɑnfədəns; 'kɒnfɪ̈dəns/ *n*

1 ▶FEELING SB/STH IS GOOD 认为某人/物好◀[U] the feeling that you can trust someone or something to be good, work well, or produce good results 信任, 信赖: [+in] *Our first priority is to maintain the customer's confidence in our product.* 我们优先考虑的是如何保持顾客对我们产品的信任。| **have confidence in** *We have every confidence in your abilities.* 我们对你的能力非常有信心。| **win/gain/lose sb's confidence (in)** *Opinion polls show that voters have lost confidence in the administration.* 民意调查显示选民对当局已失去信任。| **inspire/restore/undermine confidence (in)** (=make people feel more or less confident about something or someone) 激起/恢复/破坏信任 *These miscarriages of justice have undermined confidence in our legal system.* 这些冤案错案破坏了人们对我们司法制度的信任。| **show confidence (in)** *Middle-aged people generally do not show as much confidence in what the future holds as do the young.* 总的来说, 中年人不像青年人那样对未来充满希望。

2 ▶BELIEF IN YOURSELF 自信◀[U] the belief that you have the ability to do things well or deal with situations successfully 自信, 信心: *Joyce always had an abundance of confidence. She seemed ... fear no one.* 乔伊丝总是满怀信心, 她好像不畏惧任何人。| **la[ck confidence/be lacking in confidence]** *She's a good student but ...ks confidence in herself.* 她是好学生, 但缺乏自信。| **lack ...idence** *A lack of confidence seems to be her main proble[m]* ...自信心看来是她的主要问题。| **give sb confidence** *Living ... in a foreign country for a year gave her a lot of con[fidence]* ...自在国外生活了一年大大地增强了她的自信。| **give s[b confi]dence to do sth** *Good training will give a beginner th[e confidence] to enjoy skiing.* 良好的训练会使初学者有信心来享... | **restore/lose confidence** *Going back to work re[stored my confi]dence and made me feel more capable.* 回到工作岗... 自己更加能干了。| **boost/shake sb['s confidence]** (=make someone feel more or less confident) 增强... 并使我觉得... *Julie's confidence was badly shaken by her ca[r] ...* 动摇了朱莉的自信心。

3 ▶FEELING STH IS TRUE 确信某事确实...◀ ... that something is definite or true 确信, 坚信: ... *anyone say with confidence that the recession is ...* 有人能确切地说萧条已经结束? | **have confidence** ... *time he had little confidence that God existed.* 在那时... 相信上帝存在。

4 ▶FEELING OF TRUST 信任感◀[U] a feeling of trust [in] someone, so that you can tell them something and be sure they will not tell other people 信赖, 信任: **have/gain/get sb's confidence** (=make someone feel they can trust you) 拥有/获得/得到某人的信任 *It took me a long time to gain his confidence, but he trusts me now.* 我花了很长时间来赢得他的信任, 不过现在他很信任我。| **in (strict) confidence** (=if you tell someone something in confidence, you tell them in secret and they must not tell anyone else) 必须〔绝对〕保密 *I'm giving you this information in the strictest confidence.* 我告诉你这个消息, 你要绝对保密。| **take sb into your confidence** (=tell someone something secret) 将秘密告诉某人 *Tanya took Liane into her confidence about her marital problems.* 塔尼娅向利安娜坦露了她的婚姻问题。

5 ▶A SECRET 秘密◀[C] a secret or a piece of information that is private or personal 知心话; 秘密: *They spent their evenings drinking wine by the fire and sharing confidences.* 他们每天晚上都坐在火炉旁一边喝酒, 一边闲谈心腹事。—see also 另见 VOTE OF CONFIDENCE, VOTE OF NO CONFIDENCE

confidence-build·ing /'···, ·'/ *adj* an event, action etc that is confidence-building increases your confidence 增强自信心的: *The outdoor training is meant to be a confidence-building exercise for youngsters.* 户外训练是用来增强青少年自信心的一种训练方式。

confidence trick /'···, ·/ *n* [C] *formal* a dishonest trick played on someone in order to get their money; CON² (1)【正式】诈骗 —**confidence trickster** *n* [C]

2 3 **con·fi·dent** /`kɑnfədənt; 'kɒnfɪ̈dənt/ *adj* **1** sure that you can do something or deal with a situation successfully 有信心的: *He gave her a confident smile.* 他自信地对她微笑。| **be confident about** *Joyce is very confident about using computers.* 乔伊丝对使用电脑非常自信。**2** [not before noun 不用于名词前] very sure that something is going to happen or that you will be able to do something 确信的; 有把握的: **be confident (that)** *We are confident that next year's profits will be higher.* 我们确信明年的利润会增加。—see also 另见 SELF-CONFIDENT —**confidently** *adv*

con·fi·den·tial /ˌkɑnfə`dɛnʃəl; ˌkɒnfɪ̈'denʃəl◂/ *adj* **1** spoken or written in secret and intended to be kept secret 机密的; 机要的: *a confidential naval report on the failure of equipment* 有关设备失灵的海军机要报告 | **keep sth confidential** *Doctors are required to keep patients' records completely confidential.* 医生必须对病人的病历绝对保密。| **strictly confidential** (=completely confidential) 绝密的 *What I'm telling you is strictly confidential.* 我告诉你的是绝密的事。**2** a confidential way of speaking or behaving shows that you do not want other people to know what you are saying〔言谈举止〕神秘的: *His voice sank into a confidential whisper as he mentioned who was involved.* 当说到有谁涉及时, 他把声音压低, 悄声低语起来。**3** a confidential secretary or CLERK¹ (1) is one who is trusted with secret information〔秘书、人员〕机要的, 心腹的, 极受信任的 —**confidentially** *adv*

con·fi·den·ti·al·i·ty /ˌkɑnfəˌdɛnʃɪ`ælɪtɪ; ˌkɒnfɪ̈denʃi'ælɪ̈ti/ *n* [U] a situation in which you trust someone not to tell secret or private information to anyone else 机密, 秘密; 保密: *The relationship between attorneys and their clients is based on confidentiality.* 律师和委托人之间的关系是建立在保密的基础之上的。| **breach of confidentiality** (=an occasion when someone tells a secret) 违反保密责任 *It is a breach of confidentiality for a priest to reveal what someone has said in the confessional.* 神父把某人告解所说的事情泄露出来是违反了保密的原则。

con·fid·ing /kən`faɪdɪŋ; kən'faɪdɪŋ/ *adj* behaving in a way that shows you want to tell someone about something that is private or secret 信任他人的: *She allowed a confiding note to enter her voice.* 她让语调流露出一种对人的信任。—**confidingly** *adv*: *She spoke gaily, innocently, and confidingly.* 她愉快地与人交谈, 那么天真, 那么信赖别人。

con·fig·u·ra·tion /kənˌfɪgjə`reʃən; kənˌfɪgjʊ̈'reɪʃən/ *n* [C, U] **1** *formal or technical* the shape or arrangement of the parts of something; LAYOUT【正式或术语】构造, 结构; 布局: [+of] *the configuration of pistons in an engine* 发动机内活塞的构造 **2** *technical* the combination of equipment needed to run a computer system【术语】〔电脑设备的〕配置

con·fig·ure /kən`fɪgjɚ; kən'fɪgə/ *v* [T] *technical* to arrange [so]mething, especially computer equipment, so that it works with the equipment【术语】配置〔尤指电脑设备〕

3 **con·fi[n]e** /kən`faɪn; kən'faɪn/ *v* [T]

...限制◀to keep someone or something within the lim... ...[particu]lar activity or subject; RESTRICT 把…局限于; 把… ...[be confin]ed to *The police cadet's duties were confined* ... [f]rom the crowd. 警官学校学员的责任只限 ... | *a former editor now confined to or-* ... 只限于编排读者来信版面的前任编

辑 | **confine yourself to sth** *We must confine ourselves to the subject at hand.* 我们的讨论应当限制在眼前的这个话题。
2 be confined to a) to affect or happen to only one group of people, or in only one place or time 局限于〔某一群体、地点或时间〕: *This disease is not just confined to children.* 这种病不只发生在儿童身上。**b)** to have to stay in a place, especially because you are ill 〔尤指因病〕只能待在〔某地〕: *an elderly woman confined to a small apartment* 只能在一套小居室内活动的老妇人 | **confined to a wheelchair** (=unable to walk) 行动只能靠轮椅 *Although confined to a wheelchair, she is very active in church life.* 虽然她只能依靠轮椅行动，她对教堂的活动仍非常积极。
3 ►KEEP SB IN A PLACE 监禁某人◄ to keep someone in a place that they cannot leave, such as a prison 监禁，禁闭: **confine sb to** *Any soldier who leaves his post will be confined to the barracks.* 任何擅离职守的士兵都将被关在营房里，不准外出。| **be confined in** *He was allegedly confined in a narrow, dark room for two months.* 据说他被监禁在一个既狭小又黑暗的房间里，关了两个月。
4 ►STOP SPREADING 阻止扩散◄ to stop something bad from spreading to another place 限制，阻止: **confine sth to sth** *Fire fighters quickly confined the blaze to the factory floor.* 消防队员很快就把火势控制在工厂的车间范围内。
5 ►STAY IN BED 卧床◄ [usually passive 一般用被动态] to make someone stay in bed because they are ill 使…卧床休息: *I had flu and was confined to bed.* 我感冒了，只得卧床休息。

con·fined /kən`faɪnd; kən'faɪnd/ *adj* a confined space or area is one that is very small 〔指空间或面积〕有限的，狭窄的: *It wasn't easy to sleep in such a confined space.* 在如此狭小的空间里睡觉实在不容易。

con·fine·ment /kən`faɪnmənt; kən'faɪnmənt/ *n* **1** [U] the act of putting someone in a room, prison etc, or the state of being there 监禁，关押，禁闭: *her years of confinement* 她坐牢的那些年 | *They were held in confinement for three weeks.* 他们被关押了三个礼拜。—see also 另见 SOLITARY CONFINEMENT **2** [C,U] an act of giving birth to a child; LYING-IN 分娩；产期

con·fines /`kɑnfaɪnz; 'kɒnfaɪnz/ *n* [plural] limits or borders 界限，范围: **within/beyond the confines of** *within the confines of the prison* 在监狱范围内

con·firm /kən`fɝm; kən'fɜːm/ *v* [T] **1** to show that something is definitely true, especially by providing more proof 证实，证明: *The new evidence has confirmed the first witness's story.* 新证据证实了第一个证人的说法。| **confirm that** *Research has confirmed that the risk is higher for women.* 研究证实对妇女来说风险更大。| **confirm what** *The new results confirm what most of us knew already.* 新成果证实我们大多数人已经知道的东西。**2** to make an idea or feeling stronger or more definite 使〔想法、感觉〕巩固，更坚定，加强: *This just confirms my fears.* 这只加深了我的恐惧。| **confirm you in your belief/opinion/view etc (that)** (=make you believe something more strongly) 使信念/意见/观点等更加确实 *The expression on his face confirmed me in my suspicions.* 他脸上的表情证实了我的怀疑。**3** to say that something is definitely true 证实: *The President refused to confirm the rumor.* 总统拒绝证实这个谣言。| **confirm that** *Walsh confirmed that the money had been paid.* 沃尔什证实那笔钱已经支付。| **confirm what** *My brother will confirm what I have told you.* 我弟弟将证实我跟你说过的话。**4** to tell someone that a possible arrangement, date, or time is now definite 肯定，确认〔安排、日期等〕: *Could you confirm the dates we discussed?* 你能确认我们讨论的日期吗? | **be confirmed in office** (=be formally accepted in a new position of responsibility, especially as leader of a country) 正式就职〔尤指担任国家领导人〕**5 be confirmed** to be made a full member of the Christian church in a special ceremony 施坚信典礼〔从而正式成为基督教会成员〕

con·fir·ma·tion /,kɑnfɚ`meʃən; ,kɒnfə'meɪʃən/ *n* [C,U] **1** a statement etc that says that something is definitely true, or the act of stating this 证实，证明: **[+of]** *There's still no official con-firmation of the report.* 这则报告仍未得到官方证实。| **co[nfir]mation that** *verbal confirmation that payment has be*... 对已经付款的口头证明 **2** a letter etc that tells yo... sible arrangement, date, time etc is now defin... 时间等的〕确认函: *I'm still waiting for co*... *about my visit.* 我仍在等他们对我拜访... gious ceremony in which someone ... Christian church 坚信礼

con·firmed /kən`fɝmd... ...ch- ...pletely ... 婚的单身 elor/alcoholic/vegetar... happy with the way of ... 汉/无可救药的酒鬼/坚...

con·fis·cate /`kɑnfɪs,ket; 'kɒnf͵skeɪt/ *v* [T] to official... private property away from someone, usually as a punish... 把…充公，没收: *Miss Williams confiscated all our sweets.* ...斯小姐没收了我们所有的糖果。—**confiscation** /,kɑnfɪs`ke... ,kɒnf͵'skeɪʃən/ *n* [C,U] *the confiscation of pornographic ma... rial* 对淫秽物品的没收 —**confiscatory** /kən`fɪskə,tɔr... 'kɒnf͵skeɪtəri/ *adj*

con·fla·gra·tion /,kɑnflə`greʃən; ,kɒnflə'greɪʃən/ *n* [C] *formal*【正式】**1** a very large fire that destroys a lot of buildings, forests etc 大火 **2** a violent situation or war 冲突；战争: *a nuclear conflagration* 核冲突

con·flate /kən`flet; kən'fleɪt/ *v* [T] *formal* to combine two or more things to form a single new thing【正式】合并，混合: *This idea conflates two issues.* 这个想法来源于两点。—**conflation** /-`fleʃən; -'fleɪʃən/ *n* [C,U]

con·flict[1] /`kɑnflɪkt; 'kɒnflɪkt/ *n* [C,U] **1** a state of disagreement or argument between people, groups, countries etc 〔意见等的〕冲突，相左: *serious political conflict* 严重的政治冲突 | **[+over]** *conflicts over wage settlements* 针对工资协议的争执 | **[+between]** *the conflict between tradition and innovation* 传统与革新的冲突 | **in conflict** *permanently in conflict with her superiors* 与她的上级处于无休止的矛盾之中 | **come into conflict** (=start arguing with) 发生争执 *She had often come into conflict with her mother-in-law.* 她经常与婆婆发生争执。**2** a situation in which you have to choose between two or more opposite needs or influences 〔在对立的需要或影响之间选择的〕矛盾，冲突: **[+between]** *a conflict between the demands of one's work and one's family* 工作和家庭之间的矛盾 | **in conflict with** *The principles of democracy are sometimes in conflict with political reality.* 民主原则有时与政治现实发生冲突。**3** fighting or a war 战斗；战争: *a violent conflict* 剧烈的武装冲突 | **armed conflict** *the frightening prospect of armed conflict* 发生武装冲突的恐怖前景 **4** a situation in which you have two opposite feelings about something 矛盾心理: *an agonizing state of inner conflict* 折磨人的内心矛盾 **5 conflict of interest/interests a)** a situation in which you cannot do your job fairly because you will be affected by the decision you make 利益冲突: *There is a growing conflict of interest between her position as a politician and her business activities.* 她作为政治家的地位和她的商务活动之间的利益冲突日益严重。**b)** a situation in which different people want different things 〔不同人之间的〕利益冲突

con·flict[2] /kən`flɪkt; kən'flɪkt/ *v* [I] if two ideas, beliefs, opinions etc conflict, they cannot exist together or both be true 矛盾，冲突，抵触: **[+with]** *This conflicts with the police evidence.* 这与警方的证据相矛盾。| **conflicting opinions/demands/interests etc** *I had rung a few friends, and been given a great deal of conflicting advice.* 我打电话给几个朋友，他们给我许多相互冲突的建议。

con·flu·ence /`kɑnfluəns; 'kɒnfluəns/ *n* [singular+of] **1** *technical* the place where two or more rivers flow together【术语】〔河的〕汇合点，合流处 **2** the point at which two or more ideas, principles etc are very similar 〔不同意见、原则的〕相似之处 —**confluent** *adj*

con·form /kən`fɔrm; kən'fɔːm/ *v* [I] **1** to beha... the way ...ave 像大多 that most other people in your group or soci... conform 促使 数人一样行事: *the pressure on schoolchi...* **rule etc** to obey a 小学生循规蹈矩的力量 **2 conform t...** *conform to the rules* ...么离开学校。| *conform* law, rule etc 遵守法律/规定等...方的安全准则 **3 conform** *or leave the school.* 你要么... *formal* to happen or develop *to the official safety sta...* ...at you expect【正式】遵照模式/ **to the pattern/m...** 见 CONFORMIST —**conformer** *n* [C] in the way that ... 范例/理想...

[con·for·ma·tion] /,kɑnfɔr`meʃən; ,kɒnfɔː'meɪʃən/ *n* [C,U] ...of something or the way in which it is formed ...造: *the conformation of the earth* 地球的构造

—**con...**

con[formi]st /kən`fɔrmɪst; kən'fɔːm͵st/ *adj* thinking and ...ke everyone else, because you do not want to be ... 墨守成规的，因循守旧的: *conformist thinking* 守旧的 ...守成规 —**conformist** *n* [C] *his refusal to be a conformist* 他拒绝...

con·for·mi·ty /kən`fɔrmətɪ; kən'fɔːm͵ti/ *n* [U] *formal*【正式】**1** behaviour that obeys the accepted rules of society or a group, and is the same as that of most other people 〔对公认准则的〕遵守，依照: *an emphasis on conformity and control* 对循规蹈矩和操纵的强调 | **[+to]** *conformity to an agreed standard of taste* 符合公认的口味标准 **2 in conformity with** *formal* in a way that obeys rules, customs etc【正式】与〔规定、习俗等〕一

致, 符合: *We must act in conformity with the local regulations.* 我们必须遵守当地的法规。

con·found /kən`faʊnd; kən'faʊnd/ *v* [T] **1** to confuse and surprise people by being unexpected〔以出乎意料的行为〕使困惑; 使惊讶: *His amazing recovery confounded the medical specialists.* 他神奇的康复使医学专家感到困惑。**2** *formal* to defeat an enemy, plan etc【正式】挫败〔敌人、计划等〕**3** *formal* if a problem etc confounds you, you cannot understand it or solve it【正式】〔问题等〕把…难住, 使不知所措: *Her question completely confounded me.* 她提的问题把我完全搞糊涂了。**4 confound it/him/them** *old-fashioned* used to show that you are annoyed【过时】讨厌, 该死

con·found·ed /kən`faʊndɪd; kən'faʊndɪ̣d/ *adj* [only before noun 仅用于名词前] *old-fashioned* used to show that you are annoyed【过时】讨厌的; 该死的: *That confounded dog has run away again!* 那条该死的狗又跑掉了!

con·fra·ter·ni·ty /ˌkɑnfrə`tɝnətɪ; ˌkɒnfrə'tɜːnɪ̣ti/ *n* [C] a group of people, especially religious people who are not priests, who work together for some good purpose〔宗教、慈善事业等的〕团体, 社团

con·frère /`kɑnfrɛr; 'kɒnfrə/ *n* [C] *French, formal* a friend or someone you work with【法, 正式】朋友; 同事

con·front /kən`frʌnt; kən'frʌnt/ *v* [T] **1** to behave in a threatening way towards someone, as though you are going to attack them 以暴力相威胁: *Opening the door, he found himself confronted by a dozen policemen with guns.* 他开门时发现自己面对着12名带枪的警察。**2** to deal with something very difficult or unpleasant in a brave and determined way 勇敢地面对; 正视: *We try to help people confront their problems.* 我们试图帮助人们正视问题。**3** [usually passive 一般用被动态] to suddenly appear and need to be dealt with 突然面临: *On my first day at work I was confronted with the task of chairing a meeting.* 我第一天上班就面临主持一个会议的任务。**4** to accuse someone of doing something by showing them the proof 对质, 当面对证: **confront sb with the evidence/proof** *When the police confronted her with the evidence, she admitted everything.* 当警察当面向她出示证据时, 她承认了一切。

con·fron·ta·tion /ˌkɑnfrʌn`teʃən; ˌkɒnfrən'teɪʃən/ *n* [C, U+with/between] **1** a situation in which there is a lot of angry disagreement between two people or groups with very different opinions 对抗, 冲突: *She had stayed in her room to avoid another confrontation.* 她待在自己的房间里以避免另一次的冲突。**2** a fight or battle 战斗, 战役

con·fron·ta·tion·al /ˌkɑnfrʌn`teʃənl; ˌkɒnfrən'teɪʃənəl◂/ *adj* intended to cause arguments or make people angry 故意寻衅的; 令人生气的: *a confrontational style of government* 对抗式的统治方式

Con·fu·cian·is·m /kən`fjuʃənɪzm; kən'fjuːʃənɪzəm/ *n* [U] a Chinese way of thought which teaches that you should be loyal to your family, friends, and rulers and treat others as you would like to be treated. Confucianism was developed from the ideas of Confucius. 孔子学说, 儒家学说, 儒教〔中国的一种思想观, 教导人们忠于家庭、朋友和君王, 主张"推己及人"的思想。儒家学说起源于孔子的思想〕—**Confucian** *adj*

Con·fu·cius /kən`fjuʃəs; kən'fjuːʃəs/ (551-479 BC) a Chinese PHILOSOPHER whose ideas encouraged justice and peace, and who taught social and moral principles which had a great influence on Chinese society 孔子〔(公元前551-前479), 中国哲学家。他宣导"仁义"、"仁政", 所传授的社会和道德准则对中国社会影响重大〕

con·fuse /kən`fjuz; kən'fjuːz/ *v* [T] **1** to make someone feel that they cannot think clearly or do not understand 使困惑; 把〔某人〕弄糊涂: *Don't give me so much information – you're confusing me!* 别告诉我这么多——你会把我弄糊涂的! **2** to think wrongly that one person, thing, or idea etc is someone or something else〔把人、物或想法〕混淆, 弄错: **confuse sb/sth with** *I always confuse you with your sister – you look so alike.* 我总是把你和你妹妹搞混, 你们太像了。| *Donald Reagan, not to be confused with former President Ronald Reagan* 唐纳德·里根, 不要把他与前总统罗纳德·里根混淆 **3 confuse the issue/matter/argument etc** to make it even more difficult to think clearly about a situation or problem or to deal with it 使问题/事情/争论等更加难以弄清或处理: *He kept asking unnecessary questions which only confused the issue.* 他不停地问些无关紧要的问题, 只能使这个问题更复杂。

3 **con·fused** /kən`fjuzd; kən'fjuːzd/ *adj* **1** unable to understand clearly what someone is saying or what is happening 困惑的, 糊涂的: *I am totally confused. Could you explain that again?* 我完全糊涂了, 你能再解释一遍吗? | **[+about]** *If you're confused about anything, phone my office.* 如果你对什么事有疑问, 给我办公室打电话。**2** not clear or not easy to understand 不清楚的; 混乱的; 分不清的: *There was an argument and a confused fight followed.* 争吵过后是一场混乱的打斗。| *a lot of confused ideas* 许多混淆的观念 —**confusedly** /-`fjuzdlɪ; -'fjuːzɪ̣dli/ *adv*

con·fus·ing /kən`fjuzɪŋ; kən'fjuːzɪŋ/ *adj* difficult to understand because there is no clear order or pattern 令人困惑的, 模糊不清的, 难懂的: *The instructions were so confusing I've done it all wrong.* 那些说明模糊不清, 我全做错了。| *It was a very confusing situation.* 这是非常混乱的局面。—**confusingly** *adv* 3

con·fu·sion /kən`fjuʒən; kən'fjuːʒən/ *n* [U] **1** a state of not understanding what is happening or what something means because it is not clear 困惑; 混乱: **[+about/over/as to]** *There was some confusion as to whether we had won or lost.* 不清楚我们究竟是输了还是赢了。| **create/lead to confusion** *This complicated situation has led to considerable confusion.* 这种复杂的局势造成了相当的混乱。**2** a situation in which someone wrongly thinks that one person, thing, or idea is someone or something else 辨别不清; 混淆, 错认: *To avoid confusion, the teams wore different colours.* 为了避免混淆, 各球队穿上不同颜色的服装。| **[+between]** *confusion between 'tax avoidance' and 'tax evasion'* "避税"和"逃税"之间的混淆 **3** a feeling of not being able to think clearly what you should say or do, especially in an embarrassing situation 慌乱; 窘迫: *His confusion at meeting her there was quite apparent.* 他在那里和她不期而遇, 明显地表现得不知所措。| **in confusion** *She stopped in confusion as everyone turned to look at her.* 当每个人转头看她时, 她窘迫地停了下来。**4** a very confusing situation, usually with a lot of noise and action, so that it is difficult to understand or control 混乱, 骚乱: *a scene of indescribable confusion* 难以形容的混乱景象 3 3

con·fute /kən`fjut; kən'fjuːt/ *v* [T] *formal* to prove that a person or belief is completely wrong【正式】驳倒, 完全否定 —**confutation** /ˌkɑnfju`teʃən; ˌkɒnfjuː'teɪʃən/ *n* [C,U]

con·ga /`kɑŋgə; 'kɒŋgə/ *n* [C,U] a Latin American dance in which people hold onto each other and dance in a line, or the music for this 康茄舞〔一种拉丁美洲舞蹈〕; 康茄舞曲

con·geal /kən`dʒil; kən'dʒiːl/ *v* [I] if a liquid such as blood congeals, it becomes thick or solid〔血液等液体〕凝结

con·ge·ni·al /kən`dʒinjəl; kən'dʒiːniəl/ *adj* pleasant in a way that makes you feel comfortable and relaxed 宜人的; 令人舒适的; 令人愉快的: **[+to]** *The club provides a social atmosphere which is congenial to the average businessman.* 俱乐部提供一种社交氛围, 使一般的商人都觉得非常舒适。—**congenially** *adv*

con·gen·i·tal /kən`dʒɛnətl; kən'dʒenɪ̣tl/ *adj* **1** a congenital medical condition or disease has affected someone since they were born〔病症等〕先天的: *congenital abnormalities* 先天畸形 | *congenital defect* 先天性缺陷 **2** existing as a part of your character and unlikely to change 天生的; 根深蒂固的: *his congenital inability to make decisions* 他优柔寡断的天性 | *a congenital liar* 生性好说谎的人 —**congenitally** *adv*

con·ger eel /ˌkɑŋgɚ `il; ˌkɒŋgər 'iːl/ *n* [C] a large fish that looks like a snake 康吉鳗

con·ges·ted /kən`dʒɛstɪd; kən'dʒestɪ̣d/ *adj* **1** a congested street, city etc is very full of traffic 交通拥挤的, 车辆阻塞的: *congested air space* 拥挤的空中交通 **2** a part of your body that is congested is very full of liquid, usually blood or MUCUS〔身体某部位〕充血[黏液]的 —**congestion** /-`dʒɛstʃən; -'dʒestʃən/ *n* [U]: *traffic congestion* 交通拥挤

con·glom·e·rate /kən`glɑmərɪt; kən'glɒmərɪ̣t/ *n* **1** [C] a large business organization consisting of several different companies that have joined together 大型联合企业: *a large multinational conglomerate* 大型跨国联合企业 **2** [C,U] *technical* a rock consisting of different sizes of stones held together by clay【术语】砾岩 **3** [C] a group of things gathered together 聚集物

con·glom·e·ra·tion /kənˌglɑmə`reʃən; kənˌglɒmə'reɪʃən/ *n* [C+of] a group of many different things gathered together 聚集物

Congo /`kɑŋgo; 'kɒŋgəʊ/ **, Democratic Republic of** a very large country in central Africa, which was called Zaïre between 1971 and 1997, and before that was called the Belgian Congo. Population: 53,625,000 (2001). Capital: Kinshasa. 刚果民主共和国〔中非第一大国。1971年至1997年间称扎伊尔, 之前称比属刚果。人口: 53,625,000 (2001), 首都: 金沙萨〕—**Congolese** /ˌkɑŋgə`liz; ˌkɒŋgə'liːz◂/ *n, adj*

Congo, Republic of a country on the Equator in the western part of central Africa, to the west of the Democratic Republic of Congo (Zaïre). Population: 2,894,000 (2001). Capital: Brazzaville. 刚果共和国〔中非西部一赤道国家, 位于刚果民主共

和国以西。人口: 2,894,000 (2001), 首都: 布拉柴维尔〕—**Congolese** *n, adj*

Con·go, the the second longest African river, which flows through both the Republic of Congo and the Democratic Republic of Congo 刚果河〔非洲第二大河, 流经刚果共和国和刚果民主共和国〕

con·grats /kənˋgræts; kən'græts/ *n* [plural] *informal* CONGRATULATIONS【非正式】祝贺, 恭喜

con·grat·u·late /kənˋgrætʃə,let; kən'grætʃʊleɪt/ *v* [T] **1** to tell someone that you are happy because they have achieved something or because something nice has happened to them 祝贺, 向…道喜: *He never even stopped to congratulate me.* 他甚至都不停下来向我祝贺。| **congratulate sb on** *She congratulated me warmly on my exam results.* 她热情地祝贺我考试取得好成绩。**2 congratulate yourself (on)** to feel pleased and proud of yourself because you have achieved something or something good has happened to you 为自己高兴, 感到自豪: *I congratulated myself on my good fortune.* 我为自己的好运气感到高兴。—**congratulation** /kən,grætʃəˋleʃən; kən,grætʃʊ'leɪʃən/ *n* [U]—**congratulatory** /kənˋgrætʃələ,torɪ; kən,grætʃʊ'leɪtəri/ *adj*

3 **con·grat·u·la·tions** /kən,grætʃəˋleʃənz; kən,grætʃʊ'leɪʃənz/ *n* [plural] **1** words saying you are happy that someone has achieved something 贺词, 恭喜: *Give Marie my congratulations and tell her I'll come soon.* 替我恭喜玛丽并告诉她我很快就来。**2** an expression used when you want to congratulate someone 恭喜, 祝贺: *"I've just passed my driving test!" "Congratulations!"* "我刚刚通过驾驶执照考试!" "恭喜你!" | [+on] *Congratulations on a superb performance!* 对这场精彩的演出表示祝贺!

> **CULTURAL NOTE 文化注释**
> People say 'Congratulations' when someone has done something special, such as winning a prize, getting a new job, getting married etc. You can also say it when someone tells you they are going to get married or have a baby. 有人取得特别成绩, 如获奖、找到新工作或结婚时, 人们会说"恭喜, 恭喜!"有人即将结婚或生子时也可以这么表示祝贺。

con·gre·gate /ˋkaŋgrɪ,get; 'kɒŋgrɪ̈geɪt/ *v* [I] to come together in a group 聚合, 聚集: *Crowds began to congregate to hear the President's speech.* 人群开始聚集起来, 聆听总统的演讲。

con·gre·ga·tion /,kaŋgrɪˋgeʃən; ,kɒŋgrɪ̈'geɪʃən/ *n* [C also+plural verb *BrE* 英] **1** a group of people gathered together in a church 会众〔在教堂里聚集的人群〕: *The congregation knelt to pray.* 会众下跪祈祷。**2** the people who usually go to a particular church 教堂会众〔通常去某教堂做礼拜的人群〕: *Several members of the congregation were sick.* 常来这里做礼拜的几个人病了。—**congregational** *adj*

Con·gre·ga·tion·al·is·m /,kaŋgrɪˋgeʃənḷ,ɪzəm; ,kɒŋgrɪ̈'geɪʃənəlɪzəm/ *n* [U] one type of Christianity, in which each congregation is responsible for making its own decisions〔基督教的〕会众制, 公理制〔一种基督教教派, 主张各教堂的会众自行管理自己的事务〕—**Congregational** *adj*—**Congregationalist** *n* [C]

con·gress /ˋkaŋgrəs; 'kɒŋgres/ *n* **1** [C,U] a formal meeting of representatives of different groups, countries etc, to discuss ideas, give information etc 代表大会: *the annual congress of the miners' union* 矿工工会的年度代表大会 **2** [C] the group of people chosen or elected to make the laws in countries 国会; 议会 **3 Congress** the group of people elected to make laws in the US, consisting of the Senate and the House of Representatives〔由参议院和众议院组成的〕美国国会: *The President has lost the support of Congress.* 总统失去了国会支持。—**congressional** /kənˋgrɛʃənḷ; kən'greʃənəl/ *adj* [only before noun 仅用于名词前]: *a congressional committee* 国会委员会

> **CULTURAL NOTE 文化注释**
> The US Congress is responsible for suggesting BILLs (=plans for new laws) and deciding whether bills will become laws. If the Senate and the House of Representatives both agree that a bill should become a law, the President is asked if he agrees with it. If the President agrees with the bill he signs it, and the bill becomes law. If he VETOes the bill (=says officially that he does not agree with it), Congress can still make it a law if two-thirds of the members of both the Senate and the House of Representatives agree. 美国国会负责提交议案, 并决定议案是否成为法律。参议院和众议院都通过议案, 则征询总统意见。如总统通过议案并签署, 该议案成为法律。如总统否决议案, 但国会两院均有三分之二议员通过议案, 该议案仍会成为法律。— see Cultural Note at BILL 见 BILL 文化注释

Congressional Med·al of Hon·or, the /·,··· · ˋ··/ also 又作 **the Medal of Honor** a special MEDAL given to members of the US armed forces who have performed acts of very great bravery. It is the highest military honour in the US. 荣誉勋章〔美国最高的军功勋章, 专门颁发给表现出大无畏精神的美国军人〕

Congressional Rec·ord, the /·,··· ˋ··/ a printed report of what is said and done in the US Congress, including all the official discussions, votes, and decisions 国会议事录〔美国国会印制的工作报告, 其中包含议事、表决以及决策等内容〕— compare 比较 HANSARD

con·gress·man /ˋkaŋgrəsmən; 'kɒŋgrɪ̈smən/ *n* [C] a man who is a member of a congress, especially the US House of Representatives 国会议员〔尤指美国众议员〕: *Congressman Stephen Richards Rojack* 斯蒂芬·理查兹·罗杰众议员

Congress Party, the /ˋ·· ,··/ an important political party in India. It was started in the 19th century to oppose British rule in India. 国民大会党, 国大党〔印度一重要政党, 该党派创立于19世纪, 目的是反对英国在印度的统治〕

con·gress·wom·an /ˋkaŋgrəs,wʊmən; 'kɒŋgrɪ̈s,wʊmən/ *n* [C] a woman who is a member of a congress, especially the US House of Representatives 女国会议员〔尤指美国众议员〕: *an interview with Congresswoman Anne Harding* 对安妮·哈丁众议员的采访

con·gru·ent /ˋkaŋgrʊənt; 'kɒŋgruənt/ *adj* **1** [+with] *formal* fitting together well; suitable【正式】相配的; 符合的; 合适的 **2** *technical* congruent triangles (TRIANGLE (1)) are the same size and shape【术语】〔三角形〕全等的—**congruence** *n* [U]—**congruently** *adv* —opposite 反义词 INCONGRUENT

con·gru·ous /ˋkaŋgruəs; 'kɒŋgruəs/ *adj* [+with] fitting together well; suitable 相配的; 符合的; 合适的—**congruity** /kənˋgruətɪ; kən'gru:ɪ̈ti/ *n* [C,U] —opposite 反义词 INCONGRUOUS

con·ic /ˋkanɪk; 'kɒnɪk/ *adj* connected with or shaped like a CONE[1] (1) 圆锥的; 圆锥形的

con·i·cal /ˋkanɪkḷ; 'kɒnɪkəl/ *adj* shaped like a CONE[1] (1) 圆锥形的: *There were several huts with conical roofs.* 有几间带圆锥形屋顶的小屋。

conic sec·tion /,·· ˋ··/ *n* [C] *technical* a shape made in GEOMETRY when an imaginary flat surface is passed through a CONE[1] (1)【术语】圆锥曲线, 二次曲线

co·ni·fer /ˋkonəfɚ; 'kəʊnɪ̈fə/ *n* [C] a tree that has leaves like needles that stay on it during the winter and brown cones (CONE[1] (3)) that contain its seeds 针叶树—**coniferous** /koˋnɪfərəs; kə'nɪfərəs/ *adj*

conj the written abbreviation of 缩写= CONJUNCTION

con·jec·ture[1] /kənˋdʒɛktʃɚ; kən'dʒektʃə/ *n formal*【正式】**1** [U] the act of thinking of reasons, explanations etc without having very much information to base them on 推测, 猜测: *She didn't know the facts, so what she said was pure conjecture.* 她并不了解实际情况, 所以她说的纯属猜测。| *conjecture about their role in the affair* 对他们在该事件中所起作用的猜测 **2** [C] an idea or opinion formed by guessing〔根据推测所形成的想法或意见的〕猜想: *My results show that this conjecture was, in fact, correct.* 我得到的结果证明这个猜想实际上是正确的。—**conjectural** *adj*

conjecture[2] *v* [I,T] *formal* to form an idea or opinion without having much information to base it on; guess【正式】推测, 猜测: [+that] *It seems reasonable to conjecture that these conditions breed violence.* 有理由推断这些情况会引发暴力。

con·join /kənˋdʒɔɪn; kən'dʒɔɪn/ *v* [I,T] *formal* to join together or make things or people do this【正式】(使) 结合; (使) 联合; (使) 连接

con·joint /kənˋdʒɔɪnt; kən'dʒɔɪnt/ *adj* joined together, united 结合的; 联合的—**conjointly** *adv*: *conjointly working for peace* 共同谋求和平

con·ju·gal /ˋkandʒʊgḷ; 'kɒndʒʊgəl/ *adj* [only before noun 仅用于名词前] *formal* connected with marriage【正式】婚姻的; 夫妻之间的: *They lived together in conjugal bliss.* 他们婚姻生活非常幸福。

con·ju·gate /ˋkandʒə,get; 'kɒndʒʊgeɪt/ *v technical*【术语】**1** [I] if a verb conjugates, it has different grammatical forms to show different tenses etc〔动词〕词形变化: *The verb 'to go' conjugates irregularly.* 动词 to go 词形变化不规则。**2** [T] if

you conjugate a verb, you state the different grammatical forms that it can have 列举〔动词〕的词形变化

con·ju·ga·tion /ˌkɑndʒəˋgeʃən; ˌkɒndʒʊˈgeɪʃən/ *n* [C] *technical*【术语】**1** a set of verbs in languages such as Latin that conjugate in the same way〔拉丁语等语言中的〕词形变化相同的一组动词 **2** the way that a particular verb conjugates 某一动词的所有词形变化

con·junc·tion /kənˋdʒʌŋkʃən; kənˈdʒʌŋkʃən/ *n* **1 in conjunction with** working, happening, or being used with someone or something else 与…共同, 连同: *The worksheets are designed to be used in conjunction with the new course books.* 这些练习活页是专供与新课本一起使用的。**2** [C] a combination of different things that have come together by chance〔不同事物偶然的〕同时发生: *a happy conjunction of events* 喜事连连 **3** [C] *technical* a word such as 'but', 'and', or 'while' that connects parts of sentences, phrases, or clauses (CLAUSE (2))【术语】连词

con·junc·tive /kənˋdʒʌŋktɪv; kənˈdʒʌŋktɪv/ also 又作 **con·junct** /ˋkɑndʒʌŋkt; ˈkɒndʒʌŋkt/ *n* [C] *technical* a word that joins phrases together【术语】连词 —**conjunctive** also 又作 **conjunct** /ˋkɑndʒʌŋkt; ˈkɒndʒʌŋkt/ *adj*: *a conjunctive adverb* 连接副词

con·junc·ti·vi·tis /kənˌdʒʌŋktəˋvaɪtɪs; kənˌdʒʌŋktɪˈvaɪtɪs/ *n* [U] a painful and infectious disease of the eye that makes it red 结膜炎

con·junc·ture /kənˋdʒʌŋktʃɚ; kənˈdʒʌŋktʃə/ *n* [C] *formal* a combination of events or situations, especially one that causes problems【正式】〔事件或情况的〕同时发生: *the historic conjuncture from which Marxism arose* 马克思主义产生的历史性因缘

con·jure /ˋkʌndʒɚ; ˈkʌndʒə/ *v* **1** [I,T] to perform clever tricks in which you seem to make things appear, disappear, or change as if by magic 变魔术; 用魔术变出: *The magician conjured a rabbit out of his hat.* 魔术师从帽子里变出一只兔子。**2** [T] to make something appear or happen unexpectedly 使〔某物〕突然出现[发生] **3 a name to conjure with a)** the name of a very important person 重要人物的名字 **b)** a very long name that is difficult to say 拗口的名字

conjure sth ↔ **up** *phr v* [T] **1** to bring a thought, picture, idea, or memory to someone's mind 使浮现于脑海; 使想起: *The word 'China' conjured up a whole new set of images in his mind.* China (中国) 这个词使他在脑海中浮现出一幅幅全新的景象。**2** to make something appear when it is not expected, as if by magic 魔术般变出〔某物〕: *Somehow we have to conjure up another $10,000.* 无论如何我们要再弄到 10,000 美元。**3** to make the spirit of a dead person appear by saying special magic words 念咒使〔鬼魂〕出现

conjurer 魔术师

con·jur·er, conjuror /ˋkʌndʒərɚ; ˈkʌndʒərə/ *especially BrE n* [C] someone who entertains people by performing clever tricks in which things appear, disappear, or change as if by magic【尤英】变戏法的人; 魔术师

con·jur·ing /ˋkʌndʒərɪŋ; ˈkʌndʒərɪŋ/ *n* [U] the skill of performing clever tricks in which you seem to make things appear, disappear, or change as if by magic 变戏法, 变魔术

conk[1] /kɑŋk; kɒŋk/ *n* [C] *BrE slang* a nose【英俚】鼻子

conk[2] *v* [T] *slang* to hit someone hard, especially on the head【俚】重击〔某人, 尤指头部〕

conk out *phr v* [I] *informal*【非正式】**1** if a machine or car conks out, it suddenly stops working〔机器、汽车〕突然失灵, 突然出故障: *Our car conked out on the way home.* 我们的车在回家的路上突然抛锚了。**2** *especially AmE* if someone conks out, they fall asleep because they are very tired【尤美】〔因疲劳而〕睡着: *I got home from work and I just conked out on the sofa.* 我下班回到家倒在沙发上就睡着了。

con·ker /ˋkɑŋkɚ; ˈkɒŋkə/ *n* [C] *BrE*【英】**1** the large shiny brown seed of the HORSE CHESTNUT tree 七叶树果 **2 conkers** *BrE* a children's game in which you try to break your opponent's conker by hitting it with your own【英】康克戏〔一种儿童游戏, 各方用自己的七叶树果努力击破对方的七叶树果〕

con·man /ˋkɑnmæn; ˈkɒnmæn/ *n* [C] someone who tries to get money from people by tricking them〔诈取钱财的〕骗子

Con·naught /ˋkɑnɔt; ˈkɒnɔːt/ a PROVINCE in the west of Ireland, including the counties (COUNTY) of Leitrim, Roscommon, Sligo, Mayo, and Galway 康诺特省〔位于爱尔兰西部, 包括利特里姆、罗斯康芒、斯莱戈、梅奥和戈尔韦等郡〕

con·nect /kəˋnɛkt; kəˈnekt/ *v* S2 W2

1 ▶JOIN 连接◀[T] to join two or more things together 连结, 连接: *This railway line connects London and Edinburgh.* 这条铁路线连接伦敦和爱丁堡。| **connect sth to/with** *Connect the speakers to the record player and plug it in.* 将扬声器连在唱机上, 再插上插头。| **connecting passage/door etc** (=one that joins two rooms, buildings etc) 通道/相通的门等 *We'd like two rooms with connecting doors.* 我们想要有门相通的两间房。

2 ▶REALIZE 意识到◀[T] to realize that two facts, events, or people are related to each other 意识到两个事实/事件/人是互相关联的 *She did not connect the two events in her mind.* 在她心里她没有把这两件事联系在一起。| **connect sb/sth with** *They did not at first connect her with the crime.* 起初他们并未将她与这宗罪案联系在一起。

3 ▶ELECTRICITY/GAS ETC 电/煤气等◀[T] to join something to the main supply of electricity, gas, or water, or to the telephone network 将某物与电源、煤气、水的主要管道或电话网络连接起来: *Has the phone been connected yet?* 电话接上了吗? —opposite 反义词 DISCONNECT

4 ▶TELEPHONES 电话◀[T] to join two telephone lines so that two people can speak 给…接通电话: *Please hold the line. I'm trying to connect you.* 请别挂, 我正在为您接通。

5 ▶TRAINS/BUSES 火车/巴士◀[I] if one train, bus etc connects with another, it arrives just before the other one leaves so that you can continue your journey〔火车、公共汽车等〕衔接, 联运: *I missed the connecting flight.* 我错过了联运航班。| [+with] *This train connects with the one to Glasgow.* 这班火车与去格拉斯哥的那班衔接。

6 ▶HIT STH 击打某物◀[I] *AmE* to succeed in hitting someone or something【美】击中: *He swung at the ball, but didn't connect.* 他向球挥去, 却没击中。

7 ▶UNDERSTAND PEOPLE 理解他人◀[I +with] *especially AmE* if people connect, they feel that they like each other and understand each other【尤美】与人关系融洽: *They valued her ability to empathize and connect with others.* 他们重视她能对别人表示同情和融洽相处。

connect sth ↔ **up** *phr v* [I,T] to join something to the main supply of electricity, gas, or water, or to the telephone network 将某物与电源、煤气、水的主要管道或电话网络连接: *Is the washing machine connected up yet?* 洗衣机接通了电源吗?

con·nect·ed /kəˋnɛktɪd; kəˈnektɪd/ *adj* **1** if two things are connected, they are joined together 连接的, 相连的: *The two continents were once connected.* 这两块大陆曾经是相连的。| [+to] *The wire is connected to an electrode.* 电线与一个电极相连。**2** if two facts, events, etc are connected, they affect each other or are related to each other 相关的, 关联的: [+with] *problems connected with drug abuse* 与滥用毒品相关的问题 | **closely connected** *The two ideas are closely connected, and should be dealt with together.* 这两种观念密切相连, 应该共同处理。**3 connected with sb** having a social or professional relationship with someone 与某人有社交[职业]关系: *Aren't they connected with his father's business in some way?* 他们与他父亲的企业难道没有什么联系吗? **4 well connected** having important or powerful friends or relatives 与权贵有关系的; 关系广的

Con·nec·ti·cut /kəˋnɛtɪkət; kəˈnetɪkət/ abbreviation 缩写为 **CT** a state in the northeastern US. It was one of the original thirteen states established under British rule. 康涅狄格州〔美国东北部一州, 原 13 个英属殖民地之一〕

con·nec·tion also 又作 **connexion** *BrE*【英】/kəˋnɛkʃən; kəˈnekʃən/ *n* S3 W2

1 ▶STH THAT CONNECTS THINGS 关联◀[C] the way in which two facts, ideas, events etc are related to each other, and one is affected or caused by the other 联系, 关联: [+between] *the connection between smoking and cancer* 吸烟与癌症间的关系 | [+with] *His statement had no connection with anything that had gone before.* 他的声明与此前发生的任何事情都无关。| **find/establish a connection** (=prove or discover that something is connected with something else) 发现/证明某事与另一件事

有联系 *Police have so far failed to establish a connection between the two murders.* 到目前为止警方还未能将两宗凶杀案联系起来。| **make a connection** (=realize that there is a connection) 意识到有联系 *The evidence was there in the file but no one made the connection.* 证据就在档案里，但没有人想到这一点。—see 见 RELATIONSHIP (USAGE)

2 ►JOINING THINGS TOGETHER 将事物连接起来◄ [U] the joining together of two or more things 连接: *Connection to the water mains takes only a few minutes.* 接上总水管只要几分钟。

3 in connection with concerning something 关于；有关: *The police are interviewing two men in connection with the robbery.* 警方正在查问与抢劫案有关的两个人。

4 ►ELECTRICAL WIRE 电线◄ [C] a wire or piece of metal joining two parts of a machine or electrical system 电线；起连接作用的金属: **loose connection** (=one that is not joined properly) 接触不良 *My radio isn't working properly – I think it's got a loose connection.* 我的收音机出毛病了，我想是线路接触不良。

5 ►TRAIN/BUS ETC 火车/公共汽车等◄ [C] a train, bus, or plane which is arranged to leave at a time which allows passengers from an earlier train, bus, or plane to use it to continue their journey 联运[衔接]火车[公共汽车、飞机等]: *If this train gets delayed we'll miss our connection to Paris.* 如果这辆火车晚点，我们就会误了去巴黎的联运火车。

6 ►ROAD/RAILWAY ETC 公路/铁路等◄ [C] a road, railway etc that joins two places and allows people to travel between them〔公路、铁路等连接两地的〕交通线: *Cheshunt has good rail connections to London, with trains every half hour.* 切森特与伦敦有便利的铁路交通线，每半个小时就有火车往返。

7 ►PEOPLE 人们◄ **connections** [plural] **a)** people who you know who can help you by giving you money, finding you a job etc〔能够帮你的〕人事关系: *He used his Mafia connections to find Pablo another job.* 他运用黑手党的关系为巴伯罗找到另一份工作。**b)** people who are related to you, but not very closely〔较远的〕亲戚: *He is English, but has Irish connections.* 他是英格兰人，却有爱尔兰的亲戚。—see 见 RELATIONSHIP (USAGE)

8 ►TELEPHONE 电话◄ if you have a bad connection on the telephone, you are unable to hear properly because there is a lot of noise in the telephone 电话连接: *We had such a bad connection we gave up.* 我们通话效果极差，只好挂断。

con·nec·tive¹ /kə'nɛktɪv; kə'nektɪv/ *adj* joining two or more things together 连接的: *a lack of connective knowledge* 缺乏融会贯通的知识

connective² *n* [C] *technical* a word that joins phrases, parts of sentences etc【术语】连词

connective tis·sue /·,·· '··/ *n* [U] parts of the body such as muscle or fat, that support or join organs and other body parts together 结缔组织〈如肌肉等〉

Con·ne·ry /'kɑnərɪ; 'kɒnəri/, **Sean** /ʃɔn; ʃɔːn/ (1930-) a Scottish film actor who is famous for appearing as James Bond, in films such as *Dr No* (1962), *From Russia with Love* (1963), and *Goldfinger* (1964). 康纳利〔(1930-)，苏格兰电影演员。他在《铁金刚勇破神秘岛》(1962)、《铁金刚勇破间谍网》(1963) 和《铁金刚大战金手指》(1964) 等影片中扮演詹姆斯·邦德这一角色，并因此而著名〕

con·ne·xion /kə'nɛkʃən; kə'nekʃən/ *n* a British spelling of CONNECTION connection 的英式拼法

conning tow·er /'·· ,··/ *n* [C] *technical* the structure on top of a SUBMARINE (=underwater ship)【术语】〔潜水艇顶部的〕瞭望塔

con·nip·tion fit /kə'nɪpʃən ,fɪt; kə'nɪpʃən ,fɪt/ *n* [C] *AmE, humorous* a way of behaving which shows that you are very angry【美，幽默】激怒；歇斯底里发作: **have/throw a conniption fit** *My mother threw a conniption fit when I didn't come home till two in the morning.* 我凌晨两点才回家，我母亲因此大发雷霆。

con·nive /kə'naɪv; kə'naɪv/ *v* [I] **1** to not try to stop something wrong from happening 放任；默许〔错误事情〕: [+at] *He would not be the first politician to connive at a shady business deal.* 他不会是第一个默许不正当商业交易的政客。**2 connive to do sth** to work together secretly to achieve something, especially something wrong; CONSPIRE 秘密合谋；串通: *They connived with their mother to deceive me.* 他们串通他们的母亲来骗我。—**connivance** *n* [C]: *We could not have escaped without the connivance of the guards.* 如果不是警卫默许，我们是逃不出来的。

con·niv·ing /kə'naɪvɪŋ; kə'naɪvɪŋ/ *adj* behaving in a way that does not prevent something wrong from happening, or actively helps it to happen 纵容的；默许的；串通的: *He knew all along, the conniving bastard!* 他一直都是知道的，这个同流合污的混蛋！

con·nois·seur /,kɑnə'sɝ; ,kɒnə'sɜː/ *n* [C] someone who knows a lot about something such as art, food, music etc〔艺术、食品、音乐等的〕鉴赏家，鉴定家: *a wine connoisseur* 葡萄酒鉴定家

Connolly /'kɑnəlɪ; 'kɒnəli/, **Maureen** /mɔ'rin; mɔː'riːn/ (1934-69) a US tennis player who in 1953 became the first woman to win the Wimbledon, US, and French championships in one year 康诺利〔(1934-1969)，美国网球运动员。她在1953年一年之内获得英国温布尔登网球公开赛、美国网球锦标赛以及法国网球锦标赛冠军，是同时荣获三项网球比赛冠军的首位女运动员〕

con·no·ta·tion /,kɑnə'teʃən; ,kɒnə'teɪʃən/ *n* [C] a feeling or an idea that a word makes you think of that is not its actual meaning 隐含意义；联想的含义: *'Bermuda', with its connotations of sun, sea and sand* Bermuda（百慕大）以及它给人对阳光、海洋和沙滩的联想 | *a negative connotation* 负面的含义 —compare 比较 DENOTATION —**connotative** /'kɑnə,tetɪv; 'kɒnəteɪtɪv/ *adj*

con·note /kə'not; kə'nəʊt/ *v* [T] *formal* if a word connotes something, it makes you think of feelings and ideas that are not its actual meaning【正式】〔字、词〕使人联想到〔某些感觉和想法〕；暗含: *The word 'plump' connotes cheerfulness.* plump（丰满）这个词使人联想到高兴、开朗。—compare 比较 DENOTE

con·nu·bi·al /kə'nubɪəl; kə'njuːbiəl/ *adj* **connubial bliss** *formal* the state of being happily married【正式】婚姻美满: *living in connubial bliss* 生活在幸福的婚姻中

con·quer /'kɑŋkɚ; 'kɒŋkə/ *v* **1** [I,T] to take land by attacking people or win it by fighting a war 征服: *The Normans conquered England in 1066.* 诺曼人于1066年征服英格兰。**2** [I,T] to defeat an enemy 击败，战胜: *The Zulus conquered all the neighbouring tribes.* 祖鲁人打败了所有相邻的部落。**3** [T] to gain control over something that is difficult, using a lot of effort 克服；制伏: *Gemma felt ashamed that she hadn't been able to conquer her fear.* 杰玛因未能克服自己的恐惧而感到羞愧。| *efforts to conquer inflation* 克服通货膨胀的努力 **4** [T] to succeed in climbing to the top of a mountain when no one has ever climbed it before 成功登上〔从未有人攀登过的山顶〕**5** [T] to become very successful in a place〔在某地〕大获成功: *English comedians find it difficult to conquer America.* 英国喜剧演员认为要征服美国观众绝非易事。| **conquer sb's hearts** (=make someone love you) 博得某人的欢心 *She had conquered the hearts of the local people.* 她赢得了当地人民的喜爱。—**conqueror** *n* [C] —**conquering** *adj*: *conquering heroes* 战胜的英雄们

con·quest /'kɑŋkwɛst; 'kɒŋkwest/ *n* **1** [singular,U] the act of defeating an army or taking land by fighting 击败，征服: *the Norman Conquest* 诺曼人的征服 **2** [C] land that is won in a war 占领地，征服的土地: *French conquests in Asia* 法国在亚洲的占领地 **3** [C] *often humorous* someone that you have persuaded to love you or to have sex with you【常幽默】爱情的俘虏: *He boasts about his many conquests.* 他吹嘘自己得到了许多女孩的芳心。**4** [singular] the act of gaining control of or dealing successfully with something that is difficult or dangerous 攻克，征服〔艰难、危险事物〕: [+of] *the conquest of space* 征服太空

con·quis·ta·dor /kɑn'kwɪstə,dɔr; kɒn'kwɪstədɔː/ *n* [C] [plural] conquerors of Mexico, Central and South America in the 16th century〔指16世纪墨西哥、中美洲、南美洲的〕征服者

Con·rad /'kɑnræd; 'kɒnræd/, **Joseph** (1857-1924) a British writer, born in Poland, who is one of the greatest writers of the early 20th century. His NOVELs are often about the sea and about COLONIALISM and the moral problems it involves. His best-known novels include *Heart of Darkness*, *Lord Jim*, *Nostromo*, and *The Secret Agent*. 康拉德〔(1857-1924)，英国作家，出生于波兰，20世纪早期最伟大的作家之一。其小说常描述大海、殖民主义以及关涉的道德问题。最著名的作品有《黑暗的中心》、《吉姆老爷》、《诺斯特罗莫》和《特务》〕

Con·rail, ConRail /'kɑnrel; 'kɒnreɪl/ *trademark* a system of railways in the US for carrying FREIGHT (=goods carried by train), which is based around the northeastern US【商标】联合铁路〔以美国东北部一带为基地的铁路货运系统〕—compare 比较 AMTRAK

con·san·guin·i·ty /,kɑnsæŋ'gwɪnətɪ; ,kɒnsæŋ'gwɪnɪti/ *n* [U] *formal* the state of being members of the same family【正式】血缘；血亲关系

con·science /'kɑnʃəns; 'kɒnʃəns/ *n* [C,U]

1 ►MIND 思想◄ the part of your mind that tells you whether what you are doing is morally right or wrong 良知，良心: *Be guided by your conscience.* 听从良心的召唤。| **a social conscience** (=a moral sense of how society should be) 社会良知 | **a guilty/bad conscience** (=feel guilty because you have done

something wrong) 负疚的心情 *It was his guilty conscience that made him offer to help.* 他是因为心中有愧才提出要帮忙的。| **a clear conscience** (=a feeling that you have done nothing wrong) 无愧良心 *Well at least I can face them all with a clear conscience.* 至少我可以问心无愧地面对他们。| **a twinge/pang of conscience** (=guilty feeling) 一阵内疚的感觉 *Ian felt a pang of conscience at having misjudged her.* 伊恩因为冤枉了她而感到负疚。| **have no conscience (about sth)** (=not feel guilty about something) (对某事) 没有负疚感 *They've no conscience at all about cheating.* 他们一点也不因为行骗而受到良心谴责。| **a prisoner of conscience** (=someone who is in prison because of their political or religious beliefs) 政治犯, 思想犯 | **a matter of conscience** (=something that you must make a moral judgment about) 良心问题 *I can't tell you what to do – it's a matter of conscience.* 我无法告诉你该如何办——这是一个事关良心的问题。

2 on your conscience if you have something on your conscience it makes you feel guilty 内疚, 受到良心的谴责: *If anything happens to her I'll always have it on my conscience.* 如果她出什么问题, 我将永远受到良心谴责。

3 prick your conscience if an action or event pricks your conscience, it makes you feel guilty 问心有愧, 使良心不安: *The dog's sad look pricked her conscience and she took him home.* 那只狗可怜的神情使她良心不安, 她便带它回家了。

4 clear your conscience to make yourself stop feeling guilty by telling someone about what you did wrong 〔承认错误〕解除内疚感: *Terry decided to clear his conscience and confess.* 特里决心解除自己心中的内疚感, 便坦白了。

5 in all conscience *formal* if you cannot in all conscience do something, you cannot do it because you think it is wrong【正式】凭良心〔不能做某些事情, 因为它是错的〕: *I couldn't in all conscience tell him that his job was safe.* 凭良心我不能对他说那份工作很保险。

6 in good conscience if you do something in good conscience, you do it because you think it is the right thing to do 凭良心〔应该做某事情, 因为它是正确的〕: *statements made in good conscience* 凭良心做出的陈述

conscience clause /ˈ··, ·/ *n* [C] a part of a law that says that the law does not have to be obeyed by people who feel that it would be morally wrong to obey it 〔法律的〕道德条款〔说明如果有人认为遵守这条法律违反道德, 可以不必遵守〕

conscience-strick·en /ˈ··, ··/ also 又作 **conscience-smitten** *adj* very sorry that you have done something wrong 良心不安的, 受良心谴责的: *Kate hurried home, conscience-stricken at leaving her mother alone.* 凯特匆忙赶回家, 因为让母亲独自一人感到十分内疚。

con·sci·en·tious /ˌkɑnʃiˈɛnʃəs; ˌkɒnʃiˈenʃəs◂/ *adj* showing a lot of care and attention 认真的; 细心负责的: *a conscientious and methodical worker* 一个工作认真, 有条不紊的人 —**conscientiously** *adv* —**conscientiousness** *n* [U]: *praised for her conscientiousness* 称赞她的认真负责

conscientious ob·jec·tor /ˌ···· ·ˈ··/ *n* [C] someone who refuses to become a soldier because of their moral or religious beliefs 〔由于道德或宗教的原因〕拒服兵役者 —see also 另见 DRAFT DODGER

CULTURAL NOTE 文化注释

During wars when men had a legal duty to fight in the armed forces, conscientious objectors in the US and UK were usually asked to prove that they belonged to a religious or PACIFIST group. During World War I and World War II, many were put into prison because they could not prove this. 战争期间男子有服兵役的义务时, 在美国和英国, 通常会要求拒服兵役者证明自己从属于某个宗教或和平主义者团体。两次世界大战期间, 很多人因无法提供此类证明而被关进监狱。

S2 W3 **con·scious** /ˈkɑnʃəs; ˈkɒnʃəs/ *adj* **1** [not before noun 不用于名词前] noticing or realizing something; AWARE 注意到的; 意识到的: **conscious of (doing) sth** *I was very conscious of the fact that I had to make a good impression.* 我非常明白必须给人留下一个好印象。| **conscious that** *I was conscious that she was ill at ease.* 我注意到她有点局促不安。**2** awake and able to understand what is happening around you 清醒的: *The driver was still conscious when the ambulance reached the scene of the accident.* 当救护车赶到事故现场时, 司机仍然神志清醒。**3 a conscious effort/decision/attempt etc** an effort etc that is deliberate and intended 特意做出的努力/决定/尝试等: *Vivien had made a conscious effort to be friendly.* 维维恩有意地努力表示友善。**4 safety-conscious/fashion-conscious etc** thinking a lot about safety, fashion etc 特别注意安全的/十分关注时尚的等: *recipes for calorie-conscious slimmers* 为特别注意热量摄取的减肥者准备的食谱 —see also 另见 SELF-CONSCIOUS —opposite 反义词 UNCONSCIOUS[1] —**consciously** *adv*

con·scious·ness /ˈkɑnʃəsnɪs; ˈkɒnʃəsnəs/ *n* **1** [U] the condition of being awake and able to understand what is happening around you 神志, 知觉: **lose consciousness** (=go into a deep sleep) 失去知觉 *David lost consciousness at eight o'clock and died a few hours later.* 戴维在8点钟失去知觉, 几小时后便去世了。| **regain consciousness** (=wake up) 恢复知觉 *She could faintly hear voices as she began to regain consciousness.* 当她开始恢复知觉时, 她能隐约听见声音。**2** [U] your mind and your thoughts 思想, 意识: *Even the most important issues eventually fade from your consciousness.* 就连最重要的事情最终都会从你的思想意识中淡出。**3** [U] someone's ideas, feelings, or opinions about politics, life etc 观念, 感觉, 意见: *The experience helped to change her political consciousness.* 这次经历有助于改变她的政治观点。**4** [singular] the state of knowing that something exists or is true; AWARENESS 感知; 察觉: *a consciousness of danger* 对危险的意识 —see also 另见 STREAM OF CONSCIOUSNESS W3

C

consciousness rais·ing /ˈ··· ,··/ *n* [U] the process of making people understand and care more about a moral, social, or political problem 〔对道德、社会或政治问题的〕意识提高

con·script[1] /kənˈskrɪpt; kənˈskrɪpt/ *v* [T+into] **1** to make someone join the army, navy etc 征召〔入伍〕: *young Frenchmen who were conscripted into the army and forced to fight in Algeria* 征召入伍被迫在阿尔及利亚作战的年轻法国人 **2** to make someone become a member of a group or take part in a particular activity 吸纳…为成员, 使加入 —compare 比较 RECRUIT[1]

con·script[2] /ˈkɑnskrɪpt; ˈkɒnskrɪpt/ *n* [C] someone who has been made to join the army, navy etc 征召入伍者 —compare 比较 RECRUIT[2]

con·scrip·tion /kənˈskrɪpʃən; kənˈskrɪpʃən/ *n* [U] the practice of making people join the army, navy etc; DRAFT[1] (2a) 征兵 —see also 另见 NATIONAL SERVICE

con·se·crate /ˈkɑnsɪˌkret; ˈkɒnsɪkreɪt/ *v* [T] **1** to officially state in a special religious ceremony that a place or building is holy and can be used for religious purposes 〔举行特别宗教仪式〕宣布〔某地〕为神圣 **2** to officially state in a special religious ceremony that someone is now a priest, BISHOP (1) etc 〔举行特别宗教仪式〕宣布〔某人〕为牧师[主教]等 —**consecrated** *adj*: *consecrated ground* 圣地 —**consecration** /ˌkɑnsɪˈkreʃən; ˌkɒnsɪˈkreɪʃən/ *n* [U]

con·sec·u·tive /kənˈsɛkjətɪv; kənˈsekjətɪv/ *adj* consecutive numbers or periods of time follow one after the other without any interruptions 连续的, 不间断的: *It had rained for four consecutive days.* 雨接连下了四天。—**consecutively** *adv*: *Number the pages consecutively.* 请用连续的数字编页码。

con·sen·sus /kənˈsɛnsəs; kənˈsensəs/ *n* [singular,U] an opinion that everyone in a group will agree with or accept 共同意见, 一致看法, 共识: **reach a consensus on** *The EC Council of Finance Ministers failed to reach a consensus on the pace of integration.* 欧共体财政部长会议未能就一体化的速度达成共识。| **consensus politics** (=political ideas and actions that everyone accepts in a general way) 代表民意的政治观点[行动]

con·sent[1] /kənˈsɛnt; kənˈsent/ *n* [U] **1** permission to do something especially by someone in authority or by someone who is responsible for something 许可, 允许: **without sb's consent** *He took the car without the owner's consent.* 他没有得到车主的许可, 就把车开走了。| **give your consent** (=allow something to happen) 许可 —see also 另见 AGE OF CONSENT **2** agreement about something 同意, 赞同: **by common consent** (=with most people agreeing) 得到大多数人的同意 *The chairman was elected by common consent.* 主席是经大多数人同意选举出来的。| **by mutual consent** (=by agreement between both the people or groups of people involved) 经双方同意 *divorce by mutual consent* 双方同意离婚 **3 with one consent** *old use* if people do something with one consent, they all agree to do it【旧】全体一致同意 —see also 另见 ASSENT, DISSENT W3

consent[2] *v* [I] to give your permission for something or agree to do something 同意, 允许: **[+to]** *Her father reluctantly consented to the marriage.* 她父亲勉强答应了这门婚事。

consenting ad·ult /ˌ·· ˈ··/ *n* [C] *law* someone who is considered to be old enough to decide whether they want to have sex【法律】〔指已到达某年龄, 可以自行决定是否与人发生性关系的〕成年人 —see also 另见 AGE OF CONSENT

con·se·quence /ˈkɑnsəˌkwɛns; ˈkɒnsɨkwəns/ *n* **1** [C] something that happens as a result of a particular action or set of conditions 后果: *the harmful social consequences of high levels of unemployment* 高失业率给社会带来的不良后果 | *The safety procedures had been ignored, with potentially tragic consequences.* 安全程序被忽视，可能带来悲惨的后果。| **take/suffer/face the consequences (of sth)** (=to accept the bad results of something you have done) 接受/承担/面对(某事的)后果 *He broke the law, and now he must face the consequences of his actions.* 他触犯了法律，现在必须承担自己的行为带来的后果。**2 as a consequence (of sth)/in consequence (of sth)** *formal* as a result of something【正式】因为; 由于: *the rise in sea levels predicted as a consequence of global warming* 由于全球气候变暖而预测的海平面升高 **3 of little/no/any consequence** *formal* of little importance or value【正式】不重要的/无足轻重的: *Your opinion is of little consequence to me.* 你的意见对我而言不重要。

Con·se·quen·ces /ˈkɑnsəˌkwɛnsɪz; ˈkɒnsɨkwənsɨz/ a game played by a small group of people, in which a story is written with each person adding a sentence without knowing what has already been written. The last sentence begins: 'The CONSEQUENCE (=result) was...' The stories are usually about famous people or friends, in amusing or embarrassing situations. 连环叙事游戏〔多人参与的一种编故事游戏。每个人依次加入一句话，但都不知道前面写了些什么。最后一句的开头为“结局是…”。故事通常讲述名人或朋友可笑或尴尬的经历〕

con·se·quent /ˈkɑnsəˌkwɛnt; ˈkɒnsɨkwənt/ *adj formal* happening as a result of a particular event or situation【正式】随之发生的; 由某事引起的: *the rise in inflation and consequent fall in demand* 通货膨胀的上升和随之而来的需求下降 —compare 比较 SUBSEQUENT

con·se·quen·tial /ˌkɑnsəˈkwɛnʃəl; ˌkɒnsɨˈkwenʃəl◂/ *adj formal*【正式】**1** happening as a direct result of a particular event or situation 随之发生的: *redundancy and the consequential loss of earnings* 裁员以及随之而来的收入损失 **2** important; SIGNIFICANT 重要的, 意义重大的: *a consequential decision* 重要的决定 —opposite 反义词 INCONSEQUENTIAL —**consequentially** *adv*

con·se·quent·ly /ˈkɑnsəˌkwɛntlɪ; ˈkɒnsɨkwəntli/ *adv* [sentence adverb 句子副词] as a result 结果, 所以: *We talked until the early hours, and consequently I overslept.* 我们聊到凌晨，结果我睡过头了。| *The bank refused to give the company more time. Consequently, it went bankrupt.* 银行拒绝给这家公司更多的宽限，结果它倒闭了。—see 见 THUS (USAGE)

con·ser·van·cy /kənˈsɝvənsɪ; kənˈsɜːvənsi/ *n* [U] *BrE*【英】**1** a group of officials who control and protect an area of land, a river etc〔河道、土地等的〕管理局, 管理机构: *the Thames Conservancy* 泰晤士河管理委员会 **2** the protection of natural things such as animals, plants, forests etc; CONSERVATION (1)〔动植物、森林等的〕保护

con·ser·va·tion /ˌkɑnsəˈveʃən; ˌkɒnsəˈveɪʃən/ *n* [U] **1** the protection of natural things such as animals, plants, forests etc, to prevent them being spoiled, or destroyed〔动植物、森林等的〕保护: *wildlife conservation* 野生生物保护 **2** the act of preventing something from being lost or wasted 保存, 保护: [+of] *conservation of energy* 能源保护

conservation a·re·a /ˌ..ˈ.. ,..ˈ../ *n* [C] **1** an area where animals and plants are protected〔动植物的〕保护区 **2** an area where interesting old buildings are protected and new buildings are carefully controlled〔保护特色古旧建筑物并且控制新建筑物的〕保护区

con·ser·va·tion·ist /ˌkɑnsəˈveʃənɪst; ˌkɒnsəˈveɪʃənɨst/ *n* [C] someone who works to protect animals, plants etc or to protect old buildings〔动植物等或古旧建筑的〕保护工作者 —**conservationism** *n* [U]

con·ser·va·tis·m /kənˈsɝvətɪzəm; kənˈsɜːvətɪzəm/ *n* [U] **1** dislike of change and new ideas 守旧, 保守主义: *people's innate conservatism in matters of language* 人们在语言方面的天生守旧 **2** also 又作 **Conservatism** the political belief that society should change as little as possible 政治保守, 因循守旧 **3 Conservatism** the political beliefs of the Conservative Party 保守党的政治主张

CULTURAL NOTE 文化注释

In Britain, conservatism is usually thought of in connection with the Conservative Party. In the US, it is usually thought of in connection with the Republican Party. 英国人常认为保守党奉行保守主义, 美国人常认为共和党奉行保守主义。

con·ser·va·tive¹ /kənˈsɝvətɪv; kənˈsɜːvətɪv/ *adj* **1 Conservative** belonging to or concerned with the Conservative Party in Britain〔英国〕保守党的: *Conservative policies* 保守党的政策 | *a Conservative MP* 保守党下议院议员 **2** not liking changes or new ideas 因循守旧的, 不喜变化的: *a very conservative attitude to education* 对于教育非常守旧的态度 **3** not very modern in style, taste etc; traditional〔式样、口味等〕不时兴的, 传统的: *a very conservative suit* 一套非常老式的衣服 **4 a conservative estimate/guess** a guess which is deliberately lower than the real amount 保守的估计/猜测: *At a conservative estimate, the holiday will cost about £1,500.* 根据保守的估计, 这次外出度假要花费约 1500 英镑。—**conservatively** *adv*

conservative² *n* [C] **1 Conservative** someone who supports or is a member of the Conservative Party in Britain 英国保守党的支持者; 保守党党员 **2** someone who does not like changes in ideas or fashion 因循守旧者, 保守者: *Aunt May is a real conservative. She's totally opposed to mothers going out to work.* 梅姨是个真正的保守派, 她完全不赞成做了母亲的妇女外出工作。

Conservative Par·ty /.'... ,..../ *n* **the Conservative Party** a British political party on the RIGHT 保守党〔英国右翼政党〕

con·ser·va·toire /kənˌsɝvəˈtwɑr; kənˈsɜːvətwɑː/ *n* [C] *BrE* a school where people are trained in music or acting【英】音乐学院; 戏剧学院; CONSERVATORY *AmE*【美】

con·ser·va·to·ry /kənˈsɝvəˌtorɪ; kənˈsɜːvətəri/ *n* [C] **1** a room with glass walls and a glass roof, where plants are grown, that is usually added on to the side of a house 温室, 玻璃暖房 **2** *AmE* a school where people are trained in music or acting【美】音乐学院; 戏剧学院; CONSERVATOIRE *BrE*【英】

con·serve¹ /kənˈsɝv; kənˈsɜːv/ *v* [T] **1** to protect something and try to prevent it from changing or being damaged 保护; 保存: *We must conserve our woodlands for future generations.* 我们必须为后代保护林地。**2** to use as little water, energy etc as possible so that it is not wasted 节约〔水、能源等〕: *conserving electricity* 节约电

con·serve² /ˈkɑnsɝv; ˈkɒnsɜːv/ *n* [C,U] *formal* fruit that is preserved by being cooked with sugar; JAM¹ (1)【正式】蜜饯; 果酱

con·sid·er /kənˈsɪdə; kənˈsɪdə/ *v*

1 ▶THINK ABOUT 考虑◀ [I,T] to think about something, especially about whether to accept something or do something 考虑, 细想〔尤指是否接受或做某事〕: *He paused to consider his options.* 他停下来考虑应该作何选择。| *Any reasonable offer will be considered.* 任何合理报价都将予以考虑。| **consider doing sth** *I'm considering applying for that job.* 我在考虑是否申请那份工作。| **consider where/how/why etc** *We're still considering where to move to.* 我们仍在考虑搬到哪里去。

2 ▶HAVE AN OPINION 有某种看法◀ [T] to think of someone or something in a particular way 对某人/某事有某种看法: **consider sb/sth (to be) wise/important etc** *A further increase in interest rates is now considered unlikely.* 进一步上调利率现在被认为不大可能。| **consider sth an honour/a duty etc** *I consider it a great honour to be invited.* 承蒙邀请深感荣幸。| **consider sb (to be) a fool/hero etc** *Liz Quinn was considered an excellent teacher.* 莉兹·奎因被认为是一位优秀的教师。

3 consider yourself lucky to think you are fortunate 自认幸运: *Consider yourself lucky you weren't in the car at the time.* 你当时不在车里, 你应该感到庆幸。

4 ▶REMEMBER TO THINK OF 记得考虑◀ [T] to remember to think carefully about something before making a judgment or a decision〔在作出判断或决定前〕仔细考虑: *Before you resign you should consider the effect it will have on your family.* 你辞职前要考虑一下这会给你家庭带来怎样的影响。| **consider that** *If you consider that she's only been studying English for six months, she speaks it very well.* 如果考虑到她学英语才六个月, 她的英语可以说讲得非常好了。| **consider what/how/who etc** *Have you considered how difficult it is for these refugees?* 你有没有考虑过这些难民会有多么艰难?

5 ▶PEOPLE'S FEELINGS 人们的感情◀ [T] to think about someone or their feelings etc and try to avoid upsetting or hurting them 体谅, 体贴: *God, you're so selfish! You've got to learn to consider other people!* 天啊, 你太自私了!你必须学会替别人着想!

6 ▶DISCUSS FORMALLY 正式讨论◀ [T] to discuss something such as a report or problem, so that you can make a decision about it 讨论: *The committee has been considering the report.* 该委员会一直在讨论这份报告。

7 ▶LOOK AT 注视◀ [T] *formal* to look at someone or something carefully【正式】仔细端详: *Henry considered the sculpture with an expert eye.* 亨利以专家的眼光审视这尊雕塑。

8 **be considering your position** *formal* to be deciding whether or not to leave your job【正式】考虑是否辞职

con·sid·e·ra·ble /kən`sɪdərəbl; kən'sɪdərəbəl/ *adj* fairly large, especially large enough to have an effect or be important 相当大的〔尤指大到足以产生某种影响的程度〕: *She has considerable influence with the President.* 她对总统有相当大的影响。| *A statue was erected at considerable public expense.* 竖起了一座雕像，花了公众不少钱。—compare 比较 INCONSIDERABLE

con·sid·e·ra·bly /kən`sɪdərəblɪ; kən'sɪdərəbli/ *adv* **considerably more/colder/higher etc** much more, much colder etc 多得多，冷得多，高得多等: *It's considerably colder today.* 今天冷多了。

con·sid·er·ate /kən`sɪdərɪt; kən'sɪdərḷt/ *adj* always thinking of what other people need or want and taking care not to upset them 关切的，体贴的；替他人着想的: *Diana is a considerate boss who is always willing to listen.* 黛安娜是一位体贴的老板，她总是乐于听取意见。| **considerate of sb (to do sth)** *It was very considerate of you to let us know you were going to be late.* 你让我们知道你会迟到，真是考虑周到。—opposite 反义词 INCONSIDERATE—**considerately** *adv*—**considerateness** *n* [U]

con·sid·e·ra·tion /kən,sɪdə`reʃən; kən,sɪdə'reɪʃən/ *n*
1 ►**THOUGHT** 思想◄ [U] *formal* careful thought and attention【正式】考虑，斟酌: **under consideration** (=being discussed and thought about so that an official decision can be made) 在讨论中，在研究中，在考虑中 *There are several amendments under consideration.* 好几项修正案正在讨论中。| **due/long consideration** *After due consideration, I have decided to tender my resignation.* 在作适当的考虑后，我决定递交辞呈。| **give sth your fullest consideration** (=think about it very carefully before making an official decision) 在作正式决定前充分考虑某事
2 **take sth into consideration** to remember to think about something important when you are making a decision or judgement 〔在作出决定或判断之前〕考虑到某事: *Your teachers will take your recent illness into consideration when marking your exams.* 你的老师在批改你的试卷时，会考虑到你最近生病这一情况的。
3 ►**STH THAT AFFECTS A DECISION** 影响决定的因素◄ [C] something that you must think about when you are planning to do something, which affects what you decide to do 须考虑的因素: *Political rather than economic considerations influenced the location of the new factory.* 影响新工厂位置的是政治因素而不是经济原因。
4 ►**KINDNESS** 善意◄ [U] the quality of thinking about other people's feelings and taking care not to upset them 体贴，体谅: **out of consideration for** *The murdered woman's name has not been released, out of consideration for her parents.* 为了保护她父母，没有公布被害妇女的姓名。| **show consideration for** *Jeff never shows any consideration for his mother's feelings.* 杰夫从来不体谅他母亲的心情。
5 **of no consideration/of little consideration** *formal* if something is of no consideration it is not at all important【正式】毫不重要的
6 **in consideration of** *formal* as payment for something【正式】〔为某事所付的〕报酬: *a small payment in consideration of your services* 作为答谢你帮忙的一点报酬
7 ►**MONEY** 金钱◄ [singular] *formal* a payment for a service【正式】服务费，酬金: **for a small consideration** *I might be able to help you, for a small consideration.* 我也许能够效劳，但要收少许费用。

con·sid·ered /kən`sɪdəd; kən'sɪdəd/ *adj* 1 **considered opinion/judgement etc** an opinion based on careful thought 仔细考虑过的意见／判断等 2 **well/poorly/highly considered** thought to be good, bad etc 评价很好／不好／很高: *Her paintings are very well considered abroad.* 她的画在国外评价很高。3 **all things considered** *usually spoken* used to say what you believe after thinking about all the facts【一般口】从各个方面考虑之后，全面考虑之后: *All things considered, I'm sure we made the right decision.* 通盘考虑之后，我认为我们的决定是正确的。

con·sid·er·ing¹ /kən`sɪdərɪŋ; kən'sɪdərɪŋ/ *prep, conjunction* used when describing a situation, before stating a fact that you know has had an effect on that situation 考虑到，鉴于〔用来描绘某一情况，常用于陈述对该情况有所影响的某事实之前〕: *Considering the strength of the opposition, we did very well to score two goals.* 考虑到对方的实力，我们能攻进两球就很不错了。| **considering that/who/how etc** *John did quite well in his exams considering how little he studied.* 考虑到约翰才学了那么一点点，他考得已算不错了。

considering² *adv spoken* used at the end of a phrase when you are expressing an opinion about something in spite of another fact【口】细细想来，通盘考虑〔用于短语末尾，表示"尽管…"〕: *Mum didn't look too bad, considering.* 从各方面看，妈妈的气色并不是太差。

con·sign /kən`saɪn; kən'saɪn/ *v* [T] *formal*【正式】1 to put someone or something somewhere, especially in order to get rid of them〔尤指为丢弃而〕移走；处置: **consign sb/sth to** *I consigned his letter to the dustbin.* 我把他的信扔进了垃圾桶。| *She preferred to take care of her mother at home, rather than consigning her to institutional care.* 她情愿在家里照顾她母亲，而不愿交给养老院照顾。| **consign sb/sth to the flames** *literary* (=burn someone or something)【文】烧毁，焚烧，火化 *The body was consigned to the flames.* 尸体被火化了。2 to send or deliver something to someone who has bought it 运送〔商品给购买者〕 3 to make someone or something be in a particular situation, especially an unpleasant one 使…陷于〔某种令人不快的境地〕: **consign sb/sth to** *consigning Cambodia to a decade of civil war* 使柬埔寨陷入10年内战

con·sign·ee /,kɑnsaɪ`ni; ,kɒnsaɪ'niː/ *n* [C] *technical* the person that something is delivered to【术语】收件人，收货人

con·sign·ment /kən`saɪnmənt; kən'saɪnmənt/ *n* 1 [C] a quantity of goods delivered at the same time 同时运送的一批货物: [+of] *a new consignment of computer games* 一批新托运的电脑游戏 2 [U] the act of delivering things 运送，托运

con·sign·or, consigner /kən`saɪnə; kən'saɪnə/ *n* [C] *technical* the person who sends goods to someone else【术语】寄件人，发货人，托运人

con·sist /kən`sɪst; kən'sɪst/ *v*

consist in sth *phr v* [T not in progressive 不用进行时] *formal* to be based on or depend upon something【正式】在于，决定于: *The beauty of Venice consists largely in the style of its ancient buildings.* 威尼斯的美丽主要在于其古建筑物的风格。

consist of sth *phr v* [T not in progressive 不用进行式] used to say what something is made of when it contains a number of parts or things 由…组成，由…构成: *Bolognaise sauce consists of minced beef, onion, tomatoes, garlic and seasoning.* 博洛尼亚肉酱由碎牛肉、洋葱、番茄、大蒜和佐料调制而成。

con·sis·ten·cy /kən`sɪstənsɪ; kən'sɪstənsi/ *n* 1 [U] the quality of always being the same or always being good 连贯性，前后一致: *Replies to these questions showed no real consistency.* 对这些问题的答案前后并不一致。—opposite 反义词 INCONSISTENCY 2 [C,U] how firm or thick a mixture is 坚实度；浓度: *Beat the butter and sugar until the mixture has the consistency of thick cream.* 将黄油和糖搅拌，直到达到稠奶油的浓度。

con·sis·tent /kən`sɪstənt; kən'sɪstənt/ *adj* 1 always having the same beliefs, behaviour, attitudes, quality etc〔信仰、行为、态度、品质等〕一贯的，一致的: *one of the most consistent players on the tennis circuit* 网球巡回赛场上状态最稳定的运动员之一 | *a consistent supporter of constitutional rights* 宪法权利一贯的支持者 2 continuing to develop in the same way 稳定发展的，持续不变的: *a consistent improvement in the country's economy* 该国经济的持续好转 3 a consistent argument or idea is organized so that each part agrees with the others〔论点或看法〕前后一致的 4 **be consistent with** if something that is said, written, or done is consistent with a particular idea or piece of information, it says the same thing or follows the same principles〔所说、所写或所做的事与某一观点或信息〕相一致的，相吻合的: *This evidence is not consistent with what you said earlier.* 这项证据与你先前所说的有矛盾。—opposite 反义词 INCONSISTENT—**consistently** *adv*: *I'm fed up with your consistently negative attitude.* 你一贯的消极态度令我感到厌烦。

con·so·la·tion /,kɑnsə`leʃən; ,kɒnsə'leɪʃən/ *n* [C,U] someone or something that makes you feel better when you are sad or disappointed 安慰；起安慰作用的人[物]: *It was some consolation for me to know that I had only failed by 2%.* 知道自己只差两分就及格，这多少是一种安慰。

consolation prize /,.'..../ *n* [C] a prize that is given to someone who has not won a competition 鼓励奖，安慰奖: *Ten runners-up each received a T-shirt as a consolation prize.* 10名冠军以下的优胜者每人得到一件T恤衫作为安慰奖。

con·sol·a·to·ry /kən`sɑlə,torɪ; kən'sɒlətəri/ *adj formal* intended to make someone feel better【正式】安慰的，抚慰的

con·sole¹ /kən`sol; kən'səʊl/ *v* [T] to make someone feel better when they are feeling sad or disappointed 安慰，慰藉，安抚: *No one could console her when Peter died.* 彼得死后没人能安慰她。| **console sb with** *Console yourself with the thought that no one was injured!* 没有人受伤，这是值得庆幸的！

con·sole² /ˋkɑnsol; ˈkɒnsəʊl/ *n* [C] **1** a flat board that contains the controls for a machine, piece of electrical equipment, computer etc〔机器、电子设备、电脑等的〕操纵台盘，控制台盘: *a games console* 游戏机操纵盘 **2** a special cupboard in which a television, computer etc is fitted〔放置电视机、电脑等的〕落地柜；电脑桌

con·sol·i·date /kənˋsɑləˌdet; kənˈsɒlɪ̵deɪt/ *v* [I,T] **1** to make your position of power stronger and more likely to continue, or maintain the same level of achievement, profit, success etc so that it seems likely to continue 加强〔实力地位〕，巩固〔成就、利润、成功等〕: *His successful negotiations with the Americans helped him to consolidate his position.* 他与美国人的成功谈判巩固了他的地位。| *Canon has consolidated its hold on the European market.* 佳能加强了它在欧洲市场的地位。**2** to join together a group of companies, organizations etc, or to become jointed together 将〔公司、组织等〕合并，联合 **3** to combine several jobs, duties etc together 将〔几个职位、职责等〕合并 —**consolidated** *adj* —**consolidation** /kənˌsɑləˋdeʃən; kənˌsɒlɪ̵ˈdeɪʃən/ *n* [C,U]

C

con·som·mé /ˌkɑnsəˋme; kənˈsɒmeɪ/ *n* [U] clear soup made from meat or vegetables 用肉或蔬菜制作的清汤

con·so·nance /ˋkɑnsənəns; ˈkɒnsənəns/ *n* **1 in consonance with** *formal* agreeing with something or existing together without any problems【正式】〔与某物〕一致[协调相处] **2** [C,U] *technical* a combination of musical notes that sound pleasant; HARMONY (1)【术语】〔音乐〕协和音，和音

con·so·nant¹ /ˋkɑnsənənt; ˈkɒnsənənt/ *n* [C] **1** a speech sound made by partly or completely stopping the flow of air through the mouth 辅音 **2** a letter that represents one of these sounds. The letters 'a', 'e', 'i', 'o', and 'u' represent vowels, and all the other letters are consonants 辅音字母〔a, e, i, o, u 五个字母代表元音，所有其他字母均是辅音〕

consonant² *adj* **1 consonant with** *formal* not seeming to show that a statement or belief is wrong【正式】一致的，符合的: *This policy is scarcely consonant with the government's declared aims.* 这项政策与政府公布的目标简直自相矛盾。**2** *technical* being a combination of musical notes that sounds pleasant【术语】协和音的

con·sort¹ /ˋkɑnsɔrt; ˈkɒnsɔːt/ *n* [C] **1 in consort (with sb)** *formal* doing something together with someone【正式】〔与某人〕一起〔做某事〕: *The prince ruled in consort with his father.* 王子与他的父亲共同执政。**2** the wife or husband of a ruler 统治者的配偶 —see also 另见 PRINCE CONSORT **3** a group of people who play music from former times or the group of old-fashioned instruments they use〔演奏往日音乐的〕一群乐师；一批老式乐器

con·sort² /kənˋsɔrt; kənˈsɔːt/ *v formal* [I+with/together] to spend time with someone who other people disapprove of【正式】与名声不好的人结交；勾结: **consorting with the enemy** (=spending time with and helping the enemies of your country) 与敌人朋比为奸

con·sor·ti·um /kənˋsɔrtɪəm; kənˈsɔːtiəm/ *n plural* **consortiums** *or* **consortia** [C] a combination of several companies, banks etc working together to buy something, build something etc〔公司、银行等为了进行购买或建筑而组成的〕财团，联合企业

con·spec·tus /kənˋspɛktəs; kənˈspektəs/ *n* [C] *formal* a short report giving the most important ideas of a subject【正式】大纲，摘要

con·spic·u·ous /kənˋspɪkjuəs; kənˈspɪkjuəs/ *adj* **1** someone or something that is conspicuous is very easy to notice, especially because they are different from everything or everyone else around them 显著的，显眼的；与众不同的: *I felt very conspicuous in my suit – everyone else was in jeans.* 我觉得自己穿套装很显眼，因为别人都是穿牛仔裤。**2** unusually good, bad, skilful etc; REMARKABLE 引人注目的: *The campaign had been a conspicuous success.* 这次活动取得了令人瞩目的成功。**3 conspicuous by your absence** used to say that people noticed that you were not in the place you should have been 缺席引人注意 —opposite 反义词 INCONSPICUOUS —**conspicuously** *adv* —**conspicuousness** *n* [U]

con·spi·ra·cy /kənˋspɪrəsɪ; kənˈspɪrəsi/ *n* [C,U] a secret plan made by two or more people to do something that is harmful or illegal 密谋，阴谋: **conspiracy to (do) sth** *a conspiracy to smuggle drugs into the country* 走私毒品到这个国家的阴谋 | **conspiracy against** *a conspiracy against the elected government* 反对民选政府的阴谋 | **conspiracy of silence** (=an agreement to keep quiet about something that should not be a secret) 对不该保密的事缄口不谈的密约 | **conspiracy theory** (=the idea that an event was caused by a conspiracy) 阴谋论〔某事件是由阴谋所导致的观点〕*conspiracy theories about President Kennedy's assassination* 关于肯尼迪总统被暗杀的种种阴谋论

con·spi·ra·tor /kənˋspɪrətɚ; kənˈspɪrətə/ *n* [C] someone who is involved in a secret plan to do something harmful or illegal 阴谋家；共谋者

con·spi·ra·to·ri·al /kənˌspɪrəˋtɔrɪəl; kənˌspɪrəˈtɔːriəl/ *adj* **1** connected with a secret plan to do something harmful or illegal 阴谋的: *conspiratorial discussions* 策划阴谋的讨论 **2 conspiratorial grin/giggle/wink etc** one between two people who know a secret 诡秘的微笑/傻笑/眨眼等〔指掌握了某一秘密的两人之间交换的神色等〕—**conspiratorially** *adv*

con·spire /kənˋspaɪr; kənˈspaɪə/ *v* [I] **1** to plan something harmful or illegal together secretly 密谋；共谋；搞阴谋: **conspire (with sb) to do sth** *He had conspired with an accomplice to rob the bank.* 他与一个同谋秘密策划抢劫这家银行。| **conspire against sb** *Mentally ill people sometimes believe that relatives are conspiring against them.* 精神病人有时会认为家人密谋暗算他。**2** if events conspire to make something happen, they happen at the same time and make something bad happen〔事件〕凑在一起，共同导致: **conspire to do sth** *Technological failure and atmospheric conditions conspired to make take-off impossible.* 技术故障和大气情况凑在一起使飞机不能起飞。

con·sta·ble /ˋkɑnstəbl̩; ˈkʌnstəbəl/ *n* [C] a British police officer of the lowest rank〔英国级别最低的〕警官 —see also 另见 PATROLMAN (1)

Constable /ˋkanstəbl̩; ˈkɒnstəbəl/, **John** (1776-1837) a British painter famous for his paintings and drawings of the Suffolk countryside, especially *The Haywain* 康斯太布尔〔(1776-1837)，英国画家。他创作的萨福克乡村油画和素描十分著名，尤其是《干草车》〕

con·stab·u·la·ry /kənˋstæbjəˌlɛrɪ; kənˈstæbjɪ̵ləri/ *n* [C] *BrE* the police force of a particular area or country【英】〔某国家或地区的〕警察部队 —see also 另见 PATROL² (2)

con·stan·cy /ˋkɑnstənsɪ; ˈkɒnstənsi/ *n* [U] *formal*【正式】**1** the quality of staying the same even though other things change 坚定不移；经久不变；持久性: *constancy of purpose* 目标坚定 **2** loyalty and faithfulness to a particular person 忠实，忠贞: *constancy between husband and wife* 夫妻间的忠诚

con·stant¹ /ˋkɑnstənt; ˈkɒnstənt/ *adj* **1** staying the same for a period of time 始终如一的，恒久不变的: *A thermostat kept the temperature constant.* 恒温器保持温度恒久不变。**2** happening all the time or regularly 持续不断的，经常发生的: *Sam was in constant pain.* 萨姆感到疼痛不止。**3** *literary* loyal and faithful【文】忠实的，忠诚的: *a constant friend* 忠实的朋友 

constant² *n* [C] *technical*【术语】**1** a number or quantity that never varies 常数，恒量 **2** *formal* something that stays the same even though other things change【正式】不变的事；恒定的事物 —compare 比较 VARIABLE¹

Con·stan·tine /ˌkɑnstəntaɪn; ˌkɒnstəntaɪn/ **the Great** also 又作 **Constantine I** (?274-337 AD) the first Christian ruler of the Roman Empire. In 330 AD he made Byzantium the capital city of the EMPIRE instead of Rome and changed the name of the new capital to Constantinople. 君士坦丁大帝，君士坦丁一世〔(?公元274-337)，罗马帝国首位基督徒皇帝。公元330年，他定都拜占庭，取代了罗马，并将拜占庭改名为君士坦丁堡。

Con·stan·ti·no·ple /ˌkɑnstæntəˋnopl̩; ˌkɒnstæntɪ̵ˈnəʊpəl/ the city on the Bosporus which was the capital of the Byzantine Empire for seven centuries from 330 AD, when it was established by Constantine the Great on the place where Byzantium had formerly stood. Later it was the capital of Turkey. It is now called Istanbul. 君士坦丁堡〔地跨博斯普鲁斯海峡的一座城市。公元330年，君士坦丁大帝在拜占庭原址上修建该城，此后一直是拜占庭帝国的首都，长达七个世纪之久。后来成为土耳其的首都，现称伊斯坦布尔〕

con·stant·ly /ˋkɑnstəntlɪ; ˈkɒnstəntli/ *adv* all the time, or very often 持续不断地；经常地: *As I walked through the town, I was constantly reminded of my childhood.* 当我步行穿过市镇时，见到的景象使我不断地回忆起我的童年。| **constantly changing** *the constantly changing membership of our group* 我们这个群体不断变化的成员 S3 W3

con·stel·la·tion /ˌkɑnstəˋleʃən; ˌkɒnstɪ̵ˈleɪʃən/ *n* [C] **1** a group of stars that forms a particular pattern and has a name 星座 **2 a constellation of** *literary* a group of people or things that are similar【文】一群〔相似的人或物〕: *a constellation of famous television performers* 一群著名电视演员

con·ster·na·tion /ˌkɑnstɚˋneʃən; ˌkɒnstəˈneɪʃən/ *n* [U] a feeling of shock or worry, especially one that makes it difficult to think about what to do; DISMAY¹ 惊愕；惊恐；惊惶失措: *The*

thought of living alone filled her with consternation. 想到要独自生活使她充满惊恐。

con·sti·pa·tion /ˌkanstəˋpeʃən; ˌkɒnstɪ̈ˈpeɪʃən/ *n* [U] the condition of finding it difficult to empty your bowels (BOWEL (1)) 便秘 —**constipated** *adj*

3 **con·sti·tu·en·cy** /kənˋstɪtʃuənsɪ; kənˈstɪtʃuənsi/ *n* [C] **1** an area of the country that elects a representative to a parliament〔选举议会议员的〕选区: *John Major, speaking from his Huntingdon constituency* 约翰·梅杰在他的亨廷顿郡选区发表讲话 **2** [also+plural verb *BrE* 英] the people who live and vote in a particular area 选区的全体选民 —compare 比较 WARD[1] (2) **3** any group that supports or is likely to support a politician or a political party〔政治家或政党的〕支持者, 拥护者: *The Unions were no longer the constituency of the Labour Party alone.* 工会不再只支持工党了。

con·sti·tu·ent[1] /kənˋstɪtʃuənt; kənˈstɪtʃuənt/ *n* [C] **1** someone who votes and lives in a particular area represented by one politician 选区的选民 **2** one of the parts that combine to form something 成分; 构成部分: *the constituents of gunpowder* 火药的成分 —compare 比较 COMPONENT

constituent[2] *adj* [only before noun 仅用于名词前] being one of the parts that makes a whole 构成的, 组成的: *the EC and its constituent members* 欧洲共同体及其成员国

3 **con·sti·tute** /ˋkanstəˌtut; ˈkɒnstɪ̈tjuːt/ *v* **1** [linking verb 连系动词, not in progressive 不用进行时] if several parts constitute something, they form it together; make up (MAKE[1]) 组成, 构成: *the 50 states that constitute the USA* 组成美国的50个州 —see also 另见 COMPRISE **2** [linking verb 连系动词, not in progressive 不用进行式] to be considered to be something 被视为: *Boarding a train without a ticket constitutes a breach of the regulations.* 无票乘火车被视为违反规章。**3** [T] *formal* to make something from a number of different parts【正式】将不同部分组成〔某物〕

2 **con·sti·tu·tion** /ˌkanstəˋtjuʃən; ˌkɒnstɪ̈ˈtjuːʃən/ *n* **1** [C] the system of basic laws and principles that a DEMOCRATIC country is governed by, which cannot easily be changed by the political party in power 宪法: *The First Amendment of the Constitution guarantees freedom of speech.* 宪法第一条修正案保证言论自由。**2** [singular] the ability of your body to fight disease and illness 体质: **have a strong/good/weak etc constitution** *She's got a strong constitution – she'll recover in no time.* 她体质很好, 很快就会痊愈。**3** [C] *formal* the way something is formed and how it is organized【正式】组成; 结构: [+of] *objections to the constitution of the committee* 对委员会组成方式的反对 **4** the system of rules and principles that an organization is governed by〔某组织的〕法规; 章程

> CULTURAL NOTE 文化注释
>
> Although the constitution of most countries is written down, the British constitution is not. 大多数国家的宪法是成文法, 英国宪法则不然。— see also 另见 CONSTITUTION OF THE UNITED STATES

3 **con·sti·tu·tion·al[1]** /ˌkanstəˋtjuʃənl; ˌkɒnstɪ̈ˈtjuːʃənəl◂/ *adj* **1** officially allowed or limited by the system of rules of a country or organization 宪法[章程]规定的; 合乎宪法[章程]的: *The government can't refuse to hold an election; it's not constitutional.* 政府不能拒绝举行选举, 那是违反宪法的。| **a constitutional monarchy** (=a country ruled by a king or queen whose power is restricted by a constitution) 君主立宪制 —opposite 反义词 UNCONSTITUTIONAL **2** connected with the constitution of a country or organization 宪法[章程]的: *a constitutional crisis* 宪法危机 | **a constitutional amendment** (=a change to the original constitution) 宪法修正 **3** connected with someone's health and their ability to fight illness 体质上的 —see also 另见 CONSTITUTIONALLY

constitutional[2] *n* [C] *old-fashioned* a walk you take because it is good for your health【过时】保健散步

Constitutional Convention, the /ˌ‥‥ ˈ‥/ the meeting of representatives in 1787 in Philadelphia that led to the writing of the Constitution of the United States 制宪会议〔1787年殖民地13州的代表在费城参加的会议。会议草拟了《美利坚合众国宪法》〕

con·sti·tu·tion·al·is·m /ˌkanstəˋtjuʃənlɪzəm; ˌkɒnstɪ̈ˈtjuːʃənəlɪzəm/ *n* [U] the belief that a government should be based on a constitution 立宪主义〔主张政府应按宪法规定组建的信仰〕—**constitutionalist** *n* [C]

con·sti·tu·tion·al·i·ty /ˌkanstəˌtjuʃənˋælətɪ; ˌkɒnstɪ̈tjuːʃəˈnælɪ̈ti/ *n* [U] the quality of being acceptable according to the constitution 符合宪法, 合宪性: *The senator questioned the constitutionality of the proposed law.* 这位参议员质疑这项法案是否合乎宪法。

con·sti·tu·tion·al·ly /ˌkanstəˋtjuʃənlɪ; ˌkɒnstɪ̈ˈtjuːʃənəli/ *adv* **1** in a way that obeys the rules of a country 依照宪法: *The government must always act constitutionally.* 政府必须时刻依照宪法行事。**2** in a way that is related to someone's character or health and physical ability 就体质而言; 就性格而言

Constitution of the U·nit·ed States, the /‥ˌ‥ ‥ˌ‥ˈ‥/ also 又作 **Constitution** the highest law of the government of the US, often unofficially called **the Constitution**. The Constitution was first written at the Constitutional Convention of 1787, and it officially came into use in 1789. It consists of seven articles and 27 AMENDMENTS (=additions and changes to the original).《美国宪法》〔美国的最高政府法律, 非正式名称为the Constitution。《美国宪法》草拟于1787年的制宪会议, 1789年正式生效。《美国宪法》由7大条款和27条修正案构成〕

> CULTURAL NOTE 文化注释
>
> **The Constitution** The Constitution of the United States describes how the US government should be formed and what rights citizens and states should have, such as the right to vote and the right to carry weapons. US citizens believe that the Constitution is very important, because it protects their political freedoms. The first ten AMENDMENTS (=additions) to the Constitution were added in 1791, and these are known as the Bill of Rights. 宪法: 美国宪法规定了政府的组建形式, 以及公民和各州享有的权利, 如投票权、携带武器权。美国公民认为宪法非常重要, 因为它保护了他们的政治自由。最初的十条修正案于1791年提出, 称为《人权法案》。
>
> **The Preamble** Most Americans recognize the PREAMBLE (=beginning statement) of the Constitution, which reads: "We the people of the United States, in order to form a more perfect union, establish justice, insure domestic tranquility, provide for the common defense, promote the general welfare, and secure the blessings of liberty to ourselves and our posterity, do ordain and establish this Constitution for the United States of America." 序言: 大多数美国人熟悉宪法的序言: "我们, 合众国的公民, 为结成更好的同盟, 建立正义, 保障国内稳定, 提供共同防卫, 推动普遍福利, 保证我们及子孙后代享有自由之福, 制定和确立美利坚合众国宪法。"
>
> **The Constitution and the law** In the US, all local and national laws must agree with the Constitution. If someone thinks a law is UNCONSTITUTIONAL (=against the rules and principles stated in the Constitution), they can ask a court of law to decide whether it agrees with the Constitution or not. If the court decides a law is unconstitutional, that law can no longer be used. The US Supreme Court examines cases where a law or legal decision may be against the principles of the Constitution, in order to decide if it is unconstitutional, and the decision of the Supreme Court is final and cannot be changed. 宪法和法律: 美国的地方法和国家法必须与宪法相符。如果有人认为一项法律违背宪法, 可以要求法庭裁定该法律是否违宪。如法庭裁定某项法律违宪, 该法律即告失效。美国最高法院审理某项法律或法律裁决可能违反宪法的案件, 以裁定其是否违宪。最高法院的裁决是最终裁决, 不可更改。

con·strain /kənˋstren; kənˈstreɪn/ *v* [T] **1** to stop someone from doing what they want to do 限制, 阻止〔某人做他想做的事〕: **constrain by** *Many women feel constrained by their family's demand.* 许多妇女感觉她们受到家庭生活的束缚。**2** to prevent something from developing and improving 阻止; 抑制; 使〔某事〕不能发展[改进]: *Our research has been constrained by lack of funding.* 我们的研究由于缺乏资金而受到限制。

con·strained /kənˋstrend; kənˈstreɪnd/ *adj* **1 constrained to do sth** feeling that you are forced to do something 被迫做某事: *In the recession companies felt constrained to make job cuts where possible.* 在经济萧条时期, 各公司都被迫尽可能地削减职位。**2** a constrained smile, manner etc seems too controlled and is not natural〔微笑、态度等〕强装出来的; 拘谨的; 不自然的 —**constrainedly** /kənˋstrenɪdlɪ; kənˈstreɪnɪ̈dli/ *adv*

con·straint /kənˋstrent; kənˈstreɪnt/ *n* **1** [C] something that limits your freedom to do what you want; RESTRICTION 限制; 束缚; 约束力: [+on] *These new policies place additional constraints on housing projects.* 这些新政策对住房建造工程设置了额外的限制。| **financial/legal/cultural etc constraints** *Finan-* 3

cial constraints limited her choice of accommodation. 财力上的限制使她不能随意选择住处。**2** [U] control over the way people are allowed to behave, so that they cannot do what they want 行为约束: *freedom from constraint* 不受限制 **3 under constraint** if you do something under constraint, you do it because you have been forced to 被强迫

con·strict /kən`strɪkt; kən'strɪkt/ *v* [T] **1** to make something smaller, narrower, or tighter 压缩; 压紧; 使收缩, 使收紧 **2** to limit someone's freedom to do what they want 限制人们的行动自由: *Poverty constricts people's choices.* 贫困限制了人们的选择余地。—**constricted** *adj* —**constriction** *n* [C,U] —**constrictive** *adj*

W3 **con·struct**[1] /kən`strʌkt; kən'strʌkt/ *v* [T] **1** to build a large building, bridge, road etc 建造, 构筑: *The Golden Gate Bridge was constructed in 1933-1937.* 金门大桥建于1933－1937年。| **be constructed of/from etc** *huge skyscrapers constructed entirely of concrete and glass* 完全用混凝土和玻璃建成的摩天大楼 **2** to form something such as a sentence, argument, or system by joining words, ideas etc together 组成, 构成〔句子、论点、体系等〕: *attempts to construct a programme that will meet the educational needs of every child* 为满足每一个儿童的教育需求而制定一项计划的尝试 **3** *technical* to draw a mathematical shape【术语】绘制几何图形, 作图. *Construct a square on this line.* 以这条线段为一边作一个正方形。

con·struct[2] /`kɑnstrʌkt; 'kɒnstrʌkt/ *n* [C] **1** an idea formed by combining pieces of knowledge 构想; 概念: *the central constructs of role theory* 角色理论的中心概念 **2** *formal* something that is built or made【正式】建造物; 构成物

S3 W2 **con·struc·tion** /kən`strʌkʃən; kən'strʌkʃən/ *n*

1 ▶BUILDINGS/ROADS ETC 建筑/道路等◀ [U] the process or method of building large buildings, bridges, roads etc 建造, 建筑: *Local labor is used in the construction of the dam.* 建筑大坝用的是本地的劳动力。| *the construction industry* 建筑业 | **construction site** (=the place where something is being constructed) 建筑工地 | **under construction** (=being built) 在建造之中 *When we got to the hotel, it was still under construction.* 我们到达酒店时, 它还在建筑之中。

2 ▶MAKING STH USING MANY PARTS 使用许多部件制作某物◀ [U] the process or method of building or making something using many parts 建造, 构造: *Titanium is used in the construction of aircraft fuselages.* 钛用来建造飞机的机身。

3 ▶PHRASE 短语◀ [C] the order in which certain words are put together in a sentence, phrase etc〔词在短语或句子中的〕结构; 句法关系: *difficult grammatical constructions* 艰深的语法结构

4 ▶STH BUILT 建造物◀ [C] *formal* something that has been built【正式】建筑物; 建造物: *a strange construction made of wood and glass* 用木头和玻璃建造的奇特建筑物

5 ▶IDEAS/KNOWLEDGE 思想/知识◀ [U] the method or process of forming something from knowledge or ideas〔对知识或思想体系的〕创立, 创建: *the construction of sociological theory* 社会学理论的创立

6 of simple/strong etc construction *formal* built in a simple way, built to be strong etc【正式】构造简单/坚固等: *Your home is not secure if the doors are not of strong construction.* 如果门建得不坚固的话, 你的房子就不安全了。

7 put a construction on *formal* to think that a statement has a particular meaning or that something was done for a particular reason【正式】理解〔话语的含意、行动的原因等〕: *The judge put an entirely different construction on his remarks.* 法官对他的陈述作了完全不同的解释。—**constructional** *adj*

con·struc·tive /kən`strʌktɪv; kən'strʌktɪv/ *adj* **1** intended to be helpful and to suggest improvements, rather than to upset or offend people 建设性的: **constructive advice/criticism** *I don't mind constructive criticism but if you're just going to insult me I'm not staying.* 我不介意建设性的批评, 但如果你只是想侮辱我, 我就不会留在这里了。**2** having a good effect or likely to produce good results 积极的, 有益的: *Young people in inner cities need constructive outlets for their energy.* 市中心贫民区的年轻人需要有积极的途径来发泄自己的精力。—**constructively** *adv* —**constructiveness** *n* [U]

con·struc·tor /kən`strʌktə; kən'strʌktə/ *n* [C] a company or person that builds things 建筑公司; 建筑商

con·strue /kən`stru; kən'struː/ *v* **1 construe sth as** to understand a remark or action in a particular way 将某事解释[理解]为: *Party leaders felt that such an action would be construed as political persecution.* 政党领导人认为那样的行为可以解释为政治迫害。**2** [I,T] to translate each word in a piece of writing, especially one in Greek or Latin〔尤指对希腊文或拉丁文文章〕逐字直译

con·sub·stan·ti·a·tion /ˌkɑnsəbˌstænʃɪ`eʃən; ˌkɒnsəbstænʃi'eɪʃən/ *n* [U] *technical* the belief that the real body and blood of Christ are present in the bread and wine offered by the priest at a Christian religious service【术语】同体论〔认为基督的圣体、圣血与圣餐共在之说〕

con·sul /`kɑnsl; 'kɒnsəl/ *n* [C] **1** a representative of the government who lives in a foreign country in order to help and protect citizens of their own country who live there 领事: *the French Consul in Addis Ababa* 法国驻亚的斯亚贝巴的领事 **2** one of the two chief public officials of the ancient Roman republic, each elected for one year〔古罗马共和国时期任期一年的〕二执政官之一 —**consular** *adj*: *a consular official* 领事馆官员 —**consulship** *n* [C,U]

con·su·late, Consulate /`kɑnslɪt; 'kɒnsjʊlɪt/ *n* [C] the official building in which a consul lives and works 领事馆

con·sult /kən`sʌlt; kən'sʌlt/ *v* [I,T] **1** to ask for information or advice from someone because it is their job to know about it 咨询; 请教: *If symptoms persist, consult a doctor without delay.* 如果症状继续存在的话, 马上去请教医生。| **consult sb about sth** *An increasing number of clients are consulting them about Social Security changes.* 越来越多的客户向他们咨询有关社会保障制度的变化。**2** to ask for someone's permission or to discuss something with someone so that you can make a decision together 取得〔某人〕的允许; 与〔某人〕商量共同决定: *I can't believe you sold the car without consulting me!* 我无法相信你不经我允许就把车给卖了! | **[+with]** *The President consulted with European leaders before taking action.* 总统在采取行动以前曾与欧洲领导人商议。**3** to look for information in a book, map, list etc 查阅: *Have you consulted a dictionary?* 你查过字典了吗? S3 W3

con·sul·tan·cy /kən`sʌltənsɪ; kən'sʌltənsi/ *n* [C] a company that gives advice and training in a particular area to people in other companies 咨询公司, 顾问公司

con·sul·tant /kən`sʌltənt; kən'sʌltənt/ *n* [C] **1** someone who has a lot of experience and whose job it is to give advice and training in a particular area 顾问: *a management consultant* 经营管理顾问 **2** *BrE* a senior hospital doctor who has a lot of knowledge about a particular kind of medical treatment【英】高级顾问医生; 会诊医生; SPECIALIST (2) *AmE*【美】 S3 W3

con·sul·ta·tion /ˌkɑnsʌl`teʃən; ˌkɒnsəl'teɪʃən/ *n* **1** [U] a discussion in which people who are affected by a decision can say what they think should be done 商量, 磋商: *Parents are demanding a greater consultation over their children's future.* 家长们要求对子女的未来进行更广泛的磋商。| **in consultation with** (=with the agreement and help of someone) 经与…协商 *The decision was made in consultation with union members.* 这项决定是通过与工会会员协商后作出的。**2** [U] advice given by a professional person 建议; 意见: *The school counselor was always available for consultation.* 学校的辅导员随时都准备接受咨询。**3** [C] a meeting with a professional person, especially a doctor, for advice or treatment〔与专业人士, 尤指医师, 进行的〕会面〔以作咨询、治疗等〕: *A follow-up consultation was arranged for two weeks' time.* 安排了两个星期的后续会面。**4** [U] the act of looking for information or help in a book 查阅: *Leaflets were regularly displayed for consultation by students.* 活页材料定期展出供学生查阅参考。 S3 W3

con·sul·ta·tive /kən`sʌltətɪv; kən'sʌltətɪv/ *adj* providing advice and suggesting solutions to problems 咨询的; 顾问的: *a consultative document* 一份咨询性的文件

con·sult·ing[1] /kən`sʌltɪŋ; kən'sʌltɪŋ/ *n* [U] the service of providing financial advice to companies 财务咨询[顾问]服务

consulting[2] *adj* providing financial or other types of advice to companies 财务咨询[顾问]的; 咨询[顾问]的: *a major international consulting firm* 一家主要的国际咨询机构

consulting room *n* [C] *BrE* a room where a doctor sees patients【英】〔医生的〕会诊室

con·sume /kən`sum; kən'sjuːm/ *v* [T] **1** to use time, energy, goods etc 消耗; 消费: *As a country, we consume a lot more than we produce.* 作为一个国家, 我们的消费远远多于生产。**2 time-consuming** something that is time-consuming takes a long time 耗费时间的: *a very time-consuming process* 非常耗费时间的过程 **3** *formal* to eat or drink something【正式】吃; 喝: *He's able to consume vast quantities of food.* 他能吃掉大量的食物。**4 consumed with** if you are consumed with a feeling, you feel it very strongly and cannot forget it 被〔某种情感〕所折磨: *He was consumed with guilt after the accident.* 那次事故以后他深感内疚。**5** *formal* if fire consumes something, it destroys it completely【正式】〔大火〕(彻底) 烧毁 —see also 另见 CONSUMING

con·sum·er /kənˈsumɚ; kənˈsjuːmə/ *n* [C] someone who buys and uses products and services 消费者: *a wider choice of goods for the consumer* 可供消费者选择的品种更多的商品 —compare 比较 PRODUCER (1)

consumer con·fi·dence /.,.. ˈ.../ *n* [U] a measure of how satisfied people are with the present economic situation, as shown by how much money they spend 消费者信任度[信心]: *Consumer confidence was reported to hit an all-time low in September.* 据报道，九月份的消费者信心跌到了历史的最低点。

consumer du·ra·bles /.,..ˈ.../ *BrE n* [plural] large things such as cars, televisions, or furniture that you do not buy often or regularly【英】耐用消费品; DURABLE GOODS *AmE*【美】

consumer goods /.ˈ.., ./ *n* [plural] goods such as food, clothes, and equipment that people buy, especially to use in the home 消费品，日常生活资料 —compare 比较 CAPITAL GOODS

con·sum·er·ism /kənˈsumərɪzəm; kənˈsjuːmərɪzəm/ *n* [U] **1** the idea or belief that the buying and selling of products is the most important or useful activity for an individual and a society 消费主义〔认为买卖商品是个人和社会最重要或最有益的活动的想法或信念〕 **2** actions to protect people from unfair prices, advertising that is not true etc 保护消费者利益的行为

consumer price in·dex /.,..ˈ., .ˈ/ *n* [C] *AmE* a list of the prices of products that is prepared to show how much prices have increased during a particular period of time【美】消费品价格指数; RETAIL PRICE INDEX *BrE*【英】

Consumer Re·ports /.,..ˈ./ a US magazine which tests and reports on the quality of particular products in order to help people to decide which one to buy. There is a similar magazine in the UK called *Which?*《消费报告》〔美国一杂志，检测并报道特定产品的品质，帮助消费者选择商品。英国也有类似的杂志名为《哪一个?》〕

Consumers' As·so·ci·a·tion, the /.ˈ.. ...,./ a British organization that helps consumers. It tests the quality of products and services, and suggests the best ones to buy and use in its own magazine, called *Which?* It also fights for the rights of consumers in the UK. 消费者协会〔英国服务消费者的一个组织。其职责是检测产品和服务品质，利用会刊《哪一个?》向消费者推荐可购买和使用的最佳产品，同时也为消费者争取合法权益〕

consumer so·ci·e·ty /.ˈ.. .,../ *n* [C] a society in which the buying of products and services is considered extremely important 消费社会

con·sum·ing /kənˈsumɪŋ; kənˈsjuːmɪŋ/ *adj* [only before noun 仅用于名词前] a consuming feeling is so strong that it controls you and often has a bad effect on your life〔感情〕强烈的，支配人的〔往往是有害的〕: *It was her consuming ambition to become party leader.* 成为政党领袖是她的强烈愿望。| **consuming passion** (=something you are extremely interested in) 极大的兴趣爱好 *Sandy's consuming passion is still the martial arts.* 桑迪最大的爱好仍然是武术。

con·sum·mate[1] /kənˈsʌmɪt; kənˈsʌmɪt/ *adj formal*【正式】**1** very skilful 技艺高超的: *a great performance from a consummate actress* 技艺高超的女演员的精彩表演 **2** complete and perfect in every way 圆满的，完美的: *a consummate example of Picasso's artistry* 毕加索艺术天才的一个完美的例证 **3** used to emphasize how bad someone or something is 极其(差)的: *a man with a consummate lack of tact* 完全不懂策略的人 —**consummately** *adv*

con·sum·mate[2] /ˈkɑnsə,met; ˈkɒnsəmeɪt/ *v* [T] *formal*【正式】**1** to make a marriage or a relationship complete by having sex 圆房，完婚 **2** to make something complete or perfect 使完成，使圆满

> **CULTURAL NOTE 文化注释**
> In English and American law a marriage is legal after the wedding, but it is not considered complete until sex has taken place, and it can be declared NULL AND VOID if one partner cannot or will not consummate the marriage in this way. 根据英美法律，婚姻自婚礼举办之后就是合法的，但如果双方未圆房，则认为婚姻并未完成，如夫妻一方不能或不愿同房，可宣告婚姻无效。

con·sum·ma·tion /,kɑnsəˈmeʃən; ,kɒnsəˈmeɪʃən/ *n* [U] *formal*【正式】**1** the act of making a marriage or relationship complete by having sex 圆房，〔经同房而〕完婚 **2** *formal* the point at which something is complete or perfect【正式】圆满；完美，极至: *the consummation of his ambitions* 他雄心壮志的实现

W3 **con·sump·tion** /kənˈsʌmpʃən; kənˈsʌmpʃən/ *n* [U]
1 ▶AMOUNT OF STH USED 消耗量◀ the amount of oil, electricity etc that is used〔油、电等的〕消耗量: *Fuel consumption has risen dramatically in the last few years.* 在过去几年中，燃料的消耗量急剧增加。
2 ▶EATING/DRINKING 吃/喝◀ *formal* the act of eating or drinking【正式】吃；喝: *The consumption of alcohol was forbidden according to their religion.* 按照他们的教义，喝酒是禁止的。| **fit/unfit for human consumption** (=safe or not safe for people to eat) 适合/不适合人类食用 *The meat was declared unfit for human consumption.* 这种肉已被宣布不适合人类食用。
3 ▶BUYING 购买◀ the act of buying and using products 购买，消费: *The consumption of luxury goods is governed by psychological values like social prestige.* 奢侈品的消费是受诸如社会声望这样的心理价值支配的。| **conspicuous consumption** (=buying expensive goods in order to show other people how rich you are) 炫耀性消费
4 ▶AMOUNT OF FOOD/DRINK 吃/喝的量◀ the amount of food or drink that is eaten or drunk〔食物的〕食用量，消耗量: *Patients are advised to cut down on their consumption of alcohol.* 病人被建议少喝酒。
5 ▶ILLNESS 疾病◀ a word used in the past for the lung disease TUBERCULOSIS〔旧称〕肺痨
6 **for sb's consumption** if a piece of information or remark is for a particular person or group's consumption, it is intended to be heard or read by them 仅供某人[某些群体]聆听[阅读]: *secret policy documents that are not for public consumption* 不供公众阅读的机密政策文件

con·sump·tive /kənˈsʌmptɪv; kənˈsʌmptɪv/ *adj* a word used in the past to describe someone who had the lung disease TUBERCULOSIS〔旧称〕患肺痨的 —**consumptive** *n* [C]

cont. the written abbreviation for 缩写 = CONTAINING, CONTENTS, CONTINUED, CONTINENT

S3 W2 **con·tact**[1] /ˈkɑntækt; ˈkɒntækt/ *n*
1 ▶COMMUNICATION 交流◀ [U] communication with a person, organization, country etc 联系，联络；交往: [**+with**] *He's not had any contact with his son for months.* 他已经有好几个月没有和他的儿子联系了。| [**+between**] *There is very little contact between the two tribes.* 这两个部落几乎没有什么交往。| **be/get/stay in contact (with)** *We stay in contact with each other by telephone.* 我们通过电话保持联系。| **make/lose contact with** (=succeed in communicating or stop communicating with someone) 与〔某人〕取得/失去联系 *I've lost contact with most of my school friends.* 我已经与大部分校友失去了联系。| **put sb in contact (with)** (=make it possible for someone to communicate with another person by giving them that person's address or telephone number) 使某人得以(与…)取得联系 *Sarah put me in contact with an expert in the field.* 莎拉帮我与该领域的一个专家取得了联系。
2 ▶TOUCH 触摸◀ [U] a state in which two people or things touch each other 接触: [**+with**] *Children need close physical contact and interaction with a caring adult.* 孩子们需要与有爱心的大人有亲密的身体接触和交流。| [**+between**] *This disease is spread by contact between the animals.* 这种疾病在动物间通过接触传播。| **in contact (with)** *For a second, his hand was in contact with mine.* 他的手很快地碰了一下我的手。| **come into contact (with)** *She screamed as her body came into contact with the water.* 当她的身体碰到水的一刹那她尖叫了起来。| **on contact (with)** (=at the moment of touching something) 与…接触的刹那 *The bomb exploded on contact with the ground.* 炸弹与地面一接触就爆炸了。| **contact points/ area/surfaces etc** *The contact points of the two surfaces must be clean and dry.* 这两个表面的接触点必须既干净又干燥。
3 **come into contact with sb** to meet someone 会见某人: *Diana dazzled everyone who came into contact with her.* 黛安娜使每个见到她的人都为之倾倒。
4 ▶PERSON WHO CAN HELP 能提供帮助的人◀ [C] a person you know who may be able to help you or give you advice about something〔能提供帮助或建议的〕熟人: *He has a lot of contacts in the media.* 在传媒界他有很多熟人。
5 ▶SITUATION/PROBLEM 局势/问题◀ [U] experience of dealing with a particular kind of situation or problem〔处理某种局面或问题的〕经验: **bring sb into contact with sth** *Pat's job brought her into contact with the problems people face when they retire.* 帕特的工作使她接触到人们退休时面临的问题。
6 **point of contact a)** a place that you go to or a person that you meet when dealing with an organization 联系点；联系人: *Primary health care teams are the first point of contact for users of the health service.* 享受医疗服务的人首先联系基层保健队。**b)** a way in which two very different things are connected 联系点；接合点: *It's difficult to find a point of contact between theory and practice.* 很难在理论和实践之间找到联系。

7 ►ELECTRICAL PART 电路元件◄ [C] an electrical part that completes a CIRCUIT (4) when it touches another part〔电路的〕触点, 接头

8 ►EYES 眼睛◄ [C] a contact lens 隐形眼镜 —see also 另见 eye contact (EYE¹ (9))

contact² *v* [T] to write to or telephone someone〔写信、打电话〕联系〔某人〕: *Give the names of two people who can be contacted in case of emergency.* 给出两个人的名字, 在紧急情况下可以给他们打电话。

contact³ *adj* [only before noun 仅用于名词前] **1** a contact number or address is a telephone number or address where someone can be found if necessary 可供联系的〔电话号码或地址〕: *The school requires a contact number for each child.* 学校要求每个孩子都有一个联络电话号码。**2** contact explosives or chemicals become active when they touch something〔炸药或化学物质〕通过接触起作用的: *Contact poisons are widely used in pest control.* 接触性毒物广泛用于防治虫害。

contact lens /ˈ‥ ·/ *n* [C] a small round piece of plastic you put on your eye to help you see clearly 隐形眼镜

con·ta·gion /kənˋtedʒən; kənˈteɪdʒən/ *n* [C,U] **1** *technical* a situation in which a disease is spread by people touching each other【术语】〔病病〕接触传染: *The danger of contagion was now very small.* 接触传染的危险现在非常小。**2** *technical* a disease that can be passed from person to person by touch【术语】接触传染病 **3** *formal* a feeling or attitude that spreads quickly from person to person【正式】〔感情、态度的〕感染, 蔓延

con·ta·gious /kənˋtedʒəs; kənˈteɪdʒəs/ *adj* **1** a disease that is contagious can be passed from person to person by touch〔疾病〕接触传染的 **2** a person who is contagious has a disease that can be passed to another person by touch 患接触传染病的: *The patient is still highly contagious.* 这个病人仍然有很强的传染性。**3** if a feeling, attitude, or action is contagious, other people quickly begin to feel it, believe it, do it etc〔感情、态度、行动〕感染性的, 蔓延的: *Her enthusiasm was contagious.* 她的热情很有感染力。—**contagiousness** *n* [U] —**contagiously** *adv*

con·tain /kənˋten; kənˈteɪn/ *v* [T] **1** to have something inside, or have something as a part 包含; 容纳; 装盛: *He opened the bag, which contained a razor, soap and a towel.* 他打开袋子, 里面有一把刮胡刀、香皂和一条毛巾。| *The letter contained important information about Boulestin's legal affairs.* 这封信含有关于布里斯汀法律事务的重要资料。**2** to keep a strong feeling or emotion under control 克制〔强烈的感情〕: *Jane couldn't contain her amusement a moment longer.* 简乐得再也忍不住了。| **contain yourself** (=keep your emotions under control) 克制自己 *He was so excited he could hardly contain himself.* 他太激动了, 再也无法控制自己。**3** to stop something from spreading or escaping 抑制, 控制: *Doctors are struggling to contain the epidemic.* 医生们正在努力控制流行病。—see also 另见 SELF-CONTAINED **4** *formal* to surround an area or an angle【正式】包围〔区域或角〕: *How big is the angle contained by these two sides?* 这两条边之间的角有多大?

con·tain·er /kənˋtenə; kənˈteɪnə/ *n* [C] **1** something such as a box or bowl that can be used for keeping things in 容器: *Ice cream comes in plastic containers.* 冰激凌是用塑料容器包装出售的。**2** a very large metal box in which goods are packed to make it easy to lift or move them onto a ship or vehicle 集装箱, 货柜: *The deck was full of big cargo containers.* 甲板上堆满了大型货物集装箱。

con·tain·ment /kənˋtenmənt; kənˈteɪnmənt/ *n* [U] **1** the act of keeping something under control 控制; 抑制: *containment of public expenditure* 控制公共支出 **2** the use of political actions to prevent an unfriendly country from becoming more powerful〔对敌国的〕遏制: *a policy of containment* 遏制政策

con·tam·i·nant /kənˋtæmənənt; kənˈtæmɪ̥nənt/ *n* [C] *technical* a poisonous substance that makes something impure【术语】污染物, 致污物

con·tam·i·nate /kənˋtæməˌnet; kənˈtæmɪ̥neɪt/ *v* [T] **1** to make a place or substance dirty and dangerous by adding something to it, for example chemicals or poison 把…弄脏, 污染: *fears that dumped waste might contaminate water supplies* 对倾倒的垃圾可能会污染水源的忧虑 **2** to influence something in a way that has a bad effect 毒害; 使变坏 —**contamination** /kənˌtæməˋneʃən; kənˌtæmɪ̥ˈneɪʃən/ *n* [U]

con·tam·i·nat·ed /kənˋtæməˌnetɪd; kənˈtæmɪ̥neɪtɪ̥d/ *adj* **1** water, food etc that is contaminated has dangerous or harmful things in it, such as chemicals or poison〔水、食物等〕被污染的: *Several outbreaks of infection have been traced to contaminated food.* 几次传染病爆发的源头都已经查明是被污染的食物。**2** influenced in a way that produces a bad effect 变坏的, 变劣的

contd. the written abbreviation for 缩写 = CONTINUED

con·tem·plate /ˋkɑntəmˌplet; ˈkɒntəmpleɪt/ *v* **1** [T] to think about something that you intend to do in the future 打算, 想, 考虑: *Aren't you a little young to be contemplating marriage?* 你想结婚是不是有点儿早了? | **contemplate doing sth** *I've never even contemplated leaving my job.* 我从来连想都没想过辞职。**2** [T] to accept the possibility that something is true 预期; 视…

containers 容器

a packet *BrE*【英】/ pack *AmE*【美】/ bag of sugar/peas 一包[袋]食糖/豌豆

a packet *BrE*【英】/ pack *AmE*【美】 of cigarettes/gum 一包香烟/口香糖

tube 圆管

sachet *BrE*【英】/ packet *AmE*【美】〔供一次用的〕小袋, 小包

a box of eggs/matches 一盒鸡蛋/火柴

can/tin *BrE*【英】罐, 桶

carton 硬纸[塑料]盒

crate 装货箱

barrel 桶

drum 大桶

churn *BrE*【英】/milk can *AmE*【美】奶桶

urn 瓮

为可能: **too dreadful/horrifying etc to contemplate** *The thought of the letter never having reached him was too terrible to contemplate.* 只要一想到那封信没有送到他那里, 便令人恐惧得不敢想下去。**3** [I,T] to think seriously about something for a long time, especially in order to understand it better 深思; 细想: *contemplating the meaning of life* 仔细思考生命的意义

con·tem·pla·tion /ˌkɑntəm`pleʃən; ˌkɒntəm'pleɪʃən/ *n* [U] quiet, serious thinking about something, especially in order to understand it better 沉思, 冥想, 默想: *The monks spend an hour in contemplation each morning.* 那些修道士每天早上默祷一个小时。

con·tem·pla·tive¹ /kən`tɛmplətɪv; kən'templətɪv/ *adj* spending a lot of time thinking seriously and quietly 沉思的, 冥想的, 默想的: *a contemplative mood* 沉思的心境 **—contemplatively** *adv*

contemplative² *n* [C] *formal* someone who spends their life thinking deeply about religious matters【正式】宗教思想家

con·tem·po·ra·ne·ous /kənˌtɛmpə`renɪəs; kənˌtempə'reɪniəs/ *adj formal* happening in the same period of time; CONTEMPORARY (2)【正式】发生于同一时期的: **[+with]** *Built in the 13th and 14th centuries, they are contemporaneous with many of the great Gothic cathedrals.* 它们建于13和14世纪, 和许多伟大的哥特式大教堂属于同一个时期。**—contemporaneously** *adv* **—contemporaneity** /kənˌtɛmpərə`niətɪ; kənˌtempərə'niːəti/ *n* [U]

W2 **con·tem·po·ra·ry¹** /kən`tɛmpəˌrɛrɪ; kən'tempərəri/ *adj* **1** belonging to the present time; MODERN 当代的: **contemporary music/art/dance etc** *an exhibition of contemporary Japanese prints* 当代日本版画的展览 **2** happening or existing in the same period of time 发生[存在]于同一时代的

contemporary² *n* [C] someone who was in a particular place or who lived at the same time as someone else 同时代的人; 同辈: *Oswald was much admired by his contemporaries at the Royal Academy.* 奥斯瓦尔德在皇家艺术学会中很受同时代人的敬仰。

con·tempt /kən`tɛmpt; kən'tempt/ *n* [U] **1** a feeling that someone or something is not important and deserves no respect 轻蔑, 轻视, 鄙视: **[+for]** *His contempt for his fellow students was quite obvious.* 他对同学的鄙视之情非常明显。| **with contempt** *He had been treated with nothing but contempt ever since he arrived.* 他从到达时起就一直受到轻视。| **hold sb in contempt** (=feel contempt for someone) 鄙视某人 *They'd always held that family in contempt.* 他们一直鄙视那家人。| **beneath contempt** (=so unacceptable that you have no respect for the person involved) 为人不齿 *That sort of behavior is simply beneath contempt.* 那种行为简直为人所不齿。**2** disobedience or disrespect towards a court of law〔对法庭的〕轻蔑罪: **in contempt of** *He was found in contempt of the order.* 他被裁定为蔑视法庭命令。| **contempt of court** (=not doing what a judge or court of law has told you to do) 蔑视法庭〔罪〕**3** complete lack of fear towards something difficult or dangerous 不顾〔困难、危险〕: *contempt for danger* 不顾危险

con·temp·ti·ble /kən`tɛmptəbl; kən'temptəbəl/ *adj* so unacceptable that you have no respect for the person involved 可鄙的; 卑劣的: *They were portrayed as contemptible cowards.* 他们被刻画为可鄙的胆小鬼。**—contemptibly** *adv*

con·temp·tu·ous /kən`tɛmptʃuəs; kən'temptʃuəs/ *adj* **1** showing that you feel that someone or something is not important and deserves no respect 轻蔑的, 表示轻蔑的; 傲慢不恭的: *Cordelia threw him a contemptuous look.* 科迪莉娅轻蔑地朝他看了看。| **be contemptuous of** *He was openly contemptuous of his elder brother.* 他公开蔑视他大哥。**2** not feeling any fear in a dangerous situation 不顾危险的: *Contemptuous of the risks, she ran into the burning building.* 她不顾危险冲进燃烧着的大楼。**—contemptuously** *adv*

con·tend /kən`tɛnd; kən'tend/ *v* **1** [I] to compete against someone in order to gain something 竞争; 奋争: *contending for the World Heavyweight Title* 竞争世界重量级冠军 **2** [T+that] to argue or state that something is true 声称, 断言, 主张: *Some astronomers contend that the universe may be younger than previously believed.* 有些天文学家声称宇宙可能比原先认为的要年轻。

contend with sth *phr v* [T] **have to contend with sth/have sth to contend with** to have to deal with something difficult or unpleasant 必须处理[应付]某事: *He had to contend with a lot of shouting and jeering from the audience.* 他不得不应付观众发出的大喊大叫和嘲笑声。

con·tend·er /kən`tɛndɚ; kən'tendə/ *n* [C] someone who takes part in a competition or a situation in which they have to compete with other people 竞争者: *a serious contender for the Democratic nomination* 大有希望获得民主党提名的人

con·tent¹ /`kɑntɛnt; 'kɒntent/ *n* **1 contents** [plural] **a)** the things that are inside a box, bag, room etc 容纳的东西: *The box had fallen over, and some of the contents had spilled out.* 箱子翻了, 里面的一些东西散落出来。| *The customs official rummaged through the contents of the briefcase.* 海关官员彻底搜查了公事包里的物品。**b)** the things that are written in a letter, book etc〔信、书等的〕内容: *If the contents of this letter become known to the Foreign Secretary, there would be grave consequences.* 如果信的内容被外交大臣知道的话, 会带来严重的后果。| **table of contents** (=a list at the beginning of a book, which shows the different parts into which the book is divided) 目录, 目次 | **contents page** (=the page in a book on which the table of contents appears) 目录页 **2** [singular] the amount of a substance that is contained in something 含量: *the fat content of cheese* 干酪的脂肪含量 **3** [singular] the ideas, facts, or opinions that are contained in a speech or a piece of writing〔演讲或文章的〕内容: *They said they liked the content of your article, but the style wasn't quite right for the magazine.* 他们说喜欢你文章的内容, 但是文章的风格不太适合那本杂志。 S2 W2

con·tent² /kən`tɛnt; kən'tent/ *adj* [not before noun 不用于名词前] **1** happy and satisfied 满意的, 满足的: *Tarka lay drowsy and content in the sun.* 塔卡昏昏欲睡, 心满意足地躺在阳光下。| **content to do sth** *John is quite content to watch television for hours at a stretch.* 约翰非常满足一连看几小时电视。| **[+with]** *She is content with her job at the moment.* 她现在对自己的工作非常满意。**2 not content with** if someone is not content with doing something, they do not think that it is good enough, and so want to do more 对…不满足: *Not content with sentencing him to ten years in prison, the judge ordered that he leave the country on his release.* 法官对判他入狱10年仍不满足, 还命令他服刑期满后马上离开这个国家。 W3

content³ *n* [U] **1** *literary* a feeling of quiet happiness and satisfaction【文】满意, 满足 **2 do sth to your heart's content** to do something as much as you want 尽情[心满意足]地做某事: *We sang away to our hearts' content.* 我们尽情地唱个不停。

content⁴ *v* [T] **1 content yourself with sth** to do or have something that is not what you really wanted, but is still satisfactory 使自己满足[甘心]于某事: *This is all I have, so you'll have to content yourself with £5 for the moment.* 我只有这点钱, 所以现在只能给你5英镑, 你就将就将就吧。**2** to make someone feel happy and satisfied 使满意; 使满足: *I was no longer satisfied with the life that had hitherto contented me.* 我已经不满足于过去我一直感到满意的生活了。

con·tent·ed /kən`tɛntɪd; kən'tentɪd/ *adj* happy and satisfied because your life is good 满意的, 满足的: *a fat and contented black cat* 一只肥胖而显得心满意足的黑猫 **—contentedly** *adv*: *The baby gurgled contentedly in its crib.* 婴儿在婴儿床上满足地咯咯笑。

con·ten·tion /kən`tɛnʃən; kən'tenʃən/ *n* **1** [C] *formal* an opinion that someone expresses【正式】论点, 主张: *Her main contention is that doctors should do more to encourage people to lead healthy lives.* 她的主要观点是医生应该更多地鼓励大家过健康的生活。**2** [U] *formal* argument and disagreement between people【正式】争论, 争端; 口角: *The issue of subsidies is a great source of contention in Europe.* 补贴问题在欧洲是极易引发争论的问题。**3 a bone of contention** a subject that causes disagreement or argument 引起争论的话题: *Their aunt's will has always been a bone of contention between them.* 姑母的遗嘱一直是引起他们争吵的话题。**4 in contention** *formal* being the subject of argument and disagreement【正式】是争论、不和的主题: *The issue is no longer in contention.* 这问题不再争论了。

con·ten·tious /kən`tɛnʃəs; kən'tenʃəs/ *adj* **1** causing a lot of argument and disagreement between people 引起争论的; 有争议的: *Animal welfare did not become a contentious issue until the late 1970s.* 直到20世纪70年代晚期, 动物的福利才成为一个有争议的话题。**2** someone who is contentious often argues with people 爱争论的 **—contentiously** *adv* **—contentiousness** *n* [U]

con·tent·ment /kən`tɛntmənt; kən'tentmənt/ *n* [U] the state of being happy and satisfied 满意; 满足: *He gave a sigh of contentment, turned over and went to sleep.* 他满意地舒了口气, 转身睡着了。—opposite 反义词 DISCONTENT

con·test¹ /`kɑntɛst; 'kɒntest/ *n* [C] **1** a competition 比赛, 竞赛: *a beauty contest* 选美比赛 **2** a struggle to win control or power 竞争, 争夺, 角逐: *the contest for leadership of the party* 争夺该党的领导权 **3 no contest** used to mean that you will easily be the best or win the contest 轻易获胜, 轻取

C

con·test² /kən`tɛst; kən'test/ *v* [T] **1** to say formally that you do not accept something or do not agree with it 对…提出质疑; 抗辩: *His brothers are contesting the will.* 他的兄弟对遗嘱提出质疑。**2** to compete for something or try to win it 竞争, 争夺, 角逐: *contesting a seat on the council* 争夺议会的席位

con·tes·tant /kən`tɛstənt; kən'testənt/ *n* [C] someone who competes in a contest 竞争者; 选手; 参加竞赛者: *The next contestant is Vera Walker of Lincoln.* 下一个参赛者是来自林肯的薇拉·沃克。

con·text /`kɑntɛkst; 'kɒntekst/ *n* [C] **1** the situation, events, or information that are related to something, and that help you to understand it better 场合; 环境; 周围情况; 背景: *These changes must be seen in their historical and social context.* 这些变化必须放在所处的社会和历史环境中来看待。| **in context** (=considered together with the related situation, events etc rather than considered alone) 结合环境来考虑 *I think we need to look at these events in context.* 我认为我们需要从全局来看待这些事件。**2** the words and sentences that come before and after a particular word, and that help you to understand the meaning of the word 上下文, 语境: *'Mad' can mean 'foolish', 'insane', or 'angry', depending on the context.* 在不同的上下文中, mad的意思可以是"愚蠢的"、"发疯的"或"生气的"。**3 take/quote sth out of context** to repeat a sentence or statement, without describing the situation in which it was said, with the result that it seems to mean something different 断章取义: *Jones was furious that the papers had quoted his remarks completely out of context.* 报纸引他的话完全是断章取义, 琼斯因此十分气愤。

con·tex·tu·al /kən`tɛkstʃuəl; kən'tekstʃuəl/ *adj* relating to a particular context 与上下文[环境]有关的: *contextual information* 根据上下文而确定的信息 —**contextually** *adv*

con·tex·tu·al·ize also 又作 **-ise** *BrE*【英】/kən`tɛkstʃuəlaɪz; kən'tekstʃuəlaɪz/ *v* [T] to consider something together with the situation, events, or information that relate to it, rather than alone 把…与有关的背景一并考虑 —**contextualization** /kən-ˌtɛkstʃuəlaɪ`zeʃən; kənˌtekstʃuəlaɪ'zeɪʃən/ *n* [U]

con·tig·u·ous /kən`tɪgjuəs; kən'tɪgjuəs/ *adj* [+with] *formal* next to something, or near something in time or order【正式】〔时间、顺序上〕相邻的, 相近的: [+with] *Canada is contiguous with the US along much of its border.* 加拿大的边界大部分与美国接壤。—**contiguously** *adv* —**contiguity** /ˌkɑntə`gjuətɪ; ˌkɒntɪ'gjuːɪti/ *n* [U]

con·ti·nence /`kɑntənəns; 'kɒntɪnəns/ *n* [U] *formal* the practice of controlling your desire for sex【正式】节欲

con·ti·nent¹ /`kɑntənənt; 'kɒntɪnənt/ *n* [C] **1** a large mass of land surrounded by sea 洲; 大洲; 大陆: *the continents of Asia and Africa* 亚非大陆 **2 the Continent** *especially BrE* Western Europe not including Britain【尤英】〔不包括英国的〕欧洲大陆: *a holiday on the Continent* 在欧洲大陆上度假

continent² *adj* **1** able to control your BLADDER (1) and bowels (BOWEL (1)) 有排便节制力的 **2** *old use* controlling your desire to have sex【旧】禁欲的, 自我节制性欲的 —opposite 反义词 INCONTINENT

Continent, the *BrE* Europe, not including Britain or Ireland【英】欧洲大陆〔不包括英国和爱尔兰〕

CULTURAL NOTE 文化注释

This expression is based on the old idea that Britain is separate from, and very different from, the rest of Europe. It is typically used when talking about European countries as a place for holidays, but it is now becoming less common. 这一表达方式是基于一个古老的观念, 即认为英国独立于其他欧洲国家, 极为特殊。该词主要用来指作为度假地的欧洲国家, 但现在已不太常用。

con·ti·nen·tal¹ /ˌkɑntə`nɛntl; ˌkɒntɪ'nentl◂/ *adj* **1** [only before noun 仅用于名词前] belonging to the North American continent 北美大陆的: *The continental United States does not include Hawaii.* 美国大陆不包括夏威夷。**2** relating to a large mass of land 大陆的, 大陆性的: *birds and reptiles from continental South America* 从南美大陆来的鸟类和爬行动物 **3** *especially BrE* belonging to or in the European continent【尤英】欧洲大陆的: *We visited all the major continental cities.* 我们去了所有主要的欧洲大陆城市。**4** characteristic of the warmer countries in Western Europe 具有西欧温暖国家风格的: *That café looks very continental with its tables set out on the pavement like that.* 那家咖啡馆把咖啡桌摆放在人行道上, 看起来很有西欧大陆温暖国家的风情。

continental² *n* [C] *BrE old-fashioned* someone who comes from Europe but not from Britain【英, 过时】欧洲大陆人〔不包括英国人〕

continental break·fast /ˌ‥‥ `‥/ *n* [C] a breakfast consisting of coffee and bread with butter and JAM¹ (1)〔包括咖啡、面包、黄油和果酱的〕欧洲大陆式早餐, 清淡早餐 —compare 比较 ENGLISH BREAKFAST

Continental Con·gress, the /ˌ‥‥ `‥/ a group of politicians who represented the original 13 American colonies (COLONY), and met between 1774 and 1789. They made laws for the colonies, and later formed the government of the US. The Continental Congress wrote the Declaration of Independence, and its members are often called 'The Founding Fathers'. 大陆会议〔代表美国最初13个殖民地的一批政治家。1774年至1789年间, 他们举行会议, 制定了殖民地的法律, 之后组成了美国政府。大陆会议起草了《独立宣言》, 其成员常被称为美国的"开国元勋"〕

Continental Di·vide, the /ˌ‥‥ `‥/ also 又作 **the Great Divide** the chain of high mountains that goes from north to south in North America. They divide the rivers which flow into the Pacific Ocean from those which flow into the Atlantic Ocean or the Gulf of Mexico. 北美大陆分水岭, 大分水岭〔北美洲的一系列南北走向的山脉。它们将流入太平洋的河流与流入大西洋或墨西哥湾的河流分开〕

continental drift /ˌ‥‥ `‥/ *n* [U] *technical* the very slow movement of the continents (CONTINENT¹ (1)) across the surface of the Earth【术语】大陆漂移

continental shelf /ˌ‥‥ `‥/ *n plural* **continental shelves** [C] *technical* the part of a CONTINENT¹ (1) that slopes down under the ocean and ends in a steep slope down to the bottom of the ocean【术语】大陆架

con·tin·gen·cy /kən`tɪndʒənsɪ; kən'tɪndʒənsi/ *n* **1** an event or situation that might happen in the future, especially one that might cause problems〔可能发生的〕意外事件, 不测事件: **contingency plan** (=a plan that you make in order to deal with a problem that might happen) 应变计划 *contingency plans to cope with a major computer failure* 应付重大电脑故障的应变计划 **2 contingency fee** *AmE* an amount of money that a lawyer in the US will be paid only if the person they are advising wins in court【美】胜诉酬金〔胜诉才付给律师的酬劳〕

con·tin·gent¹ /kən`tɪndʒənt; kən'tɪndʒənt/ *adj formal* dependent on something that is uncertain or that will happen in the future【正式】因情况而变的, 视条件而定的: [+on/upon] *Further investment would be contingent upon the company's profit performance.* 进一步的投资取决于公司的利润收益。—**contingently** *adv*

contingent² *n* [C also+plural verb *BrE* 英] **1** a group of people who all have the same aim or are from the same area, and who are part of a larger group 代表团: *Has the Scottish contingent arrived yet?* 苏格兰代表团到了没有? **2** a group of soldiers sent to help a larger group〔军队的〕分遣队: *A large contingent of field artillery was dispatched.* 已派出了一大队野战炮兵。

con·tin·u·al /kən`tɪnjuəl; kən'tɪnjuəl/ *adj* **1** continuing for a long time without stopping 持续的, 不间断的: *five weeks of continual rain* 一连下了五个星期的雨 | *The hostages lived in continual fear of violent death.* 人质长期生活在暴力死亡的恐惧之中。**2** repeated often and over a long period of time; frequent 多次重复的, 频繁的: *The continual trips to my mother's house took up a lot of my time.* 经常去看母亲花费了我很多的时间。**3** used to describe actions that are repeated many times over a period of time and are annoying 频繁而讨厌的: *I wish you'd stop that continual chattering!* 我希望你不要再唠叨个没完! —**continually** *adv*: *continually reassessing the situation* 再三估计形势

USAGE NOTE 用法说明: CONTINUAL

WORD CHOICE 词语辨析: **continual(ly), continuous(ly)**

Continual describes separate actions (often annoying actions you do not like) which are repeated over a period of time. continual形容在一段时间内多次重复的独立动作〔常指令人不快的动作〕: *These continual interruptions are driving me mad.* 这些没完没了的插话快使我发疯了。| *She's continually flying off to different places.* 她不停地飞往不同的地方。

Continuous especially describes things and events that go on without a break. continuous尤指没有间断的事物或事件: *The police formed a continuous line round the building.* 警察在建筑物周围围成一圈。| *This product is the result of years of continuous development.* 这个产品是几年来不停开发的结果。| *We landed after flying continuously for 16 hours.* 我们在连续飞行了16小时后着陆。

The uses just described are regarded by many as the correct ones, but native speakers often use **continuous(ly)** also,

like **continual(ly)**, to describe repeated separate actions. 以上描述的用法很多人认为是正确的，不过母语是英语的人往往也用 continuous(ly) 来形容多次重复的独立动作: *There were continuous interruptions.* 一直有人插话。As a result, **continuous(ly)** is much more frequent in spoken English. Where both might be used, **continuous(ly)** may carry less of the idea that the repeated action is annoying. 因此 continuous(ly) 在英语口语中更常用。在两个词都能用的场合，continuous(ly) 表示反复动作令人不快的信息较少: *It rained continuously all summer, which was good for the rice crop.* 整个夏天都在下雨，这对稻米有好处。Compare 比较: *It rained continually all summer, which completely spoiled our vacation.* 整个夏天不停地下雨，彻底破坏了我们的假期。

con·tin·u·ance /kən`tɪnjuəns; kən'tɪnjuəns/ *n* **1** [singular, U] the state of continuing for a long period of time 持续; 连续, 继续: *the continuance in power of the Nationalist party* (南非)国民党继续掌权 **2** [C usually singular 一般用单数] *law* the act of allowing the events in a court of law to stop for a period of time, usually so a lawyer can find more facts about the case【法律】延期审理

con·tin·u·a·tion /kən͵tɪnjʊ`eʃən; kən͵tɪnju'eɪʃən/ *n* **1** [U] the act or state of continuing for a long period without stopping 继续; 持续: *A royal child will ensure the continuation of the family line.* 皇室有后，则血脉不断。**2** [C] something that follows after something else without stopping or changing 继续部分: [+of] *The present economic policy is a continuation of the earlier one.* 现在的经济政策是以前政策的延续。**3** [C] something that is joined to something else as if it were part of it 延续物, 接续物: [+of] *The Baltic Sea is a continuation of the North Sea.* 波罗的海是北海的延伸。

[1] [1] **con·tin·ue** /kən`tɪnjʊ; kən'tɪnjuː/ *v* **1** [I,T] to keep happening, existing, or doing something for a longer period of time without stopping (使)继续; (使)延续: *He will be continuing his education in the US.* 他会在美国继续上学。| *The fighting continued for a week.* 战斗持续了一个星期。| [+with] *Continuing with this argument is very pointless.* 继续这场争论毫无意义。| **continue to do sth** *Silvina continued to work after she had had her baby.* 茜尔维娜生小孩后继续工作。| **continue doing sth** *They continued talking after the meal.* 他们饭后继续谈话。**2** [I,T] to start again after an interruption〔中断后〕再继续: *After a brief ceasefire the fighting continued.* 经过短暂的停火后战斗又继续了。| **continue doing sth** *Are you going to continue seeing her when she comes back?* 她回来后你打算再跟她见面吗? **3** [I] to walk, travel, or go further on or along 继续走[旅行, 前行]: [+down/in/after etc] *We continued along the road for some time.* 我们继续沿着这条路走了一段时间。**4** [I,T] to say something else after you have been interrupted 继续说, 接着说: *"And so," he continued, "we will try harder next time."* "因此，"他接着说，"我们下一次会更加努力。" —see also 另见 CONTINUAL, DISCONTINUE

This graph shows how common different grammar patterns of the verb **continue** are. 本图表所示动词 continue 的常见不同语法模式的使用频率。

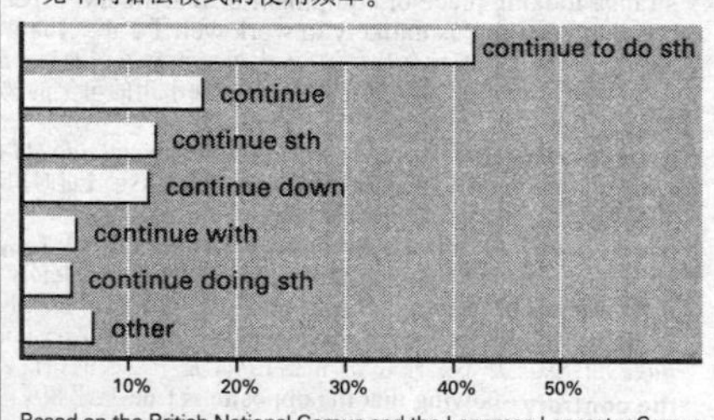

Based on the British National Corpus and the Longman Lancaster Corpus
据英国国家语料库和朗文兰开斯特语料库

con·tin·ued /kən`tɪnjud; kən'tɪnjuːd/ *adj* [only before noun 仅用于名词前] continuing to happen for a long time, or happening many times 继续的, 连续的; 反复的, 频繁的: *The continued failure of the police caused a public outcry.* 警方接连失职导致公众的强烈抗议。| *continued press speculation* 持续的媒体揣测

continuing ed·u·ca·tion /͵ ·· ·· ··'·· / *n* [U] education provided for adults outside the formal educational system, usually by means of classes that are held in the evening 继续教育, 成人教育

con·ti·nu·i·ty /͵kɑntə`nuətɪ; ͵kɒntɪ'njuːɪti/ *n* [U] **1** the continuing of an event, system etc over a long period of time, without problems happening when there is a change 连续(性), 持续(性), 连贯(性): *We should ensure continuity of care between hospital and home.* 我们应当保证医院和家庭之间保健的连续性。**2** *technical* the organization of a film or television programme to give the appearance that the action happens without pauses or interruptions【术语】〔电影的〕场景串联, 〔电视的〕节目串联

con·tin·u·o /kən`tɪnjʊo; kən'tɪnju-əʊ/ *n* [C] *technical* a musical part consisting of a line of low notes with figures showing the higher notes that are to be played with them【术语】〔音乐的〕数字低音, 通奏低音

con·tin·u·ous /kən`tɪnjʊəs; kən'tɪnjuəs/ *adj* **1** continuing to happen or exist without stopping or without any interruptions 持续的, 不间断的, 连续的: *The brain needs a continuous supply of blood.* 大脑需要不断地供血。| *The Blood Transfusion Service has a long and continuous tradition of public service.* 输血服务中心拥有长久而持续的为公众服务的传统。**2** something such as a line that is continuous does not have any spaces or holes in it〔线等〕连续的, 不间断的 **3 continuous assessment** *BrE* a way of judging how well a student is doing by looking at the work they do during the year rather than by testing them in an examination【英】〔对学生成绩的〕连续性评估〔有别于只用考试评定〕**4** *technical* the continuous form of a verb is used to show that an action or activity is continuing to happen, and is shown in English by the verb 'be', followed by a PRESENT PARTICIPLE, as in 'I was waiting for the bus'【术语】〔语法〕进行式[时]的 —**continuously** *adv* [2] [3]

con·tin·u·um /kən`tɪnjʊəm; kən'tɪnjuəm/ *n* [C] *plural* **continuums** *or* **continua** /-jʊə; -juə/ something that changes or develops very gradually, so that each part is very similar to previous and following parts; CLINE 统一体; 连续体: *a learning continuum along which all learners fit* 适合所有学习者的连续学习过程

con·tort /kən`tɔrt; kən'tɔːt/ *v* [I,T] to twist something so that it does not have its normal shape, and looks strange or unattractive, or to twist in this way (使)扭曲: [+with] *His face was contorted with rage.* 他的脸由于气愤而扭曲了。

con·tor·tion /kən`tɔrʃən; kən'tɔːʃən/ *n* [U] **1** the act of twisting something so that it does not have its normal shape, and looks strange or unattractive, or the fact of being twisted in this way 扭曲: *the involuntary contortion of muscles brought on by the illness* 由疾病引起的肌肉不由自主的扭曲 **2** [C] a twisted position or movement that looks strange 扭曲状[姿势]: *They turned as they danced with the most amazing contortions.* 他们一边跳舞一边转圈, 舞姿扭曲的幅度令人惊讶。**3** [C] complicated activity in order to do something 复杂的活动: *He went through a series of amazing contortions to get Karen a work permit.* 他费尽周折才为卡伦弄到了一个工作许可证。

con·tor·tion·ist /kən`tɔrʃənɪst; kən'tɔːʃənɪst/ *n* [C] someone who entertains people by twisting their body into strange and unnatural shapes and positions 柔体杂技演员

con·tour /`kɑntʊr; 'kɒntʊə/ *n* [C] **1** the shape of the outer edges of something such as an area of land or someone's body 外形; 轮廓: *the contours of the hills and ridges* 小山和山脊的轮廓 | *the contour of her face* 她脸部的轮廓 **2** also 又作 **contour line** a line on a map that connects points of equal height above sea level, which together with others show hills, valleys etc〔地图上的〕等高线

con·toured /`kɑntʊrd; 'kɒntʊəd/ *adj* **1** shaped to fit closely next to something else, or in a shape like this 成…的轮廓的: *The cushion was still warm, contoured to the shape of his body.* 垫子还是温的, 还留有他的坐印。**2** having an attractive, curved shape 线条迷人的; 轮廓优美的: *the smoothly contoured lines and attractive styling of this sofa* 这张沙发流畅的轮廓和迷人的风格

contra- /kɑntrə; kɒntrə/ *prefix* **1** acting to prevent something 反; 防(止): *contraceptive devices* (=against CONCEPTION) 避孕用具 **2** opposite (与…)相对: *plants in contradistinction to animals* 有别于动物的植物

con·tra·band /`kɑntrə͵bænd; 'kɒntrəbænd/ *n* [U] goods that are brought into a country illegally, especially without tax being paid on them 走私货; 禁运品: *contraband steel imported illegally into Turkey* 走私运进土耳其的钢材 —**contraband** *adj*

con·tra·bass /͵kɑntrə`bes; ͵kɒntrə'beɪs/ *n* [C] a DOUBLE BASS 低音提琴

con·tra·cep·tion /ˌkɑntrəˋsɛpʃən; ˌkɒntrəˈsepʃən/ *n* [U] the practice of making it possible for a woman to have sex without having a baby, or the methods for doing this; BIRTH CONTROL 避孕; 节（制生）育: *The pill is a popular method of contraception.* 服用避孕药是一种通用的避孕方法。

con·tra·cep·tive /ˌkɑntrəˋsɛptɪv; ˌkɒntrəˈseptɪv◂/ *n* [C] a drug, object, or method used to make it possible for a woman to have sex without having a baby 避孕药物[用具, 方法]: *You can get free contraceptives from the family planning clinic.* 你可以从计划生育门诊部免费获得避孕药。—**contraceptive** *adj* [only before noun 仅用于名词前]: *a contraceptive device* 避孕用具

2 1 **con·tract¹** /ˋkɑntrækt; ˈkɒntrækt/ *n* [C] **1** a formal written agreement between two or more people, which says what each person must do for the other 契约; 合同: *His contract of employment specifies that he must get at least one month's training.* 他的雇用合同明确写明他要接受至少一个月的培训。| **[+with]** *Tyler has just agreed a seven year contract with a Hollywood studio.* 泰勒刚刚与好莱坞的一家制片厂签订了七年的合同。| **sign a contract** *Read the contract carefully before you sign it.* 签署合同以前要仔细阅读。| **enter into a contract** *They have just entered into a lucrative contract with a clothing store.* 他们刚刚与一家服装店订立了一份利润丰厚的契约。| **be on a contract/be under contract** (=be working for someone with whom you have a contract) 跟与你订立合同的人工作 | **be in breach of contract** (=have done something that is not allowed by the contract) 违约 *If they don't get the test version of the software to us by tomorrow they'll be in breach of contract.* 如果他们到明天还没有把软件的测试版交给我们, 他们就违约了。**2 subject to contract** if an agreement is subject to contract, it has not yet been agreed formally by a contract〔达成协议但还〕须签订合约: *We've agreed to their offer on our house, subject to contract.* 我们接受了他们对房子的出价, 签订合约就成交了。**3** *informal* an agreement to kill a person for money【非正式】刺杀协议: *There is a contract out on him and he's in hiding.* 有人雇杀手杀他, 他就躲了起来。

con·tract² /kənˋtrækt; kənˈtrækt/ *v* **1** [I] to become smaller or narrower 缩小; 收缩; 缩短: *Metal contracts as it becomes cool.* 金属冷却时收缩。| *The economy continues to contract, raising fears of further political problems.* 经济继续收缩, 进一步加剧了人们对未来政治问题的恐惧。—opposite 反义词 EXPAND (1) **2** [T] *formal* to begin to have an illness【正式】感染〔疾病〕, 患〔病〕: *He contracted pneumonia.* 他得了肺炎。**3 contract to do sth** to sign a contract in which you agree formally that you will do something 签合同做…: *They contracted to work fixed hours each week.* 他们订立合同确定每个星期固定的工作时数。**4 contract a marriage/alliance etc** to agree formally that you will marry someone or have a particular kind of relationship with them 订立婚约/盟约等: *Most of the marriages were contracted when the brides were very young.* 大部分的婚约是在新娘很小的时候订立的。

contract in *phr v* [I] *formal especially BrE* to agree or promise, especially officially, to take part in something【正式, 尤英】同意参与; 订约加入: *They contracted in to the share deal.* 他们同意参与股份交易。

contract out *phr v* **1** [T **contract** sth ↔ **out**] to arrange to have a job done by a person or company outside your own organization 把〔工作等〕承包出去: *The company has contracted the catering out to an outside firm.* 这家公司已经把承办酒席包给了外面的一家公司。**2** [I] **[+of]** *formal especially BrE* to agree or promise, especially officially, not to take part in something such as a PENSION SCHEME【正式, 尤英】同意不加入〔退休金计划等〕

contract bridge /ˌ··ˈ·/ *n* [U] a form of the card game BRIDGE¹ (4), in which one of the two pairs say how many tricks (TRICK (11)) they will try to win 定约桥牌

con·trac·tion /kənˈtrækʃən; kənˈtrækʃən/ *n* **1** [C] *technical* a very strong and painful movement of a muscle, especially of the muscles around the WOMB during the process of birth【术语】挛缩〔尤指分娩时子宫收缩〕**2** [U] the process of becoming smaller or narrower 收缩; 缩小; 缩短: *the contraction of metal as it cools* 金属冷却时的收缩 **3** [C] a shortened form of a word or words〔词的〕缩略形式: *'Haven't' is a contraction of 'have not'.* haven't是have not的缩略形式。

con·trac·tor /ˋkɑntræktɚ; kənˈtræktə/ *n* [C] a person or company that makes an agreement to do work or provide goods in large amounts for another company 承包者; 承包商: *a roofing contractor* 盖屋顶的承包商

con·trac·tu·al /kənˋtræktʃuəl; kənˈtræktʃuəl/ *adj* agreed in a contract 合同规定的, 依据合同的: *College teachers have a contractual obligation to research and publish.* 大学教师依据合同有从事研究和发表作品的义务。—**contractually** *adv*

con·tra·dict /ˌkɑntrəˋdɪkt; ˌkɒntrəˈdɪkt/ *v* **1** [T] to disagree with something by saying that it is wrong or not true, especially by saying that the opposite is true 反驳; 抗辩; 否认: **contradict sb** *Don't contradict your father!* 不要顶撞你的父亲! | **flatly contradict** *The article flatly contradicts what the lobbyists have claimed.* 这篇文章与说客所宣称的完全两样。**2** [T] if one statement, story etc contradicts another statement etc, the facts in it are different so that both statements cannot be true〔说法、真相等〕与…抵触, 与…发生矛盾: *The witnesses' statements contradicted each other and the facts remained unclear.* 目击者的说法各不相同, 事实还是不清楚。**3 contradict yourself** to say something that is the opposite of what you said before 自相矛盾: *The stupid fool can't speak two sentences without contradicting himself.* 这个愚蠢的傻瓜一说话就自相矛盾。

con·tra·dic·tion /ˌkɑntrəˋdɪkʃən; ˌkɒntrəˈdɪkʃən/ *n* **1** [C] a difference between two statements, beliefs, or ideas about something that means they cannot both be true 矛盾的说法[信念、观点]: *The prosecution pointed out the contradictions in the defendant's testimony.* 控方指出了被告证词中自相矛盾的地方。| **[+between]** *There is a contradiction between the government's radical ideas and its actual urban policy.* 在政府的激进观点和其实际的城市政策之间有矛盾。**2** [U] the act of saying that someone else's opinion, statement etc is wrong or not true 反驳, 否认: *You can say what you like without fear of contradiction.* 不要怕反驳, 说你想说的。**3 a contradiction in terms** a combination of words that seem to mean opposite things, so that the phrase has no clear meaning 用词上的自相矛盾: *'Deafening silence' is a contradiction in terms.* "震耳欲聋的寂静"是用词上的自相矛盾。**4 in (direct) contradiction to** in a way that is opposite to a belief or statement 与…矛盾: *Your behavior is in direct contradiction to the principles you claim to have.* 你的行为与你所宣称的原则互相矛盾。

con·tra·dic·to·ry /ˌkɑntrəˋdɪktərɪ; ˌkɒntrəˈdɪktəri◂/ *adj* two statements, beliefs etc that are contradictory, are different and therefore cannot both be true 矛盾的; 抵触的: *The witnesses gave two completely contradictory accounts.* 目击者给了两份完全互相矛盾的证词。—see also 另见 SELF-CONTRADICTORY

con·tra·dis·tinc·tion /ˌkɑntrədɪˋstɪŋkʃən; ˌkɒntrədɪˈstɪŋkʃən/ *n* [C] **in contradistinction to** *formal* as opposed to【正式】与…相区别; 与…相对比: *plants in contradistinction to animals* 有别于动物的植物

con·tra·flow /ˋkɑntrəflo; ˈkɒntrəfləʊ/ *n* [C,U] *BrE* a temporary arrangement on a large road by which traffic in both directions uses only one side of the road because the other side is being repaired【英】〔由于公路另一侧修路而暂时实行的〕一侧双向行驶

con·trail /ˋkɑntrel; ˈkɒntreɪl/ *n* [C] *AmE* a line of white steam made in the sky by a plane【美】〔飞机在空中飞行留下的〕凝结尾流, 拉烟

con·tral·to /kənˋtrælto; kənˈtræltəʊ/ *n* [C] the lowest female singing voice, or a woman who has this voice 女低音（歌手）

con·trap·tion /kənˋtræpʃən; kənˈtræpʃən/ *n* [C] *informal* a strange looking piece of equipment or machinery, especially one that you think is unlikely to work well【非正式】奇妙的机械装置; 怪模怪样的玩意儿〔尤指不大可能正常工作的〕: *a funny old contraption for pumping up water* 抽水用的可笑的破旧玩意儿

con·tra·ri·wise /ˋkɑntrɛrɪˌwaɪz; ˈkɒntrəriwaɪz/ *adv old-fashioned* in the opposite way or direction; CONVERSE³【过时】反之, 相反地

con·tra·ry¹ /ˋkɑntrɛrɪ; ˈkɒntrəri/ *n formal*【正式】**1 on the contrary** used for showing that you disagree completely with what has just been said 正相反, 恰恰相反〔用于表示强烈不赞同别人刚说的话〕: *It wasn't a good thing; on the contrary it was a huge mistake.* 那不是件好事, 恰恰相反, 是个巨大的错误。**2 to the contrary** showing that the opposite is true 意思相反; 完全不同: *Unless there is evidence to the contrary, we ought to believe them.* 除非证据相反, 否则我们应该相信他们。**3 the contrary** the opposite of what has been said or suggested 相反; 反面; 对立面: *They say he is guilty, but I believe the contrary.* 他们说他有罪, 可我认为他无罪。

contrary² *adj* **1** contrary ideas or opinions are completely different from each other and opposed to each other 相反的, 相对的: *Two contrary views emerged in the discussion.* 讨论中出现了两个相反的意见。**2** someone who is contrary deliberately does things differently from the way that other people do them, or from the way that people expect 故意作对的, 对抗的: *Evans was*

his usual contrary self. 埃文斯依然故我，还是故意与人作对。**3 contrary to** if something is contrary to someone's belief or opinion, it is true even though that person believes or thinks the opposite 与…相反〔用于表示与别人观点相反的事实〕: *Contrary to popular belief the desert can be a beautiful place.* 正好与人们想象的相反，沙漠也可以是美丽的地方。**4** *formal* contrary weather conditions are ones that cause difficulties【正式】〔天气〕不作美的，不合人意的: *Contrary winds delayed the boats' return.* 逆风耽误了船的归航。—**contrariness** *n* [U]

con·trast¹ /ˋkɑntræst; ˈkɒntrɑːst/ *n* **1** [C,U] a difference between people, ideas, or things etc that are compared 差异，差别: **[+between]** *The contrast between the two sisters surprised him.* 两姐妹的差别让他大吃一惊。**2 in contrast/by contrast** used when you are comparing objects or situations and saying that they are completely different from each other 与…相反/相比之下: *Their old house had been large and spacious; by contrast the new London flat seemed cramped and dark.* 他们的老房子又大又宽敞，相比之下，伦敦的那套新公寓又窄又暗。| **in contrast to** *Mary was short and plump, in contrast to her mother who was tall and willowy.* 玛丽又矮又胖，与她妈妈的修长苗条形成对比。| **in sharp/marked/stark etc contrast to** *The foreign visitors were wealthy and glamorous, in complete contrast to the poverty-stricken locals.* 外国游客的富有和魅力与当地人的贫困形成鲜明的对比。**3** [C] something that is very different from something else 对照物，明显的对比物: **[+to]** *The blue skies of the holiday brochure were such a contrast to this dreary rain-sodden March day.* 度假宣传册上的蓝天与这阴雨连绵的三月天构成明显的对比。**4** [U] the differences in colour, or between light and dark, used in paintings or photographs for artistic effect〔绘画、照片中颜色、明暗的〕反差: *The artist has used contrast marvelously in his paintings.* 这个艺术家在他的绘画中巧妙地运用了颜色的反差。**5** [U] the degree of difference between the light and dark parts of a television picture〔电视画面的〕对比度，衬度: *Can you adjust the contrast please?* 请你调整一下对比度好吗?

con·trast² /kənˋtræst; kənˈtrɑːst/ *v* **1** [T] to compare two things, ideas, people etc to show how different they are from each other 使成对比〔对照〕: **contrast sth with sth** *In the film, the peaceful life of a farmer is contrasted with the violent existence of a gangster.* 电影中，农夫平静的生活与歹徒的打打杀杀形成对比。**2** [I] if two things contrast, the difference between them is very easy to see and is sometimes surprising 形成对照; 对比之下现出区别: **[+with]** *The snow was icy and white, contrasting with the brilliant blue sky.* 雪冰冷洁白，与明亮的蓝天形成对照。| **contrast sharply/strikingly with** (=be extremely different from) 与…截然不同 *These results contrast sharply with other medical tests carried out in Australia.* 这些结果与在澳大利亚进行的其他医疗检测的结果截然不同。

con·tras·ting /kənˋtræstɪŋ; kənˈtrɑːstɪŋ/ *adj* two or more things that are contrasting are different from each other, especially in a way that is interesting or attractive 对比的，对照的（尤指耐人寻味的、漂亮的）: *a blue shirt with a contrasting collar* 有截然不同颜色领子的蓝衬衫

con·tra·vene /ˌkɑntrəˋvin; ˌkɒntrəˈviːn/ *v* [T] *formal* to do something that is not allowed according to a law or rule【正式】与…相抵触，违背〔法律、法规〕: *Milk from an unhealthy cow may contravene public health regulations.* 不健康奶牛产的奶会违反公共卫生规定。

con·tra·ven·tion /ˌkɑntrəˋvɛnʃən; ˌkɒntrəˈvenʃən/ *n* **1** [C, U] the act of doing something that is not allowed by a law or rule 抵触，违反: *Sending the troops was a contravention of the treaty.* 派遣军队违反条约。**2 in contravention of** in a way that is not allowed by a law or rule 与〔法律、规定等〕抵触，与…相违: *They employed minors in contravention of the law.* 他们违法雇用未成年人。

con·tre·temps /ˋkɑntrətɑn; ˈkɒntrətɒŋ/ *n plural* **contretemps** [C] *French often humorous*【法，常幽默】**1** an argument 争论: *I had a little contretemps with Mr Willard on the phone.* 我与威拉德先生在电话里发生了一点争论。**2** an unlucky and unexpected event, especially an embarrassing one 不幸的意外事; 令人窘困的意外事

con·trib·ute /kənˋtrɪbjut; kənˈtrɪbjuːt/ *v* **1** [I,T] to give money, help, ideas etc to something that a lot of other people are also involved in 捐献; 捐助: **contribute to/towards sth** *Most people contributed something towards the new church buildings.* 大部分人都为教堂的新建筑捐了点钱。| **contribute sth to/towards sth** *The volunteers contribute huge amounts of their own time to the project.* 志愿者把自己大量的时间花在这个计划上。**2 contribute to sth** to help to cause something 对某事起促成作用: *Various factors contributed to his downfall.* 各种因素促成了他的倒台。**3** [I,T] to write articles, stories, poems etc for a newspaper or magazine〔给报纸或杂志〕撰稿; 投稿: *one of several authors contributing to the book* 为这本书撰稿的作者之一

con·tri·bu·tion /ˌkɑntrəˋbjuʃən; ˌkɒntrɨˈbjuːʃən/ *n* **1** [C] something that you give or do in order to help something be successful 捐献物; 贡献物: **[+to/towards]** *Einstein was awarded the Nobel Prize for his contribution to Quantum Theory.* 爱因斯坦因对量子论的贡献而被授予诺贝尔奖。| **make a contribution** *Day centres for the elderly make a valuable contribution to the overall service.* 照顾老人的日托所为整个服务事业作出可贵的贡献。**2** [C] an amount of money that you give in order to help pay for something 捐款: **[+to/towards]** *We are asking for contributions to disaster relief.* 我们在为赈灾募捐。| **make a contribution** *Would you like to make a contribution to the hospital rebuilding fund?* 你愿为医院重建基金捐钱吗? **3** [C] a regular payment that you make to your employer or to the government to pay for benefits that you will receive when you are no longer working, for example a PENSION¹〔保险金、养老金等的〕分摊额 **4** [C] a story, poem, or piece of writing that you write and that is printed in a magazine or newspaper 投送的稿件: *This week's issue has contributions from several well-respected journalists.* 本期周刊有几篇德高望重的新闻记者写的文章。**5** [U] the act of giving money, time, help etc 捐献: *All the money has been raised by voluntary contribution.* 这些钱都是靠自愿捐献筹措的。

con·trib·u·tor /kənˋtrɪbjətɚ; kənˈtrɪbjʊtə/ *n* [C] **1** someone who writes a story, article etc that is printed in a magazine or newspaper 撰稿人，投稿人: **[+to]** *I became a regular contributor to the paper, writing film reviews.* 我成了这份报纸的定期撰稿人，写电影评论。**2** someone who gives money, help, ideas etc to something that a lot of other people are also involved in 捐款人; 捐助人; 作出贡献的人: **[+to]** *Dr Win was a major contributor to the research.* 温博士是这项研究的主要贡献者。**3** *formal* someone or something that helps to cause something to happen【正式】导致某事的人[事]; 起作用的人[因素]: **[+to]** *Order and quiet are important contributors to a good learning environment.* 安静有序是良好的学习环境的重要因素。

con·trib·u·to·ry /kənˋtrɪbjəˌtorɪ; kənˈtrɪbjʊtəri/ *adj* **1** [only before noun 仅用于名词前] being one of the causes of a particular result 导致…: *Smoking is a contributory cause of lung cancer.* 抽烟是导致肺癌的一个因素。**2** a contributory PENSION¹ or insurance plan is one that is paid for by the workers as well as by the company〔退休金或保险金计划〕由雇主与雇员共同出钱的 —opposite 反义词 NONCONTRIBUTORY

contributory neg·li·gence /·ˌ···· ˈ···/ *n* [U] *law* failure to take enough care to avoid or prevent an accident, so that you are partly responsible for any loss or damage caused【法律】共同过失〔由于过失造成事故，因此应承担部分责任〕

con trick /ˈ· ·/ *n* [C] a CONFIDENCE TRICK 诈骗

con·trite /ˋkɑntraɪt; ˈkɒntraɪt/ *adj* feeling guilty and sorry for something bad that you have done 悔罪的，悔悟的，痛悔的: *her contrite expression* 她懊悔的表情 —**contritely** *adv* —**contrition** /kənˋtrɪʃən; kənˈtrɪʃən/ *n* [U]

con·triv·ance /kənˋtraɪvəns; kənˈtraɪvəns/ *n* **1** [C,U] a clever plan to get something for yourself by deceiving someone, or the practice of doing this 计谋; 诡计: *Their story was a clumsy contrivance to persuade me to help them.* 他们的故事是一个蹩脚的诡计，想说服我帮助他们。**2** [C] a machine or piece of equipment that has been made or invented for a special purpose 发明物，新装置: *a steam-driven contrivance used in 19th century clothing factories* 19 世纪制衣厂使用的蒸汽动力装置

con·trive /kənˋtraɪv; kənˈtraɪv/ *v* [T] **1** to arrange an event or situation in a clever way, especially secretly or by deceiving people 谋划，策划: *He managed to contrive a meeting between Janet and her ex-boyfriend.* 他设法策划珍妮特与她的前男友相会。**2** *formal* to succeed in doing something in spite of difficulties【正式】设法做到: **contrive to do sth** *She didn't speak any English, but we contrived to communicate using sign language.* 她一点英语也不会说，但是我们设法用手势语来交流。**3** to make or invent something in a clever way, especially because you need it suddenly〔尤指由于突然的需要而〕造出; 想出; 发明; 设计: *Peter had contrived a tolerable substitute for our sled.* 彼得拼凑了一种过得去的装置来代替我们的雪橇。

con·trived /kənˋtraɪvd; kənˈtraɪvd/ *adj* a story, situation etc that is contrived has been written or arranged in a way that seems false and not natural〔故事、情节等〕不自然的; 勉强的: *The film had a ridiculously contrived story line.* 这部电影的故事情节荒谬且牵强。

con·trol¹ /kən'trol; kən'trəʊl/ *n*

1 ►MAKE SB/STH DO WHAT YOU WANT 控制某人/物◄[U] the ability or power to make someone or something do what you want 掌握; 控制; 支配; 管理; 抑制: *Generally your driving's OK, but your clutch control isn't very good.* 总的来说你的驾驶还是可以的，但是你对离合器的控制不是很好。| [+of/over] *Babies are born with very little control over their movements.* 婴儿先天的运动控制能力很差。| **have control of/over** *I prefer living alone because I feel I have more control over my life.* 我宁愿一个人，因为我觉得这样更能支配自己的生活。| **under control** (=being controlled or dealt with successfully) 在控制之中 *Don't worry, everything's under control.* 不要担心，一切都在控制之中。| **out of control** (=no longer possible to be controlled) 不受控制[支配] *The car spun out of control and hit a tree.* 汽车失去控制，撞在了一棵树上。| **get out of control** (=become impossible to control) 失去控制 *The street party went on, getting louder and louder and more out of control.* 街头聚会还在继续，声音越来越大，逐渐失控。| **lose control (of)** (=not be able to control something any longer) 失去（对…的）控制 *He took a corner too fast, and lost control of the car.* 他转弯太急了，汽车失去了控制。| **beyond/outside sb's control** (=impossible for you to control) 无法/不受控制 *Ten people had been killed, and it was obvious that the situation had gotten beyond the control of the authorities.* 已经有10个人被杀了，很明显，当局已经控制不住局势了。| **take/gain control (of)** (=gain the ability to control something) 得到/取得（对…的）控制 *Students are encouraged to take control of their own learning, rather than just depending on the teacher.* 学生被鼓励要自己掌握学习，而不只是依靠老师。| **circumstances beyond sb's control** (=a situation that you cannot control) 不受控制的情况 *Tonight's performance has been cancelled due to circumstances beyond our control.* 今晚的演出取消了，因为一些不可控因素。

2 ►POLITICAL/MILITARY POWER 政治/军事权力◄[U] the power to rule or govern a place, or the fact that you have more power than other political parties 统治; 管理; 管制: **have control of/over** *By the end of the year, the rebels had control of the northern territories.* 到年底，叛乱分子已经控制了北部的领土。| **gain/take control (of)** (=get control of a place that someone else was controlling) 取得控制… *When the communists gained control they abolished the monarchy.* 共产党取得政权后废除了君主制。| **lose control** (=not be able to control a place any longer) 失去控制 *The Democrats have just lost control of Congress.* 民主党人失去了在国会的主导地位。| **be/come under sb's control** *The whole of this area came under Soviet control.* 整个地区都在苏联的控制之下。| **under the control of** (=being controlled by a political party etc) 受…的控制[支配] *The government has been overthrown and the country is now under the control of the military.* 政府被推翻了，现在整个国家都在军队的控制之下。| **under British/Communist/enemy control** *The city is now under Serbian control.* 这个城市现在在塞尔维亚人的控制之下。| **regain control** (=gain control after you had lost it) 重获支配权 *The Conservatives are hoping to regain control of the seats taken from them in the last election.* 保守党人希望重新获得在上次选举中失去的席位。| **have overall control** *BrE* (=have more members of your political party in a council than other parties have, so that you control the council) 【英】〔在议会中〕占多数席位，占支配地位 | **assume control** (=get control of a country by defeating the government using military power) 〔用军队〕取得政权 *Lij Iyasu seized the palace and assumed control of the country.* 利杰·伊亚苏攻占了皇宫并且控制了该国。

3 ►WAY OF LIMITING STH 限制措施◄[C,U] a method or law for limiting the amount or growth of something 管制（措施）: [+of] *the control of inflation* 通货膨胀的抑制 | *control of pests and diseases* 害虫和疾病控制 | [+on] *The authorities imposed strict controls on the movement of cattle.* 当局对牛的运送采取了严格的控制措施。| **arms control** (=control of the amount of weapons a country has) 军备控制 *An arms control agreement between the superpowers has just been announced.* 两个超级大国之间刚刚签订了军备控制协议。| **crowd control** *Crowd control is a problem for the police at these demonstrations.* 对警察来讲，在这些示威游行中控制人群是个难题。| **tight/rigid controls** (=strict controls) 严格的管制 *The government favours the introduction of tighter controls on immigration.* 政府赞同对移民进行更加严格的管制。| **rent/price/wage etc controls** *Rent controls ensured that no one paid too much for housing.* 租金管制保证房租不会太高。

4 ►DISEASE/FIRE ETC 疾病/火等◄[U] the ability to stop something dangerous from getting worse or affecting more people 〔对危险物的〕抑制，控制: **have sth under control** *Firefighters now have the blaze under control.* 消防队员已经使火势得到了控制。| **bring sth under control** *The plant was given six months to bring the pollution under control.* 给工厂六个月时间控制污染。| **keep sth under control** *Johnson's been struggling for years to keep his drinking under control.* 约翰逊多年来一直在努力控制自己的饮酒量。

5 ►ABILITY TO CONTROL EMOTIONS 情感克制力◄[U] the ability to remain calm even when you feel very angry, upset, or excited 克制: *It took a lot of control, but she managed not to cry.* 那需要很大的克制力，但是她终于没哭出来。| **lose control** (=become extremely angry or upset and not be able to control your behaviour) 〔情感〕失去控制 *Jim made me so mad, I just lost control and hit him.* 吉姆让我非常生气，我失去控制打了他。| **self-control** (=the ability to behave calmly even when you feel very upset, angry etc) 自我克制 | **regain control** (=succeed in behaving calmly again after you have been upset or angry) 重新平静下来 *She felt tears welling up inside her again, but she managed to regain control.* 她感到又要流泪，但是她尽量重新平静下来。

6 be in control a) to be able to control a situation, organization, or area because you have more power than anyone else 控制着〔局势、组织或地区〕: [+of] *The anti-government forces are still in control of the area.* 反政府势力现在仍控制着该地区。**b)** to be able to control your emotions, deal with problems, and organize your life well 克制住〔情感〕: *Weber's one of those guys who always seems to be in control.* 韦伯是一个仿佛总能控制住自己的人。**c)** to manage to control a difficult situation 控制了〔困难局面〕: [+of] *The police chief assured reporters that he was in control of events.* 警察总长向记者保证局面在他的控制之中。

7 ►COMPANY/ORGANIZATION 公司/组织◄[U] the power to make all the important decisions in an organization or part of an organization 控制力; 支配力: **take control (of)** *Anne Williams will take control of the research division on August 5th.* 安妮·威廉斯将在8月5日起分管研究部。| **have control of** (=own a larger part of a company than other people so that you control that company) 〔因拥有较多股本而〕控制〔公司〕 *The Johnson family has effective control of the company, owning almost 60% of the shares.* 约翰逊家族有效地控制了那家公司，掌握近60%的股份。| **lose control (of)** (=not be able to control a company etc any longer) 失去（对…的）控制 *McAllister lost control of the company in 1988.* 麦卡利斯特在1988年失去了对那家公司的控制权。| **under the control of** (=being controlled by someone) 在…的控制下 *The college was under the control of a group of trustees.* 这所大学由一群理事管理。

8 ►MACHINE/VEHICLE 机器/车辆◄[C] the thing that you press or turn to make a machine, vehicle, television etc work 〔机器、车辆、电视等的〕控制[操纵]装置: *Who's got the control for the video?* 谁拿了录像机的控制器？| *the volume control of a television set* 电视机的音量控制器 | **be at the controls** (=be controlling a vehicle or aircraft) 操纵; 驾驶 *The co-pilot is at the controls.* 副驾驶员在操纵飞机。—see also 另见 REMOTE CONTROL

9 ►SKILL 技术◄[U] the ability to make very skilful movements with a ball, pencil, tool etc 控球[运笔、使用工具等]的技巧: *Johnson passes with good control, over to Abdul-Jubber.* 约翰逊非常熟练地传给阿布杜尔·贾巴尔。

10 ►AIRCRAFT ETC 飞机等◄[U] the people who direct an activity, especially by giving instructions to an aircraft or SPACECRAFT 指挥人员; 操纵人员: *air-traffic control* 空中交通调度员

11 ►SCIENTIFIC TEST 科学测试◄*technical*【术语】[C] **a)** a person, group etc against which you compare another person or group that is very similar, in order to see if a particular quality is caused by something or happens by chance 对照人[组]: **control group/population** *A control group of nonsmoking women were compared to four groups of women smokers.* 将一个不抽烟妇女的对照组和四个抽烟妇女组进行了比较。**b)** a thing that you already know the result for that is used in a scientific test, in order to show that your method is working correctly 对照物 —see also 另见 CONTROLLED EXPERIMENT

12 ►COMPUTER 电脑◄also 又作 **control key** [singular] a particular button on a computer that allows you to do certain operations 控制键: *Press control and F2 to exit.* 按控制键和F2退出来。

13 ►YOUR BODY 身体◄the ability to control the movements of your body by using your muscles when dancing or doing physical exercise 〔跳舞或体育锻炼时对身体的〕控制力

14▶CHECKING SOMETHING 检查某物◀ [U] the process of checking that something is correct, or the place where this is done 检查; 检查站: *passport control* 护照检查（站） | *stock control* 库存管理 —see 见 BIOLOGICAL CONTROL, BIRTH CONTROL, QUALITY CONTROL, REMOTE CONTROL

S2 W1 **control²** *v* controlled, controlling [T]

1▶MAKE SB/STH DO WHAT YOU WANT 支配某人/某物◀ to make someone or something do what you want or behave in the way you want them to behave 支配; 指挥; 管理: *The teacher can't control the class.* 这老师管不住这个班。| *a huge company controlling half the world's coffee trade* 控制全球一半咖啡贸易的大公司

2▶MACHINE/PROCESS/SYSTEM 机器/过程/系统◀ to make a machine, process, or system work in a particular way 控制; 管理: *This button controls the temperature in the building.* 这个按钮控制这座建筑物内的温度。| **control how/what/which etc** *The valves in the heart control how quickly the blood is pumped around the body.* 心脏的瓣膜掌管着血液输送到身体各处的速度。

3▶LIMIT 限制◀ if a government etc controls something, it uses laws or other methods to limit the amount or growth of something 管制; 管束: *Development in areas of outstanding natural beauty is strictly controlled.* 在风景区搞开发受到严格的限制。

4▶POLITICAL/MILITARY POWER 政治/军事权力◀ to rule or govern a place, or to have more power than other political parties 统治; 支配: *The Democrats continued to control the House until 1994.* 民主党人对众议院的控制一直持续到 1994 年。| **Labour/Republican/Democrat controlled** *a Conservative-controlled council* 由保守党人控制的地方议会

5▶DISEASE/FIRE ETC 疾病/火等◀ to stop something dangerous from getting worse or affecting more people 抑制, 控制〔危险物〕: *The Ministry of Health has set up a programme to control the spread of AIDS.* 卫生部已经制定了一套抑制艾滋病传播的计划。

6▶EMOTION 情绪◀ if you control your emotions, you succeed in behaving calmly and sensibly, even though you feel angry, upset, or excited 克制, 自制: *Sarah just can't control her temper.* 莎拉根本控制不了自己的脾气。| **control yourself** (=succeed in behaving calmly and sensibly, even though you feel angry etc) 自我克制 *She annoyed me intensely, but I managed to control myself and remain polite.* 她使我非常烦, 但是我尽量克制自己并保持礼貌。

7▶VOICE/EXPRESSION 声音/表情◀ if you control your voice or the expression on your face, you make it seem normal, so that people cannot see that you are upset, angry, or excited 控制〔嗓音或表情, 以免表露情绪〕: *He controlled his voice, betraying nothing but a casual interest.* 他控制着嗓音, 只表现出泛泛的兴趣。

8▶ANIMALS 动物◀ to kill animals when there are so many of them that they cause problems 节制, 调节〔动物数量〕: *measures to control rats in the city's sewers* 节制城市下水道中老鼠数量的措施

9▶BUSINESSES/ORGANIZATIONS 企业/组织◀ to make sure that something is done correctly 确保, 保证: *The company strictly controls the quality of its products.* 这家公司严格控制其产品的质量。

USAGE NOTE 用法说明: CONTROL

WORD CHOICE 词语辨析: **control, manage, run, be in charge of, check on, inspect, monitor**

Most meanings of **control** (*n,v*) involve the idea of a person or other force having the power to change or stop something, without the people or things affected being able to do anything about it. People, organizations, machines etc **control** other people, organizations, their own or other's actions, events, etc, sometimes from far away. control 的大部分意思包含一个人或别的力量有能力改变或制止某事, 而被影响的人或物对此则无能为力。control 的主体是人、组织、机器等, 对象有时远在别处, 包括其他人、组织、主体自己或别人的行动、事件等。

Where you want to give the idea of people directing businesses etc, where the other people involved are nearby and perhaps allowed some say in the activity, you may use **manage, run**, or **be in charge of**. 指人管理商业等, 被管理的人就在附近而且或许有发言权, 可以用 manage, run 或 be in charge of: *He's managing/running an electrical shop/project group/rock band.* 他经营一家电器商店/管理一个项目组/领导一个摇滚乐队。| *Margaret is in charge of the school while Mrs Williams is away.* 威廉斯太太不在的时候玛格丽特掌管学校。

When you want to talk about people, things, or activities, in order to see if they are correct, but without directly affecting them, you may use **check on** or **inspect**. 谈论人、事物或活动, 想要知道他们是不是正确, 但是不直接影响他们, 可以用 check on 或 inspect: *We need to check on our sales.* 我们需要检查我们的销售额。| *The department is going to be inspected next week.* 这个部门下个星期要接受检查。| *a security check* 安全检查。

Control means the same as **check on** only in a few contexts, and usually only as the noun. control 与 check on 只在少数上下文中的意思一样, 而且通常只用作名词: *quality control* 质量检查 | *stock control* 库存管理

Monitor is a word meaning to watch and check on someone or something over a period of time. This can be done by a person or by a machine, often in a technical or official context. monitor 的意思是在一段时期中观察并检查某人或某物。这可以由人或机器来完成, 通常用在技术性或正式的环境中。

control key /ˈ· · ˌ/ *n* [C] a particular button on a computer that allows you to do certain operations〔电脑的〕控制键

con·trol·la·ble /kənˋtroləbḷ; kənˈtrəʊləbəl/ *adj* possible to be controlled 可管理的, 可操纵的, 可控制的: *Central heating makes the temperature of your home easily controllable.* 中央供暖系统使家中的温度可轻易控制。

con·trolled /kənˋtrold; kənˈtrəʊld/ *adj* **1** calm and not showing emotion, even if you feel angry, afraid etc 自制的, 克制的: *Her voice was resonant and controlled as she delivered her resignation speech.* 当她在作辞职演讲时声音洪亮而且是克制的。**2** a movement, action, situation etc that is controlled is one that is carefully and deliberately done in a particular way, or made to have particular qualities 受控制的; 受限制的: *The chicks are hatched in a controlled environment.* 小鸡是在一个受控制的环境中孵化的。**3** limited by a law or rule 受法律[规则]管制的: *controlled parking zones* 受管制的停车区

controlled drug /ˌ·, ˈ· ˈ/ *n* [C] *law* a drug that is illegal to possess or use【法律】管制药物

controlled ex·per·i·ment /ˌ·, · ˈ· · ·/ *n* [C] *technical* a scientific test done in a place where you can control all the things that might affect the test【术语】受控实验, 控制性实验: *a controlled experiment to determine the effects of light and nutrients on plant growth* 确定光线及各种营养素对植物生长产生的影响的控制性实验

controlled sub·stance /ˌ·, ˈ· ·/ *n* [C] *law* a drug that is illegal to possess or use【法律】管制药物: *Heroin is a controlled substance.* 海洛因是一种管制药物。

con·trol·ler /kənˋtrolɚ; kənˈtrəʊlə/ *n* [C] **1** someone who is in charge of a particular organization or part of an organization 控制者; 管理者; 指挥者: *the Controller of Channel 4* 第 4 频道的管理者 **2** also 又作 **comptroller** *formal* someone who is in charge of the money received or paid out by a company or government department【正式】审计员; 审计官

controlling in·terest /ˌ·, · · ˈ· / *n* [C usually singular 一般用单数] *technical* if you have a controlling interest in a company, you own enough shares (SHARE² (5)) to be able to make decisions about what happens to the company【术语】〔对一家公司的〕控股权益

control room /ˈ· · ˌ/ *n* [C] the room that a process, service, large machine, factory etc is controlled from 控制室

control tow·er /ˈ· ˌ· ·/ *n* [C] a tall building in an airport from which people direct the movement of aircraft on the ground and in the air〔机场的〕控制塔

con·tro·ver·sial /ˌkɑntrəˋvɝʃəl; ˌkɒntrəˈvɜːʃəl◀/ *adj* causing a lot of disagreement, because many people have strong opinions about the subject being discussed 引起争论的, 有争议的: *Contraception is still a controversial issue in this part of the world.* 在世界上的这个地方, 节育仍是个有争议的问题。| **a controversial plan/decision etc** *a highly controversial plan to flood the valley in order to build a hydro-electric dam* 一个为了建水电站而要淹没山谷的有很大争议的计划 | **a controversial figure** (=someone who does things that are controversial) 有争议的人物 *Maxwell soon became a controversial figure in the world of big business.* 马克斯韦尔很快就在大企业界成为一个有争议的人物。—**controversially** *adv*

con·tro·ver·sy /ˋkɑntrəˌvɝsɪ; ˈkɒntrəvɜːsi/ *n* [C,U] a serious argument or disagreement, especially about something such as a plan or decision, that continues for a long time 争论; 辩论; 争议: *The proposals to reduce the strength of the army have been the subject of much controversy.* 削减军队力量的提议已

经招来很多争议。| *a political controversy* 政治争论 | **[+over/about/surrounding]** *the controversy surrounding the nuclear energy program* 围绕核能项目的争论

con·tu·ma·cious /ˌkɑntjuˋmeʃəs; ˌkɒntjʊˋmeɪʃəs◂/ *adj formal* unreasonably disobedient【正式】拒不服从的 —**contumaciously** *adv*

con·tume·ly /kənˋtuməlɪ; ˈkɒntjuːmli/ *n* [C,U] disrespectful and offensive behaviour or language 谩骂; 傲慢的行为; 侮辱行为

con·tuse /kənˋtuz; kənˈtjuːz/ *v* [T] *technical* to BRUISE[2]【术语】挫伤

con·tu·sion /kənˋtjuʒən; kənˈtjuːʒən/ *n* [C,U] *technical* a BRUISE[1] or BRUISING【术语】挫伤

co·nun·drum /kəˋnʌndrəm; kəˈnʌndrəm/ *n* [C] **1** a confusing and difficult problem 难题, 复杂问题: *I don't know the answer – it's a conundrum.* 我不知道答案, 这是个难题。**2** a trick question asked for fun; RIDDLE[1] (1) 谜语

con·ur·ba·tion /ˌkɑnɚˋbeʃən; ˌkɒnɜːˈbeɪʃən/ *n* [C] a group of towns that have spread and joined together to form an area with a high population, often with a large city as its centre〔由中心大城市及卫星城镇构成的〕集合城市, 大都市圈: *urban conurbations on the west coast* 西海岸的集合城市

con·va·lesce /ˌkɑnvəˋlɛs; ˌkɒnvəˈles/ *v* [I] to spend time getting well after an illness 病后疗养; 康复: *After her operation my wife was sent abroad to convalesce.* 我妻子手术后被送到国外去疗养。

con·va·les·cence /ˌkɑnvəˋlɛsn̩s; ˌkɒnvəˈlesəns/ *n* [singular] the length of time a person spends getting well after an illness〔病后的〕康复期, 恢复期: *a long and painful convalescence* 漫长而痛苦的恢复期

con·va·les·cent /ˌkɑnvəˋlɛsn̩t; ˌkɒnvəˈlesənt◂/ *n* [C] a person spending time getting well after an illness 康复期病人 —**convalescent** *adj*: *a convalescent nursing home* 康复疗养院

con·vect /kənˋvɛkt; kənˈvekt/ *v* [I] *technical* to move heat by convection【术语】对流传热

con·vec·tion /kənˋvɛkʃən; kənˈvekʃən/ *n* [U] the movement in a gas or liquid caused by warm gas or liquid rising, and cold gas or liquid sinking〔气体、液体的〕对流: *Warm air rises by convection.* 暖空气依靠对流作用上升。

convection ov·en /ˈ·ˈ·· ˌ··/ *n* [C] a special OVEN that makes hot air move around inside it so that all the parts of the food get the same amount of heat 对流加热烤箱

con·vec·tor /kənˋvɛktɚ; kənˈvektə/ also 又作 **convector hea·ter** /ˈ·ˈ·· ˌ··/ *n* [C] an electrical heater that uses hot air 对流加热器

con·vene /kənˋvin; kənˈviːn/ *v* [I,T] *formal* if a group of people convene, or someone convenes them, they come together, especially for a formal meeting【正式】聚集, 集合; 开会: *The President's foreign policy advisers convened for an emergency session.* 总统的外交政策顾问们召开紧急会议。| *Shouldn't we convene a meeting about this?* 我们不应当为此事召集一个会议吗?

con·ve·ni·ence /kənˋvinjəns; kənˈviːniəns/ *n* **1** [U] the quality of being suitable for a particular purpose, especially because it is easy to use or saves you time 方便, 便利; 合宜: *Many women prefer the convenience of working at home while their children are small.* 很多妇女在孩子还小的时候宁可在家里工作, 因为这样比较方便。| **for convenience** *We bought this house for convenience; it's near the shops and the railway station.* 为了方便起见我们买了这座房子, 它靠近商店和火车站。**2** [U] what is easiest and best for a particular person〔个人的〕便利; 自在, 舒适: **for sb's convenience** *I'm not going to organize my day entirely for your convenience!* 我不打算完全为了你的方便而安排我的时间! | **suit sb's convenience** *We can call at your home at any time to suit your convenience.* 我们可以在任何你方便的时候去你家。| **at sb's convenience** (=at a time that is best and easiest for someone) 在某人方便的时候 *Meetings are always arranged at the management's convenience and staff are expected to fit in.* 会议总是安排在管理层最方便的时候, 而让员工去配合。**3 at your earliest convenience** *formal* as soon as possible; usually in letters【正式】尽快〔常用于书信〕: *We should be grateful if you would reply at your earliest convenience.* 盼早日回复, 非常感谢! **4** [C] something that is useful because it saves you time or means that you have less work to do 便利措施; 带来方便的装置: *The supermarket offers a bag-packing service, as a convenience to customers.* 为方便顾客, 这家超市提供装袋服务。**5** also 又作 **public convenience** [C usually plural 一般用复数] *formal* a public toilet【正式】公共厕所 **6 a marriage of convenience** a marriage that has been agreed for a particular purpose, not because the two people love each other 基于利害关系的婚姻: *In the past most royal marriages were marriages of convenience, arranged for political reasons.* 过去大部分的皇室婚姻是基于政治原因的婚姻。

convenience food /ˈ·ˈ··· ˌ·/ also 又作 **convenience foods** *n* [C,U] food that is frozen, or in tins, packages etc, and can be prepared quickly and easily 方便食品〈如速冻食品、罐装食品等〉: *People with busy lifestyles tend to rely more and more on convenience foods.* 生活节奏快的人越来越倾向于吃方便食品。

convenience store /ˈ·ˈ··· ˌ·/ *n* [C] *AmE* a shop where you can buy food, alcohol, magazines etc, that is often open 24 hours each day【美】〔常指每天营业 24 小时的〕便民店, 便利店 —see also 另见 CORNER SHOP

con·ve·ni·ent /kənˋvinjənt; kənˈviːniənt/ *adj* **1** helpful for you because it saves you time or does not spoil your plans or cause you problems 方便的; 便利的; 合宜的: *I find going to the supermarket once a month the most convenient way to shop.* 我发现一个月去超市购物一次最合适。| **convenient for sb** *Is three o'clock convenient for you?* 3点钟你方便吗? | **convenient time/moment** *I'm afraid this isn't a very convenient time – could you call back later?* 我想现在不是很合适, 你能稍后再打电话来吗? **2** near and easy to reach 附近的; 方便的: *The bus stop around the corner is probably the most convenient.* 拐角处的公共汽车站可能是最方便的了。| **convenient for sth** *Our house is very convenient for schools and stores.* 我们的房子离学校和商店很近。—opposite 反义词 INCONVENIENT

con·ve·ni·ent·ly /kənˋvinjəntlɪ; kənˈviːniəntli/ *adv* **1** in a way that is helpful for you because it saves you time or does not spoil your plans or cause you problems 方便地; 便利地; 合宜地: *The results can be summarized conveniently in the following table.* 下图概括了这些结果, 一目了然。**2** in a place that is near or easily reached 近便; 便利: *The hotel is conveniently situated near the airport.* 这家酒店坐落在机场附近, 很便利。**3** if someone has conveniently forgotten, ignored, lost etc something, they are pretending to have forgotten etc because this helps them to avoid doing something 故意〔忘记、不理会、丢失等〕: *Mary conveniently forgot that she had promised to help clean the kitchen.* 玛丽故意忘记曾答应过要帮忙打扫厨房。

con·vent /ˋkɑnvɛnt; ˈkɒnvənt/ *n* [C] a building or set of buildings where NUNS live 女修道院 —see also 另见 CONVENT SCHOOL

con·ven·tion /kənˋvɛnʃən; kənˈvenʃən/ *n* **1** [C,U] behaviour and attitudes that most people in a society consider to be normal and right 惯例; 常规; 习俗: *The handshake is a social convention.* 握手是一种社会习俗。| *She went against all convention and married outside her religion.* 她违背习俗, 与信其他宗教的人结了婚。| **by convention** *By convention, the bride's father gives her away at her wedding.* 按照习俗, 新娘的父亲在婚礼上把她交给新郎。—see 见 HABIT (USAGE) **2** [C] a formal agreement, especially between countries, about particular rules or behaviour〔国际性的〕公约; 协定: *the European Convention on Human Rights*《欧洲人权公约》—compare 比较 PACT, TREATY **3** [C] a large formal meeting for people who belong to the same profession or organization 大会, 会议: *a teacher's convention* 教师大会

CULTURAL NOTE 文化注释

In the US, the political parties hold national conventions every four years to decide who will be that party's CANDIDATE for President and Vice President. The conventions are held after the PRIMARY elections, and the person with the most votes in the primaries is usually the person chosen to run (=try to get elected) for President. At the conventions the party members also discuss what their policies (POLICY) will be. 在美国, 各政治党派每四年举行一次全国代表大会, 决定该党竞选总统和副总统的候选人。代表大会在初选后举行, 初选中得票最多者通常获选角逐总统之位。代表大会也将讨论该党未来的施政方针。

4 [C] a method or style often used in literature, art, the theatre etc to achieve a particular effect〔文学、艺术上的〕传统手法: *The omniscient narrator is a convention of the nineteenth century novel.* 无所不知的叙述者是 19 世纪小说采用的一种传统手法。

con·ven·tion·al /kənˋvɛnʃənl; kənˈvenʃənəl/ *adj* **1** [only before noun 仅用于名词前] a conventional object or way of doing something is of a type that has been used or available for a long time and is considered the usual type 按惯例的; 因袭的; 传统的: *The water purifying system fits neatly under a conventional sink unit.* 水净化系统装在传统的水槽下面, 十分简便。**2** always following the opinions and behaviour that most people

in a society consider to be normal, right, and socially acceptable but sometimes slightly boring〔观点、行为〕守旧的, 传统的: *Her opinions are rather narrow and conventional.* 她的观点相当狭窄而且守旧。| **[+in]** *John is fairly conventional in his tastes.* 约翰的趣味相当传统。—opposite 反义词 UNCONVENTIONAL **3 the conventional wisdom** the opinion that most people consider to be normal and right 公众意见, 普遍看法: *This idea has become part of the conventional wisdom of a whole generation of educationalists.* 这个观点已经成为一代教育工作者普遍看法的一部分。**4** [only before noun 仅用于名词前] conventional weapons and wars are not NUCLEAR ones〔武器、战争〕常规的, 非核子的 **5 conventional medicine** the usual form of medicine practised in most European and North American countries; WESTERN MEDICINE 传统的西方医学—**conventionally** *adv*—**conventionality** /kənˌvɛnʃənˋælətɪ; kənˌvenʃəˈnælɜti/ *n* [U]

conventional ov·en /ˌ·ˈ··ˌ··, ··/ *n* [C] an ordinary OVEN, not a MICROWAVE[1](1) 普通烤箱〔非微波炉〕: *This will take 3 minutes in a microwave, or 25 minutes in a conventional oven.* 这在微波炉中要加热3分钟, 在普通烤箱中要25分钟。

convent school /ˈ·· ,·/ *n* [C] a school for girls that is run by Roman Catholic NUNS〔由天主教会修女管理的〕女修道院学校

con·verge /kənˋvɝdʒ; kənˈvɜːdʒ/ *v* [I] **1** to come from different directions and meet at the same point 会合; 汇合; 集中: *The two streams converge here to form a river.* 两条溪流在这里汇合成一条河。**2** if groups of people converge in a particular place, they come there from many different places and meet together to form a large crowd〔人群〕聚集, 聚会, 汇集: **[+on]** *The two armies converged on the enemy capital.* 两支军队在敌人的首都会师。**3** if different ideas or aims converge, they become the same〔观点、目标〕趋同: *Here the two distinct theories converge.* 在这里两个完全不同的理论趋于一致。—opposite 反义词 DIVERGE

con·ver·sant /kənˋvɝsn̩t; kənˈvɜːsənt/ *adj* [not before noun 不用于名词前] **1** *formal* having knowledge or experience of something【正式】熟悉的; 有经验的: **[+with]** *Are you fully conversant with the facts of the case?* 你完全熟悉这个案件的情况吗? **2** *AmE* able to hold a conversation in a foreign language, but not to be able to speak it perfectly【美】有某种外语的会话能力但不精通的: **[+in]** *He's conversant in French but not really fluent.* 他会说法语但不是很流利。

1 2 **con·ver·sa·tion** /ˌkɑnvɚˋseʃən; ˌkɒnvəˈseɪʃən/ *n* **1** [C] an informal talk in which people exchange news, feelings, and thoughts〔非正式的〕谈话, 交谈, 会话: *a telephone conversation* 电话交谈 | *He stood silent in the doorway, unwilling to interrupt their conversation.* 他静静地站在门口, 不想打断他们的谈话。| **have/hold a conversation** *I had a long conversation with my brother on his birthday.* 我在弟弟生日那天和他谈了很久。| **carry on a conversation** (=have a conversation) 谈话 *It's impossible to carry on a conversation with all this noise in the background.* 在这么喧闹的环境中谈话是不可能的。| **turn a conversation to sth** (=begin talking about something) 开始谈论某事 *The conversation turned to the subject of Sarah's new boyfriend.* 谈话的主题转到莎拉的新男友身上。**2** [U] informal talk in which people exchange news, feelings, and thoughts〔非正式的〕会话, 谈话: *the buzz of conversation* 谈话的嗡嗡声 | **make conversation** (=talk to someone in an informal way that actually needs some effort to think of what to say) 搭讪, 说应酬话 *I'm not very good at making polite conversation.* 我不太擅长说应酬话。| **be in conversation with** (=be talking to someone) 与…交谈 *In today's programme, three well-known artists are in conversation with Jenny Murray.* 在今天的节目中, 有三位知名的艺术家要和珍妮·默里谈话。**3 get into conversation** *especially BrE*【尤英】also 又作 **get into a conversation** *especially AmE*【尤美】to begin to talk to someone, especially someone you do not know 开始〔与陌生人〕交谈: *I got into conversation with the bus driver today, and he told me that fares are going up again soon.* 我今天跟公共汽车司机攀谈, 他告诉我车票不久又会涨价。

con·ver·sa·tion·al /ˌkɑnvɚˋseʃənl; ˌkɒnvəˈseɪʃənəl◂/ *adj* **1** a conversational style, phrase etc is informal and commonly used in conversation〔风格、用语等〕会话(体)的, 谈话式的: *Business letters are not usually written in conversational style.* 写商业信件通常不用口语体。**2** concerning or relating to conversation 谈话的, 会谈的: *I go to evening classes to do conversational German.* 我去夜校学习德语口语。—**conversationally** *adv*

con·ver·sa·tion·al·ist /ˌkɑnvɚˋseʃənlɪst; ˌkɒnvəˈseɪʃənəlɜst/ *n* [C] someone whose conversation is intelligent, amusing, and interesting 健谈者: *a good conversationalist* 善于谈话的人

conversation piece /ˌ··ˈ·· ,·/ *n* [C] something that provides a subject for conversation, often said in a joking way about objects that seem very strange or ugly 可作话题的东西, 谈话题材

con·verse[1] /kənˋvɝs; kənˈvɜːs/ *v* [I] *formal* to talk informally, or to have a conversation【正式】谈话, 交谈: **[+with]** *It's difficult to converse rationally with people who hold extremist views.* 同持有过激观点的人是难以理性地交谈的。

con·verse[2] /ˋkɑnvɝs; ˈkɒnvɜːs/ *n formal* **the converse** the converse of a fact, word, statement etc is the opposite of it【正式】反面的事实[话语、陈述]: *I think the converse of what you just said is true.* 我认为你刚才所说的对立面是正确的。

con·verse[3] /kənˋvɝs; ˈkɒnvɜːs/ *adj formal* a converse opinion, belief, statement etc is the opposite opinion etc【正式】〔观点、信仰、陈述等〕相反的: *I hold the converse opinion.* 我持相反的意见。

con·verse·ly /kənˋvɝslɪ; kənˈvɜːsli/ *adv formal* used when one situation is the opposite of another【正式】相反地; 另一方面: *$1 will buy 100 yen. Conversely, 100 yen will buy $1.* 1美元可以换100日元; 反过来说, 100日元能换1美元。

con·ver·sion /kənˋvɝʒən; kənˈvɜːʃən/ *n* [C,U] **1** the act or process of changing something from one form, purpose, or system to a different one 转变; 转化; 转换; 换算: **[+into]** *The company buys raw material such as wool for conversion into cloth.* 这家公司买进羊毛等原材料生产成布料。| **[+of]** *The conversion of the old classrooms into a new library has greatly improved the school.* 旧教室改建成新图书馆大大改善了这所学校。| **[+to]** *The British conversion to the metric system took place in the 1970s.* 英国改用公制是在20世纪70年代。| **house conversion** (=the act or process of changing a large house into several apartments) 房屋改建 *a company that does house conversions* 从事房屋改建的公司 **2** an act of changing from one religion or belief to a different one 宗教的改变; 皈依; 归附: **[+to]** *His sudden conversion to the anti-nuclear movement may make voters suspicious.* 他突然转到反核运动一方, 可能会使选民生疑。| **[+from]** *Her conversion from the Protestant to the Catholic faith surprised many people.* 他从新教转信天主教使许多人很吃惊。**3** a score that you can make in RUGBY football by kicking the ball over the top part of the GOAL (3)〔橄榄球中将球踢过球门的横木而获得的〕附加得分

con·vert[1] /kənˋvɝt; kənˈvɜːt/ *v* **1** [I,T] to change or make something change from one form, system, or purpose to a different one (使)转变; (使)转化; (使)转换: **convert sth to/into sth** *This is part of the process of converting iron into steel.* 这是把铁炼成钢的步骤之一。| **[+to]** *The whole office converted to a new computer system last year.* 去年, 整个办公室换了一个新的电脑系统。| *Our house is a converted barn.* 我们的房子是由仓库改造的。**2** [I] to be able to be changed from one object into another 可变为另一物体: **[+to/into]** *This sofa converts to a bed.* 这张沙发可以变成床。| *I can't see how this plastic sheet converts into a tent.* 我不明白这块塑料布是怎么变成一顶帐篷的。**3** [I,T] to change or make someone change their opinion or habit (使)改变意见[习惯]: **[+to]** *I've converted to decaffeinated coffee.* 我改饮不含咖啡因的咖啡。| **convert sb to sth** *My daughter has finally converted me to Guns N' Roses.* 我的女儿终于使我转而喜欢"枪炮与玫瑰"乐队了。**4** [I,T] to change or make someone change from one religion or belief to another (使)皈依: **[+to]** *Anne has converted to Islam recently.* 安妮最近皈依了伊斯兰教。 3

con·vert[2] /ˋkɑnvɝt; ˈkɒnvɜːt/ *n* [C] someone who has been persuaded to change their opinion and accept a particular religion or belief 皈依宗教者; 改变信仰者: *a convert to Christianity* 改信基督教的人

con·vert·er, convertor /kənˋvɝtɚ; kənˈvɜːtə/ *n* [C] a machine that changes the form of things, especially one that makes steel from melted iron 转换器; 〔尤指炼钢的〕转炉

con·ver·ti·ble[1] /kənˋvɝtəbl̩; kənˈvɜːtɜbəl/ *adj* **1** an object that is convertible can be folded or arranged in a different way so that it can be used as something else 可转换的, 可改变的: *They bought a convertible sofa-bed.* 他们买了一张折叠式沙发床。**2** money that is convertible can be exchanged for the money of another country〔货币〕可兑换的 **3** a car that is convertible has a roof that you can fold back or remove〔汽车〕开篷的: *a convertible sports car* 开篷跑车 **4** *technical* a financial document such as an insurance arrangement or BOND[1] (1) that is convertible can be changed, or exchanged for something else【术语】〔证券等〕可兑换的: *convertible life insurance policy* 可兑换的人寿保险单—**convertibility** /kənˌvɝtəˋbɪlətɪ; kənˌvɜːtɜˈbɪlɜti/ *n* [U]

convertible² *n* [C] a car with a soft roof that you can fold back or remove 开篷[敞篷]汽车 —compare 比较 HARDTOP —see also 另见 CABRIOLET

con·vex /ˌkɑnˋvɛks; ˌkɒnˈveks◂/ *adj* curved outwards like the surface of the eye 凸出的; 凸面的: *a convex lens* 凸透镜 | *a convex mirror* 凸镜 —**convexly** *adv* —**convexity** /kənˋvɛksətɪ; kənˈveksə̇ti/ *n* [C,U] —opposite 反义词 CONCAVE

con·vey /kənˋve; kənˈveɪ/ *v* [T] **1** to express what you are thinking or feeling without stating it directly 传达; 表达〔想法、感情〕: *His tone conveyed an unmistakable warning.* 他的语气确定无疑地传达出警告的意味。| *Jan's office conveyed an impression of efficiency and seriousness.* 简的办公室给人留下高效和庄重的印象。**2** to communicate information or a message 传递〔信息〕; 传送; 传播: *All this information can be conveyed in a simple diagram.* 所有这些信息可以通过简单的图表来传达。| *Please convey my best wishes to her.* 请代我向她表示最好的祝愿。**3** *formal* to take or carry something from one place to another【正式】传送〔物件〕; 输送; 运送: *Your luggage will be conveyed to the hotel by taxi.* 你的行李将由出租车送到酒店。**4** *law* to legally change the possession of property from one person to another【法律】把〔财产〕让与; 转让

con·vey·ance /kənˋveəns; kənˈveɪəns/ *n* **1** [C] *formal* a vehicle【正式】运输工具; 交通工具: *There was no conveyance available, so we were obliged to walk.* 找不到交通工具了, 我们不得不步行。**2** [U] *formal* the act of taking something from one place to another【正式】传送; 运送 **3** [C] *law* a legal document that gives land, property etc from one person to another【法律】产权转让证书

con·vey·anc·ing /kənˋveənsɪŋ; kənˈveɪənsɪŋ/ *n* [U] *law* the work done, usually by a lawyer, to change the possession of property, especially a house, from one person to another【法律】财产〔尤指房子〕转让的法律手续

con·vey·or, conveyer /kənˋveə; kənˈveɪə/ *n* [C] **1** a person or thing that carries or communicates something 运送者; 传达者; 运输装置: *the conveyer of good news* 好消息的传送者 **2** a conveyor belt 传送带

conveyor belt /ˈ··· ˌ/ *n* [C] a long continuous moving band of rubber, cloth, or metal, used for moving goods or partly finished products from one place to another in a factory, or bags from one place to another in an airport 传送带, 输送带

con·vict¹ /kənˋvɪkt; kənˈvɪkt/ *v* [T] to prove or officially announce that someone is guilty of a crime after a TRIAL¹ (1) in a law court 证明[宣判]…有罪: **be convicted of sth** *Buxton was convicted of rape.* 巴克斯顿被判犯强奸罪。| *a convicted murderer* 被判有罪的谋杀犯 —opposite 反义词 ACQUIT

con·vict² /ˋkɑnvɪkt; ˈkɒnvɪkt/ *n* [C] someone who has been proved to be guilty of a crime and sent to prison 已决犯; 囚犯: *There was a report on the news about an escaped convict.* 有一则关于越狱犯的新闻报道。

3 **con·vic·tion** /kənˋvɪkʃən; kənˈvɪkʃən/ *n* **1** [C] a very strong belief or opinion 坚定的信仰[主张]: *a woman of strong political convictions* 一位有坚定政治信仰的妇女 **2** [U] the feeling of being sure about something and having no doubts 深信, 坚信: *The speech lacked style and conviction.* 这篇演讲缺乏风格和说服力。| *"Maybe it was all a mistake," said Tom, without conviction.* "或许那完全是个错误。"汤姆犹犹豫豫地说。| **carry conviction** (=show that someone feels sure about something and has no doubts) 有说服力 *Their shouts and threats carried little conviction.* 他们的喊叫和威胁几乎没有说服力。**3** [C] a decision in a court of law that someone is guilty of a crime 裁定有罪: *They had no previous convictions.* 他们没有前科。| [+for] *This was her third conviction for theft.* 这是她第三次被判犯盗窃罪。**4** [U] the process of proving that someone is guilty in a court of law 定罪: *The trial and conviction of Jimmy Malone took over three months.* 审判吉米·马隆以及给他定罪用了三个多月的时间。—opposite 反义词 ACQUITTAL —see also 另见 **have the courage of your (own) convictions** (COURAGE (2))

3 3 **con·vince** /kənˋvɪns; kənˈvɪns/ *v* [T] **1** to make someone feel certain that something is true 使确信; 使信服: *Her arguments didn't convince me.* 她的论点不能说服我。| **convince sb (that)** *I managed to convince them that the story was true.* 我终于使他们相信那故事是真的。| **convince sb of sth** *We finally convinced them of our innocence.* 我们终于使他们相信我们是无辜的。**2** to persuade someone to do something 说服, 劝服: **convince sb to do sth** *I've been trying to convince Jean to come with me.* 我一直在设法说服琼跟我们一起来。

con·vinced /kənˋvɪnst; kənˈvɪnst/ *adj* **1 be convinced** to feel certain that something is true 确信的; 信服的: *Molly agreed, but she did not sound very convinced.* 莫莉同意了, 但是她听起来不像很信服。| *I was convinced that we were doing the right thing.* 我确信我们做的事情是正确的。| **convinced of sth** *We are all convinced of his innocence.* 我们都相信他是无辜的。| **convinced (that)** *I felt convinced that they were right.* 我相信他们是正确的。**2 convinced Muslim/Christian etc** someone who believes very strongly in a particular religion 信仰坚定的穆斯林/基督徒等

con·vinc·ing /kənˋvɪnsɪŋ; kənˈvɪnsɪŋ/ *adj* **1** making you believe that something is true or right 有说服力的, 使人信服的: *You're not a very convincing liar!* 你说谎不太高明! | *There is now convincing evidence that smoking causes lung cancer.* 现在有令人信服的证据说明吸烟能导致肺癌。**2 a convincing victory/win** an occasion when a person or team wins a game by a lot of points 大胜 —**convincingly** *adv*

con·viv·i·al /kənˋvɪvɪəl; kənˈvɪviəl/ *adj* friendly and pleasantly cheerful 欢乐的; 友好的: *a convivial atmosphere* 友好的气氛 | *She seemed to be in a convivial mood.* 她看起来心情愉悦。—**convivially** *adv* —**conviviality** /kənˌvɪvɪˋælətɪ; kənˌvɪviˈælə̇ti/ *n* [U]

con·vo·ca·tion /ˌkɑnvəˋkeʃən; ˌkɒnvəˈkeɪʃən/ *n formal*【正式】**1 a)** [U] an organization of church officials or members of some universities that holds formal meetings〔由教会领袖或一些大学中的人员组成的〕会议召集团体 **b)** [C] formal meetings held in this way〔教会的正式〕会议;〔大学的〕校务会议: *He first gave the speech at a German university convocation in March.* 他第一次作这个演讲是3月份在德国一所大学的会议上。**2** [U] the process of arranging for a large meeting to be held〔大型会议的〕召集, 召开 **3** [C] *AmE* the ceremony held when students have passed their examinations and are leaving university【美】〔大学〕毕业典礼

con·voke /kənˋvok; kənˈvəʊk/ *v* [T] *formal* to tell people that they must come together for a formal meeting【正式】召开〔会议〕

con·vo·lut·ed /ˋkɑnvəˌlutɪd; ˈkɒnvəluːtə̇d/ *adj* **1** complicated and difficult to understand 不易理解的, 费解的: *The whole thing was written in the most convoluted and obscure language possible.* 通篇语言隐晦难解得无以复加。| *a convoluted argument* 错综复杂的论据 **2** *formal* having many twists and bends【正式】旋绕的, 弯曲的: *They used some convoluted glass apparatus for measuring the expansion of the gas.* 他们使用某种弯曲的玻璃器皿来测量该气体的膨胀度。—**convolutedly** *adv*

con·vo·lu·tion /ˌkɑnvəˋluʃən; ˌkɒnvəˈluːʃən/ *n* [C usually plural 一般用复数] **1** the complicated details of a story, explanation etc, which make it difficult to understand 错综复杂的细节: *It was an effort to follow the endless convolutions of the plot.* 错综复杂的情节层出不穷, 不太容易弄懂。**2** a fold or twist in something which has many of them 卷曲, 盘绕: *the many convolutions of the small intestine* 小肠的许多卷曲

con·voy¹ /ˋkɑnvɔɪ; ˈkɒnvɔɪ/ *n* [C] **1** a group of vehicles or ships travelling together 车队; 船队: *A convoy of lorries arrived bringing supplies of food and medicine.* 卡车队满载着食物和药品到达了。| **in convoy** *We decided to travel in convoy so that no-one could lose their way.* 我们决定结队而行以防有人迷路。**2** a group of armed vehicles or ships whose purpose is to travel with others in order to protect them 护送车队; 护送舰队: *They were escorted through the danger area by a naval convoy.* 在海军护航队的保护之下他们通过危险区域。| **under convoy** (=protected by a convoy) 由护送队保护 *The weapons were sent under convoy.* 武器在护送之下运走。

convoy² *v* [T] to travel with something in order to protect it 护送; 护航: *Battleships helped to convoy much-needed supplies to Britain in 1917.* 1917年, 军舰帮助护送急需物资到英国。

con·vulse /kənˋvʌls; kənˈvʌls/ *v* **1** [I] if a part of your body convulses, it moves violently and you are not able to control it〔身体某部分〕剧烈抖动: *He sat down, his shoulders convulsing with sobs.* 他坐下来, 他的肩膀由于抽泣而剧烈抖动。**2** [I] if you convulse, your body shakes violently and you are not able to control it, especially because of illness or injury 痉挛; 抽搐 **3 be convulsed with laughter/anger** to be laughing so much or feel so angry that you shake and are not able to stop yourself 笑得前仰后合/气得发抖

con·vul·sion /kənˋvʌlʃən; kənˈvʌlʃən/ *n* **1** [C usually plural 一般用复数] an act of shaking violently and uncontrollably because you are ill 惊厥; 痉挛; 抽搐: *His temperature was very high and he started having convulsions.* 他的体温很高并开始抽搐。**2 be in convulsions** *informal* to be laughing a lot【非正式】笑得前仰后合: *The story was so funny, we were in convulsions.* 这个故事太有趣了, 我们笑得前仰后合。

con·vul·sive /kənˋvʌlsɪv; kən'vʌlsɪv/ *adj* sudden, violent and impossible to control 突然的; 剧烈的; 不能控制的: *The drunken man made convulsive efforts to stand up.* 这个醉汉突然跌跌撞撞地想站起来。—**convulsively** *adv*

co·ny, coney /ˋkonɪ; 'kəʊni/ *n* **1** [C] *old use* a rabbit【旧】家兔 **2** [U] rabbit fur used for making coats 兔毛皮

coo[1] /ku; ku:/ *v* [I] **1** to make the low soft cry of a DOVE[1] (1) or PIGEON〔鸽子等〕咕咕地叫 **2** to make soft quiet sounds 低声细语: *He was cooing in her ear.* 他低声向她耳语。—see also 另见 **bill and coo** (BILL[2] (4)) —**coo** *n* [C]

coo[2] *interjection* used to express surprise 啊, 呀〔表示惊讶〕: *Coo! That must have cost a lot!* 啊, 那一定花了很多钱!

S2 **cook[1]** /kuk; kʊk/ *v* **1** [I,T] to prepare food for eating by using heat 烹调; 煮, 烧: *Mmm! That's delicious! Where did you learn to cook like that?* 嗯, 太香了! 你从哪里学的烧菜? | **cook dinner/supper/a meal etc** *I'm tired. Will you cook dinner today?* 我累了, 今天你能做晚饭吗? | **cook sth for sb** *Sarah cooked lasagne for her parents when they visited.* 莎拉在她父母来看她时给他们煮宽面条吃。| **cook sb sth** *He decided to cook his parents a special meal for their wedding anniversary.* 他决定为父母的结婚纪念日做一顿特殊的饭菜。**2** [I] to be prepared for eating by using heat 被烧煮: *The potatoes are cooking and will be ready in ten minutes.* 马铃薯正在煮, 10分钟就会好。**3** [T] *informal* to change facts, numbers etc dishonestly, for your own advantage; FALSIFY【非正式】窜改; 捏造: *I'm sure the police have been cooking the evidence to get more convictions.* 我敢肯定, 警察为了使更多人被判有罪而捏造证据。**4 be cooking** *informal* being planned in a secret way【非正式】秘密计划; 密谋: *Everyone in the office has been whispering this morning – I'm sure there's something cooking.* 今天早上办公室里的每个人都低声耳语, 肯定有事要发生了。**5 cook the books** to dishonestly change official records and figures in order to steal money 做假账: *The company accountant was charged with cooking the books.* 这家公司的会计被指控做假账。**6 cook sb's goose** to get someone into serious trouble 使某人陷入极大麻烦: *It would really cook his goose if I told his wife where he was last night.* 如果我告诉他妻子昨天晚上他在哪儿, 他麻烦就大了。**7 be cooking with gas** *AmE spoken* used to say that someone is doing something very well【美口】干得很好, 干得优秀

cook sth ↔ **up** *phr v* [T] **1** to make a meal quickly, often using food that has been left from a previous meal〔匆忙地〕煮烧, 做〔饭〕: *I volunteered to cook up a risotto using the rice from last night.* 我自愿用昨晚的米饭做鸡肉煨饭。**2** *informal* to invent a story or excuse in order to prevent someone blaming you for something【非正式】捏造; 编造: *Rachel cooked up some story about her car breaking down, to explain why she was so late.* 雷切尔编造说她的车抛锚了, 以解释她为什么迟到。

cook[2] *n* [C] **1** someone who prepares and cooks food as their job 厨师, 炊事员: *Jane works as a cook in a local restaurant.* 简在本地的一家餐馆里做厨师。—compare 比较 CHEF **2 be a good/excellent etc cook** to be good at preparing and cooking food 好的/出色的厨师: *My dad's a really good cook.* 我爸爸是一个真正出色的厨师。**3 too many cooks (spoil the broth)** used when you think there are too many people trying to do the same job at the same time, so that the job is not done well 厨师太多烧坏汤〔用来形容人多误事〕—see also 另见 **chief cook and bottle washer** (CHIEF[1] (3))

Cook, Captain James (1728-79) a British sailor and EXPLORER who sailed to Australia and New Zealand, and claimed the eastern coast of Australia for Britain. He also discovered several islands in the Pacific Ocean, including Hawaii, where he was killed. 库克〔(1728-1779), 英国航海家、探险家。他曾航行到澳大利亚和新西兰, 并宣称澳大利亚东海岸为英国所有。他还发现了太平洋中的数个岛屿, 其中包括他最后被杀的夏威夷〕

cook·book /ˋkuk,buk; 'kʊkbʊk/ *n* [C] *AmE* a book that tells you how to prepare and cook food【美】烹饪书; 食谱; COOKERY BOOK *BrE*【英】

cook-chill /,·ˈ◂/ *adj BrE* cook-chill foods have already been cooked when you buy them, and are stored at a low temperature, but not frozen【英】冷藏熟食

cooked /kukt; kʊkt/ *adj* cooked food is not raw and is ready for eating〔食物〕熟的; 煮熟的; 烧好的: *cooked meats* 熟肉

cook·er /ˋkukə; 'kʊkə/ *n* [C] *BrE*【英】**1** a large piece of equipment for cooking food on or in 厨灶; 炉具; STOVE[1] (2) *AmE*【美】—see picture on page A10 参见A10页图 **2** a fruit, especially an apple, that is suitable for cooking but not for eating raw 适宜煮食而不宜生吃的水果〔尤指苹果〕

cook·e·ry /ˋkukərɪ; 'kʊkəri/ *n* [U] *BrE* the art or skill of cooking【英】烹饪法; 烹饪术; COOKING[1] (1) *AmE*【美】: *Jane's favourite subject at school is cookery.* 简在学校最喜欢的科目是烹饪课。| *French provincial cookery* 法国的地方烹饪法

cookery book /ˈ···,·/ *n* [C] *BrE* a book that tells you how to prepare and cook food【英】烹饪书; 食谱; COOKBOOK *AmE*【美】

cook·house /ˋkuk,haus; 'kʊkhaʊs/ *n* [C] *old-fashioned* an outdoor kitchen where you cook food, especially in a military camp【过时】〔尤指军营的〕露天厨房; 野营厨房; 户外厨房

cook·ie /ˋkukɪ; 'kʊki/ *n* [C] **1** *especially AmE* a flat, dry, sweet cake usually sold in packets【尤美】小甜饼, 甜饼干; BISCUIT (1) *BrE*【英】: *Karen had a glass of milk and a cookie.* 卡伦喝了一杯牛奶, 吃了一个小甜饼。**2 tough/smart cookie** *informal* someone who is clever, successful, and strongly defends what they believe in【非正式】意志坚定/聪明能干的人 **3 that's the way the cookie crumbles** *informal* used when something unpleasant has happened to say that you must accept things the way they are, even though you do not like it【非正式】生米已煮成熟饭〔指不合意的事已发生, 不得不接受〕**4** *AmE old-fashioned* an attractive young woman【美, 过时】漂亮的年轻女子 **5** *ScotE*【苏格兰】= a BUN (1)

cookie cut·ter /ˈ··,··/ *n* [C] *AmE*【美】**1** an instrument that cuts cookies into special shapes before you bake them 饼干成型切割刀 **2** something that is almost exactly the same as other things of the same type, and is not interesting in any way 千篇一律的东西; 俗套的东西: *The new business park was totally different from the cookie cutter approach of the other buildings in the area.* 这个新的商业园完全不同于该地区其他建筑千篇一律的处理方法。

Cookie Mon·ster, the /ˈ··,··/ a character in the US television programme *Sesame Street* who loves to eat COOKIES. He always appears when anyone has cookies, and he eats all of them very quickly, loudly, and wildly. 曲奇怪物〔美国电视节目《芝麻街》中的一个角色。他喜欢吃小甜饼, 谁有小甜饼, 他就会出现。他会以很快的速度、很响的声音、很难看的吃相把小甜饼一扫而光〕

cookie sheet /ˈ·· ·/ *n* [C] *AmE* a flat piece of metal that you bake food on【美】饼干烘制板; BAKING TRAY

cook·ing[1] /ˋkukɪŋ; 'kʊkɪŋ/ *n* [U] **1** the act of making food and cooking it 烧饭, 烹饪: *I hate cooking.* 我讨厌烧饭。**2** food made in a particular way or by a particular person〔用特殊方法或由特定的人烹调的〕饭菜: *Gail's cooking is always good.* 盖尔做的菜总是很可口。| *Indian cooking* 印度菜 | **home cooking** (=good food like you get in your own house) 家庭饭菜 S3

cooking[2] *adj* [only before noun 仅用于名词前] **1** suitable for or used in cooking 烹饪用的; 适合烹饪用的: *Fry the vegetables in cooking oil.* 用食用油炒蔬菜。**2** *AmE* doing something very well【美】做得非常好的: *The band is really cooking tonight.* 这个乐队今天晚上演奏得棒极了。

cooking ap·ple /ˈ··,··/ *n* [C] a kind of apple used in cooking 煮熟吃的苹果 —compare 比较 EATING APPLE

cooking oil /ˈ·· ·/ *n* [U] oil from plants, such as sunflowers or olives (SUNFLOWER or OLIVE (2)) 烹饪油

Cook Islands /,·ˈ·/ a group of islands in the Pacific Ocean, northeast of New Zealand. It is a TERRITORY of New Zealand but has its own government. Population: 20,611 (2001). Capital: Avarua. 库克群岛〔太平洋中的一群岛屿, 位于新西兰东北。属于新西兰, 但该群岛有独立的政府。人口: 20,611 (2001), 首府: 阿瓦鲁阿〕

cook·out /ˋkuk,aut; 'kʊk-aʊt/ *n* [C] *AmE informal* a party or occasion when a meal is cooked and eaten outdoors【美, 非正式】在露天煮吃的野餐

cook·ware /ˋkukwɛr; 'kʊkweə/ *n* [U] containers and equipment used for cooking 烹饪用具, 炊具

cool[1] /kul; ku:l/ *adj* W3

1 ►TEMPERATURE 温度◄ low in temperature, but not cold, often in a way that feels pleasant 凉的, 凉爽的: *There was a cool breeze blowing off the sea.* 凉爽的微风从海上吹来。| *sipping a cool drink* 吸一口凉饮料 —see 见 COLD (USAGE)

2 ►CALM 冷静的◄ calm and not nervous, upset, embarrassed etc 冷静的; 沉着的: *Now just stay cool. Everything's OK.* 好了, 保持冷静, 一切都没事。| **(as) cool as a cucumber** (=very calm) 泰然自若, 极为冷静 *Robert walked into the exam looking cool as a cucumber.* 罗伯特走进考场时看上去泰然自若。| **cool customer** (=someone who behaves calmly in a difficult situation)〔困境中〕保持冷静的人 | **cool head** (=ability to remain calm in a difficult situation) 头脑冷静 *The job is quite demanding, so we need someone with a cool head.* 这项工作的要求很高, 所以我们需要一个头脑冷静的人。| **cool, calm, and collected** (=calm) 冷静 *Although she was nervous before the interview*

she managed to appear cool, calm and collected. 她在面试前尽管紧张，面试时却泰然自若。 **3 ►NOT FRIENDLY** 不友好的◄ behaving in a way that is not as friendly as you expect 冷漠的; 冷淡的: *Her gaze was decidedly cool.* 她的凝视显然是冷漠的。| [+towards] *The boss didn't actually say anything critical, but he was very cool towards me.* 老板实际上并没有指责我什么，但是对我却很冷淡。 **4 ►FASHIONABLE** 时髦的◄ *informal* very attractive, fashionable, relaxed etc, in a way that people admire【非正式】极有魅力的，时髦的; 放松的; 酷的: *You look really cool in those sunglasses.* 你戴着太阳镜确实很酷。 **5 it's cool** *spoken* used to say that something is not a problem【口】没问题，好办: *Don't worry about the work – it's cool!* 不要担心工作，没问题的！ **6 ►COLOUR** 颜色◄ a cool colour is one, such as blue or green, that makes you think of cool things 冷色的，〔颜色〕给人凉爽感觉的 **7 a cool million/hundred thousand etc** *informal* a surprisingly large amount of money that someone seems to earn very easily【非正式】轻易赚来的大笔钱: *He earns a cool half million every year.* 他每年轻易就赚到50万。 —**coolness** *n* [U] —**coolly** *adv* —**coolish** *adj*

3 **cool²** *v* **1** [I,T] also 又作 **cool down** to become cool or cooler, or make something do this (使)变凉: *You'll need to let your tea cool before you drink it.* 在饮用前，你需要把茶凉一凉。| *They opened the windows to cool the room down.* 他们打开窗子使房间凉快下来。 **2** [I] if a feeling, emotion, or relationship cools, it becomes less strong〔感情、情绪、关系等〕冷下来; 冷却; 变淡: *Our initial enthusiasm cooled when we saw how much work was involved.* 当我们看到要做多少工作时，我们最初的热情冷却了。 **3 cool it** *spoken*【口】**a)** used to tell someone to stop being angry, violent etc 用于要别人冷静下来: *That's enough arguing, you two – cool it!* 你们两个不要再争论了，冷静点。 **b)** to stop putting as much effort into something, or pressure on someone as you have been 沉住气; 慢慢来: *The more you chase after him, the less likely he is to go out with you. You'd better cool it a bit.* 你越追求他，他就越不会跟你来往，你最好沉住气。 **4 cool your heels** to be forced to wait 被迫等候: *The receptionist kept me cooling my heels for at least an hour.* 接待员至少让我空等了一个小时。

cool down *phr v* **1** [I,T] to become cool or cooler, or make something do this (使)冷却下来，(使)变凉: *Let the engine cool down, and then try starting it.* 让发动机冷却下来，然后再发动试试。| **cool sth ↔ down** *Blow on your cocoa to cool it down.* 吹吹你的可可饮料使它凉下来。 **2** [I] to become calm after being angry 冷静下来: *His father took a long time to cool down after their last argument.* 自从他们上一次争论之后，他父亲很长时间才冷静下来。

cool off *phr v* [I] **1** to return to a normal temperature after being hot〔温度〕凉下来; 凉快下来: *We'd been in the sun all day, so went for a swim to cool off.* 我们已经在太阳底下待了一天了，因此我们去游泳凉快凉快。 **2** to become calm after being angry 冷静下来: *Maybe you should go away and cool off before we talk anymore.* 或许你应该出去冷静一下，然后我们再来谈。

cool³ *n* **1 the cool** a temperature that is pleasantly cold 凉爽〔的气温〕: [+of] *They went for a stroll in the cool of the evening.* 他们在凉爽的夜晚出去散步。 **2 keep your cool** to remian clam in a frightening or difficult situation 保持冷静 **3 lose your cool** to stop being calm in an annoying or frightening situation 失去冷静: *I couldn't help it, I just lost my cool and started shouting at him.* 我无法自制，失去了冷静，开始对他大喊大叫。

cool⁴ *adv* **play it cool** to behave in a calm way because you do not want someone to know that you are really nervous, angry etc 冷静对待; 镇定应付: *Don't worry, just listen to what they say and play it cool.* 不要担心，好好听他们说什么，然后冷静处理。

coo·lant /ˈkulənt; ˈkuːlənt/ *n* [C,U] *technical* a liquid or gas used to cool something, especially an engine【术语】冷却剂 —see picture at 参见 ENGINE 图

cool·box /ˈkulˌbɑks; ˈkuːlbɒks/ also 又作 **cool·bag** /ˈkulˌbæg; ˈkuːlbæg/ *n* [C] *BrE* a container that keeps food and drink cool and fresh, which you use on a PICNIC¹ (1)【英】〔储藏野餐食物的〕冰盒，冰袋; COOLER (2) *AmE*【美】

cool·er /ˈkulɚ; ˈkuːlə/ *n* [C] **1** a container in which something, especially drinks, is cooled or kept cold 冷却器; 冰桶: *Mike went to fetch a bottle of wine from the cooler.* 迈克从冰桶拿来一瓶酒。 **2** *AmE* a coolbox【美】冰盒，冰袋 **3** *AmE* a machine that provides AIRCONDITIONING【美】空气调节器，空调设备 **4 the cooler** *slang* prison【俚】牢房

cool-head·ed /ˌ·ˈ··◂/ *adj* not easily excited or upset 头脑冷静的，沉着的: *We need a quick-thinking, cool-headed person for the job.* 我们需要一个思路敏捷、头脑冷静的人来做这份工作。

Coolidge /ˈkulɪdʒ; ˈkuːlɪdʒ/, **(John) Calvin** /ˈkælvɪn; ˈkælvɪn/ (1872-1933) a politician who became the US president in 1923 on the death of Warren Harding. He was re-elected as president the following year. 柯立芝〔(1872-1933)，美国政治家。1923年，沃伦·哈定去世，他继任美国总统，次年再次当选〕

coo·lie /ˈkulɪ; ˈkuːli/ *n* [C] *old-fashioned* an unskilled worker who is paid very low wages, especially in parts of Asia【过时】〔尤指在亚洲某些地区的〕苦力

cooling-off pe·ri·od /ˌ··ˈ·ˌ···/ *n* [C] **1** a period of time when two people or groups who are arguing about something can go away and think about how to improve the situation 冷却期〔争论的两个人或组织停止争吵考虑如何改善状况的时期〕 **2** a period of time after you have signed some types of sales agreement, when you can change your mind about buying something 冷却期〔在签订销售合同后，可以改变想法的一段时间〕: *a 14-day cooling-off period on a pension plan* 一个退休金计划的14天冷却期

cooling sys·tem /ˈ··ˌ··/ *n* [C] a system for keeping the temperature in a machine, engine etc low 冷却系统: *a fault in the power station's cooling system* 发电站冷却系统的故障

cooling tow·er /ˈ··ˌ··/ *n* [C] a large, round, tall building, used in industry for making water cool 冷却塔

Cool Whip /ˈ·ˌ·/ *trademark* a type of sweet white light food similar to firm cream, sold in the US, which people often put on sweet dishes such as pie or fruit【商标】"够味"蛋奶〔美国人常加在馅饼或水果等甜品上〕

coon /kun; kuːn/ *n* [C] **1** *AmE informal* a RACCOON【美，非正式】浣熊 **2** *taboo* a very offensive word for a black person【讳】黑鬼 **3 in a coon's age** *AmE informal* in a long time【美，非正式】长时间: *This is the best meal I've had in a coon's age!* 好久没吃到这样好的一顿饭了！

coon·skin /ˈkunskɪn; ˈkuːnskɪn/ *adj* made from the skin of a RACCOON 浣熊毛皮制的: *pictures of traders in coonskin caps* 戴着浣熊皮帽子的商人的图画

co-op /ˈkoɑp; ˈkəʊɒp/ *n* [C] a COOPERATIVE² 合作社 3

coop¹ /kup; kuːp/ *n* [C] a building for small animals, especially chickens 禽舍; 鸡笼

coop² *v*

coop sb/sth ↔ up *phr v* [T usually passive 一般用被动态] to restrict the freedom of someone or something by keeping them in a place that is too small 把…关在狭小的地方: [+in] *The fresh air felt good after being cooped up in the house for so long.* 在房子里关了这么久，呼吸新鲜空气的感觉非常好。

coo·per /ˈkupɚ; ˈkuːpə/ *n* [C] someone who makes barrels (BARREL¹ (1)) 制桶[修桶]工人

Cooper /ˈkupɚ; ˈkuːpə/, **James Fen·i·more** /dʒemz ˈfɛnɪmɔr; dʒeɪmz ˈfenɪmɔː/ (1789-1851) a US writer who wrote NOVELS about Native Americans and life on the American FRONTIER, including *The Deerslayer* and *The Last of the Mohicans* 库珀〔(1789-1851)，美国作家。他创作的小说以美洲的土著居民和美国的边陲生活为题材，代表作有《杀鹿者》和《最后的莫希干人》〕

co·op·e·rate also 又作 **co-operate** *BrE*【英】/koˈɑpəˌret; kəʊˈɒpəreɪt/ *v* [I] **1** if two people or groups cooperate, they work together in order to achieve a result that is good for both of them 合作，协作: *a classroom ethos which enables children to cooperate* 使得孩子们互相合作的课堂风气。| [+with] *Leopards cooperate with each other when hunting game.* 豹子在追捕猎物时互相合作。| [+in] *Russia and the US are cooperating in joint space ventures.* 俄罗斯和美国合作进行太空探索。| **cooperate to do sth** *Aid agencies and the UN are cooperating to deliver supplies to the area.* 援助机构和联合国合作向该地区派送物资。| **cooperate closely** (=work a lot together to achieve something) 亲密合作 **2** to help someone willingly when they ask for your help 配合; 协助: [+with] *I will advise my client to cooperate fully with the police.* 我会劝说我的当事人与警方全力配合的。

co·op·e·ra·tion also 又作 **co-operation** *BrE*【英】/koˌɑpəˈreʃən; kəʊˌɒpəˈreɪʃən/ *n* [U] **1** things that you do with someone else to achieve a common purpose 合作，协作: [+between] *a lack of cooperation between police and fire services* 警察和消防队之间缺少合作 | **in cooperation with** *The film was produced in cooperation with KBC of Australia.* 这部电影是与澳大利亚KBC公司联合制作的。 **2** help that is willingly given 配合: *Have your passports ready, and thank you for your cooperation.* 请把你们的护照准备好，谢谢你们的配合。| **full/**

complete cooperation *If we're going to succeed, I'll need your full cooperation.* 如果我们想成功，我需要你们的全力合作。

co·op·e·ra·tive[1] also 又作 **co-operative** *BrE*【英】/ko-ˋɑpərətiv; kəʊˈɒpərətɪv/ *adj* **1** willing to cooperate; helpful 合作的: *a cooperative witness* 合作的目击者 | *The woman in the bank wasn't very cooperative.* 银行里的那位女士不太合作。**2** done or operated by people working together 合作进行的: *The Food Stamp Program is a cooperative activity of local, state and Federal governments.* 食品券计划是由地方、州和联邦政府合作进行的。**3 cooperative factory/firm/association etc** a cooperative firm etc is operated by people working together as a cooperative 合作工厂/公司/机构等

cooperative[2] also 又作 **co-operative** *BrE*【英】*n* [C] an organization such as a company or factory in which all the people working there own an equal share of it; CO-OP 合作社: **housing/farm cooperative** *The produce is supplied by a farm cooperative.* 这些农产品是由农业合作社提供的。

Coo·pers·town /ˋkupəztaun; ˈku:pəztaʊn/ a town in the state of New York which has the Baseball Hall of Fame, a MUSEUM containing BASEBALL equipment and information about famous baseball players 库珀斯敦〔纽约州一镇。该镇建有棒球名人堂，展示棒球运动器材，介绍著名棒球运动员〕

co-opt also 又作 **co-opt** /koˋɑpt; kəʊˋɒpt/ *v* [T] *formal*【正式】**1** to add someone to an organization such as a committee, sometimes against their will, by the agreement of all the other members〔某组织的成员〕推举[增选]…为新成员〔有时被推举人并不愿意〕: *The Student's Union can have a maximum of 5 coopted members.* 学生会最多可以增选五人。| **coopt sb onto/into sth** *Mr King has been coopted onto the board.* 金先生被推选进董事会。**2** to include someone in something, especially against their will 强加于，强行拉拢: *a vision of the world which coopts and misrepresents us* 一个既强加于我们又丑化我们的世界观

co·or·di·nate[1] also 又作 **co-ordinate** *BrE*【英】/koˋɔrdn̩ˌet; kəʊˈɔ:dɪ̣neɪt/ *v* [T] **1** to organize an activity so that the people involved in it work well together and achieve a good result 协调〔多人参加的活动〕: *Harris is coordinating a campaign to make people aware of the importance of exercise.* 哈里斯正在协调一项活动，使人们意识到锻炼身体的重要性。**2** to make the movements of the parts of your body work well together when performing a particular action 协调〔身体的动作〕: *a young child unable to coordinate her movements* 无法协调动作的女童

co·or·din·ate[2] also 又作 **co-ordinate** *BrE*【英】/koˋɔrdn̩ɪt; kəʊˈɔ:dɪ̣nɪ̣t/ *n* [C] **1** *technical* one of a set of numbers which give the exact position of a point on a map, computer screen etc【术语】坐标 **2 coordinates** *plural* women's clothes that can be worn together because their colours match〔在颜色搭配上能够一起穿的〕配套女装

coordinate[3] also 又作 **co-ordinate** *BrE*【英】*adj technical*【术语】**1** equal in importance or rank 同等的；并列的: *coordinate clauses in a sentence joined by 'and'* 一个句子中用 and 连接的并列从句 —compare 比较 SUBORDINATE[1] **2** involving the use of coordinates 坐标的

coordinating con·junc·tion /ˌ· ····· ˌ·ˈ·/ *n* [C] a word such as 'and' or 'but', which joins two clauses of the same type 并列连词

co·or·di·na·tion /koˌɔrdn̩ˋeʃən; kəʊˌɔ:dɪ̣ˈneɪʃən/ *n* [U] **1** the way in which your muscles move together when you perform a movement〔肌肉的〕协调: *Too much alcohol affects your coordination.* 喝酒太多会影响你动作的协调。**2** the act of coordinating 协调，调和: *the careful coordination of research* 研究工作的精心协调

co·or·di·na·tor /koˋɔrdnˌetə; kəʊˈɔ:dɪ̣neɪtə/ *n* [C] someone who organizes the way people work in an activity 协调人

coot /kut; ku:t/ *n* [C] **1** a small black and white water bird with a short beak 白骨顶〔水鸟〕**2 old coot** *AmE informal* an old man who you think is strange or unpleasant【美，非正式】老怪人: *crazy old coot* 疯狂的老怪人

coo·ties /ˋkutɪz; ˈku:tiz/ *n* [plural] *AmE informal*【美，非正式】**1** *old use* lice (LOUSE[1] (1)) that you have in your hair【旧】体虱 **2 have cooties** *spoken* used by children to insult another child【口】有体虱〔儿童用来羞辱人的话〕: *Jenny has cooties!* 珍妮长虱子了！

[S3] **cop**[1] /kɑp; kɒp/ *n* [C] **1** *informal* a police officer【非正式】警察: *a motorcycle cop* 骑摩托车的警察 **2 not be much cop** *BrE slang* to not be very good【英俚】不大好: *The film wasn't much cop, was it?* 这部电影不怎么样，是吗? **3 it's a fair cop** *BrE spoken humorous* used when someone has discovered that you have done something wrong and you want to admit it【英口，幽默】抓得好，抓得有理〔犯错被人发现时用于承认〕

CULTURAL NOTE 文化注释

The phrase 'it's a fair cop' is supposedly used by criminals when they have been caught, but it is now really only a joke. 据认为 it's a fair cop 是罪犯在被擒获时所说的话，但现在这实际上仅是一个笑话。

cop[2] *v* **copped, copping** [T] *slang*【俚】**1 cop it** *BrE spoken* to be punished【英口】挨罚: *You'll cop it from your Mum when she finds out!* 如果你妈妈发现的话，你就倒霉了! **2 cop (a load of) this** *BrE spoken* used to say look at or listen to this【英口】听；看〔用于引人注意〕**3 cop hold of** [only in imperative 仅用于祈使句] *BrE spoken* used to tell someone to take or hold something【英口】请拿着…: *Cop hold of my bag while I go and get the tickets.* 我去取票的时候，请拿着我的提包。**4 cop a plea** *AmE* to agree to say you are guilty of a crime in order to receive a less severe punishment【美】承认有罪以求轻判 **5 cop a feel** *AmE* to touch someone in a sexual way when they do not want you to【美】〔调情时〕抚摸〔而对方并不同意〕

cop off *phr v* [I,T] *BrE slang* to meet someone and start a sexual relationship with them【英俚】与…见面并开始性关系: *So, what's the gossip? Did you cop off?* 那么，流言是什么呢? 你们发生性关系了吗? | [+with] *Who was it he copped off with at the Christmas Party?* 在圣诞晚会上他与谁勾搭上了?

cop out *phr v* [I,T] *slang* to not do something that you are supposed to do【俚】逃避〔责任〕: *It's your turn to sing – you can't cop out now.* 该你唱了，你不能赖哟。—see also 另见 COP OUT

Co·pa·ca·ban·a /ˌkopəkəˋbænə; ˌkəʊpəkəˈbænə/ a fashionable beach in Rio de Janeiro in Brazil 科帕卡巴纳〔巴西里约热内卢的一处时尚海滩〕

cope[1] /kop; kəʊp/ *v* [I] **1** to succeed in dealing with a difficult problem or situation〔成功地〕应付，对付: *I've never driven a big van before, but I'm sure I can cope.* 我从来没有驾驶过大货车，但是我一定能应付得了。| [+with] *A family and a full time job is a lot to cope with.* 照顾家庭加上一份全职工作需要花很大精力。**2** if a machine or system can cope with a particular amount of work, it can do it〔机器或系统〕能处理，能应付: *The system can cope with up to 40 terminals.* 这个系统可以处理多达40台终端机。 [S2] [W2]

cope[2] *n* [C] a long loose piece of clothing worn by priests on special occasions〔教士在特别日子穿的〕长袍，法衣

Co·pen·ha·gen /ˋkopənhegən; ˌkəʊpənˈheɪgən◂/ the capital city of Denmark, a port and industrial centre in the east of the country 哥本哈根〔丹麦首都、东部港口和工业中心〕

Copenhagen, the Battle of a naval battle between the British and the Danish in 1801. The British navy under Lord Nelson had received orders to leave the area because Danish ships were approaching. Nelson, who could not see using one of his eyes, put his telescope to that eye and said 'I see no ships'. His ships remained where they were, and in the battle that followed the Danes were defeated. 哥本哈根之战〔1801年英国和丹麦之间的一场海战。纳尔逊勋爵接到必须离开所在地区的命令，因为丹麦船只正在逼近他率领的英国海军。纳尔逊把望远镜放在他那只失明的眼睛上，说道："我什么船也没有看到。"他指挥的船只在原地未动，在接下来的战役中打败了丹麦〕

Co·per·ni·can sys·tem, the /koˋpɝnɪkən ˌsɪstəm; kəʊˈpɜ:nɪkən ˌsɪstɪ̣m/ the idea, first suggested by Copernicus, that the earth and the other PLANETS all travel in circles around the sun. Before this it was believed, according to the Ptolemaic system, that the Earth was at the centre of the universe. 哥白尼体系〔哥白尼最早提出的地球等行星围绕太阳运转的学说。之前的托勒密体系却认为，地球是宇宙的中心〕

Co·per·nic·us /koˋpɝnɪkəs; kəʊˈpɜ:nɪkəs/, **Nicholas** (1473-1543), a Polish ASTRONOMER (=person who studies the stars), who first suggested the Copernican system, in which the earth and other PLANETS are described as moving around the sun, which does not move 哥白尼〔(1473-1543)，波兰天文学家。他首次提出了哥白尼体系，即地球和其他行星围绕太阳运转，而太阳本身并不移动〕

cop·i·er /ˋkɑpɪə; ˈkɒpiə/ *n* [C] a machine that quickly makes photographic copies of documents; PHOTOCOPIER 复印机；影印机

co·pi·lot /ˋkoˌpaɪlət; ˈkəʊˌpaɪlət/ *n* [C] a pilot who shares the control of an aircraft with the main pilot〔飞机〕副驾驶员

cop·ing /ˋkopɪŋ, ˈkəʊpɪŋ/ *n* [C,U] a layer of rounded stones or bricks at the top of a wall or roof〔墙顶或屋顶的〕护顶，盖顶

co·pi·ous /ˋkopɪəs; ˈkəʊpiəs/ *adj* existing or being produced in large quantities 丰富的，大量的: *Jill sat through the meeting and made copious notes.* 吉尔参加了整个会议，并做了大量的笔记。—**copiously** *adv*: *Then she wept copiously.* 接着她泪如泉涌。

Cop·land /ˈkoplənd; ˈkəʊplənd/ **, Aa·ron** /ˈɛrən; ˈeərən/ (1900-90) a US COMPOSER of modern classical music, famous for his *Fanfare for the Common Man*, and for the music he wrote for the BALLET *Appalachian Spring* 科普兰〔(1900-1990)，美国现代古典音乐作曲家。他创作的《众人信号曲》和芭蕾舞剧《阿帕拉契之春》的音乐十分著名〕

cop out /ˈ· ·/ *n* [C] *slang* an occasion when you do or say something in order to avoid doing what you should do, or the actual words you use to make this excuse【俚】逃避责任; 逃避责任的借口

cop·per /ˈkɑpɚ; ˈkɒpə/ *n* **1** [U] a reddish-brown metal used for making wire 铜 **2 coppers** [plural] *BrE* money of low value made of this metal or of BRONZE[1] (1)【英】铜币: *He pulled a pawn ticket and a few coppers out of his pocket.* 他从口袋里掏出一张当票和几枚铜币。**3** [U] a reddish-brown colour 红棕色: *flowing copper hair* 瀑布般的红棕色头发 **4** [C] *BrE informal* a police officer【英，非正式】警察

copper beech /ˌ·· ˈ·/ *n* [C] a large tree with purple-brown leaves 紫叶欧洲山毛榉

Copperfield, David —see 见 DAVID COPPERFIELD

cop·per·head /ˈkɑpɚˌhɛd; ˈkɒpəhed/ *n* [C] a poisonous yellow and brown North American snake 铜头蝮蛇

cop·per·plate /ˈkɑpɚˌplet; ˈkɒpəpleɪt/ *n* [U] neat, regular, curving handwriting with the letters all joined together in a very specific style, used especially in the past 圆形草体〔西方字母的手写体，字体工整，笔画弯曲，字母互相连接，过去尤其常用〕

copse /kɑps; kɒps/ also 又作 **cop·pice** /ˈkɑpɪs; ˈkɒpɪs/ *n* [C] a group of trees or bushes growing close together; a small wood 矮树丛，灌木丛; 小树林

cop shop /ˈ· ·/ *n* [C] *informal* the office from which the police work; POLICE STATION【非正式】警察局

Coptic Church, the /ˌ·· ˈ·/ a Christian religious group that is separate from the Catholic, Protestant, and Orthodox churches, and was formed in Egypt in the 1st century AD. Although most Egyptians are Muslims, there is a small number of Coptic Christians. 科普特教会〔与天主教、新教和东正教会不同的一个基督教宗教团体，公元1世纪在埃及成立。尽管大多数埃及人是穆斯林，但仍有一小部分人是科普特基督教徒〕

cop·u·la /ˈkɑpjələ; ˈkɒpjʊlə/ *n* [C] *technical* a type of verb that connects the subject of a sentence to its COMPLEMENT[1] (3)【术语】连系动词; 系词: *In the sentence 'The house seems big', 'seems' is the copula.* 在句子 The house seems big 中，seems 是连系动词。

cop·u·late /ˈkɑpjəˌlet; ˈkɒpjʊleɪt/ *v* [I] *technical* to have sex【术语】交媾; 交配 —**copulation** /ˌkɑpjəˈleʃən; ˌkɒpjʊˈleɪʃən/ *n* [U]

cop·u·la·tive /ˈkɑpjəˌletɪv; ˈkɒpjʊlətɪv/ *n* [C] *technical* a word or word group that connects other word groups【术语】连系的，系词的 —**copulative** *adj*

S1 W2 **cop·y**[1] /ˈkɑpɪ; ˈkɒpi/ *n* **1** [C] something that is made to be exactly like another thing 复制件; 副本: *I haven't got the original letter, but I have got a copy.* 我没有信的原件，但有复印件。| [+of] *Please send a copy of your marriage certificate.* 请交份你的结婚证书复印件给我。| **make a copy** *I made a copy of the ad and sent it to my brother.* 我把这个广告复制了一份送给弟弟。**2** [C] one of many books, magazines etc that are all exactly the same〔书、杂志等的〕一册; 一份: [+of] *He was reading a copy of the daily newspaper.* 他在读一份日报。**3** [U] *technical* written material that is to be printed in a newspaper, magazine etc【术语】准备排印的书面材料: *All copy must be on my desk by Monday morning.* 星期一早上以前所有付印稿子必须送到我的桌子上。**4 make good copy** *informal* to be interesting news【非正式】成为〔新闻报道的〕好材料 —see also 另见 FAIR COPY, HARD COPY, SOFT COPY

S2 **copy**[2] *v* **1** [T] to make something exactly like another thing 复制，抄写: *Could you copy this letter and send it out, please?* 你能把这封信复制一份并把它投递出去吗? **2** [T] to deliberately do things that someone else has done, or do things in the same way that someone else does them 模仿; 仿效: *Street fashion tends to copy the ideas of the top fashion designers.* 街头时装往往模仿顶级时装设计师的理念。**3** [I,T] to cheat in an examination, school work etc by looking at someone else's work and writing the same thing that they have 抄袭: [+off] *If I catch anyone copying off their neighbor, they'll be sent to the principal's office!* 如果我抓住有谁抄袭邻座，我会把他送到校长室! | [+from] *Jeremy had copied from the girl next to him.* 杰里米曾抄袭他邻座的女孩。

copy sth ↔ **out** *phr v* [T] *BrE* to write something again exactly as it is written somewhere else【英】抄写: *The monks copied their manuscripts out by hand.* 修道士用手抄出文稿。| *Just copy out of the book.* 照抄这本书吧。

cop·y·book[1] /ˈkɑpɪˌbuk; ˈkɒpibʊk/ *n* [C] a book used in the past containing examples of good handwriting to copy 字帖，习字簿 —see also 另见 **blot your copybook** (BLOT[1] (2))

copybook[2] *adj* [only before noun 仅用于名词前] *BrE* completely suitable or correct【英】完全合适[正确]的: *a copybook answer* 完全正确的答案

cop·y·cat /ˈkɑpɪˌkæt; ˈkɒpikæt/ *n* [C] **1** *informal* a word used by children to criticize someone who copies other people's clothes, behaviour, work etc【非正式】模仿他人行为[衣着等]的人〔儿童用语〕**2 copycat crime/killing etc** a crime, murder etc which is similar to a famous crime that another person has done 模仿式犯罪/凶杀等

copy ed·i·tor /ˈ·· ˌ···/ *n* [C] someone whose job is to be sure that the words in a book, newspaper etc are ready to be printed 文字编辑

cop·y·ist /ˈkɑpɪɪst; ˈkɒpi-ɪst/ *n* [C] someone who made written copies of documents, books etc in the past 抄写员，誊写员

cop·y·right /ˈkɑpɪˌraɪt; ˈkɒpiraɪt/ *n* [C,U] the legal right to be the only producer or seller of a book, play, film, or record for a specific length of time 版权; 著作权: *Who owns the copyright of this book?* 谁拥有这本书的版权? | *an infringement of copyright* 侵犯版权 —**copyright** *adj* —**copyright** *v* [T]

cop·y·writ·er /ˈkɑpɪˌraɪtɚ; ˈkɒpiˌraɪtə/ *n* [C] someone who writes the words for advertisements 广告文字撰稿人

coq au vin /ˌkɑk o ˈvæn; ˌkɒk əʊ ˈvæn/ *n* [U] *French* a dish of chicken cooked in red wine【法】酒焖鸡

coq·ue·try /ˈkokɪtrɪ; ˈkɒkɪtri/ *n* [C,U] *literary* behaviour that is typical of a coquette【文】〔女人的〕卖弄风情

co·quette /koˈkɛt; kəʊˈket/ *n* [C] *literary* a woman who frequently tries to attract the attention of men without having sincere feelings for them; FLIRT[2]【文】卖弄风情的女人 —**coquettish** *adj* —**coquettishly** *adv*

cor /kɔr; kɔː/ *interjection BrE spoken* used when you are very surprised or impressed by something【英口】老天爷〔表示吃惊、震惊〕

cor- /kə, kɔr; kə, kɒ/ *prefix* the form used for CON- before r 在 r 前代替 con-: *to correlate* (=connect together) 使相互关联

cor·a·cle /ˈkɑrəkḷ; ˈkɒrəkəl/ *n* [C] a small round boat that you move with a PADDLE[1] (1) 科拉科尔小舟

cor·al[1] /ˈkɔrəl; ˈkɒrəl/ *n* [U] a hard red, white, or pink substance formed from the bones of very small sea creatures, that is often used to make jewellery 珊瑚: *a coral necklace* 珊瑚项链

coral[2] *adj* pink or reddish orange in colour 珊瑚色的，粉红色的，橘红色的

coral reef /ˌ·· ˈ·/ *n* [C] a line of hard rocks formed by coral, found in warm sea water that is not very deep 珊瑚礁

cor an·glais /ˌkɔr ɔŋˈgle; ˌkɔːr ˈɒŋgleɪ/ *n* [C] *especially BrE* a long wooden musical instrument which is like an OBOE but with a lower sound【尤英】英国管〔一种木管乐器，似双簧管〕; ENGLISH HORN *especially AmE*【尤美】

cor bli·mey /ˌkɔr ˈblaɪmɪ; ˌkɔː ˈblaɪmi/ also 又作 **blimey** *interjection BrE old-fashioned* used to express surprise【英，过时】哎呀〔表示惊讶〕

Corbusier —see 见 LE CORBUSIER

cord[1] /kɔrd; kɔːd/ *n* **1** [C,U] a piece of thick string or thin rope 粗线; 细绳; 索，带: *We need some cord to hang the picture.* 我们需要一些细绳来挂画。| *He pulled explosives and some tangled cord from his bag.* 他从他的包里掏出一些炸药和乱糟糟的细绳。**2 cords** [plural] trousers made from a thick strong cotton cloth with thin raised lines on it 灯芯绒裤子 **3** [C,U] *especially AmE* an electrical wire or wires with a protective covering, usually for connecting electrical equipment to the supply of electricity

copy out 抄写

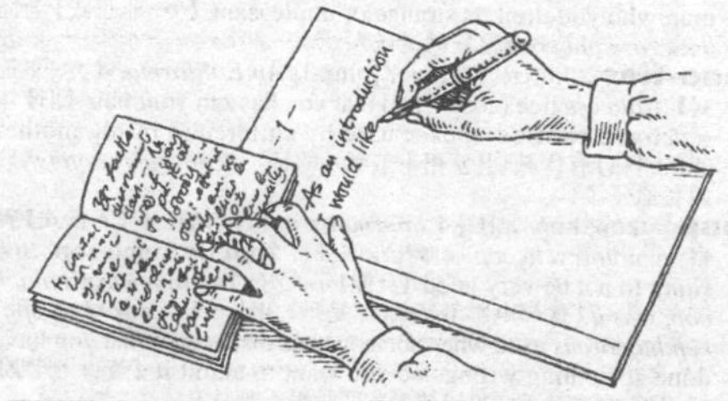

【尤美】电线: *the phone cord* 电话线 | *How much cord do you need to connect the washing machine?* 连接洗衣机你需要多少电线? **4** [C] *AmE* a specific quantity of wood cut for burning in a fire【美】考得〔木柴单位〕: [+of] *We use three cords of wood in a winter.* 一个冬天我们要用三考得的木柴。—see also 另见 **cut the cord** (CUT[1] (29)), COMMUNICATION CORD, CORDLESS, SPINAL CORD, UMBILICAL CORD, VOCAL CORDS

cord[2] *v* [T] to tie or connect something with rope, string, etc 用绳索[线]捆扎[连接]: *Bundles of hay were corded and tossed onto the wagon.* 一捆捆干草被扎好扔到马车上。

cord·age /ˋkɔrdɪdʒ; ˈkɔːdɪdʒ/ *n* [U] rope or cord in general, especially on a ship 绳索〔总称〕; 船用索具

Cor·de·li·a /kɔrˋdiljə; kɔːˈdiːliə/ a character in the play *King Lear* by William Shakespeare. She is the youngest of Lear's three daughters and the only one who really loves him. 考狄利亚〔莎士比亚戏剧《李尔王》中的人物。她是李尔王最小的三女儿, 也是唯一真正爱他的女儿〕—see also 另见 GONERIL, REGAN

cor·di·al[1] /ˋkɔrdʒəl; ˈkɔːdiəl/ *n* [C,U] **1** *BrE* sweet fruit juice that you add water to before you drink it【英】〔加水后饮用的〕果汁: *a lime cordial* 酸橙果汁 **2** *AmE old-fashioned* a strong sweet alcoholic drink; LIQUEUR【美, 过时】烈性甜酒; 甜露酒: *We were offered an after-dinner cordial.* 给我们上了一杯饭后甜露酒。

cordial[2] *adj* friendly but quite formal and polite 热诚的; 友好的〔但比较正式、有礼〕: *a cordial note from Mrs Thomas* 托马斯太太写来的热诚的便条—**cordiality** /kɔrˋdʒælətɪ; ˌkɔːdiˈælʒti/ *n* [U]

cor·di·al·ly /ˋkɔrdʒəlɪ; ˈkɔːdiəli/ *adv* **1** in a friendly but polite and formal way 热诚地; 诚挚地: *You are cordially invited to our wedding on May 9.* 热诚邀请你5月9日参加我们的婚礼。**2** **cordially disliked/hated** to dislike someone very strongly 强烈厌恶/憎恨: *He was cordially disliked by the whole street.* 整条街的人都非常讨厌他。

cor·dite /ˋkɔrdaɪt; ˈkɔːdaɪt/ *n* [U] a smokeless explosive used in bullets and bombs 无烟火药

cord·less /ˋkɔrdləs; ˈkɔːdləs/ *adj* a piece of equipment that is cordless is not connected to its power supply by wires〔设备〕无线的: *a cordless phone* 无线电话

cor·don[1] /ˋkɔrdn̩; ˈkɔːdn/ *n* [C] a line of police officers, soldiers, or vehicles put around an area to stop people going there 警戒线: *The police immediately put up a cordon around the scene of the accident.* 警察立即在事故现场周围设置了警戒线。

cordon[2] *v*

cordon sth ↔ **off** *phr v* [T] to surround and protect an area with police officers, soldiers, or vehicles 设置警戒线围起: *Police have cordoned off the street where the murder took place.* 警察在发生谋杀案的街道周围设置了警戒线。

cor·don bleu /kɔrˋdɔ̃ ˋblœ; ˌkɔːdɒn ˈblɜː/ *adj* [only before noun 仅用于名词前] concerning food cooked to the highest standard 烹饪手艺一流的: **cordon bleu chef** (=someone who is trained to prepare food to this standard) 手艺高超的厨师

cor·du·roy /ˋkɔrdəˌrɔɪ; ˈkɔːdʒərɔɪ/ *n* [U] a thick strong cotton cloth with thin raised lines on it, used for making clothes 灯芯绒, 条绒布: *a corduroy jacket* 灯芯绒夹克 —see picture on page A16 参见 A16 页图

W3 **core**[1] /kɔr; kɔː/ *n* [C]

1▶FRUIT 水果◀ the hard central part of fruit such as an apple〔苹果等的〕果心: *Remove the cores, fill with raisins and cinnamon, and bake the apples for 40 minutes.* 去除果心, 填入葡萄干和肉桂, 然后把苹果烤40分钟。

2▶CENTRAL PART 中心部分◀ the most important or central part of something〔事物的〕核心, 最重要部分: [+of] *Houston is the central core of a metropolitan area of about 2.6 million residents.* 休斯顿是大都市地区的核心部分, 有大约260万居民。

3 core values/beliefs/concerns the values etc that are most important to someone 核心价值观/最重要的信仰/最关心的问题

4▶PEOPLE 人们◀ a number of people who form a strong group which is very important to an organization〔组织的〕核心成员: *The club was beginning to develop a core of young people who were very active in the community.* 这个俱乐部开始培养一批在社区里非常活跃的年轻核心成员。

5 to the core in a way that affects all of your feelings or your character 十分地; 彻底地: *That woman is rotten to the core!* 那个女人坏透了! | *When I saw the accident, I was shaken to the core.* 我看到这起事故, 十分震惊。

6▶PLANETS 行星◀ the central part of the Earth or any other PLANET 地心; 〔天体的〕核心

7▶NUCLEAR REACTOR 核反应堆◀ the central part of a NUCLEAR REACTOR〔核反应堆的〕活性区

core[2] *v* [T] to take the centre from a piece of fruit 去掉〔水果的〕果核

core cur·ric·u·lum /ˌ· ·ˈ···/ *n* [U] the basic subjects that someone must study in school 基础课程

co·re·li·gion·ist /ˌko·rɪˋlɪdʒənɪst; ˌkəʊrɪˈlɪdʒənɪst/ *n* [C] *formal* someone who is a member of the same religion as you【正式】信奉同一宗教的人, 教友

cor·er /ˋkɔrɚ; ˈkɔːrə/ *n* [C] a specially shaped knife for taking the hard centres out of fruit 去果核的刀

co·res·pon·dent /ˌko·rɪˋspɑndənt; ˌkəʊrɪˈspɒndənt/ *n* [C] *law* someone whose name is given in a DIVORCE[1] (1) because they have had sex with the wife or husband of the person who wants the divorce【法律】共同被告〔在离婚诉讼中被指与原告的配偶通奸的人〕—compare 比较 RESPONDENT

core time /ˈ· ·/ *n* [U] the period during the middle part of the day when an office or other place of work that has FLEXITIME expects all its people to be working〔弹性工作时间制中所有人员都在上班的〕核心上班时间〔多为每天中间的一段时间〕

Cor·fu /ˋkɔrfu; ˌkɔːˈfuː/ a Greek island northwest of mainland Greece, which is a popular place for tourists to visit 科孚岛〔希腊西北沿海一岛屿, 著名旅游胜地〕

cor·gi /ˋkɔrgɪ; ˈkɔːgi/ *n plural* **corgis** [C] a small dog with short legs and a pointed nose 柯基犬〔一种腿短鼻尖的小狗〕: *the Queen's famous corgis* 女王的著名柯基犬

co·ri·an·der /ˌkɔrɪˋændɚ; ˌkɒriˈændə/ *n* [U] *BrE* a plant used to give a special taste to food, especially in Indian cooking【英】芫荽, 香菜; CILANTRO *AmE*【美】

Co·rin·thi·an /kəˋrɪnθɪən; kəˈrɪnθiən/ *adj* of a style of Greek ARCHITECTURE that uses decorations of leaves cut into stone 科林斯式建筑风格的〔一种希腊建筑的风格, 其装饰特点是在石上雕刻叶饰〕: *a Corinthian column* 科林斯式柱

Cork /kɔrk; kɔːk/ **1** the largest COUNTY in the Irish Republic 科克郡〔爱尔兰共和国最大的一个郡〕 **2** the second largest city in the Irish Republic 科克〔爱尔兰共和国第二大城市〕

cork[1] *n* **1** [U] the BARK (=outer part) of a tree from southern Europe and North Africa, used to make things 软木橡树的树皮: *cork mats* 软木橡树皮垫子 **2** [C] a long round piece of cork which is put into the top of a bottle, especially a wine bottle, to keep liquid inside 木瓶塞, 软木塞

cork[2] *v* [T] to close a bottle by blocking the hole at the top tightly with a long, round piece of cork 用软木塞塞紧 —opposite 反义词 UNCORK

cork·age /ˋkɔrkɪdʒ; ˈkɔːkɪdʒ/ *n* [U] the charge made by a hotel or restaurant for allowing people to drink alcoholic drinks which they bought somewhere else〔对自带酒水的顾客收取的〕开瓶费

corked /kɔrkt; kɔːkt/ *adj* corked wine tastes bad because a decaying cork has allowed air into the bottle〔酒由于瓶塞腐朽而〕味道不佳的, 带瓶塞味的

cork·er /ˋkɔrkɚ; ˈkɔːkə/ *n* [C] *BrE old-fashioned* someone or something you think is very good【英, 过时】出类拔萃的人[物] —**corking** *adj*

cork·screw[1] /ˋkɔrkskru; ˈkɔːkskruː/ *n* [C] a tool made of twisted metal which you use to pull a CORK[1] (2) out of a bottle〔拔木瓶塞的〕瓶塞钻 —see picture on page A10 参见 A10 页图

corkscrew[2] *adj* [only before noun 仅用于名词前] twisted or curly; SPIRAL[1] 螺旋型的: *corkscrew curls* 螺旋式的鬈发

Corleone, Vito the main character in *The Godfather*, a NOVEL and film about the MAFIA in the US. The book tells how the Corleone family become one of the most powerful criminal organizations in America. Marlon Brando played Corleone in the 1972 film of *The Godfather*. 柯里昂〔描述美国黑手党的小说及电影《教父》中的主要人物。故事讲述美国最有势力的犯罪组织柯里昂家族的发展过程。马龙·白兰度在1972年的影片《教父》中饰演柯里昂〕

cor·mo·rant /ˋkɔrmərənt; ˈkɔːmərənt/ *n* [C] a large black sea bird which has a long neck and eats fish 鸬鹚

corn /kɔrn; kɔːn/ *n* **1** [U] *BrE* grains of plants such as wheat, BARLEY, and OATS or their seeds【英】谷物; 谷粒 **2** [U] *AmE, AustrE*【美, 澳】**a)** a tall plant with large yellow grains at the top, which is cooked whole and eaten as a food; MAIZE 玉米 **b)** the grains of this plant 玉米粒 —see also 另见 SWEETCORN **3** [C] a painful area of thick hard skin on your foot 鸡眼, 肉刺 S3

corn·ball /ˋkɔrnˌbɔl; ˈkɔːnbɔːl/ *adj* [only before noun 仅用于名词前] *AmE informal* cornball humour is too simple, old-fashioned, unoriginal, and silly【美, 非正式】〔幽默感〕陈腐的, 过时的; 愚蠢的: *At lunchtime he bored us with these awful cornball jokes.* 吃午饭的时候, 他说了些糟糕的老掉牙的笑话, 让我们觉得很无趣。

Corn Belt, the /ˈ· ·/ a large area in the central part of the US which produces a lot of corn (= maize in British English) as food for cattle. It includes Iowa, Illinois, Indiana, and parts of other states. 玉米带〔美国中部盛产玉米作为牛饲料的一个大区，包括艾奥瓦州、伊利诺伊州、印第安纳州以及其他几个州的部分地区〕

corn bread /ˈ· ·/ *n* [U] bread made from CORNMEAL 玉米粉面包

corn chip /ˈ· ·/ *n* [C] crushed MAIZE formed into a small flat piece and cooked in oil, eaten especially in the US 炸玉米片

corn cir·cle /ˈ· ,· ·/ also 又作 **crop circle** *n* [C] patterns that appeared in British farm fields which some people believe were made by creatures from another world〔有些人认为是由外星人制作的〕农田圈

C

corn·cob /ˈkɔrn,kɑb; ˈkɔːnkɒb/ also 又作 **cob** *n* [C] the top part of a MAIZE plant after its yellow grains have been removed 玉米穗轴，玉米芯

corn·crake /ˈkɔrn,krek; ˈkɔːnkreɪk/ *n* [C] a European bird with a loud sharp cry 秧鸡

corn dol·ly /ˈ· ,· ·/ *n* [C] a figure made from the heads and stems of wheat plants, made especially in former times to celebrate the HARVEST[1] (1) 稻草人

cor·ne·a /ˈkɔrnɪə; ˈkɔːniə/ *n* [C] the transparent protective covering on the outer surface of your eye〔眼球的〕角膜 —**corneal** *adj*: *an operation for a corneal graft* 角膜移植手术 —see picture at 参见 EYE[1] 图

corned beef /,kɔrnd ˈbif; ,kɔːnd ˈbiːf◂/ *n* [U] *BrE*【英】**1** a kind of pressed cooked BEEF[1] (1) sold in a tin 罐装牛肉 **2** *AmE* beef that has been covered in salt water and SPICES to preserve it【美】咸牛肉

cor·ne·li·an /kɔrˈniljən; kɔːˈniːliən/ *n* [U] a red or white stone used in jewellery 红玉髓，光玉髓（石）

Cor·nell /kɔrˈnɛl; kɔːˈnel/ an important US university in Ithaca, New York. It is one of the Ivy League colleges 康奈尔大学〔美国一著名大学，位于纽约州的伊萨卡，为长春藤联合会成员〕

1 2 **cor·ner¹** /ˈkɔrnɚ; ˈkɔːnə/ *n*

1 ▶WHERE TWO LINES/EDGES MEET 角◀[C] the point at which two lines or edges meet 角；角落：*He pulled a dirty handkerchief out by its corner and waved it at me.* 他捏住脏手帕的一角拉出来向我挥动。| **in/on the corner** *Write your name in the top left-hand corner of the page.* 把你的名字写在纸的左上角。| **three-cornered/four-cornered etc** *a three-cornered hat* 三角帽

2 ▶ROADS 道路◀[C often singular 常用单数] **a)** the point where two roads meet 拐角处：**on/at the corner** *He stopped at the corner of 5th and Main to buy a newspaper.* 他在第五街和主街拐角处停下来买报纸。**b)** a point in a road where it turns sharply〔路上的〕急转弯：*I think the gas station should be just around the next corner.* 我想加油站应该就在下一个转弯处。

3 ▶CORNER OF A ROOM/BOX 房间/箱子的角落◀[C often singular 常用单数] the place inside a room or box where two walls or sides meet〔房间、箱子内部的〕角：**in/at the corner** *Jim and his cousin sat in the corner talking about people back home.* 吉姆和他的堂兄坐在角落里谈论家里人。

4 ▶MOUTH 嘴◀[C] the corners of your mouth are the sides of your mouth 嘴角：*A small smile appeared at the corners of his mouth.* 他的嘴角露出浅浅的微笑。

5 ▶DIFFICULT SITUATION 困境◀[singular] a difficult situation that is difficult to escape from 困境；绝路：**force sb into a corner** *The president is likely to be forced into a corner over his latest plans for welfare spending.* 总统有可能因为最近的福利开支计划被逼入困境。| **tight corner** (=very difficult situation) 绝路，绝境

6 ▶SPORT 体育◀[C] **a)** a kick in SOCCER that one team is allowed to take from one of the corners of their opponent's end of the field〔足球的〕角球 —see picture on page A23 参见 A23 页图 **b)** any of the four corners of the area in which the competitors fight in BOXING or WRESTLING 拳击[摔跤]场的角

7 ▶DISTANT PLACE 远方◀[C] a distant place in another part of the world 远方；天涯海角：[**+of**] *She's gone off to do voluntary work in some remote corner of the world.* 她已离开，去了世界的某个偏僻角落做志愿工作。| **the four corners of the Earth/world** (=all the distant places in the world) 四面八方，世界各地 *People came from the four corners of the world to see this spectacle.* 人们从世界各地来观看这一奇景。

8 see sth out of the corner of your eye to notice something accidentally, without turning your head towards it or looking for it 偶然看到，不经意看到：*Out of the corner of her eye she saw the dog running towards her.* 她从眼角瞟去，看到狗向她跑来。

9 just around the corner likely to happen soon 即将来临：*Economic recovery is just around the corner.* 经济很快就会恢复。

10 turn a corner to start to improve 渡过难关，转危为安：*She's been ill for a long time, but the doctors think she's turned a corner now.* 她已经病了很长时间，但是医生相信她已经渡过难关，开始康复。

11 cut corners to do things too quickly, and not as carefully as you should, especially to save money or time〔为了节省金钱或时间而〕马虎从事：*Don't try to cut corners when you're decorating.* 在装修的时候不要图省事。

12 cut a corner to go across the corner of something, especially a road, instead of keeping to the edges 抄近路，走捷径

13 have a corner on the market to have a position in which you control all of the supply of a particular type of goods 垄断：*The company had a corner on the silver market.* 这家公司垄断白银市场。—see also 另见 KITTY-CORNER

corner² *v* **1** [T] to force a person or animal into a position from which they cannot easily escape 把〔人或动物〕困住，把…逼入绝境：*As the dog was cornered, it began to growl threateningly.* 狗被逼到无路可走的时候，开始威胁似地狂吠。| *Janet cornered Marty in the hall.* 珍妮特把马蒂困在大厅里。**2 corner sb** also 又作 **back sb into a corner** to put someone into a position in which they cannot choose to do what they want to do 使某人陷入困境：*They have backed us into a corner – if we don't accept their terms, we'll lose our jobs.* 他们使我们进退维谷，如果我们不接受他们的条件就会失业。**3 corner the market** to gain control of the whole supply of a particular kind of goods 垄断：*They're trying to corner the market by buying up all the wheat in sight.* 他们企图通过买进现有的全部小麦来垄断市场。**4** [I] if a car corners, it goes around a corner or curve in the road〔车辆〕转弯

corner shop /ˈ·· ·/ *n* [C] *BrE* a small shop, usually but not always on a corner, that sells food, cigarettes, and other things needed every day【英】街头小店 —see also 另见 CONVENIENCE STORE

CULTURAL NOTE 文化注释

In the UK many corner shops are owned and run by Indian or Pakistani families. Some shops are run as a FRANCHISE. Many owners of corner shops are worried because large companies that own supermarkets are trying to open corner shops as well. This means that some corner shops may not be able to afford to stay in business. In the US, convenience stores are usually part of a group of shops owned by a company. In both countries the shops are open earlier and later than most other shops. 英国的街头小店很多是印度人或巴基斯坦人家庭开的。一些街头小店实行特许经营。很多店主担心拥有超市的大公司也会开街头小店，那样的话，一些小店将无以为继。美国的便利店通常是连锁店，归某家公司所有。在英美两国，街头小店都比大多数其他商店营业时间长。

cor·ner·stone /ˈkɔrnɚ,ston; ˈkɔːnəstəʊn/ *n* [C] **1** a stone set at one of the bottom corners of a building, often put in place at a special ceremony 基石；奠基石：*The mayor laid the cornerstone for the new city hall yesterday.* 市长昨天给新的市政大厅奠基。**2** something that is extremely important because everything else depends on it 基础；基本：[**+of/for**] *Trust and commitment are the cornerstones of any marriage.* 信任和忠诚是任何婚姻的基础。—compare 比较 FOUNDATION STONE

cor·net /ˈkɔrnɪt; ˈkɔːnɪt/ *n* [C] **1** a musical instrument like a TRUMPET[1] (1) often used in military bands 短号 **2** *BrE* a thin container shaped like a cone that you eat ICE-CREAM from【英】〔装冰激凌的〕圆锥形蛋筒 —see also 另见 CONE

corn ex·change /ˈ· ·,·/ *n* [C] a place where corn used to be bought and sold 谷物交易市场

corn·flakes /ˈkɔrn,fleks; ˈkɔːnfleɪks/ *n* [plural] small flat pieces of crushed corn, usually eaten at breakfast with milk and sugar 玉米片〔通常加牛奶和糖在早餐时吃〕

corn·flour /ˈkɔrnflauɚ; ˈkɔːnflaʊə/ *n* [U] *BrE* fine white flour made from corn, used in cooking to make liquids thick【英】〔精磨〕玉米粉；玉米面；CORNSTARCH *AmE*【美】

corn·flow·er /ˈkɔrn,flauɚ; ˈkɔːnflaʊəʳ/ *n* [C] a wild plant with blue flowers 矢车菊

cor·nice /ˈkɔrnɪs; ˈkɔːnɪs/ *n* [C] a decorative area at the top edge of a wall or PILLAR (1) 上楣，飞檐

cor·niche /kɔrˈniʃ; kɔːˈniːʃ/ *n* [C] a road built along a coast 滨海路

Corn·ing Ware/ˈkɔrnɪŋ wɛr; ˈkɔːnɪŋ weə/ *trademark* a type of glass, usually white, which does not break easily and is used for making pots, pans, and baking dishes. It is sold in the US.【商标】"康宁"器皿〔在美国销售的一种玻璃制品，通常为白色，不易碎。其制成品包括壶、锅、烤盘等〕

Cor·nish/ˈkɔrnɪʃ; ˈkɔːnɪʃ/ *adj* from or related to Cornwall 康沃尔郡的

Cornish pas·ty/, ·· ˈ· ·/ *n* [C] *BrE* a folded piece of PASTRY (1), baked with meat and potatoes in it, usually for one person to eat【英】康沃尔馅饼

Corn Laws, the/ˈ· , ·/ laws in Britain in the 19th century controlling the price of foreign corn, and making it more expensive than corn produced in Britain. This protected British farmers from competition, but hurt the ordinary people, and after much protest, the laws were changed in 1846《谷物法》〔19世纪英国一项法律，旨在控制进口谷物的价格，保护英国原产谷物的价格。该法律使英国农民免受竞争冲击，但损害了普通人的利益。遭到多次抗议之后，该法律于1846年被废除〕

corn liq·uor/ˈ· , · ·/ also 又作 **corn whiskey** *n* [U] a strong American alcoholic drink made from corn 玉米威士忌酒

corn·meal/ˈkɔrn,mil; ˈkɔːnmiːl/ *n* [U] flour made from MAIZE 玉米粉；玉米面

corn on the cob/, · · ˈ· ·/ *n* [U] the top part of a MAIZE plant, cooked and eaten whole 玉米棒子

corn pone/ˈkɔrn pon; ˈkɔːn pəʊn/ *n* [U] a kind of American bread made from cornmeal〔一种美国〕玉米饼

corn·row/ˈkɔrnro; ˈkɔːnrəʊ/ *n* [C] a way of arranging hair, especially by women of West Indian and West African origin, in which hair is put into small tight plaits (PLAIT²) in lines along your head "玉米垄"式发型〔西印度群岛和西非地区黑人妇女编成一排排辫子的发型〕

corn·starch/ˈkɔrn,stɑrtʃ; ˈkɔːnstɑːtʃ/ *n* [U] *AmE* cornflour【美】玉米粉；玉米面

corn syr·up/, · ˈ· ·/ *n* [U] a very sweet thick liquid made from MAIZE, used in cooking 玉米糖浆

cornucopia
〔象征丰饶的〕角状盛器

cor·nu·co·pi·a/,kɔrnəˈkopɪə; ,kɔːnjʊˈkəʊpiə/ *n* [singular] **1** a decorative container in the shape of an animal's horn, full of fruit and flowers, used to represent plenty〔象征丰饶的〕角饰，角状盛器 **2** a lot of good things 许多好东西，大量的好东西：*the cornucopia of delights on display* 很多令人赏心悦目的展品

Corn·wall /ˈkɔrnwɔl; ˈkɔːnwɔːl/ a COUNTY in southwest England which is a popular place for tourists. Cornwall includes Land's End and the Isles of Scilly. 康沃尔郡〔英格兰西南一郡，著名旅游胜地，包括兰兹角和锡利群岛〕—**Cornish** *adj*: *Cornish ice cream* 康沃尔式冰激凌

Corn·wal·lis/kɔrnˈwɑlɪs; kɔːnˈwɒlɪs/, **Lord Charles** (1738-1805) a British military leader who was in charge of the British army during the American Revolutionary War. He later became Governor-General of India. 康华里〔(1738-1805)，英国军事领导人。美国独立战争期间统率英国军队，后来担任印度总督〕

corn whis·key/ˈ· , · ·/ *n* [U] CORN LIQUOR 玉米威士忌酒

corn·y /ˈkɔrnɪ; ˈkɔːni/ *adj informal* not new, different, interesting, or surprising【非正式】陈旧的；平凡的；乏味的：*My dad loves telling corny jokes.* 我爸爸喜欢讲过时的笑话。| *I know it sounds corny, but I dream about her every night.* 我知道那听起来有点老套，但是我确实每天晚上都梦到她。—**cornily** *adv* —**corniness** *n* [U]

co·rol·la·ry/ˈkɔrə,lɛrɪ; kəˈrɒləri/ *n* [C] *formal* something that is the direct result of something else【正式】直接的结果；必然的推论：*This is the inevitable corollary of his determination to succeed.* 这是他一心想要成功不可避免的结果。

co·ro·na/kəˈronə; kəˈrəʊnə/ *n* [C] the shining circle of light seen around the sun when the moon passes in front of it in an ECLIPSE¹ (1) 日冕

cor·o·na·ry /ˈkɔrə,nɛrɪ; ˈkɒrənəri/ *adj* concerning or about the heart 心脏的，与心脏有关的：*coronary disease* 心脏病

cor·o·na·tion/,kɔrəˈneʃən; ,kɒrəˈneɪʃən◂/ *n* [C] the ceremony at which someone is officially made king or queen 加冕典礼

Coronation Street /·· · ·/ one of the most popular programmes on British television, which has been shown continuously since 1960. It is a SOAP OPERA set in an industrial city in northern England and its characters are working-class people who live in a street called Coronation Street. People sometimes informally call it 'Corrie'.《街头巷尾》，又译《加冕街》〔英国最受欢迎的电视节目之一，自1960年连续播出至今。这是一部以英格兰北部一工业城市为背景的肥皂剧，人物都是住在一条叫加冕街的工人阶级。人们有时非正式地称该剧为Corrie (加街)〕

cor·o·ner/ˈkɔrənə; ˈkɒrənə/ *n* [C] someone whose job is to discover the cause of someone's death, especially if they died in a sudden or unusual way〔调查死因的〕验尸官：*The coroner recorded a verdict of death by natural causes.* 验尸官判定是自然死亡。

cor·o·net/ˈkɔrənɪt; ˈkɒrənɪt/ *n* [C] **1** a small CROWN¹ (1a) worn by princes or other members of a royal family, especially on formal occasions〔王子或王族戴的〕小冠冕 **2** anything that you wear on your head that looks like a CROWN¹ (1b) 冠状头饰：*a coronet of flowers* 花环头饰

corp /kɔrp; kɔːp/ **1** the abbreviation of 缩写= CORPORAL¹ **2** the abbreviation of 缩写= CORPORATION

cor·po·ra/ˈkɔrpərə; ˈkɔːpərə/ *n* [plural] plural of CORPUS

cor·po·ral¹/ˈkɔrpərəl; ˈkɔːpərəl/ *n* [C] a low rank in the army, air force etc〔陆军、空军等的〕下士 —see table on page C6 参见C6页附录

corporal² *adj formal literary* of or about the body【正式，文】肉体的；身体的

corporal pun·ish·ment/, ··· ˈ·· ·/ *n* [U] a way of officially punishing someone by hitting them, especially in schools and prisons〔尤指学校和监狱中的〕体罚：*Corporal punishment was abolished in Britain in 1986.* 英国于1986年取消了体罚。

> **CULTURAL NOTE 文化注释**
>
> Corporal punishment is now illegal in schools in the US and the UK. In the past, boys used to be punished in this way more often than girls. They were usually hit on the hand or BUTTOCKS with a STRAP (=long thin piece of leather) or belt, a CANE *BrE* (=a long thin stick), or a PADDLE *AmE* (=a piece of wood with a handle). 体罚现在在英美学校里是非法的。在过去，男孩比女孩受到的体罚更多，常被皮带或腰带、藤条或板子打手或打屁股。

cor·po·rate/ˈkɔrpərɪt; ˈkɔːpərɪt/ *adj* [only before noun 仅用于名词前] **1** belonging to or connected with a business 公司的：*This policy is a key feature of our long-term corporate planning.* 这项政策是本公司长期计划的一个重要特色。**2** shared by or involving all the members of a group 团体的；全体的：*corporate responsibility* 集体责任 | *corporate identity* 企业标志 **3** forming a single group 合为一体的：*The university is a corporate body made up of several different colleges.* 这所大学由几个不同的学院组成。**4 corporate hospitality** ways in which companies entertain their customers in order to gain business〔为了获得商业机会而进行的〕公司招待 —**corporately** *adv* 

cor·po·ra·tion/,kɔrpəˈreʃən; ,kɔːpəˈreɪʃən/ *n* [C] **1** a big company, or a group of companies acting together as a single organization 大型公司；大企业；企业集团：*He works for a large American corporation.* 他为一家美国大公司工作。| *a multinational corporation* 跨国公司 **2** *BrE old use* a group of people elected to govern a town or city【英，旧】市镇当局；市议会 **3 corporation tax** a tax paid by companies on their profits 公司(利润)税 

cor·po·re·al/kɔrˈporɪəl; kɔːˈpɔːriəl/ *adj formal*【正式】**1** related to the body as opposed to the mind, feelings, or spirit 身体的，肉体的：*He paid little attention to corporeal needs like food.* 他很少注意各种身体的需要，如食物。**2** able to be touched; MATERIAL² (2) 物质的；有形的

corps/kɔr; kɔː/ *n* **1** a group in an army with special duties and responsibilities 特殊部队；特殊兵种：*the medical corps* 医疗部队 **2** *technical* a trained army unit made of two or more DIVISIONS (=group of soldiers)【术语】军〔军队编制单位，至少由两个师组成〕**3** a group of people who work together to do a particular job 共同工作的一群人：*the president's press corps* 总统记者团

corpse/kɔrps; kɔːps/ *n* [C] the dead body of a person 尸体：*Her corpse was found floating in the river.* 她的尸体被发现漂浮在河上。

cor·pu·lent/ˈkɔrpjələnt; ˈkɔːpjələnt/ *adj formal* very fat【正式】肥胖的；臃肿的：*He was a corpulent, pompous, and short-tempered little man.* 他是一个肥胖、自负、脾气暴躁的小男人。—**corpulence** *n* [U]

cor·pus /ˋkɔrpəs; ˈkɔːpəs/ *n plural* **corpora** /-pərə; -pərə/ *or* **corpuses** [C] **1** *formal* a collection of all the writing of a particular kind or by a particular person【正式】〔某种作品的〕总集;〔某人的〕全集: *They aim to study the entire corpus of Shakespeare's works.* 他们的目标是研究莎士比亚的全部著作。**2** *technical* a collection of information or material to be studied【术语】研究材料的汇总; 资料库: *a corpus of spoken English* 英语口语资料库 —see also 另见 HABEUS CORPUS

Cor·pus Chris·ti[1] /ˌkɔrpəs ˋkrɪstɪ; ˌkɔːpəs ˈkrɪsti/ also 又作 **the Feast of Corpus Christi** a holy day in the Roman Catholic Church, when the SACRAMENT (=the holy bread eaten at the Eucharist) is carried in PROCESSION. Corpus Christi is Latin for 'the Body of Christ'. 圣体节〔罗马天主教的一个节日〕

Corpus Christi[2] a city in southeast Texas on the Gulf of Mexico 科珀斯克里斯蒂〔得克萨斯州东南部一城市, 濒临墨西哥湾〕

cor·pus·cle /ˋkɔrpəsḷ; ˈkɔːpəsəl/ *n* [C] one of the red or white cells in the blood 血球, 血细胞

cor·ral[1] /kəˋræl; kəˈrɑːl/ *n* [C] an enclosed area where cattle, horses etc can be temporarily kept, especially in North America〔尤指北美临时关牛、马等的〕畜栏

corral[2] *v* **-ll-** [T] **1** to make animals move into a corral 把〔牲畜〕赶入畜栏: *They corralled the cattle before loading them onto the truck.* 在把牛装上车以前, 他们把牛赶入畜栏。**2** to keep people in a particular area in order to control them 把〔人〕限制在某地方: *They corralled the protesters, keeping them away from the president's car.* 他们把抗议者赶到一边, 使他们远离总统的车。

cor·rect[1] /kəˋrɛkt; kəˈrekt/ *adj* **1** without any mistakes 正确的, 无误的: *I'm not sure of the correct spelling.* 该怎么拼写我说不准。| *Make sure you replace the parts in the correct order.* 要确定按正确的顺序更换部件。**2** suitable and right for a particular situation 恰当的, 正确的: *What's the correct procedure in cases like this?* 像这种案件的正确程序是什么? | *When lifting heavy weights it is very important that your back is in the correct position.* 在举重物时, 背部保持恰当的姿势是很重要的。**3** correct behaviour is formal and polite〔行为〕合乎礼节的; 得体的: *Simpson always knew what was correct and proper.* 辛普森总是知道什么是得体和合适的。—**correctly** *adv* —**correctness** *n* [U] —opposite 反义词 INCORRECT

correct[2] *v* [T]

1 ▶SHOW STH IS WRONG 表示某事错误◀ to show someone that something is wrong, and make it right 改正; 纠正: *Correct my pronunciation if it's wrong.* 如果我的发音错了, 请予以纠正。| *I'd like to correct the impression that library work is boring.* 我希望纠正图书馆工作枯燥的印象。| **correct sb** (=tell someone that what they have said is wrong) 指出…说的话中的错误

2 ▶IMPROVE BY CHANGING 改正◀ to make something work the way it should 校正, 矫正: *Some eyesight problems are relatively easy to correct.* 有些视力问题相对来讲是容易矫正的。

3 ▶EXAMS/ESSAYS ETC 考试/文章等◀ to make marks on a piece of written work to show the mistakes in it 批改: *She spent the whole evening correcting exam papers.* 她花了整个晚上批改试卷。

4 correct me if I'm wrong *spoken* used when you are not sure that what you are going to say is true or not【口】如果我错了, 请予以纠正: *Correct me if I'm wrong, but didn't you say you were going to London today?* 如果我错了就请予以纠正, 但是你不是说过今天要去伦敦吗?

5 I stand corrected *formal spoken* used to admit that something you have said is wrong after someone has told you it is wrong【正式, 口】我承认有错, 我接受批评指正

cor·rec·tion /kəˋrɛkʃən; kəˈrekʃən/ *n* **1** [C] a change made in something in order to correct it 修改, 纠正: *The page was covered in crossings-out and corrections.* 这一页上全是叉号和所做的改正。| **make a correction** *She makes all her corrections with a green pen.* 她所有的改正都是用绿笔做的。**2** [U] the act of changing something in order to make it right or better 改正, 纠正 **3** *spoken* used to say that what you have just said is wrong and you want to change it【口】改正一下: *That figure was 30,000 ... correction, make that 31,000.* 那数字是 30,000——改正一下, 是 31,000。

correctional fa·ci·li·ty /·ˈ···, ·ˈ··/ *n* [C] *AmE technical or humorous* a prison【美, 术语或幽默】监狱

correction flu·id /·ˈ··, ·ˈ··/ *n* [U] *formal* a special white liquid used for covering written mistakes【正式】修正液, 涂改液

cor·rec·ti·tude /kəˋrɛktəˌtud; kəˈrektɪ̣tjuːd/ *n* [U] *formal* correctness of behaviour【正式】〔行为的〕正当, 端正

cor·rec·tive[1] /kəˋrɛktɪv; kəˈrektɪv/ *adj formal* intended to make a fault or mistake right again【正式】改正的; 纠正的: *corrective treatment* 矫正治疗 | *This condition may require corrective surgery.* 这种情况或许需要矫正手术。—**correctively** *adv*

corrective[2] *n* [C] *formal* something that is intended to correct a fault or mistake【正式】纠正物: [+to] *The idea is that this will function as a corrective to complacency.* 该观点认为这会对自满情绪起纠正的作用。

cor·rel·ate[1] /ˋkɔrəˌlet; ˈkɒrɪ̣leɪt/ *v* [I,T] if two or more facts, ideas etc correlate, or you correlate them, they are closely connected or one causes another (使)相互关联: *They found that the two sets of results seemed to be correlated.* 他们发现这两组结果看起来是互相关联的。| [+with] *Scientists have been unable to correlate their findings with recent increases in radioactivity levels.* 科学家不能把他们的发现和最近增长的辐射水平联系起来。

cor·re·late[2] /ˋkɔrəˌlɪt; ˈkɒrɪ̣lɪ̣t/ *n* [C] either of two things that correlate with each other 相关的事物

cor·re·la·tion /ˌkɔrəˋleʃən; ˌkɒrɪ̣ˈleɪʃən/ *n* **1** [C,U] a connection between two ideas, facts etc, especially when one may be the cause of the other 相互关系; 关联; 因果关系: [+between] *They found a strong correlation between urban deprivation and poor health.* 他们发现城市中的贫困和健康状况差有很密切的联系。| [+with] *There was also some correlation with social class.* 与社会阶级也有些关系。**2** [U] the process of correlating two or more things 联系(的过程)

cor·rel·a·tive[1] /kəˋrɛlətɪv; kəˈrelətɪv/ *adj* **1** two or more facts, ideas etc that are correlative are closely related or dependent on each other 密切相关的; 互相依赖的: *correlative theories and beliefs* 相关的理论和信仰 | *Profits were directly correlative to the popularity of the product.* 利润和产品的受欢迎程度有直接的关系。**2** *technical* two words that are correlative are frequently together but not usually used next to each other【术语】〔词语〕关联的〔指经常一起使用但一般并不连续的词〕: *'Either' and 'or' are correlative conjunctions.* either 和 or 是关联连词。

correlative[2] *n* [C] *formal* one of two or more facts, ideas etc that are closely related or that depend on each other【正式】相关物

cor·re·spond /ˌkɔrəˋspɑnd; ˌkɒrɪ̣ˈspɒnd/ *v* [I] **1** if two things or ideas correspond, the parts or information in one relate to the parts or information in the other 符合; 相一致: *The two halves of the document did not correspond.* 这份文件的前后两半不相符。| [+with/to] *The numbers correspond to distinct points on the map.* 这些数字与地图上不同的点相对应。**2** to be very similar or the same as something else 相类似, 相当: [+to] *The French 'baccalauréat' roughly corresponds to British 'A-levels'.* 法国的 baccalauréat 与英国的 A-levels 大体上相类似。**3** to write letters to someone and receive letters from them 通信: *For the next three years they corresponded regularly.* 在接下来的三年里他们经常通信。| [+with] *She stopped corresponding with him after the death of her mother.* 她母亲死后她不再与他通信。

cor·re·spon·dence /ˌkɔrəˋspɑndəns; ˌkɒrɪ̣ˈspɒndəns/ *n* [U] **1** letters exchanged between people, especially official or business letters 信件〔尤指公函或商业信函〕: *A secretary came in twice a week to deal with his correspondence.* 一个秘书每星期来两次处理他的信件。**2** the process of sending and receiving letters 通信: *All correspondence between us must cease.* 我们必须停止一切通信。**3** a relationship or connection between two or more ideas or facts 关系; 联系: [+between] *There was no correspondence between the historical facts and Johnson's account of them.* 这些历史事实和约翰逊对其表述之间没有关联。

correspondence course /··ˈ·· ˌ·/ *n* [C] a course of lessons in which the student works at home and sends completed work to their teacher by mail 函授课程: *I'm taking a correspondence course in business studies.* 我正在修读一门商务函授课程。

cor·re·spon·dent[1] /ˌkɔrəˋspɑndənt; ˌkɒrɪ̣ˈspɒndənt/ *n* [C] **1** someone who is employed by a newspaper or a television station etc to report news from a particular area or on a particular subject 新闻记者: *Our correspondent in South Africa sent this report.* 我们驻南非的记者送来了这份报道。| *the political correspondent for The Times*《泰晤士报》的政治新闻记者 **2** someone who writes letters 通信者: **good/bad correspondent** (=someone who is good or bad at writing letters regularly) 勤于/疏于写信的人 *I'm not a very good correspondent, I'm afraid.* 我想我不太勤于写信。

correspondent[2] *adj formal* being right for a particular situation【正式】适合的; 一致的: [+with] *The result was correspondent with the government's wishes in this matter.* 这个结果与政府在这件事上的愿望是一致的。

cor·re·spon·ding /ˌkɔrəˋspɑndɪŋ; ˌkɒrɪ̣ˈspɒndɪŋ◂/ *adj* [only before noun 仅用于名词前] **1** caused by or dependent on some-

thing you have already mentioned 相应的, 由此引起的: *The war, and the corresponding fall in trade, have had a devastating effect on the country.* 战争以及由此所导致的贸易量的下降对这个国家产生了致命的影响。**2** having similar qualities or a similar position to something you have already mentioned; matching; EQUIVALENT[1] 相似的; 〔位置〕对应的; 相符合的; 相等的: *The corresponding chromosome in the other parent was found to be defective.* 父母中一人身上对应的染色体被发现有缺陷。—**correspondingly** *adv*

S2 W3 **cor·ri·dor** /ˋkɔrədɚ; ˈkɒrɪ̵dɔː/ *n* [C] **1** a long, narrow passage between two rows of rooms in a building or a train, with doors leading off it 通道; 走廊: *Room 101 is at the end of the corridor.* 101房间在走廊的尽头。| *She hurried down the corridor.* 她沿着走廊匆匆而去。**2** a narrow area of land, within a bigger area, that has different qualities or features from the land that surrounds it 〔陆地上与周边地区有不同性质或特征的〕走廊; 地带: *the industrial corridor that connects Queretaro with Mexico City* 连接克雷塔罗州和墨西哥城的工业地带 | *the Polish Corridor* 波兰走廊 **3 corridors of power** the places where important government decisions are made 权力走廊, 权力核心〔政府的决策场所〕: *Who can tell what really goes on in the corridors of power?* 权力走廊里到底发生了什么, 谁能说得清?

cor·rie /ˋkɔrɪ; ˈkɒri/ *n* [C] a deep bowl-shaped area on a mountain 山侧圆形凹地 —see picture on page A12 参见A12页图

cor·rob·o·rate /kəˋrɑbəˌret; kəˈrɒbəreɪt/ *v* [T] *formal* to provide information that supports or helps to prove someone else's statement, idea etc【正式】〔提供资料〕证实: *We now have new evidence to corroborate the defendant's story.* 我们现在有新证据来证实被告人的证词。—**corroboration** /kəˌrɑbəˋreʃən; kəˌrɒbəˈreɪʃən/ *n* [U] —**corroborative** /kəˋrɑbəˌretɪv; kəˈrɒbərətɪv/ *adj*

cor·rode /kəˋrod; kəˈrəʊd/ *v* [I,T] if metal corrodes or something corrodes it, it is slowly destroyed by the effect of water, chemicals etc 腐蚀; 侵蚀: *All the electrical components have corroded.* 所有电器部件都被腐蚀了。

cor·ro·sion /kəˋroʒən; kəˈrəʊʒən/ *n* [U] **1** the gradual destruction of substances such as metal by the effect of water, chemicals etc 腐蚀; 侵蚀 **2** a substance such as RUST (=red weakened metal) that is produced by the process of corrosion 腐蚀而成之物〔如锈〕

cor·ro·sive /kəˋrosɪv; kəˈrəʊsɪv/ *adj* **1** a corrosive liquid such as an acid can destroy metal, plastic etc 腐蚀性的; 侵蚀性的: *Danger! Corrosive material.* 危险!腐蚀性物质。**2** gradually making something weaker, and possibly destroying it 有害的, 逐步起损害作用的: *Fear of unemployment is having a corrosive effect on the country's economy.* 失业的恐惧正对这个国家的经济逐步带来损害。

corrugated 有瓦楞的

corrugated iron 瓦楞铁

cor·ru·gated /ˋkɔrəˌgetɪd; ˈkɒrəgeɪtɪ̵d/ *adj* in the shape of waves or folds, or made like this in order to give something strength 起皱的, 波纹的; 有瓦楞的: *corrugated cardboard* 瓦楞纸板 | *corrugated iron* 瓦楞铁 —**corrugation** /ˌkɔrəˋgeʃən; ˌkɒrəˈgeɪʃən/ *n* [C]

cor·rupt[1] /kəˋrʌpt; kəˈrʌpt/ *adj* **1** using your power in a dishonest or illegal way in order to get an advantage for yourself 贪污受贿的, 腐败的: *Corrupt judges have taken millions of dollars in bribes.* 腐败的法官接受了几百万美元的贿赂。**2** very bad morally 有伤风化的, 道德败坏的; 邪恶的: *a corrupt society* 堕落的社会 **3** something that is corrupt is not pure or is not the way it was made or intended 讹误的; 不纯粹的 —see also 另见 INCORRUPTIBLE —**corruptly** *adv* —**corruptness** *n* [U]

corrupt[2] *v* [T] **1** to encourage someone to start behaving in an immoral or dishonest way; PERVERT[1] (2) 使道德败坏; 使腐败: *Young prisoners are being corrupted by the older, long term offenders.* 年轻囚犯被年纪较大、刑期长的囚犯带坏了。| *They say power corrupts.* 他们说权力能使人腐化。**2** to change the traditional form of something, such as a language, so that it becomes worse than it was 破坏〔语言等〕的纯洁 **3** to change the information in a computer, so that the computer does not work properly any more 使〔电脑信息〕出错 —**corruptible** *adj* —**corruptibility** /kəˌrʌptəˋbɪlətɪ; kəˌrʌptɪ̵ˈbɪlɪ̵ti/ *n* [U]

cor·rup·tion /kəˋrʌpʃən; kəˈrʌpʃən/ *n* **1** [U] dishonest, illegal, or immoral behaviour, especially from someone with power 贪污; 贿赂; 受贿; 腐败: *The Chief Executive is being investigated for alleged corruption.* 总裁由于涉嫌受贿正在接受调查。**2** [C usually singular 一般用单数] a changed form of something, for example a word 〔词等〕变化了的形式: *The word Thursday is a corruption of Thor's Day.* Thursday 是由 Thor's Day 演变而来的。

cor·sage /kɔrˋsɑʒ; kɔːˈsɑːʒ/ *n* [C] a group of small flowers that a woman fastens to her clothes on a special occasion such as a wedding 〔女服上用于婚礼等特殊场合的〕装饰花束

cor·sair /ˋkɔrsɛr; ˈkɔːseə/ *n* [C] *old use* the name of a North African PIRATE[1] (3), or their ship【旧】〔古代北非的〕海盗; 海盗船

corse /kɔrs; kɔːs/ *n* [C] *old use or poetical* a CORPSE【旧或诗】尸体

cor·set /ˋkɔrsɪt; ˈkɔːsɪ̵t/ *n* [C] **1** a tightly fitting piece of underwear that women wore in the past to make them look thinner 〔古代妇女穿来保持苗条的〕紧身褡 **2** a strong, tightly fitting piece of clothing that supports your back when it is injured 〔穿来支承受伤背部的〕围腰, 胸衣

Cor·si·ca /ˋkɔrsɪkə; ˈkɔːsɪkə/ a large island to the south of France in the Mediterranean Sea. Corsica belongs to France, but some of the people there want to have a separate government. 科西嘉岛〔地中海一大岛, 濒临法国南部。该岛归属法国, 但当地有些居民想建立一个独立政府〕—**Corsican** *n, adj*

cor·tege /kɔrˋteʒ; kɔːˈteɪʒ/ *n* [C] a line of people, cars etc that move along slowly in a funeral 送葬行列

Cor·tés /kɔrˋtɛz; ˈkɔːtez/, **Her·nán** /hɝˋnæn; hɜːˈnæn/ or 或 **Her·nan·do** /hɝˋnændo; hɜːˈnændəʊ/ (1485-1547) a Spanish soldier and CONQUISTADOR, who defeated the Aztecs in 1521 and took control of Mexico for Spain 科尔特斯〔(1485-1547), 西班牙军事家、征服者。1521年打败阿兹特克人, 为西班牙夺得墨西哥的控制权〕

cor·tex /ˋkɔrtɛks; ˈkɔːteks/ *n plural* **cortices** /-təsiz; -tɪ̵siːz/ [C] *technical* the outer layer of an organ such as your brain【术语】皮层; 皮质; 脑皮层 —**cortical** /ˋkɔrtɪkl; ˈkɔːtɪkəl/ *adj*

cor·ti·sone /ˋkɔrtɪˌson; ˈkɔːtɪ̵zəʊn/ *n* [U] a HORMONE that is used especially in the treatment of diseases such as ARTHRITIS 可的松〔用于治风湿症的激素〕

cor·us·ca·ting /ˋkɔrəsˌketɪŋ; ˈkɒrəskeɪtɪŋ/ *adj formal* flashing with light【正式】闪光的; 闪烁的: *coruscating jewels* 闪亮的珠宝

cos[1] /kəz; kəz/ *conjunction nonstandard*【不规范】an abbreviation of 缩写= because S1

cos[2] /kɑs; kɒs/ *n* the abbreviation of 缩写= COSINE

Co·sa Nos·tra /ˌkosə ˋnostrə; ˌkəʊzə ˈnɒstrə/ another name for the MAFIA (=a secret criminal organization) in the US 我们的事业〔美国黑手党的别称〕

cosh[1] /kɑʃ; kɒʃ/ *n* [C] *BrE informal* a heavy weapon in the shape of a short thick pipe【英, 非正式】〔作武器用的〕短棒

cosh[2] *v* [T] *informal especially BrE* to hit someone with a cosh【非正式, 尤英】用短棒打

Co·sì fan tut·te /koˌsi fɑn ˋtute; ˌkəʊsi fæn ˈtuti/ a humorous OPERA by Mozart in which two men play a trick on the two sisters they love in order to test whether the women really love them and will be faithful to them《女人心》〔莫扎特的一部幽默剧。剧中两个男子对自己心仪的两姐妹略施小计, 考验她们的爱情与忠贞〕

co·sig·na·to·ry /ˌkoˋsɪgnəˌtorɪ; ˌkəʊˈsɪgnətəri/ *n* [C] *formal* one of a group of people who sign a legal document for their department, organization, country etc【正式】连署人: *We will need both cosignatories to sign the cheque.* 我们需要两位连署人都签署支票。

co·sine /ˋkosaɪn; ˈkəʊsaɪn/ *n* [C] *technical* the measurement of an ACUTE (6) angle in a TRIANGLE (1) with a RIGHT ANGLE that is calculated by dividing the length of the side next to it by the length of the HYPOTENUSE【术语】〔数学的〕余弦 —compare 比较 SINE

cos·met·ic /kɑzˋmɛtɪk; kɒzˈmetɪk/ *adj* [only before noun 仅用于名词前] **1** dealing with the outside appearance rather than the important part of something; SUPERFICIAL (1) 装门面的, 表面的: *We're making a few cosmetic changes to the house before we sell it.* 我们在卖这所房子以前, 会对它的门面稍作装修。| **cosmetic exercise** (=something you do that looks good but does not achieve anything) 装门面的事 **2** intended to make your hair or skin look more attractive 化妆的, 美容的: *the cosmetic industry* 美容化妆品业 | *Are you on the diet for health or cosmetic reasons?* 你节食是为了健康还是为了美容?

cos·me·ti·cian /ˌkɑzməˋtɪʃən; ˌkɒzməˈtɪʃən/ *n* [C] someone who is professionally trained to put cosmetics on other people 美容师

cos·met·ics /kɑzˋmɛtɪks; kɒzˈmetɪks/ *n* [plural] creams, powders etc that you use on your face and body in order to look more attractive 化妆品

cosmetic sur·ge·ry /·,·· ˈ···/ *n* [U] medical operations that improve your appearance after you have been injured, or because you want to feel more attractive 整容外科手术

CULTURAL NOTE 文化注释

Cosmetic surgery is more common in the US than in the UK, and in both countries it is expensive. It is known as something famous people do, but it is also becoming more common for ordinary people to have cosmetic surgery. In the US especially, it is even becoming quite common for people to have certain treatment, such as BOTOX INJECTIONS (=that freeze some muscles in your face so that there are no lines) during their lunch break. 整容外科手术在美国比在英国普遍，两国的整容外科手术都很昂贵。做整容外科手术被看成是名人的事，但越来越多的普通人也加入其中。尤其在美国，人们甚至越来越多地进行某种治疗，如午餐休息时间做面部肌肉冷冻注射以消除皱纹。

cos·mic /ˋkɑzmɪk; ˈkɒzmɪk/ *adj* **1** connected with space or the universe 宇宙的 **2** extremely large 广大无边的；极大的：*a scandal of cosmic proportions* 特大丑闻—**cosmically** /-klɪ; -kli/ *adv*

cosmic ray /,·· ˈ·/ *n* [C usually plural 一般用复数] a stream of RADIATION (2) reaching the Earth from space 宇宙射线

Cos·mo /ˋkazmo; ˈkɒzməʊ/ an informal name for the magazine *Cosmopolitan*《大都会》〔Cosmopolitan杂志的非正式名称〕

cos·mog·o·ny /kɑzˋmɑgənɪ; kɒzˈmɒgəni/ *n* [C,U] the origin of the universe, or a set of ideas about this 宇宙起源；宇宙起源论

cos·mol·o·gy /kɑzˋmɑlədʒɪ; kɒzˈmɒlədʒi/ *n* [U] the science of the origin and structure of the universe, especially as studied in ASTRONOMY 宇宙论

cos·mo·naut /ˋkɑzmə,nɔt; ˈkɒzmənɔːt/ *n* [C] an ASTRONAUT from the former Soviet Union 〔前苏联的〕宇航员，太空人

Cos·mo·pol·i·tan /,kɑzməˋpɑlətn̩; ,kɒzməˈpɒlɪtən◂/ also 又作**Cosmo** *informal*【非正式】a monthly magazine for women, which is produced in separate EDITIONS in the US, the UK, and many other countries. It is aimed at young modern independent women and deals with subjects such as fashion, work, and sex.《大都会》〔女性月刊，在美国、英国和其他许多国家分别发行不同版本。该杂志面向现代独立的年轻女性读者，涉及时尚、工作、性等话题〕

cosmopolitan¹ *adj* **1** a cosmopolitan place consists of people from many different parts of the world 〔某地的人〕来自世界各地的：*the cosmopolitan bustle of San Francisco* 旧金山来自世界各地的人们熙熙攘攘 **2** a cosmopolitan person, belief, opinion etc shows a wide experience of different people and places 〔人〕见识广的；〔信仰、意见等〕兼容并包的：*Brigitta has such a cosmopolitan outlook on life.* 布丽吉特对生活有一种恢宏大度的观点。

cosmopolitan² *n* [C] someone who has travelled a lot and feels at home in any part of the world 游历四方的人；四海为家的人

cos·mos /ˋkɑzməs; ˈkɒzmɒs/ *n* **the cosmos** the whole universe, especially when you think of it as a system 宇宙

cos·set /ˋkɑsɪt; ˈkɒsɪt/ *v* [T] to give someone as much care and attention as you can, especially when it is too much 宠爱；娇养；纵容：*No-one in the family gets as much cossetting as that cat!* 家中没有谁比那只猫更受宠爱！

Cossutta, Carla (1932-2000) an Italian OPERA singer with a TENOR voice, who is famous for singing in Verdi OPERAS 柯素塔〔(1932-2000)，意大利男高音歌剧演唱家，以演唱威尔第歌剧闻名〕

cost¹ /kɔst; kɒst/ *n*

1 ►MONEY PAID 付出的钱◄ [C] the amount of money that you have to pay in order to buy, do, or produce something 费用；成本：*I'll give you $15 to cover the cost of the gas.* 我会给你15美元来支付汽油费用。| **at a cost of** *The new building's going up at a cost of $82 million.* 这座新建筑物要花费8200万美元。| **high/low cost** *a low cost source of electric power* 发电的低成本能源 | **full cost** *If no scholarships or other aid are available, students will have to pay the full cost of their education.* 如果得不到奖学金或别的资助，学生要支付自己的全部学习费用。| **cost of living** (=the cost of buying all the food, clothes etc that you need to live) 生活费 *The cost of living rose two percent in the last year.* 在过去的一年中生活费增加了2%。| **at no extra cost** *A cassette/radio is included at no extra cost.* 一盒磁带/一台收音机包含在内，不需另外付费。

2 ►LOSS/DAMAGE 损失/损坏◄ [C,U] something that you lose, give away, damage etc in order to achieve something 代价；牺牲：**at (a) cost to** *Duncan always puts Hannah's needs before his own, at considerable cost to himself.* 邓肯总是把汉娜的需要放在自己的需要之上，因此付出相当大的代价。| **whatever the cost** (=no matter how much work, money, risk etc is needed) 无论如何 *He's determined to win, whatever the cost.* 他无论如何决心要获胜。| **at all costs** (=whatever happens) 不惜任何代价 *We must avoid a scandal at all costs.* 我们必须不惜任何代价避免丑闻。

3 costs [plural] **a)** the money that you must regularly spend in order to continue having a home, car, business etc 费用；花费；成本：**increase costs** *Businesses protested that the new taxes would increase production costs unreasonably.* 商界抗议道，新税会不合理地增加生产成本。| **reduce/cut costs** *We've got to cut costs and we're starting with the phone bill.* 我们不得不削减成本，先从电话费开始。| **cover costs** (=make enough money to pay for the things you have bought) 支付花费 *At this rate we'll barely cover our costs.* 照这样下去我们刚刚能支付花费。| **running costs** (=the cost of owning and using a car or machine) 〔汽车或机器的〕运转费用 *Because of the engine's efficiency the car has very low running costs.* 由于发动机的高效率，这辆汽车的运转费用很低。**b) costs** also 又作**court costs** *AmE* the money that you must pay to lawyers etc if you are involved in a legal case in court, especially if you are guilty【美】诉讼费用：*Bellisario won the case and was awarded costs.* 贝利撒里奥赢了官司，诉讼费被判由败诉方支付。

4 ►PRICE PAID 支付的价格◄ [singular] *especially AmE* the price that someone pays for something that they are going to sell; COST PRICE【尤美】成本价格：**at cost** *His uncle's a car dealer and let him buy the car at cost.* 他的叔叔是汽车销售商，因此让他按成本价格购买汽车。

5 find/know/learn etc sth to your cost to realize something is true because you have had a very unpleasant experience 从不愉快的经历中得知某事：*Driving fast in wet conditions is dangerous, as my brother discovered to his cost!* 我兄弟从自己的痛苦经历中知道，雨天开快车是危险的！—see also 另见**count the cost** (COUNT¹ (9))

This graph shows some of the words most commonly used with the noun **cost**. 本图表所示为含有名词cost的一些最常用的词组。

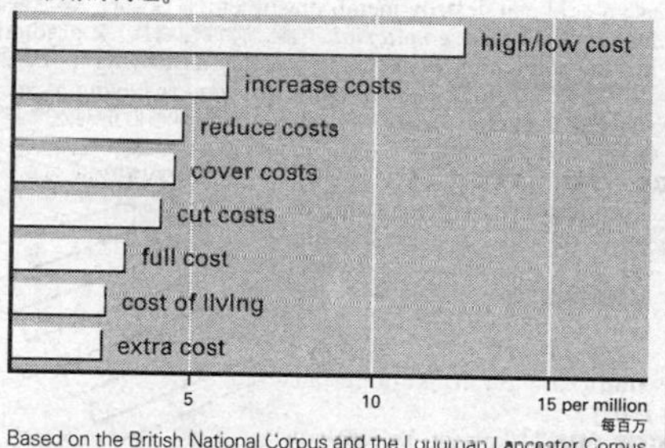

Based on the British National Corpus and the Longman Lancaster Corpus 据英国国家语料库和朗文兰开斯特语料库

USAGE NOTE 用法说明: COST

WORD CHOICE 词语辨析: **price, cost, charge, fare, fees, rent, rental**

When you are talking about the money you need to buy a particular thing, the usual word is **price**. 谈到购买某一特定物品需用的钱时一般用price: *the price of a CD/piece of land/packet of cigarettes/cauliflower* 一张激光唱片/一块地/一包香烟/花椰菜的价格

Cost (*n*) is like **price**, but is used less for objects, and more for services or activities. 名词cost和price相似，但较少用于物品，较多用于服务或活动：*the cost of having the house painted/going on holiday* 粉刷房子的费用/度假的花费。It is also used for general things. 也用于一般费用：*the cost of living* (NOT 不用 *of life*) 生活费用 | *the cost of food* 食品费用 | *the cost of production/postage* (NOT 不用 *… for postage*) 生产费用/邮费。The **cost** of something may be *high* or *low* but not *free* or *expensive*. 形容物品的费用可用high（高）或low（低），但是不能用free（免费）或expensive（昂贵）。

The amount of money you pay for something is what it **costs** (*v*) you. 你买某物花钱，动词是 cost: *How much did this CD cost you?* 这张激光唱片你花了多少钱？| *It cost £1000 to have the house painted.* 粉刷房子花了 1000 英镑。Things may **cost** *a lot* but not *cost high/expensive*. 物品可能会 cost a lot（昂贵），但是不能说 cost high/expensive。

The person who is selling goods or services to you **charges** you for them. 卖东西或提供服务的人索价，动词是 charge: *How much did he charge you for mending the car/for that CD?* 修理汽车／买那张激光唱片他要了你多少钱？ A **charge** (*n*) is a sum of money asked, especially for allowing someone to do something or for a service. 名词 charge 意指要支付的一笔钱，尤指准许某人做某事或为获得服务所需支付的钱: *There will be a small charge for admission to the museum/for reconnecting your gas supply.* 参观博物馆／重新开通煤气要付少量的钱。

A charge for travelling on a plane, train, bus etc. is the **fare**. The charge for professional services, for a course etc is the **fees** (plural). The charge for living in someone else's room or house for some time is the **rent**. In a hotel, however, you pay the **price** of the room. The charge when you rent/hire a car etc is the **rental**. 乘飞机、火车、公共汽车等旅行的费用是 fare。专业服务、课程等的费用是 fees〔复数〕。房租是 rent，但是酒店的房租是 price。租／雇用汽车的费用是 rental。

GRAMMAR 语法

Remember that the past tense and past participle of **cost** is **cost**, not *costed.* 记住 cost 的过去式和过去分词是 cost，而不是 costed。*This trip has cost her a fortune.* 这次旅行花了她一大笔钱。

cost[2] *v* [S1] [W2]

1 ►PRICE 价钱◄ *past tense and past participle* **cost** [linking verb 连系动词] to have a particular price 价钱为；使付出〔金钱〕: *Buy one of your own – they don't cost much.* 你自己也买一个吧，花不了多少钱。| **cost (sb) sth** *How much did the work cost you?* 这件成品花了你多少钱？| **cost a (small) fortune/the earth** (=cost a lot of money) 价钱昂贵 *The meal cost a small fortune, but it was well worth it.* 这顿饭价钱昂贵，但是很值。| **cost a bomb** *BrE* (=cost a lot of money)【英】昂贵 *What a fantastic dress. It must have cost a bomb!* 这件衣服真漂亮，一定很昂贵！

2 cost sb their job/life/marriage etc to do something that makes you lose your job etc 以工作／生命／婚姻等为代价: *Joe's brave action cost him his life.* 乔的英勇行为让他牺牲了生命。

3 it will cost you *spoken* used to say that something will be expensive【口】你得花大钱: *Tickets are still available, but they'll cost you!* 票仍然能买到，但是你得花大价钱！

4 ►CALCULATE COST 计算成本◄ *past tense and past participle* **costed** [T usually passive 一般用被动态] to calculate the cost of something or decide how much something should cost 计算…的成本；估计…的花费: *We'll get the plan costed before presenting it to the board.* 在提交董事会以前，我们要估计一下该计划的成本。

5 cost an arm and a leg/cost a pretty penny to have a price that is too high 昂贵: *We'd like to send the children to private school but it would cost us an arm and a leg.* 我们想把孩子送到私立学校去，但是学费非常昂贵。

6 cost sb dear/dearly to make someone suffer a lot 使某人付出沉重代价: *The delay in sending our report cost us dearly because it meant we lost the contract.* 我们的报告延误了，我们损失很大，因为那意味着我们丢掉了合同。

7 sth costs money *spoken* used to remind or warn someone that they should be careful because something is expensive【口】某物很贵的〔提醒或警告某人小心〕: *Don't leave your sneakers in the rain! Shoes cost money, you know.* 不要让雨水淋湿你的运动鞋！你知道鞋子很贵的。

Costa Bra·va, the /ˌkostə ˈbrɑvə; ˌkɒstə ˈbrɑːvə/ a region of eastern Spain, between Barcelona and the border with France, which is popular for tourism 布拉瓦海岸〔西班牙东部一地区，位于巴塞罗那与法国边境之间，是著名旅游地〕

Costa del Crime, the /ˌkostə dɛl ˈkraɪm; ˌkɒstə del ˈkraɪm/ *BrE* a humorous name for the Costa del Sol in Spain, which some people think of as a place where successful British criminals go to live【英】罪恶海岸〔西班牙太阳海岸的诨名。有些英国人认为，作案得手的英国罪犯常前往该地藏身〕

Costa del Sol, the /ˌkostə dɛl ˈsol; ˌkɒstə del ˈsɒl/ a part of the Mediterranean Sea coast in southern Spain. Many tourists go there, especially around Malaga and Marbella. 太阳海岸〔西班牙南部地中海沿岸的一部分。许多人常去那里游览，尤其是马拉加和马贝亚一带〕

co-star[1] /ˈko ˈstɑr; ˈkəʊ stɑː/ *n* [C] one of two or more famous actors that work together in a film or play 合演者；联合主演者

co-star[2] *v* [I +with] to be working in a film or play with other famous actors 合演，联袂出演

Cos·ta Ri·ca /ˈkɑstə ˈrikə; ˌkɒstə ˈriːkə/ a country in Central America between Nicaragua and Panama. Population: 3,773,000 (2001). Capital: San José. 哥斯达黎加〔中美洲一国家，位于尼加拉瓜和巴拿马之间。人口: 3,773,000 (2001)，首都: 圣何塞〕 —**Costa Rican** *n, adj*

cost-ben·e·fit a·nal·y·sis /ˌ· ˈ··· ·ˌ··· ·/ *n* [C] *technical* a way of calculating the methods or plans that will bring you the most benefits for the smallest cost【术语】成本效益分析

cost ef·fec·tive /ˌ· ·ˈ··◂/ *adj* bringing the best possible profits or advantages for the lowest possible costs 低成本高利润的；有成本效益的: *Recruitment and training have to be planned in the most cost effective way.* 招聘和培训必须要以最经济的方式来进行。—**cost effectively** *adv* —**cost effectiveness** *n* [U]

Cos·tel·lo /kɑˈstɛlo; kɒˈsteləʊ/, **Lou** /lo; ləʊ/ —see 见 ABBOTT AND COSTELLO

cos·ter·mon·ger /ˈkɑstəˌmʌŋgə; ˈkɒstəˌmʌŋgə/ *n* [C] *BrE old use* someone who sells fruit and vegetables in the street【英旧】〔在街上卖水果和蔬菜的〕小贩

cost·ing /ˈkɔstɪŋ; ˈkɒstɪŋ/ *n* [C,U] the process of calculating the cost of a future business activity, product etc, or the calculation itself 成本估算: *Have we got the costings through yet?* 我们完成成本估算了吗？

cost·ly /ˈkɔstlɪ; ˈkɒstli/ *adj* **1** too expensive and wasting a lot of money 太昂贵的，花太多钱的: *Replacing all the windows would be too costly.* 更换所有的窗户要花很多钱。**2** something that is costly causes a lot of problems or trouble 代价高的；损失大的: *Hawksworth letting that goal in proved a costly mistake.* 霍克斯沃思让球进了，这是一个代价高昂的错误。—**costliness** *n* [U]

cost-plus /ˌ· ˈ·◂/ *adj technical* a cost-plus contract gives the person selling all of their costs (COST[1] (3)) and part of the profit as well【术语】〔合同〕成本加成的，成本加利润的

cost price /ˌ· ˈ·◂/ *n* [U] the price that someone pays for something that they are going to sell 成本价格; COST[1] (4) *especially AmE*【尤美】

costume 服装

cos·tume /ˈkɑstum; ˈkɒstjʊm/ *n* **1** [C,U] a set of clothes that are typical of a particular place or historical period of time〔代表某一特定地方或历史时期的〕服装: *The dancers were all in national costume.* 跳舞的人都穿着民族服装。**2** [C] a set of clothes worn to make you look like something such as an animal, GHOST[1] (1) etc or to hide who you are 化装服；戏装: *Hallowe'en costumes* 万圣节化装服 **3** [C] *BrE* a SWIMMING COSTUME【英】游泳衣，泳装

costume dra·ma /ˈ·· ˌ·· ·/ *n* [C] a play that is about a particular time in history, in which people wear costumes from that time 古装剧

costume jew·elle·ry /ˈ·· ˌ··· ·/ *n* [U] cheap jewellery that is often designed to look expensive〔便宜但貌似昂贵的〕人造珠宝饰物

co·sy[1] *especially BrE*【尤英】, **cozy** *AmE*【美】/ˈkozɪ; ˈkəʊzi/ *adj* **1** a place that is cosy is small, comfortable, and warm 小而温暖舒适的: *a cosy room* 温暖舒适的小房间 **2** a situation that is cosy is comfortable and friendly 友好的，融洽的: *a cosy chat* 友

好的谈话 **3** having a close connection or relationship, especially one you do not approve of 密切的; 互相勾结的: *cosy deals with local councils* 与几个地方议会的默契交易 —**cosily** *adv* —**cosiness** *n* [U]

cosy² *n* [C] a covering for a teapot etc that keeps the tea inside from getting cold too quickly〔茶壶的〕保暖罩: *a tea cosy* 茶壶保暖罩

cot /kɑt; kɒt/ *n* [C] **1** *BrE* a small bed with high sides for a young child【英】〔有栏杆的〕婴儿床; CRIB¹ (1) *AmE*【美】—see picture at 参见 BED¹ 图 **2** *AmE* a CAMP BED【美】行军床, 折叠床

co·tan·gent /koˋtændʒənt; kəʊˈtændʒənt/ *n* [C] *technical* the measurement of an angle in a TRIANGLE (1) with a RIGHT ANGLE that is calculated by dividing the length of the side next to it by the length of the side opposite it【术语】〔数学的〕余切 —compare 比较 TANGENT (3)

cot death /ˈ· ,·/ *n* [C] *BrE* the sudden and unexpected death of a healthy baby while it is sleeping【英】婴儿猝死; CRIB DEATH *AmE*【美】

Côte d'A·zur /,kot dəˋzuə; ,kəʊt dæˈzjʊə/ a fashionable part of the Mediterranean coast in southeast France, including the cities of Nice and Cannes 蓝色海岸〔法国东南部地中海沿岸一时尚区域, 包括尼斯和戛纳两个城市〕

Cote d'I·voire /,kot diˋvwɑr; ,kəʊt diːˈvwɑː/ a country next to the Gulf of Guinea in West Africa, between Ghana and Liberia. Population: 16,393,000 (2001). Capital: Yamoussoukro. It is sometimes called the **Ivory Coast**. 科特迪瓦〔西非一国家, 濒临几内亚湾, 位于加纳和利比里亚之间。人口: 16,393,000 (2001), 首都: 亚穆苏克罗。该国有时也被称为"象牙海岸"〕

co·te·rie /ˋkotərɪ; ˈkəʊtəri/ *n* [C] a small group of people who enjoy doing the same things together, and do not like including others〔有共同兴趣、嗜好的排外〕小团体, 小圈子

co·ter·mi·nous /koˋtɝmənəs; kəʊˈtɜːmɪnəs/ *adj formal* coterminous countries share the same border【正式】〔国家〕有共同边界的; 毗邻的

co·til·lion /koˋtɪljən; kəˈtɪljən/ *n* [C] a formal occasion when people dance; BALL¹ (11) 正式舞会

Cots·wolds, the /ˋkɑtswoldz; ˈkɒtswəʊldz/ a hilly area of western England which has a lot of pretty villages and river valleys. It is a popular tourist area. 科茨沃尔德丘陵〔位于英格兰西部, 有许多美丽的村庄和河谷, 是大众喜爱的旅游区〕

cottage 小屋, 村舍

2 3 **cot·tage** /ˋkɑtɪdʒ; ˈkɒtɪdʒ/ *n* [C] *especially BrE* a small house in the country【尤英】小屋; 村舍: *We're staying in a holiday cottage in Dorset.* 我们在多塞特的村舍里度假。

cottage cheese /,·· ˈ·/ *n* [U] soft white cheese made from sour milk 农家鲜干酪〔一种白色软干酪, 用酸奶制成〕

cottage hos·pi·tal /,·· ˈ···/ *n BrE* a small hospital, usually in a country area【英】〔乡村的〕小医院

cottage in·dus·try /,·· ˈ···/ *n* [C] an industry that consists of people working at home 家庭小工业: *a programme to promote cottage industry in rural areas* 促进农村地区家庭小工业发展的项目

cot·tag·er /ˋkɑtɪdʒɚ; ˈkɒtɪdʒə/ *n* [C] *BrE slang* a man who looks for HOMOSEXUAL partners in a public place such as a toilet【英俚】〔在公共场所〕寻找同性恋伴侣的男子

cot·tag·ing /ˋkɑtɪdʒɪŋ; ˈkɒtɪdʒɪŋ/ *n* [U] *BrE slang* the practice of looking for male HOMOSEXUAL partners in a public place such as a toilet【英俚】〔在公共场所〕寻找男同性恋伴侣

cot·ton¹ /ˋkɑtn; ˈkɒtn/ *n* [U] **1** cloth or thread made from the white hair of the cotton plant 棉布; 棉纱: *a crisp cotton shirt* 清爽的棉衬衫 **2** a plant with white hairs on its seeds that are used for making cotton cloth and thread 棉花〔植物〕 **3** *BrE* thread used for sewing【英】〔缝纫用的〕线 **4** *AmE* COTTON WOOL【美】药棉

cotton² *v*

cotton on *phr v* [I] *informal* to begin to understand something【非正式】开始明白, 领会: *I dropped about six hints before he cottoned on.* 我暗示了大约六次他才开始醒悟。

cotton to *phr v* [T] *AmE informal* to begin to like a person, idea etc【美, 非正式】开始喜欢: *I didn't cotton to her at first, but she's really nice.* 我一开始并不喜欢她, 但是她真的很好。

Cotton Belt, the /ˈ·· ·/ an area in the southern US where cotton is grown 棉花带〔美国南部种植棉花的地区〕

Cotton Bowl, the /ˈ·· ·/ an important college football game held every year in Dallas, Texas 棉花杯〔美国大学生橄榄球重要赛事, 一年一度在得克萨斯州达拉斯市举行〕

cotton bud /,·· ˈ·/ *n* [C] *BrE* a small thin stick with COTTON WOOL at each end, used for cleaning places that are hard to reach, such as inside your ears【英】棉签; Q-TIP *AmE*【美】

cotton can·dy /,·· ˈ··/ *n* [U] *AmE* CANDYFLOSS【美】棉花糖

cotton gin /ˈ·· ·/ *n* [C] a machine that separates the seeds of a cotton plant from the cotton 轧棉机, 轧花机

cotton pick·ing /ˈ·· ,··/ *adj* [only before noun 仅用于名词前] *AmE spoken* used to emphasize that you are annoyed or surprised【美口】该死的, 糟糕透顶的〔感叹语〕: *Mind your own cotton picking business!* 别多管老子的闲事!

cotton reel /ˈ·· ·/ *n* [C] *BrE* the small object that cotton thread is wound around【英】线轴; SPOOL (2) *AmE*【美】

cot·ton·tail /ˋkɑtn,tel; ˈkɒtnteɪl/ *n* [C] *AmE* a small rabbit with a white tail【美】棉尾兔, 白尾兔

cot·ton·wood /ˋkɑtn,wʊd; ˈkɒtnwʊd/ *n* [C,U] a North American tree with seeds that look like white cotton 棉白杨, 三角叶杨

cotton wool /,·· ˈ·◂/ *n* [U] *BrE*【英】**1** a soft mass of cotton that you use especially for cleaning and protecting wounds 药棉, 脱脂棉: *Cotton wool pads are good for removing make-up.* 脱脂棉片用来抹去化妆品很好。**2 wrap sb in cotton wool** to protect someone completely from the dangers, difficulties etc of life 保护某人使其完全免于〔危险、困难等〕: *You can't wrap those kids in cotton wool all their lives.* 你不可能保护那些孩子一辈子。

cot·y·le·don /,kɑtḷˋidn; ,kɒtɪˈliːdn/ *n* [C] *technical* the first leaf that grows from a seed【术语】子叶

couch¹ /kaʊtʃ; kaʊtʃ/ *n* [C] **1** a comfortable piece of furniture for two or three people to sit on, or for one person to lie down on; SOFA 长沙发 **2** *literary* a bed【文】卧榻

couch² *v* **be couched in** *formal* to be expressed in a particular way【正式】以〔特定方式〕表达, 措辞: *The offer was couched in obscure legal jargon.* 那份提议用晦涩的法律用语写成。

cou·chette /kuˋʃɛt; kuːˈʃet/ *n* [C] **1** a narrow bed that folds down from the wall in a train〔火车上的〕可折叠卧铺 **2** a comfortable seat on a night boat or train〔夜间行驶的船、火车的〕软席 —compare 比较 SLEEPING CAR

couch po·ta·to /ˈ· ·,··/ *n* [C] *informal* someone who spends a lot of time sitting and watching television【非正式】老泡在电视机前的人

cou·gar /ˋkugɚ; ˈkuːgə/ *n* [C] a large brown wild cat from the mountains of Western North America and South America; MOUNTAIN LION 美洲狮

cough¹ /kɔf; kɒf/ *v* **1** [I] to suddenly push air out of your throat with a short sound 咳嗽, 咳: *coughing from smoking too many cigarettes* 抽烟太多而咳嗽 **2** also 又作 **cough up** [T] to get something out of your throat or lungs by coughing 咳出: *You must go to the doctor if you're coughing up blood.* 如果咳血的话你必须去看医生。**3** [I] to make a coughing sound 发出咳嗽般的声音: *The engine coughed once or twice but wouldn't start.* 发动机喀喀地响了一两声, 但是发动不起来。

cough up *phr v* [I,T **cough** sth ↔ **up**] *informal* to unwillingly give someone money, information etc【非正式】勉强给以〔钱、信息等〕: *Dad's finally coughed up for the stereo I wanted.* 爸爸终于勉强出钱买了我想要的立体声音响。

cough² *n* **1** [C] the action or sound made when you cough 咳嗽; 咳嗽声 **2** [U] a medical condition that makes you cough a lot 咳嗽病: *She's got a terrible smoker's cough.* 她由于抽烟而得了严重的咳嗽病。

cough drop /ˈ· ·/ *n* [C] *especially AmE* a cough sweet【尤美】润喉糖, 止咳糖

cough mix·ture /ˈ· ,··/ also 又作 **cough syrup** *BrE*【英】*n* [U] a thick liquid containing medicine that helps you to stop coughing 止咳药水

cough sweet /ˈ· ·/ *n* [C] *BrE* a sweet containing medicine that you suck when you have a sore throat【英】润喉糖, 止咳糖; COUGH DROP *especially AmE*【尤美】

1 1 **could**/kəd; kəd; *strong* 强读 kʊd; kʊd/ *modal verb 3rd person singular* 第三人称单数 **could** *negative short form* 否定缩略式为 **couldn't** **1** the past tense of 'can' can的过去式: *Could you hear that all right?* 你能听清楚吗? | *I couldn't get tickets after all, they were sold out.* 我最终还是没买到票, 都卖完了。| *Marcia said we could smoke, it was okay with her.* 马西娅说我们可以抽烟, 她不介意的。—see 见 CAN¹ (USAGE) **2** used to ask if someone is able or allowed to do something〔用于问某人是否能或被允许做某事〕: *Could I ask you a couple of questions?* 我能问你几个问题吗? | *What about Sam? Could he come along too?* 萨姆怎么样?他也能来吗? **3** used to express something that might be possible or might happen, when it is not certain that it will happen or be possible〔用于表示某事有可能发生〕: *Most accidents in the home could be easily prevented.* 大多数家庭事故都是很容易避免的。| *It could be weeks before the construction is actually finished.* 该建筑工程真正完成可能还要几个星期。| *If you're not careful, you could find yourself without enough stock to fill the order.* 如果你不认真的话, 可能会没有足够的存货来应付订单。**4** used to be polite when you are asking someone to do something〔用于礼貌地请某人做某事〕: *Could you pay this check into the bank for me tomorrow?* 明天你能替我把支票存进银行吗? | *Yeah, there are a couple of things you could do for me if you're going into town.* 是的, 如果你要进城的话, 或许可以替我办几件事。**5** used to suggest what you think someone should do or might be able to do〔用于表示你认为某人应当做或可能做某事〕: *We could get the bus instead.* 我们可以改乘公共汽车。| *You could always try phoning her at the office.* 你什么时候都可以试着打她办公室的电话找她。| *If you could let us know your decision as soon as possible, it would be a great help.* 如果你能尽快通知我们你的决定, 那会有很大的帮助。**6** used to show that you are annoyed about something〔用于表示懊恼〕: *You could have told me you were going to be late!* 你应当告诉我你会迟到的! | *I'm sure John could be more careful when he's washing up.* 我确信约翰洗餐具的时候可以更细心。| *How could you say such an insulting thing to her! She's my best friend!* 你怎么能对她说那种侮辱性的话呢! 她是我最好的朋友! **7 I couldn't care less** used when you are not at all interested in or concerned about something 一点也不关心, 不在乎: *I said I couldn't care less if I got paid triple time, I'm not coming in on a Sunday.* 我说我不在乎得三倍的酬金, 星期天我是不会来的。| *A lot of the students just couldn't care less about learning anything.* 很多学生对学习漠不关心。**8 I couldn't agree more** used when you completely agree with someone 完全同意: *I couldn't agree more. There's just far too much sex and violence on TV.* 我完全同意, 电视上确实有太多的色情和暴力。**9 I could have strangled/hit/killed etc sb** used to emphasize that you were very angry with someone 对某人气愤得真恨不得扼/打/杀死他〔用于加强语气〕: *I could have murdered Ryan for telling Jason that!* 瑞安居然把那件事告诉了詹森, 我真恨不得杀了他! **10 couldn't be more wonderful/exciting/boring etc** also 又作 **couldn't be better/prettier/worse etc** used to emphasize how good, exciting etc something is 非常好/令人激动/无聊等: *It couldn't have been a more restful vacation.* 那是一个非常舒心的假期。| *Things couldn't be worse, everything seems to be going wrong at once.* 事情非常糟, 好像一切都同时出毛病了。**11 I couldn't** used to politely say that you do not want any more food or drink 不需要了〔用于礼貌地表示你不再需要食物或饮料〕: *"Would you like another piece of pie?" "Oh, no thanks, I couldn't."* "你再来一块馅饼好吗?" "哦, 不, 谢谢, 我吃不下了。"

couldst /kʊdst; kʊdst/ *v* **thou couldst** *old use* you could【旧】你能

cou·lee /ˈkuːlɪ; ˈkuːli/ *n* [C] *AmE* a small valley with steep sides【美】斜壁小峡谷

2 1 **coun·cil** /ˈkaʊnsl; ˈkaʊnsəl/ *n* [C] **1** a group of people that are chosen to make rules, laws or decisions, or to give advice 委员会; 理事会: *the council for civil liberties* 民权委员会 **2** the organization that is responsible for local government in a particular region in Britain〔英国地方政府的〕政务委员会; 地方议会: *Bob Jones has been on the Borough Council for years.* 鲍勃·琼斯已在自治市议会待了很多年。| **council offices/housing/worker etc** *BrE* (=owned, employed etc by local government)【英】地方政府办公室/住房/工作人员等 *Dave's got his name down for a council flat.* 戴夫已经申请了地方政府建的公寓, 正在等候。**3** a group of people elected to the government of a city in the US〔美国的〕地方议会: *the Los Angeles city council* 洛杉矶市议会 **4 council of war** *humorous* a meeting to decide how to deal with a particular problem【幽默】紧急会议

council es·tate /ˈ‥ ˌ‥/ *n* [C] *BrE* an area consisting of streets of council houses【英】地方政府建的住房群

Council for the Pro·tec·tion of Ru·ral En·gland, the /ˌ‥ ‥ ˌ‥ ‥ ˌ‥ ˈ‥/ *n* [singular] the CPRE

council house /ˈ‥ ˌ/ *n* [C] a house or flat in Britain that is provided by the local council for a very low rent〔英国地方议会提供的〕市[郡]建住房

CULTURAL NOTE 文化注释

Council houses are usually fairly small plain houses on ESTATES (=a large area with many houses built close together). They are cheap to rent and are usually lived in by WORKING-CLASS people. But since the 1980s, people have been able to buy their houses from the council, so there are now fewer houses owned by local councils. 市、郡建住房一般是大型住宅区内的普通小房子, 租金便宜, 一般工人阶层住。但自20世纪80年代以来, 人们可以从地方政府手里买下自己的住房, 所以现在由地方政府所有的房子变少了。

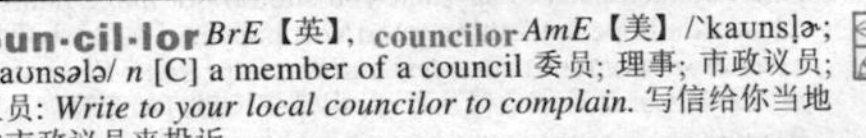

3 3 **coun·cil·lor** *BrE*【英】, **councilor** *AmE*【美】/ˈkaʊnslə; ˈkaʊnsələ/ *n* [C] a member of a council 委员; 理事; 市政议员; 议员: *Write to your local councilor to complain.* 写信给你当地的市政议员来投诉。

coun·cil·man /ˈkaʊnslmən; ˈkaʊnsəlmən/ *n* [C] a man who is a member of the government of a city in the US〔美国的〕男市议会议员

Council of Eu·rope, the /ˌ‥ ‥ ˈ‥/ an organization which was established in 1949 to develop greater unity between the countries of Europe, and to encourage DEMOCRATIC government and respect for human rights. It now consists of about 40 European countries, and its members develop policies on education, crime, health, and the environment. Complaints about cruel or unfair treatment can be settled in the Council's court, the European Court of Human Rights. Although it has close connections with the European Union, it is a separate organization. 欧洲理事会, 欧洲委员会〔成立于1949年, 旨在增进欧洲国家间紧密团结、促成民主政府以及对人权的尊重。理事会现由大约40个欧洲国家组成, 共同制定教育、惩治犯罪、卫生和环境等有关政策。欧洲理事会法庭, 即欧洲人权法庭, 负责受理有关野蛮行径或不公待遇的诉讼。欧洲理事会与欧盟关系十分密切, 但却是一个独立的组织〕

coun·cil·wom·an /ˈkaʊnslˌwʊmən; ˈkaʊnsəlˌwʊmən/ *n* [C] a woman who is a member of the government of a city in the US〔美国的〕女市议会议员

coun·sel¹ /ˈkaʊnsl; ˈkaʊnsəl/ *n technical*【术语】**1** [singular] a type of lawyer who represents you in court 辩护律师: *The judge asked counsel for the defence to explain.* 法官要求被告的辩护律师作出解释。**2 keep your own counsel** to keep your plans, opinions etc secret 不透露自己的计划[观点等] **3** [U] *literary* advice【文】忠告

counsel² *v* [T] **1** *formal* to advise someone【正式】建议: **counsel sb to do sth** *She counselled them not to accept this settlement.* 她建议他们不要接受这解决方案。**2** to listen and give support to someone with problems 忠告; 辅导: *a new unit to counsel alcoholics* 一个辅导酗酒者的新机构

coun·sel·ling *BrE*【英】, **counseling** *AmE*【美】/ˈkaʊnslɪŋ; ˈkaʊnsəlɪŋ/ *n* [U] the act of listening to people and giving them support with their problems, especially as your job 辅导〔尤指职业性的〕: *She's been undergoing counseling for depression.* 她由于精神沮丧而在接受辅导。

coun·sel·lor *BrE*【英】, **counselor** *AmE*【美】/ˈkaʊnslə; ˈkaʊnsələ/ *n* [C] someone whose job is to help and support people with problems 顾问: *Have you thought of seeing a counsellor?* 你想过要去找顾问吗? —see 见 LAWYER (USAGE)

1 3 **count¹** /kaunt; kaʊnt/ *v*

1 ▶**SAY NUMBERS** 数数◀ also 又作 **count up** [I] to say numbers in their correct order〔按顺序〕数: [+to] *Sarah can count up to five now.* 莎拉现在能数到五。| *Try to count to ten before you lose your temper.* 你要发脾气时先数到10。

2 ▶**FIND THE TOTAL** 得出总数◀ also 又作 **count up** [T] to count the people, objects, numbers etc in a group in order to find a total 计数; 点数目: *The teacher was counting the children as they got on the bus.* 在上公共汽车的时候, 老师清点学生的数目。| **count sheep** (=count imaginary sheep as a way of getting to sleep) 数羊〔睡前数数字帮助入睡的一种方法〕

3 ▶**INCLUDE** 包括◀ [T] to include someone or something in a total 把…计算在内; 包括: *There are five people in the family counting my parents.* 我家有五口人, 包括我父母在内。| **count sb/sth among** *I count Jules and Ady among my closest friends.* 我把朱尔斯和埃迪算作我最亲密的朋友。

4▶BE ALLOWED 得到许可◀ [I,T] to be officially allowed or accepted; VALID 正式被允许, 被接受; 有效: *Illegible entries do not count.* 难以辨认的参赛品无效。

5**count yourself lucky/fortunate etc** to feel that you are lucky etc 认为自己是幸运的等: *After the avalanche we counted ourselves lucky to be alive.* 我们经历了雪崩后还能活着, 真幸运。

6▶IMPORTANT 重要的◀ [I not in progressive 不用进行式] to be a very important or valuable thing 重要: *First impressions really do count.* 第一印象真的很重要。| **count for something/anything/more etc** *His promises don't count for much.* 他的承诺算不了什么。

7**be able to count sb/sth on (the fingers of) one hand** *spoken* used to emphasize how small the number of something is 【口】屈指可数: *You could have counted the number of people in the theater on one hand.* 剧院中的人很少, 你用指头就可以数过来。

8**don't count your chickens (before they're hatched)** *especially spoken* used to say that you should not make plans because you hope something good will happen 【尤口】不要指望过早: *It should be worth a few million, but I don't like to count my chickens.* 那应该会值几百万, 但是我不想打如意算盘。

9**count the cost** to start having problems as a result of your earlier decisions or mistakes 开始尝恶果: *We're now counting the cost of not taking out medical insurance.* 我们现在尝到没有买医疗保险的后果。

10**who's counting?** used to say that you are not worried about the number of times something happens 不在乎, 不担心〔某事发生的次数〕: *"But I always smoke your cigarettes." "No problem, who's counting?"* "但是我总是抽你的香烟。""没问题, 我不在乎。" —see also 另见 **stand up and be counted** (STAND[1]), **it's the thought that counts** (THOUGHT[2] (12))

count sb/sth **as** *phr v* [I] to consider or regard someone or something in a particular way 认为, 看作: *For tax purposes this counts as unearned income.* 报税时这被视为非工资收入。

count down *phr v* [I] to record the time passing until an important event happens〔重要事情发生前的〕倒数: *We're counting down to our holiday.* 我们在倒数计时, 等待假期来临。

count sb **in** *phr v* [T] *informal* to include someone in a planned activity 【非正式】把…计算在内: *Mark, can we count you in for the cricket team?* 马克, 我们能把你算在板球队里吗?

count on/upon sb/sth *phr v* [T] **1** to depend on or be certain of someone or something 依靠; 指望: *You can count on my vote.* 我准会投你一票。| *If I got into trouble I could always count on Rusty.* 如果我有麻烦, 总可以依靠拉斯蒂帮忙。| **count on doing sth** *We're all counting on winning this contract.* 我们都指望争取到这份合同。| **count on sb/sth doing sth** *Just don't count on Bev being too thrilled about the news.* 不要指望贝夫会对这个消息很高兴。| **count on sb/sth to do sth** *You can count on Dean to ruin any party.* 迪安去什么聚会都会令人扫兴。**2** to plan or expect to do something 期望, 指望, 料想: **count on (sb/sth) doing sth** *We didn't count on so many people being on vacation.* 我们没有想到会有那么多人度假。

count sb/sth **out** *phr v* [T] **1** to lay things down one by one as you count them 数, 数出: *The teller counted out ten $50 bills.* 出纳点出 10 张 50 美元面额的钞票。**2** *informal* to not include someone or something 【非正式】不包括, 不算: *If you're looking for trouble you can count me out.* 如果你要找麻烦, 别把我拉进去。

count² *n* [C]

S2 W3

1▶TOTAL 合计◀ the total that you get by counting a particular set of things, or the process of doing this 总数; 计算: *The vote was so close that we had to have several counts.* 选票数如此接近, 我们不得不计算好几次。

2▶MEASUREMENT 计算◀ a measurement that shows how much of a substance is present in the area or thing being examined〔某物存在或经计算得出的〕数字, 数目: *The pollen count is high today.* 今天的花粉数很高。| *a low sperm count* 精子数量不多

3**at the last count** used to give the latest information about a particular situation 据最新的信息: *At the last count, 46 students were interested in the trip.* 根据最新统计, 有 46 个学生对这次旅行感兴趣。

4**on all/several etc counts** in every way, in several ways etc 方方面面/在某些方面等: *Their education policy has failed on several counts.* 他们的教育政策在几个方面失败了。

5**keep count** to keep a record of the changing total of something over a period of time〔在一段时间内〕记录变化的数字: *I never manage to keep count of what I spend on the credit card.* 我从来弄不清用信用卡花了多少钱。

6**lose count** to forget a number you were calculating or a total you were trying to count 计不清数字: *Shut up – you've made me lost count now!* 闭嘴! 我都被你吵得忘记数到几了!

7**be out for the count** **a)** to be in a deep sleep 沉睡中: *There's no point in asking George – he's out for the count.* 问乔治根本没用, 他正在酣睡。**b)** if a BOXER (1) is out for the count, he has been knocked down for ten seconds or more〔拳击比赛中〕被击倒地 10 秒

8▶LAW 法律◀ *technical* one of the crimes that someone is charged with 【术语】被指控的罪状: *Davis was found not guilty on all counts.* 指控戴维斯的各项罪状都不能成立。

9▶RANK/TITLE 等级/头衔◀ a European NOBLEMAN whose rank is similar to a British EARL 伯爵〔欧洲贵族的称号, 相当于英国的 earl〕: *the Count of Monte Cristo* 基督山伯爵

count·a·ble

/ˈkauntəbl; ˈkaʊntəbəl/ *adj* a countable noun has both a singular and a plural form 可数的: *Countable nouns like 'table' or 'tables' are marked [C] in this book.* 可数名词如 table 或 tables 在本书中用 [C] 标示。—see also 另见 COUNT NOUN —compare 比较 UNCOUNTABLE

Count Basie

—see 见 Count BASIE

coun·te·nance¹

/ˈkauntənəns; ˈkaʊntn̩əns/ *n formal* 【正式】**1** [C] your face or your expression 面部表情, 面容: *the gloomy countenance of a disappointed child* 一个失望孩子的忧郁面容 **2** [U] support or approval 支持; 赞成

countenance²

v [T] to accept, support, or approve of something 支持; 赞同; 认可: **countenance doing sth** *Her father won't countenance her getting married so young.* 她父亲不赞同她那么年轻就结婚。

counter-

/kauntə; kaʊntə/ *prefix* **1** the opposite of something〔与…〕相反: *a counterproductive thing to do* (=producing results opposite to what you wanted) 适得其反的行为 **2** matching something 对应, 对等, 相当: *my counterpart in the American system* (=someone who has the same job as mine) 美国体制中与我地位相当的人 **3** done or given as a reaction to something, especially to oppose it 反, 逆: *proposals and counterproposals* 建议和反建议 **4** acting to prevent something 反, 防, 抗: *a counterinsurgency strategy* (=to prevent INSURGENTS) 反叛乱策略

coun·ter¹

/ˈkauntə; ˈkaʊntə/ *n* [C]

W3

1▶SHOP 商店◀ the place where you pay or are served in a shop, bank, restaurant etc 柜台

2**over the counter** drugs, medicines etc that are bought over the counter are ones that you can buy in a shop without a PRESCRIPTION (1) from a doctor〔买药〕不用处方

3**under the counter** if you buy something under the counter, you buy it secretly and usually illegally 秘密地, 暗地里〔通常违法地〕: *It's risky, but you can get alcohol under the counter.* 那是危险的, 但是你可以暗地里买酒。

4▶KITCHEN 厨房◀ *AmE* a flat surface on top of a piece of furniture, especially in a kitchen, used for working on, preparing food etc 【美】〔尤指厨房中的〕操作台面, 工作台; WORKSURFACE *BrE* 【英】: *Just leave my keys on the kitchen counter.* 把我的钥匙放在厨房的台面就行了。—see picture on page A10 参见 A10 页图

5▶GAME 游戏◀ a small round object that you use in some games that are played on a board 筹码

6▶EQUIPMENT 装备◀ a piece of electrical equipment that counts something 计算器, 计数器: *Set the video counter to zero before you press play.* 在你按播放键之前把录像机上的计数器拨到零。—see also 另见 GEIGER COUNTER

7▶ACTION AGAINST STH 反对◀ an action that is used to try to prevent something bad from happening, or an argument used to prove that something is wrong 制止; 反驳: [+to] *Britain began its pro-Japanese policy as a counter to Russian advances in Asia.* 英国开始执行亲日政策以对抗俄罗斯在亚洲的扩张。

counter²

v **1** [I,T] to say something in order to try to prove that what someone said was not true 反驳, 反对: [+that] *"That's not what James told me," he countered.* "詹姆斯不是这样告诉我的。"他反驳道。| **counter an argument/allegation etc** *He was determined to counter the bribery allegations.* 他决心要反驳受贿的指控。**2** [T] to do something in order to reduce the bad effects of something, or to defend yourself against them 抵消; 对抗; 制止: *One way of countering these problems would be to redistribute wealth among the poor.* 制止这类问题的一种方法是在穷人中间重新分配财富。

counter³

adv [not before noun 不用于名词前] in a way that is opposite to something 相反地: **run counter to** *The child is asked to behave in ways which run counter to his natural desires.* 孩子被要求做违背他意愿的事。—**counter** *adj*: *To publicize this*

revolting film is counter to the standards of your newspaper. 宣传这部令人反感的电影有悖贵报的标准。

coun·ter·act /ˌkaʊntəˈækt; ˌkaʊntərˈækt/ *v* [T] to reduce or prevent the bad effect of something, by doing something that has the opposite effect 抵消; 对抗: *a drug that counteracts the poison* 解毒药—**counteraction** /-ˈækʃən; -ˈækʃən/ *n* [C,U]

coun·ter·at·tack /ˈkaʊntərəˌtæk; ˈkaʊntərəˌtæk/ *n* [C] an attack that you make against someone who has attacked you, in a war, sport, or an argument 反攻, 反击: *I decided on a swift counterattack.* 我决定迅速反击。—**counterattack** *v* [I,T]—**counterattacker** *n* [C]

coun·ter·bal·ance /ˌkaʊntəˈbæləns; ˌkaʊntəˈbæləns/ *v* [T] to have an equal and opposite effect to something such as a change, feeling etc 使平衡; 抵消: *His fear of his father is counterbalanced by a genuine respect.* 他对父亲的畏惧被发自内心的尊敬抵消了。—**counterbalance** /ˈkaʊntəˌbæləns; ˈkaʊntəˌbæləns/ *n* [C]

coun·ter·clock·wise /ˌkaʊntəˈklɑkˌwaɪz; ˌkaʊntəˈklɒkwaɪz◂/ *adv AmE* moving in the opposite direction to the hands of a clock【美】逆时针方向地; ANTICLOCKWISE *BrE*【英】: *To remove the lid, turn it counterclockwise.* 要打开盖子, 请按逆时针方向转。—opposite 反义词 CLOCKWISE

coun·ter·feit¹ /ˈkaʊntəfɪt; ˈkaʊntəfɪt/ *adj* made to look exactly like something else 伪造的; 仿造的: *The task force were looking for counterfeit money.* 特警队在寻找伪币。

counterfeit² *v* [T] to copy something exactly in order to deceive people 伪造; 仿造

coun·ter·foil /ˈkaʊntəˌfɔɪl; ˈkaʊntəfɔɪl/ *n* [C] the part of something such as a cheque that you keep so that you can remember how much money you have spent〔支票等的〕存根

coun·ter·in·sur·gen·cy /ˌkaʊntərɪnˈsɝdʒənsɪ; ˌkaʊntərɪnˈsɜːdʒənsi/ *n* [U] military action against people who are fighting against their own country's government 反暴动; 反叛乱

coun·ter·in·tel·li·gence /ˌkaʊntərɪnˈtɛlədʒəns; ˌkaʊntərɪnˈtelɪdʒəns/ *n* [U] action that a country takes in order to stop other countries discovering their secrets 反情报[反间谍]活动

coun·ter·mand /ˌkaʊntəˈmænd; ˌkaʊntəˈmɑːnd/ *v* [T] to officially tell people to ignore an order, especially by giving them a different one 撤回[更改]〔命令〕: *Senior officers persuaded the general to countermand the order.* 高级军官们说服将军撤回命令。

coun·ter·mea·sure /ˈkaʊntəˌmɛʒə; ˈkaʊntəmeʒə/ *n* [C usually plural 一般用复数] an action taken to prevent another action from having a harmful effect 对策; 对付措施: *new countermeasures against terrorism* 对抗恐怖主义的新措施

coun·ter·pane /ˈkaʊntəˌpen; ˈkaʊntəpeɪn/ *n* [C] *old-fashioned* a thick cover that you put over all the other covers on a bed; BEDSPREAD【过时】床罩

coun·ter·part /ˈkaʊntəˌpɑrt; ˈkaʊntəpɑːt/ *n* [C] someone or something that has the same job or purpose as someone or something else in a different place 与另一方面地位或职务相当的人[物]: *Belgian officials are discussing this with their French counterparts.* 比利时官员与法国同级官员正在讨论这个问题。

coun·ter·point /ˈkaʊntəˌpɔɪnt; ˈkaʊntəpɔɪnt/ *n* **1** [U] a combination of two or more tunes that are played together to sound like one tune 对位法〔音乐中结合两个或两个以上旋律的方法〕 **2** [C] a tune that is one part of counterpoint 对位旋律

coun·ter·pro·duc·tive /ˌkaʊntəprəˈdʌktɪv; ˌkaʊntəprəˈdʌktɪv◂/ *adj* achieving the opposite result to the one that you want 产生相反效果的: *Sending young offenders to prison can be counterproductive.* 把少年犯送进监狱会产生适得其反的效果。

counter-rev·o·lu·tion /ˌ·· ··ˈ·· / *n* [C,U] political or military actions taken to get rid of a government that is in power because of a previous REVOLUTION (2) 反革命—**counter-revolutionary** *adj*

counter-rev·o·lu·tion·a·ry /ˌ·· ··ˈ····/ *n* [C] someone who is involved in a counter-revolution 反革命分子

coun·ter·sign /ˈkaʊntəˌsaɪn; ˈkaʊntəsaɪn/ *v* [T] to sign a paper that has already been signed by someone else 连署, 副署: *The note must be countersigned by a doctor.* 这张便条必须有一个医生连署。

coun·ter·ten·or /ˈkaʊntəˌtɛnə; ˌkaʊntəˈtenə/ *n* [C] a man who is trained to sing with a very high voice 男音最高音歌手

counter-ter·ror·ist /ˈ·· ˌ··/ *adj* **counter-terrorist operation/team/unit etc** a plan or group that tries to prevent the violent activities of political groups who use force 反恐怖主义行动/队伍/小组等—**counter-terrorist** *n* [C]

coun·ter·vail·ing /ˈkaʊntəˌvelɪŋ; ˌkaʊntəˈveɪlɪŋ◂/ *adj formal* with an equally strong but opposite effect【正式】抗衡的, 制衡的; 抵消的: *the need for countervailing forces to that of the state* 抗衡国家权力的需要

coun·tess /ˈkaʊntɪs; ˈkaʊntɪs/ *n* [C] a woman with the same rank as an EARL or a COUNT² (9) 伯爵夫人; 女伯爵

counting house /ˈ·· ·/ *n* [C] an office where accounts and money were kept in former times〔旧时的〕账房

count·less /ˈkaʊntlɪs; ˈkaʊntləs/ *adj* too many to be counted 无数的, 数不尽的: *It has saved my life, and the lives of countless others.* 它救了我的命, 也救了无数其他人的生命。| *I spent countless hours on trains and buses.* 我坐了很长时间的火车和公共汽车。

count noun /ˈ· ·/ *n* [C] *technical* a noun that has both singular and plural forms, can be used with numbers and with words such as many, few etc, or can be used with a or an【术语】可数名词 —see also 另见 NOUN

coun·tri·fied /ˈkʌntrɪˌfaɪd; ˈkʌntrifaɪd/ *adj* typical of the countryside, or made to seem typical of the countryside 乡村的, 土里土气的: *the countrified existence of the newly rich* 暴发户土里土气的生活方式

coun·try¹ /ˈkʌntrɪ; ˈkʌntri/ *n* **1** [C] an area of land that is controlled by its own government, president, king etc 国家: *Pakistan became a fully independent country shortly after the Second World War.* 第二次世界大战后不久巴基斯坦就成为一个完全独立的国家。—compare 比较 NATION (1) —see also 另见 MOTHER COUNTRY —see 见 LAND¹ (USAGE) **2 the country a)** land that is outside towns and cities, including land used for farming; the countryside 郊外; 乡村: *I've always wanted to live in the country.* 我一直想住在乡下。**b)** all the people who live in a particular country 全国人民; 全体国民: *The President has the support of over 50 per cent of the country.* 总统获得全体国民50% 以上的支持。**3 farming country/walking country etc** land that is suitable for a particular activity 农业用地/散步场所等: *The Peak District is good walking country.* 皮克区是散步的好场所。**4 go to the country** *BrE* if a Prime Minister goes to the country, they ask for a GENERAL ELECTION to be held【英】举行大选

country² *adj* [only before noun 仅用于名词前] belonging to or connected with the countryside 乡下的, 农村的: *They much preferred country life to life in the city.* 比起城市生活来他们更喜欢农村生活。

country and west·ern /ˌ·· ·ˈ··/ *n* [U] popular music in the style of music from the southern and western US〔美国的〕乡村与西部音乐

country bump·kin /ˌ·· ˈ··/ *n* [C] someone from the countryside who seems stupid 乡巴佬

country club /ˈ·· ,·/ *n* [C] a sports and social club in the countryside, especially one for rich people 乡村俱乐部〔尤指有钱的人才能加入〕

Country Code, the /ˈ·· ,·/ *BrE* a set of instructions that advise people who live in cities how to behave when they visit the countryside. For example, according to the Country Code you should always close gates in fields after using them, and you should keep your dog under control.【英】乡村行为规范〔城市居民去乡村时应注意的事项, 如应随手关好田间的门, 看管好自家的狗等〕

country danc·ing /ˌ·· ˈ··/ *n* [U] a traditional form of dance in which pairs of dancers move in rows and circles 乡村舞; 土风舞

country house /ˌ·· ˈ·/ *n* [C] *BrE* a large house in the countryside, especially one that is of historical interest【英】乡间邸宅[别墅]

Country Life /ˌ·· ˈ·/ *trademark* a British monthly magazine which contains articles about impressive homes and gardens in the country, and important social activities there【商标】《乡村生活》〔英国月刊。刊载的文章描述给人印象至深的乡村房屋和花园, 介绍重要的乡村社会活动〕

coun·try·man /ˈkʌntrɪmən; ˈkʌntrimən/ *n plural* **countrymen** /-mən; -mən/ [C] **1** someone from your own country; COMPATRIOT 同胞; 同国人: *During the war, the loyalty of fellow countrymen was all-important.* 战争期间, 国民的忠诚是很重要的。**2** a man who lives in the country rather than a town or city 乡下人

country mu·sic /ˈ·· ,··/ *n* [U] COUNTRY AND WESTERN〔美国的〕乡村与西部音乐

country seat /ˌ·· ˈ·/ *n* [C] *BrE* the countryside house of someone who is rich and owns land【英】乡绅的住宅; 庄园宅第

coun·try·side /ˈkʌntrɪˌsaɪd; ˈkʌntrisaɪd/ *n* [U] land that is outside cities and towns 郊外; 乡下, 农村: *Our new house is surrounded by the most beautiful countryside.* 我们的新房子四周是非常美丽的乡村。

Countryside Com·mis·sion, the /ˈ··· ·,··/ a British organization whose aim is to look after the countryside and prevent it being spoiled. It provides national parks, paths etc for people who want to enjoy the country. 乡村委员会〔英国一组织，旨在保护乡村环境，以免遭到破坏。同时，也开辟国家公园，修筑道路，满足人们的游览需要〕

coun·try·wom·an /ˈkʌntrɪ,wʊmən; ˈkʌntri,wʊmən/ *n plural* **countrywomen** /-,wɪmɪn; -,wɪmɪn/ [C] a woman who lives in the country rather than a town or city 乡村妇女

1 2 **coun·ty¹** /ˈkauntɪ; ˈkaʊnti/ *n* [C] an area of Great Britain, the US and some other countries that contains several towns that are governed together〔英国的〕郡；〔美国等国家的〕县

county² *adj BrE informal* belonging to or typical of people from the upper classes in Britain【英，非正式】〔英国〕上流阶层的

CULTURAL NOTE 文化注释
Many people think of county people as speaking with very upper-class ACCENTS and wearing clothes which are expensive and of good quality, but not fashionable or modern. 很多人认为上流阶层人士操上流社会口音，衣服昂贵考究，但并不入时或现代

county coun·cil /,·· ˈ··/ *n* [C] an organization consisting of a group of people who are elected to organize schools, HOUSING etc, in a county in Britain〔英国的〕郡政务委员会；郡议会

county court /,·· ˈ·/ *n* [C] *BrE* a local court of law that deals with private quarrels between people rather than with serious crimes【英】〔英国的〕郡法院

county fair /,·· ˈ·/ *n* [C] *AmE* an event that happens each year in a particular county, with games and competitions for the best farm animals, cooking etc【美】〔农、畜产品的〕县集市

county town /,·· ˈ·/ *BrE*【英】, **county seat** *AmE*【美】*n* [C] the town in a COUNTY¹ where its government is 郡[县]首府

coup /ku; kuː/ *n* [C] **1** a sudden and sometimes violent attempt by citizens or the army to take control of the government; coup d'état (军事) 政变: *There were rumours of a coup in Moscow before Gorbachev was actually overthrown.* 在戈尔巴乔夫被真正推翻以前莫斯科有谣言说会发生政变。**2** an achievement that is extremely impressive because it was very difficult 成功之举；漂亮之举: *Getting a former International as coach was a real coup for the club.* 俱乐部得到一个前国家队队员做教练确实是一个漂亮之举。

coup de grâce /ku də ˋgrɑs; ,kuː də ˈgrɑːs/ *n* [singular] *French*【法】**1** an action or event that ends or destroys something that has gradually been getting weaker 致命的打击(比喻): *The nuclear atoms delivered the coup de grâce to classical physics.* 核原子给予传统物理学致命的打击。**2** a hit or shot that kills someone or something 致命的一击

coup d'état /ku deˋtɑ; ,kuː deɪˈtɑː/ *n plural* **coups d'état** (*same pronunciation* 读音相同) [C] *French* a COUP (1)【法】(军事) 政变

cou·pé /kuˋpe; ˈkuːpeɪ/ *n* [C] *especially BrE* a car with two doors and a sloping back【尤英】双门小轿车

1 1 **cou·ple¹** /ˈkʌpl; ˈkʌpəl/ *n* **1 a couple a)** two things or people of the same kind 一对，一双: *We just need a couple more chairs so everyone can sit down.* 我们只要再有两把椅子就可以让每人都能坐下。| [+of] *There's a couple of girls waiting for you outside.* 外面有两个女孩子在等你。**b)** a small number of things 一些，几个: [+of] *I don't know why I feel so bad, I only had a couple of drinks.* 我不知道为什么感觉不舒服，我只喝了几杯酒。—see 见 PAIR¹ (USAGE) **2** [C] two people who are married or having a sexual or romantic relationship 一对夫妇；一对情侣: *This hotel is a favourite with young honeymoon couples.* 这家酒店特别受度蜜月的年轻夫妇所喜爱。| *the couple next door* 隔壁的夫妇

couple² *v* **1** [T] to join or fasten two things together, especially two vehicles 结合，连接〔尤指把两辆汽车连接在一起〕**2** [I] *formal* to have sex【正式】性交

couple with *phr v* [T usually passive 一般用被动态] if one thing is coupled with another, they happen or exist together and produce a particular result 加上: *Lack of rain coupled with high temperatures caused the crops to fail.* 雨量少加上高温导致农作物歉收。

coup·let /ˈkʌplɪt; ˈkʌplǀt/ *n* [C] two lines of poetry, one following the other, that are the same length〔同长度的〕两行诗；对句；对联: *rhyming couplets* 押韵的两行诗

coup·ling /ˈkʌplɪŋ; ˈkʌplɪŋ/ *n* [C] **1** something that connects two things together, especially two vehicles〔尤指连接两辆汽车的〕挂钩；连接装置 **2** *formal* an act of coming together to have sex【正式】性交

cou·pon /ˈkupɑn; ˈkuːpɒn/ *n* [C] **1** a small piece of printed paper that gives you the right to pay less for something or get something free 优待券；赠货券: *The coupon entitles you to 10 cents off your next purchase.* 你在下次购买时使用这张优待券可以节省 10 美分。**2** a printed form, that you write your name and address on, in order to send for information or enter a competition 查询表格；参赛表格

cour·age /ˈkɝɪdʒ; ˈkʌrɪdʒ/ *n* [U] **1** the ability to be brave when you are in danger, in pain, in a difficult situation etc 勇气，胆量，勇敢: *Sue showed great courage throughout her illness.* 休在生病期间表现出了巨大的勇气。| **summon up the courage/pluck up the courage** (=try to make yourself be brave enough) 鼓起勇气 *Liz was trying to summon up the courage to tell Paul it was all over between them.* 莉兹试图鼓起勇气告诉保罗他们之间完了。| **take courage** (=need courage) 需要勇气 *Driving again after his accident must have taken a lot of courage.* 他出事以后再驾车一定是鼓了很大的勇气。**2 have the courage of your (own) convictions** to be brave enough to say or do what you think is right even though other people may not agree or approve 有勇气去说[做]自己认为正确的事 —see also 另见 DUTCH COURAGE 3

cou·ra·geous /kəˋredʒəs; kəˈreɪdʒəs/ *adj* brave 勇敢的，有胆量的: *a courageous and independent woman* 勇敢且独立的女人 | *a courageous decision* 勇敢的决定 —**courageously** *adv* —**courageousness** *n* [U]

cour·gette /kurˋʒɛt; kʊəˈʒet/ *n* [C] *BrE* a long vegetable with a dark green skin【英】小胡瓜，密生西葫芦；ZUCCHINI *AmE*【美】—see picture on page A9 参见 A9 页图

cou·ri·er¹ /ˈkurɪə; ˈkʊriə/ *n* [C] **1** someone who is employed to take a package, documents etc somewhere〔递送包裹或文件的〕信使；快递员 **2** *BrE* someone who is employed by a travel company to help people on holiday, by giving them information, helping them with problems etc【英】旅游团领队，导游

courier² *v* [T] to send something somewhere by using a courier 由快递员[信使]递送

course¹ /kors; kɔːs/ *n* 1 1

1 of course a) used when you are mentioning something that you think other people already know, or should know 当然，自然〔用于提及你认为别人已经知道或应当知道的某事〕: *Your car insurance must, of course, be renewed every year.* 你的汽车保险当然必须要每年更新。**b)** used to say that what you or someone else has just said is not surprising 自然〔用于表示你或别人说的话不令人吃惊〕: *Hannah applied for the job and got it, of course.* 汉娜申请这份工作，自然就得到了。**c)** *spoken*【口】also 又作 **course** *informal*【非正式】used to agree with someone, or to give permission to someone 当然〔用于赞同或允许某人〕: *"Can I borrow the car tonight?" – "Yeah, course you can."* "今天晚上我能借用一下汽车吗?" "可以，当然可以。" **d)** also 又作 **course** *spoken* used to emphasize that what you are saying is true or correct【口】当然〔用于强调你所说的是真的或正确的〕: *"You promise you won't forget?" "Of course I won't!"* "你保证不会忘记?" "我当然不会忘记!" —see 见 OF COURSE (USAGE)

2 of course not/course not *spoken* used to emphasize that you are saying no to something, or that something is not true or correct【口】当然不；决不: *"Do you think they'll mind if I arrive late?" "No, of course not."* "你认为如果我迟到的话他们会介意吗?" "不，当然不会。"

3 ▶LESSONS 课◀ [C] *especially BrE* a series of lessons, or studies in a particular subject【尤英】课程: *Andy's doing a one-year journalism course.* 安迪正在修读为期一年的新闻课程。| [+on] *a course on the French Revolution* 法国革命课程 | [+in] *She's taking a course in flower arranging.* 她正在学习插花。—see also 另见 CORRESPONDENCE COURSE, CRASH COURSE, REFRESHER COURSE, SANDWICH COURSE

4 in the course of/during the course of *formal* during a process or period of time【正式】在…过程中；在…时期中: *During the course of our conversation it emerged that Bob had been in prison.* 在我们的谈话过程中得知鲍勃已经入狱了。

5 ▶ACTIONS 行动◀ [C] an action or series of actions that you could take in order to deal with a particular situation〔处理事件的〕行动；一系列行动: *In this case, the best course would be to avoid talking about it altogether.* 在这种情况下，最好是根本不要谈论这件事。| **course of action** *One possible course of action would be to increase tax on alcohol.* 一个可能的举措是提高酒类税。

6 ▶USUAL/NATURAL 通常的/自然的◀ [C] the usual or natural way that something happens, develops, or is done 自然的进

展; 通常的过程: *Once the story is begun, it must follow its course.* 一旦故事开始了, 就应该顺其自然地发展下去。| **course of history/nature etc** *When he met Sally it changed the whole course of his life.* 遇到莎莉以后, 他的一生改变了。| **in the normal course of events** *In the normal course of events a son would take over the farm from his father.* 在正常情况下, 儿子应该继承父亲的农场。

7 let sth take its course to wait for something to develop in the usual way 让某事按正常途径发展: *Just relax and let nature take its course.* 放松些顺其自然吧。

8 run its course to develop in the usual way and come to a natural end 自然发展直到终结: *The illness has run its course.* 这病自己好了。

9 ▶PLANE/BOAT 飞机/船◀ [C] the planned direction that a boat or plane takes to go somewhere 〔船或飞机的〕航向: **on/off course** (=going in the right or wrong direction) 航向正确/错误 *The ship had been blown off course in the storm.* 这艘船在暴风雨中被刮得偏离了航向。

10 ▶PART OF A MEAL 一餐的部分◀ [C] one of the separate parts of a meal 一道菜: **3-course meal/5-course meal etc** *That restaurant has excellent 3-course meals for very reasonable prices.* 那家餐馆三道菜的套餐非常好而且价钱很公道。| **first/second/main course etc** *We're having fish for the main course.* 我们的主菜是鱼。

11 be on course to be likely to achieve something because you have already had some success 可能成就〔某事〕: [+for] *The company is on course for record profits this year.* 这家公司有可能在今年取得历史上最高利润。| **be on course to do sth** *Brazil are on course to win the World Cup.* 巴西有可能赢得世界杯。

12 ▶RACE 比赛◀ [C] an area of land or water where races happen 竞赛场地; 跑道: *The course is a particularly difficult one.* 这跑道非常难跑。—see also 另见 ASSAULT COURSE, OBSTACLE COURSE

13 golf course [C] an area of land that is designed for you to play golf on 高尔夫球场

14 ▶MEDICAL TREATMENT 医治◀ [C] *especially BrE* an amount of medicine or medical treatment given or taken regularly for a fixed period of time【尤英】疗程: *If your doctor prescribes antibiotics, you should finish the course.* 如果医生开了抗生素药, 你要吃完一个疗程。| **course of injections/drugs/treatment etc** *a course of injections for weight loss* 减肥的注射疗程

15 in (the) course of time after some or enough time has passed 终于; 总有一天: *She'll get used to school in the course of time.* 她会逐渐适应学校生活的。

16 ▶RIVER 河流◀ [C] the direction a river moves in 河水的流向: *The course of the water was shown by a line of willow trees.* 一行柳树显示出水流的方向。

17 ▶BRICKS/STONE 砖/石◀ [C] a layer of bricks, stone etc 一层砖[石] —see also 另见 **in due course** (DUE[1] (6)), **as a matter of course** (MATTER[1] (18)), **be par for the course** (PAR (3)), **stay the course** (STAY[1] (7))

course² *v* **1** [I always+adv/prep] *literary* if a liquid courses somewhere, it flows rapidly【文】奔流; 快速流动: [+down/along/through etc] *He could not stop the tears coursing down his cheeks.* 他的眼泪止不住地沿着脸颊流下来。**2** [I always+adv/prep] *literary* if a feeling or thought courses through your body or mind, you feel it very strongly, or think it quickly【文】〔感情、思想〕涌动: [+down/through] *The shock was so great, it coursed down every nerve in Sam's body.* 那打击非常大, 它迅速传遍萨姆的每一根神经。**3** [I,T] to chase a rabbit with dogs as a sport 〔用猎犬〕追猎〔兔子〕

coursebook /ˈ· ·/ *n* [C] *BrE* a book that you use regularly during a set of lessons on a particular subject; TEXTBOOK[1]【英】课本

court¹ /kɔrt; kɔːt/ *n* [S1] [W1]

1 ▶LAW 法律◀ [C,U] a building or room where all the information concerning a crime is given so that it can be judged 法院; 法庭: *There was a large crowd of reporters gathered outside the court.* 法庭外聚集了一大群记者。| **in court** *He was summoned to appear in court as a witness.* 他被传唤出庭作证。| **go to court** (=start the legal process to have a case dealt with in a court) 打官司; 起诉 *She was prepared to go to court to get compensation if necessary.* 如果需要, 她准备提出起诉, 要求赔偿。| **take sb to court** (=make someone be judged in a court) 控告某人 *Davis was taken to court for assaulting a policeman.* 戴维斯被控告殴打警察。| **settle out of court** (=agree without being judged in a court) 庭外和解 *We decided to settle the matter out of court.* 我们决定庭外和解。| **court case/appearance/judge etc** *The court case lasted six weeks.* 这场诉讼持续了六个星期。

2 the court [U] the people in a court, especially the judge and the JURY (1) 全体出庭人员, 〔尤指〕法官和陪审团: *The defendant told the court that he was in Newcastle at the time of the alleged rape.* 被告对法官和陪审团说, 所述的强奸案发生时他在纽卡斯尔。

3 ▶SPORT 体育◀ an area that has been specially made for playing games such as tennis on 球场: *There are three squash courts available this evening.* 今天晚上有三个壁球场可用。| **on/off court** (=playing or not playing) 上场/不上场 *Becker and Edberg are due on court in an hour.* 贝克尔和埃德伯格该一小时后上场。—see picture at 参见 TENNIS 图

4 ▶KING/QUEEN ETC 国王/王后等◀ [C] **a)** the official place where a king or queen lives and works 宫廷: *This was one of the most splendid of the royal courts of Europe.* 这是欧洲最金碧辉煌的宫廷之一。| **court painter/jester/adviser etc** (=someone who is employed by the court to paint etc) 宫廷画师/宫廷弄臣/皇室顾问等 **b)** the royal people and the people who work for them or advise them 皇室成员、侍臣等的统称; 朝廷; 朝臣: *Several members of the court were under suspicion.* 皇室的几个成员有嫌疑。

5 hold court to speak in an interesting and amusing way so that people gather to listen to you 说笑话吸引人围观: *Gary was holding court in the pub last night.* 加里昨晚在酒馆里大说笑话。

6 pay court to *old-fashioned* to give a lot of your attention to someone in order to impress them【过时】讨好: *Stefan was dancing with everyone and paying court to all the girls.* 史蒂文与每个人都跳舞, 向每个女孩子献殷勤。

7 ▶CASTLE/LARGE HOUSE 城堡/大型房屋◀ [C] an open space that is completely or partly surrounded by buildings, especially one that is part of a castle or large house; COURTYARD 庭院, 院子

8 Court *especially BrE* used as part of the name of a short street or of an apartment building【尤英】…大院, …大楼〔用作短街道或公寓建筑的名称〕—see also 另见 **the ball is in your court** (BALL[1] (10)), **be laughed out of court** (LAUGH[1] (7))

court² *v* **1** [T] *old-fashioned* if a man courts a woman, he visits her, takes her to restaurants etc because he hopes to marry her【过时】〔男子向女子〕求爱, 追求: *Richard courted Lindsay for years before she agreed to marry him.* 理查德追了林赛多年后, 她才同意嫁给他。**2** [I,T] *old-fashioned* if a man and a woman are courting, they are having a romantic relationship and may get married【过时】〔男女〕恋爱: *We were courting for two years before we even got engaged.* 我们在订婚以前就交往了两年。**3 court danger/death/punishment etc** to behave in a way that makes danger etc more likely 招惹危险/找死/招惹惩罚等: *You realize you're simply courting danger by driving that old car?* 你知道你驾驶那辆旧车是在惹危险吗? **4** [T] to try to get something you want, especially support from other people, by doing something to please them 奉承, 讨好: *The directors are courting the support of the shareholders.* 董事由于需要支持而讨好股东。

Cour·tauld In·sti·tute, the /ˈkɔrtold ˌɪnstətjut; ˈkɔːtəʊld ˌɪnstɪtjuːt/ an art GALLERY in London. It is famous for its collection of late 19th and early 20th century paintings. 考陶尔德艺术馆〔伦敦一艺术馆, 以馆藏的19世纪末、20世纪初的油画出名〕

court card /ˈ· ·/ *n* [C] *BrE* the king, queen or JACK[1] (2) in a set of playing cards【英】〔扑克中的〕花牌; FACE CARD *AmE*【美】

cour·te·ous /ˈkɝtɪəs; ˈkɜːtiəs/ *adj* having good manners and respect for other people 有礼貌的: *The staff are always courteous and helpful.* 职员们总是彬彬有礼、乐于助人。| *I received a courteous reply from the manager.* 我从经理那里得到了礼貌的回复。—opposite 反义词 DISCOURTEOUS —**courteously** *adv* —**courteousness** *n* [U]

cour·te·san /ˈkɔrtəzn; ˌkɔːtɪˈzæn/ *n* [C] a woman in former times who had sex with rich or important men for money 〔昔日与贵族或要人周旋的〕高级妓女, 交际花

cour·te·sy /ˈkɝtəsɪ; ˈkɜːtɪsi/ *n* **1** [U] polite behaviour that shows that you have respect for other people 有礼的举止, 礼貌: *Lack of courtesy is sometimes seen as a disease of modern day society.* 缺少礼貌有时被看作是现代社会的一种病。—opposite 反义词 DISCOURTESY **2** [C] something you do or say in order to be polite 礼貌的行为[话]: *The managers exchanged courtesies before getting down to business.* 经理们谈正事前寒暄一番。**3 by courtesy of/courtesy of** by the permission or kindness of someone rather than by paying them 由于…的好意; 承蒙…的允许〔而不是由于付了钱〕: *Paul had his own flat and sports car courtesy of his celebrity father.* 因为有个名流父亲, 所以保罗拥有自己的房子和跑车。

courtesy bus /ˈ···,·/ *n* [C] a bus provided by a hotel near an airport that their guests can use to travel to and from the airport〔由机场附近的酒店提供给客人往返机场的〕免费公共汽车

courtesy call /ˈ···,·/ *n* [C] a visit to someone that you make to be polite or to show your respect for them 礼节性访问

courtesy car /ˈ···,·/ *n* [C] a car that a garage, hotel etc lends to its customers while they are having their own car fixed, are staying at the hotel etc〔修车场在客人的汽车修理期间或酒店在客人住宿时提供给客人的〕方便用车

court·house /ˈkɔrtˌhaʊs; ˈkɔːthaʊs/ *n* [C] *especially AmE* a building containing courts of law【尤美】法院（大楼）

court·ier /ˈkɔrtɪɚ; ˈkɔːtɪə/ *n* [C] someone in former times who had an important position in the COURT[1] (4b)〔昔日的〕朝臣

C

court·ly /ˈkɔrtlɪ; ˈkɔːtli/ *adj* graceful and polite 彬彬有礼的；优雅的: *He answered with a courtly bow.* 他礼貌地鞠一个躬作答。—**courtliness** *n* [U]

court-mar·tial[1] /ˌ·ˈ··/ *n* [C] **1** a military court that deals with people who break military law 军事法庭: *A court-martial found him guilty of assaulting an officer.* 他袭击军官，被军事法庭定罪。**2** an occasion on which someone is judged by one of these courts 军事法庭的审判

court-martial[2] *v past tense and past participle* **court-martialled** *BrE*【英】, **court-martialed** *AmE*【美】[T] to hear and judge someone's case in a military court 以军法审判: *Soldiers were often court-martialled for cowardice.* 士兵常常由于胆怯行为而被军事法庭审判。

Court of Ap·peal /ˌ···ˈ·/ *n* [singular] the highest court of law in Britain apart from the HOUSE OF LORDS〔英国的〕上诉法院

Court of Ap·peals /ˌ···ˈ·/ *n* [singular] one of 12 law courts in the US that deals with cases when people are not satisfied with the judgment given by a lower court〔美国的〕上诉法院 —see also 另见 APPELLATE COURT

court of en·quir·y, court of inquiry /ˌ···ˈ··/ *n* [C] *BrE* a group of people chosen to discover the facts about something or the causes of something, for example a serious accident【英】调查法庭 —compare 比较 GRAND JURY

court of law /ˌ··ˈ·/ *n* [C] a place where law cases are judged; COURT[1] (1) 法院，法庭

Court of Ses·sion, the /ˌ··ˈ··/ the most important civil court of law in the Scottish legal system〔苏格兰〕最高民事法庭

Court of St James, the /ˌ···ˈ·/ one of the old names of the official home of the British king or queen. Formally, an AMBASSADOR (=the official representative of a country) who is sent to the UK from a foreign country is called the 'Ambassador to the Court of St James'. 圣詹姆士宫〔英国国王或女王官邸旧名之一。以前，被派往英国的外国大使被称为 Ambassador to the Court of St James（驻圣詹姆士宫大使）〕

court or·der /ˌ·ˈ··/ *n* [C] an order given by a court of law that someone must do or must not do something 法院指令，庭谕

court re·port·er /ˌ··ˈ··/ *n* [C] someone who works in a court and records everything that is said during a case, on a special machine similar to a TYPEWRITER〔法院的〕书记官，证言速记员；法庭记录员

court·room /ˈkɔrtˌrum; ˈkɔːtruːm/ *n* [C] a room in a law court where cases are judged 审判室，法庭

court·ship /ˈkɔrt·ʃɪp; ˈkɔːt-ʃɪp/ *n* **1** [C,U] the period of time during which a man and woman have a romantic relationship before getting married 求爱期，恋爱期 **2** [U] special behaviour used by animals to attract each other for sex〔动物的〕求偶

court shoe /ˈ··/ *n* [C] *BrE* a type of woman's formal shoe that is very plain and has no fastening【英】浅帮鞋〔半高跟无鞋带的女鞋〕; PUMP[1] (3) *AmE*【美】—see picture at 参见 SHOE[1] 图

court·yard /ˈkɔrtˌjɑrd; ˈkɔːtjɑːd/ *n* [C] an open space that is completely or partly surrounded by buildings, especially one that is part of a castle or large house 庭院，院子

cous·cous /ˈkuskus; ˈkuːskuːs/ *n* [U] a North African dish made of crushed wheat, served with meat and vegetables 蒸粗麦粉〔北非的一道菜，与蔬菜和肉一起吃〕

3 **cous·in** /ˈkʌzn̩; ˈkʌzən/ *n* [C] **1** the child of your UNCLE or AUNT 堂[表]兄弟；堂[表]姐妹 —see also 另见 FIRST COUSIN, SECOND COUSIN, KISSING COUSIN —see picture at 参见 FAMILY 图 **2** *rare* someone who is similar to you, or something that is similar to something else【罕】同性质的人[物]；类似之物

Cous·teau /kuˈsto; kuːˈstəʊ/, **Jacques** /ʒæk; ʒæk/ (1910- 97) a French underwater EXPLORER, famous for making films about the plants and animals that live in the sea. He also helped to invent the AQUALUNG. 康斯托〔(1910-1997)，法国水下探险家。他制作的海洋动、植物影片十分著名。他也曾参与发明了水肺〕

cou·ture /kuˈtʊr; kuːˈtjʊə/ *n* [U] *French* expensive and fashionable clothes【法】昂贵的时装

cove /kov; kəʊv/ *n* [C] **1** part of the coast where the land bends around, partly enclosing the sea so the shore is protected from the wind, rain etc 小海湾 **2** *BrE old-fashioned* a man【英，过时】汉子，家伙: *He's an odd cove.* 他是个怪人。

cov·en /ˈkʌvn̩; ˈkʌvən/ *n* [C] a meeting of witches (WITCH (1)) 女巫的集会

cov·e·nant /ˈkʌvənənt; ˈkʌvənənt/ *n* a formal agreement between two or more people 盟约，契约 —**covenant** *v* [T]

Cov·ent Gar·den /ˌkʌvənt ˈgɑrdn̩; ˌkɒvənt ˈgɑːdn/ **1** an area of London once famous for its fruit and vegetable market, but which now has expensive but popular shops, eating places, etc. 科文特加登〔伦敦一城区，其蔬菜和水果市场十分有名，现已被价格不菲但颇受欢迎的商店和食府取而代之〕**2** another name for the Royal Opera House, which is next to the place where Covent Garden market used to be 科文特加登歌剧院〔英国皇家歌剧院的别称。该剧院位于科文特加登市场原址的旁边〕

Cov·en·try /ˈkɑvəntrɪ; ˈkɒvəntri/ *n* **send sb to Coventry** *BrE informal* to refuse to speak to someone in order to punish them or show disapproval【英，非正式】不理某人〔作为惩罚或表示不满〕

cov·er[1] /ˈkʌvɚ; ˈkʌvə/ *v* [T]

1 ►PUT STH OVER STH 用某物覆盖…◄ also 又作 **cover up** to put something over the top of something in order to hide or protect it 遮盖，遮蔽: *Cover the pan when the sauce boils and let it simmer.* 调味汁煮沸时把锅盖上慢慢炖。| **cover sth with sth** *They covered the tables with clean white cloths.* 他们在桌上都铺上干净的白桌布。

2 ►BE OVER STH 在…之上◄ to be on top of something or spread over something 覆盖: *Colourful pictures covered the walls.* 墙上挂着五颜六色的图画。| **be covered with sth** *If it carries on snowing the ground will be covered by morning.* 如果雪不停地下，到早上地面就会被雪覆盖。| **be covered in sth** *The children were covered in paint.* 孩子们身上满是颜料。

3 ►AN AREA 面积◄ to spread over an area 包含，包括: *The city covers 25 square miles.* 这个城市占地 25 平方英里。

4 ►DISTANCE 距离◄ to travel a particular distance 走完〔一段路程〕: *They were hoping to cover 40 miles yesterday.* 他们昨天计划走 40 英里。| **cover a lot of ground** (=travel a long way) 走很长的路 *We covered a lot of ground during those two weeks in Spain.* 在西班牙的两周期间我们到了很多地方。

5 ►DEAL WITH/INCLUDE 处理/包括◄ to include or deal with something 涉及，处理；包括: *The course covers all aspects of business and law.* 这门课程涉及商业和法律的各方面。| *Most of the key points are covered in this book.* 这本书谈到了大部分的要点。| *This scheme would cover only a few of the three million people without jobs.* 这个计划只能解决 300 万失业者中一小部分人的问题。| *development officers whose work would cover a local area* 负责一地区的开发官员

6 ►RULES 规则◄ to deal with a particular situation 处理，对待，应付: *The rules, while they cover a wide range of issues, do not cover every possible situation.* 虽然这些规定涉及广泛的问题，但是没有包含一切可能的情况。

7 ►NEWS 新闻◄ to report the details of an event for a newspaper, television, or radio 报道: *Simonson was sent to Switzerland to cover the Winter Olympics.* 西蒙森被派遣到瑞士去报道冬季奥运会。

8 ►PAY FOR STH 支付◄ money that covers a cost is enough to pay for it 够支付: *He should get enough money from the council to cover his rent.* 他应当从市政务委员会得到足够的钱来支付他的房租。| **cover the cost of sth** *You will have to pay an extra amount to cover the cost of insurance.* 你要另外付一笔钱支付保险费用。

9 ►INSURANCE 保险◄ if an insurance agreement covers someone or something, it states that money will be given to the person if they are injured, if something is damaged etc 给…保险，承保: *The policy will cover any medical expenses that you incur while you are abroad.* 这份保单承保你在国外的医疗费用。| **cover sb against sth** *We're not covered against theft.* 我们的保险不理赔失窃损失。

10 ►GUNS 枪炮◄ **a)** to protect someone by being ready to shoot anyone who attacks them 掩护: *We'll cover you while you run for it.* 你跑过去的时候我们会掩护你。**b)** to aim a gun at a person, or the door of a building with people in it, so that they cannot escape 用枪瞄准〔使人无法逃走〕: *Don't move – we've got you covered.* 不许动，我们瞄准你了。| *The police had the back entrance covered.* 警察持枪封锁了后面的出口。

11 ►SPORT 体育◄ to stay close to a member of the opposing team or a part of the field in a game, in order to prevent your

opponents from gaining points〔体育〕盯防，防守：*Who's covering second base?* 谁防守第二垒？

12 cover (all) the bases *AmE* to be prepared to deal with any situation, and be sure that nothing bad will happen and no one can criticize you【美】准备好应付各种情况；面面俱到：*Just be sure to cover all your bases if you join in their business venture.* 如果你要加入他们的企业，一定要准备好应对各种情况。

13 cover your back *BrE spoken* to be careful to do nothing that would make people criticize you【英口】不让别人抓住辫子

cover for sb *phr v* **a)** to do the work that someone else usually does because they are ill or not present 代替〔某人工作〕：*Who's going to cover for you when you're on holiday?* 你度假期间谁接替你的工作？ **b)** to prevent someone from getting into trouble by lying, especially about where they are or what they are doing 替…打掩护，替…找借口：*Cover for me, will you? Just say I'm at the dentist's.* 替我搪塞一下，就说我在看牙医，好吗？

cover up *phr v* **1** [T **cover** sth ↔ **up**] to put something over the top of something in order to hide it or protect it 遮盖，覆盖：*She put a cloth over the floor to cover up the mess.* 她用一块布铺在地板上盖住脏东西。 **2** [T **cover** sth ↔ **up**] to prevent mistakes or unpleasant facts from being known about 掩饰，隐瞒：*The whole thing was very well covered up and never reached the newspapers.* 整个事情都被巧妙地隐瞒起来，始终没有在报纸上曝光。—see also 另见 COVER-UP **3 cover up for sb** to protect someone by hiding unpleasant facts about them 为…掩盖错误；包庇：*They covered up for Kirk by refusing to answer any of the questions.* 为了袒护柯克，他们拒绝回答任何问题。 **4** [I] to put clothes on in order to keep warm or to prevent people from seeing your body 穿上衣服：*Cover up well against the cold.* 穿暖和些以御寒。 **5 cover yourself up** to put clothes, sheets etc over yourself so that your body is covered 用〔衣服、床单等〕遮盖身体：*Some religions require that women cover themselves up completely.* 有些宗教要求妇女要用服饰把自己严严实实地包起来。

[1] [2] **cover**[2] *n*

1 ▶STH THAT PROTECTS STH 保护物◀ [C] something that is put over or onto something to protect it or keep dirt etc out 覆盖物，遮盖物：*a cushion cover* 垫子套 | *Put a cover over the bowl.* 用盖子盖住碗。

2 ▶BOOKS 书◀ [C] the outer front or back page of a magazine, book etc 封面；封底：*a picture of President Clinton on the cover of Newsweek*《新闻周刊》封面上克林顿总统的照片 | **read sth from cover to cover** (=read everything in a book, magazine etc) 从头读到尾

3 ▶SHELTER/PROTECTION 遮蔽/保护◀ [U] shelter or protection from bad weather or attack 掩蔽处，掩蔽工事：*The soldiers ran for cover when the shooting began.* 射击开始后士兵跑向掩蔽工事。| **take cover** (=find shelter or protection) 找到掩护处 *Come on, we can take cover in that barn over there!* 快点儿，我们可以到那边的谷仓中躲避一下！| **break cover** (=come out from the place where you have been sheltered or protected) 从掩蔽处出来

4 covers [plural] the sheets, blankets etc on a bed 床罩；床毯：*The covers had slipped off the bed during the night.* 夜里床罩从床上滑了下来。

5 ▶INSURANCE 保险◀ [U] insurance against injury, damage etc 保险：*The policy gives you temporary medical cover for your holiday.* 这份保单为你提供假期期间的临时医疗保险。| [**+against**] *cover against fire and theft* 火险和盗窃险

6 a cover for a business that seems normal and honest, but is really used to hide illegal activities〔非法活动的〕掩饰；掩盖：*He used the shop as a cover for various illegal activities.* 他用该店铺掩护各种各样的非法活动。

7 under cover pretending to be someone else in order to do something without being noticed 隐匿地，暗地里：*She was working under cover to get information on the drug dealers.* 她秘密地打听毒贩的情况。

8 under cover of darkness hidden by darkness 在夜幕的掩护下：*They escaped under cover of darkness.* 他们在夜幕的掩护下逃跑了。

9 under plain cover/under separate cover if a letter etc is sent under plain cover or under separate cover, it is sent in a plain envelope or a separate envelope 在未写明寄件人、内容等的信封内；在另函内：*The bill will be sent to you later under separate cover.* 账单稍后将另函寄上。

cov·er·age /ˈkʌvərɪdʒ; ˈkʌvərɪdʒ/ *n* [U] **1** the way in which a subject or event is reported on television or radio, or in newspapers 新闻报道：*ABC gave the story extensive coverage in the evening news.* 美国广播公司在晚间新闻中对该事件进行了深入的报道。 **2** the amount of protection given to you by an insurance agreement 保险范围，保险项目：*Make sure your policy will give you adequate coverage in case of a break-in.* 务必使你的保单即使遭到入室盗窃也能提供充分保障。 **3** the range of subjects and facts included in a course, class etc 课程内容；一堂课的内容：*The syllabus includes coverage of all the outdoor skills.* 教学大纲的内容包含所有的户外技巧。

cov·er·alls /ˈkʌvəˌrɔlz; ˈkʌvərɔːlz/ *n* [plural] *AmE* a piece of clothing that you wear over all your clothes to protect them【美】〔穿在最外面衣裤相连的〕工作服；overalls (OVERALL[3] (3)) *BrE*【英】

cover charge /ˈ· · ·/ *n* [C] money that you have to pay in a restaurant in addition to the cost of the food and drinks〔饭店等的〕服务费

covered wag·on /ˌ·· ˈ··/ *n* [C] a large vehicle with a curved cloth top that is pulled by horses, used in former times in North America〔从前北美的〕有篷大马车，大篷车

cover girl /ˈ·· ·/ *n* [C] a young attractive woman whose photograph is on the front cover of a magazine〔杂志的〕封面女郎

cov·er·ing /ˈkʌvərɪŋ; ˈkʌvərɪŋ/ *n* [singular] something that covers or hides something 覆盖物：*a light covering of snow* 薄薄的一层雪

covering let·ter /ˌ··· ˈ··/ *n* [C] *BrE* a letter that you send with documents or a package explaining what it is or giving additional information【英】〔文件或包裹的〕附函；COVER LETTER *AmE*【美】

cov·er·let /ˈkʌvəlɪt; ˈkʌvəlɪ̀t/ *n* [C] a cloth cover for a bed; BEDSPREAD 床罩

cover let·ter /ˈ·· ˌ··/ *n* [C] *AmE* a covering letter【美】附函

cover note /ˈ·· ·/ *n* [C] *BrE* a document that proves that you have car insurance【英】汽车保单

cover sto·ry /ˈ·· ˌ··/ *n* [C] the story that goes with a picture on the cover of a magazine 封面故事〔杂志中与封面图片有关的主要文章〕

cov·ert[1] /ˈkovɚt; ˈkʌvət/ *adj* secret or hidden 秘密的；隐藏的：*illegal, covert actions of enemy agents* 敌人间谍的非法秘密活动 —opposite 反义词 OVERT —**covertly** *adv*

covert[2] *n* [C] a group of small bushes growing close together in which animals can hide〔动物藏身的〕树丛

cover-up /ˈ·· ·/ *n* [C] an attempt to prevent the public from discovering the truth about something 掩饰；隐瞒 —see also 另见 **cover up** (COVER[1])

cov·et /ˈkʌvɪt; ˈkʌvɪ̀t/ *v* [T] *formal* to have a very strong desire to have something that someone else has【正式】贪求；垂涎，觊觎：*He possessed rare and much coveted works of art.* 他拥有非常令人垂涎的稀世艺术珍品。

cov·et·ous /ˈkʌvɪtəs; ˈkʌvɪ̀təs/ *adj* having a very strong desire to have something that someone else has, especially wealth 贪婪的；垂涎的：*They began to cast covetous eyes on their neighbours' fields.* 他们开始觊觎邻居的土地。—**covetously** *adv* —**covetousness** *n* [U]

cow[1] /kaʊ; kaʊ/ *n* [C] **1** a large female animal that is kept on farms and produces milk 奶牛 —compare 比较 BULL[1] (1) **2** a male or female animal of this type 牛 **3** the female of some large land and sea animals, such as the ELEPHANT or the WHALE 大型雌性动物〈如象、鲸等〉 **4** *BrE spoken* an impolite way of saying that a woman is stupid or very unpleasant【英口】蠢女人；泼妇〔不礼貌用语〕：*Linda's a silly cow – just ignore her!* 琳达是个蠢女人，不要理她！ **5 have a cow** *AmE informal* to be very angry or surprised about something【美，非正式】非常生气；非常吃惊 **6 till the cows come home** *informal* for a very long time, or forever【非正式】长时间地；无限期地；永远 [2]

cow[2] *v* [T] to make someone behave in the way you want them to by using violence or threats 恐吓，威胁：*I was determined not to be cowed by their threats.* 我决心不被他们的威胁吓住。

cow·ard /ˈkaʊɚd; ˈkaʊəd/ *n* [C] someone who is not at all brave 胆小鬼；懦夫：*He called me a coward because I would not fight.* 因为我不肯打架，他就叫我懦夫。

CULTURAL NOTE 文化注释

Cowards are connected with the colour yellow, and people sometimes say that a coward is 'yellow' or 'yellow-bellied'. 懦夫常与黄颜色联系在一起，有时说一个人是懦夫，就说他 yellow 或 yellow-bellied。

Coward, Sir No·ël /ˈnoəl; ˈnəʊəl/ (1899-1973) a British actor, singer, and writer of songs and plays. He is famous for his clever and humorous plays, such as *Private Lives* and *Blithe*

Spirit, and his amusing song *Mad Dogs and Englishmen*. 科沃德〔(1899-1973)，英国演员、歌手、歌曲和戏剧作家。他的戏剧构思巧妙，诙谐幽默，如《私生活》和《欢乐的心灵》。他还创作了《疯狗和英格兰人》这首有趣的歌曲〕

cow·ard·ice /ˈkauədɪs; ˈkaʊədɪs/ also 又作 **cow·ard·li·ness** /ˈkauədlɪnəs; ˈkaʊədlɪnɪs/ *n* [U] lack of courage 胆小; 怯懦: *cowardice in the face of danger* 在危险面前的怯懦

cow·ard·ly /ˈkauədlɪ; ˈkaʊədli/ *adj* behaving in a way that shows that you are not brave 胆小的, 懦弱的: *That was a very cowardly thing to do.* 那样做非常懦弱。| *a cowardly attack on a defenceless man* 对无自卫能力的人懦弱的攻击

cow·bell /ˈkau,bɛl; ˈkaʊbel/ *n* [C] a bell that is put around a cow's neck so that it can be found easily 牛颈铃

cow·boy /ˈkau,bɔɪ; ˈkaʊbɔɪ/ *n* [C] **1** a man who rides a horse and is employed to look after cattle in North America〔北美的〕骑马牧人; 牛仔 **2** *BrE informal* someone who is dishonest in business, or who produces very bad quality work【英, 非正式】不诚实的商人; 低劣产品的制造商: *a firm of cowboy builders* 一家不诚实的建筑商 **3 cowboys and Indians** a game played by children who pretend to be cowboys and NATIVE AMERICANS, fighting each other 牛仔追印第安人〔一种儿童游戏〕

CULTURAL NOTE 文化注释

Americans think of cowboys as honest, independent, and strong men from the time when few people lived in the western part of the US. This romantic view of the American cowboy comes more from films and books than from real life. Cowboys still take care of cattle in the US, but they are now more likely to use OFF-ROAD VEHICLES than to ride a horse. People still think of cowboys as wearing blue JEANS, cowboy boots, and a special large hat called a STETSON. In the US, people sometimes go on VACATIONS to a DUDE RANCH where they do the work of a cowboy. Singers of COUNTRY MUSIC often dress like cowboys. 美国人认为牛仔诚实、独立、强壮，他们活跃在美国西部少有人居住的时代。对美国牛仔的这种浪漫看法更多地源于电影和书籍而不是现实生活。美国仍有牛仔在照料牛群，但现在他们更喜欢开越野车而不是骑马。现在人们仍认为牛仔穿蓝色牛仔裤、牛仔靴，戴一种叫做"史特森"高顶宽边帽。美国人有时假期会去度假牧场，干一些牛仔的活儿。乡村音乐歌手经常穿戴成牛仔的样子。

cowboy hat /ˈ· ·, ·/ *n* [C] a hat with a wide circular edge and a soft round top; STETSON 牛仔帽

cow·catch·er /ˈkau,kætʃə; ˈkaʊ,kætʃə/ *n* [C] a piece of metal on the front of a train used to push things off the track〔火车机车前的〕排障装置

cow chip /ˈ· ·/ *n* [C] *AmE* a round flat mass of dry solid waste from a cow【美】干牛粪块

cow·er /ˈkauə; ˈkaʊə/ *v* [I] to bend low and move back, especially because you are frightened 退缩, 畏缩; 蜷缩: *They were cowering in the cellars, trapped by the shelling.* 他们蜷缩在地窖里, 因遭受炮击而出不去。| *He cowered against the wall.* 他蜷缩在墙根。

Cowes /kauz; kaʊz/ an English holiday town and sailing centre on the Isle of Wight in the English Channel. Every year there is a REGATTA (=series of boat races) there, known as **Cowes Week**. 考斯〔英格兰度假小镇、帆船运动中心, 位于英吉利海峡的绯特岛。该中心每年都举办"考斯赛船会"〕

cow·girl /ˈkau,gɜl; ˈkaʊgɜːl/ *n* [C] a woman who rides a horse and is employed to look after cattle in North America〔北美的〕牧牛女工

cow·hand /ˈkau,hænd; ˈkaʊhænd/ *n* [C] someone who is employed to look after cattle 牧场工人, 牧牛工

cow·hide /ˈkau,haɪd; ˈkaʊhaɪd/ *n* [C,U] the skin of a cow or the leather that is made from this 牛皮

cowl /kaul; kaʊl/ *n* [C] **1** a very large hood that covers your head and shoulders, especially worn by MONKS〔修道士等戴的〕蒙头斗篷, 风帽 **2** a cover for a chimney that protects it from wind and rain; HOOD (4)〔用于挡风雨的〕烟囱帽, 通风帽

cow·lick /ˈkau,lɪk; ˈkaʊ,lɪk/ *n* [C] hair that sticks up on top of your head 翘起的一绺头发

cow·ling /ˈkaulɪŋ; ˈkaʊlɪŋ/ *n* [C] a metal cover for an aircraft engine〔飞机的〕发动机外罩, 整流罩 —see picture at 参见 AIRCRAFT 图

cowl neck /, ·ˈ ·/ *n* [C] the neck on a piece of clothing that falls in folds at the front 胸前皱领

co-work·er /ˈko ,wɜkə; ,kəʊ ˈwɜːkə/ *n* [C] someone who works with you and has a similar position 同事, 同僚

cow·pat /ˈkau,pæt; ˈkaʊpæt/ *n* [C] *BrE* a round flat mass of solid waste from a cow【英】〔一团〕牛粪

cow pie /, ·ˈ ·/ *n* [C] *AmE* a cow CHIP【美】干牛粪块

cow·poke /ˈkau,pok; ˈkaʊpəʊk/ *n* [C] *AmE old-fashioned* a COWBOY (1)【美, 过时】牛仔, 骑马牧人

cow·pox /ˈkau,pɑks; ˈkaʊpɒks/ *n* [U] a disease that cows suffer from and that can be given to humans to protect them from SMALLPOX 牛痘

cow·rie /ˈkaurɪ; ˈkaʊri/ *n* [C] a shiny brightly-coloured tropical shell, used in former times as money in parts of Africa and Asia〔古时亚非一些地区用作货币的〕贝壳

cow·shed /ˈkau,ʃɛd; ˈkaʊʃed/ *n* [C] a building where cows live in the winter, or where their milk is taken from them 牛棚, 牛舍

cow·slip /ˈkau,slɪp; ˈkaʊ,slɪp/ *n* [U] a small European wild plant with sweet smelling yellow flowers 黄花九轮草, 野樱草

cox /kɑks; kɒks/ *n* [C] someone who controls the direction of a rowing boat, especially in races〔赛艇的〕舵手 **—cox** *v* [T]

cox·comb /ˈkɑks,kom; ˈkɒkskəʊm/ *n* [C] *old use* a stupid man who spends too much time and money on his clothes and appearance【旧】〔特别注意衣着的〕花花公子

Cox's /ˈkɑksɪz; ˈkɒksɪz/ a popular type of English apple, whose full name is 'Cox's orange pippin' 考克斯〔深受人们喜爱的一种英格兰苹果, 全名为 Cox's orange pippin〕

cox·swain /ˈkɑksn; ˈkɒksən/ *n* [C] a cox〔赛艇的〕舵手

coy /kɔɪ; kɔɪ/ *adj* **1** pretending to be shy in order to attract interest, or to avoid dealing with something difficult〔为了引人注目或逃避困难而〕装作害羞的, 故作忸怩的: *She gave him a coy smile.* 她对他含羞一笑。**2** unwilling to give information about something 含糊其辞的, 不肯表态的: [+about] *Tania was always coy about her age.* 塔妮娅对自己的年龄总是含糊其辞。**—coyly** *adv* **—coyness** *n* [U]

coy·ote /ˈkaɪot; ˈkɔɪ-əʊt/ *n* [C] a small wild dog that lives in North West America and Mexico〔北美西部和墨西哥的〕郊狼

coy·pu /ˈkɔɪpu; ˈkɔɪpuː/ *n* [C] an animal like a BEAVER, kept on farms for its fur; NUTRIA 河狸鼠

coz /kʌz; kʌz/ *n old use* a way of addressing a cousin【旧】堂[表]兄弟[姐妹]〔称呼〕

co·zy /ˈkozɪ; ˈkəʊzi/ *adj* the American spelling of COSY cosy 的美式拼法 **—cozily** *adv* **—coziness** *n* [U]

CP /,si ˈpi; ,siː ˈpiː/ the abbreviation of 缩写 = COMMUNIST PARTY

CPA /,si pi ˈe; ,siː piː ˈeɪ/ *n* [C] *AmE* Certified Public Accountant; an ACCOUNTANT who has passed all their examinations【美】注册会计师; CHARTERED ACCOUNTANT *BrE*【英】

CPR /,si pi ˈɑr; ,siː piː ˈɑː/ *n* [C] cardiopulmonary resuscitation; a method of helping someone who has stopped breathing and whose heart has stopped beating 心肺复苏

CPRE, the /,si pi ɑr ˈi; ,siː piː ɑː ˈiː/ the Council for the Protection of Rural England; an organization whose aim is to prevent farmers and DEVELOPERS (=companies that build houses, offices, shops, or roads) from destroying the countryside in England 英格兰乡村保护委员会〔英国一组织, 旨在防止农场主和开发商破坏英格兰乡村环境〕

CPS, the /,si pi ˈɛs; ,siː piː ˈes/ the abbreviation of 缩写 = the CROWN PROSECUTION SERVICE

CPU /,si pi ˈju; ,siː piː ˈjuː/ *n* the part of a computer that controls and organizes all its activities; CENTRAL PROCESSING UNIT〔电脑的〕中央处理器

CPVE /,si pi vi ˈi; ,siː piː viː ˈiː/ the abbreviation of 缩写 = the Certificate of Pre-vocational Education 职前教育证书

crab[1] /kræb; kræb/ *n* **1** [C] a sea animal whose body is covered with a shell and that has five legs on each side and two large CLAWS on the front legs 蟹 **2** [U] the flesh of this animal that you can cook and eat as food 蟹肉 **3 crabs** [plural] a medical condition in which a kind of LOUSE is in the hair around the sexual organs 生阴虱; 阴虱病 **4** [singular] *AmE informal* someone who easily becomes annoyed about unimportant things【美, 非正式】脾气乖戾的人, 易怒的人: *He's a real crab – always finding fault with everything.* 他真是一个脾气乖戾的人, 总是到处挑刺。

crab 蟹

pincer/claw 螯

crab[2] *v* **crabbed, crabbing** [I] *informal* to complain about something in an annoyed way; GRUMBLE[1] (1)【非正式】抱怨, 发牢骚

crab ap·ple/ˈ· ,··/ *n* [C] a small apple that tastes sour, or the tree that it grows on 沙果（树），花红（树）

crab·bed/ˈkræbɪd; ˈkræbɨd/ *adj* **1** writing which is crabbed is difficult to read because the letters are small and untidy〔字迹〕潦草的，难认的 **2** *old-fashioned* someone who is crabbed always behaves as if they are annoyed; BAD-TEMPERED【过时】乖戾的

crab·by/ˈkræbi; ˈkræbi/ *adj informal* someone who is crabby easily becomes annoyed about unimportant things; BAD-TEMPERED【非正式】脾气坏的，易怒的: *a rather crabby old man* 脾气很坏的老人 | *I was feeling crabby.* 我心情不好，很暴躁。

crab·grass/ˈkræbˌgræs; ˈkræbgrɑːs/ *n* [U] a kind of rough grass 马唐〔一种野草〕

crab·wise/ˈkræbwaɪz; ˈkræbwaɪz/ also 又作 **crabways**/-wez; -weɪz/ *adv* sideways, especially in a way that seems difficult 横向地〔尤指行动不灵活〕；蟹行地: *I moved crabwise along the edge of the cliff.* 我侧身沿着悬崖边挪动。

3 **crack¹** /kræk; kræk/ *v*

1 ►BREAK 断裂◄[I,T] to break or make something break so that it gets one or more lines on its surface（使）破裂；（使）裂开: *Don't put that delicate china in the dishwasher – it may crack.* 不要把那件易碎的瓷器放入洗碗机，会碎的。| *She fell off her bike and cracked a bone in her leg.* 她从自行车上摔了下来，摔断了一根腿骨。

2 ►LOUD SOUND 响声◄[I,T] to make a sudden quick sound like the sound of something breaking, or to make something do this（使）发爆裂声: *The branch cracked loudly and broke off.* 树枝啪的一声断了。| *He had a habit of cracking his knuckles.* 他有掰指节的习惯。

3 ►HIT STH 击撞某物◄[I always+adv/prep, T always+adv/prep] to hit something hard but not deliberately, especially part of your body 重击: [**+against/on**] *The rock cracked against my shoulder.* 石头重重地砸在我的肩膀上。| **crack sth against/on** *He fell, cracking his head on the wall.* 他摔倒了，头撞到墙上。

4 ►HIT SB 击打某人◄[T] to hit someone hard and deliberately on part of their body 重击〔某人〕: **crack sb over/in/on** *He cracked the burglar over the head with a vase.* 他把花瓶重重地砸在窃贼的头上。

5 ►LOSE CONTROL 失控◄also 又作 **crack up**[I] to be unable to continue doing something or working well because of great pressure〔因受大压力而〕失去控制；崩溃: *We're hoping the prisoner will crack under interrogation.* 我们希望审讯时囚犯能够屈服招供。| *The whole political system is beginning to crack up.* 整个政治制度开始崩溃。

6 ►MENTALLY ILL 精神病◄also 又作 **crack up**[I] to become mentally ill because of too much pressure（使）发疯，（使）神经错乱: *Many of the soldiers cracked up on returning from the war.* 很多士兵打仗归来就精神失常了。

7 ►VOICE 声音◄[I] if your voice cracks, it changes from one level to another suddenly because of strong emotions〔声音〕变嘶哑: *Her voice cracked as she tried to explain what had happened.* 她设法解释发生了什么事情，声音都嘶哑了。

8 ►NERVE 神经◄[I] if your nerve cracks, you no longer feel confident that you can do something difficult 失去勇气: *At the last moment his nerve cracked.* 在最后时刻他失去了勇气。

9 ►EGG/NUT 蛋/坚果◄[T] to break the outside part of something, such as an egg or a nut, in order to get what is inside it 打开，砸开〔鸡蛋、坚果等的〕壳: *The foxes crack the eggs, and suck out the yolk.* 狐狸弄破蛋壳，舔吃流出来的蛋黄。

10 ►STEAL 偷◄[T] to open a SAFE² illegally, in order to steal what is inside 非法地打开；撬开〔保险柜盗窃〕

11 ►SOLVE 解决◄[T] to find the answer to a problem or find how to use a CODE¹ (4) 解决〔难题〕；破解〔密码〕: *His skill at cracking codes proved invaluable during the war.* 他破解密码的技能在战争中证明无比重要。| *This is a national problem, we're not going to crack it here this afternoon.* 这是一个全国性问题，今天下午我们不会在这里解决它。

12 ►STOP CRIME/ENEMY 制止犯罪/敌人◄[T] to find a way of destroying an enemy or stopping something they are doing 消灭〔敌人〕；制止〔敌人做的事〕: *Police are hoping to crack the drug-smuggling ring.* 警方希望能铲除这个毒品走私团伙。

13 crack it *BrE* to succeed in some way【英】成功

14 crack a deal *AmE informal* to succeed in making a business deal, especially when this has been difficult【美，非正式】〔尤指费力地〕达成协议，做成买卖: *We finally managed to crack that deal with the Japanese.* 我们终于设法与日本人谈成了那笔交易。

15 crack a joke *informal* to tell a joke【非正式】说笑话: *He kept cracking jokes about my appearance.* 他老是拿我的长相开玩笑。

16 crack a smile *AmE informal* to smile when you have been serious, sad, or angry【美，非正式】转怒为喜；破涕为笑: *She finally cracked a smile, although she had tears in her eyes.* 她虽然眼中含着泪花，终于还是破涕为笑。

17 crack open a bottle *informal* to open a bottle of alcohol for drinking【非正式】打开一瓶酒: *Let's crack open a bottle to celebrate!* 让我们打开一瓶酒庆祝一下！

18 not all/everything it's cracked up to be *informal* not as good as people say it is【非正式】不如人们所说的那样好；名不副实: *The film wasn't all it's cracked up to be – I was quite bored in parts.* 这部电影不像人们所说的那样好，我觉得其中有些部分非常沉闷。

19 get cracking *informal* to start doing something or going somewhere as quickly as possible【非正式】抓紧时间: *The train goes at ten so let's get cracking.* 火车10点钟开，我们得赶快点儿。

20 crack the whip *informal* to make people you have control over work very hard【非正式】逼手下人努力工作

crack down *phr v* [I] to become more strict in dealing with a problem and punishing the people involved〔对…〕采取严厉措施；制裁；镇压: [**+on**] *The police are cracking down on illegal parking.* 警方在严厉打击违章停车。—see also 另见 CRACKDOWN

crack on *phr v* [I] *BrE informal* to continue working hard at something in order to try to finish it【英，非正式】继续努力: [**+with**] *I'm hoping to crack on with that translation this weekend.* 我想这个周末继续尽力翻译。

crack up *phr v informal*【非正式】**1** [I,T] to laugh a lot at something, or to make someone laugh a lot（使）捧腹大笑: *Everyone in the class just cracked up.* 班上所有的人都大笑起来。| **crack sb up** *She's so funny. She cracks me up.* 她非常滑稽，逗得我捧腹大笑。**2** [I] to become unable to think or behave sensibly because you have too many problems, too much work etc 吃不消，精神垮掉: *I must be cracking up – I've lost those papers again!* 我一定昏了头了，又把那些文件弄丢了！—see also 另见 CRACK-UP

crack² *n* [C]

1 ►THIN SPACE 狭窄的空间◄a very narrow space between two things or two parts of something 裂缝，缝隙: [**+in**] *A thin ray of light shone through a crack in the curtains.* 一缕光线透过窗帘上的缝隙照射进来。| [**+between**] *The children carefully avoided the cracks between the paving stones.* 孩子们小心地躲过砌路石间的缝隙。| **open sth a crack**(=open something very slightly) 稍稍打开 *She opened the door a crack and peeped out.* 她把门打开一条缝，向外瞟了一眼。

2 ►BREAK 断裂◄a thin line on the surface of something when it is broken but has not actually come apart 裂痕，裂口: [**+in**] *There were several cracks in the glass.* 玻璃上有几道裂纹。

3 ►PROBLEM 问题◄a fault in an idea, system, or organization 瑕疵，缺点: [**+in**] *Cracks were appearing in the government's economic policy.* 政府的经济政策出现了漏洞。

4 ►SOUND 声音◄a sudden loud very sharp sound like the sound of a stick being broken 爆裂声，噼啪声: *There was a loud crack as the wood finally broke in two.* 木头最后在爆裂声中断成两截。—see picture on page A19 参见 A19 页图

5 ►JOKE/REMARK 玩笑/话语◄a clever joke or rude remark 俏皮话；粗鲁的话: [**+about**] *I've had enough of your cracks about my weight.* 我听够了你挖苦我的体重。| **make a crack** *I wish I hadn't made that crack about lawyers.* 我不该说那些俏皮话挖苦律师。

6 ►CHANCE TO DO STH 机遇◄*informal* an opportunity or attempt to achieve something, especially for the first time【非正式】试图，尝试: [**+at**] *I'd like a crack at climbing that mountain.* 我想试试爬那座山。| **have/take a crack at sth** *Why don't you have a crack at that competition – you might win!* 为什么你不尝试参加那个竞赛，说不定你会赢的！| **a (fair) crack of the whip** *BrE* (=a chance to do something or be in control)【英】〔做事或管事的〕机会 *They'll do well if we give them a fair crack of the whip.* 如果我们给他们一个公平的机会，他们会做得很好的。

7 a crack on the head what you feel when you are hit on the head, usually not deliberately 头上挨了一下: *I got a nasty crack on the head as I went through the low doorway.* 我通过那低矮的门道时，把头撞了一下。

8 a crack in sb's voice a sudden change in the level of someone's voice, especially because they are very upset〔尤指因情绪激动而引起的〕嗓音的变化: *He noticed the crack in her voice as she tried to continue.* 他注意到她想继续说下去的时候声音都变了。

9 crack of dawn very early in the morning 大清早，黎明: *We'll have to get up at the crack of dawn tomorrow.* 我们明天得起个大早。

10▶DRUG 毒品◀ [U] a very pure form of the drug COCAINE that some people take illegally for pleasure 强效可卡因

11 **good crack** *IrE, BrE spoken* friendly, enjoyable talk in a group【爱尔兰, 英, 口】一群人友好的交谈; 尽兴的谈话: *We go there for the crack.* 我们到那里去聊天。

12 **what's the crack?** *BrE spoken* used to ask someone what is happening, or what has been happening recently【英口】发生什么事了? 最近发生了什么事? —see also 另见 **paper over the cracks** (PAPER³ (2))

crack³ *adj* [only before noun 仅用于名词前] **1** having a very high level of quality or skill, or being very highly trained 第一流的; 受过良好训练的: *A crack regiment was sent in to deal with the situation.* 派遣了一个精锐团去处理这一局势。**2 crack shot** someone who always hits what they shoot at 神枪手

C

crack·down /ˈkræk,daʊn; ˈkrækdaʊn/ *n* [C usually singular 一般用单数] severe action that is taken in order to deal with a problem 取缔; 制裁; 镇压: [+on] *They're having a crackdown on drunk driving.* 他们正在严厉查处酒后驾车。—see also 另见 **crack down** (CRACK¹)

cracked /krækt; krækt/ *adj* **1** something that is cracked has been damaged and has one or more lines on its surface 有裂缝的; 破裂的: *cracked cups and saucers* 破裂的杯子和杯托 | *Her skin was cracked and dry.* 她的皮肤皲裂且干燥。—see picture on page A18 参见 A18 页图 **2** [not before noun 不用于名词前] *informal* someone who is cracked is slightly crazy【非正式】有点疯的 **3** someone's voice that is cracked sounds rough and uncontrolled because they are upset〔因激动而嗓音〕嘶哑的

crack·er /ˈkrækɚ; ˈkrækə/ *n* [C] **1** a small thin BISCUIT often eaten with cheese 薄脆饼干 **2** also 又作 **Christmas cracker** a brightly coloured paper tube that makes a small exploding sound when you pull it apart, and that usually contains a small gift and a joke, used at Christmas in Britain 圣诞彩包爆竹 **3** a FIRECRACKER 爆竹 **4** *BrE spoken* something that is very good or very funny【英口】好东西; 有趣的事物: *Did you hear his joke? It was a real cracker!* 你听了他讲的笑话吗? 真有意思! **5** *BrE old-fashioned* a very attractive woman【英, 过时】迷人的女子

Cracker Jack /ˈ· · ·/ *trademark* a type of sweet POPCORN sold in a box with a prize inside it, which is popular with children in the US【商标】"克拉克杰克"爆米花〔以盒装出售的一种甜味爆米花。盒内有赠品, 深受美国儿童喜爱〕

crack·ers /ˈkrækɚz; ˈkrækəz/ *adj* [not before noun 不用于名词前] *BrE informal* crazy【英, 非正式】疯狂的; 精神失常的: *You lent him all that money? You must be crackers!* 你把那笔钱都借给他了? 你一定是疯了!

crack·ing /ˈkrækɪŋ; ˈkrækɪŋ/ *adj* [only before noun 仅用于名词前] **1** very fast 快速的, 飞快的: *We set off at a cracking pace.* 我们快步出发。**2** *BrE spoken* very good【英口】极好的, 出色的: *It's going to be a cracking good race.* 这会是一场精彩的比赛。

crack·le /ˈkrækḷ; ˈkrækəl/ *v* [I] to make a repeated short sharp sound like something burning in a fire 发噼啪声: *The dry sticks crackled as they caught fire.* 干枝条着火时发出噼噼啪啪的声响。| *The radio crackled so much we could hardly hear what was said.* 收音机老是噼啪作响, 我们几乎听不清说的是什么。—**crackle** *n* [C]—**crackly** *adj* —see picture on page A19 参见 A19 页图

crack·ling /ˈkræklɪŋ; ˈkræklɪŋ/ *n* **1** [singular] the sound made by something when it crackles 噼啪声; 爆裂声: *There was a silence after that, except for the crackling of the fire.* 随后, 除了火的噼啪声, 一片沉寂。**2** *BrE*【英】**cracklings** *AmE*【美】[U] the hard skin of a pig when it has been cooked and is easily broken〔烤猪肉的〕脆皮

crack·pot /ˈkræk,pɑt; ˈkrækpɒt/ *n* [C] *humorous* someone who is slightly crazy【幽默】有点精神失常的人; 有点发疯的人 —**crackpot** *adj*

crack-up /ˈ· ·/ *n* [C] *AmE informal*【美, 非正式】**1** a NERVOUS BREAKDOWN 精神崩溃 **2** a car accident 车祸 —see also 另见 **crack up** (CRACK¹)

-cracy /krəsɪ; krəsi/ *suffix* [in nouns 构成名词] another form of the suffix -OCRACY 后缀 -ocracy 的另一种形式: *bureaucracy* (=government by officials who are not elected) 官僚政治

cra·dle¹ /ˈkredḷ; ˈkreɪdl/ *n* [C]

1▶BED 床◀ a small bed for a baby, especially one that you can move gently from side to side 摇篮: *She rocked the cradle to quieten the child.* 她摇动摇篮, 让宝宝安静下来。—see picture at 参见 BED¹ 图

2 **the cradle of** the place where something important began …的发源地; …的策源地: *Athens is often regarded as the cradle of democracy.* 雅典通常被认为是民主的发源地。

3 **from/in the cradle** from or in the earliest years of your life 从/在婴儿[幼年]时期: *Sara had learned that language from the cradle.* 莎拉在幼年就学会了那门语言。

4 **from the cradle to the grave** all through your life 一辈子, 从生到死: *a promise of security from the cradle to the grave* 保证终生安稳的许诺

5 *BrE* a structure that people working on the sides of high buildings stand in which can be moved up and down【英】〔空中作业用的〕吊架, 吊篮: *a window-cleaner's cradle* 窗户清洁工的吊篮

6 the part of a telephone where the part that you hold in your hand is put when it is not being used〔电话的〕听筒架, 叉簧 —see also 另见 CAT'S CRADLE, **rob the cradle** (ROB (5))

cradle² *v* [T] to hold something gently in your hands or arms, as if to protect it 轻轻地抱着: *John cradled the baby in his arms.* 约翰把宝宝轻轻地抱在怀里。| *The wine-glass looked tiny cradled in his big hands.* 酒杯握在他的大手里看上去很小。

cradle-snatch·er *BrE*【英】, **cradle-robber** *AmE*【美】/ˈ· · ,· ·/ *n* [C] someone who has a romantic relationship with someone much younger than they are 和比自己年轻很多的人谈恋爱的人 —**cradle-snatch** *v* [I]

-craft /kræft; krɑːft/ *suffix* [in nouns 构成名词] **1** a vehicle of a particular kind 运载工具: *a spacecraft* 航天器 | *a hovercraft* 气垫船 | *several aircraft* 几架飞机 **2** skill of a particular kind 技艺: *statecraft* (=skill in government) 政治手腕 | *stagecraft* (=skill in acting or directing plays) 演技; 舞台经验; 戏剧导演技巧 3

craft¹ /kræft; krɑːft/ *n* **1** *plural* **craft** [C] **a)** a small boat 小船: *I steered the craft carefully round the rocks.* 我小心驾船绕过岩石。**b)** an aircraft or SPACECRAFT 飞机, 飞行器, 航空器; 航天器 **2** *plural* **crafts** [C] an activity, especially a traditional one that needs a lot of skill, in which you make something with your hands〔尤指传统的手工〕工艺; 手艺: *a craft such as needlework* 针线活儿一类的手艺 **3** [C] a profession, especially one needing a special skill 行业, 职业: *The anthropologist takes years to learn his craft.* 人类学家要花多年时间来学习自己的专业。**4** [U] skill in deceiving people 诡计, 手腕: *Craft and cunning were necessary for the scheme to work.* 实施阴谋需要诡计和狡猾。—see also 另见 LANDING CRAFT

craft² *v* [T usually passive 一般用被动态] to make something using a special skill, especially with your hands 手工制作, 精制: *Each doll will be crafted individually by specialists.* 每个玩具娃娃都要由专门人员来单独手工制作。| **hand-crafted** (=made by hand, not by machine) 手工制作的 *a hand-crafted silver cigarette case* 手工制作的银烟盒

craft knife /ˈ· ·/ *n* [C] *BrE* a very sharp knife used for cutting paper, thin wood etc, when the cutting needs to be exact【英】工艺刀

crafts·man /ˈkræftsmən; ˈkrɑːftsmən/ *n* [C] someone who is very skilled at a particular CRAFT¹ (2) 工匠; 手艺人

crafts·man·ship /ˈkræftsmən,ʃɪp; ˈkrɑːftsmənʃɪp/ *n* [U] **1** the special skill that someone uses to make something beautiful with their hands 手艺; 工艺, 技艺: *These works of art combine precious materials with exquisite craftsmanship.* 这些艺术品用料珍贵, 工艺精湛。**2** very detailed work that has been done using a lot of skill, so that the result is beautiful 手工艺品: *the fine craftsmanship of the carved Georgian table* 乔治时代精工雕刻的桌子

crafts·wom·an /ˈkræfts,wʊmən; ˈkrɑːfts,wʊmən/ *n* [C] a woman who is very skilled at a particular CRAFT¹ (2) 女工匠, 女手艺人

craft·y /ˈkræftɪ; ˈkrɑːfti/ *adj* good at getting what you want by clever planning and secretly deceiving people; CUNNING¹ (1,2) 诡计多端的, 狡猾的: *You crafty devil, you!* 你这个诡计多端的家伙! —**craftily** *adv* —**craftiness** *n* [U] 3

crag /kræg; kræg/ *n* [C] a high and very steep rough rock or mass of rocks 险崖, 峭壁

crag·gy /ˈkrægɪ; ˈkrægi/ *adj* **1** a mountain that is craggy is very steep and covered in rough rocks 陡峭的; 多岩石的 **2** having a face with many deep lines on it〔脸〕满是皱纹的: *craggy good looks* 布满皱纹的俊美容貌

cram /kræm; kræm/ *v* **crammed, cramming** **1** [T always+adv/prep] to force something into a small space 把…塞入〔小空间〕: **cram sth into/onto/down etc** *Jessica crammed her clothes into the bag.* 杰西卡把她的衣服塞入袋子。**2 cram into sth** if people cram into a place, they fill it〔人〕挤进某地, 挤满某地: *Thousands of people crammed into the stadium to see the final game.* 成千上万的人挤进体育场看决赛。**3 a)** [I] to prepare yourself for an examination by learning a lot of information very quickly〔为考试而〕死记硬背, 临时抱佛脚; SWOT² *BrE*【英】: *I've been cramming hard all week.* 我整个星期都在刻苦准备考试。| [+for] *He'd crammed for the test until four in the morning.* 他为准备

考试临急抱佛脚地一直复习到凌晨4点。**b)** [T] *BrE* to help someone prepare for an examination by cramming【英】〔为考试而〕填鸭式地教〔某人〕: *The college is cramming the students hard for the summer exams.* 该学院填鸭式地给学生拼命灌输知识，准备夏季考试。

crammed /kræmd; kræmd/ *adj* **crammed with/crammed full of** completely full of things or people 填满的，塞满的: *monthly reports crammed full of information* 信息丰富的每月报告

cram·mer /ˈkræmɚ; ˈkræmə/ *n* [C] *BrE* a special school that prepares people quickly for examinations【英】〔为应付考试的〕强化知识的补习学校

cramp¹ /kræmp; kræmp/ *n* **1** [C,U] a severe pain that you get in part of your body when a muscle becomes too tight, making it difficult for you to move that part of your body 痉挛；痛性痉挛，抽筋: *I woke up in the middle of the night with cramp in my leg.* 因为腿抽筋我半夜醒了。| **have/get cramp** *BrE*【英】**have/get a cramp** *AmE*【美】*The swimmer got a cramp and had to quit the race.* 该游泳运动员因抽筋不得不退出比赛。—see also 另见 WRITER'S CRAMP **2 cramps** [plural] *especially AmE* severe pains in the stomach, especially the ones that women get during MENSTRUATION【尤美】(腹) 绞痛〔尤指妇女痛经〕

cramp² *v* [T] **1** to prevent the development of someone's ability to do something 限制〔某人的能力〕；约束: *Her education was cramped by lack of money.* 由于缺钱她没受过良好教育。**2 cramp sb's style** to prevent someone from doing something they want to do, especially by going with them when they do not want you 不让某人做某事: *He left Helen in the ski lodge. He didn't want anyone cramping his style on the slopes.* 他把海伦留在滑雪区旅馆内，因为他不想有人在斜坡地上妨碍他。

cramped /kræmpt; kræmpt/ *adj* **1** a cramped room, building etc does not have enough space for the people in it 狭窄的: *I couldn't sleep on the plane, it was too cramped.* 我在飞机上睡不着，座位之间太狭窄了。| *cramped living conditions* 拥挤的居住条件 | *cramped offices* 狭小的办公室 **2** also 又作 **cramped up** unable to move properly and uncomfortable because there is not enough space〔活动〕受限制的；拥挤的: *We all felt stiff from having been cramped up in the back of the car for so long.* 挤在汽车的后面老半天，我们都感到浑身僵硬了。**3** writing that is cramped is very small and difficult to read〔字迹〕挤在一起难辨认的

cram·pon /ˈkræmpɑn; ˈkræmpɒn/ *n* [C usually plural 一般用复数] a piece of metal with sharp points on the bottom that you fasten onto your boots to help in mountain climbing in the snow〔登山鞋底上的〕防滑铁钉

cran·ber·ry /ˈkræn,bɛrɪ; ˈkrænbəri/ *n* [C] a small red sour fruit 越橘: *cranberry sauce* 越橘酱 —see picture on page A8 参见A8页图

crane¹ /kren; kreɪn/ *n* [C] **1** a large tall machine used by builders for lifting heavy things 起重机，吊车 **2** a tall water bird with very long legs 鹤

crane² *v* [I always+adv/prep, T] to look around or over something by stretching or leaning 伸长(脖子)看；探头看: *The children craned forward to see what was happening.* 孩子们伸长脖子向前看发生了什么事。| **crane your neck** *Everyone on the bus craned their necks out of the windows and stared at them.* 公共汽车上所有的人都从车窗里面伸出脖子盯着他们看。

Crane, Ich·a·bod /ˈɪkəbɑd; ˈɪkəbɒd/ the main character in the story *The Legend of Sleepy Hollow* by Washington Irving. He is chased by the Headless Horseman. 克莱恩〔华盛顿·欧文创作的小说《睡谷的传说》中的主人公，他被无头骑士追逐〕

crane fly /ˈ· ·/ *n* [C] a flying insect with long legs 大蚊; DADDY LONGLEGS (1) *BrE*【英】

cra·ni·um /ˈkrenɪəm; ˈkreɪniəm/ *n* [C] *technical* the part of your head that is made of bone and covers your brain【术语】头盖骨，颅骨

crank¹ /kræŋk; kræŋk/ *n* [C] **1** *informal* someone who has unusual ideas and behaves strangely【非正式】怪人: *I was treated like a troublemaker and a crank.* 我被看成是个惹是生非、想法古怪的人。| **crank caller/letters** *We get quite a few crank phone calls.* 我们接到很多古怪的电话。**2** *AmE informal* someone who easily gets angry or annoyed with people【美，非正式】脾气坏的人 **3** a piece of equipment with a handle that you can turn in order to move something 曲柄，曲轴

crank² also 又作 **crank up** *v* [T] **1** to make something move by turning a crank 用曲柄启动[转动]: *crank an engine* 用曲柄启动发动机 **2** *informal* to make music louder【非正式】增加〔音量〕: *Crank up the volume!* 把音量放大些!

crank sth **↔out** *phr v* [T] *informal especially AmE* to produce a lot of something very quickly【非正式，尤美】快速大量地制造: *He cranks out detective novels at the rate of three a year.* 他每年能写出三部侦探小说。

crank·shaft /ˈkræŋk,ʃæft; ˈkræŋkʃɑːft/ *n* [C] a long piece of metal in a vehicle that is connected to the engine and helps to turn the wheels〔汽车中与发动机连接的〕曲轴

crank·y /ˈkræŋkɪ; ˈkræŋki/ *adj* **1** bad-tempered 脾气坏的: *The baby's a little cranky this morning.* 今天早上宝宝脾气有点坏。**2** *BrE* having very strange ideas, or behaving strangely; ECCENTRIC¹ (1)【英】〔想法或行为〕古怪的: *She's just a cranky old woman.* 她确实是一个古怪的老太太。—**crankiness** *n* [U]

Cran·mer /ˈkrænmɚ; ˈkrænmə/, **Thom·as** (1489-1556) an English priest who was Archbishop of Canterbury, and who was one of the leaders of the REFORMATION (=the time when many Christians in Europe left the Catholic religion and started the Protestant religion) in England. When the Catholic Mary I became Queen of England, she ordered Cranmer to be killed by being burned. 克兰麦〔(1489-1556)，英国坎特伯雷大主教、宗教改革运动领袖之一。信仰天主教的玛丽一世成为英国女王之后，下令将他处以火刑〕

cran·ny /ˈkrænɪ; ˈkræni/ *n* [C] a small narrow hole in a wall or rock〔墙或岩石上的〕裂缝，缝隙: *The toad hid itself in a cranny in the wall.* 蟾蜍躲藏在墙缝里。—see also 另见 **nook and cranny** (NOOK (3))—**crannied** *adj*

crap¹ /kræp; kræp/ *n slang*【俚】**1** [U] something someone says that you think is completely wrong or untrue 废话，胡扯: *Jane doesn't really think we believe all that crap, does she?* 简不是真的认为我们会相信所有那些废话，对吗？| **be full of crap** (=often say things that are untrue or completely wrong) 满口谎言，全是废话 *We all knew Mark was full of crap, but we still had to listen to him.* 我们都知道马克说的全是废话，但是仍不得不听他说。| **cut the crap** (=used to tell someone to stop saying things that are completely wrong or untrue) 别说废话了 **2 be a load of crap** also 又作 **be a bunch of crap** *AmE*【美】to be very bad, or completely untrue 糟透了；一派胡言: *That new comedy last night was a load of crap, I thought.* 我认为昨晚的新喜剧全是胡闹。**3** [U] things that are useless or unimportant 废物: *What is all this crap doing on my desk?* 我桌上的这些破玩意儿都是些什么？**4** [singular] solid waste that is passed from your bowels 排泄物，粪便，屎; **have/take a crap** (=to pass solid waste from the BOWELS) 排便 **5 not take crap from someone** to refuse to allow someone to treat you badly or to say something unfair to you 不允许某人待自己不好[对自己说不公正的话]: *I don't have to take that crap from her – I'm leaving!* 我不必受她的气，我要走了！**6 I don't need this (kind of) crap** used when you are angry at the way someone is talking or behaving to you 少来这一套 **7 craps** [plural] *AmE* a game played for money in the US, using two DICE¹ (1)【美】双骰子赌博游戏: **shoot craps** (=play this game) 玩双骰子赌博游戏

crap² *adj slang* of very bad quality【俚】质量极糟的: *Everyone knows those cars are crap!* 大家都知道那些汽车都是蹩脚货！

crap³ *v* **crapped, crapping** [I] *spoken taboo* to pass waste matter from the bowels【口讳】拉屎

crape /krep; kreɪp/ *n* [U] **1** CREPE (1) 绉纱，绉绸，绉呢 **2** black material that people wore in former times as a sign of their sadness when someone died〔旧时〕表示哀悼的黑纱

crap·per /ˈkræpɚ; ˈkræpə/ *n* **the crapper** *BrE slang* a rude word meaning the toilet【英俚】厕所

crap·py /ˈkræpɪ; ˈkræpi/ *adj spoken slang* not very good【口俚】差的，不好的: *We arrived late and ended up staying in a crappy hotel.* 我们来晚了，结果只能住在一家很差的旅馆里。

crash¹ /kræʃ; kræʃ/ *v*

1 ▶CAR/PLANE ETC 汽车/飞机等◀ [I,T] to have an accident in a car, plane etc by violently hitting another vehicle or something such as a wall or tree (使)〔飞机、汽车等〕坠毁，撞坏: *The DC10 crashed shortly after take-off.* 那架DC10飞机起飞后不久就坠毁了。| [+into/onto etc] *The car crashed straight into a tree.* 这辆车直撞到了树上。| **crash a car/bus/plane etc** *Rick crashed his bike before he'd finished paying for it.* 里克还没有付清买那辆自行车的钱就把它撞坏了。

2 ▶HIT STH/SB HARD 重击某物/某人◀ [I always+adv/prep, T always +adv/prep] to hit something or someone extremely hard while you are moving, causing a lot of damage, or making a lot of noise〔哗啦啦地〕猛撞，猛击: [+into/through etc] *The ladder came crashing through the window.* 梯子哗啦一声就把玻璃窗撞碎了。| **crash sth down** *Rod's face went bright red and he crashed his fist down on the table.* 罗德的脸涨得通红，啪的一拳打在桌子上。| **go crashing into** *He lost his balance on the ice and went crashing into the crowd.* 他在冰上失去平

衝，撞入人群。| **come crashing down** *A branch came crashing down onto the greenhouse.* 一根树枝哗啦一声掉在温室上。

3 ►MAKE A LOUD NOISE 发出巨响◄[I] to make a sudden, loud noise 发出巨响: *The cymbals crashed, and the symphony came to an end.* 铙钹发出巨响，交响曲结束了。—see picture on page A19 参见 A19 页图

4 ►SLEEP 睡觉◄also 又作 **crash out** [I] *spoken* 【口】 **a)** to go to bed, or go to sleep very quickly, especially because you are very tired〔尤指由于很疲倦〕很快入睡: *I was so tired last night, I got home and just crashed out on the sofa.* 昨天晚上我太累了，回到家在沙发上就很快睡着了。**b)** to stay at someone's house for the night, especially when you have not planned to〔尤指事先没有准备而留在别人家里〕过夜: *Can I crash at your place on Saturday night?* 星期六晚上我能在你那儿过夜吗？

5 ►COMPUTER 电脑◄[I,T] if a computer crashes or you crash the computer, it suddenly stops working〔电脑〕瘫痪: *The system crashed at nine this morning, so we haven't been able to do anything.* 今天上午9点系统瘫痪了，因此我们什么也做不了。

6 ►FINANCIAL 金融◄[I] if a STOCK MARKET crashes, the stocks (STOCK¹ (3a)) suddenly lose a lot of value〔股票〕狂跌

7 ►PARTY 聚会◄[T] *informal* to go to a party that you have not been invited to【非正式】不请自来〔参加聚会〕: *She crashes parties all the time even though she always gets thrown out.* 尽管总是被赶出去，她还是常常不请自来地参加聚会。

8 crashing bore *BrE old-fashioned* someone who is very boring【英，过时】令人厌烦的人

3 **crash²** *n* [C] **1** a violent accident involving one or more vehicles〔汽车的〕撞车事故；〔飞机的〕失事: **plane/car etc crash** *41 people were killed in a plane crash in the Himalayas last week.* 上周喜马拉雅山的飞机失事中有41人丧生。**2** a sudden loud noise made by something falling, breaking etc 突然发出的巨响；〔东西倒下、打破等时发出的〕碰撞声: [**+of**] *Jessica heard the crash of breaking glass behind her.* 杰茜卡听到身后有玻璃被打碎的声音。| **with a crash** *There was a loud crack and the branch came down with a crash.* 伴随着巨大的断裂声，树枝啪的一声掉下来。**3** a sudden, unexpected failing of a computer or computer system〔电脑或电脑系统的〕瘫痪，失效，死机 **4** an occasion on which the stocks (STOCK¹ (3a)) in a STOCK MARKET suddenly lose a lot of value〔股票的〕狂跌: *Nobody was prepared for the crash on Black Monday in 1987.* 1987年黑色星期一的股票狂跌使所有的人都措手不及。

crash bar·ri·er /ˈ· ,··/ *n* [C] *BrE* a strong fence or wall built to keep cars apart or to keep them away from people, in order to prevent an accident【英】防撞护栏

crash course /ˈ· ·/ *n* [C] a course in which you learn the most important things about a particular subject in a very short period of time 速成班: [**+in**] *a crash course in Spanish* 西班牙语速成班

crash di·et /ˈ· ,··/ *n* [C] an attempt that someone makes to lose a lot of weight in a very short period of time 快速减肥

crash-dive /ˈ· ·/ *v* [I] if a SUBMARINE¹ crash-dives, it sinks quickly to a great depth〔潜水艇〕紧急下潜

crash hel·met /ˈ· ,··/ *n* [C] a very strong hat that covers your whole head, worn by racing car drivers, motorcyclists etc〔赛车手、摩托车手等戴的〕防护头盔，安全帽 —see picture at 参见 HELMET 图

crash-land /ˈ· ·/ *v* [I,T] to crash a plane in a controlled way because it is damaged and cannot be flown any more（使）〔飞机〕强行着陆；紧急降落

crass /kræs; kræs/ *adj* behaving in a way that shows you do not understand other people's feelings, or care about them 愚笨的，粗鲁的；冷酷的: *crass stupidity* 极端愚蠢的 | *a crass commercial adventure* 愚蠢的商业冒险 —**crassly** *adv*

-crat /kræt; kræt/ *suffix* [in nouns 构成名词] another form of the suffix -OCRAT 后缀 -ocrat 的另一种形式

Crat·chit /ˈkrætʃɪt; ˈkrætʃɪt/, **Bob** a character in the book *A Christmas Carol* by Charles Dickens. Bob Cratchit is a kind poor man who has to work very hard for his employer, Scrooge. He has a young son, **Tiny Tim**, who is very ill and cannot walk. 克拉奇特〔查尔斯·狄更斯创作的《圣诞颂歌》中的人物。他是一位心地善良的穷人，不得不替雇主斯克鲁奇卖苦力。他有个年幼的儿子，名叫小蒂姆，病得连路都走不了〕

crate¹ /kret; kreɪt/ also 又作 **crate up** *v* [T] to pack things into a crate 把…装入货箱

crate² *n* [C] **1** a box made of wood or plastic that is used for carrying fruit, bottles etc 板条箱；装货箱: *They lifted the crates onto the wagon.* 他们把箱子搬到运货车上。—see picture at 参见 CONTAINER 图 **2** *old-fashioned* a very old car or plane that does not work very well【过时】破旧的汽车[飞机]

cra·ter /ˈkretɚ; ˈkreɪtə/ *n* [C] **1** the round open part of a VOLCANO 火山口 **2** a round hole in the ground, especially made by an explosion or by something that has fallen from the sky〔尤指炸弹爆炸、流星坠落等在地上造成的〕坑: *the craters on the moon* 月球上的环形山

cra·vat /krəˈvæt; krəˈvæt/ *n* [C] a wide piece of loosely folded material that men wear around their necks〔男人戴的〕领巾 —compare 比较 TIE² (1)

crave /krev; kreɪv/ *v* **1** [T] to have an extremely strong desire for something, especially a drug 渴望，热望: *She's an insecure child who craves attention.* 她是个患得患失的孩子，渴望受到关注。**2** *formal* to ask seriously for something【正式】恳求；请求: *May I crave your pardon?* 你能原谅我吗？

cra·ven /ˈkrevən; ˈkreɪvən/ *adj formal* completely lacking courage; COWARDLY【正式】懦弱的，胆小的: *You craven coward.* 你这个胆小鬼。—**cravenly** *adv* —**cravenness** *n* [U]

crav·ing /ˈkrevɪŋ; ˈkreɪvɪŋ/ *n* [C] an extremely strong desire for something 渴望，热望: [**+for**] *a craving for some chocolate* 想吃巧克力的渴望

craw /krɔ; krɔː/ *n* [C] *AmE*【美】—see 见 **stick in your craw** (STICK¹ (12))

craw·dad /ˈkrɔ,dæd; ˈkrɔːdæd/ *n* [C] *AmE informal* a small animal like a LOBSTER that lives in rivers and streams; CRAYFISH【美，非正式】淡水螯虾

Craw·ford /ˈkrɑfɚd; ˈkrɔːfəd/, **Joan** /dʒon; dʒəʊn/ (1904-77) one of America's most famous film actresses, who usually appeared as characters who were very brave and determined, but often also very unhappy. Her films include *Mildred Pierce* (1945) and *Whatever Happened to Baby Jane?* (1962). 克劳福德〔(1904-1977)，美国最著名的电影女演员之一。她通常饰演勇敢无畏、意志坚定，但却很不快乐的角色。她出演的影片有《米尔德里德·皮尔斯》(1945) 和《婴儿简出了什么事?》(1962)〕

crawl¹ /krɔl; krɔːl/ *v* [I]

1 ►MOVE ON HANDS AND KNEES 爬行◄to move along on your hands and knees with your body close to the ground 爬，爬行: [**+along/across etc**] *She suddenly got down and crawled along behind the wall so that Carl wouldn't see her.* 她突然蹲下来，在墙后爬行，这样卡尔就看不到她了。| *Is your baby crawling yet?* 你的宝宝会爬了吗？—see picture at 参见 KNEEL 图

2 ►INSECT 昆虫◄if an insect crawls, it moves using its legs〔昆虫〕爬: [**+over/up etc**] *Watch out! There's a wasp crawling up your leg.* 小心！你的腿上有一只黄蜂在往上爬。

3 ►CARS ETC 汽车等◄if a vehicle crawls, it moves forward very slowly〔汽车〕缓慢移动: [**+by/along etc**] *The traffic was crawling by at 5 miles an hour.* 路上的车以每小时5英里的速度缓慢行驶。

4 ►TOO HELPFUL 奉承的◄to be too pleasant or helpful to someone in authority, especially because you want them to help you 巴结，奉承: **crawl to sb** *Just look at Janice – crawling to the director of studies again!* 看看贾妮丝，她又在讨好教学主任了！

5 be crawling with to be completely covered with insects, people etc 爬满〔虫子〕；挤满〔人〕: *Eugh! This floor is crawling with ants.* 哎哟！地板上爬满了蚂蚁。

6 make your skin crawl if something or someone makes your skin crawl, you think they are extremely unpleasant 使感觉不舒服；使恶心: *The way Jonathan looks at her really makes my skin crawl.* 乔纳森看她的样子真使我恶心。

crawl² *n* [singular] **1** a very slow speed 缓慢移动，徐行: *The traffic had slowed down to a crawl.* 车辆慢了下来，成了爬行。**2** a fast way of swimming in which you lie on your stomach and move one arm and then the other over your head 自由泳；爬泳

crawl·er lane /ˈ·· ,·/ *n* [C] *BrE* a special part of a road that can be used by slow vehicles so that other vehicles can go past【英】〔车辆的〕慢行道

cray·fish /ˈkre,fɪʃ; ˈkreɪ,fɪʃ/ *n* [C,U] a small animal like a LOBSTER that lives in rivers and streams, or the flesh of this animal eaten as food 淡水螯虾（肉）

Cray·o·la /kreˈolə; kreɪˈəʊlə/ *trademark* a company that makes coloured CRAYONS and other art materials for children, such as coloured pens and paints【商标】千色乐〔美国的一家公司，制造儿童用彩色蜡笔、彩色画笔、颜料等绘画用品〕

cray·on¹ /ˈkreən; ˈkreɪən/ *n* [C] a stick of coloured WAX¹(1) or CHALK¹ (2) used for writing or drawing, especially on paper 彩色蜡笔[粉笔]: *children's crayons* 儿童彩色蜡笔

crayon² *v* [I,T] to draw with a crayon 用彩色蜡笔[粉笔]画画

craze /krez; kreɪz/ *n* [C] a fashion, game, type of music etc that suddenly becomes very popular but usually only remains popular for a very short time 时尚；时髦的东西: *This computer game is the latest craze.* 这种电脑游戏是最新时尚。

crazed /krezd; kreɪzd/ *adj* behaving in a wild and uncontrolled way as if you are crazy 疯狂的, 狂野的: *a crazed expression* 疯狂的表情 | [+with] *He was crazed with grief.* 他伤心得发疯。

cra·zy¹ /ˈkrezɪ; ˈkreɪzi/ *adj informal*【非正式】
1 ▶STRANGE 奇怪的◀ behaving in a way that is very strange〔行为〕古怪的: *Don't mind her, she's crazy.* 不要管她, 她很古怪。| *The neighbours must think we're crazy.* 邻居们一定会认为我们很古怪。| *You have some crazy friends.* 你有些古怪的朋友。
2 ▶NOT SENSIBLE 不理智的◀ an action or behaviour that is crazy is not sensible and likely to cause problems〔行动或行为〕愚蠢的, 愚笨的: **it's crazy** *spoken*【口】: *I get more money if I don't work – it's crazy.* 不工作时我的收入反而更多——真是荒唐。| *That's the craziest idea I've ever heard.* 这是我所听到的最荒谬的想法。| **be crazy to do sth** *It'd be crazy to try and drive home in this weather.* 这种天气想驾车回家简直是发疯。
3 ▶ANGRY 生气的◀ angry or annoyed 生气的; 烦恼的: **drive sb crazy** (=make sb angry or annoyed) 让人生气[烦恼] *Turn that music down, it's driving me crazy!* 把音乐调小点, 实在叫我心烦!
4 be crazy about sb/sth to like someone very much, or be very interested in something 对〔某人〕着迷; 醉心于〔某物〕: *Frank is just crazy about you!* 弗兰克对你很着迷!
5 like crazy very quickly or very hard 极快地; 拼命地: *We're going to have to work like crazy to get this finished on time.* 为了按时完成工作, 我们要拼命干。
6 ▶ILL 生病的◀ mentally ill 疯狂的, 发疯的: *He lived alone and they were sure he was crazy.* 他一人独居, 他们确信他已经疯了。| **go crazy** *Kurtz had gone crazy, alone in the jungle.* 库尔茨发疯了, 独自一人在丛林里。
7 crazy as a loon *AmE informal* very strange and possibly mentally ill【美, 非正式】想法怪异的; 疯疯癫癫的 —**crazily** *adv* —**craziness** *n* [U]

crazy² *n* [C] *AmE informal* someone who is crazy【美, 非正式】疯子

crazy golf /ˌ‥ ˈ·/ *n* [U] *BrE* a game like GOLF in which the players hit the ball through various amusing OBSTACLES【英】滑稽高尔夫球运动; MINIATURE GOLF *AmE*【美】

Crazy Horse /ˌ‥ ˈ·/ (?1842-77) a Native American chief of the Sioux tribe who united his people and helped Sitting Bull to win a victory over General Custer's army in the famous battle at the Little Bighorn 疯马〔(?1842-1877) 美国苏族印第安人部落酋长。在小比格霍恩河这场著名战役中, 他组织族人援助"坐牛"打败了卡斯特将军率领的军队〕

crazy pav·ing /ˌ‥ ˈ‥/ *n* [U] *especially BrE* pieces of stone of different shapes fitted together to make a path or flat place【尤英】〔用形状不规则的石块拼铺的〕碎纹石路

crazy quilt /ˌ‥ ˈ·/ *n* [C] *AmE* a cover for a bed made from small pieces of cloth of different shapes that have been sewn together【美】百衲被, 碎布床单

creak¹ /krik; kriːk/ *v* [I] if something such as a door, bed, stair etc creaks, it makes a long high noise when someone opens it, sits on it, walks on it etc〔门、床、楼梯等〕嘎吱作响: *The window shutters creaked in the wind.* 百叶窗在风中嘎吱作响。

creak² *n* [C] the sound made by something when it creaks 吱吱嘎嘎的声音: [+of] *the creak of a door* 门的吱吱嘎嘎声

creak·y /ˈkrikɪ; ˈkriːki/ *adj* something such as a chair, bed etc that is creaky creaks when you sit on it, stand on it etc〔椅子、床等〕嘎吱作响的 —**creakily** *adv* —**creakiness** *n* [U]

cream¹ /krim; kriːm/ *n* [U] **1** a thick yellowish-white liquid that rises to the top of milk 奶油, 乳脂: *Have some cream in your coffee.* 在你的咖啡中加些奶油吧。| *strawberries and cream* 浇奶油的草莓 **2** [C,U] a food containing this 含奶油食品: *cream of chicken soup* 奶油鸡汤 | *cream cakes* 奶油蛋糕 **3** [C,U] a thick soft substance that you put on your skin in order to make it soft, treat a medical condition etc 护肤霜, 雪花膏: *Put some sun cream on before you go out.* 出去以前涂上一些防晒霜。**4 the cream of** the cream of a group of people are the best people in that group 精华, 精英: *a team representing the cream of Britain's young athletes* 代表英国优秀年轻运动员的运动队

cream² *adj* yellowish-white in colour 奶油色的, 淡黄色的: *a cream coloured carpet* 奶黄色的地毯 —**cream** *n* [U] —see picture on page A5 参见 A5 页图

cream³ *v* [T] **1** to make something into a thick soft mixture 使成奶油状: *Cream the butter and sugar together.* 把黄油和糖调成奶油状。| *creamed potatoes* 马铃薯泥 **2** to take cream from the surface of milk 从牛奶中提取奶油 **3** *AmE informal* to defeat someone completely【美, 非正式】彻底打败

cream sb/sth **off** *phr v* [T] to choose the best people or things from a group, especially so that you can use them for your own advantage 提取〔精华〕: *We cream off the best athletes and put them into a special squad.* 我们挑选最好的运动员送到特殊训练队去。

cream cheese /ˌ· ˈ·/ *n* [U] a type of soft white smooth cheese 奶油干酪

cream crack·er /ˌ· ˈ‥/ *n* [C] *BrE* a light BISCUIT (1) often eaten with cheese【英】奶油薄脆饼干

cream·er /ˈkrimə·; ˈkriːmə/ *n* **1** [U] a liquid that you can use instead of cream in drinks 代奶油, 植脂末 **2** [C] a small container for holding cream 小奶油壶

cream·e·ry /ˈkrimərɪ; ˈkriːməri/ *n* [C] *old-fashioned* a place where milk, butter, cream, and cheese are produced or sold【过时】乳制品厂; 乳制品商店

cream·y /ˈkrimɪ; ˈkriːmi/ *adj* **1** containing cream 含乳脂的; 含奶油的: *creamy milk* 含脂牛奶 **2** thick smooth and soft like cream 似奶油的; 软厚平滑的, 光滑细软的: *This make-up has a lovely creamy consistency.* 这种化妆品的质地像奶油一样柔滑。**3** yellowish-white in colour 奶油色的, 淡黄色的

crease¹ /kris; kriːs/ *n* **1** [C] a line on cloth, paper etc, made by folding, crushing or pressing it〔衣服、纸等的〕褶痕, 皱褶: *You've got a crease in your dress where you've been sitting.* 你的连衣裙坐过的地方起皱了。| *I can never get the creases straight in these trousers.* 我怎么也无法把裤子上的皱褶烫平。**2** [singular] the line where the player has to stand to hit the ball in CRICKET (2)〔板球场上击球手站在上面的〕区域线, 击球线

crease² *v* [I,T] to become marked with a line or lines, or to make a line appear on cloth, paper etc by folding or crushing it 使起皱褶; 使起皱: *Don't sit on my paper, you'll crease it!* 不要坐在我的卷子上, 你会把它弄皱的! | *This material creases really easily.* 这种材料很容易起皱。

crease (sb) up *phr v* [I,T] *BrE spoken* to laugh or make someone laugh a lot【英口】(使)〔某人〕大笑: *That guy really creases me up!* 那个人使我笑得直不起腰!

creased /krist; kriːst/ *adj* cloth or paper that is creased has a line or lines on it because it has been folded or crushed 有皱的, 有皱褶的: *She wanted to wear her black dress but it was too creased.* 她想穿她那件黑色连衣裙, 但是皱得太厉害。

cre·ate /krɪˈet; kriˈeɪt/ *v* **1** [T] to make something exist that did not exist before 创造; 创建: *Her behaviour is creating a lot of problems.* 她的行为引起了很多的麻烦。| *Government promises to create more public sector jobs.* 政府承诺在公共部门创造更多的职位。**2** [T] to invent something 发明; 创作: *The writer creates his own special language.* 这个作家创作出自己独特的语言。| [+by] *This dish was created by our chef Jean Richard.* 这道菜是由我们的厨师琼·理查德创制的。**3 create sb/sth** *BrE* to officially give someone special rank or title【英】封爵; 任命; 授予: *James I created him Duke of Buckingham.* 詹姆斯一世封他为白金汉公爵。**4** [I] *BrE old-fashioned* to be noisily angry【英, 过时】大喊大叫; 大发雷霆: *Don't tell Grandad – he'll only start creating.* 不要告诉爷爷, 他只会大发雷霆。

cre·a·tion /krɪˈeʃən; kriˈeɪʃən/ *n* **1** [U] the act of creating something 创造; 创建: [+of] *The report proposed the creation of an independent Scottish parliament.* 该报告建议成立一个独立的苏格兰议会。| *a job-creation scheme* 创造就业机会的计划 **2** [C] something that has been created 创造物; 作品; 产物: *The story was a fanciful creation.* 该故事是个富有想象力的作品。| *this year's new fashion creations from Paris* 今年来自巴黎的新时装 **3** [U] the whole universe, and all living things 宇宙; 世界; 天地万物: *Are we the only thinking species in creation?* 我们是万物中唯一有思想的物种吗? **4 the Creation** the act by God, according to the Bible, of making the universe, including the world and everything in it〔《圣经》中的〕创世

CULTURAL NOTE 文化注释

Different societies and religions have different creation stories. The creation story of Christianity is found in the first part of the Bible in the book of Genesis. It says that God created the world and everything in it in six days, and on the seventh day God rested. When God made human beings, he made a man called Adam out of the earth, and then made a woman called Eve out of one of Adam's RIBS (=one of the curved bones that surround your chest). 不同社会和宗教有不同的创世故事。基督教的创世故事见于圣经的第一部分《创世记》, 讲到上帝在六天内创造世界和万物, 第七天休息。上帝造人时, 用泥土造了一个男人, 叫做亚当, 然后又用亚当的一根肋骨造了一个女人, 叫做夏娃。

Some Christians, called FUNDAMENTALISTs, believe that this is exactly how Creation happened, and do not believe in other scientific explanations of how the world and life began. In the US, fundamentalist Christians have been upset when the scientific idea of EVOLUTION has been taught in schools. In some states, they have influenced politicians, who have then said that schools must teach the Bible story of the Creation as well as the idea of evolution. 一些称为基要派的基督徒认为世界正是这样创造出来的，不相信关于世界和生命起源的其他科学解释。美国学校里开始讲授科学的进化论时，基要派十分不安。在一些州，他们影响政界人士，后者表示学校必须在教授进化论的同时也教授圣经的创世说。— compare 比较 EVOLUTION

cre·a·tion·ist /krɪˋeʃənɪst; kriˈeɪʃənɪst/ *n* [C] someone who believes that God created the universe in the way described in the Bible 创世论者 —**creationism** *n* [U]

cre·a·tive /krɪˋetɪv; kriˈeɪtɪv/ *adj* **1** producing or using new and effective ideas, results etc 创造（性）的: *He came up with a really creative solution to the problem.* 他想出了一个解决问题的方案，很有创造性。| *I enjoy my job, but I'd like to do something more creative.* 我很喜欢我的工作，但我想做些更具创造性的工作。**2** someone who is creative is very imaginative and good at making things, painting etc 〔人〕有创造力的: *You're so creative! – I could never make my own clothes.* 你真有创造力！我从来不会给自己做衣服。—**creatively** *adv* —**creativeness** *n* [U] —**creativity** /ˌkrieˋtɪvətɪ; ˌkriːeɪˈtɪvɪti/ *n* [U]

creative ac·count·ing /ˌ· ·ˈ··/ *n* [U] the act of changing business accounts to achieve the result you want in a way that hides the truth but is not illegal 创造性会计〔指伪造账目〕

cre·a·tor /krɪˋetə; kriˈeɪtə/ *n* [C] **1** someone who made or invented a particular thing 创作者; 创造者: *Walt Disney, the creator of Mickey Mouse* 米老鼠的创造者沃尔特·迪斯尼 **2 the Creator** God 上帝, 造物主

crea·ture /ˋkritʃə; ˈkriːtʃə/ *n* [C]

1 ▶**LIVING THING** 生物◀ anything that is living, but not a plant 动物: *The crocodile is a strange-looking creature.* 鳄鱼是一种样子古怪的动物。| **living creature** *He has great respect for all living creatures.* 他对所有的生物都很尊重。

2 ▶**STRANGE** 奇怪的◀ a strange and sometimes frightening living thing 不可名状的生物, 怪物: *creatures from outer space* 来自外太空的怪物

3 stupid/adorable/horrid etc creature someone who has a particular character or quality 愚蠢/可爱/可怕等的人: *"Lady Jones is a charming creature", he sighed.* "琼斯夫人是个尤物。"他赞叹说。

4 ▶**SB CONTROLLED BY STH** 受某物控制的某人◀ someone who is controlled by, or completely in the power of a particular person or organization 受支配的人, 傀儡, 奴才: [+of] *He was a creature of the military government.* 他是军政府的傀儡。

5 a creature of habit someone who always does things in the same way or at the same times 墨守成规的人

6 ▶**STH MADE OR INVENTED** 制造或发明的东西◀ something, especially something bad, that has been made or invented by a particular person or organization 创造物〔尤指不好的东西〕; 产物

creature com·forts /ˌ·· ˈ··/ *n* [plural] all the things that make life more comfortable and enjoyable such as good food, a warm house etc 给肉体舒适感的东西; 物质享受

crè·che /kreʃ; kreʃ/ *n* [C] **1** *BrE* a place where babies are looked after while their parents are at work【英】托儿所, 日托中心 —compare 比较 DAY CARE CENTRE (1) *AmE*【美】**2** *AmE* a model of the scene of Jesus' birth, often placed in churches and homes at Christmas【美】基督诞生情景的模型〔圣诞节时在教堂或家里陈列〕; CRIB[1](3) *BrE*【英】

cre·dence /ˋkridṇs; ˈkriːdəns/ *n* [U] *formal* the acceptance of something as true【正式】相信; 信任: *The amount of credence accorded to written records will undoubtedly vary.* 对书面记录的信任度肯定会不一样。| **gain credence** (=to become more widely accepted or believed) 得到认可; 获得信任 *This doctrine gained credence in academic circles over the next few decades.* 在接下来的几十年里这一学说得到了学术界的认可。| **give credence to sth** (=to believe or accept something as true) 相信某事 *I don't give any credence to these rumors.* 我不相信这些谣言。| **lend credence to sth** (=to make something more believable) 〔提供佐证〕使某事更可信

cre·den·tials /krɪˋdɛnʃəlz; krɪˈdenʃəlz/ *n* [plural] **1** the things that show people that you have the ability to do something, are suitable for something etc, such as your education, experience, and achievements 资格; 资格的证明: *He spent the first hour trying to establish his credentials as a financial expert.* 第一个小时他设法证明自己是金融专家。**2** a letter or other document which proves your good character or your right to have a particular position 资格证书;〔品格的〕证明信, 推荐书: *The commissioner presented his credentials to the State Department.* 委员向国务院递交了资格证书。

cred·i·bil·i·ty /ˌkrɛdəˋbɪlətɪ; ˌkredɪˈbɪlɪti/ *n* [U] **1** the quality of deserving to be believed and trusted 可靠性; 可信性: *This latest scandal has damaged his credibility as a leader.* 最近的丑闻破坏了他作为领导人的可信度。| [+of] *There are serious questions about the credibility of these reports.* 这些报告的可靠性有很多重大疑问。| **gain/lose credibility** *Predictions of economic recovery have now lost all credibility.* 经济复苏的预言现在已完全不可信。**2 credibility gap** the difference between what someone, especially a politician, says and what people can believe 信用差距〔尤指政治家的言论和公众对他的信任的差距〕

cred·i·ble /ˋkrɛdəbḷ; ˈkredɪbəl/ *adj* deserving or able to be believed or trusted 可信的, 可靠的: *a credible witness* 可信的目击者 —**credibly** *adv*

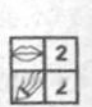

cred·it[1] /ˋkrɛdɪt; ˈkredɪt/ *n*

1 ▶**DELAYED PAYMENT** 推迟付款◀ [U] an arrangement with a shop, bank etc that makes it possible for you to buy something and pay for it later 赊购: **on credit** (=bought using this arrangement) 赊购, 记账 *stores that sell goods on credit* 可赊购商品的商店 | **interest-free credit** (=credit with no additional charge) 无息赊购 —compare 比较 DEBIT[1] (2)

2 ▶**PRAISE** 赞扬◀ [U] approval or praise that you give to someone for something they have done 赞扬; 赞许: **give (sb) credit (for sth)** *You could at least give him some credit for all the effort he's put in.* 你至少应该对他所作的所有努力给予赞扬。| **take/claim/deserve etc (the) credit** *Sam never once accepted all the credit for himself.* 萨姆从来没有把一切归功于自己。| **to sb's credit** (=making someone deserve praise or admiration) 值得赞扬[钦佩] *It is much to her credit that Joy persevered in spite of all the difficulties.* 尽管有那么多的困难, 乔伊还是挺住了, 值得赞扬。

3 be a credit to sb/sth also 又作 **do sb/sth credit** to behave so well or be so successful that everyone who is connected with you can be proud of you 为…增光: *She's a credit to the team.* 她为队里增了光。| *Your children really do you credit.* 你的孩子们真为你增光了。

4 have sth to your credit to have achieved something 成功: *She already has two successful novels to her credit.* 她已经写了两部很成功的小说。

5 be in credit to have money in your bank account 〔银行账户中〕有存款: *There are no bank charges if you stay in credit.* 只要你账户里有钱, 银行就不收费。

6 ▶**FILM** 电影◀ **the credits** [plural] the list of names of actors and other people involved shown at the beginning or end of a film or television programme 〔影片或电视节目的〕演员和摄制人员名单

7 on the credit side used to say that the things you are going to mention are the good or positive things about someone or something 好的方面; 正面: *On the credit side, the school has considerable success in sport and music.* 从好的方面来讲, 这所学校培养了很多体育和音乐人才。

8 ▶**UNIVERSITY** 大学◀ [C] a successfully completed part of a course at a university or college 学分: *The drama course should give me enough credits to finish my degree.* 戏剧课应使我得足够的学分以获得学位。

9 ▶**TRUE/CORRECT** 真的/正确的◀ [U] the belief that something is true or correct 信任

credit[2] *v* [T not in progressive 不用进行式] **1** to believe that something is true 信任; 相信: *He told me he'd just won first prize – would you credit it?* 他告诉我他刚得了头奖, 你信吗? | *I find that statement rather hard to credit.* 我觉得很难相信那个说法。**2** to add money to a bank account 把钱存入〔账户〕: [+to] *The cheque has been credited to your account.* 支票已转进你的账户了。—compare 比较 DEBIT[2] (1) **3 credit sb with sth** to believe that someone has a quality, or has done something good 相信某人有优点[做了好事]: *Do credit me with a little intelligence!* 我还是有点小聪明的, 请相信我! | *This symbol was credited with magical powers.* 这个符号被认为有魔力。**4 be credited to** if something is credited to someone or something, they have achieved it or are the reason for it 归功于…; …是某事发生的原因: *Much of their success can be credited to Wilson – an expert.* 他们的成功很大程度上归功于威尔逊——一位专家。

cred·i·ta·ble /ˋkrɛdɪtəbl; ˈkredɪ̣təbəl/ *adj* deserving praise or approval 值得赞扬的; 该称誉的: *a creditable piece of factual research* 值得称道的实况调查 | **a creditable performance** *Sue gave a very creditable performance as Lady Macbeth.* 休演麦克白夫人演得很出色。—**creditably** *adv*

credit ac·count /ˈ·· ·,·/ *n* [C] *BrE* an account with a shop which allows you to take goods and pay for them later【英】信用账户; 赊购账户; CHARGE ACCOUNT *AmE*【美】

credit card /ˈ·· ·/ *n* [C] a small plastic card that you use to buy goods or services 信用卡: *We accept all major credit cards.* 我们接受所有主要的信用卡。—compare 比较 CASH CARD, CHEQUE CARD, DEBIT CARD

credit freeze /ˈ·· ,·/ *n* [C] a period during which the government makes it more difficult for people to borrow money, to reduce the amount of money people spend 信用冻结

credit note /ˈ·· ·/ *n* [C] a document which a shop gives you when you return goods allowing you to exchange them for goods of the same value 换货凭证〔商店发出的凭证, 顾客可以据此把货物换作等价货物〕

cred·i·tor /ˋkrɛdɪtɚ; ˈkredɪ̣tə/ *n* [C] someone who money is owed to 债权人; 债主 —compare 比较 DEBTOR

credit rat·ing /ˈ·· ,··/ *n* [C] a judgement made by a financial institution about how likely a person or business is to pay their debts 信用等级, 信用评价

CULTURAL NOTE 文化注释

The credit rating of a business is based on its value and how successful it is. The ratings are done by companies whose business is to examine this type of information. Credit ratings for ordinary people are also done by special companies which examine whether people have paid back debts in the past, for example their MORTGAGE or CREDIT CARD bills. The biggest company that does this in the US is TRW. 评定一家公司的信用等级要根据其资产及业绩的情况。负责此项工作的是专门的信用审查公司, 专业公司也对普通人的信用等级进行评定, 核查他们过去是否偿还抵押贷款、信用卡等债务。美国最大的信用公司是汤普森-拉莫-伍尔德里奇公司 (TRW)。

credit voucher /ˈ·· ,··/ *n* [C] *AmE* a credit note【美】换货凭证

cred·it·wor·thy /ˋkrɛdɪt,wɝθɪ; ˈkredɪ̣t,wɜːθi/ *adj* considered to be able to repay debts 信用可靠的, 有还款能力的—**creditworthiness** *n* [U]

cre·do /ˋkrido; ˈkriːdəʊ/ *n* [C] a formal statement of the beliefs of a religion etc 教义; 信条

cre·du·li·ty /krəˋdulətɪ; krɪˈdjuːlɪ̣ti/ *n* [U] willingness or ability to believe that something is true 轻信, 易信: *childish credulity* 幼稚的轻信 | **strain/stretch credulity** *This explanation strained my credulity too far.* 我觉得这个解释太离谱。

cred·u·lous /ˋkrɛdʒələs; ˈkredjʊ̣ləs/ *adj* always believing what you are told, and therefore easily deceived 轻信的, 易上当的: *This man has coaxed millions of pounds from a credulous public.* 这个人从轻信的公众那里骗取了几百万英镑。—**credulously** *adv* —**credulousness** *n* [U]

creed /krid; kriːd/ *n* [C] **1** a set of beliefs or principles 信条, 教条: *the Marxist-Leninist creed* 马列主义信条 | *people of every creed* (=all different religious beliefs) 各种教派的人 **2 the Creed** a formal statement of belief spoken in certain Christian churches〔在某些基督教会中宣讲的〕教义

creek /krik; kriːk/ *n* [C] **1** *BrE* a long narrow area of water that flows from the sea, a river, or a lake into the land【英】〔通海、河或湖的〕小湾, 小港 **2** *AmE, AusE* a small narrow stream or river【美, 澳】小溪, 小河 **3 be up the creek** *spoken* to be in a difficult situation【口】处于困境: *If I don't get my passport by Friday, I'll be completely up the creek.* 如果到星期五还拿不到护照, 我就惨了。**4 be up shit creek (without a paddle)** *slang* an impolite way of saying that you are in serious trouble【俚】陷入严重困境, 倒了邪霉

creel /kril; kriːl/ *n* [C] a fisherman's basket for carrying fish 鱼篓, 鱼篮

creep¹ /krip; kriːp/ *v past tense and past participle* **crept** /krɛpt; krept/ [I always+adv/prep] **1** to move in a quiet, careful way, especially to avoid attracting attention 悄悄地小心行进: [+**into/over/around etc**] *Johann would creep into the gallery to listen to the singers.* 约翰会悄悄溜进楼座去听歌手唱歌。| *He crept back up the stairs, trying to avoid the ones that creaked.* 他蹑手蹑脚地回到楼上, 尽量避开会嘎吱嘎吱响的那几级楼梯。—see picture on page A24 参见 A24 页图 **2** if something such as an insect, small animal, or car creeps, it moves slowly and quietly 爬行, 匍匐: [+**down/along/away etc**] *a caterpillar creeping down my arm* 顺着我的胳膊慢慢爬下的毛毛虫 **3** to gradually enter something and change it 渐渐侵入, 逐渐融进: [+**in/into/over etc**] *Funny how religion is creeping into the environmental debate.* 很奇怪宗教怎么会融进环境辩论中去。**4** if a plant creeps it grows or climbs up or along a particular place〔植物〕攀缘, 蔓生: [+**up/over/around etc**] *ivy creeping up the walls of the building* 爬满了建筑物各面墙的常春藤 **5** if mist, clouds etc creep, they gradually fill or cover a place〔雾、云等〕弥漫: [+**into/over etc**] *Fog was creeping into the valley.* 雾飘进山谷。**6** *BrE informal* to be insincerely nice to someone, especially someone in authority, in order to gain an advantage for yourself【英, 非正式】卑躬屈膝, 巴结奉承: **creep (up) to sb** *I'm not the kind of person to creep to anybody.* 我不是那种巴结别人的人。**7 sb/sth makes my flesh creep** used to say that someone or something makes you feel strong dislike or fear 某人/某事物使我不舒服[恐惧]: *His glassy stare made my flesh creep.* 他那呆滞的凝视使我毛骨悚然。

creep up on sb/sth *phr v* [T] **1** to surprise someone by walking up behind them silently 蹑手蹑脚在后面走〔而吓人一跳〕: *Don't yell – let's creep up on them and scare them.* 别喊, 让我们悄悄从他们后面走过去吓他们一跳。**2** if a feeling or idea creeps up on you, it gradually increases〔感情或观点〕渐渐变强: *The feeling she had for Malcolm had crept up on her and taken her by surprise.* 她慢慢对马尔科姆产生了感情, 她自己也感到吃惊。**3** to seem to come sooner than you expect 不知不觉中到来: *Somehow, the end of term had crept up on us.* 不知不觉又到期末了。

creep² *n* **1** *informal especially AmE* someone who you dislike extremely【非正式, 尤美】极讨厌的人: *Get lost, you little creep!* 走开, 你这个讨厌鬼! **2** [C] *BrE informal* someone who tries to make you like them or do things for them by being insincerely nice to you【英, 非正式】献媚者; 奴颜婢膝的人: *Don't try and flatter her – she doesn't approve of creeps.* 别去奉承她, 她不喜欢拍马屁的家伙。**3 give sb the creeps** if a person or place gives you the creeps, they make you feel nervous and a little frightened, especially because they are strange〔人或地方〕使某人毛骨悚然[紧张]: *That house gives me the creeps.* 那栋房子使我毛骨悚然。

creep·er /ˋkripɚ; ˈkriːpə/ *n* [U] a plant that grows up trees or walls or along the ground 攀缘[匍匐]植物

creep·y /ˋkripɪ; ˈkriːpi/ *adj* making you feel nervous and slightly frightened 使人紧张的; 令人毛骨悚然的: *There's something creepy about the way he looks at me.* 他看我的样子使我有点紧张。| *a creepy old house* 令人毛骨悚然的老房子

creepy-crawl·y /,·· ˈ··/ *n* [C] *spoken especially BrE* an insect, especially one that you are frightened of【口, 尤英】令人讨厌的昆虫

cre·mate /ˋkrimet; krɪ̣ˈmeɪt/ *v* [T] to burn the body of a dead person at a funeral ceremony 火葬, 火化 —**cremation** /krɪˋmeʃən; krɪˈmeɪʃən/ *n* [C,U]

crem·a·to·ri·um /,kriməˋtorɪəm; ˌkreməˈtɔːriəm/**crem·a·to·ry** /ˋkrimə,torɪ; ˈkremətəri/ *especially AmE*【尤美】*n* [C] a building in which the bodies of dead people are burned at a funeral ceremony 火葬场

crème car·a·mel /,krɛm ˋkærəməl; ˌkrem ˈkærəməl/ *n* [C] a sweet food made from milk, eggs, and sugar 焦糖蛋奶

crème de la crème /,krɛm də lɑ ˋkrɛm; ˌkrem də lɑː ˈkrem/ *n* [singular] *French* the very best of a kind of thing or group of people【法】精华; 最优秀分子, 精英: *The chefs there are the crème de la crème of the culinary world.* 那里的厨师是厨艺界里最好的。

crème de menthe /,krɛm də ˋmɑnθ; ˌkrem də ˈmɒnθ/ *n* [U] a strong, sweet, green alcoholic drink 薄荷甜酒〔一种绿色的甜味烈酒〕

cren·el·lat·ed *BrE*【英】,**crenelated** *AmE*【美】/ˋkrɛnḷ,etɪd; ˈkrenəleɪtɪ̣d/ *adj technical* a wall or tower that is crenellated has BATTLEMENTS【术语】〔围墙或塔楼〕有雉堞的

cre·ole /ˋkriol; ˈkriːəʊl/ *n* **1** [C,U] a language that is a combination of a European language with one or more other languages 克里奥尔语〔一种欧洲语言和其他语言的混合语〕—compare 比较 PIDGIN **2** [C] someone descended from both Europeans and Africans 克里奥尔人〔欧洲和非洲的混血儿〕**3** [C] a white person born in the West Indies or parts of Spanish America, or descended from the original French settlers in the southern US 克里奥尔白人〔出生于西印度群岛或通用西班牙语的拉丁美洲部分地区的白人或美国南部法国移民的后裔〕**4** [U] food prepared in the hot strong-tasting style of the southern US〔美国南部的〕克里奥尔式辣味食品: *shrimp creole* 克里奥尔辣虾—**creole** *adj*

cre·o·sote /ˈkriə͵sot; ˈkriːəsəʊt/ *n* [U] a thick, brown, oily liquid used for preserving wood 杂酚油〔用于木材防护处理〕—**creosote** *v* [T]

crepe, crêpe /krep; kreɪp/ *n* **1** also 又作 **crape** [U] light, soft, thin cloth, with very small folded lines on the surface, made from cotton, silk, wool, etc. 绉纱, 绉绸, 绉呢 **2** [U] tightly pressed rubber used especially for making the bottoms of shoes〔尤用以制鞋底的〕绉橡胶: *crepe-soled shoes* 有绉胶底的鞋 **3** [C] a very thin PANCAKE (1) 薄煎饼

crepe pa·per /͵· ˈ··/ *n* [U] thin, brightly coloured paper with very small folded lines on the surface, especially used as decorations〔尤用于装饰的〕绉纸

crept /krɛpt; krept/ the past tense and past participle of CREEP[1]

cre·scen·do /krəˈʃɛndo; krȷ̈ˈʃendəʊ/ *n* [C] **1** a sound or a piece of music that becomes gradually louder〔声音或音乐的〕渐强: **rise to/reach a crescendo** (=to gradually become louder) 逐渐变响 *The violins had reached a crescendo.* 小提琴奏到了强音。| *Her voice rose to a crescendo.* 她的嗓音越来越响。—opposite 反义词 DIMINUENDO **2** a time when people are becoming more and more excited, anxious, or angry 高潮, 顶点: *A crescendo of resentment built up between the two women.* 这两个女人之间的愤恨达到了极点。| **rise to/reach a crescendo** *the clamour of telephones as the working day reached its crescendo of activity* 一天中工作最忙时的电话嘈杂声 —**crescendo** *adj*

cres·cent /ˈkrɛsn̩t; ˈkresənt/ *n* [C] **1** a curved shape, wider in the middle and pointed at the ends 新月形: **crescent moon/knife/biscuit etc** *A new crescent moon rose above the town.* 一弯新月升起在市镇上空。—see picture at 参见 SHAPE[1] 图 **2** the curved shape as a sign of the Muslim religion 新月〔伊斯兰教的象征〕**3** a word meaning a street with a curved shape, often used in the street's name 弯曲的街道〔常用作街名〕: *Turn left into Badgerly Crescent.* 向左拐进巴杰里曲街。

cress /krɛs; kres/ *n* [U] a small plant with round green leaves that can be eaten and has a slightly hot taste 水芹: *egg and cress sandwiches* 水芹鸡蛋三明治

Cres·si·da /ˈkrɛsɪdə; ˈkresɪdə/ also 又作 **Cresseid** /ˈkrɛsɪd; ˈkresɪd/ —see 见 TROILUS AND CRESSIDAS

crest¹ /krɛst; krest/ *n* **1** [C usually singular 一般用单数] the top or highest point of something such as a hill or a wave〔山〕顶;〔浪〕峰: [+of] *He climbed over the crest of the hill.* 他翻过了山顶。—see picture on page A12 参见 A12 页图 **2** [C] a special picture used as a sign of a family, town, school etc 徽章: *the school colours and crest* 学校的旗帜和徽章 | *the family crest on his notepaper* 他信笺上的家族饰章 **3** [C] a pointed group of feathers on top of a bird's head, or a raised area on the body of an animal 羽冠; 肉冠: *the dramatic feathery crest of the cockatoo* 凤头鹦鹉漂亮的羽冠 **4** [C] a decoration of bright feathers, worn, especially in former times, on top of soldiers' helmets (HELMET)〔昔日士兵的头盔上的〕羽饰 **5 be riding the crest of a wave** to be very successful, happy etc 走运; 无往不利: *The President is currently riding the crest of a wave of popularity.* 总统的声望目前已达到顶点。

crest² *v* **1** [T] to reach the top of a hill, mountain etc 到达〔山顶〕; 达到…的顶点: *They'd crested another ridge by the afternoon.* 到下午时他们爬上了另一个山顶。**2** [I] if a wave crests it reaches its highest point before it falls 形成波峰

Cres·ta Run, the /ˈkrɛstə ͵rʌn; ˈkrestə ͵rʌn/ a deep, steep path with twists in it which is cut into the ice at St Moritz in Switzerland and used for racing in BOBSLEIGHS (=a special vehicle with metal blades for riding fast over snow and ice) 克雷斯塔滑道〔在瑞士圣莫里茨山冰层中开凿出来的一条深邃、陡峭而蜿蜒的雪橇赛道〕

crest·ed /ˈkrɛstɪd; ˈkrestȷ̈d/ *adj* **1** having a crest 有羽冠的; 有羽饰的: *crested birds* 有羽冠的鸟 **2** marked by a crest 有徽章的: *the Duke's crested notepaper* 公爵有徽章的信纸

crest·fal·len /ˈkrɛst͵fɔlən; ˈkrest͵fɔːlən/ *adj* disappointed especially because you have failed to do something 沮丧的, 垂头丧气的: *The kids came back from the game looking crestfallen.* 孩子们比赛归来满脸沮丧。

cre·ta·ceous /krɪˈteʃəs; krȷ̈ˈteɪʃəs/ *adj technical*【术语】**1** similar to CHALK[1] (1) or containing chalk 似白垩的; 含白垩的 **2 the Cretaceous period** the time when rocks containing chalk were formed 白垩纪

Crete /krit; kriːt/ the largest island belonging to Greece, in the southeast Mediterranean Sea 克里特岛〔希腊最大岛屿, 位于地中海东南海域〕—**Cretan** *n, adj*

cret·in /ˈkritn; ˈkretȷ̈n/ *n* [C] *especially spoken* someone who is extremely stupid【尤口】笨蛋, 白痴: *Don't be such a cretin! Don't you know anything?* 不要那么傻了! 你什么也不知道吗? —**cretinous** *adj*

cre·vasse /krəˈvæs; krɪˈvæs/ *n* [C] a deep open crack in thick ice, especially in a GLACIER〔尤指冰川的〕裂缝, 缺口 —see picture on page A12 参见 A12 页图

crev·ice /ˈkrɛvɪs; ˈkrevȷ̈s/ *n* [C] a narrow crack, especially in rock〔尤指岩石的〕裂缝, 缺口: *He climbed the cliff, finding footholds in the crevices.* 他攀登悬崖, 在岩石裂缝里寻找踩脚的地方。

crew¹ /kru; kruː/ *n* **1** [C] all the people working on a ship, plane etc 全体船员;〔飞机上〕全体机组人员: *These planes carry over 300 passengers and crew.* 这些飞机载有三百多名乘客和机组人员。**2** [C] all the people working on a ship, plane etc except the most important officers〔除船长外的〕船员;〔除机长外的〕机组人员: *How many crew does he need to sail his yacht?* 他需要多少船员开动他的游艇? **3** [C] a group of people working together with special skills for a particular purpose 一队工作人员: *a TV camera crew* 电视摄影队 —see also 另见 GROUND CREW **4** [singular] a group of people 一群人: *We found a happy crew of foreign students in the hostel.* 在旅舍里我们发现一群快乐的外国学生。| **motley crew** (=a group of people who are a strange mixture of types) 三教九流的一群人 *My son came home from college with this motley crew.* 我儿子从大学回到家, 带了一群乱七八糟的朋友。**5** [C] a team of people who compete in rowing (ROW³) races〔划船比赛中的〕全体划船队员; 划船队: *Who will be on the college crew?* 大学划船队会有谁?

crew² *v* [I,T] to be part of the crew on a boat 当船员: *He asked me to crew for him in the sailing races.* 他要求我当他的划船比赛队员。

crew³ *old use*【旧】the past tense of CROW²

crew cut /ˈ· ·/ *n* [C] a very short hair style for men〔男子的〕平头发型, 板刷头 —see picture at 参见 HAIRSTYLE 图

Crewe /kru; kruː/ a town in Cheshire, northwest England, which is an important railway centre 克鲁〔位于英格兰西北部柴郡的一个镇, 为重要铁路枢纽〕

crew·man /ˈkrumən; ˈkruːmən/ *n plural* **crewmen** /-mən; -mən/ [C] a member, especially a male member, of a CREW¹ (2)〔尤指男的〕水手; 机组人员

crew mem·ber /ˈ· ͵··/ *n* [C] a member of a CREW¹ (2) 一名船员; 一名机组人员

crew neck /ˈ· ·/ *n* [C] a plain, round neck on a SWEATER 圆式衣领 —see picture on page A17 参见 A17 页图 —compare 比较 V-NECK

crib¹ /krɪb; krɪb/ *n especially AmE*【尤美】**1** [C] a bed for a baby or young child, especially one with bars to keep the baby from falling out〔有围栏的〕婴儿床; COT (1) *BrE*【英】—see picture at 参见 BED¹ 图 **2** [C] an open box or wooden frame holding food for animals; MANGER 饲料槽; 秣槽 **3** [C] *BrE* a model of the scene of Jesus's birth, often placed in churches and homes at Christmas【英】〔圣诞节时教堂或家中陈列的〕耶稣诞生情景的模型; CRÈCHE *AmE*【美】**4** [C] *informal*【非正式】**a)** something copied dishonestly from someone else's work, especially at school〔尤指在学校的〕抄袭, 剽窃 **b)** a book giving a translation or answers to questions, often used dishonestly by students〔学生用于作弊的〕对照本 **5** [U] the card game of cribbage 克里巴奇纸牌戏

crib² *v* **cribbed, cribbing** [I,T] to copy school or college work dishonestly from someone else 抄袭, 剽窃: **crib sth off/from sb** *He cribbed the answers off his friend.* 他抄袭朋友的答案。

crib·bage /ˈkrɪbɪdʒ; ˈkrɪbɪdʒ/ also 又作 **crib** *informal*【非正式】*n* [U] a card game in which points are shown by putting small pieces of wood in holes in a small board 克里巴奇纸牌戏〔用木钉插入木板上的小孔记分的一种纸牌戏〕

crib death /ˈ· ·/ *n* [C] *AmE*【美】COT DEATH *BrE*【英】婴儿猝死

crick¹ /krɪk; krɪk/ *n* [C] a sudden, painful stiffening of the muscles, especially in the back or the neck〔尤指背或颈的〕痛性痉挛: [+in] *Reading over your shoulder gives me a crick in my neck.* 隔着你的肩膀看书使我脖子都痉挛了。

crick² *v* [T] to do something that produces a crick in your back or neck 引起〔背或颈〕的痛性痉挛: *He bent to lift the case and cricked his back.* 他弯腰提箱子, 扭伤了背部。

Crick, Francis (1916-2004) a British BIOCHEMIST who, with the scientist J.D. Watson, discovered the double-HELIX structure of DNA. For this work he won the Nobel Prize in Medicine in 1962. 克里克〔(1916-2004), 英国生物化学家。曾与科学家 J. D. 沃森合作, 发现了 DNA (脱氧核糖核酸) 的双螺旋结构, 并因此获得 1962 年的诺贝尔医学奖〕

crick·et /ˈkrɪkɪt; ˈkrɪkȷ̈t/ *n* **1** [C] a small brown jumping insect, which makes a noise by rubbing its wings together 蟋蟀 **2** [U]

an outdoor game between two teams of 11 players in which players try to get points by hitting a ball and running between two sets of STUMPS (=special sticks) 板球 (运动)

CULTURAL NOTE 文化注释

Cricket is popular in England and in countries which used to be British colonies (COLONY). Ten international teams play each other in TEST MATCH*es* that each continue for no more than five days. These countries are: Australia, Bangladesh, England, India, New Zealand, Pakistan, South Africa, Sri Lanka, the West Indies, and Zimbabwe. England and Australia play each other in a competition consisting of five matches called The Ashes. In England and Wales, there are 18 COUNTY teams which play matches lasting no more than four days. In one-day cricket matches, each team BAT*s* once for a limited number of OVER*s*, usually 50 in an international match. 板球在英格兰和前英国殖民地很流行。10支国际球队参加预选赛，每场比赛时间不超过5天。球队来自的地方有：澳大利亚、孟加拉国、英格兰、印度、新西兰、巴基斯坦、南非、斯里兰卡、西印度群岛和津巴布韦。英格兰和澳大利亚进行5场比赛，称作"门灰板球赛"。在英格兰和威尔士，还有18支郡队，比赛时间不超过4天。为期一天的板球比赛中，每支球队在一定数量的投球轮数中各击打一次，通常国际比赛中有50轮投球。

The MCC (Marylebone Cricket Club) is responsible for the laws of cricket. The ICC (International Cricket Council) controls international cricket, and the ECB (England and Wales Cricket Board) is in charge of the game in England. Famous English cricket GROUND*s* include Lord's and The Oval (in London), Edgbaston (Birmingham), Headingly (Leeds), Old Trafford (Manchester), and Trent Bridge (Nottingham). Some of England's most famous CRICKETER*s* include Ian Botham, Geoffrey Boycott, and W.G. Grace. Many people consider the Australian BATSMAN Sir Donald Bradman to be the greatest cricketer of all time. 玛丽勒本板球俱乐部(MCC)负责制订板球规则，国际板球理事会(ICC)负责管理国际比赛，英格兰和威尔士板球委员会(ECB)负责英格兰的比赛。英国著名的板球场地包括洛兹板球场和椭圆板球场(伦敦)、埃德巴斯顿板球场(伯明翰)、黑丁利板球场(利兹)、老特拉福德板球场(曼彻斯特)和特伦特桥板球场(诺丁汉)。英国最著名的板球手有伊恩·博瑟姆、杰弗里·博伊科特和W.G.格雷斯。很多人认为澳大利亚板球手唐纳德·布拉德曼爵士是有史以来最优秀的板球手。

crick·et·er /ˈkrɪkɪtə; ˈkrɪkɪ̥tə/ *n* [C] someone who plays CRICKET (2) 板球运动员

cri·er /ˈkraɪə; ˈkraɪə/ *n* [C] a TOWN CRIER〔昔日〕沿街呼唤传报消息的人

cri·key /ˈkraɪkɪ; ˈkraɪki/ *interjection BrE informal* used to show that you are surprised or annoyed【英，非正式】哎呀〔表示惊讶或心烦〕: *Oh crikey, I'm going to miss the bus!* 哎呀，我要赶不上公共汽车了!

S2 W2 **crime** /kraɪm; kraɪm/ *n*

1 ▶CRIME IN GENERAL 犯罪◀ [U] illegal activities in general〔泛指〕违法犯罪活动: *We moved here ten years ago because there was very little crime.* 我们10年前搬到这里，因为这里的犯罪活动很少。| **crime prevention** (=work done to stop crime from happening) 防止犯罪的措施 *Neighborhood watch groups have been a very effective means of crime prevention.* 组织社区巡逻组已成为防止犯罪的一种十分有效的方法。| **serious crime** *Police need more personnel to tackle serious crime in the inner cities.* 警方需要更多的人员对付旧城区严重的犯罪。| **crime rate** (=the amount of crime in society) 犯罪率 *Voters are becoming frustrated with the growing crime rate.* 选民对上升的犯罪率感到沮丧。| **violent crime** *a worrying increase in violent crime* 暴力犯罪率令人不安的上升 | **petty crime** (=crime that is not very serious) 轻度犯罪 *Kids living on the streets are likely to be involved in petty crime.* 无家可归的孩子很容易卷入轻度犯罪。| **crime wave** (=a sudden increase in the amount of crime) 犯罪案件的突然上升 | **turn to crime** (=start doing illegal things) 走上犯罪道路 *Rich kids don't generally need to turn to crime.* 富有人家的孩子通常不需要去走犯罪道路。| **a life of crime** (=a way of living and getting money by doing illegal activities) 犯罪生涯 | **white-collar crime** (=crimes done by professional people that involve clever and complicated ways of illegally getting money) 白领犯罪

2 ▶A PARTICULAR CRIME 罪行◀ [C] a dishonest, violent, or immoral action that can be punished by law 罪，罪行: *A thirty-four year old man was charged with the crime after the murder weapon was found in his home.* 在一名34岁的男子家中发现凶器后，他被指控犯有谋杀罪。| [+against] *Crimes against the elderly are becoming more common.* 针对老人的犯罪活动越来越普遍。| **commit a crime** (=do something illegal) 犯罪 *Most crimes are committed by males under the age of 30.* 大部分案件的作案者是30岁以下的男子。| **scene of the crime** (=place where a particular crime happened) 犯罪现场 *They say a murderer always returns to the scene of the crime.* 据说杀人凶手老是会回到犯罪现场的。

3 it's a crime *spoken* used to say that you think something is completely immoral【口】(这么做是)不道德的: *It's a crime to waste all that good food.* 浪费那些美味的食物真是罪过。

4 crime against humanity a cruel crime against a lot of ordinary people, that is considered unacceptable in any situation, even a war 违反人性的罪行: *The commandant of the prison camp was found guilty of crimes against humanity.* 战俘集中营的司令官被判犯了违反人性的罪行。

5 crime of passion a crime, usually murder, that happens as a result of someone's sexual jealousy 情杀罪；桃色案件

6 crime doesn't pay used to say that it is wrong to think that being involved in crime will bring you any advantage, because you will probably be caught and punished for it 违法犯罪是没有好处的 —see also 另见 ORGANIZED CRIME, **partners in crime** (PARTNER[1] (5)), WAR CRIME, **white-collar crime** (WHITE-COLLAR (2))

This graph shows some of the words most commonly used with the noun **crime**. 本图表所示为含有名词crime的一些最常用的词组。

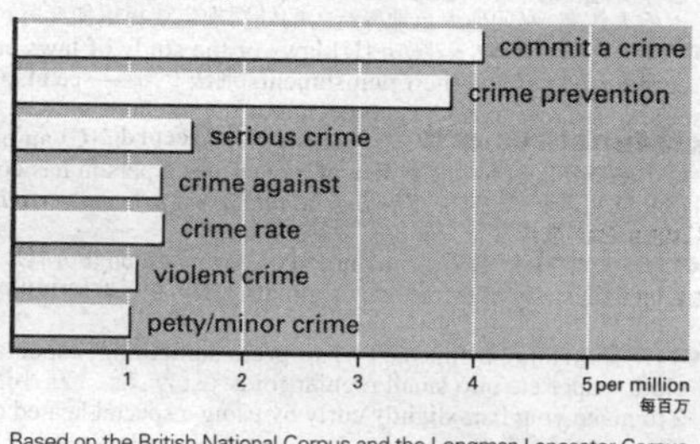

Based on the British National Corpus and the Longman Lancaster Corpus
据英国国家语料库和朗文兰开斯特语料库

Cri·me·a, the /kraɪˈmiə; kraɪˈmiːə/ a part of the Ukraine nearly surrounded by the Black Sea. The Crimean War was fought there. 克里米亚〔乌克兰的一部分，几乎被黑海包围。克里米亚战争就是在该地发生的〕

Crimean War, the /ˌ·ˌ·· ˈ·/ (1853-56) a war between Russia on one side, and Britain, France, Turkey, and Sardinia on the other. It started because Britain and France believed that Russia intended to take control of the Balkans (=southeast Europe), and it ended when the Russians were defeated and lost control of their naval base at Sevastopol 克里米亚战争〔(1853-1856)，俄国与英国、法国、土耳其、撒丁王国联军之间的一场战争。战争的起因是，英国和法国认为俄国企图争夺巴尔干半岛的控制权。战争以俄国战败并失去塞瓦斯托波尔海军基地的控制权而告终〕

crim·i·nal[1] /ˈkrɪmənl; ˈkrɪmɪ̥nəl/ *adj* **1** related to or connected with crime 犯罪的，犯法的: *criminal behaviour* 犯罪行为 | *The boy had shown criminal tendencies since early adolescence.* 这个男孩在青春期初期就表现出了犯罪的倾向。| **a criminal offence** (=a crime that can be punished by law) 刑事犯罪 | **criminal element** (=people within a particular group who are known to be involved in crime) 犯罪团伙成员 *Ray got mixed up with the local criminal element.* 雷与当地的犯罪团伙混到了一起。| **criminal negligence** (=the illegal act of not doing something you should do, with the result that someone is hurt) 刑事疏忽，过失犯罪 | **criminal damage** (=the illegal act of damaging someone else's property) 刑事毁坏，破坏罪 **2** [no comparative 无比较级] related to the part of the legal system that is concerned with crime 与犯罪有关的；刑事的: *criminal court* 刑事法庭 | *criminal case* 刑事案件 | *criminal attorney* 刑事律师 | **criminal charges** (=official statements saying that someone has done something illegal) 刑事控告 *Wharton faces criminal charges and will be tried in May.* 沃顿面临着刑事控告，将在5月受审。—compare 比较 CIVIL (3) **3** wrong, dishonest, and un- S3 W2

acceptable 罪过的; 错误的; 奸诈的; 无法容忍的: *There was a criminal lack of foresight in the planning of this venture.* 这个风险投资计划缺少远见，让人难以接受。—**criminally** *adv*

criminal² *n* [C] someone who is involved in illegal activities or has been proved guilty of a crime 罪犯: *The man is a criminal. How could the people elect him to office?* 这个人是个罪犯，人们怎么能选他当官呢? | **hardened criminal** (=someone who has been involved in crime for a long time) 惯犯 *Teenagers should not be sent to prison with hardened criminals.* 少年犯不应当与惯犯关在同一个监狱。

Criminal Cases Review Commission /,‥‥‥ ,·'·/ a British organization, set up in 1997, that investigates cases where it is believed a person might have been wrongfully CONVICT*ed* of a crime 刑事案件审查委员会〔英国一组织, 成立于1997年, 专门调查疑似误判或错判的刑事案件〕

crim·i·nal·ize also 又作 **-ise** *BrE*【英】/ˈkrɪmənḷˌaɪz; ˈkrɪmɪ̣nəlaɪz/ *v* [T] to make something illegal 立法禁止, 使…为犯罪: *The police have tried in the past to criminalize hitchhiking.* 警方曾经尝试立法禁止搭便车。

Criminal Jus·tice Bill, the /,‥'‥,·/ a series of changes to British law in 1995, officially called the **Criminal Justice and Public Order Act**, which changed the law relating to a person's right to silence (=their right to say nothing when the police arrest them, or when they are on trial in a court of law), and also made the laws against SQUATTING (=living in a building without the owner's permission) and TRESPASS*ing* (=being on someone's land without their permission) much stricter.《刑事司法法案》〔正式名称为《刑事审判和公共治安法》。1995年对英国法律所进行的一系列修订, 修改了有关个人沉默权的条款, 有关擅占他人住宅、私闯他人土地等行为的处罚规定变得更加严厉〕

criminal law /,‥'·/ *n* [U] laws or the study of laws concerning crimes and their punishments 刑法 (学) —see also 另见 CANON LAW, CIVIL LAW, COMMON LAW²

criminal rec·ord /,‥'‥/ also 又作 **record** *n* [C] an official record kept by the police of any crimes a person has committed 犯罪记录, 前科: *The defendant has no previous criminal record.* 该被告没有犯罪前科。

crim·i·nol·o·gy /ˌkrɪməˈnɑlədʒɪ; ˌkrɪmɪ̣ˈnɒlədʒi/ *n* [U] the scientific study of crime and criminals 犯罪学 —**criminologist** *n* [C]

crimp /krɪmp; krɪmp/ *v* [T] **1** to press something, especially cloth, paper etc into small regular folds 在〔布、纸〕上压小褶子 **2** to make your hair slightly curly by using a special heated tool 使〔头发〕轻微卷曲

crim·son¹ /ˈkrɪmzn̩; ˈkrɪmzən/ *adj* having a deep purplish red colour 深红色的: *a crimson sky* 深红色的天空 | *She turned crimson when he made the remark.* 他说这些话的时候, 她的脸变得通红。—**crimson** *n* [C] —see picture on page A5 参见 A5 页图

crimson² *v* [I] if your face crimsons, it becomes red because you are embarrassed〔脸〕变深红色

cringe /krɪndʒ; krɪndʒ/ *v* [I] **1** to move back or away from someone or something, especially because you are afraid or in pain 畏缩, 退缩: *The dog cringed and whimpered when the tall man appeared.* 那高个男子出现时, 狗一边后退一边发出哀鸣。**2** to feel embarrassed by something that seems stupid 感到难堪: *I cringe when I think what I used to wear in the Sixties.* 一想到我在20世纪60年代穿的衣服我就觉得很傻。| *They sing this song that makes me cringe.* 他们唱这首使我难为情的歌曲。—**cringe** *n* [C]

crin·kle¹ /ˈkrɪŋkḷ; ˈkrɪŋkəl/ *v* [I,T] also 又作 **crinkle up** to become covered with small folds, or make something do this (使) 起皱: *The heat was beginning to make the cellophane crinkle.* 高温使玻璃纸开始起皱。—compare 比较 WRINKLE² —**crinkled** *adj*

crinkle² *n* [C usually singular 一般用单数] a thin fold, especially in your skin or on cloth, paper etc〔尤指皮肤、衣服、纸等上的〕细皱纹 —compare 比较 WRINKLE¹ (1,2)

crin·kly /ˈkrɪŋklɪ; ˈkrɪŋkli/ *adj* **1** having many thin folds 多皱纹的: *Andrew stared at the old man's crinkly face.* 安德鲁盯着老人布满皱纹的脸。**2** hair that is crinkly is stiff and curly〔头发〕硬而鬈曲的 —**crinkliness** *n* [U]

crin·o·line /ˈkrɪnḷɪn; ˈkrɪnəlɪ̣n/ *n* [C] a round frame worn under a woman's skirt in former times to support it and give it shape〔旧时支撑女裙的〕裙撑; 圈环裙

cripes /kraɪps; kraɪps/ *interjection old-fashioned* used to express surprise or annoyance【过时】天哪! 啊!〔表示惊讶或烦恼〕

crip·ple¹ /ˈkrɪpḷ; ˈkrɪpəl/ *n* [C] **1** an offensive word for someone who is physically unable to use their arms or their legs properly 跛子; 手臂残废者〔侮辱用语〕**2 emotional cripple** *informal* someone who is not able to deal with their own or other people's feelings【非正式】感情残废〔不能处理自己或他人的感情的人〕—compare 比较 DISABLED

cripple² *v* [T] **1** to hurt or wound someone so that they cannot use their arms or legs properly 使〔手臂或腿〕受伤致残: *The accident crippled her for life.* 这次事故使她终生残疾。**2** to seriously damage or weaken something 严重损坏[削弱]: *The incident could easily cripple the peace talks.* 这一事件很可能使和平谈判破裂。—**crippled** *adj* —**crippling** *adj*

Cris·co /ˈkrɪsko; ˈkrɪskəʊ/ *trademark* a type of vegetable fat or vegetable oil used in cooking, which is sold in the US【商标】"克罗斯克"牌烹调油〔在美国销售的一种食用植物油〕

cri·sis /ˈkraɪsɪs; ˈkraɪsɪ̣s/ *n plural* **crises** /-siz; -siːz/ [C,U] **1** a period or moment of great danger, difficulty, or uncertainty, especially in politics or economics〔尤指政治、经济等〕危机; 紧要关头: *the energy crisis of 1972* 1972年的能源危机 | *the Cuban missile crisis* 古巴导弹危机 **2** a time when a personal emotional problem or situation has reached its worst point〔个人的〕危急之际: *In times of crisis you find out who your real friends are.* 危急时刻你就会发现谁是你真正的朋友了。| **be at a crisis point** (=be in a condition that cannot get any worse) 处于危机时刻 *I think Paul and Lucinda are at a crisis point in their marriage.* 我认为保罗和露辛达的婚姻处于危机时刻。**3** the time during a serious illness when it could get either better or worse〔重病的〕转折点: *The crisis came that night.* 病情的转折点出现在那天晚上。**4 crisis management** the skill or process of dealing with unusually dangerous or difficult situations 应付危机[困境]的技巧; 危机[困境]处理过程 **5 crisis of confidence** a situation in which people no longer believe a government, economy, system etc is working properly, and will no longer support it, work with it etc 信任危机: [+in] *a crisis of confidence in the foreign exchange when interest rates were cut* 利率下调后出现的对外汇市场的信任危机 —see also 另见 MIDLIFE CRISIS

crisp¹ /krɪsp; krɪsp/ *n* [C] *BrE* a very thin, flat round piece of potato cooked in oil and eaten cold【英】油炸 (马铃) 薯片; CHIP¹ (3b) *AmE*【美】—see also 另见 **burn sth to a crisp** (BURN¹ (4))

crisp² *adj* **1** pleasantly dry, hard, and easily broken 干而脆的; 易碎的: *crisp bacon* 松脆的熏猪肉 | *His feet broke through the crisp outer layer of snow.* 他踩碎了雪脆弱的表面。**2** a fruit, vegetable, or plant that is crisp is firm and fresh〔水果、蔬菜或植物〕新鲜而爽口的: *a crisp apple* 鲜脆的苹果 | *a crisp salad* 爽口的沙拉 **3** paper or cloth that is crisp is fresh, clean, and new〔纸或布〕清新的; 干净的; 新的: *a crisp, new five dollar bill* 簇新的5元钞票 **4** weather that is crisp is cold and dry〔天气〕干而冷的; 清爽的: *a crisp winter day* 干冷的冬日 **5** someone's behaviour or manner that is crisp is quick, confident, and shows no doubts or slowness; BRISK (1,2)〔行为、态度〕干脆利落的, 利索的: *The general's voice was crisp and clear as he addressed the meeting.* 将军在会上发言的时候声音清晰洪亮。—**crisply** *adv* —**crispness** *n* [U]

crisp³ *v* [T] to make something become crisp, especially by cooking or heating it〔尤指通过烹调或加热〕使变脆

Crisp, Quen·tin /ˈkwɛntɪn; ˈkwentɪ̣n/ (1908-99) a writer and critic who was born in the UK but went to live in the US. He is known especially for writing *The Naked Civil Servant* and for being HOMOSEXUAL, and for his clever and amusing opinions and strange clothes. 克里斯普〔(1908-1999), 英国同性恋作家、评论家。他出生于英国, 侨居在美国。他的作品《裸体公仆》十分著名。他观点机智风趣, 穿着奇异古怪〕

crisp·bread /ˈkrɪspˌbrɛd; ˈkrɪspbred/ *n* [C,U] a thin dry biscuit that is not sweet 薄脆饼干

crisp·y /ˈkrɪspɪ; ˈkrɪspi/ *adj* a word meaning CRISP² (1) used especially to talk about food〔尤指食物〕松脆的: *crispy bacon* 脆熏猪肉

criss·cross¹, criss-cross /ˈkrɪsˌkrɔs; ˈkrɪskrɒs/ *n* [C] a pattern made up of straight lines, usually a lot of them, that cross each other 线条纵横交错的图案: *the crisscross of scars on his back* 他背上纵横交错的伤疤 —**crisscross** *adj*: *trees planted in a crisscross pattern* 纵横交错种植的树木

crisscross², criss-cross *v* [I,T] to make a regularly repeated pattern of straight lines that cross each other, or to make this pattern on something (在…上) 画交错的直线; 画十字图案: *The flyovers crisscross the city above the congested streets.* 立交桥纵横交错于城市拥挤的街道上方。

cri·te·ri·on /kraɪˈtɪrɪən; kraɪˈtɪəriən/ *n plural* **criteria** /-rɪə; -riə/ [C often plural 常用复数] a standard which is established so that a judgment or decision, especially a scientific one, can be made〔判断、决定的〕标准, 准则: *More detailed criteria are*

necessary before a logical decision can be reached. 需要更详细的标准才能作出合乎逻辑的决定。| [**+for**] *What are your criteria for judging a bottle of wine?* 你用什么标准判断一瓶酒的好坏?

W3 **crit·ic** /ˈkrɪtɪk; ˈkrɪtɪk/ *n* [C] **1** someone whose job is to make judgments about the good and bad qualities of something, especially art, music, films etc〔尤指艺术、音乐、电影等的〕评论家, 批评家: *The jazz critic for the Times panned the show, calling it 'a joke'.*《泰晤士报》的爵士乐评论家严厉批评该演出, 称之为"一个玩笑"。**2** someone who expresses strong disapproval or dislike of a person, idea, organization etc 反对[憎恶]…的人: [**+of**] *He became an outspoken critic of the country's educational policies.* 他成了对该国教育政策直言不讳的批评者。**3 armchair critic** someone who does nothing themselves but criticizes others for what they do 空头批评家; 只说不做的批评家

S2 W2 **crit·i·cal** /ˈkrɪtɪkl; ˈkrɪtɪkəl/ *adj*

1 ►MAKING SEVERE JUDGMENTS 作出严厉的判断◄ someone who is critical makes severe and often unfair judgments of people or things 批评的, 批判的; 吹毛求疵的, 爱挑剔的: *I don't mean to be over critical, but isn't all of this completely unnecessary?* 我不想太挑剔, 但是所有这些不都是完全多余的吗? | [**+of**] *Pat is always very critical of her son's appearance.* 帕特对儿子的外表总是很挑剔。

2 ►IMPORTANT 重要的◄ very important because what happens in the future depends on it 紧要的, 关键性的: *We need an immediate decision on this critical issue.* 我们需要立即对这个关键问题作出决定。| **be critical to** *Parental attention is critical to the child's socialization.* 父母的关注对孩子适应社会是很重要的。| **of critical importance** (=very important) 至关重要的 *Finding the source of the gas leak was of critical importance.* 找到漏气的源头至关重要。

3 ►DANGEROUS/UNCERTAIN 危险的/不确定的◄ a critical time or moment is one that is dangerous or uncertain because a sudden change to a better or a worse condition is possible 危急的, 紧要关头的: *David is at a critical stage in the illness.* 戴维处于病情的关键时期。

4 ►MAKING FAIR JUDGMENTS 作出公正判断◄ providing careful and fair judgments of the good and bad characteristics of something 判断审慎的; 评判性的: *a critical analysis of Stevens' poem* 对斯蒂文斯的诗所作的评判性分析

5 ►ART/FILM/BOOKS ETC 艺术/电影/书等◄ produced by or resulting from the work of CRITICS 评论: *'The Piano' got a lot of critical acclaim, but I didn't like the music in it.* 电影《钢琴别恋》得到了很多好评, 但是我不喜欢其中的音乐。| *a critical success* (=the critics liked it) 受到评论家的好评

6 in a critical condition *BrE*【英】, **in critical condition** *AmE*【美】so ill that you could die 病情危急: *The patient is in critical condition at Bellvue Hospital tonight.* 今天晚上病人在贝尔维尤医院治疗, 病情危急。

7 the critical list a list of people in hospital who are so ill that they could die 病危病人名单: *He was taken off the critical list last night, so we're very relieved.* 他的名字昨晚从病危病人名单上除掉了, 因此我们大大地松了口气。

8 with a critical eye if you look at or examine something with a critical eye, you examine it carefully in order to judge its good and bad qualities 以评判[鉴别]的眼光

crit·i·cal·ly /ˈkrɪtɪklɪ; ˈkrɪtɪkli/ *adv* **1 critically ill/injured/important etc** very seriously ill, very important etc 病情严重/伤得很重/极端重要等: *10 people died and 30 were critically injured in a rail crash yesterday.* 昨天的火车相撞事故中有10人死亡, 30人受重伤。**2** in a way that shows you have thought about the good and bad qualities of something 批评性地, 批判性地: *You need to critically assess your lifestyle.* 你应该全面地评价你的生活方式。

critical mass /,… ˈ·/ *n* [C,U] *technical* the amount of a substance necessary for an ATOMIC CHAIN REACTION to start【术语】〔核连锁反应的〕临界质量

critical path a·nal·y·sis /,… ,· ˈ·-·/ *n plural* **critical path analyses** [C] *technical* a method of planning a large piece of work so that there will be few delays and the cost will be as low as possible【术语】关键途径分析法〔制订一项大型工作计划时为减少耽搁和降低花费而进行的规划方式〕

S2 W2 **crit·i·cis·m** /ˈkrɪtə,sɪzəm; ˈkrɪtɪ̇sɪzəm/ *n* **1** [C,U] the act of giving your opinion or judgment about the good and bad qualities of someone or something 评论, 批评: *Kate doesn't take any kind of criticism very well.* 凯特从来不好好接受批评。| **constructive criticism** (=intended to help someone or something improve) 建设性评论 **2** [C,U] written or spoken remarks that express your disapproval or bad opinion of someone or something 批评, 指责; 批评文: *We all felt that Wanda's criticism was unjustified.* 我们都认为万达的批评没有道理。| [**+of**] *My only criticism of the book is that it's a little too academic.* 我对这本书的唯一批评是学术气重了一点。**3 a)** [U] the activity of forming and expressing judgments about the good or bad qualities of books, films, music etc〔书、电影、音乐等〕评论: *literary criticism* 文艺评论 **b)** [C,U] the written work that results from this activity 评论文, 批评文

crit·i·cize also 又作 **-ise** *BrE*【英】/ˈkrɪtə,saɪz; ˈkrɪtɪ̇saɪz/ *v* **1** [I, T] to express your disapproval of someone or something, or to talk about their faults 批评, 指责: *Ron does nothing but criticize and complain all the time.* 罗恩什么也不干, 只是一味指责和抱怨。| **criticize sb for (doing) sth** *The report strongly criticizes the police for failing to deal with the problem quickly.* 该报告强烈指责警方没有尽快处理这个问题。**2** [T] to express judgments about the good and bad qualities of something 评论: *Criticizing your own work is very difficult.* 评论自己的作品是非常困难的。 S3 W3

cri·tique[1] /krɪˋtik; krɪˈtiːk/ *n* [C,U] an article, book etc expressing judgments about the good and bad qualities of something such as the work of a writer or artist 评论〔文章、书刊等〕: [**+of**] *The final article is a critique of John Updike's latest novel.* 最后一篇文章是评论约翰·厄普代克的最新小说的。

critique[2] *v* [I,T] *AmE* to make remarks about the good and bad qualities of something, especially artistic or literary work【美】评论〔文艺作品等〕: *I asked my professor to critique the paper before I turned it in to the examining board.* 我请教授先对我的论文进行评判, 然后再交给审查委员会。

crit·ter /ˈkrɪtɚ; ˈkrɪtə/ *n* [C] *AmE spoken* a creature, especially an animal【美口】生物, 动物: *Be careful, that horse is a mean critter!* 小心, 那匹马碰不得!

croak[1] /krok; krəʊk/ *v* **1** [I] to make a deep low sound like the sound a FROG makes 作蛙鸣声 **2** [I,T] to speak in a low, rough voice as if you have a sore throat 用低沉沙哑的声音说话: *He was shivering and croaking in a voice they barely recognized as his.* 他浑身发抖, 声音嘶哑, 他们简直辨认不出是他的声音。**3** [I] *slang* to die【俚】死亡

croak[2] *n* [C] a low sound made in an animal's or person's throat, like one that a FROG makes〔动物或人发出的〕类似蛙鸣的声音

Cro·a·tia /kroˋeʃə; krəʊˈeɪʃə/ a country in Eastern Europe between Hungary and the Adriatic Sea. Population: 4,334,000 (2001). Capital: Zagreb. It was part of Yugoslavia until 1991. 克罗地亚〔东欧一国家, 位于匈牙利和亚德里亚海之间。人口: 4,334,000 (2001), 首都: 萨格勒布。1991年以前是前南斯拉夫的一部分〕—**Croatian** *n, adj*

cro·chet /kroˋʃe; ˈkrəʊʃeɪ/ *v* [I,T] to make clothes, blankets etc from wool using a special needle with a hook at one end 用钩针编织 —compare 比较 KNIT (1) —**crochet** *n* [U] —**crotcheting** *n* [U]

crock /krɑk; krɒk/ *n* [C] **1** *old use* a clay pot【旧】瓦罐 **2 crocks** [plural] **a)** *BrE old-fashioned* plates, cups etc, especially made of baked clay【英, 过时】陶[瓦]器 **b)** pieces of broken EARTHENWARE (=baked clay) 碎瓦片 **3** *spoken*【口】**a crock of shit** *AmE taboo* something that is unbelievable, unfair, untrue etc【美讳】屁话; 骗人的东西: *You can't expect me to believe that! What a crock of shit!* 你别指望我会相信那种事! 简直是屁话! **4 old crock** *BrE slang*【英俚】**a)** an old car 旧汽车 **b)** an old person 老人: *We old crocks can't run like you.* 我们老家伙不能像你那样跑了。

crocked /krɑkt; krɒkt/ *adj* [never before noun 不用于名词前] **1** *BrE old-fashioned* injured or broken【英, 过时】受伤的; 破碎的 **2** *AmE spoken* drunk【美口】喝醉了的: *Don't mind Roger. He's always crocked by noon.* 不要介意罗杰, 中午他总是醉醺醺的。

Crocker, Betty —see 见 BETTY CROCKER

crock·e·ry /ˈkrɑkərɪ; ˈkrɒkəri/ *n* [U] *especially BrE* cups, plates etc, especially made of CHINA【尤英】陶器, 瓦器

Crock·ett /ˈkrɑkɪt; ˈkrɒkɪ̇t/, **Da·vy** /ˈdevɪ; ˈdeɪvi/ (1786-1836) a US FRONTIERSMAN who became a member of Congress and was later killed trying to defend the Alamo. 克罗克特〔(1786-1836), 美国边疆开拓者, 国会议员, 在力图保卫阿拉莫时牺牲〕

CULTURAL NOTE 文化注释

In pictures, Davy Crockett is shown wearing clothes made from brown leather and a hat made from a RACOON tail. A popular song from a 1950s US television programme about him contains the well-known words "Davy, Davy Crockett, king of the wild frontier". 在画像上, 克罗克特身穿棕色皮衣, 头戴浣熊尾巴制成的帽子。20世纪50年代美国电视节目上有一首关于他的流行歌曲唱道: "戴维, 戴维·克罗克特, 荒蛮边疆之王。"

croc·o·dile /ˋkrɑkə͵daɪl; ˈkrɒkədaɪl/ *n* **1** [C] a large REPTILE (1) with a long mouth and many sharp teeth that lives in lakes and rivers in hot wet parts of the world 鳄鱼 **2** [U] the skin of this animal, used for making things such as shoes 鳄鱼皮 **3** [singular] *BrE* a long line of people, especially school children, walking in pairs 【英】两人一排成纵队行进的一长队人〔尤指小学生〕 **4 shed crocodile tears** to pretend you feel sad, sorry, or upset when you do not really feel that way 掉鳄鱼眼泪; 假慈悲

crocodile 鳄鱼

cro·cus /ˋkrokəs; ˈkrəʊkəs/ *n* [C] a small purple, yellow, or white flower that comes up in early spring 番红花, 藏红花

Croe·sus /ˋkrisəs; ˈkriːsəs/ (?-546 BC) a king of Lydia in Asia Minor, known for being very rich. People sometimes say that someone is 'as rich as Croesus' to mean that the person is extremely rich. 克罗伊斯〔(?-公元前 546), 小亚细亚的吕底亚国王, 以十分富有而出名。人们有时会说某人 as rich as Croesus, 意指他像克罗伊斯一样有钱, 或者他极为富有〕

croft /krɔft; krɒft/ *n* [C] a very small farm in Scotland〔苏格兰的〕小农场

croft·er /ˋkrɔftɚ; ˈkrɒftə/ *n* [C] someone who lives and works on a croft〔苏格兰的〕佃农; 小农场主

croft·ing /ˋkrɔftɪŋ; ˈkrɒftɪŋ/ *n* [U] the system of farming on crofts in Scotland〔苏格兰的〕佃农制度

crois·sant /krwɑˋsɑn; ˈkwɑːsɒŋ/ *n* [C] *French* a piece of bread, shaped in a curve and usually eaten for breakfast 【法】羊角面包; 新月形面包; 牛角面包

croissant 牛角面包

Cromp·ton /ˋkrɑmptən; ˈkrɒmptən/, **Rich·mal** /ˋrɪtʃml; ˈrɪtʃməl/ (1890-1969) a British writer who wrote a famous series of humorous children's NOVELS, known as the Just William books, about the adventures of an 11-year-old English schoolboy called William Brown who always gets into trouble 克朗普顿〔(1890-1969), 英国作家, 创作过一系列著名的儿童幽默小说, 即《威廉的故事》丛书, 描述一位老是惹麻烦的 11 岁英格兰学童威廉·布朗的特殊经历〕

Crom·well /ˋkrɑmwɛl; ˈkrɒmwel/, **Ol·i·ver** /ˋɑləvɚ; ˈɒlɪvə/ (1599-1658) an English military and political leader who led the army of Parliament against King Charles I in the English Civil War. After defeating the King, he made a REPUBLIC (=a country without a king or queen) called 'the Commonwealth', and ruled as **Lord Protector** until his death. 克伦威尔〔(1599-1658), 英国军事及政治领导人。英国内战期间, 他率领议会军队反抗国王查理一世。他击败国王之后成立了共和国, 称"共和政体", 以护国公的身份掌握政权, 直至去世〕

Cromwell, Thom·as (1485-1540) an English politician who became King Henry VIII's chief adviser, and made laws that gave Henry control of all the churches in England, instead of the Pope. He also organized the Dissolution of the Monasteries. 克伦威尔〔(1485-1540), 英国政治家, 亨利八世的首席参事。他制定法律, 赋予了亨利八世统管英格兰所有教会的权力, 从而取代了教皇。他还组织了"解散隐修院运动"〕

crone /kron; krəʊn/ *n* [C] an ugly or unpleasant old woman 讨厌的丑老太婆

Cro·nus /ˋkronəs; ˈkrəʊnəs/ also 又作 **Kronos** /ˋkronɑs; ˈkrəʊnɒs/ in Greek MYTHOLOGY, a son of Uranus and one of the Titans, who became ruler of the world until he was defeated by Zeus. In Roman mythology his name is Saturn. 克洛诺斯〔希腊神话中乌拉诺斯之子, 提坦巨神之一, 被宙斯打败之前一直是世界的主宰。罗马神话中他叫萨图恩〕

cro·ny /ˋkronɪ; ˈkrəʊni/ *n* [C usually plural 一般用复数] one of a group of people, who spend a lot of time with each other and will usually help each other, even if this involves dishonesty 密友, 老朋友: *Nixon gave positions of power to many of his political cronies.* 尼克松把许多有权力的职位给了他政治上的老朋友。

crook[1] /krʊk; krʊk/ *n* [C] **1** *informal* someone who is dishonest 【非正式】骗子, 无赖: *I wouldn't buy a car from them – they're a bunch of crooks.* 我不会从他们那里买汽车的, 他们是一伙骗子。**2** a long stick with a curved end, used by people who look after sheep〔牧羊人的〕曲手杖 —see picture at 参见 STICK² 图 **3 the crook of your arm** the part of your arm where it bends, used for holding things 臂弯: *She cradled the little dog in the crook of her arm.* 她弯着手臂轻轻地抱着小狗。—see picture at 参见 BODY 图

crook[2] *v* [T] if you crook your finger or your arm, you bend it 使〔手指、手臂〕弯曲: *She beckoned me, crooking her finger.* 她勾了勾手指招呼我过去。

crook[3] *adj* [never before noun 不用于名词前] *informal AustrE* ill【非正式, 澳】有病的, 生病的

crook·ed /ˋkrʊkɪd; ˈkrʊkɪd/ *adj* **1** dishonest 不诚实的; 狡诈的: *a crooked cop* 行为不端的警察 **2** bent, twisted, or not in a straight line 弯曲的; 不直的: *Her teeth were all crooked.* 她的牙齿歪歪扭扭的。—**crookedly** *adv*—**crookedness** *n* [U]

croon /krun; kruːn/ *v* [I,T] to sing or speak in a soft gentle voice, especially about love 柔声唱〔尤指情歌〕; 柔声说〔尤指谈情说爱〕: *Sinatra crooning mellow tunes* 西纳特拉柔声哼唱着甜美的调子

crop[1] /krɑp; krɒp/ *n* [C] **1** a plant such as wheat, rice, or fruit that is grown by farmers, especially in order to be eaten 庄稼; 作物: *The main crop in China is rice.* 中国的主要作物是水稻。| *Most of the land is used for growing crops.* 这片土地大部分用以种植庄稼。| *crops being harvested in September* 9月份收获的庄稼 **2** the amount of wheat, rice, fruit etc that is produced in a season 一季的收成, 收获: *Wheat farmers have had a record crop this year.* 麦农今年的收成创了纪录。| **bumper crop** (=a very large amount of wheat, rice etc produced in a season) 大丰收 **3 a crop of** a group of people that arrive or things that happen at the same time 一群〔同时到达的人〕; 一批〔同时发生的事〕: *There was the usual crop of problems to deal with when I got back to the office.* 我回到办公室时, 照旧有一大堆问题等着处理。| *this season's crop of young players* 本赛季的年轻选手们 **4** a short whip used in horse riding 短马鞭 —see picture at 参见 WHIP¹ 图 **5** the part under a bird's throat where food is stored〔鸟的〕嗉囊 **6** a very short hairstyle 平头发型 **7 a crop of dark hair/blonde curls etc** hair that is short, thick, and attractive 一头漂亮的粗短黑发/金黄色鬈发等

crop[2] *v* [T] **1** to cut someone's hair short 剪短〔头发〕 **2** to cut a part off a photograph or picture so that it is a particular size or shape 裁切〔照片、图画〕 **3** if an animal crops grass or other plants, it makes them short by eating them〔牲畜〕啃吃〔草〕 **4** if a plant crops, it produces fruit, grain etc 结果; 结穗: *The apple trees cropped well that year.* 那年苹果收成好。

crop up *phr v* [I] **1** if something, especially a problem, crops up, it happens or appears suddenly and unexpectedly〔问题等〕突然发生[出现]: *Please let me know if anything crops up while I'm away.* 我不在的时候如果发生了什么事, 请通知我。—see 见 OCCUR (USAGE) **2** if something such as a name or a subject crops up, it appears in something you read or hear〔名字、话题等〕被提到: *Your name kept cropping up in conversation.* 你的名字在谈话中一再被提到。

crop cir·cle /ˈ· ,··/ *n* [C] a CORN CIRCLE 农田圈

crop-dust·ing /ˈ· ,··/ *n* [U] *AmE* 【美】CROP-SPRAYING 对作物喷洒杀虫剂

crop·per /ˋkrɑpɚ; ˈkrɒpə/ **come a cropper** *BrE informal*【英, 非正式】**a)** to fail in something, especially unexpectedly (意外)失败: *I came a cropper on the last question in the test.* 考试中最后一个问题我意外地没有回答上来。**b)** to accidentally fall onto the ground from a horse or bicycle〔从马或自行车上〕摔下来: *Jimmy came a cropper as he turned the corner.* 吉米拐弯的时候摔了一跤。

crop ro·ta·tion /ˈ· ·,··/ *n* [U] the practice of changing the crops that you grow in a field each year to preserve the good qualities in the soil 庄稼轮作

crop-spray·ing /ˈ· ,··/ *n* [U] the practice of spreading crops with chemicals that kill insects 对作物喷洒杀虫剂; CROP-DUSTING *AmE*【美】

cro·quet /kroˋke; ˈkrəʊkeɪ/ *n* [U] a game played on grass in which players hit balls with wooden MALLETS (=long-handled hammers) so that they roll under curved wires 槌球游戏〔在草地上用木槌击球使之穿过金属拱门〕

> **CULTURAL NOTE 文化注释**
>
> In the UK, croquet is mostly thought of as a game played by UPPER-CLASS people. It was popular in the past, but is not often played now, except in parks and gardens. In the US, croquet is usually played by families or children in their own garden. 门球在英国主要被看做上流社会的运动, 过去很流行, 但现在除了在公园或花园里, 很少见到有人玩。在美国, 通常是一家人或孩子们在自家花园里玩门球。

cro·quette /kroˋkɛt; krəʊˈket/ *n* [C] a piece of crushed meat, fish, potato etc that is made into a small round piece, covered in BREADCRUMBS, fried (FRY¹ (1)) and eaten〔外面裹面包屑做成的〕炸肉[鱼、马铃薯]丸

Cros·by /ˈkrɔzbɪ; ˈkrɒzbi/, **Bing** /bɪŋ; bɪŋ/ (1904-77) a US singer and film actor who was famous as a CROONER (=someone who sings in a soft, gentle voice). He is best known for the song *White Christmas* from the film *Holiday Inn* (1942). 克罗斯比〔(1904-1977)，美国歌手、电影演员，以低声哼唱歌曲出名。他演唱过影片《假日旅店》(1942) 的插曲《银色圣诞》，并因此而非常著名〕

cro·sier, crozier /ˈkroʒɚ; ˈkrəʊʒə/ *n* [C] a CROZIER 主教的权杖

cross- /krɔs; krɒs/ *prefix* **1** going from one side to the other; across 横穿，横跨，穿越: *a cross-Channel ferry* (=sailing from Britain to France) 横渡英吉利海峡的渡船 **2** going between two things and joining them 交叉，关联: *cross-cultural influences* 交叉文化的影响

cross out 画掉，删去

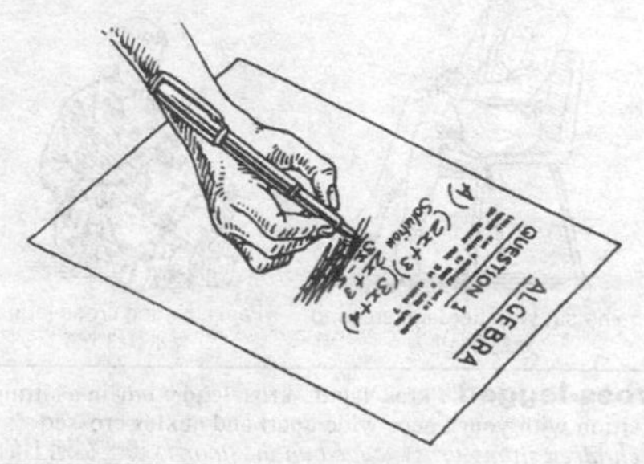

2 2 **cross¹** /krɔs; krɒs/ *v*

1 ►GO FROM ONE SIDE TO ANOTHER 从一边到另一边◄[I, T] to go or stretch from one side of something such as a road, river, room etc to the other 横穿，横渡，横跨: *It took them four weeks to cross the desert.* 他们花了四个星期横穿沙漠。| *Look both ways before you cross the road.* 过马路前要左右看看。| *The railway line from Leeds to Manchester crosses the Pennines.* 从利兹到曼彻斯特的铁路穿过奔宁山脉。

2 ►CROSS A LINE ETC 穿过界线等◄[T] if you cross a line, track etc you go over and beyond it 穿过，越过，跑过〔终点线等〕: *Two cyclists crossed the finish line together in first place.* 两名自行车选手同时越过终点线，并列第一。

3 ►TWO ROADS/LINES ETC 两条路/线等◄[T] if two or more roads, lines, etc cross, they go across each other 交叉，相交: *There's a shopping mall near where Ventura Boulevard crosses Sepulveda.* 在文图拉大道和塞普尔韦达大街交叉处附近有一个商场。| **cross sth** *Station Avenue crosses East Street about a mile down the road.* 车站大道在这条路往前约一英里处与东街相交。

4 ►LEGS/ARMS 腿/臂◄[T] if you cross your legs or arms, you put one on top of the other 交叉，叠放: *She was sitting on the floor with her legs crossed.* 她盘着腿坐在地上。

5 cross your fingers used to say that you hope something will happen in the way you want 希望如愿，但愿，祈求: *Cross your fingers that I get the job.* 为我祈求能得到那份工作。

6 cross sb's mind if an idea, thought etc crosses someone's mind, it comes into their mind for a short time〔想法、思想等〕掠过，一闪而过: *It never crossed my mind to check whether the deal was genuine.* 我从来没想过去核实这项交易是不是真的。| **the thought has crossed my mind** (=used to tell someone you have thought of the thing they are suggesting) 我动过这个念头

7 cross sb's face if an expression crosses someone's face, it appears on their face 脸上浮现出〔某种表情〕: *A look of horror crossed Ken's face when he realized what he had done.* 意识到自己做的事时，肯的脸上露出恐惧的神色。

8 cross that bridge when you come to it used to say that you will not think or worry about something until it actually happens 船到桥头自然直；不用为未发生之事担心；问题发生了再考虑解决: *Don't worry about running out of money. We'll cross that bridge when we come to it.* 别担心钱会用完，船到桥头自然直。

9 ►BREED OF PLANT/ANIMAL 种植植物/繁殖动物◄[T] to mix two or more different breeds of animal or plant to form a new breed 杂交: *This flower has been produced by crossing several different varieties.* 这种花是由几种不同的品种杂交而成的。| [**+with**] *If you cross a horse with a donkey, you get a mule.* 马与驴杂交的后代是骡子。—see also 另见 CROSS² (3), CROSSBREED¹

10 cross my heart (and hope to die) *spoken informal* used to say that you promise that you will do something or that what you are saying is true【口，非正式】〔在胸口画十字〕答应要做某事；发誓所说属实: *I didn't take it, cross my heart!* 我发誓我没有拿！

11 sb's paths cross if two people's paths cross they meet, usually unexpectedly 不期而遇，偶然遇见: *I know Irving quite well – our paths first crossed when we were at Yale.* 我和欧文很熟，我们第一次见面是在耶鲁大学。

12 ►MAKE SB ANGRY 使某人生气◄[T] to make someone angry by opposing their plans or orders 惹…生气: *Anyone who dares to cross me will find themselves in serious trouble.* 谁胆敢惹我生气，一定会给自己惹来大麻烦。

13 ►SPORT 体育◄[I,T] to kick, throw, or hit the ball across the playing area in a sport such as football, HOCKEY etc〔在足球、曲棍球等运动中〕横传（球）

14 ►CHEQUE 支票◄[T] *BrE* to draw two lines across a cheque to show that it must be paid into a bank account【英】〔在支票上〕画两条平行线〔则支票只能转入银行账户而不能支取现金〕

15 cross swords (with) to argue with someone 与…争论[辩论]；交锋: *He has crossed swords with the district attorney several times.* 他已经和地方检察官争论过数次。

16 cross yourself to move your hand across your upper body in the shape of a cross, especially as a sign of the Roman Catholic faith 用手在胸前画十字〔尤为罗马天主教信仰的象征〕

17 cross sb's palm with silver *especially BrE* to give money to someone【尤英】给…钱 —see also 另见 **dot the i's and cross the t's** (DOT² (4)), **keep your fingers crossed** (FINGER¹ (3)), **cross the Rubicon** (RUBICON)

cross sth ↔ **off** *phr v* [T] to draw a line through one or more things on a list because you have dealt with them or they are not needed any more 画掉，删去〔已经处理或无用的东西〕: *As you do each job, cross it off the list.* 每做完一件事，就把它从清单上画掉。

cross sth ↔ **out** *phr v* [T] to draw a line or lines through something you have written or drawn, usually because it is wrong 画掉，删去〔错误的内容〕

cross over *phr v* [I] **1** if an entertainer crosses over from one area of entertainment to another, they become successful in the second one as well as the first〔娱乐界人士〕转型成功 **2** *BrE old use* to die【英旧】死

cross² *n* [C] 3 3

1 ►CHRISTIAN SIGN 基督教的标记◄a) an upright post of wood with another crossing it, that people were nailed to and left to die on as a punishment in the past 十字架: *Christians believe that Jesus Christ died on a cross.* 基督徒相信耶稣基督死在十字架上。**b)** an object or picture in the shape of a cross used as a sign of the Christian faith or for decoration 十字形物体[图画]〔以示信仰或装饰〕: *Pauline wore a tiny gold cross around her neck.* 波琳脖子上戴着一个小小的金十字架。| **the Cross** (=cross that Christ died on, used as a sign of Christian faith) 十字架〔基督被钉死之处，基督教信仰的标记〕

2 ►A MARK ON PAPER 纸上的记号◄*especially BrE*【尤英】**a)** a mark (x or +) used on paper, to represent where something is, or where something should be〔在纸上标出所在位置的〕十字标记〈如 x 或 +〉: *I've put a cross on the map to mark where our house is.* 我已在地图上用十字标出我们的房子所在的位置。| *Please sign your name by the cross, to give your consent.* 请在十字标记旁边签名，以示同意。**b)** a mark (x) used on paper to show that something that has been written or printed is not correct 叉号〔以示错处〕: *There were more crosses than ticks on Mark's French homework.* 马克的法语家庭作业上叉号比勾号多。**c)** a mark (x or +) used by someone who cannot write to write their name〔不识字的人签名时画的〕十字押

3 a mixture of two things, breeds, or qualities 混合物；杂交；杂种: *Their dog is a Jack Russell cross.* 他们的狗是杰克·拉塞尔种杂交犬。| [**+between**] *He seems to think his girlfriend is a cross between Naomi Campbell and Tina Turner.* 他好像认为他的女朋友是娜奥米·坎贝尔和蒂娜·特纳的结合体。

4 ►MILITARY AWARD 军事奖赏◄a decoration in the shape of a cross worn as an honour, especially for military bravery 十字勋章: *He was awarded the George Cross.* 他被授予乔治十字勋章。

5 ►SPORT 体育◄a) a kick or hit of the ball in a sport such as football, HOCKEY etc that goes across the field〔将球〕踢[击]过场地 **b)** a way of hitting someone in the sport of BOXING in which your arm goes over theirs as they try to hit you〔拳击中〕勾拳迎击

6a (heavy) cross to bear a problem that makes you very unhappy or worried, often one that continues for a long time〔尤指长期的〕心理负担，心病；烦恼：*His mother's illness has been a very heavy cross to bear.* 母亲的病一直是他的一大心理负担。—see also 另见 **the sign of the Cross** (SIGN¹ (10))

2 **cross³** *adj especially BrE* angry or annoyed【尤英】生气的，恼怒的：**get cross** *Charlotte, Mummy will get very cross if you do it again.* 夏洛特，你再这样做，妈妈会很生气的。| **get/be cross with sb** *Alright you two, don't get cross with each other!* 好了，你们两个不要互相生气啦！—see also 另见 CROSSWIND

cross·bar /ˈkrɔs,bɑr; ˈkrɒsbɑː/ *n* [C] **1** a bar that joins two upright posts especially two GOALPOSTS〔连接两个立柱，尤指球门的〕横木 **2** the metal bar between the seat and the HANDLEBARS on a man's bicycle〔自行车的〕横梁 —see picture at 参见 BICYCLE¹ 图

cross·bones /ˈkrɔs,bonz; ˈkrɒsbəʊnz/ *n* —see 见 SKULL AND CROSSBONES

cross·bow /ˈkrɔs,bo; ˈkrɒsbəʊ/ *n* [C] a weapon like a small BOW³(1) fixed onto a longer piece of wood, used for shooting bolts (=short, heavy sticks) 十字弓，弩

cross·breed¹ /ˈkrɔs,brid; ˈkrɒsbriːd/ *v* [I,T] **a)** to make one kind of a plant or animal breed with a different breed（使）杂交 **b)** if a plant or animal crossbreeds it breeds with one of a different breed〔动植物的〕杂交繁殖—**crossbred** /ˈkrɔs,brɛd; ˈkrɒsbred/ *adj*

crossbreed² *n* [C] an animal or plant that is a mixture of breeds〔动植物的〕杂交品种 —compare 比较 INTERBREED

cross-Chan·nel /,ˑˈˑˑ◂/ *adj* travelling across the English Channel 横渡英吉利海峡的：*There are several cross-Channel ferries from Dover every day.* 每天有好几班从多佛尔出发横渡英吉利海峡的渡船。

cross·check /,krɔsˈtʃɛk; ,krɒsˈtʃek/ *v* [T] to make certain that results or calculations are correct by using a different method of calculation from the one you first used〔用不同的计算方法〕反复核对，核实—**crosscheck** *n* [C]

cross-coun·try¹ /,ˑˈˑˑ◂/ *adj* across fields or open country 越野的：*Duncan prefers cross-country skiing to down-hill.* 比起速降滑雪，邓肯更喜欢越野滑雪。—**cross-country** *adv*: *travelling cross-country* 越野旅行

cross-country² *n* [C,U] *BrE* a race that is run across countryside and fields, not on a track【英】越野赛跑

cross-cul·tu·ral /,ˑˈˑˑˑ◂/ *adj* belonging to or involving two or more different societies, countries or cultures (CULTURE (1)) 跨文化的，交叉文化间的

cross·cur·rent /ˈkrɔs,kɝənt; ˈkrɒs,kʌrənt/ *n* [C] a current in the sea, a river etc that moves across the general direction of the main current〔海、河等中的〕交叉水流，逆流

cross-dress·ing /,ˑˈˑˑ/ *n* [U] *AmE* the practice of wearing the clothes of the opposite sex, especially for sexual pleasure【美】穿异性服装—**cross-dresser** *n* [C]

crossed /krɔst; krɒst/ *adj* if a telephone line is crossed, it is connected by mistake to two or more telephones, so that you can hear other people's conversations〔电话〕串线的

crossed cheque /,ˑˈˑ/ *n* [C] a cheque in Britain that has two lines across it showing that it must be paid into a bank account 画线支票〔英国的一种支票，画有两条平行线，只能入银行账户〕

cross-ex·am·ine /,ˑˑˈˑˑ/ *v* [T] to question someone very thoroughly, especially a WITNESS in a law court 盘问〔尤指法庭上盘问证人〕—**cross-examination** /,ˑˑˑˑˈˑˑ/ *n* [C,U]—**cross-examiner** /,ˑˑˈˑˑˑ/ *n* [C]

cross-eyed /,ˑˈˑ◂/ *adj* having eyes that look in towards the nose 内斜视的，斗鸡眼的；BOSS-EYED *BrE*【英】

cross-fer·ti·lize also 又作-**ise** *BrE*【英】/,ˑˈˑˑˑ/ *v* [T] **1** to combine the male sex cells from one type of plant with female sex cells from another 使〔植物〕异体受精 **2** [often passive 常用被动态] to influence someone or something with ideas from other areas〔与不同地区的思想接触〕（使）相互影响：*Europe has been cross-fertilized by contact with many other societies.* 欧洲因与其他许多社会接触而受影响。—**cross-fertilization** /,ˑˑˑˑˈˑˑ/ *n* [U]

cross·fire /ˈkrɔs,faɪr; ˈkrɒsfaɪə/ *n* [U] **1 be caught in the crossfire** to be involved in a situation in which other people are arguing, when you do not want to be 被卷入〔不想参与的他人的〕争辩中：*I left the room to avoid being caught in the crossfire between Dad and William.* 我离开房间，以免被卷入爸爸和威廉的争辩中。**2** two or more lines of bullets being fired across a particular point 交叉火力

cross-grained /,ˑˈˑ◂/ *adj* wood that is cross-grained has lines that go across it instead of along it〔木材〕横纹的，斜纹的

cross-hatch·ing /ˈˑ,ˑˑ/ *n* [U] lines drawn across part of a picture, DIAGRAM etc to show that something is made of different material, or to produce the effect of shade〔图画、图表等中表明不同材料或阴影的〕交叉影线

cross·ing /ˈkrɔsɪŋ; ˈkrɒsɪŋ/ *n* [C] **1** a marked place where you can safely cross a road, railway, river etc〔道路、铁路的〕（人行）横道；〔河流的〕渡口 —see also 另见 LEVEL CROSSING, PEDESTRIAN CROSSING, PELICAN CROSSING, ZEBRA CROSSING **2** a place where two lines, roads, tracks etc cross 十字路口，交叉路口 **3** a journey across the sea 横渡海洋的旅程，跨海旅程：*The crossing was rough and lots of people were seasick.* 这次渡海风急浪大，许多人都晕船了。

cross-legged 盘着腿

She sat with her legs crossed. 她跷着腿坐着。

Paul is sitting cross-legged. 保尔盘腿坐着。

cross-legged /,krɔs ˈlɛgɪd; ,krɒs ˈlegd◂/ *adv* in a sitting position with your knees wide apart and ankles crossed 盘着腿：*children sitting cross-legged on the floor* 盘腿坐在地上的孩子们—**cross-legged** *adj*

cross·o·ver /ˈkrɔs,ovɚ; ˈkrɒsəʊvə/ *n* [C] the change a popular performer makes from working in one area of entertainment to another〔娱乐圈人士的〕转型，转向：[+from] *Madonna has made a crossover from rock music to the movies.* 麦当娜从摇滚乐转向电影发展。—see also 另见 **cross over** (CROSS¹)

crossover pri·ma·ry /ˈˑˑˑ,ˑˑˑ/ *n* [C] *AmE* an OPEN PRIMARY【美】开放预选

cross·patch /ˈkrɔs,pætʃ; ˈkrɒspætʃ/ *n* [C] *old-fashioned* someone who is bad-tempered【过时】脾气暴躁的人

cross·piece /ˈkrɔs,pis; ˈkrɒspiːs/ *n* [C] something that lies across another thing, especially in a building, railway track etc〔尤指建筑物、铁轨等的〕横木，横杆，横档

cross·ply /ˈkrɔs,plaɪ; ˈkrɒsplaɪ/ *adj* RADIAL 辐射状的

cross-pur·pos·es /,ˑˈˑˑˑ/ *n* **at cross-purposes** two people who are at cross-purposes do not understand each other, because they are talking about different things but do not realize it〔因未意识到而〕互相误解

cross-ques·tion /,ˑˈˑˑ/ *v* [T] to CROSS-EXAMINE someone 盘问，反诘—**cross-questioner** *n*

cross-re·fer /,ˑˑˈˑ/ *v* [I,T] to tell a reader to look in another place in the book they are reading so that they can get further information〔书中〕互见，相互参照：[+to/from] *The author cross-refers you to Chapter 10 for more details.* 作者建议你参考第10章以了解更多细节。

cross-ref·er·ence /,ˑˈˑˑˑ/ *n* [C] a note that tells the reader of a book to go to another place in the book, to get further information〔书中的〕互见，相互参照

cross·roads /ˈkrɔs,rodz; ˈkrɒsrəʊdz/ *n plural* **crossroads 1** a place where two roads meet and cross each other 十字路口，交叉路口 **2** a time in your life when you have to make a very important decision that will affect your future〔人生作出重大决定的〕关键时期，转折点：*When my marriage ended, I felt as if I had reached a crossroads in my life.* 当我的婚姻结束时，我觉得好像处于人生的十字路口。

cross-sec·tion /ˈˑ,ˑˑ/ *n* [C] **1** something that has been cut in half so that you can look at the inside, or a drawing of this 横截面（图），剖面（图）：*cross-section of a plant stem* 植物茎的横截面（图）**2** a group of people or things that is typical of a much larger group 典型；有代表性的一群：*a cross-section of the American public* 美国公众的典型代表

cross-stitch /ˈˑˑ/ *n* [C,U] a stitch in a cross shape used in decorative sewing 十字形针法〔用于装饰的缝法〕

cross street /ˈˑˑ/ *n* [C] *AmE* a smaller street that crosses the street you are on【美】〔穿过所处大街的〕小街道

cross·town /ˈkrɔs,taʊn; ˈkrɒstaʊn/ *adj* [only before noun 仅用于名词前] *AmE* moving in a direction across a town or city【美】穿过城镇的：*the crosstown bus* 穿越市区的公共汽车

cross trees /ˈ· ·/ *n* [plural] *technical* two beams fastened across the top of a ship's MAST (1)【术语】桅顶横桁

cross·walk /ˈkrɔsˌwɔk; ˈkrɒswɔːk/ *n* [C] *AmE* a special place for people to cross the road【美】人行横道; PEDESTRIAN CROSSING *BrE*【英】

cross·wind /ˈkrɔsˌwɪnd; ˈkrɒsˌwɪnd/ *n* [C] a wind that blows across the direction that you are moving in 侧风

cross·wise /ˈkrɔsˌwaɪz; ˈkrɒsˌwaɪz/ *adv* **1 lay/cut sth crosswise** to lay etc something from one corner of something to the opposite corner 斜对角地放/切某物 **2** two things that are placed crosswise are arranged to form the shape of an 'x'〔两样东西呈X形〕交叉叠放地

cross·word /ˈkrɔsˌwɜd; ˈkrɒsˌwɜːd/ also 又作 **crossword puz·zle** /ˈ· ·, ·ˈ/ *n* [C] a word game in which you write the answers to questions in a pattern of numbered boxes 纵横字谜, 纵横填字(游戏)

CULTURAL NOTE 文化注释

Crosswords are very popular in the US and the UK and appear in many different newspapers and magazines. Some crosswords are known for being very difficult, for example *The Times* crossword in the UK, and *The New York Times* crossword in the US. People who can finish these crosswords quickly are often considered to be very clever. 纵横字谜游戏在英美两国很流行, 很多报刊都有字谜游戏。有些字谜以难度大而著称, 如英国《泰晤士报》和美国《纽约时报》上的字谜游戏。能迅速填出字谜的人常被认为极其聪明。

crotch /kratʃ; krɒtʃ/ also 又作 **crutch** *BrE*【英】 *n* [C] the part of your body between the tops of your legs, or the part of a piece of clothing that covers this 胯部; 裤裆 —see picture at 参见 BODY 图

crotch·et /ˈkratʃɪt; ˈkrɒtʃɪt/ *n* [C] *BrE* a musical note which continues for a quarter of the length of a SEMIBREVE【英】四分音符; QUARTER NOTE *AmE*【美】—see picture at 参见 MUSIC 图

crotch·et·y /ˈkratʃətɪ; ˈkrɒtʃɪti/ *adj* often slightly angry or annoyed 脾气坏的; 爱发牢骚的: *a crotchety old man* 脾气坏的老人

crouch 蹲下, 蹲伏

squat 蹲(坐)

crouch/squat 蹲下

crouch 蹲伏

crouch /krautʃ; kraʊtʃ/ *v* [I] **1** also 又作 **crouch down** to lower your body close to the ground by bending your knees completely 蹲下: *My legs began to ache from crouching for so long.* 蹲了那么久我的腿开始痛了。| *The boy crouched down to fix his sandal.* 那个男孩蹲下来系凉鞋。**2** if an animal crouches it sits as low as possible, often because it is frightened or is going to attack something〔动物因为害怕或准备攻击而〕蹲伏: *The cat crouched, its eyes following the mouse as it scurried away.* 猫蹲伏着, 两眼盯着匆匆跑开的老鼠。

croup /krup; kruːp/ *n* [U] an illness in children which makes them cough and have difficulty breathing 格鲁布, 哮吼〔发生于儿童的一种疾病, 患者咳嗽, 呼吸困难〕

crou·pi·er /ˈkrupɪɚ; ˈkruːpiə/ *n* [C] someone whose job is to collect and pay out money where people play cards, ROULETTE etc for money〔赌场上的〕赌资收付人

crou·ton /ˈkrutan; ˈkruːtɒn/ *n* [C usually plural 一般用复数] a small square piece of bread cooked in fat and served with soup or on salad 油炸面包丁〔与汤一起吃或放在色拉上〕

crow¹ /kro; krəʊ/ *n* **1** [C] a large shiny black bird with a loud cry 乌鸦 **2** [singular] the loud sound a COCK¹ (1) makes 公鸡的鸣叫声 **3 as the crow flies** in a straight line 笔直地, 直线地: *ten miles from here as the crow flies* 离这里直线距离10英里 —see also 另见 **eat crow** (EAT (5))

crow² *v* [I] **1** if a COCK¹ (1) crows, it makes a loud high sound〔雄鸡〕啼叫 **2** if a baby crows, it makes a noise that shows it is happy〔婴儿〕欢叫: *The baby crowed with delight at the toy.* 婴儿看到玩具高兴得叫起来。**3** [+over/about] to talk about what you have done in a very proud way 得意洋洋地谈论

Crow, Jim —see 见 JIM CROW

crow·bar /ˈkroˌbar; ˈkrəʊbɑː/ *n* [C] a heavy iron bar used to lift or open things 铁撬棍

crowd¹ /kraud; kraʊd/ *n* **1** [C] a large group of people in a public place 人群: *A vast crowd had assembled in the main square.* 主要广场上聚集了一大群人。**2** [C] a large number of a particular kind of people or things 一群; 一堆: [+of] *a crowd of supporters* 一群支持者 | *Kemp stepped out to face a crowd of cameras.* 肯普走出去面对一大堆摄影记者。| **crowds of** *streets filled with crowds of people* 挤满了人的街道 **3** [singular] *informal* a group of people who know each other, work together etc【非正式】〔互相认识、一起工作等的〕一群人; 一伙人; 一帮人: *"Who'll be at the party?" "Oh, the usual crowd – Maura, Tom, Joe, Jen, Turi..."* "晚会有谁参加?" "哦, 平时的那一伙人, 毛拉、汤姆、乔、珍、图里…" **4 follow the crowd/go with the crowd** to always do what other people do, without thinking for yourself 随大溜, 人云亦云

crowd² *v* **1** [I,T] to gather together in large numbers, filling a particular place, or moving in a particular direction 群集, 聚集; 拥挤: *Supporters crowded the stadium.* 支持者群集在体育场里。| [+around/into etc] *We all crowded around the speaker.* 我们都聚集在演讲者周围。**2** [T] if thoughts or ideas crowd your brain, mind, head etc, they fill it〔想法或观点〕塞满〔脑子〕: *A jumble of confused thoughts crowded my brain.* 一堆杂乱无章的想法塞满了我的脑袋。**3** [T] **a)** to make someone angry by moving too close to them 挤, 逼近〔因而激怒〕: *The guy standing behind me was crowding me, so I poked him in the ribs.* 站在我后面的那个人挤我, 所以我戳了一下他的肋骨。**b)** *especially AmE* to make someone angry or upset by making too many unfair demands on them【尤美】催促; 催逼〔因而激怒烦扰〕: *Stop crowding me! I need time to make this decision.* 不要再催我了! 我需要时间来作决定。

crowd sb/sth ↔ **out** *phr v* [T] to force someone or something out of a place or situation 把…挤出, 排挤: *The bigger software firms are crowding small businesses out.* 较大的软件公司正在将小公司排挤出局。

crowd·ed /ˈkraudɪd; ˈkraʊdɪd/ *adj* too full of people or things 挤满人[物]的; 拥挤的: *Sometimes the classes were very crowded.* 有时课堂上非常拥挤。| *a crowded street* 拥挤的街道 | [+with] *It was two weeks before Christmas and the mall was crowded with shoppers.* 离圣诞节还有两个星期, 商场挤满了购物者。

crown¹ /kraun; kraʊn/ *n* **1** [C] **a)** a circle made of gold and decorated with jewels, worn by kings and queens on their heads 皇冠, 冕 **b)** a similar circle, sometimes made of other things such as leaves or flowers, worn by someone who has won a special honour〔象征特殊荣誉的〕冠帽 **2 the crown a)** the position of being king or queen 王位: *when the crown passed to George the Third...* 当王位传给乔治三世的时候… **b)** the government of a country such as Britain that is officially led by a king or queen 王国政府: *The islands are possessions of the Crown.* 这些岛屿是王国政府的。**3** [usually singular 一般用单数] the top part of a hat, head, or hill〔帽子、头或山的〕顶部: *a hat with a high crown* 高帽子 —see picture at 参见 HAT 图 **4 a)** a unit of money in several European countries 克朗〔欧洲有些国家的货币单位〕: *Swedish crowns* 瑞典克朗 **b)** an old British coin, four of which made a pound〔英国旧币的〕四分之一镑硬币 **5** [C] an artificial top for a damaged tooth 假齿冠 **6** a mark, sign, BADGE etc in the shape of a crown, used especially to show rank or quality 冠状物〔用于表示等级或质量〕**7** *informal* the fact of winning an important sports competition【非正式】获得冠军: *Can she retain her Wimbledon crown?* 她能保住她的温布尔登冠军地位吗?

crown² *v* [T] **1** to place a crown on someone's head as a sign of royal power 为…加冕, 立…为王: *The Empress was crowned ten years ago.* 女皇是在10年前加冕的。| **crown sb king/queen** *Henry was crowned king.* 亨利加冕为王。**2** to make something complete or perfect by adding success, beauty, happiness etc to it 使圆满成功; 完善: **crown sth with** *All their efforts have been crowned with success.* 他们的一切努力以圆满成功告终。**3 crowned with** *literary* having something on top【文】给…加顶, 覆盖…的顶端: *mountain peaks crowned with snow* 白雪覆盖的山峰 **4** to put a protective top on a damaged tooth 镶假牙冠 **5** *slang* to hit someone on the head【俚】打〔某人〕的头部 **6 to crown it all** *informal* used to say that the next thing that happened was the worst in a series of bad things【非正式】最糟糕的是: *And then, to crown it all, I lost my purse.* 然后, 最糟糕的是, 我丢了钱包。

crown col·o·ny /ˌ· ˈ··/ *n* [C] a COLONY[1] controlled by the British government〔英国政府的〕直辖殖民地

crown court /ˈ· ·/ *n* [C,U] a court of law in Britain that deals with serious criminal cases and is higher than a Magistrates' Court〔英国的〕刑事法院

Crown Der·by /ˌ· ˈ··/ a type of fine PORCELAIN made in the city of Derby, England in the 18th and 19th centuries 皇家王冠德比瓷器〔18、19世纪产于英格兰德比市的一种精致瓷器〕

crowned head /ˌ· ˈ·/ *n* [C usually plural 一般用复数] a king or queen 国王；女王：*All the crowned heads of Europe were present at the funeral.* 欧洲所有的君主都出席了葬礼。

crown·ing glory /ˈkraunɪŋ ˈglɔri; ˈkraʊnɪŋ glɔːri/ *n* [singular] **1** something that is more valuable, beautiful, or important than anything else you have or do 无上光荣；最有价值[最漂亮；最重要]的东西：*The hotel's crowning glory was a stunning roof garden with a panoramic view.* 这家酒店最精彩的是一个令人惊叹的屋顶花园，在那里周围的景物一览无遗。**2** *humorous* your hair【幽默】头发

C

crown jew·els /ˌ· ˈ··/ *n* [plural] the crown, sword, jewels etc worn by a king or queen for ceremonies 御宝〔国王或王后参加典礼时佩戴的王冠、宝剑、珠宝等〕

crown prince /ˌ· ˈ·◂/ *n* [C] the boy or man who is expected to become the next king 王太子，王储：*Crown Prince Frederick* 弗雷德里克王储

crown prin·cess /ˌ· ˈ··◂/ *n* [C] the girl or woman who is expected to become queen 将继承王位的公主，女王储：*the Crown Princess of Prussia* 普鲁士的女王储

Crown Pro·se·cu·tion Ser·vice, the /ˌ· ··ˈ·· ˌ··/ abbreviation 缩写为 **the CPS** the government organization in England and Wales which is responsible for bringing legal charges against criminals 刑事检察院〔英格兰、威尔士一政府机构，负责审理刑事案件〕

crow's feet /ˈ· ·/ *n* [plural] very small lines in the skin near your eyes〔眼角外的〕鱼尾纹

crow's nest /ˈ· ·/ *n* [C] a small box at the top of a ship's MAST (1) from which someone can watch for danger, land etc 桅杆瞭望台

cro·zier, crosier /ˈkroʒɚ; ˈkrəʊʒə/ *n* [C] a long stick with a decorative curved end carried by a BISHOP (1) 主教的权杖

CRT /ˌsi ɑ ˈti; ˌsiː ɑː ˈtiː/ *n* [C] the abbreviation of 缩写= CATHODE RAY TUBE

3 2 **cru·cial** /ˈkruʃəl; ˈkruːʃəl/ *adj* **1** something that is crucial is extremely important because everything else depends on it 决定性的，紧要关头的：*crucial decisions involving millions of dollars* 事关几百万美元的重要决定 **2** *slang* excellent【俚】极好的，非常好的 —**crucially** *adv*

cru·ci·ble /ˈkrusəbl; ˈkruːsɨ̣bəl/ *n* [C] a container in which substances are heated to very high temperatures 坩埚

Crucible, The a play by Arthur Miller which describes how INNOCENT women were charged with being WITCHes and cruelly punished by a court of law in Salem, Massachusetts in 1692. This play was written in 1953 to show how similar the **Salem Witch Trials** were to McCarthyism.《炼狱》〔阿瑟·米勒创作的一部戏剧。剧中的无辜女性被指控为女巫，并在1692年马萨诸塞州的赛勒姆法庭上受到残酷迫害。剧本创作于1953年，旨在表明麦卡锡主义与赛勒姆女巫审讯案何其相似〕

cru·ci·fix /ˈkrusəˌfɪks; ˈkruːsɨ̣fɪks/ *n* [C] a cross with a figure of Christ on it 有耶稣像的十字架

cru·ci·fix·ion /ˌkrusəˈfɪkʃən; ˌkruːsɨ̣ˈfɪkʃən/ *n* **1** [C,U] the act of killing someone by fastening them to a cross and leaving them to die 钉死在十字架上 **2 the Crucifixion** the death of Christ in this way 耶稣受难〔被钉死在十字架上〕**3** [C] also 又作 **Crucifixion** a picture or other object representing Christ on the cross 耶稣受难像

cru·ci·form /ˈkrusəˌfɔrm; ˈkruːsɨ̣fɔːm/ *adj* shaped like a cross 十字形的

cru·ci·fy /ˈkrusəˌfaɪ; ˈkruːsɨ̣faɪ/ *v* [T] **1** to kill someone by fastening them to a cross 把…钉在十字架上处死 **2** to criticize someone severely and cruelly for something they have done, especially in public〔尤指当众〕狠狠批评，严厉指责：*If the newspapers find out you'll be crucified.* 如果报界发现的话，你会受到严厉的指责。

crud /krʌd; krʌd/ *n* [U] *informal* something unpleasant to look at, smell, taste etc【非正式】〔难闻、难吃等〕令人厌恶的事物：*I can't eat this crud!* 我没法吃这破玩意儿！—**cruddy** *adj*

crude[1] /krud; kruːd/ *adj* **1** offensive or rude, especially in a sexual way; VULGAR (1) 粗俗的，粗野的；粗鲁的：*a crude gesture* 粗鲁的手势 | *crude jokes* 粗俗的笑话 **2** not developed to a high standard or made with great skill 粗制的：*crude tools made of stone* 粗制的石头工具 **3** crude oil, rubber etc is in its natural or raw condition before it is treated with chemicals〔石油、橡胶等〕天然的，未加提炼的 **4** done without attention to detail 粗糙的；未加修饰的；简陋的：*a crude comparison of different engines* 不同引擎间的粗略比较 **5 in crude terms** expressed in a simple way 简单地说：*In crude terms, the gulf between wealth and poverty is growing wider each year.* 简单地说，贫富之间的差距每年都在扩大。—**crudely** *adv*: *crudely built shacks* 粗糙建造的棚屋 —**crudity** also 又作 **crudeness** *n* [C,U]

crude[2] also 又作 **crude oil** /ˌ· ˈ·/ *n* [U] the oil that comes out of OIL WELLs, before it is separated into different products 原油：*1000 barrels of crude* 1000桶原油

cru·dit·és /ˌkrudəˈte; ˈkruːdɨ̣teɪ/ *n* [plural] *French* pieces of raw vegetable served before a meal【法】〔饭前吃的〕生拌凉菜 —see picture on page A15 参见A15页图

cru·el /ˈkruəl; ˈkruːəl/ *adj* **1** causing unfair or unnecessary pain or suffering 残忍的，残酷的：*a cruel twist of fate* 命运的残酷转折 | **a cruel blow** (=a sudden event that is painful and unfair) 残酷的打击 *My brother's death was a cruel blow.* 我兄弟的去世是个无情的打击。**2** deliberately making people or animals suffer 有意伤害的：*The older kids played cruel jokes on her little brother.* 大孩子们开她小弟弟恶毒的玩笑。| **cruel look/smile/laugh etc** *Cilla gave a cruel laugh and left him standing there alone.* 西莉亚冷酷地笑了笑，留下他独自一人站在那里。**3 be cruel to be kind** to do something to someone that will make them upset or unhappy in order to help them in another way 为使人今后受益而让其先吃苦头 —**cruelly** *adv*: *cruelly neglected by his parents* 父母任由他自生自灭，十分残酷 3

Cru·el·la de Vil /kruˌɛlə də ˈvɪl; kruˌelə də ˈvɪl/ a cruel and evil woman in the children's book and Disney films *One Hundred and One Dalmatians*. She pretends to be friendly in order to get the spotted fur of the DALMATIAN dogs in order to make a coat from it. 库伊拉〔儿童读物及迪斯尼影片《101忠狗》中的一个残酷邪恶的女人。她装出一副友善的样子，为的是得到大麦町犬带斑点的皮毛做狗皮大衣〕

cru·el·ty /ˈkruəltɪ; ˈkruːəlti/ *n* **1** [U] a willingness or desire to make people or animals suffer 残忍，残酷：*There was a hint of cruelty in Brian's smile.* 布赖恩的微笑流露出一丝残忍。**2** [U] behaviour that deliberately causes pain to people or animals 残忍的行为：*The children had suffered cruelty and neglect.* 这些孩子受了虐待，根本没有人管。| [+to] *cruelty to animals* 对动物的残忍 **3** [C] a cruel action 残忍的行动：*horrifying cruelties that occur in wartime* 战争时期令人发指的暴行 **4** [U] the unfairness of something that happens 不公平，不公正：*Ruth's eyes filled with tears at life's cruelty.* 鲁思由于生活的不公而双眼含满了泪水。

cru·et /ˈkruɪt; ˈkruːɨ̣t/ *n* [C] a thing that holds the containers for salt, pepper etc on a table 放调料瓶的小架

Cruft's /krʌfts; krʌfts/ a famous British competition for dogs, officially called **Cruft's Dog Show**, which is held every year in London. Judges at the show decide which is the best animal in the country for each type of dog (the 'best of breed'), and they also decide which is the best dog of all, which gets the title 'Cruft's supreme champion'. 克拉夫特狗展〔英国著名的赛狗会，正式名称为Craft's Dog Show，每年在伦敦举行。评委要评出每一犬种的"最佳"，并从参赛的各类犬中评出"克拉夫特超级冠军"〕

cruise[1] /kruz; kruːz/ *v* **1** [I] to sail along slowly, especially for pleasure〔尤指为了娱乐〕乘船巡游：*cruising in the Mediterranean* 乘船在地中海游弋 **2** [I] to move at a steady speed in a car, aircraft etc〔飞机〕巡航，〔汽车〕以快而平稳的速度行驶：*cruising at 50 miles per hour* 以每小时50英里的稳定速度行驶 **3** [I, T] to drive a car slowly through a place with no particular purpose 开车兜风：*We were out cruising Friday night, and I saw Jerry with Kimberly.* 星期五晚上我们开车兜风时，我看到杰里和金伯莉在一起。**4** [I,T] *slang* to look in a public place for a sexual partner【俚】〔在公共场所〕寻觅性伴侣：*cruising the singles bars* 在单身酒吧寻觅性伴侣

cruise[2] *n* [C] **1** a holiday on a large ship 在大船上度假：*a Caribbean cruise* 乘船在加勒比海度假 **2** a journey by boat for pleasure 乘船游览

cruise con·trol /ˈ· ·ˌ·/ *n* [C] a piece of equipment in a car that makes it go at a steady speed〔汽车的〕匀速控制器

cruise li·ner /ˈ· ˌ··/ *n* [C] a large ship for cruising 游览班轮

cruise mis·sile /ˌ· ˈ··/ *n* [C] a large explosive weapon that flies close to the ground and can be aimed at an exact point hundreds of kilometres away 巡航导弹

cruis·er /ˈkruzɚ; ˈkruːzə/ *n* [C] **1** a large fast warship 巡洋舰：*a battle cruiser* 战列巡洋舰 **2** a boat used for pleasure 游艇 **3** *AmE* a police car【美】警车

cruise ship /ˈ· ·ˌ/ *n* [C] a large ship with restaurants, bars etc that people have holidays on〔设有餐馆、酒吧等供度假的〕大型邮轮

cru·ller /ˈkrʌlɚ; ˈkrʌlə/ *n* [C] *AmE* a small piece of sweet bread with a twisted shape【美】炸面圈，炸麻花

crumb /krʌm; krʌm/ *n* [C] **1** a very small piece of dry food, especially bread or cake 食品屑；面包[蛋糕]屑：*Brush the crumbs off the table.* 把桌上的面包屑拭掉。—see picture on page A7 参见 A7 页图 **2 crumb of comfort/hope etc** a very small amount of comfort, hope etc 少许的安慰／希望等：*Marie's offer of help was our only crumb of comfort.* 玛丽提出帮助我们是我们唯一的小小安慰。**3** *AmE old-fashioned* someone who has done something unpleasant【美，过时】讨厌的人

crum·ble¹ /ˈkrʌmbḷ; ˈkrʌmbəl/ *v* **1** [I,T] also 又作 **crumble away** to break apart into little pieces, or make something do this 把…弄碎，(使)碎成细屑：*Billy crumbled the bread in his fingers.* 比利用手指把面包捻碎。**2** [I] if a building crumbles, it is old and starting to fall down〔建筑物〕破旧：*Britain's crumbling schools* 英国的破旧学校 **3** [I] also 又作 **crumble away** if your determination, courage etc crumbles, it becomes weak or fails〔决心、勇气等〕减弱，崩溃：*Brigg's resolve crumbled and he reached for the whisky bottle.* 布里格的决心动摇了，伸手去拿威士忌瓶子。**4** [I] if a military operation, government etc crumbles, it loses its power and its effectiveness〔军事行动〕挫败；〔政府〕败落，衰败：*a crumbling empire* 败落的帝国

crumble² *n* [U] a cooked dish of fruit covered with a dry mixture of flour, butter, and sugar 酥皮水果甜点心：*apple crumble* 酥皮苹果甜点心

crum·bly /ˈkrʌmblɪ; ˈkrʌmbli/ *adj* something such as food or soil that is crumbly breaks easily into small pieces〔食物、土壤等〕易碎的，脆的：*a nice, crumbly cheese* 松脆可口的干酪

crumbs /krʌmz; krʌmz/ *interjection BrE informal* used to express surprise【英，非正式】喔哟，哎呀〔用于表示惊讶〕

crum·my /ˈkrʌmɪ; ˈkrʌmi/ *adj informal*【非正式】**1** of bad quality 劣质的：*a crummy book* 糟糕的书 | *What a crummy idea!* 真是个馊主意！**2** ill or upset 生病的，身体不舒服的：*I felt pretty crummy the next morning.* 第二天早上我感觉相当不舒服。

crum·pet /ˈkrʌmpɪt; ˈkrʌmpɪ̣t/ *n* **1** [C] a small round bread with holes in one side, eaten hot with butter 小圆烤饼 **2** [U] *BrE slang* an offensive word for a sexually attractive woman【英俚】骚货〔对性感的女人的冒犯用语〕

crum·ple /ˈkrʌmpḷ; ˈkrʌmpəl/ *v* **1** [I,T] also 又作 **crumple up** to crush something so that it becomes smaller and bent, or to be crushed in this way (使)皱；扭曲：*I had crumpled up about ten sheets, trying to write the letter.* 为了写这封信，我已经把十张纸揉成一团了。**2** [I] if your face crumples you suddenly look sad or disappointed, as if you might cry〔脸容〕扭曲 **3** [I] if your body crumples, you fall in an uncontrolled way because you are unconscious, drunk etc〔身体因失去知觉、醉酒而〕倒下：*Watkins crumpled in a heap and the referee stopped the fight.* 沃特金斯重重倒了下来，不能动弹，裁判便终止了拳赛。

crum·pled /ˈkrʌmpḷd; ˈkrʌmpəld/ *adj* **1** also 又作 **crumpled up** crushed into a smaller bent shape 皱的；扭曲的：*a crumpled banknote* 皱巴巴的钞票 —see picture on page A18 参见 A18 页图 **2** cloth or clothes that are crumpled have a lot of lines or folds in them〔布、衣服〕有褶皱的：*Don't sit around in your suit. It'll get crumpled.* 不要穿着西服到处乱坐，会起皱的。**3** someone who is crumpled somewhere, is lying still in a strange position after they have fallen〔人〕歪歪扭扭地倒地不起

crumple zone /ˈ·· ·ˌ/ *n* [C] part of a car that crumples easily in an accident to protect the people inside〔汽车为发生事故时保护乘客的〕防撞压损区

crunch¹ /krʌntʃ; krʌntʃ/ *n* [singular] **1** a noise like the sound of something being crushed 嘎吱嘎吱的声音：*the crunch of footsteps on gravel* 沙砾上嘎吱嘎吱的脚步声 | *a horrible crunch* 令人恐惧的嘎吱声 —see picture on page A19 参见 A19 页图 **2** *AmE* a difficult situation caused by a lack of money【美】经济困境：*The company's in a crunch right now.* 这家公司现在资金窘迫。| **feel the crunch** (=not have enough money) 手头紧，资金不足 **3 when/if it comes to the crunch** used to say what you will do when something important happens or when a difficult decision has to be made 当关键时刻到来时，需要作出困难决定时：*If it comes to the crunch, whose side will you take?* 在关键时刻，你会站在哪一边？

crunch² *v* **1** [I] to make a sound like something being crushed 发嘎吱嘎吱声：*Our feet crunched on the frozen snow.* 我们的脚踩在冰上发出嘎吱嘎吱的声音。**2** [I always+adv/prep, T] to eat hard food in a way that makes a noise 嘎吱嘎吱地咬嚼：[+on] *The dog was crunching on a bone.* 这条狗在嘎吱嘎吱地啃骨头。| **crunch sth** *crunching a biscuit* 嘎吱嘎吱地咬饼干

crunch·y /ˈkrʌntʃɪ; ˈkrʌntʃi/ *adj* food that is crunchy is firm and fresh, and makes a noise when you bite it 脆的：*a crunchy apple* 鲜脆的苹果 —**crunchiness** *n* [U]

cru·sade¹ /kruˋsed; kruːˈseɪd/ *n* [C] **1** one of a series of wars fought in the 11th, 12th, and 13th centuries by Christian armies trying to take Palestine from the Muslims〔发生于 11、12、13 世纪的〕十字军东征 **2** a determined attempt to change something because you think you are morally right 改革运动：[+against/for] *He seems to be running a one-man crusade against cigarette smoking.* 他像是在单枪匹马进行反对吸烟的运动。

crusade² *v* [I] to take part in a CRUSADE¹ 加入十字军；从事改革运动：[+against/for] *crusading against nuclear weapons* 开展反对核武器的运动 —**crusader** *n* [C]

Cru·sades, The /kruˋsedz; kruːˈseɪdz/ eight wars led by Christian European kings in the 11th, 12th, and 13th centuries to get control of Palestine from the Saracens or Muslims 十字军东征〔发生在公元 11、12、13 世纪的八次战争。由信仰基督教的欧洲君王发起，目的是从萨拉森人或穆斯林手中夺取巴勒斯坦的控制权〕

cruse /kruz; kruːz/ *n* [C] *old use* a small pot for oil, wine etc【旧】罐，壶，坛

crush¹ /krʌʃ; krʌʃ/ *v* [T] **1** to press something so hard that it breaks or is damaged 压碎，压坏，压扁：*His leg was crushed in the accident.* 他的腿在事故中被压断了。| **be crushed to death** (=die by being crushed) 被压死 *Two people were crushed to death in the rush to escape.* 在匆忙逃跑中有两个人被压死。**2** to press something in order to break it into very small pieces, or into a powder 捣碎，弄碎，粉碎：*Crush two cloves of garlic.* 捣两瓣大蒜。—see picture on page A11 参见 A11 页图 **3 crush a rebellion/uprising/revolt etc** to use severe methods to stop people from fighting you or opposing you 平定叛乱／起义／反叛等：*The revolution was crushed within days.* 几天之内革命就被镇压了。**4 crush sb's hopes/enthusiasm/confidence etc** to make someone lose all hope, confidence etc 毁灭某人的希望／热情／信心等 **5** to make someone feel extremely upset or shocked 使非常伤心；使震惊：*Sara was crushed by their insults.* 莎拉因他们的侮辱而非常伤心。

crush up *phr v* [I] *BrE informal* if people crush up, they fit into a small space by moving closer to each other【英，非正式】挤，塞，挤入：*"Is there room for one more in your car?" "Yes, but you'll have to crush up."* "你车里还能再坐一个人吗？""可以，但是你要挤一挤。"

crush² *n* **1** [singular] a crowd of people pressed so close together that it is difficult for them to move 拥挤的人群：*There's always such a crush on the train in the mornings.* 早晨火车上总是那么拥挤。**2** [C] an uncontrollable feeling of love for someone, especially that a young person has for someone older〔尤指对年龄比自己大的人〕迷恋：**have a crush on** *Did you have a crush on one of your teachers when you were at school?* 你上学时迷恋过某位教师吗？**3 orange/lemon etc crush** a drink made by crushing the juice out of a fruit 橙汁／柠檬汁等

crush bar·ri·er /ˈ·, ···ˌ/ *n* [C] a fence used to control crowds at football matches, public events etc〔足球赛或公共活动等中的〕防挤栏杆

crush·ing /ˈkrʌʃɪŋ; ˈkrʌʃɪŋ/ *adj* **1** very hard to deal with, and making you lose hope and confidence 难以应付的，使人受不了的：*the crushing burden of debt* 使人难以承受的债务负担 | **crushing blow** (=something that makes you lose hope and confidence) 沉重的打击 *Failing his final exams was a crushing blow.* 期末考试不及格对他是个沉重的打击。| **crushing defeat** *his party's crushing defeat in the local elections* 他所属的党在地方选举中的惨败 **2** a crushing remark, reply etc contains a very strong criticism〔评论、回答等〕带有强烈批评的 —**crushingly** *adv*: *"That's fairly obvious," she replied crushingly.* "那非常明显。"她很不满地回答。

Crusoe, Robinson —see 见 ROBINSON CRUSOE

crust /krʌst; krʌst/ *n* [C,U] **1** the hard brown outer surface of bread 面包皮：*cucumber sandwiches with the crusts cut off* 去掉皮的面包做的黄瓜三明治 **2** the baked pastry on a PIE (1,2) 点心的酥皮 **3** a thin hard dry layer on the surface of something〔某物的〕硬薄外层：*the Earth's crust* 地壳

crus·ta·cean /krʌsˋteʃən; krʌˈsteɪʃən/ *n* [C] *technical* an animal such as a LOBSTER or a CRAB that has a hard outer shell and several pairs of legs, and usually lives in water【术语】甲壳纲动物〈如龙虾、螃蟹〉—**crustacean** *adj*

crust·ed /ˈkrʌstɪd; ˈkrʌstɪ̣d/ *adj* [+with] having a thin hard dry layer on the surface 有硬薄外层的：*old boots crusted with mud* 粘满泥的旧靴子

crust·y /ˈkrʌstɪ; ˈkrʌsti/ *adj* **1** bread that is crusty is pleasant to eat because it has a hard crust〔面包〕脆皮的 **2** *informal* someone who is crusty is bad-tempered【非正式】爱发脾气的, 暴躁的: *crusty old ladies in big hats* 戴着大帽子、脾气暴躁的老妇人 **3** having a thin dry hard layer of something on the surface 有薄硬外层的: *walls crusty with dirt* 覆盖着一层薄薄硬污垢的墙壁 —**crustiness** *n* [U]

crutch /krʌtʃ; krʌtʃ/ *n* [C] **1** [usually plural 一般用复数] one of a pair of long sticks that you put under your arms to help you walk when you have hurt your leg 拐杖: *walking on crutches* 拄拐杖走路 **2** something that gives you support or help 支撑物: *Joan's religion was a crutch to her when her husband died.* 琼的丈夫去世后, 她信仰的宗教对她是一种精神支柱。**3** *BrE* the part of your body between the tops of your legs【英】胯部

C

crux /krʌks; krʌks/ *n* **the crux** the most important part of a problem, question, argument etc〔问题、论据等的〕核心, 中心; 症结: *The crux of the play is his inability to accept his wife as an equal.* 这出戏的中心是他不能平等看待他的妻子。| *The crux of the matter is whether or not he'd intended to commit a crime.* 问题的核心在于他是不是故意犯罪。

cry¹ /kraɪ; kraɪ/ *v past tense and past participle* **cried** /kraɪd; kraɪd/ *present participle* **crying**

1 ▶**PRODUCE TEARS** 流泪◀ [I] to produce tears from your eyes, usually because you are unhappy or hurt 哭: *Don't cry, Laura. It's OK.* 不要哭, 劳拉, 没事的! | *I always cry at weddings.* 参加婚礼时我老是要哭。| [+over/about] *I know it's stupid to cry over something so unimportant.* 我知道为如此无关紧要的事哭泣是愚蠢的。| [+with/in] *Zack began to cry with frustration.* 扎克由于失望而哭了起来。| [+for] *The baby was crying for attention.* 宝宝哭了, 要人照顾。| **cry your eyes out/cry your heart out** *informal* (=be extremely sad and cry a lot)【非正式】哭得死去活来 | **cry yourself to sleep** (=cry until you fall asleep) 哭到睡着

2 ▶**SAY LOUDLY** 大声说◀ [T] to shout something loudly 喊叫: *"Stop!" she cried.* "停下!"她喊道。

3 ▶**ANIMALS/BIRDS** 动物/鸟类◀ [I] if animals and birds cry they make a loud sound 鸟鸣, 鸟叫;〔动物〕大声叫: *seagulls on the cliffs crying loudly* 在悬崖上大声鸣叫的海鸥

4 cry on sb's shoulder *informal* to tell someone why you are unhappy or worried【非正式】告诉某人自己的苦衷: *I've had Glen crying on my shoulder all afternoon about his love life.* 整个下午我已让格伦诉说他爱情生活中的苦楚。

5 cry over spilt milk to waste time feeling sorry about an earlier mistake or problem that cannot be changed 作无益的悔恨: *It's no use crying over spilt milk.* 牛奶洒了, 哭也无用。

6 cry into your beer *informal* to feel too much pity for yourself, especially because you think you have been treated unfairly【非正式】(尤因受不公正待遇而)感到十分委屈

7 cry wolf to ask for help when you do not need it, so that people do not believe you when you really need help 谎报险情, 发假警报

8 for crying out loud *spoken* used when you feel annoyed or impatient with someone【口】岂有此理; 天哪〔用于感到厌烦或不耐烦时〕: *For crying out loud, stop nagging me about it!* 岂有此理, 别再嘀咕个没完!

9 [T] *literary* to make something known to the public by shouting【文】当众大声宣布: **cry your wares** *market traders crying their wares* 市场上大声叫卖的小贩 —see also 另见 **cry for the moon** (MOON¹ (4))

cry off *phr v* [I] *BrE* to say that you will not do something that you have already promised to do【英】取消承诺: *Paul tried to cry off at the last moment saying he had to work late.* 保罗在最后时刻想反悔, 说他得工作到很晚。

cry out *phr v* **1** [I] to make a loud sound of fear, shock, pain etc〔由于害怕、震惊、疼痛等而〕大声喊叫, 哼: *He was in a lot of pain, but he didn't cry out.* 他痛得很厉害, 但是一声也没有喊。| [+in/with] *Even the smallest movement made him cry out in pain.* 哪怕最轻微的动作也会使他痛得直叫。**2** [I,T] to shout something loudly 大声喊叫: *Maria cried out sharply, "Don't touch it!"* 玛丽亚厉声喊道:"别碰它!" | [+for] *I was so scared, I couldn't even cry out for help.* 我害怕极了, 连喊救命都喊不出来。**3 be crying out for** *informal* to need something urgently【非正式】迫切需要: *The kitchen is crying out for a coat of paint.* 厨房急需油漆一遍。**4 cry out against** to complain strongly or protest strongly about something 强烈抱怨; 强烈抗议

cry² *n plural* **cries**

1 ▶**SOUND EXPRESSING FEELING** 表达感情的声音◀ [C] a loud sound showing fear, pain, shock etc〔因惊恐、疼痛、震惊等而发出的〕叫喊声: *a baby's cry* 婴儿的叫喊声 | **a cry of alarm/anger/despair etc** *A cry of protest rose from the crowd.* 人群中发出抗议的呼喊声。| *a cry of delight* 一声欢呼 | **give a cry/let out a cry** *Hugh let out a startled cry as he fell into the water.* 休在掉到水里的时候发出惊恐的喊叫声。

2 ▶**SHOUT** 喊叫◀ [C] a loud shout 呼喊声: [+of] *As they left the stage there were cries of "More! More!"* 他们离开舞台的时候, 人们喊道:"再来一个! 再来一个!"

3 ▶**ANIMAL/BIRD** 动物/鸟◀ [C] a sound made by a particular animal〔某种动物的〕鸣叫; 吠; 嗥叫: *the cries of seagulls wheeling over the docks* 在码头上方盘旋的海鸥发出的鸣叫声

4 ▶**TIME WHEN SB CRIES** 某人哭喊的时候◀ [singular] *especially BrE* a period of time during which you cry【尤英】哭喊时: **have a cry** *You'll feel better after you've had a good cry.* 痛哭一场后你会感觉好受些。

5 be a far cry from *informal* to be very different from something else【非正式】与…大不相同: *It was a far cry from the leafy suburbs she was used to.* 这里和她所习惯的树木茂密的郊区大不相同。

6 cry for help something someone says or does that shows that they are very unhappy and need help〔某人的所言所行表示其〕需要帮助: *Janie's suicide attempt was obviously a cry for help.* 詹妮的自杀企图显然表示她需要人帮助。

7 ▶**PHRASE** 片[短]语◀ [C] a phrase that is used to unite people in support of a particular action or idea; SLOGAN 口号: **war/battle cry** (=a phrase shouted at the enemy in a fight) 打仗[打斗]时的呐喊, 喊杀声

8 in full cry a) if someone is in full cry they are strongly or loudly criticizing someone or something 强烈谴责; 大声谴责: *The Democrats were in full cry over Reagan's defence spending plans.* 民主党人大声谴责里根的国防开支计划。**b)** if a group of dogs is in full cry, they are making loud noises as they hunt an animal〔一群猎犬〕吠叫着追赶 —see also 另见 HUE AND CRY

CULTURAL NOTE 文化注释

In the US and the UK, women are allowed by society to cry, but men do not cry very much. It is acceptable for men to cry in particular situations, for example when someone has died, but most men do not feel comfortable crying at other times. A young boy who cries is sometimes disapproved of, and called a CRYBABY. 在英美两国, 女人哭泣是社会允许的, 但男人很少哭。男人在一些特定场合哭泣是可以接受的, 如有人去世时; 但大多数男人在其他时候哭泣就会觉得不舒服。小男孩哭泣有时不被赞成, 被叫做crybaby (哭鼻子大王)。

Cry, the Be·lov·ed Coun·try /ˈ· · ·, ·· , ··/ a book by Alan Paton about a black MINISTER (=Christian priest) and his family in South Africa in the 1940s. It shows the lack of equality between black and white people, but encourages them not to hate each other.《哭吧, 亲爱的祖国》〔艾伦·佩顿所著的一部小说。小说讲述 20 世纪 40 年代一个南非黑人牧师及其家人的故事, 反映黑人与白人的不平等, 但奉劝双方不要相互憎恨〕

cry·ing /ˈkraɪɪŋ; ˈkraɪ-ɪŋ/ *adj* **1 a crying need for sth** a serious need for something 迫切需要某事物: *There is a crying need for improvements to our public transport system.* 我们的公共交通系统迫切需要改善。**2 it's a crying shame** *spoken* used to say you are angry and upset about something【口】真令人生气[伤心]: *It's a crying shame the way she works so hard to have Ken waste it all gambling.* 她辛辛苦苦挣的钱都让肯赌掉了, 真令人生气。

crypt /krɪpt; krɪpt/ *n* [C] a room under a church, used in former times for burying people〔旧时用作墓地的〕教堂地下室

cryp·tic /ˈkrɪptɪk; ˈkrɪptɪk/ *adj* deliberately mysterious, or having a secret meaning 故作神秘的; 有隐义的: **cryptic remark/comment/statement etc** *What are we supposed to understand from a cryptic remark like that?* 我们到底该如何理解那种隐晦的话呢? —**cryptically** /-klɪ; -kli/ *adv*

crypto- /krɪpto; krɪptəʊ/ *prefix formal* secret or hidden【正式】秘密的, 隐蔽的: *a crypto-Communist* 秘密共产党员

cryp·to·gram /ˈkrɪptəˌgræm; ˈkrɪptəgræm/ *n* [C] a message written in code (CODE¹ (4)) 密码文, 暗码文

cryp·to·gra·phy /krɪpˈtɑgrəfɪ; krɪpˈtɒgrəfi/ *n* [U] the study of secret writing and codes (CODE¹ (4)) 密码学 —**cryptographer** *n* [C]

crys·tal /ˈkrɪstl; ˈkrɪstl/ *n* **1** [C,U] rock that is transparent like ice, or a piece of this 水晶 **2** [U] very high quality transparent glass 水晶玻璃: *On the sideboard was his mother's collection of crystal and cut-glass.* 餐具柜上是他母亲收集的水晶玻璃和雕花玻璃器皿。**3** [C] a small regular shaped piece of a substance,

formed naturally when this substance becomes solid 结晶(体): *crystals of ice* 冰晶 | *copper sulphate crystals* 硫酸铜结晶 **4** [C] *AmE* the transparent cover on a clock or watch【美】〔钟面或表面的透明〕盖片

crystal ball /ˌ.. ˈ./ *n* [C] a glass ball that you can look into to magically see what is going to happen in the future〔占卜用的〕水晶球

crystal clear /ˌ.. ˈ.◂/ *adj* very clearly stated, easy to understand 明白的, 无疑问的, 非常清楚的: *I want to make one thing crystal clear – I do not agree with these proposals.* 有一件事我要说清楚, 我不同意这些提议。

crys·tal·line /ˈkrɪstḷˌaɪn; ˈkrɪstəlaɪn/ *adj* **1** very clear or transparent, like crystal 清澈透明的; 水晶般的 **2** made of crystals 水晶[结晶体]构成的

crys·tal·lize also 又作 **-ise** *BrE*【英】/ˈkrɪstḷˌaɪz; ˈkrɪstəlaɪz/ *v* **1** [I,T] if a liquid crystallizes, it forms crystals (CRYSTAL (3)) (使)结晶: *The liquid will crystallize at 50 degrees centigrade.* 这种液体在摄氏 50 度时结晶。**2** [I,T] if an idea, plan etc crystallizes or if you crystallize it, it becomes very clear in your mind (使)变得明朗而具体: *a number of related ideas that gradually crystallized into a practical plan* 逐渐具体化为实际计划的若干有关联的想法 —**crystallization** /ˌkrɪstḷaɪˈzeʃən; ˌkrɪstəlaɪˈzeɪʃən/ *n* [U]

crys·tal·lized /ˈkrɪstəlaɪzd; ˈkrɪstəlaɪzd/ *adj* crystallized fruit is made by a special process which covers it with sugar〔水果等〕裹糖的: *crystallized ginger* 蜜饯姜

Crystal Pal·ace, the /ˌ.. ˈ../ a large building made of glass and iron, built in Hyde Park, London to contain the Great Exhibition of 1851. The building was later moved to South London, but was destroyed by fire in 1936. The name 'Crystal Palace' is still used for a football team and a district in South London. 水晶宫〔一座以钢铁为骨架、玻璃为主要建材的大型建筑, 位于伦敦海德公园, 为举办 1851 年世界博览会而兴建。该宫后来移至伦敦南部, 1936 年毁于一场大火。"水晶宫"现也用于指称一支足球队和伦敦南部的一个区〕

crystal set /ˈ.. ./ *n* [C] a very simple old-fashioned radio 晶体管收音机

CSA, the /ˌsi ɛs ˋe; ˌsiː es ˈeɪ/ the abbreviation of 缩写= the CHILD SUPPORT AGENCY

CSE /ˌsi ɛs ˋi; ˌsiː es ˈiː/ *n* [C] Certificate of Secondary Education; an examination taken at the age of 16 in schools in Britain before 1988〔英国〕中等教育证书考试

C-section /ˋsi ˌsɛkʃən; ˈsiː ˌsekʃən/ *n* [C] *AmE informal* a CAESAREAN【美, 非正式】剖腹产

CS gas /ˌsi ɛs ˋgæs; ˌsiː es ˈgæs/ *n* [U] *BrE* TEAR GAS【英】催泪瓦斯

CSO, the /ˌsi ɛs ˋo; ˌsiː es ˈəʊ/ the abbreviation of 缩写= the CHICAGO SYMPHONY ORCHESTRA

C-SPAN /ˌsi ˋspæn; ˌsiː ˈspæn/ a CABLE television station in the US which broadcasts the meetings of the US Congress and the meetings of its various committees while they are taking place 有线公共事务网〔美国一家有线电视台, 实况转播美国国会及其委员会的会议〕

CT /ˌsi ˋti; ˌsiː ˈtiː/ the abbreviation of 缩写= CONNECTICUT

ct **1** the written abbreviation of 缩写= CARAT: *a 24ct gold necklace* 一条 24 开的金项链 **2** a written abbreviation for 缩写= CENT: *These cost 75 cts.* 这些花费了 75 美分。

CTC /ˌsi ti ˋsi ; ˌsiː tiː ˈsiː/ the abbreviation of 缩写= CITY TECHNOLOGY COLLEGE

cu the written abbreviation of 缩写= CUBIC: *40 cu m of rock* 40 立方米石头

cub /kʌb; kʌb/ *n* [C] **1** a young lion, bear etc 幼兽: *a lion cub* 小狮子 | *A fox and her cubs were crossing the field.* 一只狐狸与幼狐正在穿过田野。**2 the Cubs** *BrE* the CUB SCOUT organization【英】幼年童子军 **3** a member of the CUB SCOUT organization 幼年童子军成员

Cu·ba /ˈkjubə; ˈkjuːbə/ the largest island in the Caribbean Sea. Population: 11,184,000 (2001). Capital: Havana. Cuba has been a Communist state since 1959. 古巴〔加勒比海最大的岛国。人口: 11,184,000 (2001), 首都: 哈瓦那。1959 年起古巴成为共产党领导的国家〕—**Cuban** *n, adj*

> **CULTURAL NOTE 文化注释**
>
> There are many Cuban REFUGEES in the US. Some left Cuba when the government was taken over by the Communists in 1959, and many others came to the US as BOAT PEOPLE (=people who try to escape from their own country in boats), especially in the 1980s and 1990s. Many Cubans live in Florida, especially in Miami. The US government does not trust the Communist government in Cuba, and does not allow US citizens to visit Cuba or US companies to do business in Cuba. The US TRADE EMBARGO (=official order to stop trade with another country) has had a bad effect on the Cuban economy. 美国有很多古巴难民, 有的是在 1959 年共产党接管古巴政府时离开古巴, 其他很多人是坐船来到美国, 叫做"船民", 尤以 20 世纪 80、90 年代为多。很多古巴人住在佛罗里达州, 尤其是迈阿密。美国政府不信任古巴的共产党政府, 不允许美国公民去古巴, 也不允许美国公司在古巴开展业务。美国的贸易禁运对古巴经济产生了严重影响。— see also 另见 BAY OF PIGS, GUANTANAMO BAY

Cuban mis·sile cri·sis, the /ˌ.. ˈ.. ˌ.. ˈ../ a dangerous situation which developed in 1962 when the Soviet Union began to build bases for NUCLEAR MISSILES in Cuba. US President John F. Kennedy complained to the Soviet government, stopped all ships from going to Cuba, and threatened to take military action. This caused a lot of international anxiety, but after a few days the Soviet Union agreed to remove the missile base 古巴导弹危机〔1962年苏联着手在古巴建立核导弹基地而引发的危险局势。美国总统约翰·F.肯尼迪向苏联政府提出抗议, 禁止任何船只驶往古巴, 并以采取军事行动相威胁。这一事件引起了国际社会的担忧。数日后, 苏联同意撤除导弹基地〕

> **CULTURAL NOTE 文化注释**
>
> The Cuban missile crisis is considered to be the time when the US and the Soviet Union came closest to having a NUCLEAR WAR. Many people were very frightened when President Kennedy appeared on television to explain what was happening. 古巴导弹危机被认为是美国和苏联最接近核战争边缘的一段时期。肯尼迪总统出现在电视上解释当时发生的情况时, 许多人惶恐万分。

cub·by·hole /ˈkʌbɪˌhol; ˈkʌbihəʊl/ *n* [C] a very small space in a house, used for storing things or hiding in〔房屋内用于储藏或躲藏的〕窄小的地方

cube[1] /kjub; kjuːb/ *n* [C] **1** a solid object with six equal square sides 立方形的东西; 立方体: *a sugar cube* 一块方糖 | *an ice cube* 一小方块冰 | *Cut the meat into small cubes.* 把肉切成丁。—see picture at 参见 SHAPE[1] 图 **2 the cube of sth** the number you get when you multiply a number by itself twice, so for example 4×4×4 = 64 so the cube of 4 is 64 三次方, 立方

cube[2] *v* [T] **1** to multiply a number by itself twice 自乘两次: *4 cubed is 64.* 4 的立方是 64。**2** to cut food into cubes; DICE[2] (1) 将〔食物〕切成小方块

cube root /ˌ. ˈ./ *n* [C] *technical* the cube root of a particular number is the number that when multiplied by itself twice will give that number【术语】立方根: *4 is the cube root of 64.* 4 是 64 的立方根。

cu·bic /ˈkjubɪk; ˈkjuːbɪk/ *adj* **cubic centimetre/metre/inch etc** a measurement of space which is calculated by multiplying the length of something by its width and height 立方厘米/米/英寸等: *What's the cubic capacity of this engine?* 这台机器的容积是多少?

cu·bi·cle /ˈkjubɪkḷ; ˈkjuːbɪkəl/ *n* [C] a small part of a room that is separated from the rest of the room so that you cannot be seen by other people, cannot hear any noise etc 小室, 小房间

cub·is·m /ˈkjubɪzəm; ˈkjuːbɪzəm/ *n* [U] a 20th century style of art, in which objects and people are represented by GEOMETRIC shapes 立体派[主义]〔20世纪的一种艺术流派, 以几何图形来表现主题〕—**cubist** *adj*: *cubist paintings* 立体派油画 —**cubist** *n* [C]

cu·bit /ˈkjubɪt; ˈkjuːbḷt/ *n* [C] *biblical* an ancient measure of length equal to the length of your arm between your wrist and your elbow【圣经】腕尺, 肘尺〔古代长度单位, 相当于手腕到肘的长度〕

Cub Scout /ˈ. ./ *n* [C] *BrE*【英】**1 the Cub Scouts** the part of the SCOUT[1] (1a) organization for younger boys 幼年童子军 **2** a young boy who is a member of this organization 幼年童子军成员

cuck·old[1] /ˈkʌkḷd; ˈkʌkəld/ *n old-fashioned* an insulting name for a man whose wife has deceived him by having sex with another man【过时】"乌龟"〔妻子与人通奸的人, 侮辱用语〕

cuckold[2] *v* [T] *old-fashioned* if a wife or her LOVER cuckold her husband, they deceive him by having sex with each other【过时】给…戴绿帽子;〔妻子〕与人通奸, 与…的妻子通奸

cuck·oo[1] /ˈkuku; ˈkʊkuː/ *n* [C] a grey European bird that puts its eggs in other birds' NESTs and that makes a sound that sounds like its name 杜鹃, 布谷鸟

cuckoo² *adj* [not before noun 不用于名词前] *informal* crazy or silly【非正式】疯疯癫癫的，傻的：*You're completely cuckoo!* 你真是个傻子！

cuckoo clock /ˈ· · ·/ *n* [C] a clock with a wooden bird inside that comes out every hour and makes the sound of a cuckoo to show what time it is 杜鹃自鸣钟

cu·cum·ber /ˈkjukʌmbɚ; ˈkjuːkʌmbə/ *n* [C,U] a long thin round vegetable with a dark green skin and a light green inside usually eaten raw 黄瓜：*tomato and cucumber salad* 番茄黄瓜色拉 —see picture on page A9 参见 A9 页图

cud /kʌd; kʌd/ *n* [U] **1** food that a cow has eaten, swallowed, and brought back into its mouth to eat a second time 反刍的食物 **2 chew the cud a)** *informal* to think very hard about something before making a decision【非正式】反复思考 **b)** if a cow chews the cud, it eats cud 吃反刍的食物

cud·dle¹ /ˈkʌdḷ; ˈkʌdl/ *v* [I,T] to hold someone or something very close to you with your arms around them, especially to show that you love them〔尤指表示喜爱而〕抱，拥抱，搂抱：*Dawn and her boyfriend were cuddling on the sofa.* 唐和她的男朋友在沙发上搂搂抱抱。—see picture on page A21 参见 A21 页图

cuddle up *phr v* [I] to lie or sit very close to someone or something 紧贴着身子躺[坐]，依偎：**[+to/together]** *The children cuddled up to each other for warmth.* 孩子们互相依偎在一起取暖。

cuddle² *n* [singular] an act of cuddling someone 拥抱，紧贴着身子躺：**give sb a cuddle** *Come over here and let me give you a cuddle.* 过来，让我拥抱你一下。

cud·dly /ˈkʌdlɪ; ˈkʌdli/ *adj* someone or something that is cuddly makes you want to cuddle them 可爱的，值得拥抱的：*a cuddly little baby* 逗人爱的小宝宝

cud·gel¹ /ˈkʌdʒəl; ˈkʌdʒəl/ *n* **1** [C] a short thick stick used as a weapon〔用作武器的〕短粗棍[棒] **2 take up the cudgels** to start to fight for an idea that you believe in 努力为…奋斗，奋起捍卫

cudgel² *v* [T] **1** to hit someone with a cudgel 用棍棒打 **2 cudgel your brains** to think very hard about something 绞尽脑汁

cue¹ /kju; kjuː/ *n* [C] **1** an action or event that provides a signal 提示，暗示：*The fall in interest rates may be a cue for an upturn in consumer spending.* 利率的降低可能暗示消费的上升。**2** a word, phrase, or action in a play that is a signal for the next person to speak or act〔戏剧中暗示下一位演员接言或出场的〕尾白，提示：*She stood nervously in the wings waiting for her cue.* 她紧张地站在台侧等该她上场的尾白。| **miss your cue** (=not speak or act when you are supposed to) 漏说台词[该说的话]；该行动时没行动 **3 (right) on cue** happening or done at exactly the right moment 恰好，正好：*I had just suggested Philip's name when he walked in, right on cue.* 我刚提到菲利普的名字他就走了进来，真是凑巧。**4 take your cue from** to copy what someone else does, especially in order to behave in the right way 学别人的样：*With interest rates, the smaller banks will take their cue from the Federal Bank.* 调整利率时，小银行会仿效联邦银行。**5** a long straight wooden stick used for hitting the ball in games such as BILLIARDS and SNOOKER¹〔台球等的〕球杆

cue² *v* [T] to give someone a sign that it is the right moment for them to speak or do something especially during a performance〔尤指在表演中〕提示：*The studio manager will cue you when it's your turn to come on.* 该你上场的时候，录制室监督会提示你的。

cue ball /ˈ· ·/ *n* [C] the ball which a player hits with the CUE in a game such as BILLIARDS〔台球等的〕主球

cuff¹ /kʌf; kʌf/ *n* [C] **1** the end of a SLEEVE (=the arm of a shirt, dress etc) 袖口 —see picture on page A17 参见 A17 页图 **2** *AmE* a narrow piece of cloth turned upwards at the bottom of a trouser leg【美】〔裤脚的〕翻边；TURN-UP *BrE*【英】**3** an action in which you hit someone lightly on the head with your hand open 用手掌轻拍〔某人头部〕**4 cuffs** [plural] HANDCUFFS 手铐 —see also 另见 OFF-THE-CUFF

cuff² *v* [T] **1** to hit someone lightly, especially in a friendly way〔尤指友好地〕用掌轻拍：*She cuffed him playfully on the side of the head.* 她开玩笑地拍拍他的脑袋。**2** to put HANDCUFFS on someone 给…戴手铐

cuff link /ˈ· ·/ *n* [C] one of a pair of small round objects used for fastening shirt cuffs〔衬衫袖口的〕链扣，袖扣 —see picture on page A17 参见 A17 页图

cui·rass /kwɪˈræs; kwɪˈræs/ *n* [C] a piece of metal or leather that covers a soldier's chest and back, worn for protection in battle in former times〔旧时战争中士兵穿的〕护胸背铁甲，胸甲

Cui·sin·art /kwɪˈzɪnɑrt; kwɪˈzɨnɑːt/ *trademark* a type of food PROCESSOR sold in the US【商标】厨艺〔在美国销售的一种食品加工机〕

cui·sine /kwɪˈzin; kwɪˈziːn/ *n* [U] *French*【法】**1** a particular style of cooking 烹饪（法）：*French cuisine* 法式烹饪 | *vegetarian cuisine* 素食烹饪 **2** the food cooked in a particular restaurant or hotel, especially when it is very good 特制饭菜：*Enjoy the delicious cuisine created by our award-winning chef.* 请享用我们的获奖厨师精制的可口饭菜。

cul-de-sac /ˈkʌl də ˌsæk; ˈkʌl də ˌsæk/ *n* [C] **1** a road which is closed at one end so that there is only one way in and out 死胡同，死巷 **2** an unhelpful situation in which you cannot make any more progress 困境，死路；僵局：*These ideas lead us into a philosophical cul-de-sac.* 这些观点把我们领进了一个哲学上的死胡同。

cul·i·na·ry /ˈkjuləˌnɛrɪ; ˈkʌlɨnəri/ *adj* [only before noun 仅用于名词前] *formal* connected with cooking【正式】烹饪（用）的：*culinary herbs* 调味香料 | *culinary skills* 烹饪技术 | **culinary delights** (=food that tastes very good) 美味佳肴 *the region's culinary delights* 本地区的美味佳肴

cull¹ /kʌl; kʌl/ *v* **1** [T] *formal* to find or choose information from many different places【正式】挑选，收集，选用〔信息〕：**cull sth from** *photographs culled from various sources* 从各种来源中挑选出的照片 **2** [I,T] to kill the weakest animals in a group so that the size of the group does not increase too much 从〔一群动物中〕剔出，杀掉〔最弱者〕**3** [T] *literary* to gather flowers or fruit【文】采摘〔花或水果〕

cull² *n* [C] the act of killing the weakest animals in a group so that the size of the group does not increase too much 宰杀〔一群动物中最弱者〕

cul·len·der /ˈkʌləndɚ; ˈkʌlɨndə/ another spelling of COLANDER colander的另一种拼法

Cul·lod·en /kəˈlɑdṇ; kəˈlɒdn/ a place in northeast Scotland and also the name of a famous battle that was fought there in 1746, in which the Scots, under Bonnie Prince Charlie, were severely defeated by the English, under the Duke of Cumberland, second son of King George II 卡洛登〔苏格兰东北部一地区〕；卡洛登战役〔1746年的一场战役。英俊王子查理率领的苏格兰军队遭到英格兰王乔治二世的次子坎伯兰公爵率领的英格兰军队的重创〕

cul·mi·nate /ˈkʌlməˌnet; ˈkʌlmɨneɪt/

culminate in sth *phr v* [T] if a process culminates in something, it finally reaches the highest point of development or the most important result 达到…高峰[顶点]；最终达到：*a series of minor clashes culminating in a full scale war* 最终导致全面战争的一系列小冲突

cul·mi·na·tion /ˌkʌlməˈneʃən; ˌkʌlmɨˈneɪʃən/ *n* [U] **the culmination of** the final or highest point that is reached after a long period of effort or development 顶点，极点：*This little book represented the culmination of 15 year's work.* 这本小书是15年工作的结果。

cu·lottes /kjuˈlɑts; kjuːˈlɒts/ *n* [plural] women's trousers which stop at the knee and are shaped to look like a skirt〔女用的〕裙裤

cul·pa·ble /ˈkʌlpəbḷ; ˈkʌlpəbəl/ *adj* **1** *formal* deserving blame【正式】应受谴责[处罚]的：*Both parties were held to be to some extent culpable.* 双方都应受某种程度的谴责。**2** *technical* an action that is criminal【术语】〔行动〕有罪的：**culpable homicide/negligence etc** *He pleaded guilty to culpable homicide.* 他承认犯了杀人罪。—**culpably** *adv* —**culpability** /ˌkʌlpəˈbɪlətɪ; ˌkʌlpəˈbɪlɨti/ *n* [U]

cul·prit /ˈkʌlprɪt; ˈkʌlprɨt/ *n* [C] **1** the person who is guilty of a crime, or responsible for damage, a problem etc 罪犯；造成破坏[问题]的人：*Police finally managed to catch the culprit.* 警察最终抓住了罪犯。**2** *informal* the reason for a particular problem or difficulty【非正式】问题的起因；困难的起源：**the main culprit** *High production costs are the main culprit.* 高生产成本是主要原因。

cult /kʌlt; kʌlt/ *n* **1** [C] an extreme religious group that is not part of an established religion 异教，邪教：*Anyone who betrayed the cult could be punished by death.* 任何背叛邪教的人都可能会被处死。**2 cult film/figure/TV show etc** a film, music group etc that has become very popular but only among a particular group of people 某一群人热爱的电影/人物/电视节目等：*a cult band* 有一群狂热乐迷的乐队 | *James Dean acquired the status of a cult hero.* 詹姆斯·迪安成了某些人崇拜的英雄偶像。**3** [C] a fashionable belief, idea, or attitude that influences people's lives〔影响人们生活的〕时尚信仰[观点，态度]：*Diet, therapy, exercise ... It's all part of this cult of self-improvement.* 节食、治疗法、锻炼身体…这些都是自我改善的时尚做法。**4** [C,U] *formal* a system of religious beliefs and practices【正式】宗教信仰体系[仪式]

CULTURAL NOTE 文化注释

There are many different religious cults in the US, and some in the UK. Some cults have many members, such as the MOONIES, while others are very small. Most people think of cults as being very strange, and many people think that their members have been BRAINWASH*ed* into believing and doing what the cult leader wants them to believe or do. In the UK, and especially in the US, some cults have had arguments with the government, saying that they are churches and should not pay taxes, but the government does not consider them to be real churches. 美国有很多不同类型的极端异教信仰派别，英国也有一些。有的教派信徒众多，如文鲜明的统一教会，其他一些则人数较少。狂热教派在多数人眼中都很怪诞。很多人相信，信徒被洗了脑，听凭教主摆布。在英国，尤其是在美国，一些此类教派与政府发生争执，声称自己是教会组织，不应纳税，但政府不承认其为真正的教会组织。

cul·ti·va·ble /ˈkʌltəvəbḷ; ˈkʌltɪ̈vəbəl/ *adj* land which is cultivable can be used to grow crops〔土地〕可耕作的

cul·ti·vate /ˈkʌltəˌvet; ˈkʌltɪ̈veɪt/ *v* **1** [T] to prepare and use land for growing crops and plants 耕，耕作：*Some of the land would be impossible to cultivate.* 有些地无法耕作。**2** to develop a particular skill or quality in yourself 培养，养成：*The company have been successful in cultivating a very professional image.* 该公司在建立专业形象方面非常成功。**3** to make an effort to develop a friendly relationship with someone because you want something from them〔为了利益〕与…交往，结交〔朋友〕：*Professor Gladwyn would be an acquaintance worth cultivating.* 格拉德温教授是值得结交的朋友。

cul·ti·vat·ed /ˈkʌltəˌvetɪd; ˈkʌltɪ̈veɪtɪ̈d/ *adj* **1** someone who is cultivated is intelligent and knows a lot about music, art, literature etc 有素养的，有教养的：*It was a pleasure to talk to such a cultivated audience.* 与这么有教养的观众谈话非常高兴。**2** land that is cultivated is used for growing crops or plants〔土地〕耕作的：*cultivated fields* 耕地 **3** crops or plants that are cultivated are grown in order to be sold〔作物等〕栽培的

cul·ti·va·tion /ˌkʌltəˈveʃən; ˌkʌltɪ̈ˈveɪʃən/ *n* [U] **1** the preparation and use of land for growing crops 耕作：*different methods of soil cultivation* 不同的土地耕作法 | **under cultivation** (=used for growing crops and plants) 耕作中的 *These fields have been under cultivation for years.* 这些土地已耕作很多年了。**2** the planting and growing of plants and crops 栽培，种植：*Terraces for rice cultivation covered the hillsides.* 山坡上全是种植水稻的梯田。| [+of] *the successful cultivation of tobacco* 烟草的成功种植 **3** the deliberate development of a particular quality or skill 培养〔特性〕；学习〔技能〕

cul·ti·va·tor /ˈkʌltəˌvetɚ; ˈkʌltɪ̈veɪtə/ *n* [C] **1** *formal* someone who grows crops or plants, especially a farmer【正式】耕种者〔尤指农民〕**2** a tool or machine that is used to prepare land for growing crops 中耕机；耕耘机

W2 **cul·tu·ral** /ˈkʌltʃərəl; ˈkʌltʃərəl/ *adj* **1** belonging to or connected with a particular society and its way of life 某个社会的；文化上的：*a wide range of cultural influences* 广泛的文化影响 | **cultural heritage/traditions etc** (=ideas, customs etc that have existed in a particular society for a long time) 文化遗产/文化传统等 **2** related to art, literature, music etc 与文艺有关的，文化的：**cultural activity** *They enjoy cultural activities like going to the theatre and the opera.* 他们喜欢看戏剧、歌剧等文化活动。| **cultural centre** (=a place, usually a big city, where a lot of artistic and musical events happen) 文化中心 *Vienna is a real cultural centre for music lovers.* 维也纳确实是音乐爱好者的文化中心。| **cultural desert** *informal* (=a place such as a small town where there are no cultural activities)【非正式】文化沙漠

cul·tu·ral·ly /ˈkʌltʃərəlɪ; ˈkʌltʃərəli/ *adv* **1** in a way that is related to the ideas, beliefs, or customs of a society 社会地；人文地：*culturally approved patterns of behaviour* 社会认可的行为方式 **2** in a way that is related to art, music, literature etc 与文艺有关：*The French are a culturally sophisticated people.* 法国人民是文化底蕴很深的民族。| [sentence adverb 句子副词] *Culturally, the city has a lot to offer.* 从文艺角度看，这座城市可提供的东西很多。

Cultural Rev·o·lu·tion, the /ˌ‥ ‥ˈ‥/ a period in Chinese history, from 1966 to 1976, when its leader Mao Zedong tried to continue and develop the REVOLUTION that brought the Communists to power in China in the late 1940s. During this period educated people, including university teachers, artists, and high-ranking government officials, were criticized and physically attacked, and many of them were put in prison or forced to work on the land. The Cultural Revolution was strongly supported by young people, especially students, and many of them joined a group called the Red Guards to carry out Mao's instructions and ideas. 文化大革命〔1966年至1976年间的一段中国历史。那时，中国领导人毛泽东试图继续壮大20世纪40年代后期为共产党人夺得中国政权的革命。在此期间，包括大学教师、艺术家和高级政府官员在内的知识分子受到批判和肉体折磨，其中许多人被投进监狱或强制下田劳动。该运动受到年轻人，尤其是学生的极力支持，不少人加入了"红卫兵"组织以贯彻毛泽东的指示和思想〕

S2 W1 **cul·ture** /ˈkʌltʃɚ; ˈkʌltʃə/ *n*

1 ▶IN A SOCIETY 在社会中◀ [C,U] the ideas, beliefs, and customs that are shared and accepted by people in a society 文化：*Our culture teaches us to hide a lot of our true feelings.* 我们的文化教我们要把许多真实情感隐藏起来。| *black culture* 黑人文化 | **Western/British/Japanese etc culture** *Western culture places a high value on material acquisition.* 西方文化很看重物质的获得。

2 culture shock the feelings of shock and anxiety that someone has when they visit a foreign country or a new place for the first time 文化冲击〔指首次去国外或一个新地方的人感受到的震惊和焦虑〕：*John found life in London a bit of a culture shock at first.* 最初约翰觉得在伦敦的生活是一种文化冲击。

3 ▶IN A GROUP 在一组人中◀ [C,U] the attitudes and beliefs about something that are shared by a particular group of people or in a particular organization〔团体或组织中共同的〕态度，信仰，习俗：*Working late hours for very little money seems part of the company culture.* 工作时间长且薪酬低看来是该公司的惯例。| **drug/computer etc culture** *90's rave culture* 90年代的狂欢聚会文化 | *youth culture* 年轻人的文化 —see also 另见 SUBCULTURE

4 ▶ART/MUSIC/LITERATURE ETC 艺术/音乐/文学等◀ [U] activities that are related to art, music, literature etc 文化活动：*If it's culture you're looking for, the city has plenty of museums and art galleries.* 如果你要寻找文化，这个城市有很多博物馆和美术馆。| **popular culture** (=the music, books, films etc that are liked by most people in a society) 流行文化

5 ▶SOCIETY 社会◀ [C] a society that existed at a particular time in history〔处于历史上特定时期的〕社会：*primitive cultures* 原始社会 | *the Ancient Greek and Roman cultures* 古希腊和罗马社会 —see also 另见 CIVILIZATION

6 ▶CROPS 作物◀ [U] *technical* the practice of growing crops【术语】栽培：*strawberry culture* 草莓的种植

7 ▶SCIENCE 科学◀ [C,U] the process of growing BACTERIA for scientific use, or the bacteria produced by this 细菌培养；培养出的细菌

cul·tured /ˈkʌltʃɚd; ˈkʌltʃəd/ *adj* having had a good education so that you are interested in art, literature, music etc 有文化的，有修养的：*a well-read and cultured woman* 博览群书有教养的女人

cultured pearl /ˌ‥ ˈ‥/ *n* [C] a PEARL (1) that has been grown artificially 人工养殖珍珠

cul·vert /ˈkʌlvɚt; ˈkʌlvət/ *n* [C] a pipe that takes a stream under a road, railway line etc 排水渠，阴沟，涵洞

cum /kʌm; kʊm/ *prep* used between two nouns to show that something or someone has two purposes 兼，…两用：*a kitchen-cum-dining room* 厨房兼饭厅 | *a lunch-cum-business meeting* 工作午餐会

cum·ber·some /ˈkʌmbɚsəm; ˈkʌmbəsəm/ *adj* **1** a process or system that is cumbersome is slow and difficult〔过程或系统〕慢的，累赘的：*The technique was cumbersome and created problems with sound reproduction.* 这项技术不是很灵活，而且声音失真。**2** heavy and difficult to move 笨重的：*cumbersome equipment that slowed us down considerably* 大大降低了我们速度的笨重设备 **3** words or phrases that are cumbersome are long or complicated〔话或措辞〕冗长的；晦涩的

Cum·bri·a /ˈkʌmbrɪə; ˈkʌmbriə/ a county of northwest England just south of the border with Scotland. It is popular for its beautiful scenery, including the Lake District National Park. 坎布里亚郡〔英格兰西北部一郡，紧临苏格兰南部边界。以优美的景色著称，境内有湖区国家公园〕—**Cumbrian** *adj*

cum·in /ˈkʌmɪn; ˈkʌmɪ̈n/ *n* [U] the seeds of a plant that have a sweet smell and are used in cooking, or the plant that they grow on 小茴香；莳萝

cum lau·de /kʊm ˈlaʊdɪ; kʌm ˈlɔːdi/ *adv AmE* if you GRADUATE[3] (1) cum laude, you finish a university degree in the US and are given official praise for special achievement【美】以优等成绩〔毕业于大学〕

cum·mer·bund /ˈkʌmə˞ˌbʌnd; ˈkʌməbʌnd/ *n* [C] a wide piece of cloth that a man wears around his waist as part of a suit worn to very formal occasions〔男子在正式场合穿的〕宽腰带

Cum·mings /ˈkʌmɪŋz; ˈkʌmɪŋz/, **E.E.** (1894-1962) a US poet known for writing poems with no capital letters and for playing with the way poems are arranged on a page and with PUNCTUATION, in poems such as 'anyone lived in a little how town' 肯明斯〔(1894-1962), 美国诗人。他创作的诗歌一般不用大写, 诗行排列独出心裁, 标点符号异乎寻常, 例如 anyone lived in a little how town〕

cum·quat, kumquat /ˈkʌmkwɑt; ˈkʌmkwɒt/ *n* [C] a fruit that looks like a very small orange 金橘

cu·mu·la·tive /ˈkjumjəˌletɪv; ˈkjuːmjələtɪv/ *adj* increasing gradually as more of something is added or happens 积累的, 渐增的: *Learning is a cumulative process.* 学习是个逐渐积累的过程。| **cumulative effect (of)** *Depression is often caused by the cumulative effects of stress and over-work.* 抑郁症通常是由压力和劳累日积月累引起的。

cu·mu·lus /ˈkjumjələs; ˈkjuːmjələs/ *n* [C,U] a thick white cloud with a flat bottom edge 积云

cu·nei·form /kjuˈniəˌfɔrm; ˈkjuːnɪfɔːm/ *adj* connected with the writing used by the people of ancient Mesopotamia〔古代美索不达米亚人使用的〕楔形文字的 —**cuneiform** *n* [U]

cun·ni·lin·gus /ˌkʌnəˈlɪŋgəs; ˌkʌnɪˈlɪŋgəs/ *n* [U] the act of touching the female sex organs with the lips and tongue in order to give sexual pleasure 舔阴〔用唇和舌头刺激女性生殖器的性行为〕 —compare 比较 FELLATIO

cun·ning[1] /ˈkʌnɪŋ; ˈkʌnɪŋ/ *adj* **1** someone who is cunning is good at deceiving people in order to get what they want〔人〕狡猾的, 狡诈的: *She can be very cunning when she wants to be.* 只要她愿意, 她会非常狡猾。**2** behaviour or actions that are cunning are dishonest and unfair, and are used to get what you want〔行为或动作〕狡诈的, 狡猾的: *That was a cunning trick!* 那是一个狡猾的骗局! **3** a cunning object or piece of equipment is clever and unusual〔物体或设备〕巧妙的, 不同寻常的: *a cunning little device for keeping out draughts* 防风用的巧妙小装置 **4** *AmE old-fashioned* attractive【美, 过时】可爱的, 吸引人的: *That's a cunning little dress you're wearing.* 你穿的衣服真精致。—**cunningly** *adv*: *There was a microphone cunningly placed behind the picture.* 麦克风非常巧妙地装在了画的后面。

cunning[2] *n* [U] the ability to achieve what you want by deceiving people in a clever way 狡猾, 狡诈: *the tiger's ferocity and cunning* 老虎的凶猛和狡诈 | **low cunning** (=unpleasant dishonest methods) 令人讨厌而不诚实的方法, 花招 *She would use low cunning in order to win people's sympathy.* 她会为了赢得人们的同情耍花招。

cunt /kʌnt; kʌnt/ *n* [C] *spoken taboo*【口讳】**1** a stupid or unpleasant person 蠢人, 使人讨厌的人: *Shut up, you stupid cunt!* 闭嘴, 你这个蠢货! **2** a woman's VAGINA (=sex organ)〔女人的〕阴部, 阴道

cups 杯子

cup 杯子

mug 圆桶形有柄大杯

espresso cup 咖啡杯

tankard *BrE*【英】/ stein *AmE*【美】啤酒杯

cup[1] /kʌp; kʌp/ *n*

1 ▶**FOR DRINKING FROM** 饮具◀ [C] a small round container with a handle, that you use to drink tea, coffee etc 杯子: *a cup and saucer* 一副杯碟 | **tea cup/coffee cup** *a beautiful set of tea cups* 一套漂亮的茶杯 —compare 比较 MUG[1] (1)

2 ▶**DRINK** 饮料◀ [C] the liquid contained inside a cup〔杯中的〕液体: *Would you like another cup?* 要再来一杯吗? | **[+of]** *a nice hot cup of coffee* 一杯美味的热咖啡

3 ▶**AMOUNT OF LIQUID** 液体的量◀ [C] **a)** also 又作 **cupful** the amount of liquid a cup can hold 一杯的容量: *She came round to borrow a cupful of sugar.* 她过来借一杯糖。**b)** *AmE* an exact measure of quantity used in cooking in the US, Canada, and New Zealand【美】〔美国、加拿大、新西兰烹饪计量的〕一杯: *Stir half a cup of sugar and one cup of flour into the batter.* 将半杯糖和一杯面粉拌入面糊里搅拌。

4 ▶**ROUND THING** 圆形物◀ [C] something round and hollow that is shaped like a cup 杯状物: *acorn cups* 橡碗〔橡果的壳斗〕| **[+of]** *the cup of a flower* 花萼 | *She held it in the cup of her hand.* 她把它托在手里。

5 ▶**SPORT** 体育运动◀ **a)** [C] a specially shaped silver container that is given as a prize in a competition, especially a sports competition 奖杯: *The president of the club came to present the cup to the winners.* 俱乐部的总裁给胜者颁发奖杯。**b)** [singular] *especially BrE* a sports competition【尤英】体育比赛: *She's been picked to play in the Wightman Cup.* 她入选参加怀特曼杯网球赛。**c)** *AmE* a hole in the ground that you have to try to get the ball into in the game of GOLF【美】〔高尔夫球的〕球洞 —see picture on page A23 参见 A23 页图

6 ▶**CLOTHING** 衣服◀ [C] the part of a BRA that covers a woman's breast 乳罩杯

7 ▶**MIXED DRINK** 混合饮料◀ [C,U] *BrE* a mixed alcoholic drink【英】含酒精的混合饮料: *cider cup* 苹果酒混合饮料 | *a glass of champagne-cup* 一杯香槟混合饮料

8 **not be your cup of tea** *spoken* to not be the sort of thing that you like【口】不感兴趣的东西, 不对胃口的事物: *Jazz just isn't my cup of tea – I prefer classical music.* 我不喜欢爵士乐, 我喜欢古典音乐。

9 **in your cups** *BrE old-fashioned* drunk, or when drunk【英, 过时】喝醉了; 在喝醉时: *He sometimes attempted to speak French, in his cups.* 他有时借着酒劲试图说法语。—see also 另见 EGGCUP, LOVING CUP

cup[2] *v* **cupped, cupping** [T] **1** to hold something in your hands, so that your hands form part of a circle around it 捧: *Phil cupped her face in his hands and kissed her.* 菲尔用手捧着她的脸亲吻。**2** **cup your hand(s)** to make a shape like a cup with your hand or hands 用手作杯状: *He cupped his hands and I poured some water into them.* 他把双手合成杯状, 我便给他倒了些水。

Cup, the *BrE* an informal name for the FA Cup【英】足总杯〔英格兰足总杯的非正式名称〕

cup-bear·er /ˈ· ,··/ *n* [C] someone in a royal court who serves wine on official occasions〔宫中〕在正式场合专司斟酒的侍酒官

cup·board /ˈkʌbə˞d; ˈkʌbəd/ *n* [C] a piece of furniture with doors, and sometimes shelves, used for storing clothes, plates, food etc 橱柜, 衣柜; 碗柜, 食品柜: *It's in the kitchen cupboard.* 在厨房的碗柜里。| *The cupboard doors were open.* 橱柜的门开着。—see also 另见 AIRING CUPBOARD, **skeleton in the cupboard** (SKELETON (4)) —see picture on page A10 参见 A10 页图

cup·cake /ˈkʌpˌkek; ˈkʌpkeɪk/ *n* [C] a small round cake 杯形蛋糕

cup fi·nal /ˈ· ,··/ *n* [C] *BrE* the last and most important game in a competition, especially a football competition【英】〔尤指足球的〕决赛

Cup Final, the in the UK, the final game of the FA Cup competition【英】〔英格兰足总杯〕决赛

cup·ful /ˈkʌpfʊl; ˈkʌpfʊl/ *n* [C] the amount that a cup can hold 一杯的容量 —see 见 CUP[1] (3)

cu·pid /ˈkjupɪd; ˈkjuːpɪd/ *n* **1** the Roman god of sexual love, represented as a beautiful boy with wings who is carrying a BOW[3] (1) and ARROW (1) 丘比特〔爱神〕: *a sentimental picture with cupids around the edge* 一幅感伤的图画, 画面周围画着丘比特 **2** **play cupid** to try to arrange for two people to fall in love with each other 当月老, 做媒人: *She vowed never to play cupid again.* 她发誓再也不做红娘。

cu·pid·i·ty /kjuˈpɪdətɪ; kjuˈpɪdɪti/ *n* [U] *formal* very strong desire for something, especially money or property; GREED (2)【正式】贪心, 贪财, 贪婪: *We were astounded by the young man's cupidity.* 这个年轻人的贪婪使我们震惊。

cu·po·la /ˈkjupələ; ˈkjuːpələ/ *n* [C] a small round part on top of a building 穹顶, 圆屋顶: *a golden edifice with an onion-shaped cupola* 一幢有洋葱形屋顶的金色大楼

cup·pa /ˈkʌpə; ˈkʌpə/ *n* [C] *BrE spoken* a cup of tea【英口】一杯茶: *I'm dying for a cuppa!* 我非常想喝一杯茶!

cu·pric /ˈkjuprɪk; ˈkjuːprɪk/ *adj technical* containing COPPER (1)【术语】含铜的

cup tie /ˈ· ·/ *n* [C] *BrE* a game between two teams in a competition in which only the winning team will play any more games【英】淘汰赛: *Saturday's FA Cup tie against Spurs* 星期六对热刺队的英国足总杯比赛

cur /kɝ; kɜː/ *n* [C] **1** *old-fashioned* an unfriendly dog, especially a MONGREL【过时】恶狗, 杂种狗 **2** *old use* an unpleasant person【旧】卑劣可鄙的人

cu·ra·ble /ˈkjʊrəbl; ˈkjʊərəbəl/ *adj* an illness that is curable can be cured〔病〕可医好的 —opposite 反义词 INCURABLE (1)

cu·ra·çao /ˌkjurəˋsau; 'kjʊərəsəʊ/ *n* [U] a strong thick alcoholic drink that tastes of oranges 库拉索酒〔一种带有橙子味的醇酒〕

cu·ra·cy /ˋkjurəsɪ; 'kjʊərəsi/ *n* [U] the job or position of curate or the period of time that someone has this position 助理牧师的工作[身份, 任期]: *My first curacy was in St Luke's.* 我第一次当助理牧师是在圣路加。

cu·rate /ˋkjurɪt; 'kjʊərʒt/ *n* [C] **1** a priest of the lowest rank, whose job is to help the priest who is in charge of an area 助理牧师 **2 curate's egg** something that has good and bad parts 质量优劣兼备的东西: *The book is something of a curate's egg.* 这本书的质量不好也不坏。

cu·ra·tive /ˋkjurətɪv; 'kjʊərətɪv/ *adj* able to, or intended to cure illness 有疗效的: *the curative effects of lemon juice on scurvy victims* 柠檬汁对坏血病人的治疗效果 —**curative** *n* [C]: *This herb was once thought to be a curative.* 这种草药曾被认为能治病。

cu·ra·tor /kjuˋretɚ; kjʊ'reɪtə/ *n* [C] someone who is in charge of a MUSEUM 博物馆馆长: *He's Curator of Prints at the Metropolitan.* 他是大都会艺术博物馆版画部馆长。

curb¹ /kɝb; kɜːb/ *v* [T] to control or limit something in order to prevent it from having a harmful effect 控制, 抑制, 约束: *measures to curb the spread of the virus* 抑制病毒扩散的措施

curb² *n* [C] **1** an influence which helps to control or limit something 控制, 约束, 抑制: [+on] *We are trying to keep a curb on their activities.* 我们正设法控制他们的活动。**2** *AmE* the edge of the part of a road where people can walk【美】路缘; KERB *BrE*【英】

curb crawler /ˈ·,··/ *n* [C] the American spelling of KERB CRAWLER kerb crawler 的美式拼法

curd /kɝd; kɜːd/ *n* [U] also 又作 **curds** *plural* the thick substance that forms in milk when it becomes sour 凝乳

cur·dle /ˋkɝdl; 'kɜːdl/ *v* [I,T] **1** to become thicker or form curd, or to make a liquid do this (使)变稠; (使)凝结: *Milk may curdle in warm weather.* 天暖时牛奶会凝结。**2 make your blood curdle** to make you very frightened 使极度惊恐 —see also 另见 BLOODCURDLING

cu·r·é /kjuˋre; 'kjʊəreɪ/ *n* [C] a PARISH (1) priest in France 〔法国的〕教区神甫

cure¹ /kjur; kjʊə/ *v* [T] **1** to make someone who is ill well again 治愈〔病人〕: *The doctors did everything they could to cure her, but she died three months later.* 尽管医生尽了一切努力来治她的病, 但三个月后她还是死了。| *When I left hospital I was completely cured.* 出院时我已痊愈了。**2** to make an illness disappear completely, usually by medical treatment 治愈, 治好〔疾病〕: *an operation to cure a hernia problem* 治疗疝气的手术 **3** to remove a problem, or improve a bad situation 解决〔问题〕; 改善〔困境〕: *Attempts to cure unemployment have so far failed.* 到目前为止, 解决失业问题的种种努力都失败了。| **cure sb of** *Even whisky could not cure him of his anxieties.* 连威士忌也不能消除他的忧虑。**4** to preserve food, tobacco etc by drying it, hanging it in smoke, or covering it with salt 〔用晒、熏、腌等方法〕保存〔食品、烟草等〕: *cured ham* 腌制的火腿

cure² *n* [C] **1** a medicine or medical treatment that can cure an illness 药, 药剂; 疗法: [+for] *a cure for cancer* 治癌法 **2** something that removes a problem, or improves a bad situation 对策: *a cure for inflation* 解决通货膨胀的对策 **3** the act of making someone well again after an illness 治愈: *The new treatment effected a miraculous cure.* 这种新疗法产生了奇迹般的疗效。**4 take the cure** the practice in former times of going to a SPA (1) in order to improve your health 〔旧时〕进行矿泉治疗

cure-all /ˈ· ·/ *n* [C] something that people think will cure any problem 万应灵药, 灵丹妙药: *Privatisation is seen as a cure-all.* 私有化被视作灵丹妙药。

cu·ret·tage /kjuˋrɛtɪdʒ; kjʊə'retɪdʒ/ *n* [U] *technical* medical treatment to remove unhealthy flesh or skin【术语】刮除术

cur·few /ˋkɝfju; 'kɜːfjuː/ *n* **1** [C] a law forcing everyone to stay indoors from a particular time in the evening until a particular time in the morning 宵禁: *The military regime decided to impose a curfew.* 军政府决定实行宵禁。**2** [singular, not with *the* 不与 the 连用] the time after which everyone must stay indoors, according to this law 宵禁时间: *Anyone found in the streets after curfew will be shot.* 违反宵禁者格杀勿论。

Cu·rie /ˋkjuərɪ; 'kjʊəri/, **Ma·rie** /məˋri; 'mɑːri/ (1867-1934) a Polish scientist, who with her French husband **Pierre Curie** studied RADIOACTIVITY and discovered two new RADIOACTIVE substances, POLONIUM and RADIUM. She won two Nobel Prizes, and was the first woman ever to win one. 居里夫人〔(1867-1934), 波兰科学家。曾与其丈夫法国科学家皮埃尔·居里一起研究放射性, 发现了钋和镭两种新的放射性元素。她两度荣获诺贝尔奖, 是首位获此殊荣的女性〕

cu·ri·o /ˋkjurɪˌo; 'kjʊəriəʊ/ *n plural* **curios** [C] a small object that is valuable because it is old, beautiful, or rare 古物, 古董; 珍品: *Sue came across a shop selling curios and antiques.* 休正好碰到一家卖古董文物的商店。

cu·ri·os·i·ty /ˌkjurɪˋɑsətɪ; ˌkjʊəri'ɒsʒti/ *n* **1** [singular, U] the desire to know about something, or to know about a lot of different things 好奇心, 求知欲: [+about] *Children have a natural curiosity about the world around them.* 儿童对周围的世界有天然的好奇心。| **out of curiosity** *Just out of curiosity, how old are you?* 只是出于好奇, 请问你多大了? | **burning/bursting with curiosity** (=having an extremely strong desire to know something) 非常好奇 | **idle curiosity** (=the desire to know something that you do not need to know) 无谓的好奇, 多余的好奇 *It's not just idle curiosity.* 这并非只是无谓的好奇心。| **satisfy your curiosity** (=find out what you want to know) 满足自己的好奇心 *I just had to satisfy my curiosity, so I opened the parcel.* 我忍不住想满足自己的好奇心, 于是打开了包裹。**2** [C] something that is interesting because it is unusual or strange 奇品, 珍品: *His house was full of old maps and other curiosities.* 他的房子里装满了旧地图和其他珍品。**3 curiosity killed the cat** an expression used to tell someone not to ask questions about something that does not concern them 过于好奇会惹祸上身; 不关自己的事不要打听

cu·ri·ous /ˋkjurɪəs; 'kjʊəriəs/ *adj* **1** wanting to know about something 好奇的, 好打听的: *When I mentioned her name everyone was very curious.* 我提到她的名字时, 大家都很好奇。| [+about] *I'm curious about this book she's supposed to be writing.* 我对她据说正在写的那本书感到好奇。| **curious to see/hear/know etc** *Mandy was curious to hear what Peter had to say for himself.* 曼迪很想知道彼得自己怎么说。—opposite 反义词 INCURIOUS **2** strange or unusual 稀奇古怪的: *a curious noise coming from the cellar* 地窖里传来的怪声 | **curious that** *It's very curious that she left without saying goodbye.* 她没道别就离开了, 真奇怪。—**curiously** *adv*: *She watched curiously as I opened the box.* 她好奇地看着我打开盒子。 S3

curl¹ /kɝl; kɜːl/ *n* **1** [C] a small mass of hair that hangs in a curving shape 鬈发: *a little boy with beautiful blonde curls* 有漂亮的金黄色鬈发的小男孩 **2** [C] something that forms a curved shape 卷曲物, 螺旋状物: *A curl of smoke rose from her cigarette.* 她的香烟冒出一缕青烟。**3 a curl of your lip/mouth** a sideways and upwards movement of your lip or mouth, showing that you disapprove of someone or something 撇嘴〔表示不赞同〕

curl² *v* [I,T] **1** to form a twisted or curved shape or to make something do this 盘绕, 缠绕: *Ivy curled round the trunk of the tree.* 常春藤缠绕着树干。| **curl sth** *Maria used to curl her hair each week.* 玛丽亚过去每周烫一次发。**2** [I always+adv/prep T, always+adv/prep] to move, forming a twisted or curved shape, or to make something do this (使)弯曲: [+across/along etc] *Morning mists curled across the surface of the river.* 晨雾在河面缭绕弥漫。| **curl sth around/round/over etc** *The baby curled his fingers around my thumb.* 宝宝用手指攥着我的大拇指。**3** if you curl your lip, or if your lip curls, you move it upwards and sideways, to show that you disapprove of someone or something 〔表示反对〕撇〔嘴〕: *Her lip curled in contempt.* 她轻蔑地撇撇嘴。**4 make your hair curl** *spoken* if a story, experience etc would make your hair curl it is very surprising, frightening, or shocking【口】〔故事、经历等〕使人毛骨悚然, 使…战栗: *The stories they tell about him would make your hair curl.* 他们讲的有关他的事会使你毛骨悚然。—see also 另见 **make sb's toes curl** (TOE¹ (5))

curl up *phr v* [I] **1** to lie or sit with your arms and legs bent close to your body 蜷缩: *I just wanted to curl up and go to sleep.* 我只想蜷着身体睡觉。**2** if something flat curls up, its edges start to become curved and point upwards 卷曲: *The letter was now yellow and beginning to curl up.* 现在, 这信已发黄并开始卷曲。**3** to move upwards in the form of a curl or curls 弯曲着上升, 螺旋着上升: *Wisps of smoke were already curling up from the fireplace.* 壁炉里已袅袅升起一缕缕烟。

curl·er /ˋkɝlɚ; 'kɜːlə/ *n* [C] [usually plural 一般用复数] a small plastic or metal tube used for making hair curl 卷发夹: *Edith came to the door with her hair in curlers.* 伊迪丝带着满头发卷走到门口。

CULTURAL NOTE 文化注释

In old books and films, women are often shown wearing their curlers at bedtime or in the early morning, and not wanting anyone, especially a man they do not know, to see them like this. In Britain, curlers are thought of as being worn mostly by WORKING-CLASS women, and women

shown in curlers are often smoking a cigarette and in a rather untidy home environment. 在旧时的书籍或电影中，女人常在睡前或早晨戴着卷发夹。她们不想让别人，尤其是不认识的男人看见自己这副模样。英国人认为主要是工人阶级妇女才戴卷发夹，这些人通常的形象是叼着香烟，家里乱糟糟的。

cur·lew /ˈkɜ˞lu; ˈkɜːljuː/ *n* [C] a brown and grey bird with long legs and a curved beak, that lives near water or damp areas of land〔生活在水边或湿地的〕麻鹬

cur·li·cue, curlycue /ˈkɜ˞lɪˌkju; ˈkɜːlɪkjuː/ *n* [C] a decorative twisted pattern 花体，卷曲装饰物

curl·ing /ˈkɜ˞lɪŋ; ˈkɜːlɪŋ/ *n* [U] a winter sport played on ice by sliding flat heavy stones towards a marked point 冰壶游戏〔一种冬季运动〕

curling tongs /ˈ· · ·/ *BrE*【英】also 又作 **curling i·rons** /ˈ· · ·/ *especially AmE*【尤美】*n* [plural] a piece of electrical equipment that you heat and use to put curls in your hair 烫发钳，卷发钳

S3 **curl·y** /ˈkɜ˞lɪ; ˈkɜːli/ *adj* having a lot of curls 弯弯曲曲的：*long dark curly hair* 又长又黑的鬈发 **—curliness** *n* [U]

cur·mud·geon /kə˞ˈmʌdʒən; kɜːˈmʌdʒən/ *n* [C] *old-fashioned* an old person who is often angry or annoyed【过时】脾气坏的老人 **—curmudgeonly** *adj*

cur·rant /ˈkɜ˞ənt; ˈkʌrənt/ *n* [C] a small dried GRAPE used especially in baking cakes〔尤用于制糕点的〕葡萄干：*currant bun* 有葡萄干的小圆面包

W2 **cur·ren·cy** /ˈkɜ˞ənsɪ; ˈkʌrənsi/ *n* **1** [C,U] the system or type of money that a particular country uses 货币，通货：*The stronger currencies are under pressure in the world markets.* 强势货币在国际市场上受到压力。| *decimal currencies* 十进制货币 | **local currency** *The local currency is francs.* 当地货币是法郎。—see also 另见 HARD CURRENCY, SINGLE CURRENCY **2** [U] the state of being generally accepted or used 流传，流通；被接受，传播：**wide currency** (=accepted by many people) 广泛传播 *The idea enjoys wide currency in 20th century fiction.* 这种观点在20世纪的小说里得到广泛传播。| **gain currency** (=become accepted) 被接受 *Marxism began to gain currency.* 马克思主义开始被人们所接受。

S1 W1 **cur·rent¹** /ˈkɜ˞ənt; ˈkʌrənt/ *adj* [only before noun 仅用于名词前] happening or existing now but not expected to last for a long time 现时的，当前的，现行的：*her current boyfriend* 她的现任男友 **—currently** *adv*: *Sir Ranulph is currently occupied writing a book about his Antarctic expedition.* 雷纳夫爵士目前正忙于写一本关于他在南极探险的书。

current² *n* [C] **1** a continuous movement of water in a particular direction in the sea or in a river 流；水流：*The current was very strong.* 水流很急。**2** a flow of electricity through a wire 电流

current ac·count /ˈ· · ·/ *n* [C] *BrE* a bank account that you can take money out of at any time【英】活期存款账户；CHECKING ACCOUNT *AmE*【美】—compare 比较 DEPOSIT ACCOUNT

current af·fairs /ˌ· · ˈ·/ *n* [U] important political events or other events in society that are happening now 时事

S2 W2 **cur·rent·ly** /ˈkɜ˞əntlɪ; ˈkʌrəntli/ *adv* at the present time 现时，当前：*Two major changes are currently being considered.* 当前正在考虑两个主要的变化。| *They need more help than is currently available.* 他们对帮助的需求比当前能得到的要多。—see 见 ACTUALLY (USAGE)

W2 **cur·ric·u·lum** /kəˈrɪkjələm; kəˈrɪkjᵊləm/ *n plural* **curricula** /-lə; -lə/ or **curriculums** [C] the subjects that are taught by a school, college etc, or the things that are studied in a particular subject 课程：*Has computer studies been introduced into the school curriculum?* 电脑课列入学校课程了吗？—compare 比较 SYLLABUS

curriculum vi·tae /kəˌrɪkjələm ˈvitaɪ; kəˌrɪkjᵊləm ˈviːtaɪ/ *n* [C] **1** *BrE* a CV【英】简历；RESUMÉ² (2) *AmE*【美】**2** *AmE* a document on which a university teacher writes a list of their teaching experience and articles, books etc they have written when they are applying for a job【美】〔大学教师求职的〕简历，个人履历

Cur·ri·er and Ives /ˌkɜ˞ɪə˞ ənd ˈaɪvz; ˌkʌriə ənd ˈaɪvz/ a style of US art, named after the two men who invented it. It shows scenes from daily life in 19th century America. 柯里尔与艾夫斯〔美国的一种艺术风格，以开创此风格的两位男子的名字命名，描绘的是19世纪美国日常生活场景〕

cur·ry¹ /ˈkɜ˞ɪ; ˈkʌri/ *n* [C,U] a type of food from India consisting of meat or vegetables covered in a thick liquid with a hot taste 咖喱食品

CULTURAL NOTE 文化注释

Curry is very popular in the UK. Many different types of READY-MADE curries and curry sauces can be bought in SUPERMARKETS. There are many Indian restaurants where you can either sit down while you have your meal or order a TAKEAWAY curry. Some places in Britain are well-known for having a large number of Indian, Pakistani, or Bangladeshi restaurants, for example Brick Lane in the East End of London. These are all called Indian restaurants by most British people. One way of cooking curry, known as Balti, became especially popular in Birmingham and later spread to other places. A restaurant that serves this food is called a 'Balti House'. The STEREOTYPE of people who like eating curry in restaurants is young men who drink large amounts of LAGER with their meal and who SHOW OFF by eating curry dishes, such as Chicken Vindaloo, which contain the hottest SPICES. 咖喱食品在英国极为流行，超市里能买到很多不同类型的咖喱食品半成品和咖喱酱。有很多印度餐厅，可堂食，也可订购外卖咖喱食品。英国一些地方以印度、巴基斯坦或孟加拉国餐馆多而闻名，如伦敦东区的布里克巷，多数英国人将这些餐馆统称印度餐馆。一种叫做巴尔蒂菜系的咖喱食品在伯明翰尤其风行，后传至其他地区。提供这种菜肴的餐馆叫做巴尔蒂餐馆。喜欢在餐馆里吃咖喱食品最典型的是年轻人，他们随菜狂饮淡啤酒，吃最辣的咖喱菜（如咖喱辣鸡）炫耀。

curry² *v* [T] **1** to make meat or vegetables into curry 把〔肉、蔬菜〕做成咖喱食品 **2 curry favour with** to try to make someone like you or notice you in order to get something that you want 讨好，奉承，拍马屁：*currying favour with the teachers* 讨好老师

curry pow·der /ˈ· ·, ·ˈ·/ *n* [U] a mixture of SPICES (=dried vegetable parts with a hot taste) crushed into a fine powder, used in cooking 咖喱粉

curse¹ /kɜ˞s; kɜːs/ *v* **1** [I] to swear 咒骂：*You should have heard him cursing when he tripped over the cat.* 你真该听听他被猫绊倒时是如何咒骂的。**2** [T] to say or think bad things about someone or something because they have made you angry〔嘴上或心里〕臭骂：**curse sb/sth for (doing) sth** *I cursed myself for not buying a phrase book.* 我咒骂自己没买一本常用语手册。**3** [T] to ask God or a magical power to harm someone 诅咒：*The man had been cursed by a witch doctor and was in despair.* 那男人因受巫医的诅咒而感到绝望。

curse² *n* [C] **1** a word or words that you use when you swear or when you express anger etc 骂人话：*The convict screamed out curses at them.* 囚犯大声咒骂他们。**2** a word or sentence used to ask God or a magical power to make something happen to someone or something 诅咒，咒语：**put a curse on** *The witch doctor put a curse on him.* 巫医诅咒他。**3** something that causes trouble, harm etc 祸因，祸根：[+to] *Foxes can be a curse to farmers.* 狐狸可能成为农民的一大祸害。**4 the curse** *old-fashioned* an expression meaning MENSTRUATION【过时】月经

curs·ed /ˈkɜ˞sɪd; ˈkɜːsᵻd/ *adj* **1 be cursed with** to suffer because of a problem that you have 受折磨的，痛苦的：*She had always been cursed with ill-health.* 她总是受疾病的折磨。**2** [only before noun 仅用于名词前] *old-fashioned* unpleasant or annoying【过时】讨厌的，烦人的：*I'm sick to death of being stuck in this cursed place.* 被困在这个讨厌的地方，我简直烦死了。**3** *literary* suffering as a result of a punishment by God or a god【文】被诅咒的 **—cursedly** *adv*

cur·sive /ˈkɜ˞sɪv; ˈkɜːsɪv/ *adj* written in a flowing rounded style of writing with the letters joined together〔字迹〕草写的，〔字母间〕连笔的：*cursive script* 草体 **—cursively** *adv*

cur·sor /ˈkɜ˞sə˞; ˈkɜːsə/ *n* [C] a mark or a small light which can be moved around a computer screen to show where you are working〔电脑的〕光标

cur·so·ry /ˈkɜ˞sərɪ; ˈkɜːsəri/ *adj* quick and done without enough attention to details 粗略的，草率的，仓促的：*After only a cursory glance he tore up the note.* 他粗略看了一下纸条便将它撕掉了。**—cursorily** *adv*

curt /kɜ˞t; kɜːt/ *adj* replying with very few words in a way that does not seem polite〔人言语举止〕简慢无礼的，唐突的：*With a curt nod, he turned away and sat down.* 他匆匆点了下头，转身坐下。**—curtly** *adv* **—curtness** *n* [U]

cur·tail /kə˞ˈtel; kɜːˈteɪl/ *v* [T] *formal* to reduce something such as the amount of money you spend【正式】减少，缩减，削减：*The Government wants private firms to curtail wage rises.* 政府希望私营公司缩减工资增幅。| *Our evening's enjoyment was cur-*

tailed when Alfred became ill. 阿尔弗雷德病了，我们的晚间娱乐活动便减少了。—**curtailment** *n* [C,U]

cur·tain /ˈkɜtn; ˈkɜːtn/ *n* [C] **1** a piece of hanging cloth that can be pulled across to cover a window, door etc to divide a room etc 窗帘；门帘；帘子：**draw the curtains** (=close the curtains) 拉上帘子 **2** a sheet of heavy material that can be made to come down across the front of the stage in a theatre〔舞台上的〕幕 —see picture at 参见 THEATRE 图 **3** a thick layer of something that stops anything behind it from being seen 幕状物，帘状物：*a thick curtain of smoke* 浓厚的烟幕 | *a curtain of trailing branches* 下垂的枝条形成的幕 **4 the curtain falls on** *literary* if the curtain falls on an event or period of history, it ends【文】〔事件〕落幕；〔时代〕结束 **5 it'll be curtains for sb/sth** *informal* used to say that someone will die, or that something will end【非正式】该完蛋了：*It'll be curtains for you if they find you here!* 如果他们发现你在这儿，你就完蛋了！

curtain call /ˈ· · ·/ *n* [C] the time at the end of a performance when the actors come out to receive APPLAUSE〔演员的〕谢幕

curtain hook /ˈ· · ·/ *n* [C] a small hook which is joined to the top of a curtain so that you can hang it up 窗帘钩，门帘钩

curtain rail /ˈ· · ·/ *n* [C] a long piece of plastic or metal that you hang a curtain on 窗帘杆，门帘杆

curtain rais·er /ˈ· · ,· ·/ *n* [C] **1** a short play, film etc that is performed or shown before the main one〔正戏前的〕开场小戏；〔电影的〕开场短片 **2** a small thing that happens or is done just before something more important 前奏，引子：*a curtain raiser for the main programme of research* 主要研究项目的前奏

Curtis /ˈkɜtɪs; ˈkɜːtɪs/, **Tony** (1925-) a US actor who first became popular in the 1950s after appearing in adventure films. Later he took more serious parts in films such as *Sweet Smell of Success* (1957), and *The Boston Strangler* (1968). One of his most famous films was *Some Like It Hot* with Marilyn Monroe in 1959. 柯蒂斯〔(1925-)，美国演员，20世纪50年代以出演探险影片而出名。随后，他在影片中饰演了一些较为严肃的角色，如《成功的滋味》(1957) 和《波士顿杀人王》(1968)。他最著名的一部影片是1959年与玛丽莲·梦露合演的《热情如火》〕

Curtiz /ˈkɜtɪz; ˈkɜːtɪz/, **Michael** (1888-1962), a Hungarian-born film DIRECTOR who had a long and successful career in Hollywood. He won an Oscar for Best Director in 1943 for *Casablanca*. His other films included *The Charge of the Light Brigade* (1936), *Angels With Dirty Faces* (1938), *Yankee Doodle Dandy* (1942) and *White Christmas* (1954). 柯蒂兹〔(1888-1962)，出生于匈牙利，好莱坞有成就的资深电影导演。他拍摄过电影《卡萨布兰卡》，以此荣获1943年奥斯卡最佳导演奖。其他影片有《英烈传》(1936)、《一世之雄》(1938)、《胜利之歌》(1942) 以及《白色圣诞夜》(1954)〕

curt·sy, curtsey /ˈkɜtsɪ; ˈkɜːtsi/ *n* [C] a sign of respect that a woman makes to a more important person by bending her knees with one foot behind the other〔女子行的〕屈膝礼 —**curtsy** *v* [I] —compare 比较 BOW² (1)

cur·va·ceous, curvacious /kɜˋveʃəs; kɜːˈveɪʃəs/ *adj* having an attractively curved body shape 有曲线美的，丰满而匀称的：*curvacious female models* 身材优美的女模特儿 —**curvaceousness** *n* [U]

cur·va·ture /ˈkɜvətʃɚ; ˈkɜːvətʃə/ *n* [C,U] *technical*【术语】**1** the state of being curved, or the degree to which something is curved 弯曲(的形态)；曲率：*the curvature of the Earth's surface* 地表的曲率 **2** a medical condition in which part of someone's body curves in a way that is not natural〔人体病态的〕弯曲：*curvature of the spine* 脊柱弯曲

curve¹ /kɜv; kɜːv/ *n* [C] **1** a line which gradually bends like part of a circle 曲线，弧线：*a curve on a graph* 图表上的曲线 | *the curve of her hips* 她的臀部曲线 **2** a rounded bend in a road, river etc〔道路、河流等的〕弯曲处：*The car took the curve much too quickly.* 那辆汽车拐弯太快了。**3 curve ball** a throw in BASEBALL in which the ball spins so that it curves suddenly and is difficult to hit〔棒球的〕曲线球 **4** *AmE*【美】**throw sb a curve** to surprise someone with a question or problem that is difficult to deal with〔提出疑问或问题〕使…感到突然[棘手]；戏弄：*They threw us a curve and asked us about Longfellow when we were ready for a question on Thoreau.* 我们准备好了回答有关梭罗的问题，他们却问我们有关朗费罗的问题，这让我们措手不及。

curve² *v* [I,T] to bend or move in the shape of a curve, or to make something do this 弄弯，(使)弯曲：*The track curved into the woods.* 小路弯弯曲曲地拐进森林里。

curved /kɜvd; kɜːvd/ *adj* having a shape that is rounded and not straight 弯曲的：*a sword with a curved blade* 弯刀

curv·y /ˈkɜvɪ; ˈkɜːvi/ *adj* having a shape with several curves 弧形的，有曲线的：*her curvy red lips* 她弧形的红嘴唇 | *Eileen has a curvy figure.* 艾琳的身材曲线玲珑。

Cush·ing /ˈkʊʃɪŋ; ˈkʊʃɪŋ/, **Pe·ter** (1913-94) a British actor famous for acting in horror films, such as *Dracula* (1958) and for appearing as the character Sherlock Holmes in *The Hound of The Baskervilles* (1959) 库欣〔(1913-1994)，英国演员。他出演过《吸血鬼》(1958) 等恐怖影片，在《巴斯克维尔庄园的猎犬》(1959) 中饰演夏洛克·福尔摩斯，并因此出名〕

cush·ion¹ /ˈkʊʃən; ˈkʊʃən/ *n* [C] **1** a cloth bag filled with soft material that you put on a chair to make it more comfortable 垫子 —compare 比较 PILLOW¹ (1) **2** something that stops one thing from hitting another thing 垫形物，起垫子作用的东西；缓冲物：*The hovercraft rides on a cushion of air.* 气垫船行驶在空气垫子上。**3** something, especially money, that prevents you from being affected by a situation immediately〔尤指金钱〕起缓解作用的东西；防备不时之需的积蓄：*I have some savings – hopefully they'll act as a cushion while I'm looking for a job.* 我有一些积蓄，希望能帮助我度过找工作的那段日子。**4** the soft rubber edge of the table that is used for playing BILLIARDS or SNOOKER¹〔台球桌的〕橡皮边，弹性衬边

cushion² *v* [T] **1** to make a fall or knock less painful, for example by having something soft in the way 缓冲：*They had put mattresses on the ground to cushion his fall.* 他们已在地上铺好褥垫，以缓解他落地时的冲击。**2** to reduce the effects of something unpleasant 减轻〔令人不愉快的〕效果：**cushion the blow** *generous leaving allowances to help cushion the blow of redundancy* 慷慨的离职补贴以减轻裁员所带来的打击 | **be cushioned against** (=be protected from something unpleasant) 使…免遭困苦冲击 *The rich are cushioned against the effects of the recession.* 富人能应付经济不景气的冲击。

cush·y /ˈkʊʃɪ; ˈkʊʃi/ *adj* **cushier, cushiest** *informal* very easy【非正式】轻松的，容易的：*I wish I had a nice cushy job like her.* 我希望有份像她那样轻松的好工作。| **a cushy number** *BrE* (=an easy job)【英】轻松的工作

cusp /kʌsp; kʌsp/ *n* [C] **1** *technical* the point formed by two curves meeting【术语】尖(角)；两条曲线的交点 **2 on the cusp** someone who was born on the cusp was born near the time when one STAR SIGN ends and another one begins〔占星术〕两宫会切时段

cus·pi·dor /ˈkʌspəˌdɔr; ˈkʌspɨdɔː/ *n* [C] *AmE* a container for people to SPIT¹ (1,2) in; SPITTOON【美】痰盂

cuss¹ /kʌs; kʌs/ *v* [I,T] *AmE informal, BrE old-fashioned* to use rude words because you are annoyed by something【美，非正式；英，过时】诅咒，咒骂：*It does a fella good to cuss if he wants to.* 如果他想骂，骂一通对他是有好处的。

cuss sb **out** *phr v* [T] *AmE spoken* to swear and shout at someone because you are angry【美口】咒骂：*My Mom cussed me out for breaking the lamp.* 我打碎了灯，妈妈因此而大骂我。

cuss² *n* [C] *AmE old-fashioned* **stubborn/stupid/ornery etc cuss** a very annoying person【美，过时】讨厌的家伙，贱骨头

cuss·ed /ˈkʌsɪd; ˈkʌsɨd/ *adj* behaving in a deliberately unhelpful way 别扭的，顽固的 —**cussedness** *n* [U]

cuss word /ˈ· ·/ *n* [C] *AmE* a SWEAR WORD【美】诅咒，骂人的脏话

cus·tard /ˈkʌstɚd; ˈkʌstəd/ *n* **1** [U] *especially BrE* a yellow liquid that is eaten with sweet dishes, made with milk, sugar, eggs, and flour【尤英】牛奶蛋糊，蛋奶甜羹 **2** [C,U] a soft baked mixture of milk, sugar, and eggs 乳蛋糕

custard pie /,· · ˈ·/ *n* [C] a PIE filled with custard, which people throw at each other as a joke in films etc〔电影中当作玩笑相互扔的〕蛋奶馅饼

Cus·ter /ˈkʌstɚ; ˈkʌstə/, **Ge·ne·ral George Arm·strong** (1839-76) a US soldier who first became famous in the American Civil War. He was killed, with all the men he was in command of, by Native Americans from the Sioux tribe led by Crazy Horse and Sitting Bull, in the Battle of the Little Bighorn. This battle is also known as **Custer's Last Stand**. 卡斯特〔(1839-1876)，美国南北战争时期著名将领。小比格霍恩河战役中，他本人及全体官兵死于"疯马"和"坐牛"旗下的苏族印第安人之手。这场战役也称"卡斯特的最后抵抗"〕

cus·to·di·al /kʌsˋtodɪəl; kʌˈstəʊdiəl/ *adj formal* connected with the custody of someone【正式】监护的，看守的，监禁的：*custodial care* 看护

custodial sen·tence /,· · · · ˈ· ·/ *n* [C] *law* a period of time that someone has to spend in prison as a punishment【法律】刑期

cus·to·di·an /kʌsˋtodɪən; kʌˈstəʊdiən/ *n* [C] **1** someone who is responsible for looking after a public building or a collection of valuable objects〔公共建筑或贵重物品的〕监护人，看守人，

保管人 **2 custodian of tradition/moral values etc** someone who tries to protect a traditional set of beliefs, attitudes etc〔传统价值、道德等的〕捍卫者

cus·to·dy /ˈkʌstədɪ; ˈkʌstədi/ *n* [U] **1** the right to take care of a child, especially when the child's parents are legally separating from each other 监护权〔尤指父母离异后对孩子的监护〕: **[+of]** *In most divorce cases the mother is awarded custody of the children.* 大部分离婚案中, 孩子的监护权判归母亲。| **have custody** *a dispute over who should have custody* 关于监护权归属问题的争执 **2 in custody** being kept in prison by the police until you go to court, because the police think you are guilty 拘留, 监禁〔警方认定有罪, 庭审前的羁押〕: **hold/keep sb in custody** *A man is being held in police custody in connection with the murder.* 一名男子因涉及此桩谋杀案而被警方拘留。| **take sb into custody** (=catch someone and keep them in custody) 拘捕监禁某人 **3 in sb's custody** *formal* being kept and looked after by someone【正式】由…保管: *The silver seal was placed in the custody of the mayor.* 这枚银图章由市长保管。

cus·tom /ˈkʌstəm; ˈkʌstəm/ *n* **1** [C,U] something that is done by people in a particular society because it is traditional 风俗, 习惯, 传统: **local/tribal/ancient/Swedish etc custom** *"Why the pile of salt?" "It's an old Japanese custom."* "那堆盐是什么意思?" "那是古老的日本习俗。" | **it is the custom (for sb) to do sth** *It's the custom for the bride's father to pay for the wedding.* 根据传统, 由新娘父亲支付婚礼费用。| **the custom of doing sth** *the old French custom of serving the vegetables separate from the meat* 蔬菜与肉类分开端上桌的法国旧俗 | **by custom/according to the custom** *By custom we had to stop and speak to every person we met.* 按照习俗, 我们必须停下和遇到的每个人说几句。**2** [singular] *especially literary* something that you usually do every day, or in a particular situation【尤文】日常习惯: *He awoke early, as was his custom.* 他每天醒得很早, 这是他的习惯。—see 见 HABIT (USAGE) **3** [U] *formal* the practice of regularly using a particular shop or business【正式】〔经常性的〕惠顾, 光顾 **4 customs** [plural] the place where your bag is checked for illegal drugs, guns etc when you go into a country 海关: *She was stopped at customs and questioned.* 她在海关被拦下来接受问话。| **clear customs** (=be allowed through customs after being checked) 清关, 海关检查后放行

cus·tom·a·ry /ˈkʌstəm,ɛrɪ; ˈkʌstəməri/ *adj* **1** something that is customary is normal because it is the way something is usually done 风俗的, 惯例的: **it is customary (for sb) to do sth** *It is customary for the most important person to sit at the end of the table.* 按惯例, 最重要的人坐首席。**2** someone's customary behaviour is the way they usually do things〔人〕习惯性的: *Barbara answered with her customary frankness.* 巴巴拉以惯有的坦率回答。—**customarily** /,kʌstəˈmɛrɪlɪ; ˈkʌstəmərəli/ *adv*

custom-built /,‥ ˈ‥◂/ *adj* a custom-built car, house etc has been specially designed and made for a particular person〔汽车、房子等〕定制的, 定做的

cus·tom·er /ˈkʌstəmə; ˈkʌstəmə/ *n* [C] **1** someone who buys goods or services from a shop, company etc 顾客, 客户: *Next customer please!* 请下一位顾客! | *the customer complaints department* 客户投诉部 | **regular customer** *keeping the shop's regular customers happy* 让老客户满意 | **sb's biggest/best customer** (=someone who buys the most goods or services) 最大/最佳客户 *We don't want to lose them – they're one of our biggest customers.* 他们是我们最大的客户之一, 我们不想失去。—compare 比较 PATRON (2) —see picture on page A15 参见 A15 页图 **2 a cool customer** *informal* someone who is always calm and very confident but in an unpleasant way【非正式】一本正经的人 **3 awkward/tricky etc customer** someone who is difficult to deal with because they behave in a deliberately unhelpful way 难对付的/诡计多端的家伙

cus·tom·ize also 又作 -ise *BrE*【英】/ˈkʌstəm,aɪz; ˈkʌstəmaɪz/ *v* [T] to change something to make it more suitable for you, or to make it look special or unusual 定做, 定制; 按规格改制: *The program allows computer users to customize the menu.* 该程序允许电脑用户自定义菜单。| *a customized car* 定制的汽车

custom-made /,‥ ˈ‥◂/ *adj* a custom-made pair of shoes, shirt etc is specially made for a particular person〔鞋、衬衫等〕定制的, 定做的

Customs and Ex·cise /,‥ ‥ ˈ‥/ *n* [singular] the department of the British government that is responsible for collecting the tax on goods that are being bought or sold or have been brought into the country〔英国的〕关税及消费税务局

cut¹ /kʌt; kʌt/ *v past tense and past participle* **cut** *present participle* **cutting**

1 ▶DIVIDE WITH KNIFE ETC 用刀等分开◀ [T] to divide something into two or more pieces using a sharp tool such as a knife 切, 割: *Do you want me to cut the cake?* 要我切蛋糕吗? | *The thieves had cut the phone wires.* 小偷把电话线割断了。| **cut sth in half/in two** *cut the orange in half* 将橙子对半切开 | **cut sth into quarters/pieces/four** *Cut each one into about 6 pieces.* 把每一个切成六块左右。

2 ▶REMOVE A PIECE OF 去掉某个部分◀ [T] to use a knife to remove a piece from the main part of something 切除, 割下, 削掉: **cut sth** *I cut another slice of bread.* 我又切下一片面包。| **cut sb sth** *Cut me a big slice of that lemon cake, will you?* 把那个柠檬蛋糕切一大块给我, 好吗?

3 ▶MAKE A SHAPE 做成某形状◀ [T] to make something into a particular shape by using a sharp tool such as a knife 雕凿, 剪[割, 削, 砍]成: **cut sth into chunks/rings etc** *Cut the carrots into small cubes.* 把胡萝卜切成小方块。

4 ▶MAKE A HOLE 钻洞[孔]◀ [I,T] to make a hole in the surface of something, or to open it by using a sharp tool such as a knife 凿[挖](洞): **[+into/through etc]** *a knife that will cut through glass* 可以划开玻璃的刀 | **cut a hole in sth** *Firefighters had to cut a hole in the car roof.* 消防员不得不在车顶开个洞。| **cut sth open** *Ben cut the sack open in a great hurry to see what was inside.* 本匆忙割开袋子, 看看里面有什么。

5 ▶GRASS/HAIR ETC 草/毛发等◀ [T] to make something shorter with a knife, scissors etc in order to improve its appearance 修理, 修剪: **cut the lawn/the grass/the hedge** *I think I'll cut the grass this afternoon if it doesn't rain.* 如果不下雨, 我想下午修剪草地。| **have/get your hair cut** (=pay someone to cut your hair) 理发 *Where do you have your hair cut?* 你在哪儿理发?

6 cut sb free/loose to allow someone to escape by using a knife to cut the rope that they are tied by〔割断绳索〕让…逃走, 放走

7 ▶CROPS 农作物◀ [T] to take the top part off crops such as wheat before gathering them 收割〔庄稼〕: *cutting corn* 收割玉米

8 ▶WOUND 伤害◀ [T] to injure yourself when a sharp object or surface breaks open your skin so that you start bleeding 划破, 划伤, 割伤: **cut your finger/knee/hand etc** *Be careful not to cut your fingers with that knife – it's very sharp.* 小心, 别割破手指——那把刀很锋利。| **cut yourself (on sth)** *I cut myself quite badly on a piece of glass.* 我被一块玻璃严重划伤。| **cut sth open** (=injure part of your body by cutting it on something) 把…割伤 *He fell and cut his head open.* 他跌倒了, 把头碰破了。

9 ▶REDUCE PRICES/TIME/MONEY ETC 缩减价格/时间/钱等◀ [T] to reduce something a lot, especially prices, time, or money 削减, 裁减, 减少: *A secure home will cut the risk of burglary.* 有安全防护设备的家可减少被盗的危险。| **cut sth by a quarter/25% etc** *Marston's is to cut its workforce by 20%.* 马斯顿公司将裁员 20%。| **cut sth off/from/to etc** *The new direct service will cut 2 hours off the flying time between London and Seoul.* 新的直航将使伦敦与首尔间的航程缩短两个小时。

10 ▶FILM/SPEECH 影片/演讲◀ [T] **a)** to reduce the length of a film, speech etc 删剪, 缩短: *The original version was cut by more than 30 minutes.* 原版被删去了三十多分钟。**b)** to remove part of a film, speech, or piece of writing, for example because it might offend people 删节〔影片、演讲、文字等以免冒犯人〕, 剪掉 **c)** to put the parts of a film together so that they make a continuous story and get rid of the parts you do not want 剪辑〔影片〕 **d) Cut!** *spoken* said by the director of a film to tell everyone to stop acting, stop filming etc【口】停!〔导演口令〕

11 ▶DIVIDE AN AREA 划分区域◀ [T] to divide an area into two or more parts 划分〔区域〕: **cut sth in/into** *The river cuts the valley in two.* 那条河将山谷一分为二。

12 ▶PLAYING CARDS 打牌◀ [I,T] to divide a pack of cards into two 切(牌), 倒(牌)

13 ▶MUSIC/RECORD 音乐/唱片◀ [T] if a musician cuts a record, they make a record of their music 灌制唱片

14 ▶LINE 线条◀ [T] if a line cuts another line, they cross each other at a particular point〔一条线〕与〔另一条线〕相交

15 ▶TOOTH 牙齿◀ if a baby cuts a tooth, the tooth starts to grow 长新牙

16 cut your teeth on sth to get your first experience of doing something by practising on something simple 从〔简单的情况〕获得初步经验

17 cut in line *AmE* to unfairly go in front of other people who are waiting to buy or do something【美】插队, 不按次序排队; **jump the queue** (JUMP¹ (17)) *BrE*【英】

18 cut class *AmE informal* to deliberately not go to a class that you should go to【美, 非正式】逃课: *I cut class to go hang out in the bar.* 我逃课去泡酒吧。

19 cut corners to do something in a way that is not perfect, in order to save time, effort, or money〔做事〕抄近路，走捷径

20 cut sth short to stop doing something earlier than was planned 缩短，中断: *She had to cut short her vacation when she heard that her mother was ill.* 听说母亲病了，她不得不中断假期。

21 cut sb short to stop someone from finishing what they wanted to say 打断，插嘴: *I tried to explain, but he cut me short.* 我想解释，他却打断了我。

22 cut the crap *spoken* an impolite way of telling someone to deal with only the most important things without wasting time on unimportant details【口】闲话少说，不要瞎折腾: *I wish they'd cut the crap and get on with this meeting!* 我希望他们别纠缠琐事，快点儿开会！

23 cut sb dead to deliberately ignore someone when you meet them 不理睬，装作没看见: *I saw Ian in town but he just cut me dead!* 我在镇上看见了伊恩，他却没理睬我！

24 cut sb to the quick to upset someone very much by saying something cruel 出口伤人，说话损人

25 cut the ground from under sb's feet to make someone or their ideas seem less impressive by having better ideas yourself, doing something before they do etc 把某人的计划比下去，先发制人

26 cut your own throat to behave in a way that will harm you, especially because you are proud or angry 自取其辱，自取灭亡: *He'd just be cutting his own throat if he left now.* 他如果现在离开就等于毁了自己。

27 cut a fine figure/cut an odd figure etc *literary* to have an impressive, strange, etc appearance【文】惹人注目/怪模怪样等: *Steve cut an odd figure in his cloak and Spanish riding hat.* 斯蒂夫穿着那件斗篷，戴着那顶西班牙式骑士帽，非常惹眼。

28 it cuts both ways *informal* used to say that something has advantages but also disadvantages【非正式】有利有弊，有正反两种效果

29 cut the cord to stop depending on someone, especially your parents 摆脱〔尤指对父母的〕依赖，〔生活上〕独立

30 cut and run *informal* to leave a situation suddenly when it becomes too difficult, especially when you should have stayed【非正式】开溜，临阵脱逃: *Don't worry. He won't cut and run.* 别担心，他不会见难而逃的。

31 cut your losses to stop trying to do something that is already failing in order to prevent the situation becoming even worse 止损；及早放弃无利可图的事

32 not cut the mustard *AmE informal* to not be good enough【美，非正式】不符合要求: *Lawrence tries really hard but his work just doesn't cut the mustard.* 尽管劳伦斯工作很尽力，但仍不如人意。

33 ►ILLEGAL DRUG 非法毒品◄ [T usually passive 一般用被动态] to mix an illegal drug such as HEROIN with some other substance 混合〔毒品和其他物质〕

34 cut your coat according to your cloth to spend only as much money as you can afford 量入为出

35 cut no ice/not cut much ice if something cuts no ice with someone, it will not persuade them to change their mind 不起作用，不产生影响: *I don't expect anything I say will cut much ice with him.* 我不指望我的话能影响他。—see also 另见 **cut a long story short** (STORY (11)), **cut a swathe through** (SWATHE¹ (4)), **cut it fine** (FINE³ (5))

cut across *phr v* [T] **1** to go across an area of land instead of going around it, in order to save time 抄近路穿过，横越: *Come on, if we cut across the field we'll get there before Frank.* 快点儿，如果从田里穿过去，我们就能赶在弗兰克之前到那儿。**2** if a problem or feeling cuts across different groups of people, they are all affected by it〔问题、看法等〕影响〔不同群体的人〕: *The drug problem cuts across all social classes.* 在社会各阶层中都存在毒品问题。

cut sth ↔ **away** *phr v* [T] to remove the unwanted or unnecessary parts from something 去掉；切掉；砍掉: *Cut away all the dead wood.* 把枯木都砍掉。

cut back *phr v* **1** [I, T **cut back** sth] to reduce the numbers of something, or the time or money that is spent on something, especially because you do not have enough money 削减，缩减: *Defence spending is to be cut back.* 国防开支将被削减。| [+on] *Many schools are cutting back on staff at the moment.* 目前许多学校在裁员。**2** [T **cut** sth ↔ **back**] to remove the top part of a plant in order to help it to grow 修剪〔植物〕，打顶: *I must cut that holly bush back a bit.* 我必须修剪那冬青树丛了。—see also 另见 CUTBACK

cut down *phr v*

1 ►REDUCE 减少◄ [I,T] to reduce the amount of something that you eat, buy, use etc 减少，缩减: *You smoke too much – you should try to cut down.* 你抽烟太凶了，该少抽点儿。| **cut sth ↔ down** *The coal industry was cut down to half its former size.* 煤炭业规模缩小了一半。| [+on] *My doctor's told me to cut down on carbo-hydrates.* 我的医生告诉我要减少碳水化合物的摄入量。

2 ►TREE 树◄ [T **cut** sth ↔ **down**] to cut through the trunk of a tree so that it falls on the ground 砍倒〔树〕

3 ►KILL/INJURE 杀死/伤害◄ *literary*【文】[T **cut** sb ↔ **down**] to kill or injure someone with a sword or gun〔用剑或枪〕杀伤，砍倒，击倒: *Our men were cut down by a hail of machine-gun fire.* 我们的人被一阵机枪火力扫倒了。

4 ►MAKE SHORTER 使缩短◄ [T **cut** sth ↔ **down**] to reduce the length of something such as a piece of writing 缩短，剪短〈如文章〉: *The essay's too long – it needs cutting down a little.* 这篇文章太长了，需要缩短一些。

5 cut sb down to size to make someone realize that they are not as important, successful etc as they think they are 使有自知之明

cut in *phr v* **1** [I] to interrupt someone who is speaking by saying something 插嘴，打断别人说话: [+on] *I wish Marie would stop cutting in on our conversation all the time.* 我希望玛丽在我们谈话时别老插嘴。**2** [I] to suddenly drive into the space between two moving cars in a dangerous way 强行超车: *This idiot cut in right in front of me.* 这个傻瓜把车强行插到我的正前方。**3** [I] if a part of a machine cuts in, it starts to operate when it is needed〔机器的一部分在有需要时〕开动；接通: *The safety device cuts in automatically when needed.* 安全装置在需要时会自动接通。**4 cut sb in on** *informal* to allow someone to take part in a secret plan to make money【非正式】让〔某人〕加入秘密赚钱计划: *Come on, Joey, you said you were going to cut me in on this one!* 得了，乔伊，你说过这次也算我一份的！

cut off *phr v*

1 ►PIECE OF STH 一片◄ [T **cut** sth ↔ **off**] to separate something by cutting it from the main part 切掉；分割开: *She cut off a big piece of meat.* 她切下一大块肉。| *One of his fingers was cut off in the accident.* 他的一根手指在事故中被切断了。

2 ►STOP THE SUPPLY 停止供应◄ [T **cut** sth ↔ **off**] to stop the supply of something such as electricity, gas, water etc 中断，切断〔电、煤气、水等的〕供应: *The electricity company are threatening to cut us off.* 电力公司以停电威胁我们。| *The US has cut off aid to Cambodia.* 美国已中断对柬埔寨的援助。

3 get cut off to suddenly not be able to hear someone that you were speaking to on the telephone〔电话〕中断，掉线: *I don't know what happened – we just got cut off.* 不知出了什么事，我们的通话无缘无故中断了。

4 ►PLACE/PEOPLE 地方/人们◄ [T **cut** sb/sth ↔ **off**] to surround a place so that the people there are completely separated from other places or people 隔断；包围；隔绝: *In winter the town is often cut off by snow.* 冬天时，这座小镇常因大雪与外界隔断联系。| *They were cut off by the Russian army and forced to surrender.* 他们彻底被俄军包围，被迫投降。

5 ►STOP BEING FRIENDLY 不再友好◄ [T **cut** sb **off**] to stop having a friendly relationship with someone 中止关系: *Julia had been completely cut off by all her family and friends.* 朱莉娅的家人与朋友都与她脱离了关系。| **cut yourself off (from)** (=avoid people) 躲开所有人 *After his wife died he cut himself off completely from the rest of the world.* 妻子去世后，他彻底与外界隔绝。

6 ►MONEY/PROPERTY 金钱/财产◄ [T **cut** sb ↔ **off**] to take away someone's right to receive your money or property, especially when you die 剥夺〔某人的〕财产继承权: **cut sb off without a penny** *My parents have threatened to cut me off without a penny if I marry him.* 我父母威胁说如果我嫁给他，我就别想继承一分钱。

7 ►STOP SB TALKING 打断某人谈话◄ [T **cut** sb **off**] to prevent someone from finishing what they are saying 打断〔某人的谈话〕: *She cut me off in mid sentence.* 我刚说了半句就被她打断了。

8 be cut off a) if a place is cut off, it is difficult to get to and is a long way from any other place〔地方〕被隔绝的: *The village is so cut off from civilization that it receives almost no visitors.* 这个村庄与文明社会如此隔绝，几乎没有外人去。**b)** if someone is cut off they are lonely because they are not able to meet people〔人〕被隔绝[隔离]: [+from] *Mothers with very young children often feel cut off from the rest of the community.* 孩子太小的母亲常感觉与社会脱节。

9 cut off your nose to spite your face to do something because you are angry even though it will harm you 拿自己出气；赌气做出不顾后果的事

cut out 剪下

cut out *phr v*
1 ▶REMOVE STH 去掉某物◀ [T **cut** sth ↔ **out**] to remove something by cutting 割掉, 剪下: *I cut the advertisement out of the newspaper.* 我从报纸上剪下这则广告。| *The surgeon cut out the tumour.* 外科医生切除了肿瘤。
2 ▶MAKE STH INTO A SHAPE 将某物弄成某形状◀ [T **cut** sth ↔ **out**] to cut a piece of paper, cloth etc so that it becomes a particular shape 把〔纸、布等〕剪[切]成某形状: *The children were cutting out squares from the scraps of material.* 孩子们正用零碎材料剪出方块。
3 ▶PIECE OF WRITING/NEWS REPORT ETC 文章/新闻报道等◀ [T **cut** sth ↔ **out**] to take out part of a piece of writing, a news report etc, especially because it might offend people 截短, 删节
4 ▶STOP DOING STH 停止做某事◀ [T **cut** sth ↔ **out**] to stop doing or eating something, especially because it is harmful to you〔尤指某事有害而〕戒除, 改掉: *If you cut out the drink you'd feel much healthier.* 如果你戒酒, 就会觉得身体好很多。
5 cut it/that out *spoken* used to tell someone to stop doing something because it is annoying you【口】停止〔做某事〕: *Hey, you guys, cut it out – Mom's trying to get some sleep.* 喂, 你们别闹了, 妈妈要睡一会儿。
6 ▶STOP SB FROM DOING STH 阻止某人做某事◀ [T **cut** sb **out**] to stop someone from doing something or taking part in something 阻止, 制止: *Todd's injuries cut him out of being selected for the team.* 托德的伤势让他不能入选该队。
7 ▶MOTOR 发动机◀ [I] if a motor cuts out, it suddenly stops working 突然熄火: *The engine cut out halfway across the lake.* 开到湖中间发动机便熄了火。
8 ▶STOP STH BEING SEEN 阻止被看见◀ [T] to prevent light from reaching somewhere, or prevent a particular view from being seen 隔断〔光线或某种景色〕: *The tinted windows help cut out the glare from the sun.* 窗户的染色玻璃阻挡了耀眼的阳光。
9 cut sb out of your will to remove someone's name from the list of people who will receive your money or property when you die 取消某人的遗产继承权
10 be cut out for/cut out to be [usually in questions and negatives 一般用于疑问句和否定句] to have the qualities that you need for a particular job or activity 适合于…: *In the end I decided I wasn't cut out for the army.* 我最后得出结论, 自己不是当兵的料儿。| *Are you sure you're really cut out to be a teacher?* 你确定你真的适合做教师吗? —see also 另见 **have his/her work cut out** (WORK² (13))

cut up *phr v* **1** [T **cut** sth ↔ **up**] to cut something into small pieces 切碎, 割碎: *His mother has to cut up all his food for him.* 他妈妈不得不为他将所有的食品切碎。**2** [I] *AmE informal* if a class cuts up, the students in it behave badly【美, 非正式】〔上课时学生〕恶作剧, 胡闹 **3 be badly cut up** to have a lot of injuries because you have been in an accident or fight〔因事故或打架〕多处受伤 **4 cut up (about sth)** *informal* very upset because something bad has happened to you【非正式】伤心, 难受: *She still seems very cut up about it.* 她似乎仍为那件事感到十分伤心。**5 cut up rough** *BrE informal* to react in an angry or violent way【英, 非正式】发脾气, 发怒

S2 W2 **cut²** *n* [C]
1 ▶WOUND 伤◀ a wound that is caused when something sharp cuts your skin 伤口: *The driver escaped with a few cuts and bruises.* 司机逃过了一劫, 只割破了几处, 有一些瘀伤。
2 ▶HOLE/MARK 洞/记号◀ a hole in something, or a mark in the surface of something, made by something sharp 切口; 切痕: *The kitchen counter is covered with cuts.* 厨台上全是刀的切痕。
3 ▶REDUCTION 减少◀ [often plural 常用复数] a planned reduction in the size or amount of something〔尺寸, 数量的〕削减, 缩短: **job cuts/wage cuts/tax cuts etc** *A shorter working week will mean pay cuts for millions of workers.* 每周工作时间缩短将意味着几百万工人的工资要降低。| [**+in**] *a massive cut in public spending* 公共开支的大幅削减
4 ▶HAIR 毛发◀ [usually singular 一般用单数] **a)** the act of cutting someone's hair 剪发, 理发: *How much do they charge for a cut and blow-dry?* 理发加吹干他们要收多少钱? **b)** the style in which your hair has been cut 发式
5 ▶CLOTHES 衣服◀ [usually singular 一般用单数] the style in which your clothes have been made〔衣服的〕款式, 剪裁, 式样: *From the cut of his suit, I'd say he was pretty wealthy.* 从他的服装式样来看, 我敢说他相当富有。
6 ▶MONEY 钱◀ [singular] *informal* someone's share of something, especially money【非正式】份额〔尤指分配的金钱〕: *Investigators found that her cut of the profits amounted to more than 25%.* 调查人员发现她所占的利润份额超过25%。
7 make a cut to remove part of a speech, piece of writing etc 删节〔演说、文章等〕: *The censors made several cuts.* 审查官做了几处删节。
8 ▶FILM 电影◀ the process of putting together the different parts of a film and removing the parts that will not be shown 剪辑: *Spielberg himself oversaw the final cut.* 斯皮尔伯格亲自监督了影片的最后剪辑。
9 the cut and thrust of the violent or unpleasant way in which a particular activity is done 激烈的争斗; 交锋: *the cut and thrust of international politics* 国际政治的激烈斗争
10 be a cut above to be much better than someone else or something else 高人一等, 比别人高明: **a cut above the rest** *Just because she went to a private school, Jayne seems to think she's a cut above the rest of us.* 杰恩仅仅因为自己上过私立学校, 便认为自己比我们都高明。
11 ▶MEAT 肉◀ a piece of meat that has been cut so that you can cook it 切下的一块: *cuts of fresh lamb* 几块新鲜的羔羊肉
12 ▶ROAD 路◀ *AmE* a road that has been made through a hill【美】〔在山中开出的〕通道 —see also 另见 POWER CUT

cut and dried /ˌ· · ˈ·◂/ *adj* a decision or result that is cut and dried cannot now be changed 已成定局的; 不可改变的: *I think we can say that the result of the election is now cut and dried.* 我想我们可以说现在的选举结果已成定局。

cut·a·way /ˈkʌtəˌwe; ˈkʌtəweɪ/ *adj* a cutaway model, drawing etc is open on one side so that you can see the details inside it〔模型、图等〕剖面的

cut·back /ˈkʌtˌbæk; ˈkʌtbæk/ *n* [C usually plural 一般用复数] a reduction in something, such as the number of workers in an organization, the amount of money spent by the government etc 削减, 裁减〔员工或政府开支等〕: [**+in**] *recommended cutbacks in social programmes* 建议减少的社会福利项目 —see also 另见 **cut back** (CUT¹)

cute /kjut; kjuːt/ *adj informal*【非正式】**1** very pretty or attractive 漂亮的, 逗人喜爱的: *Jenny's such a cute little girl.* 珍妮真是一个可爱的小女孩。**2** attractive in a sexual way 性感迷人的: *an all-American type – cute, blonde and vivacious* 一个十足的美国类型: 性感、金发、活泼 **3** *especially AmE* clever and practical when dealing with people, sometimes in an unpleasant way【尤美】机灵的, 精明的〔有时贬〕: *He's one cute lawyer!* 他可是个精明的律师! | **get cute with** (=try to deceive someone) 设法欺骗〔某人〕*Don't get cute with me – I know what those tires cost.* 别骗我了, 我知道那些轮胎值多少钱。 **cutely** *adv* —**cuteness** *n* [U] S3

cute·sy /ˈkjutsɪ; ˈkjuːtsi/ *adj AmE*【美】**1** something that is cutesy is too pretty or clever in a way you think is annoying 矫揉造作的, 忸怩作态的: *That greeting card is too cutesy.* 那张贺卡太肉麻了。

cute·y /ˈkjutɪ; ˈkjuːti/ *n* [C] *spoken* someone who is attractive, kind, and helpful【口】迷人、友善、乐于帮助别人的人: *He's such a cutey!* 他真是一个热心人!

cut glass /ˌ· ˈ·◂/ *n* [U] glass that has patterns cut into its surface 雕花玻璃

cut-glass *adj* **1** made of cut glass 雕花玻璃(制品)的: *a cut-glass decanter* 雕花玻璃盛酒瓶 **2 cut-glass accent/vowel** an accent or vowel that is typical of someone from a high social class 上层社会的口音/上流社会的发音

cu·ti·cle /ˈkjutɪkl; ˈkjuːtɪkəl/ *n* [C] an outer layer of hard skin, especially around the base of your nails〔尤指指甲根部的〕角质层

cut·lass /ˈkʌtləs; ˈkʌtləs/ *n* [C] a short sword with a curved blade, used by sailors or PIRATES in former times〔旧时水手和海盗使用的〕短剑, 短弯刀 —see picture at 参见 SWORD 图

cut·ler /ˈkʌtlɚ; ˈkʌtlə/ *n* [C] someone who makes or sells cutlery 刀剪匠，刃具工人；刃具商

cut·le·ry /ˈkʌtlərɪ; ˈkʌtləri/ *n* [U] knives, forks, spoons, and other things used for eating with 刀叉等餐具；SILVERWARE *AmE*【美】：*Can you put the cutlery on the table?* 你能将刀叉摆在餐桌上吗？—see pictures on pages A10 and A15 参见 A10 页和 A15 页图

cut·let /ˈkʌtlɪt; ˈkʌtlɪ̣t/ *n* [C] **1** a small flat piece of meat on a bone, usually LAMB[1] (2) or VEAL 肉排〔通常为羔羊排或小牛肉〕：*a grilled lamb cutlet* 烤羊排 **2 vegetable/nut/prawn cutlet** a flat mass of vegetables, nuts etc covered with egg and BREADCRUMB*s* and cooked in hot fat 炸蔬菜饼/炸干果饼/炸虾饼

cut·off also 又作 **cut-off** *BrE*【英】/ˈkʌtˌɔf; ˈkʌtɒf/ *n* **1** [C] a fixed limit or level at which you decide to or have to stop doing something 停止点；截止点：**cutoff date/score/point** (=the date etc when you stop doing something) 截止日期/底线分数/截止点 *The cutoff point for this sample was a score of 50% or more.* 这个样品的最低分数不低于50%。**2 cutoffs** [plural] short trousers that you make by cutting off the bottom part of a pair of trousers〔用长裤裁剪成的〕短裤 **3** [C] a part of a pipe that you open and shut to control the flow of gas or liquid〔气体或液体流动的〕截断装置，截止阀

cut·out /ˈkʌtˌaut; ˈkʌtaʊt/ *n* [C] **1** the shape of a person, object etc that has been cut out of wood or paper 纸剪[木刻]的图形：*a life-size cardboard cutout of Margaret Thatcher* 一幅和撒切尔夫人一样大小的硬纸剪影 **2** a piece of equipment that stops a machine when something is not working properly 切断装置，保险装置

cut-price /ˌ· ˈ·◂/ *adj* **1** sold at less than the usual price 减价的，削价的：*cut-price petrol* 减价汽油 **2** a cut-price shop, supermarket etc sells goods at reduced prices 廉价的〔商店等〕：*a cut-price garage* 廉价汽车修理站

cut·purse /ˈkʌtˌpɝs; ˈkʌtpɜːs/ *n* [C] *old use* a PICKPOCKET【旧】扒手

cut-rate /ˈ· ·/ *adj* sold at less than the usual price 减价销售的

cut·ter /ˈkʌtɚ; ˈkʌtə/ *n* [C] **1** a small ship 小艇 **2** [often plural 常用复数] a tool that is used for cutting 切割器具，刀具：*wire cutters* 钢丝钳，铁丝剪

cut·throat[1] /ˈkʌtˌθrot; ˈkʌtθrəʊt/ *adj* [only before noun 仅用于名词前] a cutthroat activity involves people who are all trying to get the same thing, often behaving badly or unfairly to each other 竞争激烈的，无情的：*Cutthroat competition led to a lot of bankruptcies and mergers.* 无情的竞争导致许多公司倒闭或被合并。

cutthroat[2] *n* [C] *old use* a murderer【旧】凶手，谋杀者

cut-throat ra·zor /ˌ· · ˈ· ·/ *n* [C] a RAZOR with a very long sharp blade 剃刀 —see picture at 参见 RAZOR 图

cut·ting[1] /ˈkʌtɪŋ; ˈkʌtɪŋ/ *n* [C] **1** a stem or leaf that is cut from a plant and put in soil or water to grow into a new plant〔用来插种的〕插枝，插条 **2** *BrE* a piece of writing that is cut from a newspaper, magazine etc【英】剪报；剪下来的材料；CLIPPING (1) *AmE*【美】：**press/newspaper cuttings** *Margot had sent him a bunch of press cuttings about the wedding.* 玛戈给他寄去了许多有关那次婚礼的剪报。**3** *BrE* something that is produced by cutting, especially a passage cut through a hill for a road or railway【英】〔在山中〕开凿出来的通道；CUT[2] (12) *AmE*【美】

cutting[2] *adj* **1** very unkind and intended to upset someone 尖刻的，伤人感情的：*Danny can be so cutting at times.* 丹尼有时特别刻薄。| *Sue made a cutting remark about my clothes.* 休对我的衣服作了刻薄的评论。**2** a cutting wind is very cold and you can feel it through your clothes〔风〕刺骨的 **3 be (at) the cutting edge of sth** to be the most advanced form of an activity, in which the newest methods, systems, equipment etc are developed and used 为…最先进的，处于…的领先地位：*The information highway is the cutting edge of the electronic revolution.* 信息高速公路处于电子革命的先锋地位。

cutting board /ˈ· · ·/ *n* [C] *AmE* a large piece of wood or plastic used for cutting meat or vegetables on【美】砧板；CHOPPING BOARD *BrE*【英】

cutting room /ˈ· · ·/ *n* [C] a room where the final form of a film is prepared by cutting and putting the different parts into the correct order〔影片的〕剪辑室

Cut·ty Sark, the /ˌkʌtɪ ˈsark; ˌkʌti ˈsɑːk/ a CLIPPER (=fast sailing ship) which was built in 1869 and carried tea from China to England. It is now a MUSEUM ship at Greenwich in London. "卡蒂萨克"号〔1869年建造的一艘快速帆船，专门向英格兰运送中国茶叶。现成为船上博物馆，停泊在伦敦的格林尼治，供游客参观〕

Cuz·co /ˈkusko; ˈkʊskəʊ/ a city in southern Peru, once the most important city of the Inca people, with many palaces and temples. Much of ancient Cuzco was destroyed by the Spanish in 1533. 库斯科〔秘鲁南部一城市，曾是印加人最重要的城市，建有许多宫殿和庙宇。1533年，古城的大部分被西班牙人毁坏〕

CV /ˌsi ˈvi; ˌsiː ˈviː/ also 又作 **curriculum vitae** *n* [C] *BrE* a short written document giving your education and past employment, used when you are looking for a job【英】简历(书)；RESUME[2] (2) *AmE*【美】：*Please send a CV and brief letter to the address below.* 请按以下地址邮寄一份简历和简短的应征信。

cwt the written abbreviation of 缩写= HUNDREDWEIGHT

-cy /sɪ; si/ *suffix* [in nouns 构成名词] **1** the state or quality of being something 表示某种状态或性质：*privacy* (=state of being private) 隐私 | *accuracy* 精确 | *bankruptcy* 破产 **2** a particular rank or position 表示某种职位、职别：*a baronetcy* (=the rank of a BARONET) 准男爵爵位

cy·an /ˈsaɪæn; ˈsaɪən/ *adj* dark greenish blue 带绿的深蓝色的，青色的 —**cyan** *n* [U]

cy·a·nide /ˈsaɪəˌnaɪd; ˈsaɪənaɪd/ *n* [U] a very strong poison 氰化物

cyber- /saɪbɚ; saɪbə/ *prefix* connected with computers, especially with the sending of messages on the INTERNET 与电脑有关的，与互联网上的信息传递有关的

cy·ber·net·ics /ˌsaɪbɚˈnɛtɪks; ˌsaɪbəˈnetɪks/ *n* [U] the scientific study of the way in which information is moved about and controlled in machines, the brain and the NERVOUS SYSTEM 控制论 —**cybernetic** *adj*

cy·ber·punk /ˈsaɪbɚˌpʌŋk; ˈsaɪbəpʌŋk/ *n* [U] stories about imaginary events connected with computer science 电脑幻想故事：*cyberpunk fiction* 电脑幻想小说

cy·ber·space /ˈsaɪbɚˌspes; ˈsaɪbəspeɪs/ *n* [U] a word from SCIENCE FICTION, used to mean the place where electronic messages, information, pictures etc exist when they are sent from one computer to another 电子空间〔语出科幻小说，指信息、图像等在电脑之间传递时所处的空间〕：*We didn't meet in San Francisco – we met in cyberspace!* 我们并不是在旧金山相遇的，我们是在电子空间里认识的！

cy·borg /ˈsaɪbɔrg; ˈsaɪbɔːg/ *n* [C] a creature that is partly human and partly machine 电子人，半机械人

Cyc·la·des, the /ˈsɪklədiz; ˈsɪklədiːz/ a group of Greek islands in the Aegean Sea, including Naxos and Paros 基克拉泽斯群岛〔位于爱琴海的希腊群岛，其中包括纳克索斯岛和帕罗斯岛〕

cyc·la·men /ˈsɪkləmən; ˈsɪkləmən/ *n* [C] a plant with pink, red, or white flowers 仙客来〔一种植物〕

cy·cle[1] /ˈsaɪkl; ˈsaɪkəl/ *n* [C] **1** a number of events happening in a regularly repeated order 循环：[+of] *the cycle of the seasons* 四季的周而复始 | *the endless cycle of violence in this part of the world* 世界上这一地区永无休止的暴力事件 —see also 另见 LIFE CYCLE **2** a bicycle or MOTORCYCLE 自行车；摩托车 **3** the period of time needed for a machine to finish a process 周期：*This washing machine has a 50 minute cycle.* 这台洗衣机完成洗衣的全部程序要50分钟。**4** a group of songs, poems etc that are all about a particular important event〔表现同一重大事件的〕组歌，组诗

cycle[2] *v* [I] *especially BrE* to travel by bicycle【尤英】骑自行车：*Do you cycle to work?* 你骑自行车上班吗？

cy·clic /ˈsaɪklɪk; ˈsaɪklɪk/ also 又作 **cyc·li·cal** /ˈsaɪklɪk]; ˈsɪklɪkəl/ *adj* happening in cycles (CYCLE[1] (1)) 循环的，周期的：*the cyclical nature of history* 历史的循环本质 —**cyclically** /-klɪ; -kli/ *adv*

cy·clist /ˈsaɪklɪst; ˈsaɪklɪ̣st/ *n* [C] someone who rides a bicycle 骑自行车的人：*Andrew and Merv are very keen cyclists.* 安德鲁和默夫热衷于骑自行车。

cy·clone /ˈsaɪklon; ˈsaɪkləʊn/ *n* [C] a very violent storm that moves very rapidly in a circle 旋风，龙卷风：*Darwin was flattened by Cyclone Tracy in 1974.* 旋风特蕾西于1974年将达尔文夷为平地。—compare 比较 HURRICANE, TYPHOON

cy·clops /ˈsaɪklɑps; ˈsaɪklɒps/ *n* [singular] a very big man in ancient Greek stories who only had one eye in the middle of his forehead〔希腊神话中的〕独眼巨人

cy·der /ˈsaɪdɚ; ˈsaɪdə/ *n* [U] *BrE* another spelling of CIDER【英】cider的另一种拼法

cyg·net /ˈsɪgnɪt; ˈsɪgnɪ̣t/ *n* [C] a young SWAN[1] 幼天鹅

cyl·in·der /ˈsɪlɪndɚ; ˈsɪlɪ̣ndə/ *n* [C] **1** a shape, object, or container with circular ends and long straight sides 圆柱体；圆筒：*The gases are stored under pressure in separate cylinders.* 气体被压缩分装在几个圆筒里。—see picture at 参见 SHAPE[1] 图

2 the tube within which a PISTON moves forwards and backwards in an engine〔引擎的〕汽缸: *a four cylinder engine* 四汽缸引擎

cy·lin·dri·cal /sɪˋlɪndrɪkḷ; sɪ̈ˈlɪndrɪkəl/ *adj* in the shape of a cylinder 圆柱体的: *A huge cylindrical oil tank stood beside the engine.* 发动机旁边有一个大的圆筒形油箱。

cym·bal /ˋsɪmbḷ; ˈsɪmbəl/ *n* [C] a musical instrument made of a thin round metal plate that you play by hitting it with a stick, or by hitting two of them together 铙钹, 钗钹: *the sudden clash of cymbals* 突然的铙钹响声

Cym·ru /ˋkʌmrɪ; ˈkʌmri/ the Welsh name for Wales 威尔士〔威尔士语〕

cyn·ic /ˋsɪnɪk; ˈsɪnɪk/ *n* [C] someone who is not willing to believe that people have good, honest, or sincere reasons for doing something 愤世嫉俗的人; 讽世者; 认为人的动机皆自私者: *Even the most hardened cynic must agree that charity does some good.* 即使最顽固的愤世嫉俗者也必须承认慈善活动有一定的益处。—**cynicism** *n* [U]

cyn·i·cal /ˋsɪnɪkḷ; ˈsɪnɪkəl/ *adj* unwilling to believe that people have good, honest, or sincere reasons for doing something 愤世嫉俗的, 冷嘲热讽的: *You're just so cynical, Dave! Don't you believe in anything?* 你太愤世嫉俗了, 戴夫! 你难道什么也不信吗? | [+about] *Since her divorce she's become very cynical about men.* 离婚后, 她怀疑所有的男人。—**cynically** /-klɪ; -kli/ *adv*

cy·no·sure /ˋsaɪnə,ʃʊr; ˈsɪnəzjʊə/ *n* [usually singular 一般用单数] *formal* someone or something that everyone is interested in or attracted to【正式】引人兴趣[注目]的人[事物]

cy·pher /ˋsaɪfɚ; ˈsaɪfə/ *n* [C] another spelling of CIPHER cipher 的另一种拼法

cy·press /ˋsaɪprəs; ˈsaɪprɪ̈s/ *n* [C] a tree with dark green leaves and hard wood, that does not lose its leaves in winter 柏树; 柏属植物

Cy·prus /ˋsaɪprəs; ˈsaɪprəs/ a large island in the east Mediterranean Sea. Population: 762,887 (2001). Cyprus has a large Greek population in the south and a small Turkish population in the north. 塞浦路斯〔地中海东部一岛国。人口: 762,887 (2001)。南部地区居民是人数众多的希腊人, 北部地方是为数不多的土耳其人〕—**Cypriot** /ˋsɪprɪət; ˈsɪpriət/ *n, adj*

Cy·ril·lic /sɪˋrɪlɪk; sɪ̈ˈrɪlɪk/ *adj* Cyrillic writing is written in the alphabet used for Russian, Bulgarian, and other Slavonic languages 西里尔字母〔俄语、保加利亚语和其他斯拉夫语字母〕的: *a Cyrillic typewriter* 西里尔字母打字机

cyst /sɪst; sɪst/ *n* [C] a mass containing liquid that grows in your body or under your skin 囊肿: *an ovarian cyst* 卵巢囊肿

cys·tic fi·bro·sis /,sɪstɪk faɪˋbrosəs; ,sɪstɪk faɪˈbrəʊsɪ̈s/ *n* [U] a serious medical condition, especially in children, in which breathing and digesting (DIGEST[1] (1)) food is very difficult 囊性纤维变性〔一种严重疾病〕

cyst·i·tis /sɪsˋtaɪtɪs; sɪˈstaɪtɪ̈s/ *n* [U] an infection of the BLADDER[1] (1), especially in women〔尤指妇女的〕膀胱炎

cy·tol·o·gy /saɪˋtɑlədʒɪ; saɪˈtɒlədʒi/ *n* [U] the scientific study of cells from living things 细胞学 —**cytologist** *n* [C]

Cy Young A·ward, the /,saɪ ˋjʌŋ ə,wɔrd; ,saɪ ˈjʌŋ ə,wɔːd/ a prize given every year to the most successful PITCHER (=the player who throws the ball) in the American League and the National League of US BASEBALL. It is named after the famous pitcher Cy Young. 赛扬奖〔美国棒球联盟和全国棒球联盟每年颁发给最佳投手的一个奖项, 以著名投手赛·扬的名字命名〕

czar /zɑr; zɑː/ *n* [C] **1** another spelling of TSAR tsar 的另一种拼法 **2 banking/drug/health etc czar** *AmE* someone who is very powerful in a particular job or activity【美】银行业大王/毒品大王/卫生权威

cza·ri·na /zɑˋrinə; zɑːˈriːnə/ *n* [C] another spelling of TSARINA tsarina 的另一种拼法

Czech·o·slo·vak·i·a /,tʃɛkəsloˋvækɪə; ,tʃekəsləʊˈvækiə/ a former country in central Europe, which divided in 1993 into two separate countries, the Czech Republic and Slovakia 捷克斯洛伐克〔原为欧洲中部一国家, 1993 年分裂为捷克共和国和斯洛伐克两个独立国家〕

Czech Re·pub·lic, the /,· ·ˈ··/ a country in central Europe, between Germany, Poland, Slovakia, and Austria. Population: 10,264,000 (1994). Capital: Prague. Until 1993 it was part of Czechoslovakia. 捷克共和国〔欧洲中部一国家, 与德国、波兰、斯洛伐克以及奥地利接壤。人口: 10,264,000 (1994), 首都: 布拉格。1993 年之前为捷克斯洛伐克的一部分〕—**Czech** *n, adj*

D,d

D /di; diː/ d *plural* **D's, d's** *n* [C] **1** the fourth letter of the English alphabet 英语字母表的第四个字母 **2** the number 500 in the system of ROMAN NUMERALS 罗马数字 500

D 1 the second note in the SCALE[1] (8) of C major, or the musical KEY[2] (4) based on this note D音〔C大调音阶中的第二个音〕**2** a mark that a teacher gives to a student's work, showing that it is not very good D级, 丁级, 丁等〔表示学业成绩不太好〕—see also 另见 D AND C, D-DAY

d 1 the written abbreviation of 缩写= died 死于: *John Keats d 1821* 约翰·济慈死于1821年 **2** the abbreviation of 缩写= PENNY (4) in the system of money used in Britain before 1971 便士〔1971年前用于英国的货币体系〕

d' *spoken*【口】the short form of 缩略式= do: *D'you know how many people are going to be there?* 你知道有多少人要去那儿吗?

-'d 1 the short form of 缩略式= would: *I asked if she'd be willing to help.* 我问她是否愿意帮忙。**2** the short form of 缩略式= had: *Nobody knew where he'd gone.* 没有人知道他去了哪里。

-d /d, t; d, t/ *suffix* the form used for -ED after 'e'〔用于e之后代替 -ed 的后缀形式〕: *baked* 烘[烤]过的

DA /ˌdi ˈe; ˌdiː ˈeɪ/ *n* [C] the abbreviation of 缩写= DISTRICT ATTORNEY

dab[1] /dæb; dæb/ *n* [C] **1** a small amount of something that you put onto a surface with your hand, a cloth etc 少量, 少许〔用手、布等放在物体表面的某物〕: [+of] *Add a dab of butter and some parsley.* 加少许牛油和西芹。**2** a light touch with your hand, a cloth etc〔用手、布等的〕轻敷, 轻触: *She wiped her tears away with a dab of her handkerchief.* 她用手绢轻轻地擦掉眼泪。**3** a small flat fish 泥鲽 **4 dabs** [plural] *BrE old-fashioned* your FINGERPRINTS[1]【英, 过时】指纹

dab[2] *v* **dabbed, dabbing 1** [I,T] to touch something lightly, usually several times 轻触, 轻拍〔多次〕: [+at] *He dabbed at his bleeding lip.* 他轻轻地揩拭流血的嘴唇。**2** [T] to put a substance onto something with quick, light movements of your hand〔轻而快地〕敷, 搽: **dab sth on/onto etc** *She hastily dabbed some cream on her face.* 她匆忙地往脸上搽了些面霜。

dab·ble /ˈdæbḷ; ˈdæbəl/ *v* **1** [I] to do something or be involved in something in a way that is not very serious 涉猎, 涉足, 浅尝: [+at/in] *James dabbles in politics.* 詹姆斯浅涉政治。**2** [T+in] to move your hands, feet etc about in water〔用手、脚等〕玩水, 嬉水: *children dabbling their feet in the sea* 孩子们把双脚浸在海里玩水

dab hand /ˌ· ˈ·/ *n* **be a dab hand at** *BrE informal* to be very good at a particular activity【英, 非正式】擅长于〔某种活动〕

Dac·ca /ˈdækə; ˈdækə/ the old spelling of Dhaka, the capital of Bangladesh 达卡〔孟加拉国首都Dhaka的旧式拼法〕

Dach·au /ˈdɑkau; ˈdækaʊ/ a CONCENTRATION CAMP in southern Germany in which many Jews and other prisoners were killed during World War II 达豪集中营〔位于德国南部的一处集中营。二战期间, 许多犹太人和其他囚犯在此遭到杀害〕

dachs·hund /ˈdɑksˌhund; ˈdækshʊnd/ *n* [C] a type of small dog with short legs and a long body 猎獾狗, 腊肠狗〔一种身长腿短的狗〕—see picture at 参见 DOG[1] 图

Dac·ron /ˈdeˌkrɑn; ˈdækrɒn/ *n* [U] *trademark AmE* a kind of cloth that is not made from natural materials【商标, 美】涤纶, 的确凉

dac·tyl /ˈdæktḷ; ˈdæktɪl/ *n* [C] *technical* a repeated sound pattern in poetry, consisting of one long sound followed by two short sounds as in the word 'carefully'【术语】扬抑抑格〔即一长音后接两个短音, 如 carefully〕—**dactylic** /dækˈtɪlɪk; dækˈtɪlɪk/ *adj*

S1 W2 **dad** /dæd; dæd/ *n* [C] *informal* father【非正式】爸爸, 爹爹: *She lives with her Mom and Dad.* 她和爸爸妈妈一起生活。

Da·da·is·m /ˈdɑdɑ-ɪzəm; ˈdɑːdɑː-ɪzəm/ also 又作 **Dada** /ˈdɑdɑ; ˈdɑːdɑː/ a movement in European art and literature in the early 20th century, in which artists and writers aimed to shock people by ignoring accepted ideas and producing strange, unexpected images. Dadaism was the main influence on SURREALISM, which developed from Dadaism in the 1920s. 达达主义〔20世纪早期欧洲的文艺运动。艺术家和作家故意忽视传统思想, 塑造出人意料的怪诞形象, 以达到惊撼世人之目的。达达主义是超现实主义的主要影响因素, 20世纪20年代超现实主义发端于达达主义〕

dad·dy /ˈdædɪ; ˈdædi/ *n* [C] a word meaning father, used especially by or to young children 爸爸, 爹爹〔尤用于儿语〕: *Look, Daddy's home!* 看, 爸爸回家啦! —see also 另见 SUGAR DADDY S1

daddy long·legs /ˌdædɪ ˈlɔŋlɛgz; ˌdædi ˈlɒŋlegz/ *n* [C] **1** *BrE* a flying insect with long legs; CRANE FLY【英】长脚飞虫; 大蚊 **2** *AmE* an insect with long legs that is similar to a SPIDER【美】盲蛛〔类似蜘蛛的长脚昆虫〕

Daddy War·bucks /ˌdædɪ ˈwɔrbʌks; ˌdædi ˈwɔːbʌks/ a character in the US CARTOON STRIP *Little Orphan Annie*. He is a rich businessman who takes care of a young girl called Annie, whose parents are dead. 沃巴克斯老爹〔美国连环漫画《小孤女安妮》中的人物。他是一位富商, 照管着父母双亡的小女孩安妮〕

da·do /ˈdedo; ˈdeɪdəʊ/ *n plural* **dadoes** [C] the lower part of a wall in a room, especially when it is decorated differently to the upper part of the wall 护壁板, 墙裙〔房间墙壁下面与墙身其他部分装饰不同的部分〕

Dae·da·lus /ˈdɛdḷəs; ˈdiːdələs/ in ancient Greek stories, an inventor who designed the Labyrinth on the island of Crete, where the King of Crete kept the Minotaur. He later escaped from Crete with his son Icarus, by flying away using wings made of feathers and WAX. 代达罗斯〔古希腊神话中的发明家, 曾为克里特国王在克里特岛上设计了关押弥诺陶洛斯的迷宫。后来, 他用羽毛和蜂蜡做成翅膀与儿子伊卡洛斯一起逃离克里特岛〕

dae·mon /ˈdimən; ˈdiːmən/ *n* [C] a spirit in ancient Greek stories that is half a god and half a man〔古希腊神话中的〕半人半神的精灵, 半神 —compare 比较 DEMON

daf·fo·dil /ˈdæfədɪl; ˈdæfədɪl/ *n* [C] a tall yellow spring flower with a central tube-shaped part 水仙(花), 黄水仙

CULTURAL NOTE 文化注释

The daffodil is the national flower of Wales. On St David's Day, the Welsh national day, some Welsh people wear a daffodil on their coat. There is a famous English poem about daffodils by William Wordsworth, which most British people know. It begins: *I wandered lonely as a cloud / That floats on high o'er vales and hills / When all at once I saw a crowd/ A host of golden daffodils.* 水仙是威尔士的民族之花。每逢威尔士民族节日圣大卫节, 威尔士人在衣服上佩戴水仙花。威廉·华兹华斯有一首著名的咏水仙诗, 英国人耳熟能详, 开篇是: 独游如片云/越谷凌山岗/蓦见一簇簇/欣欣水仙黄。

Daf·fy Duck /ˌdæfɪ ˈdʌk; ˌdæfi ˈdʌk/ a black duck who is a character in CARTOON films made by Warner Bros, and who behaves in a silly way and cannot say the sound 's' properly 达菲鸭〔华纳兄弟公司制作的动画片中的黑鸭子。它举止愚蠢可笑, s音发不准〕

daft /dæft; dɑːft/ *adj BrE informal*【英, 非正式】**1** silly or not very sensible 傻的; 不明智的: *What a daft thing to say!* 真是蠢话! | **don't be daft** *spoken* (=used to tell someone not to be silly)【口】别傻了 | **as daft as a brush** (=extremely silly) 蠢透了 *Jay's a nice bloke but he's as daft as a brush.* 杰伊是个好人, 只是他太傻了。**2 be daft about** to be extremely interested in 对…着迷: *Tony's still daft about cars!* 托尼对汽车还是那么着迷! —**daftness** *n* [U]

dag /dæg; dæg/ *n* [C] *AustrE spoken* a strange or stupid person【澳口】怪人; 笨蛋

dag·ger /ˈdægə; ˈdægə/ *n* [C] **1** a short pointed knife used as a weapon 匕首, 短剑 —see picture at 参见 KNIFE[1] 图 **2 look daggers at** *BrE* to look at someone angrily【英】对〔某人〕怒目而视 —see also 另见 CLOAK-AND-DAGGER **3 be at daggers drawn** if two people are at daggers drawn, they are extremely angry with each other 拔刀相向, 势不两立, 剑拔弩张

da·go /ˈdego; ˈdeɪgəʊ/ *n* [C] an extremely offensive word for someone from Spain, Italy, Portugal etc 拉丁佬, 外国佬〔对西班牙人、意大利人、葡萄牙人等的极端冒犯用语〕

da·guer·reo·type /dəˈgɛrəˌtaɪp; dəˈgerəʊtaɪp/ *n* [C, U] an old type of photograph〔老式的〕银版照相(法)

Dag·wood /ˋdægwud; ˈdægwʊd/ a character in the US CARTOON STRIP *Blondie*. Dagwood is married to Blondie, and he is very lazy. 达格伍德〔美国连环漫画《金发女》中的人物, 十分懒惰。他与金发女是夫妻〕

Dagwood sand·wich /ˈ‥ ˌ‥/ *AmE* a very large SANDWICH with many different kinds of meat and cheese in it【美】达格伍德式三明治〔夹有多种肉类和干酪的一种特大三明治〕

dahl /dɑl; dɑːl/ *n* [C,U] an Indian dish with a hot taste, made with beans, PEAS, or LENTILS 一道印度菜〔味辣, 用蚕豆、豌豆或小扁豆煮成〕

Dahl, Ro·ald /ˋroəld; ˈrəʊəld/ (1916-90) a British writer of very popular children's books which are often both funny and frightening, such as *Charlie and the Chocolate Factory* and *James and the Giant Peach* 达尔〔(1916-1990), 英国作家。他创作的滑稽而恐怖的儿童读物十分受欢迎, 如《查理和巧克力工厂》、《詹姆斯和大桃子》〕

dah·li·a /ˋdæljə; ˈdeɪliə/ *n* [C] a large garden flower with a bright colour 大丽花, 天竺牡丹

D

Dail, the /dɔɪl; dɔɪl/ also 又作 **Dail Éi·reann** /dɔɪl ˋerən; ˌdɔɪl ˈeərən/ *formal* the lower house in the Republic of Ireland. The upper house is called the Senate, or the Seanad Éireann.【正式】爱尔兰众议院〔其参议院称 the Senate 或 the Seanad Éireann〕

S3 W2 **dai·ly¹** /ˋdelɪ; ˈdeɪli/ *adj* [only before noun 仅用于名词前] **1** happening or done every day 每日的, 每天的: *daily flights to Miami* 每天飞往迈阿密的航班 **2 daily life** the ordinary things that you usually do or experience 日常生活 **3** connected with a single day 一天的; 按天计算的: *a daily rate of pay* 日工资

daily² *adv* done or happening every day 每日, 天天: *The zoo is open daily, from 9 am to 5 pm.* 动物园每天上午9点到下午5点开放。

daily³ *n* **1** [C usually plural 一般用复数] a DAILY PAPER 日报 **2** [C] *BrE old-fashioned* a DAILY HELP【英, 过时】日工 **3 dailies** [plural] *AmE* the first prints of a film before it has been edited (EDIT (1))【美】〔未经剪辑的〕电影毛片; rushes (RUSH² (7)) *BrE*【英】

Daily Ex·press, The /ˌ‥ ˈ‥/ the former name of *The Express*《每日快报》〔《快报》旧称〕

daily help /ˌ‥ ˈ/ *n* [C] *BrE old-fashioned* someone, especially a woman, who is employed to clean someone's house【英, 过时】日工, 女佣

Daily Mail, The /ˌ‥ ˈ/ also 又作 **The Mail** a British daily TABLOID newspaper which usually supports the ideas of the Conservative Party《每日邮报》〔英国的一家小报, 通常支持保守党观点〕

Daily Mir·ror, The /ˌ‥ ˈ‥/ the former name of *The Mirror*《每日镜报》〔《镜报》的旧称〕

daily pa·per /ˌ‥ ˈ‥/ *n* [C] a newspaper that is printed and sold every day except Sunday〔除星期日外每天都发行的〕日报

Daily Plan·et, The /ˌ‥ ˈ‥/ the imaginary newspaper that Clark Kent and Lois Lane work for in the Superman stories《每日星球报》〔超人系列故事中的一家报纸, 克拉克·肯特和露易斯·莱恩在此工作〕

Daily Tel·e·graph, The /ˌ‥ ˈ‥‥/ also 又作 **The Telegraph** a serious British daily newspaper which usually supports the ideas of the Conservative Party《每日电讯报》〔英国一家通常支持保守党观点的严肃类日报〕

dain·ty¹ /ˋdentɪ; ˈdeɪnti/ *adj* **daintier, daintiest 1** small, pretty, and delicate 小巧的, 精致的: *a dainty white handkerchief* 一条精致的白手帕 **2** dainty movements are small and careful〔举止〕轻巧而优雅的 —**daintily** *adv* —**daintiness** *n* [U]

dainty² *n* [C] something small that is good to eat such as a sweet cake 精美可口的小点心〈如甜蛋糕〉

dai·qui·ri /ˋdaɪkərɪ; ˈdaɪkɪ̆ri/ *n* [C, U] a sweet alcoholic drink made with RUM¹ and fruit juice 代基里酒〔一种由朗姆酒与果汁制成的甜味酒类饮品〕

dai·ry /ˋdɛrɪ; ˈdeəri/ *n* [C] **1** a place on a farm where milk is kept and butter and cheese are made 乳品场; 牛奶场; 制酪场 **2** a company which sells milk and makes other dairy products 牛奶公司; 乳品公司

dairy cat·tle /ˈ‥ ˌ‥/ *n* [plural] cattle that are kept to produce milk rather than for their meat 奶牛, 乳牛

dairy farm /ˈ‥ ˌ/ *n* [C] a farm that has cows and produces milk 牛奶场

dai·ry·maid /ˋdɛrɪˌmed; ˈdeərimeɪd/ *n* [C] a woman who worked in a dairy in the past 牛奶场女工

dai·ry·man /ˋdɛrɪmən; ˈdeərimən/ *n* [C] a man who works in a dairy 牛奶场男工

Dairy Queen /ˈ‥ ˌ/ *trademark* also 又作 **DQ** a type of US FAST FOOD restaurant which sells ICE CREAM and other foods, and is popular with young people【商标】乳品女王〔美国一家出售冰激凌等食品的快餐店, 深受年轻人喜爱〕

da·is /ˋdeɪs; ˈdeɪɪ̆s/ *n* [singular] a low stage that you stand on when you are making a speech or performing, so that people can see and hear you 讲台

dai·sy /ˋdezɪ; ˈdeɪzi/ *n* [C] **1** a white flower with a yellow centre 雏菊(花) **2 pushing up the daisies** *humorous* someone who is pushing up the daisies is dead【幽默】死 —see also 另见 **fresh as a daisy** (FRESH (12))

daisy chain /ˈ‥ ˌ/ *n* [C] daisies tied together into a string to wear around your neck or wrist 雏菊花环

dai·sy·wheel print·er /ˋdezɪhwil ˌprɪntə; ˈdeɪziwiːl ˌprɪntə/ *n* [C] a type of PRINTER (1) that produces good quality writing〔打印效果很好的〕菊花形字盘打印机

Dak·ar /dəˋkɑr; ˈdækɑː/ the capital of Senegal, a seaport, and one of the largest industrial centres in West Africa 达喀尔〔塞内加尔首都、港口, 西非最大的工业中心之一〕

Da·ko·tas, the /dəˋkotəz; dəˈkəʊtəz/ the US states of North Dakota and South Dakota〔美国的〕南、北达科他州

Dal·ai La·ma, the /ˌdɑlaɪ ˋlɑmə; ˌdælaɪ ˈlɑːmə/ *n* [C] the leader of the Tibetan Buddhist religion 达赖喇嘛〔藏传佛教领袖〕

dale /del; deɪl/ *n* [C] a word meaning valley, used in former times or in the names of places, especially in the North of England 山谷〔过去或在地名中使用, 尤指英格兰北部的山谷〕

Dales /delz; deɪlz/ also 又作 **the Yorkshire Dales, the Dales** an area of broad, open valleys and hills in northern England. Many tourists visit the Dales. 约克谷地〔英格兰北部开阔的山谷和丘陵地区, 是许多游人观光的地方〕

Da·li, Sal·va·dor /ˋsælvədɔr; ˈsælvədɔː/ (1904-89) a Spanish painter whose work is typical of the style of SURREALISM 达利〔(1904-1989), 西班牙超现实主义画家〕

Dal·las /ˋdæləs; ˈdæləs/ a city in Texas in the US. It is a centre for business and industry and is especially famous for its rich oil businesses. It is also remembered as the place where John F. Kennedy was shot in 1963. 达拉斯〔美国得克萨斯州一城市。该市是工商业中心之一, 因拥有实力雄厚的石油公司而闻名。在人们印象中, 这里还是肯尼迪总统1963年遇刺身亡的地方〕

Dallas Cow·boys, The /ˌ‥ ˈ‥/ the main football team in Dallas, Texas 达拉斯牛仔队〔得克萨斯州达拉斯市的一支主要橄榄球队〕

dal·li·ance /ˋdælɪəns; ˈdæliəns/ *n* [U] *old-fashioned* the behaviour of two people who are dallying with each other【过时】调戏; 调情

dal·ly /ˋdælɪ; ˈdæli/ *v* [I] *old-fashioned* to waste time, or do something very slowly【过时】浪费时间, 慢吞吞做事: *Don't dally along the way!* 别在路上磨磨蹭蹭的!

dally with sb/sth *phr v* [T] **1** to think about something but not in a very serious way〔不十分认真地〕考虑〔某事〕: *They'd dallied with the idea of going on a world tour many times.* 他们多次想着要周游世界。**2** *old-fashioned* to start a romantic relationship with someone but not in a serious way【过时】〔与某人〕调情, 玩弄〔某人的〕感情

Dal·ma·tia /dælˋmeʃə; dælˈmeɪʃə/ an area of Croatia on the east coast of the Adriatic Sea 达尔马提亚〔亚得里亚海东岸克罗地亚一地区〕

dal·ma·tian /dælˋmeʃən; dælˈmeɪʃən/ *n* [C] a large dog with short white hair and black or brown spots 大麦町犬, 达尔马提亚犬, 斑点狗〔一种白毛大狗, 毛短, 带有黑色或棕色斑点〕—see picture at 参见 DOG¹ 图

dam 堤坝

dam¹ /dæm; dæm/ *n* [C] **1** a special wall built across a river, stream etc to stop the water from flowing, especially to make a lake or produce electricity 水坝, 水堤, 堤坝: *the Aswan dam in*

Egypt 埃及的阿斯旺大坝 **2** *technical* the mother of a four-legged animal, especially a horse【术语】母兽〔尤指母马〕—compare 比较 SIRE[1] (2)

dam[2] *v* **dammed, damming** [T] to stop the water in a river, stream etc from flowing by building a special wall across it 筑坝拦〔水〕, 在…中筑堤

dam sth ↔ **up** *phr v* [T] to dam a river, stream etc 建水坝于〔江、河等〕: *The stream had been dammed up.* 这条河上已筑坝拦水。

dam·age[1] /ˈdæmɪdʒ; ˈdæmɪdʒ/ *n* [U]

1 ▶PHYSICAL HARM 对物体或身体的损害◀ physical harm caused to something or someone〔对某物、某人造成的〕损害: [+to] *damage to property* 对财产造成的破坏 | **serious/severe/extensive damage** (=very bad damage) 严重损害 *The earthquake caused extensive structural damage.* 地震造成大面积的建筑物毁坏。| **minor/superficial damage** (=damage that is not very serious) 轻微损害 | **do/cause damage** *Don't you realize the damage these chemicals are doing to our environment?* 你难道没意识到这些化学物质正在破坏我们的环境吗? | **brain/liver/lung etc damage** (=damage caused to someone's brain etc) 脑/肝/肺等的损伤 *permanent brain damage from the accident* 事故造成的永久性脑损伤 | **irreparable/irreversible damage** (=damage that cannot be repaired) 无法修复的/无法挽回的损害 | **water/storm/flood etc damage** (=damage caused by water, a storm etc) 水/暴风雨/洪水等造成的损害

2 ▶EMOTIONAL HARM 情感上受到的伤害◀ harm caused to someone's emotions or mind〔对一个人感情或心理造成的〕伤害: *Such a traumatic childhood experience can cause terrible emotional damage.* 这样痛苦的童年经历容易造成极大的感情创伤。

3 ▶BAD EFFECT 不好的影响◀ a bad effect on something 坏影响: [+to] *The damage to his reputation was considerable.* 对他名誉造成的损害是巨大的。

4 ▶MONEY 钱◀ **damages** [plural] *law* money that a court orders someone to pay to someone else for harming them or their property【法律】损害赔偿金: *The court awarded him £15,000 in damages.* 法院裁定给他 15,000 英镑损害赔偿金。

5 the damage is done used to say that something bad has happened which makes it impossible to go back to the way things were before it happened 已造成的伤害无法挽回: *She immediately regretted her outburst, but the damage was done.* 她发作之后立刻就后悔了, 但是伤害已造成, 无法挽回。

6 what's the damage? *spoken* used humorously to ask how much you have to pay【口】要花多少钱?〔幽默问法〕

7 damage limitation an attempt to limit the damage to something 损失控制, 降低损失: *a damage limitation exercise to save the Prime Minister* 一项为挽救首相而采取的损失控制举措

This graph shows some of the words most commonly used with the noun **damage**. 本图表所示为含有名词 damage 的一些最常用词组。

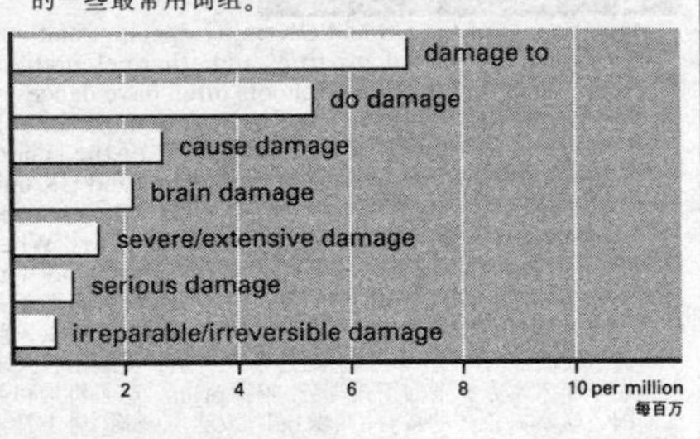

Based on the British National Corpus and the Longman Lancaster Corpus 据英国国家语料库和朗文兰开斯特语料库

damage[2] *v* [T] **1** to cause physical harm to something or to part of someone's body 损害, 损坏, 损伤〔某物或某人的身体部位〕: *Take care not to damage the timer mechanism.* 当心别弄坏计时器的机械装置。| *I've damaged a knee ligament.* 我拉伤了膝盖的韧带。**2** to have a bad effect on something or someone in a way that makes them weaker or less successful 对〔某物或某人〕有不好的影响: *Taylor felt her reputation had been damaged by the newspaper article.* 泰勒觉得她的名誉已经因为报纸上的这篇报道而受到损害。—**damaging** *adj*: *Unemployment has had a damaging effect on morale.* 失业损害了士气。

Da·mas·cus /dəˈmæskəs; dəˈmæskəs/ **1** the capital of Syria. It is one of the most ancient cities in the world and is famous for its Great Mosque. 大马士革〔叙利亚首都, 世界最古老的城市之一, 尤以大清真寺闻名〕**2 road to Damascus** a situation in which someone experiences a sudden and complete change in their opinions or beliefs. The phrase is based on the story in the New Testament of the Bible, in which St Paul, who was a soldier trying to prevent Christianity from spreading, saw a blinding light and heard God's voice while he was travelling on the road to Damascus. He immediately became a Christian. 大马士革之路〔指某人突然、彻底改变个人观点或信仰的一种情形。此短语出自《圣经·新约》的一则故事。故事中的圣保罗原是一名士兵, 力图阻碍基督教传播。然而, 在前往大马士革的途中, 他看见一道炫目的闪光, 并且听到了上帝的声音, 随即他成了一名基督教徒〕

dam·ask[1] /ˈdæməsk; ˈdæməsk/ *n* [U] a type of cloth with a pattern in it, often used to cover furniture〔经常用来铺在家具上的〕缎子, 锦缎

damask[2] *adj* **1** made of damask 缎子的, 锦缎的: *a damask tablecloth* 一块织花桌布 **2** *literary* pink【文】粉红色的: *her damask cheek* 她粉红色的面颊

damask rose /ˈ‥ ,·/ *n* [C] a pink rose with a beautiful smell 突厥蔷薇, 大马士革蔷薇〔一种粉红色、有香味的玫瑰〕

Dame /dem; deɪm/ *n* a British title of honour given to a woman as a reward for the good things she has done 女爵士, 贵夫人〔英国的荣誉头衔〕

dame *n* [C] **1** *AmE old-fashioned* a woman【美, 过时】女人 **2** a character in a PANTOMIME (=a special play at Christmas) dressed as an ugly old woman but acted by a man〔圣诞节期间演出的童话剧中常由男性扮演的〕丑老太婆 **3** a woman who has been given the British title Dame〔被授予英国女爵士头衔的〕贵夫人: *Dame Edith Evans* 伊迪丝·埃文斯(女)爵士

Dame Ed·na /ˌdem ˋɛdnə; ˌdeɪm ˈednə/ a humorous MIDDLE-AGED female character invented and performed by the male Australian COMEDIAN Barry Humphries. Her full name is 'Dame Edna Everage', and she wears unusual, brightly decorated clothes and GLASSES, and thinks that she is very attractive, amusing, and intelligent. 埃德娜夫人〔澳大利亚男喜剧演员巴里·汉弗莱塑造和扮演的一个滑稽的中年女性角色, 全名是埃德娜·埃弗里奇夫人。她穿着奇异, 装缀亮丽, 戴一副眼镜, 自以为美丽迷人、风趣聪颖〕

dam·mit /ˈdæmɪt; ˈdæmɪt/ *interjection* used to show that you are annoyed 该死, 他妈的〔表示生气〕: *Hurry up, dammit!* 快点, 该死!

damn[1] /dæm; dæm/ *adj* [only before noun 仅用于名词前] *spoken* used to show that you are angry or annoyed with someone or something【口】该死的〔表示由于某人或某事很生气〕: *I can't get this damn button undone!* 我解不开这该死的纽扣!

damn[2] *adv* [+adj/adv] *spoken*【口】**1** used to emphasize how good something is, how bad something is etc; very 非常, 很: *We've been so damn busy all day, I'm shattered!* 我们一整天忙透了, 我要累散架了! | *It's damn cold in here.* 这儿真冷。| **damn good/fine etc** *He was damn lucky he didn't have an accident.* 他还真幸运, 没出事。**2 damn well** used to emphasize how determined or sure you are about something 肯定地, 无疑地: *I damn well will go, and I'd like to see anyone try and stop me!* 我去定了, 看谁敢拦我! **3 know damn well** used to say that someone definitely knows something, especially when you are angry 清清楚楚地知道〔表示某人肯定知道某事, 尤用在说话人发火的时候〕: *Chris knew damn well we wanted to leave at 8. Where the hell is he?* 克里斯明明知道我们要在 8 点出发, 他死到哪里去了? **4 damn all** *especially BrE* nothing at all【尤英】完全没有: *Make him wash the dishes, there's damn all else he's good for.* 让他洗盘子, 别的他根本做不来。

damn[3] *interjection* used to show that you are very annoyed or disappointed 该死, 倒霉〔表示烦恼或失望〕: *Damn! I've forgotten the keys.* 该死! 我忘记带钥匙了。

damn[4] *n spoken*【口】**1 not give a damn** used to show that you do not care about something 毫不在乎: *I don't give a damn about her.* 我一点也不在乎她。**2 not worth a damn** used to say that you think something has no value at all 毫无价值: *Her promise isn't worth a damn.* 她的承诺分文不值。

damn[5] *v* [T] **1 damn you/them/it etc** *spoken* used to show that you are extremely angry with someone or something【口】该死的, 见鬼的, 他妈的〔表示极度气愤〕: *Damn you! If you think you can do this to me, you're wrong!* 该死的! 你如果以为可以这么对待我, 你就错了! **2** to state that something is very bad 贬斥; 把…说得很糟糕: *The critics damned the play on the first night.* 这出戏在首演之夜就被评论家批评得一无是处。| **damn with faint praise** (=show that you think someone or something is very bad by only praising them a little) 名褒实贬 —see also 另见 **(as) near as damn it** (NEAR[1] (5))

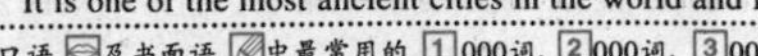

dam·na·ble /ˈdæmnəbl̩; ˈdæmnəbəl/ *adj old-fashioned* very bad or annoying【过时】极坏的；讨厌的：*This damnable heat!* 这该死的高温！—**damnably** *adv*

dam·na·tion¹ /dæmˋneʃən; dæmˈneɪʃən/ *n* [U] the act of deciding to punish someone by sending them to HELL¹ (3) for ever, or the state of being in hell for ever 遭天罚；下地狱

damnation² *interjection old-fashioned* used to show that you are very angry or annoyed【过时】该死〔表示愤怒或厌烦〕

damned¹ /dæmd; dæmd/ *adj* **1** [only before noun 仅用于名词前] *spoken* used to show that you are angry or annoyed with something【口】该死的，讨厌的〔表示某物惹人生气或厌烦〕：*a damned nuisance* 讨厌的东西 **2 be damned** be sent by God to punishment without end after death 下地狱 **3 I'll be damned** *spoken* used as a strong expression of surprise【口】真没想到〔表示极度惊奇〕 **4 I'm damned if/I'll be damned if** *spoken* used to emphasize that you do not want something to happen, or that you do not know something【口】〔强调某人决不会让某事发生或某人根本不知道某事〕：*I'll be damned if I let her come into my house.* 我决不让她进我家。| *I'm damned if I know.* 我根本就不知道。**5 damned if you do, damned if you don't** used to mean that whatever you say or do will be considered to be wrong 做也不对，不做也不对；左右都不是〔无论某人说什么或做什么都会被认为是错的〕

damned² *adv* [+adj/adv] *spoken* used to say how good something is, how bad something is etc【口】极，非常：*War is a damned expensive business.* 战争是极其耗费钱财的事情。—see also 另见 DAMN² (1)

damned³ *n* **the damned** the people who God will send to HELL¹ (3) when they die because they have been so bad〔由于做坏事而〕该下地狱的人

damned·est /ˈdæmdɪst; ˈdæmdɪ̣st/ *adj informal especially AmE*【非正式，尤美】**1 the damnedest thing/luck etc** the most unusual or surprising thing etc 最非凡[惊人]的东西/运气等：*That machine was the damnedest thing you ever saw!* 那台机器是你见过的最奇妙的玩意儿！**2 do your damnedest** to try very hard to make something work or succeed 尽最大努力：*I'll do my damnedest to fix it, but I can't promise anything.* 我会尽全力，但是我不能保证修好它。

damn-fool /ˈ· ·/ *adj* [only before noun 仅用于名词前] *spoken* very stupid【口】非常愚蠢的：*That was the biggest damn-fool mistake I ever made.* 那是我犯过的最最愚蠢的错误。

damn·ing /ˈdæmɪŋ; ˈdæmɪŋ/ *adj* **damning indictment/comment/account** something that shows someone or something is very bad 极为不利的控告/评论/叙述：*a damning indictment of the government's economic record* 对政府经济记录的强烈指责

Dam·o·cles /ˈdæmə͵kliz; ˈdæməkliːz/ —see 见 **sword of Damocles** (SWORD (3))

damp¹ /dæmp; dæmp/ *adj* **1** slightly wet, often in an unpleasant way 潮湿的：*Wipe the leather with a damp cloth.* 用块湿布把皮革擦一擦。**2 damp squib** *BrE informal* something that is intended to be exciting, effective etc, but which is disappointing【英，非正式】未达到预期效果而使人失望的事；湿水爆竹—**damply** *adv*

> **USAGE NOTE 用法说明：DAMP**
>
> WORD CHOICE 词语辨析：**damp, moist, humid**
>
> **Damp** is often used about something you would prefer to be dry. damp 通常用于最好是干爽的东西：*damp clothes/weather* 潮湿的衣服/天气 | *a damp bed/wall/room* 潮湿的床铺/墙壁/房间 | *In the rainy season everything gets damp I'm afraid.* 雨季的时候恐怕什么东西都会变潮湿的。
>
> **Moist** is used especially when something is not too wet and not too dry. moist 尤其用于说明某物不太湿也不太干：*a moist ginger cake* 一块松软的姜汁蛋糕 | *Keep houseplant soil moist – don't let it dry out.* 保持室内盆栽植物的土壤湿润，别让土干透了。
>
> **Humid** is a more technical word used mainly to describe the climate or weather, or air that feels wet. humid 较术语化一些，主要指气候、天气或空气的湿润：*It gets very humid here in the summer* (=the air is hot and damp). 这个地方的夏天非常湿热。
>
> You do not usually use these words to talk about people who get wet. 这三个词通常不用来表示人被弄湿。

damp² *n* [U] *BrE* a part or area that is slightly wet【英】潮湿的部分[地方]：*There's a patch of damp on my bedroom wall.* 我卧室的墙上有一块潮湿的地方。

damp³ *v* [T] to make a sound less loud 减低〔声响〕：*Damp the sound with the pedal after each beat.* 每拍之后用踏板来减弱音量。

damp sth ↔ **down** *phr v* [T] **1** to make a fire burn more slowly, often by covering it with ash〔常指用盖灰的方法〕封〔火〕，减弱〔火势〕**2** to control, reduce or limit something, especially a feeling 抑制〔感情〕：*damping down a child's high spirits* 打击孩子高涨的热情

damp course /ˈ· ·/ *n* [C] *BrE* a layer of material which is put into the bottom of a wall to prevent water rising through it【英】防潮层

damp·en /ˈdæmpən; ˈdæmpən/ *v* [T] **1** to make something slightly wet 使…潮湿 **2 dampen sb's enthusiasm/spirits** to make people feel less confident, happy, or ENTHUSIASTIC 打击某人的热情/情绪：*The accident had done nothing to dampen his competitive spirit.* 这次事故丝毫没有挫伤他的竞争热情。

dampen sth ↔ **down** *phr v* [T] to damp something down 减弱；控制

damp·er /ˈdæmpɚ; ˈdæmpə/ *n* [C] **1** a piece of equipment that stops a piano string from making a sound〔终止钢琴弦发出声音的〕制音器 **2** a piece of metal that is opened or closed to control how strongly a fire burns〔控制火势的〕挡板，气门，气闸 **3 put a damper on** to affect something in a way that makes people sad, disappointed, or less hopeful 使扫兴：*This unwelcome news put a damper on the celebrations.* 这个不受欢迎的消息使庆祝会颇为扫兴。

damp·ness /ˈdæmpnɪs; ˈdæmpnɪ̣s/ *n* [U] the state or condition of being slightly wet 微湿，潮湿

dam·sel /ˈdæmzl̩; ˈdæmzəl/ *n* [C] **1** *old use* a young woman who is not married【旧】未婚的少女 **2 damsel in distress** *humorous* a young woman who needs help or protection【幽默】需要帮助[保护]的年轻女子

dam·son /ˈdæmzn̩; ˈdæmzən/ *n* [C] a small bitter dark purple PLUM¹ (1) 西洋李子

dan /dæn; dæn/ *n* [C, singular] a level of skill in a fighting sport such as JUDO, including a BLACK BELT 段〔柔道等竞技运动的技艺等级〕

dance¹ /dæns; dɑːns/ *n* **1** [C] an act of dancing 舞蹈，舞：**have a dance** *Let's have one more dance before we go home.* 让我们回家之前再跳支舞吧。| **do a dance** (=move as if you are dancing) 跳跃，雀跃 *When Claire heard the news she did a little dance of excitement.* 克莱尔听到这个消息时，激动得跳了起来。**2** [C] a particular set of movements performed to music 舞蹈，舞步：*The waltz is an easy dance to learn.* 华尔兹这种舞很容易学。**3** [C] a social meeting or party for dancing 舞会：*Are you going to the dance this weekend?* 这个周末你去参加舞会吗？**4** [C] a piece of music which you can dance to 舞曲：*The band was playing a slow dance.* 乐队正在演奏一支慢舞曲。**5** [U] the activity or art of dancing 舞蹈活动；舞蹈艺术：*a course in dance and movement* 舞蹈与形体课 —see also 另见 **song and dance about** (SONG (4)), **lead sb a dance** (LEAD¹ (17))

> **CULTURAL NOTE 文化注释**
>
> Many people in the US and UK enjoy dancing, and music is usually played at parties and other celebrations so that people can dance. Schools often have dances or DISCOs for their students, and in the US most schools have a special formal dance at the end of the school year, called a PROM. CHARITY organizations and UK universities have formal dances called BALLs where women wear long dresses and men wear DINNER JACKETs. When young people want to dance, they go to NIGHTCLUBs with their friends, an activity known as CLUBBING. 很多英美人喜欢跳舞，在聚会或其他庆祝活动上常播放音乐供人跳舞。学校常为学生举办舞会或迪斯科舞会。美国学校大多在学年末举办特别的正式舞会，叫做prom。慈善机构和英国大学举办正式的舞会，叫做ball，女士穿长裙，男士着无尾晚礼服。年轻人想跳舞则和朋友去夜总会，叫做“光顾夜总会”。

dance² *v* **1** [I] to move your feet and body in a way that matches the style and speed of music 跳舞：*She danced with me until 3 am at a bar downtown.* 她和我在市中心的一个酒吧里跳舞一直跳到凌晨3点。**2 dance a waltz/rumba/tango etc** to do a particular type of dance 跳华尔兹/伦巴/探戈等 **3** [I] to move up, down, and around quickly in a way that looks like dancing 跳跃，雀跃：*Moths danced around the porch light.* 蛾子绕着门廊的灯乱舞。**4** [T always+adv/prep] to make someone or something move as if they were dancing 使…上下摆动，使…轻快移动：*She danced the baby up and down on her knee.* 她把婴儿放在膝上颠着。**5 dance attendance on** to do everything possible in order to please someone 奉承〔某人〕，讨〔某人〕欢心：*a*

movie star with several young men dancing attendance on her 被好几个年轻男子前呼后拥献殷勤的女电影明星 **6 dance to sb's tune** to do what someone wants you to do in a way that shows complete obedience〔完全〕听从某人指挥, 服从某人差遣: *They control all the funding so we have to dance to their tune.* 他们控制着所有的资金, 所以我们得听从他们指挥。—**dancing** *n* [U]: *her love of dancing* 她对舞蹈的热爱

dance-band /ˈ· ·/ *n* [C] a group of musicians who play music that you dance to 伴舞乐队

dance floor /ˈ· ·/ *n* [C] a special floor in a restaurant, hotel etc for people to dance on 舞池

dance hall /ˈ· ·/ *n* [C] a large public room where people used to pay to go and dance 舞厅

Dance of Death /ˌ· · ˈ·/ also 又作 **danse macabre** an imaginary dance which people are supposed to perform as they are being led to their death by a SKELETON (=a body consisting only of bones) representing death. It was very common in pictures and drawings in the Middle Ages, but there are also descriptions of it in music and literature. 死亡舞蹈, 骷髅舞〔一种想象中的舞蹈。据说, 人们在一具骷髅(代表死亡)的引领下走向死亡时跳这种舞。多见于中世纪的图片和绘画之中, 音乐和文学作品中也有描述〕

danc·er /ˈdænsə; ˈdɑːnsə/ *n* [C] **1** someone who dances as a profession 舞蹈演员, 舞蹈家: **ballet/ballroom etc dancer** *I want to be a ballet dancer when I grow up.* 我长大后想当一名芭蕾舞演员。**2 good/bad etc dancer** someone who dances well, badly etc 舞跳得好/差的人

Dan Dare /ˌ· ˈ·/ the main character in one of the stories in the British COMIC for boys called *The Eagle*, popular especially in the 1950s and 1960s. He is the brave captain of a spacecraft and has many exciting adventures, and his main enemy is the Mekon. 丹·戴尔, 大胆阿丹〔英国男孩子的连环漫画《鹰》杂志系列故事中的主人公。这些漫画书在20世纪50、60年代尤为畅销。阿丹是一艘太空船的船长, 勇敢无畏, 有着很多刺激的冒险经历。他的主要敌人是梅肯〕

D and C /ˌdi ənd ˈsi; ˌdiː ənd ˈsiː/ *n* [C] a medical operation to clean out the inside of a woman's WOMB 刮宫术

dan·de·li·on /ˈdændɪˌlaɪən; ˈdændḷlaɪən/ *n* [C] a wild plant with yellow flowers, and white balls of seeds that travel a long way in the air 蒲公英

dandelion clock /ˈ· · · ·, ˌ ·/ *n* [C] the soft ball of white seeds that grows on the dandelion plant 蒲公英上的白色绒球

CULTURAL NOTE 文化注释

Children in Britain often blow dandelion seeds into the air and pretend that they can tell what time it is by the number of times they need to blow to remove them all. 英国儿童经常把蒲公英种子吹向空中, 并假装能从吹掉所有种子需要的次数中说出当时是几点钟。

dan·der /ˈdændə; ˈdændə/ *n* **get sb's dander up** *old-fashioned* to make someone angry【过时】惹某人生气, 使某人发火

dan·di·fied /ˈdændɪˌfaɪd; ˈdændɪfaɪd/ *adj old-fashioned* a man who is dandified wears very fashionable clothes in a way that shows he cares too much about his appearance【过时】〔男子〕穿着非常时髦的, 过分注重外表的

dan·dle /ˈdændḷ; ˈdændl/ *v* [T] *old-fashioned* to play with a baby or small child by moving them up and down in your arms or on your knee【过时】〔在怀中或在膝上颠着〕逗〔孩子〕玩

dan·druff /ˈdændrəf; ˈdændrəf/ *n* [U] pieces of dead skin from your head that can be seen as a white dust in your hair and on your shoulders 头皮屑

dan·dy[1] /ˈdændɪ; ˈdændi/ *n* [C] *old-fashioned* a man who spends a lot of time and money on his clothes and appearance【过时】过分注重穿着打扮的男子, 花花公子

dandy[2] *adj old-fashioned especially AmE* very good【过时, 尤美】很好的: *"Let's go to the movies." "That'll be dandy."* "我们去看电影吧。""那太好了。"

Dandy, The a British COMIC (=a magazine for children that tells stories using sets of drawings), whose most famous character is Desperate Dan《英俊少年》〔英国一连环画杂志, 其最著名的人物形象是"拼命阿丹"〕

Dane /den; deɪn/ *n* [C] someone from Denmark 丹麦人

dang /dæŋ; dæŋ/ *interjection AmE spoken* a less offensive word for DAMN【美口】该死的〔damn的委婉词〕

S2 W2 **dan·ger** /ˈdendʒə; ˈdeɪndʒə/ *n* **1** [U] the possibility that someone or something will be harmed or killed 危险: *Danger! High Voltage.* 高压! 危险! | **[+of]** *Is there any danger of infection, doctor?* 医生, 有感染的危险吗? | **[+from]** *danger from radioactive sources* 来自放射源的危险 | **in danger** (=in a situation in which you may be harmed or killed) 处在危险中 *I had a sudden feeling that Petra was in danger.* 我忽然预感到彼得拉有危险。| **out of danger** (=not in danger any more) 脱离危险 *The patient is now out of danger.* 病人现在已经脱离危险。**2** [C often plural 常用复数] something or someone that may harm or kill you 威胁, 危害: *I think he enjoys the dangers of rock climbing.* 我想他喜欢攀岩过程中的种种危险。| **face dangers** (=do something that involves dangers) 面对[应付]危险的事物 *All boxers are well aware of the dangers they face in the ring.* 所有的拳击手都十分清楚, 他们在拳击场中会遇到种种危险。| **be a danger to** *The wreck is a danger to other ships.* 沉船对其他船只构成威胁。**3** [C,U] the possibility that something unpleasant will happen〔不愉快事情可能发生的〕危险: **danger that** *There is always the danger that Elizabeth will go back on her promise.* 伊丽莎白违背诺言的危险总是存在的。| **[+of]** *Is there much danger of losing money?* 赔钱的危险是不是很大? | **be in danger of** (=be in a situation in which something unpleasant may happen) 有〔不好事情发生的〕危险 *Carlos is in danger of losing his job.* 卡洛斯有丢掉工作的危险。**4 be on the danger list** to be so ill that you may die 病危 **5 there's no danger of that** used to mean that something bad will not happen 没有发生坏事的危险

danger mon·ey /ˈ· ·, ˌ· ˈ·/ *n* [U] *especially BrE* additional money that you are paid for doing dangerous work【尤英】危险工作津贴; DANGER PAY *AmE*【美】

dan·ger·ous /ˈdendʒərəs; ˈdeɪndʒərəs/ *adj* **1** able or likely to harm or kill you 危险的, 有危害的: *dangerous animals* 危险动物 | *Neil thought the man looked dangerous.* 尼尔认为那个男子看起来很危险。| **it is dangerous (for sb) to do sth** *It's dangerous for women to walk alone at night.* 女子晚上一个人走路有危险。| **highly/very dangerous** *It would be highly dangerous to attempt to cross the river just here.* 想从这儿过河会非常危险。**2** a belief, situation, or action that is dangerous involves a lot of risk, or is likely to cause problems〔信念、形势或行动〕充满风险的, 有危险的: *The business is in a dangerous financial position.* 公司的财政状况非常危急。**3 dangerous ground/territory** a situation or subject that could make someone very angry or upset 危险地带〔指能惹某人生气或不安的情形或话题〕: *You're on dangerous ground when you talk politics with Ed.* 你一和埃德谈政治, 就步入了危险境地。—**dangerously** *adv*: *driving dangerously* 危险驾驶 | *dangerously high temperatures* 危险的高温

danger pay /ˈ· ·, ˌ ·/ *n* [U] *AmE*【美】= DANGER MONEY *BrE*【英】

dan·gle /ˈdæŋgḷ; ˈdæŋgəl/ *v* **1** [I,T] to hang or swing loosely, or make something do this 悬吊, 晃动不定; 使…悬吊[晃动]: *a leather purse dangled from his belt* 他皮带上悬吊着的一个皮包 | **dangle sth** *I dangled my feet in the clear blue water.* 我把脚放到清澈碧蓝的水中摇晃着。**2 dangle sth in front of sb** to offer something good to someone in order to persuade them to do something〔为让某人做某事〕用某物诱惑某人, 用某物引诱某人: *The promise of an ice-cream cone was dangled in front of us, as a reward for washing the car.* 用吃甜筒冰激凌的许诺来诱惑我们洗车。

Dan·iel /ˈdænjəl; ˈdænjəl/ in the Old Testament of the Bible, a Jewish man who was made a prisoner by King Nebuchadnezzar of Babylon, and was put into a lions' DEN as a punishment for not changing his beliefs. The lions did not kill him, however, because God protected him. The phrase **in the lion's den** comes from this story, and is used to describe a difficult situation in which you are surrounded by people who are your enemies. 但以理〔《圣经·旧约》中的一位犹太人。他不愿改变自己的信仰, 被巴比伦的尼布甲尼撒二世关进狮子坑中。然而, 由于神佑, 狮子并没有伤害他。in the lion's den 这一短语源自该故事, 用来形容四面楚歌的险境〕

Da·nish[1] /ˈdenɪʃ; ˈdeɪnɪʃ/ *n* [U] **1** the language of Denmark 丹麦语 **2** [C] *AmE* a Danish pastry【美】丹麦甜酥皮糕饼

Danish[2] *adj* connected with the people or language of Denmark 丹麦人的; 丹麦语的

Danish blue /ˌ· · ˈ·/ a type of cheese made especially in Denmark which has blue marks in it and has a strong taste 丹麦青纹干酪

Danish pas·try /ˌ· · ˈ· ·/ *n* [C] a very sweet cake made of light PASTRY (1) 丹麦甜酥皮糕饼

dank /dæŋk; dæŋk/ *adj* unpleasantly wet and cold 湿冷的, 阴冷的: *a dank prison cell* 阴冷的牢房 —**dankness** *n* [U]

Dan·te /ˈdɑnte; ˈdænti/ (1265-1321) Dante Alighieri, an Italian poet who wrote *La Divina Commedia* (*The Divine Comedy*),

a long poem about a journey through Hell, Purgatory, and Heaven. It is one of the most important works of European literature. 但丁〔(1265-1321),但丁·阿里盖利,意大利诗人,《神曲》的作者。《神曲》是一部描写游历地狱、炼狱和天国的长诗,是欧洲最重要的文学作品之一〕

Dante's In·fer·no /,·· '··/ the first part of Dante's poem *The Divine Comedy*, in which he is led through different parts of HELL. The phrase 'Dante's Inferno' is sometimes used to describe a place where there is a lot of fire, destruction etc. 《地狱》〔但丁《神曲》长诗的第一部。诗中的他在别人的引领下游遍地狱。此短语有时用来形容一个遭遇大火或破坏的地方〕: *When the bombing finally stopped, the city looked like Dante's Inferno.* 轰炸终于结束了,那座城市看上去就像但丁笔下的地狱一样。

Dan·ton /ˈdæntn̩; ˈdæntɒn/, **Georges Jacques** /ˈʒɔrʒ ʒæk; ˈʒɔːʒ ʒæk/ (1759-94) a French politician who became one of the leaders of the French Revolution 丹东〔(1759-1794),法国政治家,法国大革命的领导人之一〕

Dan·ube, the /ˈdænjub; ˈdænjuːb/ a long and important river in Eastern Europe. It starts in the Black Forest in Germany and goes through Austria, Hungary, and Romania into the Black Sea. 多瑙河〔东欧一条重要的长河,发源于德国的黑林山,流经奥地利、匈牙利和罗马尼亚,最后注入黑海〕

Daph·ne /ˈdæfnɪ; ˈdæfni/ in ancient Greek stories, a NYMPH whom the god Apollo fell in love with. When he tried to have sex with her, she ran away, praying to the goddess of the Earth to save her, and so she was changed into a LAUREL tree. 达佛涅〔古希腊神话中阿波罗爱恋的一位水泽仙女,为躲避阿波罗的求欢,向大地女神求助,于是就被化作一棵月桂树〕

Daph·nis and Chlo·e, Daphnis and Chloë /,dæfnɪs ənd ˈkloɪ; ,dæfnɪ̤s ənd ˈkləʊi/ **1** an ancient Greek love story about a boy and a girl who are found by SHEPHERDS. They grow up in the country, fall in love with each other, and finally get married. 达佛尼斯与克洛伊〔古希腊爱情故事。故事中的牧羊人收养了一个男童和一个女童,他们在乡村一起长大,彼此相爱,最后结为夫妻〕 **2** a piece of BALLET music based on this story by Maurice Ravel 《达佛尼斯与克洛伊》〔法国作曲家莫里斯·拉威尔根据同名故事创作的芭蕾舞乐曲〕

Da Pon·te /dæ ˈpɑnte; dæ ˈpɒnteɪ/, **Lo·ren·zo** /lɔˈrɛnzo; ləˈrenzəʊ/ (1749-1838) an Italian writer and producer of OPERAS. He wrote the words for three of Mozart's greatest operas, *The Marriage of Figaro, Don Giovanni* and *Così Fan Tutte.* 达·蓬特〔(1749-1838),意大利歌剧作家、歌剧出品人。曾为莫扎特的三部最杰出歌剧《费加罗的婚礼》、《唐·乔凡尼》和《女人心》创作歌词〕

dap·per /ˈdæpɚ; ˈdæpə/ *adj* **1** a man who is dapper is small and has a neat appearance 〔指男人〕短小精悍的: *He was small, dapper, and wore a green bow tie.* 他长得短小精悍,系着绿色的蝶形领结。**2** nicely dressed 衣冠楚楚的: *You're looking very dapper in your new suit!* 你穿着新西装真精神!

dap·ple /ˈdæpl̩; ˈdæpəl/ *v* [T] *literary* to mark something with spots of colour, light, or shade【文】使〔某物〕有斑点,使〔某物〕斑驳

dap·pled /ˈdæpl̩d; ˈdæpəld/ *adj* marked with spots of colour, light, or shade 有花斑的,有亮斑的,斑驳的: *a sky dappled with clouds* 点缀着朵朵白云的天空

dapple-grey /,·· ˈ·◂/ *n* [C] a horse that is grey with spots of darker grey 灰色带黑斑的马

DAR, the /,di e ˈar; ,diː eɪ ˈɑː/ the abbreviation of 缩写 = the DAUGHTERS OF THE AMERICAN REVOLUTION

Dar·by and Joan /ˈdɑrbɪ ən ˈdʒon; ,dɑːbi ən ˈdʒəʊn/ *n* **be like Darby and Joan** *BrE humorous* used when talking about an old husband and wife who live very happily together【英,幽默】是一对恩爱的老夫妇

Dar·cy /ˈdarsɪ; ˈdɑːsi/, **Mr** the main male character in the NOVEL *Pride and Prejudice* by Jane Austen. He is attractive, intelligent, and very rich, but he seems too proud of his wealth and his importance in society. 达西〔简·奥斯丁《傲慢与偏见》的男主人公。他英俊,聪明,富有。然而,他却仗着有钱、有社会地位而过于自负〕

Dar·da·nelles, the /,dardn̩ˈɛlz; ,dɑːdəˈnelz/ the long narrow area of sea which connects the European and Asian parts of Turkey. It was called the Hellespont in ancient times. 达达尼尔海峡〔连接土耳其欧亚两部分的狭长海域,古时称作赫勒斯滂〕

3 **dare¹** /dɛr; deə/ *v*

1 ►**DO STH DANGEROUS** 做危险的事◄ [I not in progressive 不用进行时] to be brave enough to do something dangerous or that you are afraid to do 胆敢,敢于〔做危险的或一般人害怕做的事情〕: *The others used to steal things from stores, but I would never dare.* 其他人曾经偷过商店的东西,我可从来不敢。| **dare (to) do sth** *Would you dare to do a parachute jump?* 你敢跳伞吗?

2 ►**DO STH RUDE/SHOCKING ETC** 做无礼的/令人震惊的事情等◄ [I] to be confident enough, rude enough, or dishonest enough to do something that is very rude, shocking, or wrong 胆敢,竟敢〔做特别无礼的、令人震惊的或错误的事情〕: *Tell her what I really think? I wouldn't dare!* 告诉她我的真实想法?我可不敢!

3 how dare you *spoken* used to show that you are very angry and shocked about what someone has done or said【口】你竟敢,你怎么敢〔表示对他人行为、言辞的愤怒和震惊〕: *How dare you accuse me of lying!* 你竟敢指责我撒谎!

4 don't you dare! *spoken* used to warn someone not to do something because it makes you angry【口】你敢!〔用于警告某人不要做某事以免惹你生气〕: *Don't you dare talk to me like that!* 少跟我这样讲话!

5 ►**PERSUADE SB TO DO STH** 激某人做某事◄ [T] to try to persuade someone to do something dangerous or embarrassing as a way of proving that they are brave 激将,激: **dare sb to do sth** *They dared Lenny to climb to the very top branch.* 他们挑激伦尼,看他敢不敢爬到最高的树杈上去。| **I dare you!** *spoken*【口】*Go on! Ask her for her telephone number. I dare you!* 去呀!问她要电话号码。我量你不敢!

6 dare I say/suggest *formal spoken* used when adding information that you think people may not accept or believe【正式,口】我可以说〔用于添加可能不被承认或相信的信息〕: *I found him intelligent, observant, and, dare I say it, a sparkling wit!* 我认为他这个人聪明、敏锐,或许我可以说他非常风趣!

7 I dare say *spoken especially BrE* used when saying or agreeing that something may perhaps be true【口,尤英】我相信;可能: *I dare say things will improve.* 我想事情会好起来的。

dare² *n* [C] something dangerous that you have dared someone to do 激将,挑战: *a dare to run through the field with the bull in it* 跑过公牛所在的田地的挑战 | **for a dare** (=because someone has dared you to) 因受到激将 *I only did it for a dare.* 我受到激将才这么做的。

Dare, Dan —see 见 DAN DARE

dare·dev·il /ˈdɛr,dɛvl̩; ˈdeədevəl/ *n* [C] someone who likes doing dangerous things 喜欢冒险的人: *a daredevil motorcyclist* 一个胆子很大的摩托车手 —**daredevil** *adj*

daren't /dɛrnt; deənt/ *spoken*【口】the short form of 缩略式 = 'dare not' (DARE¹ (1))

dare·say /,dɛrˈse; ,deəˈseɪ◂/ *v* **I daresay** *especially BrE* used when saying or agreeing that something may perhaps be true【尤英】我想,也许: *I daresay you're right.* 也许你是对的。

Dar-es-Sa·laam /,dar ɛs səˈlam; ,dɑːr es səˈlɑːm/ the capital of Tanzania and its main port, on the Indian Ocean. It is also the main port for Zambia. 达累斯萨拉姆〔坦桑尼亚首都及其印度洋主要港口,也是赞比亚货物集散的主要港口〕

dar·ing¹ /ˈdɛrɪŋ; ˈdeərɪŋ/ *adj* **1** willing to do something that is dangerous or that involves a lot of risk 勇敢的,英勇的: *the daring lifeboatmen* 勇敢的救生艇水手 | *a daring rescue attempt* 英勇的救援努力 **2** new or unusual in a way that is sometimes shocking 大胆的;别出心裁的: *a daring film* 一部大胆的电影 | *Sometimes her outfits were more daring than usual.* 有时候,她的衣着比平时更大胆出奇。—**daringly** *adv*: *daringly close to the edge* 离悬崖边缘非常近

daring² *n* [U] courage that makes you willing to take risks 勇气,胆量: *a plan of great daring* 大胆创新的计划

Dar·jee·ling /darˈdʒilɪŋ; dɑːˈdʒiːlɪŋ/ **1** a city in the mountains of northeast India 大吉岭〔印度东北部山区的一座城市〕 **2** a delicate tea grown on the hills around Darjeeling 大吉岭茶〔产于大吉岭附近丘陵地带的一种好茶〕

dark¹ /dark; dɑːk/ *adj* S2 W1

1 ►**PLACE** 地方◄ a dark place is one where there is little or no light〔指某个地方〕黑暗的,昏暗的,无光的: *The church was dark and quiet.* 教堂里黑黑的、静静的。| *I waited for them in a dark alley.* 我在昏暗的小巷里等他们。| **go dark** (=become dark) 变暗 *Suddenly, the room went dark and somebody screamed.* 忽然,屋里的灯灭了,有人尖叫起来。—opposite 反义词 LIGHT² (3)

2 ►**COLOUR** 颜色◄ not light or pale in colour 暗色的,深色的: **dark blue/green/pink etc** *a dark blue dress* 一件深蓝色的衣服 —opposite 反义词 LIGHT² (1)

3 it gets dark when it gets dark in the evening the light disappears and night begins 天黑了,天晚了: *Come on, let's go in, it's getting dark.* 快点,我们进去吧,天快黑了。

4 ►**HAIR/EYES** 头发/眼睛◄ someone who is dark has hair and eyes that are black or brown〔头发和眼睛〕黑色的;褐色

的: *a tall, dark man* 黑眼睛黑头发的高个子男人 —opposite 反义词 FAIR[1] (5)
5 ▶THREATENING/MYSTERIOUS ETC 阴险的/神秘的等◀ threatening, mysterious, or evil 阴险的, 神秘的, 邪恶的: *the dark forces of the night* 夜晚的神秘力量 | *There was a darker side to his character.* 他性格中有邪恶的一面。
6 ▶FEELINGS/THOUGHTS 情感/思想◀ dark thoughts are sad and show that you think something very bad may happen 忧愁的, 忧郁的: *I sat there gloomily, thinking dark thoughts.* 我忧郁地坐在那儿, 想着一些不愉快的事。
7 keep sth dark *informal* to keep something secret【非正式】对某事保密: *You're getting married! You kept that dark!* 你要结婚了! 但你却守口如瓶!
8 ▶UNHAPPY TIME 不快乐的时光◀ a dark time is unhappy or without hope 无望的, 希望渺茫的: *in the dark days of the war* 在那段暗无天日的战争时期 | *Even in the darkest moments, I still had you, my love.* 即使在最无望的日子里我还有你, 亲爱的。
9 dark horse a) someone who people do not know much about who surprises everyone by winning a competition 黑马〔竞争中出乎意料获胜的人〕 **b)** *BrE* someone who does not tell people much and who has surprising qualities or abilities【英】深藏不露的人: *She's a dark horse. I didn't know she'd written a novel.* 她深藏不露, 我不知道她写过小说。
10 darkest Africa/South America etc *old-fashioned* the parts of Africa etc about which we know very little【过时】鲜为人知的非洲/南美地区等 —see also 另见 PITCH-BLACK

dark² *n* [U] **1 the dark** a situation in which there is no light 黑暗, 无光: *Children are sometimes afraid of the dark.* 孩子们有时怕黑。| **in the dark** *Be careful if you're walking home in the dark.* 晚上走路回家时小心点。**2 after dark** at night 天黑以后: *Some of my friends won't go out after dark.* 我的一些朋友天黑以后不愿外出。**3 before dark** before the time when it gets dark at night 天黑以前: *You can go out, but make sure you come home before dark.* 你可以出去, 但是你必须天黑以前回家。**4 be in the dark** *informal* to know nothing about something important because you have not been told about it【非正式】不知, 无知: *Well, I'm afraid we're in the dark as much as you are.* 恐怕我们和你们一样都被蒙在鼓里。| **keep sb in the dark** *The public was kept in the dark about the assassination attempt.* 公众对这次暗杀行动一无所知。—see also 另见 **a shot in the dark** (SHOT[1] (13))

Dark Ag·es, the /ˈ· ˌ·/ *n* the period in European history from 476 AD to about 1000 AD 黑暗时代〔欧洲历史上从公元476年到公元1000年的一段时期〕

Dark Con·ti·nent, the /ˌ· ˈ···/ a name given to Africa by Europeans in the 19th century. The name meant that Africa was then an unknown area to Europeans, but it is now considered an offensive name. 黑色大陆〔19世纪欧洲人对非洲的指称, 意思是非洲对于欧洲人来说是一个陌生的地域。此名现在有冒犯性〕

dark·en /ˈdarkən; ˈdɑːkən/ *v* [I, T] **1** to become dark, or make something dark (使…) 变暗: *the skies darkened* 天空暗了下来 | *The sun had darkened his skin.* 太阳晒黑了他的皮肤。**2** to become less happy or positive or make someone feel this way (使) 变得不乐观; (使) 不快: *The news darkened their view of the situation.* 这个消息使他们对形势的看法悲观起来。**3 never darken my door again** *old-fashioned humorous* used to tell someone that you do not want them in your house again【过时, 幽默】别再来我家了

dark glass·es /ˌ· ˈ··/ *n* [plural] glasses with dark glass in them, that you wear to protect your eyes from the sun or to hide your eyes 墨镜, 太阳镜

dark·ie /ˈdarkɪ; ˈdɑːki/ *n* [C] *old-fashioned* an offensive word for a black person【过时】黑鬼〔对黑人的冒犯用语〕

dark·ly /ˈdarklɪ; ˈdɑːkli/ *adv* **1** in an unpleasant or threatening way 不快地, 威胁地: *'Don't you be too sure,' said Marcus darkly.* "你别那么肯定。"马库斯脸色阴沉地说。**2** with a dark colour 深色地: *Philip flushed darkly.* 菲利普脸涨得通红。

W3 **dark·ness** /ˈdarknɪs; ˈdɑːknəs/ *n* [U] **1** a place or time when there is no light 黑暗: *Beyond the glittering street was darkness.* 灯火通明的街道尽头是一片黑暗。| **total darkness** (=complete darkness) 一片漆黑 *The clouds moved across the moon, leaving us in total darkness.* 云把月亮遮住了, 我们被笼罩在黑暗之中。| **darkness falls** (=it becomes night) 天色暗下来 **2 forces/powers of darkness** evil or the devil 黑势力, 恶势力 **3** the dark quality of a colour〔一种颜色的〕深, 暗

dark·room /ˈdarkˌrum; ˈdɑːkruːm/ *n* [C] a dark room where film is taken out of a camera and made into a photograph〔冲洗胶卷的〕暗室, 暗房, 黑房

dar·ling¹ /ˈdarlɪŋ; ˈdɑːlɪŋ/ *n* [C] **1** a way of speaking to someone that you love 亲爱的, 宝贝〔称呼心爱的人〕: *Hurry up, darling.* 快点, 亲爱的。**2** someone who seems very nice, generous, friendly etc 好人, 乐于助人的人: *He's such a darling.* 他真是个好人。**3 the darling of** the most popular person in a particular group or area of activity 红人, 宠儿〔某一群体或领域中最受欢迎的人〕: *She's the darling of the fashion world.* 她是时装界的红人。 S2

darling² *adj* [only before noun 仅用于名词前] *spoken* used when you love someone or something very much, or when you think something is very attractive【口】心爱的, 惹人喜爱的: *my two darling daughters* 我的两个可爱的女儿 | *What a darling little house!* 多么讨人喜欢的小屋啊!

Darling, Grace (1815-42) a British woman whose father was in charge of a LIGHTHOUSE (=a tower with a flashing light that guides ships away from dangerous rocks), and who is famous for bravely rowing out to sea in a little boat during a storm to save nine people whose boat had sunk 达琳〔(1815-1842), 英国人, 其父是海岸灯塔的守望人。她在一次风暴中勇敢地划着小船出海, 营救起九名沉船遇难者, 并因此闻名〕

Darling Buds of May, The /ˌ· ·· ˌ· ˈ·/ one of a series of humorous NOVELS by H.E. Bates about the Larkin family, a family of farmers in southern England during the 1950s《可爱的五月蓓蕾》〔H.E.贝茨创作的系列幽默小说中的一部, 讲述了20世纪50年代英格兰南部的农户拉金一家的故事〕

darn¹ /darn; dɑːn/ *v* [T] **1** to repair a hole in a piece of clothing by stitching wool over it 织补, 缝补: *darning socks* 缝补袜子 **2 darn it!** *spoken* used when you are annoyed about something【口】讨厌! 可恶! 倒霉!〔用于某人生气、厌烦的时候〕: *Darn it! I'll have to do it all myself!* 讨厌! 都得由我一个人来做! **3 I'll be darned!** *spoken* used when you are surprised about something【口】真没想到!〔表示惊讶〕: *Did they really? Well, I'll be darned!* 他们真的吗? 哎, 真没想到!

darn² *n* [C] a place where a hole in a piece of clothing has been repaired neatly with wool 缝补之处

darn³ also 又作 **darned** /darnd; dɑːnd/ *adj spoken* used to emphasize how bad, stupid, unfair etc someone or something is【口】极, 非常〔强调某人或某物是多么糟糕、愚蠢、不公平等〕: *The darn fool got lost on the way.* 这个十足的傻瓜竟然迷了路。—**darn** also 又作 **darned** *adv*: *It was a darned good movie.* 这是一部极好的电影。

darn·ing /ˈdarnɪŋ; ˈdɑːnɪŋ/ *n* [U] the practice of repairing holes in clothing by using wool 织补, 织补工作

Dar·row /ˈdæro; ˈdærəʊ/, **Clar·ence** /ˈklærəns; ˈklærəns/ (1857-1938) a US lawyer known for representing workers and members of TRADE UNIONS in court cases. In his most famous case, the Scopes Trial, he defended a teacher who was taken to court for teaching his students about EVOLUTION and the ideas of Charles Darwin. 达罗〔(1857-1938), 美国律师, 以替工人和工会会员辩护著称。在最著名的斯科普斯审判案中, 他替一名因给学生讲授进化论和达尔文思想而被指控的教师辩护〕

dart¹ /dart; dɑːt/ *v* **1** [I always+adv/prep] to move suddenly and quickly in a particular direction 突进, 猛冲: **[+forward/across/off etc]** *Jill darted forward and pulled him away from the fire.* 吉尔冲上前把他从火边拉开。**2 dart a glance/look** to look at someone or something very quickly and suddenly 瞥一眼/扫一眼: *Tom darted a terrified glance over his shoulder.* 汤姆惊恐地回头瞥了一眼。

dart² *n* **1** [C] a small pointed object that is thrown or shot as a weapon or thrown in the game of darts 镖, 飞镖: *a poisoned dart* 毒镖 **2 darts** a game in which darts are thrown at a round board with numbers on it 掷镖游戏

> **CULTURAL NOTE 文化注释**
> In the UK, darts is usually played in PUBS. Darts competitions are sometimes shown on television, and the STEREOTYPE of a darts player is a WORKING-CLASS man with a fat stomach who drinks a lot of beer. 在英国, 一般是在酒吧里玩飞镖。电视上有时会播出飞镖比赛。玩飞镖者的典型形象是大腹便便、狂饮啤酒的工人阶层男子。

3 [singular] a sudden, quick movement in a particular direction 猛冲, 突进: **make a dart at/for** *The prisoner made a dart for the door.* 犯人猛地朝门口冲去。**4** [C] a small fold put into a piece of clothing to make it fit better〔衣服上的〕缝褶

dart·board /ˈdartˌbɔrd; ˈdɑːtbɔːd/ *n* [C] a round board used in the game of darts〔掷镖游戏中的〕圆靶

Darth Va·der /ˌdarθ ˈvedɚ; ˌdɑːθ ˈveɪdə/ an evil character in the films *Star Wars, The Empire Strikes Back*, and *Return of*

the Jedi. He wears black clothes, has a black MASK that covers all of his face, and talks in a strange and frightening voice. 达斯〔电影《星球大战》、《帝国反击战》和《杰迪归来》中的一个邪恶人物。他身穿黑色衣服，头戴黑色面具，遮住整张脸，说起话来声音怪异、可怕〕

Dart·moor /ˈdɑrtmʊr; ˈdɑːtmʊə/ **1** a large area of MOOR (=wild, open country with rough grass and low bushes) in Devon, in the southwest of England, which is a National Park 达特穆尔〔位于英格兰西南德文郡的一大片漠泽，为国家公园〕 **2** Dartmoor Prison, a prison in the centre of Dartmoor, far from any towns, where many dangerous criminals are kept 达特穆尔监狱〔位于达特穆尔的中心位置，远离市镇，关押着许多重犯〕

Dart·mouth /ˈdɑrtməθ; ˈdɑːtməθ/ **1** a port in Devon, southwest England. Many officers of the British navy are trained in the Royal Naval College there. 达特茅斯〔英格兰西南德文郡一港口，许多英国海军军官在此处的皇家海军学院受训〕 **2** also 又作 **Dartmouth College** a private university in New Hampshire in the US. It is one of the universities in the Ivy League (=a group of old and respected colleges). 达特茅斯学院〔美国新罕布什尔州的一所私立大学，为常春藤盟校之一〕

D

Dar·win /ˈdɑrwɪn; ˈdɑːwɪn/ a city and important port in northern Australia 达尔文市〔澳大利亚北部城市和重要港口〕

Darwin, Charles (1809-82) a British scientist who developed the Theory of Evolution, which is the idea that plants and animals develop gradually from simpler to more complicated forms by natural selection. This is the process by which only plants and animals that are naturally suitable for life in their environment will continue to live, while all others will die. He wrote about his ideas in his book *On the Origin of Species*. 达尔文〔(1809-1882)，英国科学家，提出了进化论，即植物和动物遵循自然选择的原则由简单向复杂逐步进化的学说。在进化过程中，唯有适应自然环境的植物和动物才可继续生存，不适应就要被淘汰。他在《物种起源》中阐述了自己的这些观点〕 —**Darwinian** /dɑrˈwɪnjən; dɑːˈwɪniən/ *adj*: *the Darwinian theory of evolution* 达尔文的进化论

dash¹ /dæʃ; dæʃ/ *v* **1** [I] to go or run somewhere very quickly 猛冲: [**+into/across/behind etc**] *Olive dashed into the room, grabbed her bag and ran out again.* 奥利芙冲进屋，抓起她的手提袋又跑了出来。**2** [T always+ adv/prep] to make something move violently against a surface, usually so that it breaks 猛击，撞击: **dash sth against/onto/to etc** *The ship was dashed against the rocks.* 船猛撞在礁石上。**3 dash sb's hopes** to disappoint someone by telling them that what they want is not possible 使某人的希望破灭，让某人失望: *Budget cuts dashed hopes for several plans proposed by NASA.* 削减预算使美国太空总署提出的几个计划落了空。**4 (I) must dash/(I) have to dash** *BrE spoken* used to tell someone that you must leave quickly【英口】(我)得赶紧走了: *I must dash – I said I'd meet Daniel at eight o'clock.* 我得赶紧走了，我说好和丹尼尔 8 点钟见面。**5 dash it (all)!** *BrE spoken* used to show that you are slightly annoyed or angry about something【英口】讨厌！〔表示有些厌烦、生气〕: *Dash it! I can't find my scissors!* 讨厌！我找不着剪刀了！**6** [I always+adv/prep] if a wave or rain dashes against something it hits it hard〔波浪或大雨猛烈地〕撞击，冲击: *Stormy waves dashed against the shore.* 汹涌的海浪冲击着海岸。

dash off *phr v* **1** [I] to leave somewhere very quickly 匆匆地离开: *Harry dashed off before she had a chance to thank him.* 她还没来得及说声谢谢，哈里就匆匆地跑开了。**2** [T **dash** sth ↔ **off**] to write or draw something very quickly 匆匆地写[画]〔某物〕: *She dashed off a quick letter excusing him from school that day.* 她匆匆地写了封信，为他那天没有到校上学开脱。

dash² *n*

1 ►LINE 线条◄ [C] a line [–] used in writing and printing, for example in the sentence "Go home – they're waiting for you." 破折号 —compare 比较 HYPHEN

2 make a dash for to run very quickly in order to get away from something or in order to reach something 猛冲，飞奔: **make a dash for cover/freedom etc** *The prisoners made a dash for freedom.* 犯人们猛跑，想逃出去获得自由。| **make a dash for it** *It's pouring with rain – we'll have to make a dash for it.* 下大雨了，我们得赶紧跑去找个避雨的地方。

3 ►SMALL AMOUNT 少量◄ [singular] a very small amount of a liquid or other substance 少许，少量〔液体或其他物质〕: [**+of**] *Add salt, pepper and a dash of vinegar.* 加点盐、胡椒，再加少许醋。—see picture on page A7 参见 A7 页图

4 a mad dash *informal* an attempt to get somewhere or do something extremely quickly【非正式】急奔，狂冲: *When the alarm went there was a mad dash for the exit.* 警报一响，人们都猛冲向出口处。

5 ►SOUND 声音◄ [C] a long sound or flash of light used for sending messages in MORSE CODE〔用莫尔斯电码发报时用的〕长音；光的一长闪 —compare 比较 DOT¹ (4)

6 ►CAR 汽车◄ [C] *AmE informal* DASHBOARD【美，非正式】〔汽车的〕仪表板

7 ►STYLE 风范◄ [U] *old-fashioned* style, energy, and courage in someone such as a soldier【过时】〔如士兵般的〕帅劲，精力，干劲；勇气

8 cut a dash to look very impressive and attractive in particular clothes〔尤指穿着〕有气派，精神，漂亮: *Edmond really cut a dash in that white linen suit.* 埃德蒙穿着那套白色亚麻西装真是帅气。

dash·board /ˈdæʃˌbɔrd; ˈdæʃbɔːd/ *n* [C] the board at the front of a car that has the controls on it〔汽车的〕仪表板 —see picture on page A2 参见 A2 页图

dashed /dæʃt; dæʃt/ *adj* [only before noun 仅用于名词前] *BrE old-fashioned* used to emphasize what you are saying【英，过时】该死的，讨厌的〔强调所说的话〕: *Harry talked dashed nonsense all evening.* 哈里整个晚上讲的全都是大废话。

dash·ing /ˈdæʃɪŋ; ˈdæʃɪŋ/ *adj* a man who is dashing is very attractive, fashionable, and confident〔指人〕精神抖擞的；时髦的；有自信的 —**dashingly** *adv*

Das Kapital —see 见 Das KAPITAL

dast·ard·ly /ˈdæstɚdlɪ; ˈdæstədli/ *adj old-fashioned* very cruel or evil【过时】残酷的，邪恶的: *a dastardly plot* 阴险恶毒的阴谋

DAT /ˌdi e ˈti; ˌdiː eɪ ˈtiː/ *n* [U] digital audio tape; a system used to record music, sound, or information in DIGITAL form〔用数码形式录制音乐、声音或信息的〕数码录音磁带

da·ta /ˈdetə; ˈdeɪtə/ *n* [U, plural] **1** information or facts 资料: *We cannot tell you the results until we have looked at all the data.* 我们看过所有的资料之后才能告诉你结果。**2** information in a form that can be stored and used 数据，资料: *data retrieval system* 数据检索系统 

data bank /ˈ‥ ˌ/ *n* [C] a place, especially a computer, where information on a particular subject is stored 数据库，资料库: *a missing persons data bank* 失踪人员的数据库

da·ta·base /ˈdetəˌbes; ˈdeɪtəbeɪs/ *n* [C] a large amount of data stored in a computer system so that you can find and use it easily〔存入电脑系统中的可供随时检索、使用的〕资料库，数据库: *Put the new customers on the database.* 把新客户的资料输入数据库。

data bus /ˈ‥ ˌ/ *n* [C] *technical* an electronic path along which DATA travels from one part of a computer to another【术语】〔资料从电脑的一个部分到另一个部分的〕数据总线

data pro·cess·ing /ˌ‥ ˈ‥‥/ *n* [U] the use of computers to store and organize data, especially in business 数据处理

Data Pro·tec·tion Act, the /ˌ‥ ˈ‥ ˌ/ a British law that protects people from other people using the information about them that is stored on computers for wrong purposes, and makes it necessary for people who hold personal information on computers to REGISTER with an authority《个人资料保护法》〔英国的一项法律，旨在保护储存在电脑中的个人资料免遭滥用，要求掌握个人电子信息的有关人员须向官方登记〕

date¹ /det; deɪt/ *n* [C] **1** the numbers or words you use to talk about a particular day, month, and year 日期，日子: *The date on the letter was the 30th August 1962.* 这封信上的日期是 1962 年 8 月 30 日。| **date of birth** (=the day you were born) 出生日期 *Please write your name, address, and date of birth on the form.* 请在表格里填上你的姓名、地址和出生日期。**2** a particular day 日子〔特定的某一天〕: *a date for the next meeting* 下一次会议的日期 | **set a date** (=choose a particular date) 选定一个日子 *Have you set a date for the wedding?* 婚礼的日子定下来了吗？**3 at a later date** *formal* at some time in the future【正式】晚些时候〔将来的某个时间〕: *We'll deal with this problem at a later date.* 我们晚些时候再处理这个问题。**4 to date** up to now 迄今，至今，到目前为止: *To date there has been no improvement in his condition.* 到现在为止，他的状况还是没有改善。**5 a)** an occasion when you arrange to meet someone that you like in a romantic way〔恋人之间的〕约会: *Do you have a date tonight?* 今晚你有约会吗？| **go (out) on a date** *"So, what did he say?" "Well, we're going on a date Friday night."* "他怎么说？" "嗯，我们星期五晚上去约会。" —see also 另见 BLIND DATE **b)** *AmE* someone that you have a date with【美】约会对象: *Can I bring my date to the party?* 我可以带约会对象来参加派对吗？**6 make a date** to agree on a time to meet someone socially 约好时间: *Let's make a date to go and see 'Arcadia' one day next week.* 让我们约个时间下个星期去看"阿卡迪亚"。**7** a sweet sticky brown fruit with a long hard seed inside 椰枣，海枣 —see also 

另见 CLOSING DATE, **expiry date** (EXPIRY (2)), SELL-BY DATE, OUT-OF-DATE, UP-TO-DATE

date² *v* **1** [T] to write or print the date on something〔在某物上〕写上[印上]日期: *a newspaper dated November 23, 1963* 一份日期为1963年11月23日的报纸 **2** [T] to find out when something old such as a book, painting, building etc was made 鉴定〔古书、古画、古建筑等〕的年代: *The rocks are dated by examining the fossils found in the same layer.* 通过查看在同一岩层里发现的化石来鉴定岩石的年代。**3** [I] if clothing, art etc dates, it looks old-fashioned〔衣物、艺术等〕过时: *His designs are so successful, they've hardly dated at all.* 他的设计太成功了，现在看起来几乎一点也不过时。**4** [T] *AmE* to have a romantic relationship with someone【美】〔谈恋爱〕与…约会: **be dating sb** *Is he still dating Sarah?* 他还和萨拉好吗? **5** [T] if something that you say, do, or wear dates you, it shows that you are fairly old 显示〔某人〕老了: *Yes, I remember the moon landings – that dates me doesn't it?* 是的，我记得登月的事 —— 这说明我老了，是不是?

date from also 又作 **date back to** *phr v* [I] to have existed since a particular time in the past 自…存在至今, 追溯到…年代: *This church dates from the 13th century.* 这座教堂的历史可以追溯到13世纪。

dat·ed /ˈdetɪd; ˈdeɪtɪ̈d/ *adj* old-fashioned 过时的: *That dress looks dated now.* 那件衣服现在看起来过时了。—compare 比较 OUT-OF-DATE

date·line /ˈdet,laɪn; ˈdeɪtlaɪn/ *n* [singular] the INTERNATIONAL DATE LINE〔国际〕日界线, 国际日期变更线

date rape /ˈ· ·/ *n* [C, U] a RAPE that is done by someone the woman has met in a social situation 约会强奸

date stamp /ˈ· ·/ *n* [C] **a)** a piece of equipment used for printing the date on letters, documents etc 日期戳 **b)** the mark that it makes 日期戳印

dating a·gen·cy /ˈ·· ,···/ *n* [C] a business that helps people to meet other people, to have a romantic relationship 婚姻介绍所

da·tive /ˈdetɪv; ˈdeɪtɪv/ *n* [C] *technical* a particular form of a noun in some languages such as Latin and German, which shows that the noun is the INDIRECT OBJECT of a verb【术语】与格〔拉丁语和德语等语言中名词的特殊形式, 表示这个名词是某个动词的间接宾语〕—**dative** *adj*

daub¹ /dɔb; dɔːb/ *v* [T] to paint or cover something with a soft substance, without being very careful〔胡乱〕涂抹, 玷污: *faces daubed with black mud* 抹了黑泥的脸

daub² *n* **1** [U] *technical* mud or clay used for making walls【术语】〔抹墙的〕涂料 —see also 另见 **wattle and daub** (WATTLE (2)) **2** a small amount of a soft or sticky substance 少量软而黏的物质: [+of] *a daub of paint* 少量的涂料

daugh·ter /ˈdɔtɚ; ˈdɔːtə/ *n* [C] **1** someone's female child 女儿: *My daughter's at university now.* 我女儿现在正在读大学。—see picture at 参见 FAMILY 图 **2** *technical* something new that forms or develops when something else divides or ends【术语】产物: *a daughter language* 子语言

daughter-in-law /ˈ·· ,· ·/ *n plural* **daughters-in-law** [C] your son's wife 儿媳妇 —compare 比较 SON-IN-LAW —see picture at 参见 FAMILY 图

daugh·ter·ly /ˈdɔtɚlɪ; ˈdɔːtəli/ *adj old-fashioned* behaving in a way that a daughter is supposed to behave【过时】女儿般的; 尽女儿之道的

Daughters of the A·mer·i·can Rev·o·lu·tion, the /,· · · · ·, · · ·ˈ· ·/ also 又作 **the DAR** an organization in the US for women whose families have been in the US since the American Revolutionary War. Its members are very PATRIOTIC and generally support RIGHT-WING political ideas. 美国革命女儿〔美国一妇女组织。其成员的家族自美国独立战争起一直在美国定居, 她们十分爱国, 总体上支持右翼政治思想〕

daunt /dɔnt; dɔːnt/ *v* [T usually passive 一般用被动态] **1** to make someone feel afraid or less confident 使〔某人〕害怕, 使减少信心: *He felt utterly daunted by the prospect of moving to another country.* 他一想到要移居到别的国家就感到十分害怕。**2 nothing daunted** *formal* not at all discouraged【正式】毫不气馁, 并不畏难: *It was steep but, nothing daunted, he started climbing.* 路很陡峭, 但是他还是毫不畏惧, 开始向上攀登。

daunt·ing /ˈdɔntɪŋ; ˈdɔːntɪŋ/ *adj* frightening in a way that makes you feel less confident 使人气馁的: *It's a daunting task, but we're optimistic.* 这是一项艰巨的任务, 但是我们很乐观。| **daunting prospect** (=something daunting that you are going to do) 吓人[令人畏惧]的前景 *the daunting prospect of asking for a loan* 令人发怵的借贷一事

daunt·less /ˈdɔntlɪs; ˈdɔːntləs/ *adj literary* confident and not easily frightened【文】勇敢的, 无畏的: *dauntless optimism* 无所畏惧的乐观精神 —**dauntlessly** *adv*

dau·phin /ˈdɔfɪn; ˈdɔːfɪn/ *n* [C] the oldest son of a King of France 法国王储, 王太子

dau·phine /dɔˈfin; ˈdɔːfiːn/ *n* [C] the wife of the oldest son of a King of France 法国王太子妃

dav·en·port /ˈdævən,pɔrt; ˈdævənpɔːt/ *n* [C] *AmE* a large SOFA, especially one that can be made into a bed【美】〔尤指可以作床用的〕大沙发

Da·vid /ˈdevɪd; ˈdeɪvɪ̈d/ a STATUE of a young man made by the artist Michelangelo, which can be seen in Florence, in Italy. Many people think it is one of the best examples of the human form in art.《大卫》〔艺术家米开朗琪罗创作的一尊雕塑作品, 坐落在意大利弗罗伦萨。作品刻画的是一青年男子形象, 许多人认为它是最出色的人体艺术作品之一〕

David, King (died around 962 BC) in the Old Testament of the Bible, one of the Kings of Israel. When David was a boy, he killed the GIANT (=a very tall, strong man) Goliath by hitting him on the head with a stone thrown from his SLING. People sometimes use the names **David and Goliath** to describe a situation in which a small and less powerful person or group is fighting a much larger and more powerful person or group. 大卫〔(卒于公元前约962年),《圣经·旧约》中的一位以色列国王。孩提时代, 他用机弦甩出一粒石子打死了巨人哥利亚。人们有时借用 David and Goliath (大卫和哥利亚) 两人的名字来形容强弱之争的情形〕

David, St the PATRON SAINT of Wales, who lived in the 6th century. **St David's Day**, 1st March, is celebrated as the Welsh national day. 圣大卫〔威尔士的主保圣人, 生活于公元6世纪。3月1日圣大卫节是威尔士的民族节日〕

David Cop·per·field /,devɪd ˈkɑpɚfild; ,deɪvɪ̈d ˈkɒpəfiːld/ (1849-50) a NOVEL by Charles Dickens which describes the life of its main character, David Copperfield, from the time when he was a poor ORPHAN (=a child whose parents have both died). It is one of Dickens's most popular books, and is partly based on his own life. Many people know its characters, including Mr Micawber and Uriah Heep.《大卫·科波菲尔》, 又译《块肉余生记》〔(1849-1850), 查尔斯·狄更斯创作的一部小说, 描述了一个名叫大卫·科波菲尔的可怜孤儿的遭遇。它是狄更斯最受人欢迎的小说之一, 部分内容源于他的亲身经历。不少人都熟悉书中的人物, 比如说麦考伯先生和尤赖亚·黑普〕

Da·vies /ˈdevɪs; ˈdeɪvɪ̈s/, **Sir Pe·ter Max·well** (1934-) a British COMPOSER of modern classical music. His works include the OPERAS *Taverner* (1972), *The Martyrdom of St Magnus* (1977), *The Lighthouse* (1980), and *Resurrection* (1987). 戴维斯〔(1934-), 英国现代古典音乐作曲家。代表作有歌剧《塔弗纳》(1972)、《圣马格努斯殉难》(1977)、《灯塔》(1980)和《复活》(1987)〕

Da·vis /ˈdevɪs; ˈdeɪvɪ̈s/, **An·ge·la** /ˈændʒɪlə; ˈændʒɪ̈lə/ (1944-) a LEFT-WING black US woman who worked to achieve social and political changes in the US 戴维斯〔(1944-), 美国黑人妇女。她是一位曾致力于实现美国社会和政治变革的左翼人士〕

Davis, Jef·fer·son (1808-89) a US politician who was President of the Confederacy (=the Southern US states) during the American Civil War, from 1861 to 1865 戴维斯〔(1808-1889), 美国政治家, 1861至1865年美国内战期间任南部联邦总统〕

Davis, Miles /maɪlz; maɪlz/ (1926-91) a US musician who played the TRUMPET and led his own JAZZ band. He had an important influence on the development of jazz. 戴维斯〔(1926-1991), 美国小号演奏家、爵士乐队领队。他对爵士乐的发展产生了重要影响〕

Davis, Steve /stiv; stiːv/ (1958-) a British SNOOKER player who was extremely successful in the 1980s. He played very calmly and quietly, and was often called 'boring' as a joke. 戴维斯〔(1958-), 英国斯诺克运动员, 20世纪80年代是其事业的鼎盛时期。他打球时非常沉着冷静, 常被人戏称为"乏味的人"〕

Davis Cup, the /,· ·ˈ·/ an important international men's tennis competition, played between teams of players representing their countries 戴维斯杯〔一项重要的国际男子网球团体赛〕

dav·it /ˈdævɪt; ˈdævɪ̈t/ *n* [C] one of a pair of long curved poles that sailors swing out over the side of a ship in order to lower a boat into the water〔轮船上的〕吊艇柱, 吊艇架, 吊艇杆

Da·vy /ˈdevɪ; ˈdeɪvi/, **Sir Hum·phrey** /ˈhʌmfrɪ; ˈhʌmfri/ (1778-1829) a British scientist who invented the **Davy lamp**, an oil lamp that could be used in coal mines without causing explosions. He also discovered several ELEMENTS (=basic chemical substances), including CALCIUM, SODIUM, and POTASSIUM. 戴

维〔(1778-1829)，英国科学家，发明的戴维灯是一种可以在煤矿上使用、但不会引起爆炸的油灯。他还发现了钙、钠、钾等几种化学元素〕

daw·dle /ˈdɔdl; ˈdɔːdl/ *v* [I] to take a long time to do something or go somewhere〔做事等〕磨蹭，缓慢地做：*Don't dawdle – we're late already!* 别磨蹭了——我们已经晚了！| **[+over]** *I dawdled over a second cup of coffee.* 我慢吞吞地啜饮着第二杯咖啡。—**dawdler** *n* [C]

Dawes Plan, the /ˈdɔz ˌplæn; ˈdɔːz ˌplæn/ a plan developed by Charles G. Dawes, a US politician, to help Germany to pay its REPARATIONS (=money paid by a defeated country) after World War I 道威斯计划〔美国政治家查尔斯·G.道威斯提出的一项计划，旨在帮助德国一战后支付战争赔款〕

Daw·kins /ˈdɔkɪnz; ˈdɔːkɪnz/, **Rich·ard** (1941-) a British scientist with a special interest in EVOLUTION. In his book *The Selfish Gene*, he says that humans, plants, and animals are built by GENES (=the parts of a cell which control qualities that are passed on to a living thing from its parents) so that the genes can continue to exist. He is famous for strongly opposing the belief in God. 道金斯〔(1941-)，英国科学家，对进化论有着浓厚的兴趣。他在《自私的基因》一书中提到，人类、植物和动物都是依赖基因才存在的，所以基因得以延续。他因极力反对信仰上帝而闻名〕

dawn¹ /dɔn; dɔːn/ *n* [C, U] **1** the time at the beginning of the day when light first appears 黎明，破晓：*We talked almost until dawn.* 我们几乎一直谈到天亮。| **at dawn** *The first boats set off at dawn.* 第一批船天一亮就出发了。| **dawn breaks** (=the first light of the day appears) 破晓 *When dawn broke we were still 50 miles from Calcutta.* 破晓的时候，我们离加尔各答还有50英里。| **at the crack of dawn** (=very early in the morning) 黎明，破晓 *I was up at the crack of dawn to get the plane.* 我一大早就起来赶飞机。—compare 比较 DUSK **2 the dawn of civilization/time etc** the time when something began or first appeared 文明/时代等的开端：*People have been falling in love since the dawn of time.* 男欢女爱，自古皆然。**3 a false dawn** something that seems positive or hopeful but really is not 假曙光〔指虚幻的好迹象〕：*another false dawn on the road to recovery* 康复之路上的又一线假曙光

dawn² *v* [I] **1** if day or morning dawns, it begins 破晓，天亮：*The morning dawned fresh and clear after the storm.* 暴雨过后的清晨，天一破晓就晴空万里，空气清新。**2** *literary* if a period of time or situation dawns, it begins【文】开始：*The age of Darwin had dawned.* 达尔文时代开始了。**3** *formal* if a feeling or idea dawns, you think of it for the first time【正式】〔某种感觉或想法〕开始明白，第一次想起

dawn on sb *phr v* [T not in passive 不用被动态] if a fact dawns on you, you realize it for the first time 使开始明白〔某个事实〕，使醒悟：*Then the ghastly truth dawned on me.* 接着我突然明白了可怕的真相。| **it dawns on sb that** *It dawned on me that Joanna had been right all along.* 我突然意识到乔安娜一直都是对的。

dawn cho·rus /ˌ·ˈ··/ *n* [singular] *especially BrE* the sound of many birds singing at dawn【尤英】〔清晨〕百鸟齐鸣

dawn raid /ˌ·ˈ·/ *n* [C] an attack or operation that happens very early in the morning, especially involving the police〔尤指警方的〕凌晨突袭；拂晓袭击

day /de; deɪ/ *n*

① PERIOD OF TIME 一段时间
② THE TIME YOU ARE AWAKE 白天
③ FUTURE 将来
④ PAST 过去
⑤ SB'S LIFE/STH'S EXISTENCE 一个人的一生/一件东西的寿命
⑥ WORK 工作
⑦ EACH DAY/EVERY DAY 每天
⑧ NOW 现在
⑨ BAD THINGS HAPPEN 坏事发生
⑩ GOOD THINGS HAPPEN 好事发生
⑪ PLEASURE 快乐
⑫ SUCCESS/FAME 成功/出名
⑬ SPOKEN PHRASES 口语短语
⑭ OTHER MEANINGS 其他意思

① PERIOD OF TIME 一段时间

1 [C] a period of 24 hours〔24小时长的〕一天，一日：*We spent three days in Paris then went south.* 我们在巴黎度过三天，然后到南方去了。| *What day is it today – Tuesday?* 今天星期几——星期二？| **the day before yesterday** *I just saw Pat the day before yesterday.* 我前天刚刚见到过帕特。| **the day after tomorrow** *We're leaving for LA the day after tomorrow.* 后天我们将出发去洛杉矶。

2 [C,U] the period of time between when it becomes light in the morning and the time it becomes dark 白天，日间：*I'm usually out during the day.* 白天我通常出门。| *It rained all day.* 一整天都下着雨。| **by day** (=during the day) 在白天 *Owls usually sleep by day and hunt by night.* 猫头鹰通常白天睡觉，夜晚猎食。

day 日，天

Monday 星期一	the day before yesterday 前天
Tuesday 星期二	yesterday 昨天
Wednesday 星期三	TODAY 今天
Thursday 星期四	tomorrow 明天
Friday 星期五	the day after tomorrow 后天
Saturday 星期六	
Sunday 星期天	

② THE TIME YOU ARE AWAKE 白天

3 [C usually singular 一般用单数] the time during the day when you are awake 白天：*His day begins at six.* 他的一天从6点开始。| **long day** (=a day when you had to get up early and were busy all day) 漫长的一天〔指早上起得很早而且一整天都十分忙碌〕*It's been a very long day.* 真是漫长的一天。| **all day (long)** (=during the whole time you are awake) 一天到晚，一整天 *I've been studying all day. I'm beat!* 我一整天都在学习，我都筋疲力尽了！

③ FUTURE 将来

4 one day also 又作 **some day** at an unknown time in the future 将来有一天，有朝一日：*One day I'll buy a boat and sail around the world.* 有朝一日我要买艘船周游世界。

5 one of these days *informal* at some time in the future【非正式】这几天〔将来的某个时候〕：*I might find the time to paint the bedroom one of these days.* 这几天我或许能找到时间把卧室粉刷一下。

6 any day (now) *spoken* very soon【口】不久，很快：*She's expecting the baby any day now.* 她的孩子这几天就要出生了。

7 the day will come (when) used to emphasize that something will definitely happen at some time in the future 终有一天〔强调某事必定在将来某个时间发生〕：*The day will come when he loses his eyesight completely.* 总有一天他会完全失明。

④ PAST 过去

8 one day on a particular day in the past 有一天〔过去的某一天〕：*One day, she just didn't turn up for work, and we never saw her again.* 有一天，她没来上班，从此我们再也没见过她。

9 childhood/student/army days the time when you were a child, student, soldier etc 儿童/学生/参军时代

10 the good old days time in the past that you think was better than the present time 过去的好时光〔认为过去的时光较现在的好〕: *In the good old days people never had to lock their doors.* 在过去的好日子里，人们从来不用锁门。

11 those were the days *spoken* used to say that a time in the past was better than the present time【口】那才叫好日子〔表示过去的日子比现在好〕

12 the other day a few days ago; recently 前几天，最近: *We had a letter from Kim the other day.* 前几天我们收到了金的来信。

13 in those days during a period of time in the past 那时〔过去的一段时间〕: *Women wore long skirts in those days.* 那时妇女都穿长裙。

14 in my day used to describe what things were like when you were young 我年轻的时候: *In my day we used to have to get up at six o'clock.* 我年轻时，我们常常得6点起床。

15 in his or her day during the most successful part of someone's life 鼎盛时期，当红时期，〔某人的〕当年: *Your grandfather was a famous radio personality in his day.* 你祖父当年是广播界的名人。

16 the standards/fashion/wages etc of the day the standards etc that existed in a particular period of time in the past 过去某一时期的标准/时尚/工资等

17 five/three/nine years to the day exactly five years, three years, etc ago 正好五年/三年/九年前: *It's two years to the day since we moved here.* 我们搬到这里整整两年了。

⑤ SB'S LIFE/STH'S EXISTENCE 一个人的一生/一件东西的寿命

18 sb's days someone's life 某人的一生: *She ended her days in poverty.* 她在贫困中度过了余生。

19 sb's/sth's days are numbered someone or something will not continue to exist or be effective 某人将不久人世，活不了多长时间；某物将不再有效，支撑不了多久: *The days of the vinyl record are numbered.* 塑胶唱片的日子已屈指可数了。

⑥ WORK 工作

20 [C] the time spent working during a 24-hour period 工作日: *I work an eight-hour day.* 我一天工作八个小时。| *Did you have a good day at the office?* 你在办公室工作得愉快吗？—see also 另见 WORKING DAY

21 day off a day when you do not have to work 休息日；休假日: *I'm taking a day off next week.* 我下个礼拜将休一天假。

22 be on days *spoken* to be working during the day doing a job that you often have to do at night, for example, if you work in a hospital【口】值日班〔通常夜班的工作暂时挪到白天做〕: *I'm on days this week.* 这个星期我值日班。

⑦ EACH DAY/EVERY DAY 每天

23 day after day happening continuously for a long time so that you become annoyed or bored 日复一日，天天地: *I couldn't stand sitting at a desk day after day.* 我忍受不了日复一日地坐在桌旁。

24 from day to day if something changes from day to day it changes often 天天；每天；日益 —compare 比较 DAY-TO-DAY

25 day by day slowly and gradually 一天天，逐日，渐渐地，慢慢地: *Her health was improving day by day.* 她的身体一天天好起来了。

26 day in, day out every day for a long time 一天接一天地，日复一日，天天: *She cooked and cleaned day in, day out for forty years.* 她40年来日复一日地做饭、打扫卫生。

27 night and day also 又作 **day and night** all the time; continuously 日日夜夜，夜以继日: *He was attended by nurses night and day.* 他有护士黑天白夜地看护。

⑧ NOW 现在

28 these days used to talk about your situation, behaviour, feelings etc now, especially if they used to be different 如今，现今，当今，这年头，眼下〔尤指现在的情形、行为、感觉等和以前有所不同〕: *I don't go out much these days – once or twice a month at the most.* 如今我不太出去——最多一个月一两次。

29 in this day and age used when you are surprised or annoyed that something still happens 时至如今，在我们这个年代〔指一些令人惊讶或生气的事情仍然在发生〕: *I find it incredible that such punishments still exist in this day and age.* 这样的惩罚方式现在还有，真是难以置信。

30 to this day even now, after so much time has passed 至今: *To this day I don't know who told Katy about Duncan.* 到现在我也不知道谁把邓肯的事告诉了凯蒂。

31 up to/until/to the present day from a time in the past until now〔从过去的某一时间〕直到现在: *This tradition has continued right up until the present day.* 这种传统一直延续至今。

⑨ BAD THINGS HAPPEN 坏事发生

32 it's not my/your/his day *spoken* used when several unpleasant things have happened to someone in one day【口】我/你/他倒霉的一天〔表示一天中不愉快的事接连发生〕: *It's really not Chris's day – he overslept, his car broke down, and he spilt coffee on his new pants.* 这一天克里斯真不走运——睡过了头，车抛了锚，还把咖啡洒到了新裤子上。

33 have an off day to be less successful or happy than usual, for no particular reason 不顺利，不顺心: *His work isn't usually this bad – he must have had an off day.* 他的工作通常没这么糟——今天他一定是状态不佳。

34 it's (just) one of those days *spoken* used when everything seems to be going wrong【口】〔诸事出错的〕不幸的一天: *It's just been one of those days.* 今天真倒霉。

⑩ GOOD THINGS HAPPEN 好事发生

35 make sb's day to make someone very happy 使某人非常高兴: *Hearing her voice on the phone really made my day.* 在电话里听到她的声音真令我高兴。

36 it's your/his/my lucky day! used when something very good happens to someone 你/他/我幸运的日子！: *Ruth just found a ten pound note in the street. It must be her lucky day!* 露丝刚在街上拾到一张10英镑的钞票，今天一定是她的幸运日！

⑪ PLEASURE 快乐

37 make a day of it *spoken* to choose to spend all day doing something, usually for pleasure, when you could have spent only part of the day doing it【口】好好玩它一整天: *We were going into New York for the concert anyway, so we decided to make a day of it.* 反正我们要去纽约听音乐会，于是我们决定好好玩它一整天。

38 day out *especially BrE* a day spent at the beach, in the countryside, at the zoo etc【尤英】〔到海滩、乡村、动物园等〕外出游玩的一天，出游的一天

⑫ SUCCESS/FAME 成功/出名

39 sb's day will come used to say that someone will have a chance to succeed in the future, even if they are not successful now 某人的好日子〔将来成功的日子〕将会到来

40 have had your day to be no longer successful, powerful, or famous 不再成功[强大，有名]: *It seems as if typewriter has had its day.* 打字机的鼎盛时期似乎已经过去了。

⑬ SPOKEN PHRASES 口语短语

41 that'll be the day *spoken* used to say that you think something is very unlikely to happen【口】不太可能: *"Bill says he'll wash the dishes tonight." "That'll be the day!"* "比尔说今晚他洗碗。" "不太可能！"

⑭ OTHER MEANINGS 其他意思

42 not have all day *spoken* to not have much time available【口】时间不多了: *Hurry up, we don't have all day!* 快点，我们没那么多时间了！

43 it's not every day (that) *spoken* used to say that something does not happen often and is therefore very special【口】并不是每天都…: *Let's go out and celebrate. After all, it's not every day you get a new job.* 我们出去庆祝一下吧，毕竟并不是每天都能找到新工作。

44 (live to) see the day *spoken* to experience something that you thought would never happen【口】看到那一天: *I never thought I'd live to see the day when women became priests.* 我怎么也想不到女人还有当上神甫这一天。

45 40/50/60 etc if she's a day *spoken* used to emphasize that someone is at least as old as you are saying【口】她至少有40/50/60岁等: *She's ninety if she's a day.* 她至少有90岁。

46 from one day to the next if something changes from one day to the next, it does not stay the same for very long 从一天到下一天: *I never know where he'll be from one day to the next.* 他天天换地方，我从来不知道他会在哪儿。

47 soup/dish/fish of the day the special soup etc that a restaurant serves on a particular day〔餐厅〕某一天的特色汤/特色菜/特色鱼

D

48 **day of action** *BrE* a day when the workers in a particular place stop working for one day, to protest about something; a STRIKE[2] (1)【英】罢工日
49 **the day of reckoning** the time when you are punished or made to suffer for the things you have done wrong〔做坏事的人〕受到惩罚[报应]的日子 —see also 另见 **call it a day** (CALL[1] (22)), **carry the day** (CARRY[1] (23)), **every dog (has) its day** (DOG[1] (11)), **have a field day** (FIELD DAY (1)), HALF-DAY, **it's early days** (EARLY[1] (5)), **it's (a little) late in the day** (LATE[1] (9)), OPEN DAY, **save the day** (SAVE[1] (11)), SPEECH DAY, SPORTS DAY

USAGE NOTE 用法说明: DAY
WORD CHOICE 词语辨析: **from day to day, day by day, day after day**
Something that changes or goes on **day by day** or **from day to day** is a continuous action. day by day或者 from day to day 用来表示一个连续的动作, 如事情一天天地进行或变化: *The problem is getting worse day by day.* 这个问题变得一天比一天严重。| *We just muddle along from day to day.* 我们只是一天天地混日子。
Separate events that are repeated happen **day after day**. day after day用来表示一天天地重复某一事情: *Day after day he tramps the streets looking for work* (=he does the same thing every day). 他成天走街串巷找工作。
GRAMMAR 语法
Remember that *on* is used with days and the word **day** itself. 记住: 表示某一天或者和 day 这个词本身连用的时候要用介词 on: *on Thursday/on that day/on the same day/on the second day* (NOT 不用 **in** or 或 **at**) 在星期四/在那一天/在同一天/在第二天
On is never used with the phrase **the other day**, when you do not say the exact day when something happened. 用 the other day 表示某事发生在不确定的某一天时, 前面不用 on: *I saw Joey in Dick's Bar the other day* (=a few days ago). 前几天我在狄克酒吧看见乔伊了。Compare 比较: *We spent two days in the mountains – on one day we went hiking and on the other we went fishing.* 我们在山里度过了两天: 一天我们去远足, 另一天我们去钓鱼。
Note that you say **in those days** but **these days** (NOT 不用 **in these days**). 注意可以说 in those days, 但是在 these days 前面不加 in: *In those days not many people had TVs, but these days a lot of households have more than one.* 那时候有电视机的人家很少, 但是如今许多家庭都拥有不止一台电视机。
Remember that the phrase is **during the day**. 记住: 短语是 during the day: *I couldn't get much work done during the day* (NOT 不用 *during day* or 或 *in the day*, though you can say 然而可以说 *in the daytime*). 白天我做不了太多工作。
You do not use **the** with **all day**. all day 前面不能加 the。
SPELLING 拼法
Remember that **today** is one word. 记住: today 是一个词。

CULTURAL NOTE 文化注释
Days of the week In both the US and the UK, Monday is the first day of the working week and school week, and people often joke about how much they hate Mondays because they don't want to go back to work or school. 一周的工作日: 在英美两国, 星期一都是一周工作和学习的第一天。人们常开玩笑说多么痛恨星期一, 因为不想回去上班或上学。
The weekend The weekend consists of Friday night, Saturday, and Sunday. Most people are very happy on Friday because it is the last day of the school or working week, and they sometimes use the expression "Thank God it's Friday!" Friday nights and Saturday nights are when people usually have parties or go to theatres, restaurants etc. On Saturdays during the day, people are often busy shopping, playing or watching sports, visiting friends, and doing things that they do not have time to do during the week, such as cleaning their house. Sunday is typically a quieter day when people tend to rest and relax. Traditionally people spend time with their families and have a big meal together. Christians usually go to church on Sunday. In the past in the UK, most shops closed on Sunday, but now many of them stay open, although often for fewer hours than during the rest of the week. 周末: 周末包括星期五晚上、星期六和星期天。一到星期五, 大多数人都会非常高兴, 因为这是一周上班或上学的最后一天。人们有时会说: "谢天谢地, 到星期五了。" 星期五晚上或星期六晚上, 人们通常举办聚会, 或者去看戏、下馆子。星期六白天, 人们常忙于购物、玩乐或观看体育比赛、拜访朋友, 或做一周没来得及做的事, 如打扫房间。星期天一般比较平静, 人们更想休息和放松, 传统上家人一起度过, 吃顿大餐。基督徒一般在星期天上教堂。过去英国的商店星期天关门, 但现在很多仍旧营业, 只是营业时间较平日短。— see also 另见 WEEKEND

Day, Dor·is /ˈdɑrɪs; ˈdɒrɪ̵s/ (1924-) a US singer and film and television actress who was especially popular in the 1950s and early 1960s. Many people think of her as cheerful and morally good. 多丽丝·戴〔(1924-), 美国女歌手、影视演员, 20 世纪 50 年代和 60 年代早期尤为著名, 被认为是一位性格开朗、品行端正的女性〕
day boy /ˈ· ·/ *n* [C] *BrE* a boy DAY PUPIL【英】走读男生
day·break /ˈdeˌbrek; ˈdeɪbreɪk/ *n* [U] the time of day when light first appears 黎明, 破晓: *We arrived in Cairo at daybreak.* 天刚亮我们就到了开罗。
day camp /ˈ· ·/ *n* [C] *AmE* a place where children can go in the day during the school holidays to do sports, art etc【美】日间夏令营〔学校放假时, 孩子们白天可去的地方, 可以做体育运动、进行艺术活动等〕
day care centre *BrE*【英】, **day care center** *AmE*【美】*n* /ˈ· ·· ,· ·/ [C] **1** *AmE* a place where babies are looked after while their parents are at work【美】日间托儿所; CRÈCHE *BrE*【英】**2** a place in Britain where people who are old or ill can be looked after during the day〔英国日间照顾老人或病人的〕日间看护所
day·dream[1] /ˈdeˌdrim; ˈdeɪdriːm/ *v* [I] to think about something pleasant, especially when this makes you forget what you should be doing 做白日梦, 幻想, 梦想: *Stop daydreaming! You were meant to finish that hours ago.* 别做白日梦了! 你本来几个小时前就该做完的。—**daydreamer** *n* [C]
daydream[2] *n* [C] pleasant thoughts you have while you are awake, that make you forget what you are doing 白日梦
day girl /ˈ· ·/ *n* [C] *BrE* a girl DAY PUPIL【英】走读女生
Day-Glo, Dayglo /ˈdeglo; ˈdeɪgləʊ/ *adj trademark* having a very bright orange, green, yellow, or pink colour【商标】含"帝高"荧光加色剂的: *Dayglo socks* "帝高"牌袜子
day·light /ˈdeˌlaɪt; ˈdeɪlaɪt/ *n* [U] **1** the light produced by the sun during the day 日光, 白昼, 白天: *We'll keep working while there's still enough daylight.* 趁着天还不太黑, 我们将继续工作。**2** **daylight robbery** *BrE informal* a situation in which something costs you a lot more than it should【英, 非正式】明目张胆地索取高价, 敲竹杠: *£2.50 for a cup of coffee? It's daylight robbery!* 一杯咖啡要 2.5 英镑? 这简直是公开抢劫! **3** **see daylight** *informal* to begin to understand something that you have found difficult to understand before【非正式】开始理解, 明白〔以前不懂的事情〕: *Joan explained it again, and at last I began to see daylight.* 琼又解释了一遍, 我终于开始明白了。**4** **scare/frighten the (living) daylights out of** *informal* to frighten someone a lot【非正式】使〔某人〕非常害怕, 惊恐: *It scared the living daylights out of me when the flames shot out.* 火焰向外喷射的时候, 我吓坏了。**5** **beat/knock the (living) daylights out of** *informal* to hit someone a lot and seriously hurt them【非正式】狠打〔某人〕致重伤 —see also 另见 **in broad daylight** (BROAD[1] (6))
daylight sav·ing time /ˌ·· ˈ·· ˌ·/ also 又作 **daylight savings** /ˌ·· ˈ··/ *n* [U] *AmE* the time during the summer when clocks are one hour ahead of standard time【美】夏令时〔计时器比标准时间提早一小时〕—compare 比较 BRITISH SUMMER TIME
day nur·se·ry /ˈ· ˌ···/ *n* [C] *BrE* a place where small children can be left while their parents are at work【英】日间托儿所
Day of A·tone·ment, the /ˌ· · ·ˈ·· ·/ a Jewish holy day when Jews FAST and pray for forgiveness for their SIN (=things they have done wrong), during the past year. It is also known as Yom Kippur. 赎罪日〔犹太教圣日。此日, 犹太人禁食, 祈求上帝宽恕过去一年的罪过, 又称 Yom Kippur〕
day of judge·ment /ˌ· · ˈ··/ *n* [singular] JUDGMENT DAY 最后审判日, 世界末日
Day of the Triffids, The a science FICTION book by John Wyndham. The TRIFFID*s* are large poisonous plants that can move, and they become powerful after a bright light in the sky makes most people blind. 《三脚妖之日》〔约翰·温德姆的科

幻小说。三脚妖是可以移动的大型有毒植物。一道强光划过天空，看到强光的多数人眼睛都失明了。之后，三脚妖的威力更加强大〕

day pu·pil /ˈ· ˌ· ·/ *n* [C] *BrE* a pupil who goes to a BOARDING SCHOOL but who lives at home【英】〔寄宿学校的〕走读学生

day re·lease /ˌ· ·ˈ·/ *n* [U] *BrE* a system that allows workers to spend one day a week studying a subject at a college【英】〔准许工人一个星期有一天的时间到大学学习的〕每周一天获准请假进修制度

day re·turn /ˌ· ·ˈ·/ *n* [C] *BrE* a train or bus ticket that lets you go somewhere at a cheaper price than usual, if you go there and back on the same day【英】〔火车或公共汽车的〕当日来回票〔票价较低〕

day room /ˈ· ·/ *n* [C] a room in a hospital where patients can go to read, watch television etc〔医院里供病人去看书、看电视的〕康乐室; 阅览室

day school /ˈ· ·/ *n* [C, U] a school where the students go home in the evening rather than one where they live 日校, 走读学校 —compare 比较 BOARDING SCHOOL

day·time /ˋdeˌtaɪm; ˈdeɪtaɪm/ *n* [U] the time during the day between the time when it gets light and the time when it gets dark; DAY (2) 白天, 日间: *I can't sleep in the daytime.* 我白天睡不着觉。

day-to-day /ˌ· · ˈ·◂/ *adj* **day-to-day management/running/administration etc** work that is done as a normal part of your life, your job etc 日常[常规]的管理/运营/行政工作等: *The manager is responsible for the day-to-day running of the hotel.* 经理负责酒店的日常管理工作。

Day·to·na Beach /deˌtonə ˋbitʃ; deɪˌtəʊnə ˈbiːtʃ/ a US city on the coast of Florida. Motor races are held at the International Speedway there. 代托纳比奇〔美国佛罗里达州一海滨城市。该市的国际赛车道上举办了很多赛车比赛〕

Day·ton Ac·cords, the /ˌdetṇ əˋkɔrdz; ˌdeɪtn əˈkɔːdz/ also 又作 **the Dayton Peace Accords, the Dayton Agreements** the political agreements made in 1995 in Dayton, Ohio, in the US, between Bosnia-Herzegovina, Croatia and the Federal Republic of Yugoslavia (Serbia and Montenegro) to end the fighting between them and decide where the new borders would be between them 代顿协议〔1995年波斯尼亚和黑塞哥维那、克罗地亚以及南斯拉夫共和国（塞尔维亚和黑山）三方在美国俄亥俄州的代顿签署的一项政治协定, 目的是结束战争, 划定新的疆界〕

day trip /ˈ· ·/ *n* [C] a visit to the beach, the zoo etc when you go there and come back the same day 当天往返的旅行; 一日游

day-trip·per /ˈ· ˌ· ·/ *n* [C] *BrE* someone who visits a place for pleasure but spends only one day there【英】当天往返的游客; 一日游的游客: *Yarmouth is crowded with day-trippers at this time of year.* 每年的这个时候雅茅斯都会挤满一日游的游客。

dazed /dezd; deɪzd/ *adj* **1** unable to think clearly, especially because of a shock, accident etc〔由于震惊、意外事故等而〕茫然的, 迷乱的, 恍惚的: *Dazed survivors staggered from the wreckage.* 吓呆了的幸存者踉跄着走出废墟。**2 in a daze** unable to think clearly 处于茫然状态: *I've been wandering around in a daze all day.* 我一整天都在迷迷糊糊地四处游荡。

daz·zle /ˋdæzḷ; ˈdæzəl/ *v* [T often passive 常用被动态] **1** if a very bright light dazzles you it stops you from seeing properly for a short time〔强光等〕使…目眩, 眼花缭乱: *a deer dazzled by the headlights* 被车灯灯光照得看不清东西的鹿 **2** to make someone feel strong admiration 使〔某人〕倾倒: *As children, we were dazzled by my uncle's good looks and charm.* 小时候我们都被叔叔的英俊外表和魅力所倾倒。—**dazzle** *n* [U] *BrE*【英】

daz·zling /ˋdæzḷɪŋ; ˈdæzəlɪŋ/ *adj* **1** a light that is dazzling makes you unable to see properly for a short time 使人目眩的, 令人眼花缭乱的 **2** very impressive and attractive 给人印象深刻的; 特别吸引人的: *a dazzling display of football skills* 让人眼花缭乱的足球技巧表演

DBE /ˌdi bi ˋi; ˌdiː biː ˈiː/ *n* Dame Commander of the (Order of the) British Empire; a title given in Britain to a woman as an honour because she has done something of national importance. A woman who has a DBE can use the title **Dame** instead of **Mrs, Miss**, or **Ms**. 大英帝国二等女爵士〔英国给为国家做出重大贡献的妇女授予的一种荣誉称号, 其名字前可冠以Dame, 而不用Mrs, Miss或Ms〕: *She was awarded a DBE in 1992.* 1992年, 她被封为大英帝国二等女爵士。

dbl the written abbreviation of 缩写= double

DC /ˌdi ˋsi; ˌdiː ˈsiː/ **1** direct current; electric current that always flows in one direction 直流电 —compare 比较 AC **2** the abbreviation of 缩写= District of Columbia, in the US〔美国的〕哥伦比亚特区: *Washington, DC* 哥伦比亚特区华盛顿

D

DD /ˌdi ˋdi; ˌdiː ˈdiː/ **1** the abbreviation of 缩写= DIRECT DEBIT **2** Doctor of Divinity; an advanced university degree in THEOLOGY (=religious studies) 神学博士

D-Day /ˋdi ˌde; ˈdiː deɪ/ *n* [singular] **1** 6th June 1944; the day the British, Americans, and other armies landed in France during the Second World War 第二次世界大战盟军在法国登陆的日子〔即1944年6月6日〕**2** *informal* a day on which an important action is planned to happen or begin【非正式】重大行动要开始的日子: *So Friday is D-Day, then?* 那么星期五是开始行动的日子啦?

DDS /ˌdi di ˋɛs; ˌdiː diː ˈes/ Doctor of Dental Surgery; a university degree in DENTISTRY. DDS is written after someone's name to show that they have this degree. 牙外科医学博士〔DDS写在某人的名字后面表示拥有该学位〕

DDT /ˌdi di ˋti; ˌdiː diː ˈtiː/ *n* [U] a chemical used to kill insects that harm crops 滴滴涕〔用来杀灭危害庄稼的害虫的一种化学制品〕

DE the abbreviation of 缩写= DELAWARE

de- /di; diː/ *prefix* **1** in some verbs and nouns, shows an opposite〔构成某些动词和名词, 表示"否定"、"与…相反"之意〕: *a depopulated area* (=which all or most of the population has left)〔由于大部分人口已经离开而〕人口减少的地区 | *deindustrialization* (=becoming less industrial) 非工业化 **2** in some verbs, means to remove something or remove things from something 除去, (使)脱离〔用于构成动词〕: *to debone the fish* (=remove its bones) 剔掉鱼刺 | *The king was dethroned.* (=removed from power) 国王被废黜了。**3** in some verbs, means to make something less; reduce 降低, 贬低〔用于构成动词〕: *to devalue the currency* 使货币贬值

DEA, the /ˌdi i ˋe; ˌdiː iː ˈeɪ/ the abbreviation of 缩写= DRUG ENFORCEMENT ADMINISTRATION

dea·con /ˋdikən; ˈdiːkən/ *n* [C] a religious official, in some Christian churches, who is just below the rank of a priest 执事; 会吏〔基督教会中比牧师低一级的神职人员〕

S1 W1

dead¹ /dɛd; ded/ *adj* [no comparative 无比较级]

① NO LONGER ALIVE OR EXISTING 死去的, 不复存在的
② HAVING NO POWER/NOT WORKING 没电的/不运作的
③ HAVING NO FEELING OR ENERGY 没有知觉的, 没有精力的
④ NOT INTERESTING, USEFUL, OR IMPORTANT 没有意思的, 无用的, 不重要的
⑤ SPOKEN PHRASES 口语短语
⑥ OTHER MEANINGS 其他意思

① NO LONGER ALIVE OR EXISTING 死去的, 不复存在的

1 no longer alive 死的, 逝世的: *Her mother had been dead for ten years.* 她妈妈已经去世10年了。| *dead leaves* 枯叶 | **dead body** (=the body of a person who has died) 死尸 | **dead as a doornail/stone dead** *informal* (=completely dead with no signs of life at all)【非正式】完全死了的 | **drop dead** (=die suddenly when no-one expects it) 猝死, 暴毙 *37 years old, no health problems, and he just dropped dead at work!* 他37岁, 没有健康问题, 而在工作的时候就那么忽然死了! —compare 比较 LIVE² (1)

2 the dead people who have died, especially people who have been killed 已死的人, 死者〔尤指被害的人〕: *There wasn't even time to bury the dead.* 甚至没有时间埋葬死去的人。

3 rise from the dead/come back from the dead according to Christian beliefs, to become alive again after dying〔根据基督教的信仰〕死后重生, 再生, 复活

② **HAVING NO POWER/NOT WORKING** 没电的/不运作的
4 dead battery/engine etc an engine etc that no longer works because it has no electricity 没电的电池/熄火的引擎等
5 ▶TELEPHONES ETC 电话等◀ a telephone line, radio etc that is dead is not working and makes no sound when you try to use it〔电话线路、收音机等〕停止运作的, 没有声音的: *All the lines out of town are dead.* 城外所有的电话线路都没有声音了。| **go dead** *Suddenly the radio went dead.* 收音机忽然一下子没有声音了。

③ **HAVING NO FEELING OR ENERGY** 没有知觉的, 没有精力的
6 arm/leg etc a part of your body that is dead has no feeling in it〔胳膊、腿等身体部位〕失去知觉的, 麻木的: **go dead** *When I got up my leg had gone totally dead.* 我起来的时候腿完全麻了。
7 ▶NO EMOTION 没有感情◀ showing no emotion or sympathy 没有感情[同情心]的: *Jennie's eyes were cold and dead.* 珍妮的眼神冷酷而麻木。| [+to] *dead to all feelings of compassion* 毫无同情心
8 ▶TIRED 疲劳的◀ *spoken* very tired【口】十分疲劳的: *I can't go out tonight. I'm absolutely dead!* 今晚我不能出去了, 我累死了!
9 dead to the world very deeply asleep or unconscious 熟睡的; 失去知觉的: *Better leave Craig – he's dead to the world.* 最好别打扰克雷格 —— 他睡得正熟。

④ **NOT INTERESTING, USEFUL, OR IMPORTANT** 没有意思的, 无用的, 不重要的
10 ▶BORING 乏味的◀ a town that is dead is boring because nothing interesting or exciting happens there, and there is nothing interesting to do 没趣的, 死气沉沉的: *This place is dead after nine o'clock.* 这个地方9点之后就变得死寂一片。
11 ▶IDEA/SUBJECT 想法/话题◀ **dead and buried** an argument, problem, plan etc that is dead and buried is not worth considering again〔论点、问题、计划等〕不值得再考虑的: *You're talking as if the issue of low pay is dead and buried.* 你说话的意思好像是工资低的问题不值得再提了。
12 a dead duck *informal* a plan, idea etc that is not worth considering because it is very likely to fail【非正式】注定失败的计划[想法]等
13 be a dead loss *informal* to be completely useless【非正式】完全没用: *That building firm's a dead loss.* 那家建筑公司完全垮了。
14 dead as a dodo no longer important or useful, and no longer having any influence 不再重要的, 已失效的, 不再有影响力的: *The extreme Right of this country is as dead as a dodo.* 这个国家的极右党派已经完全失去了影响力。

⑤ **SPOKEN PHRASES** 口语短语
15 drop dead *spoken* used to rudely and angrily tell someone to go away and leave you alone【口】滚开〔用于语气粗鲁、无礼地叫某人离开, 不许来打扰你〕
16 over my dead body *spoken* used to say that you are determined not to allow something to happen【口】除非我死了〔表示坚决不让某事发生〕: *You'll marry him over my dead body!* 我死也不让你和他结婚!
17 I wouldn't be seen/caught dead *spoken* used to say that you would never wear particular clothes, go to particular places, or do particular things, because you would feel embarrassed【口】我决不; 我死也不〔坚决不穿某种衣服, 不去某些地方或不做某事〕: [+in/on/with etc] *I wouldn't be seen dead in a dress like that!* 我死也不穿那样的衣服!
18 be in dead trouble *BrE spoken* to be in serious trouble【英口】陷入大麻烦: *You'll be in dead trouble if your Dad finds out.* 你爸爸要是发现了, 你的麻烦就大了。
19 dead from the neck up *BrE spoken* very stupid【英口】没头脑的, 笨极了的

⑥ **OTHER MEANINGS** 其他意思
20 ▶LANGUAGE 语言◀ a dead language is no longer used by ordinary people〔某种语言〕不再被使用的: *What's the point of learning a dead language like Latin?* 学习像拉丁语那样已经死亡的语言有什么意义呢? —opposite 反义词 LIVING¹ (6)
21 the dead centre the exact centre 正中心
22 ▶GLASS/BOTTLE 玻璃杯/瓶子◀ *BrE informal* a glass etc that is dead is no longer being used【英, 非正式】〔表示杯子等〕不再被使用的
23 dead silence complete silence 死一般的沉寂, 死寂: *Everyone stood and waited in dead silence.* 每个人都在死一般的沉寂中站着等待。
24 ▶PLANET 行星◀ a dead PLANET (1) has no life on it〔某个行星〕没有生命存在的
25 ▶IN SPORT 在体育运动中◀ when the ball is dead in some games it is no longer on the playing area〔体育比赛中的球〕界外的
26 a dead cert *BrE spoken* something that is definitely going to happen or is definitely going to win a race【英口】必然发生的事; 赢定[稳赢]的比赛
27 in a dead faint completely unconscious 完全失去知觉的
28 dead ringer someone who looks exactly like someone else 外貌酷似的人: *Dave's a dead ringer for Paul McCartney.* 戴夫和保罗·麦卡特尼长得一模一样。
29 dead weight something that is very heavy and difficult to carry〔很难搬动的〕重物: *The boy was unconscious, a dead weight.* 这个男孩失去了知觉, 死沉死沉的。
30 dead wood the people or things within an organization that are useless or no longer needed〔一个组织内〕无用的人[物]
31 more dead than alive in a very weak physical condition 身体特别虚弱的: *They were more dead than alive when they were airlifted off the ice.* 他们被空运离开冰面的时候, 身体极度虚弱。—**deadness** *n* [U]

S3 **dead²** *adv* **1** *BrE informal* completely【英, 非正式】完全地: *Ben's dead against coming with us.* 本坚决反对和我们一起去。**2** *BrE spoken* very【英口】非常, 十分: *He was dead good-looking.* 他长得极为英俊。**3** [+adj/adv] *informal* directly or exactly【非正式】直接地, 正对着地: **dead ahead/in front/at etc** *I stared dead ahead at the doorway.* 我直盯着前面的门口看。| **dead on time** *informal* (=exactly at a particular time or the arranged time)【非正式】十分准时地 *The bus arrived dead on time.* 公共汽车准时到达。**4 dead beat** *informal* very tired【非正式】筋疲力尽的: *I can't go any further – I'm dead beat.* 我再也走不动了 —— 我都累死了。

dead³ *n* **the dead of night/winter** the middle of the night or the middle of the winter 在夜深人静的时候/在隆冬

dead beat /ˈ· ,·◂/ *n* [C] *AmE informal*【美, 非正式】**1** someone who is lazy and who has no plans in life 懒鬼; 庸庸碌碌的人 **2** someone who avoids paying their debts 赖账的人

dead bolt /ˈ· ·/ *n* [C] *AmE* a strong lock often used on doors【美】〔常用于门上的〕插锁, 嵌锁; MORTICE LOCK *BrE*【英】

dead·en /ˈdɛdn; ˈdedn/ *v* [T] to make a feeling or sound less strong 减轻〔某种感觉〕; 降低〔声响〕: *medicine to deaden the pain* 镇痛药

dead end /,· ˈ·◂/ *n* [C] **1** a street with no way out at one end 死巷, 死胡同 **2** a situation from which no more progress is possible 僵局: **come to/reach a dead end** *The negotiations have reached a dead end.* 谈判陷入了僵局。**3 dead-end job** a job with low wages and no chance of progress 工资低且无晋升机会的工作

dead·head¹ /ˈdɛd,hɛd; ˈdedhed/ *v* **1** [T] *BrE* to remove the dead flowers from a plant【英】摘去〔植物〕的枯花 **2** [I] *AmE* to drive a train, bus, or TRUCK¹ (1) with no passengers or goods【美】放空车〔火车、公共汽车或卡车在没有乘客或货物的情况下驾驶〕

deadhead² *n* [C] *AmE* a vehicle that has no passengers or goods【美】不载乘客[货物]的空车

dead heat /,· ˈ·/ *n* [C] the result of a race in which two or more competitors finish at exactly the same time 两个[多个]竞赛者同时到达终点的比赛成绩

dead let·ter /,· ˈ··/ *n* [C] **1** a law, idea that still exists but that people no longer obey, or are not interested in 形同虚设的法规, 空文; 过时的想法: *An arts education is a dead letter as far as many students are concerned.* 就许多学生而言, 艺术教育已形同虚设。**2** a letter that cannot be delivered or returned 无法投递[退回]的信, 死信

dead·line /ˈdɛd,laɪn; ˈdedlaɪn/ *n* [C] a date or time by which you have to do or complete something 截止时间; 最后期限: *The deadline is May 27th.* 截止时间是5月27日。| **work to a deadline** (=plan your work so that it can be finished by the deadline) 计划如期完成 | **meet a deadline** (=finish by the deadline) 如期完成 *The deadlines are very short and difficult to meet.* 时间非常短, 很难如期完成任务。| **tight deadline** (=a deadline that is difficult) 时间紧促〔难以如期完成任务的期限〕

dead·lock /ˈdɛd,lɑk; ˈdedlɒk/ *n* [singular,U] a situation in which a disagreement cannot be settled; STALEMATE (1) 僵局: *The talks have reached a complete deadlock.* 商谈完全陷入僵局。| **break the deadlock** (=end the deadlock) 打破僵局 —**deadlock** *v* [I,T] —**deadlocked** *adj*

dead·ly¹ /ˈdɛdlɪ; ˈdedli/ *adj*
1 ▶**VERY DANGEROUS** 非常危险的◀ likely to cause death 致命的: *a deadly poison* 致命的毒药
2 **deadly enemy** someone who will always be your enemy and will try to harm you as much as possible 不共戴天的敌人, 死敌: *The inhabitants soon came to regard the white settlers as their deadly enemy.* 居民们不久就把白人定居者视为死敌。
3 ▶**COMPLETE** 完全的◀ complete or total 完完全全的: *We sat in deadly silence.* 我们在死一般的寂静中坐着。
4 ▶**VERY EFFECTIVE** 非常有效的◀ causing harm in a very effective way 极有效的; 极精确的: *She hit the target with deadly accuracy.* 她准确无误地射中目标。
5 ▶**LIKE DEATH** 死一样的◀ [only before noun 仅用于名词前] like death in appearance 如死一样的: *His face had a deadly paleness.* 他的脸死一般的苍白。
6 ▶**BORING** 无聊的◀ *spoken* not at all interesting or exciting 【口】没趣的, 乏味的: *"How was the party?" "Pretty deadly."* "派对开得怎么样?" "没劲透了。"

deadly² *adv* **deadly serious/dull/boring etc** very serious, dull etc 非常严肃/沉闷/乏味等: *I'm deadly serious, this isn't a game!* 我是非常认真的, 这不是游戏!

deadly night·shade /,‥ ˈ‥/ *n* [C,U] a poisonous European plant; BELLADONNA 颠茄〔一种有毒的欧洲植物〕

dead-man's float /,‥ ˈ./ *n* [singular] *AmE* a way of floating in water with your body and face turned downwards 【美】〔身体和脸部朝下的〕俯卧漂浮姿势

dead·pan /ˈdɛd,pæn; ˈdedpæn/ *adj* sounding and looking completely serious when you are not really 故作严肃的: *telling a joke in a deadpan voice* 不动声色地讲笑话; 冷面孔地讲笑话 —**deadpan** *adv*

dead reck·on·ing /,. ˈ‥./ *n* [U] the practice of calculating the position of a ship or aircraft without using the sun, moon, or stars 〔不依靠太阳、月亮或星星测定船只或飞机位置的〕航位推测法

Dead Sea, the /,. ˈ./ a large lake in the Middle East. It is over 25% salt, so people can float in it very easily. 死海〔位于中东地区的大湖, 含盐量超过25%, 因此人进入水中便会浮起〕

Dead Sea Scrolls /,. . ˈ./ a collection of ancient Jewish SCROLLS (=rolls of paper containing writing) from around the time of Christ. They contain the oldest copies of parts of the Old Testament of the Bible, and were found near the Dead Sea between 1947 and 1956.《死海古卷》〔基督时代犹太教古经卷的汇编。1947至1956年间发现于死海附近, 包括《圣经·旧约》最早版本的部分内容〕

Dead·wood /ˈdɛd,wʊd; ˈdedwʊd/ a city in the Black Hills of South Dakota. It is well known for its part in the history of the American Old West. Wild Bill Hickok, a skilled gunfighter, was shot here in 1876. Both he and Calamity Jane, a woman famous for her skill in shooting, are buried in Deadwood. 死木镇〔位于南达科他州黑岗的一座城市, 以其在美国旧西部历史上所起的作用闻名。1876年神枪手野牛比尔·希科克在此遇刺身亡。他和女神枪手"患难珍妮"都安葬在死木镇〕

W3 **deaf** /dɛf; def/ *adj* 1 physically unable to hear anything or unable to hear well 耳聋的, 失聪的: *He's quite deaf and needs a hearing aid.* 他有些耳聋, 需要用助听器。| **stone deaf/deaf as a post** *informal* (=completely deaf) 【非正式】完全耳聋的 —see also 另见 TONE-DEAF 2 **the deaf** people who are deaf 耳聋的人: *a school for the deaf* 聋人学校 3 **deaf to** *literary* unwilling to hear or listen to something 【文】不愿听, 不肯听取: *She was deaf to his pleas.* 她对他的恳求充耳不闻。4 **turn a deaf ear** be unwilling to listen to what someone is saying or asking 对…充耳不闻[置若罔闻]: *The factory owners turned a deaf ear to the demands of the workers.* 工厂主对工人们提出的要求充耳不闻。5 **fall on deaf ears** if advice or a warning falls on deaf ears, everyone ignores it 〔建议、警告等〕被别人忽视; 不受注意 —**deafness** *n* [U]

deaf-aid /ˈ. ./ *n* [C] *BrE informal* a small electric machine, worn near your ear, that helps you to hear better; HEARING AID 【英, 非正式】助听器

deaf-and-dumb /,. . ˈ./ *adj* unable to hear or speak 聋哑的, 又聋又哑的 —**the deaf and dumb** *n* [plural]

deaf·en /ˈdɛfən; ˈdefən/ *v* [T usually passive 一般用被动态] 1 if a noise deafens you, it is so loud that you cannot hear anything else 使〔某人〕感到震耳欲聋: *deafened by the roar of the engine* 发动机的轰鸣声震耳欲聋 2 to make someone unable to hear 使〔某人〕耳聋

deaf·en·ing /ˈdɛfənɪŋ; ˈdefənɪŋ/ *adj* noise or music that is deafening is very loud 〔噪声或音乐〕震耳欲聋的

deaf-mute /,. ˈ./ *n* [C] someone who is unable to hear or speak 聋哑人

S1 W1 **deal¹** /dil; di:l/ *v past tense and past participle* **dealt** /dɛlt; delt/ 1 also 又作 **deal out** [I,T] to give playing cards to each of the players in a game 〔纸牌游戏中的〕发(牌): **deal sth (out) to sb** *Deal out three cards to each player.* 给每个玩牌的人发三张牌。2 [I] *informal* to buy and sell illegal drugs 【非正式】买卖非法毒品: *Many users end up dealing to support their habit.* 许多吸毒的人结果是做起非法毒品买卖来维持他们吸毒。3 **deal a blow** *literary* 【文】a) to cause harm to someone or something 给〔某人或某物〕造成损失, 伤害; 打击: **deal a crippling/decisive etc blow** (=cause very serious harm) 给予…致命的打击[伤害] *The recession dealt many small businesses a fatal blow.* 经济衰退给予许多小型企业致命的打击。b) to hit someone 打〔某人〕

deal in sth *phr v* [T] 1 to buy and sell a particular type of product 经营, 买卖〔某种产品〕: *dealing in 19th century watercolours* 从事19世纪水彩画的买卖 —see also 另见 DEALER (1) 2 to have a particular attitude to your work 〔对工作〕持有〔某种态度〕: *As a scientist, I do not deal in speculation.* 作为科学家, 我不相信猜测。

deal out sth *phr v* [T] 1 to give playing cards to each of the players in a game 发〔牌〕 2 to decide what kind of punishment someone will get 决定给予〔某人某种处罚〕

deal with sb/sth *phr v* [T] 1 to take the correct action for a piece of work, type of work etc 处理〔某项工作等〕: *Who's dealing with the Glaxo account?* 是谁在负责与葛兰素公司的业务往来? 2 to succeed in solving a problem 解决〔问题〕: *Don't worry, Mr Symes, it's already been dealt with.* 别担心, 赛姆斯先生, 问题已经解决了。3 to succeed in controlling an emotional problem so that it does not affect your life 控制〔感情〕: *It's OK, I'm dealing with it so far.* 还可以, 到现在我还能应付得了它。4 to do business with someone or have a business connection with someone 和〔某人〕做生意: *I've dealt with them for a long time.* 我和他们已经打了很长时间的交道了。5 if a book, speech, work of art etc deals with a particular subject, it is about that subject 涉及, 论及, 探讨〔某个主题〕: *These ideas are dealt with more fully in Chapter Four.* 这些观点在第四章中有较全面的阐述。

deal² *n*
1 **a great deal** also 又作 **a good deal** a large quantity of something 很多的, 大量的: [+of] *A great deal of their work is unpaid.* 他们很多工作都是没有报酬的。| **a great deal more/a great deal longer etc** (=a lot more, longer etc) 多许多/长许多等 *He knew a good deal more than I did.* 他懂的比我多很多。
2 ▶**AGREEMENT** 协议, 买卖, 交易◀ [C] an agreement or arrangement, especially in business or politics, that helps both sides involved 〔尤指生意或政治上双方的〕协议: *The band has negotiated a new deal with their record company.* 乐队和唱片公司达成了一项新的协议。| **get a good deal** (=buy something at a good price) 〔买东西〕价格便宜 *You can get some really good deals from travel agents right now.* 现在找旅行社(代办旅游)价格会非常合算。| **strike/make/cut/do a deal** (=produce or make an agreement) 达成一项协议 *The two teams did a deal and Robson was traded.* 两队达成了罗布森转队的协议。
3 **it's a deal** *spoken* used to say that you agree to do something 【口】成交〔同意做某事〕: *"OK, $500, but that's my last offer." "OK, it's a deal."* "好, 500美元, 这是我的底价。" "好, 成交。"
4 ▶**TREATMENT** 待遇◀ [C usually singular 一般用单数] treatment of a particular type that is given or received 待遇: **a better/fairer deal** *a better deal for nurses* 给护士更好的待遇 | **a new deal** (=a new and fairer system of social or political treatment) 新政(策) *The prime minister promised a new deal for farmers.* 首相许诺为农民制定新的政策。| **a rough/raw deal** (=unfair treatment) 不公平的待遇 *Women tend to get a raw deal from employers.* 妇女往往受到雇主的不公平对待。
5 ▶**GAME** 游戏◀ [singular] the process of giving out cards to players in a card game 〔纸牌游戏中的〕发牌: *It's your deal, Alison.* 该你发牌了, 艾利森。—see also 另见 DEALER (3)
6 ▶**WOOD** 木材, 木头◀ [U] *BrE* FIR or PINE¹ (2) wood used for making things 【英】冷杉木; 松木: *a deal table* 冷杉[松]木桌子
7 **a deal of** *old-fashioned* a large quantity of something 【过时】大量的 —see also 另见 **big deal** (BIG (7))

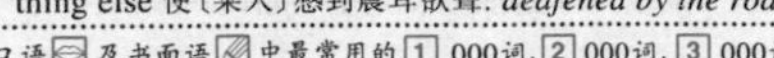

USAGE NOTE 用法说明: DEAL
GRAMMAR 语法
A great/good deal of... is usually only used with uncountable nouns. a great/good deal of 通常只用来修饰不可数名词: *a great deal of time/money/difficulty/pressure/interest* 大量时间/大量金钱/许多困难/巨大压力/很多兴趣。Compare 比较以下两个句子: *There's been a good deal of change./There have been a good many changes.* 出现了很多变化。

deal·er /ˋdilɚ; ˈdiːlə/ *n* [C] **1** someone who buys and sells a particular product, especially an expensive one〔尤指买卖贵重商品的〕商人: *a car dealer* 汽车经销商 **2** someone who sells illegal drugs 毒品贩子 **3** someone who gives out playing cards in a game〔纸牌游戏的〕发牌人 —see also 另见 DOUBLE-DEALER

deal·er·ship /ˋdilɚʃɪp; ˈdiːləʃɪp/ *n* [C] a business that sells a particular company's product, especially cars〔尤指汽车的〕特许经销商[店]: *Nissan dealerships* 日产汽车经销商[店]

D

deal·ing /ˋdilɪŋ; ˈdiːlɪŋ/ *n* **1 dealings** [plural] the business activities or relationships that you have been involved in 商业活动, 商业往来: *The secret dealings of his department were made public.* 他所在部门进行的秘密交易被曝了光。| **have dealings with** (=have a business relationship with someone) 和…有生意上的交往 *We've had dealings with ITBF for the past few years.* 我们在过去的几年中一直和ITBF公司有业务往来。**2 plain dealing/honest dealing etc** a particular way of doing business with people 朴实/诚实等的经营方式

dealt /dɛlt; delt/ *v* the past tense and past participle of DEAL[1]

dean /din; diːn/ *n* [C] **1** a priest of high rank, especially in the Anglican church, who is in charge of several priests or churches〔尤指英国国教中的〕高职牧师; 教长; 主任牧师 **2** someone in a university who is in charge of an area of study, or in charge of students and their behaviour〔大学的〕学院院长; 系主任; 学监

Dean, Dizzy (1911-74) a US BASEBALL player who was a famous PITCHER for the St Louis Cardinals team in the 1930s, helping them win the World Series in 1934. He was famous for achieving more STRIKEOUTS than any other pitcher. 迪安〔(1911-1974), 美国棒球运动员, 20世纪30年代圣路易斯红雀队的著名投手, 为该队夺得1934年美国职业棒球锦标赛冠军立下汗马功劳。他以使击球手三击未中的出局数比其他投手多而出名〕

Dean, James (1931-55) a US film actor who became extremely famous, and then died in a car crash at the age of 24. Many people think of him as a typical example of a young REBEL (=someone who refuses to follow social rules or behave in the way that other people want them to). His films include *East of Eden* (1955) and *Rebel Without a Cause* (1955). 迪安〔(1931-1955), 美国著名电影演员, 24岁时死于一场车祸。不少人视其为叛逆的年轻人的典型, 他主演的影片有《伊甸园东方》(1955) 和《无因的反叛》(1955)〕

dean·e·ry /ˋdinərɪ; ˈdiːnəri/ *n* [C,U] the area controlled by a dean or the place where a dean lives 高职牧师[主任牧师]所管辖的教区

dean's list /ˈ· ·/ *n* [C] *AmE* a list of the best students at a university【美】〔大学里〕优秀学生名单

1 **dear**[1] /dɪr; dɪə/ *interjection* The phrases 'oh dear', 'dear oh dear', 'dear dear', and 'dear me' are all used to show that you are surprised, upset, or annoyed because you have done something wrong, because something bad has happened etc. 'Oh dear' is much more common than the others. 'Dear oh dear' and 'dear dear' are used to emphasize how surprised, upset, or annoyed you are. 'Dear me' is a little old-fashioned. 天哪, 天啊〔oh dear, dear oh dear, dear dear, dear me 都用来表示惊讶、不安或恼怒的情绪, 因为自己做错事或者因为糟糕的事情已经发生等等。oh dear 比其他词组较为常见。dear oh dear 和 dear dear 用来强调一个人感到太惊讶、太不安或者太生气了。dear me 有点儿过时〕: *Oh dear I've broken the lamp.* 天啊, 我把灯打破了。| *"He's been taken into hospital." "Oh dear!"* "他被送进了医院。""我的天哪!" | *Dear oh dear, that's terrible news.* 天哪, 天哪, 那真是个可怕的消息。| *Dear, dear, I am sorry. Hope I didn't hurt you.* 天哪, 天哪, 太抱歉了, 希望没弄痛你。| *Dear me! I forgot to call Kathy and now it's too late.* 糟糕! 我忘了给凯西打电话, 现在太晚了。

2 **dear**[2] *n* [C] **1** used when speaking to someone you love 亲爱的〔用于和自己爱的人说话〕: *How did the interview go, dear?* 面试进行得怎么样, 亲爱的? **2** *spoken* a friendly way of speaking to someone you do not know, for example, to a customer in a shop【口】〔用于和不认识的人讲话, 表示友好〕: *Can I help you, dear?* 请问, 我能为您做些什么吗? **3** *spoken especially BrE* someone who is very kind and helpful【口, 尤英】好人, 可爱的人: *Be a dear and make me some coffee.* 做个好人, 给我弄点咖啡来。**4 old dear** *BrE* a fairly rude expression meaning an old woman【英】老太婆〔相当不礼貌的用法〕

Frequencies of the word **dear** in spoken and written English
单词dear在英语口语和书面语中的使用频率

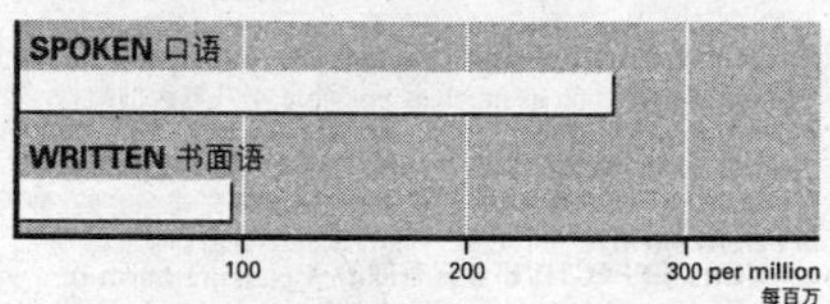

Based on the British National Corpus and the Longman Lancaster Corpus
据英国国家语料库和朗文兰开斯特语料库

This graph shows that the word **dear** is much more common in spoken English than in written English. This is because it has some special uses in spoken English and is used in some common spoken phrases. 本图表显示, 单词 dear 在英语口语中的使用频率远远高于书面语, 因为它在英语口语中有一些特殊的用法, 而且口语中一些常用短语是由 dear 构成的。

dear[3] *adj* **1 Dear** used before someone's name or title when you begin a letter〔用在信函的开头, 放在上款的人名、称谓或头衔前面〕: *Dear Madam* 尊敬的女士 | *Dear Meg* 亲爱的梅格 **2** *BrE* expensive【英】贵的, 昂贵的: *I didn't buy it because it was too dear.* 我没买它, 因为价格太贵。**3** *formal* a dear friend or relative is very important to you and you love them a lot【正式】珍贵的, 钟爱的: *Mark had become a dear friend.* 马克已成为一个亲密的朋友。| **be dear to sb** *His sister was very dear to him.* 他的妹妹是他非常钟爱的。**4 for dear life** if you run, fight, climb etc for dear life, you do it as fast or as well as you can because you are afraid 拼命地〔譬如拼命地跑、打、爬等, 用来表示因为恐惧而尽可能最快地或最好地做某事〕 2 2

dear[4] *adv* **cost sb dear** to cause a lot of trouble and suffering for someone 使某人损失惨重; 给某人带来许多麻烦和痛苦: *Carolyn's marriage to Pete cost her dear.* 与彼得的婚姻使卡罗琳痛苦不堪。

Dear Ab·by /ˌdɪr ˋæbɪ; ˌdɪər ˈæbi/ *trademark* a US newspaper COLUMN by Abigail Van Buren, which prints letters from readers asking for advice and her answers to these letters【商标】阿比信箱〔美国一家报纸的一个专栏, 由阿比盖尔·范布伦主持, 刊登读者的求助信和她的回信〕

dear·est /ˋdɪrəst; ˈdɪərɪ̌st/ *n* [C] used when speaking to someone you love〔用以称呼所爱的人〕: *Well, dearest, I was a little worried.* 我最亲爱的, 我有些担心。

dear·ie /ˋdɪrɪ; ˈdɪəri/ *n* [C] another spelling of DEARY deary 的另一种拼法

dear John let·ter /ˌ· ˈ· ˌ· ·/ *n* [C] a letter to a man from his wife or GIRLFRIEND, saying that she no longer loves him〔妻子或女朋友写给男子的〕绝交信

dear·ly /ˋdɪrlɪ; ˈdɪəli/ *adv* **1** if you love someone dearly, want something dearly etc, you do so with strong emotions 由衷地, 深情地: *James loved his sister dearly.* 詹姆斯非常疼爱他的妹妹。**2 cost sb dearly** to cause a lot of trouble or suffering 给某人带来很多麻烦[痛苦]: *Vandalism costs schools dearly.* 恣意破坏公物的行为使学校损失惨重。**3 pay dearly** to suffer a lot for something that you have done 付出沉重的代价: *They've paid dearly for not explaining beforehand.* 他们因为没有事先解释清楚而付出了沉重的代价。**4 dearly beloved** used by a priest or minister at the beginning of a Christian marriage or funeral 亲爱的兄弟姐妹〔牧师在主持基督徒的婚礼或葬礼时用的开场语〕

dearth /dɝθ; dɜːθ/ *n* [singular] *formal* a lack of something【正式】缺乏: [+of] *problems owing to the dearth of experienced personnel* 缺少富有经验的职员而引发的问题

dear·y, dearie /ˋdɪrɪ; ˈdɪəri/ *n* [C] *old-fashioned*【过时】**1** used as a way of speaking to someone you love 亲爱的〔用于称呼所爱的人〕**2 dearie me** *old-fashioned* used when you are surprised or sad about something【过时】呵, 哎呀〔用于表示惊讶或不快之情〕

death /dɛθ; deθ/ *n*
1 ►THE END OF SB'S LIFE 某人生命的结束◄ [U] the end of the life of a person or animal〔人或动物的〕死, 死亡: [+of] *The death of his mother was a great shock to him.* 他妈妈的死给他很大打击。| *shortly after Lenin's death in 1924* 列宁1924年去世后不久 | *the risk of death or serious injury at work* 工作中死

亡或受重伤的危险 | **bleed/burn/starve etc to death**(=die in a particular way) 流血而死/烧死/饿死等 *He choked to death on a fishbone.* 他被鱼刺卡住窒息而死。| **put sb to death**(=kill someone, especially after an official decision) 处死某人 *Caesar ordered the prisoners to be put to death.* 凯撒命令处死犯人。| **meet your death** *literary* (=die)【文】逝世 —see also 另见 ACCIDENTAL DEATH

2 ►**EXAMPLE OF SB DYING** 某人死亡的事例◄[C] an example of someone dying 死亡的事例: *a campaign to reduce the number of deaths on Britain's roads* 降低英国交通事故死亡人数的宣传运动 | [**+from**] *deaths from lung cancer* 肺癌导致的死亡

3 **die a horrible/terrible etc death** to die in a terrible etc way 死得很惨等: *The animals in the traps can die a slow and agonizing death.* 落入陷阱的动物可能会死得很慢、很痛苦。

4 ►**IN ART** 在艺术中◄ **Death** [singular] a creature that looks like a SKELETON (1a), used in paintings, stories etc as a sign of death and destruction 死神〔被画成或被描述成一个骷髅, 作为死亡和毁灭的象征〕

5 **scared/bored to death** *informal* extremely frightened or bored【非正式】吓得/厌烦得要死

6 **sick to death of** very unhappy with something because it has been annoying you for a long time 对…厌烦, 厌倦, 厌恶: *I am sick to death of your complaining!* 你老是抱怨, 我都烦透了!

7 **you'll catch your death (of cold)** *spoken* used as a warning to someone when you think they are likely to become ill because it is wet or cold【口】你会得重伤风; 你会得致命的感冒〔用于警告某人由于天气潮湿或寒冷, 有可能得病〕: *Don't go out without a coat! You'll catch your death of cold!* 穿上大衣再出去! 否则你会得重感冒的!

8 **at death's door** be very ill and likely to die 病入膏肓; 危在旦夕; 行将就木

9 **like death warmed up/warmed over** *informal* if someone looks or feels like death warmed up, they look or feel very ill or tired【非正式】病得不轻; 累得要命

10 ►**THE END** 终止◄[singular] the permanent end of an idea, custom etc〔观点、习俗等的〕终结: *an article lamenting the death of classical music* 一篇哀叹古典音乐衰亡的文章

11 **you'll/he'll be the death of me!** *spoken* used, especially humorously, when someone makes you very worried and anxious【口】你/他会让我担心死!〔尤作幽默用法, 表示某人带来极大的忧虑〕: *That boy is going to be the death of me!* 那个男孩早晚会让我担心死!

12 **fight to the death a)** to fight until one person is killed 力拼到底, 战斗到死; 拼个你死我活 **b)** to fight very hard to achieve something even if it means that you suffer〔为了达到某个目标而〕拼命奋斗

13 **death blow** an action or event that makes something fail or end 致命的打击: *The new evidence dealt a death blow to the prosecution case.* 新的证据给予这件公诉案件致命的打击。—see also 另见 BLACK DEATH, **kiss of death** (KISS² (2)), **a matter of life and death** (LIFE (11))

CULTURAL NOTE 文化注释

Many people in the US and the UK feel uncomfortable talking about death, and when someone has died, people sometimes say that they have 'passed away' or 'passed on' to avoid mentioning death directly. People also say that someone is 'gone' or 'no longer with us' to mean that they have died. Humorous phrases meaning 'to die' include: 'kick the bucket', 'croak' (*especially AmE*), and 'pop your clogs' (*BrE*), but it can be considered very offensive in certain situations to use these expressions. When someone dies, people send cards and letters to their family, and flowers for the grave, or give money to a CHARITY in memory of the person who has died. 英美两国有很多人在谈论死亡时会感到不自在。当有人去世时, 人们有时会说死人"去世了"(pass away)或"故去了"(pass on), 以避免直接谈论死亡, 也说某人"去了"(gone)或"离开我们了"(no longer with us)来指死亡。表示"死了"的幽默说法有kick the bucket(翘辫子)、croak(【尤美】咽气)、pop your clogs(一命呜呼)等, 但这些说法在某些场合使用极具冒犯性。人们送吊唁卡或吊唁信给死者家人, 在墓前献花, 或向慈善机构捐款以纪念死者。— see Cultural Note at FUNERAL 见 FUNERAL 文化注释

death·bed /ˈdɛθ,bɛd; ˈdeθbed/ *n* **1 on your deathbed** just before you die 临终前 **2 deathbed confession/conversion/reconciliation** something that you admit or do just before you die 临终前的忏悔/信仰改变/和解: *a deathbed conversion to Catholicism* 临终前皈依天主教 **3 be on your deathbed a)** to be close to death 临终, 生命垂危 **b)** *humorous* to be feeling very ill【幽默】病入膏肓

death camp /ˈ· ·/ *n* [C] a place where large numbers of prisoners are killed or die, usually in a war〔一般指战争中〕死亡集中营

death cer·tif·i·cate /ˈ· ·,···/ *n* [C] a legal document, signed by a doctor, that states the time and cause of someone's death 死亡证明书

death du·ty /ˈ· ,··/ *n* [U] *BrE law* tax on the money or property that you give to someone else after you die; INHERITANCE TAX【英, 法律】遗产税, 继承税

Death in Ven·ice /,· · ˈ· ·/ (1912) a NOVEL by Thomas Mann, which was made into a film in 1971, about a successful writer in Venice who falls in love with a beautiful Polish boy and therefore does not want to leave the city, even though there is CHOLERA there. He stays, and finally dies from the disease.《威尼斯之死》〔(1912), 托马斯·曼创作的一部小说, 1971年被改编成电影, 讲述一位成功的作家在威尼斯爱上一位英俊波兰男孩的故事。当时, 威尼斯霍乱流行, 但作家却不愿离开。最后, 他染上了霍乱, 离开了人世〕

death knell /ˈ· ·/ *n* [singular] **sound the death knell** to be a sign that something will soon stop existing or stop being used 敲响丧钟〔某事即将终结或停止使用的信号〕: *Plans to build a bridge across the river sounded the death knell for the ferry.* 在这条河上建桥的计划敲响了渡船的丧钟。

death·less /ˈdɛθləs; ˈdeθləs/ *adj* **deathless prose/verse/lines etc** *humorous* writing that is very bad or boring【幽默】不朽[永恒]的散文/诗篇/诗行等〔指非常差劲或乏味的作品〕

death·ly /ˈdɛθlɪ; ˈdeθli/ *adj* reminding you of death or of a dead body 死一般的: *Rachel felt deathly cold.* 雷切尔感到死一般的冰冷。| **a deathly hush** (=complete silence) 一片死寂 *A deathly hush fell over the room when the manager walked in.* 经理进屋的时候, 屋里一片死寂。—**deathly** *adv*

death mask /ˈ· ·/ *n* [C] a model of a dead person's face, made by pressing a soft substance over their face and letting it become hard 死人面具〔在死人的面部压上一种柔软的物质, 让它变硬而制成的模型〕

Death of a Sales·man /,· · · ˈ· ·/ (1949) a play by Arthur Miller about a man called Willy Loman, who kills himself because he has lost his job and feels that he has failed《推销员之死》〔(1949), 阿瑟·米勒创作的一部剧作, 讲述一名叫威利·洛曼的男子因为失业而绝望自杀的故事〕

death pen·al·ty /ˈ· ,···/ *n* [singular] punishment by killing, used in some countries for serious crimes 死刑

death rate /ˈ· ·/ *n* [C] the number of deaths for every 100 or every 1,000 people in a particular year and in a particular place 死亡率 —compare 比较 BIRTHRATE

death rat·tle /ˈ· ,··/ *n* [C] a strange noise sometimes heard from the throat or chest of someone who is dying 临终时的喉鸣〔临死的人喉头或胸中有时发出的奇怪的声响〕

death row /,dɛθ ˈro; ,deθ ˈrəʊ/ *n* [U] the part of a prison where prisoners are kept while waiting to be punished by being killed〔监狱的〕死囚区: **on death row** *a murderer on death row* 等待处决的谋杀犯

death sen·tence /ˈ· ,··/ *n* [C] the punishment of death given by a judge 死刑判决: *Gilmore received a death sentence.* 吉尔摩被判处死刑。

death's head /ˈ· ·/ *n* [C] a human SKULL used as a sign of death〔象征死亡的〕骷髅头

death squad /ˈ· ·/ *n* [C] a group of people who kill their political opponents, often because they have been ordered to by a political party〔常指受命于某一政党去谋杀政治对手的〕死亡小分队

death throes /ˈ· ·/ *n* [plural] **1** the final stages before something fails or ends〔某事失败或终结前的〕最后阶段: *The coalition seems to be in its death throes.* 这个联盟似乎到了解体的最后阶段。**2** sudden violent movements sometimes made by someone who is dying 临终前的痛苦挣扎

death toll /ˈ· ·/ *n* [C] the total number of people who die in a particular accident, war etc〔在意外事故或战争中的〕死亡总数, 死亡人数: *As the civil unrest continued, the death toll rose.* 随着内乱的持续, 死亡人数在上升。

death trap /ˈ· ·/ *n* [C] *informal* a vehicle or building that is in dangerously bad condition【非正式】死亡陷阱〔指状况十分危险的车辆或建筑物〕: *Some of those secondhand cars are real death traps.* 那些二手车中有一部分实在是死亡陷阱〔安全隐患特别大〕。

Death Val·ley /ˌ· ˈ· ·/ an area of desert in the US states of Nevada and California. It is one of the hottest places in the world, and many people died trying to cross it in the 19th century. 死谷〔美国内华达州和加利福尼亚州的沙漠地区，是世界上最炎热的地方之一。19世纪，许多人因试图穿越死谷而在中途丧生〕

death war·rant /ˈ· ˌ· ·/ *n* [C] **1** an official document stating that someone is to be killed as a punishment for their crimes 死刑执行令 **2 sign your own death warrant** to do something that seems likely to cause you very serious trouble 自讨苦吃

death wish /ˈ· ·/ *n* [singular] a desire to die 死亡愿望: *He's going out with Debbie; What does he have, a death wish?* 他正在和黛比约会；他难道想找死吗？

deb /dɛb; deb/ *n* [C] *informal* a DEBUTANTE【非正式】初次参加社交的上流社会年轻女子

de·ba·cle, débâcle /deˈbɑkl; deɪˈbɑːkəl/ *n* [C] an event or situation that is a complete failure because plans have failed〔由于计划无法实现而导致的〕惨败

de·bar /dɪˈbɑr; dɪˈbɑː/ *v* **debarred, debarring** [T] to officially prevent someone from doing something〔正式地〕阻止，禁止: [+from] *He was debarred from the golf club for stealing club funds.* 由于盗用俱乐部资金，他被赶出了高尔夫俱乐部。—compare 比较 DISBAR

de·base /dɪˈbes; dɪˈbeɪs/ *v* [T] **1** *informal* to reduce the quality or value of something【非正式】降低〔某物的品质或价值〕: *a once rational society debased by war and corruption* 一个曾经理性的社会由于战争和腐败而严重地降低了水平 **2 debase yourself** to do something that makes other people have less respect for you 降低[贬损]你的声望[身份]: *women forced to debase themselves by selling their bodies* 被迫卖身而贬低自己人格的妇女 —**debasement** *n* [C,U]

de·ba·ta·ble /dɪˈbetəbl; dɪˈbeɪtəbəl/ *adj* a question or opinion that is debatable is not clear because different people express different views about it 有争议的，可争议的: *That is a highly debatable point.* 那是个有严重争议的观点。| **it is debatable whether/how long etc** *It is debatable whether nuclear weapons actually prevent war.* 核武器是否能够真正防止战争是有争议的。

de·bate¹ /dɪˈbet; dɪˈbeɪt/ *n* **1** [C,U] discussion or argument on a subject that people have different opinions about 讨论，辩论: [+on/over/about] *As yet there has been little public debate on these issues.* 到目前为止，对于这些问题几乎还没有进行过公开讨论。| **fierce/heated/intense debate** (=discussion involving very strong opinions) 激烈的/热烈的辩论 | **the welfare/abortion etc debate** *the gun control debate in the US* 美国的枪支管制大讨论 **2** [C] a formal discussion on a subject〔就某一个话题进行的〕正式讨论: [+about/on] *a lively debate on the relevance of Marx today* 关于马克思主义对现今社会相关性问题的热烈辩论 **3 be open to debate** also 又作 **be a matter for debate** if an idea is open to debate no-one has proved yet whether it is true or false〔某种观点〕可以进行讨论的: *Whether that would have made any difference is open to debate.* 当时要是那样做是否会起作用尚待商榷。**4 under debate** being discussed 正在讨论[辩论]中: *The whole question of compensation is still under debate.* 整个赔偿问题还在讨论之中。

debate² *v* [I,T] **1** to discuss a subject formally when you are trying to make a decision or find a solution〔正式地〕讨论，辩论: *We debated for several hours before taking a vote.* 我们辩论了好几个小时才投票。| **debate whether/what/how etc** *debating whether to raise the price of school meals* 讨论是否提高学校用餐价格 | **hotly debated** (=argued about strongly) 热烈地辩论 *His conclusions are hotly debated among academics.* 他的结论在学术界引起了热烈的辩论。**2** to consider something in your own mind before reaching a decision〔作出决定前〕反复考虑，斟酌: **debate with yourself** *He debated with himself for a moment then replied.* 他考虑了一会儿才作出回答。| **debate who/what/how etc** *I wasn't feeling well and was debating whether to go to work.* 那时我身体不太舒服，所以正琢磨着去不去上班。—**debater** *n* [C]

de·bauch /dɪˈbɔtʃ; dɪˈbɔːtʃ/ *v* [T] *formal* to make someone behave in an immoral way, especially with alcohol, drugs, or sex【正式】〔尤指用酒、毒品或色情〕使〔某人〕堕落，使放荡

de·bauched /dɪˈbɔtʃt; dɪˈbɔːtʃt/ *adj* someone who is debauched is immoral because they drink a lot of alcohol, take drugs, or have an immoral attitude to sex〔因为酗酒、吸毒或者持有不健康的性观念而〕不道德的，道德败坏的，放荡的，堕落的

de·bauch·e·ry /dɪˈbɔtʃərɪ; dɪˈbɔːtʃəri/ *n* **1** [U] immoral behaviour involving drugs, alcohol, sex etc 道德败坏: *a life of total debauchery* 放荡淫逸的生活 **2** [C] an occasion when someone behaves in this way 放荡

de·ben·ture /dɪˈbɛntʃə; dɪˈbentʃə/ *n* [C] *technical* an official document given by a company, showing that it has borrowed money and that it will pay a fixed rate of INTEREST¹ (4), whether or not it makes a profit【术语】债券

de·bil·i·tate /dɪˈbɪləˌtet; dɪˈbɪləteɪt/ *v* [T] **1** if illness, heat, hunger etc debilitates someone, it makes their body or mind weak 使虚弱，使衰弱: *debilitated by fever* 因发烧身体虚弱 **2** if an action debilitates an organization or structure, it weakens its authority or effectiveness 削弱〔权威性或有效性〕

de·bil·it·at·ing /dɪˈbɪləˌtetɪŋ; dɪˈbɪləteɪtɪŋ/ *adj* **1** a debilitating disease or condition makes your body or mind weak 使〔身体或精神〕虚弱的: *debilitating heat* 使人虚弱的高温天气 **2** a debilitating action, result etc weakens an organization, structure etc 使〔组织、机构等〕削弱的: *the debilitating effect of economic decline* 经济衰退造成的削弱性后果

de·bil·i·ty /dɪˈbɪlətɪ; dɪˈbɪləti/ *n* [C,U] *formal* weakness, especially as the result of illness【正式】〔尤指疾病造成的〕虚弱，衰弱

deb·it¹ /ˈdɛbɪt; ˈdebət/ *n* [C] *technical*【术语】**1** something in a book of accounts that shows money spent or owed〔账本中的〕借方，借项 **2** a sum of money taken out of a bank account 从银行账户中提取的款项 —compare 比较 CREDIT¹ (1) —see also 另见 DIRECT DEBIT

debit² *v* [T] *technical*【术语】**1** to take money out of a bank account〔从银行账户中〕取〔款〕: *the sum of £25 debited from your account* 从你的账户中划出的25英镑的款项 **2** [+against] to record the amount of money taken from a bank account〔将取出的金额〕记入…的借方账中 —compare 比较 CREDIT² (2)

debit card /ˈ·· ˌ·/ *n* [C] a special plastic card that you can use to pay for things directly from your bank account 借记卡，借方卡 —compare 比较 CASH CARD, CHEQUE CARD, CREDIT CARD

debit note /ˈ·· ·/ *n* [C] a document sent by a company to a customer telling them how much money they owe〔公司发给顾客的〕借项清单，借项账单，借方报单，借方票，借方通知

deb·o·nair /ˌdɛbəˈnɛr; ˌdebəˈneə◂/ *adj* a man who is debonair is fashionable and well dressed and behaves in an attractively confident way〔通常指男士〕温文尔雅的，穿着入时的: *a stylish, debonair young man* 一个穿着时髦、温文尔雅的青年男子

de·bouch /dɪˈbuʃ; dɪˈbaʊtʃ/ *v* [I always+adv/prep] **1** *technical* if a river, road etc debouches somewhere, it comes out from a narrow place into a wider place【术语】〔河流〕流至较大区域；〔道路〕延伸至开阔地区 **2** *formal* if people debouch from one place to another, they move out of one place into somewhere larger【正式】〔人〕进入较开阔的地方

De·brett's /dəˈbrɛts; dəˈbrets/ also 又作 **Debrett** a book that is a guide to the British royal family and other upper-class families in the UK. It provides information about members of these families, the properties they own, and their history.《德布雷特氏贵族名鉴》〔一本介绍英国王室和其他上流社会家族的书籍，提供这些家族的成员、财产及其家史等资料〕

de·brief /ˌdiˈbrif; ˌdiːˈbriːf/ *v* [T] to talk to someone to get information from them after they have done a job that you told them to do 询问〔任务完成者〕执行情况，听取〔任务完成者〕汇报情况: *The returning bomber crews were debriefed.* 听取返回的轰炸机机组人员汇报情况。—compare 比较 BRIEF³ —**debriefing** *n* [U]

deb·ris /dəˈbri; ˈdebriː/ *n* [U] all the pieces that are left after something has been destroyed in an accident, explosion etc 碎片；残骸: *The beach was littered with debris.* 海滩上到处都是散落的残骸。

debt /dɛt; det/ *n* **1** [C] a sum of money that you owe 债务，欠款: **pay off/repay/clear your debts** *He now had enough money to pay off his father's outstanding debts.* 他现在有足够的钱来偿还他父亲尚未清还的债务。| [+of] *The company has debts of around $1,000,000.* 该公司负债大约100万美元。| **run up a debt** (=borrow money without paying it back on time) 积欠债务 *students running up massive credit card debts* 积欠大量信用卡债务的学生 **2** [U] the state of owing money 欠债，负债: *He was imprisoned for debt.* 他由于欠债而入狱。| **be in debt** (=owe money) 欠债，负债 | **£200/$1000 etc in debt** *She was still $600 in debt.* 她还欠600美元。| **go/get/run/slip etc into debt** (=spend so much money that you need to borrow money) 陷入债务之中，负债 *Malone was sinking hopelessly into debt.* 马隆无可救药地陷入债务之中。| **be heavily/deeply/up to your ears in debt** (=owe a lot of money) 债台高筑 **3 your debt to sb** the degree to which you have learned from or been influenced by someone else 受某人的影响，受某人的恩惠: *Marx's debt to earlier thinkers such as Hegel* 马克思从黑格尔等早期思想家那里受到的影响 **4 be in debt** also 又作 **owe a debt of gratitude to sb** to be

very grateful to someone for what they have done for you 感激某人, 欠某人的情 —see also 另见 BAD DEBT, NATIONAL DEBT

debt coll·ect·or /ˈ· ·, ··/ *n* [C] someone who is employed to get back the money that people owe 收债人

debt·or /ˈdɛtɚ; ˈdetə/ *n* [C] a person, group, or organization that owes money 债务人 —compare 比较 CREDITOR

de·bug /diˈbʌg; ˌdiːˈbʌg/ *v* **debugged, debugging** [T] **1** to take the mistakes out of a computer's PROGRAM (=set of instructions) 排除〔电脑程序中的错误、故障〕 **2** to find and remove secret listening equipment in a room or building 从…拆除窃听器

de·bunk /diˈbʌŋk; ˌdiːˈbʌŋk/ *v* [T] to show that an idea or belief is false 证明〔观点或观念〕错误: *debunking the myth that British cuisine is bad* 证明英国烹调很差劲这种没有根据的观念是错误的 —**debunker** *n* [C]

De·bus·sy /ˌdebjuˈsi; dəˈbjuːsi/, **Claude** /klod; kləʊd/ (1862-1918) a French COMPOSER who developed musical IMPRESSIONISM 德彪西〔(1862-1918), 法国作曲家, 印象派音乐创始人〕

de·but /dɪˈbju; ˈdeɪbjuː/ *n* [C] the first public appearance of someone such as an entertainer or a sports player or of something new and important 〔演员或运动员等的〕首次公开露面, 首次登台: *Their debut album was recorded in 1991.* 他们的首张唱片录制于 1991 年。| **make your debut** *a young actress making her debut on Broadway* 在百老汇首次登台演出的年轻女演员

deb·u·tante /ˌdɛbjuˈtɑnt; ˈdebjʊtɑːnt/ *n* [C] a young UPPER CLASS woman who goes to special parties as a way of being formally introduced to upper-class society 初次参加社交的上流社会年轻女子

Dec the written abbreviation of 缩写= DECEMBER

deca- /dɛkə; dekə/ *prefix* ten 十: *decalitre* (=ten litres)十升 | *the decathlon* (=a sports competition with 10 different events) 十项全能运动 —see table on page C4 参见 C4 页附录

S3 W2 **dec·ade** /ˈdɛked; ˈdekeɪd/ *n* [C] a period of ten years 十年; 十年期间

dec·a·dence /ˈdɛkədn̩s; ˈdekədəns/ *n* [U] the state of having low moral standards and being more concerned with pleasure than with serious matters 堕落, 颓废: *the corruption and decadence of the nobility* 贵族的腐败和颓废

dec·a·dent /ˈdɛkədn̩t; ˈdekədənt/ *adj* having low moral standards and being more concerned with your own pleasure than serious matters 堕落的, 颓废的: *Pop music was condemned as decadent and crude.* 流行音乐被指责为堕落、粗俗的音乐。—**decadently** *adv*

de·caf /ˈdikæf; ˈdiːkæf/ *n* [U] *spoken* decaffeinated coffee or tea【口】去掉咖啡因的咖啡[茶]

de·caf·fein·a·ted /diˈkæfəˌnetɪd; diːˈkæfɪ̣neɪtɪ̣d/ *adj* coffee or tea that is decaffeinated has had CAFFEINE (=a drug that keeps you awake) removed〔咖啡或茶〕除去咖啡因的

de·cal /ˈdikæl; ˈdiːkæl/ *n* [C] *AmE* a piece of paper with a pattern or picture on it that you stick onto another surface【美】贴花纸; TRANSFER² (3) *BrE*【英】

Dec·a·logue /ˈdɛkəˌlɔg; ˈdekəlɒg/ *n* [singular] the Ten Commandments〔《圣经》的〕十诫

De·cam·e·ron, the /dɪˈkæmərən; dɪ̣ˈkæmərən/ a group of amusing stories, often about sex, by the great Italian writer Boccaccio. Written in the middle of the 14th century, this work had a great influence on English literature.《十日谈》〔意大利伟大作家薄伽丘创作的一本妙趣横生的故事集, 大都与性有关。该书创作于 14 世纪中期, 对英国文学产生了重大影响〕

de·camp /dɪˈkæmp; dɪˈkæmp/ *v* [I] to leave a place quickly and usually secretly 逃走, 潜逃: *The secretary decamped with the members' money.* 那个秘书带着会员们的钱逃跑了。

de·cant /dɪˈkænt; dɪˈkænt/ *v* [T] to pour liquid, especially wine, from one container into another 将〔液体, 尤指酒〕从一个容器倒入另一个容器

de·cant·er /dɪˈkæntɚ; dɪˈkæntə/ *n* [C] a glass container for holding alcoholic drinks〔用来装酒的〕带塞玻璃瓶

de·cap·i·tate /dɪˈkæpəˌtet; dɪˈkæpɪ̣teɪt/ *v* [T] to cut off someone's head 砍…的头, 把…斩首 —**decapitation** /dɪˌkæpəˈteʃən; dɪˌkæpɪ̣ˈteɪʃən/ *n* [C,U]

de·cath·lon /dɪˈkæθlɑn; dɪˈkæθlɒn/ *n* [singular] a competition including ten different sports 十项全能运动 —compare 比较 PENTATHLON

de·cay¹ /dɪˈke; dɪˈkeɪ/ *v* **1** [I,T] to be slowly destroyed by a natural chemical process, or to make something do this (使)腐烂; (使)变坏: *The carcass was already starting to decay.*〔动物的〕尸体已经开始腐烂。**2** [I often in progressive 常用进行时] if buildings, structures, or areas decay, their condition gradually becomes worse〔可以指建筑物、结构或地区等的状况〕变坏, 破败: *The Metropole Hotel was now decaying after years of neglect.* 都会大酒店由于长年失修, 已经十分破败。**3** [I often in progressive 常用进行时] if traditional beliefs, morals, standards etc decay, people do not believe in them or support them any more〔传统观念、道德、标准等〕失去影响力, 衰败, 衰落: *Educational standards have decayed.* 教育标准已大幅度降低。

decay² *n* **1** [U] the natural chemical change that causes the slow destruction of something 腐烂, 朽烂: *The house had stood empty for years and smelled of decay.* 这座房子已经空了好多年, 有股朽烂的气味。| **tooth decay** *Use a fluoride toothpaste to fight tooth decay.* 使用含氟的牙膏预防蛀牙。**2** [singular] the part of something that has been destroyed in this way 腐烂部分, 腐蚀部分: *The dentist used a drill to remove the decay.* 牙医用牙钻除去牙齿的蛀蚀部分。**3** [U] the gradual destruction of ideas, beliefs, social or political organizations etc〔观念、信仰、社会组织或政治组织等的〕衰退, 衰败: *moral and spiritual decay* 道德和精神的颓废 **4** [U] the change from economic success to a state of being poor〔经济上的〕成功到贫穷的转变, 衰退: *urban decay* 市区的衰败 **5** [U] the gradual destruction of buildings and structures caused by a lack of care〔疏于管理而造成建筑物和大楼的〕逐渐毁坏: **fall into decay/fall into a state of decay** *the old fortress falling into a state of decay* 那个慢慢颓塌的要塞

de·cease /dɪˈsis; dɪˈsiːs/ *n* [U] *formal* death【正式】死亡: *Upon your decease the house will pass to your wife.* 你去世后, 这座房子将由你妻子继承。

de·ceased /dɪˈsist; dɪˈsiːst/ *n* **the deceased** *formal* someone who has died, especially recently【正式】死者, 已故之人〔尤指最近刚去世的人〕: *The deceased left a large sum of money to his children.* 死者留给他的孩子们一大笔钱。—**deceased** *adj*

de·ceit /dɪˈsit; dɪˈsiːt/ *n* [C,U] behaviour that is intended to make someone believe something that is not true, or an example of this behaviour 欺骗, 欺诈: *hypocrisy and deceit* 虚伪与欺骗

de·ceit·ful /dɪˈsitfəl; dɪˈsiːtfəl/ *adj* someone who is deceitful tells lies in order to get what they want 欺骗的, 撒谎的 —**deceitfully** *adv* —**deceitfulness** *n* [U]

de·ceive /dɪˈsiv; dɪˈsiːv/ *v* [T] **1** to make someone believe something that is not true in order to get what you want 欺骗: *You deceived me, and I can't forgive you.* 你欺骗了我, 我不能原谅你。| **deceive sb into doing sth** *They deceived the old man into signing the papers.* 他们骗那个老人在文件上签了字。**2 deceive yourself** to pretend to yourself that something is not true, because the truth is unpleasant 自欺欺人: *I thought she loved me, but really I was deceiving myself.* 我以为她是爱我的, 但事实上, 我是在欺骗自己。**3 are my eyes deceiving me?** *spoken* used when you see someone or something that you are very surprised to see【口】我是不是看错了?是不是我眼花了?〔表示非常惊讶〕: *Are my eyes deceiving me, or is that a genuine Persian carpet.* 我没眼花吧, 那不是正宗的波斯地毯吗。—**deceiver** *n* [C]

de·cel·e·rate /diˈsɛləˌret; ˌdiːˈseləreɪt/ *v* [I] *technical* to go slower, especially in a vehicle【术语】〔尤指车辆〕减速: *Decelerate when approaching a corner.* 驶到路口处要减速。—opposite 反义词 ACCELERATE —**deceleration** /diˌsɛləˈreʃən; ˌdiːseləˈreɪʃən/ *n* [U]

De·cem·ber /dɪˈsɛmbɚ; dɪˈsembə/ written abbreviation 缩写为 **Dec** *n* [C,U] the 12th and last month of the year, between November and January 十二月: **in December** *The course starts in December.* 课程 12 月开课。| **last/next December** *I arrived here last December.* 我是去年 12 月份到这儿的。| **on December 6th** (also 又作 **on 6th December** *BrE*【英】) *The meeting will be on December 6th* (spoken as 读作 *on the sixth of December* or 或 *on December the sixth* or 或 *AmE*【美】*on December 6th*). 会议将于 12 月 6 日举行。

CULTURAL NOTE 文化注释

In the UK and northern US, December is one of the cold winter months, when days are short and there is often snow. When people think of December, they think of Christmas, which is on December 25th, and New Year's Eve, on December 31st. 在英国和美国北部地区, 12 月是冬季最冷的月份之一, 白天短, 常下雪。12 月会让人想到 12 月 25 日的圣诞节和 12 月 31 日的新年除夕。

de·cen·cy /ˈdisn̩si; ˈdiːsənsi/ *n* [U] **1** a quality in someone's character that makes them honest and polite and makes them have respect for other people 正派, 端庄, 体面: *a judgement that reflects the decency and good sense of the American people* 反映美国人民宽容和智慧的评价 **2** acceptable behaviour, especially moral and sexual behaviour 合乎礼仪〔尤指道德和性方面的行

为]:**sense of decency** *They have no sense of honour or decency.* 他们没有荣誉感或体面感。| **common decency** (=basic standards of behaviour that everyone should follow) 基本行为标准 *It's common decency to let someone know if you are going to arrive late.* 如果你要迟到，最好通知别人，这是最起码的礼貌。| **have the decency to do sth** (=behave in a way that follows the basic standards of acceptable behaviour) 按礼节行事 *You could have had the decency to ask me before you invited all your friends to stay!* 你应该懂点道理，在把你所有的朋友请来住之前，先问问我的意见。**3 decencies** *old-fashioned* standards of behaviour that people think are acceptable【过时】文雅的行为标准

2 **de·cent** /ˋdisn̩t; ˈdiːsənt/ *adj* **1** acceptable and good enough 可接受的，相当好的，像样的：*Haven't you got a decent pair of shoes?* 你难道没有一双像样的鞋？| *a house with a decent sized yard* 院子还算大的房子 **2** treating people in a fair and kind way〔待人〕公平的；和善的：*I decided her father was a decent guy, after all.* 毕竟，我觉得她父亲还是个不错的人。| **be decent of sb to do sth** *It was decent of him to offer to help us paint the house.* 他真好，主动提出帮助我们粉刷房子。| **be decent about something** *especially BrE* (=treat someone fairly and sympathetically when they have done something wrong)【尤英】公正的；宽容的 *The lecturers were really decent about my absences.* 授课老师们对于我的缺课真的很宽容。**3** following the standards of moral behaviour accepted by most people 正派的，规矩的：*Decent citizens have nothing to fear from this legislation.* 规矩的公民无须害怕这项法规。| **do the decent thing** (=do something because you feel you ought to) 做该做的事 *When Tom found out that his girlfriend was pregnant, he did the decent thing and married her.* 汤姆发现他的女朋友怀孕时，做了该做的事，和她结了婚。**4** *usually humorous* wearing enough clothes to not show too much of your body【一般幽默】穿着得体的，不暴露太多的：*Don't come in – I'm not decent!* 别进来——我还没穿好衣服！—opposite 反义词 INDECENT (1) **5 a decent burial/funeral** if someone is given a decent burial, they are buried in an acceptable way 体面的葬礼 —**decently** *adv*

de·cen·tral·ize also 又作 **-ise** *BrE*【英】/diˋsɛntrəl͵aɪz; ͵diːˈsentrəlaɪz/ *v* [T] to move parts of a government, organization etc from one central place to several different smaller ones 分散，下放〔权力〕：*Many firms are decentralizing parts of their operations.* 许多公司正分散部分经营活动。—**decentralized** *adj*: *a decentralized economy* 分散经济 —**decentralization** /͵disɛntrələˋzeʃən; ͵diːsentrəlaɪˈzeɪʃən/ *n* [U]

de·cep·tion /dɪˋsɛpʃən; dɪˈsepʃən/ *n* [C,U] the act of deliberately making someone believe something that is not true 欺骗〔行为〕：*outrage at the government's deception* 对政府欺骗行径的愤怒

de·cep·tive /dɪˋsɛptɪv; dɪˈseptɪv/ *adj* **1** something that is deceptive seems to be one thing but is in fact very different 造成假象的，似是而非的：*A boa constrictor can move with deceptive speed.* 蟒蛇能以令人难料的速度爬行。**2** deliberately intended to make someone believe something that is not true 欺骗的，欺诈的：*deceptive behavior* 欺骗行为 —**deceptively** *adj* —**deceptiveness** *n* [U]

deci- /ˋdɛsɪ; desɪ/ *prefix* a 10th part of a unit 十分之一：*a decilitre* (=0.1 litres) 分升〔1/10 升〕—see table on page C4 参见 C4 页附录

dec·i·bel /ˋdɛsə͵bɛl; ˈdesɪbel/ *n* [C] *technical* a unit of measurement for the loudness of sound【术语】分贝〔衡量声音强度的单位〕：*The noise level in factories must not exceed 85 decibels.* 工厂的噪声水平不得超过 85 分贝。

1 1 **de·cide** /dɪˋsaɪd; dɪˈsaɪd/ *v* **1** [I,T] to make a choice or judgment about something, especially after a period of not knowing what to do or in a way that ends disagreement 决定，决断，判断：**decide to do sth** *Tina's decided to go to Prague for her holidays.* 蒂娜已决定到布拉格去度假。| **decide that** *It was eventually decided that four London hospitals should be closed.* 最后决定关闭四家伦敦医院。| **decide who/what/how etc** *I can't decide what to do.* 我不知道该做什么。| **decide whether/if** *Women now have greater freedom to decide whether or not to get married.* 妇女现在拥有较大的自由来决定自己是否结婚。| [**+between**] *I'm trying to decide between the green and the blue for the bathroom.* 我正在考虑把浴室刷成绿色的好还是蓝色的好。| **decide sth** *I'm eighteen now – I have a right to decide my own future.* 我现在 18 岁了，有权决定自己的未来。| **decide for yourself** (=make your own choice or judgment, without asking anyone else to do it for you) 自己决定 *You must decide for yourself whether to leave college.* 你必须自己决定是否退学。—see also 另见 DECISION (1) **2** [T] to be the reason for someone making a particular judgment or choice 使决定，使下决心：**decide sb to do sth** *What was it that finally decided you to give up your job?* 什么使你最终决定放弃你的工作？| **deciding factor** (=a very strong reason that forces you to make a particular decision) 决定性因素 *Money should not be the deciding factor over who runs a TV station.* 钱不应该成为选择电视台管理者的决定性因素。**3** [T] if an event, action etc decides something, it influences events so that one particular result will happen 决定〔事件的结果〕：*A goal in the last minute decided the match.* 最后一分钟的一个进球决定了比赛的胜负。| **the deciding vote** (=the person who has the deciding vote makes the final decision, because all the other votes are equally divided) 决定性一票 **4 decide in favour of/decide against a)** to choose or not choose someone or something 选择/不选择〔某人或某物〕：*After long discussion they decided in favour of the younger candidate.* 经过长时间的讨论，他们决定选那个年轻些的候选人。**b)** if a judge or JURY (1) decides in favour of someone or against someone, they say in court that someone is guilty or not guilty 作出有利于/不利于〔某人的〕裁决：*The jury decided in favour of the plaintiff.* 陪审团作出了有利于原告的裁决。

This graph shows how common the different grammar patterns of the verb **decide** are. 本图表所示为动词 decide 构成的不同语法模式的使用频率。

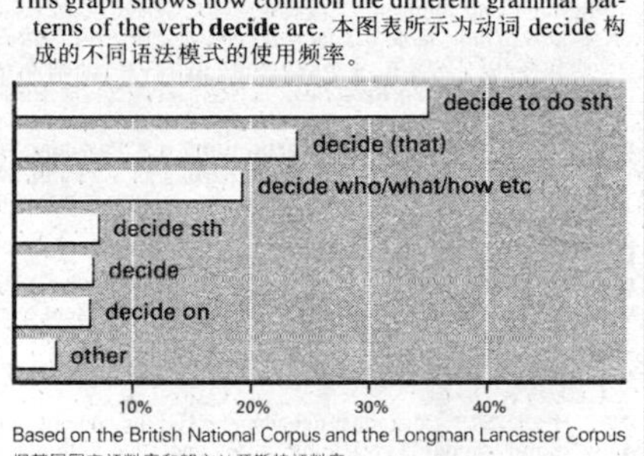

Based on the British National Corpus and the Longman Lancaster Corpus 据英国国家语料库和朗文兰开斯特语料库

decide on sth *phr v* [T] to choose one thing from many possible choices 选定：*Have you decided on a date for your wedding?* 你结婚的日子选好没有？

de·cid·ed /dɪˋsaɪdɪd; dɪˈsaɪdɪd/ *adj* definite and easily noticed 清楚的，明确的；明显的：*a decided change for the better* 明显的好转

de·cid·ed·ly /dɪˋsaɪdɪdlɪ; dɪˈsaɪdɪdli/ *adv* **1** [+adj/adv] *especially BrE* definitely or in a way that is easily noticed【尤英】肯定地，无疑地；明显地：*The man was decidedly drunk.* 这个男人肯定是喝多了。**2** in a way that shows that you are very sure and determined about what you want to do 坚决地，坚定地："*I'm not going to do it,*" *said Margaret decidedly.* "这件事，我不做。"玛格丽特坚决地说。

de·cid·er /dɪˋsaɪdɚ; dɪˈsaɪdə/ *n* [C] *informal* the last part of a game or competition, which will show who the winner is【非正式】决胜局：*This next round will be the decider.* 下一轮比赛将决定胜负。

de·cid·u·ous /dɪˋsɪdʒuəs; dɪˈsɪdʒuəs/ *adj* deciduous trees lose their leaves in winter 落叶的 —compare 比较 EVERGREEN[2]

dec·i·mal[1] /ˋdɛsəml̩; ˈdesɪməl/ *adj* a decimal system is based on the number 10 十进位的：*decimal currency* 十进币制

decimal[2] *n* [C] *technical* a FRACTION (=a number less than one) that is shown as a FULL STOP followed by the number of TENTHS, then the number of HUNDREDTHS etc, as in the numbers 0.5, 0.175, 0.661 etc【术语】小数〈如 0.5, 0.175, 0.661 等〉

dec·i·mal·ize also 又作 **-ise** *BrE*【英】/ˋdɛsəml͵aɪz; ˈdesɪməlaɪz/ *v* [I,T] to change to a decimal system of money or measurements〔将〕〔币制或度量衡〕改为十进制 —**decimalization** /͵dɛsəmələˋzeʃən; ͵desɪməlaɪˈzeɪʃən/ *n* [U]

decimal place /͵··ˈ· ˈ·/ *n* [C] *technical* one of the positions after a FULL STOP in a decimal【术语】小数点后的位数：*measurements accurate to three decimal places* 精确到小数点后三位的测量结果

decimal point /͵··ˈ· ˈ·/ *n* [C] *technical* the FULL STOP in a decimal, used to separate whole numbers from TENTHS, HUNDREDTHS, etc【术语】小数点

decimal sys·tem /ˈ··· ͵··/ *n* [singular] a system of counting that is based on the number 10 十进制

dec·i·mate /ˋdɛsə͵met; ˈdesɪmeɪt/ *v* [T usually passive 一般用被动态] to destroy a large part of something 大量毁灭：*The population has been decimated by disease.* 疾病导致大批的人死亡。—**decimation** /͵dɛsəˋmeʃən; ͵desɪˈmeɪʃən/ *n* [U]

de·ci·pher /dɪˈsaɪfɚ; dɪˈsaɪfə/ *v* [T] to find the meaning of something that is difficult to read or understand 辨认; 解释: *I can't decipher his handwriting.* 我辨认不出他写的是什么。—see also 另见 INDECIPHERABLE

de·ci·sion /dɪˈsɪʒən; dɪˈsɪʒən/ *n* **1** [C] a choice or judgment that you make after a period of discussion or thought 决定, 抉择: *The judges' decision is final.* 裁判们的决定是不可更改的。| **decision to do sth** *his wife's decision to leave him* 他妻子离开他的决定 | **make/take a decision** (=decide) 作出决定 *The committee is due to make its decision this week.* 委员会预期本周作出决定。| **come to/reach a decision** (=finally decide) 作出决定 *We finally came to a firm decision.* 我们最终作出了坚定的决定。| [**+about**] *a decision about whether to expand the business* 关于是否扩展业务的决定 | **final decision** (=a decision that will not be changed) 最后决定 *I'm afraid I don't have the final decision in these matters.* 在这些事情上恐怕我还无法作出最终的决定。| **big decision** (=an important decision) 重大决定 | **difficult/hard/tough decision** *It was a tough decision, but I decided to leave my job.* 这是个艰难的抉择, 但我还是决定辞职。**2** [U] the quality someone has that makes them able to make choices or judgments quickly and confidently 果断, 坚定, 决断: *This job requires the ability to act with speed and decision.* 这个工作需要迅速、果断的办事能力。—opposite 反义词 INDECISION **3** [U] the act of deciding something 判决, 裁决: *The burden of decision rests with the Supreme Court.* 裁定的责任在最高法院。

This graph shows some of the words most commonly used with the noun **decision**. 本图表所示为含有名词 decision 的一些最常用词组。

Based on the British National Corpus and the Longman Lancaster Corpus
据英国国家语料库和朗文兰开斯特语料库

decision-mak·ing /·ˈ··,··/ *n* [U] the process of thinking about a problem, idea etc, and then making a choice or judgment 决策: *an attempt to make workers more involved in decision-making* 让工人们更多地参与决策的尝试

de·ci·sive /dɪˈsaɪsɪv; dɪˈsaɪsɪv/ *adj* **1 a decisive step/role/battle etc** an action, event etc that has a powerful effect on the final result of something 决定性的一步/角色/战役等: *Waterloo was the decisive battle of the entire war.* 滑铁卢战役在整个战争中起了决定性作用。**2** good at making decisions quickly and with confidence 果断的, 坚决的, 决断的: *a decisive leader* 果断的领袖 | **decisive action** (=action taken quickly and confidently in order to solve a problem) 果断的行动 *She demonstrated a talent for quick, decisive action.* 她表现出做事迅速、果断的素质。**3** leading to a clear result and ending doubt 决定性的, 确定的: *a decisive election victory* 一次决定性的选举胜利 **4 play a decisive role (in sth)** to be one of the most important causes of something (在某事中) 起着至关重要的作用: *a decisive role in the recent peace process* 在最近的和平进程中起着决定性作用 **5 a decisive step** something that results in important change 决定性的一步: *The covenant at Sinai was the decisive step in the creation of Israel.* 在西奈签订的决议是创建以色列国的决定性一步。**6** definite and not able to be doubted 确定的, 明确的: *The answer was a decisive no.* 回答是非常明确的"不"。—**decisively** *adv*

de·ci·sive·ness /dɪˈsaɪsɪvnɪs; dɪˈsaɪsɪvnəs/ *n* [U] the ability to make decisions quickly with confidence and determination 果断, 决断: *David acted with speed and decisiveness.* 戴维办事迅速、果断。

deck¹ /dɛk; dek/ *n* [C] **1** the outside top level of a ship that you can walk on 甲板: **on deck** *Let's go up on deck and sit in the sun.* 让我们上去到甲板上坐坐, 晒晒太阳。| **above/below deck(s)** *Peter stayed below decks.* 彼得留在下面, 没到甲板上面来。—see picture at 参见 YACHT 图 **2** one of the levels on a ship or bus 〔船或公共汽车的〕一层: **lower/upper deck** (=on a ship) 船的下层/上层 *Our cabin is on the lower deck.* 我们的船舱在下层。| **top/bottom deck** (=on a bus) 公共汽车的顶层/底层 *The kids love riding on the top deck.* 孩子们喜欢坐公共汽车的顶层。**3** *AmE* a wooden floor built out from the back of a house, used for relaxing on【美】〔房屋后面延伸搭建供休息用的〕木制平台 **4** *especially AmE* a set of playing cards【尤美】一副纸牌; PACK² (8) *BrE*【英】**5 all hands on deck** *informal* used when everyone must work together to do something as quickly as possible【非正式】齐心合力 —see also 另见 **clear the decks** (CLEAR² (14)), **hit the deck** (HIT¹ (21)), FLIGHT DECK, TAPE DECK

deck² *v* [T] **1** also 又作 **deck sth out** to decorate something with flowers, flags etc, especially for a special occasion 〔用花、旗帜等〕装饰: [**+with**] *The street was decked with flags for the royal wedding.* 为了庆祝皇室婚礼, 人们用旗子装饰街道。**2** *slang* to hit someone so hard that they fall over【俚】将〔某人〕击倒: *Gerry just swung round and decked him.* 格里迅速转过身一下子把他打倒在地。

deck·chair /ˈdɛk,tʃɛr; ˈdektʃeə/ *n* [C] a folding chair with a long seat made of cloth, used especially on the beach 〔尤指在海滩上使用的〕折叠躺椅 —see picture at 参见 CHAIR¹ 图

deck·hand /ˈdɛk,hænd; ˈdekhænd/ *n* [C] someone who does unskilled work on a ship 舱面水手, 普通水手

deck shoe /ˈ· ·/ *n* [C] a flat shoe made of CANVAS (=heavy cloth) 平底帆布鞋 —see picture at 参见 SHOE¹ 图

de·claim /dɪˈklem; dɪˈkleɪm/ *v* [**+against/about**; T] to speak loudly, sometimes with actions, so that people will notice you 慷慨陈词 —**declamation** /,dɛkləˈmeʃən; ,dekləˈmeɪʃən/ *n* [C,U]

de·clam·a·to·ry /dɪˈklæmə,torɪ; dɪˈklæmətəri/ *adj* a declamatory speech or piece of writing expresses your feelings and opinions very strongly 激昂的, 强烈的

dec·la·ra·tion /,dɛkləˈreʃən; ,dekləˈreɪʃən/ *n* [C,U] **1** an important statement saying that something such as a war, peace etc has officially begun 重要声明; 宣言: *a ceasefire declaration* 停火声明 | [**+of**] *issue a declaration of war* 宣战 **2** an official or serious statement of what someone believes 〔官方或正式的〕宣言, 公告: [**+of**] *the United Nations Declaration of Human Rights* 联合国人权宣言 **3** a statement in which you officially give information, especially about yourself 声明, 申报: *a declaration of taxable earnings* 一份应纳税收入的申报

Declaration of In·de·pen·dence, the /·,·· · ··ˈ··/ the document written in 1776, in which the thirteen British colonies (COLONY) in America officially stated that they were an independent nation and would no longer agree to be ruled by Britain. The most famous part of it is: We hold these truths to be self-evident, that all men are created equal, that they are endowed by their Creator with certain unalienable Rights, that among these are Life, Liberty and the pursuit of Happiness. 〔美国〕《独立宣言》〔起草于1776年。美洲13个英属殖民地自此正式宣布独立, 不再受英国的统治。最著名的一段文字是: "我们坚信以下真理是不言而喻的: 人人生而平等, 造物主赋予他们某些不可转让的权利, 其中包括生命权、自由权和追求幸福的权利"〕

CULTURAL NOTE 文化注释

The Declaration of Independence is one of the most important documents in the western world. Its most famous lines officially state that all people are equal and that no government has the right to treat its citizens cruelly or prevent them from having happy lives. Because the Declaration of Independence was formally accepted in Congress on July 4, 1776, the people of the US celebrate that day as their national holiday, called the Fourth of July or Independence Day. 《独立宣言》是西方世界最重要的文献之一, 其中最著名的句子是正式宣告人人平等, 政府不得虐待公民, 不得阻碍公民追求幸福生活。由于《独立宣言》是在1776年7月4日正式被国会通过的, 因此美国人把这一天定为国庆日, 称为"七月四日"或"独立日"。

de·clar·a·tive /dɪˈklærətɪv; dɪˈklærətɪv/ *adj technical* a declarative sentence has the form of a statement【术语】陈述的, 叙述的

de·clare /dɪˈklɛr; dɪˈkleə/ *v*

1 ▶STATE OFFICIALLY 正式宣布◀ [T] to state officially and publicly that a particular situation exists or that something is true 宣布, 声明: **declare that** *The doctor finally declared that the man was dead.* 医生最终宣布该男子死亡。| **declare sth (to be) sth** *The government of New South Wales declared 8000 hectares of forest a national park.* 新南威尔士政府宣布8000公顷的森林为国家公园。| **declare sth open** *I declare this exhibition open.* 我宣布展览开幕。| **declare sth unsafe/a failure/a**

success etc *The use of certain chemicals has now been declared illegal.* 某些化学物质的使用现已被宣布为非法。| **declare sb insane/unfit/a traitor etc** (=state officially that someone is crazy etc) 正式宣布某人疯了/不合适/是叛徒等 | **declare sb the winner/the champion etc** *Ali was declared the winner of the fight.* 阿里被宣布为这场比赛的获胜者。

2 declare war (on sb) a) to decide and state officially that you will begin fighting another country 对〔某国〕宣战 **b)** *informal* to say that something is wrong and that you will do everything you can to stop it【非正式】向〔不好的事〕宣战: *Police have now declared war on drug dealers in the area.* 警方现在已经对这个地区的毒贩宣战了。

3 ▶SAY WHAT YOU THINK/FEEL 说出所想/感觉到的◀ [T] to say very clearly and publicly what you think or feel 声称, 宣称: *"On that point, I cannot agree with you," he declared.* "在那一点上我无法同意你的观点。"他宣称。| **declare that** *Jane declared that she would rather resign than change her decision.* 简宣称她宁可辞职也不改变决定。| **declare sth** *The opposition declared their support for the bill.* 反对党表示将支持这个法案。| **declare yourself (to be) sth** *She had publicly declared herself a lesbian.* 她公开声明自己是同性恋。

4 ▶MONEY/PROPERTY ETC 金钱/财产等◀ [T] to make an official statement saying how much money you have earned, what property you own etc 申报〔收入、财产等〕: *All investment income must also be declared.* 所有的投资收益也必须申报。

5 declare an interest to tell people that you are connected with something that is being discussed 宣布和…有关系: *I should declare an interest here; Mr Hackett used to work for me.* 我宣布与此事有关, 哈克特先生曾经为我工作过。

6 declare bankruptcy to state officially that you are unable to pay your debts 宣告破产

7 ▶SURPRISE 惊奇◀ (Well) I declare! *spoken old-fashioned* used as an expression of surprise【口, 过时】嘿! 真怪了!〔用于表示惊奇〕: *Well I declare! What a pretty little village.* 我的天! 多美的小村庄啊。—**declarable** *adj*

declare against sb/sth *phr v* [T] to state that you oppose someone or something 声明反对

declare for sb/sth *phr v* [T] to state that you support someone or something 声明赞成: *Paredes decided to declare for federation.* 帕雷德斯决定声明支持联邦政府。

de·clared /dɪˋklɛrd; dɪˈkleəd/ *adj* **declared wish/intention/policy etc** a wish, intention etc that you state publicly 公开表明的愿望/打算/政策等: *It is their declared intention to increase taxes.* 他们公开宣称有意增税。

de·clas·si·fied /diˋklæsə,faɪd; ,diːˈklæsɪ̈faɪd/ *adj* official information that is declassified was secret but is not secret any more〔官方信息〕不再保密的, 解除保密的

de·clen·sion /dɪˋklɛnʃən; dɪˈklenʃən/ *n* [C] *technical*【术语】**1** the set of various forms that a noun, PRONOUN, or adjective can have according to whether it is the SUBJECT[1] (5), OBJECT[1] (6) etc of a sentence in a language such as Latin or German 词形变化(表), 变格〔在某些语言, 如拉丁语或德语中, 一个名词、代词或形容词根据它们在句子中是主语还是宾语等可以有的一系列不同的形式〕**2** a particular set of nouns etc that all have the same type of these forms 词形变化相同的一组词

2 **de·cline**[1] /dɪˋklaɪn; dɪˈklaɪn/ *n* [singular,U] a gradual decrease in the quality, quantity, or importance of something 减少, 削减: [+in] *a sharp decline in profits* 利润的急剧下降 | **economic/moral etc decline** *Economic decline is often tangled up with political turmoil.* 经济衰退经常和政治动荡有关。| **fall/go into decline** (=start to decrease) 开始衰退 *The activities of Welsh mines went into decline after about 1880.* 从1880年前后起, 威尔士煤矿的开采活动开始减少。

3 **decline**[2] *v*

1 ▶BECOME LESS 变少◀ [I] to decrease in quantity or importance 减少, 下降, 衰退: *In regions such as New England textile industries had declined and unemployment was high.* 新英格兰等地区的纺织工业已经衰退, 失业率很高。| *declining prices* 下降的价格

2 ▶BECOME WORSE 变糟◀ [I] to become gradually worse in quality〔质量〕越来越差: *Do you think standards of education have declined in recent years?* 你是否觉得最近几年教育水准下降了? | *declining health* 每况愈下的健康状况

3 ▶SAY NO 说不◀ [I,T] to say no when someone invites you somewhere or offers you something 拒绝, 谢绝: *Talbot had been invited but declined on the grounds that he was too busy.* 塔尔博特获邀请, 但他以太忙为由拒绝了。| **decline an offer/proposal etc** *We declined their offer of financial help.* 我们谢绝了他们提供的经济援助。

4 ▶REFUSE 拒绝◀ to refuse to do something 拒绝〔做某事〕: **decline to do sth** *Allen angrily declined to discuss the matter.* 艾伦气愤地拒绝谈论此事。—see 见 REFUSE[1] (USAGE)

5 sb's declining years *formal* the last years of someone's life【正式】某人的晚年, 残年

6 ▶GRAMMAR 语法◀ *technical*【术语】**a)** [I] if a noun, PRONOUN, or adjective declines, its form changes according to whether it is the SUBJECT[1] (5), OBJECT[1] (6) etc of a sentence〔根据名词、代词或形容词在句中的作用, 作主语、宾语或是其他成分〕变格, 词形变化 **b)** [T] if you decline a noun etc, you show these various forms that it can take 使〔名词等〕词形变化, 使变格

Decline and Fall of the Ro·man Em·pire, The /ˌ·ˌ·ˌ·ˌ··ˌ·ˈ·/ (1776-88) a series of six historical books written by Edward Gibbon, which tell the story of the Roman Empire from the 1st century AD to the 15th century. It is one of the greatest historical works ever written in English.《罗马帝国衰亡史》〔(1776-1788), 爱德华·吉本所著的六卷本系列史书。该书记述罗马帝国公元1至15世纪的历史, 是最伟大的英文史书之一〕

de·code /ˌdiˋkod; ˌdiːˈkəʊd/ *v* [T] **1** to discover the meaning of a secret or complicated message 译〔码〕, 解〔码〕: *a computer that can decode and implement complex instructions* 能够解码和执行复杂指令的电脑 **2** *technical* to understand the meaning of a word rather than use a word to express meaning【术语】解读, 解释 —opposite 反义词 ENCODE

dé·colle·tage /deˌkɑləˋtɑʒ; ˌdeɪkɒlˈtɑːʒ/ *n* [U] *French* the top edge of a woman's dress that is cut very low to show part of her shoulders and breasts【法】〔袒胸露肩的女装的〕低领 —**décolleté** /ˌdekɑləˋte; deɪˈkɒlteɪ/ *adj*: *a satin dress, high-waisted and decolleté* 高腰低领的缎子礼服

de·col·o·nize also 又作 **-ise** *BrE*【英】/diˋkɑləˌnaɪz; ˌdiːˈkɒlənaɪz/ *v* [T] to make a former COLONY politically independent 使〔以前的殖民地〕政治独立; 使非殖民(地)化 —**decolonization** /diˌkɑlənəˋzeʃən; diːˌkɒlənaɪˈzeɪʃən/ *n* [U]

de·com·mis·sion /ˌdikəˋmɪʃən; ˌdiːkəˈmɪʃən/ *v* [T] to stop using a NUCLEAR weapon or REACTOR and prepare to take it to pieces 废弃〔核武器〕; 关闭〔核电站〕

de·com·pose /ˌdikəmˋpoz; ˌdiːkəmˈpəʊz/ *v* [I,T] **1** to decay or make something decay (使)变坏, (使)腐烂: *a partially-decomposed body* 部分腐烂的尸体 **2** *technical* to divide into smaller parts or to make something do this【术语】(使)分解 —**decomposition** /ˌdikɑmpəˋzɪʃən; ˌdiːkɒmpəˈzɪʃən/ *n* [U]

de·com·press /ˌdikəmˋprɛs; ˌdiːkəmˈpres/ *v* [T] to reduce the pressure of air on something 使减压, 减少…的气压

de·com·pres·sion cham·ber /ˌdikəmˋprɛʃən ˌtʃembɚ; ˌdiːkəmˈpreʃən ˌtʃeɪmbə/ *n* [C] a special room where people go after they have been deep under the sea, in order to slowly return to normal air pressure〔帮助从深海返回的潜水者慢慢地恢复到正常压力的〕减压室

decompression sick·ness /ˌdikəmˋprɛʃən ˌsɪknɪs; ˌdiːkəmˈpreʃən ˌsɪknɪ̈s/ *n* [U] a dangerous medical condition that people get when they come up from deep under the sea too quickly; bends (BEND[2] (3))〔因深海潜水员浮出水面太急而造成的〕潜函病, 减压病

de·con·gest·ant /ˌdikənˋdʒɛstənt; ˌdiːkənˈdʒestənt◂/ *n* [C,U] medicine that you can take if you have a cold to help you breathe more easily〔鼻〕减充血剂

de·con·struc·tion /ˌdikənˋstrʌkʃən; ˌdiːkənˈstrʌkʃən/ *n* [U] *technical* a method used in the criticism of literature which claims that there is no single explanation of the meaning of a piece of writing【术语】解构〔认为一部文学作品不仅仅有一种解释的文学评论方法〕

de·con·tam·i·nate /ˌdikənˋtæməˌnet; ˌdiːkənˈtæmɪ̈neɪt/ *v* [T] to remove a dangerous substance from somewhere 消除…的污染, 净化: *It may cost over $5 million to decontaminate the whole site.* 对这个地方全面消除污染可能要花费超过500万美元。—**decontamination** /ˌdikənˌtæməˋneʃən; ˌdiːkəntæmɪ̈ˈneɪʃən/ *n* [U]

de·cor /deˋkɔr; ˈdeɪkɔː/ *n* [C,U] the way that the inside of a building is decorated 布置, 装饰, 装修: *tacky furniture and tasteless decor* 俗气的家具和毫无品味的装修

dec·o·rate /ˋdɛkəˌret; ˈdekəreɪt/ *v especially BrE*【尤英】**1** [I,T] to make the inside of a building look more attractive by painting it, putting paper on the walls etc 装修: *I'm going to decorate the bathroom next.* 接下来我要装修浴室。**2** [T] to make something look more attractive by putting something pretty on it 装饰, 布置, 美化: **decorate sth with** *We decorated the Christmas tree with tinsel and lights.* 我们用金属箔和灯来装饰圣诞树。**3** [T+for] to give someone a MEDAL as an official sign of honour 授予…勋章[奖章] —**decorating** *n* [U]

3 **dec·o·ra·tion** /ˌdɛkəˋreʃən; ˌdekəˈreɪʃən/ *n* **1** [C often plural 常用复数] something pretty that you put onto something else in order to make it more attractive 装饰物: *Christmas decorations* 圣诞节装饰物 **2** [U] the way in which something is decorated 装饰方式: *The Rococo decoration inside the palace is delightful.* 宫殿内部的洛可可式装饰风格赏心悦目。**3** [C,U] *especially BrE* the act or process of decorating【尤英】装饰; 装修: *The decoration of the house had taken months to complete.* 装修这所房子花了好几个月的时间。**4** [C] something such as a MEDAL that is given to someone as an official sign of honour 奖章, 勋章

dec·o·ra·tive /ˋdɛkəˌretɪv; ˈdekərətɪv/ *adj* pretty or attractive, but not always necessary or useful 装饰(性)的, 作装饰用的: *a decorative panel above the door* 门楣上方装饰性的镶板 —**decoratively** *adv*

dec·o·ra·tor /ˋdɛkəˌretɚ; ˈdekəreɪtə/ *n* [C] someone who paints houses and puts paper on the walls as their job 油漆匠; 裱糊匠

dec·o·rous /ˋdɛkərəs; ˈdekərəs/ *adj formal* having the correct appearance or behaviour for a particular occasion【正式】(外表或行为)端庄得体的 —**decorously** *adv*: *A servant was hovering decorously behind them.* 一名仆人庄重地跟在他们身后。

de·co·rum /dɪˋkɔrəm; dɪˈkɔːrəm/ *n* [U] *formal* correct behaviour that shows respect【正式】端庄得体, 有礼: *I hope you will behave with suitable decorum at the prize-giving tomorrow.* 我希望你在明天的颁奖会上能表现得得体有礼。

de·coy /ˋdikɔɪ; ˈdiːkɔɪ/ *n* [C] **1** someone or something used to trick someone into going where you want them to go so that you can catch them, attack them etc 诱饵, 诱惑物: *Police have been using mocked-up patrol cars as decoys to make drivers slow down.* 警方一直使用模拟的巡逻车作伪装, 让司机减慢车速。**2** a model of a bird used to attract wild birds so that you can watch them or shoot them (观鸟或猎鸟时用以引诱鸟群的)假鸟 —**decoy** /dɪˋkɔɪ; dɪˈkɔɪ/ *v* [T]

de·crease[1] /dɪˋkris; dɪˈkriːs/ *v* [I,T] to go down to a lower level, or to make something do this (使)变小, (使)减少: *In the last ten years cars have generally decreased in size.* 过去10年里, 汽车总的说来变小了。| *making further efforts to decrease military spending* 作进一步的努力以削减军费开支 —opposite 反义词 INCREASE[1] —**decreasing** *adj*

de·crease[2] /ˋdikris; ˈdiːkriːs/ *n* [C,U] the process of reducing something, or the amount by which it reduces 减少; 减少的数量: **[+in]** *There has been a decrease in the annual birth rate for the last twenty years.* 过去20年里年出生率一直在下降。| **[+of]** *He refused to accept a decrease of 20% to his salary.* 他拒绝接受把自己的工资调降20%。

de·cree[1] /dɪˋkri; dɪˈkriː/ *n* [C] **1** an official command or decision, especially one made by the ruler of a country (尤指由国家统治者颁布的)命令, 法令: *On 13 November the Emperor issued the decree.* 11月13日皇帝颁布了敕令。**2** a judgment in a court of law (法院的)判决, 裁定

decree[2] *v* [T] to make an official judgment or give an official command 下令, 颁布命令: **decree that** *The King decreed that there should be an end to the fighting.* 国王下令结束战斗。

decree ab·sol·ute /ˌ·ˌ·ˈ···/ *n* [C] *BrE law* an order by a court of law which officially ends a marriage【英, 法律】(法院作出的)离婚判决

decree ni·si /dɪˌkri ˋnaɪsaɪ; dɪˌkriː ˈnaɪsaɪ/ *n* [C] *BrE law* an order by a court of law that a marriage will end at a particular time in the future unless there is a good reason not to end it【英, 法律】(除非有正当理由, 否则在指定日期即生效的)法院离婚判决令

decorate 装修; 装饰

de·crep·it /dɪˋkrɛpɪt; dɪˈkrepɪ̈t/ *adj* old and in bad condition 衰老的, 破旧的: *The buildings were in a decrepit state.* 这些建筑物已经破旧不堪。—**decrepitude** *n* [U]

de·crim·in·a·lize also 又作 **-ise** *BrE*【英】/diˋkrɪmɪnəˌlaɪz; diːˈkrɪmɪ̈nəlaɪz/ *v* [T] to state officially that something is not illegal any more 使(原属非法的东西)合法化: *the campaign to decriminalize cannabis* 使大麻合法化的运动 —**decriminalization** *n* [U]

de·cry /dɪˋkraɪ; dɪˈkraɪ/ *v* **decried, decrying** [T] *formal* to state publicly that you do not approve of something【正式】(公开)反对, 谴责

ded·i·cate /ˋdɛdəˌket; ˈdedɪ̈keɪt/ *v* [T] **1 a)** to say that something such as a book or film has been written, made, or sung to express love, respect etc for someone 把(作品等)献给(某人): **dedicate sth to sb** *I'd like to dedicate this song to my wife.* 我想把这首歌献给我的妻子。**b)** to state in an official ceremony that a building will be given someone's name in order to show respect for them 用…命名(建筑物, 以表达崇敬之情): **dedicate sth to sb** *a chapel dedicated to St Francis* 以圣弗朗西斯命名的教堂 **2 dedicate yourself/your life to sth** to decide to spend all your time on and put all your efforts into one particular thing 献身于/把一生献给某事: *Sheila dedicated herself to a life of religion.* 希拉献身于宗教事业。

ded·i·cat·ed /ˋdɛdəˌketɪd; ˈdedɪ̈keɪtɪ̈d/ *adj* **1** someone who is dedicated works very hard at what they do because they care a lot about it 敬业的, 有奉献精神的, 有献身精神的: *He's certainly dedicated but really not very talented.* 他确实敬业, 但是实在不大有天赋。| **[+to]** *dedicated to one's art* 献身于艺术 | **dedicated sportsman/musician/Marxist etc** *Simon has been a dedicated Marxist all his life.* 西蒙一生都是虔诚的马克思主义者。**2** made for or used for only one particular purpose 专用的: *the transmission of software code through dedicated satellite channels* 通过专用卫星频道进行的软件密码传送 **3** *technical* a dedicated computer, computer system etc is only used for one particular job, such as controlling a machine【术语】(电脑、电脑系统等)专用的 —**dedicatedly** *adv*

ded·i·ca·tion /ˌdɛdəˋkeʃən; ˌdedɪ̈ˈkeɪʃən/ *n* **1** [U] hard work or effort that someone puts into a particular activity because they care about it a lot 奉献(精神), 敬业: *The success of the festival is a tribute to the dedication of one man.* 这个庆祝活动的成功充分说明了一个人的奉献精神。| **[+to]** *singleminded dedication to her art* 她对艺术执着的奉献精神 **2** [C] an act of dedicating something to someone 奉献, 敬献 **3** [C] a ceremony in which a building is given someone's name in order to show respect for them (以某人的名字命名某个建筑物以表达对此人的尊敬的)命名典礼

de·duce /dɪˋdus; dɪˈdjuːs/ *v* [T] *formal* to make a judgment about something, based on the information that you have【正式】推理, 推断, 演绎: **deduce that** *I deduced that she was married by the ring on her finger.* 我从她手指上戴的戒指推断出她已结婚。| **[+from]** *What did Darwin deduce from the presence of these species?* 达尔文从这些物种的存在推断出了什么? —**deducible** *adj*

de·duct /dɪˋdʌkt; dɪˈdʌkt/ *v* [T] to take away an amount or part from a total; subtract 减去, 扣除: **deduct sth from** *The dues will be deducted from his weekly pay-cheques.* 会费将从他周薪中扣除。—**deductible** *adj*

de·duc·tion /dɪˋdʌkʃən; dɪˈdʌkʃən/ *n* [C,U] **1** the process of making a judgment about something, based on the information that you have (根据已知资料进行的)推理, 推断, 演绎: *His powers of deduction were impressive.* 他的推理能力令人惊叹。**2** the process of taking away an amount from a total, or the amount that is taken away 扣除; 扣除额: *After deductions for tax etc your salary is about £700 a month.* 扣除税款等之后, 你的月薪大约有700英镑。

de·duc·tive /dɪˋdʌktɪv; dɪˈdʌktɪv/ *adj* using the knowledge that you have to make a judgment about a fact or situation 推理的, 演绎的: *deductive reasoning* 演绎推理

deed /did; diːd/ *n* [C] **1** *literary* something someone does that is very good or very bad【文】行为, 行动: *heroic deeds in battle* 战场上的英雄事迹 **2** *law* an official paper that is a record of an agreement, especially an agreement concerning who owns property【法律】(尤指关于财产所有人的)契约, 证书 **3 your good deed for the day** *humorous* something kind or helpful that you do【幽默】你当天做的好事

deed poll /ˈ· ·/ *n* [C] a legal document signed by only one person, for example in order to officially change your name 平边契据, 单边契据〈如为正式改名而单方签的契约〉

deem /dim; diːm/ *v* [T not in progressive 不用进行时] *formal* to think of something in a particular way; consider【正式】认

为，视为：**deem that** *They deemed that he was no longer capable of managing the business.* 他们认为他没有能力再管理这个企业了。| **deem sth necessary/appropriate etc** *They were told to take whatever action they deemed necessary.* 他们被告知可采取任何他们认为必要的行动。

2 1 **deep¹** /dip; di:p/ *adj*

1 ▶GOING FAR DOWN 往下很深◀ going far down from the top or from the surface 深的〔从顶部或表面向下延伸〕: *a deep hole in the ground* 地底下的一个深洞 | *Come on, get in! The water's not very deep here.* 快点，进来呀！这儿的水不太深。| **2 metres/6 feet etc deep** *At this point the lake is ninety metres deep.* 此处湖水深达90米。

2 knee-deep/ankle-deep etc deep enough to come up to your knees etc 齐膝深/深到脚踝等: *Soon they were in waist-deep mud.* 不一会儿他们就陷入齐腰深的泥中。

3 ▶GOING FAR IN 往里很深◀ going far in from the outside or from the front edge of something 深处的，纵深的〔从某物的外部或前缘往里延伸〕: *He had a deep wound on his forehead.* 他额头上有道很深的伤口。| **deep in the forest/mountains etc** (=far from the edge of the forest etc) 森林/山等的深处 *The path led them deep into the forest.* 小径把他们带到森林深处。

4 ▶FEELING/BELIEF 感觉/信念◀ a deep feeling or belief is very strong and sincere 〔感情或信念等〕强烈的，深厚的: *Even Rob's parents regarded him with deep suspicion.* 连罗布的父母都对他深表怀疑。

5 run/go deep if a feeling such as hatred or anger runs deep in someone, they feel it very strongly, especially because of things that have happened in the past 〔仇恨或愤怒〕非常强烈: *Resentment against the police runs deep in the community.* 这个社区对警察的怨恨十分强烈。—see also 另见 **still waters run deep** (STILL² (5))

6 ▶SOUND 声音◀ a deep sound is very low 低沉的: *his deep voice* 他低沉的嗓音 | *There was a flash and a deep roar.* 电光一闪，紧接着听到一种沉闷的隆隆声。

7 ▶COLOUR 颜色◀ a deep colour is dark and strong 暗的，浓重的: *the deep blue sky* 深蓝色的天空 —compare 比较 LIGHT² (1), PALE¹ (2)

8 ▶BREATH ETC 呼吸等◀ a deep SIGH², GULP² etc involves taking a lot of air into your lungs before letting it out again with a loud sound 深深的: *He took a deep breath and began to sing.* 他深深地吸了口气，然后开始演唱。

9 ▶SERIOUS 严肃的◀ **a)** someone who is deep or has deep thoughts thinks very hard about things, often in a way that other people find difficult to understand 深邃的，难以理解的: *Hal seems to me to be a very deep, sensitive type of person.* 哈尔在我看来好像是个非常深沉、敏感的人。**b)** a deep book, conversation, thought etc involves serious, complicated, or mysterious subjects that are often difficult to understand 深奥的，神秘的: *a deep conversation about the meaning of life* 关于生命意义的深奥谈话

10 deep in debt owing a lot of money 负债累累；债台高筑

11 deep sleep if someone is in a deep sleep it is difficult to wake them 酣睡

12 be in deep trouble also 又作 **be in deep shit** *slang* to be in a bad situation because you have done something wrong or stupid【俚】惹上大麻烦: *Don't say another word. You're in deep shit already.* 别再说了，你已经麻烦大了。

13 in deep water in trouble or in a difficult or serious situation 处于严重困境: *He had an uneasy feeling he was getting into deep water.* 他有种不安的感觉，觉得自己正陷入严重困境。

14 to be in deep *informal* to be very involved in a situation, especially one that causes you problems【非正式】深深卷入，深深陷入

15 deep in thought/conversation etc thinking so hard, or paying attention to something so much that you do not notice anything else that is happening around you 陷入沉思/专注于谈话等

16 jump/be thrown in at the deep end to choose to do or be made to do a very difficult job without having prepared for it 〔在没有准备的情况下〕做困难的事: *Our policy is to throw trainee representatives right in at the deep end.* 我们的培训方式是把受训的代表置于困境中，让他们自己应付。

17 go off at the deep end *informal* to become angry suddenly and violently, usually without good reason【非正式】〔通常是莫名其妙地〕勃然大怒 —**deepness** *n* [U]

3 **deep²** *adv* **1** [always+adv/prep] a long way into or below the surface of something; deeply 深入地，深深地: [**+down/below etc**] *He pushed his stick deep down into the mud.* 他把手杖深深地插进泥里。| *Carl was looking deep into her eyes.* 卡尔深情地望着她的眼睛。**2 deep down a)** if you know or feel something deep down, you are sure about it even though you do not admit it 心底，内心: *I knew deep down that I would probably never see Marie again.* 我心里知道我也许再也看不到玛丽了。**b)** if someone is good, evil etc deep down, that is what they are really like even though they usually hide it 实际上: *She may seem unfriendly, but deep down she's very nice.* 她或许看起来不太友好，但是实际上她人很好。**3 deep into the night** until very late 一直到深夜: *They talked deep into the night.* 他们一直谈到深夜。**4 two/three etc deep** if things or people are two deep, there are two rows or layers of things or people 二/三等排，二/三等层: *People were standing three deep at the bar.* 人们在酒吧台前站了三圈。

deep³ *n* **the deep** *poetical* the sea【诗】海洋

deep·en /ˈdipən; ˈdi:pən/ *v* **1** [I,T] if a feeling such as love or sadness deepens, it gradually becomes stronger （使）〔感情〕加深，（使）变深: *Enid's sorrow deepened as she thought of the long years ahead without him.* 伊妮德想到未来漫长岁月中将没有他的陪伴，便愈发伤心。**2** [I] if a serious situation deepens, it gets worse 〔局势、情形〕恶化: *a deepening recession* 日益严重的衰退 **3** [I,T] if you deepen your knowledge or understanding of something, you learn more about it and understand it better （使）〔理解〕加深: *an opportunity for young people to deepen their understanding of the world* 一个让年轻人加深对世界了解的机会 **4** [I] if water deepens, it becomes deeper 〔水〕变深 **5** [I] if a colour deepens, it becomes darker 〔颜色〕变暗 **6** [I] if a sound deepens, it becomes lower 〔声音〕变低

deep freeze /ˌ· ˈ·/ *n* [C] a large metal box in which food can be stored at very low temperatures for a long time; FREEZER (1) 冰柜，冷藏箱

deep fry /ˈ· ·/ *v* [T] to cook food under the surface of hot fat or oil 油炸

deep·ly /ˈdiplɪ; ˈdi:pli/ *adv* **1** a long way into something 很深地: *The parrot dug its claws deeply into my hand.* 鹦鹉把爪子深深地抠进我的手里。**2 deeply embarrassing/worrying/involved etc** extremely or very much 令人极其尴尬的/令人十分忧虑的/深陷其中的等: *His remarks were deeply embarrassing.* 他的话令人非常尴尬。**3** if you breathe deeply you completely fill your lungs with air 〔呼吸〕深深地 **4 deeply held** a deeply held belief or opinion is one that you are very sure about and feel very strongly about 〔信仰、观念等〕坚信的 **5 deeply rooted** a deeply rooted belief, opinion etc is difficult to change 〔信仰、观念等〕根深蒂固的，难以消除的: *These traditions were deeply rooted in local custom.* 这些传统深深地扎根于当地风俗之中。 3

deep-root·ed /ˌ· ˈ··◂/ also 又作 **deeply rooted** /ˌ·· ˈ··◂/ *adj* a deep-rooted habit, idea, belief etc is so fixed in a person or society that it is very difficult to change or destroy it 〔习惯、观念、信仰等〕根深蒂固的: *a deep-rooted suspicion of lawyers* 对律师根深蒂固的不信任

deep-seat·ed /ˌ· ˈ··◂/ *adj* a deep-seated attitude, feeling, or idea is strong and is very difficult to change 〔态度、感情、观念等〕不易改变的，顽固的: *a deep-seated fear of failure* 对失败难以消除的恐惧感

deep-set /ˌ· ˈ·◂/ *adj* deep-set eyes seem to be further back into the face than most people's 〔眼睛〕深陷的，眍眼的

deep six /ˌ· ˈ·/ *v* [T] *AmE informal* to decide not to use something such as a plan【美，非正式】弃用，抛弃: *We decided to deep six the whole project.* 我们决定把整个计划搁置一边，不予采用。

Deep South /ˌ· ˈ·/ *n* [singular] the most southern states of the US 南方腹地〔指美国最南部诸州〕

CULTURAL NOTE 文化注释

People often think about the Deep South as an area where people have very CONSERVATIVE political opinions and strong Christian beliefs, and which has a history of RACIAL problems. Southern states such as Florida, Texas, and Virginia are not considered part of the Deep South. 人们通常认为，南方腹地是政治观点极为保守、笃信基督教、历来存在种族问题的地区。像佛罗里达、得克萨斯、弗吉尼亚等南部各州并不是南方腹地的组成部分。— see also Cultural Note at the SOUTH 另见 the SOUTH 文化注释

deer /dɪr; dɪə/ *n plural* **deer** or **deers** [C] a large grass eating wild animal that can run very fast and has wide branching horns 鹿

deer·stalk·er /ˈdɪrˌstɔkɚ; ˈdɪəˌstɔ:kə/ *n* [C] a type of soft hat with pieces of cloth that cover your ears 软猎帽，猎鹿帽〔软质、有遮耳〕

de·face /dɪˈfes; dɪˈfeɪs/ *v* [T] to spoil the surface or appearance of something, especially by writing or making marks on it

损坏〔某物的〕表面[外观], 涂污: *Most of the monuments had been broken or defaced.* 大多数纪念碑都被打碎或者遭到涂损。—**defacement** *n* [U]

de fac·to /dɪ `fækto; ˌdeɪ ˈfæktəʊ/ *adj Latin* really existing although not legally stated to exist【拉丁】〔法律未作规定但〕实际上存在的: *a de facto state of war* 实际上存在的战争状态 —**de facto** *adv*

def·a·ma·tion /ˌdɛfə`meʃən; ˌdefəˈmeɪʃən/ *n* [U] *formal* the act of defaming someone【正式】诽谤: **defamation of character** *Chambers sued the newspaper for defamation of character.* 钱伯斯指控这家报纸诽谤人格。

de·fame /dɪ`fem; dɪˈfeɪm/ *v* [T] *formal* to write or say something that makes people have an unfairly bad opinion of someone or something【正式】诽谤, 中伤 —**defamatory** /dɪ`fæməˌtorɪ; dɪˈfæmətəri/ *adj*

de·fault¹ /dɪ`fɔlt; dɪˈfɒlt/ *n* **1 by default** if you win a game, competition etc by default, you win it because your opponent did not play or because there were no other competitors 因对手弃权〔而获胜〕 **2** [U] *formal* failure to do something that you are supposed to do according to the law or because it is your duty【正式】违约, 未履行职责: *the risk of default by borrowers* 借方不偿还的风险 **3 in default of** *formal* because of the lack or absence of something【正式】因缺乏, 因缺席 **4** [C usually singular 一般用单数] *technical* the way in which things will be arranged on a computer screen unless you decide to change them【术语】预设值, 默认值

default² *v* [I] to not do something that you are legally supposed to, especially not to pay money you are supposed to pay 不履行, 拖欠: [+on] *He defaulted on his child support payments.* 他拖欠孩子的抚养费。—**defaulter** *n* [C]

de·feat¹ /dɪ`fit; dɪˈfiːt/ *n* **1** [C,U] failure to win or succeed 失败: *an election defeat* 竞选失败 | **serious defeat** *The government has suffered a serious defeat.* 政府严重受挫。| **admit defeat** (=stop trying to succeed) 认输 *She's told him she won't marry him, but he'll never admit defeat.* 她已经告诉他她是不会嫁给他的, 但是他永远不会放弃。**2** [U] victory over someone or something 战胜, 击败: [+of] *We made the defeat of fascism our major priority.* 我们把战胜法西斯作为首要任务。

defeat² *v* [T] **1** to win a victory over someone in a war, competition, game etc; BEAT¹ (1)〔在战争、竞争、比赛等中〕战胜, 打败: *After a long campaign Wellington's army finally defeated Napoleon.* 经过长时间的战役, 威灵顿的军队最终打败了拿破仑。| **defeat sb by 10 points/by 3 goals to 2 etc** *We defeated the other team by six runs.* 我们以六分的优势击败对手。—see 见 WIN (USAGE) **2** if something defeats you, you cannot understand it and therefore cannot answer or deal with it 把〔某人〕难住: *It was the last question on the paper that defeated me.* 考卷上的最后一个问题把我难住了。**3** to make something fail 使…失败: *It was a lack of money, not effort, that defeated their plan.* 导致他们计划失败的不是不够努力而是因为缺钱。

de·feat·ist /dɪ`fitɪst; dɪˈfiːtʃɪst/ *n* [C] someone who believes that they will not succeed 失败主义者 —**defeatist** *adj*: *a defeatist attitude* 失败主义的态度 — **defeatism** *n* [U]

def·e·cate /`dɛfəˌket; ˈdefɪkeɪt/ *v* [I] *formal* to get rid of waste matter from your BOWELS【正式】排便 —**defecation** /ˌdɛfə`keʃən; ˌdefɪˈkeɪʃən/ *n* [U]

de·fect¹ /`difɛkt; dɪˈfekt/ *n* [C] a fault or a lack of something that means that something is not perfect 缺陷, 瑕疵: *All the cars are tested for defects before they leave the factory.* 所有的汽车在出厂之前都要接受检查看有无缺陷。

de·fect² /dɪ`fɛkt; dɪˈfekt/ *v* [I] to leave your own country or a group in order to go to or join an opposing one 背叛, 叛变, 投敌, 变节: *a talented Russian actor who defected to the West* 一位投靠西方的有才华的俄罗斯演员 —**defector** *n* [C] —**defection** /dɪ`fɛkʃən; dɪˈfekʃən/ *n* [C,U]

de·fec·tive /dɪ`fɛktɪv; dɪˈfektɪv/ *adj* **1** not made properly, or not working properly 有问题的, 有毛病的, 有缺陷的: *defective components* 有毛病的部件 **2** *technical*【术语】**defective verb** a verb such as 'must' or 'can' that cannot be used in all the forms that a verb can usually be used in 不完全变化动词〔如must或can, 不能有其他动词的各种变化形式〕—**defectively** *adv* —**defectiveness** *n* [U]

de·fence *BrE*【英】, **defense** *AmE*【美】/dɪ`fɛns; dɪˈfens/ *n*

1 ▶PROTECTING 保护◀ [U] the act of protecting something or someone from attack 防御, 防护: **come to sb's defence** (=help someone by protecting them from attack) 帮助某人; 保护某人 *Several people witnessed the attack, but no one came to her defence.* 有好几个人目睹了这次袭击事件, 但是没人站出来帮助她。| **in defence of** *Hundreds gave their lives in defence of freedom.* 数以百计的人为了捍卫自由而献出了自己的生命。—see also 另见 SELF-DEFENCE

2 ▶PROTECT A COUNTRY 保卫国家◀ [U] all the systems, people, materials etc that a country uses to protect itself from attack 国防: *He's one of the President's top advisors on defense.* 他是总统的高级国防顾问之一。| **defence cuts/spending/budget etc** *There are plans to increase defence spending by 6%.* 有计划将国防支出提高6%。

3 defences *BrE*【英】, **defenses** *AmE*【美】all the armies and weapons that are available to defend a place 防御力量: *The city's defenses were not strong enough to withstand the attack.* 这个城市的防御力量不够强, 不能抵挡这次攻击。

4 ▶AGAINST CRITICISM 抵制批评◀ [C,U] something that you say or do in order to protect someone or something from criticism 〔为保护某人或某物不受批评而做的〕辩护, 答辩: **in sb's/sth's defence** *Speaking in defence of the proposal, he pointed out how much cheaper it would be.* 在为这项提议作辩护发言时, 他指出这项提议实施起来将更省钱。

5 ▶IN A LAW COURT 在法庭上◀ **a)** [C] the things that are said in a court of law to prove that someone is not guilty of a crime 〔为了证明某人没犯罪而作的〕辩护, 辩词, 答辩: *Our defense looked pretty solid.* 我们的辩护词听起来相当有力。**b) the defence** all the people who are concerned with showing in a court of law that someone is not guilty of a crime 辩方: *The defense's case is strong.* 辩方的陈述非常有说服力。—compare 比较 PROSECUTION (2)

6 ▶AGAINST ILLNESS 抵御疾病◀ [C] something that your body produces naturally as a way of preventing illness〔人体对疾病的〕抵抗力, 防御能力: *The body's immune system is its defence against infection.* 身体的免疫系统是抵御感染的武器。

7 ▶EMOTIONS 感情◀ [C] something you do or a way of behaving that prevents you from being upset or seeming weak 自我防卫: [+against] *Dean's aggressive behaviour is his defence against depression.* 迪安好斗的行为是为了防止陷入沮丧。

8 ▶SPORT 体育◀ [C] *BrE* the players in a game of football etc whose main job is to try to prevent the other team from getting points【英】防守队员, 后卫: *Barnaby cut through the heart of Arsenal's defence.* 巴纳比切入阿森纳队的防守腹地。

de·fence·less *BrE*【英】, **defenseless** *AmE*【美】/dɪ`fɛnsləs; dɪˈfensləs/ *adj* weak and unable to protect yourself from attack or harm 没有防卫能力的: *a defenceless old lady* 没有自卫能力的老太太

defence mech·a·nis·m *BrE*【英】, **defense mechanism** *AmE*【美】/ˈ·'·, ˈ···/ *n* [C] **1** a process in your brain that makes you forget things that are painful for you to think about 防卫机制〔人脑忘掉痛苦事情的机制〕 **2** a reaction in your body that protects you from an illness or danger 防御机制〔身体抵制疾病或危险的反应〕

de·fend /dɪ`fɛnd; dɪˈfend/ *v* **1** [T] to do something in order to protect someone or something from being attacked 保护, 保卫: **defend sth against/from** *They needed more troops to defend the border against possible attack.* 他们需要更多的部队来保卫边境地区免受可能的攻击。| **defend yourself** *I picked a stick up to defend myself.* 我拿起一根棍子进行自卫。**2** to do something in order to stop something being taken away or in order to make it possible for something to continue 捍卫, 维护: *The union said they would take action to defend their members' jobs.* 工会称他们将采取行动来保住会员们的工作。**3** [T] to use arguments to protect something or someone from criticism, or to prove that something is right 为…辩护, 为…辩白, 为…辩解: *How can you defend the torture of animals for scientific research?* 你怎能用科学研究的理由为折磨动物这件事辩解呢? | **defend sb against/from** *He had to defend himself against their charges.* 他必须对他们的指控为自己辩解。| **defend yourself** *As a politician, you have to be able to defend yourself when things get tough.* 作为政界人物, 在形势严峻时你必须能为自己辩解。**4** [I,T] to protect your own team's end of the field in a game such as football, to prevent your opponents from getting points〔在比赛中〕防守, 防卫 **5 defend a title/championship** to take part in a regular competition that you won the last time it was held〔冠军〕卫冕 **6** [T] to be a lawyer for someone who has been charged with a crime〔律师〕为〔被指控犯罪者〕辩护: *Who is defending the case?* 谁在为这个案子辩护? —compare 比较 PROSECUTE (2)

de·fen·dant /dɪ`fɛndənt; dɪˈfendənt/ *n* [C] *law* the person in a court of law who has been accused (ACCUSE) of doing something illegal【法律】被告: *We find the defendant not guilty.* 我们判决被告无罪。—compare 比较 PLAINTIFF

de·fend·er /dɪ`fɛndɚ; dɪˈfendə/ *n* [C] **1** one of the players in a game such as football who have to defend their team's GOAL

(3) from the opposing team 防守队员，后卫 **2 a defender of the poor/liberty/privilege etc** someone who defends a particular idea, belief, person etc 穷人/自由/特权等的守护者

Defender of the Faith /ˌ· ·· ··ˈ·/ a title used by British kings and queens since Henry VIII, who was given it by Pope Leo X in 1521 because he wrote a paper attacking the ideas of Martin Luther 信念捍卫者〔自亨利八世起英国国王和女王沿用的尊号。1521年，亨利八世撰文抨击马丁·路德的思想，教皇利奥十世因此将这一封号赐予他〕

de·fense[1] /dɪˈfɛns; dɪˈfens/ *n* the American spelling of DEFENCE defence 的美式拼法

de·fense[2] /ˈdifɛns; dɪˈfens/ *n* [C,U] *AmE* the players in a game of football etc whose main job is to try to prevent the other team from getting points【美】防守队员，后卫: *He plays defense for the New York Giants.* 他为纽约巨人队打后卫。—opposite 反义词 OFFENSE[2]

de·fen·si·ble /dɪˈfɛnsəbl; dɪˈfensəbəl/ *adj* **1** a defensible opinion or idea seems reasonable and you can easily support it〔意见或观点〕正当有理的，可辩解的: *Richmond's theories are not morally defensible.* 从道德上讲，里士满的理论是站不住脚的。**2** a defensible building or area is easy to protect against attack〔建筑物、地区等〕能防御进攻的，可防卫的 —**defensibly** *adv*

de·fen·sive[1] /dɪˈfɛnsɪv; dɪˈfensɪv/ *adj* **1** used or intended to protect people against attack 防御用的，防御性的: *The rockets are a purely defensive measure against nuclear attack.* 火箭纯粹是防止核进攻的防御性措施。—opposite 反义词 OFFENSIVE[1] (3) **2** behaving in a way that shows you think someone is criticizing you even if they are not 防备批评的，自卫的，有戒心的: *There's no need to be so defensive, I just asked how old you are!* 你没有必要这么戒备，我只是问你多大年龄！**3** *AmE* concerned with stopping the other team from getting points in a game【美】〔比赛中〕防守的，防御的: *defensive play* 防守型打法 | *the defensive coach* 防守型教练 —**defensively** *adv* —**defensiveness** *n* [U]

defensive[2] *n* **on the defensive** behaving in a way that shows that you think that someone is criticizing you even if they are not 处于防御姿态，采取守势，存有戒心

de·fer /dɪˈfɝ; dɪˈfɜː/ *v* **deferred, deferring** [T] to delay something until a later date 延期，推迟: *Let's defer the decision for a few weeks.* 我们推迟几周再作决定吧。

defer to sb/sth *phr v* [T] *formal* to agree to accept someone's opinion or decision because you have respect for that person【正式】服从，遵从，听从

def·er·ence /ˈdɛfərəns; ˈdefərəns/ *n* [U] *formal* behaviour that shows that you respect someone and are therefore willing to accept their opinions or judgment【正式】尊敬，敬重；服从: *He had the arrogance of someone who had always been accustomed to deference.* 他为人傲慢，一向习惯于别人对他尊敬和服从。| **in/out of deference to** (=done because you respect someone's beliefs, opinions etc) 出于对…的尊敬 *They were married in church out of deference to their parents' wishes.* 出于对双方父母意愿的尊重，他们在教堂结婚。—**deferential** /ˌdɛfəˈrɛnʃəl; ˌdefəˈrenʃəl◂/ *adj* —**deferentially** *adv*

de·fi·ance /dɪˈfaɪəns; dɪˈfaɪəns/ *n* [U] behaviour that shows you clearly refuse to do what someone tells you to do 违抗，挑衅的态度: *The boy gave me a look of hatred and defiance as he slammed the door.* 那个男孩"砰"的一声关上门，用仇恨和挑衅的目光看了我一眼。| **in defiance of** *The company had been dumping their waste into the sea, in defiance of government regulations.* 这家公司一直无视政府的规定，往海里倾倒垃圾。

de·fi·ant /dɪˈfaɪənt; dɪˈfaɪənt/ *adj* refusing clearly to do what someone tells you to do 违抗的，挑衅的: *He gave a short, defiant laugh.* 他挑衅地笑了一声。—**defiantly** *adv*

de·fi·cien·cy /dɪˈfɪʃənsɪ; dɪˈfɪʃənsi/ *n* [C,U] **1** a lack of something that is necessary 不足，缺乏: *The disease is caused by a vitamin deficiency.* 这种疾病是由于缺少某种维生素而引起的。**2** a weakness or fault in something 缺点，毛病

deficiency dis·ease /·ˈ·· ··ˌ·/ *n* [C,U] a disease caused by a lack of a food substance that is necessary for good health 营养缺乏症: *deficiency diseases such as rickets* 如佝偻病之类的营养缺乏症

de·fi·cient /dɪˈfɪʃənt; dɪˈfɪʃənt/ *adj* **1** not containing or having enough of something 缺乏的，不足的: *zinc deficient plants* 缺锌的植物 | [+in] *a diet deficient in calcium* 缺钙的饮食 **2** not good enough 不完美的: *Some of the methods used were deficient.* 所用的方法有一些还不够完善。

def·i·cit /ˈdɛfəsɪt; ˈdefɪsɪt/ *n* [C] the difference between the amount of something that you have and the higher amount that you need 差额，逆差，亏损，赤字: [+of] *The directors have reported a deficit of £2.5 million.* 董事们报告说亏损250万英镑。| [+in] *a deficit in magnesium* 缺镁

de·file[1] /dɪˈfaɪl; dɪˈfaɪl/ *v* [T] *formal* to make something less pure or good【正式】污损，污染，亵渎: *These disgusting videos defile and corrupt the minds of the young.* 这些令人恶心的录像带污染并腐蚀了年轻人的思想。

de·file[2] /ˈdifaɪl; dɪˈfaɪl/ *n* [C] *formal* a narrow passage, especially through mountains【正式】〔尤指山中的〕小路，狭道，隘路

de·fine /dɪˈfaɪn; dɪˈfaɪn/ *v* [T] **1** to describe something correctly and thoroughly 阐明，说明: *the ability to define clients' needs* 说明顾客需求的能力 | **define sth clearly/precisely** *The powers of the President are clearly defined in the Constitution.* 总统的权力在宪法中有明确的规定。**2** to explain exactly the meaning of a particular word or idea 给…下定义，解释: *Each of us might define the concept of freedom in a very different way.* 我们每个人可能会以极不同的方式来定义"自由"这个概念。| **define sth as** *The dictionary defines it as 'a narrow passage'.* 字典把它解释为"狭窄的通道"。| **define sth loosely/broadly** (=define something in a way that is less exact) 笼统地/大体上解释某事 **3** to show the edge or shape of something clearly 标明…界限，显出…轮廓: **sharply/clearly defined** *sharply defined footprints in the fresh snow* 新雪里轮廓清晰的脚印 **4** to have particular features or qualities that make you different or separate from other people or things 是…的特征，界定: **define sth as** *Which qualities define us as human?* 是什么特征界定了我们是人？—**definable** *adj*

def·i·nite /ˈdɛfənɪt; ˈdefɪnɪt/ *adj* **1** clearly known, seen, or stated 清楚的，明确的: *Amanda saw a definite change in her son that year.* 那一年阿曼达在她儿子身上发现了明显的变化。**2** a definite arrangement, promise etc will happen in the way that someone has said〔安排、许诺等〕确切的，确定的: *We have to set a definite date for the concert.* 我们得为音乐会定下一个确切的日期。**3 be definite (about)** to say something very firmly so that people understand exactly what you mean (对…)有把握，肯定: *She was very definite about how she felt.* 她对自己的感觉很有把握。

definite ar·ti·cle /ˌ··· ˈ···/ *n* [C usually singular 一般用单数] **1** the word 'the' in English〔英语中的〕定冠词〔即the〕**2** a word in another language that is like 'the'〔其他语言中的〕定冠词 —compare 比较 INDEFINITE ARTICLE —see also 另见 ARTICLE (4)

def·i·nite·ly /ˈdɛfənɪtlɪ; ˈdefɪnɪtli/ *adv* with no chance of being wrong; certainly 确切地，肯定地: *Max knew that he had definitely been wrong about Diana.* 马克斯知道他在黛安娜的问题上肯定是错了。| *"It's not worth that much, is it?" "No, definitely not!"* "不值那么多，对不对？""对，肯定不值！"—see 见 OF COURSE (USAGE), SURELY (USAGE)

def·i·ni·tion /ˌdɛfəˈnɪʃən; ˌdefɪˈnɪʃən/ *n* **1** [C] a phrase or sentence that says exactly what a word, phrase, or idea means 定义，释义: *a definition in a dictionary* 字典里的定义 | [+of] *No one has yet come up with a satisfactory definition of terrorism.* 关于"恐怖主义"还没有人想出一个令人满意的定义。**2 by definition** if something has a particular quality by definition, it must have that quality because all things of that type have it 从定义上讲，根据其定义: *A message that cannot be seen or heard is, by definition, not effective.* 一个看不见、听不着的信息，根据定义来说是无效的。**3** [U] the degree to which something such as a picture, sound etc is clear〔相片、声音等的〕清晰度，鲜明度: **lack definition** *The photograph lacks definition.* 这张照片清晰度不够。

de·fin·i·tive /dɪˈfɪnətɪv; dɪˈfɪnɪtɪv/ *adj* **1** [usually before noun 一般用于名词前] a definitive book, study of something etc is considered to be the best ever produced and cannot be improved 最具权威的，最可靠的: *She has written the definitive book on the poet Wordsworth.* 她写的关于诗人华兹华斯的书是最具权威性的。**2** a definitive statement, VERDICT etc will not be changed〔陈述、裁决等〕最终的，决定性的 —**definitively** *adv*

de·flate /dɪˈflet; ˌdiːˈfleɪt/ *v* **1** [I,T] if a tyre, BALLOON[1] (1, 2) etc deflates, or if you deflate it, it gets smaller because the gas inside it comes out (使)放气，(使)漏气 **2** [T] to make someone feel less important or less confident 使〔某人〕泄气: *I'd love to deflate that ego of his!* 我想挫一挫他的锐气！**3** [T] to show that a statement, argument etc is wrong 揭破 **4** [T] *technical* to change economic rules or conditions in a country so that prices fall or stop rising【术语】紧缩〔通货〕—**deflation** /dɪˈfleʃən; ˌdiːˈfleɪʃən/ *n* [U]

de·flat·ed /dɪˈfletɪd; ˌdiːˈfleɪtɪd/ *adj* feeling less cheerful or confident than before 气馁的，泄气的，灰心的: *I felt utterly deflated and let down.* 我觉得非常灰心失望。

de·fla·tion·a·ry /diˋfleʃən,ɛrɪ; ˌdiːˈfleɪʃənəri/ *adj technical* causing a situation in which prices fall or stop rising【术语】通货紧缩的: *deflationary policies* 紧缩通货的政策

de·flect /dɪˋflɛkt; dɪˈflekt/ *v* **1** [I,T] to turn in a different direction, especially after hitting something else, or to make something do this (使)转向, (使)偏斜: *The waves are deflected by the lifeboat's high narrow bows.* 救生船又高又尖的船头使海浪改变了方向。**2 deflect attention/criticism/anger etc** to stop people criticizing something, getting angry about it etc 转移注意力/批评/愤怒等: *a transparent attempt to deflect public criticism* 明显的转移公众批评的企图 **3** [T] if something deflects you from what you are doing, it takes your attention away from it 把〔某人的注意力从某事〕移开: *Nothing could deflect him from his goal.* 没有什么能使他改变目标。

de·flec·tion /dɪˋflɛkʃən; dɪˈflekʃən/ *n* [C,U] **1** the action of making something change its direction 转向, 偏差: *the deflection of the bullet* 子弹的转向 **2** *technical* the degree to which the moving part on a measuring instrument moves away from zero【术语】〔计量仪器的〕偏差(度)

de·flow·er /diˋflaʊɚ; ˌdiːˈflaʊə/ *v* [T] *literary* to have sex with a woman who has never had sex before【文】使〔女子〕失去童贞

De·foe /dɪˋfo; dɪˈfəʊ/, **Daniel** (1660-1731) a British writer whose most famous works are the NOVELs *Robinson Crusoe* and *Moll Flanders* 笛福〔(1660-1731), 英国作家。最著名的作品是小说《鲁滨逊漂流记》和《摩尔·弗兰德斯》〕

de·fog /diˋfɑg; diːˈfɒg/ *v* **defogged, defogging** [T] *AmE* to remove the CONDENSATION from the window inside a car, by using heat or warm air【美】除去〔汽车挡风玻璃上的〕雾水; DEMIST *BrE*【英】

de·fo·li·ant /diˋfolɪənt; diːˈfəʊliənt/ *n* [C,U] a chemical substance used on plants to make their leaves drop off 脱叶剂

de·fo·li·ate /diˋfolɪ,et; diːˈfəʊlieɪt/ *v* [T] to use defoliant on a plant or tree 使落叶

de·for·es·ta·tion /dɪ,fɔrəsˋteʃən; diːˌfɒrɪ̇ˈsteɪʃən/ *n* [U] the cutting or burning down of all the trees in an area 砍伐树林, 毁林 —**deforest** /diˋfɔrɪst; diːˈfɒrɪ̇st/ *v* [T usually passive 一般用被动态]

de·form /dɪˋfɔrm; dɪˈfɔːm/ *v* [T] to change the usual shape of something so that its usefulness or appearance is spoiled 使变形; 毁坏…的外观: *The heat had deformed the plastic.* 高温使得塑料变形。

de·for·ma·tion /ˌdifɔrˋmeʃən; ˌdiːfɔːˈmeɪʃən/ *n* **1** [C,U] a change in the usual shape of something, especially one that makes it worse 走样, 畸形: *deformation of the telescope's mirror* 望远镜镜片的变形 **2** [U] the process of changing the shape of something in a way that spoils its usefulness or appearance 变形

de·formed /dɪˋfɔrmd; dɪˈfɔːmd/ *adj* something that is deformed has the wrong shape, especially because it has grown or developed wrongly〔尤指发育、生长不良而〕畸形的: *a deformed foot* 一只畸形的脚

de·for·mi·ty /dɪˋfɔrmətɪ; dɪˈfɔːmɪ̇ti/ *n* [C,U] a condition in which part of someone's body is not the normal shape〔人体某部分的〕变形, 畸形

DEFRA *n* [singular] the Department for Environment, Food and Rural Affairs; a British government department〔英国〕环境、食品与农村事务部

de·fraud /dɪˋfrɔd; dɪˈfrɔːd/ *v* [T] to trick a person or organization in order to get money from them 欺骗, 骗取〔金钱〕: **defraud sb of** *She defrauded her employers of thousands of pounds.* 她从雇主那儿骗取了数千英镑。

de·fray /dɪˋfre; dɪˈfreɪ/ *v* [T] **defray costs/expenses** *formal* to pay someone's costs etc【正式】支付费用: *The company will defray any expenses you have on the journey.* 公司将为你支付旅程中的所有费用。

de·frock /diˋfrɑk; ˌdiːˈfrɒk/ *v* [T] to officially remove a priest from his job because he has done something wrong 免去〔行为不检的牧师、神甫的〕圣职 —**defrocked** *adj*

de·frost /diˋfrɔst; ˌdiːˈfrɒst/ *v* **1** [I,T] if frozen food defrosts, or if you defrost it, it gets warmer until it is not frozen (使)解冻 **2** [I,T] if a FREEZER or REFRIGERATOR defrosts, or if you defrost it, it is turned off so that the ice inside it melts (给)〔冰箱、冰柜等〕除霜 **3** [T] *AmE* to remove ice from inside the windows of a car by using heat or warm air【美】除去〔汽车玻璃上的〕霜[冰] —compare 比较 DEFOG

deft /dɛft; deft/ *adj* **1** a deft movement is skilful, and often quick〔行动〕敏捷的, 灵巧的: *With one deft movement, she flipped the pancake over.* 她敏捷地一动, 把煎饼翻了过来。**2** skilful at doing something〔做某事〕在行的, 熟练的: *a deft political operator* 手腕娴熟的政治高手 —**deftly** *adv* —**deftness** *n* [U]

de·funct /dɪˋfʌŋkt; dɪˈfʌŋkt/ *adj formal* not existing any more, or not useful any more【正式】不再存在的, 不再使用的

de·fuse /diˋfjuz; ˌdiːˈfjuːz/ *v* [T] **1** to improve a difficult or dangerous situation, for example by making people less angry or by dealing with the causes of a problem 缓和, 改善〔困难或危险局面〕: *We believe that greater economic stability might defuse the current crisis.* 我们相信较为稳定的经济或许能缓和当前的危机。| **defuse tension/anger/fears etc** *In an attempt to defuse the tension, Rob put some music on.* 为了缓和紧张的气氛, 罗布放了些音乐。**2** to remove the FUSE[1] (2) from a bomb in order to stop it exploding 拆除〔炸弹的〕引信

de·fy /dɪˋfaɪ; dɪˈfaɪ/ *v* **defied, defying** [T] **1** to refuse to obey a law or rule, or refuse to do what someone in authority tells you to do 违抗〔法律或规则〕, 公然蔑视, 拒不服从: *He defied his father's wishes and married Agnes.* 他违抗父亲的意愿, 和阿格尼丝结了婚。**2 defy description/analysis/imagination etc** to be so extreme or unusual that it is almost impossible to describe or understand 无法描述/分析/想象等: *The beauty of the scene defies description.* 这里优美的风景无法用语言描述。**3 I defy you (to)** *spoken formal* used when asking someone to do something that you think is impossible, in order to prove that you are right【口, 正式】我倒要看看…〔用于激某人做某事〕: *I defy you to think of one way in which this government has helped the poor.* 我倒要看看你能否想出这届政府为穷人做的一件好事。

De·gas /dəˋgɑ; ˈdeɪgɑː/, **Ed·gar** /ˋɛdgɚ; ˈedgə/ (1834-1917) a French IMPRESSIONIST painter, known especially for his pictures of horse racing, theatres, CAFEs, and women dancing 德加〔(1834-1917), 法国印象派画家, 尤以描绘赛马会、剧院、咖啡馆和舞女的作品闻名〕

de·gen·e·rate[1] /dɪˋdʒɛnə,ret; dɪˈdʒenəreɪt/ *v* [I] to become worse 恶化, 堕落, 退化: **[+into]** *The debate soon degenerated into petty squabbling.* 争论不多久就演变成无聊的争吵。—**degeneration** /dɪ,dʒɛnəˋreʃən; dɪˌdʒenəˈreɪʃən/ *n* [U]

de·gen·e·rate[2] /dɪˋdʒɛnərɪt; dɪˈdʒenərɪ̇t/ *adj* **1** *formal* having become worse in character or quality than before【正式】〔性格、品质上〕堕落的, 没落的, 腐化的, 退化的: *the last degenerate member of a noble family* 贵族家庭最后一个没落的成员 **2** having very low standards or moral behaviour〔道德〕败坏的, 腐败的: *The Emperor was denounced as a degenerate debauchee.* 这个皇帝被指责是个道德败坏的浪荡子。

degenerate[3] *n* [C] someone whose behaviour is considered to be morally unacceptable 堕落的人

de·gen·era·tive /dɪˋdʒɛnərətɪv; dɪˈdʒenərətɪv/ *adj* a degenerative illness gradually gets worse and cannot be stopped〔疾病〕不断恶化的

de·grad·a·tion /ˌdɛgrəˋdeʃən; ˌdegrəˈdeɪʃən/ *n* **1** [singular, U] an experience that makes you feel ashamed and angry 落魄, 丢脸: *a life of poverty and degradation* 穷困潦倒的生活 **2** [U] the process by which something changes to a worse condition 退化, 恶化

de·grade /dɪˋgred; dɪˈgreɪd/ *v* **1** [T] to treat someone without respect or make people lose their respect for someone; DEBASE 贬低〔某人〕, 使〔某人〕丢脸: *a movie that degrades women* 侮辱妇女人格的影片 | **degrade yourself** *How can you degrade yourself by writing such trash?* 你怎么能写这种垃圾作品来降低自己的身份呢? **2** [T] to make a situation or the condition of something worse 使〔局面或情况〕恶化 **3** [I,T] *technical* to change a substance, chemical etc to a simpler form【术语】(使)〔物质、化学制品等〕分解, 降解

de·grad·ing /dɪˋgredɪŋ; dɪˈgreɪdɪŋ/ *adj* a degrading experience, event etc makes you lose respect for yourself 丢脸的, 降低身份的, 有辱人格的: *We oppose flogging and other cruel, inhuman, or degrading punishments.* 我们反对鞭笞和其他残酷、野蛮或者羞辱性的惩罚方式。

de·gree /dɪˋgri; dɪˈgriː/ *n* S3 W1

1 ▶ANGLES/TEMPERATURE 角度/温度◀ [C] a unit of measurement, especially for temperature or angles 度, 度数〔尤作温度或角度的度量单位〕—see table on page C4 参见C4页附录

2 ▶AMOUNT 数量◀ [C,U] the amount of a quality that exists or how much something happens 程度: **[+of]** *People will choose the party that offers some degree of social change.* 人们将选择提出某种程度社会变革的政党。| *There are different views about the degree to which unemployment is society's fault.* 对于失业在多大程度上是社会的过错, 存在着不同的观点。

3 to a degree also 又作 **to some degree/to a certain degree**

partly 在某种程度上: *I think that's true to a degree, but the situation isn't quite as simple as that.* 我认为某种程度上说那是对的，但是情况并没那么简单。

4 ►UNIVERSITY 大学◄ [C] **a)** a course of study at a university or college〔大学的〕学位课程: *a law degree* 法律课程 | *a degree course* 学位课程 | [+in] *a degree in Economics* 经济学课程 | **take/do a degree** *Isabelle's doing her degree at the Sorbonne.* 伊莎贝尔正在巴黎大学文理学院攻读学位。**b)** a QUALIFICATION (1) given to someone who has successfully completed this course of study〔授予成功完成学业者的〕学位资格: **have/hold a degree** *Lori has a degree in Chemistry from Harvard.* 洛丽拥有哈佛大学化学学位。

5 by degrees very slowly; gradually 慢慢地; 逐渐地: *By degrees, the music drove all thoughts from his head.* 慢慢地，音乐驱散了他头脑里的种种杂念。

6 ►POSITION IN SOCIETY 社会地位◄ [U] *old use* your position in society【旧】(社会) 地位

CULTURAL NOTE 文化注释

Bachelor's degrees When students successfully complete their university courses in the US and UK, they get a BACHELOR'S DEGREE. There are two main types of bachelor's degree: a BA for ARTS subjects such as languages or history, and a B.S. (in the US) or a BSc (in the UK) for science subjects such as mathematics and chemistry. In the US, a student can study for two years in a JUNIOR COLLEGE instead of a university and get an A.A. (= Associate of Arts). This degree, however, is not as high as a bachelor's degree. In the UK, students GRADUATE with different levels of degrees, according to how well they have done in their COURSEWORK and examinations. Students with the highest grades are given a 'first'. The next level, a second class degree, is divided into two types: an upper second, or '2:1' (pronounced 'two-one') which is higher, and a lower second, or '2:2' (pronounced 'two-two') which is lower. The lowest degree in a UK university is a 'third'. In the US, students who have very high GRADES when they finish university graduate 'summa cum laude', 'magna cum laude', or 'cum laude', which mean 'with highest honours', 'with high honours', and 'with honours'. Other students are not ranked according to how well they have done. 学士学位: 英美学生顺利完成大学学业，则获学士学位。有两种学士学位: 语言或历史等文科学士学位称为文学士 (BA)，数学或化学等理科学士学位叫做理学士 (美国称B.S.，英国称BSc)。美国学生可以不在大学而在专科学校学习两年，获副文学士学位 (A.A.)，其不如文学士学位高。英国根据学生课程作业和考试成绩将其分为不同毕业等级。成绩最好的学生被授予"一级"(first) 称号; 第二等级分两种，成绩较好的称"二级一等"(2:1)，稍低的称"二级二等"(2:2); 最低等级为"三级"(third)。美国学生毕业成绩优秀，则称"最优异学业成绩"(summa cum laude)、"优异成绩"(magna cum laude) 和"优良成绩"(cum laude)。其他学生并不依成绩分级。

Higher degrees Students who want to continue studying after they graduate from university can get a higher degree such a MASTER's degree or a PhD. There are two main types of master's degree: an MA for arts subjects and an M.S. (in the US) or an MSc (in the UK) for science subjects. In Scotland, students usually spend one more year studying for their degrees than students in the rest of the UK, so they typically get a master's degree instead of a bachelor's degree when they graduate. 更高级的学位: 大学毕业后若继续深造，可获硕士学位 (master's degree) 或博士学位 (PhD)。硕士学位分两种，文科称文学硕士 (MA)，理科称理学硕士 (美国称M.S.，英国称MSc)。苏格兰学生一般比英国其他地区的学生多花一年攻读学位，因此毕业时通常获硕士学位而非学士学位。— see Feature on page F16 见F16页文化特写

de·hu·man·ize also 又作 **-ise** *BrE*【英】/diˈhjuməˌnaɪz; ˌdiːˈhjuːmənaɪz/ *v* [T often passive 常用被动态] to treat people so badly that they lose their good human qualities such as kindness etc 使〔某人〕丧失人性: *War dehumanizes people.* 战争使人们丧失人性。—**dehumanizing** *adj* —**dehumanization** /dɪˌhjumənəˈzeʃən; diːˌhjuːmənaɪˈzeɪʃən/ *n* [U]

de·hy·drate /diˈhaɪdret; ˌdiːhaɪˈdreɪt/ *v* **1** [T] to remove the liquid from a substance such as food or chemicals 使脱水，使干燥: *The substance is dehydrated and stored as powder.* 该物质被脱水并以粉末形式储存。**2** [I] to lose too much water from your body〔人体〕脱水 —**dehydrated** *adj* —**dehydration** /ˌdihaɪˈdreʃən; ˌdiːhaɪˈdreɪʃən/ *n* [U]

de-ice /ˌdiˈaɪs; ˌdiːˈaɪs/ *v* [T] to remove the ice from something 除冰; 化冻

de·i·fy /ˈdiəˌfaɪ; ˈdiːɪ̈faɪ/ *v* **deified, deifying** [T] *formal* to treat someone or something with far too much respect and admiration【正式】崇拜; 神化; 奉若神明 —**deification** /ˌdiəfəˈkeʃən; ˌdiːɪ̈fɪ̈ˈkeɪʃən/ *n* [U]

deign /den; deɪn/ *v* **deign to do something** an expression meaning to agree to do something, often used jokingly when you think someone should do that thing all the time 俯就[屈尊]做某事〔常为玩笑用法，尤用于认为某人本来就应该那么做〕: *Ah, so you've deigned to grace us with your presence I see!* 啊，你屈尊光临，我们不胜荣幸!

de·is·m /ˈdiɪzəm; ˈdiːɪzəm/ *n* [U] the belief in a God who made the world but has no influence on human lives 自然神论，理神论 —compare 比较 THEISM

De·i·ty, the /ˈdiətɪ; ˈdiːɪ̈ti/ *n formal*【正式】God 上帝

deity *n* [C] a god or GODDESS 神; 女神: *the deities of ancient Greece* 古希腊诸神

dé·jà vu /ˌdeʒɑ ˋvju; ˌdeɪʒɑː ˈvjuː/ *n* [U] *French* the feeling that you have previously experienced exactly the same thing as you are experiencing now【法】似曾经历的感觉，似曾相识的感觉: *Madeleine felt a strange sense of déjà vu as she walked into the room.* 马德琳走进房间时，有一种似曾来过的奇怪感觉。

de·jec·ted /dɪˋdʒɛktɪd; dɪˈdʒektɪ̈d/ *adj* unhappy, disappointed, or sad 抑郁的，失望的，沮丧的 —**dejectedly** /dɪˋdʒɛktɪdlɪ; dɪˈdʒektɪ̈dli/ *adv* —**dejection** /dɪˋdʒɛkʃən; dɪˈdʒekʃən/ *n* [U]

de ju·re /di ˋdʒurɪ; ˌdiː ˈdʒʊəri/ *adj law* true or right because of a law【法律】法律上的，合法的

De Klerk /də ˋklɝk; də ˈklɜːk/, **F.W.** (1936-) the President of South Africa from 1989 to 1994. He made many political changes and finally ended the system of APARTHEID. In 1990 he allowed the ANC to become a legal organization again, and let Nelson Mandela out of prison. He and Mandela won the Nobel Peace Prize in 1993. 德克勒克〔(1936-)，1989至1994年间任南非总统，曾实行诸多政治变革，最终结束了种族隔离制度。1990年，他承认南非非洲人国民大会为合法组织，并将纳尔逊·曼德拉从监狱中释放出来。1993年，他与曼德拉一起获得诺贝尔和平奖〕

De La Mare /də lɑ ˋmɛr; də lɑː ˈmeə/, **Wal·ter** /ˈwɔltɚ; ˈwɔːltə/ (1873-1956) a British writer famous especially for his poems for children 德拉马尔〔(1873-1956)，英国作家，尤以儿童诗歌闻名〕

Del·a·ware /ˈdɛləwɛr; ˈdeləweə/ abbreviation 缩写为 **DE** a small state in the northeastern US. It was one of the original thirteen colonies (COLONY) established under British rule. 特拉华州〔美国一小州名，位于东北部，为最初的13个英属殖民地之一〕

de·lay¹ /dɪˋle; dɪˈleɪ/ *n* **1** [C usually singular 一般用单数] the length of time between the moment when something should start and the moment it actually does start 延误的时间，耽搁的时间: *Sorry for the delay, Mr Weaver.* 对不起，韦弗先生，耽搁了一些时间。| [+of] *a delay of twenty minutes* 20分钟的延误 | **short/long etc delay** *There was a slight delay before the show.* 演出推迟了一小会儿。| **without delay** (=immediately) 立即，立刻，毫不耽搁 **2** [C] a situation in which someone or something is made to wait 延误，耽搁: **severe delays** *There are severe delays on Route 95 this morning because of an accident.* 由于交通事故，今天早晨95号公路上严重塞车。| [+in] *delays in transporting the goods to London* 货物运往伦敦过程中的延误 **3** [U] the situation in which something does not happen or start when it should do 推迟〔某事没有按时发生或开始〕: **be subject to delay** (=likely to be delayed) 可能推迟 2 3

delay² *v* **1** [I,T] to wait until a later time to do something 推迟，延期〔做某事〕: *She delayed for months before deciding.* 她拖延了好几个月才作决定。| **delay sth until** *Ralph decided to delay his trip until April or May.* 拉尔夫决定把他的旅行推迟到4月或5月。| **delay doing sth** *Don't delay claiming or you may lose benefit.* 索赔万勿延迟，否则你会吃亏。**2** [T often passive 常用被动态] to make someone or something late 耽误，耽搁: *The plane was badly delayed by fog.* 由于有雾，飞机严重误点。—**delayed** *adj* 3

delayed-ac·tion /ˌ· ˌ· ˈ·◂/ *adj* designed to work or start only after a fixed period of time has passed 延迟的; 定时的: *a delayed-action bomb* 定时炸弹

delaying tac·tic /ˈ··· ˌ··/ *n* [C usually plural 一般用复数] something you do deliberately in order to delay something so that you gain an advantage for yourself 拖延策略〔故意拖延某事以便为自己争得优势〕

de·lec·ta·ble /dɪˈlɛktəbl; dɪˈlektəbəl/ *adj literary* extremely pleasant to taste, smell etc【文】美味的; 好闻的: *a delectable mixture of flavours* 各种味道集于一身的美味组合 —**delectably** *adv*

de·lec·ta·tion /ˌdilɛkˈteʃən; ˌdiːlekˈteɪʃən/ *n* [U] *formal* enjoyment, pleasure, or amusement【正式】享受, 愉快; 娱乐

del·e·gate¹ /ˈdɛləgət; ˈdeləɡət/ *n* [C] someone who has been elected or chosen to speak, vote, or take decisions for a group 代表: *We sent five delegates to the conference.* 我们派了五个代表参加会议。

del·e·gate² /ˈdɛləˌget; ˈdeləɡeɪt/ *v* **1** [I,T] to give part of your power or work to someone in a lower position than you 授权, 委托权限: *A good manager knows when to delegate.* 一个好的经理知道何时该把权限下放。| **delegate sth to sb** *Minor tasks should be delegated to your assistant.* 不太重要的工作应交给你的助手去做。**2** [T] to choose someone to do a particular job, or to be a representative of a group, organization etc 委派〔某人〕做〔某项工作〕; 委任〔某人〕做代表: **delegate sb to do sth** *I've been delegated to organize the weekly meetings.* 我被指派组织每周的会议。

del·e·ga·tion /ˌdɛləˈgeʃən; ˌdeləˈɡeɪʃən/ *n* **1** [C] a group of people who represent a company, organization etc 代表团: *A small delegation had been sent to address the UN.* 一个小型代表团被派往联合国会议上发言。**2** [U] the process of giving power or work to someone else so that they are responsible for part of what you normally do 授权, 委派, 委托

de·lete /dɪˈlit; dɪˈliːt/ *v* [T] to remove a letter, word etc from a piece of writing 删除, 删掉: *His name was deleted from the list.* 他的名字被从名单上删掉了。

del·e·ter·i·ous /ˌdɛləˈtɪrɪəs; ˌdeləˈtɪəriəs◂/ *adj formal* damaging or harmful【正式】有害的: *the deleterious effects of smoking* 吸烟的害处

de·le·tion /dɪˈliʃən; dɪˈliːʃən/ *n* **1** [U] the act or process of removing something from a piece of writing 删除 **2** [C] a letter or word that has been removed from a piece of writing 删掉的字母[词]

Del·hi /ˈdɛlɪ; ˈdeli/ a large city in northern India, divided into New Delhi (the capital of India since 1911) and Old Delhi, which was the capital until 1857 德里〔印度北部一大城市, 分为新德里(1911年起为印度首都)和旧德里(1857年以前为首都)两部分〕

del·i /ˈdɛlɪ; ˈdeli/ *n* [C] *informal* a DELICATESSEN【非正式】熟食店

de·lib·e·rate¹ /dɪˈlɪbərɪt; dɪˈlɪbərət/ *adj* **1** intended or planned, and not happening accidentally 故意的, 有意的, 蓄意的: *a deliberate act of disobedience* 故意的违抗行为 **2** deliberate speech, thought, or movement is slow and careful〔讲话、思想或行动〕沉着的, 从容不迫的: *He began working in his usual deliberate and meticulous manner.* 他开始以他惯有的审慎精细的方式工作起来。—**deliberateness** *n* [U]

de·lib·e·rate² /dɪˈlɪbəˌret; dɪˈlɪbəreɪt/ *v* [I] to think about something very carefully 仔细考虑: *We really can't afford to deliberate any longer.* 我们真的没有时间再仔细考虑了。| [+on/about] *They met to deliberate on possible solutions to the problem.* 他们聚在一起仔细商讨可能解决问题的方法。

de·lib·er·ate·ly /dɪˈlɪbərɪtlɪ; dɪˈlɪbərətli/ *adv* **1** done in a way that is intended or planned 故意地, 蓄意地: *I don't think he deliberately tried to shove you.* 我想他不是故意推你的。| *They're deliberately choosing a cautious policy.* 他们有意选择了一项谨慎的政策。**2** done or said in a slow, careful way〔做事、说话〕慎重地, 从容不迫地, 不慌不忙地

de·lib·e·ra·tion /dɪˌlɪbəˈreʃən; dɪˌlɪbəˈreɪʃən/ *n* **1** [C often plural 常用复数; U] careful consideration or discussion of something 仔细考虑; 商议; 讨论: *Their deliberations went on for hours.* 他们商量了好几个小时。**2** [U] if you speak or move with deliberation, you speak or move slowly and carefully〔说话、行动〕从容, 谨慎

de·lib·e·ra·tive /dɪˈlɪbəˌretɪv; dɪˈlɪbərətɪv/ *adj* existing for the purpose of discussing or planning something 审议的; 商议的

del·i·ca·cy /ˈdɛlɪkəsɪ; ˈdelɪkəsi/ *n* **1** [C] something good to eat that is expensive or rare 珍馐, 佳肴: *Snails are considered a delicacy in France.* 在法国, 蜗牛被认为是一种美味佳肴。**2** [U] a careful and sensitive way of speaking or behaving so that you do not upset anyone; TACT〔说话、做事的〕谨慎; 敏感; 技巧 **3** [U] the quality of being easy to harm, damage, or break 脆弱

del·i·cate /ˈdɛləkət; ˈdelɪkət/ *adj*

1 ▶**EASILY DAMAGED** 容易受损的◀ easily damaged or broken; FRAGILE (1) 易坏的, 易碎的, 脆弱的: *a delicate bubble of Venetian glass* 易碎的威尼斯玻璃泡

2 ▶**NEEDING SENSITIVITY** 需要敏感性的◀ needing to be dealt with carefully or sensitively in order to avoid problems or failure 微妙的, 需要谨慎处理的: *The negotiations are at a delicate stage.* 谈判正处于微妙阶段。

3 ▶**PERSON** 人◀ someone who is delicate is hurt easily or easily becomes ill〔人〕容易生病的; 娇弱的: *a delicate child* 身体娇弱的孩子

4 ▶**PART OF THE BODY** 身体的一部分◀ a part of the body that is delicate is attractive and graceful 优美的, 优雅的: *He looked down at his long white delicate fingers.* 他低头看着自己白皙、纤长的手指。

5 ▶**SKILFULLY MADE** 制作精巧的◀ made skilfully and with attention to the smallest details 精巧的, 精致的, 精美的: *a delicate pattern of butterflies and leaves* 蝴蝶和树叶构成的精美图案

6 ▶**TASTE/SMELL/COLOUR** 味道/气味/颜色◀ a taste, smell, or colour that is delicate is pleasant and not strong 柔和的, 清淡的, 淡雅的: *a delicate shade of blue* 一抹淡蓝 —compare 比较 INDELICATE —**delicately** *adv*

del·i·cates /ˈdɛləkəts; ˈdelɪkəts/ *n* [plural] clothes that are made from material that needs careful treatment 质地柔软的服装

del·i·ca·tes·sen /ˌdɛlɪkəˈtɛsn; ˌdelɪkəˈtesən/ *n* [C] a shop that sells high quality cheeses, SALADs, cooked meats etc〔出售高品质乳酪、沙拉、熟肉等的〕熟食店

de·li·cious /dɪˈlɪʃəs; dɪˈlɪʃəs/ *adj* **1** very pleasant to taste or smell 美味的, 可口的; 芳香的: *This cake is absolutely delicious!* 这蛋糕绝对好吃! **2** *literary* extremely pleasant or enjoyable【文】绝佳的, 令人极其愉快的: *It was a delicious but unlikely fantasy.* 那是个美妙的幻想, 但不太可能实现。

de·light¹ /dɪˈlaɪt; dɪˈlaɪt/ *n* **1** [U] feelings of great pleasure and satisfaction 高兴, 快乐: **with/in delight** *The kids rushed down to the beach, shrieking with delight.* 孩子们高兴地尖叫着冲向海滩。| **to sb's delight** *To my secret delight, Sarah announced that she was leaving.* 令我暗喜的是萨拉宣布她要走了。| **scream/gasp etc of delight** *With a cry of delight he ran towards Jen.* 他欢呼一声跑向珍。**2** [C] something that makes you feel very happy or satisfied 使人高兴[满意]的事: **the delights of** *the delights of owning your own home* 拥有自己的家的种种喜悦 **3 take delight in (doing) sth** to enjoy something very much, especially something you should not do 以(做)某事为乐〔尤指做不该做的事〕: *Chris takes great delight in teasing his sister.* 克里斯特别喜欢捉弄他妹妹。

delight² *v* [T] to give someone great satisfaction and enjoyment 使愉快, 使高兴: *a book that is certain to delight any reader* 一本肯定会让所有读者喜欢的书 | **delight sb with sth** *He delighted them with his charm and sparkling wit.* 他用自己的魅力和机智诙谐让他们感到愉快。

delight in sth *phr v* [T not in passive 不用被动态] to enjoy something very much, especially something unpleasant 以…为乐, 喜欢…〔尤指不好的事〕

de·light·ed /dɪˈlaɪtɪd; dɪˈlaɪtəd/ *adj* very pleased and happy 愉快的, 高兴的: *The puppies ran around the delighted children.* 小狗们围着欢乐的孩子们跑来跑去。| **be delighted to do sth** *Thanks for the invitation. I'd be delighted to come!* 谢谢你的邀请, 我很乐意前来! | **delighted (that)** *We're delighted that you'll be there.* 你能去, 我们很高兴。| [+at/by] *Tom was delighted at the sensation he was creating.* 汤姆对他制造出来的轰动效应感到非常高兴。—**delightedly** *adv*

de·light·ful /dɪˈlaɪtfəl; dɪˈlaɪtfəl/ *adj* very pleasant 令人愉快的, 讨人喜欢的: *a delightful young man* 惹人喜爱的年轻人 —**delightfully** *adv*

De·li·lah /dɪˈlaɪlə; dəˈlaɪlə/ in the Old Testament of the Bible, a woman who persuades Samson to trust her and tell her what makes him so strong. When he tells her that it is his hair, she tricks him into having his hair cut off to make him weak. 大利拉〔《圣经·旧约》中赢得参孙信任并获知其力量之源的女人。参孙告诉她, 他的力量源于自己的头发, 她便诱骗他把头发剪掉, 从而丧失了力量〕

de·lim·it /dɪˈlɪmɪt; dɪˈlɪmət/ *v* [T] *formal* to fix or say exactly what the limits of something are【正式】确定…的界线, 界定, 限定 —**delimitation** /dɪˌlɪmɪˈteʃən; dɪˌlɪməˈteɪʃən/ *n* [C]

de·lin·e·ate /dɪˈlɪnɪˌet; dɪˈlɪnieɪt/ *v* [T] *formal* to describe or draw something carefully so that people can understand it【正式】描写, 描绘: *Make sure your ideas are clearly delineated in your speech.* 要确保在演讲中能够清楚地阐述你的观点。—**delineation** /dɪˌlɪnɪˈeʃən; dɪˌlɪniˈeɪʃən/ *n* [U]

de·lin·quen·cy /dɪˈlɪŋkwənsɪ; dɪˈlɪŋkwənsi/ *n* **1** [U] illegal or immoral behaviour, especially by young people 青少年犯罪 **2** [C] *formal* an action that is illegal or immoral【正式】违法[不道德]的行为

de·lin·quent¹ /dɪˋlɪŋkwənt; dɪˈlɪŋkwənt/ *adj* **1** behaving in a way that is illegal or that society does not approve of 违法的，有过失的: *delinquent behaviour* 违法行为 **2** *technical* a delinquent debt, account etc has not been paid on time【术语】〔债务、账目等〕到期未付的

delinquent² *n* [C] someone, especially a young person, who breaks the law or behaves in ways their society does not approve of 违法的人〔尤指青少年〕: *juvenile delinquents vandalizing telephones* 恣意破坏公用电话的少年犯

del·i·ques·cent /ˌdɛləˋkwɛsn̩t; ˌdeləˈkwesənt◂/ *adj technical* a deliquescent substance becomes a liquid because of water in the air【术语】潮解的，因受潮而溶化的

de·lir·i·ous /dɪˋlɪrɪəs; dɪˈlɪriəs/ *adj* **1** talking continuously in an excited or anxious way, especially because you are ill〔尤指由于有病而〕神智混乱的；语无伦次的；呓语的: *One patient had been babbling all night, delirious with a high fever.* 一个病人高烧烧得神志不清，整个晚上都在说胡话。**2** extremely excited or happy 特别激动的，特别高兴的 —**deliriously** *adv*

de·lir·i·um /dɪˋlɪrɪəm; dɪˈlɪriəm/ *n* **1** [C,U] a state in which someone is delirious, especially because they are very ill 精神错乱，胡言乱语，谵妄〔尤指由于生病〕: *High doses of certain drugs produce delirium.* 某些药物大剂量服用会导致精神错乱。**2** [singular] extreme excitement 狂喜

delirium tre·mens /dɪˌlɪrɪəm ˋtrimənz; dɪˌlɪriəm ˈtremənz/ *n* [U] *technical* a medical condition, caused especially by drinking too much alcohol, in which someone's body shakes and they see things that are not there【术语】〔尤指由于饮酒过度引起的〕震颤性谵妄

De·li·us /ˋdilɪəs; ˈdiːliəs/**, Fred·e·rick** /ˋfrɛdrɪk; ˈfredərɪk/ (1862-1934) a British COMPOSER whose best-known works include *On Hearing the First Cuckoo in Spring*, and the OPERA, *A Village Romeo and Juliet*. 戴流士〔(1862-1934)，英国作曲家。最著名的作品有《春闻杜鹃啼》和歌剧《乡村罗密欧和朱丽叶》〕

de·liv·er /dɪˋlɪvɚ; dɪˈlɪvə/ *v*

1 ▶TAKE STH SOMEWHERE 把某物带到某处◀ [I,T] to take goods, letters etc to the place where they have been sent 把〔货物、信件等〕送往〔某处〕: *Do you deliver on Saturdays?* 星期六你们送货吗？| **deliver sth to** *Could you deliver this letter to the accounts department?* 你能把这封信送到会计部吗？| **have sth delivered** *I'm having some flowers delivered for her birthday.* 我要派人送花给她祝贺生日。

2 deliver a speech/lecture/talk etc to make a speech etc to a lot of people 发言/授课/讲话等: *The President, as was customary, delivered the opening address.* 按照惯例，总统致开幕辞。

3 ▶DO STH YOU SHOULD DO 做应该做的事◀ [I,T] to do or provide the things you are expected to, because you are responsible for them or they are part of your job 不负所望，做该做的事: *Local councils are responsible for delivering most basic services.* 地方议会负责提供大部分基本服务。| **deliver the goods** (=do or provide what you are expected to) 履行承诺，说到做到 *They made all kinds of promises before the election, but have since failed to deliver the goods.* 他们选举前作出各种承诺，但是后来却一直没有兑现。| **deliver on a promise** *AmE* (=do what you promised to do)【美】履行诺言

4 ▶BABY 婴儿◀ [T] to help a woman give birth to a baby 给…接生；帮助〔产妇〕分娩: *Traditionally, local midwives would deliver all the babies in the area.* 过去的习俗是，当地的接生婆会给该地区所有的婴儿接生。| **deliver sb of** *formal*【正式】: *On May 14th, she was safely delivered of a daughter.* 5月14日，她平安地产下一个女婴。

5 deliver a blow/shock etc to to hit someone, give them a shock etc 给予〔某人〕打击/使〔某人〕震惊等: *He delivered a wild, desperate blow to Derek's jaw.* 他疯狂地往德里克的下巴上狠狠地打了一拳。

6 deliver a verdict/judgment/ruling etc to officially state a formal decision or judgment 作出裁决/判断/裁定等

7 ▶PERSON 人◀ [T always+adv/prep] to put someone into someone else's control 把〔某人〕交出；把〔某人〕送到…手中: **deliver sb to** *Sharett had betrayed him and delivered him to the enemy.* 沙雷特出卖了他，并把他交给了敌人。

8 ▶VOTES 投票◀ [T] *especially AmE* to get the votes or support of a particular group of people in an election【尤美】〔在竞选中〕为…拉票: *We're counting on you to deliver the blue collar vote.* 我们指望你拉到蓝领选票。

9 ▶MAKE SB FREE OF 解脱某人◀ [T] *literary or Biblical* to help someone escape from something bad or evil【文或圣经】解救，解脱〔某人〕: **deliver sb from** *Deliver us from temptation.* 让我们免受诱惑。—**deliverer** *n* [C]

deliver sth **up** *phr v* [T often passive 常用被动态] *formal* to give something to someone else【正式】把〔某物〕移交给〔某人〕: [+to] *All documents must be delivered up to the trustee.* 所有的文件必须交付给受托人。

de·liv·er·a·ble /dɪˋlɪvərəbl; dɪˈlɪvərəbəl/ *n* [C usually plural 一般用复数] something that a company has promised to have ready for a customer, especially parts of computer systems 备送货物〔尤指电脑部件〕: *a list of software deliverables* 软件备送货清单

de·liv·er·ance /dɪˋlɪvərəns; dɪˈlɪvərəns/ *n* [U+from] *formal* the state of being saved from harm or danger【正式】拯救，解救

de·liv·er·y /dɪˋlɪvərɪ; dɪˈlɪvəri/ *n* **1** [C,U] the act or process of bringing goods, letters etc to the person or place they have been sent to 送货，送信: *postal deliveries* 邮件递送 | *a delivery charge* 送货费用 | **take delivery of** (=officially accept something that has been brought or sent to you) 正式接收 **2** [C] something that is delivered 发送的东西: *Deliveries to the restaurant should be made at the back entrance.* 货物应该送到餐厅后门口。**3** [C] the process of giving birth to a child 分娩，生产: *Mrs Howell had an easy delivery.* 豪厄尔太太顺产。| **delivery room/ward etc** (=a room in a hospital for births) 产房 **4** [singular] the way in which someone speaks or performs in public〔在公共场合〕讲话方式，演说风格: *You'll have to work on your delivery.* 你还得在演说技巧上下功夫。

de·liv·er·y·man /dɪˋlɪvərɪmən; dɪˈlɪvərimən/ *n* [C] someone who delivers goods to people 送货员

dell /dɛl; del/ *n* [C] *literary* a small valley with grass and trees【文】〔有草有树的〕小山谷，幽谷

de·louse /diˋlaus; ˌdiːˈlaʊs/ *v* [T] to remove lice (LOUSE¹ (1)) or similar animals from someone's hair, clothes etc 除去〔头发上、衣服上等〕的虱子

Del·phic or·a·cle, the /ˌdɛlfɪk ˋɑrəkl; ˌdelfɪk ˈɒrəkəl/ a TEMPLE (=a holy building) in the town of Delphi in Greece where, in ancient times, a PRIESTESS gave answers from the god Apollo to questions people asked him. His answers were often mysterious and difficult to understand, and were often in the form of a RIDDLE (=a deliberately confusing question that has a clever answer). 德尔斐神谕神殿〔希腊德尔斐的一座庙宇。古时，女祭司在此传达阿波罗的神谕来回答别人的提问。问题的答案往往以谜语的形式出现，神秘莫测，难以理解〕

del·phin·i·um /dɛlˋfɪnɪəm; delˈfɪniəm/ *n* [C] a tall garden plant with many blue flowers along its stem〔沿茎部长许多蓝花的〕飞燕草

del·ta /ˋdɛltə; ˈdeltə/ *n* [C] **1** the fourth letter of the Greek alphabet 希腊字母表的第四个字母 **2** an area of low land where a river spreads into many smaller rivers near the sea〔河口的〕三角洲: *the Nile delta* 尼罗河三角洲 —see picture on page A12 参见A12页图

Delta Force /ˋ· ·, ·/ a special group of soldiers which is part of the US Army, and is specially trained to do secret and dangerous work, especially fighting TERRORISTS 德尔塔部队〔美国一特种部队，经专门训练后从事秘密和危险工作，尤其是反恐行动〕

de·lude /dɪˋlud; dɪˈluːd/ *v* [T] to make someone believe something that is not true; deceive 欺骗，哄骗: **delude sb/yourself** *You're deluding yourself if you think you'll change Rob's mind.* 如果你认为能使罗布改变主意，你就是自欺欺人。| **delude sb into doing sth** *That new job title is just a way of deluding her into thinking she's been promoted.* 那个新的工作头衔只是骗她相信自己已被提升的一种方法而已。

del·uge¹ /ˋdɛljudʒ; ˈdeljuːdʒ/ *n* **1** [C usually singular 一般用单数] a large flood, or period when there is a lot of rain 洪水；暴雨期 **2 deluge of letters/questions etc** a lot of letters, questions etc that all come at the same time 同时涌来的大量信件/问题等: *a deluge of complaints about the show* 对那场演出的大量抗议

deluge² *v* [T] **1** [usually passive 一般用被动态] to send a very large number of letters, questions etc to someone all at the same time〔大量的信件、问题等同时〕涌向〔某人〕；…如雪片飞来: **be deluged with/by** *The response has been great – we've been deluged with new orders.* 反应特别大——我们收到的新订单不计其数。**2** *formal* to cover something with a lot of water【正式】用水淹没 —see also 另见 INUNDATE

de·lu·sion /dɪˋluʒən; dɪˈluːʒən/ *n* **1** [C,U] a false belief about yourself or the situation you are in 错觉；妄想: **be under the delusion that** (=wrongly believe that) 有…的错觉 *I was still under the naive delusion that everyone was good at heart.* 我还天真地认为每个人内心都是善良的。**2 delusions of grandeur** the belief that you are much more important or powerful than you really are 妄自尊大，夸大妄想 —**delusive** /-sɪv; -sɪv/ *adj* —**delusively** *adv*

de·luxe /dɪˋlʌks; dɪ̵ˈlʌks/ *adj* [usually before noun 一般用于名词前] something that is of better quality than other things of the same type〔比同类事物〕质量高的; 豪华的: *The deluxe model costs a lot more.* 豪华型要贵很多。

delve /dɛlv; delv/ *v* [I] **1** [always+adv/prep] to search for something by putting your hand deeply into a bag, container etc〔把手伸到手提袋、容器等的深处〕搜寻, 翻找: **delve in/among/between etc** *Hank delved in his pockets for some change.* 汉克在口袋里翻找零钱。**2** *poetic* to dig【诗】挖掘

delve into *phr v* [T] to try to find more information about someone or something 探究, 探索, 钻研: *I wouldn't delve too deeply into his past if I were you.* 如果我是你的话, 我不会深究他的过去。

Dem /dɛm; dem/ the written abbreviation of 缩写= Democrat or 或 Democratic

de·mag·ne·tize also 又作 **-ise** *BrE*【英】/diˋmægnəˏtaɪz; ˌdiːˈmægnətaɪz/ *v* [T] **1** to take away the MAGNETIC qualities of something 除去〔某物〕的磁性, 使消磁 **2** *technical* to remove sounds from a MAGNETIC TAPE【术语】除去〔磁带〕的声音 —**demagnetization** /ˏdimægnətəˋzeʃən; ˌdiːmægnətaɪˈzeɪʃən/ *n* [U]

dem·a·gogue also 又作 **demagog** *AmE*【美】/ˋdɛməˏgɑg; ˈdeməgɒg/ *n* [C] someone who gives political speeches that try to persuade people by using emotional language rather than reason 蛊惑民心者, 煽动民众的政客 —**demagogy, demagogery** *n* [U] —**demagogic** /ˏdɛməˋgɑgɪk; ˌdeməˈgɒgɪk◂/ *adj* —**demagogically** /-klɪ; -kli/ *adv*

S1 W1 **de·mand¹** /dɪˋmænd; dɪˈmɑːnd/ *n*

1 ▶FIRM REQUEST 坚决要求◀ [C] a very firm request for something that you think someone should give you, or think you have a right to 要求, 请求: *The government refused to give in to the demands of the terrorists.* 政府对恐怖分子提出的要求拒绝作出让步。| [+for] *a demand for a 10% pay increase* 将工资提高 10% 的要求 —see 见 REQUEST² (USAGE)

2 demands [plural] the difficult, annoying, or tiring things that someone or something makes you do 困难的[烦人的、累人的]事情: **the demands of** *the pace and demands of modern life* 现代生活的快节奏和烦心事 | **make demands (on)** *The job makes great demands on my time.* 这项工作需要我花很多时间。

3 ▶GOODS/SERVICES 货物/服务◀ [singular,U] people's need or desire to buy or use particular goods and services 需求: [+for] *There's not much demand for oil heaters any more.* 现在燃油加热器的需求不大了。| **meet demand** (=supply or sell enough goods etc for people to buy) 满足需求 *Ford have increased production in order to meet demand.* 福特公司为了满足需求, 已提高了产量。| **be in demand** (=be wanted by a lot of people) 广受欢迎 *Her books are in great demand at the moment.* 目前, 她的书非常畅销。—see also 另见 **supply and demand** (SUPPLY¹ (5))

4 by popular demand because a lot of people have asked for something to be done, performed etc 应公众要求: *Here they are, back by popular demand, The Wild Ones!* 根据公众的要求,《飞车党》又回来了!

5 on demand *formal* done or given whenever someone asks【正式】见票即付: *This note entitles the bearer to $20 on demand.* 该票据的持有者随时有权领取 20 美元。

W2 **demand²** *v* **1** [T] to ask for something very firmly, especially something that someone does not want to give you〔坚决〕要求〔尤其是别人不想给的东西〕: *The Governor has demanded your resignation.* 州长已经要求你辞职。| **demand to know/see etc** *I demand to know what's going on!* 我要求了解正在发生什么事情! | **demand that** *Protesters went on hunger strike to demand that all political prisoners be freed.* 抗议者绝食示威, 要求释放所有政治犯。**2** [I,T] to ask a question or order something to be done very firmly 询问, 质问; 命令: *"Did you do this?" Kathryn demanded angrily.* "这是你做的吗?"凯瑟琳气愤地质问道。| **demand sth of sb** (=ask someone for something) 向某人要某物 **3** [T] to need someone's time, energy, skill etc 需要〔时间、精力、技能等〕: *There are just too many things all demanding my attention at once.* 有太多事情需要我立即处理。

S3 **de·mand·ing** /dɪˋmændɪŋ; dɪˈmɑːndɪŋ/ *adj* **1** needing a lot of ability, effort, or skill 费力的: *a demanding job* 高要求的工作 **2** expecting a lot of attention, especially in a way that is not fair 苛求的, 要求过高的: *Her mother could be very demanding at times.* 她妈妈有时会变得十分难伺候。

de·mar·cate /dɪˋmɑrket; ˈdiːmɑːkeɪt/ *v* [T] *formal* to state or fix the limits of an area, system etc【正式】标明〔一个地区、系统等〕的界线: *The development of clearly demarcated territories is fairly recent in history.* 界线分明的版图是在近代历史才出现的。

de·mar·ca·tion /ˏdimɑrˋkeʃən; ˌdiːmɑːˈkeɪʃən/ *n* [U] **1** the point at which one person's area of work, responsibility etc ends and someone else's begins〔工作范围、职权范围等的〕界限, 分界线: *There is no clear demarcation between the responsibilities of our two departments.* 我们两个部门的职责没有明显的划分。**2** a way of separating one area of land from another〔地区的〕划分, 划定, 定界

de·mean /dɪˋmin; dɪˈmiːn/ *v* [T] *formal* to do something that you think you are too good for【正式】降低…的身份, 贬低, 贬损: *Don't demean yourself by taking that job.* 不要降低你的身份去接受那份工作。—**demeaning** *adj*: *Cleaning the toilets was the most demeaning task at the camp.* 在营地, 清洗厕所是最有失身份的差事。

de·mea·nour *BrE*【英】, **demeanor** *AmE*【美】/dɪˋminɚ; dɪˈmiːnə/ *n* [singular,U] the way someone behaves or looks that gives you a general idea of their character〔能让人看出大致性格特点的〕举止, 外表, 风度: *There was certainly a large element of irony in his demeanour.* 他的举止中确实有很大的嘲讽成分。

de·men·ted /dɪˋmɛntɪd; dɪˈmentɪ̵d/ *adj* **1** behaving as if you are crazy, especially because of an upsetting experience〔由于痛苦的经历而〕疯狂的: *The woman was almost demented with grief.* 那个妇女悲痛得几乎疯掉。**2** *old-fashioned* suffering from a mental illness【过时】精神错乱的

de·men·tia /dɪˋmɛnʃə; dɪˈmenʃə/ *n* [U] *technical* an illness that affects the brain and memory, and makes you gradually lose the ability to think and behave normally【术语】痴呆

dem·e·ra·ra sug·ar /ˏdɛmərɛrəˋʃʊgɚ; ˌdeməreərəˈʃʊgə/ *n* [U] a type of rough brown sugar 德麦拉拉蔗糖〔一种褐色粗蔗糖〕

de·mer·it /diˋmɛrɪt; diːˈmerɪ̵t/ *n* [C] **1 the merits and demerits of** *formal* the good and bad qualities or features of something【正式】…的长处和短处, …的优缺点 **2** *AmE* a mark showing that a student has done something wrong at school【美】记过

de·mesne /dɪˋmen; dɪˈmeɪn/ *n* [C] *old use or law* a very big house and all the land that belongs to it, especially in former times【旧或法律】〔尤指过去〕庄园的大片房地产

demi- /dɛmɪ; demɪ/ *prefix* **1** half 一半: *a demisemiquaver* (=very short musical note) 32 分音符 **2** partly something 部分: *a demigod* (=partly human and partly a god) 半人半神

dem·i·god /ˋdɛməˏgɑd; ˈdemigɒd/ *n* [C] **1** someone who is so important and powerful that they are treated like a god 被人像神一样崇拜的人物: *a dictator with demigod status* 享有像神一样地位的独裁者 **2** a man in ancient stories, who is half god and half human〔古典神话中的〕半人半神

dem·i·john /ˋdɛməˏdʒɑn; ˈdemidʒɒn/ *n* [C] a large bottle with a short narrow neck, often used for making wine 细颈大瓶〔常用于酿酒〕

de·mil·i·ta·rize also 又作 **-ise** *BrE*【英】/diˋmɪlətəˏraɪz; ˌdiːˈmɪlɪ̵təraɪz/ *v* [T usually passive 一般用被动态] to remove the weapons, soldiers etc from a country or area so that there can be no fighting there 使非军事化, 使解除武装 —**demilitarization** /diˏmɪlətərəˋzeʃən; diːˌmɪlɪ̵təraɪˈzeɪʃən/ *n* [U]

De Mille /də ˋmɪl; də ˈmɪl/, **Ag·nes** /ˋægnɪs; ˈægnɪ̵s/ (1909-93) a US dancer and CHOREOGRAPHER who planned the dances for several musical plays on Broadway, such as *Oklahoma!* and *Carousel* 德米尔〔(1909-1993), 美国舞蹈家、编舞, 曾为《俄克拉荷马!》和《竞技表演》等百老汇音乐剧编舞〕

DeMille, Cec·il B. /ˋsɛsɪl bi; ˈsesɪ̵l biː/ (1881-1959) a US film producer and DIRECTOR who helped to establish the film industry in Hollywood. He is famous for making EPICS (=long films about people in the Bible or in history, which used hundreds of actors). His films include *Samson and Delilah* (1949) and *The Ten Commandments* (1956). 德米尔〔(1881-1959), 美国电影制片人、导演, 曾帮助创建好莱坞电影业, 以拍摄场面壮观的史诗式影片出名。拍摄的影片包括《参孙与大利拉》(1949) 和《十诫》(1956)〕

de·mise /dɪˋmaɪz; dɪˈmaɪz/ *n* [U] **1** *formal* the end of something that used to exist【正式】〔曾经存在的某物的〕终止, 结束: [+of] *the sad demise of the local newspaper* 地方报纸令人惋惜的停刊 **2** *formal or law* death【正式或法律】死亡 —**demise** *v* [I] *especially AmE*【尤美】: *The sport has continued to demise over the years.* 这些年来, 这项体育运动在持续衰退。

de·mist /diˋmɪst; ˌdiːˈmɪst/ *v* [T] *BrE* to remove mist from a car window using heat【英】除去〔汽车玻璃上的〕雾水; DEFROST (3) *AmE*【美】—**demister** *n* [C]

dem·o /ˋdɛmo; ˈdeməʊ/ *n* [C] *informal*【非正式】**1** an event at which a large group of people publicly protest about something〔为抗议某事而举行的〕游行, 示威 **2 give sb a demo** to show

someone how something works or is done 给某人示范 **3** a piece of recorded music that is sent to a record company so that they can decide whether to sell it or not 录音样带, 试样唱片: *a demo tape* 录音样带 —compare 比较 DEMONSTRATION (2)

de·mob /dɪˋmɑb; diːˈmɒb/ *v* **demobbed, demobbing** [T] *BrE informal* to demobilize【英, 非正式】遣散〔军队〕, 使〔军人〕复员

de·mo·bi·lize also 又作 **-ise** *BrE*【英】/dɪˋmobḷˌaɪz; diːˈməʊbḷlaɪz/ *v* [T usually passive 一般用被动态] to send home the members of an army, navy etc, especially at the end of a war〔尤指战争结束时〕使〔陆军、海军等的成员〕复员回家: *Unemployed demobilized soldiers drifted toward the cities.* 失业的复员士兵漫无目的地流向各个城市。—**demobilization** /diˌmobələˋzeʃən; diːˌməʊbḷlaɪˈzeɪʃən/ *n* [U]

2 **de·moc·ra·cy** /dɪˋmɑkrəsɪ; dɪˈmɒkrəsi/ *n* **1** [U] a system of government in which everyone in the country can vote to elect its members 民主政体 **2** [C] a country that has a government which has been elected by the people of the country 民主国家 **3** [U] a situation or system in which everyone is equal and has the right to vote, make decisions etc 民主作风, 民主精神

dem·o·crat /ˋdɛməˌkræt; ˈdeməkræt/ *n* [C] **1** someone who believes in, or works to achieve democracy 民主主义者, 民主人士 **2 Democrat** a member or supporter of the Democratic party of the US 美国民主党党员; 美国民主党支持者

2 **dem·o·crat·ic** /ˌdɛməˋkrætɪk; ˌdeməˈkrætɪk◂/ *adj* **1** controlled by representatives who are elected by the people of a country 民主的, 民主政体的: *a democratic government* 民主政府 **2** organized according to the principle that everyone has a right to be involved in making decisions 民主制的, 民主管理的: *a democratic management style* 民主的管理风格 —**democratically** /-klɪ; -kli/ *adv*: *democratically-elected councils* 民主选举出来的委员会

de·moc·ra·tize also 又作 **-ise** *BrE*【英】/dɪˋmɑkrəˌtaɪz; dɪˈmɒkrətaɪz/ *v* [T] to change the way in which a government, company etc is organized, so that the people in it have more power 使〔政府、公司等〕民主化 —**democratization** /dɪˌmɑkrətəˋzeʃən; dɪˌmɒkrətaɪˈzeɪʃən/ *n* [U]

dé·mo·dé /ˌdemoˋde; ˌdeɪˈməʊdeɪ/ *adj formal* not fashionable any more【正式】过时的, 不再时髦的

de·mog·ra·phy /dɪˋmɑgrəfɪ; dɪˈmɒgrəfi/ *n* [U] the study of human populations and the ways in which they change 人口学, 人口统计学 —**demographer** *n* [C] —**demographic** /ˌdɛməˋgræfɪk; ˌdeməˈgræfɪk◂/ *adj*

de·mol·ish /dɪˋmɑlɪʃ; dɪˈmɒlɪʃ/ *v* [T] **1** to completely destroy a building, especially so that the land it is on can be used for something else 拆毁, 拆除〔建筑物〕: *Several houses were demolished to make way for the new road.* 好几所房子都被拆掉以便腾出地方修新公路。**2** to prove that an idea or opinion is completely wrong 推翻, 驳倒〔想法、观点〕: *He demolished my argument in minutes.* 他几分钟内就把我的论点给驳倒了。**3** *informal especially BrE* to eat all of something very quickly【非正式, 尤英】吃光, 吞掉

dem·o·li·tion /ˌdɛməˋlɪʃən; ˌdeməˈlɪʃən/ *n* [C,U] the act, or process of demolishing a building〔房屋的〕拆除

de·mon /ˋdimən; ˈdiːmən/ *n* [C] **1** an evil spirit 魔鬼 **2** *humorous* someone who is very good at a game, especially cards【幽默】〔玩游戏, 尤指玩纸牌的〕高手: *Pete is a demon poker player.* 皮特是扑克牌高手。**3 the demon drink** *humorous* alcoholic drink【幽默】含酒精的饮料 —compare 比较 DAEMON

de·mo·ni·a·cal /ˌdiməˋnaɪəkḷ; ˌdiːməˈnaɪəkəl◂/ also 又作 **de·mo·ni·ac** /dɪˋmonɪˌæk; dɪˈməʊniæk/ *adj formal* wild, uncontrolled, and evil【正式】狂野的; 邪恶的: *demoniacal cruelty* 充满邪恶的凶残 —**demoniacally** /-klɪ; -kli/ *adv*

de·mon·ic /dɪˋmɑnɪk; dɪˈmɒnɪk/ *adj* **1** wild and cruel 疯狂的, 残忍的: *demonic laughter* 狂笑 **2** like a demon 魔鬼般的: *demonic possession* 魔鬼附身 —**demonically** /-klɪ; -kli/ *adv*

de·mon·stra·ble /dɪˋmɑnstrəbḷ; dɪˈmɒnstrəbəl/ *adj formal* able to be shown or proved【正式】可表明的, 可证实的 —**demonstrably** *adv*: *These conclusions are demonstrably wrong.* 这些结论可以证明是错误的。—**demonstrability** /dɪˌmɑnstrəˋbɪlətɪ; dɪˌmɒnstrəˈbɪlɪ̈ti/ *n* [U]

2 **dem·on·strate** /ˋdɛmənˌstret; ˈdemənstreɪt/ *v* **1** [T] to show or prove something clearly 证明, 论证, 证实: *These findings clearly demonstrate the fact that unemployment leads to poor health.* 这些调查结果清楚地证明了失业导致健康不佳这个事实。| **demonstrate that** *Edwin Hubble demonstrated that ours was not the only galaxy.* 埃德温·哈勃证实了我们所在的星系并不是唯一的星系。**2** [T] to show or describe how something works or is done 示范, 演示 **3** [I] to march through the streets with a large group of people in order to publicly protest about something〔为公开抗议某事〕游行示威: *Supporters demonstrated outside the courtroom during the trial.* 在审讯期间, 支持者们在法庭外游行示威。| **demonstrate against** *What are they demonstrating against?* 他们示威抗议什么? **4** [T] to show that you have a particular skill, quality, or ability 展示, 表露出〔某种技能、品质或能力〕: *At last she had the chance to demonstrate her musical talents.* 最后, 她终于得到了机会一展自己的音乐才华。

demonstration 游行示威

dem·on·stra·tion /ˌdɛmənˋstreʃən; ˌdemənˈstreɪʃən/ *n* **1** [C] 3
an event at which a large group of people march through the 3
streets, in order to publicly protest about something〔为抗议某事而进行的〕游行, 示威: *The new tax proposals sparked mass demonstrations.* 新的税收提议引发了大规模示威游行。| [+against] *a demonstration against the war* 反战游行 | **stage/hold a demonstration** *Students staged a demonstration to protest about the rises in tuition fees.* 学生们举行了示威游行抗议学费上涨。| **break up a demonstration** *Police used tear gas to break up the demonstration.* 警察使用催泪弹来驱散示威者。**2** [C,U] an act of explaining and showing how something works or is done 示范, 演示: **give a demonstration** *He gave a demonstration of how the program works.* 他作示范来说明这个程序是如何运作的。**3** [C] *formal* the expression of a feeling【正式】〔感情的〕表示, 表露: *a demonstration of her love* 她爱的表示

de·mon·stra·tive /dɪˋmɑnstrətɪv; dɪˈmɒnstrətɪv/ *adj* willing to show loving feelings towards people 感情外露的: *Dave's not very demonstrative, but I know he loves me.* 戴夫不太善于表露感情, 但是我知道他爱我。—**demonstratively** *adv*

demonstrative pro·noun /ˌ·,···ˋ··/ *n* [C] *technical* a PRONOUN such as 'that' or 'this' that shows which person or thing is meant, and separates it from others【术语】指示代(名)词〈如 that 或 this〉

dem·on·stra·tor /ˋdɛmənˌstretɚ; ˈdemənstreɪtə/ *n* [C] **1** someone who takes part in a DEMONSTRATION 游行者, 示威者: *Thousands of demonstrators gathered outside the Capitol building.* 数以千计的示威游行者聚集在国会大厦外面。**2** someone who shows people how something works or is done 示范人员

de·mor·al·ize also 又作 **-ise** *BrE*【英】/dɪˋmɑrəlˌaɪz; dɪˈmɒrəlaɪz/ *v* [T] to reduce or destroy someone's courage or confidence 削弱〔勇气〕, 摧毁〔自信〕: *Such a move would undermine standards in schools and demoralize teachers.* 这样的举措会降低学校的标准, 削弱教师的信心。—**demoralized** *adj*: *Defeated and demoralized, the protesters made their way home.* 抗议者受挫后垂头丧气地打道回府了。—**demoralizing** *adj*: *a series of demoralizing failures* 一连串令人泄气的失败 —**demoralization** /dɪˌmɔrələˋzeʃən; dɪˌmɒrəlaɪˈzeɪʃən/ *n* [U]: *widespread demoralization in the police force* 警察队伍中普遍存在的士气低落

de·mote /dɪˋmot; dɪˈməʊt/ *v* [T often passive 常用被动态] to make someone's rank or position lower or less important 将〔某人〕降职 —opposite 反义词 PROMOTE (2) —**demotion** /-ˋmoʃən; -ˈməʊʃən/ *n* [C,U]

de·mot·ic /dɪˋmɑtɪk; dɪˈmɒtɪk/ *adj formal* used by or popular with most ordinary people【正式】大众的, 通俗的

de·mo·ti·vate /diˋmotəˌvet; diːˈməʊtɪ̈veɪt/ *v* [T] to make someone less eager or willing to do their job 使〔某人〕失去动力, 使〔某人〕不愿〔工作〕—**demotivating** *adj*: *Lack of sufficient*

challenge at work can be very demotivating. 工作中缺乏足够的挑战会使人变得非常消极。—**demotivation** /ˌdimotə`veʃən; ˌdiːməʊtɪ̆ˈveɪʃən/ *n* [U]

de·mur[1] /dɪ`mɝ; dɪˈmɜː/ *v* **demurred, demurring** [I] *formal* to express doubt about or opposition to a plan or suggestion【正式】〔对计划或建议〕表示怀疑, 表示反对: *They demurred at the idea of working on a Sunday.* 他们对星期天上班的主意表示反对。

demur[2] *n* [U] *formal* disagreement or disapproval【正式】反对, 异议, 不赞成: **without demur** *I agreed to this without demur.* 我毫无异议地赞同此事。

de·mure /dɪ`mjʊr; dɪˈmjʊə/ *adj* a word meaning quiet, serious, and always behaving well, used especially about women in former times〔尤指旧时的妇女〕娴静的, 庄重的, 举止得体的—**demurely** *adv*: *She lowered her eyes demurely.* 她羞怯地垂下双眼。—**demureness** *n* [U]

de·mys·ti·fy /di`mɪstəˌfaɪ; ˌdiːˈmɪstɪ̆faɪ/ *v* [T] to make a subject that seems difficult or complicated easier to understand, especially by explaining it in simpler language〔尤指通过较简单的语言解释〕使〔似乎困难或复杂的问题〕容易理解: *This book attempts to demystify the whole subject of computers.* 这本书试图使电脑这门学科变得不再神秘。—**demystification** /diˌmɪstəfə`keʃən; diːˌmɪstɪ̆fɪ̆ˈkeɪʃən/ *n* [U]

den /dɛn; den/ *n* [C] **1** the home of some types of animal, for example lions or foxes (FOX[1] (1))〔某些动物的〕穴, 窝, 窟 **2** a place where secret or illegal activities take place〔进行秘密或非法活动的〕巢穴, 老窝: *a gambler's den* 赌窝 | *a den of thieves* 贼窝 **3** an enclosed and secret place where children play〔孩子们玩耍的封闭而秘密的〕集合地 **4** *especially AmE* a room in someone's house where they can relax, watch television etc【尤美】〔家中休息、看电视以及进行其他活动的〕私室 **5** *AmE* a group of CUB SCOUTS【美】幼年童子军小队 **6** *BrE old-fashioned* a small room in someone's house where they can work, read, etc without being disturbed【英, 过时】〔家中的〕书斋: *Father retreated to his den.* 爸爸躲入了自己的书房。**7 den of iniquity** *often humorous* a place where activities that you think are immoral or evil happen【常幽默】污秽之地: *Her mother saw the city as a den of iniquity.* 她妈妈把这座城市看成是个藏污纳垢之处。

De·na·li /də`nalɪ; dəˈnɑːli/ a mountain in Denali National Park in central Alaska, which is the highest point in North America. It was formerly called Mount McKinley. 迪纳利山〔阿拉斯加州中部迪纳利国家公园的一座山, 北美洲最高峰, 旧称麦金利山〕

de·na·tion·al·ize also 又作 **-ise** *BrE*【英】/di`næʃənḷˌaɪz; diːˈnæʃənəlaɪz/ *v* [T] to sell a business or industry that is owned by the state, so that it is then owned privately; PRIVATIZE 使非国有化, 使私营化 —**denationalization** /diˌnæʃənələ`zeʃən; diːˌnæʃənəlaɪˈzeɪʃən/ *n* [U]

de·ni·a·ble /dɪ`naɪəbḷ; dɪˈnaɪəbəl/ *adj* something that is deniable can be proved not to be true 可否定的, 可证明是错误的 —opposite 反义词 UNDENIABLE

de·ni·al /dɪ`naɪəl; dɪˈnaɪəl/ *n* **1** [C,U] a statement saying that something is not true 否认, 否定: [+of] *The government issued a firm denial of the rumour.* 政府对谣言予以坚决否认。**2 denial of justice/humanity/rights etc** a situation in which someone is not allowed to have justice, their rights etc 拒绝给予公平处理/人道对待/权利等: *protests against the denial of human rights* 对剥夺人权的抗议 **3** [U] *technical* a condition in which someone cannot or will not admit what they are really feeling【术语】〔对真实想法的〕拒绝承认

den·i·er /`dɛnɪɚ; ˈdeniə/ *n* [U] *BrE* a measure of how thin NYLON or silk threads are【英】旦尼尔, 旦〔尼龙或丝的纤度单位〕: *a pair of 15-denier tights* 一条 15 旦纤度的紧身裤袜

den·i·grate /`dɛnəˌgret; ˈdenɪ̆ˌgreɪt/ *v* [T] to say that something or someone is not good or important 贬低, 诋毁, 诽谤: *men who denigrate the status of women* 贬低妇女地位的男人们 —**denigration** /dɛnə`greʃən; ˌdenɪ̆ˈgreɪʃən/ *n* [U]

den·im /`dɛnəm; ˈdenɪ̆m/ *n* **1** [U] a type of strong cotton cloth, used especially to make JEANS〔尤指用于制作牛仔裤的〕粗棉布, 劳动布 —see picture on page A16 参见 A16 页图 **2 denims** [plural] *old-fashioned* a pair of trousers made of this material; JEANS【过时】牛仔裤

De Ni·ro /də `nɪro; də ˈnɪərəʊ/, **Rob·ert** /`rabɚt; ˈrɒbət/ (1943-) one of America's greatest film actors, known especially for appearing as characters who are violent or are involved in very violent situations. His films include *Taxi Driver* (1976), *Raging Bull* (1980), and *Cape Fear* (1991). 罗伯特·德尼罗〔(1943-)美国最著名的电影演员之一, 尤以饰演暴力人物或卷入暴力事件的人物闻名。他出演的影片有《出租车司机》(1976)、《愤怒的公牛》(1980) 和《海角惊魂》(1991)〕

den·i·zen /`dɛnəzṇ; ˈdenɪ̆zən/ *n* [C+of] *literary* an animal, plant, or person that lives or is found in a particular place【文】〔特定地区的〕栖息者, 居住者〔指动物、植物或人〕

Den·mark /`dɛnmark; ˈdenmɑːk/ a country in northern Europe, north of Germany and surrounded on three sides by sea. Denmark forms part of Scandinavia, and the people there are called Danes. Population: 5,353,000 (2001). Capital: Copenhagen. 丹麦〔北欧国家, 位于德国以北, 三面环海。该国是斯堪的纳维亚的一部分, 居民称 Danes (丹麦人)。人口: 5,353,000 (2001), 首都: 哥本哈根〕

den moth·er /'· ˌ··/ *n* [C] *AmE* a woman who leads a group of CUB SCOUTS【美】美国幼年童子军小队的女训导

Den·nis the Men·ace /ˌdɛnɪs ðə `mɛnɪs; ˌdenɪ̆s ðə ˈmenɪ̆s/ **1** a character in the British COMIC *The Beano*. Dennis is a young boy with thick black hair that sticks out in all directions and he wears a sweater with red and black stripes. He has a dog called **Gnasher**, and together they play tricks on people. 淘气阿丹〔英国连环漫画杂志《欢闹》中的人物。阿丹是个小男孩, 一头浓密的黑发, 蓬乱竖立。他身穿一件黑红条纹相间的套头衫。他有一条狗, 名字叫那什, 同他一起作弄人〕 **2** a character in a US CARTOON STRIP. Dennis is a little boy with light hair who is always causing problems, even though he does not intend to. He especially likes to play with his neighbour, Mr Wilson, who usually gets very annoyed with him. 淘气阿丹〔美国连环漫画中的人物。阿丹是个小男孩, 长一头浅色头发, 总是无意中惹出麻烦。他尤其喜欢同邻居威尔逊先生闹着玩, 通常惹得人家很不高兴〕

de·nom·i·nate /dɪ`naməˌnet; dɪˈnɒmɪ̆neɪt/ *v* [T] *formal* to give a name to something; DESIGNATE[1] (2)【正式】给〔某物〕命名

de·nom·i·na·tion /dɪˌnamə`neʃən; dɪˌnɒmɪ̆ˈneɪʃən/ *n* [C] **1** a religious group that is part of a larger religious organization 宗教派别: *Christians of all denominations* 各种教派的基督徒 **2** *technical* the value of a coin or NOTE[1] (5)【术语】货币面值[单位] **3** *formal* a name for a group or type【正式】〔一组或一类事物的〕名称, 种类名

de·nom·i·na·tion·al /dɪˌnamə`neʃənḷ; dɪˌnɒmɪ̆ˈneɪʃənəl/ *adj* connected with or belonging to a particular religious denomination 教派的

de·nom·i·na·tor /dɪ`naməˌnetɚ; dɪˈnɒmɪ̆neɪtə/ *n* [C] *technical* the number below the line in a FRACTION (2)【术语】〔分数的〕分母 —compare 比较 NUMERATOR —see also 另见 LOWEST COMMON DENOMINATOR

de·no·ta·tion /ˌdino`teʃən; ˌdiːnəʊˈteɪʃən/ *n* [C] *technical* the thing that is actually described by a word rather than the feelings or ideas it suggests【术语】〔词的〕指示意义, 本义〔而非隐含意义〕—compare 比较 CONNOTATION

de·note /dɪ`not; dɪˈnəʊt/ *v* [T] *formal*【正式】**1** to mean 意思是…: *The word 'family' is used here to denote the members of a household, whether or not they are related.* "家庭"这个词在这里用来指一户人家的所有成员, 而不论他们是否是亲属关系。**2** to be a sign of something; INDICATE (4) 是…的标记; 表示…: *Crosses on the map denote villages and hamlets.* 地图上的十字表示村落。—**denotative** *adj*

de·noue·ment /ˌdenu`mɑ; deɪˈnuːmɒŋ/ *n* [C] the explanation at the end of a story or play〔小说或戏剧等的〕结局, 收场; 结局[收场]的段落

de·nounce /dɪ`naʊns; dɪˈnaʊns/ *v* [T] **1** to express strong disapproval of someone or something, especially in public 谴责, 指责, 斥责: *The President's statement was denounced by all parties.* 总统的声明遭到了各党派的指责。| **denounce sb/sth as** *He denounced the waste of public money as 'criminally negligent'.* 他谴责浪费公款是"构成犯罪的玩忽职守"。**2** to give information to the police or other authority about someone's illegal political activities 告发, 检举, 举报: **denounce sb to sb** *She eventually denounced him to the secret police.* 她终于向秘密警察告发了他。—see also 另见 DENUNCIATION

dense /dɛns; dens/ *adj*

1 ▶CLOSE TOGETHER 挨在一起◀ made of several things that are closely packed together 茂密的, 密集的, 稠密的: *He forced his way through the dense crowd.* 他从密集的人群中挤过。| *Dense jungle covered the whole area.* 茂密的热带丛林覆盖了整个地区。

2 ▶SMOKE/MIST 烟/雾◀ difficult to see through or breathe in 浓密的, 不易看透[呼吸]的: *dense fog* 浓雾 | *a dense black cloud* 密密的乌云

3 ▶STUPID 愚蠢的◀ *informal* not able to understand things easily; stupid【非正式】迟钝的, 愚蠢的: *Oh, don't be so dense!* 天啊, 别那么笨!

4 ▶WRITING 写作◀ a dense piece of writing is difficult to understand because it contains a lot of information or uses complicated language〔写的东西〕不易懂的

5 ▶SUBSTANCE 物质◀ *technical* a substance that is dense has a lot of MASS[1] (6) in relation to its size【术语】密度大的: *Water is eight hundred times denser than air.* 水的密度是空气密度的800倍。—**densely** *adv*: *a densely populated area* 人口稠密的地区 —**denseness** *n* [U]

den·si·ty /ˈdɛnsətɪ; ˈdensə̇ti/ *n* [U] **1** the degree to which an area is filled with things or people 密度: *population density* 人口密度 **2** *technical* the relationship between something's MASS[1] (5) and its size【术语】密度〔质量与体积的关系〕

dent[1] /dɛnt; dent/ *n* [C] **1** a hollow area in the surface of something, usually made by something hitting it〔通常由于碰撞而造成的〕凹痕, 凹坑: [+in] *There was a dent in the door where he'd kicked it.* 他踢门的地方陷了一块。**2** a reduction in the amount of something, especially money or supplies〔尤指金钱或供应〕减少, 削减, 耗减: *The trip made a big dent in our savings.* 这次旅行花掉了我们很多积蓄。

dent 凹痕, 凹坑

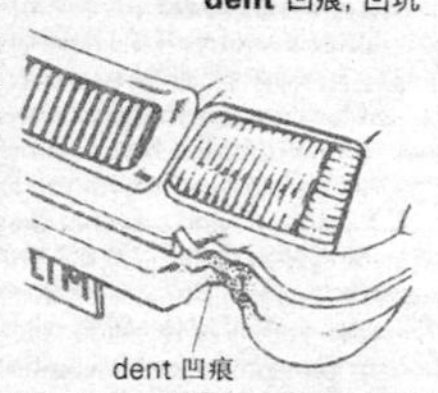

dent[2] *v* [T] **1** to make a hollow area in the surface of something, usually by hitting it 使造成凹痕: *I'm afraid I've dented the car.* 恐怕我把汽车撞出了凹痕。**2** to damage or harm something 损害, 破坏: *Diesel sales have been badly dented by environmental concerns.* 由于对环保问题的关注, 柴油的销售受到了严重影响。

den·tal /ˈdɛntl; ˈdentl/ *adj* connected with your teeth 牙齿的: *dental treatment* 牙齿的治疗

dental floss /ˌ·· ˈ·/ *n* [U] a kind of thin string that you use for cleaning between your teeth 洁牙线〔用以清洁牙缝的细线〕

dental hy·gien·ist /ˌ·· ˈ·· ·/ *n* [C] someone who works with a dentist and cleans people's teeth, or gives them advice about how to look after their teeth 牙科保健员, 牙科清洁员, 牙医助手

dental nurse /ˈ·· ·/ *n* [C] someone whose job is to help a dentist 牙科护士

dental sur·geon /ˌ·· ˈ·· ·/ *n* [C] *formal* a dentist【正式】牙科医生

den·tine /ˈdɛntin; ˈdentiːn/ also 又作 **den·tin** /ˈdɛntɪn; ˈdentɪn/ *AmE*【美】*n* [U] the type of bone that your teeth are made of 牙(本)质, 齿质 —see picture at 参见 TEETH 图

den·tist /ˈdɛntɪst; ˈdentə̇st/ *n* [C] someone whose job is to treat people's teeth 牙科医生: *I'm going to the dentist's this afternoon.* 今天下午我要去看牙医。

CULTURAL NOTE 文化注释

In Britain and the US, people usually go to see their dentist every six months when they are children (and in Britain this is paid for by the state), although often they go less frequently as adults. Many people, especially older people, connect the dentist's with pain, and some actually fear going there. 英美儿童通常每六个月去看一次牙医(英国由国家负担此项费用), 不过通常很多儿童和成年人一样去的次数并不多。很多人, 尤其是年纪较大的人, 把牙医诊所和疼痛联系起来, 有的人实际上害怕去牙科诊所。

den·tis·try /ˈdɛntɪstrɪ; ˈdentə̇stri/ *n* [U] the medical study of the mouth and teeth, or the work of a dentist 牙科学; 牙医术; 牙医业

den·tures /ˈdɛntʃɚz; ˈdentʃəz/ *n* [plural] a set of artificial teeth worn by someone who does not have their own teeth any more; FALSE TEETH (一副)假牙

de·nude /dɪˈnud; dɪˈnjuːd/ *v* [T] *formal* to remove a natural layer or part of something【正式】使〔自然层〕剥光: **denude sth of** *The trees were now denuded of their leaves.* 树木的叶子已经落光。—**denudation** /ˌdinuˈdeʃən; ˌdiːnjuːˈdeɪʃən/ *n* [U]

de·nun·ci·a·tion /dɪˌnʌnsɪˈeʃən; dɪˌnʌnsiˈeɪʃən/ *n* [C] a public statement that someone or something is wrong or bad 谴责, 斥责, 控诉

Den·ver /ˈdɛnvɚ; ˈdenvə/ the capital and largest city of the US state of Colorado, close to the Rocky Mountains. Denver is an important business, educational, and CULTURAL centre, and it is sometimes called the "**Mile High City**" because it is one mile above sea level. 丹佛〔美国科罗拉多州首府、最大的城市, 重要商业、教育和文化中心。靠近落基山脉, 因海拔有一英里之高, 所以有时也称"一英里高城"〕

Den·ver boot /ˌdɛnvɚ ˈbut; ˌdenvə ˈbuːt/ *n* [C] *AmE informal* a metal object that the police fasten to an illegally parked car so that it cannot be moved; WHEEL CLAMP【美, 非正式】丹佛扣锁, 车轮固定夹〔警察用来夹住非法停靠的汽车〕

de·ny /dɪˈnaɪ; dɪˈnaɪ/ *v* [T]

1 ▶SAY STH IS UNTRUE 说某事不是事实◀ to say that something someone has said about you is not true 否认, 否定: *I saw you, so don't try to deny it!* 我看见你了, 所以别想否认了! | **deny (that)** *Do you deny that this is your writing?* 你否认这是你的笔迹吗? | *I can't deny her remarks hurt me.* 我不能否认她的话伤害了我。| **deny doing sth** *He denied ever having been there.* 他否认曾经去了那个地方。| **flatly/categorically deny** (=deny very strongly) 坚决/断然否认 *Jackson categorically denied any involvement in the affair.* 杰克逊断然否认与此事有任何关联。

2 ▶NOT ALLOW 不允许◀ [often passive 常用被动态] to refuse to allow someone to have or do something 不允许〔某人拥有某物或做某事〕: *Permission was denied.* 没有得到准许。| **deny sb sth** *She could deny her son nothing.* 她对她儿子有求必应。| **deny sth to sb** *The campaign aims to deny contraceptive advice to girls under sixteen.* 活动旨在不许16岁以下的女孩获得有关避孕的咨询。—see 见 REFUSE[1] (USAGE)

3 there's no denying *spoken* used to say that it is very clear that something is true【口】无可否认, 不容否认: *There's no denying that this is a serious blow.* 无可否认, 这是个严重的打击。

4 ▶PRINCIPLES/BELIEFS 原则/信仰◀ *formal* to do something that is the opposite of something you strongly believe in【正式】背弃, 抛弃

5 ▶FEELINGS 感情◀ to refuse to admit that you are feeling something 拒绝承认: *I realized I'd been denying a lot of angry feelings towards my mother.* 我意识到自己一直在否认对母亲有许多愤怒的情绪。

6 deny yourself to decide not to have something that you would like, especially for moral or religious reasons〔尤指出于道德或宗教原因〕克制自己, 自制

de·o·do·rant /diˈodərənt; diːˈəʊdərənt/ *n* [C,U] a chemical substance that you put on your skin to hide or destroy unpleasant smells〔除体臭的〕防臭剂, 除臭剂

de·o·do·rize also 又作 **-ise** *BrE*【英】/diˈodəˌraɪz; diːˈəʊdəraɪz/ *v* [T] to remove or hide the unpleasant smell of something 除去…的臭气

dep the written abbreviation of 缩写= DEPART or 或 DEPARTURE

de·part /dɪˈpɑrt; dɪˈpɑːt/ *v* **1** [I] to leave, especially when you are starting a journey 离开〔尤指动身去旅行〕, 启程, 上路: *The train for Edinburgh will depart from platform 5.* 开往爱丁堡的火车将从5号站台出发。**2 depart this life** *formal* to die【正式】去世, 故去, 离开人间 —see also 另见 DEPARTURE

depart from sth *phr v* [T] to start to do something differently from the usual, traditional, or expected way 背离, 违反, 不同于〔常规等〕: *Her approach departs radically from normal educational practices.* 她的方法与通常的教育惯例大相径庭。

de·part·ed /dɪˈpɑrtɪd; dɪˈpɑːtə̇d/ *adj* [only before noun 仅用于名词前] **1** a word meaning dead, used to avoid saying this directly 已故的, 去世的〔委婉说法〕: *our dear departed father* 我们挚爱的已故的父亲 **2** *literary* a period of time that is departed has gone for ever【文】过去的, 不复再来的: *departed youth* 逝去的青春

de·part·ment /dɪˈpɑrtmənt; dɪˈpɑːtmənt/ *n* [C] **1** one of the groups of people working together to form part of a large organization such as a hospital, university, or company〔医院、大学或公司等大机构的〕科, 系, 处, 部门: **the English/sales etc department** *She's in charge of the personnel department.* 她主管人事部门。| [+of] *the Department of Genetic Research* 基因研究部门 **2** one of the parts that the government is divided into which is responsible for a particular problem or part of people's lives〔政府的〕院, 部, 司: *the State Department* 国务院 | *the Department of Transport* 交通部 **3** [C] one of the areas that sells a particular type of product in a large shop〔大商店的〕部: *the toy department* 玩具部 **4** one of the separate areas that some countries are divided into, for example in France〔法国等国家的〕行政区, 省 **5 be sb's department** *spoken* to be something that a particular person is responsible for【口】某人负责的事, 某人的职责范围: *Don't ask me – cooking's John's department.* 别问我——做饭是约翰的事。—see also 另见 FIRE DEPARTMENT, POLICE DEPARTMENT —**departmental** /ˌdɪpɑrtˈmɛntl; ˌdiːpɑːtˈmentl◂/ *adj*: *a departmental meeting* 部门会议

de·part·men·ta·lize also 又作 **-ise** *BrE*【英】/ˌdipɑrtˈmɛntlˌaɪz; ˌdiːpɑːtˈmentl-aɪz/ *v* [T] to divide something into different departments 把〔某机构〕分成不同的部门: *Most large organizations are departmentalized.* 大多数大机构都被划分成不同的部门。

Department for Cul·ture, Me·di·a and Sport, the a British government department, formerly called the Department of National Heritage, which is responsible for supporting the arts, tourism, sport etc, and for making rules about newspapers and broadcasting in the UK 文化、新闻与体育部〔英国政府部门, 以前称"民族遗产部"。其职能是支持艺术、旅游、体育等事业的发展, 制定与报纸和广播相关的法规〕

Department for Ed·u·ca·tion and Skills, the abbreviation 缩写为 DFES formerly called the Department for Education and Employment; a British government department which is responsible for the UK's education system and for organizing training programmes for people without jobs etc 教育与技能部〔英国政府部门, 以前称"教育与就业部"。其职能是管理英国的教育系统, 组织失业人员培训项目等〕

Department for Environment, Food and Ru·ral Af·fairs, the abbreviation 缩写为 DEFRA a British government department that is responsible for things such as plans for new roads and buildings, the protection of the countryside and old buildings, and the quality of the air and water in the UK. It is now also responsible for government policy on farming and the countryside. 环境、食品与乡村事务部〔英国政府部门。其职能是负责公路和建筑规划、乡村和古建筑保护以及空气质量与水质管理等事务。目前还负责制定有关农业和农村政策〕

Department for In·ter·na·tion·al De·vel·op·ment, the abbreviation 缩写为 DFID formerly called the Overseas Development Administration (ODA); a British government department that gives money, advice, and help to poorer countries 国际开发部〔英国政府部门, 以前称"海外发展管理局", 向贫穷国家提供资金、建议和援助〕

Department for Work and Pen·sions, the abbreviation 缩写为 DWP a British government department which is responsible for paying various types of BENEFIT (=money paid by the government to support people who need it, for example people who are poor, people who are too old or too sick to work, and people who cannot find jobs), and for government policy on employment 工作及抚恤金部〔英国政府部门, 负责支付各类救济金、制定就业政策〕

Department of De·fense, the the US government department which is responsible for the military forces in the US, that is, the Army, Navy, Air Force, and Marines. In the UK there is a similar department called the Ministry of Defence. 国防部〔美国政府部门, 负责陆、海、空和海军陆战队事务。英国也有一类似部门, 称 Ministry of Defence〕—see also 另见 PENTAGON

Department of Ed·u·ca·tion, the a US government department which is responsible for the education system, including education programmes, laws for schools and colleges, standards for schools and teachers etc 教育部〔美国政府部门, 负责管理美国的教育系统, 包括教育计划、有关学校的法规、学校与教师标准等〕

Department of Health, the a British government department which is responsible for health programmes in the UK and for the National Health Service 卫生部〔英国政府部门, 负责英国的健康计划和国民保健制度〕

Department of Health and Hu·man Ser·vic·es, the a US government department which is responsible for health programmes, and for providing money and support for people who are poor, people who have no jobs, and people who have stopped working because they are old 卫生与公众服务部〔美国政府部门, 负责保健计划, 资助和扶持贫困、失业和退休人员〕

Department of Hous·ing and Ur·ban De·vel·op·ment, the *n* [singular] the HUD

Department of Jus·tice, the a US government department which deals with the law. Its work includes writing laws, representing the government in a court of law, and doing criminal INVESTIGATIONs (=searching for information to solve crimes). The head of the Department of Justice is called the Attorney General. In the UK there is a similar department called the Lord Chancellor's Department. 司法部〔美国政府部门, 负责处理司法事务, 其职责包括起草法律, 代表政府出庭, 调查刑事案件。司法部长叫 Attorney General。英国也有一类似部门, 称 Lord Chancellor's Department (大法官事务部)〕

Department of La·bor, the the US government department concerned with how workers are treated by employers. It examines subjects such as fair wages, safety, and the number of hours worked each week. 劳工部〔美国政府部门, 负责劳资事务, 处理有关工资待遇、安全和周工作时间等诸多问题〕

Department of Mo·tor Ve·hic·les, the *n* [singular] the DMV

Department of Na·tion·al Her·i·tage, the /·,·· ·,··ˈ···/ the former name of the Department for Culture, Media and Sport 民族遗产部〔文化、新闻与体育部的旧称〕

Department of So·cial Se·cu·ri·ty, the abbreviation 缩写为 DSS a British government department which used to be responsible for paying various types of BENEFIT (=money paid by the government to support people who need it, for example people who are poor, people who are too old or too sick to work, and people who cannot find jobs). This department changed its name in 2001 and became the Department for Work and Pensions. 社会保障部〔英国政府部门, 过去曾负责支付各种救济金, 2001 年更名为"工作及抚恤金部"〕

Department of State, the the official name for the US State Department (美国)国务院〔the US State Department 的官方名称〕

Department of the En·vi·ron·ment, the abbreviation 缩写为 DOE a British government department that was responsible for things such as plans for new roads and buildings, the protection of the countryside and old buildings, and the quality of the air and water in the UK. It is now called the Department for Environment, Food and Rural Affairs. 环境事务部〔英国政府部门, 负责公路和建筑规划, 乡村和古建筑保护以及英国空气质量和水质管理等事务。现更名为环境、食品与乡村事务部〕

Department of the In·ter·i·or, the the part of the US government responsible for protecting the US's NATURAL RESOURCES (=land, minerals, water, natural energy etc). The person in charge of this department is called the Secretary of the Interior. 内政部〔美国政府部门, 负责保护自然资源。内政部长称 the Secretary of the Interior〕

Department of Trade and In·dus·try, the *n* [singular] the DTI

Department of Trans·port, the a British government department that deals with TRANSPORT in the UK, for example by making laws about road vehicles and planes, and by building and repairing roads. In the US there is a similar department called the Department of Transportation . 交通运输部〔英国政府部门, 负责处理交通运输事务, 如制定陆运与空运法规, 修建和维修道路等。美国也有一类似部门, 称 the Department of Transportation〕

Department of Trans·por·ta·tion, the /·,·· ·,··ˈ··/ a US government department that deals with transport in the US, for example by making laws about road vehicles and planes, and by building and repairing roads. In the UK there is a similar department called the Department of Transport. 交通运输部〔美国政府部门, 负责处理交通运输事务, 如制定陆运与空运法规，修建和维修道路等。英国也有一类似部门, 称 the Department of Transport〕

department store /·ˈ·· ·/ *n* [C] a large shop that is divided into separate departments, each selling a different type of goods 百货商店, 百货公司

de·par·ture /dɪˈpɑrtʃɚ; dɪˈpɑːtʃə/ *n* **1** [C,U] an act of leaving a place, especially at the start of a journey 离开, 起程: [+for] *I saw Simon shortly before his departure for Russia.* 在西蒙离开这儿去俄罗斯之前不久我见过他。**2** [C,U] an act of leaving an organization or position 离职: *His sudden departure from the political scene took everyone by surprise.* 他从政治舞台上突然引退, 使每个人深感惊讶。**3** [C] a flight, train etc that leaves at a particular time〔航班、火车等的〕出发: *There are several departures for New York every day.* 每天有好几个班次开往纽约。**4** [C] a way of doing something that is different from the usual, traditional, expected way〔对一般传统的〕背离, 违反: **new/fresh/radical etc departure** (=a completely new and usually better way of doing something) 新的尝试/根本上的不同〔通常指全新及较好的做事方式〕 *This approach represents a radical departure from previous policy.* 这种方法与以往的策略有着根本区别。—opposite 反义词 ARRIVAL W3

departure lounge /·ˈ·· ,·/ *n* [C] the place at an airport where people wait until their plane is ready to leave〔飞机场的〕候机室

departures board /·ˈ·· ·/ *n* [C] a board in an airport or station that shows the times at which planes or trains leave〔火车站的〕离站车次告示牌;〔飞机场的〕出发航班告示牌

de·pend /dɪˈpɛnd; dɪˈpend/ *v* **it/that depends** *spoken* used to say that you cannot give a definite answer to something, because the answer could change according to what happens【口】那得看情况: *"Are you going to visit him?" "Well, it depends."* "你要去看他吗?" "哦, 这要看情况。" S1 W2

depend on/upon *phr v* [T] **1** to need the support, help, or existence of someone or something else 依靠，依赖: *The country depends heavily on its tourist trade.* 这个国家在很大程度上依靠旅游业。| *We depend entirely on donations from the public.* 我们完全依赖公众的捐助。| **depend on sb/sth for** *Children depend on their parents for all of their material needs.* 孩子们依靠父母为他们提供所有的物质需要。| **depend on sb/sth to do sth** *I'm depending on you to get this done.* 我指望着你把这件事给办了。| **depend on sb/sth doing sth** *We're depending on him finishing the job by Friday.* 我们指望着他在星期五前完成这项工作。**2** to trust or have confidence in someone or something 信赖，相信: *You can depend on Jane – she always keeps her promises.* 你可以相信简，她一向都是信守诺言的。| **depend upon it** *spoken* (=you can be sure)【口】请放心 *Depend upon it, he'll turn up.* 请放心，他一定会来的。**3** [not in progressive 不用进行时] to change according to what else happens or whether something else changes 取决于…，视…而定: *The length of the treatment depends on the severity of the illness.* 治疗时间的长短取决于病情的严重程度。| **depending on** *The plant may grow to a height of several meters, depending on soil conditions.* 这种植物可以长到好几米高，视土壤条件而定。| **depend on who/what/how etc** *The amount you pay depends on where you live.* 付款多少取决于你居住的地区。

de·pen·da·ble /dɪˋpɛndəbl̩; dɪˈpendəbəl/ *adj* someone or something that is dependable can be trusted to do what you need or expect 可靠的，可信赖的: *Ed Duncan was a dependable, hardworking detective.* 埃德·邓肯是个可信赖的、勤奋的侦探。| *a dependable source of income* 可靠的收入来源 —**dependably** *adv* —**dependability** /dɪˌpɛndəˋbɪlətɪ; dɪˌpendəˈbɪləti/ *n* [U]

de·pen·dant /dɪˋpɛndənt; dɪˈpendənt/ *n* [C] someone, especially a child, who depends on you for food, clothes, money etc 依赖他人供养的人〔尤指孩子〕

de·pen·dence /dɪˋpɛndəns; dɪˈpendəns/ *n* [U] **1** a situation in which you depend on the help and support of someone or something else in order to exist or be successful 依赖，依靠: [+on/upon] *We need to reduce our dependence on oil as a source of energy.* 我们需要减少对石油这种能源的依赖。—opposite 反义词 INDEPENDENCE **2 drug/alcohol dependence** the state of being ADDICTED (1) to drugs or alcohol 毒瘾/酒瘾 **3** *formal* trust; RELIANCE【正式】信任，信赖: *I always place a lot of dependence on what she says.* 我总是很信赖她说的话。

de·pen·den·cy /dɪˋpɛndənsɪ; dɪˈpendənsi/ *n* **1** [U] a state of dependence 依靠，依赖 **2** [C] a country that is controlled by another country 附属国，属地

de·pen·dent /dɪˋpɛndənt; dɪˈpendənt/ *adj* **1** needing someone or something else in order to exist, be successful, be healthy etc 依赖的，依靠的: *Do you have any dependent children?* 你有没有需要扶养的孩子？| **be dependent on/upon sth (for)** *The young are totally dependent on their parents for food and shelter.* 年轻人完全依赖父母提供食宿。**2 drug/alcohol etc dependent** ADDICTED (1) to drugs, alcohol etc 有毒瘾的/有酒瘾的等 **3 be dependent on/upon** *formal* to change according to what else happens or whether something else changes【正式】取决于: *How much you get paid is dependent on how much you produce.* 你赚多少钱取决于你产出多少。

dependent clause /ˌ·ˌ·· ˈ·/ *n* [C] a CLAUSE (2) in a sentence that gives information related to the main clause, but cannot exist alone〔不能单独存在的〕从属子句，从句

de·pict /dɪˋpɪkt; dɪˈpɪkt/ *v* [T] to describe something, especially in writing or pictures, in a way that gives a clear idea of a real situation 描写；描述；描绘: *a book that depicts life in pre-revolutionary Russia* 描写革命前俄国生活的一本书 —**depiction** /dɪˋpɪkʃən; dɪˈpɪkʃən/ *n* [C,U]

de·pil·a·to·ry /dɪˋpɪləˌtorɪ; dɪˈpɪlətəri/ *n* [C] a substance that gets rid of unwanted hair from your body 脱毛剂 —**depilatory** *adj* [only before noun 仅用于名词前] *Try one of our depilatory creams.* 试用一下我们的其中一款脱毛霜。

de·plete /dɪˋplit; dɪˈpliːt/ *v* [T usually passive 一般用被动态] to reduce the amount of something that is available 削减，损耗: *Our food reserves had been severely depleted over the winter.* 经过了冬天，我们的食物储备已经消耗得差不多了。—**depletion** /dɪˋpliʃən; dɪˈpliːʃən/ *n* [U]: *the depletion of the ozone layer* 臭氧层的损耗

de·plor·a·ble /dɪˋplorəbl̩; dɪˈplɔːrəbəl/ *adj formal* very bad, unpleasant, and shocking【正式】糟透的；可悲的；极可哀叹的: *Conditions in the prison were deplorable.* 监狱的状况糟透了。| *a deplorable waste of tax-payers' money* 对纳税人钱财令人不爽的浪费 —**deplorably** *adv*

de·plore /dɪˋplor; dɪˈplɔː/ *v* [T] to disapprove very strongly of something and criticize it severely, especially publicly〔尤指公开地〕强烈反对；谴责: *The UN deplored the invasion as a 'violation of international law'.* 联合国谴责这次侵略行为"违反了国际法"。

de·ploy /dɪˋplɔɪ; dɪˈplɔɪ/ *v* [T] to organize people or things, especially soldiers, military equipment etc, so that they are in the right place and ready to be used 部署，调度〔尤指士兵、军事装备等〕: *They decided it was time to deploy more troops.* 他们认为该是部署更多部队的时候了。—**deployment** *n* [C,U]

de·pop·u·late /diˋpɑpjəˌlet; ˌdiːˈpɒpjʊ̈leɪt/ *v* [T usually passive 一般用被动态] to greatly reduce the number of people living in a particular area 减少〔某一地区〕的人口: *Many rural areas were completely depopulated by the end of the century.* 到世纪末，许多农村地区不再有人居住了。—**depopulation** /ˌdipɑpjəˋleʃən; diːˌpɒpjʊ̈ˈleɪʃən/ *n* [U]

de·port /dɪˋport; dɪˈpɔːt/ *v* [T] **1** to make someone who is not a citizen of a particular country leave that country, especially because they do not have a legal right to stay 将〔尤其是没有合法居住权的外国人〕驱逐出境 **2 deport yourself** *formal* to behave in a particular way, especially in the proper or correct way【正式】表现得体

de·por·ta·tion /ˌdiporˋteʃən; ˌdiːpɔːˈteɪʃən/ *n* [C,U] the act of deporting someone 驱逐出境: *a deportation order* 驱逐出境令

de·por·tee /ˌdiporˋti; ˌdiːpɔːˈtiː/ *n* [C] someone who has been deported or is going to be deported（将要）被驱逐出境的人

de·port·ment /dɪˋportmənt; dɪˈpɔːtmənt/ *n* [U] **1** *especially BrE* the way that someone stands and walks【尤英】举止，仪态，风度: *As a girl, she had lessons in elocution and deportment.* 她小时候曾上过言谈技巧课和仪态课。**2** *old-fashioned especially AmE* the way that a person, especially a young woman, behaves in public【过时，尤美】〔尤指年轻妇女在公共场合的〕行为，举止

de·pose /dɪˋpoz; dɪˈpəʊz/ *v* [T] **1** to remove a king, queen, or ruler from a position of power 罢免，废黜〔国王、王后或统治者〕: *The army was threatening to depose him.* 军队威胁说要罢黜他。**2** *law* to officially give information about something, after you have promised to tell the truth【法律】宣誓作证

de·pos·it[1] /dɪˋpɑzɪt; dɪˈpɒzʊ̈t/ *n* [C]

1 ▶SUM OF MONEY 金额◀ the first part of the money for a house, car, holiday etc, that you pay so that it will be kept for you〔购屋、买车、度假等的〕定金，头款，首付金: **put down a deposit (on)** (=pay a deposit) 付定金 *We put down a deposit on a house last week.* 上周我们付了房子的定金。

2 ▶RENT 租用◀ money that you pay when you rent or HIRE something, which will be given back if you do not damage the thing you are renting or hiring〔租用东西的〕押金，保证金: *You will have to pay one month's rent in advance, plus a deposit of $500.* 你得预付一个月的租金，外加500美元的押金。

3 ▶BANK 银行◀ an amount of money that is paid into a bank account 存款: **make a deposit** *I'd like to make a deposit, please.* 我想办理一下存款。

4 ▶SOIL/MINERALS 土壤/矿物质◀ a layer of a mineral, metal etc that is left in soil or rocks through a natural process 矿床: *rich deposits of gold in the hills* 山里丰富的金矿床

5 ▶LAYER 层◀ an amount or layer of a substance that gradually develops in a particular place 沉积物，沉积层: *fatty deposits on the heart* 心脏上积淀的油脂层

6 ▶ELECTION 选举◀ money paid by someone who is a CANDIDATE (1) in a political election in Britain, that will be returned to them if they get enough votes 选举保证金〔在英国参加政治选举的候选人付的保证金，如果候选人得到足够的选票，保证金将发还给他〕: **lose your deposit** (=not get enough votes)〔因选票不够而〕失去保证金

deposit[2] *v* **1** [T always+adv/prep] *formal* to put something down in a particular place【正式】把〔某物〕放在〔某地〕: [+on/in/by etc] *The female deposits her eggs directly into the water.* 这种雌性动物把卵直接产在水中。**2** [T] to leave a layer of a substance on the surface of something 沉积: *As the river slows down, it deposits a layer of soil.* 河流流速变慢时，一层泥沙便沉积下来。**3** [T] to put money or something valuable in a bank or other place where it will be safe 将〔钱等贵重物品〕存入〔银行或其他安全的地方〕: *You are advised to deposit your valuables in the hotel safe.* 建议您把贵重物品存到旅馆的保险箱里。

deposit ac·count /·ˈ·· ·ˌ·/ *n* [C] *especially BrE* a bank account that pays INTEREST[1] (4) on condition that you keep money there for a particular length of time【尤英】定期存款账户 —compare 比较 CHECKING ACCOUNT, CURRENT ACCOUNT

de·po·si·tion /ˌdɛpə`zɪʃən; ˌdepəˈzɪʃən/ *n* **1** [C] *law* a statement written for a court of law, by someone who has promised to tell the truth【法律】〔经宣誓为真实的〕证词 **2** [U] *technical* the natural process of depositing a substance in rocks or soil【术语】沉淀, 沉积 **3** [C,U] the act of removing someone from a position of power 罢免, 废黜

de·pos·i·tor /dɪ`pɑzɪtɚ; dɪˈpɒzɪ̈tə/ *n* [C] someone who puts money in a bank or other financial organization 存款人, 存户

de·pos·i·to·ry /dɪ`pɑzəˌtorɪ; dɪˈpɒzɪ̈təri/ *n* [C] a place where something can be safely kept〔可以安全存放物品的〕贮藏室, 仓库 —**depository** *adj*

deposit slip /ˈ·ˌ· ·/ *n* [C] *AmE* a form that you use to pay money into your bank account【美】存款单; PAYING-IN SLIP *BrE*【英】

dep·ot /`dipo; ˈdepəʊ/ *n* [C] **1** a place where goods are stored until they are needed 仓库, 储存处, 货场 **2** a place where buses are kept and repaired〔公共汽车的〕车库; 修车场 **3** *AmE* a railway station or bus station, especially a small one【美】〔尤指小规模的〕火车站; 公共汽车站

de·prave /dɪ`prev; dɪˈpreɪv/ *v* [T] *formal* to be an evil influence on someone, especially someone who is young or not very experienced【正式】使道德败坏〔尤指对年轻人或缺乏经验者的不良影响〕 —**depravity** /dɪ`prævətɪ; dɪˈprævɪ̈ti/ *n* [U]: *scenes of depravity* 腐化堕落的场面 —**depravation** /ˌdɛprə`veʃən; ˌdeprəˈveɪʃən/ *n* [U]

de·praved /dɪ`prevd; dɪˈpreɪvd/ *adj* completely evil or morally unacceptable 堕落的, 腐化的, 道德败坏的: *a vicious and depraved man* 一个恶毒、堕落的人

dep·re·cate /`dɛprəˌket; ˈdeprɪ̈keɪt/ *v* [T] *formal* to strongly disapprove of or criticize something【正式】坚决反对; 强烈批评 —**deprecation** /ˌdɛprə`keʃən; ˌdeprɪ̈ˈkeɪʃən/ *n* [U]

dep·re·cat·ing /`dɛprəˌketɪŋ; ˈdeprɪ̈keɪtɪŋ/ also 又作 **dep·re·ca·to·ry** /`dɛprəkəˌtorɪ; ˈdeprɪ̈keɪtəri/ *adj* **1** expressing criticism or disapproval 批评的; 反对的, 不赞成的: *She made several deprecating remarks about my dress sense.* 她好几次对我的穿着品味颇有微词。**2** words or actions that are deprecating are intended to make someone feel less annoyed or disapproving〔话语、行动〕意在使人不那么生气的; 自谦的, 谦和的: *"He's not here at the moment," She said with a deprecating smile.* "他现在不在这儿。" 她谦和地笑一笑说。—see also 另见 SELF-DEPRECATING —**deprecatingly** *adv*

de·pre·ci·ate /dɪ`priʃɪˌet; dɪˈpriːʃieɪt/ *v* **1** [I] to decrease in value or price 贬值, 跌价: *A new car will depreciate quite fast.* 新车往往很快就跌价。—opposite 反义词 APPRECIATE (4) **2** [T] *formal* to make something seem unimportant【正式】贬低〔重要性〕

de·pre·ci·a·tion /dɪˌpriʃɪ`eʃən; dɪˌpriːʃiˈeɪʃən/ *n* [U] a reduction in the value or price of something 贬值, 跌价: *the depreciation of the dollar* 美元的贬值 —**depreciatory** /dɪ`priʃɪəˌtorɪ; dɪˈpriːʃiətəri/ *adj*

dep·re·da·tion /ˌdɛprɪ`deʃən; ˌdeprɪ̈ˈdeɪʃən/ *n* [C often plural 常用复数] *formal* an act of cruelty, violence, or destruction【正式】蹂躏, 破坏

de·press /dɪ`prɛs; dɪˈpres/ *v* [T] **1** to make someone feel very unhappy 使忧愁, 使抑郁: *The thought of having to take the exam again depressed him.* 想到又要参加考试让他心情沮丧。**2** to prevent something from working properly or being as active as it usually is 使不能正常运转; 使不活跃; 使不景气: *Several factors combined to depress the American economy.* 几个因素合在一起使美国的经济不景气。**3** *formal* to press something down, especially a part of a machine【正式】按下, 压下, 推下〔尤指机器的一部分〕: *Depress the clutch fully.* 把离合器踩到底。**4** *formal* to reduce the value of prices or wages【正式】减少, 降低〔价格或工资〕: *Competition between workers will depress wage levels.* 工人们之间的竞争将会降低工资水平。

de·press·ant /dɪ`prɛsn̩t; dɪˈpresənt/ *n* [C] a substance or drug that makes your body's processes slower and makes you feel very relaxed or sleepy 抑制剂, 抑制药 —compare 比较 STIMULANT —**depressant** *adj*

de·pressed /dɪ`prɛst; dɪˈprest/ *adj* **1 a)** feeling very unhappy 忧愁的, 消沉的, 沮丧的: *She felt lonely and depressed.* 她感到孤独和沮丧。| **[+about/at]** *Carter seemed depressed about the situation.* 卡特似乎对形势感到忧虑。**b)** suffering from a medical condition in which you are so unhappy that you cannot live a normal life 患抑郁症的 **2** an area, industry etc that is depressed does not have enough economic or business activity〔地区、工业等〕不景气的, 萧条的, 经济困难的 **3** a depressed level or amount is lower than normal 低于一般水准的: *During the illness certain hormone levels are depressed.* 患病期间, 某些荷尔蒙水平低于一般水准。

de·press·ing /dɪ`prɛsɪŋ; dɪˈpresɪŋ/ *adj* making you feel very sad 令人忧愁的, 令人沮丧的: *I found the whole experience very depressing.* 我觉得这整个经历非常令人沮丧。| *It's a depressing thought.* 这是个令人沮丧的想法。—**depressingly** *adv*: *a depressingly familiar story* 令人忧伤的熟悉故事

de·pres·sion /dɪ`prɛʃən; dɪˈpreʃən/ *n* **1** [C,U] **a)** a feeling of sadness that makes you think there is no hope for the future 忧伤, 沮丧, 消沉: *She was overcome by depression.* 她抑郁成疾。| **deep/severe depression** *Peter fell into a deep depression on hearing the news.* 彼得听到这个消息后极度沮丧。**b)** a medical condition that makes you so unhappy and anxious you cannot live a normal life 抑郁症 **2 a)** [C,U] a long period during which there is very little business activity and lots of people do not have jobs 经济萧条期, 不景气时期: *the long years of economic depression* 多年的经济萧条 —compare 比较 RECESSION **3 the Depression** the period when there was not much business activity and not many jobs in the 1930s 大萧条〔指 20 世纪 30 年代的经济不景气〕 **4** [C] a part of a surface that is lower than the other parts 洼地, 坑: *The rain had collected in several depressions on the ground.* 地面上的几处洼地都积了雨水。**5** [C] *technical* a mass of air that has a low pressure and usually causes rain【术语】低气压〔通常会导致下雨〕 S3 W3

Depression, the —see 见 GREAT DEPRESSION

de·press·ive¹ /dɪ`prɛsɪv; dɪˈpresɪv/ *adj* often feeling DEPRESSED 抑郁的, 沮丧的

depressive² *n* [C] someone who suffers from DEPRESSION 抑郁症患者

dep·ri·va·tion /ˌdɛprɪ`veʃən; ˌdeprɪ̈ˈveɪʃən/ *n* **1** [C usually plural 一般用复数] something you need or usually have that you are prevented from having 丧失, 剥夺: *People suffered terrible deprivations during the war.* 战争期间, 人们遭受了严重的损失。**2** [U] a lack of something that you need or want 缺少, 缺乏: *Sleep deprivation can result in mental disorders.* 睡眠不足会导致精神疾病。

de·prive /dɪ`praɪv; dɪˈpraɪv/ *v*

deprive sb **of** sth *phr v* [T often passive 常用被动态] to take something from someone, especially something that they need or want 剥夺: *A lot of these children have been deprived of a normal home life.* 这些孩子中有许多人被剥夺了正常的家庭生活。

de·prived /dɪ`praɪvd; dɪˈpraɪvd/ *adj* not having the things that are considered to be necessary for a comfortable or happy life 贫困的, 穷苦的: *a deprived childhood* 贫苦的童年

de·pro·gram /di`progræm; ˌdiːˈprəʊgræm/ *v* [T] to help someone who has been involved in a religious CULT to stop obeying its orders and to start thinking for themselves again 使被洗脑者觉醒, 反洗脑〔旨在消除宗教崇拜〕

dept the written abbreviation of 缩写= DEPARTMENT

depth /dɛpθ; depθ/ *n* S3 W3

1 ►DISTANCE 距离◄ [C usually singular 一般用单数,U] **a)** the distance down from the top surface to the bottom of something〔从顶部到底部的〕深, 深度: *What depth is the lake?* 这湖水有多深? | **to/at a depth of** *Plant the seeds at a depth of ten centimetres.* 把种子种到 10 厘米深的地方。| **a metre/foot etc in depth** *The pond is no more than a metre in depth.* 这个池塘最多一米深。**b)** the distance from the front to the back of an object〔从前端到后端的〕深度, 纵深: *The depth of the shelves is about 35cm.* 搁板大约有 35 厘米宽。

2 ►EMOTION/SITUATION 情感/形势◄ [U] how strong an emotion is or how serious a situation is〔表明情感的〕强烈程度;〔情况的〕严重程度: *Lawmakers underestimated the depth of public feeling on this issue.* 立法者低估了公众在这个问题上的敏感程度。

3 ►KNOWLEDGE 知识◄ [U] *approving* the quality of knowing or giving a lot of details about a subject【褒】深度: *I was impressed by the depth and complexity of the book.* 这本书的深度和复杂性给我印象很深。| *The network's news coverage lacks depth.* 网络上的新闻报道缺乏深度。| **in depth** (=considering all the details) 完全地, 彻底地, 深入地 *We'll need to study the report in some depth.* 我们需要比较深入地研究这个报告。—see also 另见 IN-DEPTH

4 be out of your depth a) to be involved in a situation or activity that is too difficult for you to understand 非…所能理解, 非…力所能及: *I felt completely out of my depth when they started discussing philosophy.* 他们一讨论哲学, 我就感到一窍不通了。**b)** to be in water that is too deep for you to stand in and be able to breathe 在深得不能站立和呼吸的水中

5 be in the depths of despair/depression etc to feel very unhappy 深感绝望/沮丧等

D

6 the depths of the countryside/forest etc the middle of a place where there are not many people 偏远的乡村/森林深处等
7 the depths of winter the middle of winter, especially when it is very cold 隆冬
8 hidden depths a part of someone's character that you do not notice when you first meet them 深藏不露: *I didn't know she wrote poems – she obviously has hidden depths.* 我不知道她会写诗——很显然她是深藏不露。
9 ▶SEA 大海◀ the depths *literary* the deepest parts of the sea 【文】深海

depth charge /ˈ· ·/ *n* [C] a bomb that explodes at a particular depth under water 深水炸弹

dep·u·ta·tion /ˌdɛpjəˈteʃən; ˌdepjʊˈteɪʃən/ *n* [C] a group of people who are sent to talk to someone in authority, as representatives of a larger group〔较大的群体推选出来与当权者谈判的〕代表团

de·pute /dɪˈpjut; dɪˈpjuːt/ *v* [T] **depute sb to do sth** *formal* to tell or allow someone to do something instead of you【正式】委派某人做某事, 委派某人为代表

dep·u·tize also 又作 **-ise** *BrE*【英】/ˈdɛpjəˌtaɪz; ˈdepjʊtaɪz/ *v* [I] to do the work of someone of a higher rank than you for a short time because they are unable to do it 充当〔职位比自己高的人的〕代表: [**+for**] *Who's going to deputize for Liam while he's away?* 利亚姆不在的时候, 将由谁代理他的工作?

2 **dep·u·ty** /ˈdɛpjətɪ; ˈdepjʊti/ *n* [C] **1** someone who is directly below a manager in rank, and who is officially in charge when the manager is not there〔经理的〕副手;〔经理不在时负责工作的〕代理人 **2** a member of the LOWER HOUSE of parliament in some countries, for example France〔某些国家如法国的〕下议院议员 **3** someone whose job is to help a SHERIFF (1) in the US〔美国县治安官的〕助理: *On the third day, a deputy unlocked my cell.* 第三天的时候, 治安官的助手打开了我住的牢房。

de·rail /dɪˈrel; ˌdiːˈreɪl/ *v* **1** [T usually passive 一般用被动态] to make a train go off the railway line 使〔火车〕出轨 **2** [T] to spoil or interrupt a plan, agreement etc 破坏, 干扰〔计划、协议等〕: *The dispute has temporarily derailed the arms control agreement.* 这项争端暂时破坏了军备控制协议。—**derailment** *n* [C,U]

de·ranged /dɪˈrendʒd; dɪˈreɪndʒd/ *adj* behaving in a crazy or dangerous way 精神失常的, 疯狂的 —**derangement** *n* [C,U]

Der·by a city in Derbyshire. It is an important centre for industries such as engineering and CHINA. 德比〔英国德比郡一城市, 是重要的机械制造和瓷器工业中心〕

derby *n* [C] **1** *AmE* a man's round hard hat that is usually black【美】常礼帽〔一种男用硬质圆顶帽, 通常为黑色〕; **bowler hat** (BOWLER (2)) *BrE*【英】—see picture at 参见 HAT 图 **2** *BrE* a sports match between two teams from the same area or city【英】〔同一地区或城市的两队之间进行的〕体育比赛, 德比大赛 **3** a race that anyone can enter 赛跑, 竞赛: *a donkey derby* 骑驴大赛 **4** *AmE* a type of horse race【美】赛马

Derby, the a very important yearly horse race held at Epsom in England in May or June, on a day which is known as **Derby Day** 德比马赛〔每年5月或6月在英格兰埃普瑟姆举行的重要马赛, 比赛之日称为德比马赛日〕—see also 另见 KENTUCKY DERBY

Der·by·shire /ˈdɝbɪʃɚ; ˈdɑːbiʃə/ a COUNTY in northern central England. The Peak District National Park is mainly in Derbyshire, and is a popular place for tourists. 德比郡〔英格兰中北部一郡。皮克区国家公园主要在德比郡境内, 是一个著名旅游胜地〕

de·reg·u·late /diˈrɛgjəˌlet; ˌdiːˈregjʊleɪt/ *v* [T] to remove government rules and controls from some types of business activity 撤销政府对…的管制, 解除管制: *Data communications have largely been deregulated in Europe.* 在欧洲, 已经广泛解除对数据交流的管制。—**deregulation** /diˌrɛgjəˈleʃən; diːˌregjʊˈleɪʃən/ *n* [U]

der·e·lict[1] /ˈdɛrəˌlɪkt; ˈderɪ̈lɪkt/ *adj* a building or piece of land that is derelict is in very bad condition because it has not been used for a long time〔建筑物、土地〕破旧的, 弃置的

derelict[2] *n* [C] someone who has no money or home and who has to live on the streets 无家可归的穷人, 流浪者, 游民

der·e·lic·tion /ˌdɛrəˈlɪkʃən; ˌderɪ̈ˈlɪkʃən/ *n* **1 dereliction of duty** *formal* failure to do what you should do as part of your job【正式】失职, 玩忽职守, 渎职 **2** [U] the state of being derelict 破旧, 弃置

de·ride /dɪˈraɪd; dɪˈraɪd/ *v* [T] *formal* to make remarks or jokes that show you think someone or something is silly or useless【正式】嘲笑, 嘲弄, 讥讽: *You shouldn't deride their efforts.* 你不应该嘲笑他们的努力。| **deride sb as sth** *Wayne was derided as a mere playboy.* 人们嘲笑韦恩, 说他只不过是个花花公子。

de ri·gueur /də riˈgɝ; də riːˈgɜː/ *adj* [not before noun 不用于名词前] *French* considered to be necessary if you want to be fashionable【法】〔按照礼节、时尚等〕要求的, 必需的; 符合时尚的: *Hats are de rigueur at society weddings.* 在上流社会的婚礼上一定要戴礼帽。

de·ri·sion /dɪˈrɪʒən; dɪˈrɪʒən/ *n* [U] remarks that show you think someone or something is stupid or silly 嘲笑, 嘲弄: *There was a note of derision in his voice.* 他的声音里有一种嘲弄的语气。

de·ri·sive /dɪˈraɪsɪv; dɪˈraɪsɪv/ *adj* showing that you think someone or something is stupid or silly 嘲笑的, 嘲弄的: *derisive laughter* 嘲弄的笑声 —**derisively** *adv*

de·ri·so·ry /dɪˈraɪsərɪ; dɪˈraɪsəri/ *adj* **1** an amount of money that is derisory is so small that it is not worth considering seriously〔钱〕微不足道的, 少得可怜的: *Unions described the pay offer as derisory.* 工会称工资升价低得可怜。**2** derisive 嘲笑的, 嘲弄的: *derisory comments* 嘲弄的评论 —**derisorily** *adv*

de·riv·able /dɪˈraɪvəbl; dɪˈraɪvəbəl/ *adj formal* something that is derivable can be calculated from something else【正式】可派生的; 可推论出的

der·i·va·tion /ˌdɛrəˈveʃən; ˌderɪ̈ˈveɪʃən/ *n* **1** [C,U] the origin of something, especially a word〔尤指词语的〕起源, 出处: *the derivation of place names* 地名的起源 **2** [C] a word that comes from another word or language 派生词

de·riv·a·tive[1] /dɪˈrɪvətɪv; dɪˈrɪvətɪv/ *n* [C] something that has developed or been produced from something else 派生物; 提取物; 制成物: [**+of**] *Heroin is a derivative of morphine.* 海洛因是吗啡的提取物。

derivative[2] *adj* not new or invented, but copied or taken from something else 非独创的, 模仿他人的: *a largely derivative text* 大部分抄袭他人的文章

de·rive /dɪˈraɪv; dɪˈraɪv/ *v* **1** [T] to get something, usually a pleasant feeling, from something or someone 得到, 获得〔通常是愉快的感受〕: **derive sth from** *He derived some comfort from the fact that he wasn't the only one to fail the exam.* 得知自己并不是唯一没通过考试的人时, 他得到了一些安慰。**2** [I] to develop or come from something else 源自, 源于: [**+from**] *This word is derived from Latin.* 这个词来源于拉丁文。**3** [T] *technical* to get a chemical substance from another substance【术语】提取〔化学物质〕

der·ma·ti·tis /ˌdɝməˈtaɪtɪs; ˌdɜːməˈtaɪtɪ̈s/ *n* [U] a disease of the skin that causes redness, swelling, and pain 皮(肤)炎

der·ma·tol·o·gy /ˌdɝməˈtɑlədʒɪ; ˌdɜːməˈtɒlədʒi/ *n* [U] the part of medical science that deals with the skin, its diseases, and their treatment 皮肤学, 皮肤病学 —**dermatologist** *n* [C]

de·rog·ate /ˈdɛrəˌget; ˈderəgeɪt/ *v*
derogate from sth *phr v* [T] *formal* to make something seem less important or less good【正式】贬低, 贬损

de·rog·a·to·ry /dɪˈrɑgəˌtorɪ; dɪˈrɒgətəri/ *adj* insulting and disapproving 侮辱的; 贬义的: **derogatory remark/comment/term etc** *Many gay men still regard 'queer' as a very derogatory term.* 许多男同性恋者仍然认为 queer 是个极具侮辱性的词语。—**derogatorily** *adv*

der·rick /ˈdɛrɪk; ˈderɪk/ *n* [C] **1** a tall machine used for lifting heavy weights, used especially on ships〔尤指轮船上的〕桅杆起重机 **2** a tall tower built over an oil well to raise and lower the DRILL[1] (1) 油井架, 钻塔

der·riè·re /ˌdɛrɪˈɛr; ˈderieə/ *n* [C] *humorous* your bottom【幽默】臀部: *sitting around on your derrière* 闲坐着

der·ring-do /ˈdɛrɪŋ ˈdu; ˌderɪŋ ˈduː/ *n* [U] **deeds/acts etc of derring-do** *humorous* very brave actions like the ones that happen in adventure stories【幽默】英勇事迹

Der·ry /ˈdɛrɪ; ˈderi/ **1** a COUNTY in the west of Northern Ireland 德里〔北爱尔兰西部一郡〕 **2** another name for the city of Londonderry in Northern Ireland, used especially by the Roman Catholic population 德里〔爱尔兰北部城市伦敦德里的别称, 天主教信徒多用此名〕

derv /dɝv; dɜːv/ *n* [U] *trademark BrE* an oil product like petrol that is used in DIESEL ENGINES【商标, 英】柴油, 重油

der·vish /ˈdɝvɪʃ; ˈdɜːvɪʃ/ *n* [C] a member of a Muslim religious group, some of whom dance fast and spin around as part of a religious ceremony〔伊斯兰教的〕托钵僧, 苦行僧〔有些在宗教仪式上跳快速旋转舞〕

de·sal·i·nate /diˈsæləˌnet; diːˈsælɪ̈neɪt/ *v* [T] to remove the salt from sea water so that it can be used in homes and factories 使〔海水〕脱盐 —**desalination** /diˌsæləˈneʃən; diːˌsælɪ̈ˈneɪʃən/ *n* [U]

de·scale /diˈskel; ˌdiːˈskeɪl/ *v* [T] to remove the white substance that forms on the inside of pipes, KETTLES etc 除去〔管道和水壶等内壁上的〕水垢[水锈]

des·cant /ˈdɛskænt; ˈdeskænt/ *n* [C,U] a tune that is played or sung above the main tune in a piece of music 高音部, 上方声部

Des·cartes /deˋkɑrt; ˈdeɪkɑːt/, **Re·né** /rəˋne; rəˈneɪ/ (1596-1650) a French MATHEMATICIAN and PHILOSOPHER famous for establishing the principle of "cogito ergo sum" (=I think, therefore I am), which means "I know that I exist because I know that I think" 笛卡尔〔(1596-1650), 法国数学家、哲学家, 以提出"我思故我在"的原则而出名〕

de·scend /dɪˋsɛnd; dɪˈsend/ *v* **1** [I,T] *formal* to move from a higher level to a lower one【正式】下来, 下降: *The plane started to descend.* 飞机开始降落。| [+from] *He descended slowly from the railway carriage.* 他慢慢地从火车车厢里走出来。| **descend sth** *Mrs Danvers descended the stairs.* 丹弗斯太太走下楼梯。—opposite 反义词 ASCEND **2** [I] *literary* if darkness, night etc descends, it begins to get dark【文】〔黑暗、夜幕等〕降临 **3 in descending order** numbers, choices etc that are in descending order are arranged from the highest or most important to the lowest or least important 降序排列〔按照从大到小或从最重要的到最次要的顺序排列〕

descend from sth *phr v* [T] **1** to have developed from something that existed in the past 从〔过去的东西〕继承下来, 传下来: *These ideas descend from those of the ancient philosophers.* 这些观点是从古代哲学家的观点中传承下来的。**2 be descended from sb** to be related to someone who lived a long time ago 为某人的后裔: *My mother claims she is descended from Abraham Lincoln.* 妈妈声称自己是亚伯拉罕·林肯的后代。

descend on/upon sb/sth *phr v* [T] **1** if a feeling descends on someone, they begin to feel it 使感觉到: *Gloom descended on the office when we heard the news.* 我们听到这个消息时, 办公室里立即愁云笼罩。**2** *informal* if a large number of people descend on you, they come to your home【非正式】突然造访: *My in-laws are descending on us this weekend.* 我的亲家们忽然这个周末要来我们家。

descend to sth *phr v* [T] to behave or speak in an unpleasant way that is not what people expect from you 自降身份到…, 堕落到…: **descend to (doing) sth** *I refused to descend to petty personal attacks.* 我拒绝降低身份去进行卑劣的人身攻击。| **descend to sb's level** (=behave or speak in the same unpleasant way as someone else) 堕落到和某人一样的水平

de·scen·dant /dɪˋsɛndənt; dɪˈsendənt/ *n* [C] someone who is related to a person who lived a long time ago 后代, 后裔: **direct descendant** (=from one father or mother to the next) 直系后代 *He reckons he's a direct descendant of Napoleon Bonaparte.* 他推算自己是拿破仑·波拿巴的嫡系后代。—compare 比较 ANCESTOR (1)

de·scent /dɪˋsɛnt; dɪˈsent/ *n* **1** [C,U] *formal* the process of going down【正式】下降, 降落: *Passengers must fasten their seat belts prior to descent.* 乘客在飞机降落之前必须系好安全带。**2** [C] a path or road that goes steeply downwards〔陡峭下行的〕下坡路: *a slippery descent* 滑溜的下坡路 **3** [U] your family origins, especially in connection with the country that you come from 出身, 血统: **by descent** *They're Irish by descent.* 他们祖籍是爱尔兰。| **be of Russian/Chinese etc descent** *She's of German descent.* 她祖籍德国。**4** [singular] a gradual change towards behaviour that is wrong or not acceptable 沦落, 堕落: [+into] *her descent into a life of crime* 她堕入犯罪生涯 **5** [singular] a sudden unwanted visit or attack〔不受欢迎的〕突然到访, 突袭: *the descent on the town by a motorcycle gang* 一个摩托车团伙对该镇的突袭

S1 W1 **de·scribe** /dɪˋskraɪb; dɪˈskraɪb/ *v* [T] **1** to say what something or someone is like by giving details about them 描述, 描写, 叙述, 形容: *The police asked her to describe the two men.* 警察叫她描述一下那两个人。| *An alternative approach to the problem is described in Chapter 3.* 这个问题的另一种解决方法在第3章有所阐述。| **describe how/why/what etc** *It's difficult to describe how I feel.* 很难形容我的感受。| **describe sb/sth as** *Sarah described him as shy.* 萨拉说他很害羞。| **describe sb/sth to sb** *So describe this new boyfriend to me!* 那么, 和我详细说说你的新男朋友吧! | **describe doing sth** *He described going downstairs and finding his mother lying on the floor.* 他描述下楼时发现他妈妈躺在地板上。—see 见 SPEAK (USAGE) **2** *formal* to make a shape in the air by moving your hands in a particular way【正式】〔用手在空中〕画出〔某种形状〕: *Her hand described a circle in the air.* 她用手在空中划了一个圆圈。

S2 W2 **de·scrip·tion** /dɪˋskrɪpʃən; dɪˈskrɪpʃən/ *n* **1** [C,U] a piece of writing or speech that says what someone or something is like 描述, 描写, 叙述, 形容: *Berlin sounds fascinating from your description.* 从你的叙述来看, 柏林好像是个迷人的城市。| **detailed/accurate description** *The police have issued a detailed description of the missing woman.* 警察已经发布了这个失踪妇女的详细描述资料。| **give a description** *I gave them a description of my car.* 我给他们形容了一下我的汽车。| **brief/general description** *a brief description of what the job involves* 对这项工作内容的简要说明 | **full/complete description** *I'll need a full description of the stolen property.* 我需要一份被窃财产的完整描述资料。| **answer/fit a description** (=be like the person or thing described) 和所描述的相吻合 *A man fitting that description was seen outside the bank.* 有人在银行外面看到一名与所描述特征相符的男子。**2 be beyond/past description** to be too good, bad, big etc to be described easily 无法形容, 难以描述: *I found the play boring beyond description.* 我觉得这部戏乏味得无法形容。**3** [C] a type of thing, person etc 种类, 类型: **of every/some/that etc description** *flowers and plants of every description* 各种各样的花和植物 | **of all descriptions** *People of all descriptions came to see the show.* 形形色色的人都来观看演出。

This graph shows some of the words most commonly used with the noun **description**. 本图表所示为含有名词 description 的一些最常用词组。

Based on the British National Corpus and the Longman Lancaster Corpus
据英国国家语料库和朗文兰开斯特语料库

de·scrip·tive /dɪˋskrɪptɪv; dɪˈskrɪptɪv/ *adj* **1** giving a description of something in words or pictures 描写的, 描绘的: *The book is full of descriptive passages.* 这本书中有许多描写的段落。**2** *technical* describing how the words of a language are actually used, rather than saying how they ought to be used【术语】描写性的〔描述词语的实际使用情况而不规定它们该如何使用〕—**descriptively** *adv* —**descriptiveness** *n* [U]

de·scry /dɪˋskraɪ; dɪˈskraɪ/ *v* [T] *literary* to notice or see something, especially when it is a long way away【文】〔尤指从远处〕遥望到, 眺望到

Des·de·mo·na /ˌdɛzdɪˋmonə; ˌdezdə̇ˈməʊnə/ the main female character in the play *Othello* by William Shakespeare. She is Othello's wife, and Othello kills her because his enemy, Iago, makes him believe that she is having a sexual relationship with another man. 苔丝德蒙娜〔莎士比亚戏剧《奥赛罗》中的女主人公, 即奥赛罗之妻。奥赛罗因受敌人伊阿古之骗, 误信她与别人通奸而将她杀死〕

des·e·crate /ˋdɛsɪˌkret; ˈdesɪkreɪt/ *v* [T] to spoil or damage something holy 亵渎〔圣物〕—**desecration** /ˌdɛsɪˋkreʃən; ˌdesɪˈkreɪʃən/ *n* [U]

de·seg·re·gate /diˋsɛgrɪˌget; diːˈsegrɪgeɪt/ *v* [T] to end a system by which people of different races are kept separate 废除…的种族隔离制度 —**desegregation** /diˌsɛgrəˋgeʃən; ˌdiːsegrə̇ˈgeɪʃən/ *n* [U]

de·se·lect /ˌdisəˋlɛkt; ˌdiːsəˈlekt/ *v* [T] **1** to remove something from a list of choices on a computer〔在电脑上〕取消选定 **2** *BrE* to refuse to choose an existing Member of Parliament as a CANDIDATE (1) at the next election【英】否决〔现任议员〕担任下届候选人 —**deselection** /-ˋlɛkʃən; -ˈlekʃən/ *n* [U]

de·sen·si·tize also 又作 **-ise** *BrE*【英】/diˋsɛnsəˌtaɪz; diːˈsensə̇taɪz/ *v* [T] **1** to make someone react less strongly to something by making them become used to it〔通过使之习惯于某事物〕使〔某人〕变得不敏感: [+to] *Many children have become desensitized to violence.* 许多孩子对暴力已变得麻木了。**2** *technical* to make photographic material less sensitive to light【术语】使减少感光度 —**desensitization** /diˌsɛnsətəˋzeʃən; diːˌsensə̇taɪˈzeɪʃən/ *n* [U]

des·ert¹ /ˋdɛzət; ˈdezət/ *n* **1** [C,U] a large area of sand where it is always very hot and dry 沙漠, 荒漠: *the Sahara Desert* 撒哈拉沙漠 **2** [C] a place where there is no activity or where nothing interesting happens 荒凉的地方: *a cultural desert* 文化沙漠

de·sert² /dɪˋzɜt; dɪˈzɜːt/ *v* **1** [T] to leave someone alone and refuse to help or support them any more 遗弃, 抛弃, 离弃: *Mike just deserted her when she got pregnant.* 她怀孕后, 迈克就干脆抛弃了她。**2** [T] to leave a place so that it is completely empty

舍弃, 离开〔某地〕: *They deserted their homes and fled to the hills.* 他们舍弃家园, 逃到山上。**3** [T] if a feeling or quality deserts you, you no longer have it, especially at a time when you need it 丧失, 失去〔感觉、品质〕: *Mike's confidence seemed to have deserted him.* 迈克似乎丧失了信心。**4** [I+**from**] to leave the army without permission 擅自离开〔军队〕

de·sert·er /dɪˋzɜtə; dɪˈzɜːtə/ *n* [C] a soldier who leaves the army without permission 逃兵

de·ser·tion /dɪˋzɜʃən; dɪˈzɜːʃən/ *n* **1** [C,U] the act of leaving the army without permission 开小差, 擅离军队 **2** [U] *law* the act of leaving your wife or husband because you do not want to live with them any longer【法律】遗弃

desert is·land /ˌ‥ ˈ‥/ *n* [C] a small tropical island far from other places with no people living on it〔热带地区的〕荒岛

> **CULTURAL NOTE 文化注释**
>
> Desert islands are thought of as being rather ROMANTIC places, with sun, warm seas, and plenty of food and water available, perfect places to escape from the worries and responsibilities of ordinary life. 荒岛被看作是浪漫的地方, 有阳光、温暖的大海、充足的食物和水, 是逃避日常生活中烦恼和责任的理想去处。

Desert Is·land Discs a British radio programme in which famous people talk with the presenter about their lives and choose the eight records they would like to have with them if they were left alone on a DESERT ISLAND (=a small tropical island with no one living on it)《荒岛金曲》〔英国一档广播节目。节目邀请名人与主持人谈论自己的生活。同时, 主持人会问名人, 假如要留在一座荒无人烟的海岛上, 他自己最希望随身携带哪八张唱片〕

deserts /dɪˋzɜts; dɪˈzɜːts/ *n* **get your just deserts** to be punished in a way that you deserve 得到应得的惩罚, 罪有应得

de·serve /dɪˋzɜv; dɪˈzɜːv/ *v* [T] **1** to have earned something by good or bad actions or behaviour 应得, 应受到〔奖赏或惩罚〕: *You've been working all morning – I think you deserve a rest.* 你已经工作了一早上, 我想你该歇歇了。| **deserve to do sth** *The team deserves to win.* 这个队该赢。| **deserve it** *Yeah, I hit him but he deserved it.* 对, 我打了他, 但是他该打。| **get what you deserve** (=be punished or have something unpleasant happen in a way that you deserve) 罪有应得 | **deserve all you get** (=deserve any unpleasant things that may happen to you) 受到这一切是理所应当的 | **deserve better** (=deserve more pleasant treatment or situations than you are getting) 该得到更好一些的待遇 **2 deserve consideration/attention etc** if a suggestion, idea, or plan deserves consideration etc, it is good or sensible enough to be considered〔建议、观点、计划〕值得考虑/注意等: *These proposals deserve serious consideration.* 这些建议值得认真考虑。**3 deserve a medal** *spoken* used to say that you admire the way someone dealt with a situation or problem【口】该赏一枚勋章〔表示欣赏某人应付某种局面或处理某个问题的方式〕: *You deserve a medal for putting up with Phil for so long!* 你能忍耐菲尔这么久, 真应该赏你一枚勋章!

de·served /dɪˋzɜvd; dɪˈzɜːvd/ *adj* earned because of good or bad behaviour, skill, work etc 应得的, 理所当然的; 该受的: *a well-deserved result* 完全应得的结果

de·serv·ed·ly /dɪˋzɜvɪdlɪ; dɪˈzɜːvɪ̵dli/ *adv* **1** in a way that is right or deserved 正当地, 应得地, 理所当然地: *Her novels have been, quite deservedly, very successful.* 她的小说一直非常成功, 她受之无愧。**2 deservedly so** used to show that you agree that something is right and deserved 理应如此: *She is widely respected in the music world, and deservedly so.* 她在音乐界广受尊敬, 也理应如此。

de·serv·ing /dɪˋzɜvɪŋ; dɪˈzɜːvɪŋ/ *adj* **1** needing help and support, especially financial support〔尤指经济上的支持〕应得的, 值得的: *Grants will only be awarded to deserving applicants.* 补助金只能发给那些真正需要的申请者。| **deserving case** (=someone or something which deserves help, especially financial help) 值得帮助的人[事] **2 be deserving of** *formal* to deserve something【正式】值得…, 该得…: *This stupid-looking hat is deserving of ridicule!* 这顶样子很傻的帽子应该受到嘲笑。

de·sex·u·al·ize also 又作 **-ise** *BrE*【英】/diˋsɛkʃuəlˌaɪz; diːˈsekʃuəlaɪz/ *v* [T] to remove the sexual quality from something 除去〔某物〕的性特征, 阉割 —**desexualization** /diˌsɛkʃuələˋzeʃən; diːˌsekʃuəlaɪˈzeɪʃən/ *n* [C,U]: *desexualization of the body* 对身体的性特征的去除

dés·ha·bil·lé /ˌdɛzəˋbil; ˌdeɪzæˈbiːeɪ/ also 又作 **dishabille** *AmE*【美】—*n* [U] *literary or humorous* the state of being only partly dressed, used especially of a woman【文或幽默】〔尤指女性〕衣着仅部分遮体, 衣衫不整

des·ic·cant /ˋdɛsəkənt; ˈdesɪ̵kənt/ *n* [C,U] *technical* a substance that takes water from the air so that it keeps other things dry【术语】干燥剂

des·ic·cate /ˋdɛsəˌket; ˈdesɪ̵keɪt/ *v* [T] *formal* to remove all the water from something【正式】除去…水分, 使脱水, 使干燥 —**desiccation** /ˌdɛsəˋkeʃən; ˌdesɪ̵ˈkeɪʃən/ *n* [U]

des·ic·cat·ed /ˋdɛsəˌketɪd; ˈdesɪ̵keɪtɪ̵d/ *adj* **1** dessicated food has been dried in order to preserve it〔食物〕脱水的, 干燥的: *desiccated coconut* 椰子干 **2** *formal* completely dry【正式】干透的, 脱水的

de·sid·e·ra·tum /dɪˌsɪdəˋretəm; dɪˌzɪdəˈreɪtəm/ *n plural* **desiderata** /-tə; -tə/ [C] *Latin formal* something that is wanted or needed【拉丁, 正式】需要的东西

de·sign¹ /dɪˋzaɪn; dɪˈzaɪn/ *n*

1 ▶ARRANGEMENT OF PARTS 各部分的安排◀ [U] the way that something has been planned and made, including its appearance, how it works etc 设计〔包括其外观及运作方式等〕: *One or two changes have been made to the computer's basic design.* 对电脑的基本设计已做了一两处改动。| *the importance of good design* 良好设计的重要性

2 ▶PATTERN 图案◀ [C] a decorative pattern on something 装饰图案: *wallpaper with a floral design* 有花朵图案的墙纸

3 ▶DRAWING PLANS 绘制图表◀ [U] the art or process of making a drawing of something to show how you will make it or what it will look like 设计术, 制图术: *graphic design* 平面设计

4 ▶DRAWN PLAN 绘制的图纸◀ [C] a drawing showing how something will be made or what it will look like 设计图, 图样, 图纸: [+**for**] *The Council has just approved the design for the new sports centre.* 市议会刚刚通过新体育中心的草图。

5 ▶INTENTION 意图◀ [C] a plan that someone has in their mind〔头脑中的〕计划: *Did he have some sinister design in doing this?* 他做这事是不是有邪恶的企图? | **by design** (=intentionally) 有意地, 故意地 *Whether this happened by design or not we shall never know.* 这事的发生是否有意安排的, 我们将永远无法得知。

6 have designs on sb to want a sexual relationship with someone 对某人居心不良〔想和某人发生性关系〕: *It soon became obvious that he had designs on her.* 不久, 他对她存有不良居心就变得非常明显了。

7 have designs on sth to be interested in something because you want it for yourself, especially if it will bring you money 企图将某物据为己有〔尤指可以带来钱财的东西〕: *I reckon they have designs on their uncle's business.* 我看他们打算把他们叔叔的生意据为己有。

design² *v* **1** [I,T] to make a drawing or plan of something that will be made or built 设计: *A local architect designed the theatre.* 一名当地的建筑师设计了这座剧院。| **well/badly etc designed** *a well designed office* 设计不错的办公室 **2** [T usually passive 一般用被动态] to plan or develop something for a specific purpose〔为某种特定目的〕计划, 设计: **design sth to do sth** *These exercises are designed to develop and strengthen muscles.* 这些练习是为了增强肌肉力量而设计的。| **be designed for** *coursebooks designed for intermediate students* 为中级水平学生设计的教科书 | **be designed as** *a short film designed as an introduction to road safety* 为介绍道路安全知识而编制的电影短片 —see also 另见 DESIGNER¹

des·ig·nate¹ /ˋdɛzɪgˌnet; ˈdezɪgneɪt/ *v* [T] **1** to choose someone or something for a particular job or purpose〔为某项工作或目的〕任命, 选定, 指派: **designate sth as/for** *We're going to designate this room as a no-smoking area.* 我们准备把这个房间指定为禁烟区。| **designate sb to do sth** *She has been designated to take over the position of treasurer.* 她被选派接任财务主管的职位。**2** to show or mean something, especially by using a special name or sign〔用特殊的名字或符号〕表明, 标明, 表示: *Buildings are designated by red squares on the map.* 在地图上建筑物是用红色方块来标明的。

des·ig·nate² /ˋdɛzɪgnɪt; ˈdezɪgnɪ̵t/ *adj* [only after noun 仅用于名词后] *formal* a word used after the name of an official job showing that someone has been chosen for that job but has not yet officially started work【正式】候任的〔用在官职名称的后面〕: *the ambassador designate* 候任大使

designated dri·ver /ˌ‥‥ ˈ‥/ *n* [C] *AmE informal* someone who agrees to drive their friends and not drink alcohol when they go out together to a party, bar etc【美, 非正式】指定的司机〔指外出聚会、上酒吧等时同意开车送朋友因而不饮酒的人〕

designated hit·ter /ˌ‥‥ ˈ‥/ *n* [C] *AmE*【美】**1** someone in the game of BASEBALL whose job is usually to hit the ball, but who replaces the PITCHER (=person who throws the ball) when it is their turn to hit 指定击球手〔棒球比赛中在赛前指定的只执行

进攻任务的击球员〕 **2** *informal* someone who does a job for someone else, especially in politics or business【非正式】〔尤指在政界或生意场上〕执行指定任务的下属

CULTURAL NOTE 文化注释

The rule allowing a designated hitter was introduced in the US in 1973 but many people are opposed to it. It is used in the American League but not in the National League. 允许有指定击球手的规则是1973年开始在美国实行的，但遭到很多人反对。现在，美国棒球联盟采用此规则，全国棒球联盟则不采用。

des·ig·na·tion /ˌdɛzɪgˋneʃən; ˌdezɪgˈneɪʃən/ *n* **1** [U] the act of choosing someone or something for a particular purpose, or of giving them a particular description 任命，委派: *the designation of a student library assistant* 图书馆学生管理员的委派 **2** [C] *formal* a name or title【正式】名称，称号，头衔: *Her official designation is Systems Manager.* 她的正式头衔是系统经理。

de·sign·ed·ly /dɪˋzaɪnɪdlɪ; dɪˈzaɪnɪ̇dli/ *adv formal* on purpose; intentionally【正式】故意地，蓄意地，有计划地

de·sign·er¹ /dɪˋzaɪnɚ; dɪˈzaɪnə/ *n* [C] someone whose job is to make plans or patterns for clothes, furniture, equipment etc〔服装、家具、设备等的〕设计师，设计者: *a dress designer* 服装设计师

designer² *adj* [only before noun 仅用于名词前] **1** made by a well-known and fashionable designer 由〔著名的、时尚的〕设计师设计的: *designer jeans* 设计师品牌牛仔裤 **2** *not technical* changed by GENETIC ENGINEERING【非术语】经基因工程而改变的: *a designer virus* 一种基因被改变的病毒

designer drug /·ˌ·· ˈ·/ *n* [C] a drug similar to COCAINE or HEROIN that is produced artificially but is not illegal itself 人造毒品，化合致幻药〔类似于可卡因或海洛因的人工合成药品，但本身并不属于违禁药品〕

de·sign·ing¹ /dɪˋzaɪnɪŋ; dɪˈzaɪnɪŋ/ *adj* someone who is designing tries to deceive people in order to get what they want 工于心计的，别有用心的

designing² *n* [U] DESIGN¹ (1) 设计

de·sir·a·ble /dɪˋzaɪrəbl; dɪˈzaɪərəbəl/ *adj formal*【正式】**1** something that is desirable is worth having or doing because it is useful or popular 值得拥有的；值得做的: **highly desirable** (=very desirable) 非常想要的，很可取的 | **it is desirable that** *It is desirable that you should have some familiarity with computers.* 你应该对电脑有所熟悉，这是很有益处的。—compare 比较 UNDESIRABLE **2** someone who is desirable is very sexually attractive 性感的，引起性欲的 —**desirably** *adv* —**desirability** /dɪˌzaɪrəˋbɪlətɪ; dɪˌzaɪərəˈbɪlɪ̇ti/ *n* [U]

de·sire¹ /dɪˋzaɪr; dɪˈzaɪə/ *v* [T not in progressive 不用进行时] **1** *formal* to want or hope for something very much【正式】想要，希望: *the qualities we desire in our employees* 我们希望雇员拥有的各种素质 | **desire to do sth** *Anyone desiring to vote must come to the meeting.* 凡想投票的人都必须来参加会议。| **desire sb to do sth** *The prince desired her to be his queen.* 王子希望她能成为自己的王后。**2** **leave a lot to be desired** *especially spoken* used to say that something is not as good as you think it should be【尤口】不够好，仍有许多有待提高之处〔表明某事做得不如期望的好〕: *The standard of cooking here leaves a lot to be desired.* 这里的烹饪水平远不够好。**3** *old-fashioned* to want to have sex with someone【过时】想和〔某人〕发生性关系 —**desired** *adj*: *My remarks had the desired effect.* 我的话取得了预期的效果。

desire² *n* **1** [C,U] a strong hope or wish 渴望；欲望: [+for] *a desire for knowledge* 对知识的渴望 | **desire to do sth** *Anna has a great desire to travel.* 安娜非常向往旅游。| **desire that** *a desire that his books should reach as many people as possible* 希望他的书能够被尽可能多的人阅读的愿望 | **show/express a desire** *They did not show the slightest desire to accompany us.* 他们丝毫没有表现出陪我们的意愿。| **overwhelming/burning desire** (=very strong desire) 无法遏制的/迫切的愿望 *He fought a burning desire to break into the conversation.* 他极力遏制着想插话的强烈冲动。| **have no desire to do sth** (=used to emphasize that you do not want to do something) 不想做某事 *I have no desire to see him hurt, I assure you.* 我向你保证，我不想看见他受到伤害。**2** **sb's heart's desire** a very strong wish that someone has 某人内心的渴望 **3** [U +for] *formal* a strong wish to have sex with someone【正式】肉欲，性欲

de·sir·ous /dɪˋzaɪrəs; dɪˈzaɪərəs/ *adj formal* wanting something very much【正式】希望的，渴望的: [+of] *No one had ever been so openly desirous of my attention.* 从未有人如此公开地表示过渴望引起我的注意。

de·sist /dɪˋzɪst; dɪˈzɪst/ *v* [I] *formal* to stop doing something【正式】停止，中止；断念: [+from] *You are ordered to desist from such behaviour.* 命令你不得再有这种行为。

desk /dɛsk; desk/ *n* [C] **1** a piece of furniture like a table, usually with drawers in it, that you sit at to write and work 书桌，办公桌，写字台 **2** a place where you can get information in a hotel, airport etc〔酒店、机场等的〕询问处: *the check-in desk* 登记处 **3** an office that deals with a particular subject, especially in newspapers or television〔尤指报社或电视台负责某方面题材的〕部，司，组，室: *Lloyd is running the sports desk.* 劳埃德现在负责体育新闻组。

desk clerk /ˈ· ·/ *n* [C] *AmE* someone who works at the main desk in a hotel【美】〔旅馆的〕服务台接待员

de·skill /diˋskɪl; ˌdiːˈskɪl/ *v* [T] to remove or reduce the need for skill in a job, usually by changing to machinery〔通常指通过转为机器操作而〕降低…的技术含量

desk job /ˈ· ·/ *n* [C] a job that involves working mostly at a desk in an office 文案工作，案头工作

desk ti·dy /ˈ· ˌ··/ *n* [C] *BrE* a container for putting pens, pencils etc in, that you keep on your desk【英】笔筒

desk·top /ˋdɛsktɑp; ˈdesktɒp/ *adj* **1** **desktop computer** a computer that is small enough to be used on a desk 台式电脑，桌上型电脑 —see picture on page A14 参见A14页图 **2** **desktop publishing** the work of getting a magazine, small book etc ready to be produced, using a small computer 桌面出版〔用微型电脑工作，把杂志、小型书籍等准备好等待出版〕

Des Moines /dɪˋmɔɪn; diˈmɔɪn/ the capital city of the US state of Iowa 得梅因〔美国艾奥瓦州首府〕

des·o·late¹ /ˋdɛslɪt; ˈdesələt/ *adj* **1** a place that is desolate is empty and looks sad because there are no people there and not much activity 荒凉的，荒芜的，无人烟的: *desolate moorland* 荒凉的高沼地 **2** someone who is desolate feels very sad and lonely〔人〕凄凉的，孤独的 —**desolately** *adv* —**desolation** /ˌdɛslˋeʃən; ˌdesəˈleɪʃən/ *n* [U]

des·o·late² /ˋdɛslˌet; ˈdesəleɪt/ *v* [T usually passive 一般用被动态] *literary*【文】**1** to make someone feel very sad and lonely 使悲伤；使孤独: *Martin was desolated by his wife's death.* 妻子的死使马丁悲痛欲绝。**2** to make a place seem empty and sad 使荒凉，使荒无人烟: *He returned to the desolated camp.* 他返回到空无一人的营地。

de·spair¹ /dɪˋspɛr; dɪˈspeə/ *n* [U] **1** a feeling that you have no hope at all for the future 绝望: **in despair** *I spent ages trying to fix it, but gave up in despair.* 我花了很长时间想把它修好，但还是绝望地放弃了。| **the depths of despair** (=very strong feelings of despair) 绝望的深渊 | **drive sb to despair** *Norman's constant drinking drives his family to despair.* 诺曼没完没了地喝酒，让他的家人陷入绝望。**2** **the despair of sb** someone or something that makes someone feel very worried, upset, or unhappy 令某人绝望的人[事]: *That Jones girl is the despair of her teachers.* 那个叫琼斯的女孩在她老师们的心目中已经无可救药了。

despair² *v* [I] to feel that there is no hope that a situation will improve 绝望，感到无望: *Dirk came close to despairing in those months of unemployment.* 在失业的那几个月中，德克近乎绝望。| **despair of (doing) sth** *They despaired of finding the children alive.* 他们对能找到生还的孩子不抱任何希望了。

de·spair·ing /dɪˋspɛrɪŋ; dɪˈspeərɪŋ/ *adj* showing a feeling of despair 绝望的: *He raised his eyes in a despairing gesture.* 他绝望地抬起眼睛。—**despairingly** *adv*: *Don was shaking his head despairingly.* 唐绝望地摇着头。

de·spatch /dɪˋspætʃ; dɪˈspætʃ/ another spelling of DISPATCH dispatch 的另一种拼法

des·pe·ra·do /ˌdɛspəˋrɑdo; ˌdespəˈrɑːdəʊ/ *n* [C] *old-fashioned* a violent criminal who is not afraid of danger【过时】亡命之徒，暴徒

des·per·ate /ˋdɛspərɪt; ˈdespərɪ̇t/ *adj* **1** willing to do anything and not caring about danger, because you are in a very bad situation〔由于处在绝境而〕拼命的，不顾一切的: *We had no food left at all and were getting desperate.* 我们一点食物都没剩，十分绝望。| *an appeal from the teenager's desperate parents* 那位少年绝望的父母的恳求 **2** [not before noun 不用于名词前] needing or wanting something very much 非常需要的，极其需要的: [+for] *By then I was desperate for a holiday.* 到那时候，我已特别渴望休假了。| **desperate to do sth** *Ben was desperate to get a job.* 本急切地想找到一份工作。| **in desperate need** *We're in desperate need of help.* 我们极其需要帮助。**3** a desperate situation is very bad or serious〔局势、情形等〕危急的，严峻的: *There was a desperate shortage of doctors.* 医生人数严重不足。**4** a desperate action is something that you only do

because you are in a very bad situation〔在危急时刻〕孤注一掷的: **desperate attempt/effort/measures** *The victim had made a desperate attempt to escape.* 受害者曾经孤注一掷, 企图逃跑。

Desperate Dan a character in the British COMIC *The Dandy.* He is a very large, friendly COWBOY who eats very large meat PIES called 'cow pies'. Dan does not realize how strong he is, and he often breaks things by accident. 拼命阿丹〔英国连环漫画杂志《英俊少年》中的人物。他是个魁梧、友善的放牛郎, 吃一种叫做"奶牛馅饼"的特大肉馅饼。他十分强壮, 可自己却意识不到, 所以经常不小心损坏东西〕

des·per·ate·ly /ˈdɛspərɪtlɪ; ˈdespərᵻtli/ *adv* **1** in a desperate way 绝望地; 拼命地, 不顾一切地: *He looked round desperately for someone to help him.* 他绝望地四处张望, 希望有人能来帮他。| **try desperately** *The doctors were trying desperately to save her life.* 医生们正拼命努力, 试图挽救她的生命。**2** very much 非常地: *Joe's work is desperately important to him.* 乔的工作对他来说非常重要。| **desperately need** *He desperately needs reassurance.* 他极需安慰。

des·per·a·tion /ˌdɛspəˈreʃən; ˌdespəˈreɪʃən/ *n* [U] the state of being desperate 绝望; 拼命, 不顾一切: *a look of desperation in his eyes* 他绝望的眼神 | **in desperation** *Finally, in desperation, we went to a pawnbroker.* 最后我们实在走投无路, 就去了当铺。

des·pic·a·ble /ˈdɛspɪkəbḷ; dɪˈspɪkəbəl/ *adj* extremely unpleasant 卑鄙的: *a despicable liar* 卑鄙的撒谎者 | *It's despicable the way he treats those kids.* 他那样对待那些孩子, 真是卑鄙。—**despicably** *adv*: *grinning despicably* 无耻地咧嘴笑着

de·spise /dɪˈspaɪz; dɪˈspaɪz/ *v* [T not in progressive 不用进行时] to dislike someone or something very much 鄙视, 看不起, 藐视: *Mrs Morel had come to despise her husband.* 莫雷尔太太渐渐开始瞧不起她的丈夫。

de·spite /dɪˈspaɪt; dɪˈspaɪt/ *prep* **1** in spite of something 尽管, 不管, 任凭: *Despite all our efforts to save the school, the County decided to close it.* 尽管我们竭尽全力想保住这所学校, 县里还是决定把它关闭。| **despite the fact that** *She went to Spain despite the fact the doctor had told her to rest.* 尽管医生告诉她应该休息, 她还是去了西班牙。**2 despite yourself** if you do something despite yourself, you do it although you did not intend to 尽管并非某人的本意〔但仍被迫去做〕: *Despite herself, she found his attention rather enjoyable.* 尽管她不愿承认, 她还是喜欢他来献殷勤。

de·spoil /dɪˈspɔɪl; dɪˈspɔɪl/ *v* [T] *literary*【文】**1** to make a place much less attractive by removing or damaging things 劫掠; 破坏 **2** to steal from a place using force, especially in a war〔尤指战争中用暴力〕掠夺, 抢劫

de·spon·dent /dɪˈspɑndənt; dɪˈspɒndənt/ *adj* unhappy and not hopeful 沮丧的, 失望的: *Gill had been out of work for a year and was getting very despondent.* 吉尔失业有一年的时间了, 他变得非常消沉。—**despondency** *n* [U] —**despondently** *adv*: *He was staring despondently into the distance.* 他正沮丧地盯着远处。

des·pot /ˈdɛspət; ˈdespɒt/ *n* [C] someone such as a ruler who used power in a cruel and unfair way 专制统治者; 暴君 —**despotic** /dɪˈspɑtɪk; dɪˈspɒtɪk/ *adj* —**despotically** /-klɪ; -kli/ *adv*

des·pot·is·m /ˈdɛspətˌɪzəm; ˈdespətɪzəm/ *n* [U] rule by a despot 暴政, 专制

des res /ˌdɛz ˈrɛz; ˌdez ˈrez/ *n* [C] *BrE informal* a house that a lot of people admire and would like to live in【英, 非正式】〔许多人向往并希望入住的〕理想住宅

des·sert /dɪˈzɝt; dɪˈzɜːt/ *n* [C,U] sweet food served after the main part of a meal〔饭后的〕甜食, 甜品, 甜点: *There's ice-cream for dessert.* 饭后甜品是冰淇淋。

des·sert·spoon /dɪˈzɝtˌspun; dɪˈzɜːtspuːn/ *n* [C] **1** *especially BrE* a spoon that is between the sizes of a TEASPOON and a TABLESPOON【尤英】点心匙, 中型匙 —see picture at 参见 SPOON 图 **2** also 又作 **dessertspoonful** /-ˌful; -fʊl/ the amount held by a dessertspoon 一中匙的量

dessert wine /ˈ· ·ˌ/ *n* [C,U] a sweet wine served with dessert〔吃甜品时饮用的〕餐末甜酒

de·sta·bil·ize also 又作 **-ise** *BrE*【英】/diˈstebḷˌaɪz; diː-ˈsteɪbᵻlaɪz/ *v* [T] to make something less likely to remain politically successful 使〔政治〕不稳定, 破坏〔政治〕稳定: *an attempt to destabilize the government* 旨在破坏政府稳定的企图 —**destabilization** /diˌstebələˈzeʃən; ˌdiːsteɪbᵻlaɪˈzeɪʃən/ *n* [U]

des·ti·na·tion /ˌdɛstəˈneʃən; ˌdestᵻˈneɪʃən/ *n* [C] the place that someone or something is going to 目的地, 终点: *holiday destinations* 度假目的地

des·tined /ˈdɛstɪnd; ˈdestᵻnd/ *adj* **1** [not before noun 不用于名词前] certain to have something or do something at some time in the future 命中注定的; 预定的: **[+for]** *She seemed destined for a long and successful career.* 她似乎注定能拥有一份持久且成功的事业。| **destined to do sth** *We were destined never to meet again.* 我们命中注定无缘再相见。**2 be destined for** to be travelling towards a particular place 去, 赴〔某地〕: *a flight destined for Cairo* 飞往开罗的航班 **3 destined lover/profession etc** *literary* the person, thing etc that you will have in the future【文】命中注定的情人/职业等

des·ti·ny /ˈdɛstənɪ; ˈdestᵻni/ *n* **1** [C usually singular 一般用单数] the things that will happen to someone in the future, especially those that cannot be changed or controlled; FATE (1) 命运, 天命, 定数: **your/my/his etc destiny** *Juan accepted his destiny without complaint.* 胡安毫无怨言地认命了。**2** [U] the power that some people believe decides what will happen to them in the future 天意; 命运之神: *I'm a great believer in destiny.* 我特别相信命运。

des·ti·tute /ˈdɛstəˌtut; ˈdestᵻtjuːt/ *adj* **1** having no money, no food, and nowhere to live 穷困的, 贫困的: *Many people were so destitute they lived out of garbage cans.* 许多人贫困得靠捡垃圾箱里的东西来过活。**2 be destitute of** *formal* to be completely without something【正式】完全没有…的, 毫无…的: *a man destitute of all compassion* 毫无同情心的人 —**destitution** *n* [U]

de·stroy /dɪˈstrɔɪ; dɪˈstrɔɪ/ *v* [T] **1** to damage something so badly that it cannot be repaired or so that it no longer exists 破坏, 毁掉, 摧毁: *The school was completely destroyed by fire.* 学校被大火彻底烧毁了。| *an accident that destroyed her ballet career* 一次毁掉她芭蕾生涯的意外事故 **2** to kill an animal, especially because it is sick, or dangerous 杀死〔动物, 尤因其生病或产生危险〕 **3 destroy sb** to ruin someone's life completely so that they have no hope for the future 毁掉某人 —see also 另见 DESTRUCTION

USAGE NOTE 用法说明: DESTROY

WORD CHOICE 词语辨析: **destroy, ruin, spoil**

Destroy means to damage something so badly that it no longer exists or cannot be repaired. destroy 表示严重毁坏某物, 结果使之不复存在或无法修复: *Whole areas of the city were destroyed.* 整座城市被彻底摧毁了。| *a drug to destroy cancer cells* 杀灭癌细胞的药物 | *Their traditional way of life has been destroyed.* 他们传统的生活方式已经被破坏。

You **ruin** or (less strong) **spoil** something good or useful. It then usually still exists, but no longer has its good qualities or features. spoil 语气比 ruin 稍轻一些, 这两个词都可以用来表示毁坏某种好的或者有用的东西, 事后此物虽仍然存在, 却已失去其优良的特性或特征: *Too much sugar can ruin your teeth.* 吃糖太多能毁掉你的牙齿。| *You've completely spoiled my day.* 你把我的一天彻底地毁掉了。

de·stroy·er /dɪˈstrɔɪɚ; dɪˈstrɔɪə/ *n* [C] **1** a small fast military ship with guns 驱逐舰 **2** someone or something that destroys things or people 破坏者: *They feared photography would be the destroyer of art.* 他们担心摄影会毁掉艺术。

de·struc·tion /dɪˈstrʌkʃən; dɪˈstrʌkʃən/ *n* [U] **1** the act or process of destroying something 破坏, 摧毁, 毁坏, 消灭: *the threat of nuclear destruction* 核毁灭的威胁 **2 be sb's destruction** *formal* to be the thing that completely ruins someone's life【正式】是某人毁掉的原因: *Gambling was his destruction.* 赌博把他彻底给毁了。—see also 另见 DESTROY

de·struc·tive /dɪˈstrʌktɪv; dɪˈstrʌktɪv/ *adj* causing damage to people or things 毁灭性的, 造成破坏的: *Jealousy is a very destructive emotion.* 嫉妒是一种破坏性很强的情感。—**destructively** *adv* —**destructiveness** *n* [U]

des·ul·to·ry /ˈdɛsəlˌtorɪ; ˈdesəltəri/ *adj formal* done without any particular plan or purpose【正式】漫无目的的; 毫无计划的; 散漫的: *They talked in a desultory manner for a few minutes.* 他们漫无边际地谈了几分钟。—**desultorily** /ˈdɛsəlˌtorɪlɪ; ˈdesəltərᵻli/ *adv*

Det the written abbreviation of 缩写= DETECTIVE

de·tach /dɪˈtætʃ; dɪˈtætʃ/ *v* [T] **1** to remove a piece or part of something that is designed to be removed 拆下, 分开, 拆开, 卸下: *If you are interested in the course, detach and fill out the application form.* 如果你对这个课程感兴趣, 把申请表撕下并填好。| **detach sth from** *You can detach the hood from the jacket.* 你可以把帽兜从夹克上拆下来。**2 detach yourself** to try to be less involved in, or less concerned about a situation 使自己超然物外: *I try to detach myself from my patients.* 我尽量和我的病人保持距离。

de·tach·a·ble /dɪˋtætʃəbḷ; dɪˈtætʃəbəl/ *adj* able to be removed and put back 可拆卸的: *a detachable handle* 可拆卸的把手

de·tached /dɪˋtætʃt; dɪˈtætʃt/ *adj* **1** not reacting in an emotional way, so that you can do your job properly or make the right decisions 冷静的, 不动感情的, 客观的: *Try to take a more detached view.* 尽量采取更为客观的态度。**2** *BrE* a detached house or garage is not joined to another building on any side 【英】〔房子或车库〕单栋的, 独立的: *a large detached house on the outskirts of the town* 在城郊的一所独立式的大房子 —compare 比较 SEMI-DETACHED, TERRACED HOUSE —see picture on page A4 参见 A4 页图

de·tach·ment /dɪˋtætʃmənt; dɪˈtætʃmənt/ *n* **1** [U] the state of not reacting in an emotional way, so that you can do your job properly or make the right decisions 冷静, 超然, 客观: *Doctors need to have some degree of emotional detachment.* 医生在情绪上需要有几分冷静。**2** [C] a group of soldiers who are sent away from the main group to do a special job 分遣队, 支队

S2 W1 **de·tail**[1] /dɪˋtel; ˈdiːteɪl/ *n* **1** [C,U] a single feature, fact, or piece of information, or many small features considered together 细节, 详情: *Todd had planned the journey down to the smallest detail.* 托德把这次旅行都规划好了, 直到最小的细节。| *We need to discuss a few details before you start.* 在你开始之前, 我们需要讨论一些细节问题。| **attention to detail** *Editing requires great attention to detail.* 编辑工作需要格外注重细节。| **go into detail/details** (=include a lot of details when describing or explaining something) 叙述详情 | **read/describe etc sth in detail** (=pay attention to all the details) 详细地阅读/描述某物等 *Study the contract in detail before signing.* 签字之前要先详细地研究一下合同。| **have an eye for detail** (=be skilled at noticing details) 善于注意到细微之处 **2 details** [plural] all the additional information you need about something you already know a little about 详细情况, 详细资料: **[+of]** *Send for details of the course.* 请来函索取有关课程的详细资料。| **full/further details** *For further details, contact the personnel department.* 欲知详情, 请与人事部联系。**3** [singular,U] *technical* a specific duty in the army, or the person or group who have that duty 【术语】〔军队中的〕特遣队, 小分队: *the security detail* 安全小分队

detail[2] *v* [T] **1** to give all the facts or information about something 详述: *The paper then goes on to detail a number of joint initiatives.* 接着, 报纸详细列举了一些合作的初步行动。**2 detail sb to do sth** to officially order someone, especially soldiers, to do a particular job 指派某人〔尤指士兵〕做某事: *Vance, you're detailed to the night watch.* 万斯, 派你去值夜。

W2 **de·tailed** /dɪˋteld; ˈdiːteɪld/ *adj* including a lot of information and detail 详细的, 详尽的: *a detailed account of the development of the atom bomb* 一份研制原子弹的详尽报告

de·tail·ing /dɪˋtelɪŋ; ˈdiːteɪlɪŋ/ *n* [U] decorations that are added to something such as a car or piece of clothing 〔汽车或衣服上的〕装饰物

de·tain /dɪˋten; dɪˈteɪn/ *v* [T] **1** to officially prevent someone from leaving a place 拘留, 扣押, 羁押: *Police detained the terrorists.* 警察拘留了恐怖分子。**2** to delay someone who wants to leave, by talking to them, asking them to do something etc 〔通过与对方谈话或让其做某事等〕耽搁, 延误, 留住: *I want a quick word, but I won't detain you long.* 我想和你简单说句话, 不会耽搁你很久的。

de·tain·ee /dɪˌteˋni; ˌdiːteɪˈniː/ *n* [C] someone who is officially kept in a prison, usually because of their political views 〔通常由于所持政治观点〕被拘留者

de·tan·gle /diˋtæŋgḷ; ˌdiːˈtæŋgəl/ *v* [I,T] *especially AmE* to remove the knots in hair 【尤美】(使)〔头发〕不打结, (使)〔头发〕不绞在一块儿

W3 **de·tect** /dɪˋtɛkt; dɪˈtekt/ *v* [T] to notice or discover something, especially something that is not easy to see, hear etc 发现, 察觉〔尤指不易察觉到的事物〕: *Many forms of cancer can be cured if detected early.* 如果发现得早, 许多种癌症都是可以治愈的。| *Do I detect a note of sarcasm in your voice?* 我怎么听得出你话语里有种讽刺的意味呢? —**detectable** *adj*

de·tec·tion /dɪˋtɛkʃən; dɪˈtekʃən/ *n* [U] the process of detecting, or the fact of being detected 发现, 觉察: *the early detection of cancer* 癌症的早期发现

W3 **de·tec·tive** /dɪˋtɛktɪv; dɪˈtektɪv/ *n* [C] **1** a police officer whose job is to discover information that will result in criminals being caught 侦探, 警探 —see also 另见 STORE DETECTIVE **2** someone who is paid to discover information about someone or something 私家侦探: *She hired a detective to find out where her husband was going after work.* 她雇了一个私人侦探调查她丈夫下班后的去处。**3 detective story/novel etc** a story about a crime, often a murder, and a detective who tries to find out who did it 侦探故事/小说等

de·tec·tor /dɪˋtɛktɚ; dɪˈtektə/ *n* [C] a piece of equipment that makes a signal if it discovers something 探测器: *smoke detectors* 烟雾探测器 | *a metal detector* 金属探测器 —see also 另见 LIE DETECTOR

dé·tente /deˋtɑ̃t; deɪˈtɑːnt/ *n* [C,U] a state of more friendly political relations between countries that have previously been unfriendly 〔国家间紧张关系的〕缓和

de·ten·tion /dɪˋtɛnʃən; dɪˈtenʃən/ *n* **1** [U] the state of being kept somewhere by the police, because they think you have done something illegal 拘留, 扣留: *Willis spent over 100 days in detention.* 威利斯被扣押了一百多天。**2** [C,U] a punishment in which children who have behaved badly are forced to stay at school for a short time after the others have gone home 〔放学后〕留校惩罚; 留堂; 留课

detention cen·tre *BrE* 【英】, **detention center** *AmE* 【美】 /ˈ·· ˌ··/ *n* [C] a place where young people who have done something illegal are kept, because they are too young to go to prison 青少年管教所; 感化中心; 羁留中心

de·ter /dɪˋtɝ; dɪˈtɜː/ *v* **deterred, deterring** [T] to persuade someone not to do something, by making them realize it will be difficult or will have unpleasant results 〔通过让对方意识到做此事会有困难或会有不太好的结果〕劝说〔某人〕不做〔某事〕; 制止: *security measures aimed at deterring shoplifters* 意在防止店铺遭窃的安全措施 | **deter sb from doing sth** *a new program designed to deter kids from experimenting with drugs* 为防止孩子尝试毒品而制定的新计划 —see also 另见 DETERRENT

de·ter·gent /dɪˋtɝdʒənt; dɪˈtɜːdʒənt/ *n* [C,U] a liquid or powder that contains soap used for washing clothes, dishes etc 洗涤剂; 洗衣粉; 洗洁精; 去污剂

de·te·ri·o·rate /dɪˋtɪrɪəˌret; dɪˈtɪəriəreɪt/ *v* [I] **1** to become worse 恶化: *deteriorating health* 不断恶化的健康状况 | *Relations between the two countries have since deteriorated.* 从此, 两国的关系开始恶化。**2** **[+into]** to develop into a bad or unpleasant situation 演变成; 恶化成: *The meeting soon deteriorated into a fight.* 这次会议不久就演变成一场斗殴。—**deterioration** /dɪˌtɪrɪəˋreʃən; dɪˌtɪəriəˈreɪʃən/ *n* [U]: *environmental deterioration* 环境的恶化

de·ter·mi·nant /dɪˋtɝmənənt; dɪˈtɜːmɪnənt/ *n* [C] *formal* something that strongly influences what you do or how you behave 【正式】决定性因素: **[+of]** *Social class is a major determinant of consumer spending patterns.* 社会等级是消费者消费模式的主要决定因素。

de·ter·mi·nate /dɪˋtɝmənɪt; dɪˈtɜːmɪ̣nɪ̣t/ *adj formal* strictly controlled or limited 【正式】严格控制的, 限定的: *A firm will act in a determinate way to maximize its profits.* 一家公司将会按严格控制的方式运作, 以求利润最大化。

de·ter·mi·na·tion /dɪˌtɝməˋneʃən; dɪˌtɜːmɪ̣ˈneɪʃən/ *n* **1** [U] W3 the ability to continue trying to achieve what you have decided to do even when this is difficult 决心; 坚韧; 毅力: **determination to do sth** *Her determination to do well made her keep on studying.* 她想取得好成绩的决心使得她坚持学习下去。| **dogged determination** (=very strong determination) 坚定不移的决心 *They were admired for their dogged determination to learn the language.* 人们钦佩他们学习这门语言坚定不移的决心。**2** [U] *formal* the act of deciding something officially 【正式】〔官方的〕决定, 规定: *the determination of government policy* 政府政策的确定 **3** [C] *technical* the act of finding the exact level, amount, or causes of something 【术语】〔对水平、数量或原因的〕测定, 确定: *determination of the cause of death* 死亡原因的确定 —see also 另见 SELF-DETERMINATION

de·ter·mine /dɪˋtɝmɪn; dɪˈtɜːmɪ̣n/ *v* [T] **1** to find out the exact details or facts about something 找出, 测定, 确定: *Your parents' income is used to determine your level of financial aid.* 你父母的收入情况被用来决定你所得的经济援助水平。| **[+how/what/who etc]** *The purpose of the exercise is to determine where we want to go from here.* 这次练习的目的是决定我们该何去何从。**2** to have a strong influence or effect on something 决定, 支配: *Usually the size of the practice will determine the number of doctors.* 通常, 医务所规模的大小决定医生的人数。**3** to officially decide something 〔官方〕确定, 规定: *The date of the court case was yet to be determined.* 开庭的日期还没有确定下来。**4** *formal* to form a firm intention to do something 【正式】决心〔做某事〕: **determine to do sth** *We determined to leave at once.* 我们决心立即离开。 W1

de·ter·mined /dɪˋtɝmɪnd; dɪˈtɜːmɪ̣nd/ *adj* **1** having a strong desire to do something, so that you will not let anyone stop you 有决心的, 意志坚定的: *a determined young woman* 一位意志坚 W3

定的年轻女士 | **determined to do sth** *I am determined to find out who is responsible for this.* 我决意要弄清楚谁该对此事负责任。| **determined that** *Determined that his son would do well, Eliot sent him to a private school.* 埃利奥特坚信儿子会学业优异，因此把他送到私立学校学习。**2** showing determination, especially in a difficult situation〔尤指在困境中〕坚决的，坚定的：**determined attempts/opposition etc** *The library was closed down despite determined opposition.* 尽管受到坚决的反对，图书馆还是被关闭了。

de·ter·min·er /dɪˋtɝmɪnɚ; dɪˈtɜːmɪ̣nə/ *n* [C] *technical* a word that comes before an adjective that describes a noun, for example 'his' in 'his new car' or 'that' in 'that big tree'【术语】限定词〔置于修饰名词的形容词前，如 his new car 中的 his 或 that big tree 中的 that 都是限定词〕

de·ter·min·is·m /dɪˋtɝmən,ɪzəm; dɪˈtɜːmɪ̣nɪzəm/ *n* [U] the belief that what you do and what happens to you are caused by things that you cannot control 决定论〔相信某人所做的事或发生在某人身上的事是由他无法控制的力量决定的〕—**deterministic** /dɪ,tɝmɪˋnɪstɪk; dɪ,tɜːmɪ̣ˈnɪstɪk◂/ *adj*

de·ter·rent /dɪˋtɝənt; dɪˈterənt/ *n* [C] **1** something that makes someone less likely to do something 制止物，威慑物，威慑力量：**be a deterrent to sb** *Window locks are an effective deterrent to potential burglars.* 窗上的锁可以有效地防止窃贼从窗户潜入屋内。**2 nuclear deterrent** NUCLEAR weapons that a country has, that are supposed to prevent other countries from attacking 核威慑力量 —**deterrence** *n* [U]

de·test /dɪˋtɛst; dɪˈtest/ *v* [T not in progressive 不用进行时] to hate something or someone very much 憎恶，憎恨，嫌恶：*I detest computers.* 我讨厌电脑。—**detestation** /,ditɛˋsteʃən; ,diːteˈsteɪʃən/ *n* [U]

de·test·able /dɪˋtɛstəbḷ; dɪˈtestəbəl/ *adj* very bad, and deserving to be criticized or hated 令人憎恨的，可恶的，讨厌的：*a detestable little man* 一个讨厌的小个子男人 —**detestably** *adv*

de·throne /dɪˋθron; dɪˈθrəʊn/ *v* [T] **1** to remove a king or queen from power 废黜〔君主〕**2** to remove someone from a position of authority or importance 撵〔某人〕下台，使〔某人〕失去重要地位 —**dethronement** *n* [U]

det·o·nate /ˋdɛtə,net; ˈdetəneɪt/ *v* [I,T] to explode or make something explode, using special equipment 引爆，(使) 爆炸

det·o·na·tion /,dɛtəˋneʃən; ,detəˈneɪʃən/ *n* [C,U] an explosion, or the action of making a bomb etc explode 爆炸；引爆

det·o·na·tor /ˋdɛtə,netɚ; ˈdetəneɪtə/ *n* [C] a piece of equipment that is used to start an explosion 引爆装置，雷管

de·tour[1] /ˋditur; ˈdiːtʊə/ *n* [C] a way of going from one place to another that is longer than the usual way, for example because you want to avoid traffic problems or to visit something〔为避开交通问题或为参观某处等而走的〕绕行路线，迂回路线：**make/take a detour** *BrE*【英】: *We took a detour to avoid the town centre.* 我们绕道而行，避开了市中心。

detour[2] *v* [I,T] *especially AmE* to make a detour【尤美】绕道而行；绕过…

de·tox /ˋditɑks; ˈdiːtɒks/ *n* [U] special treatment at a hospital to help people stop drinking alcohol or taking drugs 戒酒 (治疗)；戒毒 (治疗)

de·tox·i·fi·ca·tion /di,tɑksəfəˋkeʃən; diː,tɒksɪ̣fɪ̣ˈkeɪʃən/ *n* [U] **1** the process of removing harmful chemicals or poison from something 解毒，清毒 **2** detox 戒酒；戒毒：*detoxification unit* 戒毒[戒酒]中心 —**detoxify** /diˋtɑksə,faɪ; diːˈtɒksɪ̣faɪ/ *v* [T]

de·tract /dɪˋtrækt; dɪˈtrækt/ *v*

detract from sth *phr v* [T not in progressive 不用进行时] to make something seem less good than it really is 贬损，诋毁：*One mistake is not going to detract from your achievement.* 一个错误不会抹杀你的成就。—**detraction** /dɪˋtrækʃən; dɪˈtrækʃən/ *n* [C,U]

de·trac·tor /dɪˋtræktɚ; dɪˈtræktə/ *n* [C] someone who says bad things about someone or something, in order to make them seem less good than they really are 诋毁者，贬低者：*The President's detractors expressed their usual low expectations of his policies.* 贬低总统的人照例对总统的政策表示不抱很高的期望。

det·ri·ment /ˋdɛtrəmənt; ˈdetrɪ̣mənt/ *n* [U] *formal* the state of being harmed or damaged by something【正式】损害，伤害，不利：**to the detriment of** (=resulting in harm or damage to something) 有害于…，有损于…，不利于… *He worked longer and longer hours, to the detriment of his marriage.* 他工作的时间越来越长，这不利于他的婚姻。

det·ri·men·tal /,dɛtrəˋmɛntḷ; ,detrɪ̣ˈmentl◂/ *adj formal* causing harm or damage【正式】有害的，不利的：[+to] *Smoking is detrimental to health.* 吸烟有害健康。—**detrimentally** *adv*

de·tri·tus /dɪˋtraɪtəs; dɪˈtraɪtəs/ *n* [U] *technical* pieces of waste that remain after something has been broken up or used【术语】〔某物被打碎或使用后留下的〕碎块，碎屑

De·troit /dɪˋtrɔɪt; dɪˈtrɔɪt/ a city in the US state of Michigan. It is an important centre for making cars. 底特律〔美国密歇根州一城市，是重要的汽车制造中心〕

de trop /də ˋtro; də ˈtrəʊ/ *adj* [not before noun 不用于名词前] *French* a word meaning too much or not necessary, used when you are trying too hard to sound important or educated【法】过多的，多余的，不必要的〔用于表示装腔作势，以使自己显得很重要或很有文化的样子〕

Det·tol /ˋdɛtḷ; ˈdetɒl/ *trademark* a type of liquid ANTISEPTIC sold in Britain, used especially for preventing wounds from becoming infected and for killing BACTERIA【商标】滴露〔英国销售的一种消毒液，尤用于杀菌和防止伤口感染〕

deuce /dus; djuːs/ *n* **1** the situation in tennis when both players have 40 points, after which the next player must win two points to win the game〔网球赛中〕局末平分；盘末平局，赛末点〔其后一方须连胜两分方可获胜〕**2 what/where/who etc the deuce?** *spoken old-fashioned* used to add force to a question【口，过时】到底是什么鬼东西/到底在什么鬼地方/到底是哪个家伙等〔用于加强语气〕：*What the deuce is going on?* 到底发生什么事了？**3 a deuce of** *old-fashioned* a very severe example or case of something【过时】极其糟糕的；非常严重的：*She had a deuce of a row with her father.* 她和她爸爸大吵了一场。

deuc·ed /ˋdusɪd; ˈdjuːsɪ̣d/ *adj, adv old-fashioned* very or very great【过时】很，非常：*I'm deuced glad you turned up when you did.* 看见你出现的时候，我都快高兴死了。

Deutsch·mark /ˋdɔɪtʃ,mɑrk; ˈdɔɪtʃmɑːk/ *n* [C] the former standard unit of money in Germany; MARK[2] (8) 德国马克〔原德国货币单位〕

de·val·ue /diˋvælju; diːˈvæljuː/ *v* **1** [I,T] to reduce the value that the money of one country has when it is exchanged for the money of another country (使)〔货币〕贬值 **2** [T] to make someone or something seem less important or valuable than they really are 降低〔某人的或某物的〕价值；贬低：*The skills of women were not recognized and often devalued.* 妇女的技能过去并没有得到承认，而且还经常被贬低。—**devaluation** /di,væljuˋeʃən; diː,væljuˈeɪʃən/ *n* [C,U]

dev·a·state /ˋdɛvəs,tet; ˈdevəsteɪt/ *v* [T usually passive 一般用被动态] **1** to cause so much damage to a place or area that most of it is destroyed 毁坏，摧毁，毁灭：*The bomb devastated the city centre.* 炸弹摧毁了市中心地区。**2** to make someone feel extremely shocked and sad 令〔某人〕极度震惊；使〔某人〕伤心欲绝：*Rob was devastated by the news of her death.* 罗布听到她死去的消息，悲痛欲绝。| *a country devastated by war* 被战争摧毁的国家 —**devastation** /,dɛvəsˋteʃən; ,devəˈsteɪʃən/ *n* [U]: *A cyclone came over the island, causing complete devastation.* 龙卷风袭击了该岛，造成了彻底的破坏。

dev·a·stat·ing /ˋdɛvəs,tetɪŋ; ˈdevəsteɪtɪŋ/ *adj* **1** destroying or badly damaging something 毁灭性的，破坏力极强的：*Acid rain has a devastating effect on the environment.* 酸雨对环境的破坏力极大。**2** shocking and upsetting 令人震惊的：*the devastating news of a plane crash* 令人震惊的飞机失事的消息 **3** almost impossible to argue against or deal with 难以反驳的；无法对付的：*a devastating argument in favour of legalization* 赞成合法化的强有力论点 **4** *old-fashioned* extremely attractive【过时】极富吸引力的，极漂亮的 —**devastatingly** *adv*: *Mathew looked devastatingly handsome in his white linen suit.* 马修穿上他那套白色的亚麻西装看上去帅极了。

de·vel·op /dɪˋvɛləp; dɪˈveləp/ *v*

1 ▶GROW 生长◀ [I,T] to grow or gradually change into a larger, stronger, or more advanced state, or to make someone or something do this (使) 成长；(使) 发展：*Children develop very rapidly.* 儿童长得很快。| [+into] *James has developed into a charming young man.* 詹姆斯已经长成为一个富有魅力的小伙子。| [+from] *In less than ten years it develops from a seed into a full-grown tree.* 不到10年的时间，它就从一粒种子长成一棵大树。| **develop sth** *exercises designed to develop your muscles* 为使肌肉发达而设计的锻炼

2 ▶PLAN/PRODUCT 计划/产品◀ [T] to make a new idea, plan, or product become successful over a period of time 形成〔观点〕；制订〔计划〕；研制〔产品〕：*Scientists are developing new drugs to treat arthritis.* 科学家们正在研制治疗关节炎的新药。

3 ▶START TO HAVE 开始有◀ [I,T] to gradually begin to have a quality, illness, problem etc 逐渐形成〔某种品质、疾病、问题等〕：*Some alcoholics develop liver disease.* 一些酗酒的人会得肝病。

4 ▶BECOME MORE ACTIVE 变得更加活跃◀ [I] to become more active or more of a problem, and therefore become more

noticeable〔问题等〕变得活跃, 显现: *Trouble is developing in the cities.* 一些城市里正在酝酿事端。
5▶IDEA/ARGUMENT 观点/论点◀ [T] to make an argument or idea clearer, by studying it more or by speaking or writing about it in more detail 详细阐述〔论点、观点〕: *We will develop a few of these points in the seminar.* 在研讨会上我们将详细阐述其中的一些观点。
6▶LAND 土地◀ [T] to use land for the things that people need, for example by taking minerals out of it or by building on it 开发〔土地, 如开采矿藏或修盖建筑物等〕: *We're waiting to hear if permission to develop the land will be granted.* 我们正等着看能否得到批准开发这块土地。
7▶PHOTOGRAPHY 摄影◀ [I,T] to make a photograph out of a photographic film, using chemicals 冲印, 使〔底片〕显影

de·vel·oped /dɪˋvɛləpt; dɪˈveləpt/ *adj* **1 developed country/nation/society** a rich industrial country, nation etc with a lot of business activity 发达国家/社会: *a study of farming methods used in developed countries* 对发达国家农耕方法的研究 —compare 比较 DEVELOPING, UNDERDEVELOPED **2** in a larger or more advanced state 先进的, 发达的

de·vel·op·er /dɪˋvɛləpɚ; dɪˈveləpə/ *n* **1** [C] a person or company that buys land or buildings and hopes to make a profit by building new houses, roads etc〔土地、房产等的〕开发商, 发展商: *an industrial developer* 工业用地开发公司 **2** [C,U] *technical* a chemical substance used for developing photographs【术语】〔冲印底片的〕显影剂 **3 late developer** a child whose mental or physical growth happens more slowly than other children of the same age 智力[身体]发育得比较慢的孩子

de·vel·op·ing /dɪˋvɛləpɪŋ; dɪˈveləpɪŋ/ *adj* **developing country/nation** a poor country that is trying to increase its industry and improve trade 发展中国家: *One of the basic needs in many developing countries is water.* 在许多发展中国家, 最基本的需求之一就是水。—compare 比较 DEVELOPED, UNDERDEVELOPED

[W1] **de·vel·op·ment** /dɪˋvɛləpmənt; dɪˈveləpmənt/ *n* **1** [U] the gradual growth of something, so that it becomes bigger or more advanced 发育, 成长: *an expert in child development* 儿童成长问题的专家 | [+of] *a course on the development of Greek thought* 关于古希腊思想发展的课程 **2** [C] a new event or piece of news that is likely to have an effect on the present situation 事态发展, 新情况: *recent political developments in the former Soviet Union* 前苏联的最新政治动态 **3** [C] the act or result of making a product or design better and more advanced〔产品或设计的〕发展, 进展, 进步: *There have been significant computer developments during the last decade.* 在过去的10年内, 电脑有了显著的发展。**4** [U] the process of planning and building new houses, offices etc on a piece of land〔土地的〕开发: *The land was sold for development.* 这块土地被出售供开发之用。**5** [C] a group of new buildings that have all been planned and built together on the same piece of land〔在同一块土地上建造的〕新开发的房产; 新建住宅区, 新社区: *a new housing development* 新建住宅区—**developmental** /dɪˌvɛləpˋmɛntl; dɪˌveləpˈmentl◂/ *adj*—**developmentally** *adv*

de·vi·ance /ˋdiviəns; ˈdiːviəns/ also 又作 **de·vi·an·cy** /ˋdiviənsɪ; ˈdiːviənsi/ *n* [U] deviant behaviour 反常的行为, 不正常之处: *sexual deviance* 性变态

de·vi·ant /ˋdiviənt; ˈdiːviənt/ *adj* deviant behaviour, especially sexual behaviour, is considered to be strange and morally unacceptable〔尤指性行为〕怪异的、道德上难以接受的: *Many formerly deviant activities have gradually become accepted forms of behaviour.* 许多以前被认为是离经叛道的行为方式, 已慢慢地变得可以让人接受。—**deviant** *n* [C]—**deviance, deviancy** *n* [U]

de·vi·ate¹ /ˋdivɪˌet; ˈdiːvieɪt/ *v* [I] *formal* to change what you are doing so that you are not following an expected plan, idea, or type of behaviour【正式】背离, 偏离〔原定计划、观点或行为〕: [+from] *The plane had to deviate from its normal flight path.* 飞机不得不偏离正常的航线。

de·vi·ate² /ˋdiviət; ˈdiːviȝt/ *adj AmE formal* deviant【美, 正式】怪异的; 离经叛道的

de·vi·a·tion /ˌdiviˋeʃən; ˌdiːviˈeɪʃən/ *n* **1** [C,U] a noticeable difference from what is expected or acceptable 偏离, 背离, 越轨: [+from] *deviation from the norm* 违背常态 **2** [C] *technical* a difference between a number or measurement in a set and the average of all the numbers or measurements in that set【术语】偏差, 误差 —see also 另见 STANDARD DEVIATION

de·vi·a·tion·ist /ˌdiviˋeʃənɪst; ˌdiːviˈeɪʃənȝst/ *n* [C] a word for someone who disagrees with some parts of a system of political beliefs, used to show disapproval 背离某种政治信仰的人 —**deviationism** *n* [U]

de·vice /dɪˋvaɪs; dɪˈvaɪs/ *n* [C] [W2]
1▶PIECE OF EQUIPMENT 装置◀ a piece of equipment intended for a particular purpose, for example for recording or measuring something〔用于专门用途的〕装置, 器具: [+for] *a useful device for detecting electrical activity* 用于探测电流活动的有用仪器 | *modern labour-saving devices* 节省劳力的现代化装置 —see 见 MACHINE¹ (USAGE)
2 leave sb to their own devices to leave someone alone to do whatever they want 听任某人自便, 让某人自行做想做的事情: *I just gave her a brush and paints, and left her to her own devices.* 我只给了她一支画笔和一些颜料, 就让她自己发挥了。
3▶PLAN/TRICK 计划/策略◀ a plan or trick, especially for a dishonest purpose〔尤指为不正当目的而采用的〕计划, 诡计: *Their proposal was only a device to confuse the opposition.* 他们的建议只是为迷惑反对派而使用的花招儿而已。
4▶SPECIAL METHOD 特殊方法◀ a special way of doing something that makes it easier to do〔使做某事更容易一些的〕特殊方法, 手段: *Testing yourself with information on cards is a useful device for studying.* 用卡片上的内容测试自己是一种有效的学习方法。
5▶BOMB 炸弹◀ a bomb or other explosive weapon 炸弹, 爆破装置: *an explosive device* 一个爆破装置
6▶LITERATURE/THEATRE 文学/戏剧◀ the special use of words in literature, or of words, lights etc in a play, to achieve an effect〔文学作品中的〕手法, 修辞手段;〔戏剧中灯光使用的〕技巧: *Metaphor is a common literary device.* 隐喻是一种常用的文学手法。
7▶PICTURE 图形◀ *technical* a picture or design used by a NOBLE¹ (3) family as their sign【术语】〔贵族用作家族标志的〕族徽, 纹章: *the device on his shield* 他盾牌上的族徽

dev·il /ˋdɛvl; ˈdevəl/ *n*
1▶EVIL 邪恶◀ **a) the Devil** the most powerful evil spirit in Christianity; SATAN〔基督教中的〕恶魔, 撒旦 **b)** [C] any evil spirit 魔鬼: *The villagers believed a devil had taken control of his body.* 村里的人相信他已魔鬼附身了。

> **CULTURAL NOTE 文化注释**
> In the US and UK, the Devil is typically shown with red skin, horns on his head, a long tail with a pointed end, and the legs of a goat. He is also shown holding a long fork with three points and is usually surrounded by flames. People often think of the Devil as living in Hell and ruling over the people there. 在美国和英国, 恶魔常被描绘成红发、头上长角、长尾带尖头、有山羊腿的模样。有的手持三叉长戟, 通常周身火焰围绕。人们常认为恶魔住在地狱, 统治那里的人。

2▶PERSON 人◀ [C] *informal* someone who behaves very badly, especially a child【非正式】调皮鬼, 淘气鬼〔尤指孩子〕: *Tommy's a little devil!* 汤米是个小淘气鬼!
3 speak/talk of the devil *spoken* used when someone you have just been talking about walks into the room where you are【口】说某人某人就到; 说到曹操, 曹操就到
4 play/be devil's advocate to pretend that you disagree with something so that there will be a discussion about it 假装不同意以促成一场讨论
5 be a devil *BrE spoken* used to persuade someone to do something they are not sure they should do【英口】〔用来说服某人做犹豫不决的事〕: *Go on, be a devil, have another gin and tonic.* 来, 胆子大一点, 再来一杯掺奎宁水的杜松子酒。
6 lucky/poor/silly etc devil *spoken* someone who is lucky, unlucky, silly etc【口】幸运/可怜/愚蠢等的家伙
7 what/who/why etc the devil? *spoken old-fashioned* used to show that you are surprised or annoyed【口, 过时】究竟是什么鬼名堂/哪个鬼家伙/为什么等?〔表示惊讶或恼怒〕: *What the devil d'you think you're doing?* 你到底在搞什么鬼名堂?
8 a devil of a job/mess etc *old-fashioned* a very unpleasant job, mess etc【过时】糟糕透顶的工作/烂摊子等: *We had a devil of a job trying to get the carpet clean again.* 我们要把地毯再弄干净, 真是麻烦极了。
9 go to the devil! *spoken* used to tell someone rudely to go away or stop annoying you【口】滚开! 见鬼去吧!
10 have the luck of the devil to be very lucky 运气极佳, 红运当头
11 better the devil you know (than the devil you don't) used to say that it is better to deal with someone or something you know, even if you do not like them, than to deal with someone or something new that might be worse 两害相权取其轻; 宁跟认识的魔鬼打交道〔比跟不认识的魔鬼打交道为好〕

12 be between the devil and the deep blue sea to be in a difficult situation in which you have to choose between two unpleasant things 进退维谷，左右为难
13 do sth like the devil *old-fashioned* to do something very fast or using a lot of force【过时】迅速地做某事，卖力地做某事：*They rang the bell and ran like the devil.* 他们按了门铃，之后就拼命地跑开了。
14 devil take the hindmost used to describe a situation in which people think about their own success and do not care what happens to anyone else 魔鬼专抓落后者；要鬼捉不到，抢在人前逃〔形容只顾及自己的成功而不管别人的死活〕

dev·il·ish /ˋdɛvəlɪʃ; 'devəlɪʃ/ *adj* very bad, difficult, or unpleasant 极坏的；恶毒的：*devilish schemes* 阴谋诡计

dev·il·ish·ly /ˋdɛvəlɪʃlɪ; 'devəlɪʃli/ *adv old-fashioned* [+adj/adv] a word meaning very, used to show annoyance【过时】非常，极其〔表示恼怒〕：*The collector was a devilishly hard fellow to talk to.* 这个收账人是个极难说话的家伙。

dev·illed *BrE*【英】, **deviled** *AmE*【美】/ˋdɛvḷd; 'devəld/ *adj* devilled food is cooked in or mixed with very hot pepper〔食物〕辣味的

devil-may-care /,·· · ˈ· ◂/ *adj* cheerful, careless, and willing to take risks 无忧无虑的；满不在乎的；不顾一切的：*a devil-may-care attitude to life* 天塌了也不管的生活态度

dev·il·ment /ˋdɛvḷmənt; 'devəlmənt/ *n* [U] *literary* wild or bad behaviour that causes trouble【文】恶作剧，捣蛋：*eyes blazing with devilment* 透着狡狯的眼睛

dev·il·ry /ˋdɛvḷrɪ; 'devəlri/ *n* [U] devilment 恶作剧，捣蛋

devil's food cake /ˈ· · ·,·/ *n* [C,U] an American chocolate cake 美式巧克力蛋糕

Devil's Is·land /,·· ˈ··/ an island near the coast of French Guiana in South America, which was used as a prison by France until 1938 魔岛〔南美洲法属圭亚那沿岸一岛屿，1938年前法国关押囚犯的地方〕

de·vi·ous /ˋdiviəs; 'diːviəs/ *adj* **1** using dishonest tricks and deceiving people in order to get what you want 欺诈的；不诚实的：*I wouldn't trust him – he's devious.* 我不会相信他的，他很狡诈。**2** *formal* not going in the most direct way to get to a place【正式】〔路线〕迂回的，绕弯的：*a devious route* 迂回的路线 —**deviously** *adv* —**deviousness** *n* [U]

de·vise /dɪˋvaɪz; dɪ'vaɪz/ *v* [T] to plan or invent a way of doing something, especially something complicated and clever 想出；设计；发明：*She devised a method for quicker communications between offices.* 她发明出一种加快办公室之间互相交流的方法。

de·vi·tal·ize also 又作 **-ise** *BrE*【英】/diˋvaɪtḷ,aɪz; ,diː'vaɪtlaɪz/ *v* [T] to take the power or strength away from something 使失去活力，使失去生命力 —**devitalization** /di,vaɪtḷəˋzeʃən; diː,vaɪtlaɪ'zeɪʃən/ *n* [U]

de·void /dɪˋvɔɪd; dɪ'vɔɪd/ *adj* **be devoid of** to be completely lacking in something 毫无…，完全没有…：*That man is totally devoid of all humour.* 那个人毫无幽默感。

de·vo·lu·tion /,dɛvəˋluʃən; ,diːvə'luːʃən/ *n* [U] the act of giving power from a national government to a group or organization at a lower or more local level〔中央政府向地方政府或下级组织的〕权力下放 —**devolutionary** *adj* —**devolutionist** *n* [C]

de·volve /dɪˋvɑlv; dɪ'vɒlv/ *v*
devolve on/upon sb *phr v* [T not in passive 不用被动态] *formal* to give work, responsibility etc to someone at a lower level【正式】〔工作、职责等〕下放给〔下级〕，委派给〔下级〕：**devolve sth on/upon sb** *The Governor devolved the choice upon the committee.* 州长把选择权下放给了委员会。| **it devolves on/upon sb** *It devolved upon the deputy to make a speech.* 发表讲话的任务落在了副手的头上。
devolve to sb *phr v* [T not in passive 不用被动态] *formal*【正式】**1** to give work, responsibility etc to someone at a lower level 把〔工作、职责等〕移交给〔下级〕**2** if land, goods etc devolve to someone they become the property of that person when their owner dies〔指定在自己死后〕转让〔土地、物品等〕给〔某人〕，让〔某人〕继承〔土地、物品等〕

Dev·on /ˋdɛvṇ; 'devən/ a COUNTY in southwest England famous for its natural beauty 德文郡〔英格兰西南部一郡，以优美的自然风光闻名〕

de·vote /dɪˋvot; dɪ'vəʊt/ *v* **1 devote time/effort/money etc to** to use your time, effort etc in order to do something or help something be successful 为…付出时间/努力/金钱等：*I'm devoting all my time and energy to being a mom right now.* 目前我把所有时间和精力都放在当妈妈这件事上。**2 devote yourself to** to do everything you can to achieve something or help someone 献身于…，专心致力于…：*Mother Teresa has devoted herself to caring for the poor.* 特蕾莎修女把自己的全部身心都用来照顾穷苦人。

de·vot·ed /dɪˋvotɪd; dɪ'vəʊtɪ̇d/ *adj* showing great love and loyalty for someone or something 挚爱的；忠诚的：*a devoted father* 慈爱的父亲 | [+to] *Kiko is devoted to her music.* 基科热爱她的音乐。—**devotedly** *adv*

dev·o·tee /,dɛvəˋti; ,devə'tiː/ *n* [C] **1** someone who admires someone or something very much 仰慕者，敬仰者，爱好者：[+of] *a devotee of 1930s films* 一个迷恋20世纪30年代电影的人 **2** a very religious person 虔诚的宗教信徒：*a Sikh devotee* 一个虔诚的锡克教徒

de·vo·tion /dɪˋvoʃən; dɪ'vəʊʃən/ *n* **1** [U] great love or loyalty 深爱，挚爱；忠心：[+to] *Alanna has always shown intense devotion to her children.* 阿兰娜一直非常钟爱她的孩子们。**2** [U] the act of spending a lot of time and energy on something 奉献，献身：[+to] *her total devotion to her job* 她对工作全心全意的投入 **3** [U] great loyalty to a religion〔对宗教的〕虔诚，忠信 **4 devotions** [plural] prayers and other religious acts 祈祷等宗教行为

de·vo·tion·al /dɪˋvoʃənḷ; dɪ'vəʊʃənəl/ *adj* related to or used in religious services 和宗教仪式有关的，用于宗教仪式上的：*devotional music* 宗教仪式上使用的音乐

de·vour /dɪˋvaʊr; dɪ'vaʊə/ *v* [T] **1** to eat something quickly because you are very hungry 吞食；狼吞虎咽地吃：*The boys devoured their pancakes with great joy.* 男孩子们高兴地大口吃着饼。**2** to read something quickly and eagerly 快速地阅读；贪婪地阅读：*Joseph devoured the contents of the book avidly.* 约瑟夫如饥似渴地读着书的内容。**3 be devoured by** to be filled with a strong feeling that seems to control you 充满〔强烈的，无法摆脱的情感〕：*Cindy felt devoured by jealousy.* 辛迪心里充满了妒忌。**4** to destroy someone or something 毁灭〔某人或某物〕：*beams devoured by rot* 朽烂的梁木 **5 devour sb/sth with your eyes** to look eagerly at someone or something and notice everything about them 贪婪地看某人/某物

de·vout /dɪˋvaʊt; dɪ'vaʊt/ *adj* **1** someone who is devout has a very strong belief in a religion 虔诚的，笃信宗教的：*a devout Catholic* 虔诚的天主教徒 **2** *formal* a devout hope or wish is one that you feel very strongly【正式】〔希望或愿望〕真诚的，衷心的，诚挚的：*It is my devout hope that we can work together in peace.* 我衷心希望我们能和睦地在一起工作。—**devoutly** *adv* —**devoutness** *n* [U]

dew /du; djuː/ *n* [U] the small drops of water that form on outdoor surfaces during the night 露水，露珠

dew·drop /ˋdu,drɑp; 'djuːdrɒp/ *n* [C] a small drop of dew 露珠：*dewdrops sparkling in the morning sunlight* 晨光中闪烁的露珠

Dew·ey dec·i·mal sys·tem, the /,djuɪ ˋdɛsəmḷ ,sɪstəm; ,djuːi 'desɪ̇məl ,sɪstɪ̇m/ also 又作 **the Dewey Decimal Classification** a system used by libraries for putting books into groups according to their subject. General subjects (for example, sports) are given a number, and then particular parts of this subject (for example, the Olympics) are each given a more specific number using DECIMAL numbers. The system was invented by **Melvil Dewey** (1851-1931), a US librarian. 杜威十进分类法〔图书馆按主题对图书进行分类和编目的方法。总主题（如体育）编排一个号码，次主题（如奥林匹克）编排一个更为具体的十进位号码。该方法由美国图书馆学家梅尔维尔·杜威（1851-1931）发明〕

dew·fall /ˋdu,fɔl; 'djuːfɔːl/ *n* [U] *literary* the forming of dew or the time when dew begins to appear【文】结露；开始结露的时候

dew·lap /ˋdu,læp; 'djuːlæp/ *n* [C] a hanging fold of loose skin under the throat of a cow, dog etc〔牛、狗等〕喉部垂下的松皮，垂皮，垂肉

dew·y /ˋduɪ; 'djuːi/ *adj* wet with drops of DEW 被露水所湿的，带露水的：*The dewy woodland was solitary and still.* 露水打湿的林地一片孤寂和静谧。

dewy-eyed /,·· ˈ· ◂/ *adj* having eyes that are slightly wet with tears 眼睛微湿的，眼睛含泪的

dex·ter·i·ty /dɛksˋtɛrətɪ; dek'sterɪ̇ti/ *n* [U] the ability to be very quick and skilful with your hands〔手的〕敏捷，灵巧，熟练：*He used his knife with speed and dexterity.* 他使刀又快又娴熟。

dex·ter·ous /ˋdɛkstərəs; 'dekstərəs/ also 又作 **dextrous** /ˋdɛkstrəs; 'dekstrəs/ *adj* able to use your hands in a skilful way 用手灵活的，灵巧的，熟练的：*dextrous use of the needle* 灵巧的针法 —**dexterously, dextrously** *adv*

dex·trose /ˋdɛkstros; 'dekstrəʊz/ *n* [U] a type of sugar that is in many sweet fruits 葡萄糖，右旋糖

dex·trous /ˋdɛkstrəs; 'dekstrəs/ *adj* another spelling of DEXTEROUS dexterous 的另一种拼法

DFC *n* [singular] Distinguished Flying Cross; a British MEDAL for bravery given to officers of the RAF 卓越飞行十字勋章〔英国授予英国皇家空军军官的奖章, 以表彰其英勇行为〕

DfEE, the /ˏdi ɛf i ˋi; ˌdiː ef iː ˈiː/ the abbreviation of 缩写= Department for Education and Employment; a former British government department 教育与就业部〔英国以前的一个政府部门〕

DfID, the /ˏdi ɛf aɪ ˋdi; ˌdiː ef aɪ ˈdiː/ the abbreviation of 缩写 = the DEPARTMENT FOR INTERNATIONAL DEVELOPMENT

Dhak·a /ˋdækə; ˈdækə/ the capital and the most important industrial city of Bangladesh. Its name used to be spelled Dacca. 达卡〔孟加拉国首都和最重要的工业城市。此名曾拼写为Dacca〕

dho·ti /ˋdotɪ; ˈdəʊti/ *n* [C] a piece of clothing worn by some Hindu men, consisting of a piece of cloth that is wrapped around the waist and between the legs〔印度男子用的〕缠腰布

dhow /daʊ; daʊ/ *n* [C] an Arab ship with one large sail 单桅阿拉伯帆船

DHSS, the /ˏdi etʃ ɛs ˋɛs; ˌdiː eɪtʃ es ˈes/ the former name for the DSS, a British government department 卫生和社会保障部〔英国政府部门, 社会保障部的旧称〕

DI /ˏdi ˋaɪ; ˌdiː ˈaɪ/ *n* [C] Detective Inspector; a middle rank in the British police 刑事侦缉督察〔英国的中级警衔〕

Di /daɪ; daɪ/ an informal name for Diana, Princess of Wales – used especially in newspapers 戴妃〔威尔士王妃戴安娜的非正式称呼, 多用于报纸〕

di- /daɪ, dɪ; daɪ, dɪ/ *prefix* two; twice; double 二; 两倍; 双重: *A diphthong is a vowel made up of two sounds.* 双元音是由两个音组成的元音。—compare 比较 SEMI —see also 另见 BI-, TRI-

di·a·be·tes /ˏdaɪəˋbitis; ˌdaɪəˈbiːtiːz/ *n* [U] a serious disease in which there is too much sugar in your blood 糖尿病

di·a·bet·ic[1] /ˏdaɪəˋbɛtɪk; ˌdaɪəˈbetɪk◂/ *adj* **1** having diabetes 患糖尿病的: *Sarah is diabetic.* 萨拉患有糖尿病。**2** caused by diabetes 由糖尿病引起的: *a diabetic coma* 由糖尿病引起的昏迷 **3** produced for people who have diabetes 为糖尿病患者专门制作的: *diabetic chocolate* 供糖尿病患者食用的巧克力

diabetic[2] *n* [C] someone who has diabetes 糖尿病患者

di·a·bol·i·cal /ˏdaɪəˋbɑlɪkḷ; ˌdaɪəˈbɒlɪkəl◂/ *adj* **1** also 又作 **diabolic** /ˏdaɪəˋbɑlɪk; ˌdaɪəˈbɒlɪk◂/ evil or cruel 邪恶的, 毒辣的: *diabolical abuse* 残酷的虐待 | *a diabolical plan to destroy him* 一个要毁掉他的恶毒计划 **2** *informal especially BrE* extremely unpleasant or bad【非正式, 尤英】很坏的, 糟透的: *The toilets were in a diabolical state.* 厕所的情况糟透了。—**diabolically** /-kḷɪ; -kli/ *adv*

di·achron·ic /ˏdaɪəˋkrɑnɪk; ˌdaɪəˈkrɒnɪk◂/ *adj technical* dealing with something such as a language as it changes over time【术语】历时的〔研究某物如语言长时间以来的发展情况〕: *a diachronic study* 历时的研究 —**diachronically** /-kḷɪ; -kli/ *adv*

di·a·crit·ic /ˏdaɪəˋkrɪtɪk; ˌdaɪəˈkrɪtɪk/ *n* [C] a mark placed over, under, or through a letter in some languages, to show that the letter should be pronounced differently from the letter without a mark 变音符号〔标于某些语言中的某些字母上方、下方或中间, 表示其发音与无此标志的字母有所不同〕—**diacritical** *adj*

di·a·dem /ˋdaɪəˏdɛm; ˈdaɪədem/ *n* [C] *literary* a circle of jewels, flowers etc that you wear on your head【文】镶有珠宝的环状头饰; 花冠

di·ae·re·sis, dieresis /daɪˋɛrəsɪs; daɪˈɪərǝ̇sǝ̇s/ *n plural* **diaereses** /-siz; -siːz/ [C] *technical* a sign (¨) put over the second of two VOWELs to show that it is pronounced separately from the first【术语】分音符, 隔音符〔即"¨", 置于两个元音中的第二个元音之上, 表示此元音与前一元音分开发音〕

Di·a·ghi·lev /dɪˋægɪlɛf; diˈægǝ̇lef/, **Ser·ge·i** /sɝˋge; sɜːˈgeɪ/ (1872-1929) a Russian who began the Ballet Russes, which is considered to have begun the modern style of BALLET. Many famous dancers and COMPOSERs worked with the Ballet Russes. 佳吉列夫〔(1872-1929), 俄罗斯芭蕾舞团的创建者, 也被认为是现代芭蕾的创始人。许多著名舞蹈家和作曲家都曾与俄罗斯芭蕾舞团合作过〕

di·ag·nose /ˏdaɪəgˋnos; ˈdaɪəgnəʊz/ *v* [T] to find out what is wrong with someone or something, especially what illness someone has, by examining them carefully 判断; 诊断: *diagnosing computer faults* 找出电脑的毛病 | **diagnose sth as** *The illness was diagnosed as mumps.* 所患疾病被诊断为腮腺炎。

di·ag·no·sis /ˏdaɪəgˋnosɪs; ˌdaɪəgˈnəʊsǝ̇s/ *n plural* **diagnoses** /-siz; -siːz/ [C,U] the discovery of exactly what is wrong with someone or something, by examining them closely 诊断, 判断: [+of] *diagnosis of kidney disease* 肾病的诊断 | **make/give a diagnosis** *An exact diagnosis can only be made by obtaining a blood sample.* 只有采血样才能作出准确的诊断。—compare 比较 PROGNOSIS

di·ag·nos·tic /ˏdaɪəgˋnɑstɪk; ˌdaɪəgˈnɒstɪk◂/ *adj* related to or used for diagnosis 诊断的, 判断的: *diagnostic tests* 诊断化验

di·ag·o·nal /daɪˋægənḷ; daɪˈægənəl/ *adj* **1** a diagonal line is straight and joins two opposite corners of a flat shape, usually a square 对角的, 对角线的 —compare 比较 HORIZONTAL[1] —see picture at 参见 VERTICAL 图 **2** a diagonal pattern follows a sloping direction 斜的 —**diagonal** *n* [C] —**diagonally** *adv*: *The path goes diagonally across the field.* 这条小径斜穿过田地。

di·a·gram /ˋdaɪəˏgræm; ˈdaɪəgræm/ *n* [C] a drawing or plan that shows exactly where something is, what something looks like, or how something works 图解, 图表, 示意图: *a diagram of the human body* 人体示意图 —**diagrammatic** /ˏdaɪəgrəˋmætɪk; ˌdaɪəgrəˈmætɪk◂/ *adj* —**diagrammatically** /-kḷɪ; -kli/ *adv*

dial[1] /ˋdaɪəl; ˈdaɪəl/ *n* [C] **1** the part of a machine or piece of equipment such as a watch, that is usually covered in glass and shows the time or a measurement 仪表盘, 刻度盘; 钟面, 表面: *She looked at the dial to check her speed.* 她看了看仪表, 检查一下自己的速度。**2** the wheel on a telephone with numbered holes for your fingers, that you move around in order to make a call〔电话的〕拨号盘 **3** part of a piece of equipment such as a radio, that you turn around to listen to different radio stations〔收音机等的〕调谐指示板, 调谐度盘

dial[2] *v* **dialled, dialling** *BrE*【英】, **dialed, dialing** *AmE*【美】[I,T] to move the numbered wheel or press the buttons on a telephone in order to make a telephone call 拨〔电话号码〕

di·a·lect /ˋdaɪəˏlɛkt; ˈdaɪəlekt/ *n* [C,U] a variety of a language spoken only in one area, in which words or grammar are slightly different from other forms of the same language 方言, 地方话, 土语 —compare 比较 ACCENT[1] (1), IDIOLECT

di·a·lec·tic /ˏdaɪəˋlɛktɪk; ˌdaɪəˈlektɪk/ also 又作 **dialectics** *n* [U] a method of examining and discussing ideas in order to find the truth, that follows rules developed by Socrates, Plato and Hegel 辩证法 —**dialectical** /ˏdaɪəˋlɛktɪkḷ; ˌdaɪəˈlektɪkəl◂/ *adj*

dialling code /ˋ.. ˏ./ *n* [C] *BrE* the numbers at the beginning of a telephone number that represent a specific area of a city or country【英】电话区域号码; AREA CODE *AmE*【美】

dialling tone /ˋ.. ˏ./ *n* [C] *BrE* the sound you hear when you pick up the telephone that lets you know that you can make a call【英】〔电话的〕拨号音; DIAL TONE *AmE*【美】

di·a·logue *BrE*【英】, **dialog** *AmE*【美】/ˋdaɪəˏlɔg; ˈdaɪəlɒg/ *n* [C,U] **1** a conversation in a book, play, or film〔书、戏剧、电影中的〕对话, 对白: *a boring movie full of bad dialog* 充满差劲对白的乏味电影 **2** *formal* a discussion between two groups, countries etc【正式】〔两个组织或国家等之间的〕讨论, 对话, 意见交换: *There is a need for constructive dialogue between leaders.* 领导人之间需要进行建设性的对话。—compare 比较 MONOLOGUE

dial tone /ˋ. ˏ./ *n* [C] *AmE* the sound you hear when you pick up the telephone that lets you know that you can make a call【美】〔电话的〕拨号音; DIALLING TONE *BrE*【英】

di·al·y·sis /daɪˋæləsɪs; daɪˈælǝ̇sǝ̇s/ *n* [U] the process of taking harmful substances out of someone's blood using a special machine, because their KIDNEYs do not work properly 透析, 渗析〔使用一种特殊的仪器除去肾功能不正常的病人血液中的有害物质〕

di·a·mant·é /ˏdiəmɑnˋte; ˌdiːəˈmɒnteɪ◂/ *adj* decorated with artificial diamonds 饰有人造钻石的: *a diamanté necklace* 人造钻石项链

di·am·e·ter /daɪˋæmətɚ; daɪˈæmǝ̇tə/ *n* [C] a straight line going from one side of a circle to the other side, passing through the centre of the circle 直径: **3 inches/1 metre etc in diameter** *Draw a circle six centimetres in diameter.* 画一个直径为六厘米的圆。—see picture at 参见 CIRCLE 图

di·a·met·ri·cally /ˏdaɪəˋmɛtrɪkḷɪ; ˌdaɪəˈmetrɪkli/ *adv* **diametrically opposed/opposite** completely different and opposite 截然不同的, 截然相反的: *The two ideas are diametrically opposed.* 两个观点截然相反。

di·a·mond /ˋdaɪəmənd; ˈdaɪəmənd/ *n*

1 ►**STONE** 宝石◄ [C,U] a very hard valuable stone, that usually has no colour and is used in jewellery 钻石: *Did you see the size of that diamond engagement ring?* 你有没有看到那枚订婚钻戒有多大?

CULTURAL NOTE 文化注释

In the US and the UK, a man traditionally gives a diamond ring to a woman when he asks her to marry him, and this shows that they are ENGAGED. People sometimes joke that 'diamonds are a girl's best friend', meaning that if you are rich you do not have to worry about anything. 'Dia-

D

monds are forever' is a phrase that was used as a very successful advertising SLOGAN and is also the name of a James Bond film. 按照传统，英美男子向女子求婚时通常送钻戒，来表明双方已订婚。人们有时打趣说："钻石是女孩最好的朋友。"意思是说，有钱就什么也不用愁。"钻石恒久远"是一句非常成功的广告语，也曾用作一部007影片的片名。

2 ▶**SHAPE** 形状◀[C] a shape with four straight sides of equal length that stands on one of its points 菱形 —see picture at 参见 SHAPE[1] 图
3 ▶**ON A PLAYING CARD** 在纸牌上◀[C] **a)** a diamond shape printed in red on a playing card 红方块 **b)** [C] one of the cards in the set that are printed in this way 红方块花色的纸牌: *the queen of diamonds* 红方块Q, 方块王后
4 ▶**SPORTS FIELD** 体育场地◀[C] **a)** the area in a BASEBALL field within the diamond shape formed by the four bases (BASE[2] (8)) 〔棒球赛场的〕内场〔四垒连线内呈菱形的场地〕 **b)** the whole playing field used in BASEBALL 棒球场 —see picture on page A22 参见 A22 页图

D

diamond an·ni·ver·sa·ry /ˌ···ˈ···/ *n* [C] *especially AmE* the date that is exactly 60 years after the date when two people were married【尤美】钻石婚〔结婚 60 年纪念〕; DIAMOND WEDDING *BrE*【英】

diamond in the rough /ˌ···ˈ·/ *n* [C] *AmE informal* someone who behaves in a slightly rude way, but is really kind and generous【美，非正式】外粗内秀的人; ROUGH DIAMOND *BrE*【英】

diamond ju·bi·lee /ˌ···ˈ··/ *n* [C] the date that is exactly 60 years after the date of an important event, especially of someone becoming a king or queen〔尤指国王或女王加冕的〕60 周年纪念, 60 周年庆典 —compare 比较 GOLDEN JUBILEE, SILVER JUBILEE

diamond wed·ding /ˌ···ˈ··/ *n BrE* the date that is exactly 60 years after the date when two people were married【英】钻石婚〔结婚 60 年纪念〕; DIAMOND ANNIVERSARY *AmE*【美】—compare 比较 GOLDEN WEDDING, SILVER WEDDING ANNIVERSARY

Di·an·a /daɪˈænə; daɪˈænə/ in Roman MYTHOLOGY, the goddess of hunting and the moon. In Greek mythology her name is **Artemis**. 狄安娜〔罗马神话中的狩猎和月亮女神，希腊神话中称阿尔忒尼斯〕

Diana, Princess of Wales also 又作 **Princess Di, Princess Diana, Lady Di** (1961-97) the former wife of Prince **Charles** and the mother of Prince William and Prince Harry. She was originally called **Lady Diana Spencer** and she married Prince Charles in 1981. Eventually their marriage failed and they got a DIVORCE in 1996. In 1997, she died in a car crash in Paris. 戴安娜〔(1961-1997)，查尔斯王子的前妻，小王子威廉和哈里之母，原名戴安娜·斯潘塞小姐，1981 年与查尔斯结婚。他们的婚姻最终破裂，于 1996 年离婚。1997 年，在巴黎的一场车祸中丧生〕

3 **di·a·per** /ˈdaɪpɚ; ˈdaɪəpə/ *n* [C] *AmE* a piece of soft cloth that is put between a baby's legs and fastened around its waist to hold liquid and solid waste【美】尿布，尿片; NAPPY *BrE*【英】

diaper rash /ˈ···ˌ·/ *n* [U] *AmE* sore skin between a baby's legs and on its BUTTOCKS, caused by a wet diaper【美】尿布疹; NAPPY RASH *BrE*【英】

di·aph·a·nous /daɪˈæfənəs; daɪˈæfənəs/ *adj* diaphanous cloth is so fine and thin that you can almost see through it〔布料〕半透明的，极薄的

di·a·phragm /ˈdaɪəˌfræm; ˈdaɪəfræm/ *n* [C] **1** the muscle that separates your lungs from your stomach 膈膜，横膈膜 **2** a round rubber object that some women wear inside their VAGINA so that they can have sex without having children; DUTCH CAP〔避孕用的〕子宫帽 **3** *technical* any thin piece of stretched material that is moved by sound【术语】振动膜，膜片

di·a·rist /ˈdaɪərɪst; ˈdaɪərɪst/ *n* [C] someone who keeps a diary and later sells this as a book 日记作者〔尤指日后发表日记的人〕

di·ar·rhoea, diarrhea /ˌdaɪəˈriə; ˌdaɪəˈrɪə/ *n* [U] a medical condition that makes you empty your BOWELS very often and in a very liquid form 腹泻

CULTURAL NOTE 文化注释

People from the US and the UK often suffer from diarrhoea when they go to other countries, because of the change in their food, water etc, and they sometimes joke about this, saying they had **the runs, the trots, Delhi belly** (especially in India), **Montezuma's revenge** (especially in S America) etc. 英美人去别的国家常因水土不服等原因患腹泻，他们有时开玩笑说这种情况是 the runs、the trots、Delhi belly（尤指在印度）、Montezuma's revenge（尤指在南美）等。

di·a·ry /ˈdaɪərɪ; ˈdaɪəri/ *n* [C] **1** a book in which you write down the things that happen to you each day; JOURNAL (2) 日记，日志，日记簿: **keep a diary** (=write things in a diary regularly) 记日记 **2** *BrE* a book with marked separate spaces for each day of the year, in which you write down the meetings, events etc that are planned for each day【英】〔可登记工作日程的〕日程簿，记事簿; CALENDAR (2a) *AmE*【美】: *Did you put the meeting date in your diary?* 你把开会日期写在工作记事簿上了吗？

Diary of Anne Frank /ˌ···ˌ·ˈ·/ the DIARY (=book in which you write down your thoughts, experiences etc each day) written by Anne Frank when she and her family were hiding from the NAZIS in Amsterdam during World War II. It was published after her death in a CONCENTRATION CAMP, and it has been made into a play and film.《安妮日记》〔安妮·弗兰克二战期间与家人在阿姆斯特丹躲避纳粹分子时写的日记。安妮死于集中营，后来，她的日记得以出版，并改编成戏剧和电影〕

Diary of a No·bod·y /ˌ····ˈ··/ (1892) a humorous book by George and Weedon Grossmith. It is written in the form of a diary belonging to the main character, Mr Pooter, who describes his life during the early 1890s. Mr Pooter is a very ordinary man, who often gets into embarrassing social situations and makes himself look stupid.《无名小卒日记》〔(1892)，乔治和维顿·格罗史密斯共同创作的一部幽默作品。作品以主人公波特先生写日记的形式描写了他 19 世纪 90 年代的生活。波特先生是位极其普通的男子，在社交中经常使自己陷入尴尬境地，并且出尽洋相〕

di·as·po·ra /daɪˈæspərə; daɪˈæspərə/ *n* [C] *formal*【正式】**1 the Diaspora** the movement of the Jewish people away from ancient Palestine, to settle in other countries 大流散〔指犹太人从古代巴勒斯坦流落到其他国家定居〕 **2** the spreading of people from a national group or culture to other areas〔某一国家或文化的人群向其他地区的〕流散

di·a·ton·ic scale /ˌdaɪətɑnɪk ˈskel; ˌdaɪətɒnɪk ˈskeɪl/ *n* **the diatonic scale** a set of eight musical notes that uses a fixed pattern of spaces between the notes 自然音音阶，全音阶

di·a·tribe /ˈdaɪəˌtraɪb; ˈdaɪətraɪb/ *n* [C] a long speech or piece of writing that criticizes someone or something very severely 长篇抨击: [+against] *a diatribe against contemporary American civilization* 对当代美国文明的长篇抨击

dibs /dɪbz; dɪbz/ *n* **dibs on sth** *AmE spoken* an expression used especially by children in order to claim a right to something【美口】某物归我所有〔尤指孩子们用来声明自己有权使用或拥有某物〕: *Dibs on the seat near the window!* 靠窗的位子归我！

dice[1] /daɪs; daɪs/ *n plural* **dice 1** [C usually plural 一般用复数] a small block of wood, plastic etc that has six sides with a different number of spots on each side, used in games of chance 骰子，色子: **throw/roll the dice** *She threw the dice and moved her counter across the board.* 她掷了骰子，然后把筹码移到赌台的另一边。**2** [U] any game of chance that is played with dice 掷骰子游戏 **3 no dice** *especially AmE spoken* used to refuse to do something or to say that something is not possible【尤美口】没门儿，不行〔表示拒绝做某事或说某事是不可能的〕: *"Can I borrow some cash?" "Sorry, no dice."* "我能借些钱吗？""对不起，不行。"

dice 骰子

dice[2] *v* **1** also 又作 **dice up** [T] to cut food into small square pieces 把〔食物〕切成小方块[丁]: *diced carrots* 切成丁的胡萝卜 —see picture on page A11 参见 A11 页图 **2 dice with death** to put yourself in a very dangerous situation 冒险，玩命 **3** [I +for] *literary* to play dice with someone, for money, possessions etc【文】〔为了钱或财产等〕掷骰子赌博

dic·ey /ˈdaɪsɪ; ˈdaɪsi/ *adj informal* slightly dangerous and uncertain【非正式】稍有危险的; 不肯定的; 无法预计的: *The future looks pretty dicey for small businesses.* 小型企业的前途相当难以预料。

di·chot·o·my /daɪˈkɑtəmɪ; daɪˈkɒtəmi/ *n* [C] *formal* a separation between two things or ideas that are completely opposite【正式】一分为二; 二分法: [+between] *a dichotomy between his public and private lives* 他公众生活和私人生活的两面性

dick /dɪk; dɪk/ *n* [C] **1** *slang* a PENIS【俚】阴茎 **2** *slang* a stupid annoying person, especially a man【俚】笨蛋，讨厌鬼〔尤指男人〕: *He's acting like a complete dick.* 他表现得就像个大混蛋。**3** *AmE old-fashioned* a PRIVATE DETECTIVE【美，过时】私人侦探 —see also 另见 **clever dick** (CLEVER (6)), SPOTTED DICK

dick·ens /ˋdɪkɪnz; ˈdɪkənz/ *n* **1 what/who/where the dickens** *spoken* used when asking a question to show that you are very surprised or angry【口】到底是什么/谁/在哪儿〔表示非常惊讶或愤怒〕: *What the dickens is the matter with her?* 她到底怎么回事? **2 as pretty/smart etc as the dickens** *AmE informal* very pretty, clever etc【美, 非正式】非常漂亮/聪明等: *Isn't she as cute as the dickens!* 她多么可爱啊!

Dickens, Charles (1812-70) a British writer whose NOVELs made him the most popular British writer of the 19th century, and are still very popular today. His books contain humorous characters with unusual names, many of whom have become very well known. But they also show how hard life was in Victorian England, especially for poor people and children. His books include *David Copperfield, Oliver Twist, Great Expectations, A Christmas Carol, A Tale of Two Cities,* and *The Pickwick Papers.* 狄更斯〔(1812-1870), 英国作家。他是最受人喜爱的 19 世纪英国作家, 其小说现在仍深受欢迎。小说中的人物诙谐幽默, 名字怪异, 其中的许多人物为人熟知。然而, 他的小说也再现了英国维多利亚时期的艰难时世, 尤其是穷人和小孩的艰苦生活。他的主要作品有《大卫·科波菲尔》、《雾都孤儿》、《远大前程》、《圣诞颂歌》、《双城记》和《匹克威克外传》〕

Dic·ken·si·an /dɪˋkɛnzɪən; dɪˈkenziən/ *adj* Dickensian buildings, living conditions etc are poor, dirty, and unpleasant 像狄更斯描绘的, 狄更斯笔下的〔建筑物、生活条件等贫困、脏乱、令人不愉快〕: *a single mother living in a Dickensian block of flats* 住在像狄更斯笔下的公寓房子里的单身母亲

dick·ey /ˋdɪkɪ; ˈdɪki/ *n* another spelling of DICKY² dicky² 的另一种拼法

dick·head /ˋdɪkˌhɛd; ˈdɪkhed/ *n* [C] *slang* a stupid annoying person, especially a man【俚】笨蛋, 讨厌鬼〔尤指男人〕: *Don't be such a dickhead!* 别那么讨人厌!

Dick·in·son /ˋdɪkɪnsn̩; ˈdɪkənsən/, **Em·i·ly** /ˋɛmɪlɪ; ˈeməli/ (1830-86) a US poet whose clever and original work is still very popular. She is sometimes called 'the Belle of Amherst', and was a RECLUSE (=someone who lives alone and avoids other people) for the last 25 years of her life. 迪金森〔(1830-1886), 美国诗人。她的作品巧妙独到, 至今仍颇受喜爱。有时, 人们也称她为"阿莫斯特美女"。她生命的最后 25 年在离群索居中度过〕

dick·y¹ /ˋdɪkɪ; ˈdɪki/ *adj BrE informal* weak, and likely to break or not work properly【英, 非正式】虚弱的; 不结实的, 易破的, 易坏的: **dicky heart/ticker** (=a heart that is weak and not very healthy) 虚弱的心脏

dicky², **dickey** *n* [C] a false shirt front sometimes worn by a man under a jacket〔男子穿在上衣里面的〕只有前襟的假衬衫

dick·y·bird /ˋdɪkɪˌbɝd; ˈdɪkibɜːd/ *n* [C] *BrE*【英】**1** a word meaning any small bird, used by or to children 小鸟〔儿语〕 **2 not hear a dickybird** *informal* to not hear any news about someone or something【非正式】杳无音信: *"Have you heard from them since they moved?" "No, not a dickybird."* "他们搬走后你听到过他们的消息吗?" "没有, 一点也没有。"

dicky bow /ˋdɪkɪ ˌbo; ˈdɪki bəʊ/ *n* [C] *informal* a BOW TIE【非正式】蝶形领结

dic·ta /ˋdɪktə; ˈdɪktə/ the plural of DICTUM

Dic·ta·phone /ˋdɪktəˌfon; ˈdɪktəfəʊn/ *n* [C] *trademark* an office machine on which you can record speech so that someone can listen to it and TYPE² (1) it later【商标】口述录音机〔可录下讲话然后播出给人听或供人打印出来〕

dic·tate¹ /ˋdɪktet; dɪkˈteɪt/ *v* **1** [I,T] to say words for someone else to write down 口授, 让〔某人〕听写: **dictate sth to sb** *She's dictating a letter to her secretary right now.* 她现在正在给秘书口述一封信。**2** [I,T] to tell someone exactly what they must do or how they must behave 命令, 强制规定, 指定: [+to] *I refuse to be dictated to by some mindless bureaucrat!* 我拒绝听从一些毫无头脑的官僚的指使! | **dictate who/what/how etc** *Can they dictate how the money will be spent?* 他们能强行规定如何花这些钱吗? | **as dictated by** (=according to what someone said) 如〔某人〕所指定的那样 *Federal funds have to be used as dictated by Washington.* 联邦款项得按照华盛顿规定的方法使用。| **dictate that** *The custom dictates that men should be clean-shaven.* 这儿的习俗规定男士必须把胡子刮干净。**3** [T] to control or influence something; DETERMINE (2) 支配; 影响; 决定: *Funds dictate what we can do.* 资金的多少决定我们能做些什么。

dic·tate² /ˋdɪktet; ˈdɪkteɪt/ *n* [C] *formal* an order, rule, or principle that you have to obey【正式】命令; 规定; 指示

dic·ta·tion /dɪkˋteʃən; dɪkˈteɪʃən/ *n* **1** [U] the act of saying words for someone to write down 口授, 口述, 听写: **take dictation** (=write down words that someone else is saying) 做听写 **2** [C] a piece of writing that a teacher reads out to test your ability to hear and write the words correctly 听写的文章〔老师读出来以测验学生听力和写字是否正确〕: *I hate doing French dictations.* 我讨厌做法文听写。

dic·ta·tor /ˋdɪktetɚ; dɪkˈteɪtə/ *n* [C] **1** a ruler who has complete power over a country, especially when their power has been gained by force〔尤指通过武力获取政权的〕独裁者: *the downfall of the hated dictator* 令人憎恨的独裁者的垮台 **2** someone who tells other people what they should do, in a way that seems unreasonable 霸道的人: *a real little dictator* 一个十足的小霸王

dic·ta·to·ri·al /ˌdɪktəˋtorɪəl; ˌdɪktəˈtɔːriəl◂/ *adj* **1** a dictatorial government or ruler has complete power over a country〔政府或统治者〕独裁的 **2** a dictatorial person tells other people what to do in an unreasonable way 专横的, 霸道的: *Professor Clement's dictatorial attitude* 克莱门特教授盛气凌人的态度 —**dictatorially** *adv*

dic·ta·tor·ship /dɪkˋtetɚˌʃɪp; dɪkˈteɪtəʃɪp/ *n* **1** [C,U] government by a ruler who has complete power 独裁政府, 独裁制度, 专政 **2** [C] a country that is ruled by one person who has complete power 独裁国家

dic·tion /ˋdɪkʃən; ˈdɪkʃən/ *n* [U] **1** the way in which someone pronounces words 发音法: *Actors have training in diction.* 演员接受发音法训练。**2** the choice and use of words and phrases to express meaning, especially in literature or poetry〔尤指文学或诗歌中的〕措辞, 遣词用字

dic·tion·a·ry /ˋdɪkʃənˌɛrɪ; ˈdɪkʃənəri/ *n* [C] **1** a book that gives a list of words in alphabetical order and explains their meanings in the same or another language 词典, 字典: *a German-English dictionary* 一本德英词典 **2** a book like this that deals with the words and phrases used in a particular subject 专业词典: *a science dictionary* 科学词典

Dictionary of Na·tion·al Bi·og·ra·phy, The also 又作 **the DNB** a book produced in the UK which contains short accounts of the lives of important people in British history and society, arranged in alphabetical order《英国名人词典》〔英国出版的一部词典, 简要介绍英国的历史和社会名人, 按字母顺序编排〕

dic·tum /ˋdɪktəm; ˈdɪktəm/ *n plural* **dicta** /-tə; -tə/ *or* **dictums** [C] **1** a formal statement of opinion by someone who is respected or has authority〔由受人尊敬的、有权威的人士正式发表的〕意见, 宣言 **2** a short phrase that expresses a general rule or truth 名言, 格言: *He followed the age-old dictum of 'age before beauty'.* 他遵循着"老人优先"这句古老的箴言。

did /dɪd; dɪd/ the past tense of DO¹

di·dac·tic /daɪˋdæktɪk; daɪˈdæktɪk/ *adj formal*【正式】**1** speech or writing that is didactic is intended to teach people a moral lesson 说教的: *His novel has a didactic tone.* 他的小说有一种道德说教的语气。**2** someone who is didactic is too eager to teach people things or give instructions 好说教的, 喜欢教训人的 —**didactically** /-klɪ; -kli/ *adv*

did·dle /ˋdɪdl̩; ˈdɪdl/ *v* [T] **diddle sb (out of sth)** *informal* to get money from someone by deceiving them【非正式】从某人处骗得(某物): *They'll diddle you out of your last penny if you give them the chance.* 如果你给他们机会, 他们会把你的钱骗得一分不剩。

did·dly /ˋdɪdlɪ; ˈdɪdli/ also 又作 **diddly-squat** /ˈ‥ ‧/ *n* **not know/mean diddly** *AmE informal* to know or mean nothing at all【美, 非正式】一无所知/毫无意义: *Brad? He doesn't know diddly about baseball.* 布拉德? 他对棒球一无所知。

did·dums /ˋdɪdəmz; ˈdɪdəmz/ *interjection BrE* a word used to someone who is upset or annoyed in a way you think seems childish【英】〔用于说某人孩子气地发火、无理取闹的感叹词〕

did·ge·ri·doo /ˌdɪdʒərɪˋdu; ˌdɪdʒəriˈduː/ *n* [C] a long wooden musical instrument, played especially in Australia 狄洁里都号角〔尤指在澳大利亚演奏用的一种长形木管乐器〕

did·n't /ˋdɪdn̩t; ˈdɪdnt/ the short form of 缩略式= 'did not': *You saw him, didn't you?* 你看到他了, 不是吗?

Di·do /ˋdaɪdo; ˈdaɪdəʊ/ in ancient Roman stories, the queen of Carthage who loved Aeneas, and who killed herself when he left her 狄多〔古罗马传说中的迦太基女王。她爱上了埃涅阿斯, 遭抛弃后自杀〕—see also 另见 AENEID

didst /dɪdst; dɪdst/ **thou didst** *old use*【旧】= you did

die¹ /daɪ; daɪ/ *v past tense and past participle* **died** *present participle* **dying** [I] 

1 ►BECOME DEAD 死◄ to stop living and become dead 死去, 死亡: *He was very sick and we knew he might die.* 他病得很重, 我们知道他或许会死。| **of/from** *The animals died of starvation in the snow.* 这些动物在雪中饿死了。| *My grandfather died from a heart attack.* 我爷爷死于心脏病发作。| [+for] *Do*

you believe in anything enough to die for it? 有没有什么东西让你相信到能够为它献出生命的地步？| **die happy/poor/young etc** *He died young, at the age of 27.* 他英年早逝，年仅27岁。| **die a hero/martyr/rich man etc** *Van Gogh died a broken man.* 梵高死时穷困潦倒。| **die a natural/horrible etc death** (=die in a particular way) 自然死亡/死得很惨等 | **to your dying day** (=until you die) 直到你死的那一天 | **die by your own hand** *literary* (=kill yourself)【文】自杀 | **die in your sleep** *She died peacefully in her sleep at the age of 98.* 她在睡眠中安然辞世，享年98岁。

2 ►DISAPPEAR 消失◄ to disappear or stop existing 消失，不复存在：*Our love will never die.* 我们的爱始终不渝。| **die with sb** (=disappear or be finished when someone dies) 随某人一起消失 *The family name will die with him.* 他去世的时候，家族的姓氏也随之消失。

3 ►MACHINES 机器◄ *informal* to stop working【非正式】停止运转：*The car's engine spluttered and died.* 汽车的发动机发出噼啪声，随后就熄火了。| **die on sb** (=stop working while they are using it) 某人正在使用时突然坏了 *The mower just died on me.* 我正除着草，忽然割草机坏了。

4 be dying for *spoken* to want something very much【口】极想要，渴望〔某物〕：*I'm dying for a cup of coffee.* 我真想喝一杯咖啡。

5 be dying to do sth *spoken* to want to do something very much, so that it is difficult to wait【口】迫不及待地想做某事，渴望做某事：*We're dying to get started.* 我们迫不及待地想开始。

6 be dying of hunger/thirst *spoken* to be very hungry or thirsty【口】都要饿死了/渴死了

7 I nearly died/I could have died *spoken* used to say that you felt very surprised or embarrassed【口】我太惊讶了；我尴尬极了：*I nearly died when my ex-husband walked into the room!* 我的前夫走进屋里的时候，我尴尬极了！

8 I'd rather die *spoken* used to say very strongly that you do not want to do something【口】我宁愿死〔用来强烈表示某人不想做某事〕：*I'd rather die than work for him!* 我宁愿死也不为他工作！

9 old habits die hard used to say that it takes a long time to change to a new way of doing something 积习难改

10 never say die *spoken* used to encourage someone to continue doing something that is difficult【口】永不言败，别放弃〔用于鼓励某人继续做困难的事〕

11 die laughing *spoken* to laugh a lot【口】笑死了：*I nearly died laughing when I saw him with that ridiculous haircut.* 看到他那滑稽的发型，我都要笑死了。

12 die the death *informal* to gradually fail or be destroyed【非正式】慢慢消亡，寿终正寝：*Eventually the photography club died the death.* 终于，这家摄影俱乐部无疾而终了。

13 dying breath/wish someone's very last breath or wish before they die 最后一口气/一个愿望：*No matter what you think, say nothing about it to your dying breath.* 不管你是怎么想的，至死都要守口如瓶。

14 die on the vine *literary* to fail, especially at an early stage, because of a lack of support【文】〔由于缺少支持而〕夭折

15 sth to die for something that is so nice or attractive that you would do anything to have it 特别想得到的东西：*cream cakes to die for* 特别想要的奶油蛋糕

die away *phr v* [I] if sound, wind, or light dies away, it becomes gradually weaker and finally stops〔声音、风、光等〕慢慢变弱，渐渐消失：*The strange noise died away and an absolute silence closed in upon us.* 那种奇怪的声音慢慢消失了，我们渐渐被一片寂静所笼罩。

die back *phr v* [I] if a plant dies back, it dies above the ground but remains alive at its roots〔植物〕顶死，回枯，假死〔地面以上部分枯萎，根部却仍活着〕

die down *phr v* [I] if something dies down, it becomes less strong, active, or violent 减弱，平息：*Don't worry, the gossip will soon die down.* 别担心，流言飞语不久就会消失的。

die off *phr v* [I] if a group of people, animals etc die off, they die one by one until there are no more of them 相继死去，死亡殆尽

die out *phr v* [I] to disappear or stop existing completely 灭绝，绝迹：*Smallpox has completely died out in this country.* 天花在这个国家已经绝迹了。

die² *n* [C] **1** a metal block used to press or cut something into a particular shape 金属模具，铸模，压模 **2** a DICE¹ (1) 骰子 **3 the die is cast** used to say that a decision has been taken and cannot now be changed 木已成舟，事情已成定局

die cast·ing /ˈ· ,··/ *n* [U] the process of making metal objects by forcing liquid metal into a hollow container with a particular shape, and then allowing it to become hard 压铸〔将液态金属注入特定形状的空心容器使其成形〕

die·hard /ˈdaɪ,hɑrd; ˈdaɪhɑːd/ *n* [C] someone who opposes change and refuses to accept new ideas 顽固分子，死硬派〔反对变化、拒绝新观点的人〕—see also 另见 **old habits die hard** (DIE¹ (9)) —**diehard** *adj*: *a diehard bigot* 老顽固

Di·eppe /dɪˋɛp; diˈep/ a port in northern France, on the English Channel. Boats regularly carry people and cars between Dieppe and the English port of Newhaven. 迪耶普〔法国北部一港口，濒临英吉利海峡。经常有渡轮往返于迪耶普和英国的纽黑文之间，载运乘客和车辆〕

di·e·re·sis /daɪˋɛrəsɪs; daɪˈɪərɪ̧sɪ̧s/ *n plural* **diereses** /-siz; -siːz/ [C] another spelling of DIAERESIS diaeresis 的另一种拼法

die·sel /ˈdizl̩; ˈdiːzəl/ *n* **1** [U] a type of heavy oil used instead of petrol in diesel engines 柴油 **2** [C] *informal especially AmE* a vehicle that uses diesel【非正式，尤美】内燃机车；柴油车；柴油船

diesel en·gine /ˈ·· ,··/ *n* [C] an engine that burns diesel instead of petrol used especially for buses, trains, and goods vehicles 柴油机，内燃机

diesel fu·el /ˈ·· ,··/ also 又作 **diesel oil** /ˈ·· ·/ *n* [U] DIESEL (1) 柴油

di·et¹ /ˈdaɪət; ˈdaɪət/ *n*

1 ►KIND OF FOOD 食物种类◄ [C,U] the kind of food that someone eats each day 日常饮食：*It is important to have a balanced, healthy diet.* 均衡、健康的日常饮食很重要。| *a vegetarian diet* 素食食谱 | [+of] *They exist on a diet of fish.* 他们以吃鱼为生。

> **CULTURAL NOTE 文化注释**
>
> **A healthy diet** In recent years, people in the US and UK have become more concerned about the food they eat and the effect it has on their health. People are worried about ADDITIVES (=added chemicals) in food, and many people have reduced the amount of salt, fat, and sugar that they eat in order to lose weight, lower their CHOLESTEROL levels, and reduce their risk of getting HEART DISEASE. 健康饮食：近些年，英美人越来越关注食物及其对健康的影响。人们担心食品添加剂的危害，很多人减少盐、脂肪和糖的摄入以便减肥、降低胆固醇、减少患心脏病的危险。—see Cultural Notes at HEALTHY and OBESE 见 HEALTHY 和 OBESE 文化注释

2 ►TO GET THIN 减肥◄ [C] a limited range and amount of food that you eat when you want to get thinner 节食：**go/be on a diet** *Lyn always seems to be on a diet.* 林恩似乎总是在节食。

> **CULTURAL NOTE 文化注释**
>
> **Going on a diet** Many people, especially women, regularly go on a diet (=have a period of time when they eat less than usual in order to become thinner) because they think they will look more attractive if they are thinner. They pay companies such as Weight Watchers to help them develop their own diet programmes and to give them support while they are losing weight. Most women's magazines include diet plans, and every year new books are published that contain the latest diets. 节食：很多人，尤其是女人，定期节食，因为他们认为瘦一些会让自己更好看。他们付钱给减肥顾问等公司，以帮助自己完成节食计划，并在减肥时提供帮助。大多数女性杂志都刊登节食计划，每年都有关于最新节食动向的新书出版。

3 ►FOR HEALTH 为了健康◄ [C] a limited type of food and drink that someone is allowed because they have a health problem〔基于健康考虑的〕饮食限制，规定饮食：*a salt-free diet* 无盐饮食

4 a diet of too much of an activity that you think is boring or has bad effects 多得令人生厌的：*Kids today are raised on a constant diet of pop music and television.* 今天的孩子在成长过程中不断地被灌输过多的流行音乐和电视。

5 ►MEETING 会议◄ [C] *old use* an official meeting to discuss political or church matters【旧】〔讨论政治或宗教问题的〕正式会议

diet² *v* [I] to limit the amount and type of food that you eat in order to become thinner〔为减肥而〕节食，限食，按规定进食

di·e·ta·ry /ˈdaɪə,tɛrɪ; ˈdaɪətəri/ *adj* related to someone's diet 与（规定）饮食有关的：*special dietary requirements* 特殊的饮食要求

di·e·tet·ics /ˌdaɪəˋtɛtɪks; ˌdaɪəˈtetɪks/ *n* [U] the science that is concerned with what people eat and drink and how this affects their health 饮食学，营养学

di·e·ti·cian, dietitian /ˌdaɪəˋtɪʃən; ˌdaɪəˈtɪʃən/ *n* [C] someone who is specially trained in dietetics 饮食学家，营养学家

Die·trich /ˋdɪtrɪk; ˈdiːtrɪk/, **Marle·ne** /mɑrˋlenə; mɑːˈleɪnə/ (1901-92) a German actress who became a famous film actress in the US. She was famous for being sexually attractive, and for singing in a deep, sexy voice. Her films include *The Blue Angel* (1930) and *Destry Rides Again* (1939). 黛德丽〔(1901-1992)，德国女演员，后来成为美国著名影星。她以外表性感、歌声深沉诱人闻名，演过的影片包括《蓝天使》(1930)和《碧血烟花》(1939)〕

Dieu et mon droit /ˌdju e mɑn ˋdrwɑ; ˌdjɜː eɪ mɒn ˈdrwɑː/ a French phrase meaning God and my right, which is the MOTTO on the British royal family's coat of arms 天有上帝，我有权利〔英国王室盾形纹章上的法语箴言〕

W3 **dif·fer** /ˋdɪfɚ; ˈdɪfə/ *v* **1** [I] to be different from something in quality, features etc〔在质量、特征等上〕不同于，不一样，有区别: **[+from]** *Humans differ from other mammals in their ability to speak.* 人和其他哺乳动物之不同在于人能说话。| **differ widely/greatly** *Opinions on the subject differ widely.* 在这个问题上意见分歧很大。**2** [I] if two people or groups differ about something, they have opposite opinions 有异议，〔意见〕有分歧: **[+about/on/over]** *The two lawyers differed about how to present the case.* 两个律师在如何为该案件辩护方面意见不同。**3 agree to differ** to stop arguing with someone and accept that you will never agree 承认意见分歧，保留不同意见 **4 I beg to differ** *spoken formal* used to say that you disagree with someone【口，正式】恕我不能同意，恕我不能赞同

S1 W1 **dif·fe·rence** /ˋdɪfərəns; ˈdɪfərəns/ *n* **1** [C] something that makes one thing or person different from another thing or person 差异，不同之处: **[+between]** *It's hard to see many differences between the centrist political parties.* 在各中央集权政党之间很难看出有多少差别。**2** [singular,U] the fact of being different, or an amount by which one thing is different from another 不同，差别；差额: **difference in age/size etc** *There's not much difference in price.* 价格上没有太大的区别。| **tell the difference** (=recognize that two similar things are different) 辨认出两个相似事物之间的区别 *The twins are so alike, it's difficult to tell the difference.* 这对双胞胎长得太像了，很难分出谁是谁。| **a world of difference** (=a big difference) 天壤之别 *There's a world of difference between going abroad on holiday and going there to live.* 出国旅游和到国外生活有着天壤之别。**3 your/their etc differences** the disagreements that people have 你们/他们等之间的分歧: **have your differences** *We've had our differences in the past, but we get on OK now.* 过去我们有过分歧，但是现在我们相处得不错。| **settle your differences** (=agree not to argue any more) 消除分歧 **4 difference of opinion** a slight disagreement 意见稍有不一致: *The two sides have a difference of opinion over aims and methods.* 双方在目的和方法上有些意见不一致。**5 make a (big) difference/make all the difference** to have an important effect on a thing or a situation 有(很大)影响/使大不相同: *Having a good teacher has made all the difference for Alex.* 亚历克斯有个好老师后情况完全不一样了。**6 make no difference a)** to have no effect at all on something〔对某事〕根本没有影响: *Even if you'd tried to help, it wouldn't have made the slightest difference.* 即使你设法帮忙，结果也不会有丝毫不同。**b)** to be unimportant to someone〔对某人〕不重要，无所谓: *It doesn't make any difference to me whether you go or stay.* 你是去是留对我都无所谓。**7 with a difference** used to express approval about something that is different and better 与众不同: *That was a meal with a difference!* 那顿饭就是不一样啊！—see also 另见 **split the difference** (SPLIT[1] (8))

S1 W1 **dif·fe·rent** /ˋdɪfərənt; ˈdɪfərənt/ *adj* **1** not like something or someone else, or not like before 不同的，不一样的: *You look different. Have you had your hair cut?* 你样子变了。你剪发了吗？| **[+from]** *Our two sons are very different from each other.* 我们的两个儿子彼此间一点也不像。| **[+to]** *Her jacket's a bit different to mine.* 她的上衣和我的有点不一样。| **[+than]** (*AmE* 美) *The estimate is different than we expected.* 这个估价和我们预期的有所不同。**2** [only before noun 仅用于名词前] separate; DISTINCT 分别的，各不相同的: *He took the photo from three different angles.* 他从三个不同的角度拍照。| *There are many different types of fabric.* 有许多不同种类的布料。**3** [only before noun 仅用于名词前] another 另外的: *I think she's moved to a different job now.* 我想她现在已经改做另一份工作去了。| **[+from]** *This is a different girl from the one he used to go out with.* 这个女孩不是他以前约会的那个。**4** various; several 各种不同的，几种的: *There are several different books on the subject.* 有好几本书都是关于那个主题的。**5** *spoken* unusual, often in a way that you do not like【口】与众不同的〔常指不是自己喜欢的那种类型〕: *His new jacket is certainly different, but I can't imagine wearing it myself!* 他的新夹克的确很特别，但是我自己是无论如何也不会穿那样的衣服的！—**differently** *adv*: *The two words sound the same but they're spelled differently.* 这两个词听起来一样，但是拼写却不同。

> **USAGE NOTE 用法说明: DIFFERENT**
> GRAMMAR 语法
> Teachers often prefer **different(ly) from**, but **different(ly) to** is equally common in spoken British English (though not usual in American English). **Different(ly) than** is also used, especially in American English. Note that you never say **different of**. 老师通常喜欢用 different(ly) from，但是在英国英语口语中 different(ly) to 也同样常用(尽管在美语中并不常用)。different(ly) than 也很常用，尤其是在美语中。注意：绝对不能说 different of。
> SPELLING 拼写
> The noun is **difference**. 名词是 difference: *the difference between your country and mine* (NOT 不用 *the different*) 你我两国之间的区别

dif·fe·ren·tial[1] /ˌdɪfəˋrɛnʃəl; ˌdɪfəˈrenʃəl◂/ *n* [C] **1** an amount or degree of difference between things, especially difference in the wages of people doing different types of jobs in the same industry or profession〔尤指同行业不同工作之间的〕工资差额，差别: *pay differentials* 工资差额 **2** a differential gear 差速器，差动齿轮

differential[2] *adj* based on or depending on a difference 基于差别的，依差别而定的: *differential rates of pay for skilled and unskilled workers* 熟练工人和非熟练工人间不同的工资额

differential cal·cu·lus /ˌ····ˈ···/ *n* [U] *technical* a way of measuring the speed at which an object is moving at a particular moment【术语】微分学

differential gear /ˌ····ˈ·/ *n* [C] an arrangement of gears (GEAR[1] (1)) that allows one back wheel of a car to turn faster than the other when the car goes around a corner〔车辆转弯时使车的一个后轮转动得比另一个后轮快的〕差速器，差动齿轮

dif·fe·ren·ti·ate /ˌdɪfəˋrɛnʃɪet; ˌdɪfəˈrenʃieɪt/ *v* **1** [I,T] to recognize or express the difference between things or people 辨别，区别: **[+between]** *The reviews don't even differentiate between good books and bad books.* 这些评论文章甚至连好书和坏书都不加区分。| **differentiate sb/sth from** *It's sometimes hard to differentiate one sample from another.* 有时候很难把一个样品和另一个样品区分开来。**2** [T] to be the quality, condition etc that shows the difference between things or people〔特征或条件等〕构成…间的差别，使有不同: **differentiate sth/sb from** *Its unusual nesting habits differentiate this bird from others.* 这种鸟独特的筑巢习惯使它不同于其他的鸟。| **differentiate sth** *What differentiates these two periods of history?* 是什么使这两段历史时期有所不同？**3** [I] to behave differently towards someone or something, especially in an unfair way; DISCRIMINATE (2) 区别对待〔尤指不公平对待〕: **[+between]** *He shouldn't differentiate between the quiet and the talkative children.* 他不应该区别对待安静的孩子和爱讲话的孩子。—**differentiation** /ˌdɪfəˌrɛnʃɪˋeʃən; ˌdɪfərenʃiˈeɪʃən/ *n* [U]: *socio-economic differentiation* 社会经济的区分

dif·fi·cult /ˋdɪfəˌkʌlt; ˈdɪfɪkəlt/ *adj* **1** very hard to do, understand, or deal with; not easy 困难的；不易的: *Was the exam very difficult?* 考试很难吗？| *a difficult job* 一份艰难的工作 | **difficult to do** *She finds it difficult to climb stairs.* 她觉得爬楼梯很费劲。**2** someone who is difficult never seems pleased or satisfied 难以取悦的；不易相处的；不易满足的: *Don't be so difficult!* 别这么难缠！**3** involving a lot of problems and causing a lot of trouble or worry 有困难的，有问题的，有麻烦的: *Things are a bit difficult at home at the moment.* 目前家里遇到了些麻烦。| **make life difficult for sb** (=cause problems for someone) 让某人不好过；给某人制造麻烦 *They've done everything in their power to make life difficult for me.* 他们用尽一切办法来让我的日子不好过。 S1 W1

dif·fi·cul·ty /ˋdɪfəˌkʌltɪ; ˈdɪfɪkəlti/ *n* **1** [U] the state of being hard to do, understand or deal with 困难，艰难: **have difficulty doing sth** *We have enough difficulty paying the rent as it is!* 目前我们连付租金都很困难！| **with difficulty** *With difficulty, we hauled it up the stairs.* 我们费力地把它拖上了楼梯。| **be in difficulty** (=be having problems) 有困难 *The business is in finan-* S1 W1

cial difficulty. 这家公司陷入了财务困境。| **get/run into difficulty** (=get into a difficult situation) 陷入困境 *I had to sell my sewing machine when we got into difficulty with an electric bill.* 我们付不起电费时, 我不得不把缝纫机卖掉。**2** [C] a problem or something that causes trouble 难题, 难事: *If you have any difficulties, give me a shout.* 如果你有什么困难就喊我一声。**3** [U] how difficult something is〔某事的〕难度: *The tests vary in difficulty.* 考试的难易程度有所不同。

dif·fi·dent /ˋdɪfədənt; ˈdɪfɟdənt/ *adj* shy and unwilling to make people notice you or talk about you 胆怯的, 羞怯的: *He suddenly felt diffident in the presence of these people.* 在这些人面前他忽然感到胆怯。| [+about] *She was diffident about her prize.* 她对自己获得奖项还不大好意思。—**diffidently** *adv* —**diffidence** *n* [U]

dif·fract /dɪˋfrækt; dɪˈfrækt/ *v* [T] *technical* to divide light into coloured bands or into light and dark bands【术语】使〔光〕衍射, 绕射〔将光分解成有色光带或明暗有别的光带〕—**diffraction** /dɪˋfrækʃən; dɪˈfrækʃən/ *n* [U]

diffuse 扩散

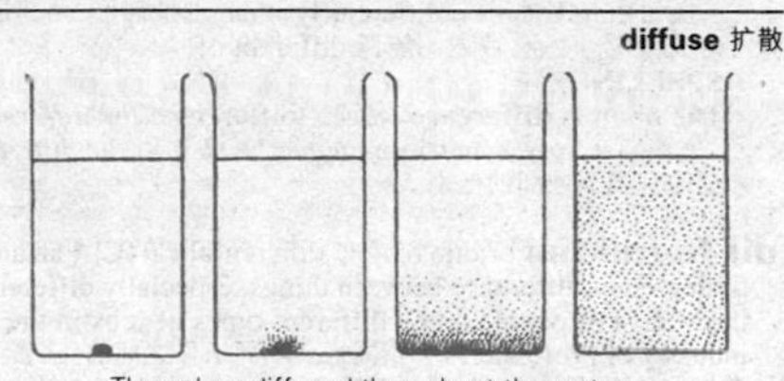

The colour diffused throughout the water.
颜料在水中扩散开来。

dif·fuse¹ /dɪˋfjuz; dɪˈfjuːz/ *v* [I,T] *formal*【正式】**1** to make heat, a gas etc spread so that it mixes with the surrounding air or water (使)〔热量、气体等〕扩散, (使)弥漫: *The kitchen stove diffused its warmth all over the house.* 厨房的炉子把热气扩散到房子的每个角落。**2** to spread ideas, information etc among a lot of people 传播, 散布〔观点、信息等〕: *Their ideas diffused quickly across Europe.* 他们的观点很快在欧洲传播开来。—**diffusion** /dɪˋfjuʒən; dɪˈfjuːʒən/ *n* [U]

dif·fuse² /dɪˋfjus; dɪˈfjuːs/ *adj* **1** scattered over a large area 散开的, 分散的: *The organization is large and diffuse.* 这个组织规模庞大且分布各地。**2** using a lot of words and not explaining things clearly and directly 堆砌辞藻的; 啰唆的: *His writing is diffuse and difficult to understand.* 他写的东西行文冗赘, 晦涩难懂。—**diffusely** *adv* —**diffuseness** *n* [U]

3 **dig¹** /dɪg; dɪg/ *v past tense and past participle* **dug** /dʌg; dʌg/ *present participle* **digging** **1** [I,T] to move earth or make a hole in it using a SPADE or your hands 挖(土); 掘(洞): *They escaped by digging an underground tunnel.* 他们挖个地道逃走了。| **dig for sth** (=dig in order to find something) 挖寻某物 *They're digging for treasure.* 他们在挖掘宝藏。**2** [T] to remove vegetables from under the earth using a SPADE 挖〔菜〕: *She's digging potatoes at the moment.* 这时候她正在挖马铃薯。**3** [T] *old-fashioned* to like something【过时】喜欢: *I really dig that dress!* 我真喜欢那件衣服! **4 dig your own grave** to do something that will cause serious problems for you in the future 自掘坟墓, 自取灭亡, 自讨苦吃 **5 dig sb in the ribs** to touch someone with your elbow, especially because you want them to notice something amusing 用肘碰某人的肋部〔让某人注意好笑的事〕

dig in *phr v* **1** [T **dig** sth ↔ **in**] to mix something into soil by digging 翻地把〔某物〕掺入土壤里: *I need to dig some manure in before I plant the potatoes.* 在种马铃薯之前我需要翻土埋进肥料。**2 dig your heels in** to refuse to do something in spite of other people's efforts to persuade you〔尽管别人苦苦相劝〕坚决不做〔某事〕, 固执己见 **3** [I] *informal* to start eating food that is in front of you【非正式】开始吃: *Dig in! There's plenty for everyone!* 尽量吃吧! 足够大家吃的! **4** [I,T] if soldiers dig in or dig themselves in, they make a protected place for themselves by digging〔士兵〕挖壕沟等掩体以隐蔽(自己)

dig into *phr v* **1** [T **dig** sth **into** sth] to mix something into soil by digging 翻土把〔某物〕混在土壤中: *Dig some fertilizer into the soil first.* 首先在翻地时把一些肥料掺到土壤里。**2** [I,T **dig** sth **into** sth] to push hard into something, or to make something do this (使)推入, (使)戳进: *Her nails were digging into his arm.* 她的指甲正往他的胳膊里抠。**3** [T **dig into** sth] to start using a supply of something, especially money 开始使用〔储备的东西, 尤指钱〕: *I'm going to have to dig into my savings again.* 我又得动用我的存款了。

dig sth ↔ **out** *phr v* [T] **1** to get something out of a place, using a SPADE or your hands 把〔某物〕挖出来: *We had to dig the car out of a snow drift.* 我们得把汽车从雪堆里挖出来。**2** to find something you have not seen for a long time, or that is not easy to find 找到, 翻出〔很久没看到的或很难找到的东西〕: *I must remember to dig out that book for you.* 我必须记着把那本书给你找出来。

dig sth ↔ **up** *phr v* [T] **1** to remove something from under the earth using a SPADE〔从地里〕挖出, 掘起: *I'll dig up that plant and move it.* 我要把那棵植物挖出来, 把它挪个地方。**2** to find hidden or forgotten information by careful searching〔通过仔细搜索、查询〕找出, 揭露: *They tried to dig up something from his past to spoil his chances of being elected.* 他们试图从他的过去挖出些东西来破坏他当选的机会。

dig² *n* **1 give sb a dig** to push someone quickly and lightly with your finger or elbow〔用手指或肘部〕触某人, 碰某人, 戳某人: *John's falling asleep – give him a dig will you?* 约翰要睡着了, 捅他一下好吗? **2** [C] a joke or remark that you make to annoy or criticize someone 挖苦, 嘲讽: [+at] *I thought that last comment was a dig at the boss.* 我认为最后那句话是在挖苦老板。**3** [C] the process of digging in an ancient place in order to find objects for study〔为找到可供研究的东西在遗址上〕发掘: *an archaeological dig* 考古发掘 **4 digs** [plural] *BrE old-fashioned* a room that you pay rent to live in【英, 过时】租住的房间

di·gest¹ /daɪˋdʒɛst; daɪˈdʒest/ *v* [T] **1** to change food that you have just eaten into substances that your body can use 消化〔食物〕: *Most babies can digest a wide range of food easily.* 大多数婴儿能容易地消化多种食物。—compare 比较 INGEST **2** to understand new information, especially when there is a lot of it or it is difficult to understand 理解, 领悟, 消化〔尤指大量新信息或难以理解的信息〕: *I struggled to digest the news.* 我费力地琢磨着那条新闻的意思。

di·gest² /ˋdaɪdʒɛst; ˈdaɪdʒest/ *n* [C] a short piece of writing that gives the most important facts from a book, report etc 摘要, 概要, 文摘

di·gest·i·ble /daɪˋdʒɛstəbl; daɪˈdʒestɟbəl/ *adj* food that is digestible can be easily digested 容易消化的, 易吸收的 —opposite 反义词 INDIGESTIBLE

di·ges·tion /dəˋdʒɛstʃən; daɪˈdʒestʃən/ *n* **1** [U] the process of digesting food 消化 **2** [C] your ability to digest food easily 消化能力: **a good/poor etc digestion** *I've always had a poor digestion.* 我一直消化不好。

di·ges·tive /daɪˋdʒɛstɪv; daɪˈdʒestɪv/ *adj* [only before noun 仅用于名词前] connected with the process of digestion 消化的: *the digestive system* 消化系统

digestive bis·cuit /.ˌ.. ˈ../ *n* [C] a type of plain, slightly sweet BISCUIT (1) that is popular in Britain 消化饼干〔一种在英国很受欢迎的、味道微甜的饼干〕

digestive system 消化系统

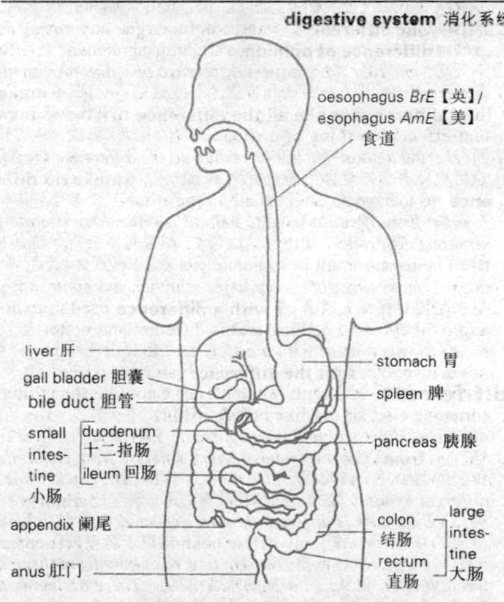

the human digestive system 人的消化系统

digestive sys·tem /.ˈ.. ˌ../ *n* [C] the system of organs in which your body digests (DIGEST¹ (1)) food 消化系统

dig·ger /ˋdɪgɚ; ˈdɪgə/ *n* [C] a large machine that digs and moves earth 挖掘机

dig·gings /ˋdɪgɪŋz; ˈdɪgɪŋz/ *n* [plural] a place where people are digging for metal, especially gold〔尤指开采黄金的〕矿区，矿场

di·git /ˋdɪdʒɪt; ˈdɪdʒ ̜ t/ *n* [C] **1** one of the written signs that represent the numbers 0 to 9〔0到9的任何一个〕数字: **three-digit/four-digit etc number** *4305 is a four-digit number.* 4305是个四位数。**2** *technical* a finger or toe【术语】手指；脚趾

di·gi·tal /ˋdɪdʒətḷ; ˈdɪdʒ ̜ tl/ *adj* **1** using a system in which information is represented in the form of changing electrical signals 数字的，数码的: **digital cassette/compact disc/audio-tape etc** *recorded on digital audiotape* 在数码录音磁带上录音的 **2** giving information in the form of numbers 数字显示的: *a digital watch* 数字显示式电子手表 **3** *formal* of the fingers and toes【正式】手指的；脚趾的

digital com·put·er /ˌ‥ ‥ˋ‥/ *n* [C] a type of computer that uses a BINARY (1) system〔使用二进制系统的〕数字计算机；数位电脑

digital re·cord·ing /ˌ‥ ‥ˋ‥/ *n* [C,U] a high quality recording of sound made by changing information about the sound into the binary system (BINARY (1)) 数码录音〔把音频信息转化成二进制系统的高质量录音方式〕

di·gi·tize also 又作 **-ise** *BrE*【英】/ˋdɪdʒəˌtaɪz; ˈdɪdʒ ̜ taɪz/ *v* [T] to put information into a digital form 把〔信息〕转变成数字形式，使〔信息〕数字化

dig·ni·fied /ˋdɪgnəˌfaɪd; ˈdɪgn ̜ faɪd/ *adj* behaving in a calm and serious way, even in a difficult situation, which makes people respect you〔举止〕庄重的，有尊严的: *a dignified old lady* 颇有威严的老太太 | *She made a dignified departure.* 她不失尊严地离去。

dig·ni·fy /ˋdɪgnəˌfaɪ; ˈdɪgn ̜ faɪ/ *v* [T] to make something or someone seem better or more important than they really are by using a particular word to describe them 使显贵；使有尊严；抬高…的身价: **dignify sb/sth with** *I cannot dignify him with the name 'physician'.* 我不能用"医师"这个称呼来高抬他。

dig·ni·ta·ry /ˋdɪgnəˌtɛrɪ; ˈdɪgn ̜ təri/ *n* [C] someone who has an important official position 显要人物，权贵: *Flowers were presented to visiting dignitaries.* 向到访的达官贵人献上了鲜花。

dig·ni·ty /ˋdɪgnətɪ; ˈdɪgn ̜ ti/ *n* **1** [U] the ability to behave in a way that shows you respect yourself and stay calm, even in a very difficult situation 庄重，尊贵，尊严，体面: *The family faced their ordeal with dignity and courage.* 这一家人以尊严和勇气面对磨难。| **human dignity** *Even in the prison camp we tried to retain some human dignity.* 即使在战俘营里我们也尽力保留一些做人的尊严。**2** [U] a calm and serious manner or quality 庄严，端庄: *The dignity of the occasion was spoilt when she fell down the steps.* 她从台阶上摔下来，破坏了这个场合的庄严气氛。**3 be beneath your dignity** if something is beneath your dignity, you think you are too good or important to do it 有失身份，有失体面: *Such arguing was beneath her dignity.* 这样的争吵有失她的身份。**4 stand on your dignity** to demand to be treated with proper respect 要求受到礼遇；摆架子: *He stood on his dignity, insisting that the car be brought to the door.* 他摆起架子，坚持让人把车开到门口。**5** [C] a high social position, rank, or title 高位，显职

di·graph /ˋdaɪgræf; ˈdaɪgrɑːf/ *n* [C] *technical* a pair of letters that represent one sound, such as 'ea' in 'head' and 'ph' in 'phrase'【术语】〔代表一个音的〕二合字母，单音双字母〈如head中的ea，phrase中的ph〉

di·gress /daɪˋgrɛs; daɪˈgres/ *v* [I] *formal* to move away from the main subject that you are talking or writing about【正式】〔说话或写作时〕偏离主题，转移话题: *Do you mind if I digress for a moment?* 我说些题外话，你不介意吧？—**digression** /daɪˋgrɛʃən; daɪˈgreʃən/ *n* [C,U]: *After several long digressions he finally reached the interesting part of the story.* 说了好几番长时间的题外话之后，他终于开始讲故事的有趣部分。

Di·jon /diˋʒɑn; ˈdiːʒɒn/ a city in eastern central France that is famous especially for producing MUSTARD 第戎〔法国中东部一城市，尤以出产芥末闻名〕

dike /daɪk; daɪk/ *n* [C] another spelling of DYKE dyke 的另一种拼法

dik·tat /dɪkˋtæt; dɪkˈtæt/ *n* [C,U] an order that is forced on people by a ruler or government〔统治者或政府强加在人民身上的〕强制命令，勒令: *government by diktat* 用专横手段统治〔人民〕的政府

di·lap·i·dat·ed /dəˋlæpəˌdetɪd; d ̜ ˈlæp ̜ deɪt ̜ d/ *adj* a dilapidated building, vehicle etc is old and in very bad condition〔建筑物、车辆等〕破烂不堪的

di·lap·i·da·tion /dəˌlæpəˋdeʃən; d ̜ ˌlæp ̜ ˈdeɪʃən/ *n* **1** [U] the state of an old building when it is in very bad condition and beginning to fall down 破旧；坍塌 **2 dilapidations** [plural] *BrE law* money that you have to pay if you damage a house that you are renting【英，法律】〔租用期间损坏房子而应支付的〕赔偿金

di·late /daɪˋlet; daɪˈleɪt/ *v* [I,T] if a part of your body dilates or if something dilates it, it becomes wider 扩张，张大，膨大: *dilated pupils* 扩大的瞳孔 —**dilation** /daɪˋleʃən; daɪˈleɪʃən/ *n* [U]: *pupil dilation during sexual arousal* 性兴奋时的瞳孔扩大

dilate on/upon sth *phr v* [T] *formal* to speak or write a lot about something【正式】详述某事，铺叙某事: *He dilated upon their piety and heroism.* 他详尽地叙述了他们的虔诚和英雄主义行为。

dil·a·to·ry /ˋdɪləˌtorɪ; ˈdɪlətəri/ *adj formal* slow and tending to delay decisions or actions【正式】拖延的，拖拉的，迟缓的: *dilatory attempts to reach an agreement* 试图拖延达成协议

Dil·bert /ˋdɪlbɚt; ˈdɪlbət/ a popular US CARTOON STRIP by Scott Adams, about a computer engineer called Dilbert who works in an office. Although he is kind, intelligent, and works hard, he is never very successful because his manager gives unreasonable orders and his company has many silly and annoying rules. Dilbert has an intelligent dog called **Dogbert**, who wears glasses and speaks, and who believes that people will only do things that give them an advantage.《呆伯特》〔斯科特·亚当斯创作的美国流行连环漫画，讲述在办公室工作的电脑工程师呆伯特的故事。他心地善良、聪明勤劳，但从未有所建树，因为公司经理的命令毫无道理，许多规章可笑而令人气恼。呆伯特有只戴眼镜、会说话的聪明小狗，叫做多格伯特，它认为人类只会做对自己有好处的事情〕

dil·do /ˋdɪldo; ˈdɪldəʊ/ *n* [C] an object shaped like a male sex organ that some women put inside their VAGINA for sexual pleasure 假阴茎〔一种性用具〕，人造男性生殖器

di·lem·ma /dəˋlɛmə; d ̜ ˈlemə/ *n* [C] a situation in which it is very difficult to decide what to do, because all the choices seem equally good or equally bad 进退两难的境地，困境: *a moral dilemma* 道德上进退两难的窘境 | **be in a dilemma** *I'm in a dilemma about this job offer.* 对于提供的这份工作我不知道是接受还是不接受。| **be on the horns of a dilemma** (=be unable to decide between two unpleasant choices) 左右为难

dil·et·tan·te /ˌdɪləˋtæntɪ; ˌdɪl ̜ ˈtænti/ *n* [C] someone who seems or pretends to be interested in a subject but is not seriously interested and does not know very much about it 半瓶醋的涉猎者，玩票式的爱好者，假行家，半吊子〔看似或假装对某个科目感兴趣，但实际上对此并非真正感兴趣或对此所知不多〕—**dilettante** *adj*

Dili /ˋdɪlɪ; ˈdɪli/ the capital of East Timor 帝力〔东帝汶首都〕

dil·i·gent /ˋdɪlədʒənt; ˈdɪl ̜ dʒənt/ *adj* someone who is diligent works hard and is careful and thorough 勤奋的，勤勉的: *Philip is a diligent worker and should do well in the examinations.* 菲利普是个勤奋的学生，他会考出好成绩的。—**diligently** *adv*: *They worked diligently all morning.* 他们整个上午工作都很勤奋。—**diligence** *n* [U]

dill /dɪl; dɪl/ *n* [U] a garden plant used to give a special taste to food 莳萝，小茴香〔用于给食物调味〕

Dil·lin·ger /ˋdɪlɪndʒɚ; ˈdɪlɪndʒə/, **John** (1903-34) a famous US robber and murderer. In 1933 and 1934 he and his GANG (=group of criminals) robbed many different banks in the US, using guns and killing many people. The FBI finally organized a trap and shot him as he was leaving a theatre. 迪林杰〔(1903-1934)，美国臭名昭著的抢劫犯和杀人犯。1933至1934年间，其团伙携带枪支抢劫了美国多家银行，并杀害了许多人。美国联邦调查局最后设置陷阱，在他离开一家剧院时将其击毙〕

dill pick·le /ˌ‥ ˋ‥/ *n* [C] a whole CUCUMBER which has been preserved in vinegar 酸黄瓜

dil·ly /ˋdɪlɪ; ˈdɪli/ *n* [C] *AmE old-fashioned* something or someone exciting or special【美，过时】惊人的人[物]；精彩的事物: *That's a dilly of a rollercoaster!* 过山车可真是惊险啊！

dilly-dal·ly /ˋ‥ ˌ‥/ *v* [I] *informal* to waste time, because you cannot decide about something【非正式】〔由于对某事犹豫不决而〕浪费时间，犹犹豫豫: *Don't dilly-dally, just get on with it!* 别磨磨蹭蹭的，继续做下去吧！

di·lute[1] /dɪˋlut; daɪˈluːt/ *v* [T] **1** to make a liquid weaker by adding water or another liquid 把〔液体〕稀释，使〔液体〕变淡: *Give the baby diluted fruit juice.* 给婴儿喝稀释的果汁。| **dilute sth with sth** *Dilute the paint with a little oil.* 用少量汽油把油漆稀释一下。**2** to make a quality, belief etc weaker or less effective 降低〔质量〕；削弱〔信念〕: *Opening NATO to new members may dilute its strength.* 把北大西洋公约组织向新成员国开放可能会削弱它的力量。—**dilution** /dɪˋluʃən; daɪˈluːʃən/ *n* [U]: *Any*

dilution of academic standards must be resisted. 任何降低学术水平的行为都必须加以抵制。

dilute² /dɪˋlut; daɪˈluːt◂/ *adj* a dilute liquid has been made weaker by the addition of water or another substance 稀释的, 冲淡的: *dilute hydrochloric acid* 稀释的盐酸

dim¹ /dɪm; dɪm/ *adj* **dimmer, dimmest**

1 ▶DARK 暗◀ fairly dark or not giving much light, so that you cannot see well 阴暗的, 昏暗的: *in the dim light of the early dawn* 在破晓的微曦下

2 ▶SHAPE 形状◀ a dim shape is one which is not easy to see because it is too far away, or there is not enough light 朦胧的, 隐约的: *The dim outline of a large building loomed up out of the mist.* 一座庞大建筑物朦胧的轮廓在雾霭中隐现出来。

3 ▶EYES 眼睛◀ *literary* dim eyes are weak and cannot see well【文】视力不好的, 弱视的: *The dim eyes of the old woman were surprisingly attractive.* 那位老太太蒙眬的双眼出奇地迷人。

4 dim recollection/awareness etc a memory or understanding of something that is not clear in your mind; VAGUE (2) 模糊的记忆/意识等: *Laura had a dim recollection of someone telling her this before.* 劳拉隐约记得以前曾有人告诉过她这事。

5 ▶FUTURE CHANCES 未来的机会◀ if your chances of success in the future are dim, they are not good〔未来成功的机会或可能〕暗淡的, 不乐观的: *Prospects for an early settlement of the dispute are dim.* 争端得到早日解决的希望渺茫。

6 in the dim and distant past *humorous* a very long time ago【幽默】很久以前

7 take a dim view of to disapprove of something 不赞成〔某事〕: *We took a dim view of his disobedience.* 我们不喜欢他的违命。

8 ▶UNINTELLIGENT 不聪明的◀ *informal especially BrE* not intelligent【非正式, 尤英】愚笨的: *You can be really dim sometimes!* 有时候你是真笨啊! —**dimly** *adv*: *a dimly lit room* 灯光暗淡的房间 | *She was only dimly aware of the risk.* 她只是隐隐约约意识到有危险。—**dimness** *n* [U]

dim² *v* **dimmed, dimming 1** [I,T] if a light dims, or if you dim it, it becomes less bright（使）变暗淡,（使）变得不亮: *The lights in the theatre began to dim.* 剧院里的灯光开始暗下来。**2** [I,T] if a feeling or quality dims or is dimmed, it grows weaker（使）〔感觉等〕变弱;（使）〔质量等〕下降: *Her beauty had not dimmed over the years.* 过了这么多年她的美貌依旧。| *His words dimmed our hopes of a peaceful settlement.* 他的话削弱了我们和平解决问题的希望。**3 dim your headlights/lights** *AmE* to lower the angle of the front lights of your car, especially when someone is driving towards you【美】〔尤其当对面有车开来的时候〕使汽车前灯灯光变暗; DIP¹ (3) *BrE*【英】

Di Mag·gi·o /də ˋmædʒɪo; də ˈmædʒiəʊ/, **Joe** /dʒo; dʒəʊ/ (1914-99), a US BASEBALL player who played for the New York Yankees team, and was one of the greatest players ever. He was also famous for being married to Marilyn Monroe. 迪马乔（1914-1999）, 美国纽约扬基队棒球运动员, 有史以来最优秀的球员之一。他也因为与玛丽莲·梦露结为夫妻而闻名

dime /daɪm; daɪm/ *n* [C] **1** a coin of the US and Canada, worth one tenth of a dollar〔美国、加拿大的〕十分硬币 —compare 比较 CENT **2 a dime a dozen** *AmE informal* very common and not valuable【美, 非正式】不值钱的, 稀松平常的: *PhDs are a dime a dozen nowadays.* 如今, 博士学位一文不值。

dime nov·el /ˈ·,··/ *n* [C] *AmE* a cheap book with a story that contains a lot of exciting events【美】廉价小说〔其中包含许多令人兴奋的故事情节〕

✎ 3 **di·men·sion** /dəˋmɛnʃən; daɪˈmenʃən/ *n* **1** [C] a part of a situation that makes you regard the situation in a particular way; ASPECT (1)〔形势的〕某一面, 某一部分: **new/different dimension** *The baby has added a new dimension to their lives.* 婴儿给他们的生活增添了新的一面。| **political/social/spiritual dimension** *We should not forget that education has an important spiritual dimension.* 我们不应该忘记精神教育是教育的一个重要部分。**2** [C] a measurement in space, for example length, height etc〔空间的〕量度, 维度〈如长度、高度等〉: *A diagram represents things in only two dimensions.* 示意图是以二维的〔平面的〕方式展现事物的。—see also 另见 FOURTH DIMENSION **3 dimensions** [plural] **a)** the size of something, especially when this is given as its length, height, and width 大小, 尺寸, 规模〔尤指某物的长、宽、高〕: *What are the room's dimensions?* 这个房间面积多少? **b)** how great or serious a problem is〔问题的〕严重程度: *We're heading for a catastrophe of enormous dimensions.* 我们正走向极其严重的灾难。

dime store /ˈ··/ *n* [C] *AmE* a shop that sells many different kinds of cheap goods, especially for the house【美】廉价〔家用品〕杂货店

di·min·ish /dəˋmɪnɪʃ; dɪ̱ˈmɪnɪʃ/ *v* **1** [I,T] to become or make something become smaller or less important（使）减少;（使）减小: *The party's share of the electorate has diminished steadily.* 这个政党拥有的选民数量正持续下降。| **diminish sth** *These drugs diminish blood flow to the brain.* 这些药物减少流向大脑的血液量。**2** [T] to deliberately make someone or something appear less important or valuable than they really are 削弱, 贬低〔重要性、价值〕: *Don't let him diminish your achievements.* 别让他贬低你的成就。**3 diminishing returns** the idea that a point can be reached at which the profits or advantages you are getting stop increasing in relation to the effort you are making 收益递减, 报酬递减

diminished re·spon·si·bil·i·ty /·,·······ˈ··/ *n* [U] *law* a state in which someone is not considered to be responsible for their actions because they are mentally ill【法律】〔由于某人精神失常而〕减轻的刑事责任

di·min·u·en·do /də,mɪnjuˋɛndo; dɪ̱,mɪnjuˈendəʊ/ *n* [C] *technical* a part in a piece of music where it becomes gradually quieter【术语】〔音乐的〕逐渐减弱, 渐弱 —opposite 反义词 CRESCENDO —**diminuendo** *adj, adv*

dim·i·nu·tion /,dɪməˋnuʃən; ,dɪmɪ̱ˈnjuːʃən/ *n* [C,U] a reduction in the size, number, or amount of something〔大小、数目、数量的〕变小, 缩小, 减少: **[+of/in]** *a diminution in value* 价值的减少

di·min·u·tive¹ /dəˋmɪnjətɪv; dɪ̱ˈmɪnjɪ̱tɪv/ *adj formal* small or short【正式】个子矮小的: *a shy diminutive man* 一个腼腆的矮个子男人

diminutive² *n* [C] a word formed by adding a diminutive suffix 由表示"小"的后缀构成的词

diminutive suf·fix /·,···ˈ··/ *n* [C] *technical* an ending that is added to a word to express smallness, for example 'ling' added to 'duck' to make 'duckling'【术语】〔加在某词后面的〕表示"小"的后缀〈如 ling, 它加在 duck（鸭子）后面便变成了 duckling（小鸭子）〉

dim·i·ty /ˋdɪmətɪ; ˈdɪmɪ̱ti/ *n* [U] a strong cotton cloth with a slightly raised pattern on it 提花棉布, 凸纹棉布

dim·mer /ˋdɪmɚ; ˈdɪmə/ also 又作 **dimmer switch** *n* [C] **1** an electric light SWITCH² (1) that can change the brightness of the light 调光器; 变光器 **2** a SWITCH for lowering the beam of a car's front lights 调节汽车前灯灯光角度的开关; DIP SWITCH *BrE*【英】

dim·ple /ˋdɪmpl̩; ˈdɪmpəl/ *n* [C] a small hollow place on your cheek or chin, especially one that forms when you smile〔脸颊上的〕酒窝;〔下巴上的〕凹痕 —see picture on page A6 参见 A6 页图

dim·pled /ˋdɪmpl̩d; ˈdɪmpəld/ *adj* having dimples 有酒窝的: *her dimpled cheeks* 她带着酒窝的双颊

dim·wit /ˋdɪm,wɪt; ˈdɪmwɪt/ *n* [C] *spoken* a stupid person【口】笨人, 傻子: *dimwits not worthy of our attention* 不值得我们关心的傻人 —**dim-witted** /,·ˈ··◂/ *adj*

din¹ /dɪn; dɪn/ *n* [singular] a loud unpleasant noise that continues for a long time〔持续很久的〕嘈杂声, 喧闹声: *The kids were making a horrendous din.* 孩子们吵得厉害。

din² *v* **dinned, dinning**

din sth into sb *phr v* [T] to make someone learn and remember something by repeating it to them again and again 再三叮嘱, 反复告诫: *Respect for our elders was dinned into us at school.* 在学校里我们被反复教导要尊敬长者。

di·nar /dɪˋnɑr; ˈdiːnɑː/ *n* [C] the standard unit of money used in the former Yugoslavia and in several muslim countries 第纳尔〔前南斯拉夫和一些穆斯林国家的货币单位〕

dine /daɪn; daɪn/ *v* [I] *formal* to eat dinner【正式】进餐: *We dined at the Ritz.* 我们在里兹大酒店用了餐。—see also 另见 **wine and dine** (WINE²)

dine on/off sth *phr v* [T] *formal* to eat a particular kind of food for dinner, especially expensive food【正式】吃〔尤指昂贵的食物〕当正餐: *We dined on lobster and strawberries.* 我们正餐吃的是龙虾和草莓。

dine out *phr v* [I] **1** *formal* to eat dinner in a restaurant or in someone else's house【正式】外出用餐〔指在餐厅或别人家吃饭〕: *They would dine out together once a month.* 他们每月一起出去吃一次饭。—see also 另见 **eat out** (EAT (1b)) **2 dine out on** *BrE humorous* to keep using a story about something that has happened to you in order to entertain people at meals【英, 幽默】〔吃饭时〕总用〔发生在自己身上的某一件事〕来逗乐

Dine, Jim /dʒɪm; dʒɪm/ (1935-) a US painter who was a leader of the pop art movement 丹因（1935- ）, 美国画家, 通俗艺术运动的领袖

din·er /ˋdaɪnɚ; ˈdaɪnə/ *n* [C] **1** someone who is eating dinner in a restaurant〔在餐厅〕用餐者 **2** *AmE* a small restaurant that serves

cheap meals【美】〔价格便宜的〕小餐馆, 小饭店: *She's a waitress in an all-night diner in North Vegas.* 她在北维加斯的一个通宵营业的小餐馆里当服务员。**3** *AmE* a DINING CAR【美】餐车

Diners Card /ˈ··· ·/ also 又作 **Diner's Club Card** *trademark* a type of charge card that can be used to pay for goods and services all over the world【商标】大来信用卡〔一种记账卡, 持此卡可在世界各地购买商品和支付服务的费用〕

Din·e·sen /ˈdɪnɪsn; ˈdɪnɪsən/, **I·sak** /ˈaɪzək; ˈaɪzək/ —see 见 Baroness Karen BLIXEN

di·nette /daɪˈnɛt; daɪˈnet/ *n* [C] *AmE* a small area, usually in or near the kitchen, where people eat meals【美】〔厨房里或靠近厨房供人们吃饭用的〕小饭厅

dinette set /·ˈ· ˌ·/ *n* [C] *AmE* a table and matching chairs【美】配套的餐桌椅

ding-a-ling /ˈdɪŋ ə lɪŋ; ˈdɪŋ ə lɪŋ/ also 又作 **ding·bat** /ˈdɪŋbæt; ˈdɪŋbæt/ *n* [C] *AmE spoken* a stupid person【美口】傻瓜, 笨蛋: *Who's that fat dingbat over there?* 那边那个肥胖的傻瓜是谁?

ding-dong /ˈdɪŋ ˌdɔŋ; ˈdɪŋ dɒŋ/ *n* **1** [U] the noise made by a bell 铃声; 叮当声 **2** [singular] *BrE informal* a noisy argument【英, 非正式】喧闹的争吵, 争辩: *They were having a real ding-dong in the kitchen.* 他们在厨房争吵得正凶呢。

din·ghy /ˈdɪŋɪ; ˈdɪŋgi/ *n* [C] **1** a small open sailing boat used especially for racing 无篷小帆船〔尤指用作比赛的小帆船〕**2** a small open boat used for pleasure or for taking people between a ship and the shore〔娱乐用的〕小游艇;〔载人往返于大船与岸边的〕小艇 —see also 另见 RUBBER DINGHY

din·gle /ˈdɪŋgl; ˈdɪŋgəl/ *n* [C] *literary* a small valley with trees in it【文】〔长满树木的〕小山谷, 幽谷: *He went alone to the dingle to clear his thoughts.* 他独自去了小幽谷整理思绪。

din·go /ˈdɪŋgo; ˈdɪŋgəʊ/ *n plural* **dingoes** [C] an Australian wild dog 澳大利亚野犬

din·gy /ˈdɪndʒɪ; ˈdɪndʒi/ *adj* a dingy room, street, or place is dark, dirty, and in bad condition 肮脏的, 邋遢的: *a dingy back street* 又黑又脏的后街 —**dingily** *adv*: *dingily furnished* 装饰暗淡破旧的 —**dinginess** *n* [U]

din·ing car /ˈ·· ·/ *n* [C] a carriage on a train where meals are served; RESTAURANT CAR〔火车上的〕餐车

dining room /ˈ·· ·/ *n* [C] a room where you eat meals in a house, hotel etc〔家里的〕饭厅;〔旅馆的〕餐厅

dining ta·ble /ˈ·· ˌ··/ *n* [C] a table for having meals on 餐桌 —compare 比较 DINNER TABLE

dink /dɪŋk; dɪŋk/ *n* [C] *informal* Double Income No Kids; one of two young people who are married to each other and who both earn a lot of money, but who have no children【非正式】丁克族〔指年轻夫妻双方都有收入但并未生育孩子〕; DINKY² *BrE*【英】

din·kum /ˈdɪŋkəm; ˈdɪŋkəm/ *adj* —see 见 FAIR DINKUM

din·ky¹ /ˈdɪŋkɪ; ˈdɪŋki/ *adj* **1** *BrE informal* small and attractive【英, 非正式】小巧的; 精致的: *What a dinky little cottage!* 多漂亮的小村舍啊! **2** *AmE* small and not very nice【美】狭小的, 简陋的: *It was a really dinky hotel room.* 那家旅馆房间真是简陋。

dinky² *n* [C] *BrE* a dink【英】丁克族〔双收入没有孩子的年轻夫妻〕

S1 W2 **din·ner** /ˈdɪnɚ; ˈdɪnə/ *n* **1** [C,U] the main meal of the day, eaten in the middle of the day or the evening〔中午或晚上吃的〕正餐, 主餐: *Would you like to come over for dinner on Friday?* 星期五过来吃晚饭好吗? | *We're having fish for dinner tonight.* 今天晚餐我们吃鱼。| **Sunday/Christmas/Thanksgiving dinner etc** (=a special meal eaten on Sunday, at Christmas, at Thanks-giving, etc) 星期日/圣诞节/感恩节等的盛餐 | **school dinner** (=a meal provided at school in the middle of the day) 学校午餐 **2** [C] a formal occasion when an evening meal is eaten, often to celebrate something〔为了庆祝某事而举行的〕晚宴: *They're giving a dinner in honour of her retirement.* 为了庆祝她退休, 他们将举行一个晚宴。**3 had more ... than you've had hot dinners** *BrE spoken humorous* used to say that someone has had a lot of experience of something and has done it many times【英口, 幽默】做过的…比你吃的饭还多, 过的桥比你走的路还多〔用来说明某人做某事已经许多次, 有着丰富的经验〕: *She's nursed more babies than you've had hot dinners.* 她哺育过的孩子比你吃过的饭还多。—see also 另见 TV DINNER, **be dressed up like a dog's dinner** (DOG¹ (9))

dinner dance /ˈ·· ˌ·/ *n* [C] a social event in the evening, that includes a formal meal and music for dancing 晚宴舞会: *the annual dinner dance* 一年一度的晚宴舞会

dinner jack·et /ˈ·· ˌ··/ *n* [C] *BrE* a black or white JACKET (1) worn by men on very formal occasions, usually with a BOW TIE【英】男子晚礼服〔正式场合穿着, 黑色或白色, 通常打蝶形领结〕; TUXEDO *AmE*【美】

dinner la·dy /ˈ·· ˌ··/ *n* [C] *BrE* a woman who serves meals to children at school【英】在学校午餐时为孩子们端饭菜的妇女

dinner par·ty /ˈ·· ˌ··/ *n* [C] a social event when people are invited to someone's house for an evening meal〔人们被邀请到某人家里吃的〕社交晚宴

dinner ser·vice /ˈ·· ˌ··/ also 又作 **dinner set** /ˈ·· ·/ *n* [C] a complete set of plates, dishes etc, used for serving a meal 成套餐具

dinner ta·ble, the /ˈ·· ˌ··/ *n* **a)** an occasion when people are eating dinner together 人们聚餐的场合: *That's not a very pleasant topic for the dinner table.* 这个话题不太适合在进餐时讨论。**b)** the table at which people eat dinner 餐桌 —compare 比较 DINING TABLE

dinner thea·ter /ˈ·· ˌ··/ *n* [C] *AmE* a restaurant in which you see a play after your meal【美】餐后可以观剧的餐厅剧院

din·ner·time /ˈdɪnɚˌtaɪm; ˈdɪnətaɪm/ *n* [singular] the time when you usually have dinner, especially in the middle of the day 用餐时间〔尤指午餐时间〕: *He always seems to call me at dinnertime.* 他似乎总是在吃饭时间打电话给我。

di·no·saur /ˈdaɪnəˌsɔr; ˈdaɪnəsɔː/ *n* [C] **1** one of a group of REPTILES that lived about 200 million years ago 恐龙 **2** *informal* something very large and old-fashioned that no longer works well or effectively【非正式】庞大而过时的东西: *one of the dinosaurs of the computer industry* 电脑产业中那种体积笨重的落后型号之一

dint /dɪnt; dɪnt/ *n* **1 by dint of** by using a particular method 通过使用…方法: *By dint of persistent questioning, I finally got to the truth.* 在不断追问后, 我终于得到真相。**2** a small hollow in the surface of something made by hitting it〔因受击打而留下的〕凹陷, 凹坑: *a dint in the car door* 车门上的凹痕

di·o·cese /ˈdaɪəˌsəs; ˈdaɪəsɪs/ *n* [C] the area under the control of a BISHOP (1), in the Christian church〔基督教的〕主教辖区, 教区 —**diocesan** /daɪˈɑsəsn; daɪˈɒsɪsən/ *adj*

Di·o·ge·nes /daɪˈɑdʒəniz; daɪˈɒdʒɪniːz/ also 又作 **Diogenes the Cynic** (?412-?323 BC) an ancient Greek PHILOSOPHER who said that the simple life was the best life and who, according to ancient stories, lived in a BARREL (=a round wooden container for liquids) 第欧根尼〔公元前?412-前?323〕, 古希腊哲学家, 又称犬儒学家第欧根尼。他认为, 简朴的生活是最理想的生活。相传, 他栖身于木桶之中〕

Di·o·ny·sus /ˌdaɪəˈnaɪsəs; ˌdaɪəˈnaɪsəs/ in Greek MYTHOLOGY, the god of wine and FERTILITY. He is usually connected with uncontrolled behaviour involving lots of drinking, parties, and sex. In Roman mythology his name is Bacchus. 狄俄尼索斯〔古希腊神话中的酒神和生育之神, 通常与酗酒、狂欢和纵欲等无节制的行为有关, 罗马神话中称巴克斯〕

di·ox·ide /daɪˈɑksaɪd; daɪˈɒksaɪd/ *n* [C,U] *technical* a chemical compound containing two atoms of oxygen to every atom of another ELEMENT (=simple substance)【术语】二氧化物 —see also 另见 CARBON DIOXIDE

di·ox·in /daɪˈɑksɪn; daɪˈɒksɪn/ *n* [C,U] a very poisonous chemical used for killing plants 二噁英〔一种剧毒化学物质, 用于灭杀植物〕

Dip the written abbreviation of 缩写= DIPLOMA

dip¹ /dɪp; dɪp/ *v* **dipped, dipping 1** [T] to put something into a liquid and quickly lift it out again 蘸, 浸: *Dip your finger in the batter and taste it.* 用手指蘸一点面糊, 尝一下。—see picture on page A11 参见 A11 页图 **2** [I] to go downwards 下降, 下落: *We watched the sun dip below the horizon.* 我们看见太阳落到地平线下。**3 dip your headlights/lights** *BrE* to lower the angle of the front lights of your car, especially when someone is driving towards you【英】降低汽车前灯角度〔尤其当对面有车开来时〕; DIM² (3) *AmE*【美】**4** [T] to make animals go through a bath containing a chemical that kills insects on their skin 让〔动物〕洗药浴〔灭虫〕—see also 另见 SKINNY-DIPPING

dip into sth *phr v* [T] **1** to read short parts of a book, magazine etc, but not the whole thing 翻阅, 浏览〔书或杂志等〕: *It's the kind of book you can dip into now and again.* 这是可以时不时翻阅一下的那种书。**2** to use some of an amount of money that you have 动用〔存款〕: **dip into your savings** *Medical bills forced her to dip into her savings.* 为了付医药费, 她不得不动用存款。| **dip into your pocket** (=pay for something with your own money)〔为买某物〕花你自己的钱 *Parents are being asked to dip into their pockets for new school books.* 父母得自掏腰包〔为孩子〕买新课本。**3** to put your hand into a bag or box in order to take out one of the things inside 把手伸进〔袋里或盒子里, 为了把里面的东西掏出来〕: *On her lap was a bag of candy which she kept dipping into.* 她不断地从腿上放着的一袋糖果里面摸出糖来吃。

dip² *n*
1 ▶**SWIM** 游泳◀ [C] *informal* a quick swim【非正式】〔为时较短的〕游泳: *Are you coming in for a dip?* 你来游一会儿吗? | **have/take a dip** *They've decided to take a dip in the lake before lunch.* 他们已经决定午餐前到湖里游一小会儿泳。
2 ▶**DECREASE** 下降◀ [C] a slight decrease in the amount of something〔某物数量上轻微的〕减少, 下降: *an unexpected dip in profits* 出乎意料的利润下降
3 ▶**IN A SURFACE** 在表面◀ [C] a place where the surface of something goes down suddenly, then goes up again 凹陷: *a dip in the road* 路上的凹陷处
4 ▶**FOOD** 食物◀ [C,U] a thick mixture that you can dip food into before you eat it〔用来蘸食物吃的〕调味酱汁: *sour cream and onion dip* 酸奶油和洋葱酱汁 — see picture on page A15 参见 A15 页图
5 ▶**FOR ANIMALS** 动物用的◀ [C,U] a liquid that contains a chemical which kills insects on sheep and other animals〔给动物洗浴用的〕药浴液〔以便杀虫〕
6 ▶**PERSON** 人◀ [C] *AmE spoken* a stupid person【美口】傻瓜, 笨蛋 —see also 另见 LUCKY DIP

diph·the·ri·a /dɪfˋθɪrɪə; dɪfˈθɪəriə/ *n* [U] a serious infectious throat disease that makes breathing difficult 白喉

diph·thong /ˋdɪfθɔŋ; ˈdɪfθɒŋ/ *n* [C] *technical*【术语】**1** a compound vowel sound made by pronouncing two vowels quickly one after the other. For example, the vowel sound in 'my' is a diphthong. 二合元音, 双元音〈如 my 中的元音便是双元音〉—see also 另见 GLIDE² (3) **2** a DIGRAPH 二合字母

di·plo·ma /dɪˋplomə; dɨˈpləʊmə/ *n* [C] **1** *BrE* a document showing that someone has successfully completed a course of study or passed an examination【英】结业证书: *I'm hoping to get my teaching diploma this year.* 我希望今年能拿到教师证书。| [+in] *a diploma in catering* 承办酒席的资格证书 **2** *AmE* a document showing that a student has successfully completed their HIGH SCHOOL, college, or university education【美】毕业文凭, 学位证书: *a master's diploma* 硕士文凭

di·plo·ma·cy /dɪˋploməsɪ; dɨˈpləʊməsi/ *n* [U] **1** the work of managing the relationships between countries 外交: *a major player in post-war diplomacy* 战后外交的主要活动家 **2** skill in dealing with people and persuading them to agree to something without upsetting them 处世之道, 交际手段: *The job requires tact and diplomacy.* 这个工作需要策略以及外交手腕。—see also 另见 **gunboat diplomacy** (GUNBOAT (2))

dip·lo·mat /ˋdɪplə,mæt; ˈdɪpləmæt/ *n* [C] **1** someone who officially represents their government in a foreign country 外交官; 外交家 **2** someone who is good at dealing with people without upsetting them 有手腕的人; 善于处理人际关系的人: *As a natural diplomat, Baxter found it easy to placate the two sides.* 作为一个天生的交际能手, 巴克斯特觉得不难安抚双方。

dip·lo·mat·ic /,dɪpləˋmætɪk; ,dɪpləˈmætɪk◂/ *adj* **1** concerning or involving the work of diplomats 外交的: *She was hoping for a diplomatic post in the Middle East.* 她盼望着能获得一个在中东工作的外交职位。**2** dealing with people politely and skilfully without upsetting them 世故的, 圆滑的: *They were always very diplomatic with awkward clients.* 他们与难缠的客户打交道一向很有策略。| *a diplomatic answer* 很圆滑的回答 —**diplomatically** /-klɪ; -kli/ *adv*: *Maria handled the situation very diplomatically.* 玛丽亚非常老道得体地处理了这个情况。

diplomatic corps /,··ˋ·· ,·/ *n* [U] all the diplomats working in a particular country〔驻某国的〕外交(使节)团

diplomatic im·mu·ni·ty /,·····ˋ···/ *n* [U] *law* a diplomat's special rights in the country where they are working, which protect them from local taxes and PROSECUTION (1)【法律】外交特权, 外交豁免权

diplomatic re·la·tions /,····ˋ··/ *n* [plural] the arrangement between two countries that each should keep representatives at an EMBASSY in the other country 外交关系: **break off diplomatic relations** *Britain broke off diplomatic relations after the crisis of 1982.* 1982 年的危机之后, 英国中断了(与该国的)外交关系。

Diplomatic Ser·vice /··ˋ·· ,··/ *n* [singular] all the people who work for their government abroad in an EMBASSY or a CONSULATE 外交部门, 外交系统

di·plo·ma·tist /dɪˋplomətɪst; dɨˈpləʊmətɨst/ *n* [C] a DIPLOMAT 外交官; 外交家

dip·per /ˋdɪpɚ; ˈdɪpə/ *n* [C] **1** a large spoon with a long handle used for taking liquid out of a container 长柄勺 **2** a small bird that feeds in mountain streams 河乌〔在山中小溪觅食的一种小鸟〕—see also 另见 BIG DIPPER

dip·py /ˋdɪpɪ; ˈdɪpi/ *adj informal* silly or crazy【非正式】笨的, 愚蠢的; 疯狂的

dip·shit /ˋdɪpʃɪt; ˈdɪpʃɪt/ *n* [C] *AmE spoken* an impolite word meaning a stupid person【美口】笨蛋, 傻瓜〔不礼貌用语〕

dip·so /ˋdɪpso; ˈdɪpsəʊ/ *n* [C] *slang* a dipsomaniac【俚】嗜酒狂患者, 间发性酒狂患者

dip·so·ma·ni·ac /,dɪpsəˋmenɪ,æk; ,dɪpsəˈmeɪniæk/ *n* [C] someone who has a very strong desire for alcoholic drinks, which they cannot control 嗜酒狂患者, 间发性酒狂患者 —**dipsomania** /-nɪə; -niə/ *n* [U]

dip·stick /ˋdɪp,stɪk; ˈdɪp,stɪk/ *n* [C] **1** a stick for measuring the amount of liquid in a container, especially the amount of oil in a car's engine〔尤指测量汽车发动机中油量的〕浸量尺, 测深尺, 量油尺 —see picture at 参见 ENGINE 图 **2** *spoken* a stupid person【口】傻瓜, 笨蛋

dip switch /ˋ· ·/ *n* [C] *BrE* a SWITCH² (1) for lowering the beam of a car's front lights【英】汽车前灯变光开关; DIMMER (2) *AmE*【美】

dip·tych /ˋdɪptɪk; ˈdɪptɪk/ *n* [C] a picture made in two parts which can be closed like a book 折合式双连画 —compare 比较 TRIPTYCH

dire /daɪr; daɪə/ *adj* **1** extremely serious, bad or terrible 极其严重的; 极糟糕的; 极可怕的人: *He was in dire trouble and he knew it.* 他麻烦大了, 他自己也知道这一点。| *That makes the situation sound dire.* 那使得局势听起来非常严峻。| **in dire need/poverty** *The country was in dire need of financial aid.* 这个国家亟须经济援助。| **dire consequences** *Increasing fuel prices will have dire consequences for the poor.* 提高燃料价格将给穷人带来严重后果。| **be in dire straits** (=be in an extremely difficult or serious situation) 处于岌岌可危的境地 **2** **dire warning/threat** a dire warning or threat warns people about something terrible that will happen in the future 大难临头的警告/威胁

di·rect¹ /dəˋrɛkt; dɨˈrekt/ *adj*
1 ▶**WITHOUT ANYTHING BETWEEN** 没有东西介入的◀ done without any other people, actions, processes etc coming between 直接的〔没有其他人、行动或过程介入〕: *Can we have direct access to the information on file?* 我们能直接获得存档的资料吗? | *She has direct control over the business.* 她直接控制这家企业。| *I'm not in direct contact with them.* 我和他们没有直接的联系。
2 ▶**FROM ONE PLACE TO ANOTHER** 从一个地方到另一个地方◀ going straight from one place to another without stopping or changing direction 笔直的, 径直的〔中间不停, 不改变方向〕: *Which is the most direct route to London?* 哪条是到伦敦最直接的路线? | *We can get a direct flight to New York.* 我们可以乘直达班机去纽约。
3 ▶**EFFECT** 效果, 结果◀ likely to change something immediately 直接的〔可能立即发生改变〕: *The change in the law will have a direct bearing on the way benefits are calculated.* 法律的变动将对利润的计算方式产生直接影响。
4 ▶**EXACT** 恰好的◀ [only before noun 仅用于名词前] exact or total 恰好的, 截然的: *Weight increases in direct proportion to mass.* 重量的增长和质量的增长成正比。| *These ideas are in direct contrast with the themes of her earlier essays.* 这些观点与她早期文章中的主旨截然相反。| **direct quote** (=what someone said in their exact words) 直接引用, 直接引语
5 ▶**BEHAVIOUR/ATTITUDE** 行为/态度◀ saying exactly what you mean in an honest clear way 率直的, 坦率的, 直言的: *If only she'd been less direct in her approach, he might have helped.* 如果她当时的方式不那么直截了当, 他或许会帮忙的。
6 **direct descendant** someone who is related to someone else through their parents and grandparents, not through their AUNTS, UNCLES, brothers, sisters etc 直系的后裔: *She claimed to be a direct descendant of Wordsworth.* 她声称是华兹华斯的直系后裔。
7 **direct result/consequence** something that happens only because of one particular thing 直接后果: *They were suffering from stress, and their physical symptoms were a direct result.* 他们正承受着精神压力, 他们身体上出现的症状便是其直接后果。
8 **direct question/answer** a question that asks for information exactly and specifically, with no possibility of misunderstanding, or an answer that gives information in this way 直截了当的问题/回答: *Now, let me ask you a direct question, and I expect a direct answer.* 现在, 让我问你一个直截了当的问题, 希望你能直截了当地回答。
9 **direct heat/sunlight** strong heat or sunlight that someone or something is not protected from〔没有任何防护的〕直接受热/日照: *Never change the film in direct sunlight.* 千万不要直接在阳光下换胶卷。—opposite 反义词 INDIRECT

direct² *v* [T]

1 ▶AIM 瞄准◀ [always+adv/prep] to aim something in a particular direction or at a particular person, group etc 把〔某物〕对准；针对：[+at/towards/away from etc] *The machine directs an X-ray beam at the patient's body.* 机器把X光射线对准病人的身体。| *For once her sarcasm was not directed at us.* 难得这一次她的讽刺不是针对我们的。| *Environmental policy was traditionally directed at pollution control.* 环保政策一向是着眼于控制污染的。| **direct your efforts towards sth** (=try hard to do one particular thing) 把精力投入到某事中〔努力做某事〕*I want to direct my efforts more towards my own projects.* 我想把精力更多地投入到自己的项目中去。| **direct your attention towards sth** *None of them had ever directed serious attention to the problem.* 他们中间从来没有人认真地注意过这个问题。

2 ▶BE IN CHARGE 负责◀ to be in charge of something or control it 负责；管理；指导；监督：*Stella had been asked to direct a research project.* 斯特拉被任命负责一个研究项目。

3 to tell someone how to get to a place 给〔某人〕指路；指挥：*A policeman stood in the middle of the road, directing the traffic.* 一名警察站在路中央指挥交通。| [+to] *Could you direct me to Trafalgar Square, please?* 你能告诉我去特拉法尔加广场怎么走吗？—see 见 LEAD¹ (USAGE)

4 *formal* to tell someone what they should do【正式】指示，命令：*We were directed to hand over our passports.* 我们被指示把护照交过去。| **direct that** *Judge Rice directed that a verdict of 'not guilty' be entered.* 赖斯法官命令把"无罪"的判决记录入册。

5 ▶ACTING 表演◀ to give the actors in a play, film, or television programme instructions about what they should do 担任〔戏剧、电影、电视节目等〕的导演：*Who directed that movie we saw last week?* 我们上周看的那部电影是谁导演的？

direct³ *adv* **1** without stopping or changing direction 中途不停地；径直地：*Can we fly direct to Chicago, or do we stop in Salt Lake City first?* 我们能否直飞芝加哥，还是要先在盐湖城停一下？ **2** without dealing with anyone else first 直接地〔和某人打交道〕：*Esther decided to contact the manager direct.* 埃丝特决定直接和经理联系。| *It is usually cheaper to buy the goods direct from the wholesaler.* 直接从批发商那里买东西通常比较便宜。

direct cur·rent /ˌ·ˈ··/ *n* [U] a flow of electricity that moves in one direction only 直流电 —compare 比较 ALTERNATING CURRENT

direct deb·it /ˌ·ˈ··/ *n* [C,U] *especially BrE* an instruction you give your bank to pay money directly out of your account regularly to a particular person or organization【尤英】直接借记，直接付款 —compare 比较 STANDING ORDER

direct de·pos·it /ˌ·ˈ···/ *n* [U] *AmE* a method of paying someone's wages directly into their bank account【美】直接存款付薪〔把某人的工资直接打入此人的账户〕

direct dis·course /ˌ·ˈ··/ *n* [U] an American form of the expression DIRECT SPEECH direct speech 的美式说法

direct hit /ˌ·ˈ·/ *n* [C] an occasion when something thrown or dropped, for example a bomb, exactly hits the object it was aimed at 直接命中〔指投射的某物，如炸弹，正好击中目标〕：*The railway station suffered two direct hits that night.* 那天晚上，火车站两次被直接击中。

di·rec·tion /dəˈrɛkʃən; dʒˈrekʃən/ *n*

1 [C] the way something or someone moves, faces, or is aimed 方向：**in the direction of** (=towards) 朝着…的方向 *The suspects were last seen heading in the direction of Miami.* 嫌疑犯最后一次被看见是朝迈阿密方向跑了。| **in sb's direction** (=towards someone) 朝着某人的方向 *Tristram glanced in her direction and their eyes met.* 特里斯特拉姆朝着她的方向瞥了一眼，结果他们四目相对。| **in the opposite direction** *The girls giggled and pointed in the opposite direction.* 女孩子们咯咯地笑着，指向相反的方向。| **change direction** *On seeing me, Maurice changed direction and went along the wharf instead.* 莫里斯看见我便调转方向，沿着码头走去。| **in a southerly/easterly etc direction** *Continue in a southerly direction until you reach the road.* 继续往南走直到走到大路上。| **in all directions** *As shots rang out, the crowd ran screaming in all directions.* 枪声响起的时候，人群尖叫着向四面八方逃散。

2 directions [plural] instructions about how to get from one place to another, or about what to do 指示；〔行路的〕指引；〔用法、操作的〕说明：*A very helpful woman gave me directions to the police station.* 一个非常肯帮忙的妇女告诉我到警察局怎么走。

3 ▶WAY STH DEVELOPS 事情发展的趋势◀ [C] the general way in which someone or something changes or develops 趋向，趋势：**take a direction** *Drayson was surprised at the direction his career had taken.* 德雷森对于他事业发展的趋向感到惊讶。| *The company is hoping to extend its operations in this direction.* 公司正盼望着朝这个方向扩充经营。

4 ▶WHERE FROM OR WHERE TO 从哪儿来或到哪儿去◀ [C] where something comes from or where something leads 方向：*The evidence all points in this direction.* 所有证据都指向这个方向。| *Help came from a wholly unexpected direction.* 援助来自一个完全没有预料到的地方。

5 ▶CONTROL 管理◀ [U] control, management, or advice 控制，监控；管理；指点：**under sb's direction** *The project progressed well, under the capable direction of Magnus Armstrong.* 由于马格努斯·阿姆斯特朗指导有方，这个项目进展顺利。

6 ▶FILM 电影◀ [U] the instructions and advice given by a film DIRECTOR (2)〔电影导演的〕指导，指示

7 ▶PURPOSE 目的◀ [U] a general purpose or aim〔总体〕目标：*Her mother felt that Rachel's life lacked direction.* 雷切尔的妈妈觉得雷切尔的生活缺少目标。

8 sense of direction a) the ability to know which way you should be going in a place you do not know well 方向感，方位感：*"Are we going north?" "Don't ask me! I've got no sense of direction at all."* "我们是在朝北走吗？""别问我！我根本没有方向感。" **b)** an idea about what your aims in life are〔生活的〕目标：*Doing the course gave her more sense of direction.* 修这门课程使得她感到更有目标了。

di·rec·tion·al /dəˈrɛkʃənl; dʒˈrekʃənəl/ *adj technical*【术语】**1** pointing in a particular direction 方向的 **2** a directional piece of equipment receives or gives out radio signals from some directions more strongly than others 定向的〔定向仪器发出或接收的无线电信号在某些方向上比其他方向强〕

di·rec·tive¹ /dəˈrɛktɪv; dʒˈrektɪv/ *n* [C] an official order or instruction 正式命令，指示：*the EU directive on paternity leave* 欧盟关于丈夫陪产假的指示

directive² *adj* giving instructions 指示的，指导的：*It is important in these cases that doctors take a less directive approach.* 在这些情况下，重要的是医生应该采取指令性不太强的态度。

di·rect·ly¹ /dəˈrɛktli; dʒˈrektli/ *adv* **1** with no other person, action, process etc between 直接地：*The new law won't directly affect us.* 新的法律不会直接影响到我们。| *I know where you can get that directly from the manufacturers.* 我知道在什么地方你可以直接从制造商那儿买到那种东西。**2** exactly 恰好，正好：*Have you noticed how he never looks directly at you?* 你有没有注意到他从未正眼看过你？| *Her practical ideas seemed directly opposed to the department's academic style.* 她的实用思想似乎和这个系的学术风格正好背道而驰。**3 speak/ask/answer etc directly** to say exactly what you mean without trying to hide anything 坦率地，直截了当地说/问/回答等：*Cindy has a job in mind, but refuses to say directly what it is.* 辛迪心里想着一种工作，但是她不肯直截了当地说那是什么工作。**4** *BrE old-fashioned* very soon【英，过时】很快地：*He should be here directly, if you don't mind waiting.* 如果你不介意多等一会儿，他应该很快就会到的。**5** *BrE old-fashioned* immediately【英，过时】立即

directly² *conjunction BrE* as soon as【英】一…就…：*I came directly I got your message.* 我一接到你的消息就来了。

direct mail /ˌ·ˈ·/ *n* [U] advertisements that are sent by post to many people 邮递广告

direct meth·od /ˌ·ˈ··/ *n* [singular,U] a method of teaching a foreign language without using the student's own language〔外语〕直接教学法〔不使用学生的本国语〕

direct ob·ject /ˌ·ˈ··/ *n* [C] *technical* the noun, noun phrase, or PRONOUN that you need to complete the meaning of a statement using a TRANSITIVE verb, for example 'Mary' in the statement 'I saw Mary'【术语】直接宾语〔指接在及物动词后面的名词、名词词组或代词，如在I saw Mary这句话中，Mary便是直接宾语〕—compare 比较 INDIRECT OBJECT

di·rec·tor /dəˈrɛktə; dʒˈrektə/ *n* [C] **1** one of the committee of top managers who control a company 董事；理事：*a former director of Gartmore Pensions Ltd* 加特莫尔退休基金有限公司的前任董事 | **board of directors** (=the committee of directors) 董事会；理事会 **2** the person who gives instructions to the actors, CAMERAMAN etc in a film or play 导演 —compare 比较 PRODUCER (2) **3** someone who is in charge of a particular activity or organization 负责人，主管：*the director of transport operations* 运输业务的主管 | *Greta has been appointed project director.* 格蕾塔被任命为项目主管。| **financial/sales/personnel director** (=a director in charge of the financial department etc) 财务部/销售部/人事部主任—see also 另见 MANAGING DIRECTOR, NON-EXECUTIVE DIRECTOR

di·rec·tor·ate /dəˈrɛktərɪt; dʒˈrektərʒt/ *n* [C] **1** the BOARD (=committee) of directors of a company 董事会；理事会 **2** a directorship 董事[主任、主管]职位

Director of Pub·lic Pros·e·cu·tions abbreviation 缩写为 the DPP in the legal system of England and Wales, the lawyer whose job is to decide whether or not a person should be charged with a crime, in cases where it is not clear. There is a similar official in Scotland called the procurator fiscal. 检察长〔英格兰和威尔士司法系统中的职位, 由律师担任。其职责是在悬而未决的情况下决定是否起诉某一责任人。苏格兰也有类似官员, 称 the procurator fiscal〕

Director of Stud·ies /,· ··· '·/ *n* [singular] a teacher in a British university or language school who is in charge of organizing the students' programmes of study〔英国大学或语言学校的〕负责编制学生学习大纲的老师, 教务长

di·rec·tor·ship /də`rɛktə,ʃɪp; dɪ'rektəʃɪp/ *n* [C] the position of being a director of a company 董事[主管]职位

di·rec·to·ry /də`rɛktərɪ; daɪ'rektəri/ *n* [C] a book or list of names, facts etc, usually arranged in alphabetical order〔通常按字母顺序排列的〕姓名地址录; 工商人名录; 电话簿: *I couldn't find your number in the telephone directory.* 我在电话簿里找不到你的号码。| *a new business directory* 新的商行名录

D

directory en·qui·ries /,· ··· '··/ *BrE*【英】, **directory assistance** /,· ··· '··/ *AmE*【美】*n* [U] a service on the British telephone network that you can use to find out someone's telephone number〔英国的〕电话查号台

direct speech /,· '·/ *n* [U] *technical* the style used to report what someone says by giving their actual words, for example 'I don't want to go,' said Julie.【术语】直接引语〔指直接引用某人说的原话, 如 'I don't want to go,' said Julie. 这里 I don't want to go 便是直接引语〕; DIRECT DISCOURSE *AmE*【美】—compare 比较 INDIRECT SPEECH, REPORTED SPEECH

direct tax /,· '·/ *n* [C,U] *technical* a tax, such as income tax, which is actually collected from the person who pays it, as opposed to a tax on goods or services【术语】直接税〔直接从纳税人征收, 如所得税; 它不同于商品税或服务税等间接税〕—opposite 反义词 INDIRECT TAX —**direct taxation** /,· · '··/ *n* [U]

dirge /dɝdʒ; dɜːdʒ/ *n* [C] **1** a slow sad song sung at a funeral 挽歌, 哀歌: *When I die, I don't want any of those awful dirges.* 我死后可不想要那种讨厌的挽歌。**2** a song or piece of music that is too slow and boring 缓慢乏味的音乐

dir·i·gi·ble /`dɪrədʒəbl; 'dɪrɪdʒəbəl/ *n* [C] an AIRSHIP 飞艇; 飞船

dirk /dɝk; dɜːk/ *n* [C] a heavy pointed knife used as a weapon in Scotland in the past〔旧时苏格兰人当作武器使用的一种沉重的〕尖刀, 短剑, 匕首

dirt /dɝt; dɜːt/ *n* [U] **1** any substance that makes things dirty, such as mud or dust 灰尘, 尘土, 脏土: *You should have seen the dirt on that car!* 可惜你没看见那车上沾了多少泥! | **dog dirt** *especially AmE* (=waste from a dog's BOWELS (1))【尤美】狗屎 **2** loose earth or soil 松土, 泥土: *Michael threw his handful of dirt onto the coffin.* 迈克尔往棺材上撒了一把土。**3** *informal* information about someone's private life or activities which could give people a bad opinion of them if it became known【非正式】〔某人私生活的〕丑事, 丑行: *Apparently, confidential files were combed for dirt on the candidates.* 很显然, 为了找出候选人的丑行, 机密档案被仔细翻查过。**4** talk, writing, films etc that are considered unpleasant or immoral because they are about sex 下流话; 下流文章; 色情电影 —see also 另见 **dish the dirt** (DISH[2] (1)), **hit the dirt** (HIT[1] (21)), **treat sb like dirt** (TREAT[1] (1))

dirt bike /'· ,·/ *n* [C] a small MOTORCYCLE for young people, usually ridden on rough paths or fields 轻型摩托车〔通常适合在粗糙的小路上或田野中行驶〕

dirt cheap /,· '·◂/ *adj, adv informal* extremely cheap【非正式】非常便宜的: *We got the cow dirt cheap because the Parsons sold off their farm.* 因为帕森一家廉价出售他们的农场, 所以我们没花几个钱就买下了这头牛。

dirt farm·er /'· ,··/ *n* [C] *AmE* a poor farmer who works to feed himself and his family, without paying anyone else to help【美】自耕农

dirt poor /,· '·◂/ *adj AmE informal* extremely poor【美, 非正式】极贫困的, 赤贫的

dirt road /'· ·/ *n* [C] a road made of hard earth 泥路, 土路

dirt track /'· ·/ *n* [C] a track used for MOTORCYCLE races〔用于摩托车比赛的〕赛道

dirt·y[1] /`dɝtɪ; 'dɜːti/ *adj* **dirtier, dirtiest**

1 ▶NOT CLEAN 不干净的◀ covered in dirt or marked with dirt 有灰尘的, 肮脏的: *Just stack the dirty dishes in the sink.* 把脏盘子堆放在水槽里就行了。| *Look how dirty your hands are! Go wash them right now!* 看看你的手有多脏! 马上去洗洗!

2 ▶IMMORAL 不道德的◀ connected with sex in a way that is considered immoral or unpleasant 下流的, 黄色的, 色情的, 猥亵的: *Mick's always telling dirty jokes.* 米克总是讲下流的笑话。| *There were a bunch of dirty magazines under his bed.* 他床底下有一堆色情杂志。| **a dirty mind** (=a mind that often thinks about sex) 经常想下流事的脑子 | **dirty weekend** *humorous* (=a weekend when a man and woman who are not married to each other go away to have sex)【幽默】风流周末〔非夫妻关系的男女周末外出过性生活〕

3 ▶UNPLEASANT 令人讨厌的◀ *spoken* used to emphasize that you think someone or something is very bad【口】可恶的, 可恨的〔强调某人或某事非常糟糕、差劲〕: *You're a dirty liar!* 你是个卑鄙的骗子! | *Yeah, they gave us all the dirty jobs.* 对, 他们把最难搞的差使都分给我们。

4 ▶DISHONEST 不诚实的◀ unfair or dishonest 不公正的; 不诚实的: *a dirty fighter* 竞争时用不公平手段的人 | *There's been some dirty business over these contracts.* 围绕这些合同有着一些不可告人的勾当。| **dirty trick** (=an unkind dishonest way of treating someone)〔对待某人的〕卑鄙手段 *I'm so sorry anyone should play such a dirty trick!* 很遗憾, 竟然有人使用这么卑劣的手段! | **do the dirty on sb** *BrE* (=treat someone in a way that is unfair or dishonest)【英】以卑劣手段耍弄某人 | **dirty pool** *AmE* (=unfair or dishonest behaviour)【美】不正当行为; 欺诈行为

5 be a dirty word if something is a dirty word, people believe it is a bad thing even if they do not know or think much about it 是不好听的字眼: *Nowadays power tends to be a slightly dirty word as far as organizations are concerned.* 如今, 就组织而言, 权力往往被看作是不太好听的字眼。

6 give sb a dirty look to look at someone in a very disapproving way 厌恶地看某人一眼: *When I went in there she gave me a dirty look and told me to take a seat.* 我进去的时候她厌恶地看了我一眼, 叫我坐下。

7 do sb's dirty work to do an unpleasant or dishonest job for someone so that they do not have to do it themselves 替某人干肮脏的工作: *I told them to do their own dirty work.* 我告诉他们自己去干自己的肮脏工作。

8 ▶DRUGS 毒品◀ *AmE slang* containing or possessing illegal drugs【美俚】含有[拥有]毒品的 —see also 另见 **wash your dirty linen in public** (WASH[1] (6)) —**dirtily** *adv*

dirty[2] *adv* [I,T] **1 dirty rotten** *spoken* extremely nasty【口】极讨厌的: *the dirty rotten bastard!* 这个特别令人厌恶的家伙! | *What a dirty rotten trick!* 多么卑劣的伎俩啊! **2 play dirty a)** to behave in a very unfair and dishonest way 耍花招儿, 使用卑鄙手段 **b)** to cheat in a game〔比赛中〕作弊 **3 talk dirty** to talk rudely about sex 说脏话, 说下流话 **4 dirty great/dirty big** *BrE spoken* extremely big【英口】特别大的: *We suddenly saw this dirty great truck coming towards us.* 忽然我们看到这辆庞然大物的卡车朝我们开过来。

dirty[3] *v* **dirtied, dirtying** [I,T] **1** to put or leave marks on something and make it no longer clean 弄脏: *Max wiped his dirtied hands on his thighs.* 马克斯把脏手在大腿上擦了擦。**2 dirty your hands on sth** to become involved in something bad that will affect people's opinion of you 因某事弄脏自己的手〔因卷入不好的事情当中而影响自己的名声〕

dirty old man /,·· · '·/ *n* [C] *informal* an older man who is too sexually interested in younger women【非正式】老色鬼, 老淫棍

dirty tricks /,·· '·/ *n* [plural] secret, dishonest, and often criminal activities by a government, political group, or company, for example spreading false information about their competitors or opponents 卑鄙手段, 卑劣伎俩: **dirty tricks campaign** (=a planned series of dirty tricks) 一系列有计划的卑劣活动 *The airline was accused of a dirty tricks campaign against their rivals.* 这家航空公司被指控对竞争对手使用一系列有预谋的卑鄙手段。

dis- /dɪs; dɪs/ *prefix* **1** shows an opposite or negative〔表示相反或否定〕: *I disapprove* (=do not approve). 我不赞成。| *his dishonesty* (=lack of honesty) 他的不诚实 | *a discontented look* 不满意的表情 **2** shows the stopping or removing of a condition〔表示停止或除去〕: *Disconnect the machine from the electricity supply.* (=so that it is no longer connected) 把机器的电源断开。| *Disinfect the wound first.* 首先要给伤口消毒。**3** [in verbs 构成动词] to remove something〔表示除掉某物〕: *a dismasted ship* 一艘折断了桅杆的船

dis·a·bil·i·ty /,dɪsə`bɪlətɪ; ,dɪsə'bɪlɪti/ *n* **1** [C] a physical problem that makes someone unable to use a part of their body properly〔身体上的〕伤残; 残障: *She manages to lead a normal life in spite of her disabilities.* 尽管她有残疾, 她仍努力过着正常人的生活。**2** [U] the state of not being able to use parts of your body properly 丧失能力: *learning to cope with disability* 学会应付生理上的缺陷

dis·a·ble /dɪs`ebl; dɪs'eɪbəl/ *v* [T] **1** [often passive 常用被动态] to make someone unable to use a part of their body properly

使丧失能力，使残废：*Carter was permanently disabled in the war.* 卡特在战争中变成终生残废。**2** to deliberately make a machine or piece of equipment impossible to use 故意毁坏〔机器设备〕；使…无法使用：*This system is designed to destroy or disable enemy ballistic missiles.* 这个系统是为摧毁敌人的弹道导弹或者使之瘫痪而设计的。—**disablement** *n* [C,U]

3 **dis·a·bled** /dɪsˋebḷd; dɪsˈeɪbəld/ *adj* **1** someone who is disabled cannot use a part of their body properly 残障的，残疾的：**severely disabled** (=unable to use most of your body) 有严重残疾的 | **disabled parking/toilet/entrance** (=for disabled people) 为伤残人士设置的停车场/厕所/入口 **2 the disabled** people who are disabled 伤残人士：*The theatre has good access for the disabled.* 这家剧院为伤残人士准备了很方便的通道。—compare 比较 CRIPPLE[1] (1), HANDICAPPED

dis·a·buse /ˌdɪsəˋbjuz; ˌdɪsəˈbjuːz/ *v* [T] *formal* to persuade someone that what they believe is untrue【正式】纠正；使…消除错误观点：[+of] *I never did anything to disabuse him of that idea.* 我从没做过任何事使他打消那个念头。

dis·ad·van·tage /ˌdɪsədˋvæntɪdʒ; ˌdɪsədˈvɑːntɪdʒ/ *n* [C,U] an unfavourable condition or quality that makes someone or something less likely to be successful or effective 不利条件，劣势：[+of] *The main disadvantage of the project is the cost.* 这个项目最主要的缺点便是费用太高。| [+to] *There are some disadvantages to his proposal.* 他的建议有几处弱点。| **be at a disadvantage** (=have a disadvantage) 处于不利境地 *I was at a disadvantage because I didn't speak French.* 我不会说法语，所以处于劣势。| **put sb at a disadvantage/be to sb's disadvantage** (=give someone a disadvantage) 置某人于不利境地/使某人处于劣势 *Her height will be very much to her disadvantage if she wants to be a dancer.* 她如果想当舞蹈演员的话，她的身高将对她很不利。

dis·ad·van·taged /ˌdɪsədˋvæntɪdʒd; ˌdɪsədˈvɑːntɪdʒd◂/ *adj* having social disadvantages, such as a lack of money or education, which make it difficult for you to succeed 社会地位低下的，处于不利社会经济地位的〈如缺钱或教育程度不够等〉：*disadvantaged kids from the ghetto* 来自贫民区的贫贱孩子

dis·ad·van·ta·geous /dɪsˌædvænˋtedʒəs; ˌdɪsædvənˈteɪdʒəs/ *adj* [+to/for] unfavourable and likely to cause problems for you 不利的；可能引发问题的 —**disadvantageously** *adv*

dis·af·fec·ted /ˌdɪsəˋfɛktɪd; ˌdɪsəˈfektɨd◂/ *adj* no longer loyal because you are not at all satisfied with your leader, ruler etc 不忠的，疏远的〔由于对领导者、统治者等不满〕：*Some of the government's most loyal supporters are now becoming disaffected.* 政府一些最忠实的支持者现在变得越来越心怀不满了。—**disaffection** /-ˋfɛkʃən; -ˈfekʃən/ *n* [U]

dis·af·fil·i·ate /ˌdɪsəˋfɪlɪˌet; ˌdɪsəˈfɪlieɪt/ *v* [I,T+from] if an organization disaffiliates from another organization or is disaffiliated from it, it breaks the official connection it has with it 脱离，正式退出〔某个组织〕；割断关系 —compare 比较 AFFILIATE[1]

2 **dis·a·gree** /ˌdɪsəˋgri; ˌdɪsəˈgriː/ *v* [T] **1** to have or express a different opinion from someone else 不同意，有分歧：[+with] *Peter may disagree with this, but I don't really care.* 彼得或许不赞成此事，但是我并不真的在乎。| [+about/on] *We often disagree about politics.* 我们经常对政治问题有不同的见解。| **I disagree** *spoken*【口】*I disagree; I think it's a bad idea.* 我反对；我认为那是个坏主意。**2** if statements or reports about the same event or situation disagree, they are different from each other〔对于同一事件或形势的几个陈述或报道〕互不相符，不一致，互不相同

disagree with sb *phr v* [T] if something such as food or weather disagrees with you, it has a bad effect on you or makes you ill〔食物、气候〕对〔某人〕有不良影响；使〔某人〕身体不适：*Seafood always disagrees with me.* 我吃海鲜总是感到不舒服。

This graph shows how common the different grammar patterns of the verb **disagree** are. 本图表所示为动词 disagree 构成的不同语法模式的使用频率。

disagree with
disagree
disagree about
disagree on
disagree (that)
other

10% 20% 30% 40% 50% 60%

Based on the British National Corpus and the Longman Lancaster Corpus
据英国国家语料库和朗文兰开斯特语料库

dis·a·gree·a·ble /ˌdɪsəˋgriəbḷ; ˌdɪsəˈgriːəbəl◂/ *adj* **1** not at all enjoyable or pleasant 令人不快的；不合意的；讨厌的：*a disagreeable experience* 一次令人不愉快的经历 **2** unfriendly and bad-tempered 不友好的；脾气坏的：*a rude, disagreeable woman* 一个不懂礼数、难相处的女人 —**disagreeably** *adv*

dis·a·gree·ment /ˌdɪsəˋgrimənt; ˌdɪsəˈgriːmənt/ *n* **1** [C,U] a situation in which people express different opinions about something and sometimes quarrel 意见不合，分歧，争论：*Just because we've had a few disagreements, it doesn't mean we aren't still friends.* 仅仅是我们有过几次意见不合并不说明我们不再是朋友。| [+about/over/as to] *There is some disagreement as to whether the disease is curable.* 关于这种疾病是否可以治愈，意见有些分歧。| [+among/between] *There is a lot of disagreement among doctors about this.* 关于此事，医生之间有着许多不同的意见。| **be in disagreement** (=disagree) 有分歧 **2** [U] differences between two statements, reports etc that ought to be similar〔两个本该相似的陈述或报道〕互不相符，不一致：[+between] *There is considerable disagreement between these two estimates.* 这两种估计很不一致。

dis·al·low /ˌdɪsəˋlaʊ; ˌdɪsəˈlaʊ/ *v* [T] to officially refuse to allow something such as a claim, because a rule has been broken〔由于违反了规则〕不准许，驳回：*Leeds had a goal disallowed for being offside.* 利兹队由于越位被判进球无效。

dis·ap·pear /ˌdɪsəˋpɪr; ˌdɪsəˈpɪə/ *v* [I] **1** to become impossible to see or find 消失，失踪：*Where are my keys? They seem to have disappeared.* 我的钥匙哪儿去了？好像失踪了。| **disappear behind/under/into etc** *Grab the cat quick! Before he disappears out the door!* 快把猫抓住！趁它还没溜出门去！| **disappear from view/sight** *David watched her car until it disappeared from view.* 戴维一直望着她的车，直到看不见为止。**2** to stop existing 不复存在：*So what happens when the rain forest disappears for ever?* 那么，热带雨林若永远消失了会怎样呢？—**disappearance** *n* [C,U]: *Her sudden disappearance was very worrying.* 她忽然失踪，很令人担忧。 2 2

dis·ap·point /ˌdɪsəˋpɔɪnt; ˌdɪsəˈpɔɪnt/ *v* [T] **1** to make someone feel sad because something they hoped for or expected did not happen 使〔某人〕失望：*I'm sorry to disappoint you, but I can't come after all.* 我很抱歉让你失望，但是我还是来不了。| *You disappoint me, Eric. I expected better.* 你令我失望，埃里克。我本想你能做得更好。**2 disappoint sb's hopes/expectations** to prevent something from happening that someone hoped for or expected 让某人的希望/期望破灭

dis·ap·point·ed /ˌdɪsəˋpɔɪntɪd; ˌdɪsəˈpɔɪntɨd◂/ *adj* **1** sad because something you hoped for did not happen, or because someone or something was not as good as you expected 失望的；沮丧的：*Dad seemed more disappointed than angry.* 与其说爸爸很生气，倒不如说他很失望。| [+about] *Nathan's really disappointed about not being able to go.* 内森对于自己去不了着实感到失望。| **disappointed in sb** *I'm disappointed in you! How could you have lied like that?* 你真让我失望！你怎么能那样撒谎呢？| **disappointed (that)** *Of course I'm disappointed I didn't get an invitation.* 我没有受到邀请，当然感到很失望。| [+with] *I have to say we're disappointed with your work.* 我不得不说你们的工作让我们很失望。| [+at] *Are you disappointed at not being chosen?* 你没被选中，是不是很失望？| **disappointed to hear/see/find** *We were disappointed to find the museum closed.* 看到博物馆已经关门，我们感到很沮丧。| **bitterly/terribly disappointed** *Gordon was bitterly disappointed when he failed that course.* 戈登那门课没及格，他非常灰心。**2 disappointed hope/plan/expectation** something you hope for, plan, or expect that does not happen or is not as good as you expected 破灭的希望/计划/期望

dis·ap·point·ing /ˌdɪsəˋpɔɪntɪŋ; ˌdɪsəˈpɔɪntɪŋ◂/ *adj* not as good as you hoped or expected 令人失望[沮丧、扫兴]的：*disappointing profit figures* 令人失望的赢利数字 | *Well, Bill was really negative about it, which was pretty disappointing.* 嗯，比尔对此事的态度很消极，这很让人扫兴。—**disappointingly** *adv*

dis·ap·point·ment /ˌdɪsəˋpɔɪntmənt; ˌdɪsəˈpɔɪntmənt/ *n* **1** [U] sadness that something is not as good as you expected it to be, or has not happened in the way you hoped it would 失望；沮丧：**to sb's (great) disappointment** *To her great disappointment none of her tomatoes grew well.* 令她十分沮丧的是，她种的番茄长得都不好。**2** [C] someone or something that is not as good as you hoped or expected 令人失望的人[事物]：*The movie was kind of a disappointment.* 那部电影有些让人失望。| **be a disappointment to sb** *Frankly, I've been a disappointment to my father; he wanted me to be a lawyer.* 说实话，我很让我父亲失望；他本想让我成为一名律师。

dis·ap·pro·ba·tion /ˌdɪsæprəˋbeʃən; ˌdɪsæprəˈbeɪʃən/ *n* [U] *formal* disapproval of someone or something because you think they are morally wrong【正式】〔认为某人或某事道德上不正确而〕反对, 不赞成; 责难

dis·ap·prov·al /ˌdɪsəˋpruvl̩; ˌdɪsəˈpruːvəl/ *n* [U] an attitude that shows you think that someone or their behaviour, ideas etc are bad or unsuitable 不赞同, 反对; 责难; 不许可: [+of] *We intend to express our disapproval of the marriage.* 我们打算反对这门婚事。| **with disapproval** *Baxter eyed our dirty clothes with obvious disapproval.* 巴克斯特打量着我们的脏衣服, 很明显是不满意。| **in disapproval** *Aunt Clarissa snorted in disapproval.* 克拉丽莎姨妈不以为然地哼了一声。

dis·ap·prove /ˌdɪsəˋpruv; ˌdɪsəˈpruːv/ *v* [I] to think that someone or their behaviour, ideas etc are bad or unsuitable 不赞成, 反对; 认为不好; 非难: [+of] *Mother disapproves of every boyfriend I bring home.* 妈妈对我带回家的每一个男朋友都不满意。| **strongly disapprove** *I strongly disapprove of couples living together before marriage.* 我坚决反对两个人未结婚便住在一起。

dis·ap·prov·ing /ˌdɪsəˋpruvɪŋ; ˌdɪsəˈpruːvɪŋ◂/ *adj* showing that you think someone or something is bad or unsuitable 不赞成的, 表示反对的: *a disapproving frown* 不满地皱着眉头 —**disapprovingly** *adv*: *Tyler shook his head disapprovingly.* 泰勒不满地摇了摇头。

dis·arm /dɪsˋɑrm; dɪsˈɑːm/ *v* **1** [I] to reduce the size of your armed forces and the number of weapons 裁军; 裁减军备: *Getting the rebels to disarm will not be easy.* 要让叛乱分子解除武装并非易事。**2** [T] to take away someone's weapons 缴〔某人〕的械, 解除〔某人〕的武装: *Captured soldiers were disarmed and put into camps.* 被俘获的士兵被缴了械, 然后关进战俘营。**3** [T] if your manner or behaviour disarms someone, it is so pleasant that it makes them stop feeling angry or disapproving towards you 消除〔某人〕的怒气[不满]: *That charm of hers can disarm even her sternest critics.* 她的那种魅力甚至可以使得对她最为苛刻的批评者也火不起来。—see also 另见 DISARMING **4** [T] to take the explosives out of a bomb, MISSILE (1) etc 拆除, 取出〔炸弹、导弹等〕的引信

dis·ar·ma·ment /dɪsˋɑrməmənt; dɪsˈɑːməmənt/ *n* [U] the reduction of the size of a country's military forces and the number of weapons that it has 裁军; 裁减军备: **nuclear disarmament** (=reduction in the number of atomic weapons) 核裁军, 核武器的裁减

dis·arm·ing /dɪsˋɑrmɪŋ; dɪsˈɑːmɪŋ/ *adj* making you trust someone or feel less angry with them than before 使人消气的, 消除敌意的, 使人不存戒心的: *Kenneth has such a disarming smile!* 肯尼思的微笑真让人倾倒! —**disarmingly** *adv*

dis·ar·range /ˌdɪsəˋrendʒ; ˌdɪsəˈreɪndʒ/ *v* [T] *formal* to make something untidy【正式】使不整齐, 弄乱 —**disarrangement** *n* [U]

dis·ar·ray /ˌdɪsəˋre; ˌdɪsəˈreɪ/ *n* [U] *formal* the state of being completely confused or untidy【正式】混乱, 凌乱: **in disarray** *Troops retreated in disarray under heavy gunfire.* 军队在猛烈的炮火下仓皇撤退。| *Manuscripts lay in wild disarray on the side table.* 手稿凌乱地放在边桌上。| **throw sth into disarray/fall into disarray** *Gray's plans have been thrown into disarray because of injuries.* 由于发生伤人事故, 格雷的计划全被打乱了。

dis·as·so·ci·ate /ˌdɪsəˋsoʃɪˌet; ˌdɪsəˈsəʊʃieɪt/ *v* [T] another form of DISSOCIATE dissociate 的另一种拼法

2 3 **di·sas·ter** /dɪˋzæstə; dɪˈzɑːstə/ *n* [C,U] **1** a sudden event such as a flood, storm, or accident which causes great damage or suffering 灾难, 灾祸〈如水灾、暴风雨、意外事故等〉: *108 people died in the mining disaster.* 在这次矿难中有108人丧生。| **natural disaster** (=caused by nature, not by an accident) 自然灾害 *The 1987 hurricane was the worst natural disaster to hit England for decades.* 1987年的飓风是数十年来袭击英格兰的最为严重的自然灾害。| **disaster area** (=a place where a disaster has happened) 灾区 | **disaster strikes** *Disaster struck on the first day, when all our equipment was stolen.* 灾难头一天就降临了, 我们所有的装备都被偷盗一空。**2** a complete failure 彻底的失败: *The party was a total disaster – half the guests didn't even turn up!* 晚会真是失败, 竟有一半的客人没有来!

CULTURAL NOTE 文化注释

In the US, if the governor or the president DECLARES (=says officially) that a place is a disaster area, it then receives money from the state or FEDERAL government to build again. 在美国, 如果州长或总统宣布某地为灾区, 该地区则会得到州政府或联邦政府的资金, 用于重建。

di·sas·trous /dɪˋzæstrəs; dɪˈzɑːstrəs/ *adj* very bad, or ending in failure 灾难性的; 以失败告终的: *Warrington's disastrous early marriage* 沃林顿以失败告终的早婚 | *Chemical leaks have had a disastrous effect on wildlife.* 化学物质泄漏对野生生物造成了灾难性的影响。—**disastrously** *adv*

dis·a·vow /ˌdɪsəˋvaʊ; ˌdɪsəˈvaʊ/ *v* [T] *formal* to state that you are not responsible for something, or that you have no knowledge of it【正式】否认, 不承认: *He later disavowed any connection with the Fascist collaborators.* 他后来否认与法西斯通敌分子有任何关系。—**disavowal** *n* [C,U]

dis·band /dɪsˋbænd; dɪsˈbænd/ *v* [I,T] if a club or organization disbands or is disbanded, its activities are officially stopped, and it no longer exists (使)〔俱乐部或组织等〕解体; 解散

dis·bar /dɪsˋbɑr; dɪsˈbɑː/ *v* **disbarred, disbarring** [T] to make a lawyer leave the bar (BAR¹ (8)) or the legal profession 取消〔某人〕的律师资格, 使〔某人〕退出律师行业 —compare 比较 DEBAR —**disbarment** *n* [U]

dis·be·lief /ˌdɪsbəˋlif; ˌdɪsbl̩ˈliːf/ *n* [U] a feeling that something is not true or does not exist 不相信, 怀疑: *My initial response was one of utter disbelief.* 我最初的反应便是根本不相信。| **stare/gasp/blink etc in disbelief** *Marta shook her head in disbelief, shocked by the damage.* 玛尔塔不相信地摇着头, 被造成的损失给吓呆了。—compare 比较 UNBELIEF, BELIEF

dis·be·lieve /ˌdɪsbəˋliv; ˌdɪsbl̩ˈliːv/ *v* [I+in,T] *formal* to not believe something or someone【正式】不相信, 怀疑〔某人或某事〕: *I see no reason to disbelieve him.* 我看没有什么理由不相信他。—**disbelieving** *adj*: *disbelieving laughter* 怀疑的笑声

dis·burse /dɪsˋbɝs; dɪsˈbɜːs/ *v* [T] *formal* to pay out money, especially from a large sum that is available for a special purpose【正式】〔从一大笔专用资金中拿出钱来〕支付, 支出: *Over $25 million has been disbursed from the fund.* 已从这项资金中支付2500多万美元。—**disbursement** *n* [C,U]

disc also 又作 **disk** *AmE*【美】/dɪsk; dɪsk/ *n* [C] **1** a round, flat shape or object〔扁平的〕圆盘状物; 圆盘形状: *a revolving metal disc* 一个旋转的金属圆盘 **2** a COMPACT DISC 激光唱片 **3** a record that you play on a RECORD PLAYER 唱片 **4** *BrE* a computer DISK【英】电脑磁盘, 磁碟 **5** a flat piece of CARTILAGE between the bones of your back 椎间盘: **slipped disc** (=one that has slipped out of its correct place) 突出的椎间盘 3

dis·card¹ /dɪsˋkɑrd; dɪsˈkɑːd/ *v* **1** [T] to get rid of something because it is useless 扔掉, 弃置: *What was more worrying was a box of used syringes that hadn't been properly discarded.* 更令人担忧的是, 一盒用过的注射器没有得到妥善弃置。**2** [I,T] to put down unwanted cards in a card game〔在牌戏中〕打出(不想要的牌) —**discarded** *adj*: *old discarded clothes* 不要的旧衣服

discard² /ˋdɪskɑrd; ˈdɪskɑːd/ *n* [C] an unwanted card that is put down in a card game〔在牌戏中〕因不要而打出的牌

disc brakes /ˈ / *n* [plural] BRAKES¹ that work by means of a pair of hard surfaces pressing against a DISC (1) in the centre of a car wheel〔汽车的〕盘式制动器, 圆盘刹车

di·scern /dɪˋsɝn; dɪˈsɜːn/ *v* [T not in progressive 不用进行时] *formal* to see, notice, or understand something only after looking at it or thinking about it carefully; PERCEIVE (2)【正式】〔仔细地看过或想过之后才〕觉察出, 弄清楚, 辨明: *In the distance I could just discern the hills near Tendaho.* 在远处我只能望见滕达霍附近的群山。| **discern who/what/how etc** *It was difficult to discern which of them was telling the truth.* 很难弄清楚他们之中谁说的是实话。—**discernible** *adj*: *There is still no discernible improvement in the economic situation.* 经济形势仍然看不出明显的好转。—**discernibly** *adv*

di·scern·ing /dɪˋsɝnɪŋ; dɪˈsɜːnɪŋ/ *adj* showing the ability to make good judgments, especially about art, music, style etc〔尤指艺术、音乐、时尚等方面〕有鉴赏力的, 有品味的, 识别能力好的: *Amanda liked to think she was discerning in her tastes.* 阿曼达自以为很有鉴赏力。| *With prices down by a third, there are many bargains around for the discerning buyer.* 价格降了三分之一, 对于那些识货的人来说, 有许多便宜货可买。

di·scern·ment /dɪˋsɝnmənt; dɪˈsɜːnmənt/ *n* [U] *formal* the ability to make good judgments about people or about art, music, style etc【正式】〔在对人或艺术、音乐、时尚等方面的〕鉴赏力, 识别能力, 品味: *I hope Pam shows more taste and discernment in choosing a husband.* 我希望帕姆选择丈夫时能更有品味和识别能力。

dis·charge¹ /dɪsˋtʃɑrdʒ; dɪsˈtʃɑːdʒ/ *v*

1 ►SEND SB AWAY 让某人走◄ [T] to officially allow a person to go or send them away, especially after being ill in hospital or working in the army, navy etc 正式准许〔某人〕离开〔尤指让住院的病人出院或让服役的人退伍等〕: [+from] *I think Oliver*

gets discharged from the RAF in August. 我想奥利弗将于今年8月从皇家空军退役。| **discharge yourself** (=leave hospital before your treatment is complete) 擅自出院
2 ▶LET STH OUT 排出某物◀ [I always+adv/prep,T] to send out gas, liquid, smoke etc, or allow it to escape 放出〔气体、液体、烟等〕: [+into] *pollutants being discharged into the atmosphere* 被排放到大气中的污染物
3 ▶SHOOT 射出◀ [T] to fire a gun or shoot an ARROW (1) etc 开〔枪、炮〕; 射〔箭〕
4 discharge a duty/promise/responsibility etc *formal* to do properly everything that is part of a particular duty etc【正式】尽职责/履行诺言/承担责任等: *the failure of the council to discharge its duty* 市议会未能履行其职责
5 discharge a debt *formal* to pay a debt【正式】清偿债务
6 ▶GOODS/PASSENGERS 货物/乘客◀ [T] to unload goods or passengers from a ship, plane etc 卸〔货〕; 让〔乘客〕下船[飞机]
7 ▶ELECTRICITY 电◀ [I,T] if a piece of electrical equipment discharges or is discharged, it sends out electricity 放〔电〕
8 ▶A WOUND 伤口◀ [I,T] to send out PUS (=infected liquid) 流〔脓〕, 出〔水〕

discharge² /ˋdɪstʃɑrdʒ; ˈdɪstʃɑːdʒ/ *n* **1** [U] the action of allowing someone to go away, especially someone who has been ill in hospital or working in the army, navy etc 准许离开〔尤指病人出院, 服役的人退伍等〕: [+from] *Patients' needs after discharge from hospital will be monitored.* 出院后病人的需求将得到监控。—see also 另见 DISHONOURABLE DISCHARGE **2** [C,U] the act of sending out gas, liquid, smoke etc, or the substance that is sent out 〔气体、液体、烟等的〕排放; 排放的物质: [+of] *the discharge of toxic waste into the sea* 有毒废物向海里的排放 | **nasal/vaginal discharge** (=a thick liquid that comes out of someone's nose or VAGINA because of illness) 鼻腔/阴道分泌物 **3** [C,U] electricity that is sent out by a piece of equipment, a storm etc 〔仪器、雷暴等释放出来的〕电 **4** [U+of] the act of doing a duty or paying a debt 〔职责的〕履行; 〔债务的〕清偿: *the discharge of the college's legal responsibilities* 学院法律责任的履行

discharged bank·rupt /ˌ·ˌ·ˈ··/ *n* [C] someone who cannot pay their debts but who has obeyed the orders of the court and can do business again 免除债务的破产者〔已执行法庭规定, 可以再做生意的破产者〕

di·sci·ple /dɪˋsaɪpl; dɪˈsaɪpəl/ *n* [C] **1** someone who believes in the ideas of a great teacher, especially a religious one, and tries to follow them 〔尤指宗教导师的〕追随者, 门徒, 信徒: *Dian Fossey, the American disciple of Louis Leakey who studied gorillas in Rwanda* 迪昂·福塞, 在卢旺达研究大猩猩的路易斯·利基的美国弟子 **2** one of the first twelve men to follow Christ 耶稣最初的十二门徒之一

di·sci·ple·ship /dɪˋsaɪplˌʃɪp; dɪˈsaɪpəlʃɪp/ *n* [U] the period of time when someone is a disciple, or the state of being one 当信徒期间; 信徒身份

dis·ci·pli·nar·i·an /ˌdɪsəplɪnˋɛrɪən; ˌdɪsɪplɪˈneəriən/ *n* [C] someone who believes people should obey orders and rules, and who makes them do this 执行纪律者: *a strict disciplinarian* 一个严格执行纪律的人

dis·ci·pli·na·ry /ˋdɪsəplɪnˌɛrɪ; ˈdɪsɪplɪnəri/ *adj* connected with the punishment of someone who has not obeyed rules, or with trying to make people obey rules 有关纪律的, 执行纪律的; 惩处的: **disciplinary action/measures** (=things you do to punish someone) 惩戒行动/措施 *The investigation led to disciplinary action against several officers.* 调查引发了对几名军官采取纪律行动。| **disciplinary hearing/committee** (=to decide if someone should be punished) 惩戒聆讯会/委员会〔决定某人是否应受到处罚〕

S3 W2 **dis·ci·pline¹** /ˋdɪsəplɪn; ˈdɪsɪplɪn/ *n* **1** [U] the practice of making people obey rules and orders, or the controlled situation that results from this practice 纪律, 纪律状况: *We have high standards of discipline at this school that must be maintained.* 在这所学校里, 我们有很高的纪律标准, 必须遵守。| *strict military discipline* 严格的军纪 | **keep discipline** *teachers who can't keep discipline in the classroom* 无法维持课堂纪律的老师们 **2** [C,U] a method of training your mind or learning to control your behaviour 〔思想或行为的〕训练, 磨练: *Learning poetry is a good discipline for the memory.* 背诗是训练记忆力的一种好方法。**3** [U] the ability to control your own behaviour and way of working 克制能力: *He'll never finish that course – he's got no discipline!* 他永远也修不完那门课程, 他一点克制能力都没有! —see also 另见 SELF-DISCIPLINE **4** [U] punishment for not obeying rules 处罚, 惩处, 处分: *That child needs discipline.* 那个孩子需要受到处罚。**5** [C] an area of knowledge such as history, chemistry, mathematics etc that is studied at a university 〔大学里学习的〕专业, 科目

discipline² *v* [T] **1** to teach someone to obey rules and control their own behaviour 训练, 管教: *At least I'm not afraid of disciplining my kids!* 至少我不害怕管教自己的孩子们! **2 discipline yourself (to do sth)** to control the way you work, how regularly you do something etc, because you know it is good for you 严格要求自己, 约束自己(去做某事): *It's a question of disciplining yourself to write every day.* 这是个约束你自己每天坚持写作的问题。**3** to punish someone in order to keep order and control 惩处〔某人〕: *One director left today and two others have been disciplined.* 一名主管今天离了职, 另外两名也已经受到了惩处。

dis·ci·plined /ˋdɪsəplɪnd; ˈdɪsɪplɪnd/ *adj* behaving in a controlled way according to strict rules 遵守纪律的: *the most disciplined, effective army in the world* 世界上最具有纪律性、效率最高的一支军队 | *a disciplined approach* 严谨有序的方法

disc jock·ey /ˈ·ˌ··/ *n* [C] someone who introduces and plays records of popular music on a radio show or at a dance club 〔电台〕音乐唱片节目主持人; 〔夜总会〕舞曲唱片播放员, 唱片骑师

dis·claim /dɪsˋklem; dɪsˈkleɪm/ *v* [T] **disclaim responsibility/knowledge etc** *formal* to state that you are not responsible for something, that you do not know anything about it, etc【正式】否认[不承认]〔对某事〕有责任/知情等: *I can't believe the insurance company disclaimed liability for the accident.* 我无法相信保险公司竟然拒绝对此意外事故负赔偿责任。

dis·claim·er /dɪsˋklemɚ; dɪsˈkleɪmə/ *n* [C] a statement that you are not responsible for something, that you are not connected with it etc 不承担责任的声明, 与某事没有关联的声明

dis·close /dɪsˋkloz; dɪsˈkləʊz/ *v* [T] **1** to make something publicly known, especially after it has been kept secret from the public 〔尤指在被隐瞒后〕透露, 揭露, 泄露; 公开〔某事〕: *The Security Service is unlikely to disclose any information.* 保安部门不可能透露任何消息。| **disclose that** *It has recently been disclosed that 30% of donations are spent on publicity.* 据最新消息透露, 30% 的捐款被用于宣传。**2** to show something by removing the thing that covers it 〔把盖在某物上的东西去掉以〕显露; 揭开: *The curtains rose, disclosing a stage bathed in red light.* 帷幕升起, 显露出笼罩在一片红光之中的舞台。

dis·clo·sure /dɪsˋkloʒɚ; dɪsˈkləʊʒə/ *n* **1** [U] the act of telling or showing something that has been kept secret 公开; 透露; 披露: *MPs called for public disclosure of the committee's findings.* 议员要求公开委员会的调查结果。**2** [C] a fact which is made known after being kept secret 被公开的秘闻; 被透露的事实: *Following sensational disclosures concerning his personal life, he has offered to resign.* 在他的私生活被大肆披露之后, 他主动提出辞职。

dis·co /ˋdɪsko; ˈdɪskəʊ/ *n* [C] a club or social event at which people dance to recorded popular music 迪斯科[的士高]舞厅, 迪斯科[的士高]舞会

dis·cog·ra·phy /dɪˋskɑgrəfɪ; dɪˈskɒgrəfi/ *n* [C] a list of the music and songs recorded by a musician or musical group 〔音乐家或音乐团体的〕录音作品目录

dis·col·or /dɪsˋkʌlɚ; dɪsˈkʌlə/ *v* [T] the American spelling of DISCOLOUR discolour 的美式拼法

dis·col·o·ra·tion /dɪsˌkʌləˋreʃən; dɪsˌkʌləˈreɪʃən/ *n* **1** [U] the process of becoming discoloured 变色; 褪色 **2** [C] a place on the surface of something where it has become discoloured 变色点, 褪色处

dis·col·our *BrE*【英】, **discolor** *AmE*【美】/dɪsˋkʌlɚ; dɪsˈkʌlə/ *v* [I,T] if something is discoloured or if it discolours, its colour changes, making it look dirty or unattractive (使)变色, 退色: *Sprinkle the apple slices with lemon juice to prevent them from discolouring.* 在苹果片上洒些柠檬汁, 防止它们变色。

dis·com·bob·u·late /ˌdɪskəmˋbɑbjəˌlet; ˌdɪskəmˈbɒbjʊleɪt/ *v* [T] *humorous* to make someone feel completely confused or upset【幽默】使〔某人〕感到困惑, 使〔某人〕极度不安

dis·com·fit /dɪsˋkʌmfɪt; dɪsˈkʌmfɪt/ *v* [T] *formal* to make someone feel slightly uncomfortable, annoyed, or embarrassed【正式】使〔某人〕窘迫, 使〔某人〕尴尬: *Expecting a handshake, Jenny was discomfited by his kiss.* 珍妮只是期待着和他握握手, 因而对于他的亲吻感到有些无所适从。—**discomfiture** *n* [U]

dis·com·fort /dɪsˋkʌmfɚt; dɪsˈkʌmfət/ *n* **1** [U] a feeling of slight pain or of being physically uncomfortable 不舒服, 不适: *You may experience some discomfort for a few days after the operation.* 手术后几天内你可能会感到有些不舒服。**2** [U] a feeling of embarrassment, shame, or slight worry 尴尬; 惭愧; 窘迫: [+at] *Paul's discomfort at facing criticism tends to make him*

too defensive. 受到批评时保罗感到很别扭，这往往使他戒心太强。**3** [C] something that makes you uncomfortable 使人感到不舒服的事情: *the discomforts of travel* 旅途中的不适

dis·com·mode /ˌdɪskə`mod; ˌdɪskə'məʊd/ *v* [T] *formal* to cause trouble or difficulties for someone; INCOMMODE【正式】给〔某人〕带来麻烦，给〔某人〕添麻烦

dis·com·pose /ˌdɪskəm`poz; ˌdɪskəm'pəʊz/ *v* [T] *formal* to make someone feel worried and no longer calm【正式】使〔某人〕焦虑，使〔某人〕不安 —**discomposure** /-`poʒɚ; -'pəʊʒə/ *n* [U]

dis·con·cert /ˌdɪskən`sɝt; ˌdɪskən'sɜːt/ *v* [T often passive 常用被动态] to make someone feel slightly confused or worried 使〔某人〕困惑；使不安: *It was that cold, steady gaze of his that disconcerted her most.* 最让她感到不安的是他那冷漠的、目不转睛的凝视。

dis·con·cert·ing /ˌdɪskən`sɝtɪŋ; ˌdɪskən'sɜːtɪŋ◂/ *adj* making you feel slightly confused or worried 令人困惑的，令人担忧的 —**disconcertingly** *adv*: *It all seemed disconcertingly familiar.* 这一切似乎熟悉得令人感到疑惑。

dis·con·nect /ˌdɪskə`nɛkt; ˌdɪskə'nekt/ *v* [T] **1** to take out the wire, pipe etc that connects a machine or piece of equipment to something 断开，切断: *Disconnect the cables before you try to move the computer.* 在你挪动电脑之前，先把连接电缆拔下来。**2** to remove the supply of power from a machine or building 切断〔电力供应〕: *You realize if we don't pay that bill soon they'll disconnect our gas?* 你有没有意识到如果我们不付煤气费，他们很快就会切断对我们的煤气供应？**3** to break the telephone connection between two people 挂断〔电话〕: *Operator? We've been disconnected.* 是接线员吗？我们的电话被中断了。—**disconnection** /-`nɛkʃən; -'nekʃən/ *n* [C,U]

dis·con·nect·ed /ˌdɪskə`nɛktɪd; ˌdɪskə'nektɪd◂/ *adj* disconnected thoughts or ideas do not seem to be related to each other〔思想或想法等〕不连贯的，无关联的

dis·con·so·late /dɪs`kɑnslɪt; dɪs'kɒnsəlɪt/ *adj* feeling extremely sad and hopeless 极度忧郁的；绝望的. *A few disconsolate men sat in the foyer with their hats in their hands.* 几个面色忧郁的男子坐在休息厅里，手里拿着他们的帽子。—**disconsolately** *adv*: *O'Grady trudged disconsolately back home.* 奥格雷迪神情沮丧地迈着沉重的步子走回家。

dis·con·tent¹ /ˌdɪskən`tɛnt; ˌdɪskən'tent/ *n* [U] a feeling of being unhappy and not satisfied with the situation you are in 不愉快；不满足；不满意: **[+with]** *There is no evidence whatsoever of customer discontent with our credit terms.* 没有任何证据显示顾客对我们的信贷条件有不满之意。—opposite 反义词 CONTENTMENT

discontent² *v* [T] to make someone feel discontented 使不愉快；使不满

dis·con·tent·ed /ˌdɪskən`tɛntɪd; ˌdɪskən'tentɪd◂/ *adj* unhappy or not satisfied with the situation you are in 不愉快的，不满的，不满足的: **[+with]** *Eva was ambitious and was discontented with her job at the post office.* 伊娃很有志向，她对自己在邮局的工作并不满足。—**discontentedly** *adv*

dis·con·tin·ue /ˌdɪskən`tɪnju; ˌdɪskən'tɪnjuː/ *v* [T] to stop doing or providing something that you have regularly done or provided until now 中止，中断，终止: *Bus Route 51 is being discontinued as of March 1st.* 51路公共汽车将从3月1日起停止运营。| *a discontinued china pattern* 不再使用的瓷器图案 | **discontinued line** (=a type of product that is no longer being produced) 已停止生产的产品 —**discontinuation** /ˌdɪskəntɪnju`eʃən; ˌdɪskəntɪnju'eɪʃən/ *n* [U] —**discontinuance** /ˌdɪskən`tɪnjuəns; ˌdɪskən'tɪnjuəns/ *n* [U]

dis·con·ti·nu·i·ty /ˌdɪskɑntə`nuətɪ; ˌdɪskɒntɪ'njuːɪti/ *n* **1** [U] the fact of a process not being continuous 不连续性，间断性 **2** [C] a sudden change or pause in a process 中断，间断

dis·con·tin·u·ous /ˌdɪskən`tɪnjuəs; ˌdɪskən'tɪnjuəs◂/ *adj* not continuous 不连续的，断续的: *Women are particularly affected because of their discontinuous employment patterns.* 妇女尤其受到影响，因为她们的就业模式是不连续的。—**discontinuously** *adv*

dis·cord /`dɪskɔrd; 'dɪskɔːd/ *n* **1** [U] *formal* disagreement or quarrelling between people【正式】不和，纷争: *marital discord* 婚姻的不和 | *discord within NATO* 北约内部的纷争 **2** [C,U] an unpleasant sound made by a group of musical notes that do not go together well 不和谐的音调，刺耳的声音 —compare 比较 HARMONY

dis·cord·ant /dɪs`kɔrdṇt; dɪs'kɔːdənt/ *adj* **1 strike/sound a discordant note** *literary* to seem strange and unsuitable in relation to everything around【文】显得不谐调／听起来突兀: *The modern decor strikes a discordant note in this 17th century building.* 这座17世纪建筑上面的现代装饰显得很不和谐。**2** a discordant sound is unpleasant because it is made up of musical notes that do not go together well〔声音〕刺耳的，嘈杂的 **3** not in agreement 不一致的，相互冲突的: *discordant results from the experiment* 不一致的实验结果

dis·co·theque /ˌdɪskə`tɛk; 'dɪskətek/ *n* [C] a DISCO 迪斯科[的士高]舞厅；迪斯科[的士高]舞会

dis·count¹ /`dɪskaunt; 'dɪskaʊnt/ *n* [C] **1** a reduction in the cost of goods that you are buying 减价，折扣: *Do I get a discount if I buy a whole case of wine?* 如果我买一整箱酒，能给我打折扣吗？| **discount price/fare** (=cheaper than the usual price) 折扣价 | **discount store/shop/warehouse** (=where you can buy goods cheaply) 廉价商店／货仓 **2 at a discount a)** bought or sold for less than the usual price〔买卖〕低于正常价，打折 **b)** *informal* not wanted or not regarded as valuable【非正式】不受欢迎的；不值钱的；受轻视的: *a ridiculous place where intelligence is at a discount* 一个聪明才智不受重视的可笑的地方 3

discount² /`dɪskaunt; dɪs'kaʊnt/ *v* [T] to regard an idea, opinion, or piece of news as unimportant or unlikely to be true 不理会，不重视〔观点、意见、消息〕: *Larry tends to discount any suggestion I make in meetings.* 拉里往往不理会我在会上提出的任何建议。| **discount the possibility of** (=think that something is very unlikely to happen) 认为〔某事〕很不可能发生 *General Hausken had not discounted the possibility of aerial attack* 豪斯肯将军并非认为空袭完全没有可能。

dis·coun·te·nance /dɪs`kauntənəns; dɪs'kaʊntɪnəns/ *v* [T] *formal* to stop someone from doing something by showing that you disapprove of their behaviour【正式】不赞成，阻止〔某人的行为〕

dis·cour·age /dɪs`kɝɪdʒ; dɪs'kʌrɪdʒ/ *v* [T] **1** to prevent or try to prevent someone from doing something by making the action difficult or unpleasant, or by showing them that it would not be a good thing to do（设法）阻止；打消…的念头: *You should install locks on all your windows to discourage burglars.* 你应该在所有的窗户上都安上锁，以防窃贼入屋。| **discourage sb from doing sth** *We ought to be focusing on discouraging kids from smoking.* 我们应把重点集中在劝阻孩子们不要吸烟。**2** to make someone think that they will not be able to succeed in doing something so that they no longer want to continue doing it 使灰心，使泄气: *Students soon get discouraged if you criticize them too often.* 如果你批评学生次数太多，他们很快就会泄气的。—opposite 反义词 ENCOURAGE

dis·cour·age·ment /dɪs`kɝɪdʒmənt; dɪs'kʌrɪdʒmənt/ *n* **1** [U] a feeling that you have lost confidence or determination and no longer want to continue doing something 气馁，泄气，失去信心 **2** [U] the act of trying to discourage someone from doing something 劝阻，阻止 **3** [C] something that discourages you 使某人气馁的事情；挫折

dis·cour·a·ging /dɪs`kɝɪdʒɪŋ; dɪs'kʌrɪdʒɪŋ/ *adj* making you lose the confidence or determination you need to continue doing something 令人失去信心的，使人气馁的，使人泄气的: *The test results so far encountered have been very discouraging.* 目前所看到的考试结果让人非常泄气。—**discouragingly** *adv*

dis·course¹ /`dɪskors; 'dɪskɔːs/ *n* **1** [C] a serious speech or piece of writing on a particular subject〔就某个题目的〕演讲，论述，著述: **[+on/upon]** *Professor Grant delivered a long discourse on aspects of moral theology.* 格兰特教授就道德神学的各个方面发表了长篇演讲。**2** [U] serious conversation between people〔严肃的〕谈话，交谈: *You can't expect meaningful discourse when you two disagree so violently.* 既然你们两位的意见分歧这么大，别指望进行什么有意义的交谈。**3** [U] the language used in particular kinds of speech or writing〔在特定类型的讲述或论著中使用的〕语言，话语: *scientific discourse* 科学话语 3

discourse² /dɪ`skors; dɪs'kɔːs/ *v*

discourse on/upon sth *phr v* [T] to make a long formal speech about something〔关于某事作长篇的、正式的〕讲述，论说: *Mrs Hitchins discoursed at length on the ignorance of the frontier people.* 希钦斯夫人详细地讲述了边疆居民的无知。

dis·cour·te·ous /dɪs`kɝtɪəs; dɪs'kɜːtiəs/ *adj formal* not polite, and not showing respect for other people【正式】不讲礼貌的；失礼的: *Cameron was not really interested, but it would be discourteous to say so.* 卡梅伦并不真正感兴趣，但是若这么说会很不礼貌。—**discourteously** *adv* —**discourteousness** *n* [U]

dis·cour·te·sy /dɪs`kɝtəsɪ; dɪs'kɜːtəsi/ *n* [C,U] *formal* an action or behaviour that is not polite【正式】粗鲁的举动

dis·cov·er /dɪs`kʌvɚ; dɪs'kʌvə/ *v* [T] **1** to find something that was hidden or that people did not know about before 发现〔隐藏的东西或以前不知道的事物〕: *I've just discovered a secret drawer in my old desk.* 我刚刚在我的旧书桌里发现了一个秘密 2 1

抽屉。| *The Curies are best known for discovering radium.* 居里夫妇最为出名的是发现了镭。—see 见 INVENT (USAGE) **2** to find out something yourself, without being told about it〔自己〕发现; 查出; 发觉: **discover that** *Police discovered that Kim's son was dealing in drugs.* 警方发现金的儿子在做毒品买卖。| **[+who/what/how etc]** *Emily's not even two, but she's discovered how to open doors.* 埃米莉还不到两岁, 但她已经弄清怎么开门了。**3** to notice someone who is very good at something and help them to become successful and well-known 发现〔某人有某方面的才能, 并帮助他成功、出名〕—**discoverer** *n* [C]

3 **dis·cov·e·ry** /dɪsˋkʌvərɪ; dɪsˈkʌvəri/ *n* **1** [C] a fact or thing that someone discovers that was hidden or not known about before 被发现的事实[事物]: *recent archaeological discoveries* 最近的考古发现 | **make a discovery** *Astronomers have made significant discoveries about our galaxy.* 天文学家对于我们的星系已作出了重大的发现。**2** [C] something that you learn or find out yourself, without being told about it〔自己〕发现, 发觉: **[+that]** *The discovery that her assistant had lied made Patty decide to fire him.* 帕蒂发现她的助手撒了谎, 这使得她决定解雇他。**3** [U] the act of discovering something 发现: **[+of]** *The discovery of oil in Alaska was a boon to the economy.* 在阿拉斯加找到石油对经济是件大好事。

Discovery, the the ship in which Captain Scott went to the Antarctic in 1901-1904 发现号〔1901 至 1904 年间斯科特船长前往南极时乘坐的船只〕

dis·cred·it¹ /dɪsˋkrɛdɪt; dɪsˈkredɪt/ *v* [T] **1** to make people stop respecting or trusting someone or something 损坏〔某人或某物〕的名声: *Black's remarks were taken out of context in an effort to discredit him.* 布莱克的话被断章取义, 他们是想破坏他的名声。**2** to make people stop believing in a particular idea 使〔人们〕不再相信〔某种观点〕: *Some of Freud's theories have now been discredited.* 弗洛伊德的一些理论现在已经不为人们所相信了。

discredit² *n* loss of other people's respect or trust 丧失名誉, 丧失信用: **to sb's discredit** *I know enough to her discredit* (=enough bad things about her) *not to vote for her.* 我知道很多关于她的不光彩的事情, 这足以让我不投她的票。| **bring discredit on/to** (=make people stop respecting someone or something) 让〔某人或某物〕蒙羞; 给〔某人或某物〕带来耻辱 *Their outrageous behaviour has brought discredit on English football.* 他们的可耻行为已经损害了英国足球的名誉。

dis·cred·i·ta·ble /dɪsˋkrɛdɪtəbḷ; dɪsˈkredɪtəbəl/ *adj* bad or wrong, and making people lose respect for you or trust in you 败坏名誉的; 丢脸的: *a discreditable secret* 有损名誉的秘密 —**discreditably** *adv*

di·screet /dɪˋskrit; dɪˈskriːt/ *adj* **1** done or said in a careful way so that you do not offend, upset, or embarrass people 言行审慎的; 谨慎小心的: *It wasn't very discreet of you to ring me up at the office.* 你往办公室给我打电话是有失谨慎的。| *That morning I began making discreet inquiries.* 那天早上我开始进行审慎的查询。**2** careful not to talk about things that other people want to keep secret 小心谨慎的〔不会泄露别人的秘密〕: *Don't worry about my secretary hearing us; he's very discreet.* 别担心我的秘书听我们的谈话; 他非常小心谨慎。—opposite 反义词 INDISCREET —compare 比较 DISCRETE —**discreetly** *adv*

di·screp·an·cy /dɪˋskrɛpənsɪ; dɪˈskrepənsi/ *n* [C,U] a difference between two amounts, details, reports etc that ought to be the same〔两个本该一样的数目、细节、报告等的〕不一致, 不符, 差异, 出入: **[+in]** *How do you explain these discrepancies in the accounts?* 你如何解释账目中这些不相符的地方? | **[+between]** *There are big discrepancies between what Margaret says and what you say.* 玛格丽特所说的和你所说的有着很大出入。

di·screte /dɪˋskrit; dɪˈskriːt/ *adj formal* separate【正式】分开的; 各别的; 互不相关的: *There are two discrete breeding groups on the island.* 岛上有两个互不相关的繁殖群体。—compare 比较 DISCREET —**discretely** *adv* —**discreteness** *n* [U]

di·scre·tion /dɪˋskrɛʃən; dɪˈskreʃən/ *n* [U] **1** the ability and right to decide exactly what should be done in a particular situation 决断能力; 处理权; 酌情决定权: *Promotions are left to the discretion of the supervisor.* 提升事宜交由主管去决定。| **at sb's discretion** (=according to someone's decision or wishes) 根据某人的决定[意愿] *The size of your payment may be changed at your discretion.* 你的付款定额可以随你的意愿而改变。**2** the ability to deal with situations in a way that does not offend or embarrass people, especially by keeping other people's secrets 谨慎; 慎重: *It's a delicate matter, Mr Nagel, that must be handled with the utmost discretion.* 这是件微妙的事情, 内格尔先生, 处理起来必须格外谨慎。| **be the soul of discretion** (=be extremely discreet) 极为谨慎 **3 discretion is the better part of valour** used to say that it is better to be careful than to take unnecessary risks 谨慎要比无谓冒险强得多〔不知进退非真勇〕

di·scre·tion·a·ry /dɪˋskrɛʃənˌɛrɪ; dɪˈskreʃənəri/ *adj* not controlled by strict rules, but left for someone to make a decision about in each particular situation 不受严格规定控制的; 自由决定的; 酌情决定的: *the court's discretionary powers* 法庭的酌情决定权

di·scrim·i·nate /dɪˋskrɪməˌnet; dɪˈskrɪmɪneɪt/ *v* **1** [I,T] to recognize a difference between things 区别, 辨别: **[+between]** *It's sometimes difficult to discriminate between edible and poisonous mushrooms.* 可食用的蘑菇和毒蘑菇有时候很难区分。| **discriminate sth from** *You must learn to discriminate fact from opinion.* 你必须学会把事实和看法区分开来。**2** [I] to treat people differently from each other in an unfair way 不公正地区别对待; 歧视: **[+against]** *Are you saying the law discriminates against the disabled?* 你是说法律歧视伤残人士吗? | **discriminate in favour of** *As an employer, she always discriminates in favour of women.* 作为雇主, 她总是优待妇女。

di·scrim·i·nat·ing /dɪˋskrɪməˌnetɪŋ; dɪˈskrɪmɪneɪtɪŋ/ *adj* able to judge what is of good quality and what is not 有鉴别能力的; 有鉴赏能力的; 识别能力强的: *We have a large wine list for those of discriminating taste.* 我们拥有种类繁多的酒可供那些有鉴赏能力的人选择。

di·scrim·i·na·tion /dɪˌskrɪməˋneʃən; dɪˌskrɪmɪˈneɪʃən/ *n* [U] **1** the practice of treating one particular group in society in an unfair way 歧视: **[+against]** *Laws have got to be tougher to stop discrimination against the disabled.* 法律应该再强硬一些以制止对伤残人士的歧视。| **[+in favour of]** *discrimination in favour of university graduates* 对大学毕业生的优待 | **racial discrimination** (=discrimination against someone who is of another race or colour) 种族歧视 | **sex discrimination** (=discrimination against women)〔对妇女的〕性别歧视 —see also 另见 POSITIVE DISCRIMINATION, REVERSE DISCRIMINATION **2** the ability to judge what is of good quality and what is not 鉴别力; 识别力; 鉴赏力

di·scur·sive /dɪˋskɝsɪv; dɪˈskɜːsɪv/ *adj* changing from one subject to another without any clear plan 东拉西扯的; 漫无边际的: *a discursive style of writing* 东拉西扯的写作风格 —**discursively** *adv* —**discursiveness** *n* [U]

dis·cus /ˋdɪskəs; ˈdɪskəs/ *n* [C] a heavy plate-shaped object which is thrown as far as possible as a sport 铁饼

di·scuss /dɪˋskʌs; dɪˈskʌs/ *v* [T] **1** to talk about something with another person or a group in order to exchange ideas or decide something 商讨, 谈论, 讨论: *Sandy won't ever discuss money.* 桑迪从不肯谈论钱。| **discuss sth with sb** *I'd like to discuss my contract with you.* 我想和你谈一下我的合同。| **discuss what/who/where etc** *We're here to discuss what we can do to prevent crime.* 我们来到这里是为了讨论我们能做些什么以防止犯罪。—see 见 SPEAK (USAGE) **2** to talk or write about something in detail and consider different ideas or opinions about it 详细阐述; 论说: *Chapter One discusses the rise of the city-state on the European continent.* 第一章详细论述了欧洲大陆上城邦的兴起。 3 1

di·scus·sion /dɪˋskʌʃən; dɪˈskʌʃən/ *n* [C,U] **1** the act of discussing something, or a conversation in which people discuss something 讨论; 谈论; 商讨: **have a discussion (about)** *Yes, on Friday we had a long discussion about the wording of the proposal.* 是的, 周五我们曾就这份提案的措辞进行了长时间的讨论。| **under discussion** (=being discussed) 在讨论中 *The section now under discussion focuses on tenants' rights.* 目前正在讨论的这部分集中探讨房客的权利问题。| **be up for discussion** (=be something that can be discussed and possibly changed) 可供讨论; 可能会改变 *Joe, I'm sorry, but item three is not up for discussion.* 乔, 对不起, 第三条是不予讨论的。**2** something that is written about a subject that considers different ideas or opinions about it〔对某一话题的〕论述, 阐述: *the report's discussion of the legislation* 该报告对立法的论述 1

dis·dain¹ /dɪsˋden; dɪsˈdeɪn/ *n* [U] a complete lack of respect that you show for someone or something because you think they are not at all worth paying attention to 鄙视; 轻视; 藐视; 不屑的态度: **[+for]** *He maintained an obvious disdain for the customs of the local people.* 他对当地人的习俗持有明显的鄙视态度。| **treat sb/sth with disdain** *Mrs Strachan's evidence was treated with disdain by the prosecution.* 斯特罗恩夫人的证据被控方所轻视。

disdain² *v* **1** [T] to have no respect for someone or something, and believe they are unimportant 鄙视; 轻视; 藐视 **2 disdain to do sth** to refuse to do something because you are too proud to do it 不屑于做某事: *Tom Butler disdained to reply to such a trivial question.* 汤姆·巴特勒不屑于回答这么一个琐碎的问题。

dis·dain·ful /dɪs`denfəl; dɪs'deɪnfəl/ *adj* showing that you do not respect someone or something and think that they are unimportant 鄙视的; 轻视的; 藐视的; 不屑的: *a long disdainful look* 轻蔑的注视 | [+of] *There are some in the sport who are disdainful of amateurs.* 体育界中有些人瞧不起业余运动员。—**disdainfully** *adv*

3 1 **dis·ease** /dɪ`ziz; dɪ'ziːz/ *n* **1** [C,U] an illness or unhealthy condition in your body, especially one caused by infection〔尤指感染而得的〕疾病, 病: **eye/liver/kidney etc disease** *Heart disease runs in our family.* 我们的家族有心脏病病史。| **cause disease** *filthy insanitary conditions that cause disease* 导致疾病的肮脏而不卫生的环境 | **infectious/contagious disease** (=easily passed from one person to another) 传染病 *vaccination against infectious diseases such as typhoid* 预防伤寒等传染性疾病的疫苗接种 | **suffer from a disease** (=have a disease) 患某种疾病 *She suffers from a rare disease of the central nervous system.* 她得了一种罕见的中枢神经系统疾病。| **catch/contract a disease** (=get a disease by being infected) 感染上疾病 **2** [C] something that is seriously wrong with society or with someone's mind, behaviour etc〔社会的〕严重弊病;〔某人头脑、行为的〕病态, 不健全: *Loneliness is a disease of our urban communities.* 寂寞是我们都市人群的一种精神疾病。—see also 另见 HEART DISEASE, SOCIAL DISEASE —**diseased** *adj*: *diseased muscles* 有病的肌肉 | *a diseased plant* 有病害的植物

USAGE NOTE 用法说明: DISEASE

WORD CHOICE 词语辨析: **disease, illness**

Though **illness** and **disease** are often used in the same way and are equally common in spoken English, **illness** is really the state, or length of time, of being unwell (usually caused by some **disease**). 尽管 illness 和 disease 两个词通常用法相同, 而且在口语中同样常用, 但 illness 真正指的是身体不舒服的状态或者身体不舒服的时间〔通常由某种 disease 引起〕: *She died after a long illness.* 她久病之后死了。| *How many working days have you missed through illness?* 你因病误了多少个工作日了?

It is **diseases** that have medical names, are related to parts of the body, and can be caught, carried and passed on if they are infectious. disease 均有医学名称, 与身体的部位有关。如果是传染性疾病的话, 可被传染、携带并且传播: *a kidney/sexually-transmitted disease/infectious disease/Alzheimer's disease* 肾病/性传播疾病/传染性疾病/早年性痴呆病。However, you would usually talk about *mental illness* or a *terminal/critical illness.* 然而, 在谈论精神病或晚期疾病/重病时通常用 illness。

This graph shows some of the words most commonly used with the noun **disease**. 本图表所示为含有名词 disease 的一些最常用词组。

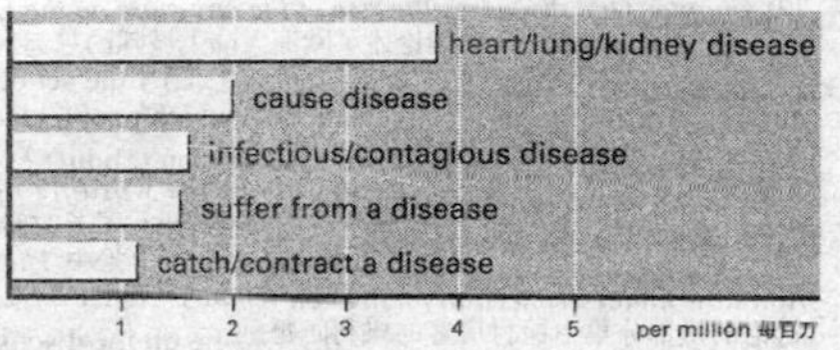

heart/lung/kidney disease
cause disease
infectious/contagious disease
suffer from a disease
catch/contract a disease
1 2 3 4 5 per million 每百万

Based on the British National Corpus and the Longman Lancaster Corpus
据英国国家语料库和朗文兰开斯特语料库

dis·em·bark /ˌdɪsɪm`bɑrk; ˌdɪsɪ̮m'bɑːk/ *v* **1** [I] to get off a ship or aircraft 下船; 下飞机 —opposite 反义词 EMBARK **2** [T] to put people or goods onto the shore from a ship 使上岸, 使登陆; 卸〔货〕—**disembarkation** /ˌdɪsɛmbɑr`keʃən; ˌdɪsembɑː'keɪʃən/ *n* [U]

dis·em·bod·ied /ˌdɪsɪm`bɑdɪd; ˌdɪsɪ̮m'bɒdid◂/ *adj* **1** existing without a body or separated from a body 无躯体而存在的; 脱离躯体的: *disembodied spirits* 游魂 **2** a disembodied sound or voice comes from someone who cannot be seen〔指声响、声音〕不知道来源的, 看不见来源的

dis·em·bow·el /ˌdɪsɪm`bauəl; ˌdɪsɪ̮m'baʊəl/ *v* **disembowelled, disembowelling** *BrE*【英】, **disemboweled, disemboweling** *AmE*【美】[T] to remove someone's bowels (BOWEL (1)) 取出〔某人〕的肠子 —**disembowelment** *n* [U]

dis·en·chant·ed /ˌdɪsɪn`tʃæntɪd; ˌdɪsɪ̮n'tʃɑːntɪ̮d/ *adj* disappointed with someone or something, and no longer believing that they are good, exciting, or right 对〔某人或某事物〕失望的; 已醒悟的; 不再着迷的; 不再抱有幻想的: [+with] *By that time I was becoming disenchanted with the whole idea.* 到那个时候, 我对那种想法不再迷恋了。—**disenchantment** *n* [U]

dis·en·fran·chise /ˌdɪsɪn`fræntʃaɪz; ˌdɪsɪn'fræntʃaɪz/ *v* [T] to take away from someone their right to vote 剥夺〔某人〕的选举权 —**disenfranchisement** /-tʃaɪzmənt; -tʃɪzmənt/ *n* [U]

dis·en·gage /ˌdɪsɪn`gedʒ; ˌdɪsɪ̮n'geɪdʒ/ *v* **1** [T] to separate something from something else that is fastened to it or holding it 使脱离, 使分开: **disengage yourself** *Sally found it difficult to disengage herself from his embrace.* 萨莉发现很难从他的怀里挣脱开。**2** [I,T] if you disengage part of a machine or if it disengages, you make it move away from another part that it was connected to (使)〔机器的某一部分与另一相连部分〕分离开, 移开, 松开: *Disengage the gears when you park the car.* 你停车时要松开排挡。**3** [I] if two armies disengage, they stop fighting〔两军〕停止交战 —**disengagement** *n* [U]

dis·en·tan·gle /ˌdɪsɪn`tæŋgḷ; ˌdɪsɪ̮n'tæŋgəl/ *v* [T] **1 disentangle yourself (from)** to escape from a difficult situation that you are involved in 从〔陷入的困境中〕解脱出来 **2** to remove knots from ropes, strings etc that have become twisted or tied together 解开〔绳子等上面〕的结 **3** to separate different ideas or pieces of information that have become confused together 理顺, 分清〔混杂的不同观念或信息〕: *It's very difficult to disentangle fact from fiction in what she's saying.* 很难分清她说的话哪些是真的, 哪些是虚构的。—**disentanglement** *n* [U]

dis·e·qui·lib·ri·um /dɪsˌikwə`lɪbrɪəm; ˌdɪsekwɪ̮'lɪbriəm/ *n* [U] *formal* a lack of balance in something【正式】失衡, 不平衡; 失调

dis·es·tab·lish /ˌdɪsə`stæblɪʃ; ˌdɪsɪ̮'stæblɪʃ/ *v* [T] *formal* to officially decide that a particular church is no longer the official church of your country【正式】废除〔教会〕的国教地位

dis·fa·vour *BrE*【英】, **disfavor** *AmE*【美】/dɪs`fevɚ; dɪs'feɪvə/ *n* [U] *formal* a feeling of dislike and disapproval【正式】不喜欢; 不赞成; 冷淡; 疏远: **look with disfavour on/upon** *The job creation program is looked upon with disfavor by the local community.* 当地社区并不赞同那个创造就业机会的计划。

dis·fig·ure /dɪs`fɪgjɚ; dɪs'fɪgə/ *v* [T] to spoil the beauty that something naturally has 毁坏〔某事物〕天生具有的美丽: *good looks marred by a disfiguring scar* 被一处丑陋的疤痕破坏了的美丽外貌 —**disfigured** *adj* —**disfigurement** *n* [C,U]

dis·fran·chise /dɪs`fræntʃaɪz; dɪs'fræntʃaɪz/ *v* [T] *especially AmE* to DISENFRANCHISE someone【尤美】剥夺〔某人〕的选举权

dis·gorge /dɪs`gɔrdʒ; dɪs'gɔːdʒ/ *v* **1** [T] *literary* if a vehicle or building disgorges people, they come out of it in a large group【文】〔车辆〕下〔客〕;〔建筑物〕使〔人流〕涌出 **2** [T] if something disgorges what was inside it, it lets it pour out 使〔某物〕大量流出, 冒出, 吐出: *Chimneys in the valley were disgorging smoke into the air.* 山谷里的烟囱正在往空中喷吐烟雾。**3** [I,T] if a river disgorges, it flows into the sea〔指河流〕流入〔大海等〕: *The Mississippi disgorges its waters into the Gulf of Mexico.* 密西西比河水汇入墨西哥湾。**4** [T] to give back something that you have taken illegally 交还, 交出, 吐出〔非法所得〕**5** [T] to bring food back up from your stomach through your mouth 呕吐出〔食物等〕

dis·grace[1] /dɪs`gres; dɪs'greɪs/ *n* **1** [U] the complete loss of other people's respect because you have done something they strongly disapprove of 丢脸; 耻辱; 出丑: *Smith faced total public disgrace after the incident.* 该事件发生之后, 史密斯面对着在公众中名誉扫地的局面。| **in disgrace** *Toranaga's father sent my mother away in disgrace.* 寅寿的父亲把我的母亲不体面地打发走了。**2 sth is a disgrace** used to say that something should not be allowed to happen because it is very wrong or unfair 某事是一种耻辱: **it's an absolute/utter disgrace** *It's an absolute disgrace, the way he treats his wife.* 他那样对待他的妻子, 简直太可耻了。**3 be a disgrace to** to have a very bad effect on people's opinion of the family or other group that you belong to 给〔某人的家庭或所属的团体〕带来耻辱: *Your conduct is a disgrace to the medical profession, and I'll see your licence is revoked.* 你的行为给医学界带来了耻辱, 我一定要让人吊销你的行医执照。

disgrace[2] *v* [T] to do something so bad that people lose respect for your family or for the group you belong to 给…丢脸; 给…带来耻辱: *How could you disgrace us all like that?* 你怎么能这样地让我们都丢脸呢? | **disgrace yourself** *Well, I'm not the one who disgraced herself at a friend's wedding!* 噢, 我可不是那个在朋友的婚礼上出洋相的女人! | **be (publicly) disgraced** (=be made to feel ashamed, especially in public) 被〔公开〕羞辱

dis·grace·ful /dɪs`gresfəl; dɪs'greɪsfəl/ *adj* extremely bad or unacceptable 可耻的；丢脸的；很差劲的：*It's a disgraceful state of affairs when decent folk are afraid to leave their homes.* 正经体面的人都害怕离开家庭，这种情形真是丢人啊。—**disgracefully** *adv*

dis·grun·tled /dɪs`grʌntḷd; dɪs'grʌntld/ *adj* annoyed, unhappy, and disappointed, especially because things have not happened in the way that you wanted〔尤因事情未像自己所想要的那样发生而〕恼火的；不高兴的；失望的；不满的：*a disgruntled client* 不满的客户

dis·guise¹ /dɪs`gaɪz; dɪs'gaɪz/ *v* [T] **1** to change someone's appearance so that they look like someone else and people cannot recognize them 装扮；假扮：**disguise yourself as** *Maybe you could disguise yourself as a waiter and sneak in there.* 或许你可以假扮成一名服务员，混进去。| **be disguised as** *He escaped across the border disguised as a priest.* 他装扮成神父越境逃走了。**2** to change the appearance, sound, taste etc of something so that people do not recognize it〔为不让别人认出来而〕改变〔某物的外表、声音、口味等〕：*There's no way you can disguise that southern accent.* 你是无法掩盖你那南方口音的。**3** to hide something so that people will not notice it〔为不让别人发现而〕隐瞒，掩盖，伪装〔某事物〕：*Try as he might, Dan couldn't disguise his feelings for Katie.* 不管丹多么努力，他都无法掩盖自己对凯蒂的感情。| **disguise the fact (that)** *There's no disguising the fact that business is bad.* 生意不好，这是无法掩盖的事实。| **thinly disguised** (=only slightly disguised) 略加掩饰的 *The speech was seen by many as a thinly disguised attack on the president.* 许多人认为这场演说是对总统稍加掩饰的攻击。

disguise² *n* **1** [C,U] something that you wear to change your appearance and hide who you are, or the act of wearing this 伪装物；假扮；伪装：*The beard, the glasses, and the German accent were all part of his disguise.* 胡子、眼镜和德国口音都是他伪装的一部分。**2 in disguise a)** wearing a disguise 穿戴伪装的物品；化了装的；假扮过的：*I kept forgetting I was in disguise, and got a lot of funny looks.* 我总是忘记我是化了装的，所以多次有人异样地看我。**b)** made to seem like something else that is better 经过伪装的〔使看起来似乎更好〕：*'Tax reform' is just a tax increase in disguise.* "税务改革"只不过是乔装打扮后的增税。—see also 另见 **blessing in disguise** (BLESSING (3))

dis·gust¹ /dɪs`gʌst; dɪs'gʌst/ *n* [U] **1** a very strong feeling of dislike that almost makes you sick, caused by something unpleasant 嫌恶，厌恶；反感；作呕；恶心：**with disgust** *Everybody except Joe looked at me with disgust.* 除了乔以外，大家都反感地看着我。**2** a feeling of annoyance and disappointment because of someone's unacceptable behaviour, the bad quality of something etc 气愤；失望：**in disgust** *Sam threw his books down in disgust and stormed out of the room.* 萨姆愤愤地把书扔下，气冲冲地冲出房间。| **much to sb's disgust** *Much to my disgust I found that there were no toilets for the disabled.* 令我非常气愤的是，我发现没有供伤残人士使用的厕所。

disgust² *v* [T] **1** to make someone feel very annoyed and disappointed about something unacceptable 使〔某人〕反感，厌恶，气愤，失望：*Enid said she was disgusted by the sex in the film.* 伊妮德说她对该影片中的性行为镜头感到恶心。| **be disgusted to find/hear/see etc** *Dear Sir: I was disgusted to see the picture on page one of Sunday's feature section.* 亲爱的先生：看到周日的特写专栏第一页上的照片，我感到很气愤。**2** to make someone feel almost sick because of something unpleasant 使〔人〕感到恶心，作呕：*The thought of dissecting a frog disgusts me.* 一想起解剖青蛙就让我感到恶心。

S2 **dis·gust·ing** /dɪs`gʌstɪŋ; dɪs'gʌstɪŋ/ *adj* **1** extremely unpleasant and making you feel sick 令人恶心的；使人极其反感的；令人厌恶的：*"Here, hold this a minute." "Yuck! It's disgusting!"* "来，把这个东西给我拿一会儿。""呸！真恶心！" **2** shocking and unacceptable 令人吃惊的；无法接受的：*Sixty pounds for a thirty-minute consultation. I think that's disgusting!* 咨询30分钟就要60英镑，我看这也太离谱了！| *Man, do you have a disgusting imagination.* 老兄，你的想象力是不是丰富得过了头。—compare 比较 NAUSEATING —**disgustingly** *adv*: *They're disgustingly rich.* 他们富得令人反感。

S3 **dish¹** /dɪʃ; dɪʃ/ *n* [C] **1** a flat round container with not very high sides, from which food is served on the table 盘子，碟子：*a serving dish* 上菜用的盘子 | *a vegetable dish* 盛蔬菜用的盘子 —compare 比较 BOWL¹ (1) **2 the dishes** all the plates, cups, bowls etc that have been used to eat a meal and need to be washed〔用餐时用过的、需要清洗的〕所有餐具〔包括盘子、杯子、碗等〕：**do/wash the dishes** *I'll just do the dishes before we go.* 我们走之前我会把碗洗好的。**3** food cooked or prepared in a particular way as a meal 烹制好的菜肴，食品，一道菜：*a wonderful pasta dish* 很棒的意大利面食 **4 be a dish** *informal* to be sexually attractive【非正式】有吸引力的；性感的；漂亮的 —see also 另见 SIDE DISH, SATELLITE DISH

dish² *v* [T] *old-fashioned*【过时】**1 dish the dirt** *informal* to spend time talking about other people's private lives and saying unkind or shocking things about them【非正式】谈论别人的私生活并说他们的坏话；揭短 **2 dish sb's hopes/chances** *especially BrE* to prevent someone from doing something that they hoped to do【尤英】使某人的希望/机会破灭；使某人不能做想做的事

dish sth ↔ **out** *phr v* [T] *informal*【非正式】**1** to give something to various people in a careless way〔随意地〕分发；提供：*We'll probably dish out some leaflets there too.* 我们很可能也上那儿分发些传单。| *Portnoy still tends to dish out unwanted advice.* 波特诺伊仍然喜欢随意地抛出人家根本不爱听的建议。**2** to serve food to people 给〔人们〕上菜，分菜：*Sam's dishing out sandwiches if you want one.* 如果你想要三明治，萨姆正在分呢。**3 sb can dish it out but they can't take it** used to say that someone is quick to criticize others but does not accept criticism well 某人很会批评别人，但自己却不能接受批评

dish up *phr v* [I,T] to put food for a meal into dishes, ready to be eaten 把〔食物〕盛到盘里〔准备让人食用〕：**dish sth ↔ up** *Could you dish up the vegetables? They're there, on the sideboard.* 请你把蔬菜盛到盘子里，好吗？蔬菜在那儿，餐具柜上。

dis·ha·bille /ˌdɪsə`bil; ˌdɪsə'biːl/ *n* [U] *AmE* the usual American form of DÉSHABILLÉ【美】déshabillé的一般美式形式

dis·har·mo·ny /dɪs`hɑrmənɪ; dɪs'hɑːməni/ *n* [U] *formal* disagreement about important things that makes people be unfriendly to each other【正式】〔在重要事情上的〕分歧，不一致；不和谐的事 —**disharmonious** /ˌdɪshɑr`monɪəs; ˌdɪshɑː'məʊniəs/ *adj*

dish·cloth /`dɪʃˌklɑθ; 'dɪʃklɒθ/ *n* [C] a cloth used for washing dishes 洗碗布 —see picture on page A10 参见A10页图

dis·heart·ened /dɪs`hɑrtṇd; dɪs'hɑːtnd/ *adj* disappointed so that you lose hope and the determination to continue doing something 沮丧的；气馁的；灰心的：*If young children don't see quick results they grow disheartened.* 如果小孩子不能很快地看到结果，他们会变得灰心的。—**dishearten** *v* [T]

dis·heart·en·ing /dɪs`hɑrtṇɪŋ; dɪs'hɑːtnɪŋ/ *adj* making you lose hope and determination 令人灰心的，令人气馁的：**be disheartening to hear/see etc sth** *It's disheartening to see what little progress has been made.* 看到只有少得可怜的一点进展，令人感到灰心丧气。—**dishearteningly** *adv*

di·shev·elled *BrE*【英】, **disheveled** *AmE*【美】/dɪ`ʃɛvḷd; dɪ'ʃevəld/ *adj* dishevelled clothes, hair etc are very untidy〔衣服、头发等〕不整齐的，凌乱的：*Pam arrived late, dishevelled and out of breath.* 帕姆迟到了，衣冠不整，上气不接下气。

dis·hon·est /dɪs`ɑnɪst; dɪs'ɒnɨst/ *adj* not honest 不老实的；不诚实的：*Unfortunately there are dishonest traders about.* 不幸的是，到处都有奸商。—**dishonestly** *adv*

dis·hon·est·y /dɪs`ɑnɪstɪ; dɪs'ɒnɨsti/ *n* [U] dishonest behaviour 不诚实的行为

dis·hon·our¹ *BrE*【英】, **dishonor** *AmE*【美】/dɪs`ɑnɚ; dɪs'ɒnə/ *n* [U] *formal* loss of respect from other people because you have behaved in a morally unacceptable way【正式】不名誉；耻辱；丢脸：**bring dishonour on** *You've brought enough dishonour on your family already without causing any more trouble.* 你已经给你的家庭带来了很多耻辱，不再惹麻烦也够瞧的了。

dishonour² *BrE*【英】, **dishonor** *AmE*【美】*v* [T] **1** *formal* to make your family, country, profession etc lose the respect of other people【正式】败坏〔家庭、国家、行业等〕的名誉 **2** if a bank dishonours a cheque, it refuses to pay out money for it〔指银行等〕拒付，拒绝承兑〔支票等〕；使〔票据〕退票

dis·hon·ou·ra·ble *BrE*【英】, **dishonorable** *AmE*【美】/dɪs`ɑnərəbḷ; dɪs'ɒnərəbəl/ *adj* not morally correct or acceptable 不名誉的；不光彩的；可耻的：*There's nothing dishonourable in charging for advice.* 收取咨询费并没有什么不光彩的。

dishonourable dis·charge /ˌ·,····'··/ *n* [C,U] an order to someone to leave the army because they have behaved in a morally unacceptable way〔因做了不光彩的事〕被开除军籍

dish·pan /`dɪʃˌpæn; 'dɪʃpæn/ *n* [C] *AmE* a large bowl which you use for washing dishes in【美】洗碗碟用的大盆

dish tow·el /'· ,··/ *n* [C] *AmE* a cloth used for drying dishes【美】〔把碗碟等擦干用的〕擦碗布；TEA TOWEL *BrE*【英】

dish·wash·er /`dɪʃˌwɑʃɚ; 'dɪʃˌwɒʃə/ *n* [C] a machine that washes dishes 洗碗机 —see picture on page A10 参见A10页图

dish·wash·ing liq·uid /`dɪʃwɑʃɪŋ ˌlɪkwɪd; 'dɪʃwɒʃɪŋ ˌlɪkwɨd/ *n* [U] *AmE* liquid soap used to wash dishes【美】洗涤液；洗洁精；WASHING-UP LIQUID *BrE*【英】—see picture on page A10 参见A10页图

dish·wa·ter /ˈdɪʃˌwɔtɚ; ˈdɪʃˌwɔːtə/ *n* [U] **1** dirty water that dishes have been washed in 洗过碗碟的水 **2 like dishwater** *informal* tea or coffee that tastes like dishwater tastes unpleasantly weak【非正式】〔茶或咖啡等〕淡而无味

dishwater blond /ˌ···ˈ·/ *adj AmE old-fashioned* dishwater blond hair is a dull brown colour【美，过时】〔指头发〕暗无光彩的，褐色的

dish·y /ˈdɪʃɪ; ˈdɪʃi/ *adj old-fashioned* sexually attractive【过时】性感的，迷人的

dis·il·lu·sion /ˌdɪsɪˈluʒən; ˌdɪsɪ̣ˈluːʒən/ *v* [T] to make someone realize that something which they thought was true or good is not really true or good 使醒悟；使不再抱幻想：*I hate to disillusion you, but you're unlikely to learn any more than I've told you already.* 我真不愿意让你失望，但你不可能了解到比我已经告诉你的还多的信息。**—disillusionment** *n* [U]

dis·il·lu·sioned /ˌdɪsɪˈluʒənd; ˌdɪsɪ̣ˈluːʒənd◂/ *adj* disappointed because you have lost your belief that someone is good, or that an idea is right 不抱幻想的；失望的；幻灭的；理想破灭的：[+by/with] *As she grew older, Laura grew increasingly disillusioned with politics.* 随着年龄的增长，劳拉对政治越来越不抱幻想了。

D

dis·in·cen·tive /ˌdɪsɪnˈsɛntɪv; ˌdɪsɪ̣nˈsentɪv/ *n* [C] something that tries to stop people from doing something 抑制因素；限制因素：[+to] *The biggest disincentive to spend is the fear of debt.* 遏制消费的最大因素是害怕负债。

dis·in·cli·na·tion /ˌdɪsɪnkləˈneʃən; ˌdɪsɪŋklɪ̣ˈneɪʃən/ *n* [U] *formal* a lack of willingness to do something【正式】不情愿；厌恶：*Very naturally there has been a disinclination to face up to these issues.* 很自然，人们不愿意正视这些问题。

dis·in·clined /ˌdɪsɪnˈklaɪnd; ˌdɪsɪnˈklaɪnd/ *adj* **be/feel disinclined to do sth** *formal* to be unwilling to do something【正式】不愿意做某事：*In the present case I feel disinclined to interfere in the matter.* 在目前情况下我不愿意介入此事。

dis·in·fect /ˌdɪsɪnˈfɛkt; ˌdɪsɪ̣nˈfekt/ *v* [T] to clean something with a chemical that destroys BACTERIA 为〔某物〕消毒，给…杀菌：*First use some iodine to disinfect the wound.* 首先，用碘酒把伤口消消毒。| *Disinfect the area thoroughly.* 把这个区域彻底消毒。

dis·in·fec·tant /ˌdɪsɪnˈfɛktənt; ˌdɪsɪ̣nˈfektənt/ *n* [C,U] a chemical that destroys BACTERIA, or a cleaning product that does this 杀菌剂；消毒剂

dis·in·for·ma·tion /ˌdɪsɪnfɚˈmeʃən; ˌdɪsɪnfəˈmeɪʃən/ *n* [U] false information which is given intentionally in order to hide the truth or confuse people, especially in political situations〔尤指在政治形势下故意透露的〕假消息，假情报：*government disinformation about the effects of nuclear testing* 政府透露的关于核试验结果的假消息 —compare 比较 MISINFORMATION

dis·in·gen·u·ous /ˌdɪsɪnˈdʒɛnjuəs; ˌdɪsɪ̣nˈdʒenjuəs◂/ *adj* not sincere and slightly dishonest 不真诚的；略有些不诚实的，不坦率的：*McEwan's claims about the incident strike me as disingenuous.* 麦克尤恩关于那个事件的声明给我的印象是不够坦诚。**—disingenuously** *adv*

dis·in·her·it /ˌdɪsɪnˈhɛrɪt; ˌdɪsɪ̣nˈherɪ̣t/ *v* [T] to take away from someone, especially your son or daughter, their legal right to receive your money or property after your death 剥夺〔尤指子女〕的继承权 **—disinheritance** *n* [U]

dis·in·te·grate /dɪsˈɪntəˌgret; dɪsˈɪntɪ̣greɪt/ *v* [I,T] **1** to break up or make something break up into very small pieces (使)粉碎；崩裂；分崩离析：*The whole plane just disintegrated in mid-air.* 整架飞机在半空中就解体了。**2** to become weaker or less united and be gradually destroyed 衰弱；瓦解；解体：*a society disintegrating under economic pressures* 在经济压力下正在瓦解中的社会 **—disintegration** /dɪsˌɪntəˈgreʃən; dɪsˌɪntɪ̣ˈgreɪʃən/ *n* [U]

dis·in·ter /ˌdɪsɪnˈtɝ; ˌdɪsɪnˈtɜː/ *v* **disinterred, disinterring** [T] *formal* to dig a dead body from a grave【正式】把〔尸体〕从坟墓中掘出 —opposite 反义词 INTER **—disinterment** *n* [U]

dis·in·terest /dɪsˈɪntrɪst; dɪsˈɪntrɪ̣st/ *n* [U] a lack of interest 无兴趣：[+in] *The exception to Balfour's disinterest in social issues was education.* 鲍尔弗对除教育以外的社会问题都不感兴趣。

dis·in·terest·ed /dɪsˈɪntrɪstɪd; dɪsˈɪntrɪ̣stɪ̣d/ *adj* **1** able to judge a situation fairly because you are not concerned with gaining any personal advantage from it; OBJECTIVE² (1) 公正无私的；无利害关系影响的；客观的：*disinterested advice* 客观的忠告 **2** sometimes used to mean 'uninterested', although many people think this is wrong〔有时用于表示〕无兴趣的；不关心的 **—disinterestedly** *adv* **—disinterestedness** *n* [U]

USAGE NOTE 用法说明: DISINTERESTED

WORD CHOICE 词语辨析: **uninterested (in), disinterested (in)**

Uninterested (in something) means not interested in it. uninterested 表示对某事物不感兴趣：*I'm completely uninterested in football.* 我对足球完全不感兴趣。| *an uninterested student* (=bored) 一个提不起兴趣的学生

If someone is **disinterested** they are able to be fair because they are not involved in a situation where other people are fighting, disagreeing etc, and not expecting to gain anything themselves from it. disinterested 用于表示某人公正无私，因为此人并没有卷入到他人的争斗或分歧中去，而且此人并没有期望从中赚取个人利益：*We need the advice of a disinterested party* (=someone who is not directly involved). 我们需要一个（与此事）没有利害关系的人给我们一些建议。

Native speakers of English also sometimes say that people are **disinterested in** things, meaning the same as **uninterested in**, though is usually considered to be incorrect. 以英语为母语的人有时也用 disinterested 来表示 uninterested（不感兴趣），尽管这种用法通常被认为是错误的：*I'm completely disinterested in football.* 我对足球毫无兴趣。

dis·in·vest·ment /ˌdɪsɪnˈvɛstmənt; ˌdɪsɪ̣nˈvestmənt/ *n* [U] *BrE technical* the act of taking your money out of a company, by selling your shares (SHARE² (5)) in it【英，术语】投资收回〔通过卖掉股份〕；减资；投资停止；DIVESTMENT *AmE*【美】

dis·joint·ed /dɪsˈdʒɔɪntɪd; dɪsˈdʒɔɪntɪ̣d/ *adj* a disjointed speech or piece of writing is one in which the words or ideas are not well connected together or arranged in a resonable order〔讲话、文章等〕不连贯的，表达混乱的；支离破碎的 **—disjointedly** *adv* **—disjointedness** *n* [U]

dis·junc·tive /dɪsˈdʒʌŋktɪv; dɪsˈdʒʌŋktɪv/ *adj technical* a disjunctive CONJUNCTION (3) expresses a choice or opposition between two ideas. For example, 'or' is a disjunctive conjunction【术语】〔连词〕转折的，反意的

dis·junc·ture /dɪsˈdʒʌŋktʃɚ; dɪsˈdʒʌŋktʃə/ *n* [C,U] a difference between two things that you would expect to be in agreement〔两个事物之间的〕不同，不一致，相悖：*a disjuncture between his private and public life* 他的私生活和公众生活的不一致

disk /dɪsk; dɪsk/ *n* [C] **1** a flat circular piece of plastic or metal used for storing computer information〔电脑的〕磁盘，磁碟 —see picture on page A14 参见 A14 页图 **2** the usual American spelling of DISC disc 的一般美式拼法 —see also 另见 COMPACT DISC, FLOPPY DISK, HARD DISK, LASER DISK

disk drive /ˈ· ·/ *n* [C] a piece of equipment in a computer system that is used to pass information to or from a disk 磁盘[碟]驱动器，磁碟机

dis·kette /dɪsˈkɛt; dɪsˈket/ *n* [C] *AmE* a FLOPPY DISK【美】软磁盘[碟]

dis·like¹ /dɪsˈlaɪk; dɪsˈlaɪk/ *v* [T, not in progressive 不用进行时] to think someone or something is unpleasant and not like them 不喜欢；讨厌：*Why do you dislike her so much?* 你为什么那么讨厌她？| **dislike doing sth** *Tom dislikes going to the dentist, that's why he's crabby.* 汤姆不喜欢去看牙医，所以他耍脾气。

dislike² *n* **1** [C,U] a feeling of not liking someone or something 不喜欢；讨厌：[+of/for] *She shared her mother's dislike of housework.* 她和她妈妈一样，不爱做家务。| **intense dislike** (=very strong dislike) 极不喜欢，强烈的反感 *His colleagues regarded him with intense dislike.* 他的同事们特别讨厌他。| **take a dislike to** (=decide that you dislike someone) 开始不喜欢〔某人〕*When the two men met, they took an instant dislike to each other.* 这两个人见面伊始就彼此讨厌对方。**2 dislikes** [plural] the things that you do not like 不喜欢的东西：**likes and dislikes** *A good hotel manager should know his regular guests' likes and dislikes.* 一个称职的酒店经理应该知道老主顾的好恶。

dis·lo·cate /ˈdɪsloˌket; ˈdɪsləkeɪt/ *v* [T] **1** to injure a joint so that the two bones at the joint are moved out of their normal position 使〔关节〕脱位，使脱臼：*I dislocated my shoulder playing football.* 踢足球时我的肩膀脱了臼。**2** to spoil the way in which a plan, system, or service is arranged, so that it cannot work normally; DISRUPT 扰乱，破坏〔计划、制度、服务等的正常安排〕**—dislocated** *adj*: *a dislocated shoulder* 脱了臼的肩膀 **—dislocation** /ˌdɪsloˈkeʃən; ˌdɪsləˈkeɪʃən/ *n* [C,U]: *The storm caused considerable dislocation of air traffic.* 这场暴风雨极大地扰乱了空中交通。

dis·lodge /dɪs`lɑdʒ; dɪs'lɒdʒ/ *v* [T] **1** to force or knock something out of its position 将〔某物〕逐出[移开]: *Ian dislodged a few stones as he climbed up the rock.* 伊恩攀岩的时候碰掉了几块石头。**2** to make someone leave a place or lose a position of power 使〔某人〕离开某地; 使〔某人〕失去权势: *the revolution that failed to dislodge the British in 1919* 未能推翻英国统治的1919年革命 —compare 比较 LODGE[1] (3) —**dislodgement** *n* [U]

dis·loy·al /dɪs`lɔɪəl; dɪs'lɔɪəl/ *adj* unfaithful to your friends, your country, or the group you belong to 不忠实的; 不忠诚的: [+to] *He felt he had been disloyal to his friends.* 他觉得自己对朋友们不忠诚。—**disloyally** *adv* —**disloyalty** *n* [C,U]

dis·mal /`dɪzml; 'dɪzməl/ *adj* **1** a dismal place, situation, thought etc has nothing pleasant in it and makes it difficult for you to feel happy and hopeful〔指某个地方、某种形势、想法等〕沉闷的; 阴郁的; 令人忧郁的; 沮丧的: *The future looks pretty dismal right now.* 现在看来, 前景相当暗淡。| *a dismal, grey November afternoon* 11月份一个阴沉、灰暗的下午 **2** bad and unsuccessful 差劲的; 不成功的; 糟糕的: *Your record so far is pretty dismal.* 你迄今为止的记录相当差。| **be a dismal failure** *His scheme was a dismal failure.* 他的计划失败得很惨。—**dismally** *adv*

dis·man·tle /dɪs`mæntl; dɪs'mæntl/ *v* **1** [T] to take a machine or piece of equipment apart so that it is in separate pieces 拆开, 拆卸〔机器、设备等〕: *Chris dismantled the bike in five minutes.* 克里斯五分钟内就把自行车给拆了。**2** [T] to gradually get rid of a system or organization 〔逐渐地〕废除〔某种制度或组织等〕: *an election promise to dismantle the existing tax legislation* 将废除现有税收法规的竞选许诺

dis·may[1] /dɪs`me; dɪs'meɪ/ *n* [U] the worry, disappointment, and unhappiness you feel when something unpleasant happens 忧虑; 失望; 沮丧; 恐慌: **with/in dismay** *Amanda read her exam results with dismay.* 阿曼达看到自己的考试成绩, 感到十分伤心。| *They stared at each other in dismay.* 他们沮丧地互相凝视着对方。| **to sb's dismay** *I found to my dismay that I had left my notes behind.* 令我沮丧的是, 我发现我忘了拿笔记了。| **fill sb with dismay** *The thought of making the journey filled him with dismay.* 一想到要出门旅行, 他就感到十分担忧。

dismay[2] *v* [T] to make someone feel worried, disappointed, and upset 使〔某人〕担忧[失望、伤心]: **be dismayed to see/hear etc** *Brenda was dismayed to find that work on the roof had not even begun.* 布伦达失望地发现屋顶的工作竟然还没开始。| **be dismayed at** *We were dismayed at the cost of the repairs.* 修理费这么贵, 令我们十分沮丧。

dis·mem·ber /dɪs`mɛmbɚ; dɪs'membə/ *v* [T] **1** to cut a body into pieces or tear it apart 肢解 **2** to divide a country, area, or organization into smaller parts 瓜分, 分割〔某个国家、地区或组织〕—**dismemberment** *n* [U]

3 **dis·miss** /dɪs`mɪs; dɪs'mɪs/ *v* [T]

1 ►IDEA 观点◄ to refuse to consider someone's idea, opinion etc, without thinking carefully about it 拒绝考虑〔某人的观点、意见等〕: **dismiss sth as** *He just laughed and dismissed my suggestion as unrealistic.* 他只是笑笑, 就以不实际为由拒绝了我的建议。| **dismiss sth out of hand** (=dismiss something completely) 全然拒绝某事物

2 ►JOB 工作◄ to remove someone from their job 解雇, 开除: **dismiss sb for** *Will they dismiss Woods for stealing the money?* 他们会因伍兹偷了钱而解雇他吗? | **dismiss sb from** *Bryant was dismissed from his post.* 布赖恩特被免职了。

3 ►SEND AWAY 打发走◄ to send someone away or allow them to go 把〔某人〕打发走; 让〔某人〕离开; 解散: *The teacher might dismiss the class early today because of the snow.* 由于下雪, 今天老师或许会提早放学。

4 ►IN A COURT 在法庭上◄ if a judge dismisses a court CASE[1] (9a), they stop it before a result is reached 驳回, 不受理〔案子〕: *The case was dismissed owing to lack of evidence.* 由于证据不足, 案子被驳回了。

5 ►SPORT 体育运动◄ to end the INNINGS of a player or a team in the game of CRICKET (2)〔板球比赛中〕迫使〔对方击球员或球队〕退场

dis·miss·al /dɪs`mɪsl; dɪs'mɪsəl/ *n* **1** [C,U] an act of removing someone from their job 解雇; 开除: **unfair dismissal** *Wilson was claiming compensation for unfair dismissal.* 威尔逊要求得到被无理解雇的赔偿金。**2** [U] a refusal to consider something seriously 不予理会; 拒绝考虑

dis·miss·ive /dɪs`mɪsɪv; dɪs'mɪsɪv/ *adj* refusing to consider someone or something seriously 不予理会的; 拒绝考虑的: [+of] *Why, I wonder, is Mr Sykes so dismissive of the protesters?* 我想知道, 为什么赛克斯先生对抗议者如此地不予理会? —**dismissively** *adv*

dis·mount /dɪs`maʊnt; dɪs'maʊnt/ *v* **1** [I+from] to get off a horse, bicycle, or MOTORCYCLE〔从马背、自行车、摩托车上〕下来 **2** [T] to take something, especially a gun, down from its base or support 把〔某物, 尤指枪炮, 从底座或支架上〕取下, 卸下

Dis·ney /`dɪznɪ; 'dɪzni/**, Walt** /wɔlt; wɔːlt/ (1901-66) a US film producer who is famous for making CARTOON films for children, and for inventing some of the best-known cartoon characters, including Mickey Mouse and Donald Duck. His cartoon films include *Snow White and the Seven Dwarfs* and *Fantasia*. His company continues to make popular films, especially for children. 迪斯尼〔(1901-1966), 美国电影制片人, 以制作儿童动画影片而出名, 塑造一些家喻户晓的卡通人物形象, 如米老鼠和唐老鸭。他制作的动画影片包括《白雪公主和七个小矮人》和《幻想曲》。目前, 其公司仍在继续推出大众喜爱的影片, 尤其是儿童电影〕

Dis·ney·land /`dɪznɪlænd; 'dɪznilænd/ *trademark*【商标】**1** a very large park near the US city of Los Angeles with many RIDE*s* (=exciting journeys in special vehicles), shops, restaurants, and hotels. Many of the shows and rides are based on Walt Disney's film characters, such as Mickey Mouse. 迪斯尼乐园〔美国洛杉矶市附近一大型公园。内有游乐场、商店、餐厅和旅馆。不少表演和滑车游戏都是根据米老鼠等迪斯尼影片的人物设计的〕**2** one of the similar parks near Paris (formerly called Eurodisney), Tokyo etc 迪斯尼乐园〔指巴黎或东京等地附近的类似公园。巴黎附近的公园旧称欧洲迪斯尼〕

Disney World, the /ˌ‥ ˈ·/ *trademark* a very large park near the US city of Orlando, Florida, with rides, games, shops etc, similar to Disneyland【商标】迪斯尼世界〔位于美国佛罗里达州奥兰多市附近一大型公园。内有游乐场、娱乐项目、商店等, 与迪斯尼乐园相似〕

dis·o·be·di·ent /ˌdɪsə`bidɪənt; ˌdɪsə'biːdiənt/ *adj* deliberately not doing what you are told to do by your parents, teacher, employer etc 不顺从的; 不服从的; 违抗的 —**disobediently** *adv* —**disobedience** *n* [U] —see also 另见 CIVIL DISOBEDIENCE

dis·o·bey /ˌdɪsə`be; ˌdɪsə'beɪ/ *v* [I,T] to refuse to do what someone with authority tells you to do, or refuse to obey a rule or law 不服从〔上级的命令〕; 不遵守〔规定或法律等〕: *Remember you're in the army; if you disobey orders you'll get a court martial.* 记住, 你是在军队里; 如果你不服从命令, 就会被送上军事法庭。

dis·o·bli·ging /ˌdɪsə`blaɪdʒɪŋ; ˌdɪsə'blaɪdʒɪŋ/ *adj formal* unwilling to help someone or do what they want【正式】不愿帮忙的; 不肯通融的 —**disoblige** *v* [T]

3 **dis·or·der** /dɪs`ɔrdɚ; dɪs'ɔːdə/ *n* **1** [U] a situation in which things or people are very untidy or disorganized 混乱; 凌乱; 杂乱; 无秩序: **in disorder** *Everything was in disorder, but nothing seemed to be stolen.* 一切都凌乱不堪, 但好像没有什么东西被偷。**2** [C,U] a situation in which many people disobey the law, especially in a violent way, and are impossible to control 动乱; 暴乱; 骚乱: **civil/public disorder** *a campaign of civil disorder* 一系列的社会骚乱 **3** [C] an illness which prevents part of your body from working properly〔身体机能的〕失调; 功能紊乱: **skin/stomach/liver etc disorder** *a rare genetic disorder* 一种罕见的基因疾病

dis·or·dered /dɪs`ɔrdɚd; dɪs'ɔːdəd/ *adj* **1** untidy or not arranged, planned, or done in a clear order 不整洁的; 杂乱的; 没有秩序的 **2** if someone is mentally disordered, their mind is not working in a normal and healthy way 精神失常的, 精神错乱的

dis·or·der·ly /dɪs`ɔrdɚlɪ; dɪs'ɔːdəli/ *adj* **1** untidy or lacking order 凌乱的; 无秩序的: *Joe left his clothes in a disorderly heap.* 乔把他的衣服乱七八糟地放成一堆。**2** behaving in a noisy violent way and causing trouble in a public place 喧闹的; 扰乱治安的; 破坏公共秩序的: **drunk and disorderly** (=behaving very badly in a public place because you have drunk too much alcohol) 酗酒后扰乱治安; 酒后失态; 发酒疯 —**disorderliness** *n* [U]

disorderly house /·ˌ‥ ˈ·/ *n* [C] *BrE law* a place where men pay to have sex; BROTHEL【英, 法律】妓院

dis·or·gan·ized also 又作 **-ised** *BrE*【英】/dɪs`ɔrgəˌnaɪzd; dɪs'ɔːgənaɪzd/ *adj* not arranged or planned in a clear order, or lacking any kind of plan or system 杂乱无章的; 组织不善的; 计划不周的: *The conference arrangements were completely disorganized.* 会议的安排毫无条理, 一片混乱。| *The whole thing's being run by a bunch of disorganized amateurs.* 整个事情正由一群组织不善的外行人在打理。—compare 比较 UNORGANIZED

dis·or·i·en·tate /dɪs`ɔrɪɛnˌtet; dɪs'ɔːriənteɪt/ also 又作 **dis·or·i·ent** /dɪs`ɔrɪˌɛnt; dɪs'ɔːriənt/ *AmE*【美】*v* [T] **1** to make

someone not know which direction they have come from or are going in 使〔某人〕迷失方向 **2** to make someone uncertain about what is happening around them and unable to think clearly 使迷惑; 晕头转向 —**disorientating, disorienting** *adj* —**disorientation** /dɪsˌɔrɪɛnˋteʃən; dɪsˌɔːriənˋteɪʃən/ *n* [U]

dis·or·i·en·tat·ed /dɪsˋɔrɪɛnˌtetɪd; dɪsˈɔːriənteɪtɪd/ also 又作 **dis·or·i·ent·ed** /dɪsˋɔrɪˌɛntɪd; dɪsˈɔːriəntɪd/ *adj, adv* **1** confused and not understanding what is happening around you 迷惑的; 头脑混乱的: *His wife said he was disoriented and begged to be allowed to sleep.* 他妻子说, 他昏沉沉的, 恳求获准睡觉。 **2** confused about which direction you are facing or which direction you should go 迷失方向的

dis·own /dɪsˋon; dɪsˈəʊn/ *v* [T not in progressive 不用进行时] to say that you no longer have any connection with someone or something; REPUDIATE (3) 声明与…断绝关系 *Frankly, I'm not surprised her family disowned her.* 老实说, 她的家人和她断绝关系, 我并不感到意外。

di·spar·age /dɪˋspærɪdʒ; dɪˈspærɪdʒ/ *v* [T] *formal* to criticize someone or something in a way that shows you do not think they are very good or important【正式】贬低, 诋毁: *Matcham's theatres were widely disparaged by architects.* 马切姆设计的剧院广遭建筑师的诋毁。—**disparagement** *n* [C,U]

di·spar·a·ging /dɪˋspærədʒɪŋ; dɪˈspærədʒɪŋ/ *adj* disparaging remarks criticize someone or something and show that you do not think they are very good〔言语等〕贬低的; 轻视的; 诋毁的; 损害名声的 —**disparagingly** *adv*

dis·pa·rate /ˋdɪspərɪt; ˈdɪspərɪt/ *adj formal* very different and not connected with each other【正式】迥然不同的; 不相干的; 全异的; 无法相比较的: *The challenge is to make disparate computer systems work together.* 难题是让迥然相异的电脑系统一起工作。—**disparately** *adv*

di·spar·i·ty /dɪsˋpærətɪ; dɪˈspærɪti/ *n* [C,U] *formal* a difference between two or more things, especially an unfair one【正式】〔两个或两个以上事物之间的〕不同; 不平等; 差异; 悬殊: [+in/between] *We are still seeing a disparity between the rates of pay for men and women.* 我们仍然可以看到男女的工资之间有着差异。—see also 另见 PARITY

dis·pas·sion·ate /dɪsˋpæʃənɪt; dɪsˈpæʃənɪt/ *adj* not influenced by emotion and therefore able to make fair decisions 不为感情所左右的; 不动感情的; 公正的: *a dispassionate view* 客观公正的见解 —**dispassionately** *adv*

di·spatch¹ also 又作 **despatch** *BrE*【英】/dɪsˋpætʃ; dɪˈspætʃ/ *v* [T] **1** *formal* to send someone or something somewhere for a particular purpose【正式】派遣; 发送: **dispatch sb/sth to** *A reporter was dispatched to Naples to cover the riot.* 一名记者被派往那不勒斯去报道暴乱之事。**2** *old-fashioned* to deliberately kill a person or animal【过时】故意杀死〔人或动物〕 **3** *old-fashioned* to finish all of something【过时】办完〔全部事情〕

dispatch² also 又作 **despatch** *BrE*【英】*n* **1** [C] a message sent between military or government officials〔在军官或政府官员之间传递的〕公文, 急件: *a dispatch from headquarters* 从总部发来的电文 **2** [C] a report sent to a newspaper from one of its writers who is in another town or country〔由身在另一城市或国家的记者发给报刊的〕报道, 电讯 **3 with dispatch** *formal* if you do something with dispatch, you do it well and quickly【正式】利落地, 迅速地 **4** [singular] the act of sending people or things to a particular place 派遣, 发送 —see also 另见 **mentioned in dispatches** (MENTION¹ (6))

dispatch box /ˋ· ·/ *n* **1** [C] a box for holding official papers〔装文件用的〕公文递送箱 **2 the dispatch box** a box on a central table in the British Parliament next to which important members of parliament stand to make speeches〔英国下议院会议厅中放置的〕案头公文箱〔重要议员在发言时便站在该箱子旁〕

dispatch rid·er /ˋ· ˌ· ·/ *n* [C] someone whose job is to take messages or packages by MOTORCYCLE or bicycle 骑摩托车[自行车]的通信员

di·spel /dɪˋspɛl; dɪˈspel/ *v* **dispelled, dispelling** [T] to stop someone believing or feeling something, especially because it is wrong or harmful 驱散, 消除: *The film aims to dispel the notion that AIDS only affects gay men.* 这部电影意在消除只有同性恋男子才会得艾滋病的错误观念。

di·spen·sa·ble /dɪˋspɛnsəbl; dɪˈspensəbəl/ *adj* easy to get rid of because not really needed〔因并不真正需要而〕可省去的; 可以丢弃的; 可有可无的: *Part-time workers are considered dispensable in times of recession.* 在经济萧条时期, 兼职工人被认为是可以不要的。—opposite 反义词 INDISPENSABLE

di·spen·sa·ry /dɪˋspɛnsərɪ; dɪˈspensəri/ *n* [C] a place where medicines are prepared and given out, especially in a hospital〔尤指医院的〕配药处, 药房 —compare 比较 PHARMACY

dis·pen·sa·tion /ˌdɪspənˋseʃən; ˌdɪspənˈseɪʃən/ *n* **1** [C,U] special permission from someone in authority or a religious leader to do something that is not usually allowed〔当权者或宗教领袖给予的〕特许: **special dispensation** *Caroline's marriage was annulled by special dispensation from the Church.* 卡罗琳的婚约是在教会的特许之下解除的。**2** [C] *formal* a religious or political system that has control over people's lives at a particular time【正式】〔某一时期控制人们生活的〕宗教[政治]制度; 教规 **3** [U] *formal* the act of providing people with something as part of an official process【正式】正式的施予; 提供; 分配: *the dispensation of justice* 正义的实施

di·spense /dɪˋspɛns; dɪˈspens/ *v* [T] **1** *formal* to give something to people, especially in fixed amounts【正式】〔尤指以固定数额〕施予; 分配〔某物〕: *Villagers dispensed tea to people involved in the accident.* 村民们送茶给遭遇这场意外事故的人们。**2** to prepare and give medicines to people 配药, 发药给〔人们〕 **3** to officially provide something for people in a society〔以官方身份〕正式提供〔某物〕; 分配, 分发; 施予: **dispense justice/punishments** (=decide whether or not someone is guilty of a crime and what punishment they should receive) 主持正义; 实施惩罚〔决定某人是否有罪, 应该得到怎样的惩罚〕

dispense with sb/sth *phr v* [T] *formal* to not use or do something that you usually use or do, because it is no longer necessary【正式】〔因已无必要〕不再使用: **can dispense with** *I think we can dispense with a translator.* 我想我们可以不用翻译人员。| **dispense with the formalities** (=not use very polite behaviour, such as introducing people to each other) 不必拘礼, 免去客套

di·spens·er /dɪˋspɛnsɚ; dɪˈspensə/ *n* [C] a machine in a public place which gives you things such as drinks or money when you press a button 自动售货机; 自动柜员机 — see also 另见 CASH DISPENSER

dispensing chem·ist /ˌ· ˋ· ˌ· ·/ *n* [C] *BrE* someone who is trained to sell medicines and advise people about them; PHARMACIST【英】配药者, 药剂师

di·sper·sal /dɪˋspɝsḷ; dɪˈspɜːsəl/ *n* [U] the act of spreading things over a wide area 散发, 散布; 传播: *the dispersal of information* 散布消息

di·sperse /dɪˋspɝs; dɪˈspɜːs/ *v* [I,T] **1** if a group of people disperses or is dispersed, they separate and go away in different directions (使)〔人群〕分散, 散开: *The police used tear gas to disperse the crowd.* 警察用催泪弹驱散人群。**2** if something disperses or is dispersed, it spreads over a wide area (使)〔某物〕消散: *The clouds dispersed as quickly as they had gathered.* 云聚集得快, 散得也快。—**dispersal** *n* [U]

Dis·per·sion, the /dɪˋspɝʒən; dɪˈspɜːʃən/ *n* the DIASPORA 大流散

dispersion *n* [U] *technical* dispersal【术语】色散; 弥散; 频散

di·spir·it·ed /dɪˋspɪrɪtɪd; dɪˈspɪrɪtɪd/ *adj* discouraged or without hope 灰心的; 沮丧的; 绝望的: *After six hours, dispirited and weary, they gave up the search.* 六个小时后, 他们又绝望又疲劳, 于是就放弃了搜寻。—**dispiritedly** *adv*

dis·place /dɪsˋples; dɪsˈpleɪs/ *v* [T] **1** to take the place of someone or something 取代, 替代: *Coal is being displaced by natural gas as a major source of energy.* 作为一种主要能源的煤正为天然气所取代。**2** to make a group of people or animals have to leave the place where they normally live 使〔人或动物的群体〕离开原来的生活之地; 使流离失所; 迫使流亡 —**displaced** *adj*

displaced per·son /ˌ· · ˋ· ·/ *n plural* **displaced persons** [C] *technical* someone who has been forced to leave their country because of war or cruel treatment; REFUGEE【术语】〔因战争或迫害而被迫离开本土的〕流亡者, 难民

dis·place·ment /dɪsˋplesmənt; dɪsˈpleɪsmənt/ *n* **1** [U] the act of forcing a group of people or animals to leave the place where they usually live〔人或动物群体的〕被迫迁徙, 流亡 **2** [singular] *technical* the weight or VOLUME (1) of liquid that something such as a ship floating on it takes the place of【术语】排水量

displacement ac·tiv·i·ty /ˋ· · ˌ· · ·/ *n* [C,U] *technical* something that is done in order to avoid doing something else that you do not want to think about【术语】替换活动, 转移活动〔为避免做不想做的事而做的另外一件事〕

di·splay¹ /dɪˋsple; dɪˈspleɪ/ *n*

1 ▶ATTRACTIVE ARRANGEMENT 吸引人的布置◀ [C,U] an attractive arrangement of objects for people to look at or buy〔物品的〕展示, 陈列: [+of] *a display of African tribal masks* 非洲部落面具展览

2 ▶PERFORMANCE 表演◀ [C] a public performance of something that is intended to entertain people〔为了娱乐人们而进行的〕公开表演: *a fireworks display* 烟花表演 | [+of] *a display of juggling* 杂耍表演

3 **be on display** something that is on display is in a public place where people can look at it 被展示，被陈列：**put sth on display** *Mapplethorpe's photographs were first put on display in New York.* 马普尔索普拍摄的照片首先在纽约展出。

4 **display of affection/temper/loyalty etc** an occasion when someone clearly shows a particular feeling, attitude, or quality 爱慕/脾气/忠诚等的流露

5 ►EQUIPMENT 设备◄ [C] a piece of equipment that can show changing information, for example the screen of a computer 显示器

2 **display²** *v* [T] **1** to show goods for sale in a shop, or paintings, historical objects etc in a public place 展示，陈列：*shop windows displaying the latest fashions* 展示最新时装的商店橱窗 **2** to clearly show a feeling, attitude, or quality by what you do or say 显示，显露〔某种情感、态度、才能等〕：*All the musicians displayed considerable skill.* 所有的音乐家都展示出相当高的技艺。**3** if a computer or notice displays information, it shows information in a way that can be clearly seen 显示〔信息等〕：*Local train and bus times are displayed on the notice-board.* 布告牌上张贴着当地火车和公共汽车的时间表。

dis·pleased /dɪsˋplizd; dɪsˈpliːzd/ *adj formal* not satisfied and annoyed【正式】不满意的；不高兴的：*"We are most displeased," said the Queen.* "我们非常不满意。"女王说道。—**displease** *v* [T]

dis·plea·sure /dɪsˋplɛʒɚ; dɪsˈpleʒə/ *n* [U] *formal* the feeling of being annoyed with someone because you do not approve of their behaviour【正式】不悦；不满；恼火：**incur sb's displeasure** (=make someone displeased) 惹某人生气

dis·port /dɪˋspɔrt; dɪˈspɔːt/ *v* [T] **disport yourself** *old-fashioned* to amuse yourself by doing active enjoyable things【过时】自娱；嬉戏；玩乐：*a charming painting of lords and ladies disporting themselves by a lake* 一幅王公贵妇在湖边嬉戏的美好画作

dis·po·sa·ble /dɪˋspozəbḷ; dɪˈspəʊzəbəl/ *adj* **1** intended to be used once or for a short time and then thrown away 一次性的；用完即可丢弃的：*disposable nappies* 一次性尿布 **2** available to be used 可使用的，可支配的：*disposable resources* 可支配的资源

disposable in·come /.,...'../ *n* [U] the amount of money you have left to spend after you have paid your taxes, bills etc 可支配收入〔完税并付清各种账款等之后所剩的钱〕

dis·pos·al /dɪˋspozḷ; dɪˈspəʊzəl/ *n* **1** [U] the act of getting rid of something 丢弃；处理：[+of] *the safe disposal of radioactive waste* 放射性废料的安全处理 **2** **at sb's disposal** available for someone to use 供某人使用，支配：*Tanner had a considerable amount of cash at his disposal.* 坦纳手头有很多现金可以支配。| **sb is at your (complete) disposal** (=someone is ready to help you in any way) 某人可随时为您效劳 **3** [C] *AmE informal* a small machine under the kitchen SINK² which breaks vegetable waste into small pieces【美，非正式】污物碾碎器〔装在厨房洗涤槽下面、把菜叶果皮等弄碎的机器〕；WASTE DISPOSAL *BrE*【英】**4** [U] *formal* the act of putting people or things in a particular place or in a particular order【正式】〔人或事物的〕安排，编排

dis·pose /dɪˋspoz; dɪˈspəʊz/ *v* [T] *formal* to arrange things or put them in their places【正式】安排，编排，处理，支配〔事物〕

dispose of sth *phr v* [T] **1** to get rid of something, especially something that is difficult to get rid of 处置，处理〔尤指难以处理的东西〕：*How did Dahmers dispose of his victims' bodies?* 达默斯是怎样将被他杀害的人毁尸灭迹的？**2** to deal with something such as a problem or question successfully 成功地处理〔问题〕，解决〔问题〕 **3** to defeat an opponent 战胜，打败〔对手〕

dispose sb **to** sth *phr v* [T usually in passive 一般用于被动态] to make someone more likely to feel or think a particular way about something 使〔某人〕较倾向于

dis·posed /dɪˋspozd; dɪˈspəʊzd/ *adj* [not before noun 不用于名词前] **1** **well/favourably/kindly disposed (to)** liking or approving of someone or something such as an idea or plan 很赞成…：*Management is favourably disposed to the idea of job-sharing.* 管理层很赞成"分工制"这一主张。**2** **be disposed to do sth** *formal* feel willing to do something or behave in a particular way【正式】愿意做某事：*Johnson disagreed, but did not feel disposed to argue.* 约翰逊不赞成，但他并不想争辩。**3** **be disposed to sth** *formal* to have a tendency towards something【正式】倾向于某事物：*a man disposed to depression* 一个趋于沮丧的人

dis·po·si·tion /ˌdɪspəˋzɪʃən; ˌdɪspəˈzɪʃən/ *n formal*【正式】**1** [C] a particular type of character which makes someone more likely to behave or react in a certain way; TEMPERAMENT 性情；性格：**have a cheerful/sunny disposition** (=have a happy character and behave in a happy way) 性格开朗；活跃 | **people of a nervous disposition** *The film is not suitable for people of a nervous disposition.* 这部电影不适合神经质的人观看。**2** [U] a tendency to behave in a particular way 意向；倾向：**have/show a disposition to do sth** *Neither side shows the slightest disposition to compromise.* 双方都丝毫没有表露出妥协的意思。**3** [C] the position or arrangement of something in a particular place 安排；布置：[+of] *a map showing the disposition of the American forces* 展示美军部署的地图 **4** [C,U] *law* the act of formally giving property to someone【法律】〔财产的〕赠予，给予，处置

dis·pos·sess /ˌdɪspəˋzɛs; ˌdɪspəˈzes/ *v* [T, usually passive 一般用被动态] *formal* to take property or land away from someone【正式】剥夺〔某人的财产、土地等〕：**be dispossessed of sth** *black South Africans who had been dispossessed of their homes* 被撵出家园的南非黑人 —**dispossession** /-ˋzɛʃən; -ˈzeʃən/ *n* [U]

dis·pos·sessed /ˌdɪspəˋzɛst; ˌdɪspəˈzest◂/ *adj* **1** having had property or land taken away 被夺走财产[土地等]的 **2** **the dispossessed** [plural] people who are dispossessed 被剥夺财产[土地]的人

dis·proof /dɪsˋpruf; dɪsˈpruːf/ *n* [C,U] *formal* a fact, argument etc that proves that something is wrong or false, or the act of proving that something is wrong or false【正式】反证；反驳；反证物；反驳的证据

dis·pro·por·tion /ˌdɪsprəˋpɔrʃən; ˌdɪsprəˈpɔːʃən/ *n* [C,U] *formal* the lack of a suitable or equal relation between two or more things【正式】不均衡；不相称；不成比例

dis·pro·por·tion·ate /ˌdɪsprəˋpɔrʃənɪt; ˌdɪsprəˈpɔːʃənə̇t◂/ *adj* too much or too little in relation to something else 不相称的；不匀称的；不成比例的：*the disproportionate amount of money being spent on defence projects* 花在防御计划上的钱与其他支出的不成比例 —**disproportionately** *adv*

dis·prove /dɪsˋpruv; dɪsˈpruːv/ *v* [T] to prove something false or wrong 证明〔某事〕是虚假[错误]的；给予…反证：*She was able to quote figures that disproved Smith's argument.* 她引用了一些数据，证明史密斯的论点是错误的。

dis·pu·ta·ble /dɪˋspjutəbḷ; dɪˈspjuːtəbəl/ *adj* something that is disputable is not definitely true or right and therefore is something that you can argue about; DEBATABLE 有争议的；可商榷的；未确定的 —opposite 反义词 INDISPUTABLE —**disputably** *adv*

dis·pu·ta·tion /ˌdɪspjuˋteʃən; ˌdɪspjʊˈteɪʃən/ *n* [C,U] *formal* a formal discussion about a subject which people cannot agree on【正式】讨论；辩论，争论

dis·pu·ta·tious /ˌdɪspjuˋteʃəs; ˌdɪspjʊˈteɪʃəs/ *adj formal* tending to argue; ARGUMENTATIVE【正式】爱争论的，好争辩的；争论性的 —**disputatiously** *adv*

dis·pute¹ /dɪˋspjut; dɪˈspjuːt/ *n* [C,U] 2

1 ►SERIOUS DISAGREEMENT 严重分歧◄ a situation in which two countries or groups of people quarrel or disagree with each other 争吵；争端：*a border dispute* 边界争端 | *A prolonged labor dispute disrupted rail services.* 久延未决的劳资争端使铁路的营运陷入混乱。

2 **be beyond dispute** if something is beyond dispute, everyone agrees that it is true or that it really happened 无可争辩；确定无疑：*It is beyond dispute that advances in medicine have enabled people to live longer.* 医学的发展使得人们更加长寿了，这是无可置疑的。

3 **be in/under dispute** if facts are in or under dispute, people do not agree about them 处在争论中；有争议

4 **be in dispute (with sb)** to disagree publicly with another person or group〔与某人或某个群体〕有分歧：*The miners were in dispute with their employers over pay.* 矿工们与雇主在工资问题上发生了纠纷。

5 **be open to dispute** if something is open to dispute, it is not completely certain and not everyone agrees about it 不确定的；有争议的：*His interpretation of the poem is open to dispute.* 他对这首诗的诠释是有争议的。

dis·pute² /dɪˋspjut; dɪˈspjuːt/ *v* **1** [T] to say that you think something such as a fact or idea is not correct or true 对〔某事〕表示异议；辩驳：*Few would dispute that travel broadens the mind.* 旅行能够开阔视野，几乎没有人会对此提出异议。**2** [I,T] to argue or disagree with someone 与〔某人〕争辩，争论，争执；有分歧：**hotly disputed** (=argued about with strong feelings or with anger) 激烈争辩的 **3** [T] to argue with another country, group etc about who owns a piece of land〔与其他国家、群体等〕争夺〔土地〕的：*The defending army disputed every inch of ground.* 防御一方的军队寸土必争。

disputed ter·ri·to·ry /.,..'..../ *n* [C,U] an area of land that is claimed by two or more countries 有争议的领土

dis·qual·i·fi·ca·tion /dɪsˌkwɑləfəˋkeʃən; dɪsˌkwɒlə̇fə̇ˈkeɪʃən/ *n* [C,U] a situation in which someone is stopped from

doing an activity or taking part in a competition because they have broken a rule 取消〔参赛〕资格: *Drug-taking is punished by instant disqualification from the game.* 服用违禁药物者会立即被取消参赛资格作为惩罚。

dis·qual·i·fy /dɪsˋkwɑləˌfaɪ; dɪsˈkwɒlɪ̈faɪ/ *v* [T] **1** to stop someone taking part in a competition because they have broken a rule 取消…的参赛资格: [+from] *Schumacher was disqualified from the race for ignoring a black flag.* 由于无视黑旗，舒马赫被取消参赛资格。**2** to prevent someone from doing a job or taking part in an activity, often unfairly〔通常不公正地〕阻止〔某人〕做某项工作[参加某项活动]; 剥夺…资格[权利]: [+from] *women in their 50's who are disqualified from working simply because of their age* 仅因年龄关系而被剥夺工作权利的五十来岁的妇女

dis·qui·et /dɪsˋkwaɪət; dɪsˈkwaɪət/ *n* [U] *formal* feelings of being anxious or not satisfied about something【正式】忧虑; 不满: [+over] *Growing disquiet was voiced over police handling of terrorist investigations.* 在警察处理对恐怖分子的调查问题上, 不满言论越来越多。

D

dis·qui·si·tion /ˌdɪskwəˋzɪʃən; ˌdɪskwɪ̈ˈzɪʃən/ *n* [C] *formal* a long speech or written report【正式】长篇演讲; 论文

Dis·rae·li /dɪzˋrelɪ; dɪzˈreɪli/, **Ben·ja·min** /ˋbɛndʒəmɪn; ˈbendʒəmɪ̈n/ (1804-81) a British politician in the Conservative Party who was Prime Minister of the UK in 1868 and from 1874 to 1880. He also wrote several NOVELs, including *Sybil.* 迪斯累里〔(1804-1881)，英国保守党政治家，1868年及1874至1880年间任英国首相。他还创作了几部小说，其中包括《西比尔》〕

dis·re·gard[1] /ˌdɪsrɪˋgɑrd; ˌdɪsrɪˈgɑːd/ *v* [T] to ignore something or treat it as unimportant 忽视; 轻视; 无视; 不顾: *The judge ordered the jury to disregard the witness's last statement.* 法官命令陪审团不要理会证人的最后陈述。

disregard[2] *n* [U] the act of ignoring something that other people think is important 忽视; 轻视; 无视: **complete/total/blatant disregard for** *Rudi drove with blatant disregard for his passengers' safety.* 鲁迪驾车时公然不顾乘客的安全。

dis·re·pair /ˌdɪsrɪˋpɛr; ˌdɪsrɪˈpeə/ *n* [U] buildings, roads etc that are in disrepair are in bad condition because they have not been repaired or looked after〔建筑物、道路等的〕破损, 失修: **be in disrepair/fall into disrepair** *a fine Georgian mansion that had been allowed to fall into disrepair* 一座年久失修的乔治王朝风格的精美宅第

dis·rep·u·ta·ble /dɪsˋrɛpjətəbl̩; dɪsˈrepjɪ̈təbəl/ *adj* a disreputable person or organization is not respected because they are thought to be involved in dishonest or illegal activities〔人或组织〕名声不好的; 不受尊敬的 **—disreputably** *adv* **—disreputableness** *n* [U]

dis·re·pute /ˌdɪsrɪˋpjut; ˌdɪsrɪˈpjuːt/ *n* [U] **bring sb/sth into disrepute** to make people stop trusting or having a good opinion of an activity, idea, organization etc 使某人/某事物丧失名誉[蒙羞]: *When one policeman is convicted of corruption, it brings the whole system into disrepute.* 如果一个警察被判犯有贪污罪, 这将使得整个警察系统都蒙受耻辱。

dis·re·spect /ˌdɪsrɪˋspɛkt; ˌdɪsrɪˈspekt/ *n* [U] **1** lack of respect for someone or for something such as the law 不尊敬, 失礼, 无礼 **2 no disrespect (to)** *spoken* used when you are criticizing someone or something to say that you do not want to seem rude【口】并不想无礼, 并无不敬〔用在批评某人或某事物的时候〕: *No disrespect to Adrian, but he's not very experienced.* 我说这话不是不尊重阿德里安, 不过他并不是很有经验。**—disrespectful** *adj* **—disrespectfully** *adv*

dis·robe /dɪsˋrob; dɪsˈrəʊb/ *v* [I] *formal or humorous* to take off your clothes【正式或幽默】宽衣; 脱衣服

dis·rupt /dɪsˋrʌpt; dɪsˈrʌpt/ *v* [T] to prevent a situation, event, system etc from continuing in its usual way by causing problems 扰乱; 使混乱: *We hope the move to Kansas won't disrupt the kids' schooling too much.* 我们希望把家搬到堪萨斯州不会过多地耽误孩子们上学。

dis·rup·tion /dɪsˋrʌpʃən; dɪsˈrʌpʃən/ *n* [C,U] a situation in which something is prevented from continuing in its normal way because of problems and difficulties 中断; 扰乱: *The strike caused widespread disruption to train services.* 罢工使铁路服务普遍陷入混乱。

dis·rup·tive /dɪsˋrʌptɪv; dɪsˈrʌptɪv/ *adj* disruptive behaviour prevents something from continuing in its usual way and causes trouble〔指行为等〕扰乱性的, 捣乱的: *a child who was disruptive in class* 一个破坏课堂秩序的孩子 **—disruptively** *adv*

diss /dɪs; dɪs/ *v* [T] *AmE slang* to make unfair and unkind remarks about someone【美俚】说〔某人〕的坏话

dis·sat·is·fac·tion /ˌdɪssætɪsˋfækʃən; dɪˌsætɪ̈sˈfækʃən/ *n* [U] a feeling of not being satisfied 不满意; 不满足

dis·sat·is·fied /dɪsˋsætɪsˌfaɪd; dɪˈsætɪ̈sfaɪd/ *adj* not satisfied because something is not as good as you had expected 不满意的; 不满足的: [+with] *If for any reason you are dissatisfied with this product, please return it to the address below.* 对这款产品如有任何不满, 请将其退回下列地址。

dis·sat·is·fy /dɪsˋsætɪsˌfaɪ; dɪˈsætɪ̈sfaɪ/ *v* [T] to fail to satisfy someone or something 使不满

dis·sect /dɪˋsɛkt; dɪˈsekt/ *v* [T] **1** to cut up the body of a dead person or animal in order to study it 解剖〔人或动物的尸体〕**2** to examine something in great detail so that you discover its faults or understand it better 剖析〔某事物〕

dis·sec·tion /dɪˋsɛkʃən; dɪˈsekʃən/ *n* [C,U] the act of cutting up the body of a dead person or animal to study it 解剖

dis·sem·ble /dɪˋsɛmbl̩; dɪˈsembəl/ *v* [I,T] *formal* to hide your true feelings, ideas, desires etc【正式】掩饰, 掩藏〔真实的情感、观点、愿望等〕

dis·sem·i·nate /dɪˋsɛməˌnet; dɪˈsemɪ̈neɪt/ *v* [T] *formal* to spread information, ideas etc to as many people as possible, especially in order to influence them【正式】散布, 广泛传播〔消息, 观点等〕**—dissemination** /dɪˌsɛməˋneʃən; dɪˌsemɪ̈ˈneɪʃən/ *n* [U]: *the dissemination of information about new tax rules* 关于新税务条例的消息的传播

dis·sen·sion /dɪˋsɛnʃən; dɪˈsenʃən/ *n* [C,U] disagreement and argument among a group of people〔某一团体内部的〕争执, 分歧: *On the issue of the single market, there was little dissension.* 在单一市场这一问题上几乎没有什么不同的意见。

dis·sent[1] /dɪˋsɛnt; dɪˈsent/ *n* **1** [U] refusal to accept an official opinion or an opinion that most people accept〔尤指对某种官方意见或多数人所持意见的〕异议; 意见的分歧: *political dissent* 不同政见 **2** [C] *AmE* a judge's written statement giving their reasons for disagreeing with the other judges in a law case【美】〔某法官表示与其他法官在某一案件中持不同见解的理由的〕书面陈述 **3** [U] *old use* a disagreement with accepted religious beliefs, especially one that makes someone leave an established church【旧】〔对公认的宗教教义的〕不赞成, 反对; 不信奉国教 — see also 另见 CONSENT[1], ASSENT[1]

dissent[2] *v* [I] to say that you strongly disagree with an official opinion or decision, or one that is accepted by most people〔对官方的观点、决定或多数人所接受的意见〕强烈反对; 持异议 **—dissenter** *n* [C]

dis·ser·ta·tion /ˌdɪsəˋteʃən; ˌdɪsəˈteɪʃən/ *n* [C] a long piece of writing about a subject, especially one that you write as part of a university degree 专题论文〔尤指大学学位论文〕

dis·ser·vice /dɪsˋsɝvɪs; dɪˈsɜːvɪ̈s/ *n* **do a disservice to** to do something that harms someone or something, especially by giving other people a bad opinion about them 对…造成损害[危害, 伤害]: *The fans' behaviour has done the game a great disservice.* 球迷们的行为对这项运动造成了很大的损害。

dis·si·dent /ˋdɪsədənt; ˈdɪsɪ̈dənt/ *n* [C] someone who publicly criticizes a government or political party, especially in a country where this is not allowed 持不同政见者 **—dissident** *adj*: *a group of dissident writers* 一群持不同政见的作家 **—dissidence** *n* [U]

dis·sim·i·lar /dɪˋsɪmələ; dɪˈsɪmɪ̈lə/ *adj* not the same 不相同的; 不相似的 **—dissimilarity** /dɪˌsɪməˋlærətɪ; dɪˌsɪmɪ̈ˈlærɪ̈ti/ *n* [C,U]

dis·sim·u·late /dɪˋsɪmjəˌlet; dɪˈsɪmjɪ̈leɪt/ *v* [I,T] *formal* to hide your true feelings or intentions, especially by lying to people【正式】〔尤指通过撒谎〕隐藏, 掩饰〔真实的感情或意图〕

dis·si·pate /ˋdɪsəˌpet; ˈdɪsɪ̈peɪt/ *v formal*【正式】**1** [I,T] to scatter or disappear, or make something do this (使)〔某事物〕消散, 消失: *England's arrogance was dissipated by a 1–0 defeat by the United States.* 英格兰队被美国队以1–0打败后, 其傲慢气焰消失殆尽。**2** [T] to gradually waste something such as money or energy by trying to do a lot of different or unnecessary things 挥霍〔金钱〕; 耗费〔精力〕; 消耗

dis·si·pat·ed /ˋdɪsəˌpetɪd; ˈdɪsɪ̈peɪtɪ̈d/ *adj* spending too much time on physical pleasures such as drinking alcohol, in a way that is harmful to your health 放荡的, 浪荡的; 无节制的, 奢靡的

dis·si·pa·tion /ˌdɪsəˋpeʃən; ˌdɪsɪ̈ˈpeɪʃən/ *n* [U] *formal*【正式】**1** the process of making something disappear or scatter 消失; 驱散; 耗尽: [+of] *the dissipation of heat* 热量的消散 **2** the enjoyment of physical pleasures such as drinking too much alcohol, that are harmful to your health 放荡; 花天酒地: *a life of luxury and dissipation* 奢侈而放荡的生活 **3** the act of wasting money, time, energy etc〔金钱、时间、精力等的〕浪费

dis·so·ci·ate /dɪˋsoʃɪˏet; dɪˈsəʊʃieɪt/ *v* [T] **1 dissociate yourself from** to do or say something to show that you do not agree with a person or organization, especially so that you avoid being criticized for their behaviour or views〔尤指为避免受到牵连或遭到批评而〕表示与…没有关系: *I wish to dissociate myself from the views expressed by Mr Irving.* 我想表明我不赞同欧文先生的观点。**2 dissociate sb/sth from** to regard two things or people as separate and not connected to each other 把某人/某物与…分开 —**dissociation** /dɪˏsoʃɪˋeʃən; dɪˌsəʊʃiˈeɪʃən/ *n* [U]

dis·so·lute /ˋdɪsəˏlut; ˈdɪsəluːt/ *adj* having an immoral way of life, for example drinking too much alcohol, having sex with many people etc〔生活〕放荡的; 道德沦丧的: *Dylan Thomas, then an intensely romantic, though dissolute figure* 迪伦·托马斯, 那时候是一个非常浪漫甚至放荡的人物 —**dissolutely** *adv* —**dissoluteness** *n* [U]

dis·so·lu·tion /ˏdɪsəˋluʃən; ˌdɪsəˈluːʃən/ *n* [U] **1** the act of formally ending a parliament〔议会的〕解散 **2** the act of formally ending a marriage or business arrangement〔婚姻关系、商务安排的〕正式解除 **3** the process by which something gradually becomes weaker and disappears〔某事物的〕衰败, 消亡: *the dissolution of the Roman Empire* 罗马帝国的衰亡

Dissolution of the Mon·as·teries /ˏ··ˏ···ˋ···/ the closing of all the monasteries (MONASTERY) in England in the 1530s, during the REFORMATION. King Henry VIII ordered the monasteries to be closed, and sold their property in order to increase his own wealth and power. 解散修道院〔指16世纪30年代宗教改革时期英格兰关闭所有修道院这一事件。当时, 国王亨利八世下令关闭所有修道院, 变卖其财产, 以增强国王个人的财力和实权〕

dissolve 溶解

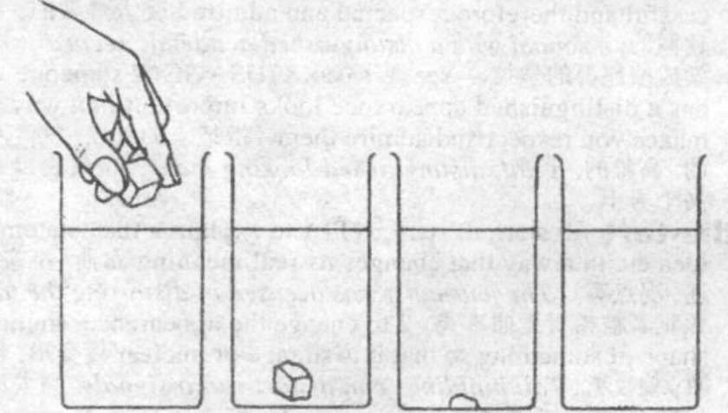

dis·solve /dɪˋzɑlv; dɪˈzɒlv/ *v*

1 ▶STH SOLID 固体物◀ a) [I] if a solid dissolves, it mixes with a liquid and becomes part of it〔固体〕溶解: **[+in]** *Sugar dissolves in water.* 糖能溶解于水。**b)** [T] to make something solid become part of a liquid by putting it in a liquid and mixing it 使〔固体〕溶解: **dissolve sth in** *Dissolve the tablets in water.* 把药片溶于水中。

2 dissolve into laughter/tears start to laugh or cry 开始哈哈大笑/泪流满面

3 ▶BECOME WEAKER 变弱◀ [I] to become weaker and disappear 变弱; 消失: *Her objections to the plan began to dissolve.* 渐渐地, 她对这项计划不再持反对意见了。

4 ▶PARLIAMENT 议会◀ [T] to formally end a parliament before an election〔在大选前〕正式解散〔议会〕

5 ▶MARRIAGE/BUSINESS/ORGANIZATION 婚姻/商务/组织◀ [T usually passive 一般用被动态] to formally end a marriage, business arrangement, or organization 解除〔婚姻关系〕; 取消〔商务安排〕; 解散〔组织〕

dis·so·nance /ˋdɪsənəns; ˈdɪsənəns/ *n* **1** [C,U] a combination of musical notes that have a strange sound because they are not in HARMONY (1)〔乐声的〕不和谐音 **2** [U] *formal* a lack of agreement between different ideas or opinions【正式】〔观点、意见的〕不一致 —**dissonant** *adj*

dis·suade /dɪˋswed; dɪˈsweɪd/ *v* [T] to persuade somebody not to do something 劝〔某人〕不要做某事; 劝阻: **dissuade sb from doing sth** *a campaign to dissuade young people from smoking* 劝年轻人不要吸烟的活动 —compare 比较 PERSUADE —**dissuasion** /dɪˋsweʒən; dɪˈsweɪʒən/ *n* [U]

S2 W2 **dis·tance¹** /ˋdɪstəns; ˈdɪstəns/ *n* [C,U]

1 ▶HOW FAR 有多远◀ the amount of space between two places or things 距离, 间距: **short/long distance** *Sylvia could only run a short distance without getting out of breath.* 西尔维娅只能跑较短的距离, 跑远了就会气喘吁吁。| **[+from]** *What's the distance from Chicago to Detroit?* 芝加哥离底特律有多远? | **at a distance of 5 metres/2 miles etc** (=5 metres etc away) 相隔5米/2英里等 *Place the rod at a distance of 40mm from the light source.* 把棒放在离光源40毫米的地方。| **some distance from/a good distance away from** (=a fairly long distance from) 离…有一段距离/很远 *Gareth's cottage is some distance from the road.* 加雷思的小屋离公路有一段距离。

2 in the distance in a place that is far away, but close enough to be seen or heard 在远处〔但可以看到或听到〕: *That's Long Island in the distance over there.* 那边远处是长岛。

3 at/from a distance a) from a place that is not very close 在远处/从不太近的地方: **follow sb from a distance** (=follow them by walking a long way behind them) 远远地跟着某人 *The detective followed him at a distance.* 侦探远远地跟着他。**b)** a long time after something happened〔时间〕相隔很久: *It's difficult to remember exactly what they looked like at this distance in time.* 时间隔了这么久, 很难确切地记清楚他们到底长得什么样。

4 within walking/driving distance near enough to walk or drive to 走路/开车去很近: **[+of]** *There are two good Chinese restaurants within walking distance of my house.* 从我家走过去不远处有两家很好的中国餐厅。

5 within spitting distance of *informal* very near【非正式】非常近

6 keep your distance a) to avoid becoming too friendly with someone or too closely involved in something 避免〔和某人〕太亲近; 避免过多地卷入〔某事〕**b)** to not go too close to someone or to another car〔与某人或其他车辆〕保持距离

7 keep sb at a distance to not become too friendly with someone 不与某人太亲近: *Ann likes to keep people at a distance.* 安喜欢与人保持一定距离。

8 ▶UNFRIENDLY FEELING 不友好的感情◀ a situation in which two people do not tell each other what they really think or feel, in a way that seems unfriendly〔两个人之间的〕疏远: **[+between]** *There was still a certain distance between me and my father.* 我和父亲之间仍然有些疏远。

9 go the distance *informal* if you go the distance in a sport or competition, you continue playing or competing until the end【非正式】〔在体育比赛或其他竞赛中〕继续比赛直到最后 —see also 另见 LONG-DISTANCE, MIDDLE DISTANCE

distance² *v* **distance yourself** to say that you are not involved with someone or something, or try to become less involved, especially to avoid being connected with them 使自己与…保持距离; 疏远〔某人〕; 不介入〔某事〕: *The Soviet Union distanced itself from the US position.* 苏联对美国的立场保持了距离。

distance learn·ing /ˋ·· ˏ··/ *n* [U] *BrE* a method of study that involves watching television programmes and sending work to teachers instead of going to a school【英】远程学习, 遥距教学〔通过收看电视节目并把作业寄给老师的学习方式〕

dis·tant /ˋdɪstənt; ˈdɪstənt/ *adj* W3

1 ▶FAR AWAY 远处的◀ far from where you are now 远处的, 远方的: *the distant sound of traffic* 远处的车辆声 | *Nora gazed at the distant hills.* 诺拉凝视着远山。

2 ▶UNFRIENDLY 不友好的◀ unfriendly and showing no emotion 不友好的; 冷淡的: *After the quarrel Susan remained cold and distant.* 那次争吵之后, 苏珊一直非常冷淡疏远。

3 ▶RELATIVE 亲属◀ [only before noun 仅用于名词前] not very closely related to you 远亲的: *a distant cousin* 一位远房表〔堂〕亲

4 in the (dim and) distant past a long time ago 很久以前, 在遥远的过去

5 in the not too distant future used when talking about what will happen in a few months or years from now 在不远的将来: *The President hopes to visit Ireland in the not too distant future.* 总统希望在不远的将来访问爱尔兰。—**distantly** *adv*

dis·taste /dɪsˋtest; dɪsˈteɪst/ *n* [U] a feeling of dislike for someone or something that you think is unpleasant or morally offensive 不喜欢, 厌恶, 反感: **[+for]** *her distaste for any form of compromise* 她对任何形式的妥协的反感

dis·taste·ful /dɪsˋtestfəl; dɪsˈteɪstfəl/ *adj* very unpleasant or morally offensive 令人生厌的; 令人反感的: *What follows is John's story. Parts of it may seem distasteful, even shocking.* 下面是约翰讲的故事, 其中有些部分也许听起来令人生厌, 甚至令人震惊。—**distastefully** *adv* —**distastefulness** *n* [U]

Di Stefano /dɪ stɛˋfɑno; dɪ steˈfɑːnəʊ/, **Alfredo** /ˏælˋfredo; ælˈfreɪdəʊ/ (1926-) a football player born in Argentina, who is considered one of the greatest players. He played international football for Argentina in the 1940s but moved to Spain and played both for the Spanish national team and for the Real

Madrid team in the 1950s. 迪·斯蒂法诺〔(1926-)，出生于阿根廷的足球运动员，被认为是最杰出的球员之一。20世纪40年代代表阿根廷参加国际比赛，20世纪50年代移居西班牙，同时效力于西班牙国家队和皇家马德里队〕

dis·tem·per /dɪsˈtɛmpɚ; dɪˈstempə/ *n* [U] **1** an infectious disease that affects dogs and cats 瘟热〔猫、狗所得的一种传染性疾病〕 **2** *BrE* a type of paint that you mix with water used for painting walls【英】〔刷墙用的〕水浆涂料

dis·tend /dɪˈstɛnd; dɪˈstend/ *v* [I,T] to swell or make something swell because of pressure from inside〔因来自内部的压力〕(使)膨胀, (使)肿胀 —**distended** *adj*: *a distended stomach* 胃胀 —**distension** /-ˈtɛnʃən; -ˈtenʃən/ *n* [U] *technical*【术语】

dis·til also 又作 **distill** *AmE*【美】/dɪˈstɪl; dɪˈstɪl/ *v* **distilled, distilling** [T] **1** to make a liquid such as water or alcohol more pure by heating it so that it becomes a gas and then letting it cool 蒸馏 **2** to make a strong alcoholic drink such as WHISKY by this method 采用蒸馏法制造〔烈性酒, 如威士忌〕 **3** to get ideas, information etc from a large amount of knowledge or experience〔从大量的知识或经验中〕提取, 提炼〔观念或信息等〕—**distillation** /ˌdɪstəˈleʃən; ˌdɪstɪˈleɪʃən/ *n* [C,U]

dis·til·ler /dɪˈstɪlɚ; dɪˈstɪlə/ *n* [C] a person or company that makes strong alcoholic drinks such as WHISKY 制酒商; 酿酒厂

dis·til·le·ry /dɪˈstɪlərɪ; dɪˈstɪləri/ *n* [C] a factory where strong alcoholic drink is produced by distilling〔采用蒸馏法的〕酿酒厂

dis·tinct /dɪˈstɪŋkt; dɪˈstɪŋkt/ *adj* **1** clearly different or belonging to a different type 明显不同的; 不同种类的: **quite/entirely distinct** (=completely distinct) 截然不同的, 完全不同的 *two entirely distinct languages* 两种完全不同的语言 | **[+from]** *The behavior of men as individuals is distinct from their behavior in a group.* 人在独处时的行为与在群体中的行为是不一样的。 **2 as distinct from** used when emphasizing that you are talking about a particular kind of thing and not something else 与…有所区别〔用于表示强调你在谈论的是某一事物〕: *childhood as distinct from adolescence* 有别于青春期的童年时期 **3** something that is distinct can clearly be seen, heard, smelled etc 清晰的, 清楚的, 明显的: *The outline of the ship became more distinct.* 船的轮廓变得更加清晰了。 **4** [only before noun 仅用于名词前] a distinct possibility, feeling, quality etc definitely exists or is definitely important and cannot be ignored〔指可能性、感觉、特征等〕确实存在的; 确实重要的; 不容忽视的: *a distinct lack of interest among the general public* 在普通大众中间明显存在的漠不关心的情况 | **have a distinct advantage** *Oxbridge graduates have a distinct advantage when applying for jobs in the civil service.* 牛津大学和剑桥大学的毕业生在申请公务员职务时有明显的优势。

dis·tinc·tion /dɪˈstɪŋkʃən; dɪˈstɪŋkʃən/ *n* **1** [C] a clear difference between two similar things 差别, 不同: **[+between]** *the distinction between formal and informal language* 正式与非正式语言之间的差别 **2 make/draw a distinction** to say that two things or groups are different or treat them in a different way 区分开来〔指区别对待〕: *The school makes no distinction between male and female students.* 学校并没有对男女学生区别对待。 **3** [U] the quality of being excellent and important 优秀; 卓越, 杰出: *No one today doubts Eliot's distinction as a poet.* 如今没有人怀疑艾略特是位杰出的诗人。 | **of (great) distinction** (=very good and very important) 卓越的 *Collingwood was a scholar of great distinction.* 科林伍德是位卓越的学者。 **4** [C] a special honour given to someone to show them respect or to reward their achievements 荣誉, 殊荣: **have the distinction of doing sth** *Dinah had the great distinction of being invited to meet the Prime Minister.* 黛娜获得殊荣, 被邀请与首相见面。 **5** [C] a special mark given to a student who has done very well 授予优秀学生的特殊分数: *Bianca got a distinction in her chemistry exam.* 比安卡的化学考试得到了优异的等级。

dis·tinc·tive /dɪˈstɪŋktɪv; dɪˈstɪŋktɪv/ *adj* having a special quality, character, or appearance that is different and easy to recognize〔特征、性格、外表等〕与众不同的: *a rock band with a distinctive sound* 声音很有特色的摇滚乐队 —**distinctively** *adv* —**distinctiveness** *n* [U]

dis·tinct·ly /dɪˈstɪŋktlɪ; dɪˈstɪŋktli/ *adv* **1** clearly 清楚地; 明白地: *I distinctly heard him say my name.* 我清楚地听见他说我的名字。 **2** used when saying that someone or something has a particular quality, character etc that is easy to recognize 明显地〔用于表示某人或某物具有某种易辨认的特征、特点等〕: *The rest of the passengers had distinctly Indian names.* 其他乘客的名字都具有明显的印度人的特征。 **3** used when emphasizing an adjective that you are using to describe something or someone 非常, 特别〔用来强调某个形容词〕: *Paul was feeling distinctly foolish.* 保罗感到非常愚蠢。 **4 distinctly remember doing sth** used to say that you definitely remember details about something very clearly 清清楚楚地记得做过某事

dis·tin·guish /dɪˈstɪŋgwɪʃ; dɪˈstɪŋgwɪʃ/ *v* **1** [I,T] to be able to recognize and understand the difference between two similar things or people 区别, 辨别: *Dogs can distinguish a greater range of sounds than humans.* 狗能辨别的音域比人类大得多。 | **[+between]** *It's important to distinguish between tax avoidance and tax evasion.* 把避税和逃税区别开是很重要的。 | **distinguish sb/sth from** *The twins are so alike it's difficult to distinguish one from the other.* 这对孪生儿长得太像了, 很难分辨谁是谁。 **2** [T not in progressive 不用进行时] to be able to see the shape of something or hear a particular sound 辨清〔某物的轮廓〕; 分清〔某种声音〕: *The light was too dim for me to distinguish anything clearly.* 光线太暗了, 我什么也看不清楚。 **3** [T not in progressive 不用进行时] *formal* to be the thing that makes someone or something different from other people or things【正式】使有别于; 使有特色: **distinguish sb/sth from** *There's not much to distinguish her from the other candidates.* 她没有太多有别于其他候选人的特点。 | **distinguishing feature/mark** (=a feature or mark that makes someone or something look different) 与众不同的特征/标记 **4 distinguish yourself** to do something so well that people notice you and remember you 表现突出: *McEnroe first distinguished himself by winning a junior tournament at Wimbledon.* 麦肯罗最初因在一次温布尔登少年网球赛中获胜而受人注目。

dis·tin·guish·a·ble /dɪˈstɪŋgwɪʃəbl; dɪˈstɪŋgwɪʃəbəl/ *adj* easily recognized as being different from other things or people 能分辨出来的, 区别得开的: **[+from]** *The copy was barely distinguishable from the original painting.* 这摹本画几乎可以乱真。

dis·tin·guished /dɪˈstɪŋgwɪʃt; dɪˈstɪŋgwɪʃt/ *adj* **1** very successful and therefore respected and admired 受人尊敬的, 令人钦佩的: *a school with a distinguished academic record* 一所教学成绩超群的学校 → see 见 FAMOUS (USAGE) **2** someone who has a distinguished appearance looks important in a way that makes you respect and admire them〔指某人的外表〕气度不凡的, 高雅的: *a tall, distinguished-looking man* 一位仪表出众的高个男士

dis·tort /dɪˈstɔrt; dɪˈstɔːt/ *v* [T] **1** to explain a fact, statement, idea etc in a way that changes its real meaning 歪曲〔事实、陈述、观点等〕: *The journalist was accused of distorting the facts.* 该记者被指责歪曲事实。 **2** to change the appearance, sound, or shape of something so that it is strange or unclear 使变形; 使失真; 使反常: *Tall buildings can distort radio signals.* 高大的建筑物会使无线电信号失真。—**distorted** *adj* —**distortion** /dɪsˈtɔrʃən; dɪˈstɔːʃən/ *n* [U]

dis·tract /dɪˈstrækt; dɪˈstrækt/ *v* [T] to make someone who is working, studying etc unable to continue what they are doing by making them look at or listen to something else 分散〔某人〕的注意力; 使〔某人〕分心: *Try not to distract the other students.* 尽量不要让其他学生分心。 | **distract sb from** *Meg was distracted from her work by the noise outside.* 外面的嘈杂声使得梅格不能专心工作。 | **distract sb's attention** (=deliberately stop someone paying attention to what they are doing) 分散某人的注意力 —**distracting** *adj*

dis·tract·ed /dɪˈstræktɪd; dɪˈstræktɪd/ *adj* anxious and unable to think clearly 心神不定的, 心烦意乱的, 精神无法集中的: *After the argument, Kathryn felt too distracted to work.* 争吵之后, 凯瑟琳感到心神不定, 无法工作。—**distractedly** *adv*

dis·trac·tion /dɪˈstrækʃən; dɪˈstrækʃən/ *n* **1** [C,U] something that makes you stop paying attention to what you are doing 使人分心的事物: *I have to study in the library — there are too many distractions at home.* 我得在图书馆学习, 因为家里分心的事太多。 **2** [C] a pleasant and not very serious activity that you do for amusement 消遣, 娱乐 **3 drive sb to distraction** to annoy someone so much, that they become angry, upset, and no longer able to think clearly 让某人烦得要命; 把某人逼疯: *The baby's constant crying was driving me to distraction.* 婴儿不停地哭, 真要把我给弄疯了。

dis·trait /dɪˈstre; dɪˈstreɪ/ *adj French* distracted【法】心神不定的, 精神无法集中的

dis·traught /dɪˈstrɔt; dɪˈstrɔːt/ *adj* so upset and worried that you cannot think clearly 忧心如焚的, 心神不定的, 忧虑欲狂的: *The distraught woman was yesterday giving police a description of her attacker.* 昨天, 那个心慌意乱的妇女向警察描述了那个袭击者的情况。

dis·tress[1] /dɪˈstrɛs; dɪˈstres/ *n* [U]

1 ►EXTREME WORRY 极度忧虑◄ a feeling of extreme worry and unhappiness 极度忧虑; 苦恼: *Luke's destructive behaviour*

caused his parents great distress. 卢克的破坏行为使他的父母深感忧虑。| **in distress** *The girl was crying and clearly in distress.* 那个女孩哭了，显然是很痛苦。

2 ►PAIN 疼痛◄ *formal* great physical pain【正式】身体上的痛苦，剧痛

3 ►LACK OF MONEY/FOOD 缺少钱/食物◄ a situation in which you suffer or have great problems because you have no money, food etc 贫困；困苦：**in distress** *charities that aid families in distress* 救助贫困家庭的慈善机构 | *acute financial distress* 严重的财务困难

4 distress signal a message sent from a ship, aircraft etc asking for help〔船、飞机等的〕求救信号

5 be in distress if a ship, aircraft etc is in distress, it is in danger of sinking or crashing〔船只、飞机等〕处于险境，遇险

distress² *v* [T] to make someone feel extremely upset and worried 使伤心，使不安，使忧虑

dis·tressed /dɪˋstrɛst; dɪˈstrest/ *adj* **1** extremely upset and shocked 极为难过的，十分不安的：**deeply distressed** *Hannah was deeply distressed by the news about her father.* 汉娜得知她父亲的消息，深感悲痛。**2** experiencing a lot of pain 十分痛苦的：*The animal was clearly distressed.* 那个动物显然很痛苦。**3** *formal* having very little money【正式】贫困的：*a family living in distressed circumstances* 生活在贫困中的一家人

dis·tress·ing /dɪˋstrɛsɪŋ; dɪˈstresɪŋ/ also 又作 **distressful** *adj* making you feel extremely upset and anxious 令人不安的，使人忧虑的：*a distressing experience* 一次痛苦的经历 —**distressingly** *adv*

W3 **dis·trib·ute** /dɪˋstrɪbjut; dɪˈstrɪbjuːt/ *v* [T] **1** to give something such as food, medicine, books etc to a large group of people, especially in a planned way〔尤指有计划地〕分发，分配，分送：**distribute sth among/to** *Clothes and blankets have been distributed among the refugees.* 已经向难民分发了衣服和毯子。| *a man distributing leaflets to passers-by* 一个派发传单给路人的男子 **2** to supply goods to shops and companies in a particular area 提供，配送〔货物〕：*Milk is distributed to the local shops by Herald's Dairies.* 牛奶是由赫拉德牛奶场提供给当地商店的。**3** to share something such as wealth or power among different people or organizations 分享〔财富或权力〕 **4** to spread something over a large area 散布；分布；撒；播：*The flowers rely on the wind to distribute their pollen.* 这些花靠风来传播花粉。

W2 **dis·tri·bu·tion** /ˌdɪstrəˋbjuʃən; ˌdɪstrɪˈbjuːʃən/ *n* **1** [U] the act of giving things to a large group of people or delivering goods to companies, shops etc 分发，分配；发送：[+of] *the distribution of aid supplies* 救济物资的分发 **2** [C,U] the way in which people, buildings etc are arranged over a large area〔人口、建筑物等的〕分布：*population distribution* 人口分布 **3** [U] *technical* the way in which wealth, property etc is shared among the members of a society【术语】〔财富、财产等的〕分配

dis·trib·u·tive /dɪˋstrɪbjətɪv; dɪˈstrɪbjʊtɪv/ *adj* **1** connected with distribution 分发的，分配的；分布的：*distributive costs* 配送费用 **2** *technical* referring to each single member of a group; distributing words in English include 'each', 'every' and 'either'.【术语】〔词〕个体的，个别的；分配的〔英语中的分配[个体]词包括 each, every 和 either〕

dis·trib·u·tor /dɪˋstrɪbjətɚ; dɪˈstrɪbjʊtə/ *n* [C] **1** a company or person that supplies shops and companies with goods 销售者；批发商；分销商 **2** the part of a car's engine that sends an electric current to the SPARK PLUGS 配电器；配电盘 —see picture at 参见 ENGINE 图

S3 W2 **dis·trict** /ˋdɪstrɪkt; ˈdɪstrɪkt/ *n* [C] **1** a particular area of a town or the countryside 地区；区域：*a semi-detached house in a pleasant suburban district* 处在景色宜人的郊区的半独立式房子 —see 见 AREA (USAGE) **2** an area of a country, city etc that has official borders 行政区：*a postal district* 邮政区

district at·tor·ney /ˌ‥ ·ˈ‥/ *n* [C] a lawyer in the US who is responsible for bringing legal charges against criminals in a particular area〔美国〕地区检察官

district coun·cil /ˌ‥ ˈ‥/ *n* [C] a group of people elected in Britain to organize local services such as education, cleaning the streets etc in a particular area〔英国〕地区行政会，区议会〔负责组织当地事务，如教育、清扫街道等〕

district court /ˌ‥ ˈ·/ *n* [C] a local court in the US where people are judged in cases involving national rather than state law〔美国〕地方法院〔审理涉及联邦法律而非州法律的案子〕

district nurse /ˌ‥ ˈ·/ *n* [C] a nurse who visits and treats people in their own homes in Britain〔英国〕社区护士〔上门为病人护理的护士〕

District of Co·lum·bi·a, the /ˌ‥ ‥ˈ‥/ abbreviation 缩写为 **D.C.** the special area in the eastern US, next to Maryland and Virginia, which includes Washington, the capital of the US 哥伦比亚特区〔美国东部一特区，与马里兰州和弗吉尼亚州交界，包括美国首都华盛顿〕

dis·trust¹ /dɪsˋtrʌst; dɪsˈtrʌst/ *n* [U] a feeling that you cannot trust someone 不信任：*The local people regard the police with suspicion and distrust.* 当地人以一种怀疑及不信任的眼光看待警察。| [+of] *Dylan's distrust of journalists makes him difficult to interview.* 迪伦对记者的不信任使他们很难采访他。—**distrustful** *adj* —**distrustfully** *adv* —compare 比较 MISTRUST¹

distrust² *v* [T] to not trust someone or something 不信任，怀疑

dis·turb /dɪˋstɝb; dɪˈstɜːb/ *v* [T]

1 ►INTERRUPT 打扰◄ to interrupt someone so that they cannot continue what they are doing by asking a question, making a noise etc 干扰，打扰；使中断：*Sorry to disturb you, but I have an urgent message from your husband.* 对不起打扰一下，我这儿有你丈夫的一份急电。

2 ►WORRY 忧虑◄ to make someone feel worried or slightly shocked 使焦虑；使惊讶：*What disturbs me most is his total lack of remorse.* 最令我不安的是他完全不感到后悔。

3 ►MOVE 移动◄ to move something or change its position 挪动，移动，改变〔某物〕的位置：*If you find a bird's nest, never disturb the eggs.* 如果你发现鸟巢，千万别动那些鸟蛋。

4 do not disturb a sign that you put on a door when you do not want anyone to interrupt you 请勿打扰〔挂在门上的牌子〕

5 disturb the peace *law* to behave in a noisy and unpleasant way in public【法律】扰乱治安

dis·turb·ance /dɪˋstɝbəns; dɪˈstɜːbəns/ *n* **1** [C,U] something that stops you from being able to continue doing something, or the act of stopping someone from being able to continue doing something 造成干扰的事物；干扰，扰乱：*The noise of the traffic is a continual disturbance.* 交通噪音是一种持续性的干扰。| *I need a place where I can work without disturbance.* 我需要一个可以静心工作的地方。**2** [C] a situation in which people fight or behave violently in public 骚乱，混乱：*There were disturbances in the crowd as fans left the stadium.* 在球迷们离开体育馆时，人群中发生了骚乱。**3** [U] a state in which someone is emotionally upset and does not behave normally 情绪困扰，精神失常：*a long history of mental disturbance* 长期的精神失常病史

dis·turbed /dɪˋstɝbd; dɪˈstɜːbd/ *adj* someone who is disturbed does not behave in a normal way, because they have had very shocking or upsetting experiences 心理不正常的，精神失常的

dis·turb·ing /dɪˋstɝbɪŋ; dɪˈstɜːbɪŋ/ *adj* making you feel worried or shocked 令人不安的；使人震惊的：*a disturbing increase in the crime rate* 令人不安的犯罪率的增长

dis·u·nite /ˌdɪsjuˋnaɪt; ˌdɪsjuːˈnaɪt/ *v* [T] *formal* to prevent people from agreeing with each other and working together【正式】使分裂；使不和 —**disunited** *adj*

dis·u·ni·ty /dɪsˋjunɪtɪ; dɪsˈjuːnɪti/ *n* [U] a situation in which a group of people cannot agree with each other or work together 不和；分裂；纷争

dis·use /dɪsˋjus; dɪsˈjuːs/ *n* [U] a situation in which something is no longer used 废弃，不用，弃置：**fall into disuse** (=stop being used) 废弃不用 *The building eventually fell into disuse.* 该建筑物最终被废弃不用了。

dis·used /ˌdɪsˋjuzd; ˌdɪsˈjuːzd◂/ *adj* no longer used 不再使用的：*a disused mine* 废弃的矿井

di·syl·lab·ic /ˌdaɪsəˋlæbɪk; ˌdaɪsɪˈlæbɪk◂/ *adj technical* having two SYLLABLES【术语】双音节的

ditch¹ /dɪtʃ; dɪtʃ/ *n* [C] a long narrow hole cut into the ground at the side of a field, road etc, especially for water to flow through〔挖在田边、路边等处的〕沟，渠〔尤用于排水〕—see also 另见 LAST-DITCH

ditch² *v* **1** [T] to get rid of something because you no longer need it 扔掉，抛弃，甩掉 **2** [T] *informal* to end a romantic relationship with someone【非正式】与〔某人〕断绝恋爱关系；抛弃〔某人〕：*Julie's ditched her boyfriend.* 朱莉把她的男朋友甩了。**3** [I,T] to deliberately crash an aircraft into the sea（使）〔飞机〕在海上降落；海上迫降

ditch·wa·ter /ˋdɪtʃˌwɔtɚ; ˈdɪtʃwɔːtə/ *n* **as dull as ditchwater** *BrE* very boring【英】极其乏味的

dith·er¹ /ˋdɪðɚ; ˈdɪðə/ *v* [I] to not do something because you are unable to decide what to do 犹豫不决：*Stop dithering, Linda, and get on with it!* 别犹豫了，琳达，快继续干啊！—**ditherer** *n* [C]

dither² *n* **be (all) in a dither** *BrE informal* to be nervous and confused because you cannot decide what to do【英，非正式】紧张；茫然不知所措

di·tran·si·tive /ˌdaɪˈtrænsətɪv; ˌdaɪˈtrænsɪ̈tɪv/ *adj technical* a ditransitive verb has an INDIRECT OBJECT and a DIRECT OBJECT. 'Give' in the sentence 'Give me the book.' is ditransitive【术语】〔动词〕带双宾语的〔即带直接宾语和间接宾语, 如 give 在句子 Give me the book 中便是个带双宾语的动词〕—compare 比较 INTRANSITIVE, TRANSITIVE —**ditransitive** *n* [C]

dit·to¹ /ˈdɪto; ˈdɪtəʊ/ *adv spoken* used to say that something is the same as something else, or that you think the same as someone else【口】我也一样: *"I'm absolutely fed up with this job." "Ditto."* "我真是烦透了这个工作。" "我也一样。"

ditto² *n plural* **dittos** [C] a mark (") you use instead of repeating what you have already written, usually immediately above in a list 同上, 同前(符号为")

dit·ty /ˈdɪtɪ; ˈdɪti/ *n* [C] *humorous* a short simple poem or song【幽默】小诗; 短歌谣

di·u·ret·ic /ˌdaɪjuˈrɛtɪk; ˌdaɪjʊˈretɪk◂/ *n* [C] a substance that increases the flow of URINE 利尿剂 —**diuretic** *adj*

di·ur·nal /daɪˈɝnḷ; daɪˈɜːnəl/ *adj technical*【术语】**1** happening in the daytime 白天的, 白昼的 **2** happening every day 每日的, 每天的

D

Div *n* the written abbreviation of 缩写 = DIVISION

di·van /ˈdaɪvæn; dɪˈvæn/ *n* [C] **1** a bed with a thick base〔底部很厚的〕矮床 **2** a long low soft seat that has no back or arms〔无靠背或扶手的〕长沙发

dive¹ /daɪv; daɪv/ *v past tense* **dived** also 又作 **dove** /dov; dəʊv/ *AmE*【美】[I]

1 ►JUMP INTO WATER 跳入水中◄ to jump into water with your head and arms first 跳水〔头和胳膊先入水〕: [+into/off etc] *Sally dived expertly into the pool.* 萨莉熟练地跳入水池。| *Diving off the cliffs is very dangerous.* 从悬崖上向下跳水是很危险的。

2 ►GO DEEPER 进入深处◄ to go deeper under water 下潜: *The submarine began to dive.* 潜水艇开始下潜。

3 ►SWIM UNDER WATER 潜水◄ to swim under water using special breathing equipment〔使用特殊呼吸器〕潜水: *frogmen diving for sunken treasure* 在水底潜游寻找沉没的宝藏的蛙人

4 ►BIRD/AIRCRAFT 鸟/飞行器◄ if a bird or an aircraft dives, it goes down through the air very quickly and steeply, head first〔指鸟、飞行器〕俯冲

5 ►JUMP FORWARDS 向前蹦跳◄ [always+adv/prep] to jump forwards or to one side in order to catch something or to avoid something〔为抓到或躲开某物〕跳跃: [+after/towards/aside etc] *Jackson dived after the ball.* 杰克逊扑过去抢球。

6 ►INTO BUILDING/CROWD 进入建筑物/人群中◄ to quickly go into a building or a crowd of people 冲进去: [+into] *We dived into a coffee shop to avoid the rain.* 我们冲进一家咖啡厅躲雨。

7 dive into your bag/pockets etc to put your hand into your bag, pockets etc so that you can get something out 把手伸入提包/衣袋等〔取出东西〕

dive in *phr v* [I] **1** to start doing something eagerly and energetically 热切地开始做某事: *Harvey dived in with several questions.* 哈维开始投入到讨论中来, 问了几个问题。**2 dive in!** *spoken* used to invite people to start eating a meal【口】开饭啦!〔用于邀请某人开始用餐〕

dive² *n* [C] **1** a jump into the water with your head and arms first 跳水 **2 make a dive for** to move quickly and suddenly towards something 扑向, 冲向 **3** *informal* a place such as a bar or club that is cheap and dirty【非正式】廉价而低级的酒吧[俱乐部]: *I've heard the new club's a bit of a dive.* 我听说新开的那家俱乐部有些低级。

dive-bomb /ˈ· ·/ *v* [I,T] to attack someone or something by flying down towards them from the air 俯冲轰炸

dive bomb·er /ˈ· ˌ· ·/ *n* [C] a type of military plane that flies low over a place and drops bombs on it 俯冲轰炸机

div·er /ˈdaɪvɚ; ˈdaɪvə/ *n* [C] **1** someone who swims or works underwater using special breathing equipment 潜水员: *a deep sea diver* 深海潜水员 **2** someone who jumps into water with their head and arms first 跳水者

di·verge /daɪˈvɝdʒ; daɪˈvɜːdʒ/ *v* [I] **1** if two lines or paths diverge, they go in different directions 岔开, 分开 **2** if two things diverge, they become different although they used to be the same 开始有分歧, 出现不一致: *Our business interests diverged and we had to sell the company.* 我们的商业利益出现了分歧, 我们不得不卖掉公司。—opposite 反义词 CONVERGE

di·ver·gence /daɪˈvɝdʒəns; daɪˈvɜːdʒəns/ *n* [C,U+between/of] a difference between two or more things such as opinions or interests〔看法或兴趣等的〕差异, 分歧

di·ver·gent /daɪˈvɝdʒənt; daɪˈvɜːdʒənt/ *adj* divergent opinions, interests etc are very different from each other〔指看法或兴趣等〕不同的, 有差异的

di·vers /ˈdaɪvɚz; ˈdaɪvəz/ *adj* [only before noun 仅用于名词前] *old-fashioned* of many different kinds【过时】各种各样的

di·verse /dəˈvɝs; daɪˈvɜːs/ *adj* very different from each other 各不相同的: *subjects as diverse as pop music and archeology* 如流行音乐和考古学一样完全不同的科目 —**diversely** *adv*

di·ver·si·fy /dəˈvɝsəˌfaɪ; daɪˈvɜːsɪ̈faɪ/ *v* **1** [I] if a business or a country's ECONOMY¹ (1) diversifies, it starts to produce a range of different products and services, instead of just one or two〔指某企业或国家的经济〕多元化; 从事多种经营: *a publishing company that is diversifying into the software market* 一家正向兼营软件方面发展的出版公司 **2** [T] to make a business or ECONOMY¹ (1) start to produce a range of different products or services 使〔企业或经济〕多元化, 使开始多种经营 **3** [I,T] to change something so that there is more variety 多元化, 使…多样化 —**diversification** /dəˌvɝsəfəˈkeʃən; dəˌvɜːsɪ̈fɪ̈ˈkeɪʃən/ *n* [U]

di·ver·sion /daɪˈvɝʒən; daɪˈvɜːʃən/ *n* **1** [C] something that stops you from paying attention to what you are doing or what is happening 分散注意力的事物; 声东击西的手段: **create a diversion** (=deliberately take someone's attention away from something else) 转移注意力 *Some of the prisoners created a diversion while Riggs climbed the wall.* 在里格斯爬墙的时候, 一些囚犯故意制造事端以转移注意力。**2** [C,U] a change in the direction or purpose of something 转向; 改变〔某事物的〕用途: [+of] *the massive diversion of resources into the military budget* 把财力大量转入军事预算 **3** [C] *formal* an activity that you do for pleasure【正式】消遣; 娱乐: *The cinema is always a pleasant diversion.* 看电影一直是非常好的娱乐方式。**4** [C] *especially BrE* a different road for traffic to travel on when the usual road cannot be used【尤英】〔正常道路不能使用时的〕分流道路

di·ver·sion·a·ry /daɪˈvɝʒənˌɛrɪ; daɪˈvɜːʃənəri/ *adj* intended to take someone's attention away from something 转移注意力的; 声东击西的

di·ver·si·ty /daɪˈvɝsətɪ; daɪˈvɜːsɪ̈ti/ *n* [singular] **1** a range of different people or things; variety〔人或事物的〕多种多样: *the cultural diversity of the United States* 美国文化的多样性 | *a diversity of opinion* 众说纷纭的看法 **2** [U] the quality of having variety and including a wide range of different people or things 多样性

di·vert /daɪˈvɝt; daɪˈvɜːt/ *v* [T] **1** to change the direction or purpose of something 转变〔方向或用途〕: *diverted traffic* 改道行驶的车辆 | **divert sth into** *The company should divert more resources into research.* 该公司应该把更多的资源转用在研究上面。**2 divert attention/criticism etc** to stop people from paying attention to something or criticizing it 转移注意力/批评等: *The tax cuts diverted attention from the real economic problems.* 减税把(人们的)注意力从真实存在的经济问题上转移了。**3** *formal* to entertain someone【正式】使消遣; 使欢娱; 使解闷

di·vert·ing /daɪˈvɝtɪŋ; daɪˈvɜːtɪŋ/ *adj formal* entertaining and amusing【正式】有趣的; 逗乐的: *a mildly diverting film comedy* 一部略带逗笑性质的喜剧片

di·vest /daɪˈvɛst; daɪˈvest/ *v*

divest sb **of** sth *phr v* [T] *formal*【正式】**1 divest yourself of** to take off something you are wearing or carrying 脱下〔所穿的衣服等〕; 放下〔所拿的东西〕: *Pedro divested himself of his overcoat and boots.* 佩德罗脱下大衣和靴子。**2** to get rid of something that you own 摆脱〔拥有的东西〕: **divest yourself of** *A new minister must divest himself of his business interests.* 一个新任部长必须脱离他的商业利益。**3** to take away someone's power, rights, etc 剥夺〔某人的权力、权利等〕: *The king was divested of all his wealth and power.* 国王被剥夺了一切财富与权力。

di·vest·ment /daɪˈvɛstmənt; daɪˈvestmənt/ *n* [U] *AmE technical* the act of taking your money out of a company or place where you had put it in order to make a profit【美, 术语】〔在某公司或某地的〕投资收回; DISINVESTMENT *BrE*【英】

di·vide¹ /dəˈvaɪd; dɪ̈ˈvaɪd/ *v*

1 ►SEPARATE 分开◄ **a)** [T] to separate something such as an area, group, or object into two or more parts 把…分成〔若干部分〕: **divide sth into** *Take the orange and divide it into quarters.* 把橘子拿去, 分成四份。| *The USA is divided into 50 states.* 美国分为50个州。| **divide sth between** *He divides his time between his house in Connecticut and New York.* 他一部分时间留在康涅狄格州家里, 另一部分时间留在纽约。**b)** [I] to become separated into two or more different parts 分开, 分成几部分: [+in/into] *The cell quickly divides in two.* 该细胞很快分裂成两个。

2 ►KEEP SEPARATE 分隔◄ also 又作 **divide off** [T] to keep two areas separate from each other 把〔两个地区〕隔开: *The Berlin Wall used to divide East and West Berlin.* 过去有柏林墙把东、西柏林给分隔开来。| **divide sth from** *The chapel is di-*

vided from the rest of the church by a screen. 一道屏风把私人祈祷室和教堂的其他部分分隔开来。

3 ▶SHARE 分享◀ also 又作 **divide up** [T] to separate something into two or more parts and share them between two or more people 分配，分享，共用：**divide sth between/among** *The money is to be divided up equally among the six grandchildren.* 这笔钱将被平分给六个孙儿、孙女。

4 ▶MATHEMATICS 数学◀ **a)** [T] to find out how many times one number is contained in another larger number 除，除以：**divide sth by sth** *Divide 21 by 3.* 21 除以 3。| **divided by sth** *6 divided by 3 is 2.* 6 除以 3 等于 2。**b)** [I] to be contained in another, usually larger, number one or more times 除尽〔一个更大的数〕：[+into] *8 divides into 64.* 64 可用 8 除尽。—compare 比较 MULTIPLY (2)

5 ▶DISAGREE 分歧◀ [T] to make people disagree with each other and form groups with opposing views 使〔人〕对立，产生分歧：**be divided over/about** (=disagree about something) 在…上有分歧 *Voters are bitterly divided over the issue of gun control.* 选民在枪支管制问题上有严重的分歧。

6 dividing line the difference between two types or groups of similar things 分界线〔指两种或两组相似事物之间的区别〕：[+between] *There's a thin dividing line between genius and madness.* 在天才与疯狂之间只有很细微的差别。

7 divide and rule to control people by making them argue or fight with each other instead of opposing you 分而治之〔让人们相互争吵或争斗而不反对自己，从而控制他们〕—**divided** *adj*

divide² *n* [C usually singular 一般用单数] **1** a difference between two groups of people, especially in their beliefs or way of life, that makes them seem separate from each other〔尤指两个群体在信仰或生活方式上的〕差异，差别：*two politicians on either side of a political divide* 两个政治立场截然相反的政治家 **2** *AmE* a line of high ground between two river systems; WATERSHED (3)【美】分水岭；分水线

divided high·way /ˌ‚ ·· ˈ· ˈ/ *n* [C] *AmE* a main road on which the traffic travelling in opposite directions is kept apart by a piece of land or a low fence【美】有分隔带的双向公路；上下行双线车道；DUAL CARRIAGEWAY *BrE*【英】

W3 **div·i·dend** /ˈdɪvəˌdɛnt; ˈdɪvɪdənd/ *n* [C] **1** a part of a company's profit that is divided among the people who have shares (SHARE² (5)) in the company 股息，红利 **2 pay dividends** if something you do pays dividends, you get an advantage from it later 产生效益；有好处；有回报：*All Ken's hard work eventually paid dividends.* 肯付出的所有努力最终有了回报。**3** *BrE* the money you can win in a national competition that involves guessing the results of football games【英】〔猜中足球比赛结果可赢得的〕彩金 **4** *technical* a number that is to be divided by another number【术语】被除数

di·vid·er /dəˈvaɪdɚ; dɪˈvaɪdə/ *n* [C] **1** something that divides something else into parts〔把某物分成几部分的〕分隔物；划分者；区划线 **2** a piece of card that separates pages in a FILE¹ (2)〔用于分隔档案中文件的〕分隔卡 **3 dividers** [plural] an instrument used for measuring or marking lines or angles, that consists of two pointed pieces of metal joined together at the top 两脚规；分线规

div·i·na·tion /ˌdɪvəˈneʃən; ˌdɪvɪˈneɪʃən/ *n* [U] the act of finding out what will happen in the future by means of special powers, or the ability to do this 占卜(术)，预测；预言

di·vine¹ /dəˈvaɪn; dɪˈvaɪn/ *adj* **1** having the qualities of a god or connected with, or coming from God 神的，上帝的；神或上帝赋予的：*the authority of divine law* 神的法律的权威 | **divine service** (=a formal ceremony involving prayers etc to God) 向上帝祈祷的仪式；礼拜 **2 divine help/intervention/inspiration/retribution** help etc from God 上帝[神]的帮助/干预/启示/惩罚 **3** *old-fashioned* very pleasant or good; WONDERFUL【过时】极好的，妙极的：*You look simply divine!* 你看起来简直美极了！

divine² *v* **1** [T] *literary* to discover or guess something【文】发现；猜出：*He must have divined from my expression that I was angry.* 他必定是从我的表情猜出我生气了。**2** [I] to search for underground water or minerals using a special Y-shaped stick〔用一丫形卜棒〕探测〔地下水、矿床〕

divine³ *n* [C] *old use* a priest【旧】牧师，神父

Divine Com·e·dy /ˌ·ˌ ˈ···/ a long poem in three parts, written around 1300 by the Italian poet Dante. It describes the poet's spiritual journey. First he is led through Hell (the **Inferno**) and Purgatory by the poet Virgil, and then he is led through Paradise by Beatrice, the woman he loves. Many people consider it to be one of the greatest poems ever written.《神曲》〔意大利诗人但丁公元1300年前后创作的一部长诗。全诗分三部分描述作者的心路历程。首先，他在诗人维吉尔的引领下穿越地狱和炼狱，然后在他所爱的女子贝雅特里齐引领下穿越天堂。许多人认为该作品是有史以来最伟大的诗作之一〕

Divine Of·fice /ˌ·ˌ ˈ··/ the daily prayers and ceremonies used by Roman Catholic priests 时辰颂祷礼〔天主教神父每日的祈祷和日课礼仪〕

di·vin·er /dəˈvaɪnɚ; dɪˈvaɪnə/ *n* [C] someone who searches for underground water or minerals using a special Y-shaped stick〔用一丫形卜棒〕探测地下水[矿床]者

divine right /ˌ·ˌ ˈ·/ *n* **1** [singular] the right given to a king or queen by God to rule a country, that in former times could not be questioned or opposed〔国王或女王统治一个国家的〕神授王权 **2 have a divine right to do sth** *informal* to be able to do what you want without having to ask permission【非正式】有神授之权〔想做什么就可做什么而不必经人允许〕：*You don't have a divine right to open all my mail, you know.* 你要知道，你无权随便拆开我所有的信件。

div·ing /ˈdaɪvɪŋ; ˈdaɪvɪŋ/ *n* [U] **1** the activity of swimming under water using special breathing equipment 潜水 **2** the activity of jumping into water with your head and arms first 跳水：*a diving competition* 跳水比赛

diving bell /ˈ· · ˌ·/ *n* [C] a metal container shaped like a bell, in which people can work under water 潜水钟〔钟形金属罩，人在其中可进行水下工作〕

diving board /ˈ· · ˌ·/ *n* [C] a board fixed above a SWIMMING POOL and used for diving〔安装在游泳池上方的〕跳(水)板

diving suit /ˈ· · ˌ·/ *n* [C] a special protective suit worn when swimming deep under water 潜水服

di·vin·ing rod /·ˈ··, ˌ·/ *n* [C] a special Y-shaped stick used to search for underground water or minerals〔用于探测地下水或矿床的〕丫形卜棒

di·vin·i·ty /dəˈvɪnətɪ; dɪˈvɪnɪti/ *n* **1** [U] the study of God and religious beliefs; THEOLOGY 神学 **2** [U] the quality or state of being like God or a god 神性；神力；神威 **3** [C] God or a god 上帝；神

divinity school /·ˈ···, ˌ·/ *n* [C] *AmE* a college where students study to become priests【美】神学院

di·vis·i·ble /dəˈvɪzəbḷ; dɪˈvɪzɪbəl/ *adj* able to be divided, especially by another number 可分的；可除尽的：*6 is divisible by 3.* 6 可被 3 除尽。

di·vi·sion /dəˈvɪʒən; dɪˈvɪʒən/ *n* S3 W1

1 ▶SEPARATING 分开◀ [C,U] the act of dividing something into different parts or the way it is divided 分开，分割：[+between] *the division between public and private life* 公众生活与私生活的分离 | [+of sth into] *the division of people into winners and losers* 把人分成成功者和失败者

2 ▶SHARING 分担◀ [C,U] the act of dividing something so that it can be shared or the way it is divided 分配；分担；分享：[+of sth between] *the division of power between church and state* 教会与国家之间的权力分配

3 ▶DISAGREEMENT 分歧◀ [C,U] a disagreement among the members of a group, especially one that makes them form smaller groups 分歧；分裂：*There are deep divisions in the party over Europe.* 该党内部在欧洲问题上有严重分歧。

4 ▶MATHEMATICS 数学◀ [U] the process of finding out how many times one number is contained in another 除；除法 —compare 比较 MULTIPLICATION (1) —see also 另见 LONG DIVISION

5 ▶PART OF AN ORGANIZATION 某组织的一部分◀ [C] a large part of an organization, company etc, consisting of several smaller parts〔机构、公司等的〕部，部门：*I work in the Computer Services Division.* 我在电脑维修部门工作。

6 ▶SPORT 体育◀ [C] *BrE* one of the groups of teams that a sports competition, especially football, is divided into【英】〔尤指足球比赛中球队被分成的〕级：**the First/Second Division** *Brighton play in the Second Division.* 布赖顿队参加乙级队比赛。

7 ▶ARMY 军队◀ [C] a part of an army larger than a BRIGADE (1) 师：*the Guards Division* 近卫师

8 ▶IN PARLIAMENT 在议会◀ [C] *technical* a process in which members of the British parliament vote for something by dividing into groups【术语】〔英国议会议员进行的〕分组表决：*MP's forced a division on the bill.* 下议院议员强行将该议案进行分组表决。

di·vi·sion·al /dəˈvɪʒənḷ; dɪˈvɪʒənəl/ *adj* connected with a DIVISION (=one of the parts into which a large organization or army is divided)〔大型机构〕部门的；〔军队〕师的：*divisional headquarters* 师指挥部

division bell /ˈ· · ˌ·/ *n* [C] a bell that is rung to tell members of the British parliament to vote〔英国议会告知议员即将进行分组表决的〕通知铃

division lob·by /ˌ·ˌ··ˌ·ˌ/ *n* [C] one of the two places to which a British Member of Parliament must go to vote 投票厅〔英国议会议员进行分组投票的两个地点之一〕

division of la·bour /ˌ·ˌ···ˈ·ˌ/ *n* [C,U] a way of organizing work in which each member of a group has a particular job to do 分工

di·vi·sive /dəˈvaɪsɪv; dɪˈvaɪsɪv/ *adj* having the effect of dividing people into groups with opposing opinions 造成不和的, 导致分裂的: *Religious schools were seen as socially divisive.* 宗教派别曾被认为是导致社会分裂的一个因素。

di·vi·sor /dəˈvaɪzɚ; dɪˈvaɪzə/ *n* [C] *technical* the number by which another number is to be divided【术语】除数

3 **di·vorce¹** /dəˈvɔrs; dɪˈvɔːs/ *n* **1** [C,U] the legal ending of a marriage 离婚: *In Britain, one in three marriages ends in divorce.* 在英国, 三分之一的婚姻以离婚告终。| **get a divorce** *Why doesn't she get a divorce?* 她为什么不离婚呢? | **divorce case** (=the legal process of divorce) 离婚诉讼 | **divorce proceedings** (=the official actions to legally end your marriage) 离婚诉讼; 离婚手续 | **divorce rate** (=the number of divorces each year) 离婚率 | **divorce settlement** (=the legal decision about how much money, property etc you get after a divorce) 离婚财产协议 —compare 比较 SEPARATION (2) **2** [C] a separation of ideas, subjects, values etc〔观念、主题、价值观等的〕分歧, 脱离: [**+between**] *the divorce between power and ideology* 权力与思想意识的分离

CULTURAL NOTE 文化注释

Divorce is legal in the US and UK. A husband or wife can get a divorce for reasons of ADULTERY (=when one of them is having sex with someone else), unreasonable behaviour such as mental or physical cruelty, DESERTION (=when one of them leaves), or SEPARATION (=when they no longer live together). Some married couples prefer a divorce in which neither the husband nor the wife is blamed for the end of the marriage. In this case, they usually get a NO-FAULT divorce, which is allowed in most US states and in the UK. In both countries, a special court decides how to divide the couple's property between them, and who will get CUSTODY of (=the legal right to take care of) their children. If one of the couple is financially dependent on the other, the court will usually order the other one to pay ALIMONY (*AmE*), or MAINTENANCE (*BrE*). In the US, a court also decides how much CHILD SUPPORT a husband or wife should pay to help support their children. In the UK, however, a government organization called the CSA (Child Support Agency) decides how much maintenance should be paid. Today in the UK around 40% of marriages end in divorce, and in the US the figure is almost 50%. It is common in both countries for people to get married again to someone else, and in the US especially, it is not unusual for people to get married three or more times. 离婚在英美是合法的。离婚的原因有很多种, 如外遇、行为悖理(如精神或肉体虐待)、遗弃、分居等。有的夫妇在双方均无过错的情况下选择离婚, 这种情况一般叫无过错离婚, 这在美国大部分州和在英国是允许的。英美两国有专门法庭裁定如何分割夫妻财产, 以及谁能获得子女的监护权。如夫妻一方在经济上依赖另一方, 法院一般裁定另一方付抚养费(美国称alimony, 英国称maintenance)。在美国, 法院还会裁定一方给予另一方抚养子女要支付的数额。不过在英国, 抚养费的数额是由一个叫做儿童抚养事务处的政府组织裁定的。今天, 在英国, 有大约40%的婚姻以离婚告终, 而在美国这一数字差不多达到了50%。在英美两国, 离婚后再婚是很普遍的事, 在美国尤其如此, 美国人结婚三次以上并不稀奇。— see Cultural Note at MARRIAGE 见 MARRIAGE 文化注释

divorce² *v* **1** [I,T] if someone divorces their husband or wife, or if two people divorce, they legally end their marriage (与…)离婚: *David's parents divorced when he was six.* 戴维的父母在他六岁时就离婚了。**2** [T] to separate two ideas, subjects, values etc completely 把…完全分开; 彻底区分: **divorce sth from** *It is difficult to divorce sport from politics.* 把体育与政治完全分开是很困难的。| **be divorced from reality** (=not based on real things or sensible thinking) 脱离现实 *Some of his ideas are completely divorced from reality.* 他的一些想法完全脱离实际。

di·vorced /dəˈvɔrst; dɪˈvɔːst/ *adj* no longer married to your former wife or husband 已离婚的: *75% of divorced women remarry.* 75%的离婚妇女再婚。| **get divorced** (=legally end your marriage) 离婚 *My parents are getting divorced.* 我父母正在办离婚。

di·vor·cee /dəˌvɔrˈsi; dɪˌvɔːˈsiː/ *n* someone who is no longer legally married to their former wife or husband 离了婚的人

div·ot /ˈdɪvət; ˈdɪvət/ *n* [C] a small piece of earth and grass that you dig out accidentally while playing sport〔体育运动时无意间〕削起的一小块泥土[草皮]

di·vulge /dəˈvʌldʒ; daɪˈvʌldʒ/ *v* [T] to give someone information, especially about something secret 泄露; 透露〔秘密〕: *Staff may not divulge confidential information.* 员工不能泄露机密资料。| **divulge sth to sb** *Do not divulge the conclusions of the report to anyone.* 不要向任何人泄露这份报告的结论。| **divulge what/where etc** *Adams refused to divulge what he had done with the money.* 亚当斯拒绝透露他是如何处理那笔钱的。| **divulge your sources** (=say who told you) 泄露消息的来源

div·vy /ˈdɪvɪ; ˈdɪvi/ *n* [C] *BrE slang* a stupid person【英俚】傻瓜

Di·wa·li /dɪˈwalɪ; dɪˈwɑːli/ *n* an important Hindu FESTIVAL (2) that is celebrated in the autumn 排灯节〔在秋季举行的印度的重大节日〕

Dix·ie /ˈdɪksɪ; ˈdɪksi/ *n* [singular] *AmE informal* the southern states of the US【美, 非正式】迪克西〔指美国南部各州〕

dix·ie·land /ˈdɪksɪˌlænd; ˈdɪksilænd/ *n* [U] a type of JAZZ¹ (1) with a strong rhythm 迪克西兰爵士乐

DIY /ˌdi aɪ ˈwaɪ; ˌdiː aɪ ˈwaɪ/ *n* [U] *especially BrE* do-it-yourself; the activity of making or repairing things yourself instead of buying them or paying someone else to do it【尤英】自己动手〔do-it-yourself的缩写, 指自己动手做东西或修理东西〕

diz·zy /ˈdɪzɪ; ˈdɪzi/ *adj* **1** feeling unable to balance, especially after spinning around or because you feel ill〔因旋转或生病而〕头晕目眩的: *Greg felt sick and dizzy in the hot sun.* 格雷格在烈日下晒得恶心头晕。| **dizzy spell** (=a short period when you feel dizzy) 一阵头晕 **2 the dizzy heights** *humorous* an important position【幽默】令人眩晕的高处〔指重要的职位〕: *Naomi had reached the dizzy heights of manageress.* 娜奥米已经高居经理的宝座。**3** *informal* careless and forgetful【非正式】粗心大意的; 心不在焉的; 糊涂健忘的: *A dizzy blonde works at the front desk.* 一个糊里糊涂的金发女郎在前台工作。**4 dizzy height/peak** *literary* a dizzy height or peak is very high【文】令人头晕的高度/顶峰 —**dizzily** *adv* —**dizziness** *n* [U]

dizzy 头晕目眩的

DJ /ˌdi ˈdʒe; ˌdiː ˈdʒeɪ◂/ *n* [C] a disc jockey; someone who plays records on a radio show or in a club〔电台〕音乐唱片节目主持人;〔夜总会〕舞曲唱片播放员, 唱片混音师

Dja·kar·ta /dʒəˈkartə; dʒəˈkɑːtə/ another spelling of Jakarta, the capital of Indonesia 雅加达〔印度尼西亚首都, Jakarta的另一种拼法〕

Dji·bou·ti /dʒɪˈbutɪ; dʒɪˈbuːti/ a small country on the coast of northeast Africa, formerly ruled by France. Population: 460,700 (2001). Capital: Djibouti. 吉布提〔非洲东北海岸一小国, 原为法属殖民地。人口: 460,700 (2001), 首都: 吉布提〕

djinn /dʒɪn; dʒɪn/ *n* [C] a magical spirit in Arab fairy stories; GENIE〔阿拉伯童话故事中的〕精灵, 神怪

DM the abbreviation of 缩写= DEUTSCHMARK

DMV /ˌdi ɛm ˈvi; ˌdiː em ˈviː/ the Department of Motor Vehicles; a government department in each of the US states, which is responsible for giving driving tests and drivers' LICENSEs. In some states the DMV has the power to collect road taxes. 机动车辆部〔美国一州政府部门, 负责主持驾照考试和颁发执照。有些州的机动车辆部还有权征收公路税〕

DNA /ˌdi ɛn ˈe; ˌdiː en ˈeɪ/ *n* [U] an acid that carries GENETIC information in a cell 脱氧核糖核酸

DNB, the /ˌdɪ ɛn ˈbi; ˌdiː en ˈbiː/ the abbreviation of 缩写= The DICTIONARY OF NATIONAL BIOGRAPHY

D-no·tice /ˈdi ˌnotɪs; ˈdiː ˌnəʊtɪs/ in the UK, an official government request to a newspaper that it should not print certain information, for reasons of national security 国防机密通知, D通告〔英国政府基于国家安全的理由要求报社不要发表某些消息的通知〕

do¹ /du; duː/ *auxiliary verb past tense* **did** /dɪd; dɪd/ *past participle* **done** /dʌn; dʌn/ *3rd person singular present tense* **does** /dəz; dəz *strong* 强读 dʌz; dʌz/ 1 1

1 ▶IN QUESTIONS/NEGATIVES 在疑问句/否定句中◀**a)** used with another verb to form questions or negatives〔与另一动词连用，构成疑问句或否定句〕: *Do you like bananas?* 你喜欢吃香蕉吗？| *I don't feel like going out tonight.* 我今天晚上不想出门。| *Ian didn't answer.* 伊恩没有回答。| *Where do you live?* 你住在哪儿？| *Doesn't Rosie look wonderful?* 罗茜看上去是不是特别精神？| *Don't just stand there – do something!* 别光站在那儿——做点事情吧！| *Why don't you come for the weekend?* (=please come) 你来我们这儿度周末好不好？| *Don't let's invite her.* (=let's not invite her) 我们别邀请她。**b)** *especially spoken* used to form QUESTION TAGS【尤口】〔用于构成附加疑问句〕: *You know Tony, don't you?* 你认识托尼，是不是？| *She didn't pay cash, did she?* 她没付现金，对不对？

2 ▶FOR EMPHASIS 表示强调◀ used to give emphasis to the main verb〔用于强调主要动词〕: *Do take care!* 一定要小心！| *"Why didn't you tell me?" "I did tell you."* "你怎么不告诉我呢？" "我确实告诉你了。" | *He owns, or did own, a yacht.* 他拥有，或者说曾经拥有，一艘游艇。

3 ▶IN POLITE REQUESTS 用于礼貌的请求◀ used as a polite way of offering someone something〔用于在给某人某物时表示礼貌〕: *Do have a cup of tea.* 来，请喝一杯茶。

4 ▶INSTEAD OF VERB 代替动词◀ used to avoid repeating another verb〔用于避免重复某一动词〕: *Omar speaks English better than he did.* (=better than he used to speak it) 奥马尔的英语说得比以前好了。| *"You broke my pencil!" "No I didn't!"* "你弄断了我的铅笔！" "我没有！" | *"You left the door open." "So I did."* (=you are right) "你没关门。" "没错。" | *"Will Kay come?" "She may do."* "凯能来吗？" "或许能来。" | *"You ought to phone your mother." "I have done."* "你应该给你妈打个电话。" "我已经打过了。" | *So he plays the piano, does he?* 那么他会弹钢琴，对吧？| **so do I** *Emma loves chocolate, and so do I.* 埃玛爱吃巧克力，我也爱吃。| **neither do I** *"I don't want any more." "Neither do I."* "我不想再要了。" "我也不想。"

5 what is sb/sth doing? used to ask why someone or something is in a particular place, when you think they should not be there 某人/某物怎么会在这[那]里？〔你认为不该在那儿〕: *What's this cake doing on the floor?* 蛋糕怎么会在地板上？| *What was that man doing in our garden anyway?* 那个人到我们的花园来干什么？

6 ▶WITH ADVERB 与副词连用◀ used to reverse the order of the subject and the verb when an adverb or adverbial phrase starts a sentence〔以副词或副词词组引出句子时用以调换主语和动词的语序〕: *Not only did I see him, I spoke to him, too.* 我不仅见到了他，还和他说话了。

Frequencies of the verb **do** in spoken and written English
动词 do 在英语口语和书面语中的使用频率

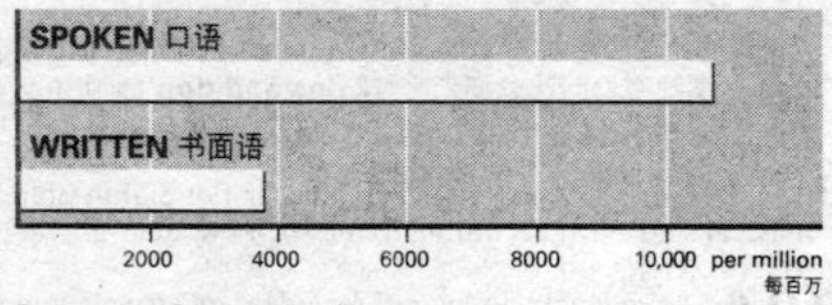

Based on the British National Corpus and the Longman Lancaster Corpus
据英国国家语料库和朗文兰开斯特语料库

This graph shows that the verb **do** is much more common in spoken English than in written English. This is because it is used to form questions and negatives and is used in some common spoken phrases. 本图表显示，动词 do 在英语口语中的使用频率远远高于书面语。因为该词用以构成疑问句和否定句，而且一些常用短语中都包含 do。

1 1 **do²** *v*

1 ▶ACTIVITY/JOB 活动/工作◀ [T] to PERFORM (2) and finish a particular activity or job 做，干；履行；完成: *Have you done your homework yet?* 你做完家庭作业了吗？| *Jo does aerobics three times a week.* 乔每星期做三次增氧健身操。| *It's a pleasure doing business with you.* 很高兴跟你做生意。| **do the dishes/washing up/laundry etc** *It's your turn to do the washing.* 轮到你洗衣服了。—see 见 JOB (USAGE), MAKE¹ (USAGE)

2 do your hair/teeth/nails to spend time making your hair look nice, brushing your teeth etc 做头发/刷牙/修剪指甲: *Jan spends ages doing her hair in the mornings.* 简早上会花很长时间做头发。

3 what do you do (for a living)? *spoken* used to ask someone what their job is【口】你是做什么工作的？

4 ▶SUCCEED/FAIL 成功/失败◀ [I] used to ask or say whether someone is being successful〔用于询问或讲述某人目前是否很成功〕: *How are you doing?* 你干得怎么样？| **[+with/in etc]** *How are you doing in your new job?* 你的新工作干得怎么样？| **do well/badly** *The children are doing very well at school.* 孩子们在学校学得很好。

5 do nothing for/do a lot for etc [T] to have a particular effect on something or someone 对…没有效果/有很大效果等: **do nothing for sb** (=not improve someone's appearance) 没有改善某人的外貌 *That colour does nothing for her.* 那种颜色并没有让她好看一些。| **do a lot for** (=have a good effect on) 对…有好的效果 *Getting the job has done a lot for her self-esteem.* 得到这份工作对她的自尊心很有好处。| **do wonders for** (=have a very good effect on) 对…有极好的效果 *Moving to the city has done wonders for my social life.* 搬到城市里极大地改善了我的社交生活。

6 ▶SPEND TIME 花时间◀ [T] *informal* to spend a period of time doing something difficult or something that you have to do【非正式】度过〔一段时间，做某种困难的或不得不做的事情〕: *I did two years of teaching before that.* 在那以前我教了两年书。

7 ▶FOOD 食物◀ [T] *informal* to make a particular kind of food【非正式】做〔某种食品〕: *I was thinking of doing a casserole tonight.* 我正考虑晚上弄一个砂锅来吃。

8 ▶A SERVICE 某项服务◀ [T] to provide a particular service 提供〔某项服务〕: *Do you do theatre bookings here?* 你们这里能订戏票吗？| *We don't do food after 2 o'clock.* 我们两点以后就不供应食物了。

9 ▶COPY 模仿◀ [T] *informal* to copy someone's behaviour, in order to entertain people【非正式】模仿〔某人的举止来逗乐〕: *He does Clinton very well.* 他模仿克林顿像极了。

10 ▶STUDY 学习◀ [T not in passive 不用被动态] *BrE* to study a particular subject in a school or university【英】〔在学校或大学里〕学习，攻读，研究〔某门课程〕: *I did French for 5 years.* 我学了5年法语。

11 do sb good to make someone feel better, more cheerful etc 对某人有好处: *A break will do you good.* 休息一下会对你有好处。

12 do 10 miles/do 20 kms etc to achieve a particular speed, distance etc 走完10英里/20公里等: *We did 300 miles on the first day.* 第一天我们走了300英里的路程。| *The car can do 120 mph.* 这车能达到120英里的时速。

13 ▶VISIT 参观◀ [T] to visit a particular place, especially when you are going to see a lot of other places 参观，游览〔某一个地方，尤指还要参观其他许多地方时〕: *Let's do the Eiffel Tower today and the Pompidou Centre tomorrow.* 咱们今天去参观埃菲尔铁塔，明天游览蓬皮杜中心。

14 ▶ENOUGH/SUITABLE 足够的/合适的◀ *especially spoken* [I,T not in progressive 不用进行时] used to say that something will be enough or be suitable【尤口】〔某物〕足够；合适: **[+for]** *Ten bottles of wine should do for the party.* 为聚会备10瓶酒应该足够了。| *That vase would do for your Mum's birthday present.* 买那个花瓶给你妈妈作生日礼物很合适。| *"I've got a saucepan." "That'll do."* "我有一个平底锅。" "那就可以了。" | **should/will do sb** *Here's £20 – that should do you.* 这里有20英镑，应该够你花的了。| **should/will do sb for** *A few sandwiches will do us for lunch.* 几块三明治就够我们午餐吃的了。

15 that will do! *spoken* used to tell a child that you want them to stop behaving in the way they are behaving【口】够了！〔用于命令孩子停止某种行为〕

16 do as you're told *spoken* used to tell a child to behave in the way you tell them to【口】告诉你怎么做，你就怎么做〔用于告诫孩子听从吩咐〕

17 would do well to do sth used to advise someone that they should do something〔建议某人〕最好做某事: *You'd do well to avoid that restaurant.* 你最好别去那家餐厅。

18 ▶CHEAT 欺骗◀ [T] *BrE spoken* to cheat someone【英口】欺骗〔某人〕: *That painting's a fake. You've been done.* 那幅画是赝品，你上当了。

19 ▶PUNISH 惩罚◀ [T] *BrE spoken* to punish someone【英口】惩罚〔某人〕: *Your Dad'll do you when he finds out.* 要是你爸知道了，他会揍你的。| **get done** *I got done for speeding yesterday.* 我昨天因超速行驶被罚了。

20 do it *informal* to have sex【非正式】性交

21 ▶HAPPEN 发生◀ [I] *spoken* to happen【口】发生: *What's doing at your place tonight?* 你们那儿今晚有什么活动？

22 do sth to death to talk about or do something so often that it becomes boring 频繁地谈论[做]某事而让人厌烦: *That joke has been done to death.* 那个笑话人人在说，真是听得腻死人了。

23 do well by sb to treat someone well 善待某人: *He's left*

do up 系上，扣上

She's doing up her blouse. 她在扣上衬衫。

She's undoing her blouse. 她在解开衬衫。

home, but he still does well by his kids. 他已经离开家另外过了，但他仍然对孩子们很好。—see also 另见 **do your bit** (BIT[1] (15)), **how do you do** (HOW[1] (10)), **nothing doing** (NOTHING[1] (13)), **do sb proud** (PROUD (4))

do away with sb/sth *phr v* [T] **1** to get rid of something so that it does not exist any longer 摆脱，废除: *The government has done away with free eye tests for everyone.* 政府已不再为大家提供免费眼科检查。**2** *informal* to kill someone【非正式】杀死，除掉〔某人〕

do sb **down** *phr v* [T] *BrE informal* to criticize someone, especially when they are not there【英，非正式】〔尤指背后〕批评〔某人〕；中伤

do for sb/sth *phr v* [T] **1 what will you do for sth?** *spoken* used to ask someone what arrangements they have made for a particular thing【口】〔用于询问某人为某事做了什么安排〕: *What will you do for transport tonight?* 今天晚上的交通你是怎么安排的？**2** *BrE slang* to kill someone【英俚】除掉，杀死〔某人〕**3** *old-fashioned* to make someone feel so tired that they cannot do anything【过时】使感到疲惫不堪；使累得动不了: *All that travelling around really did for me.* 到处旅行真把我给累死了。| **be done for** *I'm going to bed, I'm done for.* 我要上床睡觉去，我都累死了。**4** *BrE old-fashioned* to have a job cleaning someone else's house, cooking for them etc【英，过时】〔替别人〕料理家务

do in *phr v* [T] **1** [**do** sb ↔ **in**] *informal* to kill someone【非正式】杀死〔某人〕: *They say Bates did his wife in.* 他们说贝茨把他妻子给杀了。**2** [**do** sb **in**] to make someone feel extremely tired 使〔某人〕筋疲力尽: *That walk really did me in.* 走了那么多路真是把我累坏了。

do sth ↔ **out** *phr v* [T] **1** to make a room look nice by decorating it 装饰〔房间〕: *The room was beautifully done out in pastel colours.* 这个房间用柔和的色彩粉刷过。**2** *informal especially BrE* to clean a room or cupboard thoroughly【非正式，尤英】彻底清扫，清理〔房间或橱柜〕: *I'll do out the kitchen cupboards tonight.* 今晚我要把厨房的碗橱清理一下。

do sb **out of** sth *phr v* [T often passive 常用被动态] *informal* to cheat someone by not giving them something that they deserve, or something that they are owed【非正式】剥夺〔某人应得的东西〕；骗取〔某人的东西〕: *I was done out of £10 in the shop this morning.* 今天早上我在商店里被骗走了10英镑。

do over *phr v* [T] **1** [**do** sth ↔ **over**] to decorate a room, wall etc 装饰〔房间、墙壁等〕**2** [**do** sth **over**] *AmE* to do something again because you did it wrong the first time【美】把〔某事〕重新做一遍: *Your homework's full of mistakes, you'd better do it over.* 你的家庭作业错误连篇，你最好重做一遍。**3** [**do** sth ↔ **over**] *slang* to steal things from a place【俚】偷〔某处〕的东西: *The factory was done over last night.* 这家工厂昨夜被盗了。**4** [**do** sb ↔ **over**] *BrE slang* to attack and injure someone【英俚】袭击，伤害〔某人〕

do up *phr v* **1** [I,T] to fasten or tie 系上，扣上: *This skirt does up at the back.* 这条裙子在后面系扣。| **do** sth ↔ **up** *I can't do my shoelaces up.* 我鞋带系不上了。| *Do up your coat or you'll be cold.* 把大衣扣好，不然你会冻着的。—see 见 OPEN[2] (USAGE) **2** [T **do** sth ↔ **up**] to repair or redecorate a building or old car, so that it looks much better 修理〔汽车〕；重新装修〔房子〕: *They did up the house and sold it for a vast profit.* 他们把房子重新装修后卖出去，赚了不少钱。**3 do yourself up** to make yourself look neat and attractive 梳妆，打扮自己: *Sue spent ages doing herself up for her date.* 休为了赴约花了好长时间梳妆打扮。

do with sth *phr v* [T] **1 could do with** *spoken* to need or want something【口】需要，想要: *I could do with a drink.* 我想要喝一杯饮料。| *I could have done with some help this morning.* 今天早上我很需要有人来帮帮忙。**2 what you do with yourself** what you spend your time doing 怎样过的，如何打发时间的: *What do you do with yourself when you're not working?* 你不工作的时候干些什么？| **not know what to do with yourself** *June didn't know what to do with herself after she retired.* 琼退休后不知道该如何打发时间。**3 what shall we do with?/what have you done with?** *spoken* used to ask someone about arrangements that have been made or something that has been done【口】做了什么安排？/做了什么事？: *What shall we do with the kids while you're working?* 你上班的时候，孩子们怎么办？| *I can't find my pen, what have you done with it?* 我找不到钢笔，你把它弄哪去了？**4 have/be to do with** to have a connection with something 与…有关: *The programme is to do with mental illness.* 这个计划与精神病有关。| **be nothing to do with you** (=used to say that someone should not ask about something) 与某人无关 *What I do when you're out is nothing to do with you.* 你不在时我做了些什么与你无关。| **not have anything to do with** (=not have any connection with) 与…没有任何关系 *This question doesn't have anything to do with the main topic of the survey.* 这个问题与调查的主题没有任何关系。| **be something to do with** (=having some connection, but you are not sure what) 似乎与…有关 *Judy's job is something to do with marketing.* 朱迪的工作好像与市场销售有关。**5 what is someone doing with?** used to ask why someone has something 为什么某人拿某物？: *What are you doing with my diary?* 你拿我的日记干什么？

do without *phr v* **1** [I,T] to manage to live without something or someone 没有…也行；将就: *I can't afford a car, so I guess I'll just have to do without.* 我买不起汽车，所以也就只好将就着不用了。| **do without sth** *You'll have to do without your dinner if you don't get back in time.* 你如果不准时回来就别吃饭了。**2 can do without** used to say that you prefer not to have something 宁可没有…: *"Oh shut up, I can do without all this hassle."* "噢，闭嘴，我可不想再这么吵了。"

do³ *n* [C] *informal*【非正式】**1** a party or other social event 聚会；其他社交活动: *Are you going to this do at John's tonight?* 约翰家今晚举办的晚会你去吗？**2 dos and don'ts** things that you must and must not do in a particular situation 该做的和不该做的事情

do⁴, doh /do; dəʊ/ *n* [singular,U] the first or eighth note in a musical SCALE[1] (8) according to the SOL-FA system 全音阶中的第一[第八]音

D.O.A. /ˌdi o ˈe; ˌdiː əʊ ˈeɪ/ *adj AmE* dead on arrival; someone who is dead on arrival is declared to be dead as soon as they are brought to a hospital【美】〔指某人〕送到医院时已经死亡

d.o.b. the written abbreviation of 缩写= date of birth 出生日期

doc /dɑk; dɒk/ *n* [C] *spoken* a doctor【口】医生，大夫

do·cent /doˈsɛnt; dəʊˈsent/ *n* [C] *AmE*【美】**1** a university teacher 大学老师 **2** someone who guides visitors through a MUSEUM, etc〔博物馆等的〕向导；讲解员

do·cile /ˈdɑsl; ˈdəʊsaɪl/ *adj* quiet and easily controlled 安静的；容易控制的；温顺的: *a docile child* 温顺的孩子 —**docilely** *adv* —**docility** /doˈsɪlətɪ; dəʊˈsɪləti/ *n* [U]

dock¹ /dɑk; dɒk/ *n* **1** [C] a place in a port where ships are loaded and unloaded 码头: *A crowd was waiting at the dock to greet them.* 一群人在码头等着迎接他们。| **in dock** *The ship is now in dock for repairs.* 这艘船目前正在船坞里等待修理。—see also 另见 DRY DOCK **2** [C] the part of a law court where the person being tried (TRY[1] (6)) stands 被告席 **3** [C,U] a plant with thick green leaves that grows wild in Britain〔英国的〕厚叶野草；酸模

dock² *v* **1** [I,T] if a ship docks or you dock a ship, it sails into a dock (使)〔船〕进港[进码头]: *We'll be docking in about half an hour.* 大约半小时后我们就要进港了。**2 dock sb's wages/pay** to reduce the amount of money you pay someone 扣某人的工资/薪酬: *Your wages will be docked if you're away for too*

long. 如果你出去太久就会被扣工资。**3** [I] if two spaceships dock, they join together in space〔指宇宙飞船在太空〕对接 **4** [T] to cut an animal's tail short 剪短〔动物的尾巴〕

dock·er /ˈdɑkɚ; ˈdɒkə/ *n* [C] *BrE* someone whose job is loading and unloading ships; LONGSHORE-MAN, STEVEDORE【英】码头工人

dock·et /ˈdɑkɪt; ˈdɒkɪt/ *n* [C] **1** *technical* a short document used in business that shows what is in a package or describes goods that are being delivered【术语】包装单据〔如包裹单或送货单〕; 货物标签 **2** *AmE law* a list of legal cases (CASE[1] (9a)) that will take place in a particular court【美, 法律】备审案件目录表

dock·land /ˈdɑklənd; ˈdɒklənd/ also 又作 **docklands** *plural n* [U] *BrE* the area surrounding the place where ships are loaded and unloaded in a large port【英】港区; 码头区

Dock·lands /ˈdɑkləndz; ˈdɒkləndz/ a large, modern development of houses and offices in East London, along the River Thames, built mainly during the 1980s. It includes the tallest building in the UK, Canary Wharf, and the London City Airport. 船坞区, 码头区〔位于伦敦东部、泰晤士河沿岸一大型现代办公和住宅区。大部分楼宇建于20世纪80年代, 包括英国最高的建筑加纳利码头大厦和伦敦市机场〕

dock·side /ˈdɑkˌsaɪd; ˈdɒksaɪd/ *n* [singular] the area around the place in a port where ships are loaded and unloaded 码头邻区; 码头边

dock·yard /ˈdɑkˌjɑrd; ˈdɒkjɑːd/ *n* [C] a place where ships are repaired or built 船坞; 修船厂; 造船厂

S2 W1 **doc·tor**[1] /ˈdɑktɚ; ˈdɒktə/ *n* [C] **1** someone who is trained to treat people who are ill 医生, 大夫: **go to a doctor/see a doctor** *I think you'd better go to the doctor about your chest.* 我想你最好找个医生看看你的胸部。| **Doctor Smith/Brown etc** *I'd like to make an appointment to see Doctor Pugh.* 我想预约皮尤医生看病。**2** someone who holds the highest level of degree given by a university 博士: *a Doctor of Law* 法学博士 **3** *AmE* a way of addressing or referring to a DENTIST【美】〔用于称呼或指牙医〕

doctor[2] *v* [T] **1** to dishonestly change something in order to make it seem better 窜改, 伪造: *The figure had been doctored to read $5,000 instead of $500.* 数字经窜改从500元变成了5000元。**2** to add a substance, especially a drug or poison, to food or drink 将某物质〔尤指药物或毒药〕放入〔食物或饮料中〕: *Paul suspected that his drink had been doctored.* 保罗怀疑他的饮料被人做了手脚。**3** to remove the sex organs of an animal, especially a cat or dog, so that it cannot produce babies 阉割〔猫、狗等〕

doc·tor·al /ˈdɑktərəl; ˈdɒktərəl/ *adj* [only before noun 仅用于名词前] done as part of work for the university degree of DOCTOR[1] (2) 博士(学位)的: *a doctoral thesis on Kant* 一篇关于康德的博士论文

doc·tor·ate /ˈdɑktərɪt; ˈdɒktərɪt/ *n* [C] a university degree of the highest level 博士学位

Doctor of Phi·los·o·phy /ˌ·· · ·ˈ···/ *n* [C] a PHD 哲学博士

doc·tri·naire /ˌdɑktrɪˈnɛr; ˌdɒktrɪˈneə/ *adj formal* certain that your beliefs or opinions are completely correct and unable to consider the practical problems involved in making them work【正式】教条主义的; 空谈理论的; 脱离实际的: *a facile doctrinaire argument* 肤浅的、纯理论的论点

doc·trine /ˈdɑktrɪn; ˈdɒktrɪn/ *n* [C] a belief or set of beliefs that form the main part of a religion or system of ideas 信条; 教义; 主义; 学说: *the doctrine of predestination* 宿命论的学说 —**doctrinal** /ˈdɑktrɪnl; dɒkˈtraɪnl/ *adj*

doc·u·dra·ma /ˈdɑkjuˌdrɑmə; ˈdɒkjʊˌdrɑːmə/ *n* [C] *AmE* a film, usually for television, that presents a true story as a play【美】文献(电视)片, 纪实片

W2 **doc·u·ment**[1] /ˈdɑkjəmənt; ˈdɒkjʊmənt/ *n* [C] a piece of paper that gives official written information about something 文件; 公文: *legal documents* 法律文件

doc·u·ment[2] /ˈdɑkjəˌmɛnt; ˈdɒkjʊment/ *v* [T] to write about something, film it, or take photographs of it, in order to record information about it〔通过记述、拍电影或拍照片的方式来〕记载: *photographs documenting the early history of the motor car* 记录汽车早期历史的照片

doc·u·men·ta·ry[1] /ˌdɑkjəˈmɛntərɪ; ˌdɒkjʊˈmentəri◂/ *n* [C] a film or television programme that gives facts and information about something 纪录片: **[+on/about]** *a documentary about volcanoes* 关于火山的纪录片

documentary[2] *adj* **1** **documentary film/programme** a film or television programme that gives facts and information about something 纪录片/纪实(电视)节目 **2** [only before noun 仅用于名词前] documentary proof or evidence is proof in the form of documents〔证据等〕书面的; 文件形式的

doc·u·men·ta·tion /ˌdɑkjəmɛnˈteʃən; ˌdɒkjʊmənˈteɪʃən/ *n* [U] official documents that are used to prove that something is true or correct〔用于引证的〕文件证据; 证件

DOD the written abbreviation of 缩写 = the US Department of Defence 美国国防部

dod·der /ˈdɑdɚ; ˈdɒdə/ *v* [I] to walk in an unsteady way shaking slightly, especially because you are very old〔尤指因年老〕步履不稳; 走路摇晃

dod·der·ing /ˈdɑdərɪŋ; ˈdɒdərɪŋ/ *adj informal* shaking slightly and unable to walk properly because you are old or ill【非正式】〔因年老或生病而〕颤抖的, 蹒跚而行的

dod·dery /ˈdɑdərɪ; ˈdɒdəri/ *adj informal* weak and unable to walk properly or do things quickly because you are old or ill【非正式】〔因年老或生病而〕虚弱的; 步履蹒跚的; 做事缓慢的: *Some of the patients are a bit doddery.* 有些病人有点虚弱。

dod·dle /ˈdɑdl; ˈdɒdl/ *n* **be a doddle** *BrE informal* to be extremely easy【英, 非正式】…是轻而易举的事情: *The exam was a doddle!* 这次考试太简单了!

Dodge /dɑdʒ; dɒdʒ/ *trademark* a type of US car made by Chrysler【商标】道奇〔克莱斯勒公司制造的一种汽车〕

dodge[1] *v* **1** [T] to move quickly in order to avoid being hit by someone or something〔快速〕躲开, 避开, 闪开: *I managed to dodge the shot that came flying through the air.* 我设法避开了飞来的一球。—see picture on page A22 参见A22页图 **2** [I always+adv/prep] to move quickly in a particular direction to avoid someone or something 快速朝某方向移动; 躲闪: **[+into/out/behind]** *He dodged in and out of the traffic.* 他在车流中东躲西闪。**3** [T] to avoid a law or unpleasant duty in a dishonest way 逃避〔法律制裁或令人不快的责任〕: *Senator O'Brian skillfully dodged the crucial question.* 奥布赖恩参议员巧妙地回避了这一关键问题。**4** **dodge the issue** to avoid considering or discussing something that needs to be dealt with 回避问题〔对需要处理的事情不予考虑或讨论〕

dodge[2] *n* [C] **1** *informal* something dishonest you do in order to avoid a responsibility or law【非正式】〔为逃避法律或责任而使用的〕伎俩, 诡计: *Jake was full of clever dodges to avoid paying his debts.* 杰克有的是逃债的诡计。| **tax dodge** *He'll claim the car was a present as a tax dodge.* 为了逃税, 他将声称这辆车是别人送的礼物。**2** **make a dodge** to make a sudden forward or sideways movement to avoid something 躲闪, 避开

dodge ball /ˈ· ·/ *n* [U] a game played by children in which you try to avoid being hit by a large rubber ball thrown by the other players〔儿童玩的〕躲球游戏〔尽量躲开别的孩子投过来的大橡胶球〕

Dodge Cit·y /ˌ· ˈ··/ a city in the US state of Kansas. In the 19th century, Dodge City was a place where many people came to drink and play cards for money, and there was a lot of fighting and shooting. 道奇城〔美国堪萨斯州城市。19世纪, 该市是许多人饮酒和玩牌赌博的去处, 殴打和枪击事件频发〕

CULTURAL NOTE 文化注释

If someone in the US compares a place to Dodge City, they mean that it is very dangerous and full of crime. The phrase 'get out of Dodge' is sometimes used to mean to leave a very bad, dangerous, or unpleasant situation 如果某个美国人将一个地方比作道奇城, 意思是说该地极其危险, 犯罪横行。短语get out of Dodge有时用来指离开一个极为恶劣、危险或令人不快的处境: *As the drug dealers and armed gangs moved in, the neighborhood began to look like Dodge City.* 随着毒品贩子和武装帮派的到来, 该居民区开始变得像道奇城一样, 斗殴成风, 没有王法。

dodg·em car /ˈdɑdʒəm ˌkɑr; ˈdɒdʒəm kɑː/ *n* [C] *BrE* a small electric car that people drive around an enclosed area at a FUNFAIR【英】〔游乐场中的〕碰碰车; BUMPER CAR *AmE*【美】

dodg·ems /ˈdɑdʒəmz; ˈdɒdʒəmz/ *n* **the dodgems** a form of entertainment at a FUNFAIR in which people drive small electric cars around an enclosed space, chasing and hitting other cars〔游乐场中的〕碰碰车游戏: *Let's go on the dodgems.* 我们去玩碰碰车吧。

dodg·er /ˈdɑdʒɚ; ˈdɒdʒə/ *n* [C] **tax/draft dodger** someone who uses dishonest methods to avoid paying taxes or serving in the army 逃税/逃兵役的人

dodg·y /ˈdɑdʒɪ; ˈdɒdʒi/ *adj BrE informal*【英, 非正式】**1** containing false information, often for a dishonest purpose 含虚假资料的; 不可靠的: *dodgy accounts* 假账 **2** uncertain or difficult 不确定的; 困难的: *It's a dodgy situation.* 这是个困难的局面。**3**

not working properly 不好使的; 坏了的: *The gears in the car are a bit dodgy.* 这辆车的排挡有些不好使。**4** dishonest or not to be trusted 不诚实的; 不可信的: *a dodgy character* 一个不可信的家伙 —**dodginess** *n* [U]

do·do /ˈdodo; ˈdəʊdəʊ/ *n* [C] **1** a large bird that no longer exists and was unable to fly 渡渡鸟〔一种已经灭绝的、不能飞行的大鸟〕 **2** *AmE* a stupid person【美】愚蠢的人, 傻瓜 —see also 另见 **dead as a dodo** (DEAD¹ (14))

Do·do·ma /ˈdodəmɑ; ˈdəʊdəmɑː/ the capital city of Tanzania 多多马〔坦桑尼亚首都〕

DOE /ˌdi o ˈi; ˌdiː əʊ ˈiː/ the Department of Energy; a US government department 能源部〔美国政府部门〕

doe /do; dəʊ/ *n* [C] a female rabbit, DEER, etc 雌兔; 雌鹿 —compare 比较 BUCK¹ (4)

do·er /ˈduɚ; ˈduːə/ *n* [C] **1** someone who does things instead of just thinking or talking about them 实干家: *She's a doer, not a thinker.* 她不是个思想家, 而是个实干家。**2 evildoer/wrongdoer** someone who does evil or wrong 作恶的人/做错事的人

does /dəz; dəz; *strong* 强读 dʌz; dʌz/ the 3rd person singular of the present tense of DO¹ do¹ 的第三人称单数现在式

does·n't /ˈdʌzn̩t; ˈdʌzənt/ the short form of 缩略式= 'does not'

doff /dɑf; dɒf/ *v* [T] *old-fashioned* to take off a piece of clothing, especially your hat【过时】脱〔衣物, 尤指脱帽〕: *Everyone called him 'Sir' and doffed their hats.* 大家都称呼他"先生", 并向他脱帽致意。—opposite 反义词 DON²

dogs 狗

poodle 卷毛狗, 贵妇犬
pekinese 京巴, 狮子狗
dachshund 腊肠狗
spaniel 西班牙猎犬
collie 柯利牧羊犬
greyhound 灵提
Afghan 阿富汗猎犬
German shepherd 德国牧羊犬/Alsatian *BrE*【英】阿尔萨斯狼狗
Labrador 拉布拉多猎犬
pit bull terrier 斗牛㹴狗
dalmatian 大麦町犬, 斑点狗

dog¹ /dɔg; dɒg/ *n* [C]

1 ►ANIMAL 动物◄ a very common animal that people keep as a pet or to guard a building 狗: *I could hear a dog barking.* 我能听见狗吠声。

2 ►MALE ANIMAL 雄性动物◄ a male dog, FOX¹ (1) etc 公狗; 雄狐等 —compare 比较 BITCH¹ (1)

3 be going to the dogs *informal* if an organization is going to the dogs, it is getting much worse and will be difficult to improve【非正式】〔组织〕每况愈下, 趋于衰败; 一蹶不振: *This country's really going to the dogs!* 这个国家确实在走向崩溃!

4 ►WOMAN 妇女◄ *slang* an offensive word used by men meaning an unattractive woman【俚】丑婆娘, 丑女人〔冒犯用词〕

5 it's dog eat dog an expression used to describe a situation in which people compete strongly and will do anything to get what they want 残酷无情的竞争: *Show business isn't all glamour, it's dog eat dog out there.* 娱乐业并不是光有迷人的一面, 其中的竞争十分残酷。| *Advertising is a dog-eat-dog business.* 广告业的竞争十分残酷。

6 it's a dog's life *spoken* used to say that life is difficult and full of hard work and worry, with very little pleasure【口】苦难的生活

7 not have a dog's chance *informal* to have no chance of being successful【非正式】毫无成功的机会; 毫无希望

8 make a dog's breakfast of sth *BrE informal* to do something very badly【英, 非正式】把某事弄得一团糟: *You've made a real dog's breakfast of putting those shelves up.* 你把那些书架做得太差劲了。

9 be dressed up like a dog's dinner *BrE informal* to be wearing expensive clothes that you think are suitable for a social event, but that other people think are silly【英, 非正式】穿得花里胡哨; 打扮炫丽

10 dog in the manger someone who will not let other people use or have something, even though they do not need it themselves 狗占马槽, 占着茅坑不拉屎的人

11 every dog has its day an expression used to mean that even the most unimportant person has a time in their life when they are successful and noticed 凡人皆有得意时

12 sth is a dog *AmE informal* used to say that something is very poor quality【美, 非正式】某物质量低劣: *This radio is a dog.* 这个收音机质量很差。

13 the dogs *BrE informal* a sports event which consists of a series of races for dogs【英, 非正式】跑狗比赛

14 put on the dog *AmE old-fashioned* to pretend to be richer than you really are or to know more than you really do【美, 过时】摆阔气; 摆架子; 装腔作势 —see also 另见 DOGHOUSE, **the hair of the dog** (HAIR (10)), SHAGGY DOG STORY, **as sick as a dog** (SICK¹ (1)), **let sleeping dogs lie** (SLEEP¹ (6)), **the tail wagging the dog** (TAIL¹ (11)), **top dog** (TOP² (7)), **treat someone like a dog** (TREAT¹ (1))

CULTURAL NOTE 文化注释

Dogs are very popular pets in both the US and the UK. People often give them a lot of attention and consider them to be part of the family. Newspapers sometimes have articles about dogs who have done clever things such as saving a child's life, or travelling miles to find their owners after they have been lost. There are also many television shows, films, and stories about dogs, including **Lassie** and **Scooby Doo**. Because dogs are generally considered to be loyal and friendly, they are sometimes called 'man's best friend'. In the US and the UK, people can be made to pay a FINE if they do not clean up the waste left by their dogs on the pavement or in a park. In the US, some parks have built special areas for people to walk their dogs, so that the rest of the park stays clean. A famous British competition for dogs, called Cruft's, is held every year in Birmingham. 狗在英美两国都是受人喜爱的宠物。人们很关注狗, 视之为家庭的一员。报纸上有时刊登一些文章讲述狗是如何聪明, 如救孩子的命, 或在走失时找到几英里外的主人。还有很多关于狗的电视节目、电影和故事, 包括小狗拉茜和斯库比·杜。因为狗被普遍认为忠诚、友善, 它们有时被称为"人类最好的朋友"。英美人可能会因自家的狗在人行道或公园便溺而未加清理受到罚款。美国的一些公园有专门的遛狗区, 这样公园的其他部分就会保持清洁。英国每年在伯明翰举办一项重要的狗类比赛, 叫做"克拉夫特狗赛"。— see also 另见 CRUFT'S

dog² *v* **dogged, dogging** [T] **1** if a problem or bad luck dogs you, it causes trouble for a long time〔问题或噩运〕紧随〔某人〕: *Maradona had been dogged by injury all season.* 马拉多纳整个赛季不断受伤。**2** to follow close behind someone 跟踪, 紧跟〔某人〕: *A mob of youths had been dogging us for some time.* 一群年轻人已经跟着我们好一段时间了。

dog bis·cuit /ˈ· ˌ··/ *n* [C] a small dry hard BISCUIT for dogs〔喂狗的〕小块硬饼干

dog·cart /ˈdɔgˌkɑrt; ˈdɒgkɑːt/ *n* [C] **1** a vehicle pulled by a horse, that has two wheels and two seats〔双轮双座的〕马车 **2** a small vehicle pulled by a large dog 狗拉小车

dog·catch·er /ˈdɔgˌkætʃɚ; ˈdɒgˌkætʃə/ *n* [C] *AmE* someone whose job is to collect dogs without owners【美】捕狗员〔专职捕捉没有主人的狗〕; DOG WARDEN *BrE*【英】

dog col·lar /'· ,··/ *n* [C] **1** a collar worn by dogs, onto which a LEAD (=length of leather, rope, chain etc) can be fastened 狗项圈〔可以系拴狗绳〕 **2** a stiff round white collar worn by priests 牧师戴的白色硬圆领，牧师领

dog days /'· ·/ *n* [plural] *literary* the hottest days of the year 【文】盛夏，三伏天，酷暑期：*the dog days of summer* 盛夏的日子；夏三伏

doge /dodʒ; dəudʒ/ *n* [C] the highest government official in Venice and in Genoa in the past〔旧时威尼斯和热那亚的〕总督；首长

dog-eared /'· ·/ *adj* dog-eared books or papers have been used so much that the corners are turned over or torn〔书或纸等因翻得多而形成〕折角的：*a dog-eared novel* 一本翻得卷了角的小说 —see picture on page A18 参见A18页图

dog-end /'· ·/ *n* [C] **1** *BrE informal* the small part of a cigarette that is left after it has been smoked【英，非正式】烟蒂，烟头 **2** something left over and not considered to be worth very much〔不值钱的〕剩余物品

dog·fight /'dɔg,faɪt; 'dɒgfaɪt/ *n* [C] **1** an organized fight between dogs 斗狗 **2** a fight between armed aircraft〔战斗机的〕空战

dog·fish /'dɔg,fɪʃ; 'dɒg,fɪʃ/ *n* [C] *plural* **dogfish** a kind of small SHARK (1) 角鲨，星鲨

dog·ged /'dɔgɪd; 'dɒgǀd/ *adj* dogged actions or behaviour show that you are very determined to continue doing something 坚持不懈的，顽强的，不屈不挠的：*her dogged determination to succeed* 她那不屈不挠务要成功的决心 —**doggedly** *adv* —**doggedness** *n* [U]

Dog·ger Bank /,dɑgɚ 'bæŋk; ,dɒgə 'bæŋk/ an area of the North Sea, about 70 miles (110 kilometres) off the coast of northeast England, where the sea is not very deep because there is a large SANDBANK under the water. A lot of boats go there to catch fish. 多格滩〔位于北海地区，距离英格兰东北海岸约70英里处。由于水下是一大片沙坝，这片海域不是很深，大量船只到此捕鱼〕

dog·ge·rel /'dɔgərəl; 'dɒgərəl/ *n* [U] poetry that is silly or funny and not intended to be serious 打油诗，蹩脚诗

dog·gie /'dɔgɪ; 'dɒgi/ *n* [C] another spelling of DOGGY doggy 的另一种拼法

dog·go /'dɔgo; 'dɒgəu/ *adv* **lie doggo** *old-fashioned* to stay quiet and still so that people will not notice you or find you【过时】悄悄隐蔽着；隐伏不动

dog·gone /'dɔg,gɔn; 'dɒgɒn/ *v* [T] **doggone it** *AmE old-fashioned spoken* used when you are slightly annoyed that something has happened【美，过时，口】该死的；讨厌的；去他的〔用于表示对发生的事有些生气〕：*The door blew open and, doggone it, if the chickens didn't get loose!* 门被风吹开了，该死，鸡都跑了！—**doggone, doggoned** *adj*: *That doggone cat!* 那只讨厌的猫！

dog·gy, doggie /'dɔgɪ; 'dɒgi/ *n* [C] **1** a word meaning dog, used especially by or to young children 小狗〔尤为儿语〕 **2** **doggy style/fashion** a position in which two people have sex that is similar to the position that dogs or other animals use〔指人像狗或其他动物那样的〕做爱方式

doggy bag /'·· ,·/ *n* [C] a small bag for taking home food that is left over from a meal, especially from a restaurant 狗食袋〔顾客把在餐厅吃剩的食品打包带走的小袋子〕

> **CULTURAL NOTE 文化注释**
>
> The amount of food provided in restaurants is usually much greater in the US than in Britain, and it is considered quite acceptable to take some of it home in a doggy bag. 美国餐馆的菜量通常比英国的大，因此把吃剩的饭菜装袋带回家是可以接受的。

doggy pad·dle /'·· ,··/ *n* DOG PADDLE 狗爬式游泳（法）

dog han·dler /'· ,··/ *n* [C] a police officer who works with a trained dog 携带警犬值勤的警察

dog·house /'dɔg,haus; 'dɒghaus/ *n* **be in the doghouse** *informal* to be in a situation in which someone is annoyed with you because you have done something wrong【非正式】〔因做错事而〕惹得某人生气：*I'm in the doghouse because I forgot Sam's birthday.* 由于我把萨姆的生日给忘了，所以很受埋怨。

do·gie /'dogɪ; 'dəugi/ *n* [C] *AmE* a baby cow without a mother【美】〔无母牛的〕牛犊

dog·leg /'dɔg,lɛg; 'dɒgleg/ *n* [C] a place in a road, path etc where it changes direction suddenly〔道路等的〕急转弯

dog-like /'· ·/ *adj* faithful and loving without asking for anything for yourself〔像狗一样〕忠诚的，无私的：*dog-like fidelity* 像狗一样的忠诚

dog·ma /'dɔgmə; 'dɒgmə/ *n* [C,U] a fixed belief, or set of beliefs that people are expected to accept without question 教条；教义；教理：*party dogma* 党派的信条

dog·mat·ic /dɔg'mætɪk; dɒg'mætɪk/ *adj* having ideas or beliefs that you are completely certain about and expect other people to accept without question 自以为是的；固执己见的；武断的：*Her staff find her bossy and dogmatic.* 她的员工发现她是个爱指挥别人、自以为是的人。—**dogmatically** /-klɪ; -kli/ *adv*

dog·ma·tise /'dɔgmə,taɪz; 'dɒgmətaɪz/ *v* a British spelling of DOGMATIZE dogmatize 的英式拼法

dog·ma·tis·m /'dɔgmə,tɪzəm; 'dɒgmətɪzəm/ *n* [U] attitudes or behaviour that are dogmatic 教条主义；武断 —**dogmatist** *n* [C]

dog·ma·tize /'dɔgmə,taɪz; 'dɒgmətaɪz/ *v* also 又作 **-ise** *BrE*【英】[I+**about**] to speak, write, or act in a dogmatic way 教条式地说[写]；武断地行事

do-good·er /,· '··/ *n* [C] someone who thinks they are being helpful but who annoys other people because they get involved in situations where they are not wanted〔自以为〕专做好事的人〔其实是多管闲事〕

dog pad·dle /'· ,··/ also 又作 **doggy paddle** *informal n* [singular] a simple way of swimming by moving your legs and arms like a swimming dog【非正式】狗爬式游泳（法）

dogs·bod·y /'dɔgz,bɑdɪ; 'dɒgz,bɒdi/ *n* [C] *BrE* someone who has to do all the jobs that nobody else wants to do【英】勤杂工，打杂的人：*I'm just the general dogsbody around here.* 我只不过是这里的普通杂工罢了。

dog·sled /'dɔg,slɛd; 'dɒgsled/ *n* [C] a SLEDGE (=low flat vehicle on metal blades) pulled by dogs over snow 狗拉雪橇

dog tag /'· ,·/ *n* [C] *AmE* a small piece of metal that soldiers wear around their necks with their name, blood type, and number written on it【美】身份识别牌〔士兵挂在颈部标有名字、血型和部队番号的牌子〕

dog-tired /,· '·◂/ *adj informal* extremely tired【非正式】筋疲力尽的

dog war·den /'· ,··/ *n* [C] *BrE* someone whose job is to collect dogs without owners【英】捕狗员〔专职捕捉没有主人的狗的人〕；DOGCATCHER *AmE*【美】

dog·wood /'dɔg,wud; 'dɒgwud/ *n* [C,U] a tree or bush with red or pink berries (BERRY) and red stems 狗木〔一种红茎、长着红色或粉红色浆果的树木或灌木〕

DoH /,di o 'ɛtʃ; ,diː əu 'eɪtʃ/ *n* the abbreviation of 缩写= the DEPARTMENT OF HEALTH

doh, do /do; dəu/ *n* [singular, U] the first or eighth note in the SOL-FA musical SCALE¹ (8) 全音阶中的第一[第八]音

Do·ha /'dohə; 'dəuhə/ the capital city of Qatar 多哈〔卡塔尔首都〕

doi·ly /'dɔɪlɪ; 'dɔɪli/ *n* [C] a circle of paper or cloth with a pattern cut into it that you put on a plate before putting cakes etc on it〔衬在盘中蛋糕等点心下面的刻花纸或布做的〕圆形垫子

do·ing /'duɪŋ; 'duːɪŋ/ *n* **1 be sb's doing** if something bad is someone's doing, they did it 是某人干的坏事：*This mess is all your doing.* 这一团糟全都是你搞的。**2 take some doing** to be hard work 费点劲，得花些功夫：*Sorting this lot out is going to take some doing.* 把这些东西都整理好得费些工夫。**3 doings** *BrE*【英】**a)** [plural] things that someone does〔某人〕做的事情 **b)** [C] *informal* a small thing whose name you have forgotten or do not know【非正式】那东西〔指忘了或叫不出名称的小东西〕：*Pass me that doings.* 把那个东西递给我。

do-it-your·self /,· · · '·◂/ *n* [U] DIY 自己动手（做）

Dol·by /'dolbɪ; 'dɒlbi/ *n* [U] *trademark* a system for reducing unwanted noise when you record music or sounds【商标】杜比[道尔贝]（降噪）系统

dol·drums /'dɑldrəmz; 'dɒldrəmz/ *n* **1 be in the doldrums** *informal*【非正式】**a)** to be feeling sad 无精打采；伤心；郁闷：*Fay's really in the doldrums today.* 费伊今天心情实在不佳。**b)** to not be growing or improving 没发展，无进展，停滞：*The car industry has been in the doldrums for several years.* 数年来汽车工业一直停滞不前。**2 the doldrums** an area in the ocean just north of the EQUATOR where the weather can be so calm that sailing ships cannot move 赤道以北海域的无风带〔帆船无法行驶〕

dole¹ /dol; dəul/ *n* [U] *BrE*【英】**1** money given by the government in Britain to people who are unemployed〔英国政府发放给失业人士的〕失业救济金：**be/go on the dole** (=be or become unemployed and receive money from the government) 领取政府失业救济金 *Kevin was on the dole for a year before he got a job.* 凯文领了一年的失业救济金才又找到工作。**2 the dole queue a)** the line of people waiting to claim this money each week 每周等待领取失业救济金的队伍 **b)** the number of people who are unemployed and claiming money from the state 向政

府领取救济金的失业人口: *As two factories closed today, 500 people joined the dole queue.* 随着今天两家工厂的倒闭，又有500人加入了领取失业救济金的行列。

dole² *v*

dole sth ↔ **out** *phr v* [T] *informal* to give money or food to more than one person 【非正式】发放，分发〔钱、食物等〕: [+to] *Vera was doling out candy to all the kids.* 维拉正在给所有的孩子派发糖果。

dole·ful /ˈdolfəl; ˈdəʊlfəl/ *adj* very sad 哀伤的: *a doleful song about lost love* 一首关于失去爱情的哀伤歌曲 —**dolefully** *adv* —**dolefulness** *n* [U]

Do·lit·tle /ˈdulɪtl; ˈduːlɪtl/ a character in books for children by Hugh Lofting and in a film based on these books. Dr Dolittle is a man who can understand what animals are saying and can talk to them using their language. 多利特尔〔休·洛夫廷所著儿童系列读物及据此改编的一部电影中的人物。兽医多利特尔能听懂兽语，而且能用兽语同动物交谈〕

S3 **doll¹** /dɑl; dɒl/ *n* **1** [C] a child's toy that looks like a small person 玩偶，玩具娃娃 **2** [C] *slang* a word meaning an attractive young woman, that is now usually considered offensive 【俚】漂亮的年轻女子〔现通常被视为具有冒犯之意〕 **3** [singular] *AmE informal* a very nice person 【美，非正式】人好人: *Jim's a real doll – he let me borrow his car.* 吉姆真是个大好人——他让我用他的车。

doll² *v*

doll sb **up** *phr v* [T] *informal* if a woman dolls herself up, she gets ready for a social occasion by putting on attractive clothes and MAKE-UP (1) 【非正式】〔指妇女为参加某个社交活动而〕把…打扮起来: **doll yourself up** *I can't be bothered to doll myself up tonight.* 今晚我懒得打扮自己。| **be/get dolled up** *The girls were all dolled up for a party.* 女孩子们都打扮得漂漂亮亮的去参加派对。

S1 W3 **dol·lar** /ˈdɑlɚ; ˈdɒlə/ *n* [C] **1** the standard unit of money in the US, Australia, Canada, and other countries, for which the sign is $ 元，圆〔美国、澳大利亚、加拿大等国的货币单位，符号为$〕: *This book costs ten dollars.* 买这本书得花十元。**2** a piece of paper or coin worth this amount of money 一元的纸币[硬币] **3 the dollar** the value of US money in relation to the money of other countries〔和其他国家货币相关的〕美元价值: *The pound has risen against the dollar.* 英镑对美元的比价上升了。—see also 另见 **you can bet your bottom dollar** (BET¹ (4)), **feel/look like a million dollars** (MILLION (4))

dollars-and-cents /ˌ· · ˈ·/ *adj AmE* considered in a financial way 【美】金钱的; 经济的: *It's an interesting idea, but from a dollars-and-cents point of view it just won't work.* 这是个有趣的想法，但是从金钱的角度来看并不可行。

doll house /ˈ· ·/ *n* [C] *AmE* 【美】= a DOLL'S HOUSE *BrE* 【英】

dol·lop¹ /ˈdɑləp; ˈdɒləp/ *n* [C] a mass of soft food, usually dropped from a spoon 一团，一块〔软质食物〕: [+of] *a large dollop of cream* 一大团奶油 —see picture on page A7 参见A7页图

dollop² *v* [T always+adv/prep] *informal* to drop a mass of soft food onto a surface 【非正式】把〔一团软质食物〕舀到…上: **dollop sth onto/into** *May dolloped the mixture into the frying pan.* 梅把混合物舀到煎锅里。

doll's house /ˈ· ·/ *n* [C] *BrE* a child's toy house with small furniture in it 【英】玩具房子; DOLL HOUSE *AmE* 【美】

dol·ly /ˈdɑlɪ; ˈdɒli/ *n* [C] **1** another word for a DOLL¹, used by and to children 玩具娃娃〔儿语〕 **2** *technical* a flat frame on wheels used for moving heavy objects 【术语】〔用来移动重物的〕手推车

dolly bird /ˈ· · ·/ *n* [C] *BrE old-fashioned* a pretty young woman, especially one who wears fashionable clothes 【英，过时】〔尤指身穿时髦衣服的〕漂亮的年轻女子

Dolly the sheep /ˌ· · ˈ·/ a sheep who was CLONEd by British scientists in 1996. They took a cell from her body and then developed it artificially so that it became a new sheep that was an exact copy of her. 多利羊〔1996年英国科学家通过克隆技术复制的一只羊〕

dol·men /ˈdalmɛn; ˈdɒlmen/ *n* [C] *technical* two or more large upright stones supporting a large flat piece of stone, built in ancient times 【术语】〔古时建造的〕石桌坟〔由两块或多块竖立的石头支撑起大块扁平的石板构成〕

dol·our *BrE* 【英】, **dolor** *AmE* 【美】 /ˈdolɚ; ˈdɒlə/ *n* [U] *literary* great sadness 【文】哀伤，悲痛 —**dolorous** *adj*

dol·phin /ˈdɑlfɪn; ˈdɒlfɪn/ *n* [C] a very intelligent sea animal like a fish with a long grey pointed nose 海豚

dolphin 海豚

dol·phi·na·ri·um /ˌdɑlfɪˈnɛrɪəm; ˌdɒlfɪˈneəriəm/ *n* [C] a pool where dolphins are kept and people can go to see them 海豚馆，海豚池

dolt /dolt; dəʊlt/ *n* [C] *old-fashioned* a silly or stupid person 【过时】愚蠢的人，傻瓜，笨蛋 —**doltish** *adj* —**doltishly** *adv*

-dom /dəm; dəm/ *suffix* [in U nouns 构成不可数名词] **1** the state of being something 作为某事物的状态: *freedom* 自由 **2 a)** [in C nouns 构成可数名词] a particular rank 职位: *He was rewarded with a dukedom.* (=was made a DUKE) 他被封为公爵。**b)** an area ruled by a particular type of person 某种人所管辖的区域: *kingdom* 王国 **3** [in U nouns 构成不可数名词] *informal* all the people who share the same set of interests, have the same job, etc 【非正式】拥有同样利益、工作等的群体: *officialdom* (=all officials) 官员〔总称〕| *yuppiedom*〔全体〕雅皮士

do·main /doˈmen; dəˈmeɪn/ *n* [C] *formal* 【正式】

1 ▶ACTIVITY/KNOWLEDGE 活动/知识◀ an area of activity, interest, or knowledge〔活动、兴趣、知识的〕领域，范围，范畴: *This problem lies outside the domain of medical science.* 这个问题不属于医学范畴。

2 sb/sth's domain an area of activity controlled by someone 由某人/某事物控制的领地: *Mortgages were until recently the domain of building societies.* 直到最近房屋抵押贷款还是由房屋互助会经管的。

3 ▶LAND 土地◀ an area of land owned and controlled by one person or government 领地; 领土; 版图: *feudal domains* 封建领地

4 in the public domain if information is in the public domain, it is not kept secret 属公共所有的; 为公众所知晓的: *Details of the arms deals must be brought into the public domain.* 武器交易的细节必须公诸于众。

5 ▶QUANTITIES 数量◀ *technical* the set of possible quantities by which something can vary 【术语】〔数学的〕域; 整环

dome /dom; dəʊm/ *n* [C] **1** a round roof on a base like a circle 穹顶; 圆屋顶; 拱顶 **2** a shape like a ball cut in half 半球形状: *the dome of his bald head* 他那圆圆的光头顶

domed /domd; dəʊmd/ *adj* covered with a dome or shaped like a dome 有穹顶的; 半球形的: *a high domed ceiling* 高高的穹形屋顶

Domes·day Book also 又作 **Doomsday Book** /ˈdumzdeˌbuk; ˈduːmzdeɪ ˌbʊk/ a record of all the lands of England, showing their size, value, ownership etc, made in 1086 on the orders of William the Conqueror. The Domesday Book has been very valuable in the study of English history. 《末日审判书》〔1086年奉威廉一世之命对英格兰土地面积、价值、所有权等所做的调查清册，对研究英格兰历史颇有价值〕

do·mes·tic¹ /dəˈmɛstɪk; dəˈmestɪk/ *adj* W2

1 ▶WITHIN ONE COUNTRY 国内的◀ happening within a country and not involving any other countries 国内的; 本国的: *the domestic market* 国内市场 | *Domestic flights go from Terminal 1.* 国内航班从一号航站楼出发。

2 ▶USED AT HOME 家用的◀ used in the house or home 家中使用的，家用的: **domestic appliance/equipment etc** *Electricity charges can be at business or domestic rate.* 电费可分为企业用电和家庭用电两种费率。

3 ▶ABOUT FAMILY AND HOME 关于家庭的◀ [only before noun 仅用于名词前] concerning family relationships and life at home 涉及家庭关系和生活的; 家事的: **domestic life** *I suspect Tony's domestic life isn't very happy.* 我怀疑托尼的家庭生活不是很幸福。| **domestic violence/problem/trouble etc** (=violence etc between members of the same family) 家庭暴力/问题/麻烦等

4 ▶PERSON 人◀ someone who is domestic enjoys spending time at home and is good at cooking, cleaning etc 喜爱操持家务的，善于烹饪、清洁等家务的

5 ▶ANIMAL 动物◀ a domestic animal lives on a farm or in someone's home 驯养的; 家养的 —**domestically** /-klɪ; -kli/ *adv*

domestic² *n* [C] a servant who works in a large house 仆人，佣人

do·mes·ti·cate /dəˈmɛstəˌket; dəˈmestɪkeɪt/ *v* [T] to make an animal able to live with people as a pet or work for them on a farm 驯养〔动物〕—compare 比较 TAME² (2) —**domestication** /dəˌmɛstəˈkeʃən; dəˌmestɪˈkeɪʃən/ *n* [U]

do·mes·ti·cat·ed /dəˈmɛstəˌketɪd; dəˈmestɪkeɪtɪd/ *adj* someone who is domesticated enjoys spending time at home and doing work in the home 喜爱操持家务的: *Ray's very domesticated – he loves cooking.* 雷很喜欢做家务——他喜爱烹饪。

do·mes·tic·i·ty /ˌdomɛsˈtɪsətɪ; ˌdəʊmesˈtɪsɪti/ *n* [U] life at home with your family 家庭生活; 家庭小天地: *a scene of happy domesticity* 一派幸福家庭的景象

domestic sci·ence /ˌ·ˌ··ˈ··/ *n* [U] *BrE old-fashioned* the study in schools of cooking, SEWING etc【英, 过时】家政学〔学习烹饪、缝纫等〕

domestic ser·vice /ˌ·ˌ··ˈ··/ *n* [U] the work of a servant in a large house〔用人做的〕家务

CULTURAL NOTE 文化注释

In Britain it is no longer common for people to have servants living in their houses, although many people employ someone to help them clean their house for a few hours each week. 在英国, 家里住着用人的现象已不多见了, 不过很多人雇人帮自己打扫屋子, 每周就几个小时而已。

dom·i·cile /ˈdɑməsl; ˈdɒmɪsaɪl/ *n* [C] *law* a place where someone lives【法律】住处, 住所: *His last known domicile was 11 Park Road, London, N8.* 他最后一处为人所知的住所是在伦敦N8区, 公园路11号。

dom·i·ciled /ˈdɑməsld; ˈdɒmɪsaɪld/ *adj law*【法律】**be domiciled in** to live in a particular place 在…居住的

dom·i·cil·i·a·ry /ˌdɑməˈsɪlɪˌɛrɪ; ˌdɒmɪˈsɪliəri/ *adj law*【法律】**domiciliary services/care/visits etc** care or services at someone's home 上门服务/护理/拜访等

dom·i·nance /ˈdɑmənəns; ˈdɒmɪnəns/ *n* [U] the fact of being more powerful, more important, or more noticeable than other people or things 优势; 显要; 突出: *military dominance* 军事上的优势 | [+of] *Japan's dominance of the market* 日本在市场的独霸地位

W3 **dom·i·nant¹** /ˈdɑmənənt; ˈdɒmɪnənt/ *adj* **1** stronger, more powerful, or more noticeable than other people or things 强大的; 有优势的; 突出的: *The dominant male gorilla is the largest in the group.* 这只占支配地位的雄性大猩猩是这群大猩猩中个头最大的。| *a dominant personality* 霸道的性格 **2** *technical* a dominant physical feature can appear in a child even if it has been passed on from only one parent【术语】〔遗传特性〕显性的: *Brown eyes are dominant.* 棕色眼睛是显性的。—compare 比较 RECESSIVE **3** high and easily seen 高耸的; 显眼的: *The castle was built in a dominant position on a hill.* 城堡建在山上一处居高临下的地方。

dominant² *n* [singular] the fifth note of a musical SCALE¹ (8) of eight notes 全音阶的第五音

W3 **dom·i·nate** /ˈdɑməˌnet; ˈdɒmɪneɪt/ *v* **1** [I,T] to have power and control over someone or something 支配, 控制: *a society in which males dominate* 一个由男性支配一切的社会 | **dominate sth** *Sue's very nice, but she does tend to dominate the conversation.* 休的人品很好, 但喜欢在谈话中占上风。**2** [I,T] to be the most important feature of something 成为(…的)最主要特征; (在…中)占最重要的地位: *Education issues dominated the election campaign.* 教育问题成为竞选活动中的主题。**3** [T] to be very large and easily noticed 耸立于; 比…高, 俯视: *The cathedral dominates the city.* 大教堂高高矗立, 俯瞰整个城市。—**domination** /ˌdɑməˈneʃən; ˌdɒmɪˈneɪʃən/ *n* [U]: *a fight to free the country from foreign domination* 为把国家从外国统治下解放出来而进行的斗争

dom·i·na·trix /ˌdɑməˈnetrɪks; ˌdɒmɪˈneɪtrɪks/ *n* [C] a woman who is the stronger partner in a sado-masochistic (SADOMASOCHISM) sexual relationship〔在性关系上的〕女性施虐狂; 母夜叉

dom·i·neer·ing /ˌdɑməˈnɪrɪŋ; dɒmɪˈnɪərɪŋ◂/ *adj* someone who is domineering tries to control other people without considering how they feel or what they want 专横的, 霸道的: *a domineering mother* 专横的母亲—**domineer** *v* [I]

Do·min·go /dəˈmɪŋgo; dəˈmɪŋgəʊ/, **Pla·ci·do** /ˈplæsɪdo; ˈplæsɪdəʊ/ (1941-) a Spanish OPERA singer who is one of the greatest TENORS (=men with high singing voices) of the 20th century 多明戈〔(1941-), 西班牙歌剧演唱家, 20世纪最出色的男高音之一〕

Dom·i·ni·ca /dəˈmɪnɪkə; ˌdɒmɪˈniːkə/ an island in the Caribbean Sea which has been a member of the British Commonwealth since 1978. Population: 70,786 (2001). Capital: Roseau. 多米尼克〔加勒比海一岛屿, 自1978年起加入英联邦。人口: 70,786 (2001), 首都: 罗索〕—**Dominican** *n, adj*

Do·min·i·can /dəˈmɪnɪkən; dəˈmɪnɪkən/ *n* [C] a member of a Christian religious group who leads a holy life〔基督教〕多明我会修道士[修女]—**Dominican** *adj*

Do·min·i·can Re·pub·lic /dəˈmɪnɪkən rɪˈpʌblɪk; dəˌmɪnɪkən rɪˈpʌblɪk/ a country in the Caribbean Sea on the island of Hispaniola, which it shares with Haiti. Population: 8,581,000 (2001). Capital: Santo Domingo. It was the place where Christopher Columbus first landed after crossing the Atlantic Ocean. 多米尼加共和国〔加勒比海国家, 与海地同位于伊斯帕尼奥拉岛。人口: 8,581,000 (2001), 首都: 圣多明各。这是克里斯多弗·哥伦布穿越大西洋后最早登陆的地方〕

do·min·ion /dəˈmɪnjən; dəˈmɪnjən/ *n* **1** [U] *literary* the power or right to rule people【文】统治权; 管辖权: **have/hold dominion over** *Alexander the Great held dominion over a vast area.* 亚历山大大帝曾统治过辽阔的疆域。**2** [C] *formal* the land owned or controlled by one person or a government【正式】领地; 领土; 版图: *the king's dominion* 国王的领地 **3** [C] one of the countries that was a member of the British COMMONWEALTH in the past〔旧时〕英联邦的自治领 —see also 另见 COLONY (1), PROTECTORATE

Dominion Day /ˈ·ˌ··ˌ·/ a national holiday in Canada, in memory of the beginning of the Dominion of Canada in 1867 自治领日〔加拿大一全国性假日, 纪念1867年加拿大自治领成立〕

Do·min·ions /dəˈmɪnjənz; dəˈmɪnjənz/ an old British name, which is no longer used, for the countries of Australia, Canada, and New Zealand, which had their own governments but were still part of the British Empire in the early part of the 20th century 自治领〔英国对澳大利亚、加拿大和新西兰的旧称。20世纪初, 这些国家建立了自己的政府, 但仍归属大英帝国。此名称现已废弃不用〕

dom·i·no /ˈdɑməno; ˈdɒmɪnəʊ/ *n plural* **dominoes** **1** [C] one of a set of small flat pieces of wood, plastic etc, with different numbers of spots on, used for playing a game 多米诺骨牌 **2** **dominoes** [U] the game played using dominoes 多米诺骨牌游戏 **3 the domino effect** a situation in which one event or action causes several other things to happen one after the other 多米诺(骨牌)效应〔指一个事件或行动导致其他事情接连发生〕

Dom Perignon *trademark* a type of CHAMPAGNE【商标】唐裴利侬香槟王〔一种香槟酒〕

don¹ /dɑn; dɒn/ *n* [C] *BrE* a university teacher, especially one who teaches at the universities of Oxford or Cambridge【英】〔尤指牛津大学或剑桥大学的〕大学教师

don² *v* **donned, donning** [T] *formal* to put on a hat, coat etc【正式】戴上〔帽子〕; 穿上〔衣服等〕—opposite 反义词 DOFF

Don·ald Duck /ˈdɑnḷd ˈdʌk; ˌdɒnəld ˈdʌk/ a character in CARTOONS made by Walt Disney. He is one of the most famous of all Disney's characters. 唐老鸭〔沃尔特·迪斯尼塑造的一卡通形象, 是迪斯尼最著名的角色之一〕

do·nate /ˈdonet; dəʊˈneɪt/ *v* [I,T] **1** to give something, especially money, to a person or an organization in order to help them 捐赠, 捐献〔尤指钱〕: **donate sth to sb/sth** *Last year he donated $1,000 to cancer research.* 去年他捐了1,000美元支持癌症研究。**2 donate blood** to allow some blood to be removed from your body so that it can be used in a hospital to help someone who is ill or injured 捐血, 献血

Don·atel·lo /ˌdɑnəˈtɛlo; ˌdɒnəˈteləʊ/ (1386-1466) an Italian SCULPTOR of the RENAISSANCE period 多那太罗〔(1386-1466), 文艺复兴时期意大利雕塑家〕

do·na·tion /doˈneʃən; dəʊˈneɪʃən/ *n* **1** [C] something, especially money, that you give to a person or an organization in order to help them 捐赠物〔尤指捐款〕: *All donations will be gratefully received.* 我们将十分感激地接受所有的捐赠。| **make a donation** (=give money) 捐款 **2** [U] the act of giving something, especially money, to help a person or an organization 捐助〔尤指钱〕

Don·cas·ter /ˈdɑŋkəstɚ; ˈdɒŋkəstə/ an industrial town in South Yorkshire in northern England. A well-known horse race, the St Leger, takes place there every year. 唐克斯特〔英格兰北部南约克郡一工业城镇, 著名的圣莱杰赛马会每年在此举办〕

done¹ /dʌn; dʌn/ the past participle of DO¹

done² *adj* [not before noun 不用于名词前, no comparative 无比较级]

1 ▶FINISHED 完成的◀ finished or completed 完成的, 终了的: *The job's nearly done.* 工作快做完了。| *As soon as I'm done I'll give you a call.* 我一忙完就给你打电话。| **over and done with** (=completely finished) 结束, 了结 *I'll be glad when this wedding is over and done with!* 等婚礼办完, 一切都了结了, 我就高兴了!

2 ▶COOKED 煮熟的◀ cooked enough to eat 煮熟的, 煮好的: *Is the pasta done yet?* 意大利面食做好了没有? —compare 比较 OVERDONE, UNDERDONE

3 be done for *informal* to be in serious trouble or likely to fail【非正式】遭殃了; 完蛋了: *If we're caught we're done for.* 要是被抓住, 我们就完了。

4 done in *informal* extremely tired【非正式】累坏了的; 筋疲力尽的: *I've got to sit down – I'm done in.* 我得坐下来 — 我太累了。

5 be done/be the done thing to be socially acceptable 得体的, 合乎礼仪的: *It just isn't the done thing to call teachers by their first names.* 直呼老师的名字是不礼貌的。
6 be/have done with it to finish dealing with something or someone, and never deal with them again 与某事[某人]了结关系: *I know it's unfair but let's just pay the fine and have done with it.* 我知道这不公平, 但是我们就交一下罚款, 把这事给了结算了。
7 be done *BrE informal* to be deceived or cheated【英, 非正式】上当, 受骗: *You paid £50 for that! You were done mate!* 你买那东西竟然花了50英镑! 你上当了, 老兄!
8 be/get done *BrE informal* to be caught by the police for doing something illegal, but usually not too serious【英, 非正式】〔因做不太严重的违法事情而〕被警察逮着: **[+for]** *I got done for speeding on the M1 last night.* 我昨晚因为在一号高速公路上超速行驶被警察逮住了。—see also 另见 **be hard done by** (HARD² (5))

done³ *interjection* used to agree to and accept the conditions of a deal 好, 行, 成交〔用于表示同意或接受某交易的条件〕: *"I'll give you $90 a day for the job." "Done!"* "这项工作我一天给你90美元。" "行!"

Don·e·gal /ˌdɑnɪ gɔl; ˌdɒnɪˈgɔːl/ a COUNTY in northwest Ireland, on the coast of the Atlantic Ocean 多尼戈尔郡〔爱尔兰西北部一郡, 位于大西洋沿岸〕

dong /dɑŋ; dɒŋ/ *n* [C] *taboo slang* the male sex organ【讳, 俚】男性性器官

Don Gio·van·ni /ˌdɑn dʒoˋvɑnɪ; ˌdɒn dʒəʊˈvɑːni/ **1** (1787) an OPERA by Mozart with words by Lorenzo Da Ponte, about a man called Don Giovanni who is known for having very many lovers. He kills the father of one of his former lovers, but does not feel guilty about his immoral behaviour. At the end of the opera he is taken down to hell by the ghost of the man he murdered.《唐·乔凡尼》〔(1787), 莫扎特创作的一部歌剧, 由洛伦佐·达·蓬特作词, 讲述一位名叫唐·乔凡尼的男子的故事。他拥有众多情人, 并以此出名。他杀死了一位旧情人的父亲, 但丝毫没有内疚感。在歌剧的末尾, 他被死者的灵魂带到地狱〕 **2** another name for Don Juan 唐·乔凡尼〔《唐璜》的别名〕

don·jon /ˈdɑndʒən; ˈdɒndʒən/ *n* [C] the strong main tower of a MEDIEVAL castle〔中世纪〕坚固的城堡主塔

Don Ju·an /ˌdɑn ˋdʒuən; ˌdɒn ˈhwɑːn/ *n* [C] a man who is good at persuading women to have sex with him 唐璜; 善于勾引女性的人, 风流浪荡子, 花花公子

don·key /ˈdɑŋkɪ; ˈdɒŋki/ *n* [C] **1** a grey or brown animal like a horse, but smaller and with long ears 驴 **2** a stupid person 蠢人, 笨蛋 **3 donkey's years** *BrE informal* a very long time【英, 非正式】很久, 多年: *It's donkey's years since I went to the pictures.* 我已经很久没看电影了。

CULTURAL NOTE 文化注释

People often think about donkeys as being STUBBORN (=they are determined to do what they want and it is difficult to make them do anything else). People also think that donkeys are strong and hard working because they can carry heavy loads for long distances over rough ground. A traditional activity in some UK SEASIDE towns such as Blackpool is for children to go on a ride on a donkey along the beach. In the US, the Democratic Party has a donkey as its party symbol. 人们常把驴看做是固执的, 也认为它强壮耐劳, 因为它能背负重物远涉崎岖道路。在英国一些滨海城镇, 如布莱克普, 有一项传统活动就是让孩子沿着海滩骑驴。在美国, 民主党把驴视作该党的标志。— see Cultural Note at SEASIDE 见 SEASIDE 文化注释

donkey der·by /ˈ· ·, ·ˈ/ *n* [C] *BrE* a race on donkeys done for amusement or to raise money【英】〔为娱乐或筹款而举办的〕骑驴大赛

donkey en·gine /ˈ· ·, ·ˈ/ *n* [C] a small additional engine used for special jobs, especially on a ship〔尤指船上的〕辅助发动机

donkey jack·et /ˈ· ·, ·ˈ/ *n* [C] *BrE* a short thick coat, usually very dark blue, that has a piece of leather or plastic across the shoulders【英】厚实的短大衣〔通常为深蓝色, 肩部有一块皮革或塑料〕—see picture at 参见 COAT¹ 图

don·key·work /ˈdɑŋkɪˌwɝk; ˈdɒŋkiwɜːk/ *n* [U] *informal* hard boring work【非正式】艰苦而乏味的工作; GRUNT WORK *AmE*【美】: *Why do I always have to do the donkeywork?* 为什么那些没意思的苦差事老是得由我来干?

Donne /dʌn; dʌn/, **John** (?1572-1631) an English poet famous for his love poetry, and for being the greatest writer of METAPHYSICAL poetry, which combines strong feelings with clever arrangements of words and ideas 多恩〔(?1572-1631), 英国诗人, 以写爱情诗著称, 是最伟大的玄学派诗人。他的诗歌将强烈的情感融入工巧的构思和谴词之中〕

don·nish /ˈdɑnɪʃ; ˈdɒnɪʃ/ *adj especially BrE* clever, serious, and more interested in ideas than real life【尤英】聪明而严肃的; 学究式的 —**donnishly** *adv*

do·nor /ˈdonɚ; ˈdəʊnə/ *n* [C] **1** a person, group etc that gives something, especially money, to an organization in order to help people 捐赠者: *Funding for the clinic has come mostly from private donors.* 诊所的资金大多来自私人捐赠者。**2** someone who gives a part of their body so that it can be used in the medical treatment of someone else 捐献器官者: *The search is under way for a suitable donor.* 正在寻找一个合适的器官捐献者。**3 donor card** a card that you carry to show that when you die, a doctor can take parts of your body to use in the medical treatment of someone else 器官捐赠卡〔随身携带, 上面写明死后器官可捐赠〕

do-noth·ing /ˈ· ·ˌ·/ *n* [C] *informal* a lazy person【非正式】懒人; 无所事事者

Don Quix·ote /ˌdɑn ˋkwɪksət; ˌdɒn ˈkwɪksət/ **1** the main character in the humorous book *Don Quixote de la Mancha* by Miguel de Cervantes. Don Quixote wants to be a KNIGHT like the characters he admires in old stories, but when he tries to copy their adventures and behaviour, he makes many stupid mistakes. 唐吉诃德〔米格尔·德·塞万提斯的幽默小说《唐吉诃德》中的主人公。他崇拜骑士传说中的人物, 也想成为一名骑士。然而, 在试图模仿骑士的冒险活动和行为举止时, 他却犯了不少愚蠢的错误〕 **2** someone who is determined to change what is wrong, but who does it in a way that is silly or not practical 愚侠; 唐吉诃德似的人物: 不切实际的理想主义者〔指一个人决意改变不正确的事情, 但做事方式却显愚笨或不切实际〕 —see 见 QUIXOTIC

don't /dont; dəʊnt/ **1** the short form of 缩略式= 'do not': *Don't worry!* 别担心! | *You know him, don't you?* 你认识他, 对不对? —see also 另见 **dos and don'ts** (DO³ (2)) **2** *spoken* an incorrect short form of 'does not'【口】〔does not 不正确的缩略式〕: *She don't like it.* 她不喜欢它。

do·nut /ˈdonʌt; ˈdəʊnʌt/ *n* [C] an American spelling of DOUGHNUT doughnut 的美式拼法

doo·dah /ˈduˌdɑ; ˈduːdɑː/ *BrE*【英】, **doo·dad** /ˈduˌdæd; ˈduːdæd/ *AmE*【美】 *n* [C] *informal* a small object whose name you have forgotten or do not know【非正式】〔忘记或不知名称的〕小东西, 小玩意儿: *Where's the control doodah for the TV?* 控制电视的那玩意哪去了?

doo·dle /ˈdudḷ; ˈduːdl/ *v* [I] to draw shapes, lines, or patterns without really thinking about what you are doing〔心不在焉地〕乱涂, 乱画: *I always doodle when I'm on the phone.* 我在打电话时总喜欢随手乱画点什么。—**doodle** *n* [C]

doo·dle·bug /ˈdudḷˌbʌg; ˈduːdlbʌg/ *n* [C] a flying bomb used by the Germans in World War II〔德军在第二次世界大战中使用的〕V 型飞弹

doo-doo /ˈdudu; ˈduːduː/ *n* [U] *informal* a word for solid waste from your body, used by or to children【非正式】〔儿语〕㞎㞎〔指粪便〕—**doo-doo** *v* [I]

doo·fer /ˈdufɚ; ˈduːfə/ also 又作 **doo·fah** /ˈdufə; ˈduːfə/ *n* [C] *informal* a small object whose name you have forgotten or do not know【非正式】〔忘记或不知名称的〕小东西, 小玩意儿

doo·fus /ˈdufəs; ˈduːfəs/ *n* [C] *AmE informal* a silly or stupid person【美, 非正式】蠢人; 笨蛋

doo·hick·ey /ˈduˌhɪkɪ; ˈduːˌhɪki/ *n* [C] *AmE informal* a small object whose name you have forgotten or do not know, especially a part of a machine【美, 非正式】〔忘记或不知其名称的〕小物件〔尤指机器的小部件〕

doo·lal·ly /duˋlælɪ; duːˈlæli/ *adj informal* crazy【非正式】疯狂的

Doo·lit·tle /ˈdulɪtḷ; ˈduːlɪtl/, **E·li·za** /ɪˈlaɪzə; ɪˈlaɪzə/ a character in the play *Pygmalion* by George Bernard Shaw and in the film *My Fair Lady*, which is based on Shaw's play. She is a working class London flower seller who is taught by Professor Henry Higgins how to speak and behave like a woman of the highest social class. 杜利特尔〔乔治·萧伯纳剧本《皮格马利翁》(又译《卖花女》)及据此改编的电影《窈窕淑女》中的人物。她是伦敦街头的卖花女, 属工人阶级。亨利·希金斯教授教她如何像上流社会的淑女一样说话和做事〕

doom¹ /dum; duːm/ *v* [T usually passive 一般用被动态] to make someone or something certain to fail, die, be destroyed etc 注定〔失败、死亡、毁灭等〕: **doom sth to sth** *The species is doomed to extinction.* 这一物种注定要灭绝。| **doom sb/sth to do sth**

Marx's theory was that capitalist economies are eventually doomed to collapse. 根据马克思的理论，资本主义的经济体系最终注定会崩溃。| **doomed to failure** *The marriage seems doomed to failure.* 这场婚姻似乎注定长不了。—**doomed** *adj*

doom² *n* [U] the end of something especially by destruction or death, that will soon come and that you cannot avoid〔不可避免的〕毁灭；死亡；终结；劫数：*a terrible sense of impending doom* 一种末日即将来临的骇人感觉 | **meet your doom** *Thousands of soldiers met their doom on this very field.* 数以千计的士兵就是在这个战场上丧生的。| **spell doom for** (=mean that something will end) 意味着〔某事〕将终结 *The budget cuts spelled doom for the mining community.* 缩减预算意味着这个矿区要完结了。| **doom and gloom** (=a feeling that the future will be terrible) 悲观情绪

Dooms·day /ˈdumzˌde; ˈduːmzdeɪ/ *n* [singular] **1 till/until Doomsday** *informal* forever【非正式】直到永远：*You could wait till Doomsday and he'd never show up.* 你可以永远等下去，但他是不会出现的。**2** the last day of the Earth's existence 世界末日

Doomsday Book, The /ˈ· · ,·/ another spelling of *The Domesday Book*《末日审判书》〔The Domesday Book 的另一个拼法〕

doom·ster /ˈdumstɚ; ˈduːmstə/ *n* [C] *informal* someone who always thinks something bad is going to happen【非正式】预言灾难者，末日论者

Doones·bu·ry /ˈdunzbɛrɪ; ˈduːnzbəri/ a humorous US CARTOON STRIP (=a set of drawings that tell a story in a newspaper or magazine) about politics and life in the US《杜恩斯比利》〔反映美国政治和生活方式的连环漫画〕

1 1 **door** /dɔr; dɔː/ *n* [C] **1** the large flat object that you open and close at the entrance to a building, room, vehicle etc 门：**open/close/shut/slam the door** *Could you open the door for me?* 请你帮我开门好吗？| *Close the door behind you.* 进来时把门关上。| **knock on/at the door** *Knock on the door and see if they're home.* 敲一下门看他们在不在家。| **kitchen/bathroom/bedroom etc door** *Don't forget to lock the office door.* 别忘了把办公室的门锁上。| **front/back/side door** *Is the front door open?* 前门是开着的吗？| **revolving/sliding/swing doors** *Nathan got stuck in the revolving doors!* 内森被卡在旋转门里了！—compare 比较 GATE¹ (1) —see picture on page A2 参见 A2 页图 **2** the space made by an open door; DOORWAY 门口，出入口，门道：*Rick turned around and ran out of the door.* 里克一转身跑出了门。| *I glanced through the open door.* 我从敞开的门往外望了一眼。**3 at the door** if someone is at the door they are waiting for you to open it so they can come inside 在门口，在门外：*There's somebody at the door.* 门外有人。**4 answer the door** to open the door to see who is there 应门 **5 show/see sb to the door** to take someone to the main way out of a building 把某人送到门口：*Good-bye, Mr Carter. My secretary will show you to the door.* 再见，卡特先生。我的秘书会送你到门口。**6 two/three doors down etc** a place that is a particular number of houses or buildings away from where you are 再走两/三个门面等：*The Rigbys live two doors down from us.* 里格比住的地方和我们家隔两户。**7 (from) door to door a)** between one place and another 两地之间：*My commute takes forty minutes, door to door.* 从我家到工作的地方需要四十分钟。**b)** going to each house in a street or area to sell something, collect money or ask for votes 挨家挨户〔推销东西、筹钱或拉选票〕：*Joe sold vacuum cleaners door to door for years.* 乔多年来一直挨家挨户推销吸尘器。—see also 另见 DOOR-TO-DOOR **8 out of doors** outside; OUTDOORS 外面，户外，室外 **9 behind closed doors** where other people cannot see you; secretly 秘密地，不让别人看见地：*The meeting took place behind closed doors.* 会议是秘密举行的。**10 show sb the door** to make it clear to someone that you want them to leave 下逐客令：*I'm warning you, if he gets drunk I'll show him the door.* 我警告你，如果他喝醉了，我就撵他走。**11 lay sth at sb's door** to say that something is someone's fault 把某事归咎于某人 **12 be on the door** to work at the entrance to a theatre, club, etc collecting tickets 在〔剧院、俱乐部等〕门口把门〔收票〕**13 an open door policy** willingness to allow people to come in 开放政策〔允许人们进来〕：*an open door policy for immigration* 对移民的开放政策 **14 open doors for sb** to give someone an opportunity they would not have had otherwise 给某人提供不易得到的机会：*I think your new job will really open doors for you.* 我认为你的新工作确实会为你提供机会。**15 open the door to** to make something possible 使…有可能发生：*You're opening the door to trouble by hitchhiking.* 你搭便车会惹麻烦上身的。**16 shut/close the door on** to make something impossible 使…不可能发生：*Sasha's accident shut the door on her ballet career.* 莎莎所遭遇的事故使她的芭蕾舞生涯永远结束了。—see also 另见 BACK DOOR, FRONT DOOR, NEXT DOOR, **at death's door** (DEATH (8))

door·bell /ˈdɔrˌbɛl; ˈdɔːbel/ *n* [C] a button outside a house that you push to make a sound so that people inside know you are there 门铃：**ring the doorbell** (=push the button) 按门铃

do-or-die /ˌ· · ˈ·/ *adj* very determined 拼死的：*a do-or-die attitude* 破釜沉舟的态度

door·jamb /ˈdɔrˌdʒæm; ˈdɔːdʒæm/ *n* [C] one of two upright posts on either side of a doorway; DOORPOST 门柱；门侧柱

door·keep·er /ˈdɔrˌkipɚ; ˈdɔːˌkiːpə/ *n* [C] someone who guards the main door of a large building and lets people in and out 看门人，守门人，门卫

door·knob /ˈdɔrˌnɑb; ˈdɔːnɒb/ *n* [C] a round handle that you turn to open a door 球形门把手

door·knock·er /ˈdɔrˌnɑkɚ; ˈdɔːˌnɒkə/ *n* [C] a heavy metal ring or bar on a door that visitors use to knock with 门环；敲门器

door·man /ˈdɔrˌmæn; ˈdɔːmæn/ *n plural* **doormen** /-mɛn; -men/ [C] a man in a hotel or theatre who watches the door, helps people find taxis, and usually wears a uniform〔酒店、剧院的〕门卫，门童 —compare 比较 PORTER (2)

door·mat /ˈdɔrˌmæt; ˈdɔːmæt/ *n* [C] **1** a piece of material just inside a door for you to clean your shoes on〔门口的〕擦鞋垫 **2** *informal* someone who lets other people treat them badly and never complains【非正式】逆来顺受的人，甘受屈辱的人：*Ted lets Tracy treat him like a doormat.* 特德甘心忍受特蕾西的欺侮。

door·nail /ˈdɔrˌnel; ˈdɔːneɪl/ *n* [singular] —see 见 **dead as a doornail** (DEAD¹ (1))

door·plate /ˈdɔrˌplet; ˈdɔːpleɪt/ *n* [C] a flat piece of metal fixed to the door of a house or building showing the name of the person or company that works inside〔钉在门上的金属〕门牌，户名牌

door·post /ˈdɔrˌpost; ˈdɔːpəʊst/ *n* [C] one of two upright posts on either side of a doorway; DOORJAMB 门柱，门侧柱

door prize /ˈ· ·/ *n* [C] *AmE* a prize given to someone who has the winning number on their ticket for a show, dance, or party【美】〔演出、舞会、晚会的〕门票对号奖

door·sill /ˈdɔrˌsɪl; ˈdɔːˌsɪl/ *n* [C] the part of a door frame that you step across when you go through a doorway 门槛

door·step¹ /ˈdɔrˌstɛp; ˈdɔːstep/ *n* [C] **1** a step just outside a door to a house or building 门阶 **2 on your doorstep** very near to where you live or are staying 在某人住所[逗留处]近旁：*Wow! You've got the beach right on your doorstep!* 哇！你住的地方离海滩这么近！**3** *BrE informal* a very thick piece of bread cut from a loaf【英，非正式】厚面包片

doorstep² *v* [I] if politicians wanting votes or JOURNALISTS looking for a news story go doorstepping, they visit people who do not want to see them〔政客〕上门〔拉选票〕；〔记者〕造访〔找新闻等〕

door·stop /ˈdɔrˌstɑp; ˈdɔːstɒp/ also 又作 **door·stop·per** /-ˌstɑpɚ; -ˌstɒpə/ *n* [C] **1** something you put under or against a door to keep it open〔让门保持敞开的〕制门器 **2** a rubber object fixed to a wall to stop a door hitting it when it is opened〔防止门撞墙的〕门碰头

door-to-door /ˌ· · ˈ·◂/ *adj* visiting each house in a street or area, usually to sell something, collect money, or ask for votes 挨家挨户的

door·way /ˈdɔrˌwe; ˈdɔːweɪ/ *n* [C] the space where the door opens into a room or building 门口，出入口：*I looked up and there was Paolo, standing in the doorway.* 我一抬头，看见保罗站在门口。

door·yard /ˈdɔrˌjɑrd; ˈdɔːjɑːd/ *n* [C] *AmE* an area in front of the door of a house【美】门前庭院

doo·zy, doozie /ˈduzɪ; ˈduːzi/ *n* [C] *AmE informal* something that is so good, bad, strange etc that you can hardly believe it【美，非正式】极好[极坏、极奇怪]的东西：*I've heard lies before, but that one was a real doozy!* 以前我也听到过各种谎言，但那个谎言才真叫离谱！

dope¹ /dop; dəʊp/ *n informal*【非正式】**1** [U] a drug that is not legal, especially MARIJUANA 毒品〔尤指大麻〕：*a dope dealer* 毒品贩子 **2** [C] someone who is stupid 蠢人，傻瓜：*Pam, you dope!* 帕姆，你这个傻瓜！**3 the dope on** new information about someone or something, especially information that not many people know 有关…的内幕消息：*Give me all the dope on the new teacher.* 给我讲讲那个新老师的所有情况。**4** [U] medicine, especially medicine that makes you sleep easily〔尤指使人易入睡的〕药物

dope² *v* [T] *informal*【非正式】**1** also 又作 **dope up** to give someone a drug, often in their food or drink, to make them sleep

or feel better 使服麻醉品[药品]〔通常放在食物或饮料中〕: *They dope the elephants in order to tag them.* 他们把大象麻醉了，以便为它们挂上标签。| *If we dope you up enough you'll still be able to sing with a cold.* 如果我们给你服用足量的药剂，即使你感冒了，仍然可以唱歌。**2** to give an animal a drug that makes it perform better in a race or competition 给〔动物〕服用兴奋剂

dope·head /ˈdop,hɛd; ˈdəʊphed/ *n* [C] *slang* someone who takes a lot of drugs【俚】吸毒鬼；白面客

Dop·ey /ˈdopɪ; ˈdəʊpi/ one of the seven DWARFs in the story of Snow White. He is called Dopey because he is rather stupid. 糊涂蛋〔《白雪公主》中的七个小矮人之一，因糊涂而得名〕

dopey, dopy *adj informal*【非正式】**1** slow to react mentally or physically, as if you have taken a drug 昏昏沉沉的，迷迷糊糊的: *I'm still a little dopey from the anesthetic.* 由于麻醉药的作用，我还有点昏昏沉沉的。**2** slightly stupid 有些愚笨的: *Dan gave me a dopey grin.* 丹向我咧嘴傻笑了一下。

dop·pel·gang·er /ˈdɑpḷ,gæŋɚ; ˈdɒpəlgæŋə/ *n* [C] *German*【德】**1** a spirit that looks exactly like a living person〔外形和活人一样的〕幽灵 **2** someone who looks exactly like someone else〔与另一人〕外貌极相似的人

do·py /ˈdopɪ; ˈdəʊpi/ *adj* another spelling of DOPEY dopey 的另一种拼法

Dor·ches·ter /ˈdɔrtʃɛstɚ; ˈdɔːtʃɪstə/ a market town in Dorset, southern England. The local government of Dorset is based there and the writer Thomas Hardy was born nearby. 多切斯特〔英格兰南部多西特郡一集市城镇。这里是多西特郡地方政府所在地，作家托马斯·哈代出生在附近〕

Dor·dogne, the /dɔrˋdoɪn; dɔːˈdɔɪn/ an area in southwest France around the River Dordogne, which is a popular place for tourists 多尔多涅〔法国西南部一地区，位于多尔多涅河一带，为著名旅游胜地〕

Do·ri·an Gray /,dɔrɪən ˋgre; ,dɔːriən ˈgreɪ/ the main character in the NOVEL *The Picture of Dorian Gray* by Oscar Wilde 道林·格雷〔奥斯卡·王尔德小说《道林·格雷的肖像》的主人公〕

Dor·ic /ˈdɔrɪk; ˈdɒrɪk/ *adj* in the oldest and most simple of the Greek building styles 陶立克式的〔古希腊建筑中最古老的、最简单的式样〕: *a Doric column* 陶立克式圆柱 —compare 比较 CORINTHIAN, IONIC

dork /dɔrk; dɔːk/ *n* [C] *AmE informal* someone who you think is stupid, because they behave strangely or wear strange clothes【美，非正式】傻瓜，呆子: *You look a real dork in that outfit.* 你穿上那套衣服看起来傻透了。—**dorky** *adj*

dorm /dɔrm; dɔːm/ *n* [C] *informal* a dormitory【非正式】寝室；宿舍

dor·mant /ˈdɔrmənt; ˈdɔːmənt/ *adj* not active or not growing at the present time but able to be active later 蛰伏的，休眠的: *The seeds remain dormant in the soil all winter.* 整个冬天种子在土壤里呈休眠状态。| **lie dormant** *Stress may activate the virus which has lain dormant in the blood.* 紧张有可能激活潜伏在血液中的病毒。—**dormancy** *n* [U]

dor·mer /ˈdɔrmɚ; ˈdɔːmə/ also 又作 **dormer win·dow** /ˈ‥ ,‥/ *n* [C] a window built upright in the slope of a roof〔建在斜屋顶上的〕竖天窗；老虎窗；屋顶窗

dor·mi·to·ry¹ /ˈdɔrmə,torɪ; ˈdɔːmḷtəri/ *n* [C] **1** a large room in a BOARDING SCHOOL OR HOSTEL for several people to sleep in 宿舍；寝室 **2** *AmE* a large building in a college or university where students live【美】〔大学里的〕学生宿舍楼; HALL OF RESIDENCE *BrE*【英】

dormitory² *adj* [only before noun 仅用于名词前] *especially BrE* a dormitory town is a place from which people travel into a city to work every day【尤英】〔指每天去市区工作的人的〕郊外住宅区的

dor·mo·bile /ˈdɔrmə,bil; ˈdɔːməbiːl/ *n* [C] *trademark BrE* a vehicle big enough to live in when you travel, with cooking equipment and beds in it【商标，英】野营车〔旅行时供居住用，内有烹饪用具、床〕

dor·mouse /ˈdɔr,maus; ˈdɔːmaʊs/ *n* [C] a small European forest animal with a long furry tail 榛睡鼠〔一种欧洲森林小动物，长有毛茸茸的长尾巴〕

dor·sal /ˈdɔrsḷ; ˈdɔːsəl/ *adj* [only before noun 仅用于名词前] *technical* on or related to the back of an animal or fish【术语】〔动物或鱼〕背部的: *a shark's dorsal fin* 鲨鱼的背鳍 —see picture at 参见 FISH¹ 图

Dor·set /ˈdɔrsɪt; ˈdɔːsḷt/ a COUNTY in southwest England, with many popular holiday towns on its coast. The writer Thomas Hardy set most of his NOVELs in Dorset, which he called 'Wessex'. 多塞特郡〔英格兰西南部一郡，沿海有不少有名的度假小镇。作家托马斯·哈代的大部分小说以该郡为背景，书中称"威塞克斯"〕

do·ry /ˈdɔrɪ; ˈdɔːri/ *n* **1** [C] a rowing boat that has a flat bottom and is used for fishing 平底小渔船 **2** [C,U] a flat sea fish that can be eaten, or the flesh of this fish 海鲂；海鲂肉

DOS /dɑs; dɒs/ *n* [U] *trademark* Disk Operating System; SOFTWARE that is loaded onto a computer system to make all the different parts work together【商标】磁盘操作系统

dos·age /ˈdosɪdʒ; ˈdəʊsɪdʒ/ *n* [C usually singular 一般用单数] the amount of medicine that you should take at one time〔一次用药的〕剂量，服用量: *Do not exceed the recommended dosage.* 不要超过规定的剂量。

dose¹ /dos; dəʊs/ *n* [C] **1** a measured amount of a medicine〔药物的〕一剂，一服；一次服用量: [+of] *a dose of antibiotics* 一剂抗生素药物 **2** an amount of something unpleasant that you experience at one time 一次；一番；一回〔指不愉快的经历〕: [+of] *Workers were exposed to a large dose of radiation.* 工人们暴露在大剂量的辐射之下。| *a bad dose of flu* 一次严重的流感 | **in small doses** (=for a short time) 一小会儿，短时间地 *I can only tolerate Joseph in small doses.* 我只能容忍约瑟夫一小会儿。**3 like a dose of salts** *BrE informal* very quickly and easily【英，非正式】很快且很轻易地: *The new owners went through the company like a dose of salts, stripping it of its assets.* 那些新来的老板们很快就把公司的财产侵吞一空。**4 have a dose** *slang* to be infected with VENEREAL DISEASE【俚】得性病，染上花柳病

dose² also 又作 **dose up** *v* [T] to give someone medicine 给〔某人〕服药: **dose sb with** *Sumi dosed herself with aspirin and went to bed.* 苏米自己服用了阿司匹林，然后就上床睡觉了。

dosh /dɑʃ; dɒʃ/ *n* [U] *BrE spoken* money【英口】钞票，钱

do-si-do /,do sɪ ˋdo; ,dəʊ si ˈdəʊ/ *n* [singular] an action in COUNTRY DANCING in which partners pass each other sideways〔乡村舞蹈中〕舞伴互从身侧背对背交换位置的舞步 —**do-si-do** *v* [I]

doss¹ /dɑs; dɒs/ *v*

doss around/about *phr v* [I] *BrE informal* to do very little【英，非正式】几乎不做什么事；闲混: *We just dossed around all day Saturday.* 星期六一整天我们是在闲散中度过的。

doss down *phr v* [I] *BrE informal* to sleep somewhere that is not your usual place or not a real bed【英，非正式】〔在别处〕过夜；将就着睡: *Hundreds dossed down in the theatre because of the blizzards.* 由于暴风雪，数百人只好在剧院里将就着过夜。

doss² *n* **a doss** *BrE informal* work that does not need much effort【英，非正式】不费力的工作: *This job's a real doss.* 这份工作真是轻松得很。

doss·er /ˈdɑsɚ; ˈdɒsə/ *n* [C] *BrE informal* someone who has nowhere to live and sleeps in the street or in cheap HOSTELS【英，非正式】居无定所的人，露宿街头者；住廉价客栈的人

doss-house /ˈ· ·/ *n* [C] *BrE slang* a place where people who have nowhere to live can stay cheaply【英俚】〔供居无定所者居住的〕廉价客栈; FLOPHOUSE *AmE*【美】

dos·si·er /ˈdɑsɪ,e; ˈdɒsieɪ/ *n* [C] a set of papers containing detailed information on a person or subject; FILE¹ (1)〔有关一人或一事的〕档案，卷宗: **keep a dossier on** *The secret police kept dossiers on all opponents of the regime.* 秘密警察对所有反对当局的人都存有档案。

dost /dʌst; dʌst/ *v* **thou dost** *old use or biblical*【旧或圣经】= you do

Dos·toy·ev·sky /,dɑstəˋjɛfskɪ; ,dɒstɔɪˈefski/, **Fy·o·dor** /ˈfiədɔr; ˈfiːədɔː/ also 又作 **Dostoevsky** /,dɑstəˋjɛfskɪ; ,dɒstɔɪˈefski/ (1821-81) a Russian writer who many people consider to be one of the greatest writers ever. His NOVELs include *Crime and Punishment*, and *The Brothers Karamazov*. 陀思妥耶夫斯基〔(1821-1881)，俄国作家。许多人认为，他是有史以来最伟大的作家之一。他的小说有《罪与罚》和《卡拉马佐夫兄弟》〕

dot¹ /dɑt; dɒt/ *n* [C] **1** a small round mark or spot 点，小圆点 **2 on the dot** *informal* exactly at a particular time【非正式】正好在某一时间: **on the dot of five (o'clock)/at five (o'clock) on the dot** *Mr Green arrived at six on the dot.* 格林先生正好在6点钟到达。**3** something that looks like a small spot because it is so far away〔因相距很远〕看似一个小点的物体: *The plane was just a dot in the sky.* 飞机当时只是天空中的一个小点。**4** a short sound or flash of light used when sending messages by MORSE CODE 摩尔斯电码的点 —compare 比较 DASH² —see also 另见 **the year dot** (YEAR (11))

dot² *v* **dotted, dotting** [T] **1** to mark something by putting a dot on it or above it 在〔某物上面或上方〕加点: *She never dots her i's.* 她从来不在i上面加点。—see picture on page A16 参见 A16 页图 **2** [often passive 常用被动态] to spread things over a wide area and quite far apart〔星罗棋布地〕布满；分布: **be dotted with** *The lake was dotted with sailboats.* 湖面上星星点点地密布着帆船。| **be dotted about/around etc** *The company now has over*

20 stores dotted around the country. 该公司现有二十多家商店遍布全国。**3** to put a very small amount of something on a surface or in several places on a surface 点；点缀：*Dot some rouge on your cheeks, then blend carefully.* 往你的脸颊上点些胭脂，然后再仔细抹匀。**4 dot the i's and cross the t's** *informal* to pay attention to all the details when you are finishing something【非正式】〔即将完成某事时〕注意完成所有的细节：*Well, we haven't dotted the i's and crossed the t's, but the contract's nearly ready.* 我们还没有把合同的细节弄好，但已经快拟好了。—see also 另见 DOTTED LINE

do·tage /ˈdotɪdʒ; ˈdəʊtɪdʒ/ *n* **in your dotage** in your old age 在某人之老年，年迈昏聩

dote /dot; dəʊt/ *v*

dote on/upon sb *phr v* [T] to love someone and to show this by your actions 溺爱，宠爱：*I can't help doting on my granddaughter.* 我不免宠爱我的孙女。—**doting** *adj* [only before noun 仅用于名词前]：*a doting parent* 溺爱孩子的父亲[母亲] —**dotingly** *adv*

doth /dʌθ; dʌθ/ *old use or biblical*【旧或圣经】= does

dot-ma·trix print·er /ˈ· ··, ·ˈ·/ *n* [C] a machine connected to a computer that prints letters, numbers etc using many small dots 点阵式打印机

dot·ted line /ˌ·· ˈ·/ *n* [C] **1** a series of printed or drawn DOTs that form a line 虚线，点线：*Cut along the dotted lines.* 沿虚线剪下。**2 sign on the dotted line** *informal* to officially agree to something, especially by signing a contract【非正式】正式同意〔尤指在合同上签字〕

dot·ty /ˈdɑtɪ; ˈdɒti/ *adj informal especially BrE*【非正式，尤英】**1** slightly crazy or likely to behave strangely 疯疯癫癫的；〔行为〕古怪的 **2 dotty about sb/sth** very fond of or interested in someone or something 对某人/某物喜爱的[感兴趣的，着迷的]：*Gemma's dotty about horses.* 杰玛非常喜欢马。

1 2 **doub·le¹** /ˈdʌbl; ˈdʌbəl/ *adj*

1 ▶OF TWO PARTS 两部分的◀ consisting of two parts that are similar or exactly the same 成对的，成双的：*You can't park on double yellow lines.* 你不可以在双黄线上停车。

2 double l/s/9 etc *BrE spoken* used when you are spelling a word or telling someone a number, to show that a letter or number is repeated【英口】两个l/s/9等〔用在拼写单词或告诉某人某个数字时，表示应该重复某个字母或数字〕：*My number is 869 34 double 2.* 我的号码是8693422。| *That's Robbins with a double 'b'.* 是有两个"b"的Robbins。

3 ▶TWICE AS BIG 两倍大◀ twice as big, twice as much, or twice as many as usual, or twice as big, much, or many as something else 双倍的，两倍的：*Leave the dough in a warm place to rise until it is double in bulk.* 把湿面团放在暖和的地方发酵，一直发到以前两倍那么大。| *I'll have a double whisky please.* 我要一杯双份威士忌。

4 ▶FOR TWO PEOPLE 双人的◀ made to be used by two people 供两人使用的：*a double room* 双人房间 —compare 比较 SINGLE¹ (4)

5 ▶WITH TWO DIFFERENT USES 双重用途的◀ combining two different uses or qualities; DUAL 有两种用途的，双重的：*a double-action corkscrew* 双重功能的瓶塞钻 | *the double advantage of money and a good education* 既有钱又受过良好教育的双重优势

6 ▶DECEIVING 欺诈的◀ seeming to be one thing while actually being another; deceiving 两面派的，表里不一的；欺诈的：*There was a double meaning in Sybil's words.* 西比尔的话口不对心。| **lead a double life** (=pretend to be one type of person but really be another) 过着双重人格的生活

7 ▶FLOWER 花◀ a double flower has more than the usual number of PETALs 双瓣的；重瓣的 —see also 另见 DOUBLY, **double figures** (FIGURE¹ (1b))

double² *n*

1 ▶TWICE THE SIZE 两倍◀ [C,U] something that is twice the size, quantity, value, or strength of something else 两倍，双倍(的量、数)：*Scotch and water, please – make it a double.* 请来苏格兰威士忌加水——要双份的。| *"What did they offer you?" "Ten thousand." "I'll give you double."* "他们给你什么？""一万块钱。""我给你这个数的两倍。"

2 ▶SIMILAR PERSON 相似的人◀ [C] someone who looks very much like someone else 极为相似的人：*Caroline's her mother's double.* 卡罗琳和她母亲长得一模一样。

3 ▶IN FILMS 在电影中◀ [C] an actor who takes the place of another actor in a film because the acting involves something very dangerous 替身演员：*a stunt double* 特技替身演员

4 at the double *BrE*【英】，**on the double** *AmE*【美】very quickly and without any delay 飞快地，快步地：*The firemen came around on the double.* 消防人员快速赶来。

5 ▶TENNIS 网球◀ doubles [U] a game played between two pairs of players 双打：*the men's doubles* 男子双打 —compare 比较 **singles** (SINGLE² (3)) —see also 另见 MIXED DOUBLES

6 double or nothing *AmE*【美】，**double or quits** *BrE*【英】a decision in a game when you must decide to do something that will either win you twice as much money or make you lose it all〔下注的一种方式〕要么赢双倍，要么输得精光；一赌决输赢

7 ▶IN RACING 在比赛中◀ [C] a BET² (1) on the results of two races in which any money won on the first race is risked on the second 复式押注〔下注于两场比赛，第一场若赢将自动转押到第二场上〕

8 ▶A THROW 投掷◀ [C] a throw in the game of darts (DART² (2)) that hits a point between the two outer circles on the board, and has twice the usual value〔投镖游戏中的〕投中加倍记分圈

9 ▶A HIT 击打◀ [C] a hit which allows the BATTER² (3) in BASEBALL to reach second BASE¹ (8)〔棒球的〕二垒打

double³ *v* **1** [I,T] to become twice as much or as many, or to make something twice as big (使)加倍：*Unemployment more than doubled in 1921.* 失业率在1921年增加了一倍多。| *The Federal government has doubled its tax on liquor.* 联邦政府把酒税提高了一倍。**2** also 又作 **double sth over** [T] to fold something in half 把某物对折：*Take a sheet of paper and double it.* 拿一张纸，然后把它对折。**3** [I] if a BATTER² (3) in a game of BASEBALL doubles, he hits the ball far enough to get to second BASE¹ (8)〔棒球比赛中〕击出二垒打 **4 double your fists** *AmE* to curl your fingers tightly to make FISTs ready to fight【美】握紧拳头〔准备打斗〕

double as sb/sth *phr v* [T] to have a second use, job, or purpose as something else 兼任，兼作：*Our local police chief doubles as the fire chief.* 我们当地的警察局长兼任消防队长。

double back *phr v* [I] to turn around and go back the way you have come 原路折回：*I doubled back along the main highway to LA.* 我沿着去洛杉矶的干线公路折回。

double up *phr v* **1** also 又作 **double over** [I,T **double** sb **up**] to suddenly bend at the waist because you are laughing too much or are in pain and cannot stand up〔笑、痛得〕弯下腰；使…直不起身：*Emilio doubled over, grabbing his leg.* 埃米利奥弯下身，抱住自己的腿。| **be doubled up/over with** *We leant against the table, doubled over with laughter.* 我们靠在桌边，笑得直不起身。**2** [I] to share something, especially a bedroom〔尤指卧室的〕共用：*There aren't enough textbooks. Can you double up?* 课本不够了，你们能合着用吗？| [**+with sb**] *You'll have to double up with Susie while Aunt Clara is visiting.* 克拉拉姨妈来的时候你得和苏茜同住一屋。

double⁴ *adv* **1 see double** to have something wrong with your eyes so that you see two things instead of one〔因眼睛有问题〕看到重影：*I was feeling dizzy and seeing double.* 我感到头晕，看东西都是双的。**2 be bent double** to be bent over a long way 弯得很厉害：*The trees were almost bent double in the wind.* 树木被风吹得快要折断了。**3 fold sth double** to fold something in half to make it twice as thick 将某物对折〔使其比以前厚一倍〕

double⁵ *predeterminer* twice as much or twice as many 是…两倍那么多：*It's worth double the amount I paid for it.* 这东西值我所付价钱的两倍。

double-act /ˈ·· ·/ *n* [C] two actors, especially COMEDIANS, who perform together 一起演出的两个演员〔尤指滑稽演员〕

double a·gent /ˌ·· ˈ··/ *n* [C] someone who finds out an enemy country's secrets for their own country but who also gives secrets to the enemy 双重间谍 —compare 比较 SPY¹

double-bar·relled *BrE*【英】，**double-barreled** *AmE*【美】/ˌ·· ˈ··◂/ *adj* **1** a double-barrelelled gun has two places where the BULLETs come out〔枪、炮〕双管的 **2** *BrE* a double-barrelled family name has two parts【英】〔姓氏〕由两个姓组成的；复姓的 **3** *AmE* with two purposes【美】双重目的的：*a double-barreled plan* 双重目的的计划 **4** *AmE* very strong or using a lot of force【美】强有力的；使用大量武力的：*a double-barreled attack* 猛烈的进攻[抨击]

double bass /ˌdʌbl̩ ˈbes; ˌdʌbəl ˈbeɪs/ also 又作 **bass** *n* [C] a very large musical instrument shaped like a VIOLIN that the musician plays standing up 低音提琴

double bed /ˌ·· ˈ·/ *n* [C] a bed made for two people to sleep in 双人床 —see picture at 参见 BED¹ 图

double bill /ˌ·· ˈ·/ *n* [C] a cinema or theatre performance in which two films or plays are shown one after the other 两部电影[戏剧]连续放映[演出]；DOUBLE FEATURE *AmE*【美】

double bind /ˌ·· ˈ·/ *n* [C usually singular 一般用单数] a situation in which any choice you make will have unpleasant results 进退两难的困境

double-blind /ˌ·· ˈ·◂/ *adj technical* a double-blind EXPERIMENT¹ (1) or study compares two or more groups in which nei-

ther the scientists nor the people being studied know which group is being tested and which group is not【术语】〔两组或多组进行比较的试验或研究中〕双盲的〔指科学家和被试验者均不知道哪一组正接受测试〕

double bluff /ˌ··ˈ·/ *n* [C] an attempt to deceive someone by telling them the truth, hoping that they will think you are lying 虚实并用的诈骗术〔告诉某人实情并希望此人以为有诈〕

double boil·er /ˌ··ˈ··/ *n* [C] a pot for cooking food, consisting of one pan resting on top of another pan with hot water in it 双层蒸锅

double-book /ˌ··ˈ·/ *v* [I,T] to promise the same seat in a theatre, on a plane, etc to more than one person 重复预订〔同一座位等〕—**double-booking** *n* [U]

double-breast·ed /ˌ··ˈ··◂/ *adj* a double-breasted jacket, coat etc has two sets of buttons〔夹克、大衣等〕双排纽扣的, 对襟的 —compare 比较 SINGLE-BREASTED —see picture on page A17 参见 A17 页图

double-check /ˌ··ˈ·/ *v* [I,T] to check something again so that you are completely sure 复查, 复核

double chin /ˌ··ˈ·/ *n* [C] a fold of loose skin under someone's chin that looks like a second chin 双下巴 —see picture on page A6 参见 A6 页图

double cream /ˌ··ˈ·/ *n* [U] *BrE* very thick cream【英】高脂浓[厚]奶油 —compare 比较 SINGLE CREAM

double-cross /ˌ··ˈ·/ *v* [T] to cheat someone, especially after you have already agreed to do something dishonest with them〔尤指在已答应和某人一起干不诚实之事后〕出卖, 欺骗〔某人〕: *Shorty's murder was blamed on a gang he'd double-crossed in the past.* 矮子的被害归咎于他以前出卖过的一个团伙。—**double cross** *n* [C] —**double-crosser** *n* [C]

double date /ˌ··ˈ·/ *n* [C] *especially AmE* an arranged social meeting for two couples (COUPLE[1](2))【尤美】为两对男女安排的社交约会 —**double-date** *v* [I,T]

double-deal·er /ˌ··ˈ··/ *n* [C] *informal* someone who deceives other people【非正式】表里不一的人, 奸诈之徒 —**double-dealing** *n* [U]

double-deck·er /ˌ··ˈ··◂/ *n* [C] **1** a bus with two levels 双层公共汽车 **2** a SANDWICH[1] (1) made with three pieces of bread leaving two spaces to be filled with food〔三层面包夹两层菜或肉的〕双层三明[文]治

double-di·git /ˌ··ˈ··/ *adj AmE* related to the numbers 10 to 99, especially as a PERCENTAGE【美】两位数的〔尤指百分比〕: *double-digit inflation* 两位数的通货膨胀率 —see also 另见 DOUBLE FIGURES

double-dip[1] /ˌ··ˈ·/ *n* [C] *AmE* an ice-cream CONE[1] (4) with two balls of ice cream【美】双球冰淇淋甜筒

double-dip[2] *v* [I] *AmE* to collect pay or money from two places at once, usually in a way that is not legal or not approved of; MOONLIGHT[2] (2)【美】同时从两处领取报酬〔通常以非法或不为人所赞同的方式〕

double-dutch /ˌ··ˈ··/ *n* [U] **1** *informal* speech or writing that you cannot understand; nonsense【非正式】难懂的言语[文章]; 莫名其妙的话 **2** *AmE* a skipping (SKIP[1] (1)) game using two long ropes【美】〔使用两条长绳的〕跳绳游戏

double du·ty /ˌ··ˈ··/ *n* [U] *AmE*【美】**do double duty** to do more than one job or be used for more than one thing at the same time 有双重作用, 可以两用: *The lids on the camping pans do double duty as plates.* 野营锅的盖子又可作盘子用。

double-edged /ˌ··ˈ·◂/ *adj* **1** with two very different meanings 有两种不同含义的, 模棱两可的: *a double-edged remark* 模棱两可的话 **2** with two cutting edges 双刃的: *a double-edged sword* 双刃剑

double en·ten·dre /ˌdubḷ ɑnˈtɑndrə; ˌduːbl ɒnˈtɒndrə/ *n* [C] *French* a word or phrase that may be understood in two different ways, one of which is often sexual【法】〔常带有猥亵含意的〕双关语

double fault /ˌ··ˈ·/ *n* [C] two mistakes, one after another, when you are serving (SERVE[1] (10)) in tennis, that make you lose a point 双误〔网球连续两次发球失误〕

double fea·ture /ˌ··ˈ··/ *n* [C] *AmE* a cinema performance in which two films are shown one after the other; DOUBLE BILL【美】两部影片连续放映

double fig·ures /ˌ··ˈ··/ *n* [plural] *BrE* the numbers from 10 to 99【英】两位数: *The death toll is thought to have reached double figures.* 据信, 死亡人数达到了两位数。—see also 另见 DOUBLE-DIGIT

double first /ˌ··ˈ·/ *n* [C] a British university degree in which a student reaches the highest standard in two subjects〔英国大学中的〕双优学位〔两门学科获得优等成绩〕

double-glaz·ing /ˌ··ˈ··/ *n* [U] *especially BrE* glass on a window or door in two separate sheets with a space between them, in order to keep noise out and heat in【尤英】〔窗或门的〕双层玻璃 —**double-glaze** *v* [T]

> **CULTURAL NOTE 文化注释**
>
> In Britain, there are a lot of companies selling double-glazed windows and doors, and double-glazing salesmen are known for putting a lot of pressure on people to buy their product. 在英国, 很多公司销售双层玻璃门窗, 推销员以缠着顾客强卖自己的产品而著称。

double-head·er /ˌ··ˈ··/ *n* [C] *AmE* two BASEBALL games played one after the other【美】连续举行的两场棒球赛

double he·lix /ˌ··ˈ··/ *n* [C] *technical* a shape consisting of two parallel spirals (SPIRAL[2] (1)) that twist around the same centre, found especially in the structure of DNA【术语】双螺旋〔尤指脱氧核糖核酸结构中的双螺旋结构〕

double in·dem·ni·ty /ˌ··ˈ····/ *n* [U] *AmE law* a feature of a life insurance POLICY that allows double the value of the contract to be paid in the case of death by accident【美, 法律】〔人寿保险的〕双倍赔偿〔如遇意外死亡〕

double jeop·ar·dy /ˌ··ˈ···/ *n* [C] *AmE law* the act of taking someone to court a second time for the same offence, in some rare situations【美, 法律】〔在极个别情况下〕同一罪行的两次审理

double-joint·ed /ˌ··ˈ··◂/ *adj* able to move the joints in your fingers, arms etc backwards as well as forwards〔手指、手臂等关节〕可前后弯曲的; 可反弯的

double neg·a·tive /ˌ··ˈ···/ *n* [C] a sentence in which two negatives (NEGATIVE[2] (1)) are used when only one is needed in correct English grammar, for example in the sentence 'I don't want nobody to help me!' 双重否定〔一个句子中带有两个否定词, 而其实正确的英语语法只需要一个, 如 I don't want nobody to help me! 便是双重否定句〕

double-park /ˌ··ˈ·/ *v* [I,T] to leave a vehicle on a road beside another vehicle that is already parked there 并排停放〔汽车〕〔把车并排停放在另一辆已停在路边的车旁〕

double play /ˌ··ˈ·/ *n* [C] *AmE* the action of making two runners in a game of BASEBALL have to leave the field by throwing the ball quickly from one BASE[1] (8) to another before the runners reach either one【美】〔棒球〕双杀

double-quick /ˌ··ˈ·◂/ *adv BrE informal* as quickly as possible【英, 非正式】快速地, 极快地: *Call an ambulance double-quick!* 快叫救护车!

double stand·ard /ˌ··ˈ··/ *n* [C] a rule, principle etc that is unfair because it treats one group or type of people more severely than another in the same situation〔带有歧视性的〕双重标准

doub·let /ˈdʌblɪt; ˈdʌblɪ̣t/ *n* [C] a man's shirt, worn in Europe from about 1400 to the middle 1600s〔15 到 17 世纪中期欧洲的一种〕男用衬衫

double take /ˌ··ˈ·/ *n* [C] **do a double take** to react to something after a short delay because you are surprised 先怔后悟; 慢半拍才恍然大悟

double-talk /ˈ··ˌ·/ *n* [U] *informal* speech that seems to be serious and sincere, but has another meaning or is a mixture of sense and nonsense【非正式】不知所云的空话: *legal double-talk* 空洞的法律辞令 —**double-talk** *v* [I,T] —**double-talker** *n* [C]

double·think /ˈdʌbḷˌθɪŋk; ˈdʌbəlˌθɪŋk/ *n* [U] a dishonest belief in two opposing ideas at the same time〔同时接受两种矛盾观念的、不诚实的〕双重信念; 双重思想

double time /ˌ··ˈ·/ *n* [U] **1** double wages paid to someone when they work on a day or at a time when people do not normally work〔付给加班者的〕双倍工资 —compare 比较 **time and a half** (TIME[1] (89)) **2** *AmE* a fast military march【美】快步行进; 快步走

double-time *adv AmE informal* as quickly as possible【美, 非正式】以最快的速度: *C'mon get upstairs and clean your room – double-time!* 上楼打扫你的房间——越快越好!

double vi·sion /ˌ··ˈ··/ *n* [U] a medical condition in which you see two of everything, for example after hitting your head or drinking too much alcohol 复视〔碰撞头部或喝酒过多后会出现的一种情况〕

double wham·my /ˌ··ˈ··/ *n* [C] *informal* two bad things that happen together, or one after the other【非正式】坏事成双; 祸不单行: *the double whammy of higher prices and more taxes* 物价上涨与加税的双重打击

double whole note /ˌ‥ˈ‥ˌ/ *n* [C] *AmE* a musical note that continues for twice the length of a WHOLE NOTE【美】倍全音符; 二全音符; BREVE *BrE*【英】

dou·bloon /dʌˋblun; dʌˈbluːn/ *n* [C] a gold coin used in the past in Spain and Spanish America 达布隆〔旧时西班牙以及西班牙属美洲国家使用的金币〕

doub·ly /ˋdʌblɪ; ˈdʌbli/ *adv* **1** by twice the amount, or to twice the degree 加倍地: *Be doubly careful when driving in fog.* 在雾中开车要加倍小心。**2** in two ways or for two reasons 在两个方面; 由于双重原因造成: *You are doubly mistaken.* 你有两个方面的错误。

S1 W1 **doubt**[1] /daut; daʊt/ *n*

1 ▶UNCERTAIN FEELING 不确定的感觉◀ [C,U] a feeling or feelings of being uncertain about something 不确定, 怀疑: **[+about/as to]** *Maisie expressed private doubts about Lawrence's sanity.* 梅茜对劳伦斯的神志正常与否在私下里表示怀疑。| **[+whether/who/what etc]** *There's no doubt who was responsible for this outrage.* 谁该对这次暴行负责, 已毫无疑问。| **[+(that)]** *I have little doubt that the coup will succeed.* 这次突然行动将取得成功, 对此我毫不怀疑。| **cast doubt(s) on sth/raise doubts about sth** (=say that something may not be true or real) 对某事提出怀疑 *The new evidence cast some doubt on his reliability as a witness.* 新的证据令人怀疑他作为证人的可靠性。| **an element of doubt** (=a slight doubt) 少许怀疑 | **without a shadow of a doubt** (=there is no doubt at all) 丝毫没有怀疑

2 no doubt used when you are saying that you think something is probably true 多半, 很可能: *No doubt she was disturbed by the noise.* 多半是噪音惊扰了她。| **no doubt about it** (=it is certainly true) 确实无疑 *Someone had been eavesdropping, no doubt about it.* 确实无疑, 有人一直在偷听。

3 have your doubts (about) used to say that you have reasons for not feeling certain about something or someone (对…)持有怀疑: *"Don't you think she'd be a good candidate?" "Well, I have my doubts."* "难道你不认为她会是一个不错的候选人吗?" "嗯, 我有怀疑。"

4 if/when in doubt used when advising someone what to do 如无把握; 如有怀疑〔用于建议〕: *If in doubt, don't eat it.* 如果有怀疑, 就别吃它。

5 be in doubt if someone's or something's future or success is in doubt, they may not be able to continue or succeed〔对…的将来或成功等〕不太有把握: *The future of the public library is in doubt.* 公共图书馆的前途难以预料。

6 be in doubt about to not be certain about something 对…不确定: *He's still in some doubt about what to do.* 他对该如何行事还是犹豫不决。

7 be beyond doubt if something is beyond doubt, it is completely certain 确实无疑: *Patel's integrity is beyond doubt.* 帕特尔的诚实是确实无疑的。| **beyond reasonable doubt** *law*【法律】*Her guilt was established beyond reasonable doubt.* 她被确实证明有罪。

8 without/beyond doubt *formal* used to emphasize an opinion【正式】确实〔用于强调某个观点〕: *Sally was without doubt one of the finest swimmers in the school.* 莎莉确实是学校最优秀的游泳能手之一。

9 open to doubt something that is open to doubt has not been proved to be definitely true or real 有待证明的: *The authenticity of the relics is open to doubt.* 这些遗骸的真假有待考证。—see also 另见 SELF-DOUBT, **give sb/sth the benefit of the doubt** (BENEFIT[1] (4))

S2 **doubt**[2] *v* [T not in progressive 不用进行时] **1** to think that something may not be true 怀疑, 不确信: *Kim never doubted his story.* 金对于他讲的事情从不怀疑。| **doubt (that)** *I don't doubt that he's a brilliant scientist, but can he teach?* 我不怀疑他是个出色的科学家, 但他会教书吗? **2** *especially spoken* to think that something is unlikely【尤口】认为〔某事〕未必可能: **doubt if/whether** *You can complain, but I doubt if it'll make any difference.* 你可以抱怨, 但是我看抱怨也未必有用。| **doubt sth** *"Do you think there'll be any tickets left?" "I very much doubt it."* "你认为还会有余票吗?" "我认为很可能没有了。" | **doubt (that)** *I doubt that we'll ever see George again.* 我怀疑我们可能再也不会见到乔治了。**3** to not trust or have confidence in someone 不信任〔某人〕; 对〔某人〕没有信心: *If anyone doubts my ability to handle this, they should say so.* 如果有人怀疑我处理此事的能力, 他应该说出来。| **doubt sb's word** (=think that someone may not be telling the truth) 怀疑某人说的话 —**doubter** *n* [C]

doubt·ful /ˋdautfəl; ˈdaʊtfəl/ *adj* **1** having doubts about something 有疑问的, 感到怀疑的: *The journalist looked doubtful when he heard her story.* 记者听她讲事情经过时面有疑色。| **[+if/whether]** *I'm still doubtful whether I should accept this job.* 我还是拿不定主意该不该接受这份工作。| **doubtful about (doing) sth** *At first we were doubtful about employing Charlie.* 起初我们拿不定主意是否应该雇用查利。**2** something that is doubtful may not be true or may not happen in the way you want 难以预料的, 未定的: *The company's prospects are starting to look more doubtful.* 公司的前景看起来开始变得更难以预料了。| **[+if/whether]** *It was doubtful whether the patient would survive the operation.* 病人是否能熬过这次手术还很难说。**3** unlikely 不大可能的: **[+that]** *It now seems doubtful that the missing airmen will ever be found.* 要找到那个失踪的飞行员现在看来是不大可能了。**4** probably false or of no value; DUBIOUS 有可能是假的[没价值的]: *Pringle was given the doubtful privilege of leading the troops.* 普林格尔受命统率部队, 这对他是否是件好事还不好说。—**doubtfully** *adv*

doubt·ing Thom·as /ˌdautɪŋˋtɑməs; ˌdaʊtɪŋ ˈtɒməs/ *n* [singular] *humorous* someone who tends to doubt things if they have not seen proof of them【幽默】怀疑主义者; 有真凭实据才肯相信的人

doubt·less /ˋdautləs; ˈdaʊtləs/ *adv formal* used when saying something that you believe to be true although you have no proof【正式】无疑地, 肯定地: *Renee was doubtless reassured by the news.* 勒妮听到这个消息确实感到放心了。

douche /duʃ; duːʃ/ *n* [C usually singular 一般用单数] **1** a mixture of water and something such as VINEGAR, that a woman puts into her VAGINA to wash it 冲洗液, 灌洗液〔水与某物如醋的混合液, 供妇女清洗下体之用〕**2** water that is poured over part of someone's body 冲向身体某部位的水 —**douche** *v* [I,T]

dough /do; dəʊ/ *n* **1** [singular, U] a mixture of flour and water ready to be baked into bread, PASTRY etc〔做面包、糕点等用的〕生面团, 湿面团 **2** [U] *informal* money【非正式】钱

dough·nut /ˋdonət; ˈdəʊnʌt/ *n* [C] **1** a small round cake, often in the form of a ring 炸面圈, 多福饼 **2 do doughnuts** *AmE informal* to make a car spin around in circles【美, 非正式】让汽车转圈

dough·ty /ˋdautɪ; ˈdaʊti/ *adj* [only before noun 仅用于名词前] *literary* brave and determined【文】勇敢的, 坚决的: *a doughty fighter* 勇猛的斗士

dough·y /ˋdoɪ; ˈdəʊi/ *adj* **1** looking and feeling like DOUGH (1) 像面团的 **2** doughy skin is unhealthily pale and soft〔皮肤〕苍白的, 柔软的

Doug·las /ˋdʌgləs; ˈdʌgləs/ the capital of the Isle of Man 道格拉斯〔马恩岛首府〕

Doug·lass, Frede·rick /ˋdʌgləs; ˈdʌgləs, ˋfrɛdrɪk; ˈfredərɪk/ (1817-95) a former SLAVE in the US, who worked to get rid of SLAVERY (=the practice of having slaves), and wrote a book about his life 道格拉斯〔(1817-1895), 美国废奴主义者, 奴隶出身, 曾写过一本自传〕

Doun·reay /ˋdunre; ˈduːnreɪ/ a town in Scotland where there was a NUCLEAR power station until 1977 敦雷〔苏格兰一镇。1977年前, 此处建有一座核电站〕

dour /dur; dʊə/ *adj* **1** severe and never smiling 严厉的; 脸色阴沉的 **2** making you feel anxious or afraid; GRIM (1) 令人忧虑[恐惧]的: *a dour reminder* 严峻的提示 —**dourly** *adv*

douse, dowse /daus; daʊs/ *v* [T] **1** to put out a fire by pouring water on it 用水浇灭〔火〕**2 [+with/in]** to cover something in water or other liquid 用水[其他液体]浸没〔某物〕

dove[1] /dʌv; dʌv/ *n* [C] **1** a kind of small PIGEON (=bird) often used as a sign of peace 鸽子〔常用作和平的象征〕**2** someone in politics who prefers peace and discussion to war〔政治上的〕鸽派人物〔指主张和平与对话、反对战争的人〕—opposite 反义词 HAWK[1] (2)

dove[2] /dov; dəʊv/ *especially AmE*【尤美】a past tense of DIVE[1]

dove·cot /ˋdʌvˌkɑt; ˈdʌvkɒt/ also 又作 **dove·cote** /ˋdʌvˌkot; ˈdʌvkəʊt/ *n* [C] a small house built for doves to live in 鸽舍, 鸽房

Do·ver /ˋdovɚ; ˈdəʊvə/ **1** a port in southeast England, from which ships go across the English Channel to France carrying passengers, vehicles, and goods. 多佛尔〔英格兰东南部港口。运载旅客、车辆和货物的渡船由此出发经英吉利海峡前往法国〕**2** the capital city of the US state of Delaware 多佛(美国特拉华州首府)

CULTURAL NOTE 文化注释

High white cliffs rise above the port, and for English people who have travelled to Europe, the sight of the **white cliffs of Dover** is the first sign that they are returning home. (多佛尔)港口上方, 白色的峭壁突兀而起。英格兰人坐船归来时, 一看到多佛尔海边的白色悬崖, 就知道快要到家了。

dove·tail¹ /ˈdʌvˌtel; ˈdʌvteɪl/ *v* **1** [I,T] to fit perfectly together or to make two plans, ideas etc fit together perfectly 吻合；使〔两个计划、观点等〕吻合：[+with] *My vacation plans dovetail nicely with Joyce's.* 我的度假计划与乔伊丝的度假计划完全一致。**2** [T+together] to join two pieces of wood by means of dovetail joints 用鸠尾榫接合〔两块木头〕

dovetail² also 又作 **dovetail joint** /ˌ.. ˈ./ *n* [C] a type of JOINT² (3) fastening two pieces of wood together 鸠尾榫

dov·ish /ˈdʌvɪʃ; ˈdʌvɪʃ/ *adj* preferring peace and discussion to war 鸽派的，爱好和平的

dow·a·ger /ˈdauədʒə; ˈdaʊɪdʒə/ *n* [C] **1** a woman from a high social class who has land or a title from her dead husband 〔承袭亡夫土地或封号的〕孀居贵妇：*the dowager Duchess of Devonshire* 德文郡公爵的遗孀 **2** *informal* a respected and impressive old lady【非正式】受人钦敬的老妇人

dow·dy /ˈdaudɪ; ˈdaʊdi/ *adj* **1** unattractive or unfashionable 不漂亮的；过时的：*a dowdy frock* 款式陈旧的衣裙 **2** a dowdy woman wears dull or unfashionable clothes〔指妇女〕穿着单调[过时]的 —**dowdily** *adv* —**dowdiness** *n* [U]

dow·el /ˈdauəl; ˈdaʊəl/ *n* [C] a wooden pin for holding two pieces of wood, metal, or stone together 木钉，暗榫

Dow Jones Av·e·rage /ˌdau dʒonz ˈævrɪdʒ; ˌdaʊ dʒəʊnz ˈævərɪdʒ/ *n* [singular] a daily list of prices of shares (SHARE² (5)) on the American STOCK EXCHANGE, based on the daily average prices of 30 industrial shares 道琼斯（工业）平均指数〔指在美国证券交易所中，以特定的30种工业股票的日平均价格为依据的股票相对价格指数〕

down- /daun; daʊn/ *prefix* **1** to a lower position 向下：*to downgrade a job* (=make it lower in importance) 降低某工作的重要性 | *a downpour* (=heavy rain) 倾盆大雨 **2** in some adverbs and adjectives, means at or towards the bottom or end of something〔构成某些副词和形容词〕在[接近]某事物的底部[一端]：*downstairs* 在楼下；往楼下 | *downriver* (=nearer to its mouth) 近河口的；下游的 **3** in some adverbs and adjectives, means at or towards the lower or worst part of something〔构成某些副词和形容词〕在[面向]某事物的低层的[最差的]部分：*down-market* (=meeting the demand of the lower social groups) 面向社会低层市场的 compare 比较 UP-

down¹ /daun; daʊn/ *adv* **1** from above towards a lower place or position 从上到下，从高到低，朝下：*David bent down to tie his shoelace.* 戴维弯下身系鞋带。| *The sun beat down on their heads all day long.* 太阳一整天火辣辣地照在他们头上。**2** at a lower place or position than usual 处在比通常更低的地方[位置]：*You can't cross here, the bridge is down.* 你无法在这儿过河，桥在下游。**3** at or towards a lower position or floor 位于[朝向]低处[低层]：*We heard the sound of laughter down below.* 我们听到楼下的笑声。| *Let's go down to the kitchen.* 我们下去到厨房吧。**4** into a sitting or lying position（坐）下，（躺）下：*Please sit down.* 请坐。| *I think I'll go and lie down for a while.* 我想去躺一小会儿。**5** firmly and tightly into place or position 牢固地固定好，紧紧地附着：*Have you stuck down the envelope?* 你把信封粘牢了吗？**6** towards the south 朝南，向南方：*They drove all the way down from Boston to Miami.* 他们开车南下从波士顿一直到迈阿密。—opposite 反义词 UP¹ (4) **7** *BrE* away from a university at the end of a period of study【英】〔学习期满〕离开大学，毕业：*Sarah went down from Oxford in 1966.* 萨拉1966年从牛津大学毕业。**8** at or towards a lower level in price or amount〔价格或数量〕处于低水平，减少：*Keep your speed down.* 保持低速度。| *House prices have come down in recent months.* 最近几个月房价降下来了。**9** into a weaker, smaller, or quieter state 变弱；变小；变安静：*Would you mind turning the radio down?* 你把收音机音量调小些好吗？| *The heels of his shoes had worn down.* 他的鞋跟已经磨薄了。| [+to] *Sharif cut his report down to only three pages.* 沙里夫把他的报告删减到只有三页。**10** **be down to your last pound/dollar/litre** to be left with only a small amount of something 只剩下最后一镑/一元/一升：*We're down to our last five dollars.* 我们只剩下最后五块钱了。**11** **write/note/jot/take down** to write something on paper 记下，写下：*I'll write down the address for you.* 我替你把地址写下来。**12** **pass/hand down** to give or tell something to people in the next GENERATION (1) 把〔某物〕传给[告知]〔下一代〕：*The jewels were passed down through the family.* 这些珠宝是家传的。**13** paid to someone immediately in CASH¹ (1) 首付现金：*A top quality freezer for only £20 down and £5 a week for a year.* 一台上等品质的冰柜只需先付20英镑现金，而后每周付5英镑，一年内付清剩余款项。**14** from top to bottom 从顶部到底部：*I want you to wash my car down.* 请你把我的车彻底冲洗干净。**15** in or into the body as a result of swallowing 咽下，吞下：*Meg's been very ill and can't keep her food down.* 梅格病得很重，吃不下东西。**16** **be down to sb** if something is down to someone they are responsible for it or must make a decision about it 该由某人负责；该由某人作出决定：*It's down to Tom to decide whether to pay it or not.* 是否付款应该由汤姆来决定。—see also 另见 **be up to sb** (UP¹ (16)) **17** **be/come down to sth** to be mainly the result of one particular thing 是由于某事物的原因/归结为某事物：*Most of the problems came down to bad management.* 多数问题是由于管理不善造成的。**18** **Down!** *spoken* used to tell a jumping dog to get down【口】趴下！〔用于命令跳跃的狗〕**19** **down to** including something or someone at a low level or rank 下至〔等级低或职位低的物或人〕：*Everyone uses the cafeteria, from the managing director down to the office boy.* 上至经理下到办公室的工友，大家都在食堂用餐。**20** **down under** *informal* in or to Australia or New Zealand【非正式】位于[前往]澳大利亚或新西兰 **21** **Down with** ... *spoken* used to express opposition and a wish for someone or something to go【口】打倒…：*Down with the government!* 打倒政府！**22** **be/go down with sth** to have a particular illness 患某种疾病：*Jane's down with flu.* 简得了流感。

down² *prep* **1** towards the ground or a lower point, or in a lower position 向[位于]较低处：*The bathroom is down those stairs.* 顺着楼梯往下走便是浴室。**2** along 沿着，顺着：*The wind raced down the alley.* 风顺着胡同刮过去。**3** **down the river** in the direction of the river's current 顺流：*We sailed down the river.* 我们沿河向下游航行。**4** **down the shops/park/market etc** *BrE informal* an expression meaning to or at the shops etc, that some people think is not correct【英，非正式】前往[位于]商店/公园/市场等〔有人认为这种表达法不正确〕：*Bob's just gone down the pub.* 鲍勃刚去了酒吧。**5** **down the road/pike/line etc** *AmE* at some time in the future【美】在未来的某个时间：*You'll understand better a few years down the line when you've had some experience.* 过几年你有了经验时会更加明白的。

down³ *adj*

1 ▶**SAD** 伤心的◀ [not before noun 不用于名词前] sad and discouraged 伤心的；沮丧的：*Andy's been feeling down lately.* 安迪最近情绪很低落。

2 ▶**IN A GAME** 在比赛中◀ [not before noun 不用于名词前] behind an opponent by a certain number of points〔比分〕落后的：*Agassi was down by two sets to one.* 阿加西以1:2落后于对手。

3 ▶**COMPLETED** 完成的◀ [not before noun 不用于名词前] *informal* done or finished【非正式】完成的，做完的：*Three exercises down and two to go.* 完成了三个练习，还剩下两个。

4 **be down on sb/sth** *informal* to have a low opinion of someone or something【非正式】看不上[不齿]某人/某物：*Why is Mark so down on her at the moment?* 为什么现在马克这么嫌恶她？

5 ▶**COMPUTER** 电脑◀ [not before noun 不用于名词前] if a computer is down, it is not working 停止工作的，停机的，不运行的 —opposite 反义词 UP³ (3)

6 **have/put sb down for sth** to have or put someone's name on a list of people who want to do something 把某人的名字写在想做某事者的名单上：*Put me down to bring the desserts.* 把我登记上，我要带甜品来。

7 **down escalator/staircase** an ESCALATOR (=moving stairs) or stairs which take you down to a lower level 下行的自动扶梯/楼梯 — see also 另见 **be down on your luck** (LUCK¹ (14))

down⁴ *v* [T] **1** to drink or eat something quickly 很快吃下，喝下：*Jack downed three beers with his steak and fries.* 杰克就着牛排和炸薯条喝下了三杯啤酒。**2** to knock or force someone to the ground 将〔某人〕打倒在地：*O'Malley downed his opponent in the first round.* 奥马利第一回合就把对手击倒。**3** **down tools** *BrE* to stop working at the end of a day or to STRIKE (=protest about conditions by stopping work)【英】停工，罢工〔抗议恶劣的工作条件〕

down⁵ *n* **1** [U] soft hair like a baby's 柔毛，绒毛 **2** [U] the soft fine feathers of a bird 小鸟的绒羽 **3** [C] one of the four chances that an American football team has to move forward when it is their turn to have the ball〔美式橄榄球〕十码进攻 **4** **the downs** low round hills covered with grass, as in the south of England 草木覆盖的低圆山丘〈如英格兰南部的山丘〉**5** **have a down on sb** *BrE informal* to dislike or have a bad opinion of someone【英，非正式】讨厌某人；看不上某人：*Mark had a down on Utopians.* 马克讨厌所有乌托邦式的空想主义者。—see also 另见 **ups and downs** (UP⁴ (2))

Down, County a DISTRICT in southeast Northern Ireland, next to the Irish Sea 唐郡〔北爱尔兰东南部一郡，濒临爱尔兰海〕

down-and-out /ˌ.. ˈ./ *n* [C] *informal* someone who has no job, no money, and nowhere to live【非正式】穷困潦倒的人 —**down-and-out** *adj*

down-at-heel /ˌ· · ˈ·◂/ *adj especially BrE* dressed in old clothes and looking as if you do not have much money【尤英】穿着破旧的, 衣衫褴褛的, 看似贫穷的

down·beat¹ /ˋdaun,bit; ˈdaʊnbiːt/ *n* [C] **1** the first note in a BAR¹ (6) of music〔乐谱上的〕强拍 **2** the movement a CONDUCTOR makes to show when this note is to be played or sung 下拍〔乐队指挥表示要演奏或唱出某个音符时向下的手势〕

downbeat² *adj informal* not showing any strong feelings, especially not happy ones【非正式】无激情的; 忧郁的: *Al was surprisingly downbeat about the party.* 奇怪的是, 阿尔对那个聚会一点也不热心。—compare 比较 UPBEAT

down·cast /ˋdaun,kæst; ˈdaʊnkɑːst/ *adj* **1** sad or upset because of something bad that has happened〔因发生了坏事而〕悲哀的, 不安的: *Keith is very downcast at the moment – he misses his wife terribly.* 基思现在非常沮丧, 极度想念他的妻子。**2** downcast eyes are looking down〔指眼睛〕目光向下的, 低垂的

down·er /ˋdaunɚ; ˈdaʊnə/ *n informal*【非正式】**1** [C] a drug that makes you feel very relaxed or sleepy 镇静药; 安眠药 —compare 比较 UPPER² (2) **2** [singular] a person or situation that stops you feeling cheerful or happy 令人沮丧的人[情况]: *"Nick can't come." "What a downer."* "尼克来不了啦。""真扫兴。" **3** **be on a downer** *BrE* to be sad or experiencing a series of sad events【英】沮丧; 经历一连串伤心事: *What's up with Ruth? She's been on a downer all week.* 鲁丝怎么啦? 她这一星期心情都不好。

down·fall /ˋdaun,fɔl; ˈdaʊnfɔːl/ *n* [singular] complete loss of your money, moral standards, social position etc, or the sudden failure of an organization 衰落; 堕落; 垮台: *The scandal led to the family's downfall.* 丑闻导致了那个家族的败落。| **be sb's downfall** *That one error of judgment was his downfall.* 那一次判断错误是他失败的原因。

down·grade /ˋdaun,gred; ˈdaʊngreɪd/ *v* [T] **1** to make a job less important or move someone to a less important job 降低〔某职位〕的重要性; 降〔某人〕的职: **downgrade sb/sth to sth** *Harris was downgraded to Assistant Manager.* 哈里斯被降为副经理。—opposite 反义词 UPGRADE **2** to make something seem less important or valuable than it is 贬低, 轻视

down·heart·ed /ˌdaunˋhɑrtɪd; ˌdaʊnˈhɑːtɨd◂/ *adj* discouraged or made sad by something 情绪低落的, 沮丧的: *When no replies came, I began to feel downhearted.* 因为没有收到答复, 我开始感到沮丧。

down·hill¹ /ˋdaun,hɪl; ˌdaʊnˈhɪl◂/ *adv* [only after verb 仅用于动词后] **1** towards the bottom of a hill or lower land 向山下: *I had to run downhill as fast as I could.* 我得尽快往山下跑。**2** **go downhill** to become worse 走下坡路, 每况愈下: *They won the first game but after that things went downhill.* 他们打赢了第一场比赛, 但此后便每况愈下。

downhill² *adj* **1** on a slope that goes down to a lower point 下坡的: *downhill skiing* 下坡滑雪 | *The path was all downhill.* 小路全程都是下坡。**2** [not before noun 不用于名词前] easy to do, especially after you have been doing something difficult 容易做的〔尤指在做过困难的事情之后〕; 一帆风顺的: **all downhill/downhill all the way** *The worst is over – it's all downhill from here.* 最困难的已经过去了, 从此一切都将是一帆风顺。

down·home /ˋdaun,hom; ˈdaʊnhəʊm/ *adj AmE* related to the values and customs of people who live in the countryside【美】乡村的; 有乡村人特点的

Dow·ning Street /ˋdaunɪŋ strit; ˈdaʊnɪŋ striːt/ *n* [not with the 不与 the 连用] the street in central London that contains the official houses of the British Prime Minister, at number 10, and the Chancellor of the Exchequer (=chief financial minister) at number 11. The name Downing Street is often used to mean the Prime Minister and his/her officials, or the government of the UK. 唐宁街〔伦敦市中心的一条街道。英国首相官邸坐落在该条街的10号, 财政大臣官邸在11号。人们通常借用唐宁街这个名字指称英国首相及其内阁, 或英国政府〕: *Downing Street announced last night that peace talks with the IRA had lead to a breakthrough.* 英国政府昨晚宣布, 与爱尔兰共和军的和平会谈取得了突破性进展。

down·load /ˌdaunˋlod; ˌdaʊnˈləʊd/ *v* [T] to move information or PROGRAMs from one part of a computer system to another 下载〔信息或程序〕

down·mar·ket /ˌdaunˋmɑrkɪt; ˌdaʊnˈmɑːkɨt◂/ *adj BrE* downmarket goods or services are cheap and not of very good quality【英】〔指商品、服务等〕低档的, 廉价的; 质量不好的: *a downmarket magazine aimed at working mums* 针对有工作的母亲的低档杂志 —compare 比较 UPMARKET —**downmarket** *adv*

down pay·ment /ˌ· ˈ· ·/ *n* [C] a payment you make when you buy something that is only part of the full price, with the rest to be paid later〔分期付款购物的〕首次付款; 定金: **make a down payment** *We've made a down payment on a washing machine.* 我们买洗衣机的首期付款已经交了。—compare 比较 DEPOSIT¹

down·play /ˌdaunˋple; ˌdaʊnˈpleɪ/ *v* [T] to make something seem less important than it really is; play down (PLAY¹) 贬低; 轻视: *Officials are downplaying last month's drop in exports.* 官员们对上月出口额的下降轻描淡写。

down·pour /ˋdaun,pɔr; ˈdaʊnpɔː/ *n* [C often singular 常用单数] a lot of rain that falls in a short time 倾盆大雨 —see picture on page A13 参见 A13 页图

down·right¹ /ˋdaun,raɪt; ˈdaʊnraɪt/ *adj* [only before noun 仅用于名词前] used to emphasize that someone or something is completely bad, false, or unpleasant 彻头彻尾的, 全然的〔用于强调某人或某事物极差、极假、极讨厌〕: *That's a downright lie!* 那是彻头彻尾的谎言!

downright² *adv* [+adj/adv] used to emphasize that someone or something is completely bad, untrue, unpleasant etc 十足地, 彻底地〔用来强调某人或某事物极差、极假或极讨厌等〕: *Jed's just downright lazy.* 杰德简直是懒透了。

down·riv·er /ˌdaunˋrɪvɚ; daʊnˈrɪvə/ *adv* in the direction that the water in a river is flowing 顺流地: *The bridge was another mile downriver.* 桥在下游一英里处。—compare 比较 DOWNSTREAM

down·side /ˋdaun,saɪd; ˈdaʊnsaɪd/ *n* **the downside** the negative side of something〔某事物〕消极的一面, 负面, 反面: *The downside of the plan is that we lose a lot of time.* 这项计划的缺点是费时。

down·size /ˋdaun,saɪz; ˈdaʊnsaɪz/ *v* [I,T] if a company or organization downsizes, or downsizes its operations, it reduces the number of people it employs in order to reduce costs〔指公司、机构为缩减开支而〕裁〔员〕; 紧缩〔编制〕—**downsizing** *n* [U]

down·spout /ˋdaun,spaut; ˈdaʊnspaʊt/ *n* [C] *AmE* a pipe that carries water away from the roof of a building【美】水落管, 屋顶排水管; DRAINPIPE *BrE*【英】

Down's syn·drome /ˈ· ˌ· ·/ *n* [U] a condition that someone is born with, that stops them from developing in a normal way, both mentally and physically 唐氏综合征, 先天愚型

down·stage /ˋdaunˋstedʒ; ˌdaʊnˈsteɪdʒ◂/ *adv* towards or near the front of the stage in a theatre 向[接近]舞台前部 —**downstage** *adj* —opposite 反义词 UPSTAGE²

down·stairs /ˋdaunˋstɛrz; ˌdaʊnˈsteəz◂/ *adv* **1** towards or on a lower floor of a building, especially a house 往楼下; 在楼下: *Rosie ran downstairs.* 罗茜跑下楼去。**2** **the downstairs** the rooms on the ground floor in a house〔独立住宅中〕一层的房间: *We have still got to paint the downstairs.* 我们还得把底层的房间粉刷一下。—compare 比较 UPSTAIRS —**downstairs** *adj*: *a downstairs room* 楼下的房间 S2

down·stream /ˋdaunˋstrim; ˌdaʊnˈstriːm◂/ *adv* in the direction the water in a river or stream is flowing 顺流而下; 向下游方向: *a boat drifting downstream* 顺水漂流而下的小船 —compare 比较 DOWNRIVER, UPSTREAM

down·time /ˋdaun,taɪm; ˈdaʊntaɪm/ *n* [U] the time when a computer is not working〔电脑的〕停机时间

down-to-earth /ˌ· · ˈ·◂/ *adj* practical and direct in a sensible honest way 实事求是的, 实际的, 切实的, 务实的, 脚踏实地的: *a down-to-earth approach to health care* 切实可行的卫生保健方法

down·town /ˋdaunˋtaun; ˌdaʊnˈtaʊn◂/ *adv especially AmE* towards or in the centre or main business area of a town or city【尤美】向[在]城镇商业中心区, 向[在]市中心; CITY CENTRE *BrE*【英】: **go downtown** *I have to go downtown later.* 过一会儿我得到市中心去。—**downtown** *adj* [only before noun 仅用于名词前]: *downtown restaurants* 位于闹市区的餐厅 —compare 比较 UPTOWN S3 W3

down·trod·den /ˋdaunˋtrɑdn̩; ˈdaʊnˌtrɒdn/ *adj* downtrodden people, workers etc are treated badly and without respect by people who have power over them 被〔有权势者〕践踏的, 受压迫的

down·turn /ˋdauntɝn; ˈdaʊntɜːn/ *n* [C usually singular 一般用单数] a period or process in which business activity, production etc is reduced and conditions become worse〔指经济活动、生产等的〕下降趋势; 衰退: *a sharp economic downturn* 经济的急剧下滑 | [+in] *a downturn in shipbuilding orders* 造船订单数量的减少 —opposite 反义词 UPTURN

down·ward /ˋdaunwɚd; ˈdaʊnwəd/ *adj* [only before noun 仅用于名词前] going down to a lower level or place 向下的, 向低处的: *a gentle downward slope* 平缓往下的坡 | *Share prices continued their downward trend.* 股价持续下跌趋势。—opposite 反义词 UPWARD

down·ward·ly mo·bile /ˌ··· ˈ··/ *adj* someone who is downwardly mobile is becoming poorer〔指人〕越来越穷的; 趋向贫困的

down·wards /ˈdaʊnwɚdz; ˈdaʊnwədz/ also 又作 **downward** *adv* **1** towards a lower level or position 向下: *Nina glanced downwards.* 尼娜向下瞥了一眼。| **face downwards** (=with the front towards the ground) 脸朝下 *The body lay face downwards on the rug.* 尸体脸朝下伏在地毯上。—opposite 反义词 UPWARDS (1) **2** down to and including the lowest position in a set 一整体中下至及包括最低的职位: *Everyone from the chairman downwards is taking a pay cut.* 每个人, 上至总裁下至职位最低的人都将减薪。—opposite 反义词 UPWARDS (1)

down·wind /ˌdaʊnˈwɪnd; ˌdaʊnˈwɪnd/ *adv* in the direction that the wind is moving 顺风地

down·y /ˈdaʊnɪ; ˈdaʊni/ *adj* covered in or filled with soft fine hair or feathers 被绒羽覆盖的; 充满绒毛的: *the baby's downy head* 婴儿毛茸茸的脑袋

dow·ry /ˈdaʊrɪ; ˈdaʊəri/ *n* [C] property and money that a woman gives to her husband when they marry in some societies〔新娘的〕嫁妆

D

dowse¹ /daʊz; daʊz/ *v* [I+for] to look for water or minerals under the ground using a special stick that points to where they are; DIVINE² (2) 用一种特殊的枝椏探水[探矿]

dowse² /daʊs; daʊs/ *v* [T] another spelling of DOUSE douse 的另一种拼法

dow·ser /ˈdaʊzɚ; ˈdaʊzə/ *n* [C] someone who dowses for water or minerals 用枝椏探水[探矿]者

dows·ing rod /ˈ·· ·/ *n* [C] a special stick in the shape of a Y used by a dowser 探测水源[矿床]者使用的丫形卜棒

doy·en /ˈdɔɪən; ˈdɔɪən/ *n* [C] the oldest, most respected, or most experienced member of a group〔某团体中的〕资深者; 老前辈; 元老: **the doyen of** *the doyen of sports commentators* 体育评论员中的元老

doy·enne /dɔɪˈɛn; dɔɪˈen/ *n* [C] the oldest, most respected, or most experienced woman in a group〔某团体中的〕女老前辈: **the doyenne of** *the doyenne of gossip columnists* 漫谈专栏作家中的女元老

Doyle, Sir Arthur Conan —see 见 Sir Arthur CONAN DOYLE

doz *n* the written abbreviation of 缩写= DOZEN

doze /doz; dəʊz/ *v* [I] to sleep lightly for a short time 小睡, 打瞌睡, 打盹儿: *Pam often dozes in her chair after lunch.* 帕姆经常在午饭后坐在椅子上打盹。—**doze** *n* [singular] *especially BrE*【尤英】: *having a doze in front of the telly* 坐在电视机前打个盹儿

doze off *phr v* [I] to go to sleep, especially when you did not intend to; **drop off** (DROP¹), **nod off** (NOD¹)〔尤指在无意的情况下〕打盹, 打瞌睡: *I was just dozing off when the phone rang.* 我刚打盹, 电话就响了。

2 3 **doz·en** /ˈdʌzn; ˈdʌzən/ written abbreviation 缩写为 **doz** *determiner plural* **dozen** or **dozens** **1 a dozen/two dozen/three dozen** a group of twelve 一打/两打/三打〔每打为12个〕: *a dozen eggs* 一打鸡蛋 | *half a dozen* 半打; 六个 **2 dozens (of)** *informal* a lot of【非正式】许多; 数十个; 几打: *I've been there dozens of times.* 我到过那儿很多次了。| **dozens and dozens** *They collected dozens and dozens of shells on the beach.* 他们在海滩上捡了很多很多的贝壳。—see also 另见 BAKER'S DOZEN, **a dime a dozen** (DIME (2)), **nineteen to the dozen** (NINETEEN (2)), **six of one and half a dozen of the other** (SIX (2))

doz·y /ˈdozɪ; ˈdəʊzi/ *adj* **1** not feeling very awake 昏昏欲睡的; 困倦的: *I was feeling dozy after lunch.* 吃过午餐后我觉得有点困。**2** *BrE informal* slow to understand things; stupid【英, 非正式】迟钝的, 愚蠢的: *Those kids are really dozy!* 那些孩子们真是笨啊! —**dozily** *adv* —**doziness** *n* [U]

DP /ˌdi ˈpi; ˌdiː ˈpiː/ the abbreviation of 缩写= DATA PROCESSING

D Phil /ˌdi ˈfɪl; ˌdiː ˈfɪl/ the abbreviation of 缩写= Doctor of Philosophy

DQ /ˌdi ˈkju; ˌdiː ˈkjuː/ *informal* the abbreviation of 缩写= DAIRY QUEEN

Dr **1** the written abbreviation of 缩写= DOCTOR **2** the written abbreviation of 缩写= DRIVE² (7): *88 Park Dr* 公园大道88号

drab¹ /dræb; dræb/ *adj* not bright in colour or not interesting〔色彩〕暗淡的, 单调的; 乏味的: *The city looked drab and colourless to me.* 那座城市在我看来枯燥乏味。

drab² *n* [C] *old use* a dirty, untidy, and perhaps immoral woman【旧】邋遢的女人; 不规矩的女人 —see also 另见 DRIBS AND DRABS

drach·ma /ˈdrækmə; ˈdrækmə/ *n* [C] *plural* **drachmas** or **drachmae** /-mi; -miː/ **1** the unit of money in modern Greece 德拉克马〔现代希腊货币单位〕**2** an ancient Greek silver coin and weight 古希腊银币; 古希腊重量单位

dra·co·ni·an /drəˈkonɪən; drəˈkəʊniən/ *adj* very strict and cruel 严厉的, 残酷的: **draconian laws/measures/methods etc** *draconian measures to control population growth* 控制人口增长的严厉措施

Drac·u·la /ˈdrækjulə; ˈdrækjʊ̈lə/ a frightening character originally from the book *Dracula* by Bram Stoker, who has appeared in many horror films. Count Dracula is a VAMPIRE (=a creature who drinks people's blood in order to stay alive). 德拉库拉, 吸血鬼〔许多恐怖片中出现的可怕人物, 出自布拉姆·斯托克小说《吸血鬼》。德拉库拉伯爵是个吸血鬼〕

Dracula 吸血鬼

draft¹ /dræft; drɑːft/ *n*

1 ▶UNFINISHED FORM 未完成的形式◀ [C] a piece of writing, a drawing, or a plan that is not yet in its finished form 草稿; 草图; 草案: **make a draft** *Let's make a rough draft of the letter.* 我们写一下信的草稿吧。| **first/final draft** *the first draft of a poem* 诗的初稿 | **draft proposal/copy/version etc** *a draft copy of a newspaper article* 报纸文章的稿样

2 ▶ARMY 军队◀ **the draft** *AmE*【美】**a)** *informal* a system in which people are ordered to fight for their country when it is involved in a war; CONSCRIPTION【非正式】征兵, 征募 **b)** the group of people who are ordered to do this 被征入伍者

3 ▶MONEY 钱◀ [C] *especially BrE* a written order for money to be paid by a bank, especially from one bank to another【尤英】汇票: **by draft** *Payment must be made by bank draft.* 必须以银行汇票付款。

4 ▶SPORTS 体育运动◀ [C] a system in some American sports in which PROFESSIONAL¹ (3) teams pick players from colleges for their teams〔美国一些职业球队〕从大学选拔队员的制度

5 ▶COLD AIR/DRINKS 冷空气/饮料◀ [C] the American spelling of DRAUGHT draught 的美式拼法

draft² *v* [T] **1** to write a plan, letter, report etc that will need to be changed before it is in its finished form 起草, 草拟〔计划、信件、报告等〕: *Eva's busy drafting her speech for the conference.* 伊娃正忙着起草她在大会发言的讲演稿。**2** *AmE* to order someone to serve in their country's military during a war; CONSCRIPT¹ (1)【美】〔战时〕征召〔某人〕入伍; 征募; CALL-UP *BrE*【英】: **be drafted into sth** *Joe's been drafted into the army.* 乔已经应征入伍。

draft board /ˈ· ·/ *n* [C] *AmE* the committee that decides who will be drafted into the military【美】征兵局

draft card /ˈ· ·/ *n* [C] *AmE* a card sent to someone telling them they have been drafted【美】服兵役通知卡

draft dod·ger /ˈ· ˌ··/ *n* [C] *AmE* someone who illegally avoids joining the military even though they have been drafted【美】逃避兵役者

draft·ee /dræfˈti; drɑːfˈtiː/ *n* [C] *AmE* someone who has been drafted【美】应征入伍者

drafts·man /ˈdræftsmən; ˈdrɑːftsmən/ *n plural* **draftsmen** /-mən; -mən/ [C] **1** someone who puts a suggested law or a new law into the proper words 法案[新法律]的起草人 **2** the American spelling of DRAUGHTSMAN draughtsman 的美式拼法

draft·y /ˈdræftɪ; ˈdrɑːfti/ *adj* the American spelling of DRAUGHTY draughty 的美式拼法

drag¹ /dræg; dræg/ *v* **dragged, dragging**

1 ▶PULL ALONG THE GROUND 在地面上拖◀ [T] to pull someone or something along the ground, often because they are too heavy to carry 拖, 拉: **drag sth away/along/through etc** *Inge managed to drag the table into the kitchen.* 英奇费了很大劲把桌子拖到厨房里。| *Angry protesters were dragged away by the police.* 愤怒的抗议者被警察拖走了。| **drag a leg/foot etc** (=let it touch the ground as you move) 拖着腿/脚等〔挪动〕*a bird dragging its broken wing* 一只拖着断翅的鸟 —see picture on page A21 参见 A21 页图

2 ▶NOT GENTLY 粗鲁地◀ [T always+adv/prep] to pull someone or something somewhere in a way that hurts or damages them 硬拉, 硬拖, 硬拽: **drag sth up/over etc** *The plants had been dragged out by the roots.* 这些植物已被连根拔了起来。| *Harvey dragged her over to the window.* 哈维粗鲁地把她拖到窗前。| **drag sb to the ground** (=pull someone down to the ground) 将某人拖倒在地

3 drag yourself up/down/into etc *informal* to move somewhere with difficulty【非正式】吃力地挪上/挪下/挪进等: *Jacob could hardly drag himself up the stairs.* 雅各布上楼时几乎挪不动脚。

4 ▶PERSUADE SB TO COME 劝某人来◀ [T always+ adv/prep] *informal* if you drag someone somewhere, you persuade or force them to come when they do not want to【非正式】硬拉某人去某处: **drag sb along/away etc** *Try and drag her along to the meeting tonight.* 尽量把她也拉来参加今晚的聚会。| *Carla can't drag him away from the football on TV.* 卡拉无法把他拉开不看电视上的足球赛。

5 drag yourself away (from) to leave someone or something, or stop doing something, although you do not want to 恋恋不舍地离开〔某人或某物〕; 不情愿地停止〔做某事〕: *It's well worth a visit if you can drag yourself away from the pool.* 这个地方很值得一看, 如果你能离得开台球桌的话。

6 ▶TIME 时间◀ [I] if time or an event drags, it seems to go very slowly because nothing interesting is happening〔指时间、事情〕进行得缓慢: *Friday afternoons always drag.* 星期五下午总是过得那么慢。

7 ▶TOUCH THE GROUND 拖在地上◀ [I] if something is dragging along the ground, in the mud etc, part of it is touching the ground, the mud etc as you move〔指某物〕拖着地; 拖到泥上: [+along/in] *Your coat's dragging in the mud.* 你的大衣拖着泥了。

8 drag your feet/heels *informal* to take too much time to do something because you do not want to do it【非正式】做事拖拉; 迟迟不做: *The authorities are dragging their feet over banning cigarette advertising.* 当局在禁止香烟广告一事上迟迟不采取行动。

9 drag sb's name through the mud/mire to tell people about the bad things that someone has done, so that they will have a bad opinion of them 公开某人的坏事, 使某人出丑

10 drag (along) behind sb to go more slowly than someone so that you are always behind them〔放慢脚步以便始终〕跟在某人后面

11 ▶COMPUTER 电脑◀ [T always+adv/prep] to move something on a computer screen by pulling it along with the MOUSE (2)〔在电脑屏幕上〕用鼠标器拖动〔某物〕

12 drag a pond/river etc to look for something in a lake, river etc by pulling a heavy net along the bottom 拖着重网在池底/河底等搜寻〔某物〕: *They dragged the lake for the missing girl's body.* 他们用拖网在湖底搜寻失踪女孩的尸体。

13 ▶BOAT 船◀ [T] if a boat drags its ANCHOR¹ (1), it pulls the anchor away from its place on the sea bottom 把〔锚〕拖离海底

drag sb ↔ **down** *phr v* [T] **1** to make someone feel unhappy or discouraged 使〔某人〕感到不愉快〔沮丧〕: *All these criticisms were dragging her down.* 所有这些批评使她情绪低落。**2 drag sb down to your level** *informal often humorous* to make someone behave like you, in a worse way than they would usually behave【非正式, 常幽默】把某人带坏; 让某人行为标准下降: *"Look at this mess – it's not like you!" "I know – Ken's dragged me down to his level."* "看看这乱糟糟的样子, 你以前可不这样啊!" "我知道, 肯把我带坏了。"

drag sb/sth ↔ **in** *phr v* [T] to start to talk about someone or something that is not connected with what you are talking or arguing about 把〔不相干的人或事〕扯进谈话〔争论〕中: *Why drag Jules in? He has nothing to do with it.* 为什么把朱尔斯扯进来? 他与此事无关。

drag sb/sth **into** sth *phr v* [T] to make someone get involved in a particular situation, discussion etc even though they do not want to 把…硬扯进〔某个情况、讨论等〕之中: *I'm sorry to drag you into this mess.* 很抱歉, 把你扯进这烂摊子中来。

drag on *phr v* [I] if an event drags on, it seems to continue for longer than is necessary, often because you are bored〔指事情〕拖延地进行: [+for] *The meeting dragged on for hours.* 会议拖拖拉拉地开了好几个小时。

drag sth ↔ **out** *phr v* [T] to make a meeting, an argument etc last longer than is necessary 使〔会议、争论等〕不必要地拖长时间: *"How long can she drag this argument out?" Calvin wondered.* "她会把这场争论拖到什么时候?" 卡尔文想。

drag sth **out of** sb *phr v* [T] to make someone tell you something when they had not intended to or were not supposed to do so 迫使〔某人〕说出〔某事〕: *He'll tell me, even if I have to drag it out of him!* 他必须告诉我, 即使是逼他, 我也要他说出来!

drag sb/sth ↔ **up** *phr v* [T] **1** to mention an unpleasant subject or event, even though it is not necessary and it upsets the people who were involved in it 提起令人不愉快的话题[事情]: *The newspapers are dragging up her alleged affair again.* 报纸又把她所谓的风流韵事抖了出来。**2** *BrE informal often humorous* to RAISE¹ (4) a child so badly that when they are adult they behave badly, have bad manners etc【英, 非正式, 常幽默】不加管教地把〔孩子〕养大: *That child must have been dragged up.* 那孩子一定是没受到良好的家庭教育。

drag² *n*

1 ▶SB/STH BORING 乏味的人/事◀ a drag *informal* something or someone that is unexciting or boring【非正式】乏味无聊的人[事物]: *The party was a real drag.* 那晚会真是乏味。| *Don't be such a drag! Come out with us.* 别扫大家的兴了! 跟我们一起去吧。

2 be a drag on a person or thing that is a drag on someone makes it hard for them to make progress towards what they want 是…的累赘: *Marriage would be a drag on my career.* 婚姻会成为我事业的累赘。

3 ▶ON CIGARETTE 关于香烟◀ [C] the act of breathing in smoke from your cigarette 吸入一口烟: **take a drag on** *Pran took a deep drag on his cigarette.* 普兰深深地吸了一口香烟。

4 ▶CLOTHES 衣服◀ [U] women's clothes worn by a man, or men's clothes worn by a woman 男子穿的女服; 女子穿的男服: **in drag** *The whole performance is done in drag.* 在整场演出中, 演员们都穿着异性的服装。

5 ▶FORCE 力◀ [singular,U] the force of air that pushes against an aircraft or a vehicle that is moving forward〔作用于行进中的飞行器或车辆的〕空气阻力: *Increasing the car's height increases aerodynamic drag.* 增加汽车的高度会加大空气阻力。

6 ▶BORING JOURNEY 乏味的旅程◀ [U] *BrE informal* a long and boring journey【英, 非正式】漫长而乏味的旅程: *It's a terrible drag all the way from Tijuana.* 从蒂华纳出发的这段旅途太漫长乏味了。

7 the main drag *AmE informal* the biggest or longest street that goes through a town【美, 非正式】〔横穿城镇的〕主要街道, 主马路: *We passed the last buildings on the main drag of Encino.* 我们走过了恩西诺市主马路的最后几座楼。

8 ▶STH THAT IS PULLED 拖[拉]之物◀ [C] something that is made to be pulled along 用于拖[拉]的东西: *a drag harrow* 拖耙

drag·gled /ˈdrægḷd; ˈdrægəld/ *adj literary* BEDRAGGLED【文】弄湿的, 弄脏的

drag·gy /ˈdrægɪ; ˈdrægi/ *adj informal* boring or unpleasant【非正式】乏味的, 令人不愉快的

drag·net /ˈdrægˌnɛt; ˈdrægnet/ *n* [C] **1** a net that is pulled along the bottom of a river or lake, to bring up things that may be there 拖网 **2** a system in which the police look for criminals, using very thorough methods〔警察搜寻罪犯的〕法网, 罗网; 拉网搜捕: *a police dragnet* 警察的搜捕网

dragon 龙

drag·on /ˈdrægən; ˈdrægən/ *n* [C] **1** a large imaginary animal that has wings and a long tail and can breathe out fire 龙 **2** *informal* a woman who behaves in an angry, unfriendly way【非正式】凶狠的妇女, 悍妇: *Casey's new teacher's a real dragon.* 凯西的新老师真是个母老虎。—see also 另见 **chase the dragon** (CHASE¹ (6))

drag·on·fly /ˈdrægənˌflaɪ; ˈdrægənflaɪ/ *n* [C] a brightly coloured insect with a long thin, often coloured body and transparent wings 蜻蜓

dra·goon¹ /drəˈgun; drəˈguːn/ *n* [C] a soldier in past times who rode a horse and carried a gun and sword〔旧时骑马、佩枪剑的〕重骑兵; 龙骑兵

dragoon² *v*

dragoon sb **into** sth *phr v* [T] to force someone to do something they do not want to do 强迫〔某人〕做〔某事〕: **dragoon sb into doing sth** *Monica was dragooned into being on the management committee.* 莫妮卡被迫加入管理委员会。

drag queen /ˈ· ·/ *n* [C] *slang* a HOMOSEXUAL man who dresses as a woman【俚】着女装的同性恋男子

drag race /ˈ· ·/ *n* [C] *AmE* a car race that is won by the car that can increase its speed fastest over a very short distance【美】短程汽车加速赛 —**drag racing** *n* [U]

drag·ster /ˈdrægstɚ; ˈdrægstə/ *n* [C] a car used in drag races that is long, narrow, and low 短程汽车加速赛赛车

drain¹ /dren; dreɪn/ *v*

1 ▶LIQUID 液体◀ a) [T] to make the water or liquid flow away from something 使流走; 使排出: *Can you drain the spaghetti, please?* 请把意大利面条的水沥干, 好吗? | *Deep ditches were*

D

dug to drain the fields. 挖了深沟以排干田里的水。| **drain sth from sth** *Brad drained all the oil from the engine.* 布拉德将发动机中的机油全部放了出去。| **well/poorly etc drained** *Carrots grow best in a well drained soil.* 胡萝卜在排水性能良好的土壤中长得最好。—see picture on page A11 参见 A11 页图 **b)** [I] if liquid drains, it flows away〔液体〕流走; 流失: [+away] *I watched the bath water drain away.* 我看着浴缸里的水慢慢流光。**c)** [I] if something drains, the liquid that is in it or on it flows away and it becomes dry 流干; 沥干: *Open ditches drain very efficiently.* 明沟排水效果非常好。

2 drain a glass/cup etc to drink all the liquid in a glass, cup etc 喝干玻璃杯/茶杯等中的饮料: *Hannah drained her mug in one gulp.* 汉娜一口气就喝光一大杯饮料。

3 ▶USE TOO MUCH 消耗过多◀[T] to use too much of something so that there is not enough left 消耗太多, 耗尽: *Huge imports were draining the country's currency reserves.* 大量的进口正在消耗国家的货币储备。| **drain sb/sth of sth** *Our country is being drained of many of its best scientsists.* 我们国家许多优秀的科学家正在流失。

4 ▶MAKE TIRED 使疲劳◀[T] to make someone feel very tired and without any energy 使〔某人〕疲劳, 使筋疲力尽: *Working with sick children every day really drains you.* 每天和病童们打交道确实让人非常疲劳。

5 ▶COLOUR 颜色◀[I always+adv/prep] if the colour drains from your face, your skin becomes very pale usually because you are frightened or shocked〔因恐惧或震惊而〕脸色煞白, 面无血色: [+from/away etc] *All the colour had drained from Zelda's cheeks.* 泽尔达面如死灰。

6 ▶BE REDUCED 减少◀[I always+adv/prep] to gradually be reduced 慢慢减少: [+away/out of etc] *The family's wealth has slowly drained away.* 家里的财产已逐渐减少。

drain sth ↔ **off** *phr v* [T] to make water or a liquid flow off something, leaving it dry 使流走, 使变干: *Leave to simmer for 40 minutes then drain off the stock.* 煨 40 分钟, 之后把汤沥掉。

drain² *n* [C] **1** *especially BrE* a pipe that carries water or waste liquids away【尤英】下水管, 下水道, 排[废]水管: **blocked drains** *The drains were blocked and the streets were full of water.* 下水道堵塞了, 街道上到处是水。**2** the frame of metal bars over a drain where water etc can flow into it〔下水道开口上面的〕排水格栅: *Clear the leaves out of the drain.* 把排水格栅上的树叶清除掉。**3 a drain on sth** something that continuously uses time, money, strength etc 消耗〔时间、金钱、体力等〕的事物: *Not having anybody to rent my room is a serious drain on my financial resources.* 没有人租我的房子, 我的财源因此大减。**4 down the drain** *informal* wasted or having no result【非正式】被浪费掉; 没有结果: *The fire meant two years' hard work down the drain.* 那场火灾意味着两年的辛劳都付诸东流了。—see also 另见 BRAIN DRAIN

drain·age /ˋdrenɪdʒ; ˈdreɪnɪdʒ/ *n* [U] **1** a system of pipes or passages in the ground for carrying away water or waste liquids 排水系统; 排水管; 排水沟; 下水道: *drainage channels* 排水沟渠 **2** the process by which water or waste liquid flows away through this system 排水, 排污

drained /drend; dreɪnd/ *adj* very tired and without any energy 精疲力尽的: *Steve felt so drained he could hardly make it to the car.* 史蒂夫觉得精疲力尽, 几乎走不到汽车边上。

drain·ing board /ˋ‥ ˏ/ *n* [C] a slightly sloping area next to the kitchen SINK² where you put wet dishes to dry〔厨房洗碗槽边略呈倾斜的、可放置湿碗碟的〕滴水板 —see picture on page A10 参见 A10 页图

drain·pipe /ˋdrenˌpaɪp; ˈdreɪnpaɪp/ *n* [C] **1** *BrE* a pipe that carries rain water away from the roof of a building【英】〔排除屋顶雨水的〕排水管; 落水管 **2** *BrE* a pipe that carries waste water away from buildings【英】〔把废水排出建筑物的〕排水管; 下水道的管子; DOWNSPOUT *AmE*【美】—see picture on page A4 参见 A4 页图

drainpipe trou·sers /ˌ‥ ˋ‥/ *n* [plural] *BrE* trousers with narrow legs【英】瘦腿裤, 紧身裤

drake /drek; dreɪk/ *n* [C] a male duck 公鸭 —see also 另见 DUCKS AND DRAKES

Drake, Sir Francis (1540-96) an English sailor and EXPLORER, who was the first Englishman to sail around the world, and was one of the leaders of the English navy when it defeated the Spanish Armada in 1588 德雷克爵士〔(1540-1596), 英国水手、探险家。他是第一个完成环球航行的英国人, 1588 年打败西班牙"无敌舰队"的英国海军统帅之一〕

dram /dræm; dræm/ *n* [C] **1** also 又作 **drachm** a small unit of weight or of liquid 打兰〔重量单位或液量单位〕—see table on page C4 参见 C4 页附录 **2** a small alcoholic drink, especially WHISKY 少量的酒〔尤指威士忌〕: *Would you like a wee dram before you go?* 你走之前想喝点酒吗?

dra·ma /ˋdrɑmə; ˈdrɑːmə/ *n* **1** [C] a play for the theatre, television, radio etc 戏剧; 电视剧; 广播剧 **2** [U] plays considered as a form of literature 剧本; 戏剧作品; 戏剧学: *drama classes* 戏剧课 | **drama school** (=place for students to study drama) 戏剧学校; 戏剧学院 **3** [C,U] an exciting and unusual situation or set of events 戏剧性场面; (一连串) 戏剧性事件: *Maggie's life is always full of drama.* 玛吉的生活总是充满了戏剧性的事件。| **the drama of** *We all shared in the drama of the rescue.* 我们共同经历了惊险的救援工作。**4 make a drama out of sth** to make things seem worse than they really are 对某事大惊小怪, 对某事小题大作: *We won't make a drama out of a crisis.* 我们不会把危机夸大其词。 3

dra·mat·ic /drəˋmætɪk; drəˈmætɪk/ *adj* **1** impressive, sudden, and often surprising 给人深刻印象的; 突然的; 惊人的: *the dramatic changes taking place in Eastern Europe* 发生在东欧的巨变 **2** exciting 激动人心的: *a dramatic point in the story* 故事的一处高潮 **3** connected with drama or the theatre 戏剧的: *a dramatic production* 戏剧演出 **4** in a way that you intend to be impressive and exciting 夸张的; 像演戏似的: *Tristan immediately threw up his hands in a dramatic gesture.* 特里斯坦立即像演戏一样把双手向上甩了一下。—**dramatically** /-klɪ; -kli/ *adv*: *Output has increased dramatically.* 产量已大幅度提高。

dramatic i·ron·y /ˏ‥ ˋ‥/ *n* [U] a special effect in a play in which the people watching know something that the characters in the play do not, and can understand the real importance or meaning of what is happening 戏剧性讽示〔一种特殊的戏剧效果, 观众知道剧中人所不知道的某些情况, 因而能理解剧中正在发生之事真正的重要性或含义〕

dra·mat·ics /drəˋmætɪks; drəˈmætɪks/ *n* **1** [U] the study or practice of skills used in drama, such as acting 戏剧表演艺术[研究]; 演技; 演戏: *amateur dramatics* 业余戏剧活动 **2** [plural] behaviour that shows too much feeling, and that is often insincere; HISTRIONICS 夸张做作的行为

dram·a·tis per·so·nae /ˌdræmətɪs pɚˋsoni; ˌdræmətɪs pɜːˈsəʊnaɪ/ *n* [plural] *Latin* the characters in a play【拉丁】剧中人物

dram·a·tist /ˋdræmətɪst; ˈdræmətɪst/ *n* [C] someone who writes plays, especially serious ones; PLAYWRIGHT〔尤指严肃的〕剧作家, 编剧

dram·a·tize also 又作 **-ise** *BrE*【英】/ˋdræməˌtaɪz; ˈdræmətaɪz/ *v* **1** [T] to change a story so that it can be performed as a play 把〔小说、故事等〕改编为剧本: *a novel dramatized for television* 改编成电视剧的一部小说 **2** [I,T] to make a situation seem more exciting, terrible etc than it really is (使) 戏剧化; 戏剧性地表现: *Why do you have to dramatize everything?* 你为什么一定要把每件事都戏剧化呢? —**dramatization** /ˌdræmətəˋzeʃən; ˌdræmətaɪˈzeɪʃən/ *n* [C,U]

Dram·bu·ie /dræmˋbjuɪ; dræmˈbjuːi/ *trademark* a type of Scottish LIQUEUR (=a sweet and very strong alcoholic drink) made from WHISKY【商标】杜林标〔一种苏格兰利口酒, 以威士忌为基酒酿制而成〕

drank /dræŋk; dræŋk/ the past tense of DRINK[1]

drape¹ /drep; dreɪp/ *v* [T] **1** to cover or decorate something with folds of cloth〔用打褶的布〕披, 盖; 装饰: **drape sth over/around etc sth** *Jack emerged with a towel draped around him.* 杰克身上围着一条浴巾走了出来。| **drape sth with/in etc sth** *a coffin draped in the national flag* 覆盖着国旗的灵柩 **2** to let something hang or lie somewhere loosely 将〔某物〕随便地挂

Sir Francis Drake 德雷克爵士

[放]在〔某处〕: **drape sth over/around sth** *Mina lay back, her arms draped lazily over the cushions.* 明娜向后靠了靠, 胳膊懒散地搭在靠垫上。

drape² *n* **drapes** [plural] *especially AmE* curtains, especially long thick curtains【尤美】〔尤指长而厚重的〕窗帘, 布帘

drap·er /ˈdrepɚ; ˈdreɪpə/ *n* [C] *BrE old-fashioned* someone who sells cloth, curtains, etc【英, 过时】布商; 纺织品商

drap·er·y /ˈdrepərɪ; ˈdreɪpəri/ *n* **1** [C,U] cloth arranged in folds 打褶的布: *a casket covered with embroidered silk drapery* 盖有绣花丝质罩布的小箱子 **2** [U] *BrE* cloth and other goods sold by a draper【英】布料, 布匹; 纺织品; DRY GOODS (2) *AmE*【美】 **3** [U] *BrE* the trade of selling cloth, curtains, etc【英】布业; 帘幕业

dras·tic /ˈdræstɪk; ˈdræstɪk/ *adj* strong, sudden, and often severe 激烈的; 突然的; 严厉的: *NATO threatened more drastic action if its terms were not met.* 如果条款得不到履行, 北约威胁将要采取更为严厉的行动。—**drastically** /-klɪ; -kli/ *adv*: *The size of the army was drastically cut.* 军队被大幅裁减。

drat /dræt; dræt/ *interjection old-fashioned* used to show you are annoyed【过时】见鬼〔用来表示气愤〕: *Drat! The car won't start!* 见鬼! 车发动不起来了! —**dratted** *adj*: *Where are my dratted keys?* 该死的钥匙在哪儿?

draught¹ *BrE*【英】, **draft** *AmE*【美】/dræft; drɑːft/ *n* [C]

1 ▶COLD AIR 冷空气◀ a current of cold air flowing through a room〔穿过房间的〕一股冷风, 穿堂风: *Shut the window – there's a draught in here!* 把窗户关上 —— 有穿堂风!

2 ▶GAME 游戏◀ draughts [plural] *BrE*【英】 **a)** a game played by two people, each with 12 round pieces, on a board of 64 squares 国际跳棋; CHECKERS (2) *AmE*【美】 **b)** the pieces used in a game of draughts 国际跳棋的棋子

3 ▶SWALLOW 吞◀ the act of swallowing liquid, or the amount of liquid swallowed at one time 一饮; 一口之量: *Mick took a long draught of lager.* 米克喝了一大口淡啤酒。

4 on draught *especially BrE* a beer that is on draught is served from a large container rather than a bottle; on tap (TAP¹ (4b))【尤英】〔啤酒〕从大的容器中汲取的, 散装的

5 ▶MEDICINE 药◀ *literary* a medicine that you drink【文】〔药的〕饮剂: *a sleeping draught* 一剂安眠药水

6 ▶FIRE 火◀ the flow of air to a fire〔炉子的〕通风气流

7 ▶SHIP 船◀ the depth of water needed by a ship so that it will not touch the bottom of the sea, a river etc〔船的〕吃水深度

draught² *BrE*【英】, **draft** *AmE*【美】*adj* [only before noun 仅用于名词前] **1** a draught animal is used for pulling heavy loads〔牲畜〕负重的, 役用的 **2** a draught beer is served from a large container, not a bottle〔啤酒〕从桶中汲取的, 桶装的

draught·board /ˈdræftˌbɔrd; ˈdrɑːftbɔːd/ *n* [C] *BrE* a board with 64 squares on which the game of draughts (DRAUGHT¹ (2)) is played【英】国际跳棋棋盘; CHECKERBOARD *AmE*【美】

draughts·man *BrE*【英】, **draftsman** *AmE*【美】/ˈdræftsmən; ˈdrɑːftsmən/ *n* [C] **1** someone who draws all the parts of a new building or machine that is being planned 绘图员, 制图员 **2** someone who draws well 善于绘画的人

draugh·ty *BrE*【英】, **drafty** *AmE*【美】/ˈdræftɪ; ˈdrɑːfti/ *adj* with currents of air blowing through it 通风的; 有穿堂风的: *a draughty old house* 四面通风的老房子

S1 W1

draw¹ /drɔ; drɔː/ *v past tense* drew /dru; druː/ *past participle* drawn /drɔn; drɔːn/

① PICTURE/DESCRIPTION 图画/描绘
② MOVE 移动
③ GET/CAUSE STH 得到某物/引起某事
④ MAKE COMPARISON/JUDGMENT 进行比较/评判
⑤ MAKE SB NOTICE 引起某人注意
⑥ MONEY 钱
⑦ AIR/WATER 空气/水
⑧ BY CHANCE 碰巧
⑨ STOP/END 停止/结束
⑩ SPORT 体育运动
⑪ OTHER MEANINGS 其他意思

① PICTURE/DESCRIPTION 图画/描绘

1 ▶WITH PENCIL 用铅笔◀ [I,T] to make a picture of something with a pencil or pen〔用铅笔或钢笔〕画, 绘画: *Can I draw your portrait?* 我能给你画张肖像吗? | *I've never been able to draw well.* 我总是画不好。| **draw sb sth/draw sth for sb** *Hans drew her a map showing her how to get there.* 汉斯给她画了张图, 告诉她怎样去那儿。

2 ▶DESCRIBE 描绘◀ [T] to describe something in speech or writing〔用语言或文字〕描写, 刻画: *the vividly drawn character of Heathcliff* 刻画得惟妙惟肖的人物 —— 希思克利夫

② MOVE 移动

3 ▶MOVE IN ONE DIRECTION 往一个方向移动◀ [I always+adv/prep] to move steadily in a particular direction〔往某个方向〕稳步移动: **draw towards/past etc** *We watched from the deck as their boat drew alongside.* 我们在甲板上看着他们的船开过来与我们的船平行。

4 draw near/close to move closer in time or space〔时间、空间的〕临近: *Maria grew anxious as the men drew closer.* 当那些男人靠近的时候, 玛丽亚变得很着急。| *Christmas is drawing near.* 圣诞节即将来临。

5 draw level to move into a position where you are equal to someone else in a race, game, or competition〔在比赛、竞赛中与某人〕拉平: *Black drew level with the other runners.* 布莱克和其他赛跑选手拉平了。

6 ▶PULL 拉◀ [T always+adv/prep] to make someone or something move by pulling them gently〔轻拉〕使移动: **draw aside/up/across etc** *Drawing the covers around her, Zoe curled up in bed.* 佐薇拉过被子盖在身上, 在床上蜷成一团。| *Hussain drew me aside to whisper in my ear.* 侯赛因把我拉到一边, 在我耳边私语。

7 draw the curtains to open or close the curtains 拉开[上]窗帘

8 ▶PULL A VEHICLE 拉车◀ [T] if an animal draws a vehicle, it pulls it along〔指动物〕拉〔车〕: *a carriage drawn by six horses* 六匹马拉的车

9 ▶TAKE OUT 拿出来◀ [T always+adv/prep] to take something out of a container, cover etc〔从容器、覆盖物等中〕拿出来: **draw sth out/from etc** *Smedley drew some papers from his pocket.* 斯梅德利从口袋中掏出一些文件来。

10 draw a gun/pistol/sword etc to take a weapon from its container or from your pocket 拔出枪/手枪/剑等: *Jack drew his knife with a flourish.* 杰克挥手拔出刀来。

11 draw a tooth/cork/nail to pull a tooth etc out 拔牙/瓶塞/钉子

③ GET/CAUSE STH 得到某物/引起某事

12 ▶GET STH IMPORTANT 得到重要之物◀ [T] to get something that you need or that is important from someone or something 得到, 获取〔所需要的或重要的东西〕: *I drew a lot of comfort from her kind words.* 从她体贴的话语中我得到了许多安慰。| *Plants draw nourishment from the soil.* 植物从土壤中汲取营养。

13 ▶GET A REACTION 引起反应◀ to get a particular kind of reaction from someone because of something you have said or done〔因言行〕引起〔某种反应〕: **draw praise/criticism etc (from)** *Reagan's remarks drew an angry response from the Democrats.* 里根的话引起了民主党人愤怒的反应。| **draw fire (from)** (=be criticized)(从…)招致批评 *The new proposals drew fire from all sides for being elitist.* 新的提议由于主张精英主义而遭到了各方的批评。

④ MAKE COMPARISON/JUDGMENT 进行比较/评判

14 draw a comparison/analogy etc to compare two things, people, ideas etc 进行对照/类比等: *Do you think we can draw*

a parallel between the two novels? 你认为我们能把这两部小说相比较吗？

15 draw a distinction/line etc to say that you think two things are different and show why you think so 区分/划分等: *We have to draw a line between fantasy and reality.* 我们必须划清幻想与现实的界线。

16 draw a conclusion/moral etc (from sth) to decide that a particular fact or principle is true after thinking carefully about it（从某事物中）得出结论/获得教益等: *Now that you've heard the evidence, you can draw your own conclusions.* 既然你们已经听过了证词，你们就可以自己得出结论了。

⑤ MAKE SB NOTICE 引起某人注意

17 draw sb's attention (to sth) to deliberately make someone notice something 有意使某人注意（某事物）: *I'd like to draw your attention to the no smoking rule.* 我希望你们注意禁止吸烟的规定。

18 draw sb's eye if something draws your eye, it is so interesting that you notice it 吸引某人的目光: *The intentness of his gaze drew all eyes towards him.* 他目不转睛的凝视把所有人的目光都吸引到了他身上。

⑥ MONEY 钱

19 ►FROM YOUR BANK ACCOUNT 从银行账户◄ also 又作 **draw out** [T] to take money from your bank account〔从银行账户中〕取〔钱〕: *Hughes had drawn $8,000 in cash from a bank in Toronto.* 休斯从多伦多的一家银行中提走了8000美元现金。

20 ►BE PAID 领钱◄ [T] to receive an amount of money regularly from your employer or the government〔从雇主或政府那里〕定期领取〔一定数量的钱〕: *How long have you been drawing unemployment benefit?* 你领取失业救济金有多久了？

21 draw a cheque (on sth) *BrE*【英】, **draw a check (on sth)** *AmE*【美】to write a cheque for taking money out of a bank 开〔从某银行取款的〕支票: *a check drawn on a Swiss bank* 由一家瑞士银行支付的支票

⑦ AIR/WATER 空气/水

22 ►LIQUID 液体◄ [T] to take water, beer etc from a well or container〔从井里或容器中〕抽出，打出〔水、啤酒等〕

23 ►INTO YOUR LUNGS 进入肺里◄ [T] to take air or smoke into your lungs 吸入〔空气或烟〕: **draw breath** *I was having trouble just drawing breath, but Meg ran on up the hill.* 我连喘气都困难，梅格却一路跑着上了山。

24 ►FIRE/CHIMNEY 火/烟囱◄ [I] if a fire or CHIMNEY draws, it lets the air flow through to make the fire burn well〔火或烟囱〕通风好；通气〔使火烧得旺〕

⑧ BY CHANCE 碰巧

25 ►PLAYING CARD/TICKET 抓牌/抽签◄ [I,T] to choose a card, ticket etc by chance 随意抽牌，抽签: *I drew the ace of spades.* 我抽到了黑桃A。

26 draw the short straw used to say that someone has been unlucky because they were chosen by chance to do an unpleasant job 运气不佳: *I'm only here because I drew the short straw.* 我全是因为运气不好才到这儿来的。

27 draw lots to decide who will do something by taking pieces of paper etc out of a container 抓阄；抽签〔以决定谁来做某事〕: *We drew lots to see who would go first.* 我们抽签决定谁先去。

28 be drawn against sb *BrE* to be chosen by chance to play or compete against someone【英】抓阄决定与某人竞赛

⑨ STOP/END 停止/结束

29 draw to a halt/stop if a vehicle draws to a halt, it slows down and stops〔车辆等〕慢慢停下来

30 draw to a close/end if an event or a period of time draws to a close etc, it ends or finishes〔某事件或一段时间等〕结束，终止

31 draw a line under sth to say that something is completely finished 某事已彻底结束: *The agreement draws a line under the recent rail dispute.* 这一协议结束了最近的铁路纠纷。

⑩ SPORT 体育运动

32 ►GAME 比赛◄ [I,T] *especially BrE* to end a game or match without either side winning【尤英】(使)〔比赛〕打成平局，不分胜负: *They drew 3-3.* 他们打成三平。| *Inter drew with Juventus last night.* 昨晚国际米兰队和尤文图斯队打平了。

33 draw a bow to bend a BOW[3] (1) by pulling back the string in order to shoot an ARROW (1) 拉弓

⑪ OTHER MEANINGS 其他意思

34 [T] to attract someone 吸引〔某人〕: *Beth felt drawn to this gentle stranger.* 贝丝被这个温文尔雅的陌生人吸引住了。| **draw a crowd** *The festival is likely to draw huge crowds.* 这个节日有可能吸引大群大群的人。

35 draw the line (at sth) to refuse to do something because you disapprove of it〔因不赞同而〕拒绝〔做某事〕: *I'd really like to help you, but I draw the line at lying.* 我确实想帮助你，但撒谎的事我不干。

36 draw a blank *informal* to be unsuccessful, especially when you have been trying to find information or the answer to a problem【非正式】〔尤指在寻求消息或问题的答案时〕不成功，无结果: *Detectives hunting the missing girl have drawn a blank.* 侦探们对寻找那个失踪的女孩毫无所获。

37 ►PERSUADE SB 劝说某人◄ [T usually passive 一般用被动态] to persuade someone to talk about something 说服某人谈论某事: *She refused to be drawn on the subject of her divorce.* 她拒绝谈论她离婚的话题。

38 draw blood to make someone BLEED 使〔某人〕流血

39 draw breath to find time to have a rest when you are busy〔在忙碌时〕喘口气，歇一下: *I didn't have time to draw breath this morning.* 今天早上我连喘口气的时间都没有。

40 draw a veil over sth to deliberately keep something unpleasant or embarrassing from being known 隐瞒某事；避而不谈某事〔指不愉快或尴尬的事〕: *It might be best to draw a veil over Peter's past for now.* 现在或许最好别谈彼得的过去。

41 ►SHIP 船◄ *technical* if a ship draws a certain depth, it needs that depth of water to float in【术语】吃水 —see also 另见 be at daggers drawn (DAGGER (3))

draw back *phr v* [T] **1** to move yourself away from something 闪避，后退: *He drew back in horror when he saw the cuts on her face.* 当他看到她脸上的伤口时，他吓得直往后退。**2** to be afraid or unwilling to do something 害怕[不愿]做〔某事〕: [+from] *The company drew back from making a firm commitment.* 该公司不肯作出肯定的承诺。

draw in *phr v* **1** [I] if the days or nights draw in, it gets dark earlier in the evening and so there are fewer hours of daylight〔白昼〕变短: *In October the nights start drawing in.* 10月里天黑得越来越早了。**2** [T usually passive 一般用被动态] to involve someone in something, often when they do not really want to take part 使〔某人〕卷入〔某事〕〔通常在其不情愿的情况下〕: **draw sb in** *We invited Al along to our meetings but he was wary of getting drawn in.* 我们邀请阿尔一起来参加我们的会议，但他不想被扯进来。**3 draw your horns in** *BrE* to spend less money because you have financial problems【英】紧缩开支

draw sb **into** sth *phr v* [T] to involve someone in something, often when they do not really want to take part 将〔某人〕扯入〔某事中〕: *Homeless children often get drawn into crime.* 无家可归的儿童经常被扯进犯罪活动中。

draw sth ↔ **off** *phr v* [T] to remove some liquid from a larger supply 使流走，排掉: *We had to draw off some water from the radiator.* 我们得从散热器中放掉一些水。

draw on *phr v* **1 draw on a cigarette/cigar etc** to breathe in smoke from a cigarette etc 吸香烟/雪茄等 **2** [T] to use money, experiences etc for a particular purpose〔为某种目的〕利用，动用〔钱、经验等〕: **draw on/upon sth** *It was a challenge but luckily we had the expertise to draw on.* 这是个挑战，但幸运的是，我们可以利用我们的专长。| **draw on your savings** *I had to draw on my savings to pay for the repairs.* 我得动用存款来支付修理费。**3** [I] if a period of time draws on, it comes nearer〔指时间〕临近: *Winter is drawing on.* 冬天快到了。

draw out *phr v* **1** [T] to make someone feel less nervous and more willing to talk 使〔某人〕不紧张，使〔某人〕愿意说话: **draw sb out** *Try to draw the new boy out a bit if you can.* 可能的话，尽量哄这个新来的男孩说上几句话。**2** [T] to make an event last longer than usual 拖延: **draw sth ↔ out** *The final questions drew the meeting out for another hour.* 最后几个问题使会议又延长了一个小时。**3** [I] if the days draw out, it stays light until later in the evening and so there are more hours of daylight〔白昼〕变长: *It's nice when the days start drawing out again.* 白天又开始变长时真好。

draw up *phr v*

1 ►LIST/CONTRACT ETC 名单/合同等◄ [T] to prepare a written document 起草，草拟〔文件〕: **draw sth ↔ up** *They drew up a list of candidates.* 他们草拟了一份候选人的名单。

2 ►VEHICLE 车辆◄ [I] to arrive somewhere and stop 到达某处停下: *The taxi drew up at the gate.* 出租车在大门口停了下来。

3 draw up a chair [T] to bring a chair closer to someone or

something 把椅子拉近〔某人或某物〕: *Ben drew his chair up to the fireplace.* 本把他的椅子拉到壁炉旁。
4 draw yourself up (to your full height) to stand up very straight because you are angry or determined about something 〔因生气或下决心而〕挺直身体站立: *Drawing himself up to his full height, he ordered me out of the room.* 他挺直身体, 命令我出去。
5 draw up your knees to bring your legs closer to your body 蜷起双膝〔让腿靠紧身体〕: *I found him rolling on the floor in pain, with his knees drawn up to his chest.* 我看见他痛得双膝蜷在胸前在地板上打滚。
6 ▶SOLDIERS 士兵◀ [T usually passive 一般用被动态] to arrange people in a special order 使排好队形; 使列阵: **draw** sth **up** *troops drawn up in ranks* 排好队列的部队

draw² *n* [C] **1** *especially BrE* a game that ends with both teams having the same number of points【尤英】平局, 不分胜负 **2** the act of choosing a winning number, ticket etc in a LOTTERY (1) 抽奖; 抓阄; 抽签: *Bill picked the winning number on the first draw.* 比尔第一次抽奖就抽中了获奖号码。**3** a performer, show, sports team etc that a lot of people are willing to pay to see 有吸引力的表演者[演出, 球队等]: *Whitney Houston is always a big draw.* 惠特尼·休斯顿总是很叫座。**4 quick/fast on the draw a)** able to pull a gun out quickly in order to shoot 出枪快速 **b)** good at reacting quickly and intelligently to difficult questions or in difficult situations 〔对困难形势或问题〕反应机敏: *Amit was very quick on the draw in his interview.* 面试时, 阿米特反应非常迅速。—see also 另见 **the luck of the draw** (LUCK¹ (15))

draw·back /ˈdrɔˌbæk; ˈdrɔːbæk/ *n* [C] a disadvantage of a situation, product etc 缺点, 毛病; 不利因素: **[+of/to (doing sth)]** *One drawback of New York in the summer is the heat.* 纽约夏天的一个缺点就是炎热。

draw·bridge /ˈdrɔˌbrɪdʒ; ˈdrɔːbrɪdʒ/ *n* [C] a bridge that can be pulled up to let ships pass, or to stop people from entering or attacking a castle 吊桥; 开合桥

S3 **drawer** /drɔr; drɔː/ *n* **1** [C] part of a piece of furniture, such as a desk, that you pull out and push in and use to keep things in 抽屉: *The scissors are in the kitchen drawer.* 剪刀在厨房抽屉里。—see also 另见 BOTTOM DRAWER, TOP-DRAWER —see picture on page A10 参见 A10 页图 **2 drawers** [plural] *old-fashioned* underwear that women and girls wear between their waist and the tops of their legs; KNICKERS【过时】女用短衬裤

S2 W2 **draw·ing** /ˈdrɔɪŋ; ˈdrɔːɪŋ/ *n* **1** [C] a picture that you draw with a pencil, pen etc 图画: *She's done some beautiful charcoal drawings.* 她画了一些漂亮的炭笔画。**2** [U] the art of making pictures, plans etc with a pen or pencil 〔用笔进行的〕绘画; 制图: *Drawing has never been my strong point.* 画图从来都不是我的强项。

drawing board /ˈ‥ ˌ/ *n* **1** [C] a large flat board that artists and DESIGNERs work on 画板 **2 (go) back to the drawing board** to start working on a plan or idea again after something that you have tried has failed 失败后从头做起: *We didn't raise enough money so it's back to the drawing board.* 我们没有筹集到足够的钱, 因此又得从头开始了。

drawing pin /ˈ‥ ˌ/ *n* [C] *BrE* a short pin with a round flat head, used especially for putting notices on boards or walls【英】图钉; THUMBTACK *AmE*【美】—see picture at 参见 PIN¹ 图

drawing room /ˈ‥ ˌ/ *n* [C] *old-fashioned* a room, especially in a large house, where you can entertain guests or relax【过时】客厅, 起居室

drawl /drɔl; drɔːl/ *v* [I,T] to speak in a slow unclear way with vowel sounds that are longer than normal 拉长腔调慢吞吞地说话 —**drawl** *n* [singular]: *a Southern drawl* 〔美国〕南方拉长调的说话方式

drawn¹ /drɔn; drɔːn/ the past participle of DRAW¹

drawn² *adj* someone who looks drawn has a thin pale face, usually because they are ill or worried 脸色苍白的, 憔悴的, 愁眉苦脸的

drawn-out /ˌ‥ ˈ‥◂/ *adj* taking more time than usual or more time than you would like 拖长了的, 冗长的: **long drawn-out** *a long drawn-out dispute* 冗长的争论

draw·string /ˈdrɔˌstrɪŋ; ˈdrɔːstrɪŋ/ *n* [C] a string through the top of a bag, piece of clothing etc that you can pull tight or make loose 〔袋口、衣服的〕束带, 拉绳 —see picture on page A17 参见 A17 页图

dray /dre; dreɪ/ *n* [C] a flat CART¹ (1) with four wheels that was used in the past for carrying heavy loads, especially BARRELs of beer 〔旧时用于装运大桶啤酒的〕四轮平板车

dread¹ /drɛd; dred/ *v* **1** [T] to feel anxious or worried about something that is going to happen or you think will happen in the future 畏惧, 惧怕; 担心: *I've got an interview tomorrow and I'm dreading it.* 明天我要去面试, 我正为此担惊受怕呢。| **dread doing sth** *I'm dreading going back to work.* 我害怕回去工作。| **dread sb doing sth** *Tim dreaded his parents finding out.* 蒂姆唯恐他父母发现这事。| **dread (that)** *I'm dreading that I'll be asked to help on Sunday.* 我担心会要我星期天帮忙做事。**2 I dread to think** *spoken* used to show that you think a situation is very worrying【口】我不敢去想〔用于表示对某事十分担忧〕: *I dread to think what the children will get up to when I'm away.* 我真不敢想我不在家的时候孩子们会干出些什么事来。

dread² *n* **1** [U] a fear of something in the future 恐惧, 害怕; 担心: *The prospect of meeting Mark's relatives filled her with dread.* 要见马克的亲属使她非常担心。| **a dread of** *a dread of the unknown* 对未知事物的恐惧 **2 be/live in dread of** to continuously be very anxious or afraid of what may happen 处于对…的恐惧之中: *The people of the war-torn city live in dread of further shelling.* 饱受战争破坏的城市居民生活在再次遭到轰炸的恐惧中。

dread·ed /ˈdrɛdɪd; ˈdredɪ̣d/ also 又作 **dread** *literary*【文】*adj* [only before noun 仅用于名词前] *sometimes humorous* making you feel afraid or anxious【有时幽默】可怕的, 吓人的: *I hear the dreaded Miss Jones is going to be at the meeting.* 我听说令人生畏的琼斯小姐也将出席那个会议。

dread·ful /ˈdrɛdfəl; ˈdredfəl/ *adj especially BrE*【尤英】**1** extremely unpleasant 糟糕的, 令人极讨厌的: *We've had some dreadful weather lately.* 最近天气糟透了。**2** [only before noun 仅用于名词前] used to emphasize how bad something or someone is 极糟的〔用于强调〕: *It's a dreadful waste of money.* 那真是太浪费钱了。

dread·ful·ly /ˈdrɛdfəlɪ; ˈdredfəli/ *adv especially BrE*【尤英】**1** [+adj/adv] extremely 非常, 极其: *They're dreadfully busy at the moment.* 此刻他们非常忙。**2** very badly 糟糕地: *The team played dreadfully.* 那个球队表现得太差劲了。**3** very much 十分, 很: *Would you mind dreadfully if I didn't come?* 我不来你会很不高兴吗?

dread·locks /ˈdrɛdˌlɑks; ˈdredlɒks/ *n* [plural] a way of arranging your hair, popular with RASTAFARIANs, in which it hangs in thick lengths like pieces of rope 〔常见于牙买加拉斯塔法里教信徒的〕"骇人"长发绺; 拉斯塔法里发绺 —see picture at 参见 HAIRSTYLE 图

dread·nought /ˈdrɛdˌnɔt; ˈdrednɔːt/ *n* [C] a type of WARSHIP used at the beginning of the 20th century 无畏战舰, 弩级战舰〔20 世纪初使用的一种战舰〕

dream¹ /drim; driːm/ *n* S2 W2
1 ▶ASLEEP 睡着的◀ [C] a series of thoughts, images, and feelings that you experience when you are asleep 梦: *In my dream, I was playing football with the children.* 在梦里, 我在和孩子们踢足球。| **have a dream** *I had a really weird dream last night.* 昨晚, 我做了个特别怪异的梦。| **bad dream** (=frightening or unpleasant) 噩梦 *He claims that eating cheese late at night gives him bad dreams.* 他声称在夜里吃乳酪会让他做噩梦。| **recurring dream** (=a dream you have again and again) 反复出现的梦境
2 ▶WISH 愿望◀ [C] something you hope for and want to happen very much 梦想; 愿望; 理想: *Mike's big dream was to be a professional racing driver.* 迈克的最大梦想就是成为一名职业赛车手。| **[+of]** *a dream of becoming rich* 发财的梦想 | **dream house/car etc** (=the house, car etc you really want) 梦寐以求的房子/汽车等 *Three weeks in Barbados is my idea of a dream holiday.* 在巴巴多斯停留三个星期是我梦寐以求的绝好假期。| **the house/job of your dreams** *I have just met the man of my dreams!* 我刚刚遇到了我梦中的白马王子! | **beyond your wildest dreams** (=better than anything you ever imagined or hoped for) 做梦也想不到
3 ▶UNREAL SITUATION 不真实的情景◀ [singular] a situation that does not seem real or part of normal life 像梦一样的情景, 梦境: **be/seem like a dream** *After a few weeks back at work our vacation seems like a dream.* 回来工作了几个星期之后, 我们的假期仿佛是一个梦。
4 ▶PLEASANT THOUGHTS 遐想◀ [C usually singular 一般用单数] a set of pleasant thoughts that make you forget about what is really happening; DAYDREAM² 幻想, 遐想, 白日梦: *Peter's lost in a dream again.* 彼得又陷入幻想之中。
5 a dream come true something that you wanted to happen for a long time 梦想成真: *Finding my real mother after all these*

years was a dream come true. 这么多年后终于找到我的亲生母亲，我的梦想成真了。

6 like a dream *usually spoken* extremely well or effectively【一般口】好极了；非常有效：*The plan worked like a dream.* 这个计划进行得非常顺利。| **go like a dream** (=work perfectly) 用起来极好；性能极佳 *The new motorbike goes like a dream.* 这辆新摩托车开起来特别得心应手。

7 a dream *usually spoken* a very attractive person or thing【一般口】非常漂亮的人[物]：*Her latest boyfriend is an absolute dream.* 她的新任男友绝对够帅。

8 be/live in a dream world to have ideas or hopes that are not practical or likely to happen 生活在梦幻世界：*If you think he'll change, you're living in a dream world.* 如果你认为他会改变，你就太不实际了。

9 in your dreams *spoken* used to say that something is not likely to happen【口】妄想；在做梦〔表示某事不可能发生〕：*"I'm going to ask her to go out with me." "In your dreams!"* "我要约她出来。" "你做梦吧！"

3 **dream²** *v past tense and past participle* **dreamed** or **dreamt** /dɛmt; dremt/

1 ▶THINK ABOUT 梦想◀ [I,T] to think about something that you would like to happen 梦想，幻想，向往：[+of] *We dream of buying our own house.* 我们向往着买自己的房子。| **dream (that)** *She dreamed that one day she would be famous.* 她梦想有朝一日会成名。| [+about] *We used to dream about living abroad.* 过去我们常常梦想去国外生活。

2 ▶WHILE SLEEPING 睡觉时◀ [I,T] to have a dream while you are asleep 做梦；梦见：[+about] *I dreamt about you last night.* 我昨晚梦到你了。| **dream (that)** *It's quite common to dream that you're falling.* 做梦梦到自己从高处坠落是件常有的事。

3 ▶IMAGINE 想象◀ [I,T] to imagine that you have done, seen, or heard something that you have not 想象着做过[见过；听到]（某事）：*I was sure I posted the letter but I must have dreamt it.* 我确信自己已经把信寄出去了，但我一定是在凭空想象。

4 wouldn't dream of (doing) sth *spoken* used to say that you would never do something because you do not approve of it or think it is unpleasant【口】无论如何也不会做某事：*We wouldn't dream of letting our daughter go out on her own at night.* 我们无论如何也不会让女儿晚上独自出门。

5 who would have dreamt it? *spoken* used to express surprise about something that has happened【口】谁能料到会这样呢？〔表示惊讶、惊奇〕：*"Did you hear that Bruno's been made Managing Director?" "Yes, who would have dreamt it?"* "你听说布鲁诺被任命为总经理这件事了吗？" "听说了，谁也想不到啊！"

dream sth ↔ **away** *phr v* [T] to waste time by thinking about what may happen〔在空想中〕虚度〔光阴〕：*She would just sit in her room dreaming away the hours.* 她常常会在自己房间里坐着幻想上数小时。

dream on *phr v* [I] *spoken*【口】**dream on!** used to tell someone that they are hoping for something that will not happen 别做梦了！〔用于告诉某人希望的事情不可能发生〕：*You think I'm going to help you move house? Dream on!* 你以为我会帮你搬家？别做梦了！

dream sth ↔ **up** [T] to think of a plan or idea, especially an unusual one 虚构出，凭空想出〔不同寻常的计划、主意等〕：*Who on earth dreams up the plots for these soap operas?* 这些肥皂剧的情节到底是谁想出来的？

dream·boat /ˈdrimˌbot; ˈdriːmbəʊt/ *n* [C] *old-fashioned* someone who is very good-looking and attractive【过时】好看而有吸引力的人；梦中情人

dream·er /ˈdrimɚ; ˈdriːmə/ *n* [C] **1** someone who has ideas or plans that are not practical 空想家 **2** someone who dreams while they are asleep 做梦的人

dream·i·ly /ˈdrimɪlɪ; ˈdriːmə̆li/ *adv* thinking about pleasant things and not about what is actually happening 神情恍惚地；心不在焉地：*"I'm coming," he replied dreamily, without moving.* "我来了。" 他心不在焉地回答道，动都没有动一下。

dream·land /ˈdrimˌlænd; ˈdriːmlænd/ *n* [U] a happy place or situation that exists only in your imagination 梦境；梦乡；理想世界

dream·less /ˈdrimlɪs; ˈdriːmləs/ *adj* dreamless sleep is very deep and peaceful〔睡眠〕无梦的；安宁的

dream·like /ˈdrimˌlaɪk; ˈdriːmlaɪk/ *adj* as if happening in a dream; unreal 如梦的，虚幻的，梦幻般的：*There was a dreamlike quality about the film.* 这部电影有一种梦幻般的情调。

dreamt /drɛmt; dremt/ a past tense and past participle of DREAM²

dream tick·et /ˈ· ·· / *n* [C] a combination of people who you think will be sure to win an election for a political party〔被认为一定会为某政党赢得选举的候选人的〕梦幻组合：*Clinton and Gore were the Democrats' dream ticket.* 克林顿和戈尔是民主党的理想候选班子。

dream·y /ˈdrimɪ; ˈdriːmi/ *adj* **1** someone who is dreamy has a good imagination but is not very practical〔指人〕爱幻想的：*a bright, but dreamy child* 一个聪明但爱幻想的孩子 **2** looking as though you are thinking about something pleasant rather than things happening around you 神情恍惚的，心不在焉的：*a dreamy look* 恍惚的神情 **3** a dreamy sight, sound etc is peaceful and relaxing〔景色、声音等〕恬静的，悠闲的：*She loved the dreamy music of those old songs.* 她喜欢那些老歌优美的曲调。**4** *informal* very attractive and desirable【非正式】极富吸引力的；理想的；极好的：*a dreamy new sports car* 一辆极漂亮的新跑车 —**dreaminess** *n* [U]

drear·y /ˈdrɪrɪ; ˈdrɪəri/ also 又作 **drear** /drɪr; drɪə/ *poetical adj* not interesting or cheerful【诗】乏味的；沉闷的：*the same old dreary routine* 枯燥的老一套例行公事 | *a dreary winter's day* 沉闷的冬日

dredge /drɛdʒ; dredʒ/ *v* **1** [T] to remove mud or sand from the bottom of a river, HARBOUR¹ etc 疏浚，给…清淤 **2** [I,T] to search for something on the bottom of a river, lake, etc with a dredge〔用挖泥船、疏浚机在河底、湖底等处〕寻找，打捞 **3** [T] to cover food lightly with flour, sugar etc〔在食物上〕撒上〔面粉、糖等〕

dredge sth ↔ **up** *phr v* [T] **1** *informal* to start talking again about something that happened a long time ago【非正式】重提〔旧事〕：*Come on now, let's not dredge up old quarrels.* 好了，我们不要再提以前的争吵了。**2** to pull something up from the bottom of a river〔从河底〕捞取；打捞

dredg·er /ˈdrɛdʒɚ; ˈdredʒə/ also 又作 **dredge** *n* [C] a machine or ship used for digging or removing mud and sand from the bottom of a river, HARBOUR¹ etc 挖泥船；疏浚机

Dred Scott Case /ˌdrɛd ˈskɑt ˌkes; ˌdred ˈskɒt ˌkeɪs/ also 又作 **the Dred Scott Decision** an important decision made by the US Supreme Court in 1857. The case was brought to the Supreme Court by a SLAVE (=someone who is legally owned by another person) called Dred Scott. The Chief Justice of the Supreme Court officially decided that Dred Scott, like other slaves, could not be considered a citizen of the US. He also stated that Congress must not prevent any state from having slavery. 德雷德·斯科特案；德雷德·斯科特裁决〔1857年美国联邦最高法院作出的一项重大裁决。该案是由一位叫德雷德·斯科特的奴隶向美国最高法院提交的。美国联邦最高法院首席法官正式裁决，德雷德·斯科特与其他奴隶一样不能被视为美国公民。他还声明，国会不得阻止各州蓄奴。

CULTURAL NOTE 文化注释

These decisions made many people extremely angry, especially the ABOLITIONISTS (=people who wanted to end slavery and make it illegal) and members of Congress. The Dred Scott Case is considered to be one of the main causes of the American Civil War. 这些裁决令很多美国人极为愤怒，尤其是废奴主义者和国会议员。德雷德·斯科特案被看做是美国内战的一大导火索。

dregs /drɛgz; dregz/ *n* **1** [plural] small pieces that sink to the bottom of wine, coffee etc〔沉入酒、咖啡等物中的〕渣滓，沉淀物 —compare 比较 LEE (3) **2 the dregs of society/humanity** an offensive expression used to describe the people that you consider are the least important or useful 社会/人类渣滓

Drei·ser /ˈdraɪzɚ; ˈdraɪsə/, **The·o·dore** /ˈθiədor; ˈθiːədɔː/ (1871-1945) a US writer who wrote *Sister Carrie* and *An American Tragedy* 德莱塞〔(1871-1945)，美国作家，著有《嘉莉妹妹》和《美国的悲剧》〕

drench /drɛntʃ; drentʃ/ *v* [T] to make something or someone extremely wet 使湿透；淋透；浇透 —**drenching** *adj*

drenched /drɛntʃt; drentʃt/ *adj* **1** extremely wet 湿透的：*Come on in – you're drenched!* 快进来，你都淋透了！| [+with/in] *I came back from aerobics drenched in sweat.* 我练完健身操回来，浑身都让汗给湿透了。| **drenched to the skin** (=wearing completely wet clothes) 浑身湿透 **2** covered in something〔以某物〕覆盖着的：[+in] *women drenched in cheap perfume* 全身喷满廉价香水的女人 | **rain-drenched/sun-drenched etc** (=covered in rain, or in the effects of something such as the sun) 被雨水浸泡的/沐浴在阳光里的 *sun-drenched deserts* 沐浴在阳光里的沙漠

Dres·den /ˈdrɛzdn̩; ˈdrezdən/ **1** a city in the east of Germany which was badly bombed in World War II 德累斯顿〔德国东部一城市，二战期间曾遭到英国飞机的猛烈轰炸〕**2 fine CHINA** (=small people, animals, cups, plates, etc made from baked clay) made in Dresden. People sometimes use the expression 'Dresden

china' to talk about someone who seems very delicate or weak. 德累斯顿细瓷〔人们有时把看似柔弱的人说成是Dresden china〕: *Harry treats his wife like a piece of Dresden china.* 哈里对待娇妻就像对待德累斯顿细瓷一样。

dress¹ /dres; dres/ *n* **1** [C] a piece of clothing worn by a woman or girl that covers her body from her shoulder to somewhere on her leg 连衣裙, 套裙: *Sheila wore a long red dress.* 希拉穿了一条长的红色连衣裙。—compare 比较 SKIRT¹ (1) **2** [U] the way someone dresses 穿着, 着装: *His dress is always very formal.* 他的衣着总是很正式。**3 dress code** a standard of what you should wear for a particular situation〔某种特定场合的〕衣着标准: *This restaurant has a strict dress code – no tie, no service.* 这家餐厅有严格的衣着标准——不系领带, 恕不招待。**4 evening/national/battle etc dress** a special set of clothes that you wear for a particular occasion 晚礼服/民族服装/野战服装等 —see also 另见 DRESS SENSE, CLOTHES (USAGE)

dress 穿衣服

He got dressed. 他穿上了衣服。

He put on a jacket. 他穿上外衣。

He wore a dark suit. 他穿着黑色西装。

dress² *v*

1 ►PUT ON CLOTHES 穿上衣服◄ a) [I] to put on clothes, etc, especially before a special occasion〔尤指为某种特殊场合〕穿好衣服: *I've got to go home to dress.* 我得回家去更衣打扮一下。| **dress for** (=put on clothes you wear for a particular activity) 为…穿好衣服 *How do you normally dress for work?* 你通常穿什么衣服上班? | **dress for dinner** (=put on formal clothes for your evening meal) 为晚餐而穿上正式的服装 **b)** [T] to put clothes on yourself or someone else 给…穿衣: *I dress the kids before I go to work.* 我给孩子们穿好衣服, 然后上班。—see also 另见 DRESSED

2 ►WEAR CLOTHES 穿着衣服◄ [I] to wear a particular kind of clothes 穿衣: *Dress warmly if you're going out for a walk.* 如果你出去散步就穿得暖和些。

3 dress a wound/cut etc to clean and cover a wound etc 清洗并包扎伤口/刀口等

4 dress a salad to put a mixture of oil, VINEGAR, salt etc onto a SALAD (=cold vegetables) 给沙拉加〔油、醋、盐等〕调味品: *Don't dress the salad until just before you're ready to eat.* 沙拉要在准备吃的时候才加调味品。

5 dress poultry/crab etc to clean and prepare meat or fish so that it is ready to cook or eat 清洗并加工禽肉/螃蟹等〔以备烹饪或食用〕

6 ►MAKE CLOTHES 制作服装◄ [T] to make or choose clothes for someone 为〔某人〕制作[选择]服装: *The Princess is dressed by one of Britain's most famous designers.* 王妃的服装是由英国最著名的一位设计师设计的。

7 ►HAIR 头发◄ [T] *formal* to arrange someone's hair into a special style【正式】做〔头发〕

8 ►HORSE 马◄ [T] to brush a horse in order to make it clean 梳刷〔马的毛〕

9 dress wood/metal/leather etc *technical* to polish or put a special surface onto wood etc【术语】对木材/金属/皮革等做表面处理

10 dress stone *technical* to cut and shape stone so that it can be used in building【术语】加工石料

11 ►SOLDIERS 士兵◄ [I,T] *technical* a word used in the army to tell soldiers to form a straight line【术语】看齐; (使) 排列整齐

dress down *phr v* **1** [I] to wear clothes that are more informal than you would usually wear〔比平时〕穿着随便 **2** [T **dress sb ↔ down**] to speak angrily or severely to someone about something they have done wrong 训斥, 怒斥〔某人〕—see also 另见 DRESSING-DOWN

dress up 装扮; 打扮

The kids are dressing up in their room.
孩子们在自己的房间里装扮。

Jill's getting dressed up for the dinner party.
吉尔在为晚宴打扮。

dress up *phr v* **1** [I,T] to wear special clothes, MAKE-UP (1), etc for fun〔闹着玩地〕装扮: [+as] *He went to the party dressed up as a Chicago gangster.* 他装扮成一个芝加哥歹徒去参加晚会。| [+in] *I keep a box of old clothes for the children to dress up in.* 我保存了一箱旧衣服让孩子们穿着玩。| [**dress sb ↔ up**] *We dressed him up as a gorilla.* 我们把他装扮成大猩猩。**2** [I] to wear clothes that are more formal than you would usually wear〔比平时〕穿着正式: *It's a small informal party – you don't have to dress up.* 这是个非正式的小型聚会, 你不用穿得那么正式。**3** [T **dress sth ↔ up**] to make something sound more interesting or attractive than it really is 对…加以修饰, 美化: *It was the old offer dressed up as something new.* 这只不过是原来的那个提议, 改头换面像新的罢了。

USAGE NOTE 用法说明: DRESS

WORD CHOICE 词语辨析: **dress, get dressed, put on, dress up, dress yourself, have on, wear, dress in, be in**

If you **dress** (slightly formal) or **get dressed** you **put on** all your clothes. But you usually use **put on** if you are talking about just one piece of clothing or things like glasses and jewellery. dress〔稍正式〕或 get dressed 表示穿上所有的衣服。但是 put on 则通常表示穿上一件衣服或戴上眼镜或首饰等物品: *It's ten o'clock – isn't time you got dressed?* 10点钟了, 你是不是该穿好衣服了? | *We had to wash and dress in a freezing bathroom.* 我们只得在冰冷的浴室里洗脸并穿衣服。| *OK, you can put your shirt*

back on. 好了，你可以把衬衫重新穿上了。| *Wait a moment while I put my shoes on.* 等一会儿，我把鞋穿上。

You **dress up** only in special clothes or for a special occasion. These may be particularly good or formal ones. dress up表示为参加某个特殊的场合而穿着特殊的服装，可以是特别好的衣服或正式的衣服：*What kind of party is it? Will we have to dress up?* 那是个什么样的聚会？我们要不要穿得正式些？Or they may be unusual clothes that make you look like someone else, for example if you are acting in a play. dress up还可以表示穿上不同寻常的衣服，以使你看起来像另外一个人，如当你在演戏时：*He had to dress up as a clown.* 他不得不装扮成小丑。

You only talk about someone **dressing themselves** if a special effort is involved. 只在谈论某人穿衣需要特别费力时，才使用dressing oneself: *Can Tara dress herself yet?* (=Tara is a small child) 塔拉能自己穿衣服吗？〔塔拉是个小孩儿〕| *Since the accident he can't feed or dress himself.* 自从那次事故之后，他无法自己吃饭、穿衣。

After you have **put on** your clothes etc, you **have** them **on**. put on 表示穿戴衣物等的动作，而 have ... on 表示已穿戴上之后的状态：*They all had dark glasses on.* 他们都戴着墨镜。

Wear means to **have** clothes, jewellery etc **on** and is often used to describe someone's usual style of dressing. wear 表示穿着衣服或佩戴着珠宝，而且还经常用来描述一个人平时惯常的穿着风格：*She always wears earrings/casual clothes/black.* 她总是佩戴着耳环/穿着休闲服装/穿着黑色衣服。| *I'll be wearing a red coat.* 我将会穿着一件红外套。| *All visitors to the site must wear a protective helmet.* 所有参观现场的人都必须戴防护头盔。You can also use **dress (in)** and **be (dressed) in** to talk about what clothes someone is wearing, or their style of clothes. dress (in) 和 be (dressed) in 也可以用来表示某人正穿戴着什么服饰或表示某人的穿戴风格：*She always dresses casually/in black.* 她总是穿得很随便/身穿黑色衣服。| *The band were all (dressed) in green and red jackets.* 乐队里的人都穿着红绿相间的短上衣。

GRAMMAR 语法

You **dress in** clothes, or **dress** someone **in** them. You cannot *dress clothes* or *dress with clothes.* 穿衣服用 dress in clothes 表示，给某人穿衣服用 dress someone in clothes。不能用 dress clothes 或 dress with clothes 表示穿衣服。

dres·sage /drɛˈsɑʒ; ˈdresɑːʒ/ *n* [U] a competition in which a horse performs a complicated series of actions in answer to signals from its rider 花式骑术比赛，马术比赛

dress cir·cle /ˈ·,··/ *n* [C] the lowest of the curved rows of seats upstairs in a theatre 戏院楼上最低层前排座位

dressed /drɛst; drest/ *adj* **1 get dressed** to put your clothes on 穿上[穿好]衣服：*Go and get dressed!* 赶快把衣服穿好！**2** having your clothes on 穿好衣服的：*Aren't you dressed yet?* 你还没有穿好衣服吗？| **fully dressed** (=with all your clothes on) 穿戴齐备的 **3** wearing a particular type of clothes 穿某种类型衣服的：**[+in/as]** *The older woman was dressed in a suit.* 那位年长些的妇女穿着套装。| **well/neatly/badly etc dressed** *a very well-dressed young man* 穿着很体面的小伙子 **4 dressed to kill** *informal* wearing very attractive clothes so that everyone notices you【非正式】穿着非常漂亮的 **5 dressed (up) to the nines** *informal* wearing your best or most formal clothes【非正式】穿着盛装；衣饰华丽：*Where on earth's he going dressed up to the nines like that?* 他穿得那么考究到底要去哪儿？

dress·er /ˈdrɛsɚ; ˈdresə/ *n* [C] **1** *BrE* a large piece of furniture with open shelves for storing plates, dishes etc; WELSH DRESSER【英】碗柜，碗橱 **2** *AmE* a piece of furniture with drawers for storing clothes, sometimes with a mirror on top; CHEST OF DRAWERS【美】衣橱 **3 a fashionable/stylish/sloppy etc dresser** someone who dresses in a fashionable etc way 穿着新潮者/时髦者/邋遢者等：*Stanley was an impeccable dresser, with plenty of money.* 史丹利很有钱，穿得特别讲究，无可挑剔。**4** someone who looks after an actor's clothes in the theatre and helps them to dress for a play〔剧团的〕服装师

dress·ing /ˈdrɛsɪŋ; ˈdresɪŋ/ *n* **1** [C,U] a mixture of liquids, usually made from oil and VINEGAR, that you put on raw vegetables〔放在生的蔬菜上面的〕调料，调味酱：*a vinaigrette dressing* 香醋沙拉调料 —see also 另见 FRENCH DRESSING, SALAD DRESSING **2** [C,U] *AmE* a mixture of food that you put inside a piece of meat, for example a chicken, before you cook it; STUFFING (1)【美】调味馅料，填料 **3** [C] a special piece of material used to cover and protect a wound〔包扎、护理伤口的〕敷料；绷带：*Put the soiled dressings in this bin.* 把用过的脏绷带放到这个箱子里。—see also 另见 CROSS-DRESSING, POWER DRESSING, WINDOW DRESSING

dressing-down /,··ˈ·/ *n* **give sb a dressing-down** to talk to someone angrily because they have done something wrong 狠狠地训斥某人：*He gave the children a good dressing-down.* 他狠狠地训斥了孩子们一顿。

dressing gown /ˈ··,·/ *n* [C] *especially BrE* a piece of clothing like a long loose coat that you wear inside the house; BATHROBE【尤英】〔室内穿的长而宽松的〕晨衣，睡袍；浴袍

dressing room /ˈ··,·/ *n* [C] **1** a room where an actor or performer can get ready, before going on stage, appearing on television etc〔演员的〕化妆室 **2** a small room next to a BEDROOM〔卧室旁边的〕小梳妆室

dressing ta·ble /ˈ··,··/ *n* [C] *BrE* a piece of furniture like a table with a mirror on top, sometimes with drawers, that you use when you are doing your hair, putting on MAKE-UP (1) etc【英】梳妆台；VANITY TABLE *AmE*【美】

dressing-up /,··ˈ·/ *n* [U] a children's game in which they put on special clothes and MAKE-UP (1) and pretend that they are someone else〔儿童的〕化装游戏：*a box of dressing-up clothes* 箱化装用的衣服

dress·mak·er /ˈdrɛs,mekɚ; ˈdres,meɪkə/ *n* [C] someone who makes their own clothes, or makes clothes for other people as a job 给自己做衣服的人；裁缝 —**dressmaking** *n* [U]

dress re·hears·al /ˈ·,·,··/ *n* [C] the final practice of a play, OPERA etc, using all the clothes that will be worn for the actual performance 彩排

dress sense /ˈ··/ *n* [U] the ability to choose clothes that make you look attractive 衣着品位

dress shirt /ˈ··/ *n* [C] a formal shirt, sometimes with a special decoration at the front, that you wear under a DINNER JACKET〔前襟有特殊装饰的〕晚礼服衬衫

dress u·ni·form /ˈ·,···/ *n* [C,U] a uniform that officers in the army, navy etc wear for formal occasions or ceremonies 军礼服

dress·y /ˈdrɛsɪ; ˈdresi/ *adj* **1** dressy clothes are suitable for formal occasions〔服装〕适合正式场合穿的，讲究的：*Her outfit was just right for a summer evening – smart, but not too dressy.* 她的套装很适合夏日的傍晚穿 —— 时尚但又不过于正式。**2** someone who is dressy likes to wear very fashionable or formal clothes〔指人〕爱穿时髦[正式]服装的：*Mr Menendez is a very dressy sort of person.* 梅嫩德斯先生是一位很讲究穿着的人。

drew /dru; druː/ the past tense of DRAW[1]

Drew, Nan·cy /ˈnænsɪ; ˈnænsi/ the main character in US books for children. Nancy Drew is a brave young woman who is a DETECTIVE (=someone whose job is to discover information about crimes and catch criminals). 德鲁〔美国儿童系列读物中的主人公。她是一位勇敢的年轻女侦探〕

Drey·fus /ˈdrefəs; ˈdreɪfəs/, **Al·fred** /ˈælfrɪd; ˈælfrɨd/ (1859-1935) a French army officer who was put in prison in 1894 for selling military secrets to the Germans. He was not guilty, and many French writers and politicians protested about him being in prison, especially the writer Emile Zola, who wrote a famous newspaper article with the title "J'accuse!" (=I accuse). But the army and many newspapers persuaded the government to keep him in prison because they had an unreasonable dislike of him because he was Jewish. He was eventually let out of prison and officially judged to be not guilty. These events were called the **Dreyfus Affair**. 德雷福斯（1859-1935），法国军官，1894年被控向德国人出卖军事情报而入狱。事实上，他并没有罪，许多法国作家和政治家因此向当局提出抗议，尤其是作家埃米尔·左拉。他还在报纸上发表了著名的文章《我控诉!》。因为德雷福斯是个犹太人，所以军方以及不少报社对他心存莫名的厌恶感，说服当局将他继续关押。最终，他被无罪释放。这就是所谓的"德雷福斯事件"〕

drib·ble[1] /ˈdrɪbl; ˈdrɪbəl/ *v* **1** [I] *BrE* to let SALIVA (=natural liquid in your mouth) flow out of your mouth onto your chin【英】流口水；垂涎；DROOL (1) *AmE*【美】：*Watch out, the baby is dribbling on your shirt!* 小心，婴儿的口水淌到你的衬衫上了！**2** [I always+adv/prep] if a liquid dribbles, it flows very slowly in small irregular drops〔指液体〕慢慢滴淌：**[+down/from/out etc]** *There was a tiny hole in the pipe and water was dribbling out.* 管子上有个小洞，水正慢慢地往外滴。**3** [T] to pour something out slowly in an irregular way 使〔慢而不规则地〕往外倾注：*This artist works by dribbling paint straight from the tube.* 这位美术家直接把颜料从管子里挤出作画。**4** [I,T] to move the ball along with you, by short kicks, BOUNCEs, or hits, in a game of football, BASKETBALL etc〔足球、篮球等运动中的〕运（球），带（球）：*We've been learning how to dribble the ball.* 我们一直在学习如何运球。—see picture on page A23 参见 A23 页图

dribble² *n* **1** [U] *BrE* a flow of SALIVA (=natural liquid in your mouth) from your mouth【英】流淌的口水; SALIVA *AmE*【美】**2 a dribble of sth** a small amount of liquid 少量某物〔指液体〕: *He wiped a dribble of ice-cream from his chin.* 他擦掉下巴上的一小块冰激凌。**3** [C] the way in which you move the ball along with you in football, BASKETBALL etc 运球, 带球

drib·let /ˈdrɪblɪt; ˈdrɪblɨt/ *n* [C] a very small amount of something 少量, 一丁点

dribs and drabs /ˌdrɪbz ən ˋdræbz; ˌdrɪbz ən ˈdræbz/ *n* [plural] **in dribs and drabs** in small irregular amounts or numbers over a period of time 少量地, 零星地: *The guests arrived in dribs and drabs.* 客人们三三两两地到了。

dried /draɪd; draɪd/ *adj* dried substances, such as food or flowers, have had the water removed〔食物、花等〕干的, 除去水分的, 脱水的

dried fruit /ˌ· ˈ·/ *n* [C,U] fruit that has been dried and is used in cooking or eaten on its own 果脯, 干果

dried milk /ˌ· ˈ·/ *n* [U] milk that is made into a powder and can be used by adding water 奶粉

dri·er /ˈdraɪɚ; ˈdraɪə/ *n* [C] another spelling of DRYER dryer 的另一种拼法

drift¹ /drɪft; drɪft/ *v* [I] **1** to move slowly on water or in the air 飘移; 漂流: [**+out/towards etc**] *The rubber raft drifted out to sea.* 橡皮筏子漂向大海。**2** [always+adv/prep] to move or go somewhere without any plan or purpose〔毫无计划或漫无目的地〕漂泊: [**+around/along etc**] *Jenni spent the year drifting around Europe.* 珍妮这一年来一直在欧洲各地漂泊。| **drift from sth to sth** *The conversation drifted from one topic to another.* 谈话从一个话题转到另一个话题。**3 drift into sth** to go from one situation or condition to another without realizing it 不知不觉进入某种状况: *She was just drifting into sleep when the alarm went off.* 她迷迷糊糊地刚要睡着闹钟就响了。**4** if snow, sand etc drifts, the wind blows it into large piles〔指雪、沙等受风〕吹积: *The snow was drifting in great piles against the house.* 雪被风吹到屋旁, 积成了好几大堆。**5 let sth drift** to allow something to continue in the same way 听任某事发展下去, 听之任之: *He couldn't let the matter drift for much longer.* 他不会听任这种事情持续很久的。

drift apart *phr v* [I] if people drift apart, their relationship gradually ends〔人们之间的关系逐渐地〕疏远: *Over the years my college friends and I have drifted apart.* 这些年来, 我和大学时期的朋友都已经疏远了。

drift off *phr v* [I] to gradually fall asleep 慢慢入睡: *I was just drifting off when the phone rang.* 我迷迷糊糊地刚要睡着, 电话铃就响了。

drift² *n*

1 ▶SNOW 雪◀ [C] a large pile of snow, sand etc that has been blown by the wind〔风吹积成的〕雪堆, 沙堆: [**+of**] *The road is blocked with massive drifts of snow.* 大堆大堆的积雪把路给堵死了。

2 ▶SHIP 船◀ [U] the degree to which a ship or plane changes its direction because of the movement of the wind or water 偏移, 偏离

3 ▶GENERAL MEANING 大意◀ the drift the general meaning of what someone is saying〔话语的〕大意, 要旨: [**+of**] *So what's the drift of the argument?* 那么论点的要义是什么? | **follow/get/catch sb's drift** (=understand the general meaning) 明白[了解]某人的意思 *I didn't hear every word of her speech, but I got the drift.* 我没有听到她讲话的全部内容, 但是我知道了她的意思。

4 ▶CHANGE 变化◀ [singular] a slow change or development from one situation, opinion etc to another〔情形、意见等的〕渐变; 趋势: *the drift of public opinion towards the political left* 公共舆论转向左派政党的趋势 | **the broad/whole/general drift** (=the general change in direction) 总的趋势, 动向 *A general drift towards anarchy must be prevented at all costs.* 无论花任何代价都要制止住朝无政府状态发展的总趋势。

5 ▶MOVEMENT OF PEOPLE 人口流动◀ a slow and unplanned movement of large numbers of people〔大量人口缓慢、无计划的〕流动: [**+from/to/into**] *the drift from the countryside to the cities* 从乡村往城市的人口流动

drift·er /ˈdrɪftɚ; ˈdrɪftə/ *n* [C] **1** someone who is always moving from one job or place to another 漂泊者, 流浪者, 游民 **2** a fishing boat that uses a floating net 拖网[飘网]渔船

drift-ice /ˈ· ·/ *n* [U] pieces of broken ice floating in a sea, river etc 流冰, 浮冰

drift-net /ˈdrɪftˌnɛt; ˈdrɪftnet/ *n* [C] a large net behind a boat, used to catch fish 流网, 飘网

drift·wood /ˈdrɪftˌwʊd; ˈdrɪftwʊd/ *n* [U] wood floating in the sea or left on the shore 漂流木, 浮木〔在海上漂流或被海水冲上岸的木头〕

drills 钻

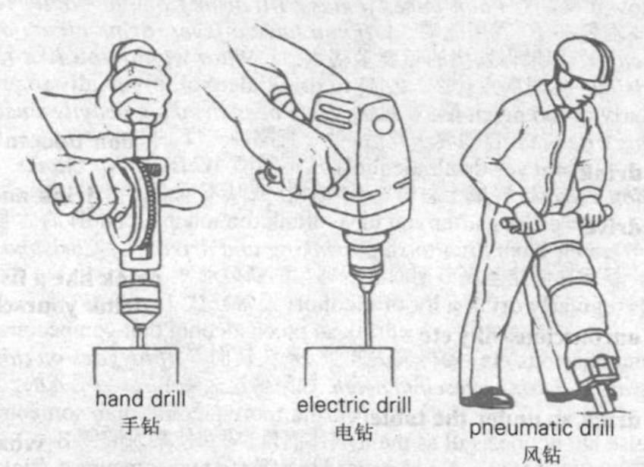

drill¹ /drɪl; drɪl/ *n*

1 ▶TOOL 工具◀ [C] a tool or machine used for making holes in something 钻; 钻床; 钻机: *an electric drill* 电钻

2 ▶WAY OF LEARNING 学习方法◀ [U] a way of learning something by repeating it many times 练习; 训练: *a pronunciation drill* 发音练习

3 fire/emergency drill a practice of the things you should do in a dangerous situation such as a fire 消防/应急演习

4 ▶MILITARY TRAINING 军事训练◀ [U] military training in which soldiers practice marching and other actions 军事操练: *rifle drill* 步枪操练

5 ▶CLOTH 布◀ [U] a type of strong cotton cloth 粗斜纹布

6 the drill *BrE old-fashioned* the correct way of doing something【英, 过时】正确的步骤; 程序: *What's the drill for getting money after four o'clock?* 4点钟之后领钱的手续是怎样的?

7 ▶SEEDS 种子◀ a) [C] a machine for planting seeds in rows 条播机 **b)** a row of seeds planted by machine 条播的一排种子

drill² *v* **1** [I,T] to make a hole in something using a drill〔用钻〕钻孔, 打眼: *You need to drill holes for the fittings.* 安装这些设备需要钻孔。| **drill for oil/water/gas etc** *The Saudi government has announced plans to drill for water in the desert.* 沙特政府已经宣布在沙漠钻井探水的计划。**2** [T] to teach someone by making them repeat something many times 教〔某人〕反复练习: *She was drilling the class in the forms of the past tense.* 她指导全班学生反复练习过去时态的各种形式。| **well-drilled** *The well-drilled cabin crew evacuated the passengers in minutes.* 训练有素的机组人员在几分钟内就疏散了乘客。**3** [I,T] to practice marching and other military actions, or to train soldiers to do this 训练, 操练 **4** [T] to plant seeds in rows 条播〔种子〕

drill sth into sb *phr v* [T] to keep telling someone something until they know it very well 向某人灌输〔某事〕: *Mother had drilled it into me not to talk to strangers.* 妈妈跟我讲了一遍又一遍, 叫我不要和陌生人说话。

drilling plat·form /ˈ·· ˌ··/ *n* [C] a large structure in the sea used for drilling for oil, gas etc 钻井平台

dri·ly /ˈdraɪlɪ; ˈdraɪli/ *adv* another spelling of DRYLY dryly 的另一种拼法

drink¹ /drɪŋk; drɪŋk/ *n* **1** [C] an amount of liquid that you drink 一杯[份]饮料: *Can I have a drink of water, please?* 我能喝杯水吗? | **soft drink** (=a non-alcoholic drink) 非酒精饮料, 软性饮料 *They sell ice-cream and soft drinks.* 他们卖冰激凌和软饮料。**2** [C,U] alcohol, or a glass or bottle of alcohol 酒; 一杯[瓶]酒: *Have another drink.* 再喝一杯。| *There were lots of food and drink left over from the party.* 晚会过后剩了许多食物和酒。| **a stiff drink** (=very strong alcohol) 烈性酒 *After that news I need a stiff drink!* 听到那则消息后我需要喝一杯烈酒! | **go out for a drink** *BrE* (=go to a PUB)【英】去酒馆喝一杯 | **take to drink** (=start drinking a lot of alcohol regularly) 开始酗酒 | **stand sb a drink** (=buy someone a drink, especially because they do not have enough money) 请某人喝一杯酒〔尤指此人没有足够的钱〕| **a drink problem** (=difficulty in limiting the amount of alcohol you drink so that it affects your life) 酗酒问题 **3 drinks** [plural] *BrE* a social occasion when you have alcoholic drinks and sometimes food【英】酒会: *Don't forget we're invited to the Jones' for drinks on Sunday.* 别忘了我们应邀到琼斯家参加星期日的酒

会。**4 the drink** *informal* the sea, a lake, or other large area of water【非正式】海; 湖; 大片水域 —see also 另见 **drive sb to drink**(DRIVE¹ (4))

drink² *v past tense* **drank**/dræŋk; dræŋk/ *past participle* **drunk** /drʌŋk; drʌŋk/ **1** [I,T] to take liquid into your mouth and swallow it 喝, 饮: *I don't need a glass, I'll drink from the bottle.* 我不需要杯子, 我用瓶喝。| *If you have a fever, drink plenty of water.* 如果你发烧的话要多喝水。| *What would you like to drink?* 你想喝点什么? **2** [I] to drink alcohol, especially regularly or too much 酗酒, 纵酒: *He's been drinking heavily since his wife died.* 自他妻子死后, 他一直酗酒无度。| **don't/doesn't drink**(=never drink alcohol) 从不喝酒 *Whisky? No thanks, I don't drink.* 要威士忌吗? 不, 谢谢, 我从不喝酒。| **drink and drive**(=driving after you have drunk too much alcohol) 酒后驾车 *a new campaign to stop drinking and driving at Christmas* 一场旨在制止圣诞节期间酒后驾车的新运动 | **drink like a fish** (=regularly drink a lot of alcohol) 经常狂饮 | **drink yourself unconscious/silly etc**(=drink so much alcohol that you become unconscious etc) 喝得失去知觉/晕头转向等 *If he goes on this way he'll drink himself to death.* 如果他这么喝下去, 会喝死的。| **drink sb under the table**(=drink more alcohol than someone else but not be as ill as them)〔比酒量〕喝到使某人醉倒 **3 what are you drinking?** *spoken* used to offer to buy someone a drink, especially in a PUB【口】你想喝点什么?〔用于表示主动给某人买酒, 尤指在酒馆中〕

drink sth ↔ **in** *phr v* [T] to look at or listen to something carefully and enjoy it 入迷地看[听], 欣赏: *We spent the day drinking in the sights and sounds of Paris.* 这一天我们尽情地享受巴黎的景色和喧嚣。

drink to sth *phr v* [T] **1** to wish someone success, good luck, good health etc before having an alcoholic drink 为〔某人的成功、好运、健康等〕祝酒, 干杯: *Let's drink to your success in your new job.* 让我们为你在新的工作中取得成功而干杯。**2 I'll drink to that!** *spoken* used to agree with what someone has said【口】我为这干一杯!〔用于表示赞同某人的话〕

drink sth ↔ **up** *phr v* [T] to drink all of something 喝光, 喝干: *Come on, drink up your milk.* 快, 把牛奶都喝了。

drink·a·ble /ˈdrɪŋkəbl; ˈdrɪŋkəbəl/ *adj* **1** water that is drinkable is safe to drink〔水〕可饮用的, 适合饮用的 **2** wine, beer etc that is drinkable is of good quality and tastes pleasant〔葡萄酒、啤酒等〕质量好的, 口感好的

drink-dri·ving /ˌ· ˈ··/ *n* [U] *BrE* driving a car after having drunk too much alcohol【英】酒后驾驶; DRUNK-DRIVING *AmE*【美】

CULTURAL NOTE 文化注释

It is illegal to drive in the US and UK if you have drunk more than the legal limit of alcohol. If the police stop you when you are driving and believe that you may have drunk too much alcohol, they will usually BREATHALYSE you (=test your breath using special equipment) to find out how much alcohol you have drunk. In the US and the UK, drink-driving is considered a very serious crime, for which you can be put in prison, lose your legal right to drive, or have to pay a large FINE. There are many advertisements, especially during the Christmas period, that try to persuade people not to drink and drive. Some large cities even offer free transportation on New Year's Eve so that people will not drive while they are drunk. 在英美, 饮用超过法定限额的酒后开车是违法的。警察通常会拦下疑似醉酒驾车者, 用呼吸测醉器对其进行醉酒测试, 确定饮酒量。英美视酒后驾车为重罪, 违反者可能会入狱、丧失驾驶资格或支付巨额罚款。有很多广告劝说人们不要酒后驾车, 圣诞节期间尤其如此。一些大城市甚至在除夕夜提供免费交通工具, 这样人们喝醉后就不会开车了。— see also 另见 MADD

drink·er /ˈdrɪŋkɚ; ˈdrɪŋkə/ *n* [C] **1** someone who regularly drinks alcohol 酒徒: *Dave has always been a bit of a drinker.* 戴夫一直是个小酒鬼。| **hard/heavy drinker**(=someone who drinks a lot) 狂饮者, 酗酒者 **2 coffee/wine/champagne etc drinker** someone who regularly drinks coffee etc 习惯喝咖啡/葡萄酒/香槟等的人: *There's no wine – we're all beer drinkers, I'm afraid.* 没有准备葡萄酒 —— 恐怕我们都习惯喝啤酒。

drink·ing foun·tain /ˈ·· ˌ··/ *n* [C] a piece of equipment in a public place that produces a stream of water for you to drink from〔公共场所的〕喷泉式饮水器; WATER FOUNTAIN *AmE*【美】

drinking-up time /ˌ·· ˈ· ·/ *n* [U] *BrE* the time, after a PUB has closed, when people are allowed to finish their drinks【英】〔酒馆关门后〕允许顾客把酒喝完的时间

drinking wa·ter /ˈ·· ˌ··/ *n* [U] water that is pure enough for you to drink 饮用水

drinks ma·chine /ˈ· ·ˌ·/ *n* [C] a machine that serves hot and cold drinks when you put money into it 自动饮料售卖机

drinks par·ty /ˈ· ˌ··/ *n* [C] *BrE* a party where you mainly talk to people and have alcoholic drinks; COCKTAIL PARTY【英】酒会

drip¹ /drɪp; drɪp/ *v* **dripped, dripping 1** [I] to produce small drops of liquid 滴水, 漏水: *The tap's dripping.* 水龙头在滴水。| *Be careful – your paintbrush is dripping.* 小心! 你的漆刷在往下滴漆。**2** [I,T] to fall or let something fall in very small drops (使) 滴下; 沥下: [**+down/from etc** *Sweat dripped from his body.* 汗从他身上滴落下来。| *Water was dripping through the ceiling.* 水正透过天花板往下滴。| **drip water/blood etc** *John came in, his arm dripping blood.* 约翰进来了, 手臂滴着血。| **be dripping with sth** *It's so hot, I'm dripping with sweat.* 天太热了, 我浑身都在滴汗。**3 be dripping with jewels/diamonds etc** to be wearing too much jewellery etc 浑身戴满了珠宝/钻石等

drip² *n* **1** [singular,U] the sound or action of a liquid falling in very small drops 滴水声; 滴落: *There was no noise except for the drip drip drip of water.* 除了滴滴答答的水声以外, 没有别的声音。**2** [C] one of the very small drops of liquid that falls from something 液滴: *I put some plastic on the floor to catch the drips.* 我把一些塑料铺在地板上接滴下来的水。**3** [C] a piece of equipment used in hospitals for putting liquids directly into your blood 滴注器; IV *AmE*【美】: *They put her on a drip to speed up the contractions.* 他们给她输液来加快子宫收缩。**4** [C] *informal* someone who is boring and has a weak character【非正式】怯懦无趣的人, 平庸乏味者

drip-dry /ˌ· ˈ·◂/ *adj* drip-dry clothing does not need ironing (IRON²)〔衣服〕滴干免烫的 **—drip-dry** *v* [I,T]

drip·ping¹ /ˈdrɪpɪŋ; ˈdrɪpɪŋ/ *n* [U] *BrE* the oily substance that comes out of meat when you cook it【英】〔烤肉时渗出的〕油

CULTURAL NOTE 文化注释

Some old people think that dripping is very tasty and have childhood memories of eating bread and dripping. Other people think it is unhealthy and unpleasant and would not want to eat it. 有些老人觉得烤肉时渗出的油很美味, 唤起童年时吃面包和渗出的油的记忆; 另一些人认为渗出的油不健康、不好吃, 因此不愿吃。

dripping² *adj* extremely wet 湿淋淋的: **dripping wet** *Take off that jacket, you're dripping wet.* 把上衣脱下来, 你都湿透了。

drip·py /ˈdrɪpɪ; ˈdrɪpi/ *adj* very emotional and weak 易动感情而软弱的: *Don't be so drippy, just call Kate and ask her out!* 别当窝囊情种了, 给凯特打电话约她出来!

drive¹ /draɪv; draɪv/ *v past tense* **drove**/drov; drəʊv/ *past participle* **driven**/ˈdrɪvən; ˈdrɪvən/

1 ▶OPERATE A VEHICLE 开车◀[I,T] to sit in a car, bus etc and make it travel from one place to another 开车; 驾驶〔轿车、公共汽车等〕: *Do you drive?* 你会开车吗? | *She drove the pick-up and got our supplies.* 她开着小货车给我们买来了日用必需品。—see picture on page A3 参见 A3 页图

2 ▶TRAVEL SOMEWHERE 去某处◀[I,T] to travel in a car 开车去 (某处): *Shall we drive or take the bus?* 我们开车去还是坐公共汽车去?

3 ▶TAKE SB SOMEWHERE 送某人去某处◀[T] to take someone somewhere in a car 开车送〔某人〕去〔某处〕: *Just tell us when you have to go, and Jim will drive you.* 你什么时候走告诉我们一声, 吉姆会开车送你。| **drive sb back/down/over etc** *Can I drive you home?* 我能开车送你回家吗?

4 ▶FEELING 感觉◀[T] to make someone feel or do something bad or unpleasant 使〔某人〕感觉不悦; 迫使〔某人〕做坏事: **drive sb to sth** *The children are driving me to despair.* 孩子们逼得我束手无策。| **drive sb to do sth** *It was hunger that drove them to steal the bread.* 他们是为饥饿所迫才去偷面包的。| **be driven by sth**(=be encouraged to do something by an unpleasant feeling or quality) 受某种不悦的感觉[品性]所驱使 *Phil, driven by jealousy, started spying on his wife.* 受嫉妒心的驱使, 菲尔开始监视他的妻子。| **drive sb to drink**(=upset someone very much) 把某人逼得借酒浇愁 *This job's enough to drive anyone to drink!* 这项工作足以把任何人逼得借酒浇愁! | **drive sb mad/crazy etc** *The noise from the neighbours is driving me mad.* 邻居家的噪音快要把我逼疯了。

5 ▶FORCE SB/STH 逼迫某人/某物◀[T] to force someone or something to go somewhere 驱赶; 驱使; 迫使…去某处: *Tourists were driven indoors by the rain.* 雨迫使游客进入室内。| *Cowhands drove the cattle into the corral.* 牛仔把牛赶进了牛栏。

6▶PROVIDE POWER 提供动力◀ [T] to provide the power for something 为〔某物〕提供动力: *a steam-driven generator* 以蒸汽为动力的发电机

7▶HIT STH INTO STH 把某物钉入某物◀ [T] to hit something, such as a nail, into something else 将〔钉子等〕敲[砸]入: *We watched Dad drive the posts into the ground.* 我们看着爸爸把木桩打入地里。

8▶SPORT 体育运动◀ [I,T] to move a ball in a game of football, GOLF etc by kicking, hitting, or bouncing (BOUNCE[1] (1)) it hard and fast 〔在足球、高尔夫球等运动中〕猛踢, 猛抽, 猛击〔球〕: *Bonds drove the ball to center field.* 邦兹猛地把球踢到中场。—see picture on page A23 参见 A23 页图

9 drive a hard bargain to make an agreement difficult by demanding a lot or refusing to give too much 极力讨价还价; 狠狠杀价

10 drive sb out of their mind to do something that makes someone feel as if they are crazy 使某人丧失理智

11 drive a coach and horses through sth to destroy an argument, plan etc completely 彻底推翻某事, 摧毁某事〔指论点、计划等〕: *The new bill will drive a coach and horses through recent trade agreements.* 这项新法案将彻底推翻最近达成的贸易协定。

12▶MAKE A HOLE 钻洞◀ [T] to make a large hole in something using heavy equipment or machinery 〔用重型设备或机器〕钻〔洞〕: *They're planning to drive a tunnel through the mountains.* 他们计划在山里开出一条隧道。

13 drive home a point to make something completely clear to someone 使清楚无误地理解: *I tried to drive home the point that we need extra people, but the boss wasn't interested.* 我尽力想说明白我们需要更多的人员, 但老板对此不感兴趣。

14 drive a wedge between to do something that makes people disagree or start to dislike each other 挑拨〔人们的关系〕, 使不和[互相厌恶]: *Lisa's lies drove a wedge between the couple.* 莉莎的谎言挑起了那对夫妇的不和。

15 drive yourself too hard to force yourself to work too hard, because you want to be successful 〔因为想成功而〕逼迫自己过分努力地工作

drive at sth *phr v* [T] **what sb is driving at** the thing someone is really trying to say 某人话语的真正意图: *He didn't mention the word 'redundancy' but I knew what he was driving at.* 他没有提"裁员"这个词, 但我知道他话里的意思。

drive sb ↔ **away** *phr v* [T] to behave in a way that forces someone to leave 赶跑〔某人〕: *Your possessiveness will drive Liz away if you're not careful.* 如果你不小心, 你的占有欲会把莉兹吓跑的。

drive off *phr v* **1** [I] if a car, driver etc drives off, they leave 〔指汽车、驾驶人员等〕开走; 驾车离开: *After the accident the other car just drove off.* 车祸之后, 另外那辆车径自扬长而去。**2** [T **drive** sb/sth ↔ **off**] to force someone or something that is attacking or threatening you to go away 赶跑, 击退〔正在威胁或攻击你的某人或某物〕: *We keep dogs in the yard to drive off intruders.* 我们在院子里养着几只狗以驱赶闯入者。**3** [I] to hit the first ball in a game of GOLF 〔高尔夫球运动中的〕发球

drive sb/sth ↔ **out** *phr v* [T] to force someone or something to leave 迫使〔某人或某物〕离开: *Downtown stores are being driven out by crime.* 犯罪活动使得市中心的商店人去店空。

drive sth ↔ **up** *phr v* [T] to force prices, costs etc to rise quickly 迫使〔价格、成本等〕快速上升: *The oil shortage drove gas prices up by 20 cents a gallon.* 石油短缺使得每加仑油价上涨了20美分。

S2 W2 **drive²** *n*

1▶IN A CAR 乘车◀ [C] a trip in a car 驱车出行: *It's a four day drive to Prague.* 开车到布拉格需要四天。| **go for a drive** *Let's go for a drive along the coast.* 我们开车到海岸边去兜兜风吧。

2▶OUTSIDE YOUR HOUSE 在房屋外边◀ [C] the area or road between your house and the street; DRIVEWAY 〔房屋与街道之间的〕私家车道: *He parked his car in the drive.* 他把车停在私家车道上。—see picture on page A3 参见 A3 页图

3▶SPORT 体育运动◀ [C] an act of hitting a ball hard, especially in tennis or GOLF 〔尤指网球或高尔夫球的〕猛击, 猛抽: *He hit a long, high drive to right field.* 他打了个高远球到右场。

4▶A FIGHT FOR STH 争取某事物的运动◀ [C] a planned effort by an organization or government to achieve a change that will improve people's lives 〔某个组织或政府为改善人民生活而作的〕有计划的努力; 运动: *a big anti-smoking drive* 大规模的反吸烟运动 | **economy drive** (=effort to reduce spending) 节约运动

5▶NATURAL NEED 自然需求◀ [C] a strong natural need which must be satisfied 基本欲求, 本能的需求: *Hunger is a human drive.* 饥饿是人类的一种原始驱动力。| *sex drive* 性欲

6▶SB'S ENERGY 某人的活力◀ [U] determination and energy that make you successfully achieve something 干劲, 魄力: *Brian has got tremendous drive.* 布赖恩干劲十足。

7 Drive used in the names of roads 路, 大道〔用于路名〕: *They live at 141 Park Drive.* 他们住在公园路141号。

8▶POWER 动力◀ [singular] the power from an engine that makes the wheels of a vehicle go round 驱动力, 传动力: *four wheel drive* 四轮驱动

9▶MILITARY ATTACK 军事进攻◀ [C] several military attacks 大规模强攻〔包括数次军事进攻〕: *a drive deep into enemy territory* 深入敌人领土的强攻战役 —see also 另见 DISK DRIVE, WHIST DRIVE

drive-by /ˈ· ·/ *adj* **drive-by shooting/killing** the act of shooting someone from a moving car 从行驶的车上射击/杀人

drive-in /ˈ· ·/ *adj* [only before noun 仅用于名词前] a drive-in restaurant, cinema etc allows you to buy food or watch a film without leaving your car 〔餐厅、电影院等〕可驾车进去的, 可坐在车上享用的 —**drive-in** *n* [C]

driv·el¹ /ˈdrɪvl; ˈdrɪvəl/ *n* [U] something that is said or written that is silly or does not mean anything 废话, 蠢话, 无聊话: *Don't talk such drivel!* 别说这样的废话!

drivel² *v* **drivelled, drivelling** [I] *BrE* 【英】**drivel on/away** to speak continuously without saying anything important 〔喋喋不休地〕说废话 —**drivelling** *adj*: *a drivelling idiot* 唠叨些废话的白痴

driv·en¹ /ˈdrɪvən; ˈdrɪvən/ the past participle of DRIVE¹

driven² *adj* trying extremely hard to achieve what you want 有紧迫感的; 迫切的 —see also 另见 **as pure as the driven snow** (PURE (8))

S1 W2 **driv·er** /ˈdraɪvɚ; ˈdraɪvə/ *n* [C] **1** someone who drives a car, bus etc 司机, 驾驶员; 开车的人 **2** a GOLF CLUB (2) with a wooden head 〔有木制槌头的〕高尔夫球杆, 发球杆 —see also 另见 **back seat driver** (BACK SEAT (2)), **Sunday driver** (SUNDAY (3))

driv·er's ed·u·ca·tion /ˌ· · ˈ· · · ·/ *n* [U] *AmE* a course that you usually take at school, that teaches you how to drive a car 【美】〔中学的〕驾驶课程

driver's lic·ense /ˈ· · ˌ· ·/ *n* [C] *AmE* an official document that allows you to drive on public roads 【美】〔汽车〕驾驶执照; DRIVING LICENCE *BrE* 【英】

drive shaft /ˈ· ·/ *n* [C] *technical* a part of a vehicle that takes power from the GEARBOX to the wheels 【术语】〔车辆的〕主动轴, 驱动轴

drive-through /ˈ· ·/ *n* [singular] *especially AmE* a restaurant, bank etc where you can buy food or do business without getting out of your car 【尤美】〔不必下车就可购买食物或做生意的〕汽车餐厅; 汽车银行

drive·way /ˈdraɪvˌwe; ˈdraɪvweɪ/ *n* [C] the area or road between your house and the street; DRIVE² (2) 〔房子与街道之间的〕私家车道 —see picture on page A3 参见 A3 页图

driv·ing /ˈdraɪvɪŋ; ˈdraɪvɪŋ/ *adj* **1 driving rain/snow** rain or snow that falls very hard and fast 暴雨/大雪 **2 driving force/ambition/politician** someone or something that produces a strong effect on people or situations 驱动力/激励向上的抱负/强有力的政治家: *Hawksworth was the driving force behind the project.* 霍克斯沃思是推动该项目的主要人物。

driving li·cence /ˈ· · ˌ· ·/ *n* [C] *BrE* an official document that allows you to drive on public roads 【英】〔汽车〕驾驶执照; DRIVER'S LICENSE *AmE* 【美】

CULTURAL NOTE 文化注释

In most parts of the US you must be at least 15 to learn to drive and 16 to get a driver's license. In the UK you must be at least 17 before you can learn to drive or get a driving licence. When you are learning to drive in either country, you must have a special document called a LEARNER'S PERMIT (in the US), or PROVISIONAL LICENCE (in the UK). This document allows you to practise driving with someone who already has a licence, and is changed into a full licence (=one which allows you to drive alone) when you pass your DRIVING TEST. People in the UK usually learn to drive by having private driving lessons. People in the US also learn by having private lessons, but many high schools offer a course called DRIVER'S EDUCATION. These classes teach students how to drive and also teach them the laws about driving in their state. In both the US and UK, you must pass a short written test about road laws as well as a practical driving test in order to get a full licence. In the UK, learner drivers have to put L-PLATES (=a flat white square with a red letter L on it) on the front

and back of their car until they pass their driving test. Some people who have just passed their driving test fix P-PLATES (=a flat white square with a green letter P on it) to warn other drivers to be careful, but this is not COMPULSORY. 在美国大部分地区，学车须满15岁，得到驾驶执照须年满16岁。在英国，学车或获得驾驶执照须年满17岁。无论在美国还是英国，学车时必须持有一种特别文件，美国称见习驾驶员许可证，英国称临时驾驶执照。该文件允许学车者在已有执照者陪同下练习驾车，通过驾驶考试则可获得正式驾驶执照。英国人通常上私人驾驶课，美国也有私人驾驶课，但很多高中提供驾驶员教育的课程，教授学生如何驾车以及本州的驾驶规章。在英美两国，要取得正式驾驶执照，都要经过简短的交通法规笔试和路考。英国的见习驾驶员须在车前和车后贴上L标牌（上有红色L字样的白色方块），直到通过驾驶考试。一些刚刚通过驾驶考试的人贴有P标牌（上有绿色P字样的白色方块），以便提醒其他驾驶员小心，但这不是强制规定。

driving range /ˈ· · ˌ·/ *n* [C] an open outdoor area where people practice hitting GOLF balls 室外高尔夫球练习场

driving school /ˈ· · ˌ·/ *n* [C] an organization that teaches you how to drive a car 驾驶学校

driving seat /ˈ· · ˌ·/ *n* **be in the driving seat** *BrE*【英】**be in the driver's seat** *AmE*【美】to be the person who is in control of a situation 掌控局面；处于主管地位：*Fiona led the meeting but Marie was the one in the driving seat.* 菲奥娜主持会议，但玛丽却是真正掌控会议的人。

driving test /ˈ· · ˌ·/ *n* [C] the official test that you must pass in order to drive a car on public roads 驾驶考试

driving un·der the in·flu·ence /ˌ· · · · ˈ· · ·/ *n* [U] *AmE* DUI【美】酒后驾驶

driz·zle¹ /ˈdrɪzl; ˈdrɪzəl/ *v* [I] to rain slightly 下蒙蒙细雨，下毛毛雨：*The rain isn't too bad – it's only drizzling.* 雨下得不太大，只是毛毛雨而已。

drizzle² *n* [singular,U] weather that is between mist and rain 蒙蒙细雨，毛毛雨：*A light drizzle had started by the time we left.* 我们离开的时候，天已经开始下毛毛雨了。—**drizzly** *adj*

droll /drol; drəʊl/ *adj old-fashioned or humorous* amusing【过时或幽默】逗乐的，有趣的：*Oh! Very droll!* 噢！太好玩了！

droll·e·ry /ˈdrolərɪ; ˈdrəʊləri/ *n* [C,U] *old-fashioned* humour【过时】幽默，诙谐

-drome /drom; drəʊm/ *suffix* [in nouns 构成名词] *old-fashioned* a large place for a particular purpose【过时】〔作某种用途的〕大地方，大场地：*an aerodrome* (=an airport) 飞机场

drom·e·da·ry /ˈdrɑməˌdɛrɪ; ˈdrɒmədəri/ *n plural* **dromedaries** [C] a CAMEL with one raised part on its back 单峰骆驼

drone¹ /dron; drəʊn/ *v* [I] to make a continuous low dull sound 发出持续的嗡嗡声，嗡嗡作响：*An airplane droned overhead.* 一架飞机在头顶上嗡嗡地飞过。

drone on *phr v* [I] to speak in a boring way, usually for a long time 令人厌烦地唠叨：**[+about]** *Tom was droning on about work.* 汤姆在没完没了地谈工作。

drone² *n* [C] **1 the drone (of)** a continuous low dull sound （…的）持续而单调的低沉声音；（…的）嗡嗡声：*the steady drone of traffic* 来往车辆发出的持续而低沉的声音 **2** a male BEE that does no work 雄蜂，公蜂 **3** someone who does a lot of dull work without many rewards 从事大量乏味工作而报酬很少的人 **4** someone who has a good life but does not work to earn it 游手好闲者：*idle drones living at the expense of society* 靠社会养活的游手好闲者

dron·go /ˈdrɑŋgo; ˈdrɒŋgəʊ/ *n* [C] *informal, especially AustrE* a boring and stupid person【非正式，尤澳】乏味的人；蠢人，笨人

drool /drul; druːl/ *v* [I] **1** to let SALIVA (=the liquid in your mouth) flow from your mouth 流口水，垂涎；DRIBBLE¹ (1) *BrE*【英】**2** to show great pleasure in looking at someone or something 痴迷地看某人或某物：**[+over]** *Janet was drooling over the two little kittens.* 珍妮特痴迷地看着那两只小猫咪。—compare 比较 SLOBBER

droop¹ /drup; druːp/ *v* [I] **1** to hang or bend downwards 低垂，下垂：*The plant needs some water – it's starting to droop.* 植物需要浇些水——它开始萎垂了。**2** to become sad or weak 情绪低落；丧失活力：*Our spirits drooped as we faced the long trip home.* 我们面临着回家的漫长路程时就无精打采了。

droop² *n* [singular] **1** an act of drooping 低垂，下垂 **2 brewer's/drinker's droop** *humorous* a condition in which a man cannot get an ERECTION (1) because he has drunk too much alcohol【幽默】男子因饮酒过多而无法勃起

drop¹ /drɑp; drɒp/ *v*

① FALL/ALLOW TO FALL 掉落/使落下
② DECREASE 下降，减少
③ STOP (DOING STH) 停止（做某事）
④ NOT USE 不使用
⑤ GO SOMEWHERE 去某处
⑥ OTHER MEANINGS 其他意思

① FALL/ALLOW TO FALL 掉落/使落下

1 [T] to stop holding or carrying something so that it falls 让〔某物〕落下：*I must have dropped my scarf on the bus.* 我一定是把围巾落在公共汽车上了。| *The dog dropped a stick at George's feet.* 狗衔来一根木棍放在乔治的脚边。

2 ▶**FALL** 落下◀ [I] to fall suddenly, especially from a high place 〔尤指从高处〕忽然落下：*A bottle rolled across the table, dropped onto the floor and smashed.* 一个瓶子从桌上滚落到地板上，摔得粉碎。| *Your button has dropped off.* 你的纽扣掉了。

3 ▶**LOWER YOUR BODY** 坐下；倒下◀ [I always+adv/prep,T] to lower yourself or part of your body suddenly （使）忽然倒下，坐下：**[+to/into/down etc]** *He dropped into a chair with a sigh.* 他叹了口气，一屁股坐在椅子上。

4 ▶**GROUND** 地面◀ [I always+adv/prep] if a path, land etc drops it goes down suddenly, forming a steep slope 〔指小径、地面等〕陡降：*At that point the path dropped sharply to the right.* 在那个地方，小径忽然向右急转直下。| **[+away]** *The cliff dropped away to the sea.* 悬崖陡然直下到海里。

5 drop anchor to lower a boat's ANCHOR¹ (1) to the bottom of the sea, lake etc so that the boat stays in the same place 抛锚〔停船〕

6 ▶**HIT** 击◀ [T] to hit someone so hard that they fall down 击倒〔某人〕：*Ali dropped him with one punch.* 阿里一拳就将他击倒了。

② DECREASE 下降，减少

7 ▶**LEVEL/AMOUNT** 水平/数量◀ [I] to fall to a lower level or amount 〔水平〕降低；〔数量〕减少：*The town's population is expected to drop in the next decade.* 预计该城镇的人口在未来十年内将会减少。| **[+to/from]** *The number of people out of work has dropped to 2 million.* 失业人数已经降低到200万。| **drop sharply** *House prices have dropped sharply in the recession.* 房价在经济衰退时期已经急剧下降。

8 ▶**TEMPERATURE** 气温◀ [I] to become colder quite quickly 骤然降温：*The temperature dropped below zero.* 气温一下子降到了零下。

9 ▶**LOWER A LEVEL/AMOUNT** 降低水平/数量◀ [T] to lower the level or amount of something 降低〔水平〕；减少〔数量〕：*Drop your speed as you approach the bend.* 接近弯道时要减速。

10 drop your voice/let your voice drop to speak more quietly 压低/放低声音：*Barbara saw the manager coming and dropped her voice to a whisper.* 芭芭拉看见经理走过来，就把声音压低成耳语。

③ STOP (DOING STH) 停止（做某事）

11 ▶**STOP DOING STH** 停止做某事◀ [T] to stop doing something or planning to do something 停止；搁置；放弃：*Plans for a new swimming pool were dropped due to lack of funding.* 由于资金短缺，建造新游泳池的计划被搁置了。

12 ▶**TO STOP TALKING** 停止谈论◀ to stop talking about something because it upsets people 〔因某事让人不安而〕停止谈论：**drop it/drop the subject** *spoken*【口】*Just drop it can't you? I'm tired of arguing.* 就此打住，行不行？我不想再争论了。| **let the matter drop** *I wish you'd let the matter drop.* 我希望你不要再提这件事。

13 drop everything to stop what you are doing in order to do something else 放下手头所有的工作〔去做别的事〕: *I can't just drop everything and go, I've got far too much work.* 我不能放下手中的工作就去，我有很多事情要做。
14 ▶RELATIONSHIP 关系◀ [T] to end a relationship with someone, usually without thinking about how the other person will feel 终止与〔某人〕的关系，将〔某人〕给甩了: *Sally drops her boyfriends as soon as she gets bored.* 萨莉一觉得厌烦就会甩了男朋友。
15 drop history/physics/German etc to decide to stop studying history etc at school or university 放弃学习历史/物理/德语等: *I wish I hadn't dropped French, it would've been useful for this job.* 我当初没有放弃学法语就好了，现在做这个工作法语会很有用。

④ NOT USE 不使用
16 ▶NOT USE 不使用◀ [T] to decide not to use something that you had planned to use 决定不使用〔原计划要用的东西〕: *This article won't be of interest to our readers. Let's drop it.* 读者不会对这篇文章感兴趣的，我们不要采用了。
17 ▶NOT INCLUDE 不包括在内◀ [T] to no longer include someone in a team or group 将〔某人〕除名，开除；使离队: [+from] *Jeff's been dropped from the team for Saturday's game.* 杰夫被队里排除在外，不参加星期六的比赛。
18 ▶WORD OR LETTER 词或字母◀ [T] to not use a particular word or letter 删掉；遗漏；略去〔某词或字母〕: *He often drops his 'h's' when he talks.* 他说话时经常不发 h 音。| *Oh, drop the 'senator', just call me Gordon.* 噢，去掉"参议员"，就叫我戈登吧。

⑤ GO SOMEWHERE 去某处
19 ▶VISIT 拜访◀ [I always+adv/prep] to visit someone informally without arranging a particular time 顺便造访，临时拜访: [+in/over/round/by] *Drop by whenever you're in the area.* 你不管什么时候来这地方，都到我这里坐坐。| **drop in on sb** *I think I'll drop in on Jill on my way home.* 我想我回家时会顺路看望一下吉尔。
20 ▶TAKE SB SOMEWHERE 送某人到某处◀ [T always+adv/prep] to take someone by car to a particular place that you are driving past〔用汽车〕顺路送某人到某处: **drop sb off/at etc** *She usually drops the kids off at school on her way to work.* 她通常在开车上班时顺路把孩子们送到学校。
21 ▶TAKE STH SOMEWHERE 把某物送到某处◀ [T always+adv/prep] to take something to a particular place and leave it there 顺便把〔某物〕送至〔某处〕: **drop sth off/at/in etc** *I'll drop the books off at your place after my class.* 上完课我会顺便把书送到你那儿。
22 drop behind/back to move slowly so that you get separated from the group you are with 落后；掉队: *Don't drop behind the others on the trail in case you get lost.* 路上别掉队，以免迷路。

⑥ OTHER MEANINGS 其他意思
23 drop sb a line/note to write a short letter to someone 给某人写短信/便条: *Drop me a line when you get to Hawaii.* 到了夏威夷给我写封短信。
24 ▶BE TIRED 疲劳◀ [I] to be extremely tired 累趴下，累倒: *They worked until they dropped.* 他们一直工作到都累趴下了。
25 (let) drop a hint/suggestion/remark etc to say something informally and without emphasizing it 无意中暗示/随口建议/漏出话语等: *He let drop a remark about his childhood which quite surprised me.* 他无意间谈起他的童年，这使我相当吃惊。
26 drop your eyes/gaze to stop looking at someone and look down, usually because you feel embarrassed or uncomfortable 垂下眼睛/目光〔通常因为尴尬〕: *She blushed and dropped her gaze.* 她脸红了，垂下目光。
27 drop dead a) to die suddenly and unexpectedly without having previously been ill 猝死，暴毙: *One day he just dropped dead in the street.* 一天，他就那样猝死在街上。**b)** *spoken* used angrily to tell someone to be quiet, stop annoying you etc【口】去你的〔用于气愤地叫某人保持安静、别再打扰等〕
28 ▶MONEY 钱◀ [T] *informal* to lose money in business, a game etc【非正式】〔做生意、玩游戏时〕输〔钱〕: *Phil dropped $200 playing poker yesterday.* 菲尔昨天玩扑克牌输了 200 美元。
29 ▶NOT CATCH 未接住◀ [T] to fail to catch a ball hit by a BATSMAN in the game of CRICKET (2)〔板球比赛中〕没接住〔击球手击来的球〕
30 ▶LOSE 失掉◀ [T] to lose a point, game etc in a sports competition〔体育比赛中〕失〔分〕，丢〔分〕: *Davison has dropped three points in the fourth round.* 戴维森在第四局比赛中丢了三分。
31 ▶DRUGS 毒品◀ [T] *informal* to swallow an illegal drug【非正式】吞服〔毒品〕: *She dropped acid in the 60s.* 她在 60 年代曾经服用过迷幻药。
32 drop names to use the names of famous or important people in conversations to make yourself seem important 把重要人物的名字挂在嘴边来炫耀自己
33 drop a stitch to let the wool fall off the needle when you are knitting (KNIT[1] (1))〔编织时〕掉一针，漏一针
34 drop a clanger/brick *BrE* to say something socially embarrassing【英】说出令人发窘的话；失言；说话失态
35 drop a bombshell *informal* to suddenly tell someone a shocking piece of news【非正式】突然告诉某人一则惊人的消息: *Then she dropped a bombshell and told me she wanted a divorce.* 接着她告诉我一个爆炸性的新闻: 她要离婚。

drop away *phr v* [I] to become lower in level or amount 逐渐减少，下降: *Sales have dropped away in recent months.* 近几个月来，销售量有所下降。

drop off *phr v* [I] **1** to begin to sleep 入睡，睡着: *Just as I was dropping off, I heard a noise in the house.* 我刚要睡着，就听见屋子里有动静。**2** to become lower in level or amount 下降；减少: *Interest in the game has dropped off recently.* 人们对这项运动的兴趣近来减退了。

drop out *phr v* [I] **1** to leave an activity, course etc before it has finished 中途退出，辍学: [+of] *He dropped out of college.* 他从大学辍学了。| *Dwyer had to drop out of the race because of injury.* 德怀尔由于受伤不得不退出比赛。**2** to move away from or refuse to take part in society because you do not agree with its principles〔因反对当前社会的道德标准而〕脱离社会；逃避现实而隐退，遁世 —see also 另见 DROPOUT (2) **3** if a word or expression drops out of a language, it is no longer used〔指某单词或表达法〕不再被使用，过时

drop[2] *n* [S2] [W3]
1 ▶LIQUID 液体◀ [C] a very small amount of liquid that falls in a round shape 珠，滴: [+of] *Big drops of rain rolled down the window.* 大滴的雨水从窗上滚落下去。| *a tear drop* 泪珠，泪滴 —see picture on page A7 参见 A7 页图
2 ▶A SMALL AMOUNT 少量◀ a drop *informal*【非正式】**a)** a small amount of liquid that you drink〔液体的〕少量，一丁点: *I like my whisky with just a drop of soda.* 我喜欢在威士忌酒中稍加点苏打水。**b)** a small amount of something〔某物的〕少量，少许: *He hasn't a drop of sense in his head.* 他毫无头脑。
3 ▶DISTANCE 距离◀ [singular] a distance from something down to the ground 下落距离；落差: *a path that ended in a vertical drop of fifty feet* 尽头是直落 50 英尺的陡峭山崖的一条小径
4 ▶LESS IN AMOUNT 数量的减少◀ [singular] if there is a drop in the amount, level, or number of something, it goes down or becomes less〔水平的〕下降；〔数量的〕减少: *a drop in interest rates* 利率的下降 | *a sudden drop in air pressure* 气压的骤然下降
5 at the drop of a hat used to say that you would do something immediately if you had the opportunity〔一有机会〕立刻，立即: *I'd go to the Far East at the drop of a hat.* 如有机会我会立刻去远东。
6 ▶DELIVER 运送◀ [C] an act of dropping or leaving something, such as food or medical supplies, especially from an aircraft 运货；空投: *an air drop to the war-torn region* 给受战争破坏地区的空投物资 —see also 另见 MAIL DROP
7 lemon/fruit/chocolate etc drop a sweet that tastes of LEMON etc 柠檬/水果/巧克力等味的糖球 —see also 另见 COUGH DROP
8 a drop in the ocean *BrE*【英】, **a drop in the bucket** *AmE*【美】a very small amount of something compared to what is actually needed or wanted 沧海一粟；杯水车薪: *The fund raising is going well, but it's really only a drop in the ocean.* 资金筹集进展顺利，但这只不过是杯水车薪罢了。
9 eye/ear etc drops a type of medicine that you put in your eye etc, one drop at a time 滴眼液/滴耳液等
10 not touched a drop used to say that you have not drunk any alcohol at all 滴酒未沾

drop cloth /ˈ· ·/ *n* [C] *AmE* a large cloth for covering furniture, floors, etc in order to protect them from dust or paint【美】〔防

止家具、地板等落灰或弄上油漆而使用的〕罩单, 罩布; DUSTSHEET *BrE*【英】

drop-dead gor·geous /ˌ· · ˈ· ·/ *adj BrE spoken* very attractive【英口】极其引人注目的

drop goal /ˈ· ·/ *n* [C] a GOAL in RUGBY football made with a dropkick〔英式橄榄球〕以抛踢法射中球门得分

drop-in cent·re /ˈ· · ˌ· ·/ *n* [C] *BrE* a place where people who have no job, nowhere to live etc can get information, relax, and talk【英】失业者活动中心

drop·kick /ˈdrɑpˌkɪk; ˈdrɒpkɪk/ *n* [C] a kick in a game such as RUGBY football, made by dropping the ball and kicking it immediately〔英式橄榄球等中的〕抛踢球 —see picture on page A22 参见 A22 页图

drop·let /ˈdrɑplɪt; ˈdrɒplɪ̣t/ *n* [C] a very small drop of liquid〔液体的〕小滴

drop·out /ˈdrɑpˌaut; ˈdrɒpaʊt/ *n* **1** [C] someone who leaves school or college before they have finished 中途辍学的学生: *a high school dropout* 中学退学生 **2** [C] someone who refuses to join ordinary society because they do not agree with its social practices, moral standards etc〔因不赞同社会习俗、道德标准等而〕逃避传统社会的人, 遁世者 **3** [C,U] *technical* a short loss of signal when an electronic machine is working【术语】〔电子器件运作时的〕短时间信号漏失

drop·per /ˈdrɑpɚ; ˈdrɒpə/ *n* [C] a short glass tube with a hollow rubber part at one end, that you use to measure out liquid one drop at a time 滴管

drop·pings /ˈdrɑpɪŋz; ˈdrɒpɪŋz/ *n* [plural] solid waste from animals or birds〔鸟兽的〕粪便

drop scone /ˈ· ·/ *n* [C] a small flat plain cake 面饼, 烙饼

drop shot /ˈ· ·/ *n* [C] a shot in a game such as tennis in which the ball falls quickly at the front of the court〔网球等的〕网前球, 短吊, 短球

drop·sy /ˈdrɑpsɪ; ˈdrɒpsi/ *n* [U] a medical condition in which liquid forms in parts of your body 水肿; 浮肿 (症)

dross /drɔs; drɒs/ *n* [U] **1** *BrE* something that is of very low quality【英】质量低劣之物: *That film was utter dross!* 那部电影简直是垃圾! **2** waste or useless substances 废料, 渣滓: *gold with impurities or dross* 含杂质的金子

drought /draut; draʊt/ *n* [C,U] a long period of dry weather when there is not enough water for plants and animals to live 干旱, 久旱, 旱灾

drove¹ /drov; drəʊv/ the past tense of DRIVE¹

drove² *n* [C] **1** a group of animals that are being moved together〔被驱赶着走的〕畜群: *a drove of cattle* 被驱赶的一群牛 **2 droves** [plural] a crowd of people 人群: **in droves** *Tourists come in droves to see the White House.* 游客们成群结队地来参观白宫。

drov·er /ˈdrovɚ; ˈdrəʊvə/ *n* [C] someone who moves cattle or sheep from one place to another in groups 赶牛羊牲畜者

drown /draun; draʊn/ *v* **1** [I,T] to die from being under water for too long or to kill someone in this way (使) 淹死, (使) 溺毙: *The woman drowned while swimming in the sea.* 那个女人在海里游泳时淹死了。**2** also 又作 **drown out** [T] to prevent a sound from being heard by making a loud noise〔用声音〕淹没: *His voice was drowned out by the traffic.* 他的声音被来往的车辆声淹没了。**3** [T] to cover something completely with liquid 把〔某物〕浸泡在〔液体〕中: **drown sth with/in** *Grant drowned his pancakes in syrup.* 格兰特把煎饼浸泡在糖浆里。**4 drown your sorrows** to drink a lot of alcohol in order to forget your problems 借酒浇愁

drowse /drauz; draʊz/ *v* [I] to be in a light sleep or feel pleasantly as though you are almost asleep 打瞌睡, 半睡半醒, 假寐: *I was drowsing in front of the television when you called.* 我正坐在电视机前打瞌睡, 忽然你打来了电话。

drow·sy /ˈdrauzɪ; ˈdraʊzi/ *adj* **1** tired and almost asleep, usually because of food, drugs, or because you are in a warm place 昏昏欲睡的, 昏昏沉沉的: *The cat lay drowsy and content in the sunshine.* 猫迷迷糊糊地在阳光下满足地躺着。**2** so peaceful that you feel relaxed and tired〔安静得让人〕放松的, 困倦的: *a drowsy summer afternoon* 一个令人昏昏欲睡的夏日午后 —**drowsily** *adv* —**drowsiness** *n* [U]: *The tablets may cause drowsiness.* 这种药片可能会引起困倦。

Dr. Pep·per /ˌdɑktə ˈpɛpɚ; ˌdɒktə ˈpepə/ *trademark* a type of sweet, non-alcoholic drink with BUBBLES【商标】"佩珀博士"〔一种不含酒精的甜味带气饮料〕

drub·bing /ˈdrʌbɪŋ; ˈdrʌbɪŋ/ *n* [C] *informal* an occasion when one team easily beats another team in sport【非正式】〔体育运动中的〕轻易取胜: **give sb a drubbing** *We gave the other team a good drubbing.* 我们把另一队打得落花流水。

drudge /drʌdʒ; drʌdʒ/ *n* [C] someone who does hard boring work 做苦工者, 干乏味工作的人 —**drudge** *v* [I]

drudg·e·ry /ˈdrʌdʒərɪ; ˈdrʌdʒəri/ *n* [U] hard boring work 苦工, 贱役, 辛苦乏味的工作

drug¹ /drʌg; drʌg/ *n* [C] **1** an illegal substance that people smoke, INJECT (1) etc to make them feel happy or excited 毒品: *He was arrested for selling drugs.* 他因贩卖毒品而被捕了。| **take/use drugs** *My cousin has been taking drugs for years.* 我表哥已经吸毒多年了。| **do drugs** *slang* (=take drugs habitually)【俚】习惯性吸毒 *Has she been doing drugs, or does she always act like this?* 她是在吸毒呢, 还是一向就这副样子? | **be on drugs** (=use drugs regularly) 经常吸毒 *My grandfather thinks all kids these days are on drugs.* 我爷爷认为现在所有的孩子都吸毒。| **illegal drugs** *They test their employees for traces of illegal drugs.* 他们对自己的雇员进行体检, 看看有没有使用毒品的迹象。| **drug abuse** (=the use of illegal drugs) 滥用毒品 *the problem of drug abuse in the inner city* 旧城区居民的滥用毒品问题 | **hard drug** (=a dangerous drug such as HEROIN, COCAINE etc) 硬毒品〈如海洛因、可卡因等危险麻醉品〉| **soft drug** (=one that is not considered very harmful such as MARIJUANA) 软毒品〈如大麻等危害性较小的麻醉品〉| **dangerous drugs** *a well-known expert on the abuse of dangerous drugs* 研究滥用危险毒品问题的著名专家 **2** a medicine or a substance for making medicines 药物; 药材: *a drug used in the treatment of cancer* 用于治疗癌症的一种药物 | **prescribe a drug** *Doctors should only prescribe drugs when it's really necessary.* 医生应该在确实必要时才开药。**3 a drug on the market** something that cannot be sold because there is too much of it available 市场上的滞销品〔滞销货〕—see also 另见 **miracle drug** (MIRACLE (3)), DESIGNER DRUG

This graph shows some of the words most commonly used with the noun **drug**. 本图表所示为含有名词 drug 的一些最常用词组。

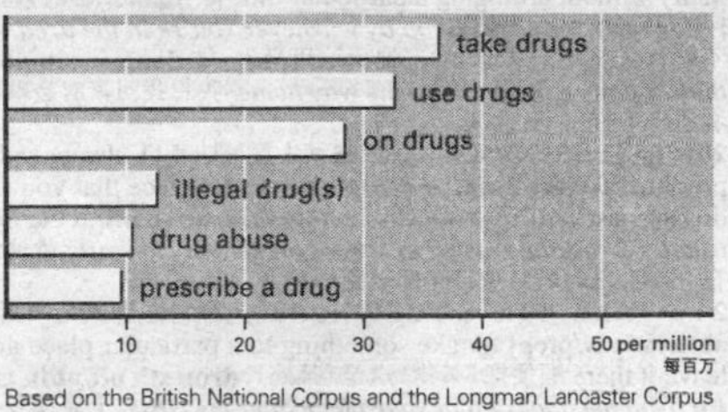

Based on the British National Corpus and the Longman Lancaster Corpus
据英国国家语料库和朗文兰开斯特语料库

CULTURAL NOTE 文化注释

Illegal drugs are considered to be a serious problem in both the US and the UK. Drugs like HEROIN, CRACK, and COCAINE are often described as **hard drugs** (=powerful drugs that seriously damage your health). Hard drugs cause a lot of crime because their users become very dependent on them and always need money to buy more drugs. Drugs like CANNABIS, ECSTASY, and LSD are often described as **soft drugs** or **recreational drugs** because many people take them for enjoyment. Some people believe that they are not very harmful, but some young people have died after taking ecstasy. Ecstasy, also called 'E' in the UK and 'X' in the US, became popular with young people in the 1990s in NIGHTCLUBS because it gave them the energy to stay awake and dance all night. The most commonly used illegal drug in both countries is cannabis. The UK government classifies (CLASSIFY) illegal drugs into different classes (A, B, and C) according to how dangerous they are and the punishment for using them. Cannabis used to be a Class B drug, but in 2004 the government changed this to Class C, a class for less harmful drugs. This change in the law caused a lot of disagreement. It is still illegal to use cannabis, but the police usually no longer ARREST people if they are found with only a small amount of the drug. 英美两国都把毒品视为一个严重的问题。海洛因、强效可卡因、可卡因常称为硬毒品。硬毒品令使用者产生严重依赖, 总需要钱买更多毒品, 因此滋生很多犯罪。大麻、摇头丸、迷幻药常称为软毒品或消遣性毒品, 因为很多人为追求快感而服用。有人认为软毒品危害不大, 但有些年轻人在服用摇头丸后死亡。摇头丸在英国又称E, 在美国又称X,

因能令人通宵不困、整夜跳舞，因此在上世纪90年代在去夜总会的年轻人中风靡一时。英美两国最常见的毒品是大麻。英国政府按毒品危害性和吸毒受惩罚的程度把毒品分为A、B、C三个不同等级。大麻曾为B级毒品，但2004年政府将其改为危害性更小的C级。对法律作出这样的修改，引起了广泛不满。现在吸食大麻仍是非法的，但如果携带的数量较少，警方一般不予逮捕。— see Cultural Note at MARIJUANA 见 MARIJUANA 文化注释

drug² *v* **drugged, drugging** [T] **1** to give someone a drug, especially in order to make them feel tired or go to sleep 使服用麻醉药；用药麻醉：*They had to drug the lion before they transported it.* 他们在运送狮子之前得先用药将它麻醉。**2** to add drugs to someone's food or drink to make them feel tired or go to sleep 在〔某人的食物或饮品〕中投放麻醉药，在…中下麻醉药 **3 be drugged up (to the eyeballs)** *especially BrE* to have been given a lot of drugs by a doctor【尤英】被〔医生〕用大量麻醉药麻醉：*I tried to speak to her after the operation, but she was drugged up to the eyeballs.* 她手术后我想和她说话，但她被麻醉得很深。**4 drugged out** *AmE* always taking and influenced by drugs【美】经常吸毒并处于毒品的影响下：*Greg's a real smart guy, it's too bad he's drugged out all the time.* 格雷格是个非常精明的人，只可惜他总是吸毒，没有清醒的时候。—**drugged** *adj*

drug ad·dict /ˈ· ˌ··/ *n* [C] someone who cannot stop taking drugs, such as HEROIN or COCAINE 吸毒者，吸毒成瘾的人—**drug addiction** /ˈ· ·ˌ··/ *n* [U]

drug bar·on /ˈ· ˌ··/ *n* [C] someone who leads an organization that deals in large quantities of illegal drugs 大毒枭

drug czar /ˈ· ·/ *n* [C] an official employed by the US government to try to stop the trade of illegal drugs〔受雇于美国政府力图制止非法毒品交易的〕毒品缉查官；首席禁毒官员

drug deal·er /ˈ· ˌ··/ *n* [C] someone who sells illegal drugs 毒品贩子，贩毒者

Drug En·force·ment Ad·min·i·stra·tion /ˌ· ·ˈ·· ···ˌ·ˈ··/ abbreviation 缩写为**DEA** a US government organization which makes sure that people and companies obey the laws about dangerous drugs. They try to catch people who bring dangerous drugs into the US and people who sell drugs within the US. 毒品管理局〔美国一政府机构。其职责是确保个人和公司遵守反毒品法，力图抓获向美国贩运毒品者和在美国境内销售毒品者〕

drug·get /ˈdrʌgɪt; ˈdrʌgɪ̈t/ *n* [C,U] rough heavy cloth used especially as a floor covering, or a piece of this material 粗毛织物；〔尤指〕粗毛地毯

drug·gie /ˈdrʌgɪ; ˈdrʌgi/ *n* [C] *informal* someone who often takes illegal drugs【非正式】吸毒者，瘾君子

drug·gist /ˈdrʌgɪst; ˈdrʌgɪ̈st/ *n* [C] *AmE old-fashioned* someone who is trained to prepare drugs and medicines, and works in a shop【美，过时】药剂师；CHEMIST (2) *BrE*【英】—compare 比较 PHARMACIST

drug mis·use /ˈ· ·ˌ·/ *n* [U] *BrE* the practice of using drugs for pleasure rather than for medical reasons【英】滥用药物〔不为治病而为享乐〕

drug re·hab·il·i·ta·tion /ˌ· ····ˈ··/ also 又作**drug rehab** /ˌdrʌg ˈrihæb; ˌdrʌg ˈriːhæb/ *AmE*【美】*n* [U] the process of helping someone to live without drugs after they have been ADDICTED to them 帮助吸毒者戒毒；吸毒康复工作

drug run·ner /ˈ· ˌ··/ *n* [C] someone who brings illegal drugs from one country to another 运毒犯

drug·store /ˈdrʌgˌstor; ˈdrʌgstɔː/ *n* [C] *AmE* a shop where you can buy medicines, beauty products etc【美】药店，药房；杂货店；PHARMACY, CHEMIST'*s BrE*【英】

dru·id /ˈdruɪd; ˈdruːɪ̈d/ *n* [C] a member of an ancient Celtic group of priests, in Britain, Ireland, and France, before the Christian religion〔在基督教之前，古代不列颠、爱尔兰和法兰西等境内凯尔特人信仰的〕德鲁伊特教的祭司

drum¹ /drʌm; drʌm/ *n* [C] **1** a musical instrument made of skin stretched over a circular frame that you hit with your hand or a stick 鼓：*the steady rhythmic beating of the drums* 节奏分明、连续不断的击鼓声 **2** something that looks like a drum, especially part of a machine 鼓状物；〔尤指机器的〕鼓轮；滚筒：*The brake drums are gone on my car.* 我车上的制动鼓坏了。**3** a large round container for storing liquids such as oil, chemicals etc〔装有如油、化学物质等液体的〕大桶：*dirty, green oil drums at the back of the yard* 在院子后面那些肮脏的绿色油桶 —see picture at 参见 CONTAINER 图 **4 the drum of** a sound like the sound a drum makes …击鼓似的声音：*the steady drum of the rain on the window* 雨打在窗户上不断发出的滴答声 **5 bang/beat the drum for sb/sth** to speak eagerly in support of someone or something 竭力支持某人/某事：*He's always banging the drum for better schools.* 他总是极力主张要创建更好的学校。

drum² *v* **drummed, drumming 1** [I] to play a drum 击鼓，打鼓 **2** [I,T] to make a sound similar to a drum by hitting a surface again and again 有节奏地击打〔使发出打鼓似的声音〕：*Rain drummed on the windows.* 雨水嗒嗒地敲着窗户。| **drum your fingers** *Drumming your fingers can be a sign of anxiety.* 用手指不断扣击东西可能是一种焦虑的表现。

drum sth **into** sb *phr v* [T] to keep telling someone something until they cannot forget it 向〔某人〕灌输〔某种观点，直到记住为止〕：*It was drummed into me to never borrow money.* 我一向被灌输不可向人借钱这一观念，已经牢记不忘了。

drum sb **out of** sth *phr v* [T] to force someone to leave an organization 迫使〔某人〕离开〔某个组织、团体等〕；开除，逐出：*He was drummed out of the army.* 他被逐出军队。

drum sth ↔**up** *phr v* [T] to obtain something by asking a lot of people for help, information etc 竭力争取；招徕；兜揽：*We managed to drum up support for the idea.* 我们尽力争取到了人们对这一主张的支持。

drum·beat /ˈdrʌmˌbit; ˈdrʌmbiːt/ *n* [C] a sound of someone hitting a drum 击鼓声

drum kit /ˈ· ·/ *n* [C] a set of drums used especially by professional musicians〔尤指专业音乐人使用的〕成套的鼓

drum ma·jor /ˌ· ˈ··/ *n* [C] the male leader of a BAND (=a group of marching musicians), especially in the army 军乐队的男指挥

drum ma·jor·ette /ˌ· ···ˈ·/ *n* [C] a MAJORETTE〔在跟随乐队行进时转动着指挥棒的〕女指挥，女领队

drum·mer /ˈdrʌmɚ; ˈdrʌmə/ *n* [C] someone who plays drums 鼓手

drum·ming /ˈdrʌmɪŋ; ˈdrʌmɪŋ/ *n* [U] the act of playing a drum or the sound a drum makes 击鼓；鼓声

drum-roll /ˈ· ·/ *n* [C] a quick continuous beating of a drum, usually used to introduce an important event 一串连续快节奏的击鼓声；一通鼓声〔通常用于宣告某重大事件时作为开始〕

drum·stick /ˈdrʌmˌstɪk; ˈdrʌmˌstɪk/ *n* [C] **1** the lower part of the leg of a chicken or other bird, cooked as food〔煮熟的鸡或其他禽类的〕小腿部 **2** a stick that you use to hit a drum 鼓槌 —see picture at 参见 STICK² 图

drunk¹ /drʌŋk; drʌŋk/ the past participle of DRINK¹

drunk² *adj* **1** [not before noun 不用于名词前] unable to control your behaviour, speech etc because you have drunk too much alcohol 喝醉的：*Graham was too drunk to remember what happened last night.* 格雷厄姆醉得太厉害了，都不记得昨晚发生了什么事。| **get drunk (on)** *As students we used to go out and get drunk most nights.* 当学生时，我们差不多每晚都出去喝得烂醉。| *I got hideously drunk on tequila last night.* 昨晚我喝龙舌兰酒喝得烂醉。| **blind drunk** (=very drunk) 醉得厉害 *I'm fed up of you coming home blind drunk.* 你常常喝得烂醉回家，真让我无法忍受。| **drunk as a skunk/lord** (=very drunk) 酩酊大醉 **2 drunk and disorderly** *law* the crime of behaving in a violent noisy way in a public place when you are drunk【法律】醉酒并扰乱治安 **3 drunk with power/happiness etc** so excited by a feeling of power etc that you behave in a strange way 为拥有权势而飘飘然/高兴得忘乎所以等 —see also 另见**roaring drunk** (ROARING (5)), PUNCH-DRUNK —compare 比较 SOBER¹ (1)

drunk³ also 又作**drunkard** /ˈdrʌŋkɚd; ˈdrʌŋkəd/ *n* [C] someone who is drunk or often gets drunk 醉鬼，酒鬼 —compare 比较 ALCOHOLIC

drunk-driv·ing /ˌ· ˈ··/ *n* [U] driving a car after having drunk too much alcohol 酒后驾驶；DRINK-DRIVING *BrE*【英】

drunk·en /ˈdrʌŋkən; ˈdrʌŋkən/ *adj* [only before noun 仅用于名词前] **1** drunk or showing that you are drunk 酒醉的，有醉态的：*drunken shouting* 酒后大喊大叫 | **be in a drunken stupor** (=almost asleep because you are so drunk) 醉得神志不清，酒醉昏迷 **2 drunken party/orgy etc** a party etc where people are drunk 纵酒宴乐等—**drunkenly** *adv*—**drunkenness** *n* [U]

drunk tank /ˈ· ·/ *n* [C] *AmE informal* a cell in a prison for people who have drunk too much alcohol【美，非正式】〔监狱中的〕酒鬼监禁室

Dru·ry Lane /ˌdrʊrɪ ˈlen; ˌdrʊəri ˈleɪn/ a street in London famous for its theatres 特鲁里街〔伦敦的一条街道，以剧院闻名〕

Druze /druz; druːz/ also 又作**Druse** *n* a religious group living mainly in parts of Lebanon, Syria, and Israel, whose beliefs include ideas from the Bible and the Koran 德鲁兹教派〔主要分布于黎巴嫩、叙利亚和以色列部分地区的宗教团体，其教义源自《圣经》和《古兰经》〕

Dr Who /ˌdɑktɚ ˈhu; ˌdɒktə ˈhuː/ a British series of television programmes, about a scientist called Dr Who, who travels with

different people through time and space in his time machine the Tardis. He fights evil people and frightening creatures from other worlds, usually in a way that is not violent. His most famous enemies are the Daleks.《无名博士》〔英国电视连续剧，讲述一位名叫无名博士的科学家与别人乘坐他的时间机器塔尔迪斯穿越时空隧道的故事。他与其他星球的坏人和可怕生物作战，但场面一般不够激烈。他最大的敌人是达莱克金属怪物〕

dry¹ /draɪ; draɪ/ *adj comparative* 比较级 **drier** *superlative* 最高级 **driest**

1 ▶**NOT WET** 不湿的◀ without water or liquid inside or on the surface 干的，干燥的: *The floor was made of hard dry earth.* 地面是干硬的泥地。| *The paint isn't dry yet – be careful!* 油漆还没干，小心！| *Can you check if the washing's dry?* 你能去看看洗的东西干了没有吗？| **shake/rub/wipe sth dry** *Give it to me and I'll wipe it dry.* 把它给我，我会把它擦干的。| **as dry as a bone** (=very dry) 干透的，十分干燥的

2 ▶**WEATHER** 天气◀ having very little rain or MOISTURE 干旱的，干燥的: *The air was dry, and the sun beat down fiercely.* 空气十分干燥，太阳毒辣辣地照着。| *the dry season* 〔热带的〕旱季

3 **run/go dry** if a lake, river etc runs dry, all the water gradually disappears, especially because there has been no rain 〔湖泊、河流等〕干涸

4 ▶**HUMOUR** 幽默◀ someone with a dry sense of humour pretends to be serious when they are really joking 〔指某人说笑话时〕冷面滑稽的

5 ▶**THIRSTY** 口渴的◀ *informal* thirsty【非正式】口干的，口渴的: *I'm really dry – do you have any orange juice?* 我很口渴，你有没有橙汁？

6 **dry mouth/skin/lips etc** without enough of the liquid that is normally in your mouth etc 口/皮肤/嘴唇等发干: *I felt nervous and dizzy and my mouth was dry.* 我感觉紧张，头晕，口发干。

7 **dry cough** a cough which does not produce any PHLEGM (1) 干咳

8 ▶**SPEECH/WRITING** 讲话/文章◀ boring 乏味的; 无趣的: *I found the lecture dry and uninspired.* 我觉得那个讲座枯燥无味。| **as dry as dust** (=very boring) 十分乏味的

9 **dry wine/sherry etc** wine etc that is not sweet 无甜味的果酒/雪利酒等: *dry white wine* 干白葡萄酒

10 **dry bread** bread eaten on its own without butter, JAM¹ (1) etc 未涂奶油、果酱等的面包

11 ▶**TOWN/COUNTRY** 城镇/国家◀ not allowing any alcohol to be sold there 禁酒的: *There are still some dry states in the US.* 在美国仍然有一些州实行禁酒。

12 ▶**VOICE** 声音◀ showing no emotion 冷漠的，没有感情的

13 **not a dry eye in the house** *often humorous* used to say that everyone was crying because something was very sad【常幽默】〔因伤心之事〕在场众人无不泪汪汪的 —see also 另见 DRIP-DRY —**dryly, drily** *adv* —**dryness** *n* [U]

dry² *v* [I,T] to make something dry or become dry (使) 变干，把…弄干: *My boots haven't dried yet.* 我的靴子还没干。| **dry sth** *Sit up and dry your eyes.* 坐起来，把眼泪擦干。—see also 另见 CUT AND DRIED, DRIED

dry off *phr v* [I,T] to become dry or make something dry, especially on the surface (使) 变干，把〔某物〕弄干: *It was lovely being able to swim and then dry off in the sun.* 游泳后能够在太阳下晒干，真好。| **dry sth ↔ off** *Put the washing near the fire to dry it off.* 把洗好的衣服放到火旁烤干。

dry out *phr v* [I,T] **1** to become or make something completely dry after it has been very wet (使) 干透; (使)〔某物〕完全变干: **dry sth ↔ out** *Dry your anorak out on the radiator.* 把带风帽的外套放在暖气上烤干。**2** to stop drinking alcohol after you have become an ALCOHOLIC〔喝酒上瘾后〕戒酒

dry up *phr v*

1 ▶**RIVER/LAKE ETC** 河流/湖泊等◀ [I,T] if something such as a river dries up, the water in it disappears (使) 干涸: *During the drought all the reservoirs dried up.* 在干旱时期，所有的水库都干涸了。| **dry sth ↔ up** *The sun has completely dried up the soil and the crops are dying.* 太阳把土地都烤干了，庄稼即将枯死。

2 ▶**SUPPLY OF STH** 供应某物◀ [I] to come to an end and have no more available 耗尽，枯竭: *The research is finishing because the money's dried up.* 研究要停止了，因为钱已用完。

3 ▶**PLATES/DISHES ETC** 盘子/碟子等◀ [I,T] to rub dry with a cloth 用布擦干: **dry sth ↔ up** *Would you mind drying up the supper things?* 你把晚饭的碗碟擦干好吗？

4 **dry up!** *spoken* used to angrily tell someone to be quiet, especially when they are complaining about something【口】住口！住嘴！: *Just dry up! I'm enjoying the film even if you're not!* 别说话了！你不爱看这部电影我还爱看呢！

5 ▶**STOP TALKING** 停止说话◀ [I] to stop talking because you have forgotten what you were going to say or what you should say when speaking or acting 忘记台词

dry·ad /ˈdraɪæd; ˈdraɪæd/ *n* [C] a female spirit in ancient Greek stories who lived in a tree 林中女仙〔古希腊神话中的树神〕

dry bat·te·ry /ˌ· ˈ···/ also 又作 **dry cell** /ˌ· ˈ·/ *n* [C] an electric BATTERY (1) containing chemicals that are not in a liquid form 干电池

dry-clean /ˌ· ˈ·/ *v* [T] to clean clothes etc with chemicals instead of water 干洗〔衣服等〕

dry clean·er's /ˌ· ˈ··/ *n plural* **dry cleaner's** [C] a shop where you can take clothes etc to be dry-cleaned 干洗店

Dry·den /ˈdraɪdn̩; ˈdraɪdən/, **John** (1631-1700) an English writer of poetry and plays. His many plays include *Marriage à la Mode* and *All for Love*. 德莱顿〔(1631-1700)，英国诗人和剧作家，创作的剧本包括《时髦的婚礼》和《一切为了爱》〕

dry dock /ˈ· ·/ *n* [C] a place where a ship can be taken out of the water for repairs 干船坞

dry·er /ˈdraɪɚ; ˈdraɪə/ *n* [C] **hairdryer/spin-dryer** a machine that dries things〔吹干头发用的〕吹风机[筒]/旋转式脱水机

dry-eyed /ˌ· ˈ·◂/ *adj* not crying 不哭的，无泪的

dry gin·ger /ˌ· ˈ··/ *n* [U] a drink that tastes of GINGER and can be mixed with WHISKY or other alcoholic drinks 姜味饮品〔可与威士忌或其他酒类饮品掺在一起饮用〕

dry goods /ˈ· ·/ *n* [plural] **1** goods such as tobacco, tea, coffee 干货〈如烟草、茶叶、咖啡等〉 **2** *AmE* things that are made from cloth such as clothes, sheets, and curtains【美】纺织品〈如衣服、床单、窗帘等〉: *a dry goods store* 纺织品商店

dry ice /ˌ· ˈ·/ *n* [U] mist produced by a machine that is used as a special effect in the theatre, DISCOs etc 固体二氧化碳，干冰〔用机器制造干冰喷雾，用于剧院、迪斯科舞厅的舞台效果〕

dry land /ˌ· ˈ·/ *n* [U] land rather than water 陆地: *After three weeks at sea we were glad to be back on dry land again.* 在海上航行三个星期后再回到陆地，我们很高兴。

dry·ly /ˈdraɪlɪ; ˈdraɪli/ *adv* if you say something dryly, you do not put any emotion in your voice, especially in order to sound funny〔指说话〕干巴巴地，冷冰冰地〔尤指为达到幽默的效果〕: *"If you're lucky," said Harrison dryly, "they'll only hang you."* "如果你们走运的话，"哈里森冷冰冰地说，"他们只不过会处你们绞刑。"

dry rot /ˌ· ˈ·/ *n* [U] a disease in wood, that turns it into powder〔木材的〕干腐，干朽

dry run /ˌ· ˈ·/ *n* [C] an event that you use as a way of practising for a more important event 演习，排练: *Both the parties are treating the local elections as a dry run.* 两党都把在地方的选举当成了一种预演。

dry-shod /ˌ· ˈ·/ *adv literary* without getting your feet wet【文】不湿脚地

dry-stone wall /ˌ· · ˈ·/ *n* [C] a wall built with pieces of stone that fit closely together and no cement〔不用水泥砌成的〕干砌墙

dry wall /ˌ· ˈ·/ *n* [U] *AmE* a hard substance used as the inside wall of a house【美】板壁墙 —**dry-wall** *v* [I,T]

DSc /ˌdi ɛs ˈsi; ˌdiː es ˈsiː/ Doctor of Science; a high-level university degree in a science subject, which is often given as an HONORARY degree (=as a special honour) 理学博士〔常作为荣誉学位授予〕

DSO *n* Distinguished Service Order; a MEDAL given to officers of the British Army and Navy for special service 特殊贡献勋章〔用于表彰有特殊贡献的英国陆军和海军军官〕

DTI /ˌdi ti ˈaɪ; ˌdiː tiː ˈaɪ/ *n* **the DTI** the abbreviation of 缩写= the Department of Trade and Industry 贸易工业部

DTP /ˌdi ti ˈpi; ˌdiː tiː ˈpiː/ *n* [U] DESKTOP PUBLISHING; the production of books, newspapers etc using computers 桌面出版〔利用电脑出版书、报纸等〕

DT's /ˌdi ˈtiz; ˌdiː ˈtiːz/ *n* **the DT's** *humorous* a condition caused by drinking too much alcohol in which your body shakes, and you see imaginary things【幽默】〔长期酗酒造成的〕震颤性谵妄(症)

du·al /ˈduəl; ˈdjuːəl/ *adj* [only before noun 仅用于名词前] **dual nationality/controls/purpose etc** having two nationalities, sets of controls etc 双重国籍/控制/目的等 —**duality** /duˈælətɪ; djuˈæləti/ *n* [U]

dual car·riage·way /ˌ·· ˈ···/ *n* [C] *BrE* a main road that has two lines of traffic travelling in each direction and has a strip of land in the centre【英】〔中间有分隔带、上下行各有两线的〕双向公路，双线车道，复式车道; DIVIDED HIGHWAY *AmE*【美】

dual cit·i·zen·ship /ˌ·· ˈ····/ *n* [U] the state of being a citizen of two countries 双重国籍

dub¹ /dʌb; dʌb/ *v* **dubbed, dubbing** [T] **1** [usually passive 一般用被动态] to give something or someone a humorous name that describes their character 把…诙谐地称为; 给…起绰号: *Mrs Thatcher was dubbed 'The Iron Lady'.* 撒切尔夫人被称为"铁娘子"。**2** to change the original spoken language of a film or television programme into another language 为〔电影或电视节目〕配音: **dub sth into sth** *It's a Swedish film dubbed into English.* 这是一部用英语配音的瑞典影片。**3** *especially BrE* to make a record out of two or more different pieces of music or sound mixed together【尤英】混合录音 **4** *literary* if a king or queen dubs someone, they give the title of KNIGHT¹ (2) to that person in a special ceremony【文】封…为爵士

CULTURAL NOTE 文化注释

This happens in a special CEREMONY in which the king or queen touches a man on the shoulder with a sword and gives him the title 'Sir' before his name. The man who is being dubbed kneels for the ceremony. At the end the king/queen says "Arise/Rise Sir ...". This ceremony is known from stories from the MIDDLE AGES and is still used regularly in Britain when men are given national honours. 授勋采取特别的仪式, 国王或女王把剑放在获得爵位的人肩上, 准许他在名字前使用"爵士"(Sir) 称号。被授勋的人跪在地上, 仪式结束时国王或女王说:"某某爵士, 请起立。"这种授勋仪式见于中世纪传说, 现在英国给予某人国家荣誉时仍旧经常采用。

dub² *n* [U] a style of poetry or music from the West Indies with a strong regular beat〔西印度群岛式〕说唱诗[乐]

Du·bai /du`baɪ; duː'baɪ/ a state on the Arabian Gulf, part of the United Arab Emirates 迪拜〔阿拉伯联合酋长国之一部分, 濒临阿拉伯湾〕

dub·bin /`dʌbɪn; 'dʌbɪ̣n/ *n* [U] a thick oily substance used to make leather softer and to stop water going through it 皮革软化防水油

du·bi·e·ty /du`baɪətɪ; djuː'baɪəti/ *n* [U] *formal* doubt【正式】疑念, 疑惑

du·bi·ous /`dubɪəs; 'djuːbiəs/ *adj* **1 be dubious** to not be sure whether something is good or true〔好坏〕不能确定的; 疑惑的: **[+about]** *I'm a bit dubious about the idea of lending Jim my car.* 我有点拿不定主意是不是该把车借给吉姆。**2** making you doubt whether someone or something is honest, safe etc 不大可靠的, 令人生疑的: *He looks like a dubious character.* 他看起来像是个不大可靠的人。| **highly dubious** *This deal sounds highly dubious to me.* 这笔交易在我看来十分靠不住。—**dubiously** *adv* —**dubiousness** *n* [U]

Dub·lin /`dʌblɪn; 'dʌblɪ̣n/ the capital of the Republic of Ireland. It is on the east coast, on the River Liffey. 都柏林〔爱尔兰共和国首都。位于该国东海岸, 地跨利菲河两岸〕

Dubya the NICKNAME of George W. Bush 大不雅〔乔治·W.布什的诨名〕

du·cal /`dukl; 'djuːkəl/ *adj* like a DUKE (1) or belonging to a duke 公爵(似)的

duc·at /`dʌkət; 'dʌkət/ *n* [C] a gold coin that was used in several European countries in the past 达克特〔旧时欧洲一些国家通用的金币〕

Du·champ /duː`ʃɑŋ; djuː'ʃɒŋ/, **Mar·cel** /mɑr`sɛl; mɑː'sel/ (1887-1968) a French painter and SCULPTOR who was important in developing the styles of CUBISM, FUTURISM, and DADAISM 杜尚〔(1887-1968), 法国画家、雕塑家。他在立体派、未来派、达达派等艺术风格的发展过程中具有举足轻重的作用〕

duch·ess /`dʌtʃɪs; 'dʌtʃɪ̣s/ *n* [C] a woman with the highest social rank outside the royal family, or the wife of a DUKE (1) 女公爵; 公爵夫人: *the Duchess of York* 约克公爵夫人

Duchess of Wind·sor /,‥‥`‥/ —see 见 Wallis SIMPSON,

Duchess of York /,‥‥`‥/ (1959-) the wife of Queen Elizabeth's second son Prince Andrew (who is called the Duke of York) until they separated in 1992. Her name is Sarah Ferguson, and she is often called 'Fergie' in newspapers. 约克公爵夫人〔(1959-), 伊丽莎白女王次子安德鲁王子(约克公爵)之妻, 1992年离婚。原名莎拉·弗格森, 报纸上经常称她为"弗吉"〕

duch·y /`dʌtʃɪ; 'dʌtʃi/ *n* [C] the land and property of a DUKE (1) or DUCHESS (1); DUKEDOM (2) 公爵[女公爵]领地

3 **duck¹** /dʌk; dʌk/ *n*

1 ►BIRD 禽鸟◄ [C] a very common water bird with short legs and a wide beak that is used for its meat, eggs, and soft feathers 鸭子; 野鸭

2 ►FEMALE BIRD 雌性禽鸟◄ [C] a female duck 母鸭

3 ►MEAT 肉◄ [U] the meat of this bird used as food 鸭肉: *roast duck with orange sauce* 配橘子酱的烤鸭(肉)

4 take to something like a duck to water to learn how to do something very easily 轻而易举地学会做某事: *Don't worry, you'll take to it like a duck to water.* 别担心, 你会很快学会的。

5 ►PERSON 人◄ also 又作 **ducks** *BrE spoken* a friendly way of speaking to someone, especially a woman or child【英口】亲爱的, 宝贝儿〔尤用于对妇女、小孩友善的称呼〕: *What can I get you, ducks?* 我能给你们弄点什么, 宝贝们?

6 ►PERSON 人◄ [C] a SCORE¹ (1) of zero by a BATSMAN in a game of CRICKET (2)〔板球中击球手〕未得分; 零分

7 duck shoot *AmE slang* a very easy job or piece of work【美俚】轻而易举的工作 —see also 另见 **a dead duck** (DEAD¹ (12)), **lame duck** (LAME¹ (3)), **like water off a duck's back** (WATER¹ (5)), DUCKS AND DRAKES

duck² *v* **1** [I,T] to lower your head or body very quickly, especially to avoid being seen or hit 迅速低下(头; 身体): *He saw a policeman coming, and ducked behind a car.* 他看见一个警察走过来, 赶紧弯腰躲在一辆汽车后面。| **duck sth** *We had to duck our heads to get through the doorway.* 我们不得不低头才能穿过那门道。**2** [T] to push someone under water for a short time as a joke 把〔某人〕猛地按入水中片刻: *The children were busy ducking each other in the swimming pool.* 孩子们在游泳池中玩得正起劲, 互相把对方按入水中。**3** [T] *informal* to try to avoid something, especially a difficult or unpleasant duty; DODGE¹ (1,2)【非正式】躲避, 推诿〔责任等〕: *His speech ducked all the major issues.* 他的讲话回避了所有主要的问题。

duck 迅速低身

duck out of sth *phr v* [T] *informal* to avoid doing something that you have to do or have promised to do【非正式】躲避, 逃避〔应该做或答应做的事情〕: **duck out of doing sth** *Don't try and duck out of cleaning the kitchen!* 别想逃避收拾厨房!

duck-billed plat·y·pus /,dʌkbɪld `plætəpəs; ,dʌkbɪld 'plætɪ̣pəs/ *n* [C] a PLATYPUS 鸭嘴兽

duck·boards /`dʌk,bɔrdz; 'dʌkbɔːdz/ *n* [plural] long narrow boards that you use to make a path over muddy ground〔在泥地上铺的〕木板道; 铺道板

duck·ing stool /`‥ ‥/ *n* [C] a seat on the end of a long pole, used to DUCK² (2) a woman in water as a punishment in the past 浸刑椅〔旧时缚在长杆一端用以惩罚妇女的一种刑具, 被罚者被捆于椅上浸入水中〕

duck·ling /`dʌklɪŋ; 'dʌklɪŋ/ *n* [C] a small young duck 小鸭, 幼鸭

ducks and drakes /,‥‥`‥/ *n* [U] a children's game in which you make flat stones jump across the surface of water〔儿童玩的〕打水漂游戏

duck·weed /`dʌk,wid; 'dʌkwiːd/ *n* [U] a plant that grows on the surface of fresh water 浮萍; 浮萍属植物

duck·y¹ /`dʌkɪ; 'dʌki/ *n BrE spoken* a friendly way of speaking to someone, especially a woman or child【英口】亲爱的, 宝贝儿〔尤用于对妇女、小孩的友善称呼〕

ducky² *adj AmE old-fashioned*【美, 过时】**1** perfect or satisfactory 极好的, 令人满意的: *That's just ducky!* 那真是好极了! **2** attractive in an amusing or interesting way; CUTE (1) 可爱的, 漂亮的: *That's a ducky dress you're wearing!* 你穿的衣服真可爱!

duct /dʌkt; dʌkt/ *n* [C] **1** a pipe or tube for carrying liquids, air, cables (CABLE¹ (1)) etc〔输送液体、气体、电缆等的〕管道, 槽: *the air duct* 输气管 **2** a thin narrow tube that carries air, liquid etc inside your body, in a plant etc〔人体或植物中输送气体、液体等的〕细管; 导管: *a tear duct* 泪腺管

duc·tile /`dʌktl; 'dʌktaɪl/ *adj* **1** ductile metals can be pressed or pulled into shape without needing to be heated〔指金属〕可锻压的, 可拉长的, 易塑的, 柔软的 **2** *formal* someone who is ductile can be easily influenced or controlled【正式】〔指人〕易受影响[控制]的, 柔顺的 —**ductility** /dʌk`tɪlətɪ; dʌk'tɪlɪ̣ti/ *n* [U]

duct·less gland /,dʌktlɪs `glænd; ,dʌktləs 'glænd/ *n* [C] an ENDOCRINE GLAND 无管腺, 内分泌腺

dud /dʌd; dʌd/ *n* [C] *informal*【非正式】**1** something that is useless, especially because it does not work correctly 无用的东西〔尤指不能正常起作用的东西〕; 废品: *Several of the fireworks were duds.* 烟火中有几个是哑炮。**2 duds** [plural] *slang* clothes【俚】衣服 —**dud** *adj*: *a dud light bulb* 坏灯泡

dud cheque /ˌ· ˈ·/ *n* [C] a cheque that is useless because the person who writes it has no money in their bank account 空头支票

dude /dud; djuːd/ *n* [C] **1** *slang especially AmE* a man【俚, 尤美】男人: *a real cool dude* 一位很帅的男士 **2** *AmE old-fashioned* an American man from a city, who is living in or visiting the countryside【美, 过时】〔指住在乡村或去乡村游览的〕城里人

dude ranch /ˈ· ·/ *n* [C] a holiday place in the US where you can ride horses and live like a COWBOY (1)〔美国西部供游客骑马和像牛仔一样生活的〕度假牧场

dud·geon /ˈdʌdʒən; ˈdʌdʒən/ *n* **in high dudgeon** *formal* angry because someone has treated you badly【正式】极为愤怒, 非常生气: *She slammed the door and flounced out in high dudgeon.* 她砰地一声关上门, 气冲冲地大步走了出去。

due¹ /du; djuː/ *adj*

1 be due to be expected to happen or arrive at a particular time 预定, 预期: *When is your baby due?* 你的预产期是什么时候? | **be due at five o'clock/thirteen hundred hours etc** *The flight from Boston is due at 9:30.* 从波士顿飞来的航班应于9点30分到达。| **be due in an hour/two days etc** *The bus is due any minute now.* 公共汽车随时都可能到来。| **be due to do sth** *The meeting isn't due to start until three.* 会议预定要到3点钟才开始。| **be due for sth** (=expect to get something) 期望应得到某事物 *I'm due for a pay rise soon.* 不久就该给我加工资了。| **due back/out/in etc** *You were due back an hour ago.* 你本该一小时前回来。

2 due to because of 由于, 因为: *The company's problems are due to a mixture of bad luck and poor management.* 该公司的问题出在运气不佳以及管理不善两个方面。| *The 15:30 train to Sheffield has been cancelled due to circumstances beyond our control.* 由于一些我们不能控制的情况, 15点30分开往谢菲尔德镇的火车已经被取消了。—see 见 OWING (USAGE)

3 ▶OWED 欠下◀ owed to someone either as a debt or because they have a right to it 欠下的, 应给的: *You're due three weeks holiday this year.* 今年你应该有三个星期的假期。| **be due to** *Treat him with the respect that is due to a world champion.* 要以一个世界冠军应得的尊重去对待他。

4 ▶MONEY 钱◀ [not before noun 不用于名词前] an amount of money that is due is the amount that should be paid now 应付的, 到期的: *The first interest payments will be due in August.* 首笔利息将在8月份支付。

5 with (all) due respect *spoken* used when you disagree with someone or criticize them in a polite way【口】恕我冒昧〔用以礼貌地反对某人或批评某人〕: *With all due respect, you don't have as much experience as she does.* 恕我冒昧, 你不如她有经验。

6 in due course at some time in the future when it is the right time, but not before 在适当[一定]的时候: *The committee will consider your application in due course.* 委员会将在适当的时候考虑你的申请。

7 ▶PROPER 适当的◀ [only before noun 仅用于名词前] *formal* proper or suitable【正式】适当的, 适宜的: *She was convicted of driving without due care and attention.* 她被判为驾车不慎。—see also 另见 DULY

due² *n* **1 give sb his/her due** used when criticizing someone to admit that not all the things they did were bad, wrong, unpleasant etc 给予某人应有的承认〔用于批评某人时〕: *John was a lousy teacher, but to give him his due he tried hard.* 约翰是个很糟的老师, 但应当承认, 他已非常努力。**2 dues** [plural] regular payments you make to an organization of which you are a member 会(员)费: **pay your dues** *All the union members have already paid their dues.* 所有工会会员都已缴纳了会费。**3 your/his etc due** the amount of money someone is owed, or something they have a right to 某人应得的钱物[权益]: *Gwen never takes more than her due.* 格温从来都只拿自己应得的那份。

due³ *adv* **due north/south/east/west** directly or exactly north etc 正北/正南/正东/正西

due date /ˈ· ·/ *n* [usually singular 一般用单数] the date on which something is supposed to happen, especially when money must be paid 预期某事应发生的日子〔尤指该付款的日子〕; 到期日

du·el¹ /ˈduəl; ˈdjuːəl/ *n* [C] **1** a fight with weapons between two people, used in the past to settle a quarrel〔旧时两男子使用武器以解决争执的〕(双人)决斗: *The officer challenged him to a duel.* 那军官向他提出决斗。**2** a situation in which two people or groups are involved in an angry disagreement〔双方进行的〕斗争; 对抗

duel² *v* **duelling, duelled** *BrE*【英】, **dueling, dueled** *AmE*【美】[I + with] to fight a duel 进行决斗

du·en·na /duˈɛnə; djuˈenə/ *n* [C] an older woman whose job was to look after the daughters in a Spanish or Portuguese family in former times; CHAPERON〔旧时西班牙人或葡萄牙人家庭中照料女孩子的〕年长保姆, 陪媪

due pro·cess /ˌ· ˈ· ·/ *n* [U] *AmE law* the correct process that should be followed in law and is designed to protect someone's legal rights【美, 法律】合法(诉讼)程序

du·et /duˈɛt; djuˈet/ *n* [C] a piece of music for two performers 二重奏(曲); 二重唱(曲) —compare 比较 QUARTET (2), SOLO² (1), TRIO (3)

duff¹ /dʌf; dʌf/ *n* **1 up the duff** *slang* PREGNANT (=with a baby growing inside you)【俚】怀孕的; 有身孕的 **2** [U] a type of cake 水果布丁: *plum duff* 葡萄干布丁

duff² *adj BrE informal* useless and broken【英, 非正式】无用的; 坏了的

duff³ *v*

duff sb ↔ up also 又作 **duff sb ↔ in** *phr v* [T] *BrE slang* to fight someone and injure them【英俚】痛打, 殴伤〔某人〕: *Let's go and duff him up!* 让我们去揍他一顿!

duf·fel bag /ˈdʌfl̩ bæg; ˈdʌfəl bæg/ *n* [C] a bag made of strong cloth, with a round bottom and a string around the top〔圆筒状〕旅行袋, 帆布袋 —see picture at 参见 BAG¹ 图

duffel coat, duffle coat /ˈdʌfl̩ kot; ˈdʌfəl kəʊt/ *n* [C] *especially BrE* a coat made of rough heavy cloth, usually with a HOOD (1) and TOGGLES (=buttons shaped like tubes)【尤英】连帽粗呢外套〔通常有棒形纽扣〕—see picture at 参见 COAT 图

duf·fer /ˈdʌfɚ; ˈdʌfə/ *n* [C] *old-fashioned* someone who is stupid or not very good at something【过时】笨蛋, 无能的人

Du·fy /duˈfi; ˈduːfi/, **Ra·oul** /rɑˈul; rɑːˈuːl/ (1877-1953) a French painter famous for his brightly coloured paintings of horse races, beaches, and boats 杜飞〔(1877-1953), 法国画家, 以描绘赛马、沙滩和船只等色彩鲜明的作品闻名〕

dug /dʌg; dʌg/ the past tense and past participle of DIG

dug·out /ˈdʌgˌaʊt; ˈdʌgaʊt/ *n* [C] **1** a small boat made by cutting out a hollow space in a tree trunk〔挖空树干做成的〕独木舟: *a dugout canoe* 独木小舟 **2** a shelter dug into the ground for soldiers to use〔供士兵使用的〕地下掩体; 防空洞 —compare 比较 TRENCH (2) **3** a low shelter at the side of a sports field, where players and team officials sit〔设在运动场边供运动员和教练用的〕休息棚

DUI /ˌdi ju ˈaɪ; ˌdiː juː ˈaɪ/ *n* [U] *AmE* driving under the influence; the crime of driving when you have had too much alcohol to drink【美】酒后驾驶: *a large number of DUI arrests on New Year's Eve* 新年前夜许多因酒后驾驶而被逮捕的人

duke /duk; djuːk/ *n* [C] **1** a man with the highest social rank outside the royal family 公爵: *the Duke of Norfolk* 诺福克公爵 —see also 另见 DUCHESS **2 dukes** [plural] *old-fashioned* FISTS【过时】拳头: *Put up your dukes and fight!* 举起拳头打吧!

duke·dom /ˈdukdəm; ˈdjuːkdəm/ *n* [C] **1** the rank of a duke 公爵爵位 **2** the land and property belonging to a duke; DUCHY 公爵的领地, 财产

Duke of Ed·in·burgh /ˌ· · ˈ· · · ·/ (1921-) the husband of the British queen, Elizabeth II. His name is Prince Philip. 爱丁堡公爵〔(1921-), 又称菲力普亲王, 英国女王伊丽莎白二世的丈夫〕

Duke of Edinburgh's a·ward /ˌ· · ˌ· · · · ˈ· ·/ also 又作 **Duke of Edinburgh's** *n* [C] a special prize given to someone who has successfully completed a number of activities in a programme that was originally set up in the UK by the Duke of Edinburgh. The programme is designed for young people, and its aim is to encourage them to achieve difficult things and do work that helps other people. The programme includes physical activities such as climbing mountains, camping, hiking (HIKE) and other outdoor activities. 爱丁堡公爵奖〔英国一项特别奖。爱丁堡公爵最初针对年轻人而设立了一个计划, 计划包括一些体力活动, 如爬山、宿营、徒步旅行等诸多户外活动, 旨在鼓励他们克服困难, 帮助他人。完成这些活动的人可获得此特别奖〕

Duke of Wel·ling·ton, the /ˌ· · ˈ· · ·/ (1769-1852) a British soldier and politician, born in Ireland, and sometimes called 'the Iron Duke'. He was a very successful military leader, and is famous for defeating Napoleon at the Battle of Waterloo in 1815. He later became Prime Minister (1828-34). 威灵顿公爵〔(1769-1852), 英国军事家、政治家, 出生于爱尔兰, 有时被称为"铁公爵"。他是一位非常出色的军事领导人, 尤以1815年滑铁卢战役中打败拿破仑而闻名。他后来成为英国首相(1828-1834)〕

Duke of Wind·sor /ˌ· · ˈ· ·/ —see 见 King EDWARD VIII

Duke of York /ˌ· · ˈ·/ —see 见 Prince ANDREW

dul·cet /ˋdʌlsɪt; ˈdʌlsɨt/ *adj* **1 sb's dulcet tones** *humorous* someone's voice【幽默】某人的嗓音: *Is the boss in yet? I thought I heard his dulcet tones.* 老板回来了吗? 我好像听到他的嗓音了。**2** *literary* dulcet sounds are soft and pleasant to hear【文】〔声音〕悦耳的, 轻柔的, 动听的

dul·ci·mer /ˋdʌlsəmɚ; ˈdʌlsɨmə/ *n* [C] **1** a musical instrument with up to 100 strings, played with light hammers 扬琴 **2** a small instrument with strings that is popular in American FOLK MUSIC, and is played across your knees 杜西莫琴〔美国的一种民间乐器〕

3 **dull¹** /dʌl; dʌl/ *adj*

1 ►BORING 乏味的◄ not interesting or exciting 无趣的, 枯燥的; 沉闷的; 无聊的: *Bill's friends are a pretty dull bunch.* 比尔的朋友都是一些乏味无趣的家伙。| *the dull routine of the office* 办公室里单调枯燥的例行公事 | **as dull as ditchwater** *BrE informal* (=very boring)【英, 非正式】非常枯燥乏味的

2 never a dull moment *often humorous* used to say that a lot of interesting things are happening or that you are very busy【常幽默】绝不会有沉闷无聊之时

3 ►COLOUR/LIGHT 颜色/光◄ not bright or shiny 暗淡的, 不鲜明的: *Nina's hair was a dull, darkish brown.* 尼娜的头发是暗褐色的。

4 ►SOUND 声音◄ not clear or loud 不清楚的, 沉闷的: *The sack hit the floor with a dull thud.* 袋子落在地上发出沉闷的响声。

5 ►PAIN 疼痛◄ a dull pain is not severe but does not stop 隐约的, 不明显的: *a dull throbbing at the base of the spine* 脊柱底部的一阵隐痛 —see graph at 参见 PAIN¹ 图表

6 ►WEATHER 天气◄ not bright and with lots of clouds 阴沉的, 昏暗的: *It'll be dry but dull today, with outbreaks of rain this evening.* 今天白天阴无雨, 傍晚将有阵雨。

7 ►NOT INTELLIGENT 不聪明的◄ not able to think quickly or understand things easily 迟钝的; 愚笨的

8 ►KNIFE/BLADE 刀/刃◄ not sharp; BLUNT¹ (1) 不锋利的, 钝的

9 ►TRADE 贸易◄ if business on the Stock Exchange is dull, few people are buying and selling 萧条的, 不景气的 —**dully** *adv* —**dullness** *n* [U]

dull² *v* [T] to make something such as pain or a feeling become less sharp, less clear etc 使〔疼痛、感觉等〕不明显, 使不清楚: *tranquillizers to dull the pain* 用于减轻疼痛的安定药 —see graph at 参见 PAIN¹ 图表

dull·ard /ˋdʌlɚd; ˈdʌləd/ *n* [C] *old-fashioned* someone who is stupid and has no imagination【过时】愚笨的人, 无想象力的人

Dul·les, John Foster (1888-1959) a US lawyer and politician in the Republican Party, who was Secretary of State (=the minister who deals with foreign policy and foreign governments) from 1953 to 1959. He strongly influenced the US's anti-Communist policy during the Cold War. 杜勒斯〔(1888-1959), 美国律师、共和党政治家。1953至1959年间任美国国务卿, 冷战时期对美国的反共政策有着强烈影响〕

du·ly /ˋdulɪ; ˈdjuːli/ *adv* **1** in the proper or expected way 适当地, 恰当地, 应当地: *Here are your travel documents, all duly signed.* 这是你的旅游证件, 都签好了。**2** at the proper time or as expected 准时地, 按时地: *The Queen duly appeared on the balcony to wave to the crowds.* 女王准时出现在阳台上, 向人群招手。

Du·mas /duˋmɑ; ˈdjuːmɑː/, **Al·ex·an·dre** /ælɪgˋzɑndrə; ˌælɪgˈzɑːndrə/ (1802-70) a French writer of NOVELs and plays. He wrote *The Count of Monte Cristo* and *The Three Musketeers.* 大仲马〔(1802-1870), 法国小说家、剧作家, 作品包括《基督山伯爵》和《三剑客》〕

3 **dumb** /dʌm; dʌm/ *adj* **1** *not technical* a word used to describe someone who is permanently unable to speak, which some people find offensive【非术语】〔指人〕哑巴的, 不能说话的〔有些人认为此词具有冒犯性〕: **deaf and dumb** (=unable to hear or speak) 聋哑的 *She's been deaf and dumb since birth.* 她生下来就又聋又哑。**2** *informal especially AmE* stupid【非正式, 尤美】愚蠢的: *What a dumb question!* 多么愚蠢的问题! | *That was a dumb thing to do!* 那件事干得真愚蠢! | **play dumb** (=pretend to be stupid) 装傻 | **dumb blonde** (=a woman who is sexually attractive, but seems stupid) 性感、漂亮但没有头脑的金发女郎 **3** unable to speak, because you are angry, surprised, shocked etc〔因愤怒、惊讶、震惊等而〕说不出话的: *He stared in dumb misery at the wreckage of the car.* 他痛苦地呆望着被撞得不像样的汽车, 说不出话来。| **be struck dumb** (=be so shocked that you cannot speak) 震惊得说不出话来 **4 dumb animals/beasts** used to emphasize that animals cannot speak and that people often treat them badly 不会说话的动物, 哑巴牲口〔用于强调动物不会说话, 但人们常虐待它们〕: *It's cruel to bait dumb animals.* 折磨不会说话的动物是残忍的。—**dumbly** *adv*: *They all stood dumbly staring at the coffin.* 他们全部站在那儿, 木然地看着棺材。—**dumbness** *n* [U]

dumb·bell /ˋdʌmˌbɛl; ˈdʌmbel/ *n* [C] **1** two weights connected by a short bar, that you can lift in each hand to strengthen your arms and shoulders 哑铃 **2** *informal especially AmE* someone who is stupid【非正式, 尤美】笨蛋, 傻瓜

dumb·found /dʌmˋfaund; dʌmˈfaʊnd/ *v* [T] to shock or surprise someone so much that they are very confused 使惊呆, 使发愣: *Pollini's piano playing continues to dumbfound the critics.* 波利尼的钢琴演奏仍然使评论家们惊羡得说不出话来。

dumb·found·ed /dʌmˋfaundɪd; dʌmˈfaʊndɨd/ *adj* so surprised that you are confused and cannot speak 惊得目瞪口呆的: *Victor stared dumbfounded as the woman continued to scream abuse at him.* 面对那个妇女不断地尖声辱骂, 维克托目瞪口呆。

Dumbo the main character in the CARTOON film *Dumbo*, made by Walt Disney in 1941. Dumbo is a young ELEPHANT with very large ears, who learns to fly. 小飞象〔迪斯尼公司1941年制作的卡通片《小飞象》中的主角。它是头长着大耳朵会飞的小象〕

dum·bo /ˋdʌmbo; ˈdʌmbəʊ/ *n* [C] *informal* someone who is stupid【非正式】傻瓜, 蠢蛋

dumb show /ˈ· ·/ *n* [C,U] a performance or action in which you do not say anything, but instead use movements to express your meaning 哑剧, 默剧; 手势

dumb·struck /ˋdʌmˌstrʌk; ˈdʌmstrʌk/ *adj* so shocked or surprised that you cannot speak 被吓呆的; 被惊呆的

dumb wait·er /ˌ·ˈ··/ *n* [C] **1** a small LIFT² (1) used to move food, plates etc from one level in a restaurant, hotel etc to another〔餐厅、酒店中在楼层间运送食物、餐具等的〕小型升降机 **2** a small table that turns around on a base, used for serving food〔餐桌上便于上菜的〕圆转台[盘]

dum-dum /ˋdʌm dʌm; ˈdʌm dʌm/ *n* [C] a soft bullet that causes serious wounds because it breaks into pieces when it hits you 达姆弹〔一种会炸成碎片、杀伤力很强的软头子弹〕

Dum·fries and Gal·lo·way /dʌmˌfris ənd ˋgæləwe; dʌmˌfriːs ənd ˈgæləweɪ/ a region in southwest Scotland, including the town of Dumfries 邓弗里斯-加洛韦〔苏格兰西南部一地区, 包括邓弗里斯镇〕

dum·my¹ /ˋdʌmɪ; ˈdʌmi/ *n* [C]

1 ►COPY 仿制◄ an object that is made to look like a tool, weapon, vehicle etc but which you cannot use〔工具、武器、车辆等的〕仿制品; 仿真物品: *Don't worry about the gun, it's a dummy.* 别担心这枪, 它是假的。

2 ►FOR CLOTHES 用于服装◄ a large model in the shape of a person, especially used when you are making clothes or to show them in a shop〔制作或陈列服装用的〕人体模型: *a dressmaker's dummy* 服装师用的人体模型

3 ►FOR BABIES 用于婴儿◄ *BrE* a specially shaped rubber object that you put in a baby's mouth for it to suck【英】橡皮奶嘴; PACIFIER (1) *AmE*【美】

4 ►STUPID PERSON 笨蛋◄ *informal especially AmE* someone who is stupid【非正式, 尤美】傻瓜, 蠢货

5 ►IN CARD GAME 在扑克牌游戏中◄ cards that are placed on the table by one player for all the other players to see in a game of BRIDGE¹ (4)〔桥牌中的〕明手牌

dummy² *adj* [only before noun 仅用于名词前] a dummy tool, weapon, vehicle etc is made to look like a real one but you cannot use it 假的, 仿真的: *a dummy rifle* 仿真步枪

dummy³ *v*

dummy up *phr v* [I] *AmE slang* to stay silent and not speak【美俚】闭口不说, 默不吭声: *When I asked her name she just dummied up.* 我问她叫什么名字, 她就是不吭声。

dummy run /ˌ··ˈ·/ *n* [C] an occasion when you practise doing something in complete detail to see if it works 演习, 预演

dump¹ /dʌmp; dʌmp/ *v*

1 ►PUT STH SOMEWHERE 将某物放置某处◄ [T always +adv/prep] to put something such as a load, bag etc somewhere in a careless, untidy way 乱放, 乱堆, 乱扔: **dump sth in/on/there etc** *Who dumped all these books on my desk?* 谁把这些书乱堆在我的书桌上?

2 ►GET RID OF 丢弃◄ [T] to get rid of someone or something that you do not want 抛弃〔某人〕; 丢弃, 扔掉〔某物〕: *I hear Lucy has dumped her boyfriend.* 我听说露西已经把她的男朋友甩了。| *Let's dump the car and walk the rest of the way.* 让我们把车丢在这儿, 剩下的路走着去。

3 ►SELL GOODS 出售货物◄ [T] to get rid of goods by selling them in a foreign country at a much lower price〔向国外〕廉价倾销〔货物〕

4 ►COPY INFORMATION 复制资讯◄ [T] *technical* to copy information stored in a computer's memory on to something

D

else such as a DISK OR MAGNETIC TAPE【术语】转储；转存；转出〔将存储在电脑中的资料转存到磁盘或磁带中〕

5 dumping ground a place where you send people or things that you want to get rid of 把想摆脱掉的人送往的地方；垃圾倾倒场：*The estate is a dumping ground for problem tenants.* 那个住宅区是个打发难缠租客的地方。

dump on sb *phr v* [T] *AmE informal*【美，非正式】**1** to criticize someone very strongly and often unfairly〔不公正地〕诋毁，贬低：*Don't dump on the teachers we've got, they're doing a good job.* 别诋毁我们的老师们，他们工作得很好。**2** to tell someone all your problems 向〔某人〕倾诉〔所有的问题〕：*Sorry to dump on you like that, I was feeling kind of low.* 我这样把所有的烦恼都倾诉给你听，很对不起，我心情有些不好。

dump² *n* [C]

1 ►WASTE 废品◄ a place where unwanted waste is taken and left 垃圾堆，垃圾场，废品堆：*the town rubbish dump* 该城镇的垃圾场

2 ►WEAPONS 武器◄ a place where military supplies are stored, or the supplies themselves 军需品存放处；军需品：*an ammunition dump* 军火（临时）存放处

3 ►UNPLEASANT PLACE 讨厌的地方◄ *informal* a place that is unpleasant to live in because it is dirty, ugly, untidy etc【非正式】脏乱的居住之地：*Do something about your room, it's a dump.* 收拾收拾你的房间，简直像个垃圾堆。

4 down in the dumps *informal* very sad and without much interest in life【非正式】伤心的，对生活失去兴趣的：*I've been feeling a bit down in the dumps lately.* 最近我感到生活有些没劲。

5 ►COMPUTER 电脑◄ *technical* the act of copying the information stored in a computer's memory onto something else, such as a DISK【术语】转储，转存，转出

dump·er truck /ˈ· · ·/ *n* [C] *BrE* a vehicle with a large open container at the back that can move up to pour sand, soil etc onto the ground【英】自动卸货车，翻斗车；DUMP TRUCK *AmE*【美】

dump·ling /ˈdʌmplɪŋ; ˈdʌmplɪŋ/ *n* [C] **1** a round lump of flour and fat mixed with water, cooked in boiling liquid and served with meat〔水煮的〕肉馅面团子，水饺：*mince and dumplings* 肉馅饺子 **2** a sweet dish made of PASTRY filled with fruit 水果馅点心，水果布丁：*apple dumplings* 苹果布丁

Dump·ster /ˈdʌmpstɚ; ˈdʌmpstə/ *n* [C] *trademark AmE* a large metal container used for waste in the US【商标，美】置垃圾的大铁桶；SKIP² (2) *BrE*【英】

dump truck /ˈ· ·/ *n* [C] *AmE*【美】= a DUMPER TRUCK *BrE*【英】

dump·y /ˈdʌmpɪ; ˈdʌmpi/ *adj informal* someone who is dumpy is fat, short, and unattractive【非正式】矮胖而丑陋的：*a dumpy little man* 矮墩墩的小个子男人

dun /dʌn; dʌn/ *n* [C,U] a dull brownish-grey colour 暗褐色，棕灰色 —**dun** *adj*

Dun·blane /dʌnˋblen; dʌnˈbleɪn/ a small town in Scotland, where in 1996 16 young children and their teacher were shot and killed in their school by a man called Thomas Hamilton, who also killed himself. Because of these murders, many people demanded stricter laws against people owning guns, and new gun-control laws were passed in 1997. 邓布兰〔苏格兰一小镇。1996年，一位名叫托马斯·汉密尔顿的男子在此地一所学校开枪打死了16名学生和一名教师，然后自杀身亡。由于这一凶案的发生，许多人要求制定更加严厉的法律，限制私人携带枪支。1997年通过了新的枪支管理法〕

Dun·can /ˋdʌŋkən; ˈdʌŋkən/ a character in the play *Macbeth* by William Shakespeare. Duncan is the king of Scotland and is murdered by Macbeth. 邓肯〔威廉·莎士比亚戏剧《麦克白》中的人物，苏格兰国王，为麦克白所杀〕

Duncan, Is·a·do·ra /ˌɪzəˋdorə; ˌɪzəˈdɔːrə/ (1878-1927) a US dancer who had a great influence on modern dance 邓肯〔(1878-1927)，美国舞蹈家，对现代舞蹈产生过深远影响〕

dunce /dʌns; dʌns/ *n* [C] *old-fashioned* someone who is slow at learning things【过时】〔学习〕迟钝的人，愚笨的人：*the dunce of the class* 这个班上的笨学生

dunce's cap /ˈ· · ·/ *n* [C] a tall pointed hat that a stupid student had to wear in school in the past 笨蛋帽〔旧时劣等生必须在学校戴的尖顶高帽〕

Dun·dee /dʌnˋdi; dʌnˈdiː/ a city on the East coast of Scotland, where the River Tay enters the sea 邓迪〔苏格兰东岸一城市，泰河由此入海〕

Dun·dee cake /dʌnˋdi ˌkek; dʌnˈdiː ˌkeɪk/ *n* [C,U] a British cake made with fruit and nuts 敦提蛋糕〔英国的一种水果果仁蛋糕〕

dun·der·head /ˋdʌndɚˌhɛd; ˈdʌndəhed/ *n* [C] *old-fashioned* someone who is stupid【过时】笨蛋，蠢人

dune /dun; djuːn/ also 又作 **sand dune** *n* [C] a hill made of sand near the sea or in the desert〔海边或沙漠中的〕沙丘

dune bug·gy /ˈ· , ··/ *n* [C] *AmE* a car with big wheels and no roof that you can drive across sand; BEACH BUGGY【美】〔装有大号轮胎适合在沙地行驶的〕沙地汽车

dung /dʌŋ; dʌŋ/ *n* [U] solid waste from animals, especially cows 动物粪；〔尤指牛的〕粪便

dun·ga·rees /ˌdʌŋgəˋriz; ˌdʌŋgəˈriːz/ *n* [plural] **1** *BrE* loose trousers that have a square piece of cloth that covers your chest, and long thin pieces that fasten over your shoulders【英】工装裤；OVERALL³ (2) *AmE*【美】**2** *AmE* heavy cotton trousers used for working in【美】粗棉布工作裤

Dun·ge·ness /ˌdʌndʒəˋnɛs; ˌdʌndʒəˈnes◂/ a place in Kent, in southeast England, next to the English Channel, where there are two NUCLEAR power stations 邓杰内斯〔位于英格兰东南部肯特郡，濒临英吉利海峡。此处建有两座核电站〕

dun·geon /ˋdʌndʒən; ˈdʌndʒən/ *n* [C] a dark underground prison used in the past, especially under a castle〔尤指旧时城堡下面的〕地牢

Dungeons and Drag·ons /ˌ· · · ˈ· ·/ *trademark* a type of ROLE playing game in which the players pretend to be a magic character or strange creature who must either do something difficult, such as finding a magic ring, or must prevent someone else from doing it【商标】龙与地下城〔一种角色扮演游戏。参与者假扮魔法师或者怪兽，要么做具有一定难度的事情，如寻找魔法指环，要么阻止他人找到魔法指环〕

dunk /dʌŋk; dʌŋk/ *v* [T] **1** to dip something that you are eating into coffee, tea etc 将〔正在吃的东西〕浸入〔咖啡、茶等中〕：*Don't dunk your biscuit in your tea!* 别把饼干往茶里蘸！**2** *AmE* to push someone under water for a short time as a joke; DUCK² (2)【美】〔玩时〕将〔某人〕按到水里片刻 **3** to throw the ball downwards into the basket in BASKETBALL〔篮球赛中〕扣篮 —see also 另见 **dunk for apples** (APPLE (3)), SLAM DUNK —**dunk** *n* [C] —see picture on page A22 参见 A22 页图

Dun·kirk /ˋdʌnkɝk; ˌdʌnˈkɜːk◂/ a port and industrial city in northern France, whose French name is Dunkerque. In 1940, during World War II, the British army was surrounded at Dunkirk by the German army, but thousands of British soldiers escaped and were brought back to England in a collection of small boats. 敦刻尔克〔法国北部港口和工业城市，法语名称Dunkerque。1940年二战期间，英国军队在此被德军包围，成千上万的英军士兵由一艘艘小船救回英国〕

Dunkirk spir·it /ˌ· ˈ· ·/ a determination to succeed despite being in a difficult or impossible situation, which many people think is a typical British quality 敦刻尔克精神〔指危难之时取胜的决心，被视为英国人的典型特性〕

> **CULTURAL NOTE 文化注释**
>
> This expression comes from the attitude shown by British people who went to Dunkirk in France in small boats to help to bring back British soldiers in World War II. 二战期间，很多英国人驾小船前往法国敦刻尔克接运英军士兵，敦刻尔克精神即指他们表现出来的这种态度。

Dún Laogh·aire /dʌn ˋlɛrə; duːn ˈleərə/ a port on the east coast of Ireland, just south of Dublin 邓莱里〔爱尔兰东海岸一港口，位于都柏林以南〕

dun·no /ˋdʌno; ˈdʌnəʊ/ *spoken* a way of saying 'I don't know', that some people think is incorrect【口】我不知道〔I don't know 的一种说法，有些人认为这种说法不正确〕：*"Do you want to come?" "I dunno, I might."* "你想来吗？""我不知道，也许吧。"

du·o /ˋduo; ˈdjuːəʊ/ *n* [C] **1** a piece of music for two performers 二重奏（曲）；二重唱（曲）**2** two people who perform together or are often seen together〔在一起表演的〕一对艺人，两人的搭档：*comedy duo Reeves and Mortimer* 一对喜剧搭档里夫斯和莫蒂默

du·o·dec·i·mal /ˌduəˋdɛsəml; ˌdjuːəˈdesəməl◂/ *adj technical* a duodecimal system of numbers is based on the number 12, instead of the usual system based on ten【术语】十二进制的

du·o·de·num /ˌduəˋdinəm; ˌdjuːəˈdiːnəm/ *n* [C] *technical* the top part of your BOWEL, below your stomach【术语】十二指肠 —**duodenal** /ˌduəˋdinl; ˌdjuːəˈdiːnl◂/ *adj*: *a duodenal ulcer* 十二指肠溃疡 —see picture at 参见 DIGESTIVE SYSTEM 图

du·o·logue /ˋduəˌlɔg; ˈdjuːəlɒg/ *n* [C] *formal* a conversation or discussion between two people, especially in a play【正式】〔尤指戏剧中二人的〕对话；商谈

dupe¹ /dup; djuːp/ *n* [C] someone who is tricked, especially into becoming involved in something illegal 受骗[上当]者〔尤指受骗参与违法之事的人〕

dupe² *v* [T usually passive 一般用被动态] to trick or deceive someone 欺骗, 哄骗: **dupe sb into doing sth** *Consumers are being duped into buying faulty electronic goods.* 消费者经常受骗购买有毛病的电子产品。

du·plex /ˈduplɛks; ˈdjuːpleks/ *n* [C] *AmE*【美】**1** a type of house divided into two parts, with two separate homes in it 毗联式住宅〔并排住两家人〕—see picture on page A4 参见 A4 页图 **2** an apartment with rooms on two levels 占两层楼的公寓; 上下两层的公寓套房

du·pli·cate¹ /ˈdupləkɪt; ˈdjuːplɪkɪt/ *n* [C] **1** an exact copy of something that you can use in the same way 复制品: *If you've lost your key I can give you a duplicate.* 如果你把钥匙丢了, 我可以给你一把配制的。**2 in duplicate** if something is written in duplicate, there are two copies of it 一式两份 —**duplicate** *adj*: *a duplicate copy* 副本

duplicate² /ˈdjupləˌket; ˈdjuːplɪkeɪt/ *v* [T] **1** to copy something exactly 复制: *It can duplicate the movements of the human hand.* 它能模仿人手的活动。| *piles of duplicated notes* 一叠叠复制的说明文稿 **2** *formal* to succeed in repeating something【正式】〔成功地〕重复: *Scientists were not able to duplicate the effect under laboratory conditions.* 科学家们无法在实验室条件下重现那种效果。—**duplication** /ˌdjupləˈkeʃən; ˌdjuːplɪˈkeɪʃən/ *n* [U]

du·pli·ca·tor /ˈdupləˌketɚ; ˈdjuːplɪkeɪtə/ *n* [C] *BrE old-fashioned* a machine used to make copies of written pages【英, 过时】复印机

du·plic·i·ty /duˈplɪsətɪ; djuːˈplɪsɪti/ *n* [U] *formal* dishonest behaviour that is intended to deceive someone【正式】欺骗行为, 奸诈行径 —**duplicitous** *adj*

Du Pré /du ˋpre; duː ˈpreɪ/**, Jac·que·line** /ˈdʒæklin; ˈdʒækəliːn/ (1945-87) a British musician who was one of the greatest ever CELLISTS (=someone who play the cello) 杜普雷〔(1945-1987), 英国音乐家, 最伟大的大提琴演奏家之一〕

dur·a·ble /ˈdurəbl̩; ˈdjʊərəbəl/ *adj* **1** staying in good condition for a long time even if used a lot 耐用的: *Plastic window frames are more durable than wood.* 塑料窗框比木质窗框耐用。**2** continuing for a long time 持久的: *a durable peace between France and Germany* 法德两国间持久的和平 —see also 另见 CONSUMER DURABLES —**durably** *adv* —**durability** /ˌdurəˈbɪlətɪ; ˌdjʊərəˈbɪlɪti/ *n* [U]

durable goods /ˈ···, ·ˈ/ *n* [plural] *AmE* large things such as cars, televisions, and furniture, that you do not buy often【美】〔大件〕耐用消费品〈如汽车、电视、家具等〉; CONSUMER DURABLES *BrE*【英】

du·ra·tion /duˈreʃən; djʊˈreɪʃən/ *n* [U] *formal* the length of time that something continues【正式】持续时间: *an illness of relatively short duration* 持续时间较短的疾病 | **for the duration (of)** *He was interned and had to stay in the US for the duration of the war.* 他遭到扣押, 战争期间不得不留在美国。

Dü·rer /ˈdjuərɚ; ˈdjʊərə/**, Al·brecht** /ˈælbrɛkt; ˈælbrekt/ (1471-1528) a German artist famous for his drawings and ENGRAVINGS, especially his very detailed pictures of himself and other people 丢勒〔(1471-1528), 德国艺术家, 以油画和雕刻, 尤其是精细的自画像和人物像闻名〕

du·ress /djʊˋrɛs; djʊˈres/ *n* [U] *formal* illegal or unfair threats【正式】胁迫; 威逼: **under duress** (=using unfair threats) 在威逼下 *The confession was obtained under duress.* 供词是在逼供之下取得的。

dur·ex /ˈdurɛks; ˈdjʊəreks/ *n trademark*【商标】**1** [C] *BrE* a rubber CONTRACEPTIVE that a man wears over his PENIS during sex【英】〔"杜蕾斯"牌〕避孕套, 保险套 **2** [U] *AustrE* clear narrow plastic that is sticky on one side and is used for fastening paper【澳】透明胶带

Dur·ham /ˈdɝəm; ˈdʌrəm/ **1** a city in northeast England on the River Wear. It has a CATHEDRAL (=large important church) and one of the UK's oldest universities. 达勒姆〔英格兰东北部城市。地跨威尔河, 市内有一座大教堂, 英国最古老的大学之一也坐落于此〕**2** also 又作 **County Durham** a COUNTY in northeast England, which used to produce a lot of coal 达勒姆郡〔英格兰东北部一郡。过去曾大量产煤〕

S1 W1 **dur·ing** /ˈdurɪŋ; ˈdjʊərɪŋ/ *prep* **1** all through a length of time 在…期间: *We didn't see a soul during the holidays.* 假期里我们一个人影也没见到。| *Children were evacuated to the country during the war.* 战争期间, 孩子们都被疏散到乡间。**2** at some point in a period of time 在〔一段时间中的〕某一时候: *Henry died during the night.* 亨利是在夜间死去的。| *There will be one ten-minute interval during the performance.* 在演出期间会有一次10分钟的休息。

> **USAGE NOTE 用法说明: DURING**
>
> WORD CHOICE 词语辨析: **during, for**
>
> If someone asks you a question beginning with *When...?*, you can answer with **during** but not **for**. 如果某人问你一个以 when 开头的问题, 你可以用 during 来回答, 但不能用 for 回答: *"When did he get those scars?" "During the last war."* "他那些疤是什么时候弄的?" "在上次战争期间。" If someone asks you a question beginning with *How long...?* you can answer with **for** but not with **during**. 如果某人问你一个以 how long 开头的问题, 你可以用 for 来回答, 但不能用 during: *"How long did you stay in Mexico City?" "For about three months."* "你在墨西哥城停留了多长时间?" "大约有三个月。"
>
> When you want to talk about the time within which something happens, you use **during**. 谈论在某一时期内发生某事要用 during: *Call me sometime during the vacation.* 假期里什么时候给我打个电话吧。| *Thieves broke in during the night.* 盗贼在夜间闯了进来。
>
> When you are talking about how long something lasts, you use **for**. 谈论某事持续多长时间要用 for: *I was only out of the room for a few minutes.* 我离开房间只有几分钟。| *They were married for 20 years.* 他们结婚有20年了。
>
> **During** is common with words for something that continues for a length of time. during 经常和表示持续一段时间的词连用: *during the program/the semester/the war/a conversation* 在节目中/这学期中/战争期间/谈话过程中。You also use it to talk about specific periods of time. during 还可以用于表示具体的某段时间: *during office hours/the day/last week/that year/the 80s* 在办公时间/白天/上个星期/那一年/〔20世纪〕80年代。**For** is more usual with phrases used to measure length of time. for 多与计量时间长度的词组连用: *for two hours/a week/many years/a long period* 两小时/一星期/许多年/很长一段时间
>
> GRAMMAR 语法
>
> **During** is never used with a clause like a **while** clause. during 从来不能引导从句, while 可以: *While I was at home, I met a nice boy* (NOT 不用 *During I was...*, but you can say 但可以说 *During my time at home,...*). 我在家时, 遇上了一个很好的男孩。Also, you would say 再举一例, 通常说: *I did the dishes while you were asleep* (NOT 不用 *during you were asleep*). 你睡觉的时候我把碗碟洗了。

Durk·heim /ˈdɝkhaɪm; ˈdɜːkhaɪm/**, É·mile** /ɛˈmil; eˈmiːl/ (1858-1917) a French university teacher who helped to establish the principles of SOCIOLOGY (=the scientific study of societies and the behaviour of people in groups) 涂尔干〔(1858-1917), 法国大学教师, 社会学原理的奠基人之一〕

Dur·rell /ˈdʌrəl; ˈdʌrəl/**, Ger·ald** /ˈdʒɛrəld; ˈdʒerəld/ (1925-95) a British writer, broadcaster and CONSERVATIONIST (=someone who works to protect rare plants and animals), who set up his own zoo on the island of Jersey, so that rare animals could be taken care of and eventually put back in their natural environment. His books include *My Family and Other Animals*. He was the brother of Lawrence Durrell. 达雷尔〔(1925-1995), 英国作家、播音员和生态环境保护主义者。他曾在泽西岛上建起了自己的动物园, 保护珍稀动物, 并最终让它们回归自然环境。著有《我的家庭与其他动物》。他是劳伦斯·达雷尔之弟〕

Durrell, Lawrence (1912-90) a British writer of NOVELS and poetry. His most famous work is a set of four NOVELS called *The Alexandria Quartet*. He was the brother of Gerald Durrell. 达雷尔〔(1921-1990), 英国小说家和诗人。最有名的作品是小说集《亚历山大四部曲》。他是杰拉尔德·达雷尔之兄〕

durst /dɝst; dɜːst/ *old use*【旧】the past tense of DARE

Du·shan·be /duˋʃæmbɪ; djuːˈʃɑːnbi/ the capital city of Tajikistan 杜尚别〔塔吉克斯坦首都〕

dusk /dʌsk; dʌsk/ *n* [U] the time before it gets dark when the sky is becoming less bright 黄昏, 傍晚: **at dusk** *The street lights go on at dusk.* 街灯在黄昏时亮了起来。—compare 比较 DAWN¹

dusk·y /ˈdʌskɪ; ˈdʌski/ *adj* dark or not very bright in colour 昏暗的, 暗淡的, 朦胧的: *The room was filled with dusky shadows.* 房间里到处都是朦胧的影子。| **dusky pink/orange/blue etc** *a dusky pink room* 暗粉色色调的房间

dust¹ /dʌst; dʌst/ *n* **1** [U] dry powder consisting of extremely small bits of earth or sand 沙尘; 尘土: *The truck drove off in a cloud of dust.* 卡车开走了, 扬起一片尘土。| *the heat and dust of an Indian town* 一个印度小城的炎热和尘土 **2** [U] dry pow- S3 W3

der consisting of extremely small bits of dirt which you find in buildings on furniture, floors etc 灰尘，尘埃: *The table was covered with a layer of dust.* 桌子上覆盖了一层灰尘。**3 coal dust/gold dust/wood dust etc** [U] powder consisting of extremely small bits of coal or gold etc 煤灰/金粉/木屑等 **4 a dust** the act of dusting something 掸灰，去尘: *Can you give the room a quick dust?* 你能把这个房间的灰尘快速清扫一遍吗？**5 let the dust settle/wait for the dust to settle** to allow or wait for a confused situation to become clear 让尘埃落定/等待烟消云散 **6 not see sb for dust** *BrE informal* if you do not see someone for dust, they leave a place very quickly in order to avoid something【英，非正式】不见某人的踪影〔指某人为逃避某事而迅速离开某处〕: *Tell him it's his turn to pay for the drinks and you won't see him for dust.* 如果你告诉他这次该他付酒钱了，他一定会逃得无影无踪。—see also 另见 **bite the dust** (BITE¹ (7)), DUSTY

dust² *v* **1** [I,T] to clean the dust from a surface by moving something such as a soft cloth across it 擦去…的灰尘，打扫: *Could you dust the dining room?* 你能把饭厅的灰尘打扫一下吗？—see picture at 参见 CLEAN 图 **2** also 又作 **dust off** [T] to remove something such as dust or dirt from your clothes by brushing them with your hands〔用手〕掸灰: *Jim got to his feet and dusted the knees of his trousers.* 吉姆站起身，掸了掸裤子的膝盖部位。**3** [T] to shake a fine powder over something 将〔粉状物〕撒于: *Dust icing sugar over the pastry.* 将糖粉撒在点心上面。

dust sth ↔ **down** *phr v* [T] to remove something such as dirt or dust from your clothes by brushing them with your hands 将〔衣服上〕的灰尘掸[拂]去: *Burt stood there dusting down his overalls.* 伯特站在那儿，在掸工装裤上的灰尘。| **dust yourself down** *The horse threw him, but Joe just laughed, picked himself up and dusted himself down.* 乔被马甩了下来，但他只是笑笑，站起来拂去身上的尘土。

dust sth ↔ **off** *phr v* [T] **1** to clean something by brushing it or wiping it with a cloth 掸〔灰〕，擦〔灰〕: *She dusted the snow off Billy's coat.* 她把比利大衣上的雪掸去。**2** to get something ready in order to use it again after not using it for a long time 把〔长期不用的东西〕备好待用，重新采用: *Investors are at last dusting off their cheque books as the economy recovers.* 随着经济的复苏，投资者终于又要把支票簿备好待用了。

3 **dust·bin** /ˈdʌstˌbɪn; ˈdʌstbɪn/ *n* [C] *BrE* a large container outside your house, used for holding food waste, empty containers etc【英】〔家庭用的〕垃圾箱；垃圾桶；GARBAGE CAN *AmE*【美】—see picture on page A4 参见 A4 页图

dustbin man /ˈ· ·, ·/ *n* [C] *BrE informal* a DUSTMAN【英，非正式】清理垃圾的工人

Dust Bowl, the /ˈ· ·/ *n* [C] a large area of the south-central US, including parts of Kansas and Oklahoma where, in the 1930s, strong winds and lack of rain caused EROSION of the soil (=when the top layer of earth is blown away), so that the land became unsuitable for farming. As a result, many farmers became very poor and had to leave their farms. 干旱尘暴区〔美国中南部广大地区，包括堪萨斯州和俄克拉何马州的一部分。20世纪30年代，那里干旱少雨，常有大风，土壤侵蚀严重，不宜耕作。结果，许多农民非常贫穷，不得不背井离乡〕

dust cart /ˈ· ·/ *n* [C] *BrE* a large vehicle that goes from house to house to collect waste from dustbins【英】垃圾车；GARBAGE TRUCK *AmE*【美】

dust cov·er /ˈ·, ··/ *n* [C] *AmE* a dust jacket【美】〔书籍的〕护封，书套

dust·er /ˈdʌstə; ˈdʌstə/ *n* [C] **1** a cloth for removing dust from furniture 抹布；尘拂，掸子 **2** *AmE* a light coat that you wear to protect your clothes while you are cleaning the house【美】〔清扫房子时穿的〕防尘罩衫 **3** *AmE informal* a DUST STORM【美，非正式】沙尘暴

dust jack·et /ˈ·, ··/ *n* [C] a paper cover of a book, which you can remove〔书籍的〕护封，书套；DUST COVER *AmE*【美】

dust·man /ˈdʌstmən; ˈdʌstmən/ *n* [C] *BrE* someone whose job is to remove waste from DUSTBINS【英】清理垃圾的工人，收垃圾的清洁工；GARBAGE COLLECTOR *AmE*【美】

dust·pan /ˈdʌstˌpæn; ˈdʌstpæn/ *n* [C] a flat container with a handle that you use with a brush to remove dust and waste from the floor 畚箕 —see picture at 参见 BRUSH¹ 图

dust·sheet /ˈdʌstˌʃit; ˈdʌst-ʃiːt/ *n* [C] *BrE* a large sheet of cloth used to protect furniture from dust or paint【英】〔防尘用的〕家具罩单，罩布；DROP CLOTH *AmE*【美】

dust storm /ˈ· ·/ *n* [C] a storm with strong winds that carries large amounts of dust 沙尘暴

dust-up /ˈdʌstˌʌp; ˈdʌst-ʌp/ *n* [C] *BrE slang* a fight【英俚】打架；斗殴

dust·y /ˈdʌstɪ; ˈdʌsti/ *adj* **1** covered with dust 布满灰尘的: *a dusty road* 满是尘土的道路 | *The shelves are really dusty.* 架子上灰尘真多。—see picture on page A18 参见 A18 页图 **2 dusty blue/pink etc** blue etc that is not bright but is slightly grey 灰蓝色/暗粉红色等: *The curtains had faded to a dusty pink.* 窗帘的颜色已经褪成了暗粉红色。**3** *literary* subjects, facts etc that are dusty are not interesting【文】〔话题、情况等〕乏味的，枯燥的

Dutch¹ /dʌtʃ; dʌtʃ/ *n* **1** [U] the language of the Netherlands 荷兰语 **2 the Dutch** [plural] people from the Netherlands 荷兰人 —see also 另见 DOUBLE-DUTCH

Dutch² *adj* **1** from or connected with the Netherlands 荷兰的 **2 go Dutch (with sb)** to share the cost of a meal in a restaurant〔在餐厅用餐时〕(和某人) 平摊费用，各付各的账 **3 talk (to sb) like a Dutch uncle** to tell someone severely that you disapprove of what they have done 严厉地批评 (某人)，训斥 (某人) **4 Dutch treat** *AmE* an occasion when you share the cost of something such as a meal in a restaurant【美】分担费用，各付各的账〈如在餐厅的用餐费用〉

Dutch auc·tion /ˌ· ˈ··/ *n* [C,U] a public sale at which the price is gradually reduced until someone will pay it〔逐渐降低价格直到有人买为止的〕荷兰式拍卖，降价式拍卖

Dutch barn /ˌ· ˈ·/ *n* [C] a farm building with a curved roof on a frame that has no walls, used for storing HAY〔无墙、仅以支架支撑弧形屋顶的〕荷兰式干草棚

Dutch cap /ˌ· ˈ·/ *n* [C] *informal* a round rubber CONTRACEPTIVE, that a woman wears inside her VAGINA during sex; DIAPHRAGM (2)【非正式】〔避孕用的〕子宫帽

Dutch cour·age /ˌ· ˈ··/ *n* [U] courage or confidence that you get when you drink alcohol 酒后之勇

Dutch elm dis·ease /ˌ· ˈ· ·ˌ·/ *n* [U] a disease that affects and kills ELM trees 荷兰榆树病

> **CULTURAL NOTE 文化注释**
>
> In the 1970s, there was an EPIDEMIC of Dutch elm disease, which killed many thousands of elm trees in Britain, the US, and many other countries. 20世纪70年代，荷兰榆树病暴发，造成英美和其他很多国家榆树大批死亡。

Dutch·man /ˈdʌtʃmən; ˈdʌtʃmən/ *n* [C] **1** someone from the Netherlands 荷兰人 **2 and I'm a Dutchman** *BrE spoken* used when someone has just said something you do not believe is true【英口】必无其事〔用于表示不相信某人刚说过的话〕: *"I've got a date with Cindy." "Oh yeah, and I'm a Dutchman!"* "我和辛迪有个约会。""是吗？鬼才相信呢！"

Dutch ov·en /ˌ· ˈ··/ *n* [C] *old-fashioned* a kind of container used for cooking【过时】荷兰炖锅[烘箱，砖灶]

Dutch Re·formed Church /ˌ· ·ˌ· ˈ·/ the main Protestant religious group in the Netherlands. It is also the main religion of the AFRIKANERS in South Africa (=white people who speak Afrikaans, whose families originally came from the Netherlands). 荷兰归正会〔荷兰主要的新教团体，也是讲阿非利堪斯语的南非白人的主要宗教〕

du·ti·able /ˈdutɪəbl; ˈdjuːtiəbəl/ *adj* dutiable goods are those that you must pay DUTY (4) on〔货物〕应纳税的

du·ti·ful /ˈdutɪfəl; ˈdjuːtɪfəl/ *adj* always doing what you are expected to do and always behaving in a loyal and obedient way 尽职尽责的；顺从的，恭敬的: *I'm not going to play the dutiful little housewife any more!* 我再也不想当贤惠的家庭小主妇了！

dut·i·ful·ly /ˈdutɪfəlɪ; ˈdjuːtɪfəli/ *adv* if you do something dutifully you do it because you think it is the correct way to behave 尽职尽责地: *I dutifully wrote down every word.* 我尽职地记下了每一个字。

du·ty /ˈdutɪ; ˈdjuːti/ *n* 1 1

1 ►STH YOU HAVE TO DO 应做的事情◄ [C,U] something that you have to do because it is morally or legally right〔道德上或法律上的〕义务，责任: [+to/towards] *Ian felt a sense of duty towards his parents.* 伊恩对他的父母有一种责任感。| **have a duty to do sth/be your duty to do sth** *The company has a duty to its shareholders to accept the highest bid.* 公司应对其股东负责，接受最高的投标价格。| *As Christians it's our duty to help the less fortunate.* 作为基督徒，帮助不幸的人是我们的责任。| **do your duty** *You must do your duty and report him to the police.* 你必须履行义务，向警方举报他。| **be (in) duty bound to do sth** (=have a duty to do something) 某事义不容辞

2 ►PART OF YOUR JOB 职责的一部分◄ [C usually plural 一般用复数,U] something you have to do as part of your job or because of your social position〔工作或社会方面的〕职责，义务: *Your duties will also include coordinating secretarial sup-*

port to the Head of Planning. 你的职责还包括协调秘书对计划部主任工作的支持。| **medical/official etc duties** *Illness prevented her from carrying out her official duties.* 由于生病, 她不能履行她的公务职责。| **report for duty** (=go somewhere and officially say you are ready to work) 报到 *Private Jones reporting for duty, Sir.* 长官, 列兵琼斯向您报到。

3 be on/off duty to be working or not working at a particular time, especially doing a job which people take turns to do so that someone is always doing it 值班[勤]/下班[不值勤]: *It was the same nurse who was on duty when you had your accident.* 你出事故时就是这个护士在值班。| **be on night duty** *Helen is on night duty all next week.* 下个星期海伦全都是值夜班。

4 ►TAX 税◄ [C,U] a tax you pay on something you buy〔购物缴纳的〕税: *The duty on wine has gone up.* 葡萄酒税已经上调。| **customs duty** (=tax paid on goods coming into the country) 关税 —see also 另见 DEATH DUTY, STAMP DUTY, TAX

5 do duty as/for sth to be used as something 用以充当/代替某物

duty-free¹ /ˌ‥ ˈ◂/ *adj* duty-free goods can be brought into a country without paying tax on them〔货物入境〕免税的: *duty-free cigarettes* 免税香烟 | *the duty-free shop* 免税商店 —**duty-free** *adv*

duty-free² *n* [C,U] *informal* alcohol, cigarettes etc that you can bring into a country without paying tax on them【非正式】〔酒、香烟等〕免税商品

Du·val·i·er /ˌduvɑlˋje; duːˈvælieɪ/, **Fran·çois** /frɑnˋswɑ; ˈfrɒnswɑː/ (1907-71) the President of Haiti from 1957 to 1971. He was called 'Papa Doc' and ruled as a DICTATOR. He had a private army of soldiers called the Tontons Macoutes, who helped him to prevent any opposition to his government. He was famous for being very violent and cruel. 杜瓦利埃〔(1907-1971), 1957至1971年任海地总统, 人称"爸爸医生"。他实行独裁统治, 拥有名为"恶魔"的私人军队, 帮助他消除反政府势力。他以残暴无情出名〕

du·vet /duˋve; ˈduːveɪ/ *n* [C] *especially BrE* a large cloth bag filled with feathers or similar material that you use to cover yourself in bed【尤英】羽绒被; 纤维棉被; COMFORTER (2) *AmE*【美】

DVLC /ˌdi vi ɛl ˋsi; ˌdiː viː el ˈsiː/ Driver and Vehicle Licensing Centre; the British government department that is responsible for collecting road tax from people who own vehicles, for giving driving tests, and for giving people their driving licences 驾驶员和车辆执照管理中心〔英国一政府部门, 负责征收养路费, 组织驾驶考试, 颁发驾驶执照〕

Dvo·řák /ˋdvɔrʒɑk; ˈdvɔːʒæk/, **An·to·nín** /ˋæntonin; ˈæntəʊniːn/ (1841-1904) a Czech COMPOSER. His most famous work is his ninth SYMPHONY, called *From the New World.* 德沃夏克〔(1841-1904), 捷克作曲家。最有名的作品是第九交响曲《自新大陆》〕

dwarf¹ /dwɔrf; dwɔːf/ *n plural* **dwarves** /dwɔrvz; dwɔːvz/ or **dwarfs** [C] **1** an imaginary creature that looks like a small man〔虚构的人物〕小矮人: *Snow White and the Seven Dwarfs* 白雪公主和七个小矮人 **2** a word that some people find offensive, for someone who does not continue growing to the normal height but stays very short 矮子, 侏儒〔一些人认为此词形容身材矮小者带有侮辱性〕

CULTURAL NOTE 文化注释

Dwarfs are often characters in children's stories and European MYTHOLOGY. They are usually described as small creatures that look like men with big heads and long beards. The most famous FAIRY TALE that has dwarfs in it is *Snow White and the Seven Dwarfs.* 小矮人是儿童故事和欧洲神话中的常见形象, 通常长相像人, 个子矮小, 大脑袋, 长胡子。关于小矮人最著名的童话是《白雪公主和七个小矮人》。

dwarf² *adj* [only before noun 仅用于名词前] a dwarf plant or animal is much smaller than the usual size〔植物或动物等〕矮小的: *a dwarf conifer* 矮小的针叶树

dwarf³ *v* [T usually passive 一般用被动态] to be so big that other things are made to seem very small〔因自身巨大而〕使…显得矮小; 使…相形见绌: *The cathedral is dwarfed by its surrounding skyscrapers.* 这座大教堂与其周围的摩天大楼相比显得格外矮小。

dwell /dwɛl; dwel/ *v past tense and past participle* **dwelt** /dwɛlt; dwelt/ or **dwelled** [I] *literary* to live in a particular place【文】〔在某一地方〕居住: *A woodsman and his family dwelt in the middle of the forest.* 一个伐木工和他的家人居住在森林深处。

dwell on/upon sth *phr v* [T] to think or talk for too long about something, especially something unpleasant 老是想着; 唠叨〔令人不愉快的事情〕: *Don't dwell on the past – try and be more positive.* 别老想着过去, 尽量乐观一些。

dwel·ler /ˋdwɛlɚ; ˈdwelə/ *n* [C] **city/town/cave/forest dweller** a person or animal that lives in a particular place 居住在城里/镇上/山洞/森林中的人[动物]: *City-dwellers suffer higher pollution levels.* 城市居民所遭受的污染程度较为严重。

dwell·ing /ˋdwɛlɪŋ; ˈdwelɪŋ/ *n* [C] *formal* a house, apartment etc where people live【正式】住宅, 寓所, 住处 [S2]

dwelling house /ˈ‥ ˌ/ *n* [C] *law* a house that people live in, not one that is being used as a shop, office etc【法律】〔与商店、办公室等相对而言的〕住宅房屋

dwelt /dwɛlt; dwelt/ a past tense and past participle of DWELL

dwin·dle /ˋdwɪndl; ˈdwɪndl/ *v* [I] also 又作 **dwindle away** to gradually become less and less or smaller and smaller 逐渐变小; 缩小; 减少: *The workforce has dwindled since its pre-war heyday.* 劳动大军在战前人数最多, 其后已日益减少。| **dwindle (away) to nothing/one/two etc** *Their supply of food had dwindled to almost nothing.* 他们的食物供应已经减少到接近于无。—**dwindling** *adj*: *a dwindling population* 逐渐减少的人口

Dyck /ˋdaɪk; ˈdaɪk/, **Sir Anthony Van** —see 见 Sir Anthony VAN DYCK

dye¹ /daɪ; daɪ/ *n* [C,U] **1** a substance you use to change the colour of your clothes, hair etc 染料: *hair dye* 染发剂 **2 dye job** *informal* someone who has had a dye job has used a substance to change the colour of their hair【非正式】〔用染料〕染发

dye² *v* **dyes, dyed, dyeing** [T] to give something a different colour using a dye〔用染料〕染: **dye sth black/blue/blonde etc** *Priscilla's hair was dyed jet black.* 普丽西拉的头发染成了乌黑色。—**dyed** *adj*

dyed-in-the-wool /ˌ‥‥ˈ◂/ *adj* having strong beliefs or opinions that will never change〔在信仰或主张等方面〕根深蒂固的, 顽固不化的: *Even dyed-in-the-wool republicans admitted he had talent.* 甚至顽固的共和党人都承认他有才能。

Dyf·ed /ˋdʌvɪd; ˈdʌvɪ̈d/ a COUNTY in southwest Wales, next to the Atlantic Ocean 达费德郡〔威尔士西南一郡, 濒临大西洋〕

dy·ing /ˋdaɪ·ɪŋ; ˈdaɪ-ɪŋ/ the present participle of DIE

dyke, dike /daɪk; daɪk/ *n* [C] **1** a wall or bank built to keep back water and prevent flooding 堤; 坝; 堰 **2** an offensive word for a LESBIAN (=woman who is sexually attracted to women) 搞同性恋的女子〔冒犯用词〕 **3** *especially BrE* a narrow passage to carry water away【尤英】排水沟, 排水渠

Dyl·an /ˋdɪlən; ˈdɪlən/, **Bob** (1941-) a US singer and songwriter who has had a great influence on popular songwriting. His early songs in the 1960s were often protest songs on the subjects of war and the Civil Rights Movement in the US, and they include *Blowin' in the Wind*, and *The Times They are A-Changing.* 鲍勃·迪伦〔(1941-), 美国歌手、词曲作家, 对流行歌曲的创作产生过重大影响。20世纪60年代, 他的早期作品通常是以战争和美国民权运动为主题的抗议歌曲, 如《在风中吹拂》和《时代在改变》〕

dy·nam·ic¹ /daɪˋnæmɪk; daɪˈnæmɪk/ *adj* **1** full of energy and new ideas, and determined to succeed 精力充沛的; 有创新思想的; 志在成功的: *a dynamic young businesswoman* 一位精力旺盛的年轻女实业家 **2** *technical* continuously moving or changing【术语】不断移动的; 不断变化的: *Markets are dynamic and a company must learn to adapt.* 市场千变万化, 因此一个公司必须学会适应变化。**3** *technical* connected with a force or power that causes movement【术语】(动)力的; 动力(学)的 **4** *technical* a dynamic verb describes an action or event, not a state【术语】〔动词〕动态的 —**dynamically** /-klɪ; -kli/ *adv*

dynamic² *n* [singular] **1 dynamics a)** [plural] the way in which things or people behave, react, and affect each other 动态: *the dynamics of capitalist economies* 资本主义经济的动态 | **group dynamics** (=the way in which the members of a group behave towards each other) 群体动态〔指某一团体成员之间的相互行为和态度〕 **b)** [U] the science concerned with the movement of objects and with the forces related to movement 动力学, 力学 **c)** [plural] changes of loudness in music〔音乐的〕力度, 力度变化 **2** *formal* something that causes action or change【正式】〔导致某种行动或变化的〕动力, 活力: *Feminism is seen as a dynamic of social change.* 女权运动被视为促进社会变革的一种动力。

dy·na·mis·m /ˋdaɪnəˌmɪzəm; ˈdaɪnəmɪzəm/ *n* [U] energy and determination to succeed 精力, 活力; 成功志向: *entrepreneurial dynamism* 企业家的志向

dy·na·mite¹ /ˋdaɪnəˌmaɪt; ˈdaɪnəmaɪt/ *n* [U] **1** a powerful explosive used especially for breaking rock〔尤指用于炸石头

的）达纳炸药，黄色炸药 **2** something or someone that is very exciting or is likely to cause a lot of trouble 很刺激的人[事物]; 易惹出许多麻烦的人[事物]: *They've only been playing together for six months but they're dynamite.* 他们在一起演奏只有六个月，但已很轰动。

dynamite² *v* [T] to damage or destroy something with dynamite 〔用炸药〕炸毁

dy·na·mo /ˈdaɪnəˌmo; ˈdaɪnəməʊ/ *n plural* **dynamos** [C] **1** a machine that changes some other form of power directly into electricity 〔尤指直流〕发电机: *bicycle lights powered by a dynamo* 以小发电机供电的自行车车灯 **2** someone who is very keen and energetic 精力充沛的人: *Gordon Strachan, Leeds midfield dynamo* 戈登·斯特罗恩，利兹队的中场干将

dyn·a·sty /ˈdaɪnəstɪ; ˈdɪnəsti/ *n* [C] **1** a family of kings or other rulers whose parents, grandparents etc have ruled the country for many years 王朝: *The Habsburg dynasty ruled in Austria from 1278 to 1918.* 哈布斯堡王朝在1278年至1918年期间统治奥地利。**2** a period of time when a particular family ruled a country or area 某一王朝的统治期间，朝，代: *Shang dynasty* 商朝

d'you /dʒə; djʊ/ *spoken*【口】the short form of 缩略式= 'do you': *D'you know what I mean?* 你知道我的意思吗？

dys·en·te·ry /ˈdɪsn̩ˌtɛrɪ; ˈdɪsəntəri/ *n* [U] a serious disease of your BOWELS (1) that makes them bleed and pass much more waste than usual 痢疾

dys·func·tion·al /dɪsˈfʌŋkʃənl; dɪsˈfʌŋkʃənəl/ *adj technical*【术语】**1** not following the normal patterns of social behaviour, especially with the result that someone cannot behave in a normal way or have a satisfactory life 与社会规范相悖的: *dysfunctional family relationships* 有问题的家庭关系 **2** not working properly or normally 不能正常运作[工作]的; 机能不良的; 有故障的

dys·lex·i·a /dɪsˈlɛksɪə; dɪsˈleksiə/ *n* [U] *technical* a difficulty with reading and writing because you are unable to see the difference between the shapes of letters; WORD BLINDNESS【术语】〔因无法分清字形而造成的〕诵读困难症 —**dyslexic** *adj*: *Two of the children in the class are dyslexic.* 班上有两个孩子患有诵读困难症。

dys·pep·si·a /dɪsˈpɛpʃə; dɪsˈpepsiə/ *n* [U] *technical* a problem that your body has in dealing with the food you eat; INDIGESTION【术语】消化不良

dys·pep·tic /dɪsˈpɛptɪk; dɪsˈpeptɪk/ *adj* **1** suffering from dyspepsia 消化不良的 **2** *old-fashioned* bad-tempered【过时】脾气坏的

E,e

E, e /i; iː/ *plural* **E's, e's** *n* [C] the fifth letter of the English alphabet 英语字母表的第五个字母

E¹ *n* **a)** the third note in the musical SCALE¹ (8) of C major E音〔C大调音阶中的第三个音〕 **b)** the musical KEY² (4) based on this note E调〔基于E音的音调〕

E² **1** the written abbreviation of 缩写= east or 或 eastern **2** *BrE technical* the written abbreviation of 缩写= earth, a connection between a piece of electrical equipment and the ground【英, 术语】地线〔电器与地连接的导线〕 **3** *slang* the abbreviation of 缩写= ECSTASY (3), an illegal drug【俚】"狂喜"迷幻药〔一种毒品〕 **4** short for 缩略式= E NUMBER **5** a very low mark for an exam or piece of school work E级, 及格〔表示学业成绩较差〕

E 111 /ˌi wʌn ɪˈlɛvən; ˌiː wʌn ɪˈlevn/ a document which is available to citizens of any country in the EU (=European Union), and which gives them the right to receive free health care when they visit other EU countries 欧盟免费医疗证〔欧盟国家给公民出具的一种证明, 赋予其访问欧盟其他国家时享受免费医疗的权利〕

1 1 **each¹** /itʃ; iːtʃ/ *determiner, pronoun* **1** every single one of two or more things or people considered separately〔两个或两个以上物、人中的〕每个, 各: *Jane had a blister on each foot.* 简每只脚上都有一个水疱。| *There are four bedrooms, each with its own shower.* 共有四间卧室, 每间都有淋浴器。| *The price is $60 for a week, then $10 for each extra day.* 一个星期的价格60美元, 此后每加一天10美元。| *My sister's got two boys and I've got one of each.* (=one son and one daughter) 我姐姐有两个儿子, 我则儿女各一个。| [+of] *I gave a piece of cake to each of the children.* 我给孩子们每人一块蛋糕。| **we/you/they each** *My wife and I each have our own bank accounts.* 我和妻子各有各的银行账户。| **one/half/a piece etc each** *Biscuits! Can we have two each, Mum?* 饼干! 妈妈, 我们每人两块行吗? **2 each and every one** an expression used to emphasize that you are talking about every single person or thing in a group 每一个, 无例外〔用于加强语气〕: *These are issues that affect each and every one of us.* 这些问题影响到我们每一个人。**3 each to his own** *old-fashioned* used to mean that we all have different ideas about how to do things, what we like etc【过时】人各不同〔人们各有不同的做事方法和爱好等〕—see also 另见 ALL, EVERY

USAGE NOTE 用法说明: EACH

WORD CHOICE 词语辨析: **each, every, both, everybody/everyone, nobody/no one, neither**

Each is used for any number of people or things considered separately, **every** for any number considered together. each 是指任何数量的人或物中的各个, every 则将任何数量的人或物当作整体来看: *Each item is carefully checked* (=probably one by one). 逐一仔细检查各项。| *Every item has been carefully checked* (=all of them). 所有各项都仔细检查过了。| *Each child was given a small gift* (=a gift of their own). 每个孩子都得到一件小礼物。| *Every child was given a small gift* (=they were all given one). 所有的孩子都得到了一件小礼物。

Both is used for two things taken together. both 是指两者都: *Both my children* (= I have two children) *go to the same school.* 我的两个孩子〔我有两个孩子〕上同一所学校。| *Each of my children* (=I have two or more children) *goes to a different school.* 我的孩子们〔我有两个或更多的孩子〕各上各的学校。

You usually use **everyone** or **everybody** rather than *every person*, though in a formal report you might read. 一般情况下使用 everyone 或 everybody 而不用 every person, 不过在正式的报告中也会看到后者: *The document was signed by every person present* (NEVER 永不用 *every persons/people*). 在场的所有人都在文件上签了名。

You do not usually use **everyone** or **everybody** followed by **not**. Instead you say **not everybody/everyone...** or **no one/nobody...**, depending on which you mean. everyone 或 everybody 后通常不接 not, 而是依说话人想表达的意思使用 not everybody/everyone... 或 no one/nobody...: *Not everybody here is a vegetarian* (=some people are but not all). 这儿并非所有人都是素食者。| *No one here is a vegetarian* (=none of the people here is a vegetarian). 这儿没有人是素食者。You would almost NEVER say 几乎从来不说: *Everyone here isn't a vegetarian.*

Similarly instead of using **both...** followed by **not...** you would say **only one...** or **neither...**. 同样, 不用 both 后接 not, 而用 only one 或 neither: *Only one of them knows the answer.* 他们中仅一人知道答案。| *Neither of them knows the answer.* 他俩谁也不知道答案。You would not usually say 通常不说: *Both of them don't know the answer.*

GRAMMAR 语法

Both is always plural. both 总是表示复数: *Both these books are mine.* 这两本书都是我的。A noun immediately after **each** or **every** is always singular. 紧跟在 each 或 every 后的名词总是单数: *each/every area of the country* (NOT 不用 *areas*) 该国的每个地区

Every, **everyone**, **everything** etc always take a singular verb. every, everyone 和 everything 等后的动词总用单数: *Every state elects its own governor.* 所有各州均选举自己的州长。

Each takes a singular verb except when it comes after a plural word. each 后面用单数动词, 除非它位于复数名词之后: *Each of them won $50.* 他们各赢了50美元。| *They each won/have each won $50.* 他们各赢了50美元。However in informal spoken English people sometimes use a plural verb, especially when there are a lot of words between **each of** and the verb. 但在非正式英语口语中, 人们有时使用动词复数形式, 尤其是在 each of 和动词之间存在很多词的情况下: *Each of the kids arriving for the first time are shown around the school.* 每个第一次来的孩子都被带着参观学校。However, some people think only the singular verb is correct. 但是一些人认为只有动词单数形式才是正确的。

Each and **every** may be followed by a plural pronoun, especially when you are talking about both males and females. each 和 every 可后跟复数代名词, 尤其当被提及者有男也有女时: *Each girl must make up her own mind.* 每个女孩都必须自己拿主意。| *Each person must make up their own mind.* 每个人都必须自己拿主意。It sounds a little formal to say 这一说法显得略微正式: *Each person must make up his or her own mind* 每个人都必须自己拿主意 and it is considered sexist to use *he* unless you are only talking about men or boys 除非仅仅谈及男性, 否则只用 he 被看作是性别歧视。

In a similar way plural pronouns (but not plural verbs) can go with **everyone**, **everybody**, **anyone**, **no one**, **someone** etc. 同样, 复数代名词〔但不是复数动词〕可与 everyone, everybody, anyone, no one 和 someone 等连用: *Has everyone finished their drinks?* 大家酒都喝光了吗? | *Somebody's left their umbrella behind.* 有人忘了拿走雨伞了。| *No one here seems to know what they are doing.* 这儿的人似乎都不知道自己在做什么。

each² *adv* for or to every one 每, 每个地: *The tickets are $5 each.* 每张票五美元。

each oth·er /ˌ·ˈ··/ *pron* [not used as the subject of a sentence 不用作句子主语] used to show that each of two or more people does something to the other or others 互相, 彼此: *Susan and Robert kissed each other passionately.* 苏珊和罗伯特深情地亲吻。| *They were holding each other's hands.* 他们彼此手拉着手。| *We had a lot to tell each other about our trip.* 关于我们的旅行, 我们有许多话要告诉对方。| *Stop arguing with each other.* 别再互相争吵了。—see also 另见 **be at each other's throats** (THROAT (5)) —compare 比较 ONE ANOTHER 1 1

each way /ˌ·ˈ·/ *adv* if you BET (=try to win money by guessing the winner of a race) money each way, you will win if the horse or dog you choose comes first, second, or third 一注三赢〔下注之马或狗获得前三名便赢〕—**each way** *adj*: *a £10 each way bet* 10英镑的一注三赢赌注

ea·ger /ˈigɚ; ˈiːgə/ *adj* **1** very keen and excited about something that is going to happen or about something you want to do 热切的, 渴望的: *There was a queue of eager schoolchildren outside the theatre.* 剧院外排着一队急切的学童。| **eager to do**

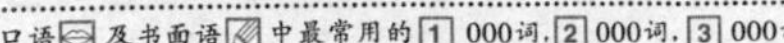

sth *Clara was eager to tell her side of the story.* 克拉拉急于诉说她对那件事的体会。| **eager for** (=eager to get or have) 急于得到 *fans eager for a glimpse of the singer* 急于见到歌手的歌迷们 **2 eager to please** willing to do anything to be helpful to people 乐于助人: *She's a very hard worker and very eager to please.* 她工作很勤奋，且非常乐于助人。**3 eager beaver** *informal* someone who is too keen and works harder than they should 【非正式】过分热心的人; 过于勤奋的人 —**eagerly** *adv*: *the eagerly awaited sequel to 'Star Wars'* 观众翘首企盼的《星球大战》续集 —**eagerness** *n* [U]: *In his eagerness to secure peace Roosevelt was duped, it was said, by Stalin.* 据说罗斯福因为渴望和平，上了斯大林的当。

ea·gle /ˈigl; ˈiːgəl/ *n* [C] a very large strong bird with a beak like a hook that eats small animals, birds etc 鹰

eagle-eyed /ˌ.. ˈ.◂/ *adj* very good at seeing or noticing things 目光锐利的; 观察敏锐的: *One eagle-eyed passer-by noticed that the window was slightly open.* 一位观察敏锐的过路人注意到窗户是微微开着的。

Eagle Scout /ˈ.. ˌ./ a boy SCOUT of the highest rank in the US 鹰徽童子军〔美国最高级别的男童子军〕

ea·glet /ˈiglɪt; ˈiːglɪ̆t/ *n* [C] a young EAGLE 小鹰

Ea·kins /ˈikɪnz, ˈiːkɪ̆nz/, **Thomas** (1844-1916) a US painter who used a very realistic style 伊肯斯〔(1844-1916)，美国现实主义画家〕

Ea·ling com·e·dy /ˌilɪŋ ˈkɑmədɪ; ˌiːlɪŋ ˈkɒmədi/ *n* [C] one of many humorous films, made mostly in black and white at **Ealing Studios** in London during the 1940s and 1950s, in which many well-known British actors appeared 伊林喜剧〔20世纪40、50年代伦敦伊林电影制片厂拍摄的喜剧片。大部分为黑白影片。众多英国著名演员参加演出〕

-ean /ɪən; iən/ *suffix* [in adjectives and nouns 构成形容词和名词] another form of the suffix -AN 后缀 -an 的另一种形式: *Mozartean* (=of or like Mozart) 莫扎特的; 像莫扎特的

ear /ɪr; ɪə/ *n*

1 ►PART OF YOUR BODY 身体部位◄ [C] one of the organs on either side of your head that you hear with 耳, 耳朵: *Lou turned to Mark and whispered something in his ear.* 卢转向马克，贴着他的耳朵小声嘀咕了几句。—see picture at 参见 HEAD[1] 图

2 ►HEARING 听觉◄ [U] the ability to hear sounds 听力: *too high-pitched to be heard by the human ear* 音调太高，人耳听不到 | **have good ears** (=be able to hear quiet noises) 听觉灵敏，听力极佳

3 ►GRAIN 谷物◄ [C] the top part of plants, such as wheat, that produces grain 穗: *an ear of corn* 玉米穗

4 long-eared/short-eared etc having long etc ears 长耳/短耳的: *a long-eared rabbit* 长耳兔

5 be all ears *informal* to be very keen to hear what someone is going to tell you【非正式】全神贯注地听，洗耳恭听: *As soon as I mentioned money, Karen was all ears.* 我一提到钱，卡伦就马上竖起了耳朵。

6 be out on your ear *informal* to be forced to leave a job, organization etc, especially because you have done something wrong【非正式】〔尤指因犯错〕被迫离职[退出某组织]: *You'd better start working harder, or you'll be out on your ear.* 你最好开始加把劲，否则将被开除。

7 be up to your ears in work/debt/problems etc to have a lot of work etc 工作/债务/问题等很多: *I'm up to my ears in work at the moment. Can we discuss this later?* 我现在忙得团团转，我们能以后讨论这事吗?

8 close/shut your ears to to refuse to listen to bad or unpleasant news 拒绝听〔坏消息或令人讨厌的消息〕

9 smile/grin etc from ear to ear to show that you are very happy or pleased by smiling so much 咧着嘴笑，眉开眼笑: *She came out of his office, grinning from ear to ear. 'I've been promoted.'* 她走出他的办公室，眉开眼笑地说:"我升职了。"

10 give sb a thick ear *BrE informal* to hit someone【英，非正式】打某人: *Behave yourself or I'll give you a thick ear!* 规矩点，要不我揍你了!

11 go in (at) one ear and out (at) the other *informal* if information goes in one ear and out the other, you forget it as soon as you have heard it【非正式】左耳进，右耳出: *I don't know why I tell her anything. It just goes in one ear and out the other.* 我不知道我为什么告诉她，我的话她只是当作耳边风。

12 have an ear for music/languages etc to be very good at learning music, copying sounds etc 善于学音乐/语言等: *She has no ear for languages at all.* 她对学语言一点也不在行。| *a good ear for dialogue* 善于听别人交谈

13 have sb's ear to be trusted by someone so that they will listen to your advice, opinions etc 获得某人信任，忠告[意见等]被某人接纳: *While Ross Perot had the ear of the nation, he did spout a number of home truths.* 当罗斯·佩罗特获得国人信任时，他的确道出了一些令人不快的事实。

14 keep your/an ear to the ground to make sure that you always know what is happening in a situation 保持关注〔以确保知晓某事态的发展动向〕: *I haven't heard any more news but I'll keep my ear to the ground.* 我还未听到更多的消息，但我将对此继续关注。

15 lend an ear to listen to what someone is saying sympathetically 同情地倾听: *I'm always ready to lend an ear, if you need to talk.* 如果你需要找人谈谈，我随时都愿意倾听。

16 play sth by ear to play music without having to read written music 不看乐谱演奏乐曲 —see also 另见 **play it by ear** (PLAY[1] (11))

17 sb's ears are burning used to say that someone thinks that people are talking about them 有人耳朵在发烧〔认为背后有人在议论时说〕

18 sb's ears are flapping *BrE* used to say that someone is trying to listen to your private conversation【英】有人在设法偷听 —see also 另见 **bend sb's ear** (BEND[1] (5)), **send sb off with a flea in their ear** (FLEA (2)), **make a pig's ear of** (PIG[1] (5)), **prick (up) your ears** (PRICK[1] (5)), **turn a deaf ear** (DEAF[1] (4)), **wet behind the ears** (WET[1] (6))

ear·ache /ˈɪrˌek; ˈɪəreɪk/ *n* [singular, U] a pain inside your ear (内)耳痛

ear drops /ˈ. ./ *n* [plural] medicine to put in your ear 滴耳药水

ear·drum /ˈ. ./ *n* [C] a tight thin skin over the inside of your ear which allows you to hear sound 鼓膜, 耳膜

ear·ful /ˈɪrfʊl; ˈɪəfʊl/ *n* **give sb an earful** *informal* to tell someone how angry you are about something they have done【非正式】斥责某人; 抱怨某人: *He gave me a real earful about being late so often.* 他着实抱怨了我一顿，说我经常迟到。

Ear·hart /ˈɛrhɑrt; ˈeəhɑːt/, **A·me·lia** /əˈmiljə; əˈmiːliə/ (1898-1937) a US pilot who was the first woman to fly across the Atlantic Ocean alone 埃尔哈特〔(1898-1937)，美国飞行员，首位独立飞越大西洋的女性〕

earhole /ˈɪrˌhol; ˈɪəhəʊl/ *n* [C] *BrE informal* your ear【英，非正式】耳朵: *If you don't shut up I'll give you a clip round the earhole!* (=hit you) 如果你不住嘴，我就抽你一个耳光!

earl /ɝl; ɜːl/ *n* [C] a man with a high social rank 伯爵: *the Earl of Warwick* 沃里克伯爵

earl·dom /ˈɝldəm; ˈɜːldəm/ *n* [C] **1** the rank of an earl 伯爵爵位 **2** the land or property belonging to an earl 伯爵的领地[财产]

Earl Grey /ˌ. ˈ./ a type of tea with a special taste and smell which come from an oil which is added to it 格雷伯爵茶〔一种通过加入某种油调制而成的具有特殊味道和香气的茶〕

ear·li·est /ˈɝlɪəst; ˈɜːliəst/ *n* **at the earliest** no earlier than the time or date mentioned 最早, 至早: *Work will begin in October at the very earliest.* 最早在10月开始工作。

ear lobe /ˈ. ./ *n* [C] the soft piece of flesh at the bottom of your ear 耳垂 —see picture at 参见 HEAD[1] 图

Earl's Court /ˌ. ˈ.◂/ **1** a large building in London used especially for EXHIBITIONS in which businesses show their new products〔伦敦〕伯爵宫会展中心: *This year's Boat Show opens at Earl's Court on Monday.* 今年的船展周一将在伯爵宫会展中心开幕。**2** the area of West London around this building 伯爵宫区〔西伦敦伯爵宫会展中心一带〕

> **CULTURAL NOTE 文化注释**
>
> Earl's Court is an area where many young people live in single rooms or small apartments. In the 1960s and 1970s, it was sometimes called Kangaroo Valley, because of the large number of young Australians who lived there. 在伯爵宫区有很多年轻人住在单间房或小公寓里。20世纪60、70年代，这里住有大量澳大利亚青年，因此有时叫做"袋鼠谷"。

ear·ly[1] /ˈɝlɪ; ˈɜːli/ *adj*

1 ►NEAR THE BEGINNING 接近开始时◄ near to the beginning of a day, year, someone's life etc 早期的, 初期的: *We've booked two weeks' holiday in early May.* 我们已定好5月初度假两周的安排。| *Her early life was miserably unhappy.* 她的早年生活十分悲惨。| **in the early days** (=at the beginning of a process, project etc) 最初, 开始时 *In the early days we used to work Saturdays as well.* 最初我们周六也上班。

2 ►BEFORE THE USUAL TIME 通常时间之前◄ arriving or happening before the usual or expected time 提早的, 提前的: *Hey, you're early! It's only five o'clock!* 嘿，你真早! 现在只有5点钟! | *The rains are early this year.* 今年雨水来得早。| **five**

minutes early/three hours early etc *The bus was ten minutes early.* 公共汽车提前了10分钟到达[开出]。| **an early grave** (=dying too soon) 过早去世
3 ►**NOT TOO LATE** 不太晚◄ near enough to the beginning of a process to prevent something bad from happening 及早的: *There is far less risk with cancer if it is detected early.* 如及早发现，癌症的危险会大大降低。
4 ►**FIRST** 最初的◄ [only before noun 仅用于名词前] being one of the first people, events, machines etc 最初的，第一批的: *Early motor cars had very poor brakes.* 早期的汽车刹车装置很差。| *early man* 原始人类
5 **it's early days** *spoken* used to say that it is too soon to be sure about what the result of something will be【口】为时还过早: *She's having a few problems with the coursework at school but it's early days yet.* 她在学业上有些困难，但最终成绩如何现在还言之过早。
6 **at/from an early age** at or since a time when you were very young 年少[早年]时/自年少[早年]时起: *At an early age she decided she wanted to be a surgeon.* 她年少时就立志当外科医生。
7 **make an early start** to start an activity, journey etc very early in the day because you have a lot to do, far to go etc 一大早就开始[出发]〔因为工作繁重、路途遥远等〕
8 **the early hours** the time between MIDNIGHT and morning 凌晨: *Order was restored in the prison in the early hours of Saturday morning.* 周六凌晨，监狱恢复了秩序。
9 **early night** if you have an early night you go to bed earlier than usual〔某晚〕比平时睡得早: *I could really do with an early night!* 我真需要早点睡了!
10 **early bird** someone who always gets up very early in the morning 早起者: *Seven? No problem! I'm a real early bird!* 7点? 没问题! 我起床早得很!
11 **the early bird catches the worm** used to say that someone is successful because they were the first to do something 捷足先登
12 **early riser** someone who always gets up early in the morning 惯于早起的人
13 **early potatoes/lettuces/avocados etc** potatoes etc that are ready to be picked before any others 早熟的马铃薯/莴苣/鳄梨等

early[2] *adv* 1 before the usual, arranged, or expected time 提早，提前: *I arrived early, to make sure of a seat.* 我提前到了，以确保有座位。| *The play ended early so we still had time for a drink.* 剧提早结束了，因此我们还有时间喝点什么。2 near the beginning of a day, week, or other period of time 在早期，在初期: *Early the following day he phoned to apologize.* 第二天一早他就打电话道歉。3 near the beginning of an event, story, process etc 在开展阶段，在早期部分: *Early in the film we see Paul's violent temper.* 在电影开头部分，我们见识了保罗暴躁的脾气。4 **early on** at an early stage in a relationship, process etc 在初期，开始不久: *I realized early on I'd never pass the exam.* 开始不久我便意识到，我绝对通不过考试。

Early Day Mo·tion /ˌ‥ ˈ‥ ˌ‥/ a proposal formally made in writing by a member of the British Parliament, and signed by other members. MPs do this in order to find out how much support there is for a particular proposal. 先期动议〔由一名议员以书面形式提出、其他议员签名的提案，其目的是为了了解支持该提案的人数多寡〕

early warn·ing sys·tem /ˌ‥ ˈ‥ ˌ‥/ *n* [C] a series of RADAR stations that give a warning when enemy aircraft are going to attack〔能及早发现敌方空袭的雷达〕预警系统

ear·mark /ˈɪrˌmɑrk; ˈɪəmɑːk/ *v* [T usually passive 一般用被动态] to decide that someone or something will be used for a particular purpose in the future 指定…的用途: **earmark sb/sth for** *80% of the funds have been earmarked for education.* 80%的资金已被指定用于教育。| *schools earmarked for closure* 被指定关闭的学校 | **earmark sb/sth as** *The building has been earmarked as a new treatment center.* 那幢建筑已被定为用作新的治疗中心。

ear·muffs /ˈɪrˌmʌfs; ˈɪəmʌfs/ *n* [plural] two pieces of material joined by a band over the top of your head, that you wear to keep your ears warm〔保暖用的〕耳套

earn /ɝn; ɜːn/ *v*
1 ►**GET MONEY** 赚钱◄ [I,T] to receive a particular amount of money for the work that you do 挣(钱): *He earns nearly £20,000 a year.* 他每年挣约20,000英镑。| *If you aren't earning you simply can't afford a holiday.* 你如果不挣钱，就当然没钱去度假。| **earn a fortune** (=earn a lot of money) 挣大钱 —see 见 GAIN[1] (USAGE)
2 ►**MAKE A PROFIT** 获利◄ [T] to make a profit from business or from putting money in a bank, lending it to a company etc 获得〔利润〕: *'Dracula' earned £7 million on its first day.*《德拉库拉》〔根据写吸血鬼的同名小说改编的恐怖电影〕第一天上映便进账700万英镑。
3 ►**GET STH YOU DESERVE** 获得所值◄ [T] to get something that you deserve, because of your qualities or actions 应获得；博得: *I think you should have a rest. You've certainly earned it.* 我想你该休息一下，这是你应得的。
4 **earn sb praise/a reputation etc** if something earns you praise, a name etc it makes other people think of you in a particular way 为某人赢得赞扬/名声等: *Her perfectionism earned her a reputation as a 'difficult' star.* 她力求完美的劲头给她带来了"难缠"明星的名声。
5 **earn a living** to make money in order to pay for the things you need 谋生: *I earned my living mainly from teaching.* 我主要以教书为生。
6 **earn your keep** to do jobs etc as a way of paying the owner of the place where you live〔为房东做工以〕换取栖身之所: *Harry is unemployed at the moment but he does lots of jobs around the house to earn his keep.* 哈里目前正失业，但他靠在房前屋后做杂活来顶房租。

earn·er /ˈɝnɚ; ˈɜːnə/ *n* 1 [C] someone who earns money for the job that they do 挣工薪者: **high earner/low earner etc** *Private childcare is still too expensive for the average earner.* 对普通工薪阶层来说，雇家庭保姆照顾孩子还是太贵。| **wage earner** *Most wage earners are paid by cheque.* 大多数挣工资的人领工资时拿的是支票。2 **a nice little earner** *BrE informal* something that earns you a lot of money【英，非正式】使人赚大钱的东西，摇钱树: *They're onto a nice little earner with that roadside café.* 他们的路边餐馆带来了滚滚财源。

ear·nest[1] /ˈɝnɪst; ˈɜːnɪ̆st/ *adj* 1 very serious and believing that what you say is very important 认真的；郑重其事的: *such an earnest young man* 如此认真的一名男青年 2 **in earnest** if something starts happening in earnest, it begins properly or as it was planned to happen 正确地；按照计划地: *On Monday your training begins in earnest!* 星期一你的训练就真正开始了! 3 **be in earnest** to really mean what you are saying, especially when expressing an intention or wish 是认真的，是诚挚的: *I'm sure he was in earnest when he said he wanted to marry her.* 我确信当他说想娶她时，他是认真的。| **be in dead/deadly/complete earnest** *I couldn't believe what he was telling me but he was in deadly earnest.* 我难以相信他对我说的话，但他却是十分诚挚的。—**earnestly** *adv* —**earnestness** *n* [U]

earnest[2] *n* [singular] **an earnest of** *formal* something that you do or give someone to show that you will do what you have promised to do【正式】…的保证

earn·ings /ˈɝnɪŋz; ˈɜːnɪŋz/ *n* [plural] 1 the money that you receive for the work that you do 薪水，工资: *He has had to pay tax on his earnings since he started at the firm.* 自进公司上班以来，他就得缴纳所得税。2 the profit that a company makes 利润: *The company's earnings have dropped by 5% in the first quarter.* 公司第一季度的利润下降了5%。

earnings-re·lat·ed /ˌ‥ ‥ˈ‥◄/ *adj* connected with the amount of money that you earn 与收入挂钩的: *an earnings-related pension scheme* 与收入挂钩的退休金计划

Earp /ɝp; ɜːp/, **Wy·att** /ˈwaɪət; ˈwaɪət/ (1848-1929) a US MARSHAL and GAMBLER (=someone who plays card games to win money etc) who fought in the famous 'Gunfight at the O.K. Corral' 厄普〔(1848-1929)，美国西部一警长。他喜好赌博，参与过著名的"O.K. 镇畜栏大决斗"〕

ear·phones /ˈɪrˌfonz; ˈɪəfəʊnz/ *n* [plural] electrical equipment that you put over your ears to listen to a radio, RECORD PLAYER etc 耳机 —see picture at 参见 PERSONAL STEREO 图

ear·piece /ˈɪrˌpis; ˈɪəpiːs/ *n* [C] 1 a piece of electrical equipment that you put into your ear to hear a recording, message etc〔录音机等的〕耳塞: *Translations are heard through an earpiece.* 通过耳塞收听翻译。2 [usually plural 一般用复数] one of the two pieces at the side of a pair of glasses that go round your ears 眼镜脚 —see picture at 参见 GLASS[1] 图 3 the part of a telephone that you listen through 电话机听筒

ear·plug /ˈɪrˌplʌg; ˈɪəplʌg/ *n* [C usually plural 一般用复数] a small piece of rubber put inside your ear to keep out noise etc〔挡噪音等的〕耳塞

ear·ring /ˈɪrˌrɪŋ; ˈɪərɪŋ/ *n* [C] a piece of jewellery that you fasten to your ear 耳环；耳饰 —see picture at 参见 JEWELLERY 图

ear·shot /ˈɪrˌʃɑt; ˈɪəʃɒt/ *n* 1 **within earshot** near enough to hear what someone is saying 在听力所及范围内: *Everyone within earshot soon knew her opinion of Reggie.* 能听到她说话的人很

快就知道了她对雷吉的看法。**2 out of earshot** not near enough to hear what someone is saying 在听力所及范围之外: *I waited for her to get out of earshot before laughing.* 等她走远了，听不见我的声音，我才笑起来。

ear-split·ting /ˈ···/ *adj* very loud 震耳欲聋的，极响的: *Suddenly an ear-splitting shriek came from the behind the door.* 突然门后传来一声刺耳的尖叫。

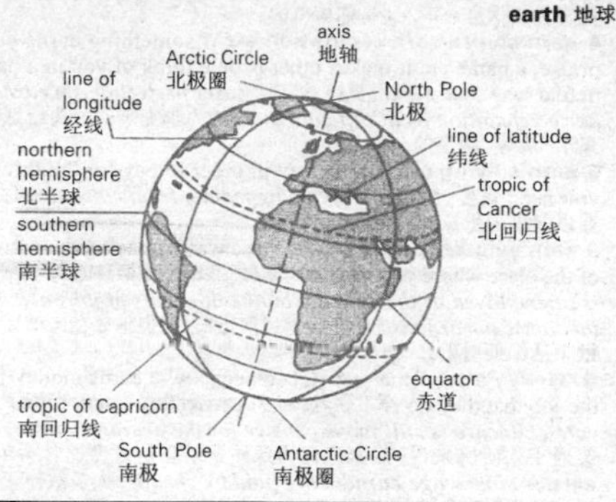

earth¹ /ɜ:θ; ɜ:θ/ *n*

1 ▶WORLD 世界◀ [singular] also 又作 **the Earth** the world that we live in 地球: *the planet Earth* 地球 | *The earth revolves around the sun.* 地球绕着太阳公转。| *The space shuttle is returning to earth.* 航天飞机正返回地球。—see 见 LAND¹ (USAGE) —see picture at 参见 SOLAR SYSTEM 图

2 ▶SOIL 土壤◀ [U] substance that plants, trees etc grow in 泥土，土壤: *footprints in the wet earth* 湿土中的脚印 | *a lump of earth* 一团泥土

3 ▶LAND 陆地◀ [singular] the hard surface of the world, as opposed to the sea 陆地; 地面: *After six months at sea, it was good to feel the earth beneath my feet again.* 在海上过了六个月后，再次踏上陆地的感觉真好。—see 见 LAND¹ (USAGE)

4 what/why/how etc on earth...? *spoken* used when you are asking a question about something that you are very surprised or annoyed about【口】究竟，到底〔用于询问令人惊讶或厌烦的事〕: *What on earth did you do that for?* 你做那事究竟为了什么?

5 cost/pay/charge the earth *informal* to cost etc a very large amount of money【非正式】花费／支付／收取一大笔钱: *What a beautiful necklace! It must have cost the earth!* 多漂亮的一串项链啊！一定很值钱了！

6 the biggest/tallest/most expensive etc on earth the biggest etc example of something that exists 世界上最大的／最高的／最贵的

7 come back/down to earth (with a bump) to stop behaving or living in a way that is not practical 回到现实，觉悟前非: *When he realized he'd spent all the money he really came back to earth with a bump.* 当他意识到钱都花光了，才猛然醒悟。

8 ▶ELECTRICITY 电◀ [C usually singular 一般用单数] *BrE* a wire that makes a piece of electrical equipment safe by connecting it with the ground【英】地线; GROUND¹ (30) *AmE*【美】

9 ▶ANIMAL'S HOME 动物居所◀ [C] the hole where a wild animal such as a FOX lives〔狐狸等野兽的〕洞穴

10 go to earth *BrE* to hide in order to escape from someone who is chasing you【英】躲藏起来

11 nothing on earth a strong way of saying 'nothing' 绝对没有什么〔用于加强语气〕: *Nothing on earth would persuade me to repeat the experience of marriage.* 绝对没什么能说服我重蹈婚姻的覆辙。

12 look/feel etc like nothing on earth *BrE* to look or feel very strange【英】看上去／摸起来非常奇怪: *It looks like smoked salmon, but tastes like nothing on earth.* 它看着像熏鲑鱼，但吃起来味道怪极了。

13 run sb/sth to earth *BrE* to find someone, especially by looking in many places【英】〔四处搜寻后终于〕找到某人／某物: *I finally ran him to earth in the stockroom.* 我最终在贮藏室找到了他。—see also 另见 DOWN-TO-EARTH, **move heaven and earth** (HEAVEN (10)), **hell on earth** (HELL¹ (1)), **promise sb the moon/the earth** (PROMISE¹ (3)), **the salt of the earth** (SALT¹ (2))

earth² *v* [T] *BrE* to make electrical equipment safe by connecting it to the ground with a wire【英】把〔电器〕接地; GROUND² (5) *AmE*【美】: *The amplifier wasn't properly earthed.* 扩音器没有妥善接地。

earth·bound /ˈɜ·θˌbaʊnd; ˈɜ:θbaʊnd/ *adj* **1** unable to move away from the surface of the Earth 不能离开地球表面的; 附着于土地的 **2** having very little imagination, thinking too much about practical things 缺乏想象力的; 太实际的

earth·en /ˈɜ·θən; ˈɜ:θən/ *adj* [only before noun 仅用于名词前] **1** an earthen pot, VASE etc is made of baked clay 陶制的 **2** an earthen floor or wall is made of earth 泥土(制)的

earth·en·ware /ˈɜ·θənˌwɛr; ˈɜ:θənweə/ *adj* an earthenware cup, plate etc is made of very hard baked clay 硬陶的 —**earthenware** *n* [U]

earth·ling /ˈɜ·θlɪŋ; ˈɜ:θlɪŋ/ *n* [C] a word used, in SCIENCE FICTION stories, by a creature from another world talking about a human 地球人〔科幻小说中外星人对地球人类的称法〕

earthly /ˈɜ·θlɪ; ˈɜ:θli/ *adj* **1 no earthly reason/use/solution etc** no reason, use etc at all 毫无缘由／用处／办法等: *There seemed to be no earthly reason for his strange behaviour.* 他奇怪的举止似乎毫无来由。**2** [only before noun 仅用于名词前] *literary* connected with life on Earth rather than in heaven【文】尘世的，人间的: *our earthly pleasures* 我们尘世间的欢乐

earth·quake /ˈɜ·θˌkwek; ˈɜ:θkweɪk/ *n* [C] a sudden shaking of the earth's surface that often causes a lot of damage 地震: *Mexico City was badly hit in the 1985 earthquake.* 1985年墨西哥城因地震严重受损。

CULTURAL NOTE 文化注释

In the US there is a major FAULT (=a crack in the rocks that form the Earth's surface) called the San Andreas Fault that runs from the north to the south of California. Serious earthquakes are common there, as well as in Alaska. 美国有一个巨大的地质断层，叫做圣安德烈亚斯断层，纵贯加利福尼亚州。该处及阿拉斯加州常有地震发生。— see also 另见 PLATE TECTONICS

earth-shat·ter·ing /ˈ·,··/ *adj* surprising or shocking and very important 惊天动地的，震惊世界的: *the day we heard the earth-shattering news of Kennedy's assassination* 我们惊闻肯尼迪遇刺消息的那天

Earth Sum·mit /ˈ·,··/ a large international meeting held in Rio de Janeiro in Brazil in 1992, at which the leaders of the countries of the United Nations discussed ways of protecting the environment and preserving the Earth's BIODIVERSITY (=all the different plants and animals on the Earth). It is sometimes also called the **Rio Summit**. 地球峰会〔1992年在巴西里约热内卢召开的一次大型国际会议。会上，联合国各成员国首脑探讨了保护地球环境和生物多样性的途径。有时也称"里约峰会"〕

earth·wards /ˈɜ·θwɚdz; ˈɜ:θwədz/ also 又作 **earth·ward** /-wɚd; -wəd/ *adv* in a direction towards the earth's surface 向地面: *The missile fell earthwards.* 导弹落向地面。—**earthward** *adj*

earth·work /ˈɜ·θˌwɜ·k; ˈɜ:θwɜ:k/ *n* [C usually plural 一般用复数] a large long pile of earth used to stop attacks in the past〔昔日的〕土垒防御工事

earth·worm /ˈɜ·θˌwɜ·m; ˈɜ:θwɜ:m/ *n* [C] a common type of long thin brown worm that lives in soil 蚯蚓

earth·y /ˈɜ·θɪ; ˈɜ:θi/ *adj* **1** talking about sex and the human body in a direct and impolite way 粗俗的，粗鄙的: *Simon has a very earthy sense of humour.* 西蒙的幽默感很粗俗。**2** tasting, smelling, or looking like earth or soil 泥土味的; 似泥土的: *a strong earthy smell* 一股很重的泥土味 —**earthiness** *n* [U]

ear trum·pet /ˈ·,··/ *n* [C] a type of tube that is wide at one end, used by old people in the past to help them hear〔昔时老年人用的〕号角状助听器

ear·wig /ˈɪrˌwɪg; ˈɪəˌwɪg/ *n* [C] a long brown insect with two curved pointed parts at the back of its body 蠼螋

ease¹ /iz; i:z/ *n* [U] **1 with ease** if you do something with ease, it is very easy for you to do it 轻易，毫不费劲: *The car travelled smoothly up the hillside, taking the bends with ease.* 小汽车顺利地爬上山，转弯轻松自如。| *It was the ease with which the burglars got into the house that worried her.* 使她担忧的是，盗贼竟能如此轻而易举地进入屋内。| **with consummate ease** (=easily and gracefully) 巧妙地 **2 at ease** feeling relaxed in a situation in which most people might feel a little nervous 不拘束; 放松: **feel/look at ease** *Nurses do all they can to make patients feel at ease.* 护士尽力使病人心情舒缓。| **put/set sb at their ease** (=try to make someone feel relaxed) 使某人

放松，使某人松弛下来 | **ill at ease** (=not relaxed) 不自在，局促不安 *You always look ill at ease in a suit.* 你穿套装看上去总有些不自然。**3** the ability to feel or behave in a natural or relaxed way 优雅自在：*He had a natural ease which made him very popular.* 他优雅自在的风度使他深受欢迎。**4 for ease of application/use etc** *formal* if something is done for ease of use, APPLICATION etc, it is done to make that process easier【正式】为使用方便：*For ease of application there is a special nozzle attached to the tube.* 为使用方便，管子上装有专用喷嘴。**5 a life of ease** a comfortable life, without problems or worries 安逸的生活：*She had a life of ease, having married her boss.* 嫁给老板后，她的生活安逸舒适。**6 stand at ease** used to tell soldiers to stand in a relaxed way with their feet apart〔军事口令〕稍息

ease[2] *v*

1 ▶MAKE EASIER 使较容易◀ [T] to make something, especially a process, happen more easily 使容易；使顺利：*a new drug designed to ease childbirth for women everywhere* 用于各地妇女助产的一种新药

2 ▶MOVE STH 移动某物◀ [T always + adv/prep] to move something slowly and carefully into another place 小心缓慢地移动；挪动：**ease sth in/onto etc** *Ease the patients slowly onto the bed.* 将病人慢慢挪到床上去。| *She eased the binoculars out of the box.* 她小心地从盒子中取出双筒望远镜。

3 ▶GET BETTER 变得较好◀ [I,T] if something unpleasant eases or you ease it, it gradually gets better 改善：*When the storm eases a little, we'll be able to go out.* 暴风雨减弱点后，我们就能外出了。| **ease the pain/pressure/stress/tension** *The cream should help ease the pain.* 这种油膏可以帮助减轻疼痛。| *an out-of-town shopping project to ease congestion in the city* 旨在改善城市拥塞状况的城外购物场所计划

4 ▶MAKE BETTER 使变得较好◀ [T] to reduce the amount or the bad effect of something 减少〔数量〕；减轻〔坏影响〕：*a plan designed to ease housing shortages* 旨在缓解住房短缺状况的计划

5 ease your grip to hold something less tightly 放松〔对某物的〕把持

6 ease your mind to make you feel less worried or nervous about something 宽慰：*It would ease my mind to know you had arrived safely.* 知道你已安全到达我就安心了。

ease out *phr v* [I] if a vehicle eases out, it slowly moves forward into the traffic〔汽车〕缓慢驶入车道，慢慢上路：*Take your time, ease out slowly and ignore the cars waiting behind you.* 别急，看准空当驶入车流，别管你后面等着的车。

ease sb ↔ **out** *phr v* [T] to deliberately try to make someone leave a job, a position of authority etc without officially saying anything 悄然使…自动离职

ease off also 又作 **ease up** *phr v* [I] **1** if something, especially something that annoys you, eases off or eases up, it gets less or better〔烦恼等〕减缓：*The noise didn't ease up for some time.* 有一阵儿噪音并未减弱。| *Why don't you wait until the traffic eases off a little?* 为什么不等到路上车少一些再走？**2 ease off on sb** to stop being unpleasant to someone, especially because they do not deserve to be treated like this 不再为难某人〔尤其是因为该人不应遭此等对待〕：*Ease off on Roger will you, he's not that bad.* 你别再为难罗杰了好吗，他没有那么坏。

ease up *phr v* [I] **1** to do something more slowly than before, especially because you have been going too fast, working too hard etc 放慢；松弛：*Dan should ease up or he'll have a nervous breakdown.* 丹该松弛一下了，否则会精神崩溃的。**2** [+on] to ease off 减缓，缓解

ea·sel /ˈizl; ˈiːzəl/ *n* [C] a wooden frame that you put a painting on while you paint it 画架

eas·i·ly /ˈizılı; ˈiːzlli/ *adv* **1** without problems or difficulties 容易地，轻易地：*This recipe can be made quickly and easily.* 这道菜做起来又快又容易。| *I'll be able to finish that easily by tonight.* 今晚我就能把它轻松完成。**2 easily the best/biggest/most stupid etc** definitely the best etc 绝对最好/最大/最蠢：*She is easily the most intelligent person in the class.* 她绝对是班上最聪明的。**3 could/can/might easily** used to say that something is possible or is very likely to happen 可能，极有可能：*I don't think we should tell her. She could easily forget and say something to Mum.* 我认为不应该告诉她，她极可能会忘记并且对妈妈说些什么。| **all too easily** (=used to say that a bad event is definitely possible) 极其容易〔指坏事完全可能发生〕*The friendly crowd can degenerate, all too easily, into an unruly mob.* 友善的人群很容易变成难以驾驭的暴徒。**4** in a relaxed way 轻松地；松弛地：*His son grinned easily back at him.* 他的儿子向他轻松地咧着嘴回笑。

eas·i·ness /ˈizınıs; ˈiːzinǝs/ *n* [U] **1** lack of difficulty 容易，无困难 **2** a feeling of being relaxed and comfortable with someone 自在；自如；无拘束

East /ist; iːst/ *n* **1 the East a)** the countries in Asia, especially China and Japan 亚洲国家；东方国家〔尤指中国和日本〕：*The martial arts originated in the East.* 武术起源于东方国家。**b)** the countries in the eastern part of Europe, especially the ones that had communist governments 东欧国家〔尤指该地区的前社会主义国家〕：*American relations with the East were at their worst in the late 1950s.* 美国与东欧国家的关系在20世纪50年代末降到了最低点。**c)** *AmE* the part of the US east of the Mississippi River, especially the states north of Washington DC【美】美国东部地区〔密西西比河以东的地区，尤指华盛顿特区以北的各州〕：*She was born in the East but now lives in Atlanta.* 她生于美国东部，但现在住在亚特兰大。| **back East** *He was born in Minneapolis but he went to college back East.* 他生在美国明尼阿波利斯，但在东部上大学。**2 East-West relations/trade etc** political relations etc between countries in eastern Europe and those in Europe and North America 东西方关系/贸易等〔指东欧国家与西欧和北美洲国家之间的政治关系等〕—compare 比较 FAR EAST, MIDDLE EAST, NEAR EAST

east[1] /ist; iːst/ abbreviation 缩写为 E *n* **1** [singular, U] the direction from which the sun rises, that is on the right of a person facing north 东，东方：*The mountains in the east get a lot of snow.* 东边的山上经常下雪。| *Which way is east?* 哪边是东？| **to the east (of)** *The sky to the east of the town was already lightening.* 镇子东面的天空已开始变亮。**2 the east** the eastern part of a country〔一个国家的〕东部地区：*The rain will spread later to the east.* 雨带将向东部移动。**3 in the east** if there is wind, rain etc in the east, it is coming from the east〔风、雨等〕来自东方，从东边来

east[2] *adj* **1** in the east or facing the east 在东方的，东部的；向东方的：*We sailed down the east coast of the island.* 我们沿着岛屿的东海岸向南航行。**2 east wind** an east wind comes from the east 东风：*a bitterly cold east wind* 刺骨的东风

east[3] *adv* towards the east 向东方，朝东面：*We zigzagged through the trees, moving east all the time.* 我们曲折行进穿过树林，一直向东前进。| *The road runs east to west.* 这条路东西向。

East An·gli·a /ˌist ˈæŋglıǝ; ˌiːst ˈæŋgliǝ/ a large area of eastern England, between the Wash and the Thames, including Norfolk, Suffolk, and parts of Essex and Cambridgeshire. The countryside is mostly flat, and a lot of wheat, flowers, and vegetables are grown there. 东英吉利亚〔英格兰东部一地区，位于沃什湾与泰晤士河之间，包括诺福克、萨福克以及埃塞克斯郡和剑桥郡的部分地区。这里的农村地区大多地势平坦，以种植小麦、花卉和蔬菜为主〕—**East Anglian** *adj*

East bloc, the also 又作 **Eastern bloc** the former name for the group of countries including the former Soviet Union and other eastern European countries with Communist governments, which had a close military and trade relationship 东欧集团〔由前苏联和其他共产党执政的东欧国家组成的集团，各成员国之间存在密切的军事和贸易关系〕—**East bloc** *adj* [only before noun] East bloc nations 东欧集团国家

east·bound /ˈistˌbaʊnd; ˈiːstbaʊnd/ *adj* travelling or leading towards the east 向东行的，朝东驶的：*A crash on the eastbound side of the freeway is blocking traffic.* 高速公路朝东方向一侧发生的车祸正阻碍着交通。

East Coast, the /ˌ· ˈ·◂/ *n* the part of the US that is next to the Atlantic Ocean, especially those states north of Washington DC 美国东海岸地区〔尤指华盛顿特区以北各州〕

CULTURAL NOTE 文化注释

People usually think about the large cities of New York, Philadelphia, and Boston as being the most important places on the East Coast, and states such as Maine, Vermont, and New Hampshire as being the areas on the East Coast that have the most traditional way of life. The STEREOTYPE of someone from the East Coast is a man or woman who thinks that he or she is more educated and more interested in art, literature, music etc than people who live in other parts of the US. 人们通常认为，纽约、费城、波士顿几大城市是东海岸最重要的地方，缅因、佛蒙特、新罕布什尔诸州是东海岸生活方式最为传统的地区。东海岸人的典型形象是：自认比别处美国人教育程度更高，更爱好艺术、文学、音乐等。

East End, the /ˌ· ˈ·◂/ *n* the eastern part of London, north of the River Thames〔泰晤士河以北的〕伦敦东区 —**East Ender** *n* [C]

CULTURAL NOTE 文化注释

People often think about the East End of London as a traditionally WORKING-CLASS area where people called COCKNEYS live. It is also known for its street markets, including Petticoat Lane and Brick Lane. The East End was badly damaged by bombs during World War II and in the 1950s many people moved out of the area to NEW TOWNS such as Milton Keynes. But since the 1980s, many businesses and MIDDLE-CLASS people have moved into parts of the East End, especially Docklands, so the character of the area has changed. House prices have greatly increased and many old buildings have been replaced by new ones. 人们通常认为伦敦东区传统上是工人阶层居住区，那里的居民被称为Cockney（伦敦佬）。这里也以衬裙巷和布里克巷市场等街头市场闻名。二战期间，伦敦东区受到轰炸，损毁严重。20世纪50年代，很多人从这里迁至密尔顿凯恩斯等新城。但自从20世纪80年代开始，很多公司和中产阶级人士搬到伦敦东区，尤其是船坞区，该区面貌为之一变，房价高涨，很多旧有建筑被新建筑取代。

East·End·ers /ist'ɛndəz; iːst'endəz/ *trademark* a popular British SOAP OPERA on television, which is about the WORKING CLASS people who live in Albert Square in the East End of London. It deals with common social problems in a realistic way.【商标】《伦敦东区人》〔英国一流行肥皂剧。该剧讲述生活在伦敦东区阿尔伯特广场的工人阶层的故事，以现实主义手法触及常见社会问题〕

Eas·ter /'istə; 'iːstə/ *n* [C,U] **1** a Christian holy day in March or April when Christians remember the death of Christ and his return to life 复活节 **2** the period of time just before and after this 复活节期间: *We spent the Easter holidays in Wales.* 我们在威尔士度过了复活节假期。

CULTURAL NOTE 文化注释

People think of Easter in connection with spring and new life. On GOOD FRIDAY Christians remember the death of Jesus Christ on the cross, and two days later, on EASTER SUNDAY, they celebrate the time when they believe Christ became alive again. Many Christians go to church on Easter Sunday, even if they do not go to church regularly. 人们认为复活节与春天和新生命有关。复活节前的星期五（受难节），基督徒怀念耶稣被钉死在十字架上。两天后，即复活节星期天，人们庆贺耶稣的复活。这一天很多基督徒会去教堂，即便他们平时并不常去教堂。

There are many Easter traditions in both the US and the UK. People paint eggs in bright colours for Easter, and often hide these eggs or small chocolate eggs for children to find. Young children believe that the eggs were hidden by the EASTER BUNNY. Sometimes children roll the coloured Easter eggs down a hill to see which ones will break. In the US some people also give EASTER BASKETS full of chocolate eggs or other sweets as presents, especially to children. In the UK, people give chocolate EASTER EGGS as presents, especially to children. In the past, people often got new clothes for Easter, and women wore special hats called EASTER BONNETS. 英美两国有很多复活节传统。人们在复活节把蛋涂上鲜艳的颜色，把这些彩蛋或巧克力做成的蛋藏起来让孩子们找。小孩子相信，彩蛋是被复活节兔子藏起来的。有时他们会把彩蛋滚下山坡，看哪些蛋先破。一些美国人还赠送装满巧克力做成的蛋和其他糖果的复活节篮子，尤其是送给孩子。英国人赠送巧克力做的复活节彩蛋作为礼物，尤其是送给孩子。过去人们常为过复活节而添置新衣，女人则戴上特别的帽子，叫做复活节软帽。

Easter Bun·ny /,..'../ *n* [singular] an imaginary rabbit that children believe brings chocolate eggs at Easter 复活节兔子〔小孩子认为该虚构的兔子会在复活节时给他们带来巧克力蛋〕

Easter egg /'.. ./ *n* [C] **1** *BrE* a chocolate egg usually given as a present at Easter【英】〔通常作礼物用的〕复活节巧克力蛋 **2** *AmE* an egg that has been coloured and decorated, usually by a child【美】〔通常由小孩子装饰的〕复活节彩蛋

Easter Is·land /'.. ,../ a small island in the Pacific Ocean, which belongs to Chile. Many tourists go to Easter Island to see the several hundred stone heads, some of which are 20 metres tall, which were made over a thousand years ago. 复活节岛〔太平洋一小岛，归属智利。岛上有数百尊石制人头像，有些高达20米，有1000多年的历史，吸引着大批游人前去参观〕

eas·ter·ly[1] /'istəlɪ; 'iːstəli/ *adj* **1** towards or in the east 向东方的; 在东方的: *an easterly course across the Pacific ocean* 向东穿过太平洋的航线 **2** easterly winds come from the east〔风〕来自东方的: *an easterly breeze* 微微的东风

easterly[2] *n* [C] a wind that blows from the east 东风

Easter Mon·day /,.. '../ the day after Easter Day, which is a public holiday in the UK 复活节后的星期一〔英国一公众假日〕

east·ern /'istən; 'iːstən/ *adj* **1** in or from the east of a country or area 在〔某国家或地区〕东部的; 来自东部的: *There were heavy snows in eastern Minnesota.* 明尼苏达州东部下了大雪。| *The eastern sky was just turning pink.* 东边的天空刚刚泛红。**2** in or from the countries in Asia, especially China and Japan 在东方国家的, 来自东方国家的〔尤指中国和日本〕: *Eastern religions* 东方宗教 **3** in or from the countries in the east part of Europe, especially the countries that used to have Communist governments 在东欧国家的, 来自东欧国家的〔尤指东欧前社会主义国家〕: *the Eastern bloc* 东欧集团 2

Eastern bloc, the /'.. ,./ another name for EAST BLOC 东欧集团〔East Bloc 的别称〕

Eastern Con·fe·rence, the /,.. '.../ a group of professional BASKETBALL teams from the eastern part of the US, which play against one another. Together with the Western Conference, a similar group from the western US, these teams form the NBA (=National Basketball Association). 东部篮球联合会〔美国东部职业篮球队团体, 与西部篮球联合会一起组成全国篮球协会〕

East·ern·er /'istənə; 'iːstənə/ *n* [C] *AmE* someone who lives in or comes from the eastern US【美】美国东部人

Eastern Eu·rope /,.. '../ the part of Europe whose countries formerly had Communist governments and close political connections with the former Soviet Union, including countries such as Poland, East Germany, Hungary and Romania 东欧〔早先由共产党执政并与前苏联有着密切政治关系的欧洲诸国, 包括波兰、东德、匈牙利和罗马尼亚等〕—**Eastern European** *n, adj*

east·ern·most /'istən,most; 'iːstənməʊst/ *adj* furthest east 最东的; 极东的: *the easternmost part of the island* 岛屿的最东端

Eastern Or·tho·dox Church, the /,.. ,... '../ —see 见 ORTHODOX CHURCH

Easter Ris·ing, the /,.. '../ the events of Easter 1916 in Ireland, when armed opponents of British rule in Ireland took control of the main Post Office in Dublin and announced that Ireland was an independent republic. They were quickly defeated by the British army, and their leaders were killed. 复活节起义〔1916年复活节期间发生在爱尔兰的事件。反对英国统治爱尔兰的武装人员占领了都柏林邮政总局, 并宣布爱尔兰为独立共和国。他们很快被英军挫败, 其领导人遭到处决〕

Easter Sun·day /,.. '../ —see 见 EASTER

East Ger·ma·ny /,. '.../ also 又作 **the German Democratic Republic** a former country in northeast Europe, which in 1990 joined again with West Germany (the Federal Republic of Germany) to become Germany 东德, 德意志民主共和国〔原欧洲东北部一国, 1990年与西德（德意志联邦共和国）再次合并成德国〕—**East German** *n, adj*

East In·di·a Com·pa·ny /,. '..., .../ one of several European companies that developed trade with India and east Asia in the 17th and 18th centuries. The British East India Company (1600-1858) was the most important of these, and was responsible for bringing India into the British Empire. 东印度公司〔指17、18世纪与印度和东亚发展贸易关系的几家欧洲公司之一。英国东印度公司（1600-1858）是其中最重要的一家, 也是它将印度纳入了英帝国的版图〕

East·man /'istmən; 'iːstmən/, **George** (1854-1932) a US inventor and businessman who started the Kodak company, and made the first camera that could be carried around and that was cheap and easy to use. 伊斯曼〔（1854-1932）, 美国发明家、商人。他创办了柯达公司, 制造了首部价格低廉、使用简单的便携式照相机〕

East Riv·er, the /'. ,../ a river flowing into New York Harbor, separating Manhattan from Long Island 伊斯特河, 东河〔位于曼哈顿与长岛之间、注入纽约港的一条河流〕

East Sea, the also 又作 **the Sea of Japan** the sea that separates Korea from Japan 东海〔也称日本海, 位于朝鲜和日本之间的海域〕

East Side, the /,. '../ *n* the south-eastern part of Manhattan in New York, lived in mostly by poor people who have come to the US from other countries 东区〔纽约市曼哈顿东南部地区, 多为贫困移民居住〕

East Sus·sex /ˌ· ˈ··/ a COUNTY in southeast England on the English Channel coast 东萨塞克斯郡〔英格兰东南部一郡, 濒临英吉利海峡〕

East Timor /ˌist ˈtimɔr; ˌiːst ˈtiːmɔː/ a TERRITORY in the southeast Indian Ocean, formerly a Portuguese COLONY, but claimed by Indonesia since 1975. In 1999 the East Timorese population voted to become independent. This led to violence between opposing groups, and the United Nations took temporary control of the country. It became an independent nation in 2002. 东帝汶〔印度洋东南部一领地, 曾为葡萄牙殖民地。1975 年被印尼占领。1999 年东帝汶人投票决定独立。此举引发了对立各方之间的暴力冲突, 联合国因此对该国实行临时管制。东帝汶 2002 年正式独立〕

east·ward /ˈistwɚd; ˈiːstwəd/ *adj, adv* going or facing towards the east 向东的[地], 朝东的[地]: *The eastward view toward the mountains was spectacular.* 向东望去, 群山景色壮美。

east·wards /ˈistwɚdz; ˈiːstwədz/ also 又作 **eastward** *adv* towards the east 向东, 朝东: *We sailed eastwards.* 我们向东航行。

East Yorkshire /ˌ· ˈ··/ a COUNTY in northeast England, which was formerly called Humberside 东约克郡〔英格兰东北部一郡, 旧称亨伯赛德〕

S1 W1 **eas·y¹** /ˈizi; ˈiːzi/ *adj*

1 ►NOT DIFFICULT 不困难◄ not difficult, and not needing much physical or mental effort 容易的, 不费力的: *The easiest way to get there is through the park.* 去那儿的捷径是穿过公园。| *It can't have been easy raising three children all by herself.* 她一个人抚养三个孩子一定不容易。| **easy to make/build/do etc** *Are the instructions easy to follow?* 这些用法说明容易理解吗? | **make things easy (for sb)** *Having a computer will definitely make things a lot easier.* 有台电脑做起事情来无疑会容易得多。| **easy as pie** (=very easy) 易如反掌, 极其容易 | **within easy (walking) distance** (=near enough to walk to) 离得很近〔步行便可到达〕

2 ►NOT WORRIED 不担心的◄ not feeling worried or anxious 不担心的; 不紧张的: *Would it make you feel easier if I phoned when I got there?* 如果我到那儿便给你打电话, 这会让你放心些吗? | **with an easy mind** *I can't go to bed with an easy mind until I know she's safe.* 在知道她安然无恙之前, 我不可能安心地去睡觉。—opposite 反义词 UNEASY

3 easy victim/prey etc someone who cannot easily defend themselves against bad treatment, attack etc 易受虐待[攻击]的人: *Elderly and frail, she was easy prey for muggers.* 她年纪大身体又弱, 很容易成为抢劫犯的目标。

4 easy on the eye/ear pleasant to look at or listen to 好看的/悦耳的: *Choose colours that are soft and easy on the eye.* 选择柔和悦目的颜色。

5 have an easy time of it to have no problems or difficulties 没有问题; 很顺心: *She hasn't had an easy time of it since Jack left.* 杰克离开后, 她没有过过舒适的日子。

6 take the easy way out to end a difficult situation in a way that seems easy, but is not the best or most sensible way 采取省事的做法〔但不是最佳或最明智的做法〕以摆脱困境: *She took the easy way out, and told him she had to visit her mother that afternoon.* 她想了个简单的办法, 对他说那天下午要去看望母亲。

7 get off easy *informal* to escape severe punishment for something that you have done wrong【非正式】逃脱重惩: *I thought I was in deep trouble, but I got off easy.* 我以为有大麻烦了, 但还是逃过了。

8 easy money money that you do not have to work hard to get 来得容易的钱

9 I'm easy *spoken* used to say that you do not mind what choice is made【口】我随便, 我无所谓〔即无论哪种选择都可以〕: *"Would you rather go out for a Chinese or an Indian meal?" "Oh, I'm easy."* "你想去吃中国菜还是印度菜?" "噢, 我无所谓。"

10 that's easy for you to say *spoken* used when someone has given you some advice that would be difficult for you to follow【口】你说得倒容易

11 be on easy street *informal, especially AmE* to be in a situation in which you have plenty of money【非正式, 尤美】手头很宽裕, 生活优裕: *They're on easy street now that he's inherited his aunt's money.* 由于他继承了姑妈的财产, 他们日子好过了。

12 on easy terms *BrE* if you buy something on easy terms, you pay for it with several small payments instead of paying the whole amount at once【英】〔购物〕分期付款

13 ►SEX 性◄ *informal* someone, especially a woman, who is easy has a lot of sexual partners【非正式】淫荡的〔尤指女性〕

14 a woman of easy virtue *old-fashioned* a woman who has sex with a lot of men【过时】水性杨花的女人

15 eggs over easy *AmE* eggs cooked on a hot surface and turned over quickly before serving【美】嫩煎蛋 —see also 另见 EASE, EASILY

S2 **easy²** *adv* **1 take it easy a)** also 又作 **take things easy** to relax and not do very much 放松; 悠着点: *The doctor says I'm going to have to take it easy for a few weeks.* 医生说我得休息几个星期。**b)** *spoken* used to tell someone to become less upset or angry【口】〔劝人〕别烦恼; 不要生气: *Just take it easy and tell us what happened.* 别急, 告诉我们发生了什么事。**2 go easy on/with sth** to not use too much of something 节省使用某物, 对某物节制: *Go easy on that whiskey if you're driving!* 如果你要开车, 威士忌少喝点! **3 go easy on sb** to be more gentle and less strict or angry with someone 温和对待某人; 对某人宽容: *Go easy on Peter for a while – he's having a hard time at school.* 对彼得宽容一阵儿吧, 他现在在学校功课正忙。**4 rest/breathe easy** to stop worrying 不再担心, 停止忧虑: *You can rest easy now – they've gone.* 他们已经走了, 你现在不用担心了。**5 easy does it** *spoken* used to tell someone to be careful, especially when they are moving something【口】〔告诉别人, 尤其是搬东西的人〕小心点 **6 easier said than done** *especially spoken* used when it would be difficult to actually do what someone has suggested【尤口】说来容易做来难: *I should treat Jim like any other client, but that's easier said than done.* 我应当像对待其他客户那样对待吉姆, 但这说起来容易做起来难。**7 stand easy** a command telling soldiers who are already standing at ease (EASE¹ (6)) to relax more〔军事口令〕稍息〔比 stand at ease 更随便自由些〕 **8 easy come, easy go** *spoken* used when something, especially money, was easily obtained and is quickly used or spent【口】来得容易, 去得快〔尤指钱财〕

easy chair /ˌ·· ˈ·/ *n* [C] a large comfortable chair 安乐椅

easy-go·ing /ˌ·· ˈ··◂/ *adj* not easily upset, annoyed, or worried 脾气随和的, 温和的: *Her easy-going nature made her popular.* 她生性随和, 受人喜爱。

easy lis·ten·ing /ˌ·· ˈ···/ *n* [U] music that is relaxing to listen to and has nice tunes, but is not very unusual 悠扬悦耳的〔但风格并不独特的〕音乐

easy-pea·sy /ˌizi ˈpizi; ˌiːzi ˈpiːzi◂/ *adj BrE* a word meaning very easy, used especially by children【英】极容易的〔尤为儿童用语〕

Easy Rid·er /ˌ·· ˈ··/ (1969) a US film about two young men who take illegal drugs and travel across the southern states of the US on MOTORCYCLEs. The subject of the film, and its music, made it very popular with young people.《逍遥骑士》〔(1969), 美国电影。影片讲述两个吸毒的年轻人骑摩托车穿越美国南部各州的故事。该片的主题和音乐深受年轻人喜爱〕

S1 W1 **eat** /it; iːt/ *v past tense* **ate** /et; eɪt/ *past participle* **eaten** /ˈitn; ˈiːtn/

1 ►FOOD 食物◄ a) [I,T] to put food in your mouth and swallow it 吃: *Vegetarians don't eat meat.* 素食者不吃肉。| **something to eat** (=some food) 一些食物 *Would you like something to eat?* 想吃点什么吗? | **eat like a bird** (=eat very little) 吃得很少 | **eat like a horse** (=eat a lot) 吃得很多 | **eat right** *AmE* (=eat food that keeps you healthy)【美】保持健康的饮食习惯 | **I couldn't eat another thing** *spoken* (=I am full)【口】我饱了, 我再也吃不下了 **b)** [I,T] to have a meal 吃饭, 就餐: *We usually eat at seven.* 通常我们 7 点吃饭。| *Do you want to eat at Musso's Restaurant before the movie?* 看电影前你想去莫索餐厅吃饭吗? | **eat out** (=have a meal in a restaurant, not at home) 下馆子, 出去吃饭 *Do you fancy eating out tonight?* 今晚你想出去吃饭吗?

2 eat your heart out a) used to compare two things and say that one is much better 强多了: *He's the new teen idol – eat your heart out, Michael Jackson!* 他是少年的新偶像, 你去嫉妒吧——迈克尔·杰克逊! **b)** *BrE* to be unhappy about something or to want someone or something very much【英】沮丧; 渴求〔某人或某物〕: *She's not coming back so it's no use lying here eating your heart out.* 她不会回来了, 因此你躺在这里苦苦想她也没用。

3 eat sb alive/eat sb for breakfast to be very angry with someone, especially someone that you have power over 对某人大发脾气: *You can't tell him that – he'll eat you alive!* 你不能告诉他那件事, 他会气得活吞了你!

4 eat sb out of house and home *humorous* to eat a lot of someone's supply of food, so that they have to buy more【幽默】把某人吃穷

5 eat crow *AmE*【美】also 又作 **eat humble pie** to be forced to admit that you were wrong and say that you are sorry 被迫认错

6 have sb eating out of your hand to have made someone very willing to believe you or do what you want 使某人俯首听

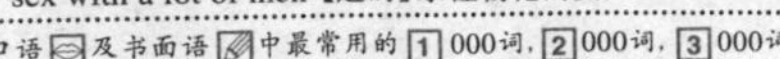

命，使某人百依百顺: *The clients were suspicious at first, but he soon had them eating out of his hand.* 客户们开始有些怀疑，但很快他就使他们言听计从了。

7 what's eating him/her/you? *spoken* used to ask why someone seems annoyed or upset【口】是什么让他/她/你烦心?: *What's eating Sally today? She just yelled at me.* 今天萨莉为什么心烦呀? 她对我大喊大叫的。

8 eat your words to admit that what you said was wrong 承认自己说错了话: *I had to eat my words when he turned up on time after all.* 他还是准时到了，我只好承认说错了话。

9 I could eat a horse *spoken* used to say you are very hungry【口】我饿极了

10 I'll eat my hat *spoken old-fashioned* used to say that you think something is not true or will not happen【口，过时】我敢打赌〔表示认为某事不是真的或不可能发生〕: *If the Democrats win the election, I'll eat my hat!* 如果民主党选举赢了，我把脑袋给你!

11 ▶USE/DAMAGE 使用/损坏◀ [I always+adv/prep, T] to damage, destroy, or use a lot of something 损坏; 毁坏; 大量消耗: *Work alone ate 72 hours of my week.* 每周光工作就占了我72个小时。—see also 另见 EATS

eat sth ↔ **away** *phr v* [T] to gradually remove or reduce the amount of something 侵蚀; 消耗: *The wooden parts had been eaten away by damp.* 木制部件已被湿气侵蚀殆尽。

eat away at sth/sb *phr v* [T] **1** to gradually remove or reduce the amount of something 侵蚀; 消耗: *Rust had eaten away at the metal frame.* 金属框架已锈蚀了。**2** to make someone feel very worried over a long period of time 困扰，烦扰: *The thought of mother alone like that was eating away at her.* 一想起母亲孤身一人的情景，她心里就不好受。

eat into sth *phr v* [T] **1** to gradually reduce the amount of time, money etc that is available 消耗〔时间、金钱等〕: *All these car expenses are eating into our savings.* 汽车上的这些消费在逐步耗去我们的积蓄。**2** to damage or destroy something 侵蚀; 腐蚀: *Acid eats into the metal, damaging its surface.* 酸腐蚀金属，损坏其表面。

eat up *phr v* **1** [I,T **eat** sth ↔ **up**] *especially spoken* to eat all of something【尤口】吃完，吃光: *Come on, eat it up, there's a good girl.* 乖，把它吃光，这才是好女孩。**2** [T **eat** sth ↔ **up**] *informal* to use all of something until it is gone【非正式】用光; 耗尽: *A big car just eats up money.* 开辆大汽车只会耗光你的钱。**3 be eaten up with jealousy/anger/curiosity etc** to be very jealous, angry etc, so that you cannot think about anything else 嫉妒/愤怒/好奇之极

eat·a·ble /ˋitəbl̩; ˈiːtəbəl/ *adj* in a good enough condition to be eaten 能食用的，可吃的 —see also 另见 EDIBLE

eat·er /ˋitə; ˈiːtə/ *n* [C] **big/light/fussy etc eater** someone who eats a lot, not much, only particular things etc 食量大/食量不大/挑食的人: *I've never been a big eater.* 我向来吃得不多。

eat·e·ry /ˋitəri; ˈiːtəri/ *n* [C] *informal especially AmE* a restaurant or other place to eat【非正式，尤美】餐馆; 饮食店: *one of the best Knoxville eateries* 诺克斯维尔最好的餐馆之一

eating ap·ple /ˋ· ·,· ·/ *n* [C] an apple that you eat raw rather than cooked 生吃的苹果

eating dis·or·der /ˋ· · ·,· ·/ *n* [C] a medical condition in which you do not eat normal amounts or at normal times 饮食失调症

eats /its; iːts/ *n* [plural] *informal* food, especially for a party【非正式】〔尤指用于聚会的〕食品，吃食: *You get the drink, and I'll organize the eats.* 你搞喝的，我弄吃的。

eau-de-co·logne /ˌo də kəˋlon; ˌəʊ də kəˈləʊn/ *n* [U] a sweet-smelling liquid used to make you feel fresh and smell nice 科隆香水，古龙香水

eaves /ivz; iːvz/ *n* [plural] the edges of a roof that stick out beyond the walls 屋檐: *Birds had nested under the eaves.* 鸟儿在屋檐下筑了巢。

eaves·drop /ˋivzˌdrɑp; ˈiːvzdrɒp/ *v* **eavesdropped, eavesdropping** [I] to listen secretly to other people's conversations 偷听别人的谈话: *There was Helena eavesdropping outside the door.* 当时海伦娜正在门外偷听。—compare 比较 OVERHEAR —**eavesdropper** *n* [C]

eavesdrop 偷听

ebb¹ /ɛb; eb/ *n* **1** [singular] also 又作 **ebb tide** the flow of the sea away from the shore, when the TIDE¹ (1) goes out 落潮，退潮 —opposite 反义词 FLOOD TIDE **2 be at a low ebb** to be in a bad state or condition 处于低潮; 处于衰退状态: *By March 1933, the economy was at its lowest ebb.* 到1933年3月，经济衰退至最低点。**3 ebb and flow** a situation or state in which something increases and decreases in a kind of pattern〔有规律的〕涨落，起伏: *I relaxed into the ebb and flow of the music.* 我随着起伏的音乐放松下来。

ebb² *v* [I] **1** if the TIDE ebbs, it flows away from the shore〔潮水〕落，退 **2** also 又作 **ebb away** to gradually decrease 衰退; 逐渐减少: *Linda's enthusiasm began to ebb away.* 琳达的热情开始减退。

Eb·o·ny /ˋɛbənɪ; ˈebəni/ *trademark* a US monthly magazine especially for African Americans【商标】《黑檀》〔专门面向非洲裔美国人读者的一种月刊〕

ebony¹ *n* [U] a hard black wood 乌木; 黑檀

ebony² *adj literary* black【文】乌黑的: *Sunlight glinted on her ebony hair.* 太阳光下，她乌黑的头发油光闪亮。

e·bul·li·ent /ɪˋbʌljənt; ɪˈbʌliənt/ *adj formal* very happy and excited【正式】兴高采烈的: *An ebullient three-year-old bounced around the room.* 一个三岁人的孩子在房间里高兴地跑来跑去。—**ebullience** *n* [U]

EC, the /ˌiˋsi; ˌiː ˈsiː◂/ *n* the European Community; the former name for the EU 欧洲共同体〔欧盟的旧称〕

ec·cen·tric¹ /ɪkˋsɛntrɪk; ɪkˈsentrɪk/ *adj* **1** behaving or appearing in a way that is unusual and different from most people〔行为或装束〕怪异的，古怪的: *students dressed in eccentric clothing* 衣着怪异的学生 | *an eccentric old woman* 一个古怪的老妇人 **2** *technical* eccentric circles do not have the same centre point【术语】圆不同心的 —compare 比较 CONCENTRIC —**eccentrically** /-klɪ; -kli/ *adv* —see picture at 参见 CONCENTRIC 图

eccentric² *n* [C] someone who behaves in a way that is different from what is usual or socially accepted 行为古怪的人: *I was regarded as something of an eccentric.* 那时人们认为我有点古怪。

ec·cen·tri·ci·ty /ˌɛksənˋtrɪsɪtɪ; ˌeksenˈtrɪsəti/ *n* **1** [U] strange or unusual behaviour 古怪行为; 反常行为: *Kate's mother had a reputation for eccentricity.* 凯特的妈妈是个出了名的怪人。**2** [C] an opinion or action that is strange or unusual 古怪的想法; 怪异的动作: *I found his eccentricities amusing rather than irritating.* 我觉得他的怪癖挺好笑，并不烦人。

Ec·cles cake /ˋɛkl̩z ˌkek; ˈekəlz keɪk/ *n* [C] *BrE* a round cake filled with CURRANTS (=type of dried fruit)【英】葡萄干馅饼

ec·cle·si·as·tic /ɪˌklizɪˋæstɪk; ɪˌkliːziˈæstɪk◂/ *n* [C] *formal* a priest, usually in the Christian church【正式】〔常指基督教的〕牧师，神父

ec·cle·si·as·ti·cal /ɪˌklizɪˋæstɪkl̩; ɪˌkliːziˈæstɪkəl/ also 又作 **ecclesiastic** *adj* connected with the Christian church or its priests 基督教的; 基督教士的: *ecclesiastical history* 基督教教会历史

ECG /ˌi si ˋdʒi; ˌiː siː ˈdʒiː/ *n* [C] *especially BrE*【尤英】**1** an electrocardiograph; a piece of equipment that records electrical changes in your heart 心电图仪 **2** an electrocardiogram; a drawing produced by an electrocardiograph 心电图

ech·e·lon /ˋɛʃəˌlɑn; ˈeʃəlɒn/ *n* [C] **1** also 又作 **echelons** a rank or level of responsibility in an organization, business etc, or the people at that level〔组织、企业等的〕梯队，阶层: *the upper echelons of government* 政府高层 **2** *technical* a line of ships, soldiers, planes etc arranged in a pattern that looks like a series of steps【术语】〔船只、士兵和飞机等的〕梯形编队

ech·o¹ /ˋɛko; ˈekəʊ/ *v present tense* **echoes** *past tense and past participle* **echoed** **1** [I often+adv/prep] if a sound echoes, you hear it again because it was made near something such as a wall or hill〔声音〕回响，发出回声: *The thunder echoed over the mountains.* 雷声在山峦间回响。| *Our shouts echoed through the silent streets.* 我们的喊声在寂静的大街上发出回声。**2** [I] if a place echoes, it is filled with sounds that are repeated or are similar to each other〔场所〕充满回声: [**+with**] *The hall echoed with laughter and stamping feet.* 大厅内回荡着笑声和跺脚声。**3** [T] *literary* to repeat what someone else has just said【文】重复〔别人的话〕: *"Paula's dead!" "Dead?" echoed Teri, stunned.* "葆拉死了!""死了?"特里重复道，惊呆了。**4** [T] to repeat an idea or opinion because you agree with it 附和: *The article simply echoed the NRA's arguments against gun control.* 这篇文章只是附和了全国步枪射击运动协会反对枪支管制的观点。

echo[2] *n plural* **echoes** [C] **1** a sound that you hear again after a loud noise, because it was made near something such as a wall 回声, 回音: *The echo of the bells died away, and the valley was quiet again.* 钟声的回音逐渐消失, 山谷又恢复了宁静。**2** something that is very similar to something that has happened or been said before 十分相似的东西, 如出一辙的事物: **[+of]** *This crash has chilling echoes of the Lockerbie disaster.* 这次失事与洛克比空难有惊人的相似之处。

éclair /eˋklɛr; ɪˈkleə/ *n* [C] a long cake covered with chocolate and filled with cream〔外涂巧克力、内填奶油的〕长条酥卷

é·clat /eˋklɑ; eɪˈklɑː/ *n* [U] *literary*【文】**1** praise and admiration 赞扬, 喝彩: *Miller's new play has been greeted with great éclat.* 米勒的新剧赢得一片喝彩。**2** a way of doing something with a lot of style, especially in order to attract attention〔尤指为吸引注意的〕炫耀

e·clec·tic[1] /ɪkˋlɛktɪk; ɪˈklektɪk/ *adj* including a mixture of many different things or people, especially so that you can use the best of all of them 兼收并蓄的; 博采众长的: *galleries with an eclectic range of styles and artists* 收藏各个流派和艺术家作品的美术馆 —**eclectically** /-klɪ; -kli/ *adv* —**eclecticism** /-tɪˌsɪzəm; -tɪsɪzəm/ *n* [U]

eclectic[2] *n* [C] *formal* someone who chooses the best or most useful parts from many different ideas, methods etc【正式】博采众长的人

e·clipse[1] /ɪˋklɪps; ɪˈklɪps/ *n* **1** [C] an occasion when the sun or the moon seems to disappear, because one of them is passing between the other one and the Earth 日蚀; 月蚀 **2** [singular] a situation in which someone loses their power or fame, because someone else has become more powerful or famous〔与他人相比之下权力或名望的〕黯然失色: *New movie studios in Hollywood soon led to the eclipse of New York as a film-making center.* 好莱坞新出现的制片厂很快就使作为电影制作中心的纽约黯然失色。**3 in/into eclipse** *formal* less famous or powerful than you should be【正式】被埋没, 湮没无闻: *Mary Shelley, the author of Frankenstein, has been too long in eclipse.*《弗兰肯斯坦》的作者玛丽·雪莱的地位长久以来得不到公正评价。

eclipse[2] *v* [T] **1** if the moon eclipses the sun or the earth eclipses the moon, it makes it seem to disappear, by passing in front of it 日[月]蚀 **2** [often passive 常用被动态] to become more important, powerful, famous etc than someone or something else, so that they are no longer noticed 使失色, 盖过: *She felt totally eclipsed by her prettier, brighter, younger sister.* 她的妹妹比她漂亮、聪明, 她觉得自己黯然失色。

e·clip·tic /ɪˋklɪptɪk; ɪˈklɪptɪk/ *n* [singular] *technical* the path along which the sun seems to move【术语】黄道

eco- /iko; iːkəʊ/ *prefix* concerned with the environment 与环境相关的, 生态的: *eco-warriors* (=people who try to stop damage to the environment) 环境卫士〔指尽力保护环境的人〕

ECO, the /ˌi si ˋo; ˌiː siː ˈəʊ/ the abbreviation of 缩写= the ENGLISH CHAMBER ORCHESTRA

e·co-friend·ly /ˋiko ˌfrɛndlɪ; ˈiːkəʊ ˌfrendli/ *adj* not harmful to the environment 不损害环境的: *eco-friendly products* 对环境无害的产品

e·co·lo·gi·cal /ˌikəˋlɑdʒɪkl̩; ˌiːkəˈlɒdʒɪkəl◂/ *adj* [only before noun 仅用于名词前] **1** connected with the way plants, animals, and people are related to each other and to their environment 生态的: *an ecological disaster* 生态灾难 **2** interested in preserving the environment 主张生态保护的: *ecological groups* 生态保护组织 —**ecologically** /-klɪ; -kli/ *adv*: *an ecologically-sound production process* 一种对生态无害的生产过程

e·col·o·gist /ɪˋkɑlədʒɪst; ɪˈkɒlədʒɪst/ *n* [C] a scientist who studies ecology 生态学家

e·col·o·gy /ɪˋkɑlədʒɪ; ɪˈkɒlədʒi/ *n* [singular, U] the way in which plants, animals, and people are related to each other and to their environment, or the scientific study of this 生态; 生态学: *the fragile ecology of the tundra* 冻原地带脆弱的生态

S3 W1 **ec·o·nom·ic** /ˌikəˋnɑmɪk; ˌekəˈnɒmɪk◂/ *adj* **1** [only before noun 仅用于名词前] connected with trade, industry, and the management of money 经济(上)的: *strategies to promote economic growth* 促进经济增长的策略 | *It makes no economic sense at all!* 经济上这绝不明智! | **economic climate** (=conditions affecting trade, industry, and business) 经济气候〔指影响贸易、工业和商业发展的条件〕**2** an economic process, activity etc produces enough profit for it to continue; PROFITABLE 产生经济效益的; 合算的: *It is no longer economic for us to run the service.* 经营这项服务不再赚钱了。| *an economic price* 合算的价格 —see 见 ECONOMIC (USAGE)

USAGE NOTE 用法说明: ECONOMIC

WORD CHOICE 词语辨析: **economy, economic, economics, economical, cheap, economically**

The adjective of the word **economy** [C], meaning the economy of a country is **economic**. economy〔指一国的经济〕的形容词是 economic: *government measures to boost the economy* 政府促进经济发展的措施 | *the various economies of South America* 南美洲各经济体 | *We are faced with a deepening economic crisis* (NOT 不用 *economical*). 我们面临日益严重的经济危机。| *economic growth/benefits/problems/policy* 经济增长/收益/问题/政策

The study of economies and their money systems is called **economics** (singular 单数形式). 对各类经济体及其货币体系的研究被称为 economics (经济学): *He's got a degree in Modern History and Economics* (NOT 不用 *economic* or 或 *economy*). 他有现代史和经济学的学位。| *Economics is my favorite subject* (NOT 不用 *are my favorite subject*). 经济学是我最喜欢的学科。

The adjective **economical** relates to the word **economy** (sense 2 [U]) meaning the careful use of money, a supply of something, effort etc that avoids any waste. economical 是 economy (名词释义 2) 的形容词, 意为"省钱的、节约的": *My new car is quite economical* (=cheap to run). 我的新车很省油。| *She was brought up to be economical with the housekeeping money* (=spend it carefully). 她从小就养成了节俭持家的习惯。

Something that is **economical** is not necessarily cheap. For example it may be more economical to buy a packet of soap powder that is twice the usual size, because even though it costs more than the small packet, it does not cost twice the amount. However, sometimes people who sell things call **cheap** things **economical** simply because this word sounds better. 经济 (economical) 的东西并不一定便宜 (cheap)。例如, 买双量包装的洗衣粉会较经济, 因为虽然它的价格比标准包装的高, 却低于两袋标准包装的价格之和。但是销售商有时会把 cheap 的商品说成是 economical, 只是因为后者好听些。

The adverb of both **economic** and **economical** is **economically**. economic 和 economical 两个词的副词形式都是 economically: *The country is not economically stable.* 这个国家的经济不稳定。| *You can live here quite economically.* 你可以很经济地生活在这儿。

ec·o·nom·i·cal /ˌikəˋnɑmɪkl̩; ˌekəˈnɒmɪkəl/ *adj* using money, time, goods etc carefully and without wasting any 经济的, 节约的: *an economical method of heating* 一种经济的供暖方法

ec·o·nom·i·cally /ˌikəˋnɑmɪklɪ; ˌekəˈnɒmɪkli/ *adv* **1** in a way that is related to systems of money, trade, or business 在经济上: *In economically advanced countries, childbearing typically begins later in life.* 在经济发达国家, 人们一般很晚才要孩子。[sentence adverb 句子副词] *Economically and politically, they've been disenfranchised.* 他们被剥夺了经济和政治上的权利。**2** in a way that uses money, goods, time etc without wasting any 经济地, 节约地: *We'll just have to shop as economically as we can from now on.* 从现在开始, 我们买东西要尽可能节省。

Economic and Mon·e·ta·ry U·nion /ˌ······ˌ·······/ —see 见 EMU

ec·o·nom·ics /ˌikəˋnɑmɪks; ˌekəˈnɒmɪks/ *n* **1** [U] the study of the way in which money and goods are produced and used 经济学 **2** [plural] the way in which money influences whether a plan, business etc will work effectively 经济情况, 经济因素; 经济意义: *The economics of the scheme will have to be looked at very carefully.* 这项计划的经济因素须认真考虑。—see also 另见 HOME ECONOMICS W3

e·con·o·mist /ɪˋkɑnəmɪst; ɪˈkɒnəmɪst/ *n* [C] someone who studies the way in which money and goods are produced and used and the systems of business and trade 经济学家

Economist, The *trademark* a British weekly magazine which reports business news and has articles about the economic situation in the UK and other countries, about large companies etc【商标】《经济学人》〔英国一周刊, 主要报导商业新闻, 刊登有关英国和其他国家的经济形势、大型公司等内容的文章〕

e·con·o·mize also 又作 **-ise** *BrE*【英】/ɪˋkɑnəˌmaɪz; ɪˈkɒnəmaɪz/ *v* [I] to reduce the amount of money, time, goods etc that you use 削减; 节省: **[+on]** *We can't economize on the central heating because the baby needs a warm house.* 我们不能减少中央供暖, 因为婴儿需要一个暖和的家。

e·con·o·my[1] /ɪˋkɑnəmɪ; ɪˈkɒnəmi/ *n* **1** [C] the system by which a country's money and goods are produced and used, or a country considered in this way 经济；经济情况；经济制度：*a capitalist economy* 资本主义经济 | *the burgeoning economies of the Pacific rim* 太平洋周边迅速发展的经济体 **2** [U] the careful use of money, time, goods etc so that nothing is wasted 节约；节俭：*For the sake of economy, I hadn't yet turned on the heating.* 为了省钱，我还未打开供暖系统。| **economy drive** (=a period of time during which you try to spend less money than usual) 节约运动；节省开支的一段日子 **3** [C] something that you do in order to spend less money 节约措施，省钱办法：*One economy would be to take sandwiches instead.* 一种省钱的办法就是改吃三明治。| **make economies** *We're trying to make a few economies this month.* 这个月我们尽力节省一点。| **false economy** (=something that seems cheaper but costs more in the end) 虚假节约〔看上去省钱，实际上费钱〕*Buying cheap tyres is a false economy – they wear out much more quickly.* 买便宜的轮胎表面上省钱，实际上并不划算 —— 因为它们磨损快得多。**4 economies of scale** *technical* the financial advantages of producing something in very large quantities【术语】规模经济 —see also 另见 BLACK ECONOMY, MARKET ECONOMY, MIXED ECONOMY

economy[2] *adj* [only before noun 仅用于名词前] **economy size/pack** a product that is cheaper, usually because you are buying a larger amount〔产品的〕经济装〔一般指比标准包装量大而便宜的包装〕

economy class /ˈ···, ·ˈ/ *n* [U] the cheapest type of seats in a plane〔飞机的〕经济舱 —**economy class** *adv*: *We flew economy class.* 我们乘坐的是经济舱。

e·co·sys·tem /ˈikoˌsɪstəm; ˈiːkəʊˌsɪstɪm/ *n* [C] all the animals and plants in a particular area, and the way in which they are related to each other and to their environment 生态系统

ec·sta·sy /ˈɛkstəsɪ; ˈekstəsi/ *n* **1** [C,U] a feeling of extreme happiness 狂喜，欣喜若狂：*His expression was one of pure ecstasy.* 他的表情是一种完完全全的欣喜若狂。| **in ecstasy/ecstasies** (=feeling extremely happy) 处于狂喜之中 | **go into ecstasies** (=become very happy and excited) 变得欣喜若狂 **2** [U] a state in which you cannot see or hear what is happening around you, because you are having a powerful religious experience 出神〔指一种宗教体验〕**3 Ecstacy** [U] an illegal drug used especially by young people to give a feeling of happiness and energy at parties "狂喜"迷幻药

ec·stat·ic /ɪkˈstætɪk; ɪkˈstætɪk/ *adj* **1** feeling extremely happy and excited 狂喜的，欣喜若狂的：*an ecstatic welcome from the thousands who lined the streets* 数千人狂热的夹道欢迎 **2** in a state in which you are having a powerful religious experience〔指处于一种宗教体验时〕出神的 —**ecstatically** /-klɪ; -kli/ *adv*

ECT /ˌi si ˈti; ˌiː siː ˈtiː/ *n* [U] electro-convulsive therapy; another word for ELECTRIC SHOCK THERAPY 电击疗法

-ectomy /ɛktəmɪ; ektəmi/ *suffix* [in nouns 构成名词] *technical* the removing of a particular part of someone's body by an operation【术语】切除术，摘除术：*an appendectomy* (=removing the APPENDIX) 阑尾切除手术

ECU /eˋku; ˈekjuː/ *n* [C] European Currency Unit; the official unit of money of the former EC〔旧时欧洲共同体的〕欧洲通货单位

Ec·ua·dor /ˈɛkwəˌdɔr; ˈekwədɔː/ a country in northern South America, between Peru and Colombia, and next to the Pacific Ocean. Population: 13,184,000 (2001). Capital: Quito. 厄瓜多尔〔南美洲北部一国，位于秘鲁和哥伦比亚之间，濒临太平洋。人口：13,184,000（2001），首都：基多〕—**Ecuadorian** /ˌɛkwəˈdorɪən; ˌekwəˈdɔːriən◂/ *n, adj*

e·cu·men·i·cal /ˌɛkjʊˈmɛnɪkl; ˌiːkjʊˈmenɪkəl◂/ *adj* supporting the idea of uniting the different branches of the Christian religion 支持基督教（不同教派）大联合的 —**ecumenically** /-klɪ; -kli/ *adv*

ec·ze·ma /ˈɛksɪmə; ˈeksɪmə/ *n* [U] a condition in which your skin becomes dry, red, and swollen 湿疹

ed 1 an abbreviation for 缩写= EDITOR **2** an abbreviation for 缩写= EDITION

-ed /d, ɪd, t; d, ɪd, t/ *suffix* **1** forms the regular past tense and past participle of verbs. The past participle form is often used as an adjective〔构成规则动词的过去式和过去分词，其中过去分词常被用作形容词〕：*I want, I wanted, I have wanted* 我想 | *I show, I showed, I have shown* 我出示 | *He walked away.* 他走开了。| *a sound that echoed through the room* 在房中回荡过的声音 | *a wanted criminal* 通缉犯 **2** [in adjectives 构成形容词] having a particular thing 有某种特征的：*a bearded man* (=a man with a beard) 留着胡子的男人 | *a kind-hearted woman* 好心的妇女

E·dam /ˈidəm; ˈiːdəm/ *n* [U] a type of yellow cheese from the Netherlands 埃丹干酪〔荷兰球形奶酪，Edam是荷兰一村名〕

ed·dy[1] /ˈɛdɪ; ˈedi/ *n* [C] a circular movement of water, wind, dust etc〔水、风、尘土等的〕旋涡：*The racing river caused swirling eddies.* 湍急的河水形成了许多旋涡。

eddy[2] *v* [I] if water, wind, dust etc eddies, it moves around with a circular movement〔水、风、尘土等〕起旋涡：*The mist eddied round the old house.* 雾旋绕在旧房子周围。

Eddy, Mary Baker (1821-1910) a US religious leader, who started a new form of Christianity called Christian Science in 1866 艾娣〔（1821-1910），美国宗教领袖，1866年创立了一个新的基督教组织，名为基督教科学派〕

E·den /ˈidn; ˈiːdn/ also 又作 **the Garden of Eden** *n* [singular] in the Bible story, the garden where Adam and Eve, the first humans lived, often seen as a place of happiness and INNOCENCE 伊甸园〔《圣经》故事中人类始祖亚当和夏娃最初居住的园子，常被认为是乐土和纯洁清净的地方〕

Eden, Sir Anthony (1897-1977) a British politician in the Conservative Party, who was Prime Minister from 1955 to 1957. He gave up this position after the Suez Crisis, when British military forces failed in an attempt to get back control of the Suez Canal from Egypt. 艾登〔（1897-1977），英国保守党政治家，1955至1957年间任英国首相。苏伊士运河危机期间，英军未能从埃及人手中夺回苏伊士运河的控制权。之后，他辞去首相职务〕

edge 边缘

on the edge of a cliff 在悬崖边缘

at the water's edge 在水边

edge[1] /ɛdʒ; edʒ/ *n* [C] **1** the part of an object that is furthest from its centre 边缘：*Just leave it on the edge of your plate.* 把它放在你盘子边上就行了。| *Suli stood at the water's edge.* 苏利站在水边上。**2** the thin sharp part of a blade or tool that cuts 刀口；刃：*Careful – that knife has a very sharp edge!* 小心点，那把刀很锋利！**3 have the edge on/over** to be slightly better than someone or something, because you have an advantage that they do not have 稍微胜过…：*Marcia has the edge over the other students, having spent a year in England.* 马西娅在英格兰待过一年，所以比其他学生稍好一些。**4 be on edge** to be nervous, especially because you are expecting something unpleasant to happen 惴惴不安；烦躁：*I've been on edge ever since I got her letter.* 收到她的信以后我就惴惴不安。**5 be on the edge** *informal* to be behaving in a way that makes it seem as if you are going crazy【非正式】举止疯癫；行为几近疯狂 **6 take the edge off** to make something less bad, good, strong etc 削弱；减轻：*Try this. It should take the edge off the pain.* 试试这个，它会缓解疼痛。—see also 另见 **be (at) the cutting edge of** (CUTTING[2] (3))

edge[2] *v* **1** [I always+adv/prep, T always+adv/prep] to move gradually with several small movements, or to make something do this（使）徐徐移动：*The car edged forwards at walking pace.* 汽车以行人步行的速度徐徐移动。| **edge sth in/across/towards etc** *Hetty edged her chair closer to mine.* 赫蒂把椅子向我挪近一些。| **edge your way in/through/towards etc** (=move somewhere carefully with small movements) 缓慢而小心地进入/穿过/移向等 *Slowly, we edge our way towards the front of the crowd.* 我们慢慢地向人群前面移动。—see picture on page A24 参见A24页图 **2** [T] to put something on the edge or border of

something 加边于; 在…的边上镶: **edge sth with** *The sleeves were edged with lace.* 袖子上镶了网眼花边。**3** [I always+adv/prep, T always+adv/prep] to develop gradually, or to make something do this (使)缓慢发展: **edge (sth) in/up/towards** *Prices have been static for months, but are now beginning to edge up.* 物价稳定了几个月, 但现在开始慢慢上涨了。**4** [T] to cut the edges of an area of grass so that they are tidy and straight 修剪〔草地边缘〕

edge·ways /ˈɛdʒˌwez; ˈedʒweɪz/ also 又作 **edge·wise** /-ˌwaɪz; -waɪz/ *adv* sideways 侧着; 斜着 —see also 另见 **get a word in edgeways** (WORD[1] (31))

edg·ing /ˈɛdʒɪŋ; ˈedʒɪŋ/ *n* [C,U] something that forms an edge or border 边缘; 饰边: *a white handkerchief with blue edging* 镶蓝边的白手帕

edg·y /ˈɛdʒɪ; ˈedʒi/ *adj* nervous and worried 紧张不安的: *She's been edgy lately, waiting for the test results.* 她最近一直心绪不宁, 在等测验结果。

ed·i·ble /ˈɛdəbl̩; ˈedɪbəl/ *adj* something that is edible can be eaten 可以食用的: *These berries are edible, but those are poisonous.* 这些浆果可以吃, 但那些有毒。

e·dict /ˈidɪkt; ˈiːdɪkt/ *n* [C] *formal*【正式】**1** an official public order made by someone in a position of power 法令, 敕令: *The emperor issued an edict forbidding anyone to leave the city.* 皇帝下令禁止任何人出城。**2** *especially humorous* any order or command【尤幽默】命令

ed·i·fice /ˈɛdəfɪs; ˈedɪfɪs/ *n* [C] *formal* a building, especially a large one【正式】建筑〔尤指宏伟的建筑〕: *Their head office was an imposing edifice in Millbank.* 他们的总部大楼是位于米尔班克的一幢宏伟建筑。

ed·i·fy /ˈɛdəˌfaɪ; ˈedɪfaɪ/ *v* [T] *formal* to improve someone's mind or character by teaching them something【正式】教诲, 教导 —**edification** /ˌɛdəfəˈkeʃən; ˌedɪfɪˈkeɪʃən/ *n* [U]: *For our edification, the preacher reminded us what 'duty' meant.* 教士教导我们, 提醒我们"责任"的意义。

ed·i·fy·ing /ˈɛdəˌfaɪɪŋ; ˈedɪfaɪ-ɪŋ/ *adj formal or humorous* an edifying speech, book etc improves your mind or moral character by teaching you something【正式或幽默】教诲的; 启迪的; 陶冶情操的: *No one would claim that the film is morally edifying.* 没有人会认为那部电影有教育意义。

Ed·in·burgh /ˈɛdɪnbɜə; ˈedɪnbərə/ the capital of Scotland, in the east of the country on the River Forth. Edinburgh is a centre for business, industry, education, and the law, and the new Scottish parliament is there. It is an important CULTURAL centre, with many theatres, concert halls, and MUSEUMS. Because of this, it is sometimes called **the Athens of the North**. 爱丁堡〔苏格兰首府, 位于苏格兰东部福斯河畔, 是商业、工业、教育和司法中心, 也是新苏格兰议会所在地。该市还是一个重要文化中心, 建有许多剧院、音乐厅和博物馆。因此, 时有"北方雅典"之称〕

Edinburgh, Duke of —see 见 DUKE OF EDINBURGH

Edinburgh Fes·tiv·al, the /ˌ···ˈ···/ also 又作 **Edinburgh International Festival of Music and Drama** /ˌ···· ˌ····ˌ···ˌ··ˈ··/ an event that takes place in Edinburgh, Scotland, every year for three weeks in the summer, when there are many performances of plays and music, and other forms of entertainment. Some of these performances are given by famous people or groups, but there are also many others which are given by less well-known people, including university students, and these events are known as the **Edinburgh Fringe**. 爱丁堡艺术节, 爱丁堡国际音乐戏剧节〔每年夏季在苏格兰爱丁堡举行的为期三周的艺术节, 有大量的戏剧和音乐等娱乐活动。有些节目的表演者和表演团体享有盛名。参加演出的也有许多名气不大的人, 如在校大学生, 其演出活动被称为"爱丁堡边缘艺术节"〕

Ed·i·son /ˈɛdɪsn; ˈedɪsən/, **Thom·as Al·va** /ˈtɑməs ˈælvə; ˈtɒməs ˈælvə/ (1847-1931) a US inventor who made over 1300 electrical inventions, including the MICROPHONE, the record player, and equipment for the cinema. He is most famous for inventing the LIGHT BULB (=a glass container with a thin wire inside, which produces light by using electricity). 爱迪生〔(1847-1931), 美国发明家。他发明了1300多种电器, 包括麦克风、留声机和电影放映设备, 以发明电灯泡最为有名〕

ed·it /ˈɛdɪt; ˈedɪt/ *v* **1** [I,T] to prepare a book, piece of film etc for printing or broadcasting by deciding what to include, and making sure there are no mistakes 编辑; 剪辑: *hours and hours spent editing text* 花在编辑文本上的大量时间 **2** [T] to work as the editor of a newspaper, magazine etc 任〔报纸、杂志等〕的编辑: *She used to edit the Washington Post.* 她曾主编过《华盛顿邮报》。—**edit** *n* [C]

edit sth ↔ **out** *phr v* [T] to remove something when you are preparing a book, piece of film etc for printing or broadcasting 〔在编辑、剪辑等过程中〕删除, 去掉: *All the swear words were edited out before the film was broadcast.* 在电影播映之前所有的脏话都被去掉了。

e·di·tion /ɪˈdɪʃən; ɪˈdɪʃən/ *n* [C] the copies of a book, newspaper etc that are produced and printed at the same time〔书、报等的〕版次; 版本: *Is there a paperback edition?* 有平装本吗? | **first edition** (=the first copies of a particular book, that are often valuable) 初版 W3

ed·i·tor /ˈɛdɪtə; ˈedɪtə/ *n* [C] **1** the person who decides what should be included in a newspaper, magazine etc〔报纸、杂志等的〕主编: *the editor of the Daily Telegraph*《每日电讯报》的主编 **2** someone who prepares a book, film etc for printing or broadcasting by deciding what to include and checking for any mistakes 编辑, 剪辑者: *a TV script editor* 电视剧本编辑 —**editorial** /ˌɛdəˈtorɪəl; ˌedɪˈtɔːriəl◂/ *adj*: *Not screening the program was an editorial decision.* 不播映这个节目是编辑的决定。 W2

ed·i·to·ri·al /ˌɛdəˈtorɪəl; ˌedɪˈtɔːriəl◂/ *n* [C] a piece of writing in a newspaper that gives the editor's opinion about something, rather than reporting facts〔报纸的〕社论, 社评

ed·i·tor·ship /ˈɛdɪtəˌʃɪp; ˈedɪtəʃɪp/ *n* [U] the position of being the editor of a newspaper or magazine〔报纸、杂志的〕编辑职位

Ed·mon·ton /ˈɛdməntən; ˈedməntən/ the capital city of Alberta, western Canada, on the North Saskatchewan River 埃德蒙顿〔加拿大西部艾伯塔省省会, 位于北萨斯喀彻温河畔〕

ed·u·cate /ˈɛdʒəˌket; ˈedjʊkeɪt/ *v* [T] to teach or train someone, especially at a school, college, or university〔尤指学校〕教育; 训练: *How can our children be educated if schools are not properly funded?* 如果学校没有足够的经费, 我们的孩子怎么能得到好的教育呢? | **educate sb about/on** *a campaign to educate teenagers about the dangers of smoking* 教育青少年认识吸烟危害的运动 —see 见 TEACH (USAGE)

ed·u·cat·ed /ˈɛdʒəˌketɪd; ˈedjʊkeɪtɪd/ *adj* **1** intelligent because you have been taught or trained somewhere 受过教育的; 受过训练的: *an educated and sensitive woman* 有教养、感觉敏锐的女人 | **Harvard-educated/Oxford-educated etc** *a Harvard-educated lawyer* 在哈佛大学受过教育[毕业]的律师 **2** having a high standard of judgement about art, literature etc〔在艺术、文学等方面〕很有修养的: *She has very educated tastes.* 她很有修养。**3** **educated guess** a guess that is likely to be correct because you have enough information 有根据的猜测

ed·u·ca·tion /ˌɛdʒəˈkeʃən; ˌedjʊˈkeɪʃən/ *n* **1** [singular, U] the process by which your mind develops through learning at a school, college, or university 教育; 培养: *They had worked hard to give their son a good education.* 他们勤奋工作以便儿子能受到良好的教育。| *adult education classes* 成人教育课程 **2** [singular, U] the knowledge and skills that you gain from being taught〔通过接受教育而获得的〕知识; 技能: *a college education* 大学教育 **3** the general area of work or study connected with teaching 教育体系; 教育学: *a lecturer in higher education* 高等教育讲师 —see also 另见 FURTHER EDUCATION, HIGHER EDUCATION S1 W1

ed·u·ca·tion·al /ˌɛdʒəˈkeʃənl; ˌedjʊˈkeɪʃənəl◂/ *adj* **1** connected with education 教育的; 与教育有关的: *a fall in educational standards* 教育水平下降 **2** teaching you something you did not know before 有教育意义的: *Work experience is an important educational experience for young people.* 工作经历对于年轻人有重要的教育意义。 S2 W2

ed·u·ca·tion·al·ist /ˌɛdʒəˈkeʃənl̩ɪst; ˌedjʊˈkeɪʃənəlɪst/ also 又作 **ed·u·ca·tion·ist** /-ʃənɪst; -ʃənɪst/ *n* [C] *formal* someone who knows a lot about methods of education【正式】教育家; 教育学家

ed·u·ca·tor /ˈɛdʒəˌketə; ˈedjʊkeɪtə/ *n* [C] *formal especially AmE* a teacher【正式, 尤美】教师, 教育工作者

ed·u·tain·ment /ˌɛdʒəˈtenmənt; ˌedjʊˈteɪnmənt/ *n* [U] films, television programmes, or computer SOFTWARE that educate and entertain at the same time 寓教于乐的影片[电视节目, 电脑软件]

Ed·ward /ˈɛdwəd; ˈedwəd/, **Prince** (1964-) the youngest son of the British queen Elizabeth II. He married Sophie Rhys-Jones in 1999 and became the Earl of Wessex. 爱德华王子〔(1964-), 英国女王伊丽莎白二世的最小儿子。1999年他与索菲·里斯一琼斯结婚, 并成为韦塞克斯伯爵〕

Edward I /ˌɛdwəd ðə ˈfɜst; ˌedwəd ðə ˈfɜːst/, **King** (1239-1307) the king of England from 1272 until his death. He took part in the Crusades, and later established English control over Wales. He tried to do the same in Scotland, but was unsuccessful. 爱德华一世〔(1239-1307), 英格兰国王, 1272年起即位直至去世。他参加过十字军东征, 之后征服了威尔士。他也试图征服苏格兰, 但未能成功〕

Edward II /ˌɛdwɚd ðə ˋsɛkənd; ˌedwəd ðə ˈsekənd/, **King** (1284-1327) the king of England from 1307 until he was murdered by his enemies (including his wife) in 1327 爱德华二世〔(1284-1327)，英格兰国王。1307年即位，1327年被仇敌（包括王后）杀害〕

Edward III /ˌɛdwɚd ðə ˋθɝd; ˌedwəd ðə ˈθɜːd/, **King** (1312-77) a king of England who ruled during the Black Death and the start of the Hundred Years War 爱德华三世〔(1312-1377)，英格兰国王。在位期间，英格兰爆发了黑死病和百年战争〕

Edward IV /ˌɛdwɚd ðə ˋfɔrθ; ˌedwəd ðə ˈfɔːθ/, **King** (1442-83) the king of England from 1461 to 1483 爱德华四世〔(1442-1483)，英格兰国王，1461至1483年间在位〕

Edward V /ˌɛdwɚd ðə ˋfɪfθ; ˌedwəd ðə ˈfɪfθ/, **King** (1470-83) the king of England for a few months in 1483, until his uncle removed him from his position and became King Richard III. Edward and his brother (who are sometimes called 'the Princes in the Tower') were put in prison in the Tower of London, and many people believe that they were later murdered there. 爱德华五世〔(1470-1483)，英格兰国王。1483年即位仅几个月，就被叔父废黜。其叔父自立为王，成为理查三世。爱德华和他的弟弟被囚禁在伦敦塔内（有时也称"塔中王子"）。不少人认为，伦敦塔是他们遇害的地方〕

Edward VI /ˌɛdwɚd ðə ˋsɪksθ; ˌedwəd ðə ˈsɪksθ/, **King** (1537-53) the king of England from 1547 to 1553 爱德华六世〔(1537-1553)，英格兰国王，1547至1553年间在位〕

Edward VII /ˌɛdwɚd ðə ˋsɛvənθ; ˌedwəd ðə ˈsevənθ/, **King** (1841-1910) the British king from 1901 until his death 爱德华七世〔(1841-1910)，英国国王，1901年即位，直至去世〕

Edward VIII /ˌɛdwɚd ðɪ ˋetθ; ˌedwəd ði ˈeɪtθ/, **King** (1894-1972) the British king in 1936. He was forced to ABDICATE (=give up being king) because he wanted to marry Wallis Simpson, an American woman who had been married before. This event is known as 'the Abdication'. After he abdicated, he was given the title 'Duke of Windsor', and he and his wife lived abroad for the rest of their lives. 爱德华八世〔(1894-1972)，英国国王，1936年即位。他曾有意与一名有过婚史的美国女子沃利斯·辛普森结婚而被迫退位。这一事件史称"逊位"。他退位后被封为温莎公爵，与妻子在国外一起度过余生〕

Ed·ward·i·an /ɛdˋwɔrdɪən; edˈwɔːdiən/ *adj* connected with or coming from the time of King Edward VII of Britain (1901-1910) 英王爱德华七世(1901–1910)的; 英王爱德华七世时代的: *Edwardian furniture* 英王爱德华七世时代的家具

Ed·wards /ˋɛdwɚdz; ˈedwədz/, **Jon·a·than** /ˋdʒɑnəθən; ˈdʒɒnəθən/ (1703-58) a US Christian THEOLOGIAN and religious leader, who succeeded in persuading large numbers of people to become Christians 爱德华兹〔(1703-1758)，美国基督教神学家、宗教领袖。他曾说服大批民众信奉基督教〕

-ee /i; iː/ *suffix* [in nouns 构成名词] **1** someone who is being treated in a particular way 受动者: *the payee* (=someone who is paid) 受款人，收款人 | *a trainee* 受训者 | *an employee* 雇员 **2** someone who is in a particular state or who is doing something 处于某种情况下的人; 行动者: *an absentee* (=someone who is absent) 缺席者 | *an escapee* 逃亡者

EEC /ˌi i ˋsi; ˌiː iː ˈsiː/ *n* [singular] the European Economic Community; the former name for the EC 欧洲经济共同体〔欧洲共同体的前称〕

EEG /ˌi i ˋdʒi; ˌiː iː ˈdʒiː/ *n* **1** electroencephalograph; a piece of equipment that records the electrical activity of your brain 脑电图仪 **2** electroencephalogram; a drawing made by an electroencephalograph 脑电图

eek /ik; iːk/ *interjection* an expression of sudden fear and surprise 唷，呀〔表示突然的惊吓〕: *Eek! A mouse!* 呀！一只老鼠！

eel /il; iːl/ *n* [C] a long thin fish that looks like a snake and can be eaten 鳗; 鳝: *He wriggled like an eel to get free.* 他像鳗鱼似地扭动身体试图挣脱。

e'en /in; iːn/ *adv poetic* 【诗】the short form of 缩略式= EVEN[1]

Ee·ny, mee·ny, mi·ney, mo /ˌinɪ ˌminɪ ˌmaɪnɪ ˋmo; ˌiːni ˌmiːni ˌmaɪni ˈməʊ/ the first words of a short poem that children say as a way of choosing something when they have two or more possibilities, but do not know which one to choose. Each time they say a word they point to the next possible thing. 一、二、三、四〔一首短诗的首句。小孩子面对多种选择一时没有主意时往往会念叨这些字词。他们每念一个词，手指就会指向下一个备选之物〕

EEO Equal Employment Opportunity; a principle that some businesses follow, stating that any qualified person will be considered for a job and that a person's race, sex, or religion cannot be a reason for not getting the job 均等就业机会〔某些行业遵循的一个原则，亦即符合条件的任何人应有均等的工作机会，而且不应由于种族、性别或宗教原因而被拒聘〕

EEOC /ˌi i o ˋsi; ˌiː iː əʊ ˈsiː/ the abbreviation of 缩写= the EQUAL EMPLOYMENT OPPORTUNITIES COMMISSION

e'er /ɛr; eə/ *adv poetic* 【诗】the short form of 缩略式= EVER

-eer /ɪr; ɪə/ *suffix* [in nouns 构成名词] someone who does or makes a particular thing, often something bad 从事[做出]某事〔常为坏事〕的人: *an auctioneer* (=someone who runs AUCTION sales) 拍卖商 | *a profiteer* (=someone who makes unfair profits) 牟取暴利的商人

ee·rie /ˋɪrɪ; ˈɪəri/ *adj* strange and frightening 怪异而令人恐惧的: *the eerie sound of an owl hooting in the forest at night* 夜间森林里猫头鹰那怪异恐怖的叫声

Ee·yore /ˋior; ˈiːɔː/ a character in the Winnie the Pooh stories by A. A. Milne. He is a DONKEY (=an animal like a small horse with long ears) who usually feels sorry for himself.依唷，依儿〔米尔恩《小熊温尼普》中的一个角色。它是一头驴，常常自哀自怜〕

eff /ɛf; ef/ *v* [I] *BrE* 【英】**1 effing and blinding** *slang* swearing 【俚】诅咒: *You should have heard him effing and blinding when he hit his thumb with the hammer.* 你真该听听锤子砸到拇指时他的叫骂声。**2 eff off!** *taboo* used to tell someone to go away instead of saying **fuck off** (FUCK[1] (1))【讳】滚蛋！—see also 另见 EFFING

ef·face /ɪˋfes; ɪˈfeɪs/ *v* [T] *formal* 【正式】**1** to prevent you from remembering an unpleasant experience 使忘记〔不愉快的经历〕: *Nothing could efface the indignity of being publicly criticized.* 没有什么能让人忘记当众挨批评的耻辱。**2** to remove a mark or sign, especially by rubbing it 抹去，擦除 **3 efface yourself** to behave in a way that does not make people notice you or look at you（使）不引人注目; 不露锋芒 —see also 另见 SELF-EFFACING

ef·fect[1] /əˋfɛkt; ɪˈfekt/ *n*

1 ▶CHANGE/RESULT 改变/结果◀ [C,U] the way in which an event, action, or person changes someone or something 效应; 作用; 结果: **[+of]** *the harmful effects of smoking* 吸烟的坏处 | **have an effect on** *Inflation is having a disastrous effect on the economy.* 通货膨胀给经济带来灾难性的影响。| **have/achieve the desired effect** (=produce the result you wanted) 取得所期望的成果 *The plan failed to achieve the desired effect of diverting traffic from the city.* 该计划未能如期望的那样分流城里的车辆。| **cause and effect** (=something that happens, and the other things that happen as a result of this) 因果 —see 见 AFFECT (USAGE)

2 put/bring sth into effect to make a plan or idea happen 实施计划; 落实想法: *It won't be easy to put the changes into effect.* 把这些变化落到实处不会很容易。

3 come into effect/take effect if a new law, rule, or system comes into effect, it officially starts〔法律、规则或系统〕生效: *The new tax rates come into effect from April.* 新的税率从4月起生效。

4 take effect to start to produce results 开始起作用; 开始产生效果: *The morphine was starting to take effect and the pain eased.* 吗啡开始起作用，疼痛减轻了。

5 in effect used when you are describing what the real situation is, especially when it is different from the way that it seems to be 实际上; 事实上: *In effect, our wages will fall by 2%.* 实际上，我们的工资将下降2%。

6 to good/little effect if you do something to good effect, it is successful and does what you want it to 产生好/差的效果: *Pat rubbed the stain frantically with a cloth, but to little effect.* 帕特发疯似地用布擦污迹，却收效甚微。

7 to this/that effect used when you are giving the general meaning of what someone says, rather than the exact words 有这样/那样的意思[内容]: *I thought he was wrong and said something to that effect at dinner.* 我认为他错了，吃晚饭时我大概表达了这个意思。| **words to that effect** *Jim said he was unhappy at work, or words to that effect.* 吉姆说了些工作不顺心之类的话。| **to the effect that** *Karl's memo was to the effect that we all needed to think more about marketing possibilities.* 卡尔的便笺大意是说，我们都需要多考虑营销机会。

8 with immediate effect/with effect from starting to happen immediately, or from a particular date 立即生效/自…起开始实行: *Hoskins is appointed manager, with immediate effect.* 霍斯金斯被任命为经理，立即上任。

9 ▶IDEA/FEELING 想法/感受◀ [C usually singular 一般用单数] an idea or feeling that an artist, speaker, book etc tries to make you think of or feel〔艺术家、演讲者或书等给人的〕感受，印象: *Turner's paintings give an effect of light.* 特纳的画表现出光的效果。| **do sth for effect** (=do something deliberately to shock or surprise people) 哗众取宠

10 ▶PERSONAL THINGS 私人物品◀ **effects** [plural] *formal* the things that someone owns; BELONGINGS【正式】私人物品; 个人财产: *Don's few personal effects were in a suitcase under the bed.* 唐的几件个人物品在床下的箱子里。
11 ▶FILM 电影◀ **effects** [plural] unusual or impressive sounds or images that are artificially produced for a film, play, or radio programme 效果 —see also 另见 SOUND EFFECTS, SPECIAL EFFECT

effect[2] *v* [T] *formal* to make something happen【正式】引起; 使发生: *efforts to effect a reconciliation between the warring factions* 使交战各派达成和解的努力

ef·fec·tive /ə`fɛktɪv; ɪ'fektɪv/ *adj* **1** producing the result that was wanted or intended 产生预期效果的; 有效的: *The ads were simple, but remarkably effective.* 这些广告很简单, 但效果出奇的好。**2** impressive or interesting enough to be noticed 引人注意的; 醒目的: *an effective use of colour* 使用引人注目的颜色 **3** [no comparative 无比较级] if a law, agreement, or system becomes effective, it officially starts〔法律、协议或制度等〕生效的: *The cut in interest rates is effective from Monday.* 从星期一起利率下调正式生效。**4** [no comparative 无比较级] real rather than what is officially intended or generally believed 实际的, 事实上的: *The rebels are in effective control of the city.* 反叛者实际上已控制了城市。—**effectiveness** *n* [U]

ef·fec·tive·ly /ə`fɛktɪvlɪ; ɪ'fektɪvli/ *adv* **1** in a way that produces the result that was intended 有效地: *Children have to learn to communicate effectively.* 小孩子应该学会有效地交流。**2** [sentence adverb 句子副词] used to describe what the real situation is, especially when it is different from the way that it seems to be 实际上, 事实上: *Effectively, it has become impossible for us to help.* 事实上, 我们已不可能帮上忙了。

ef·fec·tu·al /ə`fɛktʃuəl; ɪ'fektʃuəl/ *adj formal* producing the result that was wanted or intended; EFFECTIVE (1)【正式】有效的, 奏效的 —opposite 反义词 INEFFECTUAL —**effectually** *adv*

ef·fec·tu·ate /ə`fɛktʃu͵et; ɪ'fektʃueɪt/ *v* [T] *formal* to make something happen【正式】引起; 使发生

ef·fem·i·nate /ə`fɛmənɪt; ɪ'femɨnət/ *adj* a man who is effeminate looks or behaves like a woman〔男人〕女人气的, 女性化的: *very young and handsome in an effeminate way* 非常年轻英俊又带阴柔气质 —**effeminacy** *n* [U] —**effeminately** *adv*

ef·fer·vesce /͵ɛfə`vɛs; ͵efə'ves/ *v* [I] *technical* a liquid that effervesces produces small bubbles (BUBBLE[1] (1)) of gas【术语】〔液体〕冒气泡, 起沫

ef·fer·vesc·ent /͵ɛfə`vɛsn̩t; ͵efə'vesənt◂/ *adj* **1** someone who is effervescent is very cheerful and active 兴高采烈的; 充满活力的, 活泼的: *an effervescent personality* 活泼乐观的个性 **2** a liquid that is effervescent produces small bubbles (BUBBLE[1] (1)) of gas〔液体〕冒泡的, 起沫的 —**effervescence** *n* [U]

ef·fete /ɛ`fit; ɪ'fi:t/ *adj formal*【正式】**1** weak and powerless in a way that you dislike 软弱的, 懦弱的: *an attack against effete intellectuals* 对软弱的知识分子的攻击 **2** looking or behaving like a woman 女人气的, 女性化的: *an effete, languid young man* 充满女人气又慵懒的年轻男子 —**effetely** *adv*

ef·fi·ca·cious /͵ɛfə`keʃəs; ͵efɨ'keɪʃəs◂/ *adj formal* producing the result that was intended, especially when dealing with an illness or a problem【正式】〔尤指在治病或处理问题方面〕有效的: *an equally efficacious method of treatment* 同样有效的治疗方法 —**efficaciously** *adv*

ef·fi·ca·cy /`ɛfəkəsɪ; 'efɨkəsi/ *n* [U] *formal* the quality of being able to produce the result that was intended【正式】有效性; 功效

ef·fi·cien·cy /ə`fɪʃənsɪ; ɪ'fɪʃənsi/ *n* [U] the quality of doing something well and effectively, without wasting time, money, or energy 效率; 效能: *The improvements in efficiency have been staggering.* 效率大大提高, 使人震惊。

ef·fi·cient /ə`fɪʃənt; ɪ'fɪʃənt/ *adj* a person, machine, or organization that is efficient works well and effectively without wasting time, money, or energy 有效率的; 高效能的: *an efficient heating system* 高效能的供暖系统 | *a very efficient secretary* 高效率的秘书 —**efficiently** *adv*

ef·fi·gy /`ɛfədʒɪ; 'efɨdʒi/ *n* [C] **1** a figure made of wood, paper, stone etc, that looks like a person, especially one that makes the person look ugly or funny〔尤指丑化本人的木[纸, 石等]质〕雕像; 肖像; 模拟像: [+of] *an effigy of the prime minister* 首相的模拟像 **2 burn/hang sb in effigy** to burn or hang a figure of someone at a political DEMONSTRATION (1) because you hate them〔在政治示威中〕焚烧某人的模拟像; 对某人的模拟像处以绞刑

ef·fing /`ɛfɪŋ; 'efɪŋ/ *adj* [only before noun 仅用于名词前] *BrE spoken* a rude word used to emphasize that you are angry【英口】该死的〔表达说话者的愤怒〕: *She's gone to effing bingo again.* 她又去玩该死的宾戈游戏了。—**effing** *adv* —see also 另见 **effing and blinding** (EFF (1))

ef·flo·res·cence /͵ɛflo`rɛsn̩s; ͵eflə'resəns/ *n* [U] *technical* the action of flowers, art etc forming and developing, or the period of time when this happens【术语】开花(期); 〔艺术等〕发展(期), 全盛期: *His work represents the efflorescence of a dying culture.* 他的作品代表着一种行将消失的文化的发展。

ef·flu·ent /`ɛfluənt; 'efluənt/ *n* [C,U] liquid waste, especially chemicals or SEWAGE 废液; 污水: *The effluent was being discharged straight into the sea.* 废水被直接排放到海里。

ef·flux /`ɛflʌks; 'eflʌks/ *n* [U] *technical* an outward flow of gas or liquid【术语】〔气体或液体的〕流出; 外流

ef·fort /`ɛfət; 'efət/ *n*
1 ▶PHYSICAL/MENTAL ENERGY 体力/精力◀ [U] the physical or mental energy that is needed to do something 力气, 精力: *Lou lifted the box without any apparent effort.* 卢毫不费力地把箱子搬起来。| **take/require effort** *It takes a lot of time and effort to get an exhibition ready.* 准备一次展览要花费很多时间和精力。| **take all the effort out of** (=make something much easier) 使…变得容易多了 | **put a lot of effort into** (=work very hard at something) 投入很多精力 *Frank put a lot of effort into the preparations for the party.* 弗兰克花了很大力气来准备这次聚会。
2 ▶ATTEMPT 努力◀ [C,U] an attempt to do something, especially when this involves a lot of hard work or determination 努力: **effort to do sth** *My efforts to convince Lucy to return failed.* 我试图说服露西回来但未成功。| [+at] *Further efforts at negotiation have broken down.* 为谈判所作的进一步努力已经失败了。| **concerted effort** (=a strong sincere attempt) 全力 *Jack has made a concerted effort to improve his behaviour.* 杰克尽全力改进自己的行为。| **through sb's efforts** (=because of what someone did) 通过某人的努力 *It's only through your efforts that we have managed to raise the money.* 全靠你的努力我们才筹到这笔钱。| **in an effort to do sth** (=in order to achieve something) 为做成某事 *They've been working night and day in an effort to get the bridge ready on time.* 为了使桥能准时完工, 他们一直夜以继日地工作。
3 make an effort (to do sth) to try hard to do something, especially something you do not want to do 尽力(做某事); 勉为其难(做某事): *I know you don't like her, but you could make an effort to be polite.* 我知道你不喜欢她, 但你要尽量礼貌些。| **make every effort** (=use a lot of effort and try different ways) 尽一切努力 *Every effort is being made to deal with the issues you raised at the last meeting.* 正尽一切努力处理你在上次会议上提出的问题。
4 an effort of will/imagination/concentration the determination needed to do something〔做某事所需的〕毅力/想象力/专心: *She dismissed the painful memory with a deliberate effort of will.* 她竭力从痛苦的回忆中挣脱出来。
5 be an effort to be difficult or painful to do 费力, 痛苦: *I was so weak that even standing up was an effort.* 我太虚弱了, 站起来都很费力。| *Would it be too much effort to get it yourself?* 你自己去拿会不会太费劲呢?
6 a good/bad/poor etc effort something that has been done well, badly etc 干得好/不好/差劲等: *Not a bad effort for a beginner!* 对一个新手来说不错了!

ef·fort·less /`ɛfətlɪs; 'efətləs/ *adj* something that is effortless is done in a very skilful way that makes it seem easy 不费力的, 轻松的: *a smooth, effortless volley* 轻松自如的空中截击 —**effortlessly** *adv*: *Her fingers darted effortlessly over the keys.* 她的手指在键上轻巧地敲击。

ef·fron·te·ry /ə`frʌntərɪ; ɪ'frʌntəri/ *n* [U] *formal* behaviour that you think someone should be ashamed of, although they do not seem to be【正式】厚颜无耻: *You have the effrontery to ask for a loan!* 你还有脸要借钱!

ef·ful·gence /ɛ`fʌldʒəns; ɪ'fʌldʒəns/ *n* [U] *literary* brightness of light【文】光辉, 灿烂 —**effulgent** *adj*

ef·fu·sion /ə`fjuʒən; ɪ'fju:ʒən/ *n* [C,U] *formal* an uncontrolled expression of strong feelings【正式】〔强烈感情的〕迸发: [+of] *effusions of gratitude* 感激之情的迸发

ef·fu·sive /ɛ`fjusɪv; ɪ'fju:sɪv/ *adj* showing strong excited feelings 热情的, 感情洋溢的: *Our host gave us an effusive welcome.* 主人热情地欢迎我们。—**effusively** *adv*: *"How lovely to see you," she said effusively.* "见到你太好了。"她热切地说。—**effusiveness** *n* [U]

EFL /͵i ɛf `ɛl; ͵i: ef 'el/ *n* [U] English as a Foreign Language; the way English is taught to people who do not speak it as their first language 作为外语的英语(教学)

eg, e.g. /͵i `dʒi; ͵i: 'dʒi:/ an abbreviation for 缩写= 'for example' 例如: *citrus fruits, e.g. oranges and grapefruit* 柑橘属水果, 例如橙和葡萄柚

e·gal·i·tar·i·an /ɪˌgælɪˋtɛrɪən; ɪˌgælɪˈteəriən/ *adj* believing that everyone is equal and should have equal rights 平等主义的: *an egalitarian society* 一个人人平等的社会 —**egalitarianism** *n* [U]

egg¹ /ɛg; eg/ *n*
1 ▶BIRDS 鸟类◀ [C] a round object with a hard surface, that contains a baby bird, snake, insect etc and which is made by a female bird, snake, or insect 蛋: *Blackbirds usually lay their eggs in March.* 乌鸫通常在3月产蛋。| *an ostrich egg* 鸵鸟蛋
2 ▶FOOD 食物◀ [C,U] an egg, especially one from a chicken, that is used for food〔作食物的〕蛋; 鸡蛋: *fried eggs* 煎蛋
3 ▶ANIMALS/PEOPLE 动物/人类◀ [C] a cell produced by a woman or female animal that combines with SPERM (=male cell) to make a baby 卵, 卵细胞
4 have egg on your face if someone, especially someone in authority, has egg on their face, they look silly because something embarrassing has happened〔尤指有权威的人〕丢脸, 出丑: *The Pentagon's been left with egg on its face.* 美国五角大楼丢尽了脸。
5 put all your eggs in one basket to depend completely on one thing or one course of action in order to get success 孤注一掷
6 lay an egg *AmE informal* to fail or be unsuccessful at something that you are trying to do【美, 非正式】失败, 未成功
7 as sure as eggs is eggs *BrE old-fashioned* used to tell someone that you are sure that something will happen【英, 过时】毫无疑问, 确定无疑
8 good egg *old-fashioned* someone who you can depend on to be honest, kind etc【过时】好人

egg² *v*
egg sb ↔ **on** *phr v* [T] to encourage someone to do something, especially something that they should not do 怂恿; 鼓动: *Joe didn't want to jump but his friends kept egging him on.* 乔不想跳, 可他的朋友们一个劲地鼓动他。

egg·cup /ˋɛgˌkʌp; ˈegkʌp/ *n* [C] a small container that holds a boiled egg while you eat it〔吃蛋时用的〕蛋杯

egg·head /ˋɛgˌhɛd; ˈeghed/ *n* [C] *informal*【非正式】**1** someone who is very intelligent, and only interested in theories and books 学究; 学问家 **2** *AmE* someone who has no hair【美】秃头者

egg·plant /ˋɛgˌplænt; ˈegplɑːnt/ *n* [C] *especially AmE* a large vegetable with smooth purple skin【尤美】茄子; AUBERGINE *BrE*【英】—see picture on page A9 参见 A9 页图

egg roll /ˌ· ˈ·/ *n* [C] *AmE* a SPRING ROLL【美】春卷

egg·shell /ˋɛgˌʃɛl; ˈegʃel/ *n* [C,U] **1** the hard outside part of a bird's egg 蛋壳 **2 eggshell china/paint** a type of CHINA or paint that is thin and hard, like the shell of an egg〔薄而硬的〕蛋壳细薄瓷器/蛋壳漆

egg-tim·er /ˈ· ˌ·· / *n* [C] a small glass container with sand in it that runs from one part to the other, used for measuring the time it takes to boil an egg 煮蛋计时器〔用于计量煮蛋时间的小沙漏〕

e·go /ˋigo; ˈiːgəʊ/ *n* [C] **1** the opinion that you have about yourself 自我, 自我意识: *That promotion was a real boost for her ego.* 这次升职大大增强了她的自信心。| **have a big ego** (=think that you are very clever or important) 自高自大 *big bikes and equally outsized Hollywood egos* 大型摩托车和同样大号的好莱坞自大心态 **2 ego trip** *informal* something that you do because it makes you feel important【非正式】自我表现: *This DJ work is just a big ego trip for him!* 这份当音乐节目主持人的工作是他自我展现的好机会! **3** the part of your mind with which you think and take action, according to Freudian PSYCHOLOGY〔弗洛伊德心理学中的〕自我 —compare 比较 ID, SUPEREGO

e·go·cen·tric /ˌigoˋsɛntrɪk; ˌiːgəʊˈsentrɪk◂/ *adj* thinking only about yourself and not thinking about what other people might need or want 自我中心的; 自私自利的 —**egocentrically** /-klɪ; -kli/ *adv* —**egocentricity** /ˌigosɛnˋtrɪsətɪ; ˌiːgəʊsenˈtrɪsəti/ *n* [U]

e·go·is·m /ˋigoˌɪzəm; ˈiːgəʊɪzəm/ *n* [U] egotism 自我主义; 自大的行为 —**egoist** *n* [C] —**egoistic** /ˌigoˋɪstɪk; ˌiːgəʊˈɪstɪk◂/ *adj*

e·go·ma·ni·ac /ˌigoˋmenɪæk; ˌiːgəʊˈmeɪniæk/ *n* [C] someone who thinks that they are very important, and tries to get advantages for themselves without caring about how this affects other people 利己主义者; 自大狂 —**egomania** /-nɪə; -niə/ *n* [U]

e·go·tis·m /ˋigətɪzəm; ˈiːgətɪzəm/ *n* [U] the belief that you are much better or more important than other people, or behaviour that shows this 自我主义; 自大的行为

e·go·tis·tic·al /ˌigəˋtɪstɪkḷ; ˌiːgəˈtɪstɪkəl/ *adj* believing that you are much better or more important than other people 自大的; 自负的: *He's the most selfish, egotistical individual I have ever met!* 他是我见过的最自私、最狂妄自大的人! —**egotistically** /-klɪ; -kli/ *adv* —**egotist** /ˋigəˌtɪst; ˈiːgətɪst/ *n* [C]

e·gre·gious /ɪˋgridʒəs; ɪˈgriːdʒəs/ *adj formal* an egregious ERROR, failure, problem etc is extremely bad and noticeable【正式】〔错误、失败、问题等〕极其严重的; 令人震惊的: *a most egregious error of judgement* 极其严重的误判 —**egregiously** *adv*

e·gress /ˋigrɛs; ˈiːgres/ *n* [U] *formal or law* the act of leaving a building or place, or the right to do this【正式或法律】外出; 出外权

e·gret /ˋigrɪt; ˈiːgrɪt/ *n* [C] a bird that lives near water and has long legs and long white tail feathers 白鹭

E·gypt /ˋidʒəpt; ˈiːdʒɪpt/ a country in northeast Africa, next to the Mediterranean Sea and the Red Sea. Population: 69,537,000 (2001). Capital: Cairo. 埃及〔非洲东北部一国, 濒临地中海和红海。人口: 69,537,000 (2001), 首都: 开罗〕

E·gyp·tian¹ /ɪˋdʒɪpʃən; ɪˈdʒɪpʃən/ *n* [C] someone from Egypt 埃及人

Egyptian² *adj* from or connected with Egypt 埃及的; 与埃及有关的

eh /e; eɪ/ *interjection spoken BrE, CanE*【口, 英, 加】**1** used when you want someone to repeat something because you did not hear it 嗯, 啊〔表示未听清, 请对方重复一遍〕: *Eh? She's got how many?* 嗯? 她有多少? **2** used when you want someone to reply to you or agree with something you have said 是吗, 好吗〔表示请对方应答或同意〕: *Look at these. Smart, eh?* 看看这些, 真棒, 是吧? **3** used when you are surprised by something that someone has said 啊, 嗯〔表示对对方的话感到惊讶〕

Eich·mann /ˋaɪkmən; ˈaɪkmən/**, Ad·olf** /ˋedɑlf; ˈædɒlf/ (1906-62) an Austrian Nazi who, during World War II, was one of the main people responsible for sending Jewish people to CONCENTRATION CAMPS, where millions of them died. After the war he escaped, but he was finally caught, found guilty of war crimes, and EXECUTED in 1962. 艾希曼〔(1906-1962), 奥地利纳粹分子, 二战期间将数百万犹太人送入集中营并实施屠杀的罪魁祸首之一。战后他逃往国外, 最终被捕, 因战争罪于1962年被处决〕

ei·der·down /ˋaɪdəˌdaʊn; ˈaɪdədaʊn/ *n* [C] a thick warm cover for a bed, filled with duck feathers 鸭绒被

Eif·fel Tow·er, the /ˌaɪfḷ ˋtaʊə; ˌaɪfəl ˈtaʊə/ a 300 metre-high metal tower in Paris, completed in 1889. It is often used as a symbol representing Paris or France. 埃菲尔铁塔〔巴黎一座高300米的铁塔, 建于1889年, 经常作为巴黎或法国的象征〕

Ei·ger, the /ˋaɪgə; ˈaɪgə/ a mountain in the Alps in Switzerland. Its north side is famous for being very difficult to climb. 艾格尔山〔位于瑞士阿尔卑斯山, 其北麓因难以攀登而闻名〕

eight /et; eɪt/ *number* **1** 8 八 **2** a team of eight people who row a racing boat〔划船比赛中的〕八人划船队 **3 have had one over the eight** *BrE old-fashioned* to be drunk【英, 过时】喝醉 —**eighth** *number*

eigh·teen /eˋtin; ˌeɪˈtiːn◂/ *number* 18 十八

18 /ˌeˋtin; ˌeɪˈtiːn◂/ in the UK, a film that has been accepted as suitable only for people aged 18 and older. Films that have an 18 CERTIFICATE usually contain a lot of sex or violence. In the US system, films like this have the letter X. 英国成人电影〔被认为仅适宜18岁以上的人群观看的影片。此类电影通常含有大量性或暴力画面。在美国电影分级制中, 成人影片用字母X标识〕

18-30 hol·i·days /ˌetin ˋθɜtɪ ˌhɑlədez; ˌeɪtiːn ˈθɜːti ˌhɒlɪdiz/ *n* [plural] group holidays for people between the ages of 18 and 30, especially people who are not married 18-30 青年假日〔18至30岁年龄段的青年, 尤其是未婚者的集体假日〕

> **CULTURAL NOTE 文化注释**
> The image that many people have of 18-30 holidays is that many of the people who go on them choose to spend their time drinking alcohol, having sex, and behaving badly. 很多人对"18-30青年假日"的印象是: 很多参加这种度假的人喝酒、纵欲、胡作非为, 以此打发时间。

18-wheel·er /ˌetin ˋhwilə; ˌeɪtiːn ˈwiːlə◂/ *n* [C] *AmE* a very large TRUCK (=vehicle that carries goods on roads) which has 18 wheels, used especially for moving goods over long distances【美】18轮大卡车〔一种18轮大型货运卡车, 尤用于长途货运〕

eighth /etθ; eɪtθ/ *n* [C] one of eight equal parts of something 八分之一

eighth note /ˈ· ·/ *n* [C] *AmE* a musical note that continues for an eighth of the length of a WHOLE NOTE【美】八分音符; QUAVER² (1) *BrE*【英】—see picture at 参见 MUSIC 图

800 num·ber /ˌ·· ˈ·/ also 又作 **800 line, toll-free number** *AmE*【美】— *n* a telephone number which one can telephone without paying for the call 800号码, 免费电话号码

eigh·ty /ˋetɪ; ˈeɪti/ *number* 80 八十

Ein·stein /ˋaɪnstaɪn; ˈaɪnstaɪn/, **Albert** (1879-1955) a US PHYSICIST and MATHEMATICIAN, born in Germany, who developed the theory of relativity, which completely changed the way that scientists understand space and time. He was one of the greatest scientists ever born, and people sometimes use the name Einstein to talk about someone who is very intelligent 爱因斯坦〔(1879-1955)，美国物理学家、数学家，出生于德国。他提出相对论，完全改变了科学家对时空的认识。他是有史以来最伟大的科学家之一。人们有时借用他的名字指称极其聪明的人〕: *Go and ask Simon – he's the Einstein of the family.* 去问一下西蒙吧——他是这家的爱因斯坦。| *The controls are really easy to operate, so you don't have to be an Einstein to use it.* 控制装置很容易操作，不一定非要是爱因斯坦才行。

Eire another name for the Republic of Ireland 爱尔兰〔爱尔兰共和国的别称〕

Ei·sen·hower /ˋaɪzn̩haʊɚ; ˈaɪzənhaʊə/, **Dwight Da·vid** /dwaɪt ˋdevɪd; dwaɪt ˈdeɪvɪ̮d/ (1890-1969) a US politician in the Republican Party, who was President of the US from 1953 to 1961. Eisenhower was a general in the US army during World War II, and he became the commander of all the Allied forces in Europe, leading the attack on D-day in 1944. People informally called him **Ike**. 艾森豪威尔〔(1890-1969)，美国共和党政治家，1953至1961年间任美国总统。二战期间，他是美军的将军并担任盟军在欧洲的最高统帅，1944年D日(6月6日)指挥盟军在法国登陆。昵称为艾克〕

Ei·sen·stein /ˋaɪzn̩staɪn; ˈaɪzənstaɪn/, **Ser·gei Mi·khai·lo·vich** /sɛrˋge mɪˋkaɪləvɪtʃ; ˈseəgeɪ mɪˈkaɪləvɪtʃ/ (1898-1948) a Russian film DIRECTOR. Many people consider him to be one of the greatest directors ever, and he is famous especially for *The Battleship Potemkin* (1925) and *Alexander Nevsky* (1938). 爱森斯坦〔(1898-1948)，苏联电影导演。很多人认为他是有史以来最伟大的导演之一，尤以《波将金号战舰》(1925)和《亚历山大·涅夫斯基》(1938)闻名〕

ei·stedd·fod /eˋstɛðvɑd; aɪˈstedfəd/ *n* [C] a special meeting in Wales at which there are competitions in singing, poetry, and music 威尔士诗歌音乐比赛大会

ei·ther¹ S1 W1 /ˋiðɚ; ˈaɪðə/ *conjunction* **1** used to begin a list of two or more possibilities separated by 'or' 或是，或者〔用以引出两个或多个可能的事物，用or隔开〕: *You add either one or two stock cubes.* 你加入一两块浓缩固体汤料。| *She's the kind of person you either love or hate.* 她是那种叫你不是爱就是恨的人。| *It was either pink, red, or orange.* 不是粉红色的，就是红色的，要不就是橙色的。—compare 比较 OR (1) **2** used to say that if one thing does not happen then something else will have to 要么〔表示非此即彼〕: *It's your choice! Either she leaves or I will!* 你看着办吧！要么她走，要么我走！| *£75 seems a lot to pay for a starter motor but it's either that or a new car!* 花75英镑换一个发动机启动装置似乎很贵，但是不换启动装置就得换辆新车！

either² S1 W1 *determiner* **1** one or the other of two things or people〔两物或两人中〕任一的: *I've lived in New York and Chicago but don't like either city very much.* 我在纽约和芝加哥住过，但两个城市我都不是很喜欢。| **either way** (=in one way or the other)〔两种方式中的〕任一种方式 *You can get to Edinburgh by train or plane but either way it's very expensive.* 你可以坐火车或飞机去爱丁堡，但两种方式都很贵。| *"Shall we have Indian or Chinese?" "I don't mind either way really."* "我们去吃印度菜还是中国菜?""哪种都行，我真的不介意。" | *The baby's due on the 10th but the doctor said it could be a fortnight either way.* (=it could be born two weeks early or two weeks late) 婴儿应该是10号出生，但医生说提前或推迟两周都有可能。—compare 比较 ANY, NEITHER¹ **2** one and the other of two things or people; each〔两物或两人中〕各一的；每一的: *He sat in the back of the car with a policeman on either side.* 他坐在汽车后座上，左右各坐一名警察。| *There are shops at either end of the street.* 街的两端都有商店。—compare 比较 BOTH **3 an either-or situation** a situation in which you cannot avoid having to make a decision or choice 必须作出决定[选择]的处境 —see 见 ALSO (USAGE)

either³ *pron* one or the other of two things or people〔两者中〕任一个: *There's tea or coffee – you can have either.* 有茶和咖啡，你可任选一种。| *Do either of you know where I can buy a zip round here?* 你俩谁知道附近哪儿能买到拉链?

either⁴ *adv* **1** [only in negatives 仅用于否定句] also 也: *I haven't seen the movie and my brother hasn't either.* (=both haven't seen it) 我没看过这部电影，我弟弟也没看过。| *"I can't swim." "I can't, either."* "我不会游泳。""我也不会。" **2 me either** *AmE spoken* used to say that something is also true about you【美口】我也是: *"I don't have any money right now." "Me either."* "我现在没钱。""我也没有。" —compare 比较 NEITHER³, TOO (2)

e·jac·u·late /ɪˋdʒækjə,let; ɪˈdʒækjʊ̮leɪt/ *v* [I,T] **1** when a man ejaculates, SPERM comes out of his PENIS 射精 **2** *old-fashioned* to suddenly shout or say something, especially because you are surprised【过时】〔尤指因惊奇而〕喊出；突然说出 —**ejaculation** /ɪ,dʒækjəˋleʃən; ɪ,dʒækjʊ̮ˈleɪʃən/ *n* [C,U]

e·ject /ɪˋdʒɛkt; ɪˈdʒekt/ *v* **1** [T] to make someone leave a place or building by using force〔用武力〕驱逐；赶出: **eject sb from** *The demonstrators were ejected from the hall.* 示威者被赶出大厅。**2** [T] to suddenly send something out 喷射；射出: *Ants eject formic acid when another insect tries to attack them.* 当受到其他昆虫攻击时，蚂蚁就喷出蚁酸。**3** [I] to jump out of a plane because it is going to crash〔从要坠毁的飞机中〕弹射出来 **4** [I,T] to make something come out of a machine by pressing a button〔按按钮将某物从机器中〕弹出 —**ejection** /ɪˋdʒɛkʃən; ɪˈdʒekʃən/ *n* [C,U]

e·jec·tor seat /·ˋ·· ,·/ also 又作 **ejection seat** *AmE*【美】*n* [C] a special seat that throws the pilot out of a plane when it is going to crash〔飞机上飞行员用的〕弹射座椅

eke /ik; iːk/ *v*

eke sth ↔ out *phr v* [T] *literary*【文】**1** to make a small supply of something such as food or money last longer by carefully only using small amounts of it 精打细算地维持；尽量节省使用: *Today's retired home-owner has to eke out his pension as best he can.* 如今自己拥有住房的已退休人士必须尽量节省使用退休金了。**2 eke out a living/existence** to succeed in getting the things you need to live, even though you have very little money or food 勉强度日，竭力维持生计: *They eke out a miserable existence in cardboard shacks.* 他们在纸板屋中凄惨度日。

EKG /,i ke ˋdʒi; ,iː keɪ ˈdʒiː/ *n* [C] an American form of ECG ECG的美语形式

e·lab·o·rate¹ /ɪˋlæbərɪt; ɪˈlæbərɪ̮t/ *adj* containing a lot of small details or parts that are connected with each other in a complicated way 精心制作的；复杂的: *an elaborate mosaic consisting of thousands of tiny pieces* 由数千小块拼成的精美的镶嵌图 | **elaborate plan/notes/excuses etc** (=carefully produced and full of details) 详尽的计划/详细的笔记/精心编造的借口等 —**elaborately** *adv*: *an elaborately carved wooden statue* 做工精美的木雕 —**elaborateness** *n* [U]

e·lab·o·rate² /ɪˋlæbə,ret; ɪˈlæbəreɪt/ *v* [I,T] to give more details or new information about something 详尽说明；阐述: *He said he had new evidence, but refused to elaborate any further.* 他声称有新证据，但拒绝进一步详细说明。| [+on] *Later chapters simply elaborate on her original theses.* 后面的章节只是对她最初的论点进行详述。—**elaboration** /ɪ,læbəˋreʃən; ɪ,læbəˈreɪʃən/ *n* [U]

El Alamein —see 见 ALAMEIN

é·lan /eˋlɑ̃; ˈeɪlɒn/ *n* [U] *literary* a style that is full of energy and determination【文】热忱；活力；锐气: *The attack was planned and led with great élan.* 进攻计划制定得雄心勃勃，将帅领军作战异常勇猛。

e·lapse /ɪˋlæps; ɪˈlæps/ *v* [I not in progressive 不用进行时] *formal* if a particular period of time elapses, it passes【正式】〔时间〕流逝，过去: *Several months were to elapse before his case was brought to trial.* 几个月过去了，他的案子才开审。

e·las·tic¹ /ɪˋlæstɪk; ɪˈlæstɪk/ *n* [U] a type of rubber material that can stretch and then return to its usual length or size〔橡皮〕弹力材料: *The ball was attached to the bat with a piece of elastic.* 球用一根橡皮筋连在球拍上。

elastic² *adj* **1** made of elastic 弹力材料制成的: *elastic stockings* 弹力长筒袜 **2** a material that is elastic can stretch and then go back to its usual length or size 有弹性的: *Children's bones are far more elastic.* 儿童的骨骼弹性要大得多。**3** a system or plan that is elastic can change or be changed easily〔系统或计划〕灵活的，有伸缩性的: *Language usage is too elastic to be described using just a few simple rules.* 语言的运用灵活性太大，仅用几条简单的规则难以描述。—**elasticity** /ɪ,læsˋtɪsətɪ; iːlæˈstɪsɪ̮ti/ *n* [U]

elastic band /·,·· ˋ·/ *n* [C] *BrE* a thin circular piece of stretchy rubber used for fastening things together; RUBBER BAND【英】橡皮筋

E·las·to·plast /ɪˋlæstə,plæst; ɪˈlæstəplɑːst/ *n* [C,U] *BrE trademark* a sticky bandage used to cover small cuts【英，商标】"易理妥"牌创口贴; BAND-AID *AmE*【美】

e·lat·ed /ɪˋletɪd; ɪˈleɪtɪ̮d/ *adj* extremely happy and excited, especially because you have been successful〔尤指因成功〕兴高采烈的，欢欣鼓舞的: *Elated by our victory, we sang all the way home.* 我们因胜利而欢欣鼓舞，一路唱着歌回家。

e·la·tion /ɪˋleʃən; ɪˈleɪʃən/ *n* [U] a feeling of extreme happiness and excitement 兴高采烈，得意扬扬

El·ba /ˈɛlbə; ˈelbə/ an island west of Italy where Napoleon was sent in 1814 after the failure of his attack on Russia 厄尔巴岛〔位于意大利以西一岛屿, 1814年拿破仑进攻俄国失利后被流放到该岛〕

el·bow¹ /ˈɛl,bo; ˈelbəʊ/ *n* [C] **1** the joint where your arm bends 肘 —see picture at 参见 BODY 图 **2** the part of a shirt etc that covers your elbow〔衬衫等的〕肘部 **3 elbow grease** *informal* hard work and effort, especially when cleaning or polishing something【非正式】费力的工作〔尤指擦洗等劳动〕**4 give sb the elbow** *BrE informal* to tell someone that you no longer like them or want them to work for you and that they should leave【英, 非正式】让某人离开〔或是不再喜欢他, 或是不再需要他工作〕**5** a curved part of a pipe or CHIMNEY, that is shaped like an elbow〔管子或烟囱的〕肘状弯

elbow² *v* [T] to push someone with your elbows, especially in order to move past them 用肘挤开〔某人〕: **elbow your way through** (=move through a group of people by pushing past them) 挤过〔人群〕*I began elbowing my way through the crowd.* 我开始奋力挤过人群。—see picture on page A21 参见 A21 页图

elbow-room /ˈ‥ ·/ *n* [U] enough space in which to move easily 自由活动的空间: *There's less elbow-room in the Ford.* 福特牌汽车内身体活动空间较小。

El Cid /ɛl ˋsɪd; el ˈsɪd/ (?1043-99) a Spanish soldier who fought for both Christians and Moors. Many people see him as a perfect example of CHIVALRY, Christian values, and love of his country 熙德〔(?1043-1099), 西班牙军事家。他曾为基督徒和摩尔人作战, 被认为是骑士精神、基督教价值观和爱国热情的完美典范〕

el·der¹ /ˈɛldɚ; ˈeldə/ *adj* **1 elder brother/daughter/ sister etc** [only before noun 仅用于名词前] a brother etc who is older than other brothers etc 哥哥/大女儿/姐姐等: *My elder brother looks nothing like me.* 我哥哥跟我一点都不像。—see 见 OLD (USAGE) **2 the elder a)** the older one of two people〔两人当中的〕年长者: *Sarah is the elder of the two.* 两人当中萨拉年龄大。**b)** used after someone's name to show that they are the older of two people with the same name, usually a father and son 大, 老〔用于人名后表示两个同名者中的年长者, 二人通常为父子〕: *Pitt the elder* 老皮特 —compare 比较 YOUNGER

elder² *n* [C] **1** a member of a tribe or other social group who is important and respected because they are old 长者, 长辈: *a meeting of the village elders* 村里长辈的集会 **2** someone who has an official position of responsibility in some Christian churches〔基督教某些教会中的〕长老 **3** a small wild tree with white flowers and black berries 接骨木 **4 your elders (and betters)** people who are older than you and who you should respect 你的长辈

el·der·ber·ry /ˈɛldɚ,bɛrɪ; ˈeldəbəri/ *n* [C] the fruit of the elder tree 接骨木果

el·der·ly /ˈɛldɚlɪ; ˈeldəli/ *adj* **1** old or becoming old 年老的; 渐老的: *an elderly lady with white hair* 白发的老妇人 —see 见 OLD (USAGE) **2 the elderly** people who are old, especially people who are too old to look after themselves and need special help 老人, 上了年纪的人

elder states·man /‚‥ ˈ‥/ *n* [C] someone old and respected, especially a politician, who people ask for advice because of their knowledge and experience 年高德劭的人〔尤指政界元老〕

el·dest /ˈɛldɪst; ˈeldɪst/ *adj* **1 eldest son/sister/child etc** the oldest son, etc among a group of people, especially brothers and sisters 长子/大姐/年龄最大的孩子等: *Her eldest child is at university now.* 她最大的孩子已经上大学了。**2 the eldest** the oldest one in a group of people, especially brothers and sisters〔尤指兄弟姐妹中〕年龄最大者: *I have two brothers – I'm the eldest.* 我有两个兄弟, 我是老大。

El Do·ra·do, Eldorado /‚ɛl dəˋrado; ‚el dəˈrɑːdəʊ/ a place of very great wealth. Spanish travellers of the 16th century believed there was a place with very large amounts of gold and silver somewhere in South or Central America, which they called El Dorado, but they never found it. 黄金国; 富庶之地〔16世纪的西班牙旅行家认为南美洲或中美洲有一个黄金和白银富集的地方, 称之为埃尔多拉多, 但却从未找到过〕: *For some investment managers, Russia was seen as the next Eldorado.* 对一些投资经理人来说, 俄罗斯被视为下一个大有可为的地方。

e·lect¹ /ɪˋlɛkt; ɪˈlekt/ *v* **1** [T] to choose someone for an official position by voting 选举, 推选: *the country's first democratically elected government* 该国第一个民主选举的政府 | **elect sb to** *She was elected to Parliament in 1978.* 她于1978年入选议会。| **elect sb president/mayor etc** *Ronald Reagan was first elected President in 1980.* 罗纳德·里根于1980年首次当选总统。**2 elect to do sth** *formal* to choose to do something【正式】选择做某事: *Purchasers can elect to pay in monthly instalments.* 购买者可选择逐月分期付款。

elect² *adj* **president/governor/prime minister elect** the person who has been elected as president etc, but who has not yet officially started their job 候任总统/已当选尚未就任的州长/候任首相

e·lec·tion /ɪˋlɛkʃən; ɪˈlekʃən/ *n* **1** [C] an occasion when people vote to choose someone for an official position 选举: *The Socialists won the 1948 election by a huge majority.* 社会党在1948年选举中以很大的优势获胜。**2** [singular] the fact of being elected to an official position 当选: *Within three months of his election he was forced to resign.* 当选后不到三个月他就被迫辞职。—see also 另见 GENERAL ELECTION

CULTURAL NOTE 文化注释

US presidents are elected every four years. In some states Election Day is a public holiday. Bars and public places selling alcoholic drinks are closed on election day during the times when people can vote. 美国总统每四年选举一次。选举日在一些州是公共假日。选举日的投票时间, 酒吧和公共场所停止卖酒。— see also BY-ELECTION, GENERAL ELECTION and see Feature on page F25 另见 BY-ELECTION, GENERAL ELECTION, 并见 F25 页文化特写

e·lec·tion·eer·ing /ɪ,lɛkʃəˋnɪrɪŋ; ɪ,lekʃəˈnɪərɪŋ/ *n* [U] speeches and other activities intended to persuade people to vote for a particular person or political party 竞选活动, 拉票活动

e·lec·tive¹ /ɪˋlɛktɪv; ɪˈlektɪv/ *adj formal*【正式】**1** an elective position or organization is one for which there is an election〔职位或组织〕由选举产生的 **2** elective medical treatment is treatment that you choose to have, although you do not have to〔治疗〕非必需的

elective² *n* [C] *AmE* a course that you can choose to study because you are interested in it, while you are studying for a degree in a different subject【美】选修课

e·lec·tor /ɪˋlɛktɚ; ɪˈlektə/ *n* [C] someone who has the right to vote in an election 选民, 有选举权的人: *gradually losing the support of the electors* 逐渐失去选民的支持

e·lec·to·ral /ɪˋlɛktərəl; ɪˈlektərəl/ *adj* [only before noun 仅用于名词前] connected with elections and voting 选举的, 与选举有关的: *a campaign for electoral reform* 倡导改革选举制度的运动

electoral col·lege /·,‥· ˈ‥/ *n* [singular] a group of people chosen by the votes of the people in each US state, who come together to elect the President〔由美国各州人民选举组成的〕总统选举团

electoral re·gis·ter /·,‥ ˈ‥/ also 又作 **electoral roll** /·,‥ ˈ·/ *n* [C] an official list of the people who are allowed to vote in a particular area 选民名册

e·lec·to·rate /ɪˋlɛktərɪt; ɪˈlektərɪt/ *n* [singular] all the people in a country who have the right to vote〔一个国家的〕全体选民

E·lec·tra com·plex /ɪˋlɛktrə ,kɑmplɛks; ɪˈlektrə ,kɒmpleks/ *n* [C usually singular 一般用单数] *technical* the unconscious sexual feelings that a girl is supposed to have towards her father【术语】恋父情结 —compare 比较 OEDIPUS COMPLEX

e·lec·tric /ɪˋlɛktrɪk; ɪˈlektrɪk/ *adj* **1** an electric machine, light etc works using electricity 用电的, 电动的: *an electric heater* 电热器 **2 electric current** a flow of electricity 电流 **3** an electric wire, PLUG¹ (1) etc is used for carrying electricity 用来导电的; 带电的 **4** an electric situation is one in which people are very excited because something important is going to happen 扣人心弦的, 高度刺激的: *The atmosphere in the courtroom was electric.* 法庭上的气氛十分紧张。

e·lec·tri·cal /ɪˋlɛktrɪkl; ɪˈlektrɪkəl/ *adj* related to or connected with electricity 电的, 与电有关的: *I think there's an electrical fault.* 我认为电路出了故障。| *an electrical engineer* 电气工程师 —**electrically** /-klɪ; -kli/ *adv*

electrical storm /·,‥ ˈ·/ also 又作 **electric storm** /·,‥ ˈ·/ *n* [C] a violent storm in which electricity is produced 电暴, 雷暴

electric blan·ket /·,‥ ˈ‥/ *n* [C] a special BLANKET (=large cloth on a bed) with electric wires in it, used for making the bed warm 电热毯

electric chair /·,‥ ˈ·/ *n* [C usually singular 一般用单数] a chair in which criminals are killed using electricity, in order to punish them for crimes such as murder; used in the US etc 电椅; 电刑

electric eel /·,‥ ˈ·/ *n* [C] a large South American fish that looks like a snake, and can give an electric shock 电鳗

electric eye /·,‥ ˈ·/ *n* [C] *informal* a PHOTOELECTRIC CELL【非正式】光电池

e·lec·tri·cian /ɪˌlɛk`trɪʃən; ɪˌlekˈtrɪʃən/ *n* [C] someone whose job is to deal with or repair electrical equipment 电工, 电气技师

e·lec·tri·ci·ty /ɪˌlɛk`trɪsətɪ; ɪˌlekˈtrɪsəti/ *n* [U] **1** the power that is usually used in modern buildings to provide light and to make machines work 电 **2** the supply of electricity to a particular place 电力供应: *The electricity was cut off when we didn't pay the bill.* 我们未付电费, 电力供应被切断。**3** a feeling of excitement 激情, 强烈感情: *The electricity seemed to have gone out of their relationship.* 他们之间似乎已激情不再。

e·lec·trics /ɪ`lɛktrɪks; ɪˈlektrɪks/ *n* [plural] *BrE* the parts of a machine that use electrical power【英】〔设备中的〕电动部分; 电路: *The car won't start – I think there's something wrong with the electrics.* 汽车发动不起来, 我认为是电路出了问题。

electric shock /·ˌ·· ˈ·/ *n* [C] a sudden shock to your body, caused by electricity 触电; 电击

electric shock ther·a·py /·ˌ··ˈ·ˌ···/ *n* [U] a method of treatment for mental illness that involves sending electricity through someone's brain〔医治精神病的〕电击疗法

e·lec·tri·fi·ca·tion /ɪˌlɛktrəfəˈkeʃən; ɪˌlektrəfəˈkeɪʃən/ *n* [U] the process of changing a railway so that it uses electrical power, or making electricity available in a particular area〔铁路的〕电气化;〔向某一地区的〕供电

e·lec·tri·fy /ɪ`lɛktrəˌfaɪ; ɪˈlektrəfaɪ/ *v* [T] **1** to change a railway so that it uses electrical power, or to make electricity available in a particular area 使〔铁路〕电气化; 向〔某一地区〕供电 **2** if a performance or a speech electrifies the people who are watching it, it makes them feel very interested or excited〔表演或演讲〕使激动; 使兴奋: *Her words had an electrifying effect.* 她的话激动人心。—**electrifying** *adj* —**electrified** *adj*: *electrified fences* 通电的铁丝网

electro- /ɪlɛktro; ɪlektrəʊ/ *prefix technical*【术语】**1** concerning or worked by electricity 电的; 与电有关的; 用电的: *to electrocute* (=kill by electricity) 电死; 用电刑处死 | *an electromagnet* 电磁铁, 电磁体 **2** electric and 电与…的: *electro-chemical* 电化(学)的

e·lec·tro·car·di·o·gram /ɪˌlɛktro`kɑrdɪəˌɡræm; ɪˌlektrəʊˈkɑːdiəɡræm/ *n* [C] *technical* an ECG (2)【术语】心电图

e·lec·tro·car·di·o·graph /ɪˌlɛktro`kɑrdɪəˌɡræf; ɪˌlektrəʊˈkɑːdiəɡrɑːf/ *n* [C] *technical* an ECG (1)【术语】心电图仪

electro-con·vuls·ive ther·a·py /·ˌ··ˌ··ˈ··ˌ··/ *n* [U] ELECTRIC SHOCK THERAPY 电击疗法

e·lec·tro·cute /ɪ`lɛktrəˌkjut; ɪˈlektrəkjuːt/ *v* [T usually passive 一般用被动态] to injure or kill someone by passing electricity through their body 使触电受伤[身亡]; 用电击伤[处死]: *An employee was electrocuted on the new equipment.* 一名员工被新设备电死了。—**electrocution** /ɪˌlɛktrə`kjuʃən; ɪˌlektrəˈkjuːʃən/ *n* [U]

e·lec·trode /ɪ`lɛktrod; ɪˈlektrəʊd/ *n* [C] one of the two points at which electricity enters or leaves a BATTERY (1) or other piece of electrical equipment 电极: *fuel cells with two electrodes* 带两个电极的燃料电池

e·lec·tro·en·ceph·a·lo·gram /ɪˌlɛktroɛn`sɛfələɡræm; ɪˌlektrəʊɪnˈsefələɡræm/ *n* [C] *technical* an EEG (2)【术语】脑电图

e·lec·tro·en·ceph·a·lo·graph /ɪˌlɛktroɛn`sɛfələˌɡræf; ɪˌlektrəʊɪnˈsefələɡrɑːf/ *n* [C] *technical* an EEG (1)【术语】脑电图仪

e·lec·trol·y·sis /ɪˌlɛk`trɑləsɪs; ɪˌlekˈtrɒləsəs/ *n* [U] **1** *technical* the process of separating a liquid into its chemical parts by passing an electric current through it【术语】电解 **2** the process of using electricity to destroy hair roots and to remove unwanted hairs from your face etc 电蚀除毛

e·lec·tro·lyte /ɪ`lɛktrəˌlaɪt; ɪˈlektrəlaɪt/ *n* [C] a liquid that can be separated into different chemical parts by passing electricity through it 电解液

e·lec·tro·mag·net /ɪˌlɛktro`mæɡnɪt; ɪˌlektrəʊˈmæɡnət/ *n* [C] a piece of metal that becomes MAGNETIC (=able to attract metal objects) when an electric current is turned on 电磁体, 电磁铁 —**electromagnetic** /ɪˌlɛktromæɡ`nɛtɪk; ɪˌlektrəʊmæɡˈnetɪk◂/ *adj*

e·lec·tro·mag·ne·tis·m /ɪˌlɛktro`mæɡnəˌtɪzəm; ɪˌlektrəʊˈmæɡnətɪzəm/ *n* [U] *technical* a force caused by the movement and exchange of positively and negatively charged PARTICLES (=bits of material) in atoms【术语】电磁

e·lec·tron /ɪ`lɛktrɑn; ɪˈlektrɒn/ *n* [C] a very small piece of matter that moves around the NUCLEUS (=central part) of an atom 电子: *an electron microscope* 电子显微镜

e·lec·tron·ic /ɪˌlɛk`trɑnɪk; ɪˌlekˈtrɒnɪk/ *adj* **1** electronic equipment uses things such as chips (CHIP[1] (4a)), TRANSISTORS, or valves (VALVE (3)) that have an effect on the electricity going through a piece of equipment such as a television or computer 电子的, 用电子操作的; 电子器件的: *'smart' electronic car alarms* "智能"汽车电子报警系统 **2** using electronic equipment 使用电子设备的: *electronic music* 电子音乐 —**electronically** /-klɪ; -kli/ *adv*

electronic mail /ˌ···· ˈ·/ *n* [U] E-MAIL 电子邮件(系统)

e·lec·tron·ics /ɪˌlɛk`trɑnɪks; ɪˌlekˈtrɒnɪks/ *n* [U] **1** the study of making equipment that works electronically 电子学 **2** the industry connected with making electronic equipment 电子工业

e·lec·tro·plate /ɪ`lɛktroˌplet; ɪˈlektrəʊpleɪt/ *v* [T usually passive 一般用被动态] to put a very thin layer of metal onto the surface of an object, using ELECTROLYSIS 电镀

el·e·gant /`ɛləɡənt; ˈeləɡənt/ *adj* **1** very beautiful and graceful 高雅的, 优美的: *a tall, elegant woman* 身材修长、举止优雅的女子 | *elegant handwriting* 优美的书法 **2** an idea or a plan that is elegant is very clever and simple〔想法或计划〕巧妙的, 简捷的: *an elegant solution to a problem* 解决问题的简捷方法 —**elegantly** *adv* —**elegance** *n* [U]

el·e·gi·ac /ɪ`lidʒɪˌæk; ˌeləˈdʒaɪək◂/ *adj literary*【文】**1** showing that you feel upset about someone or something that no longer exists 哀悼的; 悲伤的: *He spoke of his childhood in elegiac tones.* 他以悲伤的口吻谈他的童年。**2** connected with elegies (ELEGY) 挽歌(体)的: *elegiac verse* 挽诗

el·e·gy /`ɛlədʒɪ; ˈelədʒi/ *n* [C] a poem or song written to show sadness for someone or something that no longer exists 挽歌; 挽诗: *an elegy to Lenny's memory* 缅怀伦尼的挽歌

el·e·ment /`ɛləmənt; ˈeləmənt/ *n* [C]

1 ▶CHEMISTRY 化学◀ a simple chemical substance such as CARBON or oxygen that consists of atoms of only one kind 元素 —compare 比较 COMPOUND[1] (1)

2 an element of surprise/danger/doubt etc a small amount of a quality or feeling 有点惊奇/危险/怀疑等: *There's always an element of risk in this kind of investment.* 这类投资总有点风险。

3 ▶PEOPLE 人群◀ a group of people who form part of a larger group, especially when the rest of the group does not approve of them〔尤指遭团体中他人非议的〕一伙人: *There is a strong right-wing element in the organization.* 该组织中右翼分子众多。

4 ▶PART 部分◀ one part of a whole system, plan, piece of writing etc 部分; 部件: *Rhyme is just one of the elements of his poetry.* 押韵只是他诗歌特色的一部分。

5 ▶WEATHER 天气◀ the elements [plural] the weather, especially bad weather 天气〔尤指坏天气〕: *battling against the elements* 与恶劣天气搏斗

6 ▶HEATING 加热◀ the heating part of a piece of electrical equipment such as a KETTLE 电热元件〔如电热水壶〕

7 the elements of sth the most simple things that you have to learn first about a subject 基础原理; 纲要: *I never managed to understand even the elements of calculus.* 我连微积分的基础原理也未能掌握。

8 ▶EARTH/AIR/FIRE/WATER 土/风/火/水◀ one of the four substances (earth, air, fire, and water) from which people used to believe that everything was made 四元素〔旧时人们认为土、风、火、水是构成一切物质的四大元素〕

9 be in your element to be in a situation that you enjoy, because you are good at it 适得其所, 得心应手: *He's in his element when he's talking to large groups of people.* 面对大群人讲话他很拿手。

10 be out of your element to be in a situation that makes you uncomfortable or unhappy 不得其所, 处于不相宜的环境: *I felt out of my element surrounded by so much finery.* 身处这么多衣着华丽的人之间, 我感到很不自在。

el·e·men·tal /ˌɛlə`mɛntl̩; ˌeləˈmentl◂/ *adj* **1** an elemental feeling exists at the simplest and most basic level〔情感〕固有的, 最基本的: *Love and fear are two of the most elemental human emotions.* 爱和恐惧是人类最基本的两种情感。**2** *technical* existing as a simple chemical element that has not been combined with anything else【术语】元素的

el·e·men·ta·ry /ˌɛlə`mɛntərɪ; ˌeləˈmentəri◂/ *adj* **1** simple or basic 简单的; 基本的: *You made a very elementary mistake.* 你犯了一个非常简单的错误。**2** [only before noun 仅用于名词前] concerning the first and easiest part of a subject 基础的, 初级的: *an elementary coursebook for learners of English* 针对英语初学者的初级课本 **3** [only before noun 仅用于名词前] *AmE* elementary education is for children between 5 and 11 years old【美】小学的; PRIMARY[1] (2) *BrE*【英】

elementary par·ti·cle /ˌ······ˈ···/ *n* [C] *technical* one of the types of pieces of matter including ELECTRONS, PROTONS, and NEUTRONS that make up atoms【术语】基本粒子

elementary school /··ˈ····, ·/ *n* [C] **1** a school in the US where basic subjects are taught for the first six years of a child's education〔美国的〕小学 **2** a state school in England or Wales during the late 19th and early 20th century for children aged 5 to 13〔19世纪后期和20世纪初期英格兰或威尔士的〕公立小学

el·e·phant /ˈɛləfənt; ˈelɨfənt/ *n* [C] a very large grey animal with four legs, two TUSKS (=long curved teeth) and a TRUNK (=long nose) that it can use to pick things up 象 —see also 另见 WHITE ELEPHANT

CULTURAL NOTE 文化注释

People sometimes say, 'Elephants never forget', because they are believed to have very good memories人们有时说: "大象什么都记得。"因为他们相信大象记忆力极好: *He's got the memory of/a memory like an elephant.* 他的记性非常好。

el·e·phan·tine /ˌɛləˈfæntin; ˌelɨˈfæntaɪn◂/ *adj formal* slow, heavy, and awkward, like an elephant【正式】〔似大象一样〕迟缓的, 笨重的, 笨拙的: *She climbed the steps with heavy elephantine movements.* 她极其笨拙地爬上台阶。

Elephant Man, the (1862-90) a name given to a British man called Joseph Merrick because he was seriously DEFORMED by illness. Merrick appeared in FREAK shows, where he was found by a doctor, Sir Frederick Treves, in 1886. 象人〔(1862-1890), 一位名叫约瑟夫·梅里克的英国男子的别称。他因病头部严重畸形, 故得此名。他在马戏团表演, 1886年被医生弗雷德里克·特里夫斯爵士发现后得到救助〕

el·e·vate /ˈɛləˌvet; ˈelɨveɪt/ *v* [T] **1** *formal* to give someone or something a more important rank or position than they had before【正式】提拔, 晋升: **[+to]** *Both were later elevated to positions of authority.* 两人后来都被提拔当了领导。**2** *formal* to make someone feel happier and more sensitive【正式】使高兴; 使情绪高昂: *The beautiful countryside was enough to elevate her spirits.* 美丽的乡间景色足以让她精神焕发。**3** to improve something or make it more important 改进; 提升: *in Japan, where just-in-time delivery has been elevated to an art form* 在日本, 及时送货已上升为一种艺术 **4** *technical* to lift someone or something to a higher position【术语】抬高, 举高: *Elevate the leg.* 抬腿。**5** *technical* to increase the amount, temperature, pressure etc of something【术语】增加[提高]〔数量、温度、压力等〕: *These drugs may elevate acid levels in the blood.* 这些药可能增加血液酸度。

el·e·vat·ed /ˈɛləˌvetɪd; ˈelɨveɪtɨd/ *adj* **1** elevated thoughts, words etc seem to be intelligent or of high moral standard〔思想、话语等〕智慧的; 高尚的: *elevated philosophical language* 充满智慧的哲学语言 **2** [only before noun 仅用于名词前] an elevated position or rank is very important〔地位或级别〕高级的; 重要的 **3** higher up than other things 比〔他物〕高的: *From our elevated vantage point we could see the castle.* 从我们这个制高点可以看见城堡。**4** *formal* elevated levels, temperatures etc are higher than normal【正式】〔水平、温度等〕偏高的

elevated rail·way /ˌ····ˈ··/ *BrE*【英】, **elevated railroad** *AmE*【美】*n* [C] a railway that runs on a kind of continuous bridge above the streets in a town〔城市里的〕高架铁路

el·e·vat·ing /ˈɛləˌvetɪŋ; ˈelɨveɪtɪŋ/ *adj formal or humorous* making you feel interested in intelligent or moral subjects【正式或幽默】〔使人〕增长知识的, 提高品格的: *beach holiday that you would hardly call an elevating experience* 很难称得上对加强修养有裨益的海滩度假

el·e·va·tion /ˌɛləˈveʃən; ˌelɨˈveɪʃən/ *n* **1** [singular] a height above the level of the sea 海拔: **[+of]** *The observatory is located on Mt Hopkins at an elevation of 2,600m.* 气象台位于霍普金斯山上, 海拔2600米。**2** [U] *formal* a situation in which someone is given a more important rank or position【正式】提升, 晋升: *His sudden elevation to the Council surprised everyone.* 他突然晋升入理事会, 大家都很吃惊。**3** [C,U] *formal* an increase in the amount or level of something【正式】〔数量、水平的〕增加, 升高: *a sudden elevation of blood pressure* 血压突然升高 **4** [C] *technical* an upright side of a building, as shown in a drawing done by an ARCHITECT (=person who plans buildings)【术语】〔建筑的〕立面(图); 立视图 *the front elevation of a house* 房子的正面立视图 **5** [C] *technical* the angle made with the HORIZON by pointing a gun【术语】〔枪炮的〕射角, 仰角: *The cannon was fired at an elevation of 60 degrees.* 大炮以60度仰角射击。

el·e·va·tor /ˈɛləˌvetɚ; ˈelɨveɪtə/ *n* [C] **1** *AmE* a machine that takes people and goods from one level to another in a building【美】电梯; LIFT² (1) *BrE*【英】**2** a machine with a moving belt and containers, used for lifting grain and liquids, or for taking things off ships〔运送粮食、液体或卸船的〕升降机, 起卸机

elevator mu·sic /ˈ····, ··/ *n* [U] *AmE informal* the type of music that is played in shops and public places, and is usually thought to be boring【美, 非正式】背景音乐〔在商店等公共场所播放的音乐, 通常被认为很乏味〕

e·lev·en /ɪˈlɛvən; ɪˈlevən/ *number* **1** 11 十一 **2** a team of eleven players in football or CRICKET (2)〔由11名球员组成的〕足球队, 板球队 —**eleventh** *number*

eleven-plus, the /·ˌ··ˈ·/ *n* an examination which children in Britain aged 11 took in the past in order to decide what type of education they would have〔英国过去11岁儿童参加的〕升中学甄别考试

e·lev·en·ses /ɪˈlɛvənzɪz; ɪˈlevənzɨz/ *n* [U] *BrE informal* a cup of coffee or tea and a BISCUIT (1), that you have in the middle of the morning【英, 非正式】上午茶点〔一般为咖啡或茶再加上饼干〕

e·lev·enth /ɪˈlɛvənθ; ɪˈlevənθ/ *n* [C] **1** one of eleven equal parts of something 十一分之一 **2 the eleventh hour** the last moment before something important happens〔重大事件即将发生前的〕最后一刻, 最后时刻: *War was averted at the eleventh hour.* 战争在最后时刻得以避免。

elf /ɛlf; elf/ *n plural* **elves** /ɛlvz; elvz/ [C] an imaginary creature like a small person with pointed ears 小精灵〔传说中的精灵, 形似小人, 耳尖〕

el·fin /ˈɛlfɪn; ˈelfɨn/ *adj* someone who looks elfin is small and delicate〔指人〕小巧的: *dark hair and a white elfin face* 黑头发和白皙的小脸

El·gar /ˈɛlgar; ˈelgɑː/, **Sir Edward** (1857-1934) a British COMPOSER of CLASSICAL music, famous for his *Enigma Variations* and *Cello Concerto*. He also wrote the music for the PATRIOTIC song *Land of Hope and Glory*. 埃尔加〔(1857-1934), 英国古典音乐作曲家。他以《迷幻变奏曲》和《大提琴协奏曲》闻名。他还为爱国歌曲《希望和荣耀的土地》作曲〕

El·gin Mar·bles, the /ˌɛlgɪn ˈmarblz; ˌelgɪn ˈmɑːbəlz/ a set of ancient Greek SCULPTURES from the Parthenon in Athens, which were brought to Britain by the Earl of Elgin in 1803, and are kept in the British Museum in London 埃尔金大理石雕塑〔指雅典帕台农神庙中的古希腊雕塑, 1803年由埃尔金伯爵运回英国, 现存于伦敦大英博物馆〕

CULTURAL NOTE 文化注释

The Greek government has asked Britain to return the Elgin Marbles to Greece. Some British people now think that Elgin had no right to bring the sculptures to Britain, and that they should be given back. 希腊政府一直要求英国归还埃尔金大理石雕塑。现在有的英国人认为埃尔金无权把这些雕塑带到英国, 因此理应归还。

El Grec·o /ˌɛl ˈgrɛko; ˌel ˈgrekəʊ/ (1541-1614) a Spanish artist famous for his religious paintings. He was called El Greco, which means 'the Greek', because he was born in Crete. 埃尔·格列柯〔(1541-1614), 西班牙艺术家, 以宗教类绘画作品闻名。他出生于(希腊的)克里特岛, 因而被称为El Greco, 即"希腊人"〕

e·li·cit /ɪˈlɪsɪt; ɪˈlɪsɨt/ *v* [T] to succeed in getting information or a reaction from someone, especially when this is difficult〔从某人处〕套出〔信息〕; 引起〔某人的反应〕: *My attempts at conversation didn't elicit much response.* 我试图跟他搭讪, 但他爱理不理的。| **elicit sth from sb** *By patient questioning we managed to elicit enough information from the witnesses.* 经耐心盘问, 我们从目击者处探得了足够的信息。—**elicitation** /ɪˌlɪsəˈteʃən; ɪˌlɪsɨˈteɪʃən/ *n* [U]

e·lide /ɪˈlaɪd; ɪˈlaɪd/ *v* [T] to leave out the sound of a letter or of a part of a word 省略〔一个字母或音节的〕发音 —**elision** /ɪˈlɪʒən; ɪˈlɪʒən/ *n* [C,U]

el·i·gi·ble /ˈɛlɪdʒəbl; ˈelɨdʒɨbəl/ *adj* **1** someone who is eligible for something is able or allowed to do it, for example because they are the right age 合格的; 有资格的: **[+for]** *Are you eligible for social security benefits?* 你有资格享受社会福利了吗? | **eligible to do sth** *Anyone over the age of 18 is eligible to vote.* 超过18岁就有选举资格。**2** rich, attractive, and not married, and therefore desirable for marriage〔作为婚姻对象〕理想的, 合适的: *a rich eligible bachelor* 一个富有的合意的单身汉 —**eligibility** /ˌɛlədʒəˈbɪlɪtɪ; ˌelɨdʒɨˈbɪlɨti/ *n* [U]

e·lim·i·nate /ɪˈlɪməˌnet; ɪˈlɪmɨneɪt/ *v* [T] **1** to completely get rid of something that is unnecessary or unwanted 消除, 根除:

Under the agreement, all trade barriers will be eliminated. 根据该协议，所有的贸易壁垒都将被消除。| **eliminate sth from** *Police have eliminated Morris from their enquiries.* 警察已将莫里斯排除在调查对象之外。**2** [usually passive 一般用被动态] to defeat a team or person in a competition, so that they no longer take part in it 淘汰: *Our team was eliminated in the first round.* 我们队第一轮就被淘汰了。**3** to kill someone in order to prevent them from causing trouble 消灭; 铲除: *a ruthless dictator who eliminated all his rivals* 铲除所有异己的残酷的独裁者

e·lim·i·na·tion /ɪˌlɪmə`neʃən; ɪˌlɪmɪˈneɪʃən/ *n* [U]
1 ▶REMOVAL OF STH 除掉某物◀ the removal or destruction of something 消除, 根除: [+of] *the elimination of smallpox with worldwide vaccination* 通过世界范围内的接种疫苗消除天花
2 process of elimination a way of discovering the cause of something by carefully examining each possibility until only one is left 排除法: *The identity of the murderer was arrived at by a process of elimination.* 通过排除法，杀人凶手的身份最终被确定。
3 ▶DEFEAT 失败◀ the defeat of a team or player in a competition, so that they may no longer take part 淘汰
4 ▶KILLING 杀害◀ a situation in which someone is killed in order to prevent them from causing trouble 消灭, 铲除: [+of] *the elimination of dissidents* 铲除持不同政见者
5 ▶BODY PROCESS 身体机能◀ *technical* the process of getting rid of substances that your body no longer needs【术语】排泄

El·i·ot /`ɛlɪət; ˈeliət/, **George** (1819-80) British woman writer, whose real name was Mary Ann or Marian Evans. She wrote some of the greatest English NOVELS, including *Middlemarch*, *The Mill on the Floss*, and *Silas Marner*. Her novels give a detailed picture of many different characters at all levels of English society. 艾略特〔(1819-1880)，英国女作家，真名玛丽·安或玛丽安·埃文斯。她创作了一些英格兰最伟大的小说，包括《米德尔马奇》、《弗洛斯河上的磨坊》和《织工马南》。她的小说详细勾画了英格兰社会各阶层的人物形象〕

Eliot, T.S. (1888-1965) a US poet and writer of plays, who lived in England for most of his life. He is one of the most important writers of the 20th century, and he won the Nobel Prize for Literature in 1948. His works include *The Cocktail Party*, *The Waste Land*, and *The Lovesong of J. Alfred Prufrock*. 艾略特〔(1888-1965)，美国诗人、剧作家。他一生中大部分时间都居住在英格兰，是20世纪最重要的作家之一，1948年获诺贝尔文学奖。其作品包括《鸡尾酒会》、《荒原》和《普鲁弗洛克的情歌》〕

e·lite /ɪ`lit; eɪˈliːt/ *n* [C] **1** a group of people who have a lot of power and influence because they have money, knowledge, or special skills（社会）精英; 上层人士: *a small privileged elite* 少数特权阶层 **2 elite corps/squad/college etc** a group of people that contains the best, most educated etc people of a larger group 精锐军团; 精英小组/大学等: *an elite corps of officers* 军官中的精英小组

e·lit·ist /e`litɪst; eɪˈliːtɪst/ *adj* based on a system in which small groups of people have a lot of power or advantages 精英统治的: *an elitist education system* 精英教育体制 **—elitism** *n* [U] **—elitist** *n* [C]

e·lix·ir /ɪ`lɪksə; ɪˈlɪksə/ *n* **1** [C] *literary* a magical liquid that is supposed to cure people of illness, make them younger etc【文】灵丹妙药; 不老药 **2** [C] something that is supposed to solve problems as if by magic〔解决问题的〕灵丹妙药: *Don't imagine that lowering inflation is an elixir for all our economic ills.* 不要以为降低通货膨胀是医治所有经济弊病的灵丹妙药。

E·liz·a·be·than /ɪˌlɪzə`biθən; ɪˌlɪzəˈbiːθən◂/ *adj* connected to the period 1558-1603 when Elizabeth I was queen of England〔英格兰女王〕伊丽莎白一世时代的: *Elizabethan drama* 伊丽莎白一世时代的戏剧 **—Elizabethan** *n* [C]: *The Earl of Essex was a famous Elizabethan.* 埃塞克斯伯爵是伊丽莎白一世时代的一位名流。

E·liz·a·beth I /ɪˌlɪzəbəθ ðə `fɜst; ɪˌlɪzəbəθ ðə ˈfɜːst/, **Queen** (1533-1603) the queen of England from 1558 until her death. She never married, and is sometimes called 'the Virgin Queen'. While she was queen, England's power in the world increased, and the period is sometimes called 'the Elizabethan age', which people think of as a great period in English history. 伊丽莎白一世〔(1533-1603)，英格兰女王，1558年即位直至去世。她终身未婚，有时也称"童贞女王"。在位期间，英格兰国力不断增强。这一时期时有"伊丽莎白时代"之称，被认为是英格兰历史上的一个伟大时期〕

Elizabeth II /ɪˌlɪzəbəθ ðə `sɛkənd; ɪˌlɪzəbəθ ðə ˈsekənd/, **Queen** (1926-) the British queen since 1952, and also head of the British Commonwealth. She is married to the Duke of Edinburgh, and they have four children. 伊丽莎白二世〔(1926-)，英国女王、英联邦首脑，1952年开始即位。她与爱丁堡公爵成婚，有四个孩子〕

Elk /ɛlk; elk/ **1 the Elks** an organization for men which does CHARITY work in many small towns and cities in the US. Its official name is the **Benevolent and Protective Order of Elks**. 麋鹿会〔一男性慈善机构，在美国众多小城镇设有分会，正式名称为麋鹿慈善互助会〕**2** a member of this organization 麋鹿会会员

elk *n* [C] a very large European and Asian DEER with big flat horns 驼鹿; 麋

El·ling·ton /`ɛlɪŋtən; ˈelɪŋtən/, **Duke** (1899-1974) a US JAZZ COMPOSER and piano player, who was also a very successful band leader 埃林顿公爵〔(1899-1974)，美国爵士乐作曲家、钢琴演奏家。他也是一位十分出色的乐队领队〕

el·lipse /ɪ`lɪps; ɪˈlɪps/ *n* [C] a curved shape like a circle, but with two slightly longer and flatter sides 椭圆

el·lip·sis /ɪ`lɪpsɪs; ɪˈlɪpsɪs/ *n plural* **ellipses** /-siz; -siːz/ [C,U] an occasion when words are deliberately left out of a sentence, though the meaning can still be understood〔不影响意义的句子成分的〕省略

el·lip·ti·cal /ɪ`lɪptɪkl; ɪˈlɪptɪkəl/ also 又作 **el·lip·tic** /-tɪk; -tɪk/ *adj* **1** having the shape of an ellipse 椭圆的; 椭圆形的: *The earth's orbit is elliptical.* 地球的轨道是椭圆形的。**2** elliptical speech or writing is difficult to understand because more is meant than is actually said〔言辞或文章〕晦涩的, 隐晦的: *an elliptical remark* 隐晦的评论

El·lis Is·land /`ɛlɪs ˌaɪlənd; ˈelɪs ˌaɪlənd/ a small island close to New York City, which for over 50 years (1892-1943) was the main centre for dealing with people arriving in the US who wanted to settle in the country as IMMIGRANTS. Millions of people, mostly from Europe, passed through Ellis Island to become US citizens. 埃利斯岛〔纽约市附近一小岛。五十多年间(1892-1943)该岛曾是美国入境移民的主要检查站。数百万人经由该岛成为美国公民，大部分是欧洲人〕

elm /ɛlm; elm/ *n* [C,U] a type of large tree with broad leaves, or the wood from this tree 榆树; 榆木

El Ni·ño /ɛl `ninjo; el ˈniːnjəʊ/ a change in the weather that happens every three to seven years, caused by a rise in the temperature of a large area of the Pacific Ocean off the west coast of South America. El Niño has severe effects on the weather in many parts of the world, and can cause DROUGHT (=complete lack of rain) in some places and heavy rain and violent storms in other places. 厄尔尼诺〔南美洲西海岸太平洋水温上升而引起的一种天气变化，每三至七年发生一次。它对世界许多地区的天气有着严重影响。有的地区因此干旱缺雨，有的地区暴雨和强风暴肆虐〕

el·o·cu·tion /ˌɛlə`kjuʃən; ˌeləˈkjuːʃən/ *n* [U] good clear speaking in public, involving voice control, pronunciation etc 演讲技巧; 演讲术: *elocution lessons* 演讲技巧课程 **—elocutionary** *adj* **—elocutionist** *n* [C]

e·lon·gate /ɪ`lɔŋget; ˈiːlɒŋgeɪt/ *v* [I,T] to become longer, or make something longer than normal（使）拉长 **—elongation** /ˌɪlɔŋ`geʃən; ˌiːlɒŋˈgeɪʃən/ *n* [C,U]

e·lon·gat·ed /ɪ`lɔŋgetɪd; ˈiːlɒŋgeɪtɪd/ *adj* longer than normal 拉长的, 偏长的: *tribeswomen with rings around their elongated necks* 拉长的脖子上戴着项圈的部落妇女

e·lope /ɪ`lop; ɪˈləʊp/ *v* [I] to leave your home secretly in order to get married 私奔 **—elopement** *n* [C,U]

el·o·quent /`ɛləkwənt; ˈeləkwənt/ *adj* **1** able to express your ideas and opinions well, especially in a way that influences people 雄辩的, 能言善辩的: *an eloquent appeal for support* 能打动人心的求助呼吁 **2** showing a feeling or meaning without using words 清楚表明的; 形象地显示的: *The photographs are an eloquent reminder of the horrors of war.* 这些照片形象地提醒人们不要忘记战争的恐怖。**—eloquently** *adv* **—eloquence** *n* [U]

El Pas·o /ɛl `pæso; el ˈpæsəʊ/ a city in Texas in the US, next to the Rio Grande and the border with Mexico 埃尔帕索〔美国得克萨斯州一城市，濒临格兰德河，地处美墨边境〕

El Sal·va·dor /ɛl `sælvədɔr; el ˈsælvədɔː/ a country in central America, between Guatemala and Honduras, on the coast of the Pacific Ocean. Population: 6,238,000 (2001). Capital: San Salvador. 萨尔瓦多〔中美洲一国家，位于危地马拉和洪都拉斯之间，濒临太平洋。人口: 6,238,000 (2001)，首都: 圣萨尔瓦多〕**—Salvadorean** *n, adj*

else /ɛls; els/ *adv* **1 who/what/why etc else** or **anything/someone/anywhere etc else** **a)** besides or in addition to someone, something etc 另外, 其他: *I've said I'm sorry. What*

else can I do? 我已经说过对不起了，还让我做什么呢？| *Who else was at the party?* 出席晚会的还有什么人？| *Do you want anything else to eat?* 你还要吃点别的吗？**b)** apart from or instead of something, someone etc 除去；其他：*Everyone else but me was invited.* 除我之外，其他人都被邀请了。| *In the end she married somebody else.* 结果她嫁给了别人。| *It's not in my drawer, where else could it be?* 它不在我的抽屉里，可又能在哪儿呢？**2 or else** or otherwise 否则，要不：*You must pay £100 or else go to prison.* 你必须付 100 英镑，否则就得入狱。| *Your book must be here, or else you've lost it.* 你的书应该在这里，要不就是你弄丢了。

Frequencies of the word **else** in spoken and written English
单词 else 在英语口语和书面语中的使用频率

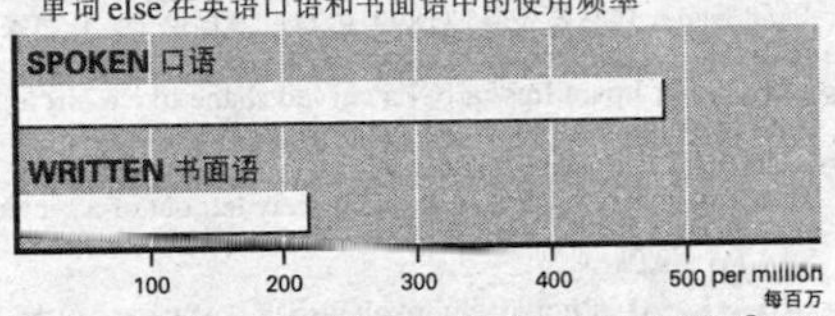

Based on the British National Corpus and the Longman Lancaster Corpus
据英国国家语料库和朗文兰开斯特语料库

This graph shows that the word **else** is much more common in spoken English than in written English. This is because it is used a lot in questions and is used in some common spoken phrases. 本图表显示，else 一词在英语口语中使用的频率要大大高于书面语，因为它大量用于疑问句和一些常见口语短语中。

else (*adv*) **SPOKEN PHRASES**
含 else 的口语短语

3 anything else? used to ask someone if they want to buy another thing, say another thing etc 还要别的吗？；还有别的吗？：*"Twenty Marlborough and a box of matches please." "Anything else?" "No, thanks."* "请来一包 20 支装的万宝路香烟和一包火柴。" "还要别的吗？" "不要了，谢谢。" **4 there's nothing else** used to say that the thing you have mentioned is the only one that exists, is possible etc 没有别的；没有其他可能〔用来表示你刚才所提的是唯一存在或可能的〕：*You'll have to have bread and cheese. There's nothing else, I'm afraid.* 你只好吃面包和干酪，恐怕别的什么也没有。| *The club was closed, so we just went home. There was nothing else to do.* 俱乐部关门了，所以我们只好回家，因为别无他事可做。**5 what else?/who else?/where else? etc** used to say that it is obvious that the thing, person, place etc that has been mentioned is the only one possible 还能有别的什么/什么人/什么地方？〔用来表示你刚才提及的事物、人、地方等是显而易见的唯一可能〕：*"Are you giving him computer games for his birthday?" "Of course, what else?"* "你准备送他电脑游戏作生日礼物吗？" "当然，要不还能送什么？" **6 what else can you do/say?** used to say that it is impossible to do or say anything apart from what you have mentioned 你还能做/说什么？：*I had to give it to her. What else could I do?* 我只能把那给她，还能怎么办呢？**7 or else** used to threaten someone 要不然〔用于表示威胁〕：*You'd better do it, or else!* 你最好去做，要不然够你受的！**8 if nothing else** used to say that something is worth doing, good for you etc for one reason, even if there are no other reasons 起码，即使不是出于别的原因〔表示某事值得做或有好处〕：*He said that if nothing else, teaching taught him how to deal with people.* 他说教书起码让他学会了如何与人打交道。

else·where /ˋɛls,hwɛr; elsˈweə/ *adv* in or to another place 在别处；去别处：*outbreaks of rioting elsewhere in the region* 该地区别处爆发的骚乱

ELT /,i ɛl ˋti; ,iː el ˈtiː/ *n* [U] *especially BrE* English Language Teaching; the teaching of the English language to people whose first language is not English【尤英】英语（语言）教学；〔英语并非母语的〕英语教学

e·lu·ci·date /ɪˋlusə,det; ɪˈluːsɪ̈deɪt/ *v* [I,T] *formal* to explain something that is difficult to understand very clearly, by providing more information【正式】阐明，解释：*His theory is further elucidated in a series of articles published between 1976 and 1980.* 他的理论在1976年至1980年发表的一系列文章中得到了进一步阐述。—**elucidation** /ɪ,lusəˋdeʃən; ɪ,luːsɪ̈ˈdeɪʃən/ *n* [C,U] **elucidatory** /ɪˋlusədə,torɪ; ɪˈluːsɪ̈deɪtəri/ *adj*

e·lude /ɪˋlud; ɪˈluːd/ *v* [T] **1** to escape from someone or something, especially by tricking them〔机敏地〕逃避，躲避：*The fleeing rebels managed to elude their pursuers.* 逃跑的叛乱分子摆脱了追踪者。**2** if something that you want eludes you, you fail to find or achieve it 找不到，错过：*Success had so far eluded him.* 成功至今与他无缘。**3** if a fact or the answer to a problem eludes you, you cannot remember or solve it 忘记；把…难倒：*The exact terminology eludes me for the moment.* 确切的术语我一时想不起来。

e·lu·sive /ɪˋlusɪv; ɪˈluːsɪv/ *adj* **1** an elusive person or animal is difficult to find or not often seen〔人或动物〕难找的；常见不到的：*an elusive man who was never in his office* 从来不在办公室的一个难找的人 **2** an elusive result is difficult to achieve 困难的，难实现的：*Success in the business world has so far proved elusive.* 到目前为止，想在商界获得成功仍是困难重重。**3** an elusive idea or quality is difficult to describe or understand 难以表述的；难懂的：*The meaning of the poem was somewhat elusive.* 这首诗的含义有点难以捉摸。—**elusively** *adv* —**elusiveness** *n* [U]

elves /ɛlvz; elvz/ *n* the plural of ELF

El·vis /ˋɛlvɪs; ˈelvɪ̈s/ also 又作 **Elvis the Pelvis** /,‥ ‥ ˈ‥/ —see 见 Elvis PRESLEY

E·ly·sée Pal·ace /elɪ,ze ˋpælɪs; eɪ,liːzeɪ ˈpælɪ̈s/ the official home of the President of France, in Paris. Its name is sometimes used to mean the President and his advisors 爱丽舍宫〔法国总统官邸，位于巴黎。该名称有时用于指称法国总统及其顾问〕：*Rumours of a split in the government were swiftly denied by the Elysée Palace.* 爱丽舍宫迅速否认了有关政府分裂的谣传。

E·lys·i·um /ɪˋlɪʒɪəm; ɪˈlɪziəm/ also 又作 **the Elysian Fields** *literary* a place of complete happiness. According to ancient Greek stories, Elysium is the place where good people go after their death. PARADISE【文】极乐世界；天堂〔古希腊传说中善人死后的归宿〕

'em /əm; əm/ *pron spoken* sometimes used as a short form of 'them'【口】〔有时用作 them 的缩略形式〕：*Go on, Bill, you tell 'em!* 你说吧，比尔，告诉他们！

em- /ɪm; ɪm/ *prefix* the form used for EN- before b, m, or p en- 的变体〔用在字母 b, m, p 之前〕：*an embittered man* (=made bitter) 一个痛苦的男人 | *empowerment* 授权

e·ma·ci·a·ted /ɪˋmeʃɪ,etɪd; ɪˈmeɪʃieɪtɪ̈d/ *adj* extremely thin from lack of food or illness〔因饥饿或疾病〕极其消瘦的，憔悴的：*The prisoners were ill and emaciated.* 囚犯们疾病缠身，骨瘦如柴。—**emaciation** /ɪ,meʃɪˋeʃən; ɪ,meɪʃiˈeɪʃən/ *n* [U]: *in an advanced state of emaciation* 处于极其瘦弱的状态

e-mail /ˋi mel; ˈiː meɪl/ *n* [U] a system that allows people to send messages to each other by computer; ELECTRONIC MAIL 电子邮件系统；电子邮件 —**e-mail** *v* [T]: *Will you e-mail me about it?* 你能就此事给我发个电子邮件吗？—see picture on page A14 参见 A14 页图

em·a·nate /ˋɛmə,net; ˈeməneɪt/ *v*

emanate from sth *phr v* [T not in passive 不用被动态] to flow or come from 散发自；来自：*Delicious smells emanated from the kitchen.* 从厨房散发出诱人的香味。—**emanation** /,ɛməˋneʃən; ,eməˈneɪʃən/ *n* [C,U]

e·man·ci·pate /ɪˋmænsə,pet; ɪˈmænsɪ̈peɪt/ *v* [T] *formal* to make someone free from social, political, or legal restrictions that limit what they can do【正式】解放，使不受〔社会、政治或法律的〕束缚：*Learning will emancipate the oppressed and engender social change.* 知识可以解放受压迫者，引发社会变革。—**emancipation** /ɪ,mænsəˋpeʃən; ɪ,mænsɪ̈ˈpeɪʃən/ *n* [U] *the emancipation of slaves* 奴隶的解放

e·man·ci·pat·ed /ɪˋmænsə,petɪd; ɪˈmænsɪ̈peɪtɪ̈d/ *adj* **1** socially, politically, or legally free 解放了的；不受束缚的 **2** an emancipated woman is not influenced by old-fashioned ideas about how women should behave〔妇女〕思想解放的，不受传统观念束缚的

Emancipation Proc·la·ma·tion, the /·‥ˈ‥ ‥ˈ‥/ an announcement made in the US by President Abraham Lincoln which ordered the end of SLAVERY (=the practice of owning people as property) in the Confederate States (=the southern states of the US) from January 1st 1863. The Proclamation was made during the Civil War. Soon after the war, slavery was completely ended by the **13th Amendment** to the US Constitution.《解放宣言》〔美国总统亚伯拉罕·林肯发布的一项法令，规定自 1863 年 1 月 1 日起废止南部邦联各州的奴隶制。该宣言在美国南北战争期间制定。战后不久，美国宪法《第十三条修正案》完全废止了奴隶制〕

e·mas·cu·late /ɪˋmæskjə,let; ɪˈmæskjɪ̈leɪt/ *v* [T often passive 常用被动态] **1** to make someone or something weaker or less effective 使衰弱；使效力减弱：*The bill has been emasculated by Congress.* 国会削弱了这个法案的效力。**2** to make a man feel less male 使缺少男子气：*Some men feel emasculated if they*

work for a woman. 在女人手下工作，有些男人会觉得没有男子气。**3** *technical* to remove all or part of a male's sex organs; CASTRATE【术语】阉割；去势 —**emasculation** /ɪˌmæskjəˋleʃən; ɪˌmæskjʊˈleɪʃən/ *n* [U]

em·balm /ɪmˋbɑm; ɪmˈbɑːm/ *v* [T] to treat a dead body with chemicals, oils etc to prevent it from decaying〔用药物、油等对尸体〕进行防腐处理: *ancient Egyptian embalming techniques* 古埃及防腐术 —**embalmer** *n* [C]

CULTURAL NOTE 文化注释

Dead bodies are almost always buried or CREMATEd in Western society. In the US a body must by law be embalmed before it is buried. 在西方通常将尸体土葬或火化。在美国，法律规定土葬前尸体须经防腐处理。

em·bank·ment /ɪmˋbæŋkmənt; ɪmˈbæŋkmənt/ *n* [C] **1** a wide wall of stones or earth built to keep the water in a river from flowing over its banks, or to support a road or railway over low ground 河堤；路堤 **2** a slope of earth, stone etc that rises from either side of a railway or road〔铁路、公路的〕堤坡

Embankment, the also 又作 **the Thames Embankment** a road along the north bank of the River Thames in London〔伦敦泰晤士河北岸的〕河堤街

em·bar·go[1] /ɪmˋbɑrgo; ɪmˈbɑːgəʊ/ *n plural* **embargoes** [C] an official order stopping trade with another country 贸易禁令；禁运: **put/impose an embargo on** *an embargo imposed on wheat exports* 小麦出口禁令 | **trade/oil/arms etc embargo** *They're accused of trying to break the oil embargo.* 他们被指控试图违反石油禁运的规定。| [+on] *an embargo on wheat exports* 小麦出口禁运

embargo[2] *v* [T] to stop trade with another country by an official order 禁止〔与另一国家〕通商；下令禁运: *a decision to embargo the Southern States* 对南方各州实行禁运的决定

em·bark /ɪmˋbɑrk; ɪmˈbɑːk/ *v* [I,T] to get onto a ship or put or take something onto a ship 上船；装船；使上船；装载 —opposite 反义词 DISEMBARK —**embarkation** /ˌɛmbɑrˋkeʃən; ˌembɑːˈkeɪʃən/ *n* [C,U]

embark on/upon sth *phr v* [T] to start something, especially something new and difficult that will take a long time 开始，着手〔尤指新的、有难度且费时的事〕: *In the 1950s China embarked on a major program of industrialization.* 20世纪50年代，中国开始实施工业化的一项重大计划。

em·bar·rass /ɪmˋbærəs; ɪmˈbærəs/ *v* [T] **1** to make someone feel anxious, ashamed, or uncomfortable, especially in a social situation〔尤指在社交场合〕使尴尬，使窘迫: *The old woman's blunt questions embarrassed her, making her momentarily tongue-tied.* 老妇人不客气地提出一些问题，使她尴尬得一时语塞。**2** to do something that causes problems for a government, political organization, or politician 给〔政府、政治组织或政治人物〕出难题；使…陷入困境: *a series of revelations that has embarrassed the government* 使政府难堪的一系列曝光事件

em·bar·rassed /ɪmˋbærəst; ɪmˈbærəst/ *adj* **1** ashamed, nervous, or uncomfortable in a social situation 难堪的，尴尬的: *I managed to spill water on one of the guests – I was so embarrassed!* 我竟把水洒到一名客人身上，难堪极了！| *an embarrassed smile* 尴尬的笑 | **[+about]** *At about the age of twelve, girls start feeling acutely embarrassed about changing their clothes in front of other people.* 大约到12岁时，女孩子便开始对当着别人的面换衣服感到极不自在。—see 见 SHAME[1] (USAGE) **2 financially embarrassed** having no money or having debts 拮据的，负债的

em·bar·ras·sing /ɪmˋbærəsɪŋ; ɪmˈbærəsɪŋ/ *adj* making you feel ashamed, nervous, or uncomfortable 令人尴尬的，使人难堪的: *The firm wants to avoid any embarrassing questions about its finances.* 这家公司力图回避有关财务方面的任何难堪问题。—**embarrassingly** *adv*

em·bar·rass·ment /ɪmˋbærəsmənt; ɪmˈbærəsmənt/ *n* **1** [U] the feeling you have when you are embarrassed 窘迫；尴尬: [+at] *He could not hide his embarrassment at his children's rudeness.* 他无法掩饰孩子们的无礼给他带来的难堪。**2** [C] an event that causes a government, political organization etc problems 使〔政府或政治机构等〕为难的事: *The allegations have been an embarrassment to the administration.* 指控令当局头痛。**3** [C] someone who behaves in a way that makes you feel ashamed and uncomfortable 使人难堪的人，令人不快的人: [+to] *His mother's boasting was an embarrassment to him.* 母亲的吹嘘令他无地自容。**4 financial embarrassment** debts or a lack of money that causes problems for you 欠账，拮据 **5 embarrassment of riches** so many good things that it is difficult to decide which one you want〔好东西〕多得不知道选哪个好

em·bas·sy /ˋɛmbəsɪ; ˈembəsi/ *n* [C] **1** a group of officials who represent their government in a foreign country 大使馆全体外交官员 **2** the official building used by these officials 大使馆: *the American Embassy in Paris* 巴黎的美国大使馆

em·bat·tled /ɪmˋbætḷd; ɪmˈbætld/ *adj formal*【正式】**1** surrounded by enemies, especially in war or fighting〔尤指在战争或打斗中〕被敌人包围的: *Their embattled army finally surrendered.* 他们的军队陷入包围，最终投降了。**2** an embattled person, organization, etc has many problems or difficulties 问题缠身的；困难重重的: *embattled companies fighting off takeover bids* 抵制竞价收购的内外交困的公司

em·bed /ɪmˋbɛd; ɪmˈbed/ *v* **embedded, embedding** [T usually passive 一般用被动态] **1** to fix something firmly and deeply in a surface or solid object 把…嵌入；把…插入: [+in] *Small stones were embedded in the ice.* 冰里嵌了许多小石子。**2** if ideas, attitudes, or feelings etc are embedded, you believe or feel them very strongly 深信，强烈感受〔思想、态度、感情等〕: *deeply embedded feelings of shame* 挥之不去的羞愧感

em·bel·lish /ɪmˋbɛlɪʃ; ɪmˈbelɪʃ/ *v* [T] **1** to make a story or statement more interesting by adding details that are not true 给〔故事或叙述〕添枝加叶；对…加以渲染: *She gave an embellished account of what had happened.* 她添油加醋地把发生的事描述了一番。**2** to make something more beautiful by adding decorations 装饰，修饰: [+with] *The ceiling was embellished with cherubs.* 天花板上装饰着小天使的图案。—**embellishment** *n* [C,U]

em·ber /ˋɛmbɚ; ˈembə/ *n* [C usually plural 一般用复数] a piece of wood or coal in a fire that is no longer burning but is still red and very hot〔木块或煤块的〕余烬: *glowing embers* 发光的余烬

em·bez·zle /ɪmˋbɛzḷ; ɪmˈbezəl/ *v* [I,T] to steal money from the place where you work 贪污；侵吞: *She had embezzled $10,000 by falsifying the accounts.* 她通过做假账侵吞了一万美元。—**embezzlement** *n* [U] —**embezzler** *n* [C]

em·bit·ter /ɪmˋbɪtɚ; ɪmˈbɪtə/ *v* [T] to make someone feel hate and anger for a long time because they think they have been treated unfairly 使怨恨，使怨愤: *The incident had embittered relations between the two countries.* 该事件使两国失和。—**embittered** *adj*

em·bla·zon /ɛmˋblezn̩; ɪmˈbleɪzən/ *v* [T] **1** to put a name, design etc on something so that it can easily be seen 在…上明显地刻上名字[标记等]: *The manufacturer's name was emblazoned on the packet.* 包装上明显标有生产厂家的名字。**2** to decorate a SHIELD[1] (2) or flag with a COAT OF ARMS 用纹章装饰〔盾形纹徽、旗〕

em·blem /ˋɛmbləm; ˈembləm/ *n* [C] **1** a picture or shape that is used to represent a country, group etc〔用来代表国家或团体等的〕标志，徽章；纹章: [+of] *The national emblem of England is a rose.* 英格兰的标志是一朵玫瑰花。—see picture at 参见 SIGN[1] 图 **2** something that represents an idea or principle〔代表一种观念或原则的〕标志；象征: [+of] *Expensive cars are seen as an emblem of success.* 豪华汽车被看做成功的标志。—compare 比较 SYMBOL (3)

em·ble·mat·ic /ˌɛmbləˋmætɪk; ˌembləˈmætɪk◂/ *adj formal* seeming to represent or be a sign of something【正式】象征性的；标志性的 —**emblematically** /-kḷɪ; -kli/ *adv*

em·bod·i·ment /ɪmˋbɑdɪmənt; ɪmˈbɒdɪmənt/ *n* **the embodiment of** someone or something that represents or is very typical of an idea or quality 化身，体现: *He is the embodiment of evil.* 他是邪恶的化身。

em·bod·y /ɪmˋbɑdɪ; ɪmˈbɒdi/ *v* [T] **1** if a person, thing, or organization embodies an idea or principle it clearly expresses it and shows its importance by the way it behaves or affects behaviour 体现〔思想、原则〕: *The country's constitution embodies the ideals of equality and freedom.* 这个国家的宪法体现了平等和自由的理想。**2** *formal* to include something【正式】包括，收录: *Their latest car model embodies many new improvements.* 他们的最新一款车型包含了许多新的改进。

em·bold·en /ɪmˋboldn̩; ɪmˈbəʊldən/ *v* [T] *formal* to give someone more courage【正式】使有胆量，使（较）勇敢: *Emboldened by her smile, he asked her to dance.* 她的微笑给他壮了胆，于是他邀请她跳舞。

em·bo·lis·m /ˋɛmbəˌlɪzəm; ˈembəlɪzəm/ *n* [C] *technical* something such as a hard mass of blood or a small amount of air that blocks a tube carrying blood through the body【术语】〔血管的〕栓塞，血栓: *a coronary embolism* 冠状动脉血栓

em·boss /ɪmˋbɔs; ɪmˈbɒs/ *v* [T usually passive 一般用被动态] to make a raised pattern on the surface of metal, paper, leather

E

etc 在〔金属、纸或皮革等〕表面上用浮雕图案装饰: **emboss sth with** *The firm's paper is embossed with its name and address.* 公司的信纸上凸印有公司的名称和地址。—**embossed** *adj*

em·brace[1] /ɪm`bres; ɪm'breɪs/ *v* **1** [I,T] to put your arms around someone and hold them in a friendly or loving way 抱, 拥抱: *She embraced her son tenderly.* 她温柔地拥抱着儿子。**2** [T] *formal* to include something as part of a subject, discussion etc 【正式】包括, 涉及: *This course embraces several different aspects of psychology.* 这门课程涉及心理学的几个不同方面。**3** [T] *formal* to accept and use new ideas, opinions etc eagerly 【正式】欣然接受, 采纳 **4** [T] *formal* to start to believe in a religion or political system 【正式】〔开始〕信奉; 皈依: *She embraced the Muslim faith.* 她皈依伊斯兰教。—see also 另见 ALL-EMBRACING

embrace[2] *n* [C] the act of holding someone close to you as a sign of love 拥抱: *The lovers were in a close embrace.* 这对情人紧紧拥抱在一起。

em·bro·ca·tion /ˌɛmbro`keʃən; ˌembrə'keɪʃən/ *n* [C,U] *formal* a liquid medicine that you rub on a part of your body that is stiff or ACHING after too much exercise 【正式】擦剂〔用于揉搓因运动过度导致的僵硬或胀疼部位〕

em·broi·der /ɪm`brɔɪdɚ; ɪm'brɔɪdə/ *v* **1** [I,T] to make a pattern of stitches on cloth with coloured cotton or silk threads 刺绣, 在…上刺绣: *The dress was embroidered with flowers.* 那件裙子上绣着花。—see picture on page A16 参见 A16 页图 **2** [T] to make a story or report of events more interesting or exciting by adding details, that you have invented; EMBELLISH (1) 对〔故事或报道〕加以渲染 —**embroidered** *adj*: *richly embroidered* 大加渲染的

em·broi·der·y /ɪm`brɔɪdərɪ; ɪm'brɔɪdəri/ *n* **1** [C,U] a decoration or pattern made by sewing onto cloth, or the act of making this 刺绣(法) **2** [U] imaginary details that are added to make a story seem more interesting or exciting 夸张之词; 渲染: *I just want the truth from you, with no embroidery.* 我只想你告诉我真相, 不要添枝加叶。

embroidery hoop *n* [C] a circular wooden frame used to hold cloth firmly in place while patterns are being SEWN into it; TAMBOUR 〔刺绣用的〕绷圈

em·broil /ɛm`brɔɪl; ɪm'brɔɪl/ *v* [T usually passive 一般用被动态] to involve someone in a difficult situation 使〔某人〕卷入〔困境〕: **embroil sb/sth in** *Soon they were embroiled in a fierce argument.* 很快他们就卷入了一场激烈的争论。

em·bry·o /`ɛmbrɪˌo; 'embriəʊ/ *n plural* **embryos** [C] **1** an animal or human that has not yet been born, and is in its first state of development in the mother's body 胚, 胚胎 —compare 比较 FOETUS **2 in embryo** not yet complete, but still developing 在胚胎阶段; 萌芽的, 未成熟的: *His plans were still in embryo.* 他的计划仍在酝酿中。

em·bry·ol·o·gy /ˌɛmbrɪ`ɑlədʒɪ; ˌembri'ɒlədʒi/ *n* [U] the scientific study of embryos 胚胎学 —**embryologist** *n* [C]

em·bry·on·ic /ˌɛmbrɪ`ɑnɪk; ˌembri'ɒnɪk◂/ *adj* in an undeveloped or very early stage of growth 萌芽阶段的, 刚起步的: *Britain's embryonic wind energy industry* 英国刚刚起步的利用风能的工业

em·cee, MC /ˌɛm`si; ˌem 'siː/ *n* [C] *AmE* someone who is in charge of a social event or programme and introduces various people or performers; MASTER OF CEREMONIES 【美】司仪; 节目主持人: *She's emcee of her radio show.* 她为自己的广播节目担任主持。—**emcee** *v* [I,T]

EMEA *n* European Medicines Evaluation Agency; an organization which examines the safety of new medicines 欧洲药物评审局〔检测新药安全性能的一个机构〕

e·mend /ɪ`mɛnd; ɪ'mend/ *v* [T] to take the mistakes out of something that has been written, before it is printed 〔付印前〕校订〔文稿〕, 修改〔作品〕—compare 比较 AMEND —**emendation** /ˌimɛn`deʃən; ˌiːmen'deɪʃən/ *n* [C,U]

em·e·rald[1] /`ɛmərəld; 'emərəld/ *n* [C] a bright green stone that is valuable and often used in jewellery 翡翠, 绿宝石

2 **emerald[2]** *adj* bright green 翠绿色的 —see picture on page A5 参见 A5 页图

Emerald Isle, the /ˌ, ··· '·/ a name for Ireland, used in literature, often humorously. It is called this because the countryside is very green. 绿宝石岛〔爱尔兰的别称。此名称用于文学作品, 通常是一种幽默用法。该岛因乡间绿野而得名〕

e·merge /ɪ`mɝdʒ; ɪ'mɜːdʒ/ *v* [I] **1** to appear or come out from somewhere 浮现, 出现: [**+from**] *The sun emerged from behind the clouds.* 太阳从云层后露了出来。**2** if facts emerge, they become known after being hidden or secret 显露, 暴露: *Eventually the truth emerged.* 终于真相大白。| **it emerged that** *Later it emerged that the judge had been employing an illegal immigrant.* 后来, 真相大白, 那个法官一直雇用着一名非法移民。**3** to come to the end of a difficult experience 〔从困境中〕摆脱出来, 出头: [**+from**] *She emerged from the divorce a stronger person.* 她走出离婚的阴影, 变得更坚强了。**4** to begin to be known or noticed 开始被人所知; 兴起: *a religious sect that emerged in the 1830s* 兴起于 19 世纪 30 年代的一个宗教派别 —**emergence** *n* [U]: *Japan's emergence as a world leader* 日本渐成世界大国

e·mer·gen·cy /ɪ`mɝdʒənsɪ; ɪ'mɜːdʒənsi/ *n* [C] an unexpected and dangerous situation that must be dealt with immediately 紧急情况, 不测事件: *Lifeguards are trained to deal with emergencies.* 救生员接受过处理紧急情况的训练。| **emergency meeting/repairs/exit etc** (=needed to deal with an urgent and unexpected problem) 紧急会议/抢修/太平门等 *He called an emergency meeting of the governors.* 他召集州长召开紧急会议。| *Emergency exits are clearly marked.* 太平门的标志很明显。—see also 另见 STATE OF EMERGENCY 2 3

emergency brake /'· ···, ·/ *n* [C] *AmE* a piece of equipment in a car that you pull up with your hand to stop the car from moving 【美】〔汽车〕手闸; HANDBRAKE *especially BrE* 【尤英】

emergency cord /'· ··· ·/ *n* [C] *AmE* a chain that a passenger pulls to stop a train in an emergency 【美】〔火车上的〕紧急制动索; COMMUNICATION CORD *BrE* 【英】

emergency room /'· ···, ·/ *n* [C] *AmE* a place in a hospital where people who have been hurt in accidents are taken for treatment 【美】〔医院的〕急救室, 急症室; CASUALTY (3) *BrE* 【英】

emergency services /'· ···, ··/ [plural] *BrE* the official organizations, for example the police, that deal with crime, fires, and injuries 【英】〔警方等处理犯罪、火灾、伤害的〕紧急应变机构

e·mer·gent /ɪ`mɝdʒənt; ɪ'mɜːdʒənt/ *adj* [only before noun 仅用于名词前] in the early stages of existence or development 新出现的; 处于萌芽阶段的: *the emergent nations of the world* 世界上新近建立的国家

e·mer·ging /ɪ`mɝdʒɪŋ; ɪ'mɜːdʒɪŋ/ *adj* [only before noun 仅用于名词前] in an early state of development 新兴的, 发展初期的: *the emerging Thai auto industry* 新兴的泰国汽车工业

e·mer·i·tus /ɪ`mɛrətəs; ɪ'merɪtəs/ *adj* an emeritus PROFESSOR (=university teacher) is no longer working but still has an official title 〔大学教师〕退休后仍保留头衔的, 荣誉退休的

Em·er·son /`ɛməsn̩; 'eməsən/**, Ralph Wal·do** /rælf `wɔldo; rælf 'wɔːldəʊ/ (1803-82) a US poet and writer who had great influence on the religious and PHILOSOPHICAL thought of his time 爱默生〔(1803-1882), 美国诗人、作家, 对当代宗教和哲学思想产生过重大影响〕

em·e·ry /`ɛmərɪ; 'eməri/ *n* [U] a very hard mineral that is used for polishing things and making them smooth 金刚砂

emery board /'··· ·/ *n* [C] a long narrow piece of stiff paper with emery on it, used for shaping your nails 指甲砂锉

e·met·ic /ɪ`mɛtɪk; ɪ'metɪk/ *n* [C] *technical* something that you eat or drink in order to make yourself VOMIT (=bring up food from your stomach) 【术语】催吐剂

em·i·grant /`ɛməgrənt; 'emɪgrənt/ *n* [C] someone who leaves their own country to live in another 〔移居外国的〕移民 —compare 比较 IMMIGRANT

em·i·grate /`ɛməˌgret; 'emɪgreɪt/ *v* [I] to leave your own country in order to live in another 移居外国: *Her family emigrated to America in the 1850s.* 她的家人于 19 世纪 50 年代移居美国。—**emigration** /ˌɛmə`greʃən; ˌemɪ'greɪʃən/ *n* [C,U]

ém·i·gré /`ɛməˌgre; 'emɪgreɪ/ *n* [C] *French* someone who leaves their own country to live in another, usually for political reasons 【法】〔通常指因政治原因移居国外的〕流亡者: *Russian émigrés living in Paris* 住在巴黎的俄国流亡者

em·i·nence /`ɛmənəns; 'emɪnəns/ *n* **1** [U] the quality of being famous and important 杰出, 卓越: *a scientist of great eminence* 出类拔萃的科学家 **2** [C] *formal* a hill or area of high ground 【正式】山丘; 高地 **3 Eminence** a title used when talking to or about a CARDINAL (=priest of high rank in the Roman Catholic Church) 阁下, 大人〔对天主教红衣主教的尊称〕: *Their Eminences are discussing the matter.* 主教大人们正在讨论那件事。

em·i·nent /`ɛmənənt; 'emɪnənt/ *adj* an eminent person is famous and admired by many people 〔指人〕杰出的, 显赫的: *an eminent lawyer* 杰出的律师 —see 见 FAMOUS (USAGE)

eminent do·main /ˌ··· ·'·/ *n* [U] *technical* the right of the US government to take private land for public use 【术语】〔美国政府对私有土地的〕征用权

em·i·nent·ly /`ɛmənəntlɪ; 'emɪnəntli/ *adv formal approving* to a very high degree; perfectly 【正式, 褒】非常; 完全: *eminently qualified for the job* 完全有资格做这项工作

e·mir /əˋmɪr; eˈmɪə/ *n* [C] a Muslim ruler, especially in Asia and parts of Africa 埃米尔〔尤指亚洲和非洲部分地区的穆斯林统治者〕: *the emir of Kano in Nigeria* 尼日利亚卡诺的埃米尔

e·mir·ate /əˋmɪrɪt; ˈemɪr̩ɪt/ *n* [C] the position or country of an emir 埃米尔的职位; 酋长国

em·is·sa·ry /ˋɛməˌsɛrɪ; ˈemɪ̩səri/ *n* [C] someone who is sent with an official message or to do special work, often secretly 使者; 特使; 密使: *a special emissary of the ayatollah* 〔伊斯兰教什叶派领袖〕阿亚图拉的特使

e·mis·sion /ɪˋmɪʃən; ɪˈmɪʃən/ *n* **1** [C] an amount of gas or other substance that a machine or factory produces and sends into the air 〔机器或工厂的〕排气; 排放物: *Britain has agreed to cut emissions of nitrogen oxide from power stations.* 英国同意减少发电站的一氧化氮排放量。| *emissions of CFCs* 含氯氟烃的排放物 **2** [U] the sending out of light, heat, gas etc 〔光、热、气等的〕散发

e·mit /ɪˋmɪt; ɪˈmɪt/ *v* **emitted, emitting** [T] **1** to send out heat, light, gas etc 散发〔热、光、气等〕: *The chimney emitted clouds of smoke.* 烟囱里冒出一团团烟雾。**2** to make a particular kind of sound 发出〔声响〕: *recording the whistles emitted by dolphins* 录下海豚发出的叫声

Em·men·thal, Emmental /ˋɛməntɑl; ˈeməntɑːl/ also 又作 **Emmenthaler, Emmentaler** /-tɑlɚ; -tɑːlə/, **Swiss cheese** *AmE* a type of hard, yellow, Swiss cheese with holes in it【美】〔一种黄色有孔的〕瑞士干酪

Em·my /ˋɛmɪ; ˈemi/ also 又作 **Emmy Award** /ˈ· · ·ˌ·/ *n* [C] a US prize given each year for special achievements in television. There are Emmys for actors, writers, DIRECTORS etc, and the prize is a small STATUE. 艾美奖〔美国每年给有特殊贡献的电视人颁发的奖项, 设演员奖、编剧奖、导演奖等, 奖品为一尊小型雕像〕

e·mol·li·ent /ɪˋmɑljənt; ɪˈmɒliənt/ *n* [C] *formal*【正式】**1** a substance that makes your skin softer and reduces pain 润肤剂, 护肤剂: *This is a powerful emollient against sunburn.* 这是防止晒伤的有效护肤剂。**2 emollient words/phrases etc** emollient words etc make you feel calmer when you have been angry 安抚的话语等

e·mol·u·ment /ɪˋmɑljəmənt; ɪˈmɒljʊ̈mənt/ *n* [C] *formal* money or another form of payment for work you have done【正式】酬金; 酬劳

3 **e·mo·tion** /ɪˋmoʃən; ɪˈməʊʃən/ *n* [C,U] a strong human feeling such as love, hate, anger etc 强烈的情感; 激情: *A mixture of emotions welled up inside him as she spoke.* 当她讲话时, 他百感交集。| *The accused man showed little sign of emotion as he was sentenced.* 宣判时被告并没有什么表情。

3 3 **e·mo·tion·al** /ɪˋmoʃənl̩; ɪˈməʊʃənəl/ *adj* **1** making people have strong feelings or opinions 令人激动的; 敏感的: *Abortion is a very emotional issue.* 堕胎是个非常敏感的问题。**2** showing your feelings to other people, especially by crying when you are upset 情绪激动的〔尤指伤心哭泣〕: *He became very emotional when we had to leave.* 当我们不得不离开时, 他非常伤感。**3** [only before noun 仅用于名词前] connected with your feelings and the way you control them 情绪〔上〕的, 情感〔上〕的: *We monitor the physical and emotional development of the children.* 我们监测孩子们生理和情绪的变化。**4** influenced by your feelings rather than by your thoughts or knowledge 感情用事的; 凭感情的: *an emotional response to the problem* 对问题的感性反应 —**emotionally** *adv*

e·mo·tion·al·is·m /ɪˋmoʃənl̩ˌɪzəm; ɪˈməʊʃənəlɪzəm/ *n* [U] a tendency to show or feel too much emotion 易露感情; 易动感情, 感情用事

e·mo·tive /ɪˋmotɪv; ɪˈməʊtɪv/ *adj* making people have strong feelings 使情绪激动的: **emotive issue/area/word etc** *Child abuse is an emotive subject.* 虐待儿童是一个易引发强烈感情的问题。—**emotively** *adv*

em·pan·el /ɪmˋpænl̩; ɪmˈpænl/ *v* [T] to choose the people to serve on a JURY 挑选〔陪审团成员〕

em·pa·thize also 又作 **-ise** *BrE*【英】/ˋɛmpəˌθaɪz; ˈempəθaɪz/ *v* [I] to be able to understand someone else's feelings, problems etc, especially because you have had similar experiences 移情, 有同感; 同情: **[+with]** *A founder member of the Gay Rights Movement, Mr Smith ensures that the reader empathizes with him.* 同性恋权益运动的创始人之一史密斯先生确保读者会跟他有同感。—compare 比较 SYMPATHIZE

em·pa·thy /ˋɛmpəθɪ; ˈempəθi/ *n* [U] the ability to understand other people's feelings and problems 同情; 同感: **[+with]** *a doctor who had great empathy with her patients* 对病人充满同情的医生 —compare 比较 SYMPATHY

em·pe·ror /ˋɛmpərɚ; ˈempərə/ *n* [C] the ruler of an EMPIRE 皇帝

Emperor's New Clothes, The /ˌ· · · ˈ·/ a FAIRY TALE (=old children's story) by Hans Christian Andersen about an EMPEROR who pays a lot of money for some new magic clothes which can only be seen by wise people. The clothes do not really exist, but the emperor does not admit he cannot see them, because he does not want to seem stupid. Everyone else pretends to see the clothes too, until a child shouts, "The Emperor has no clothes on!" The title is often used to describe a situation in which people are afraid to criticize something because everyone else seems to think it is good or important.《皇帝的新衣》〔汉斯·克里斯蒂安·安徒生创作的童话。故事中有一位皇帝花了不少钱叫人给他缝制几件只有聪明人才可看得见的魔衣。事实上, 这样的衣服并不存在, 可皇帝却不想显得愚蠢, 拒绝承认自己看不见新衣。其他人假装也能看得见, 直到最后有个小孩喊道: "皇帝什么也没穿!" "皇帝的新衣" 一说常用来描写别人都在赞美某事而自己却因此不敢有微词的情形〕

em·pha·sis /ˋɛmfəsɪs; ˈemfəs̩ɪs/ *n plural* **emphases** /-siz; -siːz/ [C,U] **1** special importance that is given to one part of something 重要性, 重点: *In Japan there is a lot of emphasis on politeness.* 在日本人们非常注重礼节。| **place/put emphasis on** *The course puts an emphasis on practical work.* 这门课程重视实践。**2** [C,U] if you put emphasis on a particular word or phrase, you say it slightly louder in order to make it more important 〔单词、短语的〕重音, 强调音: *The emphasis should be on the first syllable.* 重音应落在第一个音节。 3 2

em·pha·size also 又作 **-ise** *BrE*【英】/ˋɛmfəˌsaɪz; ˈemfəsaɪz/ *v* [T] to give special or additional importance to something 强调, 着重: *Logan made a speech emphasizing the need for more volunteers.* 洛根发表了谈话, 强调需要更多的志愿者。| **emphasize that** *It should be emphasized that flying is a very safe way to travel.* 应该着重指出的是, 坐飞机旅行十分安全。 2 2

em·phat·ic /ɪmˋfætɪk; ɪmˈfætɪk/ *adj* **1** an emphatic remark, opinion etc is expressed in a clear, strong way to show its importance 强调的; 有力的; 坚决的: *an emphatic denial* 断然否认 **2** clear and undoubted 明显的, 突出的: *an emphatic victory* 大胜 —**emphatically** /-klɪ; -kli/ *adv*

em·phy·se·ma /ˌɛmfɪˋsimə; ˌemf̩ɪˈsiːmə/ *n* [U] *technical* a disease that affects the lungs, making it difficult to breathe【术语】肺气肿

em·pire /ˋɛmpaɪr; ˈempaɪə/ *n* [C] **1** a group of countries that are all controlled by the ruler or government of one country 帝国: *the Roman empire* 罗马帝国 **2** a group of organizations controlled by one powerful company or person 大企业; 大集团: *an enormous business empire* 巨大的商业集团 3

Empire State Build·ing, the /ˌ· · · ˌ· ·/ a famous very tall office building in New York City, which has 102 floors. It was built in 1931, and for many years it was the tallest building in the world 帝国大厦〔纽约市一著名摩天办公大楼, 共有102层, 建于1931年。在过去多年里一直是世界上最高的建筑〕

em·pir·i·cal /ɛmˋpɪrɪkl̩; ɪmˈpɪrɪkəl/ *adj* [only before noun 仅用于名词前] based on scientific testing or practical experience, not on ideas from books 以科学实验[经验]为依据的; 经验主义的: *Scientists are hoping to find empirical evidence to confirm their theories.* 科学家希望能找到实验证据证明自己的理论。—**empirically** /-klɪ; -kli/ *adv*

em·pir·i·cis·m /ɛmˋpɪrəˌsɪzəm; ɪmˈpɪr̩ɪsɪzəm/ *n* [U] the belief in basing your ideas on practical experience 经验主义, 经验论 —**empiricist** *n* [C]

em·place·ment /ɪmˋplesmənt; ɪmˈpleɪsmənt/ *n* [C] a special position prepared for a gun or other large piece of military equipment 炮位, 炮台; 〔安置军事装备的〕阵地: *a gun emplacement* 炮台

em·ploy¹ /ɪmˋplɔɪ; ɪmˈplɔɪ/ *v* [T] **1** to pay someone to work for you 雇用: *The company employs 2,000 people worldwide.* 这家公司在全世界雇用了2000名员工。| **be employed as sth** *Dave is employed as a baggage handler at the airport.* 戴夫受雇在机场做行李搬运工。| **employ sb to do sth** *Freelance consultants have been employed to look at ways of reducing waste.* 独立顾问们受雇研究减少浪费的办法。—see also 另见 SELF-EMPLOYED, UNEMPLOYED **2** to use a particular method or skill in order to do something 使用, 运用: *The report examines teaching methods employed in the classroom.* 这个报告考查了课堂教学方法。**3 be employed in doing sth** to spend your time doing something 花时间做某事; 忙于做某事: *Her days are employed in gardening and voluntary work.* 她的时间全花在搞园艺和做义工上。 2 2

employ² *n* [U] **in sb's employ** *formal* if you are in someone's employ, you work for them【正式】受雇于某人, 为某人工作: *in the Prince's employ* 为王子工作

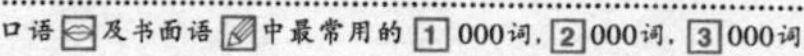
口语 及书面语 中最常用的 1 000词, 2 000词, 3 000词

em·ploy·a·ble /ɪm`plɔɪəbḷ; ɪmˈplɔɪəbəl/ *adj* suitable to be employed 适合雇用的; 可供使用的

em·ploy·ee /ɪm`plɔɪ-i; ɪmˈplɔɪ-iː/ *n* [C] someone who is paid to work for someone else 受雇者, 雇员: *bad employee relations* 很差的劳资关系

em·ploy·er /ɪm`plɔɪə; ɪmˈplɔɪə/ *n* [C] a person, company, or organization that employs people 雇用者, 雇主: *The clothing industry is a large-scale employer of women.* 服装业雇用大量女工。| *a fair employer* 公平的雇主

em·ploy·ment /ɪm`plɔɪmənt; ɪmˈplɔɪmənt/ *n* **1** [U] work that you do to earn money 职业, 工作: *students seeking employment after college* 毕业后求职的大学生 | *Are you in full-time employment?* 你是在全职工作吗? | **in employment** (=doing a job) 在业, 有工作 **2** [U] the situation or condition in which people are employed 就业(环境), 雇用(条件): *a government inquiry into employment and training* 政府对就业和培训情况的调查 | **full employment** (=a situation in which everyone in society has a job) 充分就业 —opposite 反义词 UNEMPLOYMENT **3** [U] *formal* the use of a particular method or skill to achieve something【正式】使用, 运用: [+of] *Was the employment of force justified?* 使用武力是正当的吗? **4** [C] *formal* a useful activity【正式】有益的活动: *Knitting is a pleasant evening employment.* 晚上做些编织活很舒心。

Employment Act, the /·ˈ·· ˌ·/ a set of laws made in the UK in 1989 in order to replace old laws which were unfair to women, and to encourage equal opportunities (=the same chances of employment and pay for everyone)《就业法案》〔英国于1989年制定的一套法律, 以取代过去对妇女不公的法律, 并倡导机会均等〕

employment a·gen·cy /·ˈ·· ˌ··/ *n* [C] a business that makes money by finding jobs for people 职业介绍所

em·po·ri·um /ɛm`porɪəm; ɪmˈpɔːriəm/ *n plural* **emporiums** *or* **emporia** [C] *old-fashioned* a large shop【过时】大商店; 大百货商场

em·pow·er /ɪm`pauə; ɪmˈpaʊə/ *v* [T] **1** to give someone more control over their own life or situation 使能够; 使自主: *The aim of the course is to empower women.* 这门课程的目的是教妇女如何做自己的主人。**2** *formal* to give an organization the power or legal right to do something【正式】授权〔某组织做某事〕: **be empowered to do sth** *The college is empowered to grant degrees.* 这所学院有权授予学位。—**empowerment** *n* [U]

em·press /`ɛmprɪs; ˈemprɪ̣s/ *n* [C] a female ruler of an EMPIRE, or the wife of an EMPEROR 女皇; 皇后: *the empress Josephine* 约瑟芬皇后

emp·ties /`ɛmptɪz; ˈemptiz/ *n* [plural] bottles or glasses that are empty 空瓶子; 空杯子: *We can take the empties to be recycled.* 我们可以把这些空瓶子拿去回收利用。

emp·ti·ness /`ɛmptɪnɪs; ˈemptinɪ̣s/ *n* [U] **1** a feeling of great unhappiness and loneliness 空虚; 寂寥: *She felt an emptiness in her heart when he left.* 他走后, 她心里感到空虚。**2** the state of having nothing in an area or space〔地区或空间的〕空, 无: [+of] *the silence and emptiness of the desert* 沙漠的寂静和空旷

emp·ty¹ /`ɛmptɪ; ˈempti/ *adj*

1 ►**CONTAINER** 容器◄ having nothing inside 空的: *an empty box* 空盒子 | *Your glass is empty – can I fill it up?* 你的杯子空了, 我给你倒一杯吧?

2 ►**ROOM/BUILDING** 房间/建筑物◄ an empty room, building etc does not have any people in it 无人的; 无人居住的: *The house had been empty for six months before we moved in.* 在我们搬进去之前, 这房子有六个月没人住了。| *The hall was half empty.* 大厅有一半是空的。

3 ►**NOT USED** 没人用的◄ not being used by anyone 无人用的: *I spotted an empty table in the corner.* 我发现角落里有一张桌子没人。| **be empty of** *The roads were almost empty of traffic.* 路上几乎没有车辆。

4 ►**PERSON/LIFE** 人/生活◄ unhappy because nothing interesting or important happens or because you feel your life has no purpose 寂寥的; 空虚的: *His early death left her empty and despairing.* 他的早逝使她陷入空虚和绝望。| *Her days were empty.* 她的日子过得很无聊。

5 empty words/gestures/promises etc empty words etc are not sincere or have no effect 空话/做样子/空头许诺等: *She knew her protest would be nothing more than an empty gesture.* 她知道她的抗议只是做做样子而已。

6 do sth on an empty stomach to do something without having eaten any food first 空肚子做某事: *Children shouldn't go to school on an empty stomach.* 小孩子不该空着肚子上学。

7 empty nest *AmE* the situation that parents are in when all their children have left home【美】空巢〔指子女都已长大离家〕—**emptily** *adv*

empty² *v* **1** [T] also 又作 **empty out** if you empty a container, you remove everything that is in it 倒空, 倾空: *I had to completely empty out my bag to find my keys.* 我得把包中所有东西都倒出来找我的钥匙。**2** [T] if you empty the things that are in a container, you take or pour them out of it 把…拿出来; 倾倒: *It's your turn to empty the garbage.* 该你倒垃圾了。| **empty sth onto/into etc** *Kim emptied the candies into a glass jar.* 金把糖果倒入一个玻璃罐。**3** [I] if a place empties, everyone leaves it〔场所〕变空, 人全走光: *The stores were closing, and the streets began to empty.* 商店陆续关门, 街道变得空空荡荡的。**4** [I+(out) into] if a river empties into a larger area of water, it flows into it〔河流〕流入, 注入: *The Elbe empties out into the North Sea.* 易北河注入北海。

empty-hand·ed /ˌ·· ˈ··◄/ *adj* without getting what you hoped or expected to get 一无所获的, 空手的: *I spent all morning looking for a suitable present, but came home empty-handed.* 我整个上午都在寻找一件合适的礼物, 但最后还是空手回家了。

empty-head·ed /ˌ·· ˈ··◄/ *adj informal* silly, and unable to think or behave seriously【非正式】傻的; 无头脑的: *an empty-headed blonde* 头脑简单的金发女孩

EMS /ˌi ɛm `ɛs; ˌiː em ˈes/ *n* [singular] European Monetary System; a system for limiting how much the different currencies (CURRENCY) of countries within the European Union can go up and down in value in relation to each other before the euro was adopted 欧洲货币体系

EMU /ˌi ɛm `ju; ˌiː em ˈjuː/ Economic and Monetary Union; the plan for having a single economic system and a single CURRENCY (=type of money) for all the members of the EU. Most members began using the new currency in 2002. 经济和货币联盟〔欧盟所有成员国实行单一经济体系和单一货币的计划。2002年, 多数成员国开始使用新货币〕

e·mu /`imju; ˈiːmjuː/ *n plural* **emus** *or* **emu** [C] a large Australian bird that can run very fast but cannot fly〔澳大利亚产的跑得很快却不会飞的〕鸸鹋

em·u·late /`ɛmjəˌlet; ˈemjəleɪt/ *v* [T] **1** to try to be like someone else, because you admire them 效仿, 模仿: *The local khans tried to emulate the art, culture, and pageantry of the Persian courts.* 当地的可汗们努力效仿波斯宫廷的艺术、文化和奢华。**2** if one computer or piece of electronic equipment emulates another, they both perform in the same way〔电脑等电子仪器〕仿真 —**emulation** /ˌɛmjə`leʃən; ˌemjəˈleɪʃən/ *n* [U]

e·mul·si·fi·er /ɪ`mʌlsəˌfaɪə; ɪˈmʌlsɪ̣faɪə/ *n* [C] something that is added, especially to food, to prevent liquids and solids from separating 乳化剂: *contains sunflower oil, emulsifiers, and lecithin* 含有葵花子油、乳化剂和卵磷脂

e·mul·si·fy /ɪ`mʌlsəˌfaɪ; ɪˈmʌlsɪ̣faɪ/ *v* [I,T] if two liquids emulsify, they combine to become a smooth mixture (使)〔液体〕乳化

e·mul·sion /ɪ`mʌlʃən; ɪˈmʌlʃən/ *n* [C,U] **1** a mixture of liquids that do not completely combine, such as oil and water 乳化液, 乳状液 **2** a type of paint used inside buildings on walls or ceilings, that is not shiny when it dries 乳化漆 —compare 比较 GLOSS PAINT **3** *technical* the substance on the surface of photographic film that makes it react to light【术语】〔照相胶片上的〕感光乳剂

en- /ɪn; ɪn/ *prefix* **1** to cause to become; make 使成为, 使: *enlarge* 扩大 **2** to put into a particular condition 使处于…状态: *endanger* 使处于危险 | *enriched* 浓缩的, 强化的

-en /ən; ən/ *suffix* **1** [in adjectives 构成形容词] made of something 由…制成的: *a golden crown* 金冠 | *wooden seats* 木头座位 **2** [in verbs 构成动词] to make something have a particular quality 使具有某种特性: *to darken* (=make or become dark) (使)变黑 | *ripening fruit* 即将成熟的水果 | *This strengthened his resolve.* (=made it stronger) 这增强了他的决心。

en·a·ble /ɪn`ebḷ; ɪˈneɪbəl/ *v* [T] **1** to give someone the ability or opportunity to do something 使能够; 使有机会: **enable sb to do sth** *Money from her aunt enabled Jan to buy the house.* 婶婶给简的钱使她有能力买下那幢房子。**2** *formal* to make something possible【正式】使可能: *a policy designed to enable the introduction of flexible working hours* 为引进浮动工作时间而制定的政策

en·a·bling /ɪn`eblɪŋ; ɪˈneɪblɪŋ/ *adj* [only before noun 仅用于名词前] *technical* an enabling law is one that makes something possible or gives someone special legal powers【术语】〔指法律〕使可能的; 授予权力的

en·act /ɪn`ækt; ɪˈnækt/ *v* [T] **1** to make a proposal into law 将…制定成法律: *Congress refused to enact the bill.* 国会拒绝通过该法案。**2** *formal* to act in a play, story etc【正式】上演; 扮演: *a drama enacted on a darkened stage* 在灯光暗淡的舞台上上演的戏剧 —**enactment** *n* [C,U]

e·nam·el[1] /ɪ`næml; ɪ'næməl/ *n* [U] **1** a glass-like substance that is put onto metal, clay etc for decoration or protection 瓷釉; 搪瓷; 珐琅 **2** the hard, smooth outer surface of your teeth〔牙齿的〕珐琅质, 釉质 —see picture at 参见 TEETH 图 **3** paint that is usually used on wood, and that produces a shiny surface 亮漆, 光漆, 瓷漆 —**enamel** *adj*

enamel[2] *v* [T] to cover or decorate something with enamel 给…上瓷漆[搪瓷]

en·am·oured *BrE*【英】, **enamored** *AmE*【美】/ɪn`æmə·d; ɪ'næməd/ *adj* [not before noun 不用于名词前] **1** liking something very much〔对某物〕喜爱的, 迷恋的: [+of/with] *You don't seem very enamoured with your job.* 看起来你不太喜欢你的工作。**2** *formal* in love with, or very fond of someone【正式】〔对某人〕倾心的, 迷恋的: [+of/with] *He was greatly enamoured of Elizabeth.* 他十分倾心于伊丽莎白。

en bloc /ɛn `blɑk; ɒn 'blɒk/ *adv* all together as a single unit, rather than separately 整个, 全部, 一起: *You cannot dismiss these stories en bloc.* 你不能把这些说法一股脑儿全给否定了。

en·camp /ɪn`kæmp; ɪn'kæmp/ *v* [I,T] *formal* to make a camp or put someone in a camp【正式】扎营, 宿营: *The soldiers were encamped near Damascus.* 士兵们在大马士革附近安营。

en·camp·ment /ɪn`kæmpmənt; ɪn'kæmpmənt/ *n* [C] a large temporary camp, especially of soldiers〔尤指军队的〕临时营地: *a military encampment* 军营

en·cap·su·late /ɛn`kæpsə͵let; ɪn'kæpsjʊleɪt/ *v* [T] to put the main facts or ideas of something in a short form or a small space 压缩, 概括: [+in] *Her whole philosophy can be encapsulated in this one sentence.* 她的全部哲学理论可以概括成这一句话。—**encapsulation** /ɛn͵kæpsə`leʃən; ɪn͵kæpsjʊ'leɪʃən/ *n* [C,U]

En·car·ta /ɛn`kɑrtə; en'kɑːtə/ *trademark* a type of ENCYCLOPEDIA (=a product with articles about many different subjects) which is produced only on a CD-ROM, and is not available as a printed book. It is a MULTIMEDIA product, with pictures, sound, pieces of film etc.【商标】《因卡特百科全书》〔一种只以光盘为载体的多媒体电子百科全书, 不以纸介质书的形式出现, 融文字、图片、声音、电影片段等为一体〕

en·case /ɪn`kes; ɪn'keɪs/ *v* [T often passive 常用被动态] to cover or surround something completely 把…包住; 把…围住: [+in] *His broken leg was encased in plaster.* 他的断腿打着石膏。| *her sleek legs encased in sheer black stockings* 她那双裹在黑色透明长统袜中的秀腿

-ence /əns; əns/ *suffix* [in nouns 构成名词] another form of the suffix -ANCE 后缀 -ance 的另一种形式: *its existence* (=the fact that it exists) 它的存在 | *reference* 参考 | *occurrence* 发生

en·chant /ɪn`tʃænt; ɪn'tʃɑːnt/ *v* [T often passive 常用被动态] **1** to make someone feel very interested, happy, and excited 使陶醉, 使入迷: [+by/with] *Venice enchanted me instantly.* 我一下子就被威尼斯迷住了。**2** *literary* to use magic on something【文】对…用魔法

en·chant·ed /ɪn`tʃæntɪd; ɪn'tʃɑːntɪ̈d/ *adj* an enchanted object or place has been changed by magic, so that it has special powers〔物体或场所〕施了魔法的: *an enchanted castle* 施了魔法的城堡 —see also 另见 DISENCHANTED

en·chant·er /ɪn`tʃæntə·; ɪn'tʃɑːntə/ *n* [C] *literary* someone who uses magic on people and things【文】魔法师

en·chant·ing /ɪn`tʃæntɪŋ; ɪn'tʃɑːntɪŋ/ *adj* very attractive 可爱的; 令人着迷的: *The child looked enchanting in a pale blue dress.* 那个孩子穿着浅蓝色连衣裙, 十分可爱。| *an enchanting romantic comedy* 引人入胜的浪漫喜剧 —**enchantingly** *adj*

en·chant·ment /ɪn`tʃæntmənt; ɪn'tʃɑːntmənt/ *n* **1** [C,U] a feeling of mystery that strongly interests or attracts you 着迷; 陶醉: *The forest had an air of enchantment.* 森林散发着迷人的气息。**2** [C] *literary* a change caused by magic; SPELL[2] (1)【文】着魔, (被施) 魔法, 咒语

en·chant·ress /ɪn`tʃæntrɪs; ɪn'tʃɑːntrɪ̈s/ *n* [C] *literary*【文】**1** a woman that men find very attractive and interesting 迷人的女子 **2** a woman who uses magic on people and things 女巫, 女魔法师

en·chi·la·da /͵ɛntʃɪ`lɑdə; ͵entʃɪ̈'lɑːdə/ *n* [C] **1** a Mexican food consisting of a flat piece of bread rolled around meat and covered with a hot-tasting thick liquid〔墨西哥式〕辣椒肉馅玉米卷饼 **2 the whole enchilada** *AmE informal* the whole situation; everything【美, 非正式】全部事情, 整桩事情: *Come on. Let's hear it – the whole enchilada.* 来, 让我们听一听整个事情的经过。

en·cir·cle /ɪn`sɝkl; ɪn'sɜːkəl/ *v* [T] to surround someone or something completely 围绕, 环绕: *a luscious garden, encircled by walled parkland* 四周有围墙的邸园中赏心悦目的花园 —**encirclement** *n* [U]

en·clave /`ɛnklev; 'enkleɪv/ *n* [C] a place or a group of people that is surrounded by people or areas that are different 聚居地; 身处异地的一群人: *the Italian-American enclave in New York* 纽约的意大利裔美国人聚居地

en·close /ɪn`kloz; ɪn'kləʊz/ *v* [T] **1** to put something inside an envelope as well as a letter 随信附上, 随信装入: *Please enclose a cheque with your order.* 请您随订单附上支票。| **please find enclosed** (=used in business letters to say that you are sending something as well as a letter) 兹附上… *Please find enclosed an agenda for the meeting.* 兹附上会议议程表。**2** [often passive 常用被动态] to surround something, especially with a fence or wall, in order to make it separate〔用篱笆或围墙〕围起来: *A high wall enclosed the courtyard.* 一堵高墙围着院子。

en·clo·sure /ɪn`kloʒə·; ɪn'kləʊʒə/ *n* **1** [C] an area surrounded by a wall or fence, and used for a particular purpose〔用于特定目的的〕围地, 围场: *the bear enclosure at the zoo* 动物园中的熊馆 **2** [U] the act of making an area separate by putting a wall or fence around it 围住; 圈起来: *the enclosure of arable land for pasture* 将可耕地圈起来用作牧场 **3** [C] something that is put inside an envelope as well as a letter〔信中的〕附件, 装入物

en·code /ɪn`kod; ɪn'kəʊd/ *v* [T] to put a message or other information into a CODE[1] (4) 把…译成电码[密码] —opposite 反义词 DECODE

en·com·pass /ɪn`kʌmpəs; ɪn'kʌmpəs/ *v* [T] **1** to include a wide range of ideas, subjects, etc 包含, 包括: *The study encompasses social, political, and economic aspects of the situation.* 这项研究包含了该情况的社会、政治和经济等方方面面。**2** to completely cover or surround something 覆盖; 围住: *The houses encompassed about one hundred square metres.* 房子占地约 100 平方米。

en·core[1] /`ɑŋkɔr; 'ɒŋkɔː/ *n* [C] an additional or repeated part of a performance, especially a musical one 加演节目; 重演[奏, 唱]: *The audience demanded an encore.* 听众要求再来一个。

encore[2] *interjection* used when you have enjoyed a musical performance very much and want the performer to sing or play more 再唱一首; 再来一个: *Pavarotti's performance, greeted by roars of 'Encore!'* 帕瓦罗蒂的演唱会, 听众要求"再来一个"的声音如潮。

en·coun·ter[1] /ɪn`kaʊntə·; ɪn'kaʊntə/ *v* [T] **1** to experience problems, difficulties, or opposition when you are trying to do something 遇到, 遭遇〔问题、困难、反对〕: *We encountered a serious setback when two members of the expedition were injured.* 两名远征队员受伤了, 我们严重受挫。**2** to meet someone or experience something unexpectedly 偶然碰到〔某人〕; 突然遇到〔某事〕: *I first encountered him at summer school.* 我第一次遇到他是在暑期班里。 W3

encounter[2] *n* [C] **1** an occasion when you meet someone, especially in an unplanned or unexpected way 相遇, 邂逅: *She didn't remember our encounter last summer.* 她记不起我们去年夏天那次相遇了。| **chance encounter** (=a meeting caused by luck or chance) 巧遇 **2** a short dangerous struggle or meeting between two people or groups 遭遇战; 冲突: *one of the bloodiest encounters of the American Civil War* 美国南北战争期间最惨烈的遭遇战之一 | **close encounter** (=situation that could have been dangerous or unpleasant) 差一点酿成祸事; 几乎导致不愉快 *a close encounter with a poisonous snake* 险遇一条毒蛇

en·cour·age /ɪn`kɝɪdʒ; ɪn'kʌrɪdʒ/ *v* [T] **1** to say or do something that helps someone have the courage or confidence to do something 鼓励, 激励: *Haldene encouraged him in his work.* 霍尔丹鼓励他好好工作。| **encourage sb to do sth** *Patricia encouraged me to apply for the job.* 帕特里夏鼓励我申请那份工作。**2** to make something more likely to happen or make people more likely to do something 促进, 激发: *a meeting format that will encourage debate* 鼓励辩论的会议安排 | **encourage sb to do sth** *A good public transport encourages people to leave their cars at home.* 良好的公共交通会促使人们将汽车留在家中。—opposite 反义词 DISCOURAGE —**encouragement** *n* [C,U] S2 W1

en·cour·aged /ɪn`kɝɪdʒd; ɪn'kʌrɪdʒd/ *adj* [not before noun 不用于名词前] feeling more hopeful and confident 受到鼓舞的, 更有信心的: *She felt encouraged by the many letters of support.* 许多支持信使她很受鼓舞。

en·cour·ag·ing /ɪn`kɝɪdʒɪŋ; ɪn'kʌrɪ̈dʒɪŋ/ *adj* giving you hope and confidence 令人鼓舞的, 振奋人心的: *The results of the survey have been very encouraging.* 调查结果非常令人鼓舞。—**encouragingly** *adv* S3

en·croach /ɪn`krotʃ; ɪn'krəʊtʃ/ *v*

encroach on/upon sth *phr v* [T] **1** to gradually take more control of someone's time, possessions, rights etc than you should 逐步侵占[侵犯]; 蚕食: *a government that is encroach-*

ing on the rights of individuals 正逐步侵犯公民个人权利的政府 **2** to gradually cover more and more land 侵占〔土地〕: *houses encroaching upon farmland* 正渐渐侵占耕地的住房 —**encroachment** *n* [C,U]

en·crust·ed /ɪnˋkrʌstɪd; ɪnˈkrʌstɪ̣d/ *adj* covered with a thin hard layer of something 覆有薄薄一层硬外层的, 结外壳的: **[+with/in]** *boots thickly encrusted with mud* 外面沾了厚厚一层泥的靴子 —**encrustation** /ˌɪnkrʌsˋteʃən; ˌɪnkrʌˈsteɪʃən/ *n* [C,U]

en·cum·ber /ɪnˋkʌmbɚ; ɪnˈkʌmbə/ *v* [T] *formal* to make it difficult for someone to move easily or for something to happen in the usual way【正式】妨碍, 阻碍: **[+by/with]** *I was too encumbered by suitcases to run.* 我提着手提箱, 跑不动。—**encumbrance** *n* [C]

-ency /ənsɪ; ənsi/ *suffix* [in nouns 构成名词] another form of the suffix -ANCY 后缀 -ancy 的另一种形式: *a tendency* 趋势

en·cyc·li·cal /ɛnˋsɪklɪk]; ɪnˈsɪklɪkəl/ *n* [C] *technical* a letter sent by the Pope to all Roman Catholic BISHOPS or to members of the Roman Catholic Church【术语】罗马教皇〔给全体主教或教徒〕的通谕

Encyclopaedia Bri·tan·ni·ca, the /ɪnˌsaɪkləˌpidɪə brɪˋtænɪkə; ɪnˌsaɪkləˌpiːdiə brɪˈtænɪkə/ an ENCYCLOPEDIA (=a book containing articles about many different subjects), which consists of many VOLUMES (=separate books that are part of a set) and is now also available as a CD-ROM.《不列颠百科全书》〔由多卷组成的百科全书, 现也有光盘版〕

en·cy·clo·pe·di·a also 又作 **encyclopaedia** *BrE*【英】/ɪnˌsaɪkləˋpidɪə; ɪnˌsaɪkləˈpiːdiə/ *n* [C] a book or set of books containing facts about many different subjects, or about one particular subject 百科全书; 〔某一学科的〕专科全书, 大全

en·cy·clo·pe·dic also 又作 **encyclopaedic** *BrE*【英】/ɪnˌsaɪkləˋpidɪk; ɪnˌsaɪkləˈpiːdɪk◂/ *adj* encyclopedic knowledge, memory etc has a very large amount of information in it〔知识、记忆等〕百科全书式的, 渊博的

end¹ /ɛnd; end/ *n* [C]

1 ▶LAST PART 最后部分◀ the last part of something such as a period of time, activity, book, or film 最后部分; 末尾: *He's leaving at the end of October.* 他计划于 10 月底离开。| *I found the end of the movie very disappointing.* 我觉得电影的结尾十分令人失望。| **from beginning to end** *Her story was a pack of lies from beginning to end.* 她的故事彻头彻尾都是谎言。

2 ▶FURTHEST POINT 最远端◀ the furthest point of a place or object 端; 尽头: *He sat at one end of the table and I sat at the other.* 他坐在桌子的一端, 我坐在另一端。| *The street is closed off at both ends.* 街道两头都被封锁了。| *a long pole with a hole at one end* 一端有个洞的长杆 | **end to end** (=in a line with the ends touching) 首尾相接地; 头对头地 *Put the two tables end to end.* 把两张桌子拼接在一起。

3 ▶FINISHED 结束◀ a situation in which something is finished or no longer exists 结束; 结局; 完结: *the end of all my dreams* 我所有梦想的完结 | **be at an end** (=finished) 结束了 *The long hot summer was at last at an end.* 漫长的酷暑终于过去了。| **come to an end** (=finished and no longer continuing) 完结 *That job came to an end last month.* 那项工作上个月完成了。| **put an end to** *Winning the competition put an end to his financial problems.* 在比赛中获胜使他的财政问题随之消失。| **to the end of time** *literary* (=for ever)【文】永远

4 ▶AIM 目的◀ [usually plural 一般用复数] the result that you hope to achieve 目的, 目标: *She'll stop at nothing to achieve her own ends.* 什么也挡不住她去达到个人目的。| **to that end** *formal*【正式】*Joel wants to buy a car and is saving money to that end.* 乔尔想买一辆汽车, 并正为此攒钱。| **an end in itself** (=something you aim to do because you want to, not in order to get other advantages) 自发想做的事情, 本身就是目的 *Learning to play the piano was an end in itself for me.* 我学钢琴不是为了别的目的, 只是因为想学。| **the end justifies the means** (=the result you want makes acceptable the bad things you do in order to get it) 只要能达到目的, 可以采取任何手段

5 in the end after a period of time; finally 后来; 终于: *In the end, I decided that I wouldn't go after all.* 最终我决定还是不去。—see 见 LASTLY (USAGE)

6 days/hours/weeks etc on end for many days, hours etc without stopping 连续数天/数小时/数周等: *It snowed for days on end.* 雪一连下了好几天。

7 no end *spoken* very much【口】非常: *Thanks for the letter – it cheered me up no end.* 谢谢来信, 这使我非常高兴。

8 no end of *spoken* a lot of something【口】大量的, 许多: *We've had no end of problems with the house since we moved.* 我们搬进去以后, 房子的麻烦不断。

9 put/stand sth on end to put something in a position so that its longest edge is upright 把…竖起来 —see also 另见 **make sb's hair stand on end** (HAIR (6))

10 ▶PART OF AN ACTIVITY 活动的一部分◀ *informal* the particular part of a job, activity, place etc that you are involved in, or that affects you【非正式】〔工作、活动、场所等相关的〕部分; 方面: *She works in the sales end of things.* 她做销售方面的工作。| *Let's hope they keep their end of the bargain.* 希望他们能信守协议。| **at your end** *spoken* (=where you are)【口】在你(们)那儿 *What's the weather like at your end?* 你们那里天气如何?

11 ▶SPORT 体育◀ one of the two halves of a sports field that a team defends or attacks 半边球场, 半场: *The teams change ends at half-time.* 中场时两队交换场地。

12 ▶DEATH 死亡◀ [C usually singular 一般用单数] a word meaning death, used because you want to avoid saying this directly 生命的尽头〔死亡的委婉说法〕: *James was with his father at the end.* 父亲临终时詹姆斯陪在身边。

13 at the end of the day *spoken* used to give your opinion after you have discussed all the possibilities of a situation or problem【口】最终; 到头来; 不管怎么说: *At the end of the day, it's his responsibility, and there's nothing you can do.* 不管怎么说这是他的责任, 你帮不了什么。

14 be at the end of your tether/rope to have no more PATIENCE or strength to deal with something 忍无可忍; 无能为力: *I'm at the end of my tether with their constant arguing.* 他们没完没了地争吵, 我已忍无可忍。

15 it's not the end of the world *spoken* used to say that a possible problem is not too serious or bad【口】还未到世界末日〔表示事情并不那么可怕〕: *After all, it's not the end of the world if you fail this test.* 不管怎么说, 就算你这次考试不及格, 那也不是什么世界末日。

16 hold/keep your end up *BrE informal* to continue to be brave or act effectively in a difficult situation【英, 非正式】坚持, 不泄气

17 make (both) ends meet to have just enough money to buy what you need 收支仅能相抵: *Since Mike lost his job, we can hardly make ends meet.* 自从迈克失业以后, 我们简直难以维持生计。

18 the end of the road/line the end of a process or activity 进程的尽头/活动的结局: *I tried to tell him that this defeat was not the end of the road, that football was only a game.* 我尽量对他讲, 这次失败并不代表一切, 毕竟足球比赛只是一种游戏。

19 the (absolute) end *BrE spoken* used to show disapproval of someone or something in an amused way【英口】糟糕透了的人[物]〔用于表示好笑的责难〕: *Look at this untidy room – you're the absolute end!* 看看这乱七八糟的屋子, 你简直糟透了!

20 living end *AmE spoken* used as an expression of strong approval or disapproval【美口】顶呱呱, 十足的混蛋: *What will she do next? She's the living end!* 她下一步要干什么? 她这混蛋!

21 do sth to the bitter end to keep doing something until you have tried every possible method 尽一切努力做某事; *We'll fight this decision to the bitter end.* 这个决定我们要反对到底。

22 go to the ends of the earth to do everything you can, even if it is very difficult, in order to have or achieve something 竭尽所能: *I'd go to the ends of the earth to be with him.* 哪怕走到天边我也要和他在一起。

23 get/have your end away *BrE slang* to have sex【英俚】性交 —see also 另见 **be-all and end all** (BE² (10)), DEAD END, **go off at the deep end** (DEEP¹ (17)), **be at a loose end** (LOOSE¹ (14)), ODDS AND ENDS, **be on the sharp end of sth** (SHARP¹ (21)), **come to a sticky end** (STICKY (8)), **the tail end of a queue/meeting etc** (TAIL¹ (9)), **jump/be thrown in at the deep end** (DEEP¹ (16)), **get the wrong end of the stick** (WRONG¹ (12)), **at your wit's end** (WIT (6))

end² *v* **1** [I] to finish or stop 结束; 停止: *World War II ended in 1945.* 第二次世界大战于 1945 年结束。| *The film ended with the heroine dying.* 在电影结束时, 女主角快去世了。**2** [T] to make something finish or stop 使结束; 使停止: *Jane decided it was time to end the relationship with Bob.* 简决定该结束与鲍勃的关系了。**3 end your days/life** if you end your days in a particular place or doing a particular thing, you spend the last part of your life there or doing that〔在某处或在进行某种活动过程中〕度过余生 **4 end it all** to kill yourself 自杀

end in sth *phr v* [T not in passive 不用被动态] to have in a particular result, or finish in a particular way 结果为…; 以…结束[告终]: *Their marriage ended in divorce.* 他们的婚姻以离婚告终。| **it'll all end in tears** *BrE spoken* (=used to warn that a situation will end in an unpleasant or unhappy way)【英口】将

以不快[悲剧]收场 *This game will end in tears. I know it.* 这场比赛将以悲剧收场，我确信。

end up *phr v* [I] *informal*【非正式】**1** to come to be in a particular situation or state, especially when you did not plan it 结果为…；以…结束〔尤指意料之外〕: *He'll end up in prison if he's not careful.* 如果他不小心，最后可能会锒铛入狱。| **end up doing sth** *We were going to go out, but ended up watching videos.* 我们原计划外出，但结果却是在家看录像。**2** to arrive in a place you did not plan to go to 意外到达〔某处〕: *We got to Rome okay, but our luggage ended up in Paris.* 我们顺利到达罗马，但我们的行李却被送到了巴黎。

en·dan·ger /ɪn`dendʒɚ; ɪn'deɪndʒə/ *v* [T] to put someone or something in a dangerous situation where they can be hurt, damaged, or destroyed 使处于险境；危及: *Smoking during pregnancy can endanger your baby's health.* 怀孕期间吸烟会危及胎儿的健康。| *If unemployment continues to rise, social stability may be endangered.* 失业率持续上升将会危及社会安定。

endangered spe·cies /·,··'··/ *n* [C] a type of animal or plant that may soon no longer exist 濒于灭绝的物种: *The whale is an endangered species.* 鲸鱼是一种濒于灭绝的动物。

en·dear /ɪn`dɪr; ɪn'dɪə/ *v*

endear sb **to** sb *phr v* [T] to make someone popular and liked 使受欢迎，使被喜爱: *Diana's friendly disposition endears her to everyone she meets.* 黛安娜性情友善，因而人缘很好。

en·dear·ing /ɪn`dɪrɪŋ; ɪn'dɪərɪŋ/ *adj* making someone love or like you 惹人喜爱的，引人爱慕的: *an endearing smile* 可爱的微笑 —**endearingly** *adv*

en·dear·ment /ɪn`dɪrmənt; ɪn'dɪəmənt/ *n* [C] an action or word that expresses your love for someone 表示爱慕的举动[言语]: *whispering endearments to her* 向她悄悄说着情话 | **term of endearment** (=a way you address someone you love) 爱称

en·deav·our[1] *BrE*【英】, **endeavor** *AmE*【美】/ɪn`dɛvɚ; ɪn'devə/ *v* [I] *formal* to try very hard【正式】努力；奋力: **endeavour to do sth** *We always endeavor to give our customers excellent service.* 我们总是竭尽全力向顾客提供优质的服务。

endeavour[2] *BrE*【英】, **endeavor** *AmE*【美】*n* [C,U] *formal* an attempt or effort, especially to do something new or difficult【正式】尝试；努力: *The expedition was an outstanding example of human endeavour.* 这次远征是人类奋勇进取的突出例证。| **best endeavours** *Despite our best endeavours, we couldn't get the machine started.* 我们虽然尽了最大努力，但还是无法开动机器。

en·dem·ic /ɛn`dɛmɪk; en'demɪk/ *adj* an endemic disease is always present in a particular place, or among a particular group of people〔疾病〕地方性的；某些人常有的: *Violent crime is now endemic in parts of Chicago.* 暴力犯罪现在成了芝加哥一些地区无法根除的问题。—compare 比较 PANDEMIC

end game /'· ·/ *n* [C] *technical* something that happens at the end of an activity, especially a game of CHESS【术语】〔尤指棋赛的〕残局；结束阶段；尾声

end·ing /`ɛndɪŋ; 'endɪŋ/ *n* [C] **1** the way in which of a story, film, etc finishes〔故事、电影等的〕结局，结尾: *The story has a happy ending.* 这个故事结局美满。**2** the last part of a word〔单词的〕词尾: *Verbal nouns have the ending -ing.* 动名词以 -ing 结尾。

en·dive /`ɛndaɪv; 'endɪv/ *n* [C,U] **1** a plant with curly green leaves that you eat raw 苣荬菜 **2** *AmE* a plant with bitter tasting leaves that is eaten raw【美】菊苣；CHICORY *BrE*【英】

end·less /`ɛndlɪs; 'endləs/ *adj* **1** something unpleasant that is endless continues, or seems to continue, for a long time〔不愉快的事情〕永无休止的，无穷尽的: *the endless round of meetings and interviews* 没完没了的会议和采访 **2** *technical* an endless belt, chain etc is circular with the ends joined【术语】〔带、链等〕环状的，两端连接的 —**endlessly** *adv*: *Sue was endlessly patient.* 休是个极有耐心的人。

en·do·crine gland /`ɛndo,kraɪn `glænd; 'endəʊkrɪn ,glænd/ *n* [C] *technical* an organ of your body that puts HORMONES into your blood【术语】内分泌腺

en·dorse /ɪn`dɔrs; ɪn'dɔːs/ *v* [T] **1** to express formal support or approval for someone or something〔正式〕赞同；认可；支持: *The committee has endorsed our proposals.* 委员会已经表态支持我们的建议。**2** to sign your name on the back of a cheque〔在支票背面〕签名，背书 **3** to say in an advertisement that you use a particular product and like it〔在广告中〕代言〔这种产品〕: *big names who endorsed American Express* 为美国运通公司做广告的名人 **4** [usually passive 一般用被动态] *BrE* to write a driving offence on someone's DRIVING LICENCE【英】〔在驾驶执照上〕注明司机违章: *His licence was endorsed for speeding.* 他因超速驾驶，执照被注上违章记录。—**endorsement** *n* [C,U]

en·dow /ɪn`daʊ; ɪn'daʊ/ *v* [T] to give a college, hospital etc a large sum of money that will provide it with an income 向〔院校、医院等〕捐款，资助

endow sb **with** sth *phr v* [T] **1 be endowed with** to naturally have a good feature or quality 天生赋有: *She was endowed with both looks and brains.* 她天生漂亮又聪明。**2** *formal* to give someone something【正式】给予，赋予 —see also 另见 WELL-ENDOWED

en·dow·ment /ɪn`daʊmənt; ɪn'daʊmənt/ *n* **1** [C,U] a sum of money that is given to a place such as a college or hospital to give it an income, or the giving of this money 捐赠的款项；捐款（的行为），资助: *an endowment of land and investments given to the college* 给该大学的土地捐赠和投资 **2** [C] a quality or ability that someone has naturally 天赋，天资: *Man has already changed dogs' genetic endowments by breeding them selectively.* 人类已通过选择性育种的方式改变了狗的基因品质。

endowment pol·i·cy /·'·· ,···/ *n* [C] *technical* an insurance arrangement that pays you an agreed sum of money after a period of time【术语】养老保险〔指保险公司应允在一段时间后支付一笔约定的钱款〕

end prod·uct /'· ,··/ *n* [C usually singular 一般用单数] something that is produced by an industrial process, or by a particular activity 最终产品，制成品: *Desktop publishing can produce a very high quality end product.* 桌面排版系统可以制作出高质量的产品。—compare 比较 BY-PRODUCT

end re·sult /,· ·'·/ *n* [C usually singular 一般用单数] the final result of a process or activity 最终结果: *If present trends continue, the end result will inevitably be socialized medicine.* 如果现在的趋势持续下去，最终必将走向公费医疗制。

en·due /ɪn`dju; ɪn'djuː/ *v* [T] *formal*【正式】

endue sb **with** sth *phr v* [T] to make someone have a lot of a good quality 大量赋予〔某人〕以〔某种优良的品质〕: *endued with a spirit of public service* 极富公共服务精神

en·dur·ance /ɪn`djurəns; ɪn'djʊərəns/ *n* [U] the ability to suffer difficulties or pain with strength and patience（忍）耐力: *The marathon really tested his endurance.* 马拉松赛跑真正考验了他的耐力。

en·dure /ɪn`djur; ɪn'djʊə/ *v* **1** [T] to suffer something painful or deal with a very unpleasant situation for a long time with strength and patience 忍耐；容忍；坚持: *There are limits to what the human body can endure.* 人体的耐力是有限度的。| *Bosnians have now endured several years of war.* 波斯尼亚人已忍受了数年的战争。—see graph at 参见 BEAR[1] 图表 **2** [I] to remain alive or continue to exist 生活下去；持续存在: *a city built to endure* 建筑牢固、历世长存的城市 —**endurable** *adj*

en·dur·ing /ɪn`djurɪŋ; ɪn'djʊərɪŋ/ *adj* continuing to exist for a long time 持久的，持续的: *the enduring appeal of the short story* 短篇小说经久不衰的感染力

end us·er /'· ,··/ *n* [C] the person who actually uses a particular product〔产品的〕最终使用者: *researching end users' preferences* 调查终端用户的喜好

end·ways /`ɛnd,wez; 'endweɪz/ also 又作 **end·wise** /-,waɪz; -waɪz/ *adv AmE*【美】**1** with the end forward 末端朝前: *The box looks narrow when you look at it endways.* 这盒子从末端看较窄。**2** with the ends touching each other 两端相接: *Put the tables together endways.* 把桌子接排成一行。

end zone /'· ·/ *n* [C] the place at the end of an American football field where you take the ball to get points〔美式橄榄球的〕球门区 —see picture on page A22 参见 A22 页图

en·e·ma /`ɛnəmə; 'enɪmə/ *n* [C] a liquid that is put into someone's RECTUM in order to make them empty their BOWELS 灌肠剂

en·e·my /`ɛnəmɪ; 'enəmi/ *n* [C] **1** someone who hates you and wants to harm you 敌人，仇敌: *She's a dangerous enemy to have.* 有她这样的敌人是很危险的。| **be enemies** (=hate and oppose each other) 互为仇敌，互相敌视 *Jake and Paul have been enemies for years.* 杰克和保罗已是多年的宿敌了。| **make an enemy (of sb)** *He's a ruthless businessman and has made a lot of enemies.* 他是个无情的商人，树敌很多。| **sworn enemies** (=enemies determined never to end their quarrel) 死敌，不共戴天的仇敌 **2** someone who opposes you and wants to prevent you doing something 反对者: *political enemies* 政敌 | *Greenpeace, an enemy of the chemical industry, is pressing for more environmental legislation.* 绿色和平组织是化学工业的反对者，正敦促更多的环保立法。**3** someone you are fighting in a war 敌兵，敌军: *Our enemies were hidden in the trenches.* 敌军躲在战壕里。| **enemy forces** (=the army, navy etc of the country that you are fighting) 敌国的军队 | **enemy soldiers/aircraft** *Enemy aircraft were spotted overhead.* 发现了空中的敌机。**4** W2

be your own worst enemy to behave in a way that causes problems for yourself 自作自受, 自己害自己 **5** *literary* something that changes something else or makes it weaker【文】改变物; 危害物: *Jealousy is the enemy of love.* 妒忌是爱情的大敌。

en·er·get·ic /ˌɛnɚˈdʒɛtɪk; ˌenəˈdʒetɪk◂/ *adj* very active because you have a lot of energy 充满活力的, 精力充沛的: *an able and energetic politician* 能干又充满活力的政治家 —**energetically** /-klɪ; -kli/ *adv*: *He fought energetically against apartheid.* 他积极地与种族隔离进行斗争。

en·er·gize also 又作 **-ise** *BrE*【英】/ˈɛnɚˌdʒaɪz; ˈenədʒaɪz/ *v* [T] **1** to make someone feel more determined and energetic 使增强决心, 使充满活力 **2** [usually passive 一般用被动态] to make a machine work 使〔机器〕运转: *electric motors energized by solar cells* 使用太阳能电池的电动机 —**energizing** *adj*

en·er·gy /ˈɛnɚdʒɪ; ˈenədʒi/ *n* [C,U] **1** the physical and mental strength that makes you able to be active 力量, 活力: *The task will take an enormous amount of time and energy.* 完成那项任务需要大量时间和精力。| **be full of energy** *She came back full of energy after her vacation.* 度假归来后她精力充沛。| **nervous energy** (=energy that you have because you feel nervous) 亢奋; 兴奋不安 **2** power that is used to provide heat, drive machines etc such as oil and coal 能, 能量; 能源: *the world's energy resources* 世界的能源 **3 energies** the effort that you use to do things 精力: **apply/devote your energies to** *She's devoting all her energies to the wedding preparations.* 她把所有精力都花在准备婚礼上了。

en·er·vat·ed /ˈɛnɚˌvetɪd; ˈenəveɪtɪd/ *adj formal* having lost energy and feeling weak【正式】无力的; 没精打采的: *I was utterly enervated by the argument.* 我被这场争论搞得精疲力竭。| *reclining on the chaise longue, languid and enervated* 靠在躺椅上, 倦怠无力

en·er·vat·ing /ˈɛnɚˌvetɪŋ; ˈenəveɪtɪŋ/ *adj* making you feel weak 使无力的, 使没精打采的: *Extreme heat can be very enervating.* 酷热会使人浑身乏力。

en·fant ter·ri·ble /ˌɑnfɑn tɛˈribl; ˌɒnfɒn teˈriːblə/ *n* [C] *French* someone who behaves in a way that shocks and amuses other people【法】莽撞而令人发笑的人: *Ken Russell, the enfant terrible of the British film industry* 肯·拉塞尔, 英国电影界中那个常有惊人之举的人

en·fee·ble /ɪnˈfibl; ɪnˈfiːbəl/ *v* [T] *formal* to make someone weak【正式】使衰弱, 使无力 —**enfeebled** *adj*

en·fold /ɪnˈfold; ɪnˈfəʊld/ *v* [T] *formal* to enclose or surround something【正式】围住, 包住: *He enfolded her in his arms.* 他搂住她。

en·force /ɪnˈfɔrs; ɪnˈfɔːs/ *v* [T] **1** to make people obey a rule or law 执行〔法律〕, 实施: *Governments make laws and the police enforce them.* 政府制定法律, 警察负责执行。**2** to make something happen, especially by threats or force; IMPOSE〔强迫〕实行; 把…强加于: *The unions hope to enforce a closed shop.* 工会希望实行只雇用工会会员的制度。—**enforceable** *adj* —**enforcement** *n* [U] *law enforcement agencies in the US* 美国的执法机构

en·forced /ɪnˈforst; ɪnˈfɔːst/ *adj* made to happen or exist by law, or by conditions that you cannot control 依法强制的; 强迫的: *a period of enforced isolation* 强制隔离期

en·fran·chise /ɛnˈfræntʃaɪz; ɪnˈfræntʃaɪz/ *v* [T] **1** to give a group of people the right to vote 给予…选举权 —opposite 反义词 DISENFRANCHISE **2** to free a slave 解放〔奴隶〕—**enfranchisement** /-tʃɪz-; -tʃɪz-/ *n* [U]

en·gage /ɪnˈgedʒ; ɪnˈgeɪdʒ/ *v formal*【正式】**1** [T] to attract someone and keep their interest 吸引〔某人的兴趣〕: *The new toy didn't engage the child's interest for long.* 这个新玩具对孩子的吸引力没有维持多久。**2** [T] to arrange to employ someone 安排雇用, 聘请: **engage sb to do sth** *His father engaged a private tutor to improve his maths.* 他爸爸请了一位家庭教师给他补习数学。**3** [I,T] to make one part fit into another part of a machine (使)〔机器〕啮合, 接合: *She engaged the clutch and the car moved forwards.* 她踩下离合器, 汽车便朝前开了。| [+with] *The wheel engages with the cog and turns it.* 轮子咬住轮齿并带动它转动。—opposite 反义词 DISENGAGE (2) **4** [T] to begin to fight with an enemy 开始与〔敌人〕交战: *The two armies engaged at dawn.* 两军在拂晓时分开始交火。

engage in *formal*【正式】*phr v* [T] **1** to take part or become involved in an activity 参加; 参与: *a politician engaged in various business activities* 参与各种商业活动的政治家 **2 engage sb in conversation** to start talking to someone and involve them in a conversation 与某人攀谈; 使某人加入谈话中

en·gaged /ɪnˈgedʒd; ɪnˈgeɪdʒd/ *adj* **1** having agreed to get married 已订婚的: *They've been engaged for six months.* 他们订婚已经六个月了。| [+to] *Have you met the man she's engaged to?* 你见过她的未婚夫吗? | **get engaged** (=agree to marry someone) 订婚 *Siobhan and Ray have just got engaged.* 西沃恩和雷刚刚订婚。**2** *BrE* an engaged telephone is being used【英】电话占线的; BUSY[1] (7) *AmE*【美】: **engaged line/number** *I can't get through – her line's engaged.* 我打不通, 她的电话占线。| **engaged tone** (=the sound you hear when the telephone is engaged)〔电话占线的〕忙音 **3** a public toilet that is engaged is being used〔公共厕所〕使用中的 —opposite 反义词 VACANT (1) **4 be otherwise engaged** *formal* to be unable to do something because you have arranged to do something else【正式】另外有约, 另外有事

en·gage·ment /ɪnˈgedʒmənt; ɪnˈgeɪdʒmənt/ *n* **1** [C] an agreement to marry someone 订婚, 婚约: *They've officially announced their engagement.* 他们已正式宣布订婚。| **break off your engagement** (=say you no longer want to marry someone) 解除婚约 **2** [C] an arrangement to do something or meet someone 约定; 约会: *He has engagements this month at various clubs.* 他本月与数家俱乐部有约。| **prior/previous engagement** (=an arrangement you have already made) 已定好的约会 *I won't be able to make it – I have a prior engagement.* 我不能去了, 我已另有约在先。**3** [C] *technical* a battle between armies, navies etc【术语】〔陆军、海军等的〕战斗, 交火 **4** [U] the fitting together of the working parts of a machine〔机器部件的〕啮合, 衔接

CULTURAL NOTE 文化注释

Traditionally, it is the custom in the US and the UK for a man and woman who are going to get married to get engaged first. The man buys the woman an ENGAGEMENT RING, traditionally a gold ring with a diamond on it. They tell their family and friends and sometimes have a party. There is usually a period of time between the engagement and the wedding, so that the two people can make wedding plans, save money, find somewhere to live etc. Now, however, people who decide to get married often live together first, and sometimes do not get formally engaged at all. 按英美传统, 男女结婚前要先订婚。男方为女方买订婚戒指, 常为带钻石的金戒。订婚要告知双方亲朋, 有时举办聚会。订婚和结婚之间通常有一段时间, 供新人制定结婚计划、存钱、找住处等。不过, 现在人们有结婚的打算后经常先同居, 有时根本不经过正式订婚。

engagement ring /ˈ· · · ·/ *n* [C] a ring that a man gives to a woman when they decide to marry〔男方给女方的〕订婚戒指

en·gag·ing /ɪnˈgedʒɪŋ; ɪnˈgeɪdʒɪŋ/ *adj* attracting someone's attention and interest 动人的, 迷人的: *an engaging smile* 迷人的微笑 —**engagingly** *adv*

En·gels /ˈɛŋəls; ˈeŋgəlz/, **Frie·drich** /ˈfridrɪk; ˈfriːdrɪk/ (1820-95) a German political thinker and REVOLUTIONARY who, together with Karl Marx, wrote *The Communist Manifesto* and developed the political system of COMMUNISM 恩格斯〔(1820-1895), 德国政治思想家、革命家, 与卡尔·马克思一起写成《共产党宣言》并发展了共产主义政治体系〕

en·gen·der /ɪnˈdʒɛndɚ; ɪnˈdʒendə/ *v* [T] *formal* to be the cause of a situation or feeling【正式】导致〔某种情形或感觉〕: *Racial inequality engenders conflict.* 种族不平等导致冲突。

en·gine /ˈɛndʒən; ˈendʒɪn/ *n* [C] **1** a piece of machinery with moving parts that changes power from steam, electricity, oil etc, into movement 发动机, 引擎: *the engine of a car* 汽车发动机 | *a jet engine* 喷气发动机 **2** a vehicle that pulls a railway train 火车头, 机车 **3 engine of change/destruction etc** *formal* something that causes change etc【正式】变革/毁灭等的原动力: *a newspaper that was the engine of cultural change* 推动文化变革的一家报纸 —see also 另见 FIRE ENGINE

engine driv·er /ˈ· ,· ·/ *n* [C] *BrE* someone who drives a train【英】火车司机; ENGINEER[1] (5) *AmE*【美】

en·gi·neer[1] /ˌɛndʒəˈnɪr; ˌendʒɪˈnɪə/ *n* [C] **1** someone who designs the way roads, bridges, machines etc are built 工程师, 工程[机械]设计人员: *Mike's an electrical engineer.* 迈克是一名电气工程师。**2** someone who controls the engines on a ship or aircraft〔船或飞机上控制发动机的〕机师, 机工 **3** *BrE* someone who repairs electrical or mechanical equipment【英】〔负责维修的〕机械师, 修理工: *The engineer's coming to fix the phone today.* 修理工今天来修电话。**4** a soldier in the army who designs and builds roads, bridges etc〔军队的〕工兵, 工程兵 **5** *AmE* someone who drives a train【美】火车司机

engineer[2] *v* [T] **1** to arrange something by clever secret planning 策划, 谋划: *He had powerful enemies who engineered his downfall.* 他的敌人势力强大, 策划了他的垮台。**2** [often passive

常用被动态] to design and plan the construction of roads, bridges, machines, etc 设计〔公路、桥梁、机器等〕: *This new jet engine is superbly engineered.* 这个新喷气发动机设计精良。

2 **en·gi·neer·ing** /ˌɛndʒəˋnɪrɪŋ; ˌendʒɪˈnɪərɪŋ/ *n* [U] the profession and activity of designing the way roads, bridges, machines etc are built 工程师行业; 工程设计 —see also 另见 CIVIL ENGINEERING

En·gland /ˋɪŋglənd; ˈɪŋglənd/ **1** the largest country in Britain; population 49,138,831 (2001). The capital is London. 英格兰〔英国最大的行政区域。人口: 49,138,831 (2001), 首府: 伦敦〕 —compare 比较 BRITAIN, UNITED KINGDOM **2 ... for England** *BrE spoken* a humorous way of saying that someone does a lot or too much of a particular activity【英, 口】没完没了地; 过分地〔语气幽默〕: *You know Brian, he could flirt for England.* 你知道布莱恩这个人吧, 他就爱打情骂俏。| *They say men can't communicate, but Lee and his mates talk for England when they get together.* 有人说男人不善交际, 可李和伙伴们在一起的时候总是说个不停。

En·glish¹ /ˋɪŋglɪʃ; ˈɪŋglɪʃ/ *n* [U] **1** the language of Britain, the US, Australia, and some other countries 英语 **2** English language and literature as a subject of study 英语语言和文学 (课程): *a professor of English* 英语教授 **3 the English** people from England, or sometimes from all of Britain 英格兰人; 英国人

English² *adj* from or connected with England or Britain 英格兰的; 英国的

English break·fast /ˌ‥ˈ‥/ *n* [C] *BrE* a large cooked breakfast consisting of BACON, eggs, TOAST¹ (1) etc【英】英国式早餐〔包括熏肉、蛋和烤面包等〕 —compare 比较 CONTINENTAL BREAKFAST

CULTURAL NOTE 文化注释

This meal is thought of as a typical English breakfast, but in fact not many English people eat a cooked breakfast every day. Hotels and BED AND BREAKFASTS in the UK usually serve a 'full English breakfast', which also includes CEREAL or fruit juice. 这种早餐被看成典型的英式早餐, 但事实上每天吃这种烹制早餐的英国人并不多。英国的酒店和小旅馆一般提供"全套英式早餐", 另含麦片或果汁。

English Cham·ber Or·ches·tra, the /ˌ‥ˈ‥ˌ‥/ also 又作 **the ECO** a British CHAMBER ORCHESTRA (=a small group of musicians) based in London 英国室内乐团〔总部设在伦敦〕

English Chan·nel, the /ˌ‥ˈ‥/ also 又作 **the Channel** the narrow piece of water between southern England and northern France, which French people call 'La Manche' 英吉利海峡〔英国南部与法国北部之间的狭长水域, 法国人称拉芒什海峡〕

English Her·i·tage /ˌ‥ˈ‥/ a British government organization which takes care of many old buildings and other places that are important in English history 英国遗产委员会〔英国一政府机构, 负责保护众多古建筑和历史名胜〕 —compare 比较 NATIONAL TRUST

English horn /ˌ‥ˈ/ *especially AmE* COR ANGLAIS【尤美】英国管

En·glish·man /ˋɪŋglɪʃmən; ˈɪŋglɪʃmən/ *n* [C] a man from England 英格兰男人

English muf·fin /ˌ‥ˈ‥/ *n* [C] *AmE* a round flat piece of bread that you TOAST² (2) before eating it【美】英式松饼; MUFFIN *BrE*【英】

English Na·tion·al Op·er·a, the /ˌ‥ˌ‥ˈ‥/ also 又作 **the ENO** an OPERA company which performs operas in English at a theatre called the London Coliseum 英国国家歌剧团〔在伦敦大剧院演出英语歌剧的一家歌剧团〕

English Tour·ist Board, the /ˌ‥ˈ‥ˌ/ a British organization that tries to encourage tourists to go on holiday in England, and provides information about hotels, places to visit etc 英格兰旅游局〔英国一机构, 鼓励游客去英格兰度假, 并提供酒店、景点等旅游资讯〕

En·glish·wom·an /ˋɪŋglɪʃˌwʊmən; ˈɪŋglɪʃˌwʊmən/ *n* [C] a woman from England 英格兰女人

en·grave /ɪnˋgrev; ɪnˈgreɪv/ *v* [T] **1** to cut words or pictures on metal, wood, glass etc〔在金属、木、玻璃等上〕雕刻〔文字或图案〕: **engrave sth on** *a silver pocket watch with the initials HTS engraved on the back* 背面刻着HTS三个首字母的银制怀表 | **engrave sth with** *a pendant engraved with a simple geometric design* 雕刻有简单几何图案的项链坠 **2 be engraved in your memory/mind/heart** *formal* to be impossible to forget【正式】铭刻在记忆里/脑海中/心中: *That day would be engraved in his memory for ever.* 那一天将永远铭刻在他的记忆里。**3** to prepare a special metal plate for printing〔为印刷而〕镌版, 制版 **4** to print something using a specially prepared metal plate 用镌版印 —**engraver** *n* [C]

en·grav·ing /ɪnˋgrevɪŋ; ɪnˈgreɪvɪŋ/ *n* **1** [C] a picture printed from an engraved metal plate 金属版画: *an old engraving of London Bridge* 一幅伦敦桥的旧金属版画 **2** [U] the art or work of engraving things 雕刻术; 雕刻工作; 镌版术; 镌版工作

en·gross /ɪnˋgros; ɪnˈgrəʊs/ *v* [T] **1** if something engrosses you, you are extremely interested in it 使非常感兴趣; 使全神贯

engine 发动机

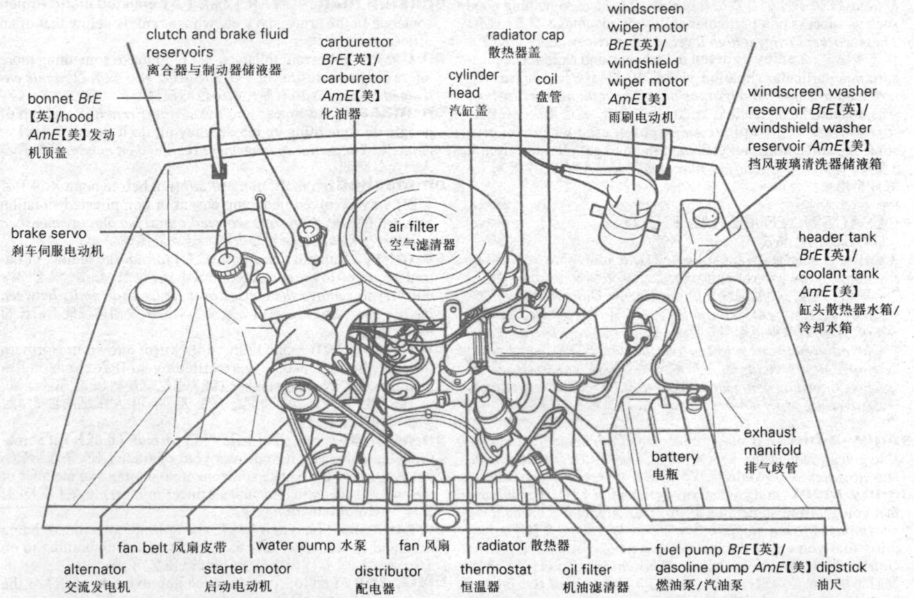

clutch and brake fluid reservoirs 离合器与制动器储液器
carburettor *BrE*【英】/ carburetor *AmE*【美】化油器
radiator cap 散热器盖
windscreen wiper motor *BrE*【英】/ windshield wiper motor *AmE*【美】雨刷电动机
bonnet *BrE*【英】/hood *AmE*【美】发动机顶盖
cylinder head 汽缸盖
coil 盘管
windscreen washer reservoir *BrE*【英】/ windshield washer reservoir *AmE*【美】挡风玻璃清洗器储液箱
brake servo 刹车伺服电动机
air filter 空气滤清器
header tank *BrE*【英】/ coolant tank *AmE*【美】缸头散热器水箱/冷却水箱
exhaust manifold 排气歧管
battery 电瓶
fan belt 风扇皮带
water pump 水泵
fan 风扇
radiator 散热器
fuel pump *BrE*【英】/ gasoline pump *AmE*【美】燃油泵/汽油泵
dipstick 油尺
alternator 交流发电机
starter motor 启动电动机
distributor 配电器
thermostat 恒温器
oil filter 机油滤清器

注: *Their revolutionary talk engrossed him, and he listened intently.* 他们的革命性的谈话使他着迷，他入神地听着。**2 engross yourself in/with** to become very interested in something and spend a lot of time doing it 专注于，专心致志于

en·grossed /ɪnˋgrost; ɪnˈgrəʊst/ *adj* so interested in something that you do not notice anything else 全神贯注的，专心致志的: [+in/with] *I tried to attract her attention but she was engrossed in conversation with Stephen.* 我试图引起她的注意，但她一直专心地和斯蒂芬说话。

en·gross·ing /ɪnˋgrosɪŋ; ɪŋˈgrəʊsɪŋ/ *adj* so interesting that you do not notice anything else 引人入胜的; 使人着迷的: *an engrossing story* 引人入胜的故事

en·gulf /ɪnˋgʌlf; ɪnˈgʌlf/ *v* [T] **1** if a feeling, especially an unpleasant one, engulfs you, you feel it extremely strongly〔尤指不愉快的情感〕吞没; 包围: *I knew I was very near death, and a terrifying panic engulfed me.* 知道自己很快要死了，我陷入极大的恐慌。**2** if a war/social change etc engulfs a place, it affects it so much that it changes completely〔战争或社会变革等〕彻底改变; 吞噬: *a war that engulfed the whole of Europe* 蔓延到整个欧洲的战争 **3** to completely surround or cover something 完全包围; 遮住: *Thick white smoke engulfed the courtyard.* 白色的浓烟吞没了庭院。**4 be engulfed in flames** if a building is engulfed in flames, the whole building is burning 被大火吞没

3 **en·hance** /ɪnˋhæns; ɪnˈhɑːns/ *v* [T] to improve something 提高; 改进; 增强: *The flavor of most foods can be enhanced by good cooking.* 好的烹饪可以使大多数食物增味。—**enhancement** *n* [C,U]: *much needed enhancements* 亟须的改进

e·nig·ma /ɪˋnɪgmə; ɪˈnɪgmə/ *n* [C] someone or something that is strange or mysterious and difficult to understand or explain 费解的事物; 不可理解的人: *The neighbours had come to regard him as something of an enigma.* 邻居们都已把他当作一个谜一样的人。

en·ig·mat·ic /ˌɛnɪgˋmætɪk; ˌenɪgˈmætɪk◂/ *adj* rather mysterious and difficult to understand or explain 费解的; 难捉摸的: *an enigmatic smile* 令人难以捉摸的微笑 —**enigmatically** /-klɪ; -kli/ *adv*: *"You'll find out soon enough," she said enigmatically.* "你很快就会发现的。"她神秘地说。

en·join /ɪnˋdʒɔɪn; ɪnˈdʒɔɪn/ *v* [T] **1** *formal* to order someone to do something【正式】命令，责令 **2** *AmE law* to legally prevent someone from going near a person or place【美，法律】依法阻止〔某人〕接近〔某人或某地〕

1 1 **en·joy** /ɪnˋdʒɔɪ; ɪnˈdʒɔɪ/ *v* [T] **1** to get pleasure from something 喜欢; 享受…的乐趣: *Did you enjoy the movie?* 你喜欢那部电影吗? | **enjoy doing sth** *Young children enjoy helping with household tasks.* 小孩子们喜欢帮着做家务。**2** to have something good such as success or a particular ability or advantage 享有; 拥有: *These workers enjoy a high level of job security.* 这些工人的工作非常稳定。**3 enjoy yourself** to be happy and experience pleasure in a particular situation 过得愉快; 感到快乐: *She was determined to enjoy herself at the party, even though her ex-boyfriend would be there.* 尽管她的前男友会来，她还是决心在晚会上痛痛快快地玩。**4 enjoy!** *AmE spoken* used when you give someone something and you want them to get pleasure from it【美口】好好享用吧: *Here's your steak – enjoy!* 你的牛排来了，好好享用吧!

> **USAGE NOTE 用法说明: ENJOY**
>
> GRAMMAR 语法
>
> **Enjoy** is nearly always followed by a noun phrase, a pronoun, or by a verb with *-ing*. 绝大多数情况下，enjoy 后跟名词短语、代名词或是加 ing 的动词: *Did you enjoy the movie? Yes, I enjoyed it a lot* (NOT 不用 *I enjoyed with/of it*). 你喜欢那电影吗? 是的，我非常喜欢。| *I really enjoyed myself last night at the theater* (NOT 不用 *I enjoyed at the theater*). 我昨晚看戏看得很开心。| *He enjoys travelling very much* (NOT 不用 *He enjoys very much travelling* or *He enjoys to travel*). 他非常喜欢旅行。

3 **en·joy·a·ble** /ɪnˋdʒɔɪəbl; ɪnˈdʒɔɪəbəl/ *adj* something enjoyable gives you pleasure 使人愉快的，令人快乐的: *games to make learning more enjoyable* 寓教于乐的游戏 —**enjoyably** *adv*

en·joy·ment /ɪnˋdʒɔɪmənt; ɪnˈdʒɔɪmənt/ *n* **1** [U] the pleasure that you get from something 愉快，乐趣: *Acting has brought me enormous enjoyment.* 演戏给我带来巨大的快乐。**2** [C] something that you enjoy doing; AMUSEMENT (2) 乐事，消遣，娱乐: *Golf and bridge were just some of his enjoyments.* 打高尔夫球和打桥牌仅是他消遣方式的一部分。**3** [U] *formal* the fact of having something【正式】拥有，享有

en·large /ɪnˋlardʒ; ɪnˈlɑːdʒ/ *v* [I,T] to become bigger or to make something bigger (使) 增大，扩大: *We're planning to enlarge the garden.* 我们正打算扩大花园。| *Travel enlarges the mind.* 旅游使人心胸开阔。

enlarge on/upon sth *phr v* [T] to provide more facts or details about something you have already mentioned 详述; 详细说明: *Mrs Maughan did not enlarge on what she meant by 'unsuitable'.* 莫恩夫人并未具体讲她所谓的"不合适"是什么意思。

en·large·ment /ɪnˋlardʒmənt; ɪnˈlɑːdʒmənt/ *n* **1** [C] a photograph that has been printed again in a larger size 放大的照片 **2** [C,U] an increase in size or amount 扩大，增大

en·lar·ger /ɪnˋlardʒɚ; ɪnˈlɑːdʒə/ *n* [C] a piece of equipment for making photographs larger〔照片〕放大机

en·light·en /ɪnˋlaɪtn̩; ɪnˈlaɪtn/ *v* [T] *formal* to explain something to someone【正式】指导，教导; 启迪: *Baldwin enlightened her as to the nature of the experiment.* 鲍德温给她讲解了这个实验的性质。—**enlightening** *adj*: *an enlightening explanation* 启发性的解释

en·light·ened /ɪnˋlaɪtn̩d; ɪnˈlaɪtənd/ *adj* **1** treating people in a kind and sensible way and understanding their needs and problems 开明的: *The more enlightened factory owners built homes for their workers in Britain in the 19th century.* 在 19 世纪的英国，较开明的工厂主为工人建造住所。**2** showing a good understanding of something and not believing things about it that are false 有见识的: *enlightened opinions* 明智的意见

en·light·en·ment /ɪnˋlaɪtn̩mənt; ɪnˈlaɪtnmənt/ *n* [U] **1** *formal* the state of understanding something clearly or the act of making someone understand something clearly【正式】领悟; 启发，开导 **2** the state in the BUDDHIST and HINDU religions, of no longer having any human desires, so that you are united spiritually with the universe〔佛教或印度教的〕觉悟，般若〔指摆脱欲望达到最高的精神境界〕

Enlightenment, the *n* a period in the eighteenth century when many writers and scientists believed that science and knowledge, not religion, could improve people's lives 启蒙运动〔18 世纪欧洲的许多作家和科学家认为，科学和知识可改善人民的生活，而并非宗教〕

en·list /ɪnˋlɪst; ɪnˈlɪst/ *v* **1 enlist sb's help** to persuade someone to help you 求到某人的帮助: *I enlisted the help of a local artist to do a painting for her birthday.* 我请一名当地画家帮忙，为她生日画幅画。**2** [I] to join the army, navy etc 参军，入伍: *In the first year of the war a million men enlisted voluntarily.* 战争的第一年，有一百万人自愿参军。—see 见 JOIN[1] (USAGE) **3** [T+in/into] to persuade people to join your organisation 劝说〔某人〕加入〔组织〕—**enlistment** *n* [C,U]

enlisted man /ˌ· ˈ· ·/ *n* [C] *AmE*【美】**enlisted man/woman** someone in the army, navy etc whose rank is below that of an officer 士兵/女兵

en·liv·en /ɪnˋlaɪvən; ɪnˈlaɪvən/ *v* [T] to make something more interesting or amusing 使…较生动活泼，使…较有趣: *a talk enlivened by photos* 因有照片而生色的演说

en masse /ˌanˋmæs; ˌɒnˈmæs/ *adv French* if a group of people do something en masse, they all do it together【法】一起，全体: *The senior management resigned en masse.* 高级管理人员全体辞职。

en·meshed /ɛnˋmɛʃt; ɪnˈmeʃt/ *adj* [not before noun 不用于名词前] very involved in an unpleasant or complicated situation 陷入的; 卷入的: *Congress worried about becoming enmeshed in a foreign war.* 国会担心会陷入一场外国战争。

en·mi·ty /ˋɛnmətɪ; ˈenmɪ̥ti/ *n* [C,U] *formal* the feeling of hatred or anger towards someone【正式】仇恨; 怨恨; 愤怒: *We must try to remove the causes of distrust and enmity between the two communities.* 我们必须设法消除两个团体彼此不信任和敌视的根源。

En·nis·kil·len /ˌɛnɪsˋkɪlɪn; ˌenɪ̥sˈkɪlɪ̥n/ a town in Northern Ireland where 11 people were killed by an IRA bomb on Remembrance Day in November 1987 恩尼斯基林〔北爱尔兰一镇。在 1987 年 11 月阵亡将士纪念日那天，有 11 人在此被北爱尔兰共和军的炸弹炸死〕

en·no·ble /ɪˋnobl̩; ɪˈnəʊbəl/ *v* [T] *formal*【正式】**1** if something ennobles you it improves your character 使〔某人〕高尚; 使〔某人〕崇高 **2** to make someone a NOBLEMAN (=a member of the part of society that includes princes, DUKEs) etc 封〔某人〕为贵族 —**ennoblement** *n* [U]

en·nui /ˋanwi; ɒnˈwiː/ *n* [U] *French formal* a feeling of being tired and bored, especially as a result of having nothing to do【法，正式】〔尤指因无所事事引起的〕倦怠，无聊

ENO, the /ˌi ɛn ˋo; ˌiː en ˈəʊ/ the abbreviation of 缩写= the ENGLISH NATIONAL OPERA

e·nor·mi·ty /ɪˋnɔrməti; ɪˈnɔːmɪ̆ti/ *n* **1** [singular] the enormity of a situation, event etc is how serious it is or how big an effect it will have 严重(性);〔后果的〕深远: *the enormity of his crimes* 他罪行的严重性 **2** [U] the enormity of a problem, subject, job etc is how large or difficult it is〔问题、主题、工作等〕巨大; 艰巨: *Don't be put off by the enormity of the task.* 不要被任务的艰巨吓倒。**3** [C] an extremely serious and cruel act 极其凶残的暴行

e·nor·mous /ɪˋnɔrməs; ɪˈnɔːməs/ *adj* extremely large in size or in amount〔尺寸、数量〕巨大的, 庞大的: *an enormous bouquet of flowers* 巨大的花束 | *The amount of paperwork involved is enormous.* 需要做的文书工作量非常大。—**enormously** *adv*: *enormously fat* 极其肥胖 —**enormousness** *n* [U]

enough 足够

Joel wasn't tall enough to play.
乔尔不够高, 不适合打球。

There wasn't enough cake for everyone.
蛋糕不够分给每个人吃。

e·nough¹ /əˋnʌf; ɪˈnʌf/ *adv* **1** to the necessary degree 足够(地): *Her sentence was light because the judge said she had suffered enough already.* 她的刑罚轻, 因为法官说她已经吃够苦头了。| *Are the carrots cooked enough?* 胡萝卜煮熟了吗? **2 tall/kind/fast etc enough** as tall, kind, fast etc as is necessary 足够高/友好/快等: *I didn't bring a big enough bag.* 我带来的包不够大。| *Is your tea sweet enough?* 你的茶够甜吗? | [+for] *Is it warm enough for you?* 你觉得够暖和吗? | **mad/tall/silly etc enough to do sth** *Is the water hot enough for a bath?* 这水用来洗澡够热吗? | *He said he would never see her again and I was gullible enough to believe him.* 他说他再也不会见她, 而我竟轻信了。| *Would you be kind enough to let us know when you are arriving?* 请你通知我们你到达的时间, 好吗? | **not good enough** (=not satisfactory or acceptable) 不令人满意; 不够好 *I'm going to go up to that school and tell them it's just not good enough.* 我要到那个学校去, 告诉他们这让人无法接受。**3 difficult/happy/busy etc enough** rather difficult, happy etc 相当困难/高兴/忙碌等: *I was happy enough in Bordeaux, but I missed my family.* 我在波尔多过得不错, 但还是想家。| *It's bad enough doing this without you giving me orders all the time.* 且不说你没完没了地指挥我, 做这件事本身就够难为人。| *It was natural enough that she should be annoyed.* 她感到厌烦, 这再正常不过了。**4 strangely/oddly/curiously enough** although this is strange, odd etc 令人奇怪的是, 说来奇怪: *Funnily enough, I bumped into her only yesterday.* 说来好笑, 我昨天刚好碰见她。**5 near enough** *BrE spoken* nearly【英口】几乎; 差不多: *Your jacket's near enough dry now.* 你的夹克现在差不多干了。| *This bottle's near enough finished.* 这瓶酒快喝完了。| *That's £3,000 near enough, isn't it?* 那大约是3000英镑, 是不是? —see also 另见 **fair enough** (FAIR¹ (17)), **sure enough** (SURE² (2))

enough² *determiner, pron* **1** as much or as many as may be necessary 充分, 足够: *Move over, I don't have enough room.* 挪一挪, 我的地方不够。| *Not enough is known about what really happened.* 究竟发生了什么事还没有弄清楚。| *Leave the potatoes if you've had enough.* 如果你吃饱了, 就把马铃薯剩下吧。| [+for] *There aren't enough chairs for everyone.* 椅子不够每人一把。| **enough to do/eat etc** *Erica was worried that the children weren't getting enough to eat.* 埃丽卡担心孩子们吃不饱。| **enough sth to do sth** *There's enough material left to make matching pillows.* 剩下的材料做配套的枕头足够了。| **more than enough** (=too much) 太多, 过多 *No, thank you, I've had more than enough.* 不, 谢谢, 我已经吃太多了。| **not nearly enough/nowhere near enough** (=much less than enough) 太少; 差得太远 *There was nowhere near enough wine to go round.* 酒太少, 根本不够大家喝。| **that's enough** *spoken* (=stop behaving like that)【口】不要那样 *Now, David, that's quite enough – be a good boy.* 噢, 戴维, 行了, 乖点儿吧。| **enough is enough** *spoken* (=there is no need to say or do any more)【口】适可而止; 不必再… *I could lend him another $20 but, really, enough's enough.* 我可以再借给他20美元, 但凡事皆应适可而止。| **time/food etc enough** *There'll be time enough to get to know each other later on.* 以后会有足够的时间相互了解。**2 have had enough (of sth)** *spoken* to be thoroughly tired or sick of something and want it to stop【口】受够了: *When I got in from work I just sat down and cried. I'd had enough.* 下班后回到家, 我就坐下哭了起来。我受够了。| *I've just about had enough of your sass.* 你的无礼我已经快要受够了。**3 enough said** *spoken* there is no need to say any more, I understand everything【口】不用再说了〔我都明白了〕: *"I saw her coming out of his room at 6 o'clock this morning." "Enough said."* "今早6点钟我看见她从他房间出来。""不用再说了。" —see 见 ADEQUATE (USAGE)

E

> **USAGE NOTE 用法说明: ENOUGH**
> GRAMMAR 语法
> **Enough** comes after adjectives and adverbs. enough 用在形容词和副词之后: *She's not old enough* (NOT 不用 *She's not enough old*). 她年纪不够大。| *He didn't pack the bowls carefully enough and they broke.* 他在包装碗的时候不够小心, 结果碗都碎了。| *Well I've done my best, and I hope it's good enough.* 我已经尽力了, 我希望结果会令人满意。
> **Enough** usually comes before a plural or uncountable noun. enough 通常用在复数名词或不可数名词前: *enough people/money* 足够的人/钱。It is only used after the noun in slightly formal or old-fashioned English. 只有在稍正式或过时的英语中, 才用于名词后面: *There was money enough for all.* 钱足够所有人花。However, *time enough* is still fairly common. 但是, time enough 的用法还很常见: *There'll be time enough for that later.* 以后会有足够的时间做那件事。

en pas·sant /ˌɑn pɑˋsɑn; ˌɒn ˈpæsɒn/ *adv French formal* if you say or mention something en passant, you say a few words about it while you are talking about something else【法, 正式】顺便提到: *She happened to mention en passant, that she'd seen Joan.* 她顺便提到她见过琼。

en·quire /ɪnˋkwaɪr; ɪnˈkwaɪə/ *v* [I,T] *especially BrE*【尤英】another spelling of INQUIRE inquire 的另一种拼法

en·qui·ry /ɪnˋkwaɪrɪ; ɪnˈkwaɪəri/ *n* [C,U] *especially BrE*【尤英】another spelling of INQUIRY inquiry 的另一种拼法

en·rage /ɪnˋredʒ; ɪnˈreɪdʒ/ *v* [T] to make someone extremely angry 使〔某人〕非常愤怒; 激怒: *She asked him to leave, enraged by his sexist comments.* 他带有性别歧视的言论激怒了她, 她叫他离开。

en·rap·tured /ɪnˋræptʃɚd; ɪnˈræptʃəd/ *adj formal* feeling such pleasure and happiness that you can think of nothing else【正式】着迷的; 心花怒放的: *The orchestra played before an enraptured audience.* 管弦乐队的演奏使听众如醉如痴。

en·rich /ɪnˋrɪtʃ; ɪnˈrɪtʃ/ *v* [T] **1** to improve the quality of something, especially by adding things to it 使丰富, 充实; 富集, 强化: *a fertilizer that enriches the soil* 使土壤肥沃的肥料 | *Education can enrich your life.* 教育可以使生活充实。**2** to make someone richer 使〔某人〕更富裕 —**enrichment** *n* [U]

en·rol *BrE*【英】, **enroll** *AmE*【美】/ɪnˋrol; ɪnˈrəʊl/ *v* **enrolled, enrolling** [I,T] to officially arrange to join a school, university or course, or arrange for someone else to 招(生), 吸收(成员); 注册(学习): [+on *BrE* 英, +in *AmE* 美] *There were 500 people enrolled in the Western Civilization class.* 有500人注册学习西方文明课。—see 见 JOIN¹ (USAGE) —**enrolment** *n* [C,U]

Enrolled Nurse /ˌ· ˈ· ˈ·/ *n* [C] a nurse who has passed an examination in England, Scotland, or Wales〔英格兰、苏格兰和威尔士的〕登记护士

en route /ˌɑn ˋrut; ˌɒn ˈruːt/ *adv French* on the way【法】在路上; 在途中: *We were going to the Florida Keys but we stopped en route to visit Miami.* 我们计划到佛罗里达群岛去, 途中顺道停下游览了迈阿密。| **[+from/for/to]** *a boat en route to the Bahamas* 去巴哈马群岛途中的一艘船

en·sconce /ɛnˋskɑns; ɪnˈskɒns/ *v* [T] to put yourself in a comfortable and safe place 安顿: **ensconce yourself** *He ensconced himself in an armchair in front of the fire.* 他安坐在炉火前的扶手椅里。| *safely ensconced in the penthouse suite* 安全地在顶楼套房安顿下来

en·sem·ble /ɑnˋsɑmbḷ; ɒnˈsɒmbəl/ *n* **1** [C] a small group of musicians who play together regularly〔经常在一起演奏的〕小乐队, 合奏组: *The ensemble will play an all-Bach program tonight.* 合奏组今晚要演奏清一色的巴赫曲目。**2** [C usually singular 一般用单数] a set of clothes that are worn together 套服: *The leggings combined with a long black tunic made an attractive ensemble.* 黑色的长紧身外衣配上绑腿精神极了。**3** [C usually singular 一般用单数] a set of things that go together to form a whole 成套的东西

en·shrine /ɪnˋʃraɪn; ɪnˈʃraɪn/ *v* [T usually passive 一般用被动态] *formal* if something such as a law, tradition, or right is enshrined in something, it is preserved, especially in written form, so that people will remember and respect it【正式】铭记; 珍藏〔指法律、传统或权利保存下来, 尤指用书面形式保存以使人铭记、珍视〕: **enshrine sth in** *Ancient practices and customs are enshrined in local folk literature.* 古代的风俗习惯传承于当地的民间文学之中。| *inalienable rights enshrined in the Constitution* 载入宪法的不可剥夺的权利

en·shroud /ɪnˋʃraʊd; ɪnˈʃraʊd/ *v* [T] *formal*【正式】**1** if something such as mystery enshrouds something, it makes it difficult to understand or explain 使有神秘色彩; 使费解: *corn circles and the mystery that enshrouds them* 麦田怪圈以及这一现象所笼罩的神秘色彩 **2** to cover or hide something 遮盖; 遮掩: *hills enshrouded in mist* 雾气笼罩的群山

en·sign /ˋɛnsaɪn; ˈensaɪn/ *n* [C] **1** a flag on a ship that shows what country the ship belongs to〔表示船只国籍的〕旗 **2** a low rank in the US navy, or an officer who has this rank〔美国〕海军少尉 —see table on page C6 参见 C6 页附录 **3** an officer of low rank in the British army in the past〔英国旧时〕步兵少尉 **4** *AmE* a small piece of metal on your uniform that shows your rank【美】〔军装上表示等级的〕徽章, 标志

en·slave /ɪnˋslev; ɪnˈsleɪv/ *v* [T usually passive 一般用被动态] **1** *formal* to trap someone in a situation that they cannot easily escape from【正式】束缚; 制约: *enslaved by marriage and trapped by taboos and prejudice* 受到婚姻约束并陷于禁忌和偏见之中 **2** to make someone into a slave 使成为奴隶, 奴役 —**enslavement** *n* [U]

en·snare /ɛnˋsnɛr; ɪnˈsneə/ *v* [T] *formal* to force or trick someone into doing something that they do not want to do【正式】强迫[欺骗]〔某人做某事〕, 使入圈套: *ensnared into a loveless relationship* 受骗陷入一种没有爱的关系之中

en·sue /ɪnˋsu; ɪnˈsjuː/ *v* [I] to happen as a result of something 因而发生, 继而发生: *Serious problems will ensue if something is not done about gang rivalry now.* 如果不采取措施制止帮派争斗, 会发生严重的问题。

en·su·ing /ɪnˋsuɪŋ; ɪnˈsjuːɪŋ/ *adj* [only before noun 仅用于名词前] happening after a particular action or event, especially as a result of it 随后的; 因而发生的: **the ensuing battle/argument/panic etc** *Japan attacked Port Arthur and in the ensuing Russo-Japanese war the Russians were defeated.* 日本袭击了旅顺, 在接下来的日俄战争中俄国人被打败了。| **the ensuing year/six months/weeks etc** (=the time after an event) 随后的一年/半年/几星期等

en suite /ˌɑn ˋswit; ˌɒn ˈswiːt◂/ *adj BrE* an en suite bathroom is joined onto a bedroom【英】〔浴室和卧室〕成套的, 构成一体的: *four bedrooms, two with en suite bathrooms* 四间卧室, 两间带浴室

S3 W1 **en·sure** *especially BrE*【尤英】/ɪnˋʃʊr; ɪnˈʃʊə/ *v* [T] to make it certain that something will happen 确保, 保证: *All the necessary steps had been taken to ensure their safety.* 已采取所有必要措施来确保他们的安全。| **[+that]** *His wife ensured that he took all his pills every day.* 他妻子确保他每天服下所有该服的药片。—compare 比较 INSURE —see 见 INSURE (USAGE)

-ent /ənt; ənt/ *suffix* [in adjectives and nouns 构成形容词和名词] another form of the suffix -ANT 后缀 -ant 的另一种形式: *different* 不同的 | *residents* 居民

en·tail /ɪnˋtel; ɪnˈteɪl/ *v* [T] **1** to make it necessary to do something 使必须〔做某事〕; 需要: *Changing the computer system would entail substantial periods of retraining.* 更换电脑系统就需要进行相当长时间的再培训。| **entail doing sth** *My job entailed being on call 24 hours a day.* 我的工作需要一天 24 小时随叫随到。**2** *old use* to arrange for your property to become the property of a particular person, especially your son, after your death【旧】遗赠〔财产〕; 限定继承

en·tan·gle /ɪnˋtæŋgḷ; ɪnˈtæŋgəl/ *v* [T always+adv/prep] to make something become twisted or caught in a rope, net etc〔用绳、网等〕缠住; 套住

en·tan·gled /ɪnˋtæŋgḷd; ɪnˈtæŋgəld/ *adj* **1** involved in an argument, or a situation that is difficult to escape from, or a relationship that causes problems etc 卷入…的; 陷于…的: **[+in]** *Military observers fear that the US could get entangled in another Vietnam.* 军事观察员们担心美国会陷入另一场越南战争。| **[+with]** *Sue became romantically entangled with a work colleague.* 休与一个同事陷入感情纠葛中。**2** twisted or caught in something such as a rope or net 被缠住的, 被绕住的: **[+in/with]** *Penguins and seals have been found entangled in lengths of fishing net.* 发现企鹅和海豹缠在一段段的渔网里。

en·tan·gle·ment /ɪnˋtæŋgḷmənt; ɪnˈtæŋgəlmənt/ *n* [C] **1** a difficult situation or relationship that is hard to escape from 纠缠; 纠葛: *emotional entanglements* 情感纠葛 **2** [C often plural 常用复数] a fence made of BARBED WIRE that prevents enemy soldiers from getting too close〔阻止敌人接近的〕带刺铁丝网围栏

En·teb·be /ɛnˋtɛbɪ; enˈtebi/ a town in southern Uganda. It has an important international airport, where in 1976 Israeli soldiers saved 103 passengers who were on a plane which had been HIJACKed (=taken illegal control of, by threatening violence). 恩德培〔乌干达南部一镇, 建有一座重要的国际机场。1976 年, 以色列士兵在此从一架被劫持的飞机上救出 103 名乘客〕

entendre *n* —see 见 DOUBLE ENTENDRE

en·tente /ɑnˋtɑnt; ɒnˈtɒnt/ *n* [C,U] *French* a situation in which two countries have friendly relations with each other【法】〔两国间的〕友好关系, 和解

Entente Cor·di·ale /ɑnˌtɑnt kɔrdɪˋɑl; ɒnˌtɒnt kɔːdiˈɑːl/ *French* a political agreement and feeling of friendship between two or more countries. The name 'Entente Cordiale' was originally used for an agreement between Britain and France in 1904.【法】〔两国或多国间的〕协约; 协议; 谅解〔源于 1904 年的《英法协约》〕

en·ter /ˋɛntɚ; ˈentə/ *v* S1 W1

1 ►**GO INTO** 进入◄ **a)** [I,T] to go or come into a place 进入〔某处〕: *Silence fell as I entered the room.* 我一进屋大家就安静下来。| *Adie was one of the few reporters who had dared to enter the war zone.* 阿迪是仅有的几个敢于进入交战区的记者之一。**b)** [T] if an object enters part of something, it goes inside it 进入〔某物中〕: *The bullet had entered his brain through the back of his skull.* 子弹穿过他的颅骨后部进入大脑。

2 ►**START WORKING** 开始工作◄ [I,T] to start working in a particular profession or organization 开始从事〔某职业〕; 加入〔某组织〕: *Andrea is studying law as a preparation for entering politics.* 安德烈娅正在学习法律, 为以后从政作准备。| *He entered the Church as a young man.* 他加入教会时很年轻。

3 ►**START TO TAKE PART IN** 开始参加◄ [T] to start to take part in an activity, for example a course or a game 开始参加〔活动〕: *Her doctor recommended that she enter a drug treatment program.* 她的医生建议她接受戒毒治疗。

4 ►**COMPUTER** 电脑◄ [T] **a)** to put information into a computer by pressing the keys 输入〔信息〕: *If a command is entered incorrectly, the machine will not recognize it.* 如果命令输入不正确, 机器就不能辨别。**b)** if you enter a computer system, you are given permission to use it by the computer 进入〔电脑系统〕

5 ►**WRITE INFORMATION** 写下信息◄ [T] to write information on a particular part of a form, document etc〔在表格、文件等中〕写下, 填上: *Enter your name in the space provided.* 在空白处填上你的姓名。

6 ►**COMPETITION/EXAMINATION** 竞赛/考试◄ [I,T] to arrange to take part in a race, competition, examination etc, or to arrange for someone else to take part 报名参加〔赛跑、竞赛、考试等〕; 安排〔某人〕参加: *I've entered you and Dan in the sack race.* 我已经安排你和丹参加套袋赛跑。

7 ►**PERIOD OF TIME** 时期◄ [T] **a)** to begin a period of time when something happens 进入…时期: *The economy entered a period of recession in the mid 1980s.* 20 世纪80 年代中期, 经济步入衰退期。**b)** **enter its third week/sixth day/second year etc** if something enters its third week, its sixth day etc, it continues for a third week, a sixth day etc 进入第三周/第六天/第二年等: *The talks have now entered their third week.* 会谈已进入第三周。

8 it never entered my mind/head *spoken* used when you are very surprised by what has happened【口】我从未想到: *It never entered my head that he would have a gun.* 我从未想到他会有枪。

9 ►CHANGE 改变◄ [T] if a particular quality enters something, it starts to exist in it and change it, especially suddenly〔尤指突然〕具有某种特质: *A note of panic entered her voice.* 她的声音突然透出一丝恐慌。

10 enter sb's life if someone or something enters your life, you start to know them or be affected by them 进入某人的生活: *By the time Angie entered his life, he was almost 30.* 安吉走进他的生活时, 他已差不多30岁了。

11 ►START DISCUSSING 开始讨论◄ [T] to start to discuss or study a particular subject 开始讨论; 开始研究: *Here we enter a disputed and delicate area of the law.* 这里我们开始研究法律当中一个充满争议且十分微妙的领域。

12 enter a plea of guilty/not guilty *law* to say that you are guilty or not guilty of a particular crime in a court【法律】〔在法庭上〕承认/否认有罪

13 enter an offer/complaint/objection etc *formal* to officially make an offer, complaint etc【正式】正式提出建议/申诉/反对等

enter into sth *phr v* [T] **1** to start doing something, especially discussing or studying something 开始做某事〔尤指讨论或研究某事〕: *This is not the place to enter into a detailed discussion of economic policy.* 这里不是详细讨论经济政策的地方。**2** to affect a situation and be something that you must consider when you make a choice 十分有影响; 干系重大: *Money doesn't enter into it – it's the principle I object to.* 钱在这件事上无关紧要, 我反对的是原则。**3 enter into an agreement/contract etc** *formal* to officially make an agreement to do something【正式】达成协议/合同等 **4 enter into the spirit of it/things** to take part in a game, party etc in an eager way 急切地参加, 兴致勃勃地参与; 进入角色

enter upon sth *phr v* [T] *formal* to start doing something or being involved in it【正式】开始做某事; 开始参与某事

Frequencies of **enter** and **go/come in** in spoken and written English 在英语口语和书面语中 enter 和 go/come in 的使用频率

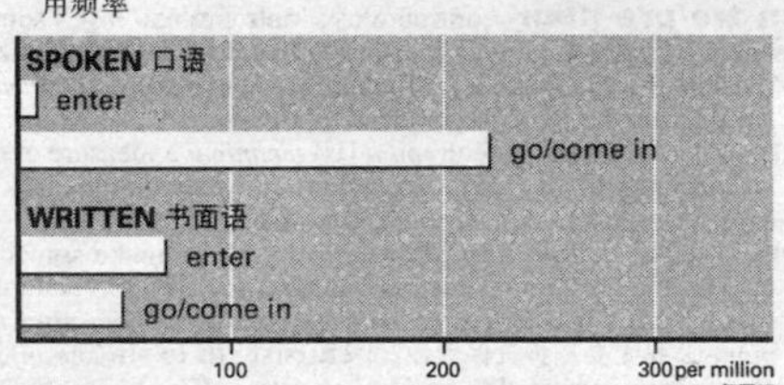

Based on the British National Corpus and the Longman Lancaster Corpus 据英国国家语料库和朗文兰开斯特语料库

This graph shows that it is much more usual in spoken English to use the expressions **go in** and **come in**, rather than the word **enter**. This is because **enter** is a formal word when used in this meaning and is more common in written English. 本图表显示, 在英语口语中 go in 和 come in 的使用频率要远远高于 enter, 这是因为 enter 用于此义时较正式, 所以它更常见于英语书面语中。

en·te·ri·tis /ˌɛntəˋraɪtɪs; ˌentəˈraɪtɪ̥s/ *n* [U] a painful infection in your INTESTINES 肠炎

2 **en·ter·prise** /ˋɛntəˌpraɪz; ˈentəpraɪz/ *n* **1** [C] a large and complicated piece of work, especially one that is done with a group of other people〔尤指与人合作的〕大型而复杂的工作: *a joint scientific enterprise* 联合科学事业 **2** [U] the ability to think of new activities or ideas and make them work 创业能力, 开创能力: *a woman with enterprise and creativity* 富有开创精神的妇女 **3** [C] a company, organization, or business 企业, 公司; 组织: *state-owned enterprises* 国有企业 **4** [U] the practice of starting and running small companies 创立和经营小企业(的行为): *a knowledge of American capitalist enterprise* 美国资本主义企业经营之道 —see also 另见 FREE ENTERPRISE, PRIVATE ENTERPRISE

CULTURAL NOTE 文化注释

In the UK, this word is often connected with the period of CONSERVATIVE government beginning in 1979, and especially with the political ideas of Margaret Thatcher, the aims of which were to encourage people to open their own businesses and to depend less on the state. 在英国, 该词常与 1979 年以后保守党执政期有关, 尤与撒切尔夫人的政治观点有关。其目的是鼓励人们自己创业, 较少依靠国家。

enterprise cul·ture /ˈ··· ,··/ *n* [C,U] a society or attitude in which starting successful businesses is believed to be very important 企业文化〔高度重视开创成功企业的社会或态度〕

en·ter·pris·ing /ˋɛntəˌpraɪzɪŋ; ˈentəpraɪzɪŋ/ *adj* showing the ability to think of new activities or ideas and make them work 富于创业精神的; 具有开创能力的: *An enterprising young student was selling copies of the answers to the test.* 一名很有事业头脑的年轻学生正在出售测验答案的复印件。—**enterprisingly** *adv*

en·ter·tain /ˌɛntəˋten; ˌentəˈteɪn/ *v* **1** [I,T] to invite people to your home for a meal or party or take your company's customers to have a meal, drinks etc 招待, 款待, 请客: *The restaurant is mainly used by executives entertaining clients.* 这家饭店主要是公司老总们用来宴请客户的地方。**2** [T] to do something that amuses or interests people 使〔某人〕快乐; 使〔某人〕有兴趣: **entertain sb with** *He entertained us with a stream of anecdotes about the Yukon.* 他讲了一连串有关育空地区的趣事引我们开心。**3 entertain an idea/hope/doubt etc** to think that something might be true, even for a short period of time 怀有想法/希望/疑惑等

en·ter·tain·er /ˌɛntəˋtenə; ˌentəˈteɪnə/ *n* [C] someone who tells jokes, sings etc to amuse people〔以讲笑话、唱歌等来逗乐的〕表演者, 艺人: *street entertainers* 街头艺人

en·ter·tain·ing[1] /ˌɛntəˋtenɪŋ; ˌentəˈteɪnɪŋ◂/ *adj* amusing and interesting 使人愉快的, 有趣的: *very entertaining storyteller* 妙趣横生的说书人 | *an entertaining evening* 一个令人开心的夜晚

entertaining[2] *n* [U] the practice of inviting people for meals or to parties, especially for business reasons〔尤指出于生意原因的〕宴请; 招待客户

en·ter·tain·ment /ˌɛntəˋtenmənt; ˌentəˈteɪnmənt/ *n* **1** [U] things such as films, television, performances etc that amuse or interest people 娱乐节目: *providing entertainment for tourists* 为游客提供娱乐节目 **2** [C] a performance or show 娱乐表演: *a musical entertainment* 音乐演出 3

en·thral also 又作 **enthrall** *especially AmE*【尤美】/ɛnˋθrɔl; ɪnˈθrɔːl/ *v* [T] to make someone so interested and excited that they listen to or watch something very carefully 迷住〔某人〕, 使〔某人〕着迷

en·thralled /ɛnˋθrɔld; ɪnˈθrɔːld/ *adj* so interested that you pay a lot of attention to what you are seeing or hearing 着迷的, 被强烈吸引的: *Richard listened, enthralled by the Captain's stories.* 理查德听着, 完全被船长的故事吸引住了。

en·thrall·ing /ɛnˋθrɔlɪŋ; ɪnˈθrɔːlɪŋ/ *adj* extremely interesting 迷人的, 非常有趣的

en·throne /ɪnˋθron; ɪnˈθrəʊn/ *v* [T usually passive 一般用被动态] to have a ceremony to show that a new king or queen is beginning to rule 为…举行登基仪式 —**enthronement** *n* [C,U]

en·thuse /ɪnˋθjuz; ɪnˈθjuːz/ *v* **1** [I] to talk about something in a very interested or excited way 津津乐道地讲述, 兴奋地说: **[+about/over]** *Jenny spent the entire evening enthusing about her new car.* 珍妮整个晚上都在津津乐道地大谈她的新汽车。**2** [T] to make someone interested in something or excited by it 使〔某人〕对…感兴趣, 激起〔某人〕热情

en·thu·si·as·m /ɪnˋθjuzɪˌæzəm; ɪnˈθjuːziæzəm/ *n* **1** [U] a strong feeling of interest and enjoyment about something and an eagerness to be involved in it 热情, 热忱: *Although she's a beginner, she played with great enthusiasm.* 虽然她是个新手, 但演奏时却充满了激情。| **[+for]** *He shares your enthusiasm for jazz.* 他与你一样爱好爵士乐。| **lack of enthusiasm** *the government's lack of enthusiasm for women's rights* 政府对维护妇女权益的不热心 **2** [C] *formal* an activity or subject that someone is very interested in【正式】热衷的活动; 热爱的事物 3

en·thu·si·ast /ɪnˋθjuzɪˌæst; ɪnˈθjuːziæst/ *n* [C] someone who is very interested in a particular activity or subject 热衷者, 热心的人: *a golfing enthusiast* 高尔夫球迷

en·thu·si·as·tic /ɪnˌθjuzɪˋæstɪk; ɪnˌθjuːziˈæstɪk◂/ *adj* showing a lot of interest and excitement about something〔对某事物〕热心的, 热衷的: *The singer got an enthusiastic reception.* 那个歌手受到了热情欢迎。| **[+about]** *I was less than enthusiastic about the idea of Bob coming to visit.* 我对鲍勃来访的事一点都不起劲。—**enthusiastically** /-klɪ; -kli/ *adv* 3

en·tice /ɪnˋtaɪs; ɪnˈtaɪs/ *v* [T] to persuade someone to do something by offering them something if they will do it 诱惑; 诱使: **entice sb away/across/down etc** *He tried to entice the dog away from its post by the door.* 他试图诱使守在门旁的那条狗离开。| **entice sb** *Banks are offering low interest rates in an attempt to*

entice new customers. 银行在降低利率以吸引新客户。—**enticement** *n* [C,U]

en·ti·cing /ɪn`taɪsɪŋ; ɪn'taɪsɪŋ/ *adj* very pleasant or interesting so that you feel strongly attracted 有吸引力的; 迷人的; 有诱惑力的: *It was a hot day and the water looked enticing.* 天气热, 水看起来十分诱人。—**enticingly** *adv*

en·tire /ɪn`taɪr; ɪn'taɪə/ *adj* [only before noun 仅用于名词前] the entire group, amount, period of time etc is used when you want to emphasize what you are saying 全部的, 整个的: *the entire staff* 所有职员 | *We spent the entire afternoon gossiping.* 我们整个下午都在聊天。

en·tire·ly /ɪn`taɪrlɪ; ɪn'taɪəli/ *adv* completely and in every possible way 完全地, 彻底地: *an entirely different matter* 完全不同的事 | *She devoted herself entirely to her research.* 她全心全意地投入到研究当中。| **consist/depend entirely etc** *The programme consists entirely of taped interviews with survivors of the Holocaust.* 这个节目全部由犹太人大屠杀的幸存者的访谈录音组成。

en·tir·e·ty /ɪn`taɪrtɪ; ɪn'taɪərəti/ *n* [U] **in its/their entirety** *formal* as a whole and including every part【正式】整体, 全部: *The correspondence has been published in its entirety for the first time.* 那些信件第一次被全文发表。

en·ti·tle /ɪn`taɪtl; ɪn'taɪtl/ *v* [T] **1** if something entitles you to something, it gives you the official right to have or do it 给予〔某人获得某物或做某事的〕权利: **be entitled to sth** *Mothers under 16 were entitled to a maternity grant of £25 a week.* 不满16岁的母亲有资格每周领取25英镑的育儿补贴。**2 be entitled sth** if a book, play etc is entitled something, that is its name 给〔书、剧等〕命名, 起名: *an autobiography entitled "Myself, My Two Countries"* 一本名为《我自己, 我的两个祖国》的自传 **3 be entitled to do something** *Ricardo believes his daughter is perfectly entitled to marry whoever she chooses.* 里卡多相信他的女儿完全有权选择要嫁给谁。

en·ti·tle·ment /ɪn`taɪtḷmənt; ɪn'taɪtlmənt/ *n* [C,U] the official right to have or receive something, or the amount that you receive〔拥有或获得某物的〕权利; 津贴: *welfare entitlements* 福利待遇 | **[+to]** *The amount of money you earn does not affect your entitlement to child benefit.* 你挣的钱并不影响你领取子女津贴。

en·ti·ty /`ɛntətɪ; 'entəti/ *n* [C] *formal* something that exists as a single and complete unit【正式】实体: *The mind and body are seen as separate entities.* 心灵和身体被看成是各自独立的实体。

en·tomb /ɪn`tum; ɪn'tuːm/ *v* [T often in passive 常用被动态] *formal* to bury or trap someone under the ground【正式】埋葬, 掩埋

en·to·mol·o·gy /ˌɛntə`mɑlədʒɪ; ˌentə'mɒlədʒi/ *n* [U] the scientific study of insects 昆虫学 —**entomologist** *n* [C] —**entomological** /ˌɛntəmə`lɑdʒɪkḷ; ˌentəmə'lɒdʒɪkəl◂/ *adj*

en·tou·rage /ˌɑntu`rɑʒ; 'ɒntʊrɑːʒ/ *n* [C usually singular 一般用单数, also plural verb *BrE* 英] a group of people who travel with an important person 随从, 随行人员: *the popstar and her entourage* 流行歌星和她的随行人员

en·trails /`ɛntrəlz; 'entreɪlz/ *n* [plural] the inside parts of an animal or person's body, especially their BOWELS 内脏〔尤指肠〕

en·trance /`ɛntrəns; 'entrəns/ *n* **1** [C] a door, gate etc that you go through to enter a place〔门等的〕入口, 通道: **[+to/of]** *the main entrance to the school* 学校的大门 —opposite 反义词 EXIT[1] **2** [C usually singular 一般用单数] the act of entering a place or room 进入, 进门: *Their conversation was interrupted by the entrance of four visitors.* 他们的谈话因进来了四个来访者而被打断。**3** [U] permission to become a member of or become involved in a profession, university, society etc〔某行业、大学、社团等的〕进入许可: *entrance examinations* 入学考试 | **gain entrance to** *By some chance he gained entrance to the Indian Civil Service.* 机缘巧合, 他加入了(殖民时代的)印度文职部门。**4** [U] the right or ability to go into a place〔某场所的〕进入权; 进入〔某场所的〕本领: *entrance fees* 入场费 | **gain entrance to** *No one is sure how the men gained entrance to the factory.* 没人确切知道那些人是怎么进入工厂的。**5 make your/an entrance a)** to come on to the stage in a play 登台, 出场〔表演戏剧〕: *The hero doesn't make his entrance until Act II, Scene 2.* 男主角直到第二幕第二场才出台。**b)** to enter a room, especially in a way that makes everyone notice you 进入房间〔尤指以引人注目的方式进入〕: *Lady Elizabeth made a noisy entrance.* 伊莉莎白小姐进屋时动静很大。

en·tranced /ɪn`trænst; ɪn'trɑːnst/ *adj* very interested in and pleased with something so that you pay a lot of attention to it 着迷的, 非常喜爱的: *entranced by the sweetness of her voice* 被她甜美的声音迷住 —**entrance** *v* [T]

en·tran·cing /ɪn`trænsɪŋ; ɪn'trɑːnsɪŋ/ *adj* very interesting and attractive 使人着迷的, 迷人的

en·trant /`ɛntrənt; 'entrənt/ *n* [C] *formal* someone entering a competition, university, or profession【正式】参赛者; 大学新生; 新成员: *The winning entrant will receive a £500 scholarship.* 比赛获胜者将赢得500英镑的奖学金。

en·trap /ɪn`træp; ɪn'træp/ *v* [T] *formal* to trap someone, especially by tricking or deceiving them【正式】使〔某人〕陷入圈套; 诱捕: *cunning and devious questions intended to entrap her* 旨在让她上当的狡诈问题

en·trap·ment /ɪn`træpmənt; ɪn'træpmənt/ *n* [U] the practice of trapping someone by tricking them, especially to show that they are guilty of a crime 诱捕

en·treat /ɪn`trit; ɪn'triːt/ *v* [T] *formal* to ask someone to do something for you in a way that shows you are very upset【正式】恳求; 乞求

en·trea·ty /ɪn`tritɪ; ɪn'triːti/ *n* [C,U] *formal* a serious request in which you ask someone to do something for you【正式】恳求; 乞求

en·trée /`ɑntre; 'ɒntreɪ/ *n French*【法】**1** [C] the main dish of a meal 主菜, 正菜 **2** [C,U] *formal* the right or freedom to enter a place or to join a group of people【正式】进场权, 进入[参加]许可: **[+to/into]** *The letter provided an easy entrée to the court at Turin.* 凭这封信容易进入都灵的宫廷。

en·trenched /ɪn`trɛntʃt; ɪn'trentʃt/ *adj* strongly established and not likely to change 牢固的: **entrenched attitudes/habits/positions etc** *The government's attitude now seems less entrenched.* 政府的态度现在似乎不那么强硬了。| **deeply/firmly entrenched** *deeply entrenched racial views* 顽固的种族偏见

en·trench·ment /ɪn`trɛntʃmənt; ɪn'trentʃmənt/ *n* **1** [U] the process in which an attitude, belief etc becomes firmly established〔态度、信念等的〕牢固确立 **2** [C] a system of TRENCH*es* (=long deep holes) dug by soldiers for defence or protection 堑壕

en·tre nous /ˌɑntrə `nu; ˌɒntrə 'nuː/ *adv French spoken* an expression used to tell someone that what you are going to say is secret and they must not tell anyone else【法口】你知我知, 不得外传

en·tre·pre·neur /ˌɑntrəprə`nɝ; ˌɒntrəprə'nɜː/ *n* [C] someone who starts a company, arranges business deals, and takes risks in order to make a profit 企业家 —**entrepreneurial** *adj*: *entrepreneurial skills* 企业家的技能

en·tro·py /`ɛntrəpɪ; 'entrəpi/ *n* [U] *technical* a measure of the lack of order in a system, that includes the idea that the lack of order increases over a period of time【术语】熵

en·trust, intrust /ɪn`trʌst; ɪn'trʌst/ *v* [T] to make someone responsible for doing something important 委托, 交代: **entrust sb with sth** *I was entrusted with the task of looking after the money.* 我受委托负责保管钱。| **entrust sth to sb** *The infant Prince was entrusted to an English nurse, Miss Shaw.* 年幼的王子被托付给一位姓肖的英国护士照料。

en·try /`ɛntrɪ; 'entri/ *n*

1 ▶COMPETITION 竞赛◀ [C] **a)** a set of answers, a song or picture etc that is intended to win a competition 参赛的事物[作品]: *Over a thousand entries were received within the first week of the competition.* 竞赛第一周内就收到了一千多件参赛作品。**b)** [usually singular 一般用单数] the number of people or things taking part in a competition 参赛者[物]的数量: *We've attracted a record entry this year.* 今年我们吸引到的参赛者数量创造了纪录。

2 ▶BECOMING INVOLVED 参与◀ [C,U] a situation in which someone starts to take part in a system, a particular kind of work etc, or joins a group of people 参加, 加入: *the entry of women into the paid labour force* 妇女加入有偿劳动者队伍 | **gain entry** (=become involved) 加入, 参与 *More Eastern European countries hope to gain entry to the European Union in the next few years.* 更多的东欧国家希望在今后几年内加入欧盟。

3 ▶RIGHT TO ENTER 进入权◀ [U] the right to enter a place, building etc 进入某地[楼房等]的权利: *an entry visa* 入境签证 | **no entry** (=a phrase written on signs to show that you are not allowed to go into a place or through a particular door) 禁止入内

4 ▶ACT OF ENTERING 进入的动作◀ [C,U] the act of going into something 进入〔的动作〕: **[+into]** *the triumphal entry of the Russian army into the city* 俄国军队的胜利进城 | **gain entry** (=get into a place, especially when this is difficult or illegal)〔尤指克服困难或非法地〕进入 *The thieves gained entry through an open kitchen window.* 窃贼是从厨房一扇开着的窗户进来的。

5 ▶**DOOR** 门◀ [C] a door, gate, or passage that you go through to enter a place 门; 入口; 通道 —see also 另见 ENTRANCE (1)
6 ▶**STH WRITTEN** 文字◀ [C] a short piece of writing in an ENCYCLOPAEDIA, DIARY etc〔百科全书〕条目;〔日记的〕一则: *The journal's last few entries described the events vividly.* 日记最后几天的记录生动描述了所发生的事。
7 ▶**COMPUTER** 电脑◀ [U] the act of writing of information onto a computer 输入, 录入: *data entry* 数据输入

en·try·phone /ˋɛntrɪˏfon; ˈentrifəʊn/ *n* [C] a type of telephone outside a building that allows visitors to ask someone inside to open the door〔楼房外让访客叫楼内的人开门的〕对讲机

en·try·way /ˋɛntrɪˏwe; ˈentriweɪ/ *n* [C] *AmE* a passage or small room you go through to enter a place【美】〔作为入口的〕通道; 小房间

en·twine /ɪnˋtwaɪn; ɪnˈtwaɪn/ *v* [I,T often passive 常用被动态] **1** to twist two things together or to wind one thing around another (使) 交错; (使) 缠绕: *They walked together with their arms entwined.* 他们挽着胳膊一起走。**2 be entwined** to be closely connected with each other in a complicated way 紧密联系在一起: *The meaning of art and the meaning of life are almost inextricably entwined.* 艺术和生活的含义几乎是密不可分的。

E num·ber /ˋi ˏnʌmbɚ; ˈiː ˌnʌmbə/ *n* [C] *BrE* a number representing a chemical that has been added to a food, shown on the outside of a container【英】〔容器上标明食品所含特定化学品的〕E 数

e·nu·me·rate /ɪˋnjuməˏret; ɪˈnjuːməreɪt/ *v* [T] *formal* to name a list of things one by one【正式】数, 点; 列举

e·nun·ci·ate /ɪˋnʌnsɪˏet; ɪˈnʌnsieɪt/ *v* **1** [I,T] to pronounce words clearly and carefully〔清晰仔细地〕发 (音); 念 (字) —see also 另见 ARTICULATE² (2) **2** [T] *formal* to express an idea clearly and exactly【正式】〔清楚准确地〕阐明; 阐述: *the theory Darwin was to enunciate decades later* 数十年后达尔文将会阐述的理论 —**enunciation** /ɪˏnʌnsɪˋeʃən; ɪˌnʌnsiˈeɪʃən/ *n* [U]

e·nure /ɪˋnjur; ɪˈnjʊə/ *v* [T] another spelling of INURE inure 的另一种拼法

en·vel·op /ɪnˋvɛləp; ɪnˈveləp/ *v* [T] to wrap something up or cover it completely 包住; 覆盖: *mountain peaks enveloped in thick mist* 隐没在浓雾中的群峰 —**enveloping** *adj* —**envelopment** *n* [U]

S3 **en·ve·lope** /ˋɛnvəˏlop; ˈenvələʊp/ *n* [C] **1** a thin paper cover in which you put a letter 信封 **2** a layer of something that surrounds something else 外裹物; 外层: [+of] *an envelope of gases around the planet* 包围着行星的大气层

en·vi·a·ble /ˋɛnvɪəbl; ˈenviəbəl/ *adj* an enviable quality, position, or possession is good and other people would like to have it 令人羡慕的: *Now he was in the enviable position of not having to work for a living.* 现在他已不必为生计而工作, 着实令人羡慕。—**enviably** *adv*

en·vi·ous /ˋɛnvɪəs; ˈenviəs/ *adj* wanting something that someone else has 妒忌的; 羡慕的: *an envious look* 艳羡的神色 | [+of] *Her colleagues were envious of her success.* 她的同事都羡慕她的成功。—see also 另见 JEALOUS —**enviously** *adv*

S1 W1 **en·vi·ron·ment** /ɪnˋvaɪrənmənt; ɪnˈvaɪərənmənt/ *n* [C,U] **1** all the situations, events, people etc that influence the way in which people live or work 环境, 周围状况: *a helpful learning environment* 有益的学习环境 | *a more competitive economic environment* 竞争更激烈的经济环境 **2 the environment** the air, water, and land in which people, animals, and plants live 自然环境: *More legislation is needed to protect the environment.* 需要制定更多法律来保护环境。—see also 另见 ECOLOGY

> **CULTURAL NOTE 文化注释**
>
> **Environmental Protest** Environmental protesters who take direct action in order to protest against damage being done to the environment of a particular place are sometimes called ECO-WARRIORS. In the UK, they protest against developments such as new roads (for example, the M6 Toll Road in Warwickshire) and new airport RUNWAYS (for example, at Manchester Airport) which would result in the countryside, especially WOODLAND, being destroyed. Sometimes protesters climb up trees to delay builders from starting work in these areas. American protesters also protest against development in certain areas, and also against WILDERNESS areas being used by private companies for MINING or logging (LOG). 环保抗议: 采取直接行动抗议某地破坏环境的环保主义者常被称为"环保斗士"。英国的环保主义者抗议一些开发项目, 如修建新路 (例如沃里克郡的 M6 收费公路) 和机场跑道 (例如曼彻斯特机场), 因为这会破坏乡村面貌, 尤其破坏林地。有时抗议者爬到树上阻挠建筑工人在这些区域动工。美国环保抗议者也反对开发某些区域, 尤其抗议私有公司把荒野开发成矿场或伐木场。
>
> Greenpeace is a large GLOBAL organization which protests against many different types of damage to the environment. There are also many different groups which protest about specific environmental issues. For example, in the UK, Reclaim The Streets is a loosely organized political movement consisting of independent groups of people who protest against the damaging effects of cars on the roads by holding entertainment events in streets and stopping cars from driving through. 绿色和平组织是一个大型国际组织, 抗议各种破坏环境的行为。还有很多其他团体抗议特定的环境问题, 如英国的"街道开垦组织"是一个组织松散的政治运动, 由独立的群体组成, 他们在街上举办娱乐活动, 不让汽车经过, 来抗议汽车行驶 (给环境) 带来的破坏。

Environment A·gen·cy, the /·ˈ··· ˌ···/ a British government organization whose aim is to make sure that rivers and water supplies are clean, and that factories, farmers etc do not harm the environment with their waste materials 环境署〔英国一政府部门。其宗旨是确保河流和供水清洁, 工厂、农场的废弃物不会危害环境〕

en·vi·ron·ment·al /ɪnˏvaɪrənˋmɛntl; ɪnˌvaɪərənˈmentl◂/ *adj* concerning or affecting the air, land, or water on Earth 自然环境的; 影响自然环境的: *the environmental damage caused by the chemical industry* 化学工业对环境造成的危害 —**environmentally** *adv* S1 W2

en·vi·ron·men·tal·ist /ɪnˏvaɪrənˋmɛntḷɪst; ɪnˌvaɪərənˈmentəl-ɪst/ *n* [C] someone who is concerned about protecting the environment 环境保护主义者, 环境保护论者 —**environmentalism** *n* [U]

environmentally friend·ly /·ˌ·····ˈ··◂/ also 又作 **environment friendly** /·ˌ···ˈ··/ *adj* soaps, containers etc that are environmentally friendly do not harm the environment〔肥皂、容器等〕对环境无害的, 不损害环境的

Environmental Pro·tec·tion A·gen·cy, the /·ˌ···· ·ˈ·· ˌ···/ abbreviation 缩写为 **the EPA** a US government organization whose aim is to protect the land, air, and water from pollution, for example by dangerous chemicals, smoke, or industrial waste 环境保护局〔美国一政府部门。其宗旨是保护土地、空气和水源, 以免被有害化学物质、烟雾或工业废弃物污染〕

en·vi·rons /ɪnˋvaɪrənz; ˈenvɪrənz/ *n* [plural] *formal* the area surrounding a place【正式】附近的地方; 周围环境: *Geneva and its immediate environs* 日内瓦及其近郊

en·vis·age /ɛnˋvɪzɪdʒ; ɪnˈvɪzɪdʒ/ also 又作 **en·vi·sion** *AmE*【美】/ɛnˋvɪʒən; ɪnˈvɪʒən/ *v* [T] to imagine that something will happen in the future 展望; 设想: *I don't envisage any major problems.* 我想不会有什么大问题。

en·voy /ˋɛnvɔɪ; ˈenvɔɪ/ *n* [C] someone who is sent to another country as an official representative 使者, 代表; 外交官: *A special envoy was sent to try to secure the release of the hostages.* 派了一名特使以设法让人质获释。

en·vy¹ /ˋɛnvɪ; ˈenvi/ *v* **envied, envying** [T] to wish that you had someone else's possessions, abilities etc 羡慕: *Evelyn was good-looking, rich, and intelligent – all the girls envied her.* 伊夫琳漂亮、富有而且聪明, 所有的女孩都羡慕她。| **envy sb (for) sth** *He envied Rosalind for her youth and strength.* 他羡慕罗莎琳德的青春和活力。—compare 比较 JEALOUS

envy² *n* [U] **1** the feeling of wanting something that someone else has 忌妒; 羡慕: *He stared with envy at Robert's new car.* 他羡慕地盯着罗伯特的新汽车。| **green with envy** (=envying someone a lot) 忌妒极了, 羡慕极了 **2 be the envy of** to be something that other people admire and want to have very much 是令人羡慕[忌妒]的事物: *Britain's National Health Service was once the envy of the world.* 英国的国民保健制度曾一度为世人所羡慕。—compare 比较 JEALOUSY

en·zyme /ˋɛnzaɪm; ˈenzaɪm/ *n* [C] *technical* a chemical substance produced by living cells in plants and animals, that causes changes in other chemical substances without being changed itself【术语】酶: *the digestive enzymes in your stomach* 胃中的消化酶

e·on /ˋiən; ˈiːən/ *n* [C] another spelling of AEON aeon 的另一种拼法

E·os /ˋiɑs; ˈiːɒs/ in Greek MYTHOLOGY, the GODDESS of the DAWN (=the beginning of the day when light first appears). In Roman mythology her name is Aurora. 厄俄斯〔希腊神话中的曙光女神, 罗马神话中称奥罗拉〕

EPA, the /ˌi pi ˋe; ˌiː piː ˈeɪ/ the abbreviation of 缩写= the ENVIRONMENTAL PROTECTION AGENCY

ep·au·let, epaulette /ˋɛpəˌlɛt; ˌepəˈlet/ *n* [C] a small piece of cloth decorating the shoulder of a coat or shirt, especially on a uniform〔尤指制服上的〕肩饰, 肩章

Ep·cot Cen·ter, the /ˋɛpkɑt ˌsɛntɚ; ˈepkɒt ˌsentə/ the Experimental Prototype Community of Tomorrow Center; a part of Walt Disney World in Orlando, Florida in the US, where visitors can see some of the machines and equipment which may be used in the future 未来世界, 艾波卡特中心〔美国佛罗里达州奥兰多的沃尔特·迪斯尼世界的一部分, 游客在此可看到未来也许会使用的机器和设备〕

é·pée /eˋpe; ˈepeɪ/ *n* [C] *French* a narrow sword with a sharp point, used in the sport of FENCING (1)【法】〔击剑比赛用的〕重剑

e·phem·e·ra /əˋfɛmərə; ɪˈfemərə/ *n* [plural] things that are only popular or important for a short time 短暂流行的事物; 仅在短期内重要的事物: *records, pictures of pop-stars, and other such ephemera* 唱片、流行歌星照片以及诸如此类只会短暂流行的东西

e·phem·e·ral /əˋfɛmərəl; ɪˈfemərəl/ *adj* popular or important for only a short time 短暂流行的; 只重要一时的: *Fashions are by nature fickle and ephemeral.* 在本质上, 时装式样变化无常, 流行时间短暂。—**ephemerally** *adv*

ep·ic[1] /ˋɛpɪk; ˈepɪk/ *n* [C] **1** a book, poem, or film that tells a long story 长篇叙事性小说、诗歌、电影等作品; 史诗般的作品: *Universal Pictures' dinosaur epic "Jurassic Park"*〔美国〕环球影片公司讲述恐龙的史诗般作品《侏罗纪公园》**2** a long poem that tells the story of what gods or important people did in ancient times〔讲述神仙或古代重要人物故事的〕史诗: *Homer's epic "Iliad"* 荷马的史诗《伊利亚特》

epic[2] *adj* **1** epic stories or poems are full of brave actions and events 英雄的, 英勇的: *Phileas Fogg's epic journey around the world* 菲利斯·福格勇敢的环球旅行 **2** very big or impressive 巨大的, 宏伟的: **of epic proportions** *They organized a banquet of epic proportions.* 他们组织了盛大的宴会。

ep·i·cen·tre *BrE*【英】, **epicenter** *AmE*【美】/ˋɛpɪˌsɛntɚ; ˈepɪˌsentə/ *n* [C] a place on the surface of the Earth that is above the point where an EARTHQUAKE begins inside the Earth 震中, 震央

ep·i·cure /ˋɛpɪˌkjʊr; ˈepɪkjʊə/ *n* [C] *formal* someone who enjoys good food and drink; GOURMET【正式】美食家

ep·i·cu·re·an /ˌɛpɪkjuˋriən; ˌepɪkjʊˈriːən◂/ *adj formal* gaining pleasure from the senses, especially through good food and drink【正式】〔尤指在吃喝上〕爱奢侈享受的 —**epicurean** *n* [C]

ep·i·dem·ic /ˌɛpəˋdɛmɪk; ˌepɪ̈ˈdemɪk◂/ *n* [C] **1** a large number of cases of a particular infectious disease occurring at the same time 流行病, 传染病: *a flu epidemic* 流行性感冒 **2** a sudden increase in the amount of times that something bad happens〔坏事的〕发生次数陡增; 频率突增: *the recent epidemic of car thefts* 近来频繁发生的汽车被盗案件 —**epidemic** *adj*: *Violence is reaching epidemic proportions in the inner cities.* 市中心贫民区的暴力事件几近泛滥。

ep·i·der·mis /ˌɛpəˋdɝmɪs; ˌepɪ̈ˈdɜːmɪ̈s/ *n* [C,U] *technical* the outside layer of your skin【术语】表皮

ep·i·dur·al /ˌɛpəˋdjurəl; ˌepɪˈdjuːrəl◂/ *n* [C] a medical process in which a drug is put into your lower back to prevent you feeling pain, especially when you are having a baby 硬脊膜外注射(麻醉)

ep·i·glot·tis /ˌɛpəˋglɑtɪs; ˌepɪ̈ˈglɒtɪ̈s/ *n* [C] a thin piece of flesh at the back of your throat〔喉后部的〕会厌 —see picture at 参见 RESPIRATORY 图

ep·i·gram /ˋɛpəˌgræm; ˈepɪ̈græm/ *n* [C] a short sentence that expresses an idea in a clever or amusing way 警句, 隽语

ep·i·gram·mat·ic /ˌɛpəgrəˋmætɪk; ˌepɪ̈grəˈmætɪk◂/ *adj* expressed in a way that is short, clever, and amusing 隽语式的, 简练幽默的 —**epigrammatically** /-kḷɪ; -kli/ *adv*

ep·i·lep·sy /ˋɛpəˌlɛpsɪ; ˈepɪ̈lepsi/ *n* [U] a medical condition in the brain that can suddenly make you become unconscious or unable to control your movements 癫痫, 羊痫疯

ep·i·lep·tic[1] /ˌɛpəˋlɛptɪk; ˌepɪ̈ˈleptɪk◂/ *adj* caused by epilepsy 癫痫的: *an epileptic fit* 癫痫发作

epileptic[2] *n* [C] someone who has epilepsy 癫痫患者

ep·i·logue also 又作 **epilog** *AmE*【美】/ˋɛpəˌlɔg; ˈepɪ̈lɒg/ *n* **1** [C] a speech or piece of writing added to the end of a book, film, or play〔书的〕跋, 后记;〔电影、戏剧的〕收场白 **2** [singular] *literary* something that happens at the end of a series of events【文】〔一系列事件的〕尾声, 结尾 —compare 比较 PROLOGUE

E·piph·a·ny /ɪˋpɪfənɪ; ɪˈpɪfəni/ *n* [not with *the* 不与 the 连用] a Christian holy day on January 6th that celebrates the Three Kings coming to see the baby Jesus〔基督教1月6日的〕显现节〔为纪念三博士拜见圣婴耶稣的节日〕

epiphany *n* [C] *literary* a moment of sudden very strong emotions【文】一阵突发的强烈情感

e·pis·co·pa·cy /ɪˋpɪskəpəsɪ; ɪˈpɪskəpəsi/ also 又作 **e·pis·co·pate** /ɪˋpɪskəpɪt; ɪˈpɪskəpət/ *n* [U] *technical*【术语】**1** the rank of a BISHOP (=a priest of high rank in charge of a large area), or the time during which someone is bishop 主教职位; 主教任期 **2** all the bishops, or the system of the church government by bishops 全体主教; 主教统辖制度

e·pis·co·pal /ɪˋpɪskəpḷ; ɪˈpɪskəpəl/ *adj* **1** connected with a BISHOP 主教的 **2** an episcopal church is governed by BISHOPS〔教会由〕主教管辖的

Episcopal Church /·ˌ··· ˈ·/ *n* [singular] a PROTESTANT church in the US that developed from the Anglican Church 美国新教圣公会

E·pis·co·pa·li·an /ɪˌpɪskəˋpelɪən; ɪˌpɪskəˈpeɪliən◂/ *n* [C] a member of an episcopal church 美国新教圣公会教徒 —**Episcopalian** *adj*

ep·i·sode /ˋɛpəˌsod; ˈepɪ̈səʊd/ *n* [C] **1** an event or a short period of time during which something specific happened 一段经历; 一段时期: *one of the saddest episodes in his tormented life* 他苦难一生中最悲伤的时期之一 **2** a television or radio programme that is one of a series of programmes telling one story〔电视连续剧或广播连载节目中的〕一集, 一节: *Watch next week's thrilling episode!* 请下周收看精彩剧集!

ep·i·sod·ic /ˌɛpɪˋsɑdɪk; ˌepɪ̈ˈsɒdɪk◂/ *adj formal*【正式】**1** happening at times that are not regular 不定期〔发生〕的: *episodic headaches* 阵发性头痛 **2** consisting of many different parts when different things happen 由许多片段组成的: *an episodic account of how a group of humble people are affected by the war* 对一群卑微的人如何受战争影响的片段式的描述 —**episodically** /-kḷɪ; -kli/ *adv*

E·pis·tle /ɪˋpɪsḷ; ɪˈpɪsəl/ *n* [C] one of the letters written by the first Christians which are in the New Testament of the Bible〔《圣经·新约》中的〕使徒书信

epistle *n* [C] *formal* a long or important letter【正式】〔长或重要的〕书信

e·pis·to·la·ry /ɪˋpɪstəˌlɛrɪ; ɪˈpɪstələri/ *adj formal* written in the form of a series of letters【正式】书信体的: *an epistolary novel* 书信体小说

ep·i·taph /ˋɛpəˌtæf; ˈepɪ̈tɑːf/ *n* [C] a short piece of writing on the stone over someone's grave 墓志铭

ep·i·thet /ˋɛpəˌθɛt; ˈepɪ̈θet/ *n* [C] an adjective or short phrase used to describe someone, especially when praising or blaming them〔尤其是褒贬人时使用的〕表述词语: *He hardly deserves the epithet 'fascist'.* 用"法西斯分子"这个词来形容他并不恰当。

e·pit·o·me /ɪˋpɪtəmɪ; ɪˈpɪtəmi/ *n* **the epitome of** the best possible example of something …的典型[典范]: *Jan's behaviour seemed to me to be the very epitome of selfishness.* 在我看来, 简的所作所为是自私自利的典型。

e·pit·o·mize also 又作 **-ise** *BrE*【英】/ɪˋpɪtəˌmaɪz; ɪˈpɪtəmaɪz/ *v* [T] to be a very typical example of something 成为…的典型: *This fiasco epitomizes the lack of regulation in the industry.* 这次困局突显了该行业缺乏规范的问题。

e·poch /ˋɛpək; ˈiːpɒk/ *n* [C] a period of history, especially one in which important events take place〔尤指重要事件发生的〕时代, 纪元: *the beginning of a new epoch in the history of mankind* 人类历史新纪元的开始

epoch-mak·ing /ˈ·· ˌ··/ *adj* very important in changing or developing people's lives 划时代的, 开创新纪元的

e·pon·y·mous /ɛˋpɑnəməs; ɪˈpɒnɪ̈məs/ *adj technical* the eponymous character in a book, film, or play is the character whose name forms its title【术语】〔以作品中的人物〕使〔书、电影或戏剧〕得名的;〔人物与作品〕同名的: *Hester, the book's eponymous heroine* 与本书同名的女主人公赫斯特 —**eponymously** *adv*

e·pox·y res·in /ɛpˋɑksɪ ˋrɛzṇ; ɪˌpɒksi ˈrezɪ̈n/ *n* [U] a type of RESIN used as a glue 环氧树脂

Ep·som /ˋɛpsəm; ˈepsəm/ a town in southeast England which is famous for its RACECOURSE (=place where people go to watch horse races). One of the most famous British horse races, the Derby, takes place at Epsom each year. 埃普瑟姆〔英格兰东南一镇, 以赛马场出名。英国最著名的马赛之一德比马赛每年在此举行〕

Epsom salts /ˌɛpsəm ˋsɔlts; ˌepsəm ˈsɔːlts/ *n* [plural,U] a white powder that can be mixed with water and used as a kind of medicine 泻盐

Ep·stein /ˈɛpˌstaɪn; ˈepstaɪn/, **Jacob** /ˈdʒekəb; ˈdʒeɪkəb/ (1880-1959) a British SCULPTOR, especially of religious subjects 爱泼斯坦〔(1880-1959)，英国雕刻家。其雕塑作品以宗教主题为主〕

Epstein-Barr vi·rus /ˌɛpstaɪn ˋbɑr ˌvaɪrəs; ˌepstaɪn ˈbɑː ˌvaɪərəs/ also 又作 **EBV** *n* [U] *AmE* an illness that makes you feel very tired and weak and can last for a long period of time【美】爱泼斯坦－巴尔病毒; ME *BrE*【英】

eq·ua·ble /ˈɛkwəbḷ; ˈekwəbəl/ *adj* **1** *formal* calm and not easily annoyed【正式】平和的, 性情温和的: *Mary's equable temperament made her easy to work with.* 玛丽性情温和, 很容易共事。**2** *technical* having weather or conditions that are neither too hot nor too cold【术语】天气冷热适中的: *an equable climate* 温和的气候 —**equably** *adv* —**equability** /ˌɛkwəˋbɪlətɪ; ˌekwəˈbɪləti/ *n* [U]

S1 W2 **e·qual**[1] /ˈikwəl; ˈiːkwəl/ *adj*

1 ►SAME 相同◄ the same in size, value, amount, number etc as something else〔在大小、价值、数量、数字等方面〕相等的: *Jennifer cut the cake into six equal pieces.* 珍妮弗将蛋糕切成六等份。| [+to] *A pound is roughly equal to 500 grams.* 1磅约等于500克。| **of equal power/strength/weight** *Choose two stones of roughly equal weight and size.* 选两块重量和大小都差不多的石头。

2 ►SAME RIGHTS/CHANCES 同等权利/机会◄ having the same rights, opportunities etc as everyone else, whatever your race, religion, or sex 平等的: *Our constitution states that all men are equal.* 我们的宪法规定人人平等。| **equal opportunities** (=the same chances of employment, pay etc for everyone) 平等的机会 *This company is an equal opportunity employer.* 这家公司平等地对待员工。| **equal rights** (=the same rights for everyone) 平等权利 *a clear statement guaranteeing equal rights for women* 确保妇女享有平等权利的明确声明

3 ►BE ABLE 能够◄ **be equal to** to have the ability to deal with a problem, piece of work etc successfully 胜任的, 能应付的: *I'm sure Barbara's quite equal to the task.* 我确信芭芭拉完全有能力承担这项任务。

4 ►AS GOOD AS 同等出色◄ having as high a standard or quality as something else 同样出色的, 水平[质量]一样高的: *religious architecture equal to any in the world* 堪与世界上任何同类建筑媲美的宗教建筑

5 on equal terms with neither side having any advantage over the other 地位平等, 互不占优: *a new law to enable small businesses to compete on equal terms with large multinational corporations* 确保小公司能与跨国大公司平等竞争的新法律

6 all (other) things being equal *spoken* used when saying what you would normally choose, unless there were special facts to consider【口】假若所有(其他)情况相同: *I'd rather go by train, all other things being equal.* 如果其他所有情况都一样, 我宁愿坐火车去。

S2 **equal**[2] *v* **equalled, equalling** *BrE*【英】, **equaled, equaling** *AmE*【美】**1** [linking verb 连系动词] to be exactly the same in size, number, or amount as something else〔在大小、数字、数量等方面〕等于, 与…相同: *Two plus two equals four.* 二加二等于四。| *Trade should balance when supply equals demand.* 供需相当时贸易便达到平衡。**2** [T] to be as good as or get to the same standard as someone or something else 比得上, 达到: *Thompson equalled the world record.* 汤普森平了世界纪录。**3** [T] to produce a particular result or effect 产生, 得出〔特定结果或效果〕: *A highly-trained workforce equals high productivity.* 高素质的劳动力创造高生产力。

S3 **equal**[3] *n* [C] **1** someone who is as important, intelligent etc as you are, or who has the same rights and opportunities as you do 同等的人: *It's a relief to find a boss who treats employees as equals.* 能碰到一个平等对待员工的老板真是令人宽慰。**2 be without equal** also 又作 **have no equal** *formal* to be better than everyone or everything else of the same type【正式】最杰出, 首屈一指: *His paintings are without equal in the Western world.* 他的画在西方世界无与伦比。

Equal Em·ploy·ment Op·por·tu·ni·ties Com·mis·sion, the /ˌ‥ ‥ˌ‥ ‥ˈ‥ ‥ ‥ˌ‥ˈ‥/ abbreviation 缩写为 **the EEOC** a US government organization whose aim is to make sure that people are not prevented from getting jobs because of their race, religion, age, sex etc, and to make sure that all workers are treated fairly and equally 均等就业机会委员会〔美国一政府部门。其宗旨是确保民众不会因种族、宗教、年龄、性别等原因而找不到工作, 并且确保所有从业者受到公正和平等的待遇〕

e·qual·i·ty /ɪˋkwɑlətɪ; ɪˈkwɒlɪ̣ti/ *n* [U] a position or situation in which people have the same rights, advantages etc 平等: *Women have yet to achieve full equality with men in the workplace.* 妇女仍需争取与男人在职业方面完全平等。| **racial/sexual equality** (=equality between all races or between men and women) 种族/男女平等

e·qual·ize also 又作 **-ise** *BrE*【英】/ˈikwəlˌaɪz; ˈiːkwəlaɪz/ *v* **1** [T] to make two or more things the same in size, value, amount etc〔在大小、价值、数量等方面〕使相等; 使平等 **2** [I] *BrE* to get a point in a game, especially football, so that you have the same number of points as your opponent【英】〔尤指足球〕打成平局, 扳平比分; TIE[1] (2) *AmE*【美】: *England equalized a few minutes before the end of the game.* 英格兰队在比赛结束前几分钟时将比分扳平。—**equalization** /ˌikwələˋzeʃən; ˌiːkwəlaɪˈzeɪʃən/ *n* [U]

e·qual·iz·er /ˈikwəlˌaɪzɚ; ˈiːkwəlaɪzə/ *n* [C] **1** *BrE* a GOAL (2) that makes the points of each team in a game equal【英】〔足球赛中〕扳平比分的一个进球 **2** *AmE slang* a gun【美俚】枪

S2 W2 **eq·ual·ly** /ˈikwəlɪ; ˈiːkwəli/ *adv* **1** [+adj/adv] to the same degree or amount 相等地, 相同地: *An equally acceptable solution could surely be found elsewhere.* 在别处肯定能找到同样可以接受的解决方案。**2** in equal parts or amounts 均等地, 平均地: *We try to divide the work equally.* 我们尽量平分工作。**3** [sentence adverb 句子副词] used when introducing a second idea or statement that is as important as your first one 同样〔重要〕地: *I want to encourage her to do well, but equally I don't want to make her feel pressurized.* 我想鼓励她好好干, 但同时我也不想让她有太大压力。

Equal Op·por·tu·nit·ies Com·mis·sion, the /ˌ‥ ‥ˈ‥ ‥ ‥ˌ‥ˈ‥/ a British government organization whose aim is to make sure that women and men have the same opportunities in education and jobs, and that people are not treated unfairly because of their sex 均等机会委员会〔英国一政府部门。其宗旨是确保男女享有同等的受教育和就业机会, 并且不会因性别原因而受到不公待遇〕

Equal Pay Act, the /ˌ‥ ˈ‥ ‥/ a law in the UK, passed in 1970, which says that men and women should get equal pay for doing the same work, and should have the same conditions of employment《同工同酬法》〔英国于1970年通过的一项法律。该法规定男女应同工同酬, 享有同等的就业条件〕

Equal Rights A·mend·ment, the /ˌ‥ ‥ ‥ˈ‥ ‥/ *n* the ERA

equals sign /ˈ‥ ‥/ *BrE*【英】, **equal sign** *AmE*【美】*n* [C] a sign used in mathematics to show that two things are the same size, number, or amount〔数学中的〕等号: *In the equation x=y, x is to the left of the equals sign.* 在等式 x=y 中, x 在等号的左侧。

eq·ua·nim·i·ty /ˌikwəˋnɪmətɪ; ˌiːkwəˈnɪmɪ̣ti/ *n* [U] *formal* calmness, especially in the way that you react to things【正式】〔尤指对某事的反应〕平和, 镇静, 沉着: *He received the news with surprising equanimity.* 他接到消息时显得异常镇静。

e·quate /ɪˋkwet; ɪˈkweɪt/ *v* [T] to consider that two or more things are similar or connected 等同: **equate sth with** *Some people equate nationalism with fascism.* 有些人将民族主义和法西斯主义等同起来。

e·qua·tion /ɪˋkweʒən; ɪˈkweɪʒən/ *n* **1** [C] a statement in mathematics, showing that two quantities are equal 等式, 方程式: *In the equation 2x + 1 = 7, what is x?* 在 2x+1=7 这个方程式中, x 是多少? **2** [C] **enter into the equation/be part of the equation** to be a fact that affects a particular problem, situation, idea etc 成为影响因素: *We hadn't realized that cost would enter into the equation at all.* 我们压根儿未曾想到成本会成为影响因素。**3** [singular] the act of equating two things 将两事物等同 W3

e·qua·tor, Equator /ɪˋkwetɚ; ɪˈkweɪtə/ *n* [singular, U] an imaginary line drawn around the middle of the Earth that is exactly the same distance from the North Pole and the South Pole 赤道 —see picture at 参见 EARTH[1] 图

eq·ua·to·ri·al /ˌikwəˋtorɪəl; ˌekwəˈtɔːriəl◄/ *adj* **1** connected with or near the equator 赤道的; 赤道附近的: *the equatorial rainforest* 赤道雨林 **2** very hot and wet 非常湿热的: *an equatorial climate* 又湿又热的气候

Equatorial Guin·ea /ˌ‥‥‥ ˈ‥/ a small country in west central Africa, between Cameroon and Gabon. Population: 486,060 (2001). Capital: Malabo. The capital city is on an island 125 miles (200 km) from the main part of the country. 赤道几内亚〔中非西部一小国, 位于喀麦隆和加蓬之间。人口: 486,060 (2001), 首都: 马拉博。首都位于距该国主体部分 125 英里 (200 公里) 的一座海岛上〕

e·quer·ry /ˈɛkwərɪ; ɪˈkweri/ *n* [C] a male official in a royal court, who serves a member of the royal family 王宫侍卫官

e·ques·tri·an /ɪˋkwɛstrɪən; ɪˈkwestriən/ *adj* connected with horse riding 骑马的, 骑术的: *equestrian events* 马术比赛项目 —**equestrian** *n* [C]

equi- /ɪkwə; ekwɨ/ *prefix* equal or equally 相等的; 相等地: *equidistant* 等距离的 | *an equilateral triangle* (=with equal sides) 等边三角形

e·qui·dis·tant /ˌikwəˋdɪstənt; ˌiːkwɨˈdɪstənt◂/ *adj* at an equal distance from or between two places 等距离的

e·qui·lat·e·ral tri·an·gle /ˌikwəlætərəl ˋtraɪæŋgl; ˌiːkwɨlætərəl ˈtraɪæŋgəl/ *n* [C] *technical* a TRIANGLE (1) whose three sides are all the same length【术语】等边三角形 —see picture at 参见 SHAPE[1] 图

e·qui·lib·ri·um /ˌikwəˋlɪbrɪəm; ˌiːkwɨˈlɪbriəm/ *n* [singular, U] **1** a balance between opposing forces or influences〔相反的力量或影响〕平衡, 均衡: *They were anxious not to upset the trading equilibrium.* 他们小心地维持贸易均衡。**2** a calm balance of emotions, attitudes, feelings etc〔情绪、态度、感情等的〕平静, 安宁: *Setting up a home helped to re-establish some kind of equilibrium in her life.* 成家帮助她的生活恢复了一些平静。

eq·uine /ˋikwaɪn; ˈekwaɪn/ *adj* connected with horses, or looking like a horse 马的; 似马的

eq·ui·noc·tial /ˌikwəˋnɑkʃəl; ˌiːkwɨˈnɒkʃəl◂/ *adj* connected with the equinox 春分的; 秋分的

eq·ui·nox /ˋikwəˌnɑks; ˈiːkwɨnɒks/ *n* [C] one of the two times in a year when all places in the world have a day and night of equal length 春分; 秋分 —compare 比较 SOLSTICE

e·quip /ɪˋkwɪp; ɪˈkwɪp/ *v* **equipped, equipping** [T] **1** to provide a person, group, building etc with the things that are needed for a particular kind of activity or work 装备, 配备: **equip sb with** *The boys equipped themselves with torches and rope, and set off.* 男孩们带上火把和绳索就出发了。| **be equipped to do sth** *The emergency services are equipped to deal with disasters of this kind.* 应急人员配有装备, 可处理此类灾难事件。| **equip sb/sth** *It cost $100,000 to equip the gym.* 配备体育馆花费了10万美元。| **well/ poorly/fully etc equipped** *It was a modern, bright, well equipped hospital.* 那是一家现代化、明亮且设备完善的医院。**2** if education or training equips you to do something, it prepares you and makes you able to do it 使有准备, 使能够〔做某事〕: **equip sb for** *We want our son to have an education that will equip him for later life.* 我们想让儿子接受可为他以后生活打基础的教育。

2 2 **e·quip·ment** /ɪˋkwɪpmənt; ɪˈkwɪpmənt/ *n* **1** [U] all the special tools, machines, clothes etc that you need for a particular activity 装备, 设备, 用具: *Dentists must take great care in sterilizing all their equipment.* 牙医在给所有用具消毒时必须十分仔细。| **office/video/sports etc equipment** *fire-fighting equipment* 消防设备 | **piece of equipment** *a very delicate piece of equipment* 一件非常精密的设备 **2** [singular] the process of equipping someone or something 装备〔某人或物的〕过程

eq·ui·poise /ˋɛkwəˌpɔɪz; ˈekwɨpɔɪz/ *n* [U] *formal* a balance between different influences, especially mental or emotional influences【正式】平衡; 均势〔尤指思想或情感上的影响〕

eq·ui·ta·ble /ˋɛkwɪtəbl; ˈekwɨtəbəl/ *adj formal* an equitable action, process etc treats everyone in an equal way; fair【正式】公平合理的; 公正的: *an equitable division of wealth* 财富的合理分配 —**equitably** *adv*

Equity **1** a TRADE UNION in the UK for actors and actresses in film, theatre, TV, and radio〔英国〕演员工会 **2** a trade union in the US for actors and actresses who perform in the theatre. Its full name is the Actor's Equity Association.〔美国〕戏剧演员工会〔全称为 Actor's Equity Association〕

eq·ui·ty /ˋɛkwətɪ; ˈekwɨti/ *n* **1** [U] *formal* a situation in which no one has an unfair advantage; fairness【正式】公平; 公正: *a society run on the principles of equity and justice* 以公平、正义为原则的社会 **2** [U] *technical* the value of a piece of property or of a company's shares (SHARE[2] (5)) after debts have been paid【术语】〔付清债务后的〕财产净值; 股本值 **3** **equities** [plural] *technical* business shares (SHARE[2] (5)) that give you some of the company's profits rather than a fixed regular payment【术语】〔分享红利而非固定股息的〕股票 **4** [U] *law* the principle that a fair judgement must be made in a situation where the existing laws do not provide an answer【法律】衡平法〔一种原则, 指现存法律不适用时, 应当作出公正的裁决〕

3 **e·quiv·a·lent**[1] /ɪˋkwɪvələnt; ɪˈkwɪvələnt/ *adj* having the same value, purpose, job etc as a person or thing of a different kind 等同的, 等价的, 相当的: [+to] *It's equivalent to the rank of captain in our army.* 这相当于我们军队中的上尉军衔。| *Alternatively, we could give you an equivalent amount in company shares.* 或者我们可以给你等价的公司股票。—**equivalently** *adv* —**equivalence** *n* [U]

equivalent[2] *n* [C] something that is equivalent to something else 等同物; 等价物; 对应物: *Some Japanese words have no English equivalents.* 一些日语词在英语中没有对应的词。| *It's the French equivalent of the IRS.* 这是法国相当于美国国内税务局的机构。

e·quiv·o·cal /ɪˋkwɪvəkl; ɪˈkwɪvəkəl/ *adj* **1** words or statements that are equivocal have more than one possible meaning and are deliberately unclear; AMBIGUOUS〔词语、声明故意〕模棱两可的; 含糊的: *His answer was evasive and equivocal.* 他的回答含糊其辞, 模棱两可。**2** equivocal actions or behaviour are mysterious or difficult to understand〔行为〕神秘的; 费解的 —**equivocally** /-klɪ; -kli/ *adv*

e·quiv·o·cate /ɪˋkwɪvəˌket; ɪˈkwɪvəkeɪt/ *v* [I] *formal* to say something that has more than one possible meaning, in order to avoid giving a clear or direct answer【正式】含糊其辞, 说模棱两可的话 —**equivocation** /ɪˌkwɪvəˋkeʃən; ɪˌkwɪvəˈkeɪʃən/ *n* [C,U]

er /ɚ; ɜː/ *interjection* a sound you make when you do not know exactly what to say next 嗯, 哦〔表示犹豫、迟疑〕: *Well, er – I'm not really sure.* 嗯, 哦 — 我不太有把握。

-er[1] /ɚ; ə/ *suffix* forms the comparative of many short adjectives and adverbs〔附在许多短小的形容词或副词后, 构成比较级〕: *hot, hotter* 热, 较热 | *dry, drier* 干燥, 较干燥 | *My car is fast, but hers is faster.* 我的汽车很快, 但她的汽车更快。| *Her car goes faster than mine.* 她的汽车跑得比我的快。—see also 另见 -EST

-er[2] *suffix* [in nouns 构成名词] **1** someone who does something or who is doing something (正在) 做某事的人: *a dancer* (=someone who dances or is dancing) 舞蹈演员; 跳舞的人 | *the diners* (=people having dinner) 就餐者 **2** something that does something 用于做某事的器械: *a screwdriver* (=tool for driving in screws) 螺丝刀 **3** someone who makes a particular kind of thing 专做某种物品的人: *a hatter* (=someone who makes hats) 制帽匠 **4** someone who lives in or comes from a particular place 住在[来自]某地的人: *a Londoner* (=someone from London) 伦敦人 | *the villagers* (=people who live in the village) 村民 **5** someone skilled in or studying a particular subject 精于[研究]某学科的人: *a geographer* (=someone who studies GEOGRAPHY) 地理学家 **6** something that has something 拥有某物的东西: *a three-wheeler car* (=with three wheels) 三轮汽车 —see also 另见 -AR, -OR

e·ra /ˋɪrə; ˈɪərə/ *n* [C] a long period of time in history that is different in some way from other periods 时代, 年代: *In the Victorian era such behaviour was socially unacceptable.* 在维多利亚时代, 这种行为是不为社会所接受的。

ERA, the /ˌi ˋar ˋe; ˌiː ˈɑːr ˈeɪ/ the Equal Rights Amendment; a suggested change to US law, which was intended to give women the same legal rights as men. Although the suggested law was agreed to by Congress, not enough states agreed in time for it to become a law.《平等权利修正案》〔建议修正美国宪法的一项议案, 旨在赋予女性与男性相同的权利。尽管该议案在美国国会已获通过, 但同意适时使之成为法律的州数尚且不足〕

e·rad·i·cate /ɪˋrædɪˌket; ɪˈrædɨkeɪt/ *v* [T] to completely get rid of something such as a disease or a social problem 根除; 消灭: [+from] *Smallpox has now been eradicated from the world.* 天花已经在世界上根除了。—**eradication** /ɪˌrædɪˋkeʃən; ɪˌrædɨˈkeɪʃən/ *n* [U]

e·rase /ɪˋres; ɪˈreɪz/ *v* [T] **1** to remove information from a computer memory or recorded sounds from a tape 删除〔电脑文件〕; 3
抹去〔磁带录音〕: *Unfortunately, the tape has been erased.* 不幸的是, 磁带录音已被抹掉了。**2** to remove marks or writing so that they can no longer be seen 擦掉; 抹去〔痕迹或文字〕**3** *formal* to get rid of or destroy something so that it no longer exists【正式】消除, 消灭: *The World Bank has agreed to erase the debt.* 世界银行已同意免除这笔债务。| *the 163 villages erased by the eruption of Krakatoa* 被喀拉喀托火山喷发所毁灭的163个村庄 **4** **erase sth from your mind/memory** to make yourself forget something bad that has happened 忘却〔坏事〕

e·ras·er /ɪˋresɚ; ɪˈreɪzə/ *n* [C] *especially AmE*【尤美】**1** a rubber object used to remove pencil or pen marks from paper 橡皮; RUBBER (2a) *BrE*【英】**2** a thing you use for cleaning marks from a BLACKBOARD 黑板擦

Erasmus /ɪˋræzməs; ɪˈræzməs/**, Desiderius** /ˌdɛzɪˋdɪrɪəs; ˌdezɪˈdɪːriəs/ (1466-1536) a Catholic Christian writer, teacher and priest, born in the Netherlands. He believed that the Catholic Church should become more simple, and that people should have a clearer understanding of the New Testament. His ideas had an important influence and helped to start the Reformation 伊拉斯谟〔(1466-1536), 天主教作家、教师、牧师, 出生于荷兰。他认为天主教会应简单一些, 人们应更清楚地理解《圣经·新约》。他的观点具有重要影响, 推动了宗教改革〕

e·ra·sure /ɪˋreʒɚ; ɪˈreɪʒə/ *n formal*【正式】**1** [C] a mark that is left when words or letters are removed with an eraser〔用橡皮擦去字后留下的〕痕迹, 字印 **2** [U] the act of completely removing or destroying something 根除, 消除

ere /ɛr; eə/ *preposition, conjunction, old use or poetic* before【旧或诗】在…之前: **ere long** (=soon) 不久, 很快

Erebus /ˋɛrəbəs; ˈerɪbəs/, **Mount** a mountain that is an active VOLCANO on Ross Island in Antarctica 厄瑞波斯山〔南极洲罗斯岛上的一座活火山〕

e·rect[1] /ɪˋrɛkt; ɪˈrekt/ *adj* **1** in a straight upright position 直立的, 垂直的: *She held her head erect.* 她昂着头。**2** an erect PENIS or NIPPLE is stiff and bigger than it usually is〔阴茎〕勃起的;〔乳头〕挺起的 —**erectly** *adv* —**erectness** *n* [U]

erect[2] *v* [T] **1** *formal* to build a building, wall, STATUE etc【正式】建造, 建立: *an imposing town hall, erected in 1892* 建于1892年的气势宏伟的市政厅 **2** to fix all the pieces of something together, and put it in an upright position 搭建, 竖起: *We had to sleep in hastily erected bunk beds.* 我们只能睡在匆匆搭成的双层床上。**3** to establish something such as a system or institution 创建, 确立〔体系或制度〕

e·rec·tile /ɪˋrɛktɪl; ɪˈrektaɪl/ *adj technical* connected with a man's erection【术语】〔阴茎〕勃起的

e·rec·tion /ɪˋrɛkʃən; ɪˈrekʃən/ *n* **1** [C] if a man has an erection, his PENIS increases in size and becomes stiff and upright because he is sexually excited〔阴茎〕勃起 **2** [U] the act of building something or putting it in an upright position 建造, 建立; 竖立: *the erection of a new temple* 建造新寺庙 **3** [C] *formal* something that has been built, especially a large structure【正式】竖立物; 建筑物〔尤指结构庞大者〕

E·rec·tor Set /·ˋ·· ˌ·/ *trademark* a type of children's toy, sold in the US, which has many small parts that can be connected together in order to build things such as cars, bridges, and machines. There is a similar type of toy in the UK called Meccano.【商标】伊雷克特组合〔在美国销售的一种建筑拼装儿童玩具, 有许多小型部件, 可组合成玩具汽车、桥梁和机器等。英国也有类似产品, 名为麦卡诺组装缩微玩具〕

Erewhon a book by the British writer Samuel Butler, published in 1872. Erewhon was an imaginary land discovered by a traveller, and Butler used it for a SATIRE on British HYPOCRISY and the way society thought about crime and religion. Many years later he wrote a second book, called *Erewhon Revisited*.《乌有乡》〔英国作家塞缪尔·巴特勒1872年出版的一本书。乌有乡是一名旅行家发现的一个假想之地, 巴特勒借以讽刺英国人的伪善及英国社会对犯罪和宗教的看法。多年之后, 他写了另一本书, 名为《重访乌有乡》〕

erg /ɝg; ɜːg/ *n* [C] *technical* a unit used to measure work or energy【术语】尔格〔功或能量单位〕

er·go /ˋɝgo; ˈɜːgəʊ/ *adv Latin formal* [sentence adverb 句子副词] therefore【拉丁, 正式】因此, 所以

er·go·nom·ics /ˌɝgəˋnɑmɪks; ˌɜːgəˈnɒmɪks/ *n* [U] the study of how the design of equipment affects how well people can do their work 工效学, 人类工程学: *the ergonomics of computer hardware* 电脑硬件设计中的人类工程学 —**ergonomic** *adj* —**ergonomically** /-klɪ; -kli/ *adv*

Er·ics·son, Eriksson /ˋɛrɪksn̩; ˈerɪksən/, **Leif** /lif; liːf/ (10th century AD) an EXPLORER from Norway, who was probably the first European to discover America. He landed in Newfoundland in the late 10th century. 埃里克松〔(公元10世纪) 挪威探险家。他可能是发现美洲的第一位欧洲人, 公元10世纪晚期曾到达纽芬兰岛〕

Eric the Red (?950-?1001) a Norwegian sailor who discovered Greenland in about 981 红发艾瑞克〔(?950- ?1001), 挪威航海家, 大约在981年发现了格陵兰岛〕

E·rie /ˋɪrɪ; ˈɪəri/, **Lake** one of the Great Lakes of North America, between the US and Canada. There is a lot of industry on the southern side. 伊利湖〔北美五大湖之一, 位于美国和加拿大之间, 南岸有不少工业企业〕

Erie Ca·nal, the /ˌ·· ·ˋ·/ a CANAL (=artificial river) in the US state of New York which connects Lake Erie and the Hudson River. Built in the early 19th century, the canal allowed trade between New York City and the states of the Midwest. 伊利运河〔美国纽约州一条连接伊利湖与哈得孙河的运河。运河修筑于19世纪早期, 促进了纽约市与美国中西部各州之间的贸易〕

Er·i·tre·a /ˌɛrɪˋtriə; ˌerɪ̣ˈtreɪə/ a country in northeast Africa, south of Sudan and north of Ethiopia, which became independent from Ethiopia in 1995 after a long war. Population: 4,298,000 (2001). Capital: Asmara. 厄立特里亚〔非洲东北部一国, 位于苏丹以南, 埃塞俄比亚以北。长期战争之后, 1995年脱离埃塞俄比亚获得独立。人口: 4,298,000 (2001), 首都: 阿斯马拉〕

ERM /ˌi ɑr ˋɛm; ˌiː ɑːr ˈem/ *n* **1** [U] the abbreviation of 缩写= EXCHANGE RATE MECHANISM **2** [singular] the abbreviation of 缩写= the EUROPEAN EXCHANGE RATE MECHANISM

er·mine /ˋɝmɪn; ˈɜːmɪ̣n/ *n* **1** [U] an expensive white fur, used especially for the clothes of judges, kings, and queens 白鼬皮〔尤用于法官、国王和女王的服饰中〕**2** [C] a small thin animal of the WEASEL[1] family whose fur is white in winter 白鼬

Er·nie /ˋɝnɪ; ˈɜːni/ Electronic Random Number Indicating Equipment; the computer which chooses the prize-winning numbers of PREMIUM BONDs in the UK. Its name is the short form of the man's name 'Ernest'. 欧尼电子摇奖机〔即电子随机编号指示器, 指英国有奖债券抽号开奖使用的电脑装置。品名是男性名字"欧内斯特"的简称〕

Ernst /ɛrnst; eənst/, **Max** /mæks; mæks/ (1891-1976) a German painter who lived in Germany, France, and then the US. He was an important figure in Dadaism and Surrealism 恩斯特〔(1891-1976), 德国画家。他曾住在德国、法国, 后迁居美国。他是达达主义和超现实主义的一个重要人物〕

e·rode /ɪˋrod; ɪˈrəʊd/ *v* also 又作 **erode away 1** [I,T] if the wind, rain etc erodes something such as rock or soil, or if they erode, their surface is gradually destroyed〔风、雨等〕侵蚀, 腐蚀: *East-facing cliffs are being constantly eroded by heavy seas.* 朝东的悬崖正不断受到汹涌海浪的侵蚀。**2** [I,T] to gradually destroy or reduce something such as someone's power, rights or confidence 逐步损害, 削弱〔权力、权利或信心〕: *She feels that her personal authority has been eroded.* 她觉得自己的威信已被削弱。

e·ro·ge·nous zone /ɪˌrɑdʒənəs ˋzon; ɪˌrɒdʒənəs ˈzəʊn/ *n* [C] a part of your body that gives you sexual pleasure when it is touched 性敏感区

E·ros /ˋɛrɑs; ˈɪərɒs/ **1** in Greek MYTHOLOGY, the god of sexual and romantic love. He is usually shown in pictures as a beautiful boy with wings, holding a BOW and ARROW. In Roman mythology his name is Cupid. 厄洛斯〔希腊神话中的爱神, 在绘画作品中通常被描绘成一个长着翅膀、手持弓箭的英俊男孩, 罗马神话中称丘比特〕**2** a statue of Eros at Piccadilly Circus in central London 爱神雕像〔位于伦敦市中心的皮卡迪利广场的厄洛斯雕像〕**3** [U] sexual love 性爱

e·ro·sion /ɪˋroʒən; ɪˈrəʊʒən/ *n* [U] **1** the process of being gradually destroyed by rain, wind, the sea etc〔风、雨、海水等的〕侵蚀, 腐蚀: *soil erosion* 土壤(受到的)侵蚀 | *the erosion of the coastline* 海岸线(遭受的)侵蚀 **2** the process of gradually destroying or reducing something 逐步毁坏, 削弱: *the erosion of civil liberties* 公民自由的逐渐削弱 —**erosive** /ɪˋrosɪv; ɪˈrəʊsɪv/ *adj*

e·rot·ic /ɪˋrɑtɪk; ɪˈrɒtɪk/ *adj* **1** an erotic book, film etc shows people having sex, and is often intended to make people reading or looking at it have feelings of sexual pleasure 色情的 **2** erotic dreams, experiences, or activities involve feelings of sexual excitement (引起)性欲的 —**erotically** /-klɪ; -kli/ *adv*

e·rot·i·ca /ɪˋrɑtɪkə; ɪˈrɒtɪkə/ *n* [plural] erotic writing, drawings etc 色情文学, 色情艺术 —compare 比较 PORNOGRAPHY

e·rot·i·cis·m /ɪˋrɑtəˌsɪzəm; ɪˈrɒtɪ̣sɪzəm/ *n* [U] a style or quality that expresses strong feelings of sexual love and desire, especially in works of art 色情; 性欲〔尤指文艺作品〕: *the eroticism of Donne's early love poems*〔英国玄学派诗人〕多恩早期爱情诗中展现的色情

err /ɝ; ɜː/ *v* [I] **1 err on the side of caution** to be too careful rather than risk making mistakes 宁愿过于谨慎也不要冒险犯错 **2** *formal or old use* a word meaning to make a mistake【正式或旧】犯错误

er·rand /ˋɛrənd; ˈerənd/ *n* [C] **1** a short journey in order to do something for someone, for example delivering or getting something for them〔短程〕差事; 跑腿: *I have a couple of errands for you.* 我有几件差事要你去办一下。| **send sb on an errand** *His mother sent him on an errand.* 他妈妈让他出去办件事。| **run an errand** *Uncle Pio has made me run errands for him all morning.* 皮奥叔叔整个上午都在让我为他跑腿。**2 errand of mercy** *literary or humorous* a journey made in order to help someone who is in a very difficult or dangerous situation【文或幽默】帮助受困者之行; 雪中送炭之行 —see also 另见 **(send sb on) a fool's errand** (FOOL[1] (10))

er·rant /ˋɛrənt; ˈerənt/ *adj* [only before noun 仅用于名词前] *usually humorous* an errant husband, wife, son etc has done something wrong【一般幽默】〔家庭成员等〕犯错的; 迷途的 —see also 另见 KNIGHT-ERRANT

er·rat·ic /əˋrætɪk; ɪˈrætɪk/ *adj* erratic actions, movements etc seem to have no pattern or plan〔行为、动作等〕不规则的; 不确定的; 无计划的: *The bus service into town was highly erratic.*

E

驶往市区的公共汽车班次极不固定。—**erratically** /-klɪ; -kli/ *adv*: *The car was weaving erratically across the road.* 汽车左拐右拐地穿过马路。

er·ra·tum /ɪ`retəm; eˈrɑːtəm/ *n plural* **errata** /-tə; -tə/ [C] *Latin technical* a mistake in a book, shown in a list added after it is printed【拉丁, 术语】〔书中勘误表列出的〕错误

er·ro·ne·ous /ə`ronɪəs; ɪˈrəʊniəs/ *adj formal* erroneous ideas, statements etc are wrong because they are based on information that is not correct【正式】〔想法、声明等〕错误的, 不正确的 —**erroneously** *adv*

er·ror /`ɛrɚ; ˈerə/ *n* **1** [C,U] a mistake, especially a mistake in speaking or writing or a mistake that causes serious problems 错误, 谬误〔尤指口误、笔误或重大过失〕: *an essay full of spelling errors* 满是拼写错误的文章 | *Heath committed a grave error by making concessions to the right wing of the party.* 希思向党内右翼势力妥协, 犯了一个严重的错误。| **computer/driver etc error** *Mrs Leigh's huge phone bill was the result of a computer error.* 莉夫人的巨额电话账单是由于电脑出错造成的。| **human error** (=made by a person rather than a machine) 人为错误〔而非机器出错〕| **commit an error** (=make a mistake) 犯错误 *Heath committed an error by making concessions to extremists.* 希思向极端分了作出了让步, 犯了个错误。| **a grave error** (=a serious mistake) 严重的失误 **2 error of judgement** a mistake in the way that you examine a situation and decide what to do 判断失误 **3 see the error of your ways** *literary or humorous* to realize that you have been behaving badly and decide to stop【文或幽默】意识到自己的过失准备改正, 知错即改 **4 be in error** to have made a mistake, especially when making an official decision〔尤指在作正式决定时〕犯错, 失误: *The company has admitted that they were in error.* 这家公司承认犯错误了。**5 in error** if you do something in error, it is wrong but you did not intend to do it 失误: *The letter was opened in error.* 信被误拆了。—compare 比较 MISTAKE —see also 另见 **by trial and error** (TRIAL[1] (3))

Frequencies of the nouns **error** and **mistake** in spoken and written English 名词 error 和 mistake 在英语口语和书面语中的使用频率

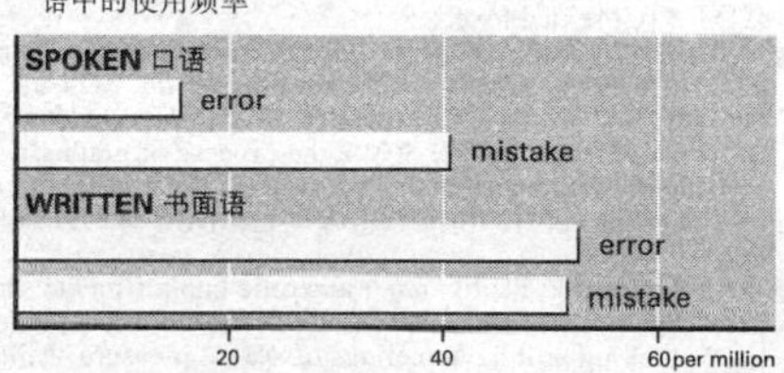

Based on the British National Corpus and the Longman Lancaster Corpus
据英国国家语料库和朗文兰开斯特语料库

This graph shows that the adverb **mistake** is more common in spoken English than the word **error**. This is because **error** is not used in a very general way. It is used when describing particular types of mistake, for example in the expressions **computer error** or **error of judgement**, and sounds formal when used on its own. It is therefore more common in written English. 本图表显示, 在英语口语中 mistake 比 error 常用, 这是因为 error 并不是很通用。当描述某些类型的错误时才使用 error, 如电脑错误或判断失误等, 单独使用时显得较正式, 因此它更常用于书面语。

er·satz /ɛr`zɑts; ˈeəzæts/ *adj* [usually before noun 一般用于名词前] artificial, and not as good as the real thing 代用的, 人造的: *ersatz coffee* 代用咖啡

Erse /ɝs; ɜːs/ *n* [U] a GAELIC language spoken in Ireland〔爱尔兰口头使用的〕盖耳语

erst·while /`ɝst,hwaɪl; ˈɜːstwaɪl/ *adj* [only before noun 仅用于名词前] your erstwhile friends, supporters, enemies etc were your friends etc until recently 从前的; 过去的〔指不久以前〕: *He has won over many of his erstwhile critics.* 他把许多不久前还批评他的人争取到自己这边。

er·u·dite /`ɛru,daɪt; ˈerʊdaɪt/ *adj* showing a lot of knowledge based on careful study 博学的, 学问精深的 —**eruditely** *adv* —**erudition** /,ɛru`dɪʃən; ,erʊˈdɪʃən/ *n* [U]

e·rupt /ɪ`rʌpt; ɪˈrʌpt/ *v* [I] **1** if a VOLCANO erupts, it explodes and sends smoke, fire, and rock into the sky〔火山〕爆发, 喷发 **2** if fighting, violence, loud noises etc erupt, they start suddenly〔搏斗、暴力事件、噪音等〕突然发生; 爆发: *Gang violence can erupt for no apparent reason.* 有时没有什么明显的原因也会爆发犯罪集团之间的暴力事件。**3 erupt into laughter/shouting etc** to suddenly start laughing or shouting 突然大笑/叫起来等 **4** if spots erupt on your body, they suddenly appear on your skin〔皮肤丘疹〕突然大片出现, 冒出 —**eruption** /ɪ`rʌpʃən; ɪˈrʌpʃən/ *n* [C,U]

-ery /ərɪ; əri/ *suffix* also 又作 **-ry** [in nouns 构成名词] **1 a)** the art, behaviour, or condition of something or of being something 技艺; 行为; 状态: *slavery* (=being a slave) 奴隶身份 | *bravery* (=being brave) 勇气 **b)** a collection of things of a particular kind 某类事物: *modern machinery* (=machines) 现代机械 | *in all her finery* (=fine clothes) 穿着她所有的华丽服饰 **2** a place where a particular thing lives or is done, made, or sold 场所: *a rookery* (=where birds called ROOKs live) 秃鼻乌鸦结巢处 | *a bakery* (=where bread is baked) 面包房 | *an oil refinery* 炼油厂

-es /əz; ɪz/ *suffix* the form used for -s when it is added to a word ending with s, z, ch, sh, or y 后缀 -s 的变体〔加在以字母 s, z, ch, sh 或 y 结尾的词后面〕: *glasses* 眼镜 | *buzzes* 嗡嗡声 | *watches* 手表 | *ladies* 女士们

ESA, the /,i ɛs `e; ,iː es ˈeɪ/ *n* the abbreviation of 缩写= the EUROPEAN SPACE AGENCY

E·sau /`isɔ; ˈiːsɔː/ in the Old Testament of the Bible, the son of Isaac, and the older brother of Jacob, whose TWIN (=one of two children born at the same time) he was. Esau was very hungry and so he sold his BIRTHRIGHT (=the property or possessions that he had a right to receive from his parents) to Jacob for 'a mess of pottage', that is, for some soup that Jacob had made. 以扫〔《圣经·旧约》中以撒之子, 雅各之孪生兄长。他在极其饥饿之时将长子名分卖给雅各以求得一碗汤〕

es·ca·late /`ɛskə,let; ˈeskəleɪt/ *v* **1** [I,T] if fighting, violence, or an unpleasant situation escalates, or if someone escalates it, it becomes much worse (使)〔战斗、暴力或不好的情况等〕升级; (使) 恶化: *They don't want the fighting to escalate into a full-scale war.* 他们不想让这场战斗升级为全面战争。**2** [I] if prices or costs escalate, they become much higher〔价格或成本〕大量增加, 升高 —**escalation** /,ɛskə`leʃən; ,eskəˈleɪʃən/ *n* [C,U]

es·ca·la·tor /`ɛskə,letɚ; ˈeskəleɪtə/ *n* [C] a set of stairs that move and carry people from one level within a building to another 自动扶梯

escalator 自动扶梯

es·ca·lope /ɛ`skɑləp; ˈeskəlɒp/ *n* [C] *BrE* a thin piece of meat, especially VEAL (=meat from a young cow), cooked in hot fat【英】油煎薄肉片〔尤指小牛肉〕

es·ca·pade /`ɛskə,ped; ˈeskəpeɪd/ *n* [C] an adventure or series of events that are exciting or contain some risk 冒险行为, 越轨行为: *Have you heard about Jane's latest escapade?* 你听说过简最近胡闹的事儿了吗?

es·cape[1] /ə`skep; ɪˈskeɪp/ *v*

1 ▶PERSON/PLACE 人/地点◀ [I,T] to get away from a place when someone is trying to catch you or stop you leaving 逃走; 逃离〔某地〕; 逃脱〔某人的追捕或阻拦〕: *Anyone trying to escape will be shot!* 谁想逃走就把他毙了! | **[+from/through/over etc]** *Two men have escaped from Durham jail.* 两名男子从达勒姆监狱逃脱。| **escape sb's clutches** (=escape from them) 从某人手中逃脱 *They managed to escape the clutches of the enemy soldiers and flee to Switzerland.* 他们设法从敌兵手中逃了出来, 跑到了瑞士。

2 ▶DANGER 危险◀ [I,T] to get away from a dangerous situation that is likely to harm you if you do not leave 逃离〔险境〕: *Only four people managed to escape before the roof collapsed.* 只有四个人抢在屋顶塌下之前逃了出来。| **escape from/through/into etc** *The dog escaped through the back window of the bus.* 狗从公共汽车的后窗逃走了。| **escape sth** *refugees escaping war and famine* 躲避战争和饥荒的难民

3 ▶GAS/LIQUID ETC 气体/液体等◀ [I] if gas, liquid, light, heat etc escapes from somewhere, it comes out when you do not want it to〔气体、液体、光、热等〕泄漏, 逸出: *Screw the top back firmly to prevent any fumes escaping.* 将盖子往回拧紧以防漏气。

4 ▶AVOID 避免◀ [I,T] to succeed in avoiding being involved in an unpleasant, difficult, or dangerous situation 逃避, 避开: *The back seat passengers escaped death by inches.* 后座的乘客死里逃生。

5 ►SOUND 声音◄ [I,T] if a sound escapes from someone's mouth, they accidentally make that sound 意外发出（声音）

6 escape sb's attention/notice if something escapes your attention or notice, you do not see it or realize that it is there 逃过某人的注意；被某人忽视

7 the name/date/title escapes me *spoken* used when you cannot remember something【口】我记不起这个名字/日期/题目：*I've met him before, but his name escapes me.* 我以前见过他，但想不起他的名字了。

8 there's no escaping (the fact) used to emphasize that something is definitely important or will definitely happen 不可否认的是；毫无疑问：*There's no escaping the fact that she did actually lie to you.* 不可否认的是，她的确对你撒了谎。—**escaped** *adj* [only before noun 仅用于名词前]: *escaped prisoners* 越狱犯

escape² *n* **1** [C,U] the act of getting away from a place where you do not want to be, or from an unpleasant or dangerous situation 逃离，逃脱：*They had been planning their escape for months.* 为逃跑他们已计划数月了。| **[+from]** *the story of Papillon's daring escape from Devil's Island* 帕皮伦从魔鬼岛英勇逃脱的故事 | **make your escape** *The party was boring – we couldn't wait to make our escape.* 晚会很无聊，我们迫不及待要逃走。| **a lucky escape** (=a situation in which you were lucky to have avoided something unpleasant) 幸运逃脱 **2** [singular, U] a way of getting away from an unpleasant situation, especially by doing something else to avoid thinking about it 逃避〔现实〕，回避：*Teenagers turn to drugs as a form of escape.* 青少年使用毒品以逃避现实。**3 an escape of gas/liquid etc** an amount of gas, liquid etc that comes out of the place where it is being kept as a result of an accident 气体/液体等泄漏：*escapes of radiation from the generating plant* 发电厂的辐射泄漏 —see also 另见 FIRE ESCAPE

es·cap·ee /ɪ,ske`pi; ˌeskeɪ'piː/ *n* [C] *literary* someone who has escaped from somewhere【文】逃离者，逃脱者

escape ve·lo·ci·ty /'·· ,··/ *n* [C,U] the speed that a ROCKET[1] (1) must travel at in order to get into space 逃逸速度〔火箭进入太空所需的速度〕

es·cap·is·m /ɪ`skepɪzəm; ɪ'skeɪpɪzəm/ *n* [U] something that helps you to forget about your normal life and think of more pleasant things 帮助人逃避现实的事物：*It's not intended to be a serious movie – it's sheer escapism.* 这部电影本来就不严肃，纯粹是为了让人逃避现实。—**escapist** *adj*

es·ca·pol·o·gy /ˌɛskə`pɑlədʒɪ; ˌeskə'pɒlədʒi/ *n* [U] the skill of escaping from ropes, chains etc as part of a performance 脱逃术，脱身术 —**escapologist** *n* [C]

e·scarp·ment /ɛ`skɑrpmənt; ɪ'skɑːpmənt/ *n* [C] a high steep slope or cliff that joins two levels on a hill or mountain 陡坡；峭壁

Esch·er /`ɛʃɚ; 'eʃə/, **M. C.** (1898-1970) a Dutch artist famous for his very detailed drawings that trick your eyes and make you think you are seeing something that is impossible 埃歇尔〔(1898-1970)，荷兰画家。其绘画作品十分细腻，让人有视觉错位和不可思议之感，他也因此闻名〕

es·chew /ɛs`tʃu; ɪs'tʃuː/ *v* [T] *formal* to deliberately avoid doing or using something, usually for moral, religious, or practical reasons【正式】〔通常为道德、宗教或实际原因而〕回避，避开：*a meek, lamb-like saviour who eschews violence* 回避冲突、温顺如羔羊般的救世主

Es·co·ri·al, Escurial /ɛ`skorɪəl; e'skɔːriæl/, **El** a former palace near Madrid, in Spain, built in the 16th century for King Philip II. The buildings include a fine church, a famous library, and a collection of art. 埃斯科里亚尔宫〔原为国王腓力二世的皇宫，建于16世纪，位于西班牙的马德里。皇宫里有一座漂亮的教堂，一个著名的图书馆，还藏有一些艺术品〕

Es·cort /`ɛskɔrt; 'eskɔːt/ *trademark* a middle-sized car made by Ford and sold especially in the UK and Europe【商标】护航舰〔福特公司制造的一款中型汽车，主要在英国和欧洲出售〕

es·cort¹ /`ɛskɔrt; 'eskɔːt/ *n* [C] **1** a person or a group of people or vehicles that go with someone in order to protect or guard them 护卫者；护送车辆：*a motorcycle escort* 摩托车护卫队 | **under escort** (=protected or guarded by an escort) 在护送[押送]下 *The suspects arrived under armed escort.* 嫌疑犯们在武装人员的押送下到达。**2** someone, especially a man, who takes someone to a formal social event 陪伴别人出席正式社交场合的人〔尤指男性〕：*Her escort was a handsome young officer.* 陪她一起来的是一名英俊的年轻军官。**3** someone who is paid to go out with someone socially 受雇陪同某人参加社交的人：*She works for an escort agency.* 她在一家社交陪伴服务社工作。

e·scort² /ɪ`skɔrt; ɪ'skɔːt/ *v* [T] **1** to go with someone to protect or guard them 护送，护卫：*The visitors were escorted by marine guards to the airport.* 来访者由海军陆战队队员护送到机场。**2** to go with someone and show them a place 引导〔某人〕游览，导游：**escort sb round** *BrE*【英】**/around** *The Queen was escorted round the factory by two of the managers.* 女王在两名经理的陪同下参观了工厂。

es·cri·toire /ˌɛskrɪ`twɑr; ˌeskrᵻ'twɑː/ *n* [C] *French* a small writing desk【法】小写字台

es·crow /`ɛskro; 'eskrəʊ/ *n* [U] *law* an object such as a written contract, money etc that is held by someone while an agreement is being fulfilled【法律】履行协议期间交由某人保管的物品〈如合同、钱款等〉

e·scutch·eon /ɪ`skʌtʃən; ɪ'skʌtʃən/ *n* [C] *formal* a SHIELD[1] (2) on which someone's COAT OF ARMS (=FAMILY SIGN) is painted【正式】饰有纹章的盾，形纹徽

-ese /iz; iːz/ *suffix* **1** [in nouns 构成名词] the people or language of a particular country or place 某国[地方]的人[语言]：*The Viennese* (=people from Vienna) *are so charming.* 维也纳人非常可爱。| *learning Japanese* (=the language of Japan) 学习日语 **2** [in adjectives 构成形容词] belonging to a particular country or place 属于某国[地方]的：*Chinese music* 中国音乐 **3** [in nouns 构成名词] language or words used by a particular group, especially when it sounds ugly or is difficult to understand 特定人群的语言[用词]〔尤指难听或难懂〕：*journalese* (=language used in newspapers) 新闻文体 | *officialese* (=language used in office or legal writing) 公文文体，官腔

Es·ki·mo /`ɛskə,mo; 'eskᵻməʊ/ *n* [C] the old name for an INUIT. The Inuit people consider the name Eskimo offensive. 爱斯基摩人〔因纽特人旧称，因纽特人认为该名称是冒犯用语〕—compare 比较 INUIT

CULTURAL NOTE 文化注释

The STEREOTYPE of an Eskimo is someone who lives in an IGLOO (=a small round house made of ice), wears furs to keep warm, and catches fish through a hole in the ice. Modern Inuit people do not live like this, however. 爱斯基摩人的典型形象是住在圆形小冰屋里，穿戴毛皮保暖，在冰上凿洞捕鱼。不过，现在的因纽特人并不是这样生活。

ESL /ˌi ɛs `ɛl; ˌiː es 'el/ *n* [U] the abbreviation of 缩写= English as a Second Language; the teaching of English to students living in an English-speaking country 作为第二语言的英语（课程）

ESOL /`isol; 'iːsɒl/ the abbreviation of 缩写= English for Speakers of Other Languages 操其他语种者的英语（课程）

e·soph·a·gus /ɪ`sɑfəgəs; ɪ'sɒfəgəs/ *n* [C] the American spelling of OESOPHAGUS oesophagus 的美式拼法

es·o·ter·ic /ˌɛsə`tɛrɪk; ˌesə'terɪk◄/ *adj* known and understood by only a few people who have special knowledge about something 深奥的，只有内行才懂的：*an esoteric form of Buddhism* 佛教密法 —**esoterically** /-klɪ; -kli/ *adv*

ESP /ˌi ɛs `pi; ˌiː es 'piː/ *n* [U] **1** the abbreviation of 缩写= extrasensory perception; the ability to know what will happen in the future, or to know what another person is thinking 超感知觉〔即可预知未来或感知他人所思的能力〕**2** the abbreviation of 缩写= English for special purposes; the teaching of English to business people, scientists etc 专业英语课程〔即针对商业人士、科学家等专业人员的课程〕

esp the written abbreviation of 缩写= especially

es·pa·drille /ˌɛspə`drɪl; ˌespə'drɪl/ *n* [C] *French* a light shoe that is made of cloth and rope【法】〔用布和绳带制成的〕轻便鞋，帆布便鞋 —see picture on page A17 参见A17页图

es·pe·cial /ə`spɛʃəl; ɪ'speʃəl/ *adj formal*【正式】= SPECIAL

es·pe·cial·ly /ə`spɛʃəlɪ; ɪ'speʃəli/ also 又作 **specially** *spoken*【口】*adv* **1** [sentence adverb 句子副词] used to emphasize that something is more important or happens more with one particular thing than with others 尤其：*Crime is growing at a rapid rate, especially in urban areas.* 犯罪率正迅速上升，尤其是在城镇中。**2** [+adj/adv] to a particularly high degree or much more than usual 特别，格外：*I was feeling especially tired that evening.* 那天晚上我感到特别累。| *"Do you feel like going out for a drink?" "Not especially, no."* "你想出去喝一杯吗？""不是特别想。" **3** for a particular person, purpose etc 专门（地）：**[+for]** *I bought these chocolates especially for you.* 这些巧克力是我专门为你买的。

USAGE NOTE 用法说明：ESPECIALLY

WORD CHOICE 词语辨析：**especially, specially, special**

Especially is most often used to emphasize something, or to say that something is more worth mentioning or more important than the other things you are talking about. es-

pecially 通常用于强调某事物，或表示该事物比其他被谈论的事物更值得一提或更重要: *It can be especially difficult for drivers to see cyclists at night.* 汽车司机夜间特别不容易看见骑车人。| *The town is especially crowded in the summer* (=much more than in winter). 这个城镇夏天时人格外多〔比冬天时多许多〕。| *I hate interruptions, especially when I'm trying to work* (=I do not mind as much at other times). 我不喜欢被打断，尤其是在工作时间。

Specially is usually used when you do something that is different from what you usually do for a particular purpose. It is often used with the passive form of a verb. specially 通常用于表示因为某个特殊目的，所做之事异于平常。它常与被动态的动词连用: *a specially made/designed/adapted etc car* 特别制造/设计/改装等的汽车 | *I bought it specially for you.* 这是我特地为你买的。

Special is the adjective for both **specially** and **especially**. special 是 specially 和 especially 两个词的形容词形式。

SPELLING 拼法

In spoken English **especially** is often shortened to **specially**, but it is usually written in full. 在英语口语中，especially 常简化为 specially，但书写时通常不简化。

Specially may be written (and heard) as **especially** in slightly formal English. **Special** is hardly ever written **especial**, which is very formal. 在稍正式的英语口语和书面语中，specially 可以说成或写作 especially。special 几乎从不写作 especial，因为 especial 是非常正式的用语。

GRAMMAR 语法

Specially and **especially** are not common at the start of a sentence or clause. specially 和 especially 两词通常不用于句子或分句的开头。You would usually say 一般都说: *I especially like New York* (NOT 不用 *especially I like New York*). 我特别喜欢纽约。

Es·pe·ran·to /ˌɛspəˈrɑnto; ˌespəˈræntəʊ/ *n* [U] an artificial language invented in 1871 to help people from different countries in the world speak to each other 世界语

es·pi·o·nage /ˈɛspɪənɑdʒ; ˈespiənɑːʒ/ *n* [U] the activity of secretly finding out a country's or company's secrets 谍报活动，间谍行为: *Some of the embassy staff were certainly involved in espionage.* 使馆中的一些人肯定参与了谍报活动。

es·pla·nade /ˌɛspləˈned; ˌespləˈneɪd/ *n* [C] *especially BrE* a wide street next to the sea in a town【尤英】滨海大道

ESPN /ˌi ɛs pi ˈɛn; ˌiː es piː ˈen/ a cable television station in the US which broadcasts only sports 娱乐体育节目网〔美国一有线体育电视台〕

es·pouse /ɪˈspaʊz; ɪˈspaʊz/ *v* [T] *formal* to support an idea, belief etc especially a political one【正式】支持，拥护〔某观点、信仰，尤指政治主张〕: *This government claims to espouse the principle of freedom of choice.* 该政府声称支持自由选择原则。—**espousal** *n* [singular, U]

es·pres·so /ɛsˈprɛso; eˈspresəʊ/ *n* [C,U] a strong black Italian coffee 蒸馏咖啡〔一种意大利浓咖啡，不加牛奶〕

esprit de corps /ɛˈspri də ˈkɔr; eˌspriː də ˈkɔː/ *n* [U] *French* feelings of loyalty towards people who are all involved in the same activity as you【法】团队精神，集体成员之间的团结

es·py /əˈspaɪ; ɪˈspaɪ/ *v* [T] *literary* to suddenly see someone or something【文】突然看见

Esq *especially BrE*【尤英】a written abbreviation of 缩写= esquire

-esque /ɛsk; esk/ *suffix* [in adjectives 构成形容词] **1** in the manner or style of a particular person, group, or place …式样[风格]的: *Kafkaesque* (=in the style of the writer Franz Kafka, or like the situations or characters in his books) 卡夫卡式的〔指奥地利小说家卡夫卡的风格或与他小说中的情景或人物相似的〕 **2** like something 似…般的: *picturesque* (=pleasant to look at) (风景)如画的

Es·quire /ˈɛskwaɪɚ; ɪˈskwaɪə/ *trademark* a magazine for men, produced in the US and UK, with articles on fashion, sports, cars etc. and pictures of attractive women【商标】《君子》〔在美国和英国出版的男性杂志，刊有时装、体育、汽车等文章和靓女照片〕

es·quire *n* a title that can be written after a man's name, especially on the address of an official letter …先生〔写在男子姓名后的尊称，尤用于正式信件的地址中〕

-ess /ɛs; es/ *suffix* [in nouns 构成名词] a female 女性; 雌性: *an actress* (=a female actor) 女演员 | *a waitress* 女侍者 | *two lionesses* 两头母狮子

es·say¹ /ˈɛse; ˈeseɪ/ *n* [C] **1** a short piece of writing by a student as part of a course of study〔学生为某门课程所写的〕短文，论说文: **[+on/about]** *an essay on the causes of the French Revolution* 一篇关于法国大革命的起因的短文 **2** a short piece of writing giving someone's ideas about politics, society etc〔关于政治、社会等的〕小品文，散文 **3** *formal* an attempt to do something【正式】尝试; 企图

essay² *v* [T] *formal* to attempt to do something【正式】试图; 企图

es·say·ist /ˈɛseɪst; ˈeseɪ-ɪ̣st/ *n* [C] someone who writes essays, especially as a form of literature 散文家

es·sence /ˈɛsn̩s; ˈesəns/ *n* **1** [singular] the most basic and important quality of something 本质，实质; 要素: **[+of]** *In his paintings Picasso tries to capture the essence of his subjects.* 毕加索在画中努力抓住所选对象的本质。**2** [U]a liquid obtained from a plant, flower etc that has a strong smell or taste and is used especially in cooking 香精，精油: *vanilla essence* 香草香精 **3 in essence** used when talking about the most basic and important part of something, especially an idea, belief, or argument 本质上，实质上: *In essence, you are saying that people do not really have free will.* 实质上你是在说，人们并不真正拥有自由意志。**4 speed/time is of the essence** used to say that it is important to do something as quickly as possible 速度/时间是至关重要的

es·sen·tial¹ /əˈsɛnʃəl; ɪˈsenʃəl/ *adj* **1** extremely important and necessary in order to do something correctly or successfully 绝对重要的; 必不可少的: *If you're going walking in the mountains, strong boots are essential.* 在山间行走，结实的靴子是必不可少的。| **[+for/to]** *Good food and plenty of exercise are essential for a healthy life.* 要健康地生活，吃得好并做大量的锻炼是最重要的。| **it is essential (that)** *It is essential that the oil is checked every 10,000 km.* 每行驶10,000公里就必须检查一下润滑油。| **it is essential to do sth** *It's essential to read the small print at the bottom of any document.* 阅读任何文件时，看清楚页脚处的小字非常重要。**2** the essential parts, qualities, or features of something are the most important, typical, or noticeable ones 最重要的; 最典型的; 最显著的: *The essential character of the village has not changed in over 300 years.* 这个村庄最显著的特征三百多年来一直未变。| **essential difference/feature/point etc** *The essential difference between man and apes is intelligence.* 人和猿最根本的区别在于智力。

essential² *n* **1** [C usually plural 一般用复数] something that is important because it is necessary for life or for doing something 必需品; 不可缺的东西: *The charity provides homeless people with essentials like food and clothing.* 慈善机构为无家可归者提供了食品和衣物等生活必需品。| **bare essentials** (=the most necessary things) 最必要的东西 *We don't have much room for luggage so we're only taking the bare essentials.* 我们没有多少地方放行李，所以只带最要紧的东西。**2 the essentials** [plural] the basic and most important information or facts about a particular subject 要点，要素: *the essentials of English grammar* 英语语法的要点

es·sen·tial·ly /əˈsɛnʃəlɪ; ɪˈsenʃəli/ *adv* used when stating the most basic facts about something 本质上，根本上: *Eisenhower was essentially a moderate in politics.* 艾森豪威尔在政治上基本属于温和派。| [sentence adverb 句子副词] *Essentially, the plan is worthwhile, but some changes will have to be made.* 从根本上讲，这个计划值得做，但必须做些修改。

essential oil /·ˌ·· ˈ·/ *n* [C] an oil from a plant that has a strong smell and is used for making PERFUME¹ (1) or in AROMATHERAPY (香)精油〔用于香水制造或芳香疗法〕

Es·sex /ˈɛsɪks; ˈesɪ̣ks/ a COUNTY in southeast England, between East London and the North Sea 埃塞克斯郡〔英格兰东南部一郡，位于东伦敦与北海之间〕

CULTURAL NOTE 文化注释

People in Britain often make jokes about young men and women who live in Essex, and this was especially true in the 1980s. In these jokes, Essex men are badly educated, and often dishonest, but they earn a lot of money, drive fast cars, and they talk loudly and have RIGHT WING political opinions. Essex girls are stupid, wear clothes such as short skirts, talk loudly, and are too willing to have sex. 英国人常拿埃塞克斯年轻人打趣，上世纪80年代尤其如此。在这些玩笑里，埃塞克斯男人教育程度低，经常撒谎，但他们很能挣钱，开快车，大声说话，政治观点右倾。埃塞克斯郡的姑娘则很愚蠢，穿短裙一类衣服，大声说话，性欲很强。

Essex, the Earl of (1566-1601) an English soldier and politician. For many years he was a close friend and adviser of Queen Elizabeth I, but after their friendship ended she ordered him to be put in prison and, later, to be killed. 埃塞克斯伯爵〔(1566-1601)，英国军事家、政治家。多年来，他一直是女王伊

丽莎白一世的密友与顾问。然而，他们之间断绝友情之后，他被女王打入牢狱，而后遭到杀害〕

est **1** the written abbreviation of 缩写= established: *H.Perkins and Company, est. 1869* H.珀金斯公司，成立于1869年 **2** the written abbreviation for 缩写= ESTIMATED

-est /ɪst; ɨst/ *suffix* **1** forms the SUPERLATIVE of many shorter adjectives and adverbs〔附在许多较短小的形容词和副词后面，构成最高级〕: *cold, colder, coldest* 冷，更冷，最冷 | *dry, drier, driest* 干燥，更干燥，最干燥 | *Our soap washes whitest.* 我们的肥皂洗起东西来最干净。—see also 另见 -ER **2** also 又作 **-st** *old use or Biblical* forms the second person singular of verbs【旧或圣经】〔用以构成动词的第二人称单数〕: *thou goest* 你走

es·tab·lish /ə`stæblɪʃ; ɪ'stæblɪʃ/ *v* [T] **1** to start a company, organization, system, situation etc that is intended to exist or continue for a long time 建立，设立: *My grandfather established the family business in 1938.* 我的祖父于1938年创立了这个家族企业。**2** to find out facts that will prove that something is true 证实，确定: *Attorneys are trying to establish the validity of his claim.* 律师们正努力证实他的说法是正确的。| **establish that** *It has been firmly established that she was not there at the time of the crime.* 有确凿的证据证明案发时她不在场。| **establish a link/connection** *establishing a link between ozone depletion and the use of CFC gases* 确定臭氧层遭破坏和使用含氯氟烃二者之间有关联 **3** to make people accept that you can do something, or that you have a particular quality 使被接受；使得到承认: **establish yourself as/in** *They have established themselves as the most powerful political party in the country.* 他们已经在国内确立了自己最有影响力的政党的地位。**4 establish links/contacts/trust etc** to start having a relationship with someone or to start discussions with them 建立关系/联系/信任等: *We decided to try and establish contacts with similar groups in the US.* 我们决定设法与美国的同类团体建立联系。

es·tab·lished /ə`stæblɪʃt; ɪ'stæblɪʃt/ *adj* [only before noun 仅用于名词前] **1** already in use or existing for a long period of time 早已确立的；早已投入使用的: *established anti-cancer drugs* 已投入使用的抗癌药物 | **well established** *well-established teaching methods* 被广泛采用的教学方法 **2** known to do a particular job well, because you have done it for a long time 资深的: *an established political figure* 资深政界人物

es·tab·lish·ment /ə`stæblɪʃmənt; ɪ'stæblɪʃmənt/ *n* **1** [C] *formal* an institution, especially a business, shop etc【正式】机构；单位〔尤指企业、商店等〕: *The hotel is a well-run establishment.* 这家旅馆经营良好。**2 the Establishment** the group of people in a society who have a lot of power and influence and are often opposed to any kind of change or new ideas 统治集团，权势集团: *It's no good fighting the Establishment; it will always win in the end.* 同当权者斗没有用，到头来赢的总是他们。**3 the medical/legal/military etc establishment** a powerful controlling group within a particular type of activity 医学界/法律界/军界等的当权派 **4** [U] the act of establishing an organization, relationship, or system 建立，设立: [+of] *Since the establishment of the club three years ago, membership has doubled.* 自从三年前该俱乐部成立，会员数已增加了一倍。

CULTURAL NOTE 文化注释

In both the US and the UK, people think of the Establishment as relating to people who have traditional and CONSERVATIVE values, who usually belong to the UPPER CLASS or the UPPER MIDDLE CLASS and who have important jobs in the government, or in banks and large companies, or who work as lawyers or judges in a court of law. It is usually regarded as being opposed to change and new ideas, and as always supporting traditional ideas, behaviour, and ways of doing things. 在英美两国，权势集团被认为是那些有传统和保守价值观的人，他们通常属于上流社会或中上阶层，在政府、银行、大公司中担当要职，或任律师或法官。通常认为他们反对变革和新观念，总是支持传统观念、行为和行事方法。

es·tate /ə`stet; ɪ'steɪt/ *n* **1** [C] *BrE* an area where houses or buildings of a similar type have all been built together in a planned way【英】有计划地建有同类建筑物的地区: **council/industrial/housing etc estate** *Rachel was brought up on a bleak post-war council estate in Liverpool.* 雷切尔在利物浦一个破旧的战后市建住宅区内长大。**2** [singular] *law* all of someone's property and money, especially everything that is left after they die【法律】个人全部财产〔尤指遗产〕: *She left her estate to her husband.* 她把财产留给了丈夫。**3** [C] a large area of land in the country, usually with one large house on it and one owner〔在乡村附近有宅邸的〕一大片私有土地，庄园: *workers on the Osborne estate* 奥斯本庄园的雇工 **4** [singular] *old-fashioned* a condition or state of life【过时】〔人生的〕状况，状态: *the holy estate of matrimony* 神圣的婚姻状况 —see also 另见 FOURTH ESTATE, REAL ESTATE

estate a·gent /·'··,··/ *n* [C] *BrE* someone whose business is to buy and sell houses or land for people【英】房地产经纪人; REAL ESTATE AGENT or REALTOR *AmE*【美】—**estate agency** *n* [C]

CULTURAL NOTE 文化注释

Estate agents are generally unpopular in the UK. Many people think that they typically describe houses as much better than they really are, and that they charge a lot of money for doing very little work. 房地产经纪人在英国普遍不受欢迎，很多人认为房地产经纪人总是把房子描述得言过其实，没做多少事，却要很高的报酬。

estate car /·'· ·/ *n* [C] *BrE* a car with a door at the back, folding back seats, and a lot of room for boxes, cases etc【英】旅行车，客货两用车; STATION WAGON *AmE*【美】

estate tax /·'· ·/ *n* [C,U] a tax in the US on the money and possessions of a dead person〔美国的〕遗产税 —see also 另见 INHERITANCE TAX

es·teem¹ /ə`stim; ɪ'stiːm/ *n* [U] a feeling of respect and admiration for someone 尊敬，敬重: **hold sb in high/great esteem** *She was an actress who was held in high esteem by everyone who knew her.* 她是一名让所有认识她的人都十分尊重的演员。| **a token of sb's esteem** (=a sign of their esteem) 某人表达敬意的象征 *Please accept this gift as a small token of our affection and esteem.* 区区薄礼，聊表敬意，请笑纳。—see also 另见 SELF-ESTEEM

esteem² *v* [T] **1** to respect and admire someone 尊敬，尊重: **highly esteemed** (=greatly respected) 极受尊重的 *a highly esteemed artist and critic* 极受尊重的艺术家兼批评家 **2 esteem it an honour/ favour/pleasure etc** *old-fashioned* used as a very polite way of saying you think something is an honour etc【过时】将某事物看作一种荣耀/恩惠/乐趣等 **3 esteem someone worthy/reliable etc** *old-fashioned* to believe that someone has a particular quality【过时】认为某人值得信赖/可靠等: *He esteemed the assistant trustworthy enough to look after the shop.* 他认为可以信赖这个助手，托付其照看店铺。

es·thete /`ɛsθit; 'iːsθiːt/ *n* [C] an American spelling of AESTHETE aesthete 的美式拼法 —**esthetic** /ˌɛs`θɛtɪk; iːs'θetɪk/ *adj* —**esthetical** *adj* —**esthetically** /-kḷɪ; -kli/ *adv* —**esthetics** *n* [U]

es·ti·ma·ble /`ɛstəməbḷ; 'estɨməbəl/ *adj formal* deserving respect and admiration【正式】值得尊敬的

es·ti·mate¹ /`ɛstəmɪt; 'estɨmɨt/ *n* [C] **1** a calculation of the value, size, amount etc of something 估计，估算: **a rough estimate** (=not very exact) 粗略估计 *At a rough estimate I'd say it's about 150 miles.* 粗略估计，我觉得约有150英里。| **a conservative estimate** (=deliberately rather low) 保守的估计 *That seems a conservative estimate to me.* 我觉得那是一个保守的估计。—see also 另见 GUESSTIMATE **2** a statement of how much it will probably cost to build or repair something 估价，报价: *We got two or three estimates so we could pick the cheapest.* 我们收到两三家的报价，可以选择最低的一家。 S3 W2

estimate² /`ɛstəˌmet; 'estɨmeɪt/ *v* [T] to try to judge the value, size, speed, cost etc of something, partly by calculating and partly by guessing 估计，估算: *The mechanic estimated the cost of repairs at $150.* 修理工估计维修费用为150美元。| *Iraq is estimated to have over 100 such weapons.* 估计伊拉克有一百多件这样的武器。| **estimate that** *It is estimated that between 70 and 90 per cent of car crimes occur in the daytime.* 据估计，70%到90%的汽车犯罪发生在白天。| **estimate how many/what etc** *It is difficult to estimate how many deaths are caused by passive smoking each year.* 很难估算每年有多少人死于被动吸烟。—**estimated** *adj* an estimated number, cost etc has been partly calculated and partly guessed 估计的，估算的: *The concert was watched on TV by an estimated one billion people.* 估计有10亿人通过电视收看了这场音乐会。—**estimator** *n* [C] S3 W3

es·ti·ma·tion /ˌɛstə`meʃən; ˌestɨ'meɪʃən/ *n* [U] **1** your opinion of the value, nature etc of someone or something 判断，看法: **in my/your etc estimation** *This will simply lead, in our estimation, to further problems.* 根据我们判断，这样只会引发更多的问题。**2** respect or admiration for someone; ESTEEM¹ 尊敬，尊重: **go up/come down in sb's estimation** (=be respected more or less by someone) 在某人心目中的地位升高/下降

Es·to·ni·a /ɛ`stonɪə; e'stəʊniə/ a small country on the Baltic Sea, between Russia and Latvia, which was part of the former

Soviet Union until 1991. Population: 1,423,000 (2001). Capital: Tallinn. 爱沙尼亚〔波罗的海一小国，位于俄罗斯和拉脱维亚之间，1991年前是前苏联的一部分。人口：1,423,000（2001），首都：塔林〕—**Estonian** *n, adj*

es·tranged /ɪˋstrendʒd; ɪˈstreɪndʒd/ *adj* **1** an expression used especially in newspaper reports meaning no longer living with your husband or wife〔与配偶〕分居的〔尤用于新闻报道中〕: **estranged husband/wife** *She was shot in bed by her estranged husband.* 她被已分居的丈夫枪杀在床上。**2** no longer having any connection with a relative or good friend, because of an argument〔因争吵而与亲戚或好朋友〕疏远的，不再联系的: **[+from]** *Mollie became increasingly estranged from her son.* 莫莉与儿子越来越疏远。**3** no longer feeling any connection with something that used to be important in your life 与〔曾经重要的事物〕远离的，决裂的: **[+from]** *estranged from their religious traditions* 背离了他们的宗教传统 —**estrangement** /əˋstrendʒmənt; ɪˈstreɪndʒmənt/ *n* [C,U]

es·tro·gen /ˋɛstrədʒən; ˈiːstrədʒən/ *n* [U] the usual American spelling of OESTROGEN oestrogen 的一般美式拼法

es·tu·a·ry /ˋɛstʃʊˌɛrɪ; ˈestʃuəri/ *n* [C] the wide part of a river where it goes into the sea 河口: *the Thames estuary* 泰晤士河河口

Estuary En·glish /ˈ····, ··/ *n* [U] a way of speaking English that is common in the London area and is now starting to spread to other areas of England. In Estuary English the letters 't', 'l', and 'h' are often pronounced as a GLOTTAL STOP, and /l/ like /w/. 河口英语〔在伦敦地区流行，现已开始传至英格兰其他地区，其特点是字母 t, l 和 h 常发声门闭塞音；/l/ 的发音和 /w/ 相似〕

E.T. /ˌiˋti; ˌiːˈtiː/ (1982) a very popular US film made by Steven Spielberg about a creature called E.T. ('the Extra Terrestrial'), who comes to Earth from another part of the universe. He is small and ugly, but very kind and intelligent, and he becomes friends with a boy called Elliot, who helps him to get home. 《外星人》〔（1982），一部深受人们喜爱的美国电影，由斯蒂芬·斯皮尔伯格制作，讲述一个外星人来到地球的故事。外星人个子矮小，相貌丑陋，但十分善良，极具智慧。他与一个名字叫做艾略特的小男孩成了朋友，并在其帮助下回了家〕

ETA /ˌi ti ˋe; ˌiː tiː ˈeɪ/ *n* the abbreviation for 缩写= estimated time of arrival; the time when a plane, ship etc is expected to arrive〔飞机、船等〕估计到达时间: *What's our ETA?* 估计我们什么时候到？

et al /ˌɛt ˋæl; ˌet ˈæl/ *adv Latin* written after a list of names to mean that other people are also involved in something【拉丁】以及其他〔有关的〕人；等人: *'The Human Embryo' by Brodsky, Rosenblum, et al* 布罗德斯基、罗森布拉姆等人所著的《人类胚胎》

etc /ˌɛt ˋsɛtərə; et ˈsetərə/ *adv Latin* the written abbreviation for 缩写= et cetera, used after a list to show that there are many other similar things or people that you could have added【拉丁】等等；以及其他〔类似的〕事物[人]: *loans taken out to cover the cost of repairs, new equipment etc* 支付修理、购置新设备等等费用的贷款 | **etc etc** (=used when you are rather bored or annoyed by the list you are giving) 等等〔用于表示对所列出的事物感到厌烦〕*The letter says pay at once, they've reminded us before etc etc.* 信中说了些要立刻付款、之前已提醒过我们之类的话。

et cet·e·ra /ˌɛt ˋsɛtərə; et ˈsetərə/ *adv Latin* the full form of etc【拉丁】etc 的全拼形式

etch /ɛtʃ; etʃ/ *v* **1** [I,T] to cut lines on a metal plate, piece of glass, stone etc to form a picture 蚀刻；凿刻 **2 be etched on your memory/mind** *literary* if an experience, name etc is etched on your memory or mind, you cannot forget it and you think of it often【文】〔经历、姓名等〕铭刻在记忆中/脑海里: *a terrible event that is etched forever on my memory* 永远留在我记忆里的可怕事件 **3** [T usually passive 一般用被动态] if someone's face is etched with pain, sadness etc you can see these feelings from their expression〔脸上〕刻着〔痛苦、悲伤等〕**4** [T] to make lines or patterns appear on something very clearly 使〔线条或图案〕清晰: *deep furrows etched in the sand* 沙地上清晰的深沟 —**etched** *adj*: *etched glass* 刻有图案的玻璃 —**etcher** *n* [C,U]

etch·ing /ˋɛtʃɪŋ; ˈetʃɪŋ/ *n* [C] a picture made by printing from an etched metal plate 刻版画；蚀刻画

e·ter·nal /ɪˋtɝnl; ɪˈtɜːnəl/ *adj* **1** continuing for ever and having no end 永远的；永恒的: *the Christian promise of eternal life* 基督教承诺的永生 **2** *informal* seeming to continue for ever, especially because of being boring or annoying【非正式】似乎无休无止的；没完没了的: *Why can't you stop your eternal complaining!* 你为什么就不能停止你那没完没了的抱怨呢！**3 eternal truths** principles that are always true 永恒的真理

Eternal Cit·y, the /·,·· ˈ··/ a name used in literature for Rome 不朽城〔文学作品中罗马的别称〕

e·ter·nal·ly /ɪˋtɝnl̩ɪ; ɪˈtɜːnəl-i/ *adv* **1** for ever 永远，永久地 **2 eternally grateful** used to say that you are very grateful 感激不尽的 **3** *informal* very often【非正式】频繁地，不断地: *She seems to be eternally asking me for help.* 她似乎总是在向我求助。

eternal tri·an·gle /·,·· ˈ···/ *n* [singular] the difficult situation that occurs when two people have a sexual relationship with the same person 三角性关系，三角恋爱

e·ter·ni·ty /ɪˋtɝnətɪ; ɪˈtɜːnɪ̣ti/ *n* **1 an eternity** a period of time that seems very long because you are annoyed, anxious etc 似乎很漫长的一段时间: *Every moment seemed like an eternity.* 每一瞬间都似乎无穷无尽。**2** [U]the whole of time without any end 永恒: **for all eternity** *a little animal preserved for all eternity as a fossil* 作为化石得以永远保存下来的小动物 **3** [U] the state of existence after death that some people believe continues for ever 永生

-eth /ɪθ; ɪ̣θ/ *suffix* also 又作 **-th** *old use or Biblical* forms the third person singular of verbs【旧或圣经】〔构成动词的第三人称单数〕: *he goeth* 他走

eth·a·nol /ˋɛθənol; ˈeθənɒl/ *n* [U] *technical* ETHYL ALCOHOL【术语】乙醇

Eth·el·red II /ˌɛθəlrɛd ðə ˋsɛkənd; ˌeθəlred ðə ˈsekənd/ also 又作 **Ethelred the Unready** (?968-1016) an English king who lost his KINGDOM to the Danes 艾特尔雷德二世〔（?968-1016），英格兰国王。丹麦人夺去了他的王国〕

e·ther /ˋiθɚ; ˈiːθə/ *n* **1** [U] a clear liquid used in the past as an ANAESTHETIC to make people sleep before an operation 醚；乙醚 **2 the ether** *BrE*【英】**a)** the air through which radio waves travel 以太，能媒: *Messages are flying through the ether.* 信息在以太空间中传输。**b)** also 又作 **aether** *poetic* the upper part of the sky【诗】苍天，苍穹

e·the·re·al /ɪˋθɪrɪəl; ɪˈθɪəriəl/ *adj* very delicate and light, in a way that does not seem real 缥缈的；超凡的: *ethereal beauty* 超凡的美丽 —**ethereally** *adv*

e·ther·net /ˋiθɚˌnɛt; ˈiːθənet/ *n* [U] a special system of wires used for connecting computer networks around the world 以太网

eth·ic /ˋɛθɪk; ˈeθɪk/ *n* **1** [C] a general idea or belief that influences people's behaviour and attitudes 伦理；道德体系: *The modern ethic seems to be to get as much money as you can without worrying how you get it.* 现代的道德观似乎是不择手段尽量弄钱。—see also 另见 WORK ETHIC **2 ethics** [plural] moral rules or principles of behaviour for deciding what is right and wrong 道德标准，道德规范: *The ethics of his actions are suspect, but technically he is within the law.* 他的行为是否合乎道德规范值得怀疑，但从严格的法律意义上讲他并没有违法。| **professional ethics** (=the moral rules relating to a particular profession) 职业道德 | **a code of ethics** (=a set of moral rules) 道德准则

eth·i·cal /ˋɛθɪkl; ˈeθɪkəl/ *adj* [no comparative 无比较级] **1** connected with principles of what is right and wrong 关于伦理的: *The use of animals in scientific tests raises some difficult ethical questions.* 用动物做科学实验引发了一些棘手的道德问题。**2** morally good or correct 合乎道德的；正确的: *Is it ethical to use drugs to control prisoners' behaviour?* 用药物来控制犯人的行为合乎道德吗？—opposite 反义词 UNETHICAL —**ethically** /-klɪ; -kli/ *adv*

E·thi·o·pi·a /ˌiθɪˋopɪə; ˌiːθiˈəʊpiə/ a country in northeast Africa on the Red Sea. Population: 65,892,000 (2001). Capital: Addis Ababa. The northern part of the country, Eritrea, fought for independence during the 1970s and 1980s, and became independent in 1993. 埃塞俄比亚〔非洲东北部一国家，濒临红海。人口：65,892,000（2001），首都：亚的斯亚贝巴。20世纪70、80年代，该国北部地方的厄立特里亚为独立而斗争。1993年正式独立〕—**Ethiopian** *n, adj*

eth·nic[1] /ˋɛθnɪk; ˈeθnɪk/ *adj* **1** connected with a particular race, nation, or tribe and their customs and traditions 种族[民族、部落]的；具有种族[民族、部落]特色的: *The city's population includes a wide range of different ethnic groups.* 这座城市居住着许多不同种族的人。| *ethnic Turks living in Bulgaria* 居住在保加利亚的土耳其人 | **ethnic violence/divisions/unrest** (=violence etc between people from different races, tribes etc) 种族[部落]冲突/分裂/骚乱 **2 ethnic cooking/fashion/design etc** cooking, fashion etc from countries that are a long way from Britain or the US, which seems very different and unusual〔对英国或美国来说具有〕异国风情的烹调/时尚/设计等: *the delights of ethnic cooking* 品尝外国菜肴的乐趣 **3 ethnic cleansing** the action of forcing people to leave their homes because of their RACIAL or national group 种族清洗 —**ethnically** /-klɪ; -kli/ *adv*

ethnic² *n* [C] *AmE* someone who belongs to a different race from the main group living in a particular country【美】少数民族的一员

ethnic mi·nor·i·ty /,‥ ·'‥·/ *n* [C] a group of people of a different race from the main group in a country 少数民族

eth·no·cen·tric /ˌɛθnoˈsɛntrɪk; ˌeθnəʊˈsentrɪk◂/ *adj* based on the idea that your own race, nation, group etc is better than any other 种族[民族、集团等]优越感的: *ethnocentric insensitivity* 种族优越感导致的麻木 —**ethnocentrism** *n* [U] —**ethnocentricity** /ˌɛθnosɛnˈtrɪsətɪ; ˌeθnəʊsenˈtrɪsɪ̈ti/ *n* [U]

eth·nog·ra·pher /ɛθˈnɑgrəfɚ; eθˈnɒgrəfə/ *n* [C] someone who studies ethnography 人种学家

eth·nog·ra·phy /ɛθˈnɑgrəfɪ; eθˈnɒgrəfi/ *n* [U] the scientific study of different races of people 人种志，人种论 —**ethnographic** /ˌɛθnəˈgræfɪk; ˌeθnəˈgræfɪk◂/ *adj* —**ethnographically** /-klɪ; -kli/ *adv*

eth·nol·o·gy /ɛθˈnɑlədʒɪ; eθˈnɒlədʒi/ *n* [U] the scientific study and comparison of the origins and organization of different races of people 人种学，民族学 —compare 比较 ANTHROPOLOGY, SOCIOLOGY —**ethnologist** *n* [C] —**ethnological** /ˌɛθnəˈlɑdʒɪkl; ˌeθnəˈlɒdʒɪkəl◂/ *adj* —**ethnologically** /-klɪ; -kli/ *adv*

e·thos /ˈiθɑs; ˈiːθɒs/ *n* [singular] the set of ideas and moral attitudes belonging to a person or group〔个人或团体的〕精神特质: *the competitive spirit in the American ethos* 美国精神中的竞争意识

eth·yl al·co·hol /ˌiθəl ˈælkəhɔl; ˌeθəl ˈælkəhɒl/ *n* [U] *technical* the type of alcohol in alcoholic drinks【术语】食用酒精

e·ti·o·lat·ed /ˈitɪəˌletɪd; ˈiːtiəleɪtɪ̈d/ *adj* **1** *literary* pale and weak【文】苍白无力的 **2** *technical* a plant that is etiolated is white because it has not received enough light【术语】〔植物因缺乏阳光而〕发黄的，变白的 —**etiolation** /ˌitɪəˈleʃən; ˌiːtiəˈleɪʃən/ *n* [U]

et·i·ol·o·gy /ˌitɪˈɑlədʒɪ; ˌetiˈɒlədʒi/ *n* [C,U] *technical* the cause of a disease or the scientific study of this【术语】病因（学），病源（学） —**etiological** /ˌitɪəˈlɑdʒɪkl; ˌetiəˈlɒdʒɪkəl◂/ *adj* —**etiologically** /-klɪ; -kli/ *adv*

et·i·quette /ˈɛtɪkɛt; ˈetɪket/ *n* [U] the formal rules for polite behaviour in society or in a particular group 礼仪，礼节: *a breach of professional etiquette* 违反职业礼仪规范

Et·na /ˈɛtnə; ˈetnə/ also 又作 **Mount Etna** a mountain in Sicily, southern Italy, which is the highest VOLCANO in Europe. Mount Etna is an active volcano, which ERUPTs every few years. 埃特纳火山〔意大利南部西西里岛的一座活火山，是欧洲海拔最高的火山，每几年就爆发一次〕

E·ton /ˈitn̩; ˈiːtn/ also 又作 **Eton College** the most famous English PUBLIC SCHOOL (=a school that is paid for by the parents and not by the government) for boys, officially called Eton College and established in the 15th century. Eton is close to the town of Windsor, to the west of London. 伊顿公学〔英国最著名的男子公学，正式名称为 Eton College，创建于 15 世纪。该校距离伦敦以西的温莎镇很近〕 —**Etonian** *n, adj*

CULTURAL NOTE 文化注释

Eton is the most famous PUBLIC SCHOOL in the UK, and many important leaders in business and the government were educated there. Men who have been educated at Eton are called 'Old Etonians', and they often want to send their sons to Eton too. As soon as a son is born, some parents 'put his name down for Eton' (=tell the school that they want him to be accepted as a student there). 伊顿公学是英国最有名的公学，很多商界和政界领袖都出自伊顿。曾在伊顿就学的人叫做"老伊顿人"，他们往往也想让自己的儿子上伊顿公学。有些家长在儿子刚一出生就去学校为他预约入学。

-ette /ɛt; et/ *suffix* [in nouns 构成名词] **1** a small thing of a particular type 小: *a kitchenette* (=small kitchen) 小厨房 | *a snackette* (=a very small meal) 小吃 **2** a woman who is doing a particular job〔做某种工作的〕女（性）: *an usherette* (=female USHER) 女引座员 **3** something that is not real, but is IMITATION (2) 仿（制）〔的东西〕: *flannelette* 棉法兰绒 | *chairs covered with leatherette* 铺有人造革的椅子

et·y·mol·o·gy /ˌɛtəˈmɑlədʒɪ; ˌetɪ̈ˈmɒlədʒi/ *n* **1** [U] the study of the origins, history, and changing meanings of words 词源学 **2** [C] a description of the history of a particular word 词源 —**etymologist** *n* [C] —**etymological** /ˌɛtəməˈlɑdʒɪk]; ˌetɪ̈məˈlɒdʒɪkəl◂/ *adj* —**etymologically** /-klɪ; -kli/ *adv*

EU /ˌi ˈju; ˌiː ˈjuː/ *n* [singular] the abbreviation of 缩写= the EUROPEAN UNION

CULTURAL NOTE 文化注释

After 10 new countries joined in 2004, the number of countries in the EU reached 25, so now the majority of countries in Europe belong to the EU. Several other countries, including Turkey and Romania, are still trying to join. In 2002, a SINGLE CURRENCY (=one type of money for the whole of Europe), called the EURO, was introduced in all but three of the countries that belonged to the EU at that time. The UK decided not to use the Euro, but it may start using it in the future. The main offices of the EU are in Brussels, and people sometimes just say 'Brussels' when they mean the EU. 继 2004 年欧盟新增 10 个成员国后，欧盟成员国增至 25 个，现在大多数欧洲国家都是欧盟成员。其他一些国家，如土耳其和罗马尼亚，正在争取加入。2002 年，除 3 个国家外，欧盟采用统一货币欧元。英国当时决定不使用欧元，但将来可能采用。欧盟主要办公地在布鲁塞尔，人们有时用布鲁塞尔指代欧盟。

People in the UK are divided in their attitudes towards the EU. Some people, known as EUROSCEPTICs, do not really like being part of the EU or think that the EU should only be concerned with trade, and not with social issues. They do not like the EU making laws that affect Britain. Eurosceptics are afraid that the UK will lose control over its own political and economic affairs, and that the traditional British way of life will gradually be lost and become more European. Eurosceptics are especially opposed to the idea of joining the single currency. 英国人对欧盟态度不一。一些人叫做疑欧派（Eurosceptic），对成为欧盟一分子并不热衷，或者认为欧盟只应处理贸易问题而不是社会问题。他们不喜欢欧盟制定的影响英国的法律。疑欧派害怕英国丧失对本国政治和经济事务的控制权，传统的英国生活方式逐渐丧失，变得更欧洲化。他们尤其反对加入单一货币体系。

Other people, known as 'pro-Europeans' or 'Europhiles', think that the UK should take a more active part in the EU, and should join the Euro. They believe that being in the EU helps British businesses, and will help to make the ECONOMY stronger. These people sometimes disapprovingly call their opponents 'Little Englanders'. 其他人被称为亲欧派（pro-European 或 Europhile），主张英国应在欧盟内发挥更积极的作用，应当加入欧元体系。他们相信加入欧盟对英国企业有利，让英国经济更强大。这些人有时将对手蔑称为"小英格兰人"。

A lot of British people, whether they support the EU or not, make jokes about some of the laws that are passed in Brussels. Sometimes newspapers report on what are seen as silly laws, but often these reports are not actually true. For example, newspapers reported that the EU wanted to call British chocolate 'vegelate', because it does not have a very high amount of real chocolate in it. This was not true. 无论是否支持欧盟，很多英国人讽刺布鲁塞尔通过的一些法律。有时候报纸会报道一些被视为愚蠢的法律，但通常这些报道并不属实。例如，报纸上说，因为英国巧克力不含多少真正的巧克力成分，欧盟准备将其叫做 vegelate，这并不属实。

eu·ca·lyp·tus /ˌjukəˈlɪptəs; juːkəˈlɪptəs/ *n* [C,U] a tall tree that produces an oil with a strong smell, used in medicines 桉树

Eu·cha·rist, the /ˈjukərɪst; ˈjuːkərɪ̈st/ *n* the holy bread and wine, representing Christ's body and blood, used during a Christian ceremony, or the ceremony itself〔基督教〕圣餐中的面包和葡萄酒；圣餐仪式 —**Eucharistic** /ˌjukəˈrɪstɪk; juːkəˈrɪstɪk◂/ *adj*

Eu·clid /ˈjuklɪd; ˈjuːklɪd/ (about 300 BC) a Greek MATHEMATICIAN who developed a system of GEOMETRY (=the study of angles, shapes, lines etc and their relationships with each other) that has been known ever since as Euclidean geometry 欧几里得〔约公元前 300 年〕，希腊数学家，建立了几何学体系，自此以欧几里得几何得名〕

eu·clid·e·an, Euclidean /juˈklɪdɪən; juːˈklɪdiən/ *adj* related to the GEOMETRY described by Euclid 欧几里得几何的

eu·gen·ics /juˈdʒɛnɪks; juːˈdʒenɪks/ *n* [plural] the study of methods to improve the mental and physical abilities of human beings by choosing who should become parents 优生学；人种改良学

eu·lo·gize also 又作 -ise *BrE*【英】/ˈjuləˌdʒaɪz; ˈjuːlədʒaɪz/ *v* [I,T] to praise someone or something very much 歌颂，赞美: *a poem eulogizing the bravery of the nation's warriors* 歌颂民族战士英勇事迹的诗 —**eulogist** *n* [C] —**eulogistic** /ˌjuləˈdʒɪstɪk; juːləˈdʒɪstɪk◂/ *adj* —**eulogistically** /-klɪ; -kli/ *adv*

eu·lo·gy /ˈjulədʒɪ; ˈjuːlədʒi/ *n* [C, U] a speech or piece of writing in which you praise someone or something very much, especially at a funeral 颂词; 颂文〔尤指葬礼上的悼词或悼文〕

eu·nuch /ˈjunʌk; ˈjuːnək/ *n* [C] a man who has had his TESTICLES removed, especially someone who guarded a king's wives in some Eastern countries in the past 阉人〔尤指过去的宦官〕

eu·phe·mis·m /ˈjufəˌmɪzəm; ˈjuːfɪ̈mɪzəm/ *n* [C] a polite word or expression that you use instead of a more direct one to avoid shocking or upsetting someone 委婉语; 委婉说法: *'Pass away' is a euphemism for 'die'.* "过去"是"死"的委婉说法。

eu·phe·mis·tic /ˌjufəˈmɪstɪk; ˌjuːfɪ̈ˈmɪstɪk◂/ *adj* euphemistic language uses polite words and expressions to avoid shocking or upsetting people 〔言语〕委婉的; 婉言的: *a euphemistic expression such as 'powder room' for 'toilet'* 例如将"厕所"说成"化妆间"的委婉说法 —**euphemistically** /-klɪ; -kli/ *adv*

eu·pho·ni·ous /juˈfonɪəs; juːˈfəʊniəs/ *adj formal* words or sounds that are euphonious are pleasant to listen to【正式】悦耳的, 动听的

eu·pho·ri·a /juˈfɔrɪə; juːˈfɔːriə/ *n* [U] a short but extremely strong feeling of happiness and excitement 狂喜; 兴奋异常: *the current state of euphoria after Ireland's amazing victory over England last Saturday* 上周六爱尔兰队奇迹般战胜英格兰队后引发的狂喜

eu·phor·ic /juˈfɑrɪk; juːˈfɒrɪk/ *adj* feeling very happy and excited 非常高兴的; 极其兴奋的 —**euphorically** /-klɪ; -kli/ *adv*

E

Eu·phra·tes, the /juˈfretiz; juːˈfreɪtiːz/ a long river which flows from Turkey through Syria and Iraq into the Persian Gulf 幼发拉底河〔从土耳其流经叙利亚和伊拉克后注入波斯湾的一条长河〕

Eu·ra·sian[1] /juˈreʒən; jʊˈreɪʒən/ *adj* concerned with both Europe and Asia 欧亚大陆的; 与欧洲和亚洲有关的

Eurasian[2] *n* [C] *old-fashioned* someone who has one European parent and one Asian parent【过时】欧亚混血儿

Eu·re·ka /juˈrikə; jʊˈriːkə/ *interjection often humorous* used to show how happy you are that you have discovered the answer to a problem, found something etc【常幽默】我发现了!〔因找到问题的解决方法或发现某物等时而发出的欢呼〕

> **CULTURAL NOTE 文化注释**
> Eureka means "I've found it!" in Greek. It originally came from the story of the Greek scientist Archimedes who shouted "Eureka" when he was taking a bath and suddenly thought of a way of measuring DENSITY. Most Americans think of Eureka as being shouted when people found gold in the streams and mountains of California during the GOLD RUSH in the 1840s. "尤里卡"在希腊语中是"我发现了"的意思。这起源于一个故事: 古希腊科学家阿基米德在洗澡时突然想到测量物体密度的办法, 大叫"尤里卡!"美国人大多相信, 19世纪40年代淘金热中, 有人在加利福尼亚的溪流中或山上找到金子, 就大喊"尤里卡!"

Eu·rip·i·des /juˈrɪpɪdiz; juːˈrɪpɪ̈diːz/ (?480-406 BC) an ancient Greek writer of plays 欧里庇得斯〔(公元前?480-前406), 古希腊剧作家〕

Eu·ro /ˈjuro; ˈjʊərəʊ/ *adj* [only before noun 仅用于名词前] European, especially connected with the European Union 欧洲的〔尤指欧盟的〕: *There's some new Euro directive on import regulations.* 欧盟对进口制度有了一些新指示。

Euro- /juro; jʊərəʊ/ *prefix* **1 a)** European, especially western European 欧洲的〔尤指西欧的〕: *Eurocommunism* 欧洲共产主义 **b)** European and 欧洲和…的: *Euro-American relations* 欧美关系 **2** of the European Union 欧盟的: *the Europarliament* 欧洲议会

Eu·ro·cheque /ˈjurotʃɛk; ˈjʊərəʊtʃek/ *n* [C] *trademark* a special cheque that can be used in different banks or shops, especially in Europe【商标】〔尤指欧洲的〕通用支票

Eu·ro·crat /ˈjurəkræt; ˈjʊərəʊkræt/ *n* [C] *informal* a government official of the European Union, especially one who makes decisions you do not like【非正式】欧盟官员〔尤指所作决定不受欢迎的官员〕

> **CULTURAL NOTE 文化注释**
> This word is used especially in newspapers when they are criticizing European officials for making too many complicated rules about things that they should not be involved in, or for being paid too much. 该词尤见于报刊, 用以批评欧洲政界人士, 说他们在本不该干预的事务上制定了太多复杂的规章, 或者说他们报酬太高。

Eu·ro·dis·ney /ˈjuroˌdɪznɪ; ˈjʊərəʊˌdɪzni/ *trademark* the former name for Disneyland Paris【商标】欧洲迪斯尼乐园〔巴黎迪斯尼乐园的旧称〕

Eu·ro·dol·lar /ˈjuroˌdɑlə; ˈjʊərəʊˌdɒlə/ *n* [C usually plural 一般用复数] *technical* a US dollar that has been put in a European bank or lent to a European customer to help trade and provide an international money system【术语】欧洲美元〔指存于欧洲银行或借给欧洲客户以帮助促进贸易和建立国际货币体系的美元〕

Eu·ro·fight·er /ˈjuroˌfaɪtə; ˈjʊərəʊˌfaɪtə/ a fast military aircraft developed by several European countries working together, including France, Germany, Italy, Spain, and the UK 欧洲战斗机〔法国、德国、意大利、西班牙和英国联合研发的一种高速军用飞机〕

Euroland /ˈjuroˌlænd; ˈjuːərəʊˌlænd/ a name used informally by politicians, news reporters etc to describe the area of Europe in which the Euro is used as the standard unit of money 欧元区〔政治家、新闻记者等使用的非正式名称, 指以欧元为标准货币单位的欧洲地区〕

Eu·rope /ˈjurəp; ˈjʊərəp/ *n* **1** the large land mass that lies north of the Mediterranean and goes as far east as the Ural Mountains 欧洲 **2** the European Union 欧盟: *Britain's future lies in Europe.* 英国的未来系于欧盟。 **3** *BrE* the CONTINENT[1] (1) of Europe not including Britain【英】〔不包括英国在内的〕欧洲大陆: *a rail link to Europe through the Channel Tunnel* 通过(英吉利海峡)海底隧道与欧洲大陆连接的铁路

Eu·ro·pe·an[1] /ˌjurəˈpiən; ˌjʊərəˈpiːən◂/ *n* [C] someone from Europe 欧洲人

European[2] *adj* from or connected with Europe 欧洲的: *European law* 欧洲的法律

European Com·mis·sion, the /ˌ····ˈ··/ also 又作 **the Commission** a group of 20 officials, chosen by the countries in the EU (=the European Union), who suggest plans for the EU, carry out decisions that the EU has made, and make sure that the EU's laws are obeyed 欧洲委员会, 欧盟执行委员会〔由欧盟成员国选任的20名官员组成的一个委员会。其职责是为欧盟建议拟采取的计划, 执行欧盟的决定, 确保欧盟的法律得以遵守〕

European Com·mu·ni·ty, the /ˌ····ˈ···/ the former name of the EU (=the European Union) 欧洲经济共同体〔欧盟的旧称〕

European Con·ven·tion on Hu·man Rights, the /ˌ····ˌ··ˌ··ˈ·/ an official agreement signed by the UK and most other European countries, in which they promise to allow every citizen their HUMAN RIGHTS, such as the right to be free, to express their political opinions, and to be treated fairly. If someone thinks that one of these countries is breaking this agreement, they can officially complain to the European Human Rights Commission. If they are still not satisfied, they can take their case to a special court called the European Court of Human Rights.《欧洲人权公约》〔英国与其他大多数欧洲国家签署的一份正式协议。各签署国保证给每个公民赋予人权, 如自由权、表达个人政见的权利和享受公正待遇的权利。如果有人认为其中一国在违反该协议, 那么就可向欧洲人权委员会投诉。如果得不到满意答复, 还可上诉至欧洲人权法庭〕

European Court of Hu·man Rights, the /ˌ····ˌ··ˌ··ˈ·/ the court of law for the Council of Europe, based in Strasbourg in France 欧洲人权法庭〔欧洲理事会下设的法庭, 总部在法国的斯特拉斯堡〕

European Court of Jus·tice, the /ˌ····ˌ··ˈ··/ the court of law for the EU (=the European Union), based in Luxembourg 欧洲法庭〔欧盟下设的法庭, 总部在卢森堡〕

European Cup, the /ˌ····ˈ·/ **1** also 又作 **European Champions Cup** a football competition in which all the teams in Europe that have been most successful in their own countries play one another, to find the best team in Europe 欧洲杯赛〔欧洲各国足球联赛前几名球队之间的比赛, 又称欧洲冠军杯赛〕: *How many times have Real Madrid won the European Cup?* 皇家马德里队获得过多少次欧洲杯赛冠军? **2** the cup given to the team that wins the competition 欧洲杯〔奖杯〕

European Cup·win·ners' Cup, the /ˌ····ˈ··ˌ··ˌ·/ a football competition held in the past that involved all the teams in Europe that won the cup final in their own country. Since 1998, these teams have entered the UEFA Cup instead. 欧洲优胜者杯赛〔过去欧洲各国足球杯赛冠军队之间进行的比赛。自1998年起, 这些球队开始参加欧洲联盟杯赛〕

European Cur·ren·cy Unit /ˌ····ˈ···ˌ·/ *n* [C] an ECU〔欧洲共同体的〕欧洲货币单位

European Ex·change Rate Mech·a·nis·m /ˌ····ˌ·ˌ··ˌ··/ *n* [singular] the ERM; a system for controlling the

EXCHANGE RATE between the money of the different countries of the European Union 欧洲汇率机制

European Mas·ters, the /ˌ···ˈ··/ an important GOLF competition that takes place in different European countries 欧洲高尔夫大师赛

European Mon·e·ta·ry Sys·tem /ˌ····ˈ····ˌ·/ *n* [singular] the EMS; a system for limiting how much the different currencies (CURRENCY (1)) of countries within the European Union can go up or down in value in relation to each other 欧洲货币体系〔限制在欧盟范围内不同货币彼此之间汇率升降幅度的体系〕

European O·pen, the /ˌ····ˈ··/ an important GOLF competition played in Europe by players from all over the world 欧洲高尔夫球公开赛: *Sandy Lyle finished second in the European Open.* 桑迪·莱尔在欧洲高尔夫球公开赛中获亚军。

European Par·lia·ment, the /ˌ····ˈ···/ a parliament whose members are elected by the citizens of the EU (=the European Union). Its members are called Euro MPs or MEPs. 欧洲议会〔由欧盟成员国公民选举产生的议会, 其议员称 Euro MP 或 MEP〕

European Space A·gen·cy, the /ˌ····ˈ·ˌ··/ abbreviation 缩写为 **the ESA** an organization formed in 1975 to manage Europe's space programme 欧洲航天局〔管理欧洲航天计划的一个机构, 成立于 1975 年〕

European Su·per Cup /ˈ····ˈ···/ a football match, officially called the UEFA Super Cup, played each year between the winners of the European Cup and the UEFA Cup 欧洲超级杯赛〔正式名称为欧洲足联超级杯赛, 指欧冠的冠军队与欧洲联盟杯冠军队之间的足球比赛〕

European U·nion /ˌ····ˈ··/ *n* [singular] a European political and economic organization that encourages trade and friendship between the countries that are members 欧洲联盟〔欧盟的全称〕

Eu·ro·star /ˈjuroˌstɑr; ˈjʊərəʊˌstɑː/ *trademark* the railway service between London and France or Belgium, using the TUNNEL under the English Channel【商标】欧洲之星〔取道英吉利海底隧道, 通行于伦敦与法国或比利时之间的高速列车〕: *You can get to Paris by Eurostar in only 3 hours.* 乘坐欧洲之星去巴黎只要三小时。—compare 比较 LE SHUTTLE

Eu·ro·vi·sion Song Con·test, the /ˌjurovɪʒən ˈsɔŋ ˌkɑntest; ˌjʊərəʊvɪʒən ˈsɒŋ ˌkɒntest/ a competition shown on television each year, in which singers or groups of singers representing European countries sing specially written songs, and judges vote for the song which they think is the best 欧洲歌曲电视大奖赛〔一年一度的歌曲电视比赛。欧洲各国的歌手或演唱组合代表本国演唱专门创作的歌曲, 评委投票评出最佳歌曲〕

CULTURAL NOTE 文化注释

Some countries, such as Norway, are known for sometimes getting no points at all (often humorously called **nuls points**, because the points are read out in French as well as English). The Eurovision Song Contest is very popular, but many British people make jokes about it, and in the UK, Terry Wogan is known for his humorous COMMENTARY. 挪威等一些国家以有时一分不得而著称(因此常被幽默地称为 nuls points (零分), 因为比分是用英法两种语言播报的)。欧洲电视歌曲大奖赛很受欢迎, 但很多英国人拿它来开玩笑, 特里·沃根以其幽默的述评著称。

Euro-zone the group of European countries that use the EURO as a standard unit of money 欧元区〔以欧元为标准货币单位的欧洲国家〕: *trade among the countries of the Euro-zone* 欧元区各国之间的贸易

Eu·ry·di·ce /juˈrɪdɪsɪ; jʊəˈrɪdɪsi/ —see 见 ORPHEUS AND EURYDICE

Eu·sta·chian tube /jusˈteʃən ˌtub; juːˈsteɪʃən ˌtjuːb/ *n* [C] one of the pair of tubes that join your ears to your throat 耳咽管, 欧氏管〔连接咽喉与耳朵的管〕

eu·tha·na·si·a /ˌjuθəˈneʒə; ˌjuːθəˈneɪziə/ *n* [U] the painless killing of people who are very ill or very old in order to stop them suffering; MERCY KILLING 安乐死

e·vac·u·ate /ɪˈvækjuˌet; ɪˈvækjueɪt/ *v* **1** [T] to send people to a safe place from a dangerous place 撤离, 撤出: **evacuate sb from/to** *The villagers were evacuated to the countryside.* 村镇居民被撤到农村。**2** [I,T] to empty a place by making all the people leave 撤空〔某地〕, 让所有人撤离〔某地〕: *The whole building has been evacuated.* 整幢大楼里的人都已被疏散。**3** *formal* to empty your BOWELS【正式】大便 —**evacuation** /ɪˌvækjuˈeʃən; ɪˌvækjuˈeɪʃən/ *n* [C,U]

e·vac·u·ee /ɪˈvækjuˌi; ɪˌvækjuˈiː/ *n* [C] someone who is sent away from a place because it is dangerous, for example because there is a war 被撤离者, 被疏散者

e·vade /ɪˈved; ɪˈveɪd/ *v* [T] **1 evade the subject/question/issue etc** to avoid talking about something, especially because you are trying to hide something 回避主题/问题/议题等: *Stop trying to evade the issue.* 不要再试图回避这个问题了。**2** to find a way of not doing something you should do 逃避〔该做的事〕: **evade your responsibilities/duty/problems** *You can't go on evading your responsibilities forever.* 你不能永远都逃避责任。**3** to avoid doing something that you should do according to the law such as paying tax 规避, 逃避〔依法该做的事〕: *If you try to evade paying taxes you risk going to prison.* 如果你试图逃税, 你就有坐牢的危险。**4** to escape from someone who is trying to catch you 躲避〔某人的追捕〕: *Williams succeeded in evading capture for several days.* 威廉斯好几天都躲过了追捕。**5** *formal* if success, the truth etc evades you, you cannot achieve it or understand it【正式】难倒; 使困惑

e·val·u·ate /ɪˈvæljuˌet; ɪˈvæljueɪt/ *v* [T] to carefully consider something to see how useful or valuable it is 评估, 评价: *evaluating the success of the training scheme* 评估训练计划的成果

e·val·u·a·tion /ɪˌvæljuˈeʃən; ɪˌvæljuˈeɪʃən/ *n* [C,U] the act of considering something to decide how useful or valuable it is, or a document in which this is done 评估, 评价; 评估报告: *an intensive evaluation of the health care program* 对医疗保健制度深入仔细的评估 W3

e·van·gel·i·cal /ˌivænˈdʒɛlɪk]; ˌiːvænˈdʒelɪkəl◂/ *adj* **1** evangelical Christians believe that they should persuade as many people as possible to become Christians 福音传道者的, 基督教福音派的 **2** very eager to persuade people to accept your ideas and beliefs 狂热宣传自己的主张和信仰的: *Andrew talks about green issues with almost evangelical fervour.* 安德鲁谈到环保问题时近乎狂热。

e·van·ge·list /ɪˈvændʒəlɪst; ɪˈvændʒəlɪst/ *n* [C] **1** someone who travels around speaking at meetings to persuade people to become Christians 巡回布道者 **2 Evangelist** one of the four writers of the books in the Bible called the Gospels《圣经》福音书的四位作者之一 —**evangelism** /ɪˈvændʒəlɪzəm; ɪˈvændʒəlɪzəm/ *n* [U] —**evangelistic** /ɪˌvændʒəˈlɪstɪk; ɪˌvændʒəˈlɪstɪk◂/ *adj*

e·van·ge·lize also 又作 **-ise** *BrE*【英】/ɪˈvændʒəˌlaɪz; ɪˈvændʒəlaɪz/ *v* [I,T] to try to persuade people to become Christians 劝(人)皈依基督教

e·vap·o·rate /ɪˈvæpəˌret; ɪˈvæpəreɪt/ *v* **1** [I,T] if a liquid evaporates or if something evaporates it, it changes into steam (使)〔液体〕汽化, (使)蒸发 **2** [I] if a feeling evaporates, it slowly disappears〔感觉〕逐渐消逝: *Hopes of reaching an agreement are beginning to evaporate.* 达成协议的希望开始破灭。—**evaporation** /ɪˌvæpəˈreʃən; ɪˌvæpəˈreɪʃən/ *n* [U]

evaporated milk /ˌ····ˈ·/ *n* [U] milk which has been made thicker by removing some of the water 淡炼乳

e·va·sion /ɪˈveʒən; ɪˈveɪʒən/ *n* [C, U] **1** the act of avoiding doing something that you should do, or an example of this behaviour 回避; 逃避: *tax evasion* 逃税 **2** an act of deliberately avoiding talking about something or dealing with something 遁词; 借口: *His speech was full of lies and evasions.* 他的演讲充满了谎言和遁词。

e·va·sive /ɪˈvesɪv; ɪˈveɪsɪv/ *adj* **1** not willing to answer questions directly 模棱两可的, 推托的, 回避的: *Paul's being very evasive about the new contract.* 保罗对新合同含糊其辞。**2 evasive action** action to avoid being injured or harmed〔为免受伤害而采取的〕规避动作 —**evasively** *adv* —**evasiveness** *n* [U]

Eve the first woman, according to the Jewish, Christian, and Islamic religions. In the Old Testament of the Bible, Eve lived in the Garden of Eden with Adam, the first man, and persuaded him to eat a fruit which God had forbidden them to eat. 夏娃〔犹太教、基督教和伊斯兰教的女性始祖。《圣经·旧约》中, 她与男性始祖亚当住在伊甸园, 说服他偷吃了禁果〕

eve /iv; iːv/ *n* **1** [C usually singular 一般用单数] the night or day before an important religious day or holiday 前夕; 前一天: **Christmas Eve** (=24th December) 圣诞节前夕 | **New Year's Eve** (=31st December) 除夕 **2 the eve of** the time just before an important event〔重大事件的〕前夕, 前一刻: *on the eve of the election* 在选举前夕 **3** [C] *poetic* evening【诗】傍晚: *one summer's eve* 夏日傍晚

e·ven¹ /ˈivən; ˈiːvən/ *adv* **1** used to emphasize something that is unexpected or surprising in what you are saying 甚至; 即使: *Even the younger children enjoyed the concert.* 连较小的孩子也喜欢这场音乐会。| *We've all been naughty sometimes – even Mummy!* 我们都有顽皮的时候, 甚至妈妈也这样! | **not even** S1 W1

Henry's a strict vegetarian – he doesn't even eat cheese. 亨利是个严格的素食者 —— 甚至连干酪都不吃。| *I never even saw the kid until I hit him.* 我在撞到那个小孩前甚至都未曾看见他。**2 even bigger/better/brighter etc** used to emphasize that someone or something is bigger, better etc than before, or than someone or something else you have just mentioned〔比从前或刚才提到的其他人或事物〕更大/好/明亮等: *New Jet now washes even whiter.* 现在用新耶特洗得更干净。| *Diane knows even less about it than I do.* 关于此事黛安娜知道的甚至比我还少。**3** used to add a stronger, more exact word to what you are saying 甚至可以说; 更确切地说: *Molly looked depressed, even suicidal.* 莫莉看上去情绪低落, 甚至可以说是有些自杀倾向。| *The bride looked beautiful, radiant even.* 新娘非常漂亮, 更确切地说是光彩照人。**4 even so** *spoken* used to introduce something that is the opposite or very different from what you have been saying【口】即使如此, 即使这样: *I myself don't believe in ghosts. Even so, I wouldn't like to be alone in that room at night.* 我并不相信鬼神。即便如此, 我也不愿意夜里一个人待在那个房间里。**5 even if** no matter if 即便, 纵然: *Charlie's going to have problems finding a job even if she gets her A levels.* 即便查莉通过了高级程度考试, 她以后找工作也成问题。**6 even though** used to emphasize that although something happens or is true, something else also happens or is true 虽然, 尽管: *Even though they loved each other, they decided to part.* 他们虽爱对方, 但还是决定分手。| *I can still remember, even though it was so long ago.* 虽然这是很久以前的事, 我还是记得。**7 even now/then** in spite of what has happened, what you have done, or what is true 即使到这/那时; 即使这/那样: *I explained it all to him again, but even then he didn't understand.* 我又全部给他解释了一遍, 可即使那样他还是不懂。| *Even now I find it hard to believe her story.* 即使到现在我还是难以相信她的说法。**8 even as** used to emphasize that something happens at the same moment as something else 正当, 恰好在…时候: *I tried to phone her, but even as I was phoning she was leaving the building.* 我试图打电话给她, 但我打电话的时候, 她正离开大楼。| *Even as we watched the car skidded out of control.* 就在我们看着的时候, 汽车打滑失去了控制。

even² *adj*

1 ▶SURFACE 表面◀ completely flat with all parts at the same height 平的, 平坦的: *The floor must be completely even before we lay the tiles.* 先要把地面弄得十分平坦才能铺地砖。| *an even stretch of road* 一段平坦的道路

2 ▶NOT CHANGING 无变化◀ an even rate, temperature etc is steady and does not change much〔比率、温度等〕平稳的, 无大波动的: *We were travelling at an even speed.* 我们以匀速行驶。| *an even rhythm* 平稳的节奏

3 ▶DIVIDED EQUALLY 均分◀ divided equally, so that there is the same amount of something in each place, for each person etc 平分的, 均分的: *an even distribution of wealth* 财富均分

4 even number a number that can be divided exactly by two 偶数: *2, 4, 6 and 8 are even numbers.* 2, 4, 6, 8 是偶数。—opposite 反义词 **odd number** (ODD (6))

5 ▶COMPETITION 竞赛◀ having teams or competitors that are equally good so that everyone has a chance of winning 势均力敌的, 水平相当的: *This year's Superbowl was a very even contest.* 今年的超级碗赛两队水平非常接近。

6 ▶LINE OF THINGS 物品排列◀ regularly spaced and neat-looking 排列整齐的, 摆放均匀的: *even rows of gleaming white teeth* 两排整齐的闪亮洁白的牙齿

7 be even *informal* to no longer owe someone something, especially money【非正式】互不欠〔钱〕的, 两讫的: *If you give me $5 for the ticket, we'll be even.* 如果你给我5块钱票钱, 我们就两讫了。

8 have an even chance (of) to be just as likely to happen as to not happen 有一半机会…, …的可能性有一半: *Derek has an even chance of getting the job.* 德里克有一半的可能得到那份工作。

9 get even with *informal* to harm someone just as much as they have harmed you【非正式】对…进行〔同等〕报复; 以眼还眼, 以牙还牙: *He's not getting away with this, I'll get even with him one day.* 不能就这样放他过去, 总有一天我会找他算账。—compare 比较 UNEVEN —see also 另见 EVEN-TEMPERED, **break even** (BREAK¹ (9)) —**evenness** *n* [U]

even³ *v*

even out *phr v* [I,T] if two amounts, levels etc even out, or if you even them out, the differences between them become smaller (使)相等; (使)平均: *You have to wait until the water level in the pipes evens out.* 你得等一等, 直到每根管子中的水位一样高。| **even** sth ↔ **out** *They even out your payments over the whole year.* 他们将你的付款分摊到全年各个月。

even up *phr v* [T **even** sth ↔ **up**] to make a situation or competition more equal 拉平; 使平衡

even⁴ *n* [U] *poetic* evening【诗】傍晚

even-hand·ed /ˌ··ˈ··◂/ *adj* giving fair and equal treatment to everyone; IMPARTIAL 公正的; 不偏不倚的: *even-handed justice* 公正无私 —**even-handedly** *adv*

eve·ning¹ /ˈivnɪŋ; ˈiːvnɪŋ/ *n* **1** [C,U] the early part of the night between the end of the day and the time you go to bed 傍晚; 晚上: *We always go swimming on Friday evenings.* 周五晚上我们总是去游泳。| **in the evening** *Mick often goes to the pub in the evening.* 米克晚上常去酒吧。| **for the evening** *I'm going out for the evening.* 我今晚要出去。| **early/late evening** *It happened in the early evening, around half past six.* 事情发生在傍晚时分, 大约6点半左右。**2 a musical/poetry etc evening** an event involving music, poetry etc that takes place in the evening 音乐/诗歌等晚会 **3 the evening of your life** *literary* the last part of your life【文】晚年

evening² *interjection informal* used to greet someone when you meet them in the evening【非正式】晚上好: *Evening Joe, everything all right?* 晚上好, 乔, 一切都好吗?

evening class /ˈ·· ˌ·/ *n* [C] a course of study for adults in the evening〔成人参加的〕夜校, 夜间课程

evening dress /ˈ·· ˌ·/ *n* **1** [U] special clothes worn for formal meals, parties etc in the evening 晚礼服 **2** also 又作 **evening gown** *especially AmE*【尤美】[C] a dress worn by women to formal meals, parties etc in the evening 女士晚礼服

eve·nings /ˈivnɪŋz; ˈiːvnɪŋz/ *adv especially AmE* during the evening【尤美】在晚上: *I'm always at home evenings.* 晚上我一定在家。

Evening Stan·dard, The /ˌ·· ˈ··/ also 又作 **The Standard** a TABLOID newspaper sold in London in the afternoon from Monday to Friday《标准晚报》〔星期一至星期五下午在伦敦出售的一种小报〕

evening star /ˌ·· ˈ·/ *n* [singular] the PLANET Venus, seen as a bright star in the western sky in the evening 黄昏星〔指金星〕

e·ven·ly /ˈivənlɪ; ˈiːvənli/ *adv* **1** with equal amounts or numbers of something in every part of a particular area, or divided equally among a group of people 平均地, 均匀地: *Support for the Liberals is fairly evenly spread across the country.* 自由党的支持者在全国分布较平均。| *Spread the butter evenly over the toast.* 将黄油均匀地涂在烤面包上。**2** in a steady or regular way 平稳地; 有规律地: *breathing deeply and evenly* 呼吸又深又平稳 | **evenly spaced** *rows of evenly spaced desks* 一排排摆放整齐的桌子 **3** dealing with or affecting all parts of something in the same way 均匀地: *Cook the meat quickly for about 3 minutes, until evenly browned.* 将肉炒约三分钟, 直至其变成均匀褐色。**4 evenly matched** if two competitors are evenly matched, they have an equal chance of winning 势均力敌的: *The two wrestlers were very evenly matched.* 两名摔跤选手实力非常接近。**5** if you say something evenly, you say it in a calm way without getting angry or upset 心平气和地: *"You can do whatever you like," she said evenly.* "你想做什么就可以做什么。"她心平气和地说。

e·vens /ˈivənz; ˈiːvənz/ *adj technical* if the ODDS (=probability that a horse will win a race) of a horse in a race are evens, then it is equally likely that it will win or lose【术语】〔赛马〕输赢机会相等的: *Black Flag is the evens favourite.* 名为"黑旗"的赛马是热门, 赔率大约是一比一。

e·ven·song /ˈivənˌsɔŋ; ˈiːvənsɒŋ/ *n* [U] the evening religious ceremony in the Church of England〔英国国教的〕晚祷

e·vent /ɪˈvɛnt; ɪˈvent/ *n*

1 ▶INTERESTING/EXCITING 有趣的/令人兴奋的◀ [C] something that happens, especially something important, interesting or unusual〔尤指重要、有意思或不寻常的〕事件: *the most important events of 1994* 1994年最重大的事件 | *The article discusses the events which led up to the prime minister's resignation.* 这篇文章讨论了导致首相辞职的一系列事件。| **sequence of events** (=the order in which events happened) 事件发生的顺序 *reconstructing the sequence of events on the night of the murder* 再现谋杀案发当晚事件的全过程 | **course of events** (=the way that each event caused the next one, without being planned)〔未经计划的〕事件发展的过程 *Nothing you could have done would have changed the course of events.* 不管你曾做过什么, 也无法改变事件的进程。

2 ▶COMPETITION/PERFORMANCE/PARTY 竞赛/演出/聚会◀ [C] an important performance, sports competition, party etc which has been arranged for a particular date and time〔事先安排好的〕演出; 赛事; 聚会: *the biggest event of the racing season* 本赛季最大的一场赛事 | **social/sporting/fund-raising etc event**

The Christie Ball soon became the social event of the year. 克里斯蒂舞会很快就成了一年中最重大的社交活动。

3 ►IN A SPORTS COMPETITION 在体育比赛中◄ [C] any of the races, competitions etc arranged as part of a day's sports 运动项目: *The next event will be the 100 metres.* 下一个比赛项目将是100米跑。—see also 另见 FIELD EVENT, THREE-DAY EVENT

4 in any/either event also 又作 **at all events** used just before or after a statement to emphasize that it will happen in spite of anything else that may happen 不管是哪种情况, 无论如何: *I'll probably see you tomorrow but I'll phone in any event.* 我明天可能会与你见面, 但无论如何我都会给你打电话。

5 in the event used to emphasize what actually happened in a situation as opposed to what you thought might happen 结果, 到头来: *We were afraid he would be nervous on stage, but in the event he sang beautifully.* 我们担心他在台上会怯场, 结果他唱得好极了。

6 in the event of rain/fire/an accident etc also 又作 **in the event that** used to tell people what they should do or what will happen if something else happens 万一下雨/起火/发生意外等; 假若发生…的情况: *Britain agreed to support the US in the event of war.* 英国同意, 一旦发生战争将支持美国。

7 in the normal course of events if things happen in the normal way 如果一切正常: *In the normal course of events, John will inherit the money from his uncle.* 如果一切正常, 约翰将继承他叔叔的财产。

even-tem·pered /,.. '..◄/ *adj* not becoming angry easily; calm 性情平和的; 沉着的

e·vent·ful /ɪ'vɛntfəl; ɪ'ventfəl/ *adj* full of interesting or important events 充满大事的; 多变故的: *She's led quite an eventful life.* 她一生历尽沧桑。| *an eventful holiday* 不平凡的假期 —**eventfully** *adv*

e·ven·tide /'ivən,taɪd; 'iːvəntaɪd/ *n* [U] *poetic* evening【诗】傍晚

e·ven·tu·al /ɪ'vɛntʃuəl; ɪ'ventʃuəl/ *adj* [only before noun 仅用于名词前] happening or achieving something at the end of a process 最终发生的; 最后获得的: *Sweden were the eventual winners of the tournament.* 瑞典是锦标赛的最后赢家。| *the eventual outcome* 最后结果

e·ven·tu·al·i·ty /ɪ,vɛntʃu'æləti; ɪ,ventʃu'ælɪ̇ti/ *n* [C] *formal* a possible event or result, especially an unpleasant one【正式】可能发生的事件[结果]〔尤指不愉快的事件〕: *We must be prepared for every eventuality.* 我们必须作好应付各种情况的准备。

1 2 **e·ven·tu·al·ly** /ɪ'vɛntʃuəli; ɪ'ventʃuəli/ *adv* after a long time, especially after a long delay or a lot of problems 终于, 最终: *He worked so hard that eventually he made himself ill.* 他工作太努力, 最终病倒了。| *She eventually passed her driving test.* 她终于通过了驾照考试。| *"Did you manage to contact Roger?" "Well yes, eventually."* "你与罗杰联系上了吗?" "噢, 是的, 最终联系上了。"

e·ven·tu·ate /ɪ'vɛntʃu,et; ɪ'ventʃueɪt/ *v formal* to happen as a result of something【正式】终于发生; 因而发生

eventuate in sth *phr v* [T] *formal* to be the final cause of something【正式】最终导致: *The scandal finally eventuated in the resignation of the prime minister.* 该丑闻最终导致首相辞职。

1 1 **ev·er** /'ɛvɚ; 'evə/ *adv* **1** a word meaning at any time; used mostly in questions, negatives, comparisons, or sentences with 'if' 在任何时候〔一般用于疑问句、否定句、比较级和最高级或带 if 的句子中〕: *Nothing ever makes Ted angry.* 从来没有什么事情会使特德生气。| *"Do you ever get to the theatre?" "No, never."* "你有时会去看话剧吗?" "不, 从来不会。" | *I don't remember ever seeing him before.* 我不记得以前见过他。| *If you're ever in Seattle, come and see me.* 如果你到西雅图, 来看我吧。| **have you ever** *"Have you ever been to Paris?" "Yes, I have."* "你去过巴黎吗?" "是的, 我去过。" | *That's the biggest fish I've ever seen.* 那是我见过的最大的鱼。| **hotter/thinner/taller etc than ever** (=hotter, thinner etc than before) 比以前任何时候都热/瘦/高等 *It's colder than ever today.* 天气从没有像今天这样冷。| **as friendly/cheerful/boring etc as ever** (=as friendly, cheerful etc as in the past) 与往常一样友好/快活/烦人等 *Magda was pale and thin, but her eyes were as bright as ever.* 玛格达苍白消瘦, 但她的眼睛和往常一样明亮。| **hardly ever** (=almost never) 几乎从来不 *I hardly ever see Sara these days.* 最近我几乎没有见过莎拉。| **never ever** *spoken* (=used to emphasize that something has never happened or someone has never done something)【口】从不, 决不, 永不: *I never ever said anything like that!* 我从未说过那样的话! | **rarely, if ever** (=probably never) 几乎从不, 极少 *Brian rarely, if ever, gets to bed before 3 am.* 布赖恩难得在凌晨3点钟以前上床睡觉。| **if ever there was one** *spoken* (=used when saying that someone or something is a typical example of something)【口】非常典型〔用于强调某人或某物是典型〕*Joe's great, a real Northern comic if ever there was one.* 乔是个伟大的、真正的北方喜剧演员, 非常典型。**2** a word meaning always; used especially with expressions of time 总是〔尤用于表示时间的用语中〕: *Ever optimistic, Gemma decided to give him another chance.* 一向乐观的杰玛决定再给他一次机会。| *His company is making ever larger profits.* 他的公司的利润一直在增加。| **ever since** (=continuously since) 从那以后一直 *Paul came here for a holiday several years ago and he's been here ever since.* 保罗几年前来这里度假, 从那以后他就一直待在这个地方。| **for ever** *He said he would love her for ever.* 他说会永远爱她。| **for ever and ever** (=always, used especially in children's stories) 永远, 一直〔尤用于童话故事中〕| **happily ever after** (=used at the end of children's stories) 从此一直幸福地…〔用于童话故事的结尾〕*The prince and princess got married and lived happily ever after.* 王子和公主结了婚, 从此一直过着幸福的生活。| **as ever** *especially BrE* (=as usually happens)【尤英】同往常一样 *As ever, Kim refused to admit she was wrong.* 同往常一样, 金拒绝承认她犯了错误。| **ever-growing/ever-increasing/ever-present etc** (=always growing etc) 不断增长的/不断增加的/始终存在的等 *the ever-increasing problems of our inner cities* 我们旧城区不断增加的问题 **3 how/what/who etc ever** *BrE old-fashioned* used to add force to a question【英, 过时】究竟如何/什么/谁等〔用于加强问句的语气〕: *How ever shall we get there?* 我们到底怎样才能到达那里? | *Whatever are you doing?* 你到底在干什么? **4 did you ever!** *old-fashioned* used to show your surprise, disbelief etc【过时】你看到过[听到过]〔这种事〕吗: *Did you ever hear of such a thing!* 你听到过这种事吗! **5 ever so cold/wet/nice etc** *BrE spoken* very cold, wet etc【英口】非常冷/湿/好等: *The assistant was ever so helpful.* 这个助手帮了大忙。| *Thanks ever so much.* 非常感谢。**6 ever such a nice boy/cold day/pretty colour etc** *BrE* a very nice, cold etc person or thing【英】如此可爱的男孩/非常冷的一天/十分漂亮的颜色等: *You'll like her, she's ever such a nice girl.* 你会喜欢她的, 她是一个如此可爱的姑娘。**7 Was sb ever** *AmE spoken* used to add force to a statement【美口】非常〔用于加强语气〕: *Was he ever mad!* (=he was very angry) 他气疯了! **8 Yours ever/Ever yours** *informal* used at the end of a letter above the signature【非正式】你永远的朋友〔信尾签名前的套语〕**9 ever and anon** *poetical* from time to time【诗】时而, 不时地

Ev·e·rage /'ɛvərɪdʒ; 'evərɪdʒ/, **Dame Edna** —see 见 DAME EDNA

Ev·e·rest /'ɛvərɪst; 'evərɪ̇st/ also 又作 **Mount Everest**, **Qomolangma** the highest mountain in the world. Everest is in the Himalayas, on the border between China and Nepal. 珠穆朗玛峰〔世界最高峰, 位于中国与尼泊尔边界的喜马拉雅山〕

CULTURAL NOTE 文化注释

Everest was first climbed in 1953 by Sir Edmund Hillary, from New Zealand, and Tenzing Norgay, from Nepal, who were members of a British team. In recent years many people have climbed Everest, and some ENVIRONMENTALISTS (=people who are concerned about protecting the environment) are worried that the mountain is being damaged. People sometimes mention the name 'Everest' when they are talking about an extremely difficult achievement 首次登上珠穆朗玛峰是在1953年, 登山者是新西兰人埃德蒙·希拉里爵士和尼泊尔人丹增·诺尔盖, 他们当时是一支英国登山队的成员。近年来, 攀登珠穆朗玛峰的人很多, 一些环保主义者担心此山遭到破坏。有时该词指极难取得的成绩: *Cancer researchers have made some progress, but they still have an Everest to climb.* 癌症研究人员已经取得了一些进展, 但面前还有一座珠穆朗玛峰要攀登。

Ev·er·glades /'ɛvɚgledz; 'evəgleɪdz/ an area of low, wet, warm land in the US state of Florida, covering about 5,000 square miles. The Everglades, which is a National Park, is famous for its special plants and animals, especially ALLIGATORS. 大沼泽地〔位于美国佛罗里达州的低洼暖湿地带, 面积约为5000平方英里。大沼泽地为国家公园, 以特种动植物, 尤其是短吻鳄闻名〕

ev·er·green[1] /'ɛvɚ,grin; 'evəgriːn/ *n* [C] a tree or bush that does not lose its leaves in winter 常青树, 常绿树

evergreen[2] *adj* **1** an evergreen tree or bush does not lose its leaves in winter〔树木或灌木〕常青的, 常绿的 **2** an evergreen sportsman, singer etc is very good even though they are fairly old〔运动员、歌手等〕永葆青春的; 持久的; 经久不衰的: *the evergreen Perry Como* 事业常青的〔美国歌手〕佩里·科摩

ev·er·last·ing /ˌɛvɚˈlæstɪŋ; ˌevəˈlɑːstɪŋ◂/ *adj* a word used especially in religious writing, meaning continuing to exist for ever; ETERNAL (1) 永久的, 永恒的〔尤用于宗教文章中〕: *life everlasting* 永生 | *the Buddhist's search for everlasting peace* 佛教徒对永恒宁静的追寻 —**everlastingly** *adv*

ev·er·more /ˌɛvɚˈmɔr; ˌevəˈmɔː/ *adv* **for evermore** *literary* if you do something for evermore you continue to do it for ever【文】永远, 始终: *I will love you for evermore.* 我将永远爱你。

Ev·er·ton /ˈɛvɚtn̩; ˈevətən/ one of the two main football teams in the city of Liverpool in northwest England 埃弗顿队〔英格兰西北部城市利物浦的两支主要足球队之一〕

ev·ery /ˈɛvrɪ; ˈevri/ *determiner* **1** each one of a group of things or people that make a group or set 每个, 所有的: *Every student has to fill in a questionnaire.* (=all the students) 每个学生都得填写一份问卷。| **every single** *Unfortunately the President disagreed with every single thing his aides said.* 不幸的是, 总统对助手们所说的每一件事都不同意。**2** used to emphasize that you are talking about the whole of something 全部, 整体〔用于强调〕: *Victor ate every bit of his meal.* 维克托把饭菜全吃光了。| *What a wonderful movie! I enjoyed every minute of it.* 多棒的一部电影!我觉得每一分钟都很精彩。| **every word** (=everything someone says or writes) 每一句话 *I know every word of his songs by heart.* 我对他的歌中的每一句歌词都了然于胸。**3 every time** each time; WHENEVER (1) 每次; 无论何时: *Every time I see him, he looks miserable.* 每次我看见他, 他都是一副愁眉苦脸的样子。**4 every day/every 3 weeks/every 10 years etc** used to say that something happens at regular periods of time, after a certain distance etc 每天/每三个星期/每十年等〔用于表示事物按一定的时间或距离间隔发生〕: *Richard visits his mother every week.* 理查德每周都去看望妈妈。| *You should change the oil every 5,000 miles.* 你应该每行5000英里换一次机油。| *Freda had to stop to rest every hundred yards or so.* 弗雷达不得不每走一百码左右就停下来休息一次。**5 one in every hundred/two in every thousand etc** used when saying how often something affects a particular group of people or things 每百个中的一个/每千个中两个等: *Thirty children in every hundred born in Mali will die before the age of five.* 马里儿童每百人中有30个在5岁前夭折。**6 in every way** in all ways 在各个方面, 在所有方面: *My new job's better than my old one in every way.* 我的新工作在各方面都比旧工作要好。**7 every other** the first, third, fifth etc or the second, fourth, sixth etc of things that can be counted 每隔一…: *Apply the ointment every other day.* 药膏每隔一天涂一次。| *I see Harold every other Friday.* 每隔一周的周五我都见到哈罗德。**8 every bit as** used when saying strongly that someone is just as good, important as someone else 完全同样地: *She was every bit as rude as her sister.* 她和她妹妹一样无礼。**9 every Tom, Dick, and Harry** *spoken* an expression meaning everyone or anyone used especially when talking about people you don't approve of【口】所有人; 任何人〔尤指说话者不满意的人〕: *She didn't want every Tom, Dick, and Harry knowing about her private affairs.* 她不想让张三李四等不相干的人知道她的私事。**10 every hope/chance/reason etc** as much hope, chance, reason etc as possible 一切希望; 所有机会; 充分理由: *There is every chance that you will succeed.* (=you probably will) 你完全有机会取得成功。| *We have every reason to believe that Hodges is telling the truth.* 我们有充分理由相信霍奇斯讲的是真话。| *The airline takes every possible precaution to ensure the safety of its passengers.* 航空公司采取一切可能措施确保旅客的安全。**11 every last drop/bit/scrap etc** *informal* every single drop, piece etc【非正式】每一滴/点/片等: *Robert had to pick up every last bit of paper from the floor.* 罗伯特不得不把地上的所有纸屑都捡起来。**12 every now and then/again** also 又作 **every so often** sometimes but not often 偶尔, 有时: *I still see her every now and then.* 我仍偶尔能看见她。**13 every which way** *AmE informal* in every direction【美, 非正式】朝各个方向: *The rain came down and the crowd in the field ran every which way.* 下雨了, 田里的人四散避雨。—see 见 EACH[1] (USAGE)

USAGE NOTE 用法说明: EVERY

SPELLING 拼法

Everyone written as one word is only used about people and can never be followed by **of**. **Every one** can be used about anything and is always used with an *of* phrase either stated or suggested. 写作单词的 everyone 仅用于人, 后面不能接 of; every one 可用于表示人或物, 后面总是跟 of 短语, 有时 of 短语省略: *Every one of your tires needs replacing.* 你汽车的所有轮胎都需要换了。| *There are five thousand people living here and almost every one (of them) has their own car* (=every one of the group mentioned has a car). 有5000人居住在这儿, 几乎每个人都有汽车。

Everybody is written as one word. **Every body** would mean 'every dead body'. everybody 是一个单词; 分开写成 every body 意为"每一具尸体"。

Every day is spelled as two words as an adverb but only one word as an adjective. every day 用作副词, 如果合在一起写成 everyday, 就变成了形容词: *She swims every day.* 她每天游泳。| *the everyday life of Scottish Highlanders* 苏格兰高地人的日常生活。Note that you never say **every days**. 注意, 永远不要说 every days。

Everything and **everywhere** are single words; **every time** is two words. everything 和 everywhere 都是单词, 而 every time 由两个单词组成。

ev·ery·bod·y /ˈɛvrɪˌbɑdɪ; ˈevribɒdi/ *pron* everyone 每个人, 人人

ev·ery·day /ˈɛvrɪˈde; ˈevrideɪ/ *adj* [only before noun 仅用于名词前] ordinary, usual, or happening every day 日常的; 通常的; 每天的: *The book is written in simple everyday language.* 这本书用简单的日常用语写成。| **everyday life** *Stress is just part of everyday life.* 压力是日常生活的一部分。

Ev·ery·man /ˈɛvrɪˌmæn; ˈevrimæn/ *n* [singular] *literary* a typical, ordinary person【文】普通人, 凡夫俗子: *This character is a symbol for Everyman.* 这个角色是普通人的代表。

ev·ery·one /ˈɛvrɪˌwʌn; ˈevriwʌn/ *pron* every person; everybody 每个人, 人人: *If everyone is ready, I'll begin.* 如果大家都准备好了, 我就开始。| *They gave a prize to everyone who passed the exam.* 他们给每个考试及格的人发了奖。| *Has everyone finished their drinks?* 大家都把酒喝光了吗? | *The canteen's almost empty. Where is everyone?* (=the people who are usually here) 食堂几乎没有人, 人都去哪儿了? | **everyone else** (=all the other people) 所有其他人 *I usually stay up after everyone else has gone to bed.* 在别人都上床睡觉后, 我一般仍不休息。| **everyone but Ann/Mark/me etc** (=all of the people except Ann, Mark etc) 除安/马克/我等之外的所有人 *Everyone but Peter got there on time.* 除了彼得, 所有人都准时到达那里。—see 见 EACH[1] (USAGE)

ev·ery·place /ˈɛvrɪˌples; ˈevripleɪs/ *adv AmE* in, at, or to every place; everywhere【美】在各个地方; 到各个地方; 处处

ev·ery·thing /ˈɛvrɪˌθɪŋ; ˈevriθɪŋ/ *pron* **1** each thing or all things 每件事物; 所有事物: *Everything is ready for the party.* 聚会的准备工作已全部就绪。| *I've forgotten everything I learned at school.* 学校里学的东西我全忘光了。| **everything else** (=all the other things) 其他所有事物 *There's only bread left; they've eaten everything else.* 只剩面包了, 他们吃光了其余所有东西。**2** used when talking in general about your life or about a situation 一切, 所有事物: *I'm OK – how's everything with you?* 我还行, 你一切都好吗? | *Everything's much better now we're allowed to work at home.* 现在我们可以在家工作, 一切都好多了。**3 be/mean everything (to sb)** to be the thing that is most important to you and that you care about the most (对某人来说)是/意味着最重要的: *Money isn't everything.* 金钱不是最重要的。| *Her daughter means everything to her now.* 现在女儿对她来说比什么都重要。**4 and everything** *spoken* and so on【口】等等, 以及其他: *Tina's worried about her work and everything.* 蒂娜担心她的工作以及其他情况。**5 have everything going for you** to have all the qualities that are likely to give you an advantage over other people and make you succeed 拥有一切有利条件: *You shouldn't worry so much – you've got everything going for you.* 你不必这么担心, 一切都对你有利。**6 everything but the kitchen sink** *informal* all the equipment that you need and also a lot of things that you do not need【非正式】需要的一切设备和许多不需要的东西: *"What's he got in that bag?" "Everything but the kitchen sink!"* "他那个包里装着什么?" "什么都有!"

ev·ery·where /ˈɛvrɪˌhwɛr; ˈevriweə/ also 又作 **everyplace** *AmE*【美】*adv* **1** in, at, or to every place 在各个地方; 到各个地方; 处处: *I've looked everywhere but I can't find it.* 我到处都找过了, 但就是找不到。| *His dog used to follow him everywhere.* 过去他走到哪里, 他的狗就跟到哪里。| *It must have rained overnight – there are puddles everywhere.* 夜里一定下过雨, 到处都是小水洼。| **everywhere else** (=in, at, or to every other place) 在其他所有地方; 到其他所有地方 *It must be in here – I've looked everywhere else.* 它一定在这里, 别的地方我都找过了。**2 be everywhere** to be very common 非常普遍, 到处都是: *Girls with long straight hair were everywhere in the 1960s.* 在20世纪60年代, 到处可见留着长长直发的女孩子。

e·vict /ɪˋvɪkt; ɪˈvɪkt/ *v* [T] to legally force someone to leave the house they are living in〔依法从房屋里〕驱逐, 赶走: *We were evicted for non-payment of rent.* 我们未付房租, 被赶出来了。—**eviction** /ɪˋvɪkʃən; ɪˈvɪkʃən/ *n* [C,U]

[3] [1] **ev·i·dence¹** /ˋɛvədəns; ˈevɨdəns/ *n* **1** [U] facts, objects, or signs that make you believe that something exists or is true 证据, 证明: [+of/for] *evidence of life on other planets* 其他行星上有生命的证据 | **evidence that** *There's some evidence that a small amount of alcohol is good for you.* 有证据显示, 少量饮酒有益健康。| **medical/scientific/archaeological etc evidence** *Medical evidence shows that men are more likely to have heart attacks than women.* 医学证据表明男人比女人更容易患心脏病。| **not a shred of evidence** (=no evidence at all) 毫无依据, 没有任何证据 *There is not a shred of evidence in support of these outrageous claims.* 这些蛮横的说法毫无根据。**2** [U] information given in a court of law in order to prove that someone is guilty〔法庭上证明某人有罪的〕证据; 证词: *Murrow's evidence was enough to convict Hayes of murder.* 默罗的证词足以证明海斯犯了谋杀罪。| **give evidence** *Carol was called upon to give evidence.* 卡罗尔被传唤出庭作证。**3 be in evidence** *formal* to be present and easily seen or noticed【正式】显眼, 引人瞩目: *The army is more in evidence in the cities than in rural areas.* 军队在城市中比在乡村里更显眼。—see also 另见 KING'S EVIDENCE, QUEEN'S EVIDENCE, STATE'S EVIDENCE

evidence² *v* [T usually passive 一般用被动态] *formal* to show that something exists or is true【正式】证明: *The volcano is still active, as evidenced by the recent eruption.* 最近的爆发证明, 这座火山依然活跃。

[3] **ev·i·dent** /ˋɛvədənt; ˈevɨdənt/ *adj* easily noticed or understood; OBVIOUS 明显的; 明白的: *Bob began eating his lunch with evident enjoyment.* 鲍勃开始吃午餐, 显得津津有味。| **it is evident that** *From the look on Joe's face it was evident that the news came as a complete shock.* 从乔的表情可以明显看出, 他被这个消息惊呆了。—see also 另见 SELF-EVIDENT

ev·i·dent·ly /ˋɛvədəntlɪ; ˈevɨdəntli/ *adv* **1** [sentence adverb 句子副词] used when saying that something seems likely, based on the information that you have 从现有证据来看, 看来: *Evidently she's been bullied at work and is very unhappy.* 看来她在工作中被欺侮了, 非常难过。**2** [+adj/adv] in a way that is very easy to see and understand 显然, 明显地: *Mary was evidently upset when she heard about Irene's death.* 听到艾琳的死讯, 玛丽显然十分难过。

[3] **e·vil¹** /ˋivḷ; ˈiːvəl/ *adj* **1** someone who is evil deliberately does very cruel things to harm other people 邪恶的; 危害他人的: *an evil dictator responsible for the deaths of millions* 应为几百万人的死亡负责的邪恶独裁者 | *An evil glint came into her eye when she picked up the knife.* 当她拾起刀时, 眼中闪过一丝恶毒的光。**2** very unpleasant 令人极不舒服的: *There's an evil smell coming from the drains.* 排水沟发出很难闻的气味。**3** connected with the Devil or having special powers to harm people 恶魔的; 有害人魔力的: *evil spirits* 恶鬼 **4** having a very harmful influence on people 造成巨大伤害的, 带来很坏影响的: *the evil effects of materialism* 物质主义的恶劣影响 **5 the evil eye** the power, which some people believe exists, to harm people by looking at them〔据说可以伤害人的〕邪毒眼光: *traditional symbols to ward off the evil eye* (阻挡邪毒眼光的) 避邪符号 **6 the evil hour/day etc** a time when you expect something unpleasant or difficult to happen 不祥的时刻; 倒霉的时候: *the evil hour when he would have to face his uncle's anger* 他不得不面对叔叔发脾气的不幸时刻 —**evilly** *adv*

evil² *n* **1** [C] a very harmful or unpleasant influence or effect 极坏影响[后果]: *the evils of capitalism* 资本主义的种种祸害 **2** [U] a powerful force that makes people behave in a cruel way, or wicked behaviour in general 邪恶; 恶行: *the eternal struggle between good and evil* 善与恶的永恒斗争 —see also 另见 **the lesser of two evils** (LESSER (2)), **necessary evil** (NECESSARY¹ (3))

evil-do·er /ˌ‥ˈ‥/ *n* [C] *old-fashioned* someone who does evil things【过时】恶人, 坏人

e·vince /ɪˋvɪns; ɪˈvɪns/ *v* [T] *formal* to show a feeling or quality very clearly in what you do or say【正式】〔行为或言语〕表明, 表露: *His remarks evinced a strong interest in my daughter's financial position.* 他的话表明他对我女儿的财政状况很感兴趣。

e·vis·ce·rate /ɪˋvɪsəˌret; ɪˈvɪsəreɪt/ *v* [T] *formal or technical* to cut the BOWELs or other organs out of a body【正式或术语】从…切除肠子; 从…切除内脏

e·voc·a·tive /ɪˋvɑkətɪv; ɪˈvɒkətɪv/ *adj* making people remember something by producing a feeling or memory in them 使想起〔某事〕的; 唤起记忆的: [+of] *a huge scrubbed kitchen evocative of the sun and bright colours of Provence* 一个宽敞而擦洗干净的厨房, 让人想起普罗旺斯地区的太阳和明亮色彩

e·voke /ɪˋvok; ɪˈvəʊk/ *v* [T] to produce a strong feeling or memory in someone 引起, 唤起〔某人强烈的感情或回忆〕: *a stage set intended to evoke the mood of a brothel* 意图让人产生妓院感觉的舞台布景 —**evocation** /ˌɛvoˋkeʃən; ˌevəˈkeɪʃən/ *n* [C,U]

ev·o·lu·tion /ˌɛvəˋluʃən; ˌiːvəˈluːʃən/ *n* [U] **1** the scientific idea that plants and animals develop gradually from simpler to more complicated forms 进化(论) **2** the gradual change and development of an idea, situation, or object 演变, 逐步发展: *the evolution of the computer over the past 30 years* 过去30年计算机的发展 [3]

ev·o·lu·tion·a·ry /ˌɛvəˋluʃənˌɛrɪ; ˌiːvəˈluːʃənəri◂/ *adj* **1** connected with scientific evolution 进化的; 进化论的: *evolutionary biology* 进化生物学 **2** connected with gradual change and development 演变的, 逐步发展的: *an evolutionary process* 演化过程

e·volve /ɪˋvɑlv; ɪˈvɒlv/ *v* [I,T] to develop or make something develop by gradually changing (使) 逐步发展; (使) 逐渐演变: [+from/out of etc] *Darwin believed that we evolved from apes.* 达尔文认为人类是由猿进化而来的。| **evolve sth** *evolving a new management style* 形成新的管理风格

ewe /ju; juː/ *n* [C] a female sheep 母羊

ew·er /ˋjuə; ˈjuːə/ *n* [C] a large container for water used in the past〔过去使用的〕水罐, 大口水壶

ex /ɛks; eks/ *n* [C usually singular 一般用单数] *informal* someone's former wife, husband, GIRLFRIEND, or BOYFRIEND【非正式】前妻; 前夫; 前女友; 前男友: *Unfortunately, my ex showed up at the dance.* 不幸的是, 我的前妻出现在舞会上。

ex- /ɛks; eks/ *prefix* former and still living 以前的, 前任的〔仍然在世的〕: *my ex-wife* 我的前妻 | *an ex-England cricketer* 前英格兰板球运动员 —compare 比较 LATE¹ (7)

ex·a·cer·bate /ɪgˋzæsɚˌbet; ɪgˈzæsəbeɪt/ *v* [T] to make a bad situation worse 使恶化; 使加重: *Reilly's crass comments just exacerbated the tension.* 赖利的蠢话使局势更加紧张。—**exacerbation** /ɪgˌzæsɚˋbeʃən; ɪgˌzæsəˈbeɪʃən/ *n* [U]

ex·act¹ /ɪgˋzækt; ɪgˈzækt/ *adj* **1** correct and including all the necessary details 确切的, 精确的: *exact description of the assassin* 对刺客的精确描述 | *I don't know the exact terms of the agreement.* 我不知道该协议的确切条款。| **exact replica/copy etc** *They built an exact replica of the opera house in Naples.* 他们在那不勒斯仿照该歌剧院建造了一座一模一样的复制品。| **to be exact** *spoken* (=used when giving an exact answer, statement etc)【口】确切地说 *It was more than 20 years ago – to be exact!* 确切地说, 是在二十多年以前! **2 the exact colour/moment/type etc** used to emphasize how similar or close two things are 一样的颜色/时间/类型等: *the exact colour I was looking for* 正是我要找的那种颜色 | *He came into the room at the exact moment I mentioned his name.* 就在我提到他的名字时, 他进入了房间。**3** someone who is exact is very careful and thorough in what they do〔人〕严格的; 严谨的 **4 the exact opposite** someone or something that is as different as possible from another person or thing 正好相反: *Gina's the exact opposite of her sister in character.* 吉娜和她妹妹的性格完全相反。**5** an exact science is based on calculating and measuring things rather than on opinions, guessing etc〔科学〕严密的, 精密的 [3]

exact² *v* [T] *formal* to demand and get something from someone by using threats, force etc【正式】强要, 勒索: *exacting payment* 索款

ex·act·ing /ɪgˋzæktɪŋ; ɪgˈzæktɪŋ/ *adj* exacting work is hard and involves a high level of skill〔工作〕严格的, 要求高的: *exacting but stimulating work* 要求很高但激励人心的工作 | *exacting scrutiny of the texts* 对文本的严格审读 —**exactingly** *adv*

ex·act·i·tude /ɪgˋzæktəˌtjud; ɪgˈzæktɨtjuːd/ *n* [U] *formal* the state of being exact【正式】精确, 确切

ex·act·ly /ɪgˋzæktlɪ; ɪgˈzæktli/ *adv* **1** used to emphasize that a particular number, amount, or piece of information is completely correct 精确地, 确切地: *We were wearing exactly the same clothes.* 我们穿着一模一样的衣服。| *It's exactly half past five.* 一分不差正好5:30。| **exactly where/what/when etc** *Tell me exactly what he said.* 确切地告诉我他是怎么说的。| *Exactly where does Petra live?* 彼得拉到底住在哪里? **2** used to emphasize a statement 恰好, 正好〔用于加强语气〕: *He gave exactly the reply they wanted to hear.* 他的答复恰好是他们想听的。| *That's exactly what we've been trying to tell you.* 那正是我们一直想告诉你的。 [1] [2]

Frequencies of the adverb **exactly** in spoken and written English 副词 exactly 在英语口语和书面语中的使用频率

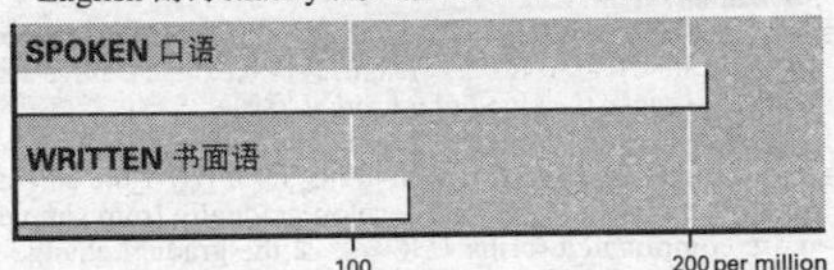

Based on the British National Corpus and the Longman Lancaster Corpus 据英国国家语料库和朗文兰开斯特语料库

This graph shows that the adverb **exactly** is much more common in spoken English than in written English. This is because it is used in some common spoken phrases. 本图表显示，副词 exactly 在英语口语中的使用频率远远高于书面语，因为一些常用的口语短语是由 exactly 构成的。

exactly (*adv*) **SPOKEN PHRASES** 含 exactly 的口语短语

3 exactly used as a reply to show that you think what someone has said is completely correct or true 正是，不错：*"So you think we should sell the house and move to the country?" "Exactly."* "这么说你认为我们应该卖掉房子搬到乡下去？""正是。" **4 not exactly a)** used as a reply to show that you think that what someone has said is not completely correct or true 不完全如此：*"You hate Lee, don't you?" "Not exactly. I just think he's a bit annoying that's all."* "你恨李，是不是？""不完全是这样，我只是觉得他有一点讨厌，仅此而已。" **b)** used when you say the opposite of what you mean, either as a humorous remark, or to show that you are annoyed 并不是，可不是〔表示幽默或厌烦〕：*Imagine calling me fat! I mean, she's not exactly thin herself, is she?* 居然说我胖！我的意思是，她自己并不见得瘦啊，不是吗？| *I wouldn't bother asking Dave, he's not exactly Einstein, is he?* 我不想问戴夫，他又不是爱因斯坦，对吧？**5 why/what/where etc exactly...?** used when asking someone to tell you the exact place, reason, thing etc 确切地说为什么/什么/何处等…：*Where exactly did you stay in Portugal?* 确切地说，你待在葡萄牙什么地方？**6 I don't know exactly/I don't exactly know** used to say that you are not sure about something 我不十分清楚：*"What does he want?" "I don't know exactly, but he said it's really urgent."* "他想要什么？""我不十分清楚，但他说真的很紧急。" **7 that's exactly what...** used to say that what someone has said, done etc is exactly the same as what you or another person said, did etc 那恰恰是…：*"I don't think he should leave his job." "That's exactly what I told him yesterday."* "我认为他不该离职。""我昨天也正是这样对他说的。"

ex·ag·ge·rate /ɪg`zædʒə,ret; ɪg'zædʒəreɪt/ *v* [I,T] to make something seem better, more important etc than it really is 夸张，言过其实：*Sue says she's seen Jurassic Park twenty times, but I'm sure she's exaggerating.* 休说《侏罗纪公园》她已看过20遍了，但我肯定她在夸张。| **exaggerate sth** *exaggerating the pain to get our sympathy* 夸大疼痛以博取我们的同情 | **greatly exaggerate** *The extent of the damage was greatly exaggerated by the press.* 损害程度被媒体极力夸大了。—**exaggeratedly** /ɪg`zædʒə,retɪdlɪ; ɪg'zædʒəreɪtɪ̣dli/ *adv*

ex·ag·ge·rat·ed /ɪg`zædʒəretɪd; ɪg'zædʒəreɪtɪ̣d/ *adj* **1** described as better, more important etc than is really true 夸大的，言过其实的：*exaggerated reports of the army's gains* 对军队战果的夸大报告 **2** an exaggerated sound or movement is emphasized to make people notice〔声音或动作〕强调的；夸张的；引人注目的：*exaggerated movements of his arms* 他手臂幅度很大的动作

ex·ag·ge·ra·tion /ɪg,zædʒə`reʃən; ɪg,zædʒə'reɪʃən/ *n* [C,U] a statement or way of saying something that makes something seem better, more important etc than it really is 夸张，夸大，言过其实：*I can say without exaggeration he's the best operator in the business.* 我可以毫不夸张地说，他是整个行业中最好的管理人员。| **it is no exaggeration** *It is no exaggeration to say your life will be changed forever.* 说你的生活将被永远改变，这一点也不夸张。

ex·alt /ɪg`zɔlt; ɪg'zɔːlt/ *v* [T] *formal*【正式】**1** to put someone or something into a high rank or position 提升，提拔 **2** to praise someone, especially God 赞扬；歌颂〔尤指歌颂上帝〕：*Exalt ye the Lord.* 赞美你，我的主！

ex·al·ta·tion /,ɪgzɔl`teʃən; ,egzɔːl'teɪʃən/ *n formal*【正式】**1** [C,U] a very strong feeling of happiness, power etc 异常兴奋；扬扬得意 **2** [U] the state of being put into a high rank or position 晋升，被提拔

ex·alt·ed /ɪg`zɔltɪd; ɪg'zɔːltɪ̣d/ *adj* **1** having a very high rank and highly respected 显贵的，高贵的：*I felt shy in such exalted company.* 我与如此显贵的人在一起，觉得不好意思。**2** *formal* filled with a great feeling of joy【正式】异常兴奋的，兴高采烈的

ex·am /ɪg`zæm; ɪg'zæm/ *n* [C] **1** a spoken or written test of knowledge, especially an important one 考试〔尤指重要考试〕：*How did you do in your exams?* 你考试考得怎么样？| *an oral exam* 口试 | **pass/fail an exam** (=succeed/not succeed) 考试通过/未通过 *Did you pass the exam?* 你考试通过了吗？| **chemistry/French etc exam** (=an exam in a particular subject) 化学/法语等科目的考试 | **take/sit an exam** *He failed his English exam and had to take it again.* 他英语考试不及格，只好再考一次。**2** *AmE* a set of medical tests【美】医学检查：*an eye exam* 眼睛检查 **3** *AmE* the paper on which the questions for an exam are written【美】考试卷：*Do not open your exams until I tell you.* 在未听到指令前请勿打开试卷。

ex·am·i·na·tion /ɪg,zæmə`neʃən; ɪg,zæmɪ̣'neɪʃən/ *n* **1** [C] *formal* a spoken or written test of knowledge【正式】考试：*The examination results will be announced in September.* 考试成绩将于9月公布。**2** [C,U] the process of looking at something carefully in order to see what it is like 检查，审查：*a detailed examination of population statistics* 对人口统计数字的详细审查 | **be under examination** *The proposals are still under examination.* 那些建议还在审查之中。| **on closer examination** *On closer examination the vases were seen to be cracked in several places.* 经细细检查发现，这些花瓶上有几处裂纹。**3** a set of medical tests 医学检查 **4** [C,U] the process of asking questions to get specific information, especially in a court of law 查问〔尤指法庭讯问〕—see also 另见 CROSS-EXAMINE

ex·am·ine /ɪg`zæmɪn; ɪg'zæmɪ̣n/ *v* [T] **1** to look at something carefully, in order to make a decision, find something, check something etc〔仔细地〕检查，审查：*After examining the evidence, I can find no truth in these claims.* 检查过证据后，我发现这些说法都不成立。| **examine sth for** *The police will have to examine the weapon for fingerprints.* 警察得检查凶器看有没有指纹。**2** if a doctor examines you, they look at your body to check that you are healthy 检查〔身体〕**3** *formal* to ask someone questions to test their knowledge of a subject【正式】考核，对…进行考试：**examine sb on** *You will be examined on American history.* 你将接受美国历史的考试。**4** *technical* to officially ask someone questions in a law court【术语】〔在法庭上〕查问，讯问

Frequencies of the verbs **examine, take/have a look at** and **inspect** in spoken and written English 动词（短语）examine, take/have a look at 和 inspect 在英语口语和书面语中的使用频率

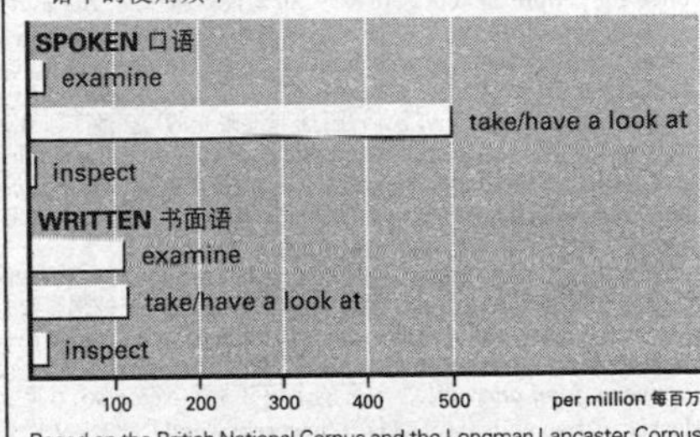

Based on the British National Corpus and the Longman Lancaster Corpus 据英国国家语料库和朗文兰开斯特语料库

This graph shows that the expressions **have a look at** and **take a look at** are much more common in spoken English than the words **examine** or **inspect**. This is because **have a look at** and **take a look at** are much more general than **examine** or **inspect**, which mean to look at something carefully in order to find out about it or check if it is satisfactory. They are more common in written English. 本图表显示，在英语口语中动词短语 have a look at 和 take a look at 的使用频率远远高于 examine 及 inspect，因为 have a look at 和 take a look at 的含义更广，而 examine 和 inspect 侧重于表示仔细检查某事物以找出信息或决定其是否令人满意，因此这两个词在书面语中更常用些。

ex·am·in·er /ɪgˋzæmɪnɚ; ɪgˈzæmɨnə/ *n* [C] someone from a university, college, or professional institution who tests students' knowledge or ability 考官，主考人

exam pa·per /·ˈ· ,··/ *n* [C] **1** *BrE* the paper on which the questions for an EXAM are written【英】考卷 **2** *AmE* the papers on which you write the answers to a test or exam【美】答题纸，答卷

S1 W1 **ex·am·ple** /ɪgˋzæmpḷ; ɪgˈzɑːmpəl/ *n* [C] **1 for example** used before mentioning a specific thing, person, place etc in order to explain what you mean or to support an argument 例如，举例来说：*Many countries, for example, Mexico and Japan, have a lot of earthquakes.* 许多国家，如墨西哥和日本，经常发生地震。| *Look at John, for example, now there's someone who's overcome his physical disabilities.* 例如约翰，就是一个已经战胜了自身残疾的人。**2** a thing, person, situation etc that you mention to show what you mean or to show that something is true 例子，例证：*The two examples on this page show the behaviour patterns of severely depressed patients.* 本页的两个例子显示了情绪极度低落的病人的行为方式。| **[+of]** *a wonderful example of High Gothic architecture* 全盛期哥特式建筑风格的极好实例 | **give an example** *I don't really understand what you mean, could you give me an example?* 我不大明白你的意思，你能举例说明一下吗？| **good example** (=example that shows something clearly)〔将事情说清楚的〕好例子；恰当的例子 | **classic/typical example** *a classic example of what not to do* 不当行为的典型实例 | **prime example** (=example of something you do not like or do not approve of)〔坏的〕典型，〔不好方面的〕代表 *Franco, a prime example of a man hungry for power* 佛朗哥，权欲熏心者的典型 **3 set an example** to behave in a sensible way so that other people will copy you 树立榜样：*It's my duty as an officer to set an example to the troops.* 作为军官，我有责任为士兵树立好榜样。**4 be an example to** if someone's behaviour is an example to you, it is so good that you should copy it 是…效仿的好榜样：*Her courage is an example to us all.* 她的勇气是我们所有人的榜样。**5 follow sb's example** to copy someone's behaviour yourself 效仿某人，学某人的样子：*I suggest you follow Rosie's example and start doing regular exercise.* 我建议你效仿罗西，经常锻炼身体。**6 make an example of** to punish someone so that other people are afraid to do the same thing 惩罚某人以警戒他人，杀鸡吓猴

This graph shows some of the words most commonly used with the noun **example**. 本图表所示为几个与名词example构成的最常见搭配词的使用频率。

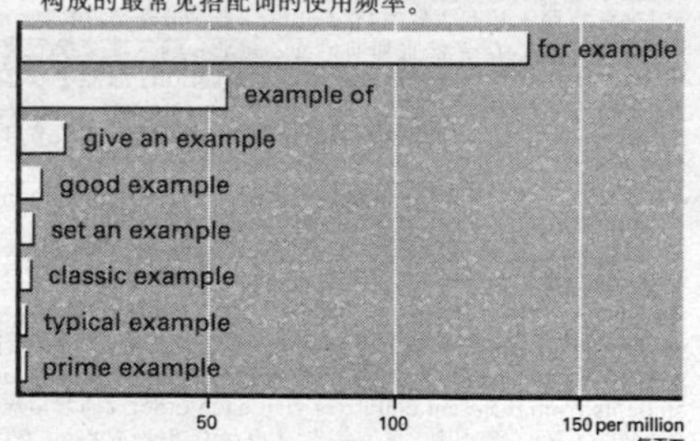

Based on the British National Corpus and the Longman Lancaster Corpus
据英国国家语料库和朗文兰开斯特语料库

examine 检查

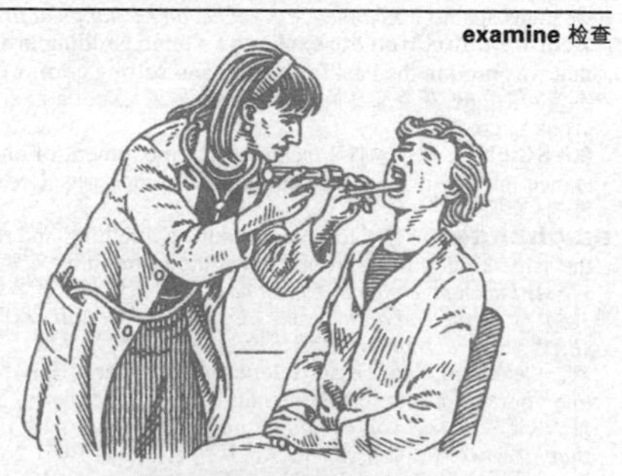

examining a patient 为病人做检查

ex·as·pe·rate /ɛgˋzæspə,ret; ɪgˈzɑːspəreɪt/ *v* [T usually passive 一般用被动态] to make someone very annoyed by continuing to do something that upsets them 使恼怒；使烦恼

ex·as·pe·rat·ed /ɛgˋzæspə,retɪd; ɪgˈzɑːspəreɪtɨd/ *adj* very annoyed and upset 恼怒的；极厌烦的：*He gave an exasperated snort.* 他恼怒地哼了一声。—**exasperatedly** *adv* —**exasperation** /ɪg,zæspəˋreʃən; ɪg,zɑːspəˈreɪʃən/ *n* [U]

ex·as·pe·rat·ing /ɪgˋzæspə,retɪŋ; ɪgˈzɑːspəreɪtɪŋ/ *adj* extremely annoying 令人极其厌烦的，使人恼怒的：*You have this exasperating habit of never looking at me!* 你从来不看我，我对你这个习惯十分不满！—**exasperatingly** *adv*

Ex·cal·i·bur /ɛkˋskælɪbɚ; ekˈskælɨbə/ the name of the SWORD belonging to King Arthur〔亚瑟王的〕神剑，石剑

ex·ca·vate /ˋɛkskə,vet; ˈekskəveɪt/ *v* [I,T] **1** to make a hole in the ground by digging up soil etc 挖掘；开凿 **2** discover something that was buried in the earth in an earlier time by digging for it 挖出；发掘：*Schliemann excavated the ancient city of Troy.* 谢里曼发掘出特洛伊古城。—**excavation** /,ɛkskəˋveʃən; ,ekskəˈveɪʃən/ *n* [C,U]

ex·ca·va·tor /ˋɛkskə,vetɚ; ˈekskəveɪtə/ *n* [C] **1** a large machine that digs and moves earth and soil 挖土机，电铲；STEAM SHOVEL *AmE*【美】**2** someone who digs to find things that have been buried under the ground for a long time 发掘者

ex·ceed /ɪkˋsid; ɪkˈsiːd/ *v* [T] **1** to be more than a number or amount, especially a fixed number 超过，超出〔尤指超过一固定值〕：*Working hours must not exceed 42 hours a week.* 工作时间每周不得超过42小时。**2** to go beyond an official or legal limit 超越〔政府或法律规定的范围〕：*He was fined for exceeding the speed limit.* 他因超速行驶而被罚款。 W3

E

ex·ceed·ing·ly /ɪkˋsidɪŋlɪ; ɪkˈsiːdɪŋli/ *adv* extremely 非常，极其：*I'd like to say thank you. You've been exceedingly kind.* 我想说声谢谢，你真是太好了。

ex·cel /ɪkˋsɛl; ɪkˈsel/ *v* **excelled, excelling** [I, not in progressive 不用进行时] to do something very well, or much better than most people 优于，擅长，胜过他人：**[+at/in]** *I never excelled at sport.* 我从来不擅长体育运动。| **excel yourself** (=do better than you usually do) 比平常做得好，超水平发挥 *Dinner was fantastic! Joe's really excelled himself this time.* 晚饭好吃极了！乔这顿饭做得特别出色。

ex·cel·lence /ˋɛksḷəns; ˈeksələns/ *n* [U] the quality of being excellent 卓越，杰出

Ex·cel·len·cy /ˋɛksḷənsɪ; ˈeksələnsi/ *n* **Your Excellency/His Excellency** a way of talking to or about people who hold high positions in the state or the church 阁下：*His Excellency the Spanish ambassador* 西班牙大使阁下

ex·cel·lent /ˋɛksḷənt; ˈeksələnt/ *adj* extremely good or of very high quality 卓越的；极好的：*Edward made an excellent speech.* 爱德华的演讲十分精彩。| *You've got some excellent CDs here.* 你这里有些非常棒的激光唱片。—**excellently** *adv* S1 W2

ex·cept¹ /ɪkˋsɛpt; ɪkˈsept/ *conjunction* **1 except for a)** apart from 除…之外：*Except for one old lady, the bus was empty.* 除了一位老妇人，公共汽车上没有别的乘客。| *The roads were clear except for a few cars.* 除了几辆汽车之外，马路上空荡荡的。**b) except for John/her/me etc** leaving out or not including John, her etc 除了约翰/她/我等之外：*The children are all asleep except for Lorna.* 除了洛娜，孩子们都睡着了。**c)** if someone or something had not happened or existed 要不是由于：*Nina would have left him years ago except for the children.* 要不是为了孩子们，尼娜几年前就离开他了。**2 except do sth** apart from doing something 除了做某事：*Tom does everything around the house except cook.* 除了做饭之外，屋里屋外的活汤姆都干。| *a computer that can do everything except talk* 除了不会讲话别的什么都能做的电脑 **3** *spoken* but【口】但是，只是：*I'd love to go, except it's too expensive.* 我很想去，但太贵了。| *It doesn't matter that I had to wait, except you did say four o'clock.* 我不介意等，但你讲好是4点钟。 S2 W2

except² *prep* used to introduce the only thing or person in a group about which a statement is not true 除…之外：*Everyone except Adam went to the concert.* 除了亚当，大家都去听音乐会了。| *You can have any of the cakes except this one.* 你可以拿任何一块蛋糕，但这块除外。| *We're open every day except Monday.* 除了周一，我们天天开门。| **[+in/to/up etc]** *I can take my vacation at any time except in August.* 我可以在8月之外的任何时间休假。| *Peter's not going anywhere except to work.* 彼得除了上班，哪儿也不去。| **[+(that)]** *The house was just as I left it except that everything was covered with dust.* 除了积满灰尘之外，这房子与我离开时没什么两样。| *I've got one exactly the same except it's silver.* 我有一个一模一样的，但我的是银的。| **[+what/how/why etc]** *I don't know anything about the*

case except what I read in the newspaper.* 除了在报纸上读到的报道之外，我对这个案子一无所知。| **except by doing sth** *You can't get credit except by making special arrangements with the management.* 不与管理部门作出特殊安排就得不到信贷。

except³ *v* [T+from] *formal* to not include something when you are talking about or considering a number or group of things【正式】把…排除在外，不计

ex·cept·ed /ɪk`sɛptɪd; ɪk'septɨd/ *adj* **Paul/football/biology excepted** used to say that you are not including a particular person, subject, or thing in a statement about something 除了保罗/足球/生物学之外: *We want every one at the meeting, David and Steven excepted of course.* 我们希望每个人都出席会议，当然戴维和史蒂文除外。| *History excepted, Peter has made good progress in all subjects this term.* 除了历史之外，彼得这学期所有学科都有很大进步。—see also 另见 **present company excepted** (PRESENT¹ (5))

ex·cept·ing /ɪk`sɛptɪŋ; ɪk'septɪŋ/ *prep* used to introduce the only thing or person in a group about which a statement is not true 除…之外: *O'Rourke answered all the questions excepting the last one.* 除了最后一个问题外，奥罗克回答了所有问题。| **always excepting** *Dogs are not allowed in here, always excepting guide dogs.* 狗不得入内，但导盲犬例外。

2 2 **ex·cep·tion** /ɪk`sɛpʃən; ɪk'sepʃən/ *n* [C,U] **1** something or someone that is not included in a rule, does not follow the expected pattern etc 例外，除外: *With one or two notable exceptions, there are few women conductors.* 除了一两个突出的例外，几乎没有女指挥。| **no exception** (=used to emphasize that a law or rule concerns someone or something) 无例外 *The law applies to all European countries, Britain is no exception.* 这项法律适用于所有欧洲国家，英国也不例外。| **minor exception** (=one that is not very important) 不太重要的例外 | **exception to a rule** *The spelling of this word is an interesting exception to the rule.* 这个单词的拼法是该规则一个有趣的例外。| **the exception that proves the rule** (=used to say that the fact that something is not true or does not exist in one situation emphasizes the fact that it is true or exists in general) 证明普通规律的例外〔虽然是例外，但反过来证明了一个普遍存在的规律或现象〕 *Most people here are very dedicated; I'm afraid Rhea's the exception that proves the rule.* 这里的大多数人都十分投入，恐怕雷亚是个例外，但也反过来证明了其他人的专注精神。**2 make an exception** used to say that on one particular occasion the normal rules or standards do not have to be obeyed 按例外处理，作为例外: *We don't usually give credit, but as you're a regular customer we'll make an exception this time.* 我们一般不赊账，但因为你是老顾客，这次我们就破个例。**3 take exception to sth** to be angry or upset because of something 因某事而生气[烦恼]: *Tom took great exception to my remark about Americans.* 汤姆对我有关美国人的评论极为不满。**4 without exception** used to say that something is true of all the people or things in a group 毫无例外: *Every type of plant, without exception, contains some kind of salt.* 所有植物都毫无例外地含有某种盐分。**5 with the exception of** used to introduce the only thing, person, or place about which a statement is not true 除…之外: *I think everyone, with the possible exception of Fauzi, will pass the exam.* 我想或许除了福齐之外，所有人都会通过考试。

ex·cep·tion·a·ble /ɪk`sɛpʃənəbḷ; ɪk'sepʃənəbəl/ *adj formal* making you feel offended and angry【正式】引起反感的；令人气愤的: *a highly exceptionable remark* 令人异常气愤的话

ex·cep·tion·al /ɪk`sɛpʃənḷ; ɪk'sepʃənəl/ *adj* **1** unusually good 非常好的，杰出的: *Richard is an exceptional student.* 理查德是个出类拔萃的学生。| *exceptional bravery* 非凡的勇气 **2** unusual and likely not to happen often 罕见的，不寻常的: *This is an exceptional case; I've never seen anything like it before.* 这是一个不寻常的案例，我从没见过这样的事。| **in exceptional circumstances** *Promotion in the first year is only given in exceptional circumstances.* 只有在特殊情况下，第一年才会得到提升。

ex·cep·tion·al·ly /ɪk`sɛpʃənḷɪ; ɪk'sepʃənəli/ *adv* [+adj/adv] used to emphasize a quality that you are describing 特别，非常: *She defended her position exceptionally well.* 她出色地捍卫了自己的立场。| *an exceptionally talented player* 一名极有天分的选手

ex·cerpt /`ɛksɝpt; 'eksɜːpt/ *n* [C+from] a short piece taken from a book, poem, piece of music etc〔书籍、诗歌、音乐等的〕摘录，节录

ex·cess¹ /ɪk`sɛs; ɪk'ses/ *n* **1** [singular, U] a larger amount of something than is allowed or needed 过多，过量: *Scrape any excess off with a spatula.* 用铲子将多余的部分刮去。| **an excess of** *It was an excess of enthusiasm that caused the problem.* 是过度热情导致了问题。**2 in excess of** more than a particular amount 超过，多于: *The car reached speeds in excess of 100 miles per hour.* 这辆汽车的时速超过了100英里。**3 do sth to excess** to do something too much or too often, so that it may harm you 做某事过度[过分]: *Drinking is OK as long as you don't do it to excess.* 饮酒可以，但不要过量。**4 excesses** [plural] harmful or thoughtless actions that are socially or morally unacceptable 过分的行为；过激行为: *The government was unable to curb the excesses of the secret police.* 政府无法约束秘密警察过分的行为。**5** [U] behaviour which is not acceptable because it is too harmful or extreme 有害的行为；极端行径: *The minister preached a long sermon against the dangers of excess.* 牧师长篇布道，告诫极端行为的危害。

ex·cess² /`ɛksɛs; 'ekses/ *adj* [only before noun 仅用于名词前] **1** additional and not wanted or needed because there is already enough of something 过多的，不要的: *Cut any excess fat from the meat.* 将肉中不要的肥肉切掉。**2 excess baggage/luggage** bags or cases that weigh more than the legal limit that you can take on a plane〔超过航班免费承运范围的〕超重行李

ex·ces·sive /ɪk`sɛsɪv; ɪk'sesɪv/ *adj* much more than is reasonable or necessary 过度的；过多的: *Boyd's wife left him because of his excessive drinking.* 博伊德的妻子因为他酗酒而离开了他。| *$15 for two cokes seems a little excessive.* 两杯可乐就要15美元，似乎有点过分。

ex·change¹ /ɪks`tʃendʒ; ɪks'tʃeɪndʒ/ *n* 3 1

1 ►GIVING/RECEIVING 给予/接受◄ [C,U] the act of exchanging one thing for another or doing something to someone at the same time as they do it to you 交换，互换: *an exchange of political prisoners* 互换政治犯 | *an honest exchange of information* 坦诚的信息交换 | **fair exchange** (=an exchange in which the things given and received are of equal value) 公平的交换，等价交换 *Four of my cassettes for your Madonna CD is a fair exchange.* 我用四盒磁带换你的麦当娜激光唱片很公平。—see also 另见 PART-EXCHANGE

2 in exchange if you do or give something in exchange for something else, you do it or give it in order to get that thing 作为交换: *They have offered to release the hostages, but what do they want in exchange?* 他们提出可以释放人质，但他们想要什么作为交换？| [+for] *I've offered to paint the kitchen in exchange for a week's accommodation.* 我提出愿意粉刷厨房，条件是让我免费住一周。

3 ►ARGUMENT 争论◄ [C] a short conversation, usually between two people who are angry with each other 短时间的交谈〔通常指两人相互生气时〕: *a quiet exchange between the judge and the clerk* 法官和书记员之间平心静气地交换意见 | **heated exchange** (=a very angry conversation) 激烈争吵 *The DJ was fired after a heated exchange on air with a call-in listener.* 在和一名打进电话的收听者大吵一顿之后，音乐节目主持人被解雇了。

4 ►MONEY 钱◄ [U] **a)** a process in which you change money from one CURRENCY to another〔货币的〕兑换: *Most capital cities have extensive exchange facilities.* 大部分首都城市都有大量外汇兑换处。**b)** [C] the EXCHANGE RATE 汇率，兑换率

5 ►BETWEEN FAMILIES/SCHOOLS 家庭/学校间◄ [C] an arrangement in which someone changes their job, home etc with someone else usually for a short period of time, or in which students from different countries visit each other〔通常指短期的〕交换工作；交换住所；交换学生: *I'm only here for one term. I'm on an exchange with Dr Fisher.* 我只在这儿待一个学期，是与费希尔教授交换工作。

6 ►WAR 战争◄ [C,U] an event during a war when armies use weapons against each other 交火，交战: *an exchange of fire* 交火

7 corn/wool/cotton etc exchange a large building in a town, that was used in the past for buying and selling corn, wool etc 玉米/羊毛/棉花等交易所 —see also 另见 LABOUR EXCHANGE, STOCK EXCHANGE

8 ►SCIENCE 科学◄ [U] *technical* the movement of one substance into the place where another substance was【术语】〔物质的〕交换

ex·change² *v* [T] **1** to give someone something and receive the same kind of thing from them at the same time 交换，交易: *We still exchange gifts at Christmas.* 我们依然在圣诞节时交换礼物。| *At the end of the game players traditionally exchange shirts with each other.* 按照传统，比赛结束时两队队员互换球衣。| **exchange addresses/telephone numbers** (=give someone your address or telephone number and take theirs) 互换地址/电话号码 *Did you exchange phone numbers with the guy that hit you?* 你和那个撞你的家伙互换电话号码了吗？**2** to give someone something so that they will give you something that is better, more suitable, or more useful for you 调换〔指换取更

好、更适合或更有用的东西）: *The store will not exchange goods without a receipt.* 这家商店没有发票不予调换商品。| **exchange sth for** *Where can I exchange my dollars for pounds?* 我在哪可以用美元兑换英镑? **3** if two people exchange something, they do something to each other 相互做某事: **exchange looks/glances** (=look at each other) 对视/互瞥 *Sally and I exchange amused glances when we heard this.* 听到这话时，我与莎莉开心地交换了一下眼色。| **exchange greetings/insults** (=greet or insult each other) 互打招呼/相互谩骂 | **exchange words** (=talk to someone) 交谈 *Until this evening I had never so much as exchanged a word with him.* 在今天晚上之前，我甚至连一句话都未跟他说过。| **exchange blows** (=fight) 打架 *Students exchanged blows with locals, and police were called in.* 学生与当地居民打了起来，叫来了警察。**4 exchange information/ideas** if two people or a group of people exchange information, ideas etc they discuss something 交流信息/想法: *We envision an artistic community where people are free to exchange ideas.* 我们设想着一个人们可以自由交流思想的艺术团体。**5 exchange houses** to go and live in someone else's house while they come and live in yours, usually for a holiday〔通常指为度假〕交换住所: *We exchanged houses with an American family for three weeks.* 我们与一个美国家庭互换住处，住了三个星期。**6 exchange contracts** *especially BrE* to complete the final stage of buying a house by signing a contract with the person you are buying it from【尤英】〔与卖方签署并〕交换购房契约 —**exchangeable** *adj*

Exchange and Mart /ɪks,tʃendʒ ənd ˋmɑrt; ɪks,tʃeɪndʒ ənd ˈmɑːt/ *trademark* a British weekly magazine, which is made up of advertisements from people who want to sell things such as cars, musical instruments, or articles for the home【商标】《交易和市场》〔英国一周刊，刊登个人转让汽车、乐器或家庭用品的广告〕

exchange rate /ˌ·ˈ· ·/ *n* [C] the value of the money of one country compared to the money of another country 汇率，兑换率: *a more favourable exchange rate in the bank than in the hotel* 银行汇率高于酒店提供的汇率

exchange rate mech·a·nis·m /ˌ·ˈ· ·, ·ˌ··/ *n* [U] a system for controlling the exchange rate between the money of one country and that of another; ERM 汇率机制

Ex·cheq·uer, the /ɪksˈtʃɛkɚ; ɪksˈtʃekə/ *n* the British government department that is responsible for collecting taxes and paying out public money; TREASURY (1) 英国财政部

ex·cise¹ /ɪkˋsaɪz; ˈeksaɪz/ *n* [C,U] the government tax that is put on the goods that are produced and used inside a country 国内货物税; 消费税: *excises on gasoline and cigarettes* 汽油和香烟税 | **excise officer** (=someone who collects excise) 消费税税务官 | **excise duty** (=the money paid as excise) 消费税金 —see also 另见 CUSTOMS AND EXCISE

ex·cise² /ɪkˋsaɪz; ɪkˈsaɪz/ *v* [T] *formal* to remove or get rid of something, especially by cutting it out【正式】切除; 去除: *The tumour was excised.* 肿瘤被切除了。—**excision** /ɪkˋsɪʒən; ɪkˈsɪʒən/ *n* [C,U]

ex·ci·ta·ble /ɪkˋsaɪtəbḷ; ɪkˈsaɪtəbəl/ *adj* becoming excited too easily 易激动的: *A puppy is naturally affectionate and excitable.* 小狗生性亲热好动。—**excitability** /ɪk,saɪtəˋbɪlətɪ; ɪk,saɪtəˈbɪlɪ̣ti/ *n* [U]

ex·cite /ɪkˋsaɪt; ɪkˈsaɪt/ *v* [T] **1 excite interest/suspicion/jealousy etc** to make someone feel a particular emotion 引起[激起]兴趣/怀疑/忌妒等: *The court case has excited a lot of public interest.* 这场官司引起了公众的极大兴趣。**2 excite comment/rumour etc** if something excites comment etc, it makes people talk about it 引发评论/谣言等: *The book excited very little comment on this side of the Atlantic.* 这本书在大西洋这一边并未引起多大反响。**3** [not in progressive or passive 不用进行时或被动态] to make someone feel happy, interested, or hopeful because something good has happened or is going to happen 使兴奋，使激动: *His playing is technically brilliant, but it doesn't excite me.* 他的演奏技巧娴熟，但无法让我兴奋起来。**4** [not in progressive 不用进行时] to make someone feel nervous so that they cannot relax 刺激，使紧张: *The doctor warned us not to excite Douglas, who had been very ill.* 医生警告我们不要刺激道格拉斯，他的病很重。**5** to make someone feel sexual desire 使产生性欲 **6** *technical* to make an organ, nerve etc in your body react or increase its activity【术语】刺激〔身体某器官或神经等〕

ex·cit·ed /ɪkˋsaɪtɪd; ɪkˈsaɪtɪ̣d/ *adj* **1** happy, interested, or hopeful because something good has happened or will happen 兴奋的，激动的: *Steve's flying home tomorrow – we're all really excited.* 史蒂夫明天就坐飞机回家了，我们都非常激动。| *excited crowds of shoppers* 兴奋的购物人群 | **[+about]** *The kids are so excited about Christmas.* 要到圣诞节了，孩子们十分激动。| **[+by]** *We were all excited by the prospect of a party.* 想到要举行一场聚会，我们都很兴奋。| **[+at]** *He got very excited at finding such perfect specimens.* 能找到这样完美的标本，他感到异常高兴。| **get/feel/look etc excited** *Maria's starting to get pretty excited about the wedding.* 玛丽亚开始变得对婚礼十分热心。**2** very nervous and upset about something so that you cannot relax 紧张不安的: *When Thierry gets excited he starts to stutter.* 蒂里一紧张就口吃。| **[+about]** *There's no point getting excited about it. We can't change things.* 没必要紧张，我们改变不了什么。**3** feeling sexual desire 性冲动的，有性欲的 **4 nothing to get excited about** *spoken* used to say that a film, book etc is not very good or enjoyable and rather disappointing【口】〔电影、书等〕不带劲的，令人失望的: *Unfortunately Doyle's latest novel is nothing to get excited about.* 遗憾的是，多伊尔的新小说一点都不带劲儿。—**excitedly** *adv*: *Squirrels chattering excitedly in the branches above.* 松鼠在上面的树枝上吱吱叫个不休。

ex·cite·ment /ɪkˋsaɪtmənt; ɪkˈsaɪtmənt/ *n* **1** [U] the feeling of being excited 兴奋; 激动: *squeals of excitement* 因兴奋而发出的尖叫声 | **[+of]** *The new job held none of the excitement of her career in the police.* 与她原来的警察工作相比，新工作一点也不令人兴奋。| **[+at]** *their excitement at the discovery* 他们发现(某事物)时的兴奋心情 | *The news that Ms Street had eloped with Jean caused great excitement.* 斯特里特女士与琼私奔的消息引起一片哗然。| *his eyes shining with excitement* 他的目光闪烁着兴奋 | **in (sb's) excitement** *In my excitement, I had forgotten to turn off the taps.* 由于激动，我忘了关水龙头。| **mounting excitement** (=a feeling of excitement that increases) 越来越激动[兴奋] **2** [C] an exciting event or situation 令人兴奋的事[情况]: *I found it difficult to sleep after the excitements of the day.* 兴奋了一整天后，我发现晚上很难入睡。

ex·cit·ing /ɪkˋsaɪtɪŋ; ɪkˈsaɪtɪŋ/ *adj* making you feel excited 令人兴奋的; 使人激动的; 刺激的: *an exciting discovery* 激动人心的发现 | **find sth exciting** *Stuart found the atmosphere of the college enormously exciting.* 斯图尔特发现该大学的氛围很让人兴奋。—**excitingly** *adv*: *excitingly different band* 卓尔不群的乐队

ex·claim /ɪkˋsklem; ɪkˈskleɪm/ *v* [I,T] to say something suddenly and loudly because you are surprised, angry, or excited〔因惊讶、愤怒或兴奋而〕呼喊; 惊叫: *"Look at you!" she exclaimed when we came in, covered in mud.* 我们浑身是泥走进来，她惊呼道:"瞧瞧你们这样子!" | **[+at/over]** *They all exclaimed at his ignorance.* 他们都猛烈谴责他的无知。

ex·cla·ma·tion /ˌɛkskləˋmeʃən; ˌekskləˈmeɪʃən/ *n* [C] a sound, word, or short sentence that you say suddenly and loudly because you are surprised, excited, or angry 惊叫，呼喊: **[+of]** *horrified exclamations of disgust* 厌恶的惊叫

exclamation mark /ˌ·ˈ·· ·/ *BrE*【英】, **exclamation point** *AmE*【美】 *n* [C] the mark '!' that you write after a sentence or word that expresses surprise, anger, or excitement 感叹号，惊叹号 —see picture at 参见 PUNCTUATION MARK 图

ex·clude /ɪkˋsklud; ɪkˈskluːd/ *v* [T] **1** to deliberately not include something, especially a particular group of people or things〔故意〕不包括; 把…排除在外: *a special diet that excludes dairy products* 不包含奶制品的特别食谱 | **exclude sb/sth from sth** *If we exclude uncompleted projects from the calculations, the total spent is still more than $15 billion.* 即使我们在计算中除去未完成的项目，总支出还是超过150亿美元。| **specifically/explicitly exclude sth** *The provisions of the Act specifically excluded minors.* 这项法律的条款明确将未成年人排除在外。**2** to not allow someone to take part in something or not allow them to enter a place 不准…参与〔某事〕; 不准…进入: **exclude sb from (doing) sth** *navigation laws to exclude foreign vessels from trading in English ports* 禁止外国船只在英国港口进行交易的航海法 **3** to deliberately not pay attention to someone so that they feel lonely or unwanted 排斥〔某人〕; 不理睬〔某人〕: *We're not trying to exclude her, it's just that we have nothing in common with her.* 我们并非想排斥她，只是我们与她毫无共同语言。**4** to decide that something is not a possibility 认为…不可能; 排除…的可能性: *Social workers have excluded sexual abuse as a reason for the child's disappearance.* 社工人员排除了这个孩子失踪是因为遭受性虐待的可能性。| **exclude the possibility of/that** *At this stage we cannot entirely exclude the possibility of staff cuts.* 在这个阶段，我们不能完全排除裁员的可能性。—opposite 反义词 INCLUDE

ex·clud·ing /ɪkˋskludɪŋ; ɪkˈskluːdɪŋ/ *prep* a word meaning not including, used especially when you are making a list or calculating a total 不包括，除去: *Television is watched in 97 per cent of American homes (excluding Alaska and Hawaii).* 在美国，97%的家庭收看电视(不包括阿拉斯加和夏威夷两个州)。

E

ex·clu·sion /ɪk`skluʒən; ɪk'skluːʒən/ *n* [U] **1** a situation in which someone or something is not allowed to take part in an activity, be a member of an organization etc 被排除在外[被拒绝]的状态: *the country's exclusion from the United Nations* 该国被排除在联合国之外 **2 to the exclusion of** if you do something to the exclusion of something else, you only do the first thing and do not do the second thing at all 排除掉, 不涉及: *Your essays tend to concentrate on one theme to the exclusion of everything else.* 你的文章往往集中于一个主题, 而不提别的。**3 exclusion zone** an area that the government does not allow people to enter, because it is dangerous or because secret things happen there 禁区: *the military exclusion zone* 军事禁区

ex·clu·sive¹ /ɪk`sklusɪv; ɪk'skluːsɪv/ *adj* **1** exclusive places, organizations, clothes etc are so expensive that not many people can afford to use or buy them 高级的; 昂贵的: *Bel Air is an exclusive suburb of Los Angeles.* 贝莱尔是洛杉矶郊外一处高级住宅区。| *an exclusive girls' school* 贵族女子学校 **2** available only to particular people, so that only they can have, do, or use something 独有的; 独做的; 独享的: **be exclusive to sb** *This offer is exclusive to readers of The Sun.* 只有《太阳报》的读者才能获此优待。| **exclusive access/rights/use etc** *Rafferty managed to gain exclusive control of the company.* 拉弗蒂设法取得了对那个公司的专控权。**3 exclusive report/interview/coverage** a report, interview etc which is only printed in one newspaper or broadcast by one television programme 独家报道/采访/披露: *Tune in to our exclusive coverage of Wimbledon.* 请收看我们对温布尔登网球赛的独家报道。**4 mutually exclusive** if two things are mutually exclusive, you cannot have or do both of them 相互排斥的, 互不相容的: *Lesbianism and motherhood are not mutually exclusive.* 女性的同性恋关系和母亲身份并不是相互排斥的。**5 exclusive of** not including 不包括, 排除…在外: *Our prices are exclusive of sales tax.* 我们的价格不包括销售税。—**exclusively** *adv* —**exclusiveness** *n* [U]

exclusive² *n* [C] an important or exciting story that is printed in only one newspaper, because that newspaper was the first to find out about it 独家新闻, 独家报道: *a New York Post exclusive about the Kennedy marriage* 《纽约邮报》有关肯尼迪婚姻的独家新闻

ex·com·mu·ni·cate /ˌɛkskə`mjunəˌket; ˌekskə'mjuːnɪ̣keɪt/ *v* [T] to punish someone by no longer allowing them to be a member of the Roman Catholic church 开除…的〔罗马天主教〕教籍 —**excommunication** /ˌɛkskəˌmjunə`keʃən; ˌekskəmjuːnɪ̣'keɪʃən/ *n* [C,U]

ex·co·ri·ate /ɪk`skorɪˌet; ɪk'skɔːrieɪt/ *v* [T] *formal* to express a very bad opinion of a book, play etc【正式】严厉批评; 痛斥〔书、戏剧等〕: *an excoriating review in the Times* 《泰晤士报》刊登的一篇措辞严厉的评论 —**excoriation** /ɪksˌkorɪ`eʃən; ekˌskɔːri'eɪʃən/ *n* [C,U]

ex·cre·ment /`ɛkskrɪmənt; 'ekskrɪ̣mənt/ *n* [U] *formal* the solid waste material that you get rid of through your BOWELS【正式】粪; 大便

ex·cres·cence /ɪk`skrɛsn̩s; ɪk'skresəns/ *n* [C] *formal*【正式】**1** something such as an ugly building that makes the surrounding area seem less attractive 破坏周围景致的东西〈如丑陋的建筑〉: *The new museum is nothing but an excrescence on the urban landscape.* 新博物馆破坏了市区的景色。**2** an ugly growth on an animal or plant 瘤; 赘生物

ex·cre·ta /ɛk`skritə; ɪk'skriːtə/ *n* [plural] *formal* the solid or liquid waste material that people and animals produce and get rid of from their bodies【正式】排泄物

ex·crete /ɛk`skrit; ɪk'skriːt/ *v* [I,T] *formal* to get rid of waste material from your body through your BOWELS, your skin etc【正式】排泄 —compare 比较 SECRETE (1)

ex·cre·tion /ɪk`skriʃən; ɪk'skriːʃən/ *n* **1** [U] the process of getting rid of waste material from your body 排泄 **2** [C,U] the waste material that people or animals get rid of from their bodies 排泄物

ex·cru·ci·at·ing /ɪk`skruʃɪˌetɪŋ; ɪk'skruːʃieɪtɪŋ/ *adj* **1** extremely painful, so that you are unable to move or do something 使人极疼痛的: *When I bend my arm the pain is excruciating.* 弯胳膊的时候, 我疼得简直受不了。**2** extremely unpleasant, because it is boring, embarrassing, or sad 令人难以忍受的: *Helena described the events of the night before in excruciating detail.* 海伦娜详细地描述了头天晚上发生的那些令人极不愉快的事。—**excruciatingly** *adv*

ex·cul·pate /`ɛkskʌlˌpet; 'ekskʌlpeɪt/ *v* [T] *formal* to prove that someone is not guilty of something【正式】证明〔某人〕无罪; 为…开脱 —**exculpation** /ˌɛkskʌl`peʃən; ˌekskʌl'peɪʃən/ *n* [U]

ex·cur·sion /ɪk`skɝʒən; ɪk'skɜːʃən/ *n* [C] **1** a short journey arranged so that a group of people can visit a place, especially while they are on holiday〔尤指一群人度假时的〕短途旅行: *a day's excursion to the island* 去岛上的一天旅行 **2** a short journey made for a particular purpose〔有特定目的的〕短途出行: *a shopping excursion* 购物游 **3 excursion into sth** *formal* an attempt to experience or learn about something that is new to you【正式】尝试[涉猎]某事: *Neither of his brief excursions into marriage had been a success.* 他的两次短暂婚姻尝试均以失败告终。

ex·cu·sa·ble /ɪk`skjuzəbl; ɪk'skjuːzəbəl/ *adj* behaviour that is excusable can be forgiven〔行为〕可原谅的: *an excusable reaction of anger* 可以原谅的生气的反应

ex·cuse¹ /ɪk`skjuz; ɪk'skjuːz/ *v* [T] **1 excuse me** *spoken*【口】 S3 **a)** used when you want to get someone's attention politely, especially when you want to ask a question 劳驾〔用于礼貌地引起人注意, 尤其是发问时〕: *Excuse me, can you tell me the way to the museum please?* 劳驾, 你能告诉我去博物馆怎么走吗? **b)** used to say that you are sorry for doing something rude or embarrassing 对不起: *Oh, excuse me. I didn't know anyone was in here.* 噢, 对不起, 我不知道里面有人。**c)** used to ask someone politely to move so that you can walk past 借光: *Excuse me, could I just squeeze past you?* 借光, 能让我从你这儿过去吗? **d)** used when you want to politely tell someone that you are leaving a place 抱歉〔用于礼貌地表示要离开〕: *Excuse me a moment, Mr Jonson. I'll be right back.* 抱歉, 琼森先生, 我离开一下, 马上就回来。**e)** used when you disagree with someone but want to be polite about it 请原谅〔用于礼貌地表示反对〕: *Excuse me, but I don't think that's what he meant at all.* 请原谅, 不过我认为他绝对不是这个意思。**f)** *AmE* used to say you are sorry when you hit someone accidentally, make a small mistake etc【美】对不起〔用于意外撞到某人或犯小错误等时表示歉意〕: *Oh, excuse me, did I spell your name wrong?* 啊, 对不起, 我是不是把你的名字拼写错了? **g)** *especially AmE* used to ask someone to repeat something that they have just said【尤美】请再说一遍: *"What time is it?" "Excuse me?" "I asked you what time it is."* "现在几点了?" "对不起, 你说什么?" "我问你现在几点了。" **2** to forgive someone for doing something that is not seriously wrong, such as being rude or careless 原谅〔某人的小错〕: *I'll excuse you this time, but try and be prompt in the future.* 这次我原谅你, 但你以后要麻利些。| *Please excuse my bad handwriting.* 请原谅我的字写得不好。| **excuse sb for (doing) sth** *I cannot excuse them for treating their animals so badly.* 他们这样虐待自己的动物, 我不能原谅他们。**3** to allow someone not to do something that they are supposed to do 免除〔某人〕的职责: *Ball was excused guard duty that night.* 保尔被免除了那天夜里的警卫任务。| **excuse sb from (doing) sth** *Can I be excused from swimming today? I have a cold.* 我今天能不去游泳吗? 我感冒了。**4** to give reasons for someone's careless or offensive behaviour in order to make it seem more acceptable 为…开脱; 给…找理由: *Nothing can excuse that kind of rudeness.* 什么也无法为那种粗鲁行为开脱。| **sb can be excused for doing sth** (=used to say that you understand why someone has done something and think they should not be blamed for it) 某人做某事情有可原 *His poetry means a lot to him, so perhaps he can be excused for neglecting his work in order to write.* 诗歌对他极为重要, 所以他因为写诗而疏忽了工作或许也是情有可原的。**5** to give someone permission to leave a place 准许…离开: *May I please be excused from the table?* 我可以离开饭桌了吗? | **excuse yourself** *Richard politely excused himself, claiming he had too much work to do.* 理查德礼貌地告辞, 说他有太多的工作要做。**6 excuse me for living!** *spoken* used when someone has offended you or told you that you have done something wrong【口】实在对不住了!

USAGE NOTE 用法说明: EXCUSE

WORD CHOICE 词语辨析: **excuse me, I'm sorry, I beg your pardon, pardon me**

In British English, you say **(I'm) sorry** to a person if you accidentally touch them, or push against them, or get in their way (for example, if you step on someone's foot). You might also hear the rather old-fashioned expression **I beg your pardon**. 如果你无意间碰到或挤到别人, 或是挡了他们的路(如踩了他们的脚), 英国英语说(I'm) sorry, 也有人使用相当过时的说法I beg your pardon。

In American English you say **Excuse me** or **Pardon me**. 在同样情况下, 美国英语说Excuse me 或 Pardon me。

ex·cuse² /ɪk`skjus; ɪk'skju:s/ *n* [C] **1** a reason that you give to explain careless or offensive behaviour〔辩解的〕理由: [+for] *What's your excuse for being late this time?* 你迟到了，这次还有什么理由？| **there is no excuse for sth** *There is no excuse for such rudeness.* 这种无礼行为怎么说都不对。| **make an excuse** *Fay's always making excuses for his erratic moods.* 费伊总是为他的情绪起伏不定找借口。| **have an excuse** *I'm sure Mike has a good excuse for not repaying the money.* 我确信迈克不还钱一定有充分的理由。**2** a false reason that you give to explain why you are doing something or not doing something 虚假的理由; 托词; 借口: **excuse to do sth** *She wanted an excuse to be at the bus stop when Billy got off.* 她想找个理由，好让比利下车时自己正好在公共汽车站。| [+for] *The conference is an excellent excuse for a few days' holiday by the sea.* 参加这个会议为在海边度几天假提供了绝好的借口。| **find/have an excuse** *Now at last I had an excuse to call him.* 现在我终于有借口给他打电话了。| **make an excuse** *I made an excuse at the first possible moment, and got up to leave.* 一有机会我就找了个借口起身离开了。| **give sb an excuse** *The arrival of the doctor gave them an excuse to leave.* 医生的到来使他们有借口离开。**3 make your excuses** to explain why you are not able to do something 解释为何不能做某事: *Please make my excuses at the meeting tomorrow. I have an appointment with an important client.* 请在明天的会上替我解释一下不能到会的原因，我要约见一个重要客户。**4 a poor/rotten etc excuse for sth** used when you think someone is very bad at something they are doing or at their job 做事极差; 极不称职: *Derico is a rotten excuse for a lawyer, why on earth did you hire him?* 德里克是个极糟糕的律师，你干吗雇用他？**5** *AmE* a note written by your doctor or one of your parents saying that you were ill on a particular day【美】病假条; SICK NOTE *BrE*【英】

USAGE NOTE 用法说明: EXCUSE

WORD CHOICE 词语辨析: **reason, explanation, excuse, pretext**

If you call something a **reason**, either you believe it, or you are just repeating what someone else has said. 所谓 reason (原因)，可以是你自己相信确有其事，也可以只是重复别人的话: *His reason for being late was that his car broke down* (=either you know the car did break down which made him late, or that was simply the reason he gave you). 他迟到的原因是汽车抛锚了〔也许你知道他的汽车的确抛锚了才迟到的，也许抛锚之说只是他告诉你的话而已〕。

If you call something an **explanation**, you are just repeating what someone else has said. 所谓 explanation (解释)，只是在重复别人的话: *His explanation for being late was that his car broke down* (=that was the reason he gave – it may or may not be true). 他迟到了，他的解释是汽车抛锚了〔这是他给你的原因，可能是真的也可能是假的〕。An **explanation** often sounds more like a personal opinion, a **reason** more like a fact. 通常，explanation 听起来更像是个人见解，而 reason 更像是事实。

If you call something an **excuse** it suggests that you may not believe it is true or, if it is true, you do not believe that it really explains what happened. 所谓excuse (借口) 暗指你可能并不相信那是真的; 即使是真的，也不相信足以解释所发生的事: *His excuse for being late was that his car broke down* (=perhaps the car broke down, or perhaps it did not OR you think it did break down, but that is not really a good enough reason for being late). 他迟到的借口是汽车抛锚了〔也许汽车真的抛锚了，也许没有; 或者你相信汽车的确抛锚了，但认为这并不构成他迟到的充分理由〕。If you say *My excuse is ...*, you are giving a reason that you know is not really good enough to explain what you did. 如果你说 My excuse is ...，你知道你所给的理由其实并不足以解释自己的行为。

If you call something a **pretext**, you definitely do not think that it is true or the real reason. 所谓 pretext (托词)，表明你绝对不相信真有其事或者认为那绝对不是真正的原因: *His pretext for being late was that his car broke down* (=you do not believe it broke down OR it did, but you know there was another reason why he was really late). 他迟到了，他托词说是汽车抛锚了〔你不相信他的汽车真的抛锚了，或者你相信汽车抛锚了，但你相信他之所以迟到肯定另有原因〕。

ex-di·rec·to·ry /ˌ. ·'···◂/ *adj BrE* deliberately not given in the public telephone book【英】〔故意〕使电话号码不列入电话簿的; UNLISTED (2) *AmE*【美】: **go ex-directory** *After a number of threatening calls, Amy went ex-directory.* 接到数个威胁电话后，埃米不再将自己的电话号码列入电话簿了。

ex·ec /ɪg`zɛk; ɪg'zek/ *n* [C] *informal* an EXECUTIVE¹ (1)【非正式】主管

ex·e·cra·ble /`ɛksɪkrəbl̩; 'eksə̇krəbəl/ *adj formal* extremely bad【正式】极坏的, 极差的: *execrable handwriting* 极差劲的书法 —**execrably** *adv*: *execrably bad* 极差的

ex·e·crate /`ɛksɪˌkret; 'eksə̇kreɪt/ *v* [T] *literary* to express strong disapproval or hatred for someone or something【文】憎恶; 诅咒

ex·e·cute /`ɛksɪˌkjut; 'eksə̇kju:t/ *v* [T] **1** to kill someone, especially legally as a punishment for a serious crime〔尤指依法〕将…处死: **be executed for sth** *He was executed for treason.* 他因叛国罪被处死。—see 见 KILL¹ (USAGE) **2** *formal* to do something that you have carefully planned or that you have agreed to do【正式】实行; 执行; 履行: *The directors make the decisions, but the managers have to execute them.* 董事们作出决定，但要由经理们来执行。**3** *formal* to perform a difficult action or movement【正式】完成, 表演〔高难动作〕: *The skaters' routine was perfectly executed.* 那些滑冰选手把整套动作完成得非常出色。**4** *law* to make sure that the instructions in someone's WILL² (2) are followed【法律】确保〔遗嘱〕得到执行 **5** *formal* to make a work of art such as a painting【正式】创作〔绘画等艺术作品〕

ex·e·cu·tion /ˌɛksɪ`kjuʃən; ˌeksə̇'kju:ʃən/ *n* **1** [C,U] the act of killing someone, especially as a legal punishment for a serious crime (依法) 处死[处决]: *a public execution* 当众处死 **2** [U] *formal* a process in which you do something that has been carefully planned or agreed【正式】实施; 执行: [+of] *the formulation and execution of urban policy* 城市政策的制定与实施 **3** [U] *formal* the performance of a difficult action or movement【正式】〔高难动作的〕表演 **4** [U] *formal* the act of making a work of art such as a painting【正式】〔绘画等艺术作品的〕创作, 制作

ex·e·cu·tion·er /ˌɛksɪ`kjuʃənɚ; ˌeksə̇'kju:ʃənə/ *n* [C] someone who legally kills someone else as a punishment for a serious crime 死刑执行人, 行刑人: *a public executioner, also called at that time, the hangman* 公共行刑人，那时又被称作刽子手

ex·ec·u·tive¹ /ɪg`zɛkjutɪv; ɪg'zekjə̇tɪv/ *n* **1** [C] someone who has an important job as a manager in a company or business〔公司或商业机构中的〕主管, 行政人员: *a publishing executive* 一个出版业的主管人员 **2 the executive** the part of a government that is responsible for making sure that new laws and other decisions are done in the way they have been planned〔政府的〕行政部门 —compare 比较 JUDICIARY, LEGISLATURE **3** [C] the group of people in a political organization, society etc that makes the rules and makes sure that they work in the way they were planned〔政治组织、团体等的〕执行委员会: *the executive of the union* 工会的执行委员会 S3 W2

executive² *adj* [only before noun 仅用于名词前] **1** connected with making decisions and organizing, especially within a company or a government〔尤指公司或政府〕行政的, 管理的: *Clancy has been given full executive powers on this matter.* 在这方面克兰西已被授予绝对执行权。| **executive body/committee** (=a group of people who make decisions etc) 主管机构/委员会 **2** for the use of people who have important jobs in the management of a company or business 供〔公司或商业机构〕主管人员使用的: *the executive dining room* 经理人员饭厅 **3** expensive and of high quality, so that only someone with a good job can afford it 高档的; 经理级的: *an executive car* 高档汽车

executive priv·i·lege /ˌ. ··· '···/ *n* [C] *AmE* the right of a president or other government leader to keep official records and papers secret【美】行政特权〔指总统或其他政府领导人保守官方机密不向外透露的权利〕

ex·ec·u·tor /ɪg`zɛkjətɚ; ɪg'zekjə̇tə/ *n* [C] a person, lawyer, or bank that deals with the instructions in someone's WILL² (2) 遗嘱执行人[律师、银行]

ex·e·ge·sis /ˌɛksə`dʒisɪs; ˌeksə̇'dʒi:sə̇s/ *n* [C,U] *formal* a detailed explanation of a piece of writing, especially one from the Bible【正式】〔尤指对《圣经》内容的〕详细解释; 诠释

ex·em·plar /ɪg`zɛmplɚ; ɪg'zemplə/ *n* [C] *formal* a good or typical example【正式】模范; 典型

ex·em·pla·ry /ɪg`zɛmplərɪ; ɪg'zempləri/ *adj* **1** excellent and providing a good example for people to follow 模范的, (可做) 楷模的: *praised for their exemplary behaviour* 他们的模范行为受到表扬 **2** [only before noun 仅用于名词前] severe and intended to be a warning 警戒性的, 惩戒性的: *an exemplary punishment* 警戒性的惩罚

E

ex·em·pli·fy /ɪg`zɛmplə͵faɪ; ɪg'zemplɪ̣faɪ/ *v* [T] **1** to be a very typical example of something 是…的范例: *Los Angeles exemplifies America's diversity.* 洛杉矶是美国(文化)多元性的典范。**2** to give an example of something 举例说明 —**exemplification** /ɪg͵zɛmpləfə`keʃən; ɪg͵zemplɪ̣fɪ'keɪʃən/ *n* [C,U]

ex·empt¹ /ɪg`zɛmpt; ɪg'zempt/ *v* [T] to give someone special permission not to do something that they would normally have to do 免除, 豁免: *a special clause exempting children* 将儿童免除在外的特殊条款 | **exempt sb from** *Marty's bad health exempts him from military service.* 马蒂因身体差而豁免服兵役。

exempt² *adj* having special permission not to do something you would normally have to do 被免除(义务)的, 被豁免的: **[+from]** *The interest is exempt from income tax.* 利息收入免征所得税。

ex·emp·tion /ɪg`zɛmpʃən; ɪg'zempʃən/ *n* **1** [C] *AmE* the amount of money that you are allowed to earn each year before you start to pay tax【美】〔年收入中的〕免税额, 可免税部分; PERSONAL ALLOWANCE *BrE*【英】**2** [C,U] permission not to do something you would normally have to do 免除, 豁免

1 2 **ex·er·cise¹** /`ɛksɚ͵saɪz; 'eksəsaɪz/ *n*

1 ►FOR HEALTH 为了健康◄ [U] physical activities that you do in order to stay healthy and become stronger 运动, 锻炼: *I could use some exercise – let's go for a swim.* 我想锻炼一下身体, 咱们去游泳吧。| **do/take exercise** (=exercise regularly) 经常性地锻炼[运动] *Do at least fifteen minutes exercise each day.* 每天至少锻炼15分钟。| **get exercise** (=do exercise as part of your daily life) 身体得到锻炼〔作为日常生活的一部分〕*You don't get much exercise sitting at a desk all day like this.* 像这样整天坐在桌子前, 你的身体得不到多少锻炼。

2 ►MOVEMENT 动作◄ [C] a movement or set of movements that you do regularly in order to keep a particular part of your body strong and healthy 练习, 体操: *The doctor gave me some exercises to help with my back.* 医生教我做一些练习来增强背部力量。| **do exercises** *Jan does her exercises every morning.* 简每天都做早操。

3 ►FOR A SKILL 为获得技能◄ [C usually plural 一般用复数] an activity or process that helps you practise a particular skill such as playing a musical instrument or singing 练习, 训练

4 ►IN A BOOK 在书中◄ [C] a set of questions in a book which test a student's skill or knowledge 练习, 习题: *Do Exercises 3 and 4 on page 51 for homework.* 家庭作业是51页上的练习3和4。

5 ►ARMY/NAVY ETC 陆军/海军等◄ [C] an activity that trains soldiers, pilots etc for war when there is still peace 训练, 演练: *a naval exercise* 海军演练

6 ►FOR A RESULT 为达到某结果◄ [singular] an activity that is intended to have a particular result 活动; 任务: *Getting everyone to agree was quite a difficult exercise.* 要让大家都同意是一项困难的任务。| **an exercise in awareness/self-control etc** (=something that you do in order to gain or develop a particular quality) 提高认识/增强自制力等的活动 *The ceremony was an exercise in self-congratulation for a leader desperate to regain popularity.* 这个仪式是一个急于重获民众支持的领导人自吹自擂之举。

7 the exercise of power/influence/authority etc *formal* the use of power, influence etc in order to achieve something【正式】运用权力/施加影响/行使权威等

3 2 **exercise²** *v* **1** [I] to walk, do sports etc in order to stay healthy and become stronger 运动, 锻炼: *It's important to exercise regularly.* 经常锻炼身体十分重要。**2** [T] to make a particular part of your body move in order to make it stronger 锻炼〔身体某一部分〕: *Swimming exercises all the major muscle groups.* 游泳能使身体所有的主要肌群得到锻炼。**3 exercise power/influence/caution etc** *formal* to use power, influence etc【正式】运用权力/施加影响/小心谨慎等: *I intend to exercise my right to vote.* 我打算行使我的选举权。**4** [T] to make an animal walk or run in order to keep it healthy and strong 遛〔动物〕: *Don's out exercising the horses.* 唐出去遛马了。**5** [T often passive 常用被动态] *formal* to make someone think about a subject or problem and consider how to deal with it【正式】使关注; 使致力于〔解决问题〕: *Scientists continue to be exercised about the ethics of genetic engineering.* 科学家们持续关注基因工程的伦理问题。

exercise bike /'···, ·/ *n* [C] a bicycle that does not move and is used for indoor exercise 自行车式健身器

exercise book /'···, ·/ *n* [C] a small book that students write their work in 练习本[簿]

ex·ert /ɪg`zɝt; ɪg'zɜːt/ *v* [T] **1 exert pressure/control/influence** to use your power, influence etc in order to have a particular effect 施加压力/控制/影响: *Photography has exerted a profound influence on art in this century.* 在本世纪, 摄影术对艺术产生了重大影响。**2 exert yourself** to make a strong physical or mental effort 尽力, 努力: *He won both games without even seeming to exert himself.* 他毫不费力地赢得了那两场比赛。

ex·er·tion /ɪg`zɝʃən; ɪg'zɜːʃən/ *n* [C,U] strong physical or mental effort 用力气; 花心思: *The afternoon's exertions had left us feeling exhausted.* 下午太用劲, 我们感到精疲力竭。| *mental exertion* 费心思

ex·e·unt /`ɛksɪənt; 'eksiʌnt/ *v Latin* a word written in the instructions of a play to tell two or more actors to leave the stage【拉丁】〔舞台指示〕至少两个角色退场, 下场

ex gra·tia /͵ɛks `greʃə; ͵eks 'greɪʃə/ *adj Latin* an ex gratia payment is one made to help someone or as a gift, not because you have a legal duty to do it【拉丁】出于帮助的; 作为优惠的〔非出于法律义务的〕: *an ex gratia payment of £15,000* 15,000英镑的补助款项

ex·hale /ɛks`hel; eks'heɪl/ *v* [I,T] to breathe air, smoke etc out of your mouth 呼出: *Take a deep breath, then exhale slowly.* 深深吸一口气, 然后慢慢呼出。—**exhalation** /͵ɛksə`leʃən; ͵ekshə'leɪʃən/ *n* [U]

ex·haust¹ /ɪg`zɔst; ɪg'zɔːst/ *v* [T] **1** to make someone extremely tired so that they have no energy left 使精疲力竭: *I find a full day's teaching exhausts me.* 我讲了一整天课, 觉得精疲力竭。| **exhaust sb to do sth** *It exhausted him even to talk very long.* 讲话时间长一些他都会感到没有力气。**2** to use all of something 用完, 耗尽: *We've nearly exhausted our coal reserves.* 我们储备的煤快要用完了。**3 exhaust a subject/topic etc** to talk about something so much that you have nothing more to say about it 详尽无遗地论述某主题/话题等: *Once we'd exhausted the subject of Jill's wedding, we had nothing to say to each other.* 谈完吉尔的婚礼以后, 我们彼此就无话可说了。

exhaust² *n* **1** [C] a pipe on a car or machine through which gas or steam passes; EXHAUST PIPE 排气管 **2** [U] the gas or steam produced when an engine is working〔发动机排出的〕废气

ex·haust·ed /ɪg`zɔstɪd; ɪg'zɔːstɪ̣d/ *adj* **1** extremely tired and having no energy 筋疲力尽的; 疲惫不堪的: *Man, I'm exhausted!* 老兄, 我实在太累了! | **[+from/by]** *Jill lay on the grass, exhausted by her long run.* 吉尔躺在草地上, 长跑使她精疲力竭。| *What's wrong? You look absolutely exhausted.* 怎么了? 你一副疲惫不堪的样子。**2** having or containing no more of a particular thing or substance 耗尽的; 枯竭的: *an exhausted coal mine* 矿源枯竭的煤矿

ex·haust·ing /ɪg`zɔstɪŋ; ɪg'zɔːstɪŋ/ *adj* making you feel extremely tired 使人精疲力竭的: *an exhausting journey* 令人疲惫不堪的旅程

ex·haus·tion /ɪg`zɔstʃən; ɪg'zɔːstʃən/ *n* [U] **1** extreme tiredness 精疲力竭: **nervous exhaustion** (=a medical condition in which you feel very sad or anxious because you have been working too hard or have been very worried) 神经衰弱 **2** the act of using all the available substances, materials etc so that there are none left 用光, 耗尽: **[+of]** *the exhaustion of oil supplies* 石油供应的耗尽

ex·haus·tive /ɪg`zɔstɪv; ɪg'zɔːstɪv/ *adj* extremely thorough 全面的, 彻底的: *an exhaustive search for the missing boy* 对失踪男孩展开的彻底搜寻 —**exhaustively** *adv*: *examined the issue exhaustively without result* 对问题进行了彻底调查却毫无结果

exhaust pipe /·'· ·/ *n* [C] a pipe on a car or a machine through which gas or steam passes 排气管 —see picture on page A2 参见A2页图

ex·hib·it¹ /ɪg`zɪbɪt; ɪg'zɪbɪ̣t/ *v* **1** [I,T] to put something in a public place so that people can go to see it 展出, 展览: *David's going to exhibit his roses at the flower show.* 戴维准备将自己的玫瑰花在花展中展出。**2** [T] *formal* to show a particular quality, emotion, or ability so that people notice it easily【正式】展示〔气质、情感或能力〕: *Moira's exhibiting classic signs of depression.* 莫伊拉表现出典型的抑郁迹象。**3** [T] *formal* to show someone something【正式】出示, 展示出: *He rolled up his trouser leg to exhibit his wounded knee.* 他卷起裤腿露出受伤的膝盖。

exhibit² *n* [C] **1** something, for example a painting, that you put in a public place so that people can go to see it 展品, 展出物: *Many exhibits were donated by local millionaire John Severi.* 许多展品都是由当地的百万富翁约翰·塞弗里捐赠的。**2** an object, piece of clothing etc that is used in a court of law to prove that someone is guilty or not guilty〔法庭上出示的〕证物: *Exhibit A is the blood-stained hammer found next to the victim's body.* 证物A是在受害者身边发现的一把带血迹的锤子。**3** an EXHIBITION (1) 展览会: *a big exhibit in Milan* 在米兰举行的大型展览

2 **ex·hi·bi·tion** /ˌɛksəˋbɪʃən; ˌeksᵻˈbɪʃən/ *n* **1** [C] a public show where you put things so that people can go to see them 展览(会): [+of] *an exhibition of black and white photographs* 黑白照片展览 **2** [U] the act of showing something such as a painting in a public place 展出, 展览: [+of] *She never agreed to the public exhibition of her sculptures while she was still alive.* 她从未同意在生前公开展出自己的雕塑作品。| **on exhibition** also 又作 **on exhibit** (=being shown) 展出中 *A collection of paintings by David Hockney is on exhibition at the Museum of Contemporary Art.* 戴维·霍克尼的一批绘画作品正在当代艺术馆展出。**3 an exhibition of rudeness/jealousy/temper etc** very rude, embarrassing, or offensive behaviour 显露出无礼/嫉妒/坏脾气等: *I've never seen such an exhibition of jealousy in my entire life.* 我一生中从未见过如此嫉妒的表现。**4 make an exhibition of yourself** behave in a silly or embarrassing way 出洋相, 出丑: *Sam made a real exhibition of himself, getting drunk and then taking all his clothes off.* 萨姆喝醉了酒后又脱掉所有的衣服, 出尽了洋相。**5** [C] *BrE* a small amount of money given as a prize to a student 【英】〔小额〕奖学金: *Michael won an exhibition at Cambridge.* 迈克尔在剑桥大学获得了一小笔奖学金。

ex·hi·bi·tion·is·m /ˌɛksəˋbɪʃənˌɪzəm; ˌeksᵻˈbɪʃənɪzəm/ *n* [U] **1** behaviour that is intended to make people notice or admire you, but which most people think is silly 表现癖: *Look at those idiots standing on the statue. It's just pure exhibitionism.* 看看那些站在雕像上的笨蛋, 纯粹是表现癖。**2** behaviour in which someone shows their PENIS or breasts to people in a public place because they have mental problems 露阴癖; 露乳癖 —**exhibitionist** *n* [C] —**exhibitionistic** /ˌɛksəbɪʃəˋnɪstɪk; ˌeksᵻbɪʃəˈnɪstɪk/ *adj*

ex·hib·i·tor /ɪgˋzɪbɪtɚ; ɪgˈzɪbᵻtə/ *n* [C] someone who is showing something, for example a painting, in a public place so that people can go to see it 参展者, 展出者: *a book exhibitor at TESOL* 在英语外语教学大会上参展的书商

ex·hil·a·rate /ɪgˋzɪləˌret; ɪgˈzɪləreɪt/ *v* [T] to make someone feel very excited and happy 使兴高采烈, 使感到激动 —**exhilaration** /ɪgˌzɪləˋreʃən; ɪgˌzɪləˈreɪʃən/ *n* [U]

ex·hil·a·rat·ed /ɪgˋzɪləˌretɪd; ɪgˈzɪləreɪtᵻd/ *adj* feeling extremely happy and excited 兴高采烈的, 异常兴奋的: *I am always exhilarated by the bustle and noise of New York.* 纽约的繁华喧闹总令我兴奋。

ex·hil·a·rat·ing /ɪgˋzɪləˌretɪŋ; ɪgˈzɪləreɪtɪŋ/ *adj* making you feel very excited and happy 使人兴高采烈的, 令人极度兴奋的: *Racing down the ski slope for the first time was an exhilarating experience.* 第一次急速滑下雪坡真是万分刺激。—**exhilaratingly** *adv*

ex·hort /ɪgˋzɔrt; ɪgˈzɔːt/ *v* [T] *formal* to try very hard to persuade someone to do something 【正式】规劝; 恳请; 激励: **exhort sb to do sth** *He exhorted the troops to prepare for battle.* 他激励军队做好战斗准备。—**exhortation** /ˌɛgzɚˋteʃən; ˌeksɔːˈteɪʃən/ *n* [C,U]

ex·hume /ɪgˋzjum; ɪgˈzjuːm/ *v* [T usually passive 一般用被动态] *formal* to remove a dead body from a grave, especially in order to check the cause of death 【正式】〔尤指为验尸而从墓内〕掘出〔尸体〕—**exhumation** /ˌɛkshjʊˋmeʃən; ˌekshjʊˈmeɪʃən/ *n* [C,U]

ex·i·gen·cy /ˋɛksədʒənsɪ; ˈeksᵻdʒənsi/ also 又作 **ex·i·gence** /ˋɛksədʒəns; ˈeksᵻdʒəns/ *n* [C usually plural 一般用复数] *formal* something that you must do to deal with an urgent situation 【正式】应急措施; 应急情况: *the exigencies of war* 战时急需

ex·i·gent /ˋɛksədʒənt; ˈeksᵻdʒənt/ *adj formal* 【正式】**1** demanding a lot of attention from other people in a way that is unreasonable 苛求的, 要求过多的 **2** an exigent situation is urgent, so that you must deal with it very quickly 〔情况〕紧急的, 急迫的

ex·ig·u·ous /ɪgˋzɪgjʊəs; ɪgˈzɪguəs/ *adj formal* very small in amount 【正式】极少的; 微薄的: *exiguous earnings* 微薄的收入

ex·ile[1] /ˋɛgzaɪl; ˈeksaɪl/ *n* **1** [singular, U] a situation in which you are forced to leave your country to live in another country, especially for political reasons 〔尤指因政治原因的〕流放, 流亡: *After a long period of enforced exile he returned to rule his country again.* 被迫流亡国外很长一段时间后, 他回国再次执政。| **be in exile** *Some of her best works were written while she was in exile.* 她的一些最好的作品是在她流亡期间写的。| **go into exile** *He was forced to go into exile to escape imprisonment after the coup.* 政变后为逃避拘捕, 他被迫流亡国外。| **send sb into exile** (=force someone to leave) 放逐某人 **2** [C] someone who has been forced to live in exile 被流放者; 流亡者 —see also 另见 TAX EXILE

exile[2] *v* [T usually passive 一般用被动态] to force someone to leave their country, especially for political reasons 〔尤指因政治原因而〕放逐, 流放〔某人〕: *After the war he was exiled and the other leaders imprisoned.* 战后他被流放国外, 其他领导人则被捕入狱。| **exile sb to** *After publishing the novel he was arrested and exiled to Siberia.* 小说发表后他被捕并被流放至西伯利亚。—**exiled** *adj* [only before noun 仅用于名词前]

ex·ist /ɪgˋzɪst; ɪgˈzɪst/ *v* [I not in progressive 不用进行时] **1** if someone or something exists, that person or thing is real and has not been imagined by someone 存在; 实际上有: *Do fairies really exist?* 真的有神仙吗? | *Stop pretending the problem doesn't exist.* 别再假装不存在这个问题了。| *Tom acts as if I don't exist at times.* 有时汤姆表现得就像我不存在一样。**2** to happen or be present in a particular situation or place 出现, 发生; 在场, 存在: *The custom of arranged marriages still exists in many countries.* 许多国家仍然存在着包办婚姻的习俗。**3** to stay alive, especially in a difficult situation when you do not have enough money, food etc 维持生存〔尤指勉强糊口〕: [+on] *The hostages existed on bread and water for over 5 months.* 人质靠面包和水生存了五个多月。 3 1

ex·ist·ence /ɪgˋzɪstəns; ɪgˈzɪstəns/ *n* **1** [U] the state of existing 存在; 实有: *It is impossible to prove the existence of God.* 无法证明上帝的存在。| **be in existence** (=exist at a particular time) 〔在某一时间〕存在 *There are three different versions of his health record currently in existence.* 目前他有三份不同的健康记录。| **come into existence** (=start to exist) 产生, 出现, 开始存在 *Scientists have many theories about how the universe first came into existence.* 关于宇宙是如何产生的, 科学家们有许多种理论。**2** [C usually singular 一般用单数] the type of life that someone has, especially when it is bad or unhappy 生活, 生活方式〔尤指不幸的生活〕: *Pablo led a lonely existence when he first moved to San Juan.* 巴勃罗刚搬到圣胡安时, 生活很孤独。| *I don't call this a life, it's an existence.* 我认为这不叫生活, 这只是勉强维生。| **eke out an existence** (=get just enough food or money to live on) 勉强糊口 *Farmers eked out a primitive existence on the dry, stony land.* 农民们在干旱多石的土地上勉强维持简单原始的生活。| **sb's/sth's very existence** (=the fact that something exists at all, especially when something could prevent it from existing) 某人的生命; 某物的存在〔尤指当生命、存在成问题时〕*a drug on which his very existence depended* 维系他生命的药物 3 2

ex·ist·ent /ɪgˋzɪstənt; ɪgˈzɪstənt/ *adj formal* existing now 【正式】现存的, 现有的: *The existent pension scheme will not change.* 现有的退休金制度不会改变。—opposite 反义词 NONEXISTENT

ex·is·ten·tial /ˌɛgzɪsˋtɛnʃəl; ˌegzɪˈstenʃəl◂/ *adj* [only before noun 仅用于名词前] connected with the existence of humans or existentialism 关于(人类)存在的; 存在主义的: *the existential notion that man is in control of his own life* 认为人能主宰自己生命的存在主义观点

ex·is·ten·tial·is·m /ˌɛgzɪsˋtɛnʃəlɪzm; ˌegzɪˈstenʃəlɪzəm/ *n* [U] the modern belief that people are responsible for their own actions and experiences 存在主义: *Sartre, the high priest of French existentialism* 法国存在主义的宗师萨特 —**existentialist** *adj* —**existentialist** *n* [C]

ex·ist·ing /ɪgˋzɪstɪŋ; ɪgˈzɪstɪŋ/ *adj* [only before noun 仅用于名词前] existing systems, situations etc are the present ones being used now 正在使用的; 现存的: *Changes will be made to the existing laws.* 将对现有的法律进行修改。 3 2

EXIT /ˋɛgzɪt; ˈegzᵻt/ a British organization which aims to change the law against helping seriously ill people to die if they wish to. The organization gives advice to such people and their families. The Hemlock Society is a similar organization in the US. "退场"自愿安乐死协会〔英国一组织, 旨在改变禁止对重症病人实行安乐死的法律。该组织向重症病人及其家人提供建议。美国有一类似组织, 名为毒芹协会〕

ex·it[1] /ˋɛgzɪt; ˈegzᵻt/ *n* [C] **1** a door or space through which you can leave a place, especially a room in a big building 出口〔尤指大建筑物的出口〕: *We made for the nearest exit.* 我们走向最近的出口。| *an exit sign* 出口通道标志 | **emergency/fire exit** (=a special door used only when there is a fire etc) 太平门; 紧急出口; 失火通道出口 **2** [usually singular 一般用单数] the act of leaving a place, especially a room 离去〔尤指离开房间〕: **make an exit** (=go out) 出去, 离开 *They made a swift exit when they saw the police approaching.* 看见警察来了, 他们便迅速离去。**3** a place on a MOTORWAY or FREEWAY where vehicles can leave it 高速公路出口: *Take exit 13 into Lynchburg.* 从13号出口开出到林奇堡。**4** [usually singular 一般用单数] an occasion when someone stops being involved in a situation, event, etc, often because they have not been successful or have done something wrong 退出〔常指因未成功或做错事而停止参与某局势或事件〕: *Manchester United's early exit from the championship* 曼联队早早退出冠军的争夺 3

exit² *v* **1** [I] to leave a place 离去, 离开: [+from/through] *I exited through a side window.* 我从侧面的一扇窗户离开。**2** [I, T] to stop using a computer PROGRAM¹ (1) 退出（软件）: *You exit the system by pressing the F3 button.* 你按 F3 键就能退出系统。**3** [I,T] *Latin* a word used in the instructions of a play to tell an actor to leave the stage【拉丁】退场, 下场〔剧本里的舞台指示〕: *Exit Hamlet, bearing the body of Polonius.* 哈姆雷特扛着波洛尼厄斯的尸体退场。

exit poll /ˈ· ·/ *n* [C] a process of asking people how they have voted in an election in order to discover the likely result of the election〔投票场所之外的〕投票后民意调查

Ex·moor /ˋɛksmur; ˈeksmʊə/ a MOOR (=area of open country with rough grass and low bushes, but no farmland) in Devon and Somerset in southwest England, famous for its wild ponies (PONY=small horses). It is a National Park and is popular with tourists. 埃克斯穆尔〔位于英格兰西南德文郡和萨默塞特郡的一片漠泽, 以矮种野马著称。该地为国家公园, 深受游客喜爱〕

Exodus /ˈɛksədəs; ˈeksədəs/ the second book of the Old Testament of the Bible, which tells the story of the Exodus, which is the journey out of Egypt to the Promised Land, made by Moses and the Israelites《出埃及记》〔《圣经·旧约》的第二卷, 讲述摩西和以色列人从埃及出走, 前往应许之地迦南的故事〕

ex·o·dus /ˋɛksədəs; ˈeksədəs/ *n* [singular] a situation in which a lot of people leave a particular place at the same time〔大批人同时〕离开; 涌离: [+from/to] *the exodus of Jews from Eastern Europe* 犹太人大批涌离东欧 | **mass exodus** *often humorous* (=when everybody goes somewhere)【常幽默】全体出动, 所有人都去〔某处〕*I joined in the mass exodus to the bar every lunchtime.* 每天午饭时间我都加入涌向酒吧的人群。

ex·of·fi·ci·o /ˌɛks əˋfɪʃɪˌo; ˌeks əˈfɪʃiəʊ/ *adj Latin formal* an ex-officio member of an organization is only a member because of their rank or position【拉丁, 正式】〔因级别或职位而成为某组织〕当然成员的: *The Mayor is an ex-officio member of the Parish Council.* 市长是教区议会的当然成员。—**ex officio** *adv*

ex·on·e·rate /ɪgˋzɑnəˌret; ɪgˈzɒnəreɪt/ *v* [T] to state officially that someone who has been blamed for something is not responsible for it 免除对…的指控[责备]: *The report did not exonerate the social workers involved in the Cleveland child abuse case.* 这份报告并未替克利夫兰虐待儿童案件涉及的社工洗脱干系。| **exonerate sb from/of** *Recent medical evidence has exonerated Dr Lamont from all blame.* 最近的医学证据表明对拉蒙特医生的所有责难都不成立。—**exoneration** /ɪgˌzɑnəˋreʃən; ɪgˌzɒnəˈreɪʃən/ *n* [U]

ex·or·bi·tant /ɪgˋzɔrbətənt; ɪgˈzɔːbɪ̣tənt/ *adj* an exorbitant price, rate, demand etc is much higher than is reasonable or usual〔价格、费用、要求等〕过高的; 过分的: *It's a good restaurant but the prices are exorbitant.* 这家饭店不错, 但价格实在太高了。—**exorbitance** *n* [U] —**exorbitantly** *adv*

ex·or·cis·m /ˋɛksɔrˌsɪzəm; ˈeksɔːsɪzəm/ *n* [C,U] **1** a process during which someone forces evil spirits to leave a place or someone's body by using special words and ceremonies 驱邪, 驱魔 **2** the act of making yourself forget a bad memory or experience〔对不好的回忆或经历的〕设法忘却, 淡忘

ex·or·cist /ˋɛksɔrˌsɪst; ˈeksɔːsɪ̣st/ *n* [C] someone who forces evil spirits to leave a place or someone's body 驱魔师

ex·or·cize also 又作 **-ise** *BrE*【英】/ˋɛksɔrˌsaɪz; ˈeksɔːsaɪz/ *v* [T] to force evil spirits to leave a place or someone's body by using special words and ceremonies〔通过念咒语或做法事〕驱除〔邪魔〕: *prayers to exorcize ghosts* 驱鬼的祷词

ex·ot·ic /ɪgˋzɑtɪk; ɪgˈzɒtɪk/ *adj approving* seeming unusual and exciting because of being connected with a foreign country【褒】异国风情的, 外国情调的: *exotic birds* 外国的奇异鸟类 | *Zara is an exotic name. Where's she from?* 扎拉是一个颇具外国味的名字, 她是哪国人? —**exotically** /-klɪ; -kli/ *adv*

ex·ot·ic·a /ɪgˋzɑtɪkə; ɪgˈzɒtɪkə/ *n* [plural] unusual and exciting things that come from foreign countries〔来自外国的〕奇异事物

exotic danc·er /ˌ· ·· ˈ··/ *n* [C] a dancer who takes off their clothes while dancing 脱衣舞演员; 跳艳舞者 —see also 另见 STRIPTEASE

ex·pand /ɪkˋspænd; ɪkˈspænd/ *v* **1** [I,T] to become larger in size, number, or amount, or to make something become larger（使）扩大; 增加: *Water expands as it freezes.* 水结冰时会膨胀。| *The population of the town expanded rapidly in the 1960s.* 20 世纪 60 年代, 这个镇子的人口迅速增加。| **expand sth** *exercises designed to expand the chest muscles* 为扩展胸肌而设计的练习 —opposite 反义词 CONTRACT² (1) **2** [T] to increase the amount or range of an activity 增加〔活动量〕; 扩展〔活动范围〕: *As children grow older they expand their interests and become more confident.* 儿童在成长过程中兴趣会变广, 人也会变得更自信。**3** [I,T] if a company, business etc expands or if someone expands it, they open new shops, factories etc 扩展（业务）**4** [I] to become more confident or friendly 变得更自信[友善]: *After a few whiskies he started to expand a little.* 几杯威士忌下肚, 他开始多了些信心。

expand on/upon sth *phr v* [T] to add more details or information to something that you have already said 详述, 进一步说明: *Payne later expanded on his initial statement, saying he hadn't meant it the way it sounded.* 佩恩后来对他最初的声明解释称, 那句话表面的意思并非他的本意。

ex·pand·a·ble /ɪkˋspændəbḷ; ɪkˈspændəbəl/ *adj* able to be made larger 可扩大的, 可放大的: *an expandable waistband* 能放宽的腰带

ex·panse /ɪkˋspæns; ɪkˈspæns/ *n* [C] a very large area of water, sky, land etc 宽广的空间: [+of] *Vast expanses of sand stretched out in front of us.* 在我们面前是广袤的沙地。

ex·pan·sion /ɪkˋspænʃən; ɪkˈspænʃən/ *n* **1** [U] the act or process of increasing in size, range, amount etc〔尺寸、范围、数量等的〕扩大; 增加: *the expansion of gases* 气体的膨胀 **2** [U] the act or process of making a company or business larger by opening new shops, factories etc〔公司或企业的〕扩张: *The industry has just undergone a period of rapid expansion.* 该产业刚经历了一轮快速扩张。**3** [C] a detailed idea, story etc that is based on one that is simpler or more general 详述, 展开, 扩充: *The novel is an expansion of a short story he wrote about forty years ago.* 这部小说由他大约四十年前写的一篇短篇小说扩展而成。

ex·pan·sion·is·m /ɪksˋpænʃənɪzm; ɪkˈspænʃənɪzəm/ *n* [U] a process in which the amount of land and power that a country has increases 扩张（主义）—**expansionary** *adj* —**expansionist** *adj* —**expansionist** *n* [C]

ex·pan·sive /ɪkˋspænsɪv; ɪkˈspænsɪv/ *adj* **1** very friendly and willing to talk a lot 友善健谈的: *After a couple of drinks she suddenly became more expansive.* 喝了几杯酒后她突然变得友好健谈起来。**2** very large and wide in area〔面积〕广阔的, 辽阔的: *a broad expansive valley* 宽广的山谷 **3** expansive behaviour or ideas are confident but not always practical〔行为或想法〕自信但不一定实在的: *He made an expansive gesture and said, "Who cares anyway?"* 他做了个有些轻浮的手势说: "谁会在乎呢?" —**expansively** *adv* —**expansiveness** *n* [U]

ex·pat /ˌɛksˋpæt; ˌeksˈpæt/ *n* [C] *informal* an expatriate【非正式】居住国外的人; 侨民

ex·pa·ti·ate /ɪkˋspeʃɪˌet; ɪkˈspeɪʃieɪt/ *v*

expatiate on/upon sth *phr v* [T] *formal* to speak or write in detail about a particular subject【正式】详述, 阐述: *He began to expatiate on the topic of the free market economy.* 他就自由市场经济的题目开始详细论述。

ex·pat·ri·ate¹ /ɛksˋpetrɪˌet; eksˈpætriət/ *n* [C] someone who lives in a foreign country 居住国外的人; 侨民: *British expatriates living in Spain* 在西班牙的英国侨民 —**expatriate** *adj* [only before noun 仅用于名词前]

CULTURAL NOTE 文化注释

British people use the words 'expatriate', or 'expat' to refer to people who have gone from the UK to another country either to work for a time or to live somewhere permanently at the end of their working lives. They are typically thought of as people who never really become part of the society in the country where they are living, and who spend most of their time with other expatriates. Spain and Greece are thought of as countries that have large numbers of British expatriates. 英国人用侨民 (expatriate 或 expat) 一词指短期出国就业或退休后出国定居的人。通常认为, 他们从未真正融入当地社会, 大多数时间还是和其他侨民来往。西班牙和希腊被认为住有大量英国侨民。

ex·pat·ri·ate² /ɛksˋpetrɪˌet; eksˈpætrieɪt/ *v* [T] to force someone to leave their own country and go to live in another country, especially because they have broken the law〔尤指依法〕使移居国外, 把…逐出本国 —compare 比较 EXILE²

ex·pect /ɪkˋspɛkt; ɪkˈspekt/ *v* [T]

1 ►**THINK STH WILL HAPPEN** 认为某事会发生◄ to think that something will happen because it seems likely or has been planned 预料, 预期: **expect (that)** *The troops expect the attack will come at dawn.* 部队预料进攻将于拂晓发起。| **expect to do sth** *The rent was much more than we had expected to pay.* 租金比我们预计要付的多得多。| **expect sb/sth to do sth** *He'd been out celebrating and expected his girlfriend to drive him home.* 他出去庆祝, 以为女朋友会开车送他回家。| **fully expect** (=be

completely sure something will happen) 完全相信, 确信〔某事会发生〕*Smedley fully expected to be paid for giving me this information.* 斯梅德利确信向我提供这个信息会得到报酬。| **half expect** (=think it is possible that something will happen) 认为〔某事〕有可能 *I half expected to see her at the party.* 我觉得可能会在聚会上看见她。| **as expected** (=in the way that was planned) 按计划进行 *The ascent of the mountain is proceeding as expected.* 登山活动正在按计划进行。| **is (only) to be expected** (=used to say that you are not surprised that an unpleasant situation or remark etc has happened or been said) 在预料之中, 并不意外 *Some resentment of the new baby was only to be expected.* 新生婴儿的哥哥、姐姐有点吃醋不足为奇。
2 ►BE WAITING FOR 等待◄ to believe that someone or something is going to arrive 期待, 预料: *We're expecting Alison home any minute now.* 我们想艾利森现在随时会到家。| *Snow is expected by the weekend.* 预计周末会下雪。
3 ►DEMAND 要求◄ to demand that someone does something because it is a duty or seems reasonable 要求; 期望〔某人做某事〕: *The officer expects complete obedience from his troops.* 这位军官要求部下绝对服从。| **expect sb to do sth** *You can't expect kids to be quiet all the time.* 你不能指望孩子们一直保持安静。| **expect a lot/too much of sb** (=think someone can do more than perhaps is possible) 对某人要求很高/过高 *The school expects a lot of its students.* 这所学校对学生要求很高。
4 ►WANT STH TO HAPPEN 想要某事发生◄ to think it is reasonable that something should happen or exist 期待, 期望〔某事发生或某物存在〕: *A job and somewhere to live – is that too much to expect?* 有份工作, 有地方住 —— 这是不是期望过多了? | *We had expected to be consulted at the very least.* 我们原本料想起码会与我们商量商量。
5 be expecting if a woman is expecting, she is going to have a baby 怀孕
6 What else can/do you expect? *spoken* used to say that you are not surprised by something unpleasant or disappointing because it has happened before【口】这不奇怪? 你还能指望怎么样?: *Tracey didn't leave a forwarding address, but then what can you expect?* 特蕾西没留下转寄地址, 你又能指望什么呢?
7 I expect *spoken especially BrE* used to introduce or agree with a statement that you think is probably true【口, 尤英】我觉得, 依我看: *I expect Mum will phone tonight.* 我觉得妈妈今晚会打电话。| **I expect so** *"Do you think Ruth will get to art college?" "Yes, I expect so."* "你觉得鲁思能进艺术学院吗?" "我看会。"

This graph shows how common the different grammar patterns of the verb **expect** are. 本图表所示为动词 expect 构成的不同语法模式的使用频率。

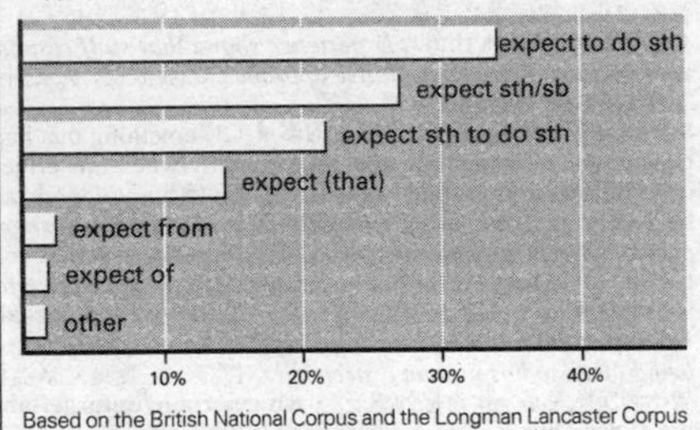

Based on the British National Corpus and the Longman Lancaster Corpus
据英国国家语料库和朗文兰开斯特语料库

ex·pec·tan·cy /ɪkˈspɛktənsɪ; ɪkˈspektənsi/ *n* [U] the feeling that something pleasant or exciting is going to happen 期待, 期望: *I saw the look of expectancy in the children's eyes.* 我从孩子们眼中看到了期待的神情。—see also 另见 LIFE EXPECTANCY

ex·pec·tant /ɪkˈspɛktənt; ɪkˈspektənt/ *adj* [usually before noun 一般用于名词前] **1** hopeful that something good or exciting will happen 期待的, 期望的: *a row of expectant faces* 一张张满怀期待的面孔 **2 expectant mother** a woman who is going to have a baby 孕妇 —**expectantly** *adv*

S2 W2 **ex·pec·ta·tion** /ˌɛkspɛkˈteʃən; ˌekspekˈteɪʃən/ *n* [C,U] **1** the belief that something will happen because it is likely or planned 预料, 预期: **your expectation is that** *My expectation is that interest rates will go up.* 我预期利率将上调。| **against/contrary to (all) expectations** *Against all expectations, Mike finished high school with top grades.* 出乎所有人的预料, 迈克中学毕业时成绩优异。| **in expectation of** (=thinking that something will happen) 预计 *They closed the windows in expectation of rain.* 他们预计会下雨, 把窗都关上了。**2** [usually plural 一般用复数] a belief that something good will happen in the future 期待, 期望: **have high expectations** (=believe that something good will happen or that someone will be successful in the future) 怀有很高的期望 *The school has high expectations for his future career.* 学校对他未来事业成功怀有很高的期望。| **beyond (your) expectations** (=better than you expected) 没有想到; 比预期的更好 *Paulito has succeeded beyond our expectations.* 保利托取得的成就比我们预期的还要高。| **fall short of/not come up to sb's expectations** (=not be as good or as successful as you expected) 未达到期望, 没有预期的那样好 *If profits fall short of expectations, how will you repay your loan?* 如果利润少于预期, 你怎么还贷款呢? | *The film just didn't come up to our expectations.* 这部电影没我们想象的那么好。| **(not) live up to sb's expectations** (=(not) be as good as people expected) (未) 达到期望 *The show lived up to all our expectations – it was wonderful!* 这场演出不负众望 —— 精彩极了! | **arouse expectations** (=make you think that something good is going to happen) 引起期望, 使充满期望 *The ceasefire has aroused expectations of an end to the war.* 停火使人们对结束战争充满了希望。**3** the belief that something ought to happen or that someone should behave in a particular way 期待; 希望: *Some have totally unrealistic expectations of both medical and nursing staff.* 有些人对医护人员的期望完全不切实际。**4 expectation of life** the number of years that someone is likely to live; LIFE EXPECTANCY 预期寿命

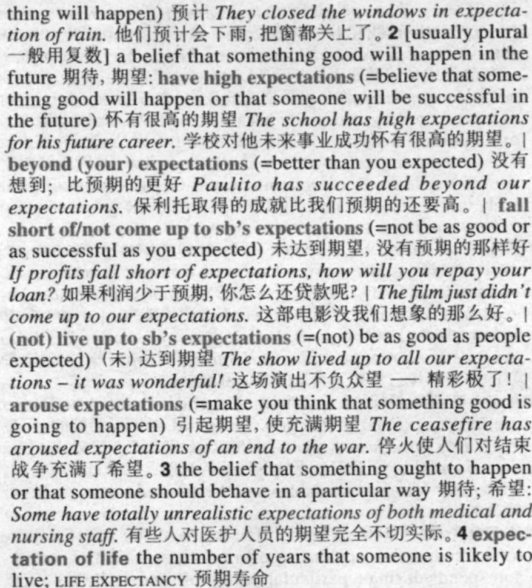

ex·pec·ted /ɪkˈspɛktɪd; ɪkˈspektɪ̈d/ *adj* [only before noun 仅用于名词前] an event or person that is expected is one you think will happen or are waiting for 预料中的; 被等待的: *The expected storm never occurred so we had the barbecue after all.* 预料中的暴风雨没有来, 所以我们最终还是举行了烧烤野餐。 S3 W2

ex·pec·to·rant /ɪkˈspɛktərənt; ɪkˈspektərənt/ *n* [U] *formal* a type of cough medicine that you take to help get rid of PHLEGM (=a sticky substance) in your lungs【正式】祛痰剂

ex·pec·to·rate /ɪkˈspɛktəˌret; ɪkˈspektəreɪt/ *v* [I] *formal* to force liquid out of your mouth; SPIT[1] (1)【正式】咳出; 吐出

ex·pe·di·en·cy /ɪkˈspidɪənsɪ; ɪkˈspiːdiənsi/ also 又作 **ex·pe·di·ence** /-dɪəns; -diəns/ *n* [C,U] what it is useful or necessary to do in a particular situation, even if it is morally wrong 不得已而做的事; 权宜之计: *Not burying the dead soldiers was unfortunately a matter of expediency.* 不掩埋死亡士兵的尸体也是不得已的事。

ex·pe·di·ent[1] /ɪkˈspidɪənt; ɪkˈspiːdiənt/ *n* [C] a clever and effective way of dealing with a problem, even though it may be morally wrong 应急对策; 权宜之计: **by the expedient of** *Moore escaped by the simple expedient of lying down in a clump of grass.* 穆尔急中生智, 躺倒在草丛中得以脱身。

expedient[2] *adj* helping you to deal with a problem quickly and effectively, although sometimes in a way that is morally wrong 权宜之计的: **be expedient to do sth** *We have decided it would be expedient to appoint a committee to investigate the problem.* 我们认为指定一个委员会来调查这个问题是权宜之计。—opposite 反义词 INEXPEDIENT —**expediently** *adv*

ex·pe·dite /ˈɛkspɪˌdaɪt; ˈekspɪ̈daɪt/ *v* [T] to make a process happen more quickly 促进, 加快〔进程〕: *strategies to expedite the decision-making process* 加快决策进程的策略

ex·pe·di·tion /ˌɛkspɪˈdɪʃən; ˌekspɪ̈ˈdɪʃən/ *n* **1** [C] a long journey, especially one made by a group of people, to a place that is dangerous or that has not been visited before〔尤指一队人的〕远征; 探险: *Brown led an expedition to the top of Kilimanjaro.* 布朗带队赴乞力马扎罗山顶探险。**2** [C] the group of people that make this journey 远征队; 探险队: *He was the youngest member of the British Everest expedition in 1974.* 他是 1974 年英国珠穆朗玛峰探险队中最年轻的成员。**3** [C] *often humorous* a short journey, usually made for a particular purpose【常幽默】〔有特定目的的〕短途出行: **a shopping expedition** *a shopping expedition to the mall* 去购物中心买东西 **4** [U] the act of doing something more quickly than you would usually〔与平时相比的〕快速行事, 动作敏捷

ex·pe·di·tion·a·ry /ˌɛkspɪˈdɪʃənˌɛrɪ; ˌekspɪ̈ˈdɪʃənəri◄/ *adj* **expeditionary army/force etc** an army etc that is sent to a battle in another country 远征军/部队等

ex·pe·di·tious /ˌɛkspɪˈdɪʃəs; ˌekspɪ̈ˈdɪʃəs◄/ *adj formal* quick and effective【正式】迅速而有效的 —**expeditiously** *adv*: *Complaints must be dealt with expeditiously.* 一定要迅速有效地处理投诉事件。

ex·pel /ɪkˈspɛl; ɪkˈspel/ *v* **expelled, expelling** [T] **1** to dismiss someone officially from a school or organization〔从学校或组

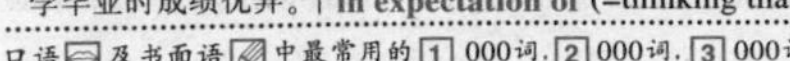

织中正式〕开除: **expel sb from** *I was expelled from school when I was fourteen.* 我在14岁时被学校开除了。| **expel sb for doing sth** *Three party members were expelled for accepting bribes.* 三名政党成员因受贿而被开除。| **get expelled** *You can get expelled for smoking.* 你会因吸烟而被开除。**2** to force a foreigner to leave a country, especially because they have broken the law or for political reasons〔尤指因犯法或政治原因〕驱逐〔外国人〕: *The government is trying to expel all journalists.* 政府正试图驱逐所有外国记者。**3** to force air, water, or gas etc out of your body or out of a container 排出〔空气、水或气体等〕—see also 另见 EXPULSION

ex·pend /ɪk`spɛnd; ɪk'spend/ *v* [T] **expend time/money/resources etc** to use or spend a lot of time etc in order to do something 耗费时间/金钱/资源等: *Try not to expend more energy than necessary.* 尽量不要耗费不必要的精力。| **expend sth in/on (doing) sth** *A great deal of time and money has been expended on creating a pleasant office atmosphere.* 为创造舒心的办公环境已花费了大量的时间和金钱。

ex·pen·da·ble /ɪk`spɛndəbḷ; ɪk'spendəbəl/ *adj* **1** no longer useful or important so that you can get rid of it 可扔掉的, 可废弃的: *This government seems to think skilled shipyard workers are expendable.* 该政府似乎认为熟练的造船工人是可有可无的。**2** a soldier who is expendable could be allowed to die〔士兵〕可牺牲的

W2 **ex·pen·di·ture** /ɪk`spɛndɪtʃɚ; ɪk'spendɪtʃə/ *n* **1** [C,U] the total amount of money that a government, organization, or person spends during a particular period of time 开支(额), 支出(额): *welfare expenditures* 福利开支 | **[+on]** *The total expenditure on defence has dropped since 1989.* 1989年以来国防总开支已有所下降。| **public expenditure** (=the amount of money a government spends on services for the public) 公共开支 —compare 比较 INCOME **2** [U] the act of spending or using time, money, energy etc〔时间、金钱、能量等的〕耗费, 花费: *The work should be produced with minimum expenditure of time and money.* 这项工作应以最少的时间和金钱来完成。

S3 W2 **ex·pense** /ɪk`spɛns; ɪk'spens/ *n* [C,U] **1** the amount of money that you have to spend on something 花销, 花费: **household/medical/living etc expenses** (=the money that you spend for a particular purpose) 家庭/医疗/生活等的支出 *The students share all the household expenses.* 学生们分担所有的日用开支。| **go to great expense** also 又作 **go to a lot of expense** (=spend a lot of money on something) 花大价钱〔在某事物上〕*We went to a lot of expense to provide the safety equipment so please take care of it.* 我们在安全设施上花了很多钱, 所以请好好照管。| **spare no expense** (=spend as much money as is necessary to get the best or most expensive things) 不惜费用, 不惜代价 *Julie's parents had spared no expense for her wedding.* 朱莉的父母不惜金钱, 就是要把她的婚礼办好。| **at great/little/no expense** *We were wined and dined at great expense.* 花大钱设了酒宴款待我们。| **think of the expense** (=it's too expensive) 想想要花的钱〔太贵了〕*I'd love to go to the Caribbean but think of the expense!* 我非常想去加勒比海度假, 但那得多少钱呀! **2 expenses** [plural] money that you spend while you are doing your job on things such as travel and food, and which your employer then pays to you 业务费用: **be on expenses** (=if the cost of something is on expenses, the person that you work for pays for it rather than you) 可以报销 *Come on, have another drink. It's all on expenses, you know.* 来吧, 再喝一杯, 反正能报销, 你知道。| **all expenses paid** (=something, especially a holiday or journey that is all paid for by someone else)〔尤指度假或旅行〕免费的, 别人支付的 *The prize is an all expenses paid trip to Rio.* 奖品为全程免费到里约热内卢度假。**3 at sb's expense a)** if you do something at someone's expense, they pay for you to do it 由某人付费: *Bill's just been on a computing course, all at the company's expense.* 比尔刚开始学习一个电脑课程, 费用全部由公司支付。**b)** if you make jokes at someone's expense, you laugh about them 嘲笑某人: *Louis kept making jokes at his wife's expense.* 路易斯不断地嘲笑妻子。**4 at the expense of** if something is done at the expense of something else, it is only achieved by harming the other thing 以(损害)…为代价: *High production rates are often achieved at the expense of quality of work.* 高产出率常常是以产品质量下降为代价的。

expense ac·count /·'· ·,·/ *n* [C] a system that allows someone who works for a company to spend the company's money rather than their own on hotels, meals etc 费用账户〔由公司支付食宿费等〕

S1 W2 **ex·pen·sive** /ɪk`spɛnsɪv; ɪk'spensɪv/ *adj* **1** costing a lot of money 昂贵的, 花钱多的: *That's a very expensive camera. Is it insured?* 那台照相机非常贵, 买保险了吗? | *the most expensive restaurant in town* 城里最贵的餐馆 | **expensive to produce/run/buy etc** *Cadillacs are beautiful cars but expensive to run.* 凯迪拉克牌汽车很漂亮, 但用起来很费钱。| **prohibitively expensive** (=so expensive that most people cannot afford it) 极昂贵的, 大多数人不敢问津的 **2 expensive mistake** a mistake that puts you in a very bad situation 代价昂贵的错误: *Losing your temper with the client was a very expensive mistake; we've lost the contract.* 你对客户发脾气是个代价昂贵的错误, 我们的合同签不成了。—**expensively** *adv*

S1 W1 **ex·pe·ri·ence**[1] /ɪk`spɪrɪəns; ɪk'spɪəriəns/ *n*

1 ►**KNOWLEDGE/SKILL** 知识/技能◄ [U] knowledge or skill gained while doing a job 经验: **[+in]** *Karl has considerable experience in modern methods of diagnosis.* 卡尔在现代诊断方法方面非常有经验。| **political/teaching/computing etc experience** *The job requires no secretarial experience.* 这个职位无需秘书工作的经验。| **previous experience** *The interviewer asked if I had any previous experience.* 面试考官问我以前是否做过这方面的工作。| **lack of experience** *He didn't get the post, due to lack of experience.* 他因缺乏工作经验而未能获得那个职位。| **get/gain experience** *Fran is gaining valuable experience working for her father's firm.* 弗兰在她父亲的公司上班, 正在积累宝贵的工作经验。| **practical experience** (=experience gained by actually doing something, rather than knowledge from books etc) 实践经验 *good judgements based on sound practical experience* 以充足的实际经验为基础的良好判断 | **have experience on your side** (=have an advantage over other people because you know more about a particular thing than they do or have been doing it for longer) 比别人更有经验 *Sampras is a skilful player, but Becker has experience on his side.* 桑普拉斯是一名技术出色的球员, 但贝克尔经验丰富些。| **first-hand experience of** (=experience gained by actually doing something) …的第一手经验; …的亲身体验 *Kevin has first-hand experience of living in Italy.* 凯文对意大利的生活有亲身体验。

2 ►**OF LIFE** 关于生活◄ [U] the state of knowing, or having learnt a lot, about life and the world from events that have happened to you and people you have met 经历; 阅历: **in your experience** *In my experience, these things never last very long.* 从我的经验来看, 这些事情从未长久过。| **past/personal experience** *Past experience told her that none of the students would have prepared the lesson.* 过去的经验告诉她, 没有一个学生会预习功课。| **know from bitter experience** (=know what is likely to happen in a particular situation because you have learned from unpleasant or difficult experiences) 有过经验教训 *Rita knew from bitter experience not to rely on Martin in a crisis.* 惨痛的教训告诉丽塔, 危难时刻不能依赖马丁。| **learn from (your) experience** *There's no point telling teenagers anything – you just have to let them learn from their experience.* 教导青少年该如何做毫无意义 — 你只能让他们从实践中学习。| **experience shows that...** *Experience shows that staff respond very well to a more consultative approach.* 经验表明, 员工们会非常欢迎更具协商性的方式。

3 ►**STH THAT HAPPENS** 发生的事◄ [C] something that happens to you or something you do, especially when this affects or influences you in some way 往事, 经历; 感受: *childhood experiences* 儿时的经历 | **[+of/with]** *This was my first experience of living with other people.* 这是我第一次与别人住在一起的经历。| **[+for]** *Failing an exam was a new experience for me.* 考试不过关对我来说还是第一次。| **a bad/strange/dreadful experience** *It was a strange experience to see my father being taken to hospital on a stretcher.* 对我来说, 看见父亲被担架抬到医院去是一次奇怪的感受。| **a memorable/unforgettable experience** *Reaching the top of Mt Whitney was an unforgettable experience.* 登上惠特尼峰是一次难忘的经历。| **quite an experience** (=very interesting, exciting etc) 非常带劲儿[刺激]的事 *Parachuting is quite an experience, let me tell you.* 听我说, 跳伞是件非常刺激的事。| **religious experience** (=a situation in which you feel, hear, or see something that affects you strongly and makes you believe in God) 宗教体验〔使人信仰上帝的体验〕*She claimed to have had some sort of religious experience while in Africa.* 她声称在非洲期间感受到某种宗教体验。

4 the black/female/Russian etc experience [U] events or knowledge shared by the members of a particular society or group of people 黑人/女性/俄罗斯人等的经验[体验]: *No writer has ever expressed the black experience with such passion as Toni Morisson.* 没有作家像托尼·莫里森那样以充满激情的笔调描述了黑人社群的体验。

5 work experience a) a system in which a student can work for a company in order to learn about a job〔学生到公司进行的〕工作实习 **b)** the period of time during which a student does

this 实习期: *Ella is about to do work experience with a clothing manufacturer.* 埃拉将去一家服装生产企业进行实习。

experience² *v* [T] **1** if you experience a problem or situation, it happens to you or affects you 经历; 体验: *Children need to experience things for themselves in order to learn from them.* 儿童需要自己经历事情以便从中学习。| *Germany experienced a period of enormous growth in the 60s.* 德国在60年代经历了一段时间的经济腾飞。| **experience sth at first hand** (=know about something because it has affected you directly, rather than just reading or hearing about it) 亲身经历[体验] *During the war they experienced at first hand the horror of night bombing raids.* 在战争期间,他们亲身体验了夜间空袭的恐惧。**2** to feel a particular emotion or physical sensation 体会到; 感受到: *Many women experience feelings of nausea during pregnancy.* 许多妇女在怀孕期间会有恶心想吐的感觉。

ex·pe·ri·enced /ɪk`spɪrɪənst; ɪk'spɪəriənst/ *adj* possessing skills or knowledge because you have done something often or for a long time 经验丰富的, 有经验的: *an experienced pilot* 经验丰富的飞行员 | **[+in]** *Blake's very experienced in microsurgery.* 布莱克在显微外科方面极富经验。

ex·per·i·en·tial /ɪk͵spɪrɪ`enʃəl; ɪk͵spɪəri'enʃəl◂/ *adj* based on or connected with experience 由经验得来的; 与经验相关的: *experiential approaches to learning* 学习上的经验方法

ex·per·i·ment¹ /ɪk`spɛrəmənt; ɪk'sperɪ̵mənt/ *n* [C,U] **1** a thorough test using scientific methods to discover how someone or something reacts under certain conditions 实验: **[+in/on/with]** *experiments on sleep deprivation* 剥夺睡眠实验 | **do/conduct/carry out/perform an experiment** (=do an experiment) 做实验 *Joule carried out a series of simple experiments to test his theory.* 焦耳做了一系列简单的实验来验证他的理论。**2** a process in which a new idea or method is tested to see if it is useful or effective 试验: *an experiment in private enterprise* 私有制企业的试验 | **by experiment** *Find out by experiment what foods the baby likes.* 通过试验来弄清楚婴儿喜欢吃什么。

ex·per·i·ment² /ɪk`spɛrə͵mɛnt; ɪk'sperɪ̵ment/ *v* [I] **1** to try various ideas, methods etc to see whether they will work or what effect they will have 试验; 试用: **[+with/on]** *I'm seeing children of 6 experiment with drugs.* 我看见六岁大的孩子在试吸毒品。**2** to test something using scientific methods to see if it is true or to obtain more information about it 用…做实验: **[+with/on]** *activists protesting against experimenting on animals* 抗议用动物做实验的积极分子 —**experimenter** *n* [C]

ex·per·i·men·tal /ɪk͵spɛrə`mɛntḷ; ɪk͵sperɪ̵'mentl◂/ *adj* **1** used for, connected with, or resulting from experiments 用于做实验的; 实验的; 实验得出的: *experimental animals* 用于实验的动物 | *experimental data* 实验数据 **2** using new ideas or methods 试验(性)的: *experimental teaching techniques* 试验性的教学技巧

ex·per·i·men·tal·ly /ɪk͵spɛrə`mɛntḷɪ; ɪk͵sperɪ̵'mentli/ *adv* **1** in a way that is connected with experiments 实验地: *data obtained experimentally* 实验获得的数据 **2** in a way that involves using new ideas or methods 作为试验地: *The Americans experimentally exploded the first nuclear weapon in the history of mankind.* 美国人试爆了人类历史上第一颗核武器。**3** if you do something experimentally you do it in order to see or feel what something is like 试探(性)地: *He ran his fingers experimentally over the animal's back.* 他试探着用手指抚摸那动物的后背。

ex·pe·ri·men·ta·tion /ɪk͵spɛrəmɛn`teʃən; ɪk͵sperɪ̵men'teɪʃən/ *n* [U] the process of testing various ideas, methods etc to see whether they will work or what effect they have 试验: *There is often a period of sexual experimentation during adolescence.* 人在青春期常会经历一个性体验阶段。| **[+with/in]** *experimentation with different combinations of chemicals* 试验不同的化学物质组合

ex·pert¹ /`ɛkspɝt; 'ekspɜːt/ *n* [C] someone who has a special skill or special knowledge of a subject 专家, 内行: **[+on/in/at]** *He's an expert in electronic music.* 他是电子音乐方面的行家。

expert² *adj* having a special skill or special knowledge of a subject 专家的, 内行的: *Ministers depend on civil servants for expert advice.* 部长需要公务员提供内行的意见。—**expertly** *adv* —**expertness** *n* [U]

ex·per·tise /͵ɛkspɚ`tiz; ͵ekspɜː'tiːz/ *n* [U] special skills or knowledge in a particular subject 专门技能[知识]: *trainee engineers with varying degrees of computer expertise* 电脑专业技能参差不齐的受训工程师 | **[+in]** *expertise in the field of literary criticism* 文学批评方面的专业知识

expert sys·tem /͵·· `··/ *n* [C] a computer system containing a lot of information about one particular subject, so that it can help someone find an answer to a problem 专家系统〔指储存大量某方面的信息以便帮人解决问题的电脑系统〕

ex·pi·ate /`ɛkspɪ͵et; 'ekspieɪt/ *v* [T] *formal* to be sorry for something you have done wrong and accept your punishment willingly, or try to do something to improve what you did【正式】为〔做错事而〕甘愿受罚; 补偿 —**expiation** /͵ɛkspɪ`eʃən; ͵ekspi'eɪʃən/ *n*: *the expiation of your sins* 赎罪

ex·pir·a·tion /͵ɛkspə`reʃən; ͵ekspɪ̵'reɪʃən/ *n* [U] the American form of EXPIRY expiry 的美语形式

expiration date /··`·· ͵·/ *n* [C] *AmE* the date on which something can no longer be used or is no longer safe to eat【美】(开始)失效日期 —see also 另见 **expiry date** (EXPIRY (2)), SELL-BY DATE

ex·pire /ɪk`spaɪr; ɪk'spaɪə/ *v* [I] **1** if an official document expires, the period of time during which it can be used ends〔正式文件等〕到期, 过期, 失效: *My passport expires next week.* 我的护照下周就过期了。| **[+on/in/at]** *Our contracts are due to expire on 20 June.* 我们的合同6月20日到期。**2** if a period of time when someone has a particular position of authority expires, it ends〔任期〕届满: *The chairman's term of office expires at the end of March.* 主席的任期3月底届满。**3** *literary* if someone expires, they die【文】死亡: *Ophelia expires in Act IV of Hamlet.* 奥菲莉娅在《哈姆雷特》第四幕中死去。

ex·pir·y /ɪk`spaɪrɪ; ɪk'spaɪəri/ *n* [U] *BrE*【英】**1** the end of a period of time during which an official document can be used, or of a period of authority〔正式文件〕到期; 〔任期〕届满; EXPIRATION *AmE*【美】**2 expiry date** the date on which something can no longer be used (开始)失效日期: *Check the expiry date on your passport.* 看一下你的护照什么时候到期。

ex·plain /ɪk`splen; ɪk'spleɪn/ *v* [I,T] **1** to make something clear or easy to understand 解释, 说明: *Our lawyer carefully explained the procedure.* 我们的律师仔细解释了程序。| **explain (to sb) why/how/where etc** *The librarian will explain how to use the catalogue system.* 图书馆管理员将说明如何使用目录系统。| **explain that** *I explained that I was really a police officer.* 我解释说我的确是警察。| **explain (sth) to sb** *He briefly explained the situation to them.* 他向他们简要介绍了一下情况。**2** to give or be a reason for something 说明[是]…的原因: *Wait! I can explain everything.* 等一下!我可以解释一切。| **explain that** *She explained that she had been ill.* 她解释说她病了。| **explain why/how etc** *Perhaps genetic differences can explain why some women develop breast cancer and others do not.* 也许基因差异可以解释为什么有些妇女患乳腺癌, 另一些妇女却没有。**3 explain yourself a)** to tell someone who is angry or upset with you the reasons why you did something 作出解释; 表白: *Mr Hennessey tells me you haven't been to school for the last few days; I think you'd better explain yourself.* 亨尼西先生告诉我你有好几天没上学了, 你最好解释一下为什么。**b)** to say clearly what you mean 把自己的意思说清楚: *No, I didn't mean that. I guess I haven't explained myself very well.* 不, 我不是那个意思, 我想我是没说清楚。

explain sth ↔ **away** *phr v* [T] to tell someone the reason why you did something or why something happened in order to make it seem less important or not your fault 通过解释消除〔某事的影响〕; 辩解: *That woman finds more ways to explain away her failures than anyone I've ever met!* 那个女人是我见过的最能找办法为自己的失败开脱的人!

ex·pla·na·tion /͵ɛksplə`neʃən; ͵eksplə'neɪʃən/ *n* **1** [C,U] the reasons given for why something happened or why you did something 解释, 给出的原因: *I'm waiting to hear your explanation.* 我在等着听你的解释。| **[+for]** *He'd better have a good explanation for his behaviour!* 他真该好好解释一下自己的行为! | **[+of]** *Did Valerie give any explanation of why she was late?* 瓦莱丽有没有解释她为什么迟到? | **in explanation of** (=as a reason for) 作为解释 *In explanation of the job cuts, the firm said that orders had been much lower than expected.* 在解释裁员的原因时, 公司说定货量比预期要少得多。| **provide/come up with an explanation** *After failing to come up with an adequate explanation, Smith was arrested for robbery.* 由于未能给出充分的解释, 史密斯因抢劫罪被捕了。—see 见 EXCUSE² (USAGE) **2** [C] a statement or piece of writing intended to describe how something works or make something easier to understand 解释, 说明: *Each of the diagrams was accompanied by a simple explanation.* 每一张图表都附有简单的说明。| **[+of]** *I'll try and give you a quick explanation of how the machine works.* 我争取快速地给你解释一下机器的工作原理。

ex·plan·a·to·ry /ɪk`splænə͵torɪ; ɪk'splænətəri/ *adj* intended to describe how something works or make something easier to understand 解释的, 说明的: *explanatory notes at the end of each chapter* 每一章后的注释 —see also 另见 SELF-EXPLANATORY

ex·ple·tive /ˋɛksplətɪv; ɪkˈspliːtɪv/ *n* [C] *formal* a rude word that you use when you are angry or in pain【正式】咒骂语: *a mild expletive such as 'damn'* 像"该死"之类较轻的咒骂语

ex·pli·ca·ble /ˋɛksplɪkəbḷ; ekˈsplɪkəbəl/ *adj* [often in negatives 常用于否定句] able to be easily understood or explained 易于理解的; 容易解释的: *for no explicable reason* 原因不明 — opposite 反义词 INEXPLICABLE

ex·pli·cate /ˋɛksplɪˌket; ˈeksplɨkeɪt/ *v* [T] *formal* to explain a work of literature, an idea etc in detail【正式】详细解释〔文学作品、主张等〕—**explication** /ˌɛksplɪˋkeʃən; ˌeksplɨˈkeɪʃən/ *n* [C,U]

ex·pli·cit /ɪkˋsplɪsɪt; ɪkˈsplɪsɨt/ *adj* **1** **explicit instructions/warnings etc** an explicit instruction etc is expressed in a way that is very clear 清楚明确的指示/警告等: *There was no explicit mention in the report of Capt Kirk's involvement.* 报告中并未明确提及是否牵连到柯克上尉。| **make something explicit** *The contrast could not have been made more explicit.* 这个对比再清楚不过了。**2** **be explicit** to say something very clearly and directly 直截了当: *I don't quite understand your plan. Could you be a little more explicit, please?* 对你的计划我不太明白, 你能直截了当说清楚吗? | [+about] *Sadie was very explicit about her reasons for wanting a divorce.* 萨迪清楚地表明了她想离婚的理由。**3** language or pictures that are explicit describe or show sex or violence very clearly〔描绘性行为或暴力时〕清晰露骨的: *The film contains some very explicit love scenes.* 这部影片含有一些露骨的性行为镜头。—compare 比较 IMPLICIT —**explicitly** *adv* —**explicitness** *n* [U]

ex·plode /ɪkˋsplod; ɪkˈspləʊd/ *v*

1 ▶BURST 爆炸◀ [I,T] to burst, or to make something burst, into small pieces, usually with a loud noise and in a way that causes damage (使) 爆炸: *We sat in the bombshelter listening to the enemy shells exploding.* 我们坐在防空洞里, 听见敌人炮弹的阵阵爆炸声。—compare 比较 IMPLODE

2 ▶GET ANGRY 发怒◀ [I] to suddenly become angry or dangerous 勃然大怒; 变得危险: *These guys tend to explode at any moment over the least thing.* 这些家伙随时都会因微不足道的事而大发雷霆。| [+in/with/into] *Tensions are running high and police are afraid the situation may explode into violence.* 局势越来越紧张, 警方担心会爆发暴力行为。

3 ▶PROVE FALSE 证明错误◀ [T] to prove that something that many people think or believe, is wrong or not true 戳穿, 破除: **explode a myth/rumour etc** *The book explodes many myths about rape.* 这本书推翻了许多有关强奸的错误观点。

4 ▶GET BIGGER 变大◀ [I] to increase greatly in numbers or amount 急剧增长, 激增: *The population exploded in the early 1970s.* 20世纪70年代初期, 人口急剧增长。

5 ▶MAKE A LOUD NOISE 发出巨响◀ [I] to make a very loud noise 爆响, 发出巨大声音: *A clap of thunder exploded overhead.* 一声惊雷在头顶爆响。

6 ▶MOVE SUDDENLY 突然移动◀ [I] to suddenly begin moving or doing something very quickly 迸发, 突发: [+into] *Nancy exploded into action.* 南希突发行动。| *The engine suddenly exploded into life.* 发动机突然开动了。

ex·plod·ed /ɪkˋsplodɪd; ɪkˈspləʊdɨd/ *adj technical* an exploded drawing, model etc shows the parts of something separately but in a way that shows how they are related or put together【术语】〔图或模型〕分解的: *an exploded diagram of an engine* 发动机的分解图

3 **ex·ploit¹** /ɪkˋsplɔɪt; ɪkˈsplɔɪt/ *v* [T] **1** to treat someone unfairly in order to get money or an advantage for yourself 剥削, 利用〔某人为自己服务〕: *People who work at home are more easily exploited by employers.* 在家工作的人更容易受雇主的剥削。**2** to use something fully and effectively in order to gain an advantage or profit 充分利用; 开发〔某物〕: *Casey founded a company to exploit the mineral resources in the area.* 凯西创立了一家公司来开发当地的矿产资源。—**exploitable** *adj* —**exploiter** *n* [C]

ex·ploit² /ˋɛksplɔɪt; ˈeksplɔɪt/ *n* [C usually plural 一般用复数] brave and exciting actions that people admire 英雄业绩; 英勇行为: *the exploits of the early explorers of the Canadian forests* 加拿大森林早期拓荒者的业绩

ex·ploi·ta·tion /ˌɛksplɔɪˋteʃən; ˌeksplɔɪˈteɪʃən/ *n* [U] **1** a situation in which someone treats someone else unfairly in order to get money or an advantage for themselves 剥削: *the exploitation of children in factories in the 1900's* 20世纪最初的几年中工厂对童工的剥削 **2** a process in which materials or someone's skills are used effectively in order to gain an advantage or profit 开发, 充分利用: *guidelines on the controlled exploitation of ocean resources* 关于有节制地开发海洋资源的指导方针

ex·ploit·a·tive /ɛkˋsplɔɪtətɪv; ɪkˈsplɔɪtətɪv/ *adj* treating people unfairly to get money or an advantage 剥削的: *exploitative employers* 剥削 (雇工) 的雇主

ex·plo·ra·tion /ˌɛkspləˋreʃən; ˌekspləˈreɪʃən/ *n* [C,U] **1** an examination of an area or journey through it in order to find out what is there or what it is like〔对某地区的〕勘查, 考察: *The North Sea has been an important centre for oil exploration.* 北海已成为重要的石油勘探中心。| [+of] *the exploration of space* 宇宙空间探索 **2** an examination or discussion of something to find out more about it 研究, 探究: [+into] *an exploration into the local records* 研究当地记录

ex·plo·ra·to·ry /ɪkˋsplorəˌtorɪ; ɪkˈsplɒrətəri/ *adj* done in order to find out more about something 探索的, 考察的: *exploratory surgery* 诊察性外科手术

ex·plore /ɪkˋsplor; ɪkˈsplɔː/ *v* **1** [I,T] to travel through or examine an area in order to find out what is there or what it is like 勘查, 考察 (某地区): *Lewis and Clark explored the territory from St Louis to the Pacific.* 刘易斯和克拉克勘查了从圣路易斯到太平洋海岸之间的地区。| *exploring for gold* 勘探金矿 **2** [T] to examine or discuss something carefully in order to find out more about it 检查, 探讨: *a theme explored by Mrs. Gaskell in her later novels* 盖斯凯尔夫人后期小说探讨的主题 3 2

ex·plo·rer /ɪkˋsplorə; ɪkˈsplɔːrə/ *n* [C] someone who travels through an area about which little is known or which has not been visited before 探险者; 勘查者

ex·plo·sion /ɪkˋsploʒən; ɪkˈspləʊʒən/ *n* **1** [C] a loud sound caused by something such as a bomb bursting into small pieces 爆炸 (声): *a nuclear explosion* 核爆炸 | [+of] *The explosion of the space shuttle Challenger shocked the nation.* "挑战者"号航天飞机的爆炸震惊了整个国家。**2** [C,U] a process in which something such as a bomb is deliberately made to explode 引爆: *controlled explosion of the device* 装置的控制引爆 **3** [C] a sudden or rapid increase in the number or amount of something 激增, 急剧膨胀: *The population explosion in India caused famine and poverty.* 印度人口激增导致了饥荒和贫困。**4** [C] a sudden expression of emotion, especially anger〔感情的, 尤指愤怒的〕爆发, 迸发: *His frustration grew, and I expected an explosion at any minute.* 他越来越沮丧, 我感到他随时会爆发。**5** [C] a sudden very loud noise 突然发出的响声: *an explosion of laughter* 迸发的一阵笑声

ex·plo·sive¹ /ɪkˋsplosɪv; ɪkˈspləʊsɪv/ *adj* **1** able or likely to explode 会爆炸的: *At high temperatures this gas is explosive.* 这种气体在高温时会爆炸。| **explosive device** (=a bomb) 爆炸装置, 炸弹 **2** an explosive situation is violent or dangerous〔形势〕爆炸性的, 一触即发的: *the explosive atmosphere of the inner cities* 市中心贫民区内一触即发的气氛 **3** increasing suddenly or rapidly in amount or number〔数量或数字〕激增的: *the computer industry's explosive growth* 电脑产业的迅猛发展 **4** tending to show angry violent feelings suddenly 暴躁的: *an explosive temperament* 暴躁的脾气 **5** having great force or power, usually as the result of an explosion〔通常指因爆炸而〕力量巨大的: *The bullet hit its target with explosive force.* 子弹猛烈地击中了目标。**6** an explosive sound is sudden and loud 轰响的 —**explosively** *adv* —**explosiveness** *n* [U]

explosive² *n* [C] a substance that can cause an explosion 炸药, 爆炸物质: *Semtex, the explosive used in the Lockerbie airplane disaster* 塞姆汀, 洛克比空难中使用的炸药 — see also 另见 HIGH EXPLOSIVE, PLASTIC EXPLOSIVE

ex·po /ˋɛkspo; ˈekspəʊ/ *n* [C] *informal* an EXPOSITION (2)【非正式】展览会, 博览会

ex·po·nent /ɪkˋsponənt; ɪkˈspəʊnənt/ *n* [C] **1** someone who supports an idea, belief etc and who tries to explain it and persuade others that it is good or useful〔想法、信仰的〕倡导者, 鼓吹者, 说明者: [+of] *a leading exponent of Jungian psychology* 〔瑞士精神病学家〕荣格精神分析法的主要倡导者 **2** someone whose work or methods provide a good example of a particular skill, idea, or activity 典型代表: [+of] *The poet Goethe is a supreme exponent of the Romantic response to nature.* 诗人歌德的作品代表了浪漫主义文学对大自然的回应, 成就最高。**3** *technical* a sign written above and to the right of a number or letter to show how many times that quantity is to be multiplied by itself, for example 2^3【术语】指数, 幂

ex·po·nen·tial /ˌɛkspoˋnɛnʃəl; ˌekspəˈnenʃəl◀/ *adj* **1** **exponential growth/increase** *technical* a rate of growth that becomes faster as the amount of the thing that is growing increases【术语】指数增长 **2** *technical* using a sign that shows how many times a number is to be multiplied by itself【术语】指数的, 含有指数的: *y^n is an exponential expression.* y^n是一个指数式。—**exponentially** *adv*

ex·port[1] /ˋɛksport; ˈekspɔːt/ *n* **1** [U] the sale of goods to another country 出口: [+of] *The export of electronic equipment has risen sharply.* 电子设备出口已大幅增加。| **export market/industry/licence etc** *Export licences for arms are strictly controlled.* 武器出口许可证受到严格限制。**2** [C usually plural 一般用复数] a product that is sold to another country 出口商品: *Wheat is one of Alberta's chief exports.* 小麦是〔加拿大〕艾伯塔省的主要出口商品之一。| **invisible export** (=something that is sold to another country which is not an industrial product, food etc) 无形出口商品〔指非实物的出口〕*Selling insurance overseas is Britain's largest invisible export.* 在海外销售保险是英国最大的无形出口。—opposite 反义词 IMPORT[1] (1,2)

ex·port[2] /ɪksˋpɔrt; ɪkˈspɔːt/ *v* **1** [I,T] to sell goods to another country 出口: **export sth to sb** *In 1986 the company exported about 210,000 cases of wine to the UK.* 1986年该公司向英国出口了约21万箱葡萄酒。**2** [T] to introduce an activity, idea etc to another place or country 传播, 输送〔到另一国家或地区〕: *The influence of African music has been exported to many parts of the western world.* 非洲音乐的影响已传播到西方世界的许多地方。—opposite 反义词 IMPORT[1] —**exportation** /ˌɛksporˋteʃən; ˌekspɔːˈteɪʃən/ *n* [U]

ex·port·er /ɪkˋsportɚ; ɪkˈspɔːtə/ *n* [C] a person, company, or country that sells goods to another country 出口者〔包括个人、公司或国家〕: [+of] *Saudi Arabia, a leading exporter of oil* 沙特阿拉伯, 主要石油输出国 —opposite 反义词 IMPORTER

ex·pose /ɪkˋspoz; ɪkˈspəʊz/ *v* [T]

1 ►SHOW 显示◄ to show something that is usually covered 显露, 暴露: *The wolf opened its mouth to expose a row of sharp white teeth.* 狼张开嘴, 露出一排白色的尖牙。| **expose sth to sth** *Wounds that are exposed to the air heal more quickly.* 伤口暴露在空气中愈合得更快。

2 ►TO STH DANGEROUS 遇到危险之物◄ to put someone in a harmful situation, position etc, where they have no protection against something dangerous 使暴露于〔险境〕, 使置身于〔危险〕当中: **expose sb to sth** *The report revealed that workers had been exposed to unacceptably high levels of radiation.* 报告披露了工人们受到有害的高强度辐射。| **expose yourself to ridicule/criticism etc** (=say or do something that may make people laugh at you, criticize you etc) 使自己被取笑/批评等

3 ►TELL THE TRUTH 讲真话◄ to tell the truth about something, or show what it is really like, especially because you think it is harmful, illegal etc 揭露, 揭发: *a radical group that works to expose and condemn racism* 专门揭发和谴责种族主义的激进团体 | **expose sb as sth** *Klaus von Bulow was exposed as a liar and a cheat.* 揭发出来克劳斯·冯·布洛是一个说谎者和骗子。

4 ►SEE/EXPERIENCE 看/体验◄ to learn about beliefs, ideas etc, especially by seeing things or having new experiences 使接触〔学习新事物〕: **expose sb to sth** *Travel abroad exposes children to different languages and cultures.* 去国外旅行使孩子们接触到不同的语言和文化。

5 ►PHOTOGRAPH 照片◄ to allow light onto a piece of film in a camera in order to take a photograph 使曝光

6 ►FEELINGS 感受◄ to show other people feelings that you usually hide, especially by behaving in a particular way 显露〔情感〕: *Eric broke down and wept, exposing the vulnerable side of his nature.* 埃里克失声痛哭, 显露出他个性中脆弱的一面。

7 expose yourself if a man exposes himself, he shows his sexual organs to someone he does not know in a public place, usually because he is mentally ill〔由于病态心理而在公共场所〕裸露性器官

ex·po·sé /ˌɛkspəˋze; ekˈspəʊzeɪ/ *n* [C] a story in a newspaper or on television that shows people the truth about something, especially something dishonest or illegal〔报纸、电视节目等〕揭露: [+of] *an exposé of corrupt practices by lawyers* 对律师们腐败行为的揭露

ex·posed /ɪkˋspozd; ɪkˈspəʊzd/ *adj* **1** not protected from the weather 无遮蔽的, 暴露(于风雨中)的: *an exposed coastline* 裸露的海岸线 **2** not protected from attack; VULNERABLE 无保护的, 易受攻击的: *Fiorentina's defence looked very exposed in the second half.* 在下半场, 佛罗伦萨队的防守名存实亡。

ex·po·si·tion /ˌɛkspəˋzɪʃən; ˌekspəˈzɪʃən/ *n* **1** [C,U] a clear and detailed explanation 明确细致的解释, 详细阐述: [+of] *a lucid exposition of educational theories* 对教育理论的明白阐述 **2** [C] an important event at which industrial goods are shown 展览会, 博览会

ex post fac·to law /ˌɛks post ˋfækto ˌlɔ; ˌeks pəʊst ˈfæktəʊ ˌlɔː/ *n* [C] *law* a law that makes a particular action into a crime, and then punishes people who took that action before it had legally become a crime【法律】有追溯效力的法律

ex·pos·tu·late /ɪkˋspɑstʃəˌlet; ɪkˈspɒstʃʊleɪt/ *v* [I] *formal* to express strong disapproval, disagreement, or annoyance【正式】反对; 抗议; 反驳: **expostulate (that)** *"But that's the equivalent of saying that you drank beer but didn't swallow it," expostulated one reporter.* "但那等于是说, 你喝了啤酒但未咽下去。"一名记者反驳说。—**expostulation** /ɪkˌspɑstʃəˋleʃən; ɪkˌspɒstʃʊˈleɪʃən/ *n* [C,U]

ex·po·sure /ɪkˋspoʒɚ; ɪkˈspəʊʒə/ *n*

1 ►TO DANGER 受危害◄ [C,U] the state of being put into a situation that is harmful because you have no protection from something that is dangerous 暴露: [+to] *Skin cancer can be caused by prolonged exposure to the sun.* 长时间晒太阳会导致皮肤癌。| *Through TV, kids have regular exposure to sex and violence.* 儿童在电视中时常看到性和暴力镜头。

2 ►TRUTH 真相◄ [C,U] something that is said or written in order to tell people the truth about something illegal, dishonest, or harmful 揭发, 披露: *The exposure of George Davis' illicit financial dealings provoked a public outcry.* 乔治·戴维斯的非法金融交易被揭露后, 公众为之哗然。

3 ►MAKE FACTS KNOWN 使事实被知晓◄ [U] things that are said and written on television and in newspapers that make a person or event known to a lot of people 报道, 曝光: *The failure of their marriage has received a lot of exposure in the press recently.* 他们婚姻失败一事近来被媒体频频曝光。

4 ►BE VERY COLD 感觉非常冷◄ [U] if you have exposure you are extremely cold and ill, especially because you have been outside in very cold weather for too long without protection 受冻: *We nearly died of exposure on the mountainside.* 我们差点冻死在山腰上。

5 ►PHOTOGRAPHY 摄影◄ [C] **a)** a length of film in a camera that is used to take a photograph 底片中的一张: *I have three exposures left on this roll.* 我这卷胶卷还剩三张。**b)** the amount of time a piece of film is exposed (EXPOSE (5)) to the light when making a photograph 曝光时间

6 ►SHOW 显示◄ [C] the act of showing something that is usually hidden 显露, 暴露

7 ►DIRECTION 方向◄ [singular] the direction in which a building, hill etc faces〔建筑、山等的〕朝向: *My bedroom has a southern exposure.* 我的卧室朝南。—see also 另见 INDECENT EXPOSURE

ex·pound /ɪkˋspaund; ɪkˈspaʊnd/ *v* [I,T] *formal* to explain or talk about something in detail【正式】阐述; 详细解释: [+on] *a philosopher expounding on the illusory nature of the world* 阐述世界虚幻本质的哲学家

ex·press[1] /ɪkˋsprɛs; ɪkˈspres/ *v* [T]

1 ►IN WORDS 用话语◄ to tell people what you are feeling or thinking by using words 表达, 陈述: *Bill's never been afraid to express his opinions.* 比尔从来不怕表达自己的观点。| **express sympathy/fear/anger etc** *Parents have expressed their concerns about their children's safety.* 父母表达了对自己孩子安全的关切。| **express interest** (=say that you are interested in something) 表示有兴趣 *The public are expressing an increasing interest in green issues.* 公众对环保问题日益关注。| **express opposition to** (=say publicly that you do not agree with something) 对…表示反对 *Managers and players alike expressed opposition to the scheme.* 管理层和队员都反对该计划。| **express thanks/gratitude** (=thank someone in a speech or by writing a letter) 表示感谢/感激 *Finally, I'd like to express my sincere gratitude for your help in this matter.* 最后, 我对你在此事中给予的帮助表示诚挚的感谢。| **express yourself** (=let people know your thoughts and feelings so that they can understand) 表达自己(的想法和感受) *Young children often have difficulty expressing themselves.* 幼儿常常很难清楚地表达自己。| **can't express** *Words can't express how angry we felt.* 言语无法表达我们心中的愤怒。

2 ►IN ART/MUSIC ETC 在艺术/音乐等方面◄ to show your feelings or thoughts using art, music, films etc 描绘, 表达: *Many of Munch's paintings express a deep feeling of despair.* 蒙克的许多画作都表达一种深深的绝望。| **express yourself by/through etc** *Alain expresses himself best through his music.* 阿兰最善于用音乐来表达自己的思想。

3 ►IN BEHAVIOUR/LOOK 在行为/表情方面◄ to let people know what you are feeling or thinking by the look on your face or by your behaviour〔以表情或行为来〕表现, 显示〔感受或想法〕: *The look on Paul's face expressed his total contempt for them.* 保罗脸上的表情显示出对他们的彻底鄙视。

4 ►FEELING 感受◄ if a feeling expresses itself it can be clearly seen and understood 流露, 表露: *Major Hall's frustration expressed itself in occasional bouts of rage.* 霍尔少校偶尔发火, 表露出他的沮丧。

5 ▶**LETTER/PACKAGE** 信件/包裹◀ *BrE* to send a letter or package using a special post system so that it arrives very quickly【英】用快邮寄出

6 ▶**MATHEMATICS** 数学◀ *technical* to show a mathematical idea in a particular form【术语】〔用某种形式〕表示: *Express three-quarters as a decimal.* 用小数来表示四分之三。

express² *adj* [only before noun 仅用于名词前] **1** an express command, desire, or aim is deliberately stated for a particular reason 专门表示的, 特别指出的: *Matthew left express instructions to keep all doors locked.* 马修特别指示要把门都锁好。| *I came here with the express purpose of seeing you.* 我来这里就是为了看你。**2 express train/coach/service** a train or bus that travels very quickly 快速列车/长途汽车/客运服务: *There's an express service between London and Glasgow twice daily.* 伦敦和格拉斯哥之间每天有两班快车。**3 express post/mail/delivery** a system within the Post Office that delivers letters and packages very quickly 特快邮递 **4 express lane** *AmE* a LANE (2) on a FREEWAY used by vehicles that are travelling fast【美】〔高速公路上的〕快车道

express³ *n* **1** [C usually singular 一般用单数] a train or bus that travels from one place to another very quickly〔火车或公共汽车的〕快车: **London-Gatwick Express/Orient Express** (=a fast train or bus which does a particular journey regularly) 伦敦—盖特威克快车/东方快车 **2** [U] a post service that delivers letters and packages very quickly 邮件快递: *Send these books by express.* 把这些书用快件寄出去。

express⁴ *adv* **send/deliver sth express** to send or deliver a letter, parcel etc quickly using a special post service 用快递寄/送某物

Express, The a British daily TABLOID newspaper which usually supports the ideas of the Conservative Party《快报》〔英国一每日小报, 通常支持保守党观点〕

ex·pres·sion /ɪk`sprɛʃən; ɪk'spreʃən/ *n*

1 ▶**WORDS** 言语◀ [C] a word or group of words with a particular meaning 词; 词组; 措辞: *The expression 'in the family way' means 'pregnant'.* 词组 in the family way 的意思是"怀孕的"。| **pardon/forgive/excuse the expression** (=used when you have used a word that you think may offend someone) 原谅出言冒犯 *He doesn't know his ass from a hole in the ground if you'll pardon the expression.* 请原谅我出言冒犯, 不过他真是狗屁不懂。

2 ▶**ON SB'S FACE** 在某人脸上◀ [C] a look on someone's face that shows what they are thinking or feeling 表情: *a thoughtful expression* 若有所思的表情 | **an expression of surprise/fear/amusement** *Petra looked at her plate with an expression of disgust.* 彼得拉看着自己盘子里的食物, 脸上露出厌恶的表情。

3 ▶**SAY/WRITE** 说/写◀ [C,U] something you say or write that shows what you think or feel〔口头或书面形式的〕表达, 表示: **an expression of sympathy/thanks etc** *Mrs Mayer received their expressions of sympathy with great dignity.* 迈耶夫人接受了他们所表达的同情, 神态极其庄重。| **give expression to sth** *The minister gave expression to his anger in an attack on the government last night.* 这位部长昨晚对政府进行攻击, 表达了他的愤怒。| **freedom of expression** (=the right to express your opinions freely) 言论自由

4 ▶**ACTIONS/BEHAVIOUR** 行动/行为◀ [C,U] something you do or make that shows what you think or feel 表露, 展现: [+of] *The recent strikes are an expression of the workers' discontent.* 最近的罢工显示出工人的不满情绪。| **give expression to** *John gave expression to his love of nature in his paintings.* 约翰的画展现了他对自然的热爱。| **find expression** *Pam's latent artistic talents found their expression in music.* 帕姆的艺术潜能在音乐中得以体现。

5 ▶**EVENTS** 事件◀ [C,U] the way in which feelings and ideas are shown in particular events 体现, 展现: **find expression in sth** *The fiscal crisis has found its clearest expression in the poverty of the inner cities.* 市中心贫民区的贫困状况最清楚地显露了财政危机。

6 ▶**MUSIC** 音乐◀ [U] the quality of singing or playing a musical instrument with feeling〔唱歌或演奏时的〕感情: *Try to put a bit more expression into the slow passage.* 在演奏缓慢的段落时要尽量投入多一点的感情。

7 ▶**MATHEMATICS** 数学◀ [C] *technical* a sign or group of signs that show a mathematical idea in a particular form【术语】表达式: *x^2+4 is an algebraic expression.* x^2+4 是一个代数式。

ex·pres·sion·is·m /ɪk`sprɛʃən,ɪzəm; ɪk'spreʃənɪzəm/ *n* [U] a style of painting, writing, or music that expresses feelings rather than describing objects and experiences〔绘画、文学或音乐的〕表现主义 —**expressionist** *n* [C] —**expressionist** *adj*

ex·pres·sion·less /ɪk`sprɛʃənlɪs; ɪk'spreʃənləs/ *adj* an expressionless face or voice does not show what someone thinks or feels 无表情的, 无感情的: *a blank expressionless stare* 毫无表情的盯视 —**expressionlessly** *adv*

ex·pres·sive /ɪk`sprɛsɪv; ɪk'spresɪv/ *adj* **1** showing very clearly what someone thinks or feels 富于感情的; 明确表露想法的: *Cath threw up her arms in an expressive gesture.* 卡斯富于表情地张开双臂。**2 be expressive of sth** showing a particular feeling or influence 体现出某种感情[影响]: *The sculpture is expressive of Michelangelo's spiritual aspirations.* 这座雕塑体现了米开朗琪罗的心灵追求。—**expressively** *adv* —**expressiveness** *n* [U]

ex·press·ly /ɪk`sprɛslɪ; ɪk'spresli/ *adv formal*【正式】**1** if you say something expressly, you say it very clearly and firmly 明确地, 确切地: *I expressly forbade them to bring animals into the house.* 我明确禁止他们将动物带进屋。**2** deliberately 特意地, 故意地: *The building is expressly designed to conserve energy.* 这座建筑经特意设计以节约能源。

express post /.ˌ.ˈ./ *BrE*【英】, **express mail** *AmE*【美】*n* [U] a post service that delivers letters and parcels very quickly 快邮

ex·press·way /ɪk`sprɛs,we; ɪk'spresweɪ/ *n* [C] *AmE* a very wide road, usually in a city, on which cars can travel very quickly without stopping【美】〔通常指城市内的〕快速干道, 高速公路 —see also 另见 FREEWAY, MOTORWAY

ex·pro·pri·ate /ɛks`proprɪ,et; ɪk'sprəʊprieɪt/ *v* [T] *formal*【正式】**1** to take away private property for public use 征用, 没收〔私人财产〕**2** to take something from someone illegally in order to use it 侵占〔他人财物〕, 把…据为己有 —**expropriator** *n* [C] —**expropriation** /ɛks,proprɪ`eʃən; ɪk,sprəʊpri'eɪʃən/ *n* [C,U]

ex·pul·sion /ɪk`spʌlʃən; ɪk'spʌlʃən/ *n* [C,U] **1** the process of sending a person or group of people away from a place often by using force 驱逐, 赶走: *the expulsion of rebel forces* 驱逐叛军 **2** the act of sending someone away from a school or organization so that they can no longer go there or be a member 开除, 除名: *Tina's anti-social behaviour eventually led to her expulsion.* 蒂娜的反社会行为最终导致自己被开除。**3** the act of getting rid of a substance from your body or from a container 排出 —see also 另见 EXPEL

ex·punge /ɪk`spʌndʒ; ɪk'spʌndʒ/ *v* [T] *formal*【正式】**1** to remove a name from a list, piece of information, or book 删去, 勾销 **2** to make someone forget something unpleasant 使淡忘, 抹掉: *I tried to expunge the whole episode from my memory.* 我努力想把整件事从记忆中抹掉。

ex·pur·gat·ed /`ɛkspɚ,getɪd; 'ekspəgeɪtɪ̣d/ *adj* an expurgated book, play etc has had some parts removed because they are considered harmful or offensive 被删节的, 经删改的: *an expurgated version of the writings of de Sade* 萨德作品的删节本 —**expurgate** *v* [T] —**expurgation** /,ɛkspɚ`geʃən; ˌekspə'geɪʃən/ *n* [C,U]

ex·qui·site /`ɛkskwɪzɪt; ɪk'skwɪzɪ̣t/ *adj* **1** extremely beautiful and very delicately made 精美的, 精致的: *exquisite craftsmanship* 精美的工艺 **2** very sensitive and delicate in the way you behave or do things 细致的, 敏感的: *Darling, you have exquisite taste.* 亲爱的, 你的情趣很高雅。**3** *literary* exquisite pain or pleasure is felt very strongly【文】〔疼痛或快乐〕强烈的 —**exquisitely** *adv* —**exquisiteness** *n* [U]

ex·ser·vice·man /ˌ.ˈ..ˌ./ *n plural* **ex-servicemen** [C] *especially BrE* a man who used to be in the army, navy, or AIRFORCE【尤英】退役[退伍]男军人

ex·ser·vice·wom·an /ˌ.ˈ...ˌ./ *n plural* **ex-servicewomen** [C] *especially BrE* a woman who used to be in the army, navy, or AIRFORCE【尤英】退役[退伍]女军人

ext. the written abbreviation of 缩写= EXTENSION (2): *Contact Alison Lever on Ext. 3945.* 请与分机3945的艾利森·利弗联系。

ex·tant /ɪk`stænt; ɪk'stænt/ *adj formal* still existing in spite of being very old【正式】尚存的, 现存的: *Few of the manuscripts are extant.* 手稿大都散逸无存。

ex·tem·po·ra·ne·ous /ɪk,stɛmpə`renɪəs; ɪkˌstempə'reɪniəs◂/ *adj* spoken or done without any preparation or practice 即兴的, 无准备的: *an extemporaneous speech* 即席演讲 —**extemporaneously** *adv* —**extemporaneousness** *n* [U]

ex·tem·po·re /ɪk`stɛmpərɪ; ɪk'stempəri/ *adj* spoken or done without any preparation or practice 即兴的, 无准备的: *an extempore speech* 即席演讲 —**extempore** *adv*

ex·tem·po·rize also 又作 **-ise** *BrE*【英】/ɪk`stɛmpə,raɪz; ɪk'stempəraɪz/ *v* [I] *formal* to speak without preparation, especially during a performance; AD-LIB【正式】临场讲话; 临时编词 —**extemporization** /ɪk,stɛmpərə`zeʃən; ɪkˌstempəraɪ'zeɪʃən/ *n* [C,U]

ex·tend /ɪk`stɛnd; ɪk'stend/ *v*
1 ▶**CONTINUE** 继续◀ [I always+adv/prep] to continue for a particular distance or over a particular area 延伸, 伸展: [+across/over/through etc] *The River Nile extends as far as Lake Victoria.* 尼罗河一直延伸至维多利亚湖。| **extend 100 km/30 yards etc** *Smith Point extends a hundred yards or so into the water.* 史密斯角向水中伸出约一百码。| *The forest extended in all directions as far as the eye could see.* 森林向四面伸展, 一望无际。
2 ▶**MAKE STH BIGGER** 使某物增大◀ [T] to make a building, road etc bigger or longer 扩大; 延长〔建筑或道路等〕: *We extended the kitchen by six feet.* 我们把厨房扩大了六英尺。
3 ▶**HAPPEN/EXIST** 发生/存在◀ [I always+adv/prep] to continue to happen or exist for a certain period of time 延续, 持续: [+for/into/over etc] *The hot weather extended well into October.* 炎热的天气一直持续到10月。
4 ▶**TIME** 时间◀ [T] to increase a period of time that has been agreed, especially in order to finish a job or pay money that you owe 延长, 推延〔期限〕: *Management have agreed to extend the deadline.* 资方已同意延长最后期限。
5 ▶**CONTROL/INFLUENCE** 控制/影响◀ [I always+adv/prep, T] if you extend your control, influence etc or if it extends over something, it becomes more powerful 延伸, 扩大: *We hope to extend the effects of sanctions against the regime.* 我们希望加大对该政权的制裁力度。| [+into/over/beyond etc] *My duties at the school extend beyond just teaching.* 我在学校的职责不只是教书。| *The regulations do not extend to foreign visitors.* 这些规定不适用于外国游客。
6 ▶**OFFER HELP/THANKS** 提供帮助/表示感谢◀ [T] *formal* to offer someone help, sympathy, thanks etc【正式】提供, 给予, 表示: **extend a welcome/greeting/invitation etc** *We'd like to extend a warm welcome to our French visitors.* 我们对法国朋友的到来表示热烈欢迎。| **extend thanks to sb** (=thank someone officially)〔正式地〕向某人致谢 | **extend condolences/sympathies** (=offer sympathy to someone when someone they know or love dies) 致哀/慰唁 | **extend credit to sb** (=if a bank extends credit to someone it lends them money) 向某人提供贷款
7 ▶**ARMS/LEGS ETC** 手臂/腿等◀ [T] to stretch out a part of your body 伸开, 舒展: *a bird soaring on extended wings* 展翅高飞的鸟
8 ▶**STRENGTH/INTELLIGENCE** 力量/智力◀ [T] to make someone use all their strength, intelligence etc, in order to achieve good results 使竭尽全力: *Olympiakos won the match without ever being fully extended.* 奥林比亚高斯未用全力便轻松获胜。

extended fam·i·ly /,· ·· '···/ *n* [C] a family group that consists not only of parents and children but also of grandparents, AUNTs etc 大家庭〔指包括(外)祖父母、姑(姨)等在内的亲属〕

ex·ten·sion /ɪk`stɛnʃən; ɪk'stenʃən/ *n*
1 ▶**EXTRA ROOMS** 额外房间◀ [C] another room or rooms which are added to a building〔建筑的〕扩建部分: *The extension to the National Museum houses the Picasso collection.* 国家美术馆收藏的毕加索作品在扩建的展厅展出。
2 ▶**TELEPHONE** 电话◀ [C] **a)** one of many telephone lines in a large building which all have different numbers 分机: **extension number** *My extension number is 3821.* 我的分机号码是 3821。**b)** one of two or more telephones, usually in someone's house, which all have the same number〔共用一个号码的〕分机: *Can you put an extension in the bedroom?* 你能在卧室里安一部分机吗?
3 ▶**EXTRA TIME** 额外时间◀ [C usually singular 一般用单数] an additional period of time given to someone in order to finish a job, pay money that they owe etc 展期, 延期: *Donald's been given an extension to finish his thesis.* 唐纳德得到宽限期以完成他的论文。| *The pub's got an extension tonight.* (=it will stay open longer than usual) 酒馆今晚延时关门。
4 ▶**ELECTRIC WIRE** 电线◀ [C] also 又作 **extension lead** *BrE*【英】, **extension cord** *AmE*【美】 an additional piece of electric wire used when the wire you already have is not long enough 延长线路, 电线延长部分: *Use the extension when you cut the grass.* 割草时请使用外接电源线。
5 ▶**CONTROL/INFLUENCE** 控制/影响◀ [singular U] a process in which someone's or something's influence or control increases 扩大, 延伸: [+of] *the extension of the copyright laws to cover recorded material* 版权法范围扩大到涵盖录制的音像材料
6 ▶**MAKING STH BIGGER** 使某物变大◀ [singular U] the process of making a road, building etc bigger or longer〔道路、建筑等的〕扩建; 延长: [+of] *the proposed extension of the London–Cambridge motorway* 延长伦敦－剑桥高速公路的建议
7 **by extension** used before mentioning something that is naturally connected to or is a natural result of something else 自然地, 当然地: *My primary responsibility is to the company, and by extension to the people who work for it.* 我主要是对公司负责, 当然也就对公司的员工负责。
8 ▶**UNIVERSITY/COLLEGE** 大学/学院◀ [U] part of a British university or college that offers courses to people who are not full time students〔为非全日制学生开设的〕大学附设部分: **extension course** (=a course done by people who cannot study full time) 大学附设部分的课程
9 ▶**STRETCH ARM/LEG** 伸展手臂/腿◀ [U] **a)** a process in which you stretch a part of the body 伸展, 舒展: *I had physiotherapy to improve the extension of my right hand.* 我做理疗来帮助伸展右手。**b)** the position of a part of the body when it is stretched〔身体部分〕伸展开的状态: *Your leg should now be at full extension.* 你的腿现在应该完全伸直。

ex·ten·sive /ɪk`stɛnsɪv; ɪk'stensɪv/ *adj* **1** covering a large area 广阔的, 大面积的: *The house stands in extensive grounds.* 这栋房子占地很大。| **extensive damage/repairs etc** *The storm caused extensive damage.* 暴风雨造成了大范围的破坏。**2** containing or dealing with a lot of information and details 广泛的, 全面的: *The abortion issue has been the subject of extensive debate.* 堕胎一直是备受争议的话题。—**extensively** *adv*: *Despite reading extensively, I still failed the exam.* 虽然进行了广泛阅读, 但我考试仍不及格。—**extensiveness** *n* [U]

ex·tent /ɪk`stɛnt; ɪk'stent/ *n* **1** [singular] the limit or degree of something's influence etc 限度; 程度: *The success of a marriage depends on the extent to which you are prepared to work at it.* 婚姻的成功取决于你们努力的程度。| **to a certain extent/to some extent** (=used to say that something is partly, but not completely, true) 在某种程度上 *To a certain extent it was my fault that we lost the contract.* 我们丢掉合同在某种程度上是我的错。| **to a great/large extent** (=used to say that something is mainly true) 在很大程度上 *These policies are to a large extent responsible for the region's economic decline.* 这些政策是该地区经济衰退的主要原因。| **to a lesser/greater extent** (=used when comparing two things to say that one thing has less or more influence) 在较轻/更大程度上 *These changes will affect all managers and to a lesser extent some shop-floor workers.* 这些变化将影响到所有的管理人员, 也将在较轻程度上影响到一些车间工人。| **to such an extent/to the extent that** (=used to say that something has affected or influenced something so much that it causes something else to happen) 达到如此程度/达到…的程度 *Violence increased to the extent that residents were afraid to leave their homes.* 暴力事件多到了令居民不敢出门的程度。| **to what extent...?** (=used to ask how big an amount or influence is) 在多大程度上…? *To what extent can we blame the government for this lack of information?* 对于这种信息缺乏, 我们能在多大程度上指责政府呢? **2** [U] the size of a large area 方圆, 范围: **full extent of** *From the top window we could see the full extent of the park.* 透过最高的窗户我们可以看见公园的全景。| **in extent** *The region is over 10,000 square kilometres in extent.* 这个地区的面积超过10,000平方公里。**3** [U] the size or degree of something dangerous or difficult, such as an injury or a problem〔伤势或问题等的〕严重性; 〔困难的〕程度: *Considering the extent of his injuries he's lucky to be alive.* 就他的伤势来说, 他能活下来真是够幸运的。| *It would be foolish to underestimate the extent of the problem.* 低估该问题的困难程度是愚蠢的。

ex·ten·u·ate /ɪk`stɛnjʊ,et; ɪk'stenjueɪt/ *v* [T] *formal* to make an action, especially a crime, seem less bad or harmful by suggesting reasons for it【正式】为〔某行为, 尤指犯罪行为〕辩解: **extenuating circumstances** (=facts which explain bad or criminal behaviour) 情有可原的具体情况 —**extenuation** /ɪk,stɛnjʊ`eʃən; ɪk,stenju'eɪʃən/ *n* [U]

ex·te·ri·or¹ /ɪk`stɪrɪə; ɪk'stɪəriə/ *n* [C] **1** [usually singular 一般用单数] the appearance or outside surface of something 外观; 外表: *Sun, rain and frost had damaged the exterior of the building.* 阳光、雨水和霜侵蚀了该建筑的外表。**2 a cool/sullen etc exterior** behaviour that seems calm, unfriendly etc but which often hides a different feeling or attitude 表面上镇定/阴沉等: *Karl hid his nervousness behind a calm exterior.* 卡尔强作镇定以掩盖内心的紧张。**3** a picture, film etc of an outdoor scene 风景画; 户外景色画; (电影) 外景 —opposite 反义词 INTERIOR¹

exterior² *adj* **1** on the outside or outside surface of something 外部的; 外面的: *The exterior walls need a new coat of paint.* 外墙需要重新刷漆了。**2 exterior to** separate or divided from something 与…分离[分开]的 —opposite 反义词 INTERIOR²

ex·ter·mi·nate /ɪk`stɝmə͵net; ɪk'stɜːmɨneɪt/ *v* [T] to kill large numbers of people or animals of a particular type so that they no longer exist 灭绝, 根除 —**exterminator** *n* [C] —**extermination** /ɪk͵stɝmə`neʃən; ɪk͵stɜːmɨ'neɪʃən/ *n* [C,U]

ex·ter·nal /ɪk`stɝnl; ɪk'stɜːnl/ *adj* **1** connected with the outside of a surface or body 外面的; 外部的: *The external walls were in need of repair.* 外墙需要修补。| **for external use** (=medicine that is for external use must be put on your skin and not swallowed) 〔药〕外用的 **2** coming from outside a particular place or organization 来自外部的, 外来的: *Considerable external pressure was put on Congress to override the veto.* 要求国会推翻该否决的外界压力相当大。| *information from external sources* 来自外部的信息 **3** connected with foreign countries 外国的: *China will not tolerate any external interference in its affairs.* 中国不会容忍任何国家干涉其内政。**4** *BrE* coming from outside a particular school or university【英】来自学校[大学]之外的, 外来的: **external examination** (=not arranged by your own school or university) 校外(主持的)考试 | **external examiner** (=someone from outside a particular school or university who examines its students) 校外考官 **5 external ear/gill/genitals etc** *technical* a part of an animal's body that is on the outer surface of the body rather than inside it【术语】〔动物长在身体〕外部的耳朵/鳃/生殖器等 —opposite 反义词 INTERNAL —**externally** *adv*

ex·ter·nal·ize also 又作 **-ise** *BrE*【英】/ɪk`stɝnl͵aɪz; ɪk'stɜːnəlaɪz/ *v* [T] to express inner feelings 表露〔内心感受〕—**externalization** /ɪk͵stɝnḷə`zeʃən; ɪk͵stɜːnəlaɪ'zeɪʃən/ *n* [C,U]

ex·ter·nals /ɪk`stɝnḷz; ɪk'stɜːnlz/ *n* [plural] the outer appearance of a situation 外观, 外表; 外在形式

ex·tinct /ɪk`stɪŋkt; ɪk'stɪŋkt/ *adj* **1** an extinct animal, plant, language etc no longer exists 灭绝的, 绝种的: *Dinosaurs have been extinct for millions of years.* 恐龙已灭绝数千万年了。**2** an extinct belief or custom no longer exists 〔信仰或风俗〕已废弃的 **3** an extinct VOLCANO no longer erupts (ERUPT (1)) 〔火山〕死的, 不再活跃的

ex·tinc·tion /ɪk`stɪŋkʃən; ɪk'stɪŋkʃən/ *n* [U] **1** a situation in which a particular kind of animal, plant etc no longer exists 灭绝, 绝种: *Conservationists are trying to save the whale from extinction.* 生态环境保护主义者正努力挽救鲸类以防止其灭绝。| **face extinction/be threatened with extinction** *Many endangered species now face extinction.* 许多濒危物种现已面临灭绝。**2** a process in which a belief, way of life, feeling etc is destroyed or stops existing 〔信仰、生活方式或感情等〕遭毁灭; 消亡: *Their traditional way of life seems doomed to extinction.* 他们的传统生活方式似乎注定要消亡。

ex·tin·guish /ɪk`stɪŋgwɪʃ; ɪk'stɪŋgwɪʃ/ *v* [T] *formal*【正式】**1** to make a fire or light stop burning or shining 熄灭〔火、光〕: *Please extinguish all cigarettes.* 请把所有的香烟都熄灭。**2** to destroy an idea or feeling or make it stop existing 使〔想法或感情〕破灭; 使消亡: *All hope was almost extinguished.* 几乎所有的希望都破灭了。

ex·tin·guish·er /ɪk`stɪŋgwɪʃɚ; ɪk'stɪŋgwɪʃə/ *n* [C] *informal* a FIRE EXTINGUISHER【非正式】灭火器

ex·tir·pate /`ɛkstɚ͵pet; 'ekstɜːpeɪt/ *v* [T] *formal* to completely destroy something that is unpleasant or unwanted【正式】消灭, 根除 —**extirpation** /͵ɛkstɚ`peʃən; ͵ekstɜː'peɪʃən/ [U]

ex·tol /ɪk`stol; ɪk'stəʊl/ *v* [T] *formal* to praise something very much【正式】赞美, 颂扬: **extol the virtues/merits of** *a speech extolling the merits of free enterprise* 赞颂自由企业制度的讲话

ex·tort /ɪk`stɔrt; ɪk'stɔːt/ *v* [T] to illegally force someone to give you money by threatening them 敲诈, 勒索〔钱财〕: **extort money from/out of sb** *Landlords tried to cover their losses by extorting high rents from tenants.* 地主向佃户勒索租金以弥补自己的损失。—**extortion** /ɪk`stɔrʃən; ɪk'stɔːʃən/ *n* [U]: *Confessions were obtained by extortion.* 招供是逼出来的。—**extortioner** *n* [C] —**extortionist** *n* [C]

ex·tor·tion·ate /ɪk`stɔrʃənɪt; ɪk'stɔːʃənɨt/ *adj* an extortionate price, demand, etc is extremely high 〔价格、要求等〕过分的, 过高的: *Most drivers under 25 can only get insurance at extortionate rates.* 大多数 25 岁以下的司机要想获得保险需交付极高的保费。—**extortionately** *adv*

extra- /ɛkstrə; ekstrə/ *prefix* outside; beyond 在…之外; 超出: *extragalactic* (=outside our GALAXY) 银河系外的 | *extramarital sex* (=between people who are not married to each other) 婚外性行为

ex·tra¹ /`ɛkstrə; 'ekstrə/ *adj* more of something, in addition to the usual or standard amount or number 额外的, 另外的: *Could you get an extra loaf of bread?* 你能多拿一条面包吗? | *Alan had taken extra care with his appearance that evening.* 艾伦那天晚上格外注重仪表。| *Residents can use the gym at no extra cost.* 居民使用体育馆可不必另外付费。| **extra ten minutes/three metres/five kilos etc** *I asked for an extra day to finish the work.* 我要求额外再加一天来完成工作。

extra² *adv* **1 cost/earn/pay extra** to cost, earn, or pay more money than the usual amount 额外花费/挣得/支付: *I earn extra for working on Sunday.* 我星期天工作获取额外收入。| **be extra** (=cost an additional amount of money) 额外付费, 另外收费 *Dinner costs $15 but wine is extra.* 晚餐费为 15 美元, 但酒水另算。| **ten minutes/three metres/five kilos extra** *I got 2 metres extra to make the curtains.* 我还有两米布可以做帘子。**2** [+adj/adv] used to emphasize an adjective or adverb 特别地, 非常: *You're going to have to work extra hard to pass the exam.* 你要格外用功才能通过考试。

extra³ *n* [C] **1** something which is added to a basic product or service which improves it and also costs more 另外计价的项目: **optional extra** (=something attractive or comfortable that you can choose to have or not) 可选择的额外事物 *Tinted windows and a sunroof are optional extras.* 有色玻璃窗和活动车顶是可选的额外配件。**2** something attractive or helpful that you do not get more money for 不另收费的好东西: *Lena did a lot of little extras for him that weren't part of her job description.* 莉娜在职责范围之外为他义务提供了许多帮助。**3** an actor in a film who does not say anything but is part of a crowd 〔电影中的〕临时演员 **4** a special EDITION of a newspaper containing important news 〔报纸的〕号外: *Extra! Extra! Read all about it!* 号外!号外!来看哪!

ex·tract¹ /ɪk`strækt; ɪk'strækt/ *v* [T] **1** to remove an object from somewhere, especially by pulling it 取出, 拔出: *You'll have to have that wisdom tooth extracted.* 你得把那颗智齿拔掉。| **extract sth from sth** *Prue managed to extract the stopper from the bottle.* 普吕设法把瓶塞拔了出来。**2** to carefully remove a substance from another substance which contains it, using a machine, chemical process etc 采掘; 提炼: *47 tonnes of gold have been extracted at the mine.* 这座矿已采掘了 47 公吨黄金。| **extract sth from sth** *The nuts are crushed to extract the oil from them.* 这些坚果被碾碎榨油。**3** to skilfully remove something which is among a lot of other objects or inside something 〔灵巧地〕取出, 抽出: **extract sth from sth** *James slowly extracted a £5 note from his wallet.* 詹姆斯慢慢从钱包里抽出一张五英镑的纸币。**4** to find out information or get money from someone who does not want to give it by asking questions or using physical force 套出〔信息〕; 逼问; 索得〔钱财〕: **extract sth from sb** *I finally managed to extract the truth from her.* 我最终设法从她嘴里套出了事实真相。

ex·tract² /`ɛkstrækt; 'ekstrækt/ *n* **1** [C] a short piece of writing, music etc taken from a particular book, piece of music etc, especially in order to show what it is like 摘录; 选段: [+from] *I've only seen short extracts from the film.* 我只是看过那部电影的部分片断。**2** [C,U] a substance taken from another substance by using a special process 提炼物, 提取物: **vanilla/malt/yeast extract** *Add one teaspoon of vanilla extract.* 加入一茶匙香草精。

ex·trac·tion /ɪk`strækʃən; ɪk'strækʃən/ *n* **1** [C,U] the process of removing an object or substance from inside something else 取出; 提炼: [+of] *the extraction of uranium from uranium ore* 从铀矿石中提取铀 **2 be of French/Russian/Italian etc extraction** to be from a French, Russian etc family even though you were not born in that country 祖籍法国/俄罗斯/意大利等

ex·trac·tor /ɛk`stræktɚ; ɪk'stræktə/ also 又作 **extractor fan** /·'·· ·/ *n* [C] a machine for removing air that is hot or smells unpleasant from a kitchen, factory etc 排气扇; 抽油烟机

ex·tra·cur·ric·u·lar /͵ɛkstrəkə`rɪkjəlɚ; ͵ekstrəkə'rɪkjɨlə◂/ *adj* extracurricular activities are not part of the course that a student is doing 课外的

ex·tra·di·ta·ble /`ɛkstrə͵daɪtəbḷ; 'ekstrədaɪtəbəl/ *adj* an extraditable crime is one for which someone can be sent back to the country where the crime happened to be judged in a court of law 〔罪犯〕可引渡的: *Terrorism is an extraditable offense.* 恐怖主义罪犯可以被引渡。

ex·tra·dite /`ɛkstrə͵daɪt; 'ekstrədaɪt/ *v* [T+from/to] to use a legal process to send someone who may be guilty of a crime back to the country where the crime happened in order to judge them in a court of law 引渡 —**extradition** /͵ɛkstrə`dɪʃən; ͵ekstrə'dɪʃən/ *n* [C,U]: *an extradition order* 引渡命令

ex·tra·ju·di·cial /͵ɛkstrədʒu`dɪʃəl; ͵ekstrədʒuː'dɪʃəl◂/ *adj* beyond or outside the ordinary powers of the law 法律制裁范围以外的; 法律管辖以外的

ex·tra·mar·i·tal /ˌɛkstrə`mærətḷ; ˌekstrəˈmærɪ̣tl◂/ *adj* an extramarital sexual relationship is one that someone has with a person who is not their husband or wife 婚外(性关系)的

ex·tra·mu·ral /ˌɛkstrə`mjurəl; ˌekstrəˈmjʊərəl◂/ *adj* **1** connected with a place or organization but happening or done outside it 某地点以外的; 机构以外的: *extramural activities* 机构外的活动 **2** *especially BrE* extramural courses, studies etc involve students from outside a particular college or university【尤英】校外的, 校外学生参与的 —opposite 反义词 INTRAMURAL

ex·tra·ne·ous /ɪk`strenɪəs; ɪkˈstreɪniəs/ *adj* **1** not belonging to or directly connected with a particular subject or problem; IRRELEVANT 外部的; 无直接关系的: [+to] *Such details are extraneous to the matter in hand.* 这些细节与手头这件事没有直接关系。**2** coming from outside 外来的: *extraneous noises* 外部的噪声 —**extraneously** *adv*

ex·tra·or·di·na·ri·ly /ɪk`strɔrdṇˌɛrəlɪ; ɪkˈstrɔːdənərɪ̣li/ *adv especially BrE*【尤英】**1** [+adj/adv] extremely 极其, 极端地: **extraordinarily beautiful/difficult/successful etc** *an extraordinarily beautiful young boy* 很好看的小男孩 **2** in a way that seems strange 奇怪地: *I'm afraid Jane can behave quite extraordinarily at times.* 恐怕简有时行为颇为古怪。

ex·tra·or·di·na·ry /ɪk`strɔrdṇˌɛrɪ; ɪkˈstrɔːdənəri/ *adj* **1** very much better, more beautiful, or more impressive than usual 非凡的, 出色的: *a woman of extraordinary beauty* 容貌出众的女子 **2** very unusual or surprising because it would normally be very unlikely to happen or exist 令人惊叹的, 极不寻常的: *the extraordinary landscapes of Cappadocia* 卡帕多西亚奇特的地貌景观 | **quite/most extraordinary** *BrE* (=very unusual)【英】非常奇怪的, 令人惊奇的 *Chris's behaviour that morning was quite extraordinary.* 克里斯那天上午的行为非常奇怪。| **extraordinary thing to do/say/happen** *What an extraordinary thing to do!* 做这件事多奇怪呀! | **how extraordinary!** *BrE spoken* (=used to express surprise)【英口】太奇怪了! *"Well then Jim got down on all fours and started barking like a dog." "How extraordinary!"* "然后吉姆就手脚同时着地像狗一样叫了起来。" "太奇怪了!" **3 extraordinary meeting/session etc** a meeting which takes place in addition to the usual ones 特别会议 **4 envoy/ambassador/minister extraordinary** an official employed for a special purpose, in addition to the usual officials 特使; 特命公使

ex·trap·o·late /ɪks`træpəˌlet; ɪkˈstræpəleɪt/ *v* [I,T] **1** to make a guess about something in the future from facts that you already know 推断, 推知: **extrapolate sth from sth** *It's my job to extrapolate future developments from contemporary trends.* 我的工作是依据现时的趋势推断未来的发展。**2** *technical* to guess a value that you do not know by continuing a curve which is based on values that you already know【术语】外推 —**extrapolation** /ɛkˌstræpo`leʃən; ɪkˌstræpəˈleɪʃən/ *n* [C,U]

extra sen·so·ry per·cep·tion /ˌ‥ ‥‥ ‥ˈ‥/ *n* [U] ESP (1) 超感知觉

ex·tra·ter·res·tri·al[1] /ˌɛkstrətə`rɛstrɪəl; ˌekstrətəˈrestriəl◂/ *n* [C] a living creature that people think may exist on another PLANET 外星生物

extraterrestrial[2] *adj* connected with things that exist outside the Earth 地球外的; 宇宙的

ex·tra·ter·ri·to·ri·al /ˌɛkstrəˌtɛrə`torɪəl; ˌekstrəterɪ̣ˈtɔːriəl◂/ *adj* **1** *formal* outside a particular country【正式】境外的, 疆界以外的 **2** *law* extraterritorial rights, powers etc are governed from outside a country or area【法律】治外法权的, 不受当地法律限制的: *an extraterritorial jurisdiction treaty* 治外法权司法协议 —**extraterritoriality** /ˌɛkstrəˌtɛrətorɪ`ælətɪ; ˌekstrəterɪ̣tɔːriˈælɪ̣ti/ *n* [U]

extra time /ˌ‥ ˈ‥/ *n* [U] *especially BrE* a period of usually thirty minutes added to the end of football games to give one of the two teams a chance to win【尤英】〔足球〕加时赛; OVERTIME (4) *AmE*【美】

ex·trav·a·gant /ɪk`strævəgənt; ɪkˈstrævəgənt/ *adj* **1** spending a lot of money on things that are not necessary〔花钱〕浪费的, 无必要的: *It was very extravagant of you to spend £500 on a dress.* 花500英镑去买一件衣服, 那太奢侈了。**2 extravagant with sth** using too much of something or wasting it 大手大脚, 过度使用[浪费]某物: *We mustn't be too extravagant with the electricity.* 我们决不能滥用电力。**3** very impressive because of being very expensive, beautiful etc 豪华的; 铺张的: *Myra and Paul decided to give an extravagant dinner party.* 迈拉和保罗决定举行一次豪华晚宴。**4** ideas or behaviour that are extravagant are too extreme and are not sensible 过度的; 越轨的: *extravagant claims about the effectiveness of the system* 对系统有效性的夸大言辞 —**extravagantly** *adv* —**extravagance** *n* [C,U]

ex·trav·a·gan·za /ɪkˌstrævə`gænzə; ɪkˌstrævəˈgænzə/ *n* [C] a very large and expensive entertainment 铺张华丽的娱乐表演

ex·tra·vert /`ɛkstrəˌvɝt; ˈekstrəvɜːt/ *n* [C] another spelling of EXTROVERT extrovert 的另一种拼法

ex·treme[1] /ɪk`strim; ɪkˈstriːm/ *adj* **1** [only before noun 仅用于名词前] very great in degree 极大的; 极度的: *Extreme poverty still exists in many rural areas.* 农村许多地区仍处于赤贫状态。**2 extreme south/point/end/limit etc** the extreme south etc is the place furthest towards the south etc 最南端/端点/尽头/极限等 **3** extreme opinions, beliefs, or organizations, especially political ones, are considered by most people to be unacceptable and unreasonable 极端的, 偏激的: *extreme right-wing nationalists* 极右翼的民族主义分子 **4** very unusual and severe 极为异常的, 极严厉的: *Her ideas about raising kids have always been a little extreme.* 她关于教养孩子的主意总是有点怪僻。| **extreme example/case** *Social workers were horrified by this extreme case of cruelty.* 社会工作者们被这一极其残酷的事例惊呆了。

extreme[2] *n* [C] **1** something that goes beyond normal limits, so that it seems very unusual and unacceptable 极端: *We had every extreme of weather that weekend – gales, snow, and sunshine.* 那个周末天气经历了剧烈的变化, 一会儿刮大风, 一会儿下雪, 一会儿又阳光灿烂。| **be driven to extremes** *Driven to extremes by the rioting, the government imposed a six pm curfew.* 为对付骚乱, 政府被迫采取了下午6点开始宵禁的极端做法。| **go to extremes/take sth to extremes** (=behave in a way that goes beyond normal limits, especially in order to achieve something) 走极端 | **go to the opposite extreme/go from one extreme to the other** (=change from being extreme in one way to being extreme in a completely different way) 走到另一个极端/从一个极端走到另一个极端 **2 in the extreme** to a very great degree 极度, 非常: *My great-aunt had been generous in the extreme over the years.* 我的姨婆这些年来一直极为慷慨。

ex·treme·ly /ɪk`strimlɪ; ɪkˈstriːmli/ *adv* to a very great degree 极度, 极其: *I'm extremely sorry to have troubled you.* 给你添了麻烦, 我实在是很抱歉。

extremis *n* —see 见 IN EXTREMIS

ex·trem·is·m /ɪk`strimɪzəm; ɪkˈstriːmɪzəm/ *n* [U] opinions, ideas, and actions, especially political or religious ones, that most people think are unreasonable and unacceptable 极端主义, 极端性

ex·trem·ist /ɪk`strimɪst; ɪkˈstriːmɪ̣st/ *n* [C] someone who has extreme political opinions and aims, and who is willing to do unusual or illegal things in order to achieve them 极端主义者, 过激分子: *The bomb was planted by right-wing extremists.* 炸弹是右翼极端分子放置的。—**extremist** *adj*

ex·trem·i·ty /ɪk`strɛmətɪ; ɪkˈstremɪ̣ti/ *n* **1** [C often plural 常用复数] one of the parts of your body that is furthest away from the centre, for example your fingers and toes 人体离中心最远的部位〈如手指、脚趾〉**2** [U] the degree to which a belief, opinion, situation, or action goes beyond what is usually thought to be acceptable 极端性, 偏激: *The committee was uncomfortable about the extremity of the proposal.* 委员会因该建议太极端而感到不安。**3** [C] the part that is furthest away from the centre of something 末端, 端点: *A land-locked stretch of water formed the western extremity of the Gulf of Tajura.* 一片内陆水域构成了塔朱拉湾的最西端。

ex·tri·cate /`ɛkstrɪˌket; ˈekstrɪ̣keɪt/ *v* [T] **1** to escape from a difficult or embarrassing situation 使摆脱, 使脱离: [+from] *By 1897 his lawyers had managed to extricate him from the contract.* 到1897年时, 他的律师帮他摆脱了那份合约的束缚。| **extricate yourself** *I desperately tried to think of a way to extricate myself from Mrs. Bedford's questioning.* 我拼命想办法要摆脱贝德福德夫人的追问。**2** to remove someone or something from a place in which they are trapped 解救, 救出: *Firemen had to extricate the driver from the wreckage.* 消防队员得把司机从残骸中救出来。—**extrication** /ˌɛkstrə`keʃən; ˌekstrɪ̣ˈkeɪʃən/ *n* [U]

ex·tro·vert, extravert /`ɛkstroˌvɝt; ˈekstrəvɜːt/ *n* [C] someone who is active and confident, and who enjoys spending time with other people 性格外向的人: *Gini was an extrovert and loved to perform to a crowd.* 吉尼性格外向, 爱在众人面前表演。—**extrovert** *adj* —opposite 反义词 INTROVERT

ex·tro·vert·ed /`ɛkstroˌvɝtɪd; ˈekstrəvɜːtɪ̣d/ *adj* having a confident character and enjoying the company of other people 性格外向的 —**extroversion** /ˌɛkstro`vɝʃən; ˌekstrəˈvɜːʃən/ *n* [U] —opposite 反义词 INTROVERTED

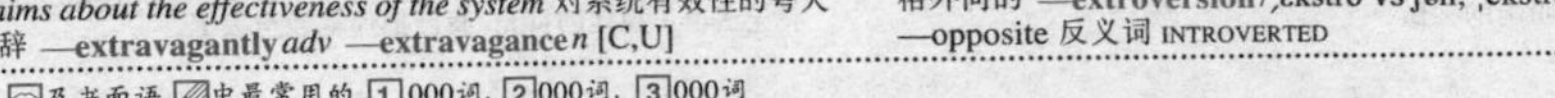

ex·trude /ɪk`strud; ɪk'stru:d/ *v* [T] *formal*【正式】**1** to push or force something out through a hole 挤出 **2** *technical* to force plastic or metal through a hole so that it has a particular shape【术语】挤压成形 —**extrusion** /ɪk`struʒən; ɪk'stru:ʒən/ *n* [C,U]

ex·u·be·rant /ɪg`zjubərənt; ɪg'zju:bərənt/ *adj* **1** happy and cheerful, and full of energy and excitement 兴高采烈的, 精神焕发的 **2** plants that are exuberant are healthy and growing very quickly〔植物〕茁壮的; 茂盛的 —**exuberance** *n* [U] —**exuberantly** *adv*

ex·ude /ɪg`zjud; ɪg'zju:d/ *v* **1** **exude confidence/sympathy etc** if you exude a particular quality, it is easy to see that you have a lot of it 充分显露信心/同情等 **2** [I,T] to flow out slowly and steadily, or to make something do this (使) 渗出; (使) 缓慢流出: *Trunkfishes exude a poisonous liquid that can kill other fish.* 箱鲀分泌一种毒液, 可以毒杀其他鱼类。

ex·ult /ɪg`zʌlt; ɪg'zʌlt/ *v* [I] *formal* to show that you are very happy and proud, especially because you have succeeded in doing something【正式】欢欣鼓舞; 洋洋得意: [**+at/in**] *They exulted at their victory.* 他们为胜利而兴高采烈。| [**+over**] *The people exulted over their fallen enemies.* 人们为击败敌人而欢欣鼓舞。—**exultation** /,ɛgzʌl`teʃən; ,egzʌl'teɪʃən/ *n* [U]

ex·ul·tant /ɪg`zʌltn̩t; ɪg'zʌltənt/ *adj formal* very happy or proud, especially because you have succeeded in doing something【正式】欢欣鼓舞的; 洋洋得意的: *Exultant crowds were dancing in the streets.* 欢腾的人群在街上跳舞。—**exultantly** *adv*

-ey /ɪ; i/ *suffix* [in adjectives 构成形容词] the form used for -Y especially after y -y 的变体〔尤用于以 y 结尾的词后面〕: *clayey soil* 黏质土壤

Eyck /aɪk; aɪk/, **Jan van** (?1390-1441) a Flemish painter, especially of religious subjects painted in a realistic way 爱克〔(?1390-1441), 佛兰德斯画家。作品以宗教题材为主, 采用现实主义绘画风格〕

E

eye[1] /aɪ; aɪ/ *n* [C]

① BODY PART 身体部位
② WATCH/SEE 注视/看见
③ LOOK AT 看
④ LOOK AFTER 照顾
⑤ WATCH FOR 小心留意
⑥ NOTICE 注意
⑦ DISAGREE/DISBELIEVE 不赞成/不相信
⑧ SURPRISE 惊奇
⑨ LOVE/SEXUAL ATTRACTION 爱/性吸引力
⑩ JUDGE 判断
⑪ SPOKEN PHRASES 口语短语
⑫ PURPOSE 目的
⑬ OTHER MEANINGS 其他意思

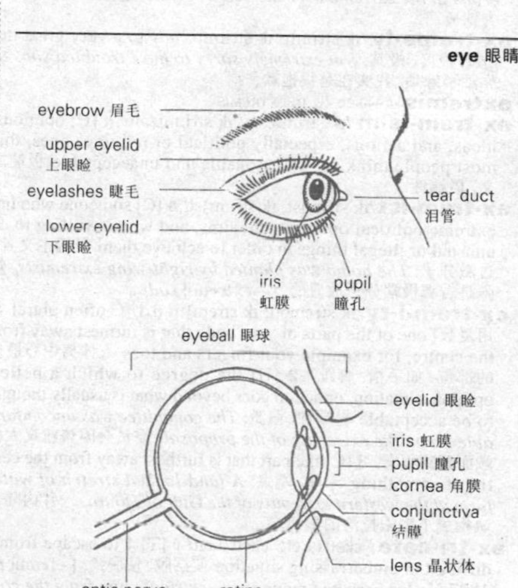

① BODY PART 身体部位

1 one of the two parts of the body that people and animals use to see 眼睛: *Annie has blue eyes.* 安妮的眼睛是蓝色的。| *Close your eyes and count to ten.* 闭上你的眼睛, 数到十。

2 blue-eyed/one-eyed/bright-eyed/wide-eyed etc having blue eyes, one eye, bright eyes, eyes that are wide open etc 蓝眼睛的/一只眼睛的/眼睛明亮的/双目圆睁的等

② WATCH/SEE 注视/看见

3 have/keep your eye on sb to be carefully watching everything that someone does, especially because you do not trust them to do things properly 注视[密切注意]某人(的举动): *I've got my eye on you now, so you do as you're told!* 我盯着你呢, 所以你要按吩咐的去做!

4 clap/lay/set eyes on sb/sth *spoken* an expression meaning to see someone or something, used especially when you are surprised or shocked【口】看见[注意到]某人/某事物〔尤用于感到惊讶时〕: *I'd never clapped eyes on him before in my life!* 我以前从没见过他!

5 the naked eye if you can see something with the naked eye, you can see it without using any artificial help such as a TELESCOPE or microscope 肉眼: *On a clear night these stars can be seen with the naked eye.* 在天气晴朗的夜晚, 凭肉眼就可以看到这些星星。| **invisible to the naked eye** (=cannot be seen without artificial help) 肉眼看不到的

6 be all eyes *especially spoken* to watch carefully what is happening or what someone is doing【尤口】全神贯注地看: *We were all eyes as he slowly drew back the curtain.* 当他慢慢拉开幕布时, 我们都目不转睛地看着。

7 in front of/before your (very) eyes *especially spoken* an expression meaning happening so that you can clearly see it, used especially when what you see is surprising or shocking【尤口】就在你眼前, 当着某人的面: *Ladies and gentlemen, before your very eyes I will now make this rabbit disappear.* 女士们, 先生们, 我现在要当着诸位的面让这只兔子消失。

③ LOOK AT 看

8 catch sb's eye a) to attract someone's attention and make them look at something 引起某人注目, 吸引某人的目光: *All of a sudden something red caught his eye.* 突然, 一个红色的东西引起了他的注意。**b)** to look at someone at the same moment that they are looking at you 碰到某人的目光: *I caught Ben's eye in the rear-view mirror and knew what he was thinking.* 我从后视镜里看到本的目光, 明白了他在想什么。

9 eye contact if you have eye contact with someone, you look directly at them and they look directly at you 对视, 相互直视: *Always establish eye contact with the customer – it inspires confidence.* 要与客户保持目光交流, 这样能增强他对你的信任。

10 cannot take your eyes off sb/sth to be unable to stop looking at someone or something, especially because they are very attractive or interesting 无法将目光从某人身上/某物上挪开: *She was so beautiful I simply couldn't take my eyes off her.* 她太漂亮了, 我简直无法将目光从她身上挪开。

11 look sb in the eye [usually in negatives 一般用于否定句] to look directly and steadily at someone because you are not embarrassed or ashamed 直视[正视]某人: *I couldn't look him in the eye afterwards, knowing that I had lost all that money.* 我无法再正视他的目光, 我已把那笔钱全丢了。

12 run/cast your eye over sth to look at something quickly without reading it in detail 匆匆看[浏览]某物: *Could you just cast your eye over this report before I hand it in?* 我把报告上交之前你能过目一下吗?

④ LOOK AFTER 照顾

13 keep your eye on sth/sb to look after someone or something and make sure that they are safe 照看[照料]某物/某人: *Mary offered to keep an eye on the baby while I went out.* 玛丽提出可以在我外出期间照看婴儿。

⑤ WATCH FOR 小心留意

14 keep an eye out for sth to hope to notice or find something 留意[想找到]某物: *Could you keep an eye out for my red pen? I seem to have mislaid it.* 你能留意一下我的那支红色钢笔吗? 我不知道放哪儿了。

15 keep your eyes open/peeled *spoken* to watch carefully for something【口】密切注意, 留神: *Keep your eyes peeled for a campsite.* 留神找一块营地。

⑥ NOTICE 注意

16 have eyes in the back of your head to know what is happening all around you, even when this might seem impossible 脑后长眼睛〔知道身边发生的一切〕: *You need to have eyes in the back of your head to be a teacher.* 作为教师, 你需要能眼观六路。

17 have eyes like a hawk to notice every small detail or everything that is happening, and therefore to be difficult to deceive 有鹰一样的眼睛; 目光犀利: *We never got away with anything in Mrs. Podell's class – she had eyes like a hawk.* 在波德尔夫人的课上, 我们干什么都瞒不过她 —— 她眼睛尖着呢。

18 have your eye on sth to have noticed something that you want to buy or have 看中某物: *I've got my eye on a nice little sports car that I'm saving up for.* 我看中了一辆漂亮的小跑车, 现在正攒钱呢。

⑦ DISAGREE/DISBELIEVE 不赞成/不相信

19 not see eye to eye to always disagree with someone 一向〔与某人〕看法不一致: *Liz never saw eye to eye with her daughter-in-law.* 莉兹与她的儿媳总想不到一块儿。

20 my eye! *spoken* used to express surprise or disagreement【口】天哪! 胡说!〔用于表示惊奇或不同意〕: *A diamond necklace, my eye! That was glass!* 一串钻石项链, 不对! 那是玻璃的!

21 in a pig's eye! *AmE spoken* used to show that you do not believe what someone is saying【美口】不可能!〔表示不相信〕: *Dan said he got up early to do all his chores. In a pig's eye he did!* 丹说他早早起来把他所有的家务活都做了。才没那回事呢!

⑧ SURPRISE 惊奇

22 not be able to believe your eyes *spoken* used when you see something very surprising【口】难以相信自己的眼睛: *I couldn't believe my eyes – there she was, stark naked!* 我简直不敢相信自己的眼睛 —— 她就在那里, 浑身一丝不挂!

23 eyes popping out of your head also 又作 **eyes out on stalks** *BrE especially spoken* used when you are very surprised or shocked by something you see【英, 尤口】双目圆睁

⑨ LOVE/SEXUAL ATTRACTION 爱/性吸引力

24 make eyes at sb/give sb the eye to look at someone in a way that shows you find them sexually attractive 眉目传情; 向某人送秋波: *Janet spent the whole evening making eyes at other men.* 珍妮特整个晚上都在向别的男人挤眉弄眼, 暗送秋波。

25 only have eyes for sb if someone only has eyes for someone else, they only love and are interested in that one person 只爱某人一个; 对某人情有独钟: *I knew it was hopeless – Mark only had eyes for his wife.* 我知道那是毫无希望的 —— 马克只爱他妻子一个人。

26 have your eye on sb to notice someone, especially because you think they are attractive 注意到某人〔尤指看中某人〕: *Mark's got his eye on that new girl in the accounts department.* 马克看中了会计部那个新来的女孩。| *I hear you've got your eye on a new player for the team.* 我听说你已经相中了一名新选手想让他加入球队。

⑩ JUDGE 判断

27 have a (good) eye for sth to be good at noticing and recognizing what is attractive, valuable, of good quality etc 对某事物有鉴赏眼光: *Gail has a good eye for colour.* 盖尔对色彩颇具眼光。

28 in the eyes of the law/the world/the police etc in the opinion or judgement of the law, the world, the police etc 从法律/世界/警察等的角度来看: *In the eyes of the law stealing is an offence, no matter what your motives.* 从法律的角度来看, 偷窃是一种犯罪行为, 无论其动机是什么。

29 to my eye *spoken* used when you want to give your opinion about the way something looks【口】我觉得, 在我看来: *To my eye the paint seemed darker than it had done in the shop.* 我觉得这漆比店中刷的要暗一些。

30 get/keep your eye in *BrE* to begin to practise or to continue practising your ability to judge the speed and direction of the ball in games such as CRICKET (2) and tennis【英】〔板球或网球等运动中〕训练判断球的速度和运动方向的眼力

⑪ SPOKEN PHRASES 口语短语

31 be up to your eyes in sth to be very busy doing something 十分忙碌地做某事: *I really can't take on anything else just now – I'm up to my eyes in paperwork as it is.* 我现在真的无法再承担别的活 —— 这些文书工作让我忙得团团转。

32 with your eyes closed/shut easily and without any difficulty 轻而易举地: *I don't know why you're so worried – you could run that place with your eyes closed!* 我不明白你为什么这么担心 —— 你闭着眼睛也能管理那个地方!

33 have eyes bigger than your stomach to take more food than you are able to eat 眼馋肚饱; 眼睛大, 肚子小: *I can't finish this cake – I must have eyes bigger than my stomach!* 这块蛋糕我吃不下了 —— 我真是眼馋肚饱啊!

34 one in the eye for *BrE* a defeat or disappointment for someone else, usually used when you are pleased about it【英】令某人高兴但令他人失望的事: *If we win the cup it'll be one in the eye for Martin – he said we wouldn't even make it to the final.* 如果我们赢得杯赛冠军, 将是对马丁的一个打击 —— 他曾说我们连决赛也进不去。

⑫ PURPOSE 目的

35 with an eye to if you do something with an eye to something else, you do it in order that the second thing will happen 指望, 期待: *Davies bought several houses, with an eye to making a quick profit.* 戴维斯买了好几幢房子, 指望着能快速获利。

36 with an eye to the main chance an expression meaning wanting to take advantage of any possible chance to succeed, usually used in a disapproving way〔为成功而〕不错过任何机会, 不惜利用任何机会〔通常含贬义〕

⑬ OTHER MEANINGS 其他意思

37 more to sth/sb than meets the eye if there is more to a situation, problem, or person than meets the eye, they are more complicated than they seem to be at first 某事/某人比(外表)看起来要复杂: *I reckon there's more to this 'relocation' business than meets the eye.* 我觉得"重新安置"这件事并不像看起来那样简单。

38 with your eyes open knowing fully what the problems, difficulties, results etc of a situation might be 心知肚明: *You went into this with your eyes open, so it's no use complaining now!* 在做这件事之前你很清楚它可能有什么后果, 所以现在抱怨没有用!

39 close/shut your eyes to sth to ignore something or pretend that you do not know it is happening 不理会[假装不知道]某事: *I closed my eyes to the fact that she wasn't supposed to be there, and bought her a drink.* 她不应该在那里, 但我不管这些, 还是给她买了杯酒喝。

40 drop/lower your eyes to move your eyes so that you are looking at a point lower than where you were looking before, especially because you are shy 往下看; 垂下眼帘〔尤指因为害羞〕: *Melissa lowered her eyes demurely as he came into the room.* 他走进房间时, 梅利莎羞涩地垂下眼帘。

41 for your eyes only used to say that something is secret and must only be seen by one particular person〔密件〕只供某人亲阅

42 an eye for an eye a system in which you punish someone by hurting them in the same way as they hurt someone else 以眼还眼, 以牙还牙: *An eye for an eye is no way to run a civilized justice system.* 文明的司法系统不允许以眼还眼、以牙还牙的行为。

43 ►NEEDLE 针◄ the hole in a needle that you put the thread through 针眼 —see picture at 参见 NEEDLE[1] 图

44 ►**CLOTHING** 服装◄ a small circle or U-shaped piece of metal used together with a hook for fastening clothes（钩）扣,（钩）环
45 ►**STORM** 暴风雨◄ the calm centre of a storm, especially a CYCLONE 风眼〔尤指气旋的中心〕
46 ►**POTATO** 马铃薯◄ a dark spot on a potato from which a new plant can grow 芽眼 —see also 另见 BLACK EYE, CAT'S EYE, PRIVATE EYE, RED EYE, **be the apple of sb's eye** (APPLE (2)), **not bat an eye/eyelid** (BAT² (2)), BIRD'S-EYE VIEW, **turn a blind eye (to)** (BLIND¹ (2b)), **see sth out of the corner of your eye** (CORNER¹ (8)), **cry your eyes out** (CRY¹ (1)), **the evil eye** (EVIL¹ (5)), **give sb the glad eye** (GLAD (8)), **in your mind's eye** (MIND¹ (43)), **here's mud in your eye** (MUD (4)), **open sb's eyes (to)** (OPEN² (3b)), **in the public eye/view** (PUBLIC¹ (4)), **make sheep's eyes at** (SHEEP (4)), **a sight for sore eyes** (SIGHT¹ (11)), **in the twinkling of an eye** (TWINKLE¹ (3)), **keep a weather eye on** (WEATHER¹ (5)), **pull the wool over sb's eyes** (WOOL (4))

eye² *present participle* **eyeing** *or* **eying** *v* [T] to look at someone or something with interest, especially because you do not trust them or because you want something 审视, 盯着看: *The child eyed me with curiosity.* 那个小孩好奇地看着我。| *Julian sat there eyeing my brandy.* 朱利安坐在那里, 眼睛盯着我的白兰地。

eye sb ↔ **up** *phr v* [T] *informal* to look at someone in a way that shows you think they are sexually attractive【非正式】〔因认为某人很性感而〕盯着看, 眼睛在〔某人〕身上打转: *They all stood in a corner, eyeing up the local girls.* 他们都站在角落里, 眼睛在那些当地女孩身上转来转去。

eye·ball¹ /ˈaɪˌbɔl; ˈaɪbɔːl/ *n* [C] **1** the round ball that forms the whole of your eye, including the part inside your head 眼球 —see picture at 参见 EYE¹ 图 **2 eyeball to eyeball** if two people are eyeball to eyeball, they are directly facing each other, especially in an angry or threatening way 面对面〔尤指怒目相视〕: *an eyeball-to-eyeball confrontation* 怒目相视的对抗

eyeball² *v* [T] *informal* to look directly and closely at something【非正式】盯住; 打量: *They eyeballed us suspiciously before speaking.* 在开口之前, 他们怀疑地打量了我们一番。

eye·brow /ˈaɪˌbraʊ; ˈaɪbraʊ/ *n* [C] **1** the line of hair above your eye 眉（毛）—see picture at 参见 EYE¹ 图 **2 raise your eyebrows** to move your eyebrows upwards in order to show surprise or disapproval 扬起眉毛〔表示惊讶或反对〕: *"Really?" she said, raising one eyebrow slightly.* "真的吗?" 她说, 一道眉微微扬起。**3 be up to your eyebrows in sth** *spoken* to be very busy doing something【口】埋头于…; 非常忙: *I'm sorry I can't come, but I'm up to my eyebrows in marking exams.* 很抱歉我不能来, 我批改试卷忙得不可开交。

eyebrow pen·cil /ˈ·· ˌ··/ *n* [C,U] a special pencil you can use to make your eyebrows darker 描眉笔

eye-catch·ing /ˈ· ˌ··/ *adj* something eye-catching is unusual or attractive in a way that makes you notice it 惹人注意的, 抢眼的: *an eye-catching new outfit* 抢眼的新衣服 —**eye-catchingly** *adv*

eye·ful /ˈaɪˌfʊl; ˈaɪfʊl/ *n* [C] **1** an amount of liquid, dust, or sand that has got into someone's eye 满眼〔的液体, 灰尘或沙子〕**2** *slang* something or someone, especially a woman, who is very attractive to look at【俚】引人注目的东西[人]〔尤指美女〕: *She's quite an eyeful!* 她可是个美人儿! **3 get an eyeful of this/that!** *spoken especially BrE* used to tell someone to look at something because it is interesting or unusual【口, 尤英】好好看一下这个/那个!

eye·glass /ˈaɪˌglæs; ˈaɪglɑːs/ *n* [C] **1** a LENS (1) for one eye, worn to help you see better with that eye; MONOCLE 单眼镜 **2 eyeglasses** *BrE old-fashioned or AmE* a pair of glasses (GLASS¹ (3))【英, 过时或美】一副眼镜

eye·lash /ˈaɪˌlæʃ; ˈaɪlæʃ/ *n* [C] **1** one of the small hairs that grow along the edge of your EYELIDS 睫（毛）—see picture at 参见 EYE¹ 图 **2 flutter your eyelashes** if a woman flutters her eyelashes, she moves them up and down very quickly, especially in order to look sexually attractive〔女人〕闪动睫毛〔尤指为了吸引异性〕

eye·less /ˈaɪləs; ˈaɪləs/ *adj* having no eyes 无眼的

eye·let /ˈaɪlɪt; ˈaɪlɨt/ *n* [C] a hole surrounded by a metal ring that is put in leather or cloth so that a string can be passed through it〔皮革或布上供穿线绳用的〕孔眼 —see picture at 参见 SHOE¹ 图

eye lev·el /ˈ· ˌ··/ *n* [singular] a height equal to the level of your eyes 齐眼的高度: *Pictures should be hung at eye level.* 画应挂在与眼睛同高的位置上。

eye·lid /ˈaɪlɪd; ˈaɪlɪd/ *n* [C] the two pieces of skin that cover your eye when it is closed 眼皮, 眼睑 —see also 另见 **not bat an eyelid** (BAT² (2)), —see picture at 参见 EYE¹ 图

eye·lin·er /ˈaɪˌlaɪnɚ; ˈaɪˌlaɪnə/ *n* [C,U] a coloured substance that you put along the edges of your eyelids to make your eyes look bigger or more noticeable〔化妆用的〕眼线膏[粉, 笔] —see picture at 参见 MAKE-UP 图

eye-o·pen·er /ˈ· ˌ···/ *n* [C] a situation, event etc from which you learn something surprising, or something that you did not know before 使人大开眼界的事物 —see also 另见 **open sb's eyes (to)** (OPEN² (3b))

eye patch /ˈ· ·/ *n* [C] a piece of material worn over one eye, usually because that eye has been damaged 眼罩〔通常在眼睛受伤时使用〕

eye pen·cil /ˈ· ˌ··/ *n* [C,U] an eyeliner 眼线笔

eye·piece /ˈaɪˌpis; ˈaɪpiːs/ *n* [C] the glass piece that you look through in a MICROSCOPE or TELESCOPE〔显微镜或望远镜的〕（接）目镜

eye shad·ow /ˈ· ˌ··/ *n* [C,U] a coloured substance that you put on your EYELIDS to make your eyes look more attractive 眼睑膏[粉], 眼影 —see picture at 参见 MAKE-UP 图

eye·sight /ˈaɪˌsaɪt; ˈaɪsaɪt/ *n* [U] your ability to see 视力

eye·sore /ˈaɪˌsɔr; ˈaɪsɔː/ *n* [C] something that is very ugly, especially a building surrounded by other things that are not ugly 不顺眼的事物, 难看的东西: *The tower block was an obvious eyesore in such a rural area.* 在这样一处乡村, 这座高楼实在有碍观瞻。

eye strain /ˈ· ·/ *n* [U] a pain you feel in your eyes, for example because you are tired or have been reading a lot 眼痛; 眼疲劳

eye tooth /ˈ· ·/ *n* [C] **1** one of the long pointed teeth at the corner of your mouth; CANINE TOOTH 上尖牙, 上犬牙 **2 give your eye teeth for sth** *spoken* used when you want something very much【口】非常希望得到某事物: *I'd give my eye teeth to be able to play the piano like that.* 要是我能像那样演奏钢琴, 我愿意付出任何代价。

eye wash /ˈ· ·/ *n* [U] **1** a special liquid used for washing your eyes when they are sore 洗眼剂, 洗眼药水 **2** *BrE spoken old-fashioned* something that you do not believe is true【英口, 过时】把戏, 骗局〔表示不相信〕: *Don't talk such eyewash!* 别再这么胡扯了!

eye·wit·ness /ˈaɪˌwɪtnɪs; ˈaɪˌwɪtnɨs/ *n* [C] someone who has seen something such as a crime happen, and is able to describe it afterwards 目击者; 见证人: *According to an eyewitness, the bomb went off at exactly three o'clock.* 一名目击者说, 炸弹是在3点整爆炸的。

ey·ing /ˈaɪ-ɪŋ; ˈaɪ-ɪŋ/ the present participle of EYE²

eyot /ˈaɪət; eɪt/ *n* [C] *BrE* a small island in a river【英】河中的小岛

ey·rie also 又作 **eyry** *BrE*【英】/ˈɛrɪ; ˈɪəri/ *n* [C] **1** the NEST of a large bird, especially an EAGLE, that is usually built high up in rocks or trees〔筑于岩石或树上等高处的〕猛禽巢〔尤指鹰巢〕**2** *informal* a room or building that is very high up【非正式】极高处的房间[建筑物]

F,f

F, f /ɛf; ef/ *plural* **F's, f's** *n* [C] the sixth letter of the English alphabet 英语字母表的第六个字母

f 1 the written abbreviation of 缩写= FORTE[2] **2** [plural] **ff** the written abbreviation of 缩写= 'following', used in a book 其后的〔用于书中〕: *see pages 54ff* 见第54页及其后几页

F[1] /ɛf; ef/ *n* **1** also 又作 **f** [C,U] the fourth note in the musical scale (SCALE[1] (8)) of C major or the musical key (KEY[2] (4)) based on this note F音〔C大调音阶中的第四个音〕; F调 **2** a mark given to a student whose work is not good enough〔学业成绩〕F级, 不及格

F[2] 1 the written abbreviation of 缩写= FAHRENHEIT: *Water boils at 212°F.* 水在212华氏度时沸腾。**2** the written abbreviation of 缩写= FEMALE **3** the written abbreviation of 缩写= FALSE

FA /ˌɛf ˋe; ˌef ˈeɪ◂/ *n* **1** the Football Association; the organization that is in charge of professional football in England〔英格兰〕足球协会; 英足总: *the FA Cup* 足总杯 **2 sweet FA** *BrE slang* nothing【英俚】什么都没有, 无

fa /fɑ; fɑː/ *n* [singular] the fourth note in a musical SCALE[1] (8) according to the SOL-FA system〔首调唱名法的〕全音阶中的第四音

FAA, the /ˌɛf e ˋe; ˌef eɪ ˈeɪ/ the abbreviation of 缩写= the FEDERAL AVIATION ADMINISTRATION

fab /fæb; fæb/ *adj informal* a word meaning extremely good, used especially in the 1960s【非正式】极好的; 极妙的〔尤用于20世纪60年代〕

Fab·er·gé /ˌfæbəˋʒe; ˌfæbəˈʒeɪ/, **Peter** (1846-1920) a Russian GOLDSMITH who made his father's jewellery business into an internationally famous company. He was most famous for producing Easter eggs decorated with jewels and ENAMEL for the Russian royal family. 法贝热〔(1846-1920), 俄国金匠。他把父亲的珠宝生意发展成为一家举世闻名的公司。他用珠宝和珐琅为俄国皇室装饰复活节彩蛋, 并以此而著名〕

Fabergé egg /ˌ···ˈ·/ one of the golden eggs decorated with jewels which were made by Peter Carl Fabergé for the Russian royal family in the late 19th century 法贝热复活节彩蛋〔19世纪末彼得·卡尔·法贝热为俄国皇室制作的嵌宝金蛋〕

Fa·bi·an /ˋfebɪən; ˈfeɪbiən/ *adj* [only before noun 仅用于名词前] connected with, or based on, the ideas of a British political group that has SOCIALIST[2] ideas and aims〔具有社会主义思想和目标的英国政治团体〕费边社的 —**Fabian** *n* [C]

fa·ble /ˋfebl; ˈfeɪbəl/ *n* **1** [C] a traditional short story that teaches a moral lesson, especially a story about animals 寓言: *the fable of the fox and the crow* 狐狸和乌鸦的寓言故事 **2** [U] such stories considered as a group; LEGEND (2) 神话传说〔总称〕: *monsters of fable and legend* 神话和传奇作品中的怪物

fa·bled /ˋfebḷd; ˈfeɪbəld/ *adj especially literary* famous and often mentioned in traditional stories; LEGENDARY【尤文】寓言[传奇]中著名的; 寓言[传奇]中的: [**+for**] *a city fabled for its wealth* 传说中以财富闻名的城市

W3 **fab·ric** /ˋfæbrɪk; ˈfæbrɪk/ *n* **1** [C,U] cloth used to make clothes, curtains etc; material 织物; 衣料: *man-made fabrics* 人造织物 —see 见 CLOTHES (USAGE) **2** [singular] the basic structure of a society, way of life etc and its relationships and traditions〔社会〕结构: *The family is the most important unit in the social fabric.* 家庭是社会结构中最重要的单位。**3 the fabric of** the basic structure of a building including the walls and the roof〔建筑物的〕基本结构〔包括墙和屋顶〕

fab·ri·cate /ˋfæbrɪˌket; ˈfæbrɪkeɪt/ *v* [T] **1** to invent a story, piece of information etc in order to deceive someone 编造, 捏造: *The police were accused of fabricating evidence.* 警方被控捏造证据。**2** *technical* to make or produce goods or equipment; MANUFACTURE[1] (1)【术语】制造, 生产: *The discs are expensive to fabricate.* 这些磁盘制造成本很昂贵。

fab·ri·ca·tion /ˌfæbrɪˋkeʃən; ˌfæbrɪˈkeɪʃən/ *n* **1** [C,U] a piece of information or story that someone has invented in order to deceive people 捏造的信息[说法]: *Officer, can't you see their story is a complete fabrication?* 长官, 你看不出他们说的事完全是捏造的吗? **2** [U] *technical* the process of making or producing something【术语】制造, 生产

fabric con·di·tion·er /ˈ·· ˌ···/ *BrE*【英】, **fabric soft·en·er** *AmE*【美】/ˈ·· ˌ···/ *n* [C,U] a chemical that you put in water when washing clothes in order to make them feel softer〔洗衣时用的〕织物柔软剂

fab·u·lous /ˋfæbjələs; ˈfæbjələs/ *adj* **1** extremely good or impressive 极好的; 绝妙的: *You look fabulous!* 你看上去好极了! | *a fabulous goal by Maradona* 马拉多纳射中的绝妙一球 **2** [only before noun 仅用于名词前] very large in amount or size 巨额的; 巨大的: *The painting was sold for a fabulous sum.* 那幅油画以天价卖出。**3** [only before noun 仅用于名词前] fabulous creatures, places etc are mentioned in traditional stories, but do not really exist 神话寓言中的, 传说中的: *dragons and other fabulous creatures* 龙和其他传说中的生物

fab·u·lous·ly /ˋfæbjələslɪ; ˈfæbjələsli/ *adv* **fabulously expensive/rich/successful etc** extremely expensive etc 极其昂贵/富有/成功等

fa·cade, façade /fəˋsɑd; fəˈsɑːd/ *n* [C] **1** the front of a building, especially a large and important one〔尤指大型或重要建筑物的〕正面: *A gang of stonemasons were restoring the facade of the cathedral.* 一群石匠正在修复大教堂的正面。**2** [usually singular 一般用单数] a way of behaving that hides your real feelings〔掩盖真实感情的〕表面: *the unpleasant reality lurking behind that facade of respectability* 隐藏在假装体面背后的令人不快的现实

face[1] /fes; feɪs/ *n* [C] S1 W1

1 ▶FRONT OF YOUR HEAD 头部的正面◀ the front part of the head from the chin to the forehead 脸, 面部: *She has such a pretty face.* 她有那么美的一张脸。| *Bob's face was covered in cuts and bruises.* 鲍勃的脸上满是划痕与擦伤。| **a sea of faces** (=a lot of faces seen together) 许许多多的脸 *The Principal looked down from the platform at the sea of faces below.* 校长从讲台上看着下面数不清的脸。—see picture at 参见 HEAD[1] 图

2 ▶EXPRESSION 表情◀ an expression on someone's face 面部表情; 脸色: *the children's happy faces* 孩子们欢快的表情 | **make/pull a face** (=change your expression to make people laugh, or to show that you are angry, disappointed etc) 做鬼脸 *Emma was making faces at me through the window.* 埃玛隔着窗子朝我做鬼脸。| **you should have seen his/her face** *spoken* (=used to say how angry, surprised etc someone looked) 你该看到他/她的神色〔用来说明某人看上去是何等生气、惊讶等〕 *You should have seen Steve's face when I told him I was resigning.* 我告诉史蒂夫我要辞职时, 你该看得到他脸上的表情。| **sb's face was a picture** *spoken* (=used to say that they looked very angry, surprised etc) 某人当时的表情极为可观〔用来说明某人看上去十分生气、惊讶等〕| **sb's face brightened/lit up** (=they started to smile and look happy) 某人面露喜色 *David's face lit up when I mentioned her name.* 我提到她的名字时, 戴维面露喜色。| **sb's face fell** (=they started to look disappointed or upset) 某人的脸色沉下来 *His face fell when I told him the news.* 我告诉他这一消息时, 他的脸色一沉。| **a face like thunder** (=a very angry expression) 震怒的表情 *Mr Neeson came striding towards us with a face like thunder.* 尼森先生怒气冲冲地大步朝我们走来。| **a long face** (=an unhappy or worried expression) 郁闷[忧虑]的表情; 愁眉苦脸

3 ▶PERSON 人◀ **a) a famous/well-known face** someone who is famous from television, magazines, films etc〔因出现在电视、杂志、电影等中而出名的〕名人 **b) new/different face** someone who you have not seen before 新人/不同的人: *There are a few new faces in class this year.* 今年班上有几张新面孔。**c) the same old faces** people that you see often, especially too often 经常看到的人; 看厌了的老面孔: *It's the same old faces at our meetings every week.* 每星期出席我们会议的老是那些人。

4 pale-faced/round-faced etc having a face that has a particular shape or colour 脸色苍白的/圆脸的等: *a pale-faced youth* 脸色苍白的青年 —see also 另见 RED-FACED

5 serious-faced/grim-faced etc showing a particular expression on your face 表情严肃的/表情严峻的等: *Negotiators emerged grim-faced after the day's talks.* 经过一天的谈判之后, 谈判者表情严峻地走了出来。—see also 另见 BAREFACED, PO-FACED, POKER-FACED, STONY-FACED

6 face to face a) if two people are face to face, they are very close and in front of each other 面对面地: **meet sb face to face** *I've never met her face to face. We've only talked on the phone.*

我从来没有当面见过她。我们只在电话中交谈过。| **come face to face with** (=suddenly meet someone who makes you very frightened, surprised etc) 突然面对面地遇见〔使你害怕、惊讶等的人〕*At that moment he came face to face with Sergeant Burke.* 那时他突然面对面地遇见了伯克中士。**b)** in a situation where you have to accept or deal with something unpleasant 面临着，面对着〔令人不愉快的事〕: **bring sb face to face with** *He was brought face to face with the truth about his daughter's disappearance.* 他不得不面对女儿失踪的事实。| **come face to face with** *This was the first time I'd ever come face to face with poverty.* 这是我第一次面对贫穷。—see also 另见 FACE-TO-FACE

7 to sb's face if you say something unpleasant to someone's face you say it to them directly 当着某人的面; 坦率地: *I told him to his face just what I thought.* 我把我的想法当面告诉了他。

8 face down/downwards with the face or front towards the ground 脸朝下, 面朝下: *The body was lying face down on the carpet.* 尸体脸朝下趴在地毯上。

9 face up/upwards with the face or front towards the sky 脸朝上, 面朝上: *She laid the cards out face upwards.* 她把纸牌面朝上摊开了。

10 in the face of in a situation where there are many problems, difficulties, or dangers 面对〔问题、困难或危险〕: *bravery in the face of danger* 面对危险时的勇气

11 on the face of it used to say that something seems true but that you think there may be other facts about it which are not yet clear 从表面上看; 乍看起来〔实情可能不同〕: *It looks, on the face of it, like a minor change in the regulations.* 这表面上看好像是对规定作了一点小变动。| *On the face of it, Norman seems the ideal man for the job.* 乍看起来, 诺曼似乎是这份工作的理想人选。

12 the face of a) the way in which an organization, system etc appears to people 〔组织、体制等的〕面貌: *recent events that changed the face of the British monarchy* 改变英国君主制面貌的一些最新事件 **b)** the general appearance of a particular place 〔某个地方的〕外观, 景观: *the changing face of the landscape* 不断变化的地貌景色

13 lose face to make other people lose their respect for you 丢脸: *He doesn't want to back down and risk losing face.* 他不想打退堂鼓, 怕会丢脸。

14 save face if you do something to save face, you do it so that people will not lose their respect for you 保全面子: *Rather than admit defeat, Franklin compromised in order to save face.* 富兰克林为了保全面子没有承认失败, 而是作了妥协。

15 blow up/go up in sb's face if a situation blows up or goes up in your face, it goes wrong, especially in an embarrassing way 当场出丑, 当众丢脸

16 disappear/vanish off the face of the earth to suddenly disappear 从地球上消失, 突然消失: *I haven't seen Paul in ages, he seems to have vanished off the face of the earth.* 我很久没见到保罗了, 他好像已经从地球上消失。

17 sb's face doesn't fit used to say that someone is not the right kind of person for a particular group, organization etc 某人不适合〔某个群体、组织等〕

18 put a brave face (on) to make an effort to behave in a happy cheerful way when you are upset or disappointed 〔虽然烦恼、失望等但〕装作若无其事的样子: *He was shattered, though he put on a brave face.* 他大为震惊, 尽管他装作若无其事的样子。

19 set your face against *especially BrE* to be very determined that something should not happen【尤英】沉下脸反对, 坚决反对

20 ▶MOUNTAIN/CLIFF 山/悬崖◀ a steep, high side of a mountain, cliff etc 〔山、悬崖等的〕正面; 陡坡面: *The cliff face was starting to crumble into the sea.* 悬崖的正面开始崩裂并坠入大海。

21 ▶CLOCK 钟◀ the front of a clock 钟面

22 ▶MINE 矿井◀ the part of a mine from which coal, stone etc is cut 〔矿井的〕采掘面

23 ▶OUTSIDE SURFACE 表面◀ one of the outside surfaces of an object or building 〔物体或建筑物的〕面, 表面: *A cube has six faces.* 立方体有六个面。

24 ▶SPORT 体育运动◀ the part of a bat (BAT[1] (2)) or racket (RACKET[1] (3)) that you use to hit the ball 〔球棒或球拍的〕击球面

25 in your face/in yer face *slang* behaviour, criticisms, remarks etc that are in your face are very direct and often shocking or surprising【俚】〔行为、批评、评论等〕当着你的面, 直截了当地, 不留情面地: *Parson's 'in your face' style of interviewing* 帕森的那种当面直言不讳的面谈方式

26 what's his face/what's her face *spoken* used as a way of talking about someone when you cannot remember their name【口】那个叫什么名字的人: *I saw old what's his face in school yesterday.* 我昨天在学校里见到了那个叫什么名字的老相识。

27 put your face on *informal humorous* to put MAKE-UP on【非正式, 幽默】〔面部〕化妆 —see also 另见 **have egg on your face** (EGG[1] (4)), **fly in the face of** (FLY[1] (28)), **a straight face** (STRAIGHT[2] (11)), **laugh in sb's face** (LAUGH[1] (12)), **not just a pretty face** (PRETTY[2] (5)), **show your face** (SHOW[1] (12)), **shut your face** (SHUT[1] (3)), **a slap in the face** (SLAP[2] (2)), **be staring sb in the face** (STARE[1] (2)), **do sth till you're blue in the face** (BLUE[1] (6)), **wipe the smile/grin off sb's face** (WIPE[1] (7)), **have sth written all over your face** (WRITE (5))

face² *v* [T] S1 W1

1 ▶DIFFICULT SITUATION 困难的局面◀ if you face a difficult situation or if it faces you, you must deal with it 面临, 面对: *The President faces the difficult task of putting the economy back on its feet.* 总统面对着恢复经济的艰巨任务。| *McManus is facing the biggest challenge of his career.* 麦克马纳斯正面临着职业生涯中的最大挑战。| **be faced with/by** *I was faced with the awful job of breaking the news to the girl's family.* 我面临着要向女孩的家人报告这一消息的可怕任务。

2 ▶ADMIT A PROBLEM EXISTS 承认问题的存在◀ to accept that a difficult situation or problem exists, even though you would prefer to ignore it 正视, 面对: **face the fact that** *Many couples refuse to face the fact that they have problems with their marriage.* 许多夫妇拒绝面对自己的婚姻出现问题这一事实。| **face facts** *It's time that we started to face a few hard facts.* 我们是时候开始面对一些铁一般的事实了。| **face the truth** *He had to face the awful truth that she no longer loved him.* 他不得不正视她不再爱他这一可怕的事实。| **(let's) face it** *spoken* (=used when saying something that someone may find difficult to accept or admit)【口】(让我们) 面对现实吧〔用于说别人难以接受或承认的话时〕: *Face it kid, you're never gonna be a rock star.* 孩子, 面对现实吧, 你永远也成不了摇滚乐歌星的。

3 can't face if you cannot face something, you feel unable to do it because it seems too unpleasant or difficult 无法面对, 无法正视: *I don't want to go back to school again – I just can't face it.* 我不想再回到学校去—— 我无法面对这事。| **can't face doing sth** *He couldn't face driving all the way to Los Angeles.* 他受不了一直开车到洛杉矶。

4 ▶BE OPPOSITE 在对面◀ to be opposite a person, building etc so that you are pointing towards them, or to point in a particular direction 面向, 面朝: *They stood facing each other for a few minutes.* 他们面对面站了好几分钟。| *Rita's apartment faces the harbor.* 丽塔的房间面朝海港。| **face north/east etc** (=point towards the north, east etc) 朝北/东等 *My bedroom faces south.* 我的卧室朝南。| **south-facing/west-facing etc** *a south-facing garden* 朝南的花园 —see 见 FRONT[1] (USAGE)

5 ▶UNPLEASANT POSSIBILITY 可能发生的不愉快的事◀ to have the possibility that something bad or unpleasant might happen to you 面临〔可能发生到自己头上的坏事或不愉快的事〕: *If he can't pay up, he's faced with losing his home.* 他如果无法付款, 将面临失去家园的后果。| *Evans could face the electric chair.* 埃文斯可能面临坐电椅的判决。

6 ▶TEAM/OPPONENT 团队/对手◀ to play against an opponent or team in a game or competition 与…比赛[竞赛]: *Martinez will face Robertson in tomorrow's final.* 马丁内斯将在明天的决赛中和罗伯逊较量。

7 ▶DIFFICULT PERSON 难相处的人◀ to deal with someone who is difficult to deal with, or talk to someone who you do not want to talk to 对付, 应付〔难对付的人或不愿意答理的人〕: *You're going to have to face him sooner or later.* 你迟早得对付他。

8 face the music *informal* to accept criticism or punishment for something you have done【非正式】〔为自己的行为〕接受批评[惩罚]; 承担后果

9 ▶BUILDING 建筑物◀ be faced with stone/concrete etc to be covered in stone, CONCRETE[2] etc 以石头/混凝土等砌面[抹面; 覆盖]的

face sb **↔ down** *phr v* [T] to deal with someone in a strong and confident way 〔用坚定和自信的方式〕压倒, 挫败, 慑服: *The police chief faced down reporters who were calling for his resignation.* 警察局长慑服了要求他辞职的记者们。

face up to sth *phr v* [T] to accept and deal with an unpleasant fact or problem 勇于接受并处理〔不愉快的事实或问题〕: *They'll never offer you another job; you might as well face up to it.* 他们绝不会再给你一份工作, 你还是接受事实吧。

face sb **with** sth *phr v* [T often passive 常用被动态] to show someone evidence that proves they have done something wrong 向某人出示〔其做了错事的证据〕; 把〔证据〕摆在〔某人〕面前

face card /ˈ· ·/ *n* [C] *AmE* the king, queen, or jack (JACK[1] (2)) in a set of playing cards【美】〔纸牌戏中的〕花牌，人头牌〔纸牌中的 K, Q, J〕; COURT CARD *BrE*【英】

face·cloth /ˈ· ·/ *n* [C] *BrE* a small piece of rough cloth used to wash the face or hands【英】〔小块园布做的〕洗脸巾；洗手巾；WASHCLOTH *AmE*【美】

face cream /ˈ· ·/ *n* [C,U] a thick cream used to clean the face or to keep it soft and smooth 洗面乳；润肤霜；面霜

face·less /ˈfeslɪs; ˈfeɪsləs/ *adj* a faceless person, organization etc consists of a lot of people who you do not know, and who do not seem interested in or to have sympathy for ordinary people 〔人或机构等〕冷漠的，没有人情味的: *faceless bureaucrats* 无人情味的官僚

face·lift /ˈfesˌlɪft; ˈfeɪslɪft/ *n* [C] **1** a medical operation in which doctors remove loose skin on someone's face in order to make them look younger 整容术；面部拉皮手术 **2** work or repairs that make a place or object look newer or better 翻新；整修: **give sth a facelift** *The new owner had given the pub a facelift.* 新业主对酒吧进行了翻修。

face-off /ˈ· ·/ *n* [C] **1** *AmE informal* a fight or argument【美，非正式】对抗，对峙；争吵: *a face-off between police and rioters* 警察与骚乱者的对抗 **2** a way of starting a game of ICE HOCKEY 〔冰球比赛的〕开球 —**faceoff** *phr v* [T]

face pack /ˈ· ·/ *n* [C] a thick cream that you spread over your face in order to clean and improve your skin 美容洁肤膏；面霜

face pow·der /ˈ· ˌ· ·/ *n* [U] powder that you put on your face in order to make it look smoother and give it more colour 扑面粉 —see picture at 参见 MAKE-UP 图

face sav·er /ˈ· ˌ· ·/ *n* [C] something that helps you not to lose other people's respect 保全面子的事物

face-sav·ing /ˈ· ˌ· ·/ *adj* [only before noun 仅用于名词前] a face-saving action or arrangement helps you not to lose other people's respect 〔行为或安排〕保全面子的: *a face-saving compromise* 保全面子的妥协

fac·et /ˈfæsɪt; ˈfæsɪ̈t/ *n* [C] **1** one of several parts of someone's character, a situation etc; ASPECT (1) 〔性格、情况等的〕（一个）方面: [+of] *discussing the many facets of the problem* 讨论这个问题的许多方面 **2 multi-faceted/many faceted** consisting of many different parts 多方面的: *a multi-faceted issue* 涉及多方面的问题 **3** one of the flat sides of a jewel 〔宝石的〕（一个）琢面，刻面，小平面

facet 刻面

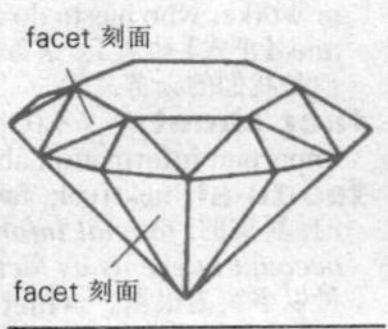

fa·ce·tious /fəˈsiʃəs; fəˈsiːʃəs/ *adj* saying things that are intended to be clever and funny but are really silly and annoying 好乱开玩笑的，故作诙谐的，不正经的: *Don't be so facetious!* 别这么没正经的！| *facetious comments* 故作诙谐的评论 —**facetiously** *adv* —**facetiousness** *n* [U]

face-to-face /ˌ· · ˈ·◂/ *adj* [only before noun 仅用于名词前] a face-to-face meeting, conversation etc is one where you are actually with another person and talking to them 〔指会晤、谈话等〕面对面的

face val·ue /ˌ· ˈ· ·/ *n* [U] **1 take sth at face value** to accept a situation or accept what someone says, without thinking there may be a hidden meaning 对〔某一情况或别人的话〕信以为真: *You shouldn't always take his remarks at face value.* 你不该总是拿他的话当真。**2** [C,U] the value or cost shown on the front of something such as a stamp or coin 〔邮票或钱币等的〕面额，票面价值

fa·cial[1] /ˈfeʃəl; ˈfeɪʃəl/ *adj* on your face or connected with your face 脸上的；面部的: *a slight facial resemblance between the two men* 两个男子的容貌有点相似 | *facial hair* 脸上的汗毛、胡须等 —**facially** *adv*: *Facially the two sisters are very similar.* 这两姐妹长相十分相似。

facial[2] *n* [C] a process in which creams are rubbed into the skin of your face in order to clean and improve your skin 面部美容

facial scrub /ˌ· · ˈ·/ *n* [C] a thick substance which you use to clean the skin on your face thoroughly 面部磨砂膏，磨砂洁面霜

fa·cile /ˈfæsl; ˈfæsaɪl/ *adj* **1** a facile remark, argument etc is too simple and shows a lack of careful thought or understanding 〔指话语、论点等〕肤浅的，未认真思考[理解]的: *facile logic* 肤浅的道理 **2** [only before noun 仅用于名词前] *formal* a facile achievement or success has been obtained too easily【正式】〔指成就或成功〕太容易得到的: *a facile victory* 轻易取得的胜利 —**facilely** *adv* —**facileness** *n* [U]

fa·cil·i·tate /fəˈsɪləˌtet; fəˈsɪlɪ̈teɪt/ *v* [T] *formal* to make it easier for a process or activity to happen【正式】使容易，使便利；有助于: *Computers can be used to facilitate language learning.* 使用电脑能为语言学习带来方便。—**facilitation** /fəˌsɪləˈteʃən; fəˌsɪlɪ̈ˈteɪʃən/ *n* [U]

fa·cil·i·tat·or /fəˈsɪləˌtetɚ; fəˈsɪlɪ̈teɪtə/ *n* [C] **1** someone who helps a group of people discuss things with each other or do something effectively 促进者，推动者；协调人 **2** *technical* something that helps a process to take place【术语】促进[方便]某过程的事物

fa·cil·i·ty /fəˈsɪlətɪ; fəˈsɪlɪ̈ti/ *n* **1 facilities** [plural] rooms, equipment, or services that are provided for a particular purpose 〔为某种目的而提供的〕设施〈如房屋、设备、服务等〉: *a 5-star hotel with fantastic facilities* 设施完善的五星级酒店 | *child-care facilities* 儿童保育设施 | *toilet facilities* 卫生间设备 **2** [usually singular 一般用单数] a special part of a piece of equipment or a system which makes it possible to do something 〔使某事得以进行的〕安排，设备，装置: *Is there a call-back facility on this phone?* 这台电话有回话装置吗？| *a bank account with an overdraft facility* 可以透支的银行账户 **3** [singular] a natural ability to do something easily and well 天赋；才能: [+for] *She has an amazing facility for mental arithmetic.* 她的心算技能令人惊叹。**4** [C] a place or building used for a particular activity or industry, or for providing a particular type of service 〔特定用途的〕场所；建筑: *a chlorine-production facility* 生产氯的工厂 **5 with great facility** *formal* very easily【正式】十分容易地，毫不费力地 S3 W1

fac·ing /ˈfesɪŋ; ˈfeɪsɪŋ/ *n* [C,U] **1** an outer surface of a wall or building made of a different material from the rest in order to make it look attractive 〔墙或建筑的〕饰面；面层 **2** material fastened to the inside of a piece of clothing to strengthen it 〔衣服的〕衬里 **3 facings** parts of a jacket, coat etc around the neck and wrists which have a different colour from the rest 〔领口或袖口的〕镶边；饰边；贴边

fac·sim·i·le /fækˈsɪməlɪ; fækˈsɪmɪ̈li/ *n* [C] **1** an exact copy of a picture, piece of writing etc 〔图片、文字作品等的〕摹本，精确的复制品 **2** *formal* a FAX[1](1)【正式】传真 —**facsimile** *adj*

fact /fækt; fækt/ *n* S1 W1

1 ▶TRUE INFORMATION 真实信息◀ [C] a piece of information that is known to be true 事实；真相: *First of all, we need to establish the facts of the case.* 首先，我们需要确定案子的事实真相。| [+about] *The book is full of interesting facts about the World Cup.* 这本书满是有关世界杯的有趣事实。| **facts and figures** (=the basic details, numbers etc concerning a particular situation or subject) 确切情况，详细的资料 | **it's a fact/that's a fact** (=used to emphasize that something is definitely true or that something definitely happened) 事实就是如此〔用于强调〕*The divorce rate in the US is now twice as high as in the 1950s – that's a fact.* 美国现在的离婚率是20世纪50年代的两倍。事实就是如此。| **it's a fact that** *It's a fact that most deaths from lung cancer are caused by smoking.* 事实是，大部分因肺癌而导致的死亡是由吸烟引起的。| **I know for a fact that** *spoken* (=used to say that you definitely know that something is true)【口】我确实知道 *I know for a fact that she earns more than I do.* 我确实知道她挣钱比我多。| **get your facts right/wrong** (=be right or wrong about something) 弄对/错事实 *We need to be sure we've got our facts right before making wild accusations.* 我们先要确保掌握的事实准确无误，不要胡乱指责人。| **stick/keep to the facts** (=only say what you know is true) 实事求是，只说确实知道的事实 *Let's just stick to the facts and not jump to any conclusions.* 我们还是实事求是吧，不要贸然下结论。| **the bare facts** (=the basic details of a situation or story) 基本情况，赤裸裸的事实 | **hard facts** (=details or pieces of information that can be proved to be true) 铁一般的事实，真实情况 *We need some hard facts not just theories and suppositions.* 我们需要一些确凿的事实，而不仅仅是理论和推测。| **the facts speak for themselves** (=they show clearly that something is true) 事实不言自明 *She obviously knows what she's doing–the facts speak for themselves.* 她显然知道自己在做什么——事实已经不言而喻。

2 the fact (that) used when talking about a situation and saying that it is true …的事实〔用于谈论某个情况并说明它是真实的〕: *He refused to help me, despite the fact that I asked him several times.* 尽管我确实求了他好几次，他还是拒绝帮助我。| **given the fact (that)/in view of the fact (that)** (=used when saying that a particular fact influences your judgement about something or someone) 鉴于，考虑到〔用于说明某一事实影响自己对某人或某事的看法〕*Given the fact that this is their first game, I think they did pretty well.* 考虑到这是他们的首次比赛，我认为他们打得很好了。| **owing to the fact (that)/due to the fact (that)** (=because) 由于，因为 *The school's poor exam record*

is largely due to the fact that it is chronically underfunded. 这所学校考试成绩差，主要是由于长期以来资金不足。

3 ►REAL EVENTS/NOT A STORY 真实事件/非虚构的故事◄ [U] situations, events etc that really happened and have not been invented 事实，实情：*Much of the novel is based on fact.* 这部小说大部分内容都是以事实为依据的。

4 in fact/in actual fact a) used to say what the real truth of a situation is, especially when this is different from what people think or say it is 事实上/实际上：*They told me it would be cheap but in fact it cost me nearly $500.* 他们对我说那是便宜货，但实际上我花了差不多500美元。| *Her teachers said she was a slow learner, whereas in actual fact she was partially deaf.* 她的老师都说她学习反应慢，然而实际上她是有点耳背。**b)** used when you are adding something, especially something surprising, to emphasize what you have just said 其实；事实上：*We live very close to Lesley's parents, in the same road in actual fact.* 我们住得离莱斯利的父母家很近，其实就在同一条路上。

5 as a matter of fact *spoken*【口】**a)** used when you are answering someone and telling them what you really think or what the real situation is 实际上；其实〔用于回复并告诉某人你的真实想法或实际情况〕：*"I didn't think you'd mind me using your office." "Well as a matter of fact I do mind."* "我原以为你不会介意我用一下你的办公室。" "哦，其实我很介意。" **b)** used to add an important fact that increases the effect of what you are saying 事实上〔用于加插某一重要情况，以增强所说话语的效果〕：*Our ELT department is doing really well. As a matter of fact we've just signed a big new contract in China.* 我们的英语教学部成绩真不错，事实上我们刚刚在中国签订了一份新的大合同。

6 in point of fact *spoken* an expression used in discussions and speeches to add another piece of information or disagree with what someone else has said【口】事实上，实际上〔用于商谈或演讲中需增添另一事实或反驳对方的一种表达法〕

7 the fact is/the fact of the matter is *spoken* used when you are telling someone what is actually true in a particular situation, especially when this is different from what people believe【口】事实是/实际情况是：*The fact of the matter is that the company is unlikely to survive the recession.* 实际情况是这家公司不大可能渡过这场经济衰退。

8 the fact remains used to emphasize that a situation is true and people must realize this 事实是，真实的情况是〔用于强调某一情况为事实，人们必须对其有认识〕：*The fact remains that the number of homeless people is rising daily.* 实际情况是无家可归者的人数每天都在增加。

9 sth is a fact of life used to say that a situation exists and must be accepted（某事）已成为必须面对的事实：*Mass unemployment seems to be a fact of life nowadays.* 大规模失业似乎已成为当今无法避免的事实。

10 the facts of life a) the details about sex and how babies are born 性知识 **b)** the way life really is, with all its problems and difficulties 严酷的生活现实；现实生活

11 after the fact after something has happened or been done, especially after a mistake has been made 情况发生后；错误发生后 —see also 另见 **as a matter of fact** (MATTER[1] (16))

fact-find·ing /ˈ· ˌ··/ *adj* **fact-finding trip/tour/mission etc** a trip during which you try to find out facts and information about something for your organization, government etc 实情调查[为弄清楚事实真相的]旅行/旅游/任务等

fac·tion /ˈfækʃən; ˈfækʃən/ *n* **1** [C] a small group of people within a larger group, who have different ideas from the other members〔团体中的〕派别，派系，小集团：*warring factions* 敌对的派系 **2** [U] *formal* disagreement or fighting within a group or a political party【正式】〔团体或政党内部的〕派系斗争，派系纠纷 **3** [C,U] a story in a film or television programme that is based on real events but is not completely true〔以真实事件为依据但又加入虚构内容的〕纪实小说；纪实电影[电视节目] **—factional** *adj*

fac·ti·tious /fækˈtɪʃəs; fækˈtɪʃəs/ *adj formal* made to happen artificially by people rather than happening naturally【正式】做作的，不自然的；虚假的

fac·tor¹ /ˈfæktə; ˈfæktə/ *n* [C]

1 ►CAUSE/INFLUENCE 原因/影响◄ one of several things that influence or cause a situation 因素，要素：*The rise in crime is mainly due to social and economic factors.* 犯罪率上升主要是由社会及经济因素造成的。| [+in] *The vaccination program has been a major factor in the improvement of health standards.* 接种疫苗计划是人类健康水平得以提高的一个主要因素。| **key/crucial factor** *The weather could be a crucial factor in tomorrow's game.* 天气情况会是明天比赛的一个至关重要的因素。| **the deciding factor** (=the most important factor) 决定性因素 *We liked both houses, but in the end the deciding factor was the location.* 这两幢房子我们都挺喜欢，但归根结底地段的好坏才是决定性因素。

2 by a factor of five/ten etc if something increases or decreases by a factor of five, ten etc it increases or decreases by five times, ten times etc 以五倍/十倍等系数（增加或减少）

3 ►LEVEL ON A SCALE 等级标准◄ a particular level on a scale of measurement of the force or effectiveness of something〔某物的〕效力等级系数：*factor 15 suntan oil* 防晒系数为15的防晒油 | *a wind chill factor of -20* 风寒指数为 -20

4 ►MATHEMATICS 数学◄ a number that divides into another number exactly 因子，因数：*3 is a factor of 15.* 3是15的因数。

5 ►LAND 土地◄ *ScotE* someone who looks after another person's land【苏格兰】代人管理土地者，地产管理人

factor² *v* [T] *AmE technical* to divide a number into factors【美，术语】将…分解为因子，把…化为因数

factor sth ↔ **in** *phr v* [T] to include a particular thing in your calculations about how long something will take, how much it will cost etc 将…计入；把…考虑在内

fac·to·ri·al /fækˈtɔrɪəl; fækˈtɔːriəl/ *n* [C] *technical* the result when you multiply a whole number by all the numbers below it【术语】阶乘，阶乘积：*factorial 3 = 3×2×1* 3的阶乘=3×2×1

fac·tor·ize also 又作 **-ise** *BrE*【英】/ˈfæktəˌraɪz, ˈfæktəraɪz/ *v* [T] *technical* to divide a number into factors【术语】把…分解成因子，把…化为因数 **—factorization** /ˌfæktərəˈzeʃən; ˌfæktəraɪˈzeɪʃən/ *n* [U]

fac·to·ry /ˈfæktərɪ; ˈfæktəri/ *n* [C] **1** a building or group of buildings in which goods are produced in large quantities, using machines 工厂，制造厂：*a car factory* 汽车制造厂 | *factory workers* 工厂工人 **2 on the factory floor** among the ordinary workers in a company 在工人[员工]当中 

factory farm /ˈ··· ˌ·/ *n* [C] *BrE* a farm where animals are kept inside, in small spaces or small CAGEs, and made to grow or produce eggs very quickly【英】〔以现代化方式饲养禽畜，以迅速提高肉、蛋产量的〕工厂化农场 **—factory farming** *n* [U]

fac·to·tum /fækˈtotəm; fækˈtəʊtəm/ *n* [C] *formal* a servant or worker who has to do many different kinds of jobs for someone【正式】勤杂工，杂务工，杂役：*He's our general factotum.* 他是我们的杂务总管。

fact sheet /ˈ· ·/ *n* [C] a piece of paper giving all the most important information about something 情况简报，资料摘要

fac·tu·al /ˈfæktʃuəl; ˈfæktʃuəl/ *adj* based on facts（基于）事实的，真实的：*factual information* 真实信息 | *Try to keep your account of events as factual as possible.* 你对事件的叙述要尽量以事实为根据。**—factually** *adv*: *The document is factually correct.* 这份文件在事实上是准确的。

fac·ul·ty /ˈfækḷtɪ; ˈfækəlti/ *n plural* **faculties** [C] **1** a natural ability, such as the ability to see, hear, or think clearly 天赋，能力：[+of] *the faculty of reason* 推理能力 | **in full possession of all your faculties** (=able to see, hear, think etc in the normal way) 心智健全的 **2** a particular skill that someone has 才能，技能：[+for] *She had a great faculty for absorbing information.* 她十分擅长汲取信息。**3** a department within a university〔大学的〕系，部，院：*the Faculty of Engineering* 工程学院 **4 the faculty** *AmE* all the teachers in a university【美】〔大学的〕全体教员：*There was a mixed reaction to the proposal among the faculty.* 教员们对这项建议的反应不一。

FA Cup, the /ˌɛf e ˈkʌp; ˌef eɪ ˈkʌp/ a football competition open to all amateur and professional football teams in the FA in England and Wales, and arranged by the FA 足总杯〔面向英格兰、威尔士足球协会所有业余和职业足球队举办的比赛，由英足总组织〕：*Liverpool won the FA Cup.* 利物浦队赢得了足总杯。

fad /fæd; fæd/ *n* [C] something that someone likes or does for a short time, or that is fashionable for a short time 一时的狂热；时尚，风尚：*The break-dancing craze soon passed, as most fads do.* 跟大多数流行时尚一样，这一阵霹雳舞热很快就过去了。**—faddy, faddish** *adj*: *She keeps trying all these faddy diets.* 她不停地尝试各种流行的节食法。**—faddiness, faddishness** *n* [U]

fade /fed; feɪd/ *v* **1** also 又作 **fade away** [I] to gradually disappear 逐渐消失：*Hopes of a peace settlement are beginning to fade.* 和平解决的希望正开始消失。| *Over the years her beauty had faded a little.* 过去几年里，她的美貌已有点失色。**2** [I, T] to lose colour and brightness, or to make something do this（使）褪色；（使）失去光泽：*the fading evening light* 逐渐苍茫的暮色 | **fade sth** *The sun had faded the curtains.* 太阳把窗帘晒得退了色。—see picture on page A18 参见A18页图 **3** also 又作 **fade away** [I] to become weaker physically, especially so that you

become very ill or die〔身体〕变得虚弱 **4** [I] if a team fades, it stops playing as well as it did before〔运动队〕水准下降: *The Broncos faded in the second half.* 野马队下半场打得较差。

fade sth ↔ **in** *phr v* [T] to make a picture or sound appear or be heard gradually 使〔画面〕淡入, 渐显; 使〔声音〕渐强 —**fade-in** /ˈ· ·/ *n* [C]

fade sth ↔ **out** *phr v* [T] to make a picture or sound disappear slowly or become quieter 使〔画面〕淡出, 渐隐; 使〔声音〕渐弱 —**fade-out** /ˈ· ·/ *n* [C]

fae·ces also 又作 **feces** *AmE*【美】/ˈfisiz; ˈfiːsiːz/ *n* [plural] *formal* solid waste material from the BOWELs【正式】粪便 —**fae·cal** /ˈfikl; ˈfiːkəl/ *adj*

Fae·roe Is·lands, the /ˈfɛro ˌaɪləndz; ˈfeərəʊ ˌaɪləndz/ also 又作 **the Faeroes, the Faroe Islands, the Faroes** a group of islands in the northeast Atlantic Ocean. They belong to Denmark, but have their own government. 法罗群岛〔大西洋东北部一群岛, 归属丹麦, 但拥有自己的政府〕

fae·ry, faerie /ˈfɛrɪ; ˈfeəri/ *n* [C] *old-use* a FAIRY(1)【旧】仙子, 小精灵

faff /fæf; fæf/ *v*

faff about/around *phr v* [I] *BrE informal* to waste time doing unnecessary things【英, 非正式】无事瞎忙: *I wish you'd stop faffing around!* 我希望你不要再无事瞎忙了。

fag[1] /fæg; fæg/ *n* [C] **1** *BrE slang* a cigarette【英俚】香烟 **2** *AmE slang* an offensive word for a HOMOSEXUAL【美俚】男同性恋者〔冒犯用语〕 **3 be a fag** *BrE informal* to be a boring or difficult thing to do【英, 非正式】烦人的活, 苦差事: *I hate ironing – it's such a fag.* 我讨厌熨衣服 —— 这是件苦差事。**4** a young student in some British PUBLIC SCHOOLs who has to do jobs for an older student〔英国一些私立中学里〕受高年级学生使唤的低年级学生

fag[2] *v* [I +**for**] to do jobs for an older student at a British PUBLIC SCHOOL〔英国私立中学里的低年级学生〕听高年级学生使唤 —**fagging** *n* [U]

fag end /ˌ· ˈ·◂/ *n* [C] *informal*【非正式】**1** *BrE* the end of a cigarette that someone has finished smoking【英】(香) 烟蒂 **2 the fag end of** *especially BrE* the last part of something, especially when it is not as good or interesting as the rest【尤英】…的末尾, 末端; 无味[没趣]的剩余部分

fagged /fægd; fægd/ *adj BrE informal*【英, 非正式】**1** also 又作 **fagged out** [not before noun 不用于名词前] extremely tired 疲惫不堪的: *I was fagged out after the journey.* 旅行后我累极了。**2 I can't be fagged** used to say that you are too tired or bored to do something 我不愿干那种累事〔用于表示自己太累或太厌烦不愿去做某事〕

fag·got /ˈfægət; ˈfægət/ *n* [C] **1** *BrE* a ball made of meat mixed with bread, which is cooked【英】〔由碎肉和面包屑做成并煮熟的〕肉丸子 **2** *AmE slang* an offensive word for a HOMOSEXUAL【美俚】男同性恋者〔冒犯用语〕 **3** a collection of small sticks for burning on a fire 柴捆, 柴把 **4** *BrE informal* an impolite word for someone you do not like, especially a woman【英, 非正式】讨厌的人〔非礼貌用语, 尤指女人〕

fag-hag /ˈ· ·/ *n* [C] *slang especially AmE* an offensive word for a woman who spends time with HOMOSEXUAL men【俚, 尤美】与男同性恋者在一起的女人〔冒犯用语〕

Fa·gin /ˈfegɪn; ˈfeɪgɪn/ a character in the book *Oliver Twist* by Charles Dickens. Fagin is the leader of a group of young thieves, who collects and then sells the objects that they have stolen. 费金〔查尔斯·狄更斯的小说《雾都孤儿》中的人物。他是一伙少年小偷的头目, 负责收缴和倒卖赃物〕

Fah·ren·heit /ˈfærənˌhaɪt; ˈfærənhaɪt/ *n* [U] a scale of temperature in which water freezes at 32° and boils at 212° 华氏温度

S2 W1 **fail**[1] /fel; feɪl/ *v*

1 ►TRY BUT FAIL 尝试但失败◄ [I] to be unsuccessful in something that you want to do 失败, 未成功: *Peace talks between the two countries have failed.* 两国间的和谈已经失败。| **fail to do sth** *Doctors failed to save the girl's life.* 医生们未能保住这女孩的性命。| **fail miserably** (=be completely unsuccessful in a way that it is embarrassing) 完全失败, 惨败: *Millions of people have tried to quit smoking and failed miserably.* 千百万人试图戒烟, 但完全失败。

2 ►NOT DO WHAT IS EXPECTED 没做应做的事◄ [I] to not do what is expected, needed, or wanted: **fail to do sth** *The letter failed to arrive.* 信没有寄到。| *The report cleverly fails to mention the real cost of this experiment.* 报告巧妙地不提这项试验的实际费用。| **fail in your duty/responsibility** *I would be failing in my duty if I didn't warn you of the consequences of your actions.* 如果我对你的行动将产生的后果不提出告诫, 那我就是失职。

3 ►EXAM/TEST 考试/测验◄ **a)** [I,T] to not pass a test or examination 不及格; 未能通过: *I failed my driving test the first time I took it.* 我第一次参加驾驶执照考试时没过关。| [+**on**] *I passed the written paper but failed on my oral.* 我通过了笔试, 但口试不及格。**b)** [T] to decide that someone has not passed a test or examination 评定〔某人〕不及格

4 I fail to see/understand *formal* used to show that you are annoyed by something that you do not accept or understand【正式】我搞不清楚/明白〔用于表示生气〕: *I fail to see why you find it so amusing.* 我不明白你为什么会觉得这很有趣。

5 ►COMPANY/BUSINESS 公司/商号◄ [I] to be unable to continue because of a lack of money〔因缺钱而〕倒闭, 破产: *A large number of small businesses failed in the recession.* 许多小型企业在经济衰退中倒闭了。

6 ►MACHINE/BODY PART 机器部件/身体部位◄ [I] if a part of a machine or an organ in your body fails, it stops working〔机件、人体器官〕失灵; 出毛病: *The rocket's engine failed a few seconds after take-off.* 火箭发射几秒钟后, 发动机便失灵了。| *My uncle's kidneys failed two days after the operation.* 我叔叔的两个肾在手术后两天便功能全失了。

7 never fail to do sth to do something so regularly that people are sure that you will do it 从来不会忘记做某事: *My grandson never fails to phone me on my birthday.* 我的孙儿从来不会忘记在我生日时打电话给我。

8 your courage/will/nerve fails (you) if your courage etc fails, or fails you, you suddenly do not have it when you need it 你的勇气/意志/胆量消失: *At the last moment my nerve failed. I walked away from her door without knocking.* 最后一刻我失去了胆量, 我没敲门就从她的门口走开了。

9 fail sb to not do what someone has trusted you to do 使某人失望: *I feel I've failed my children by not spending more time with them.* 我觉得我使孩子们失望了, 因为我没能多花些时间陪伴他们。—see also 另见 **words fail me** (WORD[1] (25))

10 ►CROPS 作物◄ [I] to not grow or produce food 歉收: *If the crops fail again this year, people will starve.* 如果今年庄稼再歉收, 人们就会挨饿。

11 ►RAINS 雨水◄ [I] to not come at the usual time of year〔在该下雨的季节〕无雨, 不下雨

12 failing sight/health sight or health that is becoming worse 衰退的视力/健康

fail[2] *n* **1 without fail a)** if you do something without fail, you always do it 必定, 总是: *Tim visits his mother every day without fail.* 蒂姆每天必去看望他的母亲。**b)** used to tell someone very firmly that they must do something 务必, 一定〔用于告诫别人一定要做某事〕: *I want that work finished by tomorrow, without fail!* 我要求那项工作必须在明天前完成, 不得有误! **2** [C] an unsuccessful result in a test or examination〔考试〕不及格: *I got a fail in history.* 我历史考试不及格。

failed /feld; feɪld/ *adj* [only before noun 仅用于名词前] **a failed actor/writer etc** someone who wanted to be an actor, writer etc but was unsuccessful 不成功[失败]的演员/作家等

fail·ing[1] /ˈfelɪŋ; ˈfeɪlɪŋ/ *n* [C] a fault or weakness 缺点, 弱点: *I love him, despite his failings.* 尽管他有种种缺点, 我还是爱他。

failing[2] *prep* used to say that if your first suggestion is not successful or possible, there is another possibility that you could try 如果不行〔用于说明如果第一个建议行不通时, 还可能做的另一件事〕: *There are two cheap hotels, but failing either of these, you may as well go back to where you were before.* 有两家廉价的旅馆; 但如果两家都不行的话, 你不妨回到你以前住的地方。| **failing that** *Try to get them to pay for the damage, or failing that, claim on their insurance.* 力争让他们赔偿损失。如果不行的话, 就要求从他们的保险赔款中赔付。

fail-safe /ˈ· ·/ *adj* **1** a fail-safe machine, piece of equipment etc contains a system that makes the machine stop working if one part of it fails〔机器、设备等〕有自动防止故障装置的; 有安全保障装置的 **2** a fail-safe plan is certain to succeed 万无一失的, 万全的

fail·ure /ˈfeljɚ; ˈfeɪljə/ *n* S2 W2

1 ►LACK OF SUCCESS 不成功◄ [C,U] a lack of success in achieving or doing something 失败: *How can we account for the failure of the League of Nations to achieve peace in Europe?* 我们怎么解释国际联盟为何无法在欧洲实现和平呢? | **end/result in failure** *Harry's ambitious plans ended in failure.* 哈里雄心勃勃的计划以失败告终。

2 ►UNSUCCESSFUL PERSON/THING 失败的人/事◄ [C] someone or something that is not successful 失败的人[事]: *I always felt a bit of a failure at school.* 我上学时总觉得自己多少是个失败者。| **a total/complete failure** *The whole thing was*

F

a total failure from start to finish. 这件事从头到尾都是个失败。| **crop failure** *a series of crop failures* 连年庄稼歉收

3 failure to do sth an act of not doing something which should be done or which people expect you to do 未能做〔应做到的〕某事: *Failure to produce proof of identity could result in prosecution.* 未能出示身份证明可能会被起诉。

4 ▶MACHINE/BODY PART 机器部件/人体部分◀ [C,U] an occasion when a machine or part of your body stops working properly 故障, 失灵; 衰竭: *engine failure* 发动机故障 | [+in] *a failure in the computer system caused by a mechanical fault* 因机械故障引起的电脑系统失灵 | **heart/kidney/liver failure** *The disease can result in terminal kidney failure.* 这种病会引起肾衰竭而不治。

5 ▶BUSINESS 企业◀ [C,U] a situation in which a business has to close because of a lack of money 倒闭, 关闭: *The number of small business failures is growing each year.* 破产的小型企业数量每年都在增加。

fain /fen; feɪn/ *adv old use* 【旧】**would fain do sth** *old use* if you would fain do something, you would like to do it 【旧】乐意地

faint¹ /fent, feɪnt/ *adj* **1** difficult to see, hear, smell etc〔指看、听、嗅等〕不清楚的, 模糊的: *a faint noise* 微弱的响声 | *the faint outline of the cliffs* 悬崖的模糊轮廓 **2 a faint hope/chance/feeling etc** a very small or slight chance etc 很小的希望/机会/感觉等: *There's still a faint hope that they might be alive.* 还有一线希望, 他们可能还活着。| *There was a faint edge of menace in his voice.* 他的声音中带有一点威胁的味道。**3** feeling weak because you are very ill, tired, or hungry〔因生病、疲倦或饥饿而〕虚弱的: [+with] *feeling faint with hunger and fatigue* 又饿又累, 感到虚弱 **4 not have the faintest idea** to not know anything at all about something〔对某事〕根本不知道, 一无所知: *They didn't seem to have the faintest idea what I was talking about.* 他们好像一点也不明白我在说什么。—see also 另见 **damn sb/sth with faint praise** (DAMN⁵ (2)) —**faintly** *adv*: *Her name sounds faintly familiar.* 她的名字听起来有一点点耳熟。| *The sun shone faintly through the clouds.* 阳光透过云层微弱地照射着。—**faintness** *n* [U]

faint² *v* [I] **1** to suddenly become unconscious for a short time 晕倒, 昏厥: *Several fans fainted in the blazing heat.* 几个球迷在炎热的气温下晕过去了。**2 I nearly/almost fainted** *spoken* used to say that you were very surprised by something 【口】我差点昏过去〔表示很惊讶〕: *I nearly fainted when they told me the price.* 他们告诉我价格时, 我差点昏过去。

faint³ *n* [C] an act of becoming unconscious 昏厥: **in a (dead) faint** *She fell down in a faint.* 她昏倒了。

faint·heart·ed /ˌ·ˈ··◂/ *adj* **1** not trying very hard, because you do not want to do something, or you are not confident that you can succeed 没有勇气的, 缺乏信心的, 怯懦的: *She made a rather faint-hearted attempt to stop him from leaving.* 她有点胆怯地试图阻止他离开。**2 not for the faint-hearted** *humorous* used to say that something is difficult and needs a lot of effort 【幽默】不是懦夫所能干的

S1 W2 **fair¹** /fɛr; feə/ *adj*

1 ▶REASONABLE AND ACCEPTABLE 合理并可接受的◀ a situation, system, or way of treating people that is fair seems reasonable and acceptable 公平的, 合理的: *a fair wage for the job* 为这份工作提供的合理工资 | *Who said life was fair?* 谁说生活是公平的? | *Everyone should have the right to a fair trial.* 每个人都应有权得到公平的审讯。| **it is fair to do sth** *It seems fair to give them their money back.* 把钱还给他们, 这似乎是应该的。| **it's fair to say that** (=used to say that a judgement about something seems reasonable) 说句公道话…; 说…才是公平的 *I think it's fair to say that she was not to blame for the accident.* 我认为, 公正地说, 这次事故不该怪她。

2 ▶TREATING EVERYONE EQUALLY 一视同仁◀ a fair situation, judgement, description etc is one in which everyone is treated equally 公正的, 公平的: *Why do you let her stay out late and not me? It's not fair!* 你为什么允许她晚回家而不让我这样做? 这不公平! | **fair to** *The old law wasn't fair to women.* 那条旧的法律对妇女不公平。| **it's only fair (that)** *You pay him $10 an hour – it's only fair that I should get the same.* 既然你给他每小时10美元, 我也该得到同样的工资, 这才是公平的。

3 ▶FAIR PERSON 公正的人◀ someone who treats everyone in a reasonable, equal way〔指人〕公平合理的, 公正的, 正直的: *The boss is a hard man – hard but fair.* 老板是个严厉的人——严厉但公正。

4 ▶QUITE BIG/FAR/A LOT 很大/远/多◀ **a fair size/number/amount/distance etc** *especially BrE* a fairly large size, number etc 【尤英】相当大的尺寸/数目/数量/距离等: *There's a fair amount of unemployment around here.* 这附近失业的人相当多。| *We had travelled a fair way by lunch time.* 到午饭时, 我们已走了相当远的一段路。

5 ▶SKIN/HAIR 皮肤/头发◀ light in colour 白皙的; 金色的: *He had blue eyes and fair hair.* 他长着蓝眼睛和金色头发。| *Both her children are very fair.* 她的两个孩子皮肤都很白皙。—opposite 反义词 DARK¹ (4) —see picture on page A6 参见A6页图

6 ▶LEVEL OF ABILITY 能力水平◀ neither particularly good nor particularly bad; average 中等的, 普通的: *Her written work is excellent but her practical work is only fair.* 她的文字功夫极佳, 但实际工作却很一般。

7 ▶ACCORDING TO THE RULES 根据规则◀ a fair fight, game, or election is one that is played or done according to the rules〔拳击、比赛、选举等〕根据规则进行的: *free and fair elections* 自由公正的选举

8 ▶WEATHER 天气◀ pleasant and not windy, rainy etc 晴朗的: *That morning the weather was fair, and the air was warm.* 那天上午天气晴朗暖和。

9 have a fair idea of to know quite a lot about what something is like 对…相当了解: *I think I have a fair idea of what the job involves.* 我想我对这项工作包含的内容有相当的了解。

10 have had more than your fair share of to have had more of something, especially something unpleasant, than seems reasonable or fair 受够了〔尤指不愉快之事〕: *Poor old Alan! He's had more than his fair share of bad luck recently.* 可怜的老艾伦! 他最近遇到的倒霉事太多了。

11 give sb a fair crack of the whip *BrE informal* to give someone the chance to do something especially to show that they are able to do it 【英, 非正式】给某人均等的机会〔以证明他能做好某事〕

12 a fair shake *AmE informal* fair treatment that allows someone the same chances as everyone else 【美, 非正式】公平的待遇; 均等的机会: *Inner city kids aren't getting a fair shake in the schools.* 市中心贫民区的孩子在学校里得不到公平的待遇。

13 by fair means or foul using any method to get what you want, including dishonest or illegal methods 不择手段, 千方百计

14 fair-to-middling not feeling very well 差强人意

15 all's fair in love and war used to say that in some situations any method of getting what you want is acceptable 情场和战场, 两者皆不厌诈〔指在某些情况下为达目的不择手段是可以接受的〕

16 ▶PLEASANT/ATTRACTIVE 悦人的/吸引人的◀ *old use* pleasant and attractive 【旧】漂亮的, 迷人的: *the fair city of Rome* 美丽的罗马城 | *a fair maiden* 美丽的少女 —see also 另见 FAIRLY, FAIRNESS

Frequencies of the adjective **fair** in spoken and written English. 形容词fair在英语口语和书面语中的使用频率

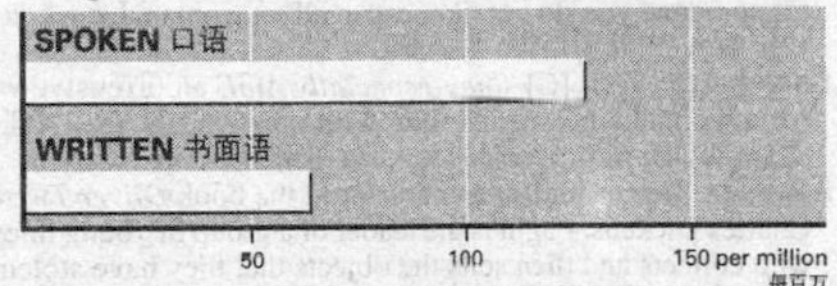

Based on the British National Corpus and the Longman Lancaster Corpus 据英国国家语料库和朗文兰开斯特语料库

This graph shows that the adjective **fair** is much more common in spoken English than in written English. This is because it is used in a lot of common spoken phrases. 本图表显示, 形容词fair在英语口语中的使用频率远远高于书面语, 因为口语中很多常用短语是由fair构成的。

fair (*adj*) **SPOKEN PHRASES** 含fair的口语短语

17 fair enough *especially BrE* used to say that you agree with someone's suggestion or that something seems reasonable 【尤英】说得对, 有道理: *"See you on Tuesday at 8." "Fair enough."* "星期二8点见。" "行。" | *Well, if you want to go on your own that's fair enough.* 好吧, 如果你要自己去, 那也可以。

18 it's/that's not fair used when you think that what is happening is unfair 这/那不公平: *It's not fair, you never let me borrow your clothes.* 这不公平, 你从来不借给我你的衣服。| **It's/that's not fair on sb** *You can't just give the clever kids attention because that's not fair on the rest of the class.*

你不能只注意那些聪明的孩子，因为那对班上的其他学生是不公平的。

19 to be fair used when adding something after someone has been criticized, which helps to explain or excuse what they did 说句公道话: *She should have phoned to tell us what her plans were although, to be fair, she's been very busy.* 她早该打电话将她的计划告诉我们。不过，说句公道话，她一直很忙。

20 fair comment *BrE* used to say that a remark or criticism seems fair【英】合理的话; 公正的评论: *"I don't mind doing the work, but you should have asked me." "Fair comment."* "我不介意做那项工作，但你应该先问我一下。" "此言有理。"

21 be fair! used to tell someone not to be unreasonable or criticize someone too much 要公道些!: *Come on, be fair, the poor girl's trying her hardest!* 算了吧，要公道些！这可怜的女孩正尽力而为！

22 fair's fair used when you think it is fair that someone should do something, especially because of something that has happened earlier 应当公道才是: *Come on, fair's fair – I paid last time so it's your turn.* 得啦，应当公平才是 —— 上次我付钱，所以这次轮到你了。

23 you can't say fairer than that *BrE* used to say that an offer you are making to someone is the best, fairest offer they can possibly get【英】这是再公道不过了，无法比这再合理了: *I'll give you £25 for it – you can't say fairer than that, can you?* 这东西我给你 25 英镑 —— 这是再公道不过了，不是吗？

24 it's a fair cop *BrE* used in a joking way when someone catches you doing something that you should not be doing【英】抓个正着，当场抓住〔用于被人发现做不该做之事时的玩笑说法〕: *"I saw you, now give me that back." "All right, it's a fair cop."* "我看见你了，把那东西还给我。" "好吧，被你抓个正着。"

25 with your own fair hands *BrE humorous* used to say that you did something by yourself without any help【英, 幽默】用自己的双手，亲自: *"Did you do all the decorating yourself?" "Yes, it's all been done with my own fair hands."* "所有的装饰都是你自己做的吗？" "是的，都是我亲手做的。"

S2 W3 **fair²** *adv* **1 play fair** to do something in a fair and honest way 公平办事，按规则做 **2 hit sth fair and square** to hit something directly in a particular place 直接击中某物; 正中某处: *I hit him fair and square on the nose.* 我不偏不倚正打中他的鼻子。 **3 tell sb fair and square** to tell someone honestly and directly 诚实地告诉某人; 直截了当地告诉某人

fair³ *n* [C] **1** a form of outdoor entertainment, at which there are large machines to ride on and games in which you can win prizes 露天游乐场〔有大型机动游戏和有奖游戏的户外活动〕; CARNIVAL (2) *AmE*【美】—see also 另见 FUNFAIR **2** *BrE* a market where animals and farm products are sold【英】〔出售动物和农产品的〕市场; 集市: *a cattle fair* 牛市场 **3** an event at which farm products and equipment are shown and entered in competitions, and where there are often games and large machines to ride on〔有农产品和农业设备展出、有竞赛，并常有娱乐活动和大型机动游戏的〕农牧集市: **state/county fair** (=a fair for the whole state or county) 州/县物产集市 **4** a regular occasion when companies show their newest products in order to advertise them〔商品〕博览会，展销会，展览会: *a trade fair* 商品交易会 | *The Frankfurt Book Fair* 法兰克福书展 **5** an outdoor event with games and things to buy, organized to get money 义卖会; FETE¹(1) *BrE*【英】

fair cop·y /ˌ· ˈ··/ *n* [C] a neat copy of a piece of writing 誊清本，清稿

fair din·kum /ˌfɛr ˋdɪŋkəm; ˌfeə ˈdɪŋkəm/ *adj AustrE spoken* real or true【澳口】真正的; 真实的

fair game /ˌ· ˈ·/ *n* [U] someone or something that is easy to criticize or deserves to be criticized 易受批评的人[物]; 该受批评的人[物]: *The behaviour of the younger royals made them fair game for the tabloid press.* 年轻的王室成员的行为使他们成了小报的批评对象。

fair·ground /ˋfɛrˌgraund; ˈfeəgraund/ *n* [C] an open space on which a fair (FAIR³ (1)) takes place 露天游乐场（会场）

fair-haired boy /ˌ·· ˈ· ·/ *n* [C] *AmE informal* someone who is likely to succeed because someone in authority likes them【美, 非正式】得宠的人; BLUE-EYED BOY *especially BrE*【尤英】: *the boss's fair-haired boy* 老板的宠儿

Fair Isle /ˈ· ·/ **1** one of the Shetland Islands 费尔岛〔设得兰群岛之一〕 **2** in shipping FORECASTs, an area of the northeast Atlantic Ocean which includes Orkney and the Shetland Islands 费尔岛海域〔见于海洋天气预报，指位于大西洋东北部包括奥克尼群岛和设得兰群岛在内的一片海域〕

S1 W2 **fair·ly** /ˋfɛrlɪ; ˈfeəli/ *adv* **1** more than a little, but much less than very 相当，颇: *The house had a fairly large garden.* 那幢房子有个相当大的花园。| *She speaks English fairly well.* 她英语讲得相当好。—see 见 RATHER (USAGE) **2** in a way that is fair and not dishonest, unreasonable etc 公正地; 诚实地: *I felt I hadn't been treated fairly.* 我觉得我没受到公正的待遇。 **3** *BrE* used to say that someone did something quickly or a lot【英】迅速地; 大量地: *He fairly raced past us on his motorcycle.* 他骑着摩托车飞快地从我们身边驶过。

fair-mind·ed /ˌ· ˈ··◂/ *adj* able to understand and judge situations fairly and always considering other people's opinions 公正的，不偏不倚的: *He's a fair-minded man – I'm sure he'll listen to what you have to say.* 他是个公正的人 —— 我确信他会倾听你说的话。

fair·ness /ˋfɛrnɪs; ˈfeənəs/ *n* [U] **1** the quality of being fair 公平，公正 **2 in fairness (to)** used after you have just criticized someone to add something more favourable which explains their behaviour 说句公道话，公正地说〔用于在批评某人后说一些有利于他的话〕: *Tardelli had a poor match, although in fairness he was playing with a knee injury.* 塔尔德利在场上表现很差，但说句公道话，他是膝部带伤参加比赛的。

fair play /ˌ· ˈ·/ *n* [U] **1** playing according to the rules of a game without cheating〔按规则进行的〕公平比赛 **2** *BrE* fair treatment of people without cheating or dishonesty【英】公正处理; 公平对待 —see also 另见 **turnabout is fair play** (TURNABOUT (2))

fair sex, the /ˌ· ˈ·/ *n old-fashioned* women【过时】妇女，女性

fair·way /ˋfɛrˌwe; ˈfeəweɪ/ *n* [C] the part of a GOLF COURSE that you hit the ball along towards the hole〔高尔夫球场上的〕球道，无障碍区 —see picture on page A23 参见 A23 页图

fair-weath·er friend /ˌ· ˌ·· ˈ·/ *n* [C] someone who only wants to be your friend when you are successful 不能共患难的朋友

fai·ry /ˋfɛrɪ; ˈfeəri/ *n* [C] **1** a small imaginary creature with magic powers, which looks like a very small person 仙子，小精灵 **2** an offensive word for a HOMOSEXUAL man 男同性恋者〔冒犯用语〕

fairy god·moth·er /ˌ·· ˈ·ˌ··/ *n* [C] a woman with magic powers who saves people from trouble, especially in children's stories〔尤指童话中帮助人的〕仙姑，仙女

fai·ry·land /ˋfɛrɪˌlænd; ˈfeərilænd/ *n* **1** [U] an imaginary place where fairies live 仙乡，仙界 **2** [singular] a place that looks very beautiful and special 仙境，幻境，美丽神奇的地方: *At night, the harbor is a fairyland.* 夜晚，港口美如仙境。

fairy lights /ˈ·· ·/ *n* [plural] *BrE* small coloured lights used especially to decorate a Christmas tree【英】〔装饰圣诞树的〕小彩灯

fairy tale /ˈ·· ·/ also 又作 **fairy sto·ry** /ˈ·· ˌ··/ *BrE*【英】*n* [C] **1** a children's story in which magical things happen 童话; 神话; 神仙故事 **2** a story that someone has invented and is difficult to believe 谎言; 骗人话; 不可信的事

fai·ry-tale /ˋfɛrɪˌtel; ˈfeəriteɪl/ *adj* [only before noun 仅用于名词前] extremely happy, lucky etc in a way that usually only happens in children's stories 童话里才有的; 童话般的; 极其美满幸福的: *a fairytale romance* 童话般的爱情故事

fait ac·com·pli /ˌfet ˌækəmˋpli; ˌfeɪt əˈkɒmpliː/ *n* [singular] *French* something that has already happened or been done and cannot be changed【法】既成事实

W2 **faith** /feθ; feɪθ/ *n*

1 ►TRUST/BELIEF IN SB/STH 信任/相信某人/某物◄ [U] a strong belief that someone or something can be trusted to be right or to do the right thing 信念; 信任; 信心: **have faith in** *I have great faith in her, she won't let me down.* 我对她很有信心，她不会让我失望的。| **destroy/restore sb's faith in** (=take away or give back their faith) 毁灭/恢复某人对…的信念[信心] *It's really restored my faith in human nature.* 此事确实恢复了我对人性的信念。| **lose faith in** *The public has quite simply lost faith in the government.* 公众已完全对政府失去信心。

2 ►RELIGION 宗教◄ a) [U] belief and trust in God 对上帝的信仰; 宗教信仰: *deep religious faith* 坚定的宗教信仰 | [**+in**] *my faith in God* 我对上帝的信仰 **b)** [C] one of the main religions in the world 宗教: *people from all faiths* 各种宗教信仰的人 | *the Jewish faith* 犹太教

3 break faith with to stop supporting or believing in a person, organization, or idea 背弃; 背信，不信守; 脱离: *How could he tell them the truth without breaking faith with the Party?* 他不脱党怎么能跟他们说明事实真相呢？

F

4 keep faith with to continue to support or believe in a person, organization, or idea 恪守对…的信仰; 信守; 不背弃

5 good faith honest and sincere intentions 真诚, 诚意, 诚信: *He proposed a second meeting as a sign of his good faith.* 他建议再举行一次会议, 以表示他的诚意。| **in good faith** (=without intending to deceive someone) 真诚地, 善意地 *The woman who sold me the car claimed she had acted in good faith.* 那个卖车给我的女人声称她是诚意出售的。

6 an act of faith something you do that shows you trust someone completely 信赖某人的行为[表示]: *Letting Sammy borrow my new camera was a real act of faith.* 让萨米借走我的新相机确实是出于对他的信任。

faith·ful¹ /ˈfeθfəl; ˈfeɪθfəl/ *adj* **1** remaining loyal to a person, belief, political party etc and continuing to support them〔对人、信念、政党等〕忠诚的, 忠实的; 守信的: *years of faithful service* 多年忠诚的服务 | [+to] *Russell remained faithful to his principles to the last.* 罗素至死忠于自己的原则。**2** representing an event or an image in a way that is exactly true or that looks exactly the same 如实的, 准确可靠的; 忠于原事[物]的: *a faithful account of what had happened* 对所发生之事的如实报道 | *a faithful reproduction of the original picture* 忠于原图的复制品 **3** loyal to your wife, boyfriend etc by not having a sexual relationship with anyone else〔爱情上〕忠贞的: [+to] *Do you think Bob's always been faithful to you?* 你认为鲍勃一直对你忠诚吗? —**faithfulness** *n* [U]

faithful² *n* **1 the faithful a)** the people who are very loyal to a leader, political party etc and continue to support them〔领袖、政党等的〕忠实信徒 **b)** the people who believe in a religion〔宗教〕教徒; 信众 **2** [C] a loyal follower, supporter, or member 忠实的追随者[支持者; 成员]: *a handful of old faithfuls at the meeting* 会上的一些多年的忠实追随者

faith·ful·ly /ˈfeθfəlɪ; ˈfeɪθfəli/ *adv* **1** in a faithful way 忠诚地, 忠实地; 如实地: *He had served the family faithfully for 40 years.* 他已忠心耿耿为这一家人服务了40年。**2 promise faithfully** to promise that you will definitely do something 真心实意地答应: *Ann promised faithfully that she would never tell.* 安真心实意地答应说她绝不会说出去。**3 Yours faithfully** especially *BrE* the usual polite way of ending a formal letter, which you have begun with Dear Sir or Dear Madam【尤英】忠实于您的〔正式信件结尾所用的客套话, 信的开端用 Dear Sir 或 Dear Madam 时用〕—compare 比较 **Yours sincerely** (SINCERELY (2))

faith heal·ing /ˈ· ˌ··/ *n* [U] a method of treating illnesses by praying〔通过祈祷来治病的〕信仰疗法 —**faith healer** *n* [C]

faith·less /ˈfeθlɪs; ˈfeɪθləs/ *adj formal* someone who is faithless cannot be trusted【正式】不忠实的, 不能信赖的, 背信弃义的, 不守信义的: *a faithless friend* 不能信赖[不忠诚]的朋友 —**faithlessly** *adv* —**faithlessness** *n* [U]

fake¹ /fek; feɪk/ *n* [C] **1** a copy of a valuable object, painting etc that is intended to deceive people 赝品, 假货: *We thought it was a genuine antique, but it was only a fake.* 我们以为那是真古董, 可实际上只是一件赝品。**2** someone who is not what they claim to be or does not have the skills they say they have 骗子, 冒充者, 假冒者: *He claimed to have natural healing powers, but he turned out to be a fake.* 他声称拥有自然治病的本领, 结果发现他只是个骗子。

fake² *adj* [usually before noun 一般用于名词前] **1** made to look like a real material or object in order to deceive people 伪造的, 假的: *fake fur* 假毛皮 **2** pretending to be something you are not in order to deceive people 冒充的, 假冒的: *A fake doctor tricked his way into a hospital last night.* 昨晚有位冒牌医生用计混进了医院。

fake³ *v* **1** [T] to make an exact copy of something, or invent figures or results, in order to deceive people 仿造; 捏造, 伪造: *He faked his father's signature on the cheque.* 他在支票上伪造父亲的签名。| *The results of these experiments were faked.* 这些实验的结果都是捏造的。**2** [I,T] to pretend to be ill, interested etc when you are not 假装, 伪装: **fake it** *I thought he was really hurt but he was faking it.* 我以为他真的受伤了, 可他是装出来的。**3** [I,T] to pretend to move in one direction, but then move in another, especially when playing sport〔比赛中〕做(…的)假动作: *He faked a pass and then handed the ball off to Perry.* 他做了个传球的假动作, 然后把球传给佩里。

fake sb **out** *phr v* [T] *AmE* to deceive someone by making them think you are planning to do something when you are really planning to do something else【美】故意欺骗〔某人〕

fa·kir /fəˈkɪr; ˈfeɪkɪə/ *n* [C] a travelling Hindu or Muslim holy man〔印度教的〕苦行者;〔伊斯兰教的〕托钵僧

fa·laf·el /ˌfəˈlæfəl; ˌfəˈlæfəl/ *n* [C,U] fried balls of an Arabic food made with CHICKPEAS 炸豆丸子, 炸豆泥

fal·con /ˈfɔlkən; ˈfɔːlkən/ *n* [C] a bird that kills and eats other animals and can be trained to hunt 猎鹰

fal·con·er /ˈfɔlkənə; ˈfɔːlkənə/ *n* [C] someone who trains falcons to hunt 放鹰狩猎者; 训练猎鹰的人, 猎鹰师

fal·con·ry /ˈfɔlkənrɪ; ˈfɔːlkənri/ *n* [U] the skill or sport of using falcons to hunt 猎鹰训练术; 放鹰狩猎运动, 鹰猎

Falk·lands /ˈfɔlkləndz; ˈfɔːlkləndz/ also 又作 **the Falkland Islands** a group of islands, under British control, in the southwest Atlantic Ocean off the coast of Argentina. The Argentinians believe that the islands belong to Argentina, and call them the Malvinas. 福克兰群岛〔阿根廷沿海一群岛, 位于大西洋西南部, 归英国管辖。阿根廷人认为这些岛屿归属阿根廷, 称其为马尔维纳斯群岛〕

Falklands War, the /ˌ·· ˈ·/ a war in the Falkland Islands between the UK and Argentina in 1982. Both countries say that the Islands belong to them. Argentina wanted control of the Islands, but the British kept control after the war. 福克兰群岛战争〔1982年英国与阿根廷在福克兰群岛爆发的一场战争。两国都声称对该群岛有所有权。阿根廷想得到群岛的控制权, 但此次战争之后英国继续控制着该岛〕

fall¹ *v* /fɔl; fɔːl/ *past tense* **fell** /fɛl; fel/ *past participle* **fallen** /ˈfɔlən, ˈfɔːlən/

1 ▶MOVE DOWNWARDS 向下移动◀ [I] to move downwards from a higher position to a lower position 落下, 降落; 跌落: *The rain had started falling again.* 雨又开始下了。| [+out of/from/on etc] *Wyatt fell from a second floor window.* 怀亚特从二楼的窗子摔下来。| [+down] *I'm always worried that one of the kids will fall down the stairs.* 我总是担心其中一个小孩会从楼梯上摔下来。| **sb's trousers/socks etc are falling down** *His shirt was all dirty and his trousers were falling down.* 他的衬衫很脏, 裤子也快掉了。| **rise and fall** *The little boat rose and fell with the movement of the waves.* 小船随着波浪起伏。

2 ▶GO DOWN ONTO THE GROUND 落到地上◀ [I] to suddenly go down onto the ground after you have been standing, walking, or running, especially without intending to 摔倒, 跌倒: *I fell and hit my head.* 我跌倒, 撞到了头。| *Careful you don't fall – the path's very icy.* 小心别摔倒── 路上结了很多冰。| [+on/into etc] *One of the horses slipped and fell into a ditch.* 有一匹马滑倒, 掉进了沟里。| **fall flat on your face** (=fall so that you are lying facing the ground) 摔了个嘴啃地 *She fell flat on her face in the mud.* 她在烂泥里摔了个嘴啃地。| **fall to your knees** (=move down from a standing position so that your body is resting on your knees) 跪下, 下跪

3 ▶TO A LOWER AMOUNT ETC 数量等下降◀ [I] to go down to a lower price, amount, level etc, especially a much lower one〔价格、数量、水平等较大幅度地〕下跌, 下降, 降低: *In winter the temperature often falls below zero.* 冬天温度经常跌到零度以下。| **fall steeply/sharply** (= by a large amount) 急剧下降 *Interest rates fell sharply.* 利率暴跌。| *falling income levels* 不断下降的收入水平

4 fall asleep/ill/silent/pregnant to become asleep, ill etc 睡着/病倒/安静下来/怀孕: *I fell asleep halfway through the film.* 电影放映了一半我就睡着了。

5 fall in love to start to love someone or something very much 爱[恋]上: [+with] *As soon as we met, we fell in love with each other.* 我们彼此一见钟情。| *Primmie fell in love with California on sight.* 普里米一眼就爱上了加利福尼亚。

6 fall to pieces/bits a) to break into many pieces 碎成许多片: *The vase fell to bits as soon as it hit the floor.* 花瓶一摔到地板上就碎了。**b)** if something such as a plan or a relationship falls to pieces, it stops working properly〔计划〕失败;〔关系〕破裂

7 be falling to pieces/bits to be in very bad condition, especially because of being very old〔尤因年久而〕快要垮掉, 快要崩溃: *The walls were all dirty and the furniture was falling to pieces.* 墙壁很脏, 家具也都快散架了。

8 fall into/out of to go into or out of a place very quickly because you are in a hurry or very tired〔因匆忙或疲倦而〕迅速进入/离开: *As soon as she got home she fell into bed.* 她一到家便一头倒到床上。

9 fall into decay/disrepair/disrepute etc to become decayed, in bad condition, no longer respected etc 朽坏/失修/名声扫地: *Over the years the old palace had fallen into decay.* 多年以来这座古老的宫殿已破烂不堪。

10 fall flat if a joke, remark, or performance falls flat, it fails to interest or amuse people〔笑话、说话或表演〕达不到预期效果; 无法逗人笑

11 fall short of to be less than the amount or standard that is needed or that you want 未达到…; 不足…; 未满…: *Unfortunately,*

the course fell far short of our expectations. 不幸的是，这个课程没有达到我们的期望。

12 **fall out of fashion/favour** to stop being popular or fashionable 不再时髦；不再受欢迎

13 **fall from grace/favour** to stop being liked by people in authority 失宠〔于权势者〕: *I don't think she'll get promotion – she's rather fallen from grace recently.* 我认为她不会得到提升——她近来已经失宠。

14 **fall into the hands of/clutches of** if something or someone falls into the hands of an enemy or dangerous person, the enemy etc gets control or possession of them 落入…的手中/控制中: *The documents fell into the hands of the KGB.* 这些文件落入克格勃的手中。

15 **fall victim/prey to** to get a very serious illness or be attacked or deceived by someone 得〔重病〕；受到…的攻击[欺骗]: *While in Africa she fell victim to a rare blood disorder.* 在非洲的时候，她得了一种罕见的血液病。

16 **fall into the habit of** to start doing something, especially something that you should not do 沾染[养成]…的习惯: *He soon fell into the habit of having a drink on the way home from work.* 他很快沾染上了在下班回家的路上去喝酒的习惯。

17 **fall into a trap/pitfall** to make a mistake that many people make 犯许多人会犯的错误: *It's easy to fall into the trap of believing that the threat of nuclear war is over.* 人们很容易犯错，认为核战争的威胁已不存在。

18 **fall back into your old ways** to start doing things or behaving in the way that you used to, especially in a way that other people disapprove of 回到过去的坏习惯；重犯已改掉的坏习惯: *I expect she'll soon fall back into her old ways.* 我想她很快就会重蹈过去的恶习。

19 **fall into a category/group etc** also 又作 **fall under a heading** to be part of a group of things or people that are similar in some way 属于某一类: *A lot of my friends fall into the same category.* 我的许多朋友都属于这一类人。

20 **fall into place** **a)** if parts of a situation that you have been trying to understand fall into place, you start to understand how they are connected with each other 变得一清二楚；变得条理清楚；变得明朗: *Gradually the clues started falling into place and it became clear who the murderer was.* 这些线索使情况逐渐明朗，凶手是谁就一清二楚了。**b)** if the parts of something that you want to happen fall into place, they start to happen in the way that you want 〔事情〕按照意愿[设想]发生；互相符合；有条有理: *We've found someone who'll lend us the money, and it looks as if things are finally falling into place.* 我们已找到愿意借钱给我们的人，看起来一切终将按部就班地实现了。

21 **fall into line** to obey someone or do what other people want you to do, especially when you do not want to do it at first 听从，服从；取得一致: *If you can persuade her, the others will soon fall into line.* 如果你能说服她，其他人很快就会一致跟上。

22 **fall into step with** **a)** to start doing something in the same way as the other members of a group 与…步调一致；与…方式一样: *The other countries on the Security Council are expected to fall into step with the US.* 预计安理会的其他成员国会与美国步调一致。**b)** to start to walk next to someone else, at the same speed as them 与…齐步行走

23 **fall by the wayside** **a)** to become unsuccessful after being successful at first 半途失败: *A lot of marriages fall by the wayside because couples cannot talk to each other.* 许多婚姻因夫妻俩无法交流而中途破裂。**b)** to stop being important and therefore be forgotten about 〔因失去重要性〕被人遗忘，被忽视: *With so many domestic problems, foreign policy issues tended to fall by the wayside.* 由于出现这么多的国内问题，外交政策问题就容易被人忽视了。

24 **night/darkness/dusk falls** *literary* used to say that the night begins and that it starts to become dark【文】夜幕降临: *We arrived at the village just as night was falling.* 夜幕降临时，我们到达了这座村子。

25 **►LIGHT/SHADOW** 光线/阴影◄ [I always+adv/prep] to shine on a surface or go onto a surface 照射（到）: *The last rays of sunlight were falling on the fields.* 夕阳的余晖照射在田野上。

26 **fall down on the job** *informal* to not do your work or duties as well as you should【非正式】工作做得不理想: *I'd be falling down on my job if I didn't take an interest in the welfare of my staff.* 如果我不关心员工的福利，我就是没有做好我的工作。

27 **it fell off the back of a lorry** *BrE humorous* used to say that something was stolen【英，幽默】被偷走了

28 **fall foul of** to do something which makes someone angry, or which breaks a rule with the result that you are punished 激怒…；同…争吵；违反（法规）〔从而受到惩处〕: *Edwards fell foul of the authorities and was ordered to leave the country.* 爱德华兹同当局发生纠纷后被勒令离境。

29 **it's as easy as falling off a log** *spoken* used to say that something is very easy to do【口】这极其简单容易

30 **fall on deaf ears** if someone's words fall on deaf ears, noone pays any attention to them 未受到注意；被置若罔闻: *His pleas fell on deaf ears.* 他的请求未受到注意。

31 **fall on hard times** to have problems because you do not have enough money 陷入贫困，境遇艰难: *middle-class families that have fallen on hard times* 生活陷入困境的中产阶级家庭

32 **►LOSE POWER** 失去权力◄ [I] if a leader or a government falls, they lose their position of power 〔领导人或政府〕垮台；失势: *The previous administration fell after only 6 months in office.* 上届政府仅执政六个月便垮台了。

33 **►BE TAKEN BY AN ENEMY** 被敌人占领◄ [I] if a place falls in a war or an election, a group of soldiers or a political party takes control of it 陷落；被攻占；被打败: [+to] *The city fell to the advancing Russian armies.* 这座城市被挺进中的俄军攻克了。

34 **►BE KILLED** 被杀死◄ [I] *literary* to be killed in a war【文】阵亡，战死

35 **►HIT** 打中，击中◄ [I always+adv/prep] to hit a particular place or a particular part of someone's body 打中，击中；撞到: [+on] *The first punch fell on his nose.* 第一拳打到他的鼻子上。

36 **►HANG DOWN** 下垂◄ [I always+adv/prep] to hang down loosely 下垂: [+to/over] *Her hair fell to her shoulders.* 她的长发垂在肩上。

37 **►VOICE/SOUND** 嗓音/声音◄ [I] if someone's voice or a sound falls, it becomes quieter or lower 〔嗓音〕变小；〔声音〕放低

38 **fall from sb's lips** *literary* if words fall from someone's lips, they say them【文】从某人的口中说出

39 **silence/sadness/calm etc falls** *literary* used to say that a group of people or a place becomes quiet, sad etc【文】安静下来/变得伤心/冷静下来: [+on/upon] *As she entered the ballroom a great silence fell on the assembled guests.* 她进入舞厅时，聚在一起的客人突然鸦雀无声了。

40 **►SPECIAL EVENT/CELEBRATION** 特殊事件/庆典◄ **fall on** to happen on a particular day or date 落在〔某一天〕: *Christmas falls on a Saturday this year.* 今年圣诞节在星期六。

41 **sb's eyes/gaze/glance fell on** used to say that someone saw something when they were looking at something else 某人的目光落在…上；〔在看别的东西时〕瞥见: *He was going through some old papers when his eyes fell on a photo of his mother.* 他正浏览一些旧文件，突然看到他母亲的一张照片。

42 **the stress/accent/beat falls on** used to say that a particular part of a word, phrase, or piece of music is emphasized or is played more loudly than the rest 重读/重音/节拍落在…: *In the word 'report', the stress falls on the second syllable.* 在 report 这个词里，重音落在第二个音节上。

43 **fall at sb's feet** to kneel in front of someone, especially to ask them to do something or to show your respect 跪在某人面前〔乞求或表示敬仰〕

44 **fall between two stools** to be neither one type of thing nor another, or be unable to choose between two ways of doing something 〔因举棋不定而〕两头落空: *The movie falls between two stools – it's neither a thriller nor a comedy.* 这部电影两头都不是——既不是惊险片也不是喜剧片。

45 **I almost fell off my chair** *spoken* used to say that you were very surprised when something happened【口】我惊讶极了 —see also 另见 **fall/land on your feet** (FOOT[1] (18)), **let drop/fall** (LET[1] (17)), **sb's face fell** (FACE[1](2)), **stand or fall by/on** (STAND[1] (46))

fall about *phr v* [I] *BrE* to laugh a lot about something【英】放声大笑: **fall about laughing** *The moment she started speaking everyone fell about laughing.* 她一开始说话，大家就放声大笑。

fall apart *phr v* [I] **1** if an organization, system etc falls apart, it stops working effectively and has a lot of problems 〔组织、制度等〕崩溃，瓦解: **be falling apart at the seams** *The Health Service is falling apart at the seams.* 医疗保健制度正在开始瓦解。**2** **be falling apart** to be in very bad condition 快散架的，破旧不堪的: *I'm not riding in your old car – it's falling apart.* 我才不坐你的旧车——它都快散架了。**3** if your life, your world etc falls apart, you suddenly have a lot of personal problems 〔生活、个人小天地等〕垮掉，崩溃: *When his wife left him his world just fell apart.* 他的妻子离开他时，他的世界就垮了。**4** to break into pieces 破碎，断裂，散开: *The book fell apart in my hands as soon as I tried to pick it up.* 我刚要把书拿起来，书就在我手里散架了。

F

fall away *phr v* [I] **1** if something such as a feeling, a quality, or a noise falls away, it gradually becomes weaker or quieter and disappears〔逐渐〕衰落, 减少; 消失: *As confidence fell away consumers kept more of their cash in their pockets.* 随着信心逐渐消失, 消费者把更多的现金留在口袋里。**2** to slope downwards 向下倾斜: *After that the road falls away to the city of Odawara.* 在那以后路就朝着小田原市的方向倾斜。**3** to become separated from something after being fixed to it 脱落, 掉出: *A piece of wood had fallen away from the foot of the door.* 一块木头已从门脚下掉了出来。**4** to stop being able to be seen as you move through an area 从〔移动着的观察者的〕视野里消失: *An hour out of London the rows of houses started to fall away and we were surrounded by beautiful countryside.* 驱车出伦敦一小时后, 一排排的房子开始从视野里消失, 我们的四周全是美丽的乡村了。

fall back *phr v* [I] **1** if soldiers fall back, they move back because they are being attacked 撤退, 退后: *He ordered the men to fall back.* 他命令士兵后撤。**2** to move backwards because you are very surprised, frightened etc〔因惊奇、惊慌等而〕后退, 退却: *They fell back in horror.* 他们吓得往后退。

fall back on *phr v* [I] **1** to use something or depend on someone's help when dealing with a difficult situation, especially after you have tried using other methods or tried to deal with it yourself〔转而〕依靠: **have sb/sth to fall back on** *Diana always had her father's money to fall back on.* 黛安娜总是还有她父亲的钱可依靠。| *In that case we'll have to fall back on our original plan.* 这么说, 我们得退而依靠我们原来的计划。**2** to use a particular method, argument etc because it seems simple and easy, not because it is the best one to use〔退而求其次地〕使用〔简单易行的方法、论点等〕: *They tend to fall back on the same tired old arguments.* 他们倾向于退而使用同样的老一套的陈腐论点。

fall behind *phr v* [I,T] **1** to go more slowly than other people so that they gradually move further ahead of you 落在〔…的〕后面: *The older walkers soon fell behind.* 年纪大一些的步行者很快就落在后面了。**2** to become less successful than someone else 落后〔于〕: *The Eisenhower administration allowed the US to fall behind the Soviet Union in the production of nuclear arms.* 艾森豪威尔政府容许美国在核武器生产方面落后于苏联。| **[+with]** *In secondary school she started falling behind with her schoolwork.* 上中学时, 她的功课开始落后了。**3** to fail to finish a piece of work or to pay someone money that you owe them at the right time 拖欠〔还款〕, 不能按时完成〔工作〕: **[+with/on]** *We fell behind with the payments on the car and it was repossessed.* 我们拖欠分期付款买车的钱, 结果车子被收回去了。| **fall behind schedule** *Preparations for the festival have fallen behind schedule because of technical difficulties.* 由于技术上的困难, 节日的准备工作已落后于原定日程。

fall down *phr v* [I] **1** if someone falls down, they fall onto the ground 跌倒, 摔倒: *Margo fell down and twisted her ankle.* 马戈跌倒了, 扭伤了踝关节。**2** if something such as a wall, building, tree etc falls down, it falls onto the ground〔墙、建筑物、树等〕倒下, 倒塌, 掉到地上: *The bridge fell down with an enormous crash.* 大桥倒塌了, 发出一声巨响。**3 be falling down** if a building is falling down, it is in very bad condition 快要塌下来, 摇摇欲坠 **4** if an argument, plan, system etc falls down, it fails to work because of a particular weakness〔因缺陷而〕失败; 不起作用: *That's where the whole argument falls down.* 那就是整个论点站不住脚的地方。

fall for *phr v* [T] *informal*【非正式】**1** to be tricked into believing something that is not true 上…的当, 受…的骗: *She'll never fall for that one!* 她永远也不会上那样的当! | **fall for sth hook, line, and sinker** (=to be completely deceived by a trick) 完全受骗, 完全上当 **2** to start to love someone 爱上〔某人〕: *That was the summer I worked at the fairground, and met and fell for Lucy.* 那年夏天我在露天游乐场工作, 遇到了露西并爱上了她。

fall in *phr v* [I] **1** if the roof, ceiling etc falls in, it falls onto the ground〔屋顶、天花板等〕坍倒, 塌下, 垮掉 **2** if a group of soldiers fall in, they form neat lines behind each other so that an officer can check them〔士兵〕列队, 集合

fall in behind sb *phr v* [T] to form a line behind someone 在…后面排成一行; 以…为排头列队

fall into sth *phr v* **1 fall into conversation/a discussion/an argument** to start talking or arguing with someone 开始交谈/讨论/争论: *I fell into conversation with a visiting Japanese professor.* 我开始和一位来访的日本教授交谈。**2** to start to have a particular mood, especially suddenly〔尤指突然〕陷入〔某种心境〕: *She's liable to fall into sudden fits of rage.* 她很容易会突然间勃然大怒。**3** to contain two or more different parts 可分为〔若干部分〕: *The agreement falls into two distinct sections.* 协议书分为两个不同的部分。

fall in with *phr v* [T] to accept someone's suggestions, decisions etc and not disagree with them 赞同, 接受〔建议、决定等〕: *I'm quite happy to fall in with whatever you decide.* 我很乐意接受你作出的任何决定。

fall off *phr v* **1** [I,T] if part of something falls off, it becomes separated from the main part 掉下, 脱落: *The door handle keeps falling off.* 门把手老是掉下来。**2** [I] if the amount, rate, or quality of something falls off, it becomes less〔数量、比率、质量〕下降; 减少: *Rising prices have caused demand for household goods to fall off dramatically.* 价格不断上涨导致家用商品的需求大幅度减少。

fall on/upon *phr v* [I] **1** *literary* to suddenly attack or get hold of someone【文】突然攻击; 抓住: *The samurai fell on him and pinned his arms tight.* 那个日本武士突然扑向他, 紧紧抓住他的双臂。**2** *literary* to eagerly start eating or using something【文】急着开始吃[用]: *The kids fell on the pizzas as if they hadn't eaten for weeks.* 孩子们扑向比萨饼大吃起来, 好像他们好几周没吃东西似的。**3** if a duty or responsibility falls on you, you are given that duty or responsibility〔责任等〕落在…的身上: *an obligation which may fall upon any citizen* 可能落到任何一位公民身上的义务

fall out *phr v* [I] **1** to have a quarrel 争吵: **[+with]** *She's fallen out with her boyfriend.* 她和男朋友吵嘴了。**2** if a group of soldiers who are standing together fall out, they leave and go to different places〔士兵〕离开队列, 解散 **3** if something such as a tooth or your hair falls out, it comes out〔牙齿或头发〕掉下, 脱落: *My dad's hair fell out when he was only 30.* 我爸爸才30岁的时候就开始掉头发了。

fall over *phr v* [I] **1** [I,T] if someone falls over or if they fall over something, they fall onto the ground 跌倒, 摔倒: *Mind you don't fall over.* 当心, 别摔倒。| *Tommy fell over one of the electric cables.* 汤米被一根电缆绊倒了。**2** if something falls over, it falls from an upright position onto its side 倒下: *The fence fell over in the wind.* 篱笆被风刮倒了。**3 be falling over yourself to do sth** to be very eager to do something, especially something you do not usually do 忙不迭地做某事, 急着做某事, 渴望做某事〔尤指一般不做的事〕: *Sylvia was falling over herself to be nice to me.* 西尔维娅急着要显出对我好。

fall through *phr v* [I] if an agreement, plan etc falls through, it is not completed successfully〔协议、计划等〕失败, 化为泡影: *The deal fell through at the last minute.* 这笔交易在最后一刻落空了。

fall to *phr v* [T] **1** if a duty falls to someone, especially an unpleasant one, it is their responsibility to do it〔责任等〕落在…的身上: **it fell to sb to do sth** *It fell to me to give her the bad news.* 这个坏消息由我负责告诉她。**2** to start doing something with a lot of effort〔用力地〕开始: *They fell to work with a will.* 他们起劲地开始干起来。**3 fall to doing something** especially *literary* to start doing something【尤文】开始做某事: *When things really started to go wrong, they fell to arguing among themselves.* 当真的开始出现问题时, 他们便互相争吵起来。**4 fall to sb's lot** *literary* to be something that someone has or must deal with【文】命定应由某人〔做某事〕; 成为某人的任务[责任]

fall² *n*

1 ▶MOVEMENT DOWNWARDS 向下移动◀ [C, singular] movement downwards towards the ground or towards a lower position 下跌; 跌落; 跌倒: *the constant fall of the rain* 下个不停的雨 | **break sb's fall** (=prevent someone from falling too quickly and hurting themselves badly) 阻止某人下跌, 减弱跌势 *Luckily there were some bushes next to the house and they broke my fall.* 幸运的是, 房子旁有些灌木, 我跌落时把我挡了一下。

2 have a fall to fall onto the ground and hurt yourself 摔伤, 跌伤: *Grandma had a bad fall and broke her hip.* 祖母摔得很重, 髋部骨折了。

3 ▶REDUCTION 减少◀ [C] a reduction in the amount, level, price etc of something〔数量、水平、价格等的〕下降, 降低, 减少: **[+in]** *the recent fall in house prices* 房价最近的下跌 | *a fall in coal output* 煤产量的减少

4 ▶AUTUMN 秋天◀ [singular] *AmE* autumn【美】秋天, 秋季: **the fall** *We met in the fall of '88.* 我们是在1988年秋天初次见面的。

5 ▶LOSE POWER/BECOME UNSUCCESSFUL 失去权力/失败◀ [singular] a situation in which someone or something loses their position of power or becomes unsuccessful 垮台, 崩溃; 灭亡: **[+from]** *Until his fall from power in 1978, the Shah remained a firm ally of the Americans.* 伊朗国王直到1978年倒台之前一直是美国人的坚定盟友。| **rise and fall** (=period of success and then failure) 兴衰 *the rise and fall of the British motorcycle industry* 英国摩托车工业的兴衰

6 fall from grace a situation in which someone stops being respected by other people or loses their position of authority, especially because they have done something wrong〔尤指做错事后〕失宠; 堕落; 不再受人尊敬; 失去权威性: *Jackson's spectacular fall from grace* 杰克逊令人吃惊的堕落
7 ▶DEFEAT 战败, 毁灭◀ [singular] a situation in which a country, city etc is defeated by an enemy〔国家、城市等的〕陷落, 沦陷; 战败, 败亡: *the fall of France in 1940* 1940 年法国的沦陷
8 falls [plural] a place where a river suddenly goes straight down over a cliff 瀑布: *Niagara Falls* 尼亚加拉大瀑布 | **the falls** *We went to see the falls.* 我们去看瀑布。
9 ▶SPORT 体育运动◀ [C] an act of forcing your opponent onto the ground in WRESTLING or JUDO〔摔跤或柔道中的〕压倒, 按倒
10 ▶AMOUNT OF SNOW ETC 降雪量等◀ [C] an amount of snow, rocks etc that has fallen onto the ground〔雪、岩石等的〕降落量: *a heavy fall of snow* 降大雪
11 the fall the occasion in the Bible when God punished Adam and Eve by making them leave the Garden of Eden〔《圣经》中亚当与夏娃的〕堕落

fal·la·cious /fəˋleʃəs; fəˈleɪʃəs/ *adj formal* containing or based on false ideas【正式】谬误的, 虚妄的: *Such an argument is misleading, if not wholly fallacious.* 这种论点如果不全是谬误的, 也是误导人的。—**fallaciously** *adv*

fal·la·cy /ˋfæləsɪ; ˈfæləsi/ *n* **1** [C] a false idea or belief, especially one that a lot of people believe is true 谬论; 谬见: *It's a common fallacy to think that crime is caused by poverty.* 认为犯罪是由贫穷引起的, 这是一种常见的谬论。**2** [C, U] *formal* a weakness in someone's argument or ideas which is caused by a mistake in their thinking【正式】错误的推理[推论] —see also 另见 PATHETIC FALLACY

fall·back /ˋfɔl͵bæk; ˈfɔːlbæk/ *n* [C] something that can be used if the usual supply, method etc fails 储备物, 备用物; 退路; 可依靠的人[物]: *It's wise to have an extra video player as a fallback.* 最好准备另一台录像播放机作为备用。

fall·en¹ /ˋfɔlən; ˈfɔːlən/ past participle of FALL¹

fallen² *adj* **1** on the ground after falling down 倒下的, 落下的, 倒在地上的: *The road was blocked by a fallen tree.* 路被倒下的一棵树堵塞了。**2 a fallen woman** *old-fashioned* a woman who has had a sexual relationship with someone she is not married to【过时】〔女子〕已失身的, 堕落的 **3 the fallen** *formal* soldiers who have been killed in a war【正式】阵亡者

fall guy /ˈ· ·/ *n* [C] *informal, especially AmE*【非正式, 尤美】
1 someone who is punished for someone else's crime or mistake; SCAPEGOAT 替罪羊, 替死鬼, 代罪羔羊, 代人受过者: *I knew what he had in mind. He'd kill Barak and set me up as the fall guy.* 我知道他的想法。他将会杀死巴拉克, 然后陷害我, 拿我当替罪羊。
2 someone who is easily tricked or made to seem stupid 易受骗上当的人, 易被愚弄的人

fal·li·ble /ˋfæləbḷ; ˈfæləbəl/ *adj* able to make mistakes or be wrong 易犯错误的; 会做错事的: *Parents are fallible, Susie, just like everyone else.* 苏西, 父母亲跟其他人一样都是会做错事的。| *These surveys are often a rather fallible guide to public opinion.* 这些调查作为衡量民意的指标经常都不太可靠。—**fallibility** /͵fæləˋbɪlətɪ; ͵fæləˈbɪləti/ *n* [U] —opposite 反义词 INFALLIBLE

falling-out /͵·· ˈ·/ *n* **have a falling-out (with)** *informal* to have a bad quarrel with someone【非正式】与…争吵, 不和

falling star /͵·· ˈ·/ *n* [C] a SHOOTING STAR 流星

fall line /ˈ· ·/ *n* [C] the natural slope of a hill straight down from top to bottom（小山的）斜坡

fal·lo·pi·an tube /fəˋlopɪən ˋtub; fə͵ləʊpiən ˈtjuːb/ *n* [C] one of the two tubes in a female through which eggs move to the UTERUS 输卵管

fall·out /ˋfɔlˋaʊt; ˈfɔːlaʊt/ *n* [U] **1** the dangerous RADIOACTIVE dust which is left in the air after a NUCLEAR (3) explosion and which slowly falls to earth〔核爆炸后的〕放射性坠尘; 沉降物; 辐射性尘埃: *There can be little lasting protection against the effects of radioactive fallout.* 几乎没有持久性的保护能够抵御放射性坠尘的影响。**2** the results or effects of a particular event, especially when they are unexpected〔尤指预料不到的〕附带影响, 附带结果: *The political fallout of the Iran-Contra affair cost him his job.* 伊朗叛军事件附带的政治影响使他失去了工作。

fallout shel·ter /ˈ·· ͵·/ *n* [C] a building under the ground in which people can shelter from a NUCLEAR (3) attack〔地下〕辐射尘掩蔽所

fal·low /ˋfælo; ˈfæləʊ/ *adj* fallow land is dug or ploughed (PLOUGH² (1)) but is not used for growing crops〔土地〕犁过而不播种的, 休闲的: *Dig over the plot in autumn and let it lie fallow over winter.* 秋天把这块地的土翻一翻, 让它休闲过冬。

fallow deer /ˈ·· ·/ *n* [C] a small European DEER which is yellowish brown with white spots 黇鹿〔产于欧洲的一种小鹿, 毛皮浅黄棕色带白斑〕

Falls Road, the /͵· ˈ·/ a street in the Roman Catholic part of Belfast in Northern Ireland where a lot of fighting has taken place since the 1960s. 福尔斯路〔北爱尔兰贝尔法斯特天主教教区的一条街道。自 20 世纪 60 年代起, 此处暴力争斗频发〕— compare 比较 SHANKHILL ROAD

false /fɔls; fɔːls/ *adj* S3 W3
1 ▶UNTRUE 不真实的◀ a statement, story, etc that is false is completely untrue 假的, 不真实的: *Please decide whether the following statements are true or false.* 请判断下面的说法是真还是假。| *false accusations* 不实的控告
2 ▶WRONG 错误的◀ based on incorrect information or ideas 不正确的, 错的: *I don't want to give you any false hopes.* 我不想给你任何虚假的希望。| *We often make false assumptions about people of other cultures.* 我们经常对其他文化的人做出不正确的假设。| **a false sense of security** (=a feeling of being safe when you are not really safe) 虚假的安全感 *It's easy to feel a false sense of security if crime never touches you personally.* 如果自己没有遇上过罪案, 就很容易产生虚假的安全感。
3 ▶NOT REAL 不是真的◀ a) not real, but intended to seem real and deceive people 伪造的; 骗人的: *a suitcase with a false bottom* 带夹层底的小提箱 | *The man had given a false name and address.* 那男子给了个假名和假地址。**b)** artificial 人造的: **false teeth/hair/eyelashes etc** *Oh no! Grandad's lost his false teeth again.* 啊, 不好! 爷爷又把假牙丢了。
4 ▶NOT SINCERE 不真诚的◀ not sincere or honest, and pretending to have feelings that you do not really have 不真诚的, 不诚实的; 装腔作势的: *She's very false.* 她很做作。| *a false laugh* 假笑 | **false modesty** *"You played brilliantly." "Not really," Ian replied with false modesty.* "你弹得真好。" "其实不太好。" 伊恩故作谦虚地答道。
5 one false move used when warning someone that if they disobey you, make a mistake, or move suddenly something very bad will happen to them 别乱动〔警告用语, 意为对方如果不听从命令、做错事或贸然行动, 就会遇到严惩〕: *One false move, and I'll shoot!* 如果乱动一下, 我就开枪!
6 under false pretences if you get something under false pretences, you get it by deceiving people 以欺诈手段, 靠欺骗: *He was accused of obtaining money under false pretences.* 他被指控以欺诈手段骗取钱财。
7 false imprisonment/arrest the illegal act of putting someone in prison or arresting (ARREST¹) them for a crime they have not done〔在某人无罪情况下的〕非法监禁/拘留
8 false economy something that you think will save money but which will really cost you more 假省钱: *It's a false economy not to have travel insurance on your belongings.* 不给自己的财物办理旅行保险是假省钱。
9 false friend a word in a foreign language that seems similar to one in your own, so that you wrongly think they both mean the same thing 假同源词〔指外语中形似意异的词〕
10 sail/fly under false colours to pretend to be something that you are not 冒充, 以假面目出现, 假装

false a·larm /͵· ·ˈ·/ *n* [C] a situation in which people think that something bad is going to happen, but this is a mistake 虚惊, 假警报: *We all thought the building was about to go up in smoke, but it was a false alarm.* 我们都以为这幢楼要被烧毁, 但这只是一场虚惊。

false dawn /͵· ˈ·/ *n* [C] a situation in which something good seems likely to happen, but it does not 假曙光, 虚幻的希望; 令人空欢喜的事: *The ceasefire turned out to be another false dawn.* 这次停战结果又是一场空欢喜。

false·hood /ˋfɔlshʊd; ˈfɔːlshʊd/ *n formal*【正式】**1** [C] a statement that is untrue 虚假的话, 谎言 **2** [U] the practice of telling lies 说谎

false start /͵· ˈ·/ *n* [C] **1** an unsuccessful attempt to begin a process or event 失败的开端: *After several false starts, the concert finally began.* 音乐会在几次延误之后终于开始了。**2** a situation at the beginning of a race when one competitor starts too soon and the race has to start again〔赛跑开始时的〕抢跑, 起跑犯规

false teeth /͵· ˈ·/ *n* [plural] a set of artificial teeth worn by someone who has lost their natural teeth〔整副的〕假牙

fal·set·to /fɔlˋsɛto; fɔːlˈsetəʊ/ *n* [C] a very high male voice〔男高音的〕假声, 假嗓 —**falsetto** *adv*

fals·ies /ˋfɔlsɪz; ˈfɔːlsiz/ *n* [plural] *informal* pieces of material inside a BRA used to make a woman's breasts look larger【非正式】〔垫在乳罩内侧使乳房显得丰满的〕衬胸, 假乳房

fal·si·fy /ˈfɔlsəˌfaɪ; ˈfɔːlsɪ̈faɪ/ *v* **falsified, falsifying** [T] to change figures, records etc so that they contain false information 篡改; 伪造〔账目、记录等〕: *Somebody had been falsifying the accounts.* 有人篡改了账目。—**falsification** /ˌfɔlsəfəˈkeʃən; ˌfɔːlsɪ̈fɪ̈ˈkeɪʃən/ *n* [C, U]

fal·si·ty /ˈfɔlsətɪ; ˈfɔːlsɪ̈ti/ *n* [U] *formal* the quality of being false or not true【正式】虚假, 不(真)实

Fal·staff /ˈfɔlstæf; ˈfɔːlstɑːf/ a character in the plays *Henry IV* (*Parts 1 and 2*) and *The Merry Wives of Windsor* by William Shakespeare. His full name is Sir John Falstaff, and he is a friend of the prince who later becomes King Henry V. Falstaff is a fat, friendly old man, who enjoys having fun, drinks too much alcohol, and is not always completely honest. 法尔斯塔夫〔威廉·莎士比亚戏剧《亨利四世》(上、下两篇)和《温莎的风流娘儿们》中的人物, 全名: 约翰·法尔斯塔夫爵士。他是亨利五世国王尚为王子时的朋友。他是个身体肥胖、性情友善的老人, 喜欢玩乐, 嗜酒成性, 有时不太诚实〕

fal·ter /ˈfɔltɚ; ˈfɔːltə/ *v* [I] **1** to become weaker and unable to continue in an effective way 变弱, 衰退: *The economy is showing signs of faltering.* 经济正出现衰退的迹象。| *My mother's iron grip upon the household never faltered.* 我母亲牢牢地管着全家从不放松。**2** to speak in a voice that sounds weak and uncertain, and keeps stopping 结巴地说, 支支吾吾地说: *Laurie's voice faltered as she tried to thank him.* 劳丽结结巴巴地对他表示感谢。**3** to become less certain and determined that you want to do something 犹豫, 踌躇: *We must not falter in our resolve.* 我们切勿动摇决心。**4** to move unsteadily because you suddenly feel weak or afraid〔因虚弱或害怕而〕蹒跚, 踉跄, 摇晃: *She faltered for a moment.* 她脚步踉跄了一会儿。

fal·ter·ing /ˈfɔltərɪŋ; ˈfɔːltərɪŋ/ *adj* nervous and uncertain or unsteady 踌躇的, 犹豫的; 摇晃的: *a baby's first faltering steps* 婴孩初学走路时摇摇晃晃的步子 —**falteringly** *adv*

fame /fem; feɪm/ *n* [U] the state of being known about by a lot of people because of your achievements 名声, 名誉, 名气: **win fame/rise to fame** *Streisand first won fame as a singer before she became an actress.* 史翠珊先作为歌手成名, 然后才成为演员。| **at the height of your fame** *The Beatles were at the height of their fame.* 甲壳虫乐队当时正处于名气最响的时候。| **claim to fame** (=the reason why someone or something is well known)〔某人或某物〕出名的原因 *The town's only claim to fame is that Queen Elizabeth I once visited it.* 该镇出名的唯一原因是女王伊丽莎白一世曾来过这里。| **fame and fortune** *He set off to find fame and fortune.* 他开始追名逐利。

famed /femd; feɪmd/ *adj especially literary* well-known【尤文】著名的, 出名的: [+for] *the island of Lontar, famed for its nutmeg and cloves* 以肉豆蔻和丁香闻名的隆塔尔岛

fa·mil·i·al /fəˈmɪljəl; fəˈmɪliəl/ *adj* [only before noun 仅用于名词前] *formal* connected with a family or typical of a family【正式】家庭的; 家庭成员特有的: *economic and familial relationships* 经济关系和家庭关系

fa·mil·i·ar¹ /fəˈmɪljɚ; fəˈmɪliə/ *adj*

1 ►EASY TO RECOGNIZE 容易辨认的◄ someone or something that is familiar is easy to recognize because you have seen or heard them many times before 熟悉的: *a familiar tune* 熟悉的曲调 | **vaguely familiar** (=a little familiar) 有点熟悉的 *Her face seems vaguely familiar, but I can't quite place her.* 她看起来有点面熟, 但我想不起她是谁。| **look/sound familiar (to sb)** *The voice on the phone sounded familiar to me.* 电话里的声音我听起来很熟悉。

2 be familiar with to know something well because you have seen it, read it, or used it many times before 通晓, 熟悉: *Are you familiar with this type of machine?* 你熟悉这种机器吗?

3 ►PLACE/SITUATION 地方/状况◄ a familiar place, situation etc is one that you know well 熟悉的: *It was a relief to be back in familiar surroundings.* 回到熟悉的环境是令人宽慰的事。

4 ►COMMON 普通的◄ a familiar sight, problem, story etc is one that you see or hear about too often because it is part of a common social problem 常见的, 普通的: **all-too-familiar** *Beggars on the streets are becoming an all-too-familiar sight.* 街道上的乞丐正成为司空见惯的景象。

5 be on familiar terms with to know someone well and be able to talk to them in an informal way 和…交情很好, 和…关系友好: *He's on familiar terms with all the teachers.* 他和所有的教师关系都很好。

6 ►TOO FRIENDLY 过分友好的◄ talking to someone as if you know them well although you do not 故作亲密的, 过分亲昵的: [+with] *I thought he was being a bit familiar with my wife.* 我认为他对我妻子有点太亲热了。

7 ►INFORMAL STYLE 非正式文体◄ informal and friendly in speech, writing, etc 非正式的; 随和的: *The novel is written in an easy, familiar style.* 这部小说是以相当轻松随便的笔调写成的。—see also 另见 FAMILIARLY

familiar² *n* [C] **1** a cat or other animal that lives with a WITCH and has magical powers〔与女巫共居的〕妖兽, 妖精 **2 familiars** *old use* close friends or companions【旧】密友, 伴侣

fa·mil·iar·ise /fəˈmɪljəˌraɪz; fəˈmɪliəraɪz/ *v* a British spelling of FAMILIARIZE familiarize 的英式拼法

fa·mil·i·ar·i·ty /fəˌmɪlɪˈærətɪ; fəˌmɪliˈærɪ̈ti/ *n* **1** [U] a good knowledge of a particular subject or place〔对某个领域或地方的〕精通, 通晓: [+with] *In fact his familiarity with the Bronx was pretty limited.* 事实上他对布朗克斯区的了解相当有限。**2** [U] a feeling of being relaxed and comfortable because you are in a place you know well or with people you know well 亲切感: *I miss the familiarity of home.* 我怀念家中的那种亲切感。**3 familiarity breeds contempt** an expression meaning that if you know someone too well, you find out their faults and respect them less 亲密生嫌隙, 亲昵生狎侮; 亲不敬, 熟生蔑

fa·mil·i·ar·ize also 又作 **-ise** *BrE*【英】/fəˈmɪljəˌraɪz; fəˈmɪliəraɪz/ *v* **familiarize yourself with sth/familiarize sb with sth** to learn about something so that you understand it, or teach someone else about something so that they understand it 使熟悉, 使通晓: *Employees must familiarize themselves with the health and safety manual.* 雇员必须熟悉健康和安全手册。—**familiarization** /fəˌmɪljərəˈzeʃən; fəˌmɪliəraɪˈzeɪʃən/ *n* [U]

fa·mil·i·ar·ly /fəˈmɪljɚlɪ; fəˈmɪliəli/ *adv* in an informal or friendly way 随和地; 亲密地: *Charles, familiarly known as Charlie* 查尔斯, 昵称查利

fam·i·ly /ˈfæməlɪ; ˈfæməli/ *n plural* **families**

1 ►PEOPLE WHO ARE CLOSELY RELATED 关系密切的人◄ [U] a group of people who are related to each other, especially a mother, a father, and their children〔由父母和孩子组成的〕家庭: *Ned comes from a big family of eight children.* 内德来自一个有八个孩子的大家庭。| *Do you know the family next door?* 你认识隔壁那家人吗? | [also+plural verb] *BrE*【英】*The family now live in London.* 那家人现在住在伦敦。| **family home/business/holiday etc** *He grew up knowing that he would take over the family business one day.* 他从小就知道他有一天要接管家里的生意的。| **nuclear family** (=a family consisting of mother, father, and their children) 核心家庭, 小家庭 | **extended family** (=all the people in a family including aunts, uncles, grandparents etc)〔包括姨婶、伯叔、祖父母等的〕大家庭 | **one-parent family/single-parent family** (=a family in which there is only one parent) 单亲家庭 | **family background** (=the sort of family you come from) 家庭背景 | **she's/he's family** *informal* (=used to say that someone is related to you)【非正式】她/他是我们的家人〔用于说明某人是自己的亲属〕

CULTURAL NOTE 文化注释

In the US and the UK, most people have a traditional idea of a typical family, called a **nuclear family**, which consists of a mother, a father, and children. Usually, the father goes out to work and the mother takes care of the home and the children. Although this type of family is often praised by politicians and often shown in advertisements, fewer and fewer real families are actually like this. Most married women now have jobs, and there are more **one-parent/single-parent families**, partly because of DIVORCE and partly because some women have children without being married. Divorce also leads to more complicated families, if parents get married to other people and have more children. Many families have **half-brothers/sisters** or **step-brothers/sisters** living in the same house. There are also some families in which the partners are HOMOSEXUAL people who are living together as if they were married. As a result of all these changes, there are now many different types of family. Another type of family, the **extended family**, which is a large family group all living together, including grandparents, COUSINS etc, used to be common in former times but is now very unusual in the US and UK. 多数英美人仍持传统观念, 认为典型的家庭是"核心家庭", 成员为父母和孩子。通常父亲外出工作, 母亲料理家务、照顾孩子。虽然政界人士赞扬这种家庭, 广告上经常展现这种家庭, 这样的家庭还是越来越少。大多数已婚女性也有工作, 单亲家庭增多, 部分因为夫妻离异, 部分因为一些女性未婚产子。若父母离婚后与有子女的人再婚, 家庭结构就会更加复杂。很多家庭里同父异母、同母异父或异父异母的兄弟姐妹住在同一屋檐下。有的家庭由同性恋人组成。这些改变现在带来了很多不同类型

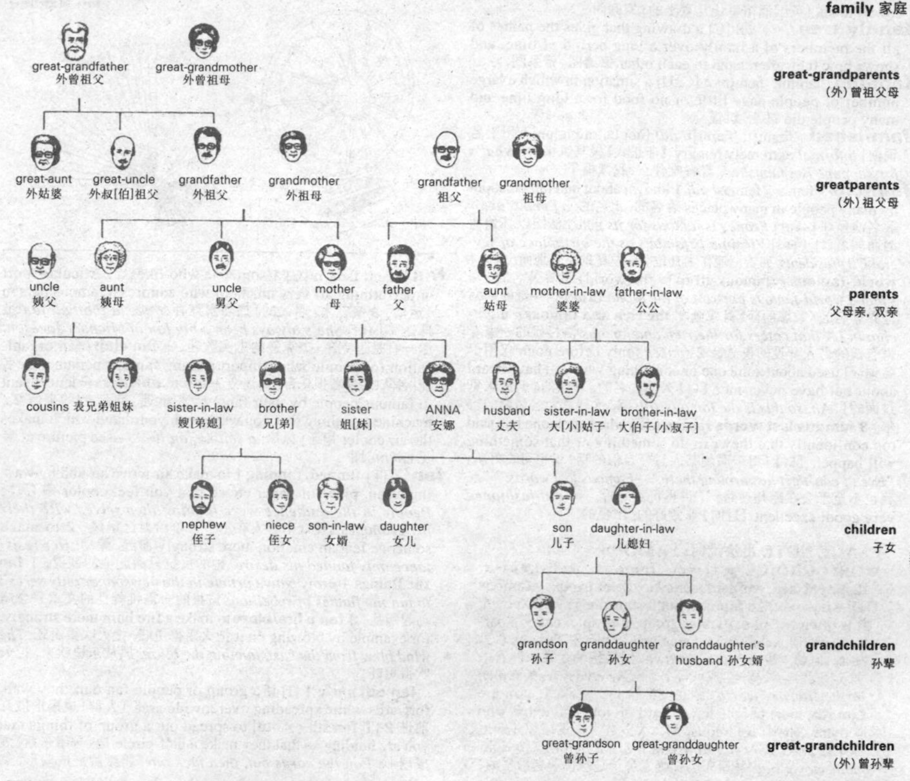

的家庭。另一种家庭类型是大家庭, 与(外)祖父母或堂表兄弟或姐妹住在一起, 这种家庭在以前常可见到, 但现在在英美已经为数极少。

2 ►ALL THE PEOPLE RELATED TO YOU 所有和你有亲属关系的人◄ [C,U] all the people you are related to, including those who are now dead 家族: *I'm moving to Detroit because I have some family there.* 我要搬到底特律, 因为我家族有一些人住在那儿。| [also+plural verb] *BrE*【英】*My family come from Scotland originally.* 我的祖籍是苏格兰。| **be in sb's family** (=be owned by someone's family, especially for a long time) 是属于某人家族的 *That painting has been in our family for 200 years.* 那幅油画属于我们家族所有已有200年了。| **run in the family** (=be a common feature in a particular family) 是一家人共有的特征, 家族世传的 *Asthma runs in the family.* 这家人个个都有哮喘病。

3 ►CHILDREN 孩子, 子女◄ [C] children 孩子, 子女: *Couples with young families wouldn't want to live here.* 子女年幼的夫妻不会愿意住在这里。| **start a family** (=have children) 开始生孩子, 生第一个孩子 *They're getting married next year, and hope to start a family straight away.* 他们准备明年结婚, 并希望马上要孩子。| **bring up/raise a family** *the problems of bringing up a family on a very low income* 靠很低的收入养家糊口的问题 | **a family film/show etc** (=suitable for children as well as adults) 老少咸宜的电影/表演等

4 family size/pack/etc a product sold in a large container packet big enough for a whole family 家庭装〔供全家人用的大包装商品〕

5 ►GROUP OF ANIMALS/THINGS 动物/事物的科、族等◄ [C] *technical* a group of related animals, plants, languages etc【术语】〔动物、植物等的〕科; 〔语言的〕语族, 语系: *The cat family includes lions and tigers.* 猫科动物包括狮子和老虎。| *Spanish and Italian are part of the Romance language family.* 西班牙语和意大利语属于罗曼语族。

6 in the family way *old-fashioned* PREGNANT【过时】怀孕; 有身孕

family cred·it /,... '../ *n* [U] money given by the government in Britain to parents who do not earn much money〔英国政府发放的〕贫困家庭救济金, 低收入家庭津贴〔发给低收入而有年幼子女的父母〕

family doc·tor /,... '../ *n* [C] a doctor trained in general medicine, who a family visits regularly 家庭医生

Family In·come Sup·port /,... '.., ./ money given by the British government to people in Britain who are unemployed and have children 失业家庭收入资助〔英国政府给需要抚养子女的失业人员提供的资助〕

family man /'..., ./ *n* [C] **1** a man who enjoys being at home with his wife and children 喜欢家庭生活的男人 **2** a man with a wife and children 有妻子儿女的男人

family name /'..., ./ *n* [C] the name someone shares with all the members of their family; SURNAME, LAST NAME 姓

family plan·ning /,... '../ *n* [U] the practice of controlling the number of children that are born using CONTRACEPTION 计划生育; 家庭计划: *a family planning clinic* 计划生育门诊部

Family Plan·ning As·so·ci·a·tion, the /,... '..., ../ abbreviation 缩写为 **FPA** a British organization which gives free advice on family planning. There is a similar organization in the US called Planned Parenthood. 计划生育协会〔英国一组织, 免费提供计划生育指导。美国也有一类似组织, 称Planned Parenthood〕

family prac·tice /,.. '../ *n* [U] *AmE* a part of medical practice in the US in which doctors learn to treat general health problems and problems connected with families and people of all ages【美】家庭保健, 普通医疗, 大众医疗 —**family practitioner** /,... '.../ *n* [C]

family room /'..., ./ *n* [C] **1** *AmE* a room in a house where the family can play games, watch television etc【美】家庭娱乐

室; 起居室 **2** a room in a PUB in Britain where children are allowed to sit〔英国酒馆里让儿童坐的〕家庭间

family tree /,··· ' ·/ *n* [C] a drawing that gives the names of all the members of a family over a long period of time, and shows how they are related to each other 家谱图; 谱系图

fam·ine /ˈfæmɪn; ˈfæmɪ̣n/ *n* [C, U] a situation in which a large number of people have little or no food for a long time and many people die 饥荒; 饥馑

fam·ished /ˈfæmɪʃt; ˈfæmɪʃt/ *adj* [not before noun 不用于名词前] *informal* extremely hungry【非正式】极其饥饿的: *What's for supper? I'm famished.* 晚餐吃什么?我饿极了。

fa·mous /ˈfeməs; ˈfeɪməs/ *adj* **1** known about and talked about by many people in many places 著名的, 出名的: *a famous actor* 著名演员 | [+for] *France is famous for its wine.* 法国以其葡萄酒而闻名。| [+as] *Virginia is famous as the birthplace of several US presidents.* 弗吉尼亚作为几位美国总统的出生地而出名。| **world-famous** (=famous all over the world) 世界著名的 *Da Vinci's world-famous portrait of the Mona Lisa* 达·芬奇的那幅世界著名的《蒙娜丽莎》肖像画 | **the rich and famous** *a nightclub in LA that caters for the rich and famous* 洛杉矶的一家专为有钱的名人开设的夜总会 **2** *spoken* [only before noun 仅用于名词前] used about someone or something who you have heard about but have never met【口】久闻大名的, 耳熟的〔但从未见过面的〕: *Ah, so this is the famous Jill.* 啊, 这就是大名鼎鼎的吉尔。**3 famous last words** *spoken* used when someone has said too confidently that they can do something or that something will happen【口】〔用于讽刺某人过分自信的话〕讲得可真好听: *"Even I can't get lost around there." "Famous last words."* "连我也不至于会在那儿迷路。""讲得可真好听。" **4** *old-fashioned* very good; excellent【过时】非常好的; 出色的

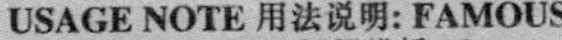

USAGE NOTE 用法说明: FAMOUS

WORD CHOICE 词语辨析: **famous, well-known, distinguished, eminent, renowned, notorious, infamous**

Well-known is like **famous**, but if someone is well-known, it is often with a particular group of people, or for a particular skill, achievement etc. well-known和 famous 意思相似, 但如果说某人 well-known, 经常指他在某一群人中著名, 或因某种技能、成就等著名: *She's very well-known in the literary world.* 她在文学界十分著名。If you are **famous**, most people have heard of you, and know who you are. 如果你是famous, 那么大多数人听说过你并知道你是什么人: *That big house in Malibu belongs to a famous movie star.* 马里布的那幢大房子是一位著名影星的。

Distinguished and **eminent** are used especially of people who are famous for serious work in science, the arts etc. distinguished和 eminent 专门用于指那些在科学、艺术等领域因作出重要贡献而出名的人: *a distinguished writer* 著名作家 | *an eminent surgeon* 杰出的外科医生

Places or people are **renowned** for a particular quality, characteristic, or skill. 地方或人因某种品质、特征或技能而出名, 则用 renowned: *Florence is renowned for its beautiful buildings.* 佛罗伦萨因其漂亮的建筑物而驰名。| *the renowned cellist, Jacqueline Du Pre* 著名大提琴家杰奎琳·杜·普蕾。If someone is **notorious** they are famous for something bad. 如果说某人notorious, 他是由于做坏事而闻名: *the notorious gangster Marco Fellini* 臭名远扬的黑手党魁马可·费里尼 | *Many politicians are notorious hypocrites.* 许多政客都是臭名远扬的伪君子。

Infamous is like **notorious** but slightly literary, and is often used about people, places, and events in the past or when they are a long way away. infamous 和notorious 相同, 但一般为书面语, 而且常与过去或远处的人、地方和事件连用: *the infamous Bastille prison* 臭名昭著的巴士底监狱

Famous Five, the /,·· ' ·/ the main characters in a series of British books for children by Enid Blyton, mostly written in the 1940s and 1950s. They are a group of two boys, two girls, and a dog called Timmy. They come from MIDDLE-CLASS families and go to private schools, but they have a lot of exciting adventures together during the school holidays. 五名人〔伊妮德·布莱顿20世纪40、50年代创作的英国儿童系列读物中的主要人物, 包括两个男孩、两个女孩和一只叫蒂米的小狗。他们出身中产阶级家庭, 上私立学校, 放假期间经历了许多激动人心的奇遇〕

fa·mous·ly /ˈfeməslɪ; ˈfeɪməsli/ *adv* **1 get on/along famously** *old-fashioned* to have a friendly relationship with someone【过时】〔与某人〕关系很好 **2** *formal* in a way that is famous【正式】著名地, 出名地; 出色地

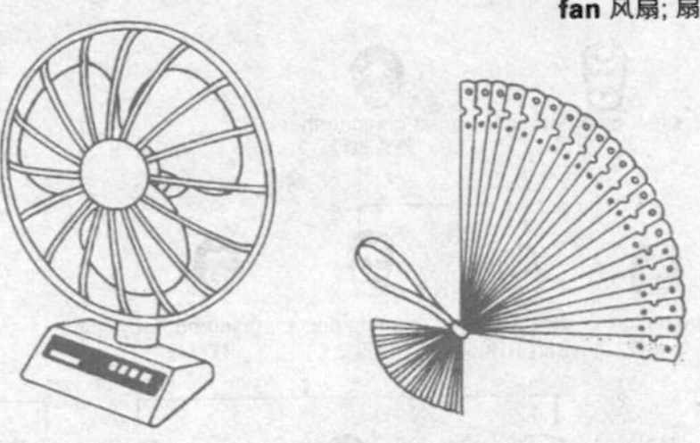

fan 风扇; 扇子

fan¹ /fæn; fæn/ *n* [C] **1** someone who likes a particular sport or performing art very much, or who admires a famous person〔运动、表演艺术、名人的〕热烈崇拜者, …迷: *a football fan* 足球迷 | [+of] *She's always been a big fan of Michael Jackson.* 她一直是迈克尔·杰克逊的忠实歌迷。| **fan club** (=an organization for people who support a team, famous person etc) 名流[名队]崇拜者俱乐部; …迷会 | **fan mail/letters** (=letters sent to famous people by their fans) 球迷[歌迷、仰慕者]的来信 **2** a machine or a thing that you wave with your hand which makes the air cooler 扇子; 风扇: *a ceiling fan* 吊扇 —see picture at 参见 ENGINE 图

fan² *v* [T] **fanned, fanning 1** to make air move around by waving a fan, piece of paper etc so that you feel cooler 扇(风): *People in the audience were fanning themselves with their programmes.* 观众中有人在用节目单给自己扇风。**2** to make someone feel an emotion more strongly 激起, 煽动: *Her resistance only fanned his desire.* 她的反抗只激起他的欲望。| **fan the flames** *A provocative article in the newspaper only served to fan the flames of rebellion.* 该报的一篇挑衅性的文章只会煽动起叛乱。**3 fan a fire/blaze** to make a fire burn more strongly, for example by blowing on it 把火扇得更旺, 把火吹得更旺: *The wind blew from the east, fanning the blaze.* 风从东边吹来, 把火吹得更旺。

fan out *phr v* **1** [I] if a group of people fan out, they walk forwards while spreading over a wide area〔人群〕成扇形散开前进 **2** [T **fan** sth ↔ **out**] to spread out a group of things that you are holding so that they make a half-circle 把〔一组东西〕展成扇形: *Fan the cards out, then pick one.* 将纸牌展成扇形, 然后选一张。

fa·nat·ic /fəˈnætɪk; fəˈnætɪk/ *n* [C] **1** someone who has extreme political or religious ideas and is often dangerous〔政治或宗教思想的〕狂热者, 盲信者: *fanatics who represent a real danger to democracy* 成为民主真正威胁的狂热者 **2** someone who likes a particular thing or activity very much〔对某种事物或活动〕入迷的人: *a health food fanatic* 极喜欢保健食品的人 —**fanatical** *adj* —**fanatically** /-klɪ; -kli/ *adv*

fa·nat·i·cis·m /fəˈnætə,sɪzəm; fəˈnætɪ̣sɪzəm/ *n* [U] extreme political or religious beliefs〔对政治或宗教〕狂热, 盲信

fan belt /' · ·/ *n* [C] the belt that operates a fan (FAN¹ (2)) which keeps a car engine cool〔汽车发动机上的〕(冷却)风扇皮带 —see picture at 参见 ENGINE 图

fan·ci·a·ble /ˈfænsɪəbl̩; ˈfænsiəbəl/ *adj BrE* sexually attractive【英】性感的; 诱惑人的

fan·ci·er /ˈfænsɪɚ; ˈfænsiə/ *n* [C] **pigeon/horse etc fancier** *especially BrE* someone who breeds and is interested in a particular kind of animal or plant【尤英】养鸽/马等(驯养)爱好者

fan·ci·ful /ˈfænsɪfəl; ˈfænsɪfəl/ *adj* **1** imagined rather than based on facts 想象的, 空想的, 幻想的: *a fanciful story* 想象出来的故事 | *The suggestion that there was a conspiracy is not entirely fanciful.* 有人在搞阴谋这一看法不完全是空想出来的。**2** full of unusual and very detailed shapes or complicated designs 奇特的, 精细的, 花哨的: *fanciful decorations* 花哨的装饰 —**fancifully** *adv*

fan·cy¹ /ˈfænsɪ; ˈfænsi/ *v* **fancied, fancying** [T]

1 ►LIKE/WANT 喜欢/想要◄ *especially BrE* to like or want something, or want to do something【尤英】喜欢, 想要: *Fancy a quick drink, Emma?* 想快快地喝一杯吗, 爱玛?

2 ►SEXUAL ATTRACTION 性吸引◄ *BrE informal* to feel sexually attracted to someone【英, 非正式】爱慕, 爱上: *All the girls fancied him like mad.* 所有的女孩子都疯狂地爱他。

3 fancy yourself *BrE informal* to behave in a way that shows you think you are very attractive or clever【英, 非正式】自以为

是, 自命不凡: *That bloke on the dance-floor really fancies himself.* 舞池里的那家伙真是自命不凡。
4 ▶THINK STH WILL BE SUCCESSFUL 认为某事会成功◀ *BrE* to think someone or something is likely to be successful in something【英】认为, 相信〔某人或某事会成功〕: **fancy sb's chances** *I don't fancy our chances of getting a ticket this late.* 我不相信我们这么晚还有机会弄到票子。
5 fancy!/fancy that! *BrE spoken* used to express your surprise or shock about something【英口】真想不到!/难以想象会有那种事!: *"The Petersons are getting divorced." "Fancy that!"* "彼德森夫妇要离婚了。""这真难以想象!"
6 ▶THINK/BELIEVE 想/相信◀ *literary* to think or believe something without being certain【文】〔不肯定地〕想; 以为: **fancy (that)** *She fancied she heard a noise downstairs.* 她觉得自己好像听到楼下有声音。

fancy[2] *n*
1 ▶DESIRE FOR 对…的欲望◀ [singular] *especially BrE*【尤英】**a)** a feeling, especially one that is not particularly strong or urgent, that you would like something or someone 喜爱: **take a fancy to** (=decide that you like someone or want to have something) 爱上 *Mr Hill took a real fancy to Clara.* 希尔先生真的爱上了克拉拉。| **a passing fancy** (=one that does not last long) 一时的兴致, 一时的爱好 *Wanting to go to Mexico was just a passing fancy.* 想去墨西哥只是一时的兴致而已。**b) take your fancy** if something takes your fancy, you like it or want to have it〔某物〕让你喜欢上, 让你看中: *Did anything take your fancy?* 你看中了什么吗?
2 tickle sb's fancy *informal* to seem attractive or amusing to someone【非正式】使某人喜欢, 吸引某人: *The idea of playing a joke on the Sergeant really tickled his fancy.* 跟中士开个玩笑的想法使他感到很有趣。
3 ▶IDEA 想法, 主意◀ [C] *old-fashioned* an idea or opinion that is not based on fact【过时】〔无根据的〕想法, 空想, 猜想, 奇想: *Oh, that was a fancy of his.* 啊, 那是他的奇想。
4 ▶IMAGINATION 想象◀ [U] *literary* imagination or something that you imagine【文】想象力; 想象出来的东西: **flight of fancy** (=when you let your imagination work in an uncontrolled way) 胡思乱想 *Pat went off on one of her flights of fancy.* 帕特又开始了胡思乱想。

S3 **fancy**[3] *adj* **1** fancy hotels, restaurants, cars etc are expensive and fashionable〔旅馆、餐厅、汽车等〕昂贵的, 豪华的: *Harry took me to a fancy restaurant for our anniversary.* 哈里带我到一家豪华的餐厅吃饭, 庆祝我们的结婚纪念日。| **fancy prices** (=very high and often unreasonable prices) 十分昂贵的价格 **2** having a lot of decoration or bright colours, or made in a complicated way 有装饰的, 花哨的, 别致的: *fancy buttons* 花哨的纽扣 | **nothing fancy** *I just want a basic sports coat – nothing fancy.* 我只要一件简单的运动外衣 —— 不带什么特别装饰的。**3** complicated and needing a lot of skill 需要复杂技巧的, 高难度的: *I can't do all that fancy stuff on the computer.* 我无法在电脑上做那些高难度的操作。**4** [only before noun 仅用于名词前] *AmE* fancy food is high quality【美】〔食品、菜肴等〕优质的, 特级的

fancy dress /,‥ ˈ·/ *n* [U] *BrE* clothes that make you look like a famous person, a character from a story etc【英】化装服: *a fancy-dress party* 化装舞会

fancy-free /,‥ ˈ·/ *adj* able to do anything you like because you do not have a family or other responsibilities〔因无家室或其他责任而〕无拘束的, 无忧无虑的: **footloose and fancy-free** *Ten years ago I was footloose and fancy-free.* 十年前我毫无牵累, 自由自在。

fancy man /ˈ‥ ·/ *n* [C] *old-fashioned* a man that a married woman has a sexual relationship with, who is not her husband【过时】情夫

fancy wom·an /ˈ‥ ,‥/ *n* [C] *old-fashioned* a woman that a married man has a sexual relationship with, who is not his wife【过时】情妇

fan·cy·work /ˈfænsɪ,wɝk; ˈfænsiwɜːk/ *n* [U] decorative sewing; EMBROIDERY 刺绣, 刺绣品; 钩编织品

fan·dan·go /fænˋdæŋgo; fænˈdæŋgəʊ/ *n* [C] a fast Spanish or South American dance, or the music for this dance 方丹戈舞〔一种西班牙或南美的快速舞〕; 方丹戈舞曲

fan·fare /ˈfæn,fɛr; ˈfænfeə/ *n* [C] a short, loud piece of music played on a TRUMPET[1] (1) to introduce an important person or event〔引导大人物进场或宣布重要事件时吹奏的〕一小段响亮的喇叭声

fang /fæŋ; fæŋ/ *n* [C] a long sharp tooth of an animal such as a snake or wild dog〔蛇、野狗等的〕尖牙; 毒牙

fan·light /ˈfæn,laɪt; ˈfænlaɪt/ *n* [C] **1** *especially BrE* a small window above a door or a larger window【尤英】〔门或大窗上方的〕楣窗, 气窗; TRANSOM (3) *AmE*【美】**2** *AmE* a window shaped like a half circle【美】扇形窗

Fan·nie Mae /,fænɪ ˋme; ,fæni ˈmeɪ/ a US financial institution which buys and sells LOANS and MORTGAGES to banks and other institutions, but does not deal directly with ordinary borrowers 房利美〔美国一金融机构。该公司购买贷款和抵押贷款, 并把它们出售给银行等金融机构, 但不直接与普通借款人发生业务往来〕

fan·ny /ˈfænɪ; ˈfæni/ *n* [C] **1** *AmE old-fashioned* the part of your body that you sit on; BOTTOM[1] (7)【美, 过时】屁股 **2** *BrE taboo* a woman's outer sex organs【英讳】女性阴部, 女性外生殖器

Fanny Hill /,fænɪ ˋhɪl; ,fæni ˈhɪl/ a book written in 1749 by John Cleland about the sexual adventures of a young woman, Fanny Hill. It is written in a very ELEGANT style but has many sex scenes.《范妮·希尔》〔约翰·克莱兰 1749 年写的一本书, 讲述一名叫范妮·希尔的年轻女子的浪荡风情史。该书语言雅致, 但有不少性爱场面〕

Fan·ta·si·a /fænˋteʒɪə; fænˈteɪziə/ *trademark* (1940) a US film made by Walt Disney, which consists of a number of different short CARTOONS, each one with its own piece of CLASSICAL music【商标】《幻想曲》〔(1940) 美国沃尔特·迪斯尼摄制的一部影片。影片由不同卡通短片组成, 每个短片都配有一曲古典音乐〕

fantasia *n* [C] **1** a piece of music that does not have a regular form or style 幻想曲; 狂想曲 **2** a piece of music consisting of a collection of well-known tunes〔名曲凑成的〕集成曲

fan·ta·size also 又作 **-ise** *BrE*【英】/ˋfæntə,saɪz; ˈfæntəsaɪz/ *v* [I,T] to imagine something strange, or very pleasant happening to you 想象, 幻想: **fantasize (that)** *I used to fantasize that my real parents were famous movie stars.* 我过去常幻想我真正的父母是著名的影星。| **[+about]** *She would fantasize about her future life with Kyle.* 她常想象自己将来与凯尔在一起的生活。

fan·tas·tic /fænˋtæstɪk; fænˈtæstɪk/ *adj* **1** extremely good, attractive, enjoyable etc 极好的, 吸引人的, 有趣的: *You look fantastic!* 你的气色好极了! | *Sounds like a fantastic idea to me.* 我觉得这主意太好了。**2** *spoken* used when someone has just told you something good【口】太好了: *"I've passed my driving test." "Fantastic!"* "我已通过驾驶考试。""太好了!" **3** a fantastic amount is extremely large〔数量〕极大的: *Teenagers spend fantastic amounts of money on clothes.* 青少年在衣着方面花大笔的钱。**4** a plan, suggestion etc that is fantastic is not likely to be possible〔计划、建议等〕不现实的, 异想天开的 **5** [only before noun 仅用于名词前] a fantastic story, creature, or place is very strange or unreal〔故事、生物或场所等〕奇异的, 荒唐的, 古怪的: *fantastic tales of dragons and fairy queens* 龙和仙后的荒诞故事 —**fantastically** /-klɪ; -kli/ *adv*: *a fantastically expensive meal* 贵得吓人的一餐 S3

fan·tas·ti·cal /fænˋtæstɪkl; fænˈtæstɪkəl/ *adj* strange and unreal 奇异的, 荒唐的, 虚构的: *a fantastical tale* 荒诞故事

fan·ta·sy /ˋfæntəsɪ; ˈfæntəsi/ *n plural* **fantasies** **1** [C,U] an exciting and unusual experience or situation you imagine happening to you but which will probably never happen 幻想, 想象: *He used to indulge in fantasies about being a famous actor.* 他过去常沉溺于当一名名演员的幻想中。| *sexual fantasies* 性幻想 | *Young children sometimes can't distinguish between fantasy and reality.* 小孩子有时不能区分幻想与现实。| **live in a fantasy world** *He lived in a fantasy world and never faced up to his problems.* 他生活在一个幻想世界里, 从来不敢直接面对自己的问题。**2** [singular, U] an idea or belief that is based only on imagination, not on real facts〔根据想象的〕空想, 怪念头: *These claims about being 'the party of law and order' are pure fantasy.* 这些声称为"遵纪守法的党"纯粹是空想。

fan·zine /ˋfænzin; ˈfænziːn/ *n* [C] a magazine written by and for people who admire and support a popular musician, a sports team etc〔仰慕和支持大众喜爱的音乐家、运动队等的〕爱好者杂志; 影[球]迷杂志

FAO, the /,ɛf e ˋo; ,ef eɪ ˈəʊ/ **1** the Food and Agriculture Organization; a part of the United Nations whose aim is to increase food production, especially in poorer countries, for example by teaching better farming skills. It is also responsible for sending food to areas where there is seriously little food. 粮农组织, 粮食及农业组织〔联合国一机构, 旨在通过传授先进的耕作技术提高世界粮食产量, 尤其要提高贫困国家的粮食产量。该组织还负责给严重缺粮的地区运送粮食〕**2** for the attention of; a note written on a letter or envelope when you want a particular person in an organization to see it or deal with it〔某某人〕亲启〔写在信封或信纸上的提示语〕

F

far¹ /fɑr; fɑː/ *adv comparative* 比较级 **farther** or **further** *superlative* 最高级 **farthest** or **furthest**

① A LONG DISTANCE 远距离
② MUCH/VERY/A LOT …得多，很
③ GIVING YOUR OPINION 发表看法
④ NOT AT ALL 根本不
⑤ TO A PARTICULAR DEGREE 到某种程度
⑥ PROGRESS/SUCCEED 进展/成功

① A LONG DISTANCE 远距离

1 ►LONG DISTANCE 远距离◄ a long distance 远：*Have you driven far?* 你驾车开了很远的路吗？| *We walked much further than we had intended.* 我们比原来计划的走得远多了。| **far away** *My parents don't live far away.* 我父母住在不远的地方。| **far above/below/across etc** *The office blocks towered far above them.* 这些办公大楼高高耸立在它们之上。| **far from/far away from** *We were sitting too far away from the stage to be able to see very much.* 我们坐的地方远离舞台，无法看清楚。

2 how far used when asking or mentioning the distance between two places or the distance someone has travelled 多远：*How far is it to the station?* 到车站有多远？| *I wonder how far we've walked today.* 我想知道今天我们已经走了多远的路。

3 as far as up to a particular point or distance 远至，一直到：*The flood waters had come up as far as the house.* 洪水一直涌到那幢房子。

4 as far as the eye can see up to the longest distance away that you can see 在肉眼看得见的范围内：*hills sweeping back as far as the eye could see* 从视野里一掠而过的小山

5 far and wide over or from a large area 四处，到处：**hunt/search far and wide** *He would hunt far and wide for rare medicinal herbs.* 他会到处寻找珍稀草药。| **travel/wander/spread etc far and wide** *Since then I have travelled far and wide.* 从那时起我就到处旅行。

② MUCH/VERY/A LOT …得多，很

6 [+adj/adv] **far stronger/far more intelligent/far more quickly etc** much stronger, more intelligent etc 强壮得多/聪明得多/快得多等：*She works far longer hours than I do.* 她每天工作的时间比我长得多。| *You'll get there far more quickly by car.* 你坐车去那儿就快多了。

7 far too much/long/soon etc much too much, long, soon etc 太多/太久/太快等：*It costs far too much money.* 这要花太多的钱。| *It's far too early to tell if she'll be OK.* 现在谈她是否安然无恙还为时过早。

8 to a great degree 很大程度上：**far above/below** *The increase in inflation is far below what experts predicted.* 通货膨胀的增长远远低于专家的预测。| **far removed** (=very different) 人相径庭的，很不一样的，差得很远的 *Life on the islands is far removed from the hustle and bustle of life in Manila.* 海岛上的生活与马尼拉熙熙攘攘的生活大不相同。

9 by far/far and away used to say that something is much better, worse etc than anything else 最；无疑；很：*The grass snake is by far the most common snake.* 这草蛇无疑是最常见的蛇。

③ GIVING YOUR OPINION 发表看法

10 as far as I'm/we're concerned *spoken* used to give your opinion about something【口】就我/我们而言：*As far as I'm concerned, it sounds like a great idea.* 就我而言，这听起来是个很好的主意。

11 as far as sth is concerned *spoken* used to give your opinion or to state facts about a particular thing【口】就某事而论，至于某事：*This has been a difficult period as far as the German economy is concerned.* 就德国经济而论，这是一个很困难的时期。

12 as far as I know/as far as I can remember *spoken* used to say that you think that something is true, although you do not know all the facts, cannot remember completely etc【口】据我所知/据我所能记得的：*As far as I can tell, the whole thing should cost about £500.* 据我所知的情况来判断，整件事应该要花大约 500 英镑。

13 I wouldn't go as far as to say *spoken* used to say that you think a particular idea or opinion is too extreme or unlikely to be true【口】我不愿意把话说得这么过分：*"Do you think they'll win?" "Oh I wouldn't go as far as to say that, but they're looking pretty good."* "你认为他们会赢吗?" "啊，我可不想这样肯定，不过他们看起来相当不错。"

④ NOT AT ALL 根本不

14 far from used to say that the opposite of something is true, or the opposite of what you expect happens 远远不，一点也不：**far from being** *Far from being a reactionary, he's actually quite liberal in his views.* 他根本不是反动分子，实际上他的观点相当开明。| **far from doing sth** *Far from helping the situation, you've just made it worse.* 你非但没让情况变好，反而把它弄得更糟。| **far from pleased/happy etc** *Michael walked in, looking far from happy.* 迈克尔走了进来，看上去一点也不快乐。

15 far from it *spoken* used to say that the opposite of what someone says is true; certainly not【口】远远不是：*"Is he a good driver?" "Far from it!"* "他是个好司机吗?" "远远谈不上!"

16 far be it from me to do sth *spoken* used when you are going to criticize someone or give them advice, and you want to pretend that you do not want to do this【口】我决不想做某事〔常用于批评人或向人提建议前，表示这样做并非情愿〕：*Far be it from me to try and run your life, but I really think you should leave him.* 我决不想控制你的生活，但我确实认为你应该离开他。

⑤ TO A PARTICULAR DEGREE 到某种程度

17 how far used to ask to what degree something is true 什么样的程度：*How far is violence caused by society?* 暴力在多大程度上是由社会所引起的？| *I'm not sure how far this will help the economy.* 这对经济的帮助有多大，我没把握。

18 as far as it goes used to say that an idea, suggestion, plan etc is satisfactory, but only to a limited degree 就其本身而言：*It's a perfectly good law as far as it goes, but it doesn't deal with the real problems.* 就其本身而言，这完全是一项好的法律，但它没有涉及到实际的问题。

19 so far up to a particular point, degree, distance etc 到某一点/程度/距离为止：*You can only trust him so far.* 你只能信任他到这个程度。| **so far and no further** *They can extend the budget so far and no further.* 他们只能将预算增加到这个程度，不能再加了。

⑥ PROGRESS/SUCCEED 进展/成功

20 how far have you got? used when asking or talking about how much of something someone has done or how much they have achieved 你进展得怎么样?：[+with] *How far did you get with the cleaning?* 你打扫得怎么样了?

21 so far so good *spoken* used to say that things have been happening successfully until now【口】到目前为止一切都好

22 sb will/should go far used to say that you think someone will be successful in the future 某人会/准能成功：*She is an excellent musician and should go far.* 她是位优秀的音乐家，将来应该能大有作为。

23 ►LONG TIME 久远◄ a long time in the past or the future, or a long time into a particular period 久，远，久远：**far back** (=a long time in the past) 久远的过去 *The story takes us far back in the past, to the time of the Pharaohs.* 这个故事将我们带到久远的过去，到法老时代。| **far into** *We worked far into the night.* 我们工作到深夜。—see also 另见 FAR-OFF

24 so far until now 到目前为止，迄今为止：*We haven't had any trouble so far.* 迄今为止我们没碰上麻烦。

25 as far as possible/so far as possible as much as possible 尽可能地：*We try to use local materials as far as possible.* 我们尽可能试着使用当地的材料。

26 go as far as to do sth to behave in a way that seems surprising or extreme 甚至做出某事：*She even went as far as to threaten to kill herself.* 她甚至威胁要自杀。

27 **go too far** also 又作 **take/carry sth too far** to do something too much or in an extreme way, especially so that people get angry〔将某事〕做得太过分: *That little brat has gone too far this time!* 那个小顽童这次做得太过分了! | *The general view was that the President had gone too far in his support for the Contras.* 人们普遍认为总统在支持反政府武装人员一事上做得太过火了。

28 **not go far a)** if money does not go far you cannot buy very much with it〔钱〕买不了多少东西; 用不多久就会完: *A dollar doesn't go very far these days.* 如今一美元买不了多少东西。**b)** if a supply of something does not go far, it is not enough 不够用, 不足: *That pot of coffee won't go far if everyone wants some.* 如果每个人都要一点, 那壶咖啡就不够了。

29 **not be far off/out/wrong** *informal* used to say that something is almost correct【非正式】基本上正确的; 没有大错误: *The weather forecast wasn't far off, just look at the rain.* 天气预报基本上正确, 瞧这雨。

30 **in so far as/in as far as/insofar as** *formal* to the degree that something affects another thing or is connected with it【正式】到…的程度; 在…的范围内; 就…而论: *The Committee's recommendations, in so far as they affect deaf people, are set out in this document.* 这份文件阐明了委员会那些会影响到聋人的建议。

[1][1] **far²** *adj comparative* 比较级 **farther** /ˈfɑrðɚ; ˈfɑːðə/ *or* **further** /ˈfɝðɚ; ˈfɜːðə/ *superlative* 最高级 **farthest** /ˈfɑrðɪst; ˈfɑːðɪ̥st/ *or* **furthest** /ˈfɝðɪst; ˈfɜːðɪ̥st/ **1** a long way away 远的, 遥远的: *You can see my house from here; it isn't far.* 我的房子不远, 你从这里可以看到。| *In the far distance she could see the outlines of tall, city buildings.* 她能看到远处城市高楼的轮廓。**2 the far end/side etc** the end or side that is furthest from you 更远的一端/一边等: *She swam to the far side of the lake.* 她游向湖的另一边。**3 the far north/south etc** the part of a country or area that is furthest in the direction of north, south etc 边远的北部/南部等: *the great plains in the far west of the country* 该国边远西部的大平原 **4 the far left/right** people who have extreme LEFT WING or RIGHT WING political opinions 极左/右分子 **5 be a far cry from** to be very different from something else 与…大不相同的: *The current economic situation is a far cry from what was predicted at the election.* 目前的经济形势与选举时预计的大相径庭。

Far·a·day /ˈfærəde; ˈfærədeɪ/, **Mi·chael** /ˈmaɪkl; ˈmaɪkəl/ (1791-1867) a British scientist who discovered the relationship between electricity and MAGNETISM and produced the first DYNAMO (=a machine that changes some other form of power into electricity) 法拉第〔(1791-1867), 英国科学家。他发现了电磁感应现象, 并制造出首台发电机〕

far·a·way /ˈfɑrəˋwe; ˈfɑːrəweɪ/ *adj* **1** [only before noun 仅用于名词前] distant 遥远的: *She was lost and alone in a faraway place.* 她孤零零一个人在一个遥远的地方迷了路。| *faraway noises* 远处的喧嚣声 **2 a faraway look** an expression on your face which shows that you are not paying attention but thinking about something very different 心不在焉的神情; 若有所思的神情

farce /fɑrs; fɑːs/ *n* **1** [singular] an event or a situation that is badly organized or that does not happen in the way that it should 闹剧场面, 一团糟的场面: *Blacks were completely shut out of the political process. For them, the right to vote was a farce.* 黑人完全被拒绝于政治进程之外。对他们来说, 选举权是一场闹剧。**2** [C] a humorous play in which people are involved in silly situations 滑稽戏, 笑剧, 闹剧 **3** [U] the style of writing or acting that is concerned with this kind of play 笑剧体裁; 滑稽戏风格

far·ci·cal /ˈfɑrsɪkl; ˈfɑːsɪkəl/ *adj* extremely silly and badly organized 笑剧的, 闹剧性的, 滑稽的: *the farcical effect of period costumes made with polyester fabrics* 聚酯纤维面料的旧时服装所产生的滑稽效果 —**farcically** /-klɪ; -kli/ *adv*

fare¹ /fɛr; feə/ *n* **1** [C] the price you pay to travel by bus, train, plane etc〔公共汽车、火车、飞机等的〕票价: **bus/train/air fare** *Air fares have shot up by 20%.* 飞机票价已猛涨 20%。| **half-fare/full-fare** *Children under 4 travel half-fare.* 四岁以下儿童可半票旅行。—see 见 COST¹ (USAGE) **2 simple/wholesome/homely etc fare** *old-fashioned* good, healthy, simple food【过时】简单/有益健康/家常的食品 **3** [C] a passenger in a taxi 出租车乘客

fare² *v* **fare well/badly/better etc** to be successful, unsuccessful etc 成功/失败/更成功等: *Although Chicago has fared better than some cities, unemployment remains a problem.* 虽说芝加哥比其他一些城市情况好些, 但失业仍是个问题。| **how did sb fare?** *He wondered how Paul had fared during the war.* 他想知道保罗在战争期间生活得如何。

Far East, the /ˌ· ˈ·◂/ *n* the countries in the east of Asia, such as China, Japan etc 远东地区 —compare 比较 MIDDLE EAST, NEAR EAST —**Far Eastern** *adj*

fare·well /ˈfɛrˋwɛl; feəˈwel/ *n* **1 farewell party/drink** a party or drink that you have because someone is leaving soon 告别会/告别酒 **2** [C,U] *old-fashioned* an act of saying goodbye to someone【过时】告别: **bid farewell to** (=say goodbye to someone) 向…告别, 向…说再见 **3** *old-fashioned* used like 'goodbye' when leaving someone for a long time【过时】再见, 再会〔旧时道别用语〕

Farewell to Arms, A /ˌ· · ˈ·/ (1929) a NOVEL by Ernest Hemingway about the romantic relationship between a US man who is working as an AMBULANCE driver and an English nurse in Italy during World War I《永别了, 武器》, 又译《战地春梦》〔(1929), 欧内斯特·海明威创作的一部小说, 讲述一战期间一位美国救护车驾驶员与一位英国护士在意大利的浪漫故事〕

far-fetched /ˌ· ˈ·◂/ *adj* extremely unlikely to be true or to happen 牵强的; 不可信的; 靠不住的: *His explanation sounds pretty far-fetched to me.* 我觉得他的解释听起来很牵强。

far-flung /ˌ· ˈ·◂/ *adj* **1** very distant 遥远的: *some far-flung corner of Ontario* 安大略省的某个偏远角落 **2** spread out over a very large area 分布广的; 散至远处的: *far-flung trading posts* 分布广的贸易站

Far from the Mad·ding Crowd /ˌfɑr frəm ðə ˌmædɪŋ ˋkraʊd; ˌfɑː frəm ðə ˌmædɪŋ ˈkraʊd/ (1874) a NOVEL by Thomas Hardy about people living in a country village in the west of England during Victorian times. The title of the book, which Hardy took from a famous poem by Thomas Gray, is often used as a phrase to mean the peacefulness and quietness of the country.《远离尘嚣》〔(1874), 托马斯·哈代创作的一部小说, 讲述维多利亚时代英格兰西部乡村居民的一个故事。书名引自托马斯·格雷的一首名诗, 常用来指乡村的平和与宁静〕

far gone /ˌ· ˈ·/ *adj* [not before noun 不用于名词前] *informal* very ill, drunk, crazy etc【非正式】〔生病、醉酒、疯狂等〕(程度)严重的: *She's pretty far gone, can you drive her home?* 她醉得不行了, 你能开车送她回家吗?

farm¹ /fɑrm; fɑːm/ *n* [C] **1** an area of land, used for growing crops or keeping animals 农场; 养殖场: **live/work on a farm** *Joe had worked on the farm all his life.* 乔一辈子都在农场干活。| **chicken/sheep/pig etc farm** *He runs a pig farm in Lincolnshire.* 他在林肯郡经营一个养猪场。**2** the main house on a farm where the farmer lives 农舍 —see also 另见 FACTORY FARM, FISH FARM, FUNNY FARM [3][2]

farm² *v* [I,T] to use land for growing crops, keeping animals etc 经营农场; 种植; 养殖: *The family has farmed there for generations.* 这一家世代都在那儿经营农场。

farm sth ↔ **out** *phr v* [T] to send work to other people instead of doing it yourself 将〔工作〕包出去: *farming out work to freelancers* 把工作外包给自由职业者

farm belt /ˈ· ·/ *n* [C] an area where there are many farms〔有许多农场的〕农场带, 农场区

farm·er /ˈfɑrmɚ; ˈfɑːmə/ *n* [C] someone who owns or manages a farm 农场主; 养殖场主 [3][2]

Farmer, Fan·nie /ˈfænɪ; ˈfæni/ (1857-1915) a US cook who wrote a COOKERY book used by many people in the US 法默〔(1857-1915), 美国厨师, 曾写过一本畅销美国的烹饪书籍〕

farm·hand /ˈfɑrmhænd; ˈfɑːmhænd/ *n* [C] someone who works on a farm 农场工人

farm·house /ˈfɑrmˌhaʊs; ˈfɑːmhaʊs/ *n* [C] the main house on a farm, where the farmer lives 农舍〔指农场主住的主要住房〕

farm·ing /ˈfɑrmɪŋ; ˈfɑːmɪŋ/ *n* [U] the practice or business of growing crops or keeping animals on a farm 农场业; 耕种; 养殖(业); 畜牧(业)

farm·land /ˈfɑrmˌlænd; ˈfɑːmlænd/ *n* [U] land used for farming 农田, 耕地; 牧地

farm·stead /ˈfɑrmˌstɛd; ˈfɑːmsted/ *n* [C] *especially AmE* a farmhouse and the buildings around it【尤美】农场的主要住房和周围建筑物, 农庄

farm·yard /ˈfɑrmˌjɑrd; ˈfɑːmjɑːd/ *n* [C] an area surrounded by farm buildings〔四周是农场建筑物的〕农家宅院

Farn·bo·rough Air Show, the /ˌfɑrnbrə ˋɛr ˌʃo; ˌfɑːnbərə ˈeə ˌʃəʊ/ a large international event, held every two years at Farnborough in the south of England, where different types of aircraft are shown and planes perform AEROBATICS to entertain the public 法恩伯勒航空展览会〔每两年一次在英格兰

南部法恩伯勒举行的大型国际展览。会上展示不同类型的飞机，还有飞机特技表演以娱乐公众〕

Faroe Islands, the also 又作 **the Faroes** —see 见 FAEROE ISLANDS

far-off /ˌ·ˈ·◂/ *adj* **1** a long way from where you are 遥远的: *a far-off country* 遥远的国家 **2** a long time ago 很久以前的: *in those far-off days when we were young* 在很久以前我们尚年轻的岁月里

far-out /ˌ·ˈ·◂/ *adj* **1** very strange or unusual 奇怪的, 异乎寻常的: *far-out ideas* 古怪的想法 **2** *old-fashioned* extremely good【过时】极好的

Far·ra·khan /ˌfærəˋkɑn; ˌfærəˈkæn/, **Louis** (1933-) the leader of the Nation of Islam, a black rights organization, since the 1970s. He was born in New York City, and his real name is Louis Eugene Walcott. 法拉汗〔(1933-) 黑人权利组织"伊斯兰国"的领袖, 20世纪70年代上任至今。他出生在纽约市, 原名路易斯·尤金·沃尔科特〕

far-reach·ing /ˌ·ˈ··◂/ *adj* having a great influence or effect〔影响〕深远的: *far-reaching reforms* 影响深远的改革

far·ri·er /ˋfærɪɚ; ˈfæriə/ *n* [C] someone who makes shoes (SHOE[1] (2)) for horses' feet 锻制马蹄铁的铁匠, 蹄铁工

Far·si /ˋfɑrzɪ; ˈfɑːzi/ *n* [U] the language of Iran; PERSIAN 现代伊朗语; 现代波斯语; 法尔斯语

Far Side, The /ˈ· ·, ·/ *trademark* a CARTOON STRIP (=a set of drawings that tell a story in a newspaper) by the US artist Gary Larson, showing strange, silly situations, especially ones involving animals that behave like human beings【商标】《在那边》〔美国艺术家加里·拉森创作的连环漫画, 展现古怪、可笑的情景, 尤其是动物拟人的情景〕

far-sight·ed /ˌ·ˈ··◂/ *adj* **1** *especially AmE* able to realize what will happen in the future and make wise decisions【尤美】有远见的, 有先见之明的: *a far-sighted economic policy* 卓有远见的经济政策 **2** *especially AmE* able to see or read things clearly only when they are far away from you; LONGSIGHTED【尤美】远视的 —opposite 反义词 SHORT-SIGHTED —**farsightedly** *adv* —**farsightedness** *n* [U]

fart[1] /fɑrt; fɑːt/ *v* [I] *taboo* to make air come out of your BOWELS (1)【讳】放屁

fart about/around *phr v* [I] *informal* to waste time not doing very much【非正式】浪费时间; 闲荡

fart[2] *n* **1** *taboo* an act of making air come out of your BOWELS (1)【讳】放屁 **2** *slang* a stupid and uninteresting person【俚】愚蠢无聊的人: *a boring old fart* 令人讨厌的无聊老家伙

far·ther[1] /ˋfɑrðɚ; ˈfɑːðə/ *adv* **1** a greater distance than before or than something else; further 更远地: *We'd better not go any farther today.* 今天我们最好不要再往前走了。| **farther away/apart etc** *The boats were drifting farther and farther apart.* 那些小船漂得越来越远。| *He heard a voice farther down the track.* 他听见小道的远处有人说话。| **farther afield** (=at or to a greater distance away) 更远处 | **farther south/north etc** *I think the state boundary is farther south than here.* 我想州界是在比这里更南的地方。**2** if you do something farther, you do it more or to a greater degree; further 在更大程度上, 更进一步: *We'd better investigate farther.* 我们最好作更进一步的调查。| **take sth farther** (=do more about it) 更进一步推进某事 *I don't think we should take this subject any farther or we'll be wasting time.* 我认为我们不应该再谈这个问题, 否则我们是在浪费时间。

farther[2] *adj* [only before noun 仅用于名词前] more distant 更远的: *A table was set at the farther end of the kitchen.* 厨房的那一头放着一张桌子。

USAGE NOTE 用法说明: FARTHER

WORD CHOICE 词语辨析: **farther, farthest, further, furthest**

When you are talking or writing about real places and distances you can use either **farther, farthest** or **further, furthest** (which are the most usual words in spoken English). 在谈到实际地点和距离时, 可以用 farther, farthest, 也可以用 further, furthest〔这些都是英语口语中最常用的单词〕: *farther/further down the road* 沿这条路继续走下去 | *What's the farthest/furthest distance you've ever run?* 你最远跑过多少距离?

Further (but not 但不用 **farther**) is also used with the meaning 'more', 'extra', 'additional' etc. further也表示"更多的"、"额外的"、"附加的"等意思(但farther不能): *a college of further education* 继续教育[进修]学院 | *For further information write to the above address.* 欲知详情, 请致函上述地址询问。

far·thest[1] /ˋfɑrðɪst; ˈfɑːðɪ̈st/ *adv* at or to the greatest distance away 最远: *Who ran farthest?* 谁跑得最远? | **farthest away/apart etc** *She lived farthest away from school of all of us.* 我们所有人里, 她住得离学校最远。

farthest[2] *adj* the most distant 最远的: *the farthest corners of the globe* 地球最偏远的角落

far·thing /ˋfɑrðɪŋ; ˈfɑːðɪŋ/ *n* [C] an old British coin that was worth one quarter of a PENNY 法寻〔英国旧时值1/4便士的硬币〕

fa·scia /ˋfeʃə; ˈfeɪʃə/ *n* [C] a long board above a shop with the shop's name on it〔挂在店门上的〕招牌; 店门匾额

fas·ci·nate /ˋfæsnˌet; ˈfæsɪ̈neɪt/ *v* [T not in progressive 不用进行式] if something fascinates you, it makes you think about it a lot, want to watch it a lot etc 迷住, 吸引; 使…着迷: *The idea of travelling through time fascinates me.* 穿越时间旅行的主意令我着迷。| **what fascinates sb is** *What fascinates me most about him is his accent. Where does it come from?* 他最使我感兴趣的是他的口音。这口音是哪的?

fas·ci·nat·ed /ˋfæsnˌetɪd; ˈfæsɪ̈neɪtɪ̈d/ *adj* [not before noun 不用于名词前] extremely interested by something or someone 被迷住的, 被吸引住的; 极感兴趣的: **[+by]** *I was fascinated by her voice.* 我被她的嗓音迷住了。| **fascinated to discover/hear/learn etc** *Listeners will be fascinated to hear that Oprah has lost more than 50lbs.* 听到奥普拉的体重减少了50多磅, 听众会大感兴趣的。

fas·ci·nat·ing /ˋfæsnˌetɪŋ; ˈfæsɪ̈neɪtɪŋ/ *adj* extremely interesting 有极大吸引力的, 迷人的: *a fascinating book* 引人入胜的书 | **find sb/sth fascinating** *I found his tale of a wild and lawless life fascinating.* 我觉得他说的那种放荡不羁、无法无天的生活很吸引人。—**fascinatingly** *adv*

fas·ci·na·tion /ˌfæsnˋeʃən; ˌfæsɪ̈ˈneɪʃən/ *n* **1** [singular, U] the state of being very interested in something, so that you want to look at it, learn about it etc 着迷, 迷恋: *The children looked on in fascination.* 孩子们入迷地观看着。| **have a fascination for/with** (=be very interested in something) 对…十分感兴趣, 酷爱 *Ken always had a fascination for stories about undersea exploration.* 肯一直特别喜欢有关海底探险的故事。**2** [C,U] something that interests you very much, or the quality of being very interesting 令人着迷的事物; 吸引力: *the fascinations of the busy street* 繁忙街道上的那些迷人事物 | **hold/have a fascination for sb** (=interest someone very much) 对某人很有吸引力 *India will always hold a great fascination for me.* 印度对我总会有非常大的吸引力。

fas·cis·m /ˋfæʃˌɪzəm; ˈfæʃɪzəm/ *n* [U] a RIGHT WING political system in which people's lives are completely controlled by the state and no political opposition is allowed, used in Germany and Italy in the 1930s and 40s 法西斯主义〔盛行于20世纪30、40年代的德国和意大利〕

fas·cist /ˋfæʃɪst; ˈfæʃɪ̈st/ *n* [C] **1** someone who supports fascism 法西斯主义支持者, 法西斯分子: *The fascists came to power in 1933.* 法西斯分子于1933年上台。**2** *informal* someone who is cruel and unfair and does not like people to argue with them【非正式】暴虐专横的人: *My last boss was a real fascist.* 我的上一个老板是个十足的法西斯。**3** *informal* someone who has extreme RIGHT WING opinions【非正式】极右分子: *They're just a bunch of fascists.* 他们只是一伙极右分子。—**fascist** *adj*: *fascist dictatorship* 法西斯专政

-fashion /fæʃən; fæʃən/ *suffix* [in adverbs 构成副词] like something, or in the way that a particular group of people does something 像…样子, 以…方式: *They ate Indian-fashion, using their fingers.* 他们像印度人那样用手指抓东西吃。

fash·ion[1] /ˋfæʃən; ˈfæʃən/ *n* **1** [singular, U] the popular style of clothes, hair, behaviour etc at a particular time, that is likely to change〔衣服、头发等的〕流行式样;〔行为等的〕时髦; 时尚: **a/the fashion for** *a fashion for alternative therapies* 各种非传统疗法的盛行 | **be the fashion** *Eastern religions such as Buddhism used to be the fashion in the 60s.* 像佛教这一类的东方宗教曾在60年代很流行。| **be in fashion** *Hats are in fashion again this year.* 今年又流行戴帽子了。| **be out of fashion/go out of fashion** (=not be popular) 不流行 *Maxiskirts went out of fashion years ago.* 超长裙几年前就不流行了。| **come into fashion** *His ideas are coming back into fashion these days.* 他的观点近来又流行起来。| **be all the fashion** (=be very popular) 很流行, 风行一时 *Psychoanalysis now seems to be all the fashion.* 精神分析疗法现在似乎很流行。| **fashion conscious** (=always wanting to wear the newest fashions) 热衷于赶时髦 *Teenage girls are very fashion conscious.* 少女们都十分热衷于赶时髦。**2** [C] a style of clothes, hair etc that is popular at a particular time 时装; 时尚: *men's fashions* 男士时装 | *This is a very popular fashion at the moment.* 这是目前十分流行的时装样式。| *High*

heels are this year's fashion. 今年时兴高跟鞋。| **the latest fashion** *They'll have all the latest fashions.* 他们将拥有所有最新的时装样式。| **a fashion for doing sth/the fashion of doing sth** *Camilla started the fashion of wearing odd socks.* 穿不成对短袜的时尚是卡米拉首先倡导起来的。**3** [U] the business or study of making and selling clothes, shoes etc in new and changing styles 时装业; 时装研究: *fashion magazines* 时装杂志 | **the fashion industry** *When I leave college I want to work in the fashion industry.* 离开大学后我想在时装业工作。**4 in a... fashion** in a particular way 以…方式: *Leave the building in an orderly fashion.* 要有秩序地走出大楼去。**5 after a fashion** if you do something after a fashion, you can do it, but not very well 不很好, 马马虎虎, 勉强凑合: *"Can you speak Russian?" "After a fashion."* "你会说俄语吗?" "勉强会一点。" **6 after the fashion of** in a style that is typical of a particular person 像〔某人〕的风格, 模仿: *Her early work is very much after the fashion of Picasso and Braque.* 她的早期作品风格很像毕加索和布拉克的。**7 like it's going out of fashion** *informal* if you eat, drink, or use something like it's going out of fashion, you eat, drink, or use a lot of it【非正式】大量地吃[喝, 用]: *Danny's been spending money like it's going out of fashion.* 丹尼在胡乱地花钱。**8 fashion victim** *BrE informal* someone who always wears or does what is fashionable, even if it does not look good on them【英, 非正式】盲目赶时髦的人; 穿戴只图时髦而不管是否合适的人 —see also 另见 **parrot fashion** (PARROT[1] (2))

fashion² *v* [T] **1** to shape or make something, using your hands or only a few tools〔用手或几件工具〕制作, 把…做成〔…形状〕: **fashion sth from sth** *He fashioned a box from a few old pieces of wood.* 他用几块旧木板做成一个箱子。**2** [usually passive 一般用被动态] to influence and form someone's ideas and opinions 影响; 形成, 塑造: *Our attitudes to politics are fashioned by the media.* 我们对政治的态度是在传媒影响下形成的。

fash·ion·a·ble /ˈfæʃənəbl; ˈfæʃənəbəl/ *adj* **1** popular, especially for a short period of time〔尤指短时期内〕时髦的, 流行的: *Pastel shades are very fashionable at the moment.* 柔和的色彩是目前最流行的。**2** popular with, or used by, rich people 受富人欢迎的, 上流人用的, 高级人士喜欢的: *She desperately wants to move to a more fashionable address.* 她不顾一切地想搬到更受上流社会欢迎的地址。**3** someone who is fashionable wears good clothes, goes to expensive restaurants etc 上流社会的; 时髦豪华的 —opposite 反义词 UNFASHIONABLE —**fashionably** *adv*: *fashionably dressed* 穿着时髦

fashion house /ˈ‥ ˌ/ *n* [C] a company that produces new and expensive styles of clothes 时装公司

fashion plate /ˈ‥ ˌ/ *n* [C] *AmE* someone who likes to wear very fashionable clothes【美】穿着很时髦的人

fashion show /ˈ‥ ˌ/ *n* [C] an event at which new styles of clothes are shown to the public 时装表演

[2] [2] **fast¹** /fæst; fɑːst/ *adj*

1 ►MOVING QUICKLY 快速移动的◄ a) moving or travelling quickly 快的, 快速的: *Burell is the fastest runner in the world.* 伯雷尔是世界上跑得最快的人。| *The first pitch was fast and hard.* 第一个投球又快又猛。**b)** able to travel or move very quickly 能非常快移动[行走]的; (动作) 敏捷的: *a fast car* 速度很快的车子 | *The horse was fast but not a good jumper.* 这匹马跑得很快, 但跳跃不行。

2 ►IN A SHORT TIME 在短时间内◄ a) doing something or happening in a short time 做得很快的; 发生得很迅速的: *a fast journey* 行程紧凑的旅行 | *IBM is shedding labour at an alarmingly fast rate.* IBM 正以令人忧虑的高速裁员。**b)** able to do something in a short time 能做得很快的: *Are you a fast reader?* 你看书很快吗? **c)** happening without delay 没有拖延的, 迅速的: *This time the response was much faster.* 这次反应迅速多了。

3 ►CLOCK 钟◄ [not before noun 不用于名词前] a clock that is fast shows a later time than the real time 偏快的, 走得快的: **five minutes/an hour etc fast** *That can't be the time – my watch must be fast.* 不可能是这个时间 —— 我的表一定是快了。

4 pull a fast one *informal* to deceive someone by using a clever trick【非正式】〔以巧妙手段〕欺骗, 诈骗: *Make sure he doesn't try and pull a fast one.* 弄清楚他不是想要诡计诈骗。

5 fast road a road on which vehicles can travel very quickly 快车道 —see also 另见 FAST LANE

6 fast film/lens a film or LENS (2) that can be used when there is little light, or when photographing something that is moving very quickly 快速感光胶卷 / 快镜头

7 ►COLOUR 颜色◄ a colour that is fast will not change when clothes are washed 不退色的 —see also 另见 COLOURFAST

8 ►SPORTS 体育运动◄ a fast surface is one on which a ball moves very quickly〔球在某一表面上滚动时〕速度快的

9 make sth fast an expression meaning to tie something firmly, used especially on ships 把某物拴牢: *He made the rope fast to the metal ring.* 他把绳子牢牢地拴在金属环上。

10 fast and furious done very quickly with a lot of effort and energy, or happening very quickly with a lot of sudden changes 迅速而剧烈的, 迅速多变的: *Political developments in South Africa have been fast and furious.* 南非的政治发展迅速且多变。

11 He's/she's etc a fast worker *informal* used to say that someone can get what they want very quickly, especially in starting a sexual relationship with another person【非正式】能很快弄到自己想要之物的人;〔尤指在性关系方面〕进展神速的人

12 fast talker someone who talks quickly and easily but is often not honest or sincere 巧舌如簧的人, 油腔滑调的人: *Nixon quickly gained a reputation as a fast talker.* 尼克松很快得到了一个口若悬河但不够真诚的名声。

13 the fast set *old-fashioned* a group of fashionable young people who spend their time doing exciting things【过时】〔进行富有刺激的各种活动以消磨时光的〕时髦[浪荡]的年轻人

14 fast friends *literary* two people who are very friendly for a long time【文】挚友

15 ►WOMAN 女子◄ *old-fashioned* becoming involved quickly in sexual relationships with men【过时】〔女子在与男子的性关系上〕放荡的 —see also 另见 FAST FOOD, FAST FORWARD, FAST LANE, **make a fast buck** (BUCK[1] (1))

fast² *adv* [2] [3]

1 ►QUICKLY 快速地◄ moving quickly〔移动〕快: *Slow down – you're going too fast.* 减速 —— 你开得太快了。| *We ran back to the house as fast as we could.* 我们拼命跑回房子。| **as fast as his legs could carry him** (=running as quickly as he could) 尽快地跑

2 ►IN A SHORT TIME 在短时间内◄ a) in a short time 迅速地: *Young kids grow up fast these days.* 现在的小孩子长得快。| **fast becoming/disappearing/developing etc** *Britain is fast becoming a sweat-shop economy based on cheap labour.* 英国的经济正迅速成为一种建立在廉价劳动力之上的血汗工厂经济。**b)** soon and without delay 很快, 立即: *The survivors needed help fast.* 幸存者需要马上得到帮助。| *He wanted to know how fast we could get it done.* 他想知道我们多快能完成这件事。

3 fast asleep sleeping very deeply 熟睡的, 酣睡的: *Shh! The baby's fast asleep!* 嘘! 宝宝睡得正香!

4 hold on fast to hold onto something very tightly 紧紧抓住: *She held on fast as they went round the bend.* 在他们绕过弯道处时, 她抓得很紧。

5 stick fast/be stuck fast to become or be firmly fixed and unable to move 紧紧夹住; 紧紧黏住; 被紧紧夹住, 被紧紧黏住: *My leg was stuck fast in the mud.* 我的脚牢牢地陷在泥里。

6 hold fast to to continue to believe in or support an idea, principle etc 坚持〔主张、原则等〕: *Bonhoeffer held fast to his beliefs till the very end.* 邦霍弗坚持自己的信念直到最后。

7 be getting/be going nowhere fast *informal* to not succeed in making progress or achieving something【非正式】失败; 不成功; 无成就: *I kept asking her the same question, but I was getting nowhere fast.* 我一直在问她同一个问题, 但总是没有结果。

8 not so fast *spoken*【口】**a)** used to tell someone to do something more slowly or carefully 不要那么快, 慢点: *Not so fast! You don't want to damage the engine.* 不要开得那么快! 别把发动机弄坏了。**b)** used to say that something has not yet happened or is not yet true 不会那么快吧: *"Henry will be manager soon." "Not so fast – he's only just been made a team leader."* "亨利很快就要当经理了。" "不会那么快吧 —— 他才刚当上组长。"

9 fast by *literary* very close to something【文】紧挨着, 贴近: *fast by the river* 紧挨着河

10 play fast and loose with *old-fashioned* to treat a sexual partner in a careless way【过时】玩弄〔异性性伙伴〕: *He felt that Lyn had played fast and loose with his emotions.* 他觉得琳恩玩弄了他的感情。—see also 另见 **stand fast** (STAND[1] (17)), **thick and fast** (THICK[2] (2))

fast³ *v* [I] to eat little or no food for a period of time, especially for religious reasons〔尤因宗教原因而〕禁食, 斋戒: *Muslims fast during Ramadan.* 穆斯林在斋月里禁食。

fast⁴ *n* [C] a period during which someone does not eat for religious reasons 禁食期, 斋戒期: **break a fast** (=eat or drink something to end your fast) 开斋

fast·ball /ˈfæstˌbɔl; ˈfɑːstbɔːl/ *n* [C] a ball that is thrown very quickly towards the BATTER[2] (3) in a game of BASEBALL〔棒球赛中投向击球手的〕快球

fast day /ˈ‥ ˌ/ *n* [C] a day when you do not eat any food, especially for religious reasons〔尤因宗教原因而不吃东西的〕禁食日, 斋戒日

F

fas·ten /ˈfæsn̩; ˈfɑːsən/ *v*

1 ►CLOTHES/BAG ETC 衣服/袋子等◄ also 又作 **fasten up a)** [T] to join together the two sides of a coat, shirt, bag etc so that it is closed 扣牢; 系牢, 缚紧; 把拉链拉好: *"I'm going now," she said, fastening her coat.* "现在我要走了。"她一边说, 一边扣上大衣。| *Fasten your seatbelt!* 系好你的安全带! —opposite 反义词 UNFASTEN **b)** [I] to become joined together with buttons, hooks etc 扣牢; 钩住; 系牢; 钉牢: *I was so fat that my skirt wouldn't fasten.* 我胖得连裙子都扣不上了。

2 ►WINDOW/GATE ETC 窗子/大门等◄ **a)** [T] to firmly close a window, gate etc so that it will not open 把〔窗、门等〕关住: *Make sure all the windows are securely fastened before you leave.* 离开前要确保所有的窗子都牢牢地关上。—opposite 反义词 UNFASTEN **b)** [I] to become firmly closed 扣牢, 关紧: *This door won't fasten.* 这门闩不上。

3 ►FIX STH TO STH 将某物固定在某物上◄ [T] to fix something firmly to another object or surface, especially using tape, a metal pin etc 〔尤指用胶带、别针等〕贴; 固定; 钉: **fasten sth to sth** *Someone had fastened a notice to my door.* 有人将一张通知贴在我的门上。| *Chains were fastened round his ankles.* 铁链拴在他的脚踝上。

4 fasten your teeth/legs/arms etc to hold something firmly with your teeth, legs, arms, etc 用你的牙齿咬住/用你的腿夹住/用你的双臂抱住等: [**+around**] *She fastened her arms around his neck.* 她双臂紧紧抱住他的脖子。| [**+onto/into**] *The snake had fastened its jaws onto his leg.* 蛇咬住他的腿。

5 fasten your eyes on to look at someone or something for a long time 注视着, 盯着: *He rose, his eyes still fastened on the piece of paper.* 他站起来, 眼睛仍紧盯着那张纸。

6 fasten your attention on to think a lot about one particular thing 集中注意力于; 认真地考虑

7 fasten blame on to blame someone or something, often unfairly 责怪, 指责, 怪罪〔常为不公正地〕

fasten on/upon sth *phr v* [T] to decide quickly and eagerly that an idea is the best one 迅速决定〔采用某一主意或方法〕: *American companies were quick to fasten on to Japanese business methods.* 美国各公司迅速决定采用日本的经营方式。

fasten onto sb *phr v* [T] to follow someone and stay with them, especially when they do not want you to 缠住, 纠缠

fasteners 扣紧物, 扣件

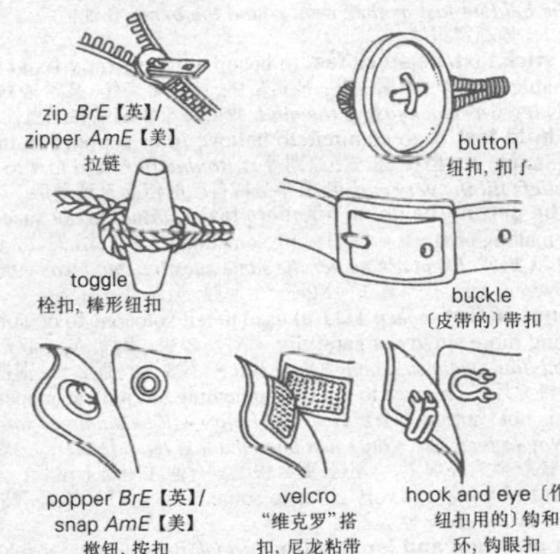

fas·ten·er /ˈfæsnə; ˈfɑːsənə/ *n* [C] *BrE* something such as a button, ZIP[1] (1) etc that you use to join something together, especially a piece of clothing【英】扣件; 扣紧物〈如纽扣、拉链等〉

fas·ten·ing /ˈfæsnɪŋ; ˈfɑːsənɪŋ/ *n* [C] something that you use to keep a door, window etc firmly shut〔门、窗等的〕紧固件, 扣件, 扣拴物, 插销

fast food /ˌ· ˈ·/ *n* [U] food such as HAMBURGERs which is prepared quickly in a restaurant 快餐食品〈如汉堡包〉

fast for·ward /ˌ· ˈ··/ *n* [U] a process in which a TAPE or VIDEO is wound forward quickly without being played〔录音带或录像带的〕快进 —**fast-forward** *v* [I,T]

fas·tid·i·ous /fæsˈtɪdɪəs; fæˈstɪdiəs/ *adj* very careful about small details in your appearance, work etc 挑剔的, 过分讲究的: *dressed with fastidious care* 穿戴得过分讲究 —compare 比较 FUSSY (1) —**fastidiously** *adv* —**fastidiousness** *n* [U]

fast lane /ˈ· ·/ *n* **1** *BrE* the part of a big road that is used by fast vehicles【英】快车道, 快线 —see picture on page A3 参见 A3 页图 **2 life in the fast lane** *informal* an exciting way of living that involves dangerous and expensive activities【非正式】刺激的生活(方式)〔涉及危险而代价昂贵的活动〕

fast·ness /ˈfæstnɪs; ˈfɑːstnəs/ *n* [C] *literary* a safe place that is difficult to reach【文】堡垒, 要塞: *mountain fastnesses* 山间要塞, 山寨

Fast·net, the /ˈfæstnɛt; ˈfɑːstnet/ a famous YACHTING race held every two years from the south of England up to the Fastnet Rock near Ireland 法斯耐特帆船赛〔每两年举行一次的著名帆船比赛。赛程从英格兰南部至爱尔兰附近的法斯耐特礁〕

fast-track /ˈ· ·/ *adj* [only before noun 仅用于名词前] someone with a fast-track job will quickly become more important in an organisation〔工作上〕提升快的, 快速成功的, 青云直上的

 2 3

fat[1] /fæt; fæt/ *adj*

1 ►FLESH 人身上的肉◄ having a lot of flesh on your body, especially too much flesh 肥胖的: *You'll get fat if you eat all that chocolate.* 如果你把那些巧克力都吃了, 你会变胖的。| *That big fat opera singer – what's his name?* 那位大胖子歌剧演员 —— 他叫什么名字? —opposite 反义词 THIN[1] (2)

2 ►THICK OR WIDE 厚或宽◄ thick or wide 厚的; 宽的: *Dobbs was smoking a fat cigar.* 多布斯正抽着一根粗大的雪茄。| *a big fat book* 又大又厚的书

3 ►MONEY 钱◄ [only before noun 仅用于名词前] *informal* containing or worth a large amount of money【非正式】巨额的: *a fat cheque* 巨额支票 | *a job in the City with a nice fat salary* 伦敦商业区里的一份工资优厚的工作

4 fat chance *informal* used to say that something is very unlikely to happen【非正式】可能性极小: [**+of**] *What, John get a job? Fat chance of that!* 什么, 约翰找到了工作? 那是不可能的!

5 a fat lot of good/use *spoken* not at all useful or helpful【口】一点用处也没有的, 全然没有帮助的: *"I don't know much about cars." "Well you're a fat lot of use aren't you?"* "我对汽车不太了解。" "你真没用, 不是吗?"

6 fat cat *informal* someone who has too much money【非正式】阔佬, 富翁, 大亨

7 in fat city *AmE informal* having plenty of money【美, 非正式】很有钱的: *We'll be in fat city if this deal goes through.* 如果这笔生意做成功, 我们就发财了。

8 grow fat on sth to become rich because of something 靠某物致富, 因某事发财: *The finance men had grown fat on managing other people's money.* 金融从业人士靠管理别人的钱发财致富。—**fatness** *n* [U]

USAGE NOTE 用法说明: FAT

WORD CHOICE 词语辨析: **fat, overweight, large, heavy, plump, chubby, stout, tubby, obese**

If you want to be polite about someone, do not say that they are **fat**. **(A little) overweight** or just **large** is a more polite way of saying the same thing. In American English, you can also say that someone is **heavy** when you want to be polite. 如果你想对别人表示有礼貌, 就不能说他们 fat (肥胖的)。用 (a little) overweight (有点超重) 或 large 来表达同样的意思较为礼貌。在美国英语中, 你想表示有礼貌时, 还可以说某人 heavy。

Plump is most often used of women and children and means slightly (and pleasantly) fat. plump 经常用来形容妇女和儿童, 意思为丰满的、胖嘟嘟的。

Chubby is most often used of babies and children and also means pleasantly fat and healthy-looking. When you are describing adults, **stout** means slightly fat and heavy and **tubby** means short and fat, especially around the stomach. chubby 经常用来指婴儿和儿童, 意思也是胖得可爱, 且看上去很健康。描述成人时, stout 表示稍胖而且略显得粗壮; tubby 表示矮胖, 尤指大腹便便。

If someone is extremely fat and unhealthy they are **obese**. **Obese** is also the word used by doctors. 如果某人特别胖而且不健康, 那就是 obese。医生也使用 obese 这个词。

CULTURAL NOTE 文化注释

In the US and the UK people who are fat are generally thought to be unattractive, and many people, especially women, often go on DIETs in order to try to lose weight. Being fat is also seen as a health problem. Some people believe they experience DISCRIMINATION (=unfair treatment,

especially at work) because they are fat. 英美人常认为人一发福就魅力不再，许多人，尤其是女人，常节食以减轻体重。肥胖也被看做是一种健康问题。一些人认为他们因肥胖遭到歧视。— see also Cultural Notes at THIN, DIET, OBESE 另见 THIN, DIET, OBESE 文化注释

fat[2] *n*
1 ►PERSON OR ANIMAL 人或动物◄ [U] a substance that is stored under the skin of people and animals, and helps to keep them warm〔人和动物皮下的〕脂肪；肥肉：*Rolls of fat bulged over his collar.* 他的衣领上鼓出了一圈圈的胖肉来。| *I didn't like the meat – there was too much fat on it.* 我不喜欢那肉——上面肥肉太多了。
2 ►IN FOOD 食物中◄ [C,U] an oily substance contained in certain foods〔某些食物中所含的〕油(脂)：*Try to reduce the amount of fat in your diet.* 要减少饮食中的油脂量。
3 ►FOR COOKING 用于烹调◄ [C,U] an oily substance taken from animals or plants and used in cooking 食用油；烹调用油：*Skim off all the fat, then add the vegetables.* 撇去所有的油，然后加进蔬菜。
4 the fat is in the fire used to say that there will be trouble because of something that has happened 闯了祸；将有麻烦
5 live off the fat of the land to get enough money to live comfortably without doing much work 过着养尊处优的生活
6 run to fat to start to become fat, especially because you are getting older or do not do much exercise〔尤因上年纪或不常运动而〕开始发胖 —see also 另见 **chew the fat** (CHEW[1] (4)), PUPPY FAT

fa·tal /ˈfetl̩; ˈfeɪtl/ *adj* **1** resulting in someone's death 致命的：*Meningitis is a serious illness, fatal in some cases.* 脑膜炎是一种严重疾病，在有些情况下是致命的。| **fatal accident/illness/injury etc** *a fatal climbing accident* 致命的攀登事故 | **prove fatal** (=be fatal) 是致命的 *If it is not treated correctly, the condition can prove fatal.* 如果处理得不正确，这情况可能会是致命的。**2** having a very bad effect, especially making someone fail or stop what they are doing 灾难性的，毁灭性的：**it is fatal to do sth** *It's always fatal to stay up late before an exam.* 考试前熬夜向来很有害。| **fatal mistake/error** *Graf made a fatal mistake halfway through the match.* 格拉夫在比赛中途犯了个致命的错误。| **fatal blow** *a fatal blow to the communist system in Eastern Europe* 对东欧共产主义制度的致命打击 | **fatal flaw** (=a serious weakness in someone or something) 严重缺陷 *There was one fatal flaw in his argument.* 他的论据有一个致命的漏洞。

fa·tal·is·m /ˈfetl̩ˌɪzəm; ˈfeɪtlɪzəm/ *n* [U] the belief that there is nothing you can do to prevent events from happening 宿命论 —**fatalist** *n* [C]

fa·tal·is·tic /ˌfetl̩ˈɪstɪk; ˌfeɪtlˈɪstɪk◄/ *adj* believing that there is nothing you can do to prevent events from happening 宿命论的：*a fatalistic attitude towards death* 对死亡听天由命的态度 —**fatalistically** /-klɪ; -kli/ *adv*

fa·tal·i·ty /feˈtæləti; fəˈtæləti/ *n* **1** [C] a death in an accident or a violent attack〔事故、暴力袭击中的〕死亡；死亡者，死亡人数：*a 50% increase in the number of traffic fatalities* 交通事故死亡人数 50% 的增长率 **2** [U] the fact that a disease is certain to cause death〔疾病的〕致命性：*New drugs have reduced the fatality of the disease.* 新药减少了这种疾病的致命性。**3** [U] the feeling that you cannot control what happens to you 不能控制自己命运的感觉；无可奈何的感觉：*Gera looked on her future with a certain degree of fatality.* 杰拉对自己的未来在某种程度上持一种无可奈何的态度。

fa·tal·ly /ˈfetl̩ɪ; ˈfeɪtəli/ *adv* **1** in a way that causes death 致命地：**fatally injured/wounded/stabbed etc** *Two officers were fatally injured in the explosion.* 两名军官在爆炸中受了致命伤。**2** in a way that will make something fail or be unable to continue 灾难性地，不幸地：**fatally flawed/weakened etc** *Bolton's idea was fatally flawed.* 博尔顿的想法存在致命的漏洞。

fate /fet; feɪt/ *n* **1** [C] the things that will happen to someone, especially unpleasant events〔尤指不好的〕命运，结局：*I wouldn't wish such a fate on my worst enemy.* 就算是我最坏的敌人，我也不希望他遇上这样可怕的结局。| **sb's fate/the fate of sb** *No one knows what the fate of the hostages will be.* 没有人知道这些人质的命运将会如何。| **seal/decide sb's fate** (=make it certain that something unpleasant will happen to someone) 决定某人的命运 *By then our fate had been sealed and we were doomed never to return home.* 到那时我们的命运已经成了定局，我们注定永远回不了家。| **leave sb to their fate** (=leave someone when something terrible could happen to them) 让某人听从命运的摆布 *He sailed away from the island, leaving the other men to their fate.* 他乘船离开了这个岛，留下其他人听从命运的摆布。| **suffer a fate** *The rest of Europe was to suffer the same fate.* 欧洲的其他地方将遭受相同的命运。**2** [U] a power that is believed to control what happens in people's lives 天命，命运，运数：*Fate plays cruel tricks sometimes.* 命运有时会残酷地捉弄人。| **by a twist of fate** (=in an unexpected way) 出乎意料地 *By a strange twist of fate, he died the day before Julia arrived.* 他在朱莉娅到达的前一天去世了，真是天意叵测。
3 a fate worse than death *often humorous* something terrible that might happen to you【常幽默】比死还糟糕的事情，极可怕的事：*Toby saw marriage as a fate worse than death.* 托比把婚姻看成是比死还不如的事。**4 the Fates** the three goddesses who, according to the ancient Greeks, controlled what happened to people〔古希腊神话中的〕命运三女神 —see also 另见 **tempt fate** (TEMPT (3))

fat·ed /ˈfetɪd; ˈfeɪtɪ̇d/ *adj* [not before noun 不用于名词前] something that is fated to happen seems certain to happen because mysterious force is controlling events 命运决定的，命中注定的：**to be fated to do sth** *She knew that their happiness was fated not to last.* 她知道他们的幸福注定不会长久。—see also 另见 ILL-FATED

fate·ful /ˈfetfəl; ˈfeɪtfəl/ *adj* having an important, especially bad, effect on future events〔对未来的发展〕重要的，决定性的；灾难性的：*that fateful day* 那灾难性的一天 | *It was a fateful decision which was to change the rest of his life.* 这个重大的决定将改变他的余生。—**fatefully** *adv*

Fates, the /fets; feɪts/ in Greek and Roman MYTHOLOGY, the three goddesses who decided what should happen in each person's life 命运三女神〔希腊和罗马神话中决定每个人命运的女神〕

fat farm /ˈ· ·/ *n* [C] *AmE informal* a place where people who are fat can go to lose weight and improve their health【美，非正式】减肥疗养地 —compare 比较 HEALTH FARM

fat-free /ˌ· ˈ·◄/ *adj* containing no fat 不含脂肪[油脂]的：*fat-free yoghurt* 脱脂酸乳酪

fat·head /ˈfætˌhɛd; ˈfæthed/ *n* [C] *informal* a stupid person【非正式】笨蛋，傻瓜 —**fatheaded** *adj*

fa·ther[1] /ˈfɑðɚ; ˈfɑːðə/ *n* [C] S1 W1
1 ►PARENT 家长◄ a male parent 父，父亲，爸爸：*Ask your father to help you.* 叫你父亲帮你。| *Andrew was very excited about becoming a father.* 安德鲁因当了父亲而兴奋不已。| **a father of two/three/four etc** (=a man with two, three etc children) 两个孩子/三个孩子/四个孩子等的父亲 *The driver, a father of four, escaped uninjured.* 司机是位有四个孩子的父亲，他没有受伤，逃过了一劫。—see picture at 参见 FAMILY 图
2 ►PRIEST 神甫◄ a priest, especially in the Roman Catholic church〔尤指天主教的〕神甫：*I have sinned, Father.* 神甫，我犯罪了。
3 fathers [plural] people related to you who lived a long time ago; ANCESTORS 祖先，先人，前辈：*We must honour the customs of our fathers.* 我们必须尊重我们祖先的风俗习惯。—see also 另见 FOREFATHERS
4 ►GOD 上帝◄ **Father** a way of addressing or talking about God, used in the Christian religion〔用于基督教〕天父，上帝，圣父：*our Heavenly Father* 我们在天上的父
5 father figure an older man who you trust and respect〔受信任和尊敬的〕父亲般的人物；〔男性〕长者
6 the father of sth the man who was responsible for starting something …的创始人，…之父：*Freud is the father of psychoanalysis.* 弗洛伊德是精神分析法之父。
7 like father like son used to say that a boy behaves like his father, especially when this behaviour is bad 有其父必有其子
8 a bit of how's your father *BrE informal humorous* the act of having sex【英，非正式，幽默】性交 —see also 另见 CITY FATHER, PILGRIM FATHERS

father[2] *v* [T] **1** to make a woman have a child〔作为父亲〕生孩子，做…的父亲：*It was rumoured that the bishop had fathered two children.* 谣传主教是两个孩子的父亲。**2** to start an important new idea or system 首先提出；创立：*Bevan fathered the concept of the National Health Service.* 比万首先提出了国民保健制度的概念。
father sth on sb *phr v* [T] *especially BrE* to claim that someone is responsible for inventing or thinking of something【尤英】宣称…是某人发明的；认为…是某人提出的：*theories fathered on Freud by his critics* 被评论家说成是弗洛伊德首创的理论

Father Brown a priest in stories by the British writer G. K. Chesterton, who solves crimes by his knowledge of human nature 布朗神甫〔英国作家切斯特顿小说中的一神甫。他谙熟人性并借以破案〕

Father Christ·mas /,‥ '‥/ *n* [singular] *BrE* an imaginary man who wears red clothes, has a long white beard, and is said to bring presents to children at Christmas; SANTA CLAUS【英】圣诞老人〔一虚构的老人，身穿红衣，留着白色长须。小孩子都相信他会送来圣诞礼物〕

fa·ther·hood /ˈfɑðɚˌhud; ˈfɑːðəhʊd/ *n* [U] the state of being a father 父亲的身份；父性

father-in-law /ˈ‥ ‥ ,‥/ *n plural* **father-in-laws** or **fathers-in-law** [C] the father of your husband or wife 公公；岳父 —see picture at 参见 FAMILY 图

fa·ther·land /ˈfɑðɚˌlænd; ˈfɑːðəlænd/ *n* [singular] a word meaning the place where someone or their family was born, used especially about Germany 祖国〔尤用于指德国〕—see also 另见 MOTHER COUNTRY, MOTHERLAND

fa·ther·ly /ˈfɑðɚlɪ; ˈfɑːðəli/ *adj* kind and gentle in a way that is considered typical of a good father 父亲般的，慈父般的：*Howard put a fatherly arm around her.* 霍华德像慈父般地用胳膊搂着她。| *fatherly advice* 父亲般的忠告

Father of the Church /,‥ ‥ 'ˌ/ *n plural* **Fathers of the Church** one of the several important teachers of the early Christian church whose writings are used to answer any difficult points of faith or practice 早期基督教著作家〔早期基督教会的重要宣教师之一。人们通过其著作可破解信仰或践行之难题〕

Father's Day /ˈ‥ ,/ *n* [C] a day on which people give cards and presents to their father 父亲节

fath·om¹ /ˈfæðəm; ˈfæðəm/ *n* [C] a unit for measuring the depth of water, equal to 1.8 metres 英寻〔测水深的单位，等于1.8米〕

fathom² *v* [T] also 又作 **fathom out** to understand what something means after thinking about it carefully 弄清楚…的意思，搞懂：*I still can't fathom out what she meant.* 我还是弄不清她的意思。

fath·om·less /ˈfæðəmlɪs; ˈfæðəmləs/ *adj literary*【文】**1** too deep to be measured 深不可测的：*the fathomless ocean* 深不可测的海洋 **2** too complicated to be understood 复杂难懂的：*a fathomless mystery* 难以理解的奥秘

fa·tigue¹ /fəˈtig; fəˈtiːg/ *n* **1** [U] very great tiredness 疲劳，疲乏，劳累：*Steve was pale with fatigue after two sleepless nights.* 史蒂夫两晚没睡，累得脸色发白。**2** [U]a weakness in metal or wood, caused when it is bent or stretched many times, which is likely to make it break; METAL FATIGUE〔金属或木头材料的〕疲劳 **3 fatigues** [plural] **a)** loose-fitting army clothes〔士兵野外作业穿的〕宽松工作服 **b)** duties that a soldier has to do such as cleaning and cooking, especially as a punishment〔士兵的〕杂役，劳动〔尤作为惩罚〕

fatigue² *v* [T] *formal* to make someone very tired【正式】使疲劳[劳累] —**fatigued** *adj*: *Fatigued after her long journey, Beth fell into a deep sleep.* 贝丝在长途旅行之后感到极度疲劳，倒头大睡起来。

fat·so /ˈfætso; ˈfætsəʊ/ *n* [C] *informal* an insulting word for someone who is fat【非正式】胖子〔侮辱性用词〕

fat·ted /ˈfætɪd; ˈfætḷd/ *adj* —see 见 **kill the fatted calf** (KILL¹ (14))

fat·ten /ˈfætṇ; ˈfætn/ *v* [I,T] to make an animal become fatter so that it is ready to eat, or to become fat and ready to eat 喂肥，养肥，(使) 变肥，长肥

fatten sb/sth ↔ **up** *phr v* [T] *often humorous* to make a person or animal fatter【常幽默】使变肥，使变胖，喂肥：*He's too thin – you ought to try fattening him up a bit.* 他太瘦了 —— 你应该把他养胖一点。

fat·ten·ing /ˈfætṇɪŋ; ˈfætnɪŋ/ *adj* likely to make you fat 易使人发胖的：*I don't eat cake – it's far too fattening.* 我不吃蛋糕 —— 它太能使人发胖。

fat·ty¹ /ˈfætɪ; ˈfæti/ **fattier, fattiest** *adj* containing a lot of fat 含脂肪多的：*Avoid fatty foods.* 避免吃多脂肪的食品。| *fatty tissue* 脂肪组织

fatty² *n* [C] *informal* an insulting word for someone who is fat【非正式】胖子〔侮辱性用词〕

fatty acid /,‥ '‥/ *n* [C] an acid that a cell needs to use food effectively 脂肪酸

fat·u·ous /ˈfætʃuəs; ˈfætʃuəs/ *adj* very silly or stupid 愚昧的；蠢的；昏庸的：*fatuous comments* 愚昧的评论 —**fatuously** *adv* —**fatuousness** *n* [U]

fat·wa /ˈfætwɑ; ˈfætwɑː/ *n* [C] an official order made by an important Islamic religious leader 法特瓦〔伊斯兰宗教领袖发出的指令〕

fau·cet /ˈfɔsɪt; ˈfɔːsḷt/ *n* [C] *AmE* the thing that you turn on and off to control the flow of water from a pipe【美】水龙头；旋塞；TAP¹ (1) *BrE*【英】—see picture on page A10 参见 A10 页图

Faulk·ner /ˈfɔlknɚ; ˈfɔːlknə/, **William** (1897-1962) a US writer of NOVELs about the South of the US, such as *The Sound and the Fury* and *As I Lay Dying*. He won the Nobel Prize for Literature in 1949. 福克纳〔(1897-1962)，美国小说家。其小说取材于美国南方，如《喧哗与骚动》和《在我弥留之际》等。1949年获诺贝尔文学奖〕

fault¹ /fɔlt; fɔːlt/ *n* [C] 2 3

1 ►RESPONSIBLE FOR MISTAKE 对错误负责◄ **be sb's fault** if something bad that has happened is someone's fault, they should be blamed for it, because they made a mistake or failed to do something 是某人的错：*I'm really sorry – it's all my fault.* 真对不起 —— 都是我的错。| **be sb's own fault** *She failed the test but it was her own fault, she didn't do any work.* 她测验不及格，但这是她自己的错，她不努力学习。| **be sb's fault (that)** *It's not my fault that the brakes didn't work properly.* 刹车不灵不是我的错。| **be sb's fault for doing sth** *He lost his job, but it was his own fault for telling lies.* 他丢了工作，但那是他自己撒谎的错。

2 at fault if a particular person, organization, or system is at fault, they are responsible for something bad that has happened〔对某事〕有过错；应当负责：*The police said that the other driver was at fault – he should have slowed down.* 警方说错在另一位司机 —— 他本来应该减速。

3 ►STH WRONG WITH STH 某事出毛病◄ **a)** something that is wrong with a machine, system, design etc, which prevents it from working properly 毛病；错误；过失：*a design fault* 设计上的错误 | [+in] *It sounds like there's a fault in one of the loudspeakers.* 听起来好像其中一个喇叭有毛病。**b)** something that is wrong with something, which could be improved〔可以改进的〕缺点，缺陷：*I suppose the book's worst fault is its total lack of good taste.* 我认为这本书的最大缺陷是毫无品味可言。| **for all its faults** (=in spite of its faults) 尽管有各种缺点 *The treaty was a great achievement for all its faults.* 条约尽管有缺点，但它是一个很大的成就。**c)** a mistake in the way that something was made, which spoils its appearance〔有损外观的〕瑕疵：[+in] *The sweater had a fault in it and I had to take it back.* 这件毛线衫有瑕疵，我只好退货。

4 ►SB'S CHARACTER 某人的性格◄ a bad or weak part of someone's character〔性格的〕缺点：*His worst fault is his arrogance.* 他的最大缺点是傲慢。| *I really like Sarah, but she does have her faults.* 我确实喜欢萨拉，不过她有她的缺点。| **for all his/her etc faults** (=in spite of someone's faults) 尽管他/她等有缺点 *For all his faults he was a good father.* 尽管他有缺点，他还算是个好父亲。

5 find fault with to criticize someone or something and complain about them 找…的岔子，对…吹毛求疵，挑剔：*I wish you'd stop trying to find fault with everything I do.* 我希望你不要再对我做的事情百般挑剔。

6 through no fault of her/my etc own used to say that something bad that happened to someone was not caused by them 不是由于她/我等自己的错：*Through no fault of her own, Lisa lost her job.* 莉萨不是由于她自己的错而丢了工作。

7 ►CRACK 裂缝◄ a large crack in the rocks that form the Earth's surface〔地表岩石的〕断层

8 generous/kind etc to a fault extremely generous, kind etc 过分大方/亲切等：*Generous to a fault, Mr Samson agreed to provide the necessary equipment free of charge.* 萨姆森先生太大方了，竟同意免费提供必需的设备。

9 ►TENNIS 网球◄ a mistake made when a player is serving (SERVE¹ (10)) 发球失误

fault² *v* [T] to find a mistake in something 找…的缺点，挑剔，找毛病：**cannot fault sth** *Richards gave a superb performance which could not be faulted.* 理查兹做了一次精彩绝伦、无懈可击的表演。| **be hard/difficult to fault** *His cooking's excellent – it's hard to fault.* 他的烹调太好了 —— 无可挑剔。

fault·less /ˈfɔltlɪs; ˈfɔːltləs/ *adj* having no mistakes; perfect 无错误的；完美无缺的：*Yasmin spoke faultless French.* 亚斯明讲一口完美的法语。—**faultlessly** *adv* —**faultlessness** *n* [U]

fault·y /ˈfɔltɪ; ˈfɔːlti/ *adj* **1** something such as a machine that is faulty has something wrong with it that stops it from working properly, or was not made properly 有毛病的；有缺点的：*If the goods are faulty you are entitled to get your money back.* 如果货物有瑕疵，你有权要求退钱。**2** a way of thinking about something that is faulty contains a mistake which results in a wrong decision〔判断〕错误的：*Through neglect or faulty judgment, Meredith had failed to take security measures.* 由于疏忽或判断失误，梅雷迪思没有采取安全措施。—**faultily** *adv*

faun /fɔn; fɔːn/ *n* [C] an ancient Roman god with the body of a man and the legs and horns of a goat 农牧神〔古罗马神话中长有人身、羊角和羊腿的神〕

fau·na /ˈfɔnə; ˈfɔːnə/ *n* [C,U] *technical* all the animals living in a particular area or period in history【术语】〔某个地区或时期的〕动物群 —compare 比较 FLORA

Fauntleroy, Little Lord —see 见 LITTLE LORD FAUNTLEROY

Fau·ré /foˈre; ˈfɔːreɪ/, **Ga·bri·el** /ˈgæbrɪəl; ˈgeɪbriəl/ (1845-1924) a French COMPOSER famous for his *Requiem* 福莱〔(1845-1924), 法国作曲家, 以创作的《安魂曲》著称〕

Faust /faust; faʊst/, **Jo·hann** /ˈjohɑn; ˈjəʊhæn/ also 又作 **Dr Faustus** a German doctor and SCHOLAR of the early 16th century, who practised magic. A story developed about him that he had 'sold his soul to the Devil' in exchange for knowledge and power. Many stories and pieces of music have been written about him, including the plays *Dr Faustus* by Christopher Marlowe and *Faust* by Goethe. 浮士德(博士)〔16世纪德国一博士、学者, 通晓魔术。据传说, 他曾"向魔鬼出卖过灵魂"以换取知识和力量。有许多小说和音乐作品都是以他为题材创作的, 其中包括克里斯多弗·马洛的《浮士德博士》和歌德的《浮士德》〕

fauv·is·m /ˈfovɪzəm; ˈfəʊvɪzəm/ *n* [U] a style of painting that uses pure bright colours, which was developed in the early 20th century 野兽派, 野兽主义〔20世纪初出现的一种画派, 使用鲜艳的色彩〕

faux /fo; fəʊ/ *adj* [only before noun 仅用于名词前] *especially AmE* artificial【尤美】人造的; 假的: *a necklace of faux pearls* 人造珍珠项链

faux pas /ˌfo ˋpɑ; ˌfəʊ ˈpɑː/ *n* [C] *French* an embarrassing mistake in a social situation【法】失礼; 失言

fa·va bean /ˈfɑvə bin; ˈfɑːvə biːn/ *n* [C] *AmE* a large flat pale green bean【美】蚕豆; BROAD BEAN *BrE*【英】

fave /fev; feɪv/ *n* [C] *informal* a favourite person or thing【非正式】受喜爱的人[事物]: *Chocolate ice cream! That's my fave.* 巧克力冰激凌! 那是我最喜欢吃的。—**fave** *adj*

fa·vor /ˈfevɚ; ˈfeɪvə/ *n,v* the American spelling of FAVOUR favour 的美式拼法

fa·vo·ra·ble /ˈfevərəbl̩; ˈfeɪvərəbəl/ *adj* the American spelling of FAVOURABLE favourable 的美式拼法

fa·vored /ˈfevɚd; ˈfeɪvəd/ *adj* the American spelling of FAVOURED favoured 的美式拼法

fa·vo·rite /ˈfevərɪt; ˈfeɪvərɪ̣t/ *adj,n* the American spelling of FAVOURITE favourite 的美式拼法

fa·vo·rit·is·m /ˈfevərɪtˌɪzəm; ˈfeɪvərɪ̣tɪzəm/ *n* [U] the American spelling of FAVOURITISM favouritism 的美式拼法

1 2 **fa·vour¹** *BrE*【英】, **favor** *AmE*【美】/ˈfevɚ; ˈfeɪvə/ *n*

1 ▶HELP 帮助◀ [C] something that you do for someone in order to help them or be kind to them 恩惠; 善意的行为: **ask a favour (of sb)** *Can I ask a favor of you?* 请你帮个忙可以吗? | **do sb a favour** *Could you do me a favour and turn off that light?* 劳您的驾, 请把那盏灯关掉好吗? | **do sth as a favour** *I'm doing this as a favour, remember, it's not part of my job.* 记住, 我是为帮忙才做这件事的, 这不是我工作的一部分。| **owe sb a favour** (=feel that you should help someone because they have helped you) 欠某人的情 *Of course I'll help you move house; I owe you a favour anyway.* 我当然会帮你搬家; 说来我还欠你的情呢。| **return a favour** (=help someone because they have helped you) 还(某人的)情 *Thanks for looking after all my things – I'll return the favour sometime!* 谢谢你帮忙照看我这些东西——我改天会还你的情!

2 do me/us a favour! *BrE spoken* used when you are annoyed because someone has asked a silly question or done something to upset people【英口】帮帮我/我们的忙吧!〔因某人问了愚蠢的问题或做了令人厌烦的事而让他停止时说的〕: *Do us a favour, Mike, and shut up!* 拜托你, 迈克, 别再说了! | *"Did you like it?" "Do me a favour!"* "你喜欢它吗?" "饶了我吧!"

3 ▶SUPPORT/APPROVAL 支持/赞许◀ [U] support or approval for something such as a plan, idea, or system 支持, 赞同, 赞许, 喜爱: **find/gain/win favour** (=be supported by a particular group of people) 受到赞许/得到赞同 *The idea may find favour with older people.* 这个想法也许会得到年纪较大的人的欢迎。| **lose favour** (=stop being supported by people) 不再受支持, 失去支持 *Plans to increase taxes have lost favour among party members.* 增税计划已失去党派成员的支持。| **look with favour on** *formal* (=use your power to help something to succeed)【正式】支持; 受…青睐 *We're hoping the President will look with favour upon such a proposal.* 我们希望总统会支持这样的建议。

4 in favour of if you are in favour of a plan, idea, or system, you agree with it and support it 同意, 支持〔计划、主意或制度等〕: *Are you in favour of the death penalty?* 你赞同死刑吗? | *Senior ministers spoke in favour of the bill.* 资历较深的部长们发言支持这项议案。| **in sb's/sth's favour** *The vote was 60-59 in his favour.* 投票结果是60比59, 他占优势。| **be all in favour of** (=completely approve of something) 完全同意, 完全支持 *I'm all in favour of people going out and enjoying themselves so long as they don't disturb other people.* 我完全支持人们出去好好玩一下, 只要他们不打扰其他人。| **come down in favour of** (=finally decide to support a plan or action) 终于决定支持 *The senate has come down in favour of the appointment of Judge Thomas.* 参议院终于决定同意对托马斯法官的任命。| **vote/decide in favour of** (=vote or decide to support something) 投票/决定支持 | **find/rule in favour of sb** *formal* (=make a legal decision that supports someone)【正式】宣判/判决某人胜诉

5 ▶CHOOSE STH INSTEAD 选择其他事物代替◀ **in favour of** if you decide not to use one plan, idea, or system in favour of another, you choose the other one because you think it is better 宁愿选择, 选…而不选〔另外一个计划、主意或系统〕: *Plans for a tunnel were rejected in favour of the bridge mainly because of the increased costs.* 修建隧道的计划被否决而选择了建桥, 主要是因为前者会使费用增加。

6 ▶UNFAIR SUPPORT 偏袒◀ [U] support that is given to one person or group and not to others in a way that seems unfair 偏袒: **show favour to sb** *Judges have to be careful not to show favour to either party in a dispute.* 法官得小心谨慎, 不能偏袒纠纷中的任何一方。

7 ▶POPULAR/LIKED 受欢迎/受喜爱◀ **in favour** if someone is in favour, people like them and approve of them at the present time 受喜爱, 受宠爱: **be in favour with** *She's very much in favour with the management at the moment.* 她目前在管理层中很得宠。| **back in favour** (=popular again) 重新受欢迎; 重新得宠 *Looks like her old boyfriend is back in favour.* 看来她以前的男朋友又得她欢心了。

8 ▶UNPOPULAR/NOT LIKED 不受欢迎/不受喜爱◀ **out of favour a)** if someone is out of favour, they are no longer liked, for example by their employers, teachers, or voters 不受欢迎, 失宠: *The boss didn't say 'hello' this morning – I think I must be out of favour.* 老板今天上午没有跟我打招呼——我想我一定失宠了。| **fall out of favour** (=stop being liked) 不再受喜爱, 失宠 *Once a presidential candidate falls out of favour it is very difficult for them to regain popularity.* 总统候选人一旦不再受欢迎, 就很难重新获得支持。**b)** methods, ideas etc that are out of favour are not fashionable or popular any more 不流行, 不时髦: **go out of favour** *Grammar-based teaching methods went out of favour in the 60s and 70s.* 以语法为基础的教学方法在60、70年代就不流行了。

9 ▶ADVANTAGE 优势◀ **in sb's favour** if something is in someone's favour, it gives them an advantage over someone else 对某人有利: *The fast surface at Wimbledon is very much in Becker's favour.* 温布尔登网球场的快速地面对贝克尔十分有利。| *The system operates in favour of the upper classes.* 这一制度的运作对上层阶级有利。| **the odds are (stacked) in sb's favour** (=someone has a big advantage) 某人占有很大的优势

10 ▶MONEY 钱◀ **in sb's favour** if a cheque is in someone's favour it should be paid to them〔支票〕开付给某人的: *He made out a cheque for £200 in her favour.* 他开了一张200英镑的支票给她。

11 ▶GIFT 礼物◀ [C] *AmE* a small gift given to guests at a party【美】〔聚会上分发给宾客的〕小礼物

12 ▶STH YOU WEAR 佩戴之物◀ [C] something you wear to show that you support a particular political party, football team etc〔佩戴在身上表示支持某个政党、足球队等的〕缎带; 徽章; 标志

13 ▶SEX 性◀ **favours** [plural] *old-fashioned* a sexual relationship that a woman agrees to have with a man【过时】〔女子同意与男子发生的〕性关系 —see also 另见 **curry favour with** (CURRY² (2)), **without fear or favour** (FEAR¹ (6))

favour² *BrE*【英】, **favor** *AmE*【美】*v* [T] 3

1 ▶PREFER 更喜欢◀ **a)** to think that a plan, idea etc is better than other plans, ideas etc 赞同, 支持〔计划、想法等〕: *The president is believed to favour further tax cuts.* 大家认为总统会支持进一步减税。**b)** to prefer something and choose it instead of something else 喜爱; 宁愿选择: *loose clothing of the type favoured in Arab countries* 阿拉伯国家中人们喜爱的那种宽松的衣服

2 ▶GIVE AN ADVANTAGE 给予好处◀ to treat someone much better than someone else, in an unfair way 偏爱; 偏袒: *a tax cut that favours rich people* 偏袒富人的减税

3 ▶HELP 帮助◀ to provide suitable conditions for something

F

to happen〔条件〕有利[有助]于: *The state of the economy does not favour the development of small businesses.* 这种经济状况不利于小企业的发展。

4 ▶LOOK LIKE 看上去像◀ *especially AmE* to look like one of your parents or grandparents【尤美】容貌像, 酷似〔父母或(外)祖父母中的某一人〕: *She favours her Aunt Jen.* 她长得像她的珍姑姑。

favour sb **with** sth *phr v* [T] *formal* to give someone something such as a look or reply【正式】给予: *The Captain favoured her with a salute.* 船长向她敬礼。

fa·vou·ra·ble *BrE*【英】, **favorable** *AmE*【美】/ˋfevərəb]; ˈfeɪvərəbəl/ *adj* **1** a favourable report, comment, or reaction shows that you think that someone or something is good or that you agree with them 赞许的, 称赞的; 同意的: *The film received favourable reviews.* 这部电影得到好评。| *Her ideas met with a favourable response.* 她的主张反应很好。**2** making people like or approve of someone or something 讨人喜欢的; 赢得赞许的: **favourable impression** *The young girl made a most favourable impression on them.* 这位少女给他们留下了非常好的印象。**3** suitable and likely to make something happen or succeed 有利的: [+for/to] *The conditions are now favourable for economic recovery.* 情况现在对于经济复苏有利。**4** favourable conditions or terms are reasonable and not too expensive or difficult 优惠的: *The bank offered to lend us the money on very favourable terms.* 银行提出以非常优惠的条件贷款给我们。—**favourably** *adv*

fa·voured *BrE*【英】, **favored** *AmE*【美】/ˋfevəd; ˈfeɪvəd/ *adj* **1** receiving special attention, help, or treatment, especially in an unfair way 受到优待的; 受宠的, 得到偏爱的: *Foreign aid seems to go mostly to favoured governments who are supporters of the US.* 外援似乎大都是给支持美国的那些特别受到优待的政府。**2** chosen by many people 由许多人选中的; 受众人喜爱的: *Brittany is a favoured holiday destination for families.* 布列塔尼是一个受人喜爱的家庭度假胜地。**3** having desirable qualities 称心的, 合意的: *a house in a favoured position* 位于好地段的房子 —see also 另见 ILL-FAVOURED, WELL-FAVOURED

fa·vou·rite¹ *BrE*【英】, **favorite** *AmE*【美】/ˋfevərɪt; ˈfeɪvərɨt/ *adj* [only before noun 仅用于名词前] **1** your favourite person or thing is the one that you like the most 最喜欢的: *Who's your favourite actor?* 谁是你最喜欢的演员? | *I'll take you to my favourite restaurant tomorrow.* 我明天带你上我最喜欢的餐馆。**2 favourite son** a politician, sports player etc who is popular with people in the area that they come from 受家乡人欢迎的政治家、运动员等

favourite² *BrE*【英】, **favorite** *AmE*【美】*n* [C] **1** something that you like more than other things of the same kind 最喜爱的东西: **my/your etc favourite** *I like all her books but this one is my favourite.* 她所有的著作我都喜欢, 但这一本是我最喜欢的。| *Which one's your favourite?* 你最喜欢哪一个? | **an old favourite/a special favourite** *This dress is an old favourite of hers.* 这件衣服是她多年来最喜欢的。**2** someone who is liked and treated better than others by a teacher or parent 受宠的人, 宠儿: *You always were Dad's favourite.* 你总是最受爸爸的宠爱。—see also 另见 FAVOURITISM **3** the horse, runner etc that is expected to win a race or competition 最有希望获胜的马[选手等]; 最被看好的竞赛者: *Italy were favourites to win the World Cup.* 意大利最有希望赢得世界杯。

fa·vou·ri·tis·m *BrE*【英】, **favoritism** *AmE*【美】/ˋfevərɪt-ˌɪzəm; ˈfeɪvərɨtɪzəm/ *n* [U] the act of treating one person or group better than others in an unfair way 偏爱; 偏袒; 徇私: *If we give her the job we'll be accused of favouritism.* 如果我们给她这份工作, 我们就会被人指责为徇私。

Fawkes /fɔks; fɔːks/, **Guy** (1570-1606) an English Roman Catholic who was killed as punishment for his part in a secret plan, known as the Gunpowder Plot, to destroy the Houses of Parliament by causing an explosion on November 5th, 1605. Guy Fawkes' Night is celebrated every year on November 5th in the UK. 福克斯〔(1570-1606), 英格兰天主教徒, 因参与1605年11月5日炸毁英国议会大厦的"火药阴谋"而被处决。英国人每年11月5日都要庆祝"盖伊·福克斯之夜"〕

fawn¹ /fɔn; fɔːn/ *n* [C] a young DEER 幼鹿

fawn² *adj* pale yellow-brown 浅黄褐色的 —**fawn** *n* [U]

fawn³ *v*

fawn on/over sb to praise someone and be friendly to them in an insincere way, because you want them to like you or give you something 巴结, 讨好: *When Madonna was in Paris she had the press fawning all over her.* 麦当娜在巴黎的时候, 传媒都巴结她。

fax¹ /fæks; fæks/ *n* **1** [C] a letter or message that is sent in electronic form down a telephone line and then printed using a special machine 传真件: *Did you get my fax?* 你收到我的传真了吗? **2** [C] also 又作 **fax machine** a machine used for sending and receiving faxes 传真机: *What's your fax number?* 你的传真号码是多少? —see picture on page A14 参见 A14 页图 **3** [U] the system of sending letters and messages using a fax machine 传真通信; 传真: *Most of our business is done by fax these days.* 如今我们的大部分业务是通过传真完成的。

fax² *v* [T] to send someone a letter or message using a fax machine 传真传输: **fax sb sth** *They've agreed to fax us their proposals tomorrow.* 他们同意明天把他们的提议传真给我们。| **fax sth (through) to sb** *The order will be faxed through to the manufacturer.* 订单将传真给厂家。

fay /fe; feɪ/ *n* [C] *poetic* a FAIRY (1)【诗】仙子, 小精灵

faze /fez; feɪz/ *v* [T] *informal* if you are fazed by a new or difficult situation, it makes you feel confused or shocked【非正式】使发窘, 使惊惶失措: *Ned seems rather fazed by the new computer system.* 内德好像被新的电脑系统吓住了。

FBI /ˌɛf bi ˋaɪ; ˌef biː ˈaɪ/ *n* [U] Federal Bureau of Investigation; the police department in the US that is controlled by the central government, and is concerned with crimes in more than one state〔美国〕联邦调查局 —compare 比较 CIA

FC /ˌɛf ˋsi; ˌef ˈsiː/ an abbreviation of 缩写= Football Club, used in names of football clubs 足球俱乐部: *Liverpool FC* 利物浦足球俱乐部

FCC, the /ˌɛf si ˋsi; ˌef siː ˈsiː/ the abbreviation of 缩写= the FEDERAL COMMUNICATIONS COMMISSION

FCO, the /ˌɛf si ˋo; ˌef siː ˈəʊ/ the Foreign and Commonwealth Office; the official name of the British Foreign Office 外交和联邦事务部〔英国外交部的正式名称〕

FDA, the /ˌɛf di ˋe; ˌef diː ˈeɪ/ Food and Drug Administration; a US government organization which makes sure that foods and drugs are safe enough to be sold. It decides which chemicals can legally be added to food, which medical drugs are safe, and how information about food and drugs should be shown on containers. 食品和药物管理局〔美国一政府机构。其职责是确保拟出售的食品和药物安全可靠。该机构决定哪些化学成分可合法加入食品, 哪些药品是安全的, 以及食物、药品包装盒上应如何标示相关信息〕

FDIC, the /ˌɛf di aɪ ˋsi; ˌef diː aɪ ˈsiː/ the Federal Deposit Insurance Corporation; a US government organization which exists to protect people's bank accounts. If your bank is a member of the FDIC and it cannot pay its debts, the FDIC will pay you the amount that you kept in the bank, up to $100,000. 联邦储蓄保险公司〔美国一政府机构, 为保护储户银行账户而设立。如果储户的开户银行是该公司的成员, 那么当银行资不抵债时, 该公司将给储户支付最高限额为10万美元的赔偿金〕

FDR /ˌɛf di ˋɑr; ˌef diː ˈɑː/ —see 见 Franklin D. ROOSEVELT

fe·al·ty /ˋfiəltɪ; ˈfiːəlti/ *n* [U] *old-fashioned* loyalty to a king, queen etc【过时】〔对国王、女王等的〕忠诚

fear¹ /fɪr; fɪə/ *n* [C,U] **1** an unpleasant feeling of being frightened or worried that something bad is going to happen 害怕, 恐惧: *The boy's eyes were full of fear.* 这男孩的眼里充满着恐惧。| *McCarthy exploited deep-seated fears about communism among the American people.* 麦卡锡利用了美国人对共产主义的那种根深蒂固的恐惧心理。| [+of] *fear of flying* 害怕飞行 | *My fear of dentists dates back to when I was a child.* 我对牙医的恐惧可追溯到我小的时候。| [+for] *fears for the future* 对未来感到的恐惧 | **fear that** *fears that his wife might leave him* 害怕他的妻子会离开他 | **in fear** (=feeling afraid) 害怕地, 提心吊胆地 *He thought he heard something and glanced round in fear.* 他以为

他听到了什么，于是提心吊胆地看了看周围。| **live in fear of** (=always be afraid of) 活在恐惧中，终日害怕 *Ordinary people live in fear of being arrested by the secret police.* 普通人终日害怕被秘密警察逮捕。| **in fear of your life** (=feeling afraid that you may be killed) 害怕会丧命 | **sb's fears are unfounded** (=there is no reason for someone to feel afraid or worried) 某人的恐惧是没有根据的 *My fears for their safety proved unfounded.* 我对他们安全的担心结果证明是没有根据的。**2 for fear of/for fear that** because you are worried that you will make something happen 因为怕…，生怕…: *Helen didn't want to get out of bed, for fear of waking her husband.* 海伦不想起床，生怕会吵醒丈夫。**3 no fear!** *BrE informal often humorous* used to say that you are definitely not going to do something【英，非正式，常幽默】当然不！绝不！〔用于说明自己绝不去做某事〕: *"Are you going to Bill's party tonight?" "No fear!"* "你今晚去参加比尔的聚会吗？""当然不去！" **4 put the fear of God into sb** *informal* to make someone feel that they must do something by telling them what will happen if they do not do it【非正式】使某人〔对不做某事的后果〕感到害怕: *The Italian manager must have put the fear of God into his team.* 这位意大利教练一定是恫吓过他的队员。**5 there's no fear of** used to say that something will definitely not happen 不会〔发生〕，不可能〔有某种事〕: *There's no fear of him changing his mind.* 他不会改变主意。**6 without fear or favour** *formal* in a fair way【正式】公平的[地]，公正的[地]，不偏袒的[地]: *to enforce the law without fear or favour* 公正地执法

2 **fear²** *v* [T] **1** a word meaning to feel frightened or worried that something bad may happen 害怕，恐惧；担心: *Fearing another earthquake, local officials ordered an evacuation.* 地方官员害怕再次发生地震，于是命令人们疏散。| **fear that** *Einstein feared that other German scientists would build a nuclear bomb first.* 爱因斯坦担心其他德国科学家会先造出原子弹。| **fear to do sth** *formal* (=be afraid to do something)【正式】害怕做某事 *Women feared to go out at night.* 妇女害怕晚上外出。**2 fear the worst** to think that the worst possible thing has happened or might happen 害怕(会)发生最坏的事: *When Tom heard about the accident he immediately feared the worst.* 汤姆听说出了事故时，立即就害怕会发生最坏的事。**3** to be afraid of someone and what they might do because they are very powerful 畏惧，害怕〔某个有权势的人〕: *The general manager was greatly feared by all his subordinates.* 总经理的所有下属都很怕他。**4 fear for** to feel worried about someone because you think they might be in danger 为…担忧: **fear for sb's safety/life** *Mary feared for her son's safety.* 玛丽为儿子的安全担忧。| **fear for sb** *He feared for his children.* 他为他的孩子担忧。**5 I fear** *formal* used when telling someone that you think that something bad has happened or is true【正式】恐怕…，很遗憾〔用于告知某种坏事已发生或成为事实〕: **I fear (that)** *I fear that we may be too late, Holmes.* 恐怕我们可能太迟了，霍姆斯。| **I fear so/I fear not** *"Is she very ill?" "I fear so."* "她病得很重吗？""恐怕是的。" **6 fear not/never fear** *formal* used to tell someone not to worry【正式】不用怕，别担心〔用于使人安心〕: *Never fear, he'll be with us soon.* 别担心，他很快会和我们在一起的。—see also 另见 GOD-FEARING

fear·ful /ˈfɪrfəl; ˈfɪəfəl/ *adj* **1** *formal* frightened that something might happen【正式】担心的，害怕的: [+of] *The defenders are fearful of another attack.* 防守队员担心会遭到又一次进攻。| **fearful that** *fearful that the disease may strike again* 担心这种疾病会再度爆发 **2** *BrE* extremely bad【英】极坏的: **be in a fearful state/condition/mess** *The room was in a fearful state.* 房间里一片狼藉。**3** *old use* [only before noun 仅用于名词前] frightening【旧】吓人的，可怕的: *fearful shapes in the darkness* 黑暗中吓人的影子 —**fearfulness** *n* [U]

fear·ful·ly /ˈfɪrfəlɪ; ˈfɪəfəli/ *adv* **1** in a way that shows you are afraid 恐惧地，害怕地: *She glanced fearfully over her shoulder.* 她提心吊胆地回头看了一眼。**2** [+adj/adv] *old-fashioned* extremely【过时】极其，非常: *She's fearfully clever.* 她非常聪明。

fear·less /ˈfɪrlɪs; ˈfɪələs/ *adj* not afraid of anything 无畏的，不怕的: *a fearless warrior* 无畏的勇士 —**fearlessly** *adv* —**fearlessness** *n* [U]

fear·some /ˈfɪrsəm; ˈfɪəsəm/ *adj* very frightening to look at 〔看上去〕可怕的，吓人的: *a woman of fearsome dimensions* 体形大得可怕的女人

fea·si·ble /ˈfizəbl; ˈfiːzəbəl/ *adj* a plan, idea, or method that is feasible is possible and is likely to work〔计划、想法或方法〕可行的，可实行的，行得通的: *Your plan is not economically feasible.* 你的计划从经济上考虑是行不通的。—**feasibly** *adv* —**feasibility** /ˌfizəˈbɪlətɪ; ˌfiːzəˈbɪləti/ *n* [U]: *a feasibility study* 可行性研究

feast¹ /fist; fiːst/ *n* [C] **1** a large meal for a lot of people, to celebrate a special occasion 盛会，宴会: *a wedding feast* 婚筵 | **hold a feast** *A great feast was held in Columbus's honour.* 为纪念哥伦布举行了盛大的宴会。**2** a very good, large meal 美味的盛筵: *Jane's mother had cooked us a real feast.* 简的母亲为我们准备了一顿十分美味的盛筵。| **midnight feast** (=a meal eaten secretly at night by children)〔儿童在晚上偷偷吃的〕午夜宴会 **3** an occasion when there are a lot of enjoyable things to see or do 节日；庆典日: [+for] *Next week's film festival should be a real feast for cinema-goers.* 下星期的电影节应该是电影迷的一个真正的盛大节日。**4** a day or period when there is a religious festival 宗教节日 —see also 另见 MOVABLE FEAST

feast² *v* **1 feast on/upon sth** to eat a lot of a particular food with great enjoyment 尽情地吃，饱餐: *flies feasting on rotting flesh* 正饱餐着臭肉的苍蝇 **2 feast your eyes on** to look at someone or something with great pleasure 尽情欣赏；饱眼福: *Travellers came to feast their eyes on the natural beauty of the region.* 游客们来尽情欣赏这个地区的自然美景。**3** [I] to eat and drink a lot to celebrate something 大吃大喝地庆祝 **4** [T usually passive 一般用被动态] to be honoured by a special meal 受到盛宴招待

Feast of Tab·er·nac·les /ˌ· · ˈ· · ·/ —see 见 SUKKOTH

Feast of Weeks, the /ˌ· · ˈ·/ a Jewish religious holiday (犹太教的)五旬节

feat /fit; fiːt/ *n* [C] something that someone does that is impressive because it needs a lot of skill, strength etc 业绩，功绩，壮举: [+of] *a remarkable feat of engineering* 一项了不起的工程壮举 | **perform/accomplish/achieve a feat** *How did they accomplish such an extraordinary feat?* 他们是怎样做出如此非凡的业绩的？| **sth is no mean feat** (=is difficult to do) 某事很难做 *Getting a degree is no mean feat!* 拿到学位可不是一件轻易可以做到的事！

feath·er¹ /ˈfɛðɚ; ˈfeðə/ *n* [C] **1** one of the things that cover a bird's body, consisting of a stem with soft hairs growing on either side 羽毛，翎: *an ostrich feather* 鸵鸟的羽毛 | **feather bed/pillow etc** (=a bed etc that is filled with feathers) 羽绒褥垫/枕头等 **2 a feather in your cap** something you have done that you should be proud of 值得自豪的成就，卓越的成就 —see also 另见 **light as a feather** (LIGHT² (4)), **birds of a feather** (BIRD (4)), **ruffle sb's feathers** (RUFFLE¹ (2)) 3

feather 羽毛

feath·er² *v* [T] **1 feather your nest** to get money by dishonest methods 营私自肥，中饱私囊 **2 feather the oars** to put the OARs flat on the surface of the water when you are rowing a boat 划平桨〔划船收桨时使桨叶与水面平行〕 **3** to put feathers on an ARROW 为〔箭〕装上翎 —see also 另见 **tar and feather sb** (TAR² (3))

feath·er bed·ding /ˌfɛðɚ ˈbɛdɪŋ; ˌfeðə ˈbedɪŋ/ *n* [U] the practice of letting workers keep their jobs even if they are not needed or do not work well〔即使不需要或工作不好也保留工人的〕超员雇佣

feather bo·a /ˌ· · ˈ· ·/ *n* [C] a long SCARF¹ (1) made of feathers and worn around a woman's neck〔妇女的〕羽毛长围巾

feath·er·brained /ˈfɛðɚˌbrend; ˈfeðəbreɪnd/ *adj* extremely silly 非常愚蠢的

feather dust·er /ˌ· · ˈ· ·/ *n* [C] a stick with feathers on the end used for removing dust 羽毛掸帚

feath·ered /ˈfɛðɚd; ˈfeðəd/ *adj* having feathers, or made from feathers 有羽毛的；羽毛做的

feath·er·weight /ˈfɛðɚˌwet; ˈfeðəweɪt/ *n* [C] a BOXER (1) who is heavier than a BANTAMWEIGHT but lighter than a LIGHTWEIGHT² (2) 次轻量级拳击运动员，羽量级拳击运动员

feath·er·y /ˈfɛðərɪ; ˈfeðəri/ *adj* **1** made of a lot of soft thin pieces〔轻柔的〕羽毛状的: *The plant has feathery leaves.* 这种植物长着羽毛状的叶子。**2** soft and light 轻柔的，轻软的

fea·ture¹ /ˈfitʃɚ; ˈfiːtʃə/ *n* [C] **1** a part of something that you notice because it seems important, interesting, or typical 特点，特征，特色: *The house has many interesting features, including a large Victorian fireplace.* 这栋房子有许多有趣的特色，包括一个维多利亚大壁炉。| [+of] *An important feature of Van Gogh's paintings is their bright colours.* 凡高的绘画的一个重要特色是色彩鲜亮。| **common feature** *Mass unemployment is a common feature of industrialized societies.* 大量失业是各工业化社会的一个共同特征。| **geographical feature** (=part of an area such as a hill, river etc) 地理特征 **2** a piece of writing about a subject in a newspaper or a magazine〔报纸或杂志上的〕特写(报道): [+on] *There was a feature on Kevin Costner in last* 2 1

week's Sunday Times. 上星期的《星期日泰晤士报》有一篇关于凯文·科斯特纳拿的特写报道。**3** [usually plural 一般用复数] the parts of someone's face such as their eyes, nose etc 面貌的一部分〔如眼、鼻等〕; 面貌（特征）; 五官: *He had fine delicate features.* 他眉清目秀。**4** a film being shown at a cinema 影片, 故事片, 正片: *There were a couple of short cartoons before the main feature.* 正片前有一些卡通短片。

3 **feature**[2] *v* **1** [T] to show a particular person or thing in a film, magazine, show etc〔在电影、杂志、表演等中〕介绍, 特载; 特别推出; 以…为主要内容: *an exhibition featuring paintings by contemporary artists* 展出当代艺术家绘画作品的展览 | **feature sb as** (=include a famous actor who plays a particular person) 由某人主演 *featuring Marlon Brando as the Godfather* 由马龙·白兰度扮演教父 **2** [I] to be included in something and be an important part of it 是…的特色: [+in] *Violence seems to feature heavily in all of his books.* 暴力似乎是他所有作品中的主要特色。**3** [T] a word meaning to include something new or unusual, used especially in advertisements 以…为特色〔尤用于广告〕: *The car features an anti-lock braking system.* 这种车装有防抱死刹车系统。**4** [T] to show or advertise a particular kind of product 展示〔某种产品〕, 为…做广告: *This week we're featuring a brand new range of frozen foods.* 这星期我们将推出一系列全新的冷冻食品。**5** to show a film, play etc 放映〔电影〕; 上演〔戏剧〕: *A popular Berkeley theater featured a porno movie called 'Slaves of Love'.* 伯克利一家大众剧院放映了一部叫做《爱情奴隶》的色情影片。

feature film /ˈ··, ·ˈ/ *n* [C] a full length film that has a story and is acted by professional actors 正片, 故事片

fea·ture·less /ˈfitʃəlɪs; ˈfiːtʃələs/ *adj* a featureless place has no interesting parts〔地方〕无特色的, 平淡无奇的: *the flat and rather featureless plains in the south* 南方那单调而毫无特色的平原

Feb the written abbreviation of 缩写= FEBRUARY

fe·brile /ˈfibrəl; ˈfiːbraɪl/ *adj* **1** *literary* full of nervous excitement or activity【文】兴奋的, 激动的, 狂热的: *a febrile imagination* 狂热的想象 **2** *medical* concerned with or caused by a fever【医】发热的, 发热引起的

Feb·ru·a·ry /ˈfɛbrʊˌɛrɪ; ˈfebruəri/ *n* [C,U] the second month of the year between January and March 二月: **in February** *The bridge will open in February 1998.* 这座桥将于1998年2月启用。| **last/next February** *Mum died last February.* 妈妈去年2月去世了。| **on February 10th** (also 又作 **on 10th February** *BrE* 英) *The meeting will be on February 10th.* (spoken as 读作 *on the tenth of February* or 或 *on February the tenth* or 或 (*AmE* 美) *on February tenth*) 会议将于2月10日举行。

fe·ces /ˈfisiz; ˈfiːsiːz/ *n* [plural] the usual American spelling of FAECES faeces 的一般美式拼法 —**fecal** /ˈfikl; ˈfiːkəl/ *adj*

feck·less /ˈfɛklɪs; ˈfekləs/ *adj* lacking determination, and not achieving anything in your life 无能的, 窝囊的, 没出息的: *a dull, rather feckless young man* 迟钝呆笨、相当没出息的年轻人 —**fecklessly** *adv* —**fecklessness** *n* [U]

fec·und /ˈfɛkənd; ˈfekənd/ *adj formal* able to produce many children, young animals, or crops; FERTILE【正式】生殖力旺盛的; 多产的 —**fecundity** /fɪˈkʌndətɪ; fɪˈkʌndʒti/ *n* [U]

fed[1] /fɛd; fed/ the past tense and past participle of FEED[1] —see also 另见 FED UP

fed[2] *n* [C] *AmE informal* an agent of the FBI【美, 非正式】联邦调查局探员[调查员]

Fed, the *AmE informal*【美, 非正式】**1** a short form of the Federal Reserve Bank 联邦储备银行 **2** a short form of the Federal Reserve System（美国）联邦储备系统

3 **fed·e·ral** /ˈfɛdərəl; ˈfedərəl/ *adj* **1** a federal country or system of government consists of a group of states which have their own government to decide their own affairs, and are controlled by a single national government which makes decisions on foreign affairs, defence etc 联邦（制）的: *Switzerland is a federal republic.* 瑞士是一个联邦共和国。**2** concerned with the central government of a country such as the US, rather than the government of one of its states〔美国等的〕联邦政府的: *federal funding* 联邦政府拨款

Federal A·vi·a·tion Ad·min·i·stra·tion, the /,··· ··'··,·/ abbreviation 缩写为 **the FAA** a US government organization which is responsible for making sure that aircraft and airports are safe for people to use. There is a similar organization in the UK called the Civil Aviation Authority. 联邦航空局〔美国一政府机构。其职责是确保飞机和机场的安全。英国也有一类似机构, 称"民用航空局"〕

Federal Bu·reau of In·ves·ti·ga·tion /,···, ·····'·/ *n* the FBI〔美国〕联邦调查局

Federal Com·mu·ni·ca·tions Com·mis·sion, the /,··· ··'··,·/ abbreviation 缩写为 **The FCC** a US government organization which makes rules that control broadcasting on radio, television, CABLE and SATELLITE TELEVISION in the US 联邦通讯委员会〔美国一政府机构。其职责是制定美国广播、电视、有线电视和卫星电视的管理办法〕

fed·e·ral·is·m /ˈfɛdərəlˌɪzəm; ˈfedərəlɪzəm/ *n* [U] belief in or support for a federal system of government 联邦主义

Federal Republic of Germany, the the official name of Germany 德意志联邦共和国〔德国的正式名称〕

Federal Re·pub·lic of Yu·go·sla·vi·a, the /,··· ,······'···/ abbreviation 缩写为 **FRY, the Republic of Yugoslavia (Serbia and Montenegro)** the official name for Serbia and Montenegro, two states of the former country of Yugoslavia, in Eastern Europe. Population: 10,406,750 (1991). Capital: Belgrade. It has existed as a country since 1992. 南斯拉夫联盟共和国〔东欧塞尔维亚和黑山共和国的正式名称。塞尔维亚和黑山是前南斯拉夫的两个州。人口: 10,406,750 (1991), 首都: 贝尔格莱德。1992年建国〕

Federal Re·serve Bank, the /,··· ·'·, ·/ also 又作 **the Fed** *informal*【非正式】abbreviation 缩写为 **FRB** the US central bank, which is divided into twelve banks, each operating in a different area of the US according to the Federal Reserve System. The 'Fed' has an important influence on US economic policy, because it fixes the rate of interest that banks must pay when they borrow money. 联邦储备银行〔美国中央银行, 共分为12家地区银行, 各自根据联邦储备体系在不同地区运作。美联储决定银行借款利率, 对美国的经济政策有着重大影响〕

Federal Re·serve Sys·tem, the /,··· ·'·, ·/ also 又作 **the Fed** *informal*【非正式】the national banking system in the US, according to which the Federal Reserve Bank operates 联邦储备系统〔即美国国家银行体系, 联邦储备银行依此运作〕

federal tax /,··· ˈ·/ *n* [C, U] *AmE* a tax in the US that is paid to the central government【美】〔美国〕联邦税

Federal Trade Com·mis·sion, the /,··· ·ˈ··/ the full name of the FTC（美国）联邦贸易委员会〔FTC的全称〕

fed·e·rate /ˈfɛdəˌret; ˈfedəreɪt/ *v* [I+with] if a group of states federate, they join together to form a federation 结成联邦[联盟]

fed·e·ra·tion /ˌfɛdəˈreʃən; ˌfedəˈreɪʃən/ *n* **1** [C] a group of organizations, clubs, or people that have joined together to form a single group 联合会; 联盟: *the National Federation of Women's Institutes*〔英国及英联邦国家〕妇女协会全国联合会 **2** [C] a group of states that have joined together to form a single group 联邦政府; 联邦共和国: *the Russian Federation* 俄罗斯联邦政府 **3** [U] the act of joining together to form a group 结成联盟[联邦]

fed up /,·ˈ·/ *adj* [not before noun 不用于名词前] *informal* annoyed or bored, and wanting something to change【非正式】厌烦的, 不满的, 无法再忍受的: [+with] *I'm really fed up with this weather – why can't it be sunny for a change?* 我真的受够了这种天气——为什么不变一下, 出出太阳? | *You look really fed up – what's the matter?* 你看来很不高兴——出了什么事? | **get fed up** *In the end she got fed up with waiting for him to decide.* 最后她等他作决定都等得不耐烦了。| *I'm getting fed up with your stupid comments.* 我听腻了你那些愚蠢的评语。| **fed up to the back teeth** (=extremely annoyed) 极其厌烦的

USAGE NOTE 用法说明: FED UP

GRAMMAR 语法

In British English, you will often hear people say **fed up of,** as well as **fed up with.** 在英国英语里, 经常会听到人们既说 fed up of, 也说 fed up with: *I'm fed up of all this waiting around.* 我讨厌这样等待。But many people consider this to be wrong. 但许多人认为这种说法是错误的。

fee /fi; fiː/ *n* [C often plural 常用复数] **1** an amount of money that you pay to a professional person for their work〔付给专业人员的〕工作酬金; 服务费: **charge a fee** *Some lawyers charge exorbitant fees.* 有些律师收费高得吓人。| **legal/medical fee** *The insurance company paid all my medical fees.* 保险公司支付了我的全部医疗费。**2** an amount of money that you pay to do something 费用: *school fees* 学费 | **entrance fee** *The entrance fees have gone up by 50%.* 入会[场]费已经上涨了50%。—see 见 COST[1] (USAGE), PAY[2] (USAGE) 2 2

fee·ble /ˈfibḷ; ˈfiːbəl/ *adj* **1** extremely weak 非常虚弱的, 无力的: *My grandfather was too feeble to sit up in bed.* 我的祖父非常虚弱, 无法在床上坐起来。| *a feeble attempt* 无力的尝试 **2** a feeble joke, excuse, argument etc is not very good or effective〔笑话、借口、论点等〕蹩脚的; 无效的, 站不住脚的: *people*

who come in late with feeble excuses 带着站不住脚的借口晚进来的人 **3** a feeble manager, teacher etc cannot control the people they are in charge of〔经理、教师等〕软弱的, 控制不住下属的

feeble-mind·ed /ˌ‥ˈ‥◂/ *adj* **1** unable to think clearly and decide what to do 无决断的, 动摇不定的, 思想糊涂的: *Her husband's so feeble-minded – he won't do a thing unless she tells him to.* 她的丈夫很优柔寡断 —— 除非她叫他做, 否则他什么事都不做。**2** *old use* having much less than average intelligence【旧】弱智的, 低能的 —**feeble-mindedly** *adv* —**feeble-mindedness** *n* [U]

1 2 **feed**[1] /fid; fiːd/ *past tense and past participle* **fed** /fɛd; fed/ *v*

1 ▶GIVE FOOD 给予食物◀ [T] **a)** to give food to a person or animal 喂养, 饲养, 为…提供食品: *Have you fed the cat?* 你喂猫了吗? | *He's so old and ill he can't feed himself any more.* 他年老多病, 再也无法自己进食。| **feed sth to sb** *Feed the food to the baby in small pieces.* 用小块的食品喂婴儿。| **feed sb on sth** *Most people feed parrots on nuts.* 大多数人用干果喂鹦鹉。**b)** to provide enough food for a group of people 养活〔一群人, 一家人〕: *You can't feed a family of five on $100 a week.* 你无法靠每周100美元来养活一家五口。

2 ▶PLANT 植物◀ [T] to give a special substance to a plant which makes it grow 给…施肥: *Feed the tomatoes once a week.* 每周给番茄施一次肥。

3 ▶ANIMAL/BABY 动物/婴儿◀ [I] if a baby or an animal feeds, they eat〔动物或婴儿〕吃 (东西): *Frogs generally feed at night.* 青蛙一般在晚上进食。—see also 另见 **feed on sth** (FEED[1])

4 ▶SUPPLY STH 供应某物◀ [T] to supply something such as FUEL[1] (1) or information to someone or something 给…供应〔燃料〕; 给…提供〔信息〕: **feed sth with** *The carburettor has to keep feeding the cylinders with petrol.* 化油器得不停地向汽缸输送汽油。| **feed sth into** *The data is then fed into a computer.* 数据随后被输入电脑。| **feed sth to sb** *US intelligence had been feeding false information to a KGB agent.* 美国情报机构过去一直在给一名克格勃间谍提供假情报。

5 ▶PUSH STH THROUGH 把某物导入◀ [T] to gradually push or put something such as a tube or a wire through a small hole〔由小孔逐渐地〕放入, 导入: **feed sth into/through** *The tube was fed down through the patient's throat into her stomach.* 软管慢慢通过病人的喉咙插入她的胃部。

6 [T] **feed sb's guilt/vanity/paranoia etc** to do something that makes someone feel more guilty etc 使某人更内疚/洋洋得意/偏执多疑等: *You shouldn't say that, you'll only feed his paranoia.* 你不该那样说话, 这只会让他更偏执猜疑。

7 feed lines/jokes to sb to say things to another performer so that they can make jokes 为某表演者提台词〔以让他作为笑料〕

8 well-fed/under-fed/poorly-fed having plenty of food or not enough food 吃得饱的/吃不饱的/吃得很差的: *exhausted, under-fed children* 疲惫不堪、食不果腹的儿童

9 feed your face *informal* to eat a lot of food【非正式】大吃一顿

10 feed sb a line *informal* to tell someone something which is not true so that they will do what you want【非正式】向某人虚报情况[撒谎]: *She tried to feed him a line about unexpected expenses.* 她企图向他虚报情况, 来解释那些意外的开支。

11 feed a meter to keep putting money into a machine so that you can have electricity, park your car etc〔为了供电或泊车等〕不断往计时器投币 —see also 另见 BREASTFEED, FORCE-FEED, SPOON-FEED, **mouth to feed** (MOUTH[1] (9))

feed off sth *phr v* [T] **1** if an animal feeds off something, it gets food from it〔动物〕从…取食: *The pigeons feed off our neighbour's crops.* 这些鸽子从我们邻居的庄稼取食。**2** an insulting way of saying that someone uses something to continue their activities 乱用; 靠…过日子〔侮辱性说法〕: *The press feeds off gossip and tittle-tattle.* 新闻界靠搜集流言飞语过活。

feed on sth *phr v* [T] **1** if an animal feeds on a particular food, it usually eats that food〔动物〕以…为食物: *Owls feed on mice and other small animals.* 猫头鹰以老鼠和其他小动物为食。**2** if a feeling or process feeds on something, it becomes stronger because of it 使〔某种感觉或过程〕变得更强烈: *Prejudice feeds on mistrust and ignorance.* 怀疑和无知会助长偏见。

feed sb **up** *phr v* [T] to give someone a lot of food to make them more healthy〔用大量食物〕养肥, 养壮〔某人〕

feed[2] *n*

1 ▶BABY 婴儿◀ [C] one of the times when you give milk to a small baby〔给婴儿的〕一次喂奶: *Is it time for Zoe's feed yet?* 到了给佐伊喂奶的时间吗?

2 ▶ANIMAL FOOD 动物的食物◀ [U] food for animals 饲料: *hen-feed* 鸡饲料

3 ▶TUBE 管道◀ [C] a tube which supplies a machine with FUEL[1] (1) 进 (燃) 料管: *There's a blockage in the petrol feed.* 汽油的输油管被阻塞了。

4 ▶MEAL 饭菜◀ [C] *old-fashioned* a big meal【过时】一顿饱餐

5 ▶PERFORMER 表演者◀ [C] *BrE* a performer who says things so that another performer can make jokes about them【英】〔喜剧演员的〕逗哏搭档 —see also 另见 CHICKENFEED

feed·back /ˈfidˌbæk; ˈfiːdbæk/ *n* [U] **1** advice, criticism etc about how successful or useful something is 反馈意见: *Most of the feedback we've received so far has been positive.* 我们迄今收到的反馈意见大都是肯定的。**2** an unpleasant high noise heard when a MICROPHONE is too close to an AMPLIFIER〔话筒太靠近放大器而产生的〕噪声 3

feed·bag /ˈfidbæg; ˈfiːdbæg/ *n* [C] *AmE* a bag put around a horse's head containing food; NOSEBAG【美】〔挂在马头上的〕饲料袋

feed·er /ˈfidɚ; ˈfiːdə/ *n* [C] **1 a slow/fussy etc feeder** a baby that eats it's food in a slow, FUSSY etc way 吃得慢的/挑食的婴儿 **2** a small road or railway line that takes traffic onto a main road or railway line〔汇入主干车道的〕支路; 公路[铁路]支线 **3** a container with food for animals or birds〔喂鸟兽的〕饲料容器 **4** *old-fashioned* a piece of cloth put under a baby's chin when he or she is eating; BIB (1)【过时】〔婴儿进食时放在下巴下的〕围嘴

feeder school /ˈ‥ ˌ‧/ *n* [C] a school from which many pupils go to a SECONDARY SCHOOL in the same area〔派学生到同一地区中学就读的〕直属学校

feeding-bot·tle /ˈ‥ ˌ‥/ *n* [C] a plastic bottle used for giving milk to a baby or young animal (塑料) 奶瓶

feeding ground /ˈ‥ ˌ‧/ *n* [C] a place where a group of animals or birds find food to eat〔动物或鸟类的〕聚食场

Feeding of the Five Thou·sand, the /ˌ‥‥ˈ‥/ a story from the Bible in which Jesus performs a MIRACLE by providing food for 5000 people with only five loaves (LOAF) of bread and two fish. People sometimes use this phrase humorously to talk about a situation in which they have to provide a meal for a lot of people. 五千人吃饱的奇迹〔《圣经》故事, 讲述耶稣仅用五块饼和两条鱼就让5000人吃饱的奇迹。人们谈到必须为许多人准备餐饭时, 有时会幽默地使用这一短语〕: *We have Beth's family and mine coming for Christmas, so it'll be like the Feeding of the Five Thousand.* 贝丝一家和我家人都要来过圣诞节, 到时候就会像要给5000人吃饱一样。

feel[1] /fil; fiːl/ *v past tense and past participle* **felt** /fɛlt; felt/ 1 1

1 ▶FEEL HAPPY/SICK ETC 感到愉快/不愉快等◀ [linking verb 连系动词, I] to experience a particular feeling or emotion 感受到, 觉得, 体会到: *You can never tell what he's feeling.* 你怎样也无法明白他此刻的感觉。| **feel fine/sick/hungry/guilty etc** *I'm feeling a little better today.* 我今天觉得身体好了一点。| *I felt a bit awkward having to ask them for money.* 向他们要钱我觉得有点别扭。| *We felt insulted by their offer.* 我们感到被他们的提议侮辱了。| **feel as if/as though** *I felt as though I'd won a million dollars.* 我觉得就像赢了一百万美元似的。

2 ▶NOTICE 注意到◀ [T not in progressive 不用进行式] to notice something that is happening to you 注意到, 感受到: *He loved feeling the sand between his toes.* 他喜欢脚趾踩在沙里的感觉。| **feel sb/sth do sth** *Terry felt the snake touch his foot.* 特里感觉那条蛇触到他的脚。| **feel yourself doing sth** *I felt myself blushing slightly.* 我觉得有点脸红。

3 ▶FEEL SMOOTH/DRY ETC 觉得光滑/干燥等◀ [linking verb 连系动词] if something feels smooth, dry, cold etc, this is the feeling it gives you, especially when you touch it〔摸上去〕感觉是…: *Her skin felt cold and rough.* 她的皮肤摸上去又凉又粗糙。| **feel as if/as though** *My leg feels as if it's broken.* 我的一条腿好像断了似的。

4 it feels good/strange etc if a situation, event etc feels good, strange etc, this is how it makes you feel〔情况、事件等使人〕觉得很好/感到奇怪等: *It felt wonderful to be wearing clean clothes again.* 再次穿上干净的衣服让我感觉好极了。| *How does it feel to be 40?* 到了40岁有什么感受?

5 ▶HAVE AN OPINION 有意见◀ [T not usually in progressive 一般不用进行式] to have a particular opinion, especially one that is based on your feelings, not on facts〔尤指根据感觉而不是事实〕以为, 认为: **feel (that)** *I can't help feeling that he deserved it.* 我不免认为他活该。| **[+about]** *How do you feel about all these changes in the curriculum?* 你认为课程的这些改动怎么样? | **feel sure/certain** (=think that something is definitely true) 确信/有把握 *She felt sure she'd made the right decision.* 她确信自己作了正确的决定。

6 feel like a) to want to have something or do something 想要: *I felt like another glass of wine.* 我想再喝一杯葡萄酒。| *He didn't feel like going to work.* 他不想去工作。**b)** to give you a particular feeling 感觉像, 摸上去像: *It's nice fabric – it feels like velvet.* 这布很好 —— 摸上去像天鹅绒。| *I was only there two days but it felt like a week!* 我在那儿只有两天, 但感觉像过了一个星期。**c)** to feel as if you are a particular kind of person 感觉自己是〔某一种人〕: *They made me feel like one of the family.* 他们使我觉得自己是他们家里的一分子。

7 ►TOUCH 摸◄ [T] to touch something with your fingers to find out about it 触摸: *She could feel a lump on her breast.* 她能摸到自己的乳房有一个肿块。| *Feel the quality of this cloth.* 摸摸这布的质地吧。—see picture on page A21 参见 A21 页图

8 feel around/on etc sth (for sth) to search for something with your fingers 〔用手指〕摸索〔某物〕: *She felt about in her bag for a pencil.* 她在袋子里摸着找铅笔。

9 feel the force/effects/benefits etc of sth to experience the good or bad results of something 感受某物的力量/受到某物的影响/感受某物的好处等: *The company is beginning to feel the effects of the strike.* 公司开始受到罢工的影响。

10 feel the need to do sth to feel that you need to do something 觉得需要做某事: *Sometimes we feel the need to get out of New York and take things easy.* 有时我们觉得需要离开纽约, 好好放松一下。

11 feel your way a) to move carefully, with your hands out in front of you because you cannot see properly 〔因看不清楚而伸出手来〕摸索前进: *He felt his way across the room, and found the light switch.* 他摸着走到房间的另一头, 找到电灯开关。**b)** to do things slowly and carefully, because you are unsure about a new situation 〔由于对新情况无把握而〕谨慎行事; 摸索行进: *He hasn't been in the job long and he's still feeling his way.* 他做这个工作还不久, 所以仍然在摸索着干。

12 feel free *spoken* used to tell someone that you are happy if they want to do something【口】尽管做, 没问题: *"Could I use your phone for a minute?" "Feel free."* "我能用一下你的电话吗?" "请便。" | **feel free to do sth** *Please feel free to make suggestions.* 请随便提建议, 不要拘束。

13 I know (just/exactly) how you feel *spoken* used to express sympathy with a remark someone has just made【口】我(十分)理解你的心情: *"Everything I do seems to go wrong!" "I know just how you feel!"* "我做的一切似乎都错了!" "我完全理解你的心情!"

14 not feel yourself *spoken* to not feel as healthy or happy as usual【口】身体不舒服; 心情不好: *Don't take any notice of her – she's not feeling quite herself today.* 别理睬她 —— 她今天很不高兴。

15 feel your age to realize that you are not as young or active as you used to be 感到老了: *It was only looking at his son that made him feel his age.* 他看着儿子才发现自己老了。

16 feel the cold to suffer because of cold weather 怕冷: *Old people tend to feel the cold more.* 老人往往更容易怕冷。

17 feel a death/a loss etc to react very strongly to a bad event, especially someone's death 对〔某人的〕死感觉到悲痛/对损失感到难过等: *Susan felt her grandmother's death more than the others.* 苏珊对她祖母的死比别人更悲痛。

feel for sb *phr v* [T] to feel sympathy for someone 同情〔某人〕: *I really feel for the parents of that little boy who was killed.* 我实在同情那个被杀男孩的父母。

feel sb ↔ **out** *phr v* [T] *AmE informal* to ask someone's opinions or feelings【美, 非正式】征求〔某人〕的看法: *Have you felt out your parents about using the cabin?* 你使用这小屋有没有征求过父母的看法?

feel sb ↔ **up** *phr v* [T] *informal* to touch someone sexually, without their permission【非正式】〔未得到允许而猥亵地〕摸弄〔某人〕

3 **feel²** *n* [singular] **1** the way that something feels when you touch it 感觉, 触觉, 手感: *I like the feel of this cloth.* 我喜欢这块布的手感。| *a soft feathery feel* 羽毛般的柔软感觉 **2** a general idea about something 〔对某事的〕一般印象, 大体感觉: *The weight adds a feel of quality to these plates.* 这些盘子的重量给它们增加了质感。**3 have a feel for** *informal* to have a natural understanding of something and skill in doing it【非正式】对…有天赋: *You've got to have a feel for the music.* 你得具备音乐天赋。

feel·er /ˈfiːlə; ˈfiːlə/ *n* [C usually plural 一般用复数] **1** one of the two long things on an insect's head which it uses to feel or touch things 〔昆虫头部的〕触角, 触须 **2 put out feelers** to start to try to discover what people think about something that you want to do 试探〔别人对你想做的事怎么想〕: *They seem to be interested in a peace settlement and have begun putting out feelers.* 他们似乎对和平解决感兴趣, 已经开始进行试探。

feel-good /ˈ· ·/ *adj* **feel-good film/programme/music etc** a film etc whose main purpose is to make you feel happy and cheerful 让人感到愉悦的影片/节目/音乐等

feel good factor /ˈ· · ˌ··/ *n* [U] *especially BrE* a feeling among ordinary people that everything is going well, and they need not worry about spending money【尤英】〔普通人的〕快乐感; 快乐因子

feel·ing¹ /ˈfiːlɪŋ; ˈfiːlɪŋ/ *n* S1 W1

1 ►ANGER/SADNESS/JOY ETC 愤怒/伤心/快乐等感觉◄ [C] something that you feel such as anger, sadness, or happiness 〔愤怒、伤心、快乐等的〕感觉: [+of] *She suddenly had a great feeling of relief.* 她突然产生一种十分宽慰的感觉。| *Feelings of guilt are common in such cases.* 内疚感在这些情况下很常见。| *It's a wonderful feeling to be back home again.* 又回到家里感觉太好了。| **the feeling's mutual** (=used to say that you have the same feeling about someone as they have about you) 这种感觉是我们彼此都有的 *"I don't ever want to see you again." "The feeling's mutual."* "我再也不想见到你。" "彼此彼此。" | **feelings are running high** (=people are very angry or excited) 人们情绪高涨; 人们十分生气[兴奋] *It was the last game of the season, and feelings were running high.* 这是这个赛季的最后一场比赛, 人们情绪高涨。

2 ►OPINION 看法◄ [C] what you think and feel about a situation 〔对某一情况的〕感想, 看法, 想法: *My own personal feeling is that we should be very careful.* 我个人的看法是, 我们应当非常小心。| [+on] *What are your feelings on the issue of abortion?* 你对堕胎这一问题有什么看法? | [+about] *I think I've already made my feelings about this perfectly clear.* 我想我已经极其清楚地阐述了对这件事的感想。| **have mixed feelings** (=not be sure what you feel or think) 心里矛盾, 感觉[想法]混乱 *Parents often have mixed feelings about their children leaving home.* 家长们对孩子长大离家一事心里通常会很矛盾。

3 have/get the feeling (that) to think that something is probably true, or will probably happen 感觉〔某事可能是真的〕; 预感〔某事会发生〕: *Leslie suddenly got the feeling that somebody was watching her.* 莱斯莉突然感觉有人在看她。| *I've got a horrible feeling I forgot to turn off the cooker.* 我突然有一种可怕的感觉我忘了关炉灶了。

4 ►GENERAL ATTITUDE 普遍态度◄ [U] a general attitude among a group of people about a subject 〔一群人对某一问题的〕普遍情绪: [+against/in favour of] *Johnson underestimated the strength of public feeling against the war in Vietnam.* 约翰逊低估了公众反对越战情绪的强烈程度。

5 ►HEAT/COLD/PAIN ETC 热/冷/痛等◄ [C] something that you feel in your body such as heat, cold, tiredness etc 〔身体上的〕感觉: *I keep getting this funny feeling* (=a strange feeling) *in my neck* 我的脖子一直有这种奇怪的感觉。| *feelings of dizziness* 头晕的感觉

6 ►ABILITY TO FEEL 感知能力◄ [U] the ability to feel pain, heat etc in part of your body 〔身体部位疼痛、热等的〕感觉, 知觉: *Herzog had lost all feeling in his toes.* 赫佐格的脚趾已经完全失去知觉。

7 ►EFFECT OF A PLACE/BOOK ETC 地方/书籍等给人的影响◄ [singular] the effect that a place, book, film etc has on people and the way it makes them feel 〔地方、书籍、电影等的〕感染力: *Glastonbury has a great feeling of history about it.* 格拉斯顿伯里这地方有一种伟大的历史感染力。

8 I know the feeling *spoken* used to say that you understand how someone feels because you have had the same experience【口】我知道那种感觉: *"It's so embarrassing when you can't remember someone's name." "I know the feeling."* "当你记不起别人的名字时是很尴尬的。" "我知道那种感觉。"

9 bad/ill feeling anger, lack of trust etc between people, especially after an argument or unfair decision 〔尤指争论或不公正的决定后人们之间的〕反感, 恶感; 不满: *The recent rail strikes have caused a lot of ill feeling.* 最近的铁路罢工引起了人们强烈的反感。

10 with feeling in a way that shows you feel very angry, happy etc 充满感情地; 情绪激动地: *Chang spoke with feeling about the injustices of the regime.* 张情绪激愤地谈论了这个政权的不公之处。

11 a feeling (for) a) an ability to do something or understand a subject, which you get from experience 〔凭经验〕做[理解]〔某事〕的能力: *It's difficult to explain – you just get this feeling for it.* 这很难解释 —— 这只是种感觉。**b)** a natural ability to do something 天分, 天赋: *She has a real feeling for the violin.* 她对小提琴真有天分。

12 ▶EMOTIONS NOT THOUGHT 感情而非思想◀ [U] a way of reacting to things using your emotions, instead of thinking about them carefully 感情: *The Romantic writers valued feeling above all else.* 浪漫派作家重视感情超过其他一切。—see also 另见 **no hard feelings** (HARD[1] (26)), **hurt sb's feelings** (HURT[1] (5))

feeling² *adj* showing strong feelings 动人的, 多情的; 表现强烈感情的; 十分激动的: *a feeling look* 带有感情的一瞥; 传情的目光 —**feelingly** *adv*

fee-pay·ing /ˈ· ,··/ *adj BrE*【英】**1 fee-paying school** a school which you have to pay to go to 收费学校 **2 fee-paying student/patient** a student or PATIENT who pays for their education or medical treatment 缴费的学生/付费的病人

feet /fit; fiːt/ the plural of FOOT —see also 另见 **cold feet** (COLD[1] (7)), **feet of clay** (FOOT[1] (24)), **have itchy feet** (ITCHY (4))

feign /fen; feɪn/ *v* [T] *formal* to pretend to have a particular feeling or to be ill, asleep etc【正式】假装〔某种感情〕、装〔病、睡等〕: *Feigning a headache, I went upstairs to my room.* 我假装头痛, 上楼到房间去了。| *Mattie watched him approach with feigned indifference.* 玛蒂假装冷漠地看着他走近。

feint¹ /fent; feɪnt/ *n* [C] a movement or an attack that is intended to deceive an opponent, especially in BOXING〔尤指拳击中的〕佯攻, 虚晃一拳

feint² *v* [I,T] to pretend to hit someone in BOXING〔拳击中〕佯攻, 虚击

feist·y /ˈfaɪstɪ; ˈfaɪsti/ *adj approving* having a strong, determined character and being willing to argue with people【褒】顽强自信的; 好争辩的: *She has the feisty image of the successful entrepreneur.* 她具有成功企业家自信好强的形象。

fe·la·fel /fəˈlɑfəl; fəˈlɑːfəl/ *n* [C] another spelling of FALAFEL falafel 的另一种拼法

feld·spar /ˈfɛld,spɑr; ˈfeldspɑː/ also 又作 **felspar** *n* [U] a kind of grey or white mineral 长石〔一种灰色或白色的矿物〕

fe·li·ci·ta·tions /fə,lɪsəˈteʃənz; fɪ,lɪsɨˈteɪʃənz/ *interjection formal* used to wish someone happiness【正式】〔用于祝愿的〕祝贺; 祝词

fe·li·ci·tous /fəˈlɪsətəs; fɪˈlɪsɨtəs/ *adj formal* well-chosen and suitable【正式】恰当的, 贴切的, 选得好的: *a felicitous choice of candidate* 候选人的恰当选择 —**felicitously** *adv*

fe·li·ci·ty /fəˈlɪsətɪ; fɪˈlɪsɨti/ *n formal*【正式】**1** [U] happiness 幸福: *domestic felicity* 家庭幸福 **2** [U] the quality of being well-chosen or suitable 恰当, 巧妙: *the felicity of this arrangement* 这种安排的恰当 **3 felicities** [plural] suitable or well-chosen remarks or details 恰当[巧妙]的话[细节]

fe·line¹ /ˈfilaɪn; ˈfiːlaɪn/ *adj* **1** connected with cats or other members of the cat family such as lions 猫的; 猫科的 **2** looking like or moving like a cat 似猫的, 无声潜行的: *She moves with feline grace.* 她轻柔无声地行走, 姿态很美。

feline² *n* [C] *technical* a cat or a member of the cat family such as a tiger【术语】猫; 猫科动物〈如虎等〉

Fe·lix the Cat /,filɪks ðə ˋkæt; ,fiːlɪks ðə ˈkæt/ a CARTOON character in films and newspapers, who first appeared in 1921. He is a black and white cat. 菲利猫, 费利克斯猫〔电影和报纸上的卡通形象, 最早出现于1921年。它是一只毛色黑白相间的猫〕

fell¹ /fɛl; fel/ the past tense of FALL[1]

fell² *n* [C] a mountain or hill in the north of England〔英格兰北部的〕山, 山冈

fell³ *v* [T] **1** to cut down a tree 砍伐〔树木〕**2** to knock someone down with great force〔用力〕击倒〔某人〕

fell⁴ *adj* **at/in one fell swoop** doing a lot of things at the same time, using only one action 一下子, 立即, 马上: *I pressed the wrong button and deleted all the files in one fell swoop.* 我按错了按钮, 一下子把全部文档都删除了。

S3 **fel·la** /ˈfɛlə; ˈfelə/ *n* [C] *spoken*【口】**1** a man 家伙: *I was talking to this fella I work with.* 我正和这个一起工作的家伙谈话。**2** a boyfriend 男朋友: *She's fine. Her new fella's lovely.* 她很好, 她那新交的男朋友很可爱。

fel·la·ti·o /fəˈleʃio; fəˈleɪʃiəʊ/ *n* [U] *formal* the practice of touching a man's PENIS with the lips and tongue to give sexual pleasure【正式】吮吸阴茎; 口交 —compare 比较 CUNNILINGUS

fel·ler /ˈfɛlɚ; ˈfelə/ *n* [C] *informal* a man【非正式】人; 男人; 家伙

Fel·li·ni /fɛˈlinɪ; feˈliːni/, **Fed·e·ri·co** /,fɛdəˈriko; ,fedəˈriːkəʊ/ (1920-93) an Italian film DIRECTOR who had an important influence on the cinema. His films, including *La Dolce Vita* (1960), and *Eight and a Half* (1963), often show a society where people are not moral, and are only interested in pleasure. 费利尼〔(1920-1993), 意大利电影导演, 曾对电影艺术产生过重大影响。其影片常揭露道德败坏、只重享乐的社会, 如《甜蜜的生活》(1960) 和《八部半》(1963)〕

fel·low¹ /ˈfɛlo; ˈfeləʊ/ *n* [C] **1** *old-fashioned* a man【过时】人; 男人: *Paul's an easy-going sort of fellow.* 保罗是个随和的家伙。**2** *old-fashioned* a friendly way of addressing a man【过时】朋友〔用于友好地称呼男人〕: *Hello my dear fellow!* 你好, 亲爱的朋友! **3** *old-fashioned*【过时】**your/his etc fellows** the people who you work with, go to school with etc 你的/他的伙伴们〔指工作上的同事或学校的同学等〕: *He's much more serious than his school fellows.* 他比他的同学严肃多了。**4** *especially BrE* a member of an important society or a college【尤英】〔重要学会的〕会员; 〔学院的〕董事; 研究员: *Fellow of the Royal College of Surgeons* 皇家外科医学院院士

fellow² *adj* **1 fellow workers/students/countrymen etc** people who work, study etc with you 同事/同学/同胞等: *She ignored her fellow passengers throughout the whole journey.* 在整个旅程中她都不理睬同行的乘客。**2 our fellow man/men** other people in general 我们的同胞; 人类: *We all have obligations to our fellow men.* 我们大家对他人都负有义务。**3 fellow feeling** a feeling of sympathy and friendship towards someone because they are like you 同情, 同感; 情谊: *As an only child myself, I had a certain fellow feeling for Laura.* 我自己也是个独生子, 因此与劳拉有某种同感。 W3

fel·low·ship /ˈfɛlo,ʃɪp; ˈfeləʊʃɪp/ *n* **1** [U] a feeling of friendship resulting from shared interests or experiences〔因共同的兴趣或经历而产生的〕友情, 友谊, 伙伴关系: *A close fellowship developed among them.* 他们之间产生了密切的伙伴情谊。**2** [C] a group of people who share an interest or belief, especially Christians who have religious ceremonies together〔具有共同兴趣或信念的〕团体; 〔基督教的〕团契 **3** [C] *BrE* a job at a university which involves making a detailed study of a particular subject【英】〔大学里的〕研究员职位; 学院院士 **4** [C] *especially AmE* money given to a student to allow them to continue their studies at an advanced level【尤美】〔为让学生能进一步深造而授予的〕奖学金 **5** [C] *AmE* a group of officials who decide which students will receive this money【美】〔决定奖学金人选的〕奖学金评选组

fellow trav·ell·er *BrE*【英】, **fellow traveler** *AmE*【美】/,·· ˈ···/ *n* [C] someone you disapprove of because they agree with the aims of the Communist Party 同路人, 同情者〔指赞成共产党的宗旨的人〕

fel·on /ˈfɛlən; ˈfelən/ *n* [C] *law* someone who is guilty of a serious crime【法律】重罪犯

fel·o·ny /ˈfɛlənɪ; ˈfeləni/ *n* [C,U] *law* a serious crime such as murder【法律】重罪〈如谋杀〉—compare 比较 MISDEMEANOUR (2)

fel·spar /ˈfɛl,spɑr; ˈfelspɑː/ *n* [U] another spelling of FELDSPAR feldspar 的另一种拼法

felt¹ /fɛlt; felt/ the past tense and past participle of FEEL[1]

felt² *n* [U] a thick soft material made of wool, hair, or fur that has been pressed flat 毛毡

felt-tip /ˈ· ·/ also 又作 **felt-tip pen** /,· ˈ· ˈ/ *n* [C] a pen that has a hard piece of felt at the end that the ink comes through 毡头笔, 毡尖笔 —see picture at 参见 PEN[1] 图

fem a written abbreviation for 缩写= FEMININE or FEMALE

fe·male¹ /ˈfi,mel; ˈfiːmeɪl/ *adj* **1** belonging to the sex that can have babies or produce eggs 女(性)的; 雌(性)的; 母的: *a female spider* 雌蜘蛛, 母蜘蛛 **2** a female plant or flower produces fruit 雌性植物的, 雌蕊的 **3** *technical* a female part of a piece of equipment has a hole into which another part fits【术语】〔零件〕阴的, 内孔的, 凹的, 母式的: *a female plug* 内凹式插头 —**femaleness** *n* [U] S3 W3

female² *n* [C] **1** a person or animal that belongs to the sex that can have babies or produce eggs 女性; 雌性动物 **2** a woman or girl 女人; 女孩: *the prettiest female in Savannah* 萨瓦纳最漂亮的女人 W

Female Eu·nuch, The /,·· ˈ··/ (1970) a book by Germaine Greer which is considered to be one of the most important books of the Women's Movement《女阉人》〔(1970), 杰曼·格里尔创作的一本书, 被认为是女权运动最重要的作品之一〕

Fem·i·dom /ˈfɛmɪdɑm; ˈfemɪdɒm/ *n* [C] *trademark* a loose rubber tube with one end closed that fits inside a woman's VAGINA when she is having sex, so that she will not have a baby【商标】女用避孕套

fem·i·nine /ˈfɛmənɪn; ˈfemɨnɨn/ *adj* **1** having qualities that are considered to be typical of women, especially by being gentle, delicate and pretty 女性的, 妇女的; 柔美的: *Dianne loved pretty feminine things.* 黛安娜喜爱漂亮的女性用品。| *his slim, feminine hand* 他的瘦长的女性般的手 **2** a feminine noun, PRONOUN etc belongs to a class of words that have different inflections (INFLECTION (2)) from MASCULINE (4) or NEUTER[1] (2) words〔名词、代词等〕阴性的

Feminine Mys·tique, The /ˌ· · ˈ· ·/ (1963) a book by Betty Friedan which discusses the way women behave in US society. It is one of the books that started the Women's Movement in the 1960s.《女性的神秘》〔(1963), 贝蒂·弗里登创作的一本书, 论述美国女性的行为方式, 被视为20世纪60年代女权运动的发轫作品之一〕

fem·i·nin·i·ty /ˌfɛməˈnɪnətɪ; ˌfeməˈnɪnəti/ *n* [U] qualities that are considered to be typical of women, especially qualities that are gentle, delicate, and pretty 女子气质〔尤指温柔、娇小、美丽等〕: *Different cultures often have different concepts of femininity and masculinity.* 不同文化通常对女子气质和男子气概有不同的概念。

fem·i·nis·m /ˈfɛməˌnɪzəm; ˈfemənɪzəm/ *n* [U] the belief that women should have the same rights and opportunities as men 女权主义 —**feminist** *adj*: *feminist principles* 女权主义原则

CULTURAL NOTE 文化注释

Feminism and the Women's Movement have tried to change the way women are treated by men and by society. Compared with the past, women today have better job and educational opportunities, and are better paid than they were. Feminism has also made people think more about how women and men share work in the home and when raising children. It has also made people think more about problems such as SEXUAL HARASSMENT at work, and the way that women are shown in magazines and newspapers, in advertisements, and on television. Feminism has helped make more people aware of these problems, but some things have not changed very much. For example, women still do most of the work in the house, even if they have paid jobs. Women have not achieved equal political power, and there are still fewer women than men in senior jobs. People often talk about the GLASS CEILING, which refers to the limit that prevents successful women from getting the most powerful jobs in an organization. 女权主义和妇女运动试图改变男人和社会对待女人的方式。与过去相比, 现在的女性有更好的工作和教育机会, 比过去薪水更高。女权主义也让人们更多地思考男女在家务和养育孩子上的分工, 思考办公室性骚扰等问题, 思考报刊、广告和电视上的女性形象。女权主义帮助更多人认识到这些问题, 但也有一些事情并无多少改变。例如, 即便女人要上班挣钱, 大多数家务还是她们来做。女人还没有取得与男人同等的政治权力, 担任高级职务的女人仍要少于男人。人们经常谈到"玻璃天花板"(glass ceiling), 就是指妨碍成功女性在某个组织内担任最高职位的限制。

fem·i·nist /ˈfɛmənɪst; ˈfemənɪst/ *n* [C] someone who supports the idea that women should have the same rights and opportunities as men 女权主义者: *If she's a sort of feminist, I can understand why she said that.* 如果她是某种女权主义者, 我会理解她为何那样说。

femme fa·tale /ˌfæm fəˈtɑl; ˌfæm fəˈtɑːl/ *n* [C] *French* a beautiful woman who men find very attractive, even though she may make them unhappy【法】引诱男子堕落的女子; 妖妇, 荡妇

fe·mur /ˈfimə; ˈfiːmə/ *n* [C] the THIGH bone 股骨 —**femoral** /ˈfɛmərəl; ˈfemərəl/ *adj* —see picture at 参见 SKELETON 图

fen /fɛn; fen/ *n* [C] an area of low flat wet land, especially in Eastern England〔尤指英格兰东部的〕沼泽地带; 湿地

fence[1] /fɛns; fens/ *n* [C] **1** a structure made of wood, metal etc that surrounds a piece of land〔木头、金属等做的〕栅栏, 围栏, 篱笆 **2** a wall or other structure that horses jump over in a race or competition〔赛马中的〕障碍物 **3** *slang* someone who buys and sells stolen goods【俚】买卖赃物的人 **4 sit on the fence** to avoid saying which side of an argument you support 保持中立, 抱骑墙态度: *The Liberals prefer to sit on the fence while the other parties fight it out.* 自由党宁可抱骑墙态度, 坐待其他党派去斗争到底。—see also 另见 **mend (your) fences** (MEND[1] (4))

fence[2] *v* **1** [T] to put a fence around something 把…用栅栏[篱笆]围起来 **2** [I] to fight with a long thin sword as a sport 击剑 **3** [I+with] to answer someone's questions in a clever way in order to get an advantage in an argument 巧妙回答; 用言辞搪塞

fence sb/sth ↔ **in** *phr v* [T] **1** to surround a place with a fence 把〔某人/某物〕用栅栏[篱笆]围住 **2** [often passive 常用被动态] to make someone feel that they cannot leave a place or do what they want 限制〔某人的〕自由, 束缚〔某人〕: *Mothers with young children often feel fenced in at home.* 有幼儿的母亲们经常觉得被束缚在家里。

fence sb/sth ↔ **off** *phr v* [T] to separate one area from another area with a fence 用栅栏[篱笆]把…隔开: *a planting area fenced off from the main garden* 用栅栏与主花园隔开的种植区

fenc·er /ˈfɛnsə; ˈfensə/ *n* [C] someone who fights with a long thin sword as a sport 击剑者, 击剑运动员

fenc·ing /ˈfɛnsɪŋ; ˈfensɪŋ/ *n* [U] **1** the sport of fighting with a long thin sword 击剑〔运动〕 **2** fences or the pieces of wood, metal etc used to make them 栅栏[篱笆]; 筑栅栏[篱笆]的材料

fend /fɛnd; fend/ *v* **fend for yourself** to look after yourself without needing help from other people 独立生活; 照料自己: *The kids had to fend for themselves while their parents were away.* 父母不在家时, 孩子们只好自己照料自己。

fend sb/sth **off** *phr v* [T] **1** to defend yourself against someone who is attacking you 挡开〔某人/某物的攻击〕: *A bag or briefcase can be used to fend off an attacker.* 提包或公文包可用来抵挡攻击者。| *fending off the blows with his sword* 他用剑挡开攻击 **2** to deal with difficult questions, especially by avoiding answering them directly 避开, 回避〔难题〕: *I did my best to fend off his critical remarks.* 我尽力招架他的批评。

fend·er /ˈfɛndə; ˈfendə/ *n* [C] **1** *AmE* a bar fixed on the front or back of a car to protect it if it hits something【美】〔汽车前面或后面的〕保险杠; BUMPER[1] (1) *BrE*【英】—see picture on page A2 参见A2页图 **2** *AmE* the side part of a car that covers the wheels【美】〔汽车轮胎上的〕挡泥板; WING[1] (6) *BrE*【英】—see picture on page A2 参见A2页图 **3** a low metal wall around a FIREPLACE that prevents burning wood or coal from falling out 壁炉挡板 **4** *AmE* a curved piece of metal over the wheel of a bicycle that prevents water and mud from flying up【美】〔自行车上的〕挡泥板; MUDGUARD *BrE*【英】—see picture at 参见 BICYCLE[1] 图 **5** an object such as an old tyre used to protect the side of a boat〔船的〕碰垫, 护舷木, 防擦垫

fender-bend·er /ˈ· · ˌ· ·/ *n* [C] *AmE informal* a car accident in which little damage is done【美, 非正式】〔损毁轻微的〕小车祸

fen·nel /ˈfɛnl; ˈfenl/ *n* [U] a pale green plant whose seeds are used to give a special taste to food and which is also used as a vegetable 茴香

Fens, the /fɛnz; fenz/ an area of flat land in eastern England which used to be partly covered by the sea and now produces good crops 费恩〔英格兰东部一平坦地区。部分土地过去曾被海水覆盖, 现为农作物丰产区〕

fe·ral /ˈfɪrəl; ˈferəl/ *adj* feral animals used to live with humans but have become wild 未驯服的, 野的; 〔驯养后脱逃〕恢复野性的: *feral cats* 野猫

Fer·di·nand and Is·a·bel·la /ˌfɜdɪnænd ənd ɪzəˈbɛlə; ˌfɜːdɪnænd ənd ɪzəˈbelə/ King Ferdinand of Spain (1452-1516), and his wife, Queen Isabella of Spain (1451-1504), who were known as the **Catholic Monarchs**. They are famous for giving Christopher Columbus the money and ships to make the journey on which he discovered America. 斐迪南与伊莎贝拉〔指西班牙国王斐迪南(1452-1516)和王后伊莎贝拉(1451-1504)。他们以"天主教君主"著称。他们因给克里斯托弗·哥伦布提供了远航需要的资金和船只出名, 哥伦布因此发现了美洲〕

Fer·gu·son /ˈfɝgəsn; ˈfɜːgəsən/, **Sa·rah** /ˈsɛrə; ˈseərə/ —see 见 DUCHESS OF YORK

Fer·man·agh /fəˈmænə; fəˈmænə/ a former COUNTY in the southwest of Northern Ireland, now a local government DISTRICT 弗马纳〔原为北爱尔兰西南一郡, 现为一地方行政区〕

fer·ment[1] /fəˈmɛnt; fəˈment/ *v* [I,T] if fruit, beer, wine etc ferments or if it is fermented, the sugar in it changes to alcohol, especially because of the action of YEAST〔水果、啤酒、葡萄酒等〕(使)发酵 —**fermented** *adj*: *fermented fruit* 发酵的水果 —**fermentation** /ˌfɝmɛnˈteʃən; ˌfɜːmenˈteɪʃən/ *n* [U]

fer·ment[2] /ˈfɝmɛnt; ˈfɜːment/ *n* [U] a situation of great excitement or trouble in a country, especially because people disagree strongly with the government 骚乱; 动乱; 激荡: **be in (a state of) ferment** *The whole of Russia was in ferment.* 其时俄罗斯全国处于动乱之中。

Fer·mi /ˈfɝmɪ; ˈfɜːmi/, **En·ri·co** /ɛnˈriko; enˈriːkəʊ/ (1901-54) a US scientist, born in Italy, who won a Nobel Prize for his work on RADIOACTIVITY and produced the first controlled NUCLEAR REACTION (=a process in which the parts in the centre of an atom are rearranged to form new substances) 费米〔(1901-1954), 美国科学家, 出生于意大利。他曾在放射性研究方面有所建树, 并因此获得诺贝尔奖。他进行了首次可控制的核反应〕

fern /fɝn; fɜːn/ *n* [C] a type of plant which has feathery green leaves, but no flowers 蕨类植物, 羊齿植物 —**ferny** *adj*

fe·ro·cious /fəˋroʃəs; fəˈrəʊʃəs/ *adj* **1** violent, dangerous, and frightening 凶猛的，凶残的: *The battle was long and ferocious.* 战斗持久而且激烈。| *ferocious dogs* 凶猛的狗 **2** very strong, severe, and unpleasant 狂暴的；猛烈的；使人不舒服的: *a ferocious headache* 剧烈的头痛 | *The heat was ferocious.* 那时热得厉害。—**ferociously** *adv* —**ferociousness** *n* [U]

fe·ro·ci·ty /fəˋrɑsətɪ; fəˈrɒsəti/ *n* [U] violence and cruelty 凶暴，残暴，凶猛

Fer·ra·ri /fəˋrɑrɪ; fəˈrɑːri/ *trademark* a very fast type of car made by the Italian company Ferrari, which produces both sports cars and racing cars【商标】法拉利〔意大利跑车和赛车制造商法拉利公司制造的一种高速、昂贵的小汽车〕

fer·ret¹ /ˋfɛrɪt; ˈferɪ̣t/ *n* [C] a small animal with a pointed nose used to hunt rats and rabbits 雪貂，白鼬

ferret² *v* [I] **1** [always+adv/prep] *informal* to search for something inside a drawer, box etc by pushing things about【非正式】〔在抽屉、箱子里〕搜找，翻寻: [**+about/around/for**] *She ferreted about in her desk for a pen.* 她在书桌抽屉里翻找钢笔。**2** to hunt rats and rabbits using a ferret 用雪貂猎鼠[猎兔]

ferret sth ↔ **out** *phr v* [T] to succeed in finding a piece of information that is difficult to find 查获；搜出: *She managed to ferret out the details of her husband's affair.* 她设法查悉丈夫婚外情的细节。

Fer·ri·er, **Kath·leen** /ˋfɛrɪɚ; ˈferiə/, /ˋkæθlin; ˈkæθliːn/ (1912-53) a British singer of OPERA and CLASSICAL music, famous for her beautiful CONTRALTO voice 费里尔〔(1912-1953)，英国歌剧和古典音乐演唱家，以优美的女低音闻名〕

fer·ris wheel /ˋfɛrɪs ˌhwil; ˈferɪ̣s ˌwiːl/ *n* [C] *especially AmE* a large upright wheel with seats on it for people to ride on in an AMUSEMENT PARK【尤美】摩天轮，大转轮〔指游乐园里设有座位的直立巨轮〕; BIG WHEEL *BrE*【英】

fer·rous /ˋfɛrəs; ˈferəs/ *adj technical* containing or connected with iron【术语】含铁的，铁的: *Ferrous metals are magnetic.* 含铁[黑色]金属有磁性。

fer·rule /ˋfɛrəl; ˈferuːl/ *n* [C] a piece of metal or rubber put on the end of a stick to make it stronger〔手杖末端的〕金属箍；橡皮箍

fer·ry¹ /ˋfɛrɪ; ˈferi/ *n* [C] a boat that carries people or goods across a river or a narrow part of a sea 渡船，摆渡(船)

ferry² *v* [T always+adv/prep] to carry people or things a short distance from one place to another in a boat or other vehicle 渡运，运送: **ferry sb/sth to/from etc** *The lifeboat ferried the crew and passengers to safety.* 救生艇把船员和乘客送到安全的地方。| *A small bus ferries tourists from their hotels to the beach.* 一辆小巴士将游客从旅馆送到海滨。

fer·ry·boat /ˋfɛrɪˌbot; ˈferibəʊt/ *n* [C] a FERRY[1] 渡船，摆渡(船)

fer·ry·man /ˋfɛrɪmən; ˈferimən/ *n* [C] someone who guides a ferry across a river 渡船工人，船夫

fer·tile /ˋfɝtl̩; ˈfɜːtaɪl/ *adj* **1** fertile land or soil produces good crops 肥沃的，富饶的: *the fertile plains of western Canada* 加拿大西部肥沃的平原 **2** able to produce babies, young animals, or new plants 可繁殖的，能生育的: *Most men remain fertile into old age.* 大多数男子直到老年还有生育能力。—opposite 反义词 INFERTILE **3** **fertile imagination/mind/brain** *often humorous* an imagination etc that is able to think of interesting and unusual ideas【常幽默】丰富的想象力，主意多[有创造性]的头脑 **4** **fertile ground** a situation where new ideas, political groups etc can easily develop and succeed 有利于〔新思想、政治组织等〕发展的环境: *Poor areas of East London became fertile ground for Mosley's fascist movement.* 伦敦东部的贫民区成了有利于莫斯利的法西斯运动的温床。

Fertile Cres·cent, the /ˌ· · ˈ· ·/ an area in the Middle East in the shape of a CRESCENT (=a curved shape) from Israel to the Gulf, including the land around the rivers Tigris and Euphrates. Several important ancient CIVILIZATIONs had their homes there, such as the Assyrian and Sumerian civilizations. 肥沃新月，新月沃地〔指中东从以色列至波斯湾的一片形似新月的地区，包括底格里斯河和幼发拉底河周围的土地。这里是亚述文明、苏美尔文明等几大古代文明的发祥地〕 —see also 另见 BABYLON, MESOPOTAMIA

fer·til·i·ty /fɚˋtɪlətɪ; fɜːˈtɪḷəti/ *n* [U] **1** the ability of the land or soil to produce good crops 肥沃；肥力: *loss of soil fertility* 土壤肥力的流失 **2** the ability of a person, animal, or plant to produce babies, young animals, or seeds 生育能力，繁殖力

fertility drug /ˈ· ˈ· · ·, ˌ· / *n* [C] a drug given to a woman to help her have a baby 助孕药，生育药

fer·ti·lize also 又作 **-ise** *BrE*【英】/ˋfɝtl̩ˌaɪz; ˈfɜːtḷaɪz/ *v* [T] **1** to make SPERM join an egg so that a young baby or animal develops, or to join particles of POLLEN so that a new plant develops 使受精，使受孕 **2** to put a substance on the soil which makes crops grow 施肥 —**fertilization** /ˌfɝtl̩əˋzeʃən; ˌfɜːtḷaɪˈzeɪʃən/ *n* [U]

fer·ti·liz·er /ˋfɝtl̩ˌaɪzɚ; ˈfɜːtḷaɪzə/ *n* [C,U] a substance that is put on the land to make crops grow 肥料

fer·vent /ˋfɝvənt; ˈfɜːvənt/ *adj* believing or feeling something very strongly and sincerely 热情的；炽热的；热烈的；强烈的: *a fervent appeal for peace* 对和平的强烈吁求 | **fervent admirer/believer/supporter etc** *Even her most fervent admirers admit that Thatcher had her faults.* 甚至连撒切尔的最狂热的倾慕者也承认她有过错。—**fervency** *n* [U] —**fervently** *adv*

fer·vid /ˋfɝvɪd; ˈfɜːvḍd/ *adj formal* believing or feeling something too strongly【正式】热烈的；激烈的；热情的 —**fervidly** *adv*

fer·vour *BrE*【英】, **fervor** *AmE*【美】/ˋfɝvɚ; ˈfɜːvə/ *n* [U] very strong belief or feeling 狂热，热诚: *religious fervour* 宗教热情

fess /fɛs; fes/ *v*

fess up [I] *AmE informal* to admit that you have done something wrong but it is not very serious【美，非正式】承认，交代: *Come on, fess up! Who ate that last cookie?* 得了，从实招来吧！谁吃了最后那块甜饼？

fes·ter /ˋfɛstɚ; ˈfestə/ *v* [I] **1** if an unpleasant feeling or problem festers, it gets more unpleasant〔不快的感觉或问题〕加剧，恶化: *The insult festered in his mind.* 那次受辱使他心中的不快日益加深。**2** if a wound festers, it becomes infected〔伤口〕溃烂，化脓: *festering sores* 溃烂的疮 **3** if rubbish or dirty objects fester, they decay and smell bad〔垃圾等〕腐烂发臭

fes·ti·val /ˋfɛstəvl̩; ˈfestḍvəl/ *n* [C] **1** an occasion when there are performances of many films, plays, pieces of music etc, which happens in the same place every year〔每年在同一地点举行的〕节庆；纪念活动: *the Newport Jazz festival* 纽波特爵士音乐节 **2** a special occasion when people celebrate something such as a religious event, and there is often a public holiday 节日，喜庆日: *Christmas is one of the main festivals in the Christian Calendar.* 圣诞节是基督教历法中的一个重要节日。

> **CULTURAL NOTE 文化注释**
>
> In Britain and the United States, many different types of festival are organized for different branches of the arts, including music, theatre, comedy, film, and literature. Some of the most well-known music festivals held in Britain are: Glastonbury (mainly rock music), the Cambridge Folk Festival, and the Brecon Jazz Festival. Festivals of classical music include the Proms held every summer at the Albert Hall in London, the Aldeburgh Festival in Suffolk, and the Glyndebourne Festival in East Sussex where OPERAs are performed. In Wales, music and poetry competitions called EISTEDDFODs are held every year. Plays, music, and other types of entertainment are performed at the Edinburgh Festival every summer. Part of this festival is called the Edinburgh Fringe, and it is known especially for performances of ALTERNATIVE COMEDY. 在英国和美国，有多种艺术的节日，包括音乐节、戏剧节、喜剧节、电影节、文学节。英国最著名的音乐节有格拉斯顿伯里音乐节（主要为摇滚音乐）、剑桥民歌节和布雷肯爵士音乐节。古典音乐节有每年夏天在伦敦艾伯特音乐厅举行的逍遥音乐会、在萨福克举办的奥尔德堡音乐节，还有在东萨赛克斯举办的格林德包恩歌剧节。威尔士每年举办的音乐和诗歌比赛，叫做"威尔士诗歌音乐比赛大会"。每年夏天的爱丁堡艺术节上演戏剧、音乐和其他娱乐活动。该艺术节的一部分叫做爱丁堡边缘艺术节，尤以演出另类戏剧著名。

Festival Hall, the /ˌ· · · ˈ· ·/ also 又作 **the Royal Festival Hall** a large concert hall used especially for performances of CLASSICAL music. It is part of the South Bank centre, on the southern side of the River Thames in London. 皇家节日音乐厅〔伦敦泰晤士河南岸一大型音乐厅，尤用于演奏古典音乐，为南岸艺术中心的一部分〕

Festival of Britain /ˌ· · · ˈ· ·/ a large EXHIBITION in London in 1951 on the bank of the River Thames to show the successes of post-war Britain 英国庆典〔1951年在英国伦敦泰晤士河河畔举行的大型展览，旨在展示英国战后取得的成就〕

Festival of Nine Les·sons and Car·ols /ˌ· · · ˌ· ˌ· · · ˈ· ·/ a service held just before Christmas in some Christian churches containing readings from the Bible and Christmas CAROLS〔圣诞节前举行的〕读经唱诗礼拜

fes·tive /ˋfɛstɪv; ˈfestɪv/ *adj* **1** looking or feeling bright and cheerful in a way that seems suitable for celebrating something

欢乐的, 欢庆的: *There was a festive atmosphere in the city.* 城里充满欢乐的节日气氛。| *John was obviously in a festive mood.* 约翰显然心情十分愉快, 像在过节似的。**2 festive occasion** a day when you celebrate something special such as a birthday 节庆场合; 纪念活动 **3 the festive season** the period around CHRISTMAS 圣诞节期间, 节期

fes·tiv·i·ty /fɛsˈtɪvətɪ; feˈstɪvəti/ *n* [U] **1 festivities** [plural] things that are done to celebrate a special occasion such as drinking, eating, dancing etc 庆祝活动, 庆典: *The festivities started with a procession through the town.* 庆祝活动以在城里的巡游开始。**2** a happy and cheerful atmosphere that exists when people celebrate something 欢乐, 欢庆: *There was an air of festivity in the village.* 村里一片欢庆气氛。

fes·toon¹ /fɛsˈtun; feˈstuːn/ *v* [T] to cover something with long pieces of material, especially for decoration 结彩于, 给…装饰花彩: **be festooned with** *Malaga was festooned with banners and flags in honour of the king's visit.* 马拉加彩旗飘扬, 欢迎国王到访。

festoon² *n* [C] *formal* a long thin piece of material, used especially for decoration【正式】花彩, 花彩装饰物

fet·a /ˈfɛtə; ˈfetə/ *n* [U] a white cheese from Greece made from sheep's milk〔希腊产的〕羊奶白干酪

fe·tal /ˈfitl̩; ˈfiːtl/ *adj* the usual American spelling of foetal (FOETUS) foetal 的一般美式拼法

2 **fetch** /fɛtʃ; fetʃ/ *v* [T] **1** to go to the place where something or someone is and bring them back 拿来; 请来; 找来: *Quick! Go and fetch a doctor.* 快!快去请医生来。| **fetch sth from** *Would you mind going to fetch the kids from school?* 你能去学校接孩子们吗? | **fetch sb sth/fetch sth for sb** *Run upstairs and fetch me my glasses, will you?* 跑上楼替我拿眼镜来, 好吗? —see 见 BRING (USAGE) **2** to be sold for a particular amount of money, especially at a public sale 卖得, 售得: *The painting is expected to fetch at least $20 million.* 这幅画预计至少能卖2000万美元。**3 fetch sb a blow/clip etc** *BrE informal* to hit someone【英, 非正式】给某人一拳/一击: *I fetched him a clip round the ear.* 我打了他一记耳光。**4 fetch and carry** to do simple and boring jobs for someone as if you were their servant 做杂务, 打杂: *Am I supposed to fetch and carry for him all day?* 难道要我整天替他打杂吗? **5** *BrE* to make people react in a particular way【英】使做出某种反应; 吸引来; 引起: *This announcement fetched a huge cheer from the audience.* 这项通知博得听众一阵极其热烈的欢呼声。

fetch up *phr v BrE informal*【英, 非正式】**1** [I always+adv/prep] to arrive somewhere without intending to〔突然〕到达: **[+in/at etc]** *I fell asleep on the train and fetched up in Glasgow.* 我在火车上睡着了, 醒来时竟到了格拉斯哥。**2** [I,T] to VOMIT¹ 呕吐: *She fetched up all over the blankets.* 她把毯子吐得一塌糊涂。

fetch·ing /ˈfɛtʃɪŋ; ˈfetʃɪŋ/ *adj* attractive, especially because the clothes you are wearing suit you〔尤指因衣着得体而〕动人的, 迷人的, 吸引人的: *Your sister looks very fetching in that dress.* 你妹妹穿那身衣服显得格外动人。—**fetchingly** *adv*

fete¹ /fet; feɪt/ *n* [C] **1** *BrE* an outdoor event where there are competitions and things to eat and drink, usually organized to get money【英】〔尤指为募捐而组织的〕游乐会: *the church fete* 教堂的游乐会 **2** *AmE* a special occasion to celebrate something【美】庆祝活动, 盛会: *Prom Night is the fete of the year for high school students.* 班级舞会之夜对高中学生来说是一年里最大的庆祝活动。

fete² *v* [T usually passive 一般用被动态] to honour someone by holding public celebrations for them〔通过举行庆祝活动来〕款待, 向…致敬: *The team was feted from coast to coast.* 这个队在全国所到之处都受到热情款待。

fet·id /ˈfɛtɪd; ˈfiːtəd/ *adj formal* having a strong, bad smell【正式】恶臭的: *the black fetid water of the lake* 湖里又黑又臭的水

fet·ish /ˈfɛtɪʃ; ˈfetɪʃ/ *n* [C] **1** something you are always thinking about or spending too much time doing 被狂热崇拜之物, 迷恋物: *Physical exercise has become something of a fetish nowadays.* 如今体育锻炼已经成为一种狂热。| **have a fetish about** *Sue has a real fetish about keeping everything tidy.* 休确有洁癖, 总是把一切弄得非常整洁。**2** an unusual object or activity which gives someone sexual pleasure〔能引起性快感的〕恋物: *a leather fetish* 皮具恋物 **3** an object that is treated like a god and is thought to have magical powers〔认为有魔力的〕神物, 崇拜物

fet·ish·ist /ˈfɛtɪʃɪst; ˈfetɪʃəst/ *n* [C] someone who gets sexual pleasure from unusual objects or activities 恋物癖者, 恋物狂者 —**fetishism** *n* [U] —**fetishistic** /ˌfɛtɪˈʃɪstɪk; ˌfetɪˈʃɪstɪk◂/ *adj*

fet·lock /ˈfɛtˌlɑk; ˈfetlɒk/ *n* [C] the back part of a horse's leg, just above the HOOF¹ (1)〔马蹄后上部的〕球节, 肢关节 —see picture at 参见 HORSE¹ 图

fet·ter¹ /ˈfɛtə; ˈfetə/ *n* **fetters** [plural] *literary*【文】**a)** the things that prevent someone from being free 桎梏, 羁绊, 束缚: *breaking the fetters of convention* 打破常规的束缚 **b)** chains that were put around a prisoner's feet in former times〔旧时的〕脚镣

fetter² *v* [T] *literary*【文】**1** to restrict someone's freedom and prevent them from doing what they want 束缚: *fettered by family responsibilities* 被家庭责任所束缚 **2** to put chains on a prisoner's hands or feet 为…上脚镣[手镣]

fet·tle /ˈfɛtl̩; ˈfetl/ *n* **in fine fettle/in good fettle** *old-fashioned* healthy or working properly【过时】健康的, 强健的; 运转良好的

fet·tuc·ci·ne /ˌfɛtuˈtʃinɪ; ˌfetʊˈtʃiːni/ *n* [U] *Italian* thin flat pieces of PASTA【意】宽面条

fe·tus /ˈfitəs; ˈfiːtəs/ *n* [C] the usual American spelling of FOETUS foetus 的一般美式拼法

feud¹ /fjud; fjuːd/ *n* [C] an angry and often violent quarrel between two people or groups that lasts for a long time〔个人间或群体间的〕长期不和, 长期争斗, 世仇: **[+over]** *a bitter feud over territory* 领土问题上的长期激烈争执

feud² *v* [I] to continue quarrelling for a long time often in a violent way 长期争斗, 结仇, 结怨: **feud (with sb) over sth** *the bitter feuding over the leadership of the EC* 关于欧洲共同体领导权的长期激烈争斗

feud·al /ˈfjudl̩; ˈfjuːdl/ *adj* [only before noun 仅用于名词前] connected with feudalism 封建的, 封建制度的: *the feudal system* 封建制度 | *feudal society* 封建社会

feu·dal·is·m /ˈfjudl̩ˌɪzəm; ˈfjuːdlɪzəm/ *n* [U] a system which existed in the Middle Ages, in which people received land and protection from a lord when they worked and fought for him 封建制度; 封建主义

feu·dal·is·tic /ˌfjudl̩ˈɪstɪk; ˌfjuːdlˈɪstɪk◂/ *adj* based on a system in which only a few people have all the power in a way that seems very old fashioned 封建制度的; 封建主义的

fe·ver /ˈfivə; ˈfiːvə/ *n* **1** [C,U] an illness or a medical condition in which you have a very high temperature 发烧, 发热: *He's in bed with a fever.* 他因发烧而卧床休息。| *Take some aspirin – it'll help the fever to go down.* 吃点阿斯匹林 — 这有助于退烧。—see also 另见 HAY FEVER, SCARLET FEVER, YELLOW FEVER **2** [singular] a situation in which people feel very excited or feel very strongly about something 高度兴奋, 狂热, 极端活跃: *a fever of excitement on Wall Street* 华尔街上异常狂热激动的气氛 | **election/carnival fever etc** (=great interest or excitement about a particular activity or event) 选举/狂欢节等的狂热 **3 fever pitch/point/heat** if people's feelings are at fever pitch etc, they are extremely excited 狂热, 异常激动, 高度活跃: *The children's excitement rose to fever pitch as Christmas approached.* 随着圣诞节的临近, 孩子们越来越激动。

fever blis·ter /ˈ‥ˌ‥/ *n* [C] *AmE* a COLD SORE【美】〔发烧引起的〕唇疱疹

fe·vered /ˈfivəd; ˈfiːvəd/ *adj* [only before noun 仅用于名词前] *literary*【文】**1** extremely excited or worried; FEVERISH (2) 高度兴奋的; 十分焦虑的: *fevered cries* 极其激动的喊叫声 **2** suffering from a fever; FEVERISH (1) 发烧的, 发热的: **fevered brow** (=a hot forehead caused by a fever) 发烧的额头 *She wiped his fevered brow.* 她擦了擦他发烧的额头。**3 a fevered imagination** someone who has a fevered imagination imagines strange things and cannot control their thoughts 狂想: *These stories are merely a product of her fevered imagination.* 这些故事只不过是她凭空臆想出来的东西。

fe·ver·ish /ˈfivərɪʃ; ˈfiːvərɪʃ/ *adj* **1** suffering from a fever 发烧的: *feeling feverish* 感到发烧 | *Her cheeks looked hot and feverish.* 她的脸颊看上去很热, 有点发烧。**2** very excited or worried about something 狂热的; 十分焦虑的: *They waited in a state of feverish anxiety for their mother to come home.* 他们焦躁不安地等着母亲回家。| **feverish activity/preparations/haste** (=activities that are done very quickly because there is not much time) 忙乱的活动/忙乱的准备工作/匆匆忙忙 *The show was about to begin and there were signs of feverish activity backstage.* 表演快要开始了, 可以看出后台在紧张忙乱着。—**feverishly** *adv*

few /fju; fjuː/ *quantifier, n* [plural] **1 a few/the few** [no comparative 无比较级] a small number (of) 少数, 一些, 几个: *I've* 1 1
got a few books on gardening. 我有几本园艺书。| *I'll pop into the supermarket and get a few bits and pieces.* 我得到超级市场去买几样零碎东西。| *only a few hundred yards past the crossroads* 过了十字路口才几百码 | *It's one of the few companies*

trying to tackle the problem. 那是想解决这个问题的少数几家公司之一。| **a few of** *I've read a few of her books.* 我读过她的几本著作。| **a few more** *There are a few more things I'd like to discuss.* 还有一些事我想讨论一下。| **a few minutes/the last few days/the next few years etc** *George arrived a few minutes later.* 乔治几分钟后到了。| *Ignore this letter if you have paid in the last few days.* 如果你前几天已经付款了，请不用理会此信。| **a few people** *There were a few people sitting at the back of the hall.* 大厅后面坐着几个人。| **only a very few** (=not many) 不多的，很少的 **2 quite a few/a good few/not a few** a fairly large number 相当多，不少: *She must have cooked a good few dinners over the years.* 这些年来，她一定做过相当多的晚餐。**3** not many; not enough 很少，不多; 不够多的: *low-paid jobs that few people want* 没有几个人想要的低工资工作 | *There may be few options open to you.* 可供你选择的办法可能很少了。| *The meals are awful, but few complain.* 饭菜一塌糊涂，但很少人抱怨。| *Which one has the fewest mistakes?* 哪个人差错最少？| **few of** *Very few of the staff come from the local area.* 工作人员中几乎没有当地人。**4 no fewer than** used to emphasize how surprisingly large a number is; at least 至少，不少于〔用于强调数目大得令人吃惊〕: *I tried to contact him no fewer than ten times.* 我至少有十次试图与他联络。**5 as few as** used to emphasize how surprisingly small a number is 少到…，只有〔用于强调数量出乎意料地小〕: *She can remember all the words accurately after reading it as few as three times.* 她只要看三遍就能一字不差地记住。**6 to name but a few** used when you are mentioning only a small number of people or things as examples of a large group 列举几个，略举几个例子: *I've visited many fascinating countries; Japan, India, Turkey, and Russia to name but a few.* 我游览过许多迷人的国家，日本、印度、土耳其和俄罗斯，就略举这几个吧。**7 the chosen few** the small number of people to be invited or selected 挑选出来[邀请]的少数几个人: *Such information is made available only to the chosen few.* 这种信息只让挑选出来的少数几个人知道。**8 precious few (of)** a very small number 极少的: *Only a small percentage of the seeds germinated and precious few of those survived.* 只有少数的种子发芽，其中存活下来的少得可怜。**9 few and far between** rare; not happening or available often 稀少的，罕见的: *Jobs are few and far between at the moment.* 职位现在已经很少了。**10 have a few (too many)** *informal* to have too much alcohol to drink【非正式】喝太多酒，喝醉，喝多了: *He looks as if he's had a few!* 他看上去是喝多了！—opposite 反义词 MANY

USAGE NOTE 用法说明: FEW
WORD CHOICE 词语辨析: **a few, few, a little, little**

When talking about amounts, you use **(a) few** with plural countable nouns, and **(a) little** with uncountable nouns. 谈论数量时，(a) few 与复数可数名词连用，(a) little 与不可数名词连用。

A few is positive and means a small number but not a lot. a few 表示肯定，指少数几个，但不多: *Yes, I do know a few words of French.* 是的，我确实懂几个法语单词。| *There are a few beers left in the fridge.* 冰箱里还剩几瓶啤酒。

Few is negative and means not many. few 表示否定，指很少: *I'm afraid I know few words of French.* 对不起，我懂的法语单词很少。**Few** used alone is fairly formal, and you would most often use it with **very**. few 单独使用时较正式，经常在前面加上 very: *Very few people come here now.* 现在很少有人到这里来。

With words for time, **a few** is almost always used. 后面带有表示时间的单词时，常常用 a few: *after a few minutes* 几分钟后 | *a few years before* 几年前

A little is positive and means some, but not a lot. a little 表示肯定，指一些，但不很多: *Fortunately he still had a little money left.* 幸运的是，他还剩下点钱。In more informal British English, **a bit** means the same thing. 在更非正式的英国英语中，a bit 具有相同的意思: *Don't worry, you've got a bit more time to get the work done.* 别担心，你还有点时间可以把工作做完。

Little is negative and means 'not much'. little 表示否定，指"很少": *Unfortunately he now had little money left.* 不幸的是，他现在身边没有什么钱了。Again, this is fairly formal, and speakers often avoid using **little** on its own. You would normally say **very little**. 同样，这较为正式，说话人常避免单独使用little，而通常用 very little。

fey /fe; feɪ/ *adj* very sensitive and behaving or talking in a strange way 疯疯癫癫的，古怪的，精神异常的: *a fey and delicate child* 一个古怪娇弱的孩子

Feyn·man /ˈfaɪnmən; ˈfaɪnmən/, **Richard Phillips** (1918-88) a US scientist who won a Nobel Prize for his work on RADIOACTIVITY 费因曼〔(1918-1988)，美国科学家。他在放射性研究方面颇有成就，并获诺贝尔奖〕

fez /fɛz; fez/ *n* [C] a round red hat with a flat top and no BRIM[1] 非斯帽，红色无边圆筒帽

ff the written abbreviation for 缩写= 'and following', meaning the pages after the one you have mentioned 及其后几页: *pages 17ff* 第 17 页及其后几页

FIA /ˌɛf aɪ ˈe; ˌef aɪ ˈeɪ/ Fédération Internationale de l'Automobile; the organization that controls Formula One car racing 国际汽联〔管理一级方程式赛车比赛的组织〕

fi·an·cé /ˌfiɑnˈse; fiˈɒnseɪ/ *n* [C] the man who a woman is going to marry and who she is ENGAGED (1) to 未婚夫

fi·an·cée /ˌfiɑnˈse; fiˈɒnseɪ/ *n* [C] the woman who a man is going to marry and who he is ENGAGED (1) to 未婚妻

Fi·an·na Fáil /ˌfiənə ˈfɔɪl; ˌfiːənə ˈfɔɪl/ one of the two main political parties in the Republic of Ireland, established in 1926 共和党〔爱尔兰共和国两大主要政党之一，创立于 1926 年〕—see also 另见 FINE GAEL

fi·as·co /fiˈæsko; fiˈæskəʊ/ *n* [C,U] an event that is completely unsuccessful, in a way that is very embarrassing or disappointing 惨败，彻底的失败: *The first lecture I ever gave was a complete fiasco.* 我的第一次讲课完全失败了。

fi·at /ˈfaɪət; ˈfiːæt/ *n* [C] *formal* an official command given by someone in a position of authority, without considering what other people want【正式】〔当权者的〕命令; 法令，谕旨: *The matter was settled by presidential fiat.* 这件事是根据总统的命令解决的。

fib[1] /fɪb; fɪb/ *n* [C] *spoken* a small unimportant lie【口】小谎，无关紧要的谎言: **tell fibs** *Don't tell fibs!* 不要撒谎！[不要说瞎话！]

fib[2] *v* **fibbed, fibbing** [I] *spoken* to tell a small unimportant lie【口】撒小谎: *I think you're fibbing.* 我想你是在撒谎。—**fibber** *n* [C]

F

fi·ber /ˈfaɪbɚ; ˈfaɪbə/ *n* [C] the American spelling of FIBRE fibre 的美式拼法

fi·ber·board /ˈfaɪbɚˌbɔrd; ˈfaɪbəbɔːd/ *n* [U] the American spelling of FIBREBOARD fibreboard 的美式拼法

fi·ber·fill /ˈfaɪbɚfɪl; ˈfaɪbəfɪl/ *n* [U] an artificial substance used to fill PILLOWS[1] (1) and DUVETS〔填塞枕头和絮被的〕合成纤维絮

fi·ber·glass /ˈfaɪbɚˌglæs; ˈfaɪbəglɑːs/ *n* [U] the American spelling of FIBREGLASS fibreglass 的美式拼法

fi·bre *BrE*【英】, **fiber** *AmE*【美】/ˈfaɪbɚ; ˈfaɪbə/ *n* **1** [U] parts of plants that you eat but cannot DIGEST[1] (1), which help food to move quickly through your body〔植物的〕纤维质，食物纤维: *Fruit and vegetables are high in fibre content.* 水果和蔬菜的纤维含量很高。**2** [U] a mass of threads used to make rope, cloth etc〔用来做绳子、布等的〕纤维: *man-made/natural fibre* 人造/天然纤维 | *Nylon is a man-made fiber.* 尼龙是一种人造纤维。**3** [C] a thin thread, or one of the thin parts like threads that form natural materials such as wood〔构成天然材料，如木材的〕(一根) 纤维 **4 nerve/muscle fibres** [plural] the thin pieces of flesh that form the nerves or muscles in your body 神经/肌肉纤维 **5 with every fibre of your being/to the very fibre of your being** *literary* if you feel something with every fibre of your being, you feel it very strongly【文】竭尽全力地，极其地，全身心地: *He wanted her with every fibre of his being.* 他非常想要她。—see also 另见 **moral fibre** (MORAL[1] (2))

fi·bre·board *BrE*【英】, **fiberboard** *AmE*【美】/ˈfaɪbɚˌbɔrd; ˈfaɪbəbɔːd/ *n* [U] board made from wood fibres pressed together 纤维板

fi·bre·glass *BrE*【英】, **fiberglass** *AmE*【美】/ˈfaɪbɚˌglæs; ˈfaɪbəglɑːs/ *n* [U] a light material made from glass threads, used for making sports cars and small boats〔制造跑车和小船的〕玻璃纤维，玻璃棉

fibre op·tics /ˌ·· ˈ··/ *n* [U] the process of using very thin threads of glass or plastic to carry information in the form of light, especially on telephone lines 纤维光学 —**fibre optic** *adj*

fi·brous /ˈfaɪbrəs; ˈfaɪbrəs/ *adj* consisting of many fibres or looking like fibres 含纤维的; 纤维状的: *The coconut has a fibrous outer covering.* 椰子有多纤维的外壳。

fib·u·la /ˈfɪbjələ; ˈfɪbjʊ̈lə/ *n* [C] *technical* the outer bone of the two bones in your leg below your knee【术语】腓骨 —see picture at 参见 SKELETON[1] 图

FICA /ˈfaɪkə; ˈfaɪkə; ˌɛf aɪ si ˈe; ˌef aɪ siː ˈeɪ/ Federal Insurance Contributions Act; in the US, money which is taken from your pay by the government to be used for Social Security《联邦社会保险捐助法》〔美国政府按一定比例从个人薪资收入中扣税，用于社会保险〕

fiche /fiʃ; fiːʃ/ *n* [C,U] a MICROFICHE 缩微胶片

fick·le /ˈfɪkl; ˈfɪkəl/ *adj* **1** someone who is fickle is always changing their mind about people or things that they like, so that you cannot depend on them 三心两意的, 靠不住的, 变化无常的: *an unpredictable and fickle lover* 一个无法捉摸、三心两意的情人 **2** something such as weather that is fickle often changes suddenly〔天气等〕变幻莫测的 **—fickleness** *n* [U]: *the fickleness of fame* 名望的起落无常

fic·tion /ˈfɪkʃən; ˈfɪkʃən/ *n* **1** [U] books and stories about imaginary people and events 小说: *popular fiction* 通俗小说 —opposite 反义词 NON-FICTION **2** [C] something that people want you to believe is true but which is not true 虚构的事, 想象的事: *preserving the fiction of his happy childhood* 保持他那快乐童年的幻象

fic·tion·al /ˈfɪkʃənl; ˈfɪkʃənəl/ *adj* fictional people or descriptions are imaginary and from a book or story 虚构的, 编造的, 小说的: *fictional characters* 虚构的人物 | *a fictional description of growing up in Detroit* 对在底特律成长的过程的虚构描写

fic·tion·al·ize also 又作 **-ise** *BrE*【英】/ˈfɪkʃənl̩aɪz; ˈfɪkʃənəlaɪz/ *v* [T] to make a film or story about a real event, changing some details and adding some imaginary characters 把…改编成电影, 把…编成小说, 使小说化: *a fictionalized account of his life in Berlin* 把他在柏林的生活用小说的笔法描述 **—fictionalization** /ˌfɪkʃənl̩əˈzeʃən; ˌfɪkʃənəlaɪˈzeɪʃən/ *n* [C,U]

fic·ti·tious /fɪkˈtɪʃəs; fɪkˈtɪʃəs/ *adj* invented by someone and not real 虚构的, 杜撰的, 捏造的: *a fictitious address* 杜撰[捏造]的地址 | *The author fills this real town with fictitious characters.* 作者给这座真实的城市装满了虚构的人物。

fic·tive /ˈfɪktɪv; ˈfɪktɪv/ *adj AmE* fictive events, people etc are imaginary and not real【美】〔事件、人等〕想象的, 虚构的, 非真实的: *the fictive world of James Bond* 詹姆斯·邦德的虚幻世界

F

fid·dle¹ /ˈfɪdl; ˈfɪdl/ *n* [C] *informal*【非正式】**1** *BrE* a dishonest way of getting money【英】欺诈, 欺骗行为: *a tax fiddle* 偷税行为 | **be on the fiddle** (=be getting money dishonestly or illegally) 搞欺诈勾当 *They suspected he was on the fiddle all along.* 他们怀疑他一直在搞欺诈勾当。**2** a VIOLIN 小提琴 **3 be a fiddle** to be difficult to do and involve complicated movements of your hands〔需要用手的〕细巧活, 难事: *This blouse is a bit of a fiddle to do up.* 扣上这件短上衣是一件比较难搞的事。—see also 另见 **fit as a fiddle** (FIT² (3)), **play second fiddle to sb** (PLAY¹ (15))

fiddle² *v* **1** [I] to keep moving something or touching it with your fingers, especially because you are bored or nervous〔尤指因厌烦或紧张而〕用手不停拨弄: **[+with]** *She sat for a time, fiddling with her glass.* 她坐了一些时候, 手不停地摆弄着玻璃杯。| *Stop fiddling will you!* 请你不要瞎拨弄了, 好不好! **2** [T] to give false information about something, in order to avoid paying money or to get extra money 篡改, 伪造〔账目等〕: *Bert had been fiddling his income tax for years.* 伯特多年来都在虚报所得税。| **fiddle the books** (=give false figures in a company's financial records) 造假账

fiddle around also 又作 **fiddle about** *BrE*【英】*phr v* [I] to waste time doing unimportant things 浪费时间, 虚度光阴: *We can't fiddle around here all day – let's move on.* 我们不能整天在这里浪费时间了 — 我们继续前进吧。

fiddle around with sth also 又作 **fiddle about with** sth *BrE*【英】*phr v* [T] **1** to keep moving the parts of something or making changes to it, especially in a way that is stupid or dangerous 乱动, 瞎搞: *Why did you let her fiddle around with the remote control?* 你为什么让她乱动遥控器呢? **2** to keep changing the positions of a group of things until you find the arrangement that you like 拨弄, 摆布〔以求取得最佳位置〕: *Is it all right if I fiddle around with these figures?* 要是我把这些数字稍作改动, 可以吗?

fiddle with sth *phr v* [T] **1** to move part of a machine in order to make it work, without knowing exactly what you should do〔在不知如何操作的情况下〕拨弄, 瞎动: *After fiddling with the tuning I finally got JFM.* 我在瞎调了一会, 终于找到了 JFM 电台。**2** to move or touch something that does not belong to you, in an annoying way 乱动〔别人的东西〕: *Don't let him fiddle with my bag.* 别让他乱动我的提包。

fiddle-fad·dle /ˈfɪdl̩ ˌfædl; ˈfɪdl ˌfædl/ *n* [U] *old-fashioned* nonsense【过时】无聊话, 废话

fid·dler /ˈfɪdlɚ; ˈfɪdlə/ *n* [C] **1** someone who plays the VIOLIN, especially someone who plays FOLK MUSIC〔尤指演奏民间音乐的〕小提琴手 **2** someone who gives false information to the government or a company, to pay less money or get more than they should 骗子, 诈骗者: *tax fiddlers* 骗税者

fid·dle·sticks /ˈfɪdl̩ˌstɪks; ˈfɪdlˌstɪks/ *interjection old-fashioned* nonsense【过时】废话!胡说!

fid·dling /ˈfɪdlɪŋ; ˈfɪdlɪŋ/ *adj* [only before noun 仅用于名词前] unimportant, and annoying 无足轻重的, 微不足道的; 令人厌烦的: *all these fiddling little jobs around the house* 家里所有这些烦人的琐碎活

fid·dly /ˈfɪdlɪ; ˈfɪdli/ *adj* **1** difficult to do because you have to deal with very small objects 精细而难做的: *He managed to fix the television, but it was a fiddly job.* 他设法修好了电视机, 这可是精细的工作。**2** unimportant, slightly difficult, and annoying 无足轻重的: *I can't be bothered with all the fiddly details.* 我懒得管这些琐碎的细节!

FIDE /ˌɛf aɪ di ˈi; ˌef aɪ diː ˈiː/ Fédération Internationale des Echecs; the world governing organization for CHESS, founded in 1924 国际象棋联合会, 国际棋联〔管理国际棋类比赛的一个组织, 始建于 1924 年〕

fi·del·i·ty /faɪˈdɛlətɪ; fɪˈdeləti/ *n* [U] **1** loyalty to your husband, girlfriend etc, shown by having sex only with them〔对丈夫、女朋友等的〕忠贞, 忠实: **[+to]** *Tom's fidelity to his wife was never in question.* 汤姆对妻子的忠贞不二从来无需怀疑。**2** the quality of not changing something when you are producing it again in a different form, by recording, translating, making a film etc〔录音、电影等的〕逼真, 不加改动;〔译文等的〕确切, 忠实: **[+to]** *the new translation's fidelity to Proust's great work* 普鲁斯特的杰作的新译文忠于原作 **3** the quality of being faithful to your friends, or of not doing anything that is against your beliefs〔对朋友、信念等的〕忠贞, 忠诚 —see also 另见 HIGH FIDELITY, FAITHFUL¹

fid·get¹ /ˈfɪdʒɪt; ˈfɪdʒɪt/ *v* [I] to keep moving your hands or feet, especially because you are bored or nervous〔因厌烦或紧张而〕坐立不安, 手足无措: *The teacher told them to stop fidgeting.* 老师叫他们别坐不住。| **fidget with sth** *Donna began fidgeting with her pencil.* 唐娜开始摆弄她的铅笔。

fidget² *n* [C] *informal*【非正式】**1** someone who keeps moving and is unable to sit or stand still 坐立不安的人: *I wish you'd sit still for a change – you're such a fidget!* 我希望你能改改, 好好坐一会儿。你真是个坐不住的人! **2 get/have the fidgets** *BrE* to be unable to stop moving【英】烦躁不安: *He gets the fidgets if he has to sit in one place for more than ten minutes.* 他如果得在一个地方坐 10 分钟以上, 就烦躁不安了。

fid·get·y /ˈfɪdʒɪtɪ; ˈfɪdʒɪti/ *adj informal* tending to fidget a lot【非正式】坐立不安的; 烦躁乱动的: *sitting with three bored, fidgety children* 与三个厌倦而烦躁的孩子同坐

fie /faɪ; faɪ/ *interjection, old use*【旧】**fie on sb** used to express anger or disapproval towards someone …真可耻〔表示生气或不赞成〕

Fied·ler /ˈfidlɚ; ˈfiːdlə/, **Arthur** (1894-1979) a US CONDUCTOR (=someone who directs a group of musicians) who was the conductor of the Boston Pops for many years 菲德勒〔(1894-1979), 美国音乐指挥家, 多年担任波士顿通俗交响乐团的指挥〕

fief /fif; fiːf/ *n* [C] an area of land that belonged to a lord in former times〔昔日的〕采邑, 封地

field¹ /fild; fiːld/ *n* [C]

1 ▶FARM 农场◀ an area of land where crops are grown or animals feed on grass 田地, 田野: *a field of wheat* 一片麦地

2 ▶SUBJECT 学科◀ a subject that people study or are involved in as part of their work〔研究或工作的〕领域, 范围: **[+of]** *He's well-known in the field of ancient history.* 他在古代史领域是很著名的。| *improvements in the field of health and safety* 卫生和安全领域中的改进 | **in his/her field** *Professor Marwick is one of the leading experts in her field.* 马威克教授在她的研究领域里是最杰出的专家之一。| **be outside your field** (=not be connected with your work or studies) 不属于你的工作范围[专业], 不是你的专长

3 ▶PRACTICAL WORK 实际工作◀ work or study that is done in the field is done in the real world rather than in a classroom or LABORATORY 现场, 实地: **in the field** *His theories haven't been tested in the field.* 他的理论还没有在实地试验过。| **field trials/testing** *field trials for an anti-cancer drug* 抗癌药的临床试验

4 baseball/soccer/sports etc field an area of ground where a sport is played 棒球场/足球场/运动场等

5 take the field to go onto the area where a sport is played so that you can take part in a game or competition〔运动员〕上场: *Supporters cheered as the team took the field.* 球队上场时, 支持者都欢呼起来。

6 ▶COMPETITORS 竞争者◀ **the field a)** all the horses or runners in a race 所有参赛马; 全体赛跑运动员: **lead/be ahead of the field** *Egyptian Prince is leading the field as they come round*

the final bend. "埃及王子"在它们绕过最后的弯道时处于领先地位。**b)** all the people, companies, or products who are competing against each other 全体竞争对手〔包括人、公司、产品等〕: **lead/be ahead of the field** *Microsoft is already way ahead of the rest of the field.* 微软公司已经遥遥领先于其他同类公司。

7 snow/ice etc field a large area covered with snow etc 雪原/冰原等

8 coal/oil/gas field a large area where coal, oil, or gas is found 煤田/油田/天然气田

9 magnetic/gravitational/force field the area in which a natural force is felt or has an effect 磁场/引力场/力场

10 field of vision/view the whole area that you are able to see without turning your head 视野: *The buildings obstructed our field of vision.* 那些建筑物挡住了我们的视野。

11 the field (of battle) the time or place where there is fighting in a war 战场, 战地: **on the field of battle** *It is always better to negotiate than to settle disputes on the field of battle.* 谈判总要比在战场上解决争端好。| **in the field** *The new tank has yet to be used in the field.* 新型坦克还没有在战场上使用过。

12 field of fire the area that you can hit by shooting from a particular position 射击范围; 火力范围

13 ►TEAM 队◄ the field the team that is throwing and catching the ball in a game such as CRICKET (2) or BASEBALL, rather than the team that is hitting 〔板球或棒球比赛中的〕防守队; 全体外场队员

14 ►COMPUTERS 电脑◄ an amount of space made available for a particular type of information 字段, 信息组: *The field for the user's name is 25 characters.* 用户名的字段是 25 个字符。—see also 另见 **play the field** (PLAY[1] (25))

field² *v* **1** [T] if you field a team, group of candidates, or an army, they represent you or fight for you in a competition, election, or war 派出〔运动队、球队、候选人或军队〕: *The Ecology Party fielded 109 candidates in the 1983 election.* 生态党推举 109 名候选人参加 1983 年的选举。**2 be fielding** the team that is fielding in a game of CRICKET (2) or BASEBALL is the one that is throwing and catching the ball, rather than the one hitting it 〔板球或棒球比赛中〕担任防守队员[外场员] **3** [T] if you field the ball in a game of CRICKET (2) or BASEBALL, you stop it after it has been hit 〔板球或棒球比赛中〕截住, 接住〔对方击出的球〕 **4 field a question** to answer a difficult question 回答难对付的问题: *The Senator had to field some tricky questions from reporters.* 参议员不得不巧妙地回答记者们提出的一些刁钻的问题。

Field, The *trademark* a British magazine which has articles about the countryside, farming, and sports such as POLO and CRICKET【商标】《原野》〔英国杂志, 刊登有关乡村、农耕以及马球、板球等体育活动的文章〕

Field and Stream /,· · '·/ *trademark* a US magazine that has articles about hunting, fishing, and other activities that are done outdoors【商标】《原野与溪流》〔美国杂志, 刊登有关狩猎、钓鱼等户外活动的文章〕

field corn /'· ·/ *n* [U] *AmE* MAIZE grown to use as grain or to feed to animals, rather than to be eaten【美】饲料玉米 —compare 比较 SWEET CORN

field day /'· ·/ *n* [C] **1 have a field day** *informal* to have a chance to do what you want, especially a chance to criticize someone【非正式】得到好机会〔尤指去批评某人的机会〕: *When the scandal finally came out, the press had a field day.* 丑闻终于传出来时, 新闻界便有机会大做文章。**2** *AmE* a day when pupils at a school have sports competitions and parents watch【美】〔有学生家长观看的〕体育比赛日, 运动日; SPORTS DAY *BrE*【英】

field·er /ˈfildɚ; ˈfiːldə/ *n* [C] one of the players who tries to catch the ball in a game of CRICKET (2) or BASEBALL 〔板球或棒球比赛中〕守场员, 外野手

field e·vent /'· ·,·/ *n* [C] a sport such as jumping or throwing the JAVELIN (1) in an ATHLETICS competition 田赛项目〈如跳高、跳远或掷标枪等〉—compare 比较 TRACK EVENT

field glass·es /'·,··/ *n* [plural] BINOCULARS 双筒望远镜

field goal /'· ·/ *n* [C] **1** the act of kicking the ball over the bar of the GOAL (3) in American football 〔美式橄榄球中〕射门得分 **2** the act of putting the ball through the circle to get points in BASKETBALL 〔篮球中的〕投球中篮得分

field hock·ey /'·,··/ *n* [U] *AmE* HOCKEY (1) played on grass【美】(草地) 曲棍球

Fiel·ding /ˈfildɪŋ; ˈfiːldɪŋ/, **Henry** (1707-54) an English writer most famous for his humorous NOVEL *Tom Jones* 菲尔丁〔(1707-1754), 英国作家, 以幽默小说《汤姆·琼斯》最为出名〕

field mar·shal /'·,··/ *n* [C] an officer of the highest rank in the British army 陆军元帅〔英国陆军中的最高将领〕—see table on page C6 参见 C6 页附录

field·mouse /ˈfildmaus; ˈfiːldmaʊs/ *n* [C] a mouse that has a long tail and lives in fields 田鼠

Fields, W.C. (1880-1946) a US film actor and COMEDIAN, famous for disliking children and animals, for becoming angry very easily, and for drinking too much alcohol. His films include *My Little Chickadee* (1940). 菲尔兹〔(1880-1946), 美国电影演员、喜剧演员。他以讨厌孩子和动物、易怒、酗酒出名, 演过的影片包括《我的小山雀》(1940)〕

fields·man /ˈfildzmən; ˈfiːldzmən/ *n* [C] *BrE* FIELDER【英】〔板球或棒球比赛中〕守场员, 外野手

field sports /'· ,·/ *n* [plural] sports that happen in the countryside, such as hunting, shooting, and fishing 野外运动〈如打猎、射击和钓鱼等〉

field test /'· ·/ *n* [C] a test of a new piece of equipment that is done in the place where it will be used rather than in a LABORATORY 〔新仪器、设备等的〕现场试验, 实地试验 —**field-test** *v* [T]

field trip /'· ·/ *n* [C] an occasion when students go somewhere to learn about a particular subject 〔学生的〕校外旅行考察; 实地调查旅行: *a geography field trip* 地理旅行考察

field·work /ˈfild,wɝk; ˈfiːldwɜːk/ *n* [U] the study of scientific or social subjects that is done outside the classroom or LABORATORY 〔科学或社会研究的〕实地考察; 野外考察 —**fieldworker** *n* [C]

fiend /find; fiːnd/ *n* [C] **1 television/fresh-air/sports fiend etc** someone who likes something much more than other people do 电视迷/最喜欢新鲜空气的人/体育迷等 **2** a very cruel or wicked person 残暴的人, 恶人, 恶魔般的人 **3** an evil spirit 恶魔, 魔鬼

fiend·ish /ˈfindɪʃ; ˈfiːndɪʃ/ *adj* **1** cruel and unpleasant 凶恶的; 残酷的: *Philip had a fiendish instinct for discovering other people's weak spots.* 菲利普有专会找出别人弱点的坏本能。**2** very clever in an unpleasant way 刁钻的, 棘手的: *a fiendish plan to take over the company* 接管公司的棘手计划 **3** extremely difficult or unpleasant 极其困难的; 令人极不愉快的: *He set us some fiendish exam questions.* 他给我们出了一些刁钻难解的考题。—**fiendishly** *adv*

fierce /fɪrs; fɪəs/ *adj* **1** a fierce person or animal is angry or ready to attack, and looks very frightening 凶猛的; 凶狠的: *armed guards accompanied by fierce dogs* 带着恶狗的武装卫兵 | *She turned round, looking fierce.* 她转过身, 看上去很凶狠。**2** fierce emotions are very strong and often angry 〔感情〕强烈的; 愤怒的: *Fierce resentment was aroused by this injustice.* 这种不公引起了强烈的不满。**3** done with a lot of energy and strong feelings, and sometimes violent 猛烈的; 激烈的: *a fierce attack on government policy* 对政府政策的猛烈抨击 | *Fighting was fiercest near the town centre.* 市中心附近的战斗最激烈。| **fierce competition** *There is fierce competition for those scholarships.* 那些奖学金的竞争很激烈。**4** fierce cold, heat, or weather is much colder, hotter etc than usual 极度的, 极端的: *a fierce wind* 一阵狂风 **5 something fierce** *AmE spoken* more loudly, strongly etc than usual【美口】极其强烈, 很厉害: *It was snowing something fierce yesterday.* 昨天雪下得非常大。—**fiercely** *adv* —**fierceness** *n* [U]

fi·er·y /ˈfaɪrɪ; ˈfaɪəri/ *adj* **1** containing or looking like fire 含有火的; 火一般的: *a fiery sunset* 火红的落日 **2** bright red 鲜红的: *a fiery blush* 满脸通红 **3** becoming angry very quickly 暴躁的, 易怒的: *He has a very fiery temper.* 他的脾气很暴躁。**4** showing or encouraging anger 激昂的; 引人发怒的: *a fiery speech* 激昂的演说 **5** fiery foods taste very strong and hot 〔食物〕辣的

fi·es·ta /fɪˈɛstə; fiˈestə/ *n* [C] *Spanish*【西】**1** a religious holiday with dancing, music etc, especially in Spain and South America 〔尤指西班牙和南美洲以舞蹈、音乐等来庆祝的〕宗教节日 **2** a party 社交聚会

FIFA /ˈfifə; ˈfiːfə/ Fédération Internationale de Football Association; the organization that controls international football and organizes the World Cup competition 国际足球联合会, 国际足联〔管理国际足球运动、组织"世界杯"比赛的一组织〕

Fife /faɪf; faɪf/ a REGION in eastern Scotland between the Firth of Tay and the Firth of Forth 法夫〔苏格兰东部一地区, 位于泰湾和福斯湾之间〕

fife *n* [C] a small musical instrument like a FLUTE, often played in military bands 〔军乐队中的〕横笛

fif·teen /ˈfɪfˈtin; ˌfɪfˈtiːn◂/ *number* 15 十五 —see table on page C1 参见 C1 页附录

fifth /fɪfθ; fɪfθ/ *n* [C] **1** one of five equal parts of something 五分之一 **2** *AmE* an amount of alcohol equal to 1/5 of an American GALLON (2), sold in bottles【美】〔瓶装销售的烈性酒〕五分之一加仑的: *a fifth of bourbon* 五分之一加仑的波旁威士忌酒 **3 fifth wheel** *AmE* someone who is with you when you do not

want them to be there【美】多余的人: *She said she didn't want to be the fifth wheel.* 她说她不想做多余的人。

Fifth A·mend·ment, the /,· ˈ· ·/ **1** a part of the Constitution of the United States which says that you do not have to give information in a court of law which could be used against you, and that you cannot be put in prison or have your property taken away without a proper legal TRIAL《美国宪法第五修正案》〔美国宪法的一部分, 规定在法庭上任何人不得被迫作不利于自己的证词, 未经合法审理, 不得被送入监狱或剥夺财产〕 **2 plead/take the Fifth (Amendment)** to refuse to give information against yourself in a court of law. People in the US sometimes use this expression humorously when they do not want to answer a question. 请求回避, 拒绝作证〔指在法庭上拒绝作出不利于自己的证词。美国人在不想回答某一问题时有时幽默地使用这一表达方式〕: *"I plead the Fifth", Jack said, when his wife wanted to know where he had been.* 妻子想知道他去过哪里时, 杰克说: "我拒绝回答。"

Fifth Av·e·nue, 5th Avenue /ˌfɪfθ ˋævənju; ˌfɪfθ ˈævə̩njuː/ a street in New York that is famous for its expensive shops 第五大道(纽约市以高档店铺著称的一条街)

fifth col·umn /,· ˈ· ·/ *n* [C] a group of people who work secretly during a war to help the enemies of the country they live in〔战时在所在国从事秘密活动、协助敌军的〕第五纵队 — **fifth columnist** *n* [C]

fif·ty /ˋfɪftɪ; ˈfɪfti/ *number* **1** 50 五十 —see table on page C1 参见 C1 页附录 **2 the fifties a)** the years between 1950 and 1959 20世纪50年代: *Standards of living rose in the fifties.* 生活水平在20世纪50年代提高了。**b)** the numbers between 50 and 59, especially when used to measure temperature 50至59之间的数字〔尤用于测量温度〕: *sunny, with temperatures in the mid fifties* 晴天, 气温55度左右 **3 be in your fifties** to be aged between 50 and 59 在50到59岁之间; 五十多岁: **early/mid/late fifties** *He must be in his early fifties by now.* 他现在肯定有五十岁出头了。**4** a piece of paper money equal to fifty dollars or fifty pounds 五十美元[英镑]票面的纸币

fifty-fif·ty /,· ·ˈ· ◂/ *adj spoken*【口】**1** divided or shared equally between two people〔两人〕平分的; 对半的: *We should divide the profits on a fifty-fifty basis.* 我们应当平分利润。| **go fifty-fifty (on sth)** (=share the cost of something equally) 均摊〔费用〕; 各出一半〔费用〕: *Let's go fifty-fifty on a new television set.* 我们一人出一半钱买一台新电视机吧。**2** having an equal chance of happening in one of two ways〔成败、利弊〕各半的: *Do you reckon our chances of success are about fifty-fifty?* 你认为我们有一半的成功机会吗?

fig¹ /fɪg; fɪg/ *n* [C] **1** a soft sweet fruit with a lot of small seeds, often eaten dried, or the tree on which this fruit grows 无花果 —see picture on page A8 参见 A8 页图 **2** *BrE* **not care/not give a fig (for sth)** to not be concerned or interested in something at all【英】(对某事)毫不在乎 **3 not worth a fig** of no value 毫无价值, 不值一文

fig² **1** the written abbreviation of 缩写= FIGURE **2** the written abbreviation of 缩写= FIGURATIVE

1 1 **fight¹** /faɪt; faɪt/ *past tense and past participle* **fought** /fɔt; fɔːt/ *v*

1 ▶**WAR** 战争◀ [I,T] to take part in a war or battle 打仗, 作战: *Did your Uncle fight in the last war?* 你叔叔参加了上一次战争吗? | **fight sb** *Vietnam fought France and then the US over 30 years.* 越南先是跟法国, 后来跟美国, 共打了三十多年的仗。| **[+against/with]** *He fought against the Russians on the Eastern Front.* 他在东线与俄国人作战。| **[+about/over/for]** *Britain and Argentina fought for control of the islands.* 英国和阿根廷为争夺这些岛屿的控制权而打仗。| **fight a war** *Neither country is capable of fighting a long war.* 这两个国家都无法打持久战。

2 ▶**HIT PEOPLE** 打人◀ [I,T] if someone fights another person, or if two people fight, they hit and kick each other in order to hurt each other 打斗, 打架, 斗殴: *Two guys were fighting in the street outside the bar.* 有两个家伙在酒吧外的街道上打架。| **fight sb** *Grant has fought most of the boys in his street.* 格兰特跟街上的大多数男孩子都打过架。| **[+with]** *Phil was fighting with Ryan in the playground.* 菲尔当时正在操场和瑞安打架。| **[+about/over/for]** *two dogs fighting over a bone* 为抢夺一块骨头而咬斗的两条狗

3 ▶**COMPETE** 竞争◀ [I,T] to compete strongly for something, especially a job or political position or in a sport 争夺, 争斗: **fight sb for sth** *Williams fought several rivals for the leadership of the party.* 威廉姆斯与几个对手争夺党的领导权。| **[+for]** *If you want the job you'll have to fight for it.* 你如果想得到这份工作就得竞争。| **fight an election** *The mayor has decided against fighting another election.* 市长已经决定不参加下一次竞选。

4 ▶**ARGUE** 争论◀ [I] to argue about something〔为…而〕争吵, 争论: *The kids fought in the back seat the whole trip.* 孩子们在整个车程中一直在后座上互相争吵。| **[+about/over]** *They're fighting about whose turn it is to do the dishes.* 他们在为该轮到谁洗碗碟而争吵。

5 ▶**SPORT** 体育运动◀ [I,T] to hit someone as a sport 与…进行拳击比赛: *Ali fought Foreman for the heavyweight title.* 阿里与福尔曼进行拳击比赛, 争夺重量级冠军。

6 ▶**EMOTION** 感情◀ [T] also 又作 **fight back/down** to try very hard not to show your feelings or not to do something you want to do 克制, 忍住, 压下去: *He fought the impulse to slap her.* 他尽力压下了想打她一巴掌的念头。

7 fight your way to push people away in order to go somewhere 打[挤; 推]出一条路; 用力开出一条路前进: *We fought our way through the crowd.* 我们从人群中挤出一条路来。

8 fight a losing battle to work hard when you cannot succeed 进行肯定要失败的斗争: *I think they're fighting a losing battle with that libel suit.* 我认为他们在那场诽谤官司中肯定会输。

9 fight shy of doing sth to try to avoid doing something or being involved in something 避免做某事, 避免参与某事; 怕惹上某事: *Jane fought shy of participating in the discussions.* 简躲闪着不参加讨论。

10 fighting spirit/words the desire to fight or words which express that desire 斗志/挑战性的言辞: *The marches aroused their fighting spirit.* 行军提高了他们的斗志。

11 have a fighting chance to have a chance to do something or achieve something if you work very hard at it 经过很大努力有可能成功: *Lewis has a fighting chance to win the gold medal.* 刘易斯如果努力拼搏还会有得金牌的机会。

12 fight fire with fire to use the same methods as your opponents in an argument〔争论中〕以火攻火, 以其人之道还治其人之身

fight back *phr v* **1** [I] to use violence against someone who has attacked you 还击, 反攻: *The rebels are fighting back.* 叛军正在还击。**2** [I] to work hard to prevent something bad happening 制止, 抑制: *Victims of discrimination often don't have the power to fight back.* 受歧视的人经常没有能力反击。**3** [T **fight** sth ↔ **back**] to try hard not to show your feelings 克制, 忍住〔不使感情流露〕: **fight back tears** *She fought back the tears until she got home.* 她在到家前一直强忍住眼泪。

fight sb/sth ↔ **off** *phr v* [T] **1** to use violence to keep someone or something away 击退, 竭力摆脱: *The stars had to fight off the crowds to get out of the auditorium.* 明星们得竭力摆脱人群, 才能走出礼堂。**2** to try hard to get rid of something 尽力克服[去掉]: *Elaine's fighting off a cold.* 伊莱恩正在治疗感冒。| *Bardot fought off the sex symbol image.* 巴多尽力摆脱掉自己的性感形象。

fight sth **out** *phr v* [T] to argue, or use violence until a disagreement is settled (通过争斗)解决〔争论〕, 平息〔不和〕: *We left them to fight it out.* 我们任由他们自行解决。

fight² *n* 2 3

1 ▶**HIT** 打, 击◀ [C] an act of fighting in which two people or groups hit, push etc each other 打斗, 打架: **[+between]** *a fight between two gangs* 两帮之间的打斗 | **[+over]** *fights over territory* 争夺领土的斗争 | **get into a fight** *He's always getting into fights with other boys.* 他老是和其他男孩打架。| **have a fight** *The cat had a fight last night.* 这只猫昨晚打架了。| **start/pick a fight** *Are you trying to start a fight?* 你是在寻衅打架吗?

2 ▶**BATTLE** 战斗◀ [C] a battle between two armies, especially the fighting that happens at one particular place and time〔两军之间的〕战斗, 战役: **[+for]** *the fight for Bunker Hill* 夺取邦克山的战斗

3 ▶**ARGUMENT** 争吵◀ [C] a quarrel or an argument 争论; 争吵: **have a fight** *They've had a fight with the neighbours.* 他们和邻居争吵了。

4 ▶**ACHIEVE/PREVENT STH** 取得某物/防止某事◀ [singular] the work of trying to achieve something, change something, or prevent something 争斗, 斗争: **[+against]** *the fight against crime* 对犯罪行为所作的斗争 | **[+for]** *We will not give up the fight for better conditions.* 我们不会放弃为争取更好条件而斗争。| **have a fight on your hands** (=have to oppose someone to achieve something) 要进行一场斗争〔方能达到目的〕 *He'll have a fight on his hands to get Malone acquitted.* 他将要进行艰巨的斗争, 以争取马隆无罪释放。

5 ▶**SPORT** 体育◀ [C] an act of fighting as a sport 拳击(运动): *Are you going to watch the big fight tonight?* 你今晚打算去看拳击大赛吗?

6 ▶**ENERGY** 精力◀ [U] the energy and desire to keep fighting for something you want to achieve 斗志: *There's still plenty of fight left in your grandmother.* 你的祖母仍然斗志旺盛。

7 put up a good fight to work very hard to fight or compete in a difficult situation〔在困难情况下〕英勇地斗争; 顽强地奋斗: *Although our team didn't win, they put up a good fight.* 虽然我们队没有赢，但队员们打得很顽强。

8 a fight to the finish a fight that continues until one side is completely defeated 打到一方被完全击败为止; 打到分清胜负为止 —see also 另见 **pick a quarrel/fight** (PICK[1] (9))

fight·er /ˈfaɪtə; ˈfaɪtə/ *n* [C] **1** someone who fights 战士，士兵，战斗者 **2** someone who keeps trying to achieve something in difficult situations 顽强拼搏者; 斗士: *James is a fighter – he'll come through it all right.* 詹姆斯是个顽强拼搏的人——他会顺利渡过困境的。**3** also 又作 **fighter plane/aircraft** a small, fast military plane that can destroy other planes 战斗机; 歼击机 —see also 另见 FREEDOM FIGHTER

fig leaf /ˈ· ·/ *n* [C] **1** the large leaf of the FIG[1] (1) tree, sometimes shown in paintings as covering people's sex organs〔有时在美术作品中用来遮盖性器官的〕无花果树叶 **2** something that is intended to hide embarrassing facts 遮羞物

fig·ment /ˈfɪgmənt; ˈfɪgmənt/ *n* [C] **a figment of sb's imagination** something that you imagine to be real, but does not exist 某人凭空想象的事物，虚构的事物: *The sinister plot is just a figment of his imagination.* 这个阴谋只是他想象出来的。

fig·u·ra·tive /ˈfɪgjərətɪv; ˈfɪgjərətɪv/ *adj* **1** if a word or phrase is used in a figurative way, it is used about something different from what it normally refers to, to give you a picture in your mind 比喻的，借喻的: *I was using the word 'battle' in its figurative sense.* 我在使用 battle（战斗）这个词的喻义。—compare 比较 LITERAL[1] (1) **2** *technical* figurative art shows objects, people, or the countryside in the way they really look【术语】具象的; 写实的 —compare 比较 ABSTRACT[1] (3) —**figuratively** *adv*: *He's up to his eyes in paperwork – figuratively speaking, of course.* 他都被案牍工作淹没了——当然这是打个比方。

S1 W1 **fig·ure**[1] /ˈfɪgjə; ˈfɪgə/ *n* [C]

1 ▶NUMBER 数字◀ **a)** a number representing an amount, especially an officially published number 数字〔尤指官方公布的数字〕: *keeping unemployment figures down* 保持失业数字于低位 **b)** a number from 0 to 10, written as a sign rather than a word〔从0到10的〕数字符号，位数: **a four/five/six figure number** (=a number in the thousands, ten thousands, hundred thousands etc) 四位数/五位数/六位数 | **double figures** (=numbers between 10 and 99) 两位数〔从10到99的数字〕: *His score is now well into double figures.* 他的得分现在已高达两位数。

2 ▶AMOUNT OF MONEY 钱的数目◀ a particular amount of money 金额，价格: *an estimated figure of $200 million* 估计为两亿美元的金额

3 father/mother/authority figure someone who is considered to be like a father etc, or to represent authority, because of their character or behaviour 父亲/母亲/权威人士形象: *He had always looked upon Sarah as a kind of mother figure.* 他一直把萨拉视为一个母亲形象。

4 figures [plural] the activity of adding, multiplying etc numbers; ARITHMETIC 计算，算术: **have a head for figures** (=be good at arithmetic) 擅长计算

5 put a figure on it/give an exact figure to say exactly how much something is worth, or how much or how many of something you are talking about 准确说出数额[数量]: *I know it's worth a lot of money but I couldn't put a figure on it.* 我知道这值很多钱，但我说不出准确的金额。

6 ▶WOMAN'S BODY 妇女的身体◀ the shape of someone's body, especially a woman's body〔尤指女人的〕体形，体态: *She has a great figure.* 她有很优美的体态。| **keep your figure** (=keep your body in an attractive shape) 保持优美的身段: *How does she manage to keep her figure when she eats so much?* 她吃得这么多，究竟是怎样保持优美的身段的？—see 见 BODY (USAGE)

CULTURAL NOTE 文化注释

In the US and the UK, a man is considered to have a good body if he has broad shoulders, strong muscles, a flat stomach, and long strong legs. A woman is considered to have a good figure if she is thin with a narrow waist, long legs, and fairly large breasts. Men and women know that most people do not look like this, but it is still what most people would like to look like. 英美人眼中，健美的男子应肩宽、肌肉强健、腹部平坦、腿长而有力; 身材好的女人应身瘦、腰细、腿长、胸较大。无论男人和女人都知道，大多数人并没有这样的身材，但这仍是大多数人追求的目标。— see also Cultural Notes at FAT, THIN 另见 FAT, THIN 文化注释

7 ▶KIND OF PERSON 人物类型◀ someone who has a particular type of character or appearance or who is important in a particular way〔具有某种性格特征或外表的〕人物: *He was the outstanding political figure of his time.* 他是他那个时代的著名政治人物。| *She stood there, a frail but defiant figure.* 她就站在那儿，人虽虚弱却傲岸不屈。—see also 另见 **cult figure** (CULT (2))

8 a fine figure of a man/woman someone who is tall and has a good body 相貌堂堂的男子/身材优美的妇女

9 ▶FAR AWAY/DIFFICULT TO SEE 在远处/很难看清◀ the shape of a person, especially one that is far away or is difficult to see〔尤指远处隐约可见的〕人影: *a dark figure in the distance* 远处的一个黑色人影

10 ▶PAINTING/MODEL 绘画/模型◀ a person in a painting or model〔绘画或模型中的〕人像; 人形: *an 18th century Maori figure* 一个18世纪的毛利人形象 —see also 另见 FIGURINE

11 ▶DRAWING 图◀ a numbered drawing or a DIAGRAM in a book〔书中有编号的〕图，图表，图解

12 ▶MATHEMATICAL SHAPE 数学中的图形◀ a GEOMETRIC shape 几何图形，几何形状: *A hexagon is a six-sided figure.* 六边形是一个有六条边的几何图形。

13 ▶ON ICE 滑冰◀ a pattern formed in FIGURE SKATING〔花样滑冰中的〕花样，花式

14 a figure of fun someone who people laugh at 被人嘲笑的人，笑柄

figure[2] *v* S2 W3 **1** [I] to be important in a process, event, or situation, and be noticed because of this〔以重要地位〕出现: *Kennedy's descendants were to figure prominently in the country's history.* 肯尼迪的后代在其后的美国历史上颇有名气。**2** [T] *informal especially AmE* to form a particular opinion after thinking about a situation【非正式，尤美】〔经过考虑后〕认为，以为: **figure that** *I figured that he was drunk and shouldn't be allowed to drive.* 我认为他喝醉了，不应该让他开车。**3 that figures/it figures** *spoken especially AmE*【口，尤美】**a)** used when something happens or someone behaves in a way that you expect, but do not like〔在预料中的不好的事发生时说的〕这是意料之中的事: *"It rained the whole weekend." "Oh, that figures."* "整个周末都下雨。" "噢，这是意料之中的事。" **b)** used to say that something is reasonable or makes sense 这是合乎情理的: *If Terry has talked to Lennox, then he knows you are here. It figures.* 如果特里跟伦诺克斯说过话，他就知道你在这里。这是合乎情理的。**4** [T] *AmE* to calculate an amount【美】计算: *Larry figured his expenses for the past month.* 拉里计算他上个月的开支。

figure sth ↔ **out** *phr v* [T] to think about a problem or situation until you find the answer or understand what has happened 想出，理解〔某事〕: **[+how/what]** *Can you figure out how to do it?* 你能想出这件事该怎么做吗？| **figure sth out** *It took me hours to figure those algebra problems out.* 我花了许多小时才推算出那些代数题。| **figure out that** *She figured out that he was leaving on Tuesday.* 她推断他会在星期二离开。

figure sb **out** *phr v* [T] to understand why someone behaves in the way they do 弄明白，看透，理解〔某人〕: *Women. I just can't figure them out.* 女人。我就是捉摸不透她们。

fig·ured /ˈfɪgjəd; ˈfɪgəd/ *adj* [only before noun 仅用于名词前] decorated with a small pattern 饰有小图案的; 有花纹的: *figured silk* 有花纹的丝绸

fig·ure·head /ˈfɪgjəˌhɛd; ˈfɪgəhed/ *n* [C] **1** someone who seems to be the leader of a country or organization but who has no real power 有名无实的领导人，挂名首脑，傀儡: *The Queen is merely a figurehead.* 女王只不过是个挂名首脑。**2** a wooden model of a woman that used to be placed on the front of ships 船首饰像

figure of eight /ˌ· · ˈ·/ *BrE*【英】, **figure eight** *AmE*【美】*n* [C] the pattern or shape of a number eight, as seen in a knot, dance etc〔绳结、舞蹈等中的〕8字形

figure of eight *BrE*【英】/**figure eight** *AmE*【美】8字形

fig·ure of speech /ˌ··· ˈ·/ *n* [C] a word or expression that is used in a different way from the normal one, to give you a picture in your mind 比喻: *When I said it was a battle to the death it was just a figure of speech.* 我说这是一场死亡之战时, 只是一种比喻。

figure skat·ing /ˈ·· ˌ··/ *n* [U] a kind of SKATING in which you cut patterns in the ice with your SKATES[1] (1) 花式溜冰, 花样滑冰 —**figure skater** *n* [C]

fig·u·rine /ˌfɪgjəˈrin; ˌfɪgjʊˈriːn/ *n* [C] a small model of a person made of CHINA (=baked clay), used as a decoration〔装饰用的瓷制〕小塑像, 小雕像

Fi·ji /ˈfidʒi; ˈfiːdʒiː/ a country in the southwest Pacific Ocean made up of two main islands and hundreds of smaller ones. Population: 844,330 (2001). Capital: Suva. 斐济〔太平洋西南部一国家, 由两大主要岛屿和几百座小岛组成。人口: 844,330 (2001), 首都: 苏瓦〕—**Fijian** /fiˈdʒiən; fiːˈdʒiːən/ *n, adj*

fil·a·ment /ˈfɪləmənt; ˈfɪləmənt/ *n* [C] a very thin thread, especially the thin wire in a LIGHT BULB 细丝;〔电灯泡内的〕灯丝

fil·bert /ˈfɪlbɚt; ˈfɪlbət/ *n* [C] *especially AmE* a HAZELNUT【尤美】榛子

filch /fɪltʃ; fɪltʃ/ *v* [T] *informal* to steal something, especially something small or not very expensive【非正式】偷〔不贵重的小东西〕: *He was sacked for filching food from the kitchen.* 他因偷厨房里的食物而被开除。

file[1] /faɪl; faɪl/ *n* [C] **1** information about a particular person or subject that is kept by an official organization〔官方机构保存的〕档案, 卷宗: **[+on]** *Mendoza read over the file on the murders again.* 门多萨从头到尾把谋杀案的文件档案再阅一遍。| **keep a file on** (=collect and store information) 保存…的档案 *The government keeps a file on known terrorists.* 政府保存着已知恐怖分子的档案。**2** a box or folded piece of heavy paper that is used to store papers in the proper order 文件夹; 文件箱: *Fran came in holding a blue file.* 弗兰拿着一个蓝色文件夹进来。**3** a collection of information on a computer that is stored under a particular name〔电脑分门别类储存信息的〕档案文件: *a spreadsheet file* 电子数据表档案 **4 on file a)** kept in a file so that it can be used later 存档: *We will keep your application on file.* 我们将把你的申请书存档。**b)** officially recorded 登记在案: *The petition has to be on file by March 3rd.* 这份请愿书须在3月3日前登记在案。**5** a metal tool with a rough surface used to smooth other surfaces or to cut through wood, metal etc 锉刀 —see also 另见 NAIL FILE —see picture at 参见 TOOL[1] 图 **6** a line of people one behind the other 纵列: **in file** *walking in file* 排成纵队行走; 鱼贯而行 —see also 另见 INDIAN FILE, SINGLE FILE, RANK AND FILE

file[2] *v* **1** [I always+adv/prep] to walk in a line of people, one behind the other 排成纵队行走: **[+past/into/through etc]** *The mourners filed past the coffin.* 送葬者排成一列走过灵柩。**2** [I always+adv/prep,T] *law* to officially record something such as a complaint, law case, official document etc【法律】把〔投诉信、法律案件、正式文件等〕登记在案; 正式提出: *Mr Genoa filed a formal complaint against the department.* 杰诺亚先生把对该部门的投诉正式登记在案。| **[+for]** *The Morrisons have filed for divorce.* 莫里森夫妇已经向法院正式申请离婚。**3** [T] to keep papers with information on them in a particular place so that you can find them easily 把…汇存起来, 把…归档[存档]: *Contributors' contracts are filed alphabetically.* 投稿人的合同按字母顺序归档。| **file sth away** *The exam papers will be filed away in my office.* 试卷将归档存放在我的办公室。**4** [I always+adv/prep,T] to cut or rub something or make something smooth, using a metal tool with a rough surface 锉, 锉平, 锉去: *She was filing her nails.* 她在锉指甲。| **[+through/away/down etc]** *I need to file down the sharp edges.* 我需要把尖利的边缘锉平。

file cab·i·net /ˈ· ˌ···/ *n* [C] *AmE* a FILING CABINET【美】档案柜; 文件柜

fil·et[1] /fɪˈle; ˈfɪlɪt/ *n* [C] the usual American spelling of FILLET[1] fillet[1] 的一般美式拼法

filet[2] *v* [T] the usual American spelling of FILLET[2] fillet[2] 的一般美式拼法

fil·i·al /ˈfɪlɪəl; ˈfɪliəl/ *adj formal* concerning the way in which a son or daughter should behave towards their parents【正式】子女般的; 孝顺的: *her filial duty* 她作为子女的责任

fil·i·bus·ter /ˈfɪləˌbʌstɚ; ˈfɪlɪbʌstə/ *v* [I] *especially AmE* to try to delay action in Congress by making very long speeches【尤美】〔在美国国会中〕以冗长的发言阻挠议事 —**filibuster** *n* [C]

fil·i·gree /ˈfɪləˌgri; ˈfɪlɪgriː/ *n* [U] delicate work made of gold or silver wire, used to decorate things 金丝[银丝]细工饰品: *silver filigree jewellery* 镶银丝的珠宝

filing cab·i·net /ˈ·· ˌ···/ *n* [C] *BrE* a piece of office furniture that has drawers for storing letters, reports etc【英】档案柜; 文件柜

fil·ings /ˈfaɪlɪŋz; ˈfaɪlɪŋz/ *n* [plural] very small sharp bits that come off a piece of metal when it is filed (FILE[2] (4)) 锉屑

fill in 填写

form 表格

fill[1] /fɪl; fɪl/ *v*

1 ►MAKE STH FULL 充满◄ **a)** also 又作 **fill up** [T] to put the right amount of a liquid, substance, or material into a container, or put in enough to make it full 装满, 注满, 填满, 充满: *I filled a saucepan and put it on the stove.* 我把深平底锅装满了, 然后把它放在灶火上。| *You've filled the bath too full.* 你把浴缸灌得太满了。| **fill sth with** *Fill the pots with earth.* 在花盆里装满泥土。| **fill sth to the brim** (=fill something completely) 把某物装得满满的 **b) be filled with** if a container is filled with something, it has had as much of something as possible put inside it 被装满: *The next drawer was filled with neat piles of shirts.* 下一个抽屉装满了叠放整齐的衬衫。

2 ►BECOME FULL 变满◄ also 又作 **fill up** [I] if a place, building, or container fills, it gradually becomes full of people, things, or a particular substance〔地方、建筑物或容器〕变满: *They opened the doors and the hall quickly started to fill.* 他们开了门, 大厅很快就开始挤满了人。| **[+with]** *The trench is filling up with water.* 沟里的水快要满了。

3 ►NOT LEAVE ANY SPACE 不留下任何空间◄ [T] if a lot of people or things fill a place, there are so many of them that there seems to be no room for anyone or anything else 挤满, 占满, 布满: *Piles of newspapers filled the garage.* 成堆的报纸占满了车库。| **be filled with** *The streets were filled with cheering crowds.* 街道上挤满了欢呼的人群。

4 ►HOLE/CRACK 孔/缝隙◄ also 又作 **fill in** [T] to put a substance in a hole or crack in order to make a surface smooth again 填补: *Fill any cracks in the wall before you paint it.* 先把墙壁的裂缝填塞好再粉刷。

5 ►SOUND/SMELL/LIGHT 声音/气味/光线◄ [T] if a sound, smell, or light fills a place or space, you notice it because it is very loud or strong 遍布, 充满: *The smell of freshly baked bread filled the room.* 房间充满了刚出炉的面包香味。| *The stage filled with light.* 舞台灯火通明。| **be filled with** *The air was filled with the sound of happy children.* 空气中充满着孩子们快乐的声音。

6 ►EMOTIONS 感情◄ [T] if an emotion fills you, you feel it very strongly 充满〔某种感情〕: *A feeling of bliss filled his body.* 他感到十分幸福。| **be filled with** *She was filled with a deep contentment.* 她感到极度心满意足。

7 fill a need/demand to give people something they want but which they have not been able to have until now 满足需要/要求: *The program helps fill a growing need among teenagers for practical advice about drugs.* 青少年需要得到有关毒品问题的切实可行的忠告, 而这项计划有助于满足他们在这方面不断增长的需求。

8 [T] if you fill a period of time with a particular activity you use most of your time doing it 占据〔时间〕: *Our days were filled with talk and music.* 我们以谈话和听音乐来打发日子。| **fill sth doing sth** *Harry filled his spare time reading and writing to friends.* 哈里把闲余时间都用来看书和给朋友写信。

9 fill yourself *informal* to eat so much food that you cannot eat any more【非正式】吃饱: **fill yourself with** *Don't fill yourself up with sweets, we're eating in an hour.* 别吃太多的糖果, 我们过一小时就要吃饭了。

10 fill a job/post/position a) to do a particular job 担任工作/职位/职务: *Women fill 30% of the senior positions.* 妇女担任了

30% 高级职位的工作。**b)** to accept someone's offer of a job 接受〔工作〕: *a shortage of trained secretaries willing to fill permanent office vacancies* 缺乏愿意担任办公室长期工作的训练有素的秘书

11 fill a role be a part of something 成为…的一部分; 起某种角色的作用: *Pop music undoubtedly fills an important role in teenagers' lives.* 流行音乐毫无疑问是青少年生活的一个重要部分。

12 fill an order *especially AmE* to supply the goods requested by a customer【尤美】供应订单; 按单配足订货

13 fill the bill *AmE* to have exactly the right qualities; **fit the bill** (FIT[1] (7))【美】完全符合要求, 正合适: *We needed an experienced reporter and Willis fills the bill.* 我们需要一个经验丰富的记者, 威利斯正合适。

14 ▶TEETH 牙齿◀ [T] to put a FILLING[2](1) in a tooth 补〔牙〕

15 ▶SAIL 帆◀ [I,T] if a sail fills or the wind fills a sail, the sail has a rounded shape rather than hanging down loosely〔帆〕张满, 张开;〔风〕把〔帆〕张满

fill in *phr v*

1 ▶DOCUMENT 文件◀ [T **fill** sth ↔ **in**] to write all the necessary information on an official document 填写〔官方文件表格〕: *Don't forget to fill in your boarding cards.* 别忘了填写你的登机证。

2 ▶TELL SB NEWS 告诉某人消息◀ [T **fill** sb ↔ **in**] to tell someone about things which have happened recently, especially because you have not seen them for a long time 向…提供最新消息: **fill sb in on sth** *Let me fill you in on what's been happening in the office over lunch.* 让我告诉你午饭时办公室里发生的事。

3 ▶CRACK/HOLE 缝/孔◀ [T **fill** sth ↔ **in**] to put a substance in a hole or crack in order to make a surface smooth again 填平〔空洞或缝隙〕: *filling in the holes in the road* 填好路上的洞

4 fill in time to use your time doing something unimportant, especially when you are waiting for something to happen 消磨时间, 打发时间: *We've got some time to fill in before the show. Let's go for a drink.* 表演开始前我们有点时间要打发。我们去喝一杯吧。

5 ▶SPACE 空间◀ [T **fill** sth ↔ **in**] to paint or draw over the space inside a shape〔绘画时〕在〔图的轮廓线〕内填色: *Somebody had filled in all the 'o's on the page.* 有人已经把这页上所有的 o 字都填黑了。

6 ▶DO SB'S JOB 做某人的工作◀ [I] to do someone's job or work because they are unable to do it〔由于某人不能工作而〕临时替代: **fill in for sb** *Sally's off sick. Can you fill in for her for a few days?* 萨莉因病请假。你能临时替她几天吗?

7 ▶HIT SB 痛打某人◀ [T **fill** sb **in**] *BrE informal* to hit someone hard and repeatedly all over their body【英, 非正式】痛打: *One more crack like that and I'll fill you in.* 再开那样的玩笑我就要好好收拾你一顿。

fill out *phr v* **1** [T **fill** sth ↔ **out**] to write all the necessary information on an official document 填写: *You haven't filled out the counterfoil.* 你还没填写支票的存根。**2** [I] **a)** if your body fills out it becomes rounded or large in a way that is considered attractive〔身体〕变圆, 变丰满, 变大: *Young Kevin has really filled out in the last six months.* 年轻的凯文最近六个月身体确实丰满起来了。**b)** a phrase meaning to become fat, used when you do not want to offend someone 发福〔意为长胖, 当不想冒犯某人时用〕: *I think Eric is filling out around the waist.* 埃里克的腰部在发福。

fill up *phr v*

1 ▶MAKE STH FULL 将某物装满◀ [T **fill** sth ↔ **up**] to put the right amount of a liquid or substance in a container or enough to make it full 装满, 使充满: *Brad just kept filling up everyone's glasses with champagne.* 布拉德不停地往大家的杯里加满香槟酒。

2 ▶BECOME FULL 变满◀ [I] to gradually become full of people, things, or a substance〔慢慢〕充满: *The church was filling up with people who had come to pay their respects.* 教堂坐满了来表示敬意的人。

3 ▶DOCUMENT 文件◀ [T **fill** sth ↔ **up**] to write all the necessary information on an official document 填写〔正式文件〕

4 fill (yourself) up *informal* to eat so much food that you cannot eat any more【非正式】吃饱: [**+with**] *Don't fill yourself up with too many cookies.* 别吃太多曲奇饼。

5 ▶STOP SB FEELING HUNGRY 使某人不觉得饿◀ [T **fill** sb **up**] *informal* food that fills you up makes you feel you have eaten a lot when you have only eaten a small amount【非正式】使…觉得饱〔实际只吃了很少的食物〕: *I used to just have a sandwich for lunch, but that doesn't fill me up anymore.* 我过去只吃一块三明治当午餐, 但现在这样吃不饱了。

fill[2] *n* **1 have your fill of sth** to no longer be able to accept an unpleasant situation 受够了某物, 对某物忍无可忍: *I've had my fill of screaming kids for one day.* 听了一天小孩的尖叫声, 我已经受够了。**2 eat/drink your fill** to eat or drink as much as you want or need 开怀大吃/开怀畅饮 **3 a fill of sth** the quantity you need to fill something 填满某物所需的量

filled gold /, · '◂/ *n* [U] *AmE* ROLLED GOLD【美】金箔, 包金

fill·er /ˈfɪlɚ; ˈfɪlə/ *n* [singular,U] **1** a substance used to fill cracks in wood, walls etc, especially before you paint them〔在木头、墙壁等上用以填平裂缝的〕填料〔尤指刷漆前使用〕; 填塞物 **2** *especially AmE* stories, information, drawings etc that are not important but are used to fill a page in a newspaper or magazine【尤美】〔报纸或杂志上的〕补白; 补足版面用的文字[图画]

filler cap /ˈ·· ·/ *n* [C] *BrE* the lid that fits over the hole in a car that you pour petrol through【英】〔汽车的〕燃油箱盖

fil·let[1] /ˈfɪlɪt; ˈfɪlʒt/ *n* [C] a piece of meat or fish without bones〔去骨的〕肉片; 鱼片; FILET[1] *AmE*【美】: *a fillet of sole* 鳎鱼片[柳]

fillet[2] *v* [T] to remove the bones from a piece of meat or fish 剔除〔肉或鱼的〕骨头; FILET[2] *AmE*【美】: *filleted sole* 去骨鳎鱼片[柳]

fill-in /ˈ· ·/ *n* [singular] *BrE informal* someone who does someone else's job when they are unable to do it【英, 非正式】临时替代的人, 替工: *I'm only here as a fill-in while Robert's away.* 我只是在罗伯特不在时来这里临时顶一会儿。

fill·ing[1] /ˈfɪlɪŋ; ˈfɪlɪŋ/ *adj* food that is filling makes your stomach feel full 耐饥的, 使人感到饱的: *That fruitcake is really filling stuff.* 那块水果蛋糕真能果腹。

filling[2] *n* **1** [C] a small amount of metal that is put into your tooth to prevent it from decaying〔补牙用的〕金属充填料 **2** [C, U] the food that is put inside a PIE, SANDWICH[1] etc〔馅饼、三明治等的〕馅: *cherry pie filling* 樱桃馅饼的馅

filling sta·tion /ˈ·· ,·/ *n* [C] a place where you can buy petrol for your car 汽车加油站; PETROL STATION *BrE*【英】

fil·lip /ˈfɪləp; ˈfɪlʒp/ *n* [singular] **give sb/sth a fillip** to do something that adds excitement or interest to something 激励[刺激]某人/某物: *All these activities and parties have given a fillip to my self-esteem.* 这些活动和聚会都增强了我的自尊心。

Fill·more /ˈfɪlmɔr; ˈfɪlmɔ/, **Mil·lard** (1800-74) the thirteenth president of the US, from 1850 to 1853 费尔莫尔〔(1800-1874), 美国第十三任总统, 1850 至 1853 年在位〕

fil·ly /ˈfɪlɪ; ˈfɪli/ *n* [C] a young female horse 小母马

film[1] /fɪlm; fɪlm/ *n* **1** [C] *especially BrE* a story that is told using sound and moving pictures, shown at a cinema or on television for entertainment【尤英】〔电影院或电视上供娱乐的〕影片, 电影; MOVIE *AmE*【美】: *Have you seen any good films recently?* 你最近看过什么好的影片吗? | *a French film* 法国影片 —see also 另见 **silent film** (SILENT (4)) **2** [U] the making of films considered as an art or a business 电影制作: *I'm interested in photography and film.* 我对摄影和电影制作感兴趣。| *the film industry* 电影业 **3** [U] the material used in a camera for taking photographs or recording moving pictures for the cinema 胶片, 软片: **roll of film** (=film in a metal container)(一卷)胶卷 *I shot five rolls of film on vacation.* 我在度假时拍了五卷胶卷。| **on film** *The whole incident was recorded on film.* 事件的整个过程都被拍摄下来。**4** [C] *BrE* a metal container with film in it that you put inside a camera to take photographs【英】胶卷 **5** [singular,U] a very thin layer of something that appears on the surface of something else 薄层, 薄膜: *a film of oil on the surface of the water* 水面上的一层油 —see also 另见 CLINGFILM

S2 W1

film[2] *v* [I,T] to use a camera to record a story or real events so that it can be shown in the cinema or on television 把…拍成电影, 拍摄〔影片〕: *The explosion had been filmed by an amateur cameraman.* 爆炸被一位业余摄影师拍摄下来了。| *filming on location in Prague* 在布拉格拍外景

film over *phr v* [I] if your eyes film over they become covered with a thin layer of liquid〔眼睛上〕盖有薄薄一层液体: *The dog's eyes had filmed over, and it was breathing heavily.* 狗的眼睛有点模糊, 正气喘吁吁。

film fes·ti·val /ˈ· ,···/ *n* [C] an event when a lot of films are shown, and sometimes prizes are given for the best ones 电影节

film star /ˈ· ·/ *n* [C] a famous actor or actress in cinema films 电影明星; MOVIE STAR *AmE*【美】

film·strip /ˈfɪlm,strɪp; ˈfɪlm,strɪp/ *n* [C] a photographic film that shows photographs, drawings etc, one at a time, not as moving pictures 幻灯片: *an educational filmstrip* 教学幻灯片

Fi·lo·fax /ˈfaɪlə,fæks; ˈfaɪləfæks/ *n* [C] *trademark* a small book in which you write addresses, things you must do etc, with pages you can add or take out【商标】活页备忘记事本

fi·lo pas·try /ˌfilo ˋpestrɪ; ˌfiːləʊ ˈpeɪstri/ *n* [U] a type of PASTRY (2) with many very thin layers 薄片酥皮

fil·ter¹ /ˋfɪltɚ; ˈfɪltə/ *n* [C] **1** a piece of equipment or a substance that you pass gas or liquid through to remove unwanted substances 过滤器: *a water filter* 滤水器 **2** a piece of glass or plastic that changes the amount or colour of light allowed into a camera or TELESCOPE[1]〔照相机或望远镜的〕滤光镜, 滤色镜 **3** a piece of equipment that only allows certain sounds to pass through it〔声音的〕滤波器; 滤音器 **4** *BrE* a light used to tell drivers they can turn right or left【英】〔指示汽车司机左转或右转的〕限阈通行灯, 〔绿色〕箭头灯, 分流信号

filter² *v* **1** [T] to clean a liquid or gas by passing it through a special substance or piece of equipment〔用特别的物质或设备〕过滤: *You need to filter the drinking water.* 你需要把饮用水过滤一下。**2** [I always+adv/prep] if people filter somewhere, they move gradually in that direction through a door, passage etc〔人群通过门、过道等〕逐渐移动; 逐渐走过: **[+in/out etc]** *Chattering noisily, the crowd began to filter into the auditorium.* 人群唧唧喳喳说着话, 开始慢慢步入会堂。**3** [I always+adv/prep] if news or information filters somewhere, people gradually hear about it from each other〔消息或信息〕慢慢传开, 走漏, 泄漏: **[+back/through etc]** *The news slowly filtered through to everyone in the office.* 这消息慢慢走漏出去, 结果办公室里每个人都知道了。**4** [I always+adv/prep] if light or sound filters into a place, it can be seen or heard only slightly〔光线或声音〕隐约地透过; 隐约地传入: **[+in/into/through]** *A few rays of sunshine filtered into the cave.* 几缕阳光映进山洞。**5** [I] *BrE* if traffic filters, cars can turn left or right while other vehicles going straight ahead must wait【英】〔车辆〕转弯〔直走的车辆必须等待〕

filter sth ↔ **out** *phr v* [T] to remove something by using a filter 滤除: *The machine filters out sediment.* 这台机器能滤除沉淀物。

F

filter tip /ˈ· · ˌ·/ *n* [C] the special end of a cigarette that removes some of the harmful substances from the smoke〔香烟〕过滤嘴 —**filter tipped** *adj*

filth /fɪlθ; fɪlθ/ *n* [U] **1** an extremely dirty substance 污物, 污秽: *Go and wash that filth off your hands!* 去把你手上的脏东西洗掉吧! **2** very rude offensive language, stories, or pictures about sex 下流话; 淫秽故事; 淫秽图片: *I don't know how you can read that filth!* 我不知道你怎么会阅读那种淫秽的东西!

3 **filth·y¹** /ˋfɪlθɪ; ˈfɪlθi/ *adj* **filthier, filthiest 1** extremely dirty 十分肮脏的, 污秽的: *Simon never cleans his house – it's absolutely filthy!* 西蒙从来不打扫房子——它脏极了! **2** showing or describing sexual acts in a very rude or offensive way 淫秽的, 下流的: *Mitch was just telling us a filthy joke when Kia walked in.* 基亚走进来时, 米奇正给我们讲下流笑话。—**filthily** *adv* —**filthiness** *n* [U]

filthy² *adv* **1 filthy dirty** very dirty 十分肮脏 **2 filthy rich** *informal* an expression meaning extremely rich, used when you think someone has too much money【非正式】腰缠万贯, 非常有钱

fil·tra·tion /fɪlˋtreʃən; fɪlˈtreɪʃən/ *n* [U] the process of being cleaned by passing through a FILTER[1] (1) 过滤

fin /fɪn; fɪn/ *n* [C] **1** one of the thin body parts that a fish uses to swim 鱼鳍 **2** part of a plane that sticks up at the back and helps it to fly smoothly〔飞机的〕垂直尾翼 —see picture at 参见 AIRCRAFT 图 **3** *BrE* a large flat rubber shoe that you wear to help you swim better【英】〔潜水、游泳用的〕脚蹼; FLIPPER (2) *AmE*【美】**4** a thin piece of metal that sticks out from something such as a car〔汽车等的〕鳍状稳定板

fi·na·gle /fəˋnegḷ; fəˈneɪgəl/ *v* [T] **finagled, finagling** *AmE informal*【美, 非正式】**1** to obtain something that is difficult to get, but not by using the usual or official methods 用欺诈手段得到; 耍花招弄到: *How he finagled four front row seats to the game I'll never know.* 他是怎样弄到比赛的四张前排票的, 我永远不会知道。**2** to trick someone into giving you something, especially money 骗取〔尤指骗钱〕: **finagle sb out of sth** *He finagled me out of ten bucks.* 他骗去了我十块钱。—**finagler** *n* [C]

1 1 **fi·nal¹** /ˋfaɪnḷ; ˈfaɪnl/ *adj* **1** [only before noun 仅用于名词前] last in a series of actions, events, parts of a story etc 最后的, 最终的: *The final episode of 'Prime Suspect' is on tonight.*《头号嫌疑犯》的最后一集于今晚播出。| **final stage/moments etc** *They scored in the final minute of the game.* 他们在比赛的最后一分钟得分。| **final demand** (=the last time you are sent a bill when you must pay)〔账单的〕最后偿付要求; 最终催付通知 **2** if a decision, offer, agreement etc is final, it cannot be changed〔决定、报价、协议等〕不可改变的, 决定性的, 最终的: **be final** *My decision is final. Do not ask me again!* 我的决定不变。不要再问我了! | **final decision/say/approval etc** *We recommended the plan to the chancellor, who had the final say.* 我们把计划推荐给校长, 他有最后决定权。| **and that's final!** *spoken* (=used to say that a decision will not be changed)【口】就这么定了! *No more money, and that's final!* 不能再多给钱了, 就这么定了! **3** [only before noun 仅用于名词前] happening at or near the end of an event or process 最后的: *They fought many battles before their final defeat.* 他们打了许多仗, 最后才被打败。**4** [only before noun 仅用于名词前] being the result at the end of a process 结果的, 最终的: *the differences between the original script and the final film* 原脚本和最终拍出来的影片之间的差别

final² *n* [C] **1 finals** *BrE* the set of examinations that university students take at the end of their time at university【英】〔大学期间〕最后一次考试, 毕业考试 **2** *AmE* an examination taken at the end of each class a student takes at university【美】〔大学〕期终考试 **3** the last and most important game, race etc in a set of games or races〔一场〕决赛: *He ran well in the heats but came in last in the final.* 他在分组预赛中跑得很好, 但在决赛中却得了最后一名。| **the finals** (=the last few games or races in a competition)〔最后几场〕决赛 *the 1994 World Cup finals* 1994 年世界杯决赛

fi·na·le /fɪˋnælɪ; fɪˈnɑːli/ *n* [C] the last part of a piece of music or a show〔演出的〕终场, 最后一幕; 〔音乐的〕终曲: *the finale of a Broadway show* 百老汇表演的终场 | **grand finale** (=very impressive end to a show)〔演出的〕大结局 *The fireworks were the grand finale of the closing ceremonies.* 闭幕仪式在烟火齐放中隆重结束。

fi·nal·ist /ˋfaɪnḷɪst; ˈfaɪnəl-ɪst/ *n* [C] one of the people or teams that reaches the final game in a competition or set of sports matches〔竞赛或体育比赛的〕决赛选手

fi·nal·i·ty /faɪˋnælətɪ; faɪˈnæləti/ *n* [U] the quality or feeling that something has when you know it is over and cannot be changed 定局, 终结: *The word 'retirement' has a horrible air of finality about it.* "退休"这个词蕴涵有终结的可怕意味。

fi·nal·ize also 又作 **-ise** *BrE*【英】/ˋfaɪnḷˌaɪz; ˈfaɪnəl-aɪz/ *v* [T] to finish the last part of a plan, business deal etc 最后定下, 使〔计划、交易等〕确定: *Jo flew out to Thailand to finalize the details of the deal.* 乔乘飞机到泰国, 把这笔交易的细节定下来。—**finalization** /ˌfaɪnələˋzeʃən; ˌfaɪnəlaɪˈzeɪʃən/ *n* [U]

fi·nal·ly /ˋfaɪnḷɪ; ˈfaɪnəli/ *adv* **1** after a long time 最后, 终于: *After several delays we finally took off at six o'clock.* 几经耽搁后, 我们终于在六点起飞了。| *Finally, to my relief, Garth brought up the subject of money.* 使我松了一口气的是, 加思终于提出了钱的问题。**2** as the last of a series of things 最后(一点): [sentence adverb 句子副词] *And finally, I'd like to thank the crew.* 最后, 我要感谢全体机组人员。**3** in a finished state 决定性地, 彻底地: *It's not finally settled yet.* 这件事还没有彻底解决。—see 见 LASTLY (USAGE) 2 1

Final So·lu·tion, the /ˌ· · ˈ· ·/ Adolf Hitler's plan to remove Jewish people from Europe by killing them all "最后解决方案"〔指阿道夫·希特勒以屠杀方式灭绝欧洲犹太人的方案〕—see also 另见 HOLOCAUST

fi·nance¹ /fəˋnæns; ˈfaɪnæns/ *n* **1** [U] the management of money, especially money controlled by a government, company, or large organization 财政, 金融: *the university's finance committee* 大学的财务委员会 | **high finance** (=financial activities involving countries or large companies)〔涉及国家或大公司的〕巨额资金活动 **2 finances a)** the money that a person, company, organization etc has available 资金, 财源, 财力: *The committee's finances are very limited.* 委员会的资金很有限。**b)** the way a person, company, organization etc manages their money 财务管理, 理财: *My finances are in a real mess.* 我的财务确实乱七八糟。**3** [U] money, especially money provided by a bank, to help run a business or buy something 资金: **[+for]** *We need to raise finance for further research.* 我们需要为进一步研究筹资。 3 2

finance² *v* [T] to provide money, especially a large amount of money, to pay for something 为…提供资金; 出资: *These concerts are financed by the Arts Council.* 这些音乐会是由艺术委员会资助的。 3

finance com·pa·ny /ˈ· ˌ· · ·/ *n* [C] *AmE* a company that lends money, especially to businesses【美】信贷公司, 金融公司, 财务公司

fi·nan·cial /fəˋnænʃəl; fəˈnænʃəl/ *adj* connected with money or the management of money 财政的, 金融的: *New York is a great financial center.* 纽约是一个大金融中心。| *financial assistance for city schools* 对市立学校的资助 | **a financial success** (=something that makes a profit) 赚钱的事 *It was a wonderful film, but not exactly a financial success.* 这是一部很好的电影, 但不一定能赚钱。—**financially** *adv* 3 1

financial aid /ˌ·ˌ··ˈ·/ *n* [U] *AmE* money given or lent to students at college or university to pay for their education【美】助学金, 助学贷款

financial in·cen·tive /ˌ·ˌ·· ·ˈ··/ *n* [C] money given to someone if they work harder or for special jobs 金钱鼓励; 奖金

financial in·sti·tu·tion /ˌ·ˌ·· ··ˈ··/ *n* [C] *technical* a business organization that lends and borrows money, for example a bank【术语】金融机构〈如银行〉: *All the big financial institutions cut their interest rates today.* 所有的大型金融机构今天都降低了利率。

financial mar·kets /ˌ·ˌ··ˈ··/ *n* [plural] *technical* banks and other financial institutions that make business contracts with each other【术语】金融市场

Financial Times, the /ˌ·ˌ··ˈ·/ *trademark* abbreviation 缩写为 **the FT** a serious British daily newspaper which contains articles about business and financial news. It is printed on pink paper.【商标】《金融时报》〔英国一份严肃类日报, 刊登商业和金融新闻, 使用粉色纸张印刷〕

Financial Times In·dex, the /ˌ·ˌ··, ·ˈ··/ —see 见 the FT 100 SHARE INDEX

financial year /ˌ·ˌ··ˈ·/ *n* [singular] the period of a year over which a company's profits and losses are calculated 财政年度, 会计年度 —compare 比较 FISCAL YEAR

fi·nan·cier /ˌfɪnənˈsɪr; fɪˈnænsɪə/ *n* [C] someone who controls or lends large sums of money 财政家, 金融家

finch /fɪntʃ; fɪntʃ/ *n* [C] a small bird with a short beak 雀科鸣禽

1 1 **find¹** /faɪnd; faɪnd/ *past tense and past participle* **found** /faʊnd; faʊnd/ *v* [T]

1 ▶BY SEARCHING 通过搜寻◀ to discover or see something that you have been searching for 发现, 找到〔一直寻找的东西〕: *I can't find the car keys.* 我找不到汽车钥匙。| *Let's hope we can find a parking space.* 但愿我们能找到一个停车的地方。| *No-one has found a solution to this problem.* 还没人找到解决这个问题的办法。| **find sb sth** *I found him a nice second-hand car.* 我替他找了辆很好的二手车。—see 见 OBTAIN (USAGE)

2 ▶ARRIVE 到达◀ to discover that someone or something is in a particular condition or doing a particular thing when you arrive or first see them 发现, 发觉〔某人或某物处在某状态或在做某事〕: *I'm sure we'll find her hard at work when we get home.* 我确信我们到家时会发现她还在努力工作。| *Michael woke up to find his bedroom ankle-deep in water.* 迈克尔醒来时发现他的卧室里有齐踝深的水。| **find sb doing sth** *Carrie went into the kitchen, where she found them giggling together.* 卡丽走进厨房, 发现她们在那儿咯咯地笑着。| [+(that)] *When I got to school I found that class was cancelled.* 我到达学校时, 发现停课了。

3 ▶BY STUDY 通过研究◀ to discover or learn something by study, tests etc 找出, 查明: *Will we ever find a cure for the disease?* 我们究竟能找到治疗这种病的药吗? | *The liquid was found to contain 7.4g of phenylamine.* 这种液体被发现含有7.4克苯胺。| [+that] *It was found that 80% of young people borrow money.* 调查发现80%的年轻人借钱。

4 ▶THINK/FEEL 认为/感觉◀ to have a particular feeling or idea about something 感到, 觉得, 认为: *I hate flying – I find it absolutely terrifying.* 我讨厌坐飞机——我觉得坐飞机非常可怕。| *Lots of women I know find him attractive.* 我认识的许多女子都觉得他很有魅力。

5 find sth easy/difficult/impossible if you find something difficult or easy it seems difficult or easy to you when you do it 觉得某事很容易/很难/是不可能的: *He said that, after Russian, I should find German easy.* 他说, 在学过俄语之后, 我应该觉得德语容易学。| **find it difficult/easy etc to do sth** *He found it almost impossible to express what he wanted to say.* 他觉得要表达他想说的话几乎是不可能的。

6 ▶BY EXPERIENCE 通过经验◀ to learn or know something by experience 学会; 知道; 发觉: [+(that)] *You might find that his work improves now he's going to a new school.* 你可能会发现他学习有所进步, 现在他要去另一所学校上学了。| *One thing I find about living in the big city is that people are more friendly than I expected.* 关于生活在大城市, 我发现那里的人比我想象的要友好。| **find sb/sth doing sth** *You find more women entering the film business now.* 你会发现现在有越来越多的女性进入电影业。

7 ▶BY CHANCE 偶然发现◀ to discover something by chance, especially something useful or interesting 偶然发现, 碰上: *I found a purse in the street.* 我在街上捡到一个钱包。| *We found a really good bar near the hotel.* 我们在旅馆附近发现一家非常好的酒吧。

8 ▶STH YOU NEED 所需的东西◀ to achieve or get something that you need 获得, 得到, 找到: *Finding accommodation in Berlin can be a nightmare.* 在柏林找地方住宿有时就像做恶梦一样。| *two lonely people who managed to find happiness together* 设法一起找到幸福的两个孤独的人

9 ▶REALIZE 意识到◀ to notice or realize a fact, often a fact that is surprising 发觉, 发现: [+(that)] *He got up to leave and found that the door was jammed.* 他站起来要离开, 但发现门卡住了打不开。| *I found I was really looking forward to going back to work.* 我发觉我确实盼望回去工作。

10 ▶ANIMALS/PLANTS 动物/植物◀ if something is found somewhere, it lives or exists there 发现…的存在〔指动植物自然地生长于某地〕: *This species is only found in West Africa.* 该物种仅见于西非。

11 ▶MONEY/TIME/ENERGY 钱/时间/精力◀ to have enough money, time, energy etc to be able to do something you want to do 设法拥有, 努力获得: *He has to find £1000 to repay the loan.* 他得去弄1000英镑来偿付贷款。| *I wouldn't mind learning a language, but I can't find the time right now.* 我不介意学一门语言, 但我现在挤不出时间来。| *David wanted to defend himself, but couldn't find the courage to speak up.* 戴维想为自己辩护, 但没有勇气说出来。

12 find your way to reach a place by discovering the right way to get there 设法到达: *Will you be able to find your way back to the house?* 你找得到回住所的路吗?

13 find its way if something finds its way somewhere, it arrives or gets there after some time〔一段时间后〕(自然)到达: *Only one of her inventions has found its way into the shops.* 她的发明只有一项最终进入了市场。

14 find yourself doing sth to gradually realize that you are doing something, although you had not intended or planned to do it 发现自己〔不知不觉地〕在做某事: *Peter, who was usually shy, found himself talking to the girls.* 彼得通常很怕羞, 但却发现自己不知不觉中已在跟女孩子们说话。

15 find yourself in/at etc a) to realize that you are in a particular situation, especially a bad one, that you did not expect 发现自己处于某种状态〔尤指没预料到的糟糕状况〕: *If you find yourself worrying about things, call me.* 如果你觉得自己为什么事烦恼, 请打电话给我。| *They suddenly found themselves without a goalkeeper.* 他们突然发现己方没有守门员。**b)** to realize that you have arrived somewhere without intending to 发现自己在不知不觉中到达: *After wandering around, we found ourselves back at the hotel.* 我们四处漫步后发现自己回到了酒店。

16 find yourself *often humorous* to discover what you are really like and what you want to do【常幽默】发现自己的真本质[真想做的事等]: *She went to India to find herself.* 她到印度去寻找真的自己。

17 find sb guilty/find sb not guilty to officially decide that someone is guilty or not guilty of something 判决某人有罪/判决某人无罪: *Galbraith was found not guilty and set free.* 加尔布雷思被判无罪而得到释放。| [+of] *A clearly innocent man has been found guilty of a serious crime.* 一个明显无辜的人被判决犯有重罪。

18 find comfort/pleasure/fulfilment in to experience a good feeling because of something 因…得到安慰/快乐/满足: *He found great satisfaction in kneading the dough and baking the bread.* 他在揉面团和烤面包中得到很大满足。

19 find fault with to criticize someone or something, often unfairly and frequently 批评, 挑剔, 找岔子: *The teacher would always find fault with our grammar.* 老师对我们的语法总是百般挑剔。

20 find favour (with) be liked or approved of by someone 得宠, 受青睐: *The recipes rapidly found favour with restaurant owners.* 这些食谱很快就受到餐馆老板的青睐。

21 find in sb's favour/find in favour of sb to judge that someone is right or not guilty 裁决〔某人〕正确; 判决〔某人〕无罪: *The Tribunal found in favour of the defendant.* 裁判庭判决被告无罪。

22 find your feet to get used to a new situation, especially one that is difficult at first 习惯新的环境〔尤指起初困难的环境〕: *Matt's only been at the school two weeks and he hasn't found his feet yet.* 马特上这所学校才两周, 还没有习惯新的环境。

23 find its mark/target if an ARROW (1), bullet etc finds its target, it hits what it is supposed to〔箭、子弹等〕射中目标

24 find your tongue to manage to speak after being too nervous to say anything〔紧张得说不出话之后〕设法说话

25 be found wanting *formal* to not be good enough【正式】不够格, 不令人满意, 不合要求: *Ryan's proposals have been examined, and found wanting by the rest of the team.* 瑞安的提议得到审议, 队里的其他人认为不很满意。

26 all found *BrE* used to mean that in addition to your wages you get food and a room【英】〔除工资外的〕膳宿供应: *The cook gets paid £90 a week all found.* 厨师每周工资 90 英镑并获供应膳宿。

find against sb *phr v* [T not in passive 不用被动态] *law* to judge that someone is wrong or guilty【法律】作出不利于〔某人〕的判决; 判决〔某人〕有罪: *The judge found against the plaintiff.* 法官作出了不利于原告的判决。

find for sb *phr v* [T not in passive 不用被动态] *law* to judge that someone is right or not guilty【法律】作出有利于〔某人〕的判决; 判决〔某人〕无罪: *The judge found for the plaintiff.* 法官作出了有利于原告的判决。

find out *phr v* **1 find** sth ↔ **out** [I,T] to learn information, after trying to discover it or by chance 了解到, 找出: **[+who/what/how etc]** *He hurried off to find out what the problem was.* 他赶忙去弄明白问题何在。| **find out sth** *We never found out her real name.* 我们从来没弄清楚她的真名。| **[+that]** *I found out that he was having an affair with another woman.* 我发现他与别的女人有染。| **[+about]** *I need to find out more about these night courses.* 我需要多了解一点这些夜间课程。| **[+if]** *A number of tests have been carried out to find out if these drugs have any effect.* 已经进行了一些测试来弄清楚这些药品是否有疗效。—see 见 KNOW¹ (USAGE) **2 find** sb **out** [T] to discover that someone has been doing something dishonest or illegal 发现〔某人〕不诚实或违法: *After years of defrauding the company, he was finally found out.* 他多年来一直诈取公司的钱财, 最后终于被揭发出来。

find² *n* **a find** something very good or valuable that you discover by chance〔偶然〕发现的好东西; 发现物: *That little Greek restaurant was a real find!* 找到那家希腊小餐馆真是一项有价值的发现!

find·er /ˈfaɪndə; ˈfaɪndə/ *n* [C] someone who finds something 发现者, 发现的人

fin de siè·cle /ˌfæn də ˈsjɛkl; ˌfæn də ˈsjeklə◂/ *adj French* typical of the end of the 19th century, especially typical of the art, literature, and attitudes of the time【法】〔尤指艺术、文学和观念〕具有 19 世纪末特征的

W2 **find·ing** /ˈfaɪndɪŋ; ˈfaɪndɪŋ/ *n* [C usually plural 一般用复数] **1** the information that someone has learnt as a result of their studies, work etc 研究[努力]的结果; 发现: *Surveys conducted in other countries reported similar findings.* 在其他国家进行的调查结果与此相似。**2** *law* a decision made by a judge or jury【法律】〔法官或陪审团的〕裁决, 判决

S1 W1 **fine¹** /faɪn; faɪn/ *adj*

1 ▶ALL RIGHT 令人满意的◀ *especially spoken*【尤口】**a)** good enough; all right 极好的, 令人满意的: *"I could make you some dinner if you like." "It's okay, a sandwich is fine, thanks."* "如果你愿意的话, 我可以给你弄点晚餐。" "好吧, 一块三明治就挺不错了, 谢谢。" | *This apartment is fine for two, but it gets very cramped with your mother here.* 这套公寓两个人住很舒适, 但你母亲住在这儿就会很拥挤。| **I'm fine** *"More coffee?" "No, I'm fine, thanks."* "再来点咖啡吗?" "不用了, 很好了, 谢谢。" **b)** healthy 健康的: *"How are you?" "Fine, thanks."* "你身体好吗?" "很好, 谢谢。" | *"Is your wife better now?" "Oh, she's fine."* "你太太现在身体好些吗?" "噢, 她很好。"

2 ▶VERY GOOD 很好的◀ of a very high quality or standard 优质的, 优秀的, 高级的: *Many people regard Beethoven's fifth symphony as his finest work.* 许多人把贝多芬的第五交响曲看成是他最优秀的作品。| *There is some fine architecture in the old city.* 老城区有些漂亮的建筑。| *fine bone china* 高级骨灰瓷 | *fine wine* 优质葡萄酒

3 ▶GRAND 华贵的◀ [usually before a noun 一般用于名词前] grand, expensive, better than others of the same kind 华丽的, 豪华的, 高贵的: *A tall woman in fine clothes got out of the carriage.* 一位穿着华丽衣服的高个子女士从马车里走出来。| *the fine ladies and gentlemen who frequent the elegant restaurants of Paris* 经常光顾巴黎这些高雅餐馆的上等男女

4 ▶NOT GOOD 不好的◀ *informal* used when you really think that something is not good or satisfactory at all【非正式】糟透的, 十分令人失望的: *"Now's a fine time to tell me!" he fumed.* "现在告诉我很不是时候!" 他怒气冲冲地说。| *That's a fine mess you've got us into!* 你使我们陷入糟糕的境地!

5 ▶WEATHER 天气◀ not raining, perhaps with the sun shining 晴朗的: *If it's fine tomorrow we'll go out.* 如果明天天气晴朗, 我们就出门。| *It was a fine evening.* 这是个天朗气清的傍晚。

6 ▶THIN 细的◀ very thin 纤细的; 薄的: *This thread's very fine – it's difficult to see.* 这条线太纤细了——很难看见。| *a fine coating of dust* 一层薄灰 —see picture at 参见 THIN 图

7 ▶SMALL 小的◀ **a)** involving differences, changes, or details that are difficult to understand or notice〔差别、改变或细节〕细微的: *the finer points of policy detail* 政策细节的细微之点 | *the fine tuning on the radio* 收音机上的微调钮 | *Scientists are now able to measure fine distinctions between levels of sleep depth.* 科学家现在能够测出不同睡眠深度的细微差别。**b)** in small grains, pieces, or drops〔颗粒〕细微的: *fine sugar* 精制食糖 | *fine drizzle* 蒙蒙细雨, 毛毛雨

8 ▶NET 网[筛]◀ having small holes 有细微网孔的: *a fine mesh* 细网眼的网

9 ▶IDEAS/SPEECHES 思想/演说◀ too grand and probably not true or unlikely to have any effect 过分夸饰的; 炫耀的: *It's all very well politicians making fine speeches, but they never get anything done.* 政客们的漂亮言辞虽然动听, 但他们从来什么事都没有做。

10 a fine woman/person a good person that you have a lot of respect for 优秀[杰出]的女性/人物: *Your father is a fine man, a real gentleman.* 你父亲是个高尚的人, 一个真正的绅士。

11 that's/it's fine by me used to say that you agree to something 行, 可以, 我同意: *"I thought we could go out to eat." "That's fine by me."* "我想我们可以出外吃饭。" "我不反对。"

12 fine features someone with fine features has a small and attractively-shaped nose, mouth etc 俊秀的五官

13 finer feelings/qualities etc feelings, qualities etc such as love, honour, loyalty and kindness〔爱、荣誉、忠诚和仁慈等〕更高尚的感情/品质等

14 a fine figure of a man/woman someone who looks big, strong and physically attractive 身材好的男子/女子: *Vellios was a fine figure of a man.* 绯利奥斯是个身材高大伟岸的男子汉。

15 a fine line if you say that there is a fine line between two different things, you mean that there is a point at which one can easily become the other 一线之隔; 极细微的分界线: *There's a fine line between bravery and recklessness.* 勇敢和鲁莽只有一线之隔。

16 not to put too fine a point on it *often humorous* used when you are criticizing something in a plain and direct way【常幽默】说得不客气一点: *That's a real yobs' pub – not to put too fine a point on it.* 说得不客气一点, 那真是一家粗野人的酒吧。

17 sb's finest hour an occasion when someone is extremely successful and proud of their achievement 某人最感春风得意的时间[场合]

fine² *interjection* used to agree to a suggestion 好, 行, 可以: *"I'll see you at eight then." "Okay. Fine."* "那么我们8点钟见面。" "行, 好的。"

fine³ *adv* **1** *spoken* in a way that is satisfactory【口】很好: *"How's it going?" "Fine, thanks."* "你好吗?" "很好, 谢谢。" | *The technician has been to fix it and it works fine now.* 技术员已经来修理过了, 现在它运转得挺好的。**2** if you cut something fine, you cut it very thin or in very small pieces〔切得〕细小地 **3 do fine** *spoken*【口】**a)** to be good enough or be satisfactory 很好, 能行, 能令人满意: *We don't need to get her anything expensive – a calendar will do fine.* 我们不需要买什么昂贵的东西给她——一本日历就可以了。**b)** to do something well or in a satisfactory way 很好地做, 令人满意地做: *"I can't draw this." "You're doing fine! Don't give up now."* "我不会画这个。" "你画得很好! 现在别放弃。" **4 sth will do me/us fine** *BrE spoken* used to say that something is satisfactory or good enough【英口】某物对我/我们很适合[已经够好了]: *Chips'll do me fine, darling.* 我吃炸薯条就好了, 亲爱的。**5 cut it fine** *informal* to leave yourself only just enough time to do something【非正式】留出刚刚好的时间; 时间抓得很紧凑

fine⁴ *v* [T] to make someone pay money as a punishment 处…以罚金: **fine sb for doing sth** *She was fined $50 for passing a stopped school bus.* 她因超越一辆停住的校车而被罚款 50 美元。

fine sth ↔ **down** *BrE* to improve something by making it thinner, smaller, or more exact【英】使〔某物〕变细[小, 精确]

fine⁵ *n* [C] money that you have to pay as a punishment 罚金, 罚款: *I got a £40 fine for speeding* 我因超速驾车而被罚款 40 英镑。| **heavy fine** (=a fine that costs you a lot of money) 一大笔罚金 *There's a heavy fine for driving drunk.* 醉酒架车的罚款很重。| **parking/library fines etc** *I forgot to return my books on time and paid $3 in library fines.* 我忘记按时还书, 被图书馆罚了3美元。

fine art /ˌ· ˈ·/ *n* [U] **1** paintings, drawings, music, SCULPTURE etc that is of very good quality 美术品〈如绘画、音乐、雕刻等〉: *the question of whether photography should be considered fine art* 摄影是否应当被看成是美术品的问题 **2 have something down to a fine art** to be extremely good at something after having practised a lot〔经过大量实践后〕对某事技术高超, 把某

事学到家: *Chris and I have got the morning routine of showers, breakfast, kids to school down to a fine art.* 我和克里斯都已经把每天早上的淋浴、早餐、送孩子上学这些事做得熟练无比了。**3 the fine arts** [plural] activities such as painting, music, and SCULPTURE that are concerned with producing beautiful rather than useful things 美术, 美艺术〈如绘画、音乐、雕刻等〉: *a student of the fine arts* 学美术的学生

Fin·e Gael /ˌfinə `gel; ˌfinə 'geɪl/ one of the two main political parties in the Republic of Ireland, established in 1933. It is more CONSERVATIVE than the other main party, Fianna Fáil. 爱尔兰统一党〔爱尔兰共和国两大主要政党之一, 创建于1933年, 比另一大政党共和党相对保守〕

fine·ly /ˈfaɪnlɪ; 'faɪnli/ *adv* **1** into very thin or very small pieces 微小地, 细微地: *Add the finely chopped onion to the butter, and fry till golden.* 把剁得很细的洋葱加到黄油里, 然后煎到金黄色为止。**2** to a very exact degree 精确地: *These instruments are very finely tuned.* 这些仪器都调得十分精确。**3** beautifully and delicately 优雅地, 雅致地: *She had an oval face with finely formed features.* 她有一张眉清目秀的鹅蛋脸。

fine print /ˌ· ˈ·/ *n* [U] SMALL PRINT 细则

fi·ne·ry /ˈfaɪnərɪ; 'faɪnəri/ *n* [U] clothes and jewellery that are beautiful or very expensive, and are worn for a special occasion 华丽的服饰: *The guests arrived in all their finery.* 客人们穿着极华丽的服饰到来。

fines herbes /ˌfin `ɛrb; ˌfiːn 'eəb/ *n* [U] *French* a mixture of thinly cut plants, added to food to improve its taste【法】〔切细混合制成的〕调味香菜

fi·nesse[1] /fəˋnɛs; fɪ'nes/ *n* [U] delicate and impressive skill 非凡[高超]的技巧: *Dario played the sonata with finesse.* 达里奥以非凡的技巧演奏了这支奏鸣曲。

finesse[2] *v* [T] **1** *AmE* to do something with style and delicate skill【美】巧妙地做: *The skier finessed the difficulties of the mountain.* 滑雪者巧妙地应付了在山上遇到的困难。**2** to handle a situation well, but in a way that is slightly deceitful 用巧妙的〔但略带欺骗性的〕手段处理好: *He finessed the deal, using his charm to cover up his lack of knowledge.* 他施展手段, 用他的魅力来掩盖他知识的贫乏, 完成了这笔交易。

fine-tooth comb /ˌ· ˈ· ·/ *n* [C] **go through/over sth with a fine-tooth comb** to examine something very carefully and thoroughly 仔细检查; 彻底地查看: *going over the evidence with a fine-tooth comb* 仔细检查证据

fine-tune /ˌ· ˈ·/ *v* [T] to make very small changes to something, especially a machine or system, so that it works as well as possible 对〔机器或系统〕进行微调, 精密调节 —**fine tuning** *n* [U]

Fin·gal's Cave /ˌfɪŋglz `kev; ˌfɪŋgəlz 'keɪv/ a CAVE (=a hole in the side of a mountain or cliff) on the island of Staffa off the west coast of Scotland. It was the subject of a famous piece of music by Felix Mendelssohn. 芬戈尔洞〔苏格兰西海岸附近斯塔法岛上一岩洞, 是费利克斯·门德尔松一首著名乐曲的主题〕

2 2 **fin·ger**[1] /ˈfɪŋgɚ; 'fɪŋgə/ *n* [C]

1 ▶PART OF YOUR HAND 手的部分◀ one of the four long thin parts on your hand, not including your thumb〔大拇指以外的〕手指: *She let sand run through her fingers.* 她让沙子从手指缝里滑落下去。| *Tim ran his finger along the windowsill.* 蒂姆用手指在窗台上抹了一下。—see also 另见 INDEX FINGER, LITTLE FINGER, MIDDLE FINGER, RING FINGER

finger 手指

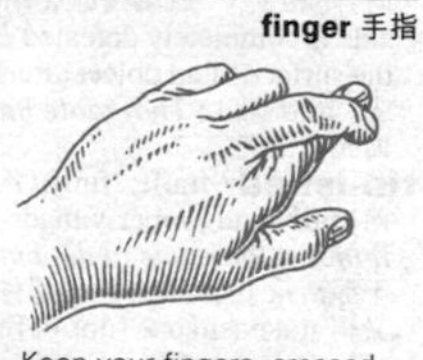

Keep your fingers crossed.
将食指与中指交叉。

2 not lift/raise a finger to not make any effort to help someone with their work 不(愿)帮忙, 不肯尽举手之劳: *We moved furniture all day long, and Sarah never lifted a finger.* 我们搬家具搬了一整天, 但萨拉一点也不帮忙。

3 keep your fingers crossed to hope that something will happen the way you want〔将食指和中指交叉〕祈求(好运): *We're all keeping our fingers crossed that Dan will actually call Megan.* 我们都在祈求丹会真的打电话给梅甘。

4 put your finger on to realize exactly what is wrong, different, or unusual about a situation 确切地明白; 弄清; 准确地指出〔错误、不同、异常之处〕: *I couldn't quite put my finger on what was different about Simone.* 我无法确切地说出西莫内有什么两样。

5 not lay a finger on sb to not hurt someone at all, especially not to hit them 不伤害某人〔尤指不动手打人〕: *Don't you dare lay a finger on me, or I'll call the police!* 你要是敢碰我一根毫毛, 我就要报警了。

6 be all fingers and thumbs *BrE* to use your hands in an awkward or careless way, so that you drop or break things【英】笨手笨脚

7 pull/take/get your finger out *BrE spoken* used to tell someone to work harder【英口】更努力地工作, 加把劲干〔用于告诫某人〕

8 be caught with your fingers in the till to be found stealing money from the place where you work 被发现在工作场所偷钱

9 ▶SHAPED LIKE A FINGER 手指状的◀ anything that is long and thin, like the shape of a finger, especially a piece of land, an area of water, or a piece of food 指状物〔尤指土地、水域、食物等〕

10 ▶DRINK 酒◀ an amount of an alcoholic drink that is as high in the glass as the width of someone's finger 一指宽, 一横指〔指玻璃杯内酒的量度〕: *Gimme three fingers of whiskey, and make it quick!* 给我三横指深的威士忌, 快点!

11 have a finger in every pie an expression meaning to be involved in many activities and have influence over them, used especially when you think someone has too much influence 多管闲事, 凡事插手

12 have/keep your finger on the pulse to always know about the most recent changes or developments in a situation or organization 了解最新变化[发展]

13 twist/wrap sb around your little finger to be able to persuade someone to do anything that you want 能任意摆布某人, 能左右某人

14 put two fingers up at sb *BrE informal* to show someone you are angry with them in a very offensive way by holding up your first two fingers with the back of your hand facing them【英, 非正式】〔手背朝对方〕向某人竖起食指和中指〔表示对其生气, 极具冒犯性〕

15 give sb the finger *AmE informal* to show someone you are angry with them in a very offensive way by holding up your middle finger with the back of your hand facing them【美, 非正式】〔手背朝对方〕向某人竖起中指〔表示对其生气, 极具冒犯性〕

16 long-fingered/delicate-fingered etc having long fingers, delicate fingers etc 手指长的/手指纤细的等: *Lee rubbed his stubby-fingered hands together.* 李搓了搓他那双手指短而粗的手。

17 two-fingered/three-fingered etc using two, three etc fingers to do something 用双指的/用三指的等: *I've become pretty fast, even with my two-fingered typing.* 即使是用双指打字, 我已经打得相当快了。—see also 另见 FISH FINGER, **have green fingers** (GREEN[1] (10)), **burn your fingers** (BURN[1] (18)), **point the finger at** (POINT[2] (7)), **let sth slip (through your fingers)** (SLIP[1] (7)), **snap your fingers** (SNAP[1] (6)), **have sticky fingers** (STICKY (7)), **work your fingers to the bone** (WORK[1] (26))

finger[2] *v* [T] **1** to touch or handle something with your fingers 用手指触碰, 拨弄, 抚摸, 触摸: *She fingered the beautiful cloth with envy.* 她羡慕地抚摸着这块漂亮的布。**2** *informal especially AmE* if someone, especially a criminal, fingers another criminal, they tell the police what they have done【非正式, 尤美】〔尤指罪犯向警察〕告发〔另一个罪犯〕

finger bowl /ˈ· · ·/ *n* [C] a small bowl in which you wash your fingers during a meal〔进餐时〕洗手指用的小碗

> **CULTURAL NOTE 文化注释**
> In Britain and the US, finger bowls are only used on formal occasions when people are eating food which is eaten with the fingers. 在英国和美国, 只有在吃饭须用手抓的正式场合才有洗手指用的小碗。

fin·ger·ing /ˈfɪŋgərɪŋ; 'fɪŋgərɪŋ/ *n* [U] the positions in which a musician puts his fingers to play a piece of music, or the order in which he uses his fingers〔音乐家弹奏乐器的〕指法

fin·ger·mark /ˈfɪŋgɚˌmark; 'fɪŋgəmɑːk/ *n* [C] a mark made by dirty fingers on something clean〔脏手留下的〕指痕, 指迹

fin·ger·nail /ˈfɪŋgɚˌnel; 'fɪŋgəneɪl/ *n* [C] the hard flat part that covers the top end of your finger 手指甲

finger-paints /ˈ· · ·/ *n* [plural] special paints that children use to paint with, using their fingers〔儿童〕作指画用的水彩颜料 —**finger painting** *n* [U]

fin·ger·plate /ˈfɪŋgɚˌplet; 'fɪŋgəpleɪt/ *n* [C] a metal or glass plate that is fastened to a door near the handle or key hole〔装在门把手上或锁眼附近的〕手污防护板

fin·ger·print¹ /ˈfɪŋgə-ˌprɪnt; ˈfɪŋgəˌprɪnt/ *n* [C] a mark made by the pattern of lines at the end of a person's finger, which can be used by the police to help find criminals 指纹: *His fingerprints were all over the gun.* 枪上满是他的指纹。| **leave (your) fingerprints** *He was careful not to leave any fingerprints.* 他小心翼翼, 避免留下指纹。| **take sb's fingerprints** (=make a picture of someone's fingerprints) 取某人的指纹 *The police questioned Beresford and took his fingerprints.* 警察审问了贝雷斯福德, 并取了他的指纹。

fingerprint² *v* [T] to press someone's finger on ink and then press it on paper in order to make a pattern of the lines at the end of the finger 取〔某人的〕指纹

fin·ger·stall /ˈfɪŋgə-ˌstɔl; ˈfɪŋgəstɔːl/ *n* [C] *BrE* a cover for your finger that protects it if it is injured【英】〔保护受伤手指的〕护指套

fin·ger·tip /ˈfɪŋgə-ˌtɪp; ˈfɪŋgəˌtɪp/ *n* [C] **1** the end of a finger 指尖 **2 have sth at your/their fingertips** to have something, especially knowledge or information, ready and available to use very easily 手头有某物〔随时可供使用〕, 对某物了如指掌: *We have all the facts and figures at our fingertips.* 我们对所有的事实和数字了如指掌。**3 to your fingertips** *BrE* in all ways【英】完全地, 彻底地: *She's British to her fingertips.* 她是地道的英国人。

fin·i·cky /ˈfɪnɪkɪ; ˈfɪnɪki/ *adj* **1** too concerned with unimportant details and small things that you like or dislike; FUSSY 过分讲究的, 爱挑剔的: *She's very finicky about what she eats.* 她太挑食了。**2** needing to be done very carefully, while paying attention to small details 需要细心做的, 细致的: *It was a finicky job, trying to get the spring back into my watch.* 把弹簧装回到我的手表里是个细致活儿。

F

fin·ish¹ /ˈfɪnɪʃ; ˈfɪnɪʃ/ *v*

1 ▶STOP DOING STH 停止做某事◀ [I,T] to come to the end of doing or making something, so that it is complete 完成, 做完: **finish sth** *You can't go anywhere until you finish your homework.* 没完成家庭作业前你哪儿也不能去。| **finish doing sth** *I finished typing the report just minutes before it was due.* 我在报告该交出前几分钟才打完它。| *"Are they still working on the road by you?" "No, they've finally finished."* "他们还在你家旁边的路上干活吗?" "不, 他们终于完工了。"

2 ▶STOP 停止◀ [I] *especially BrE* when an event, activity, or period of time finishes, it ends, especially at a particular time【尤英】〔事件、活动、时期〕结束, 终止: *The football season finishes in May.* 足球赛季在5月份结束。| *What time does school finish?* 学校什么时候放学?

3 ▶EAT 吃◀ also 又作 **finish up/off** [T] to eat or drink all the rest of something, so there is none left 吃光, 喝光〔剩下的东西〕: *Finish up your peas or you won't get any dessert.* 把豌豆吃光, 不然就不给你吃甜点。| *Sylvia finished her cigarette.* 西尔维娅抽完了那支香烟。

4 ▶END WITH/BY 以…结束, 以…告终◀ also 又作 **finish off** [I,T] to complete an event, performance, piece of work etc by doing one final thing 结束, 完成: [+with] *The party finished with a sing-song.* 聚会以唱一首歌结束。| **finish by doing sth** *She finished off her speech by thanking her sponsors.* 她以感谢赞助人结束了讲话。

5 ▶RACE 赛跑◀ [I,T] to be in a particular position at the end of a race, competition etc〔在赛跑、比赛等中〕获得名次; 到达〔终点〕: *I finished the 100 meters in sixth place.* 我在100米赛跑中得第六名。

6 ▶SURFACE 表面◀ [T] to give the surface of something, especially wood, a smooth appearance by painting, polishing, or covering it〔用油漆、抛光或贴面等方法〕使光滑; 给…最后加工, 润饰: *The furniture had been attractively finished in a walnut veneer.* 家具上贴了一层胡桃木饰面板, 十分漂亮。

7 ▶ALL SB'S STRENGTH ETC 某人全部的力气等◀ **finish sb** to take away all of someone's strength, energy etc 耗尽某人的精力, 使某人精疲力竭: *That last five-mile ride up the hill really finished me.* 骑车上山坡的那最后5英里路真把我累坏了。

8 ▶USE ALL OF STH 用完某物◀ *BrE* to use up the entire supply of something, especially food【英】用完〔尤指吃光食物〕: *The ice cream's finished, can you get some more?* 冰激凌吃完了, 你能再买一点吗?

9 put/add the finishing touches to add the final detail or details that make your work complete 做最后的润饰; 做完最后的细节工作

finish off *phr v* **1** [T **finish** sth ↔ **off**] to use or eat all of something, so there is none left 用完; 吃完: *Who finished off the cake?* 谁把蛋糕吃光了? **2** [T **finish** sb/sth ↔ **off**] to kill a person or animal when they are already weak or wounded 结束…的生命, 杀掉〔虚弱或已受伤的人或动物〕 **3** [T **finish** sb **off**] to take away all of someone's strength, energy etc 耗尽〔某人的〕精力, 使〔某人〕精疲力竭, 累垮〔某人〕: *It had already been an exhausting week, and that last argument just finished me off.* 这本来已经是令人精疲力竭的一个星期, 而最后那场争论可真把我累垮了。**4** [I,T **finish** sth ↔ **off**] to end a performance, event etc by doing one final thing 结束〔演出、事件等〕: *We finished off the evening by going out for a drink.* 我们以出去喝一杯结束了那个晚上的活动。

finish up *phr v* **1** [linking verb 连系动词] *especially BrE* to finally be in a particular place, condition etc at the end of a situation or series of events; end up (END²)【尤英】最后到达; 最后处于: *We finished up in Rome after a three week tour.* 我们最后抵达罗马, 结束了三星期的旅程。| *I finished up completely broke, tired, and hungry.* 我最后完全身无分文, 又累又饿。**2** [T **finish** sth ↔ **up**] to eat or drink all the rest of something 吃完, 喝完 **3** to end an event, situation etc by doing one final thing〔以做某件事来〕结束, 完成

finish with sth/sb *phr v* [T] **1** *especially BrE* to no longer need to use something【尤英】不再需要用〔某物〕: **be finished with** *Are you finished with the scissors?* 你用完剪刀了吗? **2** *BrE* to end a relationship with someone【英】与〔某人〕断绝关系: *Michael's finally finished with Teresa after all these years.* 迈克尔经过这些年之后, 最后与特雷莎断绝了关系。

This graph shows how common the different grammar patterns of the verb **finish** are. 本图表所示为动词 finish 构成的不同语法模式的使用频率。

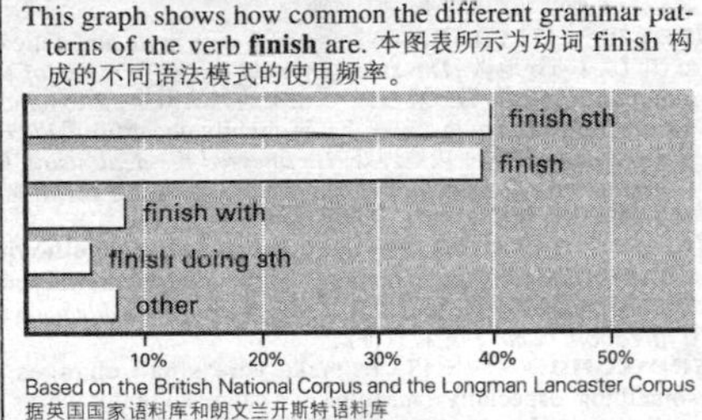

Based on the British National Corpus and the Longman Lancaster Corpus
据英国国家语料库和朗文兰开斯特语料库

finish² *n* **1** [C] the end or last part of something 终结, 最后部分: *I was watching the race but I didn't get to see the finish.* 我观看了比赛, 但没有看到最后的结果。| **from start to finish** (=from the beginning of something until the end) 自始至终, 从头到尾 *The meeting was a disaster from start to finish.* 这次会议彻头彻尾都一塌糊涂。| **a close finish** (=an end of a race where two competitors are very close to each other)〔两名选手在比赛终结时〕不相上下, 成绩接近 **2 fight to the finish** to fight until one side is completely defeated 战斗到底 **3** [C,U] the appearance of the surface of an object after it has been painted, polished etc 抛光; 光洁(度): *That table has a beautiful finish.* 那张桌子的表面光洁漂亮。

fin·ished /ˈfɪnɪʃt; ˈfɪnɪʃt/ *adj* **1** [only before noun 仅用于名词前] fully and properly made or completed 完成了的, 结束了的: *It took a long time to do, but the finished product was worth it.* 干那活花了很长时间, 但那件成品值得这样去做。—opposite 反义词 UNFINISHED **2** [not before noun 不用于名词前] no longer able to do something successfully 没有希望的, 完蛋了的: *If the bank refuses to give us money, we're finished!* 如果银行拒绝借钱给我们, 我们就完蛋了!

finishing school /ˈ··· ·/ *n* [C] a private school where rich girls go to learn social skills 精修学校〔指富家女孩学习社交技能的一种私立学校〕

fi·nite /ˈfaɪnaɪt; ˈfaɪnaɪt/ *adj* **1** having an end or a limit 有限的; 有限制的: *Earth's resources are finite.* 地球的资源是有限的。—opposite 反义词 INFINITE **2** *technical* a finite verb form shows a particular tense or subject. 'Am', 'was', and 'are' are examples of finite verb forms, but 'being' and 'been' are non-finite【术语】限定的〔动词的限定形式能显示出具体的时态或主语, 例如 "am", "was"和"are", 但 "being" 和 "been" 是动词的非限定形式〕

fink¹ /fɪŋk; fɪŋk/ *n* [C] *AmE informal old-fashioned*【美, 非正式, 过时】**1** someone who tells the police, a teacher, or a parent when someone else breaks a rule or a law 告发者, 告密者 **2** someone you dislike because they do cruel or unkind things 卑鄙的家伙, 小人

fink[2] *v* [I] *AmE informal old-fashioned* to tell the police, a teacher, or a parent that someone has broken a rule or a law【美，非正式，过时】告发，告密

Fin·land /ˈfɪnlənd; ˈfɪnlənd/ a country in northeast Europe between Russia and Sweden. Population: 5,176,000 (2001). Capital: Helsinki. People from Finland are called Finns. 芬兰〔欧洲东北部一国家，位于俄罗斯与瑞典之间。人口：5,176,000 (2001)，首都：赫尔辛基。芬兰人称作 Finns〕—**Finnish** *n, adj*

Finn, Huck·le·berry /ˈhʌkḷberɪ; ˈhʌkəlbəri/ also 又作 **Huck Finn** a character in the books *The Adventures of Tom Sawyer* and *The Adventures of Huckleberry Finn* by the 19th century US writer Mark Twain. Huckleberry Finn is a very independent young boy who runs away from his father with his friend Jim, who is a black SLAVE who has also run away. 费恩〔19 世纪美国作家马克·吐温的小说《汤姆·索耶历险记》和《哈克贝利·费恩历险记》中的人物，又称哈克·费恩。他是一个非常独立的少年，与他的黑奴朋友吉姆一起离开了父亲的家出走了〕—see also 另见 Tom SAWYER

Fin·ne·gan's Wake /ˌfɪnɪgənz ˈwek; ˌfɪnɪgənz ˈweɪk/ (1939) a book by James Joyce which is written in a strange style and language that many people find very difficult to understand《芬尼根守灵》〔(1939)，詹姆斯·乔伊斯的作品。该作品文体奇特，语言晦涩难懂〕

fi·ord /ˈfjɔrd; ˈfiːɔːd/ *n* [C] another spelling of FJORD fjord 的另一种拼法

fir /fɝ; fɜː/ *n* [C] a tree with leaves like needles that it keeps in the winter 冷杉，枞

fire 火

Lisa lit the candle. 莉萨点燃蜡烛。

He set fire to the car. 他放火烧车。

The curtain caught fire. 窗帘着火了。

[1] [1] **fire[1]** /faɪr; faɪə/ *n*

1 ▶BURNING 燃烧◀ [U] the flames, light and heat produced when something burns 火：*The warehouse was completely destroyed by fire.* 仓库全部被火烧毁。| **be on fire** (=be burning) 在燃烧，着火 *The house is on fire!* 房子着火了！| **catch fire/catch on fire** (=start to burn) 开始燃烧，着火 *Mary knocked the candle over and the table cloth caught on fire.* 玛丽打翻了蜡烛，桌布开始燃烧起来。| **set sth on fire/set fire to sth** (=make something start burning) 使某物燃烧／放火烧某物 *Sparks from the fireplace could easily set the curtains on fire.* 壁炉里爆出来的火花会很容易地使帘子燃烧起来。| *Rioters set fire to a whole row of stores.* 暴乱分子放火烧了一整排商店。

2 ▶UNCONTROLLED FIRE 无法控制的火灾◀ [C] burning material that you did not light deliberately and that burns things you do not want to be damaged 火灾，大火：*Thirty people died in a fire in downtown Chicago.* 芝加哥市中心的一场火灾烧死了 30 个人。| **start a fire** (=deliberately make a fire start burning) 放火，纵火 | **a fire breaks out** (=a fire starts suddenly) 发生火灾 *A fire broke out in the kitchens of the hotel.* 旅馆的厨房失火。| **put out a fire** (=stop a fire burning) 灭火 *It took firemen several hours to put out the fire.* 消防队员花了好几个小时才把火扑灭。| **fight a fire** (=try to stop a fire burning) 扑灭火灾 | **forest/brush fire** (=a very large fire in the forest or in an area of grass) 森林火灾／灌木丛大火等

3 ▶CONTROLLED FIRE 得到控制的火◀ [C] burning material that you have lit to provide heat, cook food etc〔为取暖、烹调等生的〕炉火，灶火：*a cheerful fire crackling in the fireplace* 壁炉中噼啪燃烧的旺火 | **make/build/light a fire** (=start one burning) 生火，点火 *You put up the tent and I'll start the fire.* 你们搭帐篷，我来生火。

4 ▶SHOOTING 射击◀ [U] an act of shooting, especially of many guns at the same time 炮火，火力，射击：*You will soon be facing enemy fire.* 你们很快会面临敌人的炮火。| **be under fire** (=be shot at) 遭到射击，遭到炮火袭击 *Our platoon was under fire from a machine gun position.* 我们排遭到来自一个机枪阵地的射击。| **come under fire** (=be shot at) 遭到射击，遭到炮火袭击 *The planes came under anti-aircraft fire.* 飞机遭到防空炮火射击。| **open fire** (=start shooting) 开火，开枪 *Troops opened fire on the rebels.* 部队朝叛乱分子开枪。| **hold your fire** (=stop shooting) 停止射击 | **be in the line of fire** (=be where you may be hit if someone shoots) 在火力线上；首当其冲；在射击范围之内

5 ▶HEATING EQUIPMENT 供暖设备◀ [C] *BrE* a machine that produces heat to warm a room, using gas or electricity as power【英】煤气取暖器；电暖器：*Turn on the fire, I'm cold.* 打开电暖器吧，我很冷。| *a gas fire* 煤气取暖器

6 ▶CRITICISM 批评◀ **under fire** being criticized very strongly for something you have done 受到抨击，遭到猛烈的批评：*The committee came under fire from fundamentalist church leaders.* 委员会遭到基要主义教会领导人的猛烈批评。

7 an open fire a fire that burns coal or wood in a FIREPLACE〔烧煤或木头的〕壁炉里的火

8 gas fired/coal fired etc *BrE* operated by burning gas, coal etc【英】燃气的／燃煤的等：*a coal fired power station* 燃煤发电厂

9 light a fire under sb *AmE spoken* to do something that makes someone who is being lazy start doing their work【美口】激起〔偷懒的人〕的工作热情

10 ▶EMOTION 激情◀ [U] a very strong emotion that makes you want to think about nothing else 狂热的情感，激情：[+of] *the fire of religious fanaticism* 宗教狂热的激情 | **be on fire with** *Harry was on fire with enthusiasm.* 哈里激情满怀。

11 ▶INJURY 伤痛◀ **be on fire** *literary* an injured part of your body that is on fire feels very painful【文】有剧痛感

12 go through fire (and water) (for sb) *old-fashioned* to do something very difficult and dangerous for someone【过时】(为某人) 赴汤蹈火

13 fire and brimstone a phrase describing Hell, used by some religious people〔一些宗教人士指的〕地狱 —see also 另见 CEASEFIRE, **add fuel to the fire/flames** (FUEL[1] (3)), **fight fire with fire** (FIGHT[1] (12)), **get on like a house on fire** (HOUSE[1] (8)), **hang fire** (HANG[1] (11)), **play with fire** (PLAY[1] (22)), **there's no smoke without fire** (SMOKE[1] (6))

USAGE NOTE 用法说明：FIRE

WORD CHOICE 词语辨析：**light, set fire to, catch fire, put out, go out, extinguish**

If you want something to burn you usually **light** it. 使某物燃烧起来，通常用 light：*She lit a cigarette/the stove/a match.* 她点燃香烟／炉火／火柴。

You can also **set fire to** things, especially things that are not supposed to be burnt. 放火烧不应该烧的东西，通常用 set fire to：*Crowds rioted through the street, breaking windows and setting fire to cars.* 人群在街道上闹事，打破窗子，放火烧汽车。

When something begins to burn, especially by accident, it **catches fire**. 尤指某物出于意外开始燃烧时，用 catch fire：*The blaze started when some oily rags caught fire.* 当一些碎油布着火时，大火开始烧起来。

To stop a fire you **put it out**, or else it may **go out** on its own (NOT 不用 *go off*). 灭火用 put out，火自动熄灭用 go out。

On official notices and instructions you may see **extinguish**. 正式通知和说明上有时用 extinguish：*Will passengers please extinguish all cigarettes.* 请乘客将香烟熄灭。

F

fire² *v*

1 ▶SHOOT 射击◀ [I,T] to shoot bullets from a gun, or to shoot small bombs 开枪, 开炮, 发射: *Roy took careful aim and fired.* 罗伊仔细瞄准, 然后开了枪。| [+at/on/into] *Police fired on the crowd.* 警察向人群开枪。| **fire a gun/weapon etc** (=make it shoot) 开枪/发射武器 *The pistol has obviously been fired recently.* 很明显, 这把手枪最近刚用过。| **fire a shot/bullet/round etc** *Who fired the bullet that killed the President?* 谁开了置总统于死地的那一枪? | **fire sth at sb** *The F16 fighter plane fired two missiles at the enemy aircraft.* F16战斗机向敌机发射了两枚导弹。

2 ▶JOB 工作◀ *especially AmE* to force someone to leave their job【尤美】开除, 解雇; SACK² (1) *BrE*【英】: **fire sb for sth** *They fired her for stealing from the company.* 他们因她在公司偷窃而开除她。

3 ▶EXCITE 激动◀ [T] also 又作 **fire up** to make someone feel very excited or interested in something; INSPIRE 使充满热情; 激发, 激励: **be fired with ambition/longing etc** *After reading Steinbeck, Joel was fired with the ambition to become a writer.* 乔尔读了斯坦贝克的小说后, 满怀壮志想当作家。| **fire sb's imagination** *Jill's imagination was fired by Granny's stories.* 奶奶的故事激发了吉尔的想象力。

4 ▶ENGINE 发动机◀ [I] if a vehicle's engine fires, the petrol is lit to make the engine work 点火; 引擎起动

5 ▶CLAY 黏土◀ [T] to bake clay pots etc in a KILN〔在窑里〕烧制: *fired earthenware* 烧制的陶器

6 fire questions (at) to ask someone a lot of questions quickly, often in order to criticize them〔对…〕提出一连串问题

7 fire away also 又作 **fire ahead** *spoken* used when you are ready to answer questions【口】请说吧〔用于准备好回答问题时〕: *"I have a few questions." "Fire away."* "我有几个问题。" "请提吧。"

8 not firing on all cylinders *informal* not thinking sensibly, or acting strangely【非正式】不明事理; 行为古怪

9 fired up *informal* excited and eager【非正式】情绪高昂的: *We've gotta get fired up for this game or we have no hope of winning!* 我们得鼓起劲头来, 不然就没有获胜的希望了!

fire back sth *phr v* [T] to quickly and angrily answer a question or remark 快速而气愤地回答[反驳]: *Claire fired back an angry response.* 克莱尔气冲冲地作了反驳。

fire off *phr v* [T] **1** to shoot a weapon, often so that there are no bullets etc left 射光〔子弹〕: *Chuck reloaded and fired off both barrels.* 查克重新装上子弹, 然后把两根枪筒中的子弹都射了出去。**2** to quickly send an angry letter to someone 气愤地匆忙寄发〔信件〕: *I fired off a furious letter to the editor.* 我向编辑发了一封急信以示愤怒。

fire a·larm /ˈ· ·,·/ *n* [C] a piece of equipment that makes a loud noise to warn people of a fire in a building〔建筑物里的〕火警钟, 火警报警器: *We were in the middle of an exam when the fire alarm went off.* 火警响起的时候, 我们的考试正进行至一半。

fire·arm /ˈfaɪr,ɑrm; ˈfaɪərɑːm/ *n* [C] a small gun that can be carried 火器〔指可携带的步枪、手枪等小型枪支〕

fire·ball /ˈfaɪr,bɔl; ˈfaɪəbɔːl/ *n* [C] a large, hot fire, such as the very hot cloud of burning gases formed by an atomic explosion〔原子弹爆炸后气体燃烧形成的〕火球

fire·bomb /ˈfaɪrbɑm; ˈfaɪəbɒm/ *n* [C] a bomb that makes a fire start burning when it explodes 燃烧弹

fire·brand /ˈfaɪr,brænd; ˈfaɪəbrænd/ *n* [C] **1** someone who tries to make people angry about a law, government etc so that they will try to change it 煽动暴乱者 **2** a large burning piece of wood 燃烧的大块木头

fire·break /ˈfaɪr,brek; ˈfaɪəbreɪk/ *n* [C] a narrow piece of land without any plants and trees on it, made to prevent fires from spreading 防火障, 防火线

fire·brick /ˈfaɪr,brɪk; ˈfaɪə,brɪk/ *n* [C] a brick that is not damaged by heat, used in chimneys 耐火砖

fire bri·gade /ˈ· ·,·/ *n* [C] **1** *BrE* an organization that works to prevent fires and stop them burning【英】消防队; 消防署; FIRE DEPARTMENT *AmE*【美】**2** *AmE* a group of people who are not paid but who work together to stop fires burning【美】〔不领报酬的〕志愿者消防队

fire·bug /ˈfaɪr,bʌg; ˈfaɪəbʌg/ *n* [C] *informal* someone who deliberately starts fires to destroy property; arsonist (ARSON)【非正式】纵火者, 放火的人

fire chief /ˈ· ,·/ *n* [C] someone who is responsible for all the organizations that stop fires burning in a city or area 消防署署长; 消防队队长

fire·crack·er /ˈfaɪr,krækɚ; ˈfaɪə,krækə/ *n* [C] a small FIREWORK that explodes loudly 鞭炮, 爆竹

fire de·part·ment /ˈ· ·,··/ *n* [C] *AmE* the organization that works to prevent fires and stop them burning【美】消防署; 消防队; FIRE SERVICE, FIRE BRIGADE *BrE*【英】

fire·dog /ˈfaɪr,dɔg; ˈfaɪədɒg/ *n* [C] *BrE* one of a pair of iron supports for burning logs in a FIREPLACE【英】〔壁炉里的〕薪架

fire door /ˈ· ,·/ *n* [C] a heavy door in a building that is kept closed to help to prevent a fire from spreading 防火安全门

fire drill /ˈ· ·/ *n* [C,U] the act of practising what people must do to leave a burning building safely 消防演习

fire-eat·er /ˈ· ,··/ *n* [C] **1** an entertainer who puts burning sticks into his mouth 吞火魔术师 **2** *informal* someone who gets angry and quarrels very easily【非正式】动辄发火吵架的人, 脾气暴躁的人

fire en·gine /ˈ· ,··/ *n* [C] a special large vehicle that carries people and equipment to stop fires burning, especially the equipment that shoots water at a fire 消防车, 救火车 —compare 比较 FIRE TRUCK *AmE*【美】

fire es·cape /ˈ· ·,·/ *n* [C] metal stairs or a metal LADDER on the outside of a tall building, that people can use to escape if there is a fire〔高楼的〕太平梯, 安全出口

fire ex·tin·guish·er /ˈ· ·,···/ *n* [C] a metal container with water or chemicals in it, used for stopping small fires 灭火器

fire extinguisher
灭火器

fire fight /ˈ· ·/ *n* [C] a short gun battle, involving soldiers or the police 交火, 枪战

fire fight·er /ˈ· ,··/ *n* [C] someone who stops fires burning, either as their job or as a special helper during forest fires or wars 消防人员

fire fight·ing /ˈ· ,··/ *n* [U] **1** the work of preventing fires and stopping them burning 消防工作 **2** the actions that are taken to find out what has caused a sudden problem in an organization, machine etc, and to correct it 发现和纠正〔组织、机器等中的〕事故隐患的措施

fire·fly /ˈfaɪr,flaɪ; ˈfaɪəflaɪ/ *n plural* **fireflies** [C] an insect with a tail that shines in the dark; LIGHTNING BUG 萤火虫

fire·guard /ˈfaɪr,gɑrd; ˈfaɪəgɑːd/ *n* [C] a large frame made of woven wire that is put in front of a FIREPLACE to protect people〔放在壁炉前保护人的〕炉栏, 挡火隔网; FIRESCREEN *AmE*【美】

fire·house /ˈfaɪr,haus; ˈfaɪəhaʊs/ *n* [C] *AmE* a small FIRE STATION, especially in a small town【美】〔尤指小城镇的〕消防站

fire hy·drant /ˈ· ,··/ *n* [C] a water pipe in a street used to get water for stopping fires burning〔街道上的〕消防栓, 消防龙头; FIREPLUG *AmE*【美】

fire i·rons /ˈ· ·,·/ *n* [plural] the metal tools used for looking after a fire in a FIREPLACE 火炉用具

fire·light /ˈfaɪr,laɪt; ˈfaɪəlaɪt/ *n* [U] the light produced by a small fire〔小火发出的〕火光: *The room glowed cozy and warm in the firelight.* 房间被炉火光照得红彤彤的, 既舒适又暖和。

fire·light·er /ˈfaɪr,laɪtɚ; ˈfaɪə,laɪtə/ *n* [C] *BrE* a piece of a substance that burns easily and helps to light a coal fire【英】〔生煤火用的〕引火物

fire·man /ˈfaɪrmən; ˈfaɪəmən/ *n* [C] **1** a man whose job is to stop fires burning; FIREFIGHTER 消防人员 **2** someone who looks after the fire in a steam railway engine or a FURNACE〔负责火车的蒸汽炉或熔炉的〕司炉工

Fire of Lon·don, the /ˌ· · ˈ··/ —see 见 the GREAT FIRE OF LONDON

fire·place /ˈfaɪr,ples; ˈfaɪəpleɪs/ *n* [C] the opening in the wall of a room, used for a wood or coal fire to heat the room 壁炉

fire·plug /ˈfaɪr,plʌg; ˈfaɪəplʌg/ *n* [C] *AmE* a FIRE HYDRANT【美】消防栓, 消防龙头

fire·pow·er /ˈfaɪr,pauɚ; ˈfaɪə,paʊə/ *n* [U] *technical* the number of weapons that an army, military vehicle etc has available【术语】〔军队、军用车辆等的〕火力

fire·proof /ˈfaɪr,pruf; ˈfaɪəpruːf/ *adj* a building, piece of cloth etc that is fireproof cannot be badly damaged by flames 防火的, 耐火的 —**fireproof** *v* [T]

fire-rais·ing /ˈ· ,··/ *n* [U] *BrE* the crime of starting a fire deliberately; ARSON【英】纵火(罪) —**fire-raiser** *n* [C]

fire sale /ˈ· ·/ *n* [C] a sale of goods that have been slightly damaged by a fire, or of goods that cannot be stored because of a fire 火灾受损物品的拍卖

fire·screen /ˈfaɪr,skrin; ˈfaɪəskriːn/ *n* [C] *AmE* a large frame made of woven wire that is put in front of a FIREPLACE to protect people【美】〔壁炉前保护人的〕炉栏, 挡火隔网; FIREGUARD *BrE*【英】

fire ser·vice /ˈ· ·, ·ˈ/ *n* [singular] *BrE* the organization that works to prevent fires and stop them burning【英】消防署; 消防队; FIRE DEPARTMENT *AmE*【美】

fire·side /ˈfaɪrˌsaɪd; ˈfaɪəsaɪd/ *n* [C usually singular 一般用单数] the area close to or around a small fire, especially in a home〔尤指家里的〕炉边: *a cat dozing in the broken armchair by the fireside* 一只趴在炉边破椅子里打瞌睡的猫

fire sta·tion /ˈ· ,· ·, ·ˈ/ *n* [C] a building where the equipment used to stop fires burning is kept, and where FIRE FIGHTERS stay until they are needed 消防站

fire·storm /ˈfaɪrˌstɔrm; ˈfaɪəstɔːm/ *n* [C] a very large fire, usually started by bombs, that is kept burning by the high winds that it causes〔通常由炸弹等引起的〕风暴性大火

fire·trap /ˈfaɪrˌtræp; ˈfaɪətræp/ *n* [C] a building that would be very dangerous if a fire started there 无消防设施的建筑物; 易引起火灾的房子

fire truck /ˈ· ·/ *n* [C] *AmE* a special vehicle that carries people and special equipment to stop fires burning【美】救火车, 消防车 —compare 比较 FIRE ENGINE

fire·watch·er /ˈfaɪrˌwɑtʃɚ; ˈfaɪəwɒtʃə/ *n* [C] *BrE* someone who watched for FIRE BOMBS in British cities during the Second World War【英】〔第二次世界大战期间英国城市里的〕火灾警戒员

fire·wat·er /ˈfaɪrˌwɔtɚ; ˈfaɪəˌwɔːtə/ *n* [U] strong alcoholic drink, such as WHISKY 烈酒〈如威士忌〉

fire·wood /ˈfaɪrˌwʊd; ˈfaɪəwʊd/ *n* [C] wood cut for burning on fires 柴火, 木柴

fire·work /ˈfaɪrˌwɝk; ˈfaɪəwɜːk/ *n* [C usually plural 一般用复数]

1 a small container filled with powder that burns or explodes to produce coloured lights, noise, and smoke 烟火, 烟花, 焰火: *a New Year's Eve fireworks display* 除夕夜的烟火表演

> **CULTURAL NOTE 文化注释**
>
> In the US fireworks are used to celebrate the Fourth of July and some other special occasions, and people go to parks or other public places to see them. There are also sometimes fireworks shows at special events such as FAIRS. In some parts of the US it is illegal to buy and light fireworks yourself. In the UK, people buy and light fireworks themselves to celebrate Guy Fawkes' Night, or they might go to organized events where a lot of fireworks are lit. Many people who originally lived in India or whose parents came from India, celebrate the Hindu FESTIVAL of Diwali with fireworks. People often buy fireworks to celebrate birthdays or New Year's Day, and some people complain about the noise that fireworks cause. 美国燃放烟花庆祝7月4日国庆日和其他特殊场合, 人们到公园或其他公共场合看烟花。有时集市等一些特别活动也会有烟花表演。在美国的一些地方, 私自购买和燃放烟花是非法的。在英国, 人们自行购买和燃放烟花庆贺盖伊·福克斯之夜, 或去参加有组织的大型烟花表演活动。很多原本住在印度或父母来自印度的人用燃放烟花来庆祝印度排灯节。人们经常购买烟花燃放来庆祝生日或新年, 有些人则抱怨烟花产生的噪音。

2 there will be fireworks *spoken* used to say that someone will be angry【口】有人会发火的; 有人将会大怒的: *There'll be fireworks if I get home late again.* 如果我再迟回家, 有人会发火的。

fir·ing line /ˈ·· ˌ·/ *n* **be in the firing line** to be in a position or situation in which you can be attacked or blamed for something, often unfairly 首当其冲地受到攻击[责备]

firing squad /ˈ·· ,·/ *n* [C] a group of soldiers with the duty of killing someone by shooting them as a punishment〔执行枪决的〕行刑队

firm¹ /fɝm; fɜːm/ *n* [C] a business or company, especially a small one〔尤指较小的〕公司, 商行, 事务所: **electronics/advertising/law etc firm** *She works for an electronics firm.* 她在一家电子公司工作。| **a firm of accountants/solicitors etc** *Kevin is with a firm of accountants in Birmingham.* 凯文在伯明翰的一家会计师事务所工作。 S1 W1

firm² *adj* S2 W2

1 ▶HARD 硬的◀ not completely hard, but not soft and not easy to bend into a different shape 坚实的: *The sofa cushions are fairly firm.* 沙发的座垫相当硬。| *a firm green apple* 坚实的青苹果

2 ▶NOT LIKELY TO MOVE 不易移动的◀ strong or fixed in position, and not likely to move or break 牢固的, 稳固的: *The ladder felt strong and firm.* 梯子感觉很结实稳固。

3 ▶NOT LIKELY TO CHANGE 不易变化的◀ firm decisions, beliefs etc are not likely to change, because you are sure about them〔决定、信念等〕坚定的, 不变的: *The client hasn't reached a firm decision on the matter yet.* 客户对这件事还没有作出肯定的决定。

4 ▶STRONG AND IN CONTROL 坚决的◀ behaving or speaking in a way that is strong and that shows you are not likely to change your answer, belief etc 强有力的, 坚决的: *Cal replied with a polite but firm 'no'.* 卡尔用礼貌又坚决的"不"字作答。| *The country needs firm leadership.* 国家需要强有力的领导。| **be firm with sb** *You need to be firm with her, or she'll try to take control.* 你需要对她强硬些, 不然她会想控制一切。

5 a firm grip/hold/grasp if you have something in a firm hold you are holding it tightly and strongly 紧握, 紧紧抓住, 牢牢握住: *He took a firm grip of my arm and marched me towards the door.* 他紧紧抓着我的手臂, 拉我往门口走去。| **a firm handshake** (=in which you hold the other person's hand strongly or tightly) 紧紧的握手

6 take a firm stand/line to state your opinion clearly and not be persuaded to change it 采取坚定立场; 坚定不移地表态

7 stand/hold firm to not change your actions or opinions 坚持下去, 坚定不移: *Gothard is urging Christians to stand firm against divorce.* 戈瑟德强烈要求基督教徒坚定不移地反对离婚。

8 ▶MONEY 货币◀ not falling in value〔价格〕坚挺的: *The pound was still firm against the dollar this morning.* 今天上午英镑对美元的汇价仍然很坚挺。—see also 另见 FIRM OFFER —**firmly** *adv* —**firmness** *n* [U]

firm³ *v* [T] to press down on soil to make it harder or more solid 使变硬; 使坚固 W3

firm sth ↔ **up** *phr v* [T] **1** to make arrangements, ideas etc more definite and exact 把〔安排、想法等〕确定下来: *We're hoping to firm up the deal later this month.* 我们希望能在这个月晚些时候把这笔买卖确定下来。**2** to make a part of your body have more muscle and less fat by exercising〔通过锻炼〕使〔身体〕结实

fir·ma·ment /ˈfɝməmənt; ˈfɜːməmənt/ *n* [singular] *literary* the sky or heaven【文】天空, 苍穹

firm of·fer /ˌ· ˈ··/ *n* [C] a price suggested for a service or for goods that becomes legally fixed if it is accepted〔价格、报价〕实盘, 固定报价

firm·ware /ˈfɝmˌwɛr; ˈfɜːmweə/ *n* [U] *technical* instructions to computers that are stored on chips (CHIP¹ (4a)) so that they can be done much faster, and cannot be changed or lost【术语】〔电脑的〕固件 —compare 比较 HARDWARE, SOFTWARE

first /fɝst; fɜːst/ *number*

① BEFORE 在…前
② THE FIRST TIME STH HAPPENS OR IS DONE 某事首次发生或完成的时间
③ BEGINNING 最初, 开始
④ MAIN/IMPORTANT 主要的/重要的
⑤ THE FIRST REASON/FACT ETC 首要原因/事实等
⑥ BEST 最好的
⑦ MORNING 早上, 上午
⑧ NOT KNOW 不知道
⑨ OTHER MEANINGS 其他意思

① BEFORE 在…前

1 before anything or anyone else 最先, 最早: *She reached the top of the hill first.* 她最先到达山顶。| *It's mine, I saw it first.* 这是我的, 我先看到的。—see 见 FIRSTLY (USAGE)

2 the first someone or something that is before other people or things 第一个人[东西]; 第一件事: **be (the) first to do sth** *My*

sister said I'd be first to get married, but she was wrong. 妹妹说我会最先结婚，可她说错了。| **come (in) first** (=win a race)〔比赛〕得第一名 *Lewis came first in the 100m race.* 刘易斯在100米比赛中得第一名。

3 before doing anything else, or before anything else happens 首先：*I always read the funnies first.* 我总是先看连环漫画。| *First I have to clean up the house, then I'll come shopping with you.* 我得先打扫房子，然后和你去购物。| **first of all** *First of all we'd better make sure we have everything we need.* 首先我们最好确实弄清我们所需要的东西都有了。

4 make the first move to be the person who does something when everyone is nervous and uncomfortable about starting to do something〔当别人都紧张踌躇时〕首先采取行动，率先挺身而出：*Barney really likes Hannah, but he's too shy to make the first move.* 巴尼确实喜欢汉娜，但他太腼腆不敢采取主动。

5 do/say sth in the first place *spoken* used to say that someone said or did something before【口】起初就做/说某事：*I don't really want to go..." "Oh Well, why didn't you say so in the first place?"* "我确实不想去…" "嗬，那你为什么不早说呢？"

6 in the first instance *especially BrE* before you do anything else【尤英】首先，最初．*It is important in the first instance to be sure that there is a demand for the product you wish to sell.* 重要的是，要先确切地弄清楚你想出售的产品是有需求的。

② THE FIRST TIME STH HAPPENS OR IS DONE 某事首次发生或完成的时间

7 happening or done before other events or actions of the same kind 首次的，最早的，第一次的：*He made his first appearance on the stage in the 1950s.* 他在20世纪50年代首次登台演出。| *My first reaction was that the story couldn't possibly be true.* 我最初的反应是，这个说法不可能是真的。| **the first time** *The first time I flew in a plane I was really nervous.* 我第一次乘飞机时确实很紧张。

8 done for the first time 首次：*The book was first published in Australia last year.* 这本书去年在澳大利亚首次出版。

9 the first someone who does something that has never been done or happened before 第一个人：*No one had ever settled in the valley before; he was the first.* 以前没有人在这个山谷住过，他是第一个。| **be the first to do sth** *She was the first to see the importance of the nineteenth century writers in this context.* 她是第一个看到19世纪作家在这方面的重要性的。

10 a first something that has never been done or happened before 先例，前所未有的事情：*Roger Bannister's four-minute mile was a notable first in the history of athletics.* 罗杰·班尼斯特4分钟跑完1英里，这是田径运动史上的杰出先例。

11 at first glance/sight the first time that you see something, before you notice much detail 乍一看，最初看到时：*At first glance the twins look identical.* 这对双胞胎乍一看完全一样。

12 first come, first served used to say that people who arrive, ask etc before other people, will be dealt with or given something before them 先到先得，先来先接待[供应]

③ BEGINNING 最初，开始

13 the first the people or things at the beginning of a row, line, series, period of time etc〔一行、一列、一系列、一段时间等中〕第一个[批、件]：*the first Monday of every month* 每月的第一个星期一 | *for the first six months of my time in Nepal* 我在尼泊尔的头六个月 | *the first chapter of the book* 本书的第一章

14 at the beginning of a situation or activity 最初时：*When we were first married, we lived in Toronto.* 我们刚结婚时住在多伦多。| *We first became friends when we were teenagers.* 我们早在十几岁的时候就成了朋友。

15 at first in the beginning 开始时，起先，起初：*Alistair felt tired at first, but soon got used to the long working hours.* 阿利斯泰尔起先感到累，但很快就适应了长时间的工作。—compare 比较 **at last** (LAST[3] (2)) —see 见 FIRSTLY (USAGE)

16 from the (very) first from the beginning 从一开始：*The relationship was doomed to failure from the first.* 这关系从一开始就注定是要失败的。

④ MAIN/IMPORTANT 主要的/重要的

17 being the most important or main thing 首要的，主要的：*The first priority is to maintain the standard of work.* 最优先的考虑是保持工作的水准。

18 first things first used to tell someone to deal with things in order of importance 要紧的事情应当先做；凡事应有轻重缓急

19 put sth first to make something the most important thing 把某事摆在最重要的位置：*Rob seems to put money first, and happiness second in his life.* 罗布似乎把金钱放在人生的首位，而把幸福放在第二位。

20 come first to be the most important thing to someone 成为〔某人〕最重要的东西：[+with] *Alma's family will always come first with her.* 在阿尔玛的心中，家庭总是放在第一位。

21 first and foremost as the main reason for or purpose of something 首要的：*The aim of the exercise was first and foremost to give confidence to the students.* 这个练习的目的最主要是给学生一点信心。

22 first among equals someone who leads a group of people but is not considered to be more important than them 一群平等的人中的领导者

⑤ THE FIRST REASON/FACT ETC 首要原因/事实等

23 used to give an important fact or reason that will be followed by others 首先，第一〔用于表达最重要的事实或原因〕：*Well, first, the building is too small, and second, it isn't in a very good location.* 嗯，首先，这座楼太小；其次，所处的位置不是很好。

24 first of all *spoken* used to introduce the first thing that you are going to talk about【口】首先，第一〔用于引入要谈论的第一件事〕：*First of all I'd like to welcome you to the meeting.* 首先，我欢迎各位参加这次会议。

25 first off *spoken* used to introduce a fact, reason, or statement that will be followed by others, especially when you are annoyed with someone【口】首先〔尤用于表示对某人生气时〕：*First off, you should have told me where you were going.* 首先，你本该先告诉我你要去哪儿。

26 in the first place *spoken* used to give a fact or reason that proves what you are saying in an argument【口】首先，第一〔用于举出能证明自己论点的事实或理由〕：*Well, in the first place, Quinn would never say any such thing.* 嗯，首先，奎因是绝对不会说这种话的。—see 见 FIRSTLY (USAGE)

⑥ BEST 最好的

27 first choice the thing or person you like best 最好的选择：*Frances was our first choice as a name for the baby.* "弗朗西丝"是我们给婴儿起名字时的最佳选择。

28 come first/win first prize to be the best in a competition 名列第一/获一等奖：*My jam won first prize at the county fair.* 我的果酱在县里的商品评比会上获一等奖。

29 a first the highest level of university degree you can get in Britain〔英国大学的〕一级荣誉学位：**get a first (in)** *Helen got a first in Law.* 海伦获得法学的一级荣誉学位。

30 of the first water *old-fashioned* of the highest quality【过时】第一流的，上等的，质量最高的：*a jewel of the first water* 质量一流的宝石

⑦ MORNING 早上，上午

31 first thing as soon as you get up in the morning, or as soon as you start work 早晨一醒来；一上班：*The boss was here first thing, but he's gone to Newcastle now.* 老板一上班就来这里，但现在他去了纽卡斯尔。| *I'll phone him first thing Monday.* 我星期一一起床就打电话给他。

32 at first light very early in the morning 一大早；天一亮：*They left at first light and were in the mountains by nightfall.* 他们一大早就启程，傍晚时分到了山里。

⑧ NOT KNOW 不知道

33 not have the first idea about/not know the first thing about to not know anything about a subject, or not know how to do something 对…一窍不通/一无所知：*I wouldn't have the first idea about what to do in an emergency.* 发生紧急情况时该怎么做，我一无所知。| *I don't know the first thing about cars.* 我对汽车一窍不通。

34 the first I (have) heard/I knew etc of it *spoken* used when you have just found out about something that other people already know, and are slightly annoyed about it【口】我头一次听到/我头一次知道〔表示不满〕：*Andrew's been promoted? That's the first I've heard about it.* 安德鲁升职了？这事我头一次听到。

⑨ OTHER MEANINGS 其他意思

35 (at) first hand if you hear or experience something at first hand, you hear etc it directly, not through other people 第一手的，直接的：*The school had to deal first hand with the social problems of the area.* 学校得直接应付该地区的社会问题。

36 first a) first gear; the lowest GEAR[1] (1) in a car, bicycle, or

other vehicle, that you use to begin moving〔汽车、自行车或其他交通工具的〕第一挡，头挡，最低挡: **be in first** *Put the car in first when you park on a hill.* 车停在坡道上时要调到第一挡。**b)** *AmE* FIRST BASE【美】一垒; 一垒手的防卫位置

37 I'd die/kill myself etc first *spoken* used to emphasize how strongly you do not want to do something【口】我就是死/自杀; 我宁可死也不…: *I'll never take him back. I'd die first!* 我宁可死也不会让他回来!

first aid /,· '·/ *n* [U] simple medical treatment that is given as soon as possible to someone who is injured or who suddenly becomes ill 急救: **give first aid** *Being given first aid at the scene of the accident probably saved his life.* 他在事故现场得到了急救，这可能救了他的命。

first aid·er /,· '··/ *n* [C] *BrE* someone who is trained to give first aid【英】急救员

first aid kit /,· '·, ·/ *n* [C] a special box containing BANDAGES and medicines to treat people who are injured or become ill suddenly 急救箱

First A·mend·ment, the /,· ·'··/ a part of the Constitution of the United States which gives US citizens the right of freedom of speech, freedom of the PRESS (=newspapers, radio, and television), freedom of religion, and freedom of ASSEMBLY (=the right of any group to meet together). Many cases concerning these rights have been taken to the Supreme Court.《美国宪法第一修正案》〔美国宪法的一部分，赋予美国公民言论自由、新闻自由、宗教信仰自由和集会自由的权利。涉及这些权利的许多案件最后被上诉至联邦最高法院审理〕

first base /,· '·/ *n* [C] **1 a)** the first of the four places in a game of BASEBALL (1) that a player must touch before gaining a point〔棒球赛中的〕一垒 **b)** the position of a defending player near this place〔棒球赛中的〕一垒手的防卫位置: *He plays first base for the Red Sox.* 他在红袜队打一垒。**2** *AmE informal* the first stage of success in an attempt to achieve something【美，非正式】成功的第一步，初步成功: **get to/reach first base** 获得初步成功: *You've gotten to first base if you've landed an interview.* 如果你能得到面试机会，那你就获得了初步的成功。**3 get to first base** *AmE spoken* an expression meaning to kiss or hug someone in a sexual way, used especially by young men【美口】〔求爱方面〕跨出第一步〔尤为青年男子所使用〕

first·born /ˈfɜst`bɔrn; ˈfɜːstbɔːn/ *n* [singular] *literary* your first child【文】头胎的孩子 —**firstborn** *adj*: *her firstborn son* 她的头一个儿子

first class /,· '·◂/ *n* **1** [U] the best and most expensive seats or rooms in a train, boat etc〔火车、船等的〕头等舱位[车厢]: *We prefer to travel in first class.* 我们喜欢乘坐头等舱[车厢]旅行。—compare 比较 BUSINESS CLASS, CABIN CLASS, ECONOMY CLASS, TOURIST CLASS **2** [U] **a)** a class of mail in Britain, used for letters and parcels, that is quicker and more expensive than second class mail〔英国的优先投递的〕第一类邮件〔邮费比第二类邮件昂贵〕—compare 比较 SECOND CLASS (1) **b)** the class of mail used in the US for ordinary business and personal letters〔美国递送普通商业和私人信函的〕第一类邮件; 普通平邮 **3** [C] the highest standard for a degree from a British university〔英国大学的〕一级荣誉学位

first-class *adj* **1** of very good quality and much better than other things of the same type 第一流的，优等的: *This is a first-class wine.* 这是一流的葡萄酒。**2** using the first class of mail 优先投递的，第一类的; 平邮的 **3** using the first class of seats and rooms in a plane, train etc〔飞机舱位或火车车厢〕头等的: *a first-class passenger* 头等舱旅客 —**first class** *adv*: *If I send the letter first class it should arrive tomorrow.* 如果我把信作为第一类邮件投寄，明天就会寄到。

First Com·mu·nion /,· ·'··/ when someone receives Holy Communion for the first time 第一次领受圣餐(的仪式): *Rachel's making her First Communion on Saturday.* 雷切尔将在星期六第一次领受圣餐。

first cous·in /,· '··/ *n* [C] a child of your AUNT or UNCLE; COUSIN (1) 堂兄弟[姐妹]，表兄弟[姐妹]

first-de·gree /,· ·'·◂/ *adj* [always before noun 总用于名词前] **1 first-degree murder** *AmE* murder of the most serious type, in which someone deliberately kills someone else【美】一级谋杀罪; 最严重的凶杀 —compare 比较 MANSLAUGHTER **2 first-degree burn** a burn that is not very serious 一度烧伤，第一度灼伤

first e·di·tion /,· ·'··/ *n* [C] one of the copies of a book that was produced the first time the book was printed〔书的〕第一版，初版

first-ev·er /,· '··◂/ *adj* [always before noun 总用于名词前] happening for the first time 第一次的: *It was the day that Michael Jackson gave his first-ever televised interview.* 就是在这一天，迈克尔·杰克逊生平第一次接受了电视采访。

first fam·i·ly /,· '···/ *n* [C usually singular 一般用单数] the family of the President of the US 第一家庭〔指美国总统的家庭〕

first floor /,· '·◂/ *n* [C] **1** *BrE* the floor of a building just above the one at the bottom level【英】二楼〔指底层上面的楼层〕**2** *AmE* the floor of a building at the bottom level【美】一楼，底层 —compare 比较 GROUND FLOOR (1) *BrE*【英】—see 见 FLOOR[1] (USAGE)

first-foot·ing /,· '··/ *n* [U] *ScotE* the custom in Scotland of visiting people as soon as the New Year has begun【苏格兰】第一个登门拜年(的习俗) —**first-footer** *n* [C]

first fruits /,· '·/ *n* [plural] the first good result of something 最初成果: *One of the first fruits of Mao's visit to Moscow was a new treaty with the Russians.* 毛泽东到莫斯科访问的一项最初成果是与苏联签订了一项新条约。

first gear /,· '·/ *n* [C] the lowest GEAR[1] (1) in a car or other motor vehicle, used when starting to move or when going up or down a very steep hill〔汽车或其他机动车辆的〕一挡，头挡，最低挡

first gen·e·ra·tion /,· ··'··◂/ *n* [singular] **1** the children of people who have moved to live in a new country 移民的第一代孩子 **2** the first type of a machine to be developed 第一代机器: *The first generation of computers were huge and slow.* 第一代电脑体积庞大，而且速度慢。**3** the first people to do something 第一批人: *the first generation of environmentalists* 第一代环境保护主义者 —**first-generation** *adj*

first half /,· '·/ *n* [C] the first of two equal periods of time that a sports match is divided into〔体育比赛的〕上半场，上半时

first-hand /,· '·◂/ *adj* **first-hand experience/knowledge/account** experience etc that has been learned or gained by doing something yourself 亲身经验/直接得来的知识/第一手报道: *journalists with first-hand experience of working in war zones* 具有战地实际工作经验的新闻记者 —compare 比较 SECOND-HAND —see also 另见 **(at) first hand** (FIRST[1] (35))

first la·dy /,· '··/ *n* [C usually singular 一般用单数] the wife of the President of the US, or of the GOVERNOR of a US state〔美国〕第一夫人，总统夫人; 州长夫人

first lan·guage /,· '··/ *n* [C] the language that you first learn as a child 母语，第一语言 —compare 比较 SECOND LANGUAGE

first lieu·ten·ant /,· ·'··◂/ *n* [C] a middle rank in the US army, Marines, or Air Force, or someone who has this rank〔美国陆军、海军陆战队或空军的〕中尉 —see table on page C6 参见 C6 页附录

first·ly /ˈfɜstlɪ; ˈfɜːstli/ *adv* [sentence adverb 句子副词] used to say that the fact or reason that you are going to mention is the first one and will be followed by others 第一，首先: *Firstly, I would like to thank everyone who has contributed to this success.* 首先，我要感谢对这次成功作出贡献的每一个人。 S 2

USAGE NOTE 用法说明: FIRSTLY

WORD CHOICE 词语辨析: **firstly, first (of all), in the first place, to start/begin with, at first, in the beginning**

Firstly/first (of all)/in the first place/to start with/to begin with are often used to introduce a series of reasons, ideas, remarks etc. firstly/first (of all)/in the first place/to start with/to begin with 常用于列举一系列原因、看法、意见等: *There are three reasons why I don't like him: first(ly)/to start with he's rude, second(ly) he's a liar, and third(ly)/finally he owes me money.* 我不喜欢他有三个原因: 首先/第一，他粗暴无礼; 第二，他撒谎; 第三/最后，他欠我钱不还。

You use **first (of all)** (NOT 不用 *firstly*) to introduce a series of actions, often in order of time. 人们常用first (of all)〔而不是 firstly〕列举往往根据时间顺序依次列出一系列的动作: *First of all I get dressed, next I bring in the paper, then I fix breakfast.* 首先，我穿上衣服，接着把报纸拿进来，然后做早餐。

At first can only be used for a period of time, often when you are comparing it with a later period. **To start/begin with** and **in the beginning** can be used in this way too. at first 只可用于表示一段时间，常与稍后的一段时间作比较，to start/begin with和in the beginning 也可以这样用: *You'll find it difficult at first/to begin with, but later/soon it'll get easier.* 起初/开始你会觉得很难，但后来/很快就会感到容易起来。

first mate /ˌ· ˈ·/ *n* [C] the officer on a non-military ship who has the rank just below captain〔非军用船只上级别仅次于船长的〕大副

First Minister /ˌ· ˈ···/ the most important minister in the Scottish Parliament, similar to the Prime Minister in the UK parliament. The minister is elected by the members of the Scottish Parliament, but would normally be the leader of the largest political party. 首席大臣〔苏格兰议会最重要的官员，类似英国议会的首相。首席大臣由苏格兰议员选举产生，但通常都是最大政党的领袖〕

first name /ˈ· ·/ *n* [C] **1** the name or names that come before your family name 名字: *Her first name's Helen, but I don't know her surname.* 她的名字叫海伦，但我不知道她姓什么。**2 be on first name terms (with sb)** *BrE*【英】, **be on a first name basis** *AmE*【美】to know someone well enough to call them by their first name〔因熟悉某人而〕直呼其名，以名相称 —compare 比较 SURNAME

first night /ˌ· ˈ·/ *n* [C] the evening when the first public performance of a show, play etc is given〔演出、戏剧等的〕首演[首映]之夜

first of·fend·er /ˌ· ·ˈ··/ *n* [C] someone who is guilty of breaking the law for the first time 初次犯法者，初犯

first of·fi·cer /ˌ· ˈ···◂/ *n* [C] FIRST MATE 大副

first per·son /ˌ· ˈ··◂/ *n* [singular] **1** *technical* a form of a verb or a pronoun that is used to show that you are the speaker. For example, 'I', 'me', 'we', and 'us' are first person pronouns, and 'I am' is the first person singular of the verb 'to be'.【术语】第一人称〈例如，I, me, we 和 us 都是第一人称代词，I am 是动词 to be 的第一人称单数形式〉**2** a way of telling a story in which the writer or speaker tells it as though he were involved in the story〔叙述中的〕第一人称: *a first person narrative* 第一人称叙述 —compare 比较 SECOND PERSON, THIRD PERSON

F

first-rate /ˌ· ˈ·◂/ *adj* of the very best quality 第一流的，极好的: *He's a first-rate surgeon.* 他是第一流的外科医生。

First Read·ing /ˌfɜst ˈridɪŋ; ˌfɜːst ˈriːdɪŋ/ **1** the first time that a suggested new law is introduced in Parliament in the UK〔议案在英国议会中的〕初读: *The new transport bill will get its first reading in the House of Commons tomorrow.* 新的交通议案明天将在下议院进行初读。**2** the first time that a suggested new law is introduced to Congress in the US〔议案在美国国会中的〕初读

first re·fus·al /ˌ· ·ˈ··/ *n* **have/give sb first refusal on sth** *BrE* to let someone decide whether to buy something before you offer to sell it to other people【英】让某人对某物有优先购买权: *I'll let you have first refusal on the car.* 我会让你优先决定是否买这辆车。

First Secretary /ˌ· ˈ···/ the most important minister in the Welsh Assembly, similar to the Prime Minister in the UK parliament. The minister is elected by the Welsh Assembly Members, but would normally be the leader of the largest political party. 首席大臣〔威尔士国民议会最重要的官员，类似英国议会的首相。首席大臣由威尔士国民议会成员选举产生，但通常都是最大政党的领袖〕

first strike /ˌ· ˈ·◂/ *n* [C] an attack made on your enemy before they attack you 先发制人的打击

first-string /ˌ· ˈ·◂/ *adj* [only before noun 仅用于名词前] a first-string player in a team plays when the game begins because they are the most skilled〔运动员〕主力的；首发阵容的，先上场的 —compare 比较 SECOND-STRING

first-time buy·er /ˌ· · ˈ··/ *n* [C] someone who is buying a house or an apartment for the first time〔房子或公寓的〕首次购买者；首次置业者

First World /ˌ· ˈ·◂/ *n* [singular] the rich industrial countries of the world 第一世界〔指世界上富有的工业国家〕—compare 比较 THIRD WORLD —**first world** *adj* [always before noun 总用于名词前]

First World War /ˌ· · ˈ·/ *n* [singular] the big war fought in Europe between 1914 and 1918 第一次世界大战

firth /fɝθ; fɜːθ/ *n* [C] a narrow area of sea between two areas of land, or the place where a river flows into the sea, especially in Scotland〔尤指苏格兰的狭长的〕港湾，河口湾: *the Firth of Forth* 福思湾

fis·cal[1] /ˈfɪskl; ˈfɪskəl/ *adj formal* connected with money, taxes, debts, etc owned and managed by the government【正式】〔政府〕财政的，公款的: *a fiscal crisis* 财政危机 —**fiscally** *adv*

fiscal[2] *n* [C] *informal* PROCURATOR FISCAL【非正式】〔地方〕检察官

fiscal year /ˌ·· ˈ·/ *n* [C] the period of a year which the government uses to calculate how much tax a person or business must pay 财政年度，会计年度，税年 —compare 比较 FINANCIAL YEAR

CULTURAL NOTE 文化注释

In Britain, the fiscal year for companies starts on 1st April and for private persons it starts on 6th April. In the US, the government fiscal year starts on October 1st; for INDIVIDUALs it is the same as the CALENDAR YEAR. Businesses may start their own fiscal years. 英国公司的财政年度从4月1日算起，私人财政年度从4月6日算起。美国政府的财政年度从10月1日算起，个人财政年度与公历年相同，公司可自行确定自己的财政年度。— compare 比较 FINANCIAL YEAR

fish 鱼

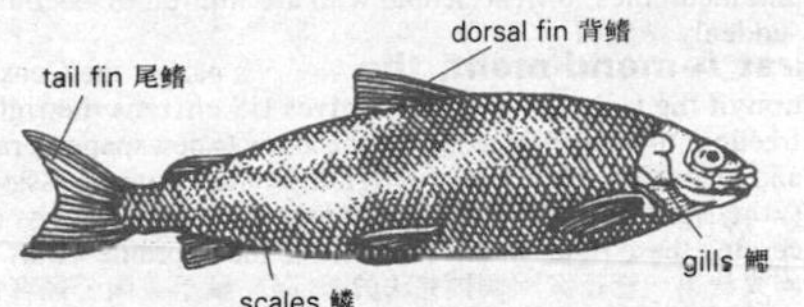

fish[1] /fɪʃ; fɪʃ/ *n plural* **fish** or **fishes** [C] **1** an animal that lives in water, and uses its FINS (1) and tail to swim 鱼: *The lake is well stocked with fish.* 这个湖里有许多鱼。| **catch a fish** *Ronny caught three huge fish this afternoon.* 罗尼今天下午捕到三条大鱼。**2** [U] the flesh of a fish used as food 鱼肉: *White wine is traditionally drunk with fish.* 在吃鱼的时候照例是喝白葡萄酒的。**3 like a fish out of water** feeling uncomfortable because you are in an unfamiliar place or situation 如离水之鱼，感到生疏[不自在]: *I felt like a fish out of water in my new school.* 我在新学校里感到很不适应。**4 there are plenty more fish in the sea** used to tell someone whose relationship has ended that there are other people they can have a relationship with 海里的鱼多得很〔用于告诉某人不必为结束同他人的某种关系而烦恼，还可以同许多其他的人建立同样的关系〕**5 neither fish nor fowl** neither one thing nor another 不伦不类，非驴非马 **6 have other/bigger fish to fry** *informal* to have other things to do, especially more important things【非正式】另有（更重要的）事要做: *I can't deal with this now, I've got other fish to fry!* 我现在不能处理这件事，我另有更重要的事要做！**7 an odd fish/a queer fish** *BrE old-fashioned* someone who is slightly strange or crazy【英，过时】古怪的人 **8 a cold fish** an unfriendly person who seems to have no strong feelings 态度冷冰冰的人，不热情的人 **9 a big fish in a little pond** someone who is important or who has influence over a very small area 小塘中的大鱼，小地方的要人 —see also 另见 **drink like a fish** (DRINK[2] (2)), **a fine/pretty kettle of fish** (KETTLE (4))

fish[2] *v* **1** [I] to try to catch fish 捕鱼，钓鱼: [+for] *We're fishing for trout.* 我们正在捕鳟鱼。**2** [T always+adv/prep] also 又作 **fish out** to find something after searching through a bag, pocket etc, and take it out 掏出，找出: **fish sth ↔ out** *Eric fished a peppermint out of the bag.* 埃里克从袋子里掏出一块薄荷糖。**3** [I always +adv/prep] *informal* to search for something in a bag, pocket etc【非正式】寻找，摸索: [+about/around] *She fished around in her purse and pulled out a photo.* 她在钱包里寻找着，拿出了一张照片。| [+for] *Chris fished in his pocket for a coin.* 克里斯在口袋里摸找硬币。**4** [T] to try to catch fish in a particular area of water 在…中捕鱼: *Other nations are forbidden to fish the waters within 200 miles of the coast.* 禁止其他国家在距海岸 200 英里的海域内捕鱼。**5** [T] also 又作 **fish out** to pull someone or something out of water〔从水里〕捞出，拖出: **fish sb out** *Police frogmen fished the body out of the East River a week later.* 警方的蛙人一星期后从东河中打捞出尸体。**6 fish for compliments** to try to make someone say something nice about you, usually by asking a question〔一般通过提问〕讨别人的恭维: *It's sickening the way he's always fishing for compliments when she's around.* 她在场的时候他总是讨人恭维，真恶心。**7 fish for information/news/gossip etc** to try to find out secret information 探听消息/新闻/流言飞语等: *Reporters were hanging around fishing for information on the Congressman's resignation.* 记者们都在附近徘徊，探听有关那位国会议员辞职的消息。**8 fish in troubled waters** to try to gain an advantage from other people's problems 趁火打劫，混水摸鱼 **9 fish or cut bait** *AmE spoken* used to tell someone to do what they say they will, or stop talking about it【美口】要么说干就干，要么索性不要说

fish and chips /ˌ· · ˈ·/ *n* [U] a meal consisting of fish covered with a mixture of flour and milk and cooked in oil and long, thin pieces of potato cooked in oil 炸鱼薯条

CULTURAL NOTE 文化注释

Fish and chips are very popular in the UK, and are considered to be a typically British meal. They are bought in a FISH AND CHIP SHOP, which is also sometimes called a CHIPPY, rather than cooked at home, and they are a quick, fairly cheap meal. The food is usually wrapped in paper and eaten at home or in the street. The chips usually have salt and VINEGAR and sometimes tomato KETCHUP on them. 炸鱼薯条在英国非常流行，被认为是典型的英餐。这些食物不用在自己家里做，可以在炸鱼薯条商店（有时也称作chippy）买到，是一种省时而且相对便宜的膳食。这些食物通常用纸包装，拿回家里吃或在街上吃。薯条上常放盐和醋，有时还放番茄酱。

fish·cake /ˈfɪʃˌkek; ˈfɪʃkeɪk/ *n* [C] a small round flat food consisting of cooked fish mixed with cooked potato〔用鱼和马铃薯做成的〕鱼饼

fish·er·man /ˈfɪʃɚmən; ˈfɪʃəmən/ *n plural* **fishermen** /-mən; -mən/ [C] someone who catches fish as a sport or as a job 钓鱼者；渔民，渔夫 —compare 比较 ANGLER

fish·e·ry /ˈfɪʃərɪ; ˈfɪʃəri/ *n* [C] a part of the sea where fish are caught as a business 渔场

fish-eye lens /ˌ· · ˈ·/ *n* [C] a type of curved LENS (=piece of glass on the front of a camera) that allows you to take photographs of a wide area 鱼眼镜头，超广角镜头

fish farm /ˈ· ·/ *n* [C] an area of water used for breeding fish as a business 养鱼场 —**fish farming** *n* [U]

fish fin·ger /ˌ· ˈ· ·/ *n* [C] *BrE* a long piece of fish covered with small pieces of dried bread and cooked【英】〔裹着面包屑的〕鱼条；FISH STICK *AmE*【美】

3 **fish·ing** /ˈfɪʃɪŋ; ˈfɪʃɪŋ/ *n* [U] **1** the sport or business of catching fish 钓鱼；捕鱼：*Fishing is one of his hobbies.* 钓鱼是他的一项业余爱好。| **go fishing** *Terry's going fishing at Lake Arrowhead next weekend.* 特里下周末要到阿罗黑德湖钓鱼。**2 be on a fishing expedition** *AmE* to try to find out secret information【美】在探听秘密消息

fishing line /ˈ· · ·/ *n* [U] very long string made of strong material and used to catch fish 钓线，钓丝

fishing rod /ˈ· · ·/ *n* [C] a long thin pole with a long string and a hook fixed to it, used for catching fish 钓竿

fishing tack·le /ˈ· ·, · ·/ *n* [U] equipment used for fishing 钓具；捕鱼索具

fish ket·tle /ˈ· , · ·/ *n* [C] a long, deep dish used for cooking whole fish〔长而深的〕煮鱼锅

fish mar·ket /ˈ· , · ·/ *n* [C] a special market that only sells fish 鱼市场

fish meal /ˈ· ·/ *n* [U] dried fish crushed into a powder and put on the land to help plants grow〔用作肥料的〕鱼粉

fish·mon·ger /ˈfɪʃˌmʌŋgɚ; ˈfɪʃmʌŋgə/ *n* [C] *especially BrE* someone who sells fish【尤英】鱼商，鱼贩

fish·net stock·ings /ˌfɪʃnɛt ˈstɑkɪŋz; ˌfɪʃnet ˈstɒkɪŋz/ also 又作 **fishnet tights** /ˌ· · ˈ·/ *BrE*【英】—*n* [plural] STOCKINGS with a pattern of small holes that make them look like a net 鱼网丝袜，网眼长袜

fish slice /ˈ· ·/ *n* [C] *BrE* a kitchen tool used especially for turning food when cooking, with a wide flat part and a handle【英】煎鱼铲，锅铲 —see picture on page A10 参见A10页图

fish stick /ˈ· ·/ *n* [C] *AmE* a long piece of fish covered with small pieces of dried bread and cooked【美】〔裹面包屑的〕鱼条；FISH FINGER *BrE*【英】

fish·tail /ˈfɪʃˌtel; ˈfɪʃteɪl/ *v* [I] *AmE* if a vehicle or aircraft fishtails, it slides from side to side, usually because the tyres are sliding on water or ice【美】〔车〕摆尾行驶；〔飞机〕摆尾飞行

fish·wife /ˈfɪʃˌwaɪf; ˈfɪʃwaɪf/ *plural* **fishwives** /-ˌwaɪvz; -waɪvz/ *n* [C] an insulting word for a woman with a loud voice 说话粗野的女人，泼妇〔具冒犯性的词语〕

fish·y /ˈfɪʃɪ; ˈfɪʃi/ *adj* **1** *informal* seeming bad or dishonest【非正式】可疑的，靠不住的：*There's something very fishy about his business deals.* 他的商业交易很靠不住。**2** tasting or smelling of fish 鱼的；鱼味的；鱼腥气的

fis·sile /ˈfɪsl̩; ˈfɪsaɪl/ *adj* **1** *technical* able to be split by atomic fission【术语】〔原子〕可裂变的 **2** tending to split along natural lines of weakness 易裂开的，可分裂的

fis·sion /ˈfɪʃən; ˈfɪʃən/ *n* [U] *technical*【术语】**1** the process of splitting an atom to produce large amounts of energy or an explosion〔原子的〕裂变 —compare 比较 FUSION (2) **2** the process of dividing a cell into two or more parts〔细胞的〕分裂

fis·sure /ˈfɪʃɚ; ˈfɪʃə/ *n* [C] a deep crack, especially in rock or earth〔尤指岩石或土地的〕裂缝，裂隙

fist /fɪst; fɪst/ *n* [C] **1** the hand when the fingers are curled in towards the PALM, especially in order to express anger or hit someone 拳，拳头：*She held the money tightly in her fist.* 她紧紧把钱握在手中。| **clench your fist** (=hold your fist very tightly closed) 握紧拳头 *Malcolm clenched his fists angrily.* 马尔科姆愤怒地握紧拳头。| **fist fight** (=a fight in which you use your bare hands to hit someone) 拳斗，斗殴 *The argument quickly turned into an all-out fist fight.* 争论很快变成一场激烈的拳斗。—see also 另见 HAM-FISTED, TIGHT-FISTED, **hand over fist** (HAND[1] (37)) —see picture at 参见 BODY 图 **2 make a good/bad fist of** *BrE informal* to make a successful or unsuccessful attempt to do something【英，非正式】做成/做不成〔某事〕

fist·ful /ˈfɪstfʊl; ˈfɪstfʊl/ *n* [C] an amount that is as much as you can hold in your hand 一把，一握：**[+of]** *a child clutching a fistful of toffees* 紧紧握着一把太妃糖的小孩

Fistful of Dol·lars, A /ˌ· · ˈ· ·/ (1964) the first SPAGHETTI WESTERN (=a film about the American west in the 19th century, made in Europe by an Italian director). It was made by Sergio Leone with Clint Eastwood as its main character.《荒野大镖客》〔(1964)，第一部由意大利人执导在欧洲拍摄反映19世纪美国西部生活的影片，由瑟古欧·莱昂内导演，克林特·伊斯特伍德主演〕

fis·ti·cuffs /ˈfɪstɪˌkʌfs; ˈfɪstɪkʌfs/ *n* [plural] *old-fashioned* a fight in which you use your bare hands to hit someone【过时】拳斗，斗殴

fit[1] /fɪt; fɪt/ *v past tense* **fitted** also 又作 **fit** *AmE*【美】*past participle* **fit** 1 2

1 ▶RIGHT SIZE 合适的尺寸◀ [I,T not in progressive 不用进行式] to be the right size and shape for someone or something (使) 合适，合身：*The dress fits perfectly.* 这件连衣裙十分合身。| **fit sb** *The jacket fitted me pretty well but the trousers were too small.* 我穿这件上衣很合身，但裤子太小了。| **fit (sb) like a glove** (=fit the shape of sb's body perfectly) 非常合身 —see 见 CLOTHES (USAGE)

2 ▶FIT A SPACE 容纳于…◀ [I always+adv/prep, not in progressive 不用进行式] to be the right size and shape for a particular space, and not be too big 适合；容得下：**[+in/into/under etc]** *Will my tennis racket fit in your bag?* 我的网球拍能装进你的袋子吗？

3 ▶EQUIPMENT/PART 设备/部件◀ [T] to put a small piece of equipment into a place, or a new part onto a machine, so that it is ready to be used 安装：**fit sth on/to etc** *Anti-theft devices are fitted to all our cars.* 我们所有的汽车上都安装了防盗装置。| **fit sth** *The plumber fit the sink this morning.* 管子工今天上午安装了洗涤槽。

4 ▶PUT IN PLACE 放在适当的位置◀ [I always+adv/prep,T always+adv/prep] to put or join something in a particular place where it is meant to go (把…) 放在适当的位置：**[+in/over/together]** *The plastic cover fits neatly over the frame.* 这块塑料罩盖在框架上正好合适。| **fit sth ↔ in/onto/together etc** *She fit a piece into the jigsaw puzzle.* 她在拼图上拼进一块。

5 ▶FIND A PLACE FOR 为…找地方◀ [I always+adv/prep,T always+adv/prep] to find enough space for something in a room, vehicle, container etc〔房间、车辆、容器等〕装得下：**fit sb/sth ↔ in** *Can you fit in another passenger?* 能再装一名乘客吗？

6 ▶MATCH 符合◀ [I,T not in progressive 不用进行式] if something fits a system, idea etc, it says the same thing or follows the same principles 符合，适合：**fit in with** *Sonny's behaviour didn't fit in with what I knew of him.* 桑尼的行为与我对他的了解不相符。| **[+in/into]** *educational videos designed to fit into the syllabus* 配合课程大纲而制作的教学录像带 | **fit sth** *a phenomenon that didn't fit the expected pattern* 与所预期的方式不相符的现象

7 ▶SUITABLE 合适的◀ [T not in progressive 不用进行式] to have the qualities, experience etc that are suitable for a particular job, situation etc 适合〔某项工作、某情况等〕：*The punishment should fit the crime.* 应当按罪量刑。| *The music fits the words perfectly.* 音乐和歌词配得很好。| **fit sb for sth** *Webb's negotiating skills fitted him for the task.* 韦布的谈判技巧使他能胜任这项任务。| **fit the bill** (=have exactly the right qualities) 正合适；正符合要求 *We wanted an experienced sportscaster, and Waggoner fit the bill.* 我们需要一名经验丰富的体育节目主持人，瓦戈纳正符合要求。

8 ▶DESCRIPTION 描写◀ [T not in progressive 不用进行式] if a description fits someone or something, it describes them ex-

actly 与…完全吻合[相称]: *Police said the car fits the description of the stolen vehicle.* 警方说这辆车与对那辆被盗的车的描述完全吻合。

9 ►DECIDE GROUP 判别群体◄ [I,T] to belong to a particular group or set of ideas (使)属于〔某个群体或某种思想〕: **[+into]** *A lot of people didn't fit into the categories the researchers had devised.* 许多人无法归纳到研究人员所定的类别中去。—see also 另见 **sb's face doesn't fit** (FACE[1] (17)), **if the cap fits** (CAP[1] (4))

fit in *phr v* **1** [I] to be accepted by other people in a group because you have the same attitudes and interests〔因为有共同的看法、趣味等〕被他人接受, 相处融洽: *At first I felt awkward, but I soon learned to fit in.* 开头我感到不自在, 但很快就学会适应了。| **[+with]** *Larry doesn't seem to fit in with the other children.* 拉里好像和别的孩子们相处得不融洽。**2** [T **fit** sth/sb ↔ **in**] to manage to do something or see someone, even though you have a lot of other things to do 安排时间做〔某事〕, 安排时间见〔某人〕; 找出…的时间: *The doctor said he can fit me in at 4:30.* 医生说他可以安排在 4:30 与我见面。**3** [T **fit** sth ↔ **in/into**] to find a time when something can happen without causing problems 安插〔时间〕: *How is the extra work going to fit into the schedule?* 额外的工作怎样才能安插在时间表里? | **[+with]** *Nancy tried to fit her holidays in with Alex's.* 南希试着把她的假期和亚历克斯的假期配合起来。

fit sb/sth ↔ **out** *phr v* [T] **1** to provide a room or building with equipment or decorations 装备, 配备; 布置: *snug mountain cabins fitted out with pine furniture* 配有松木家具的温暖舒适的山间小屋 **2** to dress someone, especially in a particular type of clothing 给…穿衣〔尤指特定式样的衣服〕: *Jennifer was fitted out like a Queen.* 珍妮弗穿得像女王。

fit sb/sth ↔ **up** *phr v* [T] **1** to provide a room or building with equipment or decorations 装备, 配备; 布置: *The bedroom is fitted up as an office.* 这间卧室被布置成办公室。**2** *BrE spoken* to make someone seem guilty of a crime they have not done, FRAME[2] (3)【英口】诬陷, 陷害: **fit sb up for sth** *Watson had been fitted up for the murder.* 沃森被诬陷犯有谋杀罪。

USAGE NOTE 用法说明: FIT

WORD CHOICE 词语辨析: **fit, suit, fit in, match, go together/with**

If something is not too big and not too small for a person or other thing, it **fits** (them). 如果某件东西对某人或其他东西 fits (正合适), 即这件东西对其来说不大也不小: *A size 12 dress should fit.* 12号的连衣裙应该会合身。| *You can't put those shelves in there, they won't fit.* 你不能把那些架子放在那儿, 它们的大小不合适。

If clothes or other personal things are the right style, colour etc for someone, you say they **suit** them. 如果衣服或其他个人物品的式样、颜色等正适合某人, 可以说 suit: *Casual clothes really don't suit her.* 她确实不适合穿休闲服。| *A green dress won't suit me.* 绿色连衣裙不适合我。| *That new haircut suits you!* 那种新发式很适合你! Schools, places, times, situations etc may also **suit** people. 学校、地方、时间、情况等也可能 suit (适合) 人: *A management position would suit him down to the ground.* 管理的职位会完全适合他。| *California doesn't suit everyone.* 加利福尼亚并不适合每个人。| *Will ten o'clock suit you?* 10 点钟你觉得合适吗?

If people **fit in** they have a good social relationship with the other people in a group, and share the same attitudes, interests etc. 如果人们 fit in (相处融洽), 是说他们在一起时关系很好, 有共同的看法、兴趣等: *Laura fits in perfectly at the tennis club.* 劳拉在网球俱乐部与大家相处得十分融洽。

If things are almost the same in some way and look good together, they **match**. 如果事物很相似, 放在一起看上去很协调, 可以说它们 match (相配): *The curtains don't match the carpet* (=they are not the same pattern/colour). 窗帘与地毯不相配 (=它们的花样/颜色不一样)。

If things look right together in style, colour etc, they **go together** or **go with** each other. 如果事物放在一起, 在式样、颜色等方面看上去恰当, 可以说它们 go together 或 go with (协调): *The curtains don't go with the carpet* (=they are not the same colour and do not look good together either). 窗帘与地毯不协调 (=它们颜色不一样, 看上去也不相配)。Things can **go together** in other ways too. 事物也可以在其他方面 go together (相配): *Fish and white wine go particularly well together.* 鱼和白葡萄酒相配得特别好。

In British English the usual past form of **fit** is **fitted**, but in the first meaning you can also use **fit** in more informal English. 在英国英语中, fit 通常的过去式是 fitted, 但用作第一种意思时, 在较非正式的英语中也可以用 fit: *Two years ago, these pants fit me perfectly.* 两年前, 这裤子我穿着很合身。In American English, the usual past form is **fit**, but you can also use **fitted** for all the meanings. 在美国英语中, fit 的过去式通常用 fit, 但所有义项都可用 fitted 作为过去式。

fit² *adj* **fitter, fittest**

1 having the qualities that are suitable for a particular job, occasion, purpose etc 适合的, 合适的: **[+for]** *I don't think Carol is the fittest person for the job.* 我不认为卡罗尔是最适合这项工作的人。| **fit to do sth** *She's not fit to look after children.* 她不适合照看小孩。| **fit to eat/drink** *This food isn't fit to eat.* 这种食物不宜食用。| **be in a fit state** *We're trying to get the house into a fit state for visitors.* 我们正在把屋子弄得像样些, 准备客人来访。| **fit for a King** (=of the highest quality) 高质量的, 精美的, 最高级的 *food fit for a King* 精美的食品; 最高级的食品

2 ►STRONG 强壮的◄ *especially BrE* healthy and strong because you exercise regularly【尤英】〔因经常锻炼而〕健壮的: *Sandy's very fit – he runs almost 30 miles a week.* 桑迪十分健壮 —— 他每星期跑差不多 30 英里。| **keep fit** (=exercise in order to stay strong)〔为了保持强壮而〕锻炼身体 *She keeps fit by swimming every morning.* 她每天上午游泳锻炼身体。| **physically fit** *AmE*【美】*Rowers have to be extremely physically fit.* 划船运动选手的身体必须特别健壮。—opposite 反义词 UNFIT (1)

3 ►HEALTHY 健康的◄ *especially BrE* healthy after having been ill【尤英】〔病后〕健康的: *I'm glad to see you looking fit again.* 我很高兴看到你气色完全好了。| **fit as a fiddle** (=completely healthy) 身体非常好的 *She's 86, but as fit as a fiddle.* 她 86 岁, 但身体好极了。| **fighting fit** (=extremely healthy) 非常健康的 | **be in a fit state/condition** (=be healthy enough, after being ill or drunk, to be able to do something)〔生病或酔酒恢复后〕身体状况良好 *Brog was in no fit state to drive when he left the party.* 布罗格离开聚会时情况欠佳 (酒醉了), 不能开车。

4 fit to drop extremely tired after using a lot of effort or energy〔付出大量气力、精力后〕累得快要瘫倒在地上的: *We worked till we were fit to drop.* 我们一直工作, 直到累得快要瘫倒在地上。

5 fit to be tied *spoken especially AmE* very angry, anxious, or upset【口, 尤美】十分恼火[着急, 烦恼]的: *The teacher will be fit to be tied when she sees the mess you've made.* 老师看到你们弄得这样一团糟会非常生气的。

6 fit to wake the dead a noise that is fit to wake the dead is extremely loud〔噪音〕非常大声的: *They were screaming fit to wake the dead.* 他们高声尖叫。

7 laughing/coughing fit to burst *informal* laughing or coughing a lot【非正式】笑破肚皮/使劲大声咳嗽: *The girls were laughing fit to burst.* 女孩子们笑破了肚皮。

8 see/think fit (to do sth) an expression meaning to decide that it is right or suitable to do a particular thing, used especially when you do not agree with this decision 认为〔做某事〕恰当: *You know the situation best. Do whatever you think fit.* 你最了解情况。你认为怎么恰当就怎么干。

fit³ *n*

1 ►EMOTION 情感◄ [C] a very strong and uncontrollable emotion〔感情〕冲动, 一阵发作: **[+of]** *In a fit of temper he slammed his hands down on the keyboard.* 他突然发起脾气, 用双手猛击键盘。| *a fit of depression* 一阵沮丧

2 be a good/tight/close etc fit to fit a person or a particular space well, tightly, closely etc 非常适合/很紧/很密切: *This jacket is a beautiful fit.* 这件夹克衫非常合身。

3 ►LOSE CONSCIOUSNESS 失去知觉◄ [C] a short period of time when someone loses consciousness and cannot control their body because their brain is not working properly 昏厥; 一时失去知觉; 痉挛: *an epileptic fit* 癫痫发作 | **have a fit** *The baby's having a fit! Call the doctor!* 婴儿痉挛了! 叫医生来!

4 ►SUITABLE 适合的◄ [singular] *formal* a relationship between two things or systems in which they match each other or are suitable for each other【正式】〔事物或制度之间〕匹配: **[+between]** *We must be sure that there's a fit between the needs of the children and the education they receive.* 我们必须确保儿童的需要和他们受到的教育相匹配。

5 ►LAUGH/COUGH 笑/咳嗽◄ a period during which you laugh or cough a lot 一阵大笑; 一阵咳嗽: *a coughing fit* 一阵咳嗽 | **[+of]** *a fit of the giggles* 一阵咯咯笑 | **in fits (of laughter)** (=laughing a lot) 一阵阵大笑 *The show was hilarious – we were all in fits.* 表演十分滑稽 —— 我们一阵阵地捧腹大笑。| **have sb**

in fits(=make someone laugh a lot) 使某人一阵阵地大笑 *Cyril had us in fits from the minute we walked in the door.* 西里尔从我们一进门就开始把我们逗得一阵阵大笑。

6 in/by fits and starts repeatedly starting and stopping 一阵一阵地, 断断续续地: *The old car moved in fits and starts up the road.* 这辆旧车时走时停地在路上行驶。| *Beverley tends to do things in fits and starts.* 贝弗莉做事情往往是断断续续的。

7 have/throw a fit *informal* to be very angry or shocked【非正式】大发脾气; 大吃一惊: *If your mother finds out about this she'll have a fit.* 如果你母亲知道这事, 她会大发脾气的。

fit·ful /ˈfɪtfəl; ˈfɪtfəl/ *adj* happening irregularly for short periods of time 不规则的, 间歇的, 一阵一阵的: *fitful showers of rain* 一阵一阵的雨 —**fitfully** *adv*: *She slept fitfully.* 她睡睡醒醒。

fit·ment /ˈfɪtmənt; ˈfɪtmənt/ *n* [C] *BrE* a piece of furniture that is made especially for a particular space in a room【英】〔房间某个地方定制的〕家具, 设备: *bathroom fitments* 浴室设备

fit·ness /ˈfɪtnəs; ˈfɪtnɪs/ *n* [U] **1** the state of being healthy and strong so that you are able to do hard work or sport 健壮; 健康: *She's following an exercise programme to improve her fitness.* 她按照锻炼计划来增强体质。| **physical fitness** *Running marathons requires a high level of physical fitness.* 跑马拉松需要有十分健壮的身体。**2** the degree to which someone or something is suitable or good enough for a particular situation or purpose 适合, 恰当: [+for] *We examine candidates' fitness for the job.* 我们考核应征者是否胜任这项工作。| **fitness to do sth** *The police questioned his fitness to drive.* 警方怀疑他是否有资格开车。

fit·ted /ˈfɪtɪd; ˈfɪtɪd/ *adj* **1 be fitted with** to have or include something as a permanent part 配备: *Is your car fitted with automatic locks?* 你的车子装了自动锁吗? **2** [only before noun 仅用于名词前] *BrE* made or cut to fit a particular space【英】按照特定空间做的, 配好大小的: *a fitted carpet* 定做的地毯 | *fitted cupboards* 定做的碗橱 **3** having the right qualities or experience for a particular job 适合的, 称职的: *Elinor is well fitted to be the sales manager.* 埃莉诺非常适合担任销售经理。

fitted kit·chen /ˌ.. ˈ../ *n* [C] *BrE* a kitchen that has cupboards that fit exactly into a particular space【英】装有定制家具的厨房, 碗橱尺寸合适的厨房

fitted sheet /ˌ.. ˈ./ *n* [C] a sheet that fits exactly over the MATTRESS on a bed 尺寸正好合适的床单

fit·ter /ˈfɪtə; ˈfɪtə/ *n* [C] *BrE* someone who puts together or repairs machines or electrical equipment【英】装配工, 修理工: *a gas fitter* 煤气装配工

fit·ting[1] /ˈfɪtɪŋ; ˈfɪtɪŋ/ *n* [C] **1** [usually plural 一般用复数] a piece of furniture that is usually included in a house but can be moved if necessary, such as a COOKER (1)〔房间内必要时可移动的〕设备, 家具〈如厨灶〉—compare 比较 FIXTURE (1) **2** [usually plural 一般用复数] a part of a piece of equipment that makes it possible for you to use it 配件, 装置: *a sink with chrome fittings* (=handle and taps) 带铬合金配件的洗碗槽 | *the light fittings* 电灯装置 **3** an occasion when you put on a piece of clothing that is being made for you, to see if it fits properly 试穿, 试衣

fitting[2] *adj formal* right for a particular situation or occasion; APPROPRIATE[1]【正式】合适的, 恰当的: *I thought the memorial was a fitting tribute to the President.* 我认为这座纪念碑表现了对总统的一种恰当的敬意。| **it is fitting that** *It was not fitting that he remarried so soon after his wife's death.* 他在妻子死后这么快就再婚, 这是不合宜的。

fitting room /ˈ.. ./ *n* [C] an area in a shop where you can put on clothes to see how they look〔商店里的〕试衣室

Fitz·ger·ald /fɪtsˋdʒɛrəld; fɪtsˈdʒerəld/, **El·la** /ˋɛlə; ˈelə/ (1918-96) a US JAZZ singer, called 'The First Lady of Jazz' because of her beautiful voice and her skill in SCAT singing 菲茨杰拉德〔(1918-1996), 美国爵士乐歌手。她因优美的嗓音和高超(模拟乐器)的拟声技巧而被誉为"爵士乐第一夫人"〕

Fitzgerald, F. Scott (1896-1940) a US writer whose NOVELS include *The Great Gatsby* and *Tender is the Night*. 菲茨杰拉德〔(1896-1940), 美国作家。他的小说包括《了不起的盖茨比》和《夜色温柔》〕

five /faɪv; faɪv/ *number* **1** 5 五 —see table on page C1 参见 C1 页附录 **2** a piece of paper money worth $5 or £5 五美元钞票; 五英镑钞票: *Do you have two fives for a ten?* 你有两张五美元的钞票来换一张十美元的吗? —see also 另见 FIVER **3 give sb (a) five** to hit the inside of someone's hand with your hand to show that you are very pleased about something 与某人击掌〔表示十分高兴〕 **4 take five** used to tell people to stop working for a few minutes 停下来休息几分钟 **5 five-day/five-month/five-year** happening or continuing for five days, months, or years 五天的/五个月的/五年的: *I've got a five-month contract in Bahrain.* 我在巴林有一项五个月的合同。**6 fives** [U] a British ball game in which the ball is hit with the hand against any of three walls〔英国的〕墙手球 —compare 比较 HANDBALL (1) —see also 另见 HIGH FIVE, NINE-TO-FIVE

five-and-ten /ˌ. . ˈ./ also 又作 **five-and-dime** *n* [C] *AmE old-fashioned* a shop that sells many different types of inexpensive goods, especially for the house; DIME STORE【美, 过时】五分一角店, 〔出售廉价日用商品的〕杂货店, 小零售店

five o'clock shad·ow /ˌ. . . ˈ. ./ *n* [singular] the dark colour on a man's chin where the hair has grown a little bit during the day〔早上刮过后当天又长出的〕短胡子茬

fiv·er /ˈfaɪvə; ˈfaɪvə/ *n* [C] *BrE* £5 or a five pound note【英】五英镑(钞票): *It's only a fiver to get in.* 只要五英镑就可以进去。

five-spot /ˈ. ./ *n* [C] *AmE old-fashioned* a piece of paper money worth $5【美, 过时】五美元钞票: *It only costs a five-spot.* 这只需花费五美元。

five-star /ˈ. ./ *adj* [only before noun 仅用于名词前] a five-star hotel or restaurant is very good〔酒店或餐厅〕五星级的, 第一流的

five star gen·e·ral /ˈ. . ˈ. . ./ *n* [C] *AmE* a GENERAL who commands an army【美】五星上将

five-stones /ˈ. ./ *n* [U] *BrE* a children's game in which the players try to pick up small objects between throwing one of them into the air and catching it【英】五石游戏〔一种儿童玩的小物件抛接游戏〕

fix[1] /fɪks; fɪks/ *v* [T] (S2, W2)

1 ►REPAIR 修理◄ to repair something that is broken or not working properly 修理; MEND[1] (1b) *BrE*【英】: *Dad's outside fixing the brakes on the Chevy.* 爸爸在外面修理那辆雪佛兰汽车的刹车。

2 ►LIMIT 限制◄ to decide on a limit for something, especially prices, costs etc, so that they do not change 确定, 决定〔价格、成本等〕: [+at] *The interest rate has been fixed at 6.5%.* 利率已经定为6.5%。

3 fix a time/day/place etc to decide on a particular time etc when something will happen 确定时间/日期/地点等: *Have you fixed a date for the wedding yet?* 你确定了婚礼的日期吗?

4 ►ARRANGE 安排◄ also 又作 **fix up** to make arrangements for something 安排: *If you want to meet the big boss, I can fix it.* 如果你想见那位大老板, 我可以安排一下。

5 ►FASTEN 使牢固◄ to fasten something firmly to something else, so that it stays there permanently 使固定[牢固]: **fix sth to/on** *We fixed the shelves to the wall using screws.* 我们用螺钉把架子装在墙上。

6 ►MAKE FOOD 准备食物◄ *informal especially AmE* to prepare a meal or drinks【非正式, 尤美】准备〔食物或饮料〕: *I watched the kids while he fixed dinner.* 他做晚饭时我照看孩子。| **fix sb sth** *I'll fix you a whisky sour.* 我给你倒一杯威士忌酸味酒。

7 fix your attention/eyes/mind etc on to think about or look at someone or something carefully 把注意力/双眼/思想等集中在…: *Aziz tried to fix his mind on the job at hand.* 阿齐斯努力想把思想集中在手头的工作上。

8 ►HAIR ETC 头发等◄ *especially AmE* to make your hair or MAKE-UP look neat and attractive【尤美】使〔头发、化妆〕整洁[漂亮], 美容: *Who fixed your hair for the wedding?* 你婚礼时的发式是谁给你梳的? | **fix your face** (=put make-up on your face) 化妆 *Hold on. Let me just fix my face before we go out.* 等等, 让我在我们出去之前化一下妆。

9 ►CAT/DOG 猫/狗◄ *AmE informal* to do a medical operation on a cat or dog so that it cannot have babies; NEUTER[2]【美, 非正式】阉割〔猫、狗〕

10 ►RESULT OF COMPETITION 竞赛的结果◄ to arrange an election, game etc dishonestly, so that you get the result you want 用不正当的手段操纵〔选举、比赛等的〕结果: *The fight must have been fixed. Nobody goes down that easily!* 这场拳击赛肯定是有人操纵的。没有人会那么容易倒下去的!

11 ►PUNISH 惩罚◄ *informal* to punish someone for something they have done【非正式】惩罚, 收拾: *I'll fix him for taking my car without my permission!* 他未经许可开我的车, 我得教训教训他!

12 fix sb with a stare/glare/look etc to look directly into someone's eyes for a long time 瞪眼看[凝视]某人: *Rachel fixed him with an icy stare.* 雷切尔冷冰冰地盯着他看了一会儿。

13 ►PAINTINGS/PHOTOGRAPHS 绘画/照片◄ to use a chemical process on paintings, photographs etc that makes the colours or images permanent 定影〔使颜色或图像持久〕

14 be fixing to do sth *AmE spoken* an expression meaning to prepare to do something, used in some parts of the US【美口】正准备[正打算]做某事: *I'm fixing to go to the store. Do you need anything?* 我正准备上商店去。你需要什么东西吗?

F

15 ▸CURE 治愈◂ *AmE informal* to make a part of the body that is damaged completely better【美, 非正式】治愈: *They'll fix your leg for you.* 他们会为你把腿治好的。

fix on sth/sb *phr v* [T] to choose a suitable thing or person especially after thinking about it carefully〔尤指经过认真考虑后〕选定, 确定: *We've finally fixed on a place to have the concert.* 我们最后确定了举行音乐会的地点。

fix sb/sth ↔**up** *phr v* [T] **1** to arrange a meeting, event etc, especially by persuading someone to agree to it〔尤指说服某人后〕安排: *We'll have to fix up a time to meet.* 我们得安排一个见面的时间。| **fix up to do sth** *BrE*【英】*I've fixed up to be in Toronto for the next conference.* 我已经安排好到多伦多参加下次会议。**2** to improve something or make it suitable 修理; 整理: *We fixed up the guest bedroom before my parents came to stay.* 我们在父母来住之前收拾了客房。**3** to provide someone with something they want 供给, 提供: [**+with**] *Can you fix me up with a bed for the night?* 你能弄张床让我过夜吗? **4** to find a suitable romantic partner for someone 为〔某人〕找女[男]友: *Bring your brother too. I'm sure we can find someone to fix him up with.* 把你的兄弟也带来吧。我确信我们能找个人陪他。

fix² *n* **1 be in a fix** to have a problem that is difficult to solve 处于困境, 遇到难题: *We were in a real fix. The car broke down and there wasn't a phone in sight.* 我们遇到大麻烦了。车子抛锚了, 而且看不到有电话。**2** [singular] an amount of something, especially an illegal drug, that you often use and badly want〔一剂〕上瘾的东西, 毒品: *addicts looking for a fix* 寻找一剂毒品的瘾君子 | *I need my fix of caffeine in the morning or I can't think.* 我清早需要一点咖啡因, 不然就无法思考问题。**3** [singular] something that has been dishonestly arranged 受操纵的事情: *The election was a fix!* 这次选举是受人操纵的! **4 get a fix on sb/sth a)** to find out exactly where someone or something is 确定某人/某物的位置: *The search boat can't get a fix on the yacht's position.* 搜救船无法确定游艇的位置。**b)** to understand what someone or something is really like 弄明白某人/某事到底如何: *I sat and stared for a while, trying to get a fix on the situation.* 我坐下来, 呆看了一会儿, 想弄清情况。

fix·a·ted /ˈfɪkˌsetɪd; fɪkˈseɪtɪ̣d/ *adj* **1** always thinking or talking about one particular thing〔思考或谈话〕专注的; 依恋的: [**+on**] *Jeremy seems to be fixated on this idea of travelling around the world.* 杰里米似乎一心想要周游世界。**2** *technical* having stopped developing emotionally or mentally【术语】〔情感或精神〕停止发展的, 固着的

fix·a·tion /fɪksˈeʃən; fɪkˈseɪʃən/ *n* [C] **1** an unnaturally strong interest in or love for someone or something 不正常的依恋, 固恋: [**+about/with**] *Trevor's got this fixation about cleanliness.* 特雷弗有洁癖。**2** *technical* a kind of mental illness in which someone's mind or emotions stop developing, so that they are like a child【术语】〔心理或情感〕固着

fix·a·tive /ˈfɪksətɪv; ˈfɪksətɪv/ *n* [C,U] **1** a substance used to glue things together or to hold things such as hair or false teeth in place 固定剂 **2** a chemical used on a painting or photograph so that the colours do not change 定色剂, 定影剂

S3 W3 **fixed** /fɪkst; fɪkst/ *adj* **1** firmly fastened to a particular position 固定的: **be fixed to/in/on** *The tables are fixed to the floor.* 这些桌子都固定在地板上。**2** times, amounts, meanings etc that are fixed cannot be changed〔时间、数量、意思等〕确定的, 不变的: *The classes begin and end at fixed times.* 上下课的时间都是固定的。| *fixed prices* 固定价格 **3 have fixed ideas/opinions** to have very definite ideas or opinions which are often unreasonable 有固执的想法/看法: [**+about/on**] *He has very fixed ideas about how a wife should behave.* 他对一个妻子应如何表现有很固执的想法。**4 how are you fixed for** *spoken* used to ask someone how much of something they have【口】你有多少…?: *How are you fixed for cash?* 你有多少现金? **5 fixed expression/smile/frown etc** a fixed smile, expression etc does not change and does not seem to express real emotions 固定[僵化]的表情/微笑/皱眉等 **6 have no fixed abode/address** *law BrE* to not have a permanent place to live【法律, 英】无固定住所[住址], 居无定所

fixed as·sets /ˌ· ˈ· ·/ *n* [plural] *technical* land, buildings, or equipment that a business owns and uses【术语】固定资产

fixed cap·i·tal /ˌ· ˈ· · ·/ *n* [U] *technical* buildings or machines that a business owns and that can be used for a long time to produce goods【术语】固定资本

fixed charge /ˌ· ˈ·/ *n* [C] a cost that does not change for a long time 固定费用, 固定收费

fixed costs /ˌ· ˈ·/ *n* [plural] *technical* costs, such as rent, that a business has to pay even when it is not producing anything【术语】固定成本

fix·ed·ly /ˈfɪksɪdlɪ; ˈfɪksɪ̣dli/ *adv* looking at, or thinking about only one thing 固定地; 专注地: *Anna stared fixedly ahead, trying to concentrate on the road.* 安娜凝视前方, 力求把注意力集中在道路上。

fix·er /ˈfɪksɚ; ˈfɪksə/ *n* [C] someone who is good at arranging events, situations etc for other people so that they have the results they want, especially by using dishonest or illegal methods 代人行贿[疏通]者

fix·ings, the /ˈfɪksɪŋz; ˈfɪksɪŋz/ *n AmE* the vegetables, bread etc that are eaten with meat at a large meal【美】〔主菜以外的〕配菜; TRIMMINGS (3) *BrE*【英】: *turkey with all the fixings* 火鸡肉加各种配菜

fix·i·ty /ˈfɪksətɪ; ˈfɪksɪ̣ti/ *n* [U] *formal* the state of not changing【正式】固定性, 稳定性: *fixity of purpose* 目标的固定性

fix·ture /ˈfɪkstʃɚ; ˈfɪkstʃə/ *n* [C] **1** [usually plural 一般用复数] a piece of equipment that is fixed inside a house or building and is sold as part of the house〔房屋或建筑物内的〕固定装修物; 固定附着物: **the fixtures and fittings** *BrE* (=all the pieces of equipment that are normally included as part of a house or building)【英】〔房屋的〕固定装置和设备 **2 be a (permanent) fixture** to be always present and not likely to move or go away 是固定存在物; 是永不离去的人[物]: *The dog became a permanent fixture in our lives.* 这条狗成为我们生活中不可缺少的一部分。**3** *BrE* a sports match that has been arranged for a particular time and place【英】〔预定举行的〕体育比赛: *a list of this season's fixtures* 本赛季各场比赛一览表

fizz¹ /fɪz; fɪz/ *v* [I] if a liquid fizzes, it produces a lot of BUBBLES[1] (1) and makes a continuous sound〔液体〕冒泡并嘶嘶作响: *champagne fizzing out of the bottle* 冒着气泡嘶嘶地流出瓶子的香槟酒 —see picture on page A19 参见 A19 页图

fizz² *n* [singular,U] **1** the BUBBLES[1] (1) of gas in some kinds of drinks or the sound that they make 饮料的泡沫; 嘶嘶声 **2** *BrE informal* CHAMPAGNE【英, 非正式】香槟酒

fiz·zle /ˈfɪzl; ˈfɪzəl/ *v*

fizzle out *phr v* [I] *informal* to gradually stop happening, especially because people become less interested in something【非正式】〔因越来越不感兴趣而〕终于失败, 渐停; 夭折: *Their romance just fizzled out.* 他们的罗曼史逐渐结束了。

fiz·zy /ˈfɪzɪ; ˈfɪzi/ *adj* **1** a fizzy liquid contains BUBBLES[1] (1) of gas〔液体〕起泡的 —opposite 反义词 FLAT[1] (4) **2 fizzy drink** *BrE* a sweet, non-alcoholic drink with BUBBLES of gas; SOFT DRINK【英】汽水

fjord, fiord /ˈfjɔrd; ˈfiːɔːd/ *n* [C] a narrow area of sea between high cliffs on the coast of Norway〔挪威海岸边的〕峡湾

FL the written abbreviation of 缩写= FLORIDA

flab /flæb; flæb/ *n* [U] *informal* soft, loose fat on a person's body【非正式】〔人体上〕松弛的脂肪[肌肉]

flab·ber·gas·ted /ˈflæbɚˌgæstɪd; ˈflæbəgɑːstɪ̣d/ *adj informal* extremely surprised or shocked【非正式】大吃一惊的, 目瞪口呆的: *Teachers were flabbergasted at the decision to close down the school.* 教师们对关闭学校的决定大吃一惊。

flab·by /ˈflæbɪ; ˈflæbi/ *adj informal*【非正式】**1** having soft, loose fat rather than strong muscles 松弛的, 松垂的: *She's getting old and flabby.* 她年纪大了, 肌肉松弛。**2** a flabby argument, excuse etc is weak and not effective〔论点、借口等〕无力的 —**flabbiness** *n* [U]

flac·cid /ˈflæksɪd; ˈflæsɪ̣d/ *adj technical* soft and weak instead of firm【术语】软弱的; 松垂的 —**flaccidity** /flækˈsɪdətɪ; flæˈsɪdɪ̣ti/ *n* [U]

flack /flæk, flæk/ *n* [U] another spelling of FLAK flak 的另一种拼法

flag¹ /flæg; flæg/ *n* [C] **1** a piece of cloth with a coloured pattern or picture on it that represents a country or organization 旗, 旗帜: *The children waved their flags as the Queen went by.* 女王走过时, 孩子们挥动着旗子。| *the flag of Texas* 得克萨斯州的州旗 | **a flag flies** (=a flag is shown on a pole) 挂起旗子 *Flags were flying at half-mast for the death of the Premier.* 为总理去世而下半旗致哀。**2** a coloured piece of cloth used as a signal 信号旗: *The flag went down, and the race began.* 信号旗一落下, 比赛便开始了。**3 under the flag of** if a group of people do something under the flag of a particular country or organization, they do it as representatives of that country or organization 在…的旗帜下; 代表… **4 the flag** an expression meaning a country or organization and its beliefs, values, and people 国家; 组织; 国家或组织代表的信仰、价值、人民等: *loyalty to the flag* 对国家的忠诚 **5 keep the flag flying** to achieve success on behalf of your country in a competition〔比赛中〕代表祖国获胜 **6** a FLAGSTONE〔铺地板或路的〕石板 —see also 另见 **fly the flag** (FLY[1](27))

CULTURAL NOTE 文化注释

In the US the national flag is very important and people are expected to treat it with respect. There is a flag in every school classroom, and children stand looking at the flag and say the Pledge of Allegiance (=a promise to be loyal to the country and the flag) every morning. They are usually taught how to fold the flag correctly. They are also taught that the flag may not be flown when it is raining or snowing, and that it should be taken down before dark each day. Many people put a flag in front of their houses on the Fourth of July and on Flag Day. After the attacks on the World Trade Center and the Pentagon on September 11, 2001, many people put flags on their houses and towns put a lot of flags along the streets to show their support for the country. 在美国，国旗十分重要，人们应敬重国旗。每个学校课堂都挂有国旗，学生每天起立注视国旗，背诵效忠词，通常还要学习如何正确折叠国旗。学生会学到：雨雪天不能升旗，每天天黑前要降旗。很多人在7月4日或国旗日这天在自己房屋前升旗。2001年9月11日世界贸易中心和五角大楼遭到袭击以后，很多人在房上插上国旗，城镇的街道上也竖立很多国旗，以示对国家的支持。

In the 1960s some people burned the flag as a protest against the Vietnam War and some Americans felt very strongly that this was wrong. People have burned the flag to protest against other political events, too. In the 1990s, however, the Supreme Court decided that burning the flag could be seen as an act of free speech, which is protected in the US CONSTITUTION. 20世纪60年代，很多人焚烧国旗抗议越南战争，一些美国人对此做法极不认同。人们也会焚烧国旗抗议其他政治事件。不过，20世纪90年代，美国最高法院裁定，焚烧国旗可以看做是一种言论自由行为的表现，受美国宪法保护。

In the UK, the flag is flown over official buildings, but ordinary people do not usually put the British flag on their houses. However, sometimes when there is an important football or RUGBY match being played by the English, Scottish, or Welsh national teams, some people put the English, Scottish, or Welsh flag on their houses. 在英国，国旗一般悬挂在政府建筑物上，但普通人一般不在自己房子上悬挂国旗。不过，有时英格兰、苏格兰或威尔士国家队有重要的足球或橄榄球赛事，有人会在房上悬挂英格兰、苏格兰或威尔士民族之旗。— see also 另见 STARS AND STRIPES, UNION JACK, Betsy ROSS

flag² **flagged, flagging** *v* **1** [T] make a mark against something to show that it is important〔用特殊记号〕标示，标出〔表示重要〕: *I've flagged the parts I want to comment on.* 我已经特别标示出我要评论的部分。**2** [I] to become tired or weak 疲倦；变虚弱: *By ten o'clock I was beginning to flag and went up to bed.* 到10点钟，我开始感到疲倦，就上床睡觉去了。

flag sb/sth ↔ **down** *phr v* [T] to make the driver of a vehicle stop by waving at them 挥手[打信号]使〔某人〕停车: *I flagged down a taxi.* 我挥手招呼一辆出租车停下。

Flag Day /ˈ· ·/ June 14th, a day in the US when people fly the US flag, remembering the day in 1777 when the Stars and Stripes (=US flag) was officially accepted and first used（美国的）国旗（纪念）日〔（6月14日），这一天美国人会升国旗，以纪念1777年星条旗被正式批准和首次投入使用的日子〕

fla·gel·lant /ˈflædʒələnt; ˈflædʒɪ̈lənt/ *n* [C] *formal* someone who whips themselves as a religious punishment【正式】自行鞭笞以赎罪的宗教信仰者

fla·gel·late /ˈflædʒəˌlet; ˈflædʒɪ̈leɪt/ *v* [T] *formal* to whip yourself or someone else, especially as a religious punishment【正式】鞭打，鞭笞〔尤作为宗教上的一种处罚〕

flag foot·ball /ˈ· ˌ· ·/ *n* [U] *AmE* a game like American football in which players tear off flags from around other players' waists instead of knocking them down【美】美式夺旗橄榄球 — compare 比较 TOUCH FOOTBALL

flagged /flægd; flægd/ *adj* covered with FLAGSTONES〔指道路、地面等〕铺石板的

flag·ging /ˈflægɪŋ; ˈflægɪŋ/ *adj* becoming tired, weaker, or less interested 疲倦的；逐渐衰弱的；失去兴趣的: *concern for the United States' flagging economy* 对美国逐渐衰退的经济的关注

flag·on /ˈflægən; ˈflægən/ *n* [C] a large container for liquids〔盛装液体的〕大肚壶

flag·pole /ˈflægˌpol; ˈflægpəʊl/ *n* [C] a tall pole on which a flag hangs; FLAGSTAFF 旗杆

fla·grant /ˈflegrənt; ˈfleɪgrənt/ *adj* **flagrant abuse/violation etc** a flagrant action is shocking because it is done in a way that is easily noticed and shows no respect for laws, truth etc 明目张胆的滥用/公然违反等: *flagrant disregard for human rights* 对人权的公然漠视 —**flagrantly** *adv*

flag·ship /ˈflægˌʃɪp; ˈflægʃɪp/ *n* [C] **1** the most important ship in a group of ships belonging to the navy, on which the ADMIRAL sails 旗舰 **2** the best and most important product, building etc that a company owns or produces〔某公司拥有或生产的产品、建筑等中〕最重要者: *the flagship of the new Ford range* 新福特汽车系列中的旗舰产品

flag·staff /ˈflægˌstæf; ˈflægstɑːf/ *n* [C] a tall pole on which a flag hangs; FLAGPOLE 旗杆

flag·stone /ˈflægˌston; ˈflægstəʊn/ *n* [C] a smooth flat piece of stone used for floors, paths etc〔铺地板或路等的〕石板

flag stop /ˈ· ·/ *n* [C] *AmE* a place where buses stop only if they are asked to do so【美】公共汽车招呼站

flag-wav·ing /ˈ· ˌ· ·/ *n* [U] the expression of strong national feelings, especially when these feelings seem too extreme 爱国情绪的强烈表现；沙文主义表现

flail¹ /flel; fleɪl/ *v* **1** [I,T] to wave your arms or legs in an uncontrolled way 胡乱地挥动〔手臂或腿〕: *His arms flailed above the surface of the water.* 他的双臂在水面上胡乱地挥动。**2** [T] to beat someone or something violently, usually with a stick〔用棍子〕敲打，殴打 **3** [I,T] to beat grain with a flail 用连枷打〔谷〕

flail² *n* [C] a tool consisting of a stick that swings from a long handle, used in the past to separate grain from wheat by beating it 连枷〔旧时用作打谷的农具〕

flair /flɛr; fleə/ *n* **1** [singular] a natural ability to do something very well 天赋，天分，才能: **have a flair for** *Carla has an instinctive flair for business.* 卡拉有经商的天分。**2** [U] a way of doing things that is interesting and shows imagination 独特的处事风格；时髦派头；新奇的创意: *Bates's advertising campaigns tended to lack flair.* 贝茨的广告攻势往往缺乏新意。

flak, flack /flæk; flæk/ *n* [U] **1** *informal* strong criticism【非正式】强烈的批评，抨击: **get/take flak** *The administration has taken a lot of flak over its decision to pull troops out of Somalia.* 政府从索马里撤军的决定遭到大量的批评。**2** bullets or shells (SHELL¹ (3)) that are shot from guns on the ground at enemy aircraft 高射炮火 —see also 另见 FLAK JACKET

flake¹ /flek; fleɪk/ *n* [C +of] **1** a very small flat thin piece that breaks away easily from something else 小薄片: *soap flakes* 肥皂片 —see also 另见 SNOWFLAKE —see picture on page A7 参见A7页图 **2** *AmE informal* someone who seems crazy【美，非正式】古怪的人；疯疯癫癫的人

flake² *v* **1** [I] also 又作 **flake off** to break off in small thin pieces（成片）剥落: *The paint is beginning to flake off.* 油漆开始剥落了。**2** [I,T] to break fish or another food into small thin pieces, or to break in this way（使）碎裂成小薄片: *Poach the fish until it flakes easily.* 把鱼加水煮到鱼肉容易分成薄片为止。

flake out *phr v* [I] *informal* to fall asleep because you are extremely tired【非正式】(累得)睡着: *Karl got home at eight o'clock and flaked out on the sofa.* 卡尔八点钟回到家，累得在沙发上睡着了。

flak jack·et /ˈ· ˌ· ·/ *n* [C] a special coat made of heavy material with metal inside it to protect soldiers and policemen from bullets〔有金属片的〕防弹衣

flak·y /ˈfleki; ˈfleɪki/ *adj* **1** tending to break into small thin pieces 易碎裂成薄片的: *rich, flaky pastry* 重油酥饼 **2** *informal especially AmE* slightly crazy【非正式，尤美】古怪的；疯疯癫癫的: *Carrie's pretty flaky but she's fun to be with.* 卡丽相当古怪，可是和她在一起很有趣。—**flakiness** *n* [U]

flam·bé /flɑmˋbe; ˈflɒmbeɪ/ also 又作 **flam·béed** /flɑmˋbed; ˈflɒmbeɪd/ *adj French* food that is flambéed has an alcoholic drink such as BRANDY poured over it to produce flames【法】〔食物〕浇酒〈如白兰地〉点燃后食用的 —see picture on page A15 参见A15页图

flam·boy·ant /flæmˋbɔɪənt; flæmˈbɔɪənt/ *adj* **1** behaving or dressing in a confident or surprising way that makes people notice you〔行为或衣着〕炫耀的，浮夸的: *his flamboyant stage personality* 他那极为造作的舞台风格 | *flamboyant gestures* 浮夸的姿态 **2** brightly coloured and easily noticed 色彩艳丽的: *flamboyant clothes* 色彩艳丽的衣服 —**flamboyantly** *adv* — **flamboyance** *n* [U]

flame¹ /flem; fleɪm/ *n* [C,U] **1** hot bright burning gas that you see when something is on fire 火焰，烈焰: *the flame of a candle* 烛火 | *Flames poured out of the windows of the building.* 火焰从大楼的窗户里不断冒出。—see picture at 参见 CANDLE 图 **2 in flames** burning strongly 熊熊燃烧: *The house was in flames by*

the time we arrived. 我们到达时，房子已在熊熊燃烧。**3 go up in flames/burst into flames** to begin burning suddenly and strongly 突然着火/失火: *I was driving along and the engine just burst into flames.* 我正开着车，发动机突然燃烧起来。**4 a flame of passion/desire/vengeance etc** *literary* a strong feeling【文】激情/欲火/强烈的复仇心等 —see also 另见 **old flame** (OLD¹ (13)), **naked flame** (NAKED (3)), **fan the flames** (FAN² (2)), **add fuel to the fire/flames** (FUEL¹ (3))

flame² *v* [I] **1** *literary* to become suddenly bright with light or colour, especially red or orange【文】变成火红色: *Her cheeks flamed for an instant.* 她的双颊马上通红了。**2** also 又作 **flame up** to suddenly burn more strongly or brightly 突然更炽烈地燃烧; (突然)爆发

fla·men·co /flə`mɛŋko; flə'meŋkəʊ/ *n* [C,U] a fast, exciting Spanish dance, or the GUITAR music that is played for this dance〔西班牙〕弗拉明科舞[音乐]

flamenco
弗拉明科舞

flame·proof /`flem,pruf; 'fleɪmpru:f/ also 又作 **flame re·sist·ant** /`· ·,··/ *adj* specially made or treated with chemicals so it does not burn easily 防火的，耐火的; 不易燃的

flame throw·er /`·,··/ *n* [C] a machine like a gun that shoots flames or burning liquid, used as a weapon or for clearing plants 喷火器; 火焰喷射器〔用作武器或清理植物〕

flam·ing /`flemɪŋ; 'fleɪmɪŋ/ *adj* [only before noun 仅用于名词前] **1 a flaming argument/row/temper** a very angry argument or temper 激烈的争论/激烈的争吵/火暴的脾气: *He had had a flaming row with his wife earlier that evening.* 在那天傍晚时分，他曾和妻子大吵了一场。**2** *BrE informal* used to emphasize what you are saying, especially when you feel annoyed【英，非正式】十足的，该死的〔尤用于不耐烦时加强语气〕: *You flaming idiot!* 你这十足的笨蛋! **3** covered with flames 燃烧着的，被火焰吞噬的

fla·min·go /flə`mɪŋgo; flə'mɪŋgəʊ/ *n* [C] a tropical bird that has very long thin legs, pink feathers, and a long neck 红鹳，火烈鸟

flam·ma·ble /`flæməbl; 'flæməbəl/ *adj* easily set on fire 易燃的: *Caution! Highly flammable chemicals.* 小心! 高度易燃化学品。—opposite 反义词 NONFLAMMABLE

flan /flæn; flæn/ *n* [C] *especially BrE*【尤英】**1** a round PIE (1) or cake that is filled with fruit, cheese etc 果馅饼，果酱饼 **2** *AmE* a sweet baked CUSTARD made with eggs【美】〔烤制的〕蛋奶糕 —compare 比较 PIE, QUICHE

Flan·ders /`flændəz; 'flɑ:ndəz/ a flat area consisting of what is now part of Belgium, the Netherlands, and northern France. Important battles were fought here in the First World War. 佛兰德〔包括现在的比利时、荷兰和法国北部的一部分平坦地区。一战期间，这里打过多场重大战役〕

Flanders, Moll —see 见 MOLL FLANDERS

flange /flændʒ; flændʒ/ *n* [C] the flat edge that stands out from the main surface of an object such as a railway wheel, to keep it in the right position 凸缘，法兰，〔火车的〕轮缘

flank¹ /flæŋk; flæŋk/ *n* [C] **1** the side of an animal's or person's body, between the RIBS¹ (1) and the HIP¹ (1) 胁部，胁腹 —see picture at 参见 HORSE¹ 图 **2** the side of an army in a battle or war〔军队在战役或战争中的〕侧翼: *We were attacked on our left flank.* 我们的左翼受到攻击。**3** the side of a hill, mountain, or very large building〔山或大建筑物的〕侧面

flank² *v* **be flanked by** to have something or someone on both sides 两侧有…: *Yeltsin emerged, flanked by his bodyguards.* 叶利钦出现了，两侧都有他的保镖。

flan·nel¹ /`flænl; 'flænl/ *n* **1** [U] soft cloth, usually made of cotton or wool, used for making clothes〔制衣用的〕法兰绒: *a flannel suit* 法兰绒套装 **2** [C] *BrE* a piece of cloth you use to wash yourself【英】〔洗澡用的〕法兰绒布块; WASHCLOTH *AmE*【美】**3** [U] *BrE informal* something that someone says that has no real meaning or is not sincere【英，非正式】废话，胡说，奉承话，兜圈子的说话 **4 flannels** [plural] *especially BrE* men's trousers made of flannel【尤英】法兰绒男装裤子

flannel² *v* [I] *BrE* to say things that are not sincere to avoid answering a question directly【英】〔为避开直接回答而〕兜圈子说

flan·nel·ette /,flænl`ɛt; ,flænəl'et/ *n* [U] soft cotton cloth used especially for night clothes, sheets etc〔尤用来做睡衣、被单等的〕绒布，棉法兰绒

flap¹ /flæp; flæp/ *n* **1** [C] a thin flat piece of cloth, paper, skin etc that is fixed by one edge to a surface, which you can lift up easily〔布、纸、皮等做的〕片状垂悬物〈如口袋盖等〉: *He lifted the tent flap slowly to see what was making the noise.* 他慢慢提起帐篷的布帘，看看是什么在发出声音。—see also 另见 CAT FLAP **2** [singular] the noisy movement of something such as cloth in the air 拍打声: *the flap of the sails* 帆的拍动声 **3** [singular] *informal* a situation in which people feel very excited, angry, or worried about something【非正式】慌乱，激动; 生气; 焦急: **be in a flap** *Rafi's in a bit of a flap over the wedding plans.* 拉菲对婚礼的安排略有点着急。—see also 另见 UNFLAPPABLE **4** [C] a part of the wing of an aircraft that can be raised or lowered to help the aircraft go up or down〔飞机的〕襟翼，副翼

flap² *v* **1** [I] if a bird flaps its wings, it moves its wings up and down in order to fly〔鸟〕振翼，扑动翅膀 **2** [I,T] if a piece of cloth, paper etc flaps it moves around quickly and noisily〔布、纸等〕呼啦呼啦地飘动，(使)摆动: *The flags were flapping in the breeze.* 旗帜在微风中飘扬。**3** [I] *BrE informal* to behave in an excited, nervous, or angry way【英，非正式】慌乱，激动，紧张; 生气: *There's no need to flap!* 不必紧张![不要生气!]

flap·jack /`flæp,dʒæk; 'flæpdʒæk/ *n* [C] **1** *BrE* a cake made of OATS, sugar, SYRUP, and butter【英】甜燕麦饼 **2** *AmE* a thick round unsweetened cake made of flour, milk, and eggs, cooked in a pan and eaten for breakfast; PANCAKE (2)【美】煎饼，烙饼

flap·per /`flæpɚ; 'flæpə/ *n* [C] a fashionable young woman in the late 1920s who wore short dresses, had short hair, and had ideas that were considered very modern〔20世纪20年代后期穿短裙、束短发、思想被认为十分现代的〕时髦女子

flare¹ /flɛr; fleə/ *v* **1** also 又作 **flare up** [I] to suddenly begin to burn, or to burn more brightly for a short time 突然烧起来;〔短暂地〕烧旺: *The match flared in the darkness.* 火柴在黑暗中猛然一闪。**2** also 又作 **flare up** [I] if strong feelings flare or flare up, people suddenly become angry, violent etc 突然爆发: *Violence has flared up again in the Middle East.* 中东突然又爆发了暴力事件。**3** also 又作 **flare up** [I] if a disease or illness flares up, it suddenly becomes worse〔疾病〕突然加剧: *My asthma tends to flare up on smoggy days.* 在烟雾天我的气喘就会加剧。**4** [I,T] to become wider towards the bottom end or edge, or to make something do this 张开，(使)展开: [+out] *The dress flared out from the hips.* 这件连衣裙从腰下开始展宽。| *flared trousers* 喇叭裤 | *The bull flared its nostrils and charged.* 公牛张大了鼻孔向前冲去。—see picture on page A17 参见 A17 页图

flare out at sb *phr v* [T] *AmE* to say something suddenly in an angry way【美】突然痛斥: *I said something about the weather and he flared out at me for no reason.* 我谈了谈天气，他却无缘无故地突然骂起我来。

flare² *n* **1** [C] a piece of equipment that produces a bright flame, or the flame itself, used outdoors as a signal 闪光信号，信号灯，信号弹: *Flares marked the landing site.* 信号灯标示了着陆地点。**2** [C usually singular 一般用单数] a sudden bright flame 闪光 **3 flares** [plural] trousers that become wide below the knee 喇叭裤

flare path /`· ·/ *n* [C] a path for aircraft to land on that is lit with special lights〔指引飞机着陆的〕照明跑道

flare-up /`· ·/ *n* [C] **1** a situation in which someone suddenly becomes angry or violent〔怒气或暴力事件的〕突然爆发: *Apart from one or two flare-ups the match went fairly smoothly.* 除了出现一两次争吵外，比赛进行得还很顺利。**2** a situation in which someone suddenly has problems because of a disease or illness after not having any problems for a long time〔疾病的〕突然发作: *a flare-up of her arthritis* 她关节炎的突然发作

flash¹ /flæʃ; flæʃ/ *v*

1 ►SHINE 发光◄ [I,T] to shine suddenly and brightly for a short time, or to make something shine in this way (使)闪光，闪亮: *The lightning flashed.* 闪电大作。| **flash sth into/at/towards** *Why is that guy flashing his headlights at me?* 那家伙为什么朝我闪前灯呢? | **flash on and off** (=shine for a short time and then stop shining) 一亮一灭 *Red warning lights flashed on and off.* 红色警告灯一闪一灭。

2 ►MOVE QUICKLY 迅速移动◄ [I always+adv/prep] to move very quickly 飞驰，掠过: [+by/past/through] *A couple of police cars flashed past, sirens wailing.* 几辆警车飞驰而过，警笛声呼啸着。

3 ►SHOW STH QUICKLY 快速亮出某物◄ [T] to show something to someone for only a short time 亮出〔随即收起〕: *He flashed his identification card.* 他出示了一下自己的身份证。

4 ►MEMORIES/IMAGES 记忆/印象◄ [I always+adv/prep] if thoughts, images, memories etc flash through your mind, you suddenly think of them or remember them 闪现: [+across/

through/into] *The possibility that Frank was lying flashed through my mind.* 我脑中忽然闪过一个念头，弗兰克可能是在撒谎。

5 ▶TIME 时间◀ [I always+adv/prep] if a period of time flashes by, past etc, it seems to end very quickly 一闪而过，飞逝：[+by/past] *Our vacation seemed to just flash by.* 我们的假期似乎只是一闪而过。

6 ▶PICTURES 图片◀ [I always+adv/prep] to be shown quickly on television or on a film〔在电视或电影中〕闪现：[+across/onto/past etc] *Images of the war flashed across the screen.* 战争的图像在屏幕上闪现。

7 ▶EYES 眼睛◀ [I] if your eyes flash, they seem to be very bright for a moment, especially because of a sudden emotion〔尤指由于突如其来的感情而〕闪耀，发亮：[+with] *Janet's blue eyes flashed with anger.* 珍妮特的蓝眼睛冒出了怒火。

8 ▶NEWS/INFORMATION 新闻/消息◀ [T always+adv/prep] to send news or information somewhere quickly by radio, computer, or SATELLITE (1)〔通过收音机、电脑或卫星〕迅速播出；传送：**flash sth to/throughout/all over etc** *News can be flashed all over the world within seconds of its happening.* 新闻可以在事情发生后的几秒钟之内发送到世界各地。

9 flash a smile/glance/look etc at sb to smile or look at someone quickly and for a short time 对某人一笑/一瞥/一看等

10 ▶SEX ORGANS 性器官◀ [I,T] if a man flashes, he shows his sexual organs in public〔男子〕当众暴露性器官，露阴

11 your life flashes before your eyes if your life flashes before your eyes, you suddenly remember many events from your life, especially because you are in great danger and might die〔尤指处于极度危险或临终时〕平生之事都闪现在眼前

flash sth **around** *phr v* [T] to show people that you have a lot of money in order to try and make them admire you 炫耀〔金钱〕: *wealthy clients flashing their credit cards around and buying everything in sight* 炫耀着信用卡、见到什么买什么的富有顾客

flash[2] *n*

1 ▶LIGHT 光◀ [C] a bright light that shines for a short time and then stops shining〔一闪而后消失的〕闪光：*flashes of lightning in the valley* 峡谷里的闪电光

2 ▶CAMERA 照相机◀ [C,U] a special bright light used when taking photographs indoors or when there is not much light 闪光灯：*Did the flash go off?* 闪光灯熄灭了吗？

3 in a flash/like a flash/quick as a flash very quickly 一会儿，马上：*Just wait here. I'll be back in a flash.* 就在这里等我。我马上就回来。

4 flash of brilliance/inspiration/intuition/anger if someone has a flash of brilliance, anger etc, they suddenly have a clever idea or suddenly have a particular feeling 才华/灵感/直觉/怒气的闪现：*Her essays show occasional flashes of brilliance.* 她的论文偶尔显露出她的才华。

5 ▶BRIGHT COLOUR/STH SHINY 艳丽的颜色/闪亮的东西◀ [C] if there is a flash of something brightly coloured or shiny, it appears suddenly for a short time 闪现物；惹人注目的东西：[+of] *The bird stood watching for the underwater flash of a turning fish.* 那只鸟站着，注视着水中瞬间一闪转身的一尾游鱼。

6 ▶LOOK 看◀ *BrE humorous* a quick look; GLIMPSE[2] (1)【英，幽默】一瞥

7 ▶SIGNAL 信号◀ the act of shining a light as a signal〔信号灯的〕闪亮：*Two flashes mean danger.* 两闪表示危险。

8 a flash in the pan a sudden success that ends quickly and is unlikely to happen again 昙花一现：*Rival record companies assumed the group would be a flash in the pan.* 作为竞争对手的几家唱片公司认为这个演唱组合只不过是昙花一现而已。

9 ▶MILITARY 军队的◀ a small piece of coloured cloth worn on the shoulder of a military uniform〔军装上的〕肩章 —see also 另见 NEWSFLASH

flash[3] *adj* **1** [only before noun 仅用于名词前] happening very quickly or suddenly, and lasting for only a short time 闪现的，突发的，短暂的：*Flash fires swept through the Los Angeles foothills last night.* 昨晚瞬间出现的山火横扫了洛杉矶的丘陵地带。—see also 另见 FLASH FLOOD **2** *BrE informal* looking very new, bright, and expensive-looking【英，非正式】奢华的，华丽的：*a big flash car* 一辆奢华的大车子 **3** *informal* [not before noun 不用于名词前] liking to have expensive clothes and possessions so that other people notice you【非正式】爱炫耀的：*Who was that flash geezer we saw you with last night?* 昨晚我们看见和你在一起的那个爱炫耀的家伙是谁？

flash·back /ˈflæʃ,bæk; ˈflæʃbæk/ *n* **1** [C,U] a scene in a film, play, book etc that shows something that happened before that point in the story〔书中的〕倒叙；〔戏剧的〕闪回场景；〔电影的〕闪回镜头：*The events of the hero's childhood are shown as a series of flashbacks.* 主人公的童年往事用一连串闪回镜头展现出来。**2** [C] a sudden very clear memory of something that happened to you in the past〔往事〕突然记起 **3** [C] *technical* a burning gas or liquid that moves back into a tube or container【术语】火舌回闪；回火〔指火循管道向气瓶或油罐退回〕

flash bulb /ˈ· ·/ *n* [C] a small BULB (=a bright light) used when you take photographs indoors or when it is dark outside〔摄影用的〕闪光灯泡

flash burn /ˈ· ·/ *n* [C] a burn that you get from being near a sudden, very hot flame, for example an explosion〔爆炸造成的〕闪光烧伤

flash·card /ˈflæʃkɑrd; ˈflæʃkɑːd/ *n* [C] a card with a word or picture on it, used in teaching〔上面有单词或图画，用于教学的〕抽认卡

flash·er /ˈflæʃɚ; ˈflæʃə/ *n* [C] a man who shows his sexual organs to women in public〔公开在女子前〕露阴的男子，暴露狂

flash flood /, · ˈ·/ *n* [C] a sudden flood that is caused by a lot of rain falling in a short period of time 暴洪，骤发的洪水

flash freeze /, · ˈ·/ *v* [T] to freeze food quickly so that the quality is not damaged 将〔食品〕速冻

Flash Gor·don /, · ˈ· ·/ a character who originally appeared in a US COMIC and films in the 1930s. Flash Gordon is a brave HERO who travels through space and saves the Earth from many dangers. 飞侠哥顿〔最早出现在20世纪30年代美国连环漫画和影片中的人物。他是一位勇敢无畏的英雄，穿越宇宙，拯救地球于危难之中〕

flash·gun /ˈflæʃ,gʌn; ˈflæʃgʌn/ *n* [C] a piece of equipment that lights a special bright light when you press the button on a camera to take a photograph〔摄影用的〕闪光枪

flash·light /ˈflæʃ,laɪt; ˈflæʃlaɪt/ *n* [C] a small electric light that you can carry in your hand 手电筒; TORCH[1] (1) *BrE*【英】

Flash·man /ˈflæʃmən; ˈflæʃmən/ a character in the 19th century NOVEL *Tom Brown's Schooldays* who is a cruel BULLY and treats the younger boys at his school very badly 弗莱希曼〔19世纪小说《汤姆·布朗的学生时代》中的人物。他是个心狠手辣的流氓，在学校常欺侮低年级的男生〕

flash·point /ˈflæʃ,pɔɪnt; ˈflæʃpɔɪnt/ *n* [C] **1** a place where trouble or violence might easily develop suddenly and be hard to control〔动乱或暴力的〕爆发点，一触即发的地点：*Beirut is one of the flashpoints of the Middle East.* 贝鲁特是中东的一个战争热点。**2** [usually singular 一般用单数] *technical* the lowest temperature at which a liquid such as oil will produce enough gas to burn if a flame is put near it【术语】燃点，闪点，引火点

flash·y /ˈflæʃɪ; ˈflæʃi/ *adj informal* too big, bright, or expensive in a way that other people disapprove of【非正式】俗艳的，华而不实的：*Marc always drove large flashy cars.* 马克总是开豪华而俗气的大车子。

flask /flæsk; flɑːsk/ *n* [C] **1** *BrE* a special type of bottle that you use to keep liquids either hot or cold, for example when travelling【英】保温瓶 **2** a flat bottle usually used to carry alcohol 扁平小酒瓶 **3** a glass bottle with a narrow top, used in a LABORATORY〔实验室用的〕烧瓶

flasks 保温瓶；瓶子

thermos flask 保温瓶　hip flask 扁平小酒瓶

flat[1] /flæt; flæt/ *adj* **flatter, flattest**

1 ▶SURFACE 表面◀ smooth and level, without raised or hollow areas, and not sloping or curving 平的，平坦的：*a flat-bottomed boat* 平底船 | *a perfectly flat sandy beach* 十分平坦的沙滩 | **flat as a pancake** (=very flat) 非常平坦的 *The countryside near there is flat as a pancake.* 那儿附近的乡间地势非常平坦。

2 flat rate/price/fee etc a flat rate, price, amount of money etc is fixed and does not change or have anything added to it 统一[固定]的收费率/价格/费用等：*We charge a flat fee for car hire.* 我们的租车费是固定不变的。

3 ▶TYRE/BALL 轮胎/球◀ having no air or not enough air in it 没气的，气不足的

4 ▶DRINK 饮料◀ having lost its BUBBLES[1] (1) of gas and so not tasting fresh 跑了气的：*This Coke must have been opened ages ago – it's completely flat!* 这瓶可乐一定是老早就打开的——气全跑光了！—opposite 反义词 FIZZY (1)

5 ▶NOT INTERESTING 没有趣味的◀ [not before noun 不用于名词前] a performance, book etc that is flat seems rather boring〔演出、书等〕沉闷乏味的，平淡的

F

S2 W2

6 ▶BATTERY 蓄电池◀ *BrE* a flat BATTERY (1) has lost its electrical power【英】电用完了的: **go flat** (=become flat) 电用完, 没电了 *Have you checked that the batteries haven't gone flat?* 你检查过电池有没有电吗?

7 ▶BUSINESS/TRADE 生意/贸易◀ not busy 不景气的, 不兴旺的: *The building industry's been completely flat for several years.* 建筑业已经萧条了好几年。

8 E flat/B flat/A flat etc a musical note that is one SEMITONE lower than the note E, B, A etc 降E调/降B调/降A调等〔音乐中降半音〕

9 ▶MUSICAL SOUND 音乐声◀ if a musical note is flat, it is played or sung at a slightly lower pitch (PITCH¹ (3)) than it should be 降音的; 偏低的: *The guitar was flat through the whole song.* 吉他的音调在整首歌里都偏低。

10 ▶VOICE 嗓音◀ not showing much emotion, or not changing much in sound as you speak 平淡的, 无变化的: *"He's dead," she said in a flat voice.* "他死了。"她语调平淡地说道。

11 flat refusal/denial etc a refusal etc that is definite and which someone will definitely not change 断然拒绝/否认等: *Our requests were met with a flat refusal.* 我们的要求遭到断然拒绝。

12 and that's flat! *spoken* used to say that you will definitely not change what you have just said【口】绝无二话; 不必多说了: *I won't go, and that's flat!* 我不去, 绝无二话!

13 be flat on your back a) to be lying down so that all of your back is touching the floor 平躺在地上: *Arthur was flat on his back under the car.* 阿瑟平躺在车子下。**b)** to be very ill so that you have to stay in bed for a period of time 卧病在床

14 ▶SHOES 鞋◀ flat shoes have very low heels〔鞋〕平底的, 无后跟的 —see picture on page A17 参见A17页图

15 ▶NOT DEEP 不深的◀ not very deep, thick, or high, especially in comparison to its width or length〔尤指与宽或长相比〕浅的; 薄的; 矮的: *a round, flat apple tart* 一块又圆又薄的苹果饼

16 ▶LIGHT 光◀ having little variety of light and dark 无深浅反差的, 无明暗的, 缺乏层次的: *Flat lighting is typical of Avedon's portraits.* 缺乏明暗层次变化是埃夫登拍摄的肖像照的典型特征。—**flatness** *n* [U] —see also 另见 **fall/go into a flat spin** (SPIN² (4))

2 3 **flat²** *n* [C]

1 ▶PLACE TO LIVE 住的地方◀ *BrE* a place for people to live that consists of a set of rooms that are part of a larger building【英】一套住房; 一套公寓房; APARTMENT *AmE*【美】: *They have a flat in Crouch End.* 他们在克劳奇恩德有一套住房。| *a ground-floor flat* 底层的住房 | **a block of flats** (=a large building with many flats in it) 公寓楼

2 ▶TYRE 轮胎◀ *especially AmE* a tyre that does not have enough air inside【尤美】扁胎; PUNCTURE *BrE*【英】

3 ▶MUSIC 音乐◀ **a)** a musical note that is one SEMITONE lower than a particular note〔音符的〕降半音 **b)** the sign (♭) in written music that shows that a note is one SEMITONE lower than a particular note 降号 —compare 比较 SHARP³, NATURAL² (2) —see picture at 参见 MUSIC 图

4 ▶LAND 土地◀ **flats** [plural] an area of land that is at a low level, especially near water 低洼沼泽地; 浅滩: *mud flats* 淤泥滩

5 the flat of sb's hand/a knife/a sword etc the flat part or flat side of something 手掌/刀面/剑面等

6 on the flat *BrE* on ground that is level and does not slope【英】在平地上: *It's much easier walking on the flat.* 在平地上走路容易多了。

This graph shows how common the nouns **flat** and **apartment** are in British and American English. 本图表所示为名词flat和apartment在英国英语和美国英语中的使用频率。

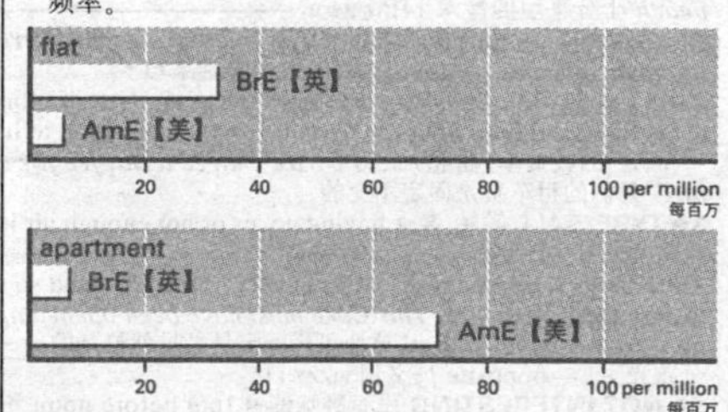

Based on the British National Corpus and the Longman Lancaster Corpus
据英国国家语料库和朗文兰开斯特语料库

In British English **flat** is used to mean a place where people live, which has a set of rooms including a kitchen and bathroom, and is part of a larger building. Americans use **apartment** for this meaning. In both British and American English **apartment** can be used to mean a large room with expensive furniture, decorations etc, used especially by an important person such as a president or prince. 在英国英语中, flat用来表示属于大楼一部分的一套房间(包括厨房和浴室), 作为人们的住所。美国人用apartment来表示这个意思。在英国英语和美国英语中, apartment可用来指有昂贵家具、装饰豪华的大房间, 特别是像总统或王子这样的大人物使用的大房间。

flat³ *adv*

1 ▶FLAT POSITION 平直的姿势◀ in a position in which the surface of something is against another surface without curving or sloping 平直地, 平坦地: **lie flat** *He lay flat on the floor to look for it under the bed.* 他平躺在地上, 向床底下寻找它。

2 three minutes/10 seconds etc flat *informal* used to emphasize that something happens or is done very quickly【非正式】正好三分钟/十秒钟等〔用于强调事情发生的速度或做事的速度很快〕: *I was dressed in five minutes flat.* 我只用了五分钟就穿好衣服了。

3 fall flat *informal*【非正式】**a)** if a joke or story falls flat, people are not amused by it〔笑话或故事〕不逗乐; 不好笑; 没引人笑: *Oh Dear! My joke about fat people fell completely flat, didn't it?* 啊, 亲爱的!我说的那些有关胖人的笑话一点都不好笑, 是吗? **b)** if something you have planned falls flat it is unsuccessful〔计划中所做的事〕完全失败

4 ▶MUSIC 音乐◀ if you sing or play music flat, you sing or play slightly lower than the correct note so that the sound is unpleasant 降音[调]地, 音调偏低 —compare 比较 SHARP² (4)

5 fall flat on your face a) to fall so that you are lying on your front on the ground 摔趴在地上 **b)** *informal* to not have the result you wanted or expected, especially when this is embarrassing【非正式】达不到预期的效果〔尤指造成窘迫〕: *It is a wonderful theory, but falls flat on its face when put into practice.* 这是一种美妙的理论, 但付诸实行时却完全行不通。

6 flat out a) *informal* as fast as possible【非正式】以最快速度, 以全速: *They were working flat out to get the job done on time.* 他们正以最快速度工作, 争取按时完工。**b)** *AmE spoken* in a direct way【美口】坦率地, 直截了当地: **ask/tell sb flat out** *She asked him flat out whether he'd been seeing another woman.* 她直截了当地问他是否在跟另一个女人约会。

7 tell sb flat *BrE spoken* to tell someone something directly and definitely【英口】直截了当地告诉某人: *I told him flat that I didn't want to see him again.* 我直截了当地告诉他我不想再见到他了。

8 go flat against *BrE spoken* to directly disobey someone or ignore them【英口】公然不服从, 公然漠视: *I don't know why you bother to ask – you'll go flat against my advice anyway!* 我不知道你干嘛还要问我 —— 你反正根本不会听我的话的! —see also 另见 **flat broke** (BROKE² (1))

flat cap /ˌ· ˈ·◂/ *n* [C] *BrE* a cap made of cloth, with a stiff piece that sticks out at the front【英】(低顶)鸭舌帽 —see picture at 参见 CAP 图

flat·car /ˈflæt,kɑr; ˈflætkɑː/ *n* [C] *AmE* a railway carriage without a roof or sides, used for carrying goods【美】〔铁路上运货的〕平板车, 敞车

flat-chest·ed /ˌ· ˈ··◂/ *adj* a woman who is flat-chested has small breasts〔妇女〕乳房小的, 平胸的

Flat Earth So·ci·e·ty, the /ˌ· ˈ· ·ˌ···/ an organization which believes that the Earth is flat and that science cannot be trusted. People sometimes mention its name when they are talking about someone whose ideas are impractical or unscientific. 地平说协会〔该组织认为地球是平的, 科学不可信。人们有时借用该名称指称想法不切实际或不科学的人〕

flat feet /ˌ· ˈ·/ *n* [plural] a medical condition in which someone's feet rest flat on the ground because the middle of each foot is not as curved as it should be (扁)平足

flat·fish /ˈflæt,fɪʃ; ˈflæt,fɪʃ/ *n* [C] a type of sea fish with a thin flat body such as COD or PLAICE 比目鱼〈如鳕、鲽〉

flat-foot·ed /ˌ· ˈ··◂/ *adj* **1** having flat feet (扁)平足的 **2** *informal* moving in an awkward way; CLUMSY (1)【非正式】拖着脚步走的, 蹒跚而行的 **3** *informal* dealing with situations in a way that is not sensitive to other people's thoughts or feelings【非正式】〔对别人的想法和感情〕不敏感的; 麻木漠然的: *Her husband's grasp on life is flat-footed and practical.* 她的丈夫对生活的看法是淡然的, 很注重实际。**4 catch sb flat-footed** *AmE old-fashioned* to find someone not working at a time when they should be【美, 过时】当场捉住某人偷懒

flat i·ron /ˈ· ·ˌ·/ *n* [C] a type of iron used in the past that was not heated by electricity〔旧时不用电的〕熨斗; 烙铁

Flat I·ron Build·ing, the /ˈ· · ·, · ·/ a tall office building in New York City, which is shaped like a very large IRON (=the thing you use for making clothes smooth) 熨斗大厦〔纽约市一座形似大熨斗的办公大厦〕

flat·let /ˈflætlɪt; ˈflætlɨt/ *n* [C] *BrE* a small apartment【英】小套房, 小公寓房

flat·ly /ˈflætlɪ; ˈflætli/ *adv* **1 flatly refuse/deny/oppose etc** to say something in a direct and definite way that is not likely to change 断然拒绝/否认/反对等: *She flatly refused to tell us where he was.* 她断然拒绝告诉我们他在哪儿。**2** without showing any emotion 平淡地: *"Aunt Alicia has changed her will," she said flatly.* "艾丽西亚姑姑已经改了遗嘱。"她平淡地说道。

flat·mate /ˈflætˌmet; ˈflætmeɪt/ *n* [C] *BrE* someone who shares a flat with one or more other people【英】合住公寓套房者; ROOMMATE (2) *AmE*【美】

flat rac·ing /ˈ· ˌ· ·/ *n* [U] horse racing without any fences on flat ground〔无障碍物的〕平地赛马 —compare 比较 STEEPLECHASE (1)

flat share /ˈ· · ·/ *n* [C] *BrE* an arrangement in which two or more people share an apartment【英】合住公寓套房

flat·ten /ˈflætn̩; ˈflætn/ *v* **1** [I,T] also 又作 **flatten out** to make something flat or flatter or to become flat or flatter (使) 变平: *Noah flattened the cardboard boxes before throwing them away.* 诺厄先把纸箱弄平后才扔掉。| *The land flattened out as we neared the coast.* 我们接近海岸时, 地势变得低平了。**2** [T] to destroy a building or town by knocking it down, bombing it etc 夷平; 炸平: *Dresden was flattened in the war.* 德累斯顿在战争中被夷为平地。**3 flatten yourself against** to press your body against something 把身体紧贴在…: *I flattened myself against the wall.* 我把身体紧贴在墙上。**4** [T] *informal* to defeat someone completely and easily in a game, argument etc【非正式】〔在比赛、争论中〕轻而易举地击败[击倒, 驳倒]: *We flattened them 6-0.* 我们以6-0彻底击败他们。**5** [T] *informal* to hit someone very hard【非正式】猛打〔某人〕; 殴击〔某人〕

flat·tened /ˈflætn̩d; ˈflætnd/ *adj* [not before noun 不用于名词前] unhappy and embarrassed because of what someone has said about you〔因某人说的有关自己的话而感到〕沮丧的; 丢脸的

flat·ter /ˈflætɚ; ˈflætə/ *v* [T] **1** to praise someone in an insincere way in order to please them or get something from them 奉承, 讨好, 向…谄媚: *He flattered her, saying how beautiful her eyes were.* 他奉承她, 说她的眼睛有多美丽。**2 be flattered** to be pleased because someone has shown you that they like or admire you〔因被喜欢或看重而〕感到荣幸[高兴]: *I was flattered to be asked to write an article for the magazine.* 我很高兴获邀为那本杂志写了一篇文章。**3** to make someone look more attractive, thinner, or younger than they really are 使形象胜过〔本人〕: *outfits designed to flatter the fuller figure* 使丰满的身材更显婀娜而设计的套装 **4 flatter yourself** if you flatter yourself that something is true about your abilities or achievements, you make yourself believe it is true, although it is not 自以为是, 自鸣得意: **flatter yourself that** *She flatters herself that she could have been a model.* 她自以为本来是可以当上模特儿的。

flat·ter·er /ˈflætərɚ; ˈflætərə/ *n* [C] someone who flatters people 阿谀奉承者, 拍马屁的人

flat·ter·ing /ˈflætərɪŋ; ˈflætərɪŋ/ *adj* clothes, pictures etc that are flattering make someone look more attractive than they really are〔衣服、照片等〕使比本人更漂亮的: *You look great! That colour is very flattering on you.* 你看上去太美了! 那种颜色让你更加漂亮。

flat·ter·y /ˈflætərɪ; ˈflætəri/ *n* [U] insincere praise 奉承, 恭维: *She uses a mixture of charm and flattery to get what she wants.* 她用魅力加恭维来达到自己的目的。| **flattery will get you nowhere!** *humorous spoken* (=flattery will not help you get what you want from me)【幽默, 口】恭维话行不通!

flat·top /ˈflætˌtɑp; ˈflæt-tɒp/ *n* [C] a type of hair style that is very short and looks flat on top〔指发式〕平顶头 —see picture at 参见 HAIRSTYLE 图

flat·u·lence /ˈflætʃələns; ˈflætjʊləns/ *n* [U] too much gas in the stomach 肠胃气胀 —**flatulent** *adj*

flat·ware /ˈflætˌwɛr; ˈflætˌweə/ *n* [U] *AmE* a word for knives, forks, and spoons; CUTLERY【美】(扁平) 餐具〔指刀、叉和匙〕

Flau·bert /floˈbɛr; ˈfləʊbeə/, **Gus·tave** /ˈgʌstav; ˈgʊstɑːv/ (1821-80) a French writer whose most famous work is the NOVEL *Madame Bovary* 福楼拜〔(1821-1880), 法国作家, 以小说《包法利夫人》最为有名〕

flaunt /flɔnt; flɔːnt/ *v* [T] **1** to show your money, success, beauty etc so that other people notice it 夸耀, 炫耀: *In New York the rich flaunt their wealth while the poor starve on the streets.* 在纽约, 富人炫耀自己的财富, 而穷人则流落街头挨饿。**2 if you've got it, flaunt it** *humorous spoken* used to tell someone not to hide their beauty, wealth, or abilities【幽默, 口】〔美丽、财富或能力〕如果拥有, 就要展示出来

flau·tist /ˈflɔtɪst; ˈflɔːtɨst/ *n* [C] *BrE* someone who plays the FLUTE【英】吹长笛的人; 长笛手; FLUTIST *AmE*【美】

fla·vor·ful /ˈflevɚfʊl; ˈfleɪvəfʊl/ *adj AmE* having a strong pleasant taste【美】味浓而可口的: *a flavorful Mexican dish* 美味可口的墨西哥菜

fla·vour[1] *BrE*【英】, **flavor** *AmE*【美】/ˈflevɚ; ˈfleɪvə/ *n* **1** [C] the particular taste of a food or drink 味, 味道: *Which flavor do you want – chocolate or vanilla?* 你要哪种味道的, 巧克力味还是香草味? **2** [U] the quality of tasting good or pleasant 美味, 味道: *A pinch of herbs will add flavour to any dish.* 一撮香草会给菜肴增添味道。**3** [singular] a quality or feature that makes something have a particular style or character 特色, 特点: *The stories have a strong regional flavour.* 这些故事有很强的地区特色。**4** [singular] an idea of what the typical qualities of something are 特色; 情调; 风味: *Marston's book gives you a flavour of life in the 16th century.* 马斯顿的书让你体会到16世纪的生活特色。**5 flavour of the month** the idea, person, style etc that is the most popular one for a short time 当前最受欢迎的思想[人物、风格等]: *Health care reform seems to be the political flavor of the month.* 医疗改革似乎是本月最受欢迎的政治话题。

flavour[2] *BrE*【英】, **flavor** *AmE*【美】—*v* [T] to give something a particular taste or more taste 加味于…, 使更有…味道

fla·voured *BrE*【英】, **flavored** *AmE*【美】/ˈflevɚd; ˈfleɪvəd/ *adj* **1 strawberry-flavoured/chocolate-flavoured etc** tasting of strawberries, chocolate etc 草莓味的/巧克力味的等 **2** having had a flavour added 加味的, 调味的: *flavored milk* 加了味道的牛奶

fla·vour·ing *BrE*【英】, **flavoring** *AmE*【美】/ˈflevərɪŋ; ˈfleɪvərɪŋ/ *n* [C,U] a substance used to increase the flavour of something 调味剂; 调味品: *This yoghurt contains no artificial flavourings.* 这种酸奶不含人造调味剂。

flaw /flɔ; flɔː/ *n* [C] **1** a mistake, mark, or weakness that makes something imperfect; DEFECT[1] 瑕疵, 缺点: *a slight flaw in the glass* 玻璃杯上的一小点瑕疵 **2** a mistake in an argument, plan, or set of ideas〔论点、计划或思想中的〕错误, 缺陷: **fundamental flaw** (=a very important mistake or weakness) 根本性的错误 *The lack of reliable statistics was a fundamental flaw in Walton's argument.* 缺乏可靠统计数字是沃尔顿论点的根本缺陷。| **fatal flaw** (=a very important weakness that makes something certain to fail) 致命的弱点 **3** a fault in someone's character〔性格上的〕缺点: *Jealousy is Othello's major flaw.* 妒忌是奥塞罗的主要缺点。

flawed /flɔd; flɔːd/ *adj* having a mistake or weakness 有缺点的, 有瑕疵的, 有错误的: *In many cases the data was incomplete or flawed.* 在许多情况下, 数据要么不完整, 要么有错误。

flaw·less /ˈflɔlɪs; ˈflɔːləs/ *adj* having no mistakes, marks, or weaknesses; PERFECT[1] (2) 无缺点的, 无痕的, 无瑕的: *Peterson's flawless performance as the hero* 扮演英雄的彼得森那完美的演出 —**flawlessly** *adv*

flax /flæks; flæks/ *n* [U] **1** a plant with blue flowers, used for making cloth and oil 亚麻 **2** the thread made from this plant, used for making LINEN (2) 亚麻纤维

flax·en /ˈflæksn̩; ˈflæksən/ *adj literary* flaxen hair is light in colour【文】〔头发〕亚麻色的, 淡黄色的

flay /fle; fleɪ/ *v* [T] **1** to criticize someone very severely 严厉批评, 痛斥: *I came out of the meeting feeling thoroughly flayed and harassed.* 我从会场走出来, 感觉受到彻底的严厉批评, 十分烦恼。**2** *literary* to whip or beat someone very severely【文】鞭打, 猛击

flea /fli; fliː/ *n* [C] **1** a very small insect without wings that jumps and bites animals and people to eat their blood 跳蚤 **2 send sb off with a flea in their ear** to talk angrily to someone, especially because they have done something you disapprove of〔尤指因某人做了你不赞成的事而〕用讥诮话气走某人

flea·bag /ˈfliˌbæg; ˈfliːbæg/ *n* [C] **1** *BrE* a dirty animal or person that you dislike【英】肮脏邋遢的动物[人] **2** *AmE* a cheap dirty hotel【美】廉价但肮脏的旅馆

flea·bite /ˈfliˌbaɪt; ˈfliːbaɪt/ *n* [C] the bite of a flea 蚤咬

flea col·lar /ˈ· ˌ· ·/ *n* [C] a special collar, worn by a dog or cat, that contains chemicals to keep fleas away from them〔给猫狗戴的含化学剂的〕灭蚤项圈

flea mar·ket /ˈ· ˌ· ·/ *n* [C] a market where old or used goods are sold 跳蚤市场〔卖旧货的市场〕

flea·pit /ˈfliˌpɪt; ˈfliːˌpɪt/ *n* [C] *old-fashioned humorous* a cheap dirty cinema or theatre【过时，幽默】蚤窝〔指廉价肮脏的电影院或剧院〕

fleck /flɛk; flek/ *n* [C] a small mark or spot 斑点；微粒：[+of] *flecks of dust* 尘土粒

flecked /flɛkt; flekt/ *adj* having small marks or spots 有斑点的：*red cloth flecked with white* 有小白点的红布

fledged /flɛdʒd; fledʒd/ *adj* —see 见 FULLY-FLEDGED

fledg·ling¹, fledgeling /ˈflɛdʒlɪŋ; ˈfledʒlɪŋ/ *n* [C] a young bird that is learning to fly 学飞的小鸟

fledgling², fledgeling *adj* [only before noun 仅用于名词前] a fledgling state, or organization, has only recently been formed and is still developing〔国家或组织〕新形成的：*a fledgling republic* 新建立的共和国

flee /fli; fliː/ *past tense and past participle* **fled** /flɛd; fled/ *v* [I, T] to leave somewhere very quickly in order to escape from danger 逃，逃走：*When they saw the police car, his attackers turned and fled.* 攻击他的人看到警车后转身就逃。| **flee the country/city** *We were forced to flee the country.* 我们被迫逃离这个国家。| [+from/to/into] *Many German artists fled to America at the beginning of World War II.* 第二次世界大战初期，许多德国艺术家逃到美国。

fleece¹ /flis; fliːs/ *n* [C] **1** the woolly coat of a sheep〔剪下而仍连在一起的〕羊毛 **2** an artificial soft material used to make warm coats〔用于制保暖衣服的〕人造柔软面料

fleece² *v* [T] *informal* to charge someone too much money for something【非正式】向…过多收费；高价欺诈；敲…的竹杠

fleec·y /ˈflisɪ; ˈfliːsi/ *adj* soft and woolly, or looking soft and woolly 羊毛的；羊毛似的；毛茸茸的：*fleecy white towels* 毛茸茸的白毛巾

fleet¹ /flit; fliːt/ *n* [C] **1** a group of ships, or all the ships in a navy 船队；舰队：*the US seventh fleet* 美国第七舰队 **2** a group of planes, cars etc that are controlled by one company〔某家公司控制的〕机群，车队：*a fleet of taxis* 出租车队

fleet² *adj literary* fast, quick【文】快速的，迅捷的：**fleet of foot** (=fast at running) 跑得快的，飞毛腿（的）

fleet ad·mi·ral /ˌ· ˈ···/ *n* [C] the highest rank in the US navy, or someone who holds this rank〔美国的〕海军五星上将 —see table on page C6 参见 C6 页附录

fleet·ing /ˈflitɪŋ; ˈfliːtɪŋ/ *adj* [usually before noun 一般用于名词前] lasting for only a short time 短暂的，飞逝的：**fleeting glimpse/impression/glance etc** *I caught a fleeting glimpse of them as they drove past.* 他们开车驶过时，我飞快地看了他们一眼。| **fleeting moment** *For one fleeting moment, I thought I recognized her.* 刹那间我觉得我认出了她。—**fleetingly** *adv*

Fleet Street /ˈ· ·/ *n* [singular] a street in London where many important newspaper offices used to be, often used as a name for the British newspaper industry 舰队街〔伦敦的一条街，过去为大报馆的办公所在地，常用来泛指英国报业界〕

Flem·ing /ˈflɛmɪŋ; ˈflemɪŋ/, **I·an** /ˈiən; ˈiːən/ (1908-64) a British writer who invented the character of James Bond and wrote many NOVELs about him 弗莱明〔(1908-1964)，英国作家。他塑造了詹姆斯·邦德这一人物形象，创作了许多有关邦德的小说〕

Flem·ing, Sir Al·ex·an·der /ˌælɪgˈzændə; ˌælɪgˈzɑːndə/ (1881-1955) a British scientist who discovered PENICILLIN, a substance that is used as a medicine to destroy BACTERIA (=very small living things related to plants, some of which cause disease) 弗莱明〔(1881-1955)，英国科学家，发现了青霉素[盘尼西林]〕

Fleming, Victor (1883-1949), a US film DIRECTOR who won an Oscar as best DIRECTOR for *Gone With the Wind* in 1939. His other films included *Captains Courageous* (1937), *The Wizard of Oz* (1939) and *Dr Jekyll and Mr Hyde* (1941). 弗莱明〔(1883-1949)，美国电影导演，1939年因电影《乱世佳人》获得奥斯卡最佳导演奖。他导演的其他电影包括《勇敢的船长》(1937)、《绿野仙踪》(1939) 和《化身博士》(1941)〕

Flem·ish /ˈflɛmɪʃ; ˈflemɪʃ/ *n* [U] a language like German spoken in northern Belgium 佛兰芒语〔比利时北部地区使用，近似德语〕

3 **flesh¹** /flɛʃ; fleʃ/ *n* [U] **1** the soft part of the body of a person or animal that is between the skin and the bones〔人或动物的〕肉：**flesh wound** (=a slight injury from a knife or bullet) 皮肉之伤 **2** the soft part of a fruit or vegetable that can be eaten 果肉，蔬菜的可食部分：*Cut the melon in half and scoop out the flesh.* 把瓜切成两半，然后挖出瓜肉。**3 in the flesh** if you see or meet someone in the flesh, you see or meet someone who you previously had only seen in pictures or films 本人：*Fans flocked to see their heroes in the flesh.* 影迷们成群结队去看他们的英雄本人。**4 make sb's flesh creep/crawl** to make someone feel frightened 使某人毛骨悚然[胆战心惊]：*The way he always stared at her made her flesh creep.* 他总是盯着她看的样子使她毛骨悚然。**5 your own flesh and blood** someone who is part of your family 亲人，亲骨肉：*I couldn't see my own flesh and blood insulted in this way.* 我不能眼睁睁看着我的亲人这样受侮辱。**6 the spirit is willing but the flesh is weak** used to say that you would like to do something, but are not strong enough, either physically or mentally, to do it 心有余而力不足，力不从心 **7 the flesh** *literary* the physical human body, as opposed to the mind or spirit【文】〔相对于心灵或精神的〕肉体：**the pleasures of the flesh** (=things such as drinking, eating a lot, or having sex) 肉体上的享受 **8 put flesh on** to give more details about something to make it clear, more interesting etc 充实，加细节于…：*I'll try to put some flesh on the plan Margaret has outlined.* 我将尽力使玛格丽特勾画的计划更为充实。**9 more than flesh and blood can stand/bear** used to describe something that you find too unpleasant to think about 常人所忍受不了的 **10 go the way of all flesh** *literary* to die【文】谢世，去世 —see also 另见 **get your pound of flesh** (POUND¹ (6)), **press the flesh** (PRESS² (15))

flesh² *v*

flesh sth ↔ **out** *phr v* [T] to add more details to something in order to improve it 使充实，使完善：*You need to flesh out your argument with a few more examples.* 你需要再多用几个案例来充实你的论点。

flesh-col·oured *BrE*【英】, **flesh-colored** *AmE*【美】/ˈ· ˌ··/ *adj* having a pinkish colour like that of white people's skin 肉色的，(白人) 肤色的：*flesh-coloured tights* 肉色紧身裤

flesh·ly /ˈflɛʃlɪ; ˈfleʃli/ *adj* [only before noun 仅用于名词前] *literary* physical, especially sexual【文】肉体的；〔尤指〕肉欲的

flesh·pots /ˈflɛʃˌpɑts; ˈfleʃpɒts/ *n* [plural] *humorous* areas where there are many places that people go to for pleasure, especially sexual pleasure【幽默】满足肉欲的场所；寻欢作乐的地方

flesh·y /ˈflɛʃɪ; ˈfleʃi/ *adj* **1** having a lot of flesh 多肉的：*the fleshy part of your hand* 你手掌上肉多的部分 **2** having a soft, thick inner part 肉质的：*a plant with dark green fleshy leaves* 带深绿色多肉质叶子的植物

flew /flu; fluː/ the past tense of FLY¹

flex¹ /flɛks; fleks/ *v* [T] **1** to tighten your muscles or bend part of your body 收紧〔肌肉〕；屈曲〔身体部位〕**2 flex your muscles** to show your ability to do something, especially your skill or power 展示你的实力〔尤指技艺或权势〕

flex² *n* [C] *BrE* an electrical wire covered with plastic, used to connect electrical equipment to an electricity supply【英】〔电器用〕花线，皮线；CORD¹ (3) *AmE*【美】—see also 另见 LEAD² (8)

flex·ib·il·i·ty /ˌflɛksəˈbɪlətɪ; ˌfleksəˈbɪləti/ *n* [U] **1** the ability to change or be changed easily to suit a different situation 灵活性 **2** the ability to bend or be bent easily 弹性，柔性

flex·i·ble /ˈflɛksəbl; ˈfleksəbəl/ *adj* **1** a person, plan etc that is flexible can change or be changed easily to suit any new situation 灵活的，可变通的：*We can be flexible about your starting date.* 我们对你开始的日期可灵活处理。—opposite 反义词 INFLEXIBLE **2** something that is flexible can bend or be bent easily 易弯曲的，有弹性的：*shoes with flexible rubber soles* 带弹性橡胶底的鞋 —**flexibly** *adv*

flex·i·time /ˈflɛksɪtaɪm; ˈfleksitaɪm/ *BrE*【英】, **flex·time** /ˈflɛkstaɪm; ˈflekstaɪm/ *AmE*【美】—*n* [U] a system in which people work a fixed number of hours each week or month, but can change the times at which they start and finish each day 弹性工作时间制

flick¹ /flɪk; flɪk/ *v* **1** [T] to make something move away by hitting or pushing it suddenly or quickly, especially with your thumb and finger〔尤指用大拇指和另一手指〕弹去，拂去：**flick sth from/off etc** *Papa flicked the ash from his cigar.* 爸爸弹去雪茄烟上的烟灰。| **flick sth ↔ away/off etc** *I flicked away the dandruff from his shoulders.* 我轻轻拂去他肩上的头皮屑。—see picture on page A20 参见 A20 页图 **2** [I always+adv/prep,T] to move with a sudden, quick movement or to make something move in this way 晃动，拍动；抖掉：[+from/up/down] *The cow's tail flicked from side to side.* 母牛的尾巴左右甩动。**3** [T] to make a light, machine etc stop or start working by pressing or moving a button 按动键钮啪地开动[关闭]：**flick sth ↔ on/off** *Sandra flicked the TV on.* 桑德拉啪地打开电视。**4** [T] if you flick something such as a whip or rope, you move it so that the end moves quickly away from you 用〔鞭或绳等〕轻拂，轻快地甩打：*Ricky flicked a towel at his sister's bare legs.* 里基用毛巾轻轻拍打他妹妹赤裸的双腿。

flick through sth *phr v* [T] to look at a book, magazine, set of photographs etc quickly 很快地浏览〔书、杂志、照片等〕

flick² *n* **1** [C] a short, light, sudden movement or hit with a part of your body, whip etc 轻打, 轻弹; 抖动: *With a flick of the wrist, Frye sent the ball into the opposite court.* 弗赖伊一抖手腕, 把球打到对方的球场。**2 a flick of a switch** used to emphasize how easy it is to start a machine and use it (只要) 轻轻一拨开关 (就行了)〔用来强调开动和使用机器很容易〕: *All it takes is a flick of a switch.* 所需要做的只是轻轻一拨开关。**3** [C usually singular 一般用单数] *old-fashioned especially AmE* a film【过时, 尤美】电影 **4 the flicks** *BrE old-fashioned* the cinema【英, 过时】电影院 **5 have a flick through** to look at a book, magazine, set of pictures etc very quickly 很快浏览〔书、杂志、照片等〕: *I had a quick flick through your report.* 我很快翻看了你的报告。

flick·er¹ /ˈflɪkɚ; ˈflɪkə/ *v* [I] **1** to burn or shine with an unsteady light that goes on and off quickly〔光〕闪烁, 摇曳: *The candle flickered.* 烛光摇曳着。**2** [always+adv/prep] if an emotion or expression flickers on someone's face or through their mind, it exists or is shown for only a short time〔感情或表情〕闪现: [+**across/through/on etc**] *A puzzled smile flickered across the lady's face.* 那位女士的脸上掠过一丝困惑的微笑。**3** to quickly make a sudden small movement or series of movements 抖动, 颤动: *Polly's eyelids flickered for a moment, then she slept.* 波莉的眼皮眨了一会儿, 然后她就睡了。

flicker² *n* [C] **1** an unsteady light that goes on and off quickly〔光的〕闪烁, 摇曳: *the flicker of the firelight* 火光的闪烁 **2 a flicker of interest/remorse/guilt etc** a feeling or expression that continues for a very short time 一时的兴趣/悔恨/内疚等 **3** a quick sudden movement or series of movements〔一次或一系列的〕抖动, 颤动

flick knife /ˈ· ·/ *n* [C] *BrE* a knife with a blade inside the handle that moves quickly into position when you press a button【英】弹簧刀; SWITCHBLADE *AmE*【美】

fli·er /ˈflaɪɚ; ˈflaɪə/ *n* another spelling of FLYER flyer 的另一种拼法

flies /flaɪz; flaɪz/ —see 见 FLY³

S3 W2 **flight** /flaɪt; flaɪt/ *n*

1 ▶TRAVEL 旅行◀ [C] a journey in a plane or space vehicle〔乘坐飞机或太空飞船的〕飞行: *It's an hour's flight to Paris from here.* 从这里坐飞机到巴黎要一小时。

2 ▶PLANE 飞机◀ [C] a plane making a particular journey 班机, 航班: *TWA Flight 284* 环球航空公司284号航班 | **call a flight** (=tell people the plane is ready to leave)〔机场中的广播系统〕通知旅客某班机即将起飞 *I've got to run – my flight's been called.* 我得快点走了——已经广播我的班机即将起飞了。—see also 另见 CHARTER FLIGHT

3 ▶FLYING 飞行◀ [U] the act of flying through the air 飞行, 飞翔: **in flight** *pelicans in flight* 飞翔中的鹈鹕

4 ▶STAIRS 楼梯◀ [C] a set of stairs between one floor and the next〔两个楼层间的〕一段楼梯: *Bert lives two flights down from here.* 伯特住在从这里下两层楼的地方。| **flight of stairs** *She tripped and fell down a whole flight of stairs.* 她绊了一跤, 从楼梯上摔下来, 摔了整整一段楼梯。

5 ▶ESCAPE 逃跑◀ [U] the act of escaping from a dangerous situation or a difficult problem〔从险[困]境中的〕逃走, 逃跑: [+**from**] *Donald Wood's hasty flight from South Africa early in 1978* 1978 年初唐纳德·伍德匆忙逃离南非

6 take (to) flight to run away in order to try and escape from someone 逃跑: *The rest of the gang took flight.* 其余的歹徒逃跑了。

7 put sb to flight *old-fashioned* make someone run away in order to try and escape【过时】使某人溃逃; 把某人赶得仓皇逃命

8 flight of imagination/fancy/fantasy thoughts, ideas etc that are full of imagination but that are not practical or sensible 驰骋的想象/幻想

9 ▶BIRDS 鸟类◀ [C] a group of birds all flying together 一群飞鸟: *a flight of swallows* 一群飞燕 —see also 另见 IN-FLIGHT, TOP-FLIGHT

flight at·tend·ant /ˈ· ·,·/ *n* [C] someone who looks after the comfort and safety of the passengers on a plane; STEWARD (1) or STEWARDESS 空中服务员

flight deck /ˈ· ·/ *n* [C] **1** the flat surface of a ship which military aircraft use to fly into the air from〔航空母舰的〕飞行甲板 **2** the room in a plane where the pilot sits to control the plane〔飞机的〕驾驶舱

Flight into E·gypt, the /,· · ˈ··/ a story in the Bible in which Joseph, Mary, and the baby Jesus run away to Egypt to escape from King Herod, who has ordered all male babies to be killed 逃往埃及〔《圣经》故事。希律王下令杀死所有男婴, 约瑟、马利亚和刚出生的耶稣因此逃往埃及〕

flight·less /ˈflaɪtləs; ˈflaɪtləs/ *adj* unable to fly 不能飞的: *a flightless bird* 一种不能飞的鸟

flight lieu·ten·ant /,· ·ˈ··/ *n* [C] *BrE* a middle rank in the British air force, or someone who holds this rank【英】空军上尉 —see table on page C7 参见 C7 页附录

flight path /ˈ· ·/ *n* [C] the course that a plane or space vehicle travels along〔飞机或太空飞船的〕飞行路线

flight re·cord·er /ˈ· ·,··/ *n* [C] a piece of equipment in an aircraft that records details such as the plane's speed and direction; BLACK BOX 飞行记录仪, 黑匣子

flight ser·geant /ˈ· ,··/ *n* [C] *BrE* a middle rank in the British air force, or someone who holds this rank【英】空军上士 —see table on page C7 参见 C7 页附录

flight sim·u·la·tor /ˈ· ,····/ *n* [C] a machine that imitates the movements of an aircraft, used to train pilots〔训练飞行员的〕飞行模拟器

flight·y /ˈflaɪtɪ; ˈflaɪti/ *adj* a woman who is flighty changes her ideas or activities a lot without finishing them or being serious about them〔女子〕反复无常的, 轻浮的, 见异思迁的 —**flightiness** *n* [U]

flim·flam /ˈflɪm,flæm; ˈflɪmflæm/ *n informal*【非正式】**1** [U] stories, information etc that do not seem serious or true 胡扯, 废话, 鬼话, 怪谈: *all this psychic flimflam* 所有这些有关通灵的鬼话 **2** [C usually singular 一般用单数] a trick intended to cheat someone 欺诈手段; 鬼把戏 —**flimflam** *v* [T]

flim·sy /ˈflɪmzɪ; ˈflɪmzi/ *adj* **1** flimsy cloth or clothing is light and thin, and can tear easily〔布或衣服〕轻而薄的, 易撕破的, 易磨损的: *a flimsy summer dress* 一件轻而薄的夏装连衣裙 **2** flimsy equipment, buildings etc are not well-made and are easily broken〔设备、建筑物等〕不结实的, 易损坏的 **3** a flimsy argument, excuse etc is not believable〔论点、借口等〕不可信的: *The evidence against him is extremely flimsy.* 不利于他的那些证据十分不足信。—**flimsily** *adv* —**flimsiness** *n* [U]

flinch /flɪntʃ; flɪntʃ/ *v* [I] **1** to make a sudden small backward movement when you are shocked by pain or afraid of something〔因疼痛或害怕而〕退缩, 畏缩 **2 sb didn't (even) flinch** used to say that someone did not seem surprised about something 某人对某事丝毫不感到惊奇[不退缩] **3** to avoid doing something because you dislike it or are afraid of it〔因厌恶或害怕而〕回避: **never flinch from doing sth** *He never flinched from doing his duty.* 他从来不逃避自己的责任。

fling¹ /flɪŋ; flɪŋ/ *v past tense and past participle* **flung** /flʌŋ; flʌŋ/ [T]

1 ▶THROW 扔◀ [always+adv/prep] to throw something quickly with a lot of force〔用力地〕扔, 抛, 掷, 丢: **fling sth at/into/on etc** *Spectators flung bottles and cans at the marchers.* 观众向游行者扔瓶子和罐子。| **fling sth ↔ down** *Sammy flings down his coat and stomps upstairs.* 萨米扔下大衣, 重步走到楼上去。

2 ▶BODY 身体◀ [always+adv/prep] to move yourself or part of your body suddenly and with a lot of force〔突然〕扑向; 猛动, 急伸: [+**down/through/towards etc**] *Ian flung himself down on his bed.* 伊恩一下扑倒在床上。| **fling sth around/towards etc** *Flinging his arms around her, he kissed her.* 他张开双臂抱住她, 吻了她。| **fling sth ↔ back/out etc** *Katie flung back her head and laughed.* 凯蒂猛然仰起头, 大笑起来。

3 fling yourself into to begin to do something using a lot of effort 全力投入, 投身于: *After the divorce he flung himself into his work and tried to forget her.* 他离婚后全力投入工作, 努力把她忘掉。

4 fling a door/window etc open to quickly and suddenly open a door, window etc 猛力打开门/窗等: *We flung open all the windows.* 我们猛地打开所有的窗。

5 fling sb in prison/jail to put someone in prison, often without having a good reason〔常指没有充分理由而〕把某人投入监狱: *Opposition leaders were flung into jail.* 反对派领导人被投入监狱。

fling sth **↔ off** *phr v* to quickly remove a piece of clothing, a sheet, or a cover 匆忙地脱掉, 掀掉〔衣、被等〕: *Tom flung off his blanket in the middle of the night.* 汤姆在半夜一下子掀开了毛毯。

fling sb/sth **↔ out** *phr v* [T] *especially BrE*【尤英】**1** to suddenly make someone leave an organization or place 突然赶走[开除] **2** [**fling** sth **↔ out**] to get rid of something you no longer want or need 丢弃, 甩掉〔不再需要的东西〕

fling² *n* [C usually singular 一般用单数] **1** a short and not very serious sexual relationship 一时的放纵[行乐]: **have a fling** *They*

F

had a brief fling years ago. 他们几年前有过一段很短暂的风流韵事。**2** a short period of time during which you enjoy yourself without worrying about anything 一阵的尽情享乐: **have your fling** *I'm going to have my fling first and see a bit of the world.* 我要先尽情玩一下, 见见世面。

flint /flɪnt; flɪnt/ *n* **1** [C,U] a type of smooth hard stone, usually black or grey in colour, or a piece of this stone 燧石, 火石 **2** [C] a piece of this stone or a small piece of metal that makes a small flame when you strike it with steel 打火石〔打火机用的电石〕

flint·lock /ˈflɪnt,lɑk; ˈflɪntlɒk/ *n* [C] a gun used in the past 〔旧时用的〕燧发机, 明火枪

Flint·stones, The /ˈflɪntstonz; ˈflɪntstəʊnz/ a humorous US television CARTOON programme, about a family from the Stone Age who live in a town called Bedrock. Fred Flintstone is the father, and is married to Wilma. They have a daughter called Pebbles and a pet DINOSAUR called Dino. Their best friends are Barney and Betty Rubble.《聪明笨伯》〔美国卡通电视喜剧, 讲述石器时代生活在基岩镇的一家人的故事。父亲董辉与母亲慧玛有个名叫佩博丝的女儿和一只宠物恐龙迪诺, 他们最要好的朋友是巴尼和贝蒂〕

flint·y /ˈflɪntɪ; ˈflɪnti/ *adj* a flinty expression or person does not show emotions 强硬的; 冷酷的; 铁石心肠的: *Duvall gave him a flinty stare.* 杜瓦尔冷冷地瞪了他一眼。

flip[1] /flɪp; flɪp/ **flipped, flipping** *v* **1** [T] to turn something over or into a different position with a quick, sudden movement〔突然很快地〕翻倒, 翻动: **flip sth ↔ open** *Paula flipped the lid of the printer open.* 葆拉迅速翻开打印机的盖。**2** [T] to make a flat object such as a coin go upwards and turn over in the air; TOSS[1] (4) 抛掷[硬币等]: *We flipped a coin to see who would go first.* 我们抛掷硬币, 看由谁先去。**3** [I] *informal* also 又作 **flip out** to suddenly become very angry or upset【非正式】大发雷霆; 心烦意乱: *Dad flipped when he found out I'd been skipping school.* 爸爸发现我在逃学, 顿时大发雷霆。| **flip your lid** (=suddenly become very angry) 大发雷霆, 暴跳如雷 **4** [I] *AmE informal* to feel very excited and like something very much【美, 非正式】着迷: [**+over**] *Krissy really flipped over our kitten.* 克里西对我们的小猫着了迷。**5** *especially AmE* [T] to quickly start or stop electrical equipment by pressing or moving a button【尤美】轻压〔按钮〕, 轻轻拨动〔按钮〕: *Who flipped the switch?* 谁按动了开关? | **flip sth ↔ on/off** *Josie flipped on the radio.* 乔西啪地打开收音机。

flip sb ↔ **off** *phr v* [T] *AmE* also 又作 **flip sb the bird** to make a rude sign at someone by raising your middle finger and keeping your other fingers down【美】〔朝某人〕伸出中指〔一种侮辱性的手势〕

flip out *phr v* [I] *informal*【非正式】**1** to suddenly become very angry or upset 大发雷霆; 心烦意乱: *Francie will flip out if you get a scratch on her new car.* 要是你划损了弗朗茜的新车, 她会大发雷霆。**2** to suddenly start behaving in a crazy way 突然发疯, 失去理智[自我控制]: *The paper says a veteran flipped out and gunned down a bunch of people.* 报上说一位老兵失去理智, 开枪打倒了一群人。

flip over *phr v* [I,T] to turn something from one side onto the other 翻转: *Larry flipped over onto his other side, trying to get comfortable.* 拉里把身体翻到另一侧, 想让自己舒服点。| **flip sth ↔ over** *Mary flipped over the cushions on the couch.* 玛丽翻转沙发上的坐垫。

flip through sth *phr v* [T] to look at a book, magazine etc quickly 快速浏览[翻阅]〔书、杂志等〕

flip[2] *n* [C] **1** a quick, light hit with your thumb or finger, especially one that makes an object turn over in the air〔用拇指或别的手指〕轻抛, 轻弹: *a flip of the coin* 捻掷硬币 **2** a movement in which you jump up and turn over in the air, so that your feet go over your head 筋斗, 空翻

flip[3] *adj informal* FLIPPANT【非正式】轻率的, 轻浮的

flip chart /ˈ· ·/ *n* [C] large pieces of paper that are connected at the top so that the pages can be turned over to present information to groups of people〔顶部互相连着的〕翻页挂图

flip-flop[1] /ˈ· ·/ *n* [C] a type of open shoe, usually made of rubber, with only a V-shaped band across the front to hold your feet〔一般用橡胶制的〕平底人字拖鞋; THONGS (2) *AmE*【美】—see picture at 参见 SHOE[1] 图

flip-flop[2] *v* [I] *AmE informal* to change your opinion about something【美, 非正式】改变观点

flip·pant /ˈflɪpənt; ˈflɪpənt/ *adj* not being serious about something that other people think you should be serious about, so that they think you do not care 轻率的, 轻浮的: *A hospital is hardly the place for such flippant remarks.* 医院绝不是说这种轻率话的地方。—**flippantly** *adv* —**flippancy** *n* [U]

flip·per /ˈflɪpɚ; ˈflɪpə/ *n* [C] **1** a flat part on the body of some large sea animals such as SEALS, used for swimming〔海豹等的〕鳍状肢, 鳍足 **2** a large flat rubber shoe worn to help you swim faster〔使人能游快些的〕脚蹼, 鸭脚板

flip·ping /ˈflɪpɪŋ; ˈflɪpɪŋ/ *adj BrE spoken* used to emphasize what you are saying when you are annoyed【英口】该死的, 讨厌的〔用作强调〕: *I'm not flipping waiting any longer.* 见鬼的, 我不再等了。—**flipping** *adv*

flip side /ˈ· ·/ *n* [singular] **1** the side of a record that has a song on it that is less popular than the one on the other side (唱片的)反面〔上面的歌曲不像正面的那么流行〕**2** the bad effects of something, after you have just described the good effects 负面, 反面, 不好的方面〔用于对比刚描述过的好的方面〕: *The flip side is that it may cause more pollution.* 负面影响是这可能造成更多污染。

flirt[1] /flɝt; flɜːt/ *v* [I] to behave towards and talk to someone as though you are sexually attracted to them, but not in a very serious way 调情, 打情骂俏: [**+with**] *Tony flirted with every woman at the party.* 托尼跟聚会上的每一个女人调情。

flirt with sth *phr v* [T not in passive 不用被动态] **1** to consider doing something, but not be very serious about it 不认真地考虑 **2** to take an unnecessary risk and not be worried about it 轻率从事, 不认真对待: *The Prince has always enjoyed flirting with danger.* 王子总是喜欢不假思索便去冒险。

flirt[2] *n* [C] someone who often behaves towards and talks to people as though she or he is sexually attracted to them, but not in a very serious way 调情者

flir·ta·tion /flɝˋteʃən; flɜːˈteɪʃən/ *n* **1** [C] a short period of time during which you are interested in something 一时的兴趣, 一时的爱好: [**+with**] *a brief flirtation with Eastern religions* 对东方各种宗教的一时兴趣 **2** [U] behaviour that shows a sexual attraction to someone, though not in a serious way 调情 **3** [C] a short sexual relationship which is not serious 短暂的风流韵事

flir·ta·tious /flɝˋteʃəs; flɜːˈteɪʃəs/ *adj* behaving in a way that deliberately tries to attract sexual attention, but not in a serious way (爱)调情的, 卖弄风骚的: *a flirtatious young girl* 一位卖弄风骚的年轻姑娘 —**flirtatiously** *adv* —**flirtatiousness** *n* [U]

flit /flɪt; flɪt/ *v* **flitted, flitting** [I always+adv/prep] to move lightly or quickly and not stay in one place for very long 轻快地行进, 掠过: *birds flitting about from branch to branch* 在树枝间飞来飞去的鸟儿 —see also 另见 **do a moonlight flit** (MOONLIGHT[1] (2))

float[1] /flot; fləʊt/ *v*

1 ►ON WATER 在水上◄[I] **a)** to stay or move on the surface of a liquid without sinking 浮; 漂: *Wood usually floats.* 木头通常会浮起来。| *Annie was floating on her back in the pool.* 安妮脸朝上地浮在池水上。| [**+along/down/past etc**] *The logs floated down the river.* 原木在河上顺水漂流。**b)** [T] to put something on the surface of a liquid so that it does not sink 使浮起: *Pour the coffee and brandy into a mug, then float the cream on top.* 把咖啡和白兰地倒入大杯, 然后把奶油放进去, 让它浮在面上。

2 ►IN THE AIR 在空中◄[I always+adv/prep] if something floats, especially something very light or filled with air, it moves slowly in the air or stays up in the air 飘浮: [**+up/down/through etc**] *He watched the balloon float up into the sky.* 他看着气球升上天空。

3 ►MUSIC/SOUNDS/SMELLS ETC 音乐/声音/气味等◄[I always+adv/prep] if sounds, smells etc float somewhere, people in another place can hear or smell them〔声音、气味等〕飘: [**+down/towards/into etc**] *The sound of her voice came floating down from an upstairs window.* 她的声音从楼上的窗子里飘下来。

4 ►MONEY 货币◄[I,T] *technical* if a country floats its money or its money floats, the value of the money is allowed to change freely in relation to money from other countries【术语】(使)浮动: *Russia floated the ruble on the foreign exchange market.* 俄罗斯让卢布在外汇市场上自由浮动。

5 ►SUGGEST 建议◄[T] to suggest an idea or plan, especially in order to find out what people think about it〔尤指为了解人们的想法而〕提出〔建议或计划〕: *The idea was first floated in a speech given by the President a few months ago.* 这种想法是几个月前总统在一次讲话中首次提出来的。

6 ►COMPANY 公司◄[T] to sell shares (SHARE[2] (5)) in a company or business to the public for the first time 首次公开发行〔股票〕—see also 另见 FLOTATION (1)

7 ►CHEQUE 支票◄*AmE* [T] to write a cheque that you do not have enough money in the bank to pay【美】开〔空头支票〕; BOUNCE[1] (3) *BrE*【英】

8 ▶MOVE GRACEFULLY 优雅地走动◀ [I] to move gracefully and lightly 飘然移动: *Rachel floated around the bedroom in a lace nightgown.* 雷切尔穿着花边睡衣在卧室里飘然走动。

9 ▶NO DEFINITE PURPOSE 无明确目的◀ [I always+adv/prep] to keep changing what you are doing without having any particular ideas or plans 不断改变; 游荡: *Dean seems to float from job to job, never getting anywhere.* 迪安似乎不断地变换工作, 一直是一事无成。—**floater** *n* [C]

float² *n* [C] **1** a large vehicle that is decorated to be part of a PARADE¹ (1) 〔游行时用的〕彩车: *a procession of Carnival floats* 狂欢节彩车的巡游队伍 —see also 另见 MILK FLOAT **2** *AmE* a SOFT DRINK¹ (1) that has ice cream floating in it【美】浮有冰淇淋的饮料 **3** a light object that floats on the surface of the water, used especially for catching fish 〔尤指钓鱼用的〕漂浮物; 鱼漂, 浮子 **4** a light object used when swimming to support your body 〔游泳时用的〕救生衣; 救生圈 **5** a small amount of money that someone in a shop keeps so that they have enough money to give change to people 〔商店的〕备用零钱

floa·ta·tion /flo`teʃən; fləʊ'teɪʃən/ *n* [C] a British spelling of FLOTATION flotation 的英式拼法

float·ing /`flotɪŋ; 'fləʊtɪŋ/ *adj* **1 floating population** if a city has a floating population, the number of people who live there keeps changing because people move into and out of it 流动人口 **2** *technical* an organ or part of your body that is floating is not properly connected or is not in the usual place【术语】〔指身体器官〕浮游的, 不在正常位置的

floating vot·er /,‥'‥/ *n* [C] someone who is not sure which political party to vote for at an election 不固定投某一政党票的投票人, 无党派投票人

flock¹ /flɑk; flɒk/ *n* **1** [C] a group of sheep, goats, or birds 畜群; 鸟群 —compare 比较 HERD¹ (1) **2** [C usually singular 一般用单数] a large group of the same kind of people 〔同类型的〕一大群人: **[+of]** *a flock of tourists* 一大群游客 **3** [C usually singular 一般用单数] *formal or humorous* a priest's flock is the group of people who regularly attend his church【正式或幽默】〔经常到某位牧师所属教堂礼拜的〕全体教徒[会众] **4** [U] small pieces of wool, cotton etc used for filling CUSHIONS¹ (1) 〔填充垫子的〕絮屑, 毛棉填料 **5** also 又作 **flock·ing** /`flɑkɪŋ; 'flɒkɪŋ/ *AmE* a soft substance used to make patterns on the surface of wallpaper, curtains, etc【美】〔供在墙纸、窗帘等表面制作图案的〕植绒材料; 柔软贴料

flock² *v* [I always+adv/prep] to go to a place in large numbers because something interesting or exciting is happening there 成群结队; 蜂拥而至: **flock to/into/around etc** *Californians are flocking to enrol in special aerobics classes.* 加利福尼亚人正成群结队参加特别有氧健身操训练班。

Flod·den /`flɑdn; 'flɒdn/ a hillside in Northumberland in the north of England, where there was a battle between England and Scotland in 1513. The Scots were severely defeated and their king, James IV, was killed. 佛洛顿〔位于英格兰北部诺森伯兰的一个山坡。1513 年英格兰与苏格兰在此交战, 苏格兰人受重创, 国王詹姆斯四世阵亡〕

floe /flo; fləʊ/ *n* [C] —see 见 ICE FLOE

flog /flɑg; flɒg/ *v* **flogged, flogging** [T] **1** to beat a person or animal with a whip or stick 鞭打; 棒打: *Thieves were flogged in public.* 小偷被当众鞭打。**2** *especially BrE informal* to sell【尤英, 非正式】出售, 卖 **3 be flogging a dead horse** *spoken* to be wasting time or effort by trying to do something that is impossible【口】浪费时间, 徒劳, 白费劲 **4 flog sth to death** *especially BrE informal* to repeat a story, complaint, idea etc so often that people become bored with it【尤英, 非正式】把某事反复说得使人厌烦

flog·ging /`flɑgɪŋ; 'flɒgɪŋ/ *n* [C] a punishment in which someone is severely beaten with a whip or stick 〔作为惩罚的〕鞭笞

3 **flood¹** /flʌd; flʌd/ *v*

1 ▶COVER WITH WATER 被水淹◀ [I,T] to make a place become covered, or to become covered with water (被)淹没: *Three days of heavy rain flooded many Eastern cities.* 三天的大雨淹了东部的许多城市。| *The basement flooded and everything got soaked.* 地下室被水淹了, 所有的东西都湿透了。

2 ▶GO/ARRIVE IN LARGE AMOUNTS/NUMBERS 大量/大批去/到达◀ [I] to arrive or go somewhere in large numbers 〔大量地〕涌到, 涌去: **[+in/into/out/across etc]** *Letters came flooding in from irate viewers.* 愤怒的观众的来信如潮水般涌至。| *Refugees flooded across the border.* 大批的难民涌过边界。

3 be flooded with to receive so many things such as letters, complaints, or inquiries that you cannot deal with them 大量收到: *We've been flooded with offers of help.* 许多人表示愿意帮助我们。

4 ▶SEND LARGE AMOUNTS/NUMBERS 大量地发送◀ [T] to send a large number of things such as letters or complaints to an organization so that it is difficult for people there to deal with them 大量地寄送〔信件、投诉等〕: **flood sth with** *Campaigners flooded Congress with letters of protest.* 参加运动的人的抗议信如潮水般涌到国会。

5 flood the market to sell something in very large numbers or amounts, so that the price goes down 〔用某物〕充斥市场〔以造成价格下跌〕: **[+with]** *Japanese companies were accused of flooding the market with cheap steel.* 日本公司因以廉价钢材充斥市场而受指责。

6 ▶RIVER 河流◀ [I,T] if a river floods, it is too full, and spreads water over the land around it (使)泛滥

7 ▶ENGINE 发动机◀ [I,T] if an engine floods or you flood it, it has too much petrol in it, so that it will not start (使)溢油; (使)燃油过多

8 ▶LIGHT 光线◀ [I,T] if light floods a place or floods into it, it makes it very light and bright 照亮, (使)明亮: *The sunset flooded the canyon with rose-colored light.* 落日那玫瑰色的光芒照遍峡谷。

9 ▶FEELING 感觉◀ [I,T] if a feeling or memory floods over someone or floods back, they feel or remember it very strongly 〔感情或回忆〕涌上心头: **[+over/back]** *I felt happiness and relief flooding over me.* 我感到心里充满快乐和宽慰。

10 flood with tears if someone's face floods with tears, they cry a lot 泪流满面

flood sb ↔ **out** *phr v* **be flooded out** to be forced to leave your home because of floods 因洪水被迫离开家园

flood² *n* **1** [C,U] a very large amount of water that covers an area that is usually dry 洪水; 水灾: *Floods in Bangladesh caused over 1000 deaths.* 孟加拉的洪水夺去一千多人的生命。—see picture on page A13 参见 A13 页图 **2 flood of** a very large number of things or people that arrive at the same time 大量的: *A TV show featuring sexy home videos was halted after a flood of complaints.* 在人们提出大量投诉之后, 一个播放色情家庭录像的电视节目被停播了。**3 in floods of tears** crying a lot 泪如雨下 **4 the Flood** the great flood described in the Bible story, that covered the world 〔《圣经》故事中毁灭世界的〕大洪水: **before the Flood** (=a very long time ago) 很久很久以前, 在大洪水以前 **5 be in flood** a river that is in flood has much more water in it than usual 〔河水〕上涨, 泛滥 —see also 另见 FLASH FLOOD 3

Flood, the 1 a story told in the Old Testament of the Bible about a great flood that covered the whole world. According to the story, God caused the Flood because he was angry with the people on Earth and wanted to punish them. Only one man, Noah, and his family were saved. God told Noah to build an ARK (=a large boat) and to take two of every kind of animal on the ark with him. When the rain stopped and the water level began to go down, Noah sent out a DOVE to look for land, and the bird returned carrying an OLIVE branch to show that the land was reappearing. 大洪水〔《圣经·旧约》中讲述洪水席卷整个世界的故事。该故事称, 上帝对世人感到不满, 想要惩罚他们, 就引发了洪水。只有诺亚和他全家得救。上帝吩咐诺亚建造一只方舟, 每种动物各带上一对。大雨停止, 洪水开始退去。诺亚放飞一只鸽子去寻找陆地, 鸽子回来时嘴里叼着一支橄榄枝, 可见陆地重现了〕**2 before the Flood** a very long time ago 很久以前

flood·gate /`flʌd,get; 'flʌdgeɪt/ *n* [C usually plural 一般用复数] **1 open the floodgates a)** to suddenly make it possible for a lot of people to do something by removing laws and rules which had previously prevented or controlled it 放开限制: *worries that a Labour government would open the floodgates to immigration* 对工党政府会放开移民限制的忧虑 **b)** to make someone show their true feelings which they have been trying not to show 打开心扉 **2** a gate used to control the flow of water from a large lake, river etc 泄水闸; 防洪闸

flood·ing /`flʌdɪŋ; 'flʌdɪŋ/ *n* [U] a situation in which an area of land becomes covered with water, for example because of heavy rain 水灾, 洪水泛滥

flood·light /`flʌd,laɪt; 'flʌdlaɪt/ *n* [C usually plural 一般用复数] a very bright light, used to light the outside of buildings, sports grounds etc at night 泛光灯

flood·lit /`flʌd,lɪt; 'flʌdlɪt/ *adj* surrounded by floodlights so that people can see at night 泛光灯照明的

flood plain /'· ·/ *n* [C] the large area of flat land on either side of a river that is sometimes covered with water 〔河边的〕洪泛区, 泛滥平原

flood tide /'· ·/ *n* [C] the flow of the TIDE¹ (1) in towards the land 涨潮, 升潮 —opposite 反义词 EBB¹ (1)

F

floor¹ /flɔr; flɔː/ *n*
1 ▶**FLAT SURFACE** 平面◀ [C] the flat surface on which you stand indoors 地板；室内的地面：*Amos ran inside, spreading mud all over the kitchen floor.* 阿莫斯跑进屋里，把厨房的地板踩得都是泥浆。—see picture on page A10 参见A10页图 —see 见 LAND¹ (USAGE)
2 ▶**LEVEL IN BUILDING** 建筑物的楼层◀ [C] one of the levels in a building〔楼房的〕层：*Our office is on the top floor.* 我们的办公室在顶层。| *a two-bedroomed ground floor flat* 有两个卧室的底层住房
3 ▶**OCEAN/FOREST/CAVE FLOOR ETC** 海底/森林地面/山洞底等◀ [singular] the ground at the bottom of the ocean, the forest etc〔海洋等的〕底；〔森林等的〕地面：*creatures that live on the ocean floor* 生活在海底的生物
4 the floor a) the people attending a public meeting 全体与会者：*Are there any questions from the floor?* 与会者有问题要提吗？**b)** the part of a parliament, public meeting place etc where people sit〔议会的〕议员席：*The delegates crowded the floor of the House.* 代表们挤满了议院的议员席。
5 take the floor a) to begin speaking at an important public meeting〔在重要的公开会议上〕开始发言 **b)** to begin dancing〔在舞会上〕开始跳舞
6 have the floor to be speaking or have the right to speak at an important public meeting 发言；有发言权：*The Senator from Wyoming had the floor.* 怀俄明州的参议员有发言权。
7 ▶**DANCE** 跳舞◀ an area where people dance 舞池，舞场：**dance floor** *Couples were already gliding over the dance floor.* 一对对的舞伴已经在舞池中翩然起舞。
8 ▶**WHERE PEOPLE WORK** 工作场所◀ [C] a large area in a building where a lot of people do their jobs〔工作场所的〕大厅：*The stock market floor was wildly busy.* 证券交易所的大厅里忙得不可开交。| **shop floor** (=the area in a factory where people work using machines) 工厂的车间 *The manager's office is above the shop floor.* 经理办公室在工作车间的上面。
9 ▶**CAR** 汽车◀ [C] *BrE* the part of a car that forms its inside floor【英】〔汽车〕底板；FLOORBOARD (2) *AmE*【美】
10 go through the floor if a price, amount etc goes through the floor, it becomes very low〔价格、数量等〕降到很低的水平：*In the past few years share prices have gone through the floor.* 过去几年来，股票价格已降到了很低的水平。
11 ▶**LIMIT** 限度◀ [singular] an officially agreed limit so that something cannot go below a certain value 最低额，底限：**put a floor under** *The French government tried to put a floor under the value of the Franc.* 法国政府试图限定法郎的最低价值。—see also 另见 **be/get in on the ground floor** (GROUND FLOOR (2)), **wipe the floor with** (WIPE¹ (5))
12 [C] *BrE* the area of the stock exchange where people buy and sell shares (SHARE² (5))【英】〔证券交易所的〕交易厅

USAGE NOTE 用法说明：FLOOR
In American English the bottom floor of a building (at ground level) is called the **first floor**. In British English this is called the **ground floor**. 建筑物的最低层（地面的一层）在美国英语中叫作 first floor（一楼），在英国英语中叫作 ground floor（底层）。
The next level up is called the **second floor** in American English and the **first floor** in British English. 再往上一层，美国英语叫作 second floor（二楼），英国英语叫作 first floor（一楼）。
GRAMMAR 语法
People say 人们说 *He lives on the second/ninth etc floor* (NOT 不用 *at/in the second/ninth etc floor*). 他住在二/九楼。

floor² *v* [T] **1** to surprise or shock someone so much that they do not know what to say or do 使惊讶得不知所措；难倒：*Her last question completely floored me.* 她的最后一个问题完全把我难倒了。**2** to hit someone so hard that they fall down 把…打倒在地：*The Champion floored Watson with a single punch.* 冠军一拳就把沃森打倒在地。**3 floor it** *AmE informal* to make a car go as fast as possible【美，非正式】踩足油门，全速行驶

floor·board /ˈflɔr,bɔrd; ˈflɔːbɔːd/ *n* [C] **1** [usually plural 一般用复数] a board in a wooden floor 木地板 —see picture at 参见 BOARD 图 **2** *AmE* the floor in a car【美】〔汽车〕底板

floor·ing /ˈflɔrɪŋ; ˈflɔːrɪŋ/ *n* [U] material used to make or cover floors 铺地面的材料

floor lamp /ˈ· ·/ *n* [C] *AmE* a lamp at the top of a tall pole on a flat base that stands on the floor of a room【美】落地灯；STANDARD LAMP *BrE*【英】—see picture at 参见 LIGHT¹ 图

floor-length /ˈ· ·/ *adj* long enough to reach the floor〔衣裙〕拖到地的：*a floor-length evening gown* 长裙拖地的晚礼服

floor mod·el /ˈ· ,··/ *n* [C] *AmE* a piece of furniture or equipment for the home, such as a washing machine, that has been in a store for people to look at and is often sold at a cheaper price【美】〔售价较低的家具或家用设备的〕陈列样品

floor plan /ˈ· ·/ *n* [C] a drawing of the shape of a room or area in a building and the position of things in it, as seen from above 楼层平面图，楼面布置图

floor show /ˈ· ·/ *n* [C] a performance by singers, dancers etc at a NIGHTCLUB〔夜总会舞池内的〕娱乐表演

floo·zy, floozie /ˈfluzɪ; ˈfluːzi/ *n* [C] *old-fashioned* a woman who is sexually immoral and who you disapprove of【过时】荡妇，不规矩的女子

flop¹ /flɑp; flɒp/ *v* **flopped, flopping** [I] **1** [always+adv/prep] also 又作 **flop down** to sit or lie down in a relaxed way, by letting all your weight fall heavily onto a chair etc 猛然坐下，猛然躺下：[+in/onto/across etc] *"I'm exhausted," said Max, flopping into a chair.* "我累坏了。"马克斯说着，一屁股坐在椅子上。**2** [always+adv/prep] to move or fall in an awkward, or uncontrolled way 笨拙地移动；摔倒；重重地落下：[+around/along/onto etc] *A bird with an injured wing flopped helplessly along the ground.* 一只翅膀受伤的鸟无助地在地面上扑腾着。**3** *informal* if something such as a product, play, or plan flops, it is not successful because people do not like it【非正式】〔产品、戏剧或计划等因无人喜欢而〕失败，砸锅：*Despite all the media hype 'Heaven's Gate' flopped at the box office.* 尽管传媒吹捧得天花乱坠，《天堂之门》的票房成绩却一塌糊涂。

flop² *n* **1** [C] *informal* a film, play, product etc that is not successful【非正式】〔电影、戏剧、产品等的〕失败：*The show was a flop and lasted only one night.* 演出很失败，只演了一个晚上。**2** [singular] the movement or noise that something makes when it falls heavily 重坠；重坠声，扑通声：*He fell with a flop into the water.* 他扑通一声掉进水里。**3** *AmE* a flophouse【美】廉价旅馆 —see also 另见 BELLY FLOP, FLIP-FLOP

flop·house /ˈflɑp,haus; ˈflɒphaʊs/ *n* [C] *AmE slang* a cheap hotel, that often has many beds in one room【美俚】廉价旅馆；DOSS HOUSE *BrE*【英】

flop·py /ˈflɑpɪ; ˈflɒpi/ *adj* soft and often hanging loosely downwards 松软的；垂下的；松垂的：*a dog with long, floppy ears* 耷拉着长耳朵的狗 —**floppiness** *n* [U]

floppy disk /,·· ˈ·/ also 又作 **floppy** *n* [C] a square piece of plastic on which information for a computer is stored; DISKETTE 软（磁）盘，软磁碟 —compare 比较 HARD DISK

flo·ra /ˈflɔrə; ˈflɔːrə/ *n* [U] all the plants of a particular place or country〔某个地方或国家的〕植物群：*the flora of the Alps* 阿尔卑斯山脉的植物群 —compare 比较 FAUNA

flo·ral /ˈflɔrəl; ˈflɔːrəl/ *adj* decorated with or made of flowers 花的；花卉图案的；用花制作的：*floral dresses* 花卉图案的连衣裙 | **floral tributes** (=flowers at a funeral)〔葬礼上〕敬献的鲜花 —see picture on page A16 参见A16页图

Flor·ence /ˈflɔrəns; ˈflɒrəns/ a city in western central Italy, which was very rich and powerful in the 14th and 15th centuries. It is famous for its art and fine buildings. 佛罗伦萨〔意大利中西部一城市，14、15世纪十分富强，以艺术和精巧的建筑著称〕—**Florentine** *n, adj*

flor·id /ˈflɔrɪd; ˈflɒrɨd/ *adj literary*【文】**1** having a red face〔脸色〕红润的：*florid cheeks* 红润的脸颊 **2** having a lot of unnecessary decoration or detail 过分华丽的，花哨的，华而不实的：*florid language* 词藻华丽的语言 —**floridly** *adv*

Flor·i·da /ˈflɔrɪdə; ˈflɒrɨdə/ abbreviation 缩写为 **FL** a state in the southeastern US. Florida has warm weather all year round, and many older people go there to live when they have stopped working. 佛罗里达〔美国东南部一州。这里四季气候温暖，许多人退休后来此居住〕

Florida Keys, the /,··· ˈ·/ a group of small islands off the coast of southern Florida, where many tourists go 佛罗里达群岛〔与佛罗里达州南部海岸隔海相望的一群小岛，吸引着许多游人前去观光〕

flor·in /ˈflɔrɪn; ˈflɒrɨn/ *n* [C] a coin used in Britain before 1971, ten of which made one pound (£1) 弗罗林〔英国1971年以前使用的硬币，等于1/10英镑〕

flor·ist /ˈflɔrɪst; ˈflɒrɨst/ *n* [C] **1** someone who owns or works in a shop that sells flowers 花商；花店主人[店员] **2** also 又作 **florist's** a shop that sells flowers 花店

floss¹ /flɔs; flɒs/ *n* [U] **1** thin silk used for sewing〔缝纫用的〕（绣花）丝线 **2** DENTAL FLOSS 洁牙线 —see also 另见 CANDYFLOSS

floss² *v* [T] to clean between your teeth with DENTAL FLOSS 用洁牙线清洁〔牙缝〕

flo·ta·tion /floˋteʃən; fləʊˈteɪʃən/ *n* [C,U] **1** the act of offering shares (SHARE[2] (5)) in a company to the public for the first time〔公司股票的〕发行，上市：*a massive flotation of government bonds* 政府债券的大量发行 **2 flotation chamber/compartment etc** a container filled with air or gas, fixed to something to make it float 浮室／浮舱等

flo·til·la /floˋtɪlə; fləˈtɪlə/ *n* [C] a group of small ships 小船队；小舰队

flot·sam /ˋflɑtsəm; ˈflɒtsəm/ *n* [U] **1** broken pieces of wood, plastic etc from a wrecked ship floating in the sea or scattered on the shore〔遇难船只的〕漂浮残骸；水面[海面]飘浮物 —compare 比较 JETSAM **2** also 又作 **flotsam and jet·sam** /ˌ‥ˈ‥/ people who do not have jobs or homes 流离失所的人；流浪者；无业游民；失业者

flounce[1] /flauns; flaʊns/ *v* [I always+adv/prep] to move in a way that shows that you are angry 怒气冲冲地走：[+out/off/past etc] *Sandra flounced out of the room.* 桑德拉怒冲冲地走出房间。

flounce[2] *n* **1** [C] a band of cloth on clothing that is stitched into folds as a decoration〔镶在衣服上作装饰的〕荷叶边 **2** [singular] a sudden quick movement that shows people that you are annoyed〔表示生气的〕骤动，急动

flounced /flaunst; flaʊnst/ *adj* a flounced skirt or dress is one that is decorated with flounces〔裙子或连衣裙〕镶荷叶边的

floun·der[1] /ˋflaundə; ˈflaʊndə/ *v* [I] **1** [always+adv/prep] to move awkwardly or with difficulty, especially in water, mud etc〔尤指在水、泥等中〕挣扎，踉跄，艰难地移动 **2** to be unable to decide what to say or do so that you find it difficult to continue 胡乱地[困难地]说话[做事]：*He left his interviewer floundering by answering every question with the word 'no'.* 他用"不"字来回答每个问题，使采访者难以继续。**3** to have a lot of problems and have difficulty continuing 遇到许多问题[困难]：*Brando's career was floundering when he was offered the role.* 白兰度被派演这个角色时，他的事业正在困厄之中。

flounder[2] *n* [C] a small flat fish, used as food 鲆；鲽

flour[1] /flaur; flaʊə/ *n* [U] a powder made by crushing grain, especially wheat, and used for making bread, cakes etc 面粉；谷物磨成的粉〔尤指小麦粉〕—see also 另见 PLAIN FLOUR, SELF-RAISING FLOUR

flour[2] *v* [T] to cover a surface with flour 在…上撒面粉

flour·ish[1] /ˋflɝɪʃ; ˈflʌrɪʃ/ *v* **1** [I] to grow well and be very healthy; THRIVE 生长茂盛：*The plants flourished in the warm sun.* 这些植物在温暖的阳光下生长茂盛。**2** [I] to develop well and be successful 繁荣，兴旺，成功：*Russia's flourishing black market economy* 俄罗斯繁荣的黑市经济 **3** [T] to wave something in your hand in order to make people notice it〔为引起注意〕挥动〔手中的东西〕：*Ellie ran in, flourishing her acceptance letter.* 埃莉挥动着录取通知书跑进来。

flour·ish[2] *n* **1 with a flourish** with a large confident movement that makes people notice you 用引人注意的动作，挥舞：*Mr Darcy swept back his hat with a flourish.* 达西先生用一个夸张的动作把帽子一挥放在背后。**2** [C] something such as a decoration or detail that is not necessary 不必要的装饰；过分华丽的词藻：*His speech was full of rhetorical flourishes.* 他的讲话充满浮夸华丽的词藻。**3** [C] a curved line when writing, which is done for decoration〔手写花体字的〕花饰 **4** [C] a loud part of a piece of music, played especially when an important person enters〔尤指重要人物进场时演奏的〕响亮的乐曲：*a flourish of trumpets* 响亮的小号乐曲

flour·mill /ˋflaurˌmɪl; ˈflaʊəˌmɪl/ *n* [C] a place where flour is made from grain 面粉厂

flour·y /ˋflaurɪ; ˈflaʊəri/ *adj* covered with or tasting of flour 盖有面粉的；(似) 面粉味的

flout /flaut; flaʊt/ *v* [T] to deliberately disobey a law, rule etc 公然无视，违抗〔法律、规定等〕：*Countries that flout the agreement will have sanctions imposed on them.* 违反协议的国家将受到制裁。

S2 W2 **flow[1]** /flo; fləʊ/ *n*

1 ▶MOVEMENT OF LIQUID 液体的流动◀ [C usually singular 一般用单数] a smooth steady movement or supply of liquid 流动：*Smoking affects the flow of blood to the brain.* 吸烟会影响血液往大脑的流动。

2 ▶SUPPLY/MOVEMENT 供应/移动◀ [C usually singular 一般用单数] a continuous supply or movement of something from one place to another 不断的供应[输送]：[+of] *the flow of arms into Bosnia* 源源不断地进入波斯尼亚的武器输送

3 in full flow if someone is in full flow, they are busy talking about something and seem likely to continue for a long time 滔滔不绝；口若悬河

4 ▶WORDS/IDEAS 词语/想法◀ [U] the continuous stream of words or ideas when someone is speaking, writing, or thinking about something 流畅，连贯：**break/interrupt sb's flow** *You've interrupted my flow now – I don't know what I was going to say next.* 你现在已把我的话打断了——我不知我刚才接下去要说什么。

5 ▶OF THE SEA 大海的◀ [singular] the movement of the TIDE[1] (1) towards the land 涨潮：*the ebb and flow of the tide* 潮水的涨落

6 go with the flow to decide to do the same thing as other people, and not ask if you can do something different 随大溜；随波逐流；从众：*I don't mind, I'll just go with the flow.* 我没关系，我随大家好了。

7 go against the flow to do something very different from what other people are doing 逆潮流，背道而驰 —see also 另见 CASH FLOW, **ebb and flow** (EBB[1] (3))

flow[2] *v* [I] S3

1 ▶LIQUID 液体◀ if a liquid flows, it moves in a steady continuous stream 流动，流淌：[+over/down/through etc] *A great river flowed along the valley.* 一条大河流过山谷。

2 ▶GOODS/INFORMATION/PEOPLE ETC 商品/消息/人等◀ if goods, information, people etc flow, they move or are supplied continuously in large numbers from one place to another 流动；流传：[+in/out/through/from etc] *Money has been flowing into the country from Western aid agencies.* 钱源源不断地从西方援助机构流进该国。

3 ▶TRAFFIC 交通◀ if traffic flows, it moves easily from one place to another〔车辆〕畅通无阻

4 ▶ALCOHOL 酒◀ if alcohol flows at a party, people drink a lot and there is a lot available 大量供应；饮之不尽：**flow freely** *The champagne flowed freely and everyone had a good time.* 香槟酒大量供应，大家玩得很开心。

5 ▶WORDS/IDEAS 词语/想法◀ if conversation or ideas flow, people talk or have ideas steadily and continuously, without anything stopping or interrupting them〔说话或思考〕流畅：**flow easily/freely** *The wine loosened our tongues, and conversation flowed freely.* 葡萄酒使我们打开了话匣子，大家的话多了起来。

6 flow from to come from a particular idea, place, or person 来自，产生于，源于：*the political wrangle that has flowed from this decision* 这项决定所产生的政治争论

7 ▶FEELINGS 感情◀ if an emotion flows, someone feels it strongly 强烈地感到：[+through/into/from etc] *Compassion for Mattie flowed through her.* 她对马蒂深感同情。

8 ▶CLOTHES/HAIR 衣服/头发◀ if clothing, hair etc flows, it falls or hangs loosely and gracefully〔衣服、头发等〕飘垂，飘拂

9 ▶SEA 大海◀ if the TIDE[1] (1) flows, it moves towards the land〔潮〕涨 —compare 比较 EBB[2] (1)

flow chart /ˈ· ·/ also 又作 **flow di·a·gram** /ˈ· ˌ‥/ *n* [C] a drawing that uses shapes and lines to show how a series of actions or parts of a system are connected with each other 流程图；作业图：*a flow chart of the company's managerial structure* 公司的管理结构图

flow·er[1] /ˋflauə; ˈflaʊə/ *n* **1** [C] the coloured part of a plant or tree that produces seeds or fruit 花，花朵：*Fruit trees produce flowers in the spring.* 果树在春天开花。**2** [C] a small plant that is grown for the beauty of this part 开花植物，花卉：*He grows flowers in the front garden.* 他在前面的园子里种花。**3 in flower** a plant or tree that is in flower has flowers on it 在开花：**come into flower** (=start to have flowers) 开始开花 *Roses usually come into flower in May or June.* 玫瑰通常在五、六月份开始开花。**4 the flower of** *literary* the best part or most perfect part of something【文】精华，精英，最好的部分：*The flower of the nation's youth was lost in the war.* 这个国家的青年精英在战争中损失殆尽。**5** *BrE old-fashioned* used to address someone in a friendly and informal way【英，过时】花儿〔英国旧时一种友好的非正式称呼语〕 S2 W2

CULTURAL NOTE 文化注释

Flowers are often given to someone as a sign of love, to say thank you, or to say sorry. They are also often given to women as a present or at celebrations such as birthdays and GRADUATIONS. There are usually flowers at a wedding, and the BRIDE carries flowers. Flowers are often given to people who are ill, and they are also put on graves. Some flowers have special meanings. For example, red roses represent romantic love, and white lilies (LILY) are often used when someone has died. 送花可表示爱意、感谢或歉意。赠送女性礼物经常送花，庆祝生日或毕业等也经常送花。婚礼上通常都有花，新娘手里捧着花。看病人也常送花，或把花放在坟墓前。有的花代表特别意义，例如，红玫瑰表示爱情，白百合常用在丧事上。

F

flower² *v* [I] **1** to produce flowers 开花 **2** *formal* to develop and reach a high level of achievement【正式】繁荣, 兴旺: *English painting flowered briefly during the Renaissance.* 英国绘画艺术在文艺复兴时期出现了短暂的繁荣。

flower ar·rang·ing /ˈ‥ ‚‥/ *n* [U] the art of arranging flowers in an attractive way 插花〔艺术〕

flow·er·bed /ˈflauɚ͵bɛd; ˈflaʊəbed/ *n* [C] an area of ground in which flowers are grown 花坛

flower child /ˈ‥ ‚/ *n plural* **flower children** [C] a young person in the 1960s and 70s who was against war and wanted peace and love in society "花孩儿"; 执花嬉皮士〔指20世纪60年代和70年代反对战争、主张和平与爱的年轻人〕

flow·ered /ˈflauɚd; ˈflaʊəd/ *adj* decorated with pictures of flowers 用花卉图案装饰的: *flowered curtains* 有花卉图案的窗帘

flower girl /ˈ‥ ‚/ *n* [C] **1** *BrE* a girl or woman who sells flowers in a street market【英】〔街市上的〕卖花女 **2** *AmE* a young girl who carries flowers in a wedding ceremony【美】〔婚礼中的〕女花童 —compare 比较 BRIDESMAID

flow·er·ing /ˈflauərɪŋ; ˈflaʊərɪŋ/ *n* **the flowering of** a successful period in the development of something 顶峰时期, 繁荣时期

flow·er·less /ˈflauɚləs; ˈflaʊələs/ *adj* not producing flowers 不开花的, 无花的

flower peo·ple /ˈ‥ ‚‥/ *n* [plural] *BrE* young people in the 1960s and 70s who were against war and wanted peace and love in society【英】"花孩儿"; 执花嬉皮士〔指 20 世纪 60 年代和 70 年代反对战争、主张和平与爱的年轻人〕

flow·er·pot /ˈflauɚ͵pɑt; ˈflaʊəpɒt/ *n* [C] a plastic or clay pot in which you grow plants〔塑料或陶瓷〕花盆

flower pow·er /ˈ‥ ‚‥/ *n* [U] the ideas of young people in the 1960s and 70s who believed that peace and love were the most important things in life "权力归花儿"〔指20 世纪 60 年代和 70 年代年轻人的主张, 认为和平与爱是生活中最重要的东西〕

flower show /ˈ‥ ‚/ *n* [C] a show at which people can look at different kinds of flowers and plants 花展

flow·er·y /ˈflauərɪ; ˈflaʊəri/ *adj* **1** decorated with pictures of flowers 用花卉图案装饰的: *a flowery pattern* 花卉图案 **2** flowery speech or writing uses complicated and rare words instead of simple clear language〔演说或文章〕词藻华丽的

flow·ing /ˈfloɪŋ; ˈfləʊɪŋ/ *adj* moving, curving, or hanging gracefully 流动的, 流畅的, 飘拂的: *long flowing white hair* 长长的飘拂的白发

flown /flon; fləʊn/ the past participle of FLY¹

flow sheet /ˈ· ‚/ *n* [C] an American form of FLOW CHART flow chart 的美语形式

fl. oz. *n* the written abbreviation of 缩写 = FLUID OUNCE

flu /flu; fluː/ *n* [C,U] a common infectious disease which is like a bad COLD² (2) but is more serious; INFLUENZA 流行性感冒, 流感: **the flu** *Darby's been in bed with the flu.* 达比患流感, 卧床休息了。| **flu** *BrE*【英】*Kate's got flu.* 凯特患了流感。

flub /flʌb; flʌb/ *v* [I,T] *AmE* to make a stupid mistake, or fail to do something by making a mistake【美】犯愚蠢的错误; 搞坏; 搞得一团糟: *He flubbed his first try at the SAT.* 他第一次考学业能力倾向测验就不及格了。

fluc·tu·ate /ˈflʌktʃu͵et; ˈflʌktʃueɪt/ *v* [I] if something such as a price or amount fluctuates, it changes very often from a high level to a low one and back again〔价格或数量〕波动, 上下变动, 涨落: [+between] *The present output of oil fluctuates between 3 and 5 million gallons per week.* 现在每周的石油产量在300万到500万加仑之间波动。| **fluctuate wildly** *House prices fluctuated wildly in the 80s.* 20 世纪 80 年代房价狂涨暴跌。

fluc·tu·a·tion /͵flʌktʃuˈeʃən; ͵flʌktʃuˈeɪʃən/ *n* [C,U] sudden changes in something such as the price, amount, or level of something〔价格、数量或水平等的〕波动: *price fluctuations* 价格波动

flue /flu; fluː/ *n* [C] a metal pipe or tube, especially in a CHIMNEY, that lets smoke or heat from a fire out of a building〔尤指烟囱的〕烟道

flu·ent /ˈfluənt; ˈfluːənt/ *adj* **1** able to speak a language very well 熟练的, 流利的: *"Can she speak Arabic?" "Yes, she's fluent."* "她会讲阿拉伯语吗?" "会, 她说得很流利。" **2 fluent French/Japanese etc** someone who speaks fluent French etc speaks it like a person from that country 流利的法语/日语等 **3** speaking, writing, or playing a musical instrument confidently and without long pauses〔说话、写作、演奏乐器等〕熟练的, 流畅的 —**fluently** *adv* —**fluency** *n* [U]

fluff¹ /flʌf; flʌf/ *n* [U] **1** soft, light bits of thread or wool that have come from wool, cotton, or other materials〔羊毛、棉或其他材料产生的〕绒毛; 蓬松毛; 碎絮 **2** soft light hair or feathers, especially from a young bird or animal〔尤指幼鸟或动物身上的〕绒毛, 软毛 —compare 比较 DOWN⁵ (2) —see also 另见 **bit of fluff** (BIT¹ (19))

fluff² *v* [T] **1** also 又作 **fluff up, fluff out** to make something soft appear larger by shaking or brushing it 抖开, 拍松: *Sue fluffed the pillows for me.* 休替我拍松了枕头。**2** also 又作 **fluff up, fluff out** if a bird fluffs its feathers, it raises them and makes itself look bigger〔鸟〕抖松〔羽毛〕**3** *informal* to make a mistake or do something badly【非正式】出错, 把…搞糟: *Rupert fluffed the catch.* 鲁珀特没有接住球。| **fluff your lines** (=make a mistake when speaking in a play)〔演戏时〕念错台词

fluff·y /ˈflʌfɪ; ˈflʌfi/ *adj* **1** made of or covered with something soft and light, such as wool, hair or feathers 绒毛的; 覆有绒毛的; 毛茸茸的: *a fluffy little kitten* 毛茸茸的小猫 **2** food that is fluffy is made soft and light by shaking, or beating so that air is mixed into it〔食物〕轻软的, 松软的: *Cream the butter and sugar until fluffy.* 将黄油和糖搅拌到松软成奶油状为止。—**fluffiness** *n* [U]

flu·id¹ /ˈfluɪd; ˈfluːɪ̇d/ *n* [C,U] *technical* a liquid【术语】液(体): *The doctor told him to drink a litre of fluid a day.* 医生告诉他每天喝一升液体。

fluid² *adj* **1** fluid movements are relaxed and graceful〔动作〕优美自然的; 优雅的; 流畅的: *fluid and expressive gestures* 流畅优美且富有表情的姿势 **2** [not before noun 不用于名词前] a situation or system that is fluid is likely to change often, or is able to change 不固定的, 易变的 —**fluidity** /fluˈɪdətɪ; fluˈɪdɪ̇ti/ *n* [U]

fluid ounce /͵‥ ˈ‥/ *n* [C] a unit for measuring liquids, equal to 0.0284 of a litre 液盎司, 液量盎司〔等于 0.0284 升〕—see table on page C5 参见 C5 页附录

fluke /fluk; fluːk/ *n* [C] *informal* something that is unlikely or surprising and only happens because of luck【非正式】侥幸, 偶然, 意外: *It was a complete fluke, meeting my sister at the airport.* 我在机场遇到妹妹, 这完全是偶然。—**fluky, flukey** *adj*

flum·moxed /ˈflʌməkst; ˈflʌməkst/ *adj* completely confused by something 弄得不知所措的: *I was totally flummoxed by his last question.* 我被他最后一个问题弄得晕头转向。—**flummox** *v* [T]

flung /flʌŋ; flʌŋ/ the past tense and past participle of FLING¹

flunk /flʌŋk; flʌŋk/ *v informal especially AmE*【非正式, 尤美】**1** [I,T] to fail a test〔在考试中〕不及格: *Tony flunked chemistry last semester.* 托尼上学期化学考试不及格。**2** [T] to give someone low marks on a test so that they fail it 给…打不及格分数

flunk out *phr v* [I] *informal especially AmE* to be forced to leave a school or college because your work is not good enough【非正式, 尤美】〔因学业不好而〕被迫退学: *Ben messed around and flunked out of college.* 本在大学里瞎混, 后来被迫退学了。

flun·key, flunky /ˈflʌŋkɪ; ˈflʌŋki/ *n* [C] someone who is always with an important person and treats them with too much respect 阿谀奉承的人, 马屁精: *The Stones were surrounded by the usual flunkeys and hangers-on.* 斯通一家人的周围常有一批阿谀奉承的人和马屁精围着。

flu·o·res·cent /͵fluoˈrɛsn̩t; fluəˈresənt/ *adj* **1** fluorescent colours are very bright and easy to see, even in the dark〔色彩〕荧光的: *a fluorescent pink T-shirt* 有荧光的粉红色 T 恤衫 **2** a fluorescent substance produces a bright white light when electricity or other types of power pass through it〔物质〕发荧光的 —**fluorescence** *n* [U]

fluorescent light /·‚‥ ˈ·/ a fluorescent light produces light when electricity is passed through a gas-filled tube 荧光灯, 日光灯

flu·o·ri·date /ˈfluərə͵det; ˈflʊərɪ̇deɪt/ *v* [T] to add fluoride to water in order to protect people's teeth〔为保护牙齿〕向〔水中〕加入氟化物 —**fluoridation** /͵fluərəˈdeʃən; ͵flʊərɪ̇ˈdeɪʃən/ *n* [U]

flu·o·ride /ˈfluə͵raɪd; ˈflʊəraɪd/ *n* [U] a chemical compound of fluorine, especially one that helps to protect teeth against decay〔尤指有助于防止龋齿的〕氟化物

flu·o·rine /ˈfluə͵rin; ˈflʊəriːn/ *n* [U] a chemical substance that is usually in the form of a poisonous gas 氟

fluo·ro·car·bon /͵fluroˈkɑrbən; ͵flʊərəʊˈkɑːbən/ *n* [C] any chemical that contains the substances fluorine and CARBON (1) 碳氟化合物: *damage to the ozone layer caused by fluorocarbons* 碳氟化合物对臭氧层造成的破坏 —see also 另见 CFC

flur·ried /ˈflɝɪd; ˈflʌrid/ *adj* confused and nervous or excited 慌张的; 激动不安的: *the flurried activity surrounding the wedding* 围绕这场婚礼的忙乱的活动

flur·ry /ˈflɝɪ; ˈflʌri/ *n* **1** [singular] an occasion when there is suddenly a lot of activity within a short period of time 紧张慌乱; 激动不安: [+of] *After a quiet spell there was a sudden flurry of phone calls.* 经过一段平静之后, 电话突然响个不停。**2** [C] if

there is a flurry of snow, rain, or wind, it suddenly starts snowing etc for a short time 阵雪; 阵雨; 阵风: *Snow flurries are expected overnight.* 整个晚上都可能有阵阵小雪。

flush¹ /flʌʃ; flʌʃ/ *n* **1** [singular] a red colour that appears on your face or body, especially because you are embarrassed, ill, or excited〔尤指因尴尬、生病或激动而引起的〕脸红, 潮红: *"How can you tell?" he said as a flush crept up his neck.* "你怎么知道?"他说着, 脖子开始变得通红。—see also 另见 HOT FLUSH **2 a flush of pride/embarrassment etc** a sudden feeling of pride, excitement, or another emotion 一阵自豪感/尴尬等 **3 the first flush of youth/success etc** the beginning of a period of time when you feel excited because you are young, successful etc 首次感到充满青春活力的/首次感到成功的(一阵)喜悦 **4** [C] a set of cards that someone has in a card game that are all of the same suit (SUIT¹ (3))〔纸牌戏中的〕同花牌 **5** [C] the part of a toilet that cleans it with a sudden flow of water〔马桶里的〕冲洗装置 **6** [C] the act of cleaning something by forcing water through it〔用水〕冲洗, 冲水

flush² *v* **1** [I,T] if you flush a toilet or if it flushes, you make water go through it to clean it〔用水〕冲洗〔马桶〕;〔马桶〕被冲洗: **flush sth down the toilet** *Mandy accidentally flushed her ring down the toilet.* 曼迪不小心把戒指从马桶里冲下去了。**2** [I] to become red in the face 脸红,〔脸〕发红: *Flushing slightly, Lesley looked away.* 莱斯莉有点脸红, 朝别处看去。**3** also 又作 **flush out** [T] to clean something by forcing water or another liquid through it〔用水或其他液体〕冲洗, 冲出: *Try flushing out the blockage with boiling water.* 试一试用沸水冲掉堵塞物。**4** [T always+adv/prep] to make someone leave the place where they are hiding 使〔某人〕离开隐蔽之处: **flush sb from/out of** *The police managed to flush the gang from their hideout.* 警方设法把这伙匪徒赶出躲藏处。

flush³ *adj* **1** if two surfaces are flush they are at exactly the same level, so that the place where they meet is flat 在同一平面上的, 齐平的: [**+with**] *Make sure that the cupboard is flush with the wall.* 要确保碗橱是嵌在墙中的。**2** [not before noun 不用于名词前] *informal* if someone is flush they suddenly have plenty of money for a short time【非正式】突然很有钱的, 暴富的

flush⁴ *adv* fitting together so that the place where two surfaces meet is flat 齐平地: *The door should fit flush into its frame.* 门应该刚好齐平地装进门框内。

flushed /flʌʃt; flʌʃt/ *adj* **1** red in the face 脸红的: *Nona was hot and flushed.* 诺娜身上发热, 脸上发红。| [**+with**] *Her face flushed with pride.* 她洋洋得意, 脸上发红。**2 flushed with success/excitement** excited and eager because you have achieved something 因成功而满脸喜色/因激动而满脸通红

flus·ter /ˈflʌstə; ˈflʌstə/ *v* [T] to make someone nervous and confused by making them hurry or interrupting them〔催促或打断某人〕使紧张, 使困惑 —**fluster** *n* [singular] *BrE*【英】

flus·tered /ˈflʌstəd; ˈflʌstəd/ *adj* confused and nervous 慌乱的, 紧张的: *Elijah got really flustered during the interview.* 伊莱贾在面试时十分紧张。

flute /flut; fluːt/ *n* [C] a musical instrument that you play by holding it across your lips, blowing into it, and pressing keys (KEY² (3)) with your fingers to change the notes 长笛

flut·ed /ˈflutɪd; ˈfluːtɪ̈d/ *adj* decorated with long narrow curves that curve inwards 饰有长凹槽的: *fluted columns* 刻有凹槽的柱子

flut·ist /ˈflutɪst; ˈfluːtɪ̈st/ *n* [C] *AmE* someone who plays the flute【美】吹长笛的人; 长笛手; FLAUTIST *BrE*【英】

flut·ter¹ /ˈflʌtə; ˈflʌtə/ *v* **1** [I,T] if a bird or insect flutters its wings or if its wings flutter, its wings move quickly and lightly up and down 振(翼), 拍打(翅膀): *butterflies fluttering from flower to flower* 在花丛中扑翅飞舞的蝴蝶 **2** [I] to wave or move gently in the air〔在空中〕飘扬, 飘动: *Dead leaves fluttered slowly to the ground.* 枯叶慢慢飘落到地上。**3** [I,T] if your heart or your stomach flutters, you feel very excited or nervous〔因激动或紧张〕(使)〔心脏或胃〕怦怦跳, 颤抖, 悸动 **4 flutter your eyelashes (at sb)** if a woman flutters her eyelashes at a man, she uses her sexual attractiveness to influence him〔女性〕(朝某人)眨眼, 抛媚眼

flutter² *n* **1** [singular] the state of being nervous, confused or excited 不安, 困惑, 激动: **in a flutter** *We're all in a flutter of excitement at the moment.* 我们此时此刻都兴奋得心怦怦直跳。| **cause a flutter** (=make people excited or interested) 令人兴奋; 引起兴趣 *News of her arrest caused quite a flutter in the office.* 她被捕的消息在办公室引起一阵不小的轰动。**2 have a flutter** *BrE informal* to risk a small amount of money on the result of a horse race; BET² (1)【英, 非正式】〔赛马时〕下一笔小赌注 **3** [singular] a fluttering movement 拍动; 飘动: *a flutter of wings* 翅膀的拍动 **4** [C] *technical* an irregular heart beat【术语】〔心脏〕不规则的跳动, 振颤; 悸动 **5** [U] *technical* a shaking movement that stops a machine working properly【术语】〔机器的〕抖动, 颤动

flu·vi·al /ˈfluvɪəl; ˈfluːviəl/ *adj technical* relating to or produced by rivers【术语】河流的; 生长在河中的

flux /flʌks; flʌks/ *n* [U] **1 be in (a state of) flux** to be changing a lot so that you cannot be sure what will happen 处于不断变化中: *The education system is in a state of flux, with new requirements constantly being added.* 教育体制处于不断变化中, 人们不断地增加新的要求。**2** a substance that is added to a metal to help it melt or when sticking two pieces of metal together; SOLDER¹ 助熔剂, 焊剂

fly¹ /flaɪ; flaɪ/ *v past tense* flew /flu; fluː/ *past participle* flown /flon; fləʊn/

① PLANE 飞机
② BIRDS/INSECTS ETC 鸟/昆虫等
③ FLOAT 飘动
④ MOVE FREELY 自由活动
⑤ MOVE/GO FAST 迅速移动/迅速去
⑥ TIME GOES QUICKLY 时间过得很快
⑦ ANGRY 生气的
⑧ ATTACK 攻击
⑨ OTHER MEANINGS 其他意思

① PLANE 飞机

1 [I] to travel by plane 乘飞机: *You can fly direct from London to Tokyo in under 12 hours now.* 你现在可以在12小时内从伦敦直飞到东京。| **fly on** (=continue flying to another place) 继续飞行 *The first stop is San Francisco, and from there we're flying on to Hawaii.* 第一站是旧金山, 然后我们从那里继续飞到夏威夷。

2 [I] to move through the air in order to go from one place to another〔飞机〕飞行: *These planes can fly at incredibly high speeds.* 这些飞机能以难以置信的高速度飞行。

3 [T] to carry or send goods or people by plane 空运〔货物或乘客〕: **fly sth into/out of** *US planes have been flying food and medical supplies into the area.* 美国飞机一直在把食品和药品空运到该地区。

4 [I,T] to use a particular AIRLINE or use a particular type of ticket when flying 乘坐〔某家航空公司的〕飞机; 用〔某类票〕飞行: *We usually fly economy class.* 我们乘飞机通常坐经济舱。

5 [I,T] to control a plane through the air 驾驶〔飞机〕: *The Prince has his own private jet which he flies himself.* 王子有私人喷气式飞机, 由他自己驾驶。

6 fly a mission to fly a plane in a war, especially in order to attack an enemy〔战时〕驾机执行任务; 驾机出击

7 [T] to cross an area of water in a plane (乘飞机)飞越〔水域〕: *the first woman to fly the Atlantic* 第一位飞越大西洋的女性

② BIRDS/INSECTS ETC 鸟/昆虫等

8 [I] to move through the air using wings 飞: [**+up/into etc**] *a flock of seagulls flying overhead* 在头上飞翔的一群海鸥

③ FLOAT 飘动

9 [I always+adv/prep] to float high in the air 飘动: *I watched the balloons fly up into the sky.* 我看着气球飘向空中。

④ MOVE FREELY 自由活动

10 [I] if your hair, coat etc is flying, it moves freely and loosely in the air〔头发、衣服等〕飘拂, 飞扬: *long hair flying in the wind* 在风中飘拂的长发

⑤ **MOVE/GO FAST** 迅速移动/迅速去

11 [I always+adv/prep] to go somewhere very quickly 飞跑，飞奔，冲: [+**down/across/out of etc**] *She flew down the stairs to find out what had happened.* 她冲下楼去看看发生了什么事。

12 [I always+adv/prep] to move suddenly and very quickly 突然快速地移动: [+**open/shut/back etc**] *The door suddenly flew open.* 门突然打开了。| *Sparks were flying everywhere.* 火花四处飞溅。

13 send sb/sth flying to knock someone or something so that they fall through the air 使某人人仰马翻；把某物撞得飞散: *He crashed into the table and sent the glasses flying.* 他撞到桌子，把玻璃杯都撞飞了。

14 go flying to suddenly fall through the air after being knocked by something or someone〔被撞而〕飞落: *The boat rocked to the side and I went flying across the room.* 船摇摆得倾侧了，我从房间的一边飞落到另一边。

15 I must fly *spoken* used to say that you must leave quickly【口】我得赶紧走了

⑥ **TIME GOES QUICKLY** 时间过得很快

16 time flies *spoken* used to say that a period of time passes or something happens in an unexpectedly short time【口】时间飞逝: *Is it August already? How time flies!* 已经8月了吗？时间过得多快！| **Time flies when you are having fun!** (=often used humorously to mean that something has been very boring) 人若快乐，时间就过得快！〔常幽默地用来表示厌烦某事〕

17 fly by/past if a period of time flies by or past, it passes very quickly without you noticing〔时间〕飞逝: *We've been so busy, the week has just flown by.* 我们很忙，整个星期就这么飞逝而过。

F

⑦ **ANGRY** 生气的

18 fly into a temper/rage to suddenly become extremely angry 勃然大怒: *My father flew into a rage and demanded his money back.* 我父亲勃然大怒，要求取回他的钱。

19 fly off the handle *informal* to become very angry suddenly and unexpectedly about something that does not seem very important【非正式】〔为不太重要的事〕大发雷霆: *There's no need to fly off the handle like that.* 不必那样大发雷霆。

20 let fly to suddenly start shouting at someone because you feel very angry about something 破口大骂: [+**at**] *The woman let fly a torrent of abuse at him.* 那个女人对他大骂一通。

21 go fly a kite *spoken* used to say that you think that someone is being very annoying【口】走开〔用于表示某人很烦时〕

⑧ **ATTACK** 攻击

22 let fly to suddenly attack someone 突然攻击，突袭: [+**with**] *The soldiers let fly with a hail of machine-gun fire.* 士兵们突然用机关枪猛烈射击。

⑨ **OTHER MEANINGS** 其他意思

23 ▶ESCAPE 逃走◀ [T] to leave somewhere in order to escape 逃离: *They were forced to fly the country in 1939.* 1939年他们被迫逃到国外。

24 fly the coop *informal especially AmE* to leave or escape【非正式，尤美】离开，逃走，离巢: *All my children have flown the coop now.* 我的所有孩子现在都离家走了。

25 fly by the seat of your pants *informal* to do something by guessing how to do it because you have very little knowledge or experience【非正式】凭猜测做事

26 ▶FLAG 旗帜◀ [I,T] if a flag flies, or if you fly it, it is fixed to a pole or a building, ship etc 飘扬，悬挂: *a ship flying the Dutch flag* 一艘挂着荷兰国旗的船

27 fly the flag to behave in a way that shows that you are proud of your country, organization etc 挥舞旗帜〔以某种行动表明为自己的祖国、组织等而骄傲〕

28 fly in the face of to be the opposite of what most people think is reasonable, sensible, or normal 违反，违抗: *Eysenck's claim flies in the face of all the evidence.* 艾森克的声称与所有的证据相违背。

29 rumours/accusations etc are flying if RUMOURS, ACCUSATIONS etc are flying about something, a lot of people are saying things about it 谣言四起/人人都在谴责等: *Rumours were flying round the capital about a possible military takeover.* 可能进行军事接管的谣言在首都四处传开。

30 ▶PLAN 计划◀ *AmE* [I] a plan that will fly is good or useful【美】〔计划〕行得通 —see also 另见 **the bird has flown** (BIRD (7)), **as the crow flies** (CROW[1] (3)), **sparks fly** (SPARK[1] (6))

fly at sb also 又作 **fly into sb** *AmE phr v* [T] to suddenly rush towards someone because you are very angry with them【美】〔因生气而〕冲向[扑向]某人: *The old man flew at her in rage.* 那位老人怒气冲冲地冲向她。

fly² *v past tense and past participle* **flied** [I] *AmE* to hit a ball in BASEBALL high into the air, especially so that the ball is caught by the other team【美】〔棒球中〕击腾空球，击高飞球〔尤指球被对方接住时〕

fly³ *n* [C]

1 ▶INSECT 昆虫◀ a small flying insect with two wings 蝇，苍蝇: *The flies kept buzzing around us.* 苍蝇老在我们周围嗡嗡叫。

2 ▶TROUSERS 裤子◀ also 又作 **flies** *BrE*【英】the part at the front of a pair of trousers which you can open and which consists of a ZIP[1] (1) or a row of buttons〔裤子前面的〕拉锁盖，钮扣盖: *He did up his fly.* 他扣上了裤扣。

3 sb wouldn't hurt a fly/sb wouldn't harm a fly *spoken* used to say that someone is very gentle and is not likely to hurt anyone【口】某人不会伤害人，某人心地善良

4 be going down like flies/be dropping like flies *informal* used to say that a lot of people are becoming ill with a particular disease【非正式】纷纷病倒

5 fly in the ointment *informal* the only thing that spoils something and prevents it from being successful【非正式】美中不足之处

6 be a fly on the wall to be able to watch what happens without other people knowing that you are there 做墙壁上的一只苍蝇，做不被察觉的观察者: *I wish I'd been a fly on the wall during that conversation.* 我真希望自己是墙壁上的一只苍蝇，能听到那次谈话。—see also 另见 FLY-ON-THE-WALL

7 there are no flies on sb *BrE spoken* used to say that someone is not stupid and cannot be tricked【英口】某人很机灵，某人不会上当受骗

8 ▶FISHING 钓鱼◀ a hook that is made to look like a fly, used for catching fish 假蝇钓钩

9 ▶BASEBALL 棒球◀ a fly ball 腾空球，高飞球

fly⁴ *adj old-fashioned especially BrE* clever and not easily tricked【过时，尤英】机灵的，聪明的；不易上当受骗的: *He's a fly old bird.* 他是个精明不易受骗的老家伙。

fly·a·way /ˈflaɪəˌwe; ˈflaɪəweɪ/ *adj* **flyaway hair** hair that is soft and thin and becomes untidy easily〔头发〕飘拂的；柔软而纤细的；易散开的

fly ball /ˈ· ·/ *n* [C] a ball that has been hit high into the air in a game of BASEBALL〔棒球中的〕腾空球，高飞球

fly·blown /ˈflaɪˌblon; ˈflaɪbləʊn/ *adj* **1** *especially BrE* old, dirty, and in bad condition【尤英】肮脏破旧的 **2** *BrE* meat that is flyblown has flies' eggs in it and is not suitable for eating【尤英】〔肉类〕沾有蝇卵的

fly·boy /ˈflaɪˌbɔɪ; ˈflaɪbɔɪ/ *n* [C] *AmE informal* a pilot【美，非正式】飞机驾驶员

fly·by /ˈflaɪˌbaɪ, ˈflaɪbaɪ/ *n* [C] *AmE* a group of planes that fly close together on a special occasion for people to watch【美】〔表演性的〕低空编队飞行

fly-by-night /ˈ· · ˌ·/ *adj* [only before noun 仅用于名词前] *informal* a fly-by-night company, businessman is not well established and may only be interested in making quick profits【非正式】〔只求迅速获利而〕不讲信用的；不可靠的〔公司、商人等〕

fly·catch·er /ˈflaɪˌkætʃɚ; ˈflaɪˌkætʃə/ *n* [C] a small bird that catches flies in the air 鹟，捕蝇鸟

fly-drive hol·i·day /ˈ· ·ˌ··· / *n* [C] a holiday arranged at a fixed price that includes your flight, a car to drive, and a place to stay 空陆联游假期〔指包括机票、租汽车和住宿的全包度假旅游〕

fly·er /ˈflaɪɚ; ˈflaɪə/ *n* [C] **1** a sheet of paper advertising something, which is given to people in the street or is pushed through their door〔广告〕传单 **2** *informal* a pilot【非正式】飞机驾驶员 **3** *informal* a FLYING START【非正式】快速起跑

fly·fish·ing /ˈflaɪˌfɪʃɪŋ; ˈflaɪˌfɪʃɪŋ/ *n* [U] the sport of fishing in a river or lake with special hooks that are made to look like flies 用假蝇钩钓鱼

fly half /ˌ· ˈ·/ *n* [C] a fast-running player in RUGBY whose job is to pass the ball to a line of players〔英式橄榄球赛中的〕外侧前卫

fly·ing¹ /ˈflaɪɪŋ; ˈflaɪ-ɪŋ/ *adj* **1 with flying colours** if you pass a test with flying colours, you are very successful in it 出色地，很成功地，大获全胜地〔通过考试〕**2 a flying visit** a quick visit because you are in a hurry 短暂访问: *They've been down*

here for a flying visit. 他们到这里进行短暂访问。**3 a flying jump/leap** a long high jump made while you are running 急行起跳

flying² *n* [U] the activity of travelling by plane 乘飞机旅行; 飞行: *fear of flying* 害怕乘飞机旅行

flying but·tress /,.. '../ *n* [C] a half ARCH¹ (1) joined to the top of the outside wall of a large building such as a church in order to support it 拱扶垛, 飞(扶)拱

flying doc·tor /,.. '../ *n* [C] a doctor, especially in Australia, who goes by plane to visit sick people who live a long way from the nearest town〔尤指澳大利亚的〕飞行医生〔乘飞机到偏远地区出诊的医生〕

Flying Dutch·man, The /,.. '../ **1** in old stories, a GHOST ship which appears in stormy weather and is a sign that something very bad is going to happen "漂泊的荷兰人", 鬼船〔传说中的鬼船, 现于风暴天气, 为不祥之兆〕**2** the CAPTAIN of this ship 鬼船船长 **3** an OPERA by Richard Wagner based on these stories《漂泊的荷兰人》〔理查德·瓦格纳根据鬼船的传说创作的一部歌剧〕

flying fish /,.. '. / *n* [C] a tropical sea fish that can jump out of the water 飞鱼〔热带海鱼〕

flying fox /,.. './ *n* [C] a FRUIT BAT 狐蝠, 热带大蝙蝠

flying of·fic·er /'.. ,.../ *n* [C] a rank in the British air-force〔英国的〕空军中尉 —see table on page C7 参见 C7 页附录

flying pick·et /,.. '../ *n* [C] someone who travels to different factories, mines etc during a strike (STRIKE² (1)) and tries to persuade workers to stop working, although they do not work there themselves〔罢工期间到各处工厂、矿山等劝说工人罢工的〕流动宣传员

flying sau·cer /,.. '../ *n* [C] a round-shaped SPACECRAFT carrying creatures from space; UFO 飞碟, 不明飞行物

Flying Scots·man, The /,.. '../ a fast train that runs between London and Edinburgh "苏格兰飞人"号〔运行于伦敦和爱丁堡之间的一列快车〕

flying squad /'.. ./ *n* [C] a special group of police officers in Britain whose job is to travel quickly to the place where there has been a serious crime〔英国的〕闪电行动队, 快速特警队

flying start /,.. './ *n* **1 get off to a flying start** *informal* to begin very well【非正式】开始时进展顺利; 顺利地开始: *He's got off to a flying start in his new job.* 他的新工作一开始就进展顺利。**2** a start to a race in which the competitors are already moving very quickly 快速起跑

flying tack·le /,.. '../ *n* [C] a way of stopping someone from running by putting your arms around their legs and making them fall over〔抱住对方的腿、使之摔倒的〕鱼跃擒抱

fly leaf /'. ./ *n* [C] a page at the beginning or end of a book, on which there is usually no printing〔书籍前后的〕空白页, 扉页, 衬页

Fly·mo /'flaɪmo; 'flaɪməʊ/ *trademark* a type of LAWN MOWER with a ROTARY blade that creates a strong current of air which lifts the MOWER a little way above the ground【商标】飞磨〔一种带旋转刀片的割草机, 工作时产生一股强气流, 将机器从地面稍微抬起〕

Flynn /flɪn; flɪn/, **Er·rol** /'ɛrəl; 'erəl/ (1909-59) a US film actor who is thought of as a typical example of a SWASHBUCKLING character (=someone who is brave and strong, and who enjoys adventures, sword-fighting etc). He was known for being sexually attractive, for having many lovers, and for drinking a lot of alcohol. His films include *Captain Blood* (1935) and *The Adventures of Robin Hood* (1938). 弗林〔(1909-1959), 美国电影演员, 被视为江湖人物的典型形象。他以性感、情人多和酗酒出名, 演过的影片包括《铁血舰长》(1935) 和《盗侠罗宾汉》(1938)〕

fly-on-the-wall /,. . . '. ◂/ *adj* [only before noun 仅用于名词前] a fly-on-the-wall television programme shows people's daily lives in a very natural way, because they forget they are being filmed〔拍摄电视节目时〕不被觉察的; 隐秘拍摄的

fly·o·ver /'flaɪ,ovɚ; 'flaɪ-əʊvə/ *n* [C] **1** *BrE* a bridge that carries a road over another road【英】立交桥, 高架公路; OVERPASS *AmE*【美】—see picture on page A3 参见 A3 页图 **2** *AmE* a flypast【美】〔表演性的〕低空编队飞行

Flyover Country the middle part of the US, which some people consider to be boring and which they only see when they are flying over it in a plane between the east and west coasts – used humorously 飞越之地〔美国中部地区。有人认为这一带乏味无聊, 只是在坐飞机穿梭于东西海岸之间时才看一眼。这是一种幽默的用法〕

fly·pa·per /'flaɪ,pepɚ; 'flaɪ,peɪpə/ *n* [C,U] paper covered with a sticky substance used to catch flies 粘蝇纸

fly·past /'flaɪ,pæst; 'flaɪpɑːst/ *n* [C] *BrE* a group of planes that fly close together on a special occasion for people to watch【英】〔表演性的〕低空编队飞行

fly·sheet /'flaɪ,ʃit; 'flaɪʃiːt/ also 又作 **fly** *n* [C] a sheet of material that is put over a tent to protect it from the rain〔帐篷上的〕防雨篷顶

fly·specked /'flaɪ,spɛkt; 'flaɪspekt/ *adj especially AmE* covered with small spots of waste matter from flies【尤美】满布蝇屎的

fly·swat·ter /'flaɪ,swɑtɚ; 'flaɪ,swɒtə/ *n* [C] a square net fixed to a handle and used for killing flies (苍) 蝇拍

fly·weight /'flaɪ,wet; 'flaɪweɪt/ *n* [C] a BOXER (1) who belongs to the lightest class of boxers and weighs 51 kilos〔体重 51 公斤的〕次最轻量级拳击手

fly·wheel /'flaɪ,hwil; 'flaɪwiːl/ *n* [C] a heavy wheel that keeps a machine working at a steady speed because of its weight 飞轮, 惯性轮

fly·whisk /'flaɪ,hwɪsk; 'flaɪ,wɪsk/ *n* [C] *BrE* a small brush, used in former times for keeping flies away【英】〔旧时驱蝇的〕掸子, 蝇拂

FM /,ɛf 'ɛm; ,ef 'em◂/ *n* [U] frequency modulation; a system used for broadcasting radio programmes which produces a very clear sound 调频; 调频广播系统 —compare 比较 AM

fnarr /fnɑr; fnɑː/ *interjection BrE spoken humorous* used to say that what has just been said also has a sexual meaning although this was not intended【英口, 幽默】别说荤话: *"He's got a big one, hasn't he?" "Fnarr!"* "他的家伙很大, 不是吗?" "别说荤话!"

FO the Foreign Office; the British government department responsible for foreign affairs, that is officially called the Foreign and Commonwealth Office 外交部〔英国政府一部门, 负责外交事务, 正式名称为Foreign and Commonwealth Office (外交和联邦事务部)〕—see also 另见 FCO

foal¹ /fol; fəʊl/ *n* [C] a very young horse 马驹

foal² *v* [I] to give birth to a foal 产驹

foam¹ /fom; fəʊm/ *n* [U] **1** a mass of small BUBBLEs¹ (1) on the surface of something, such as the sea or coffee, which are formed when air mixes with a liquid〔空气与液体混合时产生的〕泡沫 **2** a substance used for cleaning or shaving (SHAVE¹ (1)) which consists of a mass of small BUBBLEs¹ (1)〔清洗或剃须用的〕泡沫(剂) **3** foam rubber 泡沫橡胶, 海绵橡胶: *a foam mattress* 海绵橡胶床垫 —**foamy** *adj*

foam² *v* [I] **1** to produce foam 起泡沫: *When he opened the can it foamed all over his hand.* 他打开罐子时弄得满手泡沫。**2 foam at the mouth** to make a mass of small BUBBLEs¹ (1) come out of your mouth because you are very angry or ill〔发怒时〕唾沫四溅; 〔生病时〕口吐白沫

foam rub·ber /,. '..◂/ *n* [U] soft rubber full of air bubbles used in PILLOWs, chair seats etc〔用在枕头、椅座等中的〕泡沫橡胶, 海绵橡胶

fob¹ /fɑb; fɒb/ *v* **fobbing, fobbed**

fob sb ↔ **off** [T] **1** to try to stop someone complaining or asking questions by giving them explanations, excuses etc that are obviously untrue〔用借口等〕搪塞, 哄骗: **fob sb off with** *He tried to fob her off with some story about losing her telephone number.* 他想用丢失电话号码的假话来搪塞她。**2** to make someone accept something that is not as good as the thing they wanted 骗〔某人〕接受〔次货、劣质品等〕: **fob sb off with** *Don't let them fob you off with some cheap imported brand.* 别让他们用便宜的进口牌子货色把你骗了。

fob sth ↔ **off on** sb [T] to persuade someone into accepting something by a trick or deceit 骗〔某人〕接受〔某事物〕: *You can't just fob all your difficult jobs off on to me!* 你不能骗我接受你的这些艰难的工作!

fob² *n* [C] **1** a small object fixed to a key ring as a decoration 钥匙圈上的小饰物 **2** a short chain or piece of cloth to which a fob watch is fastened 怀表短链; 怀表带

fob watch /'. ./ *n* [C] a watch that fits into a pocket, or is pinned to a woman's dress 怀表; 挂表

fo·cal /'fokl; 'fəʊkəl/ *adj* [only before noun 仅用于名词前] **1** the focal point, issue etc is the thing that people pay most attention to 最受关注的; 焦点的 **2 focal attention/awareness** the main part of your attention when you are looking at or thinking about something 重点注意力; 焦点意识

focal length /,.. './ *n* [C] *technical* the distance between the centre of a lens and the focal point【术语】焦距

focal point /'.. ./ *n* [C] **1** the person or thing that you pay most attention to〔注意力的〕焦点, 重点: *The man on horseback acts as the focal point of the picture.* 骑在马背上的那个人是那

F

幅图画的焦点。**2** *technical* the point on a LENS or a mirror where light RAYS (1) meet【术语】聚焦点

fo'c'sle /fəʊksl; 'fəʊksəl/ *n* [C] *BrE* the front part of a ship, where the sailors live【英】〔船艏的〕水手舱; FORECASTLE *AmE*【美】

fo·cus¹ /'fokəs; 'fəʊkəs/ *v* **focussing, focussed** or **focused** **1** [I,T] to pay special attention to a particular person or thing instead of others (使) 集中注意力于…: [**+on**] *Modern medicine has tended to focus too much on developing highly complicated surgical techniques.* 现代医学常趋向于过分注意发展十分复杂的外科技术。| **focus attention on** *The recent wave of bombings has focussed public attention on the region.* 最近一连串的爆炸案把公众的注意力集中到该地区。**2** [T] to change the position of the LENS (2) on a camera, TELESCOPE¹ etc, so that you can see something clearly 调节〔照相机、望远镜等〕的焦距: **focus sth on** *He focused his binoculars on the building opposite.* 他对准对面的建筑物调节双目望远镜的焦距。**3** [I,T] if your eyes focus, or if you focus your eyes, you gradually become able to see something clearly (使) 逐渐看清 **4** [I,T] if you focus beams of light or if they focus, they pass through a LENS and meet at a point (使)〔光线〕聚焦; (使) 集中

focus² *n* **1** [singular] the subject or situation that people pay special attention to 〔话题或情况的〕焦点, 重点: [**+on**] *The focus of the conference shifted from population growth to the education of women.* 会议的重点从人口增长转移到妇女教育上。| **the focus is on sth** *The focus of recent legislation has been on environmental issues.* 最近立法的焦点是环境问题。| **the focus of attention** *The war in Bosnia had now become the focus of worldwide media attention.* 波斯尼亚的战争此时已成为全世界媒体关注的焦点。**2** [U] special attention that is given to one particular subject or situation 〔注意力的〕集中点, 中心点: [**+on**] *grammar based teaching, with its focus on accuracy rather than fluency* 以语法为基础的教学法, 其重点放在准确度而不是流利程度上 | **bring/throw sth into focus** (=make people notice something and pay special attention to it) 使明确, 使清楚; 使特别注意 *The case has brought the problem of child abuse sharply into focus.* 这个案例已经使虐待儿童的问题十分突出。**3** **in focus/out of focus** if a photograph or an instrument such as a TELESCOPE¹ is in focus, the edges of the things you are looking at can be seen clearly, if it is out of focus they cannot be seen clearly 〔照片或望远镜等〕焦点对准[没有对准]的, 清晰[不清晰]的 **4** [C] *technical plural* **foci** the point where beams of light or waves of sound meet after their direction has been changed【术语】〔光、声的〕焦点

fo·cussed *BrE*【英】, **focused** *AmE*【美】/'fokəst; 'fəʊkəst/ *adj* paying careful attention to what you are doing, in a way that shows you are determined to succeed 集中注意力的; 聚精会神的: *This year she's a much more focused player.* 今年她更聚精会神地参加比赛。

fod·der /'fɑdə; 'fɒdə/ *n* [C,U] food for farm animals 饲料, 秣 —see also 另见 CANNON FODDER

FoE /ˌɛf o 'i; ˌef əʊ 'iː/ the abbreviation of 缩写= FRIENDS OF THE EARTH

foe /fo; fəʊ/ *n* [C] *literary* an enemy【文】敌人, 仇敌

foe·tal, fetal /'fitl; 'fiːtl/ *adj* [only before noun 仅用于名词前] connected with a foetus 胎儿的, 胚胎的: *foetal abnormalities* 胎儿的畸形

foetal po·si·tion /'‥ ·,‥/ *n* [C] the body position of an unborn child inside its mother, in which the body is curled, and the legs are pulled up against the chest 胎姿, 胎位

foe·tus, fetus /'fitəs; 'fiːtəs/ *n* [C] a young human or animal before birth 胎儿, 胚胎 —compare 比较 EMBRYO (1)

fog¹ /fɑg; fɒg/ *n* [C,U] **1** cloudy air near the ground which is difficult to see through 雾: *Thick fog is making driving conditions hazardous.* 浓雾正使路面情况变得很危险。| **fog bank** (=a large area of fog) 雾阵, 雾堤 —compare 比较 MIST¹ (1) **2** **in a fog** *informal* confused and unable to think clearly【非正式】困惑的, 迷惘的: *Sorry, what did you say? – My mind's in a fog at the moment.* 对不起, 你说什么? — 我的头脑现在十分混乱。

fog² *v* **fogged, fogging** **1** [I,T] if something made of glass fogs up or becomes fogged up, it becomes covered in small drops of water that make it difficult to see through (使)〔玻璃制品因有微小水滴〕变得模糊 **2** **fog the issue** to make a subject, problem etc become unclear and more complicated 使问题变得模糊不清: *I think we're just fogging the issue by looking at all these details.* 我认为我们察看这些细节只会使问题变得模糊不清。

fog·bound /'fɑg,baund; 'fɒgbaʊnd/ *adj* prevented from travelling or working normally because of fog 被雾所困的; 因雾受阻的: *Moscow airport was fogbound.* 莫斯科机场大雾弥天, 不能使用。

fogey, fogy /'fogɪ; 'fəʊgi/ *n plural* **fogeys** or **fogies** [C] someone who has old-fashioned ideas and dislikes change 守旧者: **old fogey** *Don't be such an old fogey!* 别这样老顽固!

Fogg /fɑg; fɒg/**, Phil·e·as** /'fɪlɪəs; 'fɪliəs/ the main character in the book *Around the World In Eighty Days* by Jules Verne. Phileas Fogg is an Englishman who travels around the world and has many adventures. 福格〔儒勒·凡尔纳《八十天环游地球》中的主人公。他是英格兰人, 环游世界, 有许多冒险经历〕

fog·gy /'fɑgɪ; 'fɒgi/ *adj* **1** very misty because of fog 多雾的: *a foggy day in November* 11月的一个多雾的日子 **2** **not have the foggiest (idea)** *spoken* to not know at all【口】完全不知道; 全然不明白: *None of us had the foggiest idea about how to put the tent up.* 我们完全不知道怎样搭帐篷。**3** **a foggy memory/recollection** an unclear memory of something that happened in the past 模糊的记忆: *I only have a foggy recollection of my grandmother.* 我对祖母只有模糊的记忆。—**foggily** *adv* —**fogginess** *n* [U]

Foggy Bot·tom /'‥ ,‥/ a humorous name given to the US State Department because of the FOG (=thick mist) that often surrounds its offices in Washington, D.C. 雾谷〔美国国务院的谑称。位于华盛顿特区的办公区经常雾气环绕, 故名〕

fog·horn /'fɑg,hɔrn; 'fɒghɔːn/ *n* [C] **1** a piece of equipment that makes a loud noise, which is used by ships in fog to warn other ships of their position 〔雾天向其他船只发出以示自己船只方位的〕雾角, 雾笛 **2** **a voice like a foghorn** *humorous* a very loud, unpleasant voice【幽默】响亮刺耳的嗓音

fog lamp /'· ·/ *BrE*【英】, **fog light** /'· ·/ *AmE*【美】—*n* [C] a strong light on the front of a car that helps drivers to see in fog 雾灯〔汽车在雾中使用的车前强光灯〕

foi·ble /'fɔɪbl; 'fɔɪbəl/ *n* [C] a habit or feature of someone's character which is a little strange or silly 怪癖: *We all have our little foibles.* 我们大家都各有一些小怪癖。

foie gras /ˌfwɑ 'grɑ; ˌfwɑː 'grɑː/ *n* [U] PATE DE FOIE GRAS (=type of food made from LIVER) 鹅肝酱

foil¹ /fɔɪl; fɔɪl/ *n* **1** [U] metal sheets that are as thin as paper, used for wrapping food 〔包裹食品用的〕铝箔, 金属薄片: *Cover the chicken with silver foil and bake in a hot oven.* 用铝箔把鸡包起来, 放在高温烤箱里烤。—see also 另见 TINFOIL **2** [U] paper that is covered with very thin sheets of metal 锡纸, 铝箔纸: *Cigarettes are wrapped in foil to keep them fresh.* 香烟用铝箔纸包装以保持新鲜。**3** **be a foil to** to emphasize another person or thing's good qualities, by being very different from them 衬托出…; 作为…的陪衬: *His quiet determination is a perfect foil to Eva's energetic enthusiasm.* 他那种不露声色的决心正好衬托出伊娃的积极热情。**4** [C] a light narrow sword used in FENCING (1) 〔击剑中的〕轻剑, 花剑

foil² *v* [T often passive 常用被动态] to prevent something bad that someone is planning to do 挫败〔阴谋〕: *A massive arms-smuggling plan has been foiled by the CIA.* 一项大规模的武器走私计划被中央情报局粉碎了。

foist /fɔɪst; fɔɪst/ *v*

foist sth **on/upon** sb *phr v* [T] to force someone to accept or have to deal with something that they do not want 把…强加于, 把…硬塞给: *I keep getting work foisted on me at the last minute.* 我老是被人在最后一刻硬塞工作给我。

Fok·ker /'fɑkə; 'fɒkə/ *trademark*【商标】**1** a type of military aircraft used by the Germans in World War I and designed by **Anthony Fokker** (1890-1939), a Dutch aircraft designer who later moved to the US and made planes for the US aircraft industry 福克尔〔一战期间德国人使用的一种军用飞机。该飞机由荷兰设计师安东尼·福克尔 (1890-1939) 设计。他后来移居美国, 跻身于美国飞机制造业〕**2** a type of plane made by the US company Fokker. Its best-known aircraft is the Fokker Friendship. 福克尔〔美国福克尔公司制造的一种飞机, 以"福克尔-友谊"最为有名〕

-fold /fold; fəʊld/ *suffix* **1** [in adjectives 构成形容词] of a particular number of kinds …种的; …倍的: *A window has a twofold purpose – to allow light into the room and let people see out.* 窗户有双重用途 — 让光线进入房间和让人看到外面的东西。**2** [in adverbs 构成副词] a particular number of times …倍: *The value of the house has increased fourfold.* (=it is now worth four times as much as before) 房子的价值已是原先的四倍。

fold¹ /fold; fəʊld/ *v*

1 ►**BEND** 折叠◄ [T] to bend a piece of paper, cloth etc by laying or pressing one part over another 折叠, 对折: *Fold the paper along the dotted line.* 沿虚线将纸折起来。| **fold sth in two/half** *The woman folded the tickets in two and tore them in half.* 那个女人把票对折起来, 然后撕成两半。

2▶**MAKE STH SMALLER/NEATER** 使某物更小/更整齐◀ [T] also 又作 **fold up** to fold something several times so that it makes a small neat shape 折起，叠好：*I wish you kids would fold up your clothes!* 我希望你们这些孩子能把衣服叠好！

3▶**FURNITURE ETC** 家具等◀ **a)** [I] if something such as a piece of furniture folds in a particular way, it is designed so that part of it can be folded to make it smaller 可折叠：[+**away/up/down etc**] *a useful little bed that folds away when you don't need it* 一张有用的小床，不需要时可以折好收起 **b)** [T] to fold or bend part of something such as a piece of furniture to make it smaller 折叠，折起：**fold** sth ↔ **down/up/away etc** *Can you fold up these chairs while I clean the floor?* 你能在我刷洗地板时把这些椅子折起来吗？

4 **fold your arms/legs etc** to bend your arms or legs, especially so that they are resting against your body 交叉[交叠]双臂/双腿等：*George stood silently with his arms folded.* 乔治交叉着双臂一言不发地站着。

5▶**BUSINESS** 企业◀ [I] also 又作 **fold up** if an organization folds or folds up, it closes because it does not have enough money to continue 倒闭，歇业

6▶**COVER** 覆盖◀ [T] to cover something, especially by wrapping it in material or putting your hand over it 包，裹：**fold sth in sth** *a silver dagger folded in a piece of white cloth* 裹在一块白布里的一把银色匕首

7 **fold sb in your arms** *especially literary* to hold someone closely by putting your arms around them【尤文】(用双臂) 抱住某人

fold sth **in** *phr v* [T] to gently mix another substance into a mixture when you are preparing food (烹制食物时) 拌入，把…调入：*Fold in the sugar and whisk until stiff.* 拌入糖，搅拌到发稠为止。

fold² *n* [C]

1▶**LINE** 线条◀ a line made in paper or material when you fold one part of it over another (纸张或材料上的) 褶，裥；折痕：*Bend back the card and cut along the fold.* 把折叠的卡片恢复原状，然后沿折痕剪开。

2▶**LOOSE SKIN/MATERIAL** 松弛的皮肤/材料◀ [usually plural 一般用复数] **a)** a rounded shape made by folded material 材料的折叠处，褶子：*Ahmed had a dagger concealed in the folds of his robe.* 阿梅德在长袍的褶层里藏着一把匕首。**b)** an area of loose folded skin 皱皮：*The old dog had thick folds of skin around its neck.* 那条老狗的脖子上有堆垒的皱皮。

3 **the fold** the group of people that you belong to and share the same beliefs and ideas as 同一群体的人，志同道合的人：**return/come back to the fold** *Many Democrats who voted Republican in the 80s have now returned to the fold.* 许多在20世纪80年代投共和党票的民主党人现在已经回头了。| **stray from/leave the fold** *a former advocate of free market economics who had strayed from the fold* 以前提倡自由市场经济而已经脱离这一学派的人

4▶**SHEEP** 羊◀ a small area of a field surrounded by a wall or fence where sheep are kept for safety 羊栏

5▶**ROCK** 岩石◀ *technical* a bend in layers of rock, caused by underground movements in the earth【术语】(岩石的) 褶皱

6▶**VALLEY** 山谷◀ *literary* a small narrow valley【文】小山谷

fold·a·way /ˈfoldəˌwe; ˈfəʊldəweɪ/ *adj* [only before noun 仅用于名词前] a foldaway bed, table etc can be folded up so it uses less space (床、桌等) 可折叠 (存放) 的

fold·er /ˈfoldɚ; ˈfəʊldə/ *n* [C] **1** a container for keeping loose papers in, made of folded card 文件夹 **2** a picture of a folder on a computer screen, which shows you where information can be stored (电脑屏幕上的图示，表示信息储存位置的) 文件夹

fold·ing /ˈfoldɪŋ; ˈfəʊldɪŋ/ *adj* [only before noun 仅用于名词前] a folding bicycle, bed, chair etc has parts that you can bend or fold together to make it easier to carry or store 可折叠的；折叠式的

fo·li·age /ˈfolɪɪdʒ; ˈfəʊli-ɪdʒ/ *n* [U] the leaves of a plant (植物的) 叶子，叶

Fo·lies-Ber·gère, the /foˌli bɛrˈʒɛr; ˌfɒli beəˈʒeə/ a theatre in Paris known from the end of the 19th century for its music and dance shows, especially those containing women wearing very few clothes 女神游乐厅 (巴黎一剧院。自19世纪末起，以音乐舞蹈表演，尤其以穿着暴露的女子表演闻名)

fo·li·o /ˈfolɪˌo; ˈfəʊliəʊ/ *n plural* **folios** *technical*【术语】**1** [C] a book made with very large sheets of paper 对开本 **2** [C] a single numbered sheet of paper from a book (书本中有页码的) 一张

folk¹ /fok; fəʊk/ *n* **1** **folks** [plural] **a)** *especially AmE* your parents and family【尤美】家人，家属，亲属：*Is it OK if I call my folks?* 我打电话给家人可以吗？| **the folks back home** *Wait till the folks back home hear about this!* 等到爸妈都得知此事就麻烦了！**b)** used when addressing a group of people in a friendly way 各位，大伙儿：*That's all for now, folks.* 各位，到此为止。**c)** *AmE* people【美】人，人们：*Folks around here don't take too kindly to strangers.* 这里的人对陌生人不太友好。**2** **country folk/farming folk/fisher folk etc** [plural] *literary* people who live in a particular area or do a particular kind of work【文】乡下人/农民/渔民等：*simple country folk* 纯朴的乡下人 **3** [plural] *BrE old-fashioned* people【英，过时】人，人们：**young folk/old folk** *Young folk these days don't know the meaning of work.* 当今的年轻人不懂得工作的意义。**4** [U] FOLK MUSIC 民间音乐 2

folk² *adj* [only before noun 仅用于名词前] **1** folk art, stories, customs etc are traditional and typical of the ordinary people who live in a particular area 民间的，民俗的：*folk tales* 民间故事，民间传说 | *an old Spanish folk song* 一首古老的西班牙民间歌曲 **2** **folk science/psychology/wisdom etc** science etc that is based on simple ideas that ordinary people can understand and does not involve a high level of technical knowledge 民间科学/民间心理学/民间智慧等 **3** **folk medicine/remedy** a traditional type of medical treatment that uses plants etc rather than modern scientific methods 民间传统医学/民间疗法

F

folk dance /ˈ· ˌ·/ *n* [C] a traditional dance from a particular area, or a piece of music for this dance 民间舞蹈[舞曲]；土风舞 —**folk dancer** *n* [C]

folk he·ro /ˈ· ˌ··/ *n* [C] someone who people in a particular place admire very much because of something they have done 民间英雄，人们心目中的英雄；百姓心里的英雄：*Casey Jones is a well-known American folk hero.* 凯西·琼斯是美国人心目中的著名英雄。

folk·lore /ˈfokˌlɔr; ˈfəʊklɔː/ *n* [U] the traditional stories, customs etc of a particular area or country 民间传说；民俗：*According to local folklore, the cave was once occupied by a witch.* 根据当地的民间传说，一位女巫曾经住在这个山洞里。

folk mu·sic /ˈ· ˌ··/ *n* [U] **1** traditional music that has been played by ordinary people in a particular area for a long time 民间音乐 **2** a style of popular music in which people sing and play GUITARS, without any electronic equipment (用吉他伴奏而无电子器材的) 仿民间音乐

folk·sy /ˈfoksɪ; ˈfəʊksi/ *adj informal*【非正式】**1** *especially AmE* friendly and informal【尤美】友好的，随和的，无拘束的：*The town had a certain folksy charm.* 这个城镇有种很吸引人的友好的气氛。**2** in a style that is typical of traditional countryside styles or customs 民间风格的，民俗风格的

fol·li·cle /ˈfɑlɪkl; ˈfɒlɪkəl/ *n* [C] one of the small holes in the skin that hairs grow from 小囊，毛囊

1 1

fol·low /ˈfɑlo; ˈfɒləʊ/ *v*

① GO BEHIND 跟在后面	④ UNDERSTAND 理解
② AFTER/NEXT 在后面/接在后面的	⑤ DO THE SAME AS 仿效
③ OBEY RULES/TEACHINGS ETC 遵守规则/听从教导等	⑥ BE INTERESTED IN 对…感兴趣
	⑦ OTHER MEANINGS 其他意思

① **GO BEHIND** 跟在后面

1 [I,T] to walk, drive, run etc behind someone else, going in the same direction as them 跟着，跟随：**follow sb/sth** *If you'll just follow me, I'll show you to the office.* 请跟我来，我会带你到办公室。| *Tom Selleck walked in, followed by a crowd of photographers.* 汤姆·塞莱克走进来，后面跟着一大群摄影家。| **follow** *I knew the way, so I went first, and the others followed.* 我知道路，所以我先走，其他人随后。

2 [T] to go closely behind someone in order to watch them and find out where they go 跟踪: *Marlowe looked over his shoulder to make sure no-one was following him.* 马洛回过头看，想确定没有人在跟踪他。

② **AFTER/NEXT** 在后面/接在后面的
3 [I,T] to happen directly after an event or period 接着…发生: *There was a major increase in immigration in the years that followed the First World War.* 第一次世界大战后几年，移民人数大幅增加。| **be (closely) followed by** *The lightning was followed by a great crash of thunder.* 闪电之后紧接着是轰隆隆的一阵雷声。| **in the days/weeks etc that followed** *We saw a lot of each other in the months that followed.* 此后的几个月里，我们多次见面。| **there follows** (=after that there is) 随后出现 *There followed a long and embarrassing silence.* 随后出现长时间的令人尴尬的沉默。| **follow shortly** (=happen soon) 很快发生 *The late night movie will follow shortly.* 深夜电影马上就要开始。—see also 另见 FOLLOWING[1]
4 [I,T] to come directly after something else, for example in a book or a series of things 紧随…之后: *A full report of the results follows this chapter.* 本章之后是一份全面的结果报告。| **be followed by** *In English the letter 'Q' is always followed by a 'U'.* 在英语拼写中，字母Q后面总会有字母U。| **there follows** (=after that there is) 随后是 *There follows a long description of the writer's early life.* 然后是对作家早年生活的详尽描述。
5 [I,T] to do an important job after someone else 继任〔重要职位〕: **be followed by** *Ivan was followed by a succession of weak rulers.* 伊凡的后继者都是一个个懦弱昏庸的统治者。
6 a hard act to follow *spoken* someone who is so good at something that it will be difficult for the next person to be as good or as successful 【口】令人望尘莫及的人
7 as follows used to introduce a list of names, things, instructions etc that come next 如下: *The results are as follows: First was Sweden, then Germany, then Ireland.* 结果如下：第一名是瑞典，第二名是德国，然后是爱尔兰。
8 to follow after the main part of a meal〔主菜后〕下一道菜: *We're having the poached salmon, with chocolate mousse to follow.* 我们正在吃水煮鲑鱼，下一道菜吃巧克力奶油冻。

③ **OBEY RULES/TEACHINGS ETC** 遵守规则/听从教导等
9 follow sb's orders/wishes/advice etc to do something in the way that someone has told you to do it, advised you to do it etc 服从某人的命令/遵照某人的愿望/听从某人的忠告等: *If you'd followed my advice, none of this would have happened.* 如果当初你听从我的忠告，这种事就不会发生了。| **follow sb's orders etc to the letter** (=do exactly what someone told you to do) 不折不扣地服从某人的命令
10 follow the instructions/a diagram etc to do something according to the rules or instructions that say how it should be done 按照使用说明/图表去做等: *Did you follow the instructions on the package?* 你是按照包装上的使用说明做的吗？
11 follow the signs/sb's directions to go in the direction that the signs say you should go or that someone has told you to go 沿着标志所指的方向行进/沿着某人指示的方向行进: *Follow the signs for the airport, then turn off when you see the hotel.* 沿着标志指示向机场方向行进，然后在看到旅馆时拐上另一条路。
12 [T] to believe in and obey a particular set of religious or political ideas, or a leader who teaches these ideas 信奉，追随: *They still follow the teachings of Mahatma Gandhi.* 他们仍然遵从圣雄甘地的教导。

④ **UNDERSTAND** 理解
13 [I,T] to understand something such as an explanation or story 领会，听懂: *I didn't quite follow what he was saying.* 我不太明白他说的话。| **easy/hard to follow** *I must admit I found the plot a bit hard to follow.* 我必须承认我觉得情节有点难懂。

⑤ **DO THE SAME AS** 仿效
14 [I,T] to do the same thing as someone else after they have done it 仿效: *We all had to follow the teacher.* 我们都得仿效老师。| **follow sb into** (=do the same job as someone else especially a member of your family) 跟〔家中〕某人一样从事〔某种行业〕 *None of my children seem to want to follow me into journalism.* 我的孩子们似乎没有一个想跟我一样从事新闻工作。| **follow sb's example** (=do the same as them because it is a good thing to do) 以某人为榜样 *They have an excellent childcare policy, and we're hoping other companies will follow their example.* 他们有一个很好的儿童保育政策，我们希望其他公司能以他们为榜样。
15 follow suit to do the same as someone else has just done 跟着做，照着做，仿效: *The Russian team pulled out of the Los Angeles Olympics, and several Eastern European countries followed suit.* 苏联队退出洛杉矶奥运会，几个东欧国家也跟着退出了。
16 follow (in) sb's footsteps to do the same job as someone else who did it before you 步某人的后尘，继承某人的事业: *My father was a jazz player, and I wanted to follow in his footsteps.* 我父亲是个爵士乐演奏家，我想继承他的事业。
17 follow the herd/crowd to do the same thing as other people, without really thinking about what you want to do 随大溜

⑥ **BE INTERESTED IN** 对…感兴趣
18 [T] to be interested in a particular sports team, and be concerned about its performance and results 关注〔某一球队〕；拥护: *The President follows the Red Sox.* 总统拥护红袜队。
19 [T] to be interested in the way a situation or set of events develops, and try to find out the latest information about it 密切关注: *Have you been following that crime series on TV?* 你一直留意那部描写犯罪的电视系列片吗？

⑦ **OTHER MEANINGS** 其他意思
20 follow your instincts/feelings to do something in the way that you feel is best 凭本能行事/跟着感觉走
21 follow your nose a) to do something in the way that you feel is right, without asking or checking 凭直觉行事；跟着感觉走 **b)** to go straight forward 朝…直走: *Turn left at the bank, then just follow your nose.* 在银行处左拐，然后一直往前走。
22 ►GO IN A PARTICULAR DIRECTION 朝某个方向行进◄ [T] **a)** to continue along a particular road, river etc 沿着…继续行进: *Follow the main road until you get to the coast.* 沿着大路往前走到海岸。**b)** to go in the same direction as something else, especially something that is very close 顺着…行进: *The railway follows the road for several miles, and then branches off.* 铁路顺着公路延伸好几英里，然后岔开。
23 follow a trend/pattern/course etc to continue to happen or develop in a particular way 按照某种趋势/按照某一模式/遵循某一进程等: *In Australia, the weather follows a fairly predictable pattern.* 在澳大利亚，天气常按照基本上可预料的模式变化。
24 it follows (that) [I] it must be true as a result of something else that is true 是…的必然结果: *Just because you're rich, it doesn't necessarily follow that you're happy.* 富有本身并不一定带来幸福。
25 ►WATCH/LISTEN CAREFULLY 仔细观察/仔细听◄ [T] to carefully watch someone move or listen to them speaking 注视；倾听: **follow sb with your eyes** *The men all followed her with their eyes as she entered the bar.* 她进入酒吧时，男人们都注视着她。
26 ►THINK ABOUT/STUDY 考虑/研究◄ [T] to study or think about a particular idea or subject and try to find out more about it 考虑，研究: *It turned out we were both following the same line of research.* 原来我们俩考虑的是同样的研究途径。
27 ►BE ABOUT 关于◄ [T] to show or describe someone's life or a series of events, for example in a film or book 展现，描写: *The film follows Rocky's career as a boxer from his early days.* 这部电影描述了洛奇从青年时期起当拳击手的经历。
28 follow a profession/trade/way of life *formal* to do a particular job or have a particular way of life 【正式】从事某种职业/从事某种行业/遵循某种生活方式

follow sb **around** also 又作 **follow** sb **about** *BrE* 【英】 *phr v* [T] to keep following someone everywhere they go 到处跟随: *I wish you'd stop following me around.* 我希望你不要到处跟着我。

follow through *phr v* **1** [I,T] to do what needs to be done after the main part of something is finished, in order to make sure it is complete or successful〔在把一件事基本上做完后〕进行到底；执行: **follow sth ↔ through** *The success of any healthcare program depends on how it is followed through.* 任何一项保健计划的成功均取决于它如何执行。**2** [I] to continue moving your arm after you have hit the ball in tennis, GOLF etc〔网球、高尔夫球等击球后〕做随球动作 —see also 另见 FOLLOW-THROUGH

follow up *phr v* **1** [T **follow** sth ↔ **up**] to do something as a result of something you have found out, someone has suggested etc 跟进〔线索、建议等〕: *The police were criticized for failing to follow up the complaint.* 警方因没有对投诉进行追查而受到批评。**2 follow (sth) up with** to do something in addition to what you have already done in order to make sure of success 以…继续做〔某事〕; 采取后续行动: *The train drivers have voted to follow up their one-day strike with a series of 48-hour stoppages.* 火车司机已经投票决定在罢工一天之后举行一连串的48小时停工作为后续行动。—see also 另见 FOLLOW-UP[1]

fol·low·er /ˈfɑloɚ; ˈfɒləʊə/ *n* [C] someone who believes in a particular system of ideas, or who supports a leader who teaches these ideas 信徒, 追随者, 支持者: *Marx and his followers were convinced that capitalism would destroy itself.* 马克思及其支持者确信资本主义会自我毁灭。| [+of] *followers of Sun Myung Moon, better known as Moonies* 文鲜明的信徒, 更知名的称呼是 Moonies —see also 另见 CAMP FOLLOWER

2 1 **fol·low·ing[1]** /ˈfɑloɪŋ; ˈfɒləʊɪŋ/ *adj* **1 the following afternoon/month/page/chapter etc** the next afternoon, month etc 第二天下午/下个月/下页/下章等: *He was sick in the evening, but the following day he was better.* 他晚上生病了, 但第二天就好一些了。**2 the following example/way etc** the example, way etc that will be mentioned next 以下的例子/方式等: *Payment may be made in any of the following ways: cheque, cash, or credit card.* 可用以下任何一种方式付款: 支票、现金或信用卡。**3 a following wind** a wind that is blowing in the same direction as a ship, and helps it to move faster 顺风

following[2] *n* [C] **1** [usually singular 一般用单数] a group of people who support or admire someone 一批追随者[支持者, 崇拜者]: *The band has a big following in Europe.* 这支乐队在欧洲有一大批崇拜者。**2 the following** the people or things that you are going to mention 下列的人, 下列的事物: *The following have been selected to play in tomorrow's game: Louise Carus, Fiona Douglas…* 下列选手已被挑选参加明天的比赛: 路易斯·卡勒斯、菲奥娜·道格拉斯… —see also 另见 FOLLOWING[1]

following[3] *prep* after an event or as a result of it 在…以后; 由于: *Following the speech, there will be a few minutes for questions.* 演讲后将留出几分钟时间让大家提问。| *Thousands of refugees left the country following the outbreak of civil war.* 由于内战爆发, 数以千计的难民逃到国外去。

follow-my-lead·er /ˌ‥ ·ˈ‥/ *BrE*【英】, **follow-the-leader** *AmE*【美】—*n* [U] a children's game in which one of the players does actions which all the other players must copy 跟领袖, 猴子学样〔参加者要模仿领头人做动作的儿童游戏〕

follow-through /ˌ‥ ·ˈ·/ *n* [singular] **1** movement of your arm after you have hit the ball in tennis, GOLF etc 随球动作〔网球、高尔夫球等运动中击球后的挥臂动作〕—see picture on page A23 参见 A23 页图 **2** the things that someone does in order to complete a plan 〔计划的〕贯彻〔工作〕: *The budget has to cover not only the main project but the follow-through.* 预算不仅要包括主体工程, 还要包括贯彻的工作。

follow-up[1] /ˈ‥ ·/ *adj* [only before noun 仅用于名词前] a follow-up visit, examination, study etc is done to make sure that an earlier one was effective, or to continue a plan of action that was started earlier 〔访问、考试、研究等〕后续的; 跟进的; 随访的: *a follow-up story on the Watergate break-in* 有关水门入室安装窃听器事件的后续报道 —see also 另见 **follow up** (FOLLOW[1])

follow-up[2] *n* **1** [C,U] something that is done to make sure that earlier actions have been successful or effective 后续行动; 跟进行动; 随访: *preventative treatment and follow-up several weeks later* 预防性治疗以及几星期后的后续治疗 **2** [C] a book, film, article etc that comes after another one that has the same subject or characters 〔书、电影的〕续集; 〔文章的〕续篇: *Spielberg says he's planning to do a follow-up next year.* 斯皮尔伯格说他打算明年拍一部续集。

fol·ly /ˈfɑlɪ; ˈfɒli/ *n* **1** [C,U] *formal* a very stupid thing to do, especially one that is likely to have serious results【正式】〔尤指可能导致严重后果的〕蠢事, 荒唐事: **it would be folly to do sth** *It would be sheer folly to reduce spending on health education.* 减少健康教育的开支全然是一件蠢事。| **the folly of** *a writer who satirized the follies of aristocratic society* 一位讽刺贵族社会荒唐事的作家 **2** [C] *BrE* an unusual building that was built in former times as a decoration, not to be used or lived in【英】〔古代不住人的〕怪异的装饰性建筑物

Fol·som Pris·on /ˌfolsəm ˈprɪzn; ˌfəʊlsəm ˈprɪzən/ also 又作 **Folsom** an old prison in California that was very strict and unpleasant, where many violent criminals were sent 福尔瑟姆监狱〔加利福尼亚的一座旧监狱。狱规严, 条件差, 关押着许多暴力犯罪服刑人员〕

fo·ment /foˈmɛnt; fəʊˈment/ *v formal*【正式】**foment revolution/trouble/discord etc** to cause trouble and make people start fighting each other or opposing the government 挑起, 煽动: *They were accused of fomenting rebellion.* 他们被指控犯有煽动叛乱罪。—**fomentation** /ˌfomɛnˈteʃən; fəʊmenˈteɪʃən/ *n* [U]

fond /fɑnd; fɒnd/ *adj* **1 be fond of sb** to like someone very much, especially when you have known them for a long time and almost feel love for them 喜欢某人: *Joe's quite fond of her, isn't he?* 乔很喜欢她, 不是吗? | **grow fond of** *Over the years we've grown very fond of each other.* 这些年来, 我们渐渐互相喜欢对方。**2 be fond of sth** to like something, especially something you have liked for a long time 喜欢某物, 爱好某物: *I'm not very fond of country music.* 我不太喜欢乡村音乐。| **grow fond of** *I'd grown fond of the place and it was difficult to leave.* 我已爱上这个地方, 很难离开它。**3 be fond of doing sth a)** to enjoy doing something very much 喜欢做某事: *Jilly's very fond of drawing.* 吉利非常喜欢画图画。**b)** to do something often, especially something that annoys other people 老爱做某事: *My Grandfather was very fond of handing out advice to all my friends.* 我的祖父很爱给我的朋友提出忠告。**4** [only before noun 仅用于名词前] a fond look, smile, action etc shows you like someone very much 深情的, 柔情的: *He gave her a fond look.* 他深情地看了她一眼。| **a fond farewell** *As we parted we said a fond farewell.* 我们分手时深情地相互道别。**5 have fond memories of** to remember something with great pleasure 愉快地记着: *Marie still had fond memories of their time together.* 玛丽仍愉快地记着他们在一起的时光。**6 a fond belief/hope** a belief or hope that something will happen, which seems silly because it is very unlikely to happen 轻信, 愚蠢的看法/痴心妄想: **in the fond hope/belief that** *They sent him to another school in the fond hope that his behaviour would improve.* 他们把他送到另一所学校, 天真地希望他的行为会有所改善。—see also 另见 FONDLY —**fondness** *n* [U]: *His wife had a great fondness for expensive clothes.* 他的妻子非常喜欢购买昂贵的衣服。

Fon·da /ˈfɑndə; ˈfɒndə/**, Henry** (1905-82) a US film actor known especially for appearing as characters who have strong moral beliefs and a strong sense of honour. His films include *The Grapes of Wrath* (1940) and *Twelve Angry Men* (1957). He was the father of Jane Fonda and Peter Fonda, who are also actors. 亨利·方达〔(1905-1982), 美国电影演员, 尤以饰演道德感和荣誉感强的人物闻名。演出的影片包括《愤怒的葡萄》(1940) 和《十二怒汉》(1957)。他是简·方达和彼得·方达的父亲, 他们也都是演员〕

fon·dant /ˈfɑndənt; ˈfɒndənt/ *n* [C,U] a sweet made of small grains of sugar 糖霜糖, 方旦糖〔一种软糖〕

fon·dle /ˈfɑndl̩; ˈfɒndl/ *v* [T] to gently touch and move your fingers over part of someone's body in a way that shows love 爱抚, 抚摸: *She fondled the puppy's neck.* 她爱抚着小狗的脖子。

fond·ly /ˈfɑndlɪ; ˈfɒndli/ *adv* **1 fondly imagine/believe/hope etc** to believe something that is untrue, hope for something that will probably not happen etc 天真地以为/盲目地相信/痴心地希望等: *Some people still fondly believe that modern science can solve all the world's problems.* 有些人仍然天真地相信现代科学能解决世界上所有的问题。**2** in a way that shows you like someone very much 深情地, 柔情地: *He turned to see her smiling fondly at him.* 他转过身, 看见她柔情地朝他微笑着。

fon·due /ˈfɑndu; ˈfɒndjuː/ *n* [C,U] a dish made of small pieces of food that you put in melted cheese or chocolate 〔放入融化的乳酪或巧克力的〕涮制菜肴, 火锅

fondue 涮制菜肴, 火锅

font /fant; fɒnt/ *n* [C] **1** a large stone container in a church, that holds the water used for the ceremony of BAPTISM (1)〔教堂里的〕洗礼盆, 圣水盂 **2** *technical* a set of letters of a particular size and type, used for printing books, newspapers etc【术语】〔用于印刷书籍、报纸等, 同样大小和式样的〕一副铅字

Fon·teyn /fɑnˈten; fɒnˈteɪn/, **Dame Mar·got** /ˈmɑrgo; ˈmɑːgəʊ/ (1919-91) one of the UK's greatest BALLET dancers, who worked with the Royal Ballet and often danced with Rudolf Nureyev 芳廷〔(1919-1991), 英国最杰出芭蕾舞演员之一、英国皇家芭蕾舞团演员。她常与鲁道夫·努里耶夫搭档〕

food /fud; fuːd/ *n* **1** [U] things that people and animals eat, such as vegetables or meat 食物: *The food's great and it's not that expensive.* 这里的食物太好吃了, 而且不是那么贵。| *There are food shortages in many areas.* 许多地区出现食物短缺。**2** [C,U] a particular type of food〔某一种〕食品: **junk food/health food etc** *All he ever eats is junk food.* 他吃的都是"垃圾"食品。| *Try to cut down on sweet and fatty foods.* 尽量少吃甜食和脂肪多的食品。| **dog food/pet food/baby food** (=food for dogs etc) 狗食/宠物食品/婴儿食品 | **be off your food** (=feel ill and not want to eat anything) 生病不想吃东西, 没有食欲 **3 food for thought** something that makes you think carefully 引人深思的事物: *The teacher's advice certainly gave me food for thought.* 老师的忠告理所当然令我深思。

Food and Ag·ri·cul·ture Or·gan·i·za·tion, the /ˌ· · ˌ· · · · · · ˌ· · ˈ· ·/ the full name of the FAO (联合国) 粮食及农业组织〔FAO的全称〕

Food and Drug Ad·min·i·stra·tion, the /ˌ· · ˈ· · · · · ˈ· ·/ the full name of the FDA (美国) 食品和药物管理局〔FDA的全称〕

food bank /ˈ· ·/ *n* [C] *AmE* a place that gives food to poor people【美】〔向穷人分发粮食的〕食物赈济处

food chain, the /ˈ· ·/ *n* all animals and plants considered as a group in which one type of animal eats another and then is eaten by another animal 食物链: *Pollution is affecting many creatures lower down the food chain.* 污染正影响着在食物链下层的许多生物。

food cou·pon /ˈ· ˌ· ·/ *n* [C] a FOOD STAMP 食品券, 粮食券

food·ie /ˈfudɪ; ˈfuːdi/ *n* [C] *informal* someone who is very interested in cooking and eating food【非正式】美食家; 爱吃的人

food poi·son·ing /ˈ· ˌ· · ·/ *n* [U] a painful stomach illness caused by eating food that contains harmful BACTERIA 食物中毒

food pro·cess·or /ˈ· ˌ· · ·/ *n* [C] a piece of electrical equipment that helps to prepare food in various ways, such as cutting and mixing 食品加工器, 多功能食品切碎搅拌机 —see picture on page A10 参见A10页图

food stamp /ˈ· ·/ *n* [C] an official piece of paper that the US government gives to poor people so they can buy food〔美国政府发给穷人的〕食物券, 粮食券

food·stuff /ˈfudˌstʌf; ˈfuːdstʌf/ *n* [C usually plural 一般用复数,U] a word meaning food, used especially when talking about the business of producing or selling food〔尤指商业生产或销售的〕食品: *A wide variety of foodstuffs is available in the local market.* 在当地市场可买到各式各样的食品。

fool¹ /ful; fuːl/ *n*

1 ►STUPID PERSON 蠢人◄ [C] a stupid person or someone who has done something stupid 蠢人, 傻子, 笨蛋: *What a fool she had been to think that he would stay.* 她竟然那么傻, 以为他会留下来。

2 any fool can *spoken* used to say that it is very easy to do something or to see that something is true【口】任何人都会〔用于表示某事很简单〕: *Any fool can see that the painting's a fake.* 任何人都能看出这张画是赝品。

3 be no fool/nobody's fool to be difficult to trick or deceive, because you have a lot of experience and knowledge about something 不会轻易上当, 为人精明; 不是傻瓜: *Katherine was nobody's fool when it came to money.* 凯瑟琳在钱的问题上一点也不傻。

4 make a fool of yourself to do something stupid that you feel embarrassed about afterwards and that makes you seem silly 出丑, 出洋相: *Sorry I made such a fool of myself last night. I must have been drunk.* 对不起, 我昨天晚上出丑了。我一定是喝醉了。

5 ►FOOD 食品◄ gooseberry fool/strawberry fool etc *BrE* a sweet food made of soft cooked fruit mixed with cream【英】奶油醋栗泥/奶油草莓泥等

6 make a fool of sb to deliberately try to make someone seem stupid 愚弄某人, 使某人显得愚蠢: *I suddenly realised that I was being made a fool of.* 我突然意识到我正在被人愚弄。

7 more fool you/him etc *BrE spoken* used to say that you think someone was stupid to do something and it is their own fault if this causes trouble【英口】这是你自己傻/那是他自己傻等: *"Jim smashed up my car." "More fool you for letting him borrow it!"* "吉姆把我的车撞坏了。""你真傻, 竟让他借你的车去开!"

8 be living in a fool's paradise to feel happy and satisfied, and believe there are no problems, when in fact this is not true 陶醉在幻想之中, 黄粱美梦

9 play/act the fool to behave in a silly way, especially in order to make people laugh 装傻; 逗人笑: *Stop playing the fool! You'll fall.* 别逗人笑了! 你会摔倒的。

10 (send sb on) a fool's errand to make someone go somewhere or do something for no good reason (派某人去做) 徒劳无益的事

11 ►ENTERTAINER 表演者◄ [C] a man whose job was to entertain a king or other powerful person in former times, by doing tricks, singing funny songs etc〔古时候供国王或其他权势人物娱乐的〕弄臣, 小丑 —see also 另见 APRIL FOOL

fool² *v* **1** [T] to trick someone into believing something 欺骗: *You can't fool me with that old excuse.* 你那个老一套的借口是骗不了我的。| **fool sb into doing sth** *Don't be fooled into believing their promises.* 别给骗得竟然相信他们的诺言。**2 you could have fooled me** *spoken* used to show that you do not believe what someone has told you【口】我不会相信你的话[上你的当], 我才不信你呢: *"Look, we're doing our best to fix it." "Well, you could have fooled me."* "看, 我们正尽力修理它。""嘿, 我才不信你呢。" **3 sb is just fooling** *spoken* used to say that someone is not serious and is only pretending that something is true【口】某人只是在闹着玩而已: *Don't pay any attention to Henry. He's just fooling.* 别理会亨利, 他只是闹着玩而已。

fool around also 又作 **fool about** *BrE*【英】*phr v* [I] **1** to waste time behaving in a silly way 闲荡, 游手好闲: *He spent the whole afternoon just fooling around.* 他整个下午都在闲荡。**2** to behave in a careless and irresponsible way 乱弄, 瞎弄: [+with] *Some idiot's been fooling around with the electricity supply!* 不知道哪个傻子一直在乱弄电源! **3** to have a sexual relationship with someone else's wife, boyfriend etc 玩弄, 搞不正当的性关系: *Anthony's been fooling around with one of the secretaries.* 安东尼一直在跟一个秘书鬼混。

fool³ *adj* [only before noun 仅用于名词前] *AmE informal* silly or stupid【美, 非正式】愚蠢的, 傻的: *What did you say a fool thing like that for?* 你为什么要说那种蠢话?

fool·e·ry /ˈfulərɪ; ˈfuːləri/ *n* [C,U] *BrE old-fashioned* silly or stupid behaviour【英, 过时】愚蠢的行为, 蠢事

fool·har·dy /ˈfulˌhardɪ; ˈfuːlhɑːdi/ *adj* taking stupid and unnecessary risks 鲁莽的, 蛮干的: *a foolhardy attempt to capture more territory* 想占领更多领土的鲁莽企图 —**foolhardiness** *n* [U]

fool·ish /ˈfulɪʃ; ˈfuːlɪʃ/ *adj* **1** a foolish action, remark etc is stupid and shows that someone is not thinking sensibly〔行为、评论等〕愚蠢的, 傻的: *I've never heard anything so foolish in all my life.* 我这辈子从没听到过这么愚蠢的话。| **it is foolish (of sb) to do sth** *It was foolish of them to expect the economy to recover so quickly.* 他们竟指望经济会这么快复苏, 真愚蠢。**2** a foolish person behaves in a silly way or looks silly〔人〕愚笨的, 傻瓜似的: *I was young and foolish at the time.* 我当时年轻而且傻乎乎的。| *a foolish grin* 傻笑 —**foolishly** *adv*: *She foolishly agreed to go with them.* 她傻乎乎地同意跟他们去。—**foolishness** *n* [U]

fool·proof /ˈfulˌpruf; ˈfuːlpruːf/ *adj* a foolproof method, plan, system etc is certain to be successful〔方法、计划、系统等〕肯定成功的, 万无一失的: *a foolproof way of preventing credit card fraud* 防止利用信用卡诈骗的一种万无一失的方法

fools·cap /ˈfulˌskæp; ˈfuːlskæp/ *n* [U] a large size of paper, especially paper for writing on 大裁, 大页纸〔尤指书写用纸〕

fool's gold /ˌ· ˈ·/ *n* [U] **1** a kind of yellow metal that exists in some rocks and looks like gold 愚人金〔指一种存在于岩石中形似黄金的黄色金属〕**2** something that you think will be very exciting, very attractive etc but in fact is not 虚幻的东西, 华而不实的东西

foot¹ /fʊt; fʊt/ *n plural* **feet** /fit; fiːt/ [C]

1 ►BODY PART 身体部位◄ the part of your body that you stand on and walk on 脚, 足: *I have a really bad pain in my foot.* 我的脚痛得很厉害。

2 on foot if you go somewhere on foot, you walk there 步行: *It takes about*

foot 脚

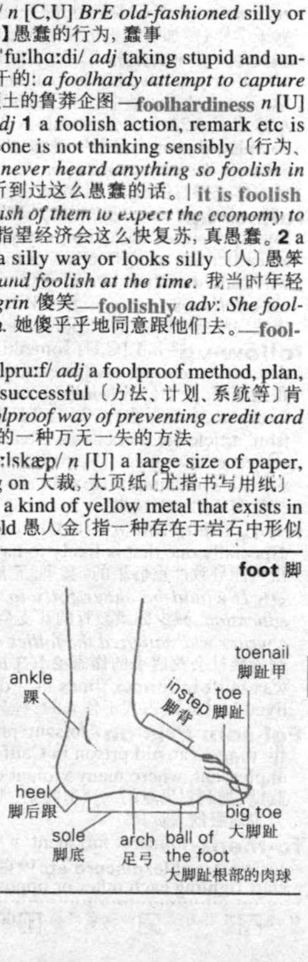

30 minutes on foot, or 10 minutes if you go by car. 步行去需要大约30分钟，如果坐车去，则需要10分钟。

3 ►MEASUREMENT 尺寸◄*written abbreviation* 缩写为 **ft** *plural* **foot** or **feet** a unit for measuring length, equal to 12 inches (INCH[1] (1)) or about 30 centimetres 英尺〔等于12英寸，约30厘米〕: *He's six feet tall, with blonde hair and a moustache.* 他身高6英尺，长着一头金发，留着小胡子。—see table on page C4 参见C4页附录

4 ►BOTTOM PART 底部◄ **the foot of** the lowest part of something such as a mountain, tree, or set of stairs, or the end of a bed where your feet go …的底部，…下端: *a stunningly beautiful lake at the foot of the mountain* 山脚下一个极其美丽的湖

5 get/jump/rise to your feet etc to stand up after you have been sitting 站起身来/跳起身来/站起身来等: *Mike leapt to his feet and ran towards the window.* 迈克跳起身来，向窗口跑去。

6 be on your feet a) to be standing for a long time without having time to sit down〔长时间〕站立着: *The worst thing about working in the shop is that you're on your feet all day.* 在商店里工作最糟糕的事情是要整天站着。**b)** to stand up 站起来: *As soon as the bell rang the class were on their feet and out of the door.* 铃一响，全班学生都站起来，跑到门外去。**c)** to feel better again after being ill and in bed〔生病卧床后〕恢复健康: *We'll soon have you on your feet again.* 我们很快就会使你恢复健康。

7 be rushed off your feet/be run off your feet to be very busy 非常忙碌，忙得脚不沾地: *Just before Christmas, most of the salespeople are rushed off their feet.* 圣诞节前，大多数售货员都很忙碌。

8 set foot in to go to or enter a place 去; 进入，踏进: *She swore she would never set foot in his house ever again.* 她发誓不再进入他的房子。

9 be/get under your feet to annoy you by always being in the same place as you and preventing you from doing what you want 妨碍着你，阻碍着你: *I hate summer vacation. The kids are under my feet all day long.* 我不喜欢暑假。孩子们整天缠着我。

10 put your foot down a) to say very firmly that someone must do something or must stop doing something 果断行事; 坚持立场; 坚决阻止: *You'll just have to put your foot down and tell him he can't stay out on school nights.* 你得果断一点，告诉他上课期间晚上不能在外面逗留。**b)** *informal* to make a car go faster【非正式】加快车速; 踩下油门

11 put your feet up *informal* to relax, especially by sitting with your feet supported on something【非正式】搁起脚休息

12 put your foot in it *especially BrE*【尤英】, **put your foot in your mouth** *especially AmE*【尤美】to say something without thinking carefully, so that you embarrass or upset someone 失言，讲错话;〔因说话随便而〕招惹麻烦: *I've really put my foot in it this time. I didn't realize that was her husband!* 我这次确实讲错话了。我没想到那人是她的丈夫!

13 have two left feet *informal* to be very CLUMSY (1)【非正式】笨拙的，笨手笨脚的: *Dan's got two left feet when it comes to dancing.* 丹跳起舞来笨手笨脚的。

14 get off on the wrong foot to start a relationship badly, usually by having an argument〔关系〕刚开始处得不好: *Simon and I got off on the wrong foot but we're good friends now.* 西蒙和我刚开始很不投机，但现在我们是好朋友。

15 not put a foot wrong *especially BrE* to do everything right and make no mistakes, especially in your job【尤英】〔尤指工作中〕做事正确无误

16 have/keep both feet on the ground to think in a sensible and practical way and not have ideas or aims that will be impossible to achieve 注重实际，脚踏实地

17 put sth back on its feet to improve the situation of a country, organization etc 改善〔国家、组织等〕的状况: *It was Larry who put the club back on its feet.* 是拉里使俱乐部有起色的。

18 fall/land on your feet to get into a good situation because you are lucky after being in a difficult situation 幸免于难，化险为夷: *Don't worry about Nina, she always falls on her feet.* 别为尼娜担心，她总是能化险为夷的。

19 get your foot in the door to get your first opportunity to work in a particular organization or industry 获得机会进入，有幸加入

20 have a foot in both camps to be involved with or connected with two opposing groups of people 脚踏两只船，骑墙

21 have one foot in the grave *humorous* to be very old or very ill【幽默】〔老得或病得〕一只脚已踏进坟墓; 离死不远

22 ...my foot! *BrE old-fashioned* used to show that you do not believe something that someone has just said【英，过时】算了吧，去你的，得了〔表示不相信对方的话〕: *£50 my foot! It'll cost £200 at least.* 去你的50英镑! 这至少值200英镑。

23 leave feet first *humorous* to die before you leave a place or job【幽默】还没离开〔某地或某工作〕就死去

24 feet of clay someone that you admire who has feet of clay has faults that you did not realize they had〔偶像的〕没觉察到的弱点，内在缺点

25 foot soldier/patrol a soldier or group of soldiers that walks and does not use a horse or a vehicle 步兵

26 foot passenger a passenger on a ship who has not brought a car with them〔汽车渡轮上的〕步行旅客，无车旅客

27 -footed/fʊtɪd; fʊtɪ̣d/ **a) left-footed/right-footed** using your left foot or right foot when you kick the ball〔踢球时〕用左脚的/用右脚的 **b) flat-footed/four-footed** having a particular kind or number of feet 平足的/四足的

28 foot pedal/brake/pump etc a machine or control that you operate using your feet 踏板/脚刹车/脚踏泵等

29 ►SOCK 袜◄ **the foot** the part of a sock that covers your foot 袜底: *There's a hole in the foot of my stocking.* 我的袜底有个洞。

30 ►POETRY 诗◄*technical* a part of a line of poetry in which there is one strong BEAT[2] (3) and one or two weaker ones【术语】音步 —see also 另见 **the boot is on the other foot** (BOOT[1] (6)), **get/have cold feet** (COLD[1] (7)), **drag your feet/heels** (DRAG[1] (8)), **find your feet** (FIND[1] (22)), **from head to foot** (HEAD[1] (2)), **stand on your own (two) feet** (STAND[1] (31)), **sweep sb off their feet** (SWEEP[1] (12))

foot[2] *v* **foot the bill** to pay for something, especially something expensive that you do not want to pay for 付账〔尤指不情愿为昂贵的东西支付时〕: *He ordered a load of drinks and then left me to foot the bill!* 他要了一大堆酒水，然后让我来付账!

foot·age /ˈfʊtɪdʒ; ˈfʊtɪdʒ/ *n* [U] cinema film showing a particular event〔某个事件的〕影片: *old footage from the First World War* 第一次世界大战的旧影片

foot and mouth dis·ease /ˌ· · ˈ· ·ˌ·/ *n* [U] a serious disease that kills cows and sheep 口蹄疫〔一种导致牛、羊死亡的严重传染病〕

foot·ball /ˈfʊtˌbɔl; ˈfʊtbɔːl/ *n* **1** [U] *BrE* a game played by two teams of eleven players who try to kick a round ball into their opponents' GOAL (3); SOCCER【英】足球(比赛): *watching football on TV* 在电视上看足球比赛 | *a football club* 足球俱乐部 **2** [U] *AmE* a game played by two teams of eleven players who carry or kick an OVAL (=egg shaped) ball【美】(美式)足球，橄榄球(比赛); AMERICAN FOOTBALL *BrE*【英】: *college football games* 大学橄榄球比赛 **3** [C] a ball used in these games 足球; 橄榄球 —see also 另见 FLAG FOOTBALL, **political football** (POLITICAL (5))

CULTURAL NOTE 文化注释

Football in the US Football (called 'American football' in British English) is a very popular sport in the US. Many people, especially men, support a particular team, usually the team from the city where they live, and go to watch them play or watch their games on television. The football SEASON (=the time of year when football is played) starts in early autumn and finishes at the end of January. The organization that controls professional football is called the NFL (=National Football League). The NFL is divided into two CONFERENCES, the AFC (=American Football Conference) and the NFC (=National Football Conference). Each conference is separated into three divisions: the Eastern, Central, and Western divisions. In January the two teams that have won the most games in each conference play against each other in the Super Bowl to decide which is the best professional football team in the US, and this is an important national event. 美国橄榄球运动: 美式橄榄球(英式英语称American football)在美国极受欢迎。很多人，尤其是男人，支持某个球队，通常是其居住地的球队，并去现场或在电视上观看该球队的比赛。橄榄球赛季8月初开始，次年1月底结束。管理职业橄榄球的机构叫做全国橄榄球联盟(NFL)，分美国橄榄球联合会(AFC)和国家橄榄球联合会(NFC)两大联合会，每个联合会又分东部、中部和西部三个分会。1月份，在两大联合会中获胜场次最多的两支球队参加"超级杯"决赛，决出全美最佳职业橄榄球队，这是一项重要的全国性体育赛事。

College Football Colleges in the US also have football teams with student players, and students and other people support the college teams. Many college football players later become professional players. On January 1st, the winning teams from the two main conferences, the Pac 10 and the Big Ten play against each other in the Rose

Bowl in Pasadena, California. 大学橄榄球运动：美国大学也有大学生组成的橄榄球队，拥有学生等支持者。很多大学生橄榄球队员后来成为职业选手。次年1月1日，两个大学联合会——"太平洋十强"和"十强"——的冠军队在加利福尼亚的帕萨迪纳参加"玫瑰碗"比赛。

Football in the UK Football (called soccer in the US) is the most popular sport in the UK. The football season is between August and May. Many people, especially men, support a particular team and go to watch them play or watch the games on television. Professional football is controlled by the Football League and the FA (=the Football Association). In England and Wales the teams are organized into four DIVISIONS: the Premiership, controlled by the FA, and the 1st, 2nd, and 3rd Divisions, controlled by the Football League. In Scotland the teams are organized into three DIVISIONS: the Scottish Premier League, and the 1st and 2nd Divisions. Teams play regularly against other teams in their division. At the end of the season the team with the most points in the Premiership (or the Scottish Premier League) becomes the League Champion. In each division, the teams that have performed least well are sent down to the division below, and the teams with the most points go up to the division above. 英国足球运动：足球（美国称soccer）是英国最受欢迎的运动。足球赛季在8月至次年5月之间。很多人，尤其是男人，支持某个球队，并去现场或在电视上观看该球队的比赛。管理职业球队的组织是足球联盟和足球协会。在英格兰和威尔士，球队分四组：超级联赛队归足球协会管理，甲级队、乙级队和丙级队归足球联盟管理。苏格兰的球队分为三组：苏格兰超级联赛队、甲级队和乙级队。同组球队定期比赛。赛季结束时，超级联赛队（或苏格兰超级联赛队）中积分最高的球队成为联赛冠军。每组积分最低的球队降一级，积分最高的球队升一级。

The FA Cup The FA Cup often just called 'the cup', is the other main football competition in the UK. It is a KNOCKOUT competition (=one in which a losing team no longer takes part, and a winning team goes on to the next ROUND), and it involves many small AMATEUR clubs as well as the professional teams. There is always a lot of interest when a 'non-league' (=amateur) team beats a well-known professional team, and the newspapers call these teams 'giantkillers'. The two teams left in the competition at the end play in the FA Cup FINAL in May. This was held at Wembley Stadium in London from 1923 to 2000, and at the Millennium Stadium in Cardiff while Wembley Stadium was being rebuilt. This is an important national event, and millions of people watch it on television. 足总杯：足总杯常称the cup，是英国另一项重要的足球赛事。它采用淘汰制，不仅包括职业足球俱乐部，也包括很多小的业余足球俱乐部。业余球队击败知名的职业球队时，会引起很大关注，报纸上称这些球队为"巨人杀手"。5月份举行"足总杯"决赛。从1923年到2000年，决赛都在伦敦的温布利球场举行。温布利球场重建期间则在加的夫的千年球场举行。这是一项全国性的重大赛事，电视观众多达数百万人。—see also 另见 WORLD CUP

Football As·so·ci·a·tion, the /'‥ ‥,‥/ the full name of the FA〔英格兰〕足球协会；英足总〔FA的全称〕

foot·bal·ler /ˈfʊtˌbɔlɚ; ˈfʊtbɔːlə/ *n* [C] *BrE* someone who plays football, especially a professional player【英】〔尤指职业的〕足球员；橄榄球员

Football League, the /,‥ '‥/ an organization of professional football teams in England and Wales. It consists of three 'Divisions': Divisions One, Two, and Three, but does not include the FA Premiership, which is the highest division. Professional football in Scotland is controlled by a similar organization called the Scottish Football League. 英格兰足球联盟〔英格兰和威尔士的职业足球队组织。该组织分英冠联赛、英甲联赛和英乙联赛三个级别，但不包括最高级别的英超联赛。苏格兰也有管理职业足球队的一个类似组织，称苏格兰足球联盟〕

football pools /'‥ ,‥/ *n* —see 见 **the pools** (POOL[1] (4))

foot·bridge /ˈfʊtˌbrɪdʒ; ˈfʊtˌbrɪdʒ/ *n* [C] a narrow bridge used by people who are walking 人行桥，步行桥

foot·er /ˈfʊtɚ; ˈfʊtə/ *n* **1 six-footer/eighteen-footer etc** someone or something that measures six feet tall, eighteen feet long etc 6英尺高的人[东西]/18英尺长的东西 **2** [U] *BrE* a game of football【英】（一场）足球[橄榄球]比赛

foot·fall /ˈfʊtˌfɔl; ˈfʊtfɔːl/ *n* [C,U] *literary* the sound of each step when someone is walking【文】脚步声：*heavy footfalls* 沉重的脚步声

foot fault /'‥ ‥/ *n* [C] a mistake in tennis when the person who is serving (SERVE[1] (10)) is not standing behind the line〔网球的〕脚步犯规〔发球踩线犯规〕

foot·hill /ˈfʊtˌhɪl; ˈfʊtˌhɪl/ *n* [C usually plural 一般用复数] one of the smaller hills below a group of high mountains 山麓丘陵：*the foothills of the Himalayas* 喜马拉雅山脉的丘陵地带

foot·hold /ˈfʊtˌhold; ˈfʊthəʊld/ *n* [C] **1** a position from which you can start to make progress and achieve your aims 稳固的基础；立足点：**gain/establish a foothold** *Extreme right wing parties gained a foothold in the latest European elections.* 极右党派在最近的欧洲各国选举中取得了稳固的基础。**2** a small hole or crack where you can safely put your foot when climbing a steep rock〔攀登陡峭的岩石时的〕立脚点

footie /ˈfʊtɪ; fʊti/ *n* [U] *BrE* a game of football【英】足球运动

foot·ing /ˈfʊtɪŋ; ˈfʊtɪŋ/ *n* [U] **1** the conditions or arrangements under which something exists or operates 状况；基础；立足处：**on a legal/scientific/official etc footing** *The article attempts to put their work on a more scientific footing.* 这篇文章企图把他们的工作置于更科学的基础上。| **on a sound/firm/solid footing** *new reforms that will put the country back on a firm financial footing* 将使国家恢复到稳固的财政基础上的新改革 | **on an equal footing/on the same footing** (=in the same situation or state as someone else) 以平等的地位/在相同的状况下 *The new law puts women on an equal footing with men.* 新法律使妇女享有与男子平等的地位。| **on a war footing** (=ready to go to war at any time) 处于准备战争状态 **2** the position of your feet when you are standing firmly on a SLIPPERY or dangerous surface〔在易滑或危险表面的〕立足处，立足点：*struggling to keep her footing on the slippery path* 挣扎着在滑溜的小道上站稳 | **lose/miss your footing** (=fall because you are no longer balanced) 失足，摔倒；未能站稳

foo·tle /ˈfutl; ˈfuːtl/ *v* **footle around/about** to waste time doing unimportant things when you should be working 闲混

foot·lights /ˈfʊtˌlaɪts; ˈfʊtlaɪts/ *n* [plural] a row of lights along the front of the stage in a theatre〔剧场舞台前的〕脚灯 —see picture at 参见 THEATRE 图

foot·ling /ˈfutlɪŋ; ˈfuːtlɪŋ/ *adj* [only before noun 仅用于名词前] *old-fashioned* unimportant and annoying【过时】无足轻重的；讨厌的

foot lock·er /'‥ ,‥/ *n* [C] *AmE* a strong box that soldiers have at the end of their beds to keep their possessions in【美】〔士兵用来存放物品的〕床脚柜

foot·loose /ˈfʊtˌlus; ˈfʊtluːs/ *adj* **1** able to move around freely because you have no permanent work or home〔无固定工作或住所而〕可到处走动的：*footloose students traveling around Europe* 在欧洲到处游逛的学生 **2 footloose and fancy free** able to do what you want and enjoy yourself because you have no responsibilities 自由自在的，无拘无束的

foot·man /ˈfʊtmən; ˈfʊtmən/ *plural* **footmen** /-mən; -mən/ *n* [C] a male servant in former times who opened the front door, announced the names of visitors etc〔旧时的〕男仆

foot·mark /ˈfʊtˌmark; ˈfʊtmɑːk/ *n* [C] a mark made by someone's shoe or foot 脚印，足迹

foot·note /ˈfʊtˌnot; ˈfʊtnəʊt/ *n* [C] a note at the bottom of the page in a book, which gives more information about something 脚注

foot·path /ˈfʊtˌpæθ; ˈfʊtpɑːθ/ *n* [C] *especially BrE* a narrow path for people to walk along, especially in the countryside【尤英】〔尤指乡间的〕人行小径，人行道；TRAIL[2] (4) *AmE*【美】

foot·print /ˈfʊtˌprɪnt; ˈfʊtˌprɪnt/ *n* [C] a mark made by a foot or shoe 脚印，足迹：*the footprints of a deer* 鹿的足迹

footprint 脚印

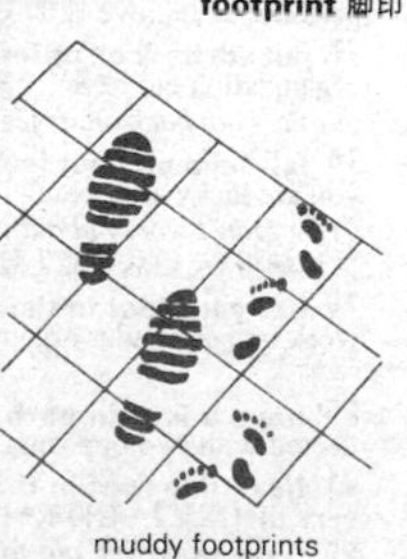

muddy footprints
泥脚印

foot·rest /ˈfʊtˌrɛst; ˈfʊtrest/ *n* [C] a small piece of furniture that you can rest your feet on when you are sitting down 搁脚架；搁脚垫；脚凳

foot·sie /ˈfʊtsɪ; ˈfʊtsi/ *n* **play footsie** *informal*【非正式】**a)** to secretly touch another person's feet with your feet under a table to show that you find them sexually attractive〔暗中在桌下〕碰脚调情 **b)** *AmE* to work together and help each other in a dishonest way【美】勾搭，狼狈为奸：*politicians playing footsie with each other* 狼狈为奸的政客

Footsie, the an informal name for the FT 100 Share Index (英国)富时100指数〔《金融时报》100种股票价格指数的别称〕

foot·slog·ging /ˈfutˌslɑgɪŋ; ˈfutslɒgɪŋ/ *n* [U] *BrE informal* a lot of walking around, which makes you very tired【英,非正式】长途费力的步行

foot·sore /ˈfutˌsɔr; ˈfutsɔː/ *adj* having feet that hurt because you have walked a long distance〔因走长路而〕脚痛的

foot·step /ˈfutˌstɛp; ˈfutstep/ *n* [C] the sound made when someone walks a single step 脚步声: *heavy footsteps on the stairs* 楼梯上沉重的脚步声 —see also 另见 **follow (in) sb's footsteps** (FOLLOW (16))

foot·stool /ˈfutˌstul; ˈfutstuːl/ *n* [C] a low piece of furniture used to support your feet when you are sitting down〔坐时搁脚的〕脚凳

foot·wear /ˈfutˌwɛr; ˈfutweə/ *n* [U] things that people wear on their feet, such as shoes or boots 鞋类〈如鞋、靴等〉

foot·work /ˈfutˌwɝk; ˈfutwɜːk/ *n* [U] skilful use of your feet when dancing or playing a sport〔舞蹈、运动中的〕步法; 腿脚功夫

fop /fɑp; fɒp/ *n* [C] *old-fashioned* a man who is too interested in his clothes and appearance【过时】〔过分讲究衣着和外表的〕纨绔子弟 —**foppish** *adj* —**foppishness** *n* [U]

1 1 **for[1]** /fɚ; fə; *strong* 强读 fɔr; fɔː/ *prep* **1** intended to be given to or belong to a particular person 给,为: *I've got a present for you.* 我有一件礼物要送给你。| *Save some for Arthur.* 留一些给阿瑟吧。**2** intended to be used in a particular situation 适合于〔某一场合使用〕: *We've bought some new chairs for the office.* 我们买了一些办公室用的新椅子。| *a name-plate for the door* 门上的姓名标牌 **3** used to show the purpose of an object, action, etc 为了; 供: *a knife for cutting bread* 切面包的刀子 | *What did you do that for?* 你为什么要那样做? | *a space just large enough for a table and two chairs* 正好能摆一张桌子和两把椅子的空间 | **for sale/hire/rent** (=available to be bought, hired) 供出售的/供出租的 *House for sale.* 有房屋出售。| *They have tools and garden equipment for hire.* 他们有工具和园艺设备出租。**4** if you do something for someone, you do it instead of them in order to help them 代替; 代表: *I looked after the kids for her.* 我替她照看小孩。| *Let me lift that for you.* 让我替你提那个吧。**5** if something is done for someone, or if they are given something for a problem, they are helped or their situation is improved 为,帮,替: *The doctor knew that there was nothing he could do for her.* 医生知道他无法为她做什么事了。| *I've found it for you.* 我已经帮你找到了它。| *I'll do what I can for you.* 我将尽力帮你。| *What can I do for you?* (=can I help you?) 我能帮你做点什么吗?[可以为您效劳吗?] **6** if something is arranged for a particular time, it is planned that it should happen then 在…〔时间〕: *I've invited them for 9 o'clock.* 我已经邀请他们九点来。| *I've made an appointment for 18th October.* 我已经约定了10月18日见面。| *It's time for supper.* 是吃晚饭的时候了。**7** if you buy someone something, or arrange an event for their birthday etc, you do it to celebrate that occasion 为〔庆祝一个日子〕而…: *What did you get for your birthday?* 你收到什么生日礼物? **8** used to express a length of time〔表示时间长度〕达,计: *Bake the cake for 40 minutes.* 将蛋糕烤40分钟。| *They had been walking for a good half hour.* 他们已步行了足有半小时。| *I've been meaning to ask you for ages.* 我老早就想问你了。| *He's been off work for a long time.* 他已经很久不工作了。| **for a while** *I'm borrowing it for a while.* 我借用它一会儿。—see 见 DURING (USAGE), SINCE[3] (USAGE) **9 for now/for the moment** used to say that you are suggesting something as a temporary solution, but it may be changed later 暂时; 目前,眼下: *I think for now we're just going to have to keep the cats in the house.* 我想暂时我们只能把猫留在房子里。**10** used to express distance〔用于表示距离〕达,计: *We walked for miles.* 我们已经走了好几英里。| *Factories and warehouses stretched for quite a distance along the canal.* 沿着运河好一段距离都是工厂和仓库。**11** used to state where a person, vehicle etc is going 往; 到…〔表示去向〕: *I set off for work.* 我动身上班去了。| *the night before leaving for New York* 去纽约之前的那个晚上 | *the train for Manchester* 开往曼彻斯特的火车 | **I'm for bed/home** *BrE* (=I'm going to bed/going home)【英】我打算去睡觉/我打算回家 **12** used to show a price or amount〔表示价格或数量〕达,计: *a cheque for a hundred pounds* 一百英镑的支票 | *The diamond was insured for two thousand dollars.* 这颗钻石投保2000美元。**13** in order to have, do, get, or obtain something 为了要; 为了做; 为了得到: *She decided to look for a job.* 她决定找份工作。| *Mother was too ill to get up for dinner.* 母亲病得无法起床吃晚饭。| *the qualifications necessary for entry to university* 进入大学所必备的资格 | *I paid $3 for it.* 我付了3美元买这个东西。| *an expert whom you can rely on for advice* 一位可以信赖其忠告的专家 | *For further details, write to this address.* 欲了解进一步详情,请致函下列地址查询。| *Let's go for a walk.* 我们去散步吧。| *We just did it for fun.* 我们这样做只是为了好玩。| *waiting for the bus* 等公共汽车 | *legislating for equality* 为平等而立法 | **run for your life** (=to save your life) 逃命 **14 now for** *spoken* used to say what you're going to have or do now【口】现在做吧: *Now for some fun!* 现在娱乐一下吧! **15** because of or as a result of something 由于,因为: *if, for any reason, you cannot attend...* 如果由于某种原因你无法出席… | *a reward for bravery* 因英勇而得到的嘉奖 | *We could hardly see for the mist.* 由于起雾,我们都看不清了。| *A certain amount must be deducted for depreciation.* 因有折旧,必须扣除一些金额。| **for doing sth** *He got a ticket for driving through a red light.* 他因驾车闯红灯而收到罚款通知单。**16** as to or concerning something 关于; 至于: *I felt sorry for him.* 我为他感到惋惜。| *He has a talent for upsetting people.* 他有使人生气的本领。| *I'm sure she's the ideal person for the job.* 我确信她是做这项工作的理想人选。| *We had pasta for lunch.* 午餐我们吃了意大利面食。| *Fortunately for him, he can swim.* 幸运的是,他会游泳。| *The success rates for each task are given in Table 4.* 每项任务的成功率在表4中列出。| **too... for me/her etc** (=more than I can deal with) 对我/她来说太… *You're too quick for me!* 对我来说你太快了! | **he's a great one for** (=he always wants or is concerned with) 他总是想要; 他总是关心 *He's a great one for details.* 他是最喜欢关心细节的人。| **Are you all right for money?** (=do you have enough?) 你的钱够用吗? | **...is not for me** (=is not suitable or appropriate for me) …不适合我 *City life is not for me.* 城市生活不适合我。**17** if you work for a company, play for a team etc, this is the one in which you work, play etc 为…〔工作、打球等〕: *surveyors working for property services* 为物业服务机构工作的测绘员 | *He writes for a weekly paper.* 他为一家周刊撰稿。| *She plays for the A team.* 她为A队出赛。**18** in favour of, supporting, or in agreement with something 赞成; 支持; 同意: *discussing the case for and against nuclear energy* 讨论支持和反对核能的理由 | *How many people voted for the proposal?* 多少人投票赞成这项提议? | *Three cheers for the captain.* 为队长欢呼三声吧。| **I'm all for** (=I approve of) 我完全同意; 我完全赞成 *I'm all for people enjoying themselves.* 我完全赞成人们多享乐。**19** representing, meaning, or as a sign of something 表示; 意思是; 是…的符号: *What's the word for 'happy' in French?* 法语中表示"happy"的单词是什么? | *Red is for danger.* 红色表示危险。**20** used after a comparative form to mean after, as a result of, or because of〔用于比较级后〕在…后; 作为…的结果; 由于,因为: *You'll feel better for a break.* 你休息后就会感觉好一些。**21** used to say that a particular feature of someone or something is surprising when you consider what they are 就…而言〔表示在这种情况下,所说的特点是令人惊讶的〕: *It's cold for the time of year.* 就一年中这个时候来说,天气算是冷的。| *She looks young for her age.* 就她的年龄而言,她看上去算是年轻的。**22 for sb/sth to do sth a)** used to introduce a phrase that is used instead of a CLAUSE (2)〔用于引出代替从句的短语〕: *It is really unusual for Michael to get cross.* 迈克尔发脾气确实是不寻常的。| **I can't bear for sb/sth to** *I can't bear for you to be unhappy.* 看着你不高兴我受不了。| **nothing worse/easier than for sb/sth to** *There's nothing worse than for a parent to ill-treat a child.* 没有什么比父母虐待小孩更恶劣的了。**b)** used when you are describing what someone should do, might do, or has done〔用于描写某人应该做、可能做或已经做的事〕: *The plan is for us to leave in the morning.* 按照计划我们是在上午离开。| **a need/desire/chance for sb/sth to** *There is an urgent need for someone to tackle this problem.* 急需有人来解决这个问题。| *There will be another opportunity for them to do it again.* 他们将有另一次机会再做这事。**c)** used when you are explaining a reason for something〔用来解释理由〕由于,为了: *He must have had some bad news for him to be so quiet.* (=as/since he is so quiet) 他这么沉默不语,一定是听到了什么坏消息。| *I've sent off my coat for it to be cleaned.* (=in order that it may be cleaned) 我已经把大衣送去清洗了。**d)** used when you are saying what someone or something is able to do〔用来说明某人或某物能做某事〕: *It's easy for a computer to keep a record of this information.* 电脑保存这种资料的记录很容易。| *It's impossible for me to get money out of Dorothy.* 要我从多萝西那里拿到钱是不可能的。| **large/difficult/near enough for sb/sth to** *The dolphin was near enough for me to reach out and touch it.* 海豚近得我伸手就可以摸到。| **too large/difficult/near for sb/sth to** *It's too difficult for me to explain.* 这太难了,我无法解释。**23 for each/every** used to say that each of one kind of thing has or will have something of another kind 每…就有: *For each mistake, you'll lose half a point.* 你每犯一个错误,就要扣去半

分。| *For every three people who agree, you'll find five who don't.* 每有三个人同意，就有五个人不同意。**24 for all a)** in spite of 虽然，尽管：*For all his efforts, he still came last.* 尽管他很努力，但还是最后一名。| *She still loves him for all that.* 尽管如此，她还是爱他。**b)** considering how little 尽管：*For all the success you've had, you might just as well have not bothered!* 尽管你已经获得一点成功，你还是不去费事干为好！**25 for all I know/care** *spoken* used to say that you do not really know or care【口】就我所知/我不介意：*For all I know, he could be dead.* 就我所知，他可能死了。| *He can jump into the river for all I care!* 他可以跳河，我才不管呢！**26 I wouldn't do it for anything** *informal* used to emphasize that you definitely would not do it【非正式】我决不做这事：*I would not go through that again for anything.* 我决不肯再经历那样的事了。**27 I for one believe/think that...** *spoken* this is my opinion, even if no one else agrees【口】我个人认为〔即使别人都不同意〕：*I for one believe that she's making a big mistake.* 我个人认为她正在犯一个大错误。**28 for one thing... (and for another)** used when you are giving reasons for a statement you have made〔用于说明理由〕一是…（二是…）：*No, I'm not going to buy it; for one thing I don't like the colour, and for another it's far too expensive.* 不，我不打算买这东西了；一是我不喜欢这颜色，二是太贵了。**29 if it weren't for/if it hadn't been for** if a particular thing had not happened, if someone had not done something, or if a situation was different 要不是：*If it hadn't been for you, I would not be alive now.* 要不是你，我早就死了。**30 (well,) that's/there's ... for you!** *spoken*【口】**a)** used to say that it is typical that something has been a disappointment; you cannot expect anything better of that type of thing 那正是…的特点！〔说明某物只可能是这么差劲〕：*That's foreign hotels for you!* 外国旅馆就是这份德行！**b)** used to say that something is the complete opposite of what you were saying 那还能算是…？那恰好跟…相反！：*I gave it to her and she just threw it away; there's gratitude for you!* 我把它给了她，她却扔掉；这就是所谓的好心有好报！**31 be (in) for it** to be likely to be blamed or punished 要挨骂；要受罚：*You'll be in for it if she finds out what you've done!* 要是她发现你做了这种事，你就要挨骂了！

F

S2 W1 **for²** *conjunction formal* used to introduce the reason for something; because【正式】因为：*He found it increasingly difficult to read, for his eyes were failing.* 他觉得阅读越来越费劲，因为他的视力越来越差。

for·age¹ /ˋfɔrɪdʒ; ˈfɒrɪdʒ/ *v* [I] **1** to go around searching for food or other supplies 四处搜寻〔食物、粮秣等〕：[+for] *The children are forced to forage for scraps in the streets.* 孩子们被迫在街上到处寻找残羹剩饭。| **a foraging party** (=group of soldiers searching for food etc) 粮秣征收队 **2** to search for something with your hands in a bag, drawer etc〔用手在袋子、抽屉等〕搜寻，翻找：*She foraged around in her purse, and finally produced her ticket.* 她在钱包里找来找去，终于翻出票来。—**forager** *n* [C]

forage² *n* **1** [singular] an act of searching for food 搜寻食物 **2** [U] food supplies for horses and cattle〔马和牛的〕饲料

for·ay¹ /ˋfɔre; ˈfɒreɪ/ *n* [C] **1** a short attempt at doing a particular job or activity, especially one that is very different from what you usually do〔尤对某项非本行的艰难工作或活动的〕短暂尝试：*After a brief unsuccessful foray into politics, he went back to his law practice.* 他短暂参政失败之后，又回来做律师了。**2** a short sudden attack by a group of soldiers〔一队士兵的〕突袭：*their nightly forays into enemy territory* 他们深入敌人领土的每夜突袭 **3** a short journey somewhere in order to get something or do something〔为得到某物或做某事而进行的〕短暂旅行：*her twice-weekly foray to the shops* 她的一周两次到商店购物

foray² *v* [I+into] to go out and make a sudden attack against the enemy, especially in order to get food or supplies〔尤指为得到食品或粮秣〕进行突袭

for·bade /fɚˋbed; fəˈbeɪd/ the past tense of FORBID

for·bear¹ /fɔrˋbɛr; fɔːˈbeə/ *past tense* **forbore** /-ˋbɔr; -ˈbɔː/ *past participle* **forborne** /-ˋbɔrn; -ˈbɔːn/ *v* [I] *formal* to not do something, even though you could do it if you wanted to【正式】克制；忍耐：[+from] *He forbore from making suggestions for fear of insulting her.* 他因怕侮辱她而克制住不提建议。| **forbear to do sth** *Clara forbore to mention that the result was likely to be the same.* 克拉拉抑制住自己，没有说结果可能相同。

for·bear² /ˋfɔr͵bɛr; ˈfɔːbeə/ *n* [C] a FOREBEAR 祖先，祖宗

for·bear·ance /fɔrˋbɛrəns; fɔːˈbeərəns/ *n* [U] *formal* patience, self-control, and willingness to forgive someone【正式】忍耐，自制；宽容：*Higgins accepted the decision with commendable forbearance.* 希金斯以值得称赞的宽大态度接受了这项决定。

for·bear·ing /fɔrˋbɛrɪŋ; fɔːˈbeərɪŋ/ *adj formal* patient and willing to forgive【正式】宽容的；有忍耐心的

for·bid /fɚˋbɪd; fəˈbɪd/ *past tense* **forbade** /-ˋbed; -ˈbeɪd/ *past participle* **forbidden** /-ˋbɪdn̩; -ˈbɪdn/ *v* [T] **1** to tell someone that they definitely must not do something 不许，禁止：*You may not go to the party – I absolutely forbid it!* 你不可以去参加聚会——我绝对不许你去！| **forbid sb from doing sth** *Women are forbidden from going out without a veil.* 禁止妇女不戴面纱外出。| **strictly forbid** *The law strictly forbids racial or sexual discrimination.* 这项法律严禁种族或性别歧视。| **forbid sb to do sth** *He was forbidden to leave the base as a punishment.* 他被禁止离开基地以作惩罚。**2 God/Heaven forbid** *spoken* used to emphasize that you hope that something will not happen【口】但愿不会发生这样的事：*Who would run the business if, God forbid, you were to die?* 如果你死了——但愿不会发生这样的事——谁来管理生意呢？**3** *formal* to make it impossible for someone to do something【正式】阻止；妨碍，使〔某人〕不可能做某事：*Lack of space forbids the listing of all those who contributed.* 篇幅不够，无法列出所有捐款人的名字。

Frequencies of **forbid, say sb can't** and **not let/allow** in spoken and written English. forbid, say sb can't 和 not let/allow 在英语口语和书面语中的使用频率

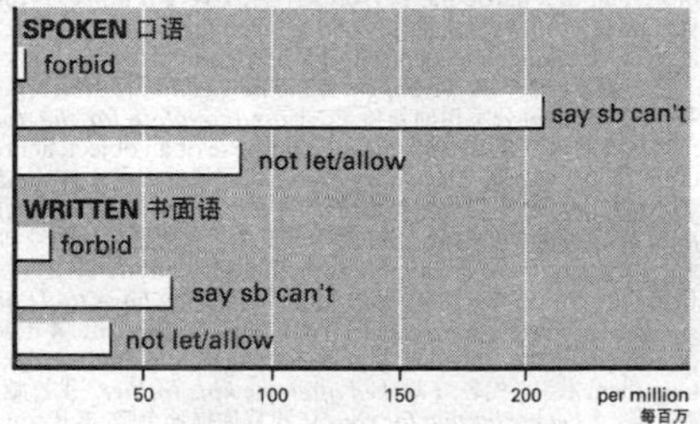

Based on the British National Corpus and the Longman Lancaster Corpus 据英国国家语料库和朗文兰开斯特语料库

This graph shows that it is much more usual in both spoken and written English to use the expressions **say sb can't** and **not let/allow**, rather than **forbid**. **Forbid** is less general. It is usually used when a government, law or person in authority orders someone not to do something. It is much more common in written English than in spoken English. 本图表显示，在英语口语和书面语中更经常使用的是 say sb can't 和 not let/allow，而不是 forbid。forbid 使用不太普遍。当政府、法律或权威人士命令某人不要做某事时，则通常使用 forbid。forbid 在英语书面语中的使用频率远远高于口语。

for·bid·den /fɚˋbɪdn̩; fəˈbɪdn/ *adj* **1** not allowed, especially because of an official rule〔尤指因官方规定而〕被禁止的；**strictly forbidden** *You can't smoke here – it's strictly forbidden.* 你不能在这里吸烟——这是严格禁止的。| **it is forbidden to do sth** *It is forbidden to marry someone who is not a member of the same faith.* 禁止与宗教信仰不同的人结婚。**2** a forbidden place is one that you are not allowed to go to〔地方〕禁止的：*the Great Mosque, whose precincts are forbidden to Christians* 禁止基督教徒进入其区域的大清真寺 **3** a forbidden activity, object etc is one that seems exciting because you are not allowed to do it or have it 禁戒的：*the forbidden sensual pleasures of the old city* 古城中的那些禁戒的肉欲快事 | **forbidden fruit** (=something forbidden that gives great pleasure) 禁果，禁止享受的快乐

Forbidden Cit·y, the /·, ···/ an area in Beijing, China, that is surrounded by a wall. In the past, no one except the IMPERIAL (=royal) family and their servants was allowed to enter it, but it is now open to the public and a lot of tourists go there. 紫禁城〔中国北京一区域。四面围墙环绕，过去只有皇室及其仆人才能进去，现已对公众开放，吸引着大批游客〕

for·bid·ding /fɚˋbɪdɪŋ; fəˈbɪdɪŋ/ *adj* having a frightening or unfriendly appearance〔外表〕可怕的，令人生畏的：*Despite her forbidding manner she's actually quite a kind person.* 虽然她的态度令人生畏，但她实际上是个相当和蔼的人。—**forbiddingly** *adv*

for·bore /fɔrˋbɔr; fɔːˈbɔː/ the past tense of FORBEAR

for·borne /fɔrˋbɔrn; fɔːˈbɔːn/ the past participle of FORBEAR

force¹ /fɔrs; fɔːs/ *n* S3 W1

1 ►MILITARY 军事◄ a) [C] a group of people who have been trained to fight in a war〔经训练的〕战斗队伍，部队：*forces loyal*

to President Aquino 忠于阿基诺总统的部队 | *a highly efficient fighting force* 一支效率十分高的战斗部队 **b) the forces** the army, navy, and air force 陆海空三军部队; 军队: *Both her sons are in the forces.* 她的两个儿子都在军队里。**c)** [U] military action used as a way of achieving your aims 军事行动; 武力: *After World War I the use of force to settle conflicts was prohibited.* 第一次世界大战后禁止使用武力解决争端。| **by force (of arms)** *The Serbs were accused of imposing these boundaries by force.* 塞尔维亚人被指责用武力强划这些边界。

2 ▶VIOLENCE 暴力◀ [U] violent physical action used to get what you want〔为得到某物而使用的〕暴力, 武力: *The question is whether the police used reasonable force when arresting him.* 问题是警方在逮捕他时是否是合理使用武力。| **by force** *Her ex-husband tried to get the children back by force.* 她的前夫企图强行要回孩子。

3 ▶PHYSICAL POWER 体力◀a) [U] the amount of physical power that is used or produced when something moves or hits something else 力, 力量: *waves hitting the rocks with tremendous force* 以巨大的力量拍击岩石的波涛 | *The force of the explosion blew out all the windows.* 爆炸力把所有的窗子都炸破了。| **brute force** (=simple physical force) 蛮力 *They kicked the door open by sheer brute force.* 他们全凭蛮力把门踢开。**b)** [C,U] *technical* power that produces movement in another object, for example by pulling it or pushing it【术语】〔作用于另一个物体使其移动的〕力: *the force of gravity* 地心引力

4 ▶STRONG INFLUENCE 强烈的影响◀ [C] something or someone that has a strong influence on the way events develop, on people's lives, or on the way people think〔对事件的发展、人们的生活或思维方式〕有影响力的人[事物]: *Mrs Thatcher is no longer the force she once was in British politics.* 撒切尔夫人再也不像以前那样对英国政界具有影响力了。| **driving force** (=person or thing that has the strongest influence on the way things happen) 推动力 *The need for short-term profits seems to be the driving force behind these mergers.* 对短期利润的追求似乎是推动这些合并产生的力量。| **a force for peace/progress/good etc** (=someone whose actions make peace, progress etc more likely to happen) 和平/进步/正义等的力量 | **a force to be reckoned with** (=a company, organization etc with a lot of power and influence) 需要认真对付的公司[组织] *Within just a few months, Microsoft became a force to be reckoned with in the global software market.* 仅在数月之内, 微软便成为全球软件市场中一股不可忽视的力量。| **forces beyond sb's control** *The fall in coffee prices was due to forces beyond their control.* 咖啡价格下降是由他们无法控制的力量引起的。| **the forces of evil/oppression** *the fight against the forces of oppression* 反抗压迫势力的斗争

5 ▶POWERFUL EFFECT 威力◀ [U] the powerful effect of what someone says or does〔某人说的话或做的事产生的〕威力, 影响力: *Even after 30 years, the play has lost none of its force.* 甚至在30年之后, 这出戏的影响力一点也没有失去。| *the force of public opinion* 舆论的威力

6 ▶ORGANIZED GROUP 有组织的群体◀ [C] a group of people who have been trained and organized for a specific purpose〔为某个目的而训练和组织的〕一群人, 队伍, 群体: *the company's sales force* 公司的销售队伍

7 join/combine forces to join together so that you can deal with a problem, defend yourselves etc〔为解决问题、保护自己而〕联合; 合作; 同心协力: *Local churches have joined forces to help the homeless.* 当地各个教堂联合起来帮助无家可归的人。| **[+with]** *The Nationalists joined forces with the Communists.* 国民党人与共产党人通力合作。

8 ▶LAW/RULE 法律/规则◀ in force a) if a law or a rule is in force, it exists and must be obeyed 生效; 有效; 实施: **come into force** (=start to operate) 开始生效, 开始实施 *The new law on drink-driving comes into force next month.* 有关酒后驾车的新法律下月开始生效。**b)** in a large group, especially in order to protest about something 大批地, 成群结队地, 人数众多地〔尤指为抗议某事〕: *Villagers turned out in force to protest about the new road.* 大批村民出动抗议修建这条新路。

9 by/from force of habit if you do something by force of habit, you do it because you have always done the same thing in the past 由于习惯, 因习惯的力量, 全因习惯

10 force of circumstance(s) the effect of a situation on what you do or decide 形势的影响: *Force of circumstance compelled him to leave Italy.* 形势迫使他离开意大利。

11 the forces of nature natural forces such as wind, rain, or EARTHQUAKES 自然力〈如风、雨或地震〉

12 ▶WIND 风◀a) force 8/9/10 etc a unit for measuring the strength of the wind 风力8/9/10级 **b) gale/hurricane force wind** extremely strong wind that does a lot of damage〔能造成大量破坏的〕大风/飓风

13 ▶POLICE 警察◀ the force a word meaning the police force, used especially by police officers 警察部队: *He resigned after 17 years in the force.* 他在警察部门服务17年后辞职。—see also 另见 LABOUR FORCE, TASK FORCE, TOUR DE FORCE

force² *v* [T] (S2, W1)

1 ▶MAKE SB DO STH 迫使某人做某事◀a) to make someone do something that they do not want to do, especially by threatening them〔尤指用威胁的手段〕强制, 逼迫, 迫使: **force sb to do sth** *Government troops have forced the rebels to surrender.* 政府军已迫使叛乱分子投降。| **force sb** *Nobody forced me – it was my own decision.* 没有人逼我 —— 这是我自己的决定。| **force sb/sth (into) doing sth** *These women are forced into accepting low-paid jobs.* 这些妇女被迫接受低工资的工作。**b)** if a situation forces you to do something, it makes you do it, even though you do not want to 迫使: **force sb to do sth** *The high cost of borrowing is forcing many companies to close.* 高昂的借贷成本正迫使许多公司倒闭。| **force sb into (doing) sth** *Bad health forced her into taking early retirement.* 她身体不好, 迫不得已要早早退休。

2 force yourself (to do sth) a) to make yourself do something that you do not want to do 勉强自己(做某事): *I forced myself to get out of bed.* 我强迫自己起床。**b)** *BrE spoken* used when trying to persuade someone to do something that they seem unwilling to do, because you know they will enjoy it【英口】别客气〔敦促某人做表面看来不愿做的事〕: *"I couldn't eat another thing!" "Go on! Force yourself!"* "我不能再吃了!" "再吃点吧! 别客气!"

3 ▶MAKE SB/STH MOVE 使某人/某物移动◀ to make someone or something move in a particular direction or into a different position, especially using physical force〔尤指用物理力量〕用力推动: **force sth into/out of** *Firemen attempted to enter the building but were forced back by the flames.* 消防队员企图进入大楼, 但被火焰顶了回来。

4 force your way in/out/through etc to push and use physical force to get into, out of, or through something 强行进入/挤出/通过等: *The doctor forced his way through the crowd.* 医生挤过人群。

5 ▶OPEN STH 打开某物◀ to use physical force to open something〔用物理力量〕砸开, 撬开: **force sth ↔ open** *Robbers forced open the safe in the manager's office.* 盗贼撬开了经理办公室里的保险箱。| **force the lock/window/door** (=open it using force, often causing damage) 撬开锁/窗户/门

6 force sb's hand to make someone do something unwillingly or earlier than they had intended 迫使某人采取行动; 迫使某人提前行动: *We didn't want to raise our prices but the fall in the dollar forced our hand.* 我们并不想提价, 但美元汇率下跌迫使我们不得不这样做。

7 force the issue to do something that makes it necessary for someone to make decisions or take action, instead of waiting for the situation to develop 迫使〔不再观望〕作出决定; 迫使采取行动: *Rather than trying to force the issue, we gave them another day to decide.* 我们没有强迫他们立即采取行动, 而是再给他们一天的时间作决定。

8 force a smile/laugh etc to make yourself smile, laugh etc even though you feel upset or annoyed 强作笑颜/勉强一笑等

9 force the pace to make the other runners in a race have to run faster by running ahead of them〔跑在前头〕促使[催促]他人跑得更快

force sth ↔ **back** *phr v* [T] to try hard to stop yourself from showing your emotions 强忍住〔感情的流露〕: *Janet forced back her tears.* 珍妮特强忍住泪水。

force sth ↔ **down** *phr v* [T] **1** to make yourself swallow something that you do not want to eat or drink 强吞下: *I managed to force down a piece of stale bread.* 我勉强吞下一片不新鲜的面包。**2** to make a plane have to land by threatening to attack it 迫使〔飞机〕降落

force sth **on/upon** sb *phr v* [T] to make someone accept something even though they do not want it 把〔某事〕强加于〔某人〕, 迫使〔某人〕接受: *children with piano lessons forced upon them* 被迫上钢琴课的儿童

force sth ↔ **out of** sb *phr v* [T] to make someone tell you something by asking them many times, threatening them etc〔通过多次要求、威胁等〕强迫〔某人〕说出: *I wasn't going to tell him, but he forced it out of me.* 我不想告诉他, 但他逼我说了出来。

forced /fɔrst; fɔːst/ *adj* **1** done unwillingly and with effort, not because of any sincere feeling 强迫的, 勉强的: *Their smiles seemed rather forced.* 他们的微笑似乎相当勉强。**2** done sud-

denly and quickly, because the situation makes it necessary 紧急的: *a forced march back to base* 返回基地的强行军 | **a forced landing** (=when an aircraft has to land quickly because of an unexpected problem)〔飞机因出现意外问题而做出的〕迫降, 紧急降落

force-feed /ˈ· ·/ *v* [T] to force someone to eat by putting food or liquid down their throat 给…强灌〔食物〕, 强喂

force·ful /ˈfɔrsfəl; ˈfɔːsfəl/ *adj* **1** a forceful person expresses their opinions very strongly and clearly and people are easily persuaded by them〔观点〕有力的, 有说服力的: *She has a strong character, very forceful and determined.* 她个性坚强, 观点非常鲜明有力, 态度坚决。**2** forceful arguments, reasons etc are strongly and clearly expressed, and help persuade you that something is true〔论据、理由等〕有力的, 有说服力的 —**forcefully** *adv*: *Dole spoke out forcefully against the plan.* 多尔大胆发言, 坚决反对这项计划。—**forcefulness** *n* [U]

force ma·jeure /ˌfɔrs mɑˈʒɝ; ˌfɔːs mæˈʒɜː/ *n* [U] *French formal* unexpected events that prevent you from doing what you intended or promised【法, 正式】不可抗力: *The company tried to escape its obligations by claiming force majeure.* 公司声称出现不可抗力, 企图以此来逃避责任。

for·ceps /ˈfɔrsəps; ˈfɔːseps/ *n* [plural] a medical instrument used for picking up and holding things〔医用的〕钳子, 镊子

for·ci·ble /ˈfɔrsəbl; ˈfɔːsəbəl/ *adj* done using physical force, especially as a result of an official order〔尤指由于官方命令而〕强行的; 用暴力的: *forcible seizure of their assets* 强行没收他们的财产 —**forcibly** *adv*: *Police threatened to have the protesters forcibly removed.* 警方威胁要强行带走这些抗议者。

Ford /fɔrd; fɔːd/ **1** *trademark* one of the world's largest car companies, which is based in the US and has factories in many countries【商标】福特公司〔世界上最大的汽车制造商之一。总部在美国, 在许多国家设有工厂〕**2** a car made by this company "福特"汽车

ford¹ *n* [C] a place where a river is not deep, so that you can walk or drive across it 浅滩, 浅水处, 津〔河流可涉水而过之处〕

ford² *v* [T] to walk or drive across a river at a place where the water is not deep 涉水而过

Ford, Ford Mad·dox /fɔrd ˈmædəks; fɔːd ˈmædəks/(1873-1939) a British writer of many poems, articles, and NOVELS, including *The Good Soldier* and *Parade's End*, which relate his experiences as an army officer in France in World War I 福特〔(1873-1939), 英国作家。作品有诗歌、随笔、小说, 其中小说包括《好兵》和《行进的目的》, 讲述一战期间他在法国担任军官的经历〕

Ford, Ger·ald /ˈdʒɛrəld; ˈdʒerəld/ (1913-2006) a US politician in the Republican Party who became President of the US in 1974 after Richard NIXON was forced to RESIGN (=leave his job) because of WATERGATE. 福特〔(1913-2006), 美国共和党政治家。1974年理查德·尼克松因水门事件被迫辞职后, 他就任美国总统〕

Ford, Har·rison (1942-) a US actor who is famous for appearing in films about exciting adventures, such as *Star Wars* (1977), and for appearing as the character Indiana Jones in a series of films such as *Indiana Jones* and *The Temple of Doom* 福特〔(1942-), 美国演员。他出演过《星球大战》(1977) 等惊险片, 在《魔域奇兵》等印第安纳·琼斯系列影片中扮演印第安纳·琼斯, 并因此而著称〕

Ford, Henry (1863-1947) a US businessman and engineer, who started making cars in 1896 and established the Ford Motor Company. He developed the idea of the ASSEMBLY LINE (=system in which each worker is responsible for one small part of the process of making something), and this made it possible to produce cars in large numbers. 福特〔(1863-1947), 美国实业家、工程师。1896年, 他开始制造汽车, 之后创办了福特汽车公司。他提出的流水线理念使汽车的批量生产成为可能〕

Ford, John (1895-1973) a US film DIRECTOR famous for his WESTERNS (=films about the American west in the 19th century). His films include *Stagecoach* (1939), *She Wore a Yellow Ribbon* (1949), and *The Searchers* (1956). 福特〔(1895-1973), 美国电影导演, 以导演西部片闻名。他导演的影片包括《关山飞渡》(1939)、《她系着黄丝带》(1949) 和《搜索者》(1956)〕

fore- /fɔr; fɔː/ *prefix* **1** before 预先; 先, 前: *to forewarn* 预先警告 **2** placed at the front (在…) 前面的: *her forenames* 她的名字 | *a horse's forelegs* 马的前腿 **3** the front part of something〔某物的〕前部: *his strong forearms* 他那强壮的前臂

fore¹ /fɔr; fɔː/ *n* **come to the fore** to become important or influential 变得重要; 崭露头角: *Yeltsin first came to the fore when he was the Party Chief in Moscow.* 叶利钦在莫斯科担任党的首脑时初次崭露头角。

fore² *adj* [only before noun 仅用于名词前] *technical* the fore parts of a ship, plane, or animal are the parts at the front【术语】〔船、飞机或动物〕前部的, 在头部的 —opposite 反义词 AFT

fore·arm /ˈfɔr,ɑrm; ˈfɔːrɑːm/ *n* [C] the lower part of the arm, between the hand and the elbow 前臂 —see also 另见 **forewarned is forearmed** (FOREWARN (2)) —see picture at 参见 BODY 图

fore·bear /ˈfɔr,bɛr; ˈfɔːbeə/ *n* [C usually plural 一般用复数] *formal* someone who was a member of your family a long time in the past【正式】祖先, 祖宗

fore·bod·ing /fɔrˈbodɪŋ; fɔːˈbəʊdɪŋ/ *n* [U] a feeling that something very unpleasant is going to happen soon〔对将发生不愉快事的〕预感: *She waited for news from the hospital with a grim sense of foreboding.* 她带着一种可怕的预感, 等待医院传来的消息。

fore·cast¹ /ˈfɔr,kæst; ˈfɔːkɑːst/ *n* [C] a description of what is likely to happen in the future, based on information that is available now 预测, 预报: *the company's annual sales forecast* 公司的年销售预测 | *the weather forecast* 天气预报

forecast² *past tense & past participle* **forecast** *or* **forecasted** *v* [T] to make a statement saying what is likely to happen in the future, based on information that is available now 预测, 预报: *Bad weather had been forecast for the day of the race.* 预报比赛当天天气不好。| **forecast (that)** *The Federal Reserve Bank has forecast that the economy will grow by 2% this year.* 联邦储备银行预测今年的经济会增长2%。—**forecaster** *n* [C]

fore·castle /ˈfoksl; ˈfəʊksəl/ *n* [C] *AmE* the front part of a ship, where the sailors live【美】〔船艏的〕水手舱; FO'C'SLE *BrE*【英】

fore·close /fɔrˈkloz; fɔːˈkləʊz/ *v* [I+on,T] *technical* to take away someone's property because they have failed to pay back the money that they borrowed to buy it【术语】〔因抵押人无法偿还贷款〕取消抵押品赎回权 —**foreclosure** /-ˈkloʒɚ; -ˈkləʊʒə/ *n* [U]

fore·court /ˈfɔr,kort; ˈfɔːkɔːt/ *n* [C] a large open area in front of a building such as a garage, or hotel〔车库、旅馆等的〕前院; 前庭; 前场

fore·doomed /fɔrˈdumd; fɔːˈduːmd/ *adj formal* intended by FATE (2) to be unsuccessful or unhappy【正式】命中注定的, 注定失败的

fore·fa·thers /ˈfɔr,fɑðɚz; ˈfɔː,fɑːðəz/ *n* [plural] the people, especially men, who were part of the same family as you a long time in the past 祖先, 祖宗〔尤指男性〕

fore·fin·ger /ˈfɔr,fɪŋgɚ; ˈfɔː,fɪŋgə/ *n* [C] the finger next to your thumb; INDEX FINGER 食指

fore·foot /ˈfɔr,fut; ˈfɔːfʊt/ *n* [C] one of the two front feet of a four-legged animal〔四足动物的〕前足

fore·front /ˈfɔr,frʌnt; ˈfɔːfrʌnt/ *n* **1 be in/at the forefront (of)** to have an important and leading position among a group of people, organizations etc that are trying to achieve something or are developing new ideas 位于最前列; 处于领先地位: *The Pasteur Institute has been at the forefront of research into the AIDS virus.* 巴斯德研究所在艾滋病病毒的研究上一直处于领先地位。**2 be in/at the forefront of sb's mind** to be thought about by someone and seem important to them 某人首先考虑的; 某人首先想到的

fore·gath·er /fɔrˈgæðɚ; fɔːˈgæðə/ *v* [I] to FORGATHER 聚会; 聚集

fore·go, forgo /fɔrˈgo; fɔːˈgəʊ/ *v past tense* **forewent** /-ˈwɛnt; -ˈwent/ *past participle* **foregone** /-ˈgɔn; -ˈgɒn/ [T] *formal* to decide to not do or have something, especially something enjoyable【正式】摒绝, 放弃: *The monks have to forego earthly pleasures.* 僧侣得摒弃俗世的乐趣。

fore·go·ing /fɔrˈgoɪŋ; fɔːˈgəʊɪŋ/ *adj* **the foregoing** *formal* the things that have just been mentioned【正式】刚提到的事物, 前面提到的事物, 上述事物

fore·gone con·clu·sion /,· · ˈ· ·/ *n* **be a foregone conclusion** if something is a foregone conclusion, the result of it is certain, even though it has not yet happened or been decided 预料中的结论; (成为) 定局: *The election result was a foregone conclusion.* 选举结果已成定局。

fore·ground /ˈfɔr,graund; ˈfɔːgraʊnd/ *n* **1 the foreground** the nearest part of a scene in a picture or a photograph〔图片或照片的〕前景 **2 be in the foreground** to be regarded as important and receive a lot of attention 处于最突出的地位; 成为众所瞩目的对象: *Education and health were very much in the foreground during the post-war years.* 教育和健康在战后几年是最受人关注的问题。

fore·hand /ˈfɔr,hænd; ˈfɔːhænd/ *n* [singular] a way of hitting the ball in tennis, with the flat part of your hand facing the di-

rection of the ball〔网球的〕正手击球 —**forehand** *adj* —see picture on page A23 参见 A23 页图

fore·head /ˈfɔrɪd; ˈfɒrɪ̈d/ *n* [C] the part of your face above your eyes and below your hair 额, 前额 —see picture at 参见 HEAD[1] 图

S3 W1 **for·eign** /ˈfɔrɪn; ˈfɒrɪ̈n/ *adj* **1** not from your own country or the country you are talking about 外国的, 国外的: *Can you speak any foreign languages?* 你会讲外语吗? | *foreign tourists* 外国游客 | *I thought she sounded foreign.* 我认为她说话像外国人。 **2** [only before noun 仅用于名词前] involving or dealing with other countries 对外的, 涉外的, 外事的, 外交的: *America's foreign policy* 美国的对外政策 **3 foreign body/matter/object** *formal* something that has come into something else, and that should not be there【正式】异物, 外来物体: *Make sure you remove all foreign matter from the wound.* 要确保清除伤口里的所有异物。**4 foreign to** *formal*【正式】**a)** not typical of someone's usual character 不相干的, 无关的; 不属于本身的: *Any form of cruelty is foreign to his nature.* 任何形式的残酷都与他的本性格格不入。**b)** seeming strange and unfamiliar 陌生的, 不熟悉的: *The idea of doing something just for pleasure is quite foreign to them.* 他们根本没有纯粹为了消遣而做一件事情的想法。—**foreignness** *n* [U]

foreign af·fairs /,·· ·'·/ *n* [plural] politics, business matters etc that affect or concern the relationship between your country and other countries 外交事务, 外事

for·eign·er /ˈfɔrɪnə; ˈfɒrɪ̈nə/ *n* [C] someone who comes from a different country 外国人: *Foreigners are not allowed to own land.* 外国人不得拥有土地。

foreign ex·change /,·· ·'·/ *n* [U] **1** the system of buying and selling foreign money 国际汇兑; 外汇; 外汇兑换[交易]: *The foreign exchange markets reacted quickly to the cut in German interest rates.* 外汇市场对德国利率的下调反应迅速。**2** foreign money, especially money obtained by selling goods to a foreign country 外汇, 外币: *Coffee is a valuable source of foreign exchange for Uganda.* 咖啡是乌干达宝贵的外汇来源。

Foreign Le·gion, the /,·· '··/ a part of the French army that is made up of VOLUNTEERS (=men who chose to join), most of whom are not French. In the past, the Foreign Legion were used to protect French colonies (COLONY) in North Africa. 外籍军团〔法国军队的一部分, 多数士兵为非法籍志愿者, 过去用于保卫北非的法国殖民地〕

Foreign Of·fice /'·· ,··/ *n* the British government department that is responsible for dealing with foreign affairs〔英国〕外交部

Foreign Sec·re·ta·ry /,·· '····/ the British politician who is in charge of the Foreign Office and the UK's political relationship with other countries. In the US there is a similar politician called the Secretary of State. (英国) 外交大臣〔负责外交部及英国与其他国家政治关系的政界官员。美国也有类似的官员, 称"国务卿"〕

Foreign Ser·vice, the /'·· ,··/ a part of the US State Department which employs the people who work in US embassies (EMBASSY) all over the world. In the UK there is a similar department called the Diplomatic Service. 驻外机关事务局〔美国国务院的一部分, 负责雇用美国驻外使馆工作人员。英国也有一类似部门, 称"外交人事局"〕

fore·knowl·edge /ˈfɔr,nɑlɪdʒ; fɔːˈnɒlɪdʒ/ *n* [U] *formal* knowledge that something is going to happen before it actually does【正式】预知, 事先知道: [+of] *The senator denied having any foreknowledge of the affair.* 这位参议员否认事先知道这件事。

fore·leg /ˈfɔr,lɛg; ˈfɔːleg/ *n* [C] one of the two front legs of a four-legged animal〔四足动物的〕前腿

fore·lock /ˈfɔr,lɑk; ˈfɔːlɒk/ *n* [C] **1** a piece of hair that falls over someone's forehead 额发, 前发;〔马的〕额毛 —see picture at 参见 HORSE[1] 图 **2 forelock-tugging/touching** *BrE* showing too much respect towards people in authority【英】对权势人物表示过分敬意的

fore·man /ˈfɔrmən; ˈfɔːmən/ *n plural* **foremen** /-mən; -mən/ [C] **1** a skilled worker who is in charge of a group of builders or factory workers 工头, 领班 **2** the leader of a JURY (=the group of 12 people who decide whether someone is guilty in a court of law) 陪审团团长

fore·most /ˈfɔr,most; ˈfɔːməʊst/ *adj* **foremost scientist/expert/writer etc** the most important and respected scientist, writer etc 最杰出的科学家/专家/作家等: *one of Europe's foremost authorities on childhood diseases* 欧洲最杰出的儿科疾病权威之一 —see also 另见 **first and foremost** (FIRST (21))

fore·name /ˈfɔr,nem; ˈfɔːneɪm/ *n* [C] *formal* someone's FIRST NAME【正式】名字

fo·ren·sic /fəˈrɛnsɪk; fəˈrensɪk/ *adj* [only before noun 仅用于名词前] connected with the methods used for finding out who is guilty of a crime 法庭的; 用于法庭的: **forensic science/medicine etc** *A specialist in forensic science was called as a witness.* 一位法庭科学专家被传召作证人。| **forensic evidence** (=blood, hair, FINGERPRINTS etc, used to prove that someone is guilty) 法庭证据

fore·or·dain /,fɔrɔrˈden; ,fɔːrɔːˈdeɪn/ *v* [T] *formal* to decide or arrange how something will happen before it actually happens【正式】预先决定, 预先安排, 注定: *Their love seemed foreordained.* 他们的爱情似乎是注定的。

fore·play /ˈfɔr,ple; ˈfɔːpleɪ/ *n* [U] sexual activity, such as kissing and touching the sexual organs, done before having sex〔性交前的〕性爱抚; 前戏

fore·run·ner /ˈfɔr,rʌnə; ˈfɔː,rʌnə/ *n* [C] **1** a person, organization, machine etc which existed a long time before a similar one that exists now, and which the present one is based upon 先驱, 先导, 前锋: [+of] *The suffragettes were forerunners of the modern women's movement.* 为妇女选举权而斗争的女子是现代妇女运动的先驱。**2** a sign or warning that something is going to happen 预兆, 前兆, 征兆

fore·see /fɔrˈsi; fɔːˈsiː/ *past tense* **foresaw** /-ˈsɔ; -ˈsɔː/ *past participle* **foreseen** /-ˈsin; -ˈsiːn/ *v* [T] to know that something is going to happen before it actually happens 预知; 预见, 预料: *The method was used in ways that could not have been foreseen by its inventors.* 这种方法以其发明者无从预见的各种方式得到使用。| **foresee that** *Few analysts foresaw that oil prices would rise so steeply.* 分析家中很少有人预料到油价会这么飞涨。

fore·see·a·ble /fɔrˈsiəbl; fɔːˈsiːəbəl/ *adj* **1 in the foreseeable future** fairly soon 在可预见的将来: *There is a possibility of severe water shortages in the foreseeable future.* 在可预见的将来可能会出现严重的水资源短缺。**2 for the foreseeable future** continuing in the future for as long as you can imagine 在可预见的未来(将持续…): *Their dependence on oil exports is likely to continue for the foreseeable future.* 他们对石油出口的依赖在可预见的未来时日里可能会持续下去。**3** foreseeable difficulties, events etc are ones that you can imagine happening in the future〔困难、事件等〕可预见到的: *planning for any foreseeable financial losses* 为应付任何可预见到的经济损失而制定计划

fore·shad·ow /fɔrˈʃædo; fɔːˈʃædəʊ/ *v* [T] to be a sign of something that will happen in the future 预示; 是…的预兆: *The events in Spain in the 1930s foreshadowed the rise of Nazi Germany.* 20世纪30年代西班牙发生的事件预示了纳粹德国的兴起。

fore·shore /ˈfɔr,ʃɔr; ˈfɔːʃɔː/ *n* [singular] **1** the part of the shore between the highest and lowest levels that the sea reaches〔高潮线和低潮线之间的〕前滩, 前滨 **2** the part of the shore between the edge of the sea and the part of the land that has houses, grass etc 海滩

fore·short·ened /fɔrˈʃɔrtn̩d; fɔːˈʃɔːtnd/ *adj* objects, places etc that are foreshortened appear to be smaller, shorter, or closer together than they really are〔事物、地方等显得〕缩小的; 缩短的; 紧凑的: *Some of the figures are oddly foreshortened, giving the picture a disturbing quality.* 有些人物莫名其妙地缩小了, 给图画一种令人不安的感觉。—**foreshorten** *v* [T]

fore·sight /ˈfɔr,saɪt; ˈfɔːsaɪt/ *n* [U] the ability to imagine what is likely to happen and to consider this when planning for the future 先见之明, 预见; 深谋远虑: *The report blames the accident on lack of foresight by the original planners.* 该报告把这次事故归咎于原设计者缺乏先见之明。| **have the foresight to do sth** *Luckily she had had the foresight to destroy the incriminating documents.* 幸运的是, 她有远见地销毁了可证明有罪的文件。

fore·skin /ˈfɔr,skɪn; ˈfɔː,skɪn/ *n* [C] a loose fold of skin covering the end of a man's PENIS〔阴茎的〕包皮

for·est /ˈfɔrɪst; ˈfɒrɪ̈st/ *n* [C] a large area of land that is thickly covered with trees 森林, 林区: *Much of Scandinavia is covered in dense pine forest.* 斯堪的纳维亚许多地方都覆盖着茂密的松林。| *a forest fire* 森林火灾 S2 W2

fore·stall /fɔrˈstɔl; fɔːˈstɔːl/ *v* [T] to prevent something from happening or prevent someone from doing something by doing something first 预先阻止; 抢先: *Gero urged reforms in order to forestall trouble.* 杰罗敦促进行改革以防止出现麻烦。

for·est·er /ˈfɔrɪstə; ˈfɒrɪ̈stə/ *n* [C] someone who works in a forest taking care of, planting, and cutting down the trees 护林人, 林务员, 林业工作者

Forester /ˈfɔrɪstə; ˈfɒrɪ̈stə/, **C.S.** (1899-1966) a British writer best known for his stories about the Royal Navy during the Napoleonic Wars, especially those about the character Captain

Horatio Hornblower 福雷斯特〔(1899-1966)，英国作家。他创作的小说以拿破仑战争时期英国皇家海军为题材，有关霍雷肖·霍恩布洛尔船长的小说尤为有名〕

Forest Hills /, · · ˈ · / a town in New York State known especially for the US Open tennis competition which takes place there every year 福里斯特希尔〔纽约州一镇，尤以每年举行的美国网球公开赛闻名〕

Forest of Dean /, · · ˈ · / an area in Gloucestershire, England, on the River Severn. It used to have an important iron and coal mining (MINE³) industry. 迪恩森林〔英格兰格洛斯特郡一地方，位于塞文河畔。过去，这里的钢铁工业、采煤业十分重要〕

for·est·ry /ˋfɔrɪstrɪ; ˈfɒrɪstri/ *n* [U] the science or skill of looking after large areas of trees 林学；林务

Forestry Com·mis·sion, the /ˈ · · · ·, · ˈ · / an organization that is responsible for taking care of forests in the UK. In the US there is a similar organization called the Forest Service. 林业委员会〔英国一森林管理机构。美国也有一类似机构，称“林务局”〕

Forest Ser·vice, the /ˈ · ·, · ˈ · / an organization that is responsible for taking care of forests in the US. In the UK there is a similar organization called the Forestry Commission. 林务局〔美国一森林管理机构。英国也有一类似机构，称“林业委员会”〕

fore·taste /ˋfɔr,test; ˈfɔːteɪst/ *n* **be a foretaste of** to be a sign of something more important, more impressive etc that will happen in the future 是…的前兆：*Two spectacular wins at the start of the season were a foretaste of things to come.* 该队在赛季一开始就惊人地两次获胜，预示着此后所要发生的事。

fore·tell /fɔrˋtɛl; fɔːˈtel/ *v past tense and past participle* **foretold** /-ˋtold; -ˈtəʊld/ [T] to say what will happen in the future, especially by using special magical powers〔尤指用超凡的能力〕预言；预示：*the birth of Christ, foretold by prophets* 先知们所预言的基督的诞生

fore·thought /ˋfɔr,θɔt; ˈfɔːθɔːt/ *n* [U] careful thought about what needs to be done in order to make sure things happen well in the future 事先的考虑，事先的筹划：*No one had had the forethought to bring a corkscrew.* 没有一个人事先想到要带开塞钻来。

fore·told /fɔrˋtold; fɔːˈtəʊld/ the past tense and past participle of FORETELL

S3 **for·ev·er, for ever** /fəˋɛvə; fərˈevə/ *adv* **1** continuing or lasting for all future time 永远：*Our love will last forever.* 我们的爱情将会直到永远。| *These valuable works of art have been lost forever.* 这些珍贵的艺术品已经永远丢失了。**2** *especially spoken* for a very long time【尤口】很长久地：*We'll be stuck here forever if the car won't start.* 如果车子发动不了，我们就要在这里被困到不知什么时候。| **take forever** (=take a long time) 花很长的时间 *It took forever to clean up after the party.* 聚会后收拾打扫花了很长时间。**3 be forever doing sth** *spoken* to do something many times, especially in a way that annoys people【口】老是做某事，不断做某事：*He's forever making comments about my weight.* 他老是在谈论我的体重。**4 forever and a day** *spoken* a very long time【口】很长的时间：*It's going to take me forever and a day to pay for it.* 为此我要花很长的时间还清欠款。**5 forever and ever** a phrase meaning forever, used especially in stories 永远永远，永久〔尤用于故事〕

fore·warn /fɔrˋwɔrn; fɔːˈwɔːn/ *v* [T often passive 常用被动态] **1** to warn someone about something dangerous, unpleasant, or unexpected before it happens 预先警告；事先告知：[**+of/about/against**] *She had been forewarned of the discomforts of travelling by train in the Soviet Union.* 她预先得到警告，在苏联乘火车旅行是很不舒适的。**2 forewarned is forearmed** used to say that if you know about something in advance, you can be properly prepared for it 凡事预则立，先知先戒备 —**forewarning** *n* [C,U]

fore·went, forwent /fɔrˋwɛnt; fɔːˈwent/ the past tense of FORGO

fore·wom·an /ˋfɔr,wumən; ˈfɔː,wumən/ *n* [C] **1** a female worker who is in charge of a group of other workers, especially in a factory〔尤指工厂里的〕女工头，女领班 **2** a woman who is the leader of a JURY (=a group of 12 people who decide if someone is guilty in a court of law) 陪审团女团长

fore·word /ˋfɔr,wɝd; ˈfɔːwɜːd/ *n* [C] a short piece of writing at the beginning of a book〔书的〕前言，序言

for·feit¹ /ˋfɔrfɪt; ˈfɔːfɪ̣t/ *v* [T] to lose something valuable by having it taken away from you, either as a punishment or because of a law or rule〔作为惩罚或由于法律或规则而〕失去；丧失；被没收：*By becoming a German citizen he forfeited his right to live in the US.* 由于成为德国公民，他丧失了在美国的居住权。—**forfeiture** /-fɪtʃə; -fɪ̣tʃə/ *n* [U]

forfeit² *n* [C] something that is taken away from you or something that you have to do, because you have broken a rule or made a mistake 没收物；丧失的东西；代价〔作为对某人违反规则或犯错误的惩罚〕

forfeit³ *adj* **be forfeit** *formal* to be legally or officially taken away from you as a punishment【正式】〔作为惩罚〕被没收；丧失：*Unless he returns with the prisoners as he promised, his life shall be forfeit.* 除非他按照自己的承诺把囚犯们带回来，不然他就要送命。

for·gath·er, foregather /fɔrˋgæðə; fɔːˈgæðə/ *v* [I] *formal* to meet as a group【正式】聚会；聚集

for·gave /fəˋgev; fəˈgeɪv/ the past tense of FORGIVE

forge¹ /fɔrdʒ; fɔːdʒ/ *v* [T] **1** to illegally copy something, especially something printed or written on paper, to make people think that it is real 伪造；假冒〔尤指印或写在纸上的东西〕：*Someone stole my credit card and forged my signature.* 有人偷了我的信用卡，并假冒我的签名。| *a forged passport* 假护照 **2 forge a relationship/alliance/links etc** to develop a strong relationship, with other groups or other countries〔与其他团体或国家〕建立关系 / 结盟 / 建立联系等：*Gorbachev was able to forge new links between Russia and the West.* 戈尔巴乔夫能建立俄罗斯和西方之间的新联系。**3** to make something from a piece of metal by heating the metal and shaping it 锻造；打〔铁〕

forge ahead *phr v* [I] **1** to make progress and become more and more successful 稳步前进；越来越成功：*individuals who have forged ahead in this competitive field* 在这个竞争性领域中领先的人 **2** to move forward in a strong and powerful way 突飞猛进，奋力前进

forge² *n* [C] **1** a place where metal is heated and shaped into objects 锻造车间；铁匠铺 **2** a large piece of equipment that produces high temperatures and is used for heating and shaping metal objects 锻铁炉；熔铁炉

forg·er /ˋfɔrdʒə; ˈfɔːdʒə/ *n* [C] someone who illegally copies documents, money, paintings etc, to try to make people think they are real〔文件、钱币、绘画等的〕伪造者

for·ge·ry /ˋfɔrdʒərɪ; ˈfɔːdʒəri/ *n* **1** [C] a document, painting, or piece of paper money that has been forged〔文件、绘画或纸币的〕伪造品，赝品：*The painting was actually a very clever forgery.* 实际上这幅画是件很巧妙的赝品。**2** [U] the crime of forging official documents, money etc 伪造罪

for·get /fəˋgɛt; fəˈget/ *past tense* **forgot** /-ˋgɑt; -ˈgɒt/ *past participle* **forgotten** /-ˋgɑtn̩; -ˈgɒtn/ *v*

1 ▶FACTS/INFORMATION 事实/信息◀ [I,T] to be unable to remember facts, information, or something that happened in the past 忘记，遗忘：*I'm sorry, I've forgotten your name.* 对不起，我忘了你的名字了。| [**+(that)**] *Don't forget that it's Sarah's birthday on Tuesday.* 别忘了星期二是萨拉的生日。| [**+about**] *Charles seems to have forgotten about what happened.* 查尔斯好像已忘了发生过的事。| [**+how/what/when/why etc**] *Natalie managed to forget where she'd parked the car.* 纳塔莉竟然忘记她把车泊在哪里了。

2 ▶STH YOU MUST DO 你必须做的事◀ [I,T] to not remember to do something that you have to do 忘记，忘掉〔做某件应当做的事〕：*"Did you remember to post that letter?" "Oh, sorry, I forgot."* “你记得要寄那封信吗？”“哦，对不起，我忘了。”| **forget to do sth** *Someone's forgotten to turn off their headlights.* 有人忘记关汽车前灯了。| **forget (that)** *I forgot that I was supposed to come in early this morning.* 我忘记我今天上午应该早来。| **clean forget** (=completely forget) 忘得一干二净 *He meant to invite Monica to the party but he clean forgot.* 他本打算邀请莫妮卡参加聚会，但却忘得一干二净。

3 ▶NOT BRING 没有带◀ [I,T] to not bring something that you need, because you did not remember to bring it 忘记〔带、拿〕：*Don't forget your passport.* 别忘了拿你的护照。| *I didn't forget the torch.* 我没有忘记带电筒。

4 ▶STOP THINKING ABOUT 停止想◀ [I, T] to try to stop thinking and worrying about someone or something that makes you unhappy 忘掉〔令人不愉快的人或事〕，不再去想：*Years after their divorce Olivia still could not forget John.* 离婚数年后，奥莉维亚仍忘不了约翰。| [**+about**] *I'd forget about it if I were you.* 如果我是你，我就把它忘了。

5 ▶NOT CARE ABOUT 对…不介意，不关心◀ [I,T] to not care about or give attention to someone or something 不介意；不关心；忽视：[**+about**] *Don't go off to college and forget about your old friends, okay?* 不要上了大学就忘了老朋友，好吗？

6 ▶STOP A PLAN 停止一项计划◀ [I, T] to stop trying to do something because it no longer seems possible 不再打算做；放弃：[**+about**] *We'll have to forget about going on holiday.* 我们将不得不放弃度假的计划。| *If we can't get any funding we might*

as well forget the whole thing. 如果我们不能得到资金，那就不如干脆别谈这件事了。
7 not forgetting used to add something to a list of things 也包括…在内，别忘了还有：*Bear in mind that we have to pay for all the packaging and transportation costs, not forgetting airport taxes.* 记住，我们得支付所有的包装和运输费用，还包括机场税。
8 forget yourself to do something stupid or embarrassing, especially by losing control of your emotions 忘乎所以；失去理智；行为失态

Frequencies of the verb **forget** in spoken and written English 动词forget在英语口语和书面语中的使用频率

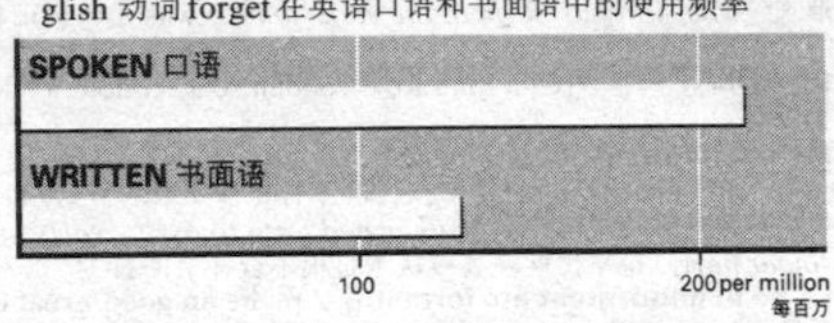

Based on the British National Corpus and the Longman Lancaster Corpus 据英国国家语料库和朗文兰开斯特语料库

This graph shows that the verb **forget** is much more common in spoken English than in written English. This is because it is used in a lot of common spoken phrases. 本图表显示，动词forget在英语口语中的使用频率远远高于书面语，因为口语中有很多常用短语是由forget构成的。

forget (*v*) **SPOKEN PHRASES**
含 forget 的口语短语

9 don't forget a) used to remind someone to do something 别忘了，要记住〔做某事〕：*We need bread, milk, and eggs. Don't forget now, will you?* 我们需要面包、牛奶和鸡蛋。可别忘了，好吗？| **don't forget to do sth** *Don't forget to lock the place up when you leave.* 离开时别忘了把这个地方锁好。**b)** used to remind someone about an important fact or detail that they should consider 别忘了〔某个重要事实或细节〕：*The kids won't be home until late, don't forget, so we'll be eating on our own.* 别忘了孩子们要很迟才回家，所以我们自己吃饭吧。| **don't forget (that)** *But don't forget you have to pay interest on the loan.* 可是不要忘记你得为贷款付利息。
10 forget it a) used when someone asks you what you just said and you do not want to repeat it 别提它了，算了〔用于不想重复刚才所说的话〕：*"What was that? I didn't hear." "Nothing, forget it."* "什么来着？我没听见。""没什么，别提它了。" **b)** used to tell someone that something is not important and they do not need to worry about it 没关系，别在意〔用于表示某物不重要〕：*"I'm really sorry, I'll get you another one." "Forget it, I've got lots of bowls."* "真的很对不起，我另外买一个给你。""没关系，我有很多碗。" **c)** used to tell someone that you refuse to do something or that it will be impossible for them to do something 休想，不可能：*"Lend me $10." "Forget it, no way."* "借给我10美元。""休想，没门儿。" | *If you're thinking of getting Roy to help, you can forget it!* 如果你想叫罗伊帮忙，那还是算了吧！**d)** used to tell someone to stop asking or talking about something, because it is annoying you 别说了：*Look, just forget it, will you. I'm not coming and that's that.* 瞧，你不要再说了好不好。我不会来，就是这样。
11 I'll never forget used to say that you will always remember something from the past, because it was sad, funny, enjoyable etc〔因某事可悲、滑稽、令人愉快等〕我永远也忘不了：*I'll never forget the look on his face when I said I'd marry him.* 我永远也忘不了我说要嫁给他时他脸上的神色。
12 I forget used to say that you cannot remember a particular detail about something you are talking about 我记不起来：**I forget what/where/how etc** *I forget what he said exactly, but it was very rude.* 我记不起他确切说过什么，不过他的话非常粗鲁。| **I forget the name/details etc** *You go down Weir Road then turn left into, I forget the name of it, but it's first left after the bank.* 你沿着威尔路往前走，然后往左拐到…，我记不起那条街的名字了，不过就是走过银行后向左第一个拐弯。
13 forget that used to tell someone to ignore what you have just said because it is not correct, important etc 那不对，错了：*Then mix the flour with 500 cls of milk, no, forget that, 50 cls of milk.* 然后将面粉和500厘升牛奶搅和，不，不对，是50厘升牛奶。
14 and don't you forget it used to remind someone angrily about an important fact that should make them behave differently 可(千万)别忘了：*Listen, I'm the boss around here, and don't you forget it!* 听着，这里我是老板，可别忘了！
15 aren't you forgetting...?/haven't you forgotten...? used to tell someone that they have forgotten to consider something important 你是不是忘了…?：*"Wait a minute – aren't you forgetting something? No? Well what about saying 'thank you'?"* "等等——你是不是忘了一件事？没有？嗯，是不是该说声'谢谢'呢？"

for·get·ful /fɚˋgɛtfəl; fəˈgetfəl/ *adj* often forgetting things 健忘的，爱忘事的，不记事的，没记性的—**forgetfulness** *n* [U]—**forgetfully** *adv*
forget-me-not /-ˈ· · ,·/ *n* [C] a small plant with pale blue flowers 勿忘(我)草，毋忘我草〔一种开淡蓝色小花的植物〕
for·get·ta·ble /fɚˋgɛtəbl̩; fəˈgetəbəl/ *adj often humorous* not very interesting or good【常幽默】易被忘记的；可抛诸脑后的；无聊的；糟糕的：*a completely forgettable movie* 一部糟糕透顶、不值一提的影片
for·giv·a·ble /fɚˋgɪvəbl̩; fəˈgɪvəbəl/ *adj* bad behaviour that is forgivable is not seriously bad and you can easily forgive it〔糟糕的行为〕可宽恕的，可原谅的：*I suppose a little over-excitement is forgivable under the circumstances.* 我认为在那种情况下有点过分激动是可以原谅的。
for·give /fɚˋgɪv; fəˈgɪv/ *v past tense* **forgave** /-ˋgev; -ˈgeɪv/ S3 *past participle* **forgiven** /-ˋgɪvən; -ˈgɪvən/ [I,T] **1** to decide not to blame someone or be angry with them although they have done something wrong 原谅；宽恕；饶恕：*Can you ever forgive me?* 你能原谅我吗？| **forgive sb for sth** *I can't forgive him for what he did to my sister.* 因为他对我妹妹所做的事，我无法原谅他。| **forgive sb sth** *forgive us our sins*〔请上帝〕赦免我们的罪 | **I'd never forgive myself** *If anything happened to the kids I'd never forgive myself.* 如果孩子们出了什么事，我永远也不能原谅自己。| **forgive and forget** (=forgive someone for something and behave as if they had never done it) 宽大为怀，不念旧恶 **2 forgive me** *spoken* used when you are going to say something or ask something that might seem rude or offensive【口】请原谅，对不起：*Forgive me, Mr Lewis, but I don't think that is relevant.* 对不起，刘易斯先生，不过我认为那是不相干的。| **forgive me for asking/saying etc** *Forgive me for saying so, but I think that's nonsense.* 请原谅我这么说，我认为那是胡说。**3 sb could be forgiven for thinking/wondering/believing etc sth** used to say that it is easy to understand why someone would think or believe something 某人认为…/想知道…/相信…等是可以理解的：*A foreign visitor could be forgiven for thinking football is a religion in this country.* 外国来访者认为足球在这个国家是一种宗教，那是可以理解的。
for·give·ness /fɚˋgɪvnɪs; fəˈgɪvnɪs/ *n* [U] the act of forgiving someone 原谅；宽恕：**ask for/beg for forgiveness** (=ask someone to forgive you) 请求原谅；恳求宽恕
for·giv·ing /fɚˋgɪvɪŋ; fəˈgɪvɪŋ/ *adj* willing to forgive 宽容的，宽大的：*My father was a kind and forgiving man.* 我父亲是个善良宽容的人。
for·go /fɔrˋgo; fɔːˈgəʊ/ *v* [T] to FOREGO 摒绝，放弃
for·got /fɚˋgɑt; fəˈgɒt/ the past tense of FORGET
for·got·ten[1] /fɚˋgɑtn̩; fəˈgɒtn/ the past participle of FORGET
forgotten[2] *adj* [usually before noun 一般用于名词前] that people have forgotten about or no longer pay much attention to 被遗忘的：*a rare plant growing in a forgotten corner of the churchyard* 生长在教堂墓地里一个被人遗忘的角落里的罕见植物

forks 叉子

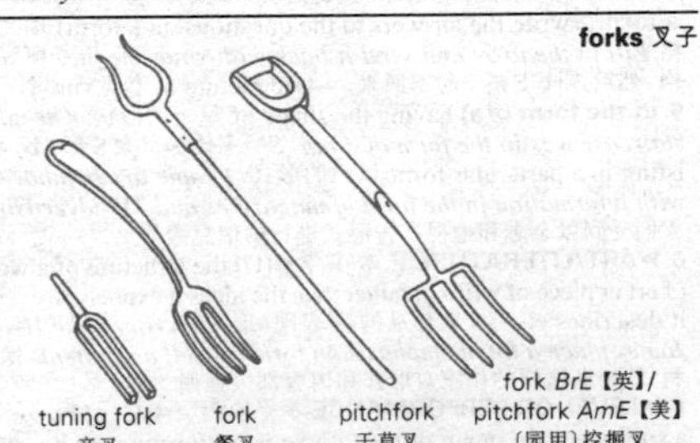

fork[1] /fɔrk; fɔːk/ *n* [C] **1** a tool used for picking up and eating food, with a handle and three or four points 餐叉，叉子：*knives*

and forks 刀叉 **2** a garden tool used for digging, with a handle and three or four points〔园用〕挖掘叉 —compare 比较 PITCHFORK[1] **3** a place where a road or river divides into two parts, or one of the parts it divides into 岔口; 岔路; 岔流: *Take the left fork then go straight on for two miles.* 走左边的岔道, 然后一直往前走两英里。**4 the forks** the parallel metal bars between which the front wheel of a bicycle or MOTORCYCLE is fixed〔自行车或摩托车的〕前叉 —see also 另见 TUNING FORK —see picture at 参见 BICYCLE 图

fork² *v* **1** [I] if a road, path, or river forks, it divides into two parts〔道路或河流〕分岔 **2 fork left/right** to travel towards the left or right part of a road when it divides into two parts 在岔口往左拐/往右拐: *Fork left at the bottom of the hill.* 在山底的岔口往左拐。**3** [T] to pick up, carry, or turn something over using a fork 叉起;〔用叉〕搬运;〔用叉〕翻耙: *He forked some bacon onto a piece of bread.* 他将一些咸肉叉到一片面包上。

fork out (sth) *phr v* [I,T] *informal* to spend a lot of money on something, not because you want to but because you have to【非正式】〔不情愿地〕付钱, 付出: [**+for/on**] *I had to fork out over £600 on my car when I had it serviced.* 我只好破费 600 多英镑请人修车。

forked /fɔrkt; fɔːkt/ *adj* having one end divided into two or more parts 叉状的; 分岔的; 有叉的: *Snakes have forked tongues.* 蛇的舌头是分叉的。

forked light·ning /ˌ. ˈ../ *n* [U] lightning that is in the form of a line of light that divides into several smaller lines near the bottom 叉状闪电 —compare 比较 SHEET LIGHTNING —see picture on page A13 参见 A13 页图

fork-lift truck /ˌ. . ˈ./ also 又作 **fork-lift** /ˈ. ./ *n* [C] a small vehicle with special equipment on the front for lifting and moving heavy things 叉车, 铲车, 叉式升降装卸车

for·lorn /fəˈlɔrn; fəˈlɔːn/ *adj* **1** seeming lonely and unhappy 孤苦伶仃的; 愁苦的; 凄凉的: *a forlorn little figure sitting outside the station* 坐在车站外的一个可怜无依的小人影 **2** a place that is forlorn seems empty and sad, and is often in bad condition〔地方〕荒凉的: *The house looked old and forlorn.* 房子看上去破旧荒凉。**3 a forlorn hope** something you hope for that is very unlikely to happen 几乎没有成功的希望: *We continued negotiating in the forlorn hope of finding a peace formula.* 我们继续谈判, 十分渺茫地希望找到一个和平方案。

form¹ /fɔrm; fɔːm/ *n*

1 ►TYPE 种类, 形式◄[C] a type of something, that exists in many different types 类型; 方式: [**+of**] *Trains are a very cost-effective form of transport.* 火车是一种成本效益很高的运输方式。| *She dislikes any form of exercise.* 她不喜欢任何一种运动。

2 ►WAY STH IS/APPEARS 形式/外形◄[C] the way in which something exists, is presented, or appears 形式, 方式: *We oppose racism in all its forms.* 我们反对所有形式的种族歧视。| **take a form/take the form of** (=happen or exist in a particular way or as a particular type) 以…的形式出现/存在 *The assignment can take any form you like – a written essay, a piece of recorded music, or whatever.* 作业可以使用你喜欢的任何方式 —— 短文写作、录制的音乐或什么的。

3 ►SHAPE 形状◄[C] a shape, especially one that you cannot see very clearly 轮廓〔尤指模糊的形状〕, 外形; 形状: [**+of**] *the shadowy forms of the divers* 潜水员模糊不清的轮廓

4 ►DOCUMENT 文件◄[C] an official document with spaces where you have to answer questions and provide information 表格: *I was interested in the job and sent off for an application form.* 我对这份工作感兴趣, 便寄信去索取申请表。| **fill in/out a form** (=write the answers to the questions on a form) 填写表格 *Fill in the form and send it back with your cheque.* 填好表格, 然后连同支票一起寄回来。—see picture at 参见 FILL 图

5 in the form of a) having the shape of 呈…的形状: *The main staircase was in the form of a big 'S'.* 主楼梯呈大 S 形。**b)** existing in a particular form 以…的形式: *People are bombarded with information in the form of magazines and TV advertising.* 人们受到以杂志和电视广告形式进行的信息轰炸。

6 ►ART/LITERATURE 艺术/文学◄[U] the structure of a work of art or piece of writing, rather than the ideas it expresses, events it describes etc〔文艺作品的〕(表现) 形式: *Writers like Henry James place a lot of emphasis on form as well as content.* 像亨利·詹姆斯这样的作家对形式和内容都很强调。

7 ►LEVEL OR PERFORMANCE 水平或表现◄[U] **a)** how well a sports person, team or race horse is performing, or has performed recently〔运动员、运动队或赛马的〕竞技状态: *Judging by her most recent form, she should easily win a medal at the Olympics.* 从她最近的竞技状态看, 她应当可以轻而易举地在奥运会上获得奖牌。**b) on present/current/past etc form** based on how well a person, team, organization etc is performing or achieving their aims 从目前的/当前的/过去的状况看: *On current form, the Democrats could lose control of the Senate in the mid-term elections.* 从当前的状况看, 民主党可能会在中期选举中失去对参议院的控制。

8 ►SCHOOL 学校◄[C] *BrE* a class in a school【英】年级: *We stopped doing Art in the fourth form.* 我们在四年级停止上美术课。—see also 另见 SIXTH FORM, FORM TEACHER

9 ►GRAMMAR 语法◄[C] a way of writing or saying a word, for example one that shows it is in the past or the plural〔词的〕形式: *'Was' is a past form of the verb 'to be'.* was 是动词 to be 的过去式。

10 ►SEAT 座位◄[C] a long low wooden seat without a back 长板凳

11 bad form *BrE old-fashioned* behaviour that is considered to be socially unacceptable【英, 过时】不合礼节要求的行为, 不礼貌的行为: *It is considered rather bad form to arrive early at a dinner party.* 过早出席晚宴被认为是很不合礼节的行为。

12 be in good/great etc form also 又作 **be on good/great etc form** *BrE* to be full of confidence and energy, so that you do something well or talk in an interesting or amusing way etc【英】〔在社交场合〕情绪良好, 兴高采烈: *Michelle was in great form at last week's conference.* 米歇尔在上星期的会议上状态大好。

form² *v*

1 ►START TO EXIST 开始存在◄[I,T often passive 常用被动态] to start to exist, or make something start to exist, especially as the result of a natural process〔尤指经过自然过程而〕形成, 产生: *The rocks were formed more than 4000 million years ago.* 这些岩石是 40 多亿年前形成的。| *Ice was beginning to form around the edges of the windows.* 窗子周围开始结冰。

2 ►BE PART OF 成为…的一部分◄[linking verb 连系动词] to be part of something, or be the thing that something is based on 成为…的一部分[基础]: *Newton's theories form the basis of modern mathematics.* 牛顿的理论构成现代数学的基础。

3 ►BE OR ACT AS STH 构成或充当某物◄[linking verb 连系动词] if something forms something, it acts as or works in a particular way 成为; 充当: *The river formed a natural boundary between the two countries.* 这条河成为两国的自然边界。

4 ►MAKE/PRODUCE 制作/生产◄[T] **a)** to make something, especially by combining two or more parts 构成: *In English the past tense is usually formed by adding 'ed'.* 在英语中, 过去式通常是通过加 ed 构成的。**b)** to make something so that it has a particular shape 形成; 塑造: *Cut off the corners of the square to form a diamond.* 切掉正方形的四角, 形成菱形。

5 ►ESTABLISH/MAKE 建立/制作◄[T] **a)** to establish an organization, committee, government etc 建立, 组成〔组织、委员会、政府等〕: *The United Nations was formed in 1945.* 联合国是 1945 年成立的。**b) form a relationship/alliance/attachment** to establish a relationship with someone 建立关系/结盟/建立感情: *She has difficulty forming long-term relationships with men.* 她难以与男子建立长期的关系。

6 form an opinion/impression/idea to use available information to develop or reach an opinion or idea 形成看法/印象/概念: *Police are trying to form an idea of what kind of person the killer is.* 警方正试图构想出杀手是属于哪一种类型的人。

7 ►DEVELOP 发展◄[T] to make someone develop into a particular type of person 培养成: *Events in early childhood often help to form our personalities in later life.* 在幼年时发生的事常对形成我们日后的个性起着作用。

8 ►LINE 队列◄[I,T] to come together and make a group or a line (把…) 编[排]成: *Film-goers began to form a line outside the cinema.* 来看电影的人开始在电影院外排成一列。

form·al¹ /ˈfɔrml; ˈfɔːməl/ *adj* **1** formal behaviour that is very polite, and is used with people you do not know well, or in official situations or at important social occasions 拘谨的; 正式的: *Our boss is very formal, she doesn't call anyone by their first name.* 我们的老板十分拘谨, 对任何人都不直呼其名。**2** formal language is used in speeches, in serious or official writing, or at official meetings or important social occasions〔语言〕规范的; 正式的; 公文的: *You shouldn't use 'Yours faithfully' in a letter to a friend – it sounds too formal.* 你在给朋友的信中不应该用 Yours faithfully —— 这听起来太正式了。**3** a formal occasion is serious and important, and people who go to it wear good clothes and behave according to strict social rules〔场合〕正式的: *I only wear this suit for formal dinners.* 我只是在参加正式宴会时才穿这套衣服。**4** a formal decision or action is made or done officially or publicly〔决定或行动〕正式的; 官方的: *On July 19th a formal*

declaration of war was made in Berlin. 7月19日柏林正式宣战。**5 formal education/training/qualification** education etc in a subject or skill gained in a school, college etc rather than practical experience of it 正规教育/训练/资格: *Many of the health workers had no formal medical training.* 许多卫生工作者没有受过正规的医学训练。—see also 另见 FORMALLY

formal² *n* [C] *AmE*【美】**1** a formal social event such as a dance, at which you have to wear formal clothes 正式的场合〈如舞会〉**2** an expensive and usually long dress that women wear at a formal occasion〔女子的〕礼服

for·mal·de·hyde /fɔrˋmældəˌhaɪd; fɔːˈmældʒhaɪd/ *n* [U] a strong-smelling gas that can be mixed with water and used for preserving things 甲醛: *frogs preserved in formaldehyde* 保存在甲醛中的青蛙

formal dress /ˌ·· ˈ·/ *n* [U] clothes worn for formal social occasions, especially a black JACKET (1), black trousers, and a BOW TIE for men, or a long dress for women〔正式社交场合穿的〕礼服

for·ma·lin /ˋfɔrməlɪn; ˈfɔːməlʒn/ *n* [U] a liquid made by mixing formaldehyde and water, used for preserving things 甲醛水(溶液), 福尔马林

for·ma·lise /ˋfɔrmḷˌaɪz; ˈfɔːməlaɪz/ *v* a British spelling of FORMALIZE formalize 的英式拼法

form·al·is·m /ˋfɔrmḷˌɪzəm; ˈfɔːməlɪzəm/ *n* [U] a style or method in art, religion, or science that pays too much attention to established rules〔艺术、宗教、科学等的〕形式主义 —**formalist** *n, adj*

for·mal·i·ty /fɔrˋmæləti; fɔːˈmælʒti/ *n* **1** [C usually plural 一般用复数] something that you must do as a formal or official part of an activity or process 正式手续: *There are a few formalities to settle before you become legal owner of the car.* 在成为合法车主之前, 要办理一些正式手续。**2 be a formality** to be something that you must do even though it has no practical importance or effects 是一种俗套; 是一种形式: *The physical exam is just a formality.* 体格检查只是例行公事而已。**3** [U] polite and formal behaviour 拘谨; 遵守礼节: *The following morning, Mr Harrison greeted her with stiff formality.* 第二天上午, 哈里森先生非常拘谨地和她打招呼。

for·mal·ize also 又作 **-ise** *BrE*【英】/ˋfɔrmḷˌaɪz; ˈfɔːməlaɪz/ *v* [T] to make a plan, decision, or idea official, especially by deciding and clearly describing all the details 使〔计划、决定或想法〕正式化; 使定形; 使形式化: *Final arrangements for the takeover have yet to be formalized.* 这次接管的最后安排还没有正式确定。—**formalization** /ˌfɔrmələˋzeʃən; ˌfɔːməlaɪˈzeɪʃən/ *n* [U]

for·mal·ly /ˋfɔrmḷɪ; ˈfɔːməli/ *adv* **1** officially 正式地: *Mr Wright has formally accepted the job.* 赖特先生已正式接受这项工作。**2** in a polite way 礼貌地: *He bowed formally to each guest in turn.* 他礼貌地依次向每个客人鞠躬。

3 **for·mat¹** /ˋfɔrmæt; ˈfɔːmæt/ *n* [C] **1** the way in which something is organized or arranged 方式, 样式: *I'd like to change the format of the meetings a little.* 我想稍微改变一下会议的方式。**2** the size, shape, design etc, in which something such as a book or magazine is produced〔书、杂志等的〕格式, 版式: *a travel show with a music video tape format* 以音乐录像带格式拍摄的旅游节目

format² *v* **formatted, formatting** [T] **1** to arrange a book, page etc according to a particular design or plan〔根据设计或计划〕为〔书刊等〕安排版式; 为…编排格式 **2** *technical* to organize the space on a computer DISK so that information can be stored on it【术语】使〔电脑磁盘〕格式化 —**formatting** *n* [U] —**formatted** *adj*

2 **for·ma·tion** /fɔrˋmeʃən; fɔːˈmeɪʃən/ *n* **1** [U] the process by which something develops into a particular thing or shape 形成: *Damp conditions are needed for the formation of mould.* 霉菌的形成需要潮湿的环境。**2** the process of starting a new organization or group 构成, 组成: *the formation of a new government* 新政府的组成 **3** the way in which a group of things are arranged to form a pattern or shape 排列方式, 样式: *The flowers had been planted in a star formation.* 这些花是排列成星形种植的。**4 in formation** if a group of planes, ships, soldiers etc are moving in formation, they are marching, flying etc in a particular order or pattern〔飞机、船只、士兵等〕排列成队, 列队, 列阵 **5** [C,U] something, especially a rock or cloud, that is formed in a particular shape, or the shape in which it is formed〔某种形状的〕形成物;〔尤指岩石或云朵的〕形成方式, 结构: *rock formations* 岩石结构

for·ma·tive /ˋfɔrmətɪv; ˈfɔːmətɪv/ *adj* [only before noun 仅用于名词前] having an important influence on the way someone's character develops 影响性格形成的, 塑造性格的: **formative influence/effect etc** *Parents have the greatest formative effect on their childrens' behaviour.* 父母对孩子的行为有最深远的影响。| **formative years/period/stages etc** (=the period when someone's character develops) 性格形成时期/阶段等

for·mer¹ /ˋfɔrmɚ; ˈfɔːmə/ *adj* [only before noun 仅用于名词前] **1** happening or existing before, but not now 以前的, 从前的: *The coal industry is now barely half its former size.* 煤炭业现在的规模几乎不到以前的一半。| *civil war in the former Yugoslavia* 前南斯拉夫的内战 | **former president/soldier/wife etc** (=someone who was a president etc, but who is not now) 前任总统/昔日的士兵/前妻等 *a former principal of the school* 学校的前任校长 **2 your former self** what you were like before you were changed by age, illness, trouble etc 以前的你〔指与现在经历衰老、疾病、苦难等后对比〕: *She seems more like her former self.* 她似乎回到了以前的她的样子。| **be a shadow of your former self** (=be much less confident, healthy, energetic etc than you used to be) 不像以前那样自信, 远不如以前自信[健康、有活力] 2 1

former² *n* **1 the former** *formal* the first of two people or things that you have just mentioned【正式】前者: *Of the two possibilities, the former seems more likely.* 在这两种可能性中, 前者似乎更有可能。—opposite 反义词 LATTER¹ **2 first/fourth/sixth former** *BrE* used in some schools to show which class a student is in, according to how many years they have been in school【英】一年级/四年级/六年级的学生

for·mer·ly /ˋfɔrmɚlɪ; ˈfɔːməli/ *adv* in earlier times 以前, 从前: *Peru was formerly ruled by the Spanish.* 秘鲁从前受西班牙统治。—compare 比较 LATTERLY

for·mi·ca /fɔrˋmaɪkə; fɔːˈmaɪkə/ *n* [U] *trademark* strong plastic made in thin sheets, used especially for covering the surfaces of tables【商标】(福米加)塑料贴面〔尤用于桌子表面〕: *formica tabletops* (福米加)桌子塑料贴面

for·mic ac·id /ˌfɔrmɪk ˋæsɪd; ˌfɔːmɪk ˈæsʒd/ *n* [U] an acid used especially for colouring cloth and in treating leather〔尤指用于染布或处理皮革的〕甲酸, 蚁酸

for·mi·da·ble /ˋfɔrmɪdəbḷ; ˈfɔːmʒdəbəl/ *adj* **1** a formidable person etc is one that you feel respect for because they are very powerful, or impressive 令人敬畏的; 令人惊叹的; 巨大的; 杰出的: *With her management skills and his marketing expertise, they make a formidable combination.* 她的管理能力和他的销售专长使他们构成一个强大有力的组合。| *The Pentium machines have formidable processing power.* 奔腾机具有惊人的处理能力。**2** difficult to deal with and needing a lot of effort or skill 难对付的: *The rally is a formidable test of both car and driver.* 这次汽车拉力赛对车子和驾驶员来说都是一次艰巨的考验。| **formidable problem/task** *the formidable task of creating a new filing system* 建立新的文件归档系统的艰难任务 —**formidably** *adv*

form·less /ˋfɔrmlɪs; ˈfɔːmləs/ *adj* **1** without a definite shape 无形状的, 无定形的: *Figures emerged out of the mist, dull and formless at first.* 人影从薄雾中出现, 开始时模糊不清而且无明确形状。**2** ideas or feelings that are formless are not clear or definite〔思想或感情〕不清楚的, 不明确的; 杂乱的: *A formless melancholy overcame her.* 一种说不清的忧郁压倒了她。—**formlessly** *adv* —**formlessness** *n* [U]

form let·ter /ˈ· ,· ·/ *n* [C] a standard letter that is sent to a number of people〔寄给许多人的〕通函, 印刷函件, 打印信件

form teach·er /ˈ· ,· ·/ *n* [C] *BrE* the teacher who is responsible for all the students in the same class at a school【英】年级主任, 班主任

for·mu·la /ˋfɔrmjələ; ˈfɔːmjʒlə/ *n plural* **formulas** *or* **formulae** /-li; -liː/ **1** [singular] a method or set of principles that you use to solve a problem or to make sure that something is successful 准则; 方案: *We're still searching for a peace formula.* 我们仍在寻求和平方案。| **[+for]** *The two sides worked out an acceptable formula for settling the strike.* 双方制定了一套解决这场罢工的可接受的方案。| **magic formula** (=a method that is certain to be successful) 成功的魔法, 秘方妙法 *There's no magic formula for a happy marriage.* 幸福的婚姻没有什么妙法。**2** [C] a series of numbers or letters that represent a mathematical or scientific rule 公式; 方程式; 分子式: *the formula for calculating distance* 计算距离的公式 **3** [C] a list of the substances used to make a medicine, FUEL¹ (1), drink etc, showing the amounts of each substance that should be used〔药品、燃料、饮料等的〕配方: *Coca-Cola's formula* 可口可乐的配方 **4 Formula One/Two/Three etc** a type of car racing, in which the different types are based on the size of the cars' engines〔赛车的〕一级/二级/三级方程式等: *a Formula One car* 一级方程式赛车 **5** [C,U] *AmE* 3

a type of liquid food for babies that is similar to milk【美】〔喂养婴儿的〕配方奶 **6** [C] a fixed and familiar series of words that seems meaningless or insincere 俗套话; 惯用语句: *a speech full of the usual formulas and cliches* 充满常用的套话和陈词滥调的演说

for·mu·la·ic /ˌfɔrmjəˋleɪk; ˌfɔːmjʊˋleɪ-ɪk◂/ *adj formal* containing or made from ideas or expressions that have been used many times before and are therefore not very imaginative【正式】公式化的; 充满俗套话的; 没有独创的: *formulaic verse* 公式化的诗节

Formula One /ˌ‥ˈ‥ ◂/ the highest level of international car racing. Formula One cars are special, very fast cars that compete for the world CHAMPIONSHIP by taking part in a series of important races, called 'Grand Prix', in several countries. 一级方程式赛车〔世界最高水平的车赛。参赛车辆均为特制的高速赛车, 通过参加在几个国家进行的一系列重要比赛, 即国际汽车大奖赛(又称"大奖赛"), 争夺世界冠军〕

for·mu·late /ˈfɔrmjəˌlet; ˈfɔːmjʊleɪt/ *v* [T] **1 formulate a plan/policy/program etc** to develop a plan or proposal, and decide all the details of how it will be done 制定计划/政策/方案等: *The government is formulating a new education policy.* 政府正制定新的教育政策。**2** to choose particular words to express your thoughts or feelings 确切地表达[阐述]: *He paused, trying to formulate an answer that would satisfy them.* 他停了一下, 力求作出一个令他们满意的回答。—**formulation** /ˌfɔrmjəˋleʃən; ˌfɔːmjʊˋleɪʃən/ *n* [C,U]

for·ni·cate /ˈfɔrnəˌket; ˈfɔːnɪkeɪt/ *v* [I] a word meaning to have sex with someone who you are not married to, used to show strong disapproval 通奸, 私通 —**fornication** /ˌfɔrnɪˋkeʃən; ˌfɔːnɪˋkeɪʃən/ *n* [U]

for·sake /fəˋsek; fəˈseɪk/ *v past tense* **forsook** /-ˋsʊk; -ˈsʊk/ *past participle* **forsaken** /-ˋsekən; -ˈseɪkən/ [T] *literary*【文】**1** to leave someone, especially when you should stay because they need you 遗弃, 抛弃, 弃之不顾: *God will never forsake you.* 上帝永远不会遗弃你的。**2** to stop doing or leave something that you have or enjoy 放弃, 摒弃; 戒掉: *We had to forsake the comfort of our hotel room and spend the night waiting at the airport.* 我们只好放弃旅馆客房的舒适享受, 在机场等一晚。—see also 另见 GODFORSAKEN

for·sooth /fəˋsuθ; fəˈsuːθ/ *adv old use* certainly【旧】确实地, 无疑地

For·ster /ˈfɔrstə; ˈfɔːstə/, **E.M.** (1879-1970) an important British writer, famous for his NOVELs *Howard's End, A Passage to India*, and *A Room with a View*. 福斯特〔(1879-1970), 一位有影响力的英国作家。他以《霍华德庄园》、《印度之行》和《看得见风景的房间》等小说而著名〕

for·swear /fɔrˋswɛr; fɔːˈsweə/ *v past tense* **forswore** /-ˋswɔr; -ˈswɔː/ *past participle* **forsworn** /-ˋswɔrn; -ˈswɔːn/ [T] *literary* to promise that you will not do or possess something【文】断然放弃; 发誓放弃: *a monk forswearing all possessions* 发誓放弃所有私产的僧侣

for·sy·thi·a /fəˋsɪθɪə; fɔːˈsaɪθiə/ *n* [C,U] a bush that is covered with bright yellow flowers in the spring 连翘, 金钟花〔一种在春天开鲜黄色花的灌木〕

fort /fɔrt; fɔːt/ *n* [C] a strong building or group of buildings used by soldiers or an army for defending an important place 堡垒, 城堡; 要塞 —see also 另见 **hold the fort** (HOLD[1] (19))

for·te[1] /fɔrt; ˈfɔːteɪ/ *n* **1 be your/their forte** to be something that you do well or are skilled at 是你/他们的专长: *Cooking has never been her forte.* 烹饪从来就不是她的强项。**2** [C] a note or line of music played or sung loudly 强音; 用强音演奏[唱出]的一段乐曲

for·te[2] /ˈfɔrte; ˈfɔːteɪ/ *adj, adv* music played or sung loudly【音乐】用强音的[地]; 响的[地]

For·te·an Times, the /ˌfɔrtɪən ˈtaɪmz; ˌfɔːtiən ˈtaɪmz/ a British magazine that gives news reports about strange and unusual events such as GHOSTs or space vehicles from other PLANETs《福特安时代》〔英国一杂志, 报导奇闻逸事, 如鬼怪或天外飞船〕

forth /fɔrθ; fɔːθ/ *adv literary*【文】**1 and so forth** used to represent other things of the type you have already mentioned without actually naming them 等等: *She started telling me about her bad back, her migraines, and so forth.* 她开始告诉我她背痛、偏头痛等等。**2 from that day/time/moment forth** *literary* beginning on that day or at that time【文】从那天起/从那时起/从那个时刻起: *From that moment forth they became close friends.* 从那时起, 他们就成了亲密的朋友。**3** [only after verb 仅用于动词后] *literary* going out from a place or point, and moving forwards or outwards【文】向外, 往外: *factory chimneys that belched forth thick smoke* 喷吐着浓烟的工厂烟囱 **4** *literary* towards a place that is in front of you; forwards【文】向前: *She stretched forth her hand.* 她把手向前伸出。—see also 另见 **back and forth** (BACK[1] (11)), **hold forth** (HOLD[1]), **put forth** (PUT)

Forth, the a river in southern central Scotland which flows into the Firth of Forth and the North Sea 福斯河〔苏格兰中南部一河流, 注入福斯湾和北海〕

Forth Bridge /ˌ· ˈ·/ **1 the Forth Bridge** a famous metal railway bridge built in 1889 over the Firth of Forth. People sometimes say that a job is 'like painting the Forth Bridge' when they mean that it seems to never end, because the metal bridge takes a long time to paint, and when the job is finished it has to start again. 福斯河铁路大桥〔福斯河上的一座著名铁路桥梁, 建于1889年。人们有时把一项工作说成 like painting the Firth of Forth, 意指工作永无休止, 因为油漆铁桥要花很长时间, 而且刚漆完又得重新开始〕**2** a road bridge built in 1964 over the Firth of Forth. It is one of the longest SUSPENSION bridges in the world. 福斯河公路大桥〔福斯河上的一座公路桥梁, 建于1964年, 是世界上最长的悬索桥之一〕

forth·com·ing /ˌfɔrθˋkʌmɪŋ; ˌfɔːθˈkʌmɪŋ◂/ *adj* **1** a forthcoming event, meeting etc is one that has been planned to happen soon 即将到来的; 即将出现的: *a potential vote-winner in the forthcoming election* 在即将举行的选举中很可能获胜的人 **2 be forthcoming** to be willing to give information about something 乐于提供信息的: **[+about]** *Jarvis was never very forthcoming about his love life.* 贾维斯一直就很不愿意透露他的爱情生活。**3** [not before noun 不用于名词前] given or offered when needed 可得到的: *When no reply was forthcoming, she wrote again.* 她没有得到答复时, 就再写了一封信去问。

forth·right /ˈfɔrθˌraɪt; ˈfɔːθraɪt/ *adj* saying honestly what you think, in a way that sometimes seems rude 直率的, 直截了当的: *She answered in her usual forthright manner.* 她和往常一样, 直截了当地回答。

forth·with /fɔrθˋwɪθ; fɔːθˈwɪð/ *adv formal* immediately【正式】立即, 马上: *These instructions must be carried out forthwith.* 这些指示必须立即执行。

for·ti·eth /ˈfɔrtɪɪθ; ˈfɔːtiəθ/ *n* [C] one of forty equal parts of something 第四十(个); 四十分之一

for·ti·fi·ca·tion /ˌfɔrtəfəˋkeʃən; ˌfɔːtɪfɪˈkeɪʃən/ *n* [U] the process of making something stronger 强化, 加强

for·ti·fi·ca·tions /ˌfɔrtəfəˋkeʃənz; ˌfɔːtɪfɪˈkeɪʃənz/ *n* [plural] towers, walls etc built around a place in order to protect it or defend it 防御工事〈如堡垒、城垣等〉: *The army destroyed most of the town's fortifications.* 军队摧毁了该城的大部分防御工事。

fortified wine /ˌ‥ˈ·/ *n* [C,U] wine such as SHERRY or PORT (3) that has strong alcohol added 加度葡萄酒

for·ti·fy /ˈfɔrtəˌfaɪ; ˈfɔːtɪfaɪ/ *v* [T] **1** to build towers, walls etc around an area or city in order to defend it 筑防御工事于; 筑堡于: *a fortified city* 设防的城市 **2** to encourage an attitude or feeling and make it stronger 激励, 鼓舞; 加强: *Recent successes had fortified the team spirit.* 最近获得的成功鼓舞了这个队的士气。**3** [often passive 常用被动态] to make someone feel physically or mentally stronger 增强体质; 振奋精神: **fortify yourself** *We had some coffee to fortify ourselves for the journey.* 我们为了旅行, 喝了些咖啡来提神。**4** [usually passive 一般用被动态] to make food or drinks more healthy by adding VITAMINs to them〔加维生素〕强化〔食品或饮料〕; 提高〔食品或饮料的〕营养价值: *fortified milk products* 强化奶产品

for·tis·si·mo /fɔrˋtɪsəˌmo; fɔːˈtɪsɪməʊ/ *adj, adv music* played or sung very loudly【音乐】非常响的[地]; 极强的[地]; 用极强音的[地] —**fortissimo** *adj* —compare 比较 FORTE[2]

for·ti·tude /ˈfɔrtəˌtud; ˈfɔːtɪtjuːd/ *n* [U] courage shown when you are in great pain or experiencing a lot of trouble 毅力, 坚忍, 刚毅, 毅勇: *She bore her illness with great fortitude.* 她以坚韧不拔的精神忍受着病痛。

Fort Knox /ˌ· ˈ·/ a military building in the US state of Kentucky which holds the government's store of gold. People often use the name 'Fort Knox' when talking about a place that is extremely well guarded or impossible to enter without permission. 诺克斯堡〔美国肯塔基州一军用建筑, 存放政府的黄金储备。人们常借用该名称形容戒备森严或未经许可无法进入的地方〕: *His house is like Fort Knox.* 他的房子就像诺克斯堡一样难以进入。

fort·night /ˈfɔrtnaɪt; ˈfɔːtnaɪt/ *n* [C usually singular 一般用单数] *BrE* two weeks【英】两星期, 十四天: *I'm going away for a fortnight's holiday.* 我要到外地度假两周。

fort·night·ly /ˈfɔrtˌnaɪtlɪ; ˈfɔːtnaɪtli/ *adj, adv BrE* happening every fortnight or once a fortnight【英】两星期一次的[地], 每两周的[地]: *We used to dread my uncle's fortnightly visits.* 我们过去都很怕叔叔每两周一次的到访。

for·tress /ˈfɔrtrɪs; ˈfɔːtr $_{\text{I}}^{\text{ə}}$s/ *n* [C] a large, strong building used for defending an important place 堡垒；要塞

for·tu·i·tous /fɔrˈtuətəs; fɔːˈtjuː $_{\text{I}}^{\text{ə}}$təs/ *adj formal* happening by chance, especially in a way that has a good result【正式】偶然的，偶然发生的〔尤指带来好结果〕: *a fortuitous meeting* 一次偶然的幸遇 —**fortuitously** *adv*

for·tu·nate /ˈfɔrtʃənɪt; ˈfɔːtʃənət/ *adj* **1** someone who is fortunate has something good happen to them, or is in a good situation; lucky 幸运的: *Think of others less fortunate than yourselves.* 想想其他不如你们那么幸运的人。| **fortunate to do sth** *He was fortunate enough to escape unharmed.* 他真是幸运，逃了出来，没有受伤。| **fortunate that** *You're fortunate that you've still got a job.* 你真幸运，总还有一份工作。| **fortunate in having** *I was fortunate in having such supportive parents.* 我有这样支持我的父母，真幸运。**2** a fortunate event is one in which something good happens by chance, especially when this saves you from trouble or danger 巧合的，偶然发生的；侥幸的: *By a fortunate coincidence, a passer-by heard her cries for help.* 真巧，一位过路的人听到她求助的呼叫。

Fortune 500, the /ˌfɔrtʃən faɪv ˈhʌndrɪd; ˌfɔːtʃən faɪv ˈhʌndr $_{\text{I}}^{\text{ə}}$d/ the 500 largest companies in the US, which are named in a yearly list in *Fortune* magazine. (美国)《财富》500强〔《财富》杂志每年评选出的美国500家最大的公司〕: *She's a vice-president of a Fortune 500 company.* 她是一家《财富》500强企业的副总裁。

for·tu·nate·ly /ˈfɔrtʃənɪtlɪ; ˈfɔːtʃənətli/ *adv* [sentence adverb 句子副词] happening because of good luck 幸运地；幸亏: *Fortunately the fire was discovered soon after it started.* 幸亏火刚着了不久就被发现了。

for·tune /ˈfɔrtʃən; ˈfɔːtʃən/ *n*

1 ►MONEY 钱◄ [C] a very large amount of money 大笔的钱，巨款: *He inherited his fortune from his father.* 他从父亲那里继承了一大笔财产。| **cost/spend/be worth a fortune** *They must have spent a fortune on that house.* 他们买那栋房子肯定花了一大笔钱。| **a small fortune** (=a lot of money) 一大笔钱 *She won a small fortune on the horses.* 她在赛马赌博中赢了一大笔钱。| **make a/your fortune** (=make a lot of money in business) 发财 *The guy who invented Post-It notes must have made a fortune by now.* 发明报事贴便条的那个人现在肯定已发财了。

2 ►CHANCE 机遇◄ [U] chance, and the good or bad influence that it has on your life 运气；机遇: *I felt it was useless to struggle against fortune.* 我觉得与运气抗争是无用的。| **ill-fortune** (=bad luck) 厄运，坏运气 *We were stoical, and did not complain of ill-fortune.* 我们处变不惊，没有怪运气不好。| **have the good fortune to do sth** *I had the good fortune to be invited to stay in Rome.* 我运气好，获邀请去罗马小住。

3 ►WHAT HAPPENS TO YOU 发生在你身上的事◄ [C usually plural 一般用复数] the good or bad things that happen in life 时运；命运: *This defeat marked a change in the team's fortunes.* 这次失败使该队的运气发生转变。| **the fortunes of war** (=things that can happen to people during a war) 战争中的命运

4 tell sb's fortune to tell someone what will happen to them in the future by looking at their hands, using cards etc 给某人算命: *She paid £5 to have her fortune told.* 她花了五英镑找人算命。

5 fortune smiles on sth/sb *literary* used to say that someone or something is lucky【文】某物/某人的运气很好 —see also 另见 SOLDIER OF FORTUNE, **fame and fortune** (FAME), **give hostages to fortune** (HOSTAGE (2)), **seek your fortune** (SEEK (4))

fortune cook·ie /ˈ‥ ˌ‥/ *n* [C] a Chinese BISCUIT that contains a piece of paper that says what will happen to you in the future 签饼，幸运曲奇饼〔据称源于中国的一种小饼，内有纸条，写着你的运气〕

fortune hunt·er /ˈ‥ ˌ‥/ *n* [C] someone who wants to marry another person only to get their money 企图通过结婚发财的人

fortune-tell·er /ˈ‥ ˌ‥/ *n* [C] someone who uses magical methods to tell people what will happen to them in the future 给人算命的人，算命者 —**fortune telling** *n* [U]

CULTURAL NOTE 文化注释

The STEREOTYPE of a fortune-teller is of a woman wearing a colourful SCARF on her head and large EARRINGS. She looks into a CRYSTAL BALL to see what is going to happen in the future and she asks people for money by asking them to 'cross my palm with silver'. 算命者的典型形象是一个裹着鲜艳头巾、戴大耳环的女人。她凝视水晶球来预知未来，她让人"把银子放在我手心上"，借此要钱。

Fort Worth /ˌ ˈ/ a city in the northeast of the US state of Texas, near Dallas. It is a centre for farming, the oil industry, and the aircraft-building industry. 沃斯堡〔美国得克萨斯州东北部一城市，位于达拉斯附近，是一个农业、石油工业和飞机制造业中心〕

for·ty /ˈfɔrtɪ; ˈfɔːti/ *number* 40 四十

forty-five /ˌ‥ ˈ◂/ *n* [C] *informal*【非正式】**1** also 又作 **45** a small record with one song on each side〔每面一首歌的〕每分钟45转的密纹唱片 **2** also 又作 **.45, Colt 45** *trademark* a small gun【商标】.45口径的手枪

Forty-five, the another name for the Jacobite Rising of 1745, when the Scottish prince, Bonnie Prince Charlie, led an attempt to bring back the Stuart family of Britain. It failed when his army was defeated at the Battle of Culloden. 1745年叛乱〔"1745年詹姆斯党人叛乱"的别称。当时，苏格兰王子"英俊查理"企图复辟斯图亚特王朝在英国的统治，但以卡洛登一役战败而告终〕

Forty-Sec·ond Street, 42nd Street /ˌ‥ˈ‥ ˌ ˈ/ **1** a street in New York City, where there are many theatres 四十二大街〔纽约市一街道，那里集中着许多剧院〕**2** a successful MUSICAL (=a show that uses singing and dancing to tell a story) that has been performed on stage and made into a film《四十二大街》〔一部优秀的音乐剧，已被搬上银幕〕

Forty Thieves, the /ˌ‥ ˈ‥/ —see 见 ALI BABA

forty winks /ˌ‥ ˈ/ *n* [U] *informal* a very short sleep【非正式】小睡，打盹儿: *Mr. Carey lay down on the sofa for forty winks.* 凯里先生躺在沙发上打个盹儿。

for·um /ˈfɔrəm; ˈfɔːrəm/ *n* [C] **1** an organization, meeting, TV programme etc where people have a chance to publicly discuss an important subject〔人们能公开讨论重要话题的〕论坛；讨论会；电视专题讨论节目: **[+for]** *The committee provided a useful forum for exposing the extent of discrimination.* 委员会提供了一个揭露歧视程度的有用的论坛。| **[+on]** *an international forum on the environment* 国际环境论坛 **2** a large outdoor public place in ancient Rome used for business and discussion〔古罗马城市中用于商业和讨论的〕广场，市场

for·ward¹ /ˈfɔrwɚd; ˈfɔːwəd/ *adv* **1** also 又作 **forwards** /-wɚdz; -wədz/ towards a place or position that is in front of you 向前: *He leaned forward slightly to try and hear what they were saying.* 他稍微向前倾身，想听听他们在说什么。| *The crowd surged forwards.* 人群向前涌去。**2** towards greater progress, improvement, or development 大有进展[改善，发展]地: *The building of the new sports stadium is going forward.* 新体育场的工程正在进行中。| *trying to find a way forward in the peace talks* 企图找出一种推动和平谈判的办法 **3** towards the future in a way that is hopeful 向将来: *This is just the moment at which companies should be looking forward.* 这正是各家公司应该展望未来的时候。**4 from that day/time/moment etc forward** beginning on that day or at that time 从那天/那时/那刻等起: *They never met again from that day forward.* 他们从那天以后就再也没见面了。**5** in or towards the front part of a ship 在船头；朝船头 —compare 比较 AFT, BACKWARDS —see also 另见 FAST FORWARD, **look forward to** (LOOK¹), **backwards and forwards** (BACKWARDS (4))

forward² *adj* **1** [only before noun 仅用于名词前] directed towards a place or position that is in front of you 向前的: *Army roadblocks prevented any further forward movement.* 军队设下的路障阻止人们继续前进。**2 forward planning/thinking** the act of making plans so that you will be prepared for what will happen in the future 预先计划/提前考虑: *Forward planning is essential if you want the venture to succeed.* 如果想让这个风险项目获得成功，预先计划是必不可少的。**3 no further forward** not having made much progress, especially compared to what was expected 无进展: *We've been trying to find a solution for weeks but we're no further forward.* 我们几周来一直在设法寻觅解决办法，但没有什么进展。**4** [only before noun 仅用于名词前] situated at or near the front of a ship, vehicle, building etc 在前部的；位于前面的: *We sat in one of the forward sections of the train.* 我们坐在火车前部的一节车厢里。**5** *formal* too confident and friendly in dealing with people you do not know very well【正式】〔与不大熟悉的人交往时〕鲁莽的；冒失的；过分主动的: *She was careful in what she said, having no wish to sound forward.* 她说话十分小心，不想让人听上去觉得她过分主动。—compare 比较 BACKWARD

forward³ *v* **1** [T] to send letters, goods etc to someone, especially when they have moved to a new address 寄发；转寄；转交；转运: *We will forward the goods on receipt of your cheque.* 我们一收到贵方的支票便发货。| **forward sth to sb** *Can you forward my mail to me, please?* 请把我的邮件转寄给我，好吗？**2** [T] *formal* to help something to develop so that it becomes

successful【正式】助长, 促进: *I see this new responsibility as a good chance to forward my career.* 我把这项新职责看作是促进自己事业发展的好机会。

forward[4] *n* [C] an attacking player on a team in sports such as football, BASKETBALL etc〔足球、篮球等运动的〕前锋

forwarding ad·dress /ˈ‥‥, ˌ/ *n* [C] an address that you leave for someone when you move to a new place so that they can send your mail to you〔邮件〕转寄地址

forward-look·ing /ˈ‥ ˌ‥/ *adj* planning for and thinking about the future in a positive way, especially by being willing to use modern methods or ideas〔尤指乐意用现代方法或思想〕向前看的; 有远见的: *forward-looking companies able to spot the trends* 能认准潮流的有远见的公司

forward mar·ket /ˈ‥ ˌ‥/ *n* [C] *technical* a market on the STOCK EXCHANGE that buys and sells products at an agreed price on a fixed date in the future; FUTURES MARKET【术语】期货市场

for·ward·ness /ˈfɔrwɚdnɪs; ˈfɔːwədnǝs/ *n* [U] behaviour that is too confident or friendly 鲁莽; 冒失; 过分主动

forward roll /ˌ‥ ˈ/ *n* [C] a movement in GYMNASTICS in which you roll over forwards onto your back so that your feet go over your head〔体操的〕前滚翻

for·wards /ˈfɔrwɚdz; ˈfɔːwədz/ *adv* FORWARD 向前

Fosse Way, the /ˌfɑs ˈwe; ˌfɒs ˈweɪ/ a road between Lincoln in eastern England and Exeter in southwest England, built in ancient times by the Romans 福斯路〔英格兰东部的林肯至英格兰西南埃克塞特的一条道路, 由古罗马人修建〕

Fos·sey /ˈfɑsɪ; ˈfɒsi/, **Dian** /ˈdaɪæn; ˈdaɪæn/ (1932-85) a US scientist who became famous for her study of mountain GORILLAS. She lived among the gorillas in Zaire (now called the Democratic Republic of Congo) during the 1960s and wrote a book called *Gorillas in the Mist* (1983). She was murdered in her forest camp in Rwanda in 1985. 佛赛〔(1932-1985), 美国科学家, 以研究大猩猩著称。20世纪60年代, 她在扎伊尔(今刚果民主共和国)与大猩猩一起生活, 并撰写了一部名为《迷雾中的大猩猩》(1983)的著作。1985年, 她在卢旺达的森林营地遇害〕

fos·sil /ˈfɑsl; ˈfɒsəl/ *n* [C] **1** an animal or plant that died many thousands of years ago and that has been preserved in rock 化石: *fossils of early reptiles* 早期爬行动物的化石 —see also 另见 LIVING FOSSIL **2** *informal* an insulting word for an old person【非正式】老顽固〔含侮辱性〕

fossil fu·el /ˈ‥ ˌ‥/ *n* [C,U] a FUEL[1] (1) such as coal or oil that is produced by the very gradual decaying of animals or plants over millions of years 矿物燃料〈如煤、石油等〉: *Environmentalists would like to see fossil fuels replaced by renewable energy sources.* 环境保护主义者很希望看到可再生能源取代矿物燃料。

fos·sil·ize also 又作 **-ise** *BrE*【英】/ˈfɑsḷˌaɪz; ˈfɒsǝlaɪz/ *v* **1 be fossilized** people, ideas, systems etc that are fossilized are very old-fashioned and never change or develop〔人、思想、体制等〕石化, 僵化, 变得陈旧: *The valley's government was a fossilized specimen of feudal rule.* 这个山谷里的政府是封建统治的化石标本。**2** [I,T] to become or form a FOSSIL by being preserved in rock 变成化石, 使成化石 —**fossilization** /ˌfɑsḷəˈzeʃən; ˌfɒsǝlaɪˈzeɪʃən/ *n* [U]

foster- /fɔstɚ; fɒstə/ *prefix* giving or receiving parental care although not of the same family 收养的: *a foster-mother* 养母 | *a foster-son* 养子 | *a foster-home* 寄养家庭 | *Danny is my foster-brother.* (=we have different parents, but he is being brought up with me in my family) 丹尼是我的义兄弟。

fos·ter[1] /ˈfɔstɚ; ˈfɒstə/ *v* **1** [I,T] to take someone else's child into your family for a period of time but without becoming their legal parent〔在一定的时间内〕抚育, 收养〔别人的孩子〕: *They fostered a little Romanian boy for a few months.* 他们收养一个罗马尼亚小男孩已有几个月。—compare 比较 ADOPT (1) **2** [T] to help a skill, feeling, idea etc develop over a period of time 促进; 培养; 助长: *These sessions are designed to foster better working relationships.* 这些会议旨在培养更好的工作关系。

CULTURAL NOTE 文化注释

Children are fostered when their parents cannot take care of them, usually because the parents are ill, because the children behave very badly, or because the parents do not take care of their children properly or hurt them. Foster parents are given some money to help them take care of a child, but they have no legal rights to keep the child, who may at some time return to his or her parents. 儿童在父母不能照料时会交给别人领养, 通常原因是父母生病、儿童行为乖戾、父母照料不当或伤害孩子。养父母会得到一些钱以养育孩子, 但他们无权拥有孩子, 孩子将来某个时候可能会回到亲生父母身边。

foster[2] *adj* **1 foster mother/father/parents** the people who foster a child 养母/养父/养父母: *It is sometimes difficult to find suitable foster parents.* 有时很难找到合适的养父母。**2 foster child** a child who is fostered 收养的孩子 **3 foster home** a private home where a child is fostered 寄养家庭

Foster, Lord Norman (1935-) a British ARCHITECT (=someone who designs buildings) who has won many prizes for his designs, and works mainly in a very modern HIGH-TECH style 福斯特〔(1935-), 英国建筑设计师。他的设计多次获奖, 作品主要采用非常现代的高科技风格〕

Foster, Ste·phen /ˈstivən; ˈstiːvən/ (1826-64) a US songwriter who wrote many popular songs, such as *Oh Susanna*, *Camptown Races*, and *Old Folks at Home*, which were often about life in the South of the US 福斯特〔(1826-1864), 美国歌曲作家, 以《噢, 苏珊娜》、《坎普敦赛马会》、《故乡的亲人》等描写美国南方生活的流行歌曲闻名〕

Fou·cault /fuˋko; ˈfuːkəʊ/, **Jean Ber·nard Léon** /ʒɑn bɛrˋnɑr leˋɑn; ʒɒn ˈbeənɑː ˈleɪɒn/ (1819-68) a French scientist who studied the speed of light. He invented **Foucault's Pendulum**, an object that swings on a wire and shows how the Earth spins around. He also invented the GYROSCOPE. 傅科〔(1819-1868), 法国科学家。他致力于光速研究, 发明了演示地球绕轴旋转的傅科摆。他还发明了陀螺仪〕

fought /fɔt; fɔːt/ the past tense and past participle of FIGHT[1]

foul[1] /faul; faʊl/ *adj*

1 ►SMELL/TASTE 气味/味道◄ a foul smell or taste is very unpleasant 难闻的, 恶臭的; 难吃的: *I gulped down some water to take the foul taste out of my mouth.* 我大口地喝水来清除嘴里的臭味。| **foul-tasting/foul-smelling** *The bags of garbage had been piled up in a foul-smelling heap.* 这一袋袋垃圾已堆成臭不可闻的一堆。

2 in a foul mood/temper *especially BrE* in a very bad mood and likely to get angry【尤英】情绪不好/发脾气: *He's in a foul mood today, isn't he?* 他今天情绪不好, 是不是?

3 ►UNPLEASANT 令人难受的◄ *especially BrE* very unpleasant【尤英】令人不快的; 糟透的: *I've had an absolutely foul day.* 我今天过得很不愉快。

4 ►AIR/WATER 空气/水◄ very dirty 肮脏的, 污浊的: *The water in the harbour was foul with oil.* 海港的水上面浮着油, 很脏。

5 foul language rude and offensive words 粗话, 骂人话, 脏话: *I've never heard such foul language in all my life!* 我这辈子还从来没听到过这样的粗言秽语!

6 ►WEATHER 天气◄ *especially BrE* if the weather is foul, it is stormy and windy, with a lot of rain or snow【尤英】恶劣的; 有风雨的; 有风雪的

7 ►EVIL 邪恶的◄ *especially literary* evil or cruel【尤文】罪恶的, 邪恶的; 残酷的: *foul deeds* 残酷的行为 —see also 另见 **by fair means or foul** (FAIR[1] (13)), **fall foul of** (FALL[1] (28)) —**foully** *adv* —**foulness** *n* [U]

foul[2] *v* **1** [I,T] **a)** if a player fouls in a game of sport, or fouls another player, they do something that is not allowed by the rules (对…)犯规, 违例: *An Everton player had been fouled in the penalty area.* 有人在禁区对一位埃弗顿队的球员犯规。**b)** to hit a ball outside the limit of the playing area in BASEBALL〔棒球中〕击〔球〕出界, 打出坏球: *On average, most batters foul at least one ball in each at bat.* 大多数击球员上场击球时, 平均每个人至少击球出界一次。**2** *formal* to make something very dirty, especially with waste【正式】弄脏, 玷污; 污染: *A thick column of black smoke rose from the wreck, fouling the air.* 一股黑色的浓烟从失事的船只升起, 污染了空气。**3** also 又作 **foul up** [I,T] if a rope, chain, or part of a machine fouls or if something fouls it, it twists or cannot move properly〔绳、链或机器部件〕缠住, 缠结: *Check that nothing can foul the moving parts.* 检查一下, 不要让任何东西缠住移动部件。

foul up *phr v informal*【非正式】**1** [T **foul** sth ↔ **up**] to spoil something 破坏; 搞糟; 弄乱: *The weather really fouled up our vacation plans.* 恶劣的天气破坏了我们的度假计划。**2** [I,T **foul** sth ↔ **up**] to do something wrong or spoil something by making mistakes〔因错误而〕搞乱, 破坏: *Glen completely fouled up the seating arrangements.* 格伦把座位安排完全搞乱了。

foul[3] *n* [C] an action in a sport that is against the rules〔体育比赛中的〕犯规(动作): *That was a foul – he touched the ball with his hand!* 那是犯规 —— 他用手触了球!

foul line /ˈ· ˌ/ *n* [C] a line marked on a sports field outside of which a ball cannot be legally played〔球场上的〕边线, 限制线

foul-mouthed /ˌ· ˈ◄/ *adj* swearing too much 满口脏话的; 恶语伤人的: *a foul-mouthed little boy* 一个口出恶言的小男孩 —**foul mouth** /ˈ· ˌ/ *n* [C]

foul play /,· ˈ·/ *n* [U] **1** if the police think someone's death was caused by foul play, they think that person was murdered 谋杀: *The police said they had no reason to suspect foul play.* 警方说他们没有理由怀疑是谋杀。**2** actions that are dishonest or unfair 奸诈的行为, 犯罪行径: *He will use any amount of foul play to get what he wants.* 他会使用各种奸诈的手段来得到自己想要的东西。

foul-up /ˈ· ·/ *n* [C] *informal* a problem caused by a stupid or careless mistake【非正式】〔因笨拙或疏忽引起的〕混乱, 一团糟: *There was a foul-up on my charter flight home and several people didn't get seats.* 我回家的包机上出了错, 有几个人没有座位。

found[1] /faund; faʊnd/ the past tense and past participle of FIND[1]

3 **found**[2] *v* [T] **1** to start something such as an organization, company, or city 创立〔组织或公司〕; 创建〔城市〕: *Founded in 1935 in Ohio, Alcoholics Anonymous is now a world-wide organization.* 嗜酒者互诫协会于1935年在俄亥俄州创立, 现在是一个世界性的组织。**2** to start something such as a school or hospital, by providing money for it〔提供资金〕创办〔学校或医院〕: *Eton College was founded by Henry VI in 1440.* 伊顿公学是1440年由亨利六世创办的。**3 be founded on a)** to be the main idea, belief etc that something else develops from 建立在…基础上: *Racism is not founded on rational thought, but on fear.* 种族主义的基础不是理性的思维, 而是恐惧。**b)** to be the solid layer of cement, stones etc that a building is built on 成为〔建筑物〕的基础, 建基: *The castle is founded on solid rock.* 这座城堡建基在坚固的岩石上。**4** *technical* to melt metal and pour it into a MOULD (=a hollow shape), to make things such as tools, parts for machines etc【术语】铸造—**founding** *n* [U]: *the founding of the University of Chicago* 芝加哥大学的创立 —see also 另见 FOUNDATION, WELL-FOUNDED

2 **foun·da·tion** /faunˋdeʃən; faʊnˈdeɪʃən/ *n*

1 ►BUILDING 建筑物◄ [C] *AmE*【美】also 又作 **foundations** [plural] *especially BrE* the solid layer of cement, bricks, stones etc that is under a building to support it【尤英】地基, 基础: **lay the foundations** (=build them) 打地基 *It should take us about three weeks to lay the foundations.* 我们需要大约三星期的时间打地基。

2 ►BASIC IDEA 基本的思想◄ [C] a basic idea, principle, situation etc that something develops from 基础; 根据; 基本原理: [+of] *All theories should be built on a foundation of factual knowledge.* 一切理论应当建立在实际知识的基础上。| **a solid/firm foundation** *He hoped that this job would serve as a firm foundation for his chosen career.* 他希望这份工作会成为他所选择的职业的有力根基。

3 ►ORGANIZATION 组织◄ [C] an organization that gives money to a CHARITY (2), for research etc 基金会: *the Carnegie Foundation* 卡内基基金会

4 ►ESTABLISHMENT 建立◄ [C,U] the establishment of an organization, business, school etc 建立; 创办: *Since its foundation in 1835, this school has served the community.* 这所学校自1835年创立以来, 就为这个社区服务。

5 lay/provide the foundation(s) for to provide the conditions that will make it possible for something to be successful 为…打下基础: *Good planning after the war laid the foundations for the nation's economic miracle.* 战后良好的规划为这个国家的经济奇迹奠定了基础。

6 be without foundation/have no foundation if a statement, idea etc is without foundation, there is no proof that it is true 没有根据: *Your accusations are completely without foundation.* 你的指控完全没有根据。

7 ►SKIN 皮肤◄ [U] a cream the same colour as your skin that you put on before the rest of your MAKE-UP〔与肤色相同的、化妆时打底用的〕粉底霜 —see picture at 参见 MAKE-UP 图

8 shake/rock sth to its foundations to completely change the way something is done or the way people think by having a completely new idea 从根本上动摇某事物; 动摇…的基础: *Darwin's theory rocked the scientific establishment to its foundations.* 达尔文的理论从根本上动摇了科学界。

foundation course /ˈ·· ,· ·/ *n* [C] *BrE* a course of study including several different subjects, taught in the first year at some universities in Britain【英】〔英国一些大学一年级的〕基础课程

foundation gar·ment /ˈ·· ,· ·/ *n* [C] a piece of clothing worn in the past by women under their clothes〔旧时妇女穿的〕紧身胸衣

foundation stone /ˈ·· · ·/ *n* [C] **1** a large stone placed at the bottom of an important building to show when it was built, usually as part of a ceremony〔建筑物奠基典礼时放置的〕基石, 奠基石 **2** the facts, ideas, principles etc that form the base from which something else develops or begins 基础; 根基; 基石: *Greek and Latin were once viewed as the foundation stones of a good education.* 希腊语和拉丁语曾经被看作是良好教育的基础。

found·er[1] /ˈfaundɚ; ˈfaʊndə/ *n* [C] someone who establishes a business, organization, school etc〔公司、组织、学校等的〕创立者, 创办人; 始创者

founder[2] *v* [I] *formal*【正式】**1** to fail after a period of time because something has gone wrong or a new problem has caused difficulties〔因出现问题于一段时间后〕失败, 崩溃, 垮掉: *Their marriage began to founder soon after the honeymoon.* 他们的婚姻在蜜月之后不久便结束了。**2** if a ship or boat founders, it fills with water and sinks〔船〕沉没

founder mem·ber /,·· ˈ··/ *n* [C] *BrE* someone who has helped to establish a new organization, club etc and is one of its first members【英】〔机构、俱乐部等的〕创立者, 创办人; CHARTER MEMBER *AmE*【美】

founding fa·ther /,·· ˈ··/ *n* [C often plural 常用复数] **1** someone who begins something such as a new way of thinking, or a new organization〔新思想或新机构的〕创立人, 开创者: *L. Threlkeld, one of the founding fathers of anthropology in Australia* 澳大利亚人类学创始人之一的思雷尔克德 **2 Founding Fathers** the group of men including George Washington, Thomas Jefferson, and Benjamin Franklin who helped to start the US as a country and to establish its government. They wrote the US's most important political documents, including *The Declaration of Independence*, *The Constitution of the United States*, and *The Bill of Rights*.（美国的）开国元勋〔指包括乔治·华盛顿、托玛斯·杰斐逊和本杰明·富兰克林在内的一批人。他们缔造了美国, 建立了美国政府, 起草了美国最重要的政治文件, 其中包括《独立宣言》、《美国宪法》和《人权法案》〕

found·ling /ˈfaundlɪŋ; ˈfaʊndlɪŋ/ *n* [C] *old use* a baby who has been left by its parents, and is found and looked after by other people【旧】弃婴, 弃儿

foun·dry /ˈfaundrɪ; ˈfaʊndri/ *n* [C] a place where metals are melted and poured into MOULDS (=hollow shapes) to make parts for machines, tools etc 铸造车间; 铸造厂: *an iron foundry* 铸铁厂

fount /faunt; faʊnt/ *n* [C] **1 the fount of all knowledge/wisdom etc** *literary or humorous* the place, person, idea etc that all knowledge, WISDOM etc comes from; SOURCE[1] (1)【文或幽默】〔一切知识、智慧的〕源头; 源泉 **2** *BrE technical* a complete set of letters of one kind and size used to print books, newspapers etc【英, 术语】〔相同字型和大小的〕一副铅字; FONT (2) *AmE*【美】

foun·tain /ˈfauntn; ˈfaʊntɪn/ *n* [C] **1** a structure from which water is sent up into the air, which is often in a small pool（人造）喷泉; 喷水池 **2** a flow of liquid, or of something bright and colourful that goes straight up into the air 喷水;〔明亮艳丽的〕喷出物: [+of] *A fountain of sparks shot high into the night sky.* 一股火花射向高高的夜空。—see also 另见 DRINKING FOUNTAIN, SODA FOUNTAIN

foun·tain·head /ˈfauntn,hɛd; ˈfaʊntɪnhed/ *n* [singular+of] the origin of something; SOURCE[1] (1) 源头

Fountain of Youth, the /,·· ˈ·/ in old stories, a flow of water which was supposed to make anyone who drank from it stay young for ever 青春泉〔古老传说中能使饮用者青春永驻的一泓泉水〕

fountain pen /ˈ·· ·/ *n* [C] a pen that you fill with ink 自来水笔, 钢笔 —see picture at 参见 PEN[1] 图

Fountains Ab·bey /,·· ˈ··/ an ABBEY, built in the 12th century, in North Yorkshire, England where Cistercian MONKS (=members of an all-male religious group) lived. It is now a RUIN and is visited by many tourists. 喷泉修道院〔英格兰约克郡北部的一座西多会修道院。建于公元12世纪, 现已成废墟。许多游客前往参观〕

four /fɔr; fɔː/ *number* **1** 4 四 **2** four o'clock 四点钟: *I'll meet you just after four, okay?* 我就四点钟后见你, 好吗? **3** a group of four people or things〔人或物〕四个一组: *The boxes were stacked in fours.* 那些箱子四个一组地堆放着。| **make up a four** (=complete a group of 4 people) 构成四人一组 *Will you make up a four for a game of cards?* 打牌三缺一, 你愿意凑个数吗? —compare 比较 FOURSOME **4 on all fours** supporting your body with your hands and knees 双手双脚着地, 趴着: *Billy was down on all fours on the ice.* 比利摔得趴在冰上。**5 from the four corners of the earth/world** from places or countries that are very far away from each other 从世界各地: *People gathered from the four corners of the earth for the ecology convention.* 人们从世界各地前来参加这次生态会议。**6 four on the floor**

AmE if a car has four on the floor, it has four GEARs worked by a GEAR LEVER【美】〔汽车〕四挡 **7** a long narrow boat rowed in races by four people 四人赛艇 **8 a coach and four** a carriage pulled by four horses 四马马车 —see also 另见 **four ply** (PLY²), **be scattered to the four winds** (SCATTER (3)) —**fourth** *number*

four-eyes /ˈ· ·/ *n* [singular] a rude way of addressing someone who wears glasses 四眼仔, 四眼儿〔对戴眼镜者的不礼貌称呼〕—**four-eyed** *adj*

four-flush-er /ˈ·,··/ *n* [C] *AmE informal* someone who cheats or tries to deceive people【美, 非正式】骗子

Four Free-doms, the /,·ˈ··/ the four things that US President Franklin Roosevelt said were worth fighting for in a speech he made in 1941, before the US entered World War II. They are Freedom of Speech and Expression, Freedom of Worship (=practising your religion), Freedom from Want (=not having enough food, money, etc), and Freedom from Fear. 四大自由〔1941 年美国参加二战之前富兰克林·罗斯福总统在演说中提到的四个值得奋斗的目标, 即言论自由、宗教信仰自由、免于匮乏的自由和免于恐惧的自由〕

Four Horse-men of the A-poc-a-lypse, the /,·,··· ·ˈ···/ in the Bible, four men who ride horses and represent the four things that cause people the greatest pain and suffering, namely war, FAMINE (=lack of food), death, and PESTILENCE (=serious disease)《启示录》四骑士〔《圣经》中代表人类四大苦难(战争、饥荒、死亡和瘟疫)的四位骑士〕

four-leaved clo-ver /,··ˈ··/ also 又作 **four-leaf clover** *n* [C] a CLOVER plant that has four leaves instead of the usual three, and is considered to be lucky 四叶苜蓿, 四叶草, 幸运草

four-let-ter word /,···ˈ·/ *n* [C] a word that is considered very rude and offensive〔由四个字母构成的〕粗俗下流词: *complaints about the use of four-letter words on TV* 对电视上使用粗俗下流词的投诉

CULTURAL NOTE 文化注释

People use the phrase 'four-letter word' when they do not want to repeat a swear word that someone else has used. Four-letter words, such as 'shit' and 'fuck', are typically words about sexual organs, sexual acts, or waste products of the body. Although they are fairly common, they are offensive to most people. Newspapers have ways of avoiding them, such as printing the first and sometimes the last letter, for example s–t or f***, or talking about 'the f-word'. When someone uses a four-letter word on television or radio, it is often covered by a BLEEP (=a high electronic sound). 人们不想重复别人说过的脏话, 就用"四个字母的词"来指代。shit 或 fuck 等四个字母的词主要和性器官、性行为或屎尿有关。虽然这些词很常用, 大多数人听到还是觉得刺耳。报纸避免使用这些词的办法是只印第一个字母, 有时也印最后一个字母, 如 s–t 或 f***, 或用"f 开头的词"。电视或广播里如果有人说了此类脏话, 一般都会用哔哔声来盖过。 see Cultural Note at SWEARWORD 见 SWEAR WORD文化注释

401K *n* in the US, a way of saving money for your retirement that is handled through the company where you work 401K 计划, 401K 条款〔美国企业针对员工退休而办理的一种存款方式〕

404 /,fɔr o ˈfɔr; ,fɔː əʊ ˈfɔː/ *adj* [not before noun 不用于名词前] someone who is 404 is stupid and unable to use computers or other complicated electronic equipment – used humorously. This word comes from the usual message which appears on the Internet when a particular page you are searching for cannot be found. 404, 笨手笨脚的〔一种幽默表达形式, 形容某人笨手笨脚, 不会使用电脑或其他复杂的电子设备。上网无法搜索到某一网页时, 屏幕上通常会出现"404"的字样, 这一习语由此而来〕

four-post-er /,·ˈ··/ also 又作 **four-poster bed** /,···ˈ·/ *n* [C] a bed with four tall posts at the corners, a cover fixed at the top of the posts, and curtains around the sides 有四根帷柱的床, 四柱大床

Four Sea-sons, The /,·ˈ··/ a piece of music by Vivaldi which represents spring, summer, autumn, and winter and is one of the best-known and most popular pieces of CLASSICAL music《四季》〔维瓦尔第创作的音乐作品, 是最著名、最受人喜爱的古典音乐作品之一〕

four-some /ˈfɔrsəm; ˈfɔːsəm/ *n* [C] a group of four people, especially two men and two women, who are together for a social occasion〔尤指社交场合二男二女的〕四人一组; 两对: **make up a foursome** (=complete a group of four people) 组成四人一组 *make up a foursome for bridge* 组成四人一组打桥牌

four-square¹ /,·ˈ·◂/ *adj* **1** a building that is foursquare is solidly and plainly built, and square in shape〔建筑物〕方形的; 稳固的 **2** *especially BrE* firm and determined【尤英】坚决的, 坚定不移的

four-square² *adv* firmly 稳固地; 坚决地: *standing four-square in the hallway* 伫立在走廊里

four-star¹ /ˈ· ·/ *n* [U] *BrE* a type of petrol with LEAD³ (1) in it【英】〔含铅的〕四星汽油

four-star² *adj* of a high standard or quality 四星级的; 高级的, 极好的: *four-star restaurants* 四星级的餐馆

four-star gen-e-ral /,··ˈ···/ *n* [C] *AmE* a GENERAL² of a high rank in the US army【美】四星上将

four-stroke /ˈ· ·/ *adj* a four-stroke engine works with two up and down movements of a PISTON〔发动机〕四冲程的

four-teen /,fɔrˈtin; ,fɔːˈtiːn◂/ *number* 14 十四 —**fourteenth** *n* [C]

Fourteenth A-mend-ment, the /,···ˈ··/ a part of the US Constitution which gave former SLAVEs the right to be US citizens. It gives all citizens the right to be protected by the law. (美国) 第十四条宪法修正案〔赋予奴隶成为美国公民的权利, 授予全体公民受法律保护的权利〕

fourth /fɔrθ; fɔːθ/ *n* [C] one of four equal parts of something; QUARTER¹ (1) 第四(个); 四分之一

fourth di-men-sion, the /,··ˈ··/ *n* **a)** an expression meaning time, used especially by scientists and writers of SCIENCE FICTION〔尤为科学家和科幻小说作家所用的〕时间, 第四维 **b)** a type of experience that is outside normal human experience 在一般人类体验范围以外的东西: *ghosts, ESP, and other aspects of the fourth dimension* 鬼魂、超感知觉和其他一般人体验范围以外的东西

fourth es-tate /,··ˈ·/ *n* [singular] newspapers, news magazines, radio, and television, the people who work for them, and the political influence that they have; the PRESS¹ 新闻界, 报界; 新闻媒体

fourth-gen-e-ra-tion lan-guage /,·····ˈ··/ also 又作 **4GL** /,fɔr dʒi ˈɛl; ,fɔː dʒiː ˈel/ *n* [singular] a computer language that is easy to use, and contains easier and faster ways of doing things〔电脑〕第四代语言

Fourth of Ju-ly /,···ˈ·/ *n* [singular] a national holiday in the US that celebrates the beginning of the United States as a nation; INDEPENDENCE DAY 美国独立纪念日〔每年的7月4日〕: *a Fourth of July picnic* 美国独立纪念日的郊游野餐

four-wheel drive /,··ˈ·/ also 又作 **4WD** /ˈfɔr dʌbḷju ˈdi; ˈfɔː dʌbəljuː ˈdiː/ *n* [C,U] a system in a car or other vehicle by which the power of the engine is given to all four wheels to make it easier to drive 四轮驱动系统 —**four-wheel drive** *adj*: *a four-wheel drive Toyota* 一辆四轮驱动的丰田汽车

fowl /faul; faʊl/ *n plural* **fowls** *or* **fowl** [C] **1** a bird, especially a chicken, that is kept for its meat and eggs 家禽〔尤指养来食用或生蛋的鸡〕**2** *old use* a bird【旧】鸟, 飞禽 —see also 另见 **neither fish nor fowl** (FISH¹ (5))

Fow-ler /ˈfaulɚ; ˈfaʊlə/, **Henry Watson** (1858-1933) a British writer of dictionaries of the English language. He is known especially for his *Dictionary of Modern English Usage*. 福勒〔(1858-1933), 英国英语词典编纂家, 尤以《现代英语惯用法词典》闻名〕

fowl pest /ˈ· ·/ *n* [U] an illness that spreads quickly among chickens and some other birds 鸡瘟, 家禽疫病

Fox /fɑks; fɒks/ also 又作 **Fox Broadcasting Company** *trademark* one of the main national television networks in the US. The others are ABC, CBS, and NBC. Fox is the newest of the main US television networks, and is part of Rupert Murdoch's company, News Corporation.【商标】福克斯〔又名福克斯广播公司, 美国主要国家电视网之一。其余为美国广播公司、哥伦比亚广播公司和全国广播公司。福克斯年资最短, 归属于鲁珀特·默多克的新闻集团〕

fox¹ *n* **1** [C] a wild animal like a dog with reddish-brown fur, a pointed face, and a thick tail 狐狸 **2** [C] *informal* someone who is clever and deceitful【非正式】狡猾的人: *He was a sly old fox.* 他是狡猾的老狐狸。**3** [U] the skin and fur of a fox, used to make clothes〔用于做衣服的〕狐皮 **4** [C] *AmE informal* someone who is sexually attractive【美, 非正式】性感的人: *She's such a fox!* 她真迷人!

fox² *v* [T] **1** *BrE informal* to be too difficult for someone to do or understand【英, 非正式】把…难住; 使猜不透: *Those childproof containers always fox me.* 那些保障小孩安全的容器总是把我难住。**2** *especially BrE* to confuse or deceive someone in a clever way【尤英】使迷惑; 欺骗

Fox, Charles James (1749-1806) a British politician who was against the SLAVE trade and the taxing of the American colo-

nies (COLONY) 福克斯〔(1749-1806), 英国政治家。他反对贩卖奴隶贸易, 反对向美国殖民地征税〕

Fox, George (1624-91), an English religious leader who started the Christian group the Society of Friends, who are also called Quakers 福克斯〔(1624-1691), 英格兰宗教领袖, 曾创立基督教公谊会, 又称贵格会〕

Fox and the Grapes, The /,· · · ˈ·/ a FABLE (=a traditional short story that teaches a moral lesson) by Aesop in which a FOX tries many times to reach some GRAPEs that are hanging above his head. When he realizes that he will never be able to reach them, he pretends that he never wanted them, saying "They're probably SOUR (=having an unpleasant acid taste) anyway". This attitude is called sour grapes.《狐狸与葡萄》〔伊索寓言故事。有一只狐狸屡次试图摘取悬在头顶上的葡萄, 当他意识到自己永远也够不着时, 便装作从来就没想要过, 说道: "葡萄可能是酸的。" 这种态度被称作"酸葡萄"〕

fox·glove /ˈfɑks,glʌv; ˈfɒksglʌv/ *n* [C] a tall plant with many bell-shaped flowers 毛地黄

fox·hole /ˈfɑks,hol; ˈfɒkshəʊl/ *n* [C] **1** a hole in the ground that soldiers use to fire from or hide from the enemy 散兵坑 **2** a hole in the ground where a fox lives〔地下的〕狐狸洞

fox·hound /ˈfɑks,haund; ˈfɒkshaʊnd/ *n* [C] a dog with a very good sense of smell, trained to hunt and kill foxes 猎狐狗, 狐猩

fox·hunt·er /ˈfɑks,hʌntɚ; ˈfɒkshʌntə/ *n* [C] a horse used in the sport of foxhunting 猎狐时用的马

fox·hunt·ing /ˈfɑks,hʌntɪŋ; ˈfɒkshʌntɪŋ/ *n* [U] the sport of hunting foxes (FOX¹ (1)) with dogs while riding on a horse〔骑马携犬的〕猎狐〔活动〕 **—fox-hunting** *adj* **—foxhunt** *n* [C]

CULTURAL NOTE 文化注释

Foxhunting takes place in the UK between November and early spring. The horse riders usually wear red coats, and the hunt is controlled by the Master of Foxhounds. Foxhunting is thought of as a sport for rich people who own land in the countryside. Many people think that foxhunting is cruel and want parliament to pass a law against it, but foxhunters say that it helps to control the number of foxes. 猎狐运动在英国的11月至初春举行。骑师通常穿红外套, 由狐提主统筹整个狩猎活动。猎狐被视为在乡村拥有土地的富人的运动。很多人认为猎狐很残忍, 希望议会通过法律予以禁止, 但猎狐者说, 这有助于控制狐狸的数量。

fox ter·ri·er /,· ˈ· · ·/ *n* [C] a small dog with short hair 狐㹴

fox·trot /ˈfɑks,trɑt; ˈfɒkstrɒt/ *n* [C] a type of formal dance with short, quick steps, or a piece of music for this dance 狐步舞〔曲〕 **—foxtrot** *v* [I]

fox·y /ˈfɑksɪ; ˈfɒksi/ *adj* **1** like a FOX¹ (1) in appearance〔外表〕似狐的: *He was a tall, thin man with a rather foxy face.* 他又高又瘦, 相貌有点像狐狸。**2** clever and deceitful 狡猾的: *That foxy bastard. How did he get away with it?* 那个狡猾的杂种。他怎么蒙混过关的? **3** *AmE informal* sexually attractive【美, 非正式】性感的, 妖艳的: *a foxy lady* 妖艳媚人的女子

foy·er /ˈfɔɪɚ; ˈfɔɪeɪ/ *n* [C] **1** a room or hall at the entrance to a public building; LOBBY¹ (1)〔公共建筑物入口处的〕休息厅, 门厅: *We met in the theatre foyer.* 我们是在剧院的门厅遇到的。**2** *AmE* a small room or hall at the entrance to a private house or flat【美】〔私人房子或公寓入口处的〕前厅, 门厅, 玄关

FPA /,ɛf pi ˈe; ,ef piː ˈeɪ/ the abbreviation of 缩写= the FAMILY PLANNING ASSOCIATION

FPO /,ɛf pi ˈo; ,ef piː ˈəʊ/ an abbreviation of 缩写='fleet post office' or 'field post office', used as part of the address of someone in the American navy or army 舰队邮局; 战地邮局〔用于美国海军或陆军地址〕

Fr 1 a written abbreviation of 缩写= Father, used in front of the name of a priest 神父〔用于教士的姓名前〕 **2** a written abbreviation of 缩写= FRANC (=a unit of French money) 法郎 **3** a written abbreviation of 缩写= French 或 France

frac·as /ˈfrekəs; ˈfrækɑː/ *n plural* **fracas or fracases** *AmE* [C] a short, noisy fight involving several people【美】喧闹的打架; 殴斗骚乱: *There was a fracas outside the courtroom as the suspect emerged.* 嫌疑人出现时, 法庭外发生一阵骚乱。

frac·tion /ˈfrækʃən; ˈfrækʃən/ *n* [C] **1** a very small amount of something 少量; 一点儿: [+of] *Gwen carefully opened the door a fraction.* 格温小心地把门稍微打开了一点儿。**2** a division or a part of a whole number in mathematics〔数学上的〕分数; 小数: *³/₄ and ¹/₂ are fractions.* ³/₄ 和 ¹/₂ 都是分数。—see also 另见 COMMON FRACTION, IMPROPER FRACTION, PROPER FRACTION, VULGAR FRACTION

frac·tion·al /ˈfrækʃənḷ; ˈfrækʃənəl/ *adj* **1** very small in amount 很少的, 少量的: *She made a fractional alteration to the floral centerpiece.* 她对餐桌中央的插花做了一点小改动。**2** connected with fractions, in mathematics〔数学上〕分数的; 小数的 **—fractionally** *adv*

frac·tious /ˈfrækʃəs; ˈfrækʃəs/ *adj* if a baby or child is fractious, they are angry or upset〔婴儿或儿童〕烦躁的; 易怒的; 发脾气的: *Babies tend to be fractious when they are teething.* 婴儿在长乳牙时往往容易烦躁。**—fractiousness** *n* [U]

frac·ture¹ /ˈfræktʃɚ; ˈfræktʃə/ *v* [I,T] if a bone or other hard substance fractures or is fractured, it breaks or cracks〔使〕断裂;〔使〕折断: *He fractured a leg in preseason training.* 他在赛季前的训练中摔断了腿。| *Under such pressure, rock will begin to fracture.* 岩石在这样的压力下会开始断裂。| *a fractured rib* 折断的肋骨

fracture² *n* [C] a crack or broken part in a bone or other hard substance 骨折; 裂缝, 裂痕: *Check all the parts to be sure there are no fractures in the metal.* 请检查所有的部件, 以确保金属没有裂缝。

fra·gile /ˈfrædʒəl; ˈfrædʒaɪl/ *adj* **1** not strong, and therefore easily broken or damaged 脆弱的; 易碎的; 易损坏的: *The parcel was marked FRAGILE–HANDLE WITH CARE.* 包裹上标着"易碎 —— 小心轻放"的字样。**2** easily damaged, spoilt, or destroyed 纤弱的; 脆弱的: *The country's fragile economy is threatened by the continued drought.* 该国脆弱的经济受到持续干旱的威胁。**3** a fragile person looks thin and delicate and is often weak or likely to become ill〔人〕瘦弱的, 弱不禁风的 **4** *BrE* if someone feels fragile they feel ill, especially because they have drunk too much alcohol【英】〔尤指喝太多酒后〕有气无力的; 虚弱的; 精神不振的 **—fragility** /frəˈdʒɪlətɪ; frəˈdʒɪlɪti/ *n* [U] —compare 比较 FRAIL

frag·ment¹ /ˈfrægmənt; ˈfrægmənt/ *n* [C] a small piece of something that has broken off or that comes from something larger 碎片, 碎块; 片断: *Roger examined the few words remaining on the charred fragment of paper.* 罗杰仔细地检查烧焦的碎纸上留下来的那几个词。| *a fragment of poetry* 诗的残篇断简 W3

frag·ment² /frægˈmɛnt; frægˈment/ *v* [I,T often passive 常用被动态] to break something, or be broken into a lot of small, separate parts〔使〕成碎片, 打碎; 分裂: *His day was fragmented by interruptions and phone calls.* 他一天中有各种事情干扰, 又有不断的电话, 弄得时间支离破碎的。**—fragmented** *adj*: *a rapidly changing and fragmented society* 一个迅速变化、四分五裂的社会 **—fragmentation** /,frægmɛnˈteʃən; ,frægmənˈteɪʃən/ *n* [U]

frag·ment·a·ry /ˈfrægmən,tɛrɪ; ˈfrægməntəri/ *adj* made of many different pieces 碎片的; 片断的; 不完整的: *We have received only fragmentary accounts of the incident.* 关于这起事件, 我们只听到了只言片语。

fra·grance /ˈfregrəns; ˈfreɪgrəns/ *n* **1** [C,U] a pleasant smell 香气, 香味, 芳香: *This soup has a delicate fragrance and a slightly sweet taste.* 这种汤闻起来有淡淡的香味, 吃起来略有点甜。—compare 比较 AROMA, SMELL² (1) **2** [C] a liquid that you put on your body to make it smell pleasant 香水: *They make soaps and fragrances based on natural ingredients.* 他们以天然配料制造肥皂和香水。

fra·grant /ˈfregrənt; ˈfreɪgrənt/ *adj* having a pleasant smell 香的, 芳香的: *The damask rose is extremely fragrant.* 大马士革蔷薇非常香。**—fragrantly** *adv*

fraid·y cat /ˈfredɪ kæt; ˈfreɪdi kæt/ *AmE informal n* [C] a word meaning someone who is too frightened to do something, used especially by children; SCAREDY-CAT【美, 非正式】胆小鬼〔尤儿语〕

frail /frel; freɪl/ *adj* **1** someone who is frail is thin and weak, especially because they are old〔尤因年老而〕瘦弱的; 衰弱的: *He was a man of about sixty, frail and bent.* 他年纪大约60岁, 瘦弱而且驼背。**2** not strongly made or built and therefore easily damaged 不坚实的; 不牢固的; 易损坏的: *It seemed impossible that these frail boats could survive in such a storm.* 这些不牢固的小船似乎不可能在这样的暴风雨中幸免于难。—compare 比较 FRAGILE

frail·ty /ˈfreltɪ; ˈfreɪlti/ *n* **1** [U] lacking in strength or health 脆弱, 虚弱: *He noticed with shock the frailty of her thin body.* 他惊讶地注意到她那纤瘦的身体非常虚弱。| *the frailty of the urban economy* 城市经济的脆弱 **2** [C] something bad or weak in your character〔性格上的〕弱点, 缺点: *human frailties* 人性的弱点

frame¹ /frem; freɪm/ *n* S3 W3

1 ►BORDER 边框◄ [C] a firm structure that holds something such as a picture or window, and provides a border for it 框架, 边框: *Stretch the embroidery on a frame before start-*

ing to sew. 先把刺绣品紧绷在框架上，然后开始缝制。| **door/window/picture frame** *He leaned against the door frame.* 他靠在门框上。
2 ▶STRUCTURE 结构◀ [C] the structure or main supporting parts of a piece of furniture, vehicle, or other object〔家具、车辆或其他物体的〕构架，骨架，支架: *a bicycle frame* 自行车车架 | *There was nothing wrong with the frame of the chair, just the upholstery.* 椅子的结构没什么问题，只是装饰料有问题。
3 ▶BODY 体格◀ [C] the structure formed by the bones of someone's body 体格；身躯；骨架: *Louise's slight frame* 路易斯瘦小的身躯
4 ▶MAIN FACTS/IDEAS 主要的事实/想法◀ [singular] the main ideas, facts etc that something is based on 构想，框架: *A clear explanation of the subject provides a frame on which a deeper understanding can be built.* 清晰地解释主题能提供一个框架，以便在此基础上作更深刻的了解。
5 ▶GLASSES 眼镜◀ the metal or plastic part of a pair of glasses (GLASS[1] (3)) that holds the lenses (LENS (1)) 眼镜框 —see picture at 参见 GLASS[1] 图
6 be in a... frame of mind to have an attitude at a particular time that helps you to do something 处于…精神状态[心情；情绪]: *Philip, I don't think you're in a proper frame of mind to enter the House of God.* 菲利普，我认为你的心情不适合进教堂。
7 ▶BOX 箱◀ [C] a large wooden box covered with glass or plastic in which young plants are grown outdoors〔木制〕温床，温箱: *cucumber frames* 黄瓜温箱
8 ▶SPORT 体育◀ [C] a complete part in the games of SNOOKER or BOWLING〔台球或保龄球的〕一轮，一局，一个回合: *I won the next three frames.* 我赢了此后的三局。
9 ▶PHOTOGRAPH 照片◀ [C] an area of a photographic film that contains one photograph, or many of these which together make a cinema or VIDEO film〔影片的〕画面，画格；〔照片的〕帧，幅 —see also 另见 CLIMBING FRAME

F

frame² *v* [T] **1** to surround something with a border so that it looks pleasant or so that you can see it clearly 给…形成框子，把…框住: *Sarah's long, dark hair framed her face.* 萨拉的黑色长发衬托着她的脸。| **be framed by** *a courtyard framed by a rectangle of tightly clipped grass* 被一圈修剪得很整洁的长方形草地围住的庭院 **2** to put a picture in a structure that will hold it firmly 给〔画等〕装框 **3** to deliberately make someone seem guilty of a crime, by providing things that seem like proof 陷害；诬告: *I'm convinced Murphy's been framed.* 我确信墨菲是被陷害了。| **frame sb for** *He told the court that the police had tried to frame him for assault.* 他告诉法庭警方想诬陷他袭击他人。**4** to organize and develop a plan, system etc 制定，构想〔计划、系统等〕: *a theory originally framed by Marx* 马克思最早构想的理论 **5 gilt-framed/wood-framed etc** having a frame or frames of a particular colour or material 镶在镀金架里的/木框里的等: *a red-framed mirror* 红框的镜子 | *wire-framed spectacles* 金属丝框的眼镜 —see also 另见 FRAME-UP

frame of ref·er·ence /,. . '.../ *n* [C usually singular 一般用单数] the knowledge, experiences, or beliefs that someone uses to understand something 参照依据；参照标准；准则

frame-up /'. ./ *n* [C] a plan to make someone seem guilty of a crime when they are not 阴谋，陷害，诬害

3 **frame·work** /ˈfremˌwɝk; ˈfreɪmwɜːk/ *n* [C] **1** the main supporting parts of a building, vehicle, or object〔建筑物、车辆、物体的〕构架，框架，结构: *airships with a rigid metal framework* 有着坚硬的金属框架的飞船 **2** a set of facts, ideas etc from which more complicated ideas are developed, or on which decisions are based 体系，体制；参照标准；准则: **[+of]** *a framework of Marxist theory* 马克思主义理论体系 | **[+for]** *This paper seeks to provide a framework for future research.* 这篇论文试图为今后的研究提供一个框架。**3 social/political/legal etc framework** the structure of a society, a legal or political system etc 社会/政治/法律等的结构[制度]: *a legal and political framework favourable to trade* 有利于贸易的法律和政治制度

franc /fræŋk; fræŋk/ *n* [C] the standard unit of money in some countries, and used in France and Belgium before EURO 法郎〔一些国家的货币单位，在法国和比利时被欧元取代〕

France /frɑns; frɑːns/ a country in western Europe and a member of the EU. Population: 59,551,000 (2001). Capital: Paris. France is famous especially for its art, good food, and fine wines. 法国〔西欧一国家，欧盟成员国。人口：59,551,000 (2001)；首都：巴黎。该国尤以艺术、佳肴和美酒闻名〕—see 见 FRENCH

fran·chise¹ /ˈfræntʃaɪz; ˈfræntʃaɪz/ *n* **1** [C] permission to sell a company's goods or service, that is given or sold to a business person〔经营某公司商品或服务的〕特许经营权: *a Benetton franchise* 贝纳通集团的特许经营权 **2** [U] the legal right to vote in your country's elections 选举权，投票权: *universal franchise* 普选权

franchise² *v* [T] to give or sell a franchise to someone 给予〔某人〕特许权；〔向某人〕出售特许权

fran·chi·see /ˌfræntʃaɪˈzi; ˌfræntʃaɪˈziː/ *n* [C] someone who is given or sold a franchise 特许经营人

Fran·cis·can /frænˋsɪskən; frænˈsɪskən/ **1 the Franciscans** a Christian religious group begun by St Francis of Assisi in 1209, whose members live a holy life according to strict rules 方济各会〔1209年由阿西西的圣·方济各创立的一个天主教宗教团体。其成员按照严格的教规过着圣洁的生活〕 **2** a member of this group 方济各会的修道士（修女）—**Franciscan** *adj*

Francis of As·si·si /ˌfrænsɪs əv əˋsisɪ; ˌfrɑːnsɪs əv əˈsiːsi/, **St** (1182-1226) an Italian Christian leader who started the Franciscan ORDER (=a group of religious men who live and pray together). He is famous for his love of nature, and is often shown in pictures surrounded by birds and animals. 阿西西的圣方济各〔(1182-1226)，意大利天主教领袖，曾创立方济各会。他以热爱大自然著称。图画中的他常被鸟儿和动物围绕〕

Francis Xa·vi·er /ˌfrænsɪs ˋzevɪɚ; ˌfrɑːnsɪs ˈzeɪviə/, **St** (1506-52) a Spanish Christian MISSIONARY (=someone who goes to a foreign country to teach people about Christianity) who travelled to India, southeast Asia, and Japan, and who helped to start the Jesuit missionary (=a group of Roman Catholic priests) 弗朗西斯·沙勿略〔(1506-1552)，西班牙天主教传教士。他到过印度、东南亚和日本，帮助当地创建天主教耶稣会〕

Fran·co /ˈfræŋko; ˈfræŋkəʊ/, **Fran·cis·co** /frænˋsɪsko; frænˈsɪskəʊ/ (1892-1975) a Spanish military leader and RIGHT-WING politician. He led the Nationalist side in the Spanish Civil War (1936-39), and ruled Spain as a DICTATOR until his death. 佛朗哥〔(1892-1975)，西班牙军事领导人、右翼政治家。他在西班牙内战(1936-1939)中领导过民族主义集团，之后在西班牙实行独裁统治，直至去世〕

Franco- /fræŋko; fræŋkəʊ/ *prefix* **1** of France 法国的: *a Francophile* (=someone who loves France) 亲法分子 **2** French and 法国和…的: *the Franco-Belgian border* 法比边界

fran·co·phone /ˈfræŋkəˌfon; ˈfræŋkəʊfəʊn/ *adj* **1** having a French-speaking population 讲法语的: *francophone countries* 讲法语的国家 **2** from a French-speaking country or population 来自讲法语的国家的，来自讲法语人口的: *francophone African literature* 非洲法语国家文学

fran·glais /ˌfrɑŋˋgle; ˈfrɒŋgleɪ/ *n* [U] a mixture of the French and English languages 英语式法语

frank¹ /fræŋk; fræŋk/ *adj* **1** honest and truthful in what you say 坦率的，坦诚的，直言不讳的: *a frank exchange of ideas* 坦率的意见交换 | **be frank with sb** *He was completely frank with her about what happened.* 他完全坦率地告诉她所发生的事。**2 to be frank** used when you are saying something true that other people may not like 坦率地说: *To be perfectly frank, I think that's a crazy idea.* 坦白相告，我认为那是个荒唐的主意。—**frankness** *n* [U]

frank² *v* [T] to print a sign on an envelope showing that the cost of sending it has been paid 在〔信封〕上盖戳记〔表示邮资已付〕

Frank, Anne (1929-1945) a Jewish girl who wrote a famous DIARY, in which she describes her life while she and her family were hiding from the Nazis in Amsterdam. The family was eventually discovered, and sent to the Nazi CONCENTRATION CAMP of Belsen, where most of them died. 弗兰克〔(1929-1945)，一犹太少女。她写有一本著名日记，描述她与家人在阿姆斯特丹躲避纳粹分子的经历。她一家人最终被发现并押送到了贝尔森集中营，大多死在那里〕

Fran·ken·stein /ˈfræŋkənˌstaɪn; ˈfræŋkɪnˌstaɪn/ a NOVEL by Mary Shelley, which was published in 1818 and tells the story of a scientist, called Frankenstein, who makes a creature by joining together bits of dead bodies. The creature is gentle at first, but later becomes violent and attacks its maker. People sometimes mistakenly call the creature Frankenstein, instead of the scientist who made it.《弗兰肯斯坦》〔玛丽·雪莱创作的一部小说，1818年出版。小说中有一位名叫弗兰肯斯坦的科学家把几具死尸的肢体和器官拼接起来造出一只怪物。这只怪物起先很温顺，但后来凶残起来，攻击造它的人。人们有时把它误称为弗兰肯斯坦〕

frank·fur·ter /ˈfræŋkfɚtɚ; ˈfræŋkfɜːtə/ also 又作 **frank** *AmE* 【美】—*n* [C] a long reddish smoked SAUSAGE; HOT DOG[1] *AmE* 【美】熏肉香肠

frank·in·cense /ˈfræŋkɪnˌsɛns; ˈfræŋkɪnsens/ *n* [U] a substance that is burnt to give a sweet smell, especially at religious ceremonies〔尤指宗教仪式上点燃的〕乳香

franking ma·chine /ˈ· · ˌ·/ *n* [C] a machine that prints signs on envelopes to show that the charge for sending them has been paid〔在信封上盖戳记、表示邮资已付的〕邮资机

Frank·lin /ˈfræŋklɪn; ˈfræŋklɪn/, **Ben·ja·min** /ˈbɛndʒəmɪn; ˈbendʒəmɪn/ (1706-90) a US politician, writer, and scientist. Franklin was involved in writing *The Declaration of Independence* and *The Constitution of the United States*. He is famous for proving that LIGHTNING is a form of electricity by doing a scientific test in which he flew a KITE during a storm, and he invented the lightning CONDUCTOR. He also wrote *Poor Richard's Almanack* (1732-57). 富兰克林〔(1706-1790), 美国政治家、作家、科学家。他参与过《独立宣言》和《美国宪法》的起草工作。他曾在暴风雨中放飞风筝做科学实验, 以此证明闪电是电的一种形式。他发明了避雷针。他还著有《穷理查德历书》(1732-1757)〕

S3 **frank·ly** /ˈfræŋklɪ; ˈfræŋkli/ *adv* **1** honestly and directly, especially in speech 坦率地, 坦诚地: *I stated my views frankly.* 我坦率地陈述了自己的观点。**2** [sentence adverb 句子副词] used to show that you are saying something direct and honest 坦率地说: *Frankly, I'm not very interested.* 坦率地说, 我不是很感兴趣。

fran·tic /ˈfræntɪk; ˈfræntɪk/ *adj* **1** extremely hurried and using a lot of energy but not very organized 紧张纷乱的: *I couldn't understand her frantic signalling.* 我无法理解她那紧张狂乱的示意手势。| **frantic activity/search/rush etc** *Before the game there was a frantic rush to get the last few seats.* 比赛前, 人们急匆匆地赶去争得最后的几个座位。**2** extremely worried and frightened about a situation, so that you cannot control your feelings〔因极端焦急恐惧而〕发疯似的; 情绪失控的: *A frantic note had crept into Jane's voice.* 简的声音开始带有慌张急迫的味道。| **get/become/grow frantic** *There was still no news of Jill, and her parents were getting frantic.* 仍然没有吉尔的消息, 她的父母急得要疯了。| **frantic with worry/grief etc** *Your mother's been frantic with worry wondering where you've been.* 你的母亲不知道你在哪里, 已经担心得要发疯了。—**frantically** /-klɪ; -kli/ *adv* —see also 另见 FRENETIC

frap·pé /fræˈpe; ˈfræpeɪ/ *n* [C,U] **1** *AmE* a thick kind of MILK SHAKE【美】一种稠的奶昔 **2** a strong alcoholic drink poured over very thin pieces of ice 利口酒刨冰 —**frappé** *adj*

frat /fræt; fræt/ *n* [C] *AmE informal*【美, 非正式】= FRATERNITY (2)

fra·ter·nal /frəˈtɝnl; frəˈtɜːnl/ *adj* **1** showing a special friendliness to other people because you share interests or ideas with them〔对志同道合的人〕友好的, 亲如手足的: *fraternal sympathy with the workers out on strike* 对罢工工人兄弟般的同情 **2** of or belonging to brothers 兄弟的; 兄弟般的: *fraternal loyalty* 兄弟般的忠诚 —**fraternally** *adv*

fra·ter·ni·ty /frəˈtɝnətɪ; frəˈtɜːnɪti/ *n* **1** **the racing/teaching/scientific fraternity** all the people who work in a particular profession 赛马界/教育界/科学界同人: *He's a member of the medical fraternity.* 他在医务界工作。**2** [C] a club of male students at an American university, usually living in the same building〔美国大学里的〕男生联谊会, 兄弟会: *a fraternity brother*〔美国大学中〕兄弟会会员 —compare 比较 SORORITY **3** [U] a feeling of friendship between members of a group 友爱; 博爱; 兄弟情谊: *the Revolutionary ideas of fraternity and equality* 博爱和平等的革命思想

frat·er·nize also 又作 **-ise** *BrE*【英】/ˈfrætɚˌnaɪz; ˈfrætənaɪz/ *v* [I] to show friendliness towards people who you are not supposed to be friendly with 与敌人友好;〔战场上〕与敌军友好交往: [**+with**] *The soldiers fraternized with the enemy on Christmas Day.* 这些士兵在圣诞节与敌人友善交往。—**fraternization** /ˌfrætɚnɪˈzeʃən; ˌfrætənaɪˈzeɪʃən/ *n* [U]

frat·ri·cide /ˈfrætrəˌsaɪd; ˈfrætrɪsaɪd/ *n* [C,U] **1** the crime of murdering your brother or sister 杀害兄弟姐妹的罪行 **2** the murder of people from your country or local area〔杀害本国人或本地人的〕自相残杀

fraud /frɔd; frɔːd/ *n* **1** [C,U] a method of illegally getting money from someone, often by using clever and complicated methods 欺诈, 诈骗: *financial losses due to theft or fraud* 由盗窃或诈骗引起的钱财损失 | **tax/share/bankruptcy etc fraud** (=fraud in a particular financial area) 骗税/股份诈骗/破产诈骗等 **2** [C] someone who deceives people to gain money, friendship etc 骗子: *She realized later that the insurance salesman had been a fraud.* 她后来意识到那个保险推销员是个骗子。

Fraud Squad /ˈ· ·/ *n* [singular] the department in the British police force that examines fraud in business〔英国警察的〕反欺诈小分队

fraud·u·lent /ˈfrɔdʒələnt; ˈfrɔːdjʊlənt/ *adj* fraudulent actions or words are intended to deceive〔行动或言语〕骗人的, 欺诈性的: *fraudulent banking practices* 欺诈性的银行业务 | *fraudulent statements* 骗人的声明 —**fraudulently** *adv* —**fraudulence** *n* [U]

fraught /frɔt; frɔːt/ *adj* **1** an activity or situation that is fraught is full of problems and is very difficult to deal with 充满问题的; 难对付的: *After the argument, relations between them were fraught.* 这场争论之后, 他们的关系很紧张。| **fraught with problems/difficulties/danger** *Any program of sudden change is likely to be fraught with pitfalls.* 任何突然改变的计划都可能会有许多缺陷。**2** full of anxiety or worry 焦虑不安的; 非常紧张的: *Julie was unhappy, fraught and depressed.* 朱莉很不高兴, 焦虑不安, 垂头丧气。**3** **fraught with meaning** showing strong feelings that are not expressed in words 意味深长的: *She gave me a long look, fraught with meaning.* 她意味深长地朝我看了很久。

fray /fre; freɪ/ *v* [I] **1** if cloth or other material frays, the threads become loose because the material is old〔布料等〕磨损, 磨破; 磨散: *That sleeve will fray if you don't darn it.* 如果你不织补, 那个袖头会散开的。—see picture on page A18 参见 A18 页图 **2** if someone's temper or nerves fray, they become annoyed 烦恼, 恼怒; 紧张: *It was only three o'clock and tempers were already beginning to fray.* 这时才三点钟, 大家便已经开始发脾气了。—**frayed** *adj*: *The carpet was badly frayed.* 地毯磨损得很厉害。

fray, the *n* a quarrel, argument, or fight 争论; 吵架; 打架; 斗殴: **join/enter the fray** *It wasn't long before all the demonstrators had joined in the fray.* 很快, 所有的游行示威者都参加了斗殴。

Fra·zer /ˈfrezɚ; ˈfreɪzə/, **Sir James George** (1854-1941) a British writer on ANTHROPOLOGY (=the scientific study of people and their societies, and the way that their customs develop), who wrote *The Golden Bough*, a book about the connections between religion and magic 弗雷泽〔(1854-1941), 英国人类学作家。他写有一部阐述宗教与巫术关系的著作, 名为《金枝》〕

fraz·zle /ˈfræzl; ˈfræzəl/ *n* [singular] *BrE informal* **be burnt to a frazzle etc** to be so burnt that there is almost nothing left【英, 非正式】被烧个精光

fraz·zled /ˈfræzld; ˈfræzəld/ *adj informal* annoyed and unable to deal with problems or difficulties, especially because you have been very busy【非正式】〔由于很忙〕烦燥的, 躁怒的: *I felt tired and frazzled.* 我感到精疲力竭, 烦躁不安。

FRB, the /ˌɛf ɑr ˈbi; ˌef ɑː ˈbiː/ the abbreviation of 缩写 = the FEDERAL RESERVE BANK

FRCM /ˌɛf ɑr si ˈɛm; ˌef ɑː siː ˈem/ Fellow of the Royal College of Music; someone who belongs to or has studied at the Royal College of Music in the UK (英国) 皇家音乐学院研究员

FRCP /ˌɛf ɑr si ˈpi; ˌef ɑː siː ˈpiː/ the abbreviation of 缩写 = Fellow of the Royal College of Physicians (in the UK) (英国) 皇家内科医师学会会员

FRCS /ˌɛf ɑr si ˈɛs; ˌef ɑː siː ˈes/ the abbreviation of 缩写 = Fellow of the Royal College of Surgeons (in the UK) (英国) 皇家外科医师学会会员

FRCVS /ˌɛf ɑr ˌsi vi ˈɛs; ˌef ɑː ˌsiː viː ˈes/ the abbreviation of 缩写 = Fellow of the Royal College of Veterinary Surgeons (in the UK) (英国) 皇家兽医外科医师学会会员

freak¹ /frik; friːk/ *n* [C] **1** **bike/fitness/film etc freak** *informal* someone who is so interested in bikes, fitness etc that other people think they are strange or unusual【非正式】自行车迷/健美迷/电影迷等: *Carrot juice is a favourite with health-food freaks.* 胡萝卜汁是健康食品迷最爱喝的。**2** someone who looks very strange or behaves in a very unusual way 怪异的人: *Women who were good at physics used to be considered freaks.* 擅长物理学的女性过去常被看作怪人。**3** something in nature, such as a strangely-shaped plant or animal, that is very unusual 畸形生物: *One of the lambs was a freak – it had two tails.* 其中一只羔羊是畸形的——它有两条尾巴。| **a freak of nature** (=something physically strange or unusual) 畸形物; 怪异的事物 *By some freak of nature there was a snowstorm in June.* 天公作怪, 6月份竟然有暴风雪。**4** **control freak** someone who always wants to control situations and other people 支配欲极强的人

freak² *adj* [only before noun 仅用于名词前] **freak accident/storm/conditions etc** an accident, storm etc that is unexpected and very unusual 反常的事故/暴风雨/状况等: *A freak wave wrecked most of the sea-front.* 一个异乎寻常的大浪損毁了大部分滨海区。

freak³ *v* [I] *informal especially AmE* to become suddenly angry or frightened, especially so that you cannot control your behaviour【非正式, 尤美】突然发怒[害怕]: *She freaked when she heard he was coming to the party.* 听说他要来参加聚会, 她突然吓得要死。

freak out *phr v* [I,T] *informal* to become very anxious, upset, or frightened, or make someone very anxious, upset or frightened【非正式】(使)暴跳如雷; (使)心烦意乱; (使)吓得要死: **freak sb out** *It freaked me out to see him so depressed.* 看到他这样垂头丧气, 我心烦意乱。

freak·ish /ˈfrikɪʃ; ˈfriːkɪʃ/ *adj* very unusual and strange 反常的, 异乎寻常的: *freakish behaviour* 反常的行为 —**freakishly** *adv* —**freakishness** *n* [U]

freak·y /ˈfrikɪ; ˈfriːki/ *adj spoken* strange and slightly frightening【口】古怪吓人的: *That science fiction film was really freaky!* 那部科幻影片真古怪吓人!

freck·le /ˈfrɛkl; ˈfrekəl/ *n* [C usually plural 一般用复数] a small brown spot on your skin, caused by the sun〔日晒引起的〕雀斑, 斑点 —see picture on page A6 参见 A6 页图

freck·led /ˈfrɛkḷd; ˈfrekəld/ *adj* having freckles 长雀斑的, 长斑点的: *a lightly freckled face* 长了一些雀斑的脸

free[1] /fri; friː/ *adj*

① ALLOWED TO DO WHAT YOU WANT 能随心所欲的
② COSTING NOTHING 免费的
③ NOT A PRISONER 不是囚犯
④ NOT BUSY 不忙的
⑤ NOT BEING USED 闲置的
⑥ WITHOUT/NOT HAVE 没有
⑦ NOT FIXED/ABLE TO MOVE 未固定的/能移动的
⑧ OTHER MEANINGS 其他意思

① ALLOWED TO DO WHAT YOU WANT 能随心所欲的

1 allowed to do whatever you want, without being controlled or restricted 自由的; 不受控制[约束]的: **free to do sth** *The children are free to decide which activity they would like to do.* 这些孩子能自由选择自己喜欢做的活动。

2 feel free *spoken* used to tell someone that they can do something【口】随便, 随意: *Feel free to ask questions.* 请随便提问吧。| *"Can I make myself some tea?" "Feel free."* "我可以自己泡点茶吗?" "请随便。"

3 without restrictions or controls 随意的, 不受限制的: *We had a free and open discussion about religion.* 我们自由开放地讨论了宗教。| *a free exchange of information* 随意的信息交换 | **free access/passage/movement etc** *free movement of people and goods between the towns* 城镇间人口和商品的自由流动 | **free speech** (=being able to say whatever you want) 言论自由

4 free election/society/press an election etc that is not controlled by the government so that people can vote, live etc how they want to 自由选举/自由社会/新闻自由

5 give sb a free hand/rein to let someone do whatever they want or need to do in a particular situation 放手让某人干: *She gave the producer a free rein with the script.* 她放手让制片人处理剧本。

6 free and easy relaxed, friendly, and without many rules 无拘束的, 随便的; 不拘礼节的: *a free and easy discussion* 无拘束的讨论

7 a free spirit someone who lives as they want to rather than in the way that society considers normal 我行我素的人

8 free agent someone who can do what they want to, and who is not controlled by anyone else 有自主权的人, 行动自由的人: *You're a free agent – you don't owe them anything.* 你是自由人—你不欠他们什么。

② COSTING NOTHING 免费的

9 costing nothing 免费的: *We were given a free lunch with lots of wine.* 我们吃了一顿免费的午餐, 喝了许多葡萄酒。| *The soft drinks are free, but you have to pay for the beer.* 软性饮料免费, 但啤酒你得付钱。| **a free gift** (=something you are given by a shop or company)〔商店或公司的〕赠品

10 a free ride something that you do not have to pay for, because someone else is paying for it 白白得到的(由别人付款的)东西: *Government employees are getting a free ride on taxpayers' money.* 政府雇员正白白得到用纳税人的钱支付的东西。

③ NOT A PRISONER 不是囚犯

11 not a prisoner 不受监禁的, 自由的: *The rapist could be free in as little as three years.* 这个强奸犯甚至可能只服刑三年就可以获得自由了。| **set sb free** (=give someone their freedom) 释放某人 *Mandela was finally set free in 1993.* 曼德拉在 1993年终于被释放。| **a free man** (=a man who was a prisoner)〔曾入狱的〕自由人

④ NOT BUSY 不忙的

12 if you are free, or have some free time, you have no work, and nothing else that you must do 空闲的; 不忙的: *Are you free next weekend?* 你下周末有空吗? | **a free day/morning/half-hour etc** *If you have a free afternoon, go and see this movie.* 如果你哪个下午有空, 该去看这部影片。| **free time** *I don't have enough free time during the week.* 我这星期没有足够的空闲时间。

⑤ NOT BEING USED 闲置的

13 something that you want to use is free if no one else is using it 闲置的, 空着的, 不在使用的: *There's a washing machine free, but you may have to wait for a dryer.* 有台洗衣机空着没人用, 不过用烘干机你可能得等着。

⑥ WITHOUT/NOT HAVE 没有

14 tax-free/duty-free etc without tax etc 免税的/免关税的等: *duty-free wine* 免税葡萄酒

15 lead-free/salt-free etc not containing lead, salt etc 无铅的/无盐的等: *lead-free petrol* 无铅汽油

16 free from/of sth without something that you do not want to have 无〔某种不想要的事物〕的: *free of obligations* 无义务的 | *free from disease* 无病的

17 free of sth/sb away from something or someone you are glad to be without 摆脱某物/某人: *I'm free of that place at last.* 我终于摆脱掉那个地方了。

⑦ NOT FIXED/ABLE TO MOVE 未固定的/能移动的

18 an action or movement that is free is graceful and not restricted 优美自如的: *a free swing of the arm* 手臂优美自如的一摆

19 loose and not fixed to anything 松动的; 未固定的: *The free end of the flag has been torn by the wind.* 旗子未固定的一端被风刮破了。

20 free hand/arm/leg etc the arm, leg etc that you are not already using 空着的手/臂/腿等: *With her free hand, she clung to the rope.* 她用空着的手紧紧抓住绳子。

21 *technical* not combined with any other simple chemical substance; pure【术语】游离的, 单体的: *free oxygen* 游离氧

⑧ OTHER MEANINGS 其他意思

22 *old-fashioned* too friendly, in a way that does not show enough respect【过时】过分亲近的; 不太有礼貌的; 过分随便的: *Your son's manner is rather free.* 你儿子的举止太随便了。

23 be free with to be generous with something 慷慨使用; 随意使用: *Mr. Leath is free with his money.* 利思先生花钱大手大脚。| *free with criticism* 随意批评人的

24 make free with to use something that belongs to someone else when you should not 擅自使用〔他人的物品〕: *I wonder if he knows that Jenny is making free with his money?* 我弄不清楚他是否知道珍妮正擅自花他的钱。

25 a translation that is free gives a general idea of a piece of writing rather than exactly translating every word〔翻译〕根据大意的, 非逐字逐句的

free[2] *v* [T] **1** to allow someone to leave prison or somewhere they have been kept by force; RELEASE[1] (1) 释放, 使自由: *Lincoln freed the slaves.* 林肯解放了奴隶。| *persuading the terrorists to free the hostages* 劝说恐怖分子释放人质 **2** to move or loosen something or someone that is fixed or trapped 救出, 使解脱出来: *After three hours the firemen freed her from the wreckage.* 三小时后消防队员把她从残骸中救出来。**3** also 又作 **free up** to make something available so that it can be used 腾

出; 使…可用: *This would free resources that are badly needed.* 这就会腾出急需的资源。**4** to help someone by removing something unpleasant 使〔某人〕解除; 使脱离: **[+from]** *They aim to free the country from its enormous debts.* 他们旨在解除这个国家的巨额债务。**5** to make someone no longer be restricted by unfair rules, a cruel government etc 解放: **[+from]** *marching to free the capital city from the rebels* 进军去解放叛乱分子控制的首都 **6** to help someone to do something, by removing restrictions or making them responsible for fewer things 使脱身; 使有时间: **free sb to do sth** *freeing teachers to concentrate on particular subjects* 让教师有时间专注某些科目 | **free sth** *Writing frees the imagination.* 写作能发挥想象力。

free[3] *adv* **1** without payment 免费地: *This card allows you to travel free for a month.* 这张卡能让你免费旅游一个月。| **for free** *They let me have these chillies for free.* 他们免费送我这些辣椒。| **free of charge** *You may park here free of charge after 6 p.m.* 下午六点后这里可以免费泊车。**2** not fixed or held in a particular place or position 不固定地; 松脱地: *The window had swung free in the wind.* 窗子被风吹得来回摆动。| **pull/struggle free** (=move to get away from somewhere) 拉出来/挣脱开 *Ken grabbed her around the waist, but she managed to struggle free.* 肯抓住她的腰, 可她设法挣脱开了。**3 break free** to escape from a place or a situation 挣脱, 逃脱: *At last he's broken free and started a new life in New York.* 他终于逃离, 在纽约开始新的生活。**4 run free** if an animal runs free it is allowed to go where it wants to, without being controlled〔动物〕乱跑, 自由走动: *a zoo where the animals can run free* 动物可以自由走动的动物园 **5 walk free** if a criminal walks free, they are not put in prison〔罪犯〕不受监禁; 逍遥法外 **6 I'll tell you that for free** *spoken* used to emphasize what you are saying, in an angry way【口】〔用于生气地强调所说的话〕我坦白告诉你: *I'm not going to offer to help you out again, I'll tell you that for free!* 我再也不会主动帮你了, 我坦白告诉你! —compare 比较 FREELY —see also 另见 SCOT-FREE

-free /fri; friː/ *suffix* [in adjectives and adverbs 构成形容词和副词] without something that you do not want 无…的: *a salt-free diet* 无盐饮食 | *a trouble-free journey* 无忧无虑的旅行 | *We bought the cigarettes duty-free.* 我们买了些免税香烟。| *They live in the house rent-free.* 他们住在这栋房子里, 免交房租。

free as·so·ci·a·tion /,· ···'·· / *n* [U] *technical* a method of finding out about someone's mind by asking them to say the first word they think of when you say a particular word【术语】自由联想〔让某人从听到的某个词中举出第一个联想到的词来, 以测验其心理活动〕

free·bie, freebee /ˈfribi; ˈfriːbiː/ *n* [C] *informal* something that you are given free, usually something small and not expensive【非正式】〔通常小而不值钱的〕免费物, 赠品

free·boot·er /ˈfriˌbutə; ˈfriːbuːtə/ *n* [C] someone who joins in a war in order to steal other people's goods and money〔参加战争的〕掠夺者; 海盗 —**freeboot** *v* [I]

free·born /ˈfriˌbɔrn; ˌfriːˈbɔːn◂/ *adj* not born as a slave 生来自由的, 自由民的

Free Church /,· '·◂/ any of the Protestant religious groups in the UK that are not part of the Church of England. The Free Churches include the Baptists, the Methodists, the United Reformed Church and the Church of Scotland.（英国）自由教会〔指（英国）国教会之外的任何新教宗教团体, 包括浸礼会、卫理公会、联合归正会和苏格兰长老会〕

Free Church of Scot·land, the /,· · · ·,· ·/ a small group of Protestant Christians mainly in the Highlands of Scotland, who are against any form of work on Sundays. Its members are sometimes called **wee frees**. 苏格兰自由教会〔主要分布于苏格兰高地的小型新教教会, 反对在星期天从事任何形式的工作。其成员有时称作 wee frees（极少数自由者）〕

free col·lec·tive bar·gain·ing /,· ····'··/ *n* [U] *BrE* talks between TRADE UNIONs and employers about pay or working conditions that are not controlled by law【英】〔劳资之间的〕自由集体谈判

2 **free·dom** /ˈfridəm; ˈfriːdəm/ *n* **1** [C,U] the right to do what
2 you want without being controlled or restricted by anyone 自由权利: *The protest is about the infringement of our democratic freedoms.* 抗议是针对我们的民主自由权利受到侵犯而举行的。| **freedom of speech/expression/choice etc** (=the legal right to choose, express yourself etc) 言论/表达/选择等的自由 *The journalists claimed they were being denied the right to freedom of expression.* 这些新闻记者声称他们正被剥夺自由表达的权利。**2** [U] the state of being free and allowed to do what you want 自由, 自主: *Kids have too much freedom these days.* 如今小孩子们太自由了。| **freedom to do sth** *Women have gained the freedom to decide whether or not to marry.* 女子已经能自主决定结婚还是不结婚。| **complete freedom** *The teachers are given complete freedom in their choice of teaching methods.* 教师可以完全自由地选择教学方法。**3** [U] the state of being free because you are not in prison 未受监禁, 在狱外: *One of the escaped prisoners was arrested again after only 48 hours of freedom.* 其中一个逃犯在越狱只有48小时后又被捕了。**4 freedom from** the state of not being affected by something that makes you worried, unhappy, afraid etc 从…中摆脱; 不受…之苦: *The new supplies will ensure temporary freedom from starvation and disease.* 新的供应品将保证能暂时摆脱饥饿和疾病。| *freedom from worry* 无忧无虑 **5 freedom of information** the availability to everyone of information that a government has about people and organizations 信息自由, 资讯自由; 知情权 **6 freedom of the city** an honour in Britain that gives someone the right to be a full member of a city〔英国的〕荣誉市民权 —compare 比较 LIBERTY

freedom fight·er /ˈ·· ,··/ *n* [C] someone who fights in a war against an unfair or dishonest government, army etc〔反对不公平或不诚实政府、军方等的〕自由战士 —compare 比较 GUERRILLA, TERRORIST

Freedom of In·for·ma·tion Act /,·· · ··'·· ,·/ a law that makes government information freely available to ordinary citizens and makes it illegal for government departments to keep information secret unless this is really necessary.《信息自由公开法案》〔该法规定, 普通公民可免费获取政府信息; 政府部门除非确有必要, 不得隐匿信息〕

free en·ter·prise /,· '···/ *n* [U] the principle and practice of allowing private business to operate without much government control 自由企业制 —see also 另见 PRIVATE ENTERPRISE

free-fall /ˈ· ·/ *n* [U] **1** part of a jump or fall from an aircraft that is made before the PARACHUTE[1] is opened〔降落伞打开前的〕自由降落 **2** a very fast and uncontrolled fall in the value of something〔某物价值的〕暴跌: **in free-fall** *The pound sterling was in free-fall.* 英镑在暴跌。—**free-falling** *adj*

free-float·ing /,· '··◂/ *adj* not connected to or influenced by anything 自由浮动的; 无联系的; 不受影响的: *free-floating anxiety* 无缘无故的忧虑

free-for-all /,· · ' ·/ *n* [singular] *informal* a noisy quarrel or fight that a lot of people join【非正式】大吵大闹; 群架; 混战: *Once a few people had been noticed stealing the supplies, there was a free-for-all.* 一旦发现有少数人在偷供应品, 便会出现一场哄抢。

Free French, the /,· '·/ *n* French people during World War II who opposed the Vichy government, because it was controlled by the Nazis, and who worked, mostly from outside France, to try and defeat it. Their leader was General de Gaulle.自由法国〔二战期间反对充当纳粹傀儡的维希政府的法国人。他们大多旅居海外, 致力于推翻傀儡政府的事业, 其首领是戴高乐将军〕—**Free French** *adj*

free·hand /ˈfriˌhænd; ˈfriːhænd/ *adj* drawn with your hand and a pen or pencil 徒手画的: *a freehand sketch* 徒手画的草图 —**freehand** *adv*

free·hold /ˈfriˌhold; ˈfriːhəʊld/ *n* [C,U] complete ownership of a building for an unlimited time〔土地或房产的〕终身保有权: *They've bought the freehold of their house.* 他们买下了房子的终身保有权。—**freehold** *adj*: *The flat is a freehold property.* 这套公寓是终身保有财产。—**freehold** *adv* —compare 比较 LEASEHOLD

free·hold·er /ˈfriˌholdə; ˈfriːhəʊldə/ *n* [C] an owner of freehold land or property〔土地或房产的〕终身保有者

free house /,· '·/ *n* [C] *BrE* a PUB that can buy beer from different companies, rather than being controlled by one company【英】可出售各种牌子啤酒的酒馆 —compare 比较 TIED HOUSE *BrE*【英】

free kick /,· '·/ *n* [C] a chance for one football team to kick the ball, when the other team has done something wrong〔足球的〕任意球, 自由球

free·lance /ˈfriˌlæns; ˈfriːlɑːns/ *adj, adv* working independently for several different companies or organizations rather than being directly employed by one 独立的[地]; 做自由职业者的[地]: *a freelance journalist* 自由职业记者 | *She's working freelance.* 她现在是自由职业者。—**freelance** *v* [I]: *He's freelancing for the BBC.* 他是英国广播公司的自由撰稿人。—**freelance** also 又作 **freelancer** *n* [C]

free·loader /ˈfriˌlodə; ˈfriːləʊdər/ *n* [C] *informal* someone who takes food, drink, etc from other people, without giving anything in return【非正式】白吃白喝的人; 占便宜的人 —**freeload** *v* [I]

free love /ˌ· ˈ·/ *n* [U] an expression meaning the practice or principle of having sex with people without being faithful to one person or without being married, used especially in the 1960s and 1970s〔尤指20世纪60年代和70年代的〕自由性爱; 自由性爱主义

free·ly /ˈfrilɪ; ˈfriːli/ *adv* **1** if you can travel, speak, operate etc freely, you can do it as much as you like and in whatever way you like 自由自在地: *In France he could write freely, without fear of arrest.* 在法国他可以自由地写作, 不用害怕会被捕。**2** without any restrictions on movement 自如地, 顺利地: *breathing freely* 自如地呼吸 | *She shook the pen so that the ink flowed more freely.* 她甩了一下钢笔, 使墨水能更顺畅地流出来。**3 freely admit/acknowledge** to agree that something is true, especially when this is difficult 坦率地承认: *I freely admit I made many mistakes.* 我坦率地承认我曾犯过许多错误。**4** if a piece of writing is translated freely, the translation does not attempt to translate the original words exactly, but gives a general meaning 根据大意地〔翻译〕**5 freely available** very easy to obtain 随手可得到的: *The two research groups are making their findings freely available to each other.* 那两个研究小组正自由地相互交换研究成果。**6** generously, or in large quantities 慷慨地; 大量地: *Promises were freely given that prices would be low.* 有人作出慷慨的承诺, 说价格会下降。

free·man /ˈfrimən; ˈfriːmən/ *n* [C] someone who is not a slave 自由民, 生来并非奴隶的人

free mar·ket /ˌ· ˈ··/ *n* [C] **1** *technical* a market on the STOCK EXCHANGE in business shares (SHARE² (5)) in which the prices are not controlled or fixed【术语】〔证券交易的〕自由市场 **2** a situation in which prices are not controlled or limited in any way〔价格不受控制或限制的〕自由市场

free mar·ket e·con·o·my /ˌ· ˌ·· ·ˈ···/ *n* [C] a system of trade in which prices are allowed to rise and fall without being restricted by the government 自由市场经济

free mar·ket·eer /ˌ· ··ˈ·/ *n* [C] someone who thinks that prices should be allowed to rise and fall naturally and should not be fixed by the government 支持自由市场经济的人

Free·ma·son /ˈfriˌmesn̩; ˈfriːˌmeɪsən/ *n* [C] a man who belongs to a secret society, in which each member helps the other members to become successful 共济会成员

Free·ma·son·ry /ˈfriˌmesn̩rɪ; ˈfriːmeɪsənri/ *n* [U] the system and practices of Freemasons 共济会制度及活动

free par·don /ˌ· ˈ··/ *n* [C] *law* the official act of forgiving someone for a crime【法律】特赦, 赦免

free pe·ri·od /ˌ· ˈ···/ *n* [C] a period of time in a school day when a student does not have a class〔学校里的〕自修课, 自由活动课

free·phone /ˈfrifon; ˈfriːfəʊn/ *n* [U] *BrE* an arrangement by which a company or organization pays the cost of telephone calls made to it【英】免费电话, 对方付费电话〔由接电话的公司或组织支付电话费的办法〕

free port /ˌ· ˈ·/ *n* [C] a port where goods from all countries can be brought in and taken out without being taxed 自由港; 免税港

free·post /ˈfripost; ˈfriːpəʊst/ *n* [U] *BrE* an arrangement by which a company or organization pays the cost of letters that you send to it by post【英】免费邮递, 收件方付邮资邮递〔由收信的公司或组织付邮资的邮递办法〕

Free Pres·by·te·ri·an Church of Scot·land, the /ˌ· ···ˌ··· ˌ· · ˈ··/ a small group of Protestant Christians mainly in the Highlands of Scotland. It has similar views to the Free Church of Scotland, especially in connection with keeping Sunday for study of the Bible and worship of God. 苏格兰自由长老会〔分布于苏格兰高地的小型新教教会, 与苏格兰自由教会的教义相似, 尤其在坚持星期天读经拜神的教规方面相似〕

free-range /ˌ· ˈ·◂/ *adj* **1** farm animals that are free-range are not kept in small CAGES but are allowed to move around in a large enclosed area 放养的, 散养的: *free-range hens* 放养的母鸡 **2** food that is free-range comes from these farm animals 由放养的家禽产下的: *free-range eggs* 放养鸡生的蛋 —compare 比较 BATTERY (2)

free·si·a /ˈfriʒɪə; ˈfriːziə/ *n* [C] a plant with pleasant smelling flowers 小苍兰

free·stand·ing /ˈfriˈstændɪŋ; ˌfriːˈstændɪŋ◂/ *adj* standing alone without being fixed to a frame, wall, or other support 独立式的; 非附属的; 自力撑持的

Free State, the /ˈ· ˌ·/ a PROVINCE of South Africa, in the area south of Johannesburg and west of Lesotho, whose capital city is Bloemfontein. It used to be called the **Orange Free State** and it was an independent state in the 19th century, but became part of South Africa after the Boer War of 1899-1902. 自由邦〔南非一省。位于约翰内斯堡以南, 莱索托以西。首府: 布隆方丹。过去曾称为奥兰治自由邦, 19世纪原是一个独立的国家, 1899至1902年的布尔战争后成为南非的一部分〕

free·style /ˈfriˌstaɪl; ˈfriːstaɪl/ *n* [U] a competition in which swimmers use the CRAWL² (2) method of swimming 自由式〔游泳〕: *the 100m freestyle* 100米自由泳比赛

free·think·er /ˌfriˈθɪŋkɚ; ˌfriːˈθɪŋkə/ *n* [C] someone who has their own opinions, ideas, and beliefs, rather than accepting other people's 思想自由的人, 自由思想家 —**freethinking** *adj*

Free·town /ˈfritaʊn; ˈfriːtaʊn/ the capital city and main port of Sierra Leone, on the Atlantic coast of West Africa 弗里敦〔塞拉利昂首都、主要港口, 位于西非的大西洋沿岸〕

free trade /ˌ· ˈ·◂/ *n* [U] a situation in which the goods coming into or going out of a country are not controlled or taxed 自由贸易

free verse /ˌ· ˈ·/ *n* [U] poetry that does not have a fixed structure〔无固定格律的〕自由诗 —compare 比较 BLANK VERSE

free·way /ˈfriˌwe; ˈfriːweɪ/ *n* [C] *AmE* a very wide road in the US, usually in cities, built for fast travel【美】高速公路: *the Ventura freeway*〔通往〕文图拉〔市的〕高速公路 —compare 比较 MOTORWAY, EXPRESSWAY, HIGHWAY (1)

free·wheel /friˈhwil; ˌfriːˈwiːl/ *v* [I] to ride a bicycle or drive a vehicle downhill, without using power from your legs or the engine〔骑自行车或开汽车下坡时〕靠惯性滑行

free·wheel·ing /ˈfriˈhwilɪŋ; ˌfriːˈwiːlɪŋ◂/ *adj informal* not worried about rules or what will happen in the future【非正式】随心所欲的; 不考虑规章[后果]的: *A lot of the girls envied me my independent, freewheeling life.* 许多女孩子羡慕我的那种独立自主、随心所欲的生活。

free will /ˌ· ˈ·/ *n* [U] **1 do sth of your own free will** to do something because you want to, not because someone else has forced you to 自愿做某事: *He went of his own free will.* 他是自愿去的。**2** the belief that human effort rather than God or FATE (2) can affect what happens in life 自由意志论

freeze¹ /friz; friːz/ *v past tense* **froze** /froz; frəʊz/ *past participle* **frozen** /ˈfrozn̩; ˈfrəʊzən/

1 ▶LIQUID 液体◀ [I,T] if a liquid freezes, or something freezes it, it becomes hard and solid because the temperature is very cold〔使〕结冰; 凝固: *The water at the edge of the lake froze last night.* 湖边的水昨晚结冰了。| **freeze sth** *The cold weather can even freeze petrol in car engines.* 寒冷的天气甚至能使汽车发动机里的汽油凝固。—compare 比较 MELT (1), THAW¹ (1)

2 ▶EARTH 土地◀ [I,T] if something such as earth that contains liquid freezes, or something freezes it, it becomes hard because of cold temperatures〔使〕冻硬; 〔使〕封冻: *The ground was frozen under the thin snow.* 地面在这层薄雪的覆盖下都冻硬了。

3 ▶MACHINE/ENGINE 机器/发动机◀ also 又作 **freeze up** [I,T] if a machine, engine, pipe etc freezes, or something freezes it, the liquid inside it becomes solid with cold, so that it does not work properly〔使〕冻住; 〔使〕冻到不能正常运转: *The water pipes have frozen up.* 水管已经冻住了。

4 ▶FOOD 食品◀ [I,T] to make food extremely cold so that you can preserve it for a long time, or to be able to be preserved in this way 冷藏, 冷冻; 适合冷藏: *I'm going to freeze some of these beans.* 我打算把一些豆冷藏起来。| *Tomatoes don't freeze well.* 番茄不宜冷冻。

5 it's freezing *spoken* used to say that the temperature is extremely cold【口】太冷了: *It's freezing in here – can't we shut a few windows?* 这里面太冷了, 我们就不能关几扇窗子吗? —see 见 COLD¹ (USAGE)

6 ▶FEEL COLD 感到寒冷◀ [I] *spoken* if someone freezes, they feel very cold【口】感到很冷; 冻僵: *You'll freeze if you don't put a coat on.* 如果不穿上大衣, 你会冻僵的。| **freeze to death** *spoken* (=feel extremely cold)【口】冷得要死 *Come inside, you must be freezing to death.* 进来, 你一定冷得要死了吧。

7 ▶WAGES/PRICES 工资/价格◀ [T] if a government or company freezes wages, prices etc, they do not increase them, and keep them at a particular level〔使〕冻结〔在某种水平上〕: *Student grants were frozen at 1989 levels.* 学生助学金冻结在1989年的水平。

8 ▶MONEY/PROPERTY 钱/财产◀ [T] to legally prevent money in a bank from being spent, property from being sold etc 冻结〔存款、财产〕: *The court froze their assets.* 法庭冻结了他们的资产。

9 ▶STOP MOVING 停止移动◀ [I] to stop moving suddenly and stay completely still and quiet 突然停止; 呆住: *I froze and listened; someone was in my apartment.* 我站住不动地听着; 有

人在我的公寓里。| *"Freeze! Drop your weapons!" shouted Officer Greer.* "不许动！放下武器！"格里尔警官高声喊道。

10 freeze to death to become so cold that you die 冷死，冻死

freeze sb **out** *phr v* [T] to deliberately prevent someone from being involved in something, by making it difficult for them, being unkind to them etc〔通过刁难或用冷淡的态度等〕不让〔某人〕参加；把〔某人〕排除在外：*You've got to stop freezing me out of the decision-making.* 你不可以再继续不让我参与决策。

freeze over *phr v* [I] if an area or pool of water freezes over, its surface turns into ice 表面结冰，封冻：*We'll go skating if the lake has frozen over.* 如果湖面结了冰，我们就去溜冰。

freeze[2] *n* **1** [C] a fixing of wages, prices etc at a particular level〔工资、价格等的〕冻结：*pay freezes* 工资冻结 **2** [C] a stopping of some activity〔活动〕停止：[**+on**] *a freeze on production* 停产 **3** *BrE* [singular] a period of extremely cold weather【英】严寒期 **4** *AmE* a short period of time, especially at night, when the temperature is extremely low【美】〔尤指夜间的〕短时间的天寒地冻 —see also 另见 DEEP FREEZE

freeze-dry /ˌ· ˈ·◂/ *v* [T] to preserve food or drink by freezing and drying it very quickly 使冷冻干燥〔以保存食物或饮料〕：*freeze-dried coffee* 冷冻干燥的咖啡

freeze-frame /ˈ· ,·/ *n* [U] the process of stopping the action on a moving film at one particular place〔电影的〕定格，定帧：*Press the freeze-frame button on the video.* 按录像机上的定格按钮。—**freeze-frame** *v* [T]

freez·er /ˈfrizɚ; ˈfriːzə/ *n* [C] **1** a large machine in which food can be stored at very low temperatures for a long time; DEEP FREEZE 冷藏箱，冷冻柜，冰柜 —see picture on page A10 参见A10页图 **2** *AmE* a part of a FRIDGE in which food can be stored at very low temperatures for a long time【美】〔冰箱中的〕冷冻室，冰冻格 —compare 比较 FRIDGE

freez·ing /ˈfrizɪŋ; ˈfriːzɪŋ/ *n* [U] **above/below freezing** above or below the temperature at which water freezes 在冰点以上/以下：*It was well below freezing when we left.* 我们离开时气温已降到冰点以下了。

freezing com·part·ment /ˈ··· ,··/ *n* [C] a part of a FRIDGE in which food can be stored at very low temperatures for a long time〔冰箱中的〕冷冻室，冰冻格

freez·ing point /ˈ·· ,·/ *n* **1** [U] the temperature at which water turns into ice 冰点 **2** [C usually singular 一般用单数] the temperature at which a particular liquid freezes〔液体的〕结冰点，凝固点：*Alcohol has a lower freezing point than water.* 酒精的结冰点比水低。—compare 比较 BOILING POINT

freight[1] /fret; freɪt/ *n* **1** [U] goods that are carried by ship, train, or aircraft〔船、火车或飞机运载的〕货物；货运：*freight containers* 货柜 **2** [C] *AmE* a FREIGHT TRAIN【美】货运列车；集装箱列车

freight[2] *v* [T] to send goods by air, sea, or train〔用飞机、轮船或火车〕运送，托运〔货物〕

freight·er /ˈfretɚ; ˈfreɪtə/ *n* [C] a ship or aircraft that carries goods 货船；运货飞机

freight·lin·er /ˈfret,laɪnɚ; ˈfreɪt,laɪnə/ *n* [C] *especially BrE* a train that carries large amounts of goods in special containers【尤英】集装箱货运列车

freight train /ˈ· ·/ *n* [C] a train that carries goods 货运列车；集装箱列车

Fré·mont /ˈfrimɑnt; ˈfriːmɒnt/**, John C.** (1813-90) a US soldier, politician, and EXPLORER, who was called 'The Pathfinder' because he travelled across the western part of North America and made maps of this area. He encouraged US citizens to move to these places, which are now the states of Idaho, Nevada, Washington, Oregon, and California. 弗里蒙特（1813-1890），美国军人、政治家、探险家。他曾穿越北美西部地区，并绘制了该地区的地图，故有"寻路者"之称。他鼓励美国公民移居到该地区，即现在的爱达荷州、内华达州、华盛顿州、俄勒冈州和加利福尼亚州）

French[1] /frɛntʃ; frentʃ/ *n* **1** the language of France, and some other countries 法语：*How do you ask for directions in French?* 你怎样用法语问路？**2** the language and literature of France as a subject of study 法国语言文学：*She's studying French at London University.* 她在伦敦大学学习法国语言文学。**3 the French** the people of France 法国人：*The French celebrate 14th July.* 法国人庆祝7月14日国庆节。

French[2] *adj* **1** belonging to or involved with France or its people 法国的；法国人的：*an excellent French wine* 一种极好的法国葡萄酒 **2** belonging to or involved with the French language 法语的：*an introduction to French grammar* 法语语法入门 **3 take French leave** to leave your job without permission 未经许可离开工作，擅离职守，擅自旷工[缺席，缺勤] **4 pardon/excuse my French** *spoken* used to say sorry for swearing【口】原谅我的粗话，请原谅我言辞不恭

French and In·di·an War, the /ˌ· · ˌ··· ˈ·/ the name for several battles that took place in North America between the French and the British in the mid-18th century, before the American Revolutionary War 法国印第安人战争〔指18世纪中期，也就是美国独立战争之前法国与英国在北美进行的战争〕

French An·til·les, the /ˌfrɛntʃ ænˈtɪliz; ˌfrentʃ ænˈtɪliːz/ a group of islands in the Caribbean Sea which belong to France 法属安的列斯群岛〔加勒比海一群岛，归属法国〕

French bean /ˌ· ˈ·/ *n* [C] *BrE* a bean with a long green case that is picked when it is young and soft; GREEN BEAN【英】青菜豆

French bread /ˌ· ˈ·/ *n* [U] white bread in the shape of a thick stick 法式长条面包

French chalk /ˌ· ˈ·/ *n* [U] CHALK[1] (2) used for drawing lines on cloth when making clothes〔做衣服时在布上画线的〕滑石，画粉

French doors /ˈ· ,·/ *n* [plural] *especially AmE* FRENCH WINDOWS【尤美】落地窗，落地玻璃门

French dress·ing /ˌ· ˈ··/ *n* [U] a mixture of oil and VINEGAR that is put on raw vegetables〔用油和醋调制成的〕色拉调料

French fry /ˌ· ˈ·/ *n* [C usually plural 一般用复数] *especially AmE* a long thin piece of potato cooked in fat【尤美】炸马铃薯条，炸薯条；CHIP[1] (3a) *BrE*【英】

French Gui·a·na /ˌfrɛntʃ giˈænə; ˌfrentʃ giˈɑːnə/ a country in northeast South America which is a department of France. Population: 177,562 (2001). Capital: Cayenne. 法属圭亚那〔南美洲东北部一国家，为法国一行政区。人口：177,562（2001），首府：卡宴〕

French horn /ˌ· ˈ·/ *n* [C] a HORN[1] (4), that is shaped like a circle, with a wide bell-like opening 法国号，圆号

French kiss /ˌ· ˈ·/ *n* [C] a kiss made with your mouths open and with your tongues touching〔将舌头伸入对方嘴内的〕法式接吻，湿吻，舌吻

French let·ter /ˌ· ˈ··/ *n* [C] *informal old-fashioned* a CONDOM【非正式，过时】避孕套，阴茎套

French loaf /ˌ· ˈ·/ *n* [C] *BrE* a long thin white LOAF of bread; FRENCH STICK【英】法式长条面包

French·man /ˈfrɛntʃmən; ˈfrentʃmən/ *n plural* **Frenchmen** /-mən; -mən/ [C] a man born in France or one who has French parents 法国人

French pol·ish /ˌ· ˈ··/ *n* [U] a clear liquid put on wooden furniture to protect it and make it shine 罩光漆，亮光漆

French Pol·y·ne·si·a /ˌ· ··ˈ···/ about 130 islands in the southern Pacific Ocean, including Tahiti, which belong to France. Population: 253,506 (2001). Capital: Papeete. 法属波利尼西亚〔南太平洋中由塔希提岛等大约130个岛屿组成的法国海外领地。人口：253,506（2001），首府：帕皮提〕

French Quar·ter, the /ˈ· ,··/ a part of the city of New Orleans in Louisiana, US, which was originally lived in by French people. Many tourists now go there. 法国人居住区〔美国路易斯安那州新奥尔良市一区域。最初为法国人居住，现有不少游人前去参观〕

French Rev·o·lu·tion, the /ˌ· ···ˈ··/ the REVOLUTION which began in France in 1789. The French king and queen, and many other people of high rank were killed and France became a REPUBLIC (=a country without a king or queen). The events and ideas of the revolution had an important influence on European history. 法国大革命〔1789年始于法国的一场革命。法国国王、王后以及许多高官被处决，法国成为一个共和国。大革命时期的事件和思想对欧洲历史有着重要影响〕

French Riv·i·e·ra, the /ˌ· ··ˈ··/ also 又作 **the Riviera** an area of southeastern France on the coast of the Mediterranean Sea, which includes places such as Nice, Cannes, and St Tropez. Many rich and fashionable people live on or visit the French Riviera. 法国里维埃拉〔法国东南部地中海沿岸一地区，包括尼斯、戛纳和圣特罗佩等。许多富有的时尚人士在该地居住或前去游览〕：*They rented a villa on the French Riviera.* 他在法国里维埃拉租住了一幢别墅。—see also 另见 SOUTH OF FRANCE

French seam /ˌ· ˈ·/ *n* [C] a double SEAM (1) used when making clothes, which hides the edges that have been cut 法式线缝，来去线缝

French stick /ˌ· ˈ·/ *n* [C] a long thin white LOAF of bread 法式长条面包

French toast /ˌ· ˈ·/ *n* [U] pieces of bread put into a mixture of egg and milk and then cooked in hot oil 法式炸面包片

French West In·dies, the /ˌ· ·ˈ··/ another name for the French Antilles 法属西印度群岛〔法属安的列斯群岛的别称〕

F

French win·dows /ˌ· ˈ··/ *n* [plural] a pair of light doors made of glass in a frame, usually opening out on to a garden or BALCONY (1) 落地窗，落地玻璃门

French·wom·an /ˈfrɛntʃˌwumən; ˈfrentʃˌwʊmən/ *n plural* **Frenchwomen** /-ˌwɪmɪn; -ˌwɪmɪn/ [C] a woman born in France or one who has French parents 法国女子

fre·net·ic /frəˈnɛtɪk; frɪ̀ˈnetɪk/ *adj* frenetic actions are very fast, uncontrolled and excited 疯狂的；狂热的；激动的：*a frenetic departure* 发疯似的离去

fren·zied /ˈfrɛnzɪd; ˈfrenzid/ *adj* frenzied activity is done with a lot of anxiety or excitement and not much organization or control 狂乱的；疯狂似的；异常激动的：*frenzied efforts to find a solution* 发疯似地努力寻求解决办法 —**frenziedly** *adv*

fren·zy /ˈfrɛnzɪ; ˈfrenzi/ *n* [C,U] **1** a state of uncontrolled excitement or emotion 疯狂似的激动；疯狂；狂热：*religious frenzies* 宗教狂热 | **in a frenzy** *She pleaded with them in a frenzy to release her son.* 她发疯似地祈求他们释放她的儿子。| **a frenzy of passion/remorse etc** *They fell into a frenzy of helpless alarm at the news.* 听到这个消息，他们不知所措，惊恐万状。**2 a frenzy of preparation/activity etc** a period of sudden energetic activity 一阵慌乱的准备／一阵活跃等：*The house was in a frenzy of activity as my aunts prepared for the wedding.* 我的姑姑们在筹备这次婚礼时，家里出现一片无比热闹的景象。

adverbs of frequency 频率副词

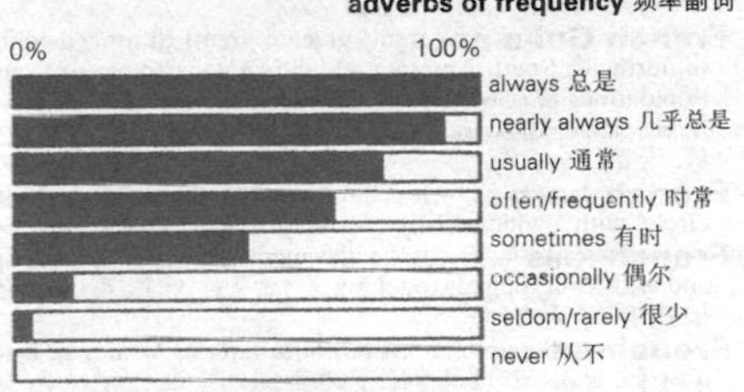

3 **fre·quen·cy** /ˈfrikwənsɪ; ˈfriːkwənsi/ *n* **1** [U] the number of times that something happens 发生的次数，发生率：**[+of]** *The frequency of mining accidents has steadily decreased over the past 20 years.* 采矿事故发生的频率在过去的20年里已逐步降低。| **high/low frequency** (=happening very often or not often) 高／低发生率 *The high frequency of cases of diarrhoea is because of poor hygiene.* 腹泻病例发生频繁是由于卫生差引起的。| **with increasing frequency** (=more and more often) 越来越频繁地 **2** [U] the fact that something happens a lot 频繁：*We are concerned about the frequency of crime in the area.* 我们对该地区频繁的犯罪活动感到担心。**3** [C] *technical* the number of radio waves for every second that a radio signal is broadcast【术语】〔无线电广播每秒钟的〕频率，周率：*This station broadcasts on three different frequencies.* 这个电台以三种不同的频率广播。**4** [C,U] the rate at which a sound WAVE² (4) moves up and down〔声波的〕振动频率：**high/low frequency** (=sounding high or low) 高／低频率 *The whistle is of such a high frequency the human ear cannot detect it.* 这种哨声频率很高，人耳觉察不出来。

3 **fre·quent¹** /ˈfrikwənt; ˈfriːkwənt/ *adj* happening often 经常发生的，频繁的：*I try to maintain frequent contact with my children.* 我尽可能和我的孩子经常保持联系。| *Her headaches are becoming less frequent.* 她不那么经常头痛了。| **a frequent visitor/user/correspondent etc** (=someone who often visits, uses something etc) 常客／长期用户／经常通信的人 *The Governor became a frequent visitor.* 总督成了常客。—opposite 反义词 INFREQUENT —see picture at 参见 FREQUENCY 图

fre·quent² /frɪˈkwɛnt; frɪˈkwent/ *v* [T] *formal* to go to a particular place often【正式】常去，常到〔某地方〕：*The bar was frequented by actors from the nearby theatre.* 这家酒吧是附近剧院的演员们经常光顾的地方。

3 2 **frequently** /ˈfrikwəntlɪ; ˈfriːkwəntli/ *adv* very often or many times 经常地，频繁地：*Sperm whales frequently dive to search for squid.* 抹香鲸经常潜入水中寻找鱿鱼。

fres·co /ˈfrɛsko; ˈfreskəʊ/ *n* [C] a painting made on a wall by using WATERCOLOUR paint on a surface of wet PLASTER¹ (1)〔用水彩颜料在湿灰浆墙面上画的〕湿壁画 —compare 比较 MURAL

2 2 **fresh** /frɛʃ; freʃ/ *adj*

1 ►NEW 新的◄ new or recently made, added etc to replace something or add to it 新的；新做的；新增的：*I'll just make some fresh coffee.* 我就新煮点咖啡吧。| *There's been no fresh news of the fighting since yesterday.* 自昨天起就没有关于战斗的新消息了。| **a fresh attempt/look/approach etc** (=done again in a new way) 再次努力／重新看／新方法等 *We need to have a fresh look at the problem.* 我们得重新看一看这个问题。| **fresh information/evidence/facts** (=new facts etc that change a situation) 新信息／新证据／新事实等：*This fresh evidence may prove his innocence.* 这项新的证据可能证明他是无辜的。| **a fresh sheet/copy/page/towel etc** (=clean, new, and not used before) 新的床单／副本／一页／毛巾等 *You'll have to start again on a fresh sheet of paper.* 你得拿一张白纸重新再画。

2 ►FOOD/FLOWERS 食品/花◄ a) fresh food is good because it was very recently produced, picked, or prepared 新鲜的：*Let's eat the bread while it's still fresh.* 我们趁面包还新鲜把它吃了吧。| *Did you get fresh or frozen peas?* 你买的是新鲜的还是冷冻的豌豆？| **fresh from the oven/sea/garden etc** *The beans are picked fresh from the garden.* 这些豆是刚从菜园里摘来的。**b)** fresh flowers have recently been picked〔花〕新摘的

3 ►COOL/CLEAN 凉快的/干净的◄ looking, feeling or tasting pleasantly clean or cool 凉爽的，清新的：*the fresh coolness of the air after rain* 雨后空气的清新凉爽 | *a fresh clean taste* 清新的味道

4 ►NOT TIRED 不疲倦的◄ full of energy because you are not tired 精神饱满的，精力充沛的：*Somehow she managed to seem fresh and lively even at the end of the day.* 即使是在一天将过去的时候，她还是设法显得神清气爽，很有活力。

5 fresh air air that is outside a building or town, and is cleaner〔室外或城外的〕新鲜空气：*Let's open the windows and have some fresh air in here!* 我们打开窗户，放点新鲜空气进来吧！

6 fresh from/fresh out of sth having just finished your education or training, and not having a lot of experience 刚从某处毕业〔经验不多〕的：*a pleasant young man, fresh from university* 刚从大学毕业、举止文雅的年轻人

7 ►WEATHER 天气◄ wind or weather that is fresh is cold〔风、天气〕凉的：*It's a bit fresh today.* 今天有点凉。

8 ►WATER 水◄ fresh water contains no salt〔水〕淡的

9 be fresh out of sth *AmE spoken* to have just used your last supplies of something【美口】刚用尽某物：*I'm fresh out of cough drops – I'll have to stop at the drug store.* 我刚吃光了止咳糖——我得在药店停一下。

10 a fresh complexion healthy-looking skin on your face〔脸上的〕好气色，健康肤色

11 fresh-made/fresh-cut/fresh-grated *especially AmE* having just been made, cut etc【尤美】新做的／新切的／新磨碎的：*fresh-ground coffee* 新磨的咖啡 —see also 另见 FRESHLY

12 fresh as a daisy *informal* not tired and ready to do things【非正式】精神饱满的

13 fresh in your/their mind recent enough to be remembered clearly〔刚过去不久因而〕记忆犹新的：*She wants to write about her visit while it's still fresh in her mind.* 她想趁记忆犹新的时候把她的这次参观感受写下来。

14 make a fresh start to start something again in a completely new and different way after being unsuccessful 从头开始，重新开始：*After the accident, they decided to make a fresh start in another town.* 事故之后他们决定在另一个城镇从头开始。

15 get/be fresh with sb a) to behave or speak rudely or without respect for someone 对某人放肆[无礼]：*Don't you get fresh with me, son!* 别对我无礼，儿子！**b)** to show someone in a rudely confident way that you think they are sexually attractive 对某人说不规矩的话／动手动脚：*He started getting fresh with me.* 他开始对我不规矩。—**freshness** *n* [U]

fresh·en /ˈfrɛʃən; ˈfreʃən/ *v* **1** [T] also 又作 **freshen up** to make something look clean, new, and attractive, or smell pleasant 使干净；使面目一新；使吸引人；使气味清新：*I think I'll freshen up the paintwork in the bathroom.* 我想我得将浴室里的油漆刷新一遍。**2** to make something feel cool 使感觉凉快：*Freshen your skin with avocado body lotion.* 用鳄梨润肤露凉快凉快皮肤吧。**3** [I] if wind or the weather freshens, it gets colder〔风、天气〕变凉

freshen (sb ↔) **up** *phr v* [I,T] to wash your hands and face in order to feel clean and comfortable 梳洗：*He hurried into the bathroom to freshen up before the meeting.* 他在开会前急忙进浴室梳洗一下。

fresh·er /ˈfrɛʃə; ˈfreʃə/ *n* [C] *BrE* a student who has just started at a college or university【英】〔学院或大学的〕一年级新生：*a freshers' party* 一年级新生聚会

fresh-faced /ˌ· ˈ·/ *adj* having a young, healthy-looking face 气色好的：*a fresh-faced youth* 气色好的年轻人

fresh·ly /ˈfrɛʃlɪ; ˈfreʃli/ *adv* **freshly ground/picked/made etc** recently ground, picked, made etc 新磨的／新摘的／新做的等：*freshly ground pepper* 新磨的胡椒粉

fresh·man /ˈfrɛʃmən; ˈfreʃmən/ *n* [C] *AmE* a student in the first year of HIGH SCHOOL or university【美】〔高中或大学的〕一年级学生

fresh·wa·ter /ˈfrɛʃˌwɔtɚ; ˈfreʃwɔːtə/ *adj* **1** having water that contains no salt 淡水的: *freshwater lakes* 淡水湖 **2** living in water that contains no salt 生活在淡水中的: *freshwater crabs* 淡水蟹 —compare 比较 SALTWATER

fret[1] /frɛt; fret/ *v* **fretted, fretting** **1** [I,T] *especially spoken* to feel worried about small or unimportant things, or to make someone feel like this【尤口】(使) 烦恼, (使) 发愁: *Don't you fret – everything will be all right.* 别烦恼——一切都会好的。| [+about/over] *Nicki was always fretting over something or other.* 尼基总是在为这为那发愁。**2** [T] to make something gradually smaller and weaker by rubbing it over a long period of time 磨细; 磨损

fret[2] *n* **1** [C] one of the raised lines on the NECK (=long straight part) of a VIOLIN, GUITAR etc〔小提琴、吉他等定音的〕品, 柱, 马 **2 be/get in a fret** *BrE informal* to become worried or anxious about something【英, 非正式】焦虑不安: *Aunt Joan always gets in a fret if we're late.* 如果我们迟到, 琼姑姑总是焦虑不安。

fret·ful /ˈfrɛtfəl; ˈfretfəl/ *adj* anxious and complaining, especially about small or unimportant things〔尤指为无足轻重的事〕烦恼的; 发牢骚的: *The child was tired and fretful.* 这孩子又疲倦又烦躁不安。—**fretfully** *adv* —**fretfulness** *n* [U]

fret·ted /ˈfrɛtɪd; ˈfretɪ̈d/ *adj* cut or shaped into complicated patterns as decoration 刻成回纹[万字]图案的

fret·work /ˈfrɛtˌwɝk; ˈfretwɜːk/ *n* [U] patterns cut into thin wood, or the activity of making these patterns 回纹格子细工, 万字浮雕细工

Freud /frɔɪd; frɔɪd/, **Sig·mund** /ˈsɪgmənd; ˈsɪgmənd/ (1856-1939) an Austrian doctor who developed a new system for understanding the way that people's minds work, and a new way of treating mental illness called PSYCHOANALYSIS. He believed that the bad experiences that people have as children can affect their mental health as adults, and that by talking to a mentally ill person about their past life and feelings, the hidden causes of their illness can be found. He wrote *The Interpretation of Dreams* and *The Ego and the Id*. His ideas, especially about the importance of sex, had a very great influence on the way that people thought in the 20th century. 弗洛伊德〔(1856-1939), 奥地利医生。他提出理解人的思维方式的新体系与治疗心理疾病的新方法, 即精神分析法。他认为孩提时代的可怕经历会影响到成年后的心理健康, 与心理疾病患者谈论过去的生活和感情, 可发现其内在的病因。他著有《释梦》和《自我与本我》。他的思想, 尤其是关于性的重要性的思想, 对20世纪的人类思维方式产生了巨大影响〕

Freud·i·an /ˈfrɔɪdɪən; ˈfrɔɪdiən/ *adj* **1** connected with or according to Sigmund Freud's ideas about the way the mind works, and the way it can be studied 弗洛伊德学说的; 根据弗洛伊德学说的 **2** a Freudian remark or action is connected with the ideas about sex that people have in their minds but do not usually talk about〔言语或行动〕与性压抑有关的

Freudian slip /ˌ‥ ˈ·/ *n* [C] something you say that is different from what you intended to say, and shows your true thoughts〔泄露真实想法的〕漏嘴, 口误, 失言

Fri the written abbreviation of 缩写= FRIDAY

fri·a·ble /ˈfraɪəbl̩; ˈfraɪəbəl/ *adj technical* friable rocks or soil are easily broken into very small pieces or into powder【术语】脆的; 易碎的

fri·ar /ˈfraɪɚ; ˈfraɪə/ *n* [C] a man who belongs to a Christian group, whose members in the past travelled around teaching about Christianity and asking for money and food〔古时基督教的〕托钵修士; 云游传道修士 —compare 比较 MONK

Fri·ar Tuck /ˌ‥ ˈ·/ a fat and cheerful MONK (=a member of an all-male religious group), who enjoys eating and drinking, and appears in old English stories about Robin Hood as one of his followers 塔克修士〔一位肥胖而快乐的男修士, 喜欢吃喝, 见于英格兰的罗宾汉传奇故事之中, 是罗宾汉的一个同伴〕

fric·as·see /ˌfrɪkəˈsi; ˈfrɪkəseɪ/ *n* [C,U] a dish made of small pieces of meat in a thick white SAUCE (1) 原汁煨肉块

fric·a·tive /ˈfrɪkətɪv; ˈfrɪkətɪv/ *n* [C] a sound, such as /f/ or /z/, made by forcing your breath through a narrow opening between your lips, or between your tongue and your lips or teeth 摩擦音〈如/f/或/z/〉

fric·tion /ˈfrɪkʃən; ˈfrɪkʃən/ *n* [U] **1** disagreement, angry feelings, or unfriendliness between people〔人们之间的〕不合, 冲突: **cause/create friction** *Restrictions on trade have caused friction between these two nations.* 贸易限制已经引起了两国之间的冲突。**2** the rubbing of one surface against another 摩擦: *Check your rope frequently, as friction against the rock can wear it down.* 要经常检查绳索, 因为与岩石摩擦会使它磨损。**3** in science, friction is the natural law that prevents one surface from sliding easily over another surface 摩擦力: *Heat can be produced by chemical reactions or friction.* 热可由化学反应或摩擦力产生。

Fri·day /ˈfraɪdɪ; ˈfraɪdi/ written abbreviation 缩写为 **Fri** *n* [C, U] the day between Thursday and Saturday. In Britain, Friday is considered the fifth day of the week, and in the US it is considered the sixth day of the week 星期五〔在英国, 星期五被认为是一周的第五天; 在美国则被认为是第六天〕: *Mom said she mailed the letter last Friday.* 妈妈说她在上星期五把信寄出了。| **on Friday** *The committee meeting is on Friday.* 委员会的会议在星期五举行。| **on a Friday** *My birthday is on a Friday this year.* 我今年的生日是在星期五。| **Friday morning/evening etc** *Can you meet me Friday morning?* 星期五上午你能来接我吗? | **on Fridays** (=each Friday) 每星期五 | **the Friday** *BrE* (=the Friday of the week being mentioned)【英】(所说到的) 那个星期五 *Mr Jones flew in on the Friday and left on the following Wednesday.* 琼斯先生在星期五乘飞机来, 在接下来的星期三离开。

fridge /frɪdʒ; frɪdʒ/ *n* [C] a special cupboard for keeping food cold; REFRIGERATOR 电冰箱, 冰柜 —see picture on page A10 参见A10页图 S2

fridge-freez·er /ˌ·ˈ‥/ *n* [C] *BrE* a large fridge with a part that keeps food frozen【英】有冷冻室的电冰箱

Frie·dan /ˈfridn̩; ˈfriːdn/, **Bet·ty** /ˈbɛtɪ; ˈbeti/ (1921-2006) a US writer and FEMINIST (=someone who supports the idea that women should have the same rights and opportunities as men) who argued against the idea that women could only be happy and satisfied if they were wives and mothers. Many people believe that her book *The Feminine Mystique* (1963) started the modern women's movement. 弗里登〔(1921-2006), 美国作家、女权主义者。她曾对女人当妻子和母亲才会快乐和满足的观点进行过反驳。许多人认为她撰写的《女性的神秘》(1963) 是现代妇女运动的发轫之作〕

Fried·man /ˈfridmən; ˈfriːdmən/, **Milton** /ˈmɪltn̩; ˈmɪltən/ (1912-2006) a US ECONOMIST who helped to develop the idea of MONETARISM, the belief that the best way for a government to manage a country's economic system is to limit the amount of money that is available to be used. He won the Nobel Prize for Economics in 1976, and his ideas had an important influence on politics in the 1980s, because the economic policies of Margaret Thatcher and Ronald Reagan were based on them. 弗里德曼〔(1912-2006), 美国经济学家。他曾提出货币主义, 即认为政府管理一国经济体系最佳的方式是限制货币流通量。1976年, 他因此获得诺贝尔经济学奖。他的思想对20世纪80年代的政治有着重大影响, 玛格丽特·撒切尔和罗纳德·里根的经济政策都是基于此思想制定的〕

Friel /fril; friːl/, **Bri·an** /ˈbraɪən; ˈbraɪən/ (1929-) an Irish writer of short stories and plays that are mostly about Irish people and the political situation in Ireland 弗里尔〔(1929-), 爱尔兰短篇小说家、剧作家。其作品大多以爱尔兰人和爱尔兰政局为题材〕

friend /frɛnd; frend/ *n* [C] S1 W1

1 ▶PERSON YOU LIKE 你喜欢的人◀ someone who you like very much and like to spend time with 朋友, 友人: *Jerry, I'd like to introduce you to my friend Lucinda.* 杰里, 我想将你介绍给我的朋友露辛达。| **be friends with sb** *My parents have been friends with the Murkets for twenty years.* 20年来我的父母和默克特一家一直是好朋友。| **friend of mine/yours/Billy's etc** *A friend of mine told me this joke yesterday.* 我的一位朋友昨天告诉我这个笑话。| **best friend** (=the friend you like best) 最好的朋友 *One of Tricia's best friends is getting married tomorrow.* 特里西娅的一位最好的朋友于明天结婚。| **good/close friend** (=one of the friends you like most) 好朋友/密友 *One of my good friends just had a baby.* 我的一位好友刚生了小孩。| **old friend** (=one you have known a long time) 老朋友 *Bruce is an old friend of mine.* 布鲁斯是我的老朋友。| **friend of a friend** *I met Stephano through a friend of a friend.* 我通过一位朋友的朋友认识了斯特凡诺。

2 make friends to meet people and become friendly with them 交朋友, 建立友好关系: *Jenny has always found it easy to make friends at school.* 珍妮在学校总是很容易交朋友。| [+with] *Have you made friends with your neighbors yet?* 你和邻居建立起友好关系了吗?

3 be just (good) friends used to say that you are not having a romantic relationship with someone 只是 (好) 朋友而已: *Ben's not her boyfriend, I think they're just good friends.* 本不是她的男朋友, 我认为他们只是好朋友而已。

4 ▶**SUPPORTER** 赞助者；支持者◀ someone who supports a theatre, arts organization, CHARITY (2) etc by giving money or help 赞助者；支持者：*We would like to invite you to become a friend of the orchestra.* 我们想请你当管弦乐队的赞助人。
5 ▶**NOT AN ENEMY** 不是敌人◀ someone who is not an enemy and will not harm you or cause trouble for you 自己人：*Who goes there? Friend or foe?* 什么人？自己人还是敌人？| *Don't worry, you're among friends.* 别担心，你是自己人。
6 **be no friend of/to** to oppose someone or something 反对，不赞成，不支持：*I'm no friend of the plan, as you know.* 你知道，我反对这项计划。
7 ▶**AT PUBLIC OCCASION** 在公共场合◀ used to address someone or a group of people in a parliament, meeting, or other formal public occasion 朋友〔在议会、会议或其他正式公共场合使用的称呼语〕：*Friends, we are gathered here today to witness the marriage of Nick and Jo.* 朋友们，今天我们聚在这里来见证尼克和乔的婚礼。
8 **Friend** a member of the Society of Friends; a QUAKER 基督教教友会[公谊会]教友
9 **our/your friend** used to talk about someone you do not know, who has done something annoying 我们的/你们的那位朋友〔指你不喜欢的不认识的人〕：*Our friend with the loud voice is back.* 我们的那位大嗓门朋友回来了。
10 **have friends in high places** to know important people who can help you 有重要人物帮忙
11 **a friend in need** someone who helps you when you need it 患难之交，真正的朋友

friend·less /ˈfrɛndlɪs; ˈfrendləs/ *adj literary* having no friends and no one to help you【文】无朋友的；孤独无助的

-friendly /frɛndlɪ; frendli/ *suffix* [in adjectives 构成形容词] **1** not difficult for particular people to use〔为某种人所〕容易使用的，方便…的：*a user-friendly computer* 用户易操作的电脑 | *a customer-friendly shopping environment* 方便顾客的购物环境 **2** not harming something 对…无害的：*eco-friendly washing powder* (=not harming the environment) 对环境无害的洗衣粉

friend·ly¹ /ˈfrɛndlɪ; ˈfrendli/ *adj* **1** behaving towards someone in a way that shows you like them and are ready to talk to them or help them 友好的，友善的：*She's cheerful and friendly the whole time.* 她整段时间都兴高采烈，态度友好。| *a friendly smile* 亲切的微笑 | [+to/towards] *The local people are always friendly to visitors.* 当地人对游客总是很友好。**2 be friendly with sb** to be friends with someone 与某人很要好：*Betty's very friendly with the Jacksons.* 贝蒂同杰克逊一家人非常要好。**3** not at war with your own country, or not opposing you 友好的，非敌对的：*friendly nations* 友好国家 **4** *BrE* a friendly game is played for pleasure or practice, and not because it is important to win【英】〔比赛〕友谊的：*a friendly match against AC Milan* 与 AC 米兰队的友谊赛 **5 environmentally friendly/ozone friendly etc** not damaging to the environment etc 对环境无害的/不破坏臭氧层的等：*environmentally friendly washing powders* 对环境无害的洗衣粉 **6 friendly fire** bombs, bullets etc that accidentally kill people who are fighting on the same side 误杀自己人的火力[炮火] —see also 另见 USER FRIENDLY —**friendliness** *n* [U]

friendly² *n* [C] *BrE* a game played for pleasure or practice, and not because it is important to win【英】友谊赛

friendly so·ci·e·ty /ˈ···,···/ *n* [C] an association in Britain that people regularly pay small amounts of money to, which then provides them with money when they become old or ill〔英国〕互济会，互助会，互助储金会

friend·ship /ˈfrɛndʃɪp; ˈfrendʃɪp/ *n* **1** [C] a relationship between friends 友谊：*Our friendship developed quickly over the weeks that followed.* 在随后的几个星期里我们的友谊发展很快。| **form a friendship** (=make friends with someone) 建立友谊 *The two boys formed a deep and lasting friendship.* 这两个男孩子建立了深厚持久的友谊。| **strike up a friendship** (=begin to be friends with someone you have just met)〔见面不久即〕结交 **2** [U] the feelings and behaviour that exist between friends 友情；友好的行为：*I could always rely on Gary for friendship and support.* 我总能依靠加里的友情和支持。

Friends of the Earth /,·····/ abbreviation 缩写为 **FOE** an international organization that tries to influence people and governments to protect the environment 地球之友〔一国际性组织，力图影响民众和政府以保护环境〕

fri·er /ˈfraɪɚ; ˈfraɪə/ *n* [C] another spelling of FRYER fryer 的另一种拼法

fries /fraɪz; fraɪz/ *n* [plural] *especially AmE* pieces of potato cut into pieces, usually long and thin, and then cooked in hot fat【尤美】炸马铃薯条

Frie·si·an /ˈfriʒən; ˈfriːziən/ *n* [C] *especially BrE* a type of cow that is black and white【尤英】霍斯坦种乳牛，黑白花牛，荷兰牛；HOLSTEIN *AmE*【美】

frieze /friz; friːz/ *n* [C] a thin border along the top of the wall of a building or in a room, usually decorated with pictures, patterns etc〔墙壁顶部沿边的〕横条装饰；雕带；饰带

frig /frɪg; frɪg/ *v*
frig about/around *phr v taboo especially BrE*【讳，尤英】**1** [I] to waste time doing unnecessary or unimportant things 闲混；虚度光阴：*Stop frigging about and help!* 不要游手好闲了，来帮个忙吧！**2** [T **frig** sb/sth **around/about**] to treat someone badly or unfairly 虐待；不公平地对待；欺压

frig·ate /ˈfrɪgɪt; ˈfrɪgɪ̇t/ *n* [C] a small, fast warship used especially for protecting other ships 护卫舰，护航舰

frig·ging /ˈfrɪgɪŋ; ˈfrɪgɪŋ/ *adj* [only before noun 仅用于名词前] *adv taboo spoken* used to emphasize something you are saying when you are angry, annoyed etc【讳，口】该死的，他妈的：*I can't open the frigging door!* 我开不了这该死的门！

fright /fraɪt; fraɪt/ *n* **1** [singular] the feeling you have when something frightens you 恐怖；惊吓：**give sb a fright** (=do something that makes someone feel afraid) 使某人吃惊，吓着某人 *You gave me such a fright creeping up on me like that!* 你偷偷朝我凑过来，吓了我一跳！| **get/have a fright** *I got an awful fright when your dog rushed out at me.* 你的狗朝我冲过来，吓了我一大跳。| **get/have the fright of your life** (=to feel extremely afraid) 感到极度恐惧 **2** [U] a feeling of fear 惊吓，恐惧：*The child was wild with fright and began to scream.* 这孩子吓坏了，开始尖叫。**3 take fright** to be very afraid of something, especially so that you run away from it 受惊吓〔尤指因而逃走〕：*The bird took fright and flew away.* 那只鸟受惊飞走了。**4 look a fright** *old-fashioned* to look untidy or unattractive【过时】很难看，怪模怪样，丑陋 —see also 另见 STAGE FRIGHT

fright·en /ˈfraɪtn; ˈfraɪtn/ *v* [T] **1** to make someone feel afraid 使害怕，使惊吓：*Don't stand so near the edge, you're frightening me!* 别那么靠边站，你要把我吓坏了！| **frighten sb to death/frighten sb out of their wits** (=make someone feel extremely afraid) 使某人吓得半死/使某人吓得魂不附体 *She'll be frightened to death when she sees the way you drive.* 看到你那样开车，她会吓得半死的。**2 frighten sb into/out of (doing) sth** to force someone to do something or not to do something by making them afraid 吓得某人做某事/吓得某人不敢做某事：*The lawyers frightened the old lady into signing the paper.* 律师们吓唬那位老太太在文件上签名。
frighten sb ↔ **away** *phr v* [T] to make a person or animal go away by making them feel afraid 吓走〔某人〕：*Terrorist activity in the area has frightened most tourists away.* 该地区的恐怖主义活动已经把大多数游客吓走。
frighten sb/sth ↔ **off** *phr v* [T] to make a person or animal so nervous or afraid that they go away or do not do something they were going to do 吓走；吓得不做：*The investors were frightened off by the company's low profits that year.* 投资者被该公司那年的低利润吓走了。

fright·ened /ˈfraɪtn̩d; ˈfraɪtnd/ *adj* feeling afraid 受惊的，害怕的：*a frightened animal* 受惊的动物 | [+of] *I was frightened of being left by myself in the house.* 我害怕自己一个人被留在屋里。| **frightened to do sth** *I'll be frightened to look out of the airplane window.* 我从飞机的舷窗往外看会害怕的。| [+that] *She's frightened that her ex-husband will find her.* 她怕前夫会找到她。

fright·en·ers /ˈfraɪtn̩ɚz; ˈfraɪtnəz/ *n* [plural] *BrE slang*【英俚】**put the frighteners on sb** to make someone do what you want by threatening them 恐吓某人〔使其做某事〕

fright·en·ing /ˈfraɪtn̩ɪŋ; ˈfraɪtn-ɪŋ/ *adj* making you feel afraid or nervous 令人害怕的，吓人的，可怕的：*That's a frightening thought.* 那是个可怕的想法。| **it is frightening (to do sth)** *It's frightening to think how easily children can be hurt.* 想到小孩很容易受到伤害，怪可怕的。—**frighteningly** *adv*

fright·ful /ˈfraɪtfəl; ˈfraɪtfəl/ *adj* **1** *especially BrE* unpleasant or bad【尤英】不愉快的；可怕的；坏的：*There's been a frightful accident on the motorway.* 高速公路上发生了一起可怕的事故。**2** *BrE old-fashioned* used to emphasize how bad something is【英，过时】极度的，极大的；很糟的：*a frightful mess* 一团糟 —**frightfulness** *n* [U]

fright·ful·ly /ˈfraɪtfəlɪ; ˈfraɪtfəli/ *adv BrE old-fashioned* very【英，过时】非常，十分

fri·gid /ˈfrɪdʒɪd; ˈfrɪdʒɪ̇d/ *adj* **1** a woman who is frigid does not like having sex〔女子〕性冷淡的 **2** not friendly or kind 冷淡的；不友好的：*The guard looked at us with a frigid stare.* 守卫冷冰冰地盯着我们。**3** a place that is frigid is very cold 寒冷的，酷寒的 —**frigidly** *adv* —**frigidity** /frɪˈdʒɪdətɪ; frɪˈdʒɪdɪ̇ti/ *n* [U]

Fri·gi·daire /ˌfrɪdʒɪˋdɛr; ˌfrɪdʒɪˈdeə/ *trademark* a type of FRIDGE made in the US. The name Frigidaire is often used in the US to mean any type of fridge.【商标】北极冰箱〔美国制造的一种电冰箱，该名称在美国常被用来指称任一种电冰箱〕

frill /frɪl; frɪl/ *n* [C] **1** a decorative edge on a piece of cloth made by another piece of cloth with many small folds in it〔布的〕饰边，褶边: *a frill on the bottom of the skirt* 裙子下摆的饰边 **2 without frills/with no frills** without attractive but unnecessary details or decorations 不带花哨装饰的，毫无矫饰的: *a no-frills deal* 无额外收费的交易

frill·y /ˋfrɪlɪ; ˈfrɪli/ *adj* having many decorative folds of cloth 有饰边的，有褶边的: *a little girl's frilly dress* 有褶边的女童连衣裙

fringe[1] /frɪndʒ; frɪndʒ/ *n* [C] **1** *BrE* the part of your hair that hangs over your forehead【英】刘海〔垂在额前的头发〕; bangs (BANG[1] (3)) *AmE*【美】—see picture on page A6 参见 A6 页图 **2** a decorative edge of hanging threads on a curtain, piece of clothing etc〔帷幕、衣服等上的〕缘穗，缘饰，流苏 **3 on the fringe of a)** at the part of something that is farthest from the centre 在…的边缘; 在…的外围: *It was easier to move around on the fringe of the crowd.* 在人群的外围比较容易走动。**b)** not quite belonging to or accepted by a group of people who share the same job, activities etc 属于…的边缘的: *a small group on the fringes of the art world* 艺术界边缘的一小群人 **4 the right wing/nationalist/radical etc fringe** a group of people within an organization or political party who have extreme ideas that most people do not agree with 右翼/民族主义/激进的极端分子等: *The terrorist fringe condemned the decision.* 恐怖主义的极端分子谴责这个决定。**5 the fringe,** also 又作 **fringe theatre** the performance of plays that are unusual or that try to make people think differently 实验戏剧（演出）; 非传统的戏剧（演出）—see also 另见 **the lunatic fringe** (LUNATIC (3))

fringe[2] *adj* [only before noun 仅用于名词前] different from the most usual or accepted way of thinking or doing things 边缘的; 非正统的，非主流的: *The environment is no longer a fringe issue in Europe.* 在欧洲，环境不再是一个边缘的问题了。

fringe[3] *v* [T] to be around the edge of something; BORDER 在…的边缘: *A line of trees fringed the pool.* 水池周围种了一行树。

Fringe, the the theatre productions in the Edinburgh Festival which are not part of the official programme 爱丁堡边缘艺术节: *a Fringe production* 爱丁堡边缘艺术节的一场演出 | *a comedian who was a great success at the Fringe* 在爱丁堡边缘艺术节演出十分成功的一位喜剧演员

fringe ben·e·fit /ˈ· ˌ···/ *n* [C usually plural 一般用复数] an additional service or advantage given with a job besides wages; PERK[1] 工资外补贴; 附加福利; 附带的好处; 边缘福利: *The pay is awful but there are several fringe benefits.* 工资很差，不过有几种工资外补贴。

fringe thea·tre /ˌ· ˈ··/ *n* [U] *BrE* plays by new writers, often on difficult subjects or written in unusual ways, that are not performed in the main theatres【英】实验戏剧

frip·pe·ry /ˋfrɪpərɪ; ˈfrɪpəri/ *n* [C] an unnecessary and useless object or decoration 多余无用的东西; 花哨的装饰品: *She spends all her money on fripperies.* 她把所有的钱都花在花哨无用的东西上。

fris·bee /ˋfrɪzbɪ; ˈfrɪzbi/ *n* [C,U] *trademark* a piece of plastic shaped like a plate that you throw to someone else to catch as a game【商标】〔游戏用的〕飞盘，飞碟

frisk /frɪsk; frɪsk/ *v* **1** [T] also 又作 **frisk down** *AmE*【美】to search someone for hidden weapons, drugs etc by feeling their body with your hands 搜〔某人〕的身: *We were frisked at the airport, can you believe it?* 我们在机场竟被搜身了，你能相信吗? —see picture on page A21 参见 A21 页图 **2** [I] to run and jump playfully 欢跃，跳蹦: *The lambs were frisking around the pen.* 羔羊在羊圈里蹦跳。

frisk·y /ˋfrɪskɪ; ˈfrɪski/ *adj* full of energy, fun, and cheerfulness 活跃的; 活泼的; 欢蹦乱跳的: *a frisky colt* 一匹欢蹦乱跳的马驹 | *He's still frisky, even at eighty years old!* 他在80岁的高龄还很活跃! —**friskily** *adv* —**friskiness** *n* [U]

fris·son /friˋsɑn; ˈfriːsɒn/ *n* [C] a sudden feeling of excitement or fear〔突然的〕兴奋感; 恐惧; 震颤: *a frisson of alarm* 一阵惊恐的战栗

frit /frɪt; frɪt/ *adj BrE dialect* frightened【英，方言】受惊的; 害怕的

frit·ter[1] /ˋfrɪtɚ; ˈfrɪtə/ *n* [C] a thin piece of fruit, vegetable, or meat covered with a mixture of eggs and flour and cooked in hot fat〔有水果、蔬菜或肉馅的〕油炸馅饼: **apple/corn/banana fritter** (=made of apple, corn etc) 油炸苹果/玉米/香蕉馅饼

fritter[2]
fritter sth ↔ **away** *phr v* [T] to waste time, money, or effort on something small or unimportant〔在微不足道的事情上〕浪费〔时间、金钱或力气〕: **[+on]** *They frittered their pocket-money away on sweets.* 他们把零用钱都浪费在买糖果上。

fritz /frɪts; frɪts/ *n* [singular] *AmE informal* **be on the fritz** if something electrical is on the fritz, it is not working properly【美，非正式】〔电器〕出故障

fri·vol·i·ty /frɪˋvɑlətɪ; frɪˈvɒlɪ̣ti/ *n* **1** [U] lack of serious or sensible thought or behaviour〔思想或行为的〕轻浮，轻佻: *Your frivolity is out of place on such a solemn occasion.* 你的轻浮举动在这种严肃的场合很不适宜。**2 frivolities** [plural] **a)** silly or amusing actions or words, especially in a situation where you should be serious or sensible 轻浮的话; 不严肃的举动; 无聊的话[行为] **b)** unimportant or unnecessary things 无关紧要的事: *Student life should be more than parties and other frivolities.* 学生生活应该不仅仅是聚会和其他无关紧要的活动。

friv·o·lous /ˋfrɪvələs; ˈfrɪvələs/ *adj* **1** not serious or sensible, especially in a way that is not suitable for a particular occasion 不严肃的; 草率的: *The court discourages frivolous law suits.* 法院不鼓励草率的诉讼。**2** a frivolous person likes having fun rather than doing serious or sensible things 轻浮的 —**frivolously** *adv*

frizz /frɪz; frɪz/ *v* [T] *informal* to make your hair curl very tightly【非正式】使〔头发〕紧紧鬈曲 —**frizz** *n* [U]

friz·zle /ˋfrɪzl; ˈfrɪzəl/ *v* [I,T] *informal* also 又作 **frizzle up** to dry or burn something, or to be dried or burnt, especially into a curly shape【非正式】(把…）烧得卷起来; (使…）干得卷起来

frizz·y /ˋfrɪzɪ; ˈfrɪzi/ *adj* frizzy hair is tightly curled〔头发〕紧紧鬈曲的

fro /fro; frəʊ/ *adv* —see 见 TO AND FRO

frock /frɑk; frɒk/ *n* [C] **1** *old-fashioned* a woman's or girl's dress【过时】〔妇女或女孩穿的〕长服: *a party frock* 宴会穿的长裙 **2** a long loose piece of clothing worn by some Christian MONKS〔基督教教士穿的〕长袍

frock coat /ˌ· ˈ·/ *n* [C] a knee-length coat for men, worn in the 19th century〔19世纪男子穿的〕长礼服

Fro·do /ˋfrodo; ˈfrəʊdəʊ/ a character in the NOVEL *The Lord of the Rings* by J.R.R. Tolkien. He is a Hobbit, a creature that looks like a human but is much smaller, and lives in a hole in the ground. 弗罗多〔J.R.R.托尔金小说《魔戒》中的霍比特人。其外表与人类相似，但身形却矮得多，生活在地下的洞穴里〕

frog /frɑg; frɒg/ *n* [C] **1** a small green animal that lives near water and has long legs for jumping 蛙 —compare 比较 TOAD **2 have a frog in your throat** *informal* to have difficulty in speaking because of a sore throat【非正式】〔因喉咙痛〕说话困难，声音沙哑 **3 Frog** *informal* an offensive word for a French person【非正式】法国佬〔具冒犯性〕

frog 蛙

frog·man /ˋfrɑgmən; ˈfrɒgmən/ *n* [C] someone who swims under water using special equipment to help them breathe, especially as a job 蛙人; 潜水员

frog·march /ˋfrɑgˌmartʃ; ˈfrɒgmɑːtʃ/ *v* [T] *BrE* to force someone to walk somewhere by having two people on either side of them who hold their arms very tightly【英】将〔某人〕反绑双臂押走

Frog Prince, The /ˌ· ˈ·/ a FAIRY TALE in which a prince, who has been changed into a FROG by an evil WITCH, tries to persuade a princess to kiss him so that he can become a prince again. She finally does, he becomes human again, and they get married.《青蛙王子》〔童话故事。故事中有一位王子被邪恶的女巫变成青蛙，他想办法说服一位公主亲吻他，好让他变回王子。最后，公主照他的话做了，王子恢复了真身，他们结为夫妇〕

frog·spawn /ˋfrɑgspɔn; ˈfrɒgspɔːn/ *n* [U] frog's eggs 蛙卵

frol·ic[1] /ˋfrɑlɪk; ˈfrɒlɪk/ *v* [I] to play in an active, happy way; FRISK (2) 嬉戏，欢快地玩耍: **[+around/about/over]** *The kids spent all day frolicking around in the surf.* 孩子们整天在欢快地玩着拍岸的浪花。

frolic[2] *n* [C often plural 常用复数] a cheerful, enjoyable game or activity 嬉戏，嬉闹: *Everyone joined in the Saturday night frolics.* 大家都参加了星期六晚上的欢闹聚会。

frol·ic·some /ˋfrɑlɪksəm; ˈfrɒlɪksəm/ *adj especially literary* active and liking to play【尤文】活跃的; 爱嬉戏的: *frolicsome kittens* 喜欢嬉戏的小猫

from /frəm; frəm; *strong* 强读 frɑm; frɒm/ *prep* **1** starting at a particular place, position, or condition 自…, 从…, 由…〔表示起点、开始位置或开始时的状况〕: *How do you get from here to Colchester?* 从这里到科尔切斯特怎么走? | *running from one side of the building to the other* 从大楼的一边跑向另一边 | *The hotel is on the main road from Caernarfon.* 旅馆位于从卡那封出来的大路上。| *dropped from a height of six feet* 从六英尺的高度落下的 | *translating from French into English* 从法语翻译成英语 | **go from A to B** (=go from one point or situation to another) 从A到B *People will choose different methods of going from A to B.* 由A到B人们会选择不同方法。| **go from bad to worse** (=get worse) 越来越糟糕 *When she arrived, things just went from bad to worse!* 她到达后, 情况每况愈下! **2 from house to house/shop to shop/place to place etc a)** calling at every house, shop, etc 挨家挨户/一家一家商店地/到处等: *She went from house to house asking if anyone had seen him.* 她挨家挨户问有没有人看见过他。**b)** in different houses, places etc 在每家每户/在各家商店/到处等: *From office to office things work differently.* 在每个办公室, 情况都不一样。| *It will vary from time to time and from place to place.* 这会因时因地而不同。| *Everything goes wrong from time to time.* (=sometimes) 不管什么东西都有出故障的时候。**3** starting at a particular time 从〔某时〕起: *He'll be here tomorrow from about seven o'clock onwards.* 明天从七点钟左右起他会在这儿。| *in a week from now* 从现在起一周内 | **from morning to night** (=without stopping) 从早到晚; 不停地 *housewives who work from morning to night* 从早到晚干个不停的家庭主妇 | **from now on** (=from this time onwards) 从现在起 *From now on, I will only be working in the mornings.* 从现在起, 我只在上午工作。—see 见 SINCE[3] (USAGE) **4** beginning at a particular limit or price 从〔某个限度或价格〕起: *The sizes range from a hundred down to twenty.* 尺寸从100号下至20号不等。| *The yield from this type of investment can be anything from five to ten percent.* 这种投资的收益从5%至10%不等。**5** if you see, watch, or do something from a place, this is where you are when you see, watch, or do it 从〔某处看或做〕: *From the top of the hill, you can see for miles.* 从山顶你可以看到好几英里远。| *There's a man watching us from behind that fence.* 有个人正从篱笆后面看着我们。**6** used to express a distance 〔表示距离〕距…, 离…: *We live about five km from Boston.* 我们住在离波士顿大约五公里的地方。| *a large Victorian house only fifty yards from my workplace* 离我的工作场所只有50码的一座维多利亚式的大房子 | *It's about an hour and a half from Scarborough.* 离斯卡伯勒大约有一个半小时的路程。**7** if something is moved or taken from a place or person, it is removed, taken away or taken out 从…移走, 从…拿走, 从…拿出: *She pulled her chair away from her desk.* 她把椅子从自己的写字台边拉开。| *I had to take that new toy away from him.* 我只好把新玩具从他那儿拿走。| *Subtract three from 15.* 从15中减去3。| *He took a knife from his pocket.* 他从口袋里掏出刀子。| *His absence from class has been noted.* 他缺课的情况已经被注意到了。**8** used to say what the origin of something is 来自…; 源自…: *He gets his good looks from his mother.* 他好看的相貌得自于他母亲的遗传。| *I'll show you a short extract from one of our training videos.* 我将给你们看我们的一个训练录像的片段。| *Do you know where the information came from?* 你知道信息的来源吗? | *an infectious disease which he got from another sick dog* 他从另一条病狗染来的传染病 | *Members are chosen from a list drawn up by the Home Secretary.* 成员是从内政大臣拟定的名单中选出来的。| *I bought it from a shop in the market.* 我从市场上的一家商店买了这东西。| *I got this from Colin.* 我是从科林那儿得到这个东西的。**9** sent or given by someone 从〔某人〕寄来; 从〔某人那里〕得到: *I've received a bill for nineteen dollars from the hospital.* 我已经收到医院寄来的一张19美元的账单。| *I had a phone call from John.* 我接到了约翰打来的电话。| *You need to get permission from the owner.* 你需要得到主人的许可。| *with lots of love from Elaine and Martin* 带着伊莱恩和马丁深深的爱[深深爱你的伊莱恩和马丁] **10 you can tell him from me...** *spoken* used to ask someone to tell another person something, when you are annoyed or determined【口】你可以替我转告他…〔不高兴时请人传话时的用语〕: *Well, you can tell him from me that I'll be making an official complaint.* 好吧, 你可以告诉他说我要正式投诉。**11** someone who comes from a particular place lives, works, or belongs there 来自〔某个地方〕: *We invited speakers from all the regions.* 我们邀请了来自各地的演讲者。| *Students from all faculties will have access to the machines.* 各院系的学生都将可以使用这些机器。| *Alison from the Job Centre is on the phone.* 我是就业服务中心的艾莉森。〔打电话时用语〕| **I'm from/I come from Devon/New York etc** (=born in Devon, New York etc) 我是德文郡人/我是纽约人等 **12** used to state the cause of something 因为…, 由于…: *mothers who are exhausted from all the sleepless nights* 由于这些不眠之夜而精疲力竭的母亲们 | *Death rates from accidents have declined.* 事故的死亡率已经下降。| **suffer from** (=be affected by; have) 患〔病〕; 因…而受苦 *Mum suffers from migraines.* 妈妈患偏头痛。**13** used to introduce the reason for, or origin of, an opinion or judgement 据…; 凭…: *From what I've read, the company seems to be in difficulties.* 据我阅读到的情况来看, 这家公司似乎遇到了困难。| *It's obvious from a quick glance that the plan has changed dramatically.* 稍微一瞥就能明显看到这个计划已经有了很大变化。| **from my point of view** (=how something affects you) 从我的观点看 *These changes are ideal from my point of view.* 从我的观点看, 这些变化很理想。| *From Clarisse's point of view, it's very distressing indeed.* 在克拉丽丝看来, 这确实十分令人苦恼。| **from memory** (=according to what I can remember) 凭我的记忆, 就我所能回忆的来说 *From memory, the film wasn't as good as the book.* 凭我的记忆来说, 这部电影不如书好。**14** used to state the substance that is used to make something 由…〔做的〕: *Bread is made from flour, water, and yeast.* 面包是由面粉、水和酵母做的。**15** used after words such as 'protect', 'prevent', or 'keep', to introduce the situation or action that is stopped, avoided, or prevented 免于〔表示阻止、避免、防止〕: *These problems have prevented me from completing the work.* 这些问题使我无法完成工作。| *people who have been disqualified from driving* 已被取消驾驶资格的人 **16** used when you are comparing things, and saying how they are similar or different 与…不同〔用于比较〕: *She's quite different from her sister.* 她和她的姐姐很不同。| *Our two cats are so alike, I can never tell one from the other.* 我们的两只猫很相像, 我从来就无法区分出来。

from·age frais /frɑˌmɑʒ ˈfre; ˌfrɒmɑːʒ ˈfreɪ/ *n* [U] *French* a soft white mild cheese you can eat with a spoon【法】液体鲜乳酪, 稀乳酪

frond /frɑnd; frɒnd/ *n* [C] a leaf of a FERN OR PALM[1] (2) 〔蕨类或棕榈树的〕叶

front 前面

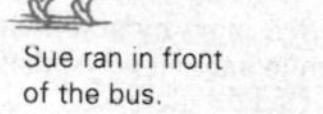

Sue ran in front of the bus.
休在公共汽车的前面跑。

Sue got a seat at/in the front of the bus.
休在公共汽车的前部找了个座位。

front[1] /frʌnt; frʌnt/ *n*

1 ▶GROUP/LINE 一群/一排◀ **the front** the front of a group or line of people or things is the position that is furthest forward in the direction that they are facing or moving 最前部, 最前面: [+of] *She always sits at the front of the class.* 她总坐在教室的最前面。| **in/at the front** *I think I can see them, they're right at the front.* 我想我可以看见他们, 他们就在最前面。| **the front of the line/queue/crowd** *TV reporters shoved their way to the front of the crowd.* 电视记者推挤到人群的最前面。

2 ▶FORWARD SIDE/SURFACE 前部/正面◀ **the front** the side or surface of something that is in the direction that it faces or moves 前部; 前面: [+of] *Where did that scratch on the front of my car come from?* 我的车子前部的那处刮痕是哪里来的? —compare 比较 REAR[1] (1)

3 the front the most important side or surface of something, that you look at first 正面; 头版: **on the front** *Get a postcard with a picture of our hotel on the front of it.* 买一张正面印着我们旅馆照片的明信片。| [+of] *She's on the front of the Radio Times.* 她出现在《广播时报》的头版上。—opposite 反义词 BACK[2] (2) —compare 比较 REAR[1] (1)

4 ▶BUILDINGS 建筑物◀ **the front** the most important side, where you go in 〔最重要的〕一面, 正面

5 ▶BOOK 书籍◀ **the front** the first pages 扉页

6 in front of sth a) near the side of something that is in the direction that it faces or moves 在某物前面: *right in front of the car* 在车子的正前面 —opposite 反义词 BEHIND[1] (1) —see pic-

ture on page A1 参见 A1 页图 **b)** near the side of a building where you go in 在〔建筑物前门的〕正前面: *She parked in front of the office.* 她在办公室前面停了车。

7 in front of sb a) ahead of someone, in the direction that they are facing or moving 在某人的前面: *Come out here in front of the class.* 出来站在全班的前面。**b)** if you say or do something in front of someone you do it where they can see or hear you 在某人的面前: *Don't swear in front of the children!* 不要当着小孩的面骂人! **c)** if you have problems or difficulties in front of you, you will soon need to deal with them 某人面临着〔难题或困难〕

8 in front a) in the most forward or leading position; ahead 在最前面的位置, 在前方: *Mrs Ramsay's horse was well in front.* 拉姆齐夫人的马遥遥领先。| *He drove straight into the car in front.* 他一下子就撞上了前面的车子。—compare 比较 BEHIND[1] (1) **b)** in the area nearest the most forward part of something, or the entrance to a building 在〔建筑物的〕前面[门前]

9 out front also 又作 **out the front/out in front** *BrE*【英】in the area near the entrance to a building 在门外, 在外面: *Hurry up! The taxi is out front.* 快! 出租车就在门外。

10 in/up front also 又作 **in the front** *especially BrE*【尤英】in the part of a car where the driver sits 在〔汽车的〕前座: *"Get in the car, kids." "Can I sit in front, Mom?"* "孩子们, 上车。" "妈妈, 我能坐在前面吗?"

11 be brought/called/hauled in front of sb to have to see someone in authority about something you have done wrong 〔因做错事〕被带到/被叫到/被拉到某人面前: *My whole section was called in front of the manager.* 我们全部门的人都被叫到经理面前。

12 sit in front of to spend time using or watching something such as a computer or television 〔花时间〕使用〔电脑〕; 观看〔电视〕: *You've spent all day just sitting in front of the television.* 你整天都在看电视。

13 ▶WEATHER 天气◀ [C] *technical* the place where two areas of air of different temperatures meet, often shown as a line on weather maps【术语】〔冷暖气流会合的〕锋, 锋面: **warm/cold front** (=an area of warm or cold air) 暖锋/冷锋

14 on the publicity/money/health front etc in a particular area 在宣传/金钱/健康等方面: *Constant effort is needed on the publicity front.* 宣传方面需要不断努力。

15 up front *informal*【非正式】**a)** money that is paid up front is paid before work is done, or goods are supplied 预先, 事先〔付款〕: *We need two hundred pounds up front.* 我们需要预付 200 英镑。**b)** directly and clearly from the start 〔一开始就〕明确地: *Jorge wanted to help her, but she'd told him up front she did not need it.* 若尔热想要帮她, 可她明确地告诉他她不需要帮助。—see also 另见 UPFRONT

16 ▶SEA 海洋◀ the front *especially BrE* the part of a town next to the sea, between the beach and the shops, hotels etc; SEAFRONT【尤英】海滨城市; 滨海地区

17 ▶BODY 身体◀ your chest, or the part of your body that faces forward 胸前; 前面: *I've spilled some soup down my front.* 我把一些汤溅到胸前了。

18 on all fronts in every area of the activity that you are involved in 在各方面: *We're making rapid progress on all fronts.* 我们在各方面进展都很快。

19 be a front for *informal* to be used for hiding a secret or illegal activity【非正式】成为〔秘密或非法活动〕的掩护者[物], 为…作掩护[当幌子]: *Could his business be a front for drug smuggling?* 他的公司会不会是毒品走私的掩护所?

20 put on/show a front to behave in a way that is braver or happier than you feel 装出〔勇敢或高兴〕的样子: *I know you're scared, but you've got to put on a brave front.* 我知道你害怕, 但你得表现出勇敢的样子。

21 ▶ORGANIZATION 组织机构◀ [singular] used in the name of a political party or unofficial military organization 阵线〔用于政党或非正式军事组织的名称〕: *the People's Liberation Front* 人民解放阵线

22 ▶WAR 战争◀ [C] a line along which fighting takes place during a war; FRONT LINE 前线, 前方: *trucks heading towards the Western Front* 向西部前线驶去的卡车 —see also 另见 HOME FRONT

23 ▶CHURCH 教堂◀ [C] a side of a large, important church building 〔大教堂的〕一面: *the west front* 朝西的一面

USAGE NOTE 用法说明: FRONT

WORD CHOICE 词语辨析: **in front of, behind, at/in the front of, at/in the back of, face, opposite, before**

In front of (opposite **behind**) is used when one thing is separate from the other. 某个东西不与另一个东西相连时, 用 in front of (反义词 behind): *A child ran out in front of the bus* (=in the road outside the bus). 一个小孩跑到了公共汽车的前面。

At/in the front of (opposite **at/in the back of**) is used when one thing is inside or part of the other. 某一个东西位于另一个东西之中或是其一部分时, 用 at/in the front of (反义词 at/in the back of): *The child took a seat at/in the front of the bus* (=in the front part of the bus). 这个小孩在公共汽车的前部坐了下来。

If a building is in front of something, it **faces** it. 如果说某建筑物在某物前面, 这栋建筑物就是面向 (face) 这个物体: *The hotel faced the Mediterranean.* 这家旅馆面向地中海。

A person or place that faces another one exactly, with a space between, is **opposite** it. If the bus stop is *opposite the station* it is not *in front of the station* but on the other side of the road. 一个人或地方正面对着另一个人或地方, 但中间有间隔, 那么这个人或地方是在对面 (opposite)。如果公共汽车站是在车站的对面 (opposite), 它不是在车站的前面 (in front of), 而是在马路的对面: *I live opposite Greg.* 我住在格雷格家的对面。

One event may happen **before** another. 一件事发生在另一件事之前时用 before: *Let's have a drink before dinner* (NOT 不用 *in front of dinner*). 我们在晚餐前先喝一杯吧。

front² *adj* [only before noun 仅用于名词前] **1** at, on, or in the front of something (在) 前面的; 前部的: *Your front teeth are going to have to be straightened.* 你的门牙得去矫正一下。| **front door/room/garden** (=at the front of a house) 前门/前厅/前花园 | **front seat/row** *Good news! I got us front row seats!* 好消息! 我给大家弄到了前排的座位! —opposite 反义词 BACK[3] (1) **2** *informal* a front man or organization acts lawfully in business as a way of hiding a secret or illegal activity【非正式】起掩护作用的, 作幌子的: *a front organization for importing heroin* 一个从事进口海洛因活动的掩护组织 **3** *technical* a front vowel sound is made by raising your tongue at the front of your mouth【术语】〔元音〕前舌音的 —opposite 反义词 BACK[3] (7)

front³ *v* **1** [I,T] if a building fronts onto the sea, a road etc, the front of the building faces it 面对, 面向: **[+onto]** *Our hotel fronts onto a main road.* 我们的旅馆面向一条大路。| **front sth** *houses fronting the lake* 面向湖的房屋 **2 be fronted by/with** to be covered or decorated at the front with something 正面饰有…的: *Victor led us into a large building fronted with marble.* 维克托把我们领进一栋正面墙由大理石砌成的大楼。**3** [T] to lead something such as a group or television programme by being the person that the public see most 领导〔一群人〕; 主持〔电视节目〕: *She's fronting a weekly current affairs program.* 她在主持一个每周时事节目。

front for sb/sth *phr v* [T] *informal* to act as the person or organization used for hiding the real nature of a secret or illegal activity【非正式】充当…的掩护, 替…作掩护: *Police suspected her of fronting for a gang of forgers.* 警方怀疑她替一帮伪造者作掩护。

front·age /ˈfrʌntɪdʒ; ˈfrʌntɪdʒ/ *n* [U] the part of a building or piece of land that is along a road, river, etc 〔建筑物的〕正面; 临路地面; 临河地面

front·al /ˈfrʌntl; ˈfrʌntl/ *adj* [only before noun 仅用于名词前] *formal*【正式】**1** at or connected with the front part of something 前面的, 正面的: *the frontal area of the brain* 大脑的前区 **2** towards the front of something 向前端的, 朝正面的: *From the frontal approach, the house looks grand and imposing.* 这座房屋从正面看上去雄伟壮丽。**3 full frontal** showing people with no clothes on, from the front 正面全裸的: *full frontal nudity* 全身正面赤裸 —**frontally** *adv*

frontal sys·tem /ˈ‥ ˌ‥/ *n* [C] *technical* a weather FRONT[1] (13)【术语】〔气象上的〕锋系

front-and-center /ˌ‥ ‥ˈ‥◂/ *adj AmE* very important and needing attention【美】重大的; 首要的; 中心的; 需要关注的: *Prayer in schools has become a front-and-center issue for the White House.* 学校祷告已经成为白宫的中心议题。

frontbench /ˌ· ˈ·◂/ *n* [C] the front row of seats on each side of the British parliament, on which the leaders of the political parties sit 〔英国议会的〕前 (排) 座 (位) 〔为各政党领导人的席位〕—compare 比较 BACKBENCH

front-bench·er /ˌfrʌntˈbɛntʃɚ; ˌfrʌntˈbentʃə◂/ *n* [C] someone who sits on a front bench in the British parliament 〔英国议会中的〕前座议员 —compare 比较 BACKBENCHER

front door /ˌ· ˈ·/ *n* [C usually singular 一般用单数] the main entrance door to a house, at the front 〔房屋的〕前门, 正门 —compare 比较 BACK DOOR (1)

fron·tier /frʌn`tɪr; ˈfrʌntɪə/ *n* **1** **the frontier** an area where people have never lived before, that not much is known about, especially in the western US before the 20th century〔尤指20世纪前美国西部的〕边远地区, 荒野地区; 边疆: *the settlement of the Oklahoma frontier* 俄克拉何马州边远地区的新拓居地 | *space, the final frontier* 太空, 最后一块未开拓的疆域 **2** [C] *especially BrE* the border of a country, where people cross from one country to another【尤英】国境, 边境: [**+between/with**] *Lille is close to the frontier between France and Belgium.* 里尔紧靠法国和比利时的边境。| **on/at the frontier** *Troops established a road block on the frontier.* 部队在边境设立了路障。**3** **the frontiers of knowledge/physics etc** the limit of what is known about something 知识/物理的新领域等: **push back the frontiers** (=discover new things) 开拓新领域 **4** **roll back the frontiers** to make something such as government power smaller 使〔政府权力等〕变小, 削减

fron·tiers·man /frʌn`tɪrzmən; ˈfrʌntɪəzmən/ *n* [C] a man who lived in the American frontier〔美国的〕边远地区居民, 边疆开拓者

fron·tis·piece /ˈfrʌntɪs,pis; ˈfrʌntɨspiːs/ *n* [C] a picture or photograph at the beginning of a book, usually opposite the page with the title on it〔书籍的〕卷首插图, 扉页画

front line /,ˈ·◂/ *n* **1** **the front line** the place where fighting happens in a war; FRONT[1] (22)〔战争中的〕前线, 前方: *troops in the front line* 前线部队 **2** **in the front line** **a)** doing something that has not been done before 在…第一线; 在…最前线: *in the front line of the fight against cancer* 在抗癌斗争的第一线 **b)** likely to be blamed for an organization's mistakes〔因所属组织的错误〕可能受指责, 可能要承担过失的责任 —**front-line** *adj* [only before noun 仅用于名词前]: *front-line conditions* 前线的形势

front man /ˈ· ·/ *n* [C usually singular 一般用单数] a person who speaks for an organization, for example an illegal one, but is not the leader of it〔某组织的〕出面人, 代表人, 发言人

front mat·ter /ˈ· ,··/ *n* [U] all the pages at the very beginning of a book, including the page with the title on it〔书籍的〕前面各页, 前件

front money /ˈ· ,··/ *n* [singular] money that is paid for something before you get it 预付款

front of·fice /,ˈ· ˈ··/ *n* [singular] *AmE* the managers of a company【美】〔公司的〕管理层, 管理部门

front page /,ˈ·ˈ/ *n* [C] the first page of a newspaper〔报纸的〕头版

front-page /ˈ· ·/ *adj* [only before noun 仅用于名词前] *informal* interesting, important, or exciting enough to be printed on the front page of a newspaper【非正式】〔报纸〕头版的: *a front-page story* 头版报道

front room /,ˈ·ˈ/ *n* [C] the main room in a house where you usually sit; LIVING ROOM 起居室, 客厅; 前厅

front-run·ner /,ˈ· ˈ··/ *n* [C] the person or thing that is most likely to succeed in a competition〔竞争中的〕领先者: *Thomson and Palmer are the front-runners for promotion.* 汤姆森和帕尔默最有希望得到提拔。

frost[1] /frɔst; frɒst/ *n* **1** [U] ice that looks white and powdery and covers things that are outside when the temperature is very cold 霜: *The grass and trees were white with frost.* 草和树上盖满了白霜。**2** [C] very cold weather, when water freezes〔天气〕严寒, 冰冻: **late/early frost** *Even in May we can sometimes get a late frost.* 即使在5月份, 我们有时都会遇到春寒冰冻的天气。| **hard frost** (=extremely cold weather) 严寒, 酷寒 *Our pipes burst in the hard frost.* 我们的管道在严寒中爆裂。—see also 另见 FROSTY, FROSTED

frost[2] *v* [T] *especially AmE* to cover a cake with a mixture of powdery sugar and liquid; ICE[2]【尤美】在〔糕饼〕上撒糖霜

frost up also 又作 **frost over** *phr v* [I] to become covered in frost 布满霜, 结霜: *The car door's all frosted up and I can't get it open.* 车门结满了霜, 我打不开它。

Frost, Robert (1874-1963) a US poet who is one of America's best known and most popular poets. Some of his best known poems are *Fire and Ice* and *Stopping by the Woods on a Snowy Evening.* 弗罗斯特 (1874-1963), 美国最有名、最受欢迎的诗人之一。他的部分代表作有《火与冰》和《雪夜林边小驻》

frost·bite /ˈfrɔst,baɪt; ˈfrɒstbaɪt/ *n* [U] a condition caused by extreme cold, that makes your fingers, toes etc swell, become darker and sometimes drop off 冻伤, 冻疮 —**frostbitten** /-bɪtn̩; -bɪtn/ *adj*

frost·ed /ˈfrɔstɪd; ˈfrɒstɨd/ *adj* covered with FROST[1] (1), or with something that looks like frost 结霜的; 有霜状表面的

frosted glass /,ˈ· ˈ·◂/ *n* [U] glass that is not transparent 磨砂玻璃: *a frosted glass screen* 磨砂玻璃屏风

frost·ing /ˈfrɔstɪŋ; ˈfrɒstɪŋ/ *n* [U] **1** *especially AmE* a sweet substance put on cakes and made from powdery sugar and liquid; ICING【尤美】〔撒在糕饼上的〕糖霜 **2** a rough surface that is not shiny 磨砂面

frost·y /ˈfrɔstɪ; ˈfrɒsti/ *adj* **1 a)** extremely cold 严寒的: *frosty air* 冷冽的空气 **b)** covered with FROST[1] (1) 覆盖着霜的, 结霜的: *She stumbled, falling heavily on the frosty ground.* 她绊了一下, 重重地摔在结霜的地面上。**2** unfriendly 不友好的; 冷淡的: *"This is a members-only club," said the doorman with frosty politeness.* "本俱乐部只接待会员。"看门人冷淡而礼貌地说道。| **frosty smile/expression/stare** *He gave me a frosty stare.* 他冷冷地瞪了我一眼。—**frostily** *adv*

froth[1] /frɔθ; frɒθ/ *n* **1** [singular, U] small BUBBLES[1] (1) that form on top of a liquid that has air mixed in it 泡沫, 泡: *He carefully wiped the froth from his moustache.* 他小心地抹去小胡子上的泡沫。**2** [singular, U] small, white BUBBLES[1] (1) of SALIVA around a person's or animal's mouth〔人或动物嘴里流出的〕白沫 **3** [U] talk or ideas that are attractive but have no real value or meaning〔华而不实的〕空谈, 空想: *The book has too much froth and not enough fact.* 这本书空话太多, 事实很少。

froth[2] *v* [I] **1** also 又作 **froth up** if a liquid froths it produces or contains BUBBLES[1] (1) on top 起泡沫; 含有泡沫: *When you first open the bottle the beer will froth for a few seconds.* 刚打开瓶子时, 啤酒会起几秒钟泡沫。**2** if someone's mouth froths, SALIVA comes out as small white BUBBLES[1] (1) 口吐白沫 **3** **froth at the mouth** **a)** *informal* to be extremely angry【非正式】气急败坏, 气得要命: *By the time I got out of the traffic jam I was frothing at the mouth.* 当我从堵塞的交通中脱身出来时, 我气得要命。**b)** to have SALIVA coming out of your mouth as small white BUBBLES[1] (1) 口吐白沫

froth·y /ˈfrɔθɪ; ˈfrɒθi/ *adj* **1** a liquid that is frothy has lots of small BUBBLES[1] (1) on top 表面起泡沫的: *a cup of hot frothy cappuccino* 一杯热腾腾、冒着泡沫的卡布奇诺咖啡 **2** a frothy book, film etc is enjoyable but not serious or important〔书、电影等〕有趣但浅薄的; 不严肃的 —**frothily** *adv*

frown[1] /fraun; fraʊn/ *v* [I] to make an angry, unhappy, or confused expression, moving your EYEBROWS together 皱眉: *She saw him frown as he read the letter.* 她看见他在读信的时候皱眉头。| [**+at**] *Mattie frowned at him disapprovingly.* 马蒂不满地朝他皱眉头。

frown on/upon sb/sth *phr v* [T usually passive 一般用被动态] to disapprove of something, especially someone's behaviour 不赞成, 反对〔尤指某人的行为〕: *Even though divorce is legal it is still frowned upon.* 尽管离婚是合法的, 人们仍然不太赞同。

frown[2] *n* [C usually singular 一般用单数] the expression on your face when you frown 皱眉: **with a frown** *He looked at her with a puzzled frown.* 他困惑不解地皱着眉头看着她。

frow·zy /ˈfrauzɪ; ˈfraʊzi/ also 又作 **frowsty** /ˈfraustɪ; ˈfraʊsti/ *BrE*【英】—*adj* **1** someone who is frowzy is not very clean or tidy and smells bad 邋遢的; 不整洁的; 肮脏难闻的: *a frowzy old woman who kept cats* 一个养了许多猫的、邋遢的老太太 **2** a house or room that is frowzy has no fresh air in it and smells bad〔房屋或房间〕气味难闻的; 霉臭的: *The air in the room had become stale and frowzy.* 房间里的空气不流通, 气味难闻。

froze /froz; frəʊz/ the past tense of FREEZE[1]

fro·zen[1] /ˈfrozn̩; ˈfrəʊzən/ the past participle of FREEZE[1]

frozen[2] *adj* **1** frozen food has been stored at a very low temperature in order to preserve it〔食物〕冷冻的, 冷藏的: *frozen meat* 冷冻肉 **2** **be frozen (stiff)** *spoken* to feel very cold【口】冻僵的, 冻坏的: *I'm frozen! Put the fire on.* 我冻僵了! 把炉子打开。**3** earth that is frozen is so cold it has become very hard〔土地〕冻硬的: *The ground was frozen beneath our feet.* 我们脚下的地都冻硬了。**4** a river, lake etc that is frozen has a layer of ice on the surface〔河、湖等〕结冰的 **5** **be frozen with fear/terror/fright** to be so afraid, shocked etc that you cannot move 被吓呆了, 被吓得无法动弹

fruc·ti·fy /ˈfrʌktə,faɪ; ˈfrʌktɨfaɪ/ *v* [I,T] *technical* to produce fruit or to make a plant produce fruit【术语】(使) 结果实 —**fructification** /,frʌktəfəˈkeʃən; ,frʌktɨfɨˈkeɪʃən/ *n* [U]

fruc·tose /ˈfrʌktos; ˈfrʌktəʊs/ *n* [U] a kind of natural sugar in fruit juices and HONEY (1)〔果汁或蜂蜜中的〕(天然) 果糖

fru·gal /ˈfrugl̩; ˈfruːgəl/ *adj* **1** careful to only buy what is necessary 节俭的, 节约的: *As children we were taught to be frugal and hard-working.* 小时候大人教我们要节俭和勤劳。**2** a frugal meal is a small meal of plain food〔膳食〕少量的, 简便的, 简单的: *We sat down to a frugal breakfast.* 我们坐下来吃了一顿简单的早餐。—**frugally** *adv* —**frugality** /fruˈgælətɪ; fruːˈgælɨti/ *n* [U]

fruit[1] /frut; fruːt/ *n plural* **fruit** or **fruits** **1** [C,U] something such as an apple, BANANA, OR STRAWBERRY that grows on a tree or other plant, and tastes sweet 水果: *fresh fruit and vegetables* 新鲜蔬果 | *a bowl of fruit* 一盘水果 —see also 另见 DRIED FRUIT, SOFT FRUIT —see picture on page A8 参见 A8 页图 **2** [C,U] *technical* the part of a plant, bush, or tree that contains the seeds【术语】果实 **3** **the fruit/fruits of sth** the good results that you have from something, after you have worked very hard 某事物的成果 **4** **bear fruit** if a plan or activity bears fruit, it produces the good results that you intended〔计划或活动〕取得成果, 有成效 **5** **in fruit** *technical* trees, plants etc that are in fruit are producing their fruit【术语】在结果实 **6** **the fruits of the earth/nature** all the natural things that the earth produces, such as fruit, vegetables, or minerals 大地/大自然的果实〈如水果、蔬菜或矿物等〉 **7** [C] *old-fashioned slang* an insulting way of talking to or about a man who is a HOMOSEXUAL【过时, 俚】男同性恋者〔侮辱性的词语〕 **8** **old fruit** *old-fashioned slang BrE* used by men as a way of addressing a man that they know well【过时, 俚, 英】老兄〔对朋友的称呼〕

fruit[2] *v* [I] *technical* if a tree or a plant fruits, it produces fruit【术语】〔树或植物〕结果实

fruit bat /ˈ· ·/ *n* [C] a large BAT[1] (1) that lives in hot countries and eats fruit 果蝠, 狐蝠〔一种热带大蝙蝠〕

fruit·cake /ˈfrutˌkek; ˈfruːtkeɪk/ *n* **1** [C,U] a cake that has dried fruit in it 水果[果脯, 果子]蛋糕 **2** [C] *informal* someone who seems to be mentally ill or behaves in a strange way【非正式】怪人, 疯子: *She's a bit of a fruitcake.* 她有点怪。—see also 另见 **nutty as a fruitcake** (NUTTY (3))

fruit·er·er /ˈfrutərə; ˈfruːtərə/ *n* [C] *BrE old-fashioned* someone who sells fruit【英, 过时】水果商

fruit fly /ˈ· ·/ *n* [C] a small fly that eats fruit or decaying plants 果蝇

fruit·ful /ˈfrutfəl; ˈfruːtfəl/ *adj* **1** something you do that is fruitful has good results 富有成效的: *Today's meeting proved more fruitful than last week's.* 今天的会议证明比上星期的有成效。—opposite 反义词 FRUITLESS **2** *literary* land that is fruitful produces a lot of corn, vegetables, fruit etc【文】〔土地〕多产的, 丰饶的; 果实累累的 —**fruitfully** *adv* —**fruitfulness** *n* [U]

fru·i·tion /fruˈɪʃən; fruːˈɪʃən/ *n* [U] *formal* the successful result of a plan, idea etc【正式】〔计划、想法等的〕实现; 完成: **come to fruition/be brought to fruition** *All his plans had come to fruition.* 他所有的计划都实现了。

fruit·less /ˈfrutlɪs; ˈfruːtləs/ *adj* failing to achieve what was wanted, especially after much effort 无成效的, 无结果的: **fruitless attempt/search/journey** *a fruitless attempt to settle the dispute* 试图解决争端的徒劳的努力 | *So far, their search has been fruitless.* 到目前为止, 他们的搜寻工作毫无结果。—opposite 反义词 FRUITFUL (1) —**fruitlessly** *adv* —**fruitlessness** *n* [U]

fruit ma·chine /ˈ· ·ˌ·/ *n* [C] *BrE* a machine in which you put a coin, that gives money back if you make three pictures of the same thing appear【英】吃角子老虎机; SLOT MACHINE *AmE*【美】

fruit sal·ad /ˌ· ˈ· ·/ *n* [C,U] a dish of many different types of fruit cut into small pieces 水果沙拉

fruit·y /ˈfrutɪ; ˈfruːti/ *adj* **1** tasting or smelling strongly of fruit 有水果味的: *a very fruity wine* 带浓郁果香的葡萄酒 **2** a voice or laugh that is fruity sounds low and pleasant〔声音〕圆润的;〔微笑〕甜美的 **3** *BrE informal* a remark, story etc that is fruity is about sex and slightly shocking or offensive【英, 非正式】〔话语、故事等〕猥亵的, 低级趣味的

frump /frʌmp; frʌmp/ *n* [C] a woman who is frumpy 衣着过时的女子

frump·y /ˈfrʌmpɪ; ˈfrʌmpi/ also 又作 **frump·ish** /ˈfrʌmpɪʃ; ˈfrʌmpɪʃ/ *adj* a woman who is frumpy looks unattractive because she dresses in old-fashioned clothes〔女子〕衣着过时的

frus·trate /ˈfrʌstret; frʌˈstreɪt/ *v* [T] **1** if something frustrates you it makes you feel annoyed or angry because you are unable to do what you want 使恼怒; 使灰心丧气: *I think the fact that he's working with amateurs really frustrates him.* 我看他和非专业人员一起干活的事实在使他感到沮丧。 **2** to prevent someone's plans, efforts or attempts from succeeding 挫败; 阻挠: *Their attempts to speak to him were frustrated by the guards.* 他们想跟他说话, 但被警卫拦住了。—compare 比较 THWART[1]

frus·trat·ed /ˈfrʌstretɪd; frʌˈstreɪtɪd/ *adj* **1** feeling annoyed, upset, and impatient, because you cannot control or change a situation, or achieve something 灰心丧气的, 泄气的, 沮丧的: **get frustrated** *He gets frustrated when he can't win.* 他赢不了的时候便垂头丧气。| [**+with/at**] *I can't understand this. I just get frustrated with it.* 我无法理解这一点。我只是对此感到沮丧。| **sexually frustrated** (=feeling dissatisfied because you cannot have sex) 性欲上不满足的 **2** **a frustrated poet/actor/dancer etc** someone who wants to develop a particular skill but has not been able to do this 失意的诗人/演员/舞蹈员等

frus·trat·ing /ˈfrʌstretɪŋ; frʌˈstreɪtɪŋ/ *adj* making you feel annoyed, upset, or impatient because you cannot do what you want to do 令人沮丧[泄气, 不快, 不耐烦]的

frus·tra·tion /frʌsˈtreʃən; frʌˈstreɪʃən/ *n* **1** [C,U] the feeling of being annoyed, upset, or impatient, because you cannot control or change a situation, or achieve something 失意; 失望; 沮丧; 受挫: *It wasn't what he said that made me cry – it was sheer frustration.* 让我哭的不是他说的话——而是彻底的失望。| **in/with frustration** *Souness watched in frustration as his team lost yet again.* 桑尼斯失望地看着他的球队又输了。**2** [U] the fact of being prevented from achieving what you are trying to achieve 受挫: [**+of**] *The frustration of his ambitions made him a bitter man.* 他的雄心壮志受挫, 使他充满怨恨。

fry[1] /fraɪ; fraɪ/ *v past and past participle* **fried** **1** [I,T] to cook something in hot fat or oil, or to be cooked in hot fat or oil 煎; 炸; 炒: *Fry the onions until they are golden.* 把洋葱炒至金黄色。—see picture on page A10 参见 A10 页图 **2** [I,T] *AmE slang* to kill someone, or to be killed, as a punishment in the ELECTRIC CHAIR【美俚】(被)以电刑处死, 坐电椅 —see also 另见 DEEP FRY, FRIES, STIR-FRY —**fried** *adj* 3

fry[2] *n* [plural] **1** very young fish 鱼苗, 鱼秧; 小鱼 —see also 另见 **small fry** (SMALL[1] (12)) **2** **fries** [plural] *AmE* long thin pieces of potato that have been cooked in fat【美】炸薯条; chips (CHIP[1] (3a)) *BrE*【英】

fry·er, frier /ˈfraɪə; ˈfraɪə/ *n* [C] **1** **deep fat fryer/deep fryer** *AmE* a big deep pan for frying food【美】油炸锅 **2** *AmE* a chicken that has been specially bred to be fried【美】〔适合油炸的〕嫩鸡

frying pan /ˈ· · ˌ·/ *n* [C] **1** a round flat pan with a long handle, used for frying food 长柄平底煎锅; SKILLET *AmE*【美】—see picture at 参见 PAN[1] 图 **2** **out of the frying pan and into the fire** to go from a bad situation to one that is even worse 跳出油锅又落入火坑〔比喻境况愈来愈糟〕

fry-up /ˈ· ·/ *n* [C] *informal BrE* a meal of fried food such as eggs, BACON, potatoes etc【非正式, 英】一份油煎食物〈如煎鸡蛋、熏肉、马铃薯等〉

FS the written abbreviation of 缩写 = the FOREIGN SERVICE

ft **1** the written abbreviation of 缩写 = FOOT[1] (3) 英尺: *a board 6ft × 4ft* 6 英尺 × 4 英尺的木板 **2** **Ft** the written abbreviation of 缩写 = FORT, used in names of places 城堡〔用于地名〕: *Ft. Lauderdale* 劳德代尔堡

FT, the /ˌɛf ˈti; ˌef ˈtiː◂/ the written abbreviation of 缩写 = the FINANCIAL TIMES

FT 100 Share In·dex, the /ˌɛf ti wʌn ˌhʌndrɪd ˈʃɛə ˌɪndɛks; ˌef tiː wʌn ˌhʌndrɪd ˈʃeər ˌɪndeks/ also 又作 **the FTSE 100** **the Footsie** the Financial Times Stock Exchange 100 Index; a number that shows whether shares in companies on the London STOCK EXCHANGE have generally risen or fallen in value on a particular day. The number is based on the share prices of 100 large and important companies. 英国《金融时报》100 指数〔反映伦敦证券交易所每日股价总体涨跌情况的资料。该资料是以 100 家大型公司的股价为基础计算的〕: *The FT 100 Share Index closed at 5124, down 40 points on the day.*《金融时报》100 指数当日收报 5124 点, 下跌 40 点。—see also 另见 DOW JONES AVERAGE, the HANG SENG INDEX, the NIKKEI INDEX

FTC, the /ˌɛf ti ˈsi; ˌef tiː ˈsiː/ the Federal Trade Commission; a US government organization that is responsible for making sure that trade between companies and their customers is fair. If two companies plan to MERGE (=join together to become a single large company), the FTC finds out whether this arrangement will be unfair to other companies or to customers in general. There is a similar organization in the UK called the Monopolies and Mergers Commission. 联邦贸易委员会〔美国一政府机构, 其职责是确保公司与客户之间的交易是公平的。如果两家公司计划合并, 那么该委员会就会查明合并总体上对其他公司或客户是否公平。英国也有一类似机构, 称"垄断与合并委员会"〕

FT Index, the /ˌɛf ti ˈɪndɛks; ˌef tiː ˈɪndeks/ —see also 另见 the FINANCIAL TIMES INDEX

fuch·sia /ˈfjuʃə; ˈfjuːʃə/ *n* **1** [C,U] a garden bush with hanging bell-shaped flowers in two colours of red, pink, or white 倒挂金钟〔花卉名〕 **2** [U] a bright pink colour 紫红色

fuck[1] /fʌk; fʌk/ *v taboo spoken*【讳, 口】**1** **Fuck off!** an offensive way of telling someone to go away 滚开!〔冒犯用语〕: *Fuck off you stupid bastard!* 滚开, 你这个笨蛋杂种! **2** [I,T] to have sex with someone (与…) 性交 **3** **fuck it/you/her/John!** used to emphasize that you are annoyed or angry at someone

or something 他妈的！/滚你妈的蛋！/滚他妈的蛋！/约翰这混蛋！〔骂人用语〕: *Oh fuck it! I'm going home early!* 嗬，他妈的！我要早回家了！

fuck around also 又作 **fuck about** *BrE*【英】*phr v* [I] *taboo spoken* to waste time or behave in a silly or careless way【讳，口】闲混；瞎搞；干蠢事

fuck sb **around** also 又作 **fuck** sb **about** *BrE*【英】*phr v* [I] *taboo spoken* to make someone angry or annoyed by wasting their time【讳，口】粗暴地对待；瞎弄；浪费时间: *The telephone company has been fucking me around all week.* 电话公司整个星期都在耍弄我。

fuck sb ↔ **off** *phr v* [T] *taboo spoken* to make someone feel annoyed or angry【讳，口】使厌烦；使生气: *Steve really fucks me off when he doesn't write down my phone messages.* 史蒂夫不记下人家给我的电话留言，使我确实很生气。

fuck sb ↔ **over** *phr v* [T] *AmE taboo* to treat someone very badly【美讳】虐待〔某人〕: *Bev had been fucked over so many times she no longer expected life to be fair.* 贝夫已经被亏待许多次了，她不再指望生活是公平的。

fuck sb ↔ **up** *phr v* [T] *taboo spoken* to make someone very unhappy and confused so that they cannot control their life【讳，口】搞糟，弄乱；毁掉: *Heroin fucks you up.* 海洛因会把你毁了。

fuck up *phr v taboo spoken* [I,T **fuck** sth ↔ **up**] to make a mistake or do something badly【讳，口】犯错误；把事情搞糟: *You really fucked up this time.* 这次你真把事情搞糟了。

fuck with sb *phr v* [T] *taboo spoken* to annoy someone or make them angry【讳，口】使某人恼怒，使某人生气: *I wouldn't fuck with Alfie if I were you.* 要是我是你，就不会激怒阿尔菲。

fuck² *interjection taboo* used when you are annoyed about something【讳】他妈的，混账，见鬼: *Fuck! I forgot my keys!* 他妈的！我忘了带钥匙！

F

fuck³ *n taboo spoken*【讳，口】**1** [C usually singular 一般用单数] the act of having sex 性交 **2 the fuck** used when you are angry to emphasize what you are saying〔发怒时用于强调〕他妈的；究竟，到底: *Get the fuck out of here!* 你他妈的滚出去！| **who/why/what etc the fuck** *What the fuck do you think you're doing?* 你他妈的究竟在做什么？**3 not care/give a fuck** to not care at all what happens 毫不在乎

fuck all /ˈ· ·/ *n* [U] *BrE taboo spoken* nothing【英，讳，口】什么都没有: *I don't know why they employ him. He does fuck all anyway.* 我不知道他们干嘛要雇他。反正他什么事也不做。

fucked up /ˌ· ˈ·/ *adj taboo* very unhappy and confused, so that you cannot control your life properly【讳】〔生活〕乱糟糟的，十分不愉快的: *She's pretty fucked up.* 她日子过得一团糟。

fuck·er /ˈfʌkə; ˈfʌkə/ also 又作 **fuck** *BrE*【英】—*n* [C] *taboo spoken* someone who you dislike very much, think is stupid etc【讳，口】讨厌透顶的人，混蛋；笨蛋

fuck·head /ˈfʌkˌhɛd; ˈfʌkhed/ *n* [C] *AmE taboo spoken* someone you dislike or think is stupid【美，讳，口】讨厌的人，混蛋；笨蛋: *Get lost, fuckhead.* 走开，混蛋。

S1 **fuck·ing** /ˈfʌkɪŋ; ˈfʌkɪŋ/ *adj* [only before noun 仅用于名词前] *taboo spoken*【讳，口】**1** used to emphasize that you are angry or annoyed 该死的: *I wish that fucking parrot would shut up!* 我希望那只该死的鹦鹉会住嘴！**2** used to emphasize your opinion of something 非常〔用于强调〕: *He's a fucking good football player.* 他足球踢得非常好。

fuck·ing A /ˌfʌkɪŋ ˈe; ˌfʌkɪŋ ˈeɪ/ *interjection AmE taboo* used when you are very surprised, shocked etc by something【美讳】他妈的〔表示惊讶、震惊等〕: *Fucking A! I never thought L.A. would be this hot.* 他妈的！我从来没想到洛杉矶会这么热。

fuck-up /ˈ· ·/ *n* [C] *taboo spoken* a situation that has been dealt with very badly【讳，口】一团糟: *Relations with the staff were bad, so any change in the schedule was seen as 'yet another fuck-up by the management'.* 公司与职员的关系很坏，因此日程表上有任何变化都被看作"管理部门又一次搞糟了"。

fud·dle¹ /ˈfʌdl; ˈfʌdl/ *v* [T] *BrE informal* if something, especially alcohol or drugs, fuddles you or your mind, it makes you unable to think clearly【英，非正式】〔尤指酒精或毒品〕使昏醉；使糊涂: *Too much drink fuddles your brain.* 喝酒太多会让你脑子糊涂。

fuddle² *n* [singular] *informal*【非正式】**in a fuddle** feeling very confused and unable to think clearly 头脑糊涂的: *Poor old Tom. Since his wife died he's been in a terrible fuddle.* 可怜的老汤姆，自从妻子去世后他就一直糊糊涂涂的。

fud·dled /ˈfʌdḷd; ˈfʌdld/ *adj* unable to think clearly, especially because you are drunk or old〔尤指由于酒醉或年老而〕头脑糊涂的，思想混乱的

fud·dy-dud·dy /ˈfʌdɪ ˌdʌdɪ; ˈfʌdi ˌdʌdi/ *n* [C] someone who has old-fashioned ideas and attitudes 守旧的人；老古董: *You're such an old fuddy-duddy. Most women wear trousers these days!* 你太顽固保守了，如今多数妇女都穿长裤了！—**fuddy-duddy** *adj*

fudge¹ /fʌdʒ; fʌdʒ/ *n* **1** [U] a soft creamy light brown sweet food 奶油软糖 **2 a fudge** *especially BrE* an attempt to deal with a situation that does not solve its problems completely, or only makes it seem better【尤英】勉强应付；作表面上的改善；敷衍了事

fudge² *v* **1** [I,T] to avoid giving exact details or a clear answer about something 回避；敷衍；搪塞: **fudge the issue** (=avoid a particular subject) 回避问题 *politicians fudging the issue of arms sales* 回避武器出售问题的政客们 **2** [T] to change important figures or facts to deceive people 捏造: *Sibley has been fudging his data for years now.* 西布利好几年来一直在捏造数据。

fudge³ *interjection* used when you are angry or annoyed, instead of saying a more offensive word 胡说，瞎说〔用于生气或烦恼时，代替更具冒犯性的词语〕: *Oh fudge! I've left my wallet at home!* 哎，妈的！我把皮夹子忘在家里了！

fudg·y /ˈfʌdʒɪ; ˈfʌdʒi/ *adj AmE* slightly sticky with a strong sweet chocolate taste【美】〔因带有浓烈巧克力甜味而〕有点黏的

fu·el¹ /ˈfjuəl; ˈfjuːəl/ *n* **1** [C,U] a substance such as coal, gas, or oil that can be burned to produce heat or energy 燃料: *Don't leave the engine switched on. It wastes fuel.* 别让发动机开着。这浪费燃料。| *Coal is one of the cheapest fuels.* 煤是最廉价的燃料之一。**2** [U] something that makes someone's anger, hatred etc worse 火上加油的东西；使〔怒气、怨恨等〕更激烈的东西: **fuel to sth** *His behaviour was only fuel to her jealousy.* 他的行为只能使她更加妒忌。**3 add fuel to the fire/flames** to make a situation a lot worse than it was already 火上浇油 S2 W2

fuel² *v past tense* **fuelled** *BrE*【英】, **fueled** *AmE*【美】**1** [T] to make a situation worse or make someone's feelings stronger 使恶化；使感情更强烈: *The attempts to stop the strike only fuelled the workers' resentment.* 制止罢工的企图只能使工人更加不满。**2** [T] to put oil, petrol etc in a vehicle 给〔车辆〕加油 **3** also 又作 **fuel up** [I] if a vehicle fuels up, fuel is put into it 加油，加燃料: *It's amazing that some planes can fuel up in mid air.* 有些飞机能在空中加油，这真令人吃惊。

fuel in·jec·tion /ˈ·· ,·ˈ·/ *n* [U] a method of putting liquid fuel directly into an engine, which allows a car to ACCELERATE more quickly 燃油喷射

fug /fʌg; fʌg/ *n* [singular] *BrE informal* air inside a room that feels heavy and unpleasant because of smoke, heat, or too many people【英，非正式】〔房间内因烟雾、热气或人多产生的〕污浊空气: *There's a terrible fug in here. Let's open a window.* 这里面空气污浊得可怕，我们开扇窗子吧。—**fuggy** *adj*

fu·gi·tive¹ /ˈfjudʒətɪv; ˈfjuːdʒɪtɪv/ *n* [C] someone who is hiding, especially from the police, and is trying to avoid being caught 逃犯；逃亡者: **[+from]** *a fugitive from justice* 在逃的罪犯

fugitive² *adj* [only before noun 仅用于名词前] **1** trying to escape 企图逃跑的 **2** *literary* lasting for a very short time【文】短暂的: *rare and fugitive visits* 难得而短暂的访问

fugue /fjug; fjuːg/ *n* [C,U] a way of writing music using a tune that is repeated regularly in different keys (KEY² (4)) by different voices, instruments etc, or a piece of music written this way 赋格（曲）

Fu·ji /ˈfudʒɪ; ˈfuːdʒi/**, Mount** also 又作 **Fujiyama** /ˌfudʒɪˈjɑmə; ˌfuːdʒiːˈjɑːmə/ a VOLCANO, about 100 km southwest of Tokyo, which is the highest mountain in Japan. Its top has the shape of a perfect CONE. 富士山〔位于东京西南100公里处的一座火山，是日本最高的山，顶部呈完美的圆锥形〕

-ful¹ /fəl; fəl/ *suffix* [in adjectives 构成形容词] **1** full of something 充满…的: *an eventful day* 多事的一天 **2** having the quality of something or causing something 有…性质的；引起…的: *restful colours* 宁神怡目的色彩 | *Is it painful?* 痛吗？—**-fully** /fəlɪ; fəli/ [in adverbs 构成副词]: *shouting cheerfully* 高兴地呼喊

-ful² /ful; fʊl/ *suffix* [in nouns 构成名词] **1** the amount of a substance needed to fill a particular container 充满…所需的量: *two cupfuls of milk* 满满两杯牛奶 **2** as much as can be carried by or contained in a particular part of the body〔身体部位〕充满…的: *carrying an armful of flowers* 抱着一抱花

Ful·bright Schol·ar·ship /ˈfulbraɪt ˌskɑləʃɪp; ˈfʊlbraɪt ˌskɒləʃɪp/ money provided for US university students and teachers so that they can study in other countries, and for students and teachers from other countries so that they can study in the US 富布赖特奖学金〔资助美国大学师生出国学习和外国师生赴美学习的一种奖学金制度〕—**Fulbright Scholar** *n*

ful·crum /ˋfʌlkrəm; ˈfʊlkrəm/ *n plural* **fulcrums** *or* **fulcra** /-krə; -krə/ [C] the point on which a LEVER (=bar) turns, balances, or is supported in turning or lifting something〔杠杆的〕支点

ful·fil *BrE*【英】, **fulfill** *AmE*【美】/fʊlˋfɪl; fʊlˈfɪl/ *v* [T] **1** if a hope, promise, wish etc is fulfilled, the thing that you had hoped, promised, wanted etc happens or is done 实现, 履行〔希望、诺言、愿望等〕: *Visiting Disneyland has fulfilled a boyhood dream.* 到迪斯尼乐园参观实现了童年的梦想。| *Eisenhower finally fulfilled his election pledge to end the war in Korea.* 艾森豪威尔终于履行他的竞选诺言, 结束了朝鲜战争。**2 fulfil a need** to provide something that someone needs 满足需要 **3 fulfil a requirement/condition** to reach a standard that is necessary, especially one that has been officially decided 符合要求/条件: *Much of the electrical equipment failed to fulfill safety requirements.* 许多电器未能符合安全要求。**4 fulfil a role/function/duty etc** to do the things you are supposed or expected to do because of your job, position in society etc 承担角色/履行职责/履行义务等: *Does the established Church fulfil any useful function in modern society?* 英国国教在现代社会发挥着什么有用的作用吗? **5** if your work fulfils you, it makes you feel satisfied because you are using all your skills, qualities etc 充分发挥〔才能等〕**6 fulfil yourself** to feel satisfied because you are using all your skills, qualities etc 充分发挥自己的才能: *She succeeded in fulfilling herself both as an actress and as a mother.* 她作为一个演员和母亲, 两者都做得十分出色。**7 fulfil your potential** to be as successful as you possibly could be 充分发挥潜能: *While he is very competent, he is not really fulfilling his potential.* 他固然很能胜任工作, 但没有真正充分发挥出他的潜力。**8 fulfil a prediction/prophecy** to happen in a way someone has said something would happen 应验预言

ful·filled /fʊlˋfɪld; fʊlˈfɪld/ *adj* satisfied with your life, job etc because you feel that it is interesting, useful, or important, and you are using all your skills 满意的; 满足的: *I'm sure I'd feel more fulfilled if I had a job that involved working with people, caring for people.* 要是我能得到一份与人打交道、关心人的工作, 我肯定会更满意。

ful·fil·ling /fʊlˋfɪlɪŋ; fʊlˈfɪlɪŋ/ *adj* a job, relationship etc that is fulfilling makes you feel satisfied because it allows you to use all your skills and qualities〔工作、关系等〕使人满意的, 使人满足的: *A career in nursing still provides one on the most fulfilling of jobs.* 护理职业仍是一种很令人满足的工作。

ful·fil·ment *BrE*【英】, **fulfillment** *AmE*【美】/fʊlˋfɪlmənt; fʊlˈfɪlmənt/ *n* [U] **1** the feeling of being satisfied, especially in your job, because you are using all your skills and qualities〔尤指工作中的〕满足感: **sense/feeling of fulfilment** *Being responsible for so many people gave her a tremendous sense of fulfilment.* 要向这么多人负责使她获得巨大的满足感。| **seek fulfilment** (=try to find it) 寻找满足 **2 fulfilment of a wish/need etc** an occasion when something that is wanted, needed etc happens or is given 愿望的实现/需要的满足等 **3 fulfilment of a promise/duty/condition etc** the action of doing what you have promised, your duty, what you have been asked to do etc 履行诺言/职责/满足条件等: *The offer of this contract is subject to the fulfilment of certain conditions.* 这份合同的要约需要首先满足某些条件。

Ful·ham /ˋfʊləm; ˈfʊləm/ an area of west London which is a fashionable place to live 富勒姆〔伦敦西部一地区, 是一处时尚居住地〕

full¹ /fʊl; fʊl/ *adj*

1 ▶CONTAINER/ROOM/PLACE ETC 容器/房间/地点等◀ also 又作 **full up** if something such as a container, room, or place is full, no more things or people can go in it 满的; 装满的; 挤满的: *a full box of cereal* 满满的一盒麦片 | *The class is full, but you can register now for next term.* 这个班已经满了, 不过你现在可以登记下学期的。| [+of] *We walked in to find the kitchen full of smoke.* 我们走进去, 发现厨房里满是烟。| **full to the brim** (=filled to the top of something) 满满的, 满到边的 *a cup full to the brim with water* 满满一杯水 | **full to bursting** *BrE* (=very full)【英】很满的 *The room was full to bursting.* 房间挤得水泄不通。

2 ▶COMPLETE/TOTAL 完整的/全部的◀ **a)** including all parts or details 完整的, 详尽的, 全面的: *Please write your full name and address on the form.* 请在表格上写下你的全名和详细地址。| *We have a full range of new cars.* 我们有各种款式的新车。| **the full story** (=everything someone knows about something)〔所知道的〕全部事实 *I still don't think he's telling us the full story.* 我仍然认为他没有把全部事实都告诉我们。**b)** the highest level or greatest amount of something 最高水平的; 最多的: *Weissman and I are in full agreement on this issue.* 威斯曼和我在这个问题上是完全一致的。

3 be full of a) to feel or express a strong emotion〔表达强烈感情〕充满…的: *children full of excitement at Christmas* 圣诞节时万分兴奋的孩子们 | *He's full of guilt about the death of his daughter.* 他对女儿的死深感内疚。**b)** to think or talk about one thing all the time 一心想着; 总是谈论: *He was full of his plans for travelling around the world.* 他总是想着他那些周游世界的计划。| **be full of yourself** (=only think about yourself) 自以为是 *Brad's all right, but he's a little too full of himself.* 布拉德不错, 可他有点自视过高。**c)** to contain many things of the same kind 有许多…的: *a sky full of stars* 布满星星的天空 | *His essay is full of mistakes.* 他的论文错误百出。

4 ▶TIME 时间◀ **a)** lasting the whole time 持续整段时间的; 整整的: *My father spent three full hours trying to explain one problem in my math book.* 爸爸花了整整三小时想解释我的数学书里的一个问题。**b)** filled with many things to do 忙碌的, 日程排得很满的: *I've had a full week. I'm looking forward to staying home tonight.* 我已经忙了整个星期。我指望着今晚能留在家里。

5 ▶FOOD 食品◀ *informal*【非正式】also 又作 **full up** *BrE* having eaten so much food that you cannot eat any more【英】饱的, 吃饱的: *No more, thanks. I'm full.* 不再吃了, 谢谢。我饱了。| **do sth on a full stomach** (=do physical activity just after a meal) 刚吃饱了就做某事

6 at full speed as fast as possible 全速地: *Parker was driving at full speed when he hit the wall.* 帕克在全速开车时撞到了墙壁上。

7 rise to your full height/draw yourself up to your full height to stand up very straight 挺直身子站起来

8 fall/lie full length to fall or lie flat, with your body stretched out 直挺挺地倒下/躺下

9 ▶CLOTHING 衣服◀ a full skirt, pair of trousers etc is made with a lot of material and fits loosely 宽松的, 肥大的: *full sleeves* 宽松的袖子 | *a dress with a full skirt* 下摆宽松的连衣裙

10 full marks *BrE* the highest number of points that you can get for school work【英】〔学校作业等〕满分

11 ▶BODY 身体◀ **a)** a full face, figure, etc is rounded or large in an attractive way 丰满的 **b)** used to mean fat when you do not want to offend someone 圆胖的, 丰腴的: *clothes for the fuller figure* 适合比较丰腴身材的衣服

12 in full view of sb so that everybody watching can see everything 使某人能看到全部; 为某人所一览无余: *The argument happened on stage in full view of the audience.* 这场争论发生在台上, 观众看得一清二楚。

13 have/lead a full life to do many different and interesting things 过着充实的生活/丰富的人生

14 full flavour *BrE*【英】, **full flavor** *AmE*【美】a pleasantly strong taste 浓味: *This wine has a wonderful full flavour.* 这种葡萄酒的味道醇厚可口。—see also 另见 FULL-BODIED

15 ▶SOUND 声音◀ a full sound is pleasantly loud or strong 洪亮的: *the full sound of the cello section* 大提琴部分的洪亮声音 —opposite 反义词 THIN¹ (7)

16 be full of crap/shit *taboo spoken* used to say that you think what someone is saying is wrong or stupid【讳, 口】一派胡言, 胡扯: *Don't listen to Jerry. He's full of crap.* 别听杰里的。他一派胡言。

17 in full a) if you pay an amount of money in full, you pay the whole amount〔付款〕全数地, 全部地: *The debt must be paid in full by 31 January 1998.* 这笔债必须在1998年1月31日前全数还清。**b)** if you write or copy something in full, you write it in its complete form 全文地; 完整地; 详细地

18 to the full in the best or most complete way 充分地; 十足地; 全面地: *To appreciate this opera to the full, you should read the story first.* 你想充分欣赏这出歌剧, 应当先读这故事。—see also 另见 FULLY, **come/turn full circle** (CIRCLE¹ (7)), **be full of beans** (BEAN¹ (4)), **(at) full belt** (BELT¹ (6)), **(at) full blast** (BLAST¹ (4)), **in full cry** (CRY² (8)), **full member** (MEMBER (1)), **(at) full pelt** (PELT² (3)), **be in full swing** (SWING² (7)), **at full tilt** (TILT² (1)), **have your hands full** (HAND¹ (32))

full² *adv* directly 直接地; 正好: [+on/in] *The ball struck him full on the chest.* 球正好打在他的胸部。—see also 另见 **know full well** (KNOW¹ (19))

full·back /ˋfʊl bæk; ˈfʊlbæk/ *n* [C] a player in a football team who plays in a particular position, or the position that they play in〔足球的〕后卫; 后卫位置

full beam /ˌ· ˈ·/ *n* [U] *BrE* lights at the front of a car that are on as brightly as possible【英】〔汽车前灯的〕远光, 强光; HIGH BEAM *AmE*【美】

full-blood·ed /ˌ· ˈ··◂/ *adj* [only before noun 仅用于名词前] **1** involving very strong feelings or emotions〔感情〕强烈的, 激烈的: **full-blooded argument/fight etc** (=an angry or violent

argument etc) 激烈的争论/吵架等 *The argument ended up as a full-blooded screaming match.* 这场争论最后演变成一次激烈的尖叫比赛。**2** having parents, grandparents etc from only one race of people 纯血统的: *There are very few full-blooded Cherokee Indians left.* 现在纯血统的切罗基印第安人所余无几了。

full blown /ˌ·ˈ·/ *adj* **1** having all of the qualities of something in its most complete or advanced stage 成熟的; 充分发展的: *The border fighting has turned into a full blown war.* 边境的冲突已经演变成一场全面战争。| *full-blown AIDS* 晚期艾滋病 **2** *often literary* a full-blown flower is completely open【常文】〔花〕盛开的, 绽放的

full board /ˌ·ˈ·/ *n* [U] a hotel that offers full board provides people with three meals a day〔旅馆提供一日三餐的〕全食宿: *A two night break costs £125 full board.* 两夜的全食宿需要 125 英镑。—compare 比较 HALF BOARD

full-bod·ied /ˌ·ˈ··◂/ *adj* tasting strong and rich〔味道〕浓郁的; 醇厚的: *a full-bodied red wine* 味道醇厚的红葡萄酒

full-court press /ˌ··ˈ·/ *n* [singular] **1** a method of attacking in the game of BASKETBALL〔篮球赛中的〕全场紧逼 **2** *AmE informal* the use of pressure or influence by one group on another【美, 非正式】〔施加压力或影响的〕全面出击, 全面攻势: *The DEA and the Justice Department put a full-court press on the drug baron.* 毒品管理局和司法部向大毒枭发动全面攻势。

full-cream /ˌ·ˈ·◂/ *adj BrE* full-cream milk has not had the cream removed【英】〔牛乳〕全脂的

full dress /ˌ·ˈ·/ *n* [U] special clothes worn for official occasions and ceremonies 礼服: *officers in full battle dress* 身穿正规战斗服的军官 —**full-dress** *adj* —see also 另见 EVENING DRESS, MORNING DRESS

Ful·ler /ˈfʊlə; ˈfʊlə/, **Rich·ard Buck·min·ster** /ˈrɪtʃəd ˈbʌkmɪnstə; ˈrɪtʃəd ˈbʌkmɪnstə/ (1895-1983) a US ARCHITECT (=someone who designs buildings) and engineer, who believed that scientific and technical developments could be used to solve many of society's problems, and who invented the GEODESIC DOME, a large, light, ball-shaped structure 富勒〔(1895-1983), 美国建筑师、工程师。他认为科技发展可解决许多社会问题。他曾发明了网格球形穹顶, 即一种体积大、重量轻的球形结构〕

ful·ler's earth /ˌfʊləz ˈɜːθ; ˌfʊləz ˈɜːθ/ *n* [U] dried clay made into a powder and used to make oil clearer and cleaner 漂白土, 漂泥

full-face /ˌ·ˈ·◂/ *adj* a full-face photograph or picture of someone shows the whole of their face〔照片或图片〕正面的 —compare 比较 PROFILE[1] (1)

full-fat /ˌ·ˈ·◂/ *adj BrE* full-fat milk or cheese has not had any of the fat taken out【英】〔乳品〕全脂的

full-fledged /ˌ·ˈ·◂/ *adj especially AmE*【尤美】**1** completely developed, trained, or established 全面发展的; 经过全面训练的; 成熟的; FULLY-FLEDGED (1) *BrE*【英】: *a full-fledged lawyer* 经过充分训练的律师 **2** a young bird is full-fledged when it has grown all its feathers and can fly〔鸟〕羽毛丰满的; FULLY-FLEDGED (2) *BrE*【英】

full-grown /ˌ·ˈ·◂/ *adj AmE* a full-grown animal, plant, or person has developed to their full size and will not grow any bigger【美】〔动物、植物或人〕完全长成的; 成熟的; 发育完全的; FULLY-GROWN *BrE*【英】: *A full-grown male elephant may weigh 2,000 pounds.* 成年的雄性大象体重可达 2000 磅。

full house /ˌ·ˈ·/ *n* [C usually singular 一般用单数] **1** an occasion at a cinema, concert hall, sports field etc when someone is sitting in every seat〔电影院、音乐厅、体育场等〕满座, 满席, 客满: *Speaking to a full house at the auditorium, he outlined his plan.* 他在满座的礼堂里对听众演说, 概述了他的计划。**2** three cards of one kind and a pair of another kind in a game of cards〔纸牌戏中的〕满堂红, 满贯〔一组牌中三张点数相同, 另外两张点数相同〕

full-length[1] /ˌ·ˈ·◂/ *adj* **1 full-length mirror/photograph/portrait** a mirror etc that shows all of a person, from their head to their feet 全身镜/照片/肖像: *a full-length portrait of the queen* 女王的全身肖像 **2 full-length skirt/dress/coat** a full length skirt etc reaches the ground, or is the longest possible for that particular type of clothing 垂地长裙/垂地连衣裙/长大衣: *a full-length evening dress* 垂地的晚礼服 **3 full-length play/book/film** a play, book etc of the normal length 足本戏剧/书/电影

full-length[2] *adv* [only after verb 仅用于动词后] someone who is lying full-length is lying flat with their legs straight out 脚伸直地; 平躺地: *Alison was stretched out full-length on the couch.* 艾莉森舒展四肢, 平躺在长沙发上。

full lock /ˌ·ˈ·/ *adv BrE* if you turn a car's STEERING WHEEL full lock, you turn it as far as it can be turned【英】完全锁定〔即把汽车方向盘转到头〕

full moon /ˌ·ˈ·/ *n* [singular] the moon when it looks completely round 满月, 圆月 —compare 比较 NEW MOON, HALF MOON

> **CULTURAL NOTE 文化注释**
> Some people believe that a full moon can make people behave strangely or dangerously. People joke that hospital CASUALTY departments are busier during full moons because people have more accidents. In stories and films people sometimes turn into werewolves (WEREWOLF) when there is a full moon. 有人相信, 满月令人做出古怪或危险的举动。人们打趣说, 因满月时事故增多, 医院的急诊室格外忙碌。在一些故事和电影里, 人有时会在月圆时变成狼人。

full·ness also 又作 **fulness** *BrE*【英】/ˈfʊlnɪs; ˈfʊlnəs/ *n* [U] **1 in the fullness of time** when the right time comes; EVENTUALLY 在适当的时候, 在时机成熟的时候; 总有一天: *I'm sure he'll tell us what's bothering him in the fullness of time.* 我肯定他会在适当的时候把他的烦恼告诉我们。**2** satisfaction 满足; 完美: *the human search for fullness in life* 人类对完美生活的追求 **3** the condition of being full 饱满; 充满; 充分

full-page /ˌ·ˈ·◂/ *adj* [only before noun 仅用于名词前] covering all of one page, especially in a newspaper or magazine〔尤指报纸或杂志〕全页的, 整版的: *a full-page advertisement* 整版广告

full pro·fes·sor /ˌ··ˈ··/ *n* [C] *AmE* a teacher at an American university who has reached the highest position and has gained TENURE (=the right to keep the job as long as they want it)【美】正教授, 终身教授 —see also 另见 ASSISTANT PROFESSOR, ASSOCIATE PROFESSOR

full-scale /ˌ·ˈ·◂/ *adj* [only before noun 仅用于名词前] **1** to the fullest amount or degree possible 最大限度的; 彻底的; 全面的: *a full-scale inquiry into the train crash* 对列车撞毁事故的全面调查 **2** a drawing, model, copy etc of something that is full-scale is the same size as the thing it represents 照原尺寸的, 与实物一样大小的

full-size /ˌ·ˈ·◂/ *adj* of the largest possible size 全尺寸的; 最大号的: *I need a full-size wrench to loosen this.* 我需要一把最大号的扳手来松开这东西。

full stop[1] /ˌ·ˈ·/ *n* **1** [C] *BrE* a point (.) that marks the end of a sentence or the shortened form of a word【英】句号; PERIOD[1] (5) *AmE*【美】—see picture at 参见 PUNCTUATION MARK 图 **2** *AmE* [singular] the state of being completely stopped, usually in a car【美】完全停止: *The car can accelerate from a full stop to 60 mph in five seconds.* 这辆车能在五秒钟内从完全停止加速到时速 60 英里。**3 come to a full stop** to stop completely, especially because of a problem or difficulty〔由于问题或困难而〕完全停顿下来: *Production came to a full stop when the generator blew up.* 发电机爆炸后, 生产完全停顿了下来。

full stop[2] *interjection BrE* used to say that you have definitely decided something, and you will not change your decision; PERIOD[1] (6)【英】就是这样, 不必多说; 没有商量: *I don't have a reason. I just don't want to go, full stop.* 我没有理由。我就是不想去, 不必多说了。

full-term /ˌ·ˈ·◂/ *adj* born after a PREGNANCY of a normal length 足月出生的: *a full-term baby* 足月出生的婴儿 —compare 比较 PREMATURE (2)

full time /ˌ·ˈ·/ *n* [U] *BrE* the end of the normal period of playing time in a sports game, especially football【英】〔尤指足球的〕比赛时间结束, 终场: *At full time neither team had scored.* 到了比赛时间结束时, 两队都没有得分。—see also 另见 HALF TIME

full-time /ˌ·ˈ·◂/ *adj, adv* **1** working or studying for the number of hours that work is usually done〔工作或学习〕全日制的[地]; 专职的[地]: *She works full-time, and has two kids.* 她全日工作, 而且有两个孩子。| **full-time staff/student** *They're looking for full-time staff at the library.* 图书馆正招聘专职工作人员。**2 full-time job a)** a job that you do for all the normal working hours in a week 全日制工作, 专职工作 **b)** hard work that you are not being paid for that takes a lot of your time〔全日而不付酬的〕艰苦工作: *Looking after three children all day is a full-time job.* 整天照顾三个小孩是件不得空闲的累活儿。—compare 比较 PART-TIME

ful·ly /ˈfʊli; ˈfʊli/ *adv* **1** completely 完全地; 充分地; 彻底地: *We are fully committed to the idea of political reform.* 我们全心全意奉行政治改革的思想。**2** used to emphasize how big, far away etc something is 足足; 至少〔强调大、远等〕: *The nearest big town is fully 300 miles away.* 最近的大城镇在足足 300 英里之外。

fully-fash·ioned /ˌ‥ˈ‥◂/ *BrE adj* clothing that is fully fashioned is made to fit the shape of the body exactly【英】〔衣服〕完全合身的, 完全照体形剪裁的

fully-fledged /ˌ‥ˈ‥◂/ *adj especially BrE*【尤英】**1** completely developed, trained, or established 全面发展的; 经过全面训练的; 成熟的; FULL-FLEDGED (1) *AmE*【美】: *After seven years of training she's now a fully-fledged doctor.* 她经过七年的训练, 现在已是个完全合格的医生。**2** a young bird is fully-fledged when it has grown all its feathers and can fly〔鸟〕羽毛丰满的; FULL-FLEDGED (2) *AmE*【美】

fully-grown /ˌ‥ˈ‥◂/ *adj* a fully-grown animal, plant, or person has developed to their full size and will not grow any bigger〔动物、植物或人〕完全长成的, 成熟的, 发育完全的; FULL-GROWN *AmE*【美】

ful·mi·nate /ˈfʌlməˌnet; ˈfʊlmɪneɪt/ *v* [I **+against/at**] *formal* to speak angrily against something【正式】怒斥; 严厉谴责: *an article fulminating against American Imperialism* 一篇严厉谴责美帝国主义的文章 —**fulmination** /ˌfʌlməˈneʃən; ˌfʊlmɪˈneɪʃən/ *n* [C,U]

ful·ness /ˈfʊlnɪs; ˈfʊlnɪs/ *n* [U] another spelling of FULLNESS fullness 的另一种拼法

ful·some /ˈfʊlsəm; ˈfʊlsəm/ *adj formal* a fulsome piece of writing, speech etc gives too much praise to be sincere【正式】〔作品或讲话等〕过分恭维的, 虚伪的, 令人厌恶的: *His speech was packed with fulsome praise for the managing director.* 他的演说充满过分恭维总经理的言辞。—**fulsomely** *adv* —**fulsomeness** *n* [U]

Ful·ton /ˈfultn̩; ˈfʊltən/, **Rob·ert** (1765-1815) a US engineer and inventor who designed and built several STEAMSHIPS (=large ships that use steam for power) 富尔顿〔(1765-1815), 美国工程师、发明家, 曾设计和制造了数艘汽船〕

Fu Man·chu /ˌfu mænˈtʃu; ˌfuː mænˈtʃuː/ the main character in the stories by Sax Rohmer and in the films based on these stories. Fu Manchu is an evil and very clever criminal. He has a very long MOUSTACHE, the ends of which hang down. A moustache that looks like this is often called a **Fu Manchu moustache**. 傅满洲〔萨克斯·罗默小说及据此改编的影片中的主人公。他是个邪恶狡猾的罪犯, 胡须很长且两端下垂。这样的胡子常被称作傅满洲式胡须〕

fum·ble /ˈfʌmbl̩; ˈfʌmbəl/ *v* **1** [I] to hold or try and move something with your hands carelessly or awkwardly 瞎弄; 笨手笨脚地摸: [**+for/with**] *Steve fumbled drunkenly with the keys, dropping them on the floor.* 史蒂夫醉酒后手忙脚乱地用钥匙开锁, 结果钥匙掉到地板上。**2** [I **+for/with**] if you fumble with your words when you are speaking, you have difficulty saying something 支支吾吾地说话, 笨嘴笨舌地说 **3** [I,T] *AmE* to drop a ball after catching it【美】接(球)不稳; 失(球) —**fumble** *n* [C]

fume /fjum; fjuːm/ *v* [I] **1** to be angry, usually without saying anything 生气, 生闷气〔通常不说话〕: *She sat in the car, fuming about what she had heard.* 她坐在车里, 对刚才听到的话感到怒不可遏。| [**+at**] *AmE* (=show you are angry by saying a lot of things to someone)【美】发怒, 怒气冲冲地说话 **2** to give off smoke or gases 冒烟; 冒气

S3 **fumes** /fjumz; fjuːmz/ *n* [plural] strong-smelling gas or smoke that is unpleasant to breathe in〔气体、烟雾的〕难闻的气味: *strong smell of paint fumes* 浓烈的油漆味

fu·mi·gate /ˈfjuməˌget; ˈfjuːmɪgeɪt/ *v* [T] to clear disease, BACTERIA, insects etc from somewhere using chemicals, smoke, or gas〔为消毒、杀菌、杀虫等而用化学品、烟或气〕熏蒸; 烟熏 —**fumigation** /ˌfjuməˈgeʃən; ˌfjuːmɪˈgeɪʃən/ *n* [U]

S2 W3 **fun¹** /fʌn; fʌn/ *adj* **1** [only before noun 仅用于名词前] a fun activity or experience is enjoyable〔活动或经历〕有趣的, 令人愉快的; 好玩的: *It was a fun night out – we'll have to do it again sometime.* 这次晚上出去很好玩 —— 我们什么时候得再去一次。**2** someone who is fun is enjoyable to be with because they are cheerful and amusing〔人〕有趣的, 能给人快乐的: **a fun person/girl/guy etc** *especially AmE*【尤美】*She's a fun person to be around.* 有她在场就很有趣。| **good/great fun** *BrE*【英】*The O'Brian boys were great fun.* 奥布赖恩家的男孩子们很有趣。

S2 **fun²** *n* [U] **1** an experience or activity that is very enjoyable and exciting 有趣的经历[活动]; 令人兴奋的经历[活动]; 乐趣: *It's no fun to be working inside when the weather's nice.* 天气晴朗的时候在屋里工作很无趣。| **good/great fun** *BrE*【英】*Why don't you come with us? It'll be great fun.* 你为什么不跟我们来呢? 会玩得很痛快的。| **have fun** (=to have an enjoyable time) 玩得[过得]很愉快 *The children were having so much fun, I hated to call them inside.* 孩子们玩得这么开心, 我舍不得把他们叫进来。| **What fun!** (=that sounds very enjoyable!) 多有趣啊! **2 for fun** also 又作 **for the fun of it** if you do something for fun, you do it because you enjoy it and not for any other reason 闹着玩地; 为了好玩: *We drove all the way to the beach, just for fun.* 我们一路老远地开车到海滩去, 只是为了好玩。**3 full of fun** playful and liking amusement 很喜欢玩的, 很爱玩闹的: *Jan's always so cheerful and full of fun.* 简总是这么高兴, 爱玩闹。**4 fun and games** playful activities 嬉闹, 欢闹: *My job isn't all fun and games you know – I work hard as well.* 我的工作不都是玩玩闹闹的, 你要知道 —— 我也努力工作的。**5 not be my idea of fun** used to talk about an activity, situation etc that is exciting or interesting to other people but is not for you 对我来说不是趣味: *Digging up old bones in a hot desert is not my idea of fun.* 在炎热的沙漠发掘古老的骨头不是我心目中好玩的事。**6 in fun** if you make a joke or say something about someone in fun, you do not intend it to be insulting 开玩笑似的[地]; 闹着玩的[地]: *Don't get upset Chris, she only said it in fun.* 不要苦恼了, 克里斯, 她那句话只是说着玩而已。**7 make fun of sb/sth** to make a joke about someone that is insulting or makes them feel bad 嘲弄某人/某物; 拿某人/某物开玩笑: *The kids at school always made fun of Jill's clothes.* 学校里的孩子总取笑吉尔穿的衣服。**8 like fun** *AmE spoken* used when you think something will not happen, or when something is not true【美口】当然不, 决不: *"I'm going to Barbara's house." "Like fun you are! Come and finish your chores first."* "我要去芭芭拉的家。" "你不能去呢! 先来干完你的家务活。" —see also 另见 FUNNY, **figure of fun** (FIGURE¹ (14)), **poke fun at** (POKE¹ (4))

S3 W1 **func·tion¹** /ˈfʌŋkʃən; ˈfʌŋkʃən/ *n* **1** [C] the purpose that something is made for, or the job that someone does〔事物的〕功能, 作用; 〔人的〕职责: *The function of a cash-machine is to provide people with cash when the bank is shut.* 自动提款机的作用是在银行关门的时候让人提取现金。| **perform a function** *In your new job you will be expected to perform many different functions.* 在新工作岗位上, 你可能要履行许多不同的职责。**2** [C] a large party or ceremonial event, especially for an important or official occasion 盛大聚会; 仪式, 典礼: *This room may be hired for weddings and other functions.* 这个房间可以被租来举行婚礼和其他仪式。**3** [U] the way in which something works or the way in which it is used 用途; 功能: *Bauhaus architects thought that function was more important than form.* 包豪斯学派的建筑师认为功能比形式重要。**4 a function of a)** if one thing is a function of another, it is produced by or varies according to the other thing 随…变化[产生]的因素 **b)** *technical* a mathematical quantity that changes according to how another mathematical quantity changes【术语】函数: *In x=5y, x is a function of y.* 在 x=5y 中, x 是 y 的函数。**5** [C] one of the basic operations performed by a computer〔电脑的〕基本功能

function² *v* [I] **1** if something functions, it works in the way it is supposed to 运转, 工作: *When the camera is functioning properly the green light comes on.* 照相机工作正常时, 绿灯就亮起来。**2** if something functions in a particular way, it works in that way〔以某种方式〕运作, 运转: *Can you explain exactly how this new system will function?* 你能解释一下这个新系统究竟是怎样运转的吗? **3 not function** if someone cannot function, they cannot do the activities that people normally do 不能正常活动: *She nurses people in their homes who are too ill to function alone.* 她上门护理生活不能自理的病人。

function as sth *phr v* [T] to be or work as something 起…作用; 用作…: *Athens functioned as a centre of trade in the thirteenth century.* 雅典在13世纪时是贸易中心。

func·tion·al /ˈfʌŋkʃənl̩; ˈfʌŋkʃənəl/ *adj* **1** designed to be useful rather than beautiful or decorative 为实用而设计的, 实用的: *It's not fast – it's just a solid, functional car.* 这辆车速度不快 —— 只是一辆结实、实用的车。**2** working in the way that something is supposed to 正常运转的: *With a few minor adjustments the filter will be functional again.* 只需几处小的调整, 过滤器将又可以用了。**3** having a useful purpose 有用途的; 有功能的 —**functionally** *adv*

func·tion·al·is·m /ˈfʌŋkʃənl̩ɪzəm; ˈfʌŋkʃənəlɪzəm/ *n* [U] the idea that the most important thing about a building, piece of furniture etc is that it is useful 功能主义, 功能论; 实用主义 —**functionalist** *n* [C] —**functionalist** *adj*

func·tion·a·ry /ˈfʌŋkʃənˌɛrɪ; ˈfʌŋkʃənəri/ *n* [C] someone who has a job doing unimportant or boring official duties〔做繁琐工作的〕职员, 工作人员; 公务人员

function key /ˈ‥ ˌ/ *n* [C] *technical* a key on the KEYBOARD¹ (1) of a computer that tells the machine to do something【术语】〔电脑的〕功能键

function word /ˈ‥ ˌ/ *n* [C] a word such as a PRONOUN or PREPOSITION that is used in place of another word or shows the relationship between two words. For example, in the sentences

'The cat is hungry. It hasn't been fed yet', 'it' is a function word. 功能词〔如代词、介词等, 用于代替一词或表明两词之间的关系。例如句子 The cat is hungry. It hasn't been fed yet 中, it 是个功能词〕

fund¹ /fʌnd; fʌnd/ *n* [C] **1** an amount of money that is collected and kept for a particular purpose 基金; 专款; 资金: *The school's funds for sports and music have been seriously depleted.* 这所学校的体育和音乐基金已消耗殆尽。| **set up a fund** (=begin to collect money) 设立基金, 开始筹款 *His grandparents set up a fund for his college education.* 他的祖父母为他设立了一个大学教育基金。—see also 另见 FUNDING, TRUST FUND —see 见 MONEY (USAGE) **2** an organization that is responsible for collecting and spending an amount of money 基金会: *We give to the Children's Fund every Christmas.* 我们每年圣诞节向儿童基金会捐款。—compare 比较 CHARITY (2) **3 a fund of** a large supply of something 大量的: *He was a large man with a strong Texan drawl and a fund of stories.* 他身材魁梧, 说话带着很浓的得克萨斯州腔, 能讲许多故事。**4 be short of funds** to have little or no money 缺钱, 手头拮据; 经费不足: *The Museum is so short of funds it may sell the painting.* 博物馆十分缺钱, 可能会把这幅画卖了。**5 in funds** having enough money to do what is necessary 手头有钱

fund² *v* [T] **1** to provide money for an activity, organization, event etc 为〔活动、组织、事件等〕提供资金; 资助: *The project is jointly funded by several local companies.* 这项目是由当地几家公司联合出资的。**2** *technical* to change the arrangements for paying a debt, so that you have more time to pay【术语】将〔短期贷款〕转为长期有息借款

fun·da·men·tal¹ /ˌfʌndəˋmɛntl; ˌfʌndəˈmentl◂/ *adj* **1** affecting the simplest and most important parts of something 根本的; 基本的; 基础的: *She's not just in a bad mood, she must have a fundamental psychological problem.* 她不仅仅是心情不好, 肯定有根本的心理问题。| **fundamental change/difference** *a fundamental difference in opinion* 看法的根本区别 | **fundamental mistake/error** *His fundamental mistake was to rely too much on other people.* 他的根本错误是过分依赖其他人。**2** very necessary and important as a part of something from which everything else develops 必不可少的; 十分重要的: [+to] *Water is fundamental to survival.* 水对生存是必不可少的。

fundamental² *n* **the fundamentals of** the most important ideas, rules etc that something is based upon 基本原理; 基本规则: *I couldn't even grasp the fundamentals of mechanics.* 我连力学的基本原理都弄不懂。

fun·da·men·tal·is·m /ˌfʌndəˋmɛntḷˌɪzəm; ˌfʌndəˈmentəlɪzəm/ *n* [U] **1** the practice of following religious laws very strictly 原教旨主义〔主张严格奉行宗教教义〕**2** a belief that some Christians have that everything in the Bible is completely true 〔基督教〕原教旨主义; 基要主义信仰

fun·da·men·tal·ist /ˌfʌndəˋmɛntḷɪst; ˌfʌndəˈmentəlɪ̇st/ *n* [C] **1** someone who follows religious laws very strictly 原教旨主义者; 基要主义者: *Muslim fundamentalists* 伊斯兰原教旨主义者 **2** a Christian who believes that everything in the Bible is completely true 信奉基要主义的基督教信徒, 基要主义者 —**fundamentalist** *adj*: *a fundamentalist doctrine* 原教旨主义[基要主义]信条

fun·da·men·tal·ly /ˌfʌndəˋmɛntḷɪ; ˌfʌndəˈmentəli/ *adv* in every way that is important or basic 根本上; 基本上: *They are good friends even though their views on many things are fundamentally different.* 他们虽然对许多事情的看法根本不同, 但还是好朋友。

fund·ing /ˋfʌndɪŋ; ˈfʌndɪŋ/ *n* [U] an amount of money used for a specific purpose 专款, 拨款: *Funding may be available from the UN.* 联合国也许会提供拨款。

fund rais·er /ˈ· ,··/ *n* [C] a person or event that collects money for a specific purpose 募捐者; 募捐活动

fu·ne·ral /ˋfjunərəl; ˈfjuːnərəl/ *n* [C] **1** a religious ceremony for burying or burning a dead person 葬礼, 丧礼: *The funeral will be held at St. Martin's church.* 葬礼将在圣马丁教堂举行。| **funeral procession/car/service etc** *The mayor gave the funeral oration.* 市长致悼词。**2 it's your funeral** *spoken* used to warn someone that they, and no one else, must deal with the result of their actions【口】你该要操心了, 你该要倒霉了: *If you show up late again, it's your funeral.* 如果你再次迟到, 那倒霉的是你自己。

CULTURAL NOTE 文化注释

In the US and UK, funerals usually take place in a church, or in a CHAPEL (=small church). The COFFIN (=special box that holds a dead person) is brought to the church in a special black car called a HEARSE. The relatives and friends of the dead person are called the mourners, and they usually follow the hearse in other black cars. At some funerals in the US, the coffin is open and people look at the dead person before the funeral service starts. In the UK the coffin is always closed. The funeral service usually includes music and prayers, and someone usually says a EULOGY (=a speech about the dead person and their good qualities). After the funeral service, the body is either buried in a cemetery, or CREMATED (=burned) in a special building called a CREMATORIUM. If the person is buried, there is usually a short ceremony beside the grave, and people traditionally throw a handful of earth into the grave. If the body is cremated, the ASHES are given to the family, who often scatter them in a pleasant place. People usually wear black clothes to a funeral, and they usually send flowers that are put around the coffin during the funeral service. After the funeral, family and friends often get together to have food and drink and talk about the person who has died. 在美国和英国, 葬礼一般在教堂或小礼拜堂举行。灵柩由特制的灵车运到教堂。死者的亲戚和朋友等吊唁者通常乘坐其他黑色车辆跟在灵车后面。在美国的一些葬礼上, 灵柩是打开的, 人们在葬礼仪式开始前瞻仰死者; 而在英国, 灵柩总是封闭的。葬礼仪式一般包括奏乐和祈祷, 通常有人致悼词。葬礼仪式后, 遗体在公墓埋葬, 或在火葬场火化。土葬通常会在坟墓前举行一个简短的仪式, 传统做法是人们各撒一把土到墓穴里。如果火化, 骨灰交与死者家属, 他们常将其撒在一个好地方。葬礼上一般穿黑衣, 葬礼仪式上通常会把花朵放在灵柩周围。葬礼后, 亲戚朋友常聚在一起吃顿饭, 并谈论死者。

funeral di·rec·tor /ˈ··· ·,··/ *n* [C] someone who is paid to organize a funeral 丧葬承办者, 殡仪业人员; UNDERTAKER *BrE*【英】

funeral home /ˈ··· ,·/ also 又作 **funeral par·lour** /ˈ··· ,··/ *especially AmE n* [C] the place where a body is kept before a funeral【尤美】殡仪馆

fu·ne·ra·ry /ˋfjunəˌrɛrɪ; ˈfjuːnərəri/ *adj* [only before noun 仅用于名词前] related to a funeral or a grave 葬礼的; 丧葬的: *a funerary urn* 骨灰瓮

fu·ne·re·al /fjuˋnɪrɪəl; fjʊˈnɪəriəl/ *adj* sad, slow, and suitable for a funeral 悲哀的; 沉重的; 适合于葬礼的: *funereal music* 哀乐 —**funereally** *adv*

fun·fair /ˋfʌnˌfɛr; ˈfʌnfeə/ *n* [C] *BrE* a noisy outdoor event where you can ride on machines, play games to win prizes etc; FAIR³ (1)【英】露天游乐场〔喧闹的大型户外活动, 有机动游戏、摊位游戏等〕

fun·gal /ˋfʌŋgəl; ˈfʌŋgəl/ also 又作 **fun·gous** /ˋfʌŋgəs; ˈfʌŋgəs/ *adj technical* connected with or caused by a fungus【术语】真菌的; 由真菌引起的: *a fungal infection* 真菌感染

fun·gi·cide /ˋfʌndʒəˌsaɪd; ˈfʌndʒɪ̇saɪd/ *n* [C,U] a chemical used for destroying fungus 杀真菌剂

fun·goid /ˋfʌŋgɔɪd; ˈfʌŋgɔɪd/ *adj technical* like a fungus【术语】真菌状[性]的: *fungoid growths* 真菌植物

fun·gus /ˋfʌŋgəs; ˈfʌŋgəs/ *n plural* **fungi** /-dʒaɪ; -dʒaɪ/ *or* **funguses 1** [C,U] a simple fast-growing type of plant, such as a MUSHROOM¹ or MOULD¹ (1) 真菌〈如伞菌或霉菌〉**2** [U] this type of plant, especially considered as a disease 真菌类植物(病)

Fungus the Bo·gey·man /,·· ˈ···/ a children's book by the British writer Raymond Briggs. It contains a lot of funny pictures of Fungus the Bogeyman, a silly creature who is smelly, dirty, ugly, and everything that children are not supposed to be. 《妖怪丰格斯》〔英国作家雷蒙德·布里格斯创作的儿童读物, 内有妖怪丰格斯的许多趣味画面。他是个浑身发臭、肮脏丑陋的傻东西, 孩子们在各方面都不应该去学他〕

fun house /ˈ· ·/ *n* [C] *AmE* a building at a FUNFAIR in which there are things that amuse or shock people【美】〔游乐场中的〕游乐宫

fu·nic·u·lar /fjuˋnɪkjələ; fjʊˈnɪkjɪ̇lə/ *n* [C] a small railway that goes up a hill or a mountain, pulled by a thick metal rope 〔登山〕缆索铁路

funk¹ /fʌŋk; fʌŋk/ *n* [U] **1** a style of music with a strong RHYTHM that is based on JAZZ and African music 〔以爵士乐和非洲音乐的强劲节奏为基础的〕乡土爵士乐 **2 in a (blue) funk** *informal* very unhappy, worried, or afraid about something【非正式】沮丧; 焦虑; 惊恐: *She's been in a funk ever since she failed that exam.* 自从她那次考试不及格后, 她就一直很沮丧。**3** *AmE informal* a strong smell that comes from someone's body【美, 非正式】〔身体发出的〕恶臭, 狐臭, 体臭

funk² *v* [T] *BrE old-fashioned* to avoid doing something because it is difficult, or because you are afraid to do it【英, 过时】〔因困难或害怕而〕逃避, 畏缩

funk·y /ˈfʌŋkɪ; ˈfʌŋki/ *adj informal*【非正式】**1** modern, fashionable, and interesting 新款的; 时髦的: *We found some really funky shoes at the market yesterday.* 我们昨天在市场上找到一些非常时髦的鞋子。**2** funky music is simple with a strong RHYTHM that is easy to dance to〔音乐〕朴实而节奏强烈的

fun·nel¹ /ˈfʌnl; ˈfʌnl/ *n* [C] **1** a tube used for pouring liquids or powders into a container with a narrow opening 漏斗: *Use a funnel to pour the oil into the bottle.* 用漏斗把油倒进瓶里。—see picture at 参见 LABORATORY 图 **2** *BrE* a metal CHIMNEY for letting smoke out from a steam engine or steam ship【英】〔蒸汽机或轮船的〕(金属) 烟囱 —compare 比较 SMOKESTACK

funnel² *v* **funnelled, funnelling** *BrE*【英】, **funneled, funneling** *AmE*【美】[I,T] to pass or be passed through a narrow opening, especially to pass a large amount of something through it (使) 流经漏斗; (使) 通过小口子: [**+through/into**] *The crowd funnelled through the narrow streets.* 人群熙熙攘攘地穿过狭小的街道。| **funnel sth into sth** *He funneled the petrol into the can.* 他用漏斗把汽油倒进罐里。

fun·nies, the /ˈfʌnɪz; ˈfʌniz/ *n AmE informal* a number of different CARTOONS (1) in newspapers or magazines【美, 非正式】〔报纸或杂志上〕(滑稽) 连环漫画栏

fun·ni·ly /ˈfʌnɪlɪ; ˈfʌnəli/ *adv* **1** in an odd or unusual way 古怪地; 异常地: *She's been behaving funnily lately.* 她近来行为古怪。**2 funnily enough** *spoken* used to say that something is unexpected or strange【口】奇怪的是; 说来也巧: *Funnily enough, I was just about to call you when you called me.* 说来也巧, 我正要打电话给你, 你就打电话给我了。**3** in an amusing way 滑稽地, 有趣地

1 3 **fun·ny** /ˈfʌnɪ; ˈfʌni/ *adj*

1 ►AMUSING 逗人笑的◄ making you laugh 使人发笑的, 有趣的; 滑稽的: *He was telling funny anecdotes about Hollywood.* 他正在讲有关好莱坞的趣闻逸事。| **hysterically/hilariously funny** *Everyone except me seemed to find her mistakes hilariously funny.* 除了我, 大家似乎都觉得她的错误极其可笑。

2 ►STRANGE 奇怪的◄ unusual and difficult to explain 古怪的; 难以解释的: *I had a funny feeling that something was going to happen.* 我莫名其妙地感觉到有事要发生了。| *It was a funny sort of day, hot but with huge rain clouds.* 这天有点奇怪, 很热但又有大片的雨云。

3 ►DISHONEST 不诚实的◄ seeming to be illegal or dishonest, although you are not exactly sure why 非法的; 不老实的; 要花招的: *There's something funny going on here.* 这里正在进行一些可疑的活动。| **funny business** (=activities that are illegal or dishonest) 非法活动; 欺骗活动 *When I checked the accounts I realized that there was some funny business going on.* 我检查账目时意识到有人做了手脚。

4 go funny *informal* if something goes funny it stops working properly【非正式】出毛病, 出故障: *I just turned it on and the picture went all funny.* 我刚一开机, 画面就出毛病了。

5 ►ILL 生病的◄ feeling slightly ill 不大舒服的: *I always feel funny after a long ride in the car.* 长时间坐汽车后我总觉得不大舒服。

6 ►CRAZY 发疯的◄ *BrE* slightly crazy【英】有点发疯的, 精神有点失常的: *After his wife died he went a bit funny.* 他在妻子去世后变得有点疯疯癫癫的。

7 see the funny side of sth to be able to laugh in a difficult or bad situation〔在困境中〕看到某事可笑的一面: *Fortunately, the patient saw the funny side of the mix-up and decided not to take us to court.* 幸好, 病人看到这回糟糕事另有可笑的一面, 决定不起诉我们。

Frequencies of the adjective **funny** in spoken and written English. 形容词 funny 在英语口语和书面语中的使用频率

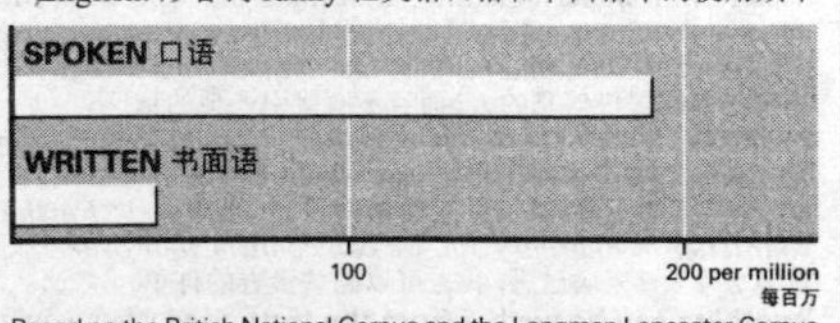

Based on the British National Corpus and the Longman Lancaster Corpus 据英国国家语料库和朗文兰开斯特语料库

This graph shows that the adjective **funny** is much more common in spoken English than in written English. This is because it is used in a lot of common spoken phrases. 本图表显示, 形容词funny在英语口语中的使用频率远远高于书面语, 因为口语中有很多常用短语是由 funny 构成的。

funny (*adj*) SPOKEN PHRASES
含 funny 的口语短语

8 it's funny used to say that you do not really understand why something happens, but it does and you think it is strange, interesting, worrying etc 真奇怪; 真有趣; 真令人担心: *It's funny, but I've known her for years and I don't even know her name.* 真奇怪, 我认识她好几年了, 却连她的名字也不知道。| **it's funny (that)** *It's funny Jack didn't come. I hope he's ok.* 杰克没来, 真奇怪, 希望他还好吧。| **it's funny how** *It's funny how you remember the words of songs, even ones you don't really like.* 真有趣, 你能记住许多歌的歌词, 甚至连你并不真正喜欢的也记得。

9 that's funny used when you are surprised by something that has happened and you can not explain it 真莫名其妙, 真怪: *That's funny! I'm sure I put my wallet down there, and now it's gone.* 真怪了! 我肯定将皮夹子放在那里的, 现在不见了。

10 the funny thing is used to say what the strangest or most amusing part of a story or situation is 最奇怪的是; 最有趣的是: *But the funny thing is, after they'd argued for ages about where to go, the car wouldn't start.* 不过最有趣的是, 他们争论了很久去什么地方之后, 车子却发动不了。| *The funny thing is, I sort of knew this would happen.* 最奇怪的是, 我有点知道会发生这事。

11 it's not funny used to tell someone not to laugh at or make jokes about something you think is very serious 这不是好笑的事, 这一点也不可笑: *It's not funny! I'm the one who's going to get blamed for this, you know.* 这不是好笑的事! 你可知道, 因为此事而该受责怪的人将是我。

12 very funny! used when someone is laughing at you or making a joke and you do not think it is funny 真滑稽!〔反话〕一点也不好笑!: *Oh very funny! Instead of laughing you could try and help.* 哼, 真滑稽! 你可以来帮忙试试, 而不是笑。| *Very funny! Who's hidden my car key?* 一点也不好笑! 谁藏了我的汽车钥匙?

13 what's so funny? used when someone is laughing and you want to know why 有什么好笑?: *Hey, what's so funny? Did I say something stupid?* 嗨, 什么事这样好笑? 我说了蠢话吗?

14 funny little used to describe something or someone that is small and unusual 又小又怪的: *I got it in that funny little shop in Market Street.* 我在市场街的那家又小又怪的商店买到这东西的。

15 funny old used to describe something or someone that is strange but that you like or think is interesting 滑稽的: *Yes, he's a funny old man – you never know what he's going to say.* 是的, 他是个很滑稽的老头 — 你永远也猜不到他会说什么。

16 I'm not being funny, but... used when you are going to say something that may seem strange or amusing but is actually serious 我不是想开玩笑, 但…: *I'm not being funny, but I quite liked it in hospital.* 我不是开玩笑, 但我曾经很喜欢住医院。

17 funny peculiar or funny ha-ha? *BrE* used when someone has described something as funny and you want to know if they mean that it is strange or amusing【英】是奇怪还是有趣?: *"You are funny, Albert." "How do you mean? Funny peculiar or funny ha-ha?"* "你很妙, 艾伯特。" "你指的是什么意思? 是奇怪还是有趣?"

funny bone /ˈ‥ ˌ/ *n* [singular] the soft part of your elbow that particularly hurts when you hit it hard〔肘部的〕鹰嘴突, 尺骨端〔受碰时会有酥麻感的敏感部位〕

funny farm /ˈ‥ ˌ/ *n* [C] *informal humorous* an expression meaning a PSYCHIATRIC HOSPITAL that some people consider offensive【非正式, 幽默】精神病院〔有些人认为该词具有冒犯义〕

funny mon·ey /ˌ‥ ˈ‥/ *n* [U] *informal* money that has been printed illegally【非正式】假钱, 假纸币 —see also 另见 COUNTERFEIT¹

funny pa·pers /ˈ‥ ˌ‥/ *n* [plural] *AmE informal* another expression meaning FUNNIES【美, 非正式】(滑稽) 连环漫画栏

fun run /ˈ· ˌ/ *n* [C] an event in which people run a long distance in order to collect money, usually for CHARITY〔为慈善募捐等而举行的〕募捐长跑活动

fur[1] /fɜ; fɜː/ *n* **1** [U] the thick soft hair that covers the bodies of some types of animal, for example cats or dogs〔猫、狗等动物的〕软毛 **2** [C,U] the fur-covered skin of an animal, especially used for making clothes〔尤指用于做衣服的〕毛皮: *Traders exchanged whiskey for furs.* 商人用威士忌酒换毛皮。| *a fur coat* 毛皮大衣 **3** [C] a coat or piece of clothing made of fur 毛皮大衣, 毛皮衣物: *She wore a small fur wrapped around her neck.* 她脖子上围着一条小毛皮围脖。**4** a hard grey chemical substance that sometimes forms on the inside of water-pipes and containers〔水管和容器内的〕水垢, 水锈; SCALE[1] (11) *AmE*【美】**5 the fur starts/begins to fly** used to say that an angry argument or fight starts 发生激烈的争论[打斗]: *The fur really started to fly when she saw the state of the kitchen.* 她看到厨房的样子时, 激烈的争吵便真正开始了。—see also 另见 FURRY

CULTURAL NOTE 文化注释

Coats and other clothing made of fur are very expensive, and in the past people wore furs to show that they were rich. Today in many Western countries, however, many people think that it is cruel to kill animals for their fur, and choose to wear FAKE FUR instead. 毛皮制成的大衣或其他衣物非常昂贵, 过去人们常穿皮草以示富有。不过现在很多西方人认为杀害动物获取皮毛太残忍, 因此选择穿戴人造毛皮服装。

fur[2] *v* [I] also 又作 **fur up** *especially BrE* to become covered with FUR[1] (4)【尤英】生水垢

fur·bish /ˈfɜbɪʃ; ˈfɜːbɪʃ/ *v* [T] also 又作 **furbish up** to improve the appearance of, or decorate something old 改善…的面貌; 翻新; 磨光; 擦亮 —compare 比较 REFURBISH (1)

Fu·ries, The /ˈfjurɪz; ˈfjʊəriz/ in Greek MYTHOLOGY, three frightening GODDESSes who had snakes instead of hair and who punished people for doing bad things, especially people who murdered members of their own family 复仇三女神〔希腊神话中头长蛇发的三位可怕女神。她们惩治罪恶之人, 尤其是杀害亲属的败类〕

fu·ri·ous /ˈfjurɪəs; ˈfjʊəriəs/ *adj* **1** [not before noun 不用于名词前] extremely angry 狂怒的, 暴怒的: *I've never been so furious in my whole life.* 我这辈子从来没有这样大发雷霆过。| **[+with/at/about etc]** *He was furious with himself for not standing up to Gillman.* 他对自己未能勇敢地面对吉尔曼而生自己的气。**2** [only before noun 仅用于名词前] done with a lot of energy, effort, or anger 猛烈的, 强烈的, 激烈的: *There was a sudden furious barking from the backyard.* 后院突然传来一阵狗的狂叫声。| **furious debate/argument** *a furious debate in Parliament over the new tax* 议会对新税种的激烈辩论 —**furiously** *adv*

furl /fɝl; fɜːl/ *v* [T] to roll or fold something such as a flag, umbrella, or sail 卷起, 折起〔旗、伞或帆等〕—**furled** *adj*: *a furled newspaper* 折起来的报纸

fur·long /ˈfɝlɔŋ; ˈfɜːlɒŋ/ *n* [C] a unit for measuring length, equal to 201 metres and used in horse racing 弗隆〔长度单位, 相当于201米, 用于赛马中〕—see table on page C4 参见 C4 页附录

fur·lough /ˈfɝlo; ˈfɜːləʊ/ *n* [C,U] a period of time when a soldier or someone working in another country can return to their own country〔军人或在国外工作的人的〕(回国) 休假: **on furlough** *a young soldier home on furlough* 回国休假的年轻士兵

fur·nace /ˈfɝnɪs; ˈfɜːnʒs/ *n* [C] **1** a large container in which a very hot fire is made, to produce power or heat, or to melt metals〔用于产生动力、热量或用以熔化金属的〕火炉; 熔炉 —see also 另见 BLAST FURNACE **2 be like a furnace** *spoken* to be extremely hot【口】热得像个火炉: *Let's open a window, it's like a furnace in here!* 我们开扇窗吧, 这里热得像个火炉!

fur·nish /ˈfɝnɪʃ; ˈfɜːnɪʃ/ *v* [T] **1** to put furniture and other things into a house or room 为〔房屋或房间〕配备家具: *The apartment was furnished in Art Deco style.* 这套公寓布置了装饰派艺术风格的家具。| **furnish sth with sth** *a room furnished with a desk and swivel chair* 摆放着书桌和转椅的房间 **2** to supply or provide something 供应, 提供: *They were asked to furnish capital for the new enterprise.* 有人要求他们为这家新企业提供资金。| **furnish sb/sth with** *The gardener furnished me with the necessary information.* 那园丁向我提供了必要的信息。—**furnished** *adj*: *a furnished flat* 配备家具的公寓套房

fur·nish·ings /ˈfɝnɪʃɪŋz; ˈfɜːnɪʃɪŋz/ *n* [plural] the furniture and other things in a room, such as curtains, baths etc〔房间里如桌椅、窗帘、浴缸等的〕家具, 室内陈设

fur·ni·ture /ˈfɝnɪtʃɚ; ˈfɜːnɪtʃə/ *n* [U] large movable objects such as chairs, tables, and beds that you use in a room to make it comfortable to live or work in〔大型可移动的〕家具: *The small room was crammed with furniture.* 那间小房间里塞满了家具。| *office furniture* 办公室家具

fu·ro·re /ˈfjurɔr; fjʊˈrɔːri/ *BrE*【英】, **fu·ror** /ˈfjurɔr; ˈfjʊərɔː/ *AmE*【美】—*n* [singular] a sudden expression of anger or excitement among a large group of people about something that has happened〔一大群人突然产生的〕骚动; 狂热: *The security leaks have caused a considerable furore within government circles.* 安全漏洞已在政府内部引起极大的骚动。

fur·ri·er /ˈfɜɪɚ; ˈfʌriə/ *n* [C] someone who makes or sells fur clothing 皮衣制造者; 皮货商

fur·row[1] /ˈfɜo; ˈfʌrəʊ/ *n* [C] **1** a deep line or fold in the skin of someone's face, especially on the forehead〔人脸部, 特别是前额的〕皱纹 **2** a long, narrow cut or hollow area in the surface of something〔某物表面的〕沟, 垄沟, 犁沟: *There were furrows in the tarmac to drain off the rainwater.* 柏油碎石路面上有许多排雨水的沟。**3** a long narrow cut made in the ground with a PLOUGH[1] (1)〔田里的〕犁沟, 垄沟

furrow[2] *v* **1** [I,T] to make the skin on your face form deep lines or folds, especially because you are worried or angry (使)〔脸部〕起皱纹〔尤指烦恼或生气时〕: *Her husband's brows were furrowed in concentration.* 她丈夫皱着眉头, 聚精会神。**2** [T] to make a deep cut or hollow area in something 犁; 在…开出沟槽 —**furrowed** *adj*: *a furrowed brow* 皱紧的眉头

fur·ry /ˈfɜɪ; ˈfɜːri/ *adj* covered with fur, or looking or feeling as if covered with fur 覆盖着毛皮的; 毛茸茸的; 柔软的: *furry little kittens* 毛茸茸的小猫 | *a large furry towel* 一条软蓬蓬的大毛巾

fur·ther[1] /ˈfɝðɚ; ˈfɜːðə/ *adv* 

1 ►MORE 更多地◄ if you do something further you do it more, or to a greater degree 进一步地; 在更大程度上; 再; 更: *I will develop this point further next week.* 我将在下星期进一步阐述这一论点。| *Things were further complicated by the fact that she did not speak Spanish.* 由于她不会说西班牙语, 事情变得更加复杂。| **[+into/away etc]** *Marcus sank further into debt.* 马库斯的债台越筑越高。| **delay/detain sth/sb further** (=make you wait) 耽搁某事/让某人久等 *After we've finished this I won't detain you any further.* 我们完成这件事后, 我就不会耽搁你了。

2 ►DISTANCE 距离◄ *especially BrE* used to say that a place is a long way from or more distant than another place; FARTHER【尤英】更远; 再往前地: *I don't think I can move a step further.* 我看我一步都走不动了。| **[+up/away/along etc]** *A little further up Main Street is an old house that's being restored.* 顺着大街往前一点是一座正在修复的老房子。—see 见 FARTHER[1] (USAGE)

3 take sth further to do something at a more serious or higher level, especially by talking about it 进一步地做某事〔尤指讨论它〕: *Would you be willing to take this research further?* 你愿意进一步从事这项研究吗? | **take the matter further** (=discuss a subject at a higher level and with more important people) 进一步讨论这事 *I'm going to take the matter further and discuss this with your parents.* 我打算把这事进一步和你的父母讨论一下。

4 ►TIME 时间◄ further back/on/ahead etc used to say how much more distant something is in the past or future 再以前/再以后/更远的未来等: *Five years further on, a cure has still not been found.* 五年过去了, 仍未找到治疗方法。| *The records don't go any further back than 1960.* 这些记录中没有早于1960年的。| **further down the road** (=in the future) 将来, 在更远的未来 *Further down the road we're looking at using up our timber resources.* 在更远的未来, 我们会看到我们的木材资源耗竭的前景。

5 go (one step) further to do or say more than before 进一步地做; 进一步地说: *Some argued that we should go one step further and get rid of him altogether.* 有人主张我们再大胆一些, 彻底把他干掉。

6 ►IN ADDITION 而且◄ [sentence adverb 句子副词] *formal* used to introduce something additional that you want to talk about; FURTHERMORE【正式】此外; 而且: *He promised not to identify his informant, and further, not to quote him directly.* 他答应不去指明提供信息的人, 而且不直接引述他的话。

7 further to *formal* used in letters or in formal speech to mention a previous subject you want to discuss more【正式】再者, 又及〔某事的更多的讨论, 用于信件或正式演说中〕: *Further to your letter of February 5th, we can confirm your order.* 又及, 贵方2月5日来函已悉, 我方可以确认贵方的订单。

8 nothing can be further from the truth used when you want to say that something is totally untrue 这完全不真实

9 sth must not go any further used to say that something you are telling someone is secret or private 某事不可外传

10 nothing is further from sb's mind *spoken* used to say that you have not been thinking about something, especially when you really have been thinking about it【口】某人的脑子里根本没有考虑〔某事〕: *"Did you come here to see Peter?" "No, nothing could be further from my mind!"* "你是来这里看彼得吗?" "不是, 我脑子里根本就没想到这回事!"

further² *adj* [only before noun 仅用于名词前] **1** more or additional 更多的; 附加的: *Are there any further questions?* 还有什么问题吗? | **a further 10 miles/5 minutes/£500 etc** *Cook gently for a further ten minutes.* 再用微火多煮十分钟。**2 until further notice** until you are told that something has changed 直至另行通知: *Lacunza ordered the suspension of the elections until further notice.* 拉昆扎命令暂停选举, 何时举行另行通知。

further³ *v* [T] to help something succeed or become successful 促进, 推动: *He dedicated his life to furthering the cause of world peace.* 他一生致力于推动世界和平事业。| **further sb's career** *Alan had been using her to further his career.* 艾伦一直在利用她来帮助自己向上爬。

fur·ther·ance /ˈfɝðərəns; ˈfɜːðərəns/ *n* [U] *formal*【正式】**1 the furtherance of** the development or progress of something …的发展, …的进展: *the furtherance of science* 科学的发展 **2 in furtherance of** in order to help something progress or become complete 为了促进…; 为了进一步完善…

further ed·u·ca·tion /ˌ‥ ‥ˈ‥/ *n* [U] *BrE* education for adults after leaving school that is not at a university【英】继续教育, 进修教育, 成人教育 —compare 比较 HIGHER EDUCATION

3 **fur·ther·more** /ˈfɝðɚˌmɔr; ˌfɜːðəˈmɔː/ *adv* [sentence adverb 句子副词] *formal* in addition to what has already been said【正式】此外; 而且; 更有甚者: *Furthermore, my aim is to provide the best service possible under these difficult circumstances.* 此外, 我的目标是在这样困难的条件下尽可能提供最好的服务。

fur·ther·most /ˈfɝðɚˌmost; ˈfɜːðəməʊst/ *adj formal* most distant【正式】最远的: *In the furthermost corner sat a tall thin man.* 在最远的角落里坐着一位瘦高个子的男人。| [+from] *in the corner furthermost from the door* 在离门最远的角落里

fur·thest /ˈfɝðɪst; ˈfɜːðɪ̈st/ *adj, adv* **1** at the greatest distance from a place or point in time; FARTHEST 最远的[地]: *There was a huge tapestry on the furthest wall.* 在最远处的墙上挂着一幅巨大的织花壁毯。| [+away/from] *He walked slowly toward the end of the jury box furthest from the judge.* 他慢慢地向陪审团席离法官最远的那端走去。—see 见 FARTHER¹ (USAGE) **2** to the greatest degree or amount or more than before 最大程度的[地]; 最大限度的[地]: *Maltby's book has probably gone furthest in explaining these events.* 莫尔特比的书可能是把这些事件解释得最详细的。

fur·tive /ˈfɝtɪv; ˈfɜːtɪv/ *adj* behaving as if you want to keep something secret 偷偷摸摸的, 鬼鬼祟祟的: *There was something furtive about his appearance.* 他的样子有点鬼鬼祟祟的。| **furtive glances/looks** *Christine kept stealing furtive glances at me.* 克里斯蒂娜不断地偷偷瞥我。—**furtively** *adv* —**furtiveness** *n* [U]

fu·ry /ˈfjʊrɪ; ˈfjʊəri/ *n* **1** [U] extreme, often uncontrolled anger 暴怒, 狂怒: *I was shaking with fury.* 我气得发抖。**2** [C] a feeling of extreme anger 暴怒, 狂怒; 激动: **in a fury** *"Go on then!" shouted Jamie in a fury. "See if I care!"* "那就继续吧!" 杰米怒不可遏地叫着, "看我在乎不在乎!" | **fly into a fury** (=quickly become very angry) 勃然大怒 *Paul flew into one of his furies.* 保罗又大怒起来。**3 much to sb's fury/to the fury of sb** if something is done much to someone's fury, it makes them very angry 使某人怒不可遏: *The report was leaked to the press, much to the president's fury.* 这个报告泄露给了报界, 这使总统怒不可遏。**4 a fury of** a state of very busy activity or strong feeling 〔感情、活动等的〕激烈, 热烈; 狂热: *She was listening with such a fury of concentration that she did not notice Arthur had left.* 她正如此聚精会神地听着, 没注意阿瑟已经离开。**5 like fury** *informal* with great effort or energy【非正式】奋力地; 使劲地; 猛烈地: *We went out and played like fury.* 我们到外面拼命地玩了一场。**6 the fury of the wind/sea/waves etc** used to describe bad weather conditions 狂风/怒海/狂浪等: *At last the fury of the storm lessened.* 暴风雨的势头终于减弱了。**7** [C] **Fury** one of the three snake-haired goddesses in ancient Greek stories, who punished crime 〔古希腊故事里的〕复仇三女神之一

furze /fɝz; fɜːz/ *n* [U] a wild bush with PRICKLY stems and bright yellow flowers 荆豆

fuse¹ /fjuz; fjuːz/ *n* [C] **1** a short thin piece of wire that is inside electrical equipment and prevents damage by melting and stopping the electricity when there is too much power 〔电器中的〕保险丝: *two 13 amp fuses* 两个 13 安培的保险丝 | **blow a fuse** (=make it melt by putting too much electricity through it) 熔断保险丝 **2** also 又作 **fuze** *AmE*【美】a thing that delays a bomb, FIREWORK etc from exploding until you are a safe distance away or makes it explode at a particular time 〔炸弹、烟火等的〕导火索, 导火线; 定时引信: *The fuse was set to go off at 6 p.m.* 引信设定在下午 6 点起爆。**3 a short fuse** if someone has a short fuse, they get angry very easily 〔人〕易发火, 脾气急躁 —see also 另见 **blow a fuse** (BLOW¹ (23))

fuse² *v* [I,T] **1** to join together, or to make something join together, to become a single thing 结合; 熔合; 合并: [+together] *The egg and sperm fuse together as one cell.* 卵子和精子结合成为一个细胞。**2** *BrE* if an electrical system or electrical equipment fuses or you fuse them, it stops working because a fuse has melted【英】(使) 因保险丝熔断而中断工作: *The lights have fused again.* 电灯又因保险丝熔断而熄灭了。**3** if metals, rocks etc fuse or you fuse them, they become joined together by being heated (使)〔金属、岩石等〕熔化在一起, 熔合 **4** *technical* if a rock or metal fuses or you fuse it, it becomes liquid by being heated【术语】(使)〔岩石或金属〕熔化: *Lead fuses at quite a low temperature.* 铅在相当低的温度下就会熔化。

fuse box /ˈ· ·/ *n* [C] a box that contains the fuses of the electrical system of a house or other building 保险丝盒

fused /fjuzd; fjuːzd/ *adj BrE* if a piece of electrical equipment is fused, it is fitted with a fuse【英】〔电器〕装有保险丝的

fu·se·lage /ˈfjuzl̩ˌɑʒ; ˈfjuːzəlɑːʒ/ *n* [C] the main part of a plane, in which people sit or goods are carried 〔飞机的〕机身 —see picture at 参见 AIRCRAFT 图

fu·si·lier /ˌfjuzl̩ˈɪr; ˌfjuːzɪ̈ˈlɪə/ *n* [C] a soldier in the past who carried a light gun called a MUSKET 〔旧时〕滑膛枪手, 火枪手

fu·sil·lade /ˌfjuzl̩ˈed; ˌfjuːzɪ̈ˈleɪd/ *n* [singular] **1** a rapid series of loud noises, especially shots from a gun 〔尤指枪炮的〕连续齐射 **2** a rapid series of questions or remarks 连珠炮似的问题; 一连串的话

fu·sion /ˈfjuʒən; ˈfjuːʒən/ *n* [U] **1** the combination or joining together of separate things, ideas, or groups 融合; 合成: *Her work is a fusion of several different styles of music.* 她的作品融合了几种不同风格的音乐。**2** a joining together of separate things by heating them 熔合; 熔化 —compare 比较 FISSION —see also 另见 NUCLEAR FUSION

fusion bomb /ˈ‥ ˌ·/ *n* [C] another word for a HYDROGEN BOMB hydrogen bomb 的另一种说法

fuss¹ /fʌs; fʌs/ *n* **1** [singular] nervous or anxious behaviour that is usually about unimportant things 〔通常指对小事〕紧张不安; 大惊小怪, 小题大作: **be a fuss** *James said he'd better be getting back or there'd be a fuss.* 詹姆斯说他最好还是回去, 不然有人就会大惊小怪。| **get/be in a fuss** *She gets in such a fuss before people come to dinner.* 她在客人来吃饭之前总是要手忙脚乱一番。**2** [singular,U] attention or excitement that is unnecessary or unwelcome 过于关心; 过于兴奋: *They wanted a quiet wedding without any fuss.* 他们想要举行一个安静的婚礼, 不想弄得沸沸扬扬。**3 make/kick up a fuss (about)** to complain or become angry about something, especially when this is not necessary 〔因…〕大吵大闹; 〔因…〕大惊小怪: *Josie kicked up a fuss because she thought the soup she ordered was too salty.* 乔西大吵大闹了一番, 因为她认为她点的汤太咸了。**4 make a fuss of** *BrE*【英】**make a fuss over** *AmE*【美】to pay a lot of attention to someone, to show that you are pleased with them or like them 对…体贴备至; 过分宠爱; 过分关心: *Make a fuss of your dog when he behaves properly.* 狗儿守规矩的时候就要宠宠它。 ⊜3

fuss² *v* **1** [I] to worry a lot about things that may not be very important 大惊小怪, 小题大作; 过于焦虑; 过于烦恼: *I wish you'd stop fussing – I'll be perfectly all right.* 我希望你不要小题大作了 — 我会很好的。**2** [I] to pay too much attention to small, unimportant details 过于讲究细节: [+with/around/about] *Paul was fussing with his clothes, trying to get his tie straight.* 保罗在不厌其烦地整理衣服, 试图把领带弄直。**3 be not fussed (about)** *BrE spoken* used when you do not think it matters what happens or is done【英口】(对…) 无所谓: *"Where do you want to go?" "I'm not fussed."* "你要去哪儿?" "我无所谓。" **4** [I] *AmE* to behave in an unhappy or angry way【美】吵闹: *The baby woke up and started to fuss.* 婴儿醒了, 开始吵闹。

fuss over sb/sth *phr v* [T] to pay a lot of or too much attention to someone, especially to show that you are pleased with them or like them 过于体贴; 过于关心

fuss·pot /ˈfʌspɑt; ˈfʌspɒt/ *BrE*【英】, **fuss·bud·get** /ˈfʌsˌbʌdʒɪt; ˈfʌsˌbʌdʒɪ̈t/ *AmE*【美】—*n* [C] someone who is very fussy 瞎忙的人; 大惊小怪的人; 爱吹毛求疵的人

fuss·y /ˈfʌsɪ; ˈfʌsi/ *adj* **1** too concerned or worried about small, usually unimportant details, and difficult to please 爱挑剔的; 过于讲究的; 难以取悦的: *Leonora was fussy about her looks.* 莉奥诺拉对自己的外表过于讲究。| **fussy eater** (=someone who

dislikes many types of food) 挑食的人 —compare 比较 FASTIDIOUS **2 not be fussy** *spoken* used when you do not mind what decision is made, where you go etc【口】无所谓, 随便: *"Do you want to go out or just rent a movie?" "I'm not fussy."* "你想出去玩还是想租部电影看?" "我无所谓。" | **[+who/what/how etc]** *Geese are not fussy whose grass they eat.* 鹅不介意吃的草是谁家的。**3** fussy clothes, objects, buildings etc are too detailed and decorated〔衣服、物体、建筑物等〕过分装饰的: *The furniture looked comfortable, nothing fussy or too elaborate.* 这家具看起来很舒适, 不过分装饰, 也不太精雕细琢。**4** with small, exact, and careful actions, sometimes showing nervousness〔动作〕过分注意细节的, 紧张的: *She patted her hair with small fussy movements.* 她拍了拍头发, 显得有点紧张。—**fussily** *adv* —**fussiness** *n* [U]

fus·ti·an /ˈfʌstʃən; ˈfʌstiən/ *n* [U] **1** a type of rough heavy cotton cloth, worn especially in the past〔尤指旧时的〕粗斜纹布 **2** *literary* words that sound important but have very little meaning【文】浮夸而无多大意义的话 —**fustian** *adj*

fus·ty /ˈfʌstɪ; ˈfʌsti/ *adj* **1** if rooms, clothes, buildings etc are fusty, they have an unpleasant smell, because they have not been used for a long time〔房间、衣服、建筑物等〕发霉味的 **2** *informal* ideas or people that are fusty are old-fashioned【非正式】〔思想或人〕过时的, 守旧的: *These fusty ideas about education should be brought up-to-date.* 这些守旧的教育思想应当予以更新。—**fustiness** *n* [U]

fu·tile /ˈfjutl; ˈfjuːtaɪl/ *adj* actions that are futile are useless because they have no chance of being successful 无用的; 徒劳的: *a futile attempt to save the paintings from the flames* 试图将那些画从大火中抢救出来的徒劳之举 | **be futile to do sth** *It was futile to continue the negotiations.* 继续谈判是无济于事的。—**futility** /fjuˋtɪlətɪ; fjuːˈtɪləti/ *n* [U]

fu·ton /ˈfutɑn; ˈfuːtɒn/ *n* [C] a flat soft CUSHION used for sleeping on, especially in Japan〔尤指日本的〕蒲团, 日本床垫 —see picture at 参见 BED[1] 图

fu·ture[1] /ˈfjutʃɚ; ˈfjuːtʃə/ *adj* [only before noun 仅用于名词前] **1** likely to happen, become, or exist at a time after the present 将来的, 未来的: *Careful accounting may help to predict future costs.* 认真的会计工作可能有助于预估将来的费用。| **future wife/husband etc** (=someone who will be your wife, husband etc) 未婚妻/夫; 未来的妻子/丈夫 **2** *technical* in grammar, being the form of a verb used to show a future act or state【术语】〔语法中的〕将来式[时]的: *the future tense* 将来时态 **3 for future reference** something kept for future reference is kept in order to be used or looked at in the future 供日后参考

future[2] *n*

1 the future the time after the present 将来, 未来: *Write an essay of 500 words describing your plans for the future.* 写一篇 500 字的文章, 描述一下你对未来的计划。| *Most science fiction stories are set in the future.* 大部分科幻小说都是以未来为背景的。

2 in future also 又作 **in the future a)** at some time in the future 在将来的某个时候: *In the future we will be using a much more sophisticated computer system.* 将来我们会使用一种更加精密的电脑系统。| **in the near/immediate future** (=soon) 在不久的将来, 不久 *The recession shows no signs of easing in the immediate future.* 这次经济衰退没有呈现不久就会缓和的迹象。| **in/for the forseeable future** (=for as long as you can imagine or plan for) 在可预见的将来 *We will not be hiring anyone else in the forseeable future.* 我们在可预见的将来不会再聘人。| **in the distant future** (=a very long time ahead in the future) 在遥远的将来 *Space travel to other planets may be possible in the distant future.* 到其他行星的太空旅行在遥远的未来有可能实现。**b)** from now until a much later time 今后: *I'll sleep in her room in future to prevent her sleepwalking.* 我今后要睡在她的房间里, 以防止她梦游。

3 ►WHAT WILL HAPPEN TO YOU 前途◄ [C] what someone or something will do or what will happen to them in the future 未来要做的事; 前途; 前景: *The islands should have the right to decide their own future.* 这些岛屿应当有权决定自己的前途。| **sth/sb's future is uncertain** *For young adults in the inner cities, the future is uncertain.* 对市中心贫民区的年轻人来说, 前途是渺茫的。

4 ►POSSIBILITY OF SUCCESS 成功的可能性◄ [singular,U] a chance or possibility of success at a later time 前途, 成功的可能性: *I'd like to discuss my future in the company.* 我想讨论一下我在公司里的前途。| **the future of sth** *Ferguson is optimistic about the future of the business.* 弗格森对公司的前途充满希望。| **a future in sth** *He felt there was no future in farming these days.* 他觉得如今种田没有前途。| **have a great/promising/bright future** (=to seem likely to do well in a job, sport etc) 前程远大/前途无量/前途光明

5 the future *technical* in grammar, the form of a verb that shows that the act or state that has been described will happen or exist at a later time【术语】〔语法中的〕将来时: *In the sentence, 'I will leave tomorrow', the verb 'will' indicates the future.* 在 I will leave tomorrow 一句中, 动词 will 表示将来。

6 futures [plural] *technical* goods, money, land etc that will be supplied or exchanged in the future at a time and price that has already been agreed【术语】〔货物、钱币、土地等的〕期货 (交易)

7 look to the future to plan for what will happen or think about what could happen in the future 计划未来, 考虑未来, 寄希望于将来

future per·fect, the /ˌ‥ ˈ‥/ *n technical*【术语】in grammar, the form of a verb that shows that the action described by the verb will be complete before a particular time in the future, formed in English by 'will have' or 'shall have'〔语法中的〕将来完成时 —**future perfect** *adj*

futures mar·ket /ˈ‥ ˌ‥/ *n* [C] *technical* the buying and selling of futures (FUTURE[2] (6)); FORWARD MARKET【术语】期货市场

fu·tur·is·m /ˈfjutʃɚˌɪzəm; ˈfjuːtʃərɪzəm/ *n* [C] a style of painting, music, and literature in the early 20th century that express the violent, active qualities of modern life, machines, science etc〔20 世纪初期绘画、音乐和文学中的〕未来主义, 未来派 —**futurist** *n* [C]

fu·tur·is·tic /ˌfjutʃɚˋɪstɪk; ˌfjuːtʃəˈrɪstɪk◄/ *adj* **1 futuristic design/building/film etc** a building, film etc that is so unusual and modern in appearance that it looks as if it belongs in the future instead of the present 未来主义设计/建筑/电影等: *The futuristic sports stadium is the pride of the city.* 那座未来派风格的体育场是该城的骄傲。**2** futuristic ideas, books etc imagine what may happen in the future, especially through scientific developments〔尤指根据科学发展〕想象的; 幻想的; 未来派的: *Orwell's disturbing futuristic novel, '1984'* 奥威尔的那部令人不安的描写未来的小说《一九八四》

fu·tu·ri·ty /fjuˋturətɪ; fjʊˈtjʊərɪti/ *n formal*【正式】**1** [U] the time after the present; FUTURE[2] (1) 将来, 未来 **2** [C] an event or possibility that may happen in the future 未来事件; 未来性

futz /fʌts; fʌts/ *v*

futz around *phr v* [I] *AmE informal* to waste time, especially by doing small, unimportant jobs slowly【美, 非正式】闲荡; 闲混: *I spent the entire day just futzing around.* 我一整天都在闲混。

fuzz[1] /fʌz; fʌz/ *n* [U] **1** thin soft hair or a hairlike substance that covers something〔覆盖在某物上的〕茸毛, 细毛: *When Jack was born he had a fuzz of black hair on his head.* 杰克出生的时候头上长着短细的黑毛发。**2** a small amount of soft material that has come from clothing etc〔衣服上脱落的小撮〕绒毛; LINT (1) *AmE*【美】**3 the fuzz** an insulting way of talking to or about the police, used especially in the 1960s and 1970s 警察〔侮辱性用语, 尤用于 20 世纪 60 年代和 70 年代〕

fuzz[2] *v* [T] to make something fuzzy 使模糊; 使成绒毛状

fuzz·y /ˈfʌzɪ; ˈfʌzi/ *adj* **1** unclear or confused and lacking details 模糊的, 不明确的: **fuzzy account/description etc** *She gave a rather fuzzy account of what had happened.* 她很模糊地描述了所发生的事。**2** if a sound or picture is fuzzy, it is unclear〔声音或图片〕不清楚的: *Some of the photos were so fuzzy it was hard to tell who was who.* 有些照片很模糊, 很难说出谁是谁。**3** having short soft hair, fur etc that stands upright 毛茸茸的: *I stroked the kitten's fuzzy back.* 我抚摸小猫毛茸茸的背。—**fuzzily** *adv* —**fuzziness** *n* [U]

f-word /ˋɛf wɝd; ˈef wɜːd/ *n* [singular] a word used when you are talking about the word FUCK but do not want to say it because it is rude. It is not used instead of the word 'fuck' 粗话〔指 fuck 一词〕: *Mommy, Billy said the f-word.* 妈妈, 比利说粗话。

fwy *AmE*【美】the written abbreviation for 缩写= FREEWAY

FX /ˌɛf ˋɛks; ˌef ˈeks/ **1** an abbreviation for 缩写= FOREIGN EXCHANGE **2** an abbreviation for 缩写= SPECIAL EFFECTS

FY *AmE*【美】the abbreviation for 缩写= FISCAL YEAR

-fy /faɪ; faɪ/ *suffix* [in verbs 构成动词] another form of the suffix -IFY 后缀 -ify 的另一种形式

G,g

G, g /dʒi; dʒiː/ *plural* **G's, g's** the seventh letter of the English alphabet 英语字母表的第七个字母

g the written abbreviation of 缩写= GRAM

G[1] *n* **1** also 又作 **g** [C,U] the fifth note in the musical SCALE[1] (8) of C MAJOR[1] (4), or the musical KEY based on this note G音〔C大调音阶中的第五个音〕; G调 **2** [C] *technical* the amount of force caused by GRAVITY (1) on an object that is lying on the Earth【术语】重力: *Astronauts endure a force of several G's during take-off.* 宇航员在起飞时要承受等于他体重好几倍的重力。**3** [U] *AmE informal* a GRAND (=$1,000)【美, 非正式】1000美元

G[2] *adj AmE* a film that is G has been officially approved as suitable for people of any age【美】〔影片〕经正式批准适合各种年龄的观众观看的; U *BrE*【英】—compare 比较 PG

G & T /ˌdʒi ən ˋti; ˌdʒiː ən ˈtiː/ *n* [C,U] gin and tonic; a popular alcoholic drink served with ice and a thin piece of LEMON (1) 加奎宁水的杜松子酒〔饮用时加冰和一薄片柠檬〕

G7, the /ˌdʒi ˋsɛvən; ˌdʒiː ˈsevən/ *n* the Group of Seven; the seven richest industrial nations in the world: Canada, France, Germany, Britain, Italy, Japan, and the US. The name changed to **G8** when Russia joined in 1997. 七国集团〔指世界七大发达工业国家: 加拿大、法国、德国、英国、意大利、日本和美国。1997年俄罗斯加入后该组织名称改为G8(八国集团)〕

GA the abbreviation of 缩写= GEORGIA

gab /gæb; gæb/ *v* **gabbed, gabbing** **[I+about]** *informal* to talk continuously, usually about things that are not important【非正式】喋喋不休, 闲聊: *You two were gabbing so much you didn't even see me!* 你们俩闲聊得那么起劲, 根本没有看见我! —see also 另见 **the gift of the gab** (GIFT (4)) —**gab** *n* [U] —**gabby** *adj*

gab·ar·dine, gaberdine /ˋgæbɚˌdin; ˈgæbədiːn/ *n* **1** [U] a strong material which does not allow water to go through and is often used for making coats 轧别丁, 华达呢〔一种防水布料, 多用于做上衣〕**2** [C] a coat made from gabardine 华达呢大衣

gab·ble[1] /ˋgæbl; ˈgæbəl/ *v* **gabbled, gabbling** [I,T] to say something so quickly that people cannot hear you or understand you properly 咕哝; 急促不清地说话: *Just calm down, stop gabbling, and tell me what has happened.* 请冷静下来, 说话别太急, 告诉我发生了什么事。| **gabble away/on** *Gina tends to gabble away when she's excited.* 吉娜一激动, 说话就会急促不清, 絮絮叨叨。

gabble[2] *n* [singular,U] a lot of talking that is difficult to understand, when several people are talking at the same time〔几个人同时说话〕混杂的说话声: *A gabble of voices came from the next room.* 隔壁房间传来嘈杂不清的说话声。

gab·er·dine /ˋgæbɚˌdin; ˈgæbədiːn/ *n* another spelling of GABARDINE gabardine的另一种拼法

ga·ble /ˋgebl; ˈgeɪbəl/ *n* [C] the upper end of a house wall where it joins with a sloping roof and makes a shape like a TRIANGLE (2) 三角墙: *the gable end of the barn* 谷仓有三角墙的一端

Gable, Clark (1901-60) a US film actor who appeared in many films especially in the 1930s and 1940s. He is most famous for appearing as the character Rhett Butler in *Gone with the Wind* (1939), and his other films include *It Happened One Night* (1934) and *Mutiny on the Bounty.* (1935). 盖博〔(1901-1960), 美国电影演员。尤其在20世纪30、40年代, 他出演过许多影片, 以扮演《乱世佳人》(1939)中的白瑞德最为出名。他出演的其他影片包括《一夜风流》(1934)和《叛舰喋血记》(1935)〕

ga·bled /ˋgebld; ˈgeɪbəld/ *adj* having one or more gables 有三角墙的: *a gabled cottage* 有三角墙的小屋

Ga·bon /gæˋbõn; gæˈbɒn/ a country in west central Africa on the Atlantic Ocean. Population: 1,221,000 (2001). Capital: Libreville. 加蓬〔中非西部一国家, 濒临大西洋。人口: 1,221,000 (2001), 首都: 利伯维尔〕—**Gabonese** /ˌgæbəˋniz; ˌgæbəˈniːz◂/ *n, adj*

Ga·bo·ro·ne /gɑbəˋron; gɑːbəˈrəʊn/ the capital city of Botswana, in the southeast of the country, formerly called Gaberones 哈博罗内〔博茨瓦纳首都, 位于该国东南部, 旧称Gaberones〕

Ga·bri·el /ˋgebrɪəl; ˈgeɪbriəl/ in the Bible, an ARCHANGEL who brings messages from God to people on Earth. In art, Gabriel is often shown blowing a TRUMPET. According to Christian belief, he was sent by God to tell Mary that she would be the mother of Jesus. In the Muslim religion, Gabriel gave Muhammad the messages from Allah which form *The Koran.* (基督教中的)加百列; (伊斯兰教中的)吉布里勒〔《圣经》中向世人传达上帝圣言的天使长。艺术作品中的他常吹着一只小号。根据基督教信仰, 他奉上帝差遣告诉马利亚她将成为耶稣之母。在伊斯兰教中, 他向穆罕默德传达真主安拉的圣言, 穆罕默德把这些圣言汇编成《古兰经》〕

gad /gæd; gæd/ *v* **gadded, gadding**

gad about/around *phr v* [I] *informal* to go out and enjoy yourself, going to many different places, especially when you should be doing something else【非正式】闲荡, 外出寻乐〔尤指本应做点别的什么事〕: *While I'm at home cooking, he's gadding about with his friends.* 我在家做饭, 而他却在跟他的朋友一起寻乐。

gad·a·bout /ˋgædəˌbaut; ˈgædəbaʊt/ *n* [C] *informal* someone who goes out a lot or travels a lot in order to enjoy themselves【非正式】游荡的人, 游手好闲的人

Gad·da·fi /gəˋdɑfɪ; gəˈdæfi/, **Colonel Mo·a·mar al** /ˌkɝnl ˋmoəmɑr æl; ˌkɜːnl ˈməʊəmɑːr æl/ also 又作 **Qaddafi** (1942-) the leader of Libya since 1969 卡扎菲〔(1942-), 利比亚领导人, 1969年就任〕

gad·fly /ˋgædˌflaɪ; ˈgædflaɪ/ *n* [C] **1** a fly that bites cattle and HORSES 虻, 牛虻 **2** someone who annoys other people by criticizing them〔爱批评别人而〕惹人讨厌的人

gad·get /ˋgædʒɪt; ˈgædʒɪt/ *n* [C] a small, useful, and cleverly-designed machine or tool 小器具, 设计精巧的机械[装置]: *a clever gadget for sharpening knives* 精巧的磨刀器具 —see 见 MACHINE[1] (USAGE)

gad·get·ry /ˋgædʒətrɪ; ˈgædʒɪtri/ *n* [U] modern gadgets in general 小巧的机械[工具]: *I don't understand how all this electronic gadgetry works.* 所有这些精巧的电子器具是如何工作的, 我不太懂。

Gads·den Pur·chase, the /ˌgædzdṇ ˋpɝtʃəs; ˌgædzdən ˈpɜːtʃɪs/ an area of land in what is now Arizona and New Mexico, which was bought by the US from Mexico in 1853 加兹登购地〔美国1853年从墨西哥购买的一片土地, 包括现在的亚利桑那州和新墨西哥州〕

Gae·lic[1] /ˋgelɪk; ˈgeɪlɪk/ *n* [U] one of the Celtic languages, especially spoken in parts of Scotland and in Ireland 盖尔语〔尤指苏格兰部分地区和爱尔兰讲的一种凯尔特语言〕

Gaelic[2] *adj* speaking Gaelic, or connected with Gaelic 讲盖尔语的; 盖尔语的

Gaelic foot·ball /ˌ‥ ˈ‥/ *n* [U] a game played in Ireland between two teams of 15 players, using a round ball that can be kicked or hit with the hands 盖尔足球〔流行于爱尔兰的一种足球运动, 两队各15人, 使用圆形球, 可足踢亦可手击〕

gaff /gæf; gæf/ *n* [C] **1** a stick with a hook at the end, used to pull big fish out of the water〔将大鱼拖出水面的〕手钩 **2** *British slang* someone's house【英俚】〔某人的〕房屋 —see also 另见 **blow the gaff** (BLOW[1] (14))

gaffe /gæf; gæf/ *n* [C] an embarrassing mistake made in a social situation or in public; FAUX PAS〔在社交场合或当众〕出丑, 失礼, 失言: *The consul's comments were a major diplomatic gaffe.* 领事的那番评论是一次重大的外交失言。

gaf·fer /ˋgæfɚ; ˈgæfə/ *n* [C] **1** the person who is in charge of the lighting in making a cinema film〔电影拍摄时负责照明的〕照明电工 **2** *informal humorous* an old man【非正式, 幽默】老头 **3** *BrE informal* a man who is in charge of people, especially in a factory【英, 非正式】〔尤指工厂里的〕工头, 领班

gag[1] /gæg; gæg/ *v* **gagged, gagging** **1** [I] to be unable to swallow and seem about to bring up food from your stomach 作呕: *The foul stench made her gag.* 那种恶臭令她想吐。| **[+on]** *He almost gagged on his first mouthful of food.* 他吃第一口便差点吐了出来。**2** [T] to put a piece of cloth over someone's mouth to stop them making a noise 用布塞进〔某人的嘴, 使其不能出声〕: *Thugs gagged her and tied her to a chair.* 暴徒用布塞住她的嘴, 把她绑在一把椅子上。| **bound and gagged** (=tied and gagged) 被捆绑着又被塞住嘴 **3** [T] to stop people saying what they want to say and expressing their opinions 压制〔某人〕言论

G

自由，限制〔某人〕发言: *an attempt to gag political activists* 压制政治活动家发言的企图 | **gagging clause/writ/order** (=a legal agreement or official order that stops you from speaking about something in public) 限制公开言论的条款/法令/命令 **4 gag me with a spoon!** *AmE spoken* used especially by older children to express a strong feeling of dislike【美口】我快吐了！〔尤指较大的孩子用来表示强烈的厌恶感〕

gag² *n* [C] **1** *informal* a joke or funny story【非正式】玩笑，笑话: *the same old gags* 老一套的笑话 **2** a piece of cloth put over someone's mouth to stop them making a noise 塞口布〔用来盖住某人的嘴使其不能发声〕 **3 gag order** an order made by the court to prevent any public reporting of a case which is still being considered by a court of law〔法庭禁止公开报道一起正在审理的案件的〕禁声令

ga·ga /ˈgɑgɑ; ˈgɑːgɑː/ *adj* [not before noun 不用于名词前] *informal*【非正式】**1** an insulting word used to describe someone who is confused because they are old〔因年老而〕糊涂的〔侮辱性用语〕: *Sid keeps forgetting my name. I think he's going a bit gaga.* 锡德老是忘记我的名字。我看他有点老糊涂了。**2** having a strong but often temporary feeling of love for someone; INFATUATED 狂热的，着迷的: **[+about/over]** *fans going gaga over the the pretty-baby looks of Sridevi* 对斯利德维漂亮宝贝般的美貌着了迷的仰慕者

Ga·ga·rin /gəˈgɑrɪn; gəˈgɑːrɪn/, **Yu·ri** /ˈjʊrɪ; ˈjʊəri/ (1934-68) a Soviet ASTRONAUT. On 12th April 1961 he became the first man in space when he travelled round the Earth in Vostok I. 加加林〔(1934-1968)，前苏联宇航员。1961年4月12日，他乘坐太空船"东方一号"完成环绕地球一周的飞行，成为第一位进入太空的人〕

gage /gedʒ; geɪdʒ/ *n* an American spelling of GAUGE gauge的美式拼法

gag·gle /ˈgægl; ˈgægəl/ *n* **1 a gaggle of tourists/children etc** a noisy group of people 喧闹的游客/儿童等: *a gaggle of teenage girls* 一群喧闹的少女 **2 a gaggle of geese** a number of geese (GOOSE¹ (1)) together 一群鹅

gai·e·ty /ˈgeətɪ; ˈgeɪəti/ *n old-fashioned*【过时】**1** [U] the fact that someone or something is cheerful and fun 快乐，欢乐，高兴: *Lars enjoyed the warmth and gaiety of these occasions.* 拉斯享受着这些场合的温暖和欢乐气氛。**2 gaieties** enjoyable events or activities 欢娱；令人欢乐的事件[活动]: *Elaine missed the gaieties of life in Paris.* 伊莱恩怀念在巴黎生活时的那些欢娱。—see also 另见 GAY¹

gai·ly /ˈgelɪ; ˈgeɪli/ *adv* **1** in a happy cheerful way 快乐地，欢乐地: *He walked past whistling gaily.* 他欢乐地吹着口哨走过去。**2** in a way that shows you do not care about, or do not realize, the effects of your actions 不顾后果地，冒失地: *They gaily went on talking after the film had started.* 电影开演后他们还毫无顾忌地说话。**3 gaily coloured/painted/decorated etc** having bright cheerful colours 色彩鲜艳/涂上艳丽油漆/装饰花哨的等: *gaily coloured tropical birds* 色彩艳丽的热带鸟

S2 W2 **gain¹** /gen; geɪn/ *v*

1 ►GET STH 得到某物◄ [T] to obtain or achieve something important or valuable 获得〔珍贵物品〕；成就〔重要事情〕: *She gained high grades in English and Math.* 她的英语和数学得了高分。| *After gaining independence in 1957, it was renamed 'Ghana'.* 1957年获得独立后，它改名为"加纳"。| *when radical left parties gained control of local authorites* 当激进的左派政党取得了对地方当局的控制权时

2 ►GET GRADUALLY 逐渐获得◄ [I,T] to gradually get more and more of a useful or valuable quality, skill etc 逐渐获得〔有用或宝贵的品质、技艺等〕: **gain experience/support/a reputation etc** *The Greens are gaining more and more support.* 绿党正获得越来越多的支持。| *You'll gain useful experience in working with computers.* 你在使用电脑的过程中会得到有用的经验。| **gain in popularity/confidence etc** (=become more popular, more confident etc) 变得越来越受欢迎/越来越有信心等 | **gain currency** (=when an idea becomes more popular)〔某种观点〕流行起来: *These ideas have gained currency in recent years.* 这些想法近几年已变得很流行。

3 ►GET AN ADVANTAGE 获益◄ [I,T] to get an advantage from a situation, opportunity, or event (使)〔从某种局势、机会或事件中〕获益，获利: **gain (sth) from** *It was the better-educated women who gained most from this expansion of opportunities.* 受过良好教育的妇女在这次机会的增加中受益最多。| **stand to gain** (=or likely to get an advantage) 可能受益 *Who is it who really stands to gain from these tax cuts?* 谁真正能从这些减税中受益？| **there's nothing to be gained** (=it will not help you) 无济于事 *There's nothing to be gained by losing your temper.* 发脾气是无济于事的。

4 gain weight/speed/height to increase in weight, speed, or height 增加体重/速度/高度: *Carrie's gained a lot of weight recently.* 卡丽的体重最近增加了很多。

5 gain access (to sth) a) to manage to enter a building 进入〔建筑物〕: *New ramps will help the disabled gain better access.* 新修的斜道将使残疾人进出更方便。**b)** to manage to see someone or use something 得以见到某人[使用某物]: *People should be able to gain easy access to this sort of information.* 人们应当能够很容易地接触到这种信息。

6 gain entrance/entry a) to enter a building that is locked 进入〔上了锁的建筑物〕: *Thieves gained entry through the skylight.* 小偷是从天窗进入的。**b)** to join or become part of a system or organization 加入，成为一部分: *At the age of 48 she gained entrance to the Civil Service.* 她在48岁时加入了公务员的行列。

7 gain ground make steady progress and become more popular, more successful etc 稳步发展；变得更受欢迎[更成功]: *The anti-smoking lobby has steadily gained ground in the last decade.* 向议员游说的反吸烟团体在过去十年中取得越来越大的成功。

8 gain time to deliberately do something to give yourself more time to think 赢得时间: *Maybe if we said you were sick we could gain some time.* 如果我们说你病了，也许可以拖延一下时间。—opposite 反义词 LOSE (12)

9 ►CLOCK 钟表◄ [I,T] if a clock or watch gains or gains time, it goes too fast〔钟表〕走得太快 —opposite 反义词 LOSE (15)

10 ►ARRIVE 到达◄ [T] *formal or literary* to reach a place after a lot of effort or difficulty【正式或文】〔经过很大努力或困难之后〕到达: *The swimmer finally gained the river bank.* 那位游泳者终于到达河岸。—see also 另见 **nothing ventured, nothing gained** (VENTURE² (4))

gain on/upon sb/sth *phr v* [T] to gradually get closer to a person, car etc that you are chasing 逼近，赶上: *Quick – they're gaining on us!* 快——他们要赶上我们了！

USAGE NOTE 用法说明: GAIN

WORD CHOICE 词语辨析: **gain, get, win, earn, make**

You can **gain** something useful or necessary whether or not you deserve it. Though you may **gain** weight, strength, a scholarship, a fortune, etc usually people speak of **gaining**, or less formally **getting**, things that you cannot touch such as experience, knowledge, education, and satisfaction. You especially **gain** (or **get**) things of this sort that other people give you, for example: support, recognition, popularity and respect. gain用于指获得有用或需要的东西，不论你是否应该得到。虽然gain可以用于指体重、力量、奖学金、财产等的获得，但更经常的是用于不可触及的东西〔此时也可用get，但不如gain正式〕，如经验、知识、教育、满足等的获得。gain(或get)尤指获得的这类东西是别人给予你的，例如：支持、承认、声望、尊敬等。

If you **win** something solid like a television or money, you get it partly by chance. win用于实在有形的东西，例如一台电视机或钱财，你在一定程度上是靠运气得到这些东西的: *Carla won $1,000 in Las Vegas!* 卡拉在拉斯韦加斯赢了1000美元！

If you **win** something you cannot touch, such as support, recognition, popularity, favour, or respect, you gain it by your own effort or abilities, usually from someone else. win用于抽象的东西，如支持、认可、声望、宠信或尊敬，你是靠自己的努力或能力从他人那里获得的: *People disliked him at first, but his reliability soon won their approval.* 人们开始时不喜欢他，但他为人可靠，很快赢得人们的认可。You can also **win** new friends. win还可以用来指赢得新朋友。

If you say that someone **wins** *a scholarship/a place at university* etc, it means they did something to get it, and probably that other people tried to get it as well (compare *gained*). *She won a prize* could mean either that she got it by luck (eg in a game), or by her own efforts. 用win来指某人赢得奖学金或大学的入学资格等，意味着此人做了某事才得到它，其他人可能也曾经设法得到它〔比较gained〕。She won a prize可能意味着她可能是靠运气得奖〔如在某项比赛中〕，也可能是靠自己的努力。

You **earn** (or less formally **get**) money for work you do. earn指通过工作挣钱〔或用不那么正式的get〕: *He earns/gets £400 a week* (NOT 不用 *gains*). 他每周挣400英镑。You can also **earn** something that you deserve such as support, recognition, popularity, or respect. earn还可以用于你应该得到的东西，如支持、认同、声望或尊敬: *The newspaper quickly earned a reputation for fair, impartial reporting.* 这家报纸很快因其公正、无偏见的报道而赢得了

声誉。| *Take a break, now you've earned it!* 休息一下吧，你该歇一会了！

You can also **make** money, especially from your own business or in a way that does not involve working. 挣钱可以用make，特别是从自己的生意或者以某种不需要工作的方式赚钱：*He made a profit of $50,000 on Wall Street last month.* 他上个月在华尔街获利50,000美元。

3 **gain²** *n* **1** [C,U] an increase in the amount or level of something〔某物数量或水平的〕增加，提高：*a gain in weekly output* 每周产量的增加 | *weight gain* 重量增加 **2** [C] an advantage or improvement, especially one achieved by planning or effort〔靠计划或努力得到的〕受益；改进：*The new machinery has produced big efficiency gains.* 新机器带来了很大的效益。| *a policy that brought Japan considerable gains in the post-war period* 使日本在战后大大受益的一项政策 **3** [U] financial profit, when this seems to be the only thing you are interested in〔财务〕收益，获利：*companies that care only about short-term gain* 只关心短期收益的公司 | **for gain** *Some of these tribes used to sell their women for gain.* 这些部落中有一部分在过去曾为了获利而出售他们的女眷。**4 ill-gotten gains** *humorous* money or advantages obtained dishonestly【幽默】不义之财；以不义的手段获得的利益 —see also 另见 CAPITAL GAINS

gain·ful /ˋgenfəl; ˈgeɪnfəl/ *adj* **gainful employment/work/activity** *formal* work or activity for which you are paid【正式】有报酬的工作/活动 —**gainfully** *adv*: *gainfully employed* 有职业有收入的

gain·say /genˋse; ˌgeɪnˈseɪ/ *v past tense and past participle* **gainsaid** /-ˋsɛd; -ˈsed/ [T usually in negatives 一般用于否定句] *formal* to say that something is not true, or to disagree with someone【正式】否认，反对：*It may be very difficult to gainsay the claim.* 反对这种主张可能很难。

Gains·bo·rough /ˋgenzbɝo; ˈgeɪnzbərə/**, Thomas** (1727-88) a British artist famous for his PORTRAITS (=pictures of people), such as *The Blue Boy*, and for his LANDSCAPES (=pictures of the countryside). 庚斯博罗〔(1727-1788)，英国艺术家，以《蓝衣少年》等肖像画和乡村风景画著名〕

gait /get; geɪt/ *n* [singular] the way someone walks 步态，步伐：*He moved off again with a slow shuffling gait.* 他缓慢地拖着脚又走开了。

gai·ter /ˋgetɚ; ˈgeɪtə/ *n* [C usually plural 一般用复数] a cloth or leather covering worn below the knee by men in past times〔旧时男人穿在膝盖以下的布质或皮质的〕护腿

gal /gæl; gæl/ *n* [C] **1** *AmE informal* a girl or woman【美，非正式】女孩，女子：*She's a great gal.* 她是个了不起的女孩。**2** *BrE old-fashioned* an UPPER-CLASS pronunciation of girl【英，过时】girl这个词的上层社会发音

gal. the written abbreviation of 缩写 = GALLON

ga·la /ˋgelə; ˈgɑːlə/ *n* [C] **1** a public entertainment or performance to celebrate a special occasion 庆典，演出盛会：**gala night/event etc** *a gala night at the opera* 歌剧院的盛大演出之夜 **2** *BrE* a sports competition, especially in swimming【英】运动会〔尤指游泳比赛〕

ga·lac·tic /gəˋlæktɪk; gəˈlæktɪk/ *adj* related to a galaxy 星系的

Gal·a·had /ˋgæləhæd; ˈgæləhæd/**, Sir** in old stories, one of King Arthur's Knights of the Round Table, who was very honest and morally good, and who found the Holy Grail. The name Sir Galahad is sometimes used to mean a man who behaves in a morally good and generous way. 加拉哈爵士〔亚瑟王的圆桌骑士之一。他无比诚实、道德高尚，并且找到了圣杯。他的名字有时用以指称道德高尚、为人慷慨的男子〕

Ga·lap·a·gos Is·lands, the /gəˋlɑpəgos ˌaɪləndz; gəˈlæpəgəs ˌaɪləndz/ a group of islands in the east Pacific Ocean which belong to Ecuador. They were visited by Charles Darwin in 1835, and the information he collected there helped him to develop his ideas about EVOLUTION. Very large rare TORTOISES live on the islands and most of the land is a national park. 加拉帕戈斯群岛〔太平洋东部一群岛，归属厄瓜多尔。1835年查尔斯·达尔文到过此地。他收集了不少资料，促成了他提出进化论。群岛上有珍稀巨型海龟，海岛的多数地区为国家公园〕

gal·ax·y /ˋgæləksɪ; ˈgæləksi/ *n* [C] **1** one of the large groups of stars that make up the universe 星系 **2 the Galaxy** the large group of stars in which our sun and its PLANETS are 银河，银河系 **3** [singular] a large number of things that are similar 一大批〔相似的东西〕：*A whole galaxy of pills and tablets was lined up on the table.* 桌子上摆着各式各样的药丸和药片。

gale /gel; geɪl/ *n* [C] **1** a very strong wind 大风：*The fence was blown down in the gale.* 篱笆在大风中被吹倒了。| **it is blowing a gale** *BrE* (=it is very windy)【英】正在刮大风 —see picture on page A13 参见A13页图 **2 a gale/gales of laughter** a sudden loud sound of laughter〔突发的〕一阵大笑声/阵阵大笑声：*Gales of laughter came from the next room.* 隔壁房间传来阵阵大笑声。

gale-force /ˈ· ·/ *adj* a gale-force wind is strong enough to be dangerous or cause damage〔风〕高强度的〔指具有危险性或可能造成灾害的大风〕—**gale-force** *adv*: *blowing gale-force* 刮大风

Gal·i·lee /ˋgælɪli; ˈgælɪ̣li/ an area in northern Israel in which the main city is Nazareth. It is best known from the New Testament of the Bible as the place where Jesus lived and taught. 加利利〔以色列北部一地区，主要城市是拿撒勒。从《圣经·新约》可知，耶稣曾在此生活和传道〕—**Galilean** /ˌgæləˋlin; ˌgælɪ̣ˈliːən◂/ *n, adj*

Galilee, the Sea of a lake in northeast Israel through which the River Jordan flows. It is mentioned in the New Testament of the Bible. 加利利海〔以色列东北部一湖泊，约旦河流经该湖。《圣经·新约》对此有所记述〕

Gal·i·le·o /ˌgælɪˋleo; ˌgælɪ̣ˈleɪəʊ/ (1564-1642) an Italian ASTRONOMER (=a scientist who studies the stars), MATHEMATICIAN, and PHYSICIST whose many discoveries had a great influence on modern science. He discovered that the PLANETS move around the Sun, and that if you drop objects of different weights in a VACUUM, they fall at the same speed. 伽利略〔(1564-1642)，意大利天文学家、数学家、物理学家。他的许多发现对现代科学有重大影响。他发现行星围绕太阳运动，还发现重量不等的两个物体在真空状态下下落，其下落速度是相同的〕

gall¹ /gɔl; gɔːl/ *n* **1 have the gall to do sth** to do something rude and unreasonable that most people would be too embarrassed to do 厚颜无耻地做某事：*Being a Tory politician, he still had the gall to be interviewed on TV and claim all the credit.* 他是个英国保守党政客，但仍敢厚着脸皮在电视上接受采访，并声称一切都归功于他。**2** [U] *old-fashioned* anger and hate that will not go away【过时】〔难以消除的〕愤恨 **3** [U] *old use* BILE【旧】胆汁 **4** [C] a swelling on a tree or plant caused by damage from insects or infection〔树或植物上的〕瘿，虫瘿 **5** [C] a painful place on an animal's skin, caused by something rubbing against it〔动物皮肤上的〕擦伤，擦伤处

gall² *v* [T] to make someone feel upset and angry because of something that is unfair〔因某事不公正而〕使恼怒，激怒：**it galls sb (that)** *It really galls me they could blame my Vicky for their own screw-up.* 他们自己把事情弄糟，竟然责怪我们的维基，这实在使我感到恼火。

gal·lant¹ /ˋgælənt; gəˈlænt/ *adj old-fashioned* a man who is gallant is kind and polite towards women【过时】〔对女子〕殷勤有礼的

gal·lant² /ˋgælənt; ˈgælənt/ *adj old use* brave【旧】勇敢的，英勇的：*gallant deeds* 英勇的行为 —**gallantly** *adv*

gal·lant³ /ˋgælənt; ˈgælənt/ *n* [C] *old use* a well-dressed young man who is kind and polite towards women【旧】时髦绅士，对女子献殷勤的穿着考究的男子

gal·lan·try /ˋgæləntrɪ; ˈgæləntri/ *n* [U] *formal*【正式】**1** courage, especially in a battle 英勇，勇敢〔尤指作战勇敢〕：*a medal for gallantry* 英雄奖章 **2** polite attention given by men to women〔男子对女子所表现的〕殷勤

gall blad·der /ˈ· ˌ··/ *n* [C] the organ in your body in which BILE is stored 胆囊 —see picture at 参见 DIGESTIVE SYSTEM 图

gal·le·on /ˋgælɪən; ˈgæliən/ *n* [C] a sailing ship used mainly by the Spanish from the 15th to the 17th century〔15世纪至17世纪主要为西班牙人用的〕帆船

gal·le·ry /ˋgælərɪ; ˈgæləri/ *n* [C] **1 a)** a large building where people can see famous pieces of art 美术馆：*an exhibition of African art at the Hayward Gallery* 海沃德美术馆的非洲艺术展览 **b)** [C] a small privately owned shop or STUDIO (3) where you can see and buy pieces of art 画廊，字画店〔陈列并出售绘画等艺术品的小型私人商店或画室〕**2 a)** [C] an upper floor or BALCONY built out from an inner wall of a hall, theatre, or church, from which people can watch a performance, DEBATE¹ (1, 2) etc〔大厅、剧场或教堂里的〕楼座，楼上旁听席：*the public gallery in Congress* 国会的旁听席 —see picture at 参见 THEATRE 图 **b) the gallery** the people sitting in a gallery 楼座观众 **3 play to the gallery** to do or say something just because you think it will please people and make you popular 哗众取宠，讨好观众 **4** [C] a level passage under the ground in a mine or CAVE¹〔矿山或山洞里的〕水平巷道，坑道 —see also 另见 PRESS GALLERY, SHOOTING GALLERY 3

gal·ley /ˋgælɪ; ˈgæli/ *n* [C] **1** a long low Greek or Roman ship with sails which was rowed by SLAVES in the past〔古代希腊、罗马由奴隶划桨的〕低舷大帆船 **2** a kitchen on a ship〔船上的〕厨

G

房: *The fire extinguishers are stored in the galley.* 灭火器存放在船上的厨房里。**3 a)** a TRAY used by printers which holds TYPE[1] (3) 活字盘 **b)** also 又作 **galley proof** a sheet of paper on which a PRINTER (2) prints a book so that mistakes can be put right before it is divided into pages 长条校样

Gal·lic /ˈgælɪk; ˈgælɪk/ *adj* typical of France or French people 法国的, 高卢的; 法国人的, 高卢人的: *Gallic charm* 法国的魅力

gal·ling /ˈgɔlɪŋ; ˈgɔːlɪŋ/ *adj* making you feel upset and angry because of something that is unfair 〔因某事不公平而〕使人恼怒的, 令人生气的: *The most galling thing is that the guy who got promoted is less qualified than me.* 最令人生气的是, 那个得到晋升的家伙, 资格根本比不上我。

Gal·lip·o·li /gəˈlɪpəlɪ; gəˈlɪpəli/ an area in Turkey on the north side of the Dardanelles, where an important battle took place during World War I. Many Australian and New Zealand soldiers landed on the coast and were killed there by the Turkish army, who were fighting on the side of the Germans. 加利波利〔土耳其一地区, 位于达达尼尔海峡北岸。一战期间, 这里发生过一场著名战役。澳大利亚和新西兰的许多士兵登陆时为德方的土耳其军队所杀〕—see also 另见 ANZAC DAY

gal·li·vant /ˈgæləˌvænt; ˈgælɪ̵vænt/ *v* [I] *informal or humorous* to spend time enjoying yourself and going from place to place for pleasure【非正式或幽默】闲逛, 游荡; 寻欢作乐: **gallivant about/around** *She spent six months gallivanting around Europe.* 她花了六个月的时间在欧洲到处游玩。

gal·lon /ˈgælən; ˈgælən/ *n* [C] **1** *BrE* a unit for measuring liquids, equal to 4.5435 litres【英】加仑〔液量单位, = 4.5435 升〕 **2** *AmE* a unit for measuring liquids, equal to 3.785 litres【美】加仑〔= 3.785 升〕—see table on page C3 参见 C3 页附录

CULTURAL NOTE 文化注释

In the US, the gallon is used as the standard liquid measure. Gas (=fuel for a car) is always bought by the gallon, and milk, water, and ice-cream are usually bought in gallon or half-gallon sizes. In the UK the gallon was used in the past, but now the litre is the standard measure for liquid. 加仑是美国标准液量单位, 汽油以加仑出售, 牛奶、水、冰淇淋通常以一加仑或半加仑出售。英国过去用加仑, 但现在公升是标准的液量单位。

gal·lop[1] /ˈgæləp; ˈgæləp/ *v* **1** [I] if a horse gallops, it moves very fast with all its feet leaving the ground together〔马〕飞奔, 疾驰: [+along/across/towards etc] *wild horses galloping over the sand* 在沙地上飞奔的野马 **2** [I,T] if you gallop, you ride very fast on a horse or you make it go very fast 骑马奔驰, 策马疾驰: [+along/across/towards etc] *I watched as Jan galloped away.* 我看着简策马奔驰而去。**3** [I always+adv/prep] to move very quickly 快速移动, 飞跑: *Ian came galloping down the stairs.* 伊恩迅速跑下楼梯。

gallop through sth *phr v* [T] *informal* to do a job, some work etc very quickly【非正式】匆匆地做完: *Neil galloped through his homework.* 尼尔匆匆做完作业。

gallop[2] *n* **1 a)** [singular] the movement of a horse at its fastest speed when all four feet leave the ground together〔马〕飞跑, 疾驰: **break into a gallop** (=begin to go very fast) 飞跑起来 **b)** [C] a ride on a horse when it is galloping 骑马奔跑 **2 at a gallop a)** at the fastest speed possible when riding a horse〔骑马〕以最快速度: *Rogers set off at a gallop.* 罗杰斯骑马奔驰而去。**b)** *informal* very quickly【非正式】急速地, 飞快地

gal·lop·ing /ˈgæləpɪŋ; ˈgæləpɪŋ/ *adj* [only before noun 仅用于名词前] rapidly increasing or developing 快速增加的; 飞速发展的: **galloping inflation** *galloping inflation of 20 to 30%* 20% 至 30% 的剧烈通货膨胀

gal·lows /ˈgæloz; ˈgæləʊz/ *n plural* **gallows** [C] a structure used for killing criminals by hanging them from a rope 绞刑架

gallows hu·mour *BrE*【英】, **gallows humor** *AmE*【美】/ˈ· · ,· ·/ *n* [U] humour which makes very unpleasant or dangerous things seem funny 绞刑架下的幽默, 大难临头的幽默

gall·stone /ˈgɔlˌston; ˈgɔːlstəʊn/ *n* [C] a hard stone which can form in your GALL BLADDER 胆(结)石

Gal·lup poll /ˈgæləp ˌpol; ˈgæləp pəʊl/ *n* [C] *trademark* a count of people's opinions on a subject, especially to find out how they will vote in an election【商标】盖洛普民意测验

ga·loot /gəˈlut; gəˈluːt/ *n* [C] *AmE informal* someone who is not at all graceful and does not dress neatly【美, 非正式】衣冠不整行为粗俗的人: *You clumsy galoot!* 你这笨蛋!

ga·lore /gəˈlɔr; gəˈlɔː/ *adj* [only after noun 仅用于名词后] in large amounts or numbers 大量的, 许多的: *There are bargains galore in the sales this year.* 今年的大减价期间有许多便宜货。

ga·losh·es /gəˈlɑʃəz; gəˈlɒʃɪ̵z/ *n* [plural] *old-fashioned* rubber shoes worn over ordinary shoes when it rains or snows【过时】〔下雨或下雪时套在普通鞋外面的〕橡胶套鞋

Gals·wor·thy /ˈgɔlzwɝðɪ; ˈgɔːlzwɜːði/, **John** (1867-1933) a British writer of books and plays who won the Nobel Prize for Literature in 1932. His most famous work is a series of NOVELS called *The Forsyte Saga*, about a wealthy English family called the Forsytes. 高尔斯华绥〔(1867-1933), 英国小说家、剧作家, 1932 年获诺贝尔文学奖。以其系列小说《福尔赛世家》最为有名, 小说讲述英格兰富户福尔赛一家人的故事〕

ga·lumph /gəˈlʌmf; gəˈlʌmf/ *v* [I always+adv/prep] *informal* to move in a noisy, heavy, and awkward way【非正式】脚步嘈杂地行进, 笨拙地行进

gal·van·ic /gælˈvænɪk; gælˈvænɪk/ *adj* **1** *formal* making people react suddenly with strong feelings or actions【正式】使人震惊的: *The bomb warning had a galvanic effect.* 炸弹的警告引起一场恐慌。**2** *technical* connected with the production of electricity by the action of acid on metal【术语】〔由化学作用〕产生电流的

gal·va·nise /ˈgælvəˌnaɪz; ˈgælvənaɪz/ *v* a British spelling of GALVANIZE galvanize 的英式拼法

gal·va·nis·m /ˈgælvəˌnɪzəm; ˈgælvənɪzəm/ *n* [U] *technical* the production of electricity by the use of chemicals, especially as in a BATTERY (1)【术语】用化学药品产生电〔尤指由原电池产生电〕

gal·va·nize also 又作 **-ise** *BrE*【英】/ˈgælvəˌnaɪz; ˈgælvənaɪz/ *v* [T] to shock or surprise someone so that they do something to solve a problem, improve a situation etc 激励, 刺激〔某人〕: **galvanize sb into (doing) sth** *The possibility of defeat finally galvanized us into action.* 失败的可能性最终促使我们采取行动。

gal·va·nized also 又作 **-ise** *BrE*【英】/ˈgælvəˌnaɪzd; ˈgælvənaɪzd/ *adj* **galvanised iron/metal etc** metal with a covering of ZINC made using electricity 镀锌铁/镀锌金属等

Gal·ves·ton /ˈgælvɪstən; ˈgælvɪstən/ a city in southeast Texas. It is the state's main cotton port and also an important fishing centre. 加尔维斯顿〔得克萨斯州东南部一城市, 是该州的主要棉花集散港口和重要渔业中心〕

Gal·way /ˈgɔlwe; ˈgɔːlweɪ/ a COUNTY in the west of the Republic of Ireland 戈尔韦郡〔爱尔兰共和国西部一郡〕

Ga·ma /ˈgɑmə; ˈgɑːmə/, **Vas·co da** /ˈvɑsko də; ˈvæskəʊ də/ (?1469-1524) a Portuguese SAILOR and EXPLORER who was the first European to discover the way to India by sea 达·伽马〔(?1469-1524), 葡萄牙航海家、探险家, 是首位发现通往印度海路的欧洲人〕

Gam·bi·a, the /ˈgæmbɪə; ˈgæmbiə/ a country in West Africa next to Senegal. Population: 1,411,000 (2001). Capital: Banjul. 冈比亚〔西非一国家, 与塞内加尔接壤。人口: 1,411,000 (2001), 首都: 班珠尔〕—**Gambian** *n, adj*

gam·bit /ˈgæmbɪt; ˈgæmbɪ̵t/ *n* [C] **1** something that you do or say which is intended to give you an advantage in an argument 精心策划的一着, 策略: *a clever debating gambit* 巧妙的辩论策略 | **opening gambit** (=the thing you say first) 开场白 **2** a planned series of moves at the beginning of a game of CHESS〔国际象棋中的〕开局时的一系列走棋

gam·ble[1] /ˈgæmbl̩; ˈgæmbəl/ *v* **1** [I] to risk money or possessions on the result of something uncertain, such as a card game, a race or a horse 赌博: *We're forbidden to drink or gamble.* 我们被禁止饮酒和赌博。| **gamble on sth** *Jack loves gambling on the horses.* 杰克喜欢赌马。| **gamble heavily** (=gamble often, using a lot of money) 豪赌 **2** [I,T] to do something that involves a lot of risk, and that will not succeed unless things happen the way you would like them to 投机, 冒险: **gamble on** *They're gambling on Johnson being fit for Saturday's game.* 他们把赌注押在约翰逊可以应付星期六的比赛。| **gamble sth on sth** *Potter gambled everything on his new play being a hit.* 波特孤注一掷, 指望他的新戏会轰动。| **gamble with** *We can't relax our safety standards – we'd be gambling with people's lives.* 我们不能放松我们的安全标准 —— 否则我们就是拿人们的生命来冒险。—**gambler** *n* [C]

gamble sth ↔ **away** *phr v* [T] to lose money by gambling 赌输掉: *Nielsen gambled his inheritance away.* 尼尔森把继承的遗产都输光了。

gamble[2] *n* [singular] an action or plan that involves a risk but that you hope will succeed 冒险, 碰运气: *We've never used this agency before, so it's a bit of a gamble.* 我们以前从来没有用过这家代理机构, 所以有点冒险。| **take a gamble** *I think she's taking a gamble setting up her own business like that.* 我认为她那样创立自己的公司是在冒险。| **a gamble pays off** (=brings success) 赌赢, 取得成功 *Ellen had to admit the gamble had paid off.* 埃伦不得不承认冒险取得了成功。

gam·bling /ˋgæmblɪŋ; ˈgæmblɪŋ/ *n* [U] **1** the practice of risking money or possessions on the result of something uncertain, such as a card game, or a horse race 赌博: *They had always strongly disapproved of gambling.* 他们一向是强烈反对赌博的。 **2 gambling den** a place where people go to gamble illegally 赌窟，赌博窝点

gam·bol /ˋgæmbl; ˈgæmbəl/ *v* [I always+adv/prep] to jump or run around in a lively active way〔活泼地〕跳跃; 嬉戏: *lambs gambolling in a field* 在田野里跳跃奔跑的羔羊 —**gambol** *n* [C]

game¹ /gem; geɪm/ *n*

1 ▶ACTIVITY OR SPORT 活动或运动◀ [C] **a)** an activity or sport in which people compete with each other according to agreed rules 游戏; 运动: *What's your favorite game?* 你最喜爱的运动是什么? | *Dan's never liked card games.* 丹从来不喜欢打牌。 **b)** an occasion when a game is played 比赛: *Did you see the game on TV last night?* 你昨天晚上在电视上看了这场比赛吗? | *Let's have a game of chess.* 我们来下盘棋吧。 **c) your game** how well you play a particular game 球技[运动技巧, 玩游戏的技巧等]; 比赛技巧: **raise/improve your game** *Liam's taking lessons to improve his game.* 利亚姆正在听课, 以改进他的比赛技巧。 **d) games** a large organized sports event 大型运动会: *the Olympic Games* 奥林匹克运动会 **e)** *BrE* organized sports as a school subject or lesson【英】体育课: *We have games on Thursdays.* 我们星期四上体育课。—compare 比较 MATCH¹ (2) —see also 另见 BALL GAME, BOARD GAME, WAR GAME

2 ▶PART OF A MATCH 比赛的一部分◀ [C] one of the parts into which a single competition is divided, for example in tennis or BRIDGE¹ (4) 一局, 一盘: *Graf leads, two games to one.* 格拉夫在三局中以2:1领先。

3 ▶CHILDREN'S GAME 儿童游戏◀ [C] a children's activity in which they play with toys, pretend to be someone else etc 游戏: *a game of hide-and-seek* 捉迷藏游戏 | *Look! Now you've spoilt our game!* 瞧! 你把我们的游戏搞砸了!

4 ▶BE A GAME 一场游戏◀ [C] to be something that you do to enjoy yourself rather than for a serious purpose 娱乐, 消遣: *Some of those kids think life's just a game.* 有些孩子认为生活就是一场游戏。

5 play games/silly games (with) to behave in a dishonest or unfair way in order to get what you want 欺骗, 耍花招: *Are you sure he's really interested, and not just playing silly games with you?* 你确信他真的感兴趣, 不是在跟你耍花招吗?

6 give the game away to spoil a surprise or secret by doing or saying something that lets someone guess what the secret is 泄露秘密: *Lynn gave the game away by laughing when Kim walked in.* 林恩在金走进来的时候笑了出来, 泄露了秘密。

7 ▶ANIMALS/BIRDS 动物/鸟◀ [U] wild animals, birds, and fish that are hunted for food, especially as a sport 猎物, 野味 —see also 另见 BIG GAME

8 beat/play sb at their own game to beat someone or fight back against them by using the same methods that they use 以其人之道还治其人之身: *Jackie decided to play Dean at his own game and left without paying the bill.* 杰基决定用同样的方法整一整迪恩, 所以没付账单就离开了。

9 what's her game/your game etc? *spoken* used to ask what the true reason for someone's behaviour is【口】她/你为什么这样做?〔用来询问某人的行为的真正原因〕: *Reg is being very nice all of a sudden. What's his game?* 雷格突然变得非常和蔼可亲。他在耍什么花招?

10 advertising/public relations etc game *informal* the profession of advertising etc【非正式】广告业/公共关系业等

11 a game of chance a game in which you risk money on the result 碰运气的游戏, 赌钱的游戏: *Poker is a game of chance.* 扑克牌是一种碰运气的游戏。

12 the game's up *spoken* used to tell someone that something wrong or dishonest that they have done has been discovered【口】事已败露, 东窗事发: *Come on, Don. The game's up. I know where you've hidden it.* 得了吧, 唐, 你已经败露了。我知道你把它藏在什么地方。

13 be on the game *slang* to be a PROSTITUTE【俚】当妓女, 卖淫

14 make game of *old-fashioned* to make fun of someone【过时】取笑, 同…开玩笑 —see also 另见 FAIR GAME, **away game/match** (AWAY²), **fun and games** (FUN² (4)), **the name of the game** (NAME¹ (13))

game² *adj* **1** willing to try something dangerous, new, or difficult〔对某些危险、新鲜或困难的事〕愿意尝试的: *If you're game, we can do it now.* 如果你愿意尝试的话, 我们现在就可以做。| [+for] *We're game for a change.* 我们愿意变一变。| **game to do sth** *"Who's game to have a try?"* 谁敢试一试? **2 game leg** *old-fashioned* an injured or painful leg【过时】受伤的腿, 疼痛的腿 —**gamely** *adv*

game·keep·er /ˋgæm͵kipɚ; ˈgeɪm͵kiːpə/ *n* [C] someone whose job is to look after wild animals and birds that are kept to be hunted on private land〔私人土地上的〕猎场看守人

game park /ˈ· ·/ *n* [C] a GAME RESERVE 野生动物保护区

game plan /ˈ· ·/ *n* [C] a plan for achieving success, especially in business or sports 方案, 策略〔尤指商业或体育比赛方面〕: *The former coach blamed the defeat on no game plan and no inspiration.* 前任教练把这次失败归咎于缺少比赛方案和激励。

game point /ˈ· ·/ *n* [C,U] the situation in a game such as tennis in which one player will win the game if they win the next point 局点〔网球等比赛中再赢一分那局即获胜的时刻〕—compare 比较 MATCH POINT

game re·serve /ˈ· ·,·/ *n* [C] a large area of land that is designed for wild animals to live in safely 野生动物保护区

game show /ˈ· ·/ *n* [C] a television programme in which people play games or answer questions to win prizes 电视有奖竞赛节目

games·man·ship /ˋgemzmən͵ʃɪp; ˈgeɪmzmənʃɪp/ *n* [U] the ability to succeed by using the rules of a game to your own advantage〔巧妙运用比赛规则的〕制胜能力

gam·ete /ˋgæmit; ˈgæmiːt/ *n* [C] a type of cell which joins with another cell, starting the development of a baby or other young creature 配子〔一种与另一细胞结合会产生胚胎的细胞〕

game war·den /ˈ· ,··/ *n* [C] someone whose job is to look after wild animals in a GAME RESERVE〔野生动物保护区的〕看守人

gam·ey, gamy /ˋgemɪ; ˈgeɪmi/ *adj* having the strong taste of wild animals that are hunted for food 有浓烈的野味味道的

ga·mine /gæˋmin; ˈgeɪmiːn/ *n* [C] a small thin girl or woman who looks like a boy 男孩气的女孩, 假小子 —**gamine** *adj*: *a gamine hairstyle* 假小子发式

gam·ing /ˋgemɪŋ; ˈgeɪmɪŋ/ *n* [U] *old-fashioned* playing cards or other games of chance for money; GAMBLING【过时】赌钱游戏, 赌博: *gaming tables* 赌桌

gam·ma /ˋgæmə; ˈgæmə/ *n* [C] the third letter of the Greek alphabet 伽玛〔希腊语字母表的第三个字母, 即Γ, γ〕

gamma glob·u·lin /͵gæmə ˋglabjulɪn; ͵gæmə ˈglɒbjʊlɪn/ *n* [U] a natural substance in your body which is a type of ANTIBODY, and gives protection against some diseases 丙种球蛋白〔人体的一种抗体, 能防止某些疾病〕

gamma ray /ˈ·· ·/ *n* [C usually plural 一般用复数] a beam of light with a short WAVELENGTH (2), that can pass through solid objects γ射线, 伽玛射线

gam·mon /ˋgæmən; ˈgæmən/ *n* [U] *BrE* meat from a pig's leg which has been preserved using salt【英】腌猪腿: *gammon steak* 腌火腿排

gam·my /ˋgæmɪ; ˈgæmi/ *adj BrE old-fashioned* a gammy leg or knee is injured or painful【英, 过时】〔腿或膝〕受伤的, 疼痛的

gam·ut /ˋgæmət; ˈgæmət/ *n* [singular] the complete range of possibilities 全部可能性; 整个范围: [+of] *College life opened up a whole gamut of new experiences.* 大学生活提供了各种全新体验。| **run the (whole) gamut** (=include or experience all the possibilities between two extremes) 包括各种可能性, 经历全部的历程 *Her feelings that day ran the whole gamut of emotions.* 她那天百感交集。

gam·y /ˋgemɪ; ˈgeɪmi/ *adj* another spelling of GAMEY gamey 的另一种拼法

-gamy /gəmɪ; gəmi/ *suffix* [in U nouns 构成不可数名词] marriage to a particular number or kind of people 结婚: *bigamy* (=being married to two people) 重婚 | *monogamy* 一夫一妻制 —**gamous** *suffix* [in adjectives 构成形容词]

Gan·dalf /ˋgandalf; ˈgændælf/ one of the main characters in the book *The Lord of the Rings* by J.R.R. Tolkien. He is a WIZARD. 甘道夫〔J.R.R. 托尔金的《指环王》中一主要人物。他是一个巫师〕

gan·der /ˋgændɚ; ˈgændə/ *n* [C] **1** a male GOOSE¹ (1a) 雄鹅 **2 have/take a gander at** *spoken* to look at something【口】看一看

Gan·dhi /ˋgandɪ; ˈgændi/, **In·di·ra** /ˋɪndɪrə; ˈɪndərə/ (1917-84) an Indian politician who was Prime Minister of India from 1966-77. She was the daughter of India's first Prime Minister, Jawaharlal Nehru. 甘地夫人〔(1917-1984), 印度政治家。她1966至1977年间任印度总理, 是印度首任总理尼赫鲁的女儿〕

Gandhi, Ma·hat·ma /məˋhatmə; məˈhætmə/ (1869-1948) an Indian lawyer and politician who successfully led the fight for India's independence from the British. Gandhi is famous especially for developing the idea of non-violent protest, and his methods have been copied in many other places. His real name was **Mohandas Karamchand Gandhi** but he was given the name 'Mahatma' (meaning 'great soul') by his followers. He was AS-

SASSINATED (=killed) soon after India gained independence. 甘地〔(1869-1948)，印度律师、政治家，成功领导了印度摆脱英国殖民统治取得独立的斗争。尤以倡导"非暴力抵抗"思想而出名。这一方法在其他许多地方被效仿。他的真名是默罕达斯·卡拉姆昌德·甘地，但其追随者称他为"圣雄"。印度独立后不久他即遭暗杀〕

gang¹ /gæŋ; gæŋ/ *n* **1** a group of young people who spend time together, and often cause trouble and fight against other groups〔常聚在一起闹事打斗的〕一帮年轻人: *a skinhead gang* 一伙光头仔 | *members of a notorious gang* 声名狼藉的帮派的成员 | **[+of]** *a gang of kids hanging around the mall* 在购物中心附近闲逛的一帮小伙子 **2** [C] a group of criminals who work together 一群合伙作案的罪犯: *Several gangs were operating in the area.* 好几个罪犯团伙在这个地区活动。| **[+of]** *a gang of smugglers* 一伙走私分子 **3** *humorous* a group of friends, especially young people【幽默】一群朋友〔尤指年轻人〕: *The whole gang will be there next weekend.* 朋友们下个周末全部都会到那儿。**4** a group of workers or prisoners doing physical work together〔干体力活的〕一群工人，一群囚犯 —see also 另见 CHAIN GANG

gang² *v*

gang up on sb *phr v* [T] to join together into a group to attack someone or oppose them 合伙打击[反对]: *I hate school! They all gang up on me!* 我讨厌上学！他们都合起伙来对付我！

gang-bang /ˈ· ,·/ *n* [C] **1** *informal* an occasion when several people have sex with each other at the same time【非正式】集体淫乱 **2** a GANG RAPE 轮奸 —**gang-bang** *v* [I,T]

gang·bust·ers /ˈgæŋ,bʌstɚz; ˈgæŋ,bʌstəz/ *n* **come on like gangbusters** *AmE informal* to begin to do something very eagerly and with a lot of energy【美，非正式】非常热情，非常起劲地开始做某事: *You can't come on like gangbusters with women – be more subtle!* 对女人你不能只凭热情冲动——应该更巧妙细微些！

Gan·ges, the /ˈgændʒiz; ˈgændʒiːz/ a long river which flows through northern India and provides water for the fields in India and Bangladesh. To the Hindus the Ganges is a holy river, and many Hindus go to the river as PILGRIMs and wash themselves in it. 恒河〔流经印度北部、为印度和孟加拉提供灌溉用水的一条长河。印度教徒把它视为圣河，许多人前去朝圣，并在河中洗浴〕—**Gangetic** /gænˈdʒɛtɪk; gænˈdʒetɪk/ *adj*: *the Gangetic plain* 恒河平原

gang·land /ˈgæŋ,lænd; ˈgæŋlænd/ *adj* **a gangland killing/murder/shooting etc** a killing etc connected with the world of organized and violent crime 黑社会凶杀/谋杀/枪杀等: *Sharp may have been the victim of a gangland revenge killing.* 夏普可能已经成了黑社会报复性凶杀的受害者。

gan·gling /ˈgæŋglɪŋ; ˈgæŋglɪŋ/ *adj* unusually tall and thin, and not at all graceful in the way you move 又高又瘦且动作笨拙的: *an awkward gangling teenager* 一位瘦长而笨手笨脚的青少年

gan·gli·on /ˈgæŋglɪən; ˈgæŋgliən/ *n* [C] *technical*【术语】**1** a painful raised area of skin that is full of liquid, often on the back of your wrist 腱鞘囊肿 **2** a mass of nerve cells 神经节

gan·gly /ˈgæŋglɪ; ˈgæŋgli/ *adj* another form of GANGLING gangling 的另一形式

gang·plank /ˈgæŋ,plæŋk; ˈgæŋplæŋk/ *n* [C] a board for walking on between a boat and the shore, or between one boat and another〔船和岸之间或船与船之间的〕跳板，步桥

gangster 歹徒，犯罪团伙成员

gang rape /ˈ· ·/ *n* [C] an occasion when several men attack a woman to force her to have sex with them 轮奸

gan·grene /ˈgæŋgrin; ˈgæŋgriːn/ *n* [U] the decay of the flesh of part of your body because blood has stopped flowing there as a result of illness or injury 坏疽 —**gangrenous** *adj*

gang·ster /ˈgæŋstɚ; ˈgæŋstə/ *n* [C] a member of a violent group of criminals 歹徒，犯罪团伙成员: *a gangster movie* 描写盗匪的影片

CULTURAL NOTE 文化注释

In Britain, the image many people have of a gangster is of a man in a SMART suit who carries a big gun hidden in a case meant for holding a VIOLIN. Most people associate the word with Al Capone and the Chicago gangsters of the 1920s and 1930s. 很多英国人对歹徒的印象是：一个穿着光鲜的男子，携带一个小提琴盒，里面却藏着一支大枪。很多人把该词与20世纪20、30年代的艾尔·卡彭和芝加哥匪帮联系在一起。

gang·way /ˈgæŋ,we; ˈgæŋweɪ/ *n* [C] **1** a space between two rows of seats in a theatre, bus, or train; AISLE (1)〔剧场、公共汽车或火车上座位间的〕过道 **2** a large GANGPLANK 大跳板，大步桥 **3 gangway!** *spoken* used to tell people in a crowd to let someone go through【口】让路！闪开！〔用来请拥挤的人群给某人让路〕

gan·ja /ˈgændʒə; ˈgændʒə/ *n* [U] *slang* MARIJUANA【俚】大麻

gan·net /ˈgænɪt; ˈgænɪt/ *n* [C] **1** a large sea bird that lives in large groups on cliffs〔群居在悬崖上的〕鲣鸟，塘鹅 **2** *BrE* someone who eats a lot【英】食量大的人

gan·try /ˈgæntrɪ; ˈgæntri/ *n* [C] a large metal frame which is used to support heavy machinery or railway signals〔支承重型机器或铁路信号灯的〕台架

Gan·y·mede /ˈgænɪmid; ˈgænɪmiːd/ in ancient Greek stories, a beautiful young boy who was taken to Olympus by Zeus and became CUPBEARER (=someone who serves wine) to the gods 该尼墨得斯〔古希腊神话中被宙斯带到奥林波斯山充当酒侍的美少年〕

gaol /dʒel; dʒeɪl/ *n,v* a British spelling of JAIL jail 的英式拼法

gaol·bird /ˈdʒel,bɝd; ˈdʒeɪlbɜːd/ *n* [C] a British spelling of JAILBIRD jailbird 的英式拼法

gaol·er /ˈdʒelɚ; ˈdʒeɪlə/ *n* [C] a British spelling of JAILER jailer 的英式拼法

gap 缺口

Ken squeezed through a gap in the fence.
肯从篱笆的一个缺口挤了过去。

gap /gæp; gæp/ *n* [C]

1 ▶A SPACE 间隔◀ a space between two objects or two parts of an object because of something that is missing 缺口；裂缝: **[+in]** *The neighbors' dog got in through a gap in the hedge.* 邻居的狗从树篱的缺口钻了进来。| **[+between]** *Lou has big gaps between her front teeth.* 卢的门牙间有很大的缝。

2 ▶DIFFERENCE 差别◀ a big difference between two situations, amounts, groups of people etc 差距；差额；差别: **[+between]** *the widening gap between the rich and the poor* 贫富之间不断扩大的差距 | **fill the gap** *Donors will be asked to fill the gap between state funding and actual costs.* 将请捐款人填补国家拨款和实际费用之间的差额。| **bridge the gap** (=reduce the amount or importance of a difference) 填补空缺，弥补差距 *His films attempt to bridge the gap between tradition and modernity.* 他的影片企图弥合传统和现代风格之间的差距。—see also 另见 **the generation gap** (GENERATION)

3 ▶STH MISSING 缺少的东西◀ something that is missing that stops something else from being good or complete 空白，缺漏: **[+in]** *There are huge gaps in my knowledge of history.* 我的历史知识很贫乏。| *Frank's death has left a big gap in my life.* 弗兰克死后，我的生活变得极度空虚。

4 ▶IN A MOUNTAIN 在山里◀ a low place between two higher parts of a mountain 山峡，山口

5 ▶IN TIME 在时间上◀ a period of time between two periods of time when nothing is happening 间隙: *an awkward gap in the conversation* 谈话中出现的一次令人尴尬的停顿

6 gap in the market an opportunity to develop a particular product and sell it because it has not been developed yet 市场空白〔开发销售一种尚无人开发的产品的机会〕

gape /gep; geɪp/ *v* [I] **1** to look at something for a long time, especially with your mouth open, because you are very surprised or shocked 瞠目结舌[目不转睛]地注视: *What are all these people gaping at?* 这些人目不转睛地都在看什么呀？—see 见 GAZE¹ (USAGE) **2** also 又作 **gape open** to come apart or open widely 裂开，敞开: *Dan stood at the door, his shirt gaping open.* 丹敞开衬衫站在门口。—**gape** *n* [C]

gap·ing /ˈgepɪŋ; ˈgeɪpɪŋ/ *adj* [only before noun 仅用于名词前] a gaping hole, wound, or mouth is very wide and open 裂开的，敞开的

gap-toothed /,· ˈ·◂/ *adj* having wide spaces between your teeth 牙齿间隙缝很大的

S2 **gar·age¹** /gəˋrɑʒ; ˈɡærɑːʒ/ *n* [C] **1** a building for keeping a car in, usually next to a house〔通常紧靠房屋的〕车库，汽车间 —compare 比较 CARPORT —see picture on page A4 参见 A4 页图 **2** a place where motor vehicles are repaired 汽车修理厂[站]: *My car's at the garage.* 我的车在修理厂。**3** *BrE* a place where you buy petrol; PETROL STATION【英】加油站

garage² *v* [T] to put or keep a vehicle in a garage 将汽车开进[停放在]车库

garage sale /ˈ· · ,·/ *n* [C] *AmE* a sale of used furniture, clothes etc from people's houses, usually held in someone's garage【美】旧物出售〔指将家里的旧家具、旧衣物等摆在自家的车库里出售〕

gar·am ma·sa·la /ˌɡarəm məˋsalə; ˌɡɑːrəm məˈsɑːlə/ *n* [U] a mixture of SPICE*s* which gives a hot taste to food, used especially in Indian cooking 有辣味的混合香料〔尤用于印度式烹调〕

garb¹ /ɡarb; ɡɑːb/ *n* [U] *formal or literary* a particular style of clothing, especially clothes that show your type of work or look unusual【正式或文】〔尤指显示工作类型或样式特别的〕制服，服装，装束: *clothed in priestly garb* 穿着牧师服装的

garb² *v* **be garbed in** *literary* to be dressed in a particular type of clothes【文】穿着…服装的: *singers garbed in costumes of gold* 穿着金色服装的歌手

S3 **gar·bage** /ˋɡarbɪdʒ; ˈɡɑːbɪdʒ/ *n* [U] **1** *especially AmE* waste material, such as paper, empty containers, and food thrown away【尤美】垃圾; RUBBISH¹ (1) *BrE*【英】: *Can you take the garbage out when you go?* 你走的时候能把垃圾带出去吗? **2** stupid words, ideas etc 蠢话，废话；愚蠢的看法: *You're talking garbage.* 你在说废话。**3 garbage in, garbage out** used to say that if you put bad information into a computer, you will get bad results〔电脑运算中〕错进，错出〔用来表示若将垃圾信息输入电脑，所输出的也是垃圾〕—see graph at 参见 RUBBISH¹ 图表

garbage can /ˈ· · ,·/ *n* [C] *AmE* a container with a lid for holding waste until it can be taken away【美】垃圾箱，垃圾桶; DUSTBIN *BrE*【英】—see picture on page A4 参见 A4 页图

garbage col·lec·tor /ˈ· · ·,· · ·/ *n* [C] *AmE* someone whose job is to remove waste from garbage cans【美】垃圾清洁工; DUSTMAN *BrE*【英】

garbage dis·po·sal /ˈ· · ·,· · ·/ *n* [C] *AmE* a small machine in the kitchen SINK which breaks vegetable waste into small pieces【美】〔厨房洗涤槽里将废弃蔬菜切碎的〕小型垃圾处理机; WASTE DISPOSAL (1) *BrE*【英】

garbage man /ˈ· · ,·/ *n* [C] *AmE* a garbage collector【美】垃圾清洁工

garbage truck /ˈ· · ,·/ *n* [C] *AmE* a large vehicle which goes from house to house to collect the contents of garbage cans【美】垃圾车; DUST CART *BrE*【英】

gar·ban·zo /ɡarˋbanzo; ɡɑːˈbænzəʊ/ also 又作 **garbanzo bean** /ˈ· · ·,·/ *n* [C] another word for CHICK-PEA, used especially in the western US 鹰嘴豆〔chick-pea 的另一名称，尤用于美国西部〕

gar·bled /ˋɡarbḷd; ˈɡɑːbəld/ *adj* a garbled statement or report is very unclear and confusing〔陈述、报告〕含混不清的，极其混乱的: *The papers had some garbled version of the story.* 对这件事报纸上有一些含糊不清的报道。| *a garbled phone message* 很不清楚的电话留言

Gar·bo /ˋɡarbo; ˈɡɑːbəʊ/, **Gret·a** /ˋɡrɛtə; ˈɡretə/ (1905-90) a US film actress, born in Sweden, who was famous for her beauty, and for saying "I want to be alone". Her films include *Queen Christina* (1933), *Anna Karenina* (1935), and *Camille* (1936). 嘉宝〔(1905-1990)，美国女电影演员，生于瑞典。她以美貌和"我喜欢一个人待着"这句名言而著称。她演过的影片包括《瑞典女王》(1933)、《安娜·卡列尼娜》(1935) 和《茶花女》(1936)〕

Gar·cì·a Lor·ca /ɡarˌsiə ˋlɔrkə; ɡɑːˌsiːə ˈlɔːkə/, **Fed·e·ri·co** /fɛdəˋriko; fedəˈriːkəʊ/ (1898-1936) a Spanish poet and writer of plays, including *Blood Wedding* and *The House of Bernarda Alba*. He was shot during the Spanish Civil War. 加西亚·洛尔卡〔(1898-1936)，西班牙诗人、剧作家。他创作的戏剧有《血婚》和《贝纳达·阿尔瓦的家》等。西班牙内战时期遭枪杀〕

Gar·cì·a Már·quez /ɡarˌsiə ˋmarkɛs; ɡɑːˌsiːə ˈmɑːkes/, **Gabriel** /ˋɡebriəl; ˈɡeɪbriəl/ (1928-) a Colombian writer whose NOVEL*s* are in the style of MAGIC REALISM, and include *One Hundred Years of Solitude* and *Love in the Time of Cholera*. He won the Nobel Prize for Literature in 1982. 加西亚·马尔克斯〔(1928-)，哥伦比亚魔幻现实主义作家。他创作的小说包括《百年孤独》和《霍乱时期的爱情》。1982 年获诺贝尔文学奖〕

gar·çon /ɡarˋsɔ̃; ˈɡɑːsɒn/ *n* [C] *French* a waiter, especially in a French restaurant【法】〔法国餐馆里的〕男服务员，男侍

Garda, the /ˋɡadə; ˈɡɑːdə/ *n* the police force in the Republic of Ireland 爱尔兰警察

S1 W1 **gar·den¹** /ˋɡardṇ; ˈɡɑːdn/ *n* **1** [C] *especially BrE* a piece of land around or next to your house where there is usually lawn (=area of grass) and an area where you grow flowers, plants, or vegetables【尤英】宅旁花园，菜园; YARD (3) *AmE*【美】: *Grace is out in the garden mowing the lawn.* 格雷斯在外面庭园的草坪上刈草。| **rose garden/herb garden etc** (=where a particular type of plant is grown) 玫瑰园/药草园等 —see picture on page A4 参见 A4 页图 **2** [C] *AmE* the part of a garden that has flowers and plants in it【美】〔庭园里的〕园圃〔指种有花木的部分〕: *We're thinking of planting a little garden in our yard.* 我们想在院子里栽种一个小花圃。**3 gardens** [plural] a large area of land where plants and flowers are grown so that the public can go and see them 公园: *the Botanic Gardens at Kew* 基尤植物园 **4 Gardens** *BrE* used in the name of streets【英】〔用于街道的名称〕: *number 211 Roland Gardens* 罗兰德街 211 号 —see also 另见 KITCHEN GARDEN, MARKET GARDEN, **lead sb up the garden path** (LEAD¹ (18))

garden² *v* [I] to work in a garden, keeping it clean, making plants grow etc 从事园艺 —**gardening** *n* [U]: *Since he's retired he's become very interested in gardening.* 他退休后对园艺很感兴趣。

> **CULTURAL NOTE 文化注释**
>
> **Gardening** Many British people enjoy gardening and spend a lot of their free time taking care of their gardens. Some people also have ALLOTMENT*s* where they grow vegetables. In the UK, there are many popular television programmes about gardening and garden design such as *Gardeners' World and Groundforce*. There is also a famous radio programme called *Gardeners' Question Time* in which members of the public can ask gardening EXPERT*s* for advice. Some of the gardeners who appear on these programmes, such as Alan Titchmarsh and Charlie Dimmock, have become very famous and have sold many books about gardening. 园艺：英国有很多人喜欢园艺，花很多业余时间照料花园。有些人还有小块租赁地，用来栽种蔬菜。英国有很多广受欢迎的有关园艺或园林设计的电视节目，如《园丁世界》和《地面力量》。还有一档著名的广播节目叫做《园丁问答》，普通人可以向园艺专家咨询。有些园丁，如艾伦·蒂奇玛什和查利·迪莫克，在节目中露面，名声大振，因此卖了很多园艺书籍。
>
> There are GARDEN CENTRE*s* in every town and city in the UK, selling plants, trees, and gardening equipment. Each year, the Royal Horticultural Society organizes the Chelsea Flower Show in London. Many British people like to visit famous public gardens such as the Royal Botanic Gardens at Kew in west London. 英国每个城镇都有园艺中心，出售植物、树木和园艺工具。每年皇家园艺协会在伦敦组织切尔西花卉展。许多英国人喜欢参观著名的公园，如伦敦西区的基尤皇家植物园。

garden cen·tre /ˈ· ·,· ·/ *n* [C] *BrE* a place that sells plants, flowers and equipment for gardens; NURSERY (4)【英】〔出售植物、花卉和园艺用具的〕花卉商店

garden cit·y /ˌ· · ˈ· ·/ *n* [C] *BrE* a town that has been designed to have a lot of trees, areas of grass, and open spaces【英】花园城市 —compare 比较 NEW TOWN

gar·den·er /ˋɡardnɚ; ˈɡɑːdnə/ *n* [C] **1** someone who enjoys growing flowers and plants 园艺爱好者: *Mom has always been a good gardener.* 母亲一直很善于种植花卉。**2** someone whose job is to work in gardens 园艺工人，园丁，花匠

garden flat /ˈ· · ,·/ *n* [C] *BrE* an apartment on the lowest floor of a house, which has a door leading to the garden【英】花园公寓〔指位于楼房最底层，有门通向花园的套房〕

gar·de·ni·a /ɡarˋdinɪə; ɡɑːˈdiːniə/ *n* [C] a large white pleasant-smelling flower that grows on a bush 栀子属植物

Garden of E·den, the /ˌ· · · ˈ· ·/ —see 见 EDEN

Garden of En·gland, the /ˌ· · · ˈ· ·/ a name for the COUNTY of Kent in southeast England, because of the fruit and vegetables it produces 英格兰花园〔英格兰东南肯特郡的别称。因出产水果和蔬菜而得名〕

garden par·ty /ˈ· · ,· ·/ *n* [C] *BrE* a formal party for a lot of people which is held in a large garden【英】〔在大花园里举行的有许多人参加的正式的〕花园招待会; LAWN PARTY *AmE*【美】

> **CULTURAL NOTE 文化注释**
>
> Every year, the British Queen holds several garden parties at Buckingham Palace. The guests are usually invited as a reward for their work or achievements, and it is considered a great honour. 每年英国女王在白金汉宫举办数场花园招待会。嘉宾一般都因工作或成就突出受邀出席，以示嘉奖，这被看作是一大荣誉。

G

gar·den-va·ri·e·ty /ˈ· · ·, · · ·/ *adj* [only before noun 仅用于名词前] *AmE* very ordinary and not very interesting【美】非常一般的, 平淡无奇的: *He's just one of your garden-variety singers.* 他只是一名不起眼的歌手。

Gar·field /ˈgɑrfild; ˈgɑːfiːld/ the main character in a humorous CARTOON STRIP (=a set of drawings that tell a story) that appears in hundreds of US newspapers and some British ones every day. Garfield is a cat who is fat and SELFISH. 加菲猫〔幽默连环漫画中的主角。它是一只肥硕而自私的猫, 出现在数百种美国报纸和部分英国报纸的版面里〕

Garfield, James (1831-81) the twentieth president of the US. In 1881, he was shot by a mentally ill man and died two months later. 加菲尔德〔(1831-1881), 美国第二十任总统。1881年, 他遭遇一精神病人枪击, 两个月后死亡〕

Garfunkel /gɑrˈfʌŋkḷ; gɑːˈfʌŋkəl/, **Art** —see 见 SIMON AND GARFUNKEL

gar·gan·tu·an /gɑrˈgæntʃuən; gɑːˈgæntʃuən/ *adj* extremely large; GIGANTIC 巨大的: *What a gargantuan bed!* 多大的一张床啊!

gar·gle¹ /ˈgɑrgḷ; ˈgɑːgəl/ *v* [I+with] to clean the inside of your mouth and throat by blowing air through water or medicine in the back of your throat 漱口, 漱喉: *Gargling with salt water may help your sore throat.* 用盐水漱口可能对你的喉咙痛有好处。

gargle² *n* **1** [C,U] liquid that you gargle with 漱口液 **2** [singular] the act of gargling 漱口

gar·goyle /ˈgɑrgɔɪl; ˈgɑːgɔɪl/ *n* [C] an ugly stone figure of a person or animal that carries rain water from the roof of an old building, especially a church〔教堂等古老建筑物屋顶上奇形怪状的石雕人物或动物形状的〕排水嘴

Gar·i·bal·di /ˌgærɪˈbɔldɪ; ˌgærɨˈbɔːldi/, **Giu·sep·pe** /dʒuˈsɛpɪ; dʒʊˈsepi/ (1807-82) an Italian military leader who helped Italy to become a united, independent country by taking control of Sicily and Naples in 1860 加里波第〔(1807-1882), 意大利军事领袖。1860年, 他率军占领了西西里和那不勒斯, 使意大利成为统一独立的国家〕

gar·ish /ˈgɛrɪʃ; ˈgeərɪʃ/ *adj* very brightly coloured in a way that is unpleasant to look at 花哨的: *Many of the rugs are too garish for my taste.* 这里许多地毯色彩太花哨, 我不喜欢。—**garishly** *adv* —**garishness** *n* [U]

gar·land¹ /ˈgɑrlənd; ˈgɑːlənd/ *n* [C] a ring of flowers or leaves that is given to someone to wear around their neck〔送给某人戴于颈部的〕花环

garland² *v* [T] *literary* to decorate someone or something, especially with flowers【文】用花环装饰

Garland, Judy (1922-69) a US film actress and singer who first appeared in films as a child. She is most famous for appearing as the character Dorothy in *The Wizard of Oz* (1939). Other films include *Meet Me in St Louis* (1944) and *A Star is Born* (1954). 嘉兰〔(1922-1969), 美国女电影演员、歌手。她最初是一名童星, 出演过数部影片。她以在影片《绿野仙踪》(1939)中扮演多萝西一角最为出名, 并曾出演《在圣路易斯与我相会》(1944)和《一个明星的诞生》(1954)〕

3 **gar·lic** /ˈgɑrlɪk; ˈgɑːlɪk/ *n* [U] a plant like a small onion, used in cooking to give a strong taste 大蒜: *a clove of garlic* (=single section of it) 蒜瓣 | *a garlic press* (=tool used to crush garlic) 捣蒜器 —**garlicky** *adj*: *his garlicky breath* 他带有大蒜味的呼吸 —see picture on page A9 参见 A9 页图

gar·ment /ˈgɑrmənt; ˈgɑːmənt/ *n* [C] *formal or technical* a piece of clothing【正式或术语】〔一件〕衣服 —see picture at 参见 CLOTHES 图

gar·ner /ˈgɑrnɚ; ˈgɑːnə/ *v* [T] *formal* to take or collect something, especially information【正式】收集〔尤指信息〕

gar·net /ˈgɑrnɪt; ˈgɑːnɨt/ *n* **1** [C] a dark red stone used as a jewel 石榴石 **2** [U] a dark red colour 石榴红色, 暗红色

gar·nish¹ /ˈgɑrnɪʃ; ˈgɑːnɪʃ/ *n* [C] something that you add to food to decorate it〔添加在食物上的〕装饰菜

garnish² *v* [T] **1** to add something to food in order to decorate it 在〔食物〕上加饰菜: **garnish sth with** *Garnish each dish with a slice of lemon.* 在每盘菜上配一片柠檬。**2** also 又作 **garnishee** *technical* to take money from someone's wages because they have not paid their debts【术语】扣发〔债务人的工资〕

gar·ret /ˈgærɪt; ˈgærɨt/ *n* [C] a small uncomfortable room at the top of a house 顶楼, 阁楼 —compare 比较 ATTIC

CULTURAL NOTE 文化注释

People often think of poor writers and artists living in garrets, as these rooms were often cheap to rent. 人们通常认为, 贫穷的作家和艺术家住在阁楼里, 因为这样的房间租金便宜。

gar·ri·son¹ /ˈgærəsn̩; ˈgærɨsən/ *n* [C] a group of soldiers living in a town or FORT and defending it 卫戍部队, 要塞驻军: *The garrison was called out when news of the enemy's advance was received.* 收到敌人推进的情报后, 卫戍部队受命出动。| *a garrison town* 有守备部队驻防的城镇

garrison² *v* [T] to send a group of soldiers to defend or guard a place 派兵驻防: *Our regiment will garrison a coastal town.* 我们团将驻防一个沿海城镇。

gar·rotte /gəˈrɑt; gəˈrɒt/ *v* [T] to kill someone using a metal collar or wire which is pulled tightly around their neck〔用金属环或金属丝〕勒杀 —**garrotte** *n* [C]

gar·ru·lous /ˈgærələs; ˈgærələs/ *adj* always talking a lot 饶舌的, 喋喋不休的: *Ian isn't normally this garrulous!* 伊恩平时没这么唠叨! —**garrulously** *adv* —**garrulousness** *n* [U]

gar·ter /ˈgɑrtɚ; ˈgɑːtə/ *n* [C] **1** a band of ELASTIC (=material that stretches) worn around your leg to keep a sock or STOCKING up 吊袜松紧带 **2** *AmE* one of four pieces of elastic fixed to a woman's underwear and to her stockings to hold them up【美】〔女子内衣和长统袜的〕吊带; SUSPENDER (1) *BrE*【英】

Garter, the Order of the the highest order of British KNIGHTHOOD. The sign of the Order of the Garter is a blue VELVET GARTER. 嘉德勋位〔英国骑士的最高荣誉, 其标识为蓝色天鹅绒袜带勋章〕

garter belt /ˈ· ·, ·ˈ/ *n* [C] *AmE* a piece of women's underwear with garters hanging down from it which fasten onto STOCKINGS (1) and hold them up【美】〔女子内衣上的〕吊袜束腰带; SUSPENDER BELT *BrE*【英】

garter snake /ˈ· ·, ·ˈ/ *n* [C] a harmless American snake with lines of colour along its back 美洲无毒束带蛇

gas¹ /gæs; gæs/ *n plural* **gases** also 又作 **gasses** **1** [C,U] a substance like air, which is not solid or liquid, and usually cannot be seen 气, 气体: *hydrogen gas* 氢气 | **a gas cylinder** (=for storing gas) 储气桶 **2** [U] a substance of this type which is burnt for heating or cooking〔供取暖、烹调用的〕可燃气: *a gas oven* 煤气炉 | *Can you light the gas for me?* 你能帮我点燃煤气炉吗? **3** [U] a substance of this type used to poison people or to control them 毒气, 麻醉气: *Police fired tear gas into the crowd.* 警察朝人群发射催泪瓦斯。**4** [U] *AmE* GASOLINE【美】汽油 **5 gas mark 4,5,6 etc** *BrE* a measurement of the temperature of a gas OVEN【英】〔测量煤气烤箱温度的〕煤气刻度4、5、6等 **6** *AmE slang* the condition of having gas in your stomach【美俚】腹胀, 胃胀; WIND¹ (9) *BrE*【英】**7** [singular] *AmE* something that is fun and makes you laugh a lot【美】有趣的事, 令人发笑的事: *The state fair was a real gas.* 这次的州博览会真是有趣。

gas² *v* **1** [T] to poison or kill someone with gas 用毒气杀死 **2** [I] *informal* to talk for a long time about unimportant or boring things【非正式】空谈, 闲聊: *They were just standing there gassing away.* 他们站在那儿聊个没完。

gas sth ↔ **up** *phr v* [I,T] *AmE* to put petrol in a car【美】给〔汽车〕加油: *We'd better gas up before we go.* 我们在走之前最好给汽车加满油。

gas·bag /ˈgæsˌbæg; ˈgæsbæg/ *n* [C] *informal* someone who talks too much; WINDBAG【非正式】夸夸其谈的人, 废话连篇的人

gas cham·ber /ˈ· ˌ· ·/ *n* [C] a large room in which people or animals are killed with poisonous gas〔用毒气杀害人或动物的〕毒气室

gas·e·ous /ˈgæsɪəs; ˈgæsiəs/ *adj* like gas or in the form of gas 似气体的, 气态的

gas-fired /ˌ· ˈ·◂/ *adj especially BrE* using gas as a fuel【尤英】燃气的: *a gas-fired central heating system* 燃气中央供暖系统

gas-guz·zler /ˈ· ˌ· ·/ *n* [C] *AmE informal* a car that uses a lot of petrol【美, 非正式】耗油量大的汽车, 油老虎 —**gas-guzzling** *adj*

gash /gæʃ; gæʃ/ *n* [C] **1** a large deep wound from a cut〔大而深的〕切口, 伤口: *a deep gash on his leg* 他腿上一处很深的伤口 **2** a long deep hole in something 深而长的裂缝: *The trench cut a brown gash through the green lawn.* 壕沟在绿色的草坪上切开一条棕色的大裂缝。—**gash** *v* [T]

gas·hold·er /ˈgæsˌholdɚ; ˈgæsˌhəʊldə/ *n* [C] a very large round metal container or building from which gas is carried in pipes to buildings 大型储气罐, 煤气供应室

gas·i·fy /ˈgæsəˌfaɪ; ˈgæsɨfaɪ/ *v* [I,T] to change into a gas, or to make something do this 成为气体, 气化 —**gasification** /ˌgæsəfəˈkeʃən; ˌgæsɨfɨˈkeɪʃən/ *n* [U]

gas·ket /ˈgæskɪt; ˈgæskɨt/ *n* [C] **1** a flat piece of material, often rubber, placed between two surfaces so that steam, oil, gas etc cannot escape 垫圈, 密封垫 **2 blow a gasket a)** if a vehicle blows a gasket, steam or gas escapes from the engine〔发动机〕漏气 **b)** *informal* to become very angry【非正式】勃然大怒

gas·light /ˈgæs,laɪt; ˈgæslaɪt/ *n* **1** [U] the light produced from burning gas 煤气灯光 **2** [C] also 又作 **gas lamp** a lamp in a house or on the street which gives light from burning gas 煤气灯

gas·man /ˈgæs,mæn; ˈgæsmæn/ *n* [C] *BrE* someone who comes to your home to see how much gas you have used or to repair your gas system【英】煤气抄表员; 煤气装置修理员

gas mask /ˈ· ·/ *n* [C] a piece of equipment worn over your face to protect you from poisonous gases 防毒面具 —see picture at 参见 MASK[1] 图

gas me·ter /ˈ· ,··/ *n* [C] a piece of equipment that measures how much gas is used in a building 煤气表

gas·o·hol /ˈgæsəhɑl; ˈgæsəhɒl/ *n* [U] *AmE* petrol with a small amount of alcohol in it, which can be used in cars and is cheaper than petrol【美】酒精－汽油混合燃料〔即加有少量酒精的汽油, 较汽油便宜, 用于汽车〕

gas·o·line, gasolene /ˈgæsl̩,in; ˈgæsəliːn/ *n* [U] *AmE* a liquid obtained from PETROLEUM, used mainly for producing power in the engines of cars【美】汽油; PETROL *BrE*【英】

gas·om·e·ter /gæsˋɑmətɚ; gæˈsɒmɪ̵tə/ *n* [C] a GASHOLDER 大型储气罐, 煤气供应室

gasp[1] /gæsp; gɑːsp/ *v* [I,T] **1** to breathe in suddenly, quickly, and in a way that can be heard, especially because you are surprised or afraid〔因惊讶或害怕, 出声地〕喘息; 喘气: *"My leg! My leg!" he gasped. "I think it's broken!"* "我的腿! 我的腿!" 他喘着气喊道, "我想是腿断了!" | [**+with**] *Ollie gasped with pain and slumped forward.* 奥利痛得直吸气, 向前栽倒。| [**+at**] *The audience gasped at the splendour of the costumes.* 如此华丽的服装让观众们惊讶得倒吸一口气。**2** [I] to breathe quickly and deeply because you are having difficulty breathing〔由于呼吸困难而〕急促地深呼吸: **gasp for air/breath** *Brendan climbed slowly, gasping for breath.* 布伦达爬得很慢, 上气不接下气。**3 be gasping** *BrE spoken* to be very thirsty【英口】非常口渴的: *Put the kettle on, love, I'm gasping.* 亲爱的, 烧壶水吧, 我渴得要命。**4 be gasping for** *BrE spoken* to feel that you urgently need something such as a drink or cigarette【英口】渴望得到〔烟、酒等〕: *I'm gasping for a pint!* 我渴望喝上一品脱啤酒。

gasp[2] *n* [C] **1** an act of taking in your breath suddenly in a way that can be heard, especially because you are surprised or afraid〔尤指因惊讶或害怕〕喘气, 抽气: [**+of**] *With a gasp of pure horror, Stormgren jumped up and ran.* 斯托姆格伦吓得倒抽了一口气, 跳起来就跑。| **give a gasp** *She gave a little gasp and clutched George's hand.* 她轻轻地吸了一口气, 抓住了乔治的手。**2** an act of taking in air quickly because you are having difficulty breathing〔因呼吸困难而〕急促呼吸: *Between gasps Michael said that he was allergic to cats.* 迈克尔上气不接下气地说他对猫过敏。**3 at your last gasp** about to die 奄奄一息, 即将断气: *He rolled his eyes as though at his last gasp.* 他转动着眼珠, 好像快要断气似的。

gas pedal /ˈ· ,··/ *n* [C] *AmE* the thing that you press with your foot to make a car go faster; ACCELERATOR (1)【美】〔汽车的〕油门 —see picture on page A2 参见 A2 页图

gas per·me·a·ble lens /,· ˈ····ˈ·/ *n* [C] a kind of CONTACT LENS that allows oxygen to reach your eyes 透氧式隐形眼镜

gas ring /ˈ· ·/ *BrE n* [C] a metal ring that gets hot when gas passes through it, used for cooking food【英】环形炉头; BURNER (2) *AmE*【美】

gas sta·tion /ˈ· ,··/ *n* [C] *AmE* a place where you can buy petrol and oil for motor vehicles【美】加油站; PETROL STATION *BrE*【英】

gas·sy /ˈgæsɪ; ˈgæsi/ *adj BrE* a gassy drink has too much gas in it【英】〔饮料等〕气过多的: *This beer is really gassy.* 这种啤酒的气实在太多。—**gassiness** *n* [U]

gas·tric /ˈgæstrɪk; ˈgæstrɪk/ *adj* [only before noun 仅用于名词前] *technical*【术语】**1** related to your stomach 胃的: *gastric ulcers* 胃溃疡 **2 gastric juices** the acids in your stomach that break food into smaller parts 胃液 **3 gastric flu** an illness that makes you VOMIT[1] and gives you DIARRHOEA 胃肠性感冒

gas·tri·tis /gæsˋtraɪtɪs; gæˈstraɪtɪ̵s/ *n* [U] an illness which makes the inside of your stomach become swollen, so that you feel a burning pain 胃炎

gas·tro·en·te·ri·tis /,gæstro,ɛntəˈraɪtɪs; ,gæstrəʊentəˈraɪtɪ̵s/ *n* [U] an illness which makes your stomach and INTESTINE become swollen 胃肠炎

gas·tro·nom·ic /,gæstrəˋnɑmɪk; ,gæstrəˈnɒmɪk◂/ *adj* [only before noun 仅用于名词前] connected with the art of cooking good food or the pleasure of eating it 烹饪法的, 美食的: *sampling the gastronomic delights of Thailand* 品尝泰国的美食 —**gastronomically** /-klɪ; -kli/ *adv*

gas·tron·o·my /gæsˋtrɑnəmɪ; gæˈstrɒnəmi/ *n* [U] the art and science of cooking and eating good food 烹饪法, 美食学

gas tur·bine /,· ˈ··/ *n* [C] an engine in which a wheel of special blades is driven round at high speed by hot gases 燃气轮机

gas·works /ˈgæs,wɝks; ˈgæswɜːks/ *n plural* **gasworks** [C] a place where gas is made from coal 煤气厂

gate[1] /get; geɪt/ *n* [C] 2 2 **1** a frame that you can open and close to get through a fence, wall etc at the entrance to a place 大门, 栅栏门: *a garden gate* 花园门 | *In front of him were the wrought-iron gates of the palace.* 他面前是宫殿的锻铁门。—compare 比较 DOOR (1) —see picture on page A4 参见 A4 页图 **2** the place where you leave an airport building to get on a plane〔机场大楼里的〕登机门: *Air France flight 76 leaves from gate 6A.* 法航76次航班从6A号门起飞。**3 Irangate/Watergate/Contragate etc** used with the name of a place or a person to give a name to an event involving dishonest behaviour by a politician or other public official 伊朗门事件/水门事件/孔特拉门事件等 **4** *BrE*【英】**a)** the number of people who go in to see a sports event, especially a football match〔体育比赛, 尤指足球比赛的〕观众人数 **b)** the amount of money that these people pay 门票收入

gate[2] *v* [T] *BrE* to prevent a student from leaving a school as a punishment for behaving badly【英】禁止离校外出〔作为对学生行为不端的一种处罚〕

gâ·teau /gɑˋto; ˈgætəʊ/ *n plural* **gâteaux** /-toz; -təʊz/ [C,U] *BrE* a large sweet cake, often filled and decorated with cream, fruit, chocolate etc【英】奶油〔水果〕大蛋糕

gate·crash /ˈget,kræʃ; ˈgeɪtkræʃ/ *v* [I,T] to go to a party that you have not been invited to 不请自到, 擅自参加〔未受邀请的聚会〕—**gatecrasher** *n* [U]

gated com·mu·ni·ty /,·· ·ˈ···/ *n* [C] *AmE* an area of shops, houses etc with a fence or wall around it and an entrance that is guarded【美】有大门的社区〔指某地区的商店、房屋等有篱笆或墙围绕, 并有人看守大门〕

gate·house /ˈget,haus; ˈgeɪthaʊs/ *n* [C] a small building next to the gate of a park or at the entrance to the land surrounding a big house 门房

gate·keep·er /ˈget,kipɚ; ˈgeɪt,kiːpə/ *n* [C] someone whose job is to open and close a gate 看门人

gate-leg ta·ble /,·· ˈ··/ *n* [C] a table that can be made larger by moving a leg out to support a folding part 可部分折叠的桌子

gate·post /ˈget,post; ˈgeɪtpəʊst/ *n* [C] **1** one of two strong upright poles fixed to the ground to support a gate 大门两边的门柱 —see picture on page A4 参见 A4 页图 **2 between you, me and the gatepost** *BrE spoken* used to say that you are going to tell someone your opinion, but you want it to be a secret【英口】你我私下说说

Gates /gets; geɪts/, **Bill** (1955-) a US computer programmer and businessman, who started the Microsoft Corporation and is famous for being the richest man in the world 盖茨〔(1955-), 美国计算机编程专家、企业家。他创立了微软公司, 以世界首富著称〕

gate·way /ˈget,we; ˈgeɪtweɪ/ *n* **1** [C] the opening in a fence, wall etc that can be closed by a gate〔篱笆或围墙上的〕出入口 **2 the gateway to a)** a place, especially a city, that you can go through in order to reach another much bigger place〔通向更广阔地区的〕通道, 门户〔尤指一座城市〕: *St Louis is the gateway to the West.* 圣路易斯是通往西部的门户。**b)** a way of achieving something 途径, 手段: *Hard work is the gateway to success.* 努力工作是获得成功的手段。**3** [C] a way of connecting two computer networks (NETWORK[1] (4)) that would otherwise not be able to be connected〔连接两个电脑网络的〕网关

Gateway Arch, the /ˈ·· ,·/ a very large ARCH in the city of St Louis, Missouri, in the US, that is sometimes used in pictures to represent St Louis 大拱门〔美国密苏里州圣路易斯市的一座大型拱门。有时出现在画中作为圣路易斯市的象征〕

gath·er[1] /ˈgæðɚ; ˈgæðə/ *v* 2 2

1 ▶COME TOGETHER 聚集◀ [I] to come together and form a group 聚集, 集合: *On Fridays the men gather together at the mosque.* 每到星期五这些男人就聚集在清真寺。| *Tens of thousands of people had gathered outside the US embassy.* 数以万计的人聚集在美国大使馆外面。| **gather around/round** *I'd like everyone to gather round so I can demonstrate how the system works.* 我想请大家聚拢过来, 这样我好演示系统是如何工作的。| **gather together** *Could the bride's family all gather together for a photo?* 请新娘全家聚在一起拍个照, 好吗? | **be gathered** *Dozens of photographers were gathered outside Jagger's villa.* 好几十名摄影师聚集在贾格尔的别墅外面。

2 ▶KNOW/THINK 了解/思考◀ [T not in progressive 不用进行时] to know something or think something is true, because of

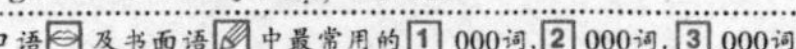

something that you have heard or seen 推断, 推测; 知道, 认为: *You two know each other, I gather.* 我想你们两人是互相认识的。| **gather (that)** *I gather you've had some problems with our sales department.* 我想你和我们的销售部有过一些争执。| **from what I can gather/as far as I can gather** (=this is what I believe to be true) 据我所知 *She's his niece, from what I can gather.* 据我所知, 她是他的侄女。

3 ►COLLECT 收集◄ [T] **a)** to search for things of the same type in several different places and collect them together 搜集, 采集: *Thelma went along the lane gathering blackberries.* 特尔玛沿着乡间小道采摘黑莓。**b)** to collect information, ideas etc for example in order to write a book or a report 收集〔信息、主意等〕: *Floyd's gathering ideas for his new novel.* 弗洛伊德正为他的新小说收集点子。

4 gather speed/force to move faster or become stronger 加快速度/加大力量: *The cart gathered speed as it coasted down the hill.* 手推车滑行下山时逐渐加快了速度。

5 gather dust if something useful gathers dust, it is not being used 闲置: *You may as well take these books – they're just gathering dust.* 你还不如把这些书拿走哩 —— 反正闲置着没人看。

6 gather momentum a) to gradually move faster, especially because of going down a hill 增加动量〔速度〕**b)** if a plan or process gathers momentum, it develops quickly and affects more and more people 势头日益增强: *A major anti-corruption campaign was gathering momentum.* 当时一场大规模的反腐败运动的势头在日益增强。

7 ►CLOTH 布◄ [T] **a)** to pull material into small folds 给…打褶裥: *The skirt is gathered at the waist.* 这条裙子的腰部有褶裥。**b)** to pull material or a piece of clothing closer to you 拉近: *Moira gathered her skirts round her and climbed the steps.* 莫伊拉提起她的裙子爬上台阶。

8 gather yourself/gather your strength to prepare yourself for something you are going to do, especially something difficult〔为某事, 尤指难事〕做好准备: *I need to rest and gather my strength for the exam.* 我需要休息一下, 为考试做好准备。

9 ►CLOUDS 云朵◄ [T] to gradually increase in number 积聚: *Storm clouds were gathering so we hurried home.* 暴风雨云在空中聚集, 所以我们赶快回家。

10 the gathering darkness/dusk/shadows etc *literary* the time in the evening when it is getting dark【文】黄昏时分: *the evening's gathering shadows* 傍晚渐浓的夜色

11 gather sb to you/gather sb up *old-fashioned* to take someone into your arms and hold them in order to protect them or show them love【过时】拥抱, 抱住

gather sth ↔ **in** *phr v* [T] to collect crops together 收〔庄稼〕: *gathering in the harvest* 在收庄稼

gather sth ↔ **together/up** *phr v* [T] to pick up lots of things from different places 集拢, 拾拢: *Paul gathered up his papers and left the room.* 保罗把他那些文件资料收集起来便离开房间。| *She gathered up some of the children's clothes and stuffed them in a bag.* 她收拾起孩子们的一些衣服, 塞进句里。

gather² *n* [C] a small fold produced by pulling cloth together 褶裥

gath·er·ing /ˋgæðrɪŋ; ˈgæðərɪŋ/ *n* [C] **1** a meeting of a group of people 集会: *a select gathering of 20 or 30 people* 20或30个特邀人士的集会 **2** a fold or group of folds in cloth 褶裥

Ga·to·rade /ˋgetəred; ˈgeɪtəreɪd/ *trademark* a type of US drink which replaces chemicals in the body that are lost when you have been exercising or playing sport【商标】"佳得乐"饮料〔美国的一种运动型饮料, 可补充人体在锻炼或比赛时损失的化学物质〕

Ga·tor Bowl, the /ˋgetɚ ˌbol; ˈgeɪtə ˌbəʊl/ an important college football game held every year in Jacksonville, Florida, in the US 盖特杯赛〔美国重要的大学生橄榄球赛事, 每年在佛罗里达州的杰克逊维尔举行〕

Gats·by /ˋgætsbɪ; ˈgætsbi/ —see 见 The GREAT GATSBY

Gat·wick /ˋgætwɪk; ˈgætwɪk/ one of the two main airports in London, UK 盖特威克机场〔英国伦敦两大主要机场之一〕

gauche /goʃ; gəʊʃ/ *adj* lacking confidence and experience in social situations, so that you often say or do the wrong thing 不善交际的: *a mature, successful business-woman, not a gauche teenager, flushing with girlish embarrassment* 一个成熟的成功女商人, 而不是一个不善交际的小姑娘, 却像姑娘般窘得涨红了脸 —**gauchely** *adv* —**gaucheness** *n* [U]

gau·cho /ˋgautʃo; ˈgaʊtʃəʊ/ *n* [C] a South American COWBOY (1)〔南美洲的〕加乌乔牧人

Gaud·i /ˋgaudi; ˈgaʊdi/ **, An·to·ni·o** /ænˋtonɪo; ænˈtəʊniəʊ/ (1852-1926) a Spanish ARCHITECT (=someone who designs buildings) who built many unusual, highly decorated buildings in Barcelona, the most famous of which is the CATHEDRAL (=large important church) called La Templo Sagrada Familia 高迪〔(1852-1926), 西班牙建筑设计师。他曾在巴塞罗那建造过许多别具一格、装饰繁复的建筑, 其中最著名的是圣家族赎罪教堂〕

gau·dy /ˋgɔdɪ; ˈgɔːdi/ *adj* clothes, colours etc that are gaudy are too bright and look cheap〔衣服、颜色等〕俗丽的: *gaudy jewelry* 俗丽的珠宝 —**gaudily** *adv* —**gaudiness** *n* [U]

gauge¹ also 又作 **gage** *AmE*【美】/gedʒ; geɪdʒ/ *n* [C]

1 ►INSTRUMENT 仪器◄ an instrument for measuring the size or amount of something 测量仪器; 量规: *a rain gauge* 雨量计 | *the fuel gauge in a car* 汽车上的燃料表

2 ►WIDTH 宽度◄ a) the width of thin metal objects such as wire, or screws〔金属线、螺钉等的〕直径; 宽度: *a narrow-gauge screw* 细径螺丝 **b)** the width of thin material such as metal or plastic sheets〔金属片或塑料片等的〕厚度: *heavy gauge black polythene* 很厚的黑色聚乙烯塑料

3 ►RAILWAY 铁道◄ the distance between the lines of a railway or between the wheels of a train〔铁轨的〕轨距; 〔火车轮的〕轮距: **broad/narrow gauge** (=with more/less than the standard distance between the rails) 宽轨距/窄轨距

4 ►GUN 枪炮◄ the width of the BARREL¹ (3) of a gun 枪管口径: *a 12-gauge shotgun* 12口径的猎枪

5 ►MEASURE 量度◄ a standard measure of weight, size etc to which objects can be compared 标准量度, 标准尺寸

gauge² *v* [T] **1** form a correct idea of how people feel about something or what they are likely to do〔对人们的情感和意图〕正确估计: *The city council failed to gauge the strength of local feeling on this issue.* 市政会未能正确估计当地人关注这个问题的热切程度。| **[+what/how etc]** *It is difficult to gauge what the other party's next move will be.* 很难判定对方下一步要做什么。**2** to calculate something by using a particular instrument or method〔用量具或方法〕测量: *The thermostat will gauge the temperature and control the heat.* 恒温器可测量温度, 控制热度。

Gau·guin /goˋgæn; ˈgəʊgæn/**, Paul** (1848-1903) a French painter who went to live in Tahiti, where he painted brightly coloured scenes which showed the life of the people there 高更〔(1848-1903), 法国画家。他曾旅居塔希提岛, 创作了反映当地人生活的色彩明快的风景画〕

Gaul /gɔl; gɔːl/ an area of western Europe in Roman times which included France, Belgium, the southern part of the Netherlands, southwest Germany, and part of North Italy 高卢〔指罗马时期西欧一地区, 包括法国、比利时、荷兰南部、德国西南部和意大利北部的部分地区〕

Gaulloise *trademark* a brand of cigarettes made in France【商标】高卢〔法国一香烟品牌〕

gaunt /gɔnt; gɔːnt/ *adj* **1** very thin and pale, especially because of illness or continued worry〔由于生病或长期烦恼〕瘦削的, 憔悴的: *I looked into her face and it was gaunt with exhaustion.* 我审视她的脸, 发觉她由于疲劳而显得很憔悴。**2** a building, mountain etc that is gaunt looks very plain and unpleasant〔建筑物、山等〕平淡无奇的, 难看的: *a gaunt cathedral* 荒凉的大教堂 —**gauntness** *n* [U]

gaunt·let /ˋgɔntlɪt; ˈgɔːntlɪ̣t/ *n* **1** [C] a long GLOVE (1) that covers someone's wrist and protects their hand, for example in a factory 长手套, 防护手套 **2** [C] a GLOVE (1) covered in metal, used for protection by soldiers in past times〔旧时士兵戴的〕铁护手套 **3 throw down the gauntlet** to invite someone to fight or compete over a disagreement 挑战〔由于争执〕**4 pick up/take up the gauntlet** to accept the invitation to fight or compete over a disagreement 接受挑战 **5 run the gauntlet** to be criticized or attacked by a lot of people 受到众人的批评[攻击]: *Once again Clinton had to run the gauntlet of the press.* 克林顿又一次受到新闻界的广泛攻击。

gauze /gɔz; gɔːz/ *n* [U] **1** very thin transparent material with very small holes in it, often used for curtains〔常用作窗帘的〕薄纱, 纱罗 **2** also 又作 **gauze bandage** *AmE* thin cotton with very small holes in it that is used for tying around a wound【美】〔包扎伤口的〕纱布 —**gauzy** *adj*

gave /gev; geɪv/ the past tense of GIVE¹

gav·el /ˋgævl̩; ˈgævəl/ *n* [C] a small hammer that the person in charge of a meeting, law court, AUCTION¹ etc hits on a table in order to get people's attention〔会议主席、法官、拍卖人等用的〕小木槌

ga·votte /gəˋvɑt; gəˈvɒt/ *n* [C] a fast, cheerful French dance, or the music for this dance 加沃特舞〔一种欢快的法国舞蹈〕; 加沃特舞曲

Gawain and the Green Knight, Sir —see 见 SIR GAWAIN AND THE GREEN KNIGHT

gawd /gɔd; gɔːd/ *interjection* used to represent the word 'god' when it is said in this way as an expression of surprise, fear etc 天哪!〔表示惊讶、恐惧时,用来代替god这个词〕

gawk /gɔk; gɔːk/ *v* [I] to look at something for a long time, in a way that looks stupid 呆呆地看: [+at] *Don't just stand there gawking at those girls!* 别站在那儿盯着那些女孩傻看!

gaw·ky /ˋgɔkɪ; ˈgɔːki/ *adj* moving in a nervous and awkward way, as if you cannot control your arms and legs 行动举止笨拙的: *a gawky, long-legged teenager* 一个举止笨拙的长腿少年 —**gawkiness** *n* [U]

gawp /gɔp; gɔːp/ *v* [I] *BrE* to look at something for a long time, especially with your mouth open because you are surprised【英】〔由于惊讶〕张口凝视: *tourists gawping at Buckingham Palace* 惊异地呆望着白金汉宫的游客

3 **gay¹** /ge; geɪ/ *adj* **1** sexually attracted to people of the same sex as yourself; HOMOSEXUAL 同性恋的: **gay rights/community etc** (=the rights etc of gay people) 同性恋者权利/同性恋者社区等 *a gay rights demonstration* 争取同性恋者权利的示威活动 **2** *old-fashioned* bright or attractive【过时】鲜艳的: *gay colours* 鲜艳的色彩 **3** *old-fashioned* cheerful and excited【过时】快乐的,兴奋的: *She felt excited and quite gay.* 她感到兴奋,非常快乐。**4** **with gay abandon** in a careless and thoughtless way 任意地,纵情地,放纵地 —see also 另见 GAILY, GAIETY—**gayness** *n* [U]

gay² *n* [C] someone who is HOMOSEXUAL, especially a man〔尤指男〕同性恋者

> **CULTURAL NOTE 文化注释**
> The word gay is used far more often than the word HOMOSEXUAL which seems very formal. Gay is the word most gay people use to describe themselves, and it is not offensive. The noun gay is often used only to mean a gay man, and LESBIAN is used to mean a gay woman. gay一词比非常正式的用语homosexual常用得多。同性恋大多自称为gay,该词并无冒犯意味。名词gay通常只指男同性恋,而用lesbian用来指女同性恋。

Gaye /ge; geɪ/, **Marvin** /ˋmɑrvɪn; ˈmɑːvɪn/ (1939-84) a US musician who wrote and performed soul music with the Motown record company. His many popular and successful songs include *I Heard It Through the Grapevine*. 盖伊〔(1939-1984),美国音乐人。他曾为汽车城唱片公司创作和表演灵乐,创作了许多大众喜欢的优秀歌曲,其中包括《我顺着葡萄藤听见的》〕

Gay Pride /ˌ· ˈ·/ a political movement that began in the U.S. and encourages gay people to be open about the fact that they are GAY and to be proud of themselves 同性恋自豪运动〔始于美国的一项政治运动,鼓励同性恋者公开身份,以己为荣〕

Ga·za Strip, the /ˌgɑzə ˋstrɪp; ˌgɑːzə ˈstrɪp/ a coastal area in the Middle East, between Egypt and Israel 加沙地带〔中东一沿海地区,位于埃及和以色列之间〕

gaze¹ /gez; geɪz/ *v* [I always+adv/prep] to look at someone or something for a long time, giving it all your attention often without realizing you are doing so〔尤指无意识地〕凝视,盯着看: [+into/at etc] *Patrick was gazing into the fire.* 帕特里克凝视着炉火。| *We gazed up at the stars.* 我们抬头凝望星空。

> **USAGE NOTE 用法说明: GAZE**
> WORD CHOICE 词语辨析: **look, gaze, stare, gape**
> These words all describe **looking** at someone or something for a long time. 这些词都描写长时间看着(look at)某人或某物。
> You may **gaze** at something interesting or beautiful without realizing you are doing it. 你可能会不知不觉地凝视(gaze at)有趣或美丽的东西: *He stood gazing at Helen/at the breathtaking landscape.* 他站在那里凝视着海伦/凝视着令人惊叹的风景。
> If you **stare** at someone or something, you look directly at them for a long time without moving your eyes, for example because you are angry, very interested, or are thinking hard about something. 如果你瞪着眼睛看(stare at)某人或某物,这表示你由于生气、很感兴趣或者努力思考什么而目不转睛地直视: *She stared at the page for several minutes, uncertain what to write.* 她盯着这一页纸好几分钟,拿不定主意要写什么。| *Why are you staring at me like that?* 你为什么那样盯着我?
> You **gape** at something with your mouth open when you are very surprised or shocked. 当你非常惊奇或震惊时,你张着口呆看(gape at)某物: *He just stood and gaped at the building began to crumble.* 他站在那里,目瞪口呆看着大楼开始倒塌。

gaze² *n* [singular] a long steady look 凝视,注视: *a curious gaze* 好奇的凝视 | **lower your gaze** *Ellen smiled uncomfortably and lowered her gaze.* 埃伦很不自在地笑一笑,低下了头。| **meet sb's gaze** (=look directly at someone who is looking at you) 与某人凝视的目光相遇 *He didn't dare to meet her gaze.* 他不敢与她凝视的目光相遇。

ga·ze·bo /gəˋzibo; gəˈziːbəʊ/ *n* [C] a small building in a garden, where you can sit and look at the view〔花园内的〕凉亭,观景亭

ga·zelle /gəˋzɛl; gəˈzel/ *n* [C] a type of small DEER, which jumps very gracefully and has large beautiful eyes 瞪羚

ga·zette¹ /gəˋzɛt; gəˈzet/ *n* [C] **1** *BrE* an official newspaper, especially one from the government giving important lists of people who have been employed by them etc【英】公报〔尤指政府公报〕**2** *AmE* a newspaper【美】报纸

gazette² *v* [T] *BrE*【英】**1 be gazetted** *formal* to be officially given a specific military job【正式】被正式任命〔某军职〕**2** to give someone an official job, especially in the military forces 正式任命〔某人担任某公职,尤指军职〕

gaz·et·teer /ˌgæzəˋtɪr; ˌgæzʒˈtɪə/ *n* [C] a list of names of places, printed as a dictionary or as a list at the end of a book of maps 地名词典;〔地图册后的〕地名索引

gaz·pa·cho /gəzˋpɑtʃo; gæzˈpætʃəʊ/ *n* [U] a cold Spanish soup made from TOMATO, GREEN PEPPER, CUCUMBER, and onion〔用番茄、青椒、黄瓜和洋葱制作的〕西班牙凉菜汤

ga·zump /gəˋzʌmp; gəˈzʌmp/ *v* [T] *BrE informal* to sell a house to another person who offers you more money than someone that you have already agreed to sell it to【英,非正式】〔房价议定后〕抬价改售他人: *We were gazumped at the last minute.* 原同意卖给我们的房子在最后一刻被以更高的价格卖给了别人。

GB /ˌdʒi ˋbi; ˌdʒiː ˈbiː/ the written abbreviation of 缩写= Great Britain

Gb the written abbreviation of 缩写= GIGABYTE

GBH /ˌdʒi bi ˋetʃ; ˌdʒiː biː ˈeɪtʃ/ *n* [U] *BrE* grievous bodily harm; the serious crime of attacking someone and injuring them【英】严重的人身伤害

GCE /ˌdʒi si ˋi; ˌdʒiː siː ˈiː◂/ *n* [C] General Certificate of Education; a school examination in one of a range of subjects, taken in England and Wales before 1988 by students aged 15 or over〔英格兰和威尔斯〕普通教育证书(考试)

GCHQ /ˌdʒi si eɪʃ ˋkju; ˌdʒiː siː eɪtʃ ˈkjuː/ Government Communication Headquarters; an organization controlled by the British government and based in Cheltenham, whose aim is to collect information about countries which may be enemies. This is done especially by listening to radio broadcasts and telephone calls from all over the world. (英国)政府通讯总部〔英国政府管辖的情报机构,总部设在切尔滕纳姆。其目的是通过监听全世界的广播和世界各地打来的电话以收集疑似敌对国的情报〕

GCSE /ˌdʒi si ɛs ˋi; ˌdʒiː siː es ˈiː/ *n* [C] General Certificate of Secondary Education; a school examination in one of a range of subjects that is taken by students aged 15 or over in Britain〔英国〕普通中等教育证书(考试)

Gdansk /gəˋdænsk; gəˈdænsk/ a city and port in Poland, known for its SHIPYARDS where protests by workers in the 1980s forced the Communist government to make changes. Gdansk was formerly known by its German name, Danzig. 格但斯克〔波兰一城市、港口,拥有众多的造船厂。20世纪80年代,在此举行过造船工人抗议活动,迫使执政的共产党政府实行改革。格但斯克以前有个德语名字,叫Danzig(但泽)〕

g'day /gəˋde; gəˈdeɪ/ *interjection AustrE & NZE* an informal way of saying 'hello'【澳和新西兰】你[你们]好〔说'hello'的一种非正式方式〕

GDP /ˌdʒi di ˋpi; ˌdʒiː diː ˈpiː/ gross domestic product; the total value of all goods and services produced in a country, in one year, except for income received from abroad 国内生产总值 —compare 比较 GNP

gear¹ /gɪr; gɪə/ *n* 3

1 ▸IN CARS ETC 在汽车里等◂ [C,U] the machinery in a vehicle that turns power from the engine into movement 排挡: *The new model has five forward gears.* 这种新型号的汽车有五个前进挡。| *driving cautiously along in third gear* 用第三挡小心驾驶前进 | **bottom gear** *BrE*【英】,**low gear** *AmE*【美】(=the gear used for driving slowly) 最低挡〔即用于慢行的排挡〕| **in gear** (=with a gear connecting the engine to the wheels, and therefore ready to move) 挂着排挡 *Don't turn off the engine while you're still in gear.* 还挂着挡时不要关发动机。

2 ▸MACHINERY 机器◂ a piece of machinery that performs a particular job〔某种用途的〕机器: *the landing gear of a plane* 飞机的起落架 | *heavy lifting gear* 重型起重机

3 ►EQUIPMENT 设备◄ a set of equipment or tools you need for a particular activity〔某种用途的〕一套设备[工具]: *He's crazy about photography – he's got all the gear.* 他对摄影很着迷——所有的器材他都有。| *We'll need camping gear when we go away.* 我们外出时需要带宿营器具。

4 ►CLOTHES 衣服◄ a set of clothes that you wear for a particular occasion or activity〔为某个场合或活动穿的〕成套服装: *Bring your rain gear.* 带上你的雨衣。| *You have to wear protective gear for this.* 为这个你得穿上防护服。

5 **change gear** *BrE*【英】, **shift gear** *AmE*【美】 **a)** to move a vehicle into a different gear 换挡 —see picture on page A3 参见 A3 页图 **b)** to start something in a different way, especially in the amount of energy or effort you use 改变方式〔做某事, 尤指精力或力气的改变〕: *The boss expects us to be able to change gear just like that.* 老板指望我们能够不问来由就忽地为他加一把劲。

6 **in top gear** *BrE*【英】, **in high gear** *AmE*【美】 **a)** the gear used at high speeds 挂最高挡 **b)** doing something with the greatest possible effort and energy 全力以赴: *During this period, Japan's export industries were in top gear.* 在这个时期, 日本的出口工业突飞猛进地发展。| *The Republican's propaganda machine moved into high gear.* 共和党的宣传机器开足了马力。

7 **be thrown out of gear** if a process is thrown out of gear, something prevents it from happening in the way that was planned 乱了套

8 ►DRUGS 毒品◄ [U] *slang* a word meaning illegal drugs, used by people who take drugs【俚】毒品

gear[2] *v* [T] **1** **be geared to** to be organized in a way that is suitable for a particular purpose or situation 适应; 使适合于〔某目的〕: *The typical career pattern was geared to men whose wives didn't work.* 典型的职业模式是为那些妻子不工作的男子设计的。| **be geared to do sth** *The course curriculum is geared to span three years.* 这门课程是按学制三年设计的。**2** **be geared up** to be well prepared for something you have to do 一切准备就绪: [+for] *The party is all geared up for the election.* 该党已为选举作好了准备。| *We need to be geared up to deal with this sort of emergency.* 我们需要为处理这种紧急情况作好准备。

G

gear·box /ˈgɪrˌbɑks; ˈgɪəbɒks/ *n* [C] a metal box containing the gears of a vehicle〔车辆的〕齿轮箱, 变速箱

gear·ing /ˈgɪrɪŋ; ˈgɪərɪŋ/ *n* [U] *technical* the relationship between the amount of money that a company is worth and the amount that it owes in debts【术语】配称, 资本搭配〔即资本和负债的关系〕

gear le·ver /ˈ· ,··/ *n* [C] a metal rod that you move in order to control the gears of a vehicle〔车辆的〕换挡杆, 变速杆 —see picture at 参见 BICYCLE[1] 图

gear shift /ˈ· ·/ *n* [C] *AmE* a gear lever【美】〔车辆的〕换挡杆, 变速杆 —see picture on page A2 参见 A2 页图

gear stick /ˈ· ·/ *n* [C] *BrE* a gear lever【英】〔车辆的〕换挡杆, 变速杆 —see picture on page A2 参见 A2 页图

geck·o /ˈgeko; ˈgekəʊ/ *n* [C] a type of small LIZARD 壁虎

GED /ˌdʒi i ˈdiː; ˌdʒiː iː ˈdiː/ General Equivalency Diploma; in the US, a DIPLOMA with the same value as a high school diploma, which people who left high school without finishing their education can study for at any age〔美国〕中学同等学历文凭〔相当于中学文凭, 中途辍学的中学生可在任何年龄补修获得〕

gee[1] /dʒi; dʒiː/ *interjection especially AmE* used to show that you are surprised or annoyed【尤美】哎呀, 哇〔用来表示惊奇或生气〕: *Aw, gee, Mom, do we have to go?* 哎呀, 妈妈, 我们非走不可吗?

gee[2] *v*

gee up *phr v* **1** [T] *BrE informal* to encourage someone to try harder【英, 非正式】激励: **gee sb ↔ up** *The team needs a captain who can gee them up a bit.* 这个队需要有个能够激励大家的队长。**2** **gee up!** used to tell a horse to go faster 快跑〔用于让马快走〕

gee·gaw /ˈdʒigɔ; ˈdʒiːgɔː/ *n* [C] another spelling of GEWGAW gewgaw 的另一种拼法

gee-gee /ˈ· ·/ *n* [C] *BrE* a word meaning a horse, used by or to children, or when talking about HORSE RACING【英】马〔儿童用语或谈论赛马时的用语〕

geek /gik; giːk/ *n* [C] *slang especially AmE* someone who is boring and wears clothes that are unfashionable【俚, 尤美】讨厌鬼〔指令人生厌、穿着不入时的人〕 —**geeky** *adj*

geese /gis; giːs/ the plural of GOOSE[1] (1)

gee whiz /ˌ· ˈ·/ *interjection AmE old-fashioned* used to show that you are surprised or annoyed【美, 过时】哎呀, 哇〔用来表示惊奇或生气〕

geez /dʒiz; dʒiːz/ *interjection* another spelling of JEEZ jeez 的另一种拼法

gee·zer /ˈgizə; ˈgiːzə/ *n* [C] *informal* a man【非正式】男子: *a funny old geezer* 一个滑稽的老人 | *Some stupid geezer had moved my bags.* 不知哪个愚蠢的家伙动了我的行李。

Geh·rig /ˈgɛrɪg; ˈgerɪg/, **Lou** /lu; luː/ (1903-41) a famous US BASEBALL player, who was called the 'Iron Horse', and who played in more CONSECUTIVE games than any other player before him. He died of a rare muscle disease which is now known as 'Lou Gehrig's disease'. 格里克〔(1903-1941), 美国著名棒球运动员。有"铁马"之称, 连续参赛场数之多是空前的。他死于一种罕见的肌肉疾病, 现称"格里克氏症"〕

Gehry /ˈgɛrɪ; ˈgeəri/, **Frank** (1929-) a US ARCHITECT (=someone who designs buildings), born in Canada, who is known for his unusual buildings with interesting shapes. He designed the Guggenheim Museum in Bilbao, Spain, which opened in 1997. 盖里〔(1929-), 美国建筑设计师, 生于加拿大, 以别具一格的设计闻名。他设计了西班牙毕尔巴鄂的古根海姆博物馆。该馆于 1997 年对外开放〕

Gei·ger count·er /ˈgaɪgə ˌkauntə; ˈgaɪgə ˌkaʊntə/ *n* [C] an instrument for finding and measuring RADIOACTIVITY 盖格计数器〔寻找和测量放射性的仪器〕

gei·sha /ˈgeʃə; ˈgeɪʃə/ also 又作 **geisha girl** /ˈ·· ·/ *n* [C] a Japanese woman who is trained in the art of dancing, singing, and providing entertainment, especially for men〔日本〕艺妓

gel[1] /dʒɛl; dʒel/ *n* [C,U] a thick, wet substance that is used in various bath or beauty products〔用于洗浴或美容产品中的〕凝胶, 冻胶: *hair gel* 发胶

gel[2] *v* **gelled, gelling** [I] **1** if a liquid gels it becomes firmer or thicker; JELL (2) 形成胶体, 胶化 **2** if an idea or plan gels it becomes clearer or more definite〔想法和计划〕变得更清楚[更明确]: *My ideas gelled as I talked the problem over.* 在讨论这个问题时我的想法变得更明确了。**3** if two or more people gel, they start working well together as a group 开始合作

gel[3] /gɛl; gel/ *n* [C] *old-fashioned* used to represent the word 'girl', when it is said in this way【过时】女孩〔用来表示 girl 这个词〕

gel·a·tine /ˈdʒɛlətin; ˈdʒelətiːn/ also 又作 **gel·a·tin** /-tṇ; -tɪn/ *AmE*【美】 *n* **1** [U] a clear substance obtained from boiled animal bones, used for making JELLY 动物胶 **2** [C] a piece of coloured plastic that is put over a light to change its colour〔改变灯光色彩的〕彩色塑料板

ge·lat·i·nous /dʒəˈlætənəs; dʒəˈlætṇəs/ *adj* in a state between solid and liquid, like a JELLY (4) 凝胶的, 凝胶状的

geld /gɛld; geld/ *v* [T] to remove the TESTICLES of a horse 割去〔马的〕睾丸

geld·ing /ˈgɛldɪŋ; ˈgeldɪŋ/ *n* [C] a horse that has been gelded 阉过的雄马, 去势的马

gel·ig·nite /ˈdʒɛlɪgˌnaɪt; ˈdʒelɪgnaɪt/ *n* [U] a very powerful explosive 葛里炸药〔一种烈性炸药〕

gem /dʒɛm; dʒem/ *n* [C] **1** a beautiful stone that has been cut into a special shape; jewel 宝石, 珠宝: *precious gems* 珍贵的宝石 **2** something that is very special or beautiful 精品: *The capital, Tallin, is an architectural gem.* 首都塔林堪称建筑瑰宝。**3** a very helpful or useful person 难能可贵的人, 非常有用的人: *Ben, you're a real gem!* 本, 你实在是个难能可贵的人!

Gem·i·ni /ˈdʒɛməˌnaɪ; ˈdʒemɪnaɪ/ *n* **1** [singular] the third sign of the ZODIAC, represented by TWINS[1] and believed to affect the character and life of people born between May 21 and June 21 双子宫[座]〔黄道第三宫, 据信该宫影响出生于 5 月 21 日至 6 月 21 日之间人们的性格和生活〕 **2** [C] someone who was born between May 21 and June 21 出生于双子宫[座]时段〔即 5 月 21 日至 6 月 21 日〕的人

Gemini Pro·gram, the /ˈ··· ,··/ (1964-66) a US government space programme which prepared for the Apollo Program "双子座"号计划〔(1964-1966), 美国政府为"阿波罗"计划服务的一项航天计划〕

Gen. a written abbreviation of 缩写 = General

gen[1] /dʒɛn; dʒen/ *n* [U] *BrE informal* information【英, 非正式】信息, 情报: [+on] *She has all the gen on cheap flights.* 她对各廉价航班信息十分灵通。

gen[2] *v* **genned, genning**

gen up *phr v* [T] *BrE informal* to learn a lot of information about something for a particular purpose【英, 非正式】了解事实; 知道详情: [+on] *It's a good idea to gen up on the company's product before the interview.* 面试前先了解该公司产品的详细情况是个好主意。

-ge·nar·i·an /dʒəˈnɛrɪən; dʒəˈneəriən/ *suffix* [in nouns and adjectives 构成名词和形容词] someone who is a particular number of DECADES (=periods of 10 years) old …十岁至…十九岁的人: *an octogenarian* (=between 80 and 89 years old) 一位八旬的老人 | *a septuagenarian ex-judge* 一位七十几岁的前任法官

gen·darme /ʒandɑrm; ˈʒɒndɑːm/ *n* [C] a French policeman 法国警察

gen·der /ˈdʒɛndɚ; ˈdʒendə/ *n* **1** [C,U] *formal* the fact of being male or female【正式】性别: *Discrimination on grounds of race or gender is forbidden.* 严禁种族或性别歧视。 **2 a)** [U] the system in some languages of marking words such as nouns, adjectives, and PRONOUNS as being MASCULINE (4), FEMININE (2), or NEUTER[1] (2) 性〔指某些语言中将名词、形容词和代词分为阳性、阴性或中性的一种系统〕 **b)** [C] a group such as FEMININE (2) into which words are divided in this system 性〔词在这种系统中所分成的类, 如阴性〕

gender bend·er /ˈ· ·, ·ˈ/ *n* [C] *informal* someone, often a popular singer or entertainer, who behaves or dresses in a way typical of someone of the opposite sex【非正式】男扮女装或女扮男装者〔尤指举止或服装模仿异性的流行歌手或演员〕

gender-spe·cif·ic /ˈ· · ·ˈ··/ *adj* for males only, or females only 限定性别的: *This law is gender-specific, singling out women.* 这项法律限定性别, 专门适用于妇女。

S2 W2 **gene** /dʒin; dʒiːn/ *n* [C] a small part of the material inside the NUCLEUS of a cell, that controls the development of the qualities that have been passed on to a living thing from its parents 基因

ge·ne·al·o·gy /ˌdʒiniˈælədʒi; ˌdʒiːniˈælədʒi/ *n* **1** [U] the study of the history of families 家谱学, 宗谱学 **2** [C] an account of the history of a family, especially when shown in a drawing that shows how each person is related to the others 家谱, 系谱图 —**genealogist** *n* [C] —**genealogical** /ˌdʒiniəˈlɑdʒɪkḷ; ˌdʒiːniəˈlɒdʒɪkəl◂/ *adj* —**genealogically** /-kḷɪ; -kli/ *adv*

gene pool /ˈ· ·/ *n* [C] all of the genes available to a particular SPECIES〔某物种的〕基因库

gen·e·ra /ˈdʒɛnərə; ˈdʒenərə/ the plural of GENUS

S1 W1 **gen·e·ral[1]** /ˈdʒɛnərəl; ˈdʒenərəl/ *adj*

1 ▶NOT DETAILED 不详细的◀ describing only the main features of something, not the details 大体的, 大致的: *a general introduction to computing* 电脑操作概论 | **general idea** *I've got a general idea of how I want the new room to look.* 新房间如何布置, 我有了一个大致的想法。| **in general terms** (=without considering specific details) 大体上, 总的说来 *The minister talked in general terms about the need for fairer taxation.* 部长笼统地谈了公平税收的必要性。

2 in general a) usually or in most situations 一般说来, 大体说来: *In general, about 10% of the candidates are eventually offered positions.* 一般说来, 大约 10% 的求职者最终得到了职位。 **b)** as a broad subject 总体上: *We're trying to raise awareness about the environment in general and air pollution in particular.* 我们正在努力从总体上增强环境意识, 特别是提高对空气污染的意识。

3 ▶AS A WHOLE 总体上◀ considered in terms of a whole situation, group, etc, not of the specific parts that it consists of; OVERALL[1] 总体的, 普遍的: *There are a few intelligent ones, but the general standard isn't very high.* 有几个很聪明, 但总体水平并不高。| *We were impressed by the quality of their work and the general air of professionalism.* 他们的工作质量和总体的专业精神给我们留下了深刻印象。| **a general anaesthetic** (=for the whole body, not one part of it) 全身麻醉剂

4 ▶ORDINARY/NOT SPECIFIC 普通的/非特定的◀ of an ordinary kind, not one particular kind 普通的: *I spend about 10 hours a week doing general cooking and cleaning.* 我每星期大约花 10 小时来做饭和扫除。| *How widespread is AIDS in the general population?* 艾滋病在普通人群中传播有多广? | *It's a good general fertilizer.* 它是一种很好的普通肥料。

5 ▶MOST PEOPLE 大多数人◀ shared by or affecting most people, or most of the people in a group 普遍的: *Keynes' view of economics gained general acceptance in the 1930's.* 凯恩斯的经济学观点在 20 世纪 30 年代被普遍接受。| *How soon can the drug be made available for general use?* 这种药需要多长时间才能够普遍使用?

6 the general area/neighbourhood/location not the exact place or direction, but somewhere near 整个地区/街区/场所: *Several bombs landed in the same general area.* 好几颗炸弹落在大概同一个地区。

7 ▶JOB 职位◀ used in the name of a job to show that the person who does this job has complete responsibility 全面负责的: *the general manager* 总经理 | *the Attorney General* 首席检察官, 司法部长

8 as a general rule used to say what happens in most cases 在一般情况下, 通常: *He doesn't give interviews as a general rule, but he's prepared to make an exception in this case.* 他通常不接受采访, 但这次他准备破例。

9 the general public ordinary people, who do not have important positions or belong to specific groups 公众: *Health education is aimed at the general public as well as at high-risk groups.* 健康教育是针对普通老百姓和高危人群的。| *The doors opened to the general public last night at the Klondyke Building.* 克朗代克大楼昨晚向公众开放。

10 in the general interest in a way that helps or brings advantage to most people 对大多数人有好处的, 符合大部分人利益的: *It's in the general interest to invest in public transportation.* 投资公共交通可为大多数人带来利益。—see also 另见 GENERALLY

general[2] *n* [C] an officer of very high rank in the army or air force〔陆军和空军的〕上将 —see table on page C6 参见 C6 页附录

General As·sem·bly, the /ˌ··· ˈ···/ **1** the group that represents all of the countries which belong to the United Nations. Its members meet regularly to discuss plans and vote on suggestions, with each country having one vote. 联合国大会〔由联合国全体成员国组成的世界性组织。其成员国定期召开会议, 讨论和表决各种提案。每个成员国有一票〕—compare 比较 the SECURITY COUNCIL **2** a group that meets to make laws in some of the states of the US 州议会〔美国某些州的立法机构〕 **3** the main group that controls some Protestant churches, especially the Church of Scotland, consisting of church leaders who meet to make decisions 总会〔管理某些新教教会, 尤其是苏格兰长老会的组织, 由数名长老组成, 经常举行决策会议〕—compare 比较 the GENERAL SYNOD

general coun·sel /ˌ··· ˈ··/ *n* [C] **1** the chief legal officer of a US company〔美国公司里的〕首席法律顾问 **2** a firm of US lawyers that gives general technical advice〔美国的〕综合性律师事务所

general de·liv·er·y /ˌ··· ·ˈ···/ *n* [U] *AmE* a post office department to which you can send letters for someone who is travelling and which will keep them until they are collected【美】邮件存局候领处; POSTE RESTANTE *BrE*【英】

general e·lec·tion /ˌ··· ·ˈ··/ *n* [C] an election in which all the people voting in a country vote at the same time to choose a government 普选, 大选

general head·quar·ters /ˌ··· ˈ···/ *n* [plural] the place from which the actions of an organization, especially a military one, are controlled 总司令部

gen·e·ral·ise /ˈdʒɛnərəlˌaɪz; ˈdʒenərəlaɪz/ *v* a British spelling of GENERALIZE generalize 的英式拼法

gen·e·ral·i·ty /ˌdʒɛnəˈrælətɪ; ˌdʒenəˈræləti/ *n* **1** [C often plural 常用复数] a very general statement that avoids mentioning details or specific cases 概括, 笼统的话: *Can we stop dealing in generalities and start suggesting practical steps to take?* 我们不要再说空话, 开始建议一下采取的实际步骤, 好吗? **2 the generality of** most of; the MAJORITY (1) of 大多数的: *Temporary workers are considerably younger than the generality of workers.* 临时工比大多数工人年轻多了。 **3** [U] *formal* the quality of being true or useful in most situations【正式】普遍性, 共通性

gen·e·ral·i·za·tion also 又作 **-isation** *BrE*【英】/ˌdʒɛnərələˈzeʃən; ˌdʒenərəlaɪˈzeɪʃən/ *n* **1** [C] a general statement or opinion that is only partly true because it is based on only a few cases or incomplete knowledge〔依据不足的〕概括, 泛论: *You're making too many generalizations about an issue that you don't really understand.* 你对一个你并不真正了解的问题作了太多的推论。| **sweeping generalization** (=saying that something is true in every case or situation) 笼统的概括: *Please! No sweeping generalizations like "all women are bad drivers".* 请不要一概而论, 说什么"所有的女子开车都不行"。 **2** [U] the act of making generalizations 归纳, 概括

gen·e·ral·ize also 又作 **-ise** *BrE*【英】/ˈdʒɛnərəlˌaɪz; ˈdʒenərəlaɪz/ *v* **1** [I] to make a general statement about a number of different things or people without mentioning any details 笼统地表达, 概括地论述: *It's difficult to generalize about the typical Republican voter.* 对共和党选民的典型特征进行概括是很难的。 **2** [I] to form a general principle or opinion after considering only a small number of facts or examples 概括, 归纳: *It's stupid to generalize and say that all young people are rude.* 泛泛而论说所有的年轻人都很粗鲁是愚蠢的。| [**+from**] *We can generalize from the samples and conclude that nitrogen levels have increased.* 我们可以从这些样品得出结论: 氮的含量已经提高了。 **3** [T] *formal* to put a principle, statement, or rule into a more general form so that it covers a larger number of examples【正式】推广, 扩大〔原则、论述或规律的〕应用范围: *I will first illustrate it by a simple example and then generalize it.* 我将先用一个简单的例子说明, 然后再把它普遍化。

G

general know·ledge /ˌ··· ˈ··/ *n* [U] knowledge of facts about many different subjects 常识, 一般知识: *a general knowledge quiz* 常识测验

gen·er·al·ly /ˈdʒɛnərəlɪ; ˈdʒenərəli/ *adv* **1** in a general way, considering without details or specific cases 大体上, 大致: *The system has generally been found very easy to use.* 人们大体上觉得这个系统很好用。| *She's not really ill, just generally rundown.* 她并不是真病了, 只是感到全身疲惫。**2** by or to most people 普遍地, 广泛地: *The plants are generally regarded as weeds.* 这些植物一般都被认为是杂草。| *So, is the plan generally acceptable?* 那么, 这项计划大多数人都可以接受吗? **3** usually or most of the time 通常地: *Jonathan says he generally gets in to work by 8.00.* 乔纳森说他通常不到8点就来工作。**4** **generally speaking** used to introduce a statement that is true in most cases but not always 一般来说: *Generally speaking, the more expensive the stereo, the better it is.* 一般说来, 立体声音响的价格越贵, 质量就越好。

General Med·i·cal Coun·cil, the —see 见 the GMC

General Mo·tors /ˌ··· ˈ··/ *trademark* abbreviation 缩写为 GM one of the world's largest car companies, which is based in the US and has factories in many countries. Its cars and TRUCKS include Chevrolets, Oldsmobiles.【商标】通用汽车公司〔世界最大的汽车制造商之一, 总部设在美国。该公司在许多国家设有制造厂, 生产的小汽车和卡车包括雪佛兰、奥兹莫比尔等〕

general prac·tice /ˌ··· ˈ··/ *n* **1** [U] the work of a doctor or lawyer who deals with all the ordinary types of illness or legal case, rather than one specific type 普通医生[普通律师]的工作 **2** [C] a group of lawyers or doctors who do all kinds of work 普通律师事务所; 普通医生诊所

general prac·ti·tion·er /ˌ··· ·ˈ···/ *n* [C] a doctor who is trained in general medicine and treats people in a particular area or town; GP〔在某一地区或城市行医的〕非专科医生, 全科医生

general-pur·pose /ˌ··· ˈ··◂/ *adj* [only before noun 仅用于名词前] a general-purpose product, vehicle etc is suitable for most situations or jobs that such things are normally used for 多用途的, 多功能的: *general-purpose glue* 多用途胶水

gen·er·al·ship /ˈdʒɛnərəlˌʃɪp; ˈdʒenərəlʃɪp/ *n* [U] the skill of leading an army, developing plans for battle etc〔军事上的〕指挥才能

general staff, the /ˌ··· ˈ·/ *n* the group of military officers who work for a commanding officer 参谋部〔指某指挥官的全体参谋〕

general store /ˈ··· ˌ·/ *n* [C] *AmE* a shop that sells a wide variety of goods, especially one in a small town【美】〔尤指小镇上的〕杂货店

general strike /ˌ··· ˈ·/ *n* [C] a time when most of the workers in a country refuse to work in order to protest about working conditions, wages, etc〔全国性的〕总罢工, 大罢工

> **CULTURAL NOTE 文化注释**
> In Britain the only general strike has been the one in 1926, when many people stopped work in support of the men who worked in the COALMINES. The strike had a great effect but was not successful in its political aims. 在英国, 唯一的一次大罢工是在1926年, 当时很多人罢工支持煤矿工人。这次罢工影响深远, 但并未达到其政治目的。

General Syn·od, the /ˌ··· ˈ··/ the group of people who govern the Church of England. It includes BISHOPS and elected representatives from among the priests and other members of the church. 英国国教总会〔管理英国国教的机构, 由主教、选举产生的牧师代表和教会其他人员组成〕

gen·e·rate /ˈdʒɛnəˌret; ˈdʒenəreɪt/ *v* [T] **1** to produce or create something 产生, 创造: *a useful technique for generating new ideas* 能产生新创意的有用技术 | *The program would generate a lot of new jobs.* 这个项目将带来许多新职位。| **generate sales/profits/income etc** *What sales volume would be required to generate an income of $96,000?* 需要多大的销售额才能产生96,000美元的收入? **2** **generate excitement/interest/ill-feeling** to produce strong feelings among a large number of people〔在一大群人之中〕引起兴奋/兴趣/敌意: *News of the Queen's visit is generating a lot of excitement.* 女王访问的消息使人们兴奋不已。**3** to produce heat, electricity, or another form of energy 产生〔热能、电能或其他能量〕: *The flowing water is used to drive turbines, which generate electricity.* 流水被用来驱动涡轮机, 以产生电力。

gen·e·ra·tion /ˌdʒɛnəˈreʃən; ˌdʒenəˈreɪʃən/ *n* **1** [C] **a)** all people of about the same age 一代(人): *My generation never knew an America before Vietnam.* 我这代人不认识越战之前的美国。| [also+plural verb *BrE* 英] *The younger generation don't know what hard work is.* 年轻一代不知道什么叫艰苦的工作。**b)** all the members of a family of about the same age〔家庭中的〕一代(人): *We're the fourth generation of Carters to live in this house.* 我们是卡特家住在这栋房子的第四代人。| *a second-generation Canadian* (=whose parents are Canadian but whose grandparents were not) 第二代加拿大人〔其父母是加拿大人, 祖父母却不是〕| **the generation gap** (=the lack of understanding between generations caused by their different attitudes and experiences) 代沟 **2** [C] the average period of time between the birth of a person and the birth of that person's children 一代人的时间〔指一个人的出生与此人的孩子出生之间的平均时间〕: *Within a generation Japan regained the status of a great power.* 日本在一代人的时间里重新获得强国的地位。**3** [C] all the members of a group of things which have been developed from a previous group〔某种事物的〕一代: *the latest generation of anti-tank missiles* 最新一代的反坦克导弹 **4** [U] the process of producing something or making something happen 产生, 发生: *the generation of electricity* 发电

Generation X also 又作 **Gen X** young people in the 1990s, seen as not having any strong beliefs, not being involved in their society, and making no plans for the future X一代〔指20世纪90年代的年轻人。他们被认为没有坚定的信仰, 没有融入自己的社会, 对未来也没有计划〕: *Generation X has its own culture, and aims to enjoy itself without making too much of an effort.* X一代人有自己的文化, 凡事不愿努力, 旨在自我享受。

Generation Y *AmE* people born in or after 1980【美】Y一代, 80后一代〔1980年或之后出生的人〕

gen·e·ra·tive /ˈdʒɛnəˌretɪv; ˈdʒenərətɪv/ *adj especially technical* able to produce something【尤术语】有生产力的, 能生成的

generative gram·mar /ˌ···· ˈ··/ *n* [C,U] the description of a language using rules that produce all the sentences of the language that are correct according to the rules of grammar 生成语法

gen·e·ra·tor /ˈdʒɛnəˌretə; ˈdʒenəreɪtə/ *n* [C] a machine that produces electricity 发电机: *a coal-powered generator* 燃煤发电机

ge·ner·ic /dʒəˈnɛrɪk; dʒ̩ˈnerɪk/ *adj* **1** **generic name/term/label etc** a word that describes a whole class of things 属名/通称等〔用来描述一类事物的词〕: *Misogyny is the generic term for all hostile feelings and actions towards women.* misogyny是所有针对妇女的敌对情感和行为的通称。**2** *technical* belonging to or typical of a GENUS【术语】属的, 类的 **3** *especially AmE* a generic product does not have a TRADEMARK【尤美】无商标的, 未注册的 (1) —**generically** /-klɪ; -kli/ *adv*

gen·e·ros·i·ty /ˌdʒɛnəˈrɑsətɪ; ˌdʒenəˈrɒsɪ̩ti/ *n* **1** [U] willingness to give money, time etc in order to help or please someone 慷慨, 大方: *an act of great generosity* 十分慷慨的行为 **2** [C] an act of being generous 慷慨大方的行为

gen·e·rous /ˈdʒɛnərəs; ˈdʒenərəs/ *adj* **1** willing to give money, spend time etc, in order to help people or give them pleasure 慷慨的, 大方的: [+to] *She's always very generous to the kids.* 她对小孩总是很大方。| **it is generous of sb (to do sth)** *What lovely presents – it's very generous of you!* 多么可爱的礼物——你非常大方啊! | **generous with your help/time/money etc** *I'd like to thank Simon, who's been very generous with his time.* 我想感谢西蒙, 他很慷慨地付出了许多时间。**2** larger than the usual or expected amount〔比通常或预想的〕量多的, 丰富的: *a generous glass of port* 一大杯波尔图葡萄酒 | *We offer a generous salary and benefits package.* 我们提供一揽子丰厚的薪水和津贴。| *generous welfare payments* 丰厚的福利津贴 **3** sympathetic in the way you deal with people, and tending not to criticize them, get angry, or treat them unkindly 宽宏大量的: *She was generous enough to overlook my little mistake.* 她非常宽宏大量, 不计较我的小错误。| *not a very generous attitude* 不很宽厚的态度 —**generously** *adv*: *Please give generously to the refugee fund.* 请为难民基金慷慨解囊。

Gen·e·sis /ˈdʒɛnəsɪs; ˈdʒenɪ̩sɪ̩s/ the first book of the Old Testament of the Bible, which describes the history of the Earth and its people. It includes the CREATION of heaven and the Earth, the story of Adam and Eve, and the story of the Flood. Many people know the first words of Genesis: In the beginning God created the heaven and the earth.《创世记》〔《圣经·旧约》的首卷, 描述地球和人类的历史, 其中有上帝创造天地的故事、亚当和夏娃的故事和大洪水的故事。许多人都熟知《创世记》的首句:"太初, 神造天地。"〕

gen·e·sis, the *n formal* the beginning or origin of something〔某事物〕的起源: *a discovery that was to be a genesis of modern physics* 成为现代物理学起源的一项发现

gene ther·a·py /ˈ· ˌ···/ *n* [U] a way of treating certain diseases by adding to the body a GENE that it does not have 基因治疗法

ge·net·ic /dʒəˋnɛtɪk; dʒɪ̀ˈnetɪk/ *adj* connected with GENEs or GENETICS 基因的，遗传学的: *genetic defects* 遗传性缺陷 | *These abnormalities may have a genetic basis.* 这些畸形可能和基因有关。

ge·net·ic·ally /dʒəˋnɛtɪkl̩ɪ; dʒəˈnetɪkli/ *adv* **1** in a way that is connected with GENETICS 遗传学上 **2 genetically engineered** a vegetable, VIRUS etc that is genetically engineered has been produced by a method that involves changing the structure of its GENEs 基因改造的

genetic code /·ˌ·· ˈ·/ *n* [C] the arrangement of GENEs that controls the way a living thing develops 遗传密码，基因密码

genetic en·gin·eer·ing /·ˌ·· ··ˈ··/ *n* [U] the science of changing the GENETIC structure of an animal, plant, or human in order to affect the way it develops 遗传[基因]工程学 —**genetic engineer** *n* [C]

genetic fin·ger·print /·ˌ·· ˈ···/ *n* [C] the pattern of GENETIC information which is different for each person or animal 基因指纹

genetic fin·ger·print·ing /·ˌ·· ˈ····/ *n* [U] the process of examining someone's GENETIC structure, especially in order to find out if they are guilty of a crime 基因指纹分析，基因鉴定〔尤用于司法的犯罪鉴定〕

ge·net·ics /dʒəˋnɛtɪks; dʒɪ̀ˈnetɪks/ *n* [plural] the study of how the nature and development of living things is affected by their GENEs (=the parts of their cells that pass on characteristics from their parents) 遗传学 —see also 另见 GENE, HEREDITY —**geneticist** /-təsɪst; -tɪ̀sɪ̀st/ *n* [C]

Ge·ne·va /dʒəˋnivə; dʒəˈniːvə/ a city in Switzerland which is the main base for the Red Cross, the World Health Organization, and several other important international organizations. It is on the shore of Lake Geneva, one of the largest lakes in Europe. 日内瓦〔瑞士一城市，国际红十字会、世界卫生组织等重要国际机构总部所在地。该市位于欧洲最大的湖泊之一日内瓦湖湖畔〕

Geneva Con·ven·tion, the /·ˌ·· ·ˈ··/ a set of agreements that establish rules for how people should be treated during wars, especially if they are wounded or taken prisoner. The Geneva Convention was first written in Geneva, Switzerland, in the 19th century and was accepted by most countries. It has been changed several times at later international meetings.《日内瓦公约》〔关于应如何对待战时受伤或被俘人员的一系列协定。《日内瓦公约》19世纪起草于瑞士日内瓦，为多数国家所接受。在之后的国际会议上对其进行过几次修订〕

Gen·ghis Khan /ˌdʒɛŋgəs ˋkɑn; ˌdʒeŋgɪ̀s ˈkɑːn/ (?1160-1227) the ruler of the Mongol people in China, who was a successful military and political leader. He took control of northern India and sent his armies as far west as the Black Sea. People think of him as a powerful leader, and people who have very RIGHT-WING political opinions are sometimes humorously described as being 'to the right of Genghis Khan'. 成吉思汗〔(?1160-1227)，中国蒙古族统治者，杰出的军事和政治领袖。他曾占领印度北部，派兵西抵黑海。有人认为他是个强有力的统治者。具有极右政治思想的人有时被幽默地说成是 to the right of Genghis Khan (观点比成吉思汗还要右倾)〕

ge·ni·al /ˋdʒinjəl; ˈdʒiːniəl/ *adj* having a cheerful and friendly character or manner 亲切的，和蔼的，友好的 —**genially** *adv* —**geniality** /ˌdʒinɪˋælətɪ; ˌdʒiːniˈælɪ̀ti/ *n* [U]

ge·nie /ˋdʒinɪ; ˈdʒiːni/ *n* [C] a magical spirit in old Arabian stories〔古代阿拉伯故事中的〕妖怪，神灵

gen·i·tal /ˋdʒɛnətl̩; ˈdʒenɪ̀tl/ *adj* connected with or affecting the outer sex organs 外生殖器的: *genital herpes* 生殖器疱疹 | *genital mutilation* 生殖器毁伤 —**genitally** *adv*

gen·i·tals /ˋdʒɛnətəlz; ˈdʒenɪ̀tlz/ also 又作 **gen·i·ta·li·a** /ˌdʒɛnəˋteljə; ˌdʒenɪ̀ˈteɪliə/ *technical n* [plural] the outer sex organs【术语】外生殖器，外阴部

gen·i·tive /ˋdʒɛnətɪv; ˈdʒenɪ̀tɪv/ *n* [C] *technical* a form of the noun in some languages, which shows a relationship of possession or origin between one thing and another【术语】〔某些语言中名词的〕属格，所有格 —**genitive** *adj*

ge·ni·us /ˋdʒinjəs; ˈdʒiːniəs/ *n* **1** [U] a very high level of intelligence, mental skill, or artistic ability, which only a few people have 天才，天赋: **a writer/work/woman etc of genius** *an imaginative novelist of great genius* 一位想象力丰富的伟大天才小说家 | *The film reveals Fellini's genius.* 这部影片展示了费里尼的天赋。| **a stroke of genius** (=a very clever idea) 天才之举 **2** [C] someone who has an unusually high level of intelligence, mental skill or artistic ability 有天才的人，天才: *a musical genius* 一位音乐天才 | *You can't compare him with a true genius like Einstein.* 你不能拿他与爱因斯坦这样的旷世奇才相比。| **be a genius at sth** *Watch your money – Lou's a genius at cards.* 当心你的钱 —— 卢是个玩牌天才。**3 have a genius for (doing) sth** to be especially good at doing something 有(做)某事的天才: *Bernard had a genius for bringing out the best in his students.* 伯纳德有让学生发挥出最佳才能的本事。| *Warhol's genius for publicity* 沃霍尔的宣传天才 **4** [U] the special quality of a particular group of people, period of time etc〔某一群体的人、某个时期等的〕特征: *the French artistic genius* 法国的艺术特征

genius lo·ci /ˌdʒinjəs ˋlosaɪ; ˌdʒiːniəs ˈləʊsaɪ/ *n* [singular] *Latin* the typical character of a place and the feelings it produces in people【拉丁】地方的风格[特色]

gen·o·cide /ˋdʒɛnəˌsaɪd; ˈdʒenəsaɪd/ *n* [U] the deliberate murder of a whole group or race of people 大屠杀，种族灭绝: *the genocide of the Jews during the Holocaust* 大屠杀时期对犹太人的种族灭绝 —**genocidal** /ˌdʒɛnəˋsaɪdl; ˌdʒenəˈsaɪdl◂/ *adj*

ge·nome /ˋdʒinom; ˈdʒiːnəʊm/ *n* [C] *technical* the total of all the GENEs that are found in one type of living thing【术语】基因组，染色体组: *the human genome* 人类基因组

gen·re /ˋʒɑnrə; ˈʒɒnrə/ *n* [C] *formal* a particular type of art, writing, music etc, which has certain characteristics that all examples of this type share【正式】〔艺术、写作、音乐等的〕类型，体裁: *Science fiction as a genre is relatively new.* 科幻小说作为一种体裁是比较新的。| *Leon's movies are outstanding examples of the genre.* 利昂的影片是这种体裁的杰出榜样。

gent /dʒɛnt; dʒent/ *n* [C] **1** *informal especially BrE* a GENTLEMAN【非正式，尤英】绅士: *Quite the gent, he was in a dress shirt, top hat, and black overcoat.* 他一派绅士风度: 着礼服衬衫，戴高顶大礼帽，穿黑色大衣。**2 the gents** [singular] *BrE* a public toilet for men【英】男厕所; MEN'S ROOM *AmE*【美】

gen·teel /dʒɛnˋtil; dʒenˈtiːl/ *adj* **1** behaving and speaking in an unnatural and very polite way, because you want people to think you belong to a high social class〔言谈举止〕假装上等人的 **2** *old-fashioned* of a high social class【过时】上流社会的: *a genteel neighbourhood* 上流社会街区 —**genteelly** *adv*

gen·tian /ˋdʒɛnʃən; ˈdʒenʃən/ *n* [C] a small plant with blue flowers that grows in mountain areas 龙胆属植物

gentian vi·o·let /ˌ·· ˈ···/ *n* [U] a purple ANTISEPTIC[2] (1) liquid that is used to treat burns or stings 龙胆紫，甲基紫〔一种杀菌剂，用于治疗烧伤、虫螫伤〕

gen·tile /ˋdʒɛntaɪl; ˈdʒentaɪl/ *n* [C] someone who is not Jewish 非犹太人 —**gentile** *adj*

gen·til·i·ty /dʒɛnˋtɪlətɪ; dʒenˈtɪlɪ̀ti/ *n* [U] *formal* the quality of appearing to belong to a high social class【正式】装出来的彬彬有礼，假斯文: *her pretensions to gentility* 她自命属于上流社会的种种装腔作势

gen·tle /ˋdʒɛntl̩; ˈdʒentl/ *adj* **1** kind and careful in your character or behaviour and not at all violent or unpleasant 和蔼友善的，温和的，不粗暴的: *Be gentle when you brush the baby's hair.* 给婴儿梳头发时要轻柔些。| *Lynne was a sweet, gentle girl.* 林恩是个可爱温和的女孩。| *a little gentle mockery* 无伤大雅的小嘲弄 | [+with] *He was incredibly gentle with her during her illness.* 在她生病期间，他对她温柔得难以置信。**2** not strong, loud, forceful, or extreme 轻柔的，轻声的，和缓的: *Take a little gentle exercise.* 做一点轻微的锻炼。| *Mother's gentle laughter* 母亲轻柔的笑声 | *the gentle warmth of the evening sun* 夕阳的和煦 **3** a gentle wind or rain is soft and light〔风、雨等〕轻柔的: *a gentle breeze clearing the mist* 吹散薄雾的微风 **4** a gentle hill or slope is not steep or sharp〔山或坡〕不陡的，平缓的: *the gentle contours of the South Downs* 南部丘陵平缓的轮廓 —see also 另见 GENTLY —**gentleness** *n* [U]

S3 W3

gen·tle·folk /ˋdʒɛntl̩ˌfok; ˈdʒentlfəʊk/ *n* [plural] *old use* people belonging to the higher social classes【旧】上流社会的人

gen·tle·man /ˋdʒɛntl̩mən; ˈdʒentlmən/ *n* [C] **1** a man who always behaves towards other people in a polite and honourable way and who can be trusted to keep his promises 绅士；彬彬有礼、言而有信的男士: *a real gentleman* 正人君子 | *Martin – always the perfect gentleman – got to his feet when my mother walked in.* 马丁始终是十足的绅士，我母亲走进来的时候他便站了起来。**2** a polite word for a man, used especially when talking to or about a man you do not know 先生〔对男士客气的称呼，尤用于你所不认识的人〕: *Could you serve this gentleman please, Ms Bath?* 巴思女士，请为这位先生服务好吗？| **ladies and gentlemen** (=used at the beginning of a speech) 女士们，先生们〔用于讲话的开头〕**3** *old-fashioned* a man from a high social class, especially one whose family owns a lot of property【过时】有身份的人；绅士〔尤指来自富裕家庭的人〕

S3 W2

gentleman farm·er /ˌ··· '··/ *n* [C] *BrE* a man belonging to a high social class who owns and runs a farm for pleasure rather than profit【英】〔经营农场作为消遣的〕乡绅

gen·tle·man·ly /ˋdʒɛntḷmənlɪ; 'dʒentlmənli/ *adj* a man who is gentlemanly is polite, honourable, and always careful to consider other people's feelings 有礼貌的, 宽容周到的, 绅士风度的

gentleman's a·gree·ment /ˌ··· ·ˋ··/ *n* [C] an agreement that is not written down, made between people who trust each other 君子协定

gen·tle·wo·man /ˋdʒɛntḷˌwumən; 'dʒentlˌwumən/ *n* [C] *old use* a woman who belongs to a high social class【旧】女士; 贵妇; 淑女

3 **gent·ly** /ˋdʒɛntlɪ; 'dʒentli/ *adv* **1** in a gentle way 轻柔地, 温柔地: *I patted her gently on the shoulder.* 我轻轻地拍了拍她的肩膀。| *The road curved gently upwards.* 路缓缓向上蜿蜒。**2 gently!** *BrE spoken* used to tell someone to be careful when they are handling something, moving something etc【英口】小心点!〔要某人触碰或移动某物时当心〕: *Gently, Sammy, you don't want to break it.* 小心点, 萨米, 别把它打破了。| **gently does it** *Careful when you lift that desk – gently does it!* 抬起那张桌子时要小心, 轻点儿搬!

gen·tri·fic·ation /ˌdʒɛntrɪfɪˋkeʃən; ˌdʒentrɪ̣fɪ̣ˈkeɪʃən/ *n* [U] the process by which a street that poor people used to live in is changed when people with more money go to live there 地区贵族化〔指较富有的人居住在原来穷人居住的地方的过程〕—**gentrify** /ˋdʒɛntrɪfaɪ; 'dʒentrɪ̣faɪ/ *v* [T usually passive 一般用被动态]

> **CULTURAL NOTE 文化注释**
>
> Gentrification is considered a bad thing by some people because it means that poor people, who may have been born and grown up in the area, can no longer afford to live there. 有人认为地区贵族化不是一件好事, 因为这意味着土生土长的穷人不能负担继续在那里生活的费用。

gen·try /ˋdʒɛntrɪ; 'dʒentri/ *n* [plural] *old-fashioned* people who belong to a high social class【过时】上流社会人士, 绅士阶层: **the landed gentry** (=the gentry who own land) 拥有土地的绅士阶层, 地主阶级

gen·u·fléct /ˋdʒɛnjuˌflɛkt; 'dʒenjʊ̣flekt/ *v* [I] to bend your knee when in church or a holy place as a sign of respect 屈膝; 跪拜〔以示礼拜〕—**genuflection** /ˌdʒɛnjuˋflɛkʃən; ˌdʒenjʊ̣ˈflekʃən/ *n* [C,U]

3 3 **gen·u·ine** /ˋdʒɛnjuɪn; 'dʒenjuɪ̣n/ *adj* **1** a genuine feeling, desire etc is one that you really feel, not one you pretend to feel in order to deceive people; sincere〔感情、欲望等〕真诚的: *The reforms are motivated by a genuine concern for the disabled.* 这些改革是出自于对残疾人的真诚关心。**2** something genuine really is what it seems to be; real〔物品〕真正的: *It's either a genuine diamond or a very good fake.* 它要么是块真钻石, 要么是一件很好的赝品。**3** someone who is genuine is honest and friendly and you feel you can trust them 真心实意的: *Dan's a real genuine guy.* 丹确实是个诚实可靠的人。**4 the genuine article** *informal* a person, or sometimes a thing, that is a true example of their type【非正式】〔某类型的人或物中〕真正的代表: *If you want to meet a real Southerner, Jake is the genuine article.* 如果你想见到一名真正的南方人, 杰克就是个典型。—**genuinely** *adv*: *He genuinely believes in what he sells.* 他真心相信他卖的东西。—**genuineness** *n* [U]

ge·nus /ˋdʒinəs; 'dʒiːnəs/ *n plural* **genera** /ˋdʒɛnərə; 'dʒenərə/ [C] *technical* one of the groups into which scientists divide animals or plants, below a FAMILY (5) and above a SPECIES【术语】〔动植物的〕属 —see also 另见 GENERIC

ge·o- /dʒio; dʒiːəʊ/ *prefix technical* concerning the Earth or its surface【术语】地球的, 地面的: *geophysics* 地球物理学 | *geopolitical* 地缘政治学的

ge·o·cen·tric /ˌdʒioˋsɛntrɪk; ˌdʒiːəʊˈsentrɪk◂/ *adj* having the Earth as the central point, or measured from the centre of the Earth 以地球为中心的, 地心的: *Ptolemy's geocentric model of the universe* 托勒密的地球中心宇宙模型

ge·o·de·sic dome /ˌdʒiodɛsɪk ˋdom; ˌdʒiːəʊdiːsɪk 'dəʊm/ *n* [C] *technical* a large building shaped like a ball, made from small flat pieces that are connected together to form POLYGONS【术语】网格球形大型建筑

ge·og·ra·phy /dʒiˋɑgrəfɪ; dʒi'ɒgrəfi/ *n* [U] **1** the study of the countries, seas, rivers, towns etc of the world 地理学: *a geography lesson* 地理课 —see also 另见 PHYSICAL GEOGRAPHY, POLITICAL GEOGRAPHY **2 the geography of** the way all the parts of a building, city etc are arranged〔建筑物、城市等的〕布局: *The geography of the old section of Boston is really complicated.* 波士顿旧区的布局确实很复杂。—**geographer** *n* [C] —**geographical** /ˌdʒiəˋgræfɪkḷ; ˌdʒiːəˈgræfɪkəl◂/ *adj*: *a geographical area* 地理区域 —**geographically** /-klɪ; -kli/ *adv*

ge·ol·o·gy /dʒiˋɑlədʒɪ; dʒi'ɒlədʒi/ *n* [U] the study of the rocks, soil etc that make up the Earth, and of the way they have changed since the Earth was formed 地质学 —**geologist** *n* [C] —**geological** /ˌdʒiəˋlɑdʒɪkḷ; ˌdʒiːəˈlɒdʒɪkəl◂/ *adj*: *geological periods* 地质时期 —**geologically** /-klɪ; -kli/ *adv*

ge·o·met·ric /ˌdʒiəˋmɛtrɪk; ˌdʒiːəˈmetrɪk◂/ also 又作 **ge·o·met·ri·cal** /-trɪkḷ; -trɪkəl/ *adj* **1** like the shapes and lines in GEOMETRY, especially in having regular patterns 几何图形的: *a geometric design* 几何图形的设计 **2** related to GEOMETRY 几何的, 几何学的 —**geometrically** /-klɪ; -kli/ *adv*

geometric pro·gres·sion /ˌ···· ·ˋ··/ *n* [U] a set of numbers in order, in which each is multiplied by a specific number to produce the next number in the series (as in 1, 2, 4, 8, 16,…) 几何级数, 等比级数〈如 1, 2, 4, 8, 16, …〉—compare 比较 ARITHMETIC PROGRESSION

ge·om·e·try /dʒiˋɑmətrɪ; dʒi'ɒmɪ̣tri/ *n* [U] the study in MATHEMATICS of the angles and shapes formed by the relationships of lines, surfaces, and solid objects in space 几何学

ge·o·phys·ics /ˌdʒioˋfɪzɪks; ˌdʒiːəʊˈfɪzɪks/ *n* [U] the study of the movements of parts of the Earth, and the forces involved with it, including the weather, the sea beds etc 地球物理学 —**geophysical** *adj* —**geophysicist** *n* [C]

ge·o·pol·i·tics /ˌdʒioˋpɑlətɪks; ˌdʒiːəʊˈpɒlɪ̣tɪks/ *n* [U] the study of the effects of a country's position, population etc on its political character and development 地理政治学, 地缘政治学 —**geopolitical** /ˌdʒiopəˋlɪtɪkḷ; ˌdʒiːəʊpəˈlɪtɪkəl◂/ *adj*

Geor·die /ˋdʒɔrdɪ; 'dʒɔːdi/ *n BrE*【英】**1** [C] someone from Tyneside in NE England〔英格兰东北部的〕泰恩赛德人 **2** [U] a way of speaking typical of people from Tyneside 泰恩赛德口音 —**Geordie** *adj*

George /dʒɔrdʒ; dʒɔːdʒ/ *n* **by George!** *old-fashioned spoken* used when you are pleasantly surprised【过时, 口】确实, 的确〔用来表示惊喜〕: *By George, I think you're right!* 可不是吗, 我认为你是对的!

George, Saint (?-303 AD) the PATRON SAINT of England. He was born in eastern Asia Minor, became a soldier in the Roman army, and was officially killed in Palestine because of his Christian beliefs. In many stories and pictures he is shown as saving the life of a woman by killing a DRAGON (=an imaginary large animal that breathes fire). **St George's Day**, 23rd April, is celebrated as the English national day. 圣乔治〔(?-公元303), 英格兰的主保圣人。他出生于小亚细亚东部, 曾在罗马军队中当过兵, 因信仰基督教在巴勒斯坦殉难。据不少故事所述, 他曾杀死一条恶龙救了一个女子的性命, 画上的他通常也是表现这一形象。4月23日的圣乔治节是英格兰的民族节日〕

George Cross, the /ˌ·ˋ·/ an honour given to British people not in the armed forces who do something extremely brave, for example saving someone else's life at great danger to themselves 乔治十字勋章〔颁发给英国平民的一项荣誉, 表彰他们舍身救人等英勇事迹〕

George I /ˌdʒɔrdʒ ðə ˋfɜst; ˌdʒɔːdʒ ðə 'fɜːst/, **King** (1660-1727) the king of Great Britain and Ireland from 1714 until his death. He was born in Germany and spent most of his time there, and he never learned to speak English. His lack of interest in government led to Britain having its first Prime Minister. 乔治一世〔(1660-1727), 大不列颠及爱尔兰国王, 1714年即位直至去世。他出生于德国, 在那里度过一生的大部分时光, 从来不会说英语。他对政府事务漠不关心, 鉴于此, 英国才有了第一位首相〕

geodesic dome 网格球形大型建筑

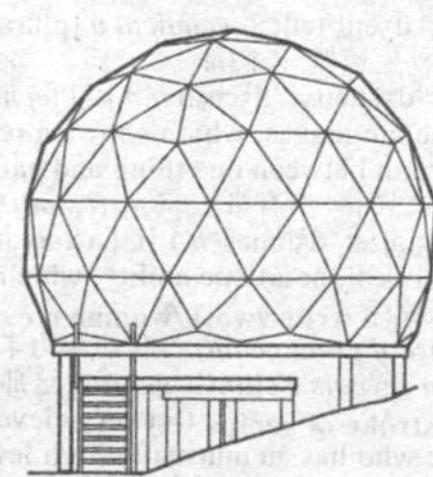

George II /ˌdʒɔrdʒ ðə ˋsɛkənd; ˌdʒɔːdʒ ðə ˈsekənd/, **King** (1683-1760) King of Great Britain and Ireland from 1727 to 1760. He was the last king to lead his men personally in battle. 乔治二世〔(1683-1760), 大不列颠及爱尔兰国王, 1727至1760年在位。他是最后一位亲自率军冲锋陷阵的国王〕

George III /ˌdʒɔrdʒ ðə ˋθɝd; ˌdʒɔːdʒ ðə ˈθɜːd/, **King** (1738-1820) the king of Great Britain and Ireland from 1760 until his death. He was the British king when the US fought to become independent of Britain, and suffered at times from a serious mental illness. 乔治三世〔(1738-1820), 大不列颠及爱尔兰国王, 1760年即位直至去世。他是美国独立战争时期在位的英国国王。他患有严重精神病, 时常遭受疾病之苦〕

George IV /ˌdʒɔrdʒ ðə ˋforθ; ˌdʒɔːdʒ ðə ˈfɔːθ/, **King** (1762-1830) the king of Great Britain and Ireland from 1820 until his death. From 1811 to 1820, he acted as king and had the title 'Prince Regent', because his father, King George III, was mentally ill and unable to rule. This period of British history is called 'the Regency'. 乔治四世〔(1762-1830), 大不列颠及爱尔兰国王, 1820年即位直至去世。1811至1820年间, 其父乔治三世患有精神病无法执政, 他出任"摄政王", 行国王之职。这一段英国历史称"摄政时期"〕

George Med·al, the /ˌ· ˋ··/ an honour in the form of a red RIBBON with five blue STRIPES. It is given for similar acts of bravery as the George Cross but is not such a high honour. 乔治奖章〔一种荣誉奖章, 饰以红绶带, 上有五道蓝色条纹。用于表彰英勇行为, 与乔治十字勋章类似, 但级别较低〕

George·town /ˋdʒɔrdʒtaʊn; ˈdʒɔːdʒtaʊn/ **1** a fashionable area of Washington, D.C., where there are many expensive shops and houses. It is also known for its university. 乔治敦区〔哥伦比亚特区华盛顿一时尚市区。该区有许多高级商店和住宅, 并以乔治敦大学闻名〕 **2** the capital city of Guyana 乔治敦〔圭亚那首都〕 **3** the capital of the Cayman Islands 乔治敦〔开曼群岛首府〕

George V /ˌdʒɔrdʒ ðə ˋfɪfθ; dʒɔːdʒ ðə ˈfɪfθ/, **King** (1865-1936) the British king from 1910 until his death 乔治五世〔(1865-1936), 英国国王, 1910年即位直至去世〕

George VI /ˌdʒɔrdʒ ðə ˋsɪksθ; dʒɔːdʒ ðə ˈsɪksθ/, **King** (1895-1952) the British king from 1936 until his death, and the father of Queen Elizabeth II 乔治六世〔(1895-1952), 英国国王, 1936年即位直至去世, 为女王伊丽莎白二世之父〕

geor·gette /dʒɔrˋdʒɛt; dʒɔːˈdʒet/ *n* [U] a light strong material, used for making clothes 乔其纱〔轻而结实的服装面料〕

Geor·gia /ˋdʒɔrdʒə; ˈdʒɔːdʒə/ abbreviation 缩写为 GA **1** a state in the southeast US, one of the original 13 states established under British rule. Its capital and largest city is Atlanta. 佐治亚州〔美国东南部一州。该州曾是英国殖民统治下最早建立的13个州之一。首府为亚特兰大, 也是该州最大城市〕 **2** a country in western Asia, east of the Black Sea. Georgia was one of the states of the former Soviet Union. Population: 4,989,000 (2001). Capital: Tbilisi 格鲁吉亚〔亚洲西部一国, 位于黑海以东, 为前苏联一加盟共和国。人口: 4,989,000 (2001), 首都: 第比利斯〕 —**Georgian** *n, adj*

Geor·gian /ˋdʒɔrdʒən; ˈdʒɔːdʒən/ *adj* **1** Georgian buildings, furniture etc come from the 18th century, when Britain was ruled by the Kings George the First, Second, and Third〔英国18世纪建筑物、家具等〕乔治一世至三世国王时期风格的: *an elegant Georgian townhouse* 一座典雅的乔治王朝时期风格的城市住宅 **2** connected with the country of Georgia, in the Caucasus 格鲁吉亚的

Geor·gie Por·gie /ˌdʒɔrdʒɪ ˋpɔrdʒɪ; ˌdʒɔːdʒi ˈpɔːdʒi/ a character in a NURSERY RHYME (=an old song or poem for young children) who is a badly-behaved little boy 乔治·波吉〔童谣中一人物。他是个调皮的小男孩〕: The rhyme goes: *Georgie Porgie pudding and pie, / Kissed the girls and made them cry. / When the boys came out to play / Georgie Porgie ran away.* 童谣如下: 乔治·波吉、布丁、派, /亲得女孩哭起来。/男孩出来找他玩, /乔治·波吉就逃开。

ge·o·sta·tion·ar·y /ˌdʒioˋsteʃənɛrɪ; ˌdʒiːəʊˈsteɪʃənəri◂/ also 又作 **geosynchronous** *adj* a geostationary spacecraft or SATELLITE (1) goes around the Earth at the same speed as the Earth moves, so that it is always above the same place on the Earth〔宇宙飞船、卫星〕与地球旋转同步的

ge·ra·ni·um /dʒəˋrenɪəm; dʒəˈreɪniəm/ *n* [C] a plant with red, pink, or white flowers and round leaves 天竺葵

ger·bil /ˋdʒɝbl; ˈdʒɜːbəl/ *n* [C] a small animal with fur, a tail and long back legs that is often kept as a pet 沙鼠

ge·ri·at·ric /ˌdʒɛrɪˋætrɪk; ˌdʒeriˈætrɪk◂/ *adj* **1** [only before noun 仅用于名词前] connected with the medical care and treatment of old people 老年医学的; 老年病学的: *The geriatric ward at the hospital is under threat of closure.* 这家医院的老年病病房濒临关闭。**2** *informal* too old to work properly or effectively【非正式】老朽的: *geriatric judges* 老朽的法官 | *another of those geriatric 1960s rock bands* 另一支老朽的20世纪60年代的摇滚乐队

ge·ri·at·rics /ˌdʒɛrɪˋætrɪks; ˌdʒeriˈætrɪks/ *n* [U] the medical treatment and care of old people 老年医学; 老年病学 —compare 比较 GERONTOLOGY —**geriatrician** /ˌdʒɛrɪəˋtrɪʃən; ˌdʒeriəˈtrɪʃən/ *n* [C]

Ger·i·tol /ˋdʒɛrɪtɑl; ˈdʒerɪtɒl/ *trademark* a type of medicine sold over-the-counter in the US which contains a lot of iron. It is usually taken by older people.【商标】"吉利妥"〔美国出售的一种非处方药, 含有大量铁元素, 一般为老年人服用〕

germ /dʒɝm; dʒɜːm/ *n* [C] **1** *not technical* a bacterium (BACTERIA) that can make you ill【非术语】病菌: *This disinfectant kills all known germs.* 这种消毒剂能杀死所有已知的病菌。**2 the germ of an idea/theory/feeling etc** the early stage of an idea, feeling etc that may develop into something bigger and more important 思想/理论/感情等的萌芽: *This doctrine contains the germ of Hegel's later philosophy.* 这一学说包含着黑格尔后期哲学的萌芽。—see also 另见 WHEATGERM, GERM WARFARE

Ger·man /ˋdʒɝmən; ˈdʒɜːmən/ *n* **1** [C] someone who comes from Germany 德国人 **2** [U] the language of Germany, Austria, and parts of Switzerland 德语〔德国、奥地利和瑞士部分地区的语言〕 —**German** *adj*

German Democratic Republic, the the official name of the former East Germany 德意志民主共和国〔前东德的正式名称〕

ger·mane /dʒɝˋmen; dʒɜːˈmeɪn/ *adj formal* an idea, remark etc that is germane to something is connected with it in an important and suitable way; RELEVANT【正式】关系密切而恰当的: [+to] *It's an interesting idea, but not really germane to the main argument.* 这是一种有趣的想法, 但跟主要论点没有多大关系。| *economic solutions germane to the present-day environment* 与当今环境息息相关的经济解决办法

Ger·man·ic /dʒɝˋmænɪk; dʒɜːˈmænɪk/ *adj* **1** connected with the language family that includes German, Dutch, Swedish and English 日耳曼语系的〔包括德、荷、瑞典、英语诸语种〕 **2** typical of Germany or the Germans 德国的, 德国人的

German mea·sles /ˌ·· ˋ··/ *n* [U] an infectious disease that causes red spots on your body, and can damage an unborn child; RUBELLA 风疹, 德国麻疹

German shep·herd /ˌ·· ˋ··/ *n* [C] a large dog rather like a WOLF that is often used by the police, for guarding property etc 德国牧羊犬, 阿尔萨斯狼狗; ALSATIAN *BrE*【英】—see picture at 参见 DOG[1] 图

German U·ni·fi·ca·tion /ˌdʒɝmən junəfəˋkeʃən; ˌdʒɜːmən juːnɪfɪˈkeɪʃən/ the uniting of East and West Germany in 1990 after they had been separated since 1945. This followed the opening of the Berlin Wall in 1989 and then the COLLAPSE of the East German government. 德国统一〔1945年二战之后德国被分割成东德和西德两个国家。随着1989年柏林墙的拆除和东德政府的垮台, 1990年实现了统一〕

Ger·man·y /ˋdʒɝmənɪ; ˈdʒɜːməni/ a country in central Europe, which was divided from 1945 until 1990 into West Germany and East Germany. Population: 83,030,000 (2001). Capital: Berlin. It is a member of the EU. 德国〔中欧一国, 1945年被分割成西德和东德, 1990年实现统一。人口: 83,030,000 (2001), 首都: 柏林。该国为欧盟成员国〕

ger·mi·cide /ˋdʒɝməˌsaɪd; ˈdʒɜːmɪsaɪd/ *n* [C,U] a substance that kills BACTERIA 杀菌剂

germinate 发芽

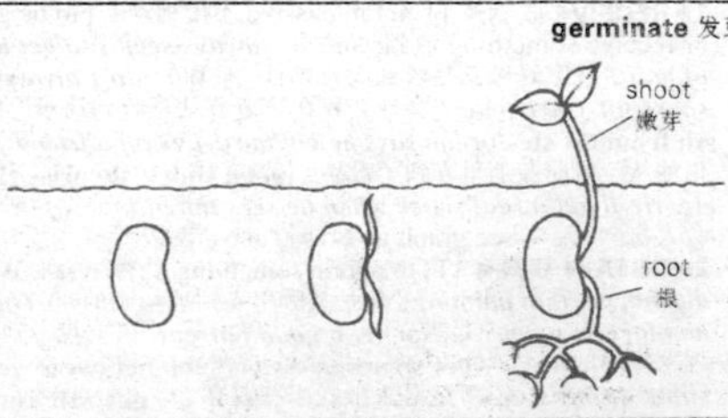

ger·mi·nate /ˋdʒɝməˌnet; ˈdʒɜːmɪneɪt/ *v* **1** [I,T] if a seed germinates or if it is germinated, it begins to grow 发芽: *Carnation seeds will germinate at a low temperature.* 康乃馨的种子在低温下会发芽。**2** [I] if an idea, feeling etc germinates, it begins to develop〔想法、感觉等〕开始形成, 萌芽: *The idea of forming a*

business partnership began to germinate in his mind. 建立一种商业伙伴关系的想法开始在他的头脑中形成。—**germination** /ˌdʒɝməˈneʃən; ˌdʒɜːmɪ̩ˈneɪʃən/ *n* [U]

germ war·fare /ˌ· ˈ· ·/ *n* [U] the use of harmful BACTERIA in war to cause illness and death among the enemy 细菌战

Ge·ro·ni·mo /dʒɪˈranɪmo; dʒɪ̩ˈrɒnɪ̩məʊ/ (1829-1909) an Apache chief who fought white settlers so that his people could continue living on their own land in New Mexico and Arizona. In 1886 the US army caught him and forced his people to move to Oklahoma. He spoke the story of his life so that it could be written down, and it became the book *Geronimo, His Own Story*. 杰罗尼莫〔(1829-1909),阿帕切族酋长。他曾与白人殖民者作斗争,以便他的族人能继续在新墨西哥州和亚利桑那州的家园居住。1886年,美国军队将他俘获,迫使其族人迁往俄克拉何马州。他口述了自己一生的经历,让人写成《杰罗尼莫自传》〕

geronimo *interjection* a word that US PARATROOPERS are known for shouting when they jump out of planes, and which children shout when they jump from a high place 杰罗尼莫!〔美国伞兵跳伞或小孩从高处跳下时发出的叫喊声〕

ger·on·toc·ra·cy /ˌdʒɛrənˈtɑkrəsɪ; ˌdʒerɒnˈtɒkrəsi/ *n* [C,U] government by old people, or a government that consists of old people 老人统治, 老人政府

ger·on·tol·o·gy /ˌdʒɛrənˈtɑlədʒɪ; ˌdʒerɒnˈtɒlədʒi/ *n* [U] the scientific study of old age and the changes it causes in the body 老年学 —compare 比较 GERIATRICS—**gerontologist** *n* [C]—**gerontological** /dʒəˌrɑntəˈlɑdʒɪk]; dʒəˌrɒntəˈlɒdʒɪkəl◂/ *adj*

ger·ry·man·der·ing /ˈdʒɛrɪˌmændərɪŋ; ˈdʒerimændərɪŋ/ *n* [U] the practice of changing the size and borders of an area for election purposes, to deliberately give one group or party an unfair advantage over the others 不公正地划分选区〔以使某团体或政党在选举中不公正地获得有利地位〕

Ger·shwin /ˈgɝʃwɪn; ˈgɜːʃwɪ̩n/, **George** (1898-1937) a US COMPOSER who wrote both CLASSICAL music and popular songs and tunes. He is famous especially for his OPERA *Porgy and Bess* and for *Rhapsody in Blue*. His brother **Ira Gershwin** (1896-1983) wrote the words for many of his popular songs. 格什温〔(1898-1937),美国作曲家。他创作有古典音乐、流行歌曲和曲调,尤以歌剧《波吉与贝丝》和《蓝色狂想曲》著称。其兄艾拉·格什温(1896-1983)为他的许多流行歌曲填词〕

ger·und /ˈdʒɛrənd; ˈdʒerənd/ *n* [C] *technical* a noun in the form of a PRESENT PARTICIPLE, that describes an action or experience, such as 'shopping', in the sentence 'I like shopping'; VERBAL NOUN【术语】动名词

ge·stalt /gəˈʃtalt; gəˈʃtɑːlt/ *n* [C] *technical* a whole thing that is different from all its parts put together and has qualities that are not present in any of its parts【术语】格式塔, 完形〔整体, 非其各个组成部分的相加, 具有后者所没有的特性〕: *gestalt psychology* 格式塔心理学

ge·sta·po /gəˈstɑpo; geˈstɑːpəʊ/ *n* [C] the secret police force used by the state in Germany during the NAZI period 盖世太保〔纳粹时期德国的秘密警察〕

ges·ta·tion /dʒɛsˈteʃən; dʒeˈsteɪʃən/ *n* **1** [U] *technical* the process by which a child or young animal develops inside its mother's body before birth【术语】怀孕, 妊娠 **2** also 又作 **gestation period** [singular] **a)** *technical* the time during which a child or young animal develops inside its mother's body【术语】怀孕期, 妊娠期 **b)** the time it takes to develop an idea, plan etc before it is made known〔想法、计划等的〕酝酿期

ges·tic·u·late /dʒɛsˈtɪkjəˌlet; dʒeˈstɪkjʊ̩leɪt/ *v* [I] to make movements with your arms and hands, usually while speaking, because you are excited, angry, or cannot think of the right words to use〔讲话时〕做手势: *Jane gesticulated wildly and shouted "Stop! Stop!"* 简发狂似地做手势, 喊着"停下!停下!"—**gesticulation** /ˌdʒɛstɪkjəˈleʃən; dʒeˌstɪkjʊ̩ˈleɪʃən/ *n* [C,U]: *Wild gesticulations of the hands accompanied his speech.* 他讲话时手发狂似地比画着。

ges·ture[1] /ˈdʒɛstʃɚ; ˈdʒestʃə/ *n* **1** [C,U] a movement of part of your body, especially your hands or head, to show what you mean or how you feel 手势, 姿势: *Jim raised his hands in a despairing gesture.* 吉姆举起双手, 做出绝望的手势。| *This form of sign language is rich in gesture.* 这种形式的手语手势很丰富。**2** [C] something that you say or do, often something small, to show your feelings or intentions 表示, 姿态: *It was a kind gesture to offer to drive me home.* 提出要开车送我回家是一种善意的表示。| **a gesture of friendship/goodwill/support etc** *The miners went on strike too, as a gesture of solidarity with the railway workers.* 矿工们也举行罢工, 作为与铁路工人团结的表示。—**gestural** *adj* 3

gesture[2] *v* [I always+adv/prep] to use a movement of your hand to tell someone something, or show them what you mean 用手势示意: [**+to/towards etc**] *"It's somewhere over there." He gestured vaguely at a group of buildings.* "在那边某个地方。"他含含糊糊地指着一群楼房。| **gesture for sb to do sth** *The lieutenant gestured for Cook to enter his office.* 中尉用手势示意库克到他的办公室去。

ge·sund·heit /gəˈzʊndhaɪt; gəˈzʊndhaɪt/ *interjection AmE* used to wish someone good health when they have just sneezed (SNEEZE[1] (1))【美】祝你健康〔对打喷嚏者的祝愿〕

G

1 1

get /gɛt; get/ *v past tense* got /gɑt; gɒt/ *past participle* got *especially BrE*【尤英】gotten /ˈgɑtn̩; ˈgɒtn/ *especially AmE*【尤美】, *present participle* getting

① RECEIVE/OBTAIN 收到/得到
② MOVE/GO/TRAVEL 移动/去/旅行
③ HAVE/OWN 有/拥有
④ BECOME/MAKE STH BECOME 成为/使某物成为
⑤ UNDERSTAND 理解
⑥ OTHER MEANINGS 其他意思

① RECEIVE/OBTAIN 收到/得到

1▶RECEIVE 收到◀ [T not in passive 不用被动态] to be given or receive something 收到: *Sharon always seems to get loads of mail.* 莎伦好像总是收到大量邮件。| *Why do I always get socks for Christmas?* 为什么我在圣诞节总是收到袜子? | **get sth from/off sb** *Jordan says he got the drugs off a friend.* 乔丹说他从一个朋友那里弄到了毒品。| **get a shock/surprise/thrill etc** *He'll get a real shock when he sees the bill.* 他见到账单时会大吃一惊。—see graph at 参见 RECEIVE 图表

2▶OBTAIN 获得◀ [T] to obtain something 获得, 得到: *Where did you get that painting?* 你是从哪里弄到那幅画的? | *There's no place in town you can get a good haircut.* 镇上找不到一个理发像样的地方。| **get sb sth** *He's just popped out to get me some stamps.* 他刚跑出去帮我买些邮票。| **get sth for sb** *Gerrard was sent to get help for his sister.* 杰勒德被派去找人帮助他姐姐。—see 见 OBTAIN (USAGE)

3▶GET BY BUYING 买到◀ [T] to buy something 买到: *That cat-basket? I got it on Harlow Market.* 那个猫篮? 我在哈洛市场买到的。| **get sth for $20/£100/50p etc** *You can't get a decent CD player for under $500.* 不花500美元无法买到一台不错的CD播放机。| **get sth free/cheap etc** *Dee gets all her clothes cheap from charity shops.* 迪伊所有的衣服都是从慈善商店廉价购买的。| **get sb sth** *While you're out, could you get me a newspaper?* 你出去的时候能帮我买份报纸吗? | **get sth for sb** *She got a ticket for Bobby as well.* 她还为博比买了一张票。—see graph at 参见 BUY 图表

4▶GET MONEY BY SELLING 售得◀ [T] to receive a particular amount of money for something when you sell it〔售卖某物〕得到…钱: *How much are you expecting to get for your house?* 你这幢房子打算卖多少钱? | **get £10/50p/$100 etc for** *Ian got $500 for that old car of his.* 伊恩的那辆旧车卖了500美元。

5▶GET AN ILLNESS 患病◀ [T not in passive 不用被动态] to catch an illness, especially one that is not very serious 得〔病, 尤指不严重的疾病〕: *It's fairly unusual for adults to get measles.* 成年人得麻疹是相当少见的。| **get sth off/from** *He seems to have got a cold off one of the kids at playgroup.* 他似乎是从幼儿游戏组的孩子那里染上感冒的。

6▶JOB 工作◀ [T] to be given or offered a new job or position, especially because of your own efforts 得到, 找到〔一份新的工

作或职位，尤指通过自己的努力）: *Why don't you get yourself a job instead of lazing around all day?* 你为什么不为自己找份工作，以免整天无所事事呢？ | **get promotion** (=be offered a more important, better paid job than the one you are already doing) 得到提升，得到晋升 *Some people have been here for years and have never got promotion.* 有些人已经在这里好几年了，但从来没晋升过。

7►EARN MONEY 挣钱◄ [T not in passive 不用被动态] to be earning a particular amount of money 挣得: *How much do you think Stewart gets?* 你认为斯图尔特挣多少钱？ | **get £3,000 / £5 $100,000 etc a day/hour/year etc** *Tracey gets five dollars an hour canning fruit.* 特雷西装水果罐头每小时挣五美元。

② MOVE/GO/TRAVEL 移动/去/旅行

8►ARRIVE 到达◄ [I always+adv/prep] to arrive somewhere 到达: *What time will we get there?* 我们什么时候到那里？ | **get to/as far as/up to etc** *Next day they got to the camp, tired and hungry.* 他们第二天到达营地，又累又饿。

9get the train/bus/ferry etc to travel somewhere on a train, bus etc 搭乘火车/公共汽车/渡船等: *I'm getting the train home tonight.* 我今天晚上乘火车回家。

10►MOVE 移动◄ [I always+adv/prep] to move to or go somewhere 移动，去: [+out of/over/into etc] *Get out of my house!* 从我家滚出去！ | *Somehow, water had gotten in through the lining.* 不知怎地，水从内衬渗了进来。

11►MAKE STH MOVE 使某物移动◄ [T] to make something move to a different place or position, especially with some difficulty〔尤指费力地〕移动: **get sth out/through/off etc** *How on earth are they going to get that piano down the stairs?* 他们究竟打算怎样把那台钢琴从楼梯搬下去？

③ HAVE/OWN 有/拥有

12have got *especially BrE* [T] to possess or own something【尤英】拥有: *What kind of car has she got?* 她有什么样的车？ | *Darren's got a Master's Degree in Linguistics.* 达伦拥有语言学硕士学位。

13 [T] to have particular features or characteristics 具有〔某种特征〕: *She's got an awful temper.* 她的脾气很坏。 | *Mr Williams is about 80, and he's got a shiny bald head.* 威廉斯先生大约80岁，他的头秃得油光闪亮。

④ BECOME/MAKE STH BECOME 成为/使某物成为

14 [linking verb 连系动词] to change from one state, feeling etc to another; become〔状态、感情等〕变成，变得: **get angry/cold/upset etc** *When I tried to talk to him about it, he just got really angry.* 我想跟他谈这件事时，他便暴跳如雷。 | *This is getting silly.* 这变得越来越荒谬了。 | **get lost/trapped/ caught etc** (=to become lost, trapped etc) 迷路/被困/被捉等 *Just think of all those people getting killed out there.* 想想在那里被屠杀的那些人们吧。 | *Nick's getting married in September.* 尼克打算9月份结婚。 | **get hot/cold/warm etc** *It's getting quite chilly out there.* 外边已经很冷了。 | *Eat your dinner before it gets cold.* 吃饭吧，免得凉了。—see 见 BECOME (USAGE)

15 [T not in passive 不用被动态] to make someone or something do something 促使[某人或某物]做某事: **get sb/sth to do sth** *Get Chris to wash his jeans occasionally.* 让克里斯偶尔洗洗牛仔裤。 | **get sth doing sth** *I wonder if Frankie could get this video working.* 我不知道弗朗姬能否把这台录像机修好。

16get going/moving/cracking etc to make yourself do something or move somewhere more quickly 赶快开始；赶快去: *What are we all waiting for? Let's get moving!* 我们还在等什么？赶快走吧！

17get to see/know/understand etc to gradually begin to see, know, understand etc 逐渐明白/知道/理解等: *I'm sure the kids will soon get to like each other.* 我相信这些孩子很快就会互相喜欢的。

18get to do sth to be able to do something, especially when this is difficult or unusual 能做某事〔尤指困难或不寻常的事〕: *Since the divorce, he hardly ever gets to see Jenny.* 自从离婚之后，他就几乎见不到珍妮了。

⑤ UNDERSTAND 理解

19 [T not in passive or progressive 不用被动态或进行时] *informal* to understand something【非正式】理解: **get the message/hint** (=to finally understand what someone has been trying to tell you, in an indirect way) 终于理解了某信息/某暗示 *I get the message – you just don't want me to come with you.* 我懂你的意思——你不想让我和你一起去。 | **get what/how/who etc** *She still doesn't get what the movie's about.* 她仍然不懂这部影片到底是想说些什么。

20get it *spoken* to understand something, especially after it has been explained to you several times【口】懂得，明白，理解〔尤用于多次解释之后〕: *Oh, the paper's supposed to go in this way up. I get it.* 啊，纸得这面朝上放进去，我明白了。

21not get it *spoken* to not understand something, especially a joke【口】不懂，不明白〔尤指笑话〕: *He just didn't get it.* 他就是不明白。

⑥ OTHER MEANINGS 其他意思

22►BRING 带来◄ [T] to bring someone or something back from somewhere; FETCH (1) 带来: *Run upstairs and get a pillow.* 跑上楼去拿个枕头来。 | **get sb/sth from** *She's just gone to get the kids from Mary-Ann's house.* 她刚去玛丽安家把孩子们带回来。 | **go and get (sb) sb/sth** *Go and get me a cloth, would you?* 去帮我拿块布来，行吗？

23►REACH A POINT 达到某一点◄ [I always+adv/prep] to reach a particular point or stage of something 到达: **get to/as far as/up to etc** *He's already got up to page 200.* 他已经读到第200页了。 | *When you get to the end of the test paper, read it through.* 试卷做完后，再通读一遍。

24►CLOTHES 衣服◄ **get sth on/off etc** to put a piece of clothing on or take it off 穿上衣服/脱去衣服等: *You'd better get those wet things off.* 你最好把那些湿衣服脱掉。

25►COOK 烹调◄ [T not in passive 不用被动态] to prepare a meal 做饭: *Who's going to get the dinner tonight?* 今天晚上谁做饭？ | **get sb dinner/lunch etc** *He expects her to get him his dinner every night.* 他指望她每天晚上给他做饭。

26you get *spoken* used to say that something happens or exists【口】〔用来表示某事确实发生、某物确实存在〕: *I didn't know you got tigers in Europe.* 我不知道欧洲有老虎。

27get the door/phone etc *spoken* to answer the door, a telephone etc【口】开门/接电话等: *Can you get the door for me? I'm in the bath!* 请你帮我去开门，好吗？我在洗澡！

28you've got me there *spoken* used to say you do not know the answer to something【口】你把我难倒了: *"So how do you spell 'rhythm' then?" "You've got me there."* "那rhythm是怎么拼的？""你把我难倒了。"

29►RADIO/TELEVISION 广播/电视◄ [T not in passive or progressive 不用被动态或进行时] to be able to receive a particular radio signal, television station etc 收听到；收看到: *Can you get satellite TV here?* 你这里可以收看卫星电视吗？

30►PUNISH 惩罚◄ [T not in passive or progressive 不用被动态或进行时] *spoken* to do something to harm or hurt someone who has harmed or hurt you【口】报复: **get sb for sth** *I'm going to get you for that!* 我要为那事报复你！

31►ATTACK 攻击◄ [T not in passive or progressive 不用被动态或进行时] to attack or harm someone 攻击，伤害: *Good luck with the diving – and mind the sharks don't get you!* 祝你潜水好运——注意别让鲨鱼袭击你！

32get sth fixed/done/mended etc to spend time and effort fixing something, finishing a job etc 把某物修理好/把某事做完/把某物补好等: *It's about time we got the kitchen repainted.* 是重新油漆一遍厨房的时候了。

33it (really) gets me *spoken* used to say that something really annoys you【口】这事(确实)使我气恼: *It really gets me the way he leaves wet towels on the bathroom floor.* 他老是把湿毛巾扔在浴室的地板上，这确实令我生气。

34get you/him/her *spoken humorous* used to say that someone is trying to seem more important, clever etc than they really are【口，幽默】瞧瞧你/他/她〔用来表示某人好像有些自以为了不起〕: *Get you, talking about going on a luxury cruise!* 你别吹牛了，说什么乘豪华游船出游呢！

get about *BrE*【英】*phr v* [I] **1** to be able to go or travel to different places 四处走动，旅行: *She's eighty now, and doesn't get about much any more.* 她现在80岁了，不再经常出门走动了。**2** if news or information gets about, it is told to a lot of people〔新闻或消息〕传开: *I don't mind you knowing, but I don't really want it to get about.* 我不介意你知道，但我确实不想让它传开。**3** *informal* if someone gets about, they have sexual relationships with a lot of different people【非正式】与许多人发生性关系

get sth ↔ **across** *phr v* [T not in passive 不用被动态] to succeed in communicating ideas, information etc to someone else 将〔想法、信息〕传达给某人: **get sth across to sb** *How can I get it across to you people how important this is?* 我怎么做才能让你们这些人理解这件事的重要性？

get along *phr v* [I] **1** if two or more people get along, they have a friendly relationship 相处融洽: *If you two are going to share a room, you'd better learn how to get along.* 如果你们两个人要同住一间房，你们最好要学会如何融洽相处。| [**+with**] *I've always found him a bit difficult to get along with.* 我总是觉得他有点难于相处。**2** to progress in something you are doing 进展: *How's your granddaughter getting along at university?* 你的孙女在大学过得怎么样？**3** *spoken* to continue with something that you were doing before【口】继续干〔以前做的事〕: *I'd like to stay and chat, but I really must be getting along.* 我想留下来聊天，但我确实必须继续干活了。

get around *phr v* **1** [I] to be able to go or travel to different places 可以四处走动[旅行] **2** [I] if news or information gets around or gets round, a lot of people come to hear about it〔新闻或消息〕传开: *It quickly got around that Joshua was back in town.* 乔舒亚已经回城的消息很快就传开了。**3** [T **get around** sb] to gently persuade someone to do what you want by being nice to them 哄: *Freddie knows exactly how to get around his mother.* 弗雷迪很善于哄他的母亲。**4** [T **get around** sth] to find a way of dealing with a problem, especially by trying to avoid it 应付[回避]某问题: *Bill's rather stupidly promised her a week in Paris – I don't know how he's going to get around that one.* 比尔很不明智地答应她在巴黎待一周，我不知道他打算如何处理这个问题。

get around to *phr v* [T not in passive 不用被动态] to finally do something that you have been intending to do for some time 终于去做〔一直打算做的事〕: *I don't know when we'll get around to doing any more decorating.* 我不知道我们什么时候会进行更多的装饰。

get at sb/sth *phr v* [T] **1** *informal* to criticize someone repeatedly in an annoying way【非正式】不断地挖苦，一再批评: *She can't think why Moira's always getting at her.* 她不知道莫伊拉为什么老是挖苦她。**2** [not in passive 不用被动态] to seem to be saying something that other people do not completely understand 暗指，暗示: *What exactly are you getting at, Helen?* 你到底想说什么，海伦？**3** to be able to reach something 能得到，能够着: *You have to use a ladder to get at the jars on the top shelves.* 你得用梯子才能够着架子最高那几格上的罐子。**4** to use threats to influence the decision of people who are involved in a court case 用恐吓来影响审判的结果: *At least eight members of the jury had been got at.* 陪审团至少有八个成员受到恐吓。**5** to find something out, especially the truth about a situation 查明真相: **get at the truth/facts/information etc** *They're prepared to use any means possible to get at the truth.* 他们准备运用各种可能的手段来查明真相。

get away *phr v* [I] **1** to succeed in leaving a place, especially when this is not easy〔尤指费力地〕走开，离开，脱身: *There's a meeting after work, but I should be able to get away by seven.* 下班后要开会，但我在7点前应该可以离开。**2** to escape from someone who is chasing you or trying to catch you 逃离，逃避: *The three men got away in a stolen car.* 那三个人乘坐一辆偷来的车逃掉了。| [**+from**] *Gillie managed to get away from the man and call the police.* 吉利设法摆脱了那个人并且报了警。**3** *informal* to take a holiday away from the place you normally live【非正式】外出度假: *Will you manage to get away this summer?* 今年夏天你能够外出度假吗？**4** **get away!** *BrE spoken* used to say you are very surprised by something or do not believe it【英口】〔用来表示你对某事十分惊讶或不相信某事〕: *"He's been invited to a garden party at Buckingham Palace." "Get away!"* "他被邀请参加白金汉宫的花园招待会。" "我才不信哩！" **5** **the one that got away** something good that you nearly had or that nearly happened, but did not 几乎到手的好东西；几乎发生的好事

get away from *phr v* [T not in passive 不用被动态] **1** to begin to talk about other things rather than the subject you are supposed to be discussing 离题: *I think we're getting away from the main issue.* 我想我们偏离了主题。**2** **there's no getting away from** *spoken* used to say that a fact must be dealt with or considered【口】不得不面对[考虑]: *There's no getting away from it – we just can't afford to move house at the moment.* 我们眼下没有钱搬家，这个问题无法回避。**3** **get away from it all** an expression used especially in advertisements meaning to have a relaxing holiday 过个轻松的假期〔尤用于广告中〕: *Get away from it all in sunny Barbados.* 在阳光灿烂的巴巴多斯过个轻松的假期。

get away with *phr v* [T not in passive 不用被动态] **a)** to not be caught or punished for something you have done wrong〔做错事而〕不被发觉[不受惩罚]: *I don't know how they manage to get away with paying such low wages.* 我不知道为什么他们支付这么低的工资仍然逍遥法外。| **get away with murder** *informal* (=repeatedly do something wrong, and not get caught or punished)【非正式】不断做坏事而不被发觉[受惩罚] *Just because he's been working here a long time, he thinks he can get away with murder.* 就因为他已在这里工作很久，他认为自己可以做错事而不受处罚。**b)** *spoken* to be able to do something, even though it is not the best thing to do【口】能做某事〔尽管这样做并不恰当〕: *I think you could just about get away with wearing navy shoes with that dress.* 我觉得你可以穿那件连衣裙，再配一双深蓝色鞋子，尽管不相配，但问题不大。

get back *phr v* **1** [I] to return to a place 回到某地: *We'll probably get back at about nine.* 我们可能在9点左右回来。**2** [I **+to**] to start doing something again or talking about something again 继续做某事[谈某事]: *Let's get back to the main point of the discussion.* 我们还是回到讨论的主要问题吧。**3** [T **get** sth ↔ **back**] to have something returned to you 取回，拿回: *Did you get your books back?* 你把你的书拿回来了吗？**4** [T **get** sb **back**] *informal* to do something to hurt or harm someone who has hurt or harmed you【非正式】报复: *Don't worry. I'll get her back for this!* 别担心，我会就这件事向她报复的！

get back at sb *phr v* [T not in passive 不用被动态] to do something to hurt or harm someone who has hurt or harmed you 报复: *He only asked Jean for a date to get back at his ex-girlfriend.* 他跟琼约会，只是为了报复以前的女朋友。

get back to sb *phr v* [T] *especially spoken* used to say that you will try to talk to someone again later, especially on the telephone【尤口】过一会儿再与某人说话〔尤用于打电话〕: *I'm a bit busy at the moment – can I get back to you?* 我现在有点忙，能过一会儿再给你打回去吗？

get behind *phr v* [I **+with**] if you get behind with a job, payments, rent etc, you have not done or paid as much of it as you should have done by now〔工作、付款、房租等〕落后；拖欠，脱期: *Try not to get too far behind with your work.* 尽量使你的工作不要落在后面太远。

get by *phr v* [I] to have enough money to buy the things you need, but no more〔钱〕勉强够花: *Her old age pension gives her barely enough to get by.* 她的养老金仅仅能供她勉强过活。| **get by on £5/$20/$100 etc** *With four kids to feed, Josie gets by on just $75 a week.* 乔西得供养四个孩子，仅靠每星期75美元生活。

get down *phr v* **1** [T not in passive 不用被动态 **get** sb **down**] to gradually make someone feel unhappy and tired 渐渐使〔某人〕不高兴[疲倦]: *All this waiting and delay is really getting her down.* 这样的等待和耽搁实在让她受不了。**2** [T **get** sth ↔ **down**] to write something, especially something that someone is saying 笔录，记下〔尤指某人说的话〕: *a group of reporters trying to get down every word he said* 想记下他的一言一语的一群记者 **3** [T] to succeed in swallowing something 吞下某物 **4** [I] *BrE* an expression used especially by children meaning to leave the table after a meal【英】餐后离开餐桌〔尤为儿童所用〕

get down to sth *phr v* [T] to finally start doing something that needs a lot of time or energy 终于开始做〔需要花费许多时间或精力的事〕: *After Christmas I'm going to get down to some serious job-hunting.* 圣诞节后我打算开始认真找工作了。| **get down to doing sth** *Isn't it time you got down to marking those papers?* 难道不是你应该评卷的时候了？

get in *phr v* **1** [I] to succeed in entering a place 进入某地: *They arrived at the stadium in good time, but they still couldn't get in.* 他们老早就到了体育场，但是仍然进不去。**2** [I] if a train, plane etc gets in at a particular time, that is the time it arrives〔火车、飞机等〕到达: *What time does the bus get in?* 公共汽车什么时候到？**3** [I] to be elected to a position of political power 当选〔政治性职务〕: *It's unlikely the Liberal Democrats will get in again.* 自由民主党再次当选是不太可能的。**4** [I] to arrive home 到家: *I'll phone her as soon as I get in.* 我一到家就会给她打电话。**5** [T **get** sth ↔ **in**] to gather together something such as crops and bring them to a sheltered place 收割: *The whole village was involved with getting the harvest in.* 整个村庄都在收割庄稼。**6** [T **get** sb ↔ **in**] to ask someone to come to your home or workplace to do a job, especially to repair something 请…来帮忙[修理]: *We'll have to get the engineer in.* 我们得把工程师请来帮忙。**7** [T **get** sth **in**] to send something to a particular place or give it to a particular person 递送，送交: *Please can you get your assignments in by Thursday.* 请你们在星期四以前把作业交上来。| *We have to get an insurance claim in as quickly as possible.* 我们得尽快把保险索赔交上去。**8** [I] to succeed in getting a place at a university, college etc 被录取: *How many of your students got in this year?* 你们今年有多少学生考上大学？

get in on *phr v* [T not in passive 不用被动态] *informal* to become involved in something that other people are doing or planning【非正式】参与〔活动〕: **get in on the act** (=get involved in something exciting, interesting, important etc) 参加: *Now the Republicans are hoping to get in on the act.* 现在共和党希望能参与进来。

get in with sb *phr v* [T] *informal* to become friendly with someone, especially someone who could be helpful to you in some way【非正式】与…拉上关系〔尤指对自己有用的人〕: *He spends all his time trying to get in with the boss.* 他把所有的时间都用来巴结老板。

get into *phr v* **1 what's got into sb** *spoken* used to express surprise that someone is behaving very differently from the way they usually behave【口】(某人)中了什么邪〔用来对某人行为异常表示惊讶〕: *I don't know what's got into Danny – he's suddenly started doing all the cooking and cleaning.* 我不知道丹尼怎么回事——他突然开始一手包办做饭和打扫卫生的活儿。**2 get (sb) into a temper/state etc** to become angry or make someone angry, become upset or make someone upset etc (使)发脾气/紧张不安等: *Don't get into a mood about it.* 别为这发脾气。**3 get (sb) into trouble/difficulties etc** to do something that causes trouble for yourself or for someone else (使某人)陷入麻烦/(使某人)遇到困难等: *That's another fine mess you've got me into.* 你让我又一次陷入难以摆脱的困境。**4** [T not in passive 不用被动态] to start doing something habitually 染上〔习惯〕, 习惯于: **get into the habit/way/routine etc of** *He had gotten into the habit of walking home through the park.* 他养成了步行穿过公园走回家的习惯。**5** [T not in passive 不用被动态] *informal* to begin to be interested in an activity or subject【非正式】开始对〔某种活动或某个话题〕感兴趣: *Lots of my friends are getting into Green politics.* 我的许多朋友开始对绿色政治感兴趣。**6 cannot get into** *informal* if you cannot get into clothes, they are too small for you【非正式】〔衣服太小〕穿不进去

get off *phr v* **1** [I] to start a journey 开始旅行, 出发: *They're planning to get off by midday.* 他们正打算中午前出发。**2** [T **get** sth **off**] to send a letter, parcel etc by mail 邮寄, 寄出: *I'll have to get this letter off by tonight.* 我得在今晚前把这封信寄出去。**3** [I] if a criminal gets off, they get little or no official punishment for their crime〔罪犯〕逃脱(应得的)惩罚: *Financial fraudsters often get off because the details of the case are too complex to be understood by juries.* 金融诈骗者经常能逃脱惩罚, 因为陪审团无法弄懂异常复杂的案情。**4** [T **get** sb **off** sth] to help someone avoid being punished for a crime or something they have done wrong 帮助〔某人〕逃避惩罚: *I'll pay anything you ask if you manage to get her off.* 要是你能让她免受惩罚, 你要什么我都答应。**5** [I **get** sb **off**] to succeed in making someone, especially a baby, go to sleep 使入睡〔尤指婴儿〕: *Guy's upstairs trying to get the baby off.* 盖伊在楼上哄孩子睡觉。| **get sb off to sleep** *Has she got the baby off to sleep yet?* 她把孩子哄睡着了吗? **6** [I] *AmE informal* to have an ORGASM【美, 非正式】达到性高潮 **7** [I,T] to finish work and leave your workplace at the end of the day 下班: *What time do you get off work?* 你什么时候下班? | [**+at**] *Shelley gets off at five-thirty.* 谢利5点半下班。**8 Get off!** *spoken* used to tell someone to stop touching you or to keep away from something【口】滚开!〔用来叫某人不要碰你或不要动某物〕**9 tell sb where to get off** *spoken* to tell someone that they are asking you for too much or are behaving in a way you will not accept【口】叫某人规矩些, 教训某人: *"She expects me to look after her kids all the time." "If I were you I'd tell her where to get off."* "她指望我随时照看她的孩子。""要是我, 我就要她别太过分了。"

get off on sth *phr v* [T not in passive 不用被动态] *informal* to become excited by something, especially sexually excited【非正式】因…感到兴奋〔尤指性兴奋〕

get off to *phr v* [T not in passive 不用被动态] to start to do something in a particular way〔以某种方式〕开始〔做某事〕: **get off to a good/bad start** *As far as school goes, Johnnie has got off to an extremely good start.* 就学业来说, 约翰尼已经有了一个非常好的开端。

get off with *phr v* [T not in passive 不用被动态] *informal* to start a sexual relationship with someone【非正式】与〔某人〕发生性关系: *She spent the whole evening trying to get off with Phil.* 她一晚上都在设法与菲尔上床。

get on *phr v*

1 [I] *especially BrE* if two or more people get on, they have a friendly relationship with each other【尤英】友好相处: [**+with**] *How does Gina get on with her colleagues?* 吉娜与她的同事相处得怎么样?

2 ▶PROGRESS 进展◀ [I] to make progress in something you are doing; GET ALONG (2) 取得进展, 进步: *He's new here, but he seems to be getting on fine.* 他是新来的, 但他好像挺适应的。

3 be getting on a) if time is getting on, it is getting late〔时间〕晚了: *Tell Rea to hurry – it's getting on.* 告诉雷快点——时候不早了。**b)** *informal* if someone is getting on, they are getting old【非正式】〔人〕变老: *We're both getting on now.* 我们俩现在都老了。

4 ▶CONTINUE DOING STH 继续做某事◀ [I] to continue with something you were doing before 继续做: [**+with**] *Get on with your work!* 继续干你的工作吧!

5 ▶ABLE TO DO STH 能做某事◀ [I] to be able to do something, in spite of problems or difficulties〔尽管有问题、有困难〕能对付下去: *I don't know how we'll manage to get on without you.* 没有你我不知道我们怎么能维持下去。

6 get it on *AmE* to have sex【美】发生性关系, 性交: *Do you think those two have got it on yet?* 你认为那两个人发生了性关系吗?

7 Get on with it! *spoken* used to tell someone to hurry【口】快一点!: *Will you lot stop messing around and get on with it!* 你们可否停止瞎胡闹, 快一点干呢?

8 let sb get on with it a) *spoken* used to say that you do not care what someone does, even though it might have bad results【口】任凭某人做他的事: *Well, if she wants to go ahead and ruin her career, let her get on with it.* 好吧, 如果她执意这样干下去, 把自己的事业毁掉, 那就随她吧。**b)** to let someone do something without your help or advice 让某人自己去做某事: *Why can't my parents ever just let me get on with it?* 为什么父母就不能让我自己去做呢?

9 Get on/along with you! *old-fashioned spoken* used to say you do not believe what someone has said【过时, 口】别胡扯!

be getting on for *phr v* [T not in passive 不用被动态] **be getting on for 90/10 o'clock/2,000 etc** to be almost that age, time, number etc 接近90岁/10点钟/2000等: *Mrs McIntyre must be getting on for 90 by now.* 麦金太尔女士现在恐怕快90岁了。| *They paid getting on for $100,000 for it.* 他们为此付了近10万美元。

get onto *phr v* [T not in passive 不用被动态] **1** to speak or write to someone, especially someone you want to help you 对…讲; 写信给; 与…接触: *I'm afraid I can't help you – you'd better get onto the Foreign Office.* 恐怕我无法帮助你, 你最好同外交和联邦事务部联系。**2** to find out about someone who has been doing something wrong 发觉, 识破〔某人进行不良勾当〕: *Why did the police fail to get onto this gang earlier?* 警方为什么没有早些发觉这伙罪犯呢? **3** to be elected as a member of a committee, a political organization etc 当选〔委员会、政治组织等的〕成员: *Very few women ever get onto industry's controlling bodies.* 很少有妇女能被选为工业管理机构的成员。**4** to begin to talk about a subject after you have been discussing something else〔讨论其他事情后〕开始谈论〔某新话题〕: *After a few minutes they got onto the subject of the election.* 几分钟后他们开始谈论选举的话题。

get out *phr v* **1** [I] to escape from somewhere 逃离, 逃走: *How on earth did the dog manage to get out?* 那条狗究竟是怎么逃走的? | [**+of**] *No-one's ever gotten out of this jail.* 从来没有人从这所监狱里逃走过。**2** [T **get** sb **out**] to help someone escape from or leave somewhere 帮〔某人〕逃跑[离开某地]: *Asylum seekers have appealed to the President to help get them out.* 寻求避难的人呼吁总统帮助他们离开。**3** [I] if information gets out, a lot of people know about it though it is meant to be secret〔本应保密的消息〕泄露: *We have to make absolutely certain that none of this gets out.* 我们得绝对保证消息一点也不会泄露出去。| **get out that** *It's bound to get out that he's retiring soon.* 他很快将退休的消息肯定会泄露出去。**4** [T **get** sth ↔ **out**] to succeed in producing or publishing something 生产, 公布, 出版, 发表: *They said they'd try and get the catalog out by the end of the month.* 他们说会尽量在月底前把目录印好。**5** [T **get** sth ↔ **out**] to succeed in saying something, especially when this is very difficult 说出〔尤指难以启齿之事〕: *I wanted to tell him I loved him, but couldn't get the words out.* 我想告诉他我爱他, 但难以说出口。

get out of *phr v* [T not in passive 不用被动态] **1** to avoid doing something you have promised to do or are supposed to do 逃避, 摆脱〔承诺或应该做的事〕: *See if you can get out of that meeting tomorrow.* 看看你明天是否能不去开那个会。| **get out of doing sth** *Danny's always trying to get out of taking the kids to school.* 丹尼总是想逃避送小孩上学的责任。**2** [**get** sb **out of**] to help someone to avoid doing something they are sup-

posed to do 帮〔某人〕逃避[摆脱]〔本应做的事情〕: *Wendy wants you to try and get her out of classes tomorrow.* 温迪要你想办法帮她不上明天的课。| **get sb out of doing sth** *OK, I'll see if I can get you out of having to testify.* 好吧，我来看看是否能帮你免于作证。**3** [**get** sth **out of** sb] to force or persuade someone to tell you something or give you something 迫使[劝说]〔某人〕说出[拿出] **4** [**get** sth **out of** sth] to gain pleasure or enjoyment from something 从…中得到快乐[享受]: *I don't know what people get out of listening to deafeningly loud music.* 我不知道人们从震耳欲聋的音乐中得到些什么乐趣。

get over *phr v* **1 a)** [T not in passive 不用被动态] to get well again after an illness 从〔疾病中〕康复过来: *She's still trying to get over that bout of flu she had.* 她还在努力从那场流感中复元过来。**b)** to begin to feel better after an upsetting emotional experience 〔从令人心烦意乱的感情经历之后〕恢复: *Some people never really get over the early death of a parent.* 有些人永远无法彻底克服父亲或母亲早逝所带来的伤痛。**2** [T **get** sth ↔ **over**] to succeed in communicating ideas, information etc to other people 把…说清楚，使理解: *There's no point in having brilliant ideas unless you can get them over.* 有了好的想法如果不说出来也就没有意义。**3** [T **get** sth **over**] to do and finish something difficult that you have to do 完成〔必须做的某困难事情〕: *Angela says she'll be in touch when she gets her exams over.* 安杰拉说她考完试就和你联系。| **get sth over with** *I'll speak first if you like – I'd rather get it over with quickly.* 如果你愿意，我想先说——我倒希望能快点结束。**4** [**get over** sth] to successfully deal with problems, difficulties etc 成功地处理问题、困难等: *Once we've got over the first few months, we should be making a reasonable profit.* 我们只要把头几个月对付过去，就会获取相当不错的利润。**5 can't/couldn't get over** *spoken* used to say that you are very surprised, shocked, or amused by something【口】对…十分惊讶；对…感到十分好笑: *Carrie couldn't get over how thin and pale he looked.* 他看上去又瘦又苍白，卡丽感到十分惊讶。| **I just can't/couldn't get over it** *They suddenly fired all the company directors. I just can't get over it.* 他们突然开除了公司所有的经理，我感到十分惊讶。

get round *phr v BrE*【英】**1** [I] if news or information gets round, it is told to a lot of people 〔新闻或消息〕传开: **get round that** *It wasn't long before it got round that Tracey was going out with James.* 不久消息就传开了，说是特蕾西已经开始和詹姆斯交往。**2** [T **get round** sth] to find a way of dealing with a problem, especially by trying to avoid it 解决；避免；回避: *There's no way your mother can stay here – we'll just have to get round it somehow.* 你的母亲绝对不能待在这里——我们要想办法解决这个问题。**3** [T **get round** sb] to gently persuade someone to do what you want by being nice to them 〔用友善的态度〕说服〔某人〕: *He's determined he won't give in – see if you can get round him.* 他决定不妥协，看看你是否能说服他。

get round to *phr v* [T not in passive 不用被动态] *BrE* to finally do something that you have been intending to do for some time, but have not because you were too busy, too lazy etc【英】终于去做〔久想做的事〕: *I haven't even got around to unpacking from my holiday yet!* 我度假回来后连行李都还没有打开！

get through *phr v* **1** [T not in passive 不用被动态] to come to the end of a difficult or unpleasant experience or period of time 消磨，度过〔艰难或不愉快的〕一段时间: *It's going to be hard to get through the next couple of days.* 度过未来这几天时间是很难的。**2** [I,T] to pass a test, examination etc 通过〔考试〕: *I'm afraid your daughter failed to get through her mid-term exams.* 很遗憾你的女儿没有通过期中考试。**3** [T **get** sb/sth **through** sth] to make sure someone or something passes an examination, test etc 保证〔某人或某事〕通过审查[考试]: *You'll never get that old car through its smog test.* 你永远也无法使那辆旧车通过烟雾测验。**4** [T **get** ↔ sth **through**] to succeed in having a plan, new law etc approved by an official group 使〔计划、新法律等〕获得批准[通过]: *Once again we failed to get the Bill through Parliament.* 我们又一次未能使该法案在议会通过。**5** [I] to succeed in reaching someone by telephone 〔电话〕与某人联系上: [**+to**] *At last I managed to get through to one of the managers.* 我终于用电话与一名经理联系上。**6** [T **get through** sth] to use a lot of something or spend a lot of money 花费，耗费: *He gets through at least $500 every weekend.* 他每个周末至少花 500 美元。

get through to *phr v* [I,T **get** sth **through to** sb] to succeed in making someone understand something, especially when this is difficult 〔尤指困难地〕使〔某人〕明白: **get it through to sb (that)** *You must try and get it through to them that this is no joke.* 你必须设法使他们明白这不是开玩笑。

get to sb *phr v* [T] *informal* to make you feel very annoyed or upset【非正式】使…生气[烦恼]: *I know they're being unfair, but don't let them get to you.* 我知道他们很不公平，但你不必为他们生气。—see 见 REACH[1] (USAGE)

get together *phr v* **1** [I] if two or more people get together, they meet each other 聚集，相聚: *We must get together some time for a drink.* 我们什么时候必须聚一聚喝一杯。| [**+with**] *It's ages since I got together with the gang from school.* 我已经很久没有跟学校那帮人相聚了。**2** [I] if two people get together, they start a romantic or sexual relationship 开始谈情说爱，开始有性关系: *Those two should get together – they have a lot in common.* 那两个人应该开始谈情说爱了——他们多投契。**3 get yourself together** to begin to be in control of your life, your emotions etc 自制；振作；集中心思: *She needs a bit of time to get herself together.* 她需要一点时间才能使自己振作起来。**4 get it together** *spoken*【口】**a)** [I] to begin to be in control of your life, your emotions etc 自制；振作；集中心思: *If this team doesn't get it together by next month, we'll all be fired.* 如果这个队到下个月还不振作起来，我们都将被开除。**b)** if two people get it together, they begin to develop a romantic or sexual relationship with each other 开始谈情说爱；开始有性关系

get up *phr v* **1** [I] to wake up and get out of your bed after sleeping, especially in the morning 〔尤指早晨〕起床: *What time did you get up this morning?* 你今天早晨什么时候起床的？**2** [T **get** sb **up**] to make someone wake up and get out of their bed, especially in the morning 叫…起床: *Get me up at seven, would you?* 7 点叫我起床，好吗？**3** [T] to stand up 起立，站起来: *No, please don't get up.* 不，请不要站起来。**4** [I] if a wind or storm gets up, it starts and gets stronger 〔风、暴风雨〕开始并增强 **5** [T **get** sth **up**] to organize something 组织: *She's getting a collection up for Sue's birthday.* 她在为休的生日组织募捐。**6 get sb up as** *BrE* to dress someone as someone or something else【英】把〔某人〕打扮[装扮]成: *He arrived at the party got up as Count Dracula.* 他装扮成吸血鬼来参加聚会。**7 get it up** *informal* to get an ERECTION (1)【非正式】勃起 **8 get up speed/steam** to begin to move or travel faster 加速前进

get up to *phr v* [T] to do something, especially something slightly bad 干〔尤指轻微的坏事〕: *Go upstairs and see what the kids are getting up to.* 上楼看看孩子们在捣什么乱。

get·a·way /ˈgɛtə,we; ˈgetəweɪ/ *n* [C] **make a getaway** to escape from somewhere after doing something criminal, or to get away from an unpleasant situation 逃跑: *The thieves made a getaway through a downstairs window.* 盗贼从楼下的一扇窗子逃走了。| **getaway car** (=a car used by criminals to escape after a crime) 罪犯做案后逃逸用的汽车

get-go /ˈ· ·/ *n* **from the get-go** *AmE informal* from the beginning【美，非正式】从一开始: *From the get-go, I knew these tapes were special.* 一开始我就知道这些磁带不一般。

Geth·sem·a·ne /gɛθˈsɛmənɪ; geθˈsemənɪ/ a garden where Jesus went with his followers, and where he was BETRAYed by one of them, Judas, and taken prisoner by the Romans 客西马尼园〔耶稣及其门徒一起去过的一个花园。耶稣在此被犹大出卖，遭罗马人拘捕〕

get-to·geth·er /ˈ· ·,·/ *n* [C] a friendly informal meeting or party 聚会；联欢会: *a family get-together* 家庭聚会

Get·ty /ˈgɛtɪ; ˈgetɪ/, **J. Paul** (1892-1976) a US businessman who owned an oil company and became one of the richest men in the world. He built the Getty Museum in Malibu, California, which has a large collection of valuable paintings and other types of art, and a second **Getty Museum** has also been built in Los Angeles. 格蒂〔(1892-1976)，美国实业家。他拥有一家石油公司，是全球巨富之一。他在加利福尼亚州马里布建起了格蒂博物馆，馆藏大量珍贵油画和其他艺术品。他还在洛杉矶兴建了另一座格蒂博物馆〕

Get·tys·burg /ˈgɛtɪz,bɝg; ˈgetɪzbɜ:g/ also 又作 **Battle of Gettysburg** a place in Pennsylvania where a very important battle in the American Civil War took place in July, 1863. Many men were killed on both sides, but the battle led the way to the Union winning the war. 葛底斯堡〔宾夕法尼亚州一地名。美国内战的一场重要战役，即葛底斯堡战役于 1863 年 7 月在此展开。南北两军伤亡惨重，但此役使联邦军乘胜追击，最终赢得内战的胜利〕

Gettysburg Ad·dress, the /,··· ˈ·/ a famous speech made by Abraham Lincoln in 1863 in the town of Gettysburg, Pennsylvania. He expressed his GRIEF for the soldiers killed in

the American Civil War, and talked about the principles that they died for, in words that are often remembered by Americans: *Four score and seven years ago, our fathers brought forth on this continent a new nation, conceived in liberty and dedicated to the proposition that all men are created equal ... We here highly resolve that these dead shall not have died in vain; that this nation, under God, shall have a new birth of freedom; and that government of the people, by the people, and for the people shall not perish from the earth.* 葛底斯堡演说〔亚伯拉罕·林肯1863年在宾夕法尼亚州葛底斯堡发表的著名演说。他对美国内战中阵亡的战士表示哀悼，并提及他们为之牺牲的信念。他的演说常为美国人民所铭记：87年前，我们的先辈在这块大陆上建立了一个新的国家，孕育在自由之中，致力于人人生来平等这一信念…。此时此地，我们坚信先烈的鲜血不会白流，我们这个国家将在神佑下获得自由的新生，我们这个民有、民治、民享的政府将永世长存〕

get·up /ˋgɛt,ʌp; ˈgetʌp/ *n* [C] *informal* a set of clothes, especially strange or unusual clothes【非正式】〔尤指奇特或不寻常的〕服装：*I hardly recognized him in that getup!* 他穿上奇装异服，我几乎认不出来了！

get-up-and-go /,· · · ˈ·/ *n* [U] *informal* energy, and determination to do things【非正式】干劲，雄心：*He was the only candidate who had some get-up-and-go.* 他是唯一一个有干劲的候选人。

gew·gaw /ˋgjugɔ; ˈgjuːgɔː/ *n* [C] a cheap brightly coloured piece of jewellery or decoration〔便宜花哨的〕珠宝，装饰品

gey·ser /ˋgaɪzɚ; ˈgiːzə/ *n* [C] **1** a natural spring of hot water that sometimes rises suddenly into the air 间歇喷泉 **2** a machine fixed to a wall over a bath or SINK and used for heating water in some British houses〔一些英国家庭里的〕热水器

Gha·na /ˋgɑnə; ˈgɑːnə/ a country in West Africa between Côte d'Ivoire and Togo. Population: 19,894,000 (2001). Capital: Accra. In 1957, Ghana, which was then called the **Gold Coast**, was the first African state to become independent from British rule. 加纳〔西非一国家，位于科特迪瓦和多哥之间。人口：19,894,000 (2001)，首都：阿克拉。1957年，时称黄金海岸的加纳是第一个摆脱英国殖民统治获得独立的非洲国家〕 —**Ghanaian** /gɑˋneən; gɑːˈneɪən/ *n, adj*

ghast·ly /ˋgæstlɪ; ˈgɑːstli/ *adj* **1** a ghastly situation, person, experience etc is one that you do not like or enjoy at all 讨厌的，令人不快的：*What ghastly weather!* 多么糟糕的天气！| *I hope they don't bring their ghastly children with them.* 我希望他们不会带他们那些讨厌的的小孩来。| *It was absolutely ghastly.* 绝对的令人厌恶。**2** making you very frightened, upset or shocked 可怕的，恐怖的：*a ghastly accident* 可怕的事故 **3 look/feel ghastly** to look or feel ill, upset, or unhappy 看上去/感觉有病[烦恼；不高兴]：*Are you alright? You look ghastly!* 你没事吧？你脸色很不好！—**ghastliness** *n* [U]

ghat /gɔt; gɔːt/ *n* [C] *IndE & PakE*【印度和巴基斯坦】**1** a set of steps leading down to a river or lake〔通向河边或湖边的〕台阶 **2** a place where dead bodies are burnt in a ceremony 举行火葬仪式的地方

Ghats /gɔts; gɔːts/ two lines of mountains in South India. The Western Ghats run along the coast of the Arabian Sea, and the Eastern Ghats run along the Bay of Bengal 高止山脉〔印度南部的两道山脉。西高止山脉与阿拉伯海岸平行，东高止山脉沿孟加拉湾延伸〕

ghee /gi; giː/ *n* [U] melted butter made from the milk of a cow or BUFFALO, used in Indian cooking〔乳牛或水牛奶制成用来做菜的〕酥油，奶油〔用于印度烹调〕

gher·kin /ˋgɝkɪn; ˈgɜːkɨn/ *n* [C] a small type of CUCUMBER that has been preserved in VINEGAR〔醋腌的〕小黄瓜

ghet·to /ˋgɛto; ˈgetəʊ/ *n plural* **ghettos** *or* **ghettoes** [C] **1** a part of a city where people of a particular race or class live separately from the main population, usually in bad conditions〔通常条件很差的〕少数民族聚居区，贫民区 **2** a part of a city where Jews were forced to live in former times〔以前的〕犹太人居住区：*She was born in a Polish ghetto.* 她出生在波兰一个犹太人区。

ghetto blast·er /ˈ· ·, ·ˌ·/ *n* [C] *informal* a large radio and TAPE RECORDER that can be carried around, and is often played very loudly in public places【非正式】便携式大型收录机，手提录音机〔通常在公共场所大声播放〕；BOOM BOX *AmE*【美】

ghet·to·ize *v* also 又作 **-ise** *BrE*【英】/ˋgɛtoaɪz; ˈgetəʊaɪz/ [T] **1** to force people to live in a ghetto 强迫人们居住在聚居区[贫民区] **2** to make part of a town become a ghetto 使成为聚居区[贫民区]

ghi /gi; giː/ *n* [U] another spelling of GHEE ghee 的另一种拼法

ghosts 鬼，幽灵

ghost¹ /gost; gəʊst/ *n* [C] **1** the spirit of a dead person that some people think they can feel or see in a place 鬼，幽灵：*The ghosts of past landlords are said to haunt this pub.* 据说前任店主的幽灵常在这家酒吧出没。| **ghost story** *We used to scare each other by telling ghost stories at night.* 我们过去经常在晚上讲鬼故事来吓唬对方。—see also 另见 HOLY GHOST **2 the ghost of a smile/sound etc** a smile etc that is so slight you are not sure it happened 一丝微笑/一点儿声音等：*He had the ghost of a smile on his lips.* 他嘴角挂着一丝微笑。**3** a GHOST WRITER 代笔人，捉刀人 **4** a second image that is not clear, especially on a television picture〔尤指电视图像的〕重像，重影 **5 give up the ghost** *humorous*【幽默】**a)** to die 死 **b)** if a machine gives up the ghost, it does not work any more and cannot be repaired〔机器〕报废：*My car's finally given up the ghost – I'm selling it for scrap.* 我的车终于报废了，我正打算把它当废铁卖掉。**6 not a ghost of a chance** not even a slight chance of doing something, or of something happening 毫无机会：*There's not a ghost of a chance of finding the missing child now.* 现在要找到那个丢失的小孩完全没有可能。

CULTURAL NOTE 文化注释

In the US and the UK, people often think about a ghost as a shapeless white figure with empty black eyes, which makes a 'woo-ooo' sound. Children often cut eye holes in a white sheet to dress as this type of ghost. In the UK, ghosts are sometimes also thought of as people dressed in Elizabethan clothes, who have had their heads cut off and are carrying them in their arms. Another type of ghost is one that looks like a normal person except that you can see through it. A POLTERGEIST is a ghost that throws things around, makes furniture move, and causes a lot of damage. People also imagine that some ghosts cannot actually be seen, but that it feels very cold when the ghost is near you. Ghosts are also thought to be able to move through walls and other objects.英美人常认为鬼魂是白色的人影，形状不定，有一双空洞的黑眼睛，发出“呜呜”的声音。儿童常在白床单上掏出两个露出眼睛的洞，扮作这种鬼魂。英国人有时认为鬼魂穿着伊丽莎白时代的服装，头被砍掉，夹在腋下。另一种鬼魂看起来像普通人，但能看穿它的身体。捉弄人的鬼是一种四处扔东西、挪动家具、造成破坏的鬼魂。人们还想象有些鬼魂实际上是看不见的，不过当它靠近你，你会感觉寒气逼人。人们还认为鬼魂能穿透墙壁和其他物体。

ghost² *v* [T] to write something as a GHOST WRITER 代人写

ghost·ly /ˋgostlɪ; ˈgəʊstli/ *adj* slightly frightening and seeming to be connected with ghosts or spirits 幽灵似的，像鬼似的：*a ghostly stare* 有点吓人的凝视 —**ghostly** *adv*: *ghostly pale* 脸色苍白得可怕 —**ghostliness** *n* [U]

ghost town /ˈ· ·/ *n* [C] a town that used to have a lot of people living and working in it, but now has very few 被废弃的城镇

ghost train /ˈ· ·/ *n* [C] a small train ride at a British FUNFAIR, that is designed to frighten you by taking you through a dark place full of SKELETONS (1) and things that jump out at you〔英国游乐场里的〕魔鬼列车，幽灵列车〔列车载着游客在黑暗中行驶，到处都是骷髅和怪物向你扑来〕

ghost writ·er /ˈ· ,· ·/ *n* [C] someone who writes a book or story for another person who then says it is their own work 代笔人，捉刀人 —**ghost-write** *v* [T]

ghoul /gul; guːl/ *n* [C] **1** an evil spirit in stories that takes bodies from graves and eats them 食尸鬼〔传说中从坟墓里挖尸体吃的魔鬼〕**2** someone who gets pleasure from unpleasant things

such as accidents that shock other people 从恐怖事件中取乐的人 —**ghoulish** *adj* —**ghoulishness** *n* [U]

GHQ /ˌdʒi etʃ ˋkju; ˌdʒiː eɪtʃ ˈkjuː/ *n* [U] General Headquarters; the place that a large military operation is controlled from 总司令部; 军事行动指挥所

GI /ˈdʒi ˋaɪ; ˌdʒiː ˈaɪ/ *n* [C] a soldier in the US army, especially during the Second World War〔尤指第二次世界大战时的〕美国兵

CULTURAL NOTE 文化注释

Many GIs came to the UK during World War II, and were seen as attractive and exciting by British women because they could provide things such as certain types of food and clothes that were not easily available in the UK at that time. Some British women, known as GI BRIDEs, married American soldiers and went to live in the US. 二战中很多美国兵来到英国, 英国女人认为美国兵迷人、刺激, 因为他们那里有当时英国不易得到的某类食品和衣物。有的英国女人嫁给美国兵, 赴美生活, 被称为美国大兵的新娘(GI bride)。

Gia·co·met·ti /ˌdʒɑkoˋmɛttɪ; ˌdʒɑːkɔːˈmetti/ (1901-66) a Swiss SCULPTOR whose most famous works include 'The Couple' (1926) and 'The Forest' (1950) 吉亚柯梅蒂〔(1901-1966), 瑞士雕塑家。最有名的作品包括《夫妇》(1926) 和《森林》(1950)〕

gi·ant¹ /ˋdʒaɪənt; ˈdʒaɪənt/ *adj* [only before noun 仅用于名词前] extremely big and much bigger than other things of the same type 巨大的, 特大的: *a giant sized box of detergent* 特大盒的洗涤剂 | *a giant supermarket just outside town* 城外的一家大型超市

giant² *n* [C] **1** a very tall, strong man in children's stories who is often bad and cruel〔儿童故事中的〕凶恶巨人 **2** a very large, successful company 兴旺的大公司: *the German chemicals giant, BASF* 德国化工产品巨头巴斯夫公司 **3** a very big man 身材特别高大的人, 巨人 **4** someone who is very good at doing something 伟人; 卓越人物: *Scorcese is a giant of the American cinema.* 斯科西斯是美国电影界的巨擘。

gi·ant·ess /ˋdʒaɪəntɪs; ˈdʒaɪəntes/ *n* [C] an extremely tall strong woman in children's stories who is often bad and cruel〔儿童故事中的〕凶残女巨人

giant kil·ler /ˈ··, ·ˈ··/ *n* [C] *BrE* a person, sports team etc that defeats a much stronger opponent【英】能打败强大对手的人[运动队]

giant pan·da /ˌ·· ˈ··/ *n* [C] a PANDA (1) 大熊猫

Giant's Cause·way, the /ˌ·· ˈ··/ a group of unusually shaped rocks on the coast of Northern Ireland, which were formed by a flow of LAVA into the sea 贾恩茨考斯韦角〔北爱尔兰沿海由火山熔岩流入海水而形成的一群奇形怪状的礁石〕

gib·ber /ˋdʒɪbɚ; ˈdʒɪbə/ *v* [I] to speak quickly in a way that no one can understand, especially because you are very frightened or shocked〔尤指由于害怕或受惊而〕说话急促不清: *The little boy was soaking wet and gibbering with agitation.* 这小男孩浑身湿透, 激动得语无伦次。

gib·ber·ing /ˋdʒɪbərɪŋ; ˈdʒɪbərɪŋ/ *adj BrE* so frightened, shocked, or excited that you speak quickly in a way that no one can understand【英】〔因害怕、受惊或激动而〕说话急促不清的: **a gibbering wreck** (=someone who is very shocked or frightened) 受惊的人, 被吓坏的人

gib·ber·ish /ˋdʒɪbərɪʃ; ˈdʒɪbərɪʃ/ *n* [U] something you write or say that has no meaning, or is very difficult to understand 胡扯; 令人费解的话: *You're talking gibberish!* 你在胡扯!

gib·bet /ˋdʒɪbɪt; ˈdʒɪbɪ̈t/ *n* [C] a wooden frame on which criminals were hanged (HANG¹ (3)) in the past with a rope around their neck 绞刑架

gib·bon /ˋgɪbən; ˈgɪbən/ *n* [C] a small animal like a monkey, with long arms and no tail, that lives in trees in Asia 长臂猿[猴]

gibe /dʒaɪb; dʒaɪb/ *n* [C] another spelling of JIBE jibe 的另一种拼法

gib·lets /ˋdʒɪblɪts; ˈdʒɪblɪ̈ts/ *n* [plural] the inside parts of a bird that can be eaten, and are taken out before the bird is cooked〔可食用家禽的〕内脏

Gi·bral·tar /dʒɪˋbrɔltɚ; dʒɪ̈ˈbrɔːltə/ a town and port on the Rock of Gibraltar on the southern coast of Spain. It has belonged to the UK since 1713, but the Spanish government would like it to belong to Spain. 直布罗陀〔位于西班牙南海岸直布罗陀岩山的一个港市。1713 年以来一直为英国所有, 但西班牙政府希望将此地划归本国版图〕—**Gibraltarian** /dʒɪbrɔlˋtɛrɪən; dʒɪ̈brɔːlˈteəriən/ *n, adj*

CULTURAL NOTE 文化注释

Although Spain wants Gibraltar back, a famous story says that Britain will only leave Gibraltar when all the Barbary APEs (=a type of monkey) that live there leave or die. 尽管西班牙想收回直布罗陀, 但有一则著名的故事说, 只有当地的叟猴全部离开或死亡, 英国人才会离开直布罗陀。

gid·dy¹ /ˋgɪdɪ; ˈgɪdi/ *adj* **1** feeling slightly sick and unable to balance, because everything seems to be moving; DIZZY (1) 头晕的, 眩晕的: *Just watching those kids spinning makes me feel giddy.* 仅仅是看那些孩子转圈就使我头晕。**2** **be giddy with sth** to be very happy because something good has happened 因〔某事而〕开心, 高兴: *Amanda was giddy with success.* 阿曼达因成功而飘飘然。**3** [only before noun 仅用于名词前] making you feel as if you may fall 令人头晕的, 令人眩晕的: *a giddy height* 令人眩晕的高度 **4** *old-fashioned* silly and not interested in serious things【过时】轻率的, 轻浮的: *Fiona's very pretty but a bit giddy.* 菲奥娜很漂亮, 但是有点轻浮。—**giddily** *adv* —**giddiness** *n* [U]

giddy² *v*

giddy up [I] used to command a horse to go faster 快走, 赶快〔对马的吆喝〕

Gid·e·on Bi·ble /ˌgɪdɪən ˋbaɪbl̩; ˌgɪdiən ˈbaɪbəl/ a Bible that is put in a hotel room or similar place by a member of a Christian organization called the **Gideons**, who encourage people to read the Bible by giving them a copy of it 基甸国际赠送的《圣经》〔基督教基甸国际会员放置在酒店客房等类似场所的《圣经》, 旨在鼓励人们阅读〕

gift /gɪft; gɪft/ *n* [C]

1 ▶OBJECT 物体◀ something that you give someone on a special occasion or to thank them 礼物: *The earrings were a gift from my aunt.* 这双耳环是我姑姑送给我的礼物。| **make sb a gift of sth** *Grandma made me a gift of her silver.* 祖母把她的银餐具作为礼物送给我。| **free gift** *Enjoy a free gift with any purchase of $20 or more.* 购物满 20 美元可获赠礼品一份。

2 ▶ABILITY 能力◀ a natural ability; TALENT (1) 天赋, 才能: *Donne's poetic gift* 多恩的诗才 | [+for] *Dee has a gift for making everyone feel at ease.* 迪伊有一种能让大家放松的本领。—see also 另见 GIFTED

3 a gift *BrE informal* something that is easier or cheaper than you expected【英, 非正式】比预料容易[便宜]的东西: *The exam paper was a gift.* 这次考试比想象的容易。

4 the gift of the gab *informal* an ability to speak confidently and to persuade people to do what you want【非正式】口才, 辩才

5 be in someone's gift *BrE informal* to be in someone's power to give a favour to someone they choose【英, 非正式】由某人授予[委派]: *The chairmanship of this committee is in the gift of the minister.* 该委员会主席是由部长委派的。

6 never/don't look a gift horse in the mouth *informal* used to tell someone to be grateful for something that has been given to them, instead of asking questions about it or finding something wrong with it【非正式】对礼物不要挑剔 —see also 另见 **God's gift to women/men etc** (GOD (15))

gift cer·tif·i·cate /ˈ· ·ˌ···/ *n* [C] *AmE* a special piece of paper that is worth a particular amount of money when it is exchanged for goods in a shop【美】购物礼券; GIFT TOKEN *BrE*【英】

gift·ed /ˋgɪftɪd; ˈgɪftɪ̈d/ *adj* having a natural ability to do one or more things extremely well 有天赋的, 有才华的: *a gifted pianist* 才华横溢的钢琴家 | **gifted child** (=one who is extremely intelligent) 天才儿童

gift shop /ˈ· ·/ *n* [C] a shop that sells small things that are suitable for giving as presents 礼品商店

gift to·ken /ˈ· ˌ··/ *n* [C] a special piece of paper that is worth a particular amount of money when it is exchanged for goods in a shop 购物礼券; GIFT CERTIFICATE *AmE*【美】

gift vou·cher /ˈ· ˌ··/ *n* [C] a gift token 购物礼券

gift-wrap /ˈ· ·/ *v* [T] to wrap a present with attractive coloured paper〔用花纸〕包装〔礼品〕: *Would you like it gift-wrapped?* 你想用花纸把它包起来吗?

gig¹ /gɪg; gɪg/ *n* [C] **1** a performance by a musician or a group of musicians playing modern popular music or JAZZ¹ (1)〔现代流行音乐或爵士乐的〕演奏会 **2** a small carriage with two wheels and pulled by one horse 双轮小马车

gig² **gigged, gigging** *v* [I] to give a performance of modern popular music or JAZZ¹ (1) 演奏现代流行音乐[爵士乐]

gig·a·byte /ˋgɪgəbaɪt; ˈgɪgəbaɪt/ *n* [C] *technical* one BILLION BYTES【术语】千兆字节

gi·gan·tic /dʒaɪˋgæntɪk; dʒaɪˈgæntɪk/ *adj* extremely big 巨大的, 庞大的: *a gigantic skyscraper* 巨大的摩天楼 —**gigantically** /-klɪ; -kli/ *adv*

gig·gle[1] /ˋgɪgl; ˈgɪgəl/ **giggled, giggling** *v* [I] to laugh quietly and often like a child, because something is funny, or because you are nervous or embarrassed 咯咯地笑, 傻笑: *If you can't stop giggling you'll have to leave the classroom.* 如果你还咯咯地笑个不停, 你就得离开教室。—**giggly** *adj*

giggle[2] *n* **1** [C] a quiet, repeated laugh 咯咯地笑, 傻笑: *She broke into a nervous giggle whenever the manager spoke to her.* 每当经理对她说话, 她就紧张得傻笑起来。**2 have (a fit of) the giggles** *informal* to be unable to stop giggling【非正式】咯咯笑个不停 **3 give sb the giggles** *informal* to make someone unable to stop giggling【非正式】让某人咯咯笑个不停 **4 a giggle** *especially BrE informal* something that you think is fun to do that will not hurt anyone or anything【尤英, 非正式】玩笑, 逗乐: *We used to hide Mum's keys for a giggle.* 我们过去经常把母亲的钥匙藏起来和她闹着玩。

gig·o·lo /ˋʒɪgəˌlo; ˈʒɪgələʊ/ *n plural* **gigolos** [C] a man who has sex with women for money 男妓

GI Joe /ˌdʒi aɪ ˋdʒo; ˌdʒiː aɪ ˈdʒəʊ/ **1** *AmE informal* a male US soldier, especially during World War II【美, 非正式】(尤指二战期间的) 美国男兵 **2** *trademark* a type of DOLL (=a child's toy like a small person) dressed as a male US soldier. A similar doll in the UK is called Action Man.【商标】玩具士兵〔形似美国男兵的小人。英国也有一种类似玩具, 称 Action Man〕

Gil·bert and Sul·li·van /ˌgɪlbət ənd ˋsʌlɪvən; ˌgɪlbət ənd ˈsʌlɪ̈vən/ two British men, **W.S. Gilbert** (1836-1911) and **Sir Arthur Sullivan** (1842-1900), who wrote many humorous OPERETTAS (=plays with songs) from 1871 to 1896. Gilbert wrote the words and Sullivan wrote the music. Their operettas, which include *The Mikado* (1885) and *The Pirates of Penzance* (1879), made fun of politicians and other well-known people of the time. 吉尔伯特和沙利文〔指英国人W.S. 吉尔伯特 (1836-1911) 和阿瑟·沙利文爵士 (1842-1900)。1871至1896年间, 他们创作了许多幽默小歌剧, 由吉尔伯特作词, 沙利文谱曲。其作品包括《日本天皇》(1885) 和《彭赞斯的海盗》(1879), 讽刺当时的政客和名人〕

gild /gɪld; gɪld/ *v* [T] **1** to cover something with a thin layer of gold or with something that looks like gold 给…镀金, 给…涂上金色: *an ornate gilded mirror* 华丽的镀金镜子 **2** *literary* to make something look as if it is covered in gold【文】给…染上金色: *The autumn sun gilded the lake.* 秋天的太阳把湖面染成金色。**3 gild the lily** *BrE* to spoil something by trying to improve it when it is already good enough【英】画蛇添足, 弄巧成拙

gill[1] /gɪl; gɪl/ *n* [C] **1** one of the organs on the sides of a fish through which it breathes 鱼鳃 —see picture at 参见 FISH[1] 图 **2** one of the thin pale lines on the bottom of a MUSHROOM[1]〔蘑菇的〕菌褶 **3 green/pale about the gills** *informal* looking sick because you are shocked, afraid, or ill【非正式】〔因受惊、害怕或生病〕脸露病容的; 面如土色的

gill[2] /dʒɪl; dʒɪl/ *n* [C] a measure of liquid equal to 0.142 litres 及耳〔液量单位, 等于0.142升〕—see table on page C5 参见 C5 页附录

Gil·les·pie /gɪˋlɛspɪ; gɪ̈ˈlespi/, **Dizzy** (1917-93) a US JAZZ musician and TRUMPET player who, with Charlie Parker, developed the BEBOP style of jazz 吉莱斯皮〔(1917-1993), 美国爵士音乐家、小号演奏家。他曾与查理·帕克一起发展了比博普爵士乐流派〕

gil·lie /ˋgɪlɪ; ˈgɪli/ *n* [C] a man who acts as a guide to someone who is fishing or shooting for sport in Scotland〔苏格兰的〕渔猎向导

gilt[1] /gɪlt; gɪlt/ *n* **1** [U] a thin shiny material, such as gold or something similar, used to cover objects for decoration 金色涂层, 镀金材料 **2** [C] a SHARE[2] (5) that is GILT-EDGED 金边股票 **3** [C] *especially AmE* a young female pig【尤美】小母猪

gilt[2] *adj* [only before noun 仅用于名词前] covered with gilt 镀金的: *gilt lettering* 镀金的字体

gilt-edged /ˌ· ˋ· ◂/ *adj technical* gilt-edged stocks (STOCK[1] (3)) or shares (SHARE[2] (5)) do not give you much INTEREST (=additional money) but are considered very safe as they are sold mainly by governments【术语】〔多为政府发行的证券、股票等〕金边的; 保险的; 优质的

gim·crack /ˋdʒɪmˌkræk; ˈdʒɪmkræk/ *adj* [only before noun 仅用于名词前] cheap and badly made 低廉劣质、粗制滥造的

gim·let /ˋgɪmlɪt; ˈgɪmlɪ̈t/ *n* [C] **1** a tool that is used to make small holes in wood so that you can put screws in easily 螺丝锥; 手钻〔用于在木头中钻孔〕**2 gimlet-eyed/gimlet eyes** if someone is gimlet-eyed, or has gimlet eyes, they look at things very hard and notice every detail 目光敏锐的/敏锐的目光 **3** an alcoholic drink made with GIN (1) or VODKA and LIME[1] (1) 琴蕾鸡尾酒〔用杜松子酒或伏特加及酸橙汁调制的一种酒〕

gim·me /ˋgɪmɪ; ˈgɪmi/ *spoken* a short form of 'give me' that many people think is incorrect【口】给我〔give me 的一种简略说法, 许多人认为这种形式不正确〕: *Gimme that! It's mine!* 把那给我! 是我的!

gim·mick /ˋgɪmɪk; ˈgɪmɪk/ *n* [C] *informal*【非正式】**1** a trick or an object that makes you notice a product and want to buy it 推销花招, 噱头〔指一种伎俩或物品, 能使你注意到某商品并愿意购买〕: *advertising gimmicks* 广告花招 **2** something unusual that someone does to make people notice them〔为引人注目而搞的〕奇招 —**gimmicky** *adj* —**gimmickry** *n* [U]

gin /dʒɪn; dʒɪn/ *n* **1** [C,U] a strong alcoholic drink made mainly from grain 杜松子酒〔用粮食酿制的烈性酒〕—see also 另见 PINK GIN, GIN AND TONIC **2** [C] a trap for catching small animals or birds〔捕猎小动物或鸟的〕陷阱, 罗网 —see also 另见 COTTON GIN

gin and ton·ic /ˌ· · ˋ··/ *n* [C,U] a popular alcoholic drink served with ice and a thin piece of LEMON (1) or LIME[1] (1) 加奎宁水的杜松子酒〔一种常见的含酒精饮料, 饮用时加冰和一片柠檬或酸橙〕

gin·ger[1] /ˋdʒɪndʒə; ˈdʒɪndʒə/ *n* [U] a root with a very strong hot taste that is used in cooking, or the plant that has this root 姜 —see picture on page A9 参见 A9 页图

ginger[2] *adj* **1** *BrE* hair or fur that is ginger is bright orange-brown in colour【英】〔头发或毛皮〕姜黄色的, 赤黄色的 —see picture on page A6 参见 A6 页图 **2** [only before noun 仅用于名词前] flavoured with ginger 姜味的

ginger[3] *v BrE*【英】

ginger sth ↔ **up** *phr v* [T] to make something more exciting 使〔某事〕更加令人兴奋

ginger ale /ˌ·· ˋ·/ *n* [C,U] a non-alcoholic drink that tastes of ginger and is often mixed with alcohol 姜味汽水〔不含酒精, 但常加酒饮用〕

ginger beer /ˌ·· ˋ·/ *n* [C,U] a non-alcoholic drink with a strong taste of ginger 姜啤〔有强烈姜味但不含酒精的饮料〕

Gin·ger·bread /ˋdʒɪndʒəˌbrɛd; ˈdʒɪndʒəbred/ a British organization which provides support and practical help for single parents and their children 姜饼协会〔英国帮助单亲家庭的一个组织〕

gingerbread *n* **1** [U] a sweet cake or BISCUIT (1) with ginger in it 姜饼 **2 gingerbread man** a piece of gingerbread in the shape of a person 人形姜饼

ginger group /ˋ·· ˌ·/ *n* [C] *BrE* a group of people within a political party or organization that tries to persuade the other members to support their ideas【英】〔政党或组织内部的〕积极派, 激进派 —compare 比较 LOBBY[1] (2)

gin·ger·ly /ˋdʒɪndʒəlɪ; ˈdʒɪndʒəli/ *adv, adj* if you move gingerly or touch something gingerly you do it in a careful way because you are afraid it will be dangerous or painful 小心翼翼地[的], 轻手轻脚地[的]: *He gingerly felt his way along the dark tunnel.* 他在漆黑的隧道里小心翼翼地摸索着前行。

Ginger Man, The a NOVEL by Irish writer J. P. Donleavy which is both funny and sad. The main character, Sebastian Dangerfield, who is a law student in Dublin, lives in a FANTASY world to escape his loneliness and an unhappy marriage.《精力充沛的人》〔爱尔兰作家唐利维的一本充满忧伤的喜剧小说。主人公塞巴斯蒂安·丹杰菲尔德是都柏林的一名法律专业学生, 生活在幻想中以摆脱孤独和不幸的婚姻〕

ginger nut /ˋ·· ˌ·/ *BrE*【英】, **ginger snap** *AmE*【美】*n* [C] a hard BISCUIT (1) with ginger in it 姜味饼干

ging·ham /ˋgɪŋəm; ˈgɪŋəm/ *n* [U] cotton cloth that has a pattern of small squares in white and one dark colour〔白色和深色相间的〕格子棉布: *a red and white gingham tablecloth* 红白相间的方格桌布 —see picture on page A16 参见 A16 页图

gin·gi·vi·tis /ˌdʒɪndʒəˋvaɪtəs; ˌdʒɪndʒɪ̈ˈvaɪtɪ̈s/ *n* [U] a medical condition in which your GUMS are red, swollen, and painful 牙龈炎

gi·nor·mous /dʒaɪˋnɔrməs; dʒaɪˈnɔːməs/ *adj BrE informal* extremely large【英, 非正式】非常大的: *Look Mum! It's ginormous!* 瞧, 妈妈! 真大啊! —**ginormously** *adv*

gin rum·my /ˌ· ˋ··/ *n* [U] a type of RUMMY (=card game for two people) 金罗美牌戏

Gins·berg /ˋgɪnzbɝg; ˈgɪnzbɜːg/, **Allen** (1926-97) a US poet and leader of the Beat Generation 金斯堡〔(1926-1997), 美国诗人、"垮掉一代"的代表人物〕

gin·seng /ˋdʒɪnsɛŋ; ˈdʒɪnseŋ/ *n* [U] medicine made from the root of a Chinese plant, that some people think keeps you young and healthy 人参; 人参制成的药品

gin sling /ˌ· ˋ·/ *n* [C] a drink made from GIN (1) mixed with water, sugar, and LEMON or LIME juice 甜味杜松子混调酒〔用水、糖和柠檬汁或酸橙汁调制〕

gin trap /ˋ· ˌ·/ *n* [C] a GIN (2)〔捕猎小动物或鸟的〕陷阱, 罗网

Giot·to /ˋdʒɑto; ˈdʒɒtəʊ/ (1266-1337) an Italian painter and ARCHITECT (=someone who designs buildings) who was one of the most important painters of his time, and painted mostly re-

ligious subjects 乔托〔(1266-1337), 意大利画家、建筑师。他是当时最有影响的画家之一, 其作品大多以宗教为题材〕

gip·sy /ˈdʒɪpsɪ; ˈdʒɪpsi/ *n* [C] a British spelling of GYPSY gypsy 的英式拼法

gi·raffe /dʒəˋræf; dʒɨˈrɑːf/ *n* [C] an extremely tall African animal with a very long neck and legs and pale brown fur with dark spots 长颈鹿

gird /gɝd; gɜːd/ *v past tense and past participle* **girded** or **girt** /gɝt; gɜːt/ [T] *literary*【文】**1 gird (up) your loins** *biblical or humorous* to get ready to do something【圣经或幽默】准备 **2** to fasten something around you 将〔某物〕围在身上

gir·der /ˈgɝdɚ; ˈgɜːdə/ *n* [C] a strong beam, made of iron or steel, that supports a floor, roof, or bridge 大梁, 桁

gir·dle /ˈgɝdl̩; ˈgɜːdl/ *n* [C] **1** a piece of women's underwear which fits tightly around her stomach, bottom, and HIPS[1] (1) and makes her look thinner〔女子的〕紧身褡 **2** *ScotE* a GRIDDLE【苏格兰】平底锅

girl /gɝl; gɜːl/ *n* [C]

1 ►CHILD 孩子◄ a female child 女孩: *Don't do that, you naughty girl!* 别那样做, 你这个调皮的女孩! | **little girl** *spoken*【口】*I used to go there on vacation when I was a little girl.* 我还是个小女孩时, 我经常到那儿度假。

2 ►DAUGHTER 女儿◄ a daughter 女儿: *They have two girls and a boy.* 他们有两个女儿, 一个儿子。

3 ►WOMAN 女性◄ a word meaning a woman, which is sometimes considered offensive by women 女人〔有时被妇女视为具有冒犯性〕: *the office girls* 办公室女勤杂员

4 girls [plural] used by a woman to address a group of other women that she knows well 姐妹们, 同伴们〔相熟女子间的友好称呼〕: *Come on girls!* 来吧, 好姐妹!

5 the girls *informal* a woman's female friends【非正式】〔女子的〕女伴们: *a night out with the girls* 跟女伴们外出玩耍一晚

6 old girl a) *informal* an old woman【非正式】老妇人: *Surely the old girl's dead by now?* 那位老妇人现在肯定已经不在了吧? **b)** *old-fashioned* used to address a woman you know well【过时】大姐〔称呼熟知的某妇女〕: *Listen, old girl, I think you need some rest.* 听我说, 大姐, 我认为你需要休息一下。—see also 另见 OLD GIRL

7 factory girl/shop girl/office girl *old-fashioned* a young woman who works in a factory, shop, office etc【过时】女工/女店员/办公室女勤杂员等

8 my girl *old-fashioned* used by an older person to address a girl or woman who is younger than they are, or when they are annoyed【过时】我的姑娘〔年长的人对年轻女性的称呼, 或说话人气恼时用语〕: *Just remember who you're talking to, my girl!* 要记得你是在跟谁说话, 我的姑娘!

9 *old-fashioned* a woman who you are having a romantic relationship with【过时】女情人, 情妇

10 ►SERVANT 女仆◄ *old-fashioned* a woman servant【过时】女仆, 女佣

girl Fri·day /ˌ· ˈ··/ *n* [C] a girl or woman worker who does several different jobs in an office 女秘书; 女助理, 女助手

girl·friend /ˈgɝlˌfrɛnd; ˈgɜːlfrend/ *n* [C] **1** a girl or woman that you have a friendly, loving relationship with, usually over a fairly long period of time 女朋友: *Shirley was his first serious girlfriend.* 雪莉是他第一位认真交往的女朋友。| **ex-girlfriend** (=a former girlfriend) 前女友 **2** a woman who you are having a romantic relationship with 女情人, 情妇 **3** *especially AmE* a woman's female friend【尤美】女子的女伴: *She's out with one of her girlfriends.* 她跟一位女伴出去了。—see also 另见 BOYFRIEND

girl·hood /ˈgɝlhʊd; ˈgɜːlhʊd/ *n* [U] the period of her life when a woman is a girl 女性的童年, 少女时期 —see also 另见 BOYHOOD

girl·ie[1], girly /ˈgɝlɪ; ˈgɜːli/ *adj informal*【非正式】**1 girlie magazine/calendar etc** a magazine etc with pictures of women with no clothes on 登有裸体女人照片的杂志/日历等 **2** a woman who is girly behaves in a silly way, for example by pretending to be shy or always thinking about how she looks〔女人〕行为愚蠢的 **3** *spoken* suitable only for girls rather than men or boys【口】只适合女孩子的: *Pink's a girlie color!* 粉红色是属于女孩子的颜色!

girlie[2] *n* [C] an offensive word used by men to address a woman who they think is less sensible or intelligent than a man 傻妞〔冒犯语, 男人认为女人不如他们聪明时使用〕

girl·ish /ˈgɝlɪʃ; ˈgɜːlɪʃ/ *adj* behaving like a girl, or looking like a girl 女孩似的, 少女似的: *a peal of girlish laughter* 一阵女孩子般的笑声 —**girlishly** *adv*

girl scout /ˌ· ˈ·/ *n* [C] a SCOUT (=member of the Girl Scouts Association in the US) 女童子军成员 —see also 另见 BOY SCOUT

girl·y /ˈgɝlɪ; ˈgɜːli/ *adj* another spelling of GIRLIE[1] girlie 的另一种拼法

gi·ro /ˈdʒaɪro; ˈdʒaɪərəʊ/ *n BrE*【英】**1** [C] a cheque paid by the government to someone who is unemployed〔政府发放的〕失业救济支票 **2** [U] a system of BANKING in Britain in which a central computer can send money from one BANK ACCOUNT to another electronically〔英国〕银行直接转账电脑系统

girt /gɝt; gɜːt/ the past participle of GIRD

girth /gɝθ; gɜːθ/ *n* **1** [C] the size of something or someone large when they are measured around their middle 围长;〔人的〕腰围: *the enormous girth of the tree* 树的巨大围长 | *Maxwell heaved his considerable girth into the long, sleek car.* 马克斯韦尔使劲把自己粗大的腰身挪进那辆线条优美的长轿车里。**2** [C] a band of leather which is passed tightly around the middle of a horse to keep a SADDLE[1] (1) or load firmly in position〔马的〕肚带 —see picture at 参见 HORSE[1] 页图

gis·mo /ˈgɪzmo; ˈgɪzməʊ/ *n* [C] another spelling of GIZMO gizmo 的另一种拼法

gist /dʒɪst; dʒɪst/ *n* **the gist** the main idea and meaning of what someone has said or written 要旨, 要点: [+of] *The gist of his argument is that full employment is impossible.* 他的论点的要旨是全民就业是不可能的。| **get the gist** (=understand the main meaning of something) 理解要点 *Don't worry about all the details – as long as you get the gist of it.* 不要担心细枝末节, 只理解要点就行了。

git /gɪt; gɪt/ *n* [C] *BrE slang* an unpleasant and annoying person, especially a man【英俚】讨厌的人〔尤指男人〕: *You miserable git!* 你这可耻的讨厌鬼!

gite /ʒit; ʒiːt/ *n* [C] *French or BrE* a holiday house in France【法或英】〔法国的〕度假别墅

CULTURAL NOTE 文化注释

Gites are quite popular with British people because they are cheaper than hotels and more comfortable than camping. They are especially popular with MIDDLE-CLASS people. 法国的度假别墅在英国很流行, 因为它比酒店便宜, 又比露营舒服。中产阶级人士尤其喜欢度假别墅。

give[1] /gɪv; gɪv/ *v past tense* **gave** /gev; geɪv/ *past participle* **given** /ˈgɪvən; ˈgɪvən/

① PROVIDE/SUPPLY 提供/供应
② TELL SB STH/PROVIDE INFORMATION 告诉某人某事/提供信息
③ DO STH 做某事
④ PRODUCE A FEELING/ILLNESS/RESULT 产生感情/传染疾病/得出结果
⑤ ALLOW 允许
⑥ JUDGE 判断
⑦ TIME 时间
⑧ THINK ABOUT STH 考虑某事
⑨ LIKE STH 喜欢某物
⑩ BEND/BREAK 弯曲/断裂
⑪ OTHER MEANINGS 其他意思

① PROVIDE/SUPPLY 提供/供应

1 [T] to provide or supply someone with something 给予, 供给: **give sb sth** *Researchers were given a £10,000 grant to continue their work.* 研究人员得到 10,000 英镑的资助以继续他们的工作。| *Can you give me a ride to the office on Tuesday?* 星期二你能让我搭你的车去办公室吗? | *He went to Las Vegas.*

He has a friend there who will give him a job. 他去了拉斯韦加斯，那里有个朋友要给他一份工作。| *The doctor gave him something for the pain.* 医生给了他一些止痛药。| **give sth to sb** *The firm gives a generous discount to companies that place large orders.* 公司给定货量大的客户优厚的折扣。
2 [T] to give something to someone by putting it near them or in their hand 交给，递给，拿给：**give sb sth** *A policeman gave me a ticket for speeding.* 警察递给我一张超速罚单。| **give sth to sb** *Why don't you give those packages to me while you find out about the train?* 你何不把那些包裹交给我，再去打听火车情况呢？
3 [T] to provide someone with something as a present〔作为礼物〕赠送：**give sb sth** *Jon always gives her flowers on her birthday.* 乔恩总是在她生日的时候给她送花。
4 [I,T] to give money, food etc in order to help people who are poor〔向穷人〕捐赠，捐助：*He gives generously to the church.* 他经常向教会慷慨解囊。| **give sth to sb** *They regularly give 5% of their income to charity.* 他们定期把收入的5%捐给慈善机构。

② TELL SB STH/PROVIDE INFORMATION 告诉某人某事/提供信息
5 [T] to tell someone information or details about something 告诉，提供〔信息〕：*a brochure giving holiday details* 提供度假资讯的小册子 | *The first chapter gives a broad outline of the topic.* 第一章对主题进行了概述。| *You will be asked to give evidence when the case is brought to trial.* 案子开始审理时，你将被要求出庭作证。| **give sb sth** *When will you be able to give us your answer?* 你什么时候能给我们答复？| **give (sb) information/a description/an example etc** *Dad gave me some information on buying a new car.* 爸爸告诉我一些有关买新车的信息。| **give (sb) advice/instructions/a warning etc** *The instructions the manufacturer gave aren't very clear.* 厂家提供的使用说明不大清楚。| **give (sb) an account/report/message etc** *The newspaper gave a disturbing account of the murder.* 报纸对这次谋杀案做了令人不安的报道。—see 见 SAY[1] (USAGE)
6 give sb your word/promise to promise to do something 答应某人，允诺某人：*I gave him my word not to repeat anything of what he'd told me.* 我答应他不把他说的话告诉给别人。
7 give sb to understand/believe *formal* to make someone believe that something will happen or is true【正式】使某人理解/相信〔某事确将发生或确有其事〕：*I was given to understand that the contract would be approved by the end of the week.* 我被告知这个合同周末前就会得到批准。
8 give it to me straight *spoken* used when you want someone to tell you something unpleasant directly【口】直接告诉我〔用于要求某人将坏消息直接告诉你〕

③ DO STH 做某事
9 give (sb/sth) a smile/laugh/shout/push etc to smile, laugh, shout etc 对〔某人/某物〕微笑/笑/喊叫/推等：*He gave me a quick smile and a hug.* 他对我微微一笑并拥抱了我一下。| *Ooh, the baby just gave a kick!* 嘀，婴儿刚刚踢了一下。
10 give (sb/sth) assistance/help/support etc to do something to help someone or something be successful 给〔某人/某物〕协助/帮助/支持等：*Committee members agreed to give the policy of increasing wheel-chair access their full support.* 委员会成员同意全力支持增加轮椅通道的政策。
11 give (sb) a hand *spoken* to help someone do something, especially something that involves physical work【口】帮助〔某人〕做某事〔尤指体力活〕：*Can you give me a hand? I need to move this box.* 你能帮我一下吗？我需要搬动这个箱子。
12 give sb a call/ring *BrE*【英】**/bell** *BrE*【英】**/buzz** to call someone on the telephone 打电话给某人：*I'll give you a call about seven, okay?* 我大约7点给你打电话，好吗？
13 give a speech/concert/performance etc to talk, play an instrument etc in front of a group of people 发表演讲/举行音乐会/进行演出等：*Seamus Heaney is giving a poetry reading Thursday evening.* 谢默斯·希尼将于星期四晚上举行诗歌朗诵会。| *She gave a performance of great beauty and sweetness.* 她的表演非常优美动人。
14 give a party/dance etc to be the person who organizes a party etc, especially at your own home〔尤指在自己家里〕举办聚会/舞会等：*Julie is giving a wedding shower for Lori next Saturday.* 朱莉下星期六要为洛丽举办结婚送礼会。
15 give sth a try/shot/go *BrE*【英】**/whirl** to be willing to attempt to do something 愿意试做某事：*I'm not usually much good at these sorts of games, but I'll give it a go.* 我通常不大擅长这类游戏，不过我愿意试试。
16 ►JOB 工作◄ [T] to ask someone to do a job or task 叫〔某人〕做〔某事〕：*My algebra teacher always gives us a lot of homework.* 代数老师总是给我们留大量的作业。| *Give Mike something to do – he's just sitting there.* 给迈克点儿事干吧 —— 他在那儿干坐着。
17 give (sb) trouble/a hard time/problems etc to do something that causes problems or makes a situation difficult for someone 给〔某人〕添麻烦/让〔某人〕吃苦头/令〔某人〕伤脑筋等：*This new computer program is giving us a little bit of trouble.* 这个新的电脑程序给我们添了一点麻烦。| *She's always giving her mother a hard time these days.* 这些日子她总是让母亲不好过。
18 give (sb) a signal/alarm/sign etc to say or do something that tells someone what to do in a particular situation 向〔某人〕发出信号/发出警报/做手势等：*The man who was controlling the traffic gave me the signal to move forward.* 管理交通的人向我发出往前走的信号。

④ PRODUCE A FEELING/ILLNESS/RESULT 产生感情/传染疾病/得出结果
19 [T] to produce a particular emotional or physical feeling (使）产生〔情感或感觉〕：**give sb sth** *He gave us quite a shock, appearing suddenly like that.* 他像那样突然出现，让我们大吃一惊。| *The heat gave me a real headache.* 高温让我头疼难耐。| *Targets help give workers a sense of achievement.* 指标有助于让工人们产生成就感。
20 [T] to infect someone with the same illness you have 传染〔疾病〕：**give sb sth** *Don't come too close – I don't want to give you my cold!* 别靠得太近 —— 我不想把感冒传给你！| **give sth to sb** *It's very unlikely a doctor could give hepatitis to a patient.* 医生不太可能会把肝炎传染给病人。
21 [T] to produce a particular effect, solution, result etc 产生〔效果、解决办法、结果等〕：*The fields that had not been fertilized gave surprisingly high yields.* 那些未施肥的田地产量高得惊人。| *The camera's focus should be set to give maximum resolution.* 相机的焦距应当调整到能够产生最高的解像度。

⑤ ALLOW 允许
22 [T] to allow something or someone to do something 允许，许可：*Women were given the vote in the early 1900's.* 妇女在20世纪初被赋予投票权。| *I gave the students the freedom to choose their own topics.* 我允许学生自由选择话题。| **give (sb) permission/consent** *Her father finally gave his consent to her marriage.* 她父亲终于同意了她的婚事。| **give sb a chance/opportunity to do sth** *These meetings give everyone a chance to express their opinions.* 这些会议给大家一个表达自己观点的机会。
23 give sb authority/responsibility/control etc to allow someone to have power or control over something 赋予某人权力/责任/控制权等：*Schools have recently been given responsibility for their own budgets.* 学校最近被授权进行独立预算。
24 [I] to be willing to change what you think or do in a situation according to what else happens 愿意〔根据情况对想法、做法〕改变；作出让步：*If only he'd give a little, we'd have this whole thing settled by now.* 当时他如果稍作让步，现在这整件事情我们已经解决了。

⑥ JUDGE 判断
25 [T] to decide how much time a criminal will have to spend in prison 判处〔犯人若干时间的〕监禁：**give sb sth** *The judge gave her two years.* 法官判决她两年监禁。| *He was given life for murdering three women.* 他因谋杀三名女子而被判处终身监禁。
26 give sth out/offside etc *BrE* to decide that a player or a ball is playing against the rules【英】判定〔球〕出界/〔球员〕越位等：*The linesman gave the ball out.* 巡边员判球出界。

⑦ TIME 时间
27 give sb time/a few weeks/all day etc to allow someone or a situation to have enough time to develop, do something etc 给某人时间/几个星期时间/一整天时间等：*Give him time. It's always hard to adjust to a new place.* 给他一些时间吧，适应新环境总是很难的。| **give sb time to do sth** *Flexible working hours could give working parents more time to spend with their children.* 弹性工作制能给上班的父母更多时间和孩子在一起。
28 I give it six weeks/a month etc *spoken* used when you think that something is not going to continue successfully for

G

very long【口】我估计不会超过六个星期/一个月等〔某事就会失败、结束〕: *Steve and Celia are going to get married? I give it six weeks.* 史蒂夫和西莉亚要结婚了吗？我估计他们的婚姻维持不了六个星期。

⑧ THINK ABOUT STH 考虑某事

29 give (sth) thought/attention/consideration etc to spend some time thinking about something carefully 思考/注意/考虑〔某事〕等: *Congress has been giving the crime bill serious consideration.* 国会一直在认真考虑这项犯罪法案。| *I'll give the matter some thought and let you know my decision next week.* 这件事我要考虑一下，下周告诉你我的决定。| **not give sth a second thought/another thought** (=not think or worry about something) 对某事不予考虑[毫不担心] *Don't give it a second thought. I'll take care of the whole thing.* 你不必担心，我会处理这件事。

30 give (sb) the impression/sense/idea etc to make someone think about something in a particular way 给〔某人〕留下印象/感觉/想法等: **give (sb) the impression that** *Paul didn't want to give Mr Bergmun the impression that he was avoiding him.* 保罗不想让伯格曼先生觉得自己在回避他。

⑨ LIKE STH 喜欢某物

31 give me sth (any day/time) *spoken* used to say that you like something much more than something else【口】我更喜欢某物: *I don't like spicy food much. Give me meat and potatoes any day.* 我不大喜欢辛辣的食物，我比较喜欢肉和马铃薯。

32 give anything/a lot/your right arm etc *spoken* used when you want something very much【口】愿意付出一切等〔表示十分想要某物〕: *I'd give my right arm for a complexion like that.* 我要是有那样的肤色该有多好。

⑩ BEND/BREAK 弯曲/断裂

33 [I] if a material gives, it bends or stretches when you put pressure on it 变曲, 伸展: *The leather will give a little after you've worn the shoes a while.* 鞋子穿了一段时间后，皮革就会略微伸展。

34 [I] if something such as a chair or shelf gives, it breaks suddenly 断裂: *The branch suddenly gave beneath him.* 树枝突然在他脚下断裂。

⑪ OTHER MEANINGS 其他意思

35 not give a damn/toss *BrE*【英】**/shit etc** *spoken* used when you do not care at all about something【口】毫不在乎: *I don't give a damn what you think.* 我对你的想法毫不在乎。

36 ▶MAKE STH HAVE A PARTICULAR QUALITY 使某物具有某种品质◀ [T not in progressive 不用进行时] to add a quality or characteristic to a person, place, thing etc 为〔某人、某地、某物等〕增添〔品质或特点〕: *The new sponsor gives the theatre some respectability.* 新的赞助者为剧院提高了一些声望。| **give a smell/taste/look etc** *Rub the salad bowl with a clove of garlic to give a delicate tang.*.用一瓣蒜头擦拭色拉碗，让它带有一种幽香。| *Her tan gave her a healthy look.* 晒黑的皮肤使她看起来很健康。

37 give (sth) coherence/form/shape etc to organize something, especially something such as an idea or situation 使〔某物〕连贯/形成/成形: *The painter takes his emotions and gives them artistic form.* 画家把自己的感情用艺术形式表现出来。

38 give (sb/sth) credit/respect/priority etc to treat something or someone in a way that shows it is important or has value 对〔某人/某物〕进行赞扬/表示尊敬/给予优先权等: *You have to give him credit for trying to learn the language.* 他努力学习这门语言，你得表扬他。| *Top priority should be given to finishing on schedule.* 应该最先考虑的是要按时完成。

39 don't give me that *spoken* used when you do not believe someone's excuse or explanation【口】别给我来那一套〔表示不相信某人的借口或解释〕: *"I'm sorry I'm late. My car broke down." "Oh, don't give me that."* "对不起，我迟到了，我的车坏了。""哦，别来那一套。"

40 give sb what for *informal* to tell someone angrily that you are annoyed with them【非正式】痛骂某人

41 ▶PAY 支付◀ [T] to be willing to pay a particular amount of money for something 愿意付〔一定数额的钱来购买某物〕: **give sb sth for** *He said he'd give us £700 for our old Ford.* 他说他愿意出700英镑买我们那辆旧福特车。

42 give as good as you get to fight or argue with someone using the same amount of skill or force that they are using 针锋相对，毫不示弱地反击[反驳]

43 give or take a few minutes/a penny/a mile etc if a number, time, or amount is correct give or take a few minutes etc, it is approximately correct 相差不了几分钟/一便士/一英里等: *You can usually predict how tall a child will be as an adult, give or take a couple of inches.* 你通常可以预计一个孩子长大后的身高，相差不了两三英寸。

44 I'll give you that *spoken* used when you accept that something is true, even though you do not like it or disagree with other parts of it【口】那点我承认，那点我接受: *Yes, he's handsome, I'll give you that, but he's really arrogant.* 是的，他长得帅，这点我承认，不过他真的很傲慢。

45 I give you the chairman/prime minister/groom etc *BrE spoken* used at the end of a speech to invite people to cheer or APPLAUD (1) a special guest【英口】我提议为主席/总理/新郎等欢呼[鼓掌]

46 What gives? *spoken* used when you want to ask what is happening【口】发生了什么事？

47 ▶SEX 性◀ [T] *old-fashioned* if a woman gives herself to a man, she has sex with him【过时】〔女子〕委身于〔男子〕—see also 另见 **give way** (way¹ (31))

give away *phr v* [T] **1** [**give** sth ↔ **away**] to give something to another person because you do not want it any longer or because they need it more than you 送掉，捐赠，分送〔将不需要的东西送给别人〕: *I need to give away some of these old baby clothes.* 我需要把这些旧的婴儿衣服送出去一些。| **give sth away to** *He gave away immense amounts of money to charity.* 他把大笔大笔的钱捐给慈善机构。**2** [**give** sth ↔ **away**] if a company gives away something, they give things to people in order to persuade them to buy that company's products〔公司为争取顾客而〕赠送，送发: *They're giving a plastic model skeleton away with a children's book on the body.* 购买一本关于身体构造的儿童书赠送塑料人体骨架模型一个。**3** [**give** sth ↔ **away**] to do something that shows what you really think or what is really true 表露，流露: *Katheryn studied the jurors' faces, but they gave away no clues as to the verdict.* 凯瑟琳打量陪审员的脸，可是他们没有透露任何判决的线索。**4** [**give** sb **away**] to show that someone is doing something wrong 败露，露马脚: **give yourself away** *Most shoplifters give themselves away by constantly looking around for cameras.* 大多数商店盗窃犯不停地四处寻找摄像头，因而露出马脚。**5** [**give** sth ↔ **away**] to tell someone something that you should keep secret 泄露〔秘密〕: *I was afraid the kids would give the whole thing away.* 恐怕孩子会把整件事说出去。| **give the game away** (=tell someone a secret plan, idea etc) 泄露秘密 **6** [**give** sth ↔ **away**] to lose something by doing something silly or stupid〔由于做了蠢事而〕丧失，丢失: *The goalkeeper gave away two goals.* 守门员丢了两个球。| *I swear the Democrats are just giving this election away.* 我断言民主党正断送这次选举。**7** [**give away** sth] to give someone something such as a prize in a ceremony〔仪式上〕颁发〔奖品等〕: *The university chancellor gave away our diplomas.* 大学校长向我们颁发毕业证书。**8** [**give** sb ↔ **away**] when a man, especially the BRIDE's father, gives the bride away, he walks with her to the front of the church and formally gives permission for her to marry〔在婚礼上，尤指新娘的父亲〕将〔新娘〕交给新郎: *She asked her eldest brother to give her away.* 她请她的长兄把她交给新郎。

give sth ↔ **back** *phr v* [T] **1** to return something to the person who owned it before 返还，归还: **give sth ↔ back to sb** *She read the letter, signed it, and gave it back to Rae.* 她读了信，签上名，然后还给雷。| **give sb back sth** *I need to give Jack back the money he lent me.* 我得把杰克借我的钱还给他。| **give sb sth back** *Mom! Tell Josh to give me my pens back!* 妈妈！告诉乔希把我的几支笔还给我！**2** if you give someone back a quality, ability, or characteristic, you make them have it again after they had lost it; RESTORE (5) 使〔某人〕恢复〔品质、能力或特点〕: *The operation gave him back his sight.* 这次手术使他恢复了视力。

give in *phr v* **1** [I] to unwillingly agree to someone's demands after they have spent a lot of time arguing with you, trying to persuade you etc 让步: *They argued back and forth until finally Buzz gave in.* 他们反复争论，直到最后布兹让步为止。| [+to] *O'Neill was giving in to pressure from London to hurry the reforms.* 伦敦施压，奥尼尔开始让步，加快进行改革。**2** [I] to stop playing, fighting etc and accept that you will be defeated 屈服，投降: *They weren't a particularly good team, but they refused to give in and accept defeat.* 他们并不是一支特别好的球队，但他们拒绝屈服，不肯认输。**3** [T **give** sth ↔ **in**] *BrE* to give something such as an official paper or piece of

work to someone【英】呈交, 交上〔公文或工作〕; **hand in** (HAND²) *AmE*【美】: *Rosa decided to give in her notice.* 罗莎决定递交辞职通知。| *You were supposed to give this work in four days ago.* 你四天前就应该交上这份作业了。

give in to *phr v* [T] to no longer control a strong emotion or desire 向〔强烈感情或欲望〕屈服: *If you feel the urge for a cigarette, try not to give in to it.* 如果烟瘾上来, 尽量要把它控制住。

give of sth *phr v* [T] if you give of yourself, your time or money, or your best, you do things for other people without expecting them to do anything for you 献出〔自身、时间或金钱, 或你最大的力量, 以帮助他人而不指望回报〕: *professionals who give of their free time to help underprivileged youngsters* 把业余时间用来帮助社会下层青年的专业人士

give off sth *phr v* [T] to produce a smell, light, heat, a sound etc 发出〔气味、光、热、声音等〕: *Chives give off a delicate oniony scent.* 细香葱发出淡淡的洋葱味。

give off 发出〔气味〕

The milk gave off a bad smell.
牛奶发出臭味。

give on/onto sth *phr v* [T not in passive 不用被动态] if a window, door, building etc gives on or onto a particular place, it leads to that place or you can see that place from it〔窗、门、建筑物等〕通向, 面朝: *a gate giving on to the main road* 通往大路的入口 | *a small window giving onto fields* 面朝田野的小窗

give out *phr v* **1** [T **give** sth ↔ **out**] to give something to a number of different people, especially to give information to people〔向多人〕分发, 发布, 公布〔信息等〕: *Students were giving out leaflets to everyone on the street.* 学生正向街上的人分发传单。| *You had no right to give my telephone number out.* 你无权公布我的电话号码。**2** [I] if a part of your body gives out, it stops working properly〔人体某一部分〕出问题: *I am so frightened that my legs give out, and I reach for the railing.* 我吓得两腿发软, 便伸手去抓栏杆。**3** [I] if a supply of something gives out, there is none left 耗尽, 用光: *My money began to give out.* 我的钱快用光了。| *predictions that the world's oil supply would soon give out* 世界石油供应快将耗尽的预测 **4** [T **give out** sth] to produce light, heat, a sound, a gas etc 发出〔光、热、声音、气体等〕: *A palm-oil lamp gave out yellowish light.* 棕榈油灯发出淡黄色的光。**5** [T **give** sth ↔ **out**] *BrE formal* to announce something, especially officially【英, 正式】〔尤指官方〕宣布, 公布, 发表: *Mr Banks gave out the last verse of the hymn.* 班克斯先生宣读了那首赞美诗的最后一节。| **give out that** *It was given out that the prime minister was to undergo minor surgery.* 据宣布, 首相将要接受一个小手术。**6** [I] *especially AmE* to end【尤美】结束: *She parked near the spot where the blacktop gave out.* 她把车子停在沥青路的尽头处。

give over *phr v* [I,T] *BrE spoken* used to tell someone angrily to stop doing something or to be quiet【英口】住手, 闭嘴〔表示愤怒地要某人停止做某事或住嘴〕: *"We're going to thrash you lot five-nil." "Oh, give over!"* "我们要把你们这帮人打成五比零。" "哼, 别胡说八道!" | **give over doing sth** *Oh, give over complaining, we're nearly there.* 哦, 别抱怨了, 我们就快到了。

give over to *phr v* [T] **1 be given over to** to be used for a particular purpose 被用于〔某一目的〕: *The best land near the village was given over to vineyards.* 村子附近最好的地被用作葡萄园。| *Two days were given over to the celebrations.* 两天时间用来搞庆祝活动。**2** [**give** sb/sth ↔ **over to**] to allow yourself or your life to be completely controlled by another person, a feeling, or an activity 受制于〔某人〕; 放任〔感情〕; 致力于〔活动〕: *a life given over to sexual excess* 纵欲过度的一生 | **give yourself over to** *After her husband's death, she gave herself over to her work.* 她丈夫去世之后, 她便完全埋头于工作。**3** [**give** sth/sb ↔ **over to**] to give the responsibility for something or someone to someone else 交托给: *His mother gave him over to his uncle's care when he was very small.* 在他很小的时候, 母亲把他交给他舅舅照看。

give up *phr v* **1** [I,T **give** sth ↔ **up**] to stop doing something or having something, especially something that you do regularly 放弃〔拥有某物或做某事, 尤指经常做的事情〕: *Shaun's giving up his karate, he's bored with it.* 肖恩打算放弃空手道, 他已经对它感到厌倦。| *When Ed left, she gave up hope of ever marrying.* 埃德离开时, 她彻底放弃了结婚的希望。| **give up doing sth** *I've given up expecting him to change.* 我已经不指望他会改变。| **give up a job/career/work etc** *Peter had given up a promising career in law to become a teacher.* 彼得放弃了很有前途的律师职业, 当了一名教师。| **give up smoking/drinking/alcohol/cigarettes etc** (=stop doing something that is unhealthy) 戒烟/戒酒等: *I gave up smoking when I got pregnant.* 我怀孕后便把烟戒了。**2** [I,T **give** sth ↔ **up**] to stop attempting to do something, especially something difficult, without completing it 放弃, 中止〔尤指难事〕: *They searched for the ball for a while, but eventually gave up and went home.* 他们找了一会儿球, 但最终还是放弃, 回家去了。| **give up doing sth** *I gave up trying to persuade him to get a degree.* 我不再试图劝说他去拿个学位。| **give it/that up** *"Give it up," Anna advised me. "You'll never get him to agree."* "放弃吧," 安娜劝我说, "你永远也无法说服他同意的。" | **I give up** *spoken* (=used when you do not know the answer to a question or joke)【口】我放弃, 我不懂〔表示不知道问题的答案或听不懂笑话〕 *"Why did the chicken cross the road?" "I give up. Why?"* "那只鸡为什么走过马路?" "不知道。为什么?" **3** [T **give** sb **up**] to allow yourself or someone else to be caught by the police or enemy soldiers 自首, 投案, 投降: **give yourself up** *The police issued a statement urging the fugitive to give himself up.* 警方发表声明, 敦促逃亡者自首。**4** [T **give up** sth] to agree to do something during the time you would normally spend doing things you enjoy 让出, 腾出〔时间〕: *The club secretary will need to give up an hour or two a week to do the correspondence.* 俱乐部的秘书每星期需要腾出一两个小时来处理信函。**5** [T **give** sth/sb ↔ **up**] to give someone else possession of something you have 放弃, 让出〔所有权〕: *thoughts that Israel might give up some of the occupied territory* 认为以色列可能让出一些被占领土的想法 | **give sth ↔ up to sb** *John gave up his seat to an elderly lady on the bus.* 约翰在公共汽车上把座位让给一位老太太。| **give sb up for adoption** (=allow your child to become legally part of someone else's family) 把孩子交托〔给他人〕抚养 **6** [T **give** sb ↔ **up**] to end a relationship with someone, especially a romantic relationship 断绝关系〔尤指爱情关系〕: *He's started going out with Emma, but he doesn't want to give up this other girl!* 他已开始和埃玛交往, 但他又不想断绝与另一女孩的关系! **7 give sb up for dead/lost etc** to believe that someone is dead and stop looking for them 认为某人已死/失踪等〔而不再寻找〕: *The ship sank and the crew were given up for dead.* 船沉了, 全体船员已无生还可能。—see also 另见 **give up the ghost** (GHOST¹ (5))

give up on sb *phr v* [T] to stop hoping that someone will change, do something etc 对〔某人〕不抱希望: *He'd been in a coma for six months, and doctors had almost given up on him.* 他已经昏迷六个月, 医生们几乎已经放弃他能活过来的希望。

give yourself **up to** sth *phr v* [T] to allow yourself to feel some emotion completely, without trying to control it 使〔自己〕陷入〔某种感情而不加控制〕: *He gave himself up to despair.* 他陷入绝望, 不能自拔。

give² *n* [U] the ability to bend or stretch when put under pressure 伸展性, 弹性: *The rope has quite a bit of give in it.* 这绳子相当有伸展性。

give-and-take /ˌ· · ˈ·/ *n* [U] a willingness between two people or groups to understand each other, and to let both of them have some of the things they want 互相忍让: *In any relationship there always has to be some give-and-take.* 在任何关系中, 互相忍让是必须的。

give·a·way¹ /ˈgɪvəˌwe; ˈgɪvəweɪ/ *n* **1** [singular] something that makes it easy for you to guess something 使人容易猜中〔露出真相〕的东西, : **be a clear/dead giveaway** *He'd been smoking dope; his glazed eyes were a dead giveaway.* 他一直在吸毒, 他那目光呆滞的眼睛彻底暴露了这一点。**2** [C] something that a shop gives you when you buy a product〔商店给顾客的〕赠品

giveaway² *adj* [only before noun 仅用于名词前] giveaway prices are extremely cheap〔价格〕极其便宜的

give·back /ˈgɪvbæk; ˈgɪvbæk/ *n* [C] *AmE* an amount of money or goods that you receive from some companies if you buy a product from them【美】〔一些公司给的〕回扣, 赠品

giv·en¹ /ˈgɪvən; ˈgɪvən/ *adj* [only before noun 仅用于名词前] **1** a given time, date etc is one that has been previously arranged〔时间、日期等〕特定的, 预定的: *At a given time we'll all start shouting and cheering.* 在预定时间我们大家都要开始高声欢呼。**2 at any given time/point etc** at any particular time, point etc 在任何特定的时间/地点等: *The distance from the centre of a circle to the edge is the same at any given point.* 从圆心到圆周上任何一点的距离都是相同的。**3 be given to (doing) sth** to tend to do something, especially something that you should not do 往往会做某事〔尤指不该做的事〕: *She is given to making wild accusations.* 她往往作出荒唐的指控。**4 take sth as given** to base your argument on the belief that something is clearly true 想当然

given² *prep* used to say that something is not surprising when you consider the situation it happened in; CONSIDERING² 如果考虑到: *Given the circumstances, you've coped well.* 考虑到各种情况, 你已经算是处理得很好了。| [+that] *Given that there was so little time, I think they've done a good job.* 考虑到时间有限, 我认为他们算是做得不错了。

given³ *n* [C] *formal* a basic fact that you accept as being true【正式】认为正确的基本事实

given⁴ the past participle of GIVE

given name /ˈ· · ˌ·/ *n* [C] *AmE* your FIRST NAME【美】名字

Gi·za /ˈgizə; ˈgiːzə/ a city in Egypt, which was important in ancient times. Buildings such as the Pyramids and the Sphinx are in Giza. 吉萨〔埃及一城市, 在古代曾十分重要, 金字塔和狮身人面像都在该市〕

giz·mo /ˈgɪzmo; ˈgɪzməʊ/ *n* [C] *informal* a word meaning a small piece of equipment, used when you cannot remember or do not know its correct name【非正式】小玩意儿, 小东西〔忘记或不知道某物的名称时用语〕

giz·zard /ˈgɪzəd; ˈgɪzəd/ *n* [C] the stomach of a bird〔鸟的〕砂囊, 胗

gla·cé /glæˋse; ˈglæseɪ/ *adj* [only before noun 仅用于名词前] glacé fruits, especially cherries (CHERRY), have been covered in sugary liquid〔水果〕糖渍的, 蜜饯的

glacé i·cing /ˌ· · ˈ· ·/ *n* [U] *BrE* a type of ICING used to decorate cakes【英】〔装饰糕饼的〕糖霜

gla·cial /ˈgleʃəl; ˈgleɪʃəl/ *adj* **1** involving ice and glaciers, or formed by glaciers 冰的, 冰川的, 冰川形成的: *a glacial valley* 冰谷 **2** a glacial look or expression is extremely unfriendly〔神色、表情〕冷峻的, 冷冰冰的 **3** extremely cold 极冷的: *a glacial wind* 刺骨的寒风 —**glacially** *adv*

gla·ci·a·tion /ˌglesɪˋeʃən; ˌgleɪsiˈeɪʃən/ *n* [U] *technical* the process in which land is covered by glaciers, or the effect this process has【术语】冰川作用

gla·ci·er /ˈgleʃə; ˈglæsiə/ *n* [C] a large mass of ice which moves slowly down a mountain valley 冰川 —see picture on page A12 参见 A12 页图

2 3 **glad** /glæd; glæd/ *adj* **gladder, gladdest 1** pleased and happy about something 高兴的: *"The doctor says she'll be well again soon." "I'm so glad."* "医生说她很快就会恢复健康。" "我真高兴。" | [+(that)] *I'm really glad I don't have to go back there again.* 我真高兴不必再回那儿了。| [+about] *Deep down he felt glad about the news.* 听到这个消息他发自内心地高兴。| **glad to know/see/hear** *We were all glad to hear you passed your exams.* 我们得知你通过了考试都很高兴。| **be/feel glad for sb** *When I heard they were getting married I felt genuinely glad for them both.* 我听到他们要结婚的消息时, 真心为他们俩高兴。**2 be glad of sth** to be grateful for something 为某事感激: *Thanks Marge, I'll be glad of the help.* 谢谢玛吉, 我非常感谢你的帮助。**3 be glad to do sth** to be very willing and eager to do something 很乐于做某事: *"Would you give me a hand?" "I'd be glad to."* "你能帮我一下忙吗?" "我很乐意。" | **be only too glad to** (=extremely willing) 非常乐意: *I'd be only too glad to let you take the kids today.* 我非常乐意今天由你来照看孩子。**4 I would be glad if** used to say you would be pleased if someone would do something for you 如果〔某人能为你做某事〕, 我将十分高兴: *I would be glad if you could arrange it for me.* 如果你能帮我安排一下, 我非常高兴。**5** making people feel happy 令人高兴的: *a glad day for everyone* 每个人都很开心的一天 **6 glad rags** *informal* your best clothes that you wear for special occasions【非正式】〔特殊场合穿的〕最好的衣服 **7 glad tidings** *old-fashioned* good news【过时】好消息 **8 give sb the glad eye** *BrE old-fashioned* to look at someone in a way that shows you are sexually attracted to them【英, 过时】向某人送秋波 —see also 另见 GLAD-HAND, GLADLY —**gladness** *n* [U]

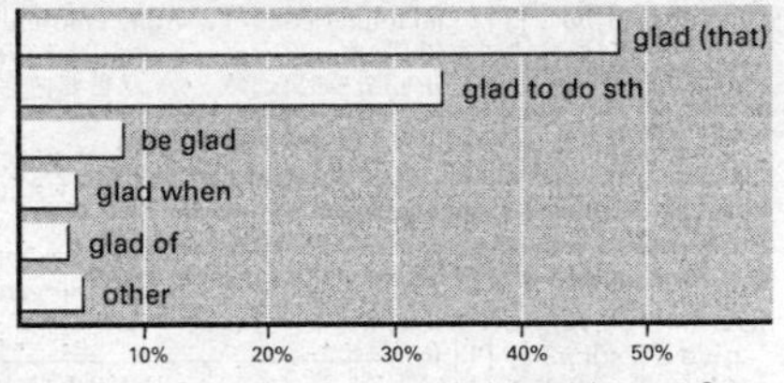
This graph shows how common the different grammar patterns of the adjective **glad** are. 本图表所示为形容词glad构成的不同语法模式的使用频率。

Based on the British National Corpus and the Longman Lancaster Corpus 据英国国家语料库和朗文兰开斯特语料库

glad·den /ˈglædn̩; ˈglædn/ *v* [T] **gladden sb's heart** *old-fashioned* to make someone feel pleased and happy【过时】使某人高兴, 使某人快乐: *It gladdened the old man's heart to see his grandchildren playing in the yard.* 老人看到自己的孙子在院子里玩, 心里很高兴。

glade /gled; gleɪd/ *n* [C] *literary* an open space in a wood or forest【文】林间空地

glad-hand /ˌ· ˈ·/ *v* [I,T] to give someone a very friendly welcome or be nice to them in order to get what you want〔为得到想要的东西而〕热烈欢迎, 态度友好: *politicians glad-handing in the crowds* 在人群中频频打招呼的政客

glad·i·a·tor /ˈglædɪˌetə; ˈglædieɪtə/ *n* [C] a soldier who fought against other men or wild animals in a public place in Roman times in order to entertain people 角斗士〔指古罗马在公共场所互相搏斗或与野兽搏斗以供人娱乐的斗士〕—**gladiatorial** /ˌglædɪəˋtɔrɪəl; ˌglædiəˈtɔːriəl◂/ *adj*

glad·i·o·lus /ˌglædɪˋoləs; ˌglædiˈəʊləs/ *plural* **gladioli** /-laɪ; -laɪ/ *n* [C] a garden plant with long leaves and brightly-coloured flowers 唐菖蒲, 剑兰

glad·ly /ˈglædlɪ; ˈglædli/ *adv* **1** willingly or eagerly 乐意地, 热切地: *I would gladly have done it for him.* 我本来很乐意为他做这事。**2** happily 高兴地, 快乐地: *"Here's Michelle!" he said gladly.* "米歇尔来了!" 他高兴地说道。

Glad·stone /ˈglædston; ˈglædstən/, **Wil·liam Ew·art** /ˈwɪljəm ˈjuət; ˈwɪljəm ˈjuːət/ (1809-98) a British politician in the Liberal Party, who was Prime Minister four times (1868-74, 1880-85, 1886, 1892-94). He established a system of primary education for all children, and also introduced secret voting rights for most males. He supported the idea of limited independence for Ireland, but did not succeed in persuading Parliament to accept this idea. 格莱斯顿〔(1809-1898), 英国自由党政治家。他曾四次出任英国首相(1868-1874, 1880-1885, 1886, 1892-1894)。他建立了全民基础教育体系, 还推行绝大多数男子不记名投票制度。他支持爱尔兰有限独立的思想, 但未能说服议会接受这一构想〕

glam·or /ˈglæmə; ˈglæmə/ *n* [U] an American spelling of GLAMOUR glamour 的美式拼法

Gla·mor·gan /gləˋmɔrgən; gləˈmɔːgən/ —see 见 MID GLAMORGAN, SOUTH GLAMORGAN, WEST GLAMORGAN

glam·o·rize also 又作 **-ise** *BrE*【英】/ˈglæməraɪz; ˈglæməraɪz/ *v* [T] to make something seem more attractive than it really is 使更吸引人, 使更有魅力; 美化: *a widespread perception that Hollywood movies tend to glamorize war* 普遍认为好莱坞电影往往美化战争 —**glamorization** /ˌglæməraɪˋzeʃən; ˌglæməraɪˈzeɪʃən/ *n* [U]

glam·or·ous /ˈglæmərəs; ˈglæmərəs/ *adj* a person, place, or activity that is glamorous seems very attractive and exciting, because it is beautiful or is connected with wealth and success〔人物、地方或活动〕有魅力的, 令人向往的, 刺激的: *a glamorous film star* 富有魅力的电影明星 | *glamorous couples in chauffeur-driven limousines* 私人司机驾驶的豪华轿车里一对对光彩夺目的夫妇 | *Tatiana's glamorous lifestyle* 塔蒂亚娜富于刺激的生活方式 —**glamorously** *adv*

glam·our *usually* 一般作 **glamor** *AmE*【美】/ˈglæmə; ˈglæmə/ *n* [U] **1** the attractive and exciting quality that something has because it is connected with wealth and success〔由财富与成功产生的〕魅力, 诱惑力: *Young actors are often dazzled by the glamor of Hollywood.* 年轻演员经常被好莱坞诱惑得眼花缭乱。**2** strong personal attractiveness〔强烈的〕个人魅力 **3 glamour girl** an actress who is beautiful but is not very good at acting 漂亮但演技不佳的女演员

3 **glance¹** /glæns; glɑːns/ *v* [I always+adv/prep] **1** to quickly look at someone or something once 一瞥, 看一眼: **[+at/towards/up etc]** *He glanced nervously at his watch.* 他紧张地看了一下手表。| *Nadine glanced round to see if there was anyone that she knew.* 娜丁快速环视一下, 看看是否有她认识的人。**2** to read something very quickly 快速阅读: **[+at/over/etc]** *Can you glance through these figures and tell me what you think of them?* 你能粗略看一下这些数字, 然后把意见告诉我吗? **3** to flash 闪耀, 闪光: *light glancing on the water* 水面上闪耀着的光

glance off *phr v* [I,T] to hit a surface at an angle and then move away from it in another direction 擦过, 掠过: *The bullet glanced off the side of the car.* 子弹从汽车边上擦过。

USAGE NOTE 用法说明: GLANCE

WORD CHOICE 词语辨析: **glance, have/take a quick look, glimpse, catch/get a glimpse of**

If you **glance** at something, you look at it quickly. glance 指对某物很快地看一眼: *After the first ten minutes the interviewer started yawning and glancing at his watch.* 头10分钟过后, 面试考官开始打哈欠, 看表。

In spoken English you often use **have/take a (quick) look**, especially to check if something is correct or working properly. 英语口语经常使用 have/take a (quick) look, 特别是检查某物是否正确, 是否运转正常时: *Could you just have a quick look at the engine for me?* 你能帮我看一眼发动机吗?

If you **glimpse** (or more commonly **catch/get a glimpse of**) someone or something, you see them by chance, for a very short time. glimpse〔或更常用的 catch/get a glimpse of〕意指偶然看到某人或某物, 而且时间很短: *I can't describe him well, I only caught a glimpse of him as he drove off.* 我无法准确描述他什么样, 我只是在他开车离开时碰巧看了他一眼。

3 **glance²** *n* [C] **1** a quick look 一瞥, 很快的一看: **give/take/shoot/throw a glance (at)** (=look at someone or something quickly)〔朝…〕一瞥, 看一眼: *He gave her a quick glance as she walked into the room.* 她走进房间时他朝她看了一眼。| **exchange glances** (=look at each other quickly) 交换目光, 互相看一眼 **2 at a glance** if you know something at a glance, you know it as soon as you see it 看一眼便知道: *He'll be able to tell if the diamonds are genuine at a glance.* 他看一眼便能认出这些钻石的真假。**3 at first glance** when you first look at something 乍一看, 最初看到时: *At first glance the place seemed deserted.* 乍一看, 这地方似乎空无一人。

glanc·ing /ˈglænsɪŋ; ˈglɑːnsɪŋ/ *adj* **a glancing blow** a hit that partly misses so that it does not have its full force 擦边而过的一击, 斜击 —**glancingly** *adv*

gland /glænd; glænd/ *n* [C] an organ of the body which produces a substance that the body needs, such as SWEAT² (1) or SALIVA 腺: *Mumps make your glands swell up.* 腮腺炎使你的淋巴腺肿大。| *the pituitary gland* 脑垂体腺

glan·du·lar /ˈglændʒələ; ˈglændjʊlə/ *adj* related to the glands, or produced by the glands 腺的, 由腺产生的

glandular fe·ver /ˌ··· ˈ··/ *n* [U] *BrE* an infectious disease which makes your LYMPH GLANDS swell up and makes you feel weak for a long time afterwards【英】腺热, 传染性单核白细胞增多症; MONONUCLEOSIS *AmE*【美】

glare¹ /glɛr; gleə/ *v* [I] **1** to look angrily at someone for a long time 怒目而视: **glare at sb** *She glared at him accusingly.* 她用责备的眼光怒视着他。**2** [always+adv/prep] to shine with a very strong bright light which hurts your eyes 发出刺眼的强光: **[+through/in]** *The sun glared through the car windscreen.* 强烈的阳光透过挡风玻璃照进车里。

glare² *n* **1** [singular] a bright unpleasant light which hurts your eyes 刺眼的强光: *the harsh glare of the desert sun* 沙漠上刺眼的阳光 **2** [C] a long angry look 怒视: *She gave him an icy glare.* 她以冷冰冰的目光怒视着他。**3 the glare of publicity** the full attention of newspapers, television etc, especially when you do not want it 众目睽睽

glar·ing /ˈglɛrɪŋ; ˈgleərɪŋ/ *adj* **1** very bad and very noticeable 糟透的; 十分显眼的: *the glaring absence of any reliable information* 可靠消息的明显缺乏 | **glaring error/mistake** *The report contained a number of glaring errors.* 报告中有许多很明显的错误。**2** too bright and difficult to look at 耀眼的: *the glaring light of the headlamps* 前灯耀眼的光 —**glaringly** *adv*

Glas·gow /ˈglæsgo; ˈglɑːzgəʊ/ the largest city in Scotland, on the River Clyde 格拉斯哥〔苏格兰第一大城市, 濒临克莱德河〕—**Glaswegian** /glæsˈwidʒɪən; glɑːzˈwiːdʒiən/ *n, adj*

Glasgow Her·ald, The /ˌ·· ˈ··/ also 又作 **The Herald** one of Scotland's main newspapers, read especially in the West of Scotland《格拉斯哥先驱报》〔苏格兰主要报纸之一, 读者主要分布在苏格兰西部地区〕

glas·nost /ˈglɑsnɑst; ˈglæznɒst/ *n* [U] *Russian* a word meaning the willingness of a country or organization to show what it is doing and discuss its decisions, used especially about the government of the former USSR【俄】公开性, 开放性〔指某国或某组织愿意公开表示目前在干些什么并公开讨论决策, 此词尤用于前苏联政府〕

glass 玻璃杯

glasses 眼镜

earpiece
眼镜腿
arm
眼镜臂
lens
镜片
hinge
铰链
bridge
鼻托
frame
眼镜框

1 1 **glass¹** /glæs; glɑːs/ *n*

1 ▶TRANSPARENT 透明的◀ [U] a transparent solid substance, for example used for making windows and bottles 玻璃: *a glass bowl* 玻璃碗 | *Polly cut herself on a piece of broken glass.* 波莉被一片碎玻璃割伤了。

2 ▶FOR DRINKING 用于喝东西◀ [C] a container used for drinking made of glass, or the drink in it 玻璃杯; 杯中的东西: *a wine glass* 葡萄酒杯 | **[+of]** *a glass of red wine* 一杯红葡萄酒

3 ▶FOR EYES 用于眼睛◀ **glasses** [plural] a set of two pieces of specially cut glass in a frame, which you wear in order to see more clearly 眼镜: *I hate wearing glasses.* 我讨厌戴眼镜。| *I need a new pair of glasses.* 我需要一副新眼镜。—see also 另见 OPERA GLASSES, FIELD GLASSES

4 ▶GLASS OBJECTS 玻璃制品◀ [U] objects which are made of glass, especially ones used for drinking and eating; GLASSWARE 玻璃器皿: *a priceless collection of Venetian glass* 一套价值连城的威尼斯玻璃器皿收藏品

5 people in glass houses shouldn't throw stones used to say that you should not criticize someone for having a fault if you have the same fault yourself 玻璃屋里的人不要扔石头〔表示你如果有某种毛病, 便不要指责别人有同样的毛病〕

6 under glass plants that are grown under glass are protected from the cold by a glass cover 在温室里: *tomatoes grown all year round under glass* 一年四季在温室里种植的番茄

7 glass ceiling an imaginary limit that prevents women from being successful, even though there are no actual laws or rules to stop them 玻璃天花板〔指妨碍妇女成功的一种无形限制〕

8 ▶MIRROR 镜子◀ *old-fashioned* a mirror【过时】镜子

9 the glass *old-fashioned* a BAROMETER (1)【过时】气压计, 晴雨计 —see also 另见 CUT GLASS, GROUND GLASS, LOOKING GLASS, MAGNIFYING GLASS, PLATE GLASS, **raise your glasses** (RAISE¹ (12)), STAINED GLASS

glass² *v*
glass sth ↔ **in** *phr v* [T] to cover something with glass, or to build a glass structure around something 用玻璃把〔某物〕罩住；围绕〔某物〕建起玻璃结构
Glass, Philip (1937-) a US COMPOSER of modern CLASSICAL music, who was influenced by Indian music, and is famous for his MINIMALIST style, in which short musical phrases are repeated again and again, with very slight changes 格拉斯〔(1937-)，美国现代古典音乐作曲家。他曾受印度音乐影响，以简约风格著称，即乐句简短，反复出现，变化细微〕
glass·blow·er /ˈglæsˌbloə; ˈglɑːsˌbləʊə/ *n* [C] someone who shapes hot glass by blowing air through a tube 吹玻璃工
glass fi·bre /ˌ· ˈ··◂/ *n* [U] FIBREGLASS 玻璃纤维
glass·ful /ˈglæsˌful; ˈglɑːsfʊl/ *n* [C] the amount of liquid a glass will hold 一玻璃杯的量
glass·house /ˈglæsˌhaʊs; ˈglɑːshaʊs/ *n* [C] *BrE*【英】**1** a building which is used for growing plants and is made of glass; GREENHOUSE 玻璃暖房，温室 **2 the glasshouse** *slang* a military prison【俚】军事监狱
glass·ware /ˈglæsˌwɛr; ˈglɑːsweə/ *n* [U] glass objects, especially ones used for drinking and eating 玻璃制品〔尤指用于饮食的玻璃器皿〕
glass wool /ˌ· ˈ·/ *n* [U] *BrE* FIBREGLASS【英】玻璃纤维
glass·y /ˈglæsɪ; ˈglɑːsi/ *adj* **1** smooth and shining, like glass〔像玻璃一样〕光滑的: *the glassy green waters of the Hudson River* 哈得孙河平滑如镜的绿色河水 **2 glassy eyes/stare** eyes that show no feeling or understanding, and do not move 目光呆滞的眼睛/眼神
glassy-eyed /ˌ·· ˈ·◂/ *adj* having still eyes and an expression that shows no feeling or understanding 目光呆滞的，眼睛无神的: *They had him doped-up. He was sort of glassy-eyed.* 他们给他用了麻醉品，他有点目光呆滞。
Glas·ton·bur·y /ˈglæstn̩bɛrɪ; ˈglæstənbəri/ a town in southwest England with one of the oldest ABBEYS (=type of religious building) in England. A large FESTIVAL of modern music is held at Glastonbury every year at midsummer. 格拉斯顿伯里〔英格兰西南一镇，这里有英格兰最古老的隐修院之一。每年仲夏在此举行大型现代音乐节〕
glau·co·ma /glɔˈkomə; glɔːˈkəʊmə/ *n* [U] an eye disease in which increased pressure inside your eye gradually makes you lose your sight 青光眼
glau·cous /ˈglɔkəs; ˈglɔːkəs/ *adj technical* a glaucous leaf or plant has a fine white powdery surface【术语】〔叶子或植物〕表面起白霜的
glaze¹ /glez; gleɪz/ *v* **1** [I] also 又作 **glaze over** if your eyes glaze over, they show no expression because you are very bored or tired〔因无聊或疲倦〕变得目光呆滞 **2** [T] to cover plates, cups etc made of clay with a thin liquid that gives them a shiny surface 给〔陶瓷碗碟等〕上釉 **3** [T] to cover fruit, cake, or meat with a liquid which gives it an attractive shiny surface 在〔水果、蛋糕或熟肉表面〕浇液浆 **4** [T] to fit glass into window frames in a house, door etc 给…装玻璃
glaze² *n* **1** [C] a liquid that is used to cover plates, cups etc made of clay and give them a shiny surface 釉 **2** [U] liquid which is put onto fruit, cake, or meat to give it an attractive shiny surface〔浇在水果、蛋糕或熟肉上使之光滑好看的〕液浆 **3** [U] a transparent covering of oil paint spread over a painting 透明色料，光油
glazed /glezd; gleɪzd/ *adj* **glazed look/eyes/expression etc** if you have a glazed look etc your eyes show no expression because you are very bored or tired〔由于无聊或疲倦而〕目光呆滞的神色/眼睛/表情等
gla·zi·er /ˈgleʒɚ; ˈgleɪziə/ *n* [C] someone whose job is to fit glass into window frames 装玻璃工
glaz·ing /ˈglezɪŋ; ˈgleɪzɪŋ/ *n* [U] glass that has been used to fill windows 窗用玻璃 —see also 另见 DOUBLE-GLAZING
gleam¹ /glim; gliːm/ *v* [I] **1** to shine softly 发微光，闪烁: *The spire of the Golden Temple gleamed in the autumn sun.* 金庙的尖塔在秋日的阳光下闪闪发光。| **[+with]** *the table's surface gleaming with wax polish* 上了蜡的桌面闪闪发亮 **2 gleam with happiness/joy etc** if your eyes or face gleam with a feeling, they show it〔眼睛或脸部〕露出喜悦的光芒等: *His face gleamed with amusement.* 他满脸开心的神色。—**gleaming** *adj*: *gleaming glass skyscrapers* 闪闪发亮的玻璃摩天楼
gleam² *n* [C] **1** a small pale light, especially one that shines for a short time〔尤指短暂的〕微光，闪光: **[+of]** *They saw the gleam of a lamp ahead.* 他们看到前面一盏灯闪烁着微光。**2** the brightness of something that shines 闪光，亮光: **[+of]** *the sudden gleam of white teeth* 突然露出光亮洁白的牙齿 **3** a sudden expression that appears for a moment on someone's face or in their eyes 闪现: **[+of]** *A gleam of satisfaction crossed her face.* 她的脸上闪现出满足的神情。
glean /glin; gliːn/ *v* **1** [T] to find out facts and information slowly and with difficulty 缓慢艰难地搜集〔事实、信息〕: **glean sth from** *I've managed to glean a few details about him from his friends.* 我已经设法从他朋友那儿弄到有关他的几点情况。**2** [I,T] to collect grain that has been left behind after the crops have been cut〔收割后〕拾落穗
glean·ings /ˈglinɪŋz; ˈgliːnɪŋz/ *n* [plural] small pieces of information that you have found out with difficulty 好不容易搜集到的零星消息
glebe /glib; gliːb/ *n* [U] **1** *poetic* earth or soil【诗】土地，大地 **2** *BrE* land given to a priest to provide part of his income【英】给予牧师的土地〔以提供其部分收入〕
glee /gli; gliː/ *n* **1** [U] a feeling of satisfaction and excitement because something good has happened to you or something bad has happened to someone else〔由于好事发生于自己，或坏事发生于他人所产生的〕满足，兴奋: *The kids watched with glee as I tried to catch the hamster.* 在我试图逮住那只仓鼠时，小孩们喜滋滋地看着。**2** [C] a song for three or four voices together 三部重唱曲，四部重唱曲
glee club /ˈ· ·/ *n* [C] *AmE* a group of people who sing together for enjoyment【美】合唱组，合唱团
glee·ful /ˈglifəl; ˈgliːfəl/ *adj* really enjoying the fact that something good has happened to you or that something bad has happened to someone else〔由于好事发生于自己或坏事发生于他人而〕心满意足的，幸灾乐祸的 —**gleefully** *adv* —**gleefulness** *n* [U]
glen /glɛn; glen/ *n* [C] a deep narrow valley in Scotland or Ireland〔苏格兰或爱尔兰的〕峡谷，幽谷
Glen·coe, Glen Coe /ˌglɛnˈko; ˌglen ˈkəʊ/ a valley in the western Highlands of Scotland, where, in 1692, members of one CLAN (=a large group of families), the Campbells, killed members of another clan, the MacDonalds, in the **Massacre of Glencoe**. It is now a popular place for people to go to SKI or climb. 格伦科〔苏格兰高地西部一谷地。1692年，那里发生了坎贝尔家族屠杀麦克唐纳家族的格伦科惨案。现为滑雪和登山胜地〕
Glenn /glɛn; glen/, **John** (1921-) the first US ASTRONAUT to make a journey in space in 1962. In 1974 he became a member of the US Senate for the Democratic Party, representing the state of Ohio. In 1998, he again went into space, becoming the oldest man to do so. 格伦〔(1921-)，1962年成为第一个完成太空飞行的美国宇航员。1974年，他成为美国民主党参议员，代表俄亥俄州。1998年，他再次进入太空，成为进入太空年龄最大的宇航员〕
glib /glɪb; glɪb/ *adj* **1** glib remarks, explanations etc are difficult to believe because they are said easily and without thinking〔评论、解释等〕轻率的: *glib generalizations about the problem of racism* 对种族主义问题的轻率概括 **2** someone who is glib says things to persuade people without being certain that they are true 能说会道的，油腔滑调的: *glib politicians with their easy solutions* 能言善辩的政客和他们认为能轻而易举解决问题的办法 —**glibly** *adv* —**glibness** *n* [U]
glide¹ /glaɪd; glaɪd/ *v* [I always+adv/prep] to move smoothly and quietly, as if no effort was being made 滑行，滑动: **[+across/over etc]** *a snake gliding across the path* 一条蛇从小道滑行而过 | *The plane glided to a halt just short of the control tower.* 飞机滑行到紧挨控制塔的地方停了下来。
glide² *n* [C] **1** a smooth, quiet movement that seems to take no effort 滑行，滑动 **2** the act of moving from one musical note to another without a break in sound 滑音，延音 **3** *technical* a vowel which is made by moving your tongue from one position to another one【术语】滑音 —see also 另见 DIPHTHONG
glid·er /ˈglaɪdɚ; ˈglaɪdə/ *n* [C] a light plane without an engine 滑翔机
glid·ing /ˈglaɪdɪŋ; ˈglaɪdɪŋ/ *n* [U] the sport of flying in a glider〔乘滑翔机飞行的〕滑翔运动 —see also 另见 HANG GLIDING
glim·mer¹ /ˈglɪmɚ; ˈglɪmə/ *n* [U] **1 a glimmer of hope/doubt/recognition** a small sign of hope, doubt etc 一线希望/一丝怀疑/似曾相识的神情 **2** a light that is not very bright 微光: *the glimmer of a candle* 蜡烛微弱的光线
glimmer² *v* [I] to shine with a light that is not very bright 发出微光: *A light glimmered at the end of the hall.* 一盏电灯在大厅尽头发出微光。
glim·mer·ing /ˈglɪmərɪŋ; ˈglɪmərɪŋ/ *n* [C often plural 常用复数] a small sign of thought or feeling 模糊的想法，一点感觉: *glimmerings of interest* 丝毫兴趣
glimpse¹ /glɪmps; glɪmps/ *n* [T] **1** to see someone or something for a moment without getting a complete view of them 一瞥，看一眼: *I glimpsed her face in the crowd, but then she was*

gone. 我在人群中瞥见她的脸，但随即她就消失了。—see 见 GLANCE[2] (USAGE) **2** to begin to understand something for a moment 开始懂得: *He glimpsed the despair that she must have felt.* 他开始体会到她肯定感受过的那种失望。

glimpse[2] *n* [C] **1** a sight of someone or something that you only have for a short time and that is not complete 一瞥，一看: **get/catch a glimpse of** *I caught only a glimpse of the president's car.* 我只瞥见总统的汽车。| **fleeting glimpse** (=a very short one) 很快的一瞥 —see 见 GLANCE[2] (USAGE) **2** a short experience of something that helps you begin to understand it〔有助于理解某事的〕一次短暂经历: *a glimpse of what life might be like in the future* 使我领会未来生活可能是什么样子的一次短暂经历

glint[1] /glɪnt; glɪnt/ *v* [I] **1** if a shiny surface glints, it gives out small flashes of light 闪烁，闪光: *Her gold bracelet glinted in the morning sunlight.* 她的金手镯在早晨的阳光里闪闪发光。**2** if your eyes glint, they shine and show an unfriendly feeling 眼睛发亮〔显示不友善的感情〕: *Derek's eyes glinted when he saw the money.* 德里克看到钱眼睛就发亮。

glint[2] *n* [C] **1** a look in someone's eyes which shows an unfriendly feeling 不友好的眼神: *There was an evil glint in her eyes.* 她露出不怀好意的眼神。**2** a flash of light from a shiny surface〔光滑的表面上发出的〕闪光

glis·ten /ˈglɪsn̩; ˈglɪsən/ *v* [I] to shine and look wet or oily〔油亮或潮湿物〕闪光: *Her dark hair glistened in the moonlight.* 她的黑发在月光下闪闪发亮。| **[+with]** *The boy's back was glistening with sweat.* 那个男孩背上的汗水闪闪发亮。

glitch /glɪtʃ; glɪtʃ/ *n* [C] **1** a small fault in the working of something 小故障，差错 **2** a false electronic signal caused by a sudden increase in the supply of electric power〔由于电源突增而产生的〕假电子信号，脉冲干扰

glit·ter[1] /ˈglɪtɚ; ˈglɪtə/ *v* [I] to shine brightly with flashing points of light 闪烁，闪光: *The blades of their swords glittered in the sunlight.* 他们的剑刃在阳光下闪闪发亮。

glitter[2] *n* [U] **1** brightness consisting of many flashing points of light 光亮，闪光: *the glitter of his gold cigarette case* 他的金烟盒发出的闪光 **2** the attractiveness of a place or a way of living which is connected with rich or famous people; GLAMOUR (1)〔地方或生活方式的〕魅力，诱惑力: *Jersey City is a world away from the glitter of Manhattan.* 泽西城远离曼哈顿的繁华魅力，是另一个世界。**3** very small pieces of shiny paper that are used for decoration〔用于装饰的〕闪光纸屑 —**glittery** *adj*

glit·te·ra·ti /ˌglɪtəˈrɑtɪ; ˌglɪtəˈrɑːti/ *n* [plural] rich, famous, and fashionable people whose activities are often reported in newspapers and magazines 知名人士，名流

glit·ter·ing /ˈglɪtərɪŋ; ˈglɪtərɪŋ/ *adj* **1** giving off many small flashes of light 闪光的: *glittering jewels* 闪光的首饰 **2** very successful, and connected with rich and famous people〔与富人、名人相连而〕辉煌的，光彩的: *a glittering career in the diplomatic service* 辉煌的外交生涯 —**glitteringly** *adv*

glitz /glɪts; glɪts/ *n* [U] the exciting, attractive quality which is connected with rich, famous and fashionable people; GLAMOUR (1)〔与富人、名人、时髦人们有关的〕魅力，富丽堂皇: *show business glitz* 娱乐行业的魅力 —**glitzy** *adj*

gloam·ing, the /ˈglomɪŋ; ˈgləʊmɪŋ/ *n* [U] *poetic* the time in the early evening when it is becoming dark; DUSK【诗】黄昏

gloat /glot; gləʊt/ *v* [I] to show in an unpleasant way that you are happy about your own success or about someone else's failure 幸灾乐祸，扬扬得意: **[+over]** *Dick was still gloating over Scotland's 5-0 defeat.* 迪克还在因苏格兰 5 比 0 告负而幸灾乐祸。—**gloat** *n* [singular]: *I bet Sam's having a gloat over that one.* 我敢打赌，萨姆肯定在为那个幸灾乐祸。—**gloatingly** *adv*

glob /glɑb; glɒb/ *n* [C] *informal* a small amount of something soft or liquid that has a round shape【非正式】〔柔软物的〕一小团，〔液体的〕一滴: *globs of mud sticking to the cat's fur* 粘在猫身上一团团的泥

3 **glo·bal** /ˈglobl̩; ˈgləʊbəl/ *adj* **1** affecting or including the whole world 全球的，世界的: *AIDS is a global problem which needs a global response.* 艾滋病是个全球问题，需要全球合力对付。**2** considering all parts of a problem or a situation together 全面的，整体的: *The report takes a global view of the company's problems.* 这份报告全面审视了公司的各种问题。—**globally** *adv*

global warm·ing /ˌ·· ˈ··/ *n* [U] a general increase in world temperatures caused by increased amounts of CARBON DIOXIDE around the Earth 全球气温变暖

globe /glob; gləʊb/ *n* [C] **1** a round object with a map of the Earth drawn on it 地球仪 **2 the globe** the world 地球，世界: *We export our goods all over the globe.* 我们的商品出口到世界各地。**3** an object shaped like a ball; SPHERE (1) 球；球状物

Globe Thea·tre, the /ˌ· ˈ··/ **1** a theatre south of the River Thames in London where William Shakespeare's plays were first performed. It was destroyed in the 17th century. 环球剧院〔伦敦泰晤士河南岸最早演出莎士比亚戏剧的一家剧院，毁于 17 世纪〕**2** an exact copy of this theatre, built in the same place and opened in 1996〔在环球剧院原址上精确仿建的一个剧院，1996 年开始投入使用〕

globe·trot·ter /ˈglobˌtrɑtɚ; ˈgləʊbtrɒtə/ *n* [C] *informal* someone who travels to many different countries【非正式】〔去许多不同国家的〕环球旅行者 —**globetrotting** *adj*

glob·u·lar /ˈglɑbjəlɚ; ˈglɒbjʊlə/ *adj* in the shape of a globule or a globe 小珠状的，球状的

glob·ule /ˈglɑbjul; ˈglɒbjuːl/ *n* [C] a small drop of a liquid, or of a solid that has been melted〔液体或熔化固体的〕一滴: *tiny globules of mercury* 细小的水银珠

glock·en·spiel /ˈglɑkənˌspil; ˈglɒkənspiːl/ *n* [C] a musical instrument consisting of many flat metal bars of different lengths, which is played with special hammers〔用小槌敲击发声的〕钟琴

glogg /glɑg; glɒg/ *n* [U] *AmE* a hot drink made with red wine and SPICES[1] (1)【美】格洛格〔一种由红葡萄酒和香料制成的热饮〕

glom /glɑm; glɒm/ *v* [I,T] *AmE informal* to take something, especially an idea, opinion etc, and make it your own【美，非正式】吸收，接受〔想法、意见等〕: **[+onto]** *Watch how the kids glom onto this new style.* 看看这些孩子怎样接纳这种新款式的。

gloom /glum; gluːm/ *n* [singular,U] **1** *especially literary* almost complete darkness【尤文】朦胧: *A tall figure appeared in the canyon's gloom.* 一个高个子人影出现在峡谷的暗处。**2** a feeling of great sadness and lack of hope 忧郁，绝望: *The officers sat sunk in gloom.* 军官们忧愁满怀地坐着。

gloom·y /ˈglumɪ; ˈgluːmi/ *adj* **1** sad because you think the situation will not improve 阴郁的，沮丧的: *When I saw their gloomy faces, I knew something was wrong.* 我看见他们那忧愁的脸时就知道出事了。**2** making you feel that things will not improve 令人沮丧的，令人扫兴的: *a gloomy economic forecast* 令人沮丧的经济预测 **3** dark, especially in a way that seems sad 阴暗的，幽暗的: *Ezra Pound's daughter visited him in his gloomy study in Carlyle Mansions.* 埃兹拉·庞德的女儿在卡莱尔大宅他那阴暗的书房里看望了他。—**gloomily** *adv* —**gloominess** *n* [U]

glop /glɑp; glɒp/ *n* [U] *AmE informal* a thick soft wet mass, especially of food that looks too unpleasant to eat【美，非正式】黏稠的糊状物质〔尤指太难看，以致难以食用的食品〕—**gloppy** *adj*

glo·ri·fied /ˈglorəˌfaɪd; ˈglɔːrɪfaɪd/ *adj* [only before noun 仅用于名词前] made to seem like something more important 被吹捧的，被美化的: *The so-called college was no more than a glorified school.* 那个所谓的学院只不过是一所被美化的学校。

glo·ri·fy /ˈglorəˌfaɪ; ˈglɔːrɪfaɪ/ *v* [T] **1** to make someone or something seem more important or better than they really are 吹捧，颂扬: *films which glorify violence* 颂扬暴力的影片 **2 glorify God/the Lord etc** to give praise and thanks to God 赞美上帝/主等 —**glorification** /ˌglorəfəˈkeʃən; ˌglɔːrɪfɪˈkeɪʃən/ *n*: **[+of]** *the glorification of war* 对战争的颂扬

glo·ri·ous /ˈglorɪəs; ˈglɔːriəs/ *adj* **1** having or deserving great fame, praise, and honour 辉煌的，光荣的，荣耀的: *It was a glorious political career while it lasted.* 在当时，那是一段光辉的政治生涯。| *a glorious victory* 光荣的胜利 **2** very beautiful, attractive, or impressive 壮丽的，吸引人的: *glorious colours* 灿烂的色彩 | *a glorious sight* 壮丽的景色 **3** extremely enjoyable; WONDERFUL 极其愉快的，极好的: *We spent three glorious weeks in Hawaii.* 我们在夏威夷度过了令人愉快的三周。**4 glorious day/summer/weather** weather etc that is very nice because it is sunny and clear 晴朗的一天/美好的夏季/宜人的天气 —**gloriously** *adv*

Glorious Rev·o·lu·tion, the /ˌ······ˈ··/ the time in British history (1688-89) when King James II was removed from power, and his daughter Mary and her husband William of Orange became joint rulers. It was also called the **Bloodless Revolution**. 光荣革命〔英国历史上 1688 年至 1689 年间，国王詹姆斯二世被废黜，其女儿玛丽和女婿奥兰治的威廉联合执政，又称"不流血革命"〕

Glorious Twelfth, the /ˌ··· ˈ·/ August 12th, the date when the season for the sport of shooting GROUSE begins 光荣 812〔8 月 12 日，指猎松鸡的季节开始的那一天〕

glo·ry[1] /ˈglorɪ; ˈglɔːri/ *n* **1** [U] the importance, honour, and praise that people give someone or something they admire a lot 光荣，荣誉: *As a child he dreamt of future glory as an Olympic champion.* 他小时候就梦想将来获得奥林匹克冠军的荣耀。| **covered in/with glory** *The team finished the season covered with glory.* 该队满载荣誉地结束了赛季。**2** [C] something that is especially beautiful, or makes you feel proud 极其漂亮的东

西; 荣耀的事, 值得骄傲的事: *the glories of Roman architecture* 罗马建筑的辉煌 | **crowning glory** (=the final completion of something successful) 至高无上的荣誉 *The Oscar was the crowning glory of her career.* 获得奥斯卡奖是她事业中的最高荣誉。**3** [U] a beautiful and impressive appearance 壮观; 辉煌: *After years of neglect the palace has been restored to its former glory.* 这座年久失修的宫殿现在又恢复了往日的辉煌。| **in all its/their etc glory** *Wild flowers in all their glory carpeted the meadow.* 野花盛开, 如地毯般把草坪铺满了。**4 bask/bathe in sb's reflected glory** to share some of the importance and praise that belongs to someone close to you 分享某人的荣誉, 沾某人的光 **5 Glory (be) to God/Jesus etc** *spoken* used to say that God deserves praise, honour, and thanks【口】荣耀归于上帝/耶稣等 **6 glory days** a time in the past when someone was admired 辉煌岁月: *his glory days on the high school football team* 他在高中足球队的威风日子 **7 to the (greater) glory of** *formal* in order to increase the honour that is given to someone or something【正式】为了(增加)…的荣耀: *Bach composed to the greater glory of God.* 巴赫为了增加上帝的荣耀而作曲。**8 go to glory** *old use* to die【旧】作古, 仙逝

glory² *v*

glory in sth *phr v* [T not in passive 不用被动态] to enjoy something very much such as praise or people's attention 因〔受到赞扬、引人注意〕而欣喜

gloss¹ /glɔs; glɒs/ *n* **1** [singular,U] shiny brightness on a surface〔表面的〕光泽, 光亮: *shoes shined to a high gloss* 擦得锃亮的鞋子 | *The gloss had gone from her dark hair.* 她的黑发已失去光泽。**2** [singular,U] a pleasant appearance of something, which is better than the truth 假象, 虚假的外表: *The General's image soon lost its gloss.* 将军的形象只是虚饰, 很快就给揭穿了。**3** [C] an explanation of a piece of writing, especially in a note at the end of a page or book 注释, 注解 **4 gloss finish/print** a surface or photograph that has been made shiny 光面〔照片等上光的表面〕—compare 比较 MATT

gloss² *v* [T] to provide an explanation of a piece of writing, especially in a note at the end of a page or book 注释, 注解

gloss over sth *phr v* [T] to deliberately avoid talking about unpleasant facts or say as little as possible about them 故意避免谈论〔不愉快的事情〕: *She glossed over the details of her divorce and changed the subject.* 她避免谈到她离婚的细节, 改变了话题。

glos·sa·ry /ˈglɑsəri; ˈglɒsəri/ *n* [C] a list of explanations of words, especially unusual ones, at the end of a book〔书末的〕词汇表

gloss paint /ˌ· ˈ·/ *n* [C,U] paint which looks shiny after it dries 有光涂料 —compare 比较 EMULSION (2)

gloss·y¹ /ˈglɔsi; ˈglɒsi/ *adj* **1** shiny and smooth 平滑而有光泽的, 光滑的: *the cat's glossy fur* 猫的光滑的毛 **2** *AmE* trying too hard to be attractive or perfect【美】虚饰的: *He may have glossy manners, but Gordon's no gentleman.* 戈登可能圆滑世故, 但他却不是正人君子。—**glossiness** *n* [U]

glossy² *n* [C] **1** *BrE* also 又作 **glossy magazine** a fashion magazine printed on good quality, shiny paper, usually with lots of colour pictures【英】〔用高级有光纸印刷的〕时尚杂志 **2** a photograph printed on shiny paper 光面照片〔指用有光纸印刷的彩色照片〕

glot·tal stop /ˌ·· ˈ·/ *n* [C] *technical* a speech sound made by completely closing and then opening your glottis, which in English may take the place of a /t/ between vowel sounds or may be used before a vowel sound【术语】喉塞音, 声门闭塞音

glot·tis /ˈglɑtɪs; ˈglɒtɪs/ *n* [C] the space between your VOCAL CORDS, which produce the sound of your voice by movements in which this space is opened and closed 声门 —**glottal** *adj* —see picture at 参见 RESPIRATORY 图

Glouces·ter /ˈglɑstɚ; ˈglɒstə/ a city in the west of England, on the River Severn. It has a famous CATHEDRAL (=an important church). 格洛斯特〔英格兰西部一城市, 濒临赛文河, 当地有一座著名教堂〕

Glouces·ter·shire /ˈglɑstɚʃɚ; ˈglɒstəʃə/ a COUNTY in the west of England, next to Wales. The Cotswolds, an area of beautiful hills and countryside, are in south and east Gloucestershire. 格洛斯特郡〔英格兰西部一郡, 毗邻威尔士。风景优美的科茨沃尔德区位于该郡的南部和东部〕

glove /glʌv; glʌv/ *n* [C] **1** a piece of clothing which covers your hand, especially one which has separate parts for each finger〔尤指有指〕手套 —compare 比较 MITTEN **2** a large leather glove used in BOXING 拳击手套 **3** a large leather glove used to catch the ball in BASEBALL 棒球手套 —see also 另见 **fit (sb) like a glove** (FIT¹ (1))

glove com·part·ment /ˈ· ·ˌ··/ also 又作 **glove box** /ˈ· ·/ *n* [C] a small shelf in a car in front of the passenger seat where small things such as maps can be kept〔汽车前排乘客座位前存放地图等小物件的〕贮物箱 —see picture on page A2 参见 A2 页图

gloved /glʌvd; glʌvd/ *adj* wearing a glove 戴手套的

glove pup·pet /ˈ· ˌ··/ *n* [C] a PUPPET (1) that you put over your hand 手套式木偶, 掌中木偶

glow¹ /glo; gləʊ/ *n* [singular] **1** a soft steady light, especially from something that is burning without flames〔尤指没有火焰的燃烧物发出的〕光亮, 光辉: *The glow from the dying fire lit his face.* 快要熄灭的火光照亮了他的脸。| *the glow of city lights on the horizon* 城市灯火在地平线上的亮光 **2** brightness of colour, especially colours like red and orange〔尤指红色和橙色的〕鲜艳: *the glow of copper pans hanging in the kitchen* 挂在厨房里的黄铜平底锅的亮光 **3** the bright colour your face or body has after exercise or when you are very pleased and excited〔运动后或兴奋时脸部或身体发出的〕红润光泽: *a healthy rosy glow in her cheeks* 她脸颊呈现的健康红润 **4 a glow of pleasure/satisfaction/happiness etc** a strong feeling of pleasure etc 强烈的愉快/满足/幸福等

glow² *v* [I] **1** to shine with a soft, steady light 发出柔和稳定的光: *We saw a lamp glowing in the garden.* 我们看见花园里有盏灯亮着。**2** to produce a red light and heat without flames〔无焰地〕发光生热: *His cigarette glowed in the dark.* 他的香烟在黑暗中发亮。**3** if your face or body glows, it is red or hot as a result of exercise or strong emotion〔由于运动或强烈情感〕面部[身体]发红[发热] **4 glow with pride/pleasure/triumph etc** to look very happy because you feel proud etc 由于自豪/愉快/胜利等容光焕发: *The boys emerged scrubbed and glowing with happiness.* 男孩子们洗得干干净净, 喜气洋洋地出现了。

glow·er /ˈglaʊɚ; ˈglaʊə/ *v* [I +at] to look angrily at someone 怒视 —**gloweringly** *adv*

glow·ing /ˈgloɪŋ; ˈgləʊɪŋ/ *adj* **1 glowing report/account/description etc** a report etc full of praise 热情赞扬的报告/叙述/描写等: *Her supervisor gave her a glowing reference.* 她的主管上司为她写了一封充满赞美的推荐信。**2 in glowing terms** using a lot of praise 以赞扬的词句: *He speaks of you in glowing terms.* 他总是以十分赞赏的口吻谈到你。—**glowingly** *adv*

glow-worm /ˈ· ·/ *n* [C] an insect which gives out light from its body 萤火虫

glu·cose /ˈglukos; ˈgluːkəʊs/ *n* [U] a natural form of sugar that exists in fruit 葡萄糖

glue¹ /glu; gluː/ *n* [C,U] a sticky substance used for joining things together 胶, 胶水

glue² *v present participle* **gluing** *or* **glueing** [T] **1** to join two things together using a special sticky substance 胶合, 黏合, 粘贴: **glue sth together** *I managed to glue the pieces back together.* 我把碎片又黏合起来了。**2 be glued to** *informal* to look at something with all your attention【非正式】盯着眼看; 审视: *Those kids are glued to the TV all day.* 那些孩子整天围着电视看。**3 glued to the spot** unable to move because you are very surprised, frightened, interested etc〔由于惊恐或极感兴趣而〕动弹不得的

glue-snif·fing /ˈ· ˌ··/ *n* [U] the habit of breathing in gases from glues or similar substances in order to produce an artificial state of excitement: SOLVENT ABUSE〔使人产生兴奋的〕吸胶毒 —**glue sniffer** *n* [C]

glue·y /ˈgluɪ; ˈgluːi/ *adj* **1** sticky like glue〔像胶一样〕有黏性的 **2** covered with glue 涂胶的

glum /glʌm; glʌm/ **glummer, glummest** *adj* sad and not talking much; GLOOMY 沉默寡言的; 忧郁的: *Hey, don't look so glum. Everything will be OK!* 嗨, 别闷闷不乐, 一切都会好的! —**glumly** *adv* —**glumness** *n* [U]

glut¹ /glʌt; glʌt/ *n* [C usually singular 一般用单数] a supply of something that is more than you need 供应过剩: [+of] *a glut of oil on the market* 市场上油的供应过剩

gloves 手套

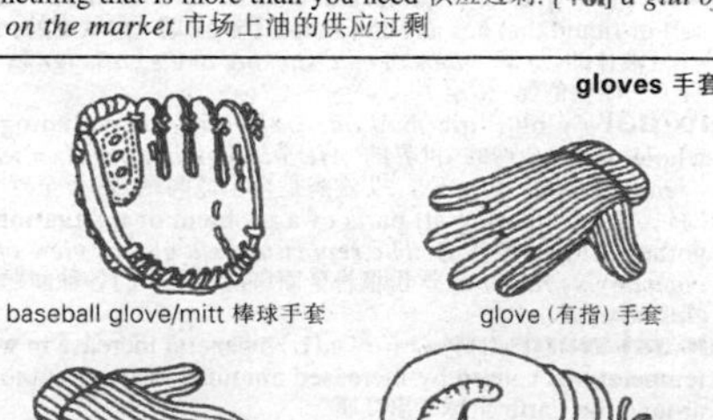

baseball glove/mitt 棒球手套　　glove (有指) 手套

mitten 连指手套

boxing glove 拳击手套

glut² *v* **glutted, glutting** [T] **1 be glutted with** to be supplied with too much of something …供应过剩; 充斥: *The shops are glutted with oranges.* 商店里的橙子供应过剩。**2 glut yourself on sth** to eat too much 过度地吃某物

glu·ten /ˈglutn̩; ˈgluːtn/ *n* [U] a sticky PROTEIN substance that is found in flour made of wheat 面筋, 麸筋

glu·ti·nous /ˈglutənəs; ˈgluːtɪnəs/ *adj* very sticky 很黏的, 黏性很大的

glut·ton /ˈglʌtn̩; ˈglʌtn/ *n* [C] **1** someone who eats too much 贪食者 **2 a glutton for punishment** someone who seems to enjoy working hard or doing something unpleasant 不辞劳苦[任劳任怨]的人 —**gluttonous** *adj* —**gluttonously** *adv*

glut·ton·y /ˈglʌtn̩ɪ; ˈglʌtəni/ *n* [U] *formal* the bad habit of eating and drinking too much【正式】暴食暴饮, 大吃大喝

gly·ce·rine /ˈglɪsərɪn; ˈglɪsərɪn/ *n* [U] a thick sweet transparent liquid made from fats and used in medicines, explosives, and foods 甘油, 丙三醇

Glynde·bourne /ˈglaɪndbɔrn; ˈglaɪndbɔːn/ a 16th-century country house in East Sussex in the south of England, famous for the **Glyndebourne Festival** that takes place there every year, when OPERAs are performed 格林德包恩庄园〔英格兰南部东萨塞克斯郡的一座16世纪的乡间别墅, 以每年在此举行的格林德包恩音乐节著称。音乐节期间, 这里上演歌剧〕

GM /ˌdʒi ˋɛm; ˌdʒiː ˈem/ **1** the abbreviation of 缩写= GENERAL MOTORS **2** the abbreviation of 缩写= GEORGE MEDAL

gm the written abbreviation of 缩写= GRAM

GMAT Graduate Management Admissions Test; a test that you take when you apply to study at a business school after you have finished your first degree 研究生管理学入学考试〔学生取得第一学位后申请在商学院学习研究生课程须参加的一种考试〕

GMC, the /ˌdʒi ɛm ˋsi; ˌdʒiː em ˈsiː/ the General Medical Council; the professional organization that all British doctors must be members of 医学委员会〔英国所有医生必须加入的一个专业团体〕

GMT /ˌdʒi ɛm ˋti; ˌdʒiː em ˈtiː/ *n* [U] Greenwich Mean Time; the time as measured at Greenwich in London, that is used as an international standard for measuring time 格林尼治标准时间

gnarled /narld; nɑːld/ *adj* **1** a gnarled tree or branch is rough and twisted with hard lumps〔树或树枝〕粗糙的; 扭曲的; 多节的 **2** gnarled hands or fingers are twisted, rough, and difficult to move, usually because they are old〔手或手指〕扭曲的; 粗糙的; 行动困难的

gnarl·y /ˈnarlɪ; ˈnɑːli/ *adj AmE slang*【美俚】**1** a word meaning very good or excellent, used by young people 很好的, 顶呱呱的〔年轻人用语〕: *"My mom said I can go out tonight!" "Gnarly, man! Let's go."* "我妈妈说今天晚上我可以出去!" "太好了, 伙计! 我们走吧。" **2** a word meaning not good enough, used by young people 不够好的〔年轻人用语〕

gnash /næʃ; næʃ/ *v* [T] **gnash your teeth** to move your teeth against each other so that they make a noise, especially because you are unhappy or angry〔不高兴或生气时〕咬牙切齿 —**gnash** *n* [C]

gnash·ers /ˈnæʃɚz; ˈnæʃəz/ *n* [plural] *BrE informal* teeth【英, 非正式】牙齿

gnat /næt; næt/ *n* [C] a small flying insect that bites〔会飞的〕叮人小虫

gnaw /nɔ; nɔː/ *v* [I always+adv/prep, T] to keep biting something hard 咬, 啃: [+away/at/on] *Val gnawed at her fingernails.* 瓦尔咬自己的手指甲。| **gnaw sth** *a dog gnawing a bone* 啃着骨头的狗 | **gnaw a hole in sth** *A rat had gnawed a hole in the box.* 老鼠在箱子上咬了一个洞。

gnaw at sb *phr v* [T] to make someone feel worried or frightened 使烦恼, 惊吓: *Something's gnawing at Celia – she's been very moody.* 有件事让西莉亚烦恼 —— 她心情很不好。

gnaw·ing /ˈnɔɪŋ; ˈnɔːɪŋ/ *adj* [only before noun 仅用于名词前] painful or worrying, especially only slightly but for a long time〔轻微但长时间〕令人痛苦的, 揪心的: *gnawing doubts about her own abilities* 怀疑自己的能力而令她揪心

gnome /nom; nəʊm/ *n* [C] **1** a creature in children's stories like a little old man with a pointed hat who lives under the ground and guards gold, jewels etc〔儿童故事里地下守护金子、珠宝等的〕土地神 **2** a stone or plastic figure representing one of these creatures 土地神石像[塑像]: *a garden gnome* 花园土地神石像

gno·mic /ˈnomɪk; ˈnəʊmɪk/ *adj* gnomic remarks are short, clever, and difficult to understand〔言论〕简短慧黠而晦涩的: *gnomic predictions about the future of the economy* 对未来经济精奥的预测 —**gnomically** /-klɪ; -kli/ *adv*

Gnos·tic Gos·pels, the /ˌnastɪk ˋgaspl̩z; ˌnɒstɪk ˈgɒspəlz/ ancient writings which some people believe had once been part of the Bible, and were taken out by early priests who disagreed with their messages 诺斯替教福音书〔古代作品。有人认为它们曾是《圣经》的一部分, 后因早期的神职人员不认同其要旨才删除的〕

GNP /ˌdʒi ɛn ˋpi; ˌdʒiː en ˈpiː/ *n* [singular] Gross National Product; the total value of all the goods and services produced in a country, usually in a single year 国民生产总值

gnu /nu; nuː/ *n* [C] a large southern African animal with a tail and curved horns; WILDEBEEST〔南非的〕牛羚

go 去, 走

Nick's gone to Pairs for the weekend.
尼克去巴黎度周末。

Derek's been to Paris three times.
德里克去过巴黎三次。

G

go¹ /go; gəʊ/ *v past tense* **went** /wɛnt; went/ *past participle* **gone** /gɔn; gɒn/ *3rd person singular present tense* **goes** /goz; gəʊz/

① TO MOVE AWAY FROM THE SPEAKER 离开说话人
② TO BE IN OR PASS INTO A PARTICULAR STATE 处于或进入某种状态
③ TO START TO DO SOMETHING OR TO DO SOMETHING 开始做某事或做某事
④ POSITION 位置
⑤ SOUND 声音
⑥ TO FINISH OR STOP 完成或结束
⑦ OTHER MEANINGS 其他意思

① **TO MOVE AWAY FROM THE SPEAKER** 离开说话人
1 ▶LEAVE SOMEWHERE 离开某地◀ [I] to leave a place to go somewhere else; DEPART 离去; 离开: *I wanted to go, but Anna wanted to stay.* 我想走, 但安娜想留下来。| *It's late; I must be*

going. 时候不早了，我该走了。| *What time does the last train go?* 最后一趟火车什么时候离开？| *The doctor hasn't gone yet.* 医生还没走。

2 go and do sth to go somewhere in order to do something 去做某事：*I'll just go and get my coat.* 我去拿一下我的大衣。| *It's time you went and saw the doctor.* 是你去看医生的时候了。

3 ▶VISIT 去◀ *past participle* 过去分词 also 又作 **been** [I] to visit a place or go to a place and then leave it 去：*Nancy has gone to Paris.* (=she is in Paris now) 南希去巴黎了。| *Nancy has been to Paris.* (=she has visited Paris in the past) 南希去过巴黎。| *The doctor hasn't been here yet.* 医生还没有来过。—see 见 VISIT¹ (USAGE)

4 ▶MOVE/TRAVEL 移动/旅行◀ [I always+adv/prep] to travel or move in a particular way, in a particular direction or a particular distance 行走；旅行：**[+by/up/to etc]** *We went by bus.* 我们是乘公共汽车去的。| *I want to go home.* 我想回家。| *Where are you going?* 你要去哪儿？| *They all went away and left me alone.* 他们都走了，留下我一个人。| **be going somewhere** (=intend to go somewhere) 打算去某地 *We're going to my parents' for Christmas.* 我们打算去我父母家过圣诞节。| **go to hospital/prison etc** (=go to hospital in order to get medical treatment, to prison as a punishment etc) 上医院/坐牢等

5 go for sth to go somewhere in order to take part in a particular activity 去参加某种活动：*Let's go for a swim before lunch.* 我们午餐前去游泳吧。

6 go shopping/swimming/fishing etc to go somewhere in order to visit the shops, swim etc 去购物/游泳/钓鱼等：*Dinah's gone skiing in Aspen.* 黛娜到阿斯彭滑雪去了。

7 go flying/laughing etc *spoken* to move in a particular way or to do something as you are moving【口】去飞行/一面走一面笑等：*The plate went crashing to the floor.* 那个盘子"砰"地掉在地板上摔碎了。

8 ▶BE SENT 送出，寄出◀ [I] to be sent or passed on 被寄出，被传递：*Make sure this package goes tonight.* 要保证这包裹今晚就寄出去。| **[+by/through/to etc]** *That letter should go by special delivery.* 那封信应该用特种快递寄出。| *Complaints must go through the proper channels.* 投诉必须通过适当的渠道。| **go before a board/committee etc** *Your suggestion will go before the committee next week.* 你的建议将于下星期提交委员会。

G

② TO BE IN OR PASS INTO A PARTICULAR STATE 处于或进入某种状态

9 ▶BECOME 变为◀ [linking verb 连系动词] to become something different and often not so good, either naturally or by changing deliberately〔自然或人为地〕变〔坏，糟〕：*The company went bankrupt last year.* 该公司去年破产了。| **go bad/sour etc** *The milk went sour.* 牛奶变酸了。| **go grey/white etc** *Jessica went bright red with shame.* 杰西卡羞得满脸通红。| **go mad/deaf/bald etc** *I think you're going crazy.* 我想你发疯了。| **go wild/mad/white etc with sth** *The crowd was going wild with excitement.* 人群激动得发狂。—see 见 BECOME (USAGE)

10 ▶BE IN A PARTICULAR STATE 处于某种状态◀ [linking verb 连系动词] to be or remain in a particular, usually bad, state 处于〔某种状态，通常指不好的状态〕：*All her complaints went unheard.* 她的一切抱怨都没人理睬。| *After these attacks he went in fear of his life.* 这些攻击之后他便为自己的生命安全担忧。| **go hungry** (=have nothing to eat) 挨饿 *When food is short it's often the mother who goes hungry.* 食物短缺时，挨饿的常常是母亲。

③ TO START TO DO SOMETHING OR TO DO SOMETHING 开始做某事或做某事

11 ▶START STH 开始某事◀ [I] to start doing something 开始：*The signal to begin a race is 'Ready, get set, go!'* 赛跑的起跑信号是"各就各位，预备，跑！"| *The preparations have been completed and we're ready to go.* 预备工作已经完成，我们准备开始。| **get going (on sth)** *You'd better get going on this contract if you want to finish on time.* 如果你想按时完成，最好开始执行合同。

12 ▶OPERATE 运转◀ [I] if a machine goes it works properly 运转，运行：*My watch isn't going.* 我的手表不走了。

13 go to church/school etc to regularly attend church, school etc 去做礼拜/上学等：*Joey's too young to go to Cubs.* 乔伊年纪太小，不能参加幼年童子军。| *Iain didn't go to university.* 伊恩没有上大学。—see graph at 参见 ATTEND 图表 —see 见 JOIN¹ (USAGE)

14 ▶HAPPEN 发生◀ [I always+adv/prep] to happen or develop in a particular way 发生，进展：**go well/smoothly/swimmingly etc** *The party went well.* 聚会开得很好。| *Everything's going fine at the moment.* 目前一切进展顺利。| **how are things going/how's it going/how goes it?** *How are things going at school, Joanna?* 在学校学习情况怎样，乔安娜？| **the way things are going** (=used before you give your opinion of what is going to happen next) 看目前的情况〔用在表达自己的意见之前〕*The way things are going, we're going to miss the bus.* 看目前的情况，我们会搭不上公共汽车。

15 be going to do sth a) to intend to do something 打算做某事：*Wendi's going to ring us from the station.* 温迪打算从车站给我们打电话。**b)** to be certain or expected to happen in the future 将要[就要；预期]做某事：*Do you think it's going to rain?* 你认为会下雨吗？—see also 另见 GONNA

16 ▶MAKE A MOVEMENT 做动作◀ [I always +adv/prep] to make a particular movement 做某种动作：**[+like/up/down etc]** *While he was describing her, he went like this with his hands.* 他在描述她时，用手这样比画。

17 don't go doing sth *spoken* used to tell someone not to do something, especially something that is wrong or bad【口】不要做某事〔用来告诫某人不要做某事，尤指错事、坏事〕：*It's a secret, so don't go telling everyone.* 这是秘密，所以不要告诉任何人。

18 have gone and done sth *spoken* used when you are surprised by what someone has done【口】居然做了某事，真的做了某事〔用来对某人所做的事表示惊讶〕：*Kay's gone and lost the car keys!* 凯真的把车钥匙丢了！| **have gone and done it** (=have really made a big mistake) 确实犯了大错误[做了大错事] *Tom's really gone and done it this time.* 汤姆这次确实做了大错事。

19 go it alone to do something, especially start a business, alone 独自干，单干〔尤指开办企业〕：*Hamish decided to go it alone and set up his own company.* 哈米什决定单干，自己开公司。

20 go one better to do something better than someone else had done it, or get something better than they have 做得比…要好；得到的比…好：*We went one better and got a colour printer.* 我们更胜一筹，获得一台彩色打印机。

21 go far to succeed in whatever you choose to do 大有前途；事事成功：*Ginny's a smart girl, and I'm sure she'll go far.* 金尼是个聪明的女孩，我肯定她大有前途。

22 go too far to go beyond the limits of what is reasonable or acceptable 太过分：*I think he went too far when he called you a fat idiot!* 他叫你大胖白痴，我认为他这样做太过分了。

23 go do sth *spoken* used to tell someone to go away when you are angry【口】滚〔生气时用来叫某人走开〕：*Go jump in the lake!* 滚开，去投湖吧！

24 here goes/here we go *spoken* used just before you do something that is exciting, dangerous etc【口】我这就开始了〔在马上就开始做刺激或危险的活动前说的话〕：*Well, here goes. Wish me luck!* 好吧，这就开始。祝我好运吧！

④ POSITION 位置

25 ▶BE PLACED 被放置◀ [I always+adv/prep, not in progressive 不用进行时] if something goes somewhere, that is its usual position 放，摆〔指摆放在通常位置〕：**[+in/under/on etc]** *Where do these plates go?* 这些盘子该放在什么地方？| *The sofa can go against the wall.* 这张沙发可靠墙放。

26 ▶FIT 适配◀ [I not in progressive 不用进行时] to fit or be contained in something 容纳，装下：*All that food won't go in this little cupboard.* 这个小食品橱装不下所有的食品。

27 ▶COLOUR 颜色◀ [I] if two colours go, they look good together 匹配，相称，和谐：*Pink and orange don't go.* 粉红色和橙黄色不相配。

28 ▶DIVIDE 除◀ [I not in progressive 不用进行时] to divide a number, especially so as to get a whole number in the answer 除〔尤指整除〕：*Three into two won't go.* 3除2除不尽。| **go into** *Two goes into ten five times.* 10除以2得5。

⑤ SOUND 声音

29 ▶SONG/STORY 歌曲/故事◀ [I always+adv/prep, T, not in progressive 不用进行时] to be said or sung in a particular way 说；唱；据传：*How does the story go?* 故事是怎么讲的？| *The tune goes something like this.* 曲调大概是这样的。| **go that** *The story goes that he was poisoned by his wife.* 据说他被妻子毒死了。

30 ▶MAKE A SOUND 发出声音◀ [T] to make a particular sound 发出〔某种声音〕：*Ducks go 'Quack'.* 鸭子的叫声是"嘎嘎"。| *The cannon suddenly went boom.* 大炮突然轰隆作响。

31 **▶WHISTLE/BELL 鸣笛/响铃◀** [I] to make a noise as a warning or signal 响, 鸣〔作为警告或信号〕: *A bell goes to mark the end of each class.* 每堂课结束时以铃响表示。
32 **▶SAY 说◀** [T] *spoken* to say something【口】说: *She goes to me: "I hope you've got a licence for that thing!"* 她对我说: "我希望你已给那玩意领了个执照!"
33 **here/there sb goes again** *spoken* used when someone has annoyed you by continuing to do something they know you do not like【口】某人又来了〔表示某人又在做你所不喜欢的事而让你生气〕: *There she goes again – complaining about the way things are run around here.* 她又来了 —— 抱怨这里的管理方式。

⑥ TO FINISH OR STOP 完成或结束
34 **▶DISAPPEAR 消失◀** [I] to no longer exist; disappear 消失: *Has your headache gone yet?* 你头痛好了吗? | *My pen's gone; who's taken it?* 我的笔不见了。谁把它拿走了?
35 **have to/must/can go** if someone or something has to go, you have to get rid of them 不得不/必须/可以去掉: *That secretary will have to go; she can't even type.* 那位秘书必须走, 她连打字都不会。
36 **▶GET WORSE 每况愈下◀** [I] to get worse or be lost altogether 每况愈下; 完全丢失: *Dad's sight is starting to go.* 爸爸的视力开始每况愈下。
37 **▶DIE 死◀** [I] used to mean to die when you do not want to say this directly 没了, 走了〔指人死, 婉辞说法〕: *Now that his wife's gone, he's all on his own.* 他的妻子没了, 他一切都要靠自己。| **dead and gone** (=dead) 去世的
38 **▶BECOME DAMAGED 损坏◀** [I] to become weak, damaged etc or stop working properly 变得不如从前; 损坏; 停止正常运转: *My old sweater had started to go at the elbows.* 我的旧运动衫肘部已经开始磨损了。| *The bulb's gone in the bathroom.* 浴室的灯泡坏了。
39 **▶BE SPENT 被花掉◀** [I] to be spent or used up 被花掉, 用完: *I don't know where all my money goes!* 我不知道我所有的钱花到哪里去了! | **[+on]** *Half her salary goes on the rent.* 她工资的一半花在房租上。| **not go far** *$20 doesn't go far these days.* 如今20美元很不经用。
40 **▶BE SOLD 被卖掉◀** [I] to be sold 卖掉: **go for sth** *That lovely house went for £30,000.* 那栋漂亮的房子卖了30,000英镑。| **go to sb** *Each lot will go to the highest bidder.* 每件货品都将卖给出价最高的人。| **Going, going, gone** (=used to say something has been sold) 要卖了, 要卖了, 成交〔用来宣布某物成交〕 *"Any more bids?" said the auctioneer; "Going ... going ... gone – to the man in the grey hat."* "还有人出价吗?"拍卖人说道, "要卖了…要卖了…成交 —— 买主是戴灰色帽子的那位男士。" | **be going cheap** (=not cost very much) 廉价出售 *I bought some mugs because they were going cheap.* 我买了几个大杯子, 因为它们都卖得很便宜。
41 **▶TIME 时间◀** [I always+adv/prep] to pass〔时间〕消逝: **[+slowly/quickly etc]** *The summer is going fast.* 夏天正飞快地过去。
42 **there goes sth** *spoken* used to show your disappointment when something stops you doing what you wanted to do【口】…消失了〔用来对不能做到你所想做的事表示失望〕: *Well, there goes my chance of stardom!* 哎, 我成为明星的机会没了。

⑦ OTHER MEANINGS 其他意思
43 **▶REACH 到达◀** [I always+adv/prep, not in progressive 不用进行时] to reach as far as is stated 到达, 通往: **[+to/from/down etc]** *Does this road go to the station?* 这条路通往车站吗? | *The valley goes from east to west.* 这个山谷呈东西走向。| *This belt won't go around my waist.* 这条皮带不够我的腰围。
44 **what sb says goes** *informal* someone is in authority and other people must do as they say【非正式】某人的话必须照办: *You might not like it, but Phil's in charge, and what he says goes.* 你可能不喜欢, 但菲尔管事, 他说了就必须照办。
45 **anything goes** used to say that anything someone says or does is acceptable 什么都行: *With this season's fashions, anything goes.* 就这个季节的时装来说, 什么样式都可以。
46 **▶HELP 帮助◀** [I] to help to make, prove, or show something 有助于: *Which qualities go to make a good teacher?* 当个好教师要有哪些素质? | **go to show** *It just goes to show, you never know what's going to happen next.* 这只是有助于说明, 你无法知道下一步会发生什么。
47 **be going** *informal* to be available to be used【非正式】可资利用的, 现成的: *Are there any jobs going in your firm?* 你们公司目前有现成职位吗? | **be going spare** *I'll have that cupcake if it's going spare.* 那块纸杯蛋糕要是没有人吃, 我就把它吃了。
48 **to go a)** still remaining before something happens 离…还剩下〔若干时间〕: *Only ten days to go to Christmas!* 离圣诞节只剩10天了! **b)** still to be dealt with before you have finished what you are doing〔在完成之前〕还要做: *Laura's sat six exams and has two more to go.* 劳拉已参加了六次考试, 还要参加两次。**c)** still to travel before you reach the place you are going to〔到达目的地之前〕还要走: *Only another five miles left to go.* 再走5英里就到了。**d)** *AmE* if you buy food from a restaurant to go, you buy it to take away and eat at home or somewhere else【美】带到餐馆外吃的, 外带的: *Two chicken dinners with corn to go.* 两份外带的鸡肉餐加玉米。—compare 比较 TAKE-OUT (1)
49 **as someone/something goes** compared with the average person or thing of that type 就某类人/事情而言: *He's not bad, as politicians go.* 就一般政治家而言, 他不算差了。| **as things go** *£100,000 for a four-bedroomed house isn't bad as things go these days.* 就现在的一般情况来说, 10万英镑买一座四间卧室的房子算不错了。
50 **there you go** *spoken* used to say that something that has happened cannot be changed or was what you expected【口】事已至此; 事情正如你所料: *Well, there you go, better luck next time.* 嗯, 事情已无法改变, 祝你下次好运。
51 **churchgoer/theatregoer etc** someone who regularly goes to church, the theatre etc 经常去做礼拜的人/看戏的人等
52 **theatregoing/churchgoing etc** the act of regularly going to the theatre, to church etc 经常去看戏/做礼拜等
53 **go it** *BrE old-fashioned*【英, 过时】**a)** to go very fast 快速行进 **b)** to behave very excitedly or carelessly 举止失措; 轻率 —see also 另见 GOING[1], GOING[2], GONE[2], GONE[3], **as far as it goes** (FAR[1] (18)), **go as far as to do sth** (FAR[1] (26)), **go halves on (sth)** (HALF[2] (12))

go about *phr v* **1** [T **go about** sth] also 又作 **set about** to begin working at something; TACKLE[1] (1) 着手〔做某事〕: *I don't know what is the best way to go about it.* 我不知道着手做此事最好的方法是什么。| **go about doing sth** *I wouldn't have the faintest idea how to go about writing a novel.* 我一点也不懂怎样着手写一本小说。**2** [T **go about** sth] to do something that you usually do 从事〔日常事务〕: *The townspeople were going about their business as usual.* 市民与平时一样都在忙着各自的事情。**3** [I] *BrE* if a ship goes about, it turns to go in the opposite direction【英】〔船〕调头行驶 **4 go about with sb** to go around with someone 常与某人结伴外出

go after sth/sb *phr v* [T not in passive 不用被动态] to try to get or catch something or someone 追逐, 追求: *I've decided to go after that job in Ohio.* 我已经决定要把俄亥俄州那份工作争取到手。

go against sb/sth *phr v* [T not in passive 不用被动态] **1** if you go against someone's wishes or ideas, you do the opposite of what they want 违背: *She went against her counsel's advice.* 她没有照律师给她的忠告去做。**2** if a decision, judgment etc goes against you, it is unfavourable to you and you lose 对…不利: *José's lawyer intimated the case might go against him.* 何塞的律师暗示他可能败诉。| *The vote went against the government.* 政府在这次表决中失利。**3** to not be in agreement with something 与…相反, 与…不符: *Such ideas went against his Calvinist upbringing.* 这些想法与他清教主义的教养格格不入。| **go against the grain** (=be hard for someone to do because it does not agree with their beliefs, ideas etc until then) 违反(某人的)信念[思想等] *It just went against the grain for men to salute a woman officer.* 过去男子不愿意向女军官敬礼。

go ahead *phr v* [I] **1** to begin 开始: *Go ahead, we're all listening.* 开始吧, 我们都在听着。| *"Do you mind if I smoke?" "No, go right ahead."* "我吸烟你介意吗?" "不, 请吧。" | **go ahead with (doing) sth** *Their solicitor is asking if you want to go ahead with the deal?* 他们的律师问你是否打算把这笔交易进行下去。| **go ahead and do sth** *The newspaper decided to go ahead and publish the story.* 这家报纸决定发表这篇报道。**2** also 又作 **go on ahead** to go somewhere before the other people in your group 先走, 先行: *You go ahead and we'll catch you up later.* 你先走, 我们随后就赶上来。| **go ahead of sb** *Kemp went ahead of the convoy to take a look.* 肯普比护送车队先走一步去看看情况。**3** to take place 发生, 举行: *The sale went ahead as planned.* 大减价按计划举行。—see also 另见 GO-AHEAD[1]

go along *phr v* [I] to continue with a plan, activity etc 继续进行〔某计划、活动〕: *I'm sure she was making her speech up as she went along.* 我确信她是一面讲, 一面编下面讲什么。

go along with sb/sth *phr v* [T] **1** to agree with or support someone or something 同意, 赞成, 支持: *They were happy to*

go along with our suggestions. 他们乐意支持我们的建议。| **not go along with sth** *informal* (=disapprove of particular behaviour or ideas)【非正式】不同意,不赞成,反对 **2 go along with you!** *BrE informal* used to say that you do not believe what someone is saying to you【英,非正式】我不信!

go around also 又作 **go round** *phr v* **1 go around doing sth** if you go around doing something, especially something people do not approve of, you often do it 经常做某事〔尤指人们不赞同的事〕: *You can't go around accusing people like that.* 你不能老是那样指责人。**2** [I,T **go around** sth] to usually dress or behave in a particular way 通常穿着; 习惯于: *She often goes around the house naked.* 她常常在屋子里一丝不挂到处走动。| **go around with your eyes shut** (=not notice what is happening around you) 不注意周围发生的事 **3** [I,T, usually in progressive 一般用进行时] if an illness, some news etc is going around it is being passed from one person to another〔疾病、消息〕流传,传播: *There's a rumor going around that Eddie's broke.* 传说埃迪破产了。| **go around the school/office etc** *A new flu bug's going around the office.* 一种新的感冒病毒在办公室传播。**4 go around with sb/go around together** also 又作 **go about** to often go out with someone 常与某人外出/常一起外出: *I used to go around with a really bad crowd.* 我过去常与一群坏人一起在外面鬼混。**5** [I] to be enough for everyone to have some 足够分配: *Is there enough ice-cream to go around?* 冰淇淋够吃吗? | *There were never enough textbooks to go around.* 课本总是不够。**6** [I] to move in a circular way 转动,旋转: *The wheels went around faster and faster.* 轮子转得越来越快。| **go around and around** (=go round in a circular way many times) 不停旋转 —see also 另见 **go around in circles** (CIRCLE¹ (6)) **7 what goes around comes around** an expression meaning that your chance will come again if you are patient 只要有耐心,机会将再来

go at sth/sb *phr v* [T not in passive 不用被动态] *informal*【非正式】**1** to start to do something with a lot of energy; TACKLE¹ (1) 开始卖力干: *Harry went at the problem like a bull at a barn door.* 哈里干劲十足地着手解决这个问题。**2** to attack someone or start to fight 攻击,打击: *The two girls went at each other like animals.* 那两个女孩子像动物一样拼命厮打起来。| **go at it** *The boxers went at it until officials pulled them apart.* 拳击运动员拳来拳往,直到裁判们把他们拉开才停下来。

go away *phr v* [I] **1** to leave a place or a person 离开,走开: *Go away! Leave me alone!* 走开!别管我! **2** to spend some time somewhere else, especially on holiday 外出〔度假〕: *Are you going away this year?* 你今年外出度假吗? **3** if a problem, unpleasant feeling etc goes away, it disappears〔问题、不愉快的感觉等〕消失: *His stutter went away once his mother was home.* 他妈妈一回家,他的口吃就消失了。

go back *phr v* [I] **1** to return to a place you have been to before or to something you were doing before 返回; 回复: *I think we ought to go back now.* 我想我们现在应该回去了。| *Once you've made the decision I'm afraid there's no going back.* 你一旦作了决定恐怕就不能反悔。| **go back for sth** (=go back to get something) 回去取某物 *I had to go back for my passport.* 我只好回去拿护照。| **go back to (doing) sth** *Melissa's decided to go back to teaching now Timmy's at school.* 既然蒂米已经开始上学,梅利莎决定回去教书。| **go back out/inside/downstairs etc** *It's cold out here – let's go back into the kitchen.* 外面很冷——我们回厨房吧。**2** [always+adv/prep] to have been made, built, or started at some time in the past 追溯: *The old dairy goes back to Tudor times.* 这座古老的乳品店可追溯到都铎王朝时代。

go back on sth *phr v* [T] to break or not succeed in keeping to an agreement or promise 违背〔约定、承诺〕: **go back on your word/promise etc** *You can rely on Sarah; she won't go back on her word.* 你可以信赖萨拉,她不会食言的。

go by *phr v* **1** [I] to pass〔时间〕过去: *Two years went by.* 两年过去了。| *Never let a good opportunity go by.* 决不要放过一次好机会。**2** [T not in passive 不用被动态 **go by** sth] to use the information or advice you get from a person, a book, a set of rules etc 依据,遵循: *Don't go by that old map; it's out of date.* 别使用那张旧地图,它已经过时了。| **go by the book** (=obey rules very strictly) 严格遵守规则 **3** [T not in passive 不用被动态 **go by** sth] to form an opinion or judgment of someone or something from something else 根据…作判断: *You can't always go by appearances.* 你不能总是以外表来判断。

go down *phr v* [I]

1 ►GO DOWNSTAIRS 下楼◄ to go to a lower floor of a building 下楼: *We went down for dinner at nine o'clock.* 我们9点下楼吃晚餐。| *The elevator was going down.* 电梯正在往下走。

2 ►BECOME LOWER 变低◄ to not be so expensive, high etc 降低,下降: *Your temperature seems to be going down.* 你的体温似乎在下降。| *Tomatoes have gone down.* (=they cost less than before) 番茄降价了。

3 ►STANDARD 标准◄ if something goes down, its quality or standard gets worse〔质量、标准〕降低,下降: *This neighbourhood has really gone down in the last few years.* (=more poor people have moved there) 这个街区最近几年居民的经济情况下降了不少。| **go down in sb's opinion/estimation** (=respect someone less) 对某人的评价下降 *Fiona's gone down in my estimation since I found out her political views.* 我知道了菲奥娜的政治观点后,对她的评价已经下降。

4 go down well/badly etc to get a particular sort of reaction from someone 反应很好/不佳等: *Matt's joke went down like a lead balloon.* 马特讲的笑话人家反应冷淡。

5 ►SINK 下沉◄ to disappear from sight or below a surface 消失,沉没: *Ten men died when the ship went down.* 船沉没时有10人死亡。| *The sun was going down behind the mountains.* 太阳正在落山。

6 ►BECOME FLATTER 变得更平◄ to become less swollen or lose air 消肿; 瘪下: *The swelling will go down if you rest your foot.* 如果让你的脚休息休息,肿块就会消退。

7 ►FOOD/DRINK 食品/饮料◄ to pass down your throat 被咽下,被吞下: *I couldn't get the pill to go down.* 我无法把药丸吞下去。| *That meringue went down very nicely.* 那种蛋白酥很顺溜就吃下去了。

8 ►BE REMEMBERED 被记住◄ [always+adv/prep] to be recorded or remembered in a particular way 被记录下来; 被记住: [**+as/in**] *The talks went down as a landmark in the peace process.* 会谈作为和平进程的里程碑名垂后世。| **go down in history** (=be remembered for many years) 载入史册 *Her work will go down in history.* 她的业绩将载入史册。

9 ►REACH 到达◄ [always+adv/prep] to reach as far as a particular place 到达,延伸到: *Some steps went down to the beach.* 有些台阶一直延伸到海滩。

10 ►GO SOUTH 往南去◄ to go further south in a country or go from a city to somewhere less important 往南去; 从城市到小地方: [**+to**] *We're going down to the country for the weekend.* 我们打算去乡下过周末。

11 ►SPORT 体育运动◄ **a)** to lose a match or competition 输了〔一场比赛或竞赛〕: *Chang went down to Sampras in the third set.* 张德培在第三盘输给了桑普拉斯。**b)** to move down to a lower position in an official list of teams or players〔在运动队或运动员的正式排名中〕降级: [**+to**] *United went down to the second division.* 联队降为了乙级队。

12 ►COMPUTER 电脑◄ to stop working for a short time 暂停运转,死机: *Overloading caused all the computers to go down.* 过载使所有的电脑都死机。

13 go down on your knees to bend your body so that your knees are on the ground, supporting your weight 下跪: *Nick went down on one knee to ask her to marry him.* 尼克单腿跪下向她求婚。

14 go down on all fours to bend your body so that your knees and your hands are on the ground, supporting your weight 匍匐,趴下

15 ►LIGHTS 灯◄ *literary* if lights go down, they become less bright【文】〔灯光〕暗下来: *The lights went down and the curtain rose on an empty stage.* 灯暗下来,帷幕开启,现出空荡的舞台。

16 ►FROM UNIVERSITY 从大学◄ *BrE* to leave a university after doing a degree or at the end of each TERM¹ (9)【英】〔获得学位后或学期末〕离开大学: [**+from**] *Emily went down from Oxford with a first class degree.* 埃米莉以一等学位从牛津大学毕业。

17 ►TO PRISON 进监狱◄ *slang* to be sent to prison【俚】入狱: *Bert went down for five years.* 伯特被判五年监禁。

go down with sth *phr v* [T not in passive 不用被动态] *informal* to become ill, especially with an infectious disease【非正式】感染上〔传染病〕: *The children have gone down with mumps.* 孩子们染上了腮腺炎。

go for sb/sth *phr v* [T not in passive 不用被动态] **1** to attack someone physically or with words 攻击; 抨击: *Lorna really went for me when I disagreed.* 我表示不同意时洛娜竟动手打我。**2** to try to get or win something 争取得到,争取赢得: *Oona's going for that job in sales.* 乌娜正争取得到那份销售工作。| *Jackson is going for his second gold medal here.* 杰克逊正在争取他在这里的第二块金牌。| **go for it** *informal* (=do everything you can to get something)【非正式】尽力争取 *If you really want the*

job, go for it! 如果你真的想要那份工作，就努力争取吧！—see also 另见 **go for broke** (BROKE² (3)) **3** to choose or take something 挑选；拿：*In a small garden, go for dwarf varieties to maximize space.* 在小花园，要选择矮生品种以尽量利用空间。**4** *informal* to like something or find something or someone attractive【非正式】喜欢；觉得…吸引人：*Annie tends to go for older men.* 安妮喜欢年纪较大的男人。**5** *spoken* to also be true about someone or something else【口】对…也适用：*I told him to work harder, and that goes for you, too.* (=you have to work harder, too) 我告诉他工作努力些，这句话对你也适用。**6** to be sold for a particular price 卖得〔某价钱〕：*How much did that Alpha Romeo go for?* 那辆阿尔法·罗密欧卖了多少钱？**7 go for nothing** to be wasted 白费：*All that hard work went for nothing when the project was dropped.* 项目被终止了，所有的艰苦工作全都白费。—see also 另见 **have a lot going for you/not have much going for you** (GOING² (4))

go in *phr v* [I] **1** to enter a building 进入户内：*Dad wants me to go in before it gets dark.* 父亲要我在天黑前进屋。**2** when the sun or the moon goes in, it becomes covered with cloud〔日、月〕被云遮住 **3** to join someone in order to start a business etc 加入〔共同办企业〕：**[+with]** *They want me to go in with them on the new venture.* 他们要我和他们一起搞这个新企业。

go in for sth *phr v* [T] **1** to do an exam or take part in a competition 参加〔考试、竞赛〕：*Are you going in for the Proficiency exam?* 你打算参加水平考试吗？**2** to like something or do something often because you enjoy it 喜欢，爱好：*I don't go in for garden gnomes.* 我不喜欢花园土地神塑像。| **go in for doing sth** *Maggie goes in for improving her mind.* 玛吉致力于提高自己的智力。**3** to choose something as your job 从事〔某种工作〕：*Have you thought of going in for nursing?* 你考虑过从事护理工作吗？

go into sth *phr v* [T]

1 ►JOB 工作◄ [not in passive 不用被动态] to enter a particular profession or business 从事〔某职业〕，进入〔某行业〕：*Sophie wants to go into the army.* 索菲想参军。| **go into partnership** *Frank's going into partnership with a friend.* 弗兰克打算与一个朋友合伙。

2 ►TIME/MONEY/EFFORT 时间/钱/力气◄ [not in passive 不用被动态] to be spent or used to get, make, or do something 用在：*Years of research have gone into this book.* 写这本书时花了许多年做研究。

3 ►EXPLAIN/DESCRIBE 解释/描述◄ to explain or describe something in detail 详细解释；详细描述：*I don't want to go into the matter now.* 我现在不想详细解释这件事。| **go into details** *Clare wouldn't go into details about her problems.* 克莱尔不愿详细说明她的问题。

4 ►CONSIDER 考虑◄ to examine something thoroughly 彻底调查；深究：*My broker is going into the question of long-term cover.* 我的经纪人正深入调查长期保险问题。

5 ►HIT 碰撞◄ [not in passive 不用被动态] if a vehicle goes into a tree, wall, or another vehicle, it hits it〔车等〕撞在…上：*His car went into a lamppost in the high street.* 他的车子撞在大街的一个路灯柱上了。

6 ►DIVIDE 除◄ [not in passive 不用被动态] *informal* if a number goes into another number, the second number can be divided by the first【非正式】可整除：*12 goes into 60 five times.* 12除60得5。

7 ►BEGIN A MOVEMENT 开始动作◄ [not in passive 不用被动态] if a vehicle or its driver goes into a particular movement, it starts to do it〔车辆、驾驶员等〕开始做〔某种动作〕：*The plane had gone into a nosedive and crashed.* 飞机开始垂直俯冲，然后坠毁。

8 ►SPEECH 演说◄ [not in passive 不用被动态] to begin a long speech, often when it is not necessary 开始〔冗长的演说〕：*Norman went into a long monologue about crime.* 诺曼开始一个人滔滔不绝地谈论起犯罪问题来。

go off *phr v*

1 ►EXPLODE 爆炸◄ [I] to explode 爆炸：*The bomb went off at 6.30 this morning.* 炸弹在上午6时30分爆炸。

2 ►MAKE A NOISE 发出响声◄ [I] to make a loud noise 发出巨响：*Our neighbor's car alarm is always going off in the middle of the night.* 我们邻居汽车的报警器总是在半夜响起来。

3 ►STOP WORKING 停止工作◄ [I] if a machine goes off, it stops working 停止运转：*The central heating goes off at 9 o'clock.* 中央供暖系统9点钟停开。| *Suddenly, all the lights went off.* 突然所有的灯都熄灭了。

4 go off well/badly etc to happen in a particular way 进展很好/很糟糕等：*The party went off swimmingly.* 聚会开得很顺利。

5 ►FOOD 食品◄ [I] *BrE* if food goes off, it goes bad【英】〔食品〕变质，腐败：*The milk's gone off.* 牛奶变质了。

6 ►STOP 停止◄ [I] *BrE* if a pain goes off, you stop feeling it【英】〔疼痛〕消失

7 ►STOP LIKING SB/STH 不再喜欢某人/某物◄ [T **go off** sb/sth] *BrE informal* to stop liking something or someone【英，非正式】不再喜欢：*Val went off coffee when she was pregnant.* 瓦尔在怀孕的时候不再喜欢喝咖啡了。| **go off doing sth** *I've gone off cooking lately.* 我最近失去了做饭的兴趣。

8 ►SLEEP 睡◄ [I] *informal* to go to sleep【非正式】入睡：**go off to sleep** *Has the baby gone off to sleep yet?* 宝宝睡着了吗？

9 ►GET WORSE 变坏◄ [I] *BrE informal* to get worse【英，非正式】变坏：*The service in this restaurant has really gone off.* 这家餐馆的服务水平确实下降了。

go off with sth/sb *phr v* [T] *informal*【非正式】**1** to leave your husband, wife, partner etc in order to have a relationship with someone else〔抛弃配偶〕移情别恋于…：*She's gone off with her husband's best friend.* 她与丈夫最好的朋友私奔了。**2** to take something away from a place without having permission 私自拿走：*Who's gone off with my pen?* 谁拿走了我的钢笔？

go on *phr v*

1 ►CONTINUE AN ACTION 继续某动作◄ [I] to continue without stopping or changing 继续下去：*We can't go on like this; I want a divorce!* 我们不能这样继续下去了，我要离婚！| **go on with sth** *Go on with your work until I come back.* 继续做你的工作，等我回来。| **go on doing sth** *You can't go on drinking so much — you're not doing yourself any good.* 你不能再喝这么多的酒 — 你是在害自己。| **go on and on** (=continue for a long time) 长时间继续下去 *The noise seemed to go on and on.* 噪音似乎没完没了。

2 ►DO STH NEXT 接着做某事◄ [I] to do something after you have finished doing something else 进而做某事：**go on to sth** *Let's go on to the next item on the agenda.* 我们转到议程的下一项吧。| **go on to do sth** *She went on to become a successful surgeon.* 她进而成为一名成功的外科医生。

3 ►HAPPEN 发生◄ to take place or happen 发生，进行：*What's going on in the kitchen?* 厨房里发生了什么事？| *There's something fishy going on here.* 这里有些事不对劲。—see also 另见 GOINGS-ON

4 ►USE AS PROOF 用作证据◄ [T not in passive 不用被动态 **go on** sth] to base an opinion or judgment on something 以〔某事〕为根据〔作出判断〕：*Police haven't much to go on in their hunt for the killer.* 警方追查杀手时没有多少线索。

5 ►BEGIN TO WORK 开始工作◄ [I] if a machine goes on, it begins to operate〔机器〕开始运转：*The heat goes on automatically at 6 o'clock.* 暖气在6点钟开始自动供应。

6 ►TIME 时间◄ [I] to pass 过去：*As time went on, I grew very fond of him.* 随着时间的推移，我变得非常喜欢他了。

7 ►CONTINUE WITH A STORY/EXPLANATION ETC 继续讲故事/解释等◄ [I] to continue talking, especially after stopping or changing to a different subject〔尤指停止或改变话题后〕接着讲，继续说：*Go on, I'm listening.* 说下去吧，我在听着。| **[+with]** *After a short pause Maria went on with her story.* 玛丽亚稍停片刻之后继续讲她的故事。| **go on to do sth** *The councillor went on to explain where the new supermarket would be.* 市议员接着解释新的超级市场会在什么地方。

8 ►BEHAVE IN THE SAME WAY 以同样的方式行事◄ [I always+adv/prep] to often behave in a particular way 常以某种方式行事：*The way she's going on she'll have a nervous breakdown.* 她这样继续下去会精神崩溃的。

9 ►COMPLAIN 抱怨◄ [I] *BrE* to continue to complain or ask someone to do something【英】不断抱怨，不断要求〔某人做某事〕：**go on at sb about sth** *I wish you'd stop going on at me about my weight!* 我希望你不要再唠叨我的体重！| **go on at sb to do sth** *Mum kept going on at him to tidy his room.* 妈妈不停地叫他整理他的房间。

10 be going on (for) to be nearly a time, age, number etc 接近〔某时间、年龄、数目等〕：*Nancy must be going on for 60, you know.* 你知道的，南希肯定快60岁了。| *Jenny's one of those wise teenagers who's 16 going on 70.* (=she seems older than she is, or thinks she is) 珍妮就是那种实际上只有16岁，但看上去很老成的聪明少女。

11 ►MEDICINE 药◄ [T not in passive 不用被动态 **go on** sth] to begin to take a type of medicine 开始服用〔某种药物〕：**go on the pill** *Dani's too young to go on the pill.* 丹尼太年轻，不能服避孕药。

12 ►GO IN FRONT OF 在其他人之前走◄ [I] to go somewhere before the other people you are with 先走，先行：*Bill went on*

in the car and I followed on foot. 比尔坐车先走，我步行跟在后面。

13 ▶TALK TOO MUCH 说太多◀ [I] *informal* to talk too much【非正式】没完没了地说，唠叨个没完：*You don't half go on!* 你真是唠叨个没完！| **go on and on** *They went on and on about the importance of safety belts.* 他们不停地唠叨安全带如何重要。

14 ▶DEVELOP 发展◀ [I] *BrE informal* to develop or make progress【英，非正式】发展，进展：*How's the work going on?* 工作进展得怎么样？

15 go on a) used to encourage someone to do something 继续吧〔用来鼓励某人去做某事〕：*Go on, have another cookie.* 来，再吃一块曲奇饼。**b)** also 又作 **go on with you** *BrE spoken* used to tell someone that you do not believe them【英口】我才不信：*I told her she had the most beautiful eyes I'd ever seen. "Oh, go on with you!" she said, blushing with pleasure.* 我告诉她说，她的眼睛是我见过最漂亮的。"嗬，我才不信呢！"她说道，高兴得涨红了脸。

16 to be going on with/to go on with *informal, BrE* if you have enough of something to be going on with, you have enough to use at present until the situation improves【非正式，英】暂时够用：*Have you got enough money to be going on with?* 你的钱暂时够用吗？

17 go on the dole *BrE informal* to begin to claim money from the government because you are not working【英，非正式】开始领取失业救济金

go out *phr v* [I]

1 ▶FOR ENTERTAINMENT 为了娱乐◀ to leave your house, especially in order to enjoy yourself 出去〔尤指娱乐〕：*Are you going out tonight?* 你今晚要出去吗？| *Let's go out for a walk.* 我们出去散步吧。| **go out doing sth** *Liam goes out drinking every Friday.* 利亚姆每个星期五都出去喝酒。| **go out to do sth** *Can I go out to play now?* 现在我能出去玩吗？| **go out and do sth** *You should go out and get some fresh air.* 你应该出去呼吸一些新鲜空气。

2 ▶WITH BOY/GIRL 和男孩/女孩◀ to spend a lot of time with someone and have a romantic relationship with them 交往；谈恋爱：**go out with sb** *Jean used to go out with my brother.* 琼与我兄弟谈过恋爱。| **go out together** *How long have you been going out together?* 你们已经交往多久了？

3 ▶FIRE/LIGHT 火/灯◀ to stop burning or shining 熄灭：*The candle spluttered and went out.* 蜡烛劈啪作响，然后就灭了。—see 见 FIRE¹ (USAGE)

4 ▶ON TV/RADIO 在电视上/广播里◀ to be broadcast on television or radio〔在电视或无线电中〕广播：*The program goes out live at 5 o'clock on Mondays.* 这个节目每周一5点现场直播。

5 ▶MOVE ABROAD 到国外◀ to travel to a place far away, often in order to live there 出国〔常指移居〕：*They've gone out to Australia.* 他们已经移居澳大利亚了。

6 ▶STRIKE 罢工◀ *BrE* also 又作 **go out on strike** to stop working because of a disagreement【英】罢工

7 go out like a light *informal* to go to sleep very quickly【非正式】很快睡着：*As soon as his head touched the pillow, he went out like a light.* 他头一碰枕头就睡着了。

8 ▶NOT BE FASHIONABLE/USED 不再流行/不再使用◀ to stop being fashionable or used 不再流行，不再用：*Flared trousers are going out again.* 喇叭裤又过时了。—opposite 反义词 **come in** (COME¹)

9 ▶SEA 海洋◀ to go back to its lower level〔潮水〕退去：*The tide's going out.* 潮水正在退去。—opposite 反义词 **come in** (COME¹)

10 ▶MAKE PUBLIC 公开◀ to let everyone know about something 公开，公布：*Word went out that the President was dead.* 总统去世的消息公布了。

11 heart/thoughts go out to sb to have a lot of sympathy for someone 十分同情某人：*Our hearts go out to the victim's family.* 我们非常同情受害者的家庭。

12 ▶TIME 时间◀ [always+adv/prep] *literary* to end【文】结束，终结：*March went out with high winds and rain.* 3月在劲风斜雨中结束。

go over *phr v*

1 ▶GO NEAR SB/STH 走近某人/某物◀ [I] to go nearer to someone or something 走近，走过去：*Blake went over and sat on the bed.* 布莱克走过去坐在床上。| [+to] *Chiara went over to the bar.* 奇阿拉向酒吧走去。| **go over to do sth** *He had gone over to say goodbye.* 他走过去道别去了。

2 ▶EXAMINE 检查◀ [T, **go over** sth] to look at something or think about something carefully 仔细审查，仔细考虑：*I had gone over and over what happened in my mind.* 我对发生的事进行了反复思考。

3 ▶SEARCH 搜查◀ [T, **go over** sth] to search something very carefully 仔细搜查：*The police have been over the apartment with a fine-tooth comb.* 警方对这套公寓房仔细搜查了一遍。

4 ▶VISIT 参观◀ [T, **go over** sth] to visit a building etc to decide whether to buy or rent it〔买房或租房前〕看〔房子〕：*We'd been over several houses before finding this one.* 我们看了好几幢房子才找到这一幢。

5 ▶REPEAT 重复◀ [T, **go over** sth] to repeat something in order to learn it or understand it 再来一遍；温习：*Maybe if I went over it all again I would see what she meant.* 也许如果我把它再看一遍，我就能明白她的意思。

6 go over well/badly etc if a speech, performance etc goes over well, the people listening like it〔演讲、表演〕获得成功/失败等：**[+with]** *His speech went over well with the Left of the party.* 他的演讲受到该党左派的欢迎。

7 ▶CHANGE 改变◀ [I] to change your beliefs, religion, habits etc 改变信仰[宗教、习惯等]：**go over from sth to sth** *Lloyd George went over to Labour in 1951.* 劳埃德·乔治于1951年改入工党。| **go over to doing sth** *I've gone over to drinking black coffee.* 我已经改喝清咖啡。

8 ▶TV/RADIO 电视/无线电广播◀ [I] to change to a broadcast from another place 转移地点播放：**[+to]** *We're going over to the White House for an important announcement.* 我们要转到白宫播放一项重要公告。

9 ▶CLEAN 清除◀ [T] to clean something 清除，打扫：*Liz went over the carpet with the hoover.* 利兹用吸尘器清扫地毯。

go round also 又作 **go around** *phr v* [I]

1 ▶BE ENOUGH 足够◀ to be enough for everyone 足够分给每个人：*Are there enough chairs to go around?* 有足够的椅子给大家坐吗？

2 ▶ILLNESS/NEWS ETC 疾病/消息等◀ if an illness, news etc goes around, it is passed from one person to another 流传，传播：*There's a lot of flu going around at the moment.* 眼下流感在大肆传播。

3 go round in your head if words, sounds etc go round in your head, you continue to hear them for a long time 在脑中萦绕：*That stupid song kept going around in my head.* 那支乏味的歌一直在我的脑中萦绕。

4 ▶DRESS/BEHAVE 穿戴/举止◀ to usually dress or behave in a particular way〔穿着、行为〕习惯于：*These shoplifters go round in pairs.* 这些盗窃商店货物的小偷总是两个人一起活动。| **go around doing sth** *You can't go around telling people what to do all the time!* 你不能老是这样对人家指手画脚！

5 go around with sb/go round together to often go out with someone 与某人交往/常在一起 —see also 另见 **go round in circles** (CIRCLE¹ (6))

go slow *phr v* [I] *BrE* to put as little effort as possible into your work, as a form of STRIKE² (1)【英】怠工 —see also 另见 GO-SLOW

go through *phr v* **1** [T, **go through** sth] to suffer or experience something bad 经受，经历〔坏事，苦事〕：*How does she keep smiling after all she's been through?* 她经历了这一切后怎么还能满脸笑容呢？**2** [T, **go through** sth] to use something and have none left; **get through** (GET) 用光：*Austria was so expensive – we went through all our money in one week.* 去奥地利一趟十分昂贵，我们在一周内花光了所有的钱。**3** [I,T, **go through** sth] if a law goes through, or goes through Parliament, it is officially accepted〔法律〕被通过：*The Bill went through Parliament without a vote.* 法案未经表决就在议会通过了。**4** [I] if a deal or agreement goes through, it is officially accepted〔交易或协定〕获正式认可：*Your application for a loan has gone through.* 你的贷款申请已被接受。**5** [T, **go through** sth] *BrE* to slowly make a hole in something【英】磨破，穿破：*My toe has gone through my sock.* 我的脚趾把袜子磨破了。**6** [T, **go through** sth] to practise something, for example a performance 练习；排练：*Let's go through the whole thing again, from the beginning.* 我们从头开始完整地练习一遍。**7** [T, **go through** sth] to look at or for something carefully 仔细检查，仔细寻找：*Dave went through his pockets looking for the keys.* 戴夫翻遍了他的衣袋找钥匙。**8** [I,T, **go through** sth] to read a document from beginning to end 从头到尾阅读：*Could you just go through this file and mark anything that's relevant?* 请你通读一下这份文件，把相关的地方标出来，好吗？

go through with sth *phr v* [T] to do something you had promised or planned to do, even though it causes problems or you are no longer sure you want to do it 做〔承诺或计划要做的事情〕；将〔某事〕进行到底：*Jenny felt she couldn't go through with the abortion.* 珍妮感到自己不能照她原来说的去做流产。

go to sth *phr v* [T, not in passive 不用被动态] **1 go to great lengths/go to a lot of trouble** to take a lot of trouble to do something〔为做某事〕费了不少气力/花了不少功夫: *They went to great lengths to make sure I felt at home.* 为了使我住得舒服，他们费了不少力气。**2 go to great expense** to spend a lot of money to do something〔为做某事〕花了很多钱 **3** to begin to experience or do something 开始经历，开始做: *Shh! Daddy's trying to go to sleep.* 嘘！爸爸正要睡觉。| *Britain and Germany went to war in 1939.* 英国和德国于1939年开战。**4** to be given to someone 被给予，送给: *All the money raised will go to local charities.* 所有筹到的钱都将捐给当地慈善机构。

go together *phr v* [I] **1** if two things go together, they look, taste etc good together〔外形、味道等〕相配，协调: *Pork and apple go well together.* 猪肉和苹果的味道很相配。—see 见 FIT[1] (USAGE) **2** if two people are going together, they are having a romantic relationship 恋爱: *I didn't know Sharon and Les were going together.* 我原来不知道莎伦和莱斯在谈恋爱。

go under *phr v* [I] **1** if a business goes under, it has serious problems and fails〔企业〕倒闭，破产，垮掉: *Many restaurants go under in the first year.* 许多餐馆在第一年就倒闭了。**2** if a ship or something that is floating goes under, it sinks beneath the surface〔船等〕沉没: *The Titanic finally went under, watched by those survivors who had found a place in the lifeboats.* 那些挤上救生艇的幸存者看着泰坦尼克号最终沉没了。

go up *phr v* [I]
1 ▶INCREASE 增加◀ *spoken* to increase in number or amount【口】增多: *I see cigarettes are going up again.* (=are getting more expensive) 我发现香烟又涨价了。
2 ▶BE BUILT 建立起来◀ *spoken* to be built【口】建立起来: *New houses are going up all around the town.* 城里到处都在建新房子。
3 ▶EXPLODE/BURN 爆炸/燃烧◀ *spoken* to explode or be destroyed in a fire【口】爆炸；被烧毁: *The whole building went up in flames.* 整座大楼在大火中烧毁。—see also 另见 **go up in smoke** (SMOKE[1] (5))
4 ▶SHOUT 叫喊◀ if a shout or a CHEER goes up, people start to shout or CHEER 开始呼喊[欢呼]
5 ▶THEATRE 剧场◀ if the curtain goes up at a theatre, it opens for the performance to start〔帷幕〕开启，演出开始: *The curtain went up on an empty stage.* 帷幕开启，显现空荡的舞台。
6 ▶REACH 到达◀ to reach as far as a particular place 到达，延伸: [+to] *The trees go right up to the beach.* 这些树一直延伸到海滩。
7 ▶TO UNIVERSITY 上大学◀ *BrE* to go to a university to begin a course of study【英】上大学: [+to] *She went up to Oxford in 1975.* 她1975年上了牛津大学。
8 ▶TO TOWN 进城◀ *BrE* to go to a town or city from a smaller place【英】进城: [+to] *I like to go up to town for Christmas shopping.* 我喜欢进城为圣诞节购物。

go with *phr v* [T not in passive 不用被动态]
1 ▶MATCH/SUIT 匹配/适合◀ if one thing goes with another, they look, taste etc good together 与…匹配，与…协调: *That shade of blue goes with your eyes.* 那种蓝色和你的眼睛很协调。—see 见 FIT[1] (USAGE)
2 ▶BE PART OF STH 成为某物的一部分◀ to be included as part of something 是…的一部分: *The house goes with the job.* 这栋房子属于这个职位。| **go with doing sth** *Responsibility goes with becoming a father.* 当了父亲也就有了责任。
3 ▶EXIST TOGETHER 共存◀ to often exist with something else 伴随: *Ill health often goes with poverty.* 贫病常相随。
4 ▶BOY/GIRL 男孩/女孩◀ *informal* to have someone as your boyfriend or girlfriend or to have a sexual relationship with someone【非正式】与某人谈恋爱；与某人发生性关系: *Is Martin still going with Jane?* 马丁还在跟简交往吗？
5 ▶AGREE 同意◀ to accept someone's idea or plan 同意，接受〔看法、计划〕: *Let's go with John's original proposal.* 我们赞成约翰原来的提议吧。

go without *phr v* [I,T] **1** to be able to live without something or without doing something 没有某物[不做某事]而能过活: *We can't afford a holiday, so we'll just have to go without.* 我们没钱度假，所以只好不去。| **go without sth** *She had gone without food to feed the children.* 她曾经没有食物喂她的孩子。**2 it goes without saying** used to say that something is so obvious that it does not need to be said 不用说，不言而喻: *It goes without saying that young doctors should work fewer hours.* 不用说，年轻医生的工作时间应该短一些。

S1 **go²** *n plural* **goes**
1 ▶TRY 尝试◀ [C] an attempt to do something 尝试: **have a go** *"I can't open this jar." "Let me have a go."* "我打不开这个罐子。""让我试试看。" | **have a go at (doing) sth** *Daisy had six goes at her driving-test before she passed.* 黛西考了六次才通过驾驶考试。| **at one go** *Ruby blew out all her candles at one go.* 鲁比一口气吹灭所有的蜡烛。| **give sth a go** (=try to do sth even though you do not think you will succeed) 试做某事 *I don't think I can make him change his mind, but I'll give it a go.* 我并不认为我能使他改变主意，但我试试看。
2 ▶IN A GAME 游戏中◀ [C] someone's turn in a game etc〔游戏中等〕轮到某人的机会: *Whose go is it?* 轮到谁了？| *If you throw a two you miss a go.* 如果掷到两点，你就要错过一轮。| **have a go on sth** *Can I have a go on your computer?* 我能用一下你的电脑吗？| **3p/5p/10p a go** *Guess the weight of the cake, 10 pence a go.* 猜一猜这蛋糕的重量，猜一次10便士。
3 make a go of sth *informal* to make a business, marriage etc succeed【非正式】使〔企业、婚姻等〕成功: **make a go of it** *Do you think they'll make a go of it with this restaurant?* 你认为他们开这家餐馆会成功吗？
4 on the go *informal* very busy or working all the time【非正式】忙个不停: *I'm on the go all day and then collapse into bed at about 10 o'clock.* 我整天忙个不停，然后大约10点就瘫倒在床上。
5 it's no go *spoken* used to say that something has not happened or that it will not happen【口】〔某事〕未发生；不会发生: *I went and asked for a rise but it was no go, I'm afraid.* 我去要求提高工资，但很遗憾，白跑一趟。—see also 另见 NO-GO AREA (2)
6 all the go *old-fashioned* very fashionable【过时】十分流行的
7 it's all go *BrE spoken* it is very busy【英口】非常忙碌: *It's all go in the toy department in December.* 玩具部在12月非常繁忙。
8 have a go at sb *spoken, especially BrE* to complain【口，尤英】抱怨: *Mark's bound to have a go at me for spending all this money.* 马克肯定会埋怨我把这笔钱都花光了。
9 have a go *spoken, especially BrE*【口，尤英】**a)** to attack someone physically 打，打架: *A whole gang of yobs were standing around, just waiting to have a go.* 一帮无赖站在周围，只等着打架。**b)** to try to catch someone who you see doing something wrong, rather than waiting for the police〔不等警察到来〕企图自行抓坏人: *The public should not be encouraged to have a go.* 不应鼓励公众自行抓坏人。
10 ▶ENERGY 活力◀ [U] *BrE* liveliness and energy【英】劲头，活力: *The children are full of go this morning.* 孩子们今天上午精力充沛。—see also 另见 GET-UP-AND-GO

goad¹ /god; gəʊd/ *v* [T] **1** to make someone do something by annoying them or encouraging them until they do it 驱使，唆使: **goad sb into (doing) sth** *Kathy goaded him into telling her what he had done.* 凯茜促使他把所干的事告诉了她。| **goad sb on** *Duval was goaded on by the need for more money.* 杜瓦尔是受需要更多的钱这一动机驱使才继续干下去的。**2** to push animals ahead of you with a sharp stick〔用尖棒〕驱赶〔牲畜〕

goad² *n* [C] **1** a sharp stick for making cattle move forward〔赶牛的〕尖棒 **2** something that forces someone to do something 驱动人行动的事物

go-a-head¹ /ˈ· · ·/ *n* **give sb the go-ahead/get the go-ahead** to give or be given permission for something to start 给予某人许可/得到准许: *The film was given the go-ahead, and production started in May.* 这部影片得到了拍摄许可，摄制工作5月份开始。

go-ahead² *adj BrE* using or encouraging new methods or ideas and therefore likely to succeed; PROGRESSIVE[1] (1)【英】开拓进取的: *This go-ahead company introduced profit-sharing.* 这家开拓进取的公司引入分红制。

goal /gol; gəʊl/ *n* [C] **1** something that you hope to achieve in the future; aim 目标，目的: **achieve a goal** *We've achieved our goal of building a shelter for the homeless.* 我们已经达到了为无家可归的人建收容所的目标。| **long-term goal/short-term goal** (=that you hope to achieve after a long or short time) 长期目标/短期目标 **2** the action of making the ball go into the scoring (SCORE[2] (1)) area in games such as football or HOCKEY, or the point won by doing this〔足球、曲棍球等〕得分: **score a goal** *Baggio scored the first goal for Italy.* 巴乔为意大利进了头一个球。**3** the area between two posts where the ball must go for a point to be won 球门: **keep goal** (=be the goalkeeper) 当守门员 —see picture on page A23 参见A23页图 S2 W1

goal·ie /ˈgolɪ; ˈgəʊli/ *n* [C] *informal* a goalkeeper【非正式】守门员 —see picture on page A23 参见 A23 页图

goal·keep·er /ˈgolˌkipɚ; ˈgəʊlˌkiːpə/ *n* [C] the player in a sports team who has to try to stop the ball going into his team's goal 守门员 —see picture on page A23 参见 A23 页图

goal·less /ˈgol·lɪs; ˈgəʊlləs/ *adj* **a goalless draw** a match where no goals are scored (SCORE[2] (1)) 无进球[零比零]的比赛

goal line /ˈ· ·/ *n* [C] a line that marks the end of a playing area, where the goal is placed 球门线, 端线

goal·mouth /ˈgolˌmaʊθ; ˈgəʊlmaʊθ/ *n* [C] the area directly in front of the GOAL (3) 球门区

goal·post /ˈgolˌpost; ˈgəʊlpəʊst/ *n* [C usually plural 一般用复数] **1** one of the two posts, with a bar along the top or across the middle, that form the GOAL (3) in games like football and HOCKEY〔足球、曲棍球等的〕球门柱 **2 move the goalposts** *BrE informal* to change the rules, limits etc while someone is trying to do something, and make it more difficult for them【英, 非正式】〔在某人做某事时〕改变规则[限制等]〔对其增大难度〕

goal·ten·der /ˈgolˌtɛndɚ; ˈgəʊlˌtendə/ *n* [C] *AmE* a GOALKEEPER【美】守门员

goat /got; gəʊt/ *n* [C] **1** an animal a little like a sheep that can climb steep hills and rocks 山羊 **2 get sb's goat** *spoken* to make someone extremely annoyed【口】使某人十分恼怒: *I'll tell you another thing that really got my goat.* 我要告诉你另一件着实令我恼怒的事。**3 act/play the goat** *BrE informal* to behave in a silly way【英, 非正式】行为愚蠢 **4 old goat** an unpleasant old man, especially one who annoys women in a sexual way 令人生厌的老头〔尤指老色鬼〕—see also 另见 BILLY GOAT

goat 山羊

goa·tee /goˈti; gəʊˈtiː/ *n* [C] a small pointed BEARD on the end of a man's chin 山羊胡子 —see picture on page A6 参见 A6 页图

goat·herd /ˈgotˌhɝd; ˈgəʊthɜːd/ *n* [C] someone who looks after a group of goats〔山羊的〕牧羊人

goat·skin /ˈgotˌskɪn; ˈgəʊtˌskɪn/ *n* **1** [C,U] leather made from the skin of a goat, or a wine container made from this 山羊皮革;〔装葡萄酒的〕山羊皮囊 **2** [C] the skin of a goat 山羊皮

gob[1] /gɑb; gɒb/ *n* [C] *informal*【非正式】**1** *BrE* an impolite word meaning your mouth【英】嘴〔粗俗用语〕: *Shut your gob!* 住嘴! **2** a mass of something wet and sticky〔黏性物的〕一块, 一团: [+of] *a gob of spit* 一团痰 **3 gobs** *AmE informal* a large amount of something【美, 非正式】大量: *gobs of money* 大量的钱

gob[2] *v* [I] *BrE informal* to blow a small amount of liquid out of your mouth; SPIT[1] (1)【英, 非正式】吐〔痰, 唾沫〕, 啐

gob·bet /ˈgɑbɛt; ˈgɒbɪ̣t/ *n* [C] a small piece of something, especially food 一小片, 一小块〔尤指食物〕

gob·ble /ˈgɑbḷ; ˈgɒbəl/ *v informal*【非正式】**1** [I,T] also 又作 **gobble up** to eat something very quickly or in a way people do not consider polite 狼吞虎咽, 大嚼〔某物〕: *Don't gobble your food!* 别大口大口地吃东西! **2** [T] also 又作 **gobble up** to finish a supply of something quickly 很快消耗掉: *Inflation has gobbled up our wage increases.* 通货膨胀抵消了我们工资的增长。**3** [I] to make a sound like a TURKEY (1) 发出像火鸡的叫声 —**gobble** *n* [C]

gob·ble·dy·gook, gobbledegook /ˈgɑbḷdɪˌguk; ˈgɒbəldiguːk/ *n* [U] *informal* complicated language, especially in an official document, that seems to have no meaning【非正式】复杂且看来并无实质意义的语言〔尤指公文用语〕

gob·bler /ˈgɑblɚ; ˈgɒblə/ *n* [C] *AmE informal* a TURKEY (1)【美, 非正式】火鸡

go-be·tween /ˈ· ·ˌ·/ *n* [C] someone who takes messages from one person or group to another, because the two sides cannot meet or do not wish to meet 中间人: *Martin acted as a go-between in the negotiations.* 马丁在谈判中充当中间人。

Go·bi Desert, the /ˌgobɪ ˈdɛzɚt; ˌgəʊbi ˈdezət/ also 又作 **the Gobi** one of the largest deserts in the world. It is partly in northern China and partly in Mongolia. 戈壁沙漠〔世界上最大的沙漠之一, 部分位于中国北部, 部分位于蒙古境内〕

gob·let /ˈgɑblɪt; ˈgɒblɪ̣t/ *n* [C] a cup made of glass or metal, with a base and a stem but no handles〔玻璃或金属制〕无柄高脚杯 —see picture at 参见 GLASS[1] 图

gob·lin /ˈgɑblɪn; ˈgɒblɪ̣n/ *n* [C] a small, often ugly creature in children's stories that likes to trick people〔童话中的〕小妖精

goblin 小妖精

gob·smacked /ˈgɑbˌsmækt; ˈgɒbsmækt/ *adj BrE spoken* very surprised, pleased, or disappointed【英口】非常吃惊[高兴, 失望]的

gob·stop·per /ˈgɑbˌstɑpɚ; ˈgɒbˌstɒpə/ *n* [C] *BrE* a large round hard sweet【英】大糖球; JAWBREAKER (1) *AmE*【美】

go-cart /ˈ· ·/ *n* [C] an American spelling of GO-KART go-kart 的美式拼法

God /gɑd; gɒd/ *n* [singular, not with *the* 不与 the 连用] **1** the BEING[2] (2) who Christians, Jews, and Muslims pray to 上帝, 主; 真主 —see also 另见 **act of God** (ACT[1] (10)) **2 God/oh God/my God/good God** *spoken* used to add force to what you are saying, when you are surprised, annoyed, or amused【口】天啊!〔惊讶、恼怒或开心时用于加强语气〕: *Oh God, how embarrassing!* 天啊, 多么令人难堪! **3 I swear/hope/wish etc to God** used to emphasize that you promise, hope or wish that something is true 我对天发誓/衷心希望: *I hope to God nothing goes wrong.* 我衷心希望一切顺利。**4 God knows** *spoken*【口】**a)** used to show that you are annoyed because you do not know something, or because you think that something is unreasonable 天晓得〔表示生气〕: **God knows who/what/how etc** *God knows what she's doing in there.* 天晓得她在那儿干什么。| **God only knows** *It'll cost God only knows how much.* 只有天晓得要花多少钱。**b)** used to add force to what you are saying 上天为证〔以强调语气〕: *God knows, it hasn't been easy.* 老天爷为证, 事情办到现在这个样子很不容易。**5 what/how/where/who in God's name** *spoken* used to add force to a question when you are angry or surprised【口】究竟什么/如何/哪里/谁〔生气或惊讶时用于加强语气〕: *Where in God's name have you been?* 你到底去了什么地方? **6 God forbid** *spoken* used to say that you very much hope that something will not happen【口】但愿〔某事〕不会发生: [+(that)] *God forbid that she should ever hurt you.* 上帝保佑, 但愿她不会伤害你。**7 honest to God** *spoken* used to emphasize that you are not lying or joking【口】绝对是真的; 绝对当真: *Honest to God, I didn't tell her!* 对老天爷说实话, 我没有告诉她! **8 God almighty** *spoken* used to express surprise, shock, annoyance, or anger【口】万能的上帝〔用来表示惊讶、震惊、恼怒或气愤〕**9 God help you/him etc** *spoken* used to warn someone【口】你/他等就有麻烦了〔用于警告某人〕: *God help you if Tom comes home and you're still here!* 要是汤姆回家而你还在这里的话, 那就只好求上帝帮助你了。**10 God help us** *spoken, usually humorous* used when you think that something bad is going to happen【口, 一般幽默】愿上帝保佑我们〔用于认为某坏事将要发生〕: *"Simon's doing the cooking." "God help us!"* "西蒙在做饭。" "上帝保佑!" **11 God bless** *spoken* used to show your affection for someone【口】上帝保佑〔用来向某人表示关爱〕: *Goodnight, Jenny – God bless.* 晚安, 珍妮——上帝保佑。**12 God willing** *spoken* used to say that you hope there will be no problems【口】如上帝许可〔用来表示希望一切顺利〕: *We'll be moving next month, God willing.* 如上帝许可, 我们下个月搬家。**13 God-given** received from God 上帝赐予的, 天赋的: *a God-given talent for singing* 天赋的歌唱才华 | **a God-given right** (=the right to do something without asking anyone else's opinion) 上帝给的权利〔指无须征求任何人意见而做某事的权利〕**14 God give me strength!** *spoken* used when you are becoming annoyed【口】上帝给我力量!〔用于开始感到恼怒时〕**15 God's gift to women/men etc** someone who thinks they are perfect or extremely attractive 上帝对女人/男人等的恩赐〔指自以为完美无缺或十分漂亮的人〕: *Paul thinks he's God's gift to the film industry.* 保罗认为他是电影界的天赐之才。**16 God rest his/her soul** also 又作 **God rest him/her** *old-fashioned* used to show respect when speaking about someone who is dead【过时】上帝让他/她安息〔用于谈及死者时表示敬意〕**17 play God** to behave as though you have the power to do whatever you like 表现得似乎自己可以随意而为: *scientists who think they can play God with their genetic experiments* 认为在做基因实验时可以随心所欲的科学家 **18 by God** *old-fashioned* used to add force when you are expressing determination or surprise【过时】老天作证〔表示决心或惊讶时用来加强语气〕

—see also 另见 **there but for the grace of God** (GRACE[1] (6)), **in the lap of the gods** (LAP[1] (5)), **thank God/goodness/heavens** (THANK (2))

USAGE NOTE 用法说明: GOD

FORMALITY AND POLITENESS 正式和礼貌

In informal spoken English the following expressions are very common. They are used in a non-religious way, but some people would consider them to be offensive. **Oh (my) God/My God/Good God/God!** are all used to show strong surprise, fear, excitement or annoyance, or to emphasize what is said. 下列词语在英语口语中十分常见。它们都用于非宗教意义, 但有些人认为这种用法是冒犯。Oh (my) God/My God/Good God/God! 都可用来表示非常吃惊、害怕、激动或恼怒, 或强调所说的话: *Oh God, what's that?* 天啊, 那是什么? | *My God, I forgot to lock the door.* 天啊, 我忘了锁门。| *God he was sexy!* 天啊, 他很性感! | *Good God no!* 啊呀, 不!

For God's sake is used to draw attention strongly to a particular point. for God's sake 用来把注意力吸引到某一点上: *How can she do that, she's only seven for God's sake!* 她怎么能做那件事呢, 天哪, 她只有七岁! It is also used with orders to make them stronger, or to show annoyance. 也可与命令连用以起强调作用, 或表示恼怒: *For God's sake shut up!* 看在上帝的分上, 住嘴!

Thank God shows you are happy and pleased about something. thank God 用来表示对某事感到高兴和满意: *Thank God you're here!* 谢天谢地你来了! | *Thank God for that!* 为那事感谢上帝!

God (only) knows is a strong way of saying 'I don't know'. God (only) knows 是 I don't know (我不知道) 的强调说法。

SPELLING 拼法

God is always written with a capital letter in these expressions. 在这些词语中, God 的第一个字母要大写。

GRAMMAR 语法

God is not used with *the*. God 不与 the 连用: *I pray to God every night* (NOT 不用 *the God*). 我每天晚上向上帝祈祷。

CULTURAL NOTE 文化注释

Some people imagine God as an old man with long hair and a long white beard. 有人把上帝想象成一个长发、长胡须的老人。

god *n* [C] **1** a male BEING who is believed to control the world or part of it, or represents a particular quality 神, 男神: *Mars, the god of war* 战神马尔斯 **2** [C] someone or something to which you give too much importance or respect 被过分重视或崇拜的人[物]: *material wealth became their god* 物质财富成为他们极度崇拜的东西 **3 the gods a)** *informal* the seats high up and at the back of a theatre【非正式】〔剧院中的〕高层后座 **b)** the force that some people believe controls their lives, bringing them good or bad luck 神, 老天爷: *The gods are against me!* 老天爷在跟我作对!

god·aw·ful /ˌ·ˈ··◂/ *adj* [only before noun 仅用于名词前] *informal* very bad or unpleasant【非正式】糟透的, 令人憎恶的

god·child /ˈgɑdˌtʃaɪld; ˈgɒdtʃaɪld/ *plural* **godchildren** /-ˌtʃɪldrən; -ˌtʃɪldrən/ *n* [C] the child that a GODPARENT promises to help and to teach Christian values to〔基督教的〕教子, 教女

god·dam·mit /ˈgɑdˋdæmɪt; gɒˈdæmɪt/ *interjection especially AmE* used to express annoyance, anger etc【尤美】该死, 要命

god·damn, goddam /ˈgɑdˋdæm; ˈgɒdæm/ also 又作 **god·damned** /-ˋdæmd; -dæmd/ *adj* [only before noun 仅用于名词前] *spoken* a word used to express annoyance or give force to an expression【口】该死〔表示恼怒或加强语气〕: *Where's the goddamn key?* 该死的钥匙到哪儿去了? —**goddamn, goddam, goddamned** *adv*: *I just did something so goddamned stupid.* 我刚才做了极其愚蠢的事。

god·daugh·ter /ˈgɑdˌdɔtə; ˈgɒdˌdɔːtə/ *n* [C] a girl that a GODPARENT promises to help and to teach Christian values to〔基督教的〕教女

god·dess /ˈgɑdɪs; ˈgɒdɪs/ *n* [C] a female BEING[3] (1) who is believed to control the world or part of it, or represents a particular quality 女神: *Aphrodite, goddess of love* 爱情女神阿佛洛狄忒

god·fa·ther /ˈgɑdˌfɑðə; ˈgɒdˌfɑːðə/ *n* [C] **1** a man who promises to help a child and to teach him or her Christian values〔基督教的〕教父 **2** *slang* the head of a criminal organization or MAFIA group【俚】〔犯罪组织或黑手党的〕首领, 教父

Godfather, The (1972) a violent US film, in which Marlon Brando appears as the leader of a powerful Mafia family, the Corleone family. Two other films, *The Godfather Part II* and *The Godfather Part III*, were made about the same family. The film is based on a book by Mario Puzo, and was made by Francis Ford Coppola.《教父》〔(1972), 美国一暴力影片。影片根据马里奥·普佐的小说改编而成, 由弗朗西斯·科波拉制作。马龙·白兰度扮演黑手党柯里昂家族的首领。《教父》(第二部) 和《教父》(第三部) 讲述的也是这一家族的故事〕

god·fear·ing /ˈ·ˌ··/ *adj old-fashioned* leading a good life following the rules of the Christian religion【过时】遵守〔基督教〕教规的; 正直善良的

god·for·sak·en /ˈgɑdfəˋsekən; ˈgɒdfəseɪkən/ *adj* a godforsaken place is far away from where people live and contains nothing interesting, attractive, or cheerful〔指地方〕被上帝遗弃的, 冷落的, 偏远的: *Do you really enjoy living in this godforsaken dump?* 你真的喜欢住在这个偏远的脏地方吗?

god·head /ˈgɑdhɛd; ˈgɒdhed/ *n* **the Godhead** *formal* a word meaning God, used by Christians to mean the Father, the Son, and the Holy Spirit【正式】上帝

Lady Godiva 戈黛娃夫人

Go·di·va, Lady /gəˋdaɪvə; gəˈdaɪvə/ an 11th-century British woman of high rank who, according to old stories, rode a horse through Coventry with no clothes on as a protest, to persuade her husband to lower the local taxes 戈黛娃夫人〔传说故事中 11 世纪一位英国贵妇人。她裸体骑马穿过考文垂以示抗议, 试图说服丈夫降低地方税赋〕

god·less /ˈgɑdlɛs; ˈgɒdləs/ *adj old-fashioned* not showing respect for God or belief in a god【过时】不敬上帝的, 不信神的 —**godlessly** *adv*

god·like /ˈgɑdˌlaɪk; ˈgɒdlaɪk/ *adj* like a god or with a quality suitable for a god 如神的, 具有神之品质的: *surveying the world with godlike calm* 用神般的冷静审视世界

god·ly /ˈgɑdlɪ; ˈgɒdli/ *adj old-fashioned* obeying God and leading a good life【过时】虔诚的, 敬畏神的 —**godliness** *n* [U]

god·moth·er /ˈgɑdˌmʌðə; ˈgɒdˌmʌðə/ *n* [C] a woman who promises to help a child, and to teach him or her Christian values〔基督教的〕教母

god·par·ent /ˈgɑdˌpɛrənt; ˈgɒdˌpeərənt/ *n* [C] someone who promises to help a child, and to teach him or her Christian values〔基督教的〕教父, 教母

God Rest You Mer·ry Gen·tle·men /ˌ·ˌ·ˌ··ˌ··ˈ··/ a religious CAROL (=traditional song) sung at Christmas《上帝一定给你快乐》〔一首圣诞颂歌〕

God Save the Queen /ˌ·ˌ·ˌ·ˈ·/ the national ANTHEM (=the official national song) of the UK. The title of the song changes to 'God Save the King' when the MONARCH is a king.《神佑女王》〔英国国歌。国王当政时, 歌名则改为《神佑国王》〕

god·send /ˈgɑdˌsɛnd; ˈgɒdsend/ *n* [singular] something good that happens to you when you really need it 天赐之物, 及时雨: *That cheque from Sandy was a real godsend.* 桑迪的那张支票真是天赐之物。

god·son /ˈgɑdˌsʌn; ˈgɒdsʌn/ *n* [C] a boy that a godparent promises to help and to teach Christian values to〔基督教的〕教子

god·speed /ˈgɑdˌspid; ˌgɒdˈspiːd/ *n* [U] *old use* used to wish someone good luck especially before a journey【旧】幸运, 顺利〔祝某人好运气, 尤用在出发旅行之前〕

God squad /ˈ··/ *n slang* an insulting way of describing Christians who try to persuade other people to become Christians【俚】上帝使团〔侮辱性词语, 指劝人入教的基督徒〕

God·thaab /ˈgɑdhɔb; ˈgɒdhɔːb/ a former name for Nuuk 戈特霍布〔努克旧称〕

God·win-Aus·ten /ˌgɑdwɪn ˋɔstɪn; ˌgɒdwɪ̣n ˈɒstɪn/, **Mount** —see 见 K2

Goeb·bels /ˈgœbəls; ˈgɜːbəlz/, **Paul Joseph** (1897-1945) a German Nazi politician who controlled German PROPAGANDA during the Second World War 戈培尔〔(1897-1945)，德国纳粹政客，二战期间负责德国的宣传工作〕

go·er /ˈgoɚ; ˈgəʊə/ *n* [C] **1 cinema-/concert-/theatre-goer** someone who regularly goes to theatres etc 常看电影/常听音乐会/常看戏的人 **2** *BrE spoken* a woman who often has sex with different men【英口】荡妇: *one of my mum's friends who's a bit of a goer* 我妈妈的一个有些放荡的朋友

Goe·ring /ˈgɝɪŋ; ˈgɜːrɪŋ/, **Her·mann Wil·helm** /ˈhɝmən ˋwɪlhɛlm; ˈhɜːmən ˈwɪlhelm/ (1893-1946) a German Nazi military commander who was in control of the German air force in the Second World War 戈林〔(1893-1946)，德国纳粹军事指挥官，二战期间任德国空军司令〕

Goe·the /ˈgɛtə; ˈgɜːtə/, **Jo·hann Wolf·gang von** /ˈjohɑn ˋwʊlfgæŋ vɑn; ˈjəʊhæn ˈwʊlfgæŋ vɒn/ (1749-1832) a German poet and scientist, and one of the best known writers of plays and books of all time, famous especially for his play *Faust* 歌德〔(1749-1832)，德国诗人、科学家，最杰出的剧作家和小说家之一，尤以剧作《浮士德》著称〕

go·fer /ˈgofɚ; ˈgəʊfə/ *n* [C] *informal* someone who carries messages or gets or takes things for their employer【非正式】勤杂工

Gog and Ma·gog /ˌgɑg ənd ˋmegɑg; ˌgɒg ənd ˈmeɪgɒg/ in old stories, the last two of a race of GIANTs living in Britain in Roman times. In the Apocalypse in the Bible they represent the future enemies of the kingdom of God. 哥革和玛各〔传说故事中的人物。他们是罗马时期生活在不列颠的巨人族中的最后两个巨人。据《圣经·启示录》，他们代表上帝王国未来的敌人〕

go-get·ter /ˌ· ˈ· ·/ *n* [C] someone who is likely to be successful because they are very determined and have a lot of energy 志在必得的人: *She's a real go-getter.* 她确实是个志在必得的人。

gog·gle /ˈgɑgḷ; ˈgɒgəl/ *v* [I] to look at something with your eyes wide open in surprise or shock〔由于惊讶、震惊〕瞪大眼睛看: **[+at]** *They were goggling at us as if we were freaks.* 他们瞪眼看着我们，好像我们是怪物似的。

goggle box /ˈ·· ·/ *n* [C usually singular 一般用单数] *BrE informal* a television【英，非正式】电视机

goggle-eyed /ˌ·· ˈ·◂/ *adj* with your eyes wide open and looking directly at something 瞪大眼睛的: *staring goggle-eyed at the women* 瞪大眼睛看那些女人

gog·gles /ˈgɑgḷz; ˈgɒgəlz/ *n* [plural] something that protects your eyes, made of two round pieces of glass or plastic with an edge that fits against your skin 护目镜

go-go danc·er /ˈ· · ˌ· ·/ *n* [C] a woman who dances with sexy movements in a bar or NIGHTCLUB〔酒吧或夜总会的〕跳色情舞蹈的舞女 —**go-go dancing** *n* [U]

go·ing¹ /ˈgoɪŋ; ˈgəʊɪŋ/ *n* [U]

1 ▶LEAVING 离开◀ the act of leaving a place 离去: *His going will be no great loss to the company.* 他的离去对公司不会造成什么大损失。

2 ▶SPEED 速度◀ the speed at which you travel or work 行走速度; 工作速度: *We climbed the mountain in three hours, which wasn't bad going.* 我们在三小时内爬上山，这样的速度还算不错。| **hard/rough/slow going** *I'm getting the work done, but it's slow going.* 我正在完成这项工作，但进展很慢。

3 heavy going if a book, play etc is heavy going, it is boring and difficult to understand〔书、戏剧等〕乏味且难懂的

4 while the going's good *especially BrE* before someone stops you from doing what you want【尤英】趁没有人阻止前: *Let's get out while the going's good.* 我们趁现在这个机会快走吧。

5 ▶GROUND 地面◀ the condition of the ground, especially for a horse race 地面状况〔特指是否适合赛马〕—see also 另见 **comings and goings** (COMING¹ (2))

going² *adj* **1** [not before noun 不用于名词前] *informal* available【非正式】可获得的，可找到的: *Are there any jobs going where you work?* 你工作的地方有空缺吗? **2 the biggest/best/nicest ... going** the biggest, best etc of a particular thing 当今最大的/最好的/最美好的: *Jim's the biggest fool going.* 吉姆是当今最大的傻瓜。**3 the going rate** the usual cost of a service or job 通常价格: *£15 per hour is the going rate for tuition.* 每小时15英镑是现行的学费。**4 have a lot going for you/not have much going for you** to have or not have many advantages and good qualities that will bring success 你有很多/你没有什么有利条件: *Stop being so depressed. You have a lot going for you.* 别这么沮丧。你有很多有利条件。**5 a going concern** a business which is making a profit and is expected to continue to do so 生意兴隆〔且将继续兴隆〕的企业

going-o·ver /ˌ·· ˈ·· ·/ *n* **1** a thorough examination of something to make sure it is all right 全面的检查: *The car needs a good going-over.* 这辆车需要好好检查一下。**2 give sb a going-over** *especially BrE* to hit someone and hurt them【尤英】把某人痛打一顿

goings-on /ˌ·· ˈ·/ *n* [plural] activities or events that are strange, especially ones that involve sex or make you think something dishonest may be happening〔怪异的，尤指色情或不正当的〕活动; 事件: *There are certainly some strange goings-on at that house, I reckon.* 我看那栋房子里肯定有怪事。

goi·tre *BrE*【英】, **goiter** *AmE*【美】/ˈgɔɪtɚ; ˈgɔɪtə/ *n* [C,U] a disease of the THYROID GLAND that makes your neck very swollen 甲状腺肿大

go-kart also 又作 **go-cart** *AmE*【美】/ˈgoˌkɑrt; ˈgəʊ kɑːt/ *n* [C] a small vehicle with an engine, made of an open frame on four wheels and used in races 微型赛车 —**go-karting** *n* [U]

Go·lan Heights, the /ˌgolɑn ˋhaɪts; ˌgəʊlæn ˈhaɪts/ a range of hills and mountains east of the Jordan River, occupied by Israel since 1967 戈兰高地〔约旦河以东的一系列丘陵和山脉，1967年起被以色列占领〕

gold¹ /gold; gəʊld/ *n* **1** [U] a valuable soft yellow metal that is an ELEMENT (=simple substance) and is used for making coins, jewellery etc 黄金: **strike gold** (=find it in the ground)〔在地下〕发现黄金 **2** [U] coins, jewellery etc made of this metal 金币，金首饰等: *Vanessa wore so much gold it's no wonder she was mugged.* 瓦妮莎戴了那么多金首饰，怪不得遭到抢劫。**3** [C, U] the colour of this metal 金色，金黄色: *The room was decorated in golds and blues.* 房间是用各种金色和蓝色来装饰的。**4** [C] *informal* a GOLD MEDAL【非正式】金质奖章，金牌 **5 gold digger** *old-fashioned slang* a woman who tries to attract rich men【过时，俚】勾引富有男子的女人 —see also 另见 **have a heart of gold** (HEART (13))

gold² *adj* **1** made of gold 金质的: *a gold chain* 金链 **2** having the colour of gold 金色的，金黄色的: *gold buttons* 金黄色的纽扣 | *gold velvet curtains* 金色的丝绒窗帘 —compare 比较 GOLDEN

Gold·berg /ˈgoldbɝg; ˈgəʊldbɜːg/, **Rube** (1883-1970) a US CARTOONIST (=an artist who draws funny pictures that tell a joke or say something humorous about the news) who drew strange and extremely complicated machines that are designed to do very simple jobs 戈德堡〔(1883-1970)，美国连环漫画家。其漫画中的机器画得怪异且极为复杂，但却用于做十分简单的工作〕—see also 另见 HEATH ROBINSON

gold·brick /ˈgoldˌbrɪk; ˈgəʊldbrɪk/ also 又作 **gold·brick·er** /-ˌbrɪkɚ; -brɪkə/ *n* [C] *AmE informal* someone who stays away from their work, especially with the false excuse that they are ill【美，非正式】装病逃避工作的人 —**goldbrick** *v* [I]

gold card /ˌ· ˈ·/ *n* [C] a special CREDIT CARD that gives you additional advantages or services, such as a high spending limit〔信用卡〕金卡

Gold Coast /ˈ· ˌ·/ *n* **1** the former name of **Ghana** before 1957 黄金海岸〔加纳旧称，1957年前使用〕**2** [C] *AmE* an expensive area of nice homes, especially one near water【美】高级(海岸)住宅区: *Chicago's Gold Coast along Lake Shore Drive* 芝加哥湖滨大道的高级住宅区

Gold Cup, the /ˌ· ˈ·/ a horse race held every March in Cheltenham, England 金杯赛〔每年3月在英格兰切尔滕纳姆举行的马赛〕

gold dust /ˈ· ·/ *n* [U] **1** gold in the form of a fine powder 金粉 **2 be like gold dust** to be very valuable and difficult to find 十分珍贵的，不可多得的: *Good secretaries are like gold dust.* 好秘书是不可多得的。

gold·en /ˈgoldṇ; ˈgəʊldən/ *adj* **1** having a bright, rich, yellow colour, like gold 金色的，金黄色的，金子般的: *golden sunlight* 金色的阳光 | *golden hair* 金黄色的头发 —see picture on page A5 参见A5页图 **2** made of gold 金质的: *a golden crown* 金王冠 **3 a golden opportunity** a good chance to get something valuable or to be very successful 绝好的机会: *Don't turn the job down – it's a golden opportunity.* 不要拒绝那份工作——这是个绝好的机会。**4 golden boy/girl** someone who is popular and successful 大受欢迎的成功男孩/女孩: *the golden girl of US tennis* 美国网球女明星 **5** [only before noun 仅用于名词前] a golden period of time is one of great happiness or success〔时期〕非常幸福的，非常成功的: *the golden summers of childhood* 童年幸福的夏天 **6 golden oldie** a popular song written several years ago that people still enjoy listening to 多年前创作而仍受喜爱的歌曲

golden age /ˈ‥ ˈ/ *n* [usually singular 一般用单数] an unusually good time of great achievement and happiness, especially in the past〔尤指过去的〕黄金时代: *the golden age of film* 电影的黄金时代

golden an·ni·ver·sa·ry /ˌ‥ ‥ˈ‥/ *n* [C] *AmE* a GOLDEN WEDDING【美】结婚50周年纪念日，金婚纪念日

golden brown /ˌ‥ ˈ◂/ *adj* a light brown colour 浅棕色的: *Bake the biscuits until golden brown.* 把饼干烘烤到浅棕色。

golden ea·gle /ˌ‥ ˈ‥/ *n* [C] a large light brown bird that lives in northern parts of the world 金雕

Golden Gate, the /ˌ‥ ˈ/ an area of water which connects San Francisco Bay in California with the Pacific Ocean. It is crossed by the Golden Gate Bridge. 金门海峡〔连接加利福尼亚州圣弗朗西斯科湾与太平洋的海域，金门桥横跨两岸〕

Golden Gate Bridge, the /ˌ‥ ˈ ˈ/ also 又作 **the Golden Gate** a bridge which crosses an area of water in San Francisco Bay in California, to connect the city of San Francisco with Marin County 金门桥〔横跨加利福尼亚金门海峡、连接圣弗朗西斯科市与马林县的一座大桥〕

Golden Glove A·wards, the /ˌ‥ ˈ ˌ/ a ceremony held every year in the US, at which prizes are given to the best BASEBALL FIELDERS in the Major Leagues "金手套"奖颁奖典礼〔每年在美国为棒球大联盟最佳外场球手颁奖的仪式〕

Golden Gloves, the /ˌ‥ ˈ/ an American competition for AMATEUR (=unpaid) boxers〔美国业余拳击手参加的〕"金手套"拳击赛

golden hand·shake /ˌ‥ ˈ‥/ *n* [C] *BrE* a large amount of money given to someone when they leave their job【英】〔离职时的一大笔〕退职金，遣散费

golden ju·bi·lee /ˌ‥ ˈ‥/ *n* [C] *BrE* the date that is exactly 50 years after some important event, especially of becoming king or queen【英】〔某重要事件，尤指国王、女王加冕〕50周年纪念日 —compare 比较 DIAMOND JUBILEE, SILVER JUBILEE

golden par·a·chute /ˌ‥ ˈ‥/ *n* [C] *BrE informal* part of a business person's contract which states that they will be paid a large sum of money when the contract ends【英，非正式】金降落伞〔指商业人员合约的一部分，规定合约终止时，他将获得一大笔钱〕

golden rai·sin /ˌ‥ ˈ‥/ *n* [C] *AmE* a small pale RAISIN (=dried fruit) used in baking【美】〔烘烤食物使用的〕无核葡萄干; SULTANA *BrE*【英】

golden re·triev·er /ˌ‥ ˈ‥/ *n* [C] a fairly large dog with silky light brown fur 金毛拾猎

golden rule /ˌ‥ ˈ/ *n* [usually singular 一般用单数] a very important principle, way of behaving etc that should be remembered 重要的原则; 重要的行为准则

Golden Rule, The an idea from the Bible that people should treat others in the way that they want to be treated themselves 为人准则〔指《圣经》中所述的观点: 你想人家怎么对待你，自己也要怎么对待人家〕

golden syr·up /ˌ‥ ˈ‥/ *n* [U] *BrE* a sweet, thick liquid made from sugar that is used in cooking【英】〔用于烹调的〕金黄色糖浆

Golden Tem·ple /ˌ‥ ˈ‥/ a TEMPLE (=a type of church) in Amritsar in India which is very important in the Sikh religion. It stands in the middle of a holy lake and contains the holy book of the Sikhs. 金庙〔印度阿姆利则一庙宇，在锡克教中极其重要。它位于一个圣湖的中心，藏有锡克教圣书〕

Golden Tri·an·gle, the /ˌ‥ ˈ‥/ an area of hills consisting of part of Laos, Thailand, and Burma. Poppies (POPPY) for making the drug OPIUM are illegally grown there. 金三角〔包括老挝、泰国、缅甸部分地区在内的丘陵地带。该地非法种植用于加工鸦片的罂粟〕

golden wed·ding /ˌ‥ ˈ‥/ also 又作 **golden wedding an·niver·sa·ry** /ˌ‥ ˈ‥ ‥ˈ‥/ *BrE informal n* [C] the date that is exactly 50 years after a wedding【英，非正式】结婚50周年纪念日，金婚纪念日; GOLDEN ANNIVERSARY *AmE*【美】—compare 比较 DIAMOND WEDDING, SILVER WEDDING, ANNIVERSARY

gold·field /ˈgoldˌfild; ˈgəʊldfiːld/ *n* [C] also 又作 **goldfields** *plural* an area of land where gold can be found 金矿区，采金地

gold·finch /ˈgoldˌfɪntʃ; ˈgəʊldˌfɪntʃ/ *n* [C] a small singing bird with yellow feathers on its wings 黄雀

gold·fish /ˈgoldˌfɪʃ; ˈgəʊldˌfɪʃ/ *n* [C] a small shiny orange fish often kept as a pet 金鱼

goldfish bowl /ˈ‥ ˌ/ *n* [C] **1** a round glass bowl in which fish are kept as pets 金鱼缸 **2 live in a goldfish bowl** to be in a situation in which people can know everything about your life 置身于没有隐私的境地

Gold·i·locks /ˈgoldɪlɑks; ˈgəʊldilɒks/ **1** the main character in the children's story *Goldilocks and the Three Bears.* Goldilocks is a young girl with golden-coloured hair who visits the house of the Three Bears while they are out. She tries sitting in each of their chairs, tastes each of their bowls of PORRIDGE, and lies in each of their beds until she finds the one she likes best. When the Bears come back, they realize that someone has been in their home. They each ask "Who's been sitting in my chair?", "Who's been eating my porridge?", and "Who's been sleeping in my bed?" until they finally find Goldilocks asleep in the baby bear's bed. Goldilocks then wakes up and runs away. 金发姑娘〔童话故事《金发姑娘和三只熊》中的主人公。她是一个满头金发的小女孩，趁三只熊外出时去它们的家里。她坐了它们的椅子，尝了它们碗里的粥，躺了它们的床，还在最舒适的一张床上睡了下来。熊一家回来后，发现有人来过，相互问道: "谁坐过我的椅子?" "谁吃过我的粥?" "谁睡过我的床?" 最后发现金发姑娘正在小熊的床上睡着。这时，金发姑娘醒来，一溜烟跑掉了〕**2** a humorous name for someone, especially a little girl, with BLONDE hair 金发姑娘〔对某人，尤其是金发小女孩的幽默指称〕

Gol·ding /ˈgoldɪŋ; ˈgəʊldɪŋ/, **William** (1911-93) a British writer who won the Nobel Prize for Literature in 1983. His most famous work is the NOVEL *Lord of the Flies.* 戈尔丁〔(1911-1993)，英国作家。1983年获诺贝尔文学奖。最著名的作品是小说《蝇王》〕

gold leaf /ˌ‥ ˈ/ *n* [U] gold which has been beaten into extremely thin sheets for use in decoration 金叶，金箔

gold med·al /ˌ‥ ˈ‥/ *n* [C] a round, flat piece of gold given to someone for a special achievement, especially for winning a race or competition 金质奖章，金牌 —see also 另见 BRONZE MEDAL, SILVER MEDAL

gold med·al·list *BrE*【英】, **gold medalist** *AmE*【美】/ˌ‥ ˈ‥/ *n* [C] someone who wins a gold medal 金质奖章获得者，金牌获得者

gold·mine /ˈgoldˌmaɪn; ˈgəʊldmaɪn/ *n* [C] **1** *informal* a business or activity that produces large profits【非正式】〔产生巨额利润的〕财源，宝库: *I bet that shop's a real goldmine.* 我敢说那家商店是个真正的金矿。**2** a deep hole or system of holes underground from which rock containing gold is taken 金矿 **3 be sitting on a goldmine** to own something very valuable, especially without realizing this 拥有非常宝贵的东西〔尤指自己并不知道〕

gold plate /ˌ‥ ˈ/ *n* [U] **1** a layer of gold on top of another metal 镀金层 **2** dishes, spoons etc made of gold 金质餐具 —**gold-plated** *adj*: *Is it solid gold or gold-plated?* 这是纯金的还是镀金的?

gold-rimmed /ˌ‥ ˈ◂/ *adj* having a gold edge or border 镶金边的: *gold-rimmed glasses* 金边玻璃杯

gold rush /ˈ‥ ˌ/ *n* [C] a situation when a lot of people hurry to a place where gold has just been discovered 淘金热〔涌向刚刚发现金子的地区〕

gold·smith /ˈgoldˌsmɪθ; ˈgəʊldˌsmɪθ/ *n* [C] someone who makes things out of gold 金匠

Goldsmith, Ol·i·ver /ˈɑlɪvɚ; ˈɒlɪvə/ (1728-74) an Irish poet and writer of NOVELS, including *The Vicar of Wakefield,* and plays, including *She Stoops to Conquer* 哥尔德斯密斯〔(1728-1774)，爱尔兰诗人、小说家。作品包括小说《威克菲尔德的牧师》和剧本《委曲求全》(又译《屈身求爱》)〕

gold stan·dard /ˈ‥ ˌ‥/ *n* **the gold standard** the use of the value of gold as a fixed standard on which to base the value of money〔货币的〕金本位

Gold·wyn /ˈgoldwɪn; ˈgəʊldwɪn/, **Sam·u·el** /ˈsæmjuəl; ˈsæmjuəl/ (1882-1974) a US film producer who started the company that became MGM and had an important part in the development of the Hollywood film industry 高德温〔(1882-1974)，美国电影制片人。他创立了后来称作米高梅的一家电影公司，对好莱坞电影业的发展起过重要作用〕

go·lem /ˈgoləm; ˈgəʊləm/ *n* [C] *AmE informal* a stupid person【美，非正式】傻瓜，蠢人

golf /gɑlf; gɒlf/ *n* [U] a game in which the players hit a small white ball into holes in the ground with a set of golf clubs using as few hits as possible 高尔夫球运动: **a round of golf** (=a game of golf) 一场高尔夫球 —**golfer** *n* [C] S2 W3

CULTURAL NOTE 文化注释

Golf was first played in Scotland and it is still a popular sport there. In England and Wales, golf is considered by many people to be a sport mainly for rich people, but in Scotland and the US it is played by people from a wider range of social classes. In the UK, the STEREO-

G

TYPE of a golfer is someone who wears a jumper and PLUS FOURS (=short loose trousers that are fastened just below the knee, that some men wore in the past). In the US, the stereotype of a golfer is of an older man who is no longer working, and who plays golf to fill up his time. Some people also think of business people making deals while playing golf together. In the UK and the US, there are public GOLF COURSE*s* and private golf courses owned by GOLF CLUB*s*, some of which are expensive to join. Some of the most famous British golf clubs are the Royal and Ancient at St Andrews (in Fife, Scotland), Muirfield (near Edinburgh, Scotland), and Wentworth (in Surrey, southern England). Some of the most famous golf courses in the US include Pebble Beach in California, Augusta National Golf Club in Georgia, and Myrtle Beach, which has many different golf courses in a fairly small area of North and South Carolina. 高尔夫最早出现在苏格兰，现在这项运动在苏格兰仍很流行。英格兰和威尔士的很多人觉得高尔夫球主要是有钱人的运动，但在苏格兰和美国，打高尔夫球的人来自社会各个阶层。英国高尔夫球手的典型形象是穿套头衫和灯笼裤。美国高尔夫球手的典型形象是一个退休的老人，打高尔夫球填补时间。还有人认为商人在一起打高尔夫球时谈生意。英美有很多公共高尔夫球场，以及归高尔夫球俱乐部所有的私人高尔夫球场，有的俱乐部入会费很昂贵。英国最著名的高尔夫球俱乐部有圣安德鲁斯皇家古典俱乐部（位于苏格兰法夫）、缪尔菲尔德俱乐部（苏格兰爱丁堡附近）和温特沃思俱乐部（位于英格兰南部萨里郡）。美国最著名的高尔夫球场有加利福尼亚的卵石滩球场、佐治亚州的奥古斯塔国家高尔夫球俱乐部球场，还有在北卡罗来纳和南卡罗来纳面积不大的区域有多家高尔夫球场的默特尔滩俱乐部。

The most important international golf competitions for professional players are called the Majors. The four Majors are: the Open (played on different golf courses in the UK), the Masters Tournament (played in Augusta, Georgia), the US Open, and the US PGA Championship. Every two years, teams from Europe and the US compete to win the Ryder Cup. 职业高尔夫球手最重要的国际赛事叫做大赛（the Majors），四大赛事分别是公开赛（在英国不同的高尔夫球场举办）、大师赛（在佐治亚州奥古斯塔举办）、美国公开赛和美国职业高尔夫球协会锦标赛。每隔两年，欧洲和美国的高尔夫球队举行比赛，争夺赖德杯。

G

golf ball /ˈ· ·/ *n* [C] **1** a small hard white ball used in the game of golf 高尔夫球 **2** a small ball in an electric TYPEWRITER that has the letters of the alphabet on it, and that moves to print them onto paper〔电动打字机的〕球形字头 **3** an electric TYPEWRITER that operates in this way 有球形字头的电动打字机 —compare 比较 DAISYWHEEL PRINTER

golf club /ˈ· ·/ *n* [C] **1** an organization of people who play golf, or the land and buildings they use 高尔夫球俱乐部 **2** a long wooden or metal stick used for hitting the ball in the game of golf 高尔夫球杆 —see picture on page A23 参见 A23 页图

golf course /ˈ· ·/ *n* [C] an area of land that golf is played on 高尔夫球场

golf·ing /ˈɡɑlfɪŋ; ˈɡɒlfɪŋ/ *n* [U] the activity of playing golf 打高尔夫球: *Ian goes golfing on Sundays.* 伊恩每星期日去打高尔夫球。

golf links /ˈ· ·/ *plural* **golf links** *n* [C] a golf course, especially by the sea〔尤指海边的〕高尔夫球场

Gol·goth·a /ˈɡɑlɡəθə; ˈɡɒlɡəθə/ the ancient Jewish name for the place near Jerusalem where, according to the New Testament of the Bible, Jesus Christ died by being crucified (CRUCIFY). Its Roman name was Calvary. 各各他〔古犹太地名，位于耶路撒冷附近。据《圣经·新约》所述，耶稣基督在这里被钉死在十字架上。罗马语称髑髅地〕

Go·li·ath /ɡəˈlaɪəθ; ɡəˈlaɪəθ/ in the Old Testament of the Bible, a GIANT (=a very big, strong man) who was killed by a boy called David, who later became King David 歌利亚〔《圣经·旧约》中被少年大卫杀死的巨人，杀人的少年即后来的大卫王〕

goliath *n* [C] a person or company that is very large, strong, and powerful; GIANT[2] 巨人; 大公司: *How can a small computer company compete with the goliaths of the industry?* 一家小电脑公司怎么能跟行业巨头竞争呢?

gol·li·wog /ˈɡɑlɪˌwɑɡ; ˈɡɒliwɒɡ/ *n* [C] a child's DOLL[1] (1) made of cloth, like a man with a black face, white eyes, and short black hair 黑脸白眼、短头发的男布娃娃

CULTURAL NOTE 文化注释

Many people who are against RACISM find golliwogs offensive because they show an old-fashioned STEREOTYPE of black people, but many other people think that golliwogs are just toys and that their appearance is not important. 很多反种族主义的人认为这种玩偶令人反感，因为它展现的是旧时黑人的典型形象。但另有很多人认为它只是玩具，外表并不重要。

gol·ly[1] /ˈɡɑlɪ; ˈɡɒli/ *interjection old-fashioned* used to express surprise【过时】天啊〔用来表示惊讶〕

golly[2] *n* [C] *informal* a golliwog【非正式】黑脸白眼、短头发男布娃娃

Go·mor·rah /ɡəˋmɔrə; ɡəˈmɒrə/ —see 见 SODOM AND GOMORRAH

-gon /ɡən; ɡən *strong* 强读 ɡɑn; ɡɒn/ *suffix* [in nouns 构成名词] a shape with a particular number of sides and angles …边形; …角形: *a hexagon* (=with six sides) 六边形 | *a polygon* (=with many sides) 多边形

go·nad /ˈɡɑnæd; ˈɡəʊnæd/ *n* [C] *technical* the male or female sex organ in which the SPERM (1) or eggs (EGG[1] (3)) are produced【术语】性腺，生殖腺; 睾丸; 卵巢

gon·do·la /ˈɡɑndələ; ˈɡɒndələ/ *n* [C] **1** a long narrow boat with a flat bottom and high points at each end, used on the CANAL*s* in Venice in Italy〔意大利威尼斯运河的〕平底船 **2** the place where passengers sit that hangs beneath an AIRSHIP or BALLOON[1] (2)〔飞船或气球下的〕吊篮，吊舱 **3** the enclosed part of a CABLE CAR where the passengers sit〔缆车的〕车厢

gon·do·lier /ˌɡɑndəˈlɪr; ˌɡɒndəˈlɪə/ *n* [C] a man who rows a gondola in Venice 威尼斯平底船船夫

Gon·dwa·na·land /ɡɑnˈdwɑnəlænd; ɡɒnˈdwɑːnəlænd/ the very large area of land that existed about 200 million years ago, before it broke apart to form Antarctica, Australia, Africa, South America, and India 冈瓦纳古大陆〔两亿年前的一块大陆，后分裂成南极洲、澳大利亚、非洲、南美洲和印度〕—see also 另见 LAURASIA, PANGAEA

gone[1] /ɡɔn; ɡɒn/ the past participle of go

gone[2] *adj informal*【非正式】**1 be gone** to be showing the effects of taking drugs or drinking alcohol〔因吸毒或饮酒而〕神志不清的: *Look at Michelle – she's totally gone!* 瞧瞧米歇尔，她完全醉了! **2 be gone on sb** to be very fond of someone and think they are very attractive 迷恋上[倾心于]某人: *Our Kate's really gone on that boy next door.* 我们的凯特真的迷恋上隔壁那个男孩了。**3 be five/six/seven etc months gone** *BrE informal* to have been PREGNANT for a particular length of time【英，非正式】已经怀孕五个月/六个月/七个月等

gone[3] *prep BrE informal* used like 'past', to mean later than a particular time or older than a particular age【英，非正式】过了〔与 past的用法相似，指过了某个时间或某一年龄〕: *When we got home it was gone midnight.* 我们到家时已经过了半夜。

gon·er /ˈɡɑnɚ; ˈɡɒnə/ *n informal*【非正式】**be a goner** someone who will soon die, or is in an impossible situation 即将死去[陷入绝境]的人: *If Mark's still inside the plane, he's a goner.* 如果马克还在飞机里，他就完了。

Gon·e·ril /ˈɡɑnərɪl; ˈɡɒnərɪl/ one of King Lear's daughters in the play *King Lear* by William Shakespeare. She and her sister Regan pretend to love their father to make him give them his land, and then treat him so cruelly that he becomes mentally ill. Goneril finally kills Regan with poison, and then kills herself. 高纳里尔〔威廉·莎士比亚戏剧《李尔王》中李尔王的一个女儿。她和妹妹里根巧言骗得父亲的国土后，把父亲虐待成精神病。高纳里尔最后毒死里根，然后自尽〕—see 见 CORDELIA, REGAN

Gone with the Wind /ˌɡɔn wɪð ðə ˋwɪnd; ˌɡɒn wɪð ðə ˈwɪnd/ (1939) a US film, based on a NOVEL by Margaret Mitchell. Many people think it is one of the greatest romantic films ever made. It tells the story of a beautiful, determined woman called Scarlett O'Hara, acted by Vivien Leigh, who lives in Georgia during the American Civil War. She marries Rhett Butler, acted by Clark Gable, but treats him badly.《飘》，又译《乱世佳人》〔(1939)，美国影片，改编自玛格丽特·米切尔的同名小说，被认为是有史以来最伟大的浪漫影片之一。影片讲述美国南北战争时期佐治亚州的一位貌美志坚的女子郝思嘉（由费雯·丽饰演）的故事。她与白瑞德（由克拉克·盖博饰演）结了婚，但却对他不好〕

gong /ɡɔŋ; ɡɒŋ/ *n* [C] a round piece of metal that hangs in a frame and that you hit with a stick to give a deep ringing sound, used for example to call people somewhere, often to announce that a meal is ready 锣

gon·na /ˈgɔnə; ˈgɒnə/ a way of saying 'going to', which many people think is incorrect 即将, 打算〔意为 going to, 许多人认为这种用法不正确〕: *This isn't gonna be easy.* 这将很不容易。

gon·or·rhe·a, gonorrhoea /ˌgɑnəˈriə; ˌgɒnəˈriːə/ *n* [U] a disease of the sex organs that is passed on during sex; VD 淋病

gon·zo jour·nal·is·m /ˈgɑnzo ˌdʒɜnḷɪzəm; ˈgɒnzəʊ ˌdʒɜːnəlɪzəm/ *n* [U] *AmE informal* reporting in newspapers which is concerned with shocking or exciting the reader and not with giving true information【美, 非正式】寻求轰动效应的新闻报道〔指一种报纸上的报道, 其目的不在于提供信息, 而在于使读者震惊或激动〕—**gonzo journalist** *n* [C]

goo /gu; guː/ *n* [U] *informal*【非正式】**1** an unpleasantly sticky substance〔令人生厌的〕黏糊糊的东西: *What's all this goo at the bottom of the bag?* 袋底的这些黏糊糊的东西是什么? **2** words or feelings that are too emotional or romantic 过分多情的话; 过分多情 —see also 另见 GOOEY

S1 W1 **good¹** /gʊd; gʊd/ *adj comparative* 比较级 **better** /ˈbɛtə; ˈbetə/ *superlative* 最高级 **best** /bɛst; best/

1 ▶OF A HIGH STANDARD 高标准的◀ of a high standard 良好的: *a good reputation* 良好的声誉 | *a good quality cloth* 优质布料 | *a good Muslim* 一名遵守教规的穆斯林 | *This book is not as good as her last one.* 这本书不如她的上一本好。| *His test scores were good, but hers were even better.* 他的考试分数很好, 可是她的更好。| *We received the best medical treatment.* 我们得到最好的医疗。| **very/extremely/pretty etc good** *Mike's done an extremely good job of painting the windows.* 迈克把窗子油漆得非常好。| **(not) good enough** *Your work's simply not good enough.* 你的工作实在不够好。| **be too good for sb** *informal*【非正式】*David doesn't deserve to have a girlfriend like Kate – she's much too good for him!* 戴维配不上有像凯特这样的女朋友, 对戴维来说凯特是太好了! —opposites 反义词 BAD¹ (2), POOR (3)

2 ▶OF THE RIGHT KIND 对头的◀ having qualities that are worth praising 值得称赞的, 良好的: *He is a good husband.* 他是个好丈夫。| *$50 is a very good price.* 50美元是个很好的价格。| *That's good news!* 那是好消息! | *They've had a really good idea.* 他们的想法确实很好。| **any good** *"Is your new doctor any good?" – "Yes, she's OK."* "你们那位新医生行吗?" "行, 她还不错。" —opposite 反义词 BAD¹ (1)

3 no good/not much good/not any good a) not very useful 不太有用: *This radio's not much good, is it?* 这台收音机不怎么好用, 是吗? | **it is no good doing sth** *It's no good talking to him – he never listens.* 跟他讲没用 — 他从来不听。| **no good for sth** *These glasses are no good for champagne.* 这些玻璃杯不适合用来喝香槟酒。| **no good to sb** *A car's not much good to me, since I can't drive!* 汽车对我没有多大用处, 因为我不会开车! **b)** bad 不好的, 坏的: *The movie wasn't much good.* 这部电影不怎么好。

4 ▶SKILFUL 熟练的◀ clever or skilful 聪明的, 熟练的: *She's a good skier.* 她是个滑雪能手。| **good at sth/doing sth** *Alfred is very good at languages.* 艾尔弗雷德很擅长学习语言。| **good with sth/sb** (=skilful at using something or dealing with someone) 擅长使用某物/与某人打交道 *My receptionist is very good with people.* 我的接待员很会与人打交道。—opposites 反义词 BAD¹ (2), POOR (5)

5 be no good at/not be much good at/not be very good at not to be skilful at something or doing something 不擅长〔做〕某事: *You're not very good at reading maps, are you?* 你不太擅长看地图, 是吗?

6 ▶STRONG 强有力的◀ strong; likely to be successful, to persuade people etc 有说服力的, 有分量的: *I want an explanation, and it had better be good!* 我需要有个解释, 最好是有说服力的解释! | *That's a good point.* 那是个很有力的论点。| *You have a fairly good chance of winning.* 你获胜的机会相当大。—opposites 反义词 POOR (3), WEAK (5)

7 ▶ENJOYABLE 令人愉快的◀ enjoyable; pleasant 令人愉快的, 合意的: *It's good to see you again.* 很高兴再次见到你。| *That was good fun.* 那非常好玩。| **have a good time/day/weekend etc** *The kids had a very good time at the zoo.* 孩子们在动物园玩得很开心。| **too much of a good thing** (=something which stops being pleasant because you have too much of it or it continues for too long) 过了头的好事 —see also 另见 **the good old days** (OLD (16))

8 ▶SUITABLE 合适的◀ a) good for sth/good for doing sth suitable for something 适合某事/适合做某事: *It's a good day for a trip to the mountains.* 今天的天气很适合到山里去玩。| *This is the best knife for cutting vegetables.* 这是最适合切菜用的刀子。| *Those cards would be good for the invitations.* 那些卡片做请柬用很合适。**b) good for sb** *especially AmE* convenient for someone【尤美】对某人是方便的: *Ten o'clock is good for me.* 10点钟对我很合适。| *So we're all meeting at the beach? That's good for me.* 那么我们大家都在海滩碰头吗? 这对我很合适。

9 ▶HELPFUL 有帮助的◀ helpful 有帮助的, 有益的: *good advice* 有益的忠告 | *That's a very good example.* 那是个很好的例子。| *She'll be a good influence on him.* 她对他会产生很好的影响。| **be good for sth** (=help it to develop or be produced) 对某物有帮助 *This weather is very good for business.* 这样的天气对生意很有帮助。| *It's been a good year for apples.* 今年是苹果的好年头。—opposites 反义词 BAD¹ (2), POOR (3)

10 ▶IN A GOOD CONDITION 状况良好◀ in a satisfactory condition for use; not broken, damaged, decayed, OUT-OF-DATE etc 状况良好的; 未坏的; 未过期的: *You need good shoes for hiking.* 徒步旅行需要穿结实的鞋子。| **good for three days/a week etc** (=to be used during that time) 能用三天/一星期等 *This ticket is good for one month.* 这张票一个月内有效。| **as good as new** (=in perfect condition, especially after being cleaned or repaired)〔通过清洗或修理〕像新的一样 *They've fixed the car, and it's as good as new.* 他们把车修好了, 现在车像新的一样。—see also 另见 **pay good money for** (MONEY (5))

11 ▶HEALTHY 有益健康的◀ healthy 有益健康的: *This water isn't good to drink.* 这水不宜饮用。| **feel good** *I don't feel too good.* 我感到不大舒服。| *He's feeling better today.* 他今天感觉好多了。| **be good for sb** *Milk is good for you.* 喝牛奶对你有好处。| *It isn't good for children to watch too much TV.* 儿童不宜看太多电视。

12 ▶SHOWING APPROVAL 表示赞许◀ Good *spoken*【口】**a)** used to show that you are pleased about something 好〔对某事感到满意〕: *Good, I'm glad you've got it under control.* 好, 我很高兴你把它控制住了。| *"Seven minus two is five." "Good."* "七减二等于五。" "对。" **b)** used when something has been decided or agreed 行, 好〔用于决定或同意某事时〕: *Good. We'll use the new one, then.* 好, 那么我们就用新的。

13 ▶CHILD 儿童◀ a word meaning well-behaved, used especially about a child 守规矩的, 乖的〔尤指儿童〕: *She's such a good baby.* 她真是一个乖孩子。| *Be a good girl, now.* 做个乖女孩, 听见了吗? | **as good as gold** (=extremely well-behaved) 十分有教养的, 非常乖的

14 ▶KIND 好心的◀ kind 好心的, 慈善的: **good about** *I had some time off work when my mother was ill, but my boss was very good about it.* 我母亲生病的时候我请了几天假, 老板对此非常谅解。| **good of sb (to do sth)** *formal*【正式】*It was good of you to come to the funeral.* 你能来参加葬礼十分感谢。| **good to sb** (=an expression meaning kind to someone, used especially to defend someone) 对某人友善的〔尤用来为某人辩护〕*Mr Hawkins has always been very good to me.* 霍金斯先生一直对我很好。

15 ▶LARGE 大的◀ large in amount, area, or range〔数量、面积或范围〕相当大的: *They stock a good range of furniture.* 他们备有各式各样的家具。| *a good crop of mangoes* 芒果大丰收 | *I've travelled a good distance.* 我走了很长一段路。| **a good while** *informal* (=quite a long time)【非正式】长时间, 很久 *We'd waited a good while by now.* 我们已经等了很久。—see also 另见 GOODISH

16 ▶MORALLY RIGHT 有道德的◀ morally right 有道德的, 高尚的: *a good man* 正派人 | *I still think it was a good thing to do.* 我仍然认为这是件该做的好事。| **my/his etc good deed for the day** *informal* (=something you do that helps someone else, especially something boring or unimportant)【非正式】我/他等做的善事〔尤指区区小事〕| **the good guys** *informal* (=the people who represent morally right behaviour, especially in films)【非正式】〔电影里的〕正派人物 | **be no good** *informal* (=be a morally bad person)【非正式】品行不端的人 *Stay away from Gerry. He's no good.* 离格里远点, 他不是好东西。—opposite 反义词 BAD¹ (3)

17 ▶COMPLETE 完整的◀ complete; thorough 完整的, 全面的, 彻底的: *Take a good look at it.* 好好地看它一眼。| *She had a good cry.* 她痛快地哭了一场。| *That needs a good washing.* 那需要好好地洗一洗。| **good and ...** *informal* (=very or completely)【非正式】非常, 完全 *Don't rush me; I'll do it when I'm good and ready.* 别催我, 我完全准备好了就会做的。

18 a good deal a lot 大量, 许多: *They went out a good deal.* 他们经常外出。| **a good deal of trouble/time etc** *I went to a good deal of trouble to get this ticket.* 我费了好大劲才弄到这张票。

19 a good deal larger/better etc also 又作 **a good bit larger/better etc** *BrE* much larger, better etc【英】大得多/好得多等: *Their kitchen is a good deal wider than ours.* 他们的厨房比我们的宽多了。

20 a good friend someone who you know very well and like very much 好朋友

21 hold good if a law, rule, reason etc holds good it is or remains effective or true〔法律、规则、理由等〕有效, 适用: *theories that hold good for all countries* 适用于各国的理论 | *These words, uttered in 1848, still hold good today.* 这些话虽然是1848年说的, 但在今天仍然适用。

22 the good good people generally; those who do what is right 好人: *Christians believe that the good go to heaven when they die.* 基督徒认为好人死后上天堂。—see also 另见 **the great and the good** (GREAT (21))

23 be too good to be true/to last *informal* to seem to be so good that you think something must be wrong, or expect something bad to happen【非正式】好得令人难以置信, 好得令人觉得有问题: *She found out he was married – I knew he was too good to be true!* 她发现他是结了婚的 —— 我就知道他不会有这么好!

24 in good time (for sth/to do sth) if you arrive somewhere in good time to do something, you arrive early enough to do it 早早地 (到某地以便不耽误做某事)

25 in her/their etc own good time *informal* someone who does something in their own good time does not do it when other people want them to, but only when they are completely ready to do it【非正式】在她/他们等认为最适合自己的时间

26 as good a time/place etc as any *usually spoken* used to say that although a time etc is not perfect, there will not be a better one【一般口】与其他时间/地点等不相上下〔用来表示某一时间等虽不完美, 但不会有更好的〕: *Well, I suppose this is as good a spot as any to set up camp.* 好吧, 我想在这个地方扎营不比其他任何地方坏。

27 good for nothing *informal* someone who is good for nothing is completely useless and worthless【非正式】〔人〕完全没用的, 一文不值的 —see also 另见 GOOD-FOR-NOTHING

28 to be good for a meal/a few drinks etc *informal* be likely to give you something【非正式】可能给一顿饭吃/几杯酒喝等: *My uncle should be good for a few bucks.* 我叔叔应当会给几块钱。

29 good offices [plural] *formal* services provided, especially by someone in a position of power, that help someone out of a difficulty【正式】〔有权势人的〕帮忙, 照顾: *Through the good offices of the ambassador we were given special permission to travel.* 由于大使的帮助, 我们获得旅行特许。

30 be in sb's good books *informal* if you are in someone's good books, they like you or approve of you more than they usually do【非正式】为某人所另眼相看: *I'll ask my boss for the day off – I'm in her good books at the moment.* 我要向老板请一天假 —— 我目前正得到她的好感。

31 the good book *old-fashioned, sometimes humorous* the Bible【过时, 有时幽默】《圣经》

32 good Samaritan someone who gives help to people in trouble 行善的人: *Mrs Hoare was the good Samaritan who came to our rescue.* 霍尔女士就是那位救援我们的善人。

33 in good faith *formal* sincerely【正式】真诚地, 诚实地: *I promised you that in good faith, but I can't do it, I'm afraid.* 我当时确是真诚地答应你办这件事, 不过现在我恐怕做不了。

34 a good three miles/ten years etc at least three miles, ten years etc, and probably more 至少三英里/十年等: *It's a good mile away.* 那里距离此地至少一英里。| *He's a good ten years younger than her.* 他比她至少小10岁。

35 be good for another three years/hundred miles etc something that is good for a particular length of time is not in good condition but will probably last for that length of time 可再对付用三年/可再走一百英里等: *Nonsense, my bike's good for a few miles yet!* 胡说, 我的自行车还能骑几英里!

36 a good few/many *informal* quite a lot of something【非正式】许多, 大量: *I've done this a good few times now.* 我到现在已经做了许多遍了。| *"How many people were there?" "Oh, a good many."* "那里有多少人?" "噢, 很多人。"

37 as good as done/finished/yours etc used to say that something is almost done etc, or definitely will be soon 可以说已经做完/完成/就是你的等: *The work is as good as finished.* 这件工作可以说已经完成。

38 as good as dead/ruined/useless etc in a state that is not much better than being dead, ruined etc 差不多死了/毁了/废了等: *If he finds out, I'm as good as dead!* 如果他发现, 我就没命了!

39 give as good as you get *BrE informal* to react to someone who attacks or harms you by doing equal damage to them【英, 非正式】以牙还牙

40 have a good thing going to be doing something that is and will continue to be successful 成功地做着某事: *They've got a good thing going with that little business of theirs.* 他们的那个小生意做得很红火。

41 be as good as your word to keep your promise 守信用, 信守诺言: *He said he'd see what he could do, and he was as good as his word.* 他答应尽力帮忙, 而且他说话算数。

42 a good word for sb/sth a favourable remark about someone or something 为某人/某事说的一句好话: **have a good word (to say) for sb/sth** *I'm afraid no one had a good word to say for her.* 恐怕没人说她的好话。| **put in a good word for sb** *When you see the CEO, put in a good word for me.* 你见到行政总裁时帮我说句好话。

43 be onto a good thing *informal* to have found a way of getting a lot without paying money or working hard【非正式】找到了不必花钱[不必努力工作]便大有所获的办法

44 make good also 又作 **make it good** an expression meaning to become successful and rich after being poor, used especially in newspapers 变富; 获得成功〔尤用于报纸上〕: *a boy from a hick town who made good in New York* 一位来自偏僻乡镇在纽约获得成功的男孩

45 make good a debt/loss etc an expression meaning to pay someone money that you owe, or provide money instead of what has been lost, used especially in business 偿还债务/赔偿损失等〔尤用于生意〕: *The loss to the company was made good by contributions from its subsidiaries.* 公司的损失由各子公司的捐助弥补了。

46 make good your escape *literary* to succeed in escaping【文】成功逃跑

47 the good life a simple, natural way of living 朴素自然的生活方式 —see also 另见 **so far so good** (FAR¹ (21)), **while the going's good** (GOING¹ (4)), **for good measure** (MEASURE¹ (9)), **bad/good sailor** (SAILOR (2)), **that's/it's all well and good** (WELL³ (5))

Frequencies of the adjective **good** in spoken and written English 形容词good在英语口语和书面语中的使用频率

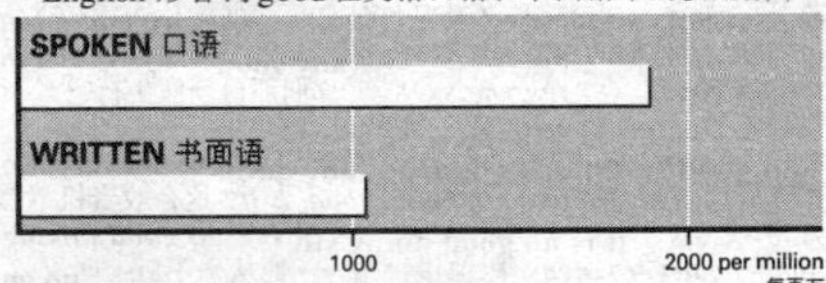

Based on the British National Corpus and the Longman Lancaster Corpus 据英国国家语料库和朗文兰开斯特语料库

This graph shows that the adjective **good** is much more common in spoken English than in written English. This is because it has some special uses in spoken English and is used in some common spoken phrases. 本图表显示, 形容词good在英语口语中的使用频率远远高于书面语, 因为它在口语中有特殊的用法, 并用在一些常见的口语短语中。

good (*adj*) **SPOKEN PHRASES**
含good的口语短语

48 good used to say that you are pleased that something happens or is done 好〔用来表示对某事发生或办成很高兴〕: *"I could do it tomorrow if you want." "Good."* "如果你需要的话, 我可以明天做。" "好。" used to tell someone that you think their work or what they are doing is good〔用来告诉某人你对他的工作满意〕: *Good, that's the way, keep going.* 干得好, 就是这样, 继续干吧。**49 oh good** used to say that you are pleased that something you didn't know about happens or is done 好啊〔用来对原来不知道的事情的发生或完成表示高兴〕: *"I've invited Danny and Marilyn to dinner tonight." "Oh good."* "我请了丹尼和玛丽莲今晚来吃饭。" "好啊。" **50 good morning/afternoon/evening** used to say hello to someone in the morning, afternoon or evening 早上好/下午好/晚上好: *Good afternoon everyone. Sorry I'm late.* 大家下午好。对不起我迟到了。**51 what a good girl/boy/dog etc** used to tell a child or animal that it has behaved well or done something well 多乖的女孩/男孩/狗等: *What a good girl! Mummy's going to give you a nice chocolate.* 多乖的孩子! 妈妈要给你一块好吃的巧克力。**52 good idea/point/question** used when someone says or suggests something interesting or important that you had not thought of before 好主意/说得对/问题提得好: *"But tomorrow's Sunday, the bank will be closed." "Yes, good point."* "不过明天是星期天, 银行会关门。" "是的, 说得对。"

53 that's no good used to say that something is not suitable or convenient 不合适, 不方便: *"I could do it next week." "That's no good. I'll be away."* "我可以下星期做。" "那不行, 下星期我不在家。" **54 that's/it's not good enough** used to say that you are not satisfied with something and you are annoyed about it 那/这不好〔表示对某事不满意和气恼〕: *Look, it's just not good enough. I've been waiting an hour!* 你瞧, 这就不怎么好。我已经等了一个小时了! **55 good luck** used to say that you hope that someone is successful or that something good happens to them 祝你好运: *"When's the exam?" "Next week." "Well, good luck and stay calm."* "考试是在什么时候?" "下星期。" "祝你好运, 不要紧张。" **56 good luck to him/them** used to say that you hope someone is successful, although you think it is very unlikely that they will be 祝他/他们好运〔表示尽管认为某人成功的可能性不大仍祝其成功〕: *Good luck to them. You've got to respect them for trying.* 祝他们好运。他们敢于一试, 你得对他们表示敬意。 **57 good for you/her** also 又作 **good on you/her** *BrE, AusE* used to say that you approve of or are pleased with what someone has done or decided 【英, 澳】干得好, 好样的: *"I told him to go away and leave me alone." "Good for you."* "我告诉他走开, 别管我。" "干得好。" **58 it's a good thing** also 又作 **it's a good job** *BrE* used to say that you are glad something happened, because there would have been problems if it had not happened 【英】这是件好事, 幸亏: *It's a good thing you were in. I lost my keys.* 幸亏你在家, 我的钥匙丢了。| **and a good thing/job too** *BrE* 【英】 *She's gone, and a good thing too.* 她走了, 这倒是好事。 **59 good old John/Karen etc** used to praise someone, especially because they have behaved in the way that you would expect them to 好样的: *Good old Roger! I knew he wouldn't let us down.* 罗杰是好样的! 我知道他不会让我们失望的! **60 good grief/god/lord/heavens/gracious!** used to express surprise, anger, or other strong feelings 天啊〔用来表示惊奇、愤怒或其他强烈感情〕: *"It's going to cost us £500 to repair it." "Good grief!"* "修理它我们得花500英镑。" "天啊!" **61 be a good laugh** *BrE* to be enjoyable or amusing 【英】令人愉快, 令人开心: *You should come to the club with us some time, it's always a good laugh.* 你应该什么时候跟我们去俱乐部玩玩, 那里总是很好玩的。 **62 be good for a laugh** to be enjoyable, or amusing to do, although not useful, important etc 可博得一笑: *Let's go watch the guys trying to skate. That should be good for a laugh.* 我们去看看那些人学滑冰。应该会挺滑稽的。 **63 that's a good one** used to tell someone that you do not believe something they have said and think it is a joke or a trick 我不信, 开玩笑吧: *You won $50,000? Very funny, that's a good one!* 你赢了50,000美元? 真好笑, 我才不信哩! **64 all in good time** used when someone wants you to hurry but you are not going to 不急, 别急: *"When are we going to open our presents, Mom?" "All in good time, Billy, all in good time."* "我们什么时候打开礼物呢, 妈妈?" "别急, 比利, 别急。" **65 if you know what's good for you** used to threaten someone that something bad will happen to them if they don't do something 你要是知道好歹: *Do as he says, if you know what's good for you!* 如果你知道好歹的话, 就照他说的做吧! **66 would you be good enough to/be so good as to...?** *formal* used to ask someone very politely to do something 【正式】你能否…?〔用来客气地请人做某事〕: *Would you be good enough to help me with my bags.* 请你帮我搬一下这些行李, 好吗? **67 good day** *BrE old-fashioned* used to say 'hello' or 'goodbye' 【英, 过时】你好; 再见 **68 very good** *BrE old-fashioned* used to tell someone in a position of authority over you that you will do what they have told you to 【英, 过时】好〔用于对有权势的人说话, 表示将按他吩咐的去做〕: *"Tell the men to come in." "Very good, sir."* "叫那些人进来。" "好的, 先生。" **69 (jolly) good show** *old-fashioned BrE* used to express your satisfaction with something 【过时, 英】太好了, 真棒

good² *n*

1 ▶ADVANTAGE 好处◀ gain or advantage 利益, 好处: **do sb (a power of/the world of) good** (=to bring someone (a lot of) advantages or improvement) 对某人有(很大的)好处 *It'll do you good to have a vacation.* 度假对你会有好处。| *That little talk with the boss certainly did him the world of good!* 与老板的那次短暂谈话确实对他有很大好处! | **for the good of** (=to help something) 为了有助于… *I hate swimming – I only go for the good of my health.* 我不喜欢游泳, 我只是为了健康才去的。| **for your/his/their own good** *Come on, drink up the medicine – it's for your own good!* 来, 把药喝下 —— 这是为你好! | **do more harm than good** *I don't think you should go – it's bound to do more harm than good.* 我认为你不应该去 —— 这肯定是弊多利少。| **the common/general good** *formal* (=the advantage of everyone in society or in a group) 【正式】公益

2 do no good/not do any good to not have any useful effect 没有用处: *Try and persuade her if you like, but I don't think it'll do any good!* 如果你愿意, 想办法说服她吧, 但我认为这没有什么用!

3 What's the good of...?/What good is...? *informal* used to say that having or doing something brings you no advantage 【非正式】…有什么用?〔表示不会带来好处〕: *What's the good of buying a boat if you're too busy to use it?* 如果你忙得没有时间划船, 买条船有什么用? | *What good is money when you haven't any friends?* 如果没有朋友, 钱有什么用?

4 ▶GOOD BEHAVIOUR 良好的行为◀ [U] actions or behaviour that are morally right or that follow religious principles 合乎道德的行为, 遵守教规的行为: *She is definitely an influence for good on those boys.* 她给那些男孩子的影响肯定是有益的。| *There's good in him, in spite of his violent behaviour.* 尽管他举止粗暴, 但他是有善心的。| **good and evil** *the eternal struggle between good and evil* 善恶之间的永恒斗争 —see also 另见 DO-GOODER

5 be up to no good *informal* to be doing or planning something wrong or dishonest 【非正式】正在做坏事, 打算做坏事: *Anyone waiting around on street corners at night must be up to no good.* 晚上在街角游荡的人肯定想干坏事。

6 for good also 又作 **for good and all** *informal* if someone closes something, leaves, stays etc for good, they close it, leave etc permanently 【非正式】永远: *We've separated from each other before, but I think it's for good this time.* 我们以前分开过, 但我觉得这次是永别。

7 be £10, $50 etc to the good to have made a profit of £10, $50 etc 净赚10英镑、50美元等

8 [singular] *technical* a particular article that is produced in order to be sold 【术语】商品: *a good that could have been obtained more cheaply elsewhere* 本来可从其他地方便宜买到的商品 —see also 另见 GOODS (1)

good³ *adv AmE* a word meaning well, which some people think is incorrect 【美】好好地〔与well意思相同, 有人认为这种用法不正确〕: *Listen to me good!* 好好听我说!

good af·ter·noon /˙,˙˙˙/ *interjection, n* [C] an expression meaning hello, used when you are greeting someone in the afternoon 下午好

Good Book, the the Christian Bible《圣经》

good·bye /gʊdˋbaɪ; gʊdˈbaɪ/ *interjection, n* [C] used when you are leaving or being left by someone 再见: *"Goodbye, John, see you tomorrow."* "再见! 约翰, 明天见。" | **say goodbye** *I just have to say goodbye to Fred.* 我得跟弗雷德道别。| **say your goodbyes** *We said our goodbyes and left.* 我们告辞后便离开了。

good day /˙ˈ˙/ *interjection, n* [C] **1** *especially AustrE, NZE* an expression meaning hello, used when you are greeting someone especially in the morning or afternoon 【尤澳, 新西兰】日安, 你好〔意思与hello同, 多用于上午或下午打招呼〕 **2** *especially BrE, old fashioned* an expression used to say hello or goodbye 【尤英, 过时】你好; 再见

good eve·ning /˙ˈ˙˙/ *interjection, n* [C] an expression meaning hello used when you are greeting someone in the evening 晚上好 —compare 比较 GOOD NIGHT

good faith /˙ˈ˙/ *n* **in good faith** if an agreement, deal etc is made in good faith, it is made honestly with no intention to deceive anyone 诚实无欺: *a contract drawn up in good faith* 真心诚意草拟的合同

good-for-noth·ing /˙˙˙ˈ˙˙◂/ *n* [C] someone who is lazy or has no skills 饭桶, 无用的人 —**good-for-nothing** *adj* [only before noun 仅用于名词前]

Good Fri·day /˙ˈ˙˙/ *n* [C,U] the Friday before the Christian holiday of EASTER 受难日〔复活节前的星期五〕

Good Friday Agreement /˙ˈ˙˙˙/ an agreement reached in 1998 on Good Friday (the first day of the Christian Easter holiday) between the political parties of Northern Ireland and the Irish Republic to end 30 years of violence between Catholic and Protestant groups. The people of Northern Ireland and the Irish Republic were then asked to vote on the agreement, and accepted it by a large majority.《耶稣受难日协定》〔北爱尔兰和爱尔兰共和国的两方政党在1998年耶稣受难日(基督教复活节假期的第一天)达成协定, 以结束天主教和新教之间长达30年的暴

力对抗。北爱尔兰和爱尔兰共和国进行了全民公决，最后以大多数投票赞成通过了该协定〕

good-heart·ed /ˌ· ˈ·· ◂/ *adj* kind and generous 好心肠的

Good House·keep·ing /ˌ· ˈ·· ·/ *trademark* a monthly magazine which contains articles and pictures about decorating your home, cooking, and fashions for women and children【商标】《家政》〔刊登有关家庭装潢、烹饪以及妇女、儿童时装等文章和图片的月刊〕

Good Hu·mor /ˌ· ˈ·· ·/ *trademark* a type of ICE CREAM sold in the US【商标】好心情〔在美国出售的一种冰淇淋〕

good-hu·moured *BrE*【英】, **good-humored** *AmE*【美】/ˌ· ˈ·· ◂/ *adj* naturally cheerful and friendly 愉快而友好的: *Jo is always remarkably good-humoured whatever happens.* 无论发生了什么事，乔总是非常开朗。—**good-humouredly** *adv*

good·ie /ˈgudɪ; ˈgʊdi/ also 又作 **goody** *n* [C] *informal humorous* someone in a book or film who is good and does things you approve of【非正式，幽默】〔书或电影中的〕好人

good·ish /ˈgudɪʃ; ˈgʊdɪʃ/ *adj* [only before noun 仅用于名词前] *BrE informal*【英，非正式】**1 a goodish distance/number etc** quite a long way, quite a lot etc 相当远/多等 **2** fairly good but not very good 尚好〔但并非很好的〕

Good King Wen·ces·las /ˌgud kɪŋ ˈwɛnsəsləs; ˌgʊd kɪŋ ˈwensələs/ a popular Christmas CAROL (=a traditional song)《好国王瓦茨拉夫》〔一首广为传唱的圣诞颂歌〕

good-look·ing /ˌ· ˈ·· ◂/ *adj* someone who is good-looking has an attractive face〔人〕好看的，漂亮的 —see 见 BEAUTIFUL (USAGE) —**good-looker** *n* [C]

good looks /ˌ· ˈ·/ *n* [plural] the attractive appearance of someone's face 美貌，漂亮的容貌: *the young actor's romantic good looks* 年轻演员漂亮而迷人的容貌 | **keep your good looks** (=still be attractive) 保持美貌 *She's certainly kept her good looks.* 她确实保持了她的美貌。

good·ly /ˈgudlɪ; ˈgʊdli/ *adj* [only before noun 仅用于名词前] **1 a goodly number/sum/amount etc** *old-fashioned* a large amount【过时】大量，许多: *a goodly number of people* 相当多的人 **2** *old use* pleasant in appearance or good in quality【旧】好看的，质量好的

G

Good·man /ˈgudmən; ˈgʊdmən/, **Benny** (1909-86) a US JAZZ musician and band leader who played the CLARINET, and who helped to make Big Band music popular in the 1930s. He was known as 'The King of Swing'. 古德曼〔(1909-1986)，美国爵士音乐家、乐队领队。他演奏单簧管，20世纪30年代积极推动大乐队音乐的普及。他享有"摇摆乐之王"的美誉〕

S2 **good mor·ning** /ˌ· ˈ·· ·/ *interjection, n* [C] an expression meaning hello, used when you are greeting someone in the morning 早上好

good-na·tured /ˌ· ˈ·· ◂/ *adj* naturally kind and helpful and not easily made angry 和蔼的，性情温和的 —**good-naturedly** *adv* —**good-naturedness** *n* [U]

S2 **good·ness** /ˈgudnɪs; ˈgʊdnɪs/ *n* [U]

1 my goodness!/goodness (gracious) me! *spoken* used when you are surprised or sometimes angry【口】〔用来表示惊讶，有时表示愤怒〕: *My goodness, you did buy a lot!* 啊呀，你买了这么多!

2 have the goodness to do sth *formal* used to show extreme politeness when asking someone to do something【正式】〔用来十分客气地〕请〔某人〕做某事: *Will you have the goodness to excuse me?* 你愿意原谅我吗?

3 for goodness' sake *spoken* used when you are annoyed or surprised【口】看在老天爷面上〔用来表示烦躁或惊讶〕: *For goodness' sake stop arguing!* 看在老天爷面上，别吵了!

4 goodness (only) knows *spoken* used to emphasize that you are not sure about something or to make a statement stronger【口】天晓得，谁也不知道〔用来强调你对某事没有把握或加强语气〕: *That bar's been closed for goodness knows how long.* 天晓得那家酒吧已经关了多久。| *Goodness knows, I tried to help him!* 天晓得，我还想办法帮过他哩!

5 ▶BEING GOOD 好◀ the quality of being good 善良的品质: *Claire has an essential goodness of character.* 克莱尔本性善良。

6 ▶BEST PART 精华部分◀ the best part, especially the part of food which is good for your health〔尤指食品的〕精华: *All the goodness of an egg is in the yolk.* 蛋的精华在蛋黄里。

S3 **good night** /ˌ· ˈ·/ *interjection, n* [C] an expression used when you are leaving or being left by someone at night, especially before going to bed or to sleep 晚安〔晚上分别时尤指就寝前用语〕: *Good night. Sleep well.* 晚安，睡个好觉。—compare 比较 GOOD EVENING —see also 另见 **kiss sb goodbye/goodnight etc** (KISS[1] (1))

goods /gudz; gʊdz/ *n* [plural] **1** things that are produced in order to be sold 商品: *The demand for goods and services is lower this year.* 今年对商品和服务的需求比较低。| *electrical goods* 电器商品 | **consumer goods** (=televisions, washing machines etc) 消费品 **2 come up with the goods/deliver the goods** to do what other people need or expect 满足要求，不负所望，履行诺言: *Tony makes a lot of promises but rarely comes up with the goods.* 托尼经常作很多承诺，但很少履行。**3** possessions which can be moved, as opposed to houses, land etc 动产: **sb's worldly goods** (=everything someone owns) 某人的家当 **4 have/get the goods on sb** *especially AmE* to have or find proof that someone is guilty of a crime【尤美】掌握[发现]某人的罪证[把柄]: *Face it, Bukowski, we got the goods on you!* 面对现实吧，布科夫斯基，我们抓住你的把柄了! **5** *BrE* heavy things which can be carried by road, train etc【英】〔用公路或火车运输的笨重的〕货物; FREIGHT[1] (2) *especially AmE*【尤美】: *a goods train* 货运列车 **6 he's/she's/it's the goods** *spoken* used to say that you really like someone or something【口】他/她/它就是我喜欢的: *Emma thinks he's the goods!* 埃玛认为他是她的意中人! —see also 另见 DRY GOODS

W2 S2

goods and chattels *n* [plural] *law* personal possessions【法律】私人财产

Good Shep·herd, the /ˌ· ˈ·· ·/ a name used for Jesus in the New Testament of the Bible 好牧人〔《圣经·新约》中耶稣的别称〕

good-tempered *adj* cheerful and not easily made angry 好脾气的，随和的

Good·will /ˈgudˈwɪl; ˌgʊdˈwɪl/ a CHARITY organization in North America that helps people who have difficulty in getting jobs because they are DISABLED, cannot read or write, have been in prison etc. It gets money by collecting old clothes, furniture, and electrical equipment, which its members repair and sell in **Goodwill shops**. 良愿会，良愿业会〔北美洲一慈善机构，旨在帮助因残疾、不识字或受过狱刑等原因而找不到工作的人。该机构募集资金的途径是，收集旧衣服、旧家具和旧电器，然后由其成员修理并在良愿会商店出售〕: *He looks as if he buys all his clothes from Goodwill.* 看来他所有的衣服都是从良愿会商店买来的。

goodwill *n* [U] **1** kind feelings towards or between people and a willingness to be helpful 好意，亲善 **2** the success of a company, and its good relationship with its customers, calculated as part of its value when it is sold〔出售公司时计算在其价值内的〕商誉: *We paid £60,000 for the store, plus £5,000 for goodwill.* 我们付60,000英镑买下这家商店，另外加5000英镑买它的商誉。

Good·win Sands, the /ˌgudwɪn ˈsændz; ˌgʊdwɪn ˈsændz/ a dangerous area of sand just under the sea near Dover in the English Channel, where many ships have sunk 古德温暗沙〔英吉利海峡一处危险的暗礁，位于多佛尔附近。许多船只在此沉没〕

good·y[1] /ˈgudɪ; ˈgʊdi/ *n plural* **goodies** [C usually plural 一般用复数] *informal*【非正式】**1** something that is nice to eat 好吃的东西: *We brought lots of goodies for the picnic.* 我们为野餐买了许多好吃的东西。**2** something attractive, pleasant, or desirable 吸引人的东西，好东西: *The CD is given away as an extra goody when you buy the CD player.* 买CD唱机的时候额外赠送这张唱片。**3** a GOODIE 好人

goody[2] *interjection* a word used especially by children to express pleasure 高兴〔儿童用语〕

goody-good·y /ˈ·· ˌ··/ also 又作 **goody-two-shoes** /ˌ·· ˈ· ·/ *AmE n* [C] someone who likes to seem very good and helpful in order to please their parents, teachers etc【美】假正经的人，假装的乖孩子〔喜欢装成品行端正、乐于助人以取悦父母、老师的人〕

goo·ey /ˈguɪ; ˈguːi/ *adj informal*【非正式】**1** sticky, soft and often sweet 黏、松软而甜的: *gooey cakes* 黏性甜饼 **2** expressing your love for someone in a way that other people think is silly; SENTIMENTAL〔以某种可笑的方式〕对〔某人〕表示喜爱的; 多愁善感的: *Babies make her go all gooey.* 只要见到婴儿，她就喜欢得不知道怎么才好。

goof[1] /guf; guːf/ also 又作 **goof up** *v* [I] *especially AmE* to make a silly mistake【尤美】犯愚蠢的错误: *The restaurant totally goofed up our reservations.* 餐馆把我们预订的座位全部弄错了。—**goof-off** /ˈ· ·/ *n* [C] —**goof-up** /ˈ· ·/ *n* [C]

goof around *phr v* [I] *AmE informal* to spend time doing silly things【美，非正式】闲荡，瞎混; MESS ABOUT *BrE*【英】

goof off *phr v* [I] *AmE informal* to waste time or avoid doing any work【美，非正式】混日子，逃避工作: *Wayne's been goofing off at school and his report card shows it.* 韦恩在学校一直是混日子，他的成绩单说明了这一点。

goof[2] *n* [C] *informal especially AmE*【非正式，尤美】**1** someone who is silly 傻瓜，蠢人 **2** a silly mistake 愚蠢的错误，差错: *a goof on the spelling test* 拼写测试上犯的错误

goof·y /ˋgufɪ; ˈguːfi/ *adj informal* stupid or silly【非正式】愚蠢的, 傻的: *a goofy grin* 傻笑 —**goofily** *adv* —**goofiness** *n* [U]

goo·gly /ˋguglɪ; ˈguːgli/ *n* **1** [C] a ball bowled (BOWL[2] (2)) in CRICKET (2) in such a way that it looks as if it will go in one direction but goes in the other〔板球的〕外曲线球, 变向球 **2 bowl sb a googly** *BrE* to ask someone a question that is intended to trick them【英】向某人提出愚弄他的问题

goo-goo eyes /ˌ· · ˈ·/ *n* [plural] *AmE humorous* a silly look that shows you love someone【美, 幽默】含情脉脉的目光: **make goo-goo eyes at sb** *Look at them, making goo-goo eyes at each other.* 瞧他们, 眉来眼去的。—**goo-goo eyed** *adj*

gook /guk; guːk/ *n* [C] *AmE* a very offensive word for someone from a country in the Far East【美】外国佬〔对远东国家人的冒犯用语〕

goo·ly, goolie /ˋgulɪ; ˈguːli/ *n* [C usually plural 一般用复数] *BrE slang* an impolite word meaning a TESTICLE【英俚】睾丸〔粗俗的词语〕

goon /gun; guːn/ *n* [C] *informal*【非正式】**1** *especially BrE* a silly or stupid person【尤英】傻瓜, 蠢人 **2** *especially AmE* a violent criminal that is paid to frighten or attack people【尤美】〔受雇佣来恐吓或袭击别人的〕暴力罪犯

goop /gup; guːp/ *n* [U] *AmE informal* a thick, slightly sticky substance【美, 非正式】浓而稍黏的物质: *What's that goop you're putting on your hair?* 你往头发上涂的黏糊糊的东西是什么?

goose[1] /gus; guːs/ *n* **1 a)** [C] *plural* **geese** /gis; giːs/ a bird that is similar to a duck but larger and makes a hissing (HISS (1)) or honking (HONK[2] (1)) noise 鹅 **b)** a female goose 雌鹅 —compare 比较 GANDER (1) **2** [U] the cooked meat of this bird 鹅肉 **3** *old-fashioned* a silly person【过时】傻瓜, 蠢人 **4 kill the goose that lays the golden egg** to destroy the thing that brings you profit or success 杀鹅取金蛋, 杀鸡取卵 —see also 另见 WILD-GOOSE CHASE, **wouldn't say boo to a goose** (BOO[2] (3)), **cook someone's goose** (COOK[1] (6))

goose[2] *v* [T] *AmE informal* to touch or press someone on their bottom as a rude joke【美, 非正式】碰或按某人的臀部〔作为一种粗俗的玩笑〕

goose·ber·ry /ˋgusˌbɛrɪ; ˈgʊzbəri/ *n* [C] **1** a small round green fruit with a sour taste that grows on a bush 醋栗 —see picture on page A8 参见 A8 页图 **2 play gooseberry** *BrE informal* to be the unwanted third person who is with two people who are having a romantic relationship and want to be alone together【英, 非正式】充当(情侣间的)"电灯泡"

goose·bumps /ˋgusˌbʌmps; ˈguːsbʌmps/ *n* [plural] *AmE* goose pimples【美】鸡皮疙瘩

goose·flesh /ˋgusflɛʃ; ˈguːsfleʃ/ *n* [U] *especially BrE* goose pimples【尤英】鸡皮疙瘩

Goose Green /ˌ· ˈ·/ a place in the Falklands where British soldiers fought with Argentinians in May 1982, and where many soldiers were killed 古斯格林〔福克兰群岛一地。1982年5月英国士兵在此与阿根廷人交战, 许多士兵阵亡〕

goose pim·ples /ˈ· ˌ··/ *n* [plural] a condition in which your skin is raised up in small points because you are cold or frightened〔因冷或害怕而〕起鸡皮疙瘩

goose·step, the /ˋgusˌstɛp; ˈguːs-step/ *n* a way of marching, used by soldiers in some countries, in which each step is taken without bending your knee〔一些国家部队的〕正步走 —**goosestep** *v* [I]

GOP, the /ˌdʒi o ˋpi; ˌdʒiː əʊ ˈpiː/ *n AmE* Grand Old Party; the Republican Party in US politics【美】老大党〔美国共和党的别称〕

go·pher /ˋgofɚ; ˈgəʊfə/ *n* [C] a North and Central American animal like a large rat that lives in holes in the ground〔生活在北美洲和中美洲的〕地鼠

Gor·ba·chev /ˋgɔrbətʃɔf; ˈgɔːbətʃɒf/, **Mi·khail** /mɪˋkaɪl; mɪˈkaɪl/ (1931-) the President of the Soviet Union from 1985 to 1991, who started the process of economic and political change which improved his country's relationship with the West and resulted in the end of Communism in the Soviet Union and Eastern Europe 戈尔巴乔夫〔(1931-), 苏联总统, 1985年至1991年在任。他曾在苏联实行经济改革和政治改革, 从而改善了苏联与西方国家的关系, 最终导致苏联及东欧的共产党政权的结束〕

Gor·bals, the /ˋgɔrblz; ˈgɔːbəlz/ an area of Glasgow in Scotland which was for many years one of the UK's worst SLUMS (=an area of old houses in bad condition) and had high rates of crime and violence 戈布尔〔苏格兰格拉斯哥一地区, 多年来一直是英国最糟糕的贫民窟之一, 犯罪和暴力事件发生率居高不下〕

Gor·di·an knot /ˋgɔrdɪən ˋnɑt; ˌgɔːdiən ˈnɒt/ *n* **cut the Gordian knot** to quickly solve a difficult problem by determined action〔大刀阔斧地〕解决难题, 快刀斩乱麻

Gor·di·mer /ˋgɔrdɪmɚ; ˈgɔːdʒmə/, **Na·dine** /nəˋdin; nəˈdiːn/ (1923-) a South African writer, whose NOVELS include *The Conservationist*, which won the Booker Prize, and *July's People*. She won the Nobel Prize for Literature in 1991. 戈迪默〔(1923-), 南非作家。其小说包括《自然资源保护论者》(获布克奖)和《朱利的族人》。她1991年获诺贝尔文学奖〕

Gor·don /ˋgɔrdn̩; ˈgɔːdn/, **Flash** —see 见 FLASH GORDON

Gordon, General Charles (1833-85) a British military leader who fought in the Crimean War and then in China. He led the British forces in the SIEGE of Khartoum, in Sudan, where he was killed by the enemy. 戈登〔(1833-1885), 英国军队指挥官。他参加过克里米亚战争, 后在中国作战。他曾在苏丹率领英国军队突破起义军对喀土穆的包围, 在突围中被杀〕

Gordon High·land·ers, the /ˌ·· ˈ···/ a Scottish REGIMENT (=a large group of soldiers) in the British army 戈登高地人团〔英国军队中的一个苏格兰兵团〕

Gor·don·stoun /ˋgɔrdn̩ztən; ˈgɔːdnztən/ a PUBLIC SCHOOL (=expensive private school) in the north of Scotland, which is famous because several members of the British royal family have been educated there, and because the pupils live without many comforts 戈登斯顿公学〔苏格兰北部的一所公学。该校出名的原因有两个: 一是几名英国王室成员曾在此接受过教育, 二是在此就读的学生生活较为俭朴〕

gore[1] /gɔr; gɔː/ *v* [T] if an animal gores someone, it wounds them with its horns or TUSKS〔动物用角或獠牙〕顶伤, 抵伤

gore[2] *n* **1** [U] *literary* blood that has flowed from a wound and become thicker and darker【文】〔伤口流出的〕已变浓发黑的血 **2** [C] a piece of material that gets wider towards the bottom, used in making a skirt 加宽下摆的裥幅〔指缝制裙子的布料〕—see also 另见 GORY

Gore-Tex /ˋgɔrtɛks; ˈgɔːteks/ *trademark* a special WATERPROOF material, usually used for making winter and sport clothes【商标】戈尔特斯〔一种特殊防水面料, 通常用于制作防寒服装或运动服装〕

gorge[1] /gɔrdʒ; gɔːdʒ/ *n* [C] **1** a deep narrow valley with steep sides 峡谷 **2 make sb's gorge rise** to make someone feel sick or very angry about something 令某人作呕; 令某人愤怒: *When they saw the burned-out homes it made their gorge rise.* 他们看见被烧毁的家园时, 感到怒火中烧。

gorge[2] *v* **1 gorge yourself on/with** to eat until you are too full to eat any more 拼命地吃, 塞饱: *We gorged ourselves on ripe plums.* 我们大嚼成熟的李子。**2 be gorged with** to have eaten so much of something that you are completely full 肚子塞满, 饱食

gor·geous /ˋgɔrdʒəs; ˈgɔːdʒəs/ *adj informal*【非正式】**1** extremely beautiful or attractive 极其漂亮的, 极其吸引人的: *a gorgeous blonde* 极其漂亮的金发女郎 | *gorgeous silks* 极其漂亮的丝绸 **2** extremely pleasant or enjoyable 令人十分愉快[开心]的: *What a gorgeous afternoon!* (=warm and sunny) 天气多好的下午! —**gorgeously** *adv* —**gorgeousness** *n* [U] S3

gor·gon /ˋgɔrgən; ˈgɔːgən/ *n* [C] **1** *informal* an ugly frightening woman【非正式】丑陋可怕的女人 **2 Gorgon** one of the three sisters in ancient Greek stories with snakes on their heads that made anyone who looked at them change into stone 戈耳工, 蛇发女怪〔古希腊传说中蛇发三姐妹中的一位, 见到她的人会变成石头〕

Gor·gon·zo·la /ˌgɔrgənˋzolə; ˌgɔːgənˈzəʊlə/ a type of Italian cheese which is white with blue marks, and which has a strong taste and smell 戈尔贡左拉干酪〔意大利一种口感和气味浓郁的白色蓝纹干酪〕

go·ril·la /gəˋrɪlə; gəˈrɪlə/ *n* [C] **1** a very large African monkey that is the largest of the APES[1] (1) 大猩猩 **2** *slang* an ugly, strong man who is employed to protect an important person【俚】〔雇来保护要人的〕彪形大汉

Gor·ky /ˋgɔrkɪ; ˈgɔːki/, **Maxim** (1868-1936) a Russian writer of NOVELS and plays. He also wrote important books about other Russian writers and about his own life. 高尔基〔(1868-1936), 俄国小说家、剧作家。他还为他自己和其他作家著书立传〕

Gor·men·ghast /ˋgɔrmənˌgæst; ˈgɔːmənɡɑːst/ (1950) a NOVEL by Mervyn Peake, full of strange characters and events. Gormenghast is also the name of the castle that belongs to the Earl of Groan in two other books by Peake, *Titus Groan* and *Titus Alone*. 《戈尔曼加斯特》, 又译《仇云盖堡》〔(1950), 默文·皮克创作的一部小说。故事充满离奇怪异的人和事。这也是一座城堡的名字, 归格罗恩伯爵所有。这座城堡见于皮克的另外两部小说《泰特斯·格罗恩》和《泰特斯独自一人》中〕

gorm·less /ˈgɔrmlɪs; ˈgɔːmləs/ *adj BrE informal* stupid, especially in appearance【英，非正式】傻乎乎的: *a gormless grin* 傻笑 —**gormlessly** *adv* —**gormlessness** *n* [U]

gorse /gɔrs; gɔːs/ *n* [U] a PRICKLY bush with bright yellow flowers, which grows in the countryside 荆豆

gor·y /ˈgɔri; ˈgɔːri/ *adj* **1** *informal* clearly describing or showing violence, blood, and killing【非正式】渲染暴力、血腥和杀戮的: *That film was too gory for me.* 我觉得那部影片过多渲染了暴力。**2 all the gory details** *often humorous* all the interesting details about an unpleasant event【常幽默】〔一次不愉快事件的〕所有有趣的细节: *Come on, I want to hear all the gory details.* 给我讲讲吧，我想听听这件可怕事情所有的细节。**3** *literary* covered in blood【文】血迹斑斑的，血淋淋的 —see also 另见 GORE[2] —**gorily** *adv* —**goriness** *n* [U]

S2 **gosh** /gɑʃ; gɒʃ/ *interjection* used to express surprise〔用来表示惊讶〕: *Gosh, it's cold.* 啊呀，真冷啊！

gos·ling /ˈgɑzlɪŋ; ˈgɒzlɪŋ/ *n* [C] a young GOOSE[1] (1) 小鹅，幼鹅

go-slow /ˌ. ˈ.◂/ *n* [C] **1** *BrE* a way of protesting against an employer by working as slowly as possible【英】怠工; SLOWDOWN[2] (2) *AmE*【美】—compare 比较 WORK-TO-RULE **2** *WAfrE* a TRAFFIC JAM【西非】交通堵塞

gos·pel /ˈgɑspḷ; ˈgɒspəl/ *n* **1 Gospel** [C] one of the four stories of Christ's life in the Bible 福音书〔《圣经》中有关耶稣生平的四福音书之一〕**2** [C usually singular 一般用单数] a particular set of ideas that someone believes in very strongly and tries to persuade other people to accept 信条，教义: **spread/preach the gospel** *spreading the gospel of monetarism* 散播货币主义的信条 **3** also 又作 **gospel truth** /ˌ.. ˈ./ [U] something that is completely true 真理，绝对真理: **take sth as gospel** *Don't take everything she says as gospel.* 别把她所说的话都当做真理。**4** also 又作 **gospel mu·sic** /ˈ.. ˌ../ [U] a style of Christian music usually performed by Black singers in which religious songs are sung strongly and loudly 福音音乐〔通常由黑人歌手有力地大声演唱的基督教歌曲〕: *a gospel choir* 福音唱诗班

gos·sa·mer /ˈgɑsəmɚ; ˈgɒsəmə/ *n* [U] **1** *literary* a very light thin material【文】薄纱 **2** light silky thread which SPIDERs leave on grass and bushes 蜘蛛丝

gos·sip[1] /ˈgɑsəp; ˈgɒsɪp/ *n* **1** [C,U] conversation or information about other people's behaviour and private lives, often including unkind or untrue remarks 流言飞语，街谈巷议，闲话: *What's the latest gossip?* 最近有些什么闲话？| **have a gossip** *Phil's in there having a gossip with Maggie.* 菲尔在那里面跟玛吉闲聊。| **idle gossip** (=gossip not based on facts) 无中生有的流言飞语 **2** [C] someone who likes talking about other people's private lives 爱谈论别人私生活的人

gossip[2] *v* [I] to spend time talking to someone about other people's behaviour and private lives or about other things that do not concern you 说闲话，说长道短: **[+about]** *Julie was gossiping about Jane and Mick's affair.* 朱莉正在聊简和米克的风流韵事。

gossip col·umn /ˈ.. ˌ../ *n* [C] a regular article in a newspaper or magazine about the behaviour and private lives of famous people〔报刊杂志上定期登载的〕关于名人行为和私生活的专栏 —**gossip columnist** *n* [C]

gos·sip·y /ˈgɑsəpɪ; ˈgɒsɪpi/ *adj informal*【非正式】**1** a gossipy person likes to gossip 爱说闲话的，爱谈论别人私生活的 **2** talk or writing that is gossipy, is informal and full of gossip 说人闲话的，充满流言飞语的，闲聊式的: *a long, gossipy letter* 闲聊式的长信

got /gɑt; gɒt/ the past tense and a participle of GET —see 见 GOTTEN (USAGE)

got·cha /ˈgɑtʃə; ˈgɒtʃə/ *interjection* **1** a word meaning 'I've got you' that is used to surprise someone, or to show them that you have gained a sudden advantage over them 抓到你了〔I've got you 的连音，用来使某人吃惊或表示你突然间占了他的上风〕

> **CULTURAL NOTE 文化注释**
> During the Falklands War *The Sun* newspaper used **Gotcha!** in its HEADLINE when the British sank an Argentine ship. Many people found this insensitive and offensive. 福克兰战争中，英国击沉一艘阿根廷舰船，《太阳报》用该词作为大字的标题。很多人觉得这样做缺乏同情心，令人反感。

2 a word meaning 'I understand' 我明白了: *"Yeah, okay, 5 o'clock, gotcha."* "是的，好，5点钟，我明白了。"

Goth·am /ˈgɑθəm; ˈgɒθəm/ also 又作 **Gotham City** **1** the city where the character Batman lives in the stories about him 哥特城〔《蝙蝠侠》故事中的蝙蝠侠居住的地方〕**2** *AmE* an informal name for New York City【美】哥特城〔纽约市别称〕

Goth·ic /ˈgɑθɪk; ˈgɒθɪk/ *adj* **1** the Gothic style of building was common in Western Europe between the 12th and 16th centuries. Its main features were pointed ARCHes[1] (1,2), tall PILLARs (1), and tall thin pointed windows. 哥特式的，哥特风格的〔指12至16世纪流行于西欧的建筑风格，其主要特征是尖形拱门、高大廊柱和又高又狭的尖形窗户〕**2** a Gothic story, film etc is about frightening things that happen in mysterious old buildings, and lonely places, and was popular in the early 19th century 哥特派的〔发生在神秘古老的建筑、偏僻地方的吓人故事、电影等，这种风格流行于19世纪初〕**3** Gothic writing, printing etc has thick decorated letters 哥特式〔粗笔画加装饰的书写和印刷字体〕

got·ta /ˈgɑtə; ˈgɒtə/ *spoken* a short form of 缩略式= 'have got to', 'has got to', 'have got a', or 或 'has got a', which most people think is incorrect【口】要，得；有〔一个、一件等，被大多数人视为不正确〕: *We gotta go now.* 我们现在得走了。

got·ten /ˈgɑtṇ; ˈgɒtn/ *AmE*【美】the past participle of GET: *You've gotten us into a lot of trouble.* 你给我们惹了许多麻烦。—see also 另见 ILL-GOTTEN

> **USAGE NOTE 用法说明: GOTTEN**
> GRAMMAR 语法
> In British English, **got** is the past participle of **get**, but in American English, **gotten** is more commonly used as the past participle. 在英国英语中用 got 是 get 的过去分词，但在美国英语中用 gotten 作为过去分词更为常见: *Kim's gotten engaged!* 基姆已经订婚了！| *He'd gotten up early that day.* 那天他起床很早。**Got** is used in British English to mean 'possess'. got 在英国英语中用来表示"拥有": *We've got two cars.* 我们有两辆车。It may also be used this way in American English, though Americans usually use 'have'. 在美国英语中也可以这样用，但美国人通常用 have: *We have two cars.* 我们有两辆车。**Got** is also used in British English to mean 'buy' or 'receive'. got 用在英国英语中也可表示"买"或"收到": *Tim has just got a new bicycle.* 蒂姆刚买了[得到]辆新自行车。In American English, you can say either: *Tim has just gotten a new bicycle.* or *Tim just got a new bicycle.* 在英国英语中，说以上两句均可。
> **Got** is used in both British and American English to mean 'must'. got 在英国英语和美国英语中都可以表示 must (必须): *I've got to talk to him.* 我必须跟他谈谈。In American English, if you say *I've gotten to talk to him*, you mean you have succeeded in talking to him 在美国英语中，如果你说 I've gotten to talk to him，意思是说你已经跟他谈过了，but in both British and American English you would usually say 不过在英国英语和美国英语中，通常说的是: *I got to talk him.* 我跟他谈过了。**Gotten** is not used in British English. 英国英语不用 gotten。

gou·ache /gʊˈɑʃ; gʊˈɑːʃ/ *n* **1** [U] a method of painting using colours that are mixed with water and made thicker with a type of GUM[1] (3) 水粉画法 **2** [C] a picture produced by this method 水粉画

Gou·da /ˈgaudə; ˈgaʊdə/ *n* [U] a yellow Dutch cheese that does not have a very strong taste 高德干酪〔味道较淡的黄色荷兰干酪〕

gouge[1] /gaudʒ; gaʊdʒ/ *v* [T] to make a deep hole or cut in the surface of something 在〔某物表面〕凿洞，凿槽: *The desks were scratched and gouged.* 这些桌子的桌面上有许多划痕并被凿了不少洞槽。

gouge sth ↔ **out** *phr v* [T] **1** to make a hole in something such as rock etc by removing material that is on the surface 掘出，挖出: *Glaciers gouged out narrow valleys during the Ice Age.* 冰川在冰期开出了窄的峡谷。**2 gouge sb's eyes out** to remove someone's eyes with a pointed weapon 挖出某人的眼睛

gouge[2] *n* [C] a hole or cut made in something, usually by a sharp tool or weapon〔利器凿成的〕孔，洞，槽

gou·lash /ˈgulæʃ; ˈguːlæʃ/ *n* [C,U] a dish from Hungary made of meat cooked in liquid with a hot tasting pepper〔匈牙利的〕辣椒炖肉

Gould /guld; guːld/**, Glenn** /glɛn; glen/ (1932-82) a Canadian PIANIST known especially for playing piano music by J.S. Bach 古尔德〔(1932-1982)，加拿大钢琴家，尤以演奏巴赫的作品闻名〕

gourd /gɔrd; gʊəd/ *n* [C] **1** a round fruit whose outer shell can be used as a container 葫芦〔果实〕**2** the container made from this fruit 葫芦〔容器〕

gour·mand /ˈgurmənd; ˈgʊəmənd/ *n* [C] someone who is too interested in eating and drinking 贪吃贪喝的人

gour·met¹ /ˈgʊrme; ˈgʊəmeɪ/ *adj* [only before noun 仅用于名词前] producing or connected with very good food and drink 制作[关于]美食佳酿的: *a gourmet cook* 能做出精美菜肴的厨师

gourmet² *n* [C] someone who knows a lot about food and wine and who enjoys good food and wine 美食家

gout /gaʊt; gaʊt/ *n* [U] a disease that makes your toes, fingers, and knees swollen and painful 痛风(病) —**gouty** *adj*

> CULTURAL NOTE 文化注释
>
> In the past, gout was often thought to be caused by drinking too much of certain kinds of alcohol, especially PORT. 过去认为痛风是喝某种酒太多造成的，尤其是喝波尔多葡萄酒。

W3 **gov·ern** /ˈgʌvən; ˈgʌvən/ *v* **1** [I,T] to officially and legally control a country and make all the decisions about taxes, laws, public services etc 管理，统治〔国家〕: *The country was governed by a small military élite.* 这个国家被少数军事头目统治。**2** [T] if rules, principles etc govern the way a system or situation works, they control how it happens or what happens〔规则、原则等〕规定，管制，制约: *rules governing the export of live animals* 管制活牲畜出口的条例 | *the laws that govern the universe* 制约宇宙的规律 **3** [T] to affect the grammar of another word and make it have a particular form〔语法中〕支配〔另一词，决定该词应具有何种形式〕**4** [T] *old-fashioned* to control a strong or dangerous emotion【过时】抑制，控制〔强烈或危险的感情〕

gov·ern·ess /ˈgʌvənɪs; ˈgʌvənɪs/ *n* [C] a female teacher who lives with a rich family and teaches their children at home〔住在富有家庭中管教孩子的〕家庭女教师

gov·ern·ing /ˈgʌvənɪŋ; ˈgʌvənɪŋ/ *adj* **1** [only before noun 仅用于名词前] having the power to control an organization, country etc 统治的，执政的，管理的: **governing body** (=the group of people controlling an institution) 主管机构 *the university's governing body* 大学的主管机构 | **governing party** (=the political party that is governing a country) 执政党 **2 governing principle** a principle that has the most important influence on something 指导原则: *Freedom of speech for all is one of the governing principles in a democracy.* 人人享有言论自由是民主国家的指导原则之一。—see also 另见 SELF-GOVERNING

S2 W1 **gov·ern·ment** /ˈgʌvənmənt; ˈgʌvənmənt/ *n* **1** also 又作 **Government** [C] the group of people who govern a country or state 政府: *The new military government does not have popular support.* 新上台的军人政府没有得到广泛的支持。| [also+plural verb *BrE* 英] *The Government are planning further cuts in public spending.* 政府正计划进一步削减公共支出。| **government policy/funding/statistics** *Government statistics show an increase in unemployment.* 政府统计数字显示失业率有所上升。| **form a government** (=become the government after an election in a parliamentary system) 组织政府，组阁 *Which party will form the next government?* 哪一个党将组织下一届政府？| **under a government** (=during the period of a government) 在某届政府执政期间 *changes in policy under the last Labour government* 上届工党政府的政策调整 **2** [U] a form or system of government 政府形式[体制]: *the return to democratic government* 恢复民主政体 | **local government** (=the government of towns, cities etc) 地方政府 | **central government** (=the government of a whole country) 中央政府 **3** [U] the act or process of governing 治理，管理: *Government has been entrusted to the elected politicians.* 治理的任务已委托给当选的政治家。| **be in government** (=be governing a country) 在执政中 *How long have the Christian Democrats been in government?* 基督教民主党已经执政多久了？**4** [U] *especially AmE* the degree to which the government controls economic and social activities【尤美】管理经济与社会活动的程度: *a pledge of less government and greater personal freedom* 减少对经济与社会活动的干预和增加个人自由的承诺

government health warn·ing /ˌ···ˈ·, ˌ·/ *n* [C] *BrE* a notice that, by law, must be put on some products, for example cigarettes, to warn people that they are dangerous to their health【英】政府健康警告〔根据法律必须印制在一些诸如香烟等的产品之上，警告人们该产品有害健康〕

W3 **gov·er·nor** /ˈgʌvənə; ˈgʌvənə/ *n* [C] **1** also 又作 **Governor** **a)** the person in charge of governing a state in the US〔美国〕州长 **b)** the person in charge of governing a country that is under the political control of another country 总督〔政治上受另一国家控制的国家首脑〕**2** *especially BrE* a member of a committee that controls an organization or institution【尤英】〔指导、监督某组织或机构的〕董事，理事: *a school governor* 学校董事 **3** *BrE* the person in charge of a prison【英】典狱长; WARDEN (2) *AmE*【美】: *After the riot the prison governor resigned.* 典狱长在暴乱后辞职。**4** a part of a machine that controls how the machine works, especially by limiting it in some way〔机器上的〕调节器 **5** *BrE* a GUVNOR【英】老板，先生 —see also 另见 GUBERNATORIAL

Governor-Gen·e·ral /ˌ··ˈ···/ *n* [C] someone who represents the King or Queen of Britain in other Commonwealth countries which are not REPUBLICS〔英联邦国家中英国以外非共和制国家的〕总督: *the Governor-General of Australia* 澳大利亚总督

Governor of the Bank of En·gland, the /ˌ····· ˌ···ˈ··/ the head of the Bank of England, who is responsible for important financial decisions, especially for fixing interest rates in the UK 英格兰银行行长〔负责制定重大金融决策，尤其是确定英国的银行利率〕

gov·ern·or·ship /ˈgʌvənəʃɪp; ˈgʌvənəʃɪp/ *n* [U] the position of being governor, or the period during which someone is governor〔州长、总督等的〕职位; 任期

govt a written abbreviation of 缩写= GOVERNMENT

gown /gaʊn; gaʊn/ *n* [C] **1** a long dress worn by a woman on formal occasions 女礼服: *Arabella wore a blue silk evening gown.* 阿拉贝拉穿着蓝色的丝绸晚礼服。**2** a long loose piece of clothing worn for special ceremonies by judges, teachers, lawyers, and members of universities〔法官、教师、律师、大学成员在特殊仪式上穿的〕长袍 **3** a long loose piece of clothing worn in a hospital by someone doing or having an operation 外科手术服 —see also 另见 DRESSING GOWN

Go·ya /ˈgɔɪə; ˈgɔɪə/, **Fran·cis·co de** /frænˈsɪsko də; frænˈsɪskəʊ də/ (1746-1828) a Spanish artist famous especially for his PORTRAITS of members of the royal families of Spain 戈雅〔(1746-1828)，西班牙艺术家，尤以西班牙皇室成员的肖像作品闻名〕

GP /ˌdʒi ˈpi; ˌdʒiː ˈpiː/ *n* [C] *especially BrE* general practitioner; a doctor who is trained in general medicine and treats people in a particular area or town【尤英】〔在某特定区域或城镇行医的〕全科医生，普通医师

GPA /ˌdʒi pi ˈe; ˌdʒiː piː ˈeɪ/ *n* [C] grade point average; the average of a student's marks over a period of time in the US education system〔美国教育体制中的〕平均分

GPO, the /ˌdʒi pi ˈo; ˌdʒiː piː ˈəʊ◂/ **1** the General Post Office; the former name of the organization that controls mail in the UK, now called the Post Office (英国) 邮政总局〔the Post Office 的旧称〕**2** Government Printing Office; a US government organization that prints government documents, maps, books etc, which it gives to national libraries and government offices, and sells to the public at low cost 政府印刷局〔美国一政府部门，负责印刷政府文件、地图、书籍等，给国家图书馆和政府机构分发印刷品，同时也以低价向公众出售〕—compare 比较 HMSO

GQ /ˌdʒi ˈkju; ˌdʒiː ˈkjuː/ *trademark* a monthly magazine for men produced in the UK and the US. It includes men's fashions and articles about successful men, health etc【商标】《智族》〔英国、美国出版的一种男性月刊，登载有关时装、事业、健康等主题的文章〕

grab¹ /græb; græb/ *v* **grabbed, grabbing** [T] S3 W3

1 ▶WITH YOUR HAND 用手◀ to take hold of someone or something with a sudden or violent movement 攫取，抓住: *The policeman grabbed his shoulder.* 警察抓住他的肩膀。| **grab sth from sb** *I managed to grab the gun from Bowen.* 我把枪从鲍恩手里抢了过来。| **grab hold of** *Kay grabbed hold of my arm to stop herself falling.* 凯抓住我的手臂，以免摔倒。

2 ▶FOOD/SLEEP 食品/睡◀ *informal* to get some food or sleep quickly because you are busy【非正式】〔因忙碌而〕赶紧，抓紧〔吃或睡〕: *I managed to grab an hour's sleep this afternoon.* 今天下午我抓紧时间睡了一个小时。| **grab a bite to eat** *Let's grab a bite to eat before we go.* 我们走之前赶紧吃点什么吧。

3 ▶GET STH FOR YOURSELF 为自己获取某物◀ to take something for yourself, especially in an unfair way〔尤指通过不公平手段〕霸占，捞取，强夺: *Bob tried to grab the profit for himself.* 鲍勃想把利润占为己有。| *Try to get there early and grab a seat.* 想办法早点到那儿占个座位。

4 how does sth grab you? *spoken* used to ask someone if they would be interested in doing a particular thing【口】你对某事是否有兴趣？*How does the idea of a trip to Spain grab you?* 你对到西班牙旅行的想法感兴趣吗？

5 grab a chance/opportunity *informal* to take the opportunity to do or have something immediately【非正式】抓住机会: *Grab your chance to travel while you're still young!* 趁你还年轻，抓住机会去旅游！

G

grab at *phr v* [T] **1** to quickly and suddenly put out your hand in order to take hold of something〔迅速伸手〕抓住: *Donny hid behind his mother, grabbing at her skirt.* 多尼藏在母亲身后，拽着她的裙子。**2** to immediately try to take an opportunity that someone offers you 抓住〔机会〕: *Melanie grabs at every invitation that comes her way.* 每次收到邀请，梅拉妮都去。

grab² *n* **1 make a grab for/at** to suddenly try to take hold of something〔猛然去〕抓: *I made a grab for the revolver.* 我迅速伸手去抓左轮手枪。**2 be up for grabs** *informal* if a job, prize, opportunity etc is up for grabs, it is available for anyone who wants to try to have it【非正式】〔工作、奖金、机会等〕人人都可以争取得到的，供争夺的 **3** [C] a piece of machinery used for taking hold of things 抓具；抓斗挖土机

grab bag /ˈ· ,·/ *n AmE*【美】**1** [C] a container filled with small presents that you put your hand in to pick one out 摸彩袋; LUCKY DIP (1) *BrE*【英】**2** [singular] *informal* a situation in which things are decided by chance【非正式】碰运气 **3** [singular] a mixture of different things or styles; RAGBAG〔各种东西或样式的〕混合: *A grab bag of different kinds of music accompanies the film.* 这部电影的配乐是由各种音乐混杂在一起的。

Gra·ble, Bet·ty (1916-73) a US actress who appeared in musical films. She became a PIN-UP for the soldiers during World War II, and in 1942 her legs were insured for $250,000. 格拉布尔〔(1916-1973)，美国音乐剧电影演员。二战期间，男兵常把她的靓照贴在墙上欣赏。1942年，她为自己的双腿投保250,000美元〕

grace¹ /gres; greɪs/ *n*

1 ▶WAY OF MOVING 移动方式◀ [U] a smooth controlled way of moving that is attractive to look at, especially because it seems natural and relaxed 优美，优雅自然: *Lena had the grace and poise of a model.* 莉娜具有模特儿般的优雅和体态。

2 ▶BEHAVIOUR 行为◀ a) [U] polite and pleasant behaviour 彬彬有礼: *Jenny answered their questions with grace and dignity.* 珍妮体面有礼地回答了他们的问题。| **have the (good) grace to do sth** (=be polite enough to do something) 有做某事的气量 *Meg didn't even have the grace to apologize.* 梅格连道歉的气量也没有。**b) graces** [plural] the skills needed to behave in a way that is considered polite and socially acceptable 风度: *social graces* 社交风度

3 ▶MORE TIME 更多的时间◀ [U] more time that is added to the period you are allowed for finishing a piece of work, paying a debt etc 宽限: **a day's/week's etc grace** *I got a day's grace to finish my essay.* 我得到一天的宽限来完成我的论文。

4 with (a) good/bad grace willingly and cheerfully, or in an unwilling and angry way 大方地/勉强地: *Kevin smiled and accepted his defeat with good grace.* 凯文微笑着，大方地接受自己的失败。

5 ▶GOD'S KINDNESS 上帝的恩典◀ [U] God's kindness shown to people because he loves them 上帝的恩典: **by/through the grace of God** (=because of God's kindness) 承蒙上帝的恩典 *By the grace of God, Alan wasn't hurt.* 承蒙上帝的恩典，艾伦没有受伤。

6 there but for the grace of God (go I) used to say how lucky you feel that you are not in the same bad situation as someone else 要不是上帝的恩典(我也遭殃)〔表示没有遭到某人那样的厄运〕

7 ▶PRAYER 祷告◀ [C,U] a prayer thanking God, said before a meal〔饭前的〕感恩祷告: **say grace** *Who will say grace?* 谁来做感恩祷告?

8 be in sb's good graces to be liked and approved by someone at a particular time 受到某人的眷顾[青睐]

9 ▶SOUL 心灵◀ [U] the state of someone's soul when it has been freed from evil, according to Christian belief 恩典，恩宠〔基督教教义，指灵魂无罪时的状态〕: **be in a state of grace** (=to have been forgiven for what you have done wrong when you die) 在恩典的状态〔死时生平所做错事得到宽恕〕

10 Your/His etc Grace used as a title for talking to or about a DUKE, DUCHESS, or ARCHBISHOP 阁下〔对公爵、公爵夫人或大主教的尊称〕

11 the Graces three beautiful Greek goddesses who often appear in art〔希腊〕美慧三女神 —see also 另见 **fall from grace** (FALL¹ (13)), **saving grace** (SAVE¹ (13))

grace² *v* [T] **1 grace sth/sb with your presence** an expression meaning to bring honour to an occasion or group of people by being present, often used jokingly when someone comes late or does not often come to meetings etc 以你的莅临来给某事/某人增光〔常用来给迟到或经常缺席的人开玩笑〕: *Ah so you've decided to grace us with your presence!* 啊，这么说你已经决定光临，给我们增辉添彩! **2** to make a place or an object look more beautiful or attractive 美化，使优美: *His portrait now graces the wall of the drawing room.* 他的画像现在给客厅的墙壁添了光彩。

Grace, W.G. (1848-1915) an English CRIKET player who many people think was the greatest player of the 19th century. He was a very tall, large man with a long thick BEARD. 格雷斯〔(1848-1915)，英国板球运动员，被视为19世纪最出色的板球选手。他身材高大，留有浓密的长须〕

grace·ful /ˈgresfəl; ˈgreɪsfəl/ *adj* **1** moving in a smooth and attractive way, or having an attractive shape〔动作、线条〕优美的，雅致的: *a slim graceful figure* 修长而优美的身材 **2** behaving in a polite and pleasant way 优雅得体的，体面的: *a graceful apology* 得体的道歉 **—gracefully** *adv*: *When I am no longer needed, I shall retire gracefully.* 当不再需要我的时候，我将体面地退休。**—gracefulness** *n* [U]

Grace·land /ˈgreslənd; ˈgreɪslənd/ the home of Elvis Presley in Memphis, Tennessee in the US, which many tourists visit 雅园〔埃尔维斯·普雷斯利在美国田纳西州孟菲斯的住宅。许多游人前去参观〕

grace·less /ˈgreslɪs; ˈgreɪsləs/ *adj* **1** not being polite, especially when someone has been kind to you 无礼貌的，不知情理的: *She was utterly graceless, showing no gratitude for all we had done.* 她没有一点礼貌，对我们所做的一切没表示任何感激。**2** moving or doing something in a way that seems awkward〔动作、行为等〕笨拙的 **3** something that is graceless is unattractive and unpleasant to look at〔外观〕难看的，不优美的: *graceless architecture* 难看的建筑 **—gracelessly** *adv* **—gracelessness** *n* [U]

Grac·es, The /ˈgresɪz; ˈgreɪsɨz/ also 又作 **The Three Graces** in Greek and Roman MYTHOLOGY, the three goddesses of CHARM and beauty who are often shown in art 美慧三女神〔希腊和罗马神话中的三位魅力和美丽女神，常见于艺术作品之中〕

gra·cious /ˈgreʃəs; ˈgreɪʃəs/ *adj* **1** behaving in a polite, kind, and generous way, especially to people of a lower class 有礼貌的；仁慈的；和蔼的，亲切的〔尤指对较低阶层的人们〕: *Thank you for your gracious hospitality.* 感谢你的盛情款待。**2** having the kind of expensive style, comfort, and beauty that only rich people can afford 豪华舒适的，华美的: *gracious colonial houses* 豪华舒适的殖民时期式样的房子 | *the gracious ease of the hotel foyer* 旅馆门厅的豪华舒适 | **gracious living** (=an easy way of life enjoyed by rich people)〔富人的〕安逸生活 **3** a word meaning kind and forgiving, used to describe God 仁慈的，宽恕的〔用于形容上帝〕**—graciously** *adv* **—graciousness** *n* [U]

gracious! *interjection old-fashioned* used to express surprise or to emphasize 'yes' or 'no'【过时】〔用来表示惊讶或对"是"与"否"加以强调〕: **good gracious!/gracious me!/goodness gracious!** *Good gracious! What have you done to your hair?* 天哪，你把头发弄成什么样子了? | *"You aren't disappointed, are you?" "Good gracious, no, of course not."* "你没有失望吧?" "啊呀，不，当然不。"

grad /græd; græd/ *n* [C] *AmE informal* a GRADUATE¹【美，非正式】毕业生

grad·a·ble /ˈgredəbl; ˈgreɪdəbəl/ *adj* an adjective which is gradable can be used in the COMPARATIVE¹ (4) or SUPERLATIVE² (1) forms, or with words such as 'very', 'fairly', and 'almost'〔形容词〕可分级的〔指可以有比较级或最高级形式或可被 very, fairly, almost 等词修饰的〕**—gradability** /ˌgredəˈbɪlətɪ; ˌgreɪdəˈbɪlɨti/ *n* [U]

gra·da·tion /greˈdeʃən; grəˈdeɪʃən/ *n* [C] *formal* a small change, or a stage in a set of changes or degrees of development【正式】小变化；层次；阶段: *There are many gradations of colour between light and dark blue.* 淡蓝和深蓝之间有许多层次。

grade¹ /gred; greɪd/ *n*

1 ▶STANDARD 标准◀ [C,U] a particular standard or level of quality that a product, material etc has〔产品、材料等的〕等级，级别: *Grade A eggs* 甲级鸡蛋 | *low-grade steel* 低等钢材

2 ▶COMPANY 公司◀ [C] the level of importance you have or the level of pay you receive in a company or organization〔职务、工资〕级别: *Wilma has a lot of responsibility but she's still on a secretarial grade.* 威尔玛负责很多事情，但她仍是秘书级别。

3 make the grade to succeed or reach the necessary standard 成功；达到标准: *Nina'll never make the grade as a professional tennis player.* 尼娜永远也达不到职业网球运动员的水平。

4 ▶SCHOOL YEAR 学年◀ [C] a particular year of a school course in the American school system〔美国学校的〕年级: *Bobby's in the second grade.* 博比读二年级。

CULTURAL NOTE 文化注释

In the US, children begin school in KINDERGARTEN, usually at age five. At age six, they enter first grade. The first years of school take place at an ELEMENTARY SCHOOL, and then children go to a JUNIOR HIGH SCHOOL or MIDDLE SCHOOL for several years, before going to HIGH SCHOOL for the last few years. There are twelve grades in the US school system. Children in a particular grade are often called first graders, second graders, eighth graders etc. The expression 'K-12' is sometimes used to talk about the US school system, meaning all the grades from kindergarten to grade 12. 美国儿童一般在五岁时上幼儿园, 六岁时上一年级。学校教育的最初阶段叫做小学 (elementary school), 然后就进入初中 (junior high school 或 middle school) 学习几年, 接着进入高中 (high school) 再上几年学。美国学校体制有12个年级。常以特定的年级称呼学生为一年级生、二年级生、八年级生等。美国学校体制有时叫做K-12, 指从幼儿园到12年级的所有年级。

5 ►MARK IN SCHOOL 学习成绩◄ [C] *especially AmE* a mark given for a particular piece of work in school, or for your work during all or part of a year【尤美】成绩; 分数: *You need good grades to go to college.* 你要有好的成绩才能上大学。

6 ►SLOPE 斜坡◄ [C] *AmE* degree of slope, especially in a road or railway【美】〔尤指道路或铁路的〕坡度; GRADIENT *BrE*【英】

grade² *v* [T] **1** to separate things, or arrange them in order according to their quality or rank 给〔物品〕分等级: *potatoes graded according to size* 根据大小分等级的马铃薯 **2** *especially AmE* to give a mark to an examination paper or to a piece of school work【尤美】给〔试卷或作业〕评分: *Matt's busy at home grading papers.* 马特正在家忙着评卷子。**3** to give a particular rank and level of pay to a job 给〔某职位〕评定级别和工资等级

grade cross·ing /ˈ· ,··/ *n* [C] *AmE* a place where a road and railway cross each other, usually with gates that shut the road while the train passes【美】〔公路、铁路〕交叉处〔通常有栅栏在火车通过时将道路关闭〕; LEVEL CROSSING *BrE*【英】

grad·ed /ˈgredɪd; ˈgreɪdɪ̆d/ *adj* designed to suit different levels of learning〔学习〕分级的: *graded coursebooks* 分级教科书

grade point av·e·rage /ˈ· ·, ···/ *n* [C] GPA 平均分

grade school /ˈ· ,·/ *n* [C] *AmE* an ELEMENTARY SCHOOL【美】小学

Grad·grind, Mr /ˈgrædgraɪnd; ˈgrædgraɪnd/ one of the main characters in the book *Hard Times* by Charles Dickens. Gradgrind is only concerned with facts, and does not consider the importance of love or imagination, especially when educating and caring for his children. 葛拉德顾兰德〔查尔斯·狄更斯小说《艰难时世》的主要人物之一, 他只讲究实际, 而不重视爱或想象的重要性, 教育和抚养孩子时尤为如此〕

gra·di·ent /ˈgredɪənt; ˈgreɪdiənt/ *n* [C] a degree of slope, especially in a road or railway〔尤指道路或铁路的〕坡度; GRADE¹ (6) *AmE*【美】: *a steep gradient* 陡坡

grad school /ˈ· ·/ *n* [C] *AmE informal* a GRADUATE SCHOOL【美, 非正式】研究生院

grad·u·al /ˈgrædʒuəl; ˈgrædʒuəl/ *adj* **1** happening, developing, or changing slowly over a long period of time 逐渐的, 逐步的: *Computerization has resulted in the gradual disappearance of many manual jobs.* 电脑化逐步取代了许多手工活。| *I noticed a gradual change in her behaviour.* 我注意到她的举止逐渐发生了变化。**2** a gradual slope is not steep〔坡〕缓的, 不陡的 — **gradualness** *n* [U]

2 3 **grad·u·al·ly** /ˈgrædʒulɪ; ˈgrædʒəli/ *adv* in a way that happens or develops slowly over a long period of time 逐渐地, 逐步地: *The rock gradually wears away due to the action of the water.* 由于水的冲刷作用, 岩石逐渐磨损。

grad·u·ate¹ /ˈgrædʒuɪt; ˈgrædʒuɪ̆t/ *n* [C] **1** someone who has completed a university degree course, especially for a first degree〔尤指完成学士学位课程的〕大学毕业生: *a history graduate* 历史系的大学毕业生 | [+of] *a graduate of Birmingham University* 伯明翰大学的毕业生 —compare 比较 UNDERGRADUATE **2** *AmE* someone who has completed a course at a college, school etc【美】毕业生: *a high-school graduate* 高中毕业生

graduate² /ˈgrædʒu,ɪt; ˈgrædʒueɪt/ *adj* **1** [only before noun 仅用于名词前] *AmE* a graduate student is studying for a MASTER'S or a DOCTORATE degree after receiving their first degree【美】攻读硕士[博士]研究生的; POSTGRADUATE² (1) *BrE*【英】**2** graduate studies or courses are done after receiving your first degree 研究生〔课程〕

graduate³ *v* **1** [I] to obtain a degree, especially a first degree, from a college or university〔尤指以学士学位〕大学毕业: [+from] *Mitch graduated from Stanford with a degree in Law.* 米奇毕业于斯坦福大学, 获法学学位。**2** [I] *AmE* to complete your education at HIGH SCHOOL【美】高中毕业: [+from] *Jerry graduated from high school last year.* 杰里去年高中毕业。**3 graduate (from sth) to** to start doing something that is bigger, better or more important (从某处) 升级到: *Bob played college baseball but never graduated to the Majors.* 鲍勃在大学是棒球队队员, 但从来没有升级加入职业棒球队。**4** [T] *especially AmE* to give a degree or DIPLOMA to someone who has completed a course【尤美】向〔毕业生〕授予学位[文凭]

grad·u·at·ed /ˈgrædʒu,etɪd; ˈgrædʒueɪtɪ̆d/ *adj* **1** divided into different levels or GRADES¹ (1) 分级的: *graduated rates of taxation* 分级税率 **2** a tool or container that is graduated has small marks on it showing measurements 标有刻度的

graduate school /ˈ··· ,·/ *n* [C] *AmE* a college or university where you can study for a MASTER'S or a DOCTORATE degree after receiving your first degree, or the period of time when you study for these degrees【美】研究生院

grad·u·a·tion /,grædʒuˈeʃən; ,grædʒuˈeɪʃən/ *n* **1** [U] the time when you complete a university degree course or your education at an American HIGH SCHOOL〔美国高中或大学的〕毕业: *After graduation Helen went into accountancy.* 海伦毕业后从事会计工作。**2** [U] a ceremony at which you receive a university degree or a DIPLOMA from an American HIGH SCHOOL〔美国大学或高中的〕毕业典礼: *graduation day* 毕业典礼日 **3** [C] a mark showing measurement on an instrument or container for measuring 刻度

Grae·co- /ˈgriko; ˈgriːkəʊ/ *prefix* another spelling of GRECO greco 的另一种拼法

graf·fi·ti /grəˈfitɪ; grəˈfiːti/ *n* [U] rude, humorous, or political writing and pictures on the walls of buildings, trains etc〔在墙上、火车上等的〕乱涂乱抹, 涂鸦

graft¹ /græft; grɑːft/ *n* **1** [C] a piece of healthy skin or bone taken from someone's body and put in or on another part of their body that has been damaged 移植皮, 移植骨: *Her severe burns were treated with skin grafts.* 她的重度烧伤得到植皮治疗。**2** [C] a piece cut from one plant and tied to or put inside a cut in another, so that it grows there〔切取于某植物的供嫁接用的〕接穗 **3** [U] *informal especially BrE* hard work【非正式, 尤英】艰苦的工作: *I was too tired to talk after a hard day's graft.* 一天艰苦的工作之后我累得连说话的力气都没有了。**4** [U] *especially AmE* the practice of obtaining money or advantage by the dishonest use of influence, especially political influence【尤美】贪污, 受贿; 〔尤指通过政治影响〕以权谋私: *Theo rose to power through graft and corruption.* 西奥靠贪污腐败上台。

graft² *v* **1** [I,T] to put a piece of skin or bone from one part of someone's body onto another part that has been damaged 移植〔皮肤、骨〕: **graft sth onto** *They grafted skin from his thigh onto his badly burned face.* 他们把他大腿的皮肤移植到他严重烧伤的脸上。**2** [I,T +on/onto] to join a part of a flower, plant, or tree onto another flower, plant, or tree〔花、草或树〕嫁接 **3 graft sth onto** to try to combine an idea, style etc with another idea or style 将〔某想法、风格等与另一想法、风格〕结合起来: *modern institutions grafted onto medieval traditions* 结合中世纪传统的现代制度 **4** [I] *informal especially BrE* to work hard【非正式, 尤英】努力地工作

graft off sb ↔ *phr v* [T] *especially AmE* to get money or advantages from someone by the dishonest use of influence, especially political influence【尤美】〔以不正当手段利用权势〕向〔某人〕索贿, 谋取私利: *politicians who graft off each other* 互相捞取好处的政客

Graham, Mar·tha /ˈmɑrθə; ˈmɑːθə/ (1894-1991) a US dancer and CHOREOGRAPHER (=someone who decides what movements dancers will do during a performance), who had an important influence on the development of modern dance 格雷厄姆〔(1894-1991), 美国舞蹈家、编舞, 对现代舞蹈的发展影响很大〕

Gra·hame /ˈgreəm; ˈgreɪəm/, **Ken·neth** (1859-1932) a British writer whose most famous work is his book for children *The Wind in the Willows* 格雷厄姆〔(1859-1932), 英国作家。他创作的儿童文学著作《杨柳风》十分著名〕

Grail, the /grel; greɪl/ *n* —see 见 HOLY GRAIL

grain /gren; greɪn/ *n*

1 ►FOOD 食物◄ **a)** [U] the seeds of crops such as corn, wheat, or rice that are gathered for use as food, or these crops themselves 谷物, 粮食 **b)** [C] a single seed of corn, wheat etc 谷粒

2 ▶**OF WOOD ETC** 木头等的◀ **the grain** the natural arrangement of the threads or FIBRES (3) in wood, flesh, rock, and cloth, or the pattern you see as a result of this 纹理: *Cut the wood in the direction of the grain.* 顺着木头的纹理把木头劈开。—see picture at 参见 KNOT[1] 图

3 **a grain of sympathy/truth/doubt etc** a small amount of truth etc 一点点同情/真实性/怀疑等: *They don't have a grain of common sense between them.* 他们两人没有一点儿共识。

4 ▶**SMALL PIECE** 颗粒◀ [C] a single, very small piece of a substance such as sand, salt etc〔沙、盐等的〕颗粒 —see picture on page A7 参见 A7 页图

5 **go against the grain** if something that you have to do goes against the grain, you do not like doing it, because it is not what you would naturally do 违背本人的意愿: *It went against the grain for her to be so strict.* 这么严格是她不愿意的。

6 ▶**MEASURE** 计量单位◀ [C] the smallest measure of weight, used for medicines, equal to .0648 gram 格令〔最小重量单位, 等于0.0648克, 用于称量药品〕—see table on page C3 参见 C3 页附录 —see also 另见 **take sth with a pinch/grain of salt** (SALT[1] (3))

grain·y /ˈgreni; ˈgreini/ *adj* a photograph that is grainy has a rough appearance, as if the images are made up of spots 颗粒状的, 似有颗粒状的〔指照片看起来很粗糙, 其图像似由颗粒组成〕

gram, gramme /græm; græm/ written abbreviation 缩写= **g** or **gm** *n* [C] the basic unit for measuring weight in the METRIC system 克〔公制基本单位〕—see table on page C3 参见 C3 页附录

-gram /græm; græm/ *suffix* [in nouns 构成名词] a message delivered as an amusing surprise 给人惊喜的有趣讯息: *On his birthday we sent him a kissagram* (=a girl who was paid to give him a message and kiss him). 他生日的那天我们雇一个能给他送去贺卡并亲吻他一下的女孩。

gram·mar /ˈgræmɚ; ˈgræmə/ *n* **1** [U] the rules by which words change their forms and are combined into sentences, or the study or use of these rules 语法(学): *I find German grammar very difficult.* 我觉得德语语法很难。| *I often have to correct his grammar.* 我经常得纠正他的语法。**2** [C] a particular description of grammar or a book that describes grammar rules 语法书: *Have you seen that new French grammar?* 你见过那本新的法语语法书吗?

gram·mar·i·an /grəˈmɛriən; grəˈmeəriən/ *n* [C] someone who studies and knows about grammar 语法学家

grammar school /ˈ··, ·/ *n* [C] **1** a school in Britain for children over the age of 11 who have to pass a special examination to go there 文法学校〔英国的一种学校, 为 11 岁以上的儿童设立, 但必须通过一种特殊考试才能录取〕—compare 比较 COMPREHENSIVE SCHOOL **2** *AmE old-fashioned* an ELEMENTARY SCHOOL【美, 过时】小学

gram·mat·i·cal /grəˈmætɪkḷ; grəˈmætɪkəl/ *adj* **1** [only before noun 仅用于名词前] concerning grammar 语法的: *grammatical rules* 语法规则 **2** correct according to the rules of grammar 语法正确的, 符合语法的 —**grammatically** /-klɪ; -kli/ *adv*

gramme /græm; græm/ *n* [C] another spelling of GRAM gram 的另一种拼法

Gram·my /ˈgræmɪ; ˈgræmi/ *n* [C] an award given by the US National Academy of Recording Arts and Sciences for special achievement in the record industry 格莱美奖〔美国国家录音艺术与科学学会给在唱片业有特殊成就的人士颁发的奖项〕

gram·o·phone /ˈgræməfon; ˈgræməfəʊn/ *n* [C] *old-fashioned* a RECORD PLAYER【过时】留声机

Gram·pi·an /ˈgræmpɪən; ˈgræmpiən/ a region in northeast Scotland, which includes the city of Aberdeen 格兰扁〔苏格兰东北部包括阿伯丁市在内的一个行政区〕

Gram·pi·an Moun·tains —see 见 the GRAMPIANS

Gram·pi·ans, the /ˈgræmpɪənz; ˈgræmpiənz/ also 又作 **the Grampian Mountains** a line of mountains that stretches across Scotland and divides the Highlands and Lowlands of Scotland. Its highest mountain is Ben Nevis. 格兰扁山脉〔横贯苏格兰并将其分为高地和低地两部分的一道山脉。最高山峰是本尼维斯山〕

gram·pus /ˈgræmpəs; ˈgræmpəs/ *n* [C] a sea animal like a WHALE 灰海豚

gran /græn; græn/ *n* [C] *BrE informal* grandmother【英, 非正式】祖母, 奶奶; 外祖母, 外婆

gra·na·ry[1] /ˈgrænərɪ; ˈgrænəri/ *n* [C] a place where grain, especially wheat, is stored 粮仓〔尤指储存小麦的仓库〕

granary[2] *adj* [only before noun 仅用于名词前] *BrE* granary bread is bread which contains whole grains of wheat【英】〔面包〕全麦的

Gran Ca·na·ri·a /ˌgræn kəˈnɑrɪə; ˌgræn kəˈnɑːriə/ also 又作 **Grand Canary** an island in the Atlantic Ocean, off the coast of northwest Africa, which is one of the Canary Islands 大加那利岛〔大西洋一岛, 位于非洲西北海岸外, 属加那利群岛〕

grand[1] /grænd; grænd/ *adj* **1** a grand building, occasion etc is very impressive 壮观的, 盛大的, 隆重的: *We attended a grand ceremony at the Palace.* 我们在王宫参加了一个隆重的典礼。| **on a grand scale** *Preparations for the wedding are taking place on a grand scale.* 婚礼的准备工作正在大规模地进行。**2** a grand plan or idea aims to achieve something very impressive 宏伟的: *As a young minister he was full of grand ideas for social reform.* 作为一位年轻的部长, 他心里充满对社会改革的宏伟想法。**3** people who are grand are rich and important but often too proud 有钱有势而神气活现的: *A very grand-looking gentleman entered the room.* 一位神气十足的绅士走进房间。**4** *informal or dialect* very good, pleasant, or enjoyable【非正式或方言】极好的, 非常愉快[令人开心]的: *We had a grand day out at the seaside.* 我们在海边度过了非常愉快的一天。| *Wasn't it grand to see Ted again?* 再次见到特德真好, 不是吗? **5 grand total** the final total you get when you add up several numbers or amounts 总计 **6 the Grand Old Man of** a man who has been involved in an activity or a profession for a long time and is highly respected〔某活动、某行业的〕元老, 老前辈: *the Grand Old Man of British theatre* 英国戏剧界的老前辈 —**grandly** *adv* —**grandness** *n* [U]

grand[2] *n* [C] **1** *plural* **grand** *informal* a thousand pounds or dollars【非正式】一千英镑, 一千美元: *That new car of his cost him fifteen grand.* 他那辆新车花了他一万五千英镑。**2** *informal* a GRAND PIANO【非正式】大钢琴

gran·dad *especially BrE*【尤英】, **granddad** *especially AmE*【尤美】/ˈgrænˌdæd; ˈgrændæd/ *n* [C] **1** *informal* grandfather【非正式】爷爷; 外公 **2** *BrE informal* an impolite way of addressing an old man【英, 非正式】老头〔对老年人的一种不礼貌的称呼〕: *Hurry up, grandad!* 快点, 老头!

gran·dad·dy, granddaddy /ˈgrænˌdædɪ; ˈgrændædi/ *n* [C] *AmE informal*【美, 非正式】**1** grandfather 爷爷; 外公 **2 the grandaddy of** the first or greatest example of something〔某一行中最杰出的〕老祖宗, 祖师爷: *Louis Armstrong, the grandaddy of all jazz trumpeters* 爵士乐号手的祖师爷路易斯·阿姆斯特朗

grandad shirt /ˈ··, ·/ *n* [C] a shirt without a collar 无领衬衫 —see picture on page A17 参见 A17 页图

Grand Ca·nal, the /ˌ· ·ˈ·/ **1** a CANAL (=an artificial river) in Venice, Italy, which is the main way through the city and has many famous buildings along its sides 大运河〔意大利威尼斯的一条运河。它是贯穿该市的主要水道, 两岸有许多著名建筑〕**2** the longest canal in China. Part of it, connecting the Yangtze and Yellow Rivers, was built in the 5th century BC. 大运河〔中国最长的运河。其连接长江与黄河的河段, 修建于公元前 5 世纪〕

Grand Ca·na·ry /ˌ· ·ˈ··/ —see 见 GRAN CANARIA

Grand Can·yon, the /ˌ· ˈ··/ a very large, deep GORGE (=a steep-sided valley cut by a river) in the US state of Arizona 大峡谷〔位于美国亚利桑那州的一个幽深而宽阔的峡谷〕

Grand Cen·tral Sta·tion /ˌ· ˌ·· ˈ··/ the main railway station in New York City. Grand Central Station is a very busy place, and in the US people often mention it humorously to say how busy another place is. 中央大火车站〔纽约市的主要火车站, 非常繁忙。美国人常幽默地借用此名来指称嘈杂拥挤的地方〕: *Our house was like Grand Central Station last night!* 我家昨晚简直就像中央大火车站!

grand·child /ˈgrændˌtʃaɪld; ˈgræntʃaɪld/ *plural* **grandchildren** /-ˌtʃɪldrən; -ˌtʃɪldrən/ *n* [C] the child of your son or daughter 孙子[女]; 外孙[女] —see picture at 参见 FAMILY 图

grand·dad /ˈgrænˌdæd; ˈgrændæd/ *n* [C] the usual American spelling of GRANDAD grandad 的一般美式拼法

grand·dad·dy /ˈgrænˌdædɪ; ˈgrændædi/ *n* [C] another spelling of GRANDADDY grandaddy 的另一种拼法

grand·daugh·ter /ˈgrændˌdɔtɚ; ˈgrænˌdɔːtə/ *n* [C] the daughter of your son or daughter 孙女; 外孙女 —see picture at 参见 FAMILY 图

gran·dee /grænˈdi; grænˈdiː/ *n* [C] **1** a Spanish or Portuguese NOBLEMAN of the highest rank in former times 大公〔以前西班牙或葡萄牙的最高爵位〕**2** a politician of the highest social class who has a lot of influence〔极有影响的〕社会最上层政客

gran·deur /ˈgrændʒɚ; ˈgrændʒə/ *n* [U] impressive beauty, power, or size 壮丽, 雄伟: *the grandeur of the mountains* 山峦的壮丽 —see also 另见 **delusions of grandeur** (DELUSION (2))

grand·fa·ther /ˈgrændˌfɑðɚ; ˈgrændˌfɑːðə/ *n* [C] the father of your father or mother 祖父; 外祖父 —see picture at 参见 FAMILY 图

grandfather clock /ˈ··· ·/ *n* [C] an old-fashioned tall clock which stands on the floor 老式的落地钟

grand fi·na·le /ˌ· ·ˈ··/ *n* [C] the last and most impressive or exciting part of a show or performance〔节目或演出的〕终曲,终场,压轴戏

gran·dil·o·quent /grænˋdɪləkwənt; grænˈdɪləkwənt/ *adj formal* using words that are too long and formal in order to sound important; POMPOUS【正式】浮夸的,华而不实的〔指使用华丽的辞藻以显得重要〕—**grandiloquence** *n* [U]

gran·di·ose /ˋgrændɪˌos; ˈgrændiəʊs/ *adj* grandiose plans sound very important or impressive, but will never really happen because they are not practical〔计划〕浮夸的,不切合实际的: *It's just another of Wheeler's grandiose schemes.* 这只是惠勒的又一个不切实际的计划。

grand ju·ry /ˌ· ˈ··/ *n* [C] *law* a group of people in the US who decide whether someone charged with a crime should be judged in a court of law【法律】〔美国的〕大陪审团 —**grand juror** *n* [C]

grand lar·ce·ny /ˌ· ˈ···/ *n* [U] *AmE law* the crime of stealing very valuable goods【美,法律】严重盗窃罪〔指盗窃十分珍贵的物品〕

[1] **grand·ma** /ˋgrændmɑ; ˈgrænmɑː/ *n* [C] *informal* grandmother【非正式】奶奶;外婆

grand mal /ˌgræn ˋmæl; ˌgrɒn ˈmæl/ *n* [U] *technical* a serious form of EPILEPSY【术语】重度癫痫发作

Grandma Mo·ses /ˌ·· ˈ··/ —see 见 Grandma MOSES

grand mas·ter /ˌ· ˈ··/ *n* [C] a CHESS player of a very high standard 国际象棋大师

[3] **grand·moth·er** /ˋgrændˌmʌðə; ˈgrænˌmʌðə/ *n* [C] the mother of your mother or father 祖母;外祖母 —see picture at 参见 FAMILY 图

Grand Na·tion·al, the /ˌ· ˈ···/ a horse race that takes place every year at the Aintree race course near Liverpool, England. Many people who are not usually interested in horse racing BET money on the horse they think will win the Grand National. 全国越野障碍大赛马〔每年在英格兰利物浦附近安特里赛马场举行的赛马比赛。许多平时对赛马不感兴趣的人也会前去参加赌马〕

Grand Old Duke of York, the /ˌ· · · · ˈ·/ a character in a British NURSERY RHYME (=an old song or poem for children) 约克老公爵〔英国一儿歌中的人物〕:

Oh the Grand Old Duke of York
He had ten thousand men,
He marched them up to the top of the hill
And he marched them down again.
约克老公爵
统兵一万多,
一令上山岗,
二令下山忙。

Grand Ole Op·ry, the /ˌgrænd ol ˋɑprɪ; ˌgrænd əʊl ˈɒpri/ a centre for country and western music in Nashville, Tennessee, known especially for the radio and television broadcasts made there for many years. In 1974, it moved to Opryland USA near Nashville, and it is still an important centre for COUNTRY AND WESTERN music. 大奥普里〔美国一个乡村音乐与西部音乐中心,位于田纳西州纳什维尔,尤以多年制作广播、电视节目著称。1974年,搬迁至纳什维尔附近的奥普里兰,至今仍是美国重要的乡村与西部音乐中心〕

grand op·e·ra /ˌ· ˈ···/ *n* [C,U] an OPERA with a serious subject in which all the words are sung 大歌剧

[1] **grand·pa** /ˋgrændpɑ; ˈgrænpɑː/ *n* [C] *informal* grandfather【非正式】爷爷;外公

grand·par·ent /ˋgrændˌpɛrənt; ˈgrænˌpeərənt/ *n* [C usually plural 一般用复数] one of the parents of your mother or father 祖父[母];外祖父[母]: *My grandparents live in Sussex.* 我的祖父母住在萨塞克斯郡。—see picture at 参见 FAMILY 图

grand pi·an·o /ˌ· ·ˈ··/ *n* [C] the type of large piano often used in concerts〔通常在音乐会上使用的〕大钢琴 —compare 比较 UPRIGHT PIANO

grand prix /grɑ̃ ˋpri; ˌgrɒn ˈpriː/ *n* [C] one of a set of international races, especially a car race 国际大奖赛〔尤指赛车〕

grand slam /ˌ· ˈ·/ *n* [C] **1** the winning of all of a set of important sports competitions in the same year〔同年各项重要比赛的〕全胜 **2** a hit in BASEBALL which gets four runs (RUN² (17)) because it is a HOME RUN and there are players on all the bases (BASE² (8))〔棒球中的〕满垒本垒打 **3** the winning of all of the tricks (TRICK¹ (11)) possible in one game of cards, especially in BRIDGE¹ (4)〔扑克牌,尤指桥牌中的〕大满贯

grand·son /ˋgrændˌsʌn; ˈgrænsʌn/ *n* [C] the son of your son or daughter 孙子;外孙 —see picture at 参见 FAMILY 图

grand·stand /ˋgrændˌstænd; ˈgrændstænd/ *n* [C] a large structure that has many rows of seats where people sit and watch sports competitions, games, or races〔体育比赛场地的〕大看台

grand·stand·ing /ˋgrændˌstændɪŋ; ˈgrædstændɪŋ/ *n* [U] *AmE* an action that is intended to make people notice and admire you【美】引人注意的动作,哗众取宠的行为: *His opening the new school is just a piece of political grandstanding.* 他主持这所新学校的成立典礼只是一种哗众取宠的政治举动。

grand tour /ˌ· ˈ·/ *n* [C] **1** *humorous* an occasion when someone takes you around a building to show it to you【幽默】参观: *They took us on a grand tour of their new house.* 他们领我们参观了他们的新居。**2 the grand tour** a trip round Europe made in former times by young English or American people from rich families as a part of their education 环欧旅行〔指旧时英美富家子弟作为其教育的一部分所作的环欧洲旅行〕

Grand U·nion Ca·nal, the /ˌ· ˌ·· ·ˈ·/ a CANAL (=an artificial river made for boats to travel on) opened in 1801, connecting London with the English Midlands 大联合运河〔1801年开通的一条运河,将伦敦与英格兰中部地区相连接〕

grange /grendʒ; greɪndʒ/ *n* [C] a large country house with farm buildings 农庄,庄园

gran·ite /ˋgrænɪt; ˈgrænɪ̣t/ *n* [U] a very hard grey rock, often used in building 花岗岩,花岗石

gran·ny¹, **grannie** /ˋgrænɪ; ˈgræni/ *n* [C] *informal* grandmother【非正式】祖母;奶奶;外婆: *Look what granny's bought you!* 瞧奶奶给你带什么来了! [3]

granny², **grannie** *adj* [only before noun 仅用于名词前] *BrE* of a style typically used by old women【英】老太太式样的: *granny shoes* 老奶奶鞋

granny flat /ˈ·· ·/ *n* [C] *BrE* a separate place inside or next to someone's house, that is designed for an old relative to live in 老奶奶住房〔指在住宅内部或隔壁专供年老亲戚居住的一套居室〕

granny knot /ˈ·· ˌ·/ *n* [C] a REEF KNOT in which the two pieces of string are crossed in the wrong way〔两条绳反向打的〕老奶奶结

gra·no·la /grəˋnolə; grəˈnəʊlə/ *n* [U] *AmE* breakfast food made from mixed nuts, grains, and seeds【美】〔用坚果、谷物和种子混合制成的〕早餐食品

grant¹ /grænt; grɑːnt/ *n* [C] an amount of money given to someone, especially by the government for a particular purpose〔政府发给的〕补助金: *We're hoping to get a grant from the local council for the project.* 我们正希望能从本地市政会为这个项目得到一笔拔款。| **student grant** (=a grant to pay for a student's education at university) 助学金 [1] [2]

grant² *v* [T] **1** *formal* to give someone something that they have asked for, especially official permission to do something【正式】给予,准予〔尤指官方授权〕: **grant sb sth** *The Norton consortium has been granted permission to build a shopping mall.* 诺顿财团已获准建立一家购物中心。| **grant sb's request** *Your request for housing benefit has been granted.* 你的住房补贴申请已经得到批准。**2** to admit that something is true although it does not make much difference to your opinion 承认〔确有某事,但不影响自己的看法〕: **I grant you** *Darren's not an intellectual, I grant you, but he does work hard.* 达伦不是一个知识分子,这不假;但他确实工作很努力。| **granted** (=used when you admit that what someone has said is true) 不错;我承认〔用来表示承认某人所说为事实〕 *Granted, we don't want to scare them, but it's time we applied some pressure.* 不错,我们不想把他们吓住,但现在是我们施加点压力的时候了。**3 take it for granted (that)** to believe that something is true without making sure 想当然地认为: *Sorry! I just took it for granted that you'd want to come.* 对不起!我想当然地认为你愿意来。**4 take sb/sth for granted** to expect that someone will always be there when you need them and never show them any special attention or thank them 视某人/某事为当然〔因而对其从不特别关注或感谢〕: *I'm sick and tired of my husband taking me for granted!* 我丈夫觉得我一切理当如此,真令我感到生气和厌倦! [2] [2]

Grant, Ca·ry /ˋkɛrɪ; ˈkæri/ (1904-86) a US film actor, who was born in the UK. He is known for being very good-looking and for appearing as characters who are confident, amusing and relaxed, in humorous films such as *Bringing Up Baby* (1938), *His Girl Friday* (1940), and *The Philadelphia Story* (1940). 格兰特〔(1904-1986),美国电影演员,出生于英国。他相貌英俊,在《育婴奇谭》(1938)、《他的女伴礼拜五》(1940)和《费城故事》(1940)等喜剧片中扮演自信诙谐、开朗轻松的角色,并因此闻名〕

Grant, Ulysses S. (1822-85) a US army leader who commanded the army of the Union (=the northern US states) during the American Civil War. His military victories, especially the one at Appomattox against General Robert E. Lee, helped the Union to win the war. He was US President from 1869 to 1877.

格兰特〔(1822-1885)，美国军事领袖，南北战争时期曾指挥北方联邦军队。他的军事成就，尤其是在阿波马托克斯打败罗伯特·E.李将军的战绩，帮助联邦军队赢得了战争。1869 至 1877 年间任美国总统〕

grant-main·tained /ˌ· ˈ· ·◂/ *adj* a grant-maintained school in Britain receives its money directly from the central government rather than from the local government 直接由中央政府资助的〔学校〕

gran·u·lar /ˈgrænjələ˞; ˈgrænjʊlə/ *adj* consisting of or covered with granules 由颗粒组成的；布满颗粒的

gran·u·lat·ed /ˈgrænjəletɪd; ˈgrænjʊleɪtɪ̇d/ *adj* granulated sugar is in the form of small white grains rather than powder 〔白糖〕砂状的

gran·ule /ˈgrænjul; ˈgrænjuːl/ *n* [C] a small hard piece of something 细粒，小粒：*coffee granules* 咖啡晶

grape /grep; greɪp/ *n* [C] a small round juicy fruit that grows on a VINE and is often used for making wine 葡萄：*a bunch of grapes* 一串葡萄 —see picture on page A8 参见 A8 页图

grape·fruit /ˈgrepˌfrut; ˈgreɪpfruːt/ *n* [C] a round yellow CITRUS fruit with a thick skin, like a large orange 西柚，葡萄柚 —see picture on page A8 参见 A8 页图

Grapes of Wrath, The /ˌ· · ˈ·/ (1939) a NOVEL by John Steinbeck which describes how a family called Joad have to leave their farm in the Dust Bowl in the US state of Oklahoma during the Great Depression of the 1930s, and the difficulties they have in moving to California and trying to work on farms there《愤怒的葡萄》〔(1939)，约翰·斯坦贝克创作的一部小说。故事发生在 20 世纪 30 年代的大萧条时期。乔德一家人被迫离开美国俄克拉何马州干旱尘暴区的农场，历经艰难才到达加利福尼亚，并想方设法在那里的农场安顿下来〕

grape·vine /ˈgrepˌvaɪn; ˈgreɪpvaɪn/ *n* [C] **1 hear sth on the grapevine** to hear about something because the information has been passed from one person to another in conversation 从传闻听到某事：*I heard about his resignation on the grapevine.* 我听说了有关他辞职的传闻。**2** a climbing plant on which grapes grow; VINE (1) 葡萄〔植物〕

graph /græf; græf/ *n* [C] a drawing that uses a line or lines to show how two or more sets of measurements are related to each other 图表〔指用线条表示两组或多组计量之间关系的图表〕：*Martin showed me a graph of their recent sales.* 马丁给我看了一张有关他们最近销售额的图表。—see picture at 参见 CHART[1] 图

graph·ic /ˈgræfɪk; ˈgræfɪk/ *adj* **1 a graphic account/description etc** a very clear description of an event that gives a lot of details, especially unpleasant ones 清楚详细的叙述/描写等〔尤指包含令人不愉快的细节的〕：*Cookson gives a graphic account of her unhappiness as a child.* 库克森详尽地描述了她童年的不幸。**2** [only before noun 仅用于名词前] connected with or including drawing, printing, or designing 绘画的，印刷的；平面造型设计的：*a graphic artist* 平面造型艺术家 | *the graphic arts* 平面造型艺术

graph·i·cally /ˈgræfɪklɪ; ˈgræfɪkli/ *adv* **1** if you describe something graphically, you describe it very clearly with a lot of detail 清晰详细地：*Stella described the scene so graphically that I could almost imagine I was there.* 斯特拉十分详尽地描述了这一场面，我几乎就像身临其境一样。**2** *formal* using a graph【正式】用图表：*statistics represented graphically* 用图表表示的统计资料

graphic de·sign /ˌ·· ·ˈ·/ *n* [U] the art of combining pictures, words, and decoration in the production of books, magazines etc〔书、杂志等的〕平面造型设计 —**graphic designer** *n* [C]

graph·ics /ˈgræfɪks; ˈgræfɪks/ *n* [plural] drawings or images that are designed to represent objects or facts, especially in a computer program〔尤指电脑程序中的〕图，图表 —see also 另见 COMPUTER GRAPHICS

graph·ite /ˈgræfaɪt; ˈgræfaɪt/ *n* [U] a soft black substance that is a kind of carbon, used in pencils, paints, and electrical equipment 石墨〔碳的一种形式，用于铅笔、油漆和电气设备中〕

gra·phol·o·gy /græˈfɑlədʒɪ; græˈfɒlədʒi/ *n* [U] the study of HANDWRITING in order to understand people's characters 笔迹学 —**graphologist** *n* [C]

graph pa·per /ˈ· ˌ··/ *n* [U] paper with many squares printed on it, used for drawing GRAPHS〔有格子的〕标绘纸，坐标纸

-gra·phy /grəfɪ; grəfi/ *suffix* used in nouns to mean the making of a copy or picture of something〔用于名词，意为制作或复制图像的技术〕：*radiography* 射线照相，X 光照相 | *photography* 摄影

grap·ple /ˈgræpl̩; ˈgræpəl/ *v* [I] to fight or struggle with someone, holding them tightly 扭打，揪斗：[+with] *Two men grappled with a guard at the door.* 两个男人和一个门卫在门口扭打。

grapple with sth *phr v* [T] to try hard to deal with a difficult problem 尽力解决〔困难问题〕：*The Government is grappling with major areas of social policy.* 政府正努力处理社会政策的主要领域。

grap·pling i·ron /ˈ·· ˌ··/ also 又作 **grappling hook** /ˈ·· ·/ *n* [C] an iron tool with several hooks that you tie to a rope and use to hold a boat still, look for objects on the bottom of a river etc 抓钩〔带若干弯钩的铁制工具，系于绳上用以固定船只或在河底寻物〕

Gras·mere /ˈgræsmɪr; ˈgræsmɪə/ a lake and village in the Lake District in northwest England. The poet William Wordsworth lived there from 1799 to 1808, and many tourists visit his home, Dove Cottage. 格拉斯米尔〔英格兰一湖泊和村庄，位于西北部湖区。诗人威廉·华兹华斯 1799 至 1808 年间曾在此居住。许多游客前去参观他的故居"鸽舍"〕

grasp¹ /græsp; grɑːsp/ *v* [T] **1** to take and hold something firmly 抓牢，握紧：*Make sure you grasp the rope with both hands.* 一定要用双手抓紧绳索。| **grasp hold of sth** *Paula grasped hold of my arm.* 葆拉紧紧抓住我的胳膊。**2** [not in progressive 不用进行时] to completely understand a fact or an idea, especially a complicated one 理解，领会〔尤指复杂的意思〕：*They failed to grasp the full significance of his remarks.* 他们没有领会他的话的全部意义。**3 grasp a chance/opportunity** to eagerly and quickly use an opportunity to do something〔急切地〕抓住机会 **4 grasp the nettle** *BrE* to deal with an unpleasant situation firmly and without delay【英】果断地处理棘手问题

grasp at sth *phr v* [T] **1** to eagerly try to use an opportunity 急切尝试利用〔一次机会〕：*He was ready to grasp at any excuse, however flimsy.* 他随时准备找个借口，不管这种借口是如何牵强。**2** to try to hold on to something 企图抓住

grasp² *n* [singular] **1** the way you hold something or your ability to hold it 抓，握：*The book slipped from his grasp and fell to the floor.* 书从他的手里滑落到地板上。| *Take a firm grasp on the rope.* 抓紧绳子。**2** your ability to understand a complicated idea or situation〔对复杂概念或棘手状况的〕理解力：**a good/poor grasp of** *You seem to have a good grasp of the subject.* 看来你对这个题目理解得很透彻。| **beyond sb's grasp** (=too difficult for them to understand) 超乎某人的理解力 **3** your ability to achieve or gain something 力所能及；把握；掌握：**within sb's grasp** *Success is now within our grasp.* 现在我们已经成功在握。**4** *especially literary* control or power【尤文】控制，权力

grasp·ing /ˈgræspɪŋ; ˈgrɑːspɪŋ/ *adj* too eager to get money and unwilling to give any of it away or spend it 贪财而吝啬的：*Hanson was a hard, grasping man.* 汉森是个苛刻贪财又吝啬的人。

grass¹ /græs; grɑːs/ *n*

1 ▶IN FIELDS 在田野◀ **a)** [U] a very common plant with thin green leaves that grows in fields and is often eaten by animals 草：*a blade of grass* 一根草 | *Please keep off the grass.* 请勿践踏草地。**b)** [C] a particular kind of grass〔专指某种草〕：*sea grasses* 大叶藻

2 ▶DRUG 毒品◀ [U] *slang* MARIJUANA【俚】大麻

3 ▶CRIMINAL 罪犯◀ [C] *BrE informal* someone, usually a criminal, who gives information about other criminals to the police; INFORMER【英，非正式】告密者，通风报信者〔通常指向警方告发其他罪犯〕；STOOLPIGEON *AmE*【美】—see also 另见 SUPERGRASS

4 not let the grass grow under your feet to not waste time or delay starting something 不浪费时间，做事不拖沓

5 put sb out to grass *informal* to make someone leave their job because they are too old to do it effectively【非正式】使某人离职〔由于年老而不能有效工作〕：*an old judge being put out to grass* 即将被迫离职的老法官 —see also 另见 GRASS ROOTS, **snake in the grass** (SNAKE[1] (3))

grass² *v* [I] *BrE informal* if a criminal grasses on other criminals, he tells the police about their activities【英，非正式】〔罪犯〕向警方告发[告密]：[+on] *That bastard must have grassed on us!* 那个杂种肯定把我们给告发了！| **grass sb up** *BrE*【英】：*I wonder who grassed us up?* 不知道谁告发了我们？

grass sth ↔ **over** *phr v* [T] to cover land with grass〔在地上〕覆盖草皮

Grass, Günter (1927-) a German writer of NOVELS and plays with strong moral ideas. His best known works include *The Tin Drum* and *The Flounder*. 格拉斯〔(1927-)，德国小说和戏剧作家，有很强的道德观念。他最著名的作品包括《铁皮鼓》和《比目鱼》〕

grass·hop·per /ˈgræsˌhɑpə˞; ˈgrɑːsˌhɒpə/ *n* [C] an insect that has long back legs for jumping and that makes short loud noises 蚱蜢，蝗虫 —see also 另见 **knee-high to a grasshopper** (KNEE-HIGH[1] (2))

grass·land /ˈgræs,lænd; ˈgrɑːslænd/ also 又作 **grasslands** [plural] *n* [U] a large area of land covered with wild grass 草原

grass roots, the /,· ˈ·/ *n* the ordinary people in an organization, rather than the leaders〔组织中除领袖外的〕普通民众, 草根阶层 —**grass roots** *adj*: *We are hoping for full participation at grass roots level.* 我们希望基层民众充分参与。

grass snake /ˈ· ·/ *n* [C] a common snake that is not poisonous 游蛇

gras·sy /ˈgræsɪ; ˈgrɑːsi/ *adj* covered with grass 长满草的: *sitting on a grassy bank* 坐在长满草的河岸上

grate[1] /gret; greɪt/ *n* [C] the metal bars and frame that hold the wood, coal etc in a FIREPLACE〔壁炉的〕金属炉架

grate[2] *v* **1** [T] to rub cheese, fruit etc against a rough or sharp surface in order to break them into small pieces 磨碎〔干酪、水果等〕: *grated carrot* 磨碎的胡萝卜 —see picture on page A11 参见 A11 页图 **2** [I] to make an unpleasant sound 发出刺耳的摩擦声: [+on/against] *the sound of chalk grating against the blackboard* 粉笔摩擦黑板的刺耳声 **3** [I] to have an annoying effect on someone's nerves 使某人感到烦躁: [+on] *Hardy's constant questions were beginning to grate on me.* 哈迪不断提出问题, 开始使我烦躁。—see also 另见 GRATING[2]

3 **grate·ful** /ˈgretfəl; ˈgreɪtfəl/ *adj* **1** feeling that you want to thank someone because of something kind that they have done 感谢的, 感激的: *Dr Cameron has received hundreds of letters from grateful patients.* 卡梅伦医生收到数百封向他表示感谢的病人来信。| [+for] *I'm so grateful for all your help.* 我非常感谢你的帮助。| **be grateful to sb for sth** *He was extremely grateful to Gladstone for his support.* 他非常感谢格拉德斯通的支持。| **be grateful that** *I'm very grateful that you didn't tell my husband about this.* 我非常感激你没有告诉我丈夫这件事。| **deeply/eternally grateful** (=extremely grateful) 非常感谢, 感激不尽 **2 be grateful for small mercies** used in a bad situation to say that things could be worse than they are 庆幸〔境况未恶化〕: *Well, be grateful for small mercies – at least you've still got a job!* 好啦, 应感到庆幸了——至少你还有个工作! **3 I would be grateful if you could/would ...** *formal* used to make requests in formal situations or letters【正式】如果你能…我将感激不尽〔用于在正式场合或信件中提出请求〕: *We would be most grateful if you could confirm these arrangements immediately.* 如蒙贵方立即确认安排事项, 我方感激不尽。—opposite 反义词 UNGRATEFUL —**gratefully** *adv*: *We gratefully accepted their offer.* 我们十分感激地接受了他们的提议。—**gratefulness** *n* [U]

grat·er /ˈgretɚ; ˈgreɪtə/ *n* [C] a tool used for grating food〔食品〕磨碎器, 擦子: *a cheese grater* 干酪磨碎器

grat·i·fy /ˈgrætə,faɪ; ˈgrætɪ̈faɪ/ *v* [T] *formal*【正式】**1 be gratified** to feel pleased and satisfied 感到高兴和满意: *I was very gratified to hear how much they liked my work.* 我非常高兴听到他们说有多喜欢我干的活儿。**2** to satisfy a desire 满足〔欲望〕: *Hoping to gratify my curiosity, I opened the door.* 为了满足我的好奇心, 我打开了门。—**gratification** /,grætəfəˈkeʃən; ,grætɪ̈fɪ̈ˈkeɪʃən/ *n* [C,U]

grat·i·fy·ing /ˈgrætə,faɪɪŋ; ˈgrætɪ̈faɪ-ɪŋ/ *adj* pleasing and satisfying 令人欣慰的, 使人满足的: *It's gratifying to know they liked our project.* 得知他们喜欢我们的项目, 真令人欣慰。—**gratifyingly** *adv*

grat·ing[1] /ˈgretɪŋ; ˈgreɪtɪŋ/ *n* [C] a metal frame with bars across it, used to cover a window or hole〔窗或洞的〕格栅: *Leaves clogged the grating over the drain.* 树叶把排水管上的格栅堵住了。

grating[2] *adj* a grating sound is hard and unpleasant〔声音〕刺耳的: *a harsh grating laugh* 刺耳难听的笑声 —**gratingly** *adv*

grat·is /ˈgrætɪs; ˈgrætɪ̈s/ *adj, adv* provided without payment; free 免费: *Medical advice was provided gratis.* 医疗咨询是免费提供的。

grat·i·tude /ˈgrætə,tjud; ˈgrætɪ̈tjuːd/ *n* [U] the feeling of being grateful 感激(之情): *Tears of gratitude filled her eyes.* 她的眼里充满感激的泪水。| *I couldn't adequately express my gratitude to Francis.* 我对弗朗西斯的感激之情难以言表。| [+for] *I didn't get a single word of gratitude for all my trouble.* 我没有听到一句对我的辛劳表示感谢的话。| **deepest gratitude** (=very great gratitude) 万分的感激 —opposite 反义词 INGRATITUDE —see also 另见 **owe a debt of gratitude to sb** (DEBT (4))

gra·tu·i·tous /grəˈtjuətəs; grəˈtjuːɪ̈təs/ *adj* **gratuitous violence/insults/cruelty etc** violence etc that is done for no reason and causes unnecessary harm or offence 不必要的暴力/无端的侮辱/无端的残酷(行为)等 —**gratuitously** *adv* —**gratuitousness** *n* [U]

gra·tu·i·ty /grəˈtjuətɪ; grəˈtjuːɪ̈ti/ *n* [C] *formal*【正式】**1** a small gift of money given to someone for a service they provided; TIP[1] (2) 小费, 赏钱 **2** *especially BrE* a large gift of money given to someone when they leave their job, especially in the army, navy etc【尤英】〔尤指陆军、海军等的〕退职金, 退伍金

grave[1] /grev; greɪv/ *n* [C] **1** the place in the ground where a dead body is buried 坟墓 —compare 比较 TOMB **2 the grave** *especially literary* death【尤文】死亡: *Had his spirit returned from the grave to haunt them?* 是不是他的鬼魂从坟墓里回来缠上了他们? **3 sb would turn/spin in their grave** used to say that someone who is dead would strongly disapprove of something happening now 某人于九泉之下不得安宁〔表示某人在九泉之下也不会赞成〕: *The way Bill plays that piece would have Mozart turning in his grave.* 比尔那样演奏那首曲子莫扎特在九泉之下也不会赞成。—see also 另见 **dig your own grave** (DIG[1] (4)), **from the cradle to the grave** (CRADLE[1] (4)), **have one foot in the grave** (FOOT[1] (21)), **silent as the grave** (SILENT (6)), **a watery grave** (WATERY (5))

grave[2] *adj* **1** very serious and worrying 严重的; 令人担忧的: *This decision may have very grave consequences.* 这一决定可能产生非常严重的后果。| *I have grave doubts about his ability.* 我对他的能力十分怀疑。**2** looking or sounding quiet and serious, especially because something important or worrying has happened〔由于发生重大事情, 表情或说话〕严肃的: *Turnbull's face was grave as he told them about the accident.* 特恩布尔向他们讲述这次事故时表情十分严肃。—**gravely** *adv*: *Adam nodded gravely.* 亚当严肃地点点头。—see also 另见 GRAVITY (2, 3)

grave[3] /grɑv; grɑːv/ *adj* a grave ACCENT[1] (4) is a mark put above a letter in some languages such as French to show the pronunciation, for example è 有沉[抑]音符〔法语等语言中加在字母之上表示发音的符号〕的 —compare 比较 ACUTE (7), CIRCUMFLEX

grave·dig·ger /ˈgrev,dɪgɚ; ˈgreɪv,dɪgə/ *n* [C] someone whose job is to dig graves 掘墓人

grav·el /ˈgrævḷ; ˈgrævəl/ *n* [U] small stones, used to make a surface for paths, roads etc 砾石, 碎石: *a gravel path* 石子小道 | *a gravel pit* (=a place where gravel is dug out of the ground) 砾石采掘坑

grav·elled /ˈgrævḷd; ˈgrævəld/ *adj* a gravelled path or road has a surface made of gravel〔小道或道路〕用砾石[碎石]铺成的

grav·el·ly /ˈgrævəlɪ; ˈgrævəli/ *adj* **1** a gravelly voice has a low, rough sound 嗓音低哑的 **2** covered with or mixed with gravel 铺砾[碎]石的; 含砾[碎]石的: *gravelly soil* 含砾石的土壤

gra·ven /ˈgrevən; ˈgreɪvən/ *adj* **graven image** *literary* an image or figure that has been made out of stone, wood, or metal【文】〔用石、木或金属制作的〕雕像

Graves /grevz; greɪvz/, **Rob·ert** /ˈrɑbɚt; ˈrɒbət/ (1895-1985) a British poet and writer whose most famous works are his NOVELs set in ancient Roman times, *I, Claudius* and *Claudius the God*, and for his description of his life as a soldier in World War I, *Goodbye to All That* 格雷夫斯〔(1895-1985), 英国诗人、作家。代表作有以古罗马时代为背景的小说《我, 克劳狄乌斯》和《神明的克劳狄乌斯》以及描述一战期间从军经历的自传《向那一切告别》〕

grave·side /ˈgrev,saɪd; ˈgreɪvsaɪd/ *n* [singular] **at the graveside** beside a grave, especially when someone is being buried there〔尤指某人下葬时〕在坟墓边上

grave·stone /ˈgrev,ston; ˈgreɪvstəʊn/ *n* [C] a stone above a grave showing details of the person buried there; HEADSTONE 墓碑

grave·yard /ˈgrev,jɑrd; ˈgreɪvjɑːd/ *n* [C] **1** an area of ground where people are buried, often next to a church〔常指挨近教堂的〕墓地 —compare 比较 CEMETERY, CHURCHYARD **2** a place where things that are no longer wanted or useful are left 垃圾场: *a graveyard for old cars* 废旧汽车堆放场

graveyard shift /ˈ· · ,·/ *n* [C] *especially AmE* a regular period of working time at night【尤美】夜班

grav·i·tas /ˈgrævɪtæs; ˈgrævɪtæs/ *n* [U] *formal* a seriousness of manner that people respect【正式】〔令人肃然起敬的〕庄严态度

grav·i·tate /ˈgrævə,tet; ˈgrævɪ̈teɪt/ *v* [I always+adv/prep] *formal* to be attracted to something and therefore move towards it or become involved with it【正式】被吸引到: [+to/towards] *Very sporty students tended to gravitate towards others with similar interests.* 酷爱体育的学生往往会因志趣相投而互相吸引。

grav·i·ta·tion /,grævəˈteʃən; ,grævɪ̈ˈteɪʃən/ *n* [U] **1** *technical* the force that causes two objects to move towards each other because of their MASS[1] (5)【术语】引力 **2** the act of gravitating towards something 受吸引

grav·i·ta·tion·al /,grævəˈteʃənḷ; ,grævɪ̈ˈteɪʃənəl◂/ *adj* connected with or resulting from the force of gravity 与引力有关

G

的; 产生于引力的: *the planet's gravitational field* 这颗行星的引力场

grav·i·ty /ˈgrævətɪ; ˈgrævɪ̵ti/ *n* [U] **1** *technical* the force that causes something to fall to the ground or to be attracted to another PLANET【术语】重力, 引力, 地心吸力 **2** *formal* the extreme and worrying seriousness of a situation【正式】(局势的) 严重性: *Carl did not seem to understand the gravity of this situation.* 卡尔似乎不理解这种情况的严重性。**3** an extremely serious way of behaving, speaking etc 严肃〔指举止、言谈等的态度〕: *The Consul spoke slowly and with great gravity.* 这位领事讲话缓慢, 而且十分严肃。—see also 另见 CENTRE OF GRAVITY

gra·vy /ˈgrevɪ; ˈgreɪvi/ *n* [U] **1** a SAUCE made from the juice that comes from meat as it cooks, mixed with flour〔调味用的〕肉汁〔由烹调肉类时产生的汁水与面粉混合制成〕**2** *slang, especially AmE* money, profit, or something that you like that is gained when you do not expect it【俚, 尤美】意外之财, 意外所得

gravy boat /ˈ·· ·/ *n* [C] a long JUG (1) that you pour gravy from〔长形有柄带嘴〕盛肉汁用的器皿

gravy train, the /ˈ·· ,·/ *n informal* an organization, activity, or business from which many people can make money or profit without much effort【非正式】不费什么气力便可从中获利的组织[活动、买卖], 美差

gray /gre; greɪ/ *adj, n, v* the usual American spelling of GREY grey 的一般美式拼法

Gray, Do·ri·an /ˈdɔrɪən; ˈdɔːriən/ the main character in the NOVEL *The Picture of Dorian Gray* by Oscar Wilde 格雷〔奥斯卡·王尔德小说《道林·格雷的肖像》中的主人公〕

Gray, Thomas (1716-71) an English poet whose best-known work, *Elegy written in a Country Churchyard*, is usually called **Gray's Elegy** 格雷〔(1716-1771), 英国诗人。其代表作《墓园挽歌》通常被称作"格雷挽歌"〕

Gray's Inn /,· ˈ·/ a London organization of law students and BARRISTERS and the buildings they use, which is one of the four Inns of Court 格雷律师学院〔英国伦敦四所律师学院之一〕

graze[1] /grez; greɪz/ *v*

1 ▶EAT GRASS 吃草◀ a) [I] if an animal grazes, it eats grass that is growing (动物) 吃草: *The sheep continued to graze.* 羊继续吃草。**b)** [T] to let animals eat grass 放牧: *fields where they used to graze their sheep* 他们过去经常牧羊的田野

2 ▶INJURE YOURSELF 伤到自己◀ [T] to break the surface of your skin by rubbing it against something 擦伤: *Oliver grazed his knee when he fell over.* 奥利弗跌倒时擦伤了膝盖。

3 ▶TOUCH STH 碰触某物◀ [T] to touch something lightly while passing it 擦过, 掠过: *As the plane climbed away, its wing seemed to graze the treetops.* 飞机爬升时, 机翼似乎擦过树梢。

4 ▶EAT 吃◀ [I] to eat small amounts of food all through the day instead of having regular meals 少食多餐

5 ▶TELEVISION 电视◀ [I] to keep changing television CHANNELs, watching only a little of each programme 不停切换频道

graze[2] *n* [C] a wound caused by rubbing that slightly breaks the surface of your skin〔皮肤的〕擦伤

GRE /,dʒi ɑr ˋi; ,dʒiː ɑːr ˈiː/ *n* [C] Graduate Record Examination; an examination taken by students in the US who have done a first degree and want to go to GRADUATE SCHOOL〔美国〕研究生入学考试

grease[1] /gris; griːs/ *n* [U] **1** animal fat that is soft after being melted〔熔化了的〕动物油脂 **2** any thick oily substance, especially one used to make parts of machines work smoothly 润滑油

grease[2] *v* [T] **1** to put grease on something 给…涂油脂: *Grease the pan before you pour the batter in.* 将面糊倒入锅里之前, 要在锅底涂上油脂。**2 grease sb's palm** to give someone money in a secret or dishonest way in order to persuade them to do something〔向某人〕行贿 **3 like greased lightning** *informal* extremely fast【非正式】闪电般, 非常快地: *He disappeared like greased lightning when the police arrived.* 警察到达时他闪电般消失了。

grease gun /ˈ· ·/ *n* [C] a tool for forcing grease into machinery 注油枪, 油枪

grease mon·key /ˈ· ,··/ *n* [C] *slang* someone who repairs car engines or other machinery; MECHANIC【俚】汽车修理工, 机器修理工

grease·paint /ˈgris,pent; ˈgriːs-peɪnt/ *n* [U] a thick soft kind of paint that actors use on their face or body〔演员涂在脸上或身上的〕油彩

grease·proof pa·per /ˈgris,pruf ˋpepə; ,griːs-pruːf ˈpeɪpə/ *n* [U] *BrE* a kind of paper that GREASE[1] (1) cannot pass through, used in cooking and for wrapping food【英】〔用于烹调、包装食品的〕防油纸, 蜡纸; WAXED PAPER *AmE*【美】

greas·er /ˈgrisə; ˈgriːsə/ *n* [C] **1** someone who puts GREASE on machinery to make it run smoothly 润滑工 **2** *AmE slang* a very offensive word for someone from Latin America, especially Mexico【美俚】拉美佬; 墨西哥佬〔对拉丁美洲人, 尤其是墨西哥人的冒犯用语〕

greas·y /ˈgrisɪ; ˈgriːsi/ *adj* **1** covered in grease or oil 多脂的, 沾油脂的: *greasy food* 多脂的食品 | *greasy hair* 油腻腻的头发 **2** slippery 滑的: *The roads are greasy after the rain.* 雨后道路很滑。**3** too polite and friendly in a way that seems insincere or unpleasant; SMARMY 谄媚的, 虚情假意的 —**greasily** *adv* —**greasiness** *n* [U]

greasy spoon /,·· ˈ·/ *n* [C] a small cheap restaurant that mainly serves fried (FRY[1] (1)) food〔主要供应油炸食品的〕廉价小餐馆

great /gret; greɪt/ *adj*

① VERY GOOD 很好
② A LOT/VERY MUCH 很多
③ LARGE 大的
④ IMPORTANT 重要的
⑤ FAMILY 家庭
⑥ OTHER MEANINGS 其他意思

① VERY GOOD 很好

1 *spoken*【口】**a)** very good; excellent 非常好的, 好极的: *We had a great time at the fair.* 我们在游乐场玩得非常愉快。| *You can come after all? Great!* 你最终还是可以来? 太好了! | *It's great to see you again!* 再次见到你太好了。**b)** used when you really think that something is not good, satisfactory or enjoyable at all〔用来表示其实认为某事不好, 不令人满意或不令人愉快〕: *"Daniel's cancelled the party." "Oh great!"* "丹尼尔取消了聚会。""那太好了!"〔此为反话〕

2 ▶IN GOOD HEALTH 身体健康◀ feeling well and happy 感到健康快乐的: *I feel great this morning!* 今天早上我感觉棒极了!

3 ▶SKILFUL/SUCCESSFUL 熟练的/成功的◀ a) considered to be one of the best in the world and therefore admired by many people 伟大的, 卓越的: *a great work of art* 伟大的艺术品 | *one of the greatest boxers of all time* 迄今最伟大的拳击手之一 **b)** able to do something well 擅长的: **[+at]** *Joanna's great at chess.* 乔安娜精通国际象棋。

4 the greats the most famous and successful performers, especially in sport or entertainment 大人物, 巨擘〔尤指体育或娱乐方面〕: **the all-time greats**: *Charlie Chaplin is one of the all-time cinema greats.* 查理·卓别林是电影史上罕见的伟大演员。

5 be no great shakes to not be very good or skilful 并不好; 并不高明: *Alex thinks he's an ace at tennis, but he's no great shakes.* 亚历克斯认为自己是网球高手, 可是他的水平并不怎么样。

6 ▶VERY SUITABLE 很合适的◀ *informal* to be very useful or suitable for something【非正式】非常有用的, 非常合适的: **[+for]** *This knife's great for peeling vegetables.* 这把刀非常适合削蔬菜皮。

7 go great guns *informal* to do something very fast and successfully【非正式】顺利地快速大干: *Their campaign began slowly, but now they're going great guns.* 他们的运动开始时进展很慢, 但现在很快。

② A LOT/VERY MUCH 很多

8 great care/pleasure/strength etc a lot of care etc 极大的关心/快乐/力气等: *Take great care with those glasses.* 拿那些玻璃杯时要非常小心。| *It gives me great pleasure to introduce tonight's speaker.* 介绍今晚的演讲人, 我非常高兴。

9 a great deal a lot 许多, 大量: *I've travelled a great deal.* 我到过很多地方。| **[+of]** *I have a great deal of work right now.* 我此刻有许多工作要做。

10 a great number/quantity/extent etc a very large number etc 许多／大量／很大程度等: *Agnes survived the accident and went on to live to a great age* (=she was very old when she died). 阿格尼丝在事故中幸免于难, 后来活到很大的年纪。| **the great many** (=very many) 非常多的 | **the great majority** (=almost all) 绝大多数 *a proposal supported by the great majority of members* 得到绝大多数成员支持的提案
11 great friend/admirer etc a very good friend, a very keen admirer etc 很要好的朋友／十分热烈的爱慕者等
12 be a great one for writing/sailing/football etc *BrE* to enjoy writing, sailing, football etc very much【英】酷爱写作／帆船运动／足球等: *Adam's a great one for football – he never misses a match.* 亚当酷爱足球 —— 他从来不错过任何一场比赛。
13 a great talker/reader etc someone who enjoys doing a lot of talking, reading etc 爱说话的人／热衷于读书的人等

③ LARGE 大的
14 ▶VERY LARGE 很大的◀ very large and impressive 巨大的, 壮观的: *The great northern plain is divided by two rivers.* 北部的大平原被两条河分开。| *a great herd of buffalo* 一大群水牛 —see 见 BIG (USAGE)
15 great big/stupid/fat etc *spoken* used to emphasize how big, stupid etc something or someone is【口】巨大的／极愚蠢的／极肥胖的等: *They live in a great big house.* 他们住在一栋巨大的房子里。
16 huge/enormous great *BrE spoken* used to emphasize how big something is【英口】巨大的, 庞大的: *There's a huge great spider in the bath.* 浴缸里有一只硕大的蜘蛛。

④ IMPORTANT 重要的
17 ▶IMPORTANT 重要的◀ [only before noun 仅用于名词前] especially important or serious 特别重要的; 格外严重的: *a great state occasion* 国家的盛典 | *the great political issues of our time* 这时代的重大政治问题
18 the great advantage of/the great thing about the most important advantage of something〔某物〕最主要优点: *The great thing about nylon is that it's extremely tough.* 尼龙的最大优点是极其牢固。
19 ▶HAVING INFLUENCE 具有影响◀ having a lot of influence or power as a result of what you have achieved 强大的, 伟大的: *We must strive to make our country great again.* 我们必须努力奋斗, 使祖国再次强大起来。| *the great man himself* 这位伟人自己
20 the Great used in the name or title of someone or something to show their importance〔用于某人的名字、头衔或某物的名称中, 以示其重要性〕: *King Alfred the Great* 阿尔弗雷德大帝
21 the great and the good *formal or humorous* people who are considered important【正式或幽默】大人物

⑤ FAMILY 家庭
22 great-grandmother/great-grandfather etc the grandmother etc of one of your parents (外)曾祖母／(外)曾祖父等 —see picture at 参见 FAMILY 图
23 great-granddaughter/great-nephew etc the GRANDDAUGHTER of your child; the GRANDSON of your brother or sister etc 曾(外)孙女／(外)侄[甥]孙等 —see picture at 参见 FAMILY 图

⑥ OTHER MEANINGS 其他意思
24 Great Scott/Great Heavens! *old-fashioned* used to express surprise【过时】天哪!〔表示惊讶〕
25 Greater used before the name of a city to mean the city and its outer areas〔用于城市名称前, 指该市及其周边地区〕: *Greater Manchester* 大曼彻斯特
26 be great with child *biblical* to be PREGNANT【圣经】怀孕 —**greatness** *n* [U]

Great Bar·ri·er Reef, the /ˌ· ·, ··· ˈ·/ the largest CORAL REEF in the world, off the northeast coast of Australia. It is around 2000 km (1250 miles) long. 大堡礁〔世界上最大的珊瑚礁, 位于澳大利亚东北沿海附近, 长约2000公里(即1250英里)〕

Great Bear, the /ˌ· ˈ·/ another name for Ursa Major, a large group of bright stars 大熊座

Great Brit·ain /ˌ· ˈ··/ another name for the United Kingdom 大不列颠〔英国的别称〕

great·coat /ˈgretˌkot; ˈgreɪtkəʊt/ *n* [C] a long heavy coat 厚大衣

Great De·pres·sion, the /ˌ· ·ˈ··/ the severe economic problems that followed the Wall Street Crash of 1929. In the early 1930s, many banks and businesses failed, and millions of people lost their jobs in the US and in the UK and the rest of Europe. 大萧条〔指1929年华尔街股灾之后出现的严重经济问题。20世纪30年代初期, 美国、英国以及欧洲其他地区的许多银行和公司相继倒闭, 数百万人失业〕

Great Di·vide, the /ˌ· ·ˈ·/ —see 见 CONTINENTAL DIVIDE

Greater Lon·don /ˌ·· ˈ··/ London and the area surrounding it, which used to be a local government area 大伦敦〔指伦敦及其周围地区, 原为地方政府一辖区〕

Greater London Authority, the /ˌ··, ··ˈ···/ a group of people who are elected to govern the city of London. It consists of the Mayor of London and the 25 members of the London Assembly. The Authority is responsible for TRANSPORT, planning, economic development, environment, the police, the EMERGENCY services, culture, and health. 大伦敦政府〔管理伦敦市的机构。该机构由选举产生的伦敦市长和25名伦敦议会议员组成, 负责交通、规划、经济发展、环境、治安、急救服务、文化和卫生等工作〕

Greater Man·ches·ter /ˌ·· ˈ···/ a former COUNTY in northwest England, that included the whole of Manchester and parts of other counties 大曼彻斯特〔原为英格兰西北部一郡, 包括整个曼彻斯特和其他郡的部分地区〕

Great Ex·hi·bi·tion, the /ˌ· ··ˈ··/ a large EXHIBITION held in Hyde Park in 1851. It was the idea of Queen Victoria's husband, Prince Albert, and it was intended to show modern achievements in industry, science, and technology. The exhibition took place in a large glass building called the 'Crystal Palace'. 大博览会〔指1851年在海德公园举办的大型展览。这是维多利亚女王的丈夫艾伯特亲王的构想, 目的是展示现代工业和科技成就。展览在大型玻璃建筑"水晶宫"举行〕

Great Ex·pec·ta·tions /ˌ· ··ˈ··/ (1861) a NOVEL by Charles Dickens about a young man called Pip who wants to become rich and successful. He is given money by an unknown person, and as a result he becomes a less nice person, but after several difficult experiences, he finally realizes that he must work hard to make enough money to live well, and he becomes a kind, generous man.《远大前程》, 又译《孤星血泪》〔(1861), 查尔斯·狄更斯创作的小说, 讲述一位名叫匹普的年轻人梦想发财和成功的故事。他得到了一位无名人士的资助, 可结果他并没有活出个人样来。历经数次挫折之后, 他终于认识到只有辛劳才能多赚钱, 过上好日子。后来, 他成了一个善良、慷慨的人〕

Great Fire of Lon·don, the /ˌ· ·, · ˈ··/ a very serious fire that destroyed most of the city of London, including the old St Paul's Cathedral, in September 1666 伦敦大火〔指1666年9月的一场火灾。火灾烧毁了大半个伦敦城, 其中包括古老的圣保罗大教堂〕

Great Gats·by, The /ˌgret ˈgætsbɪ; ˌgreɪt ˈgætsbi/ (1925) a NOVEL by F. Scott Fitzgerald about the relationship between a man called Jay Gatsby and a married woman called Daisy Buchanan. It describes how bored and disappointed people in New York were during the 1920s even though they seemed GLAMOROUS (=rich, exciting, and attractive) and happy.《了不起的盖茨比》〔(1925), F. 斯科特·菲茨杰拉德创作的一部小说, 讲述男子杰伊·盖茨比与已婚女子黛西·布坎南之间的关系。小说反映了20世纪20年代的纽约人看似体面快乐但内心空虚沮丧的矛盾心理〕

great-grand·child /ˌ· ˈ··/ *n* [C] the GRANDCHILD of your child 曾孙(女), 曾外孙(女)

Great Lakes, the /ˌ· ˈ·/ a group of five lakes along the border between the US and Canada. These lakes are Lake Superior, Lake Michigan, Lake Huron, Lake Erie, and Lake Ontario. They are connected to form the St Lawrence Seaway which can be used by large ships. 五大湖〔位于美国和加拿大交界的五个大湖, 即苏必利尔湖、密歇根湖、休伦湖、伊利湖和安大略湖。它们连在一起形成了圣罗伦斯河航道, 可通行大型船只〕

Great Leap For·ward, the /ˌ· · ˈ··/ an attempt by the Chinese government, led by Mao Zedong, to achieve very rapid industrial development between 1958 and 1960. 大跃进〔指1958至1960年间毛泽东领导的中国政府为实现工业快速发展而进行的一次尝试〕

great·ly /ˈgretlɪ; ˈgreɪtli/ *adv formal* [usually before verb or participle 一般用于动词或过去分词前] extremely or very much【正式】非常, 很: *We greatly regret the trouble we have caused.* 我们对所引起的麻烦感到非常抱歉。| *a greatly improved design* 得到极大改善的设计 W3

Great Or·mond Street Hos·pi·tal /gret ˌɔrmənd strit ˈhɑspɪtl; greɪt ˌɔːmənd striːt ˈhɒspɪtl/ a famous children's hospital in London 大奥蒙德街医院〔伦敦一家著名的儿科医院〕

Great Plains, the /ˌ· ˈ·/ a large area of flat, high land in the western central US 大平原〔位于美国中西部的一片广袤平坦的土地〕

Great Rift Val·ley, the /ˌ· ˌ· ˈ··/ a very deep, wide valley which is 3000 miles long and runs across most of East Africa and into southwest Asia 大裂谷〔经东非大部分地区延伸至亚洲西南部的一条幽深宽阔的谷地，长3000英里〕

Great Salt Lake, the /ˌ· · ˈ·/ a lake in the US state of Utah which is about 70 miles long and has strong salt water 大盐湖〔位于美国犹他州的一个湖。长约70英里，湖水含盐量高〕

Great Seal of the U·nit·ed States, the /ˌ· ˌ· · · ˌ·· ˈ·/ the official SEAL (=special circle-shaped design) printed on important documents, used to prove that a document is from the US government. The seal has two sides, and on one side is a picture of a BALD EAGLE (=the national bird of the US), and on the other side is a picture of a PYRAMID with an eye above it. Both designs are printed on the back of a one-dollar bill. 美国国玺〔加盖在重要文档上的印章，以示由美国政府签发。印章有两面，一面为秃鹰图案，另一面为金字塔图案，金字塔上方是一只眼睛，一美元纸币的背面印有这两个图案〕

Great Smok·y Moun·tains, the /ˌ· ˌ·· ˈ··/ also 又作 **the Great Smokies**, **the Smokies** a range of mountains along the border between the US states of North Carolina and Tennessee 大雾山〔位于美国北卡罗来纳州和田纳西州边界的一座山脉〕

Great Train Rob·be·ry, the /ˌ· ˈ· ˌ···/ an event in 1963 when a group of criminals robbed a British mail train and stole over £2 million, which at that time was the largest amount of money ever stolen in the UK 火车大劫案〔指1963年一帮歹徒从英国一列邮政列车上劫走200多万英镑的事件。该案是当时英国有史以来数额最大的抢劫案〕

Great Wall of Chi·na, the /ˌ· ˌ· · ˈ··/ a large strong wall that was first built across northern China during the third century BC to protect the country against enemy armies. It is over 6,300 kilometres long. 中国万里长城〔从公元前3世纪开始为抵御外敌入侵而修筑的防御墙，高大坚固，贯穿中国北部地方，绵延6300余公里〕

Great War, the /ˌ· ˈ·/ an old-fashioned name for World War I 大战〔第一次世界大战旧称〕

Great White Way, the /ˌ· · ˈ·/ a NICKNAME for Broadway in New York City, which is called this because of the large number of bright lights along it 白色大道〔纽约市百老汇大街的别称。因大街两旁灯火通明而得名〕

grebe /grib; griːb/ *n* [C] a bird similar to a duck 䴙䴘

Gre·cian /ˈgriʃən; ˈgriːʃən/ *adj literary* from ancient Greece, or having a style or appearance that is considered typical of ancient Greece【文】古希腊的；古希腊式的

Gre·co-, Graeco- /griko; griːkəʊ/ *prefix* **1** of ancient Greece; Greek 古希腊的；希腊的 **2** ancient Greek and 古希腊和: *Greco-Roman art* 古希腊－罗马艺术

Greco, El see 见 EL GRECO

Greece /gris; griːs/ a country in southeast Europe on the Mediterranean Sea, which is a member of the EU. Population: 10,624,000 (2001). Capital: Athens. 希腊〔欧洲东南部地中海沿岸一国家，为欧盟成员国。人口：10,624,000 (2001)，首都：雅典〕 —**Greek** *n, adj*

greed /grid; griːd/ *n* [U] **1** a strong desire for more food or drink than you need 贪食，贪喝: **pure greed** *It's pure greed but I'd love some more of that cake.* 这完全是贪吃，不过我很想再吃一点那块蛋糕。**2** a strong desire for more money, power, possessions etc than you need 贪婪: *a man driven by greed and envy* 受贪婪和妒忌驱使的人

greed·y /ˈgridɪ; ˈgriːdi/ *adj* **1** wanting more food or drink than you need 贪吃的，贪喝的: *Don't be greedy – leave some cake for us.* 别贪心！给我们留点蛋糕。| *You greedy pig!* 你这贪吃猪！**2** always wanting more money, possessions etc〔对金钱、财产等〕贪婪的，渴望的: **greedy for profit/power/fame etc** *The company had become too greedy for profit.* 这家公司对利润过分贪婪。—**greedily** *adv* —**greediness** *n* [U]

Greek¹ /grik; griːk/ *n* **1** [U] the language of modern or ancient Greece 希腊语；古希腊语 **2** [C] someone from Greece 希腊人 **3** [C] *AmE* a member of a SORORITY or FRATERNITY (2) at an American college or university【美】〔美国大学里的〕女生[男生]联谊会会员 **4 it's all Greek to me** *informal* used to say that you cannot understand something【非正式】我（对此）一窍不通

Greek² *adj* **1** from or connected with Greece 来自希腊的；希腊的 **2 Greek god** *informal* a very attractive man【非正式】美男子

Greek Or·tho·dox Church, the /ˌ· ˈ··· ˈ·/ the main group of Christian churches in Eastern Europe and southwest Asia, which was formed in the 11th century by separating from the Catholic Church. The Russian Orthodox Church, the main Christian group in Russia, is closely related. 希腊正教会，希腊东正教会〔东欧和亚洲西南部的主要基督教教派。该教派11世纪从天主教会分裂出来，与俄罗斯的主要基督教教派俄罗斯正教会关系密切〕 —**Greek Orthodox** *adj*: *a Greek Orthodox priest* 一位希腊正教会牧师

green¹ /grin; griːn/ *adj*
1 ▶COLOUR 颜色◀ having the colour of grass or leaves 绿色的: *Go on – the traffic lights have turned green!* 走吧——信号灯已经变绿色了！| *green eyes* 绿色的眼睛 —see picture on page A5 参见 A5 页图
2 ▶GRASSY 长满草的◀ covered with green grass 铺满绿草的，长满绿草的: *green fields* 绿油油的农田
3 ▶FRUIT/PLANT 水果/植物◀ very young, or not yet ready to be eaten 尚未成熟的: *The bananas are still green.* 香蕉还没熟。| *new green shoots on the roses* 玫瑰丛上的嫩绿色新芽
4 ▶WITHOUT EXPERIENCE 没有经验的◀ *informal* young and lacking experience【非正式】年轻而无经验的: *a new batch of very green recruits* 新招来的一批生手
5 ▶ILL 生病的◀ *informal* looking pale and unhealthy because you are ill【非正式】〔脸色〕苍白的，不健康的: *George looked a bit green the next morning.* 乔治第二天早上看上去脸色有点苍白。| **green around/about the gills** (=looking ill or frightened) 脸色苍白；面无人色
6 ▶ENVIRONMENT 环境◀ connected with the environment 环境的: *green issues* 环境问题
7 ▶POLITICS 政治◀ belonging to the Green political party 绿党的
8 green with envy wishing very much that you had something that someone else has 十分嫉妒的
9 the green-eyed monster *humorous or literary* jealousy【幽默或文】嫉妒
10 have green fingers *BrE*【英】, **have a green thumb** *AmE*【美】to be good at making plants grow 擅长园艺
11 the green stuff *AmE informal* money【美，非正式】钱

green² *n* **1** [C,U] the colour of grass and leaves 绿色: *a room decorated in pale blues and greens* 以浅蓝色和绿色装饰的房间 **2 greens** [plural] **a)** *informal* vegetables with large green leaves【非正式】绿色阔叶蔬菜；青菜: *Eat your greens.* 要吃青菜。**b)** *AmE* leaves and branches used for decoration, especially at Christmas【美】〔尤指圣诞节用于装饰的〕青枝绿叶 —compare 比较 GREENERY **3** [C] a level area of grass, especially in the middle of a village〔村庄中心部位的〕一块草地: *playing cricket on the green* 在村里草地上打板球 —see also 另见 BOWLING GREEN, VILLAGE GREEN **4** [C] a smooth flat area of grass around each hole on a GOLF COURSE 果岭〔高尔夫球场上每个球洞周围的平坦草地〕 —see picture on page A23 参见 A23 页图 **5 Green** [C] someone who supports the Green political party 绿党支持者

green³ *v* **1** to fill an area with growing plants in order to make it more attractive 绿化: *the challenge of greening the city* 绿化城市的挑战性任务 **2** to make a person or organization realize the importance of environmental problems 使〔某人、某组织〕意识到环境问题的重要性: *the greening of public opinion* 使舆论认识到环境问题如何重要

green·back /ˈgrinˌbæk; ˈgriːnbæk/ *n* [C] *AmE informal* an American BANKNOTE【美，非正式】美钞

green bean /ˌ· ˈ·/ *n* [C] a long thin green vegetable which is picked before the beans inside it grow 青菜豆，嫩菜豆; FRENCH BEAN *BrE*【英】—see picture on page A9 参见 A9 页图

green belt /ˈ· ·/ *n* [C,U] an area of land around a city where building is not allowed, in order to protect fields and woods〔城市周围的〕绿化带

Green Berets, the /ˌ· ˈ·ˈ·/ a special group of soldiers in the US Army who wear green hats. They are officially called the Special Forces, and are trained to fight in difficult conditions. 绿色贝雷帽〔美国一支受过专门训练以应对复杂情况的部队，士兵头戴绿颜色的帽子。其正式名称为"特种部队"〕

green card /ˌ· ˈ·/ *n* [C] **1** a British motor insurance document that you need when you drive abroad〔英国〕绿色保险证〔在国外开车时使用〕 **2** a document that a foreigner must have in order to work legally in the US〔美国的〕绿卡

Greene /grin; griːn/, **Graham** (1904-91) a British writer of NOVELs and plays, one of the most respected British writers of the 20th century. His books include *Brighton Rock* and *The Power and the Glory*, and the characters in his stories often

have to make difficult moral decisions. 格林〔(1904-1991), 英国小说家、剧作家, 20 世纪最受人尊敬的英国作家之一。其作品包括《布赖顿硬糖》和《权力与荣耀》。故事中的人物经常必须面对道义上的两难抉择〕

green·e·ry /ˈgrinərɪ; ˈgriːnəri/ *n* [U] green leaves and plants 绿叶; 绿色植物

green·field site /ˈgrinfild ˌsaɪt; ˈgriːnfiːld ˌsaɪt/ *n* [C] a piece of land that has never been built on before〔从未建过房子的〕地皮

green·fly /ˈgrinflaɪ; ˈgriːnflaɪ/ *n plural* **greenflies** [C] a very small green insect that feeds on and damages young plants 蚜虫

green·gage /ˈgrinˋgedʒ; ˈgriːngeɪdʒ/ *n* [C] a juicy greenish-yellow PLUM[1] (1) 青梅子, 青李子

green·gro·cer /ˈgrinˌgrosɚ; ˈgriːnˌgrəʊsə/ *n* [C] *especially BrE*【尤英】**1** someone who owns or works in a shop selling fruit and vegetables 蔬菜水果商; 菜[水果]贩 **2 greengrocer's** a greengrocer's shop 蔬菜水果店

green·horn /ˈgrinˌhɔrn; ˈgriːnhɔːn/ *n* [C] *informal* someone who lacks experience and can be easily deceived【非正式】没有经验的人, 生手, 新手; 易上当的人

green·house /ˈgrinˌhaʊs; ˈgriːnhaʊs/ *n* [C] a glass building used for growing plants that need warmth, light, and protection 温室, 暖房

greenhouse ef·fect /ˈ· · ˌ· ˌ·/ *n* [singular] the gradual warming of the air surrounding the Earth as a result of heat being trapped by POLLUTION 温室效应 —see also 另见 GLOBAL WARMING

greenhouse gas /ˈ· · ˌ·/ *n* [C] a gas, especially CARBON DIOXIDE or METHANE, that is thought to trap heat above the Earth and cause the greenhouse effect 温室气体〔被认为导致温室效应的气体, 尤指二氧化碳或甲烷〕

green·ish /ˈgrinɪʃ; ˈgriːnɪʃ/ *adj* slightly green 略带绿色的: *a greenish tinge* 一抹绿色

Green Jack·ets, the —see 见 the ROYAL GREEN JACKETS

Green·land /ˈgrinlənd; ˈgriːnlənd/ a large island in the North Atlantic Ocean, near northeast Canada. Population: 56,352 (2001). Capital: Nuuk. Nearly all of Greenland is covered by ice, and it belongs to Denmark but has its own government. 格陵兰〔北大西洋一大岛, 靠近加拿大东北部。人口: 56,352 (2001), 首府: 努克。岛上几乎全被冰层覆盖。该岛属于丹麦, 但有自己的政府〕

green light /ˈ· ·/ *n* [C] **1** the colour of a TRAFFIC LIGHT that shows cars they can go forward 交通绿灯 **2 give sb the green light** to allow a project, plan etc to begin 给某人开绿灯〔允许某工程、计划等启动〕: *The government has given the green light to Sunday trading.* 政府已经给星期日贸易开了绿灯。

green·light /ˈgrinˌlaɪt; ˈgriːnlaɪt/ *v* [T] to give official permission for something to be started 正式批准〔某事〕启动

green on·ion /ˌ· ˈ· ·/ *n* [C] *AmE* an onion with a small white round part and a long green stem, usually eaten raw【美】大葱; SPRING ONION *BrE*【英】

green pa·per /ˌ· ˈ· ·/ *n* [C] a document produced by the British government containing proposals to be discussed, that may later be used in making laws 绿皮书〔英国政府编制的一种文件, 提出建议以供讨论; 日后可能用作立法的依据〕—compare 比较 WHITE PAPER, BILL[1] (2)

Green Par·ty, the /ˈ· ˌ· ·/ a political party whose main aim is to preserve the environment. There are Green Parties in most countries of western Europe, and their members are often informally called **Greens**. 绿党〔旨在保护环境的一个政治党派。西欧大多数国家都有绿党组织, 其成员的非正式名称为 Greens〕

Green·peace /ˈgrinpis; ˈgriːnpiːs/ an international organization whose members work actively to protect the environment from damage caused by industrial processes or military activities. It uses its own boats to try to prevent governments from testing NUCLEAR weapons and other sea animals from being killed. "绿色和平"组织〔一国际性组织。其成员积极从事环保工作, 避免环境受到工业活动或军事行动的破坏。该组织成员经常划着小船出现在海域, 努力阻止各国政府进行核武器试验, 防止海洋动物遭遇捕杀〕

green pep·per /ˌ· ˈ· ·/ *n* [C] a vegetable with green flesh and white seeds that you can cook or eat raw in SALADS 青椒, 甜椒

green pound /ˌ· ˈ·/ *n* [C,U] the value of the pound STERLING when exchanged for farm products in the EC 绿色英镑〔指在欧共体内购买农产品时的英镑等值单位〕

green rev·o·lu·tion /ˌ· · · ˈ· ·/ *n* [singular] **1** an increase in the amount that is produced by crops, such as wheat, due to improved scientific methods of farming 绿色革命〔指由于改进科学耕作法而产生的诸如小麦等农作物产量的增加〕**2** the new interest in protecting the environment that has developed in many parts of the world 环境革命〔指在世界许多地方出现的对保护环境的新兴趣〕

green sal·ad /ˌ· ˈ· ·/ *n* [C] a SALAD made with LETTUCE and other raw green vegetables〔莴苣和其他绿色生蔬菜制作的〕绿色色拉, 生菜色拉

Green·sleeves /ˈgrinslivz; ˈgriːnsliːvz/ an English song from the end of the 16th century, which most people in the UK and US know. Some people believe it was written by King Henry VIII. 《绿袖子》〔16 世纪末的一首英格兰歌曲。英美国家大多数人都熟悉。有人认为这首歌是由国王亨利八世谱写的〕

green tea /ˌ· ˈ·/ *n* [U] light-coloured tea made from leaves that have been heated with steam 绿茶

Green·wich /ˈgrɪnɪdʒ; ˈgrenɪtʃ/ an area of southeast London on the River Thames. The original British Royal OBSERVATORY (=a special building from which scientists watch the moon, stars etc) is there, and the MERIDIAN (=an imaginary line which divides the eastern and western halves of the world) passes through the grounds of the Observatory. 格林尼治〔伦敦东南部一地区, 濒临泰晤士河, 原英国皇家天文台所在地。本初子午线从天文台经过〕

Green·wich Mean Time /ˈgrɪnɪdʒ ˋmin ˌtaɪm; ˌgrenɪtʃ ˈmiːn taɪm/ abbreviation 缩写为 **GMT** *n* [U] the time as measured at Greenwich in London 格林尼治 (平均) 时间

Greenwich Vil·lage /ˌ· · ˈ· ·/ a fashionable area of New York City, famous for being the home of many artists 格林尼治村〔纽约市一时尚地带, 以住有许多艺术家而闻名〕

Greer /ˈgriɚ; griːə/, **Ger·maine** /dʒɜˋmen; dʒɜːˈmeɪn/ (1939-) an Australian writer, university teacher, and FEMINIST, whose book *The Female Eunuch* (1970) made her an important figure in the women's movement 格里尔〔(1939-), 澳大利亚作家、大学教师、女权主义者。其作品《女阉人》(1970) 使她成为妇女解放运动的一个重要人物〕

greet /grit; griːt/ *v* [T] **1** to say hello to someone or welcome them 问候, 迎接, 招呼: *Mr Grimshaw got up from behind his desk to greet me.* 格里姆肖先生从桌后站起来迎接我。| **greet sb with a smile/kiss etc** *Billie greeted us with a cheerful grin.* 比利灿烂一笑给我们打招呼。**2** [always+adv/prep] to react to something in a particular way 对〔某事〕作出反应: **be greeted with** *The proposal was greeted with bursts of laughter.* 对这项提议的反应是阵阵笑声。**3** to be the first thing you see or hear when you arrive somewhere 最先映入〔某人的〕眼帘; 传入〔某人的〕耳中: *As we entered, complete chaos greeted us.* 我们走进去时, 一片混乱景象映入眼帘。

greet·ing /ˈgritɪŋ; ˈgriːtɪŋ/ *n* [C] **1** words you use or something you do when you meet someone 问候, 招呼: *I said good morning to Diane, but she didn't return my greeting.* 我向黛安娜道早安, 可是她对我的招呼没有回应。| **exchange greetings** (=greet each other) 互相问候 **2** [usually plural 一般用复数] a message saying that you hope someone will be happy, healthy etc 祝贺, 问候语, 祝愿词: *birthday greetings* 生日贺词 **3 greetings!** *formal or humorous* used to say hello to someone【正式或幽默】你好! 喂!

greet·ings card /ˈ· · ˌ·/ *n* [C] a card that you send to someone on their birthday, at Christmas etc〔生日、圣诞节等的〕贺卡

gre·gar·i·ous /grɪˈgɛrɪəs; grɪˈgeəriəs/ *adj* **1** friendly and preferring to be with others rather than alone; SOCIABLE[1] 爱交际的, 不喜独处的 **2** *technical* gregarious animals tend to live in a group【术语】〔动物〕倾向于群居的 —**gregariously** *adv* —**gregariousness** *n* [U]

Gre·go·ri·an cal·en·dar /grɛˋgorɪən ˋkæləndɚ; grɪˌgɔːriən ˈkælɪ̣ndə/ *n* [singular] the system of arranging the 365 days of the year in months and giving numbers to the years from the birth of Christ, used in the West since 1582 公历, 阳历, 格雷果里历〔自 1582 年起在西方使用的历法〕

Gregorian chant /·ˌ· · · ˈ·/ *n* [C,U] a kind of church music for voices alone 格列高利圣咏〔一种无伴奏的合唱形式的宗教音乐〕

Gregory XIII /ˌgrɛgərɪ ðə θɚˋtinθ; ˌgregəri ðə θɜːˈtiːnθ/ (1502-85) Pope from 1572 until his death. He is famous for changing the system of calculating the days of the year, by introducing the Gregorian Calendar in 1582. 格列高利十三世〔(1502-1585), 1572 年开始任教皇, 直到去世。1582 年, 他发明了格列高利历, 即现行公历, 改变了当时的日期计算方法, 并因此闻名〕

G

grem·lin /ˋgrɛmlɪn; ˈgremlᵻn/ *n* [C] an imaginary evil spirit that is blamed for problems in machinery, especially when no scientific explanation can be found〔传说中使机器设备产生无法用科学解释的故障的〕小妖精

Gre·na·da /grɪˋnedə; grəˈneɪdə/ a country in the Caribbean Sea consisting of the main island of Grenada, in the southern part of the Windward Islands, and some small islands called the **Grenadines**. It is a member of the British COMMON WEALTH. Population: 89,227 (2001). 格林纳达〔加勒比海一岛国，由向风群岛南部的主岛格林纳达及格林纳丁斯群岛组成，为英联邦成员国。人口: 89,227 (2001)〕—**Grenadian** *n, adj*

gre·nade /grɪˋned; grᵻˈneɪd/ *n* [C] a small bomb that can be thrown by hand or fired from a gun 手榴弹，枪榴弹: *a hand grenade* 手榴弹

gren·a·dier /ˌgrɛnəˋdɪr; ˌgrenəˈdɪə◂/ *n* [C] a soldier in a famous REGIMENT[1] (1) of the British army 英国著名兵团的士兵

gren·a·dine /ˌgrɛnəˋdin; ˈgrenədiːn/ *n* [U] a sweet liquid made from POMEGRANATE*s* that is used in drinks〔用于饮料的〕石榴糖浆

Gret·na Green /ˌgrɛtnə ˋgrin; ˌgretnə ˈgriːn/ a village in southern Scotland on the border with England. Until 1940, the marriage laws were less strict in Scotland than in England, and so many young English COUPLE*s*, whose parents did not want them to marry, ran away to get married in Gretna Green. 格雷特纳格林〔苏格兰南部一村庄，位于苏格兰与英格兰的边界。1940年以前，苏格兰的婚姻法比英格兰宽松，因此许多婚姻大事得不到父母应允的英格兰年轻人逃到该村成婚〕

grew /gru; gruː/ *v* the past tense of GROW

grey[1] usually 一般作 **gray** *AmE*【美】/gre; greɪ/ *adj*

1 ▶COLOUR 颜色◀ having a colour of black mixed with white, like the colour of ash 灰色的: *an old lady with grey hair* 头发灰白的老太太 | *a grey sky* 灰色的天空

2 ▶HAIR 头发◀ having grey hair (有) 灰白头发的: **go grey** *My brother went grey in his forties.* 我哥哥在四十多岁的时候头发就灰白了。—see picture on page A6 参见 A6 页图

3 ▶FACE 脸◀ looking pale because you are tired, frightened, or ill〔人由于疲倦、害怕或生病而〕脸色苍白的: *Noel's face was gray with fatigue.* 诺埃尔累得脸色苍白。

4 ▶BORING 乏味的◀ boring and unattractive; GLOOMY 单调乏味的; 暗淡的; 阴郁的: *the grey anonymous men in government offices* 政府部门里那些了无生气的无名小卒

5 ▶OF OLD PEOPLE 老年人的◀ *BrE* connected with old people【英】老年人的: *the grey vote* 老年人的投票

6 grey area an area of law or science that cannot be dealt with in a definite way because it is outside those areas that have clear rules and limits 灰色领域〔指法律或科学中未有明确规则和范围，因而难以处理的那些领域〕

grey[2] usually 一般作 **gray** *AmE*【美】*n* [C,U] the colour of smoke and rain clouds 灰色: *dull greys and browns* 各种暗灰色和棕色 —see picture on page A5 参见 A5 页图

grey[3] usually 一般作 **gray** *AmE*【美】*v* [I] if someone greys, their hair becomes grey〔头发〕开始变灰白色: *Jim's beginning to gray at the temples.* 吉姆已经开始两鬓斑白。

Grey, Lady Jane (1537-54) a woman who was queen of England for 9 days in 1553, before she was put in prison by Mary I, and later killed 格雷郡主〔(1537-1554)，1533 年只做了九天的英格兰女王。她被玛丽一世投入监狱，后遭杀害〕

Grey Cup, the /ˌ· ˈ·, ·ˈ/ a prize given to the best Canadian football team each year 格雷杯〔一年一度颁发给加拿大最佳橄榄球队的一个奖杯〕

grey·hound /ˋgreˌhaund; ˈgreɪhaʊnd/ *n* [C] a type of thin dog that can run very fast and is used in races 灵缇〔一种身体瘦长、跑得很快的犬，常用于比赛〕—see picture at 参见 DOG[1] 图

Greyhound Bus /ˌ·· ˈ·/ *trademark* a type of bus service, connecting cities in the US, operated by Greyhound Lines Inc.【商标】灰狗长途客运〔美国城市间的一种长途客运服务，由灰狗长途客运股份有限公司经营〕

grey·ish usually 一般作 **grayish** *AmE*【美】/ˋgreɪʃ; ˈgreɪ-ɪʃ/ *adj* slightly grey 略带灰色的

grey mat·ter /ˈ· ˌ··/ *n* [U] *informal* your intelligence【非正式】智力

grid /grɪd; grɪd/ *n* **1** [C] a metal frame with bars across it 金属格栅 —see also 另见 CATTLE GRID **2** [C] a pattern of straight lines that cross each other and form squares 方格图案 **3 the grid** *BrE* the network of electricity supply wires that connects POWER STATIONS【英】电力网，输电网: *the national grid* 全国电力网 **4** [C] a system of numbered squares printed on a map so that the exact position of any place can be found〔地图上的〕坐标方格 **5** [C] a set of starting positions for all the cars in a motor race〔汽车赛中的〕赛车出发点

grid·dle /ˋgrɪdl; ˈgrɪdl/ *n* [C] a round iron plate that is used for cooking flat cakes on top of a STOVE[1] (2) or over a fire〔用来烙饼的〕圆形平底锅

grid·dle·cake /ˋgrɪdlˌkek; ˈgrɪdlˌkeɪk/ *n* [C] *AmE* a PANCAKE (2)【美】烙饼，烤饼

grid·i·ron /ˋgrɪdˌaɪən; ˈgrɪdaɪən/ *n* [C] **1** an open frame of metal bars for cooking meat or fish over a very hot fire〔用来烧烤肉或鱼的〕烤架 **2** *AmE* a field marked in white lines for American football【美】〔画有白线的〕美式橄榄球场

grid·lock /ˋgrɪdlɑk; ˈgrɪdlɒk/ *n* [U] *especially AmE*【尤美】**1** a situation in which streets in a city are so full of cars that they cannot move〔街道上车辆过多造成的〕交通堵塞 **2** a situation in which nothing can happen, usually because people disagree strongly〔由于强烈的意见分歧而造成的〕僵局: *Clinton is in gridlock with the Congress.* 克林顿与国会陷入僵局。—**gridlocked** *adj*

grief /grif; griːf/ *n* **1** [U] extreme sadness, especially because someone you love has died 极度悲伤〔尤指因所爱之人去世而感受的悲痛〕: **[+over/at]** *The grief she felt over Helen's death was almost unbearable.* 她因海伦的去世而感到悲痛难当。**2** [C] something that makes you feel extremely sad 伤心事，不幸: *It was a grief to him that he had never had any children.* 他一直没有小孩，这是他的伤心事。**3 good grief!** *spoken* used when you are slightly surprised or annoyed【口】哎哟!〔用于略感惊讶或气恼之时〕: *Good grief! This must have cost you a fortune! Where did you get the money?* 哎呀！这肯定花了你很多钱！你从哪里弄到这钱的？**4 come to grief** to fail, or to be harmed or destroyed in an accident 失败；〔在事故中〕受损；被毁: *The expedition shortly came to grief on Vanikoro Reef.* 这次探险不久就在瓦尼科罗因触礁而失败。**5 give sb grief** *informal* to criticize someone in an annoying way【非正式】数落[责备]某人: *I'd better go home now – my Mum'll give me grief if I'm not back for dinner.* 我最好是现在回家——如果我不回去吃晚饭，我妈会骂我。

grief-strick·en /ˈ· ˌ··/ also 又作 **grief-struck** /ˈ· ·/ *adj* feeling very sad because of something that has happened 感到极度悲伤的，悲痛欲绝的

Grieg /grig; griːg/, **Ed·vard** /ˋɛdvɑrd; ˈedvɑːd/ (1843-1907) a Norwegian COMPOSER whose most famous works are his music for the play *Peer Gynt* and his *Piano Concerto* 格里格〔(1843-1907)，挪威作曲家。其代表作是他为戏剧《彼尔·金特》创作的音乐和《钢琴协奏曲》〕

griev·ance /ˋgrivəns; ˈgriːvəns/ *n* [C,U] something that you complain about because you feel you have been treated unfairly 不平，委屈，不满，抱怨，牢骚: **[+against]** *Anyone who has a legitimate grievance against the company can take it to the committee.* 对公司有正当不满情绪的人可以把意见提交给委员会。| **air your grievances** (=tell other people you feel you have been treated unfairly) 把你的委屈讲出来 *The meetings provide employees with an opportunity to air their grievances.* 这些会议使雇员有机会申诉自己的不满。| **nurse a grievance** (=think about it continuously) 心存不满 | **sense of grievance** (=a feeling that you have been treated unfairly) 委屈感 *Grant's deep sense of grievance at not being promoted* 格兰特对没有得到晋升而感到的极度委屈

grieve /griv; griːv/ *v* **1** [I,T] to feel extremely sad, especially because someone you love has died〔尤指所爱之人去世而〕感到悲痛[伤心]: *People need time to grieve after the death of a loved one.* 人们在所爱之人去世后需要一段哀悼的时间。| **grieve sth** *The family grieved the loss of its only son.* 这家人为他们独子的去世而伤心。**2** [T] if something grieves you, it makes you feel very unhappy 使伤心: **it grieves sb to think/say/see etc** *It grieves me to think of all the money we've spent on that ungrateful brat.* 想到我们在那个忘恩负义的小坏蛋身上所花的那些钱真让我伤心。

grieved /grivd; griːvd/ *adj literary* very sad and upset【文】悲伤的，伤心的: **be grieved (at)** *I am deeply grieved at this sad news.* 我听到这个悲惨的消息深感悲伤。

griev·ous /ˋgrivəs; ˈgriːvəs/ *adj* **1** *formal* very serious and likely to be very harmful【正式】严重的；可能很有害的: *a grievous error* 严重错误 | *a grievous shortage of hospital beds* 医院床位的严重短缺 **2** *especially literary* a grievous wound or pain is severe and hurts a lot【尤文】〔伤痛〕剧烈的 —**grievously** *adv* —**grievousness** *n* [U]

grievous bod·i·ly harm /ˌ·· ˌ··· ˈ·/ *n* [U] *BrE law* serious injury caused by a criminal attack; GBH【英，法律】〔因罪犯袭击而造成的〕身体严重受伤，重伤

grif·fin, gryphon /ˈgrɪfɪn; ˈgrɪfən/ *n* [C] an imaginary animal in stories that has a lion's body and an EAGLE's wings and head〔神话中的〕狮身鹰首兽

griffin 狮身鹰首兽

Grif·fith /ˈgrɪfɪθ; ˈgrɪfʒθ/, **D.W.** (1875-1948) one of the greatest US film DIRECTORS, famous especially for inventing new ways of making films and of using the camera. His films include *Birth of a Nation* (1915) and *Intolerance* (1916). 格里菲思〔(1875-1948)，美国最杰出的电影导演之一，尤以创新的制片与拍摄方式出名。他导演的电影包括《一个国家的诞生》(1915) 和《党同伐异》(1916)〕

grif·ter /ˈgrɪftə; ˈgrɪftə/ *n* [C] *AmE informal* someone who dishonestly obtains something, especially money【美，非正式】不当谋利者；骗子 **—grift** *v* [T]

grill¹ /grɪl; grɪl/ *v* **1** [I,T] if you grill something, or if it grills, you cook it by putting it close to very strong direct heat 烧烤，烤制：*Grill the burgers for eight minutes each side.* 把这些制作汉堡包的牛肉片每面烤八分钟。**2** [T] to ask someone a lot of difficult questions in order to make them explain their actions, opinions etc 对〔某人〕严加盘问：*I was grilled by customs officers for several hours.* 我被海关官员盘问了好几个小时。

grill² *n* [C] **1** *BrE* a part of a COOKER (1) in which very strong heat from above cooks food on a metal shelf below【英】〔炉具中热力自上而下的〕烤架；BROILER (1) *AmE*【美】：*Pop it under the grill for five minutes.* 把它放在烤架下烤上五分钟。**2** a flat frame with metal bars across it that can be put over a fire, so that food can be cooked quickly on it 栅状烤架 **3** a place where you can buy and eat grilled food 烧烤店，烧烤餐馆：*Henry J. Bean's Bar and Grill* 亨利·J. 比恩酒吧烧烤餐馆 —see also 另见 MIXED GRILL **4** a grille〔门窗的〕护栏；〔汽车散热器的〕护栅

grille, grill /grɪl; grɪl/ *n* [C] **1** a frame with metal bars or wire across it that is put in front of a window or door for protection 门窗护栏 **2** the metal bars at the front of a car that protect the RADIATOR (2)〔汽车散热器的〕护栅

gril·ling /ˈgrɪlɪŋ; ˈgrɪlɪŋ/ *n* **give sb a grilling** to ask someone a lot of difficult questions in order to make them explain their actions or opinions 盘问某人

grill pan /ˈ· ·/ *n* [C] a square flat pan, used under a GRILL² (1)〔用在烤架下的〕焙盘 —see picture at 参见 PAN¹ 图

grim /grɪm; grɪm/ *adj* **grimmer, grimmest**

1 ▶SITUATION/NEWS 情况/消息◀ making you feel worried and unhappy 令人担忧的，令人发愁的：*There's more grim news from the war zone.* 战区传来更多令人担忧的消息。| **things look grim (for)** *Things look pretty grim for farmers right now.* 对农民来说目前情况相当严峻。| **grim prospect** (=something bad that will probably happen) 堪忧的前景

2 ▶PLACE/BUILDING ETC 地点/建筑物等◀ unpleasant and unattractive 令人不愉快的，讨厌的：*a grim industrial town* 令人生厌的工业城镇

3 ▶PERSON 人◀ looking or sounding very serious because the situation is very bad〔神色或口气〕严肃的，严酷的：*The grim-faced judge sentenced Burke to life-imprisonment.* 面孔铁板的法官判处伯克终身监禁。| **grim determination** (=serious determination in spite of difficulties or dangers) 坚韧不拔的决心

4 feel grim *informal* to feel ill【非正式】感觉病了：*I felt a bit grim the morning after the party.* 聚会后的第二天早晨我感觉有点不舒服。

5 ▶OF BAD QUALITY 劣质的◀ *BrE informal* very bad in quality【英，非正式】质量很低的：*You should see some of her recent essays – they're pretty grim.* 你应该看看她最近写的一些文章——质量很差。

6 hold/hang on for grim death *BrE informal* to hold something very tightly because you are afraid【英，非正式】吓得紧紧抓住〔某物〕**—grimly** *adv*: *Arnold smiled grimly.* 阿诺德阴冷地笑了笑。**—grimness** *n* [U]

gri·mace¹ /grɪˋmes; grɪˈmeɪs/ *v* [I] to twist your face in an ugly way because you do not like something, because you are feeling pain, or because you are trying to be funny〔因感到疼痛或开玩笑而〕扭曲脸部，做怪相：*Toni muttered and grimaced at each tug of the comb.* 托妮每梳一下头发都要龇牙咧嘴地咕哝。| **[+with]** *Baggio lay grimacing with pain.* 贝吉奥躺在那里痛得嘴歪眼斜。

grimace² *n* [C] an expression you make by twisting your face because you do not like something or because you are feeling pain 脸部扭曲，怪相，鬼脸〔指不喜欢某物或感到疼痛时的面部表情〕：*Bernie gave a grimace of disgust and left the room.* 伯尼做了一个表示厌恶的鬼脸，离开了房间。

grime /graɪm; graɪm/ *n* [U] dirt that forms a black layer on surfaces〔表面的〕尘垢，污垢：*black with grime* 因污垢而发黑

Grimm /ˈgrɪm; grɪm/ two German brothers, **Jakob Grimm** (1785-1863) and **Wilhelm Grimm** (1786-1859), usually known as **The Brothers Grimm**. They studied language and wrote a German dictionary, and are famous for writing *Grimm's Fairy Tales*, a collection of nearly 200 stories which are still popular with children. 格林兄弟〔指德国人雅科布·格林 (1785-1863) 和威廉·格林 (1786-1859) 兄弟俩。一般称格林兄弟。他们研究语言，编撰过一部德语词典，以创作的《格林童话集》著称。该书收集了近 200 篇故事，至今仍受儿童喜爱〕

Grim Reap·er, the /,· ˈ··/ a name given to Death in stories and literature. He is shown in pictures as a human SKELETON in long black clothes that also cover his head, carrying a large SCYTHE (=a tool for cutting crops). 狰狞的收割者；死神〔故事和文学作品中的死神。他常被画成骷髅模样，长长的黑衣裹着脑袋，手持一把大镰刀〕

the Grim Reaper 狰狞的收割者；死神

grim·y /ˈgraɪmɪ; ˈgraɪmi/ *adj* covered with dirt 满是污垢的，蒙上灰尘的：*grimy windows* 蒙着灰尘的窗子

grin¹ /grɪn; grɪn/ *v* [I] **grinned, grinning 1** to smile widely 露着牙齿笑，咧着嘴笑：*Grinning sheepishly, James admitted he was seeing Sue.* 詹姆斯尴尬地露齿一笑，承认他正和休约会。| **[+at]** *Stop grinning at me, you stupid jackass!* 别朝我咧着嘴笑，你这傻瓜！| **[+with]** *grinning with delight* 高兴得咧着嘴笑 | **grin from ear to ear** (=grin very widely) 笑容满面 **2 grin and bear it** to accept and bear an unpleasant or difficult situation without complaining, usually because you realize there is nothing you can do to make it better 苦笑着忍受，逆来顺受〔通常因知道无法挽救而接受某一尴尬局面或困境〕

grin² *n* [C] a wide smile 露齿笑，咧嘴笑：*a broad grin* 合不拢嘴的笑 | *Take that cheeky grin off your face!* 别那样厚着脸皮笑！—see also 另见 **wipe the smile/grin off sb's face** (WIPE¹ (7))

Grinch /grɪntʃ; grɪntʃ/ **1 the Grinch** the main character in a story for children by the US writer Dr Seuss called *How the Grinch Stole Christmas*. He is a nasty, unkind green creature who almost spoils Christmas. 圣诞怪杰，格林奇〔美国作家索伊斯博士创作的儿童读物《格林奇如何偷走圣诞节》中的主角。他是个坏脾气的绿色生物，差点破坏了圣诞节的气氛〕**2** [C] *AmE* a very bad-tempered person【美】脾气极坏的人

grind¹ /graɪnd; graɪnd/ *v past tense and past participle* **ground** /graʊnd; graʊnd/

1 ▶INTO SMALL PIECES 变成碎末◀ [T] **a)** also 又作 **grind up** [T] to break something such as corn or coffee beans into small pieces or powder, either in a machine or between two hard surfaces 把〔玉米、咖啡豆等〕碾碎，磨成粉末 **b)** *AmE* to cut food, especially raw meat, into very small pieces by putting it through a machine【美】〔用机器将食物，尤指生肉〕绞碎；MINCE¹ (1) *BrE*【英】

2 ▶SMOOTH/SHARP 光滑的/锋利的◀ [T] to make something smooth or sharp by rubbing it on a hard surface or by using a machine 磨光，磨利：*a stone for grinding knives and scissors* 磨刀剪的石头 | *The lenses are ground to a high standard of precision.* 镜片被研磨到很高的精确度。

3 ▶PRESS STH DOWN 向下挤压某物◀ [T always+adv/prep] to press something down into a surface and rub it with a strong twisting movement 用力旋转地挤压：**grind sth into/in** *He dropped a cigar butt and ground it into the carpet with his heel.* 他扔下雪茄烟头，用脚后跟把它踩进地毯里。

4 grind your teeth to rub your upper and lower teeth together making a noise 把牙齿磨得嘎嘎响

5 grind to a halt a) if a vehicle grinds to a halt, it stops gradually〔车辆〕慢慢停下来：*Traffic ground to a halt as it approached the accident site.* 车辆在靠近事故现场时慢慢停了下来。**b)** if a country, organization, or process grinds to a halt, it gradually stops working〔国家、组织或进程〕逐渐停顿，慢慢瘫痪：*As more and more workers joined the strike, Britain's economy was grinding to a halt.* 由于越来越多的工人参加罢工，英国的经济逐渐趋于停滞。

6 grind the faces of the poor to make poor people work very hard and give them almost nothing in return 压榨穷人 —see also 另见 **have an axe to grind** (AXE[1] (4))

grind sb ↔ down *phr v* [T] to treat someone in a cruel way for such a long time that they lose all courage and hope; OPPRESS 长期欺压某人〔使其达到绝望地步〕: *Years of dictatorship had ground the people down.* 多年的独裁统治已使人民处于绝境。

grind on *phr v* [I] to continue for an unpleasantly long time 令人厌烦地长期持续: *Winter grinds on until March.* 冬季一直要持续到三月份。

grind sth ↔ out *phr v* [T] to produce information, writing, music etc in such large amounts that it becomes boring 大量撰写, 大量提供〔信息、文字或音乐作品等〕: *Frank just keeps grinding out detective stories.* 弗兰克不停地大量撰写侦探故事。

grind² *n* **1** [singular] something that is hard work and physically or mentally tiring 令人疲劳[厌倦]的苦事: *I find the journey to work a real grind.* 我认为每天上班的行程真辛苦。| **the daily grind** (=things that you have to do every day that are boring) 乏味的日常苦差使 **2** [C] *AmE informal* a student who never does anything except study; SWOT[1]【美, 非正式】埋头学习[死读书]的学生

grind·er /ˋgraɪndɚ; ˈgraɪndə/ *n* [C] a machine for crushing coffee beans, PEPPERCORN*s* etc into powder 研磨机, 碾磨机: *a pepper grinder* 辣椒碾磨机

grind·ing /ˋgraɪndɪŋ; ˈgraɪndɪŋ/ *adj* [only before noun 仅用于名词前] **1 grinding poverty/misery** a situation that makes your life very difficult and unhappy, and never seems to improve 贫困/痛苦不堪 **2** a grinding noise is the continuous unpleasant noise of machinery parts rubbing together〔指机器部件互相摩擦产生的声音〕持续而刺耳的

grind·stone /ˋgraɪndˏston; ˈgraɪndstəʊn/ *n* [C] a large round stone that is turned like a wheel while tools, knives etc are rubbed against it to make them sharp〔用来磨快刀等工具的〕砂轮 —see also 另见 **keep your nose to the grindstone** (NOSE[1] (15))

grin·go /ˋgrɪŋgo; ˈgrɪŋgəʊ/ *n plural* **gringos** [C] an offensive word for someone from North America, used by people in Latin American countries 外国佬〔拉丁美洲国家的人对北美洲人的冒犯用语〕

G

grip¹ /grɪp; grɪp/ *n*

1 ▶FIRM HOLD 紧握◀ [C usually singular 一般用单数] the way you hold something tightly or your ability to do this 紧握; 握紧: *Don't loosen your grip on the rope or you'll fall.* 抓住绳索别松手, 不然你会掉下去。

2 ▶POWER 权力◀ [singular] power and control over someone or something〔对某人或某事物的〕控制: **have a grip on sth** *The chancellor doesn't seem to have a very firm grip on the economy.* 这位总理看来没有牢牢地控制住经济。

3 come/get to grips with to understand and deal with a difficult problem or situation 了解并应付〔困难问题或局面〕: *I've never really got to grips with this new technology.* 我还从来没有真正了解这种新技术。

4 lose your grip to become less confident and less able to deal with a situation〔对某局面〕信心不足; 失去控制: *I handled that interview very badly – I must be losing my grip.* 今天的面试我表现很糟糕 —— 我大概是无能为力了。

5 get/keep a grip on yourself to start controlling your emotions when you have been very upset〔在生气一段时间之后〕开始控制自己的感情: *Stop being hysterical and get a grip on yourself.* 别歇斯底里的, 冷静下来。

6 be in the grip of to be experiencing a very unpleasant situation that cannot be controlled or stopped 处于〔无法控制的不利局势〕之中: *a country in the grip of famine* 饱受饥荒困扰的国家

7 ▶STOP STH SLIPPING 制止某物滑动◀ [C] **a)** a special part of a handle that has a rough surface so that you can hold it firmly without it slipping〔有粗糙表面的〕把手〔可以紧握而不滑动〕: *a racquet with a rubber grip* 带防滑橡胶手柄的球拍 —see picture on page A23 参见 A23 页图 **b)** the ability of something to stay on a surface without slipping 黏力, 防滑力: *I want some tennis shoes with a good grip.* 我要几双防滑力很好的网球鞋。

8 ▶FOR HAIR 用于头发◀ [C] *BrE* a HAIRGRIP【英】发夹

9 ▶CAMERAMAN 摄影师◀ [C] someone whose job is to move the cameras around while a television show or film is being made〔拍电视节目或电影时〕管理摄像[摄影]机的工作人员

10 ▶BAG 袋, 包◀ [C] *old-fashioned* a bag or case used for travelling【过时】旅行袋[箱]

grip² *v* **gripped, gripping 1** [I,T] to hold something very tightly 紧握: *I gripped the handrail tightly and tried not to look down.* 我紧紧抓住扶手, 尽量不往下看。**2** [T] to have a strong effect on someone or something 对〔某人或某事物〕具有强烈影响: *a country gripped by economic problems* 受经济问题严重影响的国家 | *Panic suddenly gripped me when it was my turn to speak.* 轮到我说话时, 我突然惊慌起来。**3** [T] to hold someone's attention and interest 吸引〔某人的〕注意[兴趣]: *a story that really grips you* 确实能吸引你的故事 **4** [T] if something grips a surface, it stays on it without slipping 紧附于〔某表面而不滑动〕: *Radial tires grip the road well.* 子午线轮胎在路面上防滑能力很好。—see also 另见 GRIPPING

gripe¹ /graɪp; graɪp/ *v* [I] to complain about something continuously and in an annoying way 抱怨, 发牢骚: **[+about]** *Joe came in griping about how cold it was outside.* 乔走进来, 抱怨外面太冷。

gripe² *n informal*【非正式】**1** [C] something unimportant that you complain about 抱怨〔尤指小事情〕: *My main gripe was the price of refreshments.* 我主要抱怨的是点心的价格。**2 the gripes** *old-fashioned* sudden bad stomach pains【过时】胃绞痛

gripe wa·ter /ˋ· ˏ··/ *n* [U] *BrE* a liquid medicine given to babies when they have stomach pains【英】驱风剂〔治疗小儿腹痛的药水〕

grip·ing /ˋgraɪpɪŋ; ˈgraɪpɪŋ/ *adj* a griping pain is a sudden severe pain in the stomach〔胃肠突然〕绞痛的

grip·ping /ˋgrɪpɪŋ; ˈgrɪpɪŋ/ *adj* a gripping film, story etc is very exciting and interesting〔电影、故事等〕扣人心弦的, 引人入胜的 **—grippingly** *adv*

gris·ly /ˋgrɪzlɪ; ˈgrɪzli/ *adj* extremely unpleasant, usually because death, decay, or destruction is involved〔通常因涉及死亡、腐朽、破坏而〕令人极其厌恶的: *the grisly discovery of human remains in the cellar* 地窖中尸体的可怕发现

grist /grɪst; grɪst/ *n* **(all) grist to the mill** something additional that can be used for your advantage in a particular situation 可用来〔为自己〕谋利的事: *Any publicity is good – it's all grist to the mill.* 任何宣传都是好的 —— 都可以用来谋取利益。

gris·tle /ˋgrɪsl̩; ˈgrɪsəl/ *n* [U] the part of meat that is not soft enough to eat〔肉食中的〕软骨 **—gristly** *adj*

grit¹ /grɪt; grɪt/ *n* [U] **1** very small pieces of stone or sand that are scattered on frozen roads to make them less slippery〔撒在结冰的道路上防滑用的〕沙砾, 沙粒 **2** *informal* determination and courage【非正式】坚毅, 勇气 **3 grits** *AmE* HOMINY grain that is roughly crushed before cooking, often eaten for breakfast【美】粗碾的谷物〔常于早餐食用〕**—gritty** *adj*

grit² *v* [T] **gritted, gritting 1** to scatter grit on a frozen road to make it less slippery 在结冰的道路上撒沙砾〔以防滑〕**2 grit your teeth** to use all your determination to continue in spite of difficulties 咬紧牙关, 下定决心: *Just grit your teeth and hang on – it will be over soon.* 咬紧牙关坚持下去吧, 事情很快会过去的。

grit·ter /ˋgrɪtɚ; ˈgrɪtə/ *n* [C] *BrE* a large vehicle that puts salt or sand on the roads in winter to make them less icy【英】〔冬天在道路上撒沙或盐防滑的〕撒沙车, 撒盐车; SALT TRUCK *AmE*【美】

Grizedale Forest a 9,500 acre forest between Lake Windermere and Coniston Water in the Lake District, northwest England. SCULPTOR*s* from all over the world were asked to create works in the Forest from whatever materials they found there. There are now more than 70 works throughout the Forest. 格雷兹德尔森林〔位于温德米尔湖和科尼斯顿湖之间的一片森林, 面积达 9500 英亩。林区曾邀请世界各地的雕刻家前来创作, 要求他们用可以找到的任何材料进行雕刻。整个林区现有 70 多件雕刻作品〕

griz·zle /ˋgrɪzl̩; ˈgrɪzəl/ *v* [I] *BrE informal*【英, 非正式】**1** if a baby or child grizzles, they cry quietly and continuously〔婴儿或孩子〕不停地小声哭泣 **2** to complain continuously in an annoying way 不停地抱怨

griz·zled /ˋgrɪzl̩d; ˈgrɪzəld/ *adj literary* having grey or greyish hair【文】头发花白的

griz·zly bear /ˌ·· ˋ·/ also 又作 **grizzly** *n* [C] a very large brownish-grey bear that lives in the Rocky Mountains of North America〔北美落基山脉的〕大灰熊

groan¹ /gron; grəʊn/ *v* [I] **1** to make a long deep sound because you are in pain, upset, or disappointed〔因疼痛、心烦或失望而〕呻吟, 发出低沉的声音: *The kids all groaned when I switched off the TV.* 我关掉电视时孩子们都发出不满的哼哼声。| **moan and groan** (=complain a lot) 不停地抱怨 *I'm tired of him moaning and groaning all the time.* 他一天到晚不停地发牢骚, 我都听腻了。**2** to make a sound similar to someone groaning 发出低沉的嘎吱声: *The old tree groaned in the wind.* 老树在风中嘎吱作响。**3** if a table groans with food there is a very large amount of food on it〔在桌子上〕摆放大量的食品

groan² *n* [C] **1** a long deep sound that you make when you are in pain or do not want to do something〔疼痛时的〕呻吟;〔不愿做某事时发出的〕哼哼声: *Casey let out a groan of protest at having to go to bed.* 凯西不愿上床睡觉,哼了一声表示抗议。**2** *literary* a long low sound like someone groaning【文】低沉的声响: *The door opened with a groan.* 门嘎吱一声开了。

groat /grot; grəʊt/ *n* **1 groats** [plural] grain, especially OATS with the outer shell removed 去壳谷物〔尤指去壳燕麦〕**2** [C] a former British coin that had a low value 格罗特〔英国从前的低面值硬币〕

gro·bag, growbag /ˈgrobæg; ˈgrəʊbæg/ *n* [C] *BrE* a large plastic bag containing specially prepared earth for growing vegetables【英】〔装有种植蔬菜用的特别配制的土壤的〕袋装栽培土,生长袋

gro·cer /ˈgrosɚ; ˈgrəʊsə/ *n* [C] **1** someone who owns or works in a shop that sells food such as flour, sugar, food in cans, and other things used in the home 食品杂货店主[店员] **2 grocer's** a grocer's shop 食品杂货店

gro·cer·y /ˈgrosərɪ; ˈgrəʊsəri/ *n* **1 groceries** [plural] goods sold by a grocer or a SUPERMARKET 食品杂货 **2** also 又作 **grocery store** /ˈ····/ [C] *AmE* a SUPERMARKET【美】超级市场

gro·dy /ˈgrodɪ; ˈgrəʊdi/ *adj AmE slang* a word meaning very unpleasant or offensive, used especially by children【美俚】太讨厌,真恶心〔尤为儿童用语〕

grog /grɑg; grɒg/ *n* [U] **1** a mixture of strong alcoholic drink, especially RUM¹, and water 掺水的烈性酒〔尤指朗姆酒〕**2** *informal* any alcoholic drink【非正式】烈性酒

grog·gy /ˈgrɑgɪ; ˈgrɒgi/ *adj* weak and unable to walk steadily or think clearly because you are ill or very tired〔因生病或劳累而〕身体虚弱的,行走不稳的,头脑昏沉的: *I felt really groggy after 15 hours on the plane.* 我乘了15个小时飞机之后,感到昏昏沉沉的。—**groggily** *adv*

groin /grɔɪn; grɔɪn/ *n* [C] **1** the place where the tops of your legs meet the front of your body 腹股沟 —see picture at 参见 BODY 图 **2** a GROYNE 海岸防波堤

grom·met /ˈgrɑmɪt; ˈgrɒm<u>ɪ</u>t/ *n* [C] **1** a small metal ring used to make a hole in cloth or leather stronger 金属扣眼 **2** a small piece of plastic put into a child's ear in order to remove liquid from it 去水塞〔放入儿童耳中以除去耳内液体的塑料制品〕

groom¹ /grum; gruːm/ *v* **1** [T] to take care of animals, especially horses, by cleaning and brushing them 照料〔动物,尤指刷洗马匹〕**2** [I,T] to take care of your own appearance by keeping your hair and clothes clean and tidy 修饰,打扮: *a well-groomed woman in her twenties* 打扮整洁的二十来岁的女子 **3** [T] to prepare someone for an important job or position in society by training them over a long period 培养,培训: **groom sb for sth** *Tim was being groomed for a managerial position.* 蒂姆正在受训以担任一个经理职位。| **groom sb to do sth** *Clare's father is grooming her to take his place when he retires.* 克莱尔的父亲正在培养她,以便在自己退休后她能接班。**4** [I,T] if an animal grooms itself or another animal, it cleans its own fur and skin or that of the other animal〔动物为自己或另一动物〕梳理皮毛 —**grooming** *n* [U] —see also 另见 WELL-GROOMED

groom² *n* [C] **1** a BRIDEGROOM 新郎 **2** someone whose job is to feed, clean, and take care of horses 马夫

grooms·man /ˈgrumzmən; ˈgruːmzmən/ *n* [C] *AmE* a friend of a BRIDEGROOM who has special duties at a wedding【美】男傧相; USHER¹ (1) *BrE*【英】

groove¹ /gruv; gruːv/ *n* [C] **1** a thin line cut into a surface, especially to guide the movement of something〔尤指用于引导某物的〕凹槽: *The bolt slid easily into the groove.* 插销轻松滑入槽里。**2 be in a groove** to be living or working in a situation that has been the same for a long time and that is unlikely to change 墨守成规,一成不变

groove² *v* [T] to make a long narrow track in something 在〔某物〕上开槽 —**grooved** *adj*

groov·y /ˈgruvɪ; ˈgruːvi/ *adj* a word meaning fashionable, modern, and fun, used especially in the 1960s 时髦的,新潮的,有趣的〔此词尤用于20世纪60年代〕

grope¹ /grop; grəʊp/ *v* **1** [I always+adv/prep] to try to find something that you cannot see by feeling with your hands〔在黑暗中〕摸索: [+for/through/around etc] *Ginny groped for her glasses on the bedside table.* 金尼在床边小几上摸找眼镜。| *groping around in the dark* 在黑暗中四处摸索 **2 grope your way along/across etc** to go somewhere by feeling the way with your hands because you cannot see〔因看不见而用手〕摸索着走/穿过等: *I groped my way along the wall to the door.* 我摸着墙走到门口。**3** [I] to try hard to find the right words to say, or the right solution to a problem but without any real idea of how to do this 努力搜寻〔恰当的言辞或解决办法〕: [+for] *Accusations of misconduct left Keeler groping for a response.* 行为不端的指责使得基勒不得不设法作出反应。**4** [T] *informal* to move your hands over someone's body to get sexual pleasure, especially when they do not want you to do this【非正式】〔为得到性快感〕抚摸某人的身体〔尤指当对方不愿意的时候〕

grope² *n* [C] *informal* an act of groping (GROPE¹ (4))【非正式】抚摸

gross¹ /gros; grəʊs/ *adj* [W3]

1 ▶TOTAL 总共的◀ **a)** a gross amount of money is the total amount before any tax or costs have been taken away〔扣去税或成本之前〕总的,毛的: *a gross profit of $15 million* 1500万美元的毛利 | *gross receipts* (=the gross amount of money received) 进款总额 —compare 比较 NET³ (1) **b)** a gross weight is the total weight of something, including its wrapping 毛重的

2 gross negligence/misconduct/injustice etc behaviour that is clearly wrong and unacceptable 明显的过失/行为不端/不公平等: *a gross exaggeration of the truth* 对真实情况的严重夸张

3 ▶RUDE 粗鲁的◀ behaviour that is gross is extremely rude and completely unacceptable〔行为〕极端粗鲁的,完全不能接受的

4 ▶NASTY 令人厌恶的◀ *spoken* very unpleasant to look at or think about【口】看上去[想起来]令人厌恶的: *Ooh, gross! I hate spinach!* 啊,讨厌!我讨厌吃菠菜!

5 ▶FAT 胖的◀ extremely fat and unattractive 极胖而难看的 —**grossly** *adv*: *grossly overweight* 严重超重 —**grossness** *n* [U]

gross² *adv* **earn £20,000/$30,000 etc gross** to earn £20,000 etc before tax has been taken away 税前收入20,000英镑/30,000美元等: *a junior executive earning more than $30,000 gross* 税前收入为30,000多美元的初级行政人员

gross³ *v* [T] to gain an amount as a total profit, or earn it as a total amount, before tax has been taken away 获得…的总利润[毛利,税前收入]: *This type of store may gross $8 million or more annually.* 这类商店每年可获得800万美元或更多的毛利。

gross sb **out** *phr v* [T] *spoken AmE* to make someone wish they had not seen or been told about something because it is so unpleasant【口,美】但愿某人没看过[听过]〔如此恶劣的事情〕

gross⁴ *determiner n plural* **gross** [C] a quantity of 144 things 罗〔即12打,144个〕: *a gross of candles* 一罗蜡烛

gross do·mes·tic prod·uct /,· ··· ˈ··/ *n* [singular] *technical* the GDP; the total value of all the goods and services produced in a country, except for income received from abroad【术语】国内生产总值 —compare 比较 GROSS NATIONAL PRODUCT

gross mar·gin /,· ˈ··/ *n* [C] the financial difference between what something costs to produce and what it is sold for 毛利

gross na·tion·al prod·uct /,· ··· ˈ··/ *n technical* [singular] the GNP; the total value of all the goods and services produced in a country, including income from abroad【术语】国民生产总值 —compare 比较 GROSS DOMESTIC PRODUCT

gross prof·it /,· ˈ··/ *n* [C] GROSS MARGIN 毛利

gro·tesque¹ /groˈtɛsk; grəʊˈtesk/ *adj* **1** strange or unusual in a way that is shocking or offensive 怪诞的,荒唐的: *The idea of my best friend becoming my stepmother was too grotesque to contemplate.* 我最好的朋友要成为我继母的想法过于荒唐,无法细想。**2** extremely ugly in a strange or unnatural way 极丑陋的,怪异的: *a grotesque figure with a huge head* 长着大脑袋的丑陋人形 —**grotesquely** *adv*

grotesque² *n* **1** [C] an image of someone who is strangely ugly 某人奇丑的形象 **2 the grotesque** a grotesque style in art〔艺术中的〕怪诞[奇异]风格

grot·to /ˈgrɑto; ˈgrɒtəʊ/ *n* [C] a small natural CAVE¹, or one that someone has made in their garden 天然小洞穴;人造洞室

grot·ty /ˈgrɑtɪ; ˈgrɒti/ *adj BrE informal* nasty, dirty, or unpleasant【英,非正式】令人厌恶的;肮脏的;令人不快的: *a grotty little bedsit* 一间肮脏的小卧室兼起居室 —**grottily** *adv* —**grottiness** *n* [U]

grouch¹ /grautʃ; graʊtʃ/ *n informal*【非正式】**1** [C] someone who is always complaining 总是发牢骚的人: *My grandad is such an old grouch.* 我爷爷是个牢骚佬。**2** [C] something unimportant that you complain about 所抱怨的小事: *One of his main grouches is that they never put the top back on the toothpaste.* 他主要的抱怨是,他们从来不把牙膏盖盖回去。

grouch² *v* [I+about] *informal* to complain in an angry way; GRUMBLE¹ (1)【非正式】〔怒气冲冲地〕抱怨

grouch·y /ˈgrautʃɪ; ˈgraʊtʃi/ *adj* in a bad temper, especially because you are tired〔尤指因疲倦而〕脾气坏的 —**grouchiness** *n* [U]

ground¹ /graʊnd; graʊnd/ *n*

① EARTH SURFACE 地面
② AREA 地方
③ SUBJECT 主题
④ OPINION/ATTITUDE 观点/态度
⑤ REASON 理由
⑥ SUCCESS/ADVANTAGE 成功/优势
⑦ HIDE/FIND 隐藏/找到
⑧ COLOUR/PAINT 颜色/颜料
⑨ OTHER MEANINGS 其他意思

① EARTH SURFACE 地面

1 [U] the surface of the earth 地面: *The leaf slowly fluttered to the ground.* 叶子慢慢地飘落到地上。| *The air raids were followed by military action on the ground.* 空袭之后是地面军事行动。| **below/above ground** *miners working 10-hour shifts below ground* 每一班在地下工作十小时的矿工 —compare 比较 FLOOR¹ (1) —see 见 LAND¹ (USAGE)

2 ►SOIL 土壤◄ [U] the soil on and under the surface of the earth 土, 土地: *Dig the ground over in autumn.* 秋天要翻土。| *marshy ground* 沼泽地

3 ►UNDER THE SEA 在海底◄ [U] the bottom of the sea 海底: *Our ship touched ground.* 我们的船搁浅了。

② AREA 地方

4 ►OPEN LAND 空旷之地◄ [U] an area of land without buildings or trees〔无建筑物或树木的〕空地: *a view across open ground* 空旷地带的景色 | *They're building a car lot on some waste ground across the street.* 他们正在街对面那块废弃的空地上建造停车场。

5 grounds [plural] **a)** a large area of land or sea that is used for a particular activity or sport〔用于某项活动或运动的〕一大片场地[海域]: *hunting grounds* 狩猎场 | *fishing grounds* 渔场 **b)** the land or gardens around a large house, hospital etc〔大房子、医院等周围的〕庭园, 场地

6 parade/recreation/burial etc ground an area of land that is used for a particular purpose 阅兵场/游乐场/墓地等 —see also 另见 PLAYGROUND

7 ►SPORTS 体育◄ [C] *BrE* the place where a sport such as football or CRICKET (2) is played; STADIUM【英】〔足球、板球等的〕球场; 体育场: *the team's home ground* (=where they usually play) 该队的主场

8 cover a lot of ground to travel a very long distance 走了不少路, 旅行到过很多地方: *You certainly covered a lot of ground on your travels.* 你确实去过不少地方。

③ SUBJECT 主题

9 ►AREA OF KNOWLEDGE 知识领域◄ [U] an area of knowledge, ideas, experience etc 知识[概念, 经验]领域, 范围: **go over the same ground** (=talk about the same things again) 又谈论同样的事, 老调重弹 *The article says nothing new – it just goes over the same old ground.* 这篇文章没有讲什么新内容 — 只是老调重弹。| **be on familiar ground/be on your own ground** (=be talking about or dealing with a subject you know a lot about) 谈论或处理你所熟知的领域 *Keith's on familiar ground. He's worked with this type of computer before.* 基思驾轻就熟, 他以前用过这种电脑。

10 be on dangerous/safe ground to be expressing ideas that are likely or unlikely to offend or embarrass someone 处于危险/安全境地〔指提出的看法可能或不大可能冒犯某人或使其难堪〕

11 cover a lot of ground to give information about many different parts of a subject 涉及〔某话题的〕诸多方面: *It's absurd to try to cover so much ground in such a short lecture.* 想在如此短的讲座中涉及这么大的范围是荒谬的。

④ OPINION/ATTITUDE 观点/态度

12 the middle ground the area of political opinion that most people agree about 中间立场〔为大多数人所赞同的政治观点〕: *the middle ground between two passionately opposed views* 两种激烈对立观点之间的中间立场

13 common ground an area of opinion that two people or groups share〔两人或两个团体的〕共同看法: *We hope to find some common ground as a basis for agreement.* 我们希望达成某些共识作为协议的基础。

14 shift/change your ground to begin to use different reasons or ideas to support your opinions 改变立场

15 hold your ground to continue to support a particular opinion in spite of opposition 坚持立场

16 the moral high ground an opinion that is regarded as morally better than others 高道义立场〔被视为在道义上较其他观点更为高尚的观点〕

⑤ REASON 理由

17 ►REASON 理由◄ [C usually plural 一般用复数] a reason, especially one that makes you think that something is true or correct 理由, 根据: **grounds for (doing) sth** *Jim has strong grounds for asking for more money.* 吉姆有充分的理由索要更多的钱。| **on moral/legal etc grounds** *He refused to sign the contract on moral grounds.* 他以道德为由拒绝签署那份合同。| **on grounds of** *The divorce was granted on grounds of adultery.* 因有通奸情形, 离婚得到批准。| **on the grounds that** *Zoe was awarded compensation on the grounds that the doctor had been negligent.* 佐伊被判给赔偿金, 根据是医生玩忽职守。

⑥ SUCCESS/ADVANTAGE 成功/优势

18 get off the ground if a plan, a business idea etc gets off the ground, or if you get it off the ground, it starts to be successful〔计划、经商点子等〕开始获得成功: *It took a while for the business to get off the ground, but it's making a profit now.* 这家公司经过相当一段时间之后才取得进展, 但现在已经开始赢利了。

19 gain ground a) to get an advantage and become more successful 取得优势, 变得比较有利: *The Republicans have been gaining ground in the opinion polls.* 共和党在民意测验中逐渐取得优势。**b)** if an idea, belief etc gains ground, it starts to become accepted or believed by more people〔主张、信仰等〕开始被更多的人接受: *a theory gaining ground among academics* 被学术界愈来愈多的人接受的一种理论

20 lose ground to lose an advantage and become less successful 失去优势, 失利

⑦ HIDE/FIND 隐藏/找到

21 go to ground *BrE* to hide from someone, especially the police【英】躲避〔某人, 尤指警察〕

22 run sb to ground *BrE* to succeed in finding someone after a long search【英】长期搜寻之后找到某人: *I finally ran Luke to ground in the basement store room.* 我终于在地下贮藏室找到了卢克。

⑧ COLOUR/PAINT 颜色/颜料

23 ►BACKGROUND 背景◄ [C] the colour that is the background for a design 背景: *white flowers on a blue ground* 蓝底白花

24 ►PAINT 颜料◄ [C] the first covering of paint on a painting 底色

⑨ OTHER MEANINGS 其他意思

25 fertile ground/breeding ground a situation in which it is easy for something to develop 沃土/滋生地: *The universities were a fertile ground for left-wing radicalism.* 大学是左翼激进主义的沃土。| *a breeding ground for germs* 细菌的滋生地

26 on the ground in the actual place where something, especially a war, is happening, rather than in another place where it is being discussed 在现场〔尤指战争现场, 而非讨论的场所〕: *While the politicians talked of peace, the situation on the ground remained tense.* 政治家在谈论和平的时候, 战场局势仍然很紧张。

27 on your own ground/on home ground in the place or situation that is most familiar to you 在你最熟悉的地方/在你最了解的情况下: *I wouldn't dream of meeting my ex-husband again unless I was on home ground.* 除非是在我熟知的地方, 否则我做梦也不想再见到我的前夫。

28 work/drive yourself into the ground to work so hard that you become extremely tired 拼命工作，使自己极度劳累：*Kay's working herself into the ground trying to meet her deadlines.* 凯拼命地工作，想在最后期限内完成任务。
29 grounds *plural* the small pieces of something such as coffee which sink to the bottom of a liquid 沉淀物，渣滓：*coffee grounds* 咖啡渣
30 ▶ELECTRICAL 电气的◀ [singular] *AmE* a wire that connects a piece of electrical equipment to the ground for safety 【美】地线；EARTH[1] (8) *BrE*【英】—see also 另见 **break fresh/new ground** (BREAK[1] (33)), **cut the ground from under sb's feet** (CUT[1] (25)), **have/keep both feet on the ground** (FOOT[1] (16)), **stand your ground** (STAND[1] (8)), **stand your ground** (STAND[1] (17)), **suit sb down to the ground** (SUIT[2] (1)), **be thin on the ground** (THIN[1] (12)), **hit the ground running** (HIT[1] (22))

ground² *v* **1** [T usually passive 一般用被动态] to stop an aircraft or pilot from flying 使〔飞机、飞行员〕停飞：*All planes are grounded until the fog clears.* 所有的飞机都停飞，直至雾散为止。**2** [I,T] if you ground a boat or if it grounds, it hits the bottom of the sea so that it cannot move〔船舶〕搁浅 **3 be grounded in/on** to be based on something 以…为根据，建立在…基础上：*David's values are grounded in a Protestant work ethic.* 戴维的价值观建立在新教的职业道德基础之上。**4** [T] *informal* to stop a child going out with their friends as a punishment for behaving badly【非正式】不许〔孩子〕与朋友一起出去玩〔作为表现不好的惩罚〕：*I got home at 2 am and Dad grounded me on the spot.* 我凌晨两点回家，爸爸当场罚我不准出去。**5** [T] *AmE* to make a piece of electrical equipment safe by connecting it to the ground with a wire【美】把〔电器装置〕接地〔以确保电器安全〕；EARTH[2] *BrE*【英】—see also 另见 WELL-GROUNDED

ground sb **in** sth *phr v* [T usually passive 一般用被动态] to teach someone the basic things they should know in order to be able to do something 对〔某人〕进行基本训练：*The recruits were grounded in combat techniques.* 新兵接受作战技术的基本训练。

ground³ *adj* [only before noun 仅用于名词前] ground coffee or nuts have been broken up into powder or very small pieces, using a special machine 磨成粉末的，磨碎的

ground⁴ the past tense and past participle of GRIND[1]

ground bait /ˈ· ·/ *n* [U] food that you throw onto a river, lake etc when you are fishing in order to attract fish〔捕鱼时投入河、湖等中的〕诱饵

ground beef /ˌ· ˈ·/ *n* [U] *AmE* BEEF[1] (1) that has been cut up into very small pieces, often used to make HAMBURGERS【美】〔做汉堡包的〕牛肉末；MINCE[2] *BrE*【英】

ground·break·ing /ˈgraʊndˌbrekɪŋ; ˈgraʊndˌbreɪkɪŋ/ *adj* groundbreaking work involves making new discoveries, using new methods etc 开辟新天地的

ground cloth /ˈ· ·/ *n* [C] *AmE* a piece of material that water cannot pass through which people sleep on when they are camping【美】〔野营睡觉时铺地用的〕防潮布；GROUNDSHEET *BrE*【英】

ground con·trol /ˈ· ·ˌ·/ *n* [U] the people on the ground who are responsible for guiding the flight of SPACECRAFT or aircraft〔航天、航空的〕地面控制人员

ground cov·er /ˈ· ˌ··/ *n* [U] plants that cover the soil 地被植物

ground crew /ˈ· ·/ *n* [C] the group of people who work at an airport looking after the aircraft〔机场的〕地勤人员；GROUND STAFF *BrE*【英】

ground·er /ˈgraʊndɚ; ˈgraʊndə/ *n* [C] a ball hit along the ground in BASEBALL〔棒球中的〕地滚球，地面球

ground floor /ˌ· ˈ·◂/ *n* **1** [C] *especially BrE* the floor of a building that is at ground level【尤英】〔楼房与地面齐平的〕底层；FIRST FLOOR (2) *AmE*【美】—see 见 FLOOR[1] (USAGE) **2 be/get in on the ground floor** to become involved in a plan, business activity etc from the beginning 从一开始便参加〔某计划、商务活动等〕

ground for·ces /ˈ· ˌ··/ *n* [plural] military groups that fight on the ground rather than at sea or in the air 地面部队

ground glass /ˌ· ˈ·◂/ *n* [U] **1** glass that has been made into a powder 玻璃粉 **2** glass that has been rubbed on the surface so that you cannot see through it, but light passes through it 毛玻璃，磨砂玻璃

ground·hog /ˈgraʊndˌhɑg; ˈgraʊndhɒg/ *n* [C] a small North American animal that has thick brown fur and lives in holes in the ground; WOODCHUCK 花白旱獭，美洲旱獭

Groundhog Day /ˈ·· ˌ·/ the 2nd February, celebrated in the US. On this day, according to old stories, the GROUNDHOG comes out of its hole for the first time since winter began. If it sees its shadow, it is frightened back into its hole and there will be six more weeks of winter, but if it is cloudy and the groundhog cannot see its shadow, there will be an early spring. (美国) 土拨鼠日〔即2月2日。根据古老传说，这天是入冬以来土拨鼠首次出洞的日子。土拨鼠出洞后如果看见自己的影子，就会被吓回到洞里去，这则表明冬天还将延续6周。如果出洞的那天是阴天，它看不见自己的影子，那么春天就会早早到来〕

ground·ing /ˈgraʊndɪŋ; ˈgraʊndɪŋ/ *n* **1** [singular] a training in the basic parts of a subject or skill 基础训练：[+in] *A thorough grounding in mathematics is essential for the economics course.* 严密的数学基础训练对经济学这门课程来说是必不可少的。**2** [C] *AmE* a punishment for a child's bad behaviour in which they are not allowed go out with their friends for a period of time【美】〔因孩子表现不佳〕在一定时间内不许与朋友外出的惩罚。

ground·less /ˈgraʊndlɪs; ˈgraʊndləs/ *adj* groundless fears, worries etc are unnecessary because there are no facts to base them on 无根据的：*Fortunately my suspicions proved groundless.* 幸亏我的猜疑后来证明是没有根据的。

ground lev·el /ˈ· ˌ··/ *n* [singular] the same level as the surface of the earth, rather than above it or below it 地平面

ground·nut /ˈgraʊndˌnʌt; ˈgraʊndnʌt/ *n* [C] *BrE technical* a PEANUT or peanut plant【英，术语】落花生，花生；花生植株

ground plan /ˈ· ·/ *n* [C] **1** a drawing of how a building is arranged at ground level, showing the size, position, and shape of walls, rooms etc 楼层平面图 **2** a plan of how something will happen in the future 大纲，初步计划，草案

ground rent /ˈ· ·/ *n* [C,U] rent paid to the person who owns the land that your house is built on 地租

ground rules /ˈ· ·/ *n* [plural] the basic rules or principles on which future actions or behaviour should be based 基本规则[原则]

ground·sheet /ˈgraʊndˌʃit; ˈgraʊndʃiːt/ *n* [C] *BrE* a piece of material that water cannot pass through which people sleep on when they are camping【英】〔野营睡觉时铺地用的〕防潮布；GROUND CLOTH *AmE*【美】

grounds·man /ˈgraʊndzmən; ˈgraʊndzmən/ *plural* **groundsmen** /-mən; -mən/ *n* [C] *especially BrE* a man whose job is to take care of large gardens or a sports field【尤英】大花园[运动场]的管理员

ground squir·rel /ˈ· ˌ··/ *n* [C] a North American animal that lives in the ground and often damages crops; GOPHER 地松鼠，黄鼠

ground staff /ˈ· ·/ *n* [C] *BrE*【英】**1** the people who take care of the grass and sports equipment at a sports ground〔运动场草坪和运动器材的〕管理人员 **2** the group of people who work at an airport looking after the aircraft; GROUND CREW〔机场的〕地勤人员

ground stroke /ˈ· ·/ *n* [C] a way of hitting the ball after it has hit the ground in tennis and similar games〔网球等的〕击落地球

ground·swell /ˈgraʊndswɛl; ˈgraʊndswel/ *n* **1 groundswell of support/opinion etc** a sudden increase in how strongly people feel about something 突然高涨的支持/舆论等 **2** [singular, U] the strong movement of the sea that continues after a storm or strong winds〔暴风雨或大风后的〕海涌，巨浪

ground·work /ˈgraʊndˌwɝk; ˈgraʊndwɜːk/ *n* [U] important work that has to take place before another activity, plan etc can be successful 基础，根基：*The groundwork for the peace summit was laid during last month's conference.* 和平峰会的基础是在上月那次会议期间打下的。

group¹ /grup; gruːp/ *n* [C] **1** several people or things that are all together in the same place〔人或物聚在一处的〕组，群，批：[+of] *a group of tall trees* 一片大树 | *Get into groups of four.* 分成四个人一组。| [also+plural verb *BrE* 英] *A group of us are going to London for the concert.* 我们中有一群人要去伦敦听这场音乐会。**2** several people or things that are connected with each other in some way〔人或物彼此之间有某种联系的〕团体；群体：[+of] *A group of animal rights activists claimed responsibility for the bomb.* 一个动物权利保护团体声称对这一爆炸事件负责。| *the Germanic group of languages* 日耳曼语系 | **income/ethnic etc group** (=people with the same income level, same race etc) 同一收入水平/同一种族等的群体 **3** several companies that all have the same owner 集团(公司)：*a giant textiles group* 庞大的纺织集团 **4** a number of musicians or singers who perform together, usually playing popular music〔通常演奏流行音乐的〕乐团，乐队，组合：*a rock group* 摇滚乐团 —see also 另见 AGE GROUP, BLOOD GROUP, INTEREST GROUP, PLAYGROUP

group² *v* **1** [I,T] to come together to make a group or to arrange people or things in a group 聚集成一组; 把人或物分组: [+on/in/together etc] *Can you all group around the piano?* 请大家围拢在钢琴周围好吗? **2** [T always+ adv/prep] to divide people or things into groups or types according to a system〔将人或物〕分类: *The soils can be broadly grouped according to their acidity.* 这些土壤可以按照它们的酸度粗略分类。

group cap·tain /,· '··◂/ *n* [C] a fairly high rank in the British airforce, or someone who has this rank〔英国的〕空军上校(军衔) —see table on page C7 参见 C7 页附录

group·ie /ˈgrupi; ˈgruːpi/ *n* [C] someone, especially a young woman, who follows POP muscians to their concerts, hoping to meet them 流行歌星迷〔尤指少女〕

group·ing /ˈgrupɪŋ; ˈgruːpɪŋ/ *n* [C] a set of people, things, or organizations that have the same interests, qualities, or features〔兴趣、品质或特征相同的〕派别, 小集团: *The unemployed form the largest single grouping of the electorate.* 失业者构成了这个选区最大的一个群体。

Group of Eight, the /,·· '·/ the full name of the G8 八国集团〔G8 的全称〕 —see 见 G7

Group of Sev·en, the /,· · '··/ the full name of the G7 七国集团〔G7 的全称〕

group prac·tice /,· '··/ *n* [C,U] a group of doctors who work together, in the same building〔几名医生在同一栋楼里一起工作的〕联合医疗

Group Thea·tre, the /,· '··/ a group of actors and DIRECTORS in the US who worked together from 1931 to 1940 to produce plays with a political message. Many of the people in the group, such as Elia Kazan and Lee Strasberg, became very important in the US theatre. 同仁剧团〔指 1931 至 1940 年美国的一群演员和导演。他们一起创作了具有政治寓意的戏剧, 其中伊莱业·卡赞、李·斯特拉斯伯格等人在美国戏剧界具有重要地位〕 — see also 另见 ACTORS' STUDIO

group ther·a·py /,· '···/ *n* [U] a method of treating people with emotional or PSYCHOLOGICAL problems by bringing them together in groups to talk about their problems 集体心理治疗〔把有情感或心理疾病的患者聚集在一起, 分组让他们谈论自己的问题〕

G

grouse¹ /graus; graʊs/ *n* **1** [C] *informal* a complaint, especially an unreasonable one【非正式】牢骚〔尤指无理的抱怨〕**2** [C,U] a small fat bird that is hunted and shot for food and sport, or the meat of this bird 松鸡; 松鸡肉

CULTURAL NOTE 文化注释

In Britain, grouse shooting begins every year on August 12th (known as the 'Glorious Twelfth') and ends on December 10th. It is popular especially with the ARISTOCRACY and richer classes of British society. 英国猎松鸡于 8 月 12 日开始, 称为"光荣的 12 日", 于 12 月 10 日结束。这项运动尤其受到贵族和富人的喜爱。

grouse² *v* [I +about] *informal* to complain about something in an angry way: GRUMBLE¹ (1)【非正式】〔生气地〕发牢骚, 抱怨

grove /grov; grəʊv/ *n* **1** [C] an area of land planted with a particular type of fruit tree 果园, 果树林: *an orange grove* 柑橘园 —compare 比较 ORCHARD **2** [C] *literary* a small group of trees【文】树丛, 小树林 **3 Grove** used in the names of roads …路〔用于路名〕: *Lisson Grove* 利胜路

grov·el /ˈgrɑvl; ˈgrɒvəl/ *v* **grovelled, grovelling** *BrE*【英】, **groveled, groveling** *AmE*【美】[I] **1** to behave with too much respect towards someone, because you are asking them to help or forgive you〔因有求于人而〕卑躬屈膝: *There's nothing worse than seeing a man grovel just to keep his job.* 没有什么比看到一个人只是为了保住工作而卑躬屈膝更糟糕的了。**2** to lie or move flat on the ground because you are afraid of someone, or as a way of showing obedience〔因害怕某人或表示顺从而〕匍匐在地: *That dog grovels every time you shout.* 每次你一喊, 那条狗就趴在地上。

grow out of 因长大而穿不进〔原来的衣服〕

He's grown out of his clothes.
他长大了, 衣服都穿不下了。

grow /gro; grəʊ/ *v past tense* **grew** /gru; gruː/ *past participle* **grown** /gron; grəʊn/

1 ▶PERSON/ANIMAL 人/动物◀ [I] to become bigger and develop over a period of time 成长, 长大: *How you've grown since the last time I saw you!* 自上次见到你以来, 你长高了不少啊! | **grow 2 inches/5cm etc** *Stan grew two inches in six months.* 斯坦在六个月中长高了两英寸。| **growing boy/girl** *Of course he eats a lot – he's a growing boy!* 他当然吃得多 — 他正在发育!

2 ▶PLANTS/CROPS 植物/作物◀ a) [I] to exist and develop somewhere in a natural way 自然生长: *There's corn growing in that field.* 那块田里长着玉米。| *It's too cold for orchids to grow here.* 这里太冷了, 兰花无法生长。**b)** [T] to make plants or crops grow by taking care of them 栽, 种植: *We grow all our own vegetables.* 我们吃的蔬菜都是自己种的。—see 见 RAISE¹ (USAGE)

3 ▶HAIR/NAILS 头发/指甲◀ a) [I] if hair, nails etc grow, they become longer〔头发、指甲等〕变长 **b)** [T] if you grow your hair, nails, you do not cut them 留〔长头发、长指甲〕

4 ▶INCREASE 增加◀ [I] to increase in amount, size, or degree 增多, 增大, 增强, 增长: *De Niro's reputation continues to grow.* 德尼罗的声望在继续上升。| *Fears are growing for the safety of the crew.* 人们越来越担心船员们的安全。| **growing concern/interest/disbelief etc** *Scientists view the hole in the ozone layer with growing concern.* 科学家日益关注臭氧层空洞。| **a growing number** *A growing number of people are taking part-time jobs.* 越来越多人在从事兼职工作。| **grow in strength/confidence** (=become stronger, more confident) 更加强壮[壮大]/更有信心

5 grow old/hot/worse etc to become old etc over a period of time 逐渐衰老/变热/恶化等: *She grew impatient with his constant excuses.* 因为他不断地找借口, 她越来越不耐烦了。| *I'm scared of growing old.* 我害怕衰老。

6 grow to like/fear/respect etc to gradually start to like etc someone or something 逐渐开始喜欢/害怕/尊敬等: *After a while the kids grew to like Mr Cox.* 不久之后, 孩子开始喜欢上考克斯先生了。

7 ▶IMPROVE 改善◀ [I] to improve in ability or character〔在能力或性格方面〕改善: *She's grown tremendously as a musician since Pallino took her on.* 自从帕利诺雇了她, 她作为乐师的水平大大提高。

8 ▶BUSINESS 生意◀ [T] to make something increase in size or importance 扩大, 增强: *We want to grow the export side of the business.* 我们想要扩大企业的出口业务。

9 it doesn't grow on trees *spoken* used about money, to mean that you should not waste it【口】钱不是从树上长出来的〔用以表示不可浪费金钱〕

grow apart *phr v* [I] if two people grow apart, their relationship becomes less close〔彼此的关系〕越来越疏远: *He said the couple had been growing apart for at least a year.* 他说这对夫妇不和至少有一年了。

grow away from sb *phr v* [T not in passive 不用被动态] to begin gradually to have a less close relationship with someone that you loved 与〔所爱之人〕开始逐渐疏远: *While at university she had grown away from her family.* 她在上大学时就逐渐和家人疏远起来。

grow into sb/sth *phr v* [T not in passive 不用被动态] **1** to develop over a period of time and become a particular kind of person or thing 成长为: *Susan's grown into a lovely young woman.* 苏珊已长成为一个可爱的少妇。**2** if a child grows into clothes, they become big enough to wear them〔小孩〕长得适合穿〔本来嫌大的衣服〕: *His new jacket's a bit big for him now but he'll soon grow into it.* 他的那件新上衣现在嫌大, 不过很快就会合身了。**3** to gradually learn how to do a job or deal with a situation successfully 逐渐学会[适应]〔工作或情况〕

grow on sb *phr v* [T] if someone or something grows on you, you like them more and more 越来越喜爱: *His music is difficult to listen to, but after a while it grows on you.* 他的音乐很难懂, 但不久会让你越来越喜欢。

grow out of sth *phr v* [T] **1** if a child grows out of clothes, they become too big to wear them〔小孩〕因长大而穿不进〔原来的衣服〕**2** if a child grows out of a habit, they stop doing it as they get older〔因年龄增长而〕戒除, 改掉〔原有的习惯〕: *She used to bite her nails but seems to have grown out of it.* 她过去经常咬指甲, 但现在似乎已经改掉了。**3** to develop from something small or simple into something bigger or more complicated 由〔小或简单的事〕发展成〔大或复杂的事〕: *The dispute grew out of an argument between a worker and the foreman.* 这场争执是从一名工人和工头的争论引发的。

grow up *phr v* [I] **1** develop from being a child to being an adult 长大成人: *What do you want to be when you grow up?* 你长大以后想当什么? | *I grew up on a farm.* 我是在农场里长大

的。**2 grow up!** *spoken* used to tell someone to behave more like an adult, especially when they have been behaving in a silly way【口】要像个大人样！〔尤用于某人行为幼稚可笑之时〕**3** to start to exist and become bigger or more important 形成，兴起，发展：*Trading settlements grew up along the river.* 河的两岸形成了一些贸易区。

grow·bag /ˈgrobæg; ˈgrəʊbæg/ *n* [C] another spelling of GROBAG grobag 的另一种拼法

grow·er /ˈgroə; ˈgrəʊə/ *n* [C] a person or company that grows fruit, vegetables etc in order to sell them〔水果蔬菜等的〕种植者[公司]：*apple growers* 种植苹果的果农

grow·ing pains /ˈ‥ ˌ·/ *n* [plural] **1** aches and pains that children can sometimes feel in their arms and legs when they are growing 发育期痛〔儿童发育时的四肢酸痛〕**2** problems and difficulties that are experienced at the beginning of a new activity〔某项新活动所经历的〕初期困难；发展时期的困难

growl /graul; graʊl/ *v* **1** [I] if an animal growls it makes a long deep angry sound〔动物〕吼叫：*The dog growled at any stranger who came close.* 有生人走近时，那条狗就狂吠不已。**2** [I,T] to say something in a low angry voice 怒气冲冲地低声说："*Get out of my way," he growled.* "滚开。"他咆哮道。—**growl** *n* [C]: *The bear gave a sudden growl.* 这只熊突然发出一声咆哮。

grown¹ /gron; grəʊn/ *adj* [only before noun 仅用于名词前] **grown man/woman** an expression meaning an adult man or woman, used especially when you think someone is not behaving as an adult should 成年男子/女子〔尤用于认为某人行为不像一个成年人时〕：*A grown man should know better than to shout and scream.* 成年男子应该明白不应那样喊叫。—compare 比较 FULL-GROWN, HOMEGROWN

grown² the past participle of GROW

grown-up¹ /ˌ· ˈ·◂/ *adj* **1** fully developed as an adult 成年的：*Before you know it, they'll be all grown-up and leaving home.* 转眼之间，他们就会长大成人，离开家庭。**2** behaving like an adult or typical of an adult〔行为〕符合成年人身份的；具有成年人特点的：*I expect more grown-up behaviour of you now.* 我希望你现在能表现得更像一个成年人。

grown-up² /ˈ· ·/ *n* [C] a word meaning an adult person, used especially by or to children 成年人，大人〔尤为儿语〕：*If you're frightened, tell one of the grown-ups.* 如果你害怕，就跟大人讲。

W2 **growth** /groθ; grəʊθ/ *n*

1 ►INCREASE IN AMOUNT 数量增加◄ [U] an increase in amount, size, or degree 增多，增长，增大，增强：*efforts to control population growth* 为控制人口增长所作的努力 | [+in] *During the 1970's there was rapid growth in oil production and consumption.* 在20世纪70年代，石油产量和消费迅速增长。| **growth rate** (=the speed at which something increases or grows) 增长率 *Japan's economic growth rate* 日本的经济增长率 | **growth area/industry** (=an area of business that is growing very quickly) 迅速增长的〔某企业〕领域/工业

2 ►PERSON/ANIMAL/PLANT 人/动物/植物◄ [U] the development of the physical size, strength etc of a person, animal or plant over a period of time 成长，发育，生长：*Vitamins are essential for healthy growth.* 维生素是健康成长必不可少的。

3 ►INCREASE IN IMPORTANCE 重要性的增加◄ [singular,U] the gradual development and increase of a particular feeling, idea, or way of living〔某种感觉、想法或生活方式的〕逐渐发展和扩大：[+of] *the growth of capitalism* 资本主义的发展 | *Currently there is a growth of interest in African music.* 目前对非洲音乐的兴趣有所增长。

4 ►PERSONAL DEVELOPMENT 个人发展◄ [U] the development of someone's character, intelligence or emotions〔性格、智力或感情的〕发展：**emotional/intellectual/personal etc growth** *A loving home environment is essential for a child's personal growth.* 充满爱心的家庭环境对小孩的个人发展是必不可少的。

5 ►SWELLING 肿块◄ [C] a swelling on your body or under your skin, caused by disease〔由疾病引起，体内或皮下的〕肿块，肿瘤：*a cancerous growth* 癌瘤

6 ►GROWING THING 生长物◄ [C,U] something which has grown 生长物：*I thought the tree was dead, but there are signs of new growth.* 我原以为这棵树已经死了，但它有长出新枝的迹象。

groyne, groin /grɔɪn; grɔɪn/ *n* [C] a low wall built out into the sea to prevent the sea from removing sand and stones from the shore〔海岸的〕防波堤 —see picture on page A12 参见 A12 页图

Grozny /ˈgrozni; ˈgrɔːzniː/ also 又作 **Groznyi, Groznyy** the capital city of the Republic of Chechnya, in southeast Russia on the Sunzha River 格罗兹尼〔车臣共和国的首府，位于俄罗斯东南部的孙扎河畔〕

grub¹ /grʌb; grʌb/ *n* **1** [U] *informal* food【非正式】食物：*Let's get some grub.* 我们买点吃的吧。**2** [C] an insect when it is in the form of a small soft white worm〔昆虫的〕幼虫，蛴螬

grub² [I always+adv/prep] *informal* to look for something, especially by moving things, looking under them etc【非正式】寻找〔尤指翻开别的东西，在下面寻找某物〕：[+around/about] *The dog was grubbing around under a bush looking for a bone.* 那条狗在灌木丛下面翻掘，寻找骨头。

grub sth ↔ **up/out** *phr v* [T] to dig around something and then pull it out of the ground 将…挖出：*Farmers were encouraged to grub up hedgerows.* 农民被鼓励挖掉灌木树篱。

grub·by /ˈgrʌbɪ; ˈgrʌbi/ *adj* **1** fairly dirty 肮脏的：*a grubby handkerchief* 肮脏的手帕 **2** grubby behaviour or activity is morally unpleasant〔行为或活动〕卑鄙的：*the grubby details of Harper's financial dealings* 有关哈珀金融交易的肮脏细节 —**grubbiness** *n* [U]

grub·stake /ˈgrʌbˌstek; ˈgrʌbˌsteɪk/ *n* [U] *AmE informal* money provided to develop a new business in return for a share of the profits【美，非正式】〔为分红而投资开发新业务的〕资金，贷款

grudge¹ /grʌdʒ; grʌdʒ/ *n* [C] **1** a feeling of anger or dislike you have for someone because you cannot forget that they harmed you 怀恨，怨恨：[+against] *He's had a grudge against Bob ever since he was promoted.* 自从鲍勃晋升以来他就对鲍勃怀恨在心。| **bear (sb) a grudge** (=continue to have a grudge)〔对某人〕怀有积怨 **2 grudge fight/match** a fight or competition in sport between two people who dislike each other a lot〔体育中〕冤家对头的决斗/比赛

grudge² *v* [T] **1** to do or give something very unwillingly; BEGRUDGE 勉强做〔某事〕；勉强给〔某物〕：**grudge doing sth** *I really grudge paying so much money for such poor service.* 我确实不愿意为这么差劲的服务付这么多的钱。**2 grudge sb sth** to not want someone to have something 嫉妒：*I don't grudge him his success.* 我并不嫉妒他的成功。

grudg·ing /ˈgrʌdʒɪŋ; ˈgrʌdʒɪŋ/ *adj* done or given very unwillingly 不情愿的，勉强的：*He was looking at Nick with a certain grudging respect.* 他看尼克的目光流露出一种不情愿的尊敬。—**grudgingly** *adv*: *He grudgingly admitted that he'd been wrong.* 他勉强承认他错了。

gru·el /ˈgruəl; ˈgruːəl/ *n* [U] a thin liquid food made of crushed OATS that was eaten in the past by poor or sick people〔过去穷人或病人吃的稀薄的〕燕麦粥，麦片粥

> **CULTURAL NOTE 文化注释**
>
> Formerly in Britain, gruel was often the only food a poor person could afford or would be given if they lived in the WORKHOUSE (=former state building for the homeless and unemployed). 从前在英国，燕麦粥通常是穷人唯一能负担得起的食物，也是住在救贫院里的人唯一能得到的食物。

gru·el·ling *BrE*【英】, **grueling** *AmE*【美】/ˈgruəlɪŋ; ˈgruːəlɪŋ/ *adj* very tiring because you have to use a lot of effort for a long time 非常累人的：*a gruelling 6 hour mountain hike* 非常累人的六小时爬山 —**gruellingly** *adv*

grue·some /ˈgrusəm; ˈgruːsəm/ *adj* very unpleasant and shocking, and usually connected with death or injury; GRISLY〔通常与死亡或伤害相关的〕令人厌恶的，可怕的：*Spare me all the gruesome details.* 别跟我讲那些可怕的细节。—**gruesomely** *adv*

gruff /grʌf; grʌf/ *adj* **1** unfriendly or annoyed, especially in the way you speak〔尤指说话的口气〕不友好的；生硬的：*a gruff reply* 生硬的回答 **2** a gruff voice sounds low and rough as if the speaker does not want to talk 低沉而生硬的〔指声音，好像说话者不愿意讲话〕—**gruffly** *adv* —**gruffness** *n* [U]

grum·ble¹ /ˈgrʌmbḷ; ˈgrʌmbəl/ *v* [I] **1** to keep complaining in an unhappy way 不断地发牢骚，抱怨：[+about/at etc] *The farmers are always grumbling about the weather.* 农民老是在抱怨天气。**2** to make a very low sound that gets quieter then louder continuously; RUMBLE¹ (1) 发出时高时低的隆隆声：*Is that your tummy grumbling?* 那是你的肚子在咕咕叫吗？**3 mustn't grumble** *BrE spoken* used to say that you are fairly well or that you have no serious problems【英口】还不错〔用来表示自己的情况没有什么严重问题〕："*How are you today?" "Mustn't grumble."* "你今天好吗？""还不错。" —**grumbler** *n* [C]

grumble² *n* [C] **1** something that you feel dissatisfied about and keep complaining about 牢骚，怨言：*Take your grumbles to the boss – don't bother me with them.* 有怨言去跟老板说——不要来烦我。**2 have a grumble** to complain about something 发牢骚，抱怨

grum·bling ap·pen·dix /ˌ·· ·ˈ··/ *n* [singular] *BrE not technical* a condition in which your APPENDIX (1) causes you pain from time to time【英, 非术语】阑尾阵痛

grump·y /ˈgrʌmpɪ; ˈgrʌmpi/ *adj* bad-tempered and tending to complain 脾气坏又爱发牢骚的 —**grumpily** *adv* **grumpiness** *n* [U]

Grun·dy /ˈgrʌndɪ; ˈgrʌndi/, **Mrs** an unpleasant character in a play called *Speed the Plough* (1798) by the British writer Thomas Morton. She has very strict ideas about moral and social behaviour, and tries to make sure that other people are behaving properly. 葛兰地太太〔英国作家托马斯·莫顿戏剧《加快耕地》(1798) 中令人讨厌的一个角色。她恪守近乎刻薄的道德和社会行为观念, 且试图让别人也中规中矩〕

grunge /grʌndʒ; grʌndʒ/ *n* [U] **1** *AmE informal* dirt; GRIME【美, 非正式】污物, 污垢: *What's all that grunge in the bathtub?* 浴缸里的那些脏兮兮的东西是什么? **2** a style of fashion popular with young people in the early 1990s, in which they wear clothes that look dirty and untidy 邋遢时尚〔20世纪90年代初在年轻人中流行的一种时装潮流〕 **3** a type of loud music played with electric GUITARs popular during this period〔流行于20世纪90年代的〕格朗基摇滚

grung·y /ˈgrʌndʒɪ; ˈgrʌndʒi/ *adj AmE informal* dirty and sometimes smelling bad in an offensive way【美, 非正式】肮脏的, 肮脏难闻的: *grungy jeans* 肮脏的牛仔裤

grunt[1] /grʌnt; grʌnt/ *v* **1** [I,T] to make short sounds or say a few words in a low rough voice, showing that you do not want to have a conversation〔表示不愿意讲话时〕发出哼声; 嘟哝着说: *I tried to cheer him up but he only grunted.* 我想给他打气, 可他只是嘟哝了一声。**2** [I] if an animal grunts, especially a pig, it makes short low sounds deep in its throat〔尤指猪等〕发出咕噜声

grunt[2] *n* [C] **1** a short low sound made deep in your throat like the sound a pig makes 呼噜声, 嘟哝声, 咕哝声: *Chris just gave a grunt and went back to sleep.* 克里斯只是哼了一声, 又睡着了。**2** *AmE slang* an INFANTRY soldier【美俚】步兵

grunt work /ˈ· ·/ *n* [U] *AmE informal* the hard uninteresting part of a piece of work; DONKEYWORK【美, 非正式】〔某项工作中〕困难而单调的部分

Gru·yère /gruˈjɛr; ˈgruːjeə/ *n* [U] a kind of hard cheese with holes in it, from Switzerland 格鲁耶尔干酪〔一种带孔的瑞士硬干酪〕

gryph·on /ˈgrɪfən; ˈgrɪfən/ *n* [C] another spelling of GRIFFIN griffin 的另一种拼法

g-spot /ˈdʒi spɑt; ˈdʒiː spɒt/ *n* [C] a centre of sexual feeling in a woman's VAGINA G点

Gstaad /gəˈʃtɑd; gəˈʃtɑːd/ a town in Switzerland which is a fashionable place to go to ski 格施塔德〔瑞士一小镇, 是时尚人士滑雪的去处〕

G-string /ˈdʒi strɪŋ; ˈdʒiː ˌstrɪŋ/ *n* [C] a very small piece of cloth, leather etc worn to cover your sexual organs G带, 遮羞布

GTi /ˌdʒi ti ˈaɪ; ˌdʒiː tiː ˈaɪ/ *adj* a GTi car has a special FUEL system which helps it to go at high speeds 燃油直喷(装置)〔装有特别燃料系统, 有助于高速行驶〕 compare 比较 FUEL INJECTION

gua·ca·mo·le /ˌgwɑkəˈmolɪ; ˌgwɑːkəˈməʊli/ *n* [U] a Mexican dish made with crushed AVOCADOs 鳄梨色拉〔墨西哥菜肴〕

Guadalcanal /ˌgwadḷkəˈnæl; ˌgwɑːdlkəˈnæl/ the largest island in the Solomon Islands in the southwestern Pacific Ocean. There was a lot of fighting on Guadalcanal between Japanese and Allied forces during World War II. 瓜达尔卡纳尔〔太平洋西南海域所罗门群岛中的最大岛屿。二战期间, 日军与盟军在此多次交战〕

Guadeloupe /ˈgwadḷˌup; ˈgwɑːdəluːp/ an island in the Caribbean Sea, south of Antigua and Barbuda and north of Dominica. The island is a dependency of France. Population: 431,170 (2001). Capital: Basse-Terre. 瓜德罗普岛〔加勒比海一岛屿, 位于安提瓜和巴布达以南、多米尼克以北, 是法国的属地。人口: 431,170 (2001), 首府: 巴斯特尔〕

Guam /gwɑm; gwɑːm/ an island east of the Philippines that belongs to the US. Population: 157,557 (2001). Capital: Agaña. 关岛〔菲律宾以东一岛屿, 属于美国。人口: 157,557 (2001), 首府: 阿加尼亚〕

Guang·zhou /ˌgɒɑŋˈdʒo; ˌgwɑːŋˈdʒəʊ/ a large city in southern China on the Pearl River, near Hong Kong. Its name in English was Canton. 广州〔中国南部一大城市, 位于珠江之滨, 邻近香港。过去的英文名为 Canton〕

gua·no /ˈgwano; ˈgwɑːnəʊ/ *n* [U] solid waste passed from the stomachs of sea birds that is often put on soil to help plants grow 海鸟粪

guar·an·tee[1] /ˌgærənˈti; ˌgærənˈtiː/ *v* [T] S2 W3

1 ►PROMISE STH WILL HAPPEN 许诺某事会发生◄ to promise that something will certainly happen or be done 担保, 保证: **guarantee (that)** *Take this opportunity, and I guarantee you won't regret it.* 抓住这个机会吧, 我保证你不会后悔的。| **guarantee sth** *The authorities could not guarantee the safety of the UN observers.* 当局无法保证联合国观察员的安全。| **guarantee sb sth** *Even if you complete your training I can't guarantee you a job.* 即使你完成了培训, 我也无法保证你能有工作。

2 ►A PRODUCT 产品◄ to make a formal written promise to repair or replace a product if it has a fault within a specific period of time after you buy it 保修; 包换: **guarantee sth against** *a toaster guaranteed for one year against failure of parts* 零部件保用一年的烤面包箱

3 ►LEGAL 法律上的◄ to make yourself legally responsible for the payment of money 保证付款

4 ►MAKE STH CERTAIN 确保某事◄ to make it certain that something will happen 保证〔某事必然发生〕: *She soon learned that marriage does not guarantee happiness.* 她很快就发现婚姻不能保证有幸福。

5 ►CERTAIN TO DO STH 肯定做某事◄ **be guaranteed to do sth** to be certain to behave, work, or happen in a particular way 肯定会以某种方式行事[工作, 发生]: *If you yell at him, he's guaranteed to do the opposite of what you want.* 如果你向他大喊大叫, 他肯定会跟你对着干。

6 ►PROTECT 保护◄ **guarantee sth against** *AmE* to provide complete protection against harm or damage【美】〔为免受伤害或损毁〕提供完全的保护: *Rust-shield guarantees your car against corrosion.* "防锈盾"保护你的汽车不受腐蚀。

guarantee[2] *n* [C] 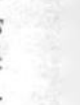 S2

1 a formal written promise to repair or replace a product without charging, if it has a fault within a specific time after you buy it 保修单; 包换单: *The television comes with a two-year guarantee.* 这台电视机有两年的保修期。| **be under guarantee** (=be protected by a guarantee) 在质保期内 *Your watch will be repaired free if it's still under guarantee.* 你的手表在质保期内可享受免费修理。

> **CULTURAL NOTE 文化注释**
>
> Not all goods have a guarantee but they must still do the job for which they were made and last a reasonable length of time, as defined in the rules of the Consumer Council in Britain, and the Consumer Protection Agency in the US. 并非所有商品都有保修单, 但依照英国消费者委员会和美国消费者保护处的规定, 商品必须能发挥其用途而且有一个合理的保用期。

2 a formal and firm promise that something will be done or will happen〔某事必将办到或发生的〕正式而坚定的承诺: **[+of]** *Is there a guarantee of work after training?* 培训结束之后是否保证就业? | **give sb a guarantee (that)** *Can you give me a guarantee that the work will be finished on time?* 你能向我保证工作会按时完成吗? **3 a)** an agreement to be responsible for someone else's promise, especially a promise to pay a debt 担保〔尤指为保证还债而作的担保〕 **b)** something valuable given to someone to keep until the owner has kept their a promise, especially to pay a debt〔尤指对债务的〕担保物; 抵押品 —compare 比较 SECURITY (4), WARRANTY

guar·an·tor /ˈgærəntɚ; ˌgærənˈtɔː/ *n* [C] *law* someone who promises that they will pay for something if the person who should pay for it does not【法律】担保人

guar·an·ty /ˈgærəntɪ; ˈgærənti/ *n* [C] *AmE law* a formal promise, especially of payment【美, 法律】〔尤指有关付款的〕保证, 保证书 —see also 另见 WARRANTY

guard[1] /gɑrd; gɑːd/ *n*

1 ►PERSON 人◄ [C] **a)** someone whose job is to guard a place, person, or object in order to protect them from attack or from thieves 卫兵, 警卫, 门卫: *The guards stopped us at the gate.* 卫兵把我们挡在门口。—see also 另见 SECURITY GUARD **b)** someone whose job is to guard prisoners and prevent them from escaping 狱吏, 监狱看守人

2 be on guard to be responsible for guarding a place or person for a specific period of time 站岗, 执勤: *Who was on guard when the fire broke out?* 火灾发生时是谁在执勤?

3 keep/stand/mount guard (over) to guard a person or place 守卫, 看守〔某人或某地〕: *Catherine kept guard over the horses while we looked for water.* 我们找水时凯瑟琳看着马。

4 ►GROUP 群◄ [singular] a group of people, especially soldiers, who guard someone or something 一队守卫〔尤指士兵〕

5 be under (armed) guard to be guarded by a group of people with weapons 在武装人员的保卫[守卫]下

6 ▶THING 事物◀ [C] something that is fitted to a machine or worn on a part of your body to protect you against damage or injury 保护装置〔指安装在机器上或戴在身体某部位以防损毁或伤害的装置〕: *a football player's mouth guard* 橄榄球员的护齿

7 catch/throw/take sb off guard to surprise someone by doing or saying something that they are not ready to deal with〔乘某人不备而做或说某事〕使人惊讶: *Senator O'Hare was caught off guard by the reporter's question.* 记者突然提出的问题让参议员奥黑尔愣住了。

8 be on your guard to pay careful attention to what is happening so that you avoid being tricked or getting into danger 警惕, 提防: *Be on your guard – they always try to cheat tourists.* 提防点——他们总是想办法欺骗游客。| **lower your guard/let your guard down** (=forget to be careful) 放松警惕

9 ▶ON A TRAIN 火车上◀ [C] *BrE* an official in charge of a train【英】列车长; CONDUCTOR (4) *AmE*【美】

10 ▶BOXING 拳击◀ [singular] the position of your hands in BOXING when you are holding them up to defend yourself〔拳击中手的〕防御姿势

11 the Guards special groups of soldiers in the British army whose original duty was to guard the king or queen〔英国〕皇家卫队, 御林军

guard² *v* [T] **1** to protect a person, place, or valuable object by staying near them and watching them 保卫, 守卫: *The Sergeant told Swift to guard the entrance to the building.* 警官叫斯威夫特守卫大楼的入口处。| **guard sb/sth against** *There is no one to guard these isolated farms against possible attack.* 这几处孤立的农场门户大开, 没有人守卫。**2** to watch a prisoner and prevent them from escaping 看守〔囚犯〕**3 guard your tongue** *old-fashioned* used to tell someone to be careful of what they say so that they do not tell a secret【过时】管住自己的嘴

guard against sth *phr v* [T] to try to prevent something from happening by being careful〔小心谨慎地〕防止…发生: *Nurses should guard against becoming too emotionally attached to their patients.* 护士应该防止对其看护的病人产生过多的感情依恋。

guard dog /ˈ· ·/ *n* [C] a dog often used by soldiers, police officers etc that is trained to guard a place 军犬; 警犬

guard·ed /ˈgɑrdɪd; ˈgɑːdɪ̣d/ *adj* a guarded statement, remark etc deliberately does not give much information about your thoughts and feelings〔言辞等〕谨慎的, 有保留的, 提防的: *"What do you want?" Her tone was guarded and hesitant.* "你想要什么?"她的语气既谨慎又犹豫。—**guardedly** *adv*

guard·house /ˈgɑrdˌhaʊs; ˈgɑːdhaʊs/ *n* [C] a building for soldiers who are guarding the entrance to a military camp〔军营入口处的〕岗哨楼, 卫兵室

guard·i·an /ˈgɑrdɪən; ˈgɑːdiən/ *n* [C] **1** someone who is legally responsible for looking after someone else's child, especially after the child's parents have died 监护人 **2** *formal* someone who guards or protects something, especially an institution or moral principle【正式】〔尤指某种制度或道德准则的〕维护者, 保卫者: [+of] *The US has represented itself as the guardian of democracy.* 美国把自己描绘成民主政治的卫士。

Guardian, The *trademark* a serious British daily newspaper that has LEFT-WING opinions【商标】《卫报》〔英国一家持左翼观点的严肃类日报〕

guardian an·gel /ˌ··· ˈ··/ *n* [C] **1** a good spirit who is believed to protect a person or place〔某人或某地的〕守护天使 **2** someone who helps or protects someone else when they are in trouble 帮助或保护有难者的好人

Guardian An·gels /ˌ··· ˈ··/ an organization whose members try to protect people from being attacked or robbed, especially when they are travelling on underground railways in big cities. The first group was started in New York City, and there are groups in other US cities as well as in other countries. The members wear red BERETS (=flat cloth hats) and do their work without being paid. 守护天使〔保护人们免受袭击或抢劫的一个组织, 尤其是在大城市乘坐地铁之时。该组织最早成立于纽约市, 目前可见于美国其他城市乃至其他国家, 成员头戴红色贝雷帽, 义务工作〕

guard·i·an·ship /ˈgɑrdɪənˌʃɪp; ˈgɑːdiənʃɪp/ *n* [U] *law* the position of being legally responsible for someone else's child, or the period during which you have this position【法律】监护人的身份[期限]

guard·rail /ˈgɑrdˌrel; ˈgɑːd-reɪl/ *n* [C] **1** a bar or RAIL that is intended to prevent people from falling from a bridge or stairs〔桥或楼梯的〕护栏 **2** *especially AmE* a bar or RAIL¹ (1) intended to prevent drivers from going off the road in a car accident【尤美】〔防止汽车在交通事故中冲出公路的〕护栏

guard·room /ˈgɑrdˌrum; ˈgɑːd-rʊm/ *n* [C] a room, especially in a GUARDHOUSE, for soldiers who are guarding a military camp 卫兵室, 警卫室

Guards, the /gɑrdz; gɑːdz/ a group of REGIMENTS (=large groups of soldiers) in the British army, originally those who guarded the king or queen 近卫军, 近卫队〔英国陆军兵团。原指保护国王或女王的兵团〕

guards·man /ˈgɑrdzmən; ˈgɑːdzmən/ *n* [C] **1** a British soldier in the Guards (GUARD¹ (11))〔英国〕皇家卫队士兵, 御林军士兵 **2** a member of the US National Guard 美国国民警卫队士兵

guard's van /ˈ· ·/ *n* [C] *BrE* the part of a train where the official in charge of it travels, usually at the back【英】〔火车〕列车长车厢〔通常在列车尾〕; CABOOSE *AmE*【美】

Gua·te·ma·la /ˌgwɑtəˈmɑlə; ˌgwɑːtəˈmɑːlə/ a country in Central America, between the Pacific and Atlantic Oceans. Population: 12,974,000 (2001). Capital: Guatemala City. 危地马拉〔中美洲国家, 位于太平洋与大西洋之间。人口: 12,974,000 (2001), 首都: 危地马拉城〕—**Guatemalan** *n, adj*

Guatemala City /ˌ··ˌ··ˈ··/ the capital city of Guatemala 危地马拉城〔危地马拉首都〕

gua·va /ˈgwɑvə; ˈgwɑːvə/ *n* [C] a small tropical fruit with pink flesh and many seeds inside 番石榴〔一种小型热带水果〕

gu·ber·na·to·ri·al /ˌgjubərnəˈtɔrɪəl; ˌguːbənəˈtɔːriəl◂/ *adj formal* connected with the position of being a GOVERNOR【正式】州长的

gue·ril·la /gəˈrɪlə; gəˈrɪlə/ *n* [C] another spelling of GUERRILLA guerrilla 的另一种拼法

Guer·ni·ca /ˈgwɛrnɪkə; ˈgɜːnɪkə/ a town in the Basque area of northern Spain, which was destroyed by bombs dropped by German aircraft in 1937, during the Spanish Civil War. The picture called 'Guernica' painted by Pablo Picasso shows the destruction of the town. 格尔尼卡〔西班牙北部巴斯克地区一镇。该镇在 1937 年西班牙内战中被德军飞机炸毁, 毕加索的作品《格尔尼卡》展现了该镇遭遇残毁的景象〕

Guern·sey /ˈgɝnzɪ; ˈgɜːnzi/ an island in the English Channel near northwest France. Guernsey is one of the Channel Islands. It is popular for holidays and famous as a place where people pay very little tax. 根西岛〔英吉利海峡一岛屿, 邻近法国西北海岸, 属海峡群岛。该岛为度假胜地, 因纳税极少而闻名〕

G

guernsey *n* [C] a SWEATER made of wool with a special pattern of raised stitches across the shoulder〔肩部有用凸针编织的图案的〕毛衣

guer·ril·la /gəˈrɪlə; gəˈrɪlə/ *n* [C] a member of an unofficial military group, especially one fighting to remove a government from power, that attacks its enemies in small groups unexpectedly 游击队员: *guerrilla warfare* 游击战 —compare 比较 FREEDOM FIGHTER, TERRORIST

guess¹ /gɛs; ges/ *v* S1 W3

1 ▶WITHOUT BEING SURE 不确信◀ [I,T] to try to answer a question or make a judgment about something without having all the necessary facts, so that you are not sure whether you are correct 猜测: *I'd say he's around 50, but I'm only guessing.* 我想他大约 50 岁, 不过我只是猜测而已。| **guess what/who/how etc** *Guess how much I had to pay – 3,000 pounds!* 猜一猜我得付多少钱——3000 英镑! | **guess at** *We can only guess at what caused the crash.* 我们只能猜测这次空难的原因。

2 ▶GUESS CORRECTLY 正确猜出◀ [I,T] to guess something correctly 猜中, 猜对: **[+from]** *"How did you know I won?" "I just guessed from the look on your face."* "你怎么知道我赢了?" "我只是从你脸上的神色猜出来的。" | **guess that** *I'd never have guessed that you two were brothers.* 我绝对不可能猜出你们俩是兄弟。| **guess sth** *You've guessed my secret.* 你已经猜中了我的秘密。| **have guessed as much** (=have guessed something before someone tells you) 早猜中了 *He told me he was leaving, but I had already guessed as much.* 他告诉我他要走了, 但我事前猜测也是这样。

3 I guess *spoken especially AmE* used to mean that you suppose something is true or likely【口, 尤美】我想, 我认为〔用来表示你认为某事是真实的或很有可能〕: *I guess I never married because I just didn't find the right girl.* 我想我从来没结过婚是因为我找不到中意的女孩。| **I guess so/not** *"She wasn't happy?" "I guess not."* "她不高兴吗?" "我想她是不高兴。"

4 keep sb guessing to not tell someone what is going to happen next〔不告诉某人下一步将发生什么〕让某人捉摸不定

5 guess what/you'll never guess *spoken* used when you are about to tell someone something that will surprise them【口】猜猜看/你永远也猜不出: *Guess what! Bradley's resigned.* 你准

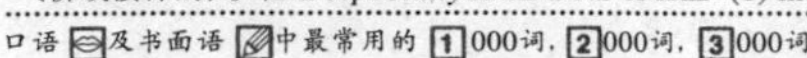

猜不到，布拉德利辞职了！| *You'll never guess who I saw today.* 你永远也猜不出我今天看见谁了。

guess² *n* [C] **1** an attempt to guess something 猜测: *If you're not sure of the answer give us your best guess.* 如果你对答案不确定，把你最有把握的猜测告诉我们。| *I'll give you three guesses.* 我让你猜三次。| **make a guess (at)** *I don't know the exact figure but I'll make a guess at it.* 我不知道准确的数字，不过我要猜测一下。| **rough guess** (=one that is unlikely to be exact) 粗略的猜测 *I'd say she's about 35, but that's only a rough guess.* 我说她大约35岁，不过那只是粗略的猜测而已。| **wild guess** (=one that is made without much thought) 乱猜 | **have a guess at** *BrE*【英】/ **take a guess at** *AmE*【美】(=try to guess something) 猜测 *Take a guess at what's in the third box and you could win a trip to Hawaii.* 猜猜第三个盒子装的是什么，你可能赢得去夏威夷旅游的机会。| **at a guess** *spoken* (=used to mean that what you are saying is just a guess)【口】凭猜测〔表示你所说的不过是一种猜测〕*The girl was twelve years old at a guess.* 我猜这个女孩有十二岁。**2** an opinion formed by guessing 猜想: **my guess is** *My guess is that there won't be many people there today.* 我猜今天那里不会有许多人。**3 be anybody's guess** to be something that no one knows 谁也不知道，谁也拿不准: *What she's going to do with her life now is anybody's guess.* 现在她的日子怎么过谁也不知道。**4 your guess is as good as mine** *spoken* used to tell someone that you do not know any more than they do about something【口】我跟你一样不知道

guess·ti·mate /ˈgɛstəˌmət; ˈgestɪ̥mɪ̥t/ *n* [C] *informal* an attempt to judge a quantity by guessing it【非正式】〔对某数量的全凭猜测的〕估计 —**guesstimate** /-təˌmet; -tɪ̥meɪt/ *v* [I,T]

Guess Who's Com·ing to Din·ner? /ˌ· · ˈ· · · ˈ· ·/ (1967) a US film about a white girl who invites her black boyfriend home to meet her parents. It was one of the first US films to deal with the subject of RACISM.《猜猜谁来吃晚餐》〔(1967)，美国影片，讲述一位白人姑娘邀请黑人男友回家见父母的故事。这是美国最早讨论种族问题的一部影片〕

guess·work /ˈgɛsˌwɝk; ˈgeswɜːk/ *n* [U] the method of trying to find the answer to something by guessing 猜测，推测: *In this study, scientific methods seem to have been replaced by guesswork.* 在这项研究里，科学的方法似乎被推测替代了。

guest¹ /gɛst; gest/ *n* [C]

1 ►AT YOUR HOUSE 在你家里◄ someone who is staying in someone else's home because they have been invited 客人，宾客: *We have guests staying with us.* 有客人住在我们家里。

2 ►AT A HOTEL 在旅馆◄ someone who is paying to stay in a hotel, GUESTHOUSE etc 旅客，宿客: *The hotel takes very good care of its guests.* 这家旅馆细心照料住宿的客人。

3 ►AT A RESTAURANT/CLUB 在餐馆/俱乐部◄ someone who is invited to a restaurant, theatre, club etc by another person who pays for them〔被邀请去餐馆、剧院、俱乐部由另一人请客的〕客人: *I'd like you to be my guest for dinner tonight.* 今天晚上我想请你吃饭。

4 ►ON A SHOW 演出◄ someone famous who is invited to take part in a show, concert etc, in addition to those who usually take part〔表演、音乐会等的〕特邀名演员[演奏者]: **make a guest appearance** *She is making her first guest appearance on the show.* 她在这场表演中作她的首次特邀演出。

5 be my guest *spoken* used to politely give someone permission to do what they have asked to do【口】请便〔用于礼貌地同意别人的请求〕: *"Do you mind if I look at your notes?" "Of course not. Be my guest."* "我想看一下你的笔记，你介意吗？""当然不介意，请便。"

6 guest of honour *BrE*【英】/**honor** *AmE*【美】the most important person who has been invited to a special occasion, especially a celebration that is given for them 贵宾

7 guest speaker someone who has been invited to make a speech at a meeting 特邀演讲人 —compare 比较 HOST¹ (1)

guest² *v* [I] to take part in a show, concert etc as a guest performer〔以特邀演员身份〕参加演出[音乐会等]

guest book /ˈ· ·/ *n* [C] a book in which everyone who comes to a formal occasion or stays at a hotel writes their name〔正式场合或旅馆的〕客人登记簿

guest·house /ˈgɛsthaus; ˈgesthaʊs/ *n* [C] a private house where people can pay to stay and have meals 家庭旅馆

> **CULTURAL NOTE 文化注释**
>
> Guesthouses are often used by people who are on holiday or working away from home and are usually cheaper than hotels. 度假或离家工作的人常住家庭旅馆。家庭旅馆通常比酒店便宜。

guest·room /ˈgɛstˌrum; ˈgest-rʊm/ *n* [C] a room in a private house that is kept for visitors to sleep in 客房〔指私人住宅中供客人使用的卧室〕

guest work·er /ˈ· ˌ··/ *n* [C] a foreign worker, usually from a poor country, working in another country for a limited period 外籍工人〔在另一国家短期工作的人，通常来自贫穷国家〕

Guevara, Ché —see 见 CHÉ GUEVARA

guff /gʌf; gʌf/ *n* [U] *informal* nonsense【非正式】胡说，废话: *Don't give me any of that guff.* 别跟我说那些废话了。

guf·faw /gʌˈfɔ; gəˈfɔː/ *v* [I] to laugh loudly 大笑 —**guffaw** *n* [C]: *A loud guffaw came from the back of the room.* 房间后部传来一阵大笑。

Gug·gen·heim Mu·se·um, the /ˈgugənhaɪm mjuˈziəm; ˈgʊgənhaɪm mjuːˈziːəm/ also 又作 **the Guggenheim** a MUSEUM in New York City that contains an important collection of modern art. It is named after the businessman who established it in 1939, Solomon R. Guggenheim, and is famous for its large circular building designed by Frank Lloyd Wright. In 1997 a new Guggenheim Museum, designed by Frank Gehry, was opened in Bilbao, Spain. 古根海姆博物馆〔纽约市一博物馆，馆藏一系列重要现代艺术品。该馆创建于1939年，以创建人所罗门·R. 古根海姆的名字命名。博物馆以弗兰克·劳埃德·赖特设计的大型圆形建筑著称。1997年，西班牙毕尔巴鄂新开了一个古根海姆博物馆，由弗兰克·盖里设计〕

guid·ance /ˈgaɪdn̩s; ˈgaɪdəns/ *n* [U] **1** help and advice given to someone about their work, education, personal life etc 指导，引导: [**+on/about**] *I went to a career counselor for guidance on how to start my job search.* 我到一位就业顾问那里去讨教如何开始找工作。**2** the process of directing a MISSILE (1) in flight〔飞行中导弹的〕制导（过程）: *electronic guidance systems* 电子制导系统

guidance coun·sel·or /ˈ· · ˌ···/ *n* [C] *AmE* someone employed in a school to give advice to students about what subjects to study and to help them with personal problems【美】辅导员〔指学校中就如何选课及个人问题向学生提供指导的人员〕—see also 另见 MARRIAGE GUIDANCE

guide¹ /gaɪd; gaɪd/ *n* [C]

1 ►PERSON 人◄ a) someone who shows you the way to a place, especially someone whose job is to show a place to tourists 向导；导游: *a tour guide* 导游 **b)** someone who advises you and influences the way you live and behave 指导者，引导者: *The medicine man was the tribe's spiritual guide.* 巫医是这个部落的精神指导。

2 ►FOR JUDGING STH 用于判断某事◄ something that provides information on which you can base your judgement, or your method of doing something〔判断或行事的〕根据: [**+to**] *The opinion polls are not a very reliable guide to how people will vote.* 根据这些民意测验来判断人们将如何投票，并不很可靠。

3 ►BOOK 书◄ a) a book that provides information on a particular subject or explains how to do something; HANDBOOK 指南；手册: [**+to**] *a guide to North American birds* 北美鸟类指南 **b)** a guidebook 旅行指南

4 ►GIRL 女孩◄ *BrE*【英】**a) the Guides** the Guides Association, which trains girls in practical skills and tries to develop their character 女童子军 **b)** a member of the Guides Association 女童子军成员

> **CULTURAL NOTE 文化注释**
>
> Originally established by **Agnes**, sister of Lord Baden-Powell, and including a junior section (the Brownie Guides), the Guides is an international movement recognizable by its uniform and known for its aim of developing good citizenship among its members. 女童子军协会最早由巴登-鲍威尔勋爵的妹妹艾格尼丝创建，包括幼年女童子军 (Brownie Guides)。该协会是一个国际性组织，有统一制服，目的是在成员当中推广良好的公民品行。

guide² *v* [T] **1** to take someone through or to a place that you know very well, showing them the way 带领，引导: [**+along/through/to etc**] *He guided us through the narrow streets to the central mosque.* 他带领我们穿过狭窄的街道，来到中央清真寺。**2** to help someone to move in a particular direction 为…引路: *She took her friend's arm to guide her.* 她挽着朋友的胳膊，为她引路。**3** to strongly influence someone's behaviour, thoughts etc 强烈影响〔行为、思想等〕: *He let himself be guided by his mother's opinion.* 他任由自己为母亲的观点所左右。**4** to show someone the right way to do something, especially something difficult or complicated 指引，指导〔尤指做困难或复杂的事〕: **guide sb through** *We need a lawyer to guide us through the*

procedure. 我们需要一位律师来指导我们完成这一手续。—see also 另见 GUIDING —see 见 LEAD[1] (USAGE)

guide·book /ˈgaɪd͵bʊk; ˈgaɪdbʊk/ *n* [C] a special book about a city, area etc that gives details about the place and its history〔关于城市、地区等的〕旅行指南

guided mis·sile /͵‥ ˈ‥/ *n* [C] a MISSILE (1) that can be controlled electronically while it is flying 导弹

guide dog /ˈ· ͵·/ *n* [C] *BrE* a dog trained to guide a blind person【英】导盲犬; SEEING EYE DOG *AmE*【美】

guided tour /͵‥ ˈ·/ *n* [C] a trip around a city, building etc led by someone who tells people about the place 有导游的游览: *a guided tour of the palace* 有导游引领的对这座宫殿的游览

guide·lines /ˈgaɪd͵laɪnz; ˈgaɪdlaɪnz/ *n* [plural] official instructions about the best way to do something, especially something that could be difficult or dangerous〔尤指可能是困难或危险的事的〕指导方针, 行动准则: **[+for/on]** *Staff have been issued with new guidelines for dealing with infectious patients.* 全体职员都发给了处理感染病人的新规定。

guid·ing /ˈgaɪdɪŋ; ˈgaɪdɪŋ/ *adj* **guiding principle/star/light** a principle, idea, or person that you follow in order to help you decide what you should do in a difficult situation 指导原则/指路星/指路明灯〔在困境中处理问题所遵循的原则、观念或所遵从的人物〕

Guiding Light /͵‥ ˈ·/ a US television SOAP OPERA, which began as a radio show in 1937 and moved on to television in 1952, and is now the longest running DRAMA. It tells of the lives of people who live in the FICTIONAL town of Springfield.《指路明灯》〔美国一电视肥皂剧, 1937年首先在电台播出, 1952年搬上电视, 现在是连续播出时间最长的一个剧。该剧讲述虚拟小镇斯普林菲尔德上人们的生活〕

guild /gɪld; gɪld/ *n* [C] **1** an organization of people who do the same job, who joined together in the past to help each other improve their businesses 同业公会; 行会 **2** a group of people with the same interest 协会: *the Women's Guild* 妇女协会

guil·der /ˈgɪldɚ; ˈgɪldə/ *n* [C] the former standard unit of money in the Netherlands; GULDEN 盾〔原荷兰货币单位〕

guild·hall /ˈgɪldˋhɔl; ͵gɪldˈhɔːl/ *n* [C] a large building in which members of a guild met in the past 行会[同业公会]会馆

guile /gaɪl; gaɪl/ *n* [U] *formal* the use of clever dishonest methods to deceive someone【正式】施诡计, 欺骗 —**guileful** *adj*

guile·less /ˈgaɪllɪs; ˈgaɪl-ləs/ *adj* behaving in an honest way, without trying to hide anything or deceive people 诚实无欺的 —**guilelessly** *adv* —**guilelessness** *n* [U]

guil·le·mot /ˈgɪlə͵mɑt; ˈgɪlǀmɒt/ *n* [C] a black and white sea bird with a narrow beak 海鸠

guil·lo·tine[1] /ˈgɪlə͵tin; ˈgɪlətiːn/ *n* [C] **1** a piece of equipment used to cut off the heads of criminals, especially in France in the past〔尤指法国以前使用的〕断头台 **2** a piece of equipment used to cut large sheets of paper 切纸机, 裁切机 **3** *BrE* the setting of a time limit on the discussion about a proposed law in the British parliament【英】〔英国议会〕对一项法律议案进行讨论的时限的规定

guillotine[2] *v* [T] **1** to cut off someone's head using a guillotine 在断头台上将…斩首 **2** *BrE* to limit the period of time allowed for the discussion of a proposed law in the British parliament【英】〔英国议会〕限制〔对一项法律议案进行讨论的时间〕

guilt /gɪlt; gɪlt/ *n* [U] **1** a strong feeling of shame and sadness because you have done something that you know is wrong 内疚, 自责: **[+about/at]** *Don't you have any feelings of guilt about leaving David?* 你离开大卫难道没有任何内疚感吗? | **sense of guilt** *He felt an enormous sense of guilt when he thought about how he'd treated her.* 他想到自己当时那样对待她, 感到非常内疚。**2** the fact of having broken an official law or moral rule 犯罪: *an admission of guilt* 承认有罪 | *It is up to the prosecution to establish the defendant's guilt.* 控方有责任证实被告有罪。**3** responsibility and blame for something bad that has happened 责任, 罪责: *The teacher said Sonia was impossible to control and that the guilt lay with her parents.* 老师说索尼娅根本不受人管教, 责任可归咎于她的父母。**4 guilt trip** a feeling of guilt about something 负疚感: **lay/put a guilt trip on sb** *AmE informal* (=make someone feel guilty about something)【美, 非正式】使某人感到内疚

guilt·less /ˈgɪltlɪs; ˈgɪltləs/ *adj* not responsible for a crime or for having done something wrong; INNOCENT[1] (1) 无罪的, 无辜的 —**guiltlessly** *adv*

guilt-rid·den /ˈ· ͵‥/ *adj* feeling so guilty about something that you cannot think about anything else 受内疚感折磨而不能自已的

guilt·y /ˈgɪltɪ; ˈgɪlti/ *adj* **guiltier, guiltiest** S2 W3

1 ►ASHAMED 羞愧的◄ feeling very ashamed and sad because you have done something that is wrong 羞愧的, 内疚的: **[+about]** *I feel really guilty about forgetting her birthday again.* 我又忘记了她的生日, 对此我确实感到内疚。| **guilty conscience** *My guilty conscience got the better of me, and I went back to apologize.* 我无法抑制内疚的心情, 便回去道歉。

2 ►OF A CRIME 关于罪行的◄ having done something that is a crime 犯有罪行的, 有罪的: **guilty of** *The jury found her guilty of murder.* 陪审团裁定她的谋杀罪名成立。| **plead guilty** *law* (=admit in a court of law that you are guilty)【法律】在法庭上认罪 | **not guilty** *law* (=not guilty of the offence you are charged with in a court of law)【法律】无罪的〔指并未犯有在法庭上被指控的罪行〕—opposite 反义词 INNOCENT[1] (1)

3 responsible for behaviour that is morally or socially unacceptable〔对道德败坏、社会唾弃的行为〕负有责任的: **guilty of doing sth** *Lately the press has been guilty of reporting scandal in order to sell papers.* 报界近来为了销售报纸而报道丑闻, 自取其咎。

4 guilty party *formal* the person who has done something illegal or wrong【正式】犯罪的一方, 有过错的一方 —**guiltily** *adv* —**guiltiness** *n* [U]

This graph shows some of the words most commonly used with the adjective **guilty**. 本图表所示为含有形容词 guilty 的一些最常用词语。

Based on the British National Corpus and the Longman Lancaster Corpus
据英国国家语料库和朗文兰开斯特语料库

Guin·ea /ˈgɪnɪ; ˈgɪni/ a country in West Africa between Senegal and Sierra Leone. Population: 7,614,000 (2001). Capital: Conakry. Guinea used to belong to France. 几内亚〔西非一国, 位于塞内加尔和塞拉利昂之间。人口: 7,614,000 (2001), 首都: 科纳克里。该国曾是法国属地〕—**Guinean** *n, adj*

guinea *n* [C] a British gold coin or unit of money used in the past, worth £1.05 几尼〔英国旧时的一种金币或货币单位, 合 1.05 英镑〕

Guinea-Bis·sau /͵gɪnɪ bɪˋsaʊ; ͵gɪni bɪˈsaʊ/ a small country in West Africa between Guinea and Senegal. Population: 1,316,000 (2001). Capital: Bissau. Guinea-Bissau used to belong to Portugal. 几内亚比绍〔西非一小国, 位于几内亚和塞内加尔之间。人口: 1,316,000 (2001), 首都: 比绍。该国曾是葡萄牙属地〕

guinea fowl /ˈ‥ ͵·/ *n* [C] a grey African bird that is often used for food 珍珠鸡〔常供食用的一种非洲灰色禽类〕

guinea pig /ˈ‥ ͵·/ *n* [C] **1** a small round animal that has fur, short ears, and no tail, which is kept as a pet 天竺鼠, 豚鼠〔一种小型宠物〕**2** someone who is used in a scientific test to see how successful or safe a new product, system etc is 供科学实验的人〔为试验某产品、系统等的效果〕

Guin·e·vere /ˈgwɪnɪvɪr; ˈgwɪnǀvɪə/ the wife of King Arthur in old stories, who had a sexual relationship with Sir Lancelot 圭尼维尔〔古老传说中亚瑟王之妻, 曾与朗斯洛爵士有奸情〕

Guin·ness /ˈgɪnɪs; ˈgɪnǀs/ *trademark* a type of STOUT (=a strong dark beer), originally made in Ireland, which has a creamy white FROTH on top of it when it is poured into a glass【商标】吉尼斯黑啤〔原产于爱尔兰的一种啤酒, 倒入杯中时会泛起乳白色的泡沫〕

Guinness, Sir Al·ec /ˈælɪk; ˈælǀk/ (1914-2000) a British actor in films and in the theatre, whose best-known films are *The Bridge on the River Kwai* (1957), *Lawrence of Arabia* (1962) and *Star Wars* (1977) 吉尼斯〔(1914-2000), 英国电影和戏剧演员。他演出的著名影片有《桂河大桥》(1957)、《阿拉伯的劳伦斯》(1962) 和《星球大战》(1977)〕

Guinness Book of Rec·ords, The /͵‥ ‥ ˈ‥ ·/ *trademark* a book produced every year, which contains facts about people, events, and things that are the biggest, fastest, longest, shortest etc【商标】《吉尼斯世界纪录大全》〔每年出版的记录世界之最的一部全书〕

guise /gaɪz; gaɪz/ *n* [C] *formal* the appearance of something that makes it seem different from how it really is, especially in order to deceive someone【正式】装扮过的外表, 伪装: **in/un-**

der the guise of *Advertising material was given to us under the guise of information.* 广告材料被伪装成资讯送到我们这里。| **in a different guise** *It's just the same set of ideas in a different guise.* 这还是老一套的想法，只是形式不同而已。

3 **gui·tar** /gɪˋtɑr; gɪˈtɑː/ *n* [C] a musical instrument that has six strings and is played by plucking (PLUCK[1] (5)) the strings 吉他 —**guitarist** *n* [C]

gu·lag /ˊgulæg; ˈguːlæg/ *n* [C] one of a group of prison camps in the former USSR, where conditions were very bad 古拉格〔前苏联劳改营〕

gulch /gʌltʃ; gʌltʃ/ *n* [C] *AmE* a narrow deep valley formed by flowing water, but usually dry【美】〔由流水冲刷形成，通常已经干涸的〕峡谷，沟壑

gul·den /ˊguldən; ˈgʊldən/ *n* [C] a GUILDER 荷兰盾

3 **gulf** /gʌlf; gʌlf/ *n* [C] **1** a large area of sea partly enclosed by land 海湾: *the Gulf of Mexico* 墨西哥湾 **2** a great difference and lack of understanding between two groups of people, especially in their beliefs, opinions, and way of life 鸿沟，分歧，隔阂: **[+between]** *The gulf between management and unions is as wide as ever.* 管理层和工会之间的分歧依旧严重。**3** a deep hollow place in the Earth's surface; CHASM (1)〔地球表面的〕深坑，深渊

Gulf of Mex·i·co, the /ˌ· · ˈ· · ·/ an area of the Atlantic Ocean south of the US, east of Mexico, and west of Cuba 墨西哥湾〔大西洋的一部分，位于美国以南，墨西哥以东，古巴以西〕

Gulf States, the /ˈ· ˌ·/ **1** the small Arab countries on the Gulf, all of which produce oil and gas. These are Bahrain, Kuwait, Qatar, and the United Arab Emirates. 海湾国家〔包括巴林、科威特、卡塔尔和阿拉伯联合酋长国。这些国家出产石油和天然气〕 **2** *AmE* the US states whose coasts are on the Gulf of Mexico. These are Alabama, Florida, Louisiana, Mississippi, and Texas.【美】墨西哥湾诸州〔包括亚拉巴马、佛罗里达、路易斯安那、密西西比和得克萨斯〕

Gulf Stream /ˈ· ·/ *n* [singular] a current of warm water that flows northeastward in the Atlantic Ocean from the Gulf of Mexico towards Europe 墨西哥湾流〔大西洋中从墨西哥湾向东北流向欧洲的暖流〕

Gulf War, the /ˌ· ˈ·/ a war which began in 1991, after Iraq attacked Kuwait and took control of it. A United Nations force led by the US, and including soldiers from Saudi Arabia, Egypt, the UK, and France, attacked Iraq and forced the Iraqi army out of Kuwait. 海湾战争〔始于1991年伊拉克侵占科威特之后的一场战争。以美国为首的联合国多国部队，其中包括沙特阿拉伯、埃及、英国和法国，对伊拉克进行打击，迫使伊拉克撤出科威特〕

Gulf War Syn·drome /ˌ· ˈ· ˌ· ·/ one or more illnesses suffered by soldiers who fought in the Gulf War, which some people believe may have been caused by chemicals or drugs used in the war. The most common illnesses are head pains, damage to the memory, and permanent tiredness. 海湾战争综合征〔参加过海湾战争的士兵所患的一种或多种疾病，据说是由战争中使用的化学物质或药物引起的。最常见的病症是头痛、记忆损伤和永久性疲劳〕

gull[1] /gʌl; gʌl/ *n* [C] **1** a large common black and white sea bird that lives near the sea; SEAGULL 海鸥 **2** *literary* someone who is easily deceived【文】易受骗的人

gull[2] *v* [T] *old use* to cheat or deceive someone【旧】欺骗，诈骗

gul·let /ˊgʌlɪt; ˈgʌlɪ̈t/ *n* [C] the tube through which food goes down your throat 食管

gul·ley /ˊgʌlɪ; ˈgʌli/ *n* [C] another spelling of GULLY gully 的另一种拼法

gul·li·ble /ˊgʌləbḷ; ˈgʌlɪ̈bəl/ *adj* too ready to believe what other people tell you, so that you are easily deceived 轻信的，易受骗上当的: *Plastic replicas were sold to gullible tourists as ancient relics.* 塑料复制品被当作古代文物卖给了轻信的游客。—**gullibly** *adv* —**gullibility** /ˌgʌləˋbɪlətɪ; ˌgʌlɪ̈ˈbɪlɪ̈ti/ *n* [U]

Gul·li·ver's Trav·els /ˌgʌlɪvəz ˋtrævḷz; ˌgʌlɪ̈vəz ˈtrævəlz/ (1726) a book by Jonathan Swift which is a SATIRE (=a humorous criticism) on Britain in the 18th century. Each of the imaginary lands that the main character Gulliver visits shows how unreasonable the British government, British customs, wars etc really are. The most famous part of the book is Gulliver's visit to the country of Lilliput, where all the people and buildings are very small.《格利佛游记》〔(1726)，乔森纳·斯威夫特创作的一部讽刺18世纪英国的小说。从主人公格利佛去过的每一处虚构的地方可以看出，英国政府、英国的习俗、战争等非常不合乎情理。小说最有名的部分是格利佛游历小人国〕

gul·ly /ˊgʌlɪ; ˈgʌli/ *n* [C] **1** a small narrow valley, usually formed by a lot of rain flowing down the side of a hill〔山坡上被雨水冲成的〕隘谷，沟壑 **2** a deep DITCH[1] 深沟

gulp[1] /gʌlp; gʌlp/ *v* **1** [T] also 又作 **gulp** sth ↔ **down** to swallow something quickly 快速吞下: *She gulped down the rest of her coffee and left.* 她匆匆喝掉剩下的咖啡便离开了。**2** [T] also 又作 **gulp** sth ↔ **in** to take in quick large breaths of air 大口吸气: *We rushed outside and gulped in the sweet fresh air.* 我们跑到外面大口呼吸甘甜的新鲜空气。**3** [I] to swallow suddenly because you are surprised or nervous〔因惊讶或紧张〕倒吸气: *I gulped when I saw the bill.* 我看到账单时倒吸一口气。

gulp sth ↔ **back** *phr v* [T] to stop yourself from expressing your feelings 抑制，忍住〔自己的感情〕: *Sandra tried to gulp back her tears.* 桑德拉竭力忍住泪水。

gulp[2] *n* [C] an act of gulping 吞咽: **take a gulp** *He took a gulp and handed the cup back to Rachel.* 他喝了一大口，然后把杯子递还给雷切尔。| **in one gulp/at a gulp** *I've seen him swallow a whole glass of vodka in one gulp.* 我见过他把整杯伏特加酒一饮而尽。

gum[1] /gʌm; gʌm/ *n* **1** [C usually plural 一般用复数] one of the two areas of firm pink flesh at the top and bottom of your mouth, in which your teeth are fixed 齿龈 —see picture at 参见 TEETH 图 **2** [U] CHEWING GUM 口香糖 **3** [U] a sticky substance found in the stems of some trees 树胶 **4** [U] *BrE* a special kind of glue used to stick light things such as paper together【英】黏胶 **5** [C] a GUM TREE 桉树 **6 by gum!** *spoken old-fashioned* used to express surprise【口，过时】哎哟!〔表示惊讶〕

gum[2] *v* **gummed, gumming** [T always+adv/prep] *BrE* to stick something to something else, using a sticky substance【英】〔用胶〕粘住: **gum sth to/down etc** *A large label had been gummed to the back of the photograph.* 一张大标签被粘贴在照片的背后。

gum sth ↔ **up** *phr v* [T] *informal* to prevent something from working properly by covering it with a sticky substance【非正式】搞糟; 使出故障〔由于黏性物质覆盖而不能正常工作〕: *Dirt had got inside the watch and gummed up the works.* 污垢进了手表里面，使机件不能正常工作。

gum·ball /ˊgʌmbɔl; ˈgʌmbɔːl/ *n* [C] *AmE* CHEWING GUM in the form of a small round brightly coloured sweet【美】彩色圆形口香糖

gum·bo /ˊgʌmbo; ˈgʌmbəʊ/ *n* [U] **1** a thick soup made with meat, fish, and OKRA (=a small green vegetable) 秋葵汤〔用肉、鱼和秋葵制作的很稠的汤〕 **2** a word used in some parts of the US for OKRA 秋葵〔此词使用于美国某些地区〕

gum·boil /ˊgʌmˌbɔɪl; ˈgʌmbɔɪl/ *n* [C] a painful swelling on your GUM[1] (1); ABSCESS 齿龈脓肿

gum·boot /ˊgʌmˌbut; ˈgʌmbuːt/ *n* [C] *BrE old-fashioned* a tall boot made of rubber worn to keep your feet dry【英，过时】长统橡胶靴

gum·drop /ˊgʌmˌdrɑp; ˈgʌmdrɒp/ *n* [C] a firm transparent sweet that is like JELLY 橡皮糖〔胶冻状的透明糖食〕

gum·my /ˊgʌmɪ; ˈgʌmi/ *adj* **1** sticky or covered in GUM[1] (3) 黏性的，涂胶的 **2** a gummy smile shows the gums (GUM[1] (1)) in your mouth 露齿龈的〔微笑〕

gump·tion /ˊgʌmpʃən; ˈgʌmpʃən/ *n* [U] the ability and determination to decide what needs doing and to do it 精明，魄力，勇气: *He probably didn't even have enough gumption to propose to her.* 他可能连向她求婚的勇气都没有。

gum·shoe /ˊgʌmˋʃu; ˈgʌmˌʃuː/ *n* [C] *AmE old-fashioned* a DETECTIVE【美，过时】侦探

gum tree /ˈ· ·/ *n* [C] **1** a tall tree which produces a strong-smelling oil used in medicine; EUCALYPTUS 桉树 **2 be up a gum tree** *BrE informal* to be in a very difficult situation【英，非正式】陷入困境

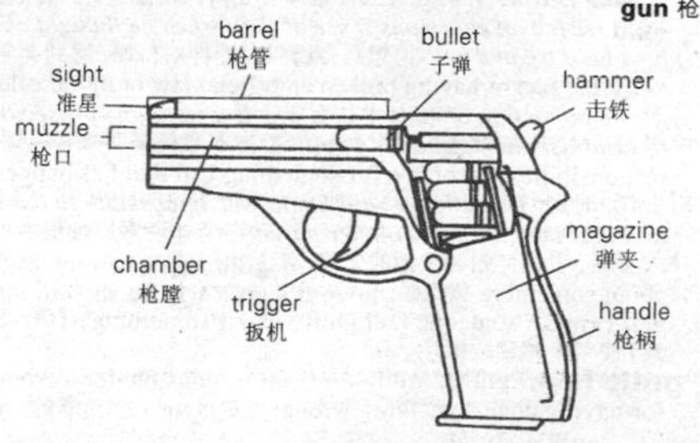

gun[1] /gʌn; gʌn/ *n* [C] **1** a weapon from which bullets or SHELLS[1] (3) are fired 枪，炮 **2** a tool used to send out a liquid, such as

paint, GREASE[1] (2), or glue, by pressure 喷射器, 喷射枪〔供喷射诸如油漆、油脂或胶水的工具〕—see also 另见 FLASHGUN, SPRAY GUN **3** *AmE informal* someone who is temporarily put in a position to do a particular job【美, 非正式】被临时安排做某项工作的人: *He was the sixth gun on the job.* 他是被临时安排做这份工作的第六个人。**4 hired gun** *AmE informal* someone who is paid to shoot someone else【美, 非正式】〔被雇佣来射杀某人的〕杀手, 刺客, 枪手 —see also 另见 SON OF A GUN, **stick to your guns** (STICK[1] (7)), **jump the gun** (JUMP[1] (11)), **go great guns** (GREAT (7)), **spike sb's guns** (SPIKE[2] (4))

CULTURAL NOTE 文化注释

Gun Culture in the UK In the UK, crimes involving guns greatly increased in the 1990s, especially in the poorer areas of cities such as London, Manchester, and Birmingham. Many murders involving guns are connected with fights between GANG*s*, and this is often related to drug DEAL*ing*. A series of murders in 2002 made many people very worried about the problem of gun crime. 英国的枪支文化: 英国涉及枪支的犯罪在20世纪90年代激增, 伦敦、曼彻斯特、伯明翰等城市的贫民区尤其如此。很多持枪杀人案与帮派火并有关, 常涉及毒品交易。2002年发生的一系列谋杀令很多人非常担心枪支犯罪问题。

The police have taken measures to try to reduce gun crime, for example arranging gun amnesties (AMNESTY) which allow people who have guns to give them to the police without being PROSECUTE*d*. After someone has been shot, it is often very difficult for the police to find WITNESS*es* because people are frightened of reporting crimes COMMITT*ed* (=done) by people from their own community. 警方采取措施试图减少枪支犯罪, 如发布枪支赦免令, 允许持枪者向警方上交枪支而不会被起诉。有人遭枪击身亡后, 警方一般很难找到目击证人, 因为人们不敢告发本地社区居民的犯罪行为。

Gun Culture in the US In the US, many ordinary people own guns, and most people who own guns say they have them to protect themselves or to HUNT with. People who own guns say that the Constitution of the US gives them the right to have a gun, because it says that people should have a 'right to bear arms'. The National Rifle Association (NRA) is a very strong organization which supports ordinary citizens owning guns and often tries to prevent any laws which would limit people buying or owning guns. There are laws about who is allowed to buy a gun, and most states have a law that says someone who is buying a gun must wait a particular number of days between paying for the gun and being allowed to have it. 美国的枪支文化: 很多普通美国人拥有枪支。很多持有枪支的人声称, 他们用枪自卫或打猎。持枪者说, 美国宪法给予他们拥有枪支的权利, 因为宪法上写着公民有"携带武器的自由"。美国全国步枪协会是个影响很大的组织, 它支持普通公民拥有枪支, 极力反对法律限制公民购买和拥有枪支。有一些法律规定什么人可以购买枪支, 大多数州的法律规定: 购买枪支者须在付款之后、获准拿到枪支前等候一段时间。

Many people in the US are either murdered or killed accidentally by guns each year. Murders are often related to crimes committed with guns or to gang activity. There have been a number of times when young people have shot other children at school, and the worst case of this was at Columbine High School in Colorado. Americans were very shocked by these events. A lot of Americans want stronger laws against people owning guns, and think that it is still too easy to buy guns. Some laws have been passed which limit the types of guns people are allowed to buy, and many people would like to make these laws even stronger. However, powerful groups such as the NRA argue against doing this, and say that only criminals would then have guns. People who want to keep owning guns also often say that "Guns don't kill people. People kill people." 每年有很多美国人死于枪杀, 或被谋杀, 或被误杀。谋杀案经常与持枪犯罪或帮派活动有关。发生过好多次校园枪击案, 最严重的一次发生在科罗拉多州科伦比纳高中。美国民众对这些事件十分震惊。很多美国人希望制定更严格的法律限制人们持有枪支, 他们认为现在购买枪支仍太过容易。一些法律已获通过, 规定人们可以购买什么类型的枪支, 很多人希望这些法律更加严厉。不过, 全国步枪协会反对这样做, 声称那样将导致只有罪犯才有枪可用。想要继续持有枪支的人也常说: "杀人的不是枪, 而是人。"

gun² *v* **1** [T] *AmE informal* to make the engine of a car go very fast by pressing the ACCELERATOR (1) very hard【美, 非正式】加速, 猛踩油门: **gun it** (=make a car go fast) 使汽车加速行驶 **2 be gunning for sb** *BrE informal* to be trying to find an opportunity to criticize or harm someone【英, 非正式】伺机批评[加害]: *Ever since I proved he'd made a mistake in the accounts he's been gunning for me.* 自从我证实他的账目有错后, 他一直在寻找机会加害于我。

gun sb ↔ **down** *phr v* [T] to shoot someone and badly injure or kill them, especially someone who cannot defend themselves 用枪击伤; 击毙〔尤指不能自卫的人〕: *Innocent civilians were gunned down in the street.* 无辜的平民被枪击倒在街上。

gun·boat /ˈgʌnˌbot; ˈgʌnbəʊt/ *n* [C] **1** a small military ship that is used near a coast〔海岸〕炮艇 **2 gunboat diplomacy** the practice of threatening to use force against another country to make them agree to your demands 炮舰外交〔指用武力威胁使另一国家屈从的做法〕

gun car·riage /ˈ· ˌ··/ *n* [C] a frame with wheels on which a heavy gun is moved around 炮架

gun con·trol /ˈ· ·ˌ·/ *n* [U] laws that restrict the possession and use of guns 枪支管制法

gun dog /ˈ· ·/ *n* [C] a dog trained to find and bring back dead birds shot for sport 猎狗〔指受过训练能寻找并带回被射杀禽鸟的犬〕; BIRD DOG *AmE*【美】

gun·fight /ˈgʌnfaɪt; ˈgʌnfaɪt/ *n* [C] a fight between people using guns 枪战, 炮战 —**gunfighter** *n* [C]

CULTURAL NOTE 文化注释

The STEREOTYPE of a gunfight in an old WESTERN film is of two men who stand in an empty street facing each other. The one who is 'quickest on the draw' (=fastest at taking out his gun and shooting) usually wins. 旧时西部电影中枪战的典型场景是: 两个男人在空无一人的街道上相对而立, 拔枪最快的人通常取胜。

gun·fire /ˈgʌnˌfaɪr; ˈgʌnfaɪə/ *n* [U] the repeated firing of guns, or the noise made by this 炮火; 炮火声: *enemy gunfire* 敌人的炮火

gunge¹ /gʌndʒ; gʌndʒ/ *n* [U] *BrE informal* any substance that is dirty, sticky, or unpleasant; GUNK[1]【英, 非正式】污秽[黏性或讨厌]的东西 —**gungy** *adj*

gunge² *v* **be gunged up with sth** *BrE informal* to be blocked with a dirty sticky substance【英, 非正式】被〔肮脏黏糊的东西〕堵塞

gung-ho /ˌgʌŋˈho; ˌgʌŋˈhəʊ/ *adj informal* very eager to do something, especially too eager【非正式】非常急切的, 莽撞的, 操之过急的: *His gung-ho attitude was not appropriate for such delicate negotiations.* 他那急切的态度在这种微妙的谈判中是不适宜的。

gunk¹ /gʌŋk; gʌŋk/ *n* [U] *informal* any substance that is dirty, sticky, or unpleasant【非正式】污秽[黏性或讨厌]的东西; GUNGE[1] *BrE*【英】: *The milk congealed into a black gunk on the stove.* 牛奶在炉子上凝结成一块黑色黏糊糊的东西。—**gunky** *adj*

gunk² *v* **be gunked up (with)** *AmE informal* to be blocked with a dirty sticky substance【美, 非正式】被〔黏性的脏东西〕堵塞: *Here's your problem. The fuel line's all gunked up.* 问题出在这里。输油管全给污垢堵塞了。

gun·man /ˈgʌnˌmæn; ˈgʌnmən/ *n* [C] a criminal or TERRORIST who uses a gun 持枪歹徒; 恐怖分子

gun·met·al /ˈgʌnˌmɛtl; ˈgʌnˌmetl/ *n* [U] a dull grey coloured metal which is a mixture of COPPER (1), TIN[1] (1), and ZINC 炮铜〔暗灰色的铜、锡、锌的合金〕

gun·nel /ˈgʌnl; ˈgʌnl/ *n* [C] a GUNWALE 舷缘, 舷边

gun·ner /ˈgʌnə; ˈgʌnə/ *n* [C] **1** a soldier, sailor etc whose job is to aim or fire a large gun〔陆军、海军的〕炮手 **2** a soldier in the British ARTILLERY (=part of the army which uses heavy guns)〔英国炮兵部队中的〕炮兵: *Gunner Smith* 炮兵史密斯

gun·ner·y /ˈgʌnərɪ; ˈgʌnəri/ *n* [U] the science and practice of shooting with heavy guns 重炮射击术, 重炮射击操作: *a gunnery officer* 重炮射击军官

gun·ny·sack /ˈgʌnɪsæk; ˈgʌnisæk/ *n* [C] *AmE* a large bag made from HEMP, in which coal, potatoes etc are stored【美】〔装贮煤、马铃薯等用的〕黄麻袋

gun·point /ˈgʌnˌpɔɪnt; ˈgʌnpɔɪnt/ *n* **at gunpoint** while threatening or being threatened with a gun 用枪威胁, 在枪口威胁下: *The frightened clerk was forced at gunpoint to hand over all the money.* 惊恐的职员在枪口威胁下被迫把所有的钱交出去。

gun·pow·der /ˈgʌnˌpaudə; ˈgʌnˌpaʊdə/ *n* [U] an explosive substance in the form of a powder 火药

G

Gunpowder Plot, the /ˈ··· ,·/ a plan by English Catholics led by Guy Fawkes to kill King James I and destroy Parliament by blowing it up with explosives on November 5th 1605. The plan failed when one of the Catholics warned a relative not to attend Parliament that day and all the people in the Plot were caught and killed. People in the UK remember the event every November 5th on Guy Fawkes' Night. 火药阴谋案〔指1605年11月5日盖伊·福克斯带领英格兰天主教徒企图炸死国王詹姆斯一世、炸毁议会大厦的计划。当时，一名同伙提醒其亲戚那天不要出席议会，计划由此败露。参与这场阴谋的人最后全被抓获并处决。每年11月5日的盖伊·福克斯之夜就是纪念这一事件〕

gun·run·ning /ˈ·,··/ *n* [U] the activity of taking guns into a country secretly and illegally, especially so that they can be used by people who want to fight against their government 私运军火〔秘密非法带入某国以供反政府分子使用〕—**gun-runner** *n* [C]

gun·ship /ˈgʌn,ʃɪp; ˈgʌnʃɪp/ *n* [C] a military HELICOPTER used to protect other helicopters and to destroy enemy guns 武装直升机

gun·shot /ˈgʌn,ʃɑt; ˈgʌnʃɒt/ *n* **1** [C] the sound made when a gun is fired 枪炮声 **2** [U] the bullets fired from a gun〔枪射出的〕子弹: **gunshot wound** (=a wound caused by a bullet) 枪伤 **3 out of/within gunshot** beyond or within the distance that can be reached by a shot fired from a gun 超出枪射程/在枪射程之内

gun-shy /ˈ· ·/ *adj* **1** a GUN DOG that is gun-shy is easily frightened by the noise of a gun〔猎狗〕易被枪声惊吓的 **2** *AmE* very careful or frightened about doing something, because of a bad experience in the past【美】〔因过去失败的经历而〕非常谨慎的，提心吊胆的

gun·sling·er /ˈgʌn,slɪŋɚ; ˈgʌn,slɪŋə/ *n* [C] *AmE* someone who is very skilful at using guns, especially a criminal【美】熟练的枪手〔尤指罪犯〕

gun·smith /ˈgʌn,smɪθ; ˈgʌn,smɪθ/ *n* [C] someone who makes and repairs guns 枪炮匠

gun·wale /ˈgʌnl̩; ˈgʌnl/ *n* [C] *technical* the upper edge of the side of a boat or small ship【术语】舷缘，舷边

gup·py /ˈgʌpɪ; ˈgʌpi/ *n plural* **guppies** [C] a small brightly-coloured tropical fish 虹鳉，孔雀鱼〔一种小型色彩亮丽热带鱼〕

gur·gle¹ /ˈgɝgl; ˈgɜːgəl/ *v* [I] **1** if something such as a stream gurgles, it makes a low sound, like water flowing through a pipe〔溪水等〕汩汩作响 **2** if a baby gurgles, it makes this kind of sound in its throat〔婴儿喉中〕发汩汩声，发咯咯声 —**gurgling** *adj*: *a gurgling stream* 汩汩流的小溪

gurgle² *n* [C] the sound of gurgling 汩汩声，咯咯声

Gur·khas, the /ˈgɝkəz; ˈgɜːkəz/ a REGIMENT (=a large group of soldiers) in the British army. Gurkhas come from Nepal, and are very brave fighters.（英国）廓尔喀兵团〔士兵来自尼泊尔，作战十分勇猛〕

gur·ney /ˈgɝnɪ; ˈgɜːni/ *n* [C] *AmE* a long narrow table with wheels used for moving sick people in a hospital【美】〔医院中移动病人用的〕轮床

gu·ru /ˈguru; ˈguruː/ *n* [C] **1** *informal* someone who knows a lot about a particular subject, and to whom people go for advice【非正式】专家，权威，大师: *one of the president's foreign policy gurus* 总统的一位外交政策专家 **2** a Hindu religious teacher or leader 古鲁〔印度教的教师或领袖〕

gush¹ /gʌʃ; gʌʃ/ *v* **1** [I always+adv/prep] if a liquid gushes from something, such as a hole or cut, it comes out in large quantities〔液体从某物〕大量涌出，喷出: [**+out/from/down etc**] *The blood began to gush out, red and frightening.* 血开始涌出，一片红色，十分吓人。| *oil gushing from the broken pipe* 从破裂的管中喷出来的石油 **2** [T] if something gushes a liquid, large quantities of that liquid come out of it 涌出，喷出〔大量液体〕: *The wound gushed blood.* 伤口大量出血。**3** [I,T] to express your admiration, pleasure etc too strongly so that people do not think you are sincere 夸张地表达〔爱慕、高兴之情〕: *"I simply loved your book," she gushed.* "我实在非常喜欢你的书。"她装模作样地说。**4** [I] if words or emotions gush out, you suddenly express them very strongly〔话语〕迸出；〔感情〕迸发: [**+out**] *All that pent up frustration gushed out in a torrent of abuse.* 被压抑的挫败感迸发出来，他突然破口大骂。

gush² *n* **1** a large quantity of liquid that suddenly flows from somewhere 涌流，喷出之物: *Gushes of water sprayed out of the pipe.* 水柱从管道喷洒出来。**2 a gush of relief/anxiety etc** a sudden feeling or expression of emotion 一阵宽慰/焦虑等

gush·er /ˈgʌʃɚ; ˈgʌʃə/ *n* [C] an OIL WELL where the natural flow of oil is very strong, so that a pump is not needed 喷油井

gush·ing /ˈgʌʃɪŋ; ˈgʌʃɪŋ/ also 又作 **gush·y** /ˈgʌʃɪ; ˈgʌʃi/ *adj informal* expressing admiration, pleasure etc strongly, so that people may think you are not sincere【非正式】夸大其词的；装腔作势的—**gushingly** *adv*

gus·set /ˈgʌsɪt; ˈgʌsɪ̣t/ *n* [C] a small piece of material stitched into a piece of clothing to make it stronger, wider, or more comfortable in a particular place〔衣服的〕衬料

gus·sy /ˈgʌsɪ; ˈgʌsi/ *v*

gussy up *phr v* [I,T] *AmE informal* to make yourself look attractive by wearing your best clothes etc【美，非正式】（把…）打扮得漂漂亮亮: **gussy yourself up** *Jolene gussied herself up for the party.* 乔利恩穿戴得漂漂亮亮地参加聚会。

gust¹ /gʌst; gʌst/ *n*[C] **1** a sudden strong movement of wind 一阵狂风: *A sudden gust of wind blew the door shut.* 一阵狂风把门吹得关上了。**2** a sudden strong feeling of anger, excitement etc 突发的一阵怒气、兴奋等: *A gust of rage swept through him.* 一阵怒火涌上他的心头。

gust² *v* [I] if the wind gusts, it blows strongly with sudden short movements〔狂风〕一阵阵劲吹: *wind gusting at up to 45 miles per hour* 时速高达45英里的狂风

gus·to /ˈgʌsto; ˈgʌstəʊ/ *n* [U] **with gusto** if you do something with gusto, you do it with a lot of eagerness and energy 精力充沛地，热忱地: *Brendon always sang hymns with great gusto.* 布伦登总是兴致勃勃地唱圣歌。

gust·y /ˈgʌstɪ; ˈgʌsti/ *adj* with wind blowing in strong sudden movements 刮阵风的: *a cold, gusty October night* 寒冷而狂风阵阵的十月夜晚

gut¹ /gʌt; gʌt/ *n*

1 ▶COURAGE 勇气◀ guts [plural] *informal* the courage and determination you need to do something difficult or unpleasant【非正式】〔做困难或不愉快事情所需要的〕勇气，魄力，决心: *Sonia succeeded through sheer guts and determination.* 索尼娅全凭着胆量和决心取得了成功。| **have the guts to do sth** *No one had the guts to tell Paul what a mistake he was making.* 没有人有胆量告诉保罗他在犯什么样的错误。

2 ▶BODY PARTS 身体器官◀ a) guts [plural] the organs inside your body 内脏 **b)** the tube through which food passes from your stomach 肠子，肠道

3 gut reaction/feeling/instinct etc *informal* a reaction or feeling that you are sure is right, although you cannot give a reason for it【非正式】本能的反应/本能的感觉/直觉等: *He had a gut feeling that Sarah was lying.* 他凭直觉感到萨拉在撒谎。

4 hate sb's guts *informal* to hate someone very much【非正式】痛恨某人

5 sweat/slog your guts out *informal* to work very hard【非正式】拼命工作

6 at gut level if you know something at gut level, you feel sure about it, though you could not give a reason 凭直觉，本能地: *She knew at gut level that he was guilty.* 她本能地知道他有罪。

7 ▶STRING 线◀ [U] a type of strong string made from the INTESTINE of an animal 肠线〔用动物肠子制成的十分结实的绳索〕—see also 另见 CATGUT

8 I'll have sb's guts for garters *BrE informal* used to say that you would like to punish someone severely for something they have done【英，非正式】〔用于表示希望严惩某人〕—see also 另见 BEER BELLY, **bust a gut** (BUST¹ (3)), **spill your guts** (SPILL¹ (4))

gut² *v* **gutted, gutting** [T] **1** [usually passive 一般用被动态] to completely destroy the inside of a building, especially by fire 毁坏〔建筑物〕内部〔尤指烧毁〕: *The kitchen was completely gutted.* 厨房里面全被烧毁。**2** to remove the organs from inside a fish or animal in order to prepare it for cooking 取出〔鱼或动物内脏，以备烹调〕**3** to change something by removing some of the most important or central parts〔通过去除重要的或中心的部分〕改变: *gutting the system from the inside so as to restructure it completely* 去除系统内部以便彻底重建 —see also 另见 GUTTED

Gu·ten·berg Bi·ble, the /,gutn̩bɝg ˈbaɪbl; ,guːtənbɜːg ˈbaɪbəl/ a Bible which was the first book ever printed in Europe using movable type. This method of printing was invented by **Johannes Gutenberg** (1397-1468), and the Bible was printed in about 1455. 谷登堡《圣经》〔欧洲第一部用活字印刷的书。这种印刷方法由约翰尼斯·谷登堡(1397-1468)发明。谷登堡《圣经》印制于1455年前后〕

Guth·rie /ˈgʌθrɪ; ˈgʌθri/, **Woody** (1912-67) a US FOLK singer and songwriter who is famous for his songs against war. He was greatly admired by younger folk singers in the 1960s, including Bob Dylan. 格思里〔(1912-1967)，美国民歌歌手、词作家，尤以其反战歌曲著名。20世纪60年代，他深受鲍勃·迪伦等年轻民歌歌手仰慕〕

gut·less /ˈgʌtləs; ˈgʌtləs/ *adj informal* lacking courage or determination【非正式】缺乏胆量的, 怯懦的—**gutlessly** *adv* **gutlessness** *n* [U]

guts·y /ˈgʌtsɪ; ˈgʌtsi/ *adj informal* brave and determined【非正式】勇敢的, 坚毅的: *a gutsy young fighter* 一位勇敢的年轻战士

gut·ted /ˈgʌtɪd; ˈgʌtɨd/ *adj* **1** seriously damaged or completely destroyed 严重受损的, 完全毁坏的 **2** *BrE spoken* very shocked or disappointed【英口】十分吃惊的, 非常失望的: *"And how did you feel when Arsenal scored?" "Totally gutted."* "阿森纳队得分时你感觉如何?" "彻底震惊。" **3** *BrE spoken* very tired; EXHAUSTED【英口】精疲力竭的: *I was gutted by the end of the week!* 到周末我就精疲力竭!

gut·ter¹ /ˈgʌtɚ; ˈgʌtə/ *n* **1** [C] the edge of a road next to the path, where water collects and flows away〔路边的〕排水沟 **2** [C] an open pipe or CHANNEL¹ (4), fixed to the edge of a roof to collect and carry away rain water〔屋檐边的〕雨水槽 —see picture on page A4 参见 A4 页图 **3 the gutter** the bad social conditions of the lowest and poorest level of society 社会最底层的恶劣环境: *Men like him usually ended up in jail – or the gutter.* 像他这样的男人, 下场通常是坐牢或穷困潦倒。**4 the gutter press** *BrE* the newspapers that print shocking stories about people's personal lives【英】〔耸人听闻地刊登人们私生活新闻的〕低级趣味报纸, 下流报纸 —compare 比较 TABLOID

gutter² *v* [I] *literary* if a CANDLE gutters it burns with an unsteady flame【文】〔烛光〕摇曳不定

gutter out *phr v* [I] *AmE* to become gradually weaker and then stop completely【美】逐渐停止: *What had been a promising film career in the end just guttered out.* 原来很有前途的电影生涯最终灰飞烟灭。

gut·ter·ing /ˈgʌtərɪŋ; ˈgʌtərɪŋ/ *n* [U] the open pipes that are fixed to the edge of the roof of a house to collect and carry away rain water〔屋檐边的〕雨水槽 —see also 另见 GUTTER¹ (2)

gut·ter·snipe /ˈgʌtɚˌsnaɪp; ˈgʌtəsnaɪp/ *n* [C] *old-fashioned* a dirty, untidy, badly-behaved child from a poor home【过时】又脏又野的穷人家孩子

gut·tur·al /ˈgʌtərəl; ˈgʌtərəl/ *adj* a guttural voice or sound is or seems to be produced deep in the throat〔声音〕喉中发出的, 像喉中发出的

guv /gʌv; gʌv/ *n BrE spoken* used by men, as a way of addressing a male customer in a shop, taxi etc【英口】先生〔男性用语, 用来称呼商店、出租车等的男性顾客〕: *Where to, guv?* 上哪儿, 先生?

guv·nor, guv'nor /ˈgʌvnɚ; ˈgʌvnə/ *n BrE spoken*【英口】**1** a man who is in a position of authority over you, usually your employer 老板, 雇主: *You'll have to speak to the guvnor about that.* 那件事你得跟老板说。**2** *old-fashioned* used as a way of addressing a man of a higher social class than you【过时】先生〔用来称呼地位比自己高的男人〕

S1 W3 **guy¹** /gaɪ; gaɪ/ *n* [C] **1** *informal* a man【非正式】男人: *Dave's a nice guy when you get to know him.* 戴夫是个好人, 你认识他后就知道。**2** a figure of a man burnt every year on Guy Fawkes' Night, in Britain〔在英国每年盖伊·福克斯之夜焚烧的〕盖伊·福克斯模拟像

> **CULTURAL NOTE 文化注释**
>
> Shortly before Guy Fawkes Night, some children make guys and ask people for money, saying 'a penny for the guy!'. They then spend the money on FIREWORKS. This was more common in the past than now. 盖伊·福克斯之夜前夕, 有些孩子制作盖伊模拟像, 向别人要钱, 嘴里说:"给盖伊一便士吧!" 然后他们把钱用来买烟花。现在这种情况已不如过去常见。

3 also 又作 **guy rope** a rope that stretches from the top or side of a tent or pole to the ground to keep it in the right position〔帐篷或杆柱的〕固定拉绳, 牵索 **4 guys** [plural] *AmE spoken* used when talking to or about a group of people, male or female【美口】大家, 各位〔用于对同一群人讲话或指一群人时〕: *Hey you guys! Where are you going?* 嗨, 你们哪! 要上哪儿去? **5 no more Mr Nice Guy!** used to say that you will stop trying to behave honestly and fairly 不再当好好先生了! —see also 另见 **wise guy** (WISE¹ (6))

guy² *v* [T] *old-fashioned* to copy how someone talks or behaves in a way that makes people laugh【过时】模仿〔某人说话或行动以使人发笑〕

Guy·an·a /gaɪˈænə; gaɪˈænə/ a country in northeast South America on the Atlantic Ocean, between Venezuela and Surinam. Population: 697,181 (2001). Capital: Georgetown. The country used to belong to the UK and was called British Guiana. It is the only English-speaking country in South America. 圭亚那〔南美洲东北部一国家, 濒临大西洋, 位于委内瑞拉和苏里南之间。人口: 697,181 (2001), 首都: 乔治敦。该国曾属于英国, 旧称英属圭亚那, 是南美洲唯一讲英语的国家〕—**Guyanese** /ˌgaɪəˈniz; ˌgaɪəˈniːz◂/ *n, adj*

Guy Fawkes' Night /ˌgaɪ ˈfɔks naɪt; ˌgaɪ ˈfɔːks naɪt/ *n* [singular] November 5th, when in Britain people light FIREWORKS and burn a GUY¹ (2) on a fire 盖伊·福克斯之夜〔即11月5日, 在英国届时人们燃放烟火并焚烧模拟人像〕

Guy's /gaɪz; gaɪz/ also 又作 **Guy's Hospital** an important hospital in London, for training doctors and nurses 盖伊医院〔伦敦一家有影响的教学医院〕

guz·zle /ˈgʌzl; ˈgʌzəl/ *v* [I,T] *informal* to eat or drink a lot of something, eagerly and quickly【非正式】滥吃, 狂饮: *They've been guzzling beer all evening.* 他们整个晚上都在狂饮啤酒。—see also 另见 GAS-GUZZLER

Gwent /gwɛnt; gwent/ a COUNTY in southeast Wales, formerly called Monmouthshire 格温特〔威尔士东南部一郡, 旧称蒙茅斯郡〕

Gwyn /gwɪn; gwɪn/, **Nell** /nɛl; nel/ (?1650-87) an English actress who became the lover of King Charles II. She sold oranges on the streets of London, and is often shown in pictures carrying a basket of oranges. 格温〔(?1650-1687), 英格兰女演员, 国王查理二世的情妇。她曾沿街卖过橘子。图画中, 她手里常提着一篮橘子〕

Nell Gwyn 内尔·格温

Gwyn·edd /ˈgwɪnɪð; ˈgwɪnɨð/ a COUNTY in northwest Wales 圭内斯〔威尔士西北部一郡〕

gym /dʒɪm; dʒɪm/ *n informal*【非正式】**1** [C] a special hall or room that has equipment for doing physical exercise; GYMNASIUM 体育馆, 健身房 **2** [U] exercises done indoors for physical development and as a sport, especially as a school subject 体操, 体育: **gym kit/shoes etc** *Do not wear your gym kit outdoors.* 在室外别穿体操服。

gym·kha·na /dʒɪmˈkɑnə; dʒɪmˈkɑːnə/ *n* [C] **1** *BrE* a sporting event at which people on horses compete in races and jumping competitions【英】赛马大会 **2** *AmE* a car race that involves difficult driving【美】汽车比赛

gym·na·si·um /dʒɪmˈneziəm; dʒɪmˈneɪziəm/ *n* [C] a special hall or room that has equipment for doing physical exercise 体育馆, 健身房

gym·nast /ˈdʒɪmnæst; ˈdʒɪmnæst/ *n* [C] someone who is very good at doing physical exercises, especially someone who competes against other people in gymnastic competitions 体操运动员

gym·nas·tics /dʒɪmˈnæstɪks; dʒɪmˈnæstɪks/ *n* [U] **1** a sport involving skilled and controlled physical exercises and movements, often performed in competitions 体操 **2 mental/intellectual/moral gymnastics** very clever thinking 非常聪明的想法 **3 verbal gymnastics** using words in a very clever way 遣词造句的高超技巧—**gymnastic** *adj*: *gymnastic skills* 体操技能

gym shoe /ˈ· ·/ *n* [C] a light shoe with a cloth top and a flat rubber bottom used for games and sport, especially at school〔特指在学校里穿用的〕体操鞋, 运动鞋, 球鞋; PLIMSOLL *BrE*【英】

gym·slip /ˈdʒɪmˌslɪp; ˈdʒɪmˌslɪp/ *n* [C] *BrE*【英】**1** a type of dress without sleeves that girls used to wear over a shirt as a part of their school uniform〔女生穿在衬衫外的〕无袖制服 **2 gymslip mother** a girl who has a baby while she is still at school 学生妈妈

gyn- /dʒaɪn; gaɪn/ *prefix technical* concerning women【术语】与妇女有关的: *gynaecology* (=treatment of women's diseases) 妇科学

gy·nae·col·o·gy *BrE*【英】, **gynecology** *AmE*【美】/ˌdʒaɪnɪˈkɑlədʒɪ; ˌgaɪnɨˈkɒlədʒi/ *n* [U] the study and treatment of medical conditions and illnesses affecting only women 妇科(学) —**gynaecologist** *n* [C]—**gynaecological** /ˌdʒaɪnɪkəˈlɑdʒɪkl; ˌgaɪnɨkəˈlɒdʒɪkəl◂/ *adj*

gyp¹ /dʒɪp; dʒɪp/ *n informal*【非正式】**1 give sb gyp** *BrE*【英】**a)** to be painful 疼痛: *My bad leg is really giving me gyp today.* 我受伤的腿今天实在疼痛得不行。**b)** to punish someone or be angry with them because of something they have done 处罚某人; 对某人生气 **2** [singular] *AmE*【美】**a)** something that you were tricked into buying 被骗买的东西 **b)** a situation in which

you feel you have been cheated 欺骗，诈骗，骗局: *What a gyp!* 好一个骗局！

gyp² *v* **gypped, gypping** [T] *informal* to cheat someone【非正式】欺骗，诈骗: *Ten quid? You've been gypped!* 十镑？你被骗了！

gyp·sum /ˋdʒɪpsəm; ˈdʒɪpsəm/ *n* [U] a soft white substance that is used to make PLASTER OF PARIS 石膏

gyp·sy also 又作 **gipsy** *BrE*【英】/ˋdʒɪpsɪ; ˈdʒɪpsi/ *n* [C] **1** a member of a dark-haired race that is thought to be of Indian origin, who usually live and travel around in CARAVANs 吉卜赛人 **2** someone who does not like to stay in the same place for a long time; TRAVELLER (2) 不喜欢长时间在同一个地方的人

CULTURAL NOTE 文化注释

Gypsies live in the UK and most European countries, but very few gypsies live in the US. Gypsies typically do not live in one place, but travel from place to place while living in a CARAVAN. In the past, their caravans were pulled by horses, and were usually brightly painted. Gypsies do various jobs to earn a living, but traditionally they are thought of as horse traders, musicians, basket makers, and FORTUNE-TELLERs. 在英国和大多数欧洲国家都有吉普赛人，但美国的吉普赛人极少。吉普赛人一般不在一地久居，而是住在大篷车里四处迁徙。大篷车过去是用马拉的，颜色鲜艳。为了谋生，吉普赛人从事各种职业，但传统上人们认为他们的职业是贩马、卖唱、制作篮子、给人算命。

In the UK, some people DISCRIMINATE against gypsies because their way of life is so different from the way most British people live. These people often complain if gypsies decide to live near them. In the US, people imagine that gypsies have a very interesting life, travelling and not worrying about money. 吉普赛人的生活方式与大多数英国人截然不同，因此遭到一些英国人的歧视。这些人看到吉普赛人决定安顿在自家住处旁边就经常抱怨。美国人则想象吉普赛人的生活很精彩，四处旅游，不用为钱发愁。—compare 比较 NEW AGE TRAVELLER

gy·rate /ˋdʒaɪret; dʒaɪˈreɪt/ *v* [I] *literary* to turn around fast in circles【文】快速旋转: *The dancers gyrated wildly to the beat of the music.* 舞蹈员随着音乐的节奏猛烈地旋转。—**gyration** /dʒaɪˋreʃən; dʒaɪˈreɪʃən/ *n*

gy·ro /ˋdʒaɪro; ˈdʒaɪrəʊ/ *n* [C] *informal* a gyroscope【非正式】陀螺仪，回转仪

gy·ro·scope /ˋdʒaɪrə,skop; ˈdʒaɪrəskəʊp/ *n* [C] a wheel that spins inside a frame and is used for keeping ships and aircraft steady or as a child's toy 陀螺仪，回转仪 —**gyroscopic** /,dʒaɪrəˋskɑpɪk; ˌdʒaɪrəˈskɒpɪk◂/ *adj*

H,h

H, h /etʃ; eɪtʃ/ *plural* **H's, h's** the 8th letter of the English alphabet 英语字母表的第八个字母 —see also 另见 H-BOMB

H_2O /ˌetʃ tu ˋo; ˌeɪtʃ tuː ˈəʊ/ *n* [U] *technical* the chemical sign for water【术语】水的化学分子式

ha[1] /hɑ; hɑː/ *interjection* used when you are surprised or have discovered something interesting〔表示惊异或发现了某些有趣的事物〕哈!: *Ha! I thought it might be you hiding there!* 哈! 我以为可能是你藏在那儿! —see also 另见 AHA, HA-HA

ha[2] the written abbreviation of 缩写= HECTARE(S)

ha·be·as cor·pus /ˋhebɪəs ˋkɔrpəs; ˌheɪbiəs ˈkɔːpəs/ *n* [U] *law* the right of someone in prison to come to a court of law so that the court can decide whether they should stay in prison【法律】人身保护状[令]〔指被拘留的人有权要求及时移交法庭, 以决定其是否应入狱〕

hab·er·dash·er /ˋhæbɚˌdæʃɚ; ˈhæbədæʃə/ *n* [C] *old-fashioned* a shopkeeper who sells haberdashery【过时】男士服饰用品商; 缝纫用品商

hab·er·dash·er·y /ˋhæbɚˌdæʃərɪ; ˈhæbədæʃəri/ *n* **1** [C] *BrE* a shop or part of a large store where things used for making clothes are sold【英】缝纫用品店[部] **2** [C] *AmE old-fashioned* a shop or part of a large store where men's clothes, especially hats, are sold【美, 过时】男士服饰用品〔尤指帽子〕店[部] **3** [U] the goods sold in these shops 男士服饰用品; 缝纫用品

3 3 **hab·it** /ˋhæbɪt; ˈhæbɪ̣t/ *n*

1 ►STH YOU DO REGULARLY 惯做的事◄ [C,U] something that you do regularly, often without thinking about it because you have done it so many times before 习惯: *Dalton was a man of regular habits.* 多尔顿是一个遵守习惯的人。| **out of habit/from habit** (=because it is a habit) 出于习惯 *After we moved I kept driving to the old house out of habit.* 我们搬家后, 出于习惯我开车时总是奔着老房子去。| **be in the habit of doing sth** *Jeff was in the habit of taking a walk after dinner.* 杰夫习惯在晚饭后散步。| **get into/get in/out of the habit** (=start/stop doing something regularly) 养成/改掉〔做某事的〕习惯 *Since I stopped taking lessons, I've gotten out of the habit of practising my saxophone.* 自从我没有上课以后, 我再也没有练萨克斯管的习惯了。| *She got in the habit of having a drink with us on Fridays.* 她养成了逢星期五和我们一起喝酒的习惯。| **eating/drinking habits** (=how often, how much, and what you eat or drink) 饮食/饮酒习惯 *When she is busy, her eating habits become erratic.* 她一忙饮食习惯就变得毫无规律了。

2 ►ANNOYING BEHAVIOUR 令人讨厌的行为◄ [C] something that someone does regularly and that other people find annoying 坏习惯: **have a habit of doing sth** *Glenna has an annoying habit of talking to herself while she's working.* 格伦纳有一个坏习惯, 就是一边工作一边自言自语。| **a bad/filthy/disgusting habit** *Don't bite your fingernails – it's a disgusting habit.* 别咬指甲, 这是个令人讨厌的习惯。

3 ►DRUGS 毒品◄ a strong physical need to keep taking a drug regularly 毒瘾: *Many of them get into petty crime to support their habit.* 他们当中有很多人为了满足毒瘾而犯轻罪。| **heroin/cocaine etc habit** *His cocaine habit ruined him physically and financially.* 他的可卡因瘾使他的身体和经济都毁了。| **kick the habit** (=stop taking a drug regularly) 戒除毒瘾

4 break the habit to stop doing something that is annoying or bad for your health 摆脱坏习惯: *a new system that's supposed to help you break the smoking habit* 一个帮助你戒烟的新方法

5 don't make a habit of (doing) sth *spoken* used to tell someone who has done something bad or wrong that they should not do it again【口】不要养成做某事的习惯: *You're ten minutes late. I hope you're not going to make a habit of this.* 你迟了十分钟。我希望你不要养成迟到的习惯。

6 I'm not in the habit of doing sth *spoken* used when you are offended because someone has suggested that you have done something that you have not done【口】我没有做某事的习惯: *I'm not in the habit of lying to my friends.* 我没有对朋友撒谎的习惯。

7 old habits die hard used to say that it is difficult to make people change their attitudes or behaviour 旧习难改

8 ►CLOTHES 衣服◄ [C] a long loose piece of clothing worn by people in some religious groups〔某些宗教团体成员穿的〕服装; 长袍: *a nun's habit* 修女服

9 habit of thought/mind the way someone usually thinks about something, or the attitudes they usually have 已成习惯的思维方式/惯常的态度 —see also 另见 **a creature of habit** (CREATURE (5)), **by/from force of habit** (FORCE[1] (9))

USAGE NOTE 用法说明: HABIT
WORD CHOICE 词语辨析: **habit, custom, tradition, practice, convention**

A **habit** is usually something someone does again and again, perhaps without them realizing it. habit (习惯) 通常指某人在可能没有意识到的情况下经常做的事情: *He has an annoying habit of biting his nails.* 他有咬指甲的坏习惯。

A **custom** is usually something which has been done for a long time by a group – for example, a school, company, or society, perhaps every year. custom (习俗) 通常指某一群人, 如学校、公司或社会, 长久以来可能每年都要做的事情: *the custom of holding exams in June* 六月份举行考试的习俗 | *a local custom* 当地习俗

A **tradition** is similar to a **custom**, but may be older and passed down from parents to their children. tradition (传统) 与 custom (习俗) 类似, 但可能更古老, 由父母传给子女: *the tradition of eating turkey at Thanksgiving* 感恩节吃火鸡的传统 | *a family tradition* 家族传统

A **practice** is the usual way of doing things in business, law etc. practice (惯例、常规做法) 指商业、法律等领域中的惯常做法: *The normal practice in this company is to send the bill as soon as the job is done.* 本公司的惯例是完成工作后马上寄出账单。

The **conventions** of a society are its generally accepted rules of behaviour. 某一社会的 conventions (常规、习俗) 指的是普遍接受的行为准则: *It is a matter of convention for people attending funerals to wear dark clothes.* 人们参加丧礼时穿深色衣服是一种社会习俗。

hab·i·ta·ble /ˋhæbɪtəbl; ˈhæbɪ̣təbəl/ *adj* good enough for people to live in 适宜居住的: *It would cost a fortune to make the place habitable.* 要想让这个地方变得适宜居住得花一大笔钱。—**habitability** /ˌhæbɪtəˋbɪlətɪ; ˌhæbɪ̣təˈbɪlɪ̣ti/ *n* [U]

hab·i·tat /ˋhæbəˌtæt; ˈhæbɪ̣tæt/ *n* [C] the natural home of a plant or animal〔植物的〕产地;〔动物的〕栖息地: *The polar bear's habitat is the icy wastes of the Arctic.* 北极熊的栖息地是冰冷的北极荒原。| **natural habitat** *Mountain areas are the natural habitat of the golden eagle.* 山区是金雕的自然栖息地。

hab·i·ta·tion /ˌhæbəˋteʃən; ˌhæbɪ̣ˈteɪʃən/ *n formal*【正式】**1 unfit for human habitation** a building that is unfit for human habitation is not safe or healthy for people to live in 不适合人类居住, 不适宜住人 **2** [U] the act of living in a place 居住: *There was no sign of habitation as far as the eye could see.* 放眼望去, 看不到有人居住的迹象。**3** [C] a house or place to live in 住宅, 住处

habit-form·ing /ˋ‥ˌ‥/ *adj* a drug or activity that is habit-forming makes you want to keep taking it, keep doing it etc 使人上瘾的; 让人形成习惯的

ha·bit·u·al /həˋbɪtʃuəl; həˈbɪtʃuəl/ *adj* **1** done as a habit or doing something from habit 已成习惯的: *My father was a habitual gambler.* 我父亲赌博成性。| *habitual drinking* 习惯性饮酒 **2** [only before noun 仅用于名词前] usual or typical of someone 习惯(性)的, 惯常的: *James took his habitual morning walk around the garden.* 詹姆斯如常地绕着花园作晨间散步去了。—**habitually** *adv*: *habitually violent behaviour* 经常性暴力行为

ha·bit·u·ate /həˋbɪtʃuˌet; həˈbɪtʃueɪt/ *v* **be/become habituated to (doing sth)** *formal* to be or gradually become used to something【正式】习惯于(做某事): *Over the centuries, these animals have become habituated to living in such a dry environment.* 经过许多世纪, 这些动物已经习惯于生活在如此干燥的环境里。

ha·bit·u·é /həˋbɪtʃʊˏe; həˈbɪtʃueɪ/ *n* [C+of] *formal* someone who regularly goes to a particular place or event【正式】经常出入某一场所[地方]的人, 常客

Habs·burg /ˋhæpsbɝg; ˈhæpsbɜːg/ another spelling of HAPSBURG 哈布斯堡王朝〔Hapsburg 的另一拼法〕

ha·ci·en·da /ˏhɑsɪˋɛndə; ˌhæsiˈendə/ *n* [C] a large farm in Spanish-speaking countries〔西班牙语国家的〕大庄园, 大农场

hack¹ /hæk; hæk/ *v* **1** [I always+adv/prep, T always+adv/prep] to cut something into pieces roughly or violently 砍, 劈: **hack away/at etc** *She hacked away at the ice, trying to make a hole.* 她在冰上凿, 想凿出一个洞来。| **hack sth into/through etc** *We had to hack a path through the jungle.* 我们只得在丛林中劈出一条路来。**2 can't hack sth** *informal* to feel that you cannot do something that is difficult or boring【非正式】〔由于困难或厌烦〕不愿做某事: *I've been doing this job for years, but I just can't hack it anymore.* 这份工作我已经干了很多年, 再也不想干了。**3** [I] *AmE* to drive a taxi【美】开出租车 **4** [I,T always+adv/prep] *BrE* to ride a horse along roads or through the country【英】〔在郊外或沿路〕骑马

hack into *phr v* [T] *informal* to secretly find a way to get into the information on someone else's computer system so that you can use or change it【非正式】侵入〔他人的电脑系统〕

hack² /hæk; hæk/ *n* [C] **1** a writer who does a lot of low quality work, especially writing newspaper articles〔写报纸文章等的〕蹩脚文人, 雇佣文人: *hack journalism* 雇佣文人写的报刊文章 —see also 另见 HACKWORK **2** an unimportant politician 二流政客, 政治仆从: *The meeting was attended by the usual old party hacks.* 参加会议的都是那些常见的老党棍。**3** *AmE informal* a taxi, or a taxi driver【美, 非正式】出租车; 出租车司机 **4** an act of hitting something roughly with a cutting tool 砍, 劈: *Just give it a hack with the axe.* 用斧头劈一下。**5** an old, tired horse 老马 **6** a horse you can pay money to ride on 供出租的马 **7** *BrE* a ride on a horse【英】骑马

hacked-off /ˏ·ˈ·/ *adj BrE informal* extremely annoyed【英, 非正式】非常生气的: *I'm really hacked-off; I left my coat on the bus.* 真是气死我了, 我把外套落在公共汽车上了。

hack·er /ˋhækɚ; ˈhækə/ *n* [C] *informal* someone who secretly uses or changes the information in other people's computer systems【非正式】私自存取或窜改（他人）电脑资料的人, 黑客 —**hacking** *n* [U]

hacking cough /ˏ·· ˈ·/ *n* [usually singular 一般用单数] a repeated painful cough with an unpleasant sound 短促频繁的干咳

hacking jacket /ˈ·· ˏ·/ *n* [C] *BrE* a woollen JACKET (1) worn when riding a horse【英】骑马外套, 夹克骑装

hack·les /ˋhækḷz; ˈhækəlz/ *n* [plural] **1 sb's hackles rise** if someone's hackles rise they begin to feel very angry, because someone's behaviour or attitude offends them 被激怒, 勃然大怒: *Laura saw the insolent look on his face, and felt her hackles rising.* 劳拉看到他脸上傲慢的表情时按捺不住心头的怒火。| **raise sb's hackles** (=make someone angry) 激怒某人 *tactless remarks that were enough to raise anyone's hackles* 足以激怒任何人的不得体的话 **2** the long feathers or hairs on the back of the neck of some animals and birds, which stand up straight when they are in danger〔某些鸟兽遇到危险时会竖起的〕颈背毛, 细长颈羽

Hackney /ˋhæknɪ; ˈhækni/ a BOROUGH of East London which is a rather poor area 哈克尼区〔伦敦东部一贫困区〕

hack·ney car·riage /ˋhæknɪ ˏkærɪdʒ; ˈhækni ˌkærɪdʒ/ *n* [C] *BrE*【英】**1** also 又作 **hackney coach** /ˈ·· ·/ *AmE*【美】a carriage pulled by a horse, used in the past like a taxi〔旧时的〕出租马车 **2** also 又作 **hackney cab** /ˈ·· ·/ *formal* a taxi【正式】出租车

hack·neyed /ˋhæknɪd; ˈhæknid/ *adj* a hackneyed phrase, statement etc is boring and does not have much meaning because it has been used so often; TRITE〔言辞等〕陈腐的, 老生常谈的

hack·saw /ˋhækˏsɔ; ˈhæksɔː/ *n* [C] a cutting tool with small teeth on its blade, used especially for cutting metal 弓锯, 钢锯 —see picture at 参见 TOOL¹ 图

hack·work /ˋhækˏwɝk; ˈhækwɜːk/ *n* [U] uninteresting work, especially writing, done to earn money rather than because you enjoy it〔职业性的〕卖文工作;〔雇佣文人的〕平庸作品

had /əd, həd; d, əd, həd; *strong* 强读 hæd; hæd/ **1** the past tense and past participle of HAVE **2 be had** *informal* to be tricked or be made to look stupid【非正式】上当受骗: *I'm afraid you've been had! This watch is a fake!* 恐怕你是上当了! 这只表是假货!

had·dock /ˋhædək; ˈhædək/ *n plural* **haddock** [C,U] a common fish that lives in northern seas and is often used as food 黑线鳕〔北大西洋产的一种食用鱼〕

Ha·des /ˋhediz; ˈheɪdiːz/ *n* [U] the land of the dead in the stories of ancient Greece; HELL¹ (3)〔希腊神话中的〕冥府, 黄泉, 地狱

hadj /hædʒ; hædʒ/ *n* [C] another spelling of HAJ haj 的另一种拼法

had·ji /ˋhædʒi; ˈhædʒi/ *n* [C] another spelling of HAJJI hajji 的另一种拼法

had·n't /ˋhædṇt; ˈhædnt/ short for 缩略式= had not: *If I hadn't seen it myself, I'd never have believed it.* 要不是我亲眼看见, 我是怎么也不会相信的。

Ha·dri·an's Wall /ˏhedrɪənz ˋwɔl; ˌheɪdriənz ˈwɔːl/ a stone wall which the Roman EMPEROR Hadrian ordered to be built across the north of England in 122 AD from the east coast to the west, in order to defend Roman Britain from attack by northern tribes such as the Picts 哈德良长城〔公元 122 年罗马皇帝哈德良为抵御皮克特等北方部族袭击罗马不列颠行省而下令建造的石砌高墙, 位于英格兰北部, 横贯东西海岸〕

hae·ma·tol·o·gy *BrE*【英】, **hematology** *AmE*【美】/ˏhiməˋtɑlədʒɪ; ˌhiːməˈtɒlədʒi/ *n* [U] the scientific study of blood 血液学

haemo- *BrE*【英】, **hemo-** *AmE*【美】/himo, himə; hiːməʊ, hiːmə/ *prefix technical* concerning the blood【术语】血液的, 与血有关的: *a hemorrhage* (=bleeding) 出血

hae·mo·glo·bin *BrE*【英】, **hemoglobin** *AmE*【美】/ˏhiməˋglobɪn; ˌhiːməˈgləʊbɪn/ *n* [U] a red substance in the blood that contains iron and carries oxygen 血红蛋白

hae·mo·phil·i·a *BrE*【英】, **hemophilia** *AmE*【美】/ˏhiməˋfɪlɪə; ˌhiːməˈfɪliə/ *n* [U] a serious disease that prevents the blood from becoming thick, so that a person loses a lot of blood easily 血友病

hae·mo·phil·i·ac *BrE*【英】, **hemophiliac** *AmE*【美】/ˏhiməˋfɪlɪˏæk; ˌhiːməˈfɪliæk/ *n* [C] a person who suffers from haemophilia 血友病患者

hae·mor·rhage¹ *BrE*【英】, **hemorrhage** *AmE*【美】/ˋhɛmərɪdʒ; ˈhemərɪdʒ/ *n* [C,U] a serious medical condition in which a person BLEEDs a lot, often inside the body 大量出血〔常指体内〕

haemorrhage² *BrE*【英】, **hemorrhage** *AmE*【美】*v* [I] to have a haemorrhage 大出血; 出血

hae·mor·rhoids *BrE*【英】, **hemorrhoids** *AmE*【美】/ˋhɛməˏrɔɪdz; ˈhemərɔɪdz/ *n* [plural] painfully swollen BLOOD VESSELS at the ANUS 痔

haft /hæft; hɑːft/ *n* [C] *technical* a long handle on an AXE¹ (1) or on other weapons【术语】〔斧、刀、枪等的〕柄, 把

hag /hæg; hæg/ *n* [C] an ugly or unpleasant woman, especially one who is old or looks like a WITCH (1) 老丑婆, 母夜叉

hag·gard /ˋhægɚd; ˈhægəd/ *adj* having lines on your face and dark marks around your eyes, especially because you are ill, worried, or have not had enough sleep〔面容〕憔悴的, 形容枯槁的: *Suddenly, he was looking much older, his face haggard and unshaven.* 他突然看起来老多了, 面容憔悴, 满面胡须。

hag·gis /ˋhægɪs; ˈhægɪ̈s/ *n* [C,U] a food eaten in Scotland, made from the heart and other organs of a sheep, cut up and boiled in a skin made from the sheep's stomach 肚包羊杂碎〔把羊杂碎放入羊肚中烧的典型苏格兰食品〕

hag·gle /ˋhægḷ; ˈhægəl/ *v* [I] to argue, especially when trying to agree about the price of something〔尤指在价格方面〕争论不休, 讨价还价: **haggle with sb over/about** *I had to haggle with the taxi driver over the fare.* 我不得不和出租车司机就车费讨价还价。—**haggling** *n* [U]

hag·i·og·ra·phy /ˏhægɪˋɑgrəfɪ; ˌhægiˈɒgrəfi/ *n* [C,U] **1** a book about the lives of SAINTS 圣徒传记 **2** a book about someone that describes them as better than they really are 把主角美化[理想化]的传记

hag·rid·den /ˈ·ˏ··/ *adj literary* always worried by problems in your life【文】受困扰的; 忧心忡忡的

Hague, the /heg; heɪg/ a city in the Netherlands. The country's government is in The Hague, but its capital city is Amsterdam. 海牙〔荷兰一城市, 国家政府所在地, 但该国首都是阿姆斯特丹〕

ha-ha¹ /ˏ·ˈ·/ *interjection* **1** used in writing to represent a shout of laughter 哈哈〔笑声〕**2** *spoken* used, sometimes angrily, to show that you do not think something is funny【口】哈哈〔表示某事并不好笑, 有时表示生气〕: *Oh, very funny, John, ha-ha.* 啊, 约翰, 很好笑, 哈哈。

ha-ha² /ˈ· ·/ *n* [C] a wall or fence set in a hole in the ground which divides parts of a park etc without spoiling the view〔界沟中不遮挡视线的〕暗墙; 隐篱

Haight-Ash·bu·ry /ˌhet ˋæʃbərɪ; ˌheɪt ˈæʃbəri/ a part of San Francisco, California, where the HIPPIE movement began in the 1960s 海特－阿什伯里〔加利福尼亚旧金山一地区。20 世纪 60 年代嬉皮士运动在此兴起〕

hai·ku /ˈhaɪku; ˈhaɪkuː/ *n* [C] *plural* **haiku** a type of Japanese poem with three lines consisting of five, seven, and five SYLLABLES 俳句〔一种三行的日本诗体〕

hail¹ /hel; heɪl/ *n* **1** [U] frozen rain drops which fall as hard balls of ice 雹, 冰雹 **2 a hail of bullets/stones** a large number of bullets, stones etc thrown or fired at someone 一阵弹雨/一阵像雹子般袭来的石块 **3 a hail of criticism/abuse** a lot of criticism etc 连珠炮般的批评/辱骂

hail² *v* [T] to call to someone in order to greet them or try to attract their attention 呼喊; 大声招呼: *She leaned out of the window and hailed the first passerby.* 她探出窗户, 招呼她看到的第一个过路人。| **hail a cab/taxi** *The hotel doorman will hail a cab for you.* 旅馆门口的侍者会替你叫出租车的。

hail sb/sth **as** sth *phr v* [T often passive 常用被动态] to describe someone or something as being very good, especially in newspapers, magazines etc 把…称作, 把…誉为: *Lang's first film was immediately hailed as a masterpiece.* 兰的第一部电影很快被誉为一部杰作。

hail from sth *phr v* [T not in passive 不用被动态] *especially humorous* to have been born in a particular place【尤幽默】出生地是, 来自: *What part of the world do you hail from?* 你来自哪里?

Hai·le Se·las·sie /ˌhaɪlɪ sɪˋlæsɪ; ˌhaɪli sə̇ˈlæsi/ (1892-1975) the EMPEROR of Ethiopia from 1930 to 1974, who is remembered especially for having modernized his country. He was removed from power by his army in 1974 but is still important to his followers, called Rastafarians, who consider him a god. He is also sometimes called **Ras Tafari**, the **Lion of Judah**. 海尔·塞拉西〔(1892-1975), 埃塞俄比亚皇帝, 1930 至 1974 年间在位。他实现了该国的现代化, 这一点尤为国人所牢记。1974 年, 他被军队废黜, 但在其追随者拉斯塔法里教教徒当中仍享有重要地位。他们尊他为神明, 有时也称他为拉斯·塔法里, 即"犹大之狮"〕

hail-fel·low-well-met /ˌ· ··· ˈ·ˈ·/ *adj old-fashioned* very friendly and cheerful, sometimes in a way that you do not trust【过时】(过分)亲热友好的, 一见如故的: *very cheerful and noisy in a hail-fellow-well-met sort of way* 过分地友好和喧闹

Hail Ma·ry /ˌhel ˋmɛrɪ; ˌheɪl ˈmeəri/ *n* [C] a special Roman Catholic prayer to Mary, the mother of Jesus 万福马利亚〔天主教对圣母马利亚的祷辞〕

hail·stone /ˈhelˌston; ˈheɪlstəʊn/ *n* [C] a small ball of frozen rain 雹块, 雹子

hail·storm /ˈhelˌstɔrm; ˈheɪlstɔːm/ *n* [C] a storm when a lot of HAIL¹ (1) falls 雹暴

Hail to the Chief /ˌ· · · ˈ·/ a tune that is played when the US President arrives to visit a place or attend a ceremony《向总统致敬》〔美国总统访问某地或出席典礼时演奏的乐曲〕

[1] [1] **hair** /hɛr; heə/ *n* **1** [U] the mass of things like fine threads that grows on your head 头发: *She brushed her hair.* 她梳理头发。| *I must get my hair cut – it's getting too long.* 我必须去理发了, 头发太长了。| **blond/red/dark hair** *Emma's the one with the red hair.* 那个红头发的是埃玛。| **short/long/shoulder-length hair** *Jane has long blond hair.* 简有一头长长的金发。| **straight/curly/wavy/thick hair** *Her long wavy hair was tied back with a bow.* 她那长长的波浪形头发用一个蝴蝶结束在脑后。| **dark-haired/fair-haired/short-haired etc** *He's a tall, fair-haired guy.* 他是一个金发的高个小伙子。—see picture at 参见 HEAD¹ 图 **2** [C] one of the long fine things like thread that grows on people's heads and on other parts of their bodies, or similar things that grow on animals〔人、动物的〕毛, 汗毛, 茸毛: *The cat has left white hairs all over the sofa.* 猫在沙发上到处留下白毛。**3 get in sb's hair** *informal* to annoy someone, especially by always being near them【非正式】〔尤指因不断烦扰而〕惹恼某人 **4 keep your hair on** *spoken* used to tell someone to keep calm and not get annoyed【口】保持冷静, 别发火 **5 let your hair down** *informal* to enjoy yourself and start to relax, especially after working very hard【非正式】尽情放松, 无拘无束〔尤指在紧张的工作过后〕: *The party gave us all a chance to really let our hair down.* 晚会给了我们一个尽情放松的机会。**6 make sb's hair stand on end** to make someone very frightened 使某人毛骨悚然 **7 not have a hair out of place** to have a very neat appearance 十分整洁 **8 not turn a hair** to remain completely calm when something bad or surprising suddenly happens 处之泰然, 面不改色, 保持镇静 **9 not harm/touch a hair of sb's head** to not harm someone in any way 丝毫无损于某人 **10 the hair of the dog (that bit you)** *humorous* an alcoholic drink that you drink to cure a headache caused by drinking too much alcohol the night before【幽默】用来解宿醉的酒 —see also 另见 **have a good/fine head of hair** (HEAD¹ (4)), **not see hide nor hair of** (HIDE² (4)), **split hairs** (SPLIT¹ (7)), **tear your hair (out)** (TEAR² (11))

hair·breadth /ˈhɛrˌbrɛdθ; ˈheəbredθ/ *n* [singular] another spelling of HAIR'S BREADTH hair's breadth 的另一种拼法

hair·brush /ˈhɛrˌbrʌʃ; ˈheəbrʌʃ/ *n* [C] a brush you use on your hair to make it smooth 毛刷, 发刷 —see picture at 参见 BRUSH¹ 图

hair·cloth /ˈhɛrˌklɔθ; ˈheəklɒθ/ *n* [U] rough material made from animal hair, especially from horses or CAMELS 马尾衬〔用马毛、驼毛等动物毛织成的粗面料〕

hair·cut /ˈhɛrˌkʌt; ˈheəkʌt/ *n* [C] **1** the act of having your hair cut by someone 理发: *I'm going for a haircut.* 我去理发。**2** the style your hair is cut in 发型, 发式: *Do you like my new haircut?* 你喜欢我的新发型吗?

hair·do /ˈhɛrˌdu; ˈheəduː/ *n plural* **hairdos** [C] *informal* a woman's haircut【非正式】女子发型

hair·dress·er /ˈhɛrˌdrɛsɚ; ˈheəˌdresə/ *n* [C] **1** a person who cuts, washes, and arranges people's hair in particular styles 理发师, 美发师 **2 the hairdresser's** the hairdresser's shop 理发店, 发廊 —compare 比较 BARBER —**hairdressing** *n* [U]

hair·dry·er, hairdrier /ˈhɛrˌdraɪɚ; ˈheəˌdraɪə/ *n* [C] a machine that blows out hot air for drying hair〔吹干头发用的〕吹风机

hair·grip /ˈhɛrˌgrɪp; ˈheəgrɪp/ *n* [C] *BrE* a very small thin piece of metal folded in half and used to hold a woman's hair in place【英】发夹; BOBBY PIN *AmE*【美】—see picture at 参见 PIN¹ 图

hair·less /ˈhɛrlɪs; ˈheələs/ *adj* with no hair 无头发的, 秃头的

hair·line /ˈhɛrˌlaɪn; ˈheəlaɪn/ *n* [C] **1** the line around your head, especially at the front, where your hair starts growing〔额上的〕发际线, 头发轮廓线: *a receding hairline* 不断往后退的发际线〔指头发不断从前额往后秃〕 **2 a hairline crack/fracture** a very thin crack 细微的裂缝/骨折: *a hairline fracture in a bone* 骨头上的细微骨折

hair·net /ˈhɛrˌnɛt; ˈheənet/ *n* [C] a very thin net that stretches over your hair to keep it in place 发网

hair·piece /ˈhɛrˌpis; ˈheəpiːs/ *n* [C] a piece of false hair used to make your own hair look thicker〔加在头发上使之显得更浓密的〕小假发

hair·pin /ˈhɛrˌpɪn; ˈheəˌpɪn/ *n* [C] a pin made of wire bent into a U-shape to hold long hair in position〔U 形〕发卡; 发针 —see picture at 参见 PIN¹ 图

hairpin bend /ˌ·· ˈ·/ *n* [C] a very sharp U-shaped curve in a road, especially on a steep hill〔尤指陡坡处的〕U 字形弯路

hair-rais·ing /ˈ· ˌ··/ *adj* frightening in a way that is exciting 惊险的; 恐怖的: *a hair-raising car chase* 一场惊险的汽车追逐

hair re·stor·er /ˈ· ·ˌ··/ *n* [C,U] a substance or liquid that is supposed to make hair grow again 毛发再生剂[液]

hair's breadth /ˈ· ·/ *n* [singular] a very small amount or distance 极小的量; 一发之差, 极细微的距离: *The bullet missed me by a hair's breadth.* 子弹以毫发之差从我身边擦过。

hair shirt /ˌ· ˈ·/ *n* [C] a shirt made of rough uncomfortable cloth containing hair, worn in the past by some religious people to punish themselves〔过去有些苦修者惩罚自己时穿的〕刚毛衬衣

hair slide /ˈ· ·/ *n* [C] *BrE* a small attractive metal or plastic object used to fasten a woman's hair in place【英】〔金属或塑料〕小发夹; BARRETTE *AmE*【美】

hair·split·ting /ˈ· ˌ··/ *n* [U] the act of paying too much attention to small differences and unimportant details, especially in an argument〔尤指在争论中的〕吹毛求疵 —see also 另见 **split hairs** (SPLIT¹ (7))

hair spray /ˈ· ·/ *n* [U] a sticky substance that is sprayed (SPRAY¹ (1)) from a container and used to keep hair in place 喷发胶, 喷发定型剂

hair·spring /ˈhɛrˌsprɪŋ; ˈheəsprɪŋ/ *n* [C] a very small spring inside a watch that helps the watch work correctly〔手表中的〕游丝, 细弹簧

H

hairstyles 发型

flattop 平顶头

crew cut 板刷头

bob 短齐发

dreadlocks 长发绺

ponytail 马尾辫

plait *BrE*【英】/pigtail/ braid *AmE*【美】辫子

bun 圆发髻

plaits *BrE*【英】/pigtails/ braids *AmE*【美】双辫子

hair·style /ˈhɛrˌstaɪl; ˈheəstaɪl/ *n* [C] the style in which someone's hair has been cut or shaped 发型，发式

hair trig·ger /ˌ· ˈ··◂/ *n* [C] **1** a TRIGGER[1] (1) on a gun that needs very little pressure to fire the gun〔枪的〕微力扳机 **2 hair trigger temper** someone who has a hair trigger temper gets very angry easily 火暴的脾气

hair·y /ˈhɛrɪ; ˈheəri/ *adj* **1** having a lot of body hair〔身体〕多毛的: *He's a skinny guy with hairy legs.* 他是个双腿多毛的瘦削男子。| *a hairy chest* 多毛的胸脯 **2** *informal* dangerous or frightening, often in a way that is exciting【非正式】惊险的；令人恐惧的: *We had to climb down the cliff, and that was pretty hairy.* 我们得爬下悬崖，真惊险啊。**—hairiness** *n* [U]

Hai·ti /ˈhetɪ; ˈheɪti/ a country in the Caribbean Sea on the island of Hispaniola, which it shares with the Dominican Republic. Population: 6,965,000 (2001). Capital: Port au Prince. 海地〔加勒比海一岛国，与多米尼加共和国同在伊斯帕尼奥拉岛上。人口：6,965,000（2001），首都：太子港〕 **—Haitian** /ˈheʃən; ˈheɪʃən/ *n, adj*

haj, hadj /hædʒ; hædʒ/ *n* [C] a journey to Mecca for religious reasons, that all Muslims try to make at least once in their life〔伊斯兰教的〕麦加朝圣

haj·ji, hadji /ˈhædʒi; ˈhædʒi/ *n* [C] used as a title for a Muslim who has made a haj 哈吉〔曾朝觐麦加的伊斯兰教徒的称号〕

hake /hek, heɪk/ *n* [C,U] a sea fish, used as food 狗鳕〔一种食用海鱼〕

ha·kim /haˋkim; hɑːˈkiːm/ *n* [C] a Muslim doctor〔伊斯兰教的〕医生

ha·lal, hallal /həˋlal; hɑːˈlɑːl/ *adj* halal meat is meat from an animal that has been killed in a way that is approved by Muslim law 哈拉〔哈拉肉指按伊斯兰教习俗屠宰的牲畜的肉〕

hal·berd /ˈhælbɚd; ˈhælbəd/ *n* [C] a weapon with a blade on a long handle, used in past times 戟〔旧时的一种武器〕

hal·cy·on days /ˌhælsɪən ˋdez; ˌhælsiən ˈdeɪz/ *n* [plural] *especially literary* a time when you are very happy【尤文】美好的时光: *She often recalled the halcyon days of her youth.* 她经常回忆起年轻时的美好时光。

hale /hel; heɪl/ *adj* **hale and hearty** someone, especially an old person, who is hale and hearty is very healthy and active〔尤指老人〕精神矍铄的，老当益壮的: *still hale and hearty at 74* 74岁高龄仍然精神矍铄

Hale, Na·than /ˈneθən; ˈneɪθən/ (1755-76) a US soldier who was caught by the British and hanged for being a SPY (=someone whose job is to find out secret information about an enemy) during the American Revolutionary War. He is known for saying, before he was hanged, "I only regret[1] that I have but one life to lose for my country." 黑尔〔(1755-1776)，美国军人。他在美国独立战争期间被英军逮捕，因间谍罪被处以绞刑。他就义前说过这样一句名言："我唯一遗憾的是，我只有一次生命可奉献给祖国。"〕

Ha·ley /ˈhelɪ; ˈheɪli/, **Bill** (1927-81) a US singer who, with his band **The Comets**, helped to make rock 'n' roll music popular in the 1950s. His most famous song was *Rock Around the Clock*, which was also the name of a film in which he and his band appeared. 哈利〔(1927-1981)，美国歌手。20世纪50年代，他与其"彗星"乐队一起带动了摇滚音乐的流行。他最有名的歌曲是《昼夜摇滚》，这也是他与其乐队共同演出的一部影片的片名〕

half[1] /hæf; hɑːf/ *predeterminer, adj* [only before noun 仅用于名词前] **1** being half of an amount, time, distance, number etc 一半的，半: *events that happened over half a century ago* 半个多世纪前发生的事情 | *Only half the guests had arrived by seven o'clock.* 七点钟时只有一半的来宾到达。| *The studio is only half a block away.* 工作室离这儿只有半个街区。| **half a mile/pound/hour etc** (=half of a unit of measurement) 半英里/磅/小时 *half a pound of butter* 半磅黄油 | *It's about half a mile down the road.* 顺路走大约半英里远。| **a half hour/mile etc** *You can't just waltz in a half hour late – we need you here on time.* 你不能晚半小时才大摇大摆地进来，我们需要你准时来到这里。**2** if something is half one thing and half something else, it is a combination of those two things 一半…一半…: *A Minotaur is a monster that is half man, half bull.* 弥诺陶洛斯是一个半人半牛的怪物。**3 half one/two/three etc** *BrE informal* thirty minutes after the hour mentioned【英，非正式】一点半/两点半/三点半等: *I rang at about half six.* 我大约在六点半打了电话。**4 half a dozen a)** six 半打，六个: *half a dozen eggs* 六只蛋 **b)** several or many 几个；多个: *The children seemed to be singing 'Happy Birthday' to half a dozen different tunes.* 孩子们好像用好几种不同的曲调在唱生日歌。**5 be half the battle** *spoken* used to say that when you have done the most difficult part of an activity, the rest is easy【口】成功了一大半: *Getting Jimmy dressed in the mornings is half the battle.* 每天早上只要给吉米穿好衣服，剩下的事情就好办了。**6 half the fun/time/trouble etc** the largest part of something 大部分乐趣/时间/麻烦等: *Half the trouble with John is that he never really listens to what you say.* 约翰最麻烦的地方在于他从不真正听你说话。| *Kids seem to think that climbing up a slide is half the fun.* 孩子们好像认为大部分的乐趣在于爬上滑梯。**7 half a minute/moment/second etc** *spoken* a very short time【口】半分钟/刻/秒等〔表示时间很短〕: *Hold on, this will only take half a second.* 等一等，一会儿就行了。**8 have half a mind to do sth** *spoken*【口】**a)** to say that you would like to do something but you probably will not do it, especially when you want to show your disapproval of what someone has done 有点想做某事〔但很可能不做〕: *I have half a mind to tell him what an idiot he is.* 我真想告诉他他有多笨。**b)** used as a not very serious threat to show your disapproval of what someone has done 说不定我会〔表示不太当真的威胁〕: *I have half a mind to tell your mother about this.* 说不定我会把此事告诉你母亲。**9 only half the story** an explanation that is not complete, used especially to say that someone is trying to keep something secret 只是〔事件的〕部分真相: *Journalists are convinced that the Congressman was only telling them half the story.* 记者们相信那个众议员只告诉了他们部分真相。**10 half measures** actions or methods that are not effective in dealing with a difficult problem 不彻底的办法: *The opposition accused the government of being satisfied with half measures.* 反对党指

责政府满足于不彻底的办法。**11 go off at half cock/half cocked** to happen without enough preparation being done, with the result that it is not successful 因准备不足而失败

1 2 **half²** *n, pron plural* **halves** /hævz; hɑːvz/ [C]

1 ▶50%◀ either of the two equal parts into which something is divided or can be divided; ½ 一半, 二分之一: *Half of 50 is 25.* 50 的一半是 25。| *An hour and a half later I was still waiting for him to arrive.* 一个半小时之后, 我还在等着他的到来。| *"How old is Samantha now?" "She's five and a half."* "萨曼莎现在多大了?" "五岁半了。" | *The trade figures improved in the second half of last year.* 贸易数字于去年下半年有所改善。| *Half of the class was working on math problems while the other half divided into reading groups.* 班上的同学有一半在做数学题, 另一半分成了几个阅读小组。| *Scott gave her a piece of chocolate and kept the other half for himself.* 斯科特给了她一块巧克力, 另一半留给了自己。| **reduce/cut sth by half** (=make something 50% smaller) 减少/削减一半 *The new policy could cut the world oil production by half.* 这个新政策将使世界石油产量减少一半。| **break/cut sth in half** (=cut something into two equal parts) 分成/切成两半 *He cut the cake in half.* 他把蛋糕切成两半。

2 ▶NUMBER 数字◀ the number ½ 〔数字〕½, 二分之一: *Three halves make 1½.* 三个二分之一相加等于 1½。

3 half past *especially BrE* thirty minutes after the hour mentioned【尤英】〔…点钟〕以后半小时: **half past one/two/three etc** *Bill came home about half past one.* 比尔大约一点半回到家。| *She said she'd be home by six or half past.* 她说她会在六点或六点半回到家。

4 ▶SPORTS EVENT 体育项目◀ either of the two parts into which a sports event is divided 半场: *The Minnesota Vikings pulled ahead to win by seven points in the second half.* 明尼苏达维京人队在下半场以七分领先而获胜。

5 ▶FOOTBALL ETC 足球等◀ a player who plays in the middle part of the field 中(前)卫

6 ▶BEER 啤酒◀ *BrE* a half of a PINT of beer【英】半品脱: *Fancy a quick half down the pub?* 想不想去酒吧待一小会儿, 喝半品脱啤酒? | *two halves of bitter* 两份半品脱苦啤酒

7 ▶TICKET 票◀ *BrE* a child's ticket, for example on a bus or train, that is cheaper than an adult's ticket【英】儿童半票: *One and a half to Waterloo, please.* 请给我一张去滑铁卢的大人票和一张儿童半票。

8 and a half *informal* used when you think that something is very unusual or surprising, or very good【非正式】棒极了, 好极了: *That was a meal and a half!* 那顿饭棒极了!

9 your better half/other half *humorous* your husband or wife【幽默】丈夫; 妻子: *Let me introduce you to my better half.* 让我把你介绍给我的另一半。

10 not do sth by halves to do something very eagerly and using a lot of care and effort 认真地做某事, 不马虎: *I'm sure it will be a fantastic wedding. Eva never does anything by halves.* 我肯定婚礼一定会办得非常出色。伊娃办事从不马虎。

11 you don't know the half of it *spoken* used to emphasize that a situation is more difficult, complicated, or unpleasant than people realize【口】比你想象的更甚: *"I know it was a dreadful time, just after the war." "You don't know the half of it."* "我知道那时情况很糟糕, 战争才刚刚结束。" "比你想象的更糟。"

12 go halves (on sth) to share something, especially the cost of something, equally between two people〔两人〕平均分摊〔费用〕; 平分, 对半分: *Do you want to go halves on a pizza?* 你要和我合买一个意大利薄饼吗?

13 how the other half lives how people who are much richer or much poorer than you manage their lives, work, money etc 富人[穷人]是怎样过日子的: *He's working for a millionaire, so he's getting a taste of how the other half lives.* 他为一个百万富翁工作, 所以感受到了富人是怎样生活的。

14 too clever/rich/virtuous etc by half *BrE informal* clever, rich etc in an annoying way【英, 非正式】聪明/富有/高尚等过了头: *That boy's too arrogant by half.* 那个男孩太傲慢了。

2 **half³** *adv* **1** partly, but not completely 部分地, 不完全地: *I was half in love with her by the end of the evening.* 晚会快结束时, 我已经有点爱上她了。| *She was standing there half-dressed, putting on her makeup in front of the mirror.* 她站在镜子前化妆, 衣服还没有穿好。| *He seemed to half expect her to come back and apologize.* 他似乎有点期待她回来道歉。| **half-finished/half-empty/half full** *Cups of half-finished tea were on the floor beside the bed.* 床边的地板上有几杯喝了一半的茶。**2** used to emphasize something, especially when a situation is extremely bad 极其, 非常〔尤指情况很糟〕: *I had been driven half out of my mind with worry.* 我担忧得发疯了。| *The kitten looked half starved.* 小猫看起来饿坏了。**3 half as much/big etc again** larger by an amount that is equal to half the original size 多少/大小等是原来的一倍半: *Roy invested his savings in a new store that was half as big again as the old one.* 罗伊把他的积蓄投资在一家大小是原来一倍半的新店。**4 not half as good/interesting etc (as)** much less good, less interesting etc than someone or something else 远不如…好/有趣等: *The movie wasn't half as entertaining as the book.* 这部电影远不如原书好看。| *She can't love you half as much as I do.* 她不可能像我这样爱你。**5 not half** *BrE spoken* used when you want to emphasize an opinion or statement【英口】极其, 非常: *She doesn't half talk once she gets started.* 她只要一打开话匣子就说个没完。| *"Did you enjoy it, then?" "Not half!"* "那么你玩得高兴吗?" "高兴极了!" **6 not half bad** an expression meaning good, used especially when you are rather surprised that something is good〔出乎意料地〕相当好, 很棒: *Actually, the party wasn't half bad.* 实际上, 晚会真的不错。**7 half and half** partly one thing and partly another 各占一半; 既是…又是…: *"What is she, then, a psychiatrist or a social worker?" "Sort of half and half."* "那么, 她到底是一位精神科医生还是社会工作者?" "两者皆是。"

half-and-half /ˌ· · ˈ·/ *n* [U] *AmE* a mixture that is half milk and half cream, used in coffee or tea【美】〔奶油和牛奶各半, 掺加于咖啡或茶中的〕稀奶油

half-arsed /ˌhæf ˋɑrst; ˌhɑːf ˈɑːst◂/ *BrE*【英】, **half-assed** /ˌhæf ˋæst; ˌhɑːf ˈæst◂/ *AmE*【美】*adj informal*【非正式】**1** done without enough attention or effort 胡乱的; 敷衍了事的: *He made a half-arsed attempt to clean up after the party.* 晚会结束后, 他敷衍了事地收拾了一下。**2** completely stupid 极愚蠢的: *What a half-assed idea!* 真是个愚蠢的主意!

half·back /ˋhæfˌbæk; ˈhɑːfbæk/ *n* [C] **1** a player in football, RUGBY, HOCKEY etc who plays in the middle part of the field〔足球、橄榄球、曲棍球的〕中(前)卫, 中场球员 **2** a player in American football who, at the start of play, is behind the front line of players and next to the FULLBACK〔美式橄榄球的〕中卫

half-baked /ˌ· ˈ·◂/ *adj* a half-baked idea, suggestion, plan etc has not been properly planned〔想法、建议、计划等〕不成熟的, 考虑不周全的: *Education has been damaged by the half-baked notions of theorists who've never been in a classroom.* 教育被那些从未进过教室的理论家们草率的观点所害。

half board /ˌ· ˈ·/ *n* [U] *especially BrE* the price of a room in a hotel that includes breakfast and dinner【尤英】〔包括早餐及晚餐的〕半食宿房价 —compare 比较 FULL BOARD

half-breed /ˈ· ·/ *n* [C] a word which is now considered offensive meaning someone whose parents are of different races, especially one white parent and one Native American parent 混血儿〔父母为不同种族, 尤指一方为白人, 另一方为美洲印第安人。此词现具冒犯性〕 **—half-breed** *adj*

half broth·er /ˈ· ˌ· ·/ *n* [C] a brother who is the son of only one of your parents 同父异母[同母异父]兄弟

half-caste /ˈ· ·/ *n* [C] a word which is now considered offensive, meaning someone whose parents are of different races 混血儿〔此词现具冒犯性〕 **—half-caste** *adj*

half cock /ˌ· ˈ·/ —see 见 **go off at half cock** (HALF¹ (11))

half-crazed /ˌ· ˈ·◂/ *adj* behaving in a slightly crazy, uncontrolled way 有点发疯的: *half-crazed with pain* 疼得快发疯了

half crown /ˌ· ˈ·◂/ *n* [C] a coin used in Britain before 1971. There were eight half crowns in £1 半克朗〔1971 年以前的英国硬币名, 合一英镑的八分之一〕

half-cup /ˈ· ·/ *n* [C] *AmE* a small container used to measure an amount of food when cooking, or the amount that this holds【美】〔用来量食物的〕小量杯: *Add a half-cup of sugar.* 加上一小杯糖。

half-cut /ˌ· ˈ·/ *adj BrE old-fashioned* drunk【英, 过时】(酒)醉的

half-day /ˈ· ·/ *n* [C] a day when you work or go to school either in the morning or the afternoon, but not all day (上)半天班[学]

half dol·lar /ˌ· ˈ· ·/ *n* [C] an American or Canadian coin worth 50 cents〔美国或加拿大的〕半元硬币

half-heart·ed /ˌ· ˈ· ·◂/ *adj* a half-hearted attempt to do something is done without much effort and without much interest in the result 半心半意的, 敷衍了事的, 不热心的: *She made a half-hearted attempt to be friendly.* 她敷衍地表示了一下友好。 **—half-heartedly** *adv* **—half-heartedness** *n* [U]

half-hol·i·day /ˌ· ˈ· · ·/ *n* [C] *BrE* a morning or afternoon in which you do not have to go to work or school; HALF DAY【英】半日假

half-hour·ly /ˌ· ˈ· ·◂/ *adj, adv* done or happening every half hour 每半小时的[地]: *the half-hourly chimes of the clock* 半小时一次的钟鸣

half-length /ˌ· ˈ·◂/ *adj* **1** a half-length coat reaches to just above the knee〔长及膝上的〕半长〔外套〕**2** a half-length painting or picture shows the top half of someone's body 半身〔画像、照片〕

half-life /ˈ· ·/ *n* [C] the half life of a RADIOACTIVE substance is the length of time it takes to lose half of its RADIOACTIVITY〔放射性物质的〕半衰期

half-light /ˈ· ·/ *n* [U] the dull grey light you see when it is almost dark but not completely dark 半明半暗的光, 灰暗的光线: *Briggs heard the commotion but in the half-light of dawn could not see anyone clearly.* 布里格斯听到了喧闹声, 但在黎明半明半暗的光线中无法看清任何人。

half-mast /ˌ· ˈ·/ *n* **at half-mast a)** a flag that is at half mast has been put at the middle of the pole in order to show respect and sadness for someone important who has died 下半旗〔表示哀悼〕**b)** *BrE humorous* if someone's trousers are at half-mast, they are too short【英, 幽默】〔裤子〕短得半吊着, 短得见踝的

half moon /ˌ· ˈ·/ *n* [C] the shape of the moon when only half of it is showing 半月(形) —compare 比较 FULL MOON, NEW MOON —see picture on page A6 参见 A6 页图

half nel·son /ˌhæf ˋnɛlsn̩; ˌhɑːf ˈnelsən/ *n* [C] a way of holding your opponent's arm behind their back in the sport of WRESTLING〔摔跤姿势〕侧面肩下握颈

half note /ˈ· ·/ *n* [C] *AmE* a musical note which continues for half the length of a WHOLE NOTE【美】〔音乐〕二分音符; MINIM *BrE*【英】—see picture at 参见 MUSIC 图

half·penny /ˋhepnɪ; ˈheɪpni/ *n* [C] a small coin worth half of one penny, used in Britain in the past〔英国旧时使用的〕半便士小硬币 —see also 另见 **not have two pennies/halfpennies to rub together** (RUB[1] (11))

half price /ˌ· ˈ·◂/ *adv* at half the usual price 以半价: *Do you like the new carpet? We got it half price in the sale.* 你喜欢那张新地毯吗? 我们在大减价时以半价买的。—**half-price** *adj*: *half-price sale items* 半价商品

half-sis·ter /ˈ· ,··/ *n* [C] a sister who is the daughter of only one of your parents 同父异母[同母异父]姊妹

half step /ˈ· ·/ *n* [C] *AmE* the difference in PITCH[1] (3) between any two notes that are next to each other on a piano【美】半音; SEMITONE *BrE*【英】

half-term /ˌ· ˈ·◂/ *n* [C] *BrE* a short holiday from school in the middle of a TERM[1] (9)【英】〔学校的〕期中假 —compare 比较 MIDTERM[2]

half-tim·bered /ˌ· ˈ··◂/ *adj* a half-timbered house is usually old and shows the wooden structure of the building on the outside walls〔古式房屋建筑〕露明木架的

half time /ˌ· ˈ·◂/ *n* [U] a short period of rest between two parts of a game, such as football or BASKETBALL〔足球、篮球比赛等的〕中场休息: *The score at half time was 34-7.* 中场休息时比分为 34 比 7。—see also 另见 FULL TIME

half·tone /ˋhæfˌton; ˌhɑːfˈtəʊn◂/ *n* **1** [U] a method of printing black and white photographs that shows different shades of grey by changing the number of black DOTs in an area of the photograph〔印刷中的〕网目凸版(制版法), 网线凸版 **2** [C] a photograph printed by this method 网版印刷的照片, 网目版图, 网线凸版画 **3** [C] *AmE* a HALF STEP【美】半音

half-truth /ˈ· ·/ *n* [C] a statement that is only partly true, especially one that is intended to keep something secret〔为了隐瞒真相的〕半真半假的陈述: *His replies were full of evasions and half-truths.* 他的回答充满推诿之词和半真半假的鬼话。

half vol·ley /ˌ· ˈ··/ *n* [C] **1** an action in tennis in which the ball is hit just after it hits the ground〔网球〕一落地就跳起即击的击球 **2** in CRICKET, a ball that can easily be hit by the BATSMAN just after it hits the ground〔板球〕落地后跳起时即被击球手轻易击中的球, 反弹球

half·way /ˋhæfˋwe; ˌhɑːfˈweɪ◂/ *adj, adv* **1** at a middle point in space or time between two things〔空间、时间的〕中间(的), 半途(的): *We reached the halfway point ten miles into our walk.* 走了十英里后, 我们到达了中间点。| *Grease the muffin tins and fill them halfway with batter.* 将松饼烤模涂上牛油, 再把面糊倒至半满。| [**+up/along etc**] *He chased Kevin halfway up the stairs.* 他追凯文一直追到楼梯的中间。| *It was a terrible film – I left halfway through.* 这部电影糟糕得很, 我半途就离场了。| **be halfway there** (=be halfway to achieving something) 完成一半 *If we can just finish this section we'll be halfway there.* 如果我们能干完这部分, 就算完成一半了。**2 halfway respectable/decent/civil etc** reasonably RESPECTABLE etc 还算正派/体面/文明等: *It's the only halfway decent hotel around here.* 这是附近唯一一家还算体面的旅馆。**3 go halfway towards doing sth** to achieve something partly but not completely 完成一部分; 做得不彻底: *These measures only go halfway towards solving the problem.* 这些措施不能彻底地解决这个问题。—see also 另见 **meet sb halfway** (MEET[1] (17))

halfway house /ˌ·· ˈ· ·/ *n* **1** [singular] something which is a combination of the qualities of two things, but may not be as good as either of those two things by themselves 介乎两者之间的东西: *His clarinet solos are a kind of halfway house between the styles of Dodds and Russell.* 他的单簧管独奏既有点多兹的风格, 又有点拉塞尔的风格。**2** [C] a place for former prisoners or people who have had mental illnesses, where they can live until they are ready to live on their own〔为刑满释放者或已痊愈的精神病人重返社会而设立的〕过渡教习所[疗养所], 重返社会训练所

half-wit /ˈ· ·/ *n* [C] *informal* a stupid person or someone who has done something stupid【非正式】傻瓜, 笨蛋 —**half-witted** *adj*: *a burly half-witted fellow with one eye* 一个独眼的傻大个 —**half-wittedly** *adv*

half-year·ly /ˌ· ˈ··/ *adj, adv* done or happening every six months 每隔半年(的), 半年一次(的): *half-yearly meetings in June and December* 于六月和十二月每隔半年开一次的会议

hal·i·but /ˋhæləbət; ˈhælɨbət/ *n* [C] a large flat sea fish used as food 大比目鱼〔食用海鱼〕

hal·i·to·sis /ˌhæləˋtosɪs; ˌhælɨˈtəʊsɨs/ *n* [U] a condition in which someone's breath smells very bad 口臭

hall /hɔl; hɔːl/ *n* [C] **1** the area just inside the door of a house or other building that leads to other rooms; HALLWAY (1)〔住宅的〕门厅,〔正门入口处的〕走廊: *We hung our coats on a rack in the entrance hall.* 我们把外套挂在门厅里的衣架上。**2** a passage in a building or house that leads to many of the rooms; CORRIDOR (1)〔建筑物内的〕走廊, 过道: *Each floor of the dorm had ten rooms on both sides of the hall.* 宿舍楼的每一层在走廊的两边都有十个房间。**3** a building or large room for public events such as meetings or dances 大厅, 会堂, 礼堂: *Five hundred people filled the lecture hall.* 来了五百人, 把演讲厅都挤满了。| *Carnegie Hall* 卡内基音乐厅 **4 Hall** *especially BrE* part of the name of some large houses in the country【尤英】〔乡间〕大庄园, 府第: *Haddon Hall* 哈登庄园 **5** *BrE* a place provided by a college or university for students to live in; HALL OF RESIDENCE【英】〔大学的〕学生宿舍 —see also 另见 CITY HALL, MUSIC HALL, TOWN HALL

hal·lal /həˋlɑl; hɑːˈlɑːl/ *adj* another spelling of HALAL halal 的另一种拼法

Hal·lé /ˋhæle; ˈhæleɪ/, **Sir Charles** (1819-95) a German PIANIST and CONDUCTOR who came to live in the UK and started the **Hallé Orchestra** in Manchester in 1857 阿莱〔(1819-1895), 德国钢琴家、音乐指挥。他后来移居英国, 并于 1857 年在曼彻斯特创立了阿莱管弦乐团〕

hal·le·lu·jah /ˌhæləˋlujə; ˌhælɨˈluːjə◂/ *interjection* **1** used as an expression of thanks, JOY, or praise to God 哈利路亚〔表示感谢、欣喜或赞美上帝〕**2** used when something has finally happened that you think should have happened before 哈利路亚〔表示期望已久的事终于发生〕: *"The bus is here!" "Well, hallelujah."* "公共汽车来了!" "啊, 哈利路亚!" —**hallelujah** *n* [C]

Hallelujah Cho·rus, the /ˌ····ˈ··/ a part of Handel's *Messiah*, which is sung by a large group of people《哈利路亚合唱曲》〔韩德尔《弥赛亚》中的合唱曲〕

Hal·ley's com·et /ˌhælɪz ˋkɑmɪt; ˌhæliz ˈkɒmɨt/ a COMET (=an object in space like a bright ball with a long tail) that moves around the Sun and passes close to the Earth every 76 years. It was named after the English ASTRONOMER Edmund Halley (1656-1742), and it last appeared close to the Earth in 1986. 哈雷彗星〔绕太阳运行的一颗彗星, 每 76 年回归一次, 以英国天文学家艾德蒙·哈雷 (1656-1742) 的姓氏命名。最近一次回归是在 1986 年〕

hal·liard /ˋhæljɚd; ˈhæljəd/ *n* [C] another spelling of HALYARD halyard 的另一种拼法

hall·mark[1] /ˋhɔlˌmɑrk; ˈhɔːlmɑːk/ *n* [C] **1** an idea, method, or quality that is typical of a particular person or thing 特点, 特征; 标志: [**+of**] *Non-violence and simplicity were the hallmarks of Gandhi's philosophy.* 非暴力和简朴是甘地哲学的特点。| **have all the hallmarks of** *The explosion had all the hallmarks of a terrorist attack.* 这次爆炸事件是一次不折不扣的恐怖袭击。**2** a mark put on silver, gold, or PLATINUM that shows the quality of the metal, and where and when it was made〔金、银或白金制品上的〕纯度印记

hallmark[2] *v* [T] to put a hallmark on silver, gold, or PLATINUM 在〔金、银或白金制品〕上打印记

hal·lo /həˋlo; həˈləʊ/ *interjection old-fashioned* a British form of HELLO【过时】hello 的英式拼法

Hall of Fame /ˌ· · ˈ·/ *n* [C] a place in the US where people can go to learn about a particular sport or activity and the famous people connected with it〔美国〕名人堂，名人纪念馆

hall of res·i·dence /ˌ· · ˈ··· / *n* [C] *BrE* a college or university building where students live【英】〔学院或大学的〕学生宿舍楼; DORMITORY[1] (2) *AmE*【美】

hal·lowed /ˈhælod; ˈhæləʊd/ *adj* **1** made holy 神圣的，奉为神圣的: **hallowed ground** (=land, especially around a church, that has been made holy)〔尤指教堂四周的〕圣地 **2** *sometimes humorous* important and respected【有时幽默】重要而受尊崇的: *a hallowed tradition* 神圣的传统 | *the hallowed portals* (=doors) *of Broadcasting House* 英国广播公司中央大楼的神圣入口

Hal·low·een, Hallowe'en /ˌhæloˈin; ˌhæləʊˈiːn◂/ *n* [U] the night of October 31st, when it was believed that the spirits of dead people appeared, and which is now celebrated by children, who dress as WITCH*es*, GHOST*s* etc 万圣节前夕〔10月31日之夜〕

CULTURAL NOTE 文化注释

Halloween is celebrated in both the US and the UK. Children dress in special clothes, for example as GHOST*s*, PRINCESS*es*, COWBOY*s*, or WITCH*es*. Children go trick-or-treating (TRICK OR TREAT), which means they go from house to house dressed in their special clothes, knocking on doors and saying 'trick or treat!' The people in the houses must then either give the children a 'treat' (usually sweets) or the children will play a trick on them. People also make JACK-O'-LANTERN*s* by cutting faces in PUMPKIN*s* and putting a light inside. Trick-or-treating is much more common in the US than in the UK, and in some areas people decorate their houses with ghosts or make their front gardens look like GRAVEYARD*s*. 英美两国都庆贺万圣节。儿童穿着特殊服装，如扮作鬼魂、公主、牛仔、巫师。儿童玩一种叫做"不请吃就捣乱"的游戏，他们穿着特殊服装挨家敲门，说道："不请吃就捣乱"，那户人家要请他们吃东西（通常给些糖果），不然那些孩子就会捉弄他们。人们还在南瓜上掏出人脸的形状，内置蜡烛，叫做"灯笼杰克"。"不请吃就捣乱"游戏在美国比在英国常见。有些地方人们用鬼魂形象装饰房屋，或把前院弄成坟地的样子。

Children and older people sometimes go to Halloween parties where they play games such as 'bobbing for apples', when they try to catch an apple floating in water by using their teeth. Food at these parties is usually made to look very strange, for example by making it an unusual colour or by making it in the shape of a witch, a ghost, or a BAT (=a small black animal like a mouse with wings). Many of these Halloween traditions originally come from the US, but they are now also common in the UK. 孩子和大人有时去参加万圣节聚会，玩游戏，如"钓苹果"，即试着咬起浮在水上的苹果。这些聚会上的食物通常样子古怪，比如颜色怪异，或形状像巫师、鬼魂或蝙蝠。这些万圣节传统很多源自美国，但现在在英国也很常见。

hal·lu·ci·nate /həˈlusn̩ˌet; həˈluːsɪ̩neɪt/ *v* [I] to see or hear things that are not really there 产生幻觉

hal·lu·ci·na·tion /həˌlusn̩ˈeʃən; həˌluːsɪ̩ˈneɪʃən/ *n* **1** [C,U] the experience of seeing or feeling something that is not really there 幻觉 **2** [C] something which you imagine you can see or hear, but which is not really there 由幻觉产生的形象[声音]: *drug-induced hallucinations* 由药物引起的幻觉

hal·lu·ci·na·to·ry /həˈlusn̩əˌtɔrɪ; həˈluːsɪ̩nətəri/ *adj formal*【正式】**1** causing hallucinations or resulting from hallucinations（引起）幻觉的; 幻觉导致的: *hallucinatory drugs* 致幻药物 **2** using strange images, sounds etc like those experienced in a hallucination 似幻觉的，幻觉般的: *a hallucinatory collage of images* 各种图像如幻觉般的拼凑

hal·lu·ci·no·gen·ic /həˌlusn̩əˈdʒɛnɪk; həˌluːsɪ̩nəˈdʒenɪk◂/ *adj* hallucinogenic drugs make people experience hallucinations 引起幻觉的，致幻的

hall·way /ˈhɔlˌwe; ˈhɔːlweɪ/ *n* [C] **1** the area just inside the door of a house or other building that leads to other rooms; HALL (1)〔住宅的〕门厅;〔正门入口处的〕走廊 **2** a passage in a building or house that leads to many of the rooms; CORRIDOR (1)〔建筑物内的〕走廊，过道

ha·lo /ˈhelo; ˈheɪləʊ/ *n* [C] **1** a bright circle that is often shown above or around the heads of holy people in religious art〔神像头上的〕光轮，光环 **2** a bright circle of light 晕，晕圈

hal·o·gen /ˈhælədʒən; ˈhælədʒen/ *n* [U] one of a group of five simple chemical substances that make compounds easily 卤素

Hals /hæls; hæls/, **Frans** /fræns; fræns/ (?1580-1666) a Dutch painter who painted many PORTRAIT*s* (=paintings of real people). His most famous portrait is *The Laughing Cavalier* 哈尔斯〔(?1580-1666)，荷兰画家。他画过不少肖像画，最有名的作品是《笑脸骑士》〕

halt[1] /hɔlt; hɔːlt/ *n* [singular] a stop or pause 停止，停住; 暂停: **bring sth to a halt** (=make something stop moving or continuing) 使…停顿; 使…中止 *Heavy snowfalls brought traffic to a halt on the Brenner Pass.* 大雪使得布伦纳山口的交通陷于停顿。| *fuel shortages that have brought the industry to a grinding halt* 使该工业慢慢地停止生产的燃料短缺 | **come/grind/crash etc to a halt** (=stop moving or continuing) 停下/慢慢停下/猛然停下 *The whole peace process seems to have ground to a halt.* 整个和平进程似乎已慢慢地停顿下来。| *Joe slammed on the brakes and the car skidded to a halt.* 乔猛踩刹车，汽车便向前滑行着停住了。| **call a halt (to)** (=officially stop an activity from continuing)〔正式〕中止，停止 *The IRA leadership has called a halt to its campaign of violence.* 爱尔兰共和军的领导层已经停止其暴力活动。

halt[2] *v* **1** [I] to stop moving 停下，停止: *The parade halted by a busy corner.* 游行队伍在一个热闹的拐角处停下了。**2 halt!** used as a military command to order someone to stop moving or soldiers to stop marching〔口令〕站住！立定！: *Company halt!* 全连立定！| *Halt! Who goes there?* 站住！是谁？**3** [T] to prevent someone or something from continuing with something 阻止: *There were calls to halt the hunting of seals.* 人们呼吁停止捕猎海豹。

hal·ter /ˈhɔltɚ; ˈhɔːltə/ *n* [C] **1** a rope or leather band that fastens around a horse's head, usually used to lead the horse〔马的〕笼头，缰绳 **2** also 又作 **halter top** a type of clothing for women that ties behind the neck and across the back, so that the arms and back are not covered〔女用的在颈及背后系带的〕袒肩露背上装，三角背心 **3** *literary* a piece of rope used to HANG[1] (3) criminals【文】绞索

hal·ter·neck /ˈhɔltɚˌnɛk; ˈhɔːltənek/ *adj* a halterneck shirt ties around the neck and behind the back, so that the arms and back are not covered〔在颈及背后系带〕袒肩露背的〔服装〕— **halterneck** *n* [C]

halt·ing /ˈhɔltɪŋ; ˈhɔːltɪŋ/ *adj* if your speech or movements are halting, you stop for a moment between words or movements, especially because you are not confident 断断续续的; 迟疑不决的: *We carried on a halting conversation in our imperfect German.* 我们用不熟练的德语断断续续地进行交谈。— **haltingly** *adv*

halve /hæv; hɑːv/ *v* [T] **1** to cut or divide something into two equal pieces 把…分成两半，对半分: *Halve the eggplant lengthwise and hollow out the center.* 把茄子纵向地切成两半，把中间挖空。**2** to reduce something by a half 将…减半: *The European Union plans to halve production of CFCs by the end of the decade.* 欧盟计划在本十年末将含氯氟烃的产量减少一半。

halves /hævz; hɑːvz/ the plural of HALF

hal·yard, halliard /ˈhæljɚd; ˈhæljəd/ *n* [C] *technical* a rope used to raise or lower a flag or sail【术语】〔用以升降旗、帆的〕吊索，升降索

ham[1] /hæm; hæm/ *n* **1** [C,U] the upper part of a pig's leg that has been preserved with salt or smoke, or the meat from this 火腿; 火腿肉: *a ham sandwich* 火腿三明治 | *a seven-pound ham* 七磅重的火腿 **2** [C] *informal* an actor who performs with too much false emotion【非正式】演技做作的演员，表演过火的演员 **3** [C] someone who receives and sends radio messages for fun rather than as their job 业余无线电爱好者 **4 hams** [plural] the upper part of a person's or animal's legs 股臀

ham[2] *v* **ham it up** *informal* to perform with too much false emotion when acting【非正式】做作地表演，表演过火

Ha·mas /ˈhɑmɑs; ˈhɑːmɑːs/ an organization of Islamic Fundamentalists (=people who follow the rules of their religion very strictly) in Palestine 哈马斯〔巴勒斯坦伊斯兰教原教旨主义者组织〕

ham·burg·er /ˈhæmbɚgɚ; ˈhæmbɜːgə/ *n* **1** [C] very small pieces of BEEF pressed together, cooked, and eaten between two round pieces of bread 汉堡包 **2** [U] *AmE* beef that has been cut into very small pieces【美】牛肉馅，碎牛肉; MINCE[2] *BrE*【英】

ham-fist·ed /ˌ·ˈ··◂/ also 又作 **ham-handed** *adj informal*【非正式】**1** not at all skilful with your hands; CLUMSY (1) 笨手笨脚的，手不灵巧的 **2** not at all skilful or careful in the way that you deal with people〔待人接物〕笨拙的，不灵巧的: *the government's ham-fisted approach towards the disabled* 政府对待残疾人士的拙劣手法 — **ham-fistedly, ham-handedly** *adv*

Ham·il·ton /ˈhæməltən; ˈhæmḷtən/ the capital city and main port of Bermuda, on Bermuda Island 汉密尔顿〔百慕大首府及主要港口，位于百慕大岛〕

Hamilton /ˈhæmɪltn̩; ˈhæmḷtən/, **Al·ex·an·der** /ˌælɪgˈzændɚ; ˌælɪgˈzɑːndə/ (?1755-1804) a US politician who helped to write *The Constitution of the United States* and was the first US Secretary of the Treasury from 1789 to 1795. Alexander Hamilton's picture is printed on the US ten-dollar bill. 汉密尔顿〔(?1755-1804)，美国政治家。他曾帮助起草了《美国宪法》，1789 至 1795 年任美国第一任财政部长。10 美元纸币上印有他的画像〕

Ham·let /ˈhæmlɪt; ˈhæmlḷt/ the main character in the play *Hamlet* by William Shakespeare, which is one of Shakespeare's most famous plays. Hamlet is the Prince of Denmark, and is a serious, unhappy young man who is unable to decide how he feels or what he should do. 哈姆雷特〔威廉·莎士比亚最著名的戏剧之一《哈姆雷特》的主人公。他是丹麦王子，也是一位严肃、忧郁、处事犹豫不决的年轻人〕—see also 另见 OPHELIA

hamlet *n* [C] a very small village 小村庄

ham·mer¹ /ˈhæmɚ; ˈhæmə/ *n* [C]

1 ▶**TOOL** 工具◀ **a)** a tool with a heavy metal part on a long handle, used for hitting nails into wood 榔头，锤子 —see picture at 参见 TOOL¹ 图 **b)** a tool like this with a wooden head used to make something flat, make a noise etc 木槌: *an auctioneer's hammer* 拍卖人的木槌

2 come/go under the hammer to be offered for sale at an AUCTION¹ 被拍卖

3 be/go at it hammer and tongs *informal* to fight or argue very loudly【非正式】激烈打斗[争吵]

4 ▶**PIANO** 钢琴◀ a wooden part of a PIANO that hits the strings inside to make a musical sound 音锤

5 ▶**GUN** 枪、炮◀ the part of a gun that hits the explosive CHARGE¹ (8) that fires a bullet 击铁 —see picture at 参见 GUN¹ 图

6 ▶**SPORT** 体育◀ a heavy metal ball on a wire with a handle that is thrown as far as possible, as a sport 链球

hammer² *v*

1 ▶**HIT STH WITH A HAMMER** 用锤击打某物◀ [I,T] to hit something with a hammer in order to force it into a particular position or shape 锤击，锤打；把…锤进: **hammer sth into/onto** *He hammered the door into its frame.* 他把门锤进门框中。| *The blacksmith then hammers the horseshoe into its final shape.* 铁匠随后将马蹄铁锤打成形。

2 ▶**HIT REPEATEDLY** 反复敲打◀ [I] to hit something many times, especially making a loud noise〔大声地〕反复敲打: [**+against/on**] *The rain was hammering against the window.* 雨不停地敲打着窗户。

3 ▶**DEFEAT** 击败◀ [T] *informal* to defeat someone completely at a sport【非正式】〔在体育比赛中〕彻底击败: *Arsenal hammered Manchester United in yesterday's game.* 阿森纳队在昨天的比赛中彻底击败了曼联队。

4 ▶**HIT HARD** 狠击◀ [T] *informal* to hit or kick something very hard【非正式】猛击；狠踢: *Robinson hammered the ball into the goal.* 鲁宾逊猛力将球攻进了球门。

5 hammer away at a) to work hard and continuously at something 接连工作，不懈地致力于: *I kept hammering away at the essay until it was done.* 我一直在埋头苦干，直到论文写好为止。 **b)** to repeat something continuously until you are sure that people understand or accept what you are saying 重复论及，反复说明: *Petersen kept hammering away at his demand for a public inquiry.* 彼得森不断要求进行一次公开调查。

6 hammer sth home to make sure that people understand what you want to say by speaking in a determined way 明确指出；强调: *an important point that needs to be hammered home* 需特别强调的一个要点

7 ▶**HEART** 心◀ [I] if your heart hammers, you feel it beating strongly and quickly〔猛烈快速地〕跳动: *She stood outside the door, her heart hammering.* 她站在门外，心在怦怦跳动。

hammer ↔ sth **in, hammer** sth **into** sb *phr v* [T] to repeat something continuously until people completely understand it 不断重复使某人明白〔某事〕，反复灌输: *The coach hammered his message into the team.* 教练向全队反复灌输他的话。

hammer out sth *phr v* [T] to decide on an agreement, contract etc after a lot of discussion and disagreement〔经详细的讨论及争议后〕得出〔协议、解决办法等〕: *The UN is trying to force the warring factions to get together and hammer out a solution.* 联合国正试图拉拢各敌对派系一起寻求解决问题的方案。

Hammer, Mike a PRIVATE DETECTIVE in books by the US writer Mickey Spillane. He is very tough and usually shoots criminals instead of having them arrested. 迈克·哈默〔美国作家米基·斯皮兰小说中的私家侦探。他行事粗暴，通常不是逮捕罪犯，而是直接将他们击毙〕

hammer and sick·le /ˌ.. . ˈ../ *n* [singular] **1** the sign of a hammer crossing a SICKLE on a red background, used as a sign of COMMUNISM 镰刀和锤头（图案）〔共产主义的标志〕 **2** the flag of the former Soviet Union 前苏联国旗

ham·mered /ˈhæmɚd; ˈhæməd/ *adj* [only before noun 仅用于名词前] **1** hammered silver, gold etc has a pattern of small hollow areas on its surface〔金、银等制品〕锻造的 **2** *informal* very drunk【非正式】喝得醉醺醺的

Hammer film /ˈ.. ˌ./ *n* [C] a HORROR FILM produced by a British company called Hammer Film Productions during the 1950s and 1960s. The films were often based on well-known stories, such as those about *Dracula* and *Frankenstein*. 哈默影片〔指 20 世纪 50、60 年代英国哈默电影制作公司制作的恐怖影片。影片通常根据《吸血僵尸》和《科学怪人》等著名小说改编而成〕

ham·mer·ing /ˈhæmərɪŋ; ˈhæmərɪŋ/ *n* [singular] **1 give/take a hammering** to attack or be attacked very severely 发起/受到猛烈攻击: *Dresden took a real hammering during the war.* 德累斯顿在战争期间受到猛烈攻击。**2** the sound of someone hitting something with a hammer or with their FISTS (=closed hands) 锤击声；拳击声: *There was a hammering at the door.* 有人在使劲敲门。

Ham·mers, the /ˈhæmɚz; ˈhæməz/ the informal name for West Ham football club 哈默斯，锤子〔西汉姆足球俱乐部的非正式名称〕

Ham·mer·stein /ˈhæmɚstaɪn; ˈhæməstaḷn/, **Oscar** (1895-1960) a US songwriter, who worked for many years with the COMPOSER Richard Rodgers to produce many famous MUSICALS (=films or plays that use singing and dancing to tell a story), such as *Oklahoma!*, *The King and I*, *South Pacific*, and *The Sound of Music* 哈默斯坦〔(1895-1960)，美国词作家。他曾与作曲家理查德·罗杰斯合作多年，创作了许多著名音乐剧，如《俄克拉荷马州》、《国王与我》、《南太平洋》以及《音乐之声》〕

ham·mock /ˈhæmək; ˈhæmək/ *n* [C] a thing for sleeping in, consisting of a long piece of cloth or a net that is hung between two trees〔帆布或网做的〕吊床

ham·per¹ /ˈhæmpɚ; ˈhæmpə/ *v* [T] to restrict someone's movements, activities, or achievements by causing difficulties for them 阻碍，妨碍；牵制: *Women's progress in the workplace is still hampered by male attitudes.* 妇女在工作上的发展仍受到男性态度的阻扰。

hamper² *n* [C] **1** a basket with a lid, often used for carrying food〔用于携带食品的〕有盖篮子: *a picnic hamper* 野餐篮子 —see picture at 参见 BASKET 图 **2** *AmE* a large basket that you put dirty clothes in until they can be washed【美】〔放置待洗脏衣物的〕洗衣筐；LAUNDRY BASKET *BrE*【英】

Hamp·shire /ˈhæmpʃɚ; ˈhæmpʃə/ a COUNTY in southern England on the English Channel 汉普郡〔英格兰南部一郡，濒临英吉利海峡〕

Hamp·stead /ˈhæmpstɛd; ˈhæmpstḷd/ an area of North London with expensive houses, where many well-known writers and INTELLECTUALS live. In the middle of Hampstead there is a large area of grassland called **Hampstead Heath** 汉普斯特德〔伦敦北部一高级住宅区，许多著名作家和知识分子在此居住。住宅区中心有一大片草地，称汉普斯特德绿地〕

Hamp·ton Court /ˌ.. ˈ./ also **Hampton Court Palace** a large building southwest of London, which belonged to King Henry VIII and was used as a royal palace until the 18th century 汉普顿宫〔伦敦西南一处大型建筑，曾属亨利八世，18 世纪以前被用作皇宫〕

ham·ster /ˈhæmstɚ; ˈhæmstə/ *n* [C] a small animal like a mouse, often kept as a pet 仓鼠〔多作宠物〕

ham·string¹ /ˈhæmˌstrɪŋ; ˈhæmˌstrɪŋ/ *n* [C] a TENDON behind your knee 腘绳肌腱，腘旁腱，腿腱

hamstring² *v past tense and past participle* **hamstrung** /-ˌstrʌŋ; -ˌstrʌŋ/ [T often passive 常用被动态] to restrict someone's activities or development so much that they cannot do the job they are supposed to do（受到）阻碍，（被…）束缚；使无能为力: *Police officers claim that they are hamstrung by regulations and paperwork.* 警察声称他们被各种规定和文案工作所束缚。

Han·cock /ˈhænkɑk; ˈhænkɒk/, **John** (1737-93) a US politician who was the president of the Continental Congress before the US became an independent country, and was the first person to write his name on *The Declaration of Independence* 汉考克〔(1737-1793)，美国政治家。美国独立前，曾任大陆会议主席，也是第一个在《独立宣言》上签名的人〕

hand¹ /hænd; hænd/ *n*

① PART OF THE BODY 人体部位
② HELP/WORK 帮助/工作
③ SKILFUL 有某种技能的
④ CONTROL 控制
⑤ DEAL WITH/BE INVOLVED IN 处理/参与
⑥ CLOSE 接近的
⑦ DIRECTLY/NOT DIRECTLY 直接的/非直接的
⑧ OTHER MEANINGS 其他意思

① PART OF THE BODY 人体部位

1 [C] the part at the end of a person's arm, including the fingers and thumb, used to pick up or keep hold of things 手: *He held the pencil in his right hand.* 他用右手握着铅笔。| *Go wash your hands.* 去洗手。| **hold hands** *They kissed and held hands.* 他们接吻并拉着手。| **take sb by the hand** (=hold sb's hand in order to take them somewhere) 牵着某人的手 *Marika took the child by the hand and led her away.* 马里卡牵着孩子的手把她带走了。—see picture at 参见 BODY 图

2 hand in hand holding each other's hand, especially to show love 手拉手〔尤指表示爱意〕: *They strolled hand in hand through the flower garden.* 他们手拉着手漫步穿过花园。

3 right-handed/left-handed using the right hand for most actions rather than the left, or the left hand rather than the right 惯用右手/左手的: *a left-handed tennis player* 左撇子网球手

4 right/left hander a player who uses mainly the right hand or mainly the left hand 惯用右手/左手的选手[球员]

② HELP/WORK 帮助/工作

5 a hand help with something you are doing, especially something that involves physical work 帮忙, 支援: **give/lend sb a hand** *It's really heavy – can you give me a hand?* 这东西真重——你能帮个忙吗? | **need a hand** *Tell me if you need a hand.* 需要帮忙就告诉我。—see 见 HELP¹ (USAGE)

6 ►WORKER 工人◄ [C] someone who does physical work on a farm, in a factory etc 〔从事体力劳动的〕工人

7 not do a hand's turn *BrE informal* to do no work at all 【英, 非正式】一点事也不做: *He never does a hand's turn to help me.* 他从不帮我。

③ SKILFUL 有某种技能的

8 a dab hand someone who is very good at doing something 能手: *She's a dab hand at making pastry.* 她是做糕点的能手。

9 good with your hands skilful at making things 手巧的, 有一双灵巧的手

10 turn your hand to to start doing something new or practising a new skill 着手做〔新的事情〕; 开始练习〔新技能〕: *Larry can turn his hand to anything.* 拉里做什么工作都行。

11 keep your hand in to keep practising something so you do not lose your skill 继续练习以保持熟练: *You should work part-time, just to keep your hand in.* 你应该做一份兼职工作, 免得生疏了。

④ CONTROL 控制

12 in the hands of/in sb's hands controlled by someone 在〔某人〕的控制之中, 由〔某人〕支配[掌管]: *The area is already in rebel hands.* 那个地区已经落入叛乱分子的手中。

13 a firm hand strict control of someone 严厉管制: *That child is a little monster. She obviously needs a firm hand.* 那个孩子是个调皮鬼, 她显然需要严加管教。

14 get out of hand to become impossible to control 失控: *Deal with the problem before it gets completely out of hand.* 在问题完全失控之前加以处理。

15 take sb/sth in hand to bring someone or something under control 控制, 管制: *It's time these young offenders were taken in hand.* 到了好好管教这些少年犯的时候了。

⑤ DEAL WITH/BE INVOLVED IN 处理/参与

16 in hand being dealt with 在处理之中: *Don't worry – all the arrangements are in hand.* 别担心, 一切都安排好了。| **have sth in hand** *Give them a call to let them know we have the matter in hand.* 打电话告诉他们我们正在处理这件事。

17 have a hand in to influence or be involved in something 插手, 参与: *I suspect John had a hand in this.* 我怀疑约翰参与了此事。

18 in the hands of/in sb's hands being dealt with by someone 由〔某人〕处理: *The whole affair is now in the hands of the police.* 整件事现在由警方负责处理。

19 in good/safe/capable hands being dealt with or looked after by someone who can be trusted 在可靠的/稳妥的/能干的人手里: *We left the project in the capable hands of our deputy manager.* 我们把这个项目交给了能干的副经理负责。

20 off your hands if something or someone is off your hands, you are not responsible for them any more 不再负责: *We have more free time now the kids are off our hands.* 现在孩子们不用我们看管了, 我们就有更多的自由时间了。

21 have sth/sb on your hands to have a difficult job, problem, or responsibility that you must deal with 手头有某事待处理〔指困难的事情或问题〕: *They'll have a battle on their hands if they try to build a road here.* 如果他们要在这里筑路, 他们将面临一场艰难的战斗。

⑥ CLOSE 接近的

22 at hand *formal* near in time or space 【正式】〔时间或空间上〕接近的, 不远的: *The great day was almost at hand.* 重要的一天即将到来。| **near/close at hand** *There are shops and buses close at hand.* 附近就有商店和公共汽车。

23 have/keep sth to hand to have or keep something where you can easily reach it 将某物放在手边

24 on hand close by and ready when needed 在手头; 在近旁: *The nurse will be on hand if you need her.* 如果你需要护士的话, 她就在附近。

⑦ DIRECTLY/NOT DIRECTLY 直接的/非直接的

25 first hand/at first hand by direct personal experience 第一手的/第一手地; 直接的/直接地: *She stayed there to experience village life at first hand.* 她留在那儿亲身体验乡村生活。| *first hand eyewitness accounts of the riot* 亲眼目击者对暴乱的描述

26 at second/third/fourth hand passed from the first person who actually saw or heard something to a second, third, or fourth person 第二/三/四(道)手: *I may have the story wrong as I heard it at second hand.* 我说的不一定对, 因为我是听别人说的。—see also 另见 SECOND HAND

27 by hand a) by a person, not a machine 手工的: *Every buttonhole is made by hand.* 所有纽扣眼都是手工做的。**b)** delivered from one person to another, not sent through the post 亲手交的, 非邮递的

⑧ OTHER MEANINGS 其他意思

28 go hand in hand to be closely connected 密切相关; 同时发生: *High unemployment and high crime often go hand in hand.* 高失业率和高犯罪率常常是密切相关的。

29 get your hands on a) to obtain something 获取, 得到: *They all want to get their hands on my money.* 他们都想得到我的钱。**b)** to catch someone you are angry with 抓住〔某人〕: *Wait until I get my hands on her, she's borrowed my best skirt.* 等我把她抓住再说, 她借走了我最好的裙子。

30 lay your hands on to find or obtain something 找到; 得到: *I'll bring some tapes if I can lay my hands on them.* 如果找得到的话, 我会带几盒录音带来。

31 have time on your hands to have a lot of time because you have no work to do 无所事事, 没事可做

32 have your hands full to be very busy or too busy 非常忙: *I'm sorry I can't help – I have my hands full with problems at home.* 对不起, 我帮不了忙。我自己家里的问题已经忙不过来了。

33 out of hand if you refuse something out of hand, you refuse immediately and completely 断然, 即时〔拒绝〕

34 hand in glove closely connected with someone, especially in a bad or illegal activity 与…勾结, 关系密切: *They suspect*

the politicians are hand in glove with the mafia. 他们怀疑那些政客与黑手党互相勾结。
35 right/left hand side the side on your right or left 右边/左边: *Keep to the left hand side of the road.* 保持左行。
36 on the one hand ... on the other hand used when comparing different or opposite facts or ideas 一方面…, 另一方面…; 从一方面来说…, 从另一方面来说…: *On the one hand I want to sell the house, but on the other hand I can't bear the thought of moving.* 一方面我想把房子卖掉, 但另一方面我又不愿搬家。
37 make/lose/spend hand over fist *informal* to gain, lose, or spend money very quickly and in large amounts【非正式】大量而迅速地赚钱/赔钱/花钱
38 give sb a (big) hand to CLAP¹ (1) loudly in order to show your approval of a performer or speaker 为某人热烈鼓掌
39 ▶CARD GAMES 纸牌游戏◀ [C] **a)** a set of playing cards held by one person in a game 一手牌: *a winning hand* 一手赢牌 **b)** a game of cards 一局牌: *We played a couple of hands of poker.* 我们打了几局扑克牌。
40 ▶ON A CLOCK 时钟上◀ [C] a long, thin piece of metal that points at the numbers on a clock 指针: *the hour hand* 时针
41 time/money in hand time or money that is available to be used 手头现有的时间/金钱: *We still have a couple of weeks in hand before the deadline.* 我们离最后限期还有两三个星期。
42 at the hands of if you suffer at the hands of someone, they treat you badly 从〔某人〕那里〔大吃苦头〕: *They suffered terribly at the hands of the secret police.* 他们吃尽了秘密警察的苦头。
43 tie/bind sb hand and foot a) to tie someone's hands and feet 捆住〔某人的〕手脚 **b)** to severely restrict someone's freedom to make decisions 束缚: *We're bound hand and foot by all these safety regulations.* 我们被这些安全规则束缚住手脚。
44 sb's hand (in marriage) *old-fashioned* permission or agreement for a man to marry a particular woman【过时】对求婚的应允: *He asked for her hand in marriage.* 他向她求婚。
45 ▶WRITING 书写◀ [singular] the way you write; HANDWRITING 笔迹: *a letter written in a neat hand* 一封笔迹工整的信
46 ▶HORSE 马◀ [C] a unit for measuring the height of a horse, equal to about 10 centimetres 一手之宽〔用于量度马匹高度的单位, 约10厘米〕—see also 另见 FREEHAND, HANDS-ON, HANDS UP, **be an old hand at** (OLD (31)), **bite the hand that feeds you** (BITE¹ (14)), **force sb's hand** (FORCE² (6)), **overplay your hand** (OVERPLAY (2)), **shake hands (with)** (SHAKE¹ (5)), **wash your hands of sth** (WASH¹ (5)), **win hands down** (WIN¹ (1))

S2 W2 **hand²** *v* [T] **1** to pass something to someone else 传, 递; 交; 给: **hand sb sth** *Can you hand me that book, please?* 请把那本书递给我, 好吗? | **hand sth to sb** *She handed her ticket to the ticket collector.* 她把票交给了检票员。**2 you have to hand it to sb** *spoken* used to say that you admire someone【口】你不得不佩服某人: *You have to hand it to her. She's really made a success of that company.* 你不得不佩服她。她的确把那家公司经营得很成功。

hand sth ↔ **around** also 又作 **hand** sth ↔ **round** *BrE*【英】*phr v* [T] to offer something to all the people in a group 分发: *She was busy handing around cups of coffee.* 她在忙着把一杯杯咖啡分给大家。

hand sth ↔ **back** *phr v* [T] **1** to pass something back to someone 交还, 交回: *Kurt examined the document and handed it back to her.* 库尔特审阅过文件后就交还给她。**2** to give something back to someone it used to belong to 归还: *The land was handed back to its original owner.* 那块土地被归还给原主。

hand sth ↔ **down** *phr v* [T] **1** to give or leave something to people who are younger than you or live after you 传给〔后代〕: *stories that were handed down from generation to generation* 代代相传的故事 | *a ring which was handed down from her grandmother* 她祖母传下来的一只戒指 —see also 另见 HAND-ME-DOWN **2** to pass something to someone who is below you 递下来: *The truck driver handed down her rucksack.* 货车司机把她的背包递了下来。**3 hand down a decision/ruling/sentence etc** to officially announce a decision, a punishment etc 公布[宣布]一项决定/裁决/判决等

hand sth ↔ **in** *phr v* [T] to give something to a person in authority 上交; 提交: *Hand your papers in at the end of the exam.* 考试结束后把试卷交上来。

hand sth ↔ **on** *phr v* [T] to give something you have finished dealing with to someone who is waiting for it 交付, 传递

hand sth ↔ **out** *phr v* [T] **1** to give something to each member of a group of people; DISTRIBUTE 分发, 散发: *Could you start handing these books out.* 请你把这些书分发出去吧。**2 hand out advice** to give advice, even if people do not want to hear it 出主意 —see also 另见 HANDOUT

hand over *phr v* **1** [T **hand** sb/sth ↔ **over**] to give someone or something to someone else to take care of or to control 把…送交; 交出: *The resistance fighters agreed to hand over the hostages.* 秘密抵抗运动的战士同意交出人质。**2** [I,T **hand** sth ↔ **over**] to give power or responsibility to someone else 移交〔权力、责任等〕: *The captain was unwilling to hand over the command of his ship.* 船长不愿把船的指挥权交出来。| *Before handing over to Jim, I'd like to thank you all for your support.* 在把工作移交给吉姆之前, 我要感谢大家对我的支持。

S3 **hand·bag** /ˈhænd͵bæg; ˈhændbæg/ *n* [C] a small bag, used by women to carry money and personal things 〔女用〕手提包, 手袋; PURSE¹ (3) *AmE*【美】—see picture at 参见 BAG¹ 图

hand·ball /ˈhænd͵bɔl; ˈhændbɔːl/ *n* **1** [U] a game, played especially in the US, in which you hit a ball against a wall with your hand 手球(戏)〔用手把球击向墙壁的美国球戏〕**2** [C] the ball used in this game 手球比赛用的球 **3** [C,U] the offence, in football, of touching the ball with your hands 〔足球比赛中的〕手球犯规

hand·bas·ket /ˈhænd͵bæskɪt; ˈhænd͵bɑːskɪ̞t/ *n* —see 见 **go to hell in a handbasket** (HELL¹ (23))

hand·bill /ˈhænd͵bɪl; ˈhænd͵bɪl/ *n* [C] a small printed notice or advertisement 传单; 广告单

hand·book /ˈhænd͵bʊk; ˈhændbʊk/ *n* [C] a short book giving information or instructions 手册, 便览, 指南

hand·brake /ˈhænd͵brek; ˈhændbreɪk/ *n* [C] *BrE* a piece of equipment in a car that you pull up with your hand to stop the car from moving【英】手刹车; 手闸; EMERGENCY BRAKE *AmE*【美】—see picture on page A2 参见 A2 页图

hand·car /ˈhænd͵kɑr; ˈhændkɑː/ *n* [C] *AmE* a small railway vehicle operated by pushing large handles up and down【美】〔铁路上的〕手泵式四轮小车

hand·cart /ˈhænd͵kɑrt; ˈhændkɑːt/ *n* [C] a small vehicle used for carrying goods, that is pushed or pulled by hand 手推车, 手拉车

hand·craft·ed /ˈhænd͵kræftɪd; ˈhænd͵krɑːftɪ̞d/ *adj* skilfully made by hand, not by machine 用手工做的

hand·cuff /ˈhænd͵kʌf; ˈhændkʌf/ *v* [T] to put handcuffs on someone 给〔某人〕戴上手铐

hand·cuffs /ˈhænd͵kʌfs; ˈhændkʌfs/ *n* [plural] a pair of metal rings joined by a chain for holding a prisoner's wrists together 手铐

Han·del /ˈhændl; ˈhændl/, **George Fred·e·rick** /dʒɔrdʒ ˈfrɛdərɪk; ˈdʒɔːdʒ ˈfredərɪk/ (1685-1759) a British COMPOSER, born in Germany, famous for his ORATORIOS, such as the *Messiah*, and his ORCHESTRAL music, particularly his *Water Music* and *Music for the Royal Fireworks* 韩德尔〔(1685-1759), 英国作曲家, 生于德国。他创作有《弥赛亚》等清唱剧和《水上音乐》、《王室焰火音乐》等管弦乐, 并因此著称〕

hand-eye co·or·di·na·tion /͵· ˈ· ·· ··͵· ˈ·/ *n* [U] the way in which your hands and eyes work together, especially in sport 〔尤指体育运动中的〕手眼协调

hand·ful /ˈhænd͵fʊl; ˈhændfʊl/ *n* **1** [C] an amount that you can hold in your hand 一把: [+of] *a handful of nuts* 一把硬壳果 **2 a handful of** a very small number of people or things 几个, 少数: *Only a handful of countries have implemented these regulations.* 只有少数国家执行了这些规定。**3 a handful** *informal* someone, especially a child, who is difficult to control【非正式】难管[控制]的人〔尤指孩子〕

hand gre·nade /ˈ· ·͵·/ *n* [C] a small bomb which is thrown by hand 手榴弹

hand·gun /ˈhænd͵gʌn; ˈhændgʌn/ *n* [C] a small gun that you hold in one hand when you fire it 手枪

hand-held /͵· ˈ·◂/ *adj* a hand-held machine or piece of electronic equipment is small enough to hold in your hand when you use it 手持的, 手提的: *a hand-held TV camera* 手提式电视摄像机

hand·i·cap /ˈhændɪ͵kæp; ˈhændikæp/ *n* [C] **1** an inability to use part of your body or mind because it has been damaged 〔身体或智力上的〕残障, 残疾: *a mental or physical handicap* 一种智力或身体上的残疾 **2** a condition or situation that makes it difficult for someone to do what they want 缺陷, 不利条件: *Not speaking the language is a real handicap.* 语言不通的确是一个不利条件。**3** a disadvantage given to the stronger competitors

in a race or competition, in order to make it fair〔比赛中加给强手的〕不利条件: *She had a handicap of 7 in golf.* 她在高尔夫球比赛中让了七杆。

hand·i·capped /ˈhændɪˌkæpt; ˈhændikæpt/ *adj* **1** having serious difficulty using part of your body or mind fully because of injury or damage 残疾的; 弱智的: **physically/mentally handicapped** *mentally handicapped children* 弱智儿童 | **visually handicapped** (=blind or partly blind) 视障的 **2 the handicapped** people who are physically or mentally handicapped 残障人士; 弱智人士: *meeting the needs of the handicapped* 满足残障人士的需要 **3 be handicapped by** to have difficulties in doing what you want to do, because of a particular problem 受…之阻, 被…妨碍: *Rescue efforts were handicapped by the darkness.* 黑暗使得救援工作受阻。—compare 比较 DISABLED

hand·i·craft /ˈhændɪˌkræft; ˈhændikrɑːft/ also 又作 **craft** *n* [C usually plural 一般用复数] a skill needing careful use of your hands, such as SEWING, making baskets etc 手工艺; 手艺

handily —see 见 HANDY

hand·i·work /ˈhændɪˌwɝk; ˈhændiwɜːk/ *n* [U] **1** work that needs skill in using your hands 手工; 手工艺(品): *When he'd cut the hedge he stood back and admired his handiwork.* 修剪完树篱后, 他后退几步欣赏自己的手艺。**2 the handiwork of** something, especially something bad, that has been done by a particular person or group〔尤指坏的〕结果; 所为: *The explosion looks like the handiwork of terrorists.* 这次爆炸看起来像是恐怖分子干的。

hand job /ˈ· ·/ *n* [C] *taboo slang* the act of exciting a man's sex organs by touching or rubbing them【讳, 俚】〔男子〕手淫

hand·ker·chief /ˈhæŋkɚtʃɪf; ˈhæŋkətʃɪf/ *n* [C] a piece of cloth or thin soft paper for drying your nose or eyes 手帕; 纸巾

2 2 **han·dle¹** /ˈhændḷ; ˈhændl/ *v*

1 ▶DEAL WITH STH 处理某事◀ [T] **a)** to deal with a difficult situation or problem 应付〔困难局面〕, 处理〔难题〕: *She couldn't handle the pressures of her new job.* 她无法应付新工作带来的压力。**b)** to deal with something by doing what is necessary 处理: *My secretary will handle all the details.* 我的秘书会处理所有的具体问题。

2 ▶DEAL WITH SB 应付某人◀ to deal with people or behave towards them in a particular way, especially to get what you want 对待, 应付〔某人〕: *She's very good at handling difficult customers.* 她很擅长对付挑剔的顾客。| **handle yourself** (=control your behaviour) 控制自己 *advice on how to handle yourself in an interview* 有关在面试中如何表现得体的建议

3 ▶HOLD 拿◀ [T] to pick up, touch, or feel something with your hands 触; 摸; 碰; 拿: *When the children handle the kittens it makes the mother cat restless.* 孩子们触摸小猫时, 母猫会觉得不安。

4 ▶CONTROL WITH YOUR HANDS 用手操纵◀ a) [T] to control the movement of a vehicle, tool etc 操纵, 操作〔车辆、工具等〕: *The windsurfer handled her board with great skill.* 那个帆板运动员熟练地操纵着她的帆板。**b) handle well/ badly etc** to be easy or difficult to drive or control 容易/不易操纵: *The car handles well, even on wet roads.* 这辆车很好驾驶, 即使是在湿滑的路面上也是如此。

5 ▶IN CHARGE OF 负责◀ [T] to be in charge of 负责: *Ms Brown handles the company's accounts.* 布朗女士负责公司的账目。

6 ▶MACHINES/SYSTEMS 机器/系统◀ [T] to have the power, equipment, or systems that are necessary to deal with a particular amount of work, number of people etc 处理〔一定数量的工作、人员等〕: *The computers are capable of handling massive amounts of data.* 电脑能处理大量的数据。

7 ▶BUY/SELL 买/卖◀ [T] to buy, sell, or deal with goods or services in business or trade 经销; 买卖; 处理: *Bennet was charged with handling stolen goods.* 贝内特被控买卖赃物。

3 **handle²** *n* [C] **1** the part of a door, drawer, window etc that you use for opening it 把手 **2** the part of an object that you use for holding it 柄: *a knife with an ivory handle* 一把带象牙柄的刀 —see pictures at 参见 GUN¹ and 和 TOOL¹ 图 **3 get a handle on** [T] to start to understand a person, situation etc 开始理解, 了解〔某人、某形势等〕: *It's difficult to get a handle on exactly how this law will affect us.* 要想确切了解这项法律将会对我们有什么影响并不容易。**4** *informal* a name used by someone, especially by a user of CB RADIOS【非正式】民用波段无线电用户的呼号 —see also 另见 **fly off the handle** (FLY¹ (19))

han·dle·bar mous·tache /ˌhændḷbɑr ˈmʌstæʃ; ˌhændlbɑː məˈstɑːʃ/ *n* [C] a long thick MOUSTACHE which curves upwards at both ends〔两端上翘的〕翘八字胡须

CULTURAL NOTE 文化注释

This kind of moustache was especially popular with men in the British airforce in the World War II. 这种胡子在二战时期的英国空军中尤为流行。

han·dle·bars /ˈhændḷbɑrz; ˈhændlbɑːz/ *n* [plural] the bar above the front wheel of a bicycle or MOTORCYCLE that you turn to control the direction it goes in〔脚踏车和摩托车等的〕把手 —see picture at 参见 BICYCLE¹ 图

han·dler /ˈhændlɚ; ˈhændlə/ *n* [C] someone who trains an animal, especially a dog 驯兽师〔尤指驯狗师〕

hand·ling /ˈhændlɪŋ; ˈhændlɪŋ/ *n* [U] **1** the way in which a problem or person is treated or dealt with 处理(方式), 应付(方式): *The President has been much criticized for his handling of health policy.* 总统对医疗卫生政策的处理受到了很多的批评。**2** the act of picking something up, or touching or feeling it with your hands 触摸; 拿[抱]起: *his gentle handling of the baby* 他温柔的抱婴儿动作

handling charge /ˈ·· ˌ·/ *n* [C] the amount charged for dealing with goods or moving them from one place to another 手续费, 搬运费

hand·loom /ˈhændlum; ˈhændluːm/ *n* [C] a small machine for weaving by hand 手织机

hand lug·gage /ˈ· ˌ··/ *n* [U] the small bags that you carry when you are travelling, especially on a plane 手提行李

hand·made /ˈhændˌmed; ˌhændˈmeɪd◂/ *adj* made by hand, not by machine 手工做的: *expensive handmade shoes* 昂贵的手工制作的鞋子

hand·maid·en /ˈhændˌmedṇ; ˈhændˌmeɪdn/ also 又作 **hand·maid** /ˈhændˌmed; ˈhændmeɪd/ *n* [C] **1** *old use* a female servant【旧】女佣, 女仆 **2** *formal* an idea, principle etc that has an important part in supporting or helping another idea etc【正式】辅助, 支持: [+of] *Militarism, Ross wrote, is the handmaiden of imperialism.* 罗斯曾写道, 军国主义是帝国主义的帮凶。

hand-me-down /ˈ· · ·ˌ·/ *n* [C usually plural 一般用复数] a piece of clothing which has been used by someone and then given to another person in the family〔年长者穿过传给年少者的〕旧衣服: *I always had to wear my sister's hand-me-downs.* 我老是得穿姐姐穿过的旧衣服。

hand·out /ˈhændˌaʊt; ˈhændaʊt/ *n* [C] **1** money or goods that are given to someone, for example because they are poor 救济品; 施舍物: *They only want a helping hand from the government, not a handout.* 他们只需要政府的帮助, 而不是施舍。**2** a piece of paper with information given to people who are attending a lesson, meeting etc〔分发给听众的〕材料; 讲义; 印刷品: *You'll find a full list of references on the last page of the handout.* 你们可以在讲义的最后一页找到一份完整的参考书目。

hand·o·ver /ˈhændˌovɚ; ˈhændəʊvə/ *n* [C] the act of making someone else responsible for something 移交: *Arrangements for the handover of prisoners have been made.* 已经作好了移交战俘的安排。—see also 另见 **hand over** (HAND²)

hand·picked /ˈhændˋpɪkt; ˌhændˈpɪkt◂/ *adj* someone who is handpicked has been carefully chosen for a special purpose〔人〕精心挑选的: *volunteers handpicked for their ability to speak Spanish* 根据其西班牙语的程度而精心挑选出来的志愿者

hand·rail /ˈhændˌrel; ˈhænd-reɪl/ *n* [C] a long bar fixed to the side of a passage or stairs for people to hold while they walk〔通道、楼梯等的〕扶手; 栏杆

hand·saw /ˈhændˌsɔ; ˈhændsɔː/ *n* [C] a small tool for cutting wood etc that has a flat blade and sharp V shaped teeth 手锯

hands·free /ˈhændzˌfri; ˈhændzfriː/ *adj* [only before noun 仅用于名词前] a handsfree machine is one that you operate without using your hands 无需用手操纵的

hand·shake /ˈhændˌʃek; ˈhændʃeɪk/ *n* [C] **a)** the act of taking someone's right hand and shaking it, which people do when they meet or leave each other or when they have made an agreement 握手 **b)** the way that someone does this 握手方式: *a nice firm handshake* 坚定有力的握手 —see also 另见 GOLDEN HANDSHAKE

CULTURAL NOTE 文化注释

FREEMASONs are said to have a special kind of handshake, and this is sometimes mentioned in stories and jokes. 共济会会员据说有某种特别的握手方式, 这在故事或笑话中有时会提到。

hands off /ˌ· ˈ·/ *interjection* used to warn someone not to touch something 别碰, 别动: *Hands off, that's my candy bar!* 别动, 那是我的糖果条!

hands-off /ˈ· ·/ *adj* [only before noun 仅用于名词前] letting other people do what they want and make decisions, without telling them what to do 放手的; 不干涉的; 不插手的: *a hands-off style of management* 放手式管理

hand·some /ˈhænsəm; ˈhænsəm/ *adj* **1 a)** a man who is handsome is attractive; GOOD-LOOKING〔男子〕英俊的, 漂亮的 **b)** a woman who is handsome is attractive in a strong healthy way〔女子〕健美的 —see 见 BEAUTIFUL (USAGE) **2** an object, building etc that is handsome is attractive in an impressive way〔建筑等〕宏伟的, 雄伟的 **3 a handsome profit/fee/sum etc** a large amount of money 丰厚的利润/大笔费用/大笔金额等: *He sold the stocks and made a handsome profit for himself.* 他卖掉了股票, 赚了一大笔钱。**4 a handsome gift/offer etc** a generous or valuable gift etc 慷慨的礼物/优惠的报价等: *She received a handsome gift of money from her aunt.* 她从姑妈那儿得到了一大笔钱作为礼物。**—handsomely** *adv*

hands-on /ˈ· ·/ *adj* [only before noun 仅用于名词前] providing practical experience of something by letting people do it themselves 实际操作的, 亲身实践的: *The computer course includes plenty of hands-on training.* 这个电脑课程包括大量实际操作训练。

hand·spring /ˈhændˌsprɪŋ; ˈhændsprɪŋ/ *n* [C] a movement in which you turn yourself over completely, first with your hands on the floor and then your feet again 手翻, 前手翻腾越

hand·stand /ˈhændˌstænd; ˈhændstænd/ *n* [C] a movement in which you put your hands on the ground and your legs into the air 手倒立

hands up /ˌ· ˈ·/ *interjection* **1** used to tell people to put one of their hands in the air if they want something or if they know the answer to a question 请举手: *Hands up everyone who wants a cup of tea.* 想要茶的人请举手。**2** used when threatening someone with a gun 举起手来!〔持枪者下的命令〕

hand to hand /ˌ· · ˈ·◂/ *adj, adv* **hand to hand fighting/combat** a way of fighting in a war using hands, knives etc rather than guns 肉搏战

hand to mouth /ˌ· · ˈ·◂/ *adv* with only just enough money and food to live and nothing for the future 勉强糊口地, 只够糊口地: *living hand to mouth* 吃了上顿没下顿 **—hand-to-mouth** *adj*: *a hand-to-mouth existence* 现挣现吃地勉强度日

hand tow·el /ˈ· ˌ··/ *n* [C] a small TOWEL[1] for drying your hands 擦手巾

hand·writ·ing /ˈhændˌraɪtɪŋ; ˈhændˌraɪtɪŋ/ *n* [U] the style of someone's writing 笔迹, 字迹; 书法; 写字风格: *I recognised her handwriting on the envelope.* 我认出了信封上她的笔迹。

hand·writ·ten /ˈhændˌrɪtn; ˌhændˈrɪtn◂/ *adj* written by hand, not printed 手写的

hand·y /ˈhændɪ; ˈhændi/ *adj* **1** useful and simple to use 简便的, 方便的: *a handy little gadget for peeling potatoes* 削马铃薯皮的简便小器具 **2** *informal* near and easy to reach【非正式】手边的; 附近的: *If there's a pen and paper handy, I'll make a shopping list.* 如果手边有笔和纸的话, 我要列一份购物清单。| **be handy for** *BrE*【英】*Theo's flat is handy for the shops.* 西奥的住处离商店很近。**3 come in handy** to be useful 迟早有用: *Take a sleeping bag with you – it might come in handy.* 带一个睡袋去吧, 可能用得着的。**4** good at using something, especially a tool 手巧的, 灵活的: **[+with]** *He's handy with a screwdriver.* 他善于使用螺丝刀。**—handily** *adv* **—handiness** *n* [U]

Handy /ˈhændɪ; ˈhændi/, **W.C.** (1873-1958) a US JAZZ musician and writer of jazz songs, thought to be the first person to write Blues music. His most famous song is *St Louis Blues*. 汉迪〔(1873-1958), 美国爵士音乐家、爵士歌曲词作家。他被认为是首位布鲁斯音乐作曲家, 以歌曲《圣路易斯布鲁斯》最为著名〕

hand·y·man /ˈhændɪˌmæn; ˈhændimæn/ *n* [C] someone who is good at doing repairs and practical jobs in the house〔尤指在做家庭小修小补活上〕手巧的人

hang[1] /hæŋ; hæŋ/ *v past tense and past participle* **hung** /hʌŋ; hʌŋ/

1 ▶HANG FROM ABOVE 从高处悬下◀ **a)** [T] to fix or put something in a position so that the bottom part is free to move and does not touch the ground 悬挂, 吊起: *Hang your coat on the hook.* 把你的外套挂在钩上。**b)** [I always+adv/prep] to be fixed in position at the top so that the bottom part is free to move and does not touch the ground 悬挂着, 吊着: **[+on/from/out of etc]** *A large handbag hung from her shoulder.* 她的肩膀上挂着一个大手袋。| *She sat there with a cigarette hanging out of her mouth.* 她坐在那里, 嘴里叼着一根烟。

2 ▶PICTURES ETC 画、照片等◀ **a)** [I always+adv/prep, T] to fix a picture, photograph etc to a wall, or to be fixed this way 挂: **[+on]** *A photograph of a handsome soldier hung on the wall.* 墙上挂着一幅一个英俊军人的照片。**b)** [I always+adv/prep, T] to show a picture publicly or be shown publicly 公开展出: *Her portrait now hangs in the National Gallery.* 她的画像目前在国家美术馆里展出。**c) be hung with** if the walls of a room are hung with pictures or decorations, the pictures etc are on the walls 挂着, 挂有: *rooms hung with rich tapestries* 挂有华丽壁毯的房间

3 ▶KILL/BE KILLED 杀死/被杀死◀ *past tense and past participle* **hanged** [I,T] to kill someone by dropping them with a rope around their neck, or to die in this way, especially as a punishment for a serious crime (被)吊死, (被)绞死: **[+for]** *They were convicted of genocide and hanged for their crimes.* 他们被判犯了灭绝种族的大屠杀罪而被处以绞刑。| *Corey hanged himself in his prison cell.* 科里在囚室里上吊自杀。

4 hang in the balance to be in a situation in which the end is not certain, and something bad may happen 前景难料; 安危难说: *The future of the airline hangs in the balance.* 该航空公司的前景无法预料。

5 hang by a thread to be in a very dangerous situation 千钧一发; 岌岌可危: *For weeks after the accident, her life hung by a thread.* 出事后的几个星期里, 她的生命一直岌岌可危。

6 ▶PAPER 纸◀ [T] to fix WALLPAPER[1] on a wall 贴[糊]〔墙纸〕

7 ▶DOOR 门◀ [T] to fix a door in position 安装〔门〕

8 ▶MIST/SMOKE/SMELL 雾气/烟/气味◀ [I+adv/prep] to stay in the air in the same place for a long time 难以散发; 滞留; 悬浮: *The smoke from the bonfires hung in the air.* 空中飘浮着篝火的烟。

9 hang in there also 又作 **hang tough** *informal, especially AmE* to remain brave and determined when you are in a difficult situation【非正式, 尤美】挺下去; 坚持到底: *You're innocent and you'll win, so hang in there!* 你是无辜的, 一定会胜利, 坚持住!

10 hang your head to look ashamed and embarrassed〔羞愧、尴尬地〕垂下头: *He hung his head and didn't answer her questions.* 他低着头, 没有回答她的问题。

11 hang fire to be delayed or prevented from happening or continuing 推迟, 延迟; 停顿: *The whole project is hanging fire until next week's meeting.* 整个项目要等到下周的会议之后再继续。

12 leave sth hanging in the air to fail to make a definite decision about a question 使某事悬而未决: *important issues left hanging in the air* 悬而未决的重大问题

13 hang a right/left *AmE spoken* used to tell the driver of a car to turn right or left【美口】〔车辆〕往右转/往左转

14 hang up your hat *informal* to leave your job, especially at the end of your working life【非正式】不再工作, 退休

15 hang loose *old-fashioned* used to tell someone to stay calm and relaxed【过时】冷静点; 放松些

16 I'll be hanged/I'm hanged if *BrE old-fashioned* used to express annoyance or to say that you will not allow something to happen【英, 过时】岂有此理; 休想: *I'll be hanged if I'll let these people order me around!* 见鬼去吧, 我才不让这些人支使我!

17 hang it/hang it all *BrE old-fashioned* used to say that you are disappointed or annoyed about something【英, 过时】见鬼, 该死〔表示失望或厌烦〕

18 hang sth *BrE old-fashioned* used to say that you are not going to do something【英, 过时】让…见鬼去吧, 去它的…〔表示不想做某事〕: *Oh hang the ironing, let's go for a drink.* 熨什么鬼衣服, 我们去喝酒吧!

hang about *phr v BrE*【英】**1** [I] *spoken* to move slowly or take too long doing something【口】动作慢吞吞; 拖延: *Don't hang about, we've got a train to catch!* 别慢吞吞的, 我们还要赶火车呢! **2** [I] to spend time somewhere without any real purpose 闲逛, 闲荡: *There are always kids hanging about down by the shops.* 商店附近总有些孩子在闲逛。**3 hang about with** to spend a lot of time with someone 厮混: *I don't know what he's doing, hanging about with that bunch.* 我不知道他到底在干什么, 整天和那伙人混在一起。**4 hang about!** *spoken* used to ask someone to wait or stop what they are doing【口】等一下, 停一下: *Hang about – I'm nearly ready.* 等等, 我快好了。

hang around *phr v* [I,T] *informal*【非正式】**1** to wait or stay somewhere with no real purpose 闲荡; 干等: *I hung around the station for an hour but he never showed up.* 我在车站附近呆等了一小时, 但他始终没有来。**2 hang around with** to spend a lot of time with someone 厮混: *He hangs around with Luke and Callum.* 他整天和卢克及卡勒姆混在一起。

hang back *phr v* [I] to be unwilling to speak or do something because you are shy 退缩, 踌躇不前: *Don't hang back – go and introduce yourself.* 别犹豫了, 走上前去自我介绍吧。

hang on *phr v* **1** [I] to hold something tightly 紧紧抓住: *We all hung on as the bus swung around a sharp bend.* 公共汽车急转弯时, 我们赶紧抓住扶手。| [+to] *Hang on to the rail or you'll fall.* 抓紧栏杆, 要不然你会摔倒的。**2 hang on!** *BrE spoken* used to ask or tell someone to wait【英口】等等!: *Hang on! I'll be back in a minute.* 等等! 我一会儿就回来。**3** [I] to continue doing something in spite of difficulties 坚持不懈, 不放弃: *I know you're tired, but try to hang on a bit longer.* 我知道你累了, 但是再坚持一会儿吧。**4** [T] **hang on** sth to depend on 依赖于, 取决于: *The team's survival in the league hangs on the result of this game.* 该队能否继续留在联赛中将取决于今场比赛。**5 hang on sb's words/every word** to pay close attention to everything someone is saying 倾听[注意]某人的谈话/每一句话

hang on to sth/sb *phr v* [T] to keep something 保留, 保存: *I'd hang on to that letter. You might need it later.* 我会保留着那封信。你以后可能会用得着。

hang out *phr v* **1** [I always+adv/prep] *informal* to spend a lot of time in a particular place or with particular people【非正式】闲荡; 厮混: *She hangs out with a pretty wild crowd.* 她经常和一群很不安分的人混在一起。| *That's the corner where all the junkies hang out.* 那是吸毒者经常聚集的一个角落。—see also 另见 HANGOUT **2** [T **hang** sth ↔ **out**] to hang clothes on a piece of string outside in order to dry them 晾晒〔衣服〕: *I've hung out the washing.* 我已经把洗好的衣服晾出去了。**3 let it all hang out** *slang* to relax and do what you like【俚】放纵自己, 做自己想做的事

hang over sth/sb *phr v* [I] if something unpleasant hangs over you, you are worried because it is likely to happen soon〔不愉快的事〕逼近; 威胁着: *The prospect of famine hangs over the whole area.* 整个地区都受到饥荒的威胁。| **be hanging over sb's head** *With the exams hanging over her head she can't sleep at night.* 随着考试的临近, 她晚上都睡不着觉。

hang round *phr v* [I,T] = **hang around** (HANG[1])

hang together *phr v* [I] **1** to help each other and work together to achieve an aim 同心协力, 团结一致: *We must hang together if we're going to get out of this mess.* 要想走出困境, 我们就必须同心协力。**2** if a plan, story, set of ideas etc hangs together, it is well-organized and makes sense〔计划、故事、想法等〕站得住脚; 前后一致; 合情合理: *The case for the defence just doesn't hang together.* 被告方的陈述根本站不住脚。

hang up 挂

Paula is hanging up her suit.
葆拉在挂衣服。

After arguing for ten minutes she hung up.
争吵了十分钟后, 她挂断了电话。

hang up *phr v* **1** [I,T] to finish a phone conversation by putting the telephone down 挂断电话: *After I hung up I realized I forgot to ask him his telephone number.* 挂了电话后我才想起忘了问他的电话号码。| **hang up on sb** (=put the phone down before they have finished speaking)〔对方没有讲完即〕挂断电话 *I was so angry that I hung up on her.* 我一气之下挂断了她的电话。**2** [T **hang** sth ↔ **up**] to hang clothes on a hook etc 挂起〔衣服〕**3 be hung up on/about** *informal* to be anxious about something when there is no reason to be【非正式】无端担心: *She's hung up about people knowing she didn't go to college.* 她老是担心别人知道她没有上过大学。—see also 另见 HANG-UP

hang² *n* **get/have the hang of something** *informal* to learn how to do something or use something【非正式】学会: *Using the computer isn't difficult once you get the hang of it.* 一旦你学会后, 使用电脑就一点不难了。

hang·ar /ˋhæŋɚ; ˈhæŋə/ *n* [C] a very large building where aircraft are kept 飞机库

hang·dog /ˋhæŋˌdɔg; ˈhæŋdɒg/ *adj* a hangdog expression on your face shows you feel sorry or ashamed about something〔表情〕羞愧的, 惭愧的

hang·er /ˋhæŋɚ; ˈhæŋə/ *n* [C] a thing for hanging clothes on, consisting of a curved piece of wood or metal with a hook on it 衣架

hanger-on /ˌ·· ˈ·/ *n* [C] someone who spends a lot of time with a person who is important, famous, or rich, because they hope to get some advantage 随从, 跟班, 依附他人者: *Hollywood celebrities and their hangers-on* 好莱坞明星及他们的跟班

hang glid·er /ˈ· ˌ·· / *n* [C] a large frame covered with cloth that you hold on to and fly slowly through the air on, without an engine 悬挂式滑翔机

hang gliding 悬挂式滑翔(运动)

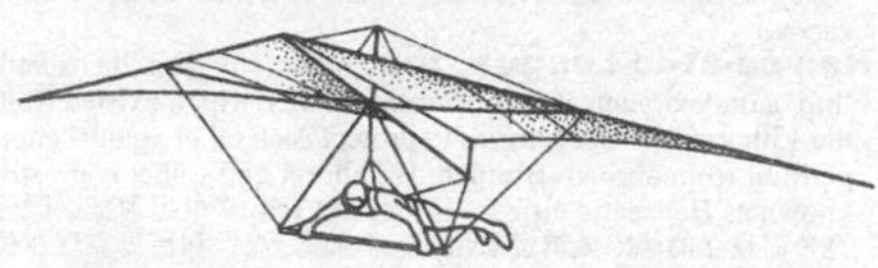

hang glid·ing /ˈ· ˌ·· / *n* [U] the sport of flying using a hang glider 悬挂式滑翔(运动)

hang·ing /ˋhæŋɪŋ; ˈhæŋɪŋ/ *n* [C,U] **1** the practice or act of punishing someone by putting a rope around their neck and hanging them until they are dead 绞刑: *public hangings* 当众执行绞刑 | *right-wingers who want to bring back hanging* 想要恢复绞刑的右翼分子 **2 it's/that's no hanging matter** used to say that a problem or mistake is not as bad as someone thinks it is 问题没那么严重, 不是什么大不了的事 **3** a large piece of cloth hung on a wall as a decoration〔挂在墙上作装饰的〕帘子, 帷幕; 悬挂物: *wall hangings* 挂在墙上的布帘

hang·man /ˋhæŋmən; ˈhæŋmən/ *n* [C] someone whose job is to kill criminals by hanging them 执行绞刑者, 刽子手

hang·nail /ˋhæŋˌnel; ˈhæŋneɪl/ *n* [C] a piece of skin that has become loose near the bottom of the fingernail〔指甲旁的〕倒刺, 甲刺

hang·out /ˋhæŋˌaʊt; ˈhæŋaʊt/ *n* [C] *informal* a place someone likes to go to often【非正式】常去的地方; 聚集处: *a favourite hangout for artists* 艺术家爱去的地方

hang·o·ver /ˋhæŋˌovɚ; ˈhæŋəʊvə/ *n* [C] **1** the HEADACHE and sickness that you get the day after you have drunk too much alcohol 宿醉 **2 a hangover from** *BrE* an attitude, habit etc from the past, that is not suitable or practical any more【英】以前遗留下来的态度[习惯]; HOLDOVER *AmE*【美】: *a hangover from her schooldays* 她学生时代遗留下来的习惯

Hang Seng In·dex, the /ˌhæŋ ˋsɛŋ ˌɪndɛks; ˌhæŋ ˈseŋ ˌɪndeks/ a number that shows how well or badly shares in companies have performed on the STOCK EXCHANGE in Hong Kong on a particular day. The number is based on the share prices of large companies. 恒生指数〔反映一天内香港证券交易所股票涨跌情况的数值。该数值以大公司股价为计算依据〕—see also 另见 DOW JONES AVERAGE, the FT 100 SHARE INDEX, the NIKKEI INDEX

hang-up /ˈ· ·/ *n* [C] *informal* if you have a hang-up about something you feel unreasonably worried or embarrassed about it【非正式】〔无端的〕担忧, 苦恼, 困扰: *She's got a real hang-up about her nose.* 她老为自己的鼻子感到苦恼。—see also 另见 **hang up** (HANG[1])

hank /hæŋk; hæŋk/ *n* [C] an amount of wool, cotton, or thread that has been wound into a loose ball 线卷, 线球

han·ker /ˋhæŋkɚ; ˈhæŋkə/ *v*

hanker after/for *phr v* [T] to secretly feel that you want something, over a long period 渴望, 追求: *Lucy had always hankered after a place of her own.* 露西一直都渴望拥有自己的住处。

han·ker·ing /ˋhæŋkərɪŋ; 'hæŋkərɪŋ/ *n* [singular] a strong wish to have something 渴望

han·kie, hanky /ˋhæŋkɪ; 'hæŋki/ *n* [C] *informal* HANDKERCHIEF【非正式】手帕

hank·y-pank·y /ˋhæŋkɪ ˋpæŋkɪ; ˌhæŋki 'pæŋki/ *n* [U] *humorous* sexual activity that is not very serious【幽默】调情, 调戏

Han·na Bar·be·ra /ˌhænə ˋbɑrbərə; ˌhænə 'bɑːbərə/ two CARTOONISTS, **William Hanna** (1910-2001) and **Joe Barbera** (1911-), who worked together for almost 50 years to make many popular cartoons, including *Tom and Jerry*, *The Flintstones*, and *Yogi Bear* 汉纳和巴伯拉〔指两位漫画家威廉·汉纳（1910-2001）和乔·巴伯拉（1911- ）。他们一起合作了近 50 年, 创作出了许多广受喜爱的漫画作品, 包括《汤姆和杰里》、《聪明笨伯》和《瑜伽熊》〕

Han·ni·bal /ˋhænəbḷ; 'hænɪ̈bəl/ (247-183 BC) a GENERAL who led the army of Carthage in its war against the Romans between 218 and 201 BC. Hannibal is famous especially for having crossed the Alps into Italy with a large army and 37 ELEPHANTS. 汉尼拔〔（公元前 247-前 183）, 公元前 218 至前 201 年统领迦太基军队抗击罗马人的一位将军, 尤以率领大军和 37 头大象越过阿尔卑斯山进兵意大利闻名〕

Ha·noi /hæˋnɔɪ; hæ'nɔɪ/ the capital city of Vietnam, on the Red River 河内〔越南首都, 濒临红河〕

Han·sard /ˋhænsɚd; 'hænsɑːd/ *n* [singular] the official written record of what happens in the British Parliament 英国议会议事录: *Read about the debate in Hansard.* 看一看议会议事录中关于这次辩论的记录吧。—compare 比较 the CONGRESSIONAL RECORD

Han·se·at·ic League, the /ˌhænsɪætɪk ˋlig; ˌhænsiætɪk 'liːg/ a trade organization of German towns, which existed from the 13th to the 17th centuries to protect each other against competition from abroad. Bremen, Hamburg, and Lübeck are still known as Hanseatic cities. 汉萨同盟〔13 至 17 世纪为抵制国外竞争而设立的德国城镇贸易组织。不来梅、汉堡和吕贝克现在仍称汉萨同盟城市〕

Han·sel and Gret·el /ˌhænsḷ ənd ˋgrɛtḷ; ˌhænsəl ənd 'gretl/ the two main characters in the FAIRY TALE *Hansel and Gretel* by the Brothers Grimm. Hansel and Gretel are a brother and sister who get lost in a forest. They find a house made of GINGERBREAD, which is owned by an evil WITCH who likes to catch children and eat them. When the witch tries to cook Hansel, Gretel pushes her into the OVEN, and Hansel and Gretel escape with the witch's money and jewels. 汉塞尔和格雷特尔〔格林童话《汉塞尔和格雷特尔》的两位主人公。他们是兄妹俩, 在森林中迷了路。他们发现了一座用姜汁饼干做成的房子。房子的主人是个爱抓小孩吃的巫婆。当巫婆试图把汉塞尔煮了吃的时候, 格雷特尔把她推进了烤炉。于是, 兄妹俩带着巫婆的钱和珠宝逃走了〕

H

han·som /ˋhænsəm; 'hænsəm/ also 又作 **hansom cab** /ˋ‥ ˏ/ *n* [C] a two-wheeled vehicle pulled by a horse, used in the past as a taxi〔旧时供出租的〕双轮马车

Ha·nuk·kah, Chanukah /ˋhɑnʊkə; 'hɑːnʊ̈kə/ *n* an eight-day Jewish holiday in December〔犹太人的〕献殿节, 光明节

ha'penny /ˋhepnɪ; 'heɪpni/ *n* [C] another spelling of HALFPENNY halfpenny 的另一种拼法

hap·haz·ard /ˌhæpˋhæzɚd; ˌhæp'hæzəd◂/ *adj* happening or done in a way that is not planned or recognized 无计划的, 没有条理的, 随意的: *The training was carried out in a haphazard fashion.* 培训活动毫无计划地进行。—**haphazardly** *adv*

hap·less /ˋhæplɪs; 'hæpləs/ *adj* [only before noun 仅用于名词前] *literary* unlucky【文】倒霉的, 不幸的: *Hapless passers-by could be dragged into the argument.* 倒霉的过路人会被拖进这场争论之中。

hap·ly /ˋhæplɪ; 'hæpli/ *adv old use* perhaps【旧】可能, 或许

hap'orth /ˋhepɚθ; 'heɪpəθ/ *n* [singular **+of**] *old-fashioned BrE* an amount that is worth half of one penny【过时, 英】价值半便士的东西

hap·pen /ˋhæpən; 'hæpən/ *v* [I] **1** if an event or situation happens, it exists and continues for a period of time, especially without being planned first（偶然）发生: *The accident happened early on Tuesday morning.* 这场意外在星期二清晨发生。| *No one knew who had fired the gun – it all happened so quickly.* 没有人知道是谁开枪的, 事情发生得太快了。| *It's impossible to predict what will happen in Cambodia in the next few months.* 无法预料今后几个月内柬埔寨会发生什么事情。| **sth is bound to happen** (=something is certain to happen) 一定会发生 | **sth happens all the time** (=something happens often) 经常发生 *This kind of thing happens all the time.* 这种事经常都会发生。| **whatever happens** *I'll look after you whatever happens.* 不管发生什么事, 我都会照顾你的。—see 见 OCCUR (USAGE) —see also 另见 **happen to 2** to be caused as the result of an event or action 发生作用; 产生结果: *She pressed hard on the brake pedal, but nothing happened.* 她使劲地往下踩刹车踏板, 可是车没有反应。| *What would happen if your parents found out?* 要是你父母发现了, 会怎么样呢? **3** to do or have something by chance 碰巧, 凑巧: **happen to do sth** *I happened to meet her on my way home.* 我在回家的路上碰巧遇见了她。| **it happens that** (=by chance, it is true that) 凑巧的是 *It happened that the new person in the office was the woman he had met at Gail's party.* 凑巧的是, 办公室里新来的人就是他在盖尔的晚会上遇到过的那个女人。**4 sb/sth happens to be** used when telling someone something in an angry way, especially because you are annoyed by something they have just said 碰巧, 凑巧〔表示恼怒〕: *That woman you're talking about just happens to be my wife!* 你正在谈论的那个女人碰巧是我的妻子! —see also 另见 **accidents will happen** (ACCIDENT (5))

happen by *phr v* [I,T] *AmE* to find a place by chance【美】偶然发现〔某处〕

happen on sb/sth, **happen upon** sb/sth *phr v* [T] to find something or meet someone by chance 偶然碰上; 偶然看到: *They were strolling through the old part of the town when they happened on a tiny Greek restaurant.* 他们在老城区里游逛时偶然看见一家希腊小餐馆。

happen to sb/sth *phr v* [T] **1** if an event happens to someone or something, they are involved in it and affected by it〔事情〕发生在…身上, 临到…头上: *A funny thing happened to me on my way home last night.* 昨晚我在回家的路上发生了一点好笑的事。**2 whatever happened to a)** used when you want to know where someone is and what they are doing, because it is a long time since you saw them〔某人〕最近怎么样?: *Whatever happened to Kate Scott?* 凯特·斯科特最近怎么样? **b)** used when saying that something such as an idea, quality, or custom seems to have disappeared or been forgotten about〔想法、特点或习俗〕怎么不见了?: *Whatever happened to the idea of the paperless office?* 怎么再也不见有人提"无纸办公室"了?

Frequencies of the verb **happen** in spoken and written English 动词 happen 在英语口语和书面语中的使用频率

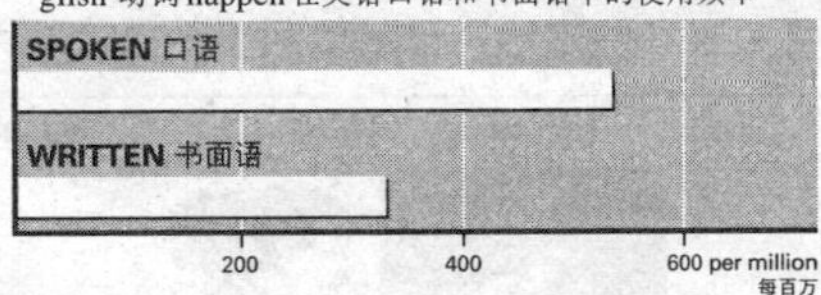

Based on the British National Corpus and the Longman Lancaster Corpus
据英国国家语料库和朗文兰开斯特语料库

This graph shows that the verb **happen** is much more common in spoken English than in written English. This is because it is used in a lot of common spoken phrases. 本图表显示, 动词 happen 在英语口语中的使用频率远远高于书面语, 因为口语中有很多常用短语是由 happen 构成的。

happen (*v*) SPOKEN PHRASES
含 happen 的口语短语

5 what's happening? a) used to ask what people are doing, or what the situation is, especially when you are worried or annoyed about this 发生什么事了?: *Hey, what's happening? Why has the light gone out?* 嗨, 发生什么事了? 灯为什么灭了? | *What's happening here, then? You'd better stop that!* 哎, 你在干什么? 快停下! **b)** *AmE* used when you meet someone you know well, to ask them how they are and what they have been doing【美】近来怎么样?: *Hey Carl, what's happening, man?* 嗨, 卡尔, 近来怎么样, 老兄? **6 what's going to happen/what happens/what will happen...?** used to ask what the result of something will be …会有什么结果?: *What happens if you push this button?* 按下这个按钮会有什么结果? | *What's going to happen when she finds out?* 一旦给她发现了, 会有什么结果? **7 whatever happens** used to say that no matter what else happens, one thing will certainly happen 不管发生什么事, 无论如何: *Whatever happens in the future, we wish you well.* 不管今后情况如何, 我们都祝你好运。**8 as it happens** used to tell someone something that you think will be useful for them, and is connected with what they have just been talking about 碰巧, 正巧〔用于告诉某人对他有用的事〕: *As it happens I know someone who might be able to give you some advice.* 我正好认识

一个人，可以给你提点意见。**9 it (just) so happens that** used to tell someone about something interesting that is connected with what you have just been talking about 真巧，碰巧〔用于告诉某人有趣的事，跟刚提及的事情有关〕: *Now, it just so happens that he had been to the same school as me.* 真巧，他和我正好上同一所学校。**10 these things happen** used to tell someone not to worry about a mistake they have made, an accident they have caused etc 这算不了什么: *These things happen: don't give it another thought.* 这算不了什么，别再想了。**11 anything can happen** used to say that it is impossible to know what will happen 什么事都可能发生，结果无法预料: *Anything can happen in a race like that.* 像这样的比赛，结果无法预料。**12 see what happens** used to say that if someone does not know what the result of doing something will be, they should try it and find out〔试一试〕看看会有什么结果: *Just turn the switch and see what happens. Is it working?* 试着打开开关，看看会有什么结果。它在转动吗？**13 what usually happens is/what tends to happen is** used to say what usually happens in a particular situation〔在某一特定情况下〕通常〔发生的事〕，往往: *What tends to happen is we meet up for a drink, then go for something to eat.* 我们通常聚在一起喝点酒，然后去吃点东西。**14 you don't/do you happen to...?** used politely to ask someone if they have or know something 你是否…？〔婉转的问法〕: *You don't happen to know his address, do you?* 你知道他的地址吗？

2 **hap·pen·ing¹** /ˈhæpənɪŋ; ˈhæpənɪŋ/ *n* [C] something that happens, especially a strange event 发生的事〔尤指怪事〕: *recent mysterious happenings on the island* 该岛上最近发生的神秘事件

happening² *adj slang* fashionable and exciting【俚】时兴的，流行的；刺激的

hap·pen·stance /ˈhæpənˌstæns; ˈhæpənstæns/ *n* [U] *AmE* something good that happens by chance【美】巧合: *It was just happenstance that we met.* 我们相遇是个巧合。

hap·pi·ly /ˈhæpɪlɪ; ˈhæpɪ̆li/ *adv* **1** in a happy way 高兴地，快乐地: *a happily married couple* 一对幸福的夫妇 **2** [sentence adverb 句子副词] fortunately 幸运地: *Happily, his injuries were not serious.* 幸好，他的伤势并不严重。**3** very willingly 很乐意地: *I'd happily go for you.* 我很乐意为你去一趟。

hap·pi·ness /ˈhæpɪnɪs; ˈhæpinɪ̆s/ *n* [U] the state of being happy 快乐，幸福: *She believes she's finally found true happiness.* 她相信自己终于找到了真正的幸福。

1 1 **hap·py** /ˈhæpɪ; ˈhæpi/ *adj* **1** having feelings of pleasure, for example because something good has happened to you 高兴的，快乐的: *Larry looked really happy when we gave him his present.* 我们把礼物送给拉里时，他看起来高兴极了。| *He was a happy child who rarely cried.* 他是一个不爱哭的快乐孩子。| **be happy to be doing sth** *They felt happy to be going home.* 他们为即将回家而感到高兴。| **happy that** *I'm happy that everything worked out well in the end.* 我很高兴到最后一切都很顺利。| **be/feel happy for sb** *I felt really happy for you when I heard you'd passed your exams.* 我听说你通过了考试，真为你感到高兴。—opposite 反义词 SAD (1) **2** a happy time, place, occasion etc is one that makes you feel happy〔使人感到〕愉快的；幸福的: *Some people say that your schooldays are the happiest time of your life.* 有人说学生时代是人一生中最愉快的日子。| **a happy ending** *The story has a happy ending.* 故事的结局很美满。**3** satisfied or not worried 对…感到满意〔放心〕的: [**+about**] *I'm not happy about Dave riding around on that motorbike.* 我对戴夫骑着那辆摩托车到处乱跑很不放心。| [**+with**] *Are you happy with your new car?* 你对新车感到满意吗？| **keep sb happy** *I pretended to agree with her, just to keep her happy.* 我假装赞同她的意见，只是为了让她高兴。**4 be happy to do sth** to be very willing to do something, especially to help someone 乐意做某事: *I'd be happy to take you in my car.* 我很乐意开车送你去。**5 Happy Birthday/Christmas/Anniversary etc** used when greeting someone on their birthday, at Christmas etc 生日/圣诞节/周年纪念日快乐 **6 the happy event** the time when a baby is born or when two people get married〔婴儿出生或新人结婚等的〕喜事 **7 a happy medium** a way of doing something that is somewhere between two possible choices and that satisfies everyone 皆大欢喜的折衷办法 **8 happy as a lark** very happy 非常快乐 **9 not a happy bunny** *BrE*【英】**/not a happy camper** *AmE*【美】*humorous* someone who is not pleased about a situation【幽默】对…感到不满意 **10** *formal* suitable【正式】恰当的，得体的: *His choice of words was not a very happy one.* 他用词不当。

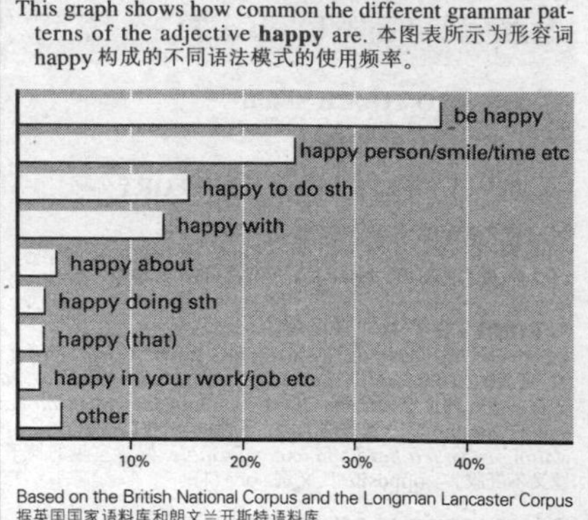
This graph shows how common the different grammar patterns of the adjective **happy** are. 本图表所示为形容词 happy 构成的不同语法模式的使用频率。

Based on the British National Corpus and the Longman Lancaster Corpus
据英国国家语料库和朗文兰开斯特语料库

happy-go-luck·y /ˌ··ˈ··◂/ *adj* not caring or worrying about what happens 无忧无虑的；逍遥自在的: *a happy-go-lucky kind of person* 无忧无虑的人

happy hour /ˈ·· ˌ·/ *n* [singular] a special time in a bar when alcoholic drinks are sold at lower prices〔酒吧中的〕优惠时间；快乐时光

Haps·burg /ˈhæpsbɝg; ˈhæpsbɜːg/ the name of an important European royal family that ruled in Austria from 1278 to 1918 and in Spain from 1516 to 1700. The German spelling of the name is Habsburg. 哈布斯堡王朝〔欧洲一主要王朝。1278 至 1918 年统治奥地利，1516 至 1700 年统治西班牙。德语拼法为 Habsburg〕 —**Habsburg** *adj*

har·a·kiri /ˌhɑrəˈkɪrɪ; ˌhærəˈkiri/ *n* [U] a way of killing yourself by cutting open your stomach, used in former times in Japan to avoid losing your honour〔旧时日本的〕剖腹自杀

ha·rangue¹ /həˈræŋ; həˈræŋ/ *v* [T] to make a loud speech that criticizes or blames someone or tries to persuade people about something 慷慨激昂地演说；高声训斥: *Mr Major was harangued by reporters.* 梅杰先生遭到记者的大声责问。

harangue² *n* [C] a loud long angry speech that criticizes or blames people, or tries to persuade them 滔滔不绝的高声训斥〔劝说〕: *The principal launched into his usual harangue about standards of behaviour.* 校长开始像往常一样滔滔不绝地谈起了行为准则。

Ha·ra·re /həˈrɑrɪ; həˈrɑːri/ the capital city of Zimbabwe, formerly called Salisbury 哈拉雷〔津巴布韦首都，旧称索尔兹伯里〕

har·ass /ˈhærəs; ˈhærəs/ *v* [T] **1** to treat someone unfairly by threatening them or being continuously unpleasant to them 骚扰: *Black teenagers are being constantly harassed by the police.* 黑人青少年经常遭到警察骚扰。**2** to annoy someone by continually interrupting them 烦扰，打扰: *Stop harassing me will you! I'm trying to work!* 别烦我了！我在干活呢！**3** to continually attack an enemy 不断攻击〔敌人〕

har·assed /ˈhærəst; ˈhærəst/ *adj* anxious and tired because you have too many problems or things to do 烦恼的；疲累的: *The waiter looked harassed so I didn't bother him.* 服务员看起来一脸烦恼的，所以我没有叫他。

har·ass·ment /ˈhærəsmənt; ˈhærəsmənt/ *n* [U] **1** unpleasant and often threatening behaviour, or offensive remarks 构成骚扰的言行: **sexual/racial harassment** (=towards someone of a different sex or race) 性/种族骚扰 *sexual harassment in the workplace* 在工作场所的性骚扰 **2** a feeling of anxiety and tiredness because you have too many problems or things to do 烦扰；疲累

har·bin·ger /ˈhɑrbɪndʒɚ; ˈhɑːbɪndʒə/ *n* [C **+of**] *literary* a sign that something is going to happen soon【文】先兆，预兆

har·bour¹ *BrE*【英】, **harbor** *AmE*【美】/ˈhɑrbɚ; ˈhɑːbə/ *n* [C] an area of water next to the land where the water is calm, so that ships are safe when they are inside it 港口，港湾，海港

harbour² *BrE*【英】, **harbor** *AmE*【美】*v* [T] **1** to protect and hide criminals that the police are searching for 窝藏，包庇〔罪犯〕**2** to keep bad thoughts, fears, or hopes in your mind for a long time 怀有〔不好的想法、恐惧等〕: **harbour a grudge** *I think he's harbouring some sort of grudge against me.* 我觉得他对我有点怀恨在心。

hard¹ /hard; hɑːd/ *adj*

① FIRM TO TOUCH 坚硬的
② DIFFICULT 困难的
③ INVOLVING WORK AND EFFORT 费力的，费劲的
④ FULL OF PROBLEMS 棘手的，艰难的
⑤ UNKIND 无情的
⑥ USING FORCE 用力气
⑦ UNFORTUNATE 不幸的
⑧ OTHER MEANINGS 其他意思

① FIRM TO TOUCH 坚硬的

1 firm and stiff, and difficult to press down, break, or cut 硬的，坚固的: *Diamond is the hardest substance known to man.* 钻石是已知的最坚硬的物质。| *The plums are much too hard to be eaten now.* 李子现在太硬，不能吃。| *The chairs in the waiting room felt hard and uncomfortable.* 候诊室里的椅子又硬又不舒服。—opposite 反义词 SOFT (1)

② DIFFICULT 困难的

2 difficult to do or understand 难做的；难懂的；困难的，不易的: *This year's exam was much harder than last year's.* 今年的考试比去年的难得多。| **be hard for sb** *It must be hard for her, bringing up three kids on her own.* 她一个人养育三个孩子一定很不容易。| **be hard to come by** (=be difficult to get or find) 不易得到[找到] *Good jobs are hard to come by these days.* 如今想找份好工作很不容易。| **the hardest thing is** *The hardest thing is going to be telling her parents.* 最难办的是如何告诉她的父母。—opposite 反义词 EASY¹ (1)

3 hard to tell/say difficult to know 难以判断/难说: *It was hard to tell whether Katie really wanted to go.* 很难说凯蒂是否真的想去。

4 find sth hard to believe to think that something is probably not true 认为某事让人难以置信: *I find it extremely hard to believe that he didn't know.* 他竟然不知道，这太让我难以置信了。

5 hard to take difficult to accept or believe 难以接受[相信]: *She found all this sudden concern for her welfare rather hard to take.* 她对所有这些突如其来的对她的幸福的关切感到有点难以置信。

③ INVOLVING WORK AND EFFORT 费力的，费劲的

6 ►A LOT OF EFFORT 许多努力◄ using or involving a lot of mental or physical effort 费神的；费力的: *It's been a long hard day.* 今天过得真累啊！| **hard work** *It's not easy running a business – it takes a great deal of hard work.* 要经营一家铺子真不容易 —— 这需要许多艰苦的努力。

7 hard going a) difficult to do and needing a lot of effort 费劲的，费力的 **b)** boring 乏味的: *I find most of Sartre pretty hard going.* 我觉得萨特人多数的作品读起来都很乏味。

8 too much like hard work used to say that you do not want to do something because it will be too much effort 太难了，太费劲了〔表示不愿做某事〕

9 make hard work of to make something you are trying to do seem more difficult than it really is 使〔某事〕看起来更难

10 hard-earned/hard-won achieved after a lot of effort 得来不易的

11 be hard at it *informal* to be very busy doing something【非正式】忙于干某事: *Sarah was hard at it on her computer.* 萨拉在电脑上忙着。

④ FULL OF PROBLEMS 棘手的，艰难的

12 a period of time that is hard is one when you do not have enough money and have a lot of problems〔日子〕艰难的，困苦的，拮据的: **times are hard** *Times were hard and we were forced to sell our home.* 那时的日子过得很艰难，我们被迫卖掉了房子。

13 have a hard life to have many problems and not have much money or comfort 生活艰难，生活拮据: *Miners used to have a very hard life.* 过去矿工们的生活十分艰难。

14 it's hard on/for sb used to say that a situation causes a lot of problems and difficulties for someone〔某人〕过得很不容易: *It's hard on the kids having their father in hospital.* 父亲住院了，孩子们过得很不容易。

⑤ UNKIND 无情的

15 showing no feelings or sympathy 冷酷的，无情的: *He had a hard face and cold blue eyes.* 他长着一张无情的脸和一双冷酷的蓝眼睛。| *I'm afraid I said some very hard things to her.* 恐怕我对她说了些很刻薄的话。| *You're a hard man, Mr Dawson.* 你是个无情的人，道森先生。

16 be hard on to treat someone in a way that is unfair, unkind, or too strict〔对某人〕严厉的；无情的；苛刻的；不公平的: *You mustn't be too hard on David – he's been under a lot of pressure lately.* 别对戴维太苛刻 —— 他最近一直压力很大。

17 a hard taskmaster/master someone who makes people work too hard 要求过分严格的上司；对别人过分苛刻的人

18 ►STRONG/NOT AFRAID 勇敢的/不害怕的◄ *informal* strong, ready to fight, and not afraid of anyone or anything【非正式】坚强的，勇敢的: *I suppose you think you're really hard, don't you!* 我想你以为自己很厉害，是吧！

19 a hard case *informal* a strong and violent person【非正式】不好惹的人

⑥ USING FORCE 用力气

20 using force 用力的: *Jane gave the door a good hard push.* 简使劲地推门。

⑦ UNFORTUNATE 不幸的

21 ►FEEL SORRY FOR SB 为某人感到遗憾的◄ **hard luck** also 又作 **hard lines** *BrE spoken* used to tell someone that you feel sorry for them【英口】真不幸！真倒霉！〔对别人表示同情〕

22 hard cheese *especially BrE spoken* used to tell someone that you do not feel sorry for them【尤英，口】活该！

23 hard-luck story a story you tell someone to make them feel sorry for you〔为博取别人同情而说的〕不幸的遭遇

⑧ OTHER MEANINGS 其他意思

24 give sb a hard time *informal*【非正式】**a)** to deliberately make someone feel uncomfortable or embarrassed〔故意〕让某人难堪或难受，给某人吃苦头: *Come on guys – stop giving me such a hard time!* 好了，别再让我难堪了！**b)** to criticize someone a lot 严厉批评某人: *My boss has been giving me a really hard time.* 我的老板近来动不动就骂我！

25 be hard on sth to have a bad effect on something 对…不利；把…用坏: *Running 50 miles a week is really hard on the knee joints.* 每周跑50英里真让膝关节受不了。

26 no hard feelings *spoken* used to tell someone who you have been arguing with that you do not feel anger towards them any more【口】我不生气，我不介意〔争吵后对人说的话〕

27 as hard as nails not feeling any emotions, especially fear or sympathy 无动于衷的，冷酷无情的

28 learn/do sth the hard way to learn about something by a bad experience or by making mistakes 以吃力的方式学习/做某事

29 hard winter a very cold winter 严冬 —opposite 反义词 MILD¹ (1)

30 ►WATER 水◄ hard water contains a lot of minerals and does not mix easily with soap〔水〕硬的，含无机盐的

31 hard facts/information/evidence etc facts, information etc that are definitely true and can be proved 确切[确凿]的事实/情报/证据等: *Police have several theories, but no hard evidence.* 警方有好几种说法，但都缺乏确实的证据。

32 take a (long) hard look at to think about something without being influenced by your feelings 冷静看待: *We need to take a long hard look at the whole system of welfare payments.* 我们需要认真仔细地审视整套福利支付制度。

33 take a hard line on/over to deal with something in a very strict way 采取强硬态度[立场]: *They've promised to take a hard*

line on law and order. 他们承诺在法律与秩序方面采取强硬立场。
34 the hard stuff *informal* strong alcohol or illegal drugs【非正式】烈酒; 烈性毒品
35 a hard left/right a sharp turn to the left or right 猛地向左/向右急转
36 ▶PRONUNCIATION 发音◀ a hard 'c' is pronounced /k/ rather than /s/; a hard 'g' is pronounced /g/ rather than /dʒ/ 发硬音的〈字母 c 发 /k/ 音而不发 /s/ 音; 字母 g 发 /g/ 音而不发 /dʒ/ 音〉 **—hardness** *n* [U]: *a material that would combine the flexibility of rubber with the hardness of glass* 能将橡胶的弹性和玻璃的硬度结合起来的一种材料 —see also 另见 **drive a hard bargain** (DRIVE[1] (9))

hard² *adv*
1 ▶USING ENERGY/EFFORT 用劲/用力◀ using a lot of effort, energy, or attention 费劲地; 费力地: *She had been working hard all morning.* 她整个上午都在努力工作。| *I tried as hard as I could to remember his name.* 我费尽全力想记起他的名字。
2 ▶WITH FORCE 用力气◀ with a lot of force 用力地; 重重地: *Tyson hit him so hard that he fell back on the ropes.* 泰森给了他一记重拳, 使他倒在栏索上。| *The boys pressed their noses hard against the window.* 男孩们将鼻子紧紧地贴在窗户上。| *It's raining hard.* 雨下得很大。
3 be hard hit/be hit hard to be badly affected by something that has happened 受到严重影响, 受到沉重打击: *The Italian economy has been particularly hard hit by the world recession.* 意大利的经济受全球经济衰退的影响尤为严重。
4 be hard put/pressed/pushed (to do sth) *informal* to have difficulty doing something【非正式】难以做到, 做某事有困难: *We'd be hard pushed to get there by 7 o'clock.* 我们很难在7点以前赶到那里。
5 be hard done by *informal* to be unfairly treated【非正式】受到不公平对待: *The other children felt hard done by because they didn't get any chocolates.* 其余的孩子都感到自己受到不公平对待, 因为他们没有得到巧克力。
6 take sth hard *informal* to feel upset about something, especially bad news【非正式】〔尤指因坏消息〕感到不快[难过]: *She's taking it very hard.* 她为此而耿耿于怀。
7 laugh hard/cry hard etc to laugh, cry etc a lot 笑/哭得很厉害: *He laughed so hard he had tears in his eyes.* 他笑得连眼泪都出来了。
8 hard on the heels of happening soon after something 紧接着: *Hard on the heels of the last week's defeat comes news of yet another disaster.* 在上周的失败后紧接着又传来不利的消息。
9 be hard on sb's heels to follow close behind or soon after someone 紧跟在某人之后: *They fled in panic with the enemy hard on their heels.* 在敌人的紧追下, 他们恐慌出逃。
10 baked/set hard made firm and stiff by being heated, glued etc 烧硬/粘牢的 —see also 另见 HARD BY, HARD UP, HARD UPON, **play hard to get** (PLAY[1] (10))

hard-and-fast /ˌ· · ˈ·◂/ *adj* **hard and fast rules/regulations** rules that are fixed and that you cannot change 不容改变的规定

hard·back /ˈhɑrdˌbæk; ˈhɑːdbæk/ *n* [C] a book that has a strong stiff cover 硬皮书, 精装本: *a hardback edition* 精装本 | **in hardback** *The book sold more than a million copies in hardback.* 这本书的精装本卖出了一百多万本。—compare 比较 PAPERBACK

hard·ball /ˈhɑrdˌbɔl; ˈhɑːdbɔːl/ *n* [U] *AmE*【美】**1** the game of BASEBALL rather than SOFTBALL 棒球 **2 play hardball** *informal* to be very determined to get what you want, especially in business or politics【非正式】〔尤指商界或政界中〕采取强硬方式

hard-bit·ten /ˌ· ˈ··◂/ *adj* not easily shocked or upset, because you have had a lot of experience 老练的; 经过磨练的: *a hard-bitten journalist* 一位老练的新闻工作者

hard·board /ˈhɑrdbɔrd; ˈhɑːdbɔːd/ *n* [U] a material made from small pieces of wood pressed together 硬质纤维板; 加压纤维板

hard-boiled /ˌ· ˈ·◂/ *adj* **1** a hard-boiled egg has been boiled until it becomes solid〔鸡蛋〕煮得老[硬]的 —compare 比较 SOFT-BOILED **2** *informal* not showing your emotions and not influenced by your feelings; TOUGH【非正式】不动感情的; 冷酷的

hard·bound /ˈhɑrdˋbaund; ˈhɑːdbaʊnd/ *adj* HARDCOVER 精装的, 硬皮的

hard by /ˌ· ˈ·/ *adv, prep old use* very near【旧】在近旁, 非常靠近: *in a house hard by the city gate* 城门边上的一座房子里

hard can·dy /ˌ· ˈ··/ *n* [C] *AmE* a hard piece of sweet food, which often tastes of fruit【美】(水果) 硬糖; BOILED SWEET *BrE*【英】

hard cash /ˌ· ˈ·/ *n* [U] money that consists of notes and coins, not cheques or CREDIT CARDS 现金, 现钞

hard ci·der /ˌ· ˈ··/ *n* [U] *AmE* an alcoholic drink made from apples【美】苹果酒; CIDER (1) *BrE*【英】

hard cop·y /ˈ· ˌ··/ *n* [U] information from a computer that is printed out onto paper 硬拷贝, 硬副本〔指电脑打印出来的信息资料〕—compare 比较 SOFT COPY

hard core /ˌ· ˈ·/ *n BrE*【英】**1 the hard core** the small central group that is most active within a group or organization〔组织中的〕核心力量, 中坚分子, 骨干: *the hard core of the Communist party* 共产党的中坚分子 **2** [singular] a group of people who cannot be persuaded to change their behaviour or beliefs 顽固分子: *a hard core of young offenders* 年轻罪犯中的顽固分子

hard-core /ˌ· ˈ·◂/ *adj* **1 hard-core pornography** magazines, films etc that show the details of sexual behaviour, often in an unpleasant way 赤裸裸的色情作品〔书刊、电影等〕**2** [only before noun 仅用于名词前] having an extremely strong belief or opinion that is unlikely to change 死硬的, 顽固不化的: *hard-core opposition to the government's educational policies* 顽固地反对政府的教育政策

hard court /ˌ· ˈ·/ *n* [C] an area for playing tennis which has a hard surface, not grass 硬地网球场

hard·cov·er /ˈhɑrdˋkʌvɚ; ˈhɑːdˌkʌvə/ *adj* a hardcover book has a strong stiff cover〔书〕硬皮的, 精装的

hard cur·ren·cy /ˌ· ˈ···/ *n* [C,U] money that will not lose value because it is from a country that has a strong ECONOMY and can be used in other countries to buy things 硬通货, 强势货币

hard disk /ˌ· ˈ·/ *n* [C] a part that is fixed inside a computer and is used for permanently storing information〔电脑〕硬磁盘 —compare 比较 FLOPPY DISK

hard-drink·ing /ˈ· ˌ··/ *adj* drinking a lot of alcohol 酗酒的, 喝酒成瘾的: *a hard-drinking man* 酒鬼

hard drugs /ˌ· ˈ·/ *n* [plural] very strong illegal drugs such as HEROIN and COCAINE 硬性毒品, 烈性毒品〈如海洛因、可卡因等〉—compare 比较 SOFT DRUG

hard-edged /ˌ· ˈ·◂/ *adj* a hard-edged report, article etc deals with unpleasant subjects or criticizes someone severely in a way that may offend some people 笔锋犀利的, 批评严厉的〔报告、文章等〕

hard·en /ˈhɑrdn; ˈhɑːdn/ *v* **1** [I,T] to become firm or stiff, or to make something firm or stiff (使) 变硬; (使) 坚固; (使) 硬化: *Make sure you give the paint enough time to dry and harden.* 你一定要让油漆有足够的时间干透和变硬。**2** [I] to become more strict and determined and less sympathetic 变得更坚定; 变得冷酷无情: *Opposition to the military regime has hardened since the massacres.* 大屠杀后, 反对军政府的力量更强硬了。| *a hardening of attitudes* 态度变得强硬 | *His face hardened.* 他的脸沉了下来。—compare 比较 SOFTEN (2) **3** [T] if an experience hardens someone, it makes them stronger and more able to deal with difficult or unpleasant situations 使变得坚强, 使更有忍耐力 **4 hardened criminal/police officer etc** a criminal etc who has had a lot of experience of things that are shocking and is therefore less affected by them 死不悔改的罪犯/见怪不怪的警官等 **5 become hardened towards/to** to become used to something shocking because you have seen it many times 对…变得麻木[不在乎] **6 harden your heart** to make yourself not feel pity or sympathy for someone 硬起心肠

hard hat /ˌ· ˈ·/ *n* [C] a protective hat, worn especially by workers in places where buildings are being built〔建筑工人的〕安全帽, 防护帽 —see picture at 参见 HAT 图

hard-head·ed /ˌ· ˈ··◂/ *adj* practical and able to make difficult decisions without letting your emotions affect your judgment 头脑清醒的, 讲究实际的, 不感情用事的: *a hard-headed business tycoon* 精明的商业巨头 **—hard-headedness** *n* [U]

hard-heart·ed /ˌ· ˈ··◂/ *adj* not caring about other people's feelings 硬心肠的, 没有同情心的 **—hard-heartedness** *n* [U]

hard-hit·ting /ˌ· ˈ··◂/ *adj* criticizing someone or something in a strong and effective way 激烈批评的: *a hard-hitting report* 措辞尖锐的报告

Hardin /ˈhɑrdn; ˈhɑrdn/, **John (Wesley)** (1856-95), a US GUNFIGHTER and OUTLAW of the Wild West. 哈丁〔(1856-1895), 美国枪手, "荒蛮西部"逃犯〕

har·di·ness /ˈhɑrdɪnɪs; ˈhɑːdinɪ̥s/ *n* [U] the ability to bear difficult or severe conditions 坚强; 耐性; 吃苦耐劳的精神

Harding /ˈhɑrdɪŋ; ˈhɑːdɪŋ/, **Warren** (1865-1923) the twenty-ninth president of the US, from 1921 to 1923 哈丁〔(1865-1923), 美国第二十九任总统, 1921 至 1923 年在任〕

hard la·bour *BrE*【英】, **hard labor** *AmE*【美】/ˌ· ˈ··/ *n* [U] punishment in prison which consists of hard physical work 苦役, 劳役

hard land·ing /ˌ· ˈ··/ *n* [singular] *technical* a sudden fall in economic activity coming after a successful period【术语】硬着陆〔指经济经过一段时期增长后的突然回落〕

hard left /ˌ· ˈ·◂/ *n* [singular] the part of a political party that believes strongly in SOCIALISM〔坚信社会主义的〕强硬左派

hard-line /ˌ· ˈ·◂/ *adj* having extreme political beliefs, and refusing to change them 立场坚定的, 不妥协的: *a hard-line Marxist* 立场坚定的马克思主义者 —see also 另见 **take a hard line on/over** (HARD[1] (33))

hard·lin·er /ˌhɑrdˈlaɪnɚ; ˌhɑːdˈlaɪnə/ *n* [C] a politician who wants political problems to be dealt with in a strong and extreme way 奉行强硬路线者: *Communist hardliners* 共产党中的强硬派

hard liq·uor /ˌ· ˈ··/ *n* [U] *especially AmE* strong alcohol such as WHISKY【尤美】烈酒〈如威士忌等〉

S2 W2 **hard·ly** /ˈhɑrdlɪ; ˈhɑːdli/ *adv* **1** almost not 几乎不; 几乎没有: *I hadn't seen him for years but he had hardly changed at all.* 我已多年没有见到他, 但他几乎一点都没变。| **can/could hardly do sth** *The children were so excited they could hardly speak.* 孩子们兴奋得几乎连话都说不出来了。| *I can hardly believe it.* 这简直让我难以置信。| **hardly anyone/anything** (=almost no one or almost nothing) 几乎没有人/东西 *Hardly anyone writes to me these days.* 现在几乎没有人给我写信了。| **hardly any** (=very few) 几乎没有 *There are hardly any cookies left.* 几乎没剩下什么饼干了。| **hardly ever** (=almost never) 几乎从未 *She hardly ever wore a hat.* 她几乎从未戴过帽子。| **hardly a day/week goes by when/without** (=used to say that something happens almost every day or every week) 几乎每天/周都… *Hardly a day goes by when I don't think of her.* 我几乎每天都在想她。—see 见 ALMOST (USAGE) **2** used to say that something had only just happened or someone had only just done something 刚刚: *The day had hardly begun, and he felt exhausted already.* 新的一天才刚刚开始, 他就已经觉得筋疲力尽了。**3** used to say that something is not at all true, possible, correct etc 很难说是…, 一点也不: *It's hardly what I'd call the perfect relationship.* 这绝对不是我所说的完美关系。| **hardly surprising** *It was hardly surprising you didn't pass your exam.* 你考试不及格, 这丝毫不让人感到意外。| **hardly the time/place/person** (=a very unsuitable time, place, person) 绝不是恰当的时候/地方/人选 *This is hardly the place to talk about our marriage problems.* 这里绝不是谈论我们的婚姻问题的地方。| **you can/could hardly do sth** (=it would not be sensible to do it) 你不应该做某事 *You could hardly blame Jane for being nervous.* 你不该责怪简过于紧张。| **could hardly be** *The message could hardly be clearer.* 这个意思再清楚不过了。| **hardly a child/beginner etc** *He was fifteen – hardly a kid.* 他已经十五岁了, 绝不是一个小孩子。

USAGE NOTE 用法说明: HARDLY

GRAMMAR 语法

Hardly is a negative word, so it is not used with another negative word. hardly 是一个否定词, 因此不与另外一个否定词连用: *hardly any pollution* 几乎没有污染 (NOT 不用 *hardly no pollution*) | *We could hardly believe our eyes.* 我们几乎无法相信自己的眼睛。(NOT 不用 *We couldn't hardly believe our eyes...*)

Hardly usually comes just before the main verb. hardly 往往紧挨着出现在主动词前: *He could hardly hear her.* 他几乎听不见她的话。(NOT 不用 *He hardly could hear her*)

Hardly is used at the beginning of sentences only in very formal or old-fashioned writing. hardly 只有在非常正式或旧式文体中才会用于句首。People would say, and usually write 人们通常会这样说, 或这样写: *The game had hardly begun when it started to rain.* 比赛刚刚开始, 天就开始下起雨来。(compare the formal 比较正式说法: *Hardly had the game begun when it started to rain...*)

Hardly is not the adverb of *hard*. hardly 不是 hard 的副词形式。You say 应该这样说: *I tried hard to remember.* 我使劲地回想。| *She works very hard.* 她工作非常努力。(NOT 不用 hardly)

hard-nosed /ˌ· ˈ·◂/ *adj* [usually before noun 一般用于名词前] not affected by emotions, and determined to get what you want 顽强的, 不屈不挠的, 倔强的: *a hard-nosed approach to business negotiations* 对商业谈判所持的一种不屈不挠的态度

hard nut /ˌ· ˈ·/ *n* [C] **1** *informal* someone who is physically or mentally very strong, or thinks that they are strong【非正式】硬汉子 **2 a hard nut to crack** someone or something that is difficult to deal with 难对付的人[事]

hard of hear·ing /ˌ· · ˈ··/ *adj* [not before noun 不用于名词前] **1** unable to hear very well 听觉不灵的, 耳背的 **2 the hard of hearing** people who are unable to hear very well 有听力障碍的人, 耳背者

hard-on /ˈ· ·/ *n* [C] *taboo* an ERECTION (1)【讳】勃起

hard pal·ate /ˌ· ˈ··/ *n* [C] the hard part of the top of your mouth that is at the front behind your teeth 硬颚 —compare 比较 SOFT PALATE

hard porn /ˌ· ˈ·/ *n* [U] *informal* magazines, films etc that show sexual behaviour in an unacceptable, sometimes violent way【非正式】赤裸裸的色情作品〔杂志、电影等〕: *sales of hard-porn videos* 色情录像带的销售 —compare 比较 SOFT PORN

hard-pressed /ˌ· ˈ·◂/ *adj* **1** having a lot of problems and not enough money or time 处于困境的; 遭受强大压力的: *Hard-pressed local authorities are finding it difficult to pay for essential services.* 处于困境的地方政府连支付最基本的公共服务费用都有困难。**2 sb would be hard-pressed to do sth** used to say that it would be difficult for someone to do something 某人难以做到某事: *They'd be hard-pressed to find a better editor.* 他们很难找到一位更好的编辑。

hard right /ˌ· ˈ·◂/ *n* [singular] the part of a political party that believes strongly in RIGHT WING political ideas 极右派

hard rock /ˌ· ˈ·/ *n* [U] a type of ROCK MUSIC that has loud electric GUITARS and a strong beat 硬摇滚乐

hard-scrab·ble /ˌ· ˈ··/ *adj AmE* hard-scrabble land is difficult to grow crops on【美】〔土地〕贫瘠的

hard sell /ˌ· ˈ·◂/ *n* [singular] a way of selling something in which there is a lot of pressure on you to buy 强行[硬性]推销(法) —compare 比较 SOFT SELL

hard·ship /ˈhɑrdʃɪp; ˈhɑːdʃɪp/ *n* [C,U] the condition of having very little money so that life is very difficult 艰苦, 贫困: *a time of great economic hardship* 经济极度困难的时期

hard shoul·der /ˌ· ˈ··/ *n* [singular] *BrE* the area at the side of a big road where you are allowed to stop if you have a problem with your car【英】〔公路旁的〕紧急停车处, 路肩; SHOULDER[1] (9) *AmE*【美】—see picture on page A3 参见 A3 页图

Hard Times /ˌ· ˈ·/ (1854) a book by Charles Dickens about life in an imaginary industrial city in northern England. One of its main characters is the businessman Thomas Gradgrind, who is only interested in facts and practical matters, and teaches his children that love and imagination have no use or value.《艰难时世》〔(1854), 查尔斯·狄更斯的小说, 讲述英格兰北部一虚构的工业城市的生活, 其中一位主人公是商人托马斯·格拉德格林德, 他只注重实际, 而且还教育他的孩子爱和想象毫无用处, 分文不值〕

hard·top /ˈhɑrdˌtɑp; ˈhɑːdtɒp/ *n* [C] a car that has a metal roof which cannot be removed 硬顶小汽车, 有固定金属车顶的汽车 —compare 比较 CONVERTIBLE[2]

hard up /ˌ· ˈ·◂/ *adj* not having enough money to buy the things you need, especially for a short period of time〔尤指短期内〕缺钱的, 手头紧的: *We were too hard up to afford new clothes.* 那时我们手头紧, 没有钱买新衣服。

hard up·on /ˈ· ·ˌ·/ also 又作 **hard on** *prep literary*【文】**1** soon after〔时间〕紧接着, 随即 **2** close behind 紧接…之后

hard·ware /ˈhɑrdˌwɛr; ˈhɑːdweə/ *n* [U] **1** computer machinery and equipment, as opposed to the programmes that make computers work〔电脑〕硬件 —compare 比较 SOFTWARE **2** equipment and tools for your home and garden〔家用或园艺用的〕金属器件[用具]; 五金制品 **3** the machinery and equipment that is needed to do something 装备, 设备: *tanks and other military hardware* 坦克和其他军事装备

hard-wearing /ˌ· ˈ··◂/ *adj BrE* clothes, materials etc that are hard-wearing will remain in good condition for a long time【英】经穿的, 耐磨的; LONGWEARING *AmE*【美】

hard-wired /ˌ· ˈ·◂/ *adj technical* computer systems that are hard-wired are controlled by HARDWARE rather than SOFTWARE and therefore cannot be easily changed by the user【术语】〔电脑作业〕硬件控制的, 硬连线的

hard·wood /ˈhɑrdˌwʊd; ˈhɑːdwʊd/ *n* **1** [C,U] strong heavy wood from trees such as OAK that take a long time to grow, used for making furniture 硬木〈如橡木〉 **2** [C] a tree that produces this kind of wood 硬木树; 阔叶树 —compare 比较 SOFTWOOD

hard-working /ˌ· ˈ··/ *adj* working with a lot of effort 努力工作的, 勤奋的: *a hard-working teacher* 一位努力工作的教师

H

har·dy /ˈhɑrdɪ; ˈhɑːdi/ *adj* **1** strong and healthy and able to bear difficult living conditions 能吃苦耐劳的; 坚强的; 强壮的: *the hardy fishermen who turned out in these arctic conditions* 在这种极度寒冷的环境中外出的吃苦耐劳的渔民 **2** a hardy plant is able to live through the winter〔植物〕耐寒的

Hardy, Ol·i·ver /ˈɑlɪvɚ; ˈɒlɪvə/ —see 见 LAUREL AND HARDY

Hardy, Thomas (1840-1928) a British writer and poet. Many of his NOVEL*s* are set in the countryside of Dorset in the southwest of England, and they often describe the unhappy side of life. His characters are often shown to be struggling against their own feelings and against FATE. His best known books include *Far From the Madding Crowd, The Mayor of Casterbridge, Tess of the D'Urbervilles*, and *Jude the Obscure*. 哈代〔(1840-1928), 英国作家、诗人。他的许多小说都是以英格兰西南部的多赛特乡村为背景, 描写生活中不幸的一面。他笔下的人物常与自己的感情和命运抗争。最有名的小说包括《远离尘嚣》、《卡斯特桥市长》、《德伯家的苔丝》和《无名的裘德》〕

Hardy Boys, the /ˈ· ·, ·/ the main characters in a series of US books known as *The Hardy Boys Mysteries*, the first of which was written in 1927. The Hardy Boys are two brave young brothers called Frank and Joe Hardy who are always getting involved in exciting, dangerous adventures in which they help to solve crimes. 哈迪小子〔美国系列丛书《哈迪小子谜案》中的主人公。丛书的第一本于1927年写成。哈迪小子是一对姓哈迪的勇敢的年轻兄弟, 一个叫弗兰克, 一个叫乔。他们总是卷入危险而刺激的事情之中, 从而协助破案〕

hardy pe·ren·ni·al /,· · ˈ· · ·/ *n* [C] **1** a hardy plant that produces flowers for several years 耐寒的多年生植物 —see also 另见 PERENNIAL[2] **2** an idea that is often suggested or discussed 经常提到或谈论到的话题

hare[1] /hɛr; heə/ *n plural* **hare** or **hares** [C] **1** an animal like a rabbit but larger, that can run very quickly 野兔 —see picture at 参见 RABBIT[1] 图 **2 run with the hare and hunt with the hounds** *old-fashioned* to try to support both sides in an argument【过时】两面讨好

hare[2] *v* [I always+adv/prep] *BrE informal* to run or go very fast【英, 非正式】飞跑, 飞奔: [+off/away] *He hared off down the road.* 他沿着马路飞快地跑掉了。

Hare and the Tor·toise, The /,· · · ˈ· ·/ another name for *The Tortoise and the Hare*《兔龟赛跑》〔《龟兔赛跑》的别名〕

hare·bell /ˈhɛr,bɛl; ˈheəbel/ *n* [C] a wild plant with bell-shaped blue flowers on a thin stem 圆叶风铃草, 蓝铃花

hare·brained /ˈhɛrˈbrend; ˈheəbreɪnd/ *adj* a harebrained person, plan etc is very silly and unlikely to succeed〔人、计划等〕愚蠢的; 轻率的; 不切实际的: *wasting public money on harebrained schemes* 将公款浪费在一些不切实际的计划上

hare cours·ing /ˈ· ,· ·/ *n* [U] the sport of chasing a HARE with dogs 用猎犬追踪野兔的狩猎

Har·e Krish·na /,hærɪ ˈkrɪʃnə; ,hæri ˈkrɪʃnə/ an international religious group that was started in the 1960s and is based on great love for the Hindu god Krishna. Its members wear loose yellow-orange ROBE*s* and the men cut off most of their hair, and they often go around city streets in groups singing the words 'Hare Krishna'. 国际黑天觉悟会〔一国际性宗教团体, 成立于20世纪60年代, 尊奉印度教黑天神。教徒身着宽松的橘黄长袍, 男子几乎不蓄发。他们常成群结队口诵"Hare Krishna"游走在城市街头〕

hare·lip /,hɛrˈlɪp; ,heəˈlɪp/ *n* [singular,U] the condition of having your top lip divided into two parts because it did not develop properly before birth 兔唇, 唇裂 —**harelipped** *adj*

har·em /ˈhɛrəm; ˈhɑːriːm/ *n* [C] **1** the group of wives or women who lived with a rich or powerful man in some Muslim societies in the past〔旧时有钱或有权的穆斯林的〕妻妾, 女眷 **2** part of a Muslim house that is separate from the rest of the house, where only women live〔穆斯林的〕女眷居住的内室, 闺房

harem pants /ˈ· ·, ·/ *n* [plural] loose-fitting women's trousers made from thin cloth 扎脚管宽松女长裤, 哈伦裤

Har·greaves /ˈhɑrgrivz; ˈhɑːgriːvz/, **James** (1720-78) a British inventor who invented machines such as the Spinning Jenny, which was used for making cotton and wool into thread, and which he used in his factory in Nottingham 哈格里夫斯〔(1720-1778), 英国发明家。他发明了珍妮纺纱机等机器, 用于加工棉线和毛线。他在诺丁汉的自办工厂里就使用了这种纺纱机〕—see also 另见 INDUSTRIAL REVOLUTION

Hari, Mata —see 见 MATA HARI

har·i·cot /ˈhærɪ,ko; ˈhærɪkəʊ/ also 又作 **haricot bean** /,· · · ˈ·/ *n* [C] a small white bean 菜豆, 扁豆

hark /hɑrk; hɑːk/ *v* **1 hark at him/her!** *BrE spoken* used when you think someone is saying something stupid or unreasonable【英口】暂且听听〔某人的蠢话〕: *Hark at him! I bet he couldn't do any better.* 听他说的! 我敢打赌他也好不到哪里去! **2 hark!** *old use* used to tell someone to listen【旧】听着! 留神听!

hark back *phr v* [I] **1** to remember and talk about things that happened in the past 回想, 谈论往事, 追溯过去 **2** to be similar to something in the past 与过去的某事相类似: [+to] *music that harks back to the early age of jazz* 类似早期爵士乐的音乐

har·ken /ˈhɑrkən; ˈhɑːkən/ *v* [I] another spelling of HEARKEN hearken的另一种拼法

Har·lem /ˈhɑrləm; ˈhɑːləm/ an area of New York City in northeast Manhattan, where many African-American and Hispanic people live 哈勒姆〔纽约市一区, 位于曼哈顿东北部, 住有大量非裔美国人和拉美裔美国人〕

Harlem Globe·trot·ters, the /,hɑrləm ˈglobtrɑtɚz; ,hɑːləm ˈgləʊbtrɒtəz/ a black US BASKETBALL team who travel around the world to play games in which they entertain people with their skill at basketball and their amusing style of playing 哈林环球旅行者篮球队〔美国一黑人篮球队。他们周游世界参加比赛, 以篮球技艺和滑稽动作取悦观众〕

har·le·quin /ˈhɑrləkwɪn; ˈhɑːlɪkwɪn/ *n* [C] **1** a character in some traditional plays who wears brightly coloured clothes and plays tricks〔身穿鲜艳服装的〕滑稽角色, 小丑 **2** a harlequin pattern is made up of DIAMOND shapes in many different colours〔由不同颜色的菱形组成的〕彩色拼块

Harlequin Ro·mance /,· · · ˈ· ·/ one of a US series of romantic NOVEL*s* about men and women who fall in love. The stories are usually simple, with a happy ending. 禾林浪漫小说〔美国的系列爱情小说之一, 描写男女相爱的故事, 通常情节简单, 结局圆满〕—compare 比较 MILLS AND BOON

Har·ley-Da·vid·son /,hɑrlɪ ˈdevɪdsn; ,hɑːli ˈdeɪvɪdsən/ *trademark* a type of large and powerful US MOTORCYCLE【商标】哈雷戴维森〔美国的一种马力强劲的大型摩托车〕

Har·ley Street /ˈhɑrlɪ strit; ˈhɑːli striːt/ a street in west central London where many well-known and expensive doctors have their offices 哈利街〔伦敦市中心西区一街名。许多收费不菲的名医在此挂牌行医〕: *a Harley Street specialist* 一位在哈利街开诊所的专科医生

har·lot /ˈhɑrlət; ˈhɑːlət/ *n* [C] *old use* a PROSTITUTE【旧】娼妓, 妓女

harm[1] /hɑrm; hɑːm/ *n* [U] **1** damage, injury, or trouble caused by someone's actions or by an event 损害; 危害; 伤害: **do harm to** *Modern farming methods have done considerable harm to the countryside.* 现代农作方式对乡村造成了很大的损害。| **do more harm than good** (=cause even more problems rather than improving the situation) 坏处多于好处, 弊大于利 *Criticizing people's work often does more harm than good.* 批评别人的工作往往弊多利少。| **where's the harm in that?** *spoken* (=used when you think that something seems a reasonable thing to do)【口】那有什么害处呢? | **no harm done** *spoken* (=used to tell someone not to worry about something they have done)【口】没事儿, 不要紧 **2 come to no harm/not come to any harm** to not be hurt or damaged 没有受到伤害[损害]: *She was relieved to see the children had come to no harm.* 她看到孩子们没有受到伤害, 舒了一口气。**3 mean no harm/not mean any harm** to have no intention of hurting or upsetting anyone 无意伤害别人: *He doesn't mean any harm – he's only joking.* 他没有恶意, 只是开个玩笑。**4 it does no harm to do sth/there's no harm in doing sth** used to suggest that someone should do something 不妨做某事: *It does no harm to ask.* 不妨问问。| *There's no harm in trying.* 试试也无妨。**5 it wouldn't do sb any harm to do sth** used to suggest that someone should do something that may be helpful or useful 做〔某事〕对〔某人〕并无害处: *It would do you no harm to get some experience first.* 你不妨先积累点经验。**6 out of harm's way a)** in a safe place 在安全的地方 **b)** if something dangerous is out of harm's way, it is in a place where it is unable to hurt anyone or damage anything 不构成伤害的, 处于不伤害人的地位 —compare 比较 HURT[3] —see also 另见 GRIEVOUS BODILY HARM

harm[2] *v* [T] **1** to damage something 危害, 伤害, 损害〔某事物〕: *Too much direct sunlight will harm the plant.* 阳光直接照射过多会伤害植物。**2 harm sb's image/reputation** to make people have a worse opinion of a person or group 损害某人的形象/名声 **3** to hurt someone 伤害〔某人〕: *The dogs look fierce, but they wouldn't harm anyone.* 这些狗看起来很凶猛, 但不会伤人。

harm·ful /ˈhɑrmfəl; ˈhɑːmfəl/ *adj* causing or likely to cause harm 有害的; 致伤的: *the harmful effects of smoking* 吸烟的害处 | [+to] *chemicals that are harmful to the environment* 对环境有害的化学品 —**harmfully** *adv* —**harmfulness** *n* [U]

harm·less /ˈhɑrmlɪs; ˈhɑːmləs/ *adj* **1** unable or unlikely to hurt anyone or cause damage 无害的; 不致伤的: *The dog seems fierce, but actually he's harmless.* 这条狗看起来很凶, 但实际上不会伤人。**2** not likely to upset or offend anyone 无恶意的: **harmless fun** *It was just a bit of harmless fun.* 这只是个无恶意的玩笑。—**harmlessly** *adv* —**harmlessness** *n* [U]

har·mon·ic /hɑrˋmɑnɪk; hɑˈmɒnɪk/ *adj technical* concerned with the way notes are played or sung together to give a pleasing sound【术语】和声的: *harmonic scales* 调和音阶

har·mon·i·ca /hɑrˋmɑnɪkə; hɑːˈmɒnɪkə/ *n* [C] a small musical instrument that you play by blowing into it and moving it from side to side; MOUTH ORGAN 口琴

har·mo·ni·ous /hɑrˋmonɪəs; hɑːˈməʊniəs/ *adj* **1** harmonious relationships, agreements etc are ones in which people are friendly and helpful to one another〔关系〕和睦的, 融洽的 **2** sounds that are harmonious are very pleasant 音调和谐的, 悦耳的 **3** parts, colours etc that are harmonious look good or work well together〔部分、颜色等〕协调的, 和谐的, 调和的: *The decor is a harmonious blend of traditional and modern.* 这种装饰风格是传统和现代的和谐统一。—**harmoniously** *adv* —**harmoniousness** *n* [U]

har·mo·ni·um /hɑrˋmonɪəm; hɑːˈməʊniəm/ *n* [C] a musical instrument like a small piano worked by pumped air 簧风琴

har·mo·nize also 又作 **-ise** *BrE*【英】/ˋhɑrməˌnaɪz; ˈhɑːmənaɪz/ *v* **1** [I] if two or more things harmonize, they work well together or look good together 和谐, 协调: **[+with]** *colours that don't seem to harmonize with each other* 看上去相互不协调的颜色 **2** [T] to make two or more sets of rules, taxes etc the same 使一致, 统一: *harmonizing Europe's widely varying immigration procedures* 统一欧洲各国间相去甚远的移民程序 **3** [I] to sing or play music in HARMONY 用和声演唱[演奏]

har·mo·ny /ˋhɑrmənɪ; ˈhɑːməni/ *n* **1** [C usually plural 一般用复数,U] notes of music combined together in a pleasant way〔音乐中的〕和声: **in harmony** *a choir singing in perfect harmony* 用完美的和声演唱的唱诗班 **2 be in harmony with** *formal* to agree with another idea, feeling etc, or look good with other things【正式】〔思想、感情等的〕和睦, 一致, 融洽: *Your suggestions are not in harmony with the aims of this project.* 你的建议与本项目的目标不符。**3 live/work in (perfect) harmony** to live or work together without fighting or disagreeing with each other 一起生活/工作得(十分)融洽 **4** [U] the pleasant effect made by different things that form an attractive whole 和谐, 协调: *the harmony of sea and sky* 海天一色 —compare 比较 DISCORD

har·ness[1] /ˋhɑrnɪs; ˈhɑːnɪs/ *n* [C,U] **1** a piece of equipment for controlling a horse, consisting of long pieces of leather held together by metal and worn over the horse's head and shoulders〔马的〕挽具, 马具 **2** a piece of equipment used to fasten someone in a place or to stop them from falling 系带: *a safety harness* 安全带 **3 be back in harness** *informal* to have come back to do your usual work【非正式】恢复正常工作 **4 in harness with** working closely with another group 与…密切合作

harness[2] *v* [T] **1** to control and use the natural force or power of something 利用〔自然界的力量〕: *harnessing the power of the wind to generate electricity* 利用风力发电 **2** to fasten two animals together, or to fasten an animal to something using a harness〔将两只动物〕系拴在一起,〔将动物〕系到某物上 **3** to put a harness on a horse 给马套上挽具

Har·old II /ˌhærəld ðə ˋsɛkənd; ˌhærəld ðə ˈsekənd/, **King** (?1022-66) the last Anglo-Saxon king of England, who became king at the beginning of 1066 but later that year died in battle against William the Conqueror at Hastings. He is supposed to have been killed by an ARROW that hit him in the eye. 哈罗德二世〔(?1022-1066), 英格兰最后一位盎格鲁-撒克逊国王, 1066年初即位, 但同年在黑斯廷斯与"征服者"威廉交战时阵亡。据信, 他是被一支箭射中眼睛而死的〕

harp[1] /hɑrp; hɑːp/ *n* [C] a large musical instrument with strings that are stretched from top to bottom of a frame with three corners 竖琴 —**harpist** *n* [C]

harp[2] *v*

harp on [I *BrE* 英, T *AmE* 美] *informal* to talk about something continuously, especially in a way that is annoying or boring【非正式】唠唠叨叨, 喋喋不休: **[+about]** *My grandfather harps on about the war all the time.* 我的祖父总是喋喋不休地说起战争的事。

Har·pers & Queen /ˌhɑrpəz ənd ˋkwin; ˌhɑːpəz ənd ˈkwiːn/ *trademark* a British magazine with articles and pictures about fashion, famous people etc【商标】《哈珀斯与名媛》〔英国一杂志, 刊登时尚、名人等方面的文章和图片〕

Harper's Ferry /ˋhɑrpəz ˋfɛrɪ; ˈhɑːpəz ˈferi/ a town in West Virginia, where the Potomac and Shenandoah Rivers meet, that was the place of many battles during the American Civil War. Just before the war, an ABOLITIONIST (=someone who wants to stop slavery) called John Brown took control of the government weapons that were kept there and tried to get slaves to fight against their owners. He was caught and hanged for TREASON (=actions against your country). 哈珀斯费里〔美国西弗吉尼亚一镇, 位于波托马克河和谢南多厄河汇合处。美国内战期间这里发生过许多次战役。内战爆发前夕, 一位名叫约翰·布朗的废奴主义者控制了存放在该镇的政府军火, 并竭力鼓动奴隶们反抗奴隶主。他因此被逮捕, 并以叛国罪处以绞刑〕

har·poon /hɑrˋpun; hɑːˈpuːn/ *n* [C] a weapon used for hunting WHALES 捕鲸叉 —**harpoon** *v* [T]

harp·si·chord /ˋhɑrpsɪˌkɔrd; ˈhɑːpsɪkɔːd/ *n* [C] a musical instrument like a PIANO, used in former times 大键琴; 古键琴〔古时类似钢琴的一种乐器〕

har·py /ˋhɑrpɪ; ˈhɑːpi/ *n* [C] *literary* a cruel or nasty woman【文】凶恶卑鄙的女人, 泼妇

har·ri·dan /ˋhærədən; ˈhærɪdən/ *n* [C] *old-fashioned* a bad-tempered, unpleasant woman【过时】泼妇, 恶婆, 母夜叉

Harrier jump jet /ˌ⋯ˋ⋅, ⋅/ *trademark* a British military plane that can take off and land by going straight up or down. The Royal Navy use the **Sea Harrier** which is very similar.【商标】鹞式飞机〔英国一种可直接起飞和降落的军用飞机。英国皇家海军使用的海鹞式飞机与之极为相似〕

Harrisburg /ˋhærɪsˌbɝg; ˈhærɪsbɜːg/ the capital city of the US state of Pennsylvania 哈里斯堡〔美国宾夕法尼亚州首府〕

Har·ri·son /ˋhærɪsən; ˈhærɪsən/, **Benjamin** /ˋbɛndʒəmɪn; ˈbendʒəmɪn/ (1833-1901) the twenty-third president of the US, from 1889 to 1893 哈里森〔(1833-1901), 美国第二十三任总统, 1889至1893年间在任〕

Harrison, George (1943-2001) a British musician and songwriter who sang and played the GUITAR in The Beatles. After The Beatles separated, he made records on his own, including *My Sweet Lord*. 哈里森〔(1943-2001), 英国音乐家、词作家。他曾在甲壳虫乐队演唱并弹奏吉他。乐队解散后, 他自己灌制唱片, 包括《亲爱的上帝》等〕

Harrison, William Henry (1773-1841) a US politician who became President in 1841, but died a month later. 哈里森〔(1773-1841), 美国政治家。1841年就任总统, 一个月后去世〕

Har·row /ˋhæro; ˈhærəʊ/ a famous British PUBLIC SCHOOL (=expensive private school) for boys, in northwest London. Men who have been educated at Harrow are known as **Old Harrovians**. 哈罗公学〔英国一著名男子公学, 位于伦敦西北部。曾在该校受过教育的人被称为Old Harrovians (老哈罗人)〕—compare 比较 ETON

harrow *n* [C] a farming machine with sharp metal blades, used to break up the earth before planting crops 耙 —**harrow** *v* [I,T]

har·rowed /ˋhærod; ˈhærəʊd/ *adj* a harrowed look or expression shows that you are very worried or afraid〔样子或表情〕苦恼的, 忧虑的, 忧伤的; 害怕的

har·row·ing /ˋhærəwɪŋ; ˈhærəʊɪŋ/ *adj* very frightening or shocking and making you feel very upset 折磨人的, 可怕的, 令人痛苦的: *a harrowing experience* 可怕的经历 | *harrowing video tapes of torture* 令人毛骨悚然的酷刑录像带

har·ry /ˋhærɪ; ˈhæri/ *v* **harried, harrying** [T] **1** to keep asking someone for something in a way that is upsetting or annoying 不断烦扰, 使苦恼 **2** to attack an enemy repeatedly 再三袭击, 侵扰〔敌人〕

Harry /ˋhærɪ; ˈhæri/, **Prince** (1984-) the younger son of Prince Charles and Princess Diana. His official name is Prince Henry. 哈里王子〔(1984-), 查尔斯王子和戴安娜王妃的次子, 正式称号为亨利王子〕

harsh /hɑrʃ; hɑːʃ/ *adj*

1 ►CONDITIONS/WEATHER 条件/天气◄ difficult to live in and very uncomfortable, cold etc 恶劣的, 艰苦的, 严峻的: *The prisoners had to endure harsh living conditions and near starvation.* 犯人们得忍受艰苦的生活条件和极度饥饿。| *the harsh winters of northern China* 中国北方的严冬 | **harsh reality** *experiencing the harsh realities of adult life* 体验成人生活的残酷现实

2 ►SOUND/LIGHT/COLOUR 声音/光线/颜色◄ unpleasant and too loud or bright 刺耳的; 刺眼的, 耀眼的: *a harsh, croaking voice* 刺耳而沙哑的声音 | *They stepped out into the harsh sunlight.* 他们走了出去, 置身于刺眼的阳光之中。

3 ►**CRUEL/STRICT** 残酷的/严苛的◄ criticizing, punishing, or treating people in a very cruel or strict way 无情的；严厉的：**harsh criticism** *Brando has had to endure some harsh criticism from the press.* 白兰度得忍受新闻界对他的严厉批评。| *a harsh, authoritarian regime* 无情独裁的政权
4 ►**LINES/SHAPES ETC** 线条/形状等◄ ugly and unpleasant to look at 难看的，丑陋的：*the harsh outline of the factories against the sky* 在天空映衬下丑陋的工厂轮廓
5 ►**CLEANING SUBSTANCE** 清洁用品◄ too strong and likely to damage the thing you are cleaning 太粗糙的；太强力的 —**harshly** *adv* —**harshness** *n* [U]

hart /hɑrt; hɑːt/ *n* [C] *especially BrE* a male DEER【尤英】公鹿

Hart, Lor·enz Mil·ton /ˈlɔrənz ˈmɪltn̩; ˈlɔrənz ˈmɪltən/ (1895-1943) a US songwriter who worked with the COMPOSER Richard Rodgers to produce MUSICAL*s* (=films or plays that use singing and dancing to tell a story), such as *Babes in Arms* and *Pal Joey* 哈特〔(1895-1943)，美国歌词作家。他曾与作曲家理查德·罗杰斯一起创作音乐剧，如《怀中佳丽》和《好伙伴宙伊》〕

Hartford /ˈhɑrtfəd; ˈhɑːtfəd/ the capital city of the US state of Connecticut 哈特福德〔美国康涅狄格州首府〕

har·um-scar·um /ˈhɛrəm ˋskɛrəm; ˌheərəm ˈskeərəm/ *adv old-fashioned* in an uncontrolled way and without thinking【过时】冒失的，鲁莽的，轻率的 —**harum-scarum** *adj*

Har·vard /ˈhɑrvəd; ˈhɑːvəd/ also 又作 **Harvard University** a famous and respected university in Cambridge, Massachusetts, established in 1636, which is the oldest university in the US 哈佛大学〔马萨诸塞州坎布里奇的一所久负盛名的大学。创建于1636年，为美国历史最悠久的一所大学〕 —compare 比较 YALE

har·vest¹ /ˈhɑrvɪst; ˈhɑːvɪ̣st/ *n* **1** [C,U] the time when crops are gathered from the fields, or the act of gathering them 收获期；收获，收割：*harvest time* 收获时节 **2** [C] the size or quality of the crops that have been gathered 收成；收获量：**a poor/bumper harvest** (=a harvest that produces few crops or a lot of crops) 歉收/丰收 **3 reap a harvest** to get good or bad results 获得成果；尝到后果：*The company is now reaping the harvest of careful planning.* 公司目前尝到了严谨规划带来的好处。

harvest² *v* [I,T] to gather crops from the fields 收获，收割

har·vest·er /ˈhɑrvɪstəː; ˈhɑːvɪ̣stə/ *n* [C] someone who gathers crops 收获者，收割者 —see also 另见 **combine harvester** (COMBINE² (1))

harvest fes·ti·val /ˌ·· ˈ···/ *n* [C] *especially BrE* an occasion in the Christian religion when people thank God for the harvest【尤英】收获感恩节 —compare 比较 THANKSGIVING

harvest moon /ˌ·· ˈ·/ *n* [usually singular 一般用单数] the FULL MOON in autumn 秋分前后的满月

Harvey /ˈhɑrvɪ; ˈhɑːvi/, **William** (1578-1657) an English doctor who discovered the CIRCULATION of the blood, that is, the way the heart makes the blood move around the body 哈维〔(1578-1657)，英国医生。他发现了血液循环原理，即心脏促使血液在体内流动的方式〕

Har·vey's Bris·tol Cream /ˌ··ˌ·· ˈ·/ *trademark* a popular and well-known type of sweet SHERRY (=a type of strong, dark wine from Spain) made by Harvey's, a company based in Bristol in England【商标】哈维雪利酒〔一种广受喜爱的名牌甜雪利酒，由总部在英格兰布里斯托尔的哈维公司生产〕

Har·well /ˈhɑrwəl; ˈhɑːwəl/ a British government centre for atomic research, near the village of Harwell in Oxfordshire, southern England 哈韦尔原子能研究所〔英国政府原子能研究中心，位于英格兰南部牛津郡哈韦尔村附近〕

Har·wich /ˈhærɪtʃ; ˈhærɪtʃ/ a port in Essex, eastern England, from which ferries (FERRY) and other ships sail to ports in Denmark, Belgium, and the Netherlands 哈里奇〔英格兰东部埃塞克斯郡一港口。渡轮和其他船只从这里开往丹麦、比利时、荷兰的一些港口〕

has /əz, həz; z, əz, həz; *strong* 强读 hæz; hæz/ the third person singular of the present tense of HAVE¹

has-been /ˈ· ·/ *n* [C] *informal* someone who was important or popular but who has now been forgotten【非正式】过时的人，已失去往日风光的人

hash¹ /hæʃ; hæʃ/ *n* **1 make a hash of** *informal* to do something very badly【非正式】把…弄糟：*I made a real hash of my exams.* 我的考试考得一团糟。**2** [U] *informal* HASHISH【非正式】大麻麻醉剂 **3** [C,U] a dish made with cooked meat and potatoes 肉末马铃薯泥

hash² *v*
hash sth ↔ up *phr v* [T] *informal* to do something very badly【非正式】把…弄得乱七八糟：*She was so nervous at the interview that she completely hashed it up.* 她面试时太紧张了，结果表现得极糟。—**hash-up** *n* [C]

hash browns /ˌ· ˈ·/ *n* [plural] potatoes that are cut into very small pieces, pressed together, and cooked in oil 煎马铃薯饼

hash·ish /ˈhæʃiʃ; ˈhæʃiːʃ/ *n* [U] the strongest form of the drug CANNABIS 大麻麻醉剂

has·n't /ˈhæznt̩; ˈhæzənt/ the short form of 缩略式= has not: *Hasn't she finished yet?* 她做完了没有？

hasp /hæsp; hɑːsp/ *n* [C] a flat metal thing used to fasten a door, lid etc〔金属〕锁搭，搭扣

Has·sam /ˈhæsəm; ˈhæsəm/, **Childe** /tʃaɪld; tʃaɪld/ (1859-1935) a US painter and maker of PRINT*s* (=printed pictures). His work was influenced by IMPRESSIONISM. 哈桑姆〔(1859-1935)，美国油画家、版画家，其作品受印象派的影响〕

Has·sel·blad /ˈhæsl̩blæd; ˈhæsəlblæd/ *trademark* a very good quality type of camera made by the Swedish company Hasselblad, often used by professional photographers. Different LENSE*s* can be fitted to the camera, which takes photos of larger than average size.【商标】哈苏照相机〔瑞典哈苏公司制造的一种高级相机，常为专业摄影师使用。该相机可安装各种不同的镜头，拍摄画面较大〕

has·sle¹ /ˈhæsl̩; ˈhæsəl/ *n* **1** [C,U] *spoken* something that is annoying, because it causes problems or is difficult to do【口】麻烦：*I don't feel like cooking tonight, it's too much hassle.* 今天晚上我不想做饭，太麻烦了。| *It's such a hassle not having a washing machine.* 没有洗衣机真是麻烦。**2** [C] *AmE informal* an argument between two people or groups【美，非正式】争论，争吵：*hassles with the management* 与管理层的争论

hassle² *v* **hassled, hassling** *informal*【非正式】**1** [T] to be continuously asking someone to do something in a way that annoys them 烦扰，不断打扰：*I wish you'd stop hassling me.* 希望你不要再烦我了。**2** [I+**with**] to argue with someone 争论，争吵

has·sock /ˈhæsək; ˈhæsək/ *n* [C] **1** a small CUSHION¹ (1) for kneeling on in a church〔教堂里的〕祈祷跪垫 **2** *AmE* a soft round piece of furniture used as a seat or for resting your feet on【美】坐垫，脚垫；POUF (1) *BrE*【英】

hast /hæst; hæst/ **thou hast** *old use* a way of saying【旧】= you have

haste /hest; heɪst/ *n* [U] **1** great speed in doing something, especially because you do not have enough time 匆忙，仓促：*I soon regretted my haste.* 我很快就对自己的仓促感到后悔。| **in your haste to do sth** *In his haste to leave he forgot his briefcase.* 他走得很匆忙，忘了带公事包。**2 in haste** quickly or in a hurry 匆忙地，急忙地：*They left in haste, without even saying goodbye.* 他们走得很匆忙，连再见都没说。**3 make haste** *old use* to hurry or do something quickly【旧】赶紧，仓促 **4 more haste less speed** *BrE* used to say that it is useless to do something too quickly【英】欲速则不达

has·ten /ˈhesn̩; ˈheɪsən/ *v* **1** [T] to make something happen faster or sooner 加速，加紧：*Her death had been hastened by large doses of pain-killing drugs.* 大剂量的止痛药加速了她的死亡。**2** [I] to do or say something quickly or without delay 抢着，急忙，赶快：**hasten to do sth** *I hastened to assure her that there was no danger.* 我赶紧向她保证不会有什么危险。**3** [I always+adv/prep] *formal* to go somewhere quickly【正式】赶到某地 **4 I hasten to add** used when you realize that what you have said may not have been understood correctly 我得赶紧补充说：*an exhausting course, which, I hasten to add, was also great fun* 整个课程十分累人，但我得说，也十分好玩

Has·tings /ˈhestɪŋz; ˈheɪstɪŋz/ a town on the southeast coast of England. 黑斯廷斯〔英格兰东南海岸一镇〕

> **CULTURAL NOTE 文化注释**
> The **Battle of Hastings** took place near the town in 1066, when King Hharold II of England was defeated and killed by the French army of William the Conqueror, the Duke of Normandy. The battle is shown in the Bayeux Tapestry. 黑斯廷斯战役于1066年发生在该镇附近，当时英格兰国王哈罗德二世被诺曼底公爵"征服者"威廉率领的法国军队击败并杀死。巴约挂毯上有这场战役的场景。— see also 另见 the NORMAN CONQUEST

hast·y /ˈhestɪ; ˈheɪsti/ *adj* done in a hurry, especially with bad results 仓促完成的；匆忙的：*He soon regretted his hasty decision.* 他很快就对自己的仓促决定感到后悔。| *a hasty breakfast* 急匆匆的一顿早餐 —**hastily** *adv* —**hastiness** *n* [U]

2 3 **hat** /hæt; hæt/ *n* [C] **1** a piece of clothing that you wear on your head 帽子: **straw/bowler/woolly etc hat** *She wore an enormous flowery hat.* 她戴着一顶大大的带花饰的帽子。**2 keep something under your hat** *informal* to keep something secret【非正式】保守秘密 **3 be wearing your manager's/teacher's etc hat** *informal* to be doing your duty as a manager etc, which is not your only duty【非正式】兼着经理/老师的工作〔指做不止一份工作〕**4 I take my hat off to** *informal* used to say you admire someone very much because of what they have done【非正式】我钦佩〔某人〕**5 pass the hat round** *BrE*【英】**/pass the hat (around)** *AmE*【美】to collect money from a group of people, especially in order to buy someone a present〔尤指为了给某人买礼物而〕筹集金钱，募捐 **6 bowler-hatted/top-hatted etc** wearing a BOWLER hat, etc 戴礼帽/高顶礼帽等的 **7 my hat!** *old-fashioned* used to express great surprise【过时】天哪！—see also 另见 HARD HAT, **at the drop of a hat** (DROP² (5)), **hang up your hat** (HANG¹ (14)), **I'll eat my hat** (EAT (10)), OLD HAT, **be talking through your hat** (TALK¹ (17)), **throw your hat into the ring** (THROW¹ (33))

hat·band /ˈhætˌbænd; ˈhætbænd/ *n* [C] a band of cloth or leather fastened around a hat 帽圈，帽带

hat box /ˈ· ·/ *n* [C] a special box used for carrying a hat in 帽盒

hatch¹ /hætʃ; hætʃ/ *v* **1** also 又作 **hatch out** [I,T] if an egg hatches or is hatched, it breaks, letting the young bird, insect etc come out〔蛋〕孵化: *The eggs take three days to hatch.* 这些蛋要三天时间才能孵化。**2** also 又作 **hatch out** [I,T] if a young bird, insect etc hatches or is hatched, it comes out of its egg〔幼禽等〕孵出，破壳而出: *All the chicks have hatched out.* 小鸡都已破壳而出。**3 hatch a plot/plan/deal etc** to form a plan etc secretly 秘密策划阴谋/计划/交易等

hatch² *n* [C] **1** a hole in a ship or aircraft, used for loading goods, or the door that covers it〔船、飞机上的〕舱口；舱门 —see picture at 参见 AIRCRAFT 图 **2** also 又作 **hatchway** a small hole in the wall or floor between two rooms, or the door that covers it〔墙、地板上的〕开口，活板门: *the hatch between the kitchen and the dining room* 厨房与餐厅之间的小窗口 **3** the act of hatching eggs 孵蛋

hatch·back /ˈhætʃbæk; ˈhætʃbæk/ *n* [C] a car with a door at the back that opens upwards 掀背式轿车〔装有向上开的后车门的小轿车〕

hat·check /ˈhætˌtʃɛk; ˈhæt-tʃek/ *n* [C] *AmE old-fashioned* the place in a restaurant, theatre etc where you can leave your coat【美，过时】〔餐馆、剧院等的〕衣帽间

hatch·er·y /ˈhætʃərı; ˈhætʃəri/ *n* [C] a place for hatching eggs, especially fish eggs〔尤指鱼的〕孵化场

hatch·et /ˈhætʃıt; ˈhætʃɪ̈t/ *n* [C] a small AXE with a short handle 短柄小斧 —see also 另见 **bury the hatchet** (BURY (8))

hatchet-faced /ˈ· ·, ·/ *adj* having an unpleasantly thin face with sharp features 尖下巴的，瘦削脸的

hatchet job /ˈ· ·, ·/ *n* **do a hatchet job on** *informal* to criticize someone severely and unfairly in a newspaper, on television etc【非正式】〔在报章、电视节目中〕尖刻地攻击，诋毁: *Republican columnists did a hatchet job on Dukakis.* 共和党的专栏作家对杜卡基斯作了尖刻的批评。

hatchet man /ˈ· ·, ·/ *n* [C] *informal* someone who is employed to make unpopular changes in an organization【非正式】受雇在某机构内进行不受欢迎的改革的人

hatch·ing /ˈhætʃıŋ; ˈhætʃɪŋ/ *n* [U] fine lines drawn on or cut into a surface〔画或刻在平面上的〕影线

hatch·way /ˈhætʃˌwe; ˈhætʃweɪ/ *n* [C] a HATCH² (2) 开口，活板门

hate¹ /het; heɪt/ *v* [T not in progressive 不用进行式] **1** to dislike someone very much and feel angry towards them 憎恨，憎恶，仇恨: *Jill really hates her stepfather.* 吉尔非常憎恨她的继父。| **hate sb's guts** *informal* (=hate someone very much)【非正式】恨透某人 **2** *informal* to dislike something very much【非正式】讨厌，不喜欢: *I hate housework.* 我讨厌做家务。| *Liz won't eat that, she hates bananas.* 莉兹不会吃的，她不喜欢香蕉。| **hate doing sth** *Paul hates having his photo taken.* 保罗不喜欢别人给他照相。| **hate to do sth** *I hate to see you making a fool of yourself.* 我不喜欢看见你出丑。| **hate sb doing sth** *Jenny's mother hates her staying out late.* 珍妮的母亲不喜欢她晚上在外面待得太晚。| **hate it when** *I hate it when people ask me for money.* 我不喜欢别人向我要钱。**3 I'd hate (sb) to do sth** *spoken* used to emphasize that you really do not want something to happen【口】我不愿发生某事: *I'd hate you to go.* 我不希望你走。**4 I hate to think what/how** *spoken* used when you feel sure that something would have a bad result【口】我不敢想…: *I hate to think what would have happened, if you hadn't called the police.* 我不敢想如果你没有报警会发生什么事。**5 I hate to ask/interrupt/disturb etc** *spoken* used to say that you are sorry that you have to ask etc【口】很抱歉，请问/打断你/打扰你等: *I hate to ask, but would you be able to give me a lift home tonight?* 很抱歉，请问你今晚能不能让我搭你的车回家？**6 I hate to (have to) say this, but...** *spoken* used when saying something that you do not want to say, for example because it is embarrassing【口】我真不好意思告诉你，但… —**hated** *adj*: *the hated dictator* 令人憎恨的独裁者 —opposite 反义词 LOVE 1 3

This graph shows how common the different grammar patterns of the verb **hate** are. 本图表所示为动词hate构成的不同语法模式的使用频率。

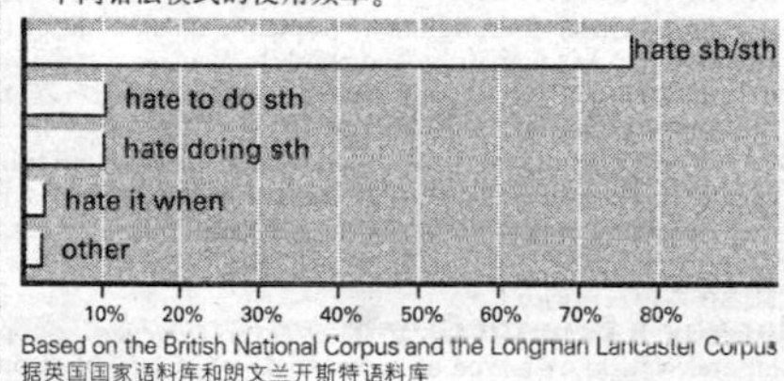

Based on the British National Corpus and the Longman Lancaster Corpus 据英国国家语料库和朗文兰开斯特语料库

hate² *n* [U] an angry unpleasant feeling that someone has when they hate someone and want to harm them 憎恨，仇恨: *Their minds were poisoned with envy and hate.* 他们的心智受到了妒忌和仇恨的毒害。—opposite 反义词 LOVE² (1)

hate·ful /ˈhetfəl; ˈheɪtfəl/ *adj old-fashioned* very bad, unpleasant, or unkind【过时】可恨的，可恶的，令人讨厌的 —**hatefully** *adv*

hath /hæθ; hæθ/ *old use*【旧】= has

Hath·a·way /ˈhæθəwe; ˈhæθəweɪ/, **Anne** (?1557-1623) the wife of William Shakespeare 哈瑟维〔?1557-1623〕，威廉·莎士比亚之妻〕

hat·pin /ˈhætˌpın; ˈhætˌpɪn/ *n* [C] a long pin that is used to make a woman's hat stay on her head〔女士用于使帽子固定在头上的〕长饰针 —see picture at 参见 PIN¹ 图

ha·tred /ˈhetrıd; ˈheɪtrɪ̈d/ *n* [U] an angry feeling of extreme dislike for someone or something 憎恨，憎恶，仇恨: *Her voice was full of hatred and contempt.* 她的声音里充满了仇恨和鄙夷。| **[+of]** *Tom's hatred of authority* 汤姆对权威的憎恶 | **[+for/towards]** *Strangely, the murderer said he never felt hatred for any of his victims.* 奇怪的是，杀人凶手声称自己从未对任何一位受害者怀有仇恨。| **deep hatred** *This experience left him with a deep hatred of politicians.* 这次经历使他对政客产生了强烈的仇恨。

hat stand /ˈhæt ˌstænd; ˈhæt stænd/ *n* [C] a tall pole with hooks at the top used to hang coats and hats on 衣帽架 —see picture on page A15 参见 A15 页图

hat·ter /ˈhætə; ˈhætə/ *n* [C] someone who makes or sells hats 制帽匠; 帽商 —see also 另见 **as mad as a hatter** (MAD (14))

hat-trick /ˈ· ·/ *n* [C] a series of three successes, especially in sports such as football when the same person scores (SCORE² (1)) three times 帽子戏法〔指一名运动员在一场比赛中连得三分, 尤指在足球比赛中连进三球〕: *Saunders scored a hat-trick in the final game of the series.* 桑德斯在联赛的决赛中上演了帽子戏法。

haugh·ty /ˈhɔtɪ; ˈhɔːti/ *adj* **haughtier, haughtiest** behaving in a proud unfriendly way 倨傲不逊的, 傲慢的, 目中无人的: *a haughty laugh* 傲然一笑 —**haughtily** *adv* —**haughtiness** *n* [U]

haul¹ /hɔl; hɔːl/ *v* **1** [I always+adv/prep,T] to pull something heavy with a continuous, steady movement 拖, 拉: **haul sth along/in/across etc** *The fishermen were hauling in their nets.* 渔民正在收网。**2 haul sb over the coals** to speak to someone angrily and severely because they have done something wrong 狠狠责备, 训斥 **3** to carry goods in a vehicle〔用车辆〕运送〔货物〕**4 haul yourself up/out of etc a)** to succeed in achieving a higher position in society, in a competition etc 提高〔社会地位〕; 取胜: *He hauled himself out of the gutter and became the world heavyweight champion.* 他努力使自己走出社会最底层, 成了世界重量级冠军。**b)** to pull yourself up, out of etc 起来; 走出: *I see you've managed to haul yourself out of bed.* 你终于起床了。**5 haul off and hit/punch sb** *AmE informal* to hit someone very hard【美, 非正式】重击 **6 haul ass** *AmE slang* to hurry【美俚】赶快

haul sb **up** *phr v* [T usually passive 一般用被动态] *informal* to officially bring someone to a court of law to be judged【非正式】传讯, 把…拉上法庭: *Campbell was hauled up in front of the magistrate.* 坎贝尔被传讯在地方法院出庭。

haul² *n* [C] **1** a large amount of goods that has been stolen, or found by the police〔一大批〕赃物, 走私物品: *The robbers' haul included a very valuable diamond ring.* 盗贼的赃物中有一枚价值不菲的钻石戒指。| *Police announced a drugs haul worth two million pounds.* 警方宣布截获了价值二百万英镑的毒品。**2 long/slow haul** something that takes a lot of time and effort 耗时费力的事: **it's been a long haul** *At last we've won our freedom but it's been a long bitter haul.* 我们终于赢得了自由, 但这是通过漫长不懈的努力才得来的。**3** the amount of fish caught when fishing with a net 一网的捕鱼量 —see also 另见 LONG-HAUL, SHORT-HAUL

haul·age /ˈhɔlɪdʒ; ˈhɔːlɪdʒ/ *n* [U] **1** the business of carrying goods by road or railway〔公路或铁路〕货运业 **2** the charge for this〔公路或铁路〕货运费

haul·i·er /ˈhɔljə; ˈhɔːliə/ *BrE*【英】, **hau·ler** *AmE*【美】/ˈhɔlə; ˈhɔːlə/ *n* [C] someone who owns or manages a haulage business 公路或铁路货运业经营者

haunch /hɔntʃ; hɔːntʃ/ *n* **1 haunches** [plural] the part of your body at the back between your waist and legs〔人的〕臀部, 胯部: *They squatted on their haunches playing dice.* 他们蹲着玩掷骰子。**2** [C] one of the back legs of a four-legged animal, especially when it is used as meat〔四腿动物的〕一条后腿〔尤指供食用的腰腿肉〕

haunt¹ /hɔnt; hɔːnt/ *v* [T not in progressive 不用进行式] **1** if the spirit of a dead person haunts a place, it appears there often〔鬼魂〕经常出没于…: *The pub is said to be haunted by the ghost of a former landlord.* 据说这个酒吧里经常有一位旧房主的鬼魂出没。**2** to make someone worry or make them sad 缠扰, 烦扰; 萦绕在…心头: *Clare was haunted by the fear that her husband was having an affair.* 克莱尔总是担心她丈夫有外遇。**3** to cause problems for someone over a long period of time〔长期〕给〔某人〕带来麻烦: *an error that would come back to haunt the US Administration for years to come* 一个会在今后几年给美国政府不断带来麻烦的失误

haunt² *n* [C] a place that someone likes to go to often〔某人〕常去的地方: **a favourite haunt** *The Café Vienna was a favourite haunt of journalists and actors.* 维也纳咖啡馆是记者和演员最爱光顾的地方。

haunt·ed /ˈhɔntɪd; ˈhɔːntɪ̣d/ *adj* **1** a haunted building is believed to be visited regularly by the spirit of a dead person 闹鬼的: *a haunted house* 闹鬼的房子 **2 haunted expression/look** a worried or frightened expression etc 担惊受怕的表情/样子

haunt·ing /ˈhɔntɪŋ; ˈhɔːntɪŋ/ *adj* sad but also beautiful and staying in your thoughts for a long time 萦绕于心的, 不易忘怀的: *a haunting melody* 令人难忘的曲调 —**hauntingly** *adv*

haute cou·ture /ˌot kuˈtur; ˌəʊt kuːˈtjʊə/ *n* [U] *French* the business of making and selling very expensive and fashionable clothes for women【法】高级女式时装业 —**haute couturier** *n* [C]

haute cui·sine /ˌot kwɪˈzin; ˌəʊt kwɪˈziːn/ *n* [U] *French* cooking of a very high standard, especially French cooking【法】(法国式)高级烹饪

hau·teur /oˈtɝ; əʊˈtɜː/ *n* [U] *formal* a proud, very unfriendly manner【正式】傲慢

Ha·van·a /həˈvænə; həˈvænə/ *n* **1** the capital of Cuba 哈瓦那〔古巴首都〕**2** [C] a type of CIGAR made in Cuba 哈瓦那雪茄〔古巴生产的一种雪茄〕

have¹ /v, əv, həv; v, əv, həv; *strong* 强读 hæv; hæv/ *auxiliary verb past tense* **had** /əd, həd; d, əd, həd; *strong* 强读 hæd; hæd/ *third person singular present tense* **has** /əz, həz; z, əz, həz; *strong* 强读 hæz; hæz/ *negative short forms* 否定缩略式为 **haven't** /ˈhævn̩t; ˈhævənt/, **hadn't** /ˈhædn̩t; ˈhædnt/, **hasn't** /ˈhæzn̩t; ˈhæzənt/ **1** used with the past participle of another verb to make the perfect tense of that verb〔与过去分词连用构成动词的完成时〕: *We have finished the decorating.* 我们已经完成了装修。| *Have you read that book yet?* 你看过那本书吗? | *We have been spending too much money.* 我们已经花钱太多了。**2 had better/best** used when telling someone what they should do 最好; 应该: *You'd better phone to say you'll be late.* 你最好打电话说一声你要晚到。| *We'd better not tell Jim about our plans just yet.* 我们最好先别把计划告诉吉姆。**3 have had it** *spoken*【口】**a)** used to say that someone will be in serious trouble for something they have done 完了, 糟了, 遇到麻烦了〔用于表示某人惹来了大祸〕: *Press the wrong button and you've had it!* 你按错按钮就完了! **b)** used to say that someone is tired〔用于表示某人〕累坏了: *We'll have to stop for the night – the kids have just about had it.* 我们得停下来过夜了 —— 孩子们已经累坏了。**c)** used to say that something is so old or damaged that it cannot be used any more 已经坏了, 不能用了: *It looks as if your stereo's had it.* 你的立体声唱机好像坏了。**d) have had it with** used to say you do not want to waste any more time on someone or something that has annoyed you 受够了, 腻烦了 **4 had sb done sth** if someone had done something 如果〔某人〕做了〔某事〕…: *Had we known about the plans for the factory, we would never have bought the house.* 假如我们知道建工厂的计划, 我们就不会买这座房子了。

have² *v* [T not usually in passive 一般不用被动态]

1 ►HAVE AN APPEARANCE/QUALITY/FEATURE 具有某种外表/特性/特征◄ [not in progressive 不用进行式] also 又作 **have got** *especially BrE*【尤英】used when saying what someone or something looks like, what qualities or features they possess etc 具有〔某种外表、特性或特征〕: *She has dark hair and brown eyes.* 她有一头深色发和一双棕色眼睛。| *I think the idea does have some good points.* 我认为这个主意的确有一些可取之处。| *You need to have a lot of patience to be a teacher.* 当教师必须有很大的耐性。

2 ►INCLUDE/CONTAIN 包括/包含◄ [not in progressive 不用进行式] also 又作 **have got** *especially BrE*【尤英】to include or contain something or a particular number of things or people 包括, 包含, 有: *Japan has a population of over 120 million.* 日本有超过1.2亿的人口。| *Our old apartment had a huge kitchen.* 我们过去住的公寓有一个大厨房。| *How many pages has it got?* 它一共有多少页?

3 ►OWN/BE ABLE TO USE 拥有/具有◄ [not in progressive 不用进行式] also 又作 **have got** *spoken BrE*【英口】**a)** to own something or have been given it to use 有, 拥有: *They used to have a Mercedes Benz.* 他们曾经拥有一辆梅赛德斯-奔驰汽车。| *Has she got a fax machine?* 她有传真机吗? | *Have you ever had your own business?* 你自己开过店吗? **b)** to own a pet or animal 养〔宠物〕: *He's a lovely dog – How long have you had him?* 这只狗真可爱, 你养了多久了?

4 ►DO STH 做某事◄ *BrE* a word meaning to do something, used in certain phrases【英】〔用在某些词组中表示做某事〕: **have a look/walk/sleep/talk/think etc** *Do you mind if I have a look at what's on television?* 我看一看电视上播放什么节目你不介意吧? | **have a holiday/bath/shower etc** *It's about time she had a holiday.* 她该去度个假了。

5 ►EAT/DRINK/SMOKE 吃/喝/抽烟◄ to eat, drink, or smoke 吃; 喝; 抽〔烟〕: *She sat down and had another drink.* 她坐下来, 又喝了一杯。| **have lunch/a meal etc** *I usually have breakfast at about 8 o'clock.* 我通常八点左右吃早餐。

6 ►HAVE AN IDEA/FEELING 有个主意/感觉◄ [not in progressive 不用进行式] also 又作 **have got** *especially BrE*【尤英】to think of an idea or experience a particular feeling 想起

〔某个主意〕; 感到: *If you have any good ideas for presents, let me know.* 如果你想到送什么礼物的好主意, 就告诉我。| *I have lots of happy memories of my time in Japan.* 在日本的那段日子给我留下了许多美好的回忆。| **have a shock/surprise etc** *When the waiter brought the bill they had a nasty shock.* 服务员拿来账单时, 他们大吃一惊。

7 ►HAVE A DISEASE/INJURY/PAIN 生病/受伤/疼痛◄ [not in progressive 不用进行式] also 又作 **have got** *especially BrE*【尤英】to suffer from a disease, injury, or pain 生病; 受伤; 疼痛: *Sarah's got a cold.* 萨拉患了感冒。| *The doctor said he had a broken leg.* 医生说他的一条腿断了。

8 ►EXPERIENCE STH 经历某事◄ to experience something or be affected by something 经历, 遇到: **have problems/difficulties/troubles etc** *We've been having a lot of difficulties with our new computer system.* 我们在新电脑系统上遇到了很多困难。| **have an accident/crash** *I'm afraid your son has had a serious accident.* 恐怕你儿子遇到了严重的事故。| **have a good/terrible etc time** *Thanks for everything – we had a great time.* 谢谢你 —— 我们玩得很开心。

9 have sth stolen/broken/taken etc if you have something stolen, broken etc, someone steals it etc 某物被盗/打破/拿走等: *She had all her jewellery stolen.* 她所有的首饰都被偷了。

10 have your hair cut/your car repaired/your house painted etc to pay a professional person to cut your hair etc for you 请人理发/修车/粉刷房子等: *Where do you normally have your hair done?* 你通常在哪里剪发? | *We'd only just had a new engine put in.* 我们刚请人换了一台新的引擎。

11 have sth ready/done/finished etc to have made something ready to be used, or have finished doing something 准备好/做好/做完某事等: [+by] *I should have the car ready by Monday.* 我会在星期一前将车准备好。

12 have sth going/working/on to make a machine operate 使机器运转/工作/开动: *She always has the TV going at full blast.* 她总是把电视机的声音开到最大。

13 ►KEEP/PUT STH IN A PARTICULAR POSITION 使某物保持/将某物放在某个位置◄ [not in progressive 不用进行式] also 又作 **have got** *especially BrE*【尤英】to keep or have put something in a particular position 保持; 放置: **have sth open/closed/out/in/over etc** *I had my eyes half-closed.* 我半闭着眼睛。| *Janice likes to have the window open at night.* 贾尼丝喜欢在晚上开着窗户。

14 ►RECEIVE 收到◄ also 又作 **have got** *especially BrE*【尤英】to receive something 收到, 接到: **have a letter/phone call/message** *I had lots of phone calls.* 我接到很多电话。| **have news/information** *Have you had any news yet from Graham?* 你有没有得到来自格雷厄姆的消息? | **have help/advice etc** *I expect he had some help from his father.* 我估计他得到了父亲的帮助。

15 can/could/may I have used when politely asking someone to give you something 能不能把…给我?: *Can I have the bill please?* 请结账。| *Could we have our ball back?* 能不能把球还给我们?

16 I'll have/we'll have *spoken* used to ask for what you want especially to eat or drink【口】我/我们想要〔尤指食物或饮料〕: *I'll have one vegetable curry and two chapatis please.* 请来一份咖喱蔬菜和两块薄煎饼。

17 have a brother/grandmother etc [not in progressive 不用进行式] also 又作 **have got** *especially BrE*【尤英】if you have a brother, grandmother etc, they are part of your family 有个兄弟/祖母等: *She has an uncle who lives in Wisconsin.* 她有一个叔叔住在威斯康星州。

18 ►KNOW SB 认识某人◄ [not in progressive 不用进行式] also 又作 **have got** *especially BrE*【尤英】to know someone because you have a relationship with them, work with them etc 认识〔某人〕: *I have a friend who looks like you.* 我有个朋友长得很像你。

19 have a duty/responsibility etc also 又作 **have got** *especially BrE*【尤英】if you have a particular duty, responsibility etc, it is yours and you must do it 有义务/责任等

20 have a job/position/role etc also 又作 **have got** *especially BrE*【尤英】if you have a particular job, position etc, it is yours and you are the one who does it 有一份工作/一个职位/一项职责等

21 ►EMPLOY/BE IN CHARGE OF 雇用/负责◄ [not in progressive 不用进行式] to employ or be in charge of a group of workers 雇用, 负责管理〔员工〕: *She had more than 20 servants who took care of her every need.* 她有二十多名佣人照顾她各方面的需要。

22 ►HAVE AN AMOUNT OF TIME 有时间◄ [not in progressive 不用进行式] also 又作 **have got** *especially BrE*【尤英】if you have a particular amount of time, it is available for you to do something 有〔时间〕: *You have 30 seconds to answer the question.* 你有30秒时间回答这个问题。| *I wish I had more time to talk to you.* 真希望能有时间和你多谈一会儿。

23 ►HAVE GOODS/ROOMS AVAILABLE 有现成的商品/房间◄ [not in progressive 不用进行式] also 又作 **have got** *especially BrE*【尤英】if a shop or a hotel has goods or rooms, they are available to you to buy or use〔商店〕供应〔商品〕;〔旅馆〕有〔房间〕: *Do you have any single rooms?* 有单人房间吗? | *They didn't have any sweaters in my size.* 他们没有我穿的尺码的毛衣。

24 ►HAVE BROUGHT STH WITH YOU 带有某物◄ [not in progressive 不用进行式] also 又作 **have got** *especially BrE*【尤英】to have brought something with you or keep something near you 带着, 有: *Have you got your pen?* 你带笔了吗? | **have sth with you** *I'm afraid I don't have my address book with me.* 我恐怕忘了带通讯录了。| **have sth on you** *How much money do you have on you?* 你身上有多少钱?

25 have sb with you also 又作 **have got** *especially BrE*【尤英】if you have someone with you, they are present with you 和某人在一起: *Luckily I had a friend with me who spoke German.* 幸好当时有个会讲德语的朋友和我在一起。

26 ►HOLD SB 捉住某人◄ **have sb by sth** also 又作 **have got** *especially BrE*【尤英】to hold someone violently by a part of their body 捉住, 紧握: *They had him by the throat.* 他们扼住了他的喉咙。

27 have visitors/guests if you have visitors or guests, they have to come to your home, office etc 来客人, 有客人: *Sorry, I didn't realize you had visitors.* 对不起, 我不知道你家来客人了。

28 have a meeting/party/concert etc to hold an event such as a meeting 举办会议/晚会/音乐会等: *We're having a party on Saturday – you're very welcome to come.* 我们会在周六开舞会, 欢迎你来。

29 have an effect/influence/result etc to cause a particular result 产生效果/影响/结果等: *This could have a disastrous effect on the world economy.* 这可能会对世界经济产生灾难性的影响。

30 have the chance/opportunity/honour etc to do sth/of doing sth to be able to do something 能有机会/很荣幸地做某事: *If you have the chance you should go and see it – it's a really good film.* 有机会你应该去看一下, 这真是一部好电影。| *I had the honour of meeting the Duke of Edinburgh.* 我很荣幸地见到了爱丁堡公爵。

31 have a baby/twins etc if a woman has a baby, it is born from her body 生孩子/双胞胎等: *Anna insisted on having the baby at home.* 安娜坚持要在家里生孩子。

32 have an operation/treatment etc to be given an operation, treatment etc for a medical problem 做手术/接受治疗等

33 ►MAKE SB DO STH 使某人做某事◄ [not in progressive 不用进行式] **a)** make someone start doing something 使〔某人〕做某事: **have sb laughing/crying etc** *Within minutes he had the whole audience laughing and clapping.* 短短几分钟内他就使全体观众发出阵阵笑声和掌声。**b)** to persuade or order someone to do something 劝说[命令]〔某人〕做某事: **have sb doing sth** *She had me doing all kinds of jobs for her.* 她指使我替她做各种各样的工作。| **have sb do sth** *AmE*【美】*I'll have Hudson show you to your room.* 我会让赫德森带你去看你的房间。

34 ►SEX 性◄ [not in progressive 不用进行式] *informal* to have sex with someone【非正式】有〔性关系〕: *I expect she's had lots of men.* 我想她有不少男人。

35 ►NOT ALLOW 不允许◄ **I won't have/we can't have** *spoken* used to say that you do not want or you refuse to allow something to happen【口】我/我们不允许[愿意]: *I won't have you walking home on your own – let me call you a taxi.* 我不会让你自己走回家的 —— 让我给你叫辆出租车吧!

36 have it coming also 又作 **have got it coming** *spoken* used to say that you are not sorry that something bad has happened to someone, because they deserve it【口】…是应得的; 活该: *I'm not surprised his wife left him – he's had it coming for years.* 他老婆离开他, 我丝毫不觉得奇怪 —— 他早就该落到这种下场。

37 I've got it *spoken* used to say you have suddenly thought of the solution to a problem or understand【口】我知道了; 我想出来了

38 you have me there also 又作 **you've got me there** *spoken* used to say that you do not know the answer to a question【口】你把我问住了, 我被难倒了

39 I'll have you know *spoken* used to start to tell someone something when you are annoyed with them【口】你给我听着〔表示不耐烦〕

40 have sb doing sth *especially in questions or negatives* to allow someone to do something or agree that they should do it 允许[同意]某人做某事〔多用于问句或否定式〕: *I wouldn't have you walking home all by yourself.* 我不会让你独个儿走回家的。
41 have done with to finish or settle an argument or a difficult situation 结束〔某事〕, 了结〔某事〕: *Let's get this sorted out and have done with it.* 我们把这事弄清楚并了结掉吧!
42 have it (that) a) to say that something is true 说, 表示: **rumour has it** (=a lot of people are saying) 谣传 *Rumour has it he's going out with Michele.* 谣传他和米歇尔在交往。**b)** to be told that something is true 得知, 获悉: **have it on good authority** (=to have been told by someone you can trust) 从可靠渠道得知
43 have it in for *spoken* to want to harm someone【口】图谋伤害〔某人〕, 有意同〔某人〕过不去: *Dean thinks his teachers have it in for him.* 迪安认为他的老师有意和他过不去。
44 have (got) it in you to have a particular quality, skill, or ability 有本事; 有两下子: *You should have seen the way Dad was dancing – I didn't know he had it in him!* 可惜你没有看到爸爸的舞姿 —— 我真没想到他还有这个本事!
45 have (got) something against sb to dislike someone for something they have done 因某事而不喜欢某人: *I don't know what she's got against me.* 我不知道她为什么不喜欢我。
46 have (got) nothing against sb *especially spoken* used to say that you do not dislike the person you are talking about【尤口】对某人没有不好的看法: *I've got nothing against Gary, but I wish he'd show a little more initiative.* 我对加里没有什么看法, 但我希望他今后能表现得更主动一些。
47 be not having any (of that) *spoken* to refuse to agree to something, listen to someone etc【口】不同意; 不接受: *I tried to explain to her, but she just wasn't having any.* 我试着向她解释, 但她根本不听。
48 you've been had *spoken* used to say that someone has been deceived, for example, by being tricked into paying too much money【口】你上当了!: *You paid £200? You've been had!* 你付了200英镑? 你上当了!
49 have sth/sb (all) to yourself to be the only person or people in a place, using something, talking to someone else etc 独自, 单独: *He couldn't wait to have Beth all to himself.* 他巴不得马上就和贝丝单独在一起。

have sb/sth in also 又作 **have got sb/sth in** *BrE*【英】*phr v* [T] **a)** to have someone in your home in order to do building work etc 雇用某人到家里干活: *She won't go to work while she's got the builders in.* 家里有建筑工人在干活时, 她就不去上班。**b)** to have something in your home that you can use, eat etc 家里有某样东西

have it off *phr v* [I+with] *BrE slang* to have sex with someone【英俚】与…发生性关系

have on also 又作 **have got on** *especially BrE*【尤英】[T] **1** [**have** sth **on**] to be wearing a piece of clothing or type of clothing 穿着, 戴着: *She had on lime-green slacks and a purple nylon shirt.* 她穿着一条酸橙绿色的便裤和一件紫色的尼龙衬衫。| **have nothing on** (=have no clothes on) 没穿衣服, 光着身子 *Jimmy had nothing on except his socks.* 吉米身上除了袜子外什么也没穿。**2 have the TV/radio/washing machine etc on** to have your television, radio etc switched on and working 开着电视机/收音机/洗衣机等: *Billie has his walkman on all day long.* 比利整天都开着他的随身听。**3 be having sb on** *especially BrE* to make someone believe something that is not true, especially as a joke【尤英】〔开玩笑地〕骗人: *He told you he's a Managing Director? He's having you on!* 他告诉你他是个总经理? 他在捉弄你呢! **4** [**have** sth **on**] to have arranged to do something, go somewhere etc, especially when this means you cannot do something else〔日程上〕已安排好做某事: *Sorry, I can't do any overtime this weekend – I've got too much on already.* 抱歉, 我这个周末不能加班, 我已经安排好有很多事要做了。**5** [**have** sth **on** sb] to know about something bad that someone has done 掌握对〔某人〕不利的证据: *What do the police have on him?* 警方掌握了他什么证据? **6** [**have nothing on sb/sth**] to not be nearly as good as someone or something else 比不上, 不如: *Supermarket vodkas are fine, but they have nothing on brands like Stolichnaya.* 超级市场里出售的各种伏特加不错, 但都比不上〔俄罗斯的〕斯托利恰耶酒这样的名牌伏特加。

have sth out *phr v* [T] **1** [**have** sth **out**] **have a tooth/your tonsils etc out** to have a tooth etc removed by a medical operation 拔牙/割除扁桃腺等 **2 have it out with sb** *informal* to settle a disagreement or difficult situation by talking to the person involved, especially when you are angry with them【非正式】与某人把某事说清楚以解决纠纷[困局]〔尤指对他愤怒时〕

have sb up *phr v* [T] *BrE informal* to take someone to court, especially to prove they are guilty of a crime【英, 非正式】〔法庭〕传讯某人; 控告某人: *Last year he was had up for drunken driving.* 他去年曾被控酒后驾驶。

have[3] *v* [**have to do sth** also 又作 **have got to do sth** *especially BrE* 尤英] **1** if you have to do something, you must do it because your situation forces you to do it, because you have arranged to do it, or because someone makes you do it 必须, 不得不: *In the end she had to go into a mental hospital.* 最后她不得不进了一家精神病院。| *I hate having to get up early in the morning.* 我讨厌一早就得起床。| *We had to do Latin every day.* 我们每天都要学拉丁语。**2** used when saying that it is important that something happens, or that something must happen if something else is to happen 必须, 一定; 只有…才…: *There has to be an end to the violence.* 必须阻止暴力活动。| *You have to believe me!* 你一定要相信我! | *There will have to be a complete ceasefire before the Government will agree to talks.* 只有完全停火后, 政府才会同意谈判。**3** used when telling someone how to do something 要, 应该: *First of all you have to mix the flour and the butter.* 首先要将面粉和黄油搅拌一下。**4** used when saying that you are sure that something will happen, or you are sure that something is true 肯定, 必定: *The price of houses has to go up sooner or later.* 房价肯定迟早会上涨。| *None of the others could have done the murder, so it had to be the husband.* 其他人都不可能是杀人犯, 那肯定是她丈夫干的。**5** *spoken* used when talking about an annoying event which caused you problems【口】不巧〔抱怨某事带来麻烦〕: *Of course it had to happen on a Sunday, when all the dentists are shut.* 这事偏偏发生在星期天, 所有的牙科诊所当时都关门了。**6** *spoken* used when talking about something annoying or surprising that someone does【口】只会, 只能〔对某人所做的事表示不悦或惊奇〕: *She has to go to Marks and Spencers – nowhere else is good enough for her.* 她只会去马克斯与斯潘塞公司买东西, 别处她都看不上。| **do you have to do sth?** (=used to ask someone to stop doing something that annoys you) 你非得要这样做吗? *Lieutenant, do you have to keep repeating everything I've just said?* 中尉, 你非得重复我刚刚讲过的一切吗? **7 I have to say/admit/confess** *spoken* used when speaking honestly about something awkward or embarrassing【口】我不得不说/承认/坦白: *I have to say I don't know the first thing about computers.* 老实说, 我对电脑一窍不通。—see also 另见 MUST[1]

ha·ven /ˈhevən; ˈheɪvən/ *n* [C] a place where people go to be safe 安全地; 避难所: *The border region was a natural haven for fugitives.* 边境地区曾是逃亡者的天然避难所。

have-nots /ˌ·ˈ·/ *n* **the have-nots** the poor people in a country or society 穷人 —see also 另见 HAVES

have·n't /ˈhævn̩t; ˈhævənt/ the short form of 缩略式= have not

hav·er·sack /ˈhævɚˌsæk; ˈhævəsæk/ *n* [C] *BrE old-fashioned* a bag that you carry on your back【英, 过时】背包

haves, the /hævz; hævz/ *n* the rich people in a country or society 有钱人, 富人: *the widening gap between the haves and the have-nots* 不断扩大的贫富差距 —see also 另见 HAVE-NOTS

Hav·i·sham /ˈhævɪʃəm; ˈhævɪʃəm/, **Miss** a character in the book *Great Expectations* by Charles Dickens. She is a strange, rich old woman who hates men because her future husband left her on their wedding day. She still wears her wedding dress and everything in her house has been left exactly as it was on her wedding day, and is now covered in COBWEBS. 哈薇夏姆小姐〔查尔斯·狄更斯小说《远大前程》中的人物。她是一位古怪、富有的老太太。她在婚礼当天遭未婚夫抛弃, 从此对男人怀恨在心。之后, 她便一直穿着结婚礼服, 家中的摆设也一如婚礼当天, 只是已结满了蜘蛛网〕

hav·oc /ˈhævək; ˈhævək/ *n* [U] a situation in which there is a lot of confusion or damage 浩劫, 大破坏: **cause/create havoc** *The Wall Street Crash created havoc and ruin.* 华尔街股市暴跌造成了严重的破坏。| **wreak havoc (on)/play havoc with** (=to cause great harm by causing a confusing situation) 对…造成破坏

Ha·vre —see 见 LE HAVRE

haw /hɔ; hɔː/ *v* —see 见 **hum and haw** (HUM[1] (4))

Ha·wai·i /həˈwaɪ-i; həˈwaɪ-i/ abbreviation 缩写为 **HI** a US state in the Pacific Ocean which consists of eight main islands, known as the **Hawaiian Islands**. Its capital city, Honolulu, is on the island of Oahu. 夏威夷〔美国一州, 位于太平洋, 由八个主要岛屿组成, 称夏威夷群岛。首府为火奴鲁鲁, 位于瓦胡岛〕—**Hawaiian** *n, adj*

CULTURAL NOTE 文化注释

In the US Hawaii is thought of as a place where people go for a holiday, especially for their HONEYMOON. The islands are known for their VOLCANOes, warm beaches, bright blue water, and PALM TREEs, and for particular foods such as MACADAMIA NUTs and PINEAPPLEs. 夏威夷被认为是美国人度假的去处, 尤其是蜜月旅行的好地方。这些岛屿以火山、温暖的海滩、清澈湛蓝的海水、棕榈树以及夏威夷果和菠萝等特色食物闻名。

When many people think of Hawaii, they think of Hawaiian women dancers, who have long dark hair, wear grass skirts and LEIs (=a circle made of flowers that you wear around your neck), and who do a dance called the 'hula' by shaking their HIPs from side to side. 很多人想起夏威夷会联想到夏威夷女子的舞蹈, 她们留着长长的乌发, 穿着草裙, 脖子上戴着花环, 摇动臀部, 跳草裙舞。

hawk[1] /hɔk; hɔːk/ *n* [C] **1** a large bird that hunts and eats small birds and animals 鹰 **2** a politician who believes in using military force 鹰派人物, 主战派人物: *Meese and other hawks in the Reaganite administration* 里根政府中米斯等主战派人物 —opposite 反义词 DOVE[1] (2) **3 watch sb like a hawk** to watch someone very carefully 仔细打量某人, 严密监视某人 **4 have eyes like a hawk** to be quick to notice things, especially small details 目光锐利; 具有鹰一般敏锐的眼力

hawk[2] *v* **1** [T] to try to sell goods by carrying them around 〔到处〕叫卖, 兜售 **2** [I] to cough up PHLEGM 咳出〔痰〕

hawk·er /ˋhɔkɚ; ˈhɔːkə/ *n* [C] someone who carries goods from place to place and tries to sell them 〔到处〕兜售商品的人, 小贩

hawk-eyed /ˈ· ·/ *adj* quick to notice small details 目光敏锐的, 善于观察的: *hawk-eyed customs officers* 有敏锐观察力的海关官员

Haw·king /ˋhɔkɪŋ; ˈhɔːkɪŋ/, **Ste·phen** /ˋstivən; ˈstiːvən/ (1942-) a British scientist who has developed important new ideas about Relativity and Black Holes. He has continued working even though he suffers from a serious disease of the NERVOUS system, and he uses a special computer system in order to talk. He wrote an extremely popular book called *A Brief History of Time* (1988), in which he explains his ideas about how the universe and time began and how they have developed. 霍金〔(1942-), 英国科学家。关于相对论和黑洞问题, 他提出过重要的新观点。他尽管患有严重的神经系统疾病, 但仍坚持工作。现在, 他使用一种特殊的电脑系统与人交谈。他撰写的《时间简史》(1988) 极其畅销, 书中阐述了他对宇宙和时间的起源与发展的看法〕

hawk·ish /ˋhɔkɪʃ; ˈhɔːkɪʃ/ *adj* supporting the use of military force 鹰派的, 主战的 —**hawkishness** *n* [U]

Hawks·moor /ˋhɔksmur; ˈhɔːksmʊə/, **Nicholas** (1661-1736) an English ARCHITECT (=someone who designs buildings) who worked with Sir Christopher Wren on St Paul's Cathedral and built many churches in London. He combined the CLASSICAL style of ancient Rome with the Gothic style. 霍克斯穆尔〔(1661-1736), 英国建筑师。他与克里斯托弗·雷恩爵士一起设计了圣保罗大教堂, 并在伦敦建造了许多教堂。他的设计融古罗马的经典风格与哥特式风格于一体〕

Ha·worth /ˋhauwəθ; ˈhaʊwəθ/ a small village in West Yorkshire, in northern England, which many tourists visit because the Brontë family, a family of famous writers, lived there. The area around the village is described in Emily Brontë's famous novel *Wuthering Heights*. 霍沃思〔英格兰北部西约克郡一小村庄。该村庄是著名作家勃朗特三姐妹的故居, 因此吸引着众多游人前去参观。埃米莉·勃朗特的名著《呼啸山庄》描写的就是村庄周围的景象〕

haw·ser /ˋhɔzɚ; ˈhɔːzə/ *n* [C] a thick rope or steel CABLE[1] (2) used on a ship 缆索; 钢缆

haw·thorn /ˋhɔˌθɔrn; ˈhɔːθɔːn/ *n* [C,U] a small tree that has small white flowers and red berries 山楂(树)

Haw·thorne /ˋhɔθɔrn; ˈhɔːθɔːn/, **Na·than·i·el** /nəˋθænɪəl; nəˈθæniəl/ (1806-64) a US writer of NOVELs and short stories, whose most famous novels are *The Scarlet Letter* and *The House of the Seven Gables*. His books are mainly concerned with subjects such as SIN (=doing wrong) and punishment. 霍桑〔(1806-1864), 美国长篇和短篇小说作家。最著名的小说有《红字》和《七个尖角阁的房子》。他的作品主要以罪与罚等为主题〕

hay /he; heɪ/ *n* [U] **1** long grass that has been cut and dried, often used as food for cattle 〔作牲畜饲料用的〕干草, 饲草 **2 hit the hay** *slang* to go to bed 【俚】上床睡觉 **3 make hay while the sun shines** do something while the conditions are favourable 晒草要趁太阳好; 抓紧时机 —see also 另见 **a roll in the hay** (ROLL[2] (10))

hay·cock /ˋhekɑk; ˈheɪkɒk/ *n* [C] a small round pile of hay left in a field to dry 〔田地里的〕小干草堆

Hay·dn /ˋhaɪdn̩; ˈhaɪdn̩/, **Joseph** (1732-1809) an Austrian COMPOSER who wrote over 100 symphonies (SYMPHONY) and the ORATORIO *The Creation* 海顿〔(1732-1809), 奥地利作曲家。他创作了 100 多首交响乐及清唱剧《创世记》〕

Hayes /hez; heɪz/, **Rutherford** /ˋrʌθɚfɚd; ˈrʌðəfəd/ (1822-1893) the nineteenth president of the US, from 1877 to 1881 海斯〔(1822-1893), 美国第十九任总统, 1877 至 1881 年间在任〕

hay fe·ver /ˈ· ˌ··/ *n* [U] a medical condition, like a bad cold (COLD[2] (2)), that is caused by POLLEN (=dust from plants) 枯草热, 花粉病

hay·loft /ˋheˌlɔft; ˈheɪlɒft/ *n* [C] the top part of a farm building where hay is stored 〔谷仓里〕贮放干草的顶阁

hay·mak·ing /ˋheˌmekɪŋ; ˈheɪˌmeɪkɪŋ/ *n* [U] the process of cutting and drying hay 制备干草〔指收割和晾晒〕

Hay·mar·ket /ˋhemɑrkɪt; ˈheɪmɑːkɪt/ a street in the West End of London, where there is a theatre also called The Haymarket 秣市街〔伦敦西区的一条街, 建有一座同名剧院〕

hay·rick /ˋherɪk; ˈheɪrɪk/ *n* [C] a haystack 干草堆

hay·ride /ˋheraɪd; ˈheɪraɪd/ *n* [C] *AmE* an organized ride in a CART filled with hay, usually as part of a social event for young people 【美】乘坐装满干草的大车出游

hay·stack /ˋheˌstæk; ˈheɪstæk/ *n* [C] a large firmly built pile of hay 干草堆 —see also 另见 **like looking for a needle in a haystack** (NEEDLE[1] (6))

Hay·wain, the /ˋhewen; ˈheɪweɪn/ a famous painting by John Constable, showing horses pulling a CART across a river 《干草车》〔约翰·康斯太布尔的名画, 描绘的是几匹马拉着大车过河的场景〕

Hay·ward Gal·le·ry, the /ˋhewɚd ˌgælərɪ; ˈheɪwəd ˌgæləri/ an art GALLERY which is part of the South Bank centre, on the southern side of the River Thames in London 海沃德美术馆〔位于伦敦泰晤士河南岸的一座艺术馆, 是南岸艺术中心的组成部分〕

hay·wire /ˋheˌwaɪr; ˈheɪwaɪə/ *adj* **go haywire** *informal* to start working in completely the wrong way 【非正式】乱七八糟的, 出差错的: *The computer went haywire and started printing numbers at random.* 这台电脑出毛病了, 开始胡乱地打印数字。

haz·ard[1] /ˋhæzɚd; ˈhæzəd/ *n* [C] **1** something that may be dangerous, cause accidents etc 危险; 隐患; 会造成危害的事物: *Ice on the road is a major hazard at this time of the year.* 每年的这个时候结冰的路面是事故的主要隐患。| **be a hazard to** *Polluted water sources are a hazard to wildlife.* 受污染的水源对野生生物造成危害。| **fire hazard** (=something that may cause a fire) 火灾隐患 | **health hazard** (=something that is likely to harm your health) 危害健康的因素 **2** a risk that cannot be avoided 〔不可避免的〕风险: **hazard of doing sth** *the economic hazards of running a small farm* 经营小农场的经济风险 | **occupational hazard** (=a danger that always exists in a job) 职业风险 *Divorce seems to be an occupational hazard for politicians.* 离婚好像是政客们的一种职业风险。

hazard[2] *v* [T] **1** to say something that is only a suggestion or guess and so might not be correct 斗胆提出; 大胆猜测: **hazard a guess** *Would you like to hazard a guess as to how much he earns?* 你想不想猜猜他挣多少钱? **2** *formal* to risk losing your money, property etc in an attempt to gain something 【正式】〔拿金钱、财产等〕冒…的风险

hazard light /ˈ·· ˌ·/ *n* [C usually plural 一般用复数] a special light on a vehicle that flashes to warn other drivers of danger 〔汽车上的〕危险警告灯

haz·ard·ous /ˋhæzɚdəs; ˈhæzədəs/ *adj* **1 hazardous chemicals/waste/substances etc** *technical* chemicals etc that are dangerous and likely to harm people's health 【术语】有害化学品/废料/物质等 **2 hazardous journey/operation/undertaking etc** a journey etc that involves danger 危险的旅程/手术/任务等

haze[1] /hez; heɪz/ *n* [singular,U] **1** smoke, dust, or MOISTURE in the air which makes it difficult to see through 烟雾, 霾: **[+of]** *a haze of cigarette smoke* 香烟的烟雾 | **heat haze** (=a haze that forms in hot weather) 热气 **2** the feeling of being very confused and unable to think clearly 懵懂, 迷糊, 迷惑

haze[2] *v* [T] *AmE* to play tricks on a new college student as part of the ceremony of joining a club 【美】〔作为入会仪式的一部分〕戏弄〔大学新生〕

haze over *phr v* [I] to become HAZY (1) 起雾: *The sky hazed over.* 天空生起雾霭。

ha·zel[1] /'hezl; 'heɪzəl/ *n* [C,U] a small tree that produces nuts 榛树

hazel[2] *adj* light brown 淡褐色的: *hazel eyes* 淡褐色的眼睛 —**hazel** *n* [U] —see picture on page A6 参见 A6 页图

ha·zel·nut /'hezḷ,nʌt; 'heɪzəlnʌt/ *n* [C] the nut of the HAZEL[1] tree 榛子, 榛实

Haz·litt /'hæzlɪt; 'hæzlḷt/, **William** (1778-1830) a British writer and CRITIC known for his ESSAYs on many subjects, especially literature. His best-known collection of essays is called *Table Talk*. 哈兹里特〔(1778-1830), 英国作家、评论家。他以创作的文学等多主题论著而闻名, 最著名的散文集是《席间杂谈》〕

haz·y /'hezɪ; 'heɪzi/ *adj* **1** not clear because of a slight mist that is caused by heat, smoke etc 雾蒙蒙的, 朦胧的: *The tower looked dim in the hazy English air.* 塔在英国雾蒙蒙的空中若隐若现。**2** an idea, memory etc that is hazy is not clear or exact〔印象、记忆等〕模糊的, 不清楚的: *My memories of the holiday are rather hazy.* 我对假期的记忆十分模糊。**3 be hazy about** to not know or understand very much about something〔对某事〕不明确, 不了解: *Most people are pretty hazy about Clinton's economic program.* 多数人对克林顿的经济计划都不甚了解。—**hazily** *adv* —**haziness** *n* [U]

HBO /,etʃ bi 'o; ,eɪtʃ biː 'əʊ/ *n* the abbreviation of 缩写= HOME BOX OFFICE

H-bomb /'etʃ ,bɑm; 'eɪtʃ bɒm/ *n* [C] a powerful NUCLEAR bomb 氢弹

HCF /,etʃ si 'ɛf; ,eɪtʃ siː 'ef/ the abbreviation of 缩写= HIGHEST COMMON FACTOR

H.E. the abbreviation of 缩写= His Excellency or Her Excellency, used in the title of an AMBASSADOR 阁下〔用于称呼大使〕

he /hi; hiː/ *pron* [used as subject of a verb 用作动词的主语] **1** used to talk about a male person or animal that has already been mentioned or is already known about 他; 它〔雄性动物〕: *"Where's Paul?" "He's gone to the cinema."* "保罗在哪儿?" "他去看电影了。" | *Be careful of that dog. He sometimes bites.* 当心那条狗, 它有时咬人。**2** used to talk about anyone, everyone, or an unknown person who may be either male or female 人, 他〔泛指男性或女性〕: *Everyone should do what he considers best.* 每个人做事都应按照自己认为最好的去做。**3 He** used when writing about God〔用于书面语〕上帝

USAGE NOTE 用法说明: HE

POLITENESS 礼貌程度

Some people, especially women, do not like the use of **he** to include both men and women in a sentence like 有些人, 特别是女性, 不喜欢使用不区分性别的 he 来表示人, 如下句: *Everyone should do what he thinks best.* 每个人都应按照自己认为最好的方法去做事。Instead they use **he or she, she or he**, or **they** 他们常使用 he or she, she or he 或 they 来代替: *Everyone should do what they think best.*

In writing **he/she** is often used, or simply **s/he**. Often you can write what you want to say in a different way in order to avoid the problem. 在书面表达中经常使用 he/she, 或者简写作 s/he。人们经常还用其他表达方法来避免出现这个问题。For example say 例如: *People should all do what they think best.* 人们都应该按照自己认为最好的方法去做事。

he- /hi; hiː/ *prefix* a male animal〔动物〕雄(性的): *a he-goat* 一只雄山羊

-head /hɛd; hed/ *suffix* [in nouns 构成名词] **1** the top of something 顶部, 上端, 口: *a pithead* (=the top of a coalmine) 矿井口 **2** the place where something begins; SOURCE[1] (1) 源头; 源泉: *a fountainhead* 泉源

head[1] /hɛd; hed/ *n*

① TOP OF BODY 头部
② MIND 头脑, 脑子
③ UNDERSTAND 理解
④ TOP PERSON 首要人物
⑤ TOP/FRONT/MOST IMPORTANT PART 上端/前端/最重要部分
⑥ CALM 冷静的
⑦ CRAZY 发疯的
⑧ INTELLIGENT/SENSIBLE 聪明的/明智的
⑨ TOO PROUD 过分自满
⑩ ALCOHOL/DRUGS 酒/毒品
⑪ FOR EACH PERSON 每人
⑫ OTHER MEANINGS 其他意思

head 头

hair 头发
temple 太阳穴
forehead 额
eyebrow 眉毛
eyelashes 睫毛
ear 耳朵
eye 眼
nose 鼻
face 脸
ear lobe 耳垂
nostril 鼻孔
cheek 颊
mouth 嘴
jaw 颌
lip 唇
neck 颈
chin 颏
Adam's apple 喉结
throat 喉

① TOP OF BODY 头部

1 [C] the top part of your body which has your eyes, mouth, brain etc in it 头, 头部: *My head aches.* 我头痛。| *He turned his head and looked at me.* 他转过头来看着我。| *severe head injuries* 严重的头部损伤

2 from head to foot/toe over your whole body 从头到脚, 全身上下: *He was shaking from head to foot.* 他在浑身发抖。| *dressed in black from head to toe* 穿着一身黑色衣服

3 a bad/sore head *informal* a pain in your head【非正式】头痛: *I woke up with a bad head the next morning.* 第二天早上醒来时我觉得头痛。

4 have a good/fine head of hair to have a lot of hair on your head 长有一头浓密的头发

② MIND 头脑, 脑子

5 [C] your mind 头脑, 脑子: *My head was full of strange thoughts.* 我脑子里全是些奇怪的想法。| **in/inside sb's head** *All the details are in my head.* 所有的细节都在我脑子里。| **do sth in your head** (=calculate something in your mind) 在脑子里计算 *I can do the figures in my head.* 我可以心算这些数字。

6 sth never entered sb's head used to say that you never thought of something 从未想过: *"Do you think she's crazy?" "The thought never entered my head!"* "你认为她疯了吗?" "我从来没有这样的想法。"

7 don't bother/trouble your head about it *spoken* used to tell someone not to worry about something【口】别多想了, 别担心

8 put sth out of your head *spoken* to stop worrying about something【口】不再为某事担心

9 can't get something out of your head to be unable to stop thinking about something 忍不住老想某事, 心里放不下某事

10 put your heads together *informal* to discuss a difficult problem together【非正式】一起想办法, 共同商量: *We'll have to put our heads together and see if we can come up with some ideas.* 我们得坐下来一起想想, 看看能不能想出什么办法来。

11 have your head in the clouds to spend too much time thinking about things that you would like to do 想入非非; 耽于空想

③ UNDERSTAND 理解

12 get your head round *BrE informal* to understand something difficult【英, 非正式】想通, 理解

13 can't make head nor tail of to be completely unable to understand something 弄不清，不能理解；被…弄糊涂：*I can't make head nor tail of this letter – does it mean anything to you?* 我给这封信弄糊涂了，你看得懂吗？

14 go over your head to be too difficult for you to understand 太高深而使某人无法理解：*The discussions went completely over my head.* 讨论的内容太深奥了，我根本无法听懂。

15 get sth into your head *informal* to understand and realize something【非正式】理解，明白：*I wish he'd get it into his head that I don't want to go out.* 我希望他能明白我不想出去。| **get sth into sb's head** (=make someone understand and realize something) 使某人理解，使某人明白

④ TOP PERSON 首要人物

16 [C] the leader or person in charge of a group or organization 首脑，首长，领袖，主管：[+of] *Eileen is head of the family now.* 艾琳现在成了一家之主了。| *the former head of the FBI, J Edgar Hoover* 前联邦调查局局长J.埃德加·胡佛

17 head waiter/chef/gardener etc the most senior waiter etc 服务员领班/厨师长/花匠领班等

18 ▶OF A SCHOOL 中小学的◀ [C] *BrE informal* the teacher who is in charge of a school【英，非正式】校长：**head teacher/the head** *We'll have to ask the head for permission.* 我们必须先征得校长的同意。

⑤ TOP/FRONT/MOST IMPORTANT PART 上端/前端/最重要部分

19 the head of the top or front of something, or the most important part of it 上端，顶部；前端；最重要的部分：**at the head of** *Write your name clearly at the head of each page.* 请将你的名字清楚地写在每页纸的上方。| **the head of the table** (=the part where the most important people sit) 首席，上座 *Frank sat proudly at the head of the table.* 弗兰克得意地坐在上座。

20 [singular] the large or wide end of a long thin object such as a tool〔细长工具的〕粗的一端，头：[+of] *the head of a hammer* 锤头

21 ▶PLANT 植物◀ [C] the top of a plant where its leaves and flowers grow 头状花序；叶球

⑥ CALM 冷静的

22 keep your head to remain calm in a difficult or dangerous situation 保持头脑冷静：*a leader with a steady nerve and the ability to keep her head in a crisis* 一位处事稳妥、能在危机中保持镇静的领导

23 lose your head to become too anxious to think or behave calmly 慌了神，失去冷静，惊惶失措：*When the engine caught fire, I just lost my head.* 发动机起火时，我都慌了神了。

24 a clear/cool head the ability to think clearly or calmly in a difficult or dangerous situation 冷静[清醒]的头脑：*You need to approach this kind of emergency with a cool head.* 你应该用冷静的头脑处理这种紧急情况。

⑦ CRAZY 发疯的

25 be out of your head/off your head *BrE spoken* to be crazy【英口】发疯的，精神错乱的

26 not be right in the head *spoken* to be mentally ill or crazy【口】发疯的，精神错乱的，脑子有问题的

27 need your head examined *spoken* to be crazy【口】发疯的，精神错乱的：*If you ask me, anyone who believes in UFO's needs their head examined!* 照我看，相信有不明飞行物的人脑子都有问题。

⑧ INTELLIGENT/SENSIBLE 聪明的/明智的

28 have your head screwed on (straight) *informal* to be sensible【非正式】明智的，理智的，有头脑

29 have a good head on your shoulders to be sensible or intelligent 明智的；聪明的

30 use your head to think about something sensibly 认真思考，动脑筋

⑨ TOO PROUD 过分自满

31 have a bighead also 又作 **have a swollen head** *BrE informal* to think you are much better, more important, more skilful etc than you are【英，非正式】自负，骄傲，自命不凡

32 go to sb's head *informal* if success goes to someone's head, it makes them feel more important than they really are【非正式】使飘飘然，冲昏头脑

⑩ ALCOHOL/DRUGS 酒/毒品

33 go to sb's head to make someone quickly feel slightly drunk〔酒〕上头，使某人微醉：*The wine went straight to my head.* 我很快就感到酒力了。

34 be out of your head *informal* to not know what you are doing because you have taken illegal drugs or drunk too much alcohol【非正式】〔酗酒或吸毒后〕神智混乱的

⑪ FOR EACH PERSON 每人

35 a head/per head for each person 每人，一个人：**$5/£10 etc a head** *The meal worked out at $50 a head.* 这顿饭算下来每人50美元。

⑫ OTHER MEANINGS 其他意思

36 ▶COIN 硬币◀ **heads** the side of a coin which has the king's or queen's head on it 正面，带人像的一面 —opposite 反义词 **tails** (TAIL¹ (5a))

37 keep your head above water to only just manage to continue to live on your income or keep your business working in spite of money problems〔靠自己的收入〕勉强度日；勉强维持经营

38 keep/get your head down to work steadily and quietly 专心工作，不分心：*He promised he would get his head down and work for his exams.* 他答应会专心学习，准备应试。

39 laugh/shout/scream your head off *informal* to laugh, shout etc very loudly【非正式】大笑/高喊/尖叫

40 be banging your head against a brick wall to keep trying to do something which seems impossible 枉费心机，白费气力，试图干不可能成功的事：*I feel as if I'm banging my head against a brick wall.* 我觉得自己完全是在白费气力。

41 take it into your head to do sth to suddenly decide to do something that does not seem sensible 突发奇想，突然打算做某事〔指不明智的事〕：*They suddenly took it into their heads to go off without telling anyone.* 他们突然心血来潮，没有告诉任何人就走了。

42 turn/stand sth on its head to consider a statement or idea in the opposite way from the way in which it was intended 倒过来想

43 give sb their head to give someone the freedom to do what they want to do 放任，听任某人自由行动

44 go head to head with *AmE* to deal with someone in a very direct and determined way【美】与某人正面交锋，与某人硬碰硬

45 come/bring sth to a head if a problem or difficult situation comes to a head, or if something brings it to a head, it suddenly becomes very bad (使)〔事情〕到了紧要关头；突然恶化：*The crisis came to a head when the bank refused to accept our cheques.* 银行拒绝接受我们的支票，这使得危机被推至极点。

46 go over sb's head to ask a more important person than the one you would normally ask 越过某人：*My boss was angry because I went over his head to the department manager.* 我的上司很生气，因为我越过他去找部门经理。

47 be over your head in debt *AmE* to owe so much money that there is no possibility of paying it all back【美】负债累累，欠了一屁股债

48 have a head for figures/facts/business etc to be good at doing calculations, remembering facts etc 擅长计算/记忆/做生意等

49 have no head for heights to be unable to look down from high places without feeling nervous 有恐高症

50 head and shoulders above the rest/others much better at something than everyone else 远远胜过其他人

51 head over heels in love loving someone very much 深深地爱着〔某人〕：*Sam was obviously head over heels in love with his new bride.* 萨姆显然深深地爱着他的新娘。

52 heads will roll *spoken* used to say that some people will be punished severely for something that has happened【口】将要受到严厉的惩罚

53 on your own head be it *spoken* used to tell someone that they will be blamed if the thing they are planning to do has bad results【口】责任自负，落到自己头上

54 heads up! *AmE spoken* used to warn people that something is falling from above【美口】当心！〔警告别人上面有东西掉下〕

55 do your head in *BrE spoken* to make you feel confused and annoyed【英口】使人烦恼，使人讨厌：*The way he keeps changing his mind about things really does my head in.* 他老是改变主意，真是烦死我了。

56 ▶BEER 啤酒◀ [C] the layer of small white BUBBLEs on the top of a glass of beer〔啤酒上面的〕泡沫
57 ▶RECORDING 录音◀ [C] the part of a TAPE RECORDER that records sound〔录音机的〕磁头
58 head of cattle/sheep etc a particular number of cows, sheep etc 牛/羊等的头数: *a small farm with 20 head of cattle* 养有20头牛的小农场
59 head of water/steam pressure that is made when water or steam is kept in an enclosed space 水压/蒸汽压力
60 ▶LAND 地方◀ a high area of land that sticks into the sea; HEADLAND 海岬, 陆岬, 角: *Beachy Head* 比奇角
61 ▶RIVER/STREAM 河/溪◀ the beginning of a river or stream 源头
62 ▶INFECTION 感染◀ [C] the white centre of a swollen spot on your skin 脓头 —see also 另见 **bite sb's head off** (BITE[1] (9)), **bury your head in the sand** (BURY (11)), **hold up your head** (HOLD[1] (38)), **nod your head** (NOD[1] (1)), **off the top of your head** (TOP[1] (16)), **shake your head** (SHAKE[1] (4)), **turn sb's head** (TURN[1] (21)), **do sth standing on your head** (STAND[1] (38))

S2 W2 **head²** *v*
1 ▶GO TOWARDS 朝…行进◀ [I] to go or make something go in a particular direction 朝…前进, 向…去: [+for/towards/across etc] *The ship was heading for Cuba.* 船正开往古巴。| *It's about time we were heading home.* 我们该动身回家了。| **head north/south etc** *We headed south towards the capital.* 我们朝南向首都进发。| **be headed (for)** *especially AmE*【尤美】*Where are you guys headed?* 你们要去哪儿?
2 ▶BE IN CHARGE 负责◀ also 又作 **head up** [T] to be in charge of a government, organization, or group of people 主管, 领导: *a delegation headed by former President Jimmy Carter* 一个由前总统吉米·卡特率领的代表团
3 be heading for also 又作 **be headed for** *especially AmE*【尤美】if you are heading for a situation, it is likely to happen to you〔注定〕遭受, 碰到, 面临: *They're heading for disaster.* 他们正面临灾难。
4 ▶BE AT THE TOP 居于首位◀ [T] **a)** to be at the top of a list or group of people or things 居于首位, 名列第一: *The movie heads the list of Oscar nominations.* 这部影片在奥斯卡提名影片中名列首位。**b) be headed** if a page is headed with a particular word or sentence, it has it on the top〔页〕最上端〔文字〕为: *The page was headed 'Expenses'.* 这一页的上端标有"开支"。
5 ▶BE AT THE FRONT 在前列◀ to be at the front of a line of people 位于队伍之首; 带领: *a procession headed by the Reverend Martin Luther King* 由马丁·路德·金牧师带领的游行队伍
6 ▶FOOTBALL 足球◀ [T] to hit the ball with your head, especially in football 用头顶〔球〕—see picture on page A23 参见A23页图

head off *phr v* **1** [T **head** sth ↔ **off**] to prevent something from happening 阻止, 防止…发生: *They've headed off several crises since they took charge.* 自接手以来, 他们已避免了几次危机。**2** [T **head** sth ↔ **off**] to stop someone moving in a particular direction by moving in front of them〔在前面〕拦截, 拦挡: *Soldiers headed them off at the border.* 士兵在边境上将他们拦截住了。**3** [I] to leave to go to another place 离开〔某地〕去〔别处〕: *I'm heading off now.* 我现在要走了。

head·ache /ˈhɛd͵ek; ˈhedeɪk/ *n* [C] **1** a pain in your head 头痛: **splitting headache** (=a very bad headache) 头痛欲裂 **2** *informal* an annoying or worrying problem【非正式】使人头痛的事, 棘手的事, 难题: *Censorship was a constant headache for Soviet newspapers.* 对苏联的各家报纸来说, 新闻审查是件让人头痛的事。—**headachy** *adj*: *a headachy feeling* 头痛的感觉

head·band /ˈhɛd͵bænd; ˈhedbænd/ *n* [C] **1** a band that you wear around your head to keep your hair off your face〔扎在头上的〕束发带 **2** a similar band around a horse's head〔扎在马头上的〕系带; 头羁 —see picture at 参见 HORSE[1] 图

head·bang·er /ˈhɛd͵bæŋɚ; ˈhedbæŋə/ *n* [C] **1** *informal* someone who enjoys HEAVY METAL music and moves their head around violently to the beat of the music【非正式】喜欢听重金属音乐的人 **2** someone who behaves in a stupid or crazy way 疯疯癫癫的人, 疯子

head·board /͵hɛdˋbord; ˈhedbɔːd/ *n* [C] the upright wooden board at the end of a bed where your head is 床头板

head boy /͵· ˈ·/ *n* [C] the boy who is chosen in a British school each year to represent the school〔英国学校里每年选出的〕男学生代表

head·butt /ˈhɛd͵bʌt; ˈhedbʌt/ *v* [T] to deliberately hit someone in the stomach with your head 以头顶〔某人的肚子〕

head·case /ˈhɛd͵kes; ˈhedkeɪs/ *n* [C] *slang* a crazy person【俚】疯子

head·cheese /ˈhɛd͵tʃiz; ˈhedtʃiːz/ *n* [U] *AmE* meat from the head of a pig boiled and pressed【美】〔用猪头肉煮成的〕碎肉冻; BRAWN (2) *BrE*【英】

head count /ˈ· ·/ *n* **do a head count** to count how many people are present 点人数

head·dress /ˈhɛd͵drɛs; ˈhed-dres/ *n* [C] something that someone wears on their head for decoration on a special occasion 头饰: *a feathered headdress* 插有羽毛的头饰

head·ed /ˈhɛdɪd; ˈhedɪ̣d/ *adj* **1 two-headed/three-headed etc** having two heads etc 有两/三个头的等 **2 headed notepaper** paper for writing letters that has your name and address printed at the top 印有抬头的信纸 **3 red-headed/grey-headed etc** having red hair etc 红头发/花白头发的等

head·er /ˈhɛdɚ; ˈhedə/ *n* [C] **1** a shot in football made by hitting the ball with your head〔足球的〕头球 **2** the top of a page, especially on a computer〔尤指电脑屏幕上的〕页首 **3 take a header** to jump or fall into water with your head going in first 头朝下跳水[掉进水里]

head·first /͵· ˈ·◂/ *adv* **1** moving forward with the rest of your body following your head 头朝前地: **fall/plunge head-first** *I fell head-first down the stairs.* 我一头栽下楼梯。**2** if you rush into something head-first, you start doing it too quickly without thinking carefully 仓促地, 鲁莽地

head·gear /ˈhɛd͵gɪr; ˈhedgɪə/ *n* [U] *informal* hats and other things that you wear on your head【非正式】帽, 头上戴的东西

head girl /͵· ˈ·/ *n* [C] the girl who is chosen in a British school each year to represent the school〔英国学校里每年选出的〕女学生代表

head·hunt·er /ˈ· ͵· ·/ *n* [C] **1** someone who finds people with the right skills and experience to do a particular job, and persuades them to leave their present jobs 物色人才者, 猎头 **2** a member of a tribe of people who cut off and keep the heads of their enemies 割取敌人首级作为战利品保存的某一部落成员 —**headhunt** *v* [T]

head·ing /ˈhɛdɪŋ; ˈhedɪŋ/ *n* [C] the title written at the top of a piece of writing 标题, 题目

head·lamp /ˈhɛd͵læmp; ˈhedlæmp/ *n* [C usually plural 一般用复数] a HEADLIGHT〔车辆的〕前灯, 车头灯

head·land /ˈhɛdlənd; ˈhedlənd/ *n* [C] an area of land that sticks out from the coast into the sea 岬, 岬角, 海岬 —see picture on page A12 参见A12页图

head·less /ˈhɛdlɪs; ˈhedləs/ *adj* without a head 无头的: *a headless corpse* 一具无头尸体

Headless Horse·man, the /͵·· ˈ·· ·/ a GHOST (=the spirit of a dead person) with no head, who rides a horse. He appears in several ghost stories, the most famous of which is *The Legend of Sleepy Hollow* (1820) by Washington Irving. 无头骑士〔指骑马的无头鬼怪, 出现在一些鬼怪小说中, 其中最著名的是华盛顿·欧文的《睡谷的传说》(1820)〕

head·light /ˈhɛd͵laɪt; ˈhedlaɪt/ *n* [C usually plural 一般用复数] one of the large lights at the front of a vehicle〔车辆的〕前灯, 车头灯 —see picture on page A2 参见A2页图

head·line¹ /ˈhɛd͵laɪn; ˈhedlaɪn/ *n* [C usually plural 一般用复数] **1** the title of a newspaper report, which is printed in large letters above the report〔报纸的〕标题, 大字标题: *an eye-catching headline* 醒目的标题 **2 the headlines** the important points of the main news stories that are read at the beginning of a news programme〔广播或电视的〕新闻提要 **3 hit the headlines/make the headlines** to be reported in newspapers or on radio and television 成了报纸上的新闻; 成为电台或电视报道的新闻: *Computer crime first hit the headlines in 1983.* 电脑犯罪在1983年首次成为媒体报道的新闻。 S3

headline² *v* [T] **1** [usually passive 一般用被动态] to give a headline to an article or story 给…加标题 **2** *AmE* to appear as the main performer in a show【美】扮演主角, 成为…的主要表演者: *Frank Sinatra headlines this month's production.* 本月推出的影片由弗兰克·西纳特拉主演。

head·lock /ˈhɛd͵lɑk; ˈhedlɒk/ *n* [C] a way of holding someone around their neck so that they cannot move〔摔跤中的〕夹头

head·long /ˈhɛd͵lɔŋ; ˈhedlɒŋ/ *adv* **1** if you rush headlong into something, you start doing it too quickly without thinking carefully 轻率地, 仓促地: **rush headlong into** *Martin just isn't the*

H

type to rush headlong into marriage. 马丁根本不是会轻率地结婚的人。**2** falling with your head first and the rest of your body following 头朝下地，头在前地 **3** running very quickly without looking where you are going〔奔跑时〕仓皇地，慌不择路地: *He fled headlong down a narrow passageway.* 他沿着一条窄路仓皇逃跑。—**headlong** *adj*: *a headlong dash for the frontier* 向边境仓皇奔逃

head·man /ˈhɛdmən; ˈhedmən/ *n plural* **headmen** /-mən; -mən/ [C] a chief of a village where a tribe lives 部落的首领，酋长

head·mas·ter /ˈhɛd,mæstɚ; ,hedˈmɑːstə/ *n* [C] *BrE* a male teacher who is in charge of a school【英】〔中小学的〕男校长

head·mis·tress /ˈhɛd,mɪstrɪs; ,hedˈmɪstrɨs/ *n* [C] *BrE* a female teacher who is in charge of a school【英】〔中小学的〕女校长

head of·fice /,· ˈ··/ *n* **1** [C] the main office of a company〔公司的〕总部，总公司，总行 **2** [singular] the managers who work there 总部管理人员

head of state /,· · ˈ·/ *n* [C] the main representative of a country, such as a queen, king, or president 国家元首

head-on /,· ˈ·◂/ *adv* **1 meet/crash etc head-on** if two vehicles meet head-on, the front part of one vehicle hits the front part of the other〔车辆〕正面相撞: *Their car collided head-on with a van.* 他们的汽车与一辆小货车迎头相撞。**2** if someone deals with a problem head-on, they deal with it in a direct and determined way 面对面地，毫不回避地: *It would be best to tackle the situation head-on.* 最好的办法是正面地解决问题。—**head-on** *adj*: *a head-on collision* 迎面相撞

head·phones /ˈhɛd,fonz; ˈhedfəʊnz/ *n* [plural] a piece of equipment that you wear over your ears to listen to a radio or recording 耳机，耳塞

head·piece /ˈhɛd,pis; ˈhedpiːs/ *n* [C] **1** something you wear on your head for protection 头盔；帽子 **2** a decorated title at the top of a page or piece of writing〔页首或文章开头的〕带花饰图案的标题

head·quar·tered /ˈhɛd,kwɔrtɚd; ˈhed,kwɔːtəd/ *adj* having your headquarters at a particular place 总部设在…的: *Many top companies are headquartered here.* 很多大公司都把总部设在这里。—**headquarter** *v* [T]

3 **head·quar·ters** /ˈhɛd,kwɔrtɚz; ˈhed,kwɔːtəz/ *n plural* **headquarters** [C] **1** the main building or offices used by a large organization 总部，总公司，总办事处 **2** *abbreviation* 缩写为 **HQ** the place from which military operations are controlled〔军队的〕司令部，指挥部，大本营

head·rest /ˈhɛd,rɛst; ˈhed-rest/ *n* [C] the top part of a chair or of the front seat in a car that supports the back of your head〔汽车座椅上的〕头靠，头垫 —see picture on page A2 参见 A2 页图

head·room /ˈhɛd,rum; ˈhed-rʊm/ *n* [U] **1** the amount of space above your head, especially when you are in a car〔车辆中乘客头顶以上的〕头顶空间 **2** the amount of space above a vehicle when it is under a bridge〔车顶与桥底之间的〕净空（高度）

head·scarf /ˈhɛdskɑrf; ˈhedskɑːf/ *n* [C] a square piece of cloth that women wear on their heads, tied under their chin〔女用〕方头巾 —see picture at 参见 SCARF[1] 图

> **CULTURAL NOTE 文化注释**
> In Britain and the US headscarves are no longer fashionable, and are worn mainly by older upper-class women. 女用方头巾在英美已不再时髦，主要是年纪较大的上层妇女才戴。

head·set /ˈhɛd,sɛt; ˈhedset/ *n* [C] a set of HEADPHONES 耳机，头戴式受话器

head·ship /ˈhɛdʃɪp; ˈhedʃɪp/ *n* [C] **1** a position of being in charge of an organization 领导地位[职务] **2** *BrE* the job of being in charge of a school【英】〔中小学的〕校长职务

head·shrink·er /ˈhɛd,ʃrɪŋkɚ; ˈhed,ʃrɪŋkə/ *n* [C] *informal* a PSYCHIATRIST or PSYCHOANALYST【非正式】精神科医生；精神分析专家

head·square /ˈhɛd,skwɛr; ˈhedskweə/ *n* [C] a HEADSCARF〔女用〕方头巾

head·stand /ˈhɛdstænd; ˈhedstænd/ *n* [C] a position in which you turn your body upside down, with your head and hands on the floor and your legs and feet in the air 倒立

head start /ˈ· ·/ *n* [C] **1** an advantage that helps you to be successful 先起步的优势；有利开端；占先: *Give your children a head start by sending them to nursery school.* 送你的孩子上幼儿园，让他们有个好的开端。**2** a start in a race in which you begin earlier or further ahead than someone else〔赛跑中〕先起动，抢先

head·stone /ˈhɛd,ston; ˈhedstəʊn/ *n* [C] a piece of stone on a grave on which the dead person's name is written; GRAVESTONE, TOMBSTONE 墓碑，墓头石

head·strong /ˈhɛd,strɔŋ; ˈhedstrɒŋ/ *adj* very determined to do what you want, even when other people advise you not to do it 任性的，固执的: *an impulsive headstrong child* 一个冲动任性的孩子

head ta·ble /,· ˈ··/ *n* [C] *AmE* a table at a formal meal where the most important people or those giving speeches sit【美】主桌〔正式宴会上最重要的客人或要发表讲话的人所坐的桌子〕; TOP TABLE *BrE*【英】

head teach·er /,· ˈ··/ *n* [C] *BrE* the teacher who is in charge of a school【英】〔中小学的〕校长; PRINCIPAL[2] (2) *AmE*【美】

head wait·er /,· ˈ··/ *n* [C] the WAITER who is in charge of the other waiters in a restaurant〔餐馆的〕服务员领班 —see picture on page A15 参见 A15 页图

head·wa·ters /ˈhɛd,wɔtɚz; ˈhedwɔːtəz/ *n* [plural] the part where a stream starts before it flows into a river 河源，上游源头

head·way /ˈhɛd,we; ˈhedweɪ/ *n* **make headway a)** to make progress towards achieving something in spite of difficulties 取得进展: [**+towards/in/with etc**] *They had made no headway towards finding a solution.* 他们尚未就解决这个问题取得任何进展。**b)** to move forwards 向前行进

head·wind /ˈhɛd,wɪnd; ˈhed,wɪnd/ *n* [C,U] a wind that blows directly towards you when you are moving 逆风，顶头风

head·word /ˈhɛd,wɝd; ˈhedwɜːd/ *n* [C] one of the words whose meaning is explained in a dictionary〔词典中的〕词目

head·y /ˈhɛdɪ; ˈhedi/ *adj* [usually before noun 一般用于名词前] **1** a heady smell, drink etc is pleasantly strong and seems to affect your senses〔气味、饮料等〕令人陶醉的: *a heady aroma* 醉人的香味 | *a heady combination of wine and brandy* 令人陶醉的葡萄酒和白兰地混合酒 **2** very exciting in a way that makes you feel as if you can do anything you want to 使人飘飘然的，使人兴奋的: *the heady atmosphere of the early sixties* 60 年代初期的狂热气氛

heal /hil; hiːl/ *v* **1** [I] also 又作 **heal up** if a wound or a broken bone heals, the flesh, skin, bone etc grows back together and becomes healthy again〔伤口或断骨〕长好，愈合: *It took three months for my arm to heal properly.* 我的胳膊过了三个月才完全长好。**2** [T] to cure someone who is ill or make a wound heal 医治；治愈 **3 heal the wounds/breach/divisions** to make people stop being angry with each other 治愈创伤/弥补裂痕/消除分歧 —see also 另见 FAITH HEALING

heal over *phr v* [I] **1** if a wound or an area of broken skin heals over, new skin grows over it and it becomes healthy again〔伤口或破损的皮肤〕愈合，痊愈 **2** [I,T] if an argument heals over or is healed over, it is forgotten 忘掉过去的争吵，重归于好

heal·er /ˈhilɚ; ˈhiːlə/ *n* [C] someone who is believed to have the natural ability to cure people 自然力治疗师

health /hɛlθ; helθ/ *n* [U] **1** your physical condition and how healthy you are 健康（状况）: *Betty's anxious about her husband's health.* 贝蒂十分担心她丈夫的健康状况。| *Smoking can seriously damage your health.* 吸烟会严重损害你的健康。| **be in good/excellent/poor health** (=be generally healthy or unhealthy) 身体好/非常好/不好 | **be good/bad for your health** *A low-fat diet is better for your health.* 低脂饮食更有利于你的健康。**2** the state of being healthy（身体）健康: *Even if you haven't got much money, at least you've got your health.* 即使你没有太多钱，但起码你拥有健康。| **sb is a picture of health** (=used to say that someone looks very healthy) 某人看起来很健康 **3** the work of providing medical services to keep people healthy 医疗保健（工作）: *The government has promised to spend more on health and education.* 政府已经承诺增加医疗保健和教育经费。**4** how successful an economy or organization is〔经济〕运行状况；〔机构〕运转状况: *The monthly trade figures are seen as an indicator of the health of the economy.* 每月的贸易数字被视为经济运行情况的指标。**5 drink (to) sb's health** to say that you wish someone will be healthy and happy, and then have a drink of alcohol 为某人的健康干杯

health and safe·ty /,· · ˈ··/ *n* [U] an area of government and law concerned with people's health and safety, especially at work 卫生与安全〔指政务和法律范畴，尤指工作场所的卫生与安全〕

Health and Safe·ty at Work Act, the /,· · ,· · · ˈ· ,·/ a set of laws made in the UK in 1974 in order to protect people at work and make sure that they do not have to work in dangerous conditions, without the proper clothing or safety equipment etc《岗位卫生与安全法》〔1974 年英国制定的一系列法规，旨在保护从业人员，确保他们不会在危险环境或在缺少防护服装或装备的情况下作业〕

Health and Safe·ty Ex·ec·u·tive, the /,· ·'· · ·, ··/ abbreviation 缩写为 HSE a British government organization that gives advice to companies about health and safety, and makes rules to prevent workers from being injured or becoming ill at work 卫生与安全执行委员会〔英国一政府机构。其职能是向公司提供卫生与安全咨询服务，制定规章制度防止工人上岗时受伤或生病〕 —compare 比较 OSHA

health care /'· ·/ *n* [U] the service of looking after the health of all the people in a country or an area 医疗保健

CULTURAL NOTE 文化注释

Health Care in the UK In the UK there is a National Health Service, the NHS, which is paid for by taxes and National Insurance (=a system of insurance run by the government), and in general people do not have to pay for medical treatment. Every person has a GP (=general practitioner), a doctor who is trained in general medicine and who treats people in their local area. People who are ill can make an appointment to see their GP, or they can call their GP to visit them at home. People have to pay part of the cost of the medicines that the doctor prescribes (PRESCRIBE), unless they are children, unemployed, or over 60 years old. If a GP decides that it is necessary, he or she will make an appointment for the patient to see a specialist doctor at a hospital. Anyone who is very ill can call an AMBULANCE and get taken to hospital for free urgent medical treatment. Although medical treatment is free in the NHS, people often have to wait for a long time before they are treated. The problem of NHS waiting lists (=lists of people who need treatment but must wait before they can have it) is discussed by a lot of politicians and ordinary people. A small number of people choose to 'go private', which means paying to have treatment done privately, and they get treated more quickly. People who do this usually have private health insurance. As the average age of the population gets older and older, the NHS is becoming more and more expensive to run, and people are worried that medical care will not be free in the future. 英国的医疗保健：英国有国民保健制度，简称NHS，费用由税收和国民保险承担，一般人们无须付医疗费。每个人都有一个当地的全科医生负责，生病时可预约去医生诊所，或打电话请医生来家出诊。医生开的药需付一定的费用，儿童、失业者或60岁以上的老人除外。若全科医生认为必要，他会为病人约医院的专科医生。病重者可叫救护车去医院，接受免费急诊治疗。国民保健制度内虽然医疗免费，但人们常常得等很长时间才能得到治疗。很多政界人士和普通百姓都会讨论候诊时间过长的问题，有人选择去看私人医生，自掏腰包以更快得到治疗。这样做的人往往有个人医疗保险。随着人口老龄化加剧，国民保健制度运作成本越来越高，人们担心将来不会再有免费医疗。

Health Care in the US Unlike the UK, the US does not have a national health care service. Most people have health insurance to pay for their medical care, and this is often paid for by their employer. People can get insurance from a regular insurance company, or they can pay to become members of an HMO (Health Maintenance Organization), a company that owns hospitals and practices (=a place where doctors work) for its members to use. The government helps to pay for some medical care for people who are on low incomes through the MEDICAID system, and for old people through the MEDICARE system. There are many people who cannot afford health insurance but are not poor enough to get government help. Health care is an important political subject in the US. The cost of medical insurance and the problems of those who cannot afford it are often discussed by politicians and ordinary people, as are cases of health insurance companies refusing to pay for treatment. When people are ill, they usually go first to an INTERNIST (=a doctor trained in general medicine), but people sometimes go to a specialist without seeing an internist first. Children are usually taken to a PEDIATRICIAN. Doctors do not go to people's homes when they are ill. Patients always make an appointment to see the doctor in the doctor's office. HMO members choose their regular doctor from a list of doctors who work for that HMO. In an EMERGENCY, HMO members contact the HMO and speak to an employee, often a nurse, who arranges for them to be taken to a hospital for treatment. 美国的医疗保健：与英国不同，美国没有全国性的卫生保健制度。大多数人购买医疗保险支付医疗费用，医疗保险一般由雇主支付。人们可以购买一般的保险公司的保险，也可以付费加入健康维护机构，这是一家公司，它拥有医院和医务所供会员使用。政府通过医疗补助制度帮助低收入者，通过国家医疗保健制度帮助老人。无力负担医疗保险但又不够条件获得政府救济的人很多。医疗在美国是一大政治话题。政界人士和普通人都会讨论医疗保险的费用问题和无力支付医疗保险问题，以及保险公司拒付医疗费的问题。人们生病时一般先去找受过全科训练的内科医生，但有时人们也略过这一步直接去看专科医生。儿童一般看儿科医生。医生不去患者家里出诊，都是由病人预约去医生诊所。健康维护机构会员可以从为该机构工作的医生名录里选择自己常看的医生。情况紧急时，健康维护机构会员可以联系该机构，告知那里的雇员（通常是护士），后者会安排他们来医院接受治疗。

health cen·ter /'· ,··/ *n* [C] *AmE* a building where students go to get medical help or advice【美】〔学生〕医疗中心，保健中心

health cen·tre /'· ,··/ *n* [C] *BrE* a building where several doctors have offices【英】〔包括几个诊所的〕医疗中心，医务所

health club /'· ·/ *n* [C] a private club where people can go to exercise in order to become physically stronger and more attractive 健身俱乐部

CULTURAL NOTE 文化注释

In the 1980s exercising to be healthy became popular in Britain, and many health clubs were established. It is usually quite expensive to be a member. In the US, the practice of going to health clubs started in the 1970s. 20世纪80年代，运动健身在英国蔚然成风，成立了很多健身俱乐部。要成为俱乐部会员，通常都要支付不菲的费用。在美国，去健身俱乐部的风气可追溯到20世纪70年代。

health farm /'· ·/ *n* [C] a place where people pay to stay so that they can lose weight 健身庄〔人们减肥的一个地方〕

health food /'· ·/ *n* [C,U] food that contains only natural substances 保健食品〔指不含化学物质的天然食品〕

CULTURAL NOTE 文化注释

Health food is a general name for food that does not contain ADDITIVE*s* (=added chemicals to improve the taste or colour etc), food that is not PROCESS*ed* (=changed from its natural state) such as BROWN RICE (=rice that still has its outer layer), and ORGANIC food (=food grown without the help of chemicals). 健康食品是不含添加剂的食品、未经加工的食品（如糙米）和有机食品的通称。

Many supermarkets sell health food, but it is sold especially in health food stores, which also sell things like VITAMIN*s* and ALTERNATIVE MEDICINE*s* (=medicines made from plants, herbs etc). 健康食品在很多超市可以买到，但尤其会在健康食品店出售，这些商店也卖维生素和替代疗法药物等。

Health food is connected in some people's minds with people who support 'Green' ideas and care a lot about the environment, and some people make fun of people who eat health food and call them 'cranks' or 'health freaks' (=people with strange or silly ideas who worry too much about what they eat and do not seem to enjoy their food). However, more and more people are becoming concerned about health and chemicals in food, and are buying more organic food. 在很多人眼中，倡导"绿色"概念、关注环境问题的人青睐健康食品。有人拿吃健康食品的人开玩笑，叫他们"怪人"或"健康狂"。不过，越来越多的人关注食品健康和食品中的化学成分，更多地购买有机食品。— see also JUNK FOOD and Cultural Notes at ADDITIVE, VEGETARIAN 另见 JUNK FOOD，并见ADDITIVE，VEGETARIAN 文化注释

health·ful /ˈhɛlθfəl; 'helθfəl/ *adj AmE* likely to make you healthy【美】有利于健康的：*healthful mountain air* 有利于健康的山间空气

Health Ser·vice, the /'· ,··/ the British National Health Service 保健制度〔英国国民医疗保健制度的简称〕

CULTURAL NOTE 文化注释

Because there is no national health service in the US, medical care is extremely expensive. Most people have some kind of health insurance, which is partly paid by their employer or by a family member's employer. 因美国没有全国性的医疗保健制度，医疗费奇贵。大多数人购买某种健

康保险，该保险有一部分由本人的雇主或一位家庭成员的雇主支付。— see also Cultural Note at HEALTH CARE 另见 HEALTH CARE 文化注释

health vis·it·or /ˈ·,···/ *n* [C] a nurse in Britain who visits people in their homes〔英国的〕卫生访问员〔指上门作健康护理的护士〕

health·y /ˈhɛlθɪ; ˈhelθi/ *adj*

1 ▶PERSON/ANIMAL 人/动物◀ physically strong and not likely to become ill 健康的，健壮的：*a healthy baby boy* 健康的男婴 | *I've always been perfectly healthy until now.* 我的身体一直非常健康。

2 ▶MAKING YOU HEALTHY 使人健康◀ likely to make you healthy 有益健康的：*a healthy diet* 健康的饮食

CULTURAL NOTE 文化注释

Many people in both the US and the UK are very interested in foods and exercise that will help them to stay healthy. People know that too much fat in your food can give you high CHOLESTEROL (=a substance that causes heart disease), so many people try not to eat too many foods that have a lot of fat or sugar in them. Food companies often advertise their foods as being low in fat, and these foods often have the word 'lite' (=light) in their names. 很多英美人对有助健康的食品和运动很感兴趣。人们了解到，体内脂肪过多会引起胆固醇升高，因此很多人尽量少吃含脂肪或糖分太多的食品。食品公司经常宣传其产品脂肪含量低，这些食品名称一般含lite（清淡）字样。— see also 另见 EXERCISE

3 ▶GOOD FOR YOUR CHARACTER 有利于人的品格◀ [usually in questions or negatives 一般用于疑问句或否定句] good for someone's mind or character 有益于精神[品格]的，有益于身心的：*I don't think it's healthy for her to spend so much time alone.* 我认为长时间独处对她的身心健康没有好处。

4 ▶SHOWING GOOD HEALTH 显示健康◀ showing that you are healthy 显示健康的：*Her face had a healthy glow.* 她容光焕发。| *a healthy skin* 健康的皮肤 | **a healthy appetite** (=a desire to eat a lot) 旺盛的食欲

5 ▶COMPANY/SOCIETY ETC 公司/社会等◀ a healthy company, society, economic system etc is working effectively and successfully 运作良好的；兴旺发达的：*The economy is looking quite healthy now.* 目前的经济看起来相当兴旺。

6 a healthy respect/contempt/curiosity etc a natural and sensible feeling 自然的尊重/鄙视/好奇心等：*a healthy contempt for silly regulations* 对可笑规矩的自然鄙视

7 ▶AMOUNT 数量◀ large and showing that someone is successful 大量的，可观的：*By the end of the year we should make a healthy profit.* 到年底我们应该会有可观的利润。—**healthily** *adv* —**healthiness** *n* [U]

Hea·ney /ˈhinɪ; ˈhiːni/**, Sea·mus** /ˈʃeməs; ˈʃeɪməs/ (1939-) an Irish poet. His collections of poems include *Death of a Naturalist*, *The Haw Lantern* and *Seeing Things*. In 1995, he won the Nobel Prize for Literature. 希尼（1939- ），爱尔兰诗人。他的诗集有《一位自然主义者之死》、《山楂灯笼》和《视幻》。1995年获诺贝尔文学奖〕

heap¹ /hip; hiːp/ *n* [C] **1** a large untidy pile of things〔大而杂乱的〕堆：*a rubbish heap* 垃圾堆 | [+of] *heaps of dead leaves* 落叶堆 | **in heaps** *Dirty clothes lay in heaps on the floor.* 脏衣服成堆地放在地上。**2 heaps of** *informal* a lot of something【非正式】大量，许多：*Don't worry, we've got heaps of time.* 别担心，我们有的是时间。**3** *humorous* an old car that is in bad condition【幽默】破旧的汽车 **4 fall/collapse in a heap** to fall down and lie without moving 瘫倒/动弹不了 **5 be struck/knocked all of a heap** *BrE old-fashioned informal* to be suddenly very surprised or confused【英，过时，非正式】被突然惊呆，被弄得慌作一团

heap² *v* [T] **1** also 又作 **heap up** to put a lot of things on top of each other in an untidy way〔杂乱地〕堆积，堆放：*The ashes from the fire were heaped in a huge pile.* 大火产生的灰烬堆成了一大堆。| **heap sth on/onto** *They had heaped all the rubbish onto the back of the truck.* 他们将所有的垃圾都堆在卡车后面的车斗里。**2 be heaped with** if a plate is heaped with food, it has a lot on it〔盘子〕堆满〔食物〕**3 heap praises/insults etc on** to praise, insult etc someone a lot 极力称赞/百般侮辱等

heaped /hipt; hiːpt/ *adj* **heaped teaspoon/tablespoon etc** an amount of something that is as much as a spoon can hold 满满的一茶匙/汤匙：*Add 3 heaped teaspoons of sugar.* 加入满满的三茶匙糖。

heaps /hips; hiːps/ *adv* **heaps better/bigger etc** *informal* much better, bigger etc【非正式】好/大得多

hear 听

Joe can't hear the phone ringing because he's listening to music.
乔听不见电话铃声，因为他在听音乐。

hear /hɪr; hɪə/ *v past tense and past participle* **heard** /hɝd; hɜːd/

1 ▶HEAR SOUNDS/WORDS ETC 听到声音/话语等◀ [I,T not in progressive 不用进行式] to know that a sound is being made, using your ears 听到，听见：*Did you hear that noise?* 你听见那个声音吗？| *I called his name, but he pretended not to hear.* 我叫他的名字，但他假装没听见。| **hear sb/sth doing sth** *I think I can hear someone knocking.* 我似乎听到有人在敲门。| **hear sb/sth do sth** *Dixon's going to resign – I heard him say so.* 狄克逊要辞职了 — 我听见他这么说的。| **hear what** *I'm sorry, I didn't hear what you said.* 对不起，我没有听到你说什么。| **be heard to say/ask/remark etc** *One delegate was heard to remark that the conference had been a waste of time.* 有人听到其中一个代表说这次会议是在浪费时间。

2 ▶LISTEN TO SB/STH 听◀ [T not usually in progressive 一般不用进行式] to listen to what someone is saying, the music they are playing etc 听，聆听，倾听：*Without waiting to hear her answer, he stood up and walked away.* 他没有听她的回答，便站起来走了。| *You can hear that broadcast again on Monday at 9.00.* 你可以在星期一9点再次收听那个广播节目。| **hear sb do sth** *Pavarotti is amazing – you should hear him sing 'Nessun dorma'.* 帕瓦罗蒂真棒，你应该听听他唱的《今夜无人入眠》。| **hear what** *Let's hear what he's got to say.* 我们听听他怎么说吧！| **I hear what you're saying** *spoken* (=used to tell someone that you have listened to their opinion)【口】我听到你的话了，我明白你的意思 *I hear what you're saying, but we can't ignore the facts.* 我明白你的意思，但我们也不能不顾事实。

3 ▶BE TOLD STH 被告知某事◀ [I,T not usually in progressive 一般不用进行式] to be told or find out a piece of information 听说，被告知，得知：**hear (that)** *I hear you've been selected to play for the A team.* 听说你已被选入A队了。| [+about] *Did you hear about the fire?* 你听说起火的事了吗？| **be glad/pleased to hear (that)** *I'm glad to hear your sister's feeling better.* 听说你姐姐好多了，我感到很高兴。| **so I've heard** *spoken* (=used to say that you already know about something)【口】我已经听说了 *"Nina's quit her job." "Yes, so I've heard."* "尼娜辞职了。""哦，我已经听说了。" | **hear sth** *We've heard such a lot about you.* 我们已经听到过很多有关你的事。| **hear what/how/who etc** *When the authorities heard what we were planning, they tried to stop us.* 当局得知我们的计划后，便试图阻止我们。| **hear anything of** (=receive any news about) 听到有关…的消息 *Have you heard anything of Bob lately?* 你最近听到鲍勃的消息没有？| **hear sth on the grapevine** (=find out about something in conversation) 从谈话中获悉 | **I've heard it said** *spoken*【口】also 又作 **I've heard tell** *old-fashioned*【过时】(=used when you are repeating something that someone else has told you) 我听人说 *I've heard it said she's a tough businesswoman.* 我听人说她是个厉害的女商人。

4 ▶IN COURT 在法庭上◀ hear a case if a court or a committee hears a case, they listen to all the evidence in order to make a decision 审理案件：*The case was heard at Teeside Crown Court on April 10.* 提塞德刑事法庭于4月10日审理了此案。

5 I won't hear of it *spoken* used to say that someone should not do something, especially because you want to help them【口】我不允许；不要提：*I've offered to pay Simon for fixing my car, but he won't hear of it.* 我提出要酬谢西蒙，因为他帮我修好了车，但他拒绝了。

6 I/we haven't heard the last of *spoken* used to say that someone or something will cause more problems for you【口】〔某人

或物〕还会给我/我们带来更多麻烦；没完没了：*I'm sure we haven't heard the last of that woman.* 那个女人肯定还会给我们带来更多麻烦。

7 I'll/he'll etc never hear the end of it *spoken* used to say that someone will criticize or make jokes about something you have done【口】我/他将会遭到没完没了的批评[取笑]：*If my Mum finds out, I'll never hear the end of it.* 如果妈妈知道了，她会唠叨个没完。

8 be hearing things to imagine you can hear a sound when really there is no sound 产生幻听：**I must be hearing things** *I must be hearing things, I could have sworn you just called my name.* 我一定是听错了，我刚才明明听见你喊我的名字。

9 (do) you hear me? *spoken* used when you are giving someone an order and want to be certain that they will obey you【口】听见了吗？明白了吗?：*Now you go straight home. You hear me?* 你马上回家去，听见了吗？

10 now hear this! *AmE old use* used to introduce an important official announcement【美，旧】请大家注意听！〔用于正式通告〕

11 you could hear a pin drop used to say that a place was extremely quiet〔安静得〕听得见针落地的声音：*After she finished telling her story you could have heard a pin drop.* 她讲完后，四周安静得连一根针掉在地上的声音都能听见。

12 I can't hear myself think *spoken* used to say that the place where you are is too noisy【口】这里太吵了

13 have you heard the one about... used when asking someone if they know a joke 你听过有关…的笑话吗?：*Have you heard the one about the turtle and the elephant?* 你听过有关乌龟和大象的笑话吗？

14 I've heard that one before *spoken* used when you do not believe someone's excuse or explanation【口】这（借口）我以前已听过了〔表示不相信某人的解释〕：*Kept late at the office, were you? I've heard that one before.* 又是在办公室加班了，是吗？这个借口我以前已听过了。

hear from sb *phr v* [T not in progressive 不用进行式] **1** to receive news from someone, usually by letter〔通常指通过信件〕得到某人的消息：*Have you heard from Sarah lately?* 你最近收到过莎拉的信吗？| **I look forward to hearing from you** (=used at the end of a letter) 盼尽早赐复〔信尾套语〕 **2** to listen to someone giving their opinion in a radio or television discussion programme 听，收听：*And now we are going to hear from some of the victims of violent crime.* 下面我们将听到几位暴力罪行的受害者讲述他们的经历。

hear of sb/sth *phr v* [T] **1 have heard of** to know that someone or something exists because you have been told about them 知道，听说过：*I've never heard of him!* 我从未听说过他！ **2** [not in progressive 不用进行式] to get news or information about someone or something 得到有关某人[事]的消息：**she/he was last heard of** (=the last time people say they saw someone) 最后一次听人说见到她/他 *He was last heard of in Lansing, Michigan in 1935.* 人们最后一次听到他的消息是1935年在密歇根州的兰辛市。—compare 比较 **hear from** (HEAR) —see also 另见 UNHEARD-OF

hear sb **out** *phr v* [T not in passive 不用被动态] to listen to all of what someone wants to tell you without interrupting them 听某人说完：*Look, I know you're angry but you could at least hear me out.* 好了，我知道你很生气，但你起码听我把话讲完吧。

Hear! Hear! /,·'·/ *interjection especially BrE* used in parliament or in a meeting to say that you agree with the person who is speaking【尤英】好哇！好哇！〔在议会或会议上对某人所说的话表示赞同的呼喊声〕

hear·er /ˈhɪrə·; ˈhɪərə/ *n* [C] someone who hears something 听者

S3 W2 **hear·ing** /ˈhɪrɪŋ; ˈhɪərɪŋ/ *n* **1** [U] the sense which you use to hear sounds 听觉：*Speak up, please. My hearing is not too good.* 请大声一点，我的听觉不太好。—see also 另见 HARD OF HEARING **2** [C] a meeting of a court or special committee to find out the facts about a case 听证会；审讯；聆讯 **3 give sb a (fair) hearing** to give someone an opportunity to explain their actions, ideas, or opinions 给某人一个（公平的）解释机会 **4 in/within sb's hearing** if you say something in someone's hearing, you say it where they can hear you 在某人听力所及的范围内：*Don't mention that in John's hearing or he'll go crazy.* 别在约翰听得见的地方提那件事，否则他会很生气的。

hearing aid /'· ·· ,·/ *n* [C] a small thing which fits into or behind your ear to make sounds louder, worn by people who cannot hear well 助听器

hear·ken, harken /ˈhɑrkən; ˈhɑːkən/ *v* [I+to] *literary* to listen【文】倾听

hear·say /ˈhɪr,se; ˈhɪəseɪ/ *n* [U] something that you have heard about from other people but do not know to be definitely true or correct 传闻，道听途说：*I wouldn't take any notice of it, it's just hearsay.* 我不会在意，这只不过是谣言而已。

hearse /hɝs; hɜːs/ *n* [C] a large car used to carry a dead body in a COFFIN at a funeral 灵车

Hearst /hɝst; hɜːst/ **, Wil·liam Ran·dolph** /ˈwɪljəm ˈrændɑlf; ˈwɪljəm ˈrændɒlf/ (1863-1951) a powerful US businessman who owned many popular newspapers 赫斯特〔(1863-1951)，美国实力雄厚的报业主，曾拥有多家大众类报纸〕

heart /hɑrt; hɑːt/ *n* S1 W1

1 ▶BODY ORGAN 人体器官◀ [C] the organ in your chest which pumps blood through your body 心（脏）：*Eating too many fatty foods is bad for the heart.* 吃太多油腻的食物对心脏不好。| *My heart was beating so fast I thought it would burst.* 我的心跳得很快，好像快要炸开了。| **have heart trouble/have a heart condition** (=have problems with your heart) 患心脏病 | **a weak heart** (=an unhealthy heart) 衰弱的心脏 —see picture at 参见 RESPIRATORY 图

2 ▶EMOTIONS/LOVE 感情/爱◀ [C] *especially literary* the part of your body that feels strong emotions and feelings【尤文】内心；心肠；爱心：*My head said no, but my heart kept saying yes.* 我的理智在说"不行"，但我的感情却一直在说"行"。| **affairs of the heart** (=matters connected with love) 与爱情相关的事 | **(deep) in your heart** (=used when saying what someone really feels) 在内心（深处） *She still loved him, deep down in her heart.* 在内心深处，她仍爱着他。| **heart and soul** (=completely) 全心全意地，完全地 *You love the boy heart and soul, don't you?* 你是全心全意地爱这个男孩的，是吗？| **break sb's heart** (=to make someone extremely sad, especially by ending a romantic relationship with them)〔尤指因断绝恋爱关系〕使某人心碎，使某人伤透了心

3 ▶YOUR CHEST 胸部◀ [C usually singular 一般用单数] the part of your chest near your heart 胸口处，心口处：*He put his hand across his heart to show where the pain was.* 他用手按着心口，指出痛楚的地方。

4 ▶SHAPE 形状◀ [C] a shape used to represent a heart 心形 —see picture at 参见 SHAPE[1] 图

> **CULTURAL NOTE 文化注释**
>
> A heart is used to represent the love between a man and a woman. It frequently appears on VALENTINE CARDS which people, especially young unmarried people, send on VALENTINE'S DAY to the man or woman they love or like romantically. 心形用来代表男女之爱情，通常出现在情人节贺卡上。人们，尤其是未婚男女，在情人节那天为自己心仪的对象赠送贺卡。

5 from the heart if you say or mean something from the heart, you really mean it or feel it very strongly 从内心；真心地：*He spoke simply but from the heart.* 他说得很简单，但却是出于真心的。| **from the bottom of my heart** *I want to thank you from the bottom of my heart.* 我衷心地感谢你。| **straight from the heart** *What she said came straight from the heart.* 她说的全是真心话。

6 in your heart of hearts if you know, feel, or believe something in your heart of hearts, you are secretly sure about it although you may not admit it 在心底里，在内心深处：*Claire knew in her heart of hearts that she would never go back there.* 克莱尔从心底里明白她永远不会再回到那儿了。

7 ▶IMPORTANT PART OF STH 重要部分◀ the most important part of a problem, question etc 实质；中心，核心；关键：**get to the heart of the matter/problem/question etc** *The new book gets to the heart of the controversy over nuclear power.* 这本新书论述了有关核能争议的中心问题。

8 ▶THE MIDDLE PART OF AN AREA 某地区的中心◀ [C] the middle of an area 中心（地区）：**in the heart of** *somewhere deep in the heart of Texas* 深入得克萨斯州腹地的某个地方

9 know/learn something by heart to know or learn something so that you can remember all of it 背诵，熟记：*You have to know all the music by heart.* 你必须把乐曲全部背下来。

10 set your heart on to want something very much 非常想得到，渴望得到：*The coach had set his heart on winning.* 教练一心一意希望能够获胜。

11 ▶CARD GAMES 纸牌游戏◀ **a)** [C] a heart shape printed in red on a playing card 红心，红桃 **b) hearts** [plural] the SUIT (=set) of playing cards that have these shapes on them 一套红桃纸牌：*the ace of hearts* 红桃A **c)** [C] one of the cards in this set 一张红桃（纸牌）：*Have you got any hearts?* 你有红桃吗？

12 kind-hearted/cold-hearted/hard-hearted etc having a kind, unkind, cruel etc character 心肠善良的/冷酷的/狠毒的/等

13 have a heart of gold to be very kind 非常仁慈，心地善良
14 have a heart of stone to be very cruel or unsympathetic 铁石心肠
15 a man/woman after my own heart someone who likes the same things or behaves in the same way that you do 喜好[处事]和我相似的[合我心意的]男人/女人: *Geoff was clear-thinking and decisive – a man after my own heart.* 杰夫是个思路清晰、行动果断的人，正合我心意。
16 at heart if you are a particular kind of person at heart, that is the kind of person that you really are 本质上，心底里；实际上: *I've always been a country boy at heart.* 我实质上一直是个乡下男孩。—see also 另见 **have sb's (best) interests at heart** (INTEREST[1] (5)), **young at heart** (YOUNG[1] (4))
17 close/dear to sb's heart very important to someone 为某人所爱/关注；对某人非常重要
18 my/his/her heart leapt *literary* used to say that someone suddenly felt happy and full of hope【文】我/他/她的心中突然充满了希望
19 my/his etc heart sank used to say that someone suddenly lost hope and began to feel sad 我/他等的心突然一沉〔指感到失望〕: *Our hearts sank when we heard the results of the voting.* 听到投票结果后，我们的心沉了下来。
20 my heart was in my mouth used to say that you suddenly felt very afraid 我突然感到很害怕；我的心都快跳出来了
21 my heart bleeds (for sb) used to say that you do not really feel any sympathy towards someone 我并不同情某人: *"He's had to sell his Ferrari." "My heart bleeds for him."* "他不得不卖掉了他的法拉利跑车。""我一点也不可怜他。"
22 my/his/her heart goes out to sb used to say that someone feels a lot of sympathy towards another person 我/他/她非常同情某人
23 my/his/her heart isn't in it used to say that someone does not really want to do something 我/他/她的心不在此事上〔指并非衷心想做某事〕: *I tried to join in the fun, but somehow my heart wasn't in it.* 我试着和他们一起玩，但不知怎么却心不在焉。
24 not have the heart to do something to be unable to do something because it will make someone unhappy 不忍心做某事: *I didn't have the heart to tell my daughter we couldn't keep the puppy.* 我真不忍心告诉女儿我们不能养那只小狗。
25 be in good heart *formal* to feel cheerful and confident【正式】情绪高昂: *Our troops are in good heart and ready for action.* 我们的部队士气高昂，准备迎接战斗。
26 take heart to feel encouraged 鼓起勇气，有了信心，受到鼓舞: *We took heart when we saw the sign, knowing that we were close to home.* 看到路标时我们都振作起来，因为知道马上就要到家了。
27 take sth to heart to be very upset by something that someone says or does to you 把某事放在心上，为某事心烦意乱: *Don't take her criticisms so much to heart.* 别太把她的批评放在心上。
28 do sth to your heart's content to do something as much as you want 痛快地[尽情地]做某事: *After I leave, Joe can sing in the shower to his heart's content.* 我走后，乔可以在淋浴时尽情地唱歌了。
29 it does your heart good to see/hear used to say that something makes you feel happy 很高兴看到/听到: *It does my heart good to see him running around again.* 看到他又能四处跑来跑去，我感到很高兴。
30 have a heart! *often humorous* used to tell someone not to be too strict or unkind【常幽默】发发善心吧！做做好事吧！
31 with all your heart with all your strength, energy or emotion 全心全意地，真心实意地: *Ben hated school with all his heart.* 本从心里痛恨上学。
32 have your heart's desire/have everything your heart could desire to get everything that you could possibly want 心想事成，要什么有什么
33 know the way to sb's heart *humorous* to know the way to please someone【幽默】知道如何讨好某人: *What a great meal! You certainly know the way to a man's heart!* 这顿饭棒极了！你太懂如何讨好男人的心了！
34 ►VEGETABLE 蔬菜◄ [C] the firm middle part of some vegetables〔某些菜的〕实心: *artichoke hearts* 洋蓟心
35 his/her heart is in the right place *informal* used to say that someone is really a kind person, even though they may not appear to be【非正式】他/她的心地还是善良的: *He's a little grouchy sometimes, but his heart's in the right place.* 他有时有点脾气不好，但心地还是善良的。—see also 另见 **a broken heart** (BROKEN[2] (10)), **cross my heart** (CROSS[1] (10)), **eat your heart out** (EAT (2)), **change of heart** (CHANGE[2] (1)), **sick at heart** (SICK[1] (9)), **strike at the heart of** (STRIKE[1] (9)), **wear your heart on your sleeve** (WEAR[1] (10)), **win sb's heart** (WIN[1] (3)), **with a heavy heart** (HEAVY[1] (25))

heart·ache /ˈhɑrtˌek; ˈhɑːteɪk/ *n* [U] a strong feeling of great sadness and anxiety 痛心，伤心

heart at·tack /ˈ· ·ˌ·/ *n* [C] a sudden serious medical condition in which someone's heart stops working, causing them great pain 心脏病发作

heart·beat /ˈhɑrtˌbit; ˈhɑːtbiːt/ *n* [C,U] the action or sound of your heart as it pumps blood through your body 心跳，心搏: *the amount of blood pumped by each heartbeat* 每次心跳的泵血量

heart·break /ˈhɑrtˌbrek; ˈhɑːtbreɪk/ *n* [U] great sadness or disappointment 心碎，悲伤；极度失望

heart·break·ing /ˈhɑrtˌbrekɪŋ; ˈhɑːtˌbreɪkɪŋ/ *adj* making you feel extremely sad or disappointed 使人心碎[悲伤；极度失望]的: *heartbreaking pictures of starving children* 令人心碎的饥饿儿童的图片 —**heartbreakingly** *adv*

heart·brok·en /ˈhɑrtˌbrokən; ˈhɑːtˌbrəʊkən/ *adj* extremely sad because of something that has happened 极度伤心的，心碎的，悲伤的: *When her parents split up she was heartbroken.* 父母离婚时，她感到很伤心。

heart·burn /ˈhɑrtˌbɝn; ˈhɑːtbɜːn/ *n* [U] an unpleasant burning feeling in your stomach or chest caused by INDIGESTION〔消化不良引起的〕胃灼热，烧心

heart dis·ease /ˈ· ·ˌ·/ *n* [C,U] an illness which prevents someone's heart from working normally 心脏病

heart·en /ˈhɑrtn̩; ˈhɑːtn/ *v* [T usually passive 一般用被动态] to make someone feel happier and more hopeful 使高兴；使振作，鼓舞: *I was heartened by the news that the operation had been a success.* 手术成功的消息使我感到很高兴。—**heartening** *adj* —**hearteningly** *adv* —opposite 反义词 DISHEARTEN

heart fail·ure /ˈ· ˌ··/ *n* [U] a serious medical condition in which someone's heart stops, often resulting in death 心力衰竭，心脏停跳

heart·felt /ˈhɑrtˌfɛlt; ˈhɑːtfelt/ *adj* very strongly felt and sincere 衷心的，诚挚的: *a heartfelt apology* 真诚的道歉

hearth /hɑrθ; hɑːθ/ *n* [C] **1** the area of floor around a FIREPLACE in a house 壁炉前的地板，壁炉边 **2 hearth and home** *literary* your home and family【文】温暖的家（庭）: *the joys of hearth and home* 温暖快乐的家庭生活

heart·i·ly /ˈhɑrtlɪ; ˈhɑːtɪli/ *adv* **1** loudly and cheerfully 开怀地: *He laughed heartily and embraced his brother.* 他开怀大笑，拥抱他的兄弟。**2** completely or very much 完全地；十分地: **heartily agree/approve of/support etc** *a sentiment with which she heartily agreed* 她完全认同的一种感情 | **heartily fed up with/sick of** *By the end we were heartily fed up with the whole thing.* 到最后我们都给这件事烦死了。**3 eat/drink heartily** to eat or drink a large amount 大吃/大喝

heart·land /ˈhɑrtlænd; ˈhɑːtlænd/ *n* [C] **1 the heartland** the central part of a country or area of land 腹地，心脏地带，中心区域: *in the Russian heartland* 在俄罗斯的心脏地带 **2** the most important part of a country or area for a particular activity, or the part where a political group has most support〔一国某项活动的〕最重要地区；〔某政党占优势的〕中心地区: *the Democratic heartlands of the Deep South* 民主党占优势的南方腹地

heart·less /ˈhɑrtlɪs; ˈhɑːtləs/ *adj* not feeling any pity 无情的，冷酷的: *How can you be so heartless?* 你怎么能如此无情呢? —**heartlessly** *adv* —**heartlessness** *n* [U]

heart-lung ma·chine /ˌ·ˈ· ·ˌ·/ *n* [C] a machine that pumps blood and oxygen around someone's body during a medical operation〔手术时用来维持血液和氧气供应的〕人工心肺机

Heart of Dark·ness /ˌ· · ˈ··/ (1902) a book by Joseph Conrad in which the main character, Marlow, travels on a river through Africa until he meets Kurtz, an educated white man who has stopped accepting Western values and has become the violent, powerful ruler of an African community《黑暗的心》〔(1902)，约瑟夫·康拉德的作品。书中的主人公马娄乘船在非洲漫游时遇到了库尔茨。库尔茨是个有文化的白人，但已不再接受西方的价值观，当上了非洲某一社会的首领，性情残暴，不可一世〕

Heart of En·gland, the /ˌ· · ˈ··/ the central area of England, which is very industrial 英格兰的心脏〔指英格兰中部地区，工业化程度较高〕

heart·rend·ing /ˈhɑrtˌrɛndɪŋ; ˈhɑːtˌrendɪŋ/ *adj* making you feel great pity 使人极度怜悯的；令人悲痛的: *heartrending stories of children being taken from their parents* 关于孩子被人从父母身边夺走的令人心酸的故事

heart-search·ing /ˈ· ˌ··/ *n* [U] the process of examining very carefully your feelings about something or your reasons for doing something 内省，反省

heart·sick /ˈhɑrtˌsɪk; ˈhɑːtˌsɪk/ *adj* very unhappy or disappointed 闷闷不乐的, 忧伤的, 沮丧的

heart·strings /ˈhɑrtˌstrɪŋz; ˈhɑːtˌstrɪŋz/ *n* [plural] **tug/tear at sb's heartstrings** to make someone feel strong love or sympathy 牵动某人的心弦〔使人感动或同情〕

heart·throb /ˈhɑrtˌθrɑb; ˈhɑːtθrɒb/ *n* [C] a famous actor, singer etc who is very attractive to women 使〔女性〕着迷的歌星[影星等], 心仪的对象: *teenage heartthrobs 'Take That'* 让青少年着迷的"接招"乐队

heart-to-heart /ˌ· · ˈ·◄/ *n* [C] a conversation in which two people say honestly and sincerely what they really feel about something 贴心的谈话, 坦率的谈心: *Why don't you have a heart-to-heart with him and sort out your problems?* 你为什么不和他坦诚地谈谈, 把问题解决掉呢? —**heart-to-heart** *adj*

heart·warm·ing /ˈhɑrtˌwɔrmɪŋ; ˈhɑːtˌwɔːmɪŋ/ *adj* making you feel happy because you see other people being happy or kind to each other 暖人心房的, 温馨感人的: *a heartwarming sight* 感人的场面 —**heartwarmingly** *adv*

heart·wood /ˈhɑrtˌwud; ˈhɑːtwʊd/ *n* [U] the older harder wood at the centre of a tree〔树干中心的〕心材

heart·y /ˈhɑrtɪ; ˈhɑːti/ *adj* **1** cheerfully friendly 热情友好的: *a hearty laugh* 开怀大笑 **2** *old-fashioned* strong and healthy【过时】健壮的 —see also 另见 **hale and hearty** (HALE) **3** a hearty meal is very large〔饭菜〕丰盛的 **4** *especially BrE* with a friendly, noisy and cheerful manner that is not sincere【尤英】假装开心友好的 —**heartiness** *n* [U] —see also 另见 HEARTILY

S2 W2 **heat**[1] /hit; hiːt/ *n*

1 [U] warmth or hotness 热, 热量, 热力: *The heat of the water caused the glass to shatter.* 水把玻璃杯烫裂了。| *Black surfaces absorb heat from the sun.* 黑色的表面吸收阳光的热量。

2 the heat a) very hot weather 酷暑, 炎热的天气: *I couldn't stand the heat.* 我无法忍受炎热的天气。| **the heat of the day** (=the hottest part of the day) 一天中最热的时候 **b)** *AmE* the system in a house that keeps it warm in the winter【美】供暖系统, 暖气设备; HEATING *BrE*【英】

3 [C usually singular 一般用单数] the hot temperature of an OVEN or a heating system〔烤箱或暖气设备的〕高温, 温度: *When the oven reaches the correct heat, the light goes off.* 烤箱达到所需温度时, 灯就会熄灭。| **turn up/turn down the heat** *She turned up the heat on the cooker.* 她调高了炉子的温度。

4 in the heat of the moment/argument/battle etc while feeling angry or excited 在最关键/辩论最激烈/战斗最激烈等的时刻: *In the heat of the argument I said a few things I regret now.* 在争论最激烈的时刻, 我说了一些令我现在感到后悔不已的话。

5 take the heat out of the situation to make a situation calmer and make people less angry and excited 使局面冷静[缓和]下来

6 the heat is on/off *spoken* used to say that a situation is very difficult, or that a difficult situation has now ended and you can relax【口】形势十分严峻/已经趋于平稳

7 on heat also 又作 **in heat** *AmE*【美】if a female animal is on heat, her body is ready to have sex with a male〔雌性动物〕发情

8 ▶IN A RACE 在比赛中◀ [C] a part of a race or competition whose winners then compete against each other in the next part 分组赛, 预赛 —see also 另见 DEAD HEAT, WHITE HEAT

heat[2] *v* [I,T] to make something become warm or hot 加热, 使变热: *Heat the milk until it boils.* 把牛奶煮开。

heat up *phr v* **1** [I,T] to become warm or hot or to make something become warm or hot (使)变热, (把…)加热: **heat sth ↔ up** *I heated up the remains of last night's supper.* 我把昨天晚饭剩下的饭菜热了一下。| **heat up** *The stove takes a while to heat up.* 炉子要过一会儿才能热起来。**2** [I] if a situation heats up, it becomes dangerous or full of problems〔形势〕激化, 加剧

heat sth **through** *phr v* [T] to heat food thoroughly 充分加热〔食物〕

heat·ed /ˈhitɪd; ˈhiːtɪ̈d/ *adj* **1** a heated SWIMMING POOL, room etc is made warm using a heater〔人工〕加热的; 有暖气的 **2 heated argument/debate/discussion etc** an argument etc that is full of angry and excited feelings 激烈的争论/辩论/讨论等 —**heatedly** *adv*

heat·er /ˈhitə; ˈhiːtə/ *n* [C] a machine for making air or water hotter 加热器; 暖气机; 暖炉: *Did you turn the heater off?* 你关掉加热器了吗? —see picture on page A2 参见 A2 页图

heat ex·haus·tion /ˈ· ·ˌ··/ *n* [U] weakness and sickness caused by doing too much work, exercise etc when it is hot 热衰竭, 中暑衰竭

heath /hiθ; hiːθ/ *n* [C] an area of open land where grass, bushes, and other small plants grow〔杂草和灌木丛生的〕荒野, 荒原

Heath, Sir Edward (1916-) a British politician in the Conservative Party, who was Prime Minister from 1970 to 1974. He disagreed with Margaret Thatcher, who followed him as Conservative leader, and supported the European Union and the idea of a single European CURRENCY (=system of money). 希思〔(1916-), 英国保守党政治家, 1970 至 1974 年间任英国首相。他与继任的保守党领导人玛格丽特·撒切尔政见相左, 支持欧盟和欧洲单一货币的构想〕

Heath·cliff /ˈhiθklɪf; ˈhiːθklɪf/ one of the main characters in the book *Wuthering Heights* (1847) by Emily Brontë. He is an attractive, proud, and often angry man with very strong emotions. He loves Catherine Earnshaw and she loves him, but they are prevented from marrying. As a result, he decides to punish the other members of her family because he believes that they are responsible for his unhappy life. 希斯克利夫〔埃米莉·勃朗特的小说《呼啸山庄》(1847) 的主人公之一。他英俊、骄傲、易怒、感情强烈。他与凯萨琳·厄恩肖相互爱慕, 但婚事遇阻。于是, 他决意要惩罚凯萨琳的家人, 在他看来自己不幸福的生活是他们造成的〕

hea·then[1] /ˈhiðən; ˈhiːðən/ *adj old-fashioned* not connected with or belonging to the Christian religion or any of the large established religions【过时】〔不信奉基督教等主要宗教的〕异教徒的

heathen[2] *n old use*【旧】**1 the heathen** *old-fashioned* people who are heathen【过时】异教徒〔总称〕**2** [C] *old-fashioned* someone who is heathen【过时】异教徒 **3** [singular] *often humorous* someone who refuses to believe in something【常幽默】无信仰的人

CULTURAL NOTE 文化注释

This word was used especially in the 19th century when Britain was building its EMPIRE. When British companies went to countries in the Empire to get cheap goods, missionaries (MISSIONARY) went to teach Christianity to the heathen, people they thought of as either wicked or not knowing about the right ways to behave 该词尤用于19世纪英国正处于帝国的形成扩张阶段。随着英国公司去英帝国国家获取廉价货物, 传教士也去那里向异教徒传播基督教, 在他们眼中异教徒要么邪恶要么不懂规矩: *They went out to Africa to convert the heathen.* 他们去非洲感化那里的异教徒。

heath·er /ˈhɛðə; ˈheðə/ *n* [U] a low plant with small purple, pink, or white flowers which grows on hills〔开紫色、粉红色或白色花的〕石南属灌木

CULTURAL NOTE 文化注释

People connect heather with Scotland where the mountainsides are purple with heather in the autumn. White heather is said to be lucky and gypsies (GYPSY) sometimes try to sell it. 石楠属灌木常与苏格兰联系在一起, 那里一到秋天山坡上满是紫色的石楠属灌木开的花。白色石楠花据说会带来好运, 吉普赛人有时会设法兜售这些花。

Heath Rob·in·son /ˌhiθ ˈrɑbɪnsn; ˌhiːθ ˈrɒbɪ̈nsən/ *adj BrE* a Heath Robinson machine, system etc is very complicated in an amusing way but not at all practical【英】〔机械、系统等〕设计精巧但却可笑而不实用的; RUBE GOLDBERG *AmE*【美】

Heath·row Air·port /ˌhiθro ˈɛrport; ˌhiːθrəʊ ˈeəpɔːt/ also 又作 **Heathrow** an international airport in London. Heathrow is the largest airport in the UK, and it is 20 miles to the west of London. 希思罗机场〔伦敦一国际机场, 是英国最大的机场, 位于伦敦以西 20 英里处〕

heat·ing /ˈhitɪŋ; ˈhiːtɪŋ/ *n* [U] *BrE* a system for making a room or building warm【英】供暖系统, 暖气设备; the heat *AmE*【美】: *a huge heating bill* 一笔高昂的暖气费 —see also 另见 CENTRAL HEATING S2

heat light·ning /ˈ· ˌ··/ *n* [U] *especially AmE* LIGHTNING[1] (1) without THUNDER or rain【尤美】〔不伴有雷声或降雨的〕热闪电

heat·proof /ˈhitpruf; ˈhiːtpruːf/ *adj* heatproof material cannot be damaged by heat 耐热的, 耐高温的; 隔热的

heat pump /ˈ· ·/ *n* [C] part of a machine that takes heat from one place to another 热泵

heat rash /ˈ· ·/ *n* [C,U] painful or ITCHY red spots on someone's skin caused by heat〔皮肤上的〕痱子

heat-re·sist·ant /ˈ· ·ˌ··/ *adj* not easily damaged by heat 抗热的, 耐热的

heat-seek·ing /ˈ· ˌ··/ *adj* a heat-seeking weapon is able to find and move towards the hot gases from an aircraft or ROCKET

and destroy it〔武器〕装有热跟踪装置的，热跟踪的〔指跟踪飞机、火箭等排出的热气〕

heat·stroke /ˈhitˌstrok; ˈhiːtstrəʊk/ *n* [U] fever and weakness caused by being outside in the heat of the sun for too long 中暑 —compare 比较 SUNSTROKE

heat wave /ˈ· ·/ *n* [C] a period of unusually hot weather, especially one that continues for a long time 一段非常炎热的时期，热浪期

heave[1] /hiv; hiːv/ *v* **1** [I,T] to pull or lift something very heavy with one great effort〔用很大力气〕拉；举，抬：**heave sth onto/into/towards etc** *He heaved the pack up onto his back.* 他使劲地将包背到了背上。| *We heaved with all our strength but couldn't shift the old piano.* 我们用尽了全力，但那架旧钢琴却纹丝不动。| **heave at/on sth** *He heaved on the rope with all his strength.* 他用尽全力拉动绳子。**2** [T] to throw something heavy using a lot of effort〔用力〕扔，抛〔重物〕**3 heave a sigh** to breathe out noisily and slowly once, because you are pleased or disappointed 长长地舒[叹]了一口气：*She heard him heave a great sigh and then saw that he was crying.* 她听见他长长地叹了一口气，然后就看见他哭了。| **heave a sigh of relief** *Paolo heaved a great sigh of relief when he heard that she had returned.* 听说她已经回来了，保罗宽慰地舒了一口气。**4** [I] if the sea or someone's chest heaves, it moves up and down with very strong movements 起伏：*Brigg's chest was heaving with exhaustion.* 布里格累得直喘气，胸脯不停地起伏着。**5** [I] *informal* to VOMIT[1]【非正式】呕吐 **6 heave into sight/view** *past tense and past participle* **hove** to appear, especially by getting closer from a distance 逐渐进入视线：*A few moments later a barge hove into view.* 过了一会儿，一艘大驳船在眼前出现了。—see also 另见 HEAVING

heave to *phr v past tense* **hove to** /ˌhov ˈtu; ˌhəʊv ˈtuː/ [I] *technical* if a ship heaves to, it stops moving【术语】〔船只〕停止移动

heave[2] *n* **1** [C] a strong pulling, pushing, or lifting movement〔猛力的〕拉；推；举：*He gave the door a good heave.* 他用力推了一下门。**2** [U] *literary* a strong rising or falling movement【文】起伏

heave-ho /ˌ· ˈ·/ *interjection* **1** *old-fashioned* used as an encouragement to a person or group of people who are pulling something, especially on ships【过时】用力拉啊〔尤指在船上拉东西时所喊的号子〕**2 give someone the (old) heave-ho** *informal* to end a relationship with someone, or to make someone leave their job【非正式】与某人断绝关系；解雇某人

3 **heav·en** /ˈhɛvən; ˈhevən/ *n* **1** also 又作 **Heaven** [singular] the place where God is believed to live and where good people are believed to go when they die 天堂，天国，极乐世界 **2** [U] *informal* a very good situation or place【非正式】极好的情况[地方]：**sheer heaven** (=perfect heaven) 绝妙的事 *It was sheer heaven being able to stay in bed all day!* 能整天躺在床上真是件绝妙的事情。| **heaven on earth** *I had imagined that being married to Max would be heaven on earth.* 我曾经幻想嫁给马克斯能让我过上天堂般美好的日子。**3 for heaven's sake** *spoken*【口】**a)** used to show that you are annoyed or angry 天哪！哎呀！〔表示厌烦或生气〕：*Oh, for heaven's sake! Do they have to make so much noise?* 啊，天哪！他们非得这么大声吗？**b)** used to emphasize a question or request 看在上帝的份上〔强调问题或要求〕：For *heaven's sake don't tell Simon about this!* 看在上帝的份上，不要把这件事告诉西蒙！**4 heaven forbid** *spoken* used to say that you very much hope something will not happen【口】但愿不要这样，但愿不会：*"Will your parents be coming to the party?" "Heaven forbid!"* "你父母会来参加聚会吗？""但愿不会！" **5 heaven help** *spoken*【口】**a)** used to say that you will be very angry with someone if they do something 饶不了〔某人〕：*Heaven help him if he ever comes back here again!* 要是他回到这里来，我一定饶不了他。**b)** used to say that it is dangerous to do something 愿上天保佑〔表示做某事很危险〕：*Heaven help anyone who goes in there at night.* 谁要是在夜里去那儿，就只能盼老天爷保佑了。**6 heaven (only) knows** *spoken*【口】**a)** used to say that you do not know and cannot imagine what is happening or what will happen 天晓得，谁知道：*We used to keep in touch, but heaven knows what they're all doing now.* 我们曾经保持联系，但天晓得他们现在在干些什么。**b)** used to emphasize what you are saying 确实，的确，无疑〔用以加强语气〕：*I just couldn't get him to stop gambling although heaven knows I tried hard enough.* 我确实努力劝过他，但还是无法使他放弃赌博。**7 what/how/why etc in heaven's name** *spoken* used when asking a surprised and angry question【口】到底[究竟]什么/怎么/为什么等：*What in heaven's name did you think you were doing?* 你到底在干什么？**8 the heavens** *literary* the sky【文】天空 **9 the heavens opened** *especially literary* it started to rain very hard【尤文】下起倾盆大雨来 **10 move heaven and earth** to try very hard to achieve something 竭尽全力，用尽各种方法 —see also 另见 **be in seventh heaven** (SEVENTH (2)), **thank heavens** (THANK (2))

CULTURAL NOTE 文化注释

People in the US and UK often think about Heaven as a place in the sky where God lives with the ANGELS, who wear long white dresses and play musical instruments called HARPS. When someone dies, people imagine that they go to the entrance of Heaven, known as the Pearly Gates. Saint Peter stands by the gates holding the keys, and asks the dead person questions to find out whether they were good or bad during their life. If they have been good, they go up to Heaven. If they have been bad, they go down to HELL. 英美人常认为天堂在天上某个地方，那里住着上帝和天使。天使穿着白色的长服，演奏竖琴。人们想象死去的人会来到天堂入口，称"珍珠之门"。圣彼得手持钥匙站在那里，向来人提问，以确定他生前是善是恶。善人上天堂，恶人则下地狱。— see Cultural Note at HELL 见 HELL 文化注释

heav·en·ly /ˈhɛvənlɪ; ˈhevənli/ *adj* **1** *old-fashioned* very beautiful, pleasant, or enjoyable【过时】极好的；非常美丽的；令人非常愉快的：*What heavenly weather!* 多好的天气啊！**2** [only before noun 仅用于名词前] *biblical* existing in or belonging to heaven【圣经】天堂的，天国的：*a heavenly choir of angels* 天使圣诗班 | **heavenly Father** (=God) 上帝，天父 | **the Heavenly Host** (=all the angels)〔所有的〕天使，众天使 **3** *literary* existing in or connected with the sky or stars【文】天体的；天空的

heavenly bod·y /ˌ··· ˈ··/ *n* [C] a star, PLANET or the moon 天体

Heavenly Twins, the /ˌ··· ˈ·/ —see 见 CASTOR AND POLLUX

Heav·ens! /ˈhɛvənz; ˈhevənz/ also 又作 **Good Heavens!, Heavens a·bove!**, /ˌ·· · ˈ·/ also 又作 **Heavens to Bet·sy!** /ˌhɛvənz tə ˈbɛtsɪ; ˌhevənz tə ˈbetsi/ *AmE*【美】—*interjection* used to express surprise, especially when you are annoyed 天哪！我的天！〔表示恼人的惊讶〕：*Good Heavens what a mess!* 天哪！多乱呀！

heaven-sent /ˌ·· ˈ·◂/ *adj* happening fortunately at exactly the right time 天赐的；最合时宜的：*a heaven-sent opportunity* 天赐良机

heav·en·ward /ˈhɛvənwəd; ˈhevənwəd/ also 又作 **heav·en·wards** /-wədz; -wədz/ *adv literary* towards the sky【文】向天上，朝天空

heav·ily /ˈhɛvɪlɪ; ˈhevəli/ *adv* 3

1 ►A LOT/IN LARGE AMOUNTS 很多/大量◄ a lot or in large amounts 很多地，大量地：*It's been raining heavily all day.* 大雨已经下了整整一天了。| **drink/smoke heavily** *Paul was drinking heavily by this time.* 这时保罗已喝了很多酒。

2 ►VERY 非常◄ very or very much 很大程度上；非常：**heavily dependent/reliant/influenced** *Japan is heavily dependent on imported oil from the Middle East.* 日本严重依赖从中东进口的石油。

3 ►SLEEP 睡眠◄ if you sleep heavily, you cannot be woken easily 沉沉地：*Joe slept heavily for eight hours.* 乔酣睡了八小时。

4 breathe heavily to breathe slowly and loudly 喘粗气

5 heavily built having a large broad body that looks strong〔身材〕粗壮的，强壮的

6 be heavily into *informal* to do something a lot or be very interested in it【非正式】对…非常着迷：*Brenda's heavily into motorbikes.* 布伦达对摩托车着了迷。

7 ►SLOWLY 缓慢地◄ if you do or say something heavily, you do it slowly, especially because you are sad or bored〔尤指因伤心或无聊而〕缓慢地〔说或做〕：*He was walking heavily, his head down.* 他低着头，拖着沉重的步伐走着。

hea·ving /ˈhivɪŋ; ˈhiːvɪŋ/ *adj BrE informal* very busy or full of people【英，非正式】热闹的；繁忙的；拥挤的：**[+with]** *The place was heaving with showbiz types.* 这个地方到处都是娱乐圈里的人。

heav·y[1] /ˈhɛvɪ; ˈhevi/ *adj* **heavier, heaviest**

1 ►WEIGHT 重量◄ weighing a lot 重的，沉重的：*I can't lift this case – it's too heavy.* 我提不起这只箱子，太重了。| *The baby seemed to be getting heavier and heavier in her arms.* 她手里抱着的婴儿好像变得越来越重了。| **how heavy?** (=how much does it weigh) 多重？*How heavy is the parcel?* 这个包裹有多重？—opposite 反义词 LIGHT[2] (4)

2 ►A LOT 许多◄ a lot or in very large amounts 很多的, 大量的: *The traffic was heavier than normal and I was late for work.* 交通异常拥挤, 结果我上班迟到了。| **heavy rain/snow** *flooding caused by heavy rain over the weekend* 周末大雨引发的洪水泛滥 | **heavy use/consumption** *the film's heavy use of special effects* 影片大量采用的特技效果

3 heavy smoker/drinker someone who smokes a lot or drinks a lot of alcohol 大量抽烟/喝酒的人

4 ►SERIOUS/SEVERE 严重的/严厉的◄ serious or severe 严重的, 严厉的: *heavy winter storms* 冬天猛烈的暴风雨 | *a heavy burden of responsibility* 沉重的责任 | **heavy fine/penalty** *heavy fines for possession of hard drugs* 对藏有硬性毒品的巨额罚款 | **a heavy cold** (=a very bad cold) 重感冒 *She's in bed with a heavy cold.* 她因重感冒而卧床不起。| **heavy losses** *Most insurance companies suffered heavy losses last year.* 大多数保险公司去年都遭受严重亏损。

5 ►NEEDING PHYSICAL EFFORT 费力的◄ needing a lot of physical strength and effort 繁重的, 费力的: *heavy manual work* 繁重的体力劳动

6 ►NEEDING MENTAL EFFORT 费神的◄ not easy or entertaining and needing a lot of mental effort 费神的, 费脑力的: *I want something to read on holiday – nothing too heavy.* 我想找一本假期里看的书, 要轻松点的。

7 heavy going difficult to understand or deal with 难懂的; 难办的: **find sth heavy going** *I found Balzac's books pretty heavy going.* 我觉得巴尔扎克的书很难懂。

8 be heavy on *informal* to use a lot or too much of something【非正式】大量消耗[使用]: *The car's rather heavy on oil.* 这辆汽车的耗油量很大。

9 heavy schedule/timetable/day etc one in which you have a lot to do in a short time 紧张[工作繁重]的日程/时间表/一天等: *I'd had a heavy day at the office.* 我今天在办公室过了非常忙碌的一天。

10 heavy sleeper someone who does not wake easily 不易醒的人, 睡得很沉的人

11 heavy breathing breathing that is slow and loud 沉重的呼吸, 喘粗气 —see also 另见 HEAVY BREATHER

12 make heavy weather of sth *BrE* to make something that you are doing seem more difficult or complicated than it really is【英】把某事弄得比实际困难, 对某事小题大做: *All Nick had to do was reorganize the files but he was making heavy weather of it.* 尼克所要做的只是重新整理一下档案, 但他却小题大做。

13 ►CLOTHES ETC 衣物等◄ clothes, jewellery, or shoes that are heavy are large, thick, and solid〔衣物〕厚重的;〔首饰〕粗重的: *a heavy winter coat* 一件冬天穿的厚大衣

14 ►BODY/FACE 身材/脸◄ having a large, broad, or thick appearance that is unattractive〔身材〕粗壮的;〔五官〕粗糙的: *a large, heavy-featured woman* 一个高大的、浓眉大眼的女人 | **heavy build** (=a large broad body) 身材粗壮的

15 ►WITH FORCE 用力◄ hitting something or falling with a lot of force or weight 用力的, 重重的: *the sound of heavy footsteps in the hall* 大厅里沉重的脚步声 | *Ali caught him with a heavy blow to the jaw.* 阿里给了他的下巴一记重拳。

16 heavy silence/atmosphere a situation in which people feel sad, anxious, or embarrassed 令人心情沉重的寂静/沉重的气氛: *A heavy silence fell upon the room.* 屋子里顿时陷入沉重的寂静之中。

17 heavy sky/clouds looking dark and grey as though it will soon rain 阴沉的天空/密布的乌云

18 heavy seas sea with big waves 波浪汹涌的大海: *The ship went down in heavy seas off the coast of Scotland.* 船在苏格兰沿海波涛汹涌的大海中沉没了。

19 ►FOOD 食物◄ solid and making your stomach feel full and uncomfortable 难消化的: *a heavy meal* 一顿不好消化的饭菜 | *heavy fruitcake* 不易消化的水果蛋糕

20 ►GROUND 地面◄ a) soil that is heavy is thick and solid〔土壤〕黏重的 **b)** a sports ground or race track that is heavy is muddy〔运动场地、跑道〕泥泞的: *The going is heavy at Epsom today.* 埃普瑟姆的场地今天很泥泞。

21 ►SMELL 气味◄ strong and usually sweet 浓烈的: *a heavy fragrance* 浓浓的香味 | **be heavy with a scent/fragrance/smell** *The garden was heavy with the scent of summer.* 花园里满是夏日浓郁的芳香。

22 be heavy with fruit/blossom etc *literary* if trees are heavy with fruit etc they have a lot of fruit etc on them【文】果实累累/鲜花满枝等

23 ►AIR 空气◄ unpleasantly warm and not at all fresh because there is no wind 闷热的: *the damp heavy atmosphere of the rainforest* 雨林中潮湿闷热的空气

24 heavy irony/sarcasm remarks that very clearly say the opposite of what you really feel 辛辣的讽刺/嘲笑

25 with a heavy heart *literary* feeling very sad【文】心情沉重地, 悲伤地: *It was with a heavy heart that Kate kissed her children goodbye.* 凯特怀着沉重的心情跟她的孩子们一一吻别。

26 ►RELATIONSHIP 关系◄ *informal* involving serious or strong emotions【非正式】感情深的, 感情认真的: *She didn't want things to get too heavy at such an early stage in their relationship.* 她不希望他们的感情在交往初期发展得太深。

27 heavy date *AmE usually humorous* a very important DATE with a BOYFRIEND or GIRLFRIEND【美, 一般幽默】〔男女朋友间的〕重要约会

28 ►SERIOUS/WORRYING 严重的/令人担忧的◄ *slang* a situation that is heavy makes you feel that people are very angry or have very strong feelings【俚】〔形势〕严峻的, 令人担忧的, 令人不安的

29 ►GUNS/WEAPONS 枪炮/武器◄ [only before noun 仅用于名词前] large and powerful 重型的: *tanks and heavy weaponry* 坦克和重型武器

30 have a heavy foot *AmE informal* to drive too fast【美, 非正式】开快车, 超速驾驶 —**heaviness** *n* [U]

heavy² *adv* **time hangs/lies heavy on your hands** if time hangs or lies heavy on your hands, it seems to pass slowly because you are bored or have nothing to do 时间过得很慢/度日如年

heavy³ *n* [C] **1** [usually plural 一般用复数] *informal* a large strong man who is paid to protect someone or to threaten other people【非正式】打手, 保镖 **2** a serious male character in a play or film, especially a bad character; VILLAIN (1)〔戏剧或电影中的〕严肃的角色〔尤指男性反派人物〕**3 the heavies** *BrE* large, serious newspapers【英】大型的严肃报纸

heavy breath·er /ˌ‥ˈ‥/ *n* [C] a man who calls a woman on the telephone and does not speak, but breathes loudly, in order to get sexual pleasure 浊重呼吸者〔在电话中不说话、对女性喘粗气进行性骚扰的男子〕—**heavy breathing** *n* [U]

heavy cream /ˌ‥ˈ‥/ *n* [U] *AmE* thick cream【美】浓稠乳脂; DOUBLE CREAM *BrE*【英】

heavy-du·ty /ˌ‥ˈ‥◂/ *adj* **1** heavy duty materials are strong and thick and not easily damaged〔材料〕耐用的, 厚实的: *heavy-duty canvas* 耐久的帆布 **2** heavy-duty machines or equipment are designed to be used for very hard work〔机器〕重型的, 干重活的 **3** *especially AmE informal* very serious, complicated, or involving strong emotions【尤美, 非正式】〔感情〕深的, 认真的: *a heavy-duty affair* 认真的恋情

heavy goods ve·hi·cle /ˌ‥ˈ‥ˌ‥/ *n* [C] an HGV 大型货运卡车, 重型卡车

heavy-hand·ed /ˌ‥ˈ‥◂/ *adj* done without thinking about other people's feelings 粗暴的; 严厉的; 高压的: *a heavy-handed style of management* 高压的管理方式 —**heavy-handedly** *adv* —**heavy-handedness** *n* [U]

heavy-heart·ed /ˌ‥ˈ‥◂/ *adj literary* very sad【文】心情沉重的

heavy hit·ter /ˌ‥ˈ‥/ *n* [C] *AmE*【美】**1** someone who has a lot of power, especially in business or politics〔尤指商界或政界〕举足轻重的人物, 有权势的人物, 大亨 **2** a BASEBALL player who hits the ball very hard〔棒球〕强击手

heavy in·dus·try /ˌ‥ˈ‥ˌ‥/ *n* [U] industry that produces large goods such as cars and machines, or materials such as coal, steel, or chemicals 重工业 —compare 比较 LIGHT INDUSTRY

heavy-lad·en /ˌ‥ˈ‥◂/ *adj literary*【文】**1** carrying or supporting something very heavy 负载沉重的 **2** having many worries or problems 心情沉重的, 忧心忡忡的

heavy met·al /ˌ‥ˈ‥◂/ *n* [U] **1** a type of ROCK[1] (2) music with a strong beat, played very loudly on electric GUITARS 重金属摇滚乐

> **CULTURAL NOTE 文化注释**
>
> The STEREOTYPE of a heavy metal FAN is a man with long hair who wears tight black clothes and a black leather JACKET. 重金属摇滚乐迷的典型形象是长发男子, 穿紧身黑衣和黑色皮夹克。

2 *technical* a metal that has a high SPECIFIC GRAVITY, such as gold, MERCURY, and LEAD[3] (1)【术语】重金属

heavy pet·ting /ˌ‥ˈ‥/ *n* [U] sexual activities without actually having sex〔没有真正性交的〕性爱活动: *teenagers who indulge in heavy petting* 沉溺于性爱游戏的青少年

heavy-set /ˌ‥ˈ◂/ *adj* someone who is heavy-set is large or broad and looks strong or fat〔身材〕粗壮的; 矮胖的

heav·y·weight /ˈhɛvɪˌwet; ˈheviweɪt/ *n* [C] **1** someone or something that is very important or has a lot of influence 重量级人物，要人，有影响力的人[事物]: *one of the heavyweights of the movie industry* 电影业巨子之一 **2** a BOXER (1) in the heaviest weight group 重量级拳手

He·bra·ic /hiˈbre·ɪk; hɪˈbreɪ-ɪk/ *adj* connected with the Hebrew language or people 希伯来语的，希伯来人的: *Hebraic literature* 希伯来文学

He·brew /ˈhibru; ˈhiːbruː/ *n* **1** [U] the language traditionally used by the Jewish people 希伯来语 **2** [C] a member of the Jewish people, especially in ancient times〔尤指古代的〕希伯来人 —**Hebrew** *adj*

Heb·ri·des, the /ˈhɛbrəˌdiz; ˈhebrɪ̈diːz/ a group of islands off the west coast of Scotland, consisting of the Inner Hebrides and Outer Hebrides 赫布里底群岛〔与苏格兰西海岸隔海相望的一群岛，包括内赫布里底群岛和外赫布里底群岛〕—**Hebridean** /ˌhɛbrɪˈdiən; ˌhebrɪ̈ˈdiːən/ *adj*

CULTURAL NOTE 文化注释

British people think of the Hebrides, especially the Outer Hebrides, as a very REMOTE place (=one far away from cities or other places where people live) that is not much affected by things happening in the rest of the UK. 英国人认为赫布里底群岛，尤其是外赫布里底群岛非常遥远，受英国其他地区影响甚小。

heck /hɛk; hek/ *interjection informal*【非正式】**1** used to show that you are annoyed or to emphasize something you are saying 唉，见鬼〔用以表示烦恼或加强语气〕: *Oh heck! I've lost my keys!* 真见鬼！我的钥匙丢了！| **a heck of a lot** *a heck of a lot of money* 很多钱 | **where/how/who etc the heck** *Where the heck are we?* 我们到底是在哪儿？**2 what the heck!** *spoken* used to say that you will do something even though you really should not do it【口】管它呢！不管它！〔用以表示将会做不应做的事〕: *It's rather expensive, but what the heck!* 这个相当贵，不过管它呢！

heck·le /ˈhɛkl̩; ˈhekəl/ *v* [I,T] to interrupt a speaker at a public meeting〔在公开集会上〕打断某人的发言，诘问，起哄 —**heckler** *n* [C] —**heckling** *n* [U]: *The speaker's voice was drowned by constant heckling.* 发言人的声音被此起彼落的起哄声淹没了。

heck·u·va /ˈhɛkəvə; ˈhekəvə/ *adj spoken* an abbreviation of 缩写= heck of a; used to emphasize that something is very big, very good etc【口】很大的；极好的: *That was a heckuva storm last night.* 昨晚的暴风雨真大啊！

H

hec·tare /ˈhɛktɛr; ˈhektɑː/ *n* [C] a unit for measuring area, equal to 10,000 square metres 公顷〔等于10,000平方米〕—see table on page C3 参见 C3 页附录

hec·tic /ˈhɛktɪk; ˈhektɪk/ *adj* very busy or full of activity 繁忙的，忙乱的: *I've had a pretty hectic day at the office.* 我在办公室里忙乱了一整天。| *a hectic social life* 繁忙的社交生活 —**hectically** /-kl̩ɪ; -kli/ *adv*

hecto- /hɛkto; hektəʊ/ *prefix* 100 times a particular unit 表示"百": *a hectometre* (=100 metres) 一百米 —see table on page C4 参见 C4 页附录

Hec·tor /ˈhɛktɚ; ˈhektə/ in ancient Greek stories, the leader of the Trojans in the Trojan War. He was killed by the Greek Achilles, who then tied his body to the back of his CHARIOT and drove around the walls of Troy to show the Trojans that he had killed their leader. 赫克托耳〔古希腊传说中特洛伊战争期间特洛伊人的首领。他死于希腊人阿喀琉斯之手。阿喀琉斯用战车拖着他的尸体环绕特洛伊城招摇，向特洛伊人炫耀是他杀了他们的首领〕—see also 另见 The ILIAD

hector *v* [I,T] to speak to someone in an angry, threatening way 吓唬，威胁: *a hectoring, bullying tone of voice* 威吓欺凌的口气

Hec·u·ba /ˈhɛkjubə; ˈhekjʊ̈bə/ in ancient Greek stories, the wife of Priam and the mother of Hector and Paris. She appears in ancient Greek literature as a typical example of an unlucky mother who experiences suffering. 赫卡柏〔古希腊传说中普里阿摩斯之妻，赫克托耳和帕里斯之母。在古希腊文学中，她承受着痛苦，是个不幸母亲的典型〕—see also 另见 The ILIAD

he'd /ɪd, hɪd; id, hid; *strong* 强读 hid; hiːd/ **1** the short form of 缩略式= he had: *By the time I got there he'd gone.* 我赶到那里时，他已经走了。**2** the short form for 缩略式= he would: *I'm sure he'd help if he could.* 我相信如果他能做到的话一定会出手帮忙的。

hedge¹ /hɛdʒ; hedʒ/ *n* [C] **1** a row of small bushes or trees growing close together, usually dividing one field or garden from another〔用灌木或矮树筑起的〕树篱 **2** something that gives you protection in case you lose money〔避免金钱损失的〕防范措施: *Buying a house will be a hedge against inflation.* 买房子是对付通货膨胀的一种防范手段。

hedge² *v* **hedged, hedging 1** [I] to avoid giving a direct answer to a question 避免作正面回答，规避: *You're hedging again – have you got the money or haven't you?* 你又在闪烁其词了，你究竟拿到钱没有？**2 hedge your bets** to reduce your chances of failure or loss by having several choices available to you 多处下注以减少风险；脚踏两只船: *It's a good idea to hedge your bets by applying to more than one college.* 同时向几所大学提出申请是个保险的好主意。**3** [T] to make a hedge around an area of land 用树篱围起〔地〕

hedge sb/sth **in** *phr v* **be hedged in a)** to be surrounded or enclosed by something 被…包围: *The building was hedged in with trees.* 大楼周围种着树木。**b)** if you feel hedged in by something, you feel that your freedom is restricted by it 受到…的束缚[限制]

hedge against sth *phr v* [T] to try to protect yourself against possible problems, especially financial loss 采取措施以防招致〔财务损失〕: *Any well-managed business will hedge against price increases.* 任何一家管理完善的企业都会采取措施防范价格上涨带来的风险。

hedge·hog /ˈhɛdʒˌhɑg; ˈhedʒhɒg/ *n* [C] a small brown European animal whose body is round and covered with sharp SPINES (=sharp needles) 刺猬

hedgehog 刺猬

spines
刺（毛）

hedge·row /ˈhɛdʒˌro; ˈhedʒrəʊ/ *n* [C] *especially BrE* a line of bushes or small trees growing along the edge of a field or road【尤英】灌木树篱，一排树篱

hedge spar·row /ˈ· ˌ··/ *n* [C] a small common bird that lives in Europe and America〔产于欧洲和美洲的〕篱雀

he·don·ist /ˈhidn̩ˌɪst; ˈhiːdən-ɪst/ *n* [C] someone who believes that pleasure is the most important thing in life 享乐主义者 —**hedonism** *n* [U] —**hedonistic** /ˌhidəˈnɪstɪk; ˌhiːdən-ˈɪstɪk◂/ *adj*

hee·bie-jee·bies /ˈhibɪ ˈdʒibɪz; ˌhiːbi ˈdʒiːbiz/ *n* **give sb the heebie-jeebies** *informal* to make someone feel nervous【非正式】使某人神经紧张，使某人坐立不安

heed¹ /hid; hiːd/ *v* [T] *formal* to pay attention to someone's advice or warning【正式】听从；注意〔别人的建议或警告〕: *If she had only heeded my warnings, none of this would have happened.* 要是她当初听从我的警告，就不会发生这种事了。

heed² *n* [U] *formal* **pay/give heed to sth** also 又作 **take heed of sth** to pay attention to something and seriously consider it【正式】注意某事；慎重考虑某事: **pay no heed to** *Tom paid no heed to her warning.* 汤姆根本没有理会她的警告。

heed·less /ˈhidlɪs; ˈhiːdləs/ *adj* **heedless of** not paying attention to something 不注意，不理会，掉以轻心: *O'Hara rode on, heedless of danger.* 奥哈拉不理会危险，继续骑车走去。

hee-haw /ˈhi ˌhɔ; ˈhiː ˌhɔː/ *n* [C] the noise made by a DONKEY 驴叫声

heel¹ /hil; hiːl/ *n* [C]

1 ▶OF YOUR FOOT 脚的◀ the back part of your foot 脚后跟，踵 —see pictures at 参见 BODY and 和 FOOT¹ 图

2 ▶OF A SHOE 鞋的◀ the raised part of a shoe that is under the back of your foot 后跟，鞋跟 —see picture at 参见 SHOE¹ 图

3 high-heeled/low-heeled etc high-heeled or low-heeled shoes have high or low heels〔鞋〕高跟/低跟的

4 ▶OF A SOCK 袜子的◀ the part of a sock that covers your heel（袜）后跟

5 ▶OF YOUR HAND 手的◀ the raised part of your hand near your wrist〔近腕处的〕手掌根: *I pressed the paper down firmly with the heel of my hand.* 我用手掌根紧紧地把纸压下去。

6 heels [plural] a pair of women's shoes with high heels〔一双〕高跟鞋

7 be on/at sb's heels to be following closely behind someone, especially in order to catch or attack them 紧跟着某人，紧随其后: *The gang were at his heels.* 那帮歹徒紧紧跟在他的身后。

8 on the heels of very soon after something〔时间上〕紧接着，在…后不久: *Kinnock's resignation came on the heels of the party's fourth defeat.* 该政党第四次竞选失败后不久，金诺克就辞职了。

9 bring sb to heel to force someone to behave in the way that you want them to 使某人就范，使某人顺从

10 call sth to heel if you call a dog to heel, you tell it to come back to you 唤〔狗〕回来

11 come to heel a) if a dog comes to heel, it comes back to its owner when the owner calls it〔狗〕被唤回来 **b)** if someone comes to heel they obey you again〔某人〕服从, 就范

12 take to your heels to start running as fast as possible 拔腿逃走: *As soon as he saw me he took to his heels.* 一看到我, 他拔腿就逃。

13 turn/spin on your heel to suddenly turn away from someone, especially in an angry or rude way〔尤指生气地、无礼地〕突然转身走掉

14 under the heel of completely controlled by a government or group 遭…践踏; 在…的统治下: *The whole country was under the heel of a tyrannical dictatorship.* 整个国家的人民都活在专制独裁的统治之下。

15 ▶BAD MAN 坏人◀ *old-fashioned* a man who behaves badly towards other people【过时】坏蛋, 坏家伙 —see also 另见 WELL-HEELED, ACHILLES' HEEL, **click your heels** (CLICK (1)), **cool your heels** (COOL[2] (4)), **dig your heels in** (DIG[1]), DOWN-AT-HEEL, **drag your heels** (DRAG[1] (8)), **be hard on sb's heels** (HARD[2] (9)), **head over heels in love** (HEAD[1] (51)), **be hot on sb's heels** (HOT[1] (15)), **kick your heels** (KICK[1] (11))

heel² *v* **1** [T] to put a heel on a shoe 给〔鞋子〕钉后跟 **2 heel!** *spoken* used when telling a dog to walk next to you【口】跟着我!〔唤狗用语〕 **3** [T] to send the ball backwards in RUGBY by hitting it with your heel〔橄榄球比赛中〕用脚后跟向后传〔球〕

heel over *phr v* [I] if something heels over, it leans to one side as if it is going to fall 倾斜(要倒): *The ship was heeling over in the wind.* 船在风中向一侧倾斜。

Heep /hip; hiːp/, **U·ri·ah** /juˋraɪə; juːˈraɪə/ a character in the book *David Copperfield* (1850) by Charles Dickens, who is a CLERK (=someone who keeps records in an office) working for a lawyer. He pretends to be very helpful, and he is known for often saying how 'umble' (=humble) he is. But in fact he is clever and dishonest, and only interested in getting advantages for himself. 希普〔查尔斯·狄更斯小说《大卫·科波菲尔》(1850)中的人物。他是一位律师的文牍员。他总是装出一副卖力的样子, 而且常常在人前夸耀自己的谦卑。事实上, 他为人精明狡诈, 自私自利〕

hef·ty /ˋhɛftɪ; ˈhefti/ *adj* **1** a hefty person, book etc is big and heavy 高大健壮的; 笨重的: *a hefty volume containing over 1200 pages* 一本一千二百多页的巨著 **2** a hefty amount of something such as money is very large 大量的, 巨额的: *a hefty fine* 巨额罚款 **3** a hefty blow, kick etc is done using a lot of force 有力的, 重重的: *a hefty punch* 一记重击 —**heftily** *adv*

He·gel /ˋhegl; ˈheɪgəl/, **Ge·org Wil·helm Fried·rich** /ˋgeɔrg ˋvɪlhɛlm ˋfridrɪk; ˈgeɪɔːg ˈvɪlhelm ˈfriːdrɪk/ (1770-1831) a German PHILOSOPHER who had great influence on European and US PHILOSOPHY with books such as *The Phenomenology of the Mind* 黑格尔〔(1770-1831), 德国哲学家。他写有《精神现象学》等著作, 对欧洲和美国哲学产生了重要影响〕

he·gem·o·ny /hɪˋdʒɛmənɪ; hɪˈgeməni/ *n* [U] *formal* a situation in which one state or country controls others【正式】〔一国对他国的〕霸权; 支配权; 领导权

He·gi·ra, Hejira /hiˋdʒaɪrə; ˈhedʒɨrə/ *n* [singular] the journey of Muhammad from Mecca to Medina in AD 622 希吉来, 海纪拉〔指公元622年穆罕默德从麦加到麦地那的逃亡〕

Hegira cal·en·dar /ˌ… ˈ…/ *n* [singular] the Muslim system of dividing a year of 354 days into 12 months and starting to count the years from the Hegira 希吉来历, 伊斯兰教历, 回历〔穆斯林历法。该历法将一年354天分为12个月, 从希吉来(海纪拉, 即公元622年)纪元〕

Hei·del·berg /ˋhedḷˌbɝg; ˈheɪdəlbɜːg/ a university town in southwest Germany 海德堡〔德国西南部的一座大学城〕

Hei·di /ˋhaɪdɪ; ˈhaɪdi/ a little girl who is the main character in the children's book *Heidi* by the Swiss writer Johanna Spyri (1827-1901). She makes the lives of people around her much happier and better. 海蒂〔瑞士作家约翰娜·施皮里(1827-1901)的儿童读物《海蒂》的主人公。她是个小女孩, 给周围人的生活增添了幸福和欢乐〕

heif·er /ˋhɛfɚ; ˈhefə/ *n* [C] a young cow that has not yet given birth to a CALF (=baby cow)〔未生过小牛的〕小母牛 —compare 比较 BULLOCK, OX, STEER

heigh-ho /ˋhe ˋho; ˌheɪ ˈhəʊ/ *interjection old-fashioned* used when you have to accept something that is boring or unpleasant【过时】唉, 嗨嗬〔表示对沉闷或不愉快的事物无奈地接受〕

height /haɪt; haɪt/ *n*

1 ▶TALL 高◀ a) [U] how tall someone is 身高: **sb's height** *State your age, height, and weight.* 说出你的年龄、身高和体重。| **be the same/right etc height** *My daughter's already about the same height as I am.* 我女儿已经几乎和我一样高了。 **b)** [C,U] the distance between the base and the top of something 高, 高度: *What's the height of the Empire State Building?* 帝国大厦有多高? | **in height** *Some of the pyramids are over 200 feet in height.* 有几座金字塔的高度超过200英尺。—see picture at 参见 LENGTH 图

2 ▶DISTANCE ABOVE THE GROUND 离地面的距离◀ [C] a particular distance above the ground〔离地面的〕高度: *It's a miracle she didn't break her neck falling from that height.* 她从那么高的地方掉下来居然没有摔断脖子, 真是个奇迹! | *at a height of 10,000 feet* 在离地面10,000英尺的高空

3 gain/lose height if an aircraft gains height or loses height, it moves higher in the sky or it drops lower in the sky〔飞机在空中〕上升/下降: *The plane was rapidly losing height.* 飞机正在快速下降。

4 ▶HIGH PLACE 高处◀ heights *plural* **a)** places that are a long way above the ground 高处: *Rachel had always been scared of heights.* 雷切尔过去一直恐高。| **have a head for heights** (=not be afraid of heights) 不恐高, 不畏高 **b)** a particular high place 高地: *the Golan Heights* 戈兰高地

5 reach/attain/rise to new heights a) to reach a very high level of achievement or success 达到新的高度, 取得新的成就: *Her career rose to new heights.* 她的事业取得了新的成就。| **take sth to new heights** *Torville and Dean took ice dancing to new heights.* 托维尔和迪安使冰上舞蹈迈向了新的境界。 **b)** to reach a very great level or degree 达到很高的水平[程度]: *War fever had reached new heights.* 战争热升级了。

6 the height of the part of a period of time that is the busiest, hottest etc, or when there is the most activity 最繁忙的时候[季节]; 高潮, 顶点: *the height of the tourist season* 旅游旺季

7 be at the height of your success/fame/powers etc to be at the time when you are most successful, famous etc 处于成功/名声/权力等的巅峰: *The Beatles were at the height of their fame.* 当时正是甲壳虫乐队最出名的时候。

8 be the height of fashion/stupidity/luxury etc to be extremely fashionable, stupid etc 是最时髦/愚蠢/奢侈的等: *Flared trousers were considered to be the height of fashion in those days.* 喇叭裤那时被认为是最时髦的。

height·en /ˋhaɪtn̩; ˈhaɪtn/ *v* [I,T] if something heightens a feeling, effect etc, or if a feeling etc heightens, it becomes stronger or increases; INTENSIFY 加强, 增加: *Lemon helps to heighten the flavour.* 柠檬使味道变得更浓。| *Berg uses music to heighten tension in the scene.* 伯格利用配乐来增强该场景的紧张气氛。| **heighten awareness** (=make people realize something more clearly) 提高意识 *an attempt to heighten their awareness of political issues* 为提高他们的政治意识所作的努力

Hei·ne /ˋhaɪnə; ˈhaɪnə/, **Hein·rich** /ˋhaɪnrɪk; ˈhaɪnrɪk/ (1797-1856) a German poet who also wrote political SATIRE (=books making fun of people in public life). Some of his poems were set to music by Schubert and Schumann. 海涅〔(1797-1856), 德国诗人, 也创作过讽喻政治的作品。有些诗歌配有舒伯特和舒曼谱写的乐曲〕

hei·nous /ˋhenəs; ˈheɪnəs/ *adj formal* very shocking and immoral【正式】极邪恶的, 令人发指的: *a heinous crime* 滔天罪行 —**heinously** *adv* —**heinousness** *n* [U]

heir /ɛr; eə/ *n* [C] **1** the person who has the legal right to receive the property or title of another person when they die 继承人: [+to] *John was the sole heir to a vast estate.* 约翰是一座大庄园的唯一继承人。| **the heir to the throne** (=the person who will become king or queen) 王位继承人 **2** the person who will take over a position or job after you 继任者, 接班人: *Jonson was his political heir as leader of the Nationalist Party.* 琼森在政治上接他的班, 成了民族主义政党的领袖。

heir ap·par·ent /ˌ· ·ˈ··/ *n* [C] an heir whose right to receive the family property, money, or title cannot be taken away 法定继承人 —compare 比较 HEIR PRESUMPTIVE

heir·ess /ˋɛrɪs; ˈeərɨs/ *n* [C] a woman who will receive a lot of money, property, or a title when an older member of her family dies〔大笔财产或某头衔的〕女继承人

CULTURAL NOTE 文化注释

People sometimes make jokes about men dreaming of marrying wealthy heiresses, and popular newspapers often have stories about unmarried wealthy heiresses and the men they are seen with 人们有时拿那些梦想娶一位富有的女继承人的男人来开玩笑。通俗报纸常常报道未婚的富有女继承人和某个男人出双入对: *He hopes to marry a rich heiress and stop working.* 他想娶一位富有的女继承人, 不再工作。

heir·loom /ˈɛr`lum; ˈeəluːm/ *n* [C] a valuable object that has been owned by a family for many years and that is passed from the older members to the younger members 祖传宝物，传家宝

heir pre·sump·tive /ˌ· ·ˈ··/ *n* [C] an HEIR whose right to receive the family property, money, or title can be taken away if someone else with a better claim is born 假定继承人〔其继承权可能因更近的亲属出生而丧失〕—compare 比较 HEIR APPARENT

Hei·sen·berg /ˈhaɪznbɝg; ˈhaɪzənbɜːg/, **Wer·ner** /ˈvɛrnɚ; ˈveənə/ (1901-76) a German PHYSICIST who studied the behaviour of atoms, and won a Nobel Prize. He is famous for developing the Uncertainty Principle. 海森伯〔(1901-1976)，德国物理学家。他研究原子的特性，获过诺贝尔奖，以提出"测不准原理"著称〕

Heis·man Tro·phy /ˈhaɪsmən ˌtrofi; ˈhaɪsmən ˌtrəʊfi/ also 又作 **Heisman Memorial Trophy** a prize given each year to the best college football player in the US 海斯曼杯，海斯曼纪念杯〔美国一年一度颁发给最佳大学生橄榄球运动员的奖杯〕

heist /haɪst; haɪst/ *n* [C] *AmE informal* an act of robbing something very valuable from a shop, bank etc 【美，非正式】〔对贵重物品的〕抢劫: *a jewelry heist* 对首饰的抢劫 —**heist** *v* [T]

He·ji·ra /hiˋdʒaɪrə; ˈhedʒɪrə/ *n* another spelling of the HEGIRA Hegira的另一种拼法

held /hɛld; held/ past tense and past participle of HOLD[1]

Hel·e·na /ˈhɛlənə; ˈhelɪnə/ the capital city of the US state of Montana 海伦娜〔美国蒙大拿州首府〕

Hel·en of Troy /ˌhɛlən əv ˋtrɔɪ; ˌhelɪn əv ˈtrɔɪ/ in ancient Greek stories, the wife of Menelaus, the king of Sparta. Helen was famous for her great beauty, and she is often mentioned in literature as a typical example of a very beautiful woman. When Helen's lover Paris took her away to Troy with him, he caused the Trojan War. The phrase 'the face that launched a thousand ships' is often used about her, since the Greeks sailed to Troy to bring her back. 特洛伊的海伦〔古希腊传说中斯巴达国王墨涅拉俄斯之妻，以美貌著称，常以美女之典范出现在文学作品之中。她的情人帕里斯把她带到特洛伊，由此引发了特洛伊战争。因为希腊人动用了一千艘船只才把她从特洛伊带了回来，所以人们通常用 the face that launched a thousand ships（千船扬帆之娇容）这一短语描述她的美貌〕—see also 另见 The ILIAD

hel·i·cop·ter /ˈhɛlɪˌkɑptɚ; ˈhelɪkɒptə/ *n* [C] a type of aircraft with large metal blades on top which turn around very quickly to make it fly 直升机

helicopter pad /ˈ····ˌ·/ *n* [C] an area where helicopters can land 直升机停机坪

he·li·o·graph /ˈhilɪəˌgræf; ˈhiːliəgrɑːf/ *n* [C] an instrument that sends messages by directing flashes of light with a mirror 日光反射信号器

he·li·o·trope /ˈhilɪəˌtrop; ˈhiːliətrəʊp/ *n* **1** [C] a garden plant that has pleasant-smelling pale purple flowers 天芥菜属植物 **2** [U] the colour of this flower 浅紫红色〔此种植物花的颜色〕

hel·i·pad /ˈhɛlɪˌpæd; ˈhelipæd/ *n* [C] a HELICOPTER PAD 直升机停机坪

hel·i·port /ˈhɛlɪˌport; ˈhelipɔːt/ *n* [C] a small airport for HELICOPTERS 供直升机用的小型机场

he·li·um /ˈhilɪəm; ˈhiːliəm/ *n* [U] a gas that is lighter than air, often used in BALLOONS 氦（气）

he·lix /ˈhilɪks; ˈhiːlɪks/ *n* [C] *technical* a line that curves and rises around a central line; SPIRAL【术语】螺线；螺旋（形）—see also 另见 DOUBLE HELIX

he'll /ɪl, hɪl; il, hil; *strong* 强读 hil; hiːl/ **1** the short form of 缩略式= he will **2** the short form of 缩略式= he shall

hell[1] /hɛl; hel/ *n*

1 ►UNPLEASANT SITUATION 糟糕的情况◄ [singular,U] *informal* a situation, experience, or place that is very unpleasant【非正式】极糟的情况[经历，地方]: *Central London was hell the Saturday before Christmas.* 圣诞节前的星期六，伦敦市中心简直乱得一团糟。| **sheer hell** (=extremely unpleasant) 糟透了 *"How was your exam?" "Sheer hell!"* "你考得怎么样?" "糟透了!" | **hell on earth** *This town is my idea of hell on earth.* 这个小镇在我看来像个人间地狱。

2 ►SUFFERING 痛苦◄ a place or situation in which people suffer very much, either physically or emotionally 令人痛苦的地方[状态]: *the hell of the battlefield* 战场这个鬼地方 | **make sb's life hell** *He'll make my life hell if I don't do what he wants.* 如果我不满足他的要求，他就不会给我好日子过。| **living hell** *Josh felt trapped in a living hell.* 乔希感觉自己像被困在活地狱里。

3 ►WHEN YOU DIE 死后◄ also 又作 **Hell** [singular] the place where the souls of bad people are believed to be punished after death, especially in the Christian and Muslim religions〔尤指基督教和伊斯兰教所说的〕地狱，阴间

CULTURAL NOTE 文化注释

Hell is thought of as a dark place that is deep under the ground and full of fire, where Satan and his followers live, and where people who have been bad during their lives burn forever. 地狱被看做是地下深处的一个黑暗地方，遍布火焰，住着撒旦及其党羽，那里生平作恶的人永受烈火焚烧之苦。— see Cultural Note at DEVIL and HEAVEN 见 DEVIL 和 HEAVEN 文化注释

4 how/what/where etc the hell? *spoken* used to show that you are very surprised or angry【口】到底怎么/什么/哪里等?〔表示惊讶或愤怒〕: *What the hell does he think he's doing?* 他到底认为自己在干什么呢? | *Where the hell have you been?* 你刚才到底上哪儿了?

5 a/one hell of a *spoken* used to emphasize the idea that something is very big, very good, very bad etc【口】〔用以加强语气〕极，非常〔大、好、坏等〕: *He's one hell of a good actor.* 他真是个好演员。| *a hell of a lot of money* 一大笔钱 | **have one hell of a time** *We had one hell of a time trying to get here.* 我们费了好大劲才赶到这里。

6 go to hell! *spoken* used to tell someone that you do not care about them or about what they think【口】见鬼去吧! 管它呢!〔表示不理会某人或其想法〕: *If John doesn't like it, he can go to hell!* 如果约翰不喜欢这样，让他见鬼去吧!

7 feel/look like hell *spoken* to feel or look very ill or tired【口】感觉/看起来不舒服[疲惫]: *I've been feeling like hell all week.* 我整整一星期都感到很不舒服。

8 beat/irritate/scare etc the hell out of sb *informal* to beat, irritate etc someone very much【非正式】把某人打得/气得/吓得半死

9 (just) for the hell of it *spoken* for no serious reason, or only for fun【口】只是为了好玩，玩玩而已: *We decided to go for a midnight swim, just for the hell of it.* 我们决定半夜去游泳，只是为了好玩。

10 what the hell! *spoken* used to say that you will do something and not worry about any problems it causes【口】管它呢!〔表示不顾后果〕: *What the hell, let's go with them.* 管它呢，我们和他们一起去吧!

11 to hell with *spoken* used to say that you do not care about something any more【口】让…见鬼去吧: *To hell with school! I'm going to leave and get a job.* 让学校见鬼去吧! 我马上就要离开学校去找工作了。

12 run/work/hurt etc like hell *informal* to run, work etc very quickly or very much【非正式】拼命地跑/拼命地工作/痛得要命等: *We ran like hell and didn't stop until we were safely home.* 我们拼命地跑，直到安全回到家。

13 like hell/the hell *spoken* used to say that you do not believe what someone has said, or that you disagree with it【口】哪有这种事，绝不会: *"Like hell you'd pay it back", Wade said wearily.* 韦德有气无力地说道："我才不信你会归还呢。"

14 from hell *informal* the worst you can imagine【非正式】最糟的: *It was disaster after disaster – the holiday from hell!* 倒霉事一件接着一件，这个假期真是糟透了!

15 mad/weird/ugly etc as hell *especially AmE spoken* very angry, strange etc【尤美，口】非常生气的/古怪的/丑陋的等: *I wouldn't ask him now, he's mad as hell.* 我现在不会去问他，他正暴跳如雷呢!

16 give sb hell *informal* to blame someone angrily【非正式】狠狠地责骂某人: *My dad gave me hell when he found out that I'd borrowed the car.* 父亲发现我借了那辆车后，把我臭骂了一顿。

17 get the hell out (of somewhere) *informal* to leave a place quickly and suddenly【非正式】赶紧离开（某地）: *Let's get the hell out of here!* 我们赶紧离开这里吧!

18 there'll be hell to pay *spoken* used to say that people will be very angry【口】〔某人〕会非常愤怒的: *There'll be hell to pay when the boss finds out.* 要是老板发现这件事，那就麻烦了。

19 catch hell *AmE spoken* to be blamed or punished【美口】挨骂，受责备[惩罚]: *You'll catch hell when your Mom comes home!* 你母亲回家后会骂你的!

20 all hell broke loose *informal* used to say that people suddenly become very noisy or angry【非正式】突然喧闹起来；一片混乱: *The rival gang arrived and all hell broke loose.* 敌对的团伙来到后，这里就乱成了一片。

21 hell's bells *spoken* also 又作 **hell's teeth** *BrE*【英】used to express great annoyance or surprise【口】见鬼了〔表示极度厌烦或惊讶〕

22 come hell or high water *informal* in spite of any problems or difficulties【非正式】无论有什么困难: *I decided I would get*

the job done by Friday, come hell or high water. 不管遇到什么困难，我都决心要在星期五之前完成这项工作。

23 go to hell in a handbasket *AmE informal* if a system or organization has gone to hell in a handbasket, it has stopped working properly【美，非正式】〔系统或机构〕无法正常运作；出了毛病：*The education system in this state has gone to hell in a handbasket.* 这个国家的教育体系出了很多问题。

24 run/go hell for leather *informal* to run away as fast as possible【非正式】拼命地跑，狂奔

25 hell on wheels *AmE informal* someone who does exactly what they want and does not care what happens as a result【美，非正式】我行我素的人；做事不顾后果的人

26 play (merry) hell with *informal* to make something stop working or happening as it should【非正式】打乱，搅乱：*The cold weather played hell with the weekend sports schedule.* 寒冷的天气打乱了周末的体育活动计划。

27 when hell freezes over *informal* used to say that something will never happen【非正式】永不，绝不可能 —see also 另见 **not a hope in hell** (HOPE² (5))

hell² *interjection* **1** *especially BrE* used to express anger or annoyance【尤英】见鬼，该死〔表示愤怒或不耐烦〕：*Oh hell! I've left my purse at home.* 真该死！我把钱包忘在家里了。**2** *AmE* used to emphasize something you are saying【美】见鬼，该死〔用来加强语气〕：*Hell, I don't know!* 见鬼，我不知道！

hell-bent /, ·ˈ·◂/ *adj* [not before noun 不用于名词前] very determined to do something, especially something that other people do not approve of 坚决的，不顾一切的：**hell-bent on (doing) sth** *They seemed hell-bent on creating a scandal.* 他们好像一意孤行要制造丑闻。

hell·cat /ˈhɛlˌkæt; ˈhelkæt/ *n* [C] *informal* a woman who has a violent temper【非正式】泼妇，悍妇

Hel·lene /ˈhɛlin; ˈheliːn/ *n* [C] *formal* a Greek, especially an ancient Greek【正式】〔尤指古代的〕希腊人

Hel·len·ic /hɛˈlɛnɪk; heˈlenɪk/ *adj* connected with the history, society, or art of the ancient Greeks 古希腊的

Hel·les·pont, the /ˈhɛləspɑnt; ˈhelɪ̯spɒnt/ a former name for the Dardanelles 赫勒斯海峡〔达达尼尔海峡旧称〕

hell-hole /ˈ· ·/ *n* [C] a very unpleasant place 地狱般的地方，环境极恶劣的地方：*His last apartment was a real hell-hole.* 他上次住的公寓就像地狱一样。

hell·ish /ˈhɛlɪʃ; ˈhelɪʃ/ *adj informal* extremely unpleasant【非正式】糟透的，极坏的：*I've had a hellish day at work.* 我今天忙得要命。—**hellishly** *adv*: *a hellishly difficult exam* 极其困难的考试

Hell·man /ˈhɛlmən; ˈhelmən/, **Lil·li·an** /ˈlɪlɪən; ˈlɪliən/ (1905-84) a US writer of plays, whose most famous works are *The Children's Hour* and *The Little Foxes*. She is also remembered for refusing to name anyone as a Communist in front of the HUAC. 海尔曼〔(1905-1984)，美国剧作家。最著名的作品是《孩子的时间》和《小狐狸》。令人记忆犹新的是，她曾面对众议院非美活动调查委员会拒绝指认共产党人〕

S1 **hel·lo** /həˈlo; həˈləʊ/ also 又作 **hallo, hullo** *BrE*【英】*interjection* **1** used as a usual greeting 喂，哈罗，你好〔问候语〕：*Hello, John! How are you?* 喂，约翰！你好吗？| **say hello to sb** *She always says hello to me in the street.* 她在街上总是和我打招呼。| **hello there** *Well, hello there! I haven't seen you for ages.* 嗨，你好！好久不见了。**2** used when answering the telephone or starting a telephone conversation 喂〔打电话用的招呼语〕：*Hello, is Rachel there please?* 喂，请问雷切尔在吗？**3** used when calling to get someone's attention 喂〔用以引起别人注意〕：*Hello! Is there anybody home?* 喂！家里有人吗？**4** *BrE* used to show that you are surprised or confused by something【英】嘿〔表示惊讶或不解〕：*Hello! What's happened here?* 嘿！出什么事了？

Hello! *trademark* a British magazine with pictures and articles about famous people, such as film actors, fashion models, and members of the British ARISTOCRACY【商标】《哈罗！》〔英国杂志，刊登电影演员、时装模特、英国贵族等名人的照片和相关报道〕

helm /hɛlm; helm/ *n* **1** [C] the wheel or TILLER which guides a ship or boat〔船的〕舵轮 **2 at the helm a)** in charge of something 掌权，领导：*The company flourished with David Finch at the helm.* 公司在戴维·芬奇的领导下兴旺起来。**b)** guiding a ship or boat 掌舵 **3** *old use* a helmet【旧】头盔

hel·met /ˈhɛlmɪt; ˈhelmɪ̯t/ *n* [C] a strong hard hat worn for protection by soldiers, MOTORCYCLE riders, the police etc 头盔，钢盔，安全帽 —see also 另见 CRASH HELMET, PITH HELMET

hel·met·ed /ˈhɛlmɪtɪd; ˈhelmɪ̯tɪ̯d/ *adj* wearing a helmet 戴头盔的

helms·man /ˈhɛlmzmən; ˈhelmzmən/ *n plural* **helmsmen** /-mən; -mən/ [C] someone who guides a ship or boat 舵手

Hél·o·ïse /ˈɛloiz; ˈeləʊiːz/ (1101-64) the pupil, lover, and wife of Peter Abelard. The love between Héloïse and Abelard is one of the most famous love stories in history, and their love letters are well known. 埃罗伊兹〔(1101-1164)，彼得·阿贝拉尔的学生、情人及妻子。他们的爱情是历史上最著名的浪漫故事之一，他们的情书也很著名〕

help¹ /hɛlp; help/ *v* S1 W1

1 ►MAKE POSSIBLE OR EASIER 使可能或容易◄ [I,T] to make it possible or easier for someone to do something by doing part of their work or by giving them something they need 帮助，帮忙：*If there's anything I can do to help, just give me a call.* 如果需要我帮忙，就给我打个电话。| *She devoted her life to helping the poor and sick.* 她一生致力于帮助穷人和病人。| **help sb (to) do sth** *We all helped him fill out the application form.* 我们大家一起帮他填写申请表。| *Andy said he would help us to move the furniture.* 安迪说他会帮我们搬家具。| **help sb with sth** *Do you mind helping me with this a minute?* 你能抽点时间帮我一把吗？| **help (to) do sth** *Part of my job is to help organize conferences.* 我其中一项工作是帮忙筹备会议。| **help sb into/out of/across etc** (=help someone move to a particular place) 扶某人进入/出去/穿过等 *He was so drunk we had to help him into the taxi.* 他醉得很厉害，我们不得不将他扶进出租车里。| **help sb on/off with sth** (=help someone put on or take off a piece of clothing) 帮某人穿/脱〔衣服〕*Here, let me help you on with your coat.* 嗨，我来帮你穿大衣吧！

2 ►BE GOOD FOR 对…有好处◄ [T] to make it easier for something to develop or be improved 有助于，助长：*The fall in oil prices should help economic development.* 油价下跌将有利于经济发展。| **help sb (to) do sth** *All this arguing isn't going to help us win the election.* 这样争论下去不会帮我们赢得选举。

3 ►MAKE BETTER 使更好◄ [I,T] to make a situation better, easier, or less painful 使〔形势〕改善，好转；减轻〔痛苦〕：*Crying won't help.* 哭无助于事。| *It helped a lot to know that someone understood how I felt.* 知道有人理解我的感受，我感觉好多了。| **help sth** *A couple of aspirin might help your headache.* 吃两片阿斯匹林可能会减轻你的头痛。

4 Help! *spoken* used to call people and ask them to help you when you are in danger【口】救命啊！〔求救声〕

5 can't help it a) to not be responsible for something unpleasant or annoying 没有办法；不是〔某人〕的过错：*I can't help it if she's late, can I?* 要是她迟到，我也没有办法，对吧？**b)** to be unable to stop doing something, or change the way that you behave 忍不住，无法控制自己：*I always get angry with him, I just can't help it.* 我老是对他发火，我就是控制不了自己。

6 can't/couldn't help doing sth to be unable to stop yourself from doing something 忍不住做某事，不能停止做某事：*I can't help thinking that we've made a big mistake.* 我不禁感到我们犯了一个大错误。| *I couldn't help hearing what you just said.* 我无意中听到了你刚刚说的那些话。

7 can't/couldn't help but do sth if you cannot help but do something, it is impossible for you not to do it 不可能不做某事：*I couldn't help but notice the bruise she had under her eye.* 我不可能注意不到她眼睛底下的青肿。

8 can't help yourself to be unable to stop yourself from doing something you should not do 忍不住，无法控制自己：*Sue doesn't always mean to be so rude but sometimes she just can't help herself.* 休不是故意要这么粗暴无礼的，但有时她就是克制不了自己。

9 help yourself (to sth) a) to take something that you want, such as food, without asking permission 自己取〔食物等〕：*Please help yourself to more; there's plenty of everything.* 请再吃点吧，还有很多呢！**b)** *informal* to steal something【非正式】偷窃：*Obviously he had been helping himself to the money.* 他显然一直在偷钱。

10 help sb to sth to serve someone food or drink 为某人取〔食物、饮料〕：*Can I help you to some dessert?* 我给你拿些甜点好吗？

11 God help him/them etc *spoken* used to say that something bad may happen to someone【口】他/他们要倒霉了：*If you trust*

helmets 头盔

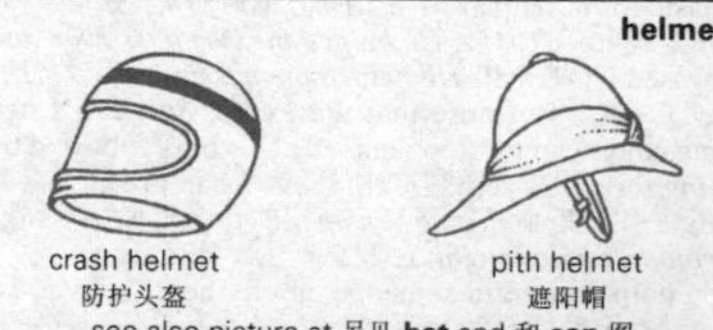

see also picture at 另见 **hat** and 和 **cap** 图

H

that man with a secret, God help you. 如果你将秘密告诉那个人，你就倒霉了！

12 a helping hand help and support 援手，帮助：**give sb a helping hand** *She's been giving me a helping hand with the children.* 她一直在帮我照顾孩子。

13 it can't be helped *spoken* used to say that there is nothing you can do to change an unpleasant situation【口】无法避免；没办法：*It's going to make a terrible noise, but never mind. It can't be helped.* 这样会发出可怕的噪音。不过别在意，这是不可避免的。

14 not if I can help it *spoken* used to say that you are not going to do something【口】不会做某事：*"Are you going to the meeting this afternoon?" "Not if I can help it."* "你今天下午去参加会议吗？""能不去就不去。"

15 so help me (God) used when making a serious promise, especially in a court of law 我发誓；上天作证〔尤指在法庭上发誓时用〕

help out *phr v* **1** [I,T] to help someone who is busy by doing some of their work for them 分担…工作，帮…一把：*Is there anything I can do to help out?* 我能帮上忙吗？| **help sb out** *If you haven't got time to finish I'll help you out.* 如果你来不及做完，我会帮你一把。**2** [T] to give help and support to someone who has problems 帮助〔某人解决难题〕：*He was obviously in some kind of trouble, but I didn't know how I could help him out.* 他显然遇到了麻烦，但我不知道应该怎样帮他。

USAGE NOTE 用法说明：HELP

WORD CHOICE 词语辨析：**help, assist, give/lend a hand, help out, come to somebody's aid/assistance, aid, give/send aid**

Help and **assist** can both describe people or institutions helping each other do a job. However, **assist** is more formal and often suggests that the person assisting is doing a simple or unimportant part of what has to be done. help和assist都可以用来表示人或机构相互帮助做某事，但assist较正式，常常暗示提供帮助的一方所做的事比较简单或占次要地位：*My company assists businesses in all their office cleaning requirements.* 我公司协助企业做办公室的清洁工作。| *You will assist the administrative officer with day-to-day organization* (Note that **assist** can never mean 'attend' or 'be present at'). 你将协助行政官员做日常的组织工作（注意assist不可用来表示"参加"或"在场"）。

In more informal English people often use **give/lend a hand** or **help out**, especially where there is something practical to do and not enough people to do it. 在较非正式的英语中，人们往往用give/lend a hand 或help out，特别是在要做具体工作而又没有足够人手的情况下：*Can you give me a hand with the drinks?* 你能帮我端一下饮料吗？| *I sometimes lend a hand/help out at the old folk's home.* 我有时在养老院里帮忙。

If someone is in danger or trouble, you may **help** them or more formally **come to their aid/assistance**. 若某人处于危险或困境之中而你施以援手，可用help，或者是更正式的come to their aid/assistance：*My car's broken down, can you help?* 我的车坏了，你能帮忙吗？| *If you get into difficulties, the lifeguard will come to your assistance.* 如果你遇到困难，救生员会来帮你。

If a person, charity, or government helps with money or other necessary things, **aid** (formal) or often **give/send aid** may be used. 若个人、慈善机构或政府通过金钱或其他必需品提供帮助，可以用aid（正式用语）或常用give/send aid：*Many projects are aided by Oxfam.* 许多项目都得到乐施会的资助。| *Aid will be sent to the area as soon as possible.* 援助物资将会尽快送往该地区。Informally **help** would be used. 在非正式场合可用help：*Please help the homeless.* 请帮帮无家可归的人吧。

GRAMMAR 语法

Help (but not **assist**) is often followed by a verb in the *to* or basic form. help（而不是assist）的后面常常跟有某动词的不定式（to）或原形：*He helped me (to) pass my exam* (=I passed NOT 不用 *He helped me passing...*). 他帮助我通过了考试。But note that the expression **can't help...** meaning 'cannot stop yourself...' is only followed by the *-ing* form of a verb. 但应注意，词组can't help… 意为"忍不住…"，后面只能接某一动词的动名词形式（-ing）：*I couldn't help laughing.* 我忍不住大笑起来。

You **help/assist/aid** someone, not *to* them. help/assist/aid直接接帮助的对象，不加to。

help² *n* **1** [U] the action of helping someone by doing part of their work or by showing them how to do it 帮助，帮忙：*If I need any help, I'll call you.* 如果我需要帮助，我会给你打电话。| **[+with]** *Do you want any help with that?* 那件事你需要帮忙吗？**2** [U] the fact of being useful or making something easier to do 有帮助的人[物]：*That map isn't much help.* 那张地图不管用。| **with the help of** *We got it open with the help of a knife.* 我们用刀子把它打开了。| **be of great/little/no help** *I'm sorry I haven't been of much help to you.* 抱歉，我没帮上你什么忙。**3 be a (big/great/real) help** also 又作 **be a lot of help a)** to be very useful, or give a lot of help（很）有用；有（很大）帮助：*Thanks. You've been a big help.* 谢谢，你帮了个大忙。**b)** often used jokingly to say that something is not useful, or someone is not helping you〔开玩笑〕帮倒忙：*A lot of help you've been! Why did you bother to come?* 你真是帮倒忙！你又何必赶来呢？**4** [U] help which people can give to save someone from danger or difficulty 救助；援助；帮助：*She screamed at them to go and get help.* 她高声叫喊，让他们去找救兵。**5** [U] advice, treatment, information, or money which is given to people who need it〔建议、治疗、资料或金钱等〕援助，帮助：*A lot of these children need professional help.* 许多这样的儿童需要专业人士的帮助。| **[+with]** *You may be able to get help with the rent.* 你可能会获得租金上的援助。| **beyond help** (=no longer able to be helped or saved) 无可救药 *I'm afraid the patient is beyond help.* 这个病人恐怕是没救了。**6 the help** *AmE* someone's servant or servants【美】佣人

help·er /ˈhɛlpɚ; ˈhelpə/ *n* [C] **1** someone who helps another person 帮手；助手：*She's the cook's helper.* 她是厨师的助手。**2** *AmE* someone who is employed to do some of the work in someone else's home【美】佣人

help·ful /ˈhɛlpfəl; ˈhelpfəl/ *adj* **1** useful in making a situation better or easier 有用的；有帮助的：**it is helpful (for sb) to do sth** *Sometimes it's helpful to make a list of everything you have to do.* 有时把你要做的事情列成清单是很有用的。| *It'd be helpful for me to know what your plans for the week are.* 了解你这星期的计划会对我很有帮助。| **helpful in doing sth** *Any information would be helpful in determining what happened.* 任何信息都会帮助我们确定到底发生了什么事情。| **helpful suggestions/hints/ideas etc** *Has anybody got any helpful suggestions?* 谁能提出一些有用的建议？**2** always willing to help people 乐于助人的：*She's a helpful child.* 她是个乐于助人的孩子。—**helpfully** *adv* —**helpfulness** *n* [U]

help·ing /ˈhɛlpɪŋ; ˈhelpɪŋ/ *n* [C] the amount of food that someone gives you or that you take; SERVING〔食物的〕一份，一客：*a huge helping of potatoes* 一大份马铃薯

help·less /ˈhɛlplɪs; ˈhelpləs/ *adj* **1** unable to look after yourself or to do anything to help yourself 无法照顾自己的；无助的：*Without proper defences we'd be helpless against an enemy attack.* 如果缺乏适当的防御手段，我们将无法抵挡敌人的进攻。| *Why is he so helpless?* 他为什么会这么无助呢？**2** unable to control a strong feeling that you have 忍不住的，情不自禁的：**[+with]** *We rolled on the floor, helpless with laughter.* 我们忍不住笑得在地上打滚儿。| **helpless rage/despair/laughter etc** *fits of helpless laughter* 阵阵开怀大笑 —**helplessly** *adv* —**helplessness** *n* [U]

help·line /ˈhɛlplaɪn; ˈhelplaɪn/ *n* [C] a telephone number that you can ring if you need advice or information 求助热线

help·mate /ˈhɛlpˌmet; ˈhelpmeɪt/ also 又作 **help·meet** /-mit; -miːt/ *n* [C] *biblical* a helpful partner, usually a wife【圣经】伙伴，伴侣〔常指妻子〕

Help the Ag·ed /ˌ· · ˈ··/ a British CHARITY organization which collects money for old people and provides them with help and advice 济老会〔英国一慈善组织，为老人筹措钱款，并提供必要的帮助和建言〕

Hel·sin·ki /hɛlˈsɪŋkɪ; helˈsɪŋki/ the capital of Finland 赫尔辛基〔芬兰首都〕

Helsinki Ac·cords, the /ˌ··· ˈ··/ also 又作 **the Helsinki Agreement** an official agreement which encourages European countries to be peaceful and to make sure all their citizens are treated fairly and have basic HUMAN RIGHTS. It was signed in 1975 by every European country except Albania, and also by the US and Canada.《赫尔辛基协定》〔又称《赫尔辛基协议》。该协议旨在促进欧洲国家和平共处、确保各国公民享有平等待遇和基本人权，1975年由除阿尔巴尼亚以外的欧洲各国、美国和加拿大共同签署〕

hel·ter·skel·ter¹ /ˈhɛltɚ ˈskɛltɚ; ˌheltə ˈskeltə/ *adv* quickly and without order or organization 慌慌张张地，手忙脚乱地：*He ran off helter-skelter down the slope.* 他慌慌张张地逃下山坡。

helter-skelter² *n* [C] *BrE* a tall structure in a FAIRGROUND which you sit on at the top and slide round and round to the bottom【英】〔游乐场内的〕螺旋滑梯

hem¹ /hɛm; hem/ *n* [C] the edge of a piece of cloth that is turned under and stitched down, especially the lower edge of a skirt, trousers etc〔衣服的〕褶边;〔裙子的〕下摆;〔裤子的〕裤脚 —see picture on page A17 参见A17页图

hem² **hemmed, hemming** *v* **1** [T] to turn under the edge of a piece of material or clothing and stitch it in place 给…缝褶边 **2 hem and haw** *AmE* to keep pausing before saying something, and avoid saying it directly【美】〔说话时〕吞吞吐吐, 支支吾吾

hem sb in *phr v* [T usually passive 一般用被动态] **1** to surround someone closely, in a way that prevents them from moving 把〔某人〕围住; 困住: *They were hemmed in by steep mountains on all sides.* 他们四周都是陡峭的高山。**2** to make someone feel that they are not free to do what they want to do 限制住: *She felt hemmed-in by the daily routine.* 她感到自己被一成不变的日常工作困住。

he-man /ˈ· ·/ *n* [C] *humorous* a strong man with powerful muscles【幽默】肌肉发达的健壮男子

He·ming·way /ˈhɛmɪŋwe; ˈhemɪŋweɪ/, **Er·nest** /ˈɝnɪst; ˈɜːnɪst/ (1899-1961) one of the great US writers of the 20th century, who won the Nobel prize for literature in 1954. He wrote many NOVELs and short stories in a simple and direct style, and his books are often about typically male activities like war and hunting. His novels include *A Farewell to Arms*, *For Whom the Bell Tolls*, and *The Old Man and the Sea*. He died by shooting himself. 海明威〔(1899-1961), 20世纪最伟大的美国作家之一, 1954年获诺贝尔文学奖。他以简洁明了的文风创作了许多长篇小说和短篇小说, 作品常描写战争、狩猎之类的男性活动。代表作包括《永别了, 武器》、《丧钟为谁而鸣》和《老人与海》。他饮弹自尽〕

hem·i·sphere /ˈhɛməsˌfɪr; ˈhemɪsfɪə/ *n* [C] **1** a half of the earth, especially one of the northern and southern halves above and below the EQUATOR〔地球的〕半球〔尤指北半球或南半球〕**2** one of the two halves of your brain〔大脑的〕半球 **3** half of a SPHERE (=an object which is round like a ball)〔球体的〕一半, 半球

hem·line /ˈhɛmlaɪn; ˈhemlaɪn/ *n* [C] the length of a dress, skirt etc〔衣裙下摆的〕底边; 裙子等的长度: *Short hemlines are in this spring.* 今春流行短裙。

hem·lock /ˈhɛmlɑk; ˈhemlɒk/ *n* [C,U] a very poisonous plant, or the poison that is made from it 毒芹; 由毒芹提取的毒药

> **CULTURAL NOTE 文化注释**
>
> When they hear this word some people think of the ancient Greek thinker Socrates, who was killed by being made to drink hemlock. 毒芹令有些人想起古希腊思想家苏格拉底, 他就是被迫喝毒芹而死去的。

Hemlock So·ci·e·ty, the /ˈ·· ·ˌ···/ an organization in the US which aims to change the law that prevents helping seriously ill people to die if they wish to. The organization gives advice to such people and their families. There is a similar organization in the UK called EXIT. 毒芹协会〔美国一组织, 旨在改变禁止对重症病人实行安乐死的法律。该组织向重症病人及其家人提供建议。英国有一类似组织, 称"退场"自愿安乐死协会〕

hemo- /himo, himə; hiːməʊ, hemə/ the American spelling of HAEMO- haemo-的美式拼法

he·mo·glo·bin /ˌhiməˈglobɪn; ˌhiːməˈgləʊbɪn/ *n* [U] the American spelling of HAEMOGLOBIN haemoglobin的美式拼法

he·mo·phil·i·a /ˌhiməˈfɪlɪə; ˌhiːməˈfɪliə/ *n* [U] the American spelling of HAEMOPHILIA haemophilia的美式拼法

he·mo·phil·i·ac /ˌhiməˈfɪlɪæk; ˌhiːməˈfɪliæk/ *n* [C] the American spelling of HAEMOPHILIAC haemophiliac的美式拼法

hem·or·rhage /ˈhɛmərɪdʒ; ˈhemərɪdʒ/ *n* [C,U] the American spelling of HAEMORRHAGE haemorrhage的美式拼法

hem·or·rhoids /ˈhɛmərɔɪdz; ˈhemərɔɪdz/ *n* [plural] the American spelling of HAEMORRHOIDS haemorrhoids的美式拼法

hemp /hɛmp; hemp/ *n* [U] a type of plant that is used to make rope and sometimes to produce the drug CANNABIS 大麻〔用以制绳, 有时制成毒品〕

hen /hɛn; hen/ *n* [C] **1** an adult female chicken 母鸡 **2** any female bird of which the male is the COCK¹ (5) 雌禽

> **CULTURAL NOTE 文化注释**
>
> A woman who worries about her children and wants to know where they are is sometimes compared to a mother hen. 担心子女、总想知道子女在哪儿的母亲有时被比做老母鸡。

hence /hɛns; hens/ *adv formal*【正式】**1** [sentence adverb 句子副词] for this reason 因此, 由此, 所以: *He's an extremely private person; hence his reluctance to give interviews.* 他是一个极端孤僻的人, 因此不愿接受采访。**2 ten days hence/five months hence etc** ten days from now, five months from now etc 十天/五个月等以后 ✍2

hence·forth /ˌhɛnsˈfɔrθ; ˌhensˈfɔːθ/ also 又作 **hence·for·ward** /ˌhɛnsˈfɔrwɚd; ˌhensˈfɔːwəd/ *adv formal* from this time on【正式】从今以后, 今后, 从现在起: *The company will henceforth be known as "Johnson and Brown."* 公司今后将称为"约翰逊－布朗公司"。

hench·man /ˈhɛntʃmən; ˈhentʃmən/ *n plural* **henchmen** /-mən; -mən/ [C] a faithful supporter, especially of a political leader or a criminal〔尤指政治领导人或罪犯的〕忠实支持者, 党羽, 喽罗, 狗腿子, 心腹

Hen·drix /ˈhɛndrɪks; ˈhendrɪks/, **Jim·i** /ˈdʒɪmɪ; ˈdʒɪmi/ (1942-70) a US GUITAR player and singer who played the guitar in a completely new way, and was famous for his exciting performances. He died as a result of taking drugs. His songs include *Purple Haze* and *Voodoo Chile*. 亨德里克斯〔(1942-1970), 美国吉他手、歌手。他采用一种全新的方式弹奏吉他, 并以激动人心的表演闻名。他最终死于吸毒, 其歌曲包括《紫雾》和《巫毒智利》〕

hen house /ˈ· ·/ *n* [C] a small building where chickens are kept 鸡舍

Hen·ley Re·gat·ta /ˌhɛnlɪ rɪˈgætə; ˌhenli rɪˈgætə/ also 又作 **Henley** a series of boat races for ROWING BOATs, held every year on the river Thames near the town of Henley in the south of England. Henley is also a fashionable social event, especially for rich and UPPER-CLASS people. 亨利赛船会〔每年在英格兰南部亨利镇附近的泰晤士河上举行的系列划船比赛。这也是一项时尚的社交活动, 对富人和上流社会人士来说尤为如此〕

hen·na /ˈhɛnə; ˈhenə/ *n* [U] a reddish-brown substance used to change the colour of hair〔红褐色的〕散沫花染发剂 —**henna** *v* [T]

hen par·ty /ˈ· ˌ··/ *n* [C] *informal BrE* a party for women only, that happens just before one of them gets married【非正式, 英】〔女性即将结婚前举行的〕只有女性朋友参加的聚会 —compare 比较 STAG PARTY

hen·pecked /ˈhɛnˌpɛkt; ˈhenpekt/ *adj* a man who is henpecked is always being told what to do by his wife, and is afraid to disagree with her〔男人〕怕老婆的, 惧内的: *a henpecked husband* 怕老婆的丈夫

Hen·ry /ˈhɛnrɪ; ˈhenri/, **John** a character in US stories and FOLK songs who worked on railways and was very strong 亨利〔美国传说故事、民歌中的一个人物。他在铁路上工作, 身体十分强壮〕

Henry, O. /o; əʊ/ (1862-1910) a US writer of short stories, whose real name was William Sydney Porter. His stories treat the everyday life of working people in a humorous way, and often have unexpected endings. 欧·亨利〔(1862-1910), 美国短篇小说家, 真名威廉·西德尼·波特。其作品以幽默的笔触描述工人阶层的日常生活, 结局往往出人意料〕

Henry, Pat·rick /ˈpætrɪk; ˈpætrɪk/ (1736-99) a US politician who was one of the leaders of the fight for independence during the American Revolutionary War. He is famous for saying 'Give me liberty, or give me death'. 亨利〔(1736-1799), 美国政治家, 独立战争领导人之一, 以"不自由, 毋宁死"这句名言而著称〕

Henry, Prince —see 见 Prince HARRY

Henry I /ˌhɛnrɪ ðə ˈfɝst; ˌhenri ðə ˈfɜːst/, **King** (1068-1135) the king of England from 1100 until his death. He was the youngest son of William the Conqueror. 亨利一世〔(1068-1135), 英格兰国王, 1100年即位直至去世, 为征服者威廉的幼子〕

Henry II /ˌhɛnrɪ ðə ˈsɛkənd; ˌhenri ðə ˈsekənd/, **King** (1133-89) the king of England from 1154 until his death. He tried to reduce the power of the Church, and as a result he quarrelled with Thomas à Becket, the Archbishop of Canterbury. Some of Henry's soldiers killed Becket in Canterbury Cathedral. 亨利二世〔(1133-1189), 英格兰国王, 1154年即位直至去世。他试图削弱教会的权力, 结果与坎特伯雷大主教托马斯·贝克特发生争执。他的卫兵在坎特伯雷大教堂杀害了大主教〕

Henry III /ˌhɛnrɪ ðə ˈθɝd; ˌhenri ðə ˈθɜːd/, **King** (1207-72) the king of England from 1216 until his death. He fought many wars in Europe, and this made him unpopular with the BARONs (=men of the highest social class). Led by Simon de Montfort, they fought against him but eventually lost. 亨利三世〔(1207-1272), 英格兰国王, 1216年即位直至去世。他在欧洲多次发动战争, 引起男爵们的不满。他们在西蒙·德·蒙特福特的带领下发动叛乱, 但最终失败〕

Henry IV /ˌhɛnrɪ ðə ˋforθ, ˌhenri ðə 'fɔːθ/, **King** (1366-1413) the king of England from 1399, when he took power from King Richard II, until his death. He spent much of his time as king fighting to gain control over Wales and Scotland, but he was unsuccessful in this. There are two plays by William Shakespeare about his life (*Henry IV, Part I*, and *Henry IV, Part II*). 亨利四世〔(1366-1413)，英格兰国王，1399年从理查二世国王手中夺取王位，在位直至去世。在位期间，他多年率军作战以夺取威尔士和苏格兰的控制权，但未能成功。威廉·莎士比亚的两部戏剧《亨利四世》(上篇)和《亨利四世》(下篇)都以他的生平为题材〕

Henry Tu·dor /ˌ‥ˈ‥/ —see 见 King HENRY VII

Henry V /ˌhɛnrɪ ðə ˋfɪfθ; ˌhenri ðə 'fɪfθ/, **King** (1387-1422) the king of England from 1413 until his death, who is remembered especially for defeating the French at the Battle of Agincourt. The events surrounding this battle are described in Shakespeare's play *Henry V*. 亨利五世〔(1387-1422)，英格兰国王，1413年即位直至去世。令人记忆犹新的是，他在阿让库尔战役中打败法国军队。围绕这场战役的诸多事件在莎士比亚戏剧《亨利五世》中有所描绘〕

Henry VI /ˌhɛnrɪ ðə ˋsɪksθ; ˌhenri ðə 'sɪksθ/, **King** (1421-71) the king of England from 1422 to 1461 and from 1470 to 1471. During Henry's rule there was great dissatisfaction with the government. This led to the Wars of the Roses, in which Henry was finally murdered. 亨利六世〔(1421-1471)，英格兰国王，1422至1461年和1470至1471年在位。在他统治期间，人民对政府强烈不满，从而引发了玫瑰战争。亨利六世最终被杀〕

Henry VII /ˌhɛnrɪ ðə ˋsɛvənθ; ˌhenri ðə 'sevənθ/, **King** also **Henry Tudor** (1457-1509) the king of England from 1485. He defeated Richard III at the battle of Bosworth Field, and married to unite the families of York and Lancaster and so ended the Wars of the Roses between the two families. 亨利七世〔(1457-1509)，英格兰国王，1485年即位。在博斯沃思原野战役中击败理查三世，并通过联姻方式让约克和兰开斯特两个家族和好，从而结束了玫瑰战争〕

Henry VIII /ˌhɛnrɪ ðɪ ˋeθ; ˌhenri ði 'eɪtθ/, **King** (1491-1547) the king of England from 1509 until his death. The fact about Henry VIII which most British people know is that he had six wives. He tried to legally end his first marriage, to Catherine of Aragon, because she did not produce any sons and he wanted to marry Anne Boleyn, but the Pope refused to allow this. Henry disobeyed the Pope and made himself the head of the church in England. This started the Reformation in England, in which the Protestant church was established. His other wives were: Anne Boleyn, who had her head cut off; Jane Seymour, who died while giving birth to a child; Anne of Cleves, whom Henry DIVORCE*d*; Catherine Howard, who had her head cut off; and Catherine Parr, who lived on after Henry's death. During Henry's time as king, many schools were established, and England became a more powerful country. 亨利八世〔(1491-1547)，英格兰国王，1509年即位直至去世。关于亨利八世，大多数英国人都知道他娶过六个妻子。他的首任妻子阿拉贡的凯萨琳没能为他生下子嗣，所以他试图依法结束与她的婚姻关系，并娶安妮·博林为妻，但是遭到了教皇的反对。亨利八世违背教皇旨意，自立为英格兰教会首脑，从而引发了英格兰的宗教改革，创立了新教教会。他的另外几位妻子是：安妮·博林(遭斩首)、简·西摩(在分娩时死亡)、克利夫斯的安妮(离婚)、凯萨琳·霍华德(遭斩首)、凯萨琳·帕尔(亨利八世死后仍活着)。执政期间，亨利八世兴建了不少学校，英格兰的国力日益强大〕

Henry Wood Prom·e·nade Con·certs, the /ˌ‥ ˈ‥ˌ‥/ the official name of the PROMS 亨利·伍德逍遥音乐会〔逍遥音乐会的正式名称〕

Hen·son /ˋhɛnsn̩; 'hensən/, **Jim** /dʒɪm; dʒɪm/ (1936-90) a US maker of PUPPET*s*, who invented the Muppets, including characters such as Kermit the Frog, Miss Piggy, and the Cookie Monster. 亨森〔(1936-1990)，美国木偶制作人。他发明提线木偶，包括青蛙凯米特、猪小姐和饼干精等角色〕

hep·a·ti·tis /ˌhɛpəˋtaɪtɪs; ˌhepə'taɪtɪs◂/ *n* [U] a disease of the LIVER (1) that causes fever and yellow colour in your skin 肝炎

hepatitis A /ˌ‥‥ˈ‥/ *n* [U] a usually less severe form of hepatitis, caused by infected food or water 甲型肝炎

hepatitis B /ˌ‥‥ˈ‥/ *n* [U] a severe form of hepatitis passed from one person to another in infected blood 乙型肝炎

Hep·burn /ˋhɛpbɝn; 'hepbɜːn/, **Au·drey** /ˋɔdrɪ; 'ɔːdri/ (1929-92) an actress, famous for being beautiful and graceful, who was born in Belgium and who appeared in both British and American films, such as *Breakfast at Tiffany's* (1961) and *My Fair Lady* (1964). She also worked for UNICEF, helping poor and sick children in places like Africa and Latin America. 赫本〔(1929-1992)，女演员，以美艳绝伦、气质优雅出名。她出生在比利时，演过许多英美影片，如《在蒂芬尼饭店进早餐》(1961)和《窈窕淑女》(1964)。同时，她还为联合国儿童基金会工作，致力于帮助非洲、拉丁美洲等地的家庭贫困和身患疾病的儿童〕

Hepburn, Kath·a·rine /ˋkæθərɪn; 'kæθərɪn/ (1909-) one of America's greatest film and theatre actresses, known for appearing as strong, brave, and determined characters. She often worked with Spencer Tracy, with whom she had a romantic relationship for many years. Her films include *The Philadephia Story* (1940), *The African Queen* (1951), *Guess Who's Coming to Dinner* (1967) and *On Golden Pond* (1981). 赫本〔(1909-)，美国最出色的电影和戏剧女演员之一，以扮演坚强勇敢、意志坚定的角色闻名。她常与斯潘塞·屈塞合作，两人的亲密关系保持了许多年。其影片包括《费城故事》(1940)、《非洲皇后号》(1951)、《猜猜谁来吃晚餐》(1967)和《金色池塘》(1981)〕

He·phaes·tus /hɪˋfistəs; hɪ'fiːstəs/ in Greek MYTHOLOGY, the god of fire and METALWORK (=making metal objects), who made weapons for the gods. In Roman mythology his name is Vulcan. 赫菲斯托斯〔古希腊神话中的火和锻冶之神，为诸神锻造武器。罗马神话中称伏尔甘〕

hep·ta·gon /ˋhɛptəˌgɑn; 'heptəgən/ *n* [C] a shape with seven sides 七边形，七角形 —**heptagonal** /hɛpˋtægənl; hep'tægənəl/ *adj*

Hep·worth /ˋhɛpwɝθ; 'hepwɜːθ/, **Bar·ba·ra** /ˋbɑrbərə; 'bɑːbərə/ (1903-75) a British SCULPTOR (=a person who makes art products out of stone, metal, and wood) who worked in an ABSTRACT style 赫普沃斯〔(1903-1975)，英国雕塑家。她的作品具有抽象艺术风格〕

her[1] /ɚ, hɚ; ə, hə; *strong* 强读 hɝ; hɜː/ *determiner* [possessive form of 'she' she 的所有格] **1** belonging to or connected with a woman, girl, or female animal that has been mentioned or is known about〔指女性或雌性动物〕她的: *Maria starts her swimming lessons on Friday.* 玛丽亚星期五开始上她的游泳课。| *It's her first child.* 这是她的第一个孩子。**2** connected with a country, ship, car etc that has been mentioned〔指国家、船只、车辆等〕她的: *Her top speed is about 110 miles an hour.* 她的最高时速大约为110英里。 S1 W1

her[2] *pron* [object form of 'she' she 的宾格] **1** a woman, girl, or female animal that has been mentioned or is known about〔指女性或雌性动物〕她: *Janet? I've not seen her for a long time.* 珍妮特？我已经很久没见过她了。| *Give her the keys.* 把钥匙给她。| *Is that her over there?* 那边是她吗？—see 见 ME (USAGE) **2** a country, ship, car etc that has been mentioned 她〔指国家、船只、车辆等〕: *God bless this ship and all who sail in her.* 愿上帝保佑这条船和船上所有的人！ S1 W1

He·ra /ˋhɪrə; 'hɪərə/ in Greek MYTHOLOGY, the GODDESS of women and marriage. She was the wife of Zeus. In Roman mythology her name is Juno. 赫拉〔古希腊神话中司妇女生活和婚姻的女神。她是宙斯之妻，罗马神话中称朱诺〕

Her·a·kles, Heracles /ˋhɛrəˌkliz; 'herəkliːz/ the Greek name for Hercules 赫拉克勒斯〔赫丘利的希腊名〕

her·ald[1] /ˋhɛrəld; 'herəld/ *v* [T] **1** to be a sign of something that is going to happen 预示…的发生: *The talks herald a new era in East-West relations.* 会谈预示着东西方关系将进入一个新的时代。**2** to say publicly that someone or something will be good or important 公开称赞: *She has been heralded as one of the country's finest musicians.* 她被誉为该国最优秀的音乐家之一。

herald[2] *n* **1** [C] someone who carried messages from a ruler in the past〔古时的〕传令官 **2 herald of** a sign that something is soon going to happen …的预兆: *primroses, the first herald of spring* 报春花，春天来临的首个预兆

Herald, The —see 见 The GLASGOW HERALD

he·ral·dic /hɛˋrældɪk; he'rældɪk/ *adj* connected with heraldry 纹章术的；纹章学的

her·ald·ry /ˋhɛrəldrɪ; 'herəldri/ *n* [U] the skill of making or the study of coats of arms (COAT OF ARMS) 纹章术；纹章学

Herald Trib·une, The /ˌ‥ˈ‥/ —see 见 The INTERNATIONAL HERALD TRIBUNE

herb /hɝb; hɜːb/ *n* [C] a small plant that is used to improve the taste of food, or to make medicine〔用于调味或制药的〕香草；药草

her·ba·ceous /hɝˋbeʃəs; hə'beɪʃəs/ *adj technical* plants that are herbaceous have soft stems rather than wood stems【术语】〔植物〕草本的

herbaceous bor·der /ˌ‥ˌ‥ˈ‥/ *n* [C] part of a garden where plants are grown that live for many years and do not need to be replaced〔花园中种植的多年生的〕绿草带，绿缘

herb·al /ˈhɝbl; ˈhɜːbəl/ *adj* made of herbs 用草本植物制成的: *herbal tea* 药草茶 | *herbal remedies* 草药

herb·al·ist /ˈhɝblɪst; ˈhɜːbəl̩st/ *n* [C] someone who grows, sells, or uses HERBS, especially to treat illness 种草药的人; 草药商; 草药医生

herbal medi·cine /ˌ‥ ˈ‥‥/ *n* **1** [U] the practice of treating illness using plants 草药治疗法, 草药医学 **2** [C,U] medicine made from plants 草药

Her·bert /ˈhɝbɚt; ˈhɜːbət/**, George** (1593-1633) an English poet who wrote poetry in the Metaphysical style 赫伯特〔(1593-1633), 英国玄学派诗人〕

herb gar·den /ˈ· ˌ‥/ *n* [C] a garden in which only HERBS are grown 百草园

herb·i·cide /ˈhɝbɪˌsaɪd; ˈhɜːbə̩saɪd/ *n* [C,U] *technical* a substance used to kill unwanted plants【术语】除草剂

her·bi·vore /ˈhɝbɪˌvɔr; ˈhɜːbə̩vɔː/ *n* [C] an animal that only eats plants 食草动物 —**herbivorous** /hɝˈbɪvərəs; hɜːˈbɪvərəs/ *adj* —compare 比较 CARNIVORE, OMNIVORE

Hercegovina —see 见 HERZEGOVINA

her·cu·le·an /hɝˈkjulɪən; ˌhɜːkjʊˈliːən◂/ *adj* needing great strength or determination 需要花很大力气[决心]的: *a herculean task* 艰巨的任务

Her·cu·les /ˈhɝkjəˌliz; ˈhɜːkjə̩liːz/ in ancient Roman stories, a HERO known for his very great strength and for performing twelve very difficult and dangerous jobs known as *the Labours of Hercules*. People sometimes use the name 'Hercules' to describe a man who is physically very strong. In ancient Greek stories, his name is Herakles. 赫丘利〔古罗马传说中的英雄。他力大无比, 完成过12件十分艰险的苦差事(人称赫丘利的苦差), 并因此著称。人们有时借用Hercules(赫丘利)这个名字来形容体格健壮的男子。古希腊神话中称赫拉克勒斯〕—see also 另见 the AUGEAN STABLES, PILLARS OF HERCULES

herd¹ /hɝd; hɜːd/ *n* **1** [C] a group of animals of one kind that lives and feeds together〔同一种类并一同栖息的〕兽群: **[+of]** *a herd of cattle* 一群牛 | [also+plural verb in *BrE* 英] *A herd of cows were descending into the valley.* 一群牛正从山上走下来, 进入山谷。—compare 比较 FLOCK¹ (1) **2 the herd** people generally, especially when thought of as being easily influenced〔易受人支配的〕民众, 老百姓, 芸芸众生: *She's never been the sort of person to follow the herd.* 她是一个从来不随大流的人。| **the herd instinct** (=the need to behave in the same way as everyone else) 群体本能, 随大溜的本能

herd² *v* **1** [I always+adv/prep, T] to come together or bring people together in a large group, especially roughly〔尤指粗暴地〕(使)集合在一起: **[+into/through etc]** *The waiting tourists were herded onto the bus.* 等待着的游客被赶进大客车里。**2** [T] to make animals move together in a group 放牧: *herding sheep* 牧羊

herds·man /ˈhɝdzmən; ˈhɜːdzmən/ *n plural* **herdsmen** /-mən; -mən/ [C] a man who looks after a herd of animals 牧人

[1] [1] **here¹** /hɪr; hɪə/ *adv* **1** in this place 在这里: *Is George here?* 乔治在这里吗? | *Kabul is four hundred miles west of here.* 喀布尔在此地以西400英里。| *I knew there would be no one here in this room.* 我早就知道这房间里没有人。| *Shall we eat here?* 我们在这里吃饭好吗? | **here and now** (=used to emphasize what you are saying) 此时此地〔用来加强语气〕*I'll tell you here and now that I am not going to resign.* 我现在就告诉你, 我不会辞职。| **on here/out here/down here/over here etc** *It's very cold out here.* 这外面很冷。| *We're over here!* 我们在这儿呢! —compare 比较 THERE² (1) **2** happening now 此时: *I'll be glad when the summer vacation is here.* 暑假来到时, 我会很高兴。**3** at this point in a discussion〔讨论中〕在这一点上: *There are many reasons for this decline, which we cannot discuss here.* 造成这种下降的原因有很多, 在此我们无法讨论。**4 here's/here is/here are/here comes etc** used when introducing something or someone, or showing them to someone 这就是…〔用以介绍某人或某物〕: *Here comes Michael now.* 这位就是迈克尔。| *Here's the shop I was telling you about.* 这就是我一直向你提起的那家商店。**5 here/here is/here's/here we are etc** used when you have just found something that you have been looking for 找到了: *Ah, here we are, here's my address book.* 哈, 找到了, 我的地址簿在这里呢。**6 here's/here/here you are etc** used when you are giving something to someone 给你〔用于把某物给某人时〕: *Here's some money for you.* 给你点钱。| *Here are your keys back.* 还你钥匙。**7 neither here nor there** not important 不重要, 无关紧要的: *The hospital needs this machine. The fact that it costs a lot of money is neither here nor there.* 医院需要这种机器, 价格昂贵这一点并不重要。**8 here and there** scattered around in several different places 到处, 各处; 零散地: *Windows were shattered and there was minor damage to buildings here and there.* 窗户都被打破了, 建筑物上到处都是轻微的损伤。**9 here, there, and everywhere** *informal* in many different places【非正式】到处, 各处; 在许多不同的地方: *We've been looking for you here, there, and everywhere.* 我们一直在到处找你。**10 here goes!** used when you are going to try to do something difficult 我这就开始〔做困难的事〕: *I've never ridden a motorbike before, so here goes!* 我以前从未骑过摩托车, 现在就试试看吧! **11 here we go (again)** *informal* used when something unpleasant is beginning to happen again【非正式】〔不愉快的事〕又发生了!: *Janet stormed off in a temper. "Here we go again," Matt thought.* 珍妮特气冲冲地走了。马特心想: "又来了!" **12 Here's to** used when you are going to drink something to wish someone good luck, show your respect for them etc 为…干杯, 祝…〔敬酒时说的祝词〕: *Here's to the happy couple.* 为这幸福的一对干杯! | *Here's to your new job.* 为你的新工作干杯! **13 here to stay** if something is here to stay, it has become a part of life and will continue to be so〔某物〕已经成为生活中的一部分

Frequencies of the word **here** in spoken and written English.
单词here在英语口语和书面语中的使用频率

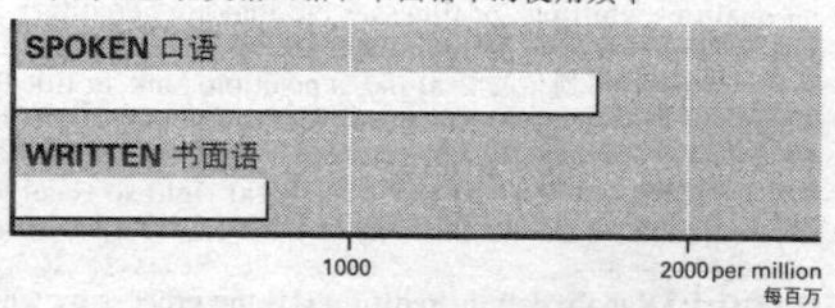

Based on the British National Corpus and the Longman Lancaster Corpus
据英国国家语料库和朗文兰开斯特语料库

This graph shows that the word **here** is much more common in spoken English than in written English. This is because it has special uses in spoken English and is used in a lot of common spoken phrases. 本图表显示, 单词here在英语口语中的使用频率远远高于书面语, 因为它在英语口语中有一些特殊的用法, 而且口语中有很多常用短语是由here构成的。

here (*adv*) **SPOKEN PHRASES**
含here的口语短语

14 a) used when you are giving or offering something to someone 喏〔把某物给某人时用〕: *Here, have my chair. I don't mind standing.* 喏, 坐我的椅子吧, 我可以站着。**b)** *BrE* used to get someone's attention or to show that you are annoyed【英】喂〔用来引起别人注意或表示不高兴〕: *Here! Just what do you think you're doing?* 喂! 你认为你这是在干什么? **15 here is a)** used when you are giving something to someone 给你…〔给别人东西时用〕: *Here's some money. Have a good time.* 给你点钱。好好玩吧! **b)** used to say that someone or something is arriving …来了: *Ah, look – here's the mailman.* 啊, 瞧! 邮递员来了。| **here it is/they are** *Here they are, late as usual.* 他们终于来了, 一如既往又迟到了。**c)** used to tell someone that you have found something, or to say where something is …在这儿〔表示发现某物〕: *Oh, here's the knife, it was under these dishes.* 啊, 刀子在这儿呢! 就在这堆盘子底下。| **here it is/they are** *Here she is, hiding behind the curtains.* 她在这儿呢, 藏在帘子后面。**16 here you are/here you go** used when you are giving something to someone 给你〔把东西给某人时用〕: *Here you are John, have some cake.* 约翰, 给你, 吃点蛋糕吧! **17 here we go** used when you are starting to do something or when something is starting to happen (我们)开始了: *Right, here we go, the game's starting.* 好了, 开始了, 游戏就要开始了。**18 here goes** used when you are going to try something and you do not know what will happen 我要开始了〔表示准备做某事并对后果不确定〕: *O.K. Here goes. Stand back everyone.* 好了, 我要开始了。大家往后站。**19 here comes** used when you can see something or someone arriving …来了: *Quick, here comes the bus. Have you got the right money?* 快, 公共汽车来了。准备好零钱了吗?

here² *interjection* **1** used when you are giving or offering something to someone〔用于把某物给某人时〕喏: *Here, have my chair. I don't mind standing.* 喏, 坐我的椅子吧。我可以站着。**2** *BrE* used to attract someone's attention or to express annoyance【英】喂!〔用来引起别人注意或表示不高兴〕: *Here! Just what do you think you're doing?* 喂! 你认为你这是在干什么?

here·a·bouts /ˌhɪrəˋbauts; ˌhɪərəˈbaʊts/ also 又作 **hereabout** *AmE*【美】*adv* somewhere near the place where you are〔在这〕附近, 在这一带: *There must be a public telephone hereabouts.* 这附近肯定有公用电话。

here·af·ter /hɪrˋæftɚ; ˌhɪərˈɑːftə/ *adv* **1** [sentence adverb 句子副词] *formal* from this time【正式】此后, 今后 **2** *formal* after death【正式】死后 **3** *law* in a later part of a legal document【法律】〔法律文件的〕在下文中, 此后

hereafter, the *n* a life after death 来世: *Do you believe in the hereafter?* 你相信有来世吗?

here·by /hɪrˋbaɪ; ˌhɪəˈbaɪ/ *adv law* a word meaning 'by this statement', used in official documents or statements【法律】特此, 兹: *I hereby declare that James Lowe is elected to serve as MP for this constituency.* 我特此宣布詹姆斯·洛已经当选为本选区的下议院议员。

Here Comes the Bride /ˌ· ·ˌ· ˋ· ˋ·/ a piece of music which is often played at the beginning of a marriage ceremony, when the bride begins to walk up the AISLE of the church《新娘来啦》〔婚礼开始, 新娘步入教堂通道时常播放的乐曲〕—compare 比较 the WEDDING MARCH

he·red·i·ta·ry /həˋrɛdəˌtɛrɪ; hɪ̣ˈredɪ̣təri/ *adj* **1** mental or physical qualities, abilities, or illnesses etc that are hereditary are passed from parent to child in the cells of the body〔品质、体格、能力、疾病等〕遗传的 **2 a)** *BrE* a position, rank, or title that is hereditary can be passed from an older to a younger person in the same family, usually when the older one dies【英】〔地位、称号等〕世袭的, 承袭的 **b)** having a legal right to receive a position, rank, or title in this way 享有承袭权的: *a hereditary peer* 世袭的贵族

he·red·i·ty /həˋrɛdətɪ; hɪ̣ˈredɪ̣ti/ *n* [U] the process by which mental or physical qualities, abilities, or illnesses pass from parents to children in the cells of the body 遗传

Her·e·ford /ˋhɛrɪfɚd; ˈherɪ̣fəd/ **1** a small city with a CATHEDRAL (=a large, important church) in Herefordshire in western England 赫里福德〔英格兰西部赫里福德郡一小城市。城中有一座大教堂〕 **2** a breed of red and white cattle, originally from Herefordshire, and used for producing BEEF 赫里福德牛〔原产于赫里福德郡的一种毛色红白相间的肉牛〕

He·re·ford·shire /ˋhɛrɪfɚdʃɚ; ˈherɪ̣fədʃə/ a COUNTY in western England, next to Wales 赫里福德郡〔英格兰西部一郡, 与威尔士相邻〕

here·in /hɪrˋɪn; ˌhɪərˈɪn/ *adv formal* in this place, situation, document etc【正式】在此地; 在这种情况下; 在本文中: *the conditions stated herein* 本文所列条件 —compare 比较 THEREIN

here·in·af·ter /ˌhɪrɪnˋæftɚ; ˌhɪərɪnˈɑːftə/ *adv law* later in this official statement, document etc【法律】〔正式文件〕在下文中: *Messrs Wilson and Cartwright, hereinafter referred to as "the insurers"...* 威尔逊先生和卡特赖特先生, 以下称"承保人"…

here·of /hɪrˋɑv; ˌhɪərˈɒv/ *adv formal or law* connected with or belonging to this【正式或法律】关于这点, 在本文中: *every part hereof* 本文中的每个部分 —compare 比较 THEREOF

her·e·sy /ˋhɛrəsɪ; ˈherɪ̣si/ *n* [C,U] **1** a belief that disagrees with the official principles of a particular religion 异教 **2** a belief, statement etc that disagrees with what a group of people believe to be right 异端邪说: *In the 1980s it became economic heresy to challenge monetarist theory.* 20世纪80年代, 质疑货币主义理论的观点被看做是经济学上的异端邪说。

her·e·tic /ˋhɛrətɪk; ˈherɪ̣tɪk/ *n* [C] someone who is guilty of heresy 异教徒; 异端分子: *Cranmer was put to death as a heretic.* 克兰默被当做异端分子处死了。—**heretical** /həˋrɛtɪkḷ; hɪ̣ˈretɪkəl/ *adj*

here·to /hɪrˋtu; ˌhɪəˈtuː/ *adv formal* to this【正式】于此, 在此, 至此: *my signature hereto appended* 在此附上本人签名

here·to·fore /ˌhɪrtəˋfɔr; ˌhɪətʊˈfɔː/ *adv formal* before this time【正式】此前, 在此之前

here·up·on /ˌhɪrəˋpɑn; ˌhɪərəˈpɒn/ *adv formal* at or after this moment【正式】此刻; 随后

here·with /hɪrˋwɪθ; ˌhɪəˈwɪð/ *adv formal* with this letter or document【正式】与此〔信或文件〕一道, 随函附上: *I enclose herewith two copies of the contract.* 随函附上合同副本两份。

her·i·ta·ble /ˋhɛrətəbḷ; ˈherɪ̣təbəl/ *adj law* property that is heritable can be passed from the older members of a family to the younger ones; HEREDITARY (2)【法律】〔财产〕可继承的

her·i·tage /ˋhɛrətɪdʒ; ˈherɪ̣tɪdʒ/ *n* [singular,U] important qualities, customs, and TRADITIONS that have been in a society for a long time 遗产; 传统: *the cultural heritage of Italy* 意大利的文化遗产 —compare 比较 INHERITANCE

her·maph·ro·dite /hɝˋmæfrəˌdaɪt; hɜːˈmæfrədaɪt/ *n* [C] a living thing that has the organs of both male and female 雌雄同体的生物 —**hermaphrodite** *adj* —**hermaphroditic** /hɝˌmæfrəˋdɪtɪk; hɜːˌmæfrəˈdɪtɪk◂/ *adj*

Her·mes /ˋhɝmiz; ˈhɜːmiːz/ in Greek MYTHOLOGY, the god who is the MESSENGER (=someone who takes messages) of the gods. He is usually shown in pictures with wings on his shoes and on his HELMET. In Roman mythology his name is Mercury. 赫耳墨斯〔古希腊神话中的神的信使。在图画中, 他的鞋子和头盔上插有翅膀。罗马神话中称墨丘利〕

her·met·ic /hɝˋmɛtɪk; hɜːˈmetɪk/ *adj technical* very tightly closed so that air cannot get in or out; AIRTIGHT【术语】密封的, 不透气的 —**hermetically** /-klɪ; -kli/ *adv*: *stored in hermetically sealed containers* 保存在密封的容器里

her·mit /ˋhɝmɪt; ˈhɜːmɪ̣t/ *n* [C] someone who lives alone and has a simple way of life, usually for religious reasons〔一般指出于宗教原因的〕隐士, 独居修道士; 遁世者 —compare 比较 RECLUSE

her·mit·age /ˋhɝmɪtɪdʒ; ˈhɜːmɪ̣tɪdʒ/ *n* [C] a place where a hermit lives or has lived 隐居处, 隐士住处

Hermitage, the a large museum in St Petersburg in Russia, known especially for its collection of Impressionist paintings 爱尔米塔什博物馆〔俄罗斯圣彼德堡一大型博物馆, 尤以收藏印象派作品闻名〕

hermit crab /ˈ· ·ˌ·/ *n* [C] a kind of CRAB[1] (1) that lives in the empty shells of other sea creatures 寄居蟹

her·ni·a /ˋhɝnɪə; ˈhɜːniə/ *n* [C,U] a medical condition in which an organ pushes through the muscles that are supposed to contain it; RUPTURE[1] (3)〔脏器的〕突出, 疝(气)

he·ro /ˋhɪro; ˈhɪərəʊ/ *n plural* **heroes** [C] **1** a man who is admired for doing something extremely brave 英雄, 豪杰, 勇士: *He had dared to speak out against injustice, and overnight he became a national hero.* 他敢于站出来抨击不公正的现象, 一夜之间就成了国家英雄。| **war hero** (=a soldier who was very brave in a war) 战争英雄 **2** the man or boy who is the main character in a book, film, play etc 男主角, 男主人公: *Indiana Jones is the hero of the film.* 印第安那·琼斯是影片的男主角。**3** someone you admire very much for their intelligence, skill etc 偶像: **sb's hero** *My hero as a boy was the great Di Maggio.* 我儿时的偶像是了不起的迪马乔。**4** *AmE* a SANDWICH made of a long LOAF of bread filled with meat, cheese etc【美】〔夹有肉、干酪等的〕长面包三明治 —see also 另见 HEROINE 3

Her·od /ˋhɛrəd; ˈherəd/ **1 Herod the Great** (74-4 BC) the king of Judea at the time when Jesus Christ was born. according to the New Testament of the Bible, he ordered that all the male babies in Bethlehem should be killed because he wanted to kill the baby who ancient stories said would become king. 希律大帝〔(公元前74-前4), 耶稣基督出生时, 他任犹太国王。据《圣经·新约》所述, 因传说中有新君王将要诞生之说, 他便下令杀死伯利恒的所有男婴〕 **2 Herod Antipas** (21 BC-AD 39) a Roman governor in Palestine, who was the son of Herod the Great. In the New Testament of the Bible, he ordered the killing of John the Baptist, and later he refused to make a decision about whether Jesus should be killed or not. 希律〔(公元前21-公元39), 巴勒斯坦的罗马统治者, 希律大帝之子。据《圣经·新约》所述, 他曾下令杀害施洗者约翰。后来, 就是否处决耶稣一事, 他不愿作出判决〕

he·ro·ic /hɪˋro·ɪk; hɪˈrəʊɪk/ *adj* **1** extremely brave or determined and admired by many people 英雄的, 英勇的: *her heroic efforts to save her family* 她为挽救全家人所作的英勇的尝试 **2** a heroic story, poem etc involves a hero〔关于〕英雄的 **3 on a heroic scale/of heroic proportions** very large or great 很大的: *a battle on a heroic scale* 大规模的战争 —**heroically** /-klɪ; -kli/ *adv*

heroic coup·let /ˌ· ·ˋ· ˋ·/ *n* [C] a pair of lines in poetry which end with the same sound and that have five beats in each line〔两行相互押韵、每行含有五个节拍的〕英雄偶句诗

he·ro·ics /hɪˋro·ɪks; hɪˈrəʊɪks/ *n* [plural] language or behaviour that is too brave for a particular situation〔过分的〕豪言壮语; 逞英雄行为: *America's present need is not heroics, but calm diplomacy.* 美国当前需要的不是逞英雄, 而是冷静的外交。

her·o·in /ˋhɛro·ɪn; ˈherəʊɪn/ *n* [U] a powerful and illegal drug made from MORPHINE 海洛因, 二乙酰吗啡: *a heroin addict* 海洛因瘾君子

her·o·ine /ˋhɛro·ɪn; ˈherəʊɪn/ *n* [C] **1** the woman or girl who is the main character in a book, film, play etc 女主角, 女主人公: *the tragic heroine of Sophocles' play*〔古希腊剧作家〕索福克勒斯戏剧中悲惨的女主角 **2** a woman who is extremely brave and is admired by many people 女英雄: *a heroine of the French Resistance* 法国抵抗运动的女英雄 **3** a woman you admire very much for her intelligence, skill etc 受崇拜的女人, 〔女〕偶像 —see also 另见 HERO

her·o·is·m /ˈhɛroˌɪzəm; ˈherəʊɪzəm/ *n* [U] very great courage 英雄气概; 大无畏精神, 英勇: *stories of heroism and self-sacrifice* 关于英勇无畏和自我牺牲的故事

her·on /ˈhɛrən; ˈherən/ *n* [C] a large bird with very long legs and a long beak, that lives near water (苍) 鹭

Heron, Patrick (1920-99), a British painter famous for his ABSTRACT paintings. He is also well-known as an art CRITIC. 赫伦〔(1920-1999), 英国画家, 因抽象作品而著名。他也是一位有名的艺术批评家〕

hero wor·ship /ˈ‥, ˌ‥/ *n* [U] great admiration for someone you think is very brave, good, skilful etc 英雄[偶像]崇拜 —**hero-worship** *v* [T]

her·pes /ˈhɝpiz; ˈhɜːpiːz/ *n* [U] a very infectious disease that causes spots on the skin, especially on the face or GENITALS 疱疹

her·ring /ˈhɛrɪŋ; ˈherɪŋ/ *n plural* **herrings** or **herring** [C] a long thin silver sea fish that can be eaten 鲱鱼 —see also 另见 RED HERRING

her·ring·bone /ˈhɛrɪŋˌbon; ˈherɪŋbəʊn/ *n* [U] a pattern consisting of a continuous line of V shapes, used in cloth etc〔织物上的〕鲱骨式图案, 人字形图案 —see picture on page A16 参见 A16 页图

herring gull /ˈ‥ ‥/ *n* [C] a large white bird that lives near the sea in Britain 银鸥

Her·ri·ot /ˈhɛrɪət; ˈheriət/, **James** (1916-95) the name that a British writer, James Alfred White, used to write stories about his life as a country VET (=animal doctor) 赫里奥特〔(1916-1995), 英国作家詹姆斯·阿尔弗雷德·怀特的笔名, 英国作家。他曾以此笔名创作小说, 讲述自己在农村当兽医的经历〕

S3 **hers** /hɝz; hɜːz/ *pron* the possessive form of 'she'; of or belonging to a female person or animal already mentioned〔she 的所有格〕她的 (所有物): *This is my coat. Hers* (=Her coat) *is over there.* 这是我的外套。她的 (外套) 在那边。| *My shoes are brown and hers are red.* 我的鞋子是棕色的, 她的 (鞋子) 是红色的。| *Paul's a friend of hers.* 保罗是她的朋友。

S2 W1 **her·self** /hɚˈsɛlf; əˈself; *strong* 强读 hɝ-; hɜː-/ *pron* **1** reflexive form of 'she'〔she 的反身代词〕她自己: *She hurt herself.* 她 (把自己) 弄伤了。| *She made herself a cup of coffee.* 她给自己煮了杯咖啡。**2** the strong form of 'she' used to emphasize the subject or object of a sentence〔she 的强调形式〕她本人: *It must be true that she's leaving because she told me so herself.* 她的确是要走了, 因为这是她亲口对我说的。| *She herself told me.* 她本人告诉我的。**3** *informal* in her usual state of mind or body【非正式】〔身心的〕正常状态: *She's feeling much more herself today.* 她今天感觉好多了。**4 (all) by herself a)** alone (她) 独自, 一个人: *She lives by herself.* 她独自居住。**b)** without help from anyone else 独力: *The little girl wrote the letter all by herself.* 这个小女孩不用别人帮助, 自己写了这封信。**5 (all) to herself** for her own use; not having to share (她) 私用的, 独用的: *She had the house to herself while her parents were gone.* 她父母不在家时, 她一个人住在这座房子里。

Her·shey bar /ˈhɝʃɪ bɑr; ˈhɜːʃi bɑː/ *trademark* a type of chocolate bar made by the Hershey company and sold especially in the US【商标】好时巧克力〔好时公司生产的一种巧克力条。主要在美国出售〕

Hershey's Kiss·es /ˌ‥ˈ‥/ *trademark* a type of small chocolate wrapped in silver-coloured paper, made by the Hershey Company and sold in the US【商标】好时巧克力糖〔好时公司生产的一种用银色纸包裹的小块巧克力, 在美国出售〕

Hert·ford·shire /ˈhɑrtfɚdʃɚ; ˈhɑːtfədʃə/ a COUNTY in south-east England, north of London 赫特福德郡〔英格兰东南部一郡, 位于伦敦以北〕

hertz /hɝts; hɜːts/ *n plural* **hertz** [C] a measurement meaning one time each second, used to measure SOUND WAVES 赫 (兹), 周/秒, 次/秒〔频率单位〕

Her·ze·go·vi·na, Hercegovina /hɝtsɪgoˈvinə; hɜːtsəgəˈviːnə/ a PROVINCE which is part of Bosnia-Herzegovina, a former republic of Yugoslavia 黑塞哥维那〔前南斯拉夫的加盟共和国波士尼亚和黑塞哥维那的一个省〕

he's /ɪz, hɪz; iz, hiz; *strong* 强读 hiz; hiːz/ **1** the short form of 缩略式= he is: *He's a writer.* 他是一位作家。| *He's reading.* 他正在看书。**2** the short form of 缩略式= he has: *He's bought a new car.* 他买了一辆新车。

hes·i·tan·cy /ˈhɛzətənsɪ; ˈhezɪ̈tənsi/ also 又作 **hes·i·tance** /-təns; -təns/ *n* [U] the quality of being uncertain or slow in doing or saying something 犹豫, 踌躇, 迟疑 (不决)

hes·i·tant /ˈhɛzətənt; ˈhezɪ̈tənt/ *adj* uncertain about what to do or say because you are nervous or unwilling 犹豫 (不决) 的, 迟疑的, 有疑虑的: *Gail gave me a hesitant little smile.* 盖尔对我犹豫地微笑了一下。| **hesitant to do sth** *The economist was hesitant to comment on government policy.* 那个经济学家不大愿意对政府的政策作出评论。—**hesitantly** *adv*

hes·i·tate /ˈhɛzəˌtet; ˈhezɪ̈teɪt/ *v* **1** [I] to pause before saying or doing something because you are not sure or nervous 犹豫, 踌躇, 迟疑 (不决): *Harriet hesitated a moment before replying.* 哈丽雅特犹豫了一下才作出回答。**2 hesitate to do sth** to be unwilling to do something because you are not sure that it is right 不愿做某事, 对…有顾虑: *Don't hesitate to contact me if you need any more information.* 如果你需要更多资料, 尽管和我联系。—**hesitatingly** *adv*

hes·i·ta·tion /ˌhɛzəˈteʃən; ˌhezɪ̈ˈteɪʃən/ *n* [C,U] the action of hesitating 踌躇, 犹豫, 迟疑 (不决): *After some hesitation one of them began to speak.* 犹豫了一会儿之后, 其中一个人开口了。| **have no hesitation in** *I would have no hesitation in declining the post.* 我会毫不犹豫地拒绝这个职位。| **after/without a moment's hesitation** *Without a moment's hesitation she kissed him.* 她毫不犹豫地亲吻了他。

Hess /hɛs; hes/, **Ru·dolf** /ˈrudɑlf; ˈruːdɒlf/ (1894-1987) a German Nazi politician who was directly below Hitler in rank. In 1941 he made a secret flight to Scotland to try to arrange a peace agreement, but he was caught and made a prisoner. In 1946 he was judged to be guilty of war crimes, and was put in Spandau Prison in Berlin until his death. 赫斯〔(1894-1987), 德国纳粹政客, 职位仅次于希特勒。1941 年, 他乘飞机秘密进入苏格兰, 试图达成一项和平协定, 但被捕入狱。1946 年被判战争罪, 关押在柏林的施潘道监狱, 直至去世〕

Hes·se /ˈhɛsə; ˈhesə/, **Her·mann** /ˈhɝmən; ˈhɜːmən/ (1877-1962) a German writer and poet. His NOVELS include *Steppenwolf*, *The Glass Bead Game*, and *Siddhartha*, and often deal with the deep struggles that go on in the human mind. He won the Nobel Prize for Literature in 1946. 海塞〔(1877-1962), 德国作家、诗人。其小说包括《草原之狼》、《玻璃球游戏》和《流浪者之歌》, 常涉及人类内心深处激烈的思想斗争。1946 年获诺贝尔文学奖〕

hes·si·an /ˈhɛʃən; ˈhesiən/ *n* [U] *BrE* thick rough cloth sometimes used for making sacks (SACK¹ (1))【英】麻袋布, 粗麻布; BURLAP *AmE*【美】

het /hɛt; het/ —see 见 HET UP

hetero- /hɛtəro, -rə; hetərəʊ, -rə/ *prefix formal or technical* other; opposite; different【正式或术语】异的; 杂的; 其他的; 相反的: *heterosexual* (=attracted to the opposite sex) 异性恋的

het·e·ro·dox /ˈhɛtərəˌdɑks; ˈhetərədɒks/ *adj formal* heterodox beliefs, practices etc are not approved of by a particular group, especially a religious one【正式】异教的, 异端的, 非正统的 —compare 比较 UNORTHODOX

het·e·ro·ge·ne·ous /ˌhɛtərəˈdʒinɪəs; ˌhetərəʊˈdʒiːniəs/ also 又作 **het·e·ro·ge·nous** /ˌhɛtəˈrɑdʒənəs; ˌhetəˈrɒdʒənəs◂/ *AmE*【美】—*adj formal* consisting of parts or members that are very different from each other【正式】由全然不同的部分[成员]组成的, 混杂的: *a heterogeneous collection of buildings* 风格各异的一组建筑 —**heterogeneity** /ˌhɛtərədʒəˈniətɪ; ˌhetərəʊdʒɪ̈ˈniːɪ̈ti/ *n* [U] —**heterogeneously** *adv*

het·e·ro·sex·u·al /ˌhɛtərəˈsɛkʃuəl; ˌhetərəˈsekʃuəl◂/ *adj* sexually attracted to people of the opposite sex 异性恋的 —compare 比较 BISEXUAL¹ (1), HOMOSEXUAL —**heterosexual** *n* [C] —**heterosexuality** /ˌhɛtərəˌsɛkʃuˈælətɪ; ˌhetərəsekʃuˈælɪ̈ti/ *n* [U] —**heterosexually** *adv*

het up /ˌhɛt ˈʌp; ˌhet ˈʌp/ *adj* [not before noun 不用于名词前] *informal* anxious, upset, or slightly angry【非正式】焦虑不安的, 慌张的, 激动的: *Why's Andy so het up?* 安迪为什么这样焦虑不安呢? | **[+about]** *Mike's very het up about his exams.* 迈克对考试感到忧心忡忡。

heu·ris·tic /hjuˈrɪstɪk; hjʊˈrɪstɪk/ *adj formal*【正式】**1** heuristic education is based on discovering and experiencing things for yourself〔教育〕启发式的 **2** helping you in the process of learning or discovery〔对学习和发现〕有启发作用的, 探索 (性) 的 —**heuristically** /-klɪ; -kli/ *adv*

heu·ris·tics /hjuˈrɪstɪks; hjʊˈrɪstɪks/ *n* [plural,U] the study of how people use their experience to find answers to questions or to improve performance 启发法, 探索法

hew /hju; hjuː/ *v past tense* **hewed** *past participle* **hewed** or **hewn** /hjun; hjuːn/ *literary*【文】**1** [I,T] to cut something with a cutting tool〔用刀、斧等〕砍, 劈: *hewn stone* 凿好的石头 **2 hew a path/channel etc** to cut a path etc through something 开辟道路/渠道等 —see also 另见 ROUGH-HEWN —**hewer** *n* [C]

hewn /hjun; hjuːn/ the past participle of hew

hex¹ /hɛks; heks/ *n* [C] *especially AmE* an evil CURSE² (2) that brings trouble【尤美】〔招致灾祸的〕恶毒的诅咒; 不祥之物

hex² *v* [T] *especially AmE* to use magic powers to make bad things happen to someone; CURSE¹ (3)【尤美】施魔法于；念恶咒〔使某人遭殃或倒霉〕

hex·a·de·ci·mal /ˌhɛksəˋdɛsəml̩; ˌheksəˈdesɪ̆məl◂/ also 又作 **hex** *adj technical* hexadecimal numbers are based on the number 16 and are mainly used on computers【术语】十六进制的

hex·a·gon /ˋhɛksəˌgɑn; ˈheksəgən/ *n* [C] a shape with six sides 六边形，六角形 —**hexagonal** /hɛkˋsægənəl; hekˈsægənəl/ *adj*

hex·a·gram /ˋhɛksəˌgræm; ˈheksəgræm/ *n* [C] a star shape with six points, made from two TRIANGLES 六角星形

hex·am·e·ter /hɛksˋæmətɚ; hekˈsæmɪ̆tə/ *n* [C] a line of poetry with six main beats 有六韵步的诗行

hey /he; heɪ/ *interjection* a shout used to get someone's attention or to express surprise, interest, or annoyance 嘿，喂〔用来引起注意或表示惊讶、兴趣或恼怒的喊声〕

hey·day /ˋheˌde; ˈheɪdeɪ/ *n* **sb's/sth's heyday** the time when someone or something was most popular, successful, or powerful 某人/某物的全盛时期，最兴盛[最有影响，最成功]的时期：*a picture of Greta Garbo in her heyday* 格丽泰·嘉宝风华正茂时期的照片

hey pres·to /ˌhe ˋprɛsto; ˌheɪ ˈprestəʊ/ *interjection especially BrE* used to say that something happens so easily that it seems to be magic【尤英】说变就变〔指某事发生得很快，如同变魔术一般〕

Hey·sel Sta·di·um Di·sas·ter, the /ˋhaɪsl̩ ˋstedɪəm dɪˌzɑrstɚ; ˈhaɪsəl ˈsteɪdiəm dɪˌzɑːstə/ the death of 39 people at a football ground in Belgium in 1985, which happened when English football supporters started fights and caused a wall to fall down. Because of this, English teams were not allowed to play in European competitions for several years. 海塞尔体育场事件〔1985年在比利时一足球场，英国球迷挑起殴斗，致使一堵墙倒塌，造成39人死亡。鉴于此，英国队在欧洲被禁赛数年〕

Hez·bo·llah /ˌhɛzbuˋlɑ; ˌhezbʊˈlɑː/ also 又作 **Hizbollah** a military group of Shiite Muslims that supports Iran. 真主党〔支持伊朗的什叶派穆斯林军事组织〕

HGV /ˌetʃ dʒi ˋvi; ˌeɪtʃ dʒiː ˈviː/ *n* [C] *BrE* a HEAVY GOODS VEHICLE; a large road vehicle used for moving goods【英】大型货运卡车，载重货车

HI the written abbreviation of 缩写＝HAWAII

1 **hi** /haɪ; haɪ/ *interjection informal* hello【非正式】哈罗，你好，喂，嘿：*Hi! How are you?* 嘿！你好吗？| **hi there!** *Hi there! I haven't seen you for ages.* 嘿！好久不见。

hi·a·tus /haɪˋetəs; haɪˈeɪtəs/ *n* [C usually singular 一般用单数] **1** *formal* a break or INTERRUPTION in an activity【正式】停顿，间断：*Talks between the two countries have resumed after a six year hiatus.* 两国间的谈判在中断了六年后又恢复了。**2** a space where something is missing, especially in a piece of writing〔尤指文稿中的〕脱漏 **3** *technical* a pause between two vowel sounds【术语】元音[母音]分立[分读]〔指相连两个元音之间的短暂停顿〕

Hi·a·wath·a /ˌhaɪəˋwɑθə; ˌhaɪəˈwɒθə/ a Native American chief who, in the 16th century, helped to unite the Iroquois tribes into a single group called the **Five Nations**. He is the subject of a long poem by Longfellow called *The Song of Hiawatha* (1855). 海华沙〔美洲印第安人一部落首领。16世纪，他联合易洛魁各部落，组成一个独立组织，称"五族联盟"。朗费罗的长诗《海华沙之歌》(1855)就是以他为主题创作的〕

hi·ber·nate /ˋhaɪbɚˌnet; ˈhaɪbəneɪt/ *v* [I] if an animal hibernates, it sleeps for the whole winter〔动物〕冬眠 —**hibernation** /ˌhaɪbɚˋneʃən; ˌhaɪbəˈneɪʃən/ *n* [U]

hi·bis·cus /haɪˋbɪskəs; haɪˈbɪskəs/ *n* [C,U] a tropical plant with large brightly coloured flowers 木槿〔热带植物〕

hic·cup¹, hiccough /ˋhɪkʌp; ˈhɪkʌp/ *n* [C] **1** [usually plural 一般用复数] a sudden, quick movement of your DIAPHRAGM (1) that happens repeatedly and uncontrollably for a short time 呃逆，打嗝(声)：**get/have hiccups** *Don't drink so fast – you'll get hiccups.* 别喝得这么快，你会打嗝的。**2** a small problem or delay 小问题；短暂的耽搁：*Fortunately, the computer problem was only a hiccup.* 幸好电脑的毛病只是一点小问题。

hiccup² *v* **hiccupped, hiccupping** [I] to have hiccups 打嗝

hick /hɪk; hɪk/ *n* [C] *AmE informal* an insulting word for someone who lives in the countryside, and is considered to be less educated than people who live in the city【美，非正式】乡巴佬〔此词具侮辱性〕

hick·ey /ˋhɪkɪ; ˈhɪki/ *n* [C] *AmE* a red mark on someone's skin caused by someone else sucking it as a sexual act【美】〔皮肤上〕用力亲吻后留下的红色痕迹，吻痕；LOVE-BITE *BrE*【英】

Hick·ok /ˋhɪkɑk; ˈhɪkɒk/, **Wild Bill** (1837-76) a US soldier who was one of the first white Americans who went to live in the western US, where he became a MARSHAL (=someone who controls a particular area and makes sure that laws are obeyed). He was famous for his skill at shooting, and for his love of GAMBLING (=playing card games for money). 希科克〔(1837-1876)，美国军人，也是最早移居美国西部的白人之一。他是当地的一名执法官，以善射击、好赌博出名〕

hick·o·ry /ˋhɪkərɪ; ˈhɪkəri/ *n* [C,U] a North American tree that produces nuts, or the wood that comes from this tree 山核桃树；山核桃木

hid /hɪd; hɪd/ the past tense of HIDE¹

hid·den¹ /ˋhɪdn̩; ˈhɪdn/ the past participle of HIDE¹

hidden² *adj* **1** difficult to see or find 隐藏的，隐秘的：*hidden passages and hidden staircases* 隐秘的通道和隐秘的楼梯 **2** not easy to notice or realize 潜在的，隐含的：*hidden problems* 潜在的问题

hidden a·gen·da /ˌ‥ ·ˈ··/ *n* [C] an intended result of a plan or activity that you do not tell other people about 隐秘的动机；不可告人的目的：*Voters suspected a hidden political agenda.* 选民怀疑背后有暗藏的政治目的。

2 2 **hide¹** /haɪd; haɪd/ *v past tense* **hid** *past participle* **hidden** /ˋhɪdn̩; ˈhɪdn/ **1** [T] to deliberately put or keep something in a place where it cannot easily be seen or found 把…藏起来，隐藏：*My girlfriend keeps hiding my cigarettes.* 我的女友总是把我的香烟藏起来。| **hide sth from sb** *The bushes hid Dave's bike completely from the passers-by.* 灌木丛将戴夫的自行车完全挡住了，路过的人根本无法发现。| **keep sth hidden** *Confidential documents are kept hidden in a secret vault.* 机密文件被藏在一个秘密的保险库里。| **hide sth in/under/behind etc** *She hides his letters under her pillow.* 她把他的信都藏在枕头下面。**2** [I] to go or stay in a place where you hope no one will find you 躲藏，藏身：*Quick – she's coming – we'd better hide!* 快，她来了，我们最好躲起来！| [**+under/behind/in etc**] *Harry hid under the bed until they had gone.* 哈里一直躲在床下，直到他们离开。| **hide from** *Kylie tried to hide from the stranger.* 凯莉设法躲过那个陌生人。**3** [T] to keep someone in a place where other people will not find them 把〔某人〕藏起来：**hide sb from** *an attempt to hide her children from their violent father* 试图将她的孩子藏起来，以躲开他们凶暴的父亲 **4** [T] to not show your feelings to people 隐藏，掩盖〔自己的感情〕：*Paul struggled to hide his disappointment at not getting the job.* 保罗竭力掩藏自己因得不到那份工作而生的失望情绪。**5** [T] to deliberately not tell people facts or information 隐瞒：*He took off his ring to hide the fact that he was married.* 他摘下戒指，想隐瞒自己已婚的事实。| **hide sth from** *Don't try to hide anything from me.* 别想瞒过我！**6 have nothing to hide** to be willing to tell people about everything you have done, because you have done nothing dishonest, illegal, or immoral 没什么可隐瞒的；光明磊落：*The company claimed that the deal was legal and that they had nothing to hide.* 公司声称这笔交易是合法的，他们是光明磊落的。**7 hide your light under a bushel** to not tell anyone that you are very good at something〔对自己的特长〕藏而不露

hide 躲藏

hide² *n* [C] **1** *BrE* a place from which you can watch animals or birds without being seen by them【英】〔可观察鸟兽的〕隐匿处，埋伏处；BLIND³ (3) *AmE*【美】**2** an animal's skin, especially when it has been removed to be used for leather〔用于制成皮革的〕兽皮：*ox hide gloves* 牛皮手套 **3 have/tan sb's hide** *spoken humorous* to punish someone severely【口，幽默】剥了某人的皮〔指严厉惩罚某人〕**4 not see hide nor hair of** *spoken* to have not seen someone at all recently【口】没有见到〔某人〕的踪影：*I haven't seen hide nor hair of him for ages.* 我已经好久没有见过他的踪影了。

hide-and-seek /ˌ· · ˈ·/ also 又作 **hide-and-go-seek** /ˌ· · · ˈ·/ *AmE*【美】— *n* [U] a children's game in which one player shuts their eyes while the others hide, and then goes to look for them 捉迷藏

hide·a·way /ˋhaɪdəˌwe; ˈhaɪdəweɪ/ *n* [C] a place where you can go when you want to be alone 躲藏处，藏匿处

hide·bound /ˋhaɪdˌbaʊnd; ˈhaɪdbaʊnd/ *adj* having old-fashioned attitudes and ideas; NARROW-MINDED 古板的，守旧的，思想褊狭的：*hidebound reactionaries* 守旧的反动分子

hid·e·ous /ˈhɪdɪəs; ˈhɪdiəs/ *adj* extremely unpleasant or ugly 极丑的, 极难看的: *a hideous dress* 一条很难看的连衣裙 —**hideously** *adv* —**hideousness** *n* [U]

hide-out /ˈ· ·/ *n* [C] a place where someone goes because they do not want anyone to find them 藏匿处, 躲藏处

hid·ing /ˈhaɪdɪŋ; ˈhaɪdɪŋ/ *n* **1 be/go into hiding** to hide somewhere because you have done something illegal or are in danger〔因犯法或躲避危险〕藏匿, 躲藏: *The gang spent weeks in hiding before they were finally caught.* 那伙罪犯藏匿了几星期后才被抓获。**2 give sb/get a good hiding** *spoken informal* 【口, 非正式】**a)** used to say that you will physically punish someone 狠揍[痛打]某人/被狠揍[痛打]: *Any more cheek from you and you'll get a good hiding.* 你要是再这么无礼, 我便狠狠揍你一顿。**b)** to defeat someone or be defeated very seriously, especially in a sports game〔尤指在体育比赛中〕打败; 大败 **3 be on a hiding to nothing** *BrE informal* to be completely wasting your time trying to do something【英, 非正式】白白浪费时间, 白费工夫

hiding place /ˈ· ·· ,·/ *n* [C] a place where you can hide or where you can hide something 藏匿处, 躲藏处, 隐藏处

hie /haɪ; haɪ/ *v* [I,T] *old use* to make yourself hurry, or go quickly【旧】(使) 赶紧, (使) 赶忙

hi·er·ar·chy /ˈhaɪəˌrɑrkɪ; ˈhaɪrɑːki/ *n* **1** [C,U] a system within an organization in which people have authority and control over the people in the rank below them, who then have authority over the people below them 等级制度: *a rigid hierarchy* 严格的等级制度 **2** [C] the group of people in an organization who have power or control〔组织、团体中的〕统治集团: *All policy decisions were made by the party's hierarchy.* 所有的政策都是由该党内的高层成员决定的。—**hierarchical** /ˌhaɪəˈrɑrkɪkḷ; haɪˈrɑːkɪkəl/ *adj* —**hierarchically** /-kḷɪ; -kli/ *adv*

hi·e·ro·glyph·ics /ˌhaɪərəˈglɪfɪks; ˌhaɪrəˈglɪfɪks/ *n* [U] a system of writing that uses pictures to represent words 象形文字 —**hieroglyphic** *adj*: *hieroglyphic script* 象形文字手稿

hi-fi /ˈhaɪ ˈfaɪ; ˈhaɪ faɪ/ *n plural* **hi-fis 1** [C] a piece of high quality electronic equipment for playing recorded music〔高保真度〕音响设备 **2** [U] a way of playing recorded music that is very clear and of very good quality 用高保真度音响设备播放音乐

Hig·gins /ˈhɪgɪnz; ˈhɪgɪnz/, **Professor Henry** a character in the play *Pygmalion* by George Bernard Shaw and in the film *My Fair Lady*, which is based on Shaw's play, who teaches a poor girl called Eliza Doolittle how to speak and behave like an UPPER-CLASS lady. 希金斯〔萧伯纳的剧作《皮格马利翁》和根据剧本改编的电影《窈窕淑女》中的一个人物。他教一个名叫伊莉莎·杜利特的穷女孩学习上流社会女子的言谈举止〕

hig·gle·dy-pig·gle·dy /ˈhɪgḷdɪ ˈpɪgḷdɪ; ˌhɪgəldi ˈpɪgəldi/ *adj* things that are higgledy-piggledy are mixed together in an untidy way 乱七八糟的, 杂乱无章的 —**higgledy-piggledy** *adv*

-high /haɪ; haɪ/ *suffix* [in adjectives 构成形容词] of a particular height …高的: *The wall was about chest-high.* (=as high as your chest) 这墙大约有齐胸高。| *a 7000 metre-high mountain* 一座7000米高的山

high¹ /haɪ; haɪ/ *adj*

① MEASUREMENT/DISTANCE 计量/距离	⑤ VERY GOOD 很好
② LARGE AMOUNT/NUMBER 大量/数值大	⑥ DRUGS/ALCOHOL 毒品/酒精
③ IMPORTANT 重要的	⑦ HAPPY 高兴的
④ SOUND 声音	⑧ PROUD 骄傲的
	⑨ OTHER MEANINGS 其他意思

high 高的

a high shelf 一个高架子

a tall building 一幢高楼

① MEASUREMENT/DISTANCE 计量/距离

1 ►FROM BOTTOM TO TOP 从底部到顶部◄ something that is high measures a long distance from its bottom to its top 高的: *the highest mountain in Japan* 日本最高的山 | *a castle surrounded by high walls* 被高墙包围着的城堡 | **100 feet/30 metres etc high** *a building 20 storeys high* 一幢20层高的大楼 | *How high is the Eiffel tower?* 埃菲尔铁塔有多高? | *a ten-foot high wall* 10英尺高的墙 | **chest/waist/knee etc high** (=as high as your chest etc) 齐胸/腰/膝高 *The grass was knee-high.* 草有齐膝高。

2 ►ABOVE THE GROUND 在地面以上◄ being a long way, or a longer way than usual, above the ground〔离地面〕高的: *a spacious room with a high ceiling* 天花板很高的一个大房间 | *a high shelf* 一个高的架子 | *high in the sky* 在高空 | **high up** *High up among the clouds, we could just see the summit of Everest.* 在高高的云端中, 我们只能看到珠穆朗玛峰的峰顶。

3 ►SEA/RIVER ETC 海/河等◄ having risen to a higher level than usual〔水位〕高的: *The river was unusually high.* 这条河的水位异乎寻常地高。| *high tide* 高[满]潮

② LARGE AMOUNT/NUMBER 大量/数值大

4 a high amount, number, or level is greater than normal〔数值、水平〕高的, 超乎寻常的: *high blood pressure* 高血压 | *high levels of radiation* 高能级辐射 | *high temperatures* 高温 | **high rent/price/tax etc** *the high cost of insurance* 昂贵的保险费 | **at high speed** (=very fast) 高速地 *A car was approaching at high speed.* 有一辆车正在高速地驶来。| **high proportion/percentage** (=a very large part of an amount) 高比例/百分比 *A high proportion of married women have part-time jobs.* 很大部分的已婚妇女都在做兼职的工作。

5 ►CONTAINING A LOT 含量高◄ containing a lot of a particular substance or quality〔含量〕高的: *an alloy with a high carbon content* 高碳合金 | **high in fat/sugar/salt etc** *Beer is high in calories.* 啤酒含的热量很高。

③ IMPORTANT 重要的

6 ►IN SOCIETY/ORGANIZATION 在社会/组织中◄ having an important or powerful position in society or in an organization〔职位或等级〕高的, 高级的; 重要的: *the highest rank in the US Navy* 美国海军中的最高军衔 | *the City's highest honour* 该市的最高荣誉 | **high up** (=in a powerful position) 居于高位 *someone high up in the civil service* 在政府文职机构担任要职的人 | **high office** *With men like Gould in high office, it was easy for the military to influence policy.* 有古尔德这样的人身居高职, 军队就很容易对政策施加影响。| **high**

H

society (=rich people of the highest social class) 上流社会 —see also 另见 HIGH-UP, HIGH-RANKING, **have friends in high places** (FRIEND (10))
7 be high on the list/agenda to be important and need to be dealt with quickly 被列为重要[优先处理]的事项

④ SOUND 声音
8 near the top of the range of sounds that humans can hear〔音调〕高的, 尖声的: *Dogs respond to sounds that are too high for the human ear.* 狗对人耳听不到的高音有反应。—see also 另见 HIGH-PITCHED

⑤ VERY GOOD 很好
9 high quality/standard/calibre etc very good quality etc 高质量/标准/水准等: *high quality goods* 高质量商品 | *a high standard of workmanship* 高水平的工艺
10 high opinion/praise/regard etc strong approval, or an expression of strong approval 高度评价/赞扬/尊重等: **have a high opinion of** *I have a high opinion of Miss Boyce's work.* 我对博伊斯小姐的工作评价很高。| **hold sb/sth in high esteem/regard** (=respect them very much) 高度尊重某人/某事 *As an educationalist, he was held in high esteem.* 作为一名教育学家, 他得到人们的高度尊敬。
11 high standards/principles rules of personal behaviour based on the belief that everyone should always be very good and honest 高尚[崇高]的标准/原则: *a man of high moral principles* 具有崇高道德原则的人
12 have high hopes/expectations to hope for or expect very good results or great success 抱有很高的希望/期望: *parents who have such high hopes for their children* 对孩子寄予如此厚望的父母
13 high point/spot the best part of an activity or occasion〔活动的〕高潮/最精彩部分: *Our visit to the Grand Canyon was definitely the high point of our vacation.* 游览大峡谷无疑是我们这次度假最精彩的部分。

⑥ DRUGS/ALCOHOL 毒品/酒精
14 [not before noun 不用于名词前] behaving in an unusually excited way because of taking drugs〔吸食毒品后〕极度兴奋的: **[+on]** *They were high on cocaine.* 他们吸食可卡因后显得极度亢奋。| **get high** (=take a drug to make yourself high) 吸毒以求得飘飘欲仙的感觉 | **high as a kite** (=very high) 飘飘欲仙的

⑦ HAPPY 高兴的
15 high spirits feelings of happiness and energy, especially when you are having fun 欢欣, 兴高采烈: *I know the kids are a bit noisy but it's just high spirits.* 我知道孩子们有点吵, 但他们只是太高兴了。| **in high spirits** *It was a bright sunny day and we set off in high spirits.* 那天阳光明媚, 我们兴高采烈地出发了。
16 ►HAPPY/EXCITED 高兴的/兴奋的◄ happy and excited 高兴的; 兴奋的: **[+on]** *We were still high on our victory over the champions.* 我们还在为击败冠军队而兴奋不已。
17 have a high old time *old-fashioned* to enjoy an occasion very much【过时】度过愉快的时光, 玩得很痛快

⑧ PROUD 骄傲的
18 be/get on your high horse to behave or talk as if you are better than other people 自高自大, 自以为是
19 high and mighty talking or behaving as if you think you are more important than other people 盛气凌人的, 不可一世的

⑨ OTHER MEANINGS 其他意思
20 it is high time used to say that something should be done now 到了该做某事的时候: *It's high time you got a job and settled down.* 你该找份工作安顿下来了。
21 ►FOOD 食物◄ cheese, meat etc that is high is not fresh and has a strong smell or taste〔干酪、肉类等〕不新鲜的; 变质的
22 high wind a strong wind 大风
23 high complexion/colouring a naturally pink or red face 自然红润的脸色
24 high drama/adventure events or situations that are very exciting 充满戏剧性的事件/极刺激的历险: *a life with moments of high drama* 具有不少刺激经历的人生
25 ►TIME 时间◄ the middle or the most important part of a particular period of time 趋于顶点的, 全盛的: *high summer* 盛夏 | *the high renaissance* 文艺复兴的全盛时期 | **high noon** (=12 o'clock in the middle of the day) 正午 —see also 另见 HIGH SEASON
26 high life/living the enjoyable life that rich people and fashionable people have〔上层社会的〕奢华生活: *the high life of a capital city* 首都的奢华生活
27 high finance the business of dealing with very large sums of money 涉及巨额资金的业务
28 high style/register the style of language used in literature 文学语言风格/语域 —see also 另见 HIGHLY, **in high dudgeon** (DUDGEON), **stink to high heaven** (STINK[1] (1))

USAGE NOTE 用法说明: HIGH
WORD CHOICE 词语辨析: **high, higher, advanced, tall**
High (opposite **low**) is used of most things, especially when you are thinking only of how far something, or its top, is from the ground. high (反义词为 low) 可用来描述大多数东西, 尤其是描述该物或其顶部离地面的高度: *a high shelf* 高架子 | *a high mountain* 高山 | *The shelf's too high, I can't reach it.* 架子太高了, 我够不着。
Many things you cannot touch may also be **high**. 很多人们无法触摸的东西也可以用 high 来描述: *a high standard* 高标准 | *a high degree of sophistication* 高精密度 | *high technology* 高科技。However, with some words related to education **higher** (or **advanced**) must be used instead. 但在某些与教育有关的词组中则要用 higher (或 advanced): *higher education* 高等教育 | *advanced teaching/techniques* 高等教学工作/高级技术 | *a higher degree/diploma* (but do not confuse this with *High School diploma* etc) 高等学位/高级文凭 (但不要将其与 High School diploma (高中毕业文凭) 等混淆起来)
Tall (opposite **short**) is used for people and animals. tall (反义词为 short) 用来描述人或动物: *Your son's getting tall, isn't he?* 你的儿子越长越高了, 不是吗?
Tall is also used for things that are high and narrow, especially when you are thinking of the complete distance from top to bottom. tall 也可用来描述一些高而窄的东西, 尤其是在考虑这个东西从顶到底的全距离时: *a tall building like the Sears Tower* 像西尔斯大厦那样的高楼 | *a tall tree/column/vase/fridge/bottle* 高的树木/柱子/花瓶/冰箱/瓶子

high² *adv*
1 ►ABOVE THE GROUND 在地面以上◄ at or to a level high above the ground〔离地面〕高高地; 在[向]高处: **[+into/above etc]** *Paula threw the ball high into the air.* 葆拉将球高高地抛向天空。| *flying high in the sky* 在高空飞翔
2 ►VALUE/COST/AMOUNT 价值/成本/数量◄ at or to a high value, cost, amount etc 高〔价值、成本、数量等〕: *The dollar stayed high after a busy day on the foreign exchanges.* 外汇市场整天交易频繁, 接近收市时美元价格仍然居高不下。| *He scored higher than anyone else in the class.* 他的分数比班上其他人都要高。
3 ►SOUND 声音◄ with a high sound 高音调地: *boy's voices, ringing high above everyone else's* 高过所有人的男孩的嗓音
4 ►ACHIEVEMENT 成就◄ to a high rank or level of achievement, especially in an organization, business etc 向高的地位[成就]: *Don't set your goals too low. You should always aim high.* 不要将你的目标定得太低。你应该永远保持着雄心壮志。
5 be left high and dry *informal* to be left without any help or without the things that you need【非正式】孤立无援, 陷入困境
6 look/search high and low to try to find someone or something by looking everywhere 到处寻找: *We looked high and low for Sandy but couldn't find her.* 我们到处寻找桑迪, 但没有找到她。
7 hold your head high to behave in a proud confident way, especially in a difficult situation〔尤指在困境中〕充满自信: *You've kept the family together, I think you can hold your head high.* 你使一家人团结起来, 我认为你应该感到自豪。
8 live high on the hog *AmE informal* to enjoy expensive food, clothes etc without worrying about the cost【美, 非正式】过奢华的生活: *They've been living high on the hog since Jim got the money from his aunt.* 自从吉姆从他的姑妈那儿得到那笔钱后, 他们就一直过着奢华的生活。—see also 另见 **be riding high** (RIDE[1] (7)), **be running high** (RUN[1] (28))

high³ *n* [C]
1 ►NUMBER/AMOUNT 数量◄ the highest price, number, temperature etc that has ever been recorded〔价格、数量、温度等的〕最高点; 最高水平: *The price of oil reached a new high this week.* 本周的石油价格创出了新高。

2 ►WEATHER 天气◄ a) the highest temperature in a particular day, week, month etc〔某月、周、日的〕最高气温: *Highs today were in the mid 20's.* 今天的最高气温为25度左右。**b)** an area of HIGH PRESSURE[2] that affects the weather 高气压(区)
3 ►DRUGS 毒品◄ a feeling of pleasure or excitement produced by some drugs〔某些毒品带来的〕极度兴奋感, 飘飘欲仙的感觉: *The high she got from cocaine never lasted.* 她从可卡因中得到的兴奋感总是转眼即逝。
4 ►EXCITEMENT 兴奋◄ a feeling of happiness or excitement you get from doing something you enjoy 兴奋感, 欢欣, 情绪高涨: **be on a high** *I've been on a high ever since we won the game last week.* 自上周我们比赛获胜以来, 我一直感到兴奋不已。
5 ►SCHOOL 学校◄ a short form of 缩略式= HIGH SCHOOL, used in the name of a school 中学〔用于学校名称中〕: *She graduated from Reseda High in 1979.* 她于1979年毕业于雷西达中学。
6 on high *biblical* in, to, or from heaven or a high place【圣经】在[从]天堂; 在[从]高处
7 from on high *humorous* from someone in a position of authority【幽默】来自上级的, 来自高层的: *an order from on high* 上头的命令

high·ball /ˈhaɪˌbɔl; ˈhaɪbɔːl/ *n* [C] *especially AmE* an alcoholic drink, especially WHISKY or BRANDY mixed with water or SODA【尤美】高杯酒〔尤指威士忌或白兰地加水或苏打水〕

high beam /ˌ· ˈ·/ *n* [U] *AmE* lights at the front of a car that are on as brightly as possible【美】〔车头开着的〕远光灯, 高灯 —see also 另见 BRIGHTS

high-born /ˌ· ˈ·◂/ *adj formal* born into the highest social class【正式】出身高贵的

high·boy /ˈhaɪˌbɔɪ; ˈhaɪbɔɪ/ *n* [C] *AmE* a piece of tall wooden furniture with many drawers【美】〔带有很多抽屉的〕高脚橱柜; TALLBOY *BrE*【英】

high·brow /ˈhaɪˌbraʊ; ˈhaɪbraʊ/ *adj* **1** a highbrow book, film etc is intended for very intelligent people who like serious subjects〔书籍、电影等〕高雅的 **2** someone who is highbrow is interested in serious or complicated ideas and subjects; INTELLECTUAL〔人〕趣味高雅的, 文化修养高的 —**highbrow** *n* [C] —compare 比较 LOWBROW

high·chair /ˌhaɪˈtʃɛr; ˌhaɪˈtʃeə/ *n* [C] a special tall chair that a young child sits in to eat〔幼儿吃饭时坐的〕高脚椅 —see picture at 参见 CHAIR[1] 图

High Church /ˌ· ˈ·◂/ *n* [U] the part of the Church of England that is closest in its beliefs to the Roman Catholic Church〔英国国教的〕高派教会〔英格兰圣公会一教派, 其信仰与天主教最相近〕—compare 比较 LOW CHURCH —**High Church** *adj*

high-class /ˌ· ˈ·◂/ *adj* [usually before noun 一般用于名词前] of good quality and style, and usually expensive 高级的, 上等的: *a high-class restaurant* 高级餐馆 —compare 比较 LOW-CLASS

high com·mand /ˌ· ·ˈ·/ *n* [singular] the most important leaders of a country's army, navy etc〔军队的〕统帅(部); 最高指挥部: *the German High Command* 德军最高指挥部

high com·mis·sion /ˌ· ·ˈ··/ *n* [C] **1** a group of people working for a government or an international organization to deal with a specific problem〔政府或国际组织的〕高级专员公署 **2** a group of people with official duties concerning the relationship of one Commonwealth country with another〔英联邦国家中负责各英联邦国家之间关系的〕高级专员公署 —**High Commissioner** *n* [C]

high court /ˌ· ˈ·◂/ *n* [C usually singular 一般用单数] a court of law in Britain that is at a higher level than ordinary courts and that can be asked to change the decisions of a lower court〔英国的〕高等法院

High Court of Jus·ti·cia·ry, the /ˌhaɪ ˌkort əv dʒʌsˈtɪʃɪˌɛrɪ; ˌhaɪ ˌkɔːt əv dʒʌˈstɪʃɪərɪ/ in the Scottish legal system, a court of law that is more important than a SHERIFF court and deals with serious crimes such as murder 苏格兰最高刑事法院〔苏格兰司法系统中高于郡法院的一级法院, 主要受理谋杀等重大刑事案件〕

high-def·i·ni·tion /ˌ· ··ˈ··◂/ *adj* [only before noun 仅用于名词前] a high-definition television or computer shows images very clearly〔电视或电脑〕高清晰度的

high·er[1] /ˈhaɪɚ; ˈhaɪə/ *adj* [the comparative of *high* high 的比较级] **1** [only before noun 仅用于名词前] more advanced in development or organization〔发展过程或组织结构〕高等的: *the higher forms of mammals, such as the primates and big cats* 高等哺乳动物, 如灵长目动物和大型猫科动物 **2** at a more advanced level of knowledge〔知识〕高等的: *higher mathematics* 高等数学 —see 见 HIGH (USAGE)

higher[2] *n* [C] the higher level of the Scottish Certificate of Education 苏格兰高等教育证书

higher ed·u·ca·tion /ˌ·· ··ˈ··/ *n* [U] college or university education as opposed to school or HIGH SCHOOL 高等教育 —compare 比较 FURTHER EDUCATION

higher-up /ˌ·· ˈ·◂/ *n* [C] *informal* someone who has a high rank in an organization【非正式】〔机构、部门的〕高层人物, 要员: *Rumour has it that the higher-ups want to push the schedule forward.* 谣传高层人物想促使日程提前进行。

highest com·mon fac·tor /ˌ·· ·· ˈ··/ *n* [C] *technical* the largest number that a set of numbers can be divided by exactly【术语】最大公因数: *the highest common factor of 12, 24 and 30 is 6.* 12、24和30的最大公因数是6。

high ex·plo·sive /ˌ· ·ˈ··◂/ *n* [C,U] a substance that explodes with great power and violence 高爆炸药, 烈性炸药

high·fa·lu·tin /ˌhaɪfəˈlutn̩; ˌhaɪfəˈluːtɪn◂/ *adj informal* highfalutin language or behaviour seems silly although it is intended to be impressive【非正式】〔言行〕浮夸的, 做作的

high fi·del·i·ty /ˌ· ·ˈ···◂/ *adj* [usually before noun 一般用于名词前] high fidelity recording equipment produces sound that is very clear〔音响设备〕高保真度的 —see also 另见 HI-FI

high five /ˌ· ˈ·/ *n* [singular] *especially AmE* the action of hitting someone's open hand with your own above your heads to show that you are pleased about something【尤美】〔两人〕举手击掌〔以示庆贺〕

high-fli·er /ˌ· ˈ··/ *n* [C] someone who is extremely successful in their job or in school〔事业或学业上〕极有成就的人: *a young businessman pegged as a high-flier by the media* 被传媒称为成功人士的年轻实业家 —**high-flying** *adj*

high-flown /ˌ· ˈ·◂/ *adj* high-flown language sounds impressive but does not have much real meaning〔言词〕浮夸的, 空洞的

High·gate /ˈhaɪget; ˈhaɪgeɪt/ an area of North London with many large expensive houses. Many famous people, including Karl Marx, are buried in **Highgate Cemetery**. 海格特〔北伦敦一地区, 建有许多大型高级住宅。卡尔·马克思等许多名人安葬在海格特墓地〕

high-grade /ˌ· ˈ·◂/ *adj* [only before noun 仅用于名词前] of the best quality 优质的, 高档的, 上等的: *high-grade beef* 优质牛肉

High·grove House /ˌhaɪgrov ˈhaus; ˌhaɪgrəʊv ˈhaʊs/ a large house in Gloucestershire, England, which is owned by Prince Charles 海格罗夫府邸〔位于英格兰格洛斯特郡的一幢大宅, 为查尔斯王子所有〕

high-hand·ed /ˌ· ˈ··◂/ *adj* using your authority in an unreasonable way 专横的, 高压的, 盛气凌人的: *high-handed and insensitive management decisions* 专横而冷漠无情的管理决策 —**high-handedly** *adv* —**high-handedness** *n* [U]

high heels /ˌ· ˈ·/ *n* [plural] women's shoes with high heels 高跟鞋 —**high-heeled** *adj* —see picture on page A17 参见 A17 页图

high jinks also 又作 **hi-jinks** *AmE*【美】/ˈhaɪ ˌdʒɪŋks; ˈhaɪ dʒɪŋks/ *n* [U] *old-fashioned* noisy or excited behaviour when people are having fun【过时】嬉闹, 狂欢作乐: *youthful high jinks* 年轻人的狂欢作乐

high jump /ˈ· ·/ *n* **1 the high jump** a sports event in which someone runs and jumps over a bar that is raised higher each time they jump 跳高〔体育比赛〕 **2 be (in) for the high jump** *BrE informal* if someone is for the high jump, they will be punished for something they have done wrong【英, 非正式】将受到惩罚 —**high jumper** *n* [C]

High·land /ˈhaɪlənd; ˈhaɪlənd/ a REGION (=local government area) of northern Scotland which includes many islands and the highest mountain in the UK, Ben Nevis 苏格兰高地行政区〔位于苏格兰北部, 包括许多岛屿和英国最高峰本尼维斯山〕

highland *adj* [only before noun 仅用于名词前] **1** coming from or connected to the Scottish Highlands 苏格兰高地的: *Highland pipers* 苏格兰高地的风笛手 **2** from or about an area with a lot of mountains 高地的, 高原的: *workers in highland Ecuador* 厄瓜多尔高原的工人们

Highland dress /ˌ·· ˈ·/ a set of clothes worn by some Scottish men on special occasions, for example at a wedding. Highland dress consists of a short black JACKET, a BOW TIE, a KILT and long socks with a small knife kept under the fold at the top of one of the socks. 苏格兰高地人套装〔一些苏格兰男子在婚礼等特殊场合穿的套装, 由黑色短上衣、领结、苏格兰短裙及长统袜组成, 其中一只袜子的褶边下挂有一把小刀〕

High·land·er /ˈhaɪləndɚ; ˈhaɪləndə/ *n* [C] someone from the Scottish Highlands 苏格兰高地人

Highland fling /ˌ·· ˈ·/ *n* [C] a fast Scottish dance, danced by one person 高地舞〔苏格兰的一种单人跳的快舞〕

Highland Games /,·· ˈ·/ also 又作 **Highland Gathering** a special event held every year in Scottish towns, with traditional Scottish sports, dancing, and music. The sports include 'tossing the caber' (=throwing a long, heavy wooden pole into the air). 苏格兰高地运动会〔一年一度在苏格兰城镇举行的特殊文体活动，其中包括苏格兰传统体育项目、舞蹈和音乐。体育项目包括"投掷木棒"等〕

high·lands /ˈhaɪləndz; ˈhaɪləndz/ *n* [plural] **1 the Highlands** an area in the north of Scotland where there are a lot of mountains 苏格兰北部的高地 **2** an area of a country where there are a lot of mountains 高地，高原：*forested highlands* 森林覆盖的高地 —compare 比较 LOWLANDS

Highlands and Is·lands, the /,·· · ˈ··/ the northern and northwestern areas of Scotland and the islands off its west coast 高地和岛屿〔苏格兰北部和西北部地区以及西海岸附近的岛屿〕

high-lev·el /,· ˈ··◂/ *adj* [only before noun 仅用于名词前] **1** done by or involving people who are in powerful positions, for example the government 〔政府〕高层的，由高层人士进行[组成]的：*officials attending a high-level conference on arms control* 参加军备控制高层会议的官员 **2** at a high level or degree 高度的：*high-level anxiety* 高度忧虑 **3** high-level words or language are very formal or technical 〔用词、语言〕非常正式的；术语的 **4** a high-level computer language is similar to human language rather than machine language 〔电脑语言〕高级的〔接近人类语言〕 —compare 比较 LOW-LEVEL

high life, the /ˈ· ·/ *n* a way of life that involves a lot of parties, and expensive food, wine, travel etc 〔上层社会的〕奢华生活

3 **high·light¹** /ˈhaɪ,laɪt; ˈhaɪlaɪt/ *v* [T] **1** to make a problem or subject easy to notice so that people pay attention to it 使…突出，使注意力集中于：*a test to highlight students' strengths and weaknesses* 能突显学生优缺点的测试 **2** to mark written words with a special coloured pen, or in a different colour on a computer, so that you can see them easily 在〔书面材料或电脑上〕画出重点 **3** to make some parts of your hair a lighter colour than the rest 将〔部分头发〕染成有光泽的浅色，挑染 —**highlighting** *n* [U]

highlight² *n* **1** [C] the most important, interesting, or enjoyable part of something such as a holiday, performance, or sports competition 最突出[精彩]的部分[场面]：*That weekend in Venice was definitely the highlight of our trip.* 在威尼斯度过的那个周末无疑是我们这次旅行最精彩的部分。**2 highlights** [plural] areas of hair that have been made a lighter colour than the rest 〔挑染后〕头发上呈浅色的部分 **3** [C] *technical* a light, bright area on a painting or photograph【术语】〔绘画、照片上的〕强光部分，最亮部分

high·light·er /ˈhaɪ,laɪtə; ˈhaɪlaɪtə/ *n* [C] a special light coloured pen used for marking words in a book, article etc 〔用来在书上、文章上画重点的〕浅色彩笔，荧光笔

2 2 **high·ly** /ˈhaɪlɪ; ˈhaɪli/ *adv* **1** [+adj, adv] very 非常，极：*highly successful* 非常成功的 | *highly skilled* 十分熟练的 **2** [+adj, adv] to a high level or standard 高度地，高水平地：*She is a highly educated woman.* 她是个受过高水平教育的女人。| *highly paid experts* 薪酬丰厚的专家 **3 highly placed** in an important or powerful position 身居高职的：*a highly placed government official* 身居高职的政府官员 **4 speak/think highly of** to tell other people how good someone is at something or to think they are very good at something 高度称赞/评价

highly strung /,·· ˈ·◂/ *especially BrE*【尤英】, also 又作 **high-strung** /,· ˈ·◂/ *AmE*【美】— *adj* nervous, and easily upset or excited 容易激动的，神经质的：*a highly strung child* 神经质的孩子

High Mass /,· ˈ·/ *n* [C,U] a very formal church ceremony in the Roman Catholic Church 〔天主教的〕大弥撒

high-mind·ed /,· ˈ··◂/ *adj* having very high moral standards or principles 品德[情操]高尚的，高洁的：*a high-minded sermon on charity* 以仁爱为题的情操高尚的布道 —**high-mindedly** *adv* —**high-mindedness** *n* [U]

High·ness /ˈhaɪnɪs; ˈhaɪnǝs/ *n* [C] **Your/Her/His Highness** used to speak to or about a king, queen, prince etc 殿下〔用于对国王、王后、王子等的尊称〕

High Noon /,· ˈ·/ a highly-praised film about the American Old West. A newly-married town MARSHAL discovers no one will help him when a man he had once sent to prison returns with three GUNMEN to kill him. His bride, a Quaker, who does not believe in violence, decides to leave him when he says he will stay and fight, but when she hears shooting she goes back to help her husband and kills one of the men. 《正午》〔美国一部颇受好评的西部影片。故事中，一位新婚不久的小镇警长以前曾把一名男子送进监狱。这名男子出狱后带着三个枪手找他报仇时，他却发现没人愿意帮助他。他的妻子是教友派信徒，反对暴力。当她听他说要留下来迎战时，便决定弃他而去。可当她一听到枪声，便又回过头来帮他，还杀死了一个枪手〕

high-oc·tane /,· ˈ··◂/ *adj* high-octane petrol is of a very high quality 〔汽油〕高辛烷值的；优质的

high-pitched /,· ˈ·◂/ *adj* a high-pitched voice or sound is higher than usual 声调高的

high-pow·ered /,· ˈ··◂/ *adj* [usually before noun 一般用于名词前] **1** a high-powered machine, vehicle, or piece of equipment is very powerful 大功率的，大马力的，强有力的：*a high-powered automobile* 大马力的汽车 **2** having a powerful and important job 干劲十足的；积极进取的：*a high-powered publisher* 劲头十足的出版商

high-pres·sure¹ /,· ˈ··◂/ *adj* [only before noun 仅用于名词前] **1** a high-pressure job or situation is one in which you need to work very hard; STRESSFUL 给人很大压力的，非常紧张的 **2 high-pressure sales/selling methods etc** very direct and often successful ways of persuading people to buy something 强有力的[强行的]推销/销售方法等：*high-pressure sales techniques* 咄咄逼人的推销手法 **3** containing or using a very high pressure or force of water, gas, air etc 〔水、天然气、大气等〕高压的

high-pressure² *n* [U] a condition of the air over a large area that affects the weather 高气压

high priest /,· ˈ·/ *n* [C] **1** *informal* someone who is famous for being the best at something such as a type of art or music【非正式】〔艺术、音乐界的〕代表人物：*the high priest of modern jazz* 现代爵士乐的代表人物 **2** a chief PRIEST in some religions 大祭司，祭司长

high-prin·ci·pled /,· ˈ···◂/ *adj* having high moral standards 品德高尚的，情操高尚的

high-pro·file /,· ˈ··◂/ *adj* [only before noun 仅用于名词前] attracting a lot of public attention, usually deliberately 〔刻意地〕引人注目的，高调的：*a high-profile public figure* 一位引人注目的公众人物 —**high profile** *n* [singular]

high-rank·ing /,· ˈ··◂/ *adj* [only before noun 仅用于名词前] having a high position in a government or other organization 〔在政府或其他机构中〕级别[地位]高的

high re·lief /,· ·ˈ·/ *n* [U] **1** a form of art in which figures cut in stone or wood stand out from the surface 高凸浮雕 —compare 比较 BAS-RELIEF **2 throw sth into high relief** to make something very clear and easy to notice 使某物突出

high-rise /ˈ· ·/ *adj* [only before noun 仅用于名词前] high-rise buildings are tall buildings with many levels 〔建筑物〕高耸的，高层的 —compare 比较 LOW-RISE —**high rise** *n* [C]: *They live in a high rise on the East Side.* 他们住在东区的一座高层大厦里。

> **CULTURAL NOTE 文化注释**
>
> In Britain, high-rise buildings are usually in inner city areas and are lived in by people who are not very rich, but in the US, some high-rise flats are very attractive and very expensive. 英国的高层建筑一般建在市中心，住户都不太富裕；但在美国，一些高层公寓很有吸引力，价格高昂。

high-risk /,· ˈ·◂/ *adj* [only before noun 仅用于名词前] involving a risk of death, injury, failure etc 高风险的：*high-risk investments* 高风险投资 | *cancer screening for women over 55 and other high-risk groups* 针对55岁以上的妇女及其他高危人群的癌症筛查

high road /ˈ· ·/ *n* [C] *BrE old use* a main road【英旧】大路，大道，大街

high rol·ler /,· ˈ··/ *n* [C] *AmE informal* someone who spends a lot of money carelessly or risks a lot of money on games, races etc【美，非正式】挥金如土的人；下大赌注赌钱的人

high school /ˈ· ·/ *n* **1** [C,U] a school in the US and Canada for children of 14 or 15 to 18 years old 〔美国和加拿大14或15至18岁学生就读的〕高中 **2** used in the names of some schools in Britain for children from 11 to 18 years old 〔英国11至18岁学生就读的〕中学〔用于校名中〕：*Leytonstone High School for Girls* 雷顿斯通女子中学 —compare 比较 SECONDARY SCHOOL

high seas, the /,· ˈ·/ *n* **a)** the areas of ocean around the world that do not belong to any particular country 公海 **b)** *literary* the sea【文】大海，海洋

high sea·son /,· ˈ··/ *n* [singular,U] *especially BrE* the time of year when businesses make a lot of money and prices are high, especially in the tourist industry; PEAK SEASON【尤英】〔商业，尤指旅游业的〕旺季 —compare 比较 LOW SEASON

high-sound·ing /ˌ· ˈ··◂/ *adj* [only before noun 仅用于名词前] high-sounding statements, principles etc seem very impressive but are often insincere〔陈述、准则等〕华而不实的, 虚夸的

high-speed /ˌ· ˈ·◂/ *adj* [only before noun 仅用于名词前] designed to travel or operate very fast 高速的, 快速的: *a high-speed train* 高速列车

high-spir·it·ed /ˌ· ˈ···◂/ *adj* **1** someone who is high-spirited has a lot of energy and enjoys fun and adventure〔人〕生气勃勃的, 活泼的; 爱冒险的 **2** a horse that is high-spirited is nervous and difficult to control〔马〕烈性的, 难驾驭的

high street /ˈ· ·/ *n* [C] *BrE* the main street of a town where most of the shops and businesses are【英】大街〔市镇商业区的主要街道〕: *Camden High Street* 卡姆登大街 | *peak sales on the high street at Christmas* 圣诞节时商业街上的销售高峰 | **high street banks/shops etc** (=the shops etc that most people use) 大型银行/商店等 —compare 比较 MAIN STREET (1)

high-strung /ˌ· ˈ·◂/ *adj* an American form of HIGHLY STRUNG highly strung 的美语形式

high ta·ble /ˌ· ˈ··/ *n* [U] *BrE* the table where the most important people at a formal occasion sit【英】贵宾桌

high·tail /ˈhaɪˌtel; ˈhaɪteɪl/ *v* **hightail it** *informal* to leave a place quickly【非正式】快速离开, 急忙逃走: *kids high-tailing it down the street on their bikes* 骑自行车飞快驶过街道的孩子们

high tea /ˌ· ˈ·/ *n* [C,U] *BrE* a meal of cold food, cakes etc eaten in the early evening【英】傍晚茶点

high-tech /ˌhaɪˈtɛk; ˌhaɪˈtek◂/ *adj* [usually before noun 一般用于名词前] **1** using high technology 高科技的: *high-tech industries* 高科技产业 —compare 比较 LOW-TECH **2** furniture, designs etc that are high-tech are made in a very modern style〔家具、设计等〕现代风格的, 摩登的 —**high tech** *n* [U]

high tech·nol·o·gy /ˌ· ·ˈ····◂/ *n* [U] the use of the most modern machines and methods in industry, business etc 高科技, 尖端技术

high-ten·sion /ˌ· ˈ··◂/ *adj* **high-tension wires/cables etc** wires etc that have a powerful electric current going through them 高压电线/电缆等

high tide /ˌ· ˈ·/ *n* **1** [C,U] the point or time at which the sea reaches its highest level 高[满]潮时 **2** [singular] the time when something is at its best or most successful 成功的顶点, 全盛时期: *The election victory marked the high tide in the party's fortunes.* 大选胜利标志着该党时运的顶点。

high-toned /ˌ· ˈ·◂/ *adj* seeming to be concerned with high moral principles 唱高调的, 自命高尚的

high trea·son /ˌ· ˈ··/ *n* [U] the crime of putting your country in great danger, for example by giving military secrets to the enemy 叛国罪, 叛逆罪

high-up /ˈ· ·/ *n* [C] *BrE* someone who has a high rank in an organization; HIGHER-UP【英】〔机构、部门的〕高层人物, 要员

high wa·ter /ˌ· ˈ··/ *n* [U] the period of time during which the water in a river or the sea is at its highest level because of the TIDE[1] (1) 高水位期, 涨潮时 —compare 比较 LOW WATER —see also 另见 **come hell or high water** (HELL[1] (22))

high water mark /ˌ· ˈ·· ·/ *n* [singular] **1** the mark that shows the highest level that the sea or a river reaches 高水位线 **2** the time when someone or something is most successful〔成功的〕顶峰, 顶点, 全盛时期: *the high water mark of Herrera's presidency* 埃雷拉担任总统时最成功的时期

2 **high·way** /ˈhaɪˌwe; ˈhaɪweɪ/ *n* [C] **1** *especially AmE* a broad main road that joins one town to another【尤美】公路 —compare 比较 FREEWAY, EXPRESSWAY, MOTORWAY **2** *BrE*【英】**a)** *old-fashioned* any road or street【过时】公路, 大街 **b) the public highway** an expression used in legal documents meaning roads〔用于法律文件中〕公路 **3 highway robbery** *AmE informal* a situation in which something costs you a lot more than it should【美, 非正式】要价太高: *It's highway robbery, charging that much for gas!* 这简直就是抢钱, 竟然要这么多煤气钱!

CULTURAL NOTE 文化注释

In the US, there are many different names for fast roads. Highways usually connect cities. Sometimes they have only two LANES, especially in country areas, but near cities they may have three or four LANES going in each direction. A road with many lanes is sometimes called a SUPERHIGHWAY. INTERSTATE highways connect cities in different states, and sometimes go through several states. FREEWAYS are roads within a city on which you can drive very fast without stopping, and they usually have three or more lanes going in each direction. EXPRESSWAYS are fast roads in or near cities. You do not have to pay to use freeways and expressways, but you have to pay a small amount of money before you can use a fast road called a TURNPIKE or a TOLLWAY. These roads are often very long, and may go from one end of a state to the other. Some highways also cost money to use. 美国的快速道路有很多名称。highway一般指城际公路, 有时只有两条车道, 在乡村地区尤其如此; 但临近市区, 单向可能会有三四条车道。有很多车道的公路有时叫 superhighway (高速公路)。州际公路连接不同州的城市, 有时跨几个州。freeway 是市内高速公路, 可以快速行驶而无须停车, 单向一般有三条以上的车道。expressway是市内或城市周边的快速公路。freeway 和 expressway 无须交费, 但要交少许费用才能使用一种叫做 turnpike 或 tollway 的高速公路。

In the UK, there is a network of fast roads, with two or three lanes in each direction, connecting most big cities. These roads are called MOTORWAYS. 英国有高速公路网, 单向两条或三条车道, 连接多数大城市。这些高速公路叫做 motorway。

Highway Code /ˌ·· ˈ·/ *n* [singular] the set of official rules and laws about driving and using roads in Britain〔英国的〕公路法规

high·way·man /ˈhaɪˌwemən; ˈhaɪweɪmən/ *n plural* **highwaymen** /-mən; -mən/ [C] someone who stopped people and carriages on the roads and robbed them especially in the 17th and 18th centuries〔尤指17、18世纪的〕拦路抢劫的强盗, 公路响马

highwayman 拦路抢劫的强盗, 公路响马

highway pa·trol /ˈ··· ˌ·/ *n* [singular] the police who make sure that people obey the rules on main roads in the US〔美国的〕公路巡逻队

high wire /ˈ· ·/ *n* [C] a tightly stretched rope or wire high above the ground that someone walks along, usually as part of a CIRCUS performance〔走钢丝表演用的〕绷索, 钢丝

hi·jack[1] /ˈhaɪˌdʒæk; ˈhaɪdʒæk/ *v* [T] **1** to use violence or threats to take control of a plane, vehicle, or ship 劫持, 抢劫〔飞机等〕 **2** to take control of something and use it for your own purposes 控制, 把持: *Some people think the party has been hijacked by right-wing extremists.* 有人认为该党已经被右翼极端分子所把持。—**hijacker** *n* [C]

hijack[2] *n* [C] *BrE* an act of hijacking a plane, vehicle etc【英】劫持事件

hi·jack·ing /ˈhaɪˌdʒækɪŋ; ˈhaɪdʒækɪŋ/ *n* **1** [C,U] the use of violence or threats to take control of a plane 劫机: *the recent series of airplane hijackings* 最近接二连三的劫机事件 **2** [U] the act of stealing goods from vehicles 盗窃车辆内物品的行为

hi·jinks /ˈhaɪˌdʒɪŋks; ˈhaɪdʒɪŋks/ *n* [plural] an American spelling of HIGH JINKS high jinks 的美式拼法

hike[1] /haɪk; haɪk/ *n* [C] **1** a long walk in the mountains or countryside〔在山区或乡间〕徒步旅行, 远足: *a hike in the woods* 在林间远足 **2** *especially AmE informal* a large increase in prices, wages, taxes etc【尤美, 非正式】〔价格、工资、税等的〕大幅度上升: *a petition against the proposed tax hikes* 反对拟议中大幅度提税的请愿书 **3 take a hike** *AmE spoken* used to tell someone rudely to go away【美口】滚开!

hike[2] *v* **1** [I,T] to walk a long way in the mountains or countryside 徒步旅行, 远足: **hike sth** *AmE*【美】*He wants to hike the Himalayas.* 他想在喜马拉雅山区作徒步旅行。| **go hiking** *The kids often go hiking at weekends.* 孩子们经常在周末去远足。—compare 比较 WALKING[1] (1) **2** also 又作 **hike sth ↔ up** [T] *especially AmE* to increase prices, taxes, fees etc, especially by a large amount【尤美】〔大幅度〕提高〔价格、税款、服务费等〕

hike sth ↔ up *phr v* **1** *especially AmE informal* to lift up a piece of your clothing【尤美, 非正式】提起, 拉起〔衣服〕: *She hiked her skirt up to climb the stairs.* 她提起裙子上楼。**2** HIKE[2] (2) 大幅度提高

hik·er /ˈhaɪkɚ; ˈhaɪkə/ *n* [C] someone who walks long distances in the mountains or country for pleasure; WALKER (1) 徒步旅行者, 远足者

hi·lar·i·ous /həˈlɛrɪəs; hɪˈleəriəs/ *adj* extremely funny 极好笑的, 极有趣的: *You should have seen that program last night – it was hilarious!* 你真该看看昨晚的节目, 好笑极了! —**hilariously** *adv*

hi·lar·i·ty /həˋlærətɪ; hɪˈlærɪ̵ti/ *n* [U] laughter, or a feeling of fun 欢笑, 欢闹: *Gloria's costume caused a good deal of hilarity.* 格洛丽亚的服装引起了阵阵大笑。

hill /hɪl; hɪl/ *n* [C] **1** an area of land that is higher than the land around it, like a mountain but smaller 小山, 小丘, 山岗 **2** a slope on a road〔路上的〕斜坡: *There's a steep hill ahead – get into low gear.* 前面有个陡坡, 把车子挂到低挡。**3 on the Hill** *AmE* on CAPITOL HILL or in the US government【美】在美国国会[政府]中 **4 over the hill** no longer young, and therefore no longer attractive or good at doing things 不再年轻: *Kathleen thinks she's over the hill, but she's only 32.* 凯瑟琳觉得自己已经老了, 但她只有32岁。**5 it doesn't amount to a hill of beans** *AmE spoken* it is not important【美口】毫无价值, 微不足道

Hill, Joe /dʒo; dʒəʊ/ (1879-1915) a US TRADE UNION leader, who tried to help workers to get better pay and more rights. He also wrote many songs on social subjects, including *Casey Jones.* 希尔〔(1879-1915), 美国一工会领导人。他致力于帮助工人争取更好的报酬和更多的权利, 也写过不少有关社会问题的歌曲, 包括《凯西·琼斯》〕

Hil·la·ry /ˋhɪlərɪ; ˈhɪləri/, **Sir Ed·mund** /ˋɛdmənd; ˈedmənd/ (1919-2008) a New Zealand mountain climber who was the first person, with Sherpa Tenzing, to reach the top of Mount Everest in 1953. He also travelled by land to the South Pole in 1958. 希拉里〔(1919-2008), 新西兰登山运动员。1953年, 他与夏尔巴人丹增一起登上珠穆朗玛峰, 成为登上该峰的第一人。1958年, 他还通过陆路前往南极〕

hill·bil·ly /ˋhɪl,bɪlɪ; ˈhɪlbɪli/ *n* [C] *AmE* an insulting word meaning an uneducated person who lives in the mountains【美】山里人, 乡巴佬〔一种带侮辱性的称呼〕

hill·ock /ˋhɪlək; ˈhɪlək/ *n* [C] a little hill 小山丘

Hills·bo·rough /ˋhɪlzbərə; ˈhɪlzbərə/ also 又作 **the Hillsborough Disaster** a serious accident which happened in 1989 during a football game at Hillsborough, in the city of Sheffield in northern England. 96 people died and several hundred were injured by being crushed when a large crowd of people moved into a small area and could not escape. This event led to changes in the design of football grounds and in the methods used for controlling large crowds safely. 希尔斯伯勒事件〔1989年在英格兰北部设菲尔德市希尔斯伯勒区的一场足球比赛中发生的严重事故。一大批人涌入一个小的区域又无法逃离, 结果造成96人死亡, 数百人被挤伤。这一事件之后, 足球场的设计及控制大量人群的方法有所改进〕

hill·side /ˋhɪl,saɪd; ˈhɪlsaɪd/ *n* [C] the sloping side of a hill〔小山的〕山坡

hill sta·tion /ˈ· ,··/ *n* [C] a town in the hills, especially in South Asia, where people go to escape the hot weather〔尤指南亚供避暑用的〕山间小镇

hill·y /ˋhɪlɪ; ˈhɪli/ *adj* having a lot of hills 多山丘的, 丘陵起伏的: *a hilly region* 丘陵地带

hilt /hɪlt; hɪlt/ *n* [C] **1** the handle of a sword or knife that is used as a weapon〔刀、剑等武器的〕柄 —see picture at 参见 SWORD 图 **2 (up) to the hilt** completely, or as much as possible 完全地, 彻底地, 最大限度地: *mortgaged up to the hilt* 已全部抵押的 | *I'd back him to the hilt any day.* 我任何时候都会全力支持他。

Hil·ton Head /,·· ˈ·/ an island off the coast of South Carolina, US, which is popular for holidays, especially with wealthy tourists 希尔顿海岬〔美国南卡罗来纳州近海一岛屿, 为著名度假胜地, 尤为有钱的游客所青睐〕

him /hɪm; ɪm; *strong* 强读 hɪm; hɪm/ *pron* object form of 'he'〔he的宾格〕他: *I don't know why he left early, I'll have to ask him about it.* 我不知道他为什么提前离开了, 我得问问他。| *It's a great movie, with Sylvester Stallone as we've never seen him before!* 这真是部好电影, 西尔维斯特·史泰龙有我们从未见过的演出! | *Imagine Ian becoming a pilot, and him so scared of flying too.* 想象一下伊恩成为一名飞行员, 而他是一个如此惧怕飞行的人。—see 见 ME (USAGE)

Him·a·lay·as, the /,hɪməˋleəz; ,hɪməˈleɪəz/ a long range of mountains in southern Asia which includes the highest mountain in the world, Mount Everest, and other mountains which only very experienced climbers try to climb 喜马拉雅山〔亚洲南部一山系, 包括世界最高峰珠穆朗玛峰以及其他山峰, 唯有经验颇丰的登山者才敢攀登〕

him·bo /ˋhɪmbo; ˈhɪmbəʊ/ *n* [C] *humorous* a young man who is sexually attractive but is not very intelligent【幽默】徒有其表的年轻男子, 没头脑的帅男

Him·mler /ˋhɪmlɚ; ˈhɪmlə/, **Hein·rich** /ˋhaɪnrɪk; ˈhaɪnrɪk/ (1900-45) a German Nazi leader who was in charge of the SS, and was responsible for organizing the killing of millions of Jews in CONCENTRATION CAMPS 希姆莱〔(1900-1945), 德国纳粹头领, 负责掌管党卫军, 曾在集中营组织杀害了上百万名犹太人〕

him·self /hɪmˋsɛlf; ɪmˈself; *strong* 强读 hɪmˋsɛlf; hɪmˈself/ *pron* **1** used to emphasize the pronoun 'he', a male name etc 他自己, 他本人〔用于强调he〕: *To her surprise it was the President himself who opened the door.* 出乎她的意料, 竟是总统本人开的门。| *It must be true, he said so himself.* 这肯定是真的, 是他自己亲口说的。| *How can he criticise her work when he has been judged so harshly himself.* 他自己得到的评价如此低, 他还有什么资格对她的工作提出批评呢。**2 not be/feel etc himself** if a man, boy etc is not himself, he does not feel or behave in the way that he usually does because he is nervous or upset 表现/感觉反常: *I think there's something on his mind – he hasn't really seemed himself lately.* 他一定有什么心事, 他近来一直表现得不大正常。**3 (all) by himself a)** alone 独自一人地: *He said he would prefer to spend some time by himself for a while.* 他说他希望独自一个人待一段时间。**b)** without help 独力地, 独自地: *My son was about 2 years old before he could walk by himself.* 我儿子快两岁时才会自己走路。**4 (all) to himself** if a man, boy etc has something to himself, he does not have to share it with anyone 独自享用[拥有]的: *When his brother got married, John finally had a bedroom to himself.* 哥哥结婚后, 约翰终于有了自己一个人用的卧室。**5 a)** the reflexive form of HE〔he的反身代词〕他自己: *I don't think he hurt himself when he fell.* 我想他摔倒时并没有伤着自己。| *His name is James but he usually calls himself Jim.* 他的名字叫詹姆斯, 但他通常称自己为吉姆。| *He spends all day by the fire, talking to himself.* 他整天都待在火炉边自言自语。**b)** the reflexive form of HE used after words like EVERYONE, ANYONE, NO ONE etc〔he的反身代词, 用于everyone, anyone, no one之类的词语之后〕自己: *Everyone should learn to respect himself.* 人人都应学会尊重自己。—see also 另见 YOURSELF

hind[1] /haɪnd; haɪnd/ *adj* **hind legs/feet** the back legs or feet of an animal with four legs〔四足动物的〕后腿 —see also 另见 **talk the hind legs off a donkey** (TALK[1] (11))

hind[2] *n* [C] a female DEER 雌鹿

Hin·de·mith /ˋhɪndəmɪt; ˈhɪndəmɪt/, **Paul** (1895-1963) a German COMPOSER (=a writer of music) who had great influence on 20th century CLASSICAL music 兴德米特〔(1895-1963), 德国作曲家, 对20世纪的古典音乐产生过重要影响〕

Hin·den·burg /ˋhɪndən,burk; ˈhɪndənbʊək/ a German AIRSHIP, which exploded when coming into land in New Jersey, USA, after crossing the Atlantic in 1937. All passengers and crew were killed, and businesses stopped using airships to carry people or goods. 兴登堡号飞艇〔德国一飞艇。1937年穿越大西洋, 进入美国新泽西州时发生爆炸, 所有乘客和船员全部遇难。之后, 企业不再使用飞艇运送乘客或货物〕

hin·der /ˋhɪndɚ; ˈhɪndə/ *v* [T] to make it difficult for someone to do something or for something to develop 阻碍, 妨碍, 阻止: *High interest rates will hinder economic growth.* 高利率将会阻碍经济增长。

Hin·di /ˋhɪndɪ; ˈhɪndi/ *n* [U] one of the official languages of India 印地语

Hindley, Myra —see 见 the MOORS MURDERERS

hind·most /ˋhaɪnd,most; ˈhaɪndməʊst/ *adj old use* furthest behind【旧】最后面的 —see also 另见 **devil take the hindmost** (DEVIL (14))

hind·quar·ters /ˋhaɪndˋkwɔrtɚz; ˈhaɪnd,kwɔːtəz/ *n* [plural] the back part of an animal, including the back legs〔动物的〕后臀及后腿 —see picture at 参见 HORSE[1] 图

hin·drance /ˋhɪndrəns; ˈhɪndrəns/ *n* **1** [C] something or someone that makes it difficult for you to do something successfully 起阻碍作用的人[事]; 障碍物; 阻碍者: **be a hindrance to** *Lack of funding was a serious hindrance to the progress of our research.* 缺少资金严重地阻碍了我们的研究进展。| **be more of a hindrance than a help** (=try to help but cause more problems) 帮倒忙 **2** [U] *formal* the act of making it difficult for someone to do something【正式】阻碍, 妨碍 —see also 另见 **without let or hindrance** (LET[2] (2))

hind·sight /ˋhaɪnd,saɪt; ˈhaɪndsaɪt/ *n* [U] the ability to understand facts about a situation only after it has happened 事后聪明, 后见之明: **with the benefit/wisdom of hindsight** (=when hindsight makes it possible to realize what mistakes were made) 通过事后总结/分析 *With the benefit of hindsight it's easy to criticize Lyndon Johnson's fateful decision.* 事后才指责林登·约翰逊的重大失误当然不难。

Hin·du /ˋhɪndu; ˈhɪnduː/ *n plural* **Hindus** [C] someone who believes in Hinduism 印度教徒 —**Hindu** *adj*: *a Hindu temple* 印度教寺庙

Hin·du·is·m /ˈhɪnduˌɪzəm; ˈhɪndu-ɪzəm/ *n* [U] the main religion in India, which includes belief in DESTINY and REINCARNATION 印度教〔印度的主要宗教〕

Hines /haɪnz; haɪnz/, **Earl** (1903-83) a US JAZZ musician, piano player, and band leader 海因斯〔(1903-1983)，美国爵士音乐家、钢琴演奏家和乐队领队〕

hinge¹ /hɪndʒ; hɪndʒ/ *n* [C] a metal part used to fasten a door to its frame, a lid to a box etc, so that it can swing open and shut 〔门、箱等上的〕铰链, 合叶 —see picture at 参见 GLASS¹ 图

hinge² *v*

hinge on/upon sth *phr v* [T not in progressive 不用进行时] if a result hinges on something happening, it depends on it completely 取决于: *The future prospects of a student hinge on his performance in these examinations.* 一个学生的发展前途取决于他在这些考试中的表现。

hinged /hɪndʒd; hɪndʒd/ *adj* joined by a hinge 用铰链连接的

hint¹ /hɪnt; hɪnt/ *n* [C] **1** something that you say or do in order to tell someone something in an indirect way, so that they can guess what you mean 暗示: **drop a hint (that)** (=give a hint) 作出暗示 *Harry was dropping hints that he wanted to be invited to the party.* 哈里一直在暗示自己希望被邀请参加这次晚会。| **a broad hint** (=one that is deliberately easy to understand) 明显的暗示 | **take a/the hint** (=understand someone's hint) 领会暗示 *I kept looking at my watch, but Laura wouldn't take the hint – she didn't leave till midnight.* 我不停地看手表, 但劳拉就是不领会这个提示, 她直到午夜才离开。**2** a very small amount or sign of something (细微的) 迹象; 少许, 微量: [+of] *There was a hint of anger in his voice.* 他的声音中带有一点恼怒。| *a sauce with a hint of garlic* 带有少许大蒜的调味汁 | **give no hint of/that** *literary*【文】*a blue sky that gave no hint of the storm to come* 没有一点要出现暴风雨迹象的蓝天 **3** a useful piece of advice about how to do something 有益的建议[指点]: [+on] *helpful hints on looking after house plants* 关于种植室内盆栽植物的好建议

hint² *v* [I,T] to say something in an indirect way, but so that someone can guess what you mean 暗示, 示意: [+at] *What are you hinting at?* 你在暗示什么? | **hint (that)** *I think she was hinting that I might be offered a contract.* 我想她在暗示我可能会获得一份合同。

hin·ter·land /ˈhɪntɚˌlænd; ˈhɪntəlænd/ *n* [singular] an area of land beyond a coast or large river 内地, 腹地

hip¹ /hɪp; hɪp/ *n* [C] **1** one of the two parts on each side of your body between the top of your leg and your waist 臀部 —see picture at 参见 BODY 图 **2** [usually plural 一般用复数] the red fruit of some kinds of ROSE bushes; ROSE HIP 〔红色的〕蔷薇果 (实)

hip² *interjection* **hip, hip, hurray!** used as a shout of approval 加油! 万岁! 〔表示赞许的喊声〕

hip³ *adj informal* doing things or done according to the latest fashion【非正式】新潮的, 赶时髦的

hip·bath /ˈhɪpˌbæθ; ˈhɪpbɑːθ/ *n* [C] a bath you can sit but not lie down in 坐浴浴盆

hip flask /ˈ· ·/ *n* [C] a small container for strong alcoholic drinks, made to fit in your pocket 〔可放在衣服口袋里的〕扁平小酒瓶 —see picture at 参见 FLASK 图

hip hop /ˈ· ·/ *n* [U] a kind of popular dance music with a regular heavy BEAT and spoken words 嘻哈乐〔节奏强烈、说唱形式的一种流行舞曲〕

hip·hug·gers /ˈhɪpˌhʌgɚz; ˈhɪpˌhʌgəz/ *n* [plural] *AmE* HIPSTERS【美】低腰裤〔裤腰低及臀部的紧身长裤〕

hip·pie, hippy /ˈhɪpɪ; ˈhɪpi/ *n* [C] someone opposed to the traditional standards of society who wears unusual clothes, has long hair, and takes drugs for pleasure 嬉皮士

hippie 嬉皮士

hip·po /ˈhɪpo; ˈhɪpəʊ/ *n* [C] *informal* a hippopotamus【非正式】河马

hip pock·et /ˌ· ˈ· ·/ *n* [C] a back pocket in a pair of trousers or a skirt 〔裤子或裙子的〕后口袋, 后兜

Hip·poc·ra·tes /hɪˈpɑkrətiz; hɪˈpɒkrətiːz/ (?460-?377 BC) a doctor in ancient Greece who wrote many books about medicine and began the study of modern medicine 希波克拉底〔(公元前?460-前?337)，古希腊医生, 写有多部医学著作, 开创了现代医学的先河〕

Hip·po·crat·ic oath /ˌhɪpəkrætɪk ˈoθ; ˌhɪpəkrætɪk ˈəʊθ/ *n* [singular] the promise made by doctors

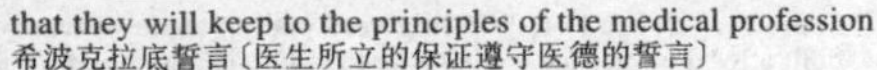
that they will keep to the principles of the medical profession 希波克拉底誓言〔医生所立的保证遵守医德的誓言〕

hip·po·pot·a·mus /ˌhɪpəˈpɑtəməs; ˌhɪpəˈpɒtəməs/ *n* [C] a large African animal with a large head, a wide mouth, and thick grey skin, that lives in and near water 河马〔产于非洲〕

hip·py /ˈhɪpɪ; ˈhɪpi/ *n* [C] another spelling of HIPPIE hippie 的另一种拼法

hip·sters /ˈhɪpstɚz; ˈhɪpstəz/ *n* [plural] *BrE* trousers that fit tightly over your HIPS and do not cover your waist【英】低腰裤; HIPHUGGERS *AmE*【美】

hire¹ /haɪr; haɪə/ *v* [T] **1** *BrE* to pay money to borrow something for a period of hours or days【英】〔短期〕租用; LET¹ (11), RENT¹ (3) *AmE*【美】: *Let's hire a car for the weekend.* 我们这个周末租辆车吧! —see 见 BORROW (USAGE) **2 a)** to employ someone for a short time to do a job for you 〔短期〕雇用〔某人〕: *I'm hiring a private detective to trace my ex-husband.* 我雇了一名私家侦探跟踪我的前夫。**b)** *especially AmE* to employ someone【尤美】雇用, 聘任: **hire and fire** (=employ and dismiss people) 聘用与解雇 S3

hire sth ↔ **out** *phr v* [T] *BrE*【英】**1** to allow someone to use something for a short time in exchange for money 〔短期〕出租; RENT¹ (3) *AmE*【美】: *a little company that hires out boats to tourists* 一家向游客出租游船的小公司 **2 hire yourself out** to arrange to work for someone 受雇于某人

USAGE NOTE 用法说明: HIRE

WORD CHOICE 词语辨析: **hire, hire out, rent, rent out, let out, employ, take on, appoint, charter**

In British English you **hire** things for just a short time and the owner **hires** them **out** to you. 在英国英语中, 短期租用物品用 hire, 而物主将物品出租则用 hire out: *Let's hire a car for the weekend.* 我们这个周末租辆车吧! | *I'll have to hire a suit for the wedding.* 我得为婚礼租一套礼服。

You **rent** things for a longer period. rent 表示租用的时间比较长: *Is that your own fax or do you rent it?* 那台传真机是你自己的还是租来的? You **rent** a house, room etc and the owner **lets** it **(out)** to you. 租用房屋等用 rent, 房主将房屋出租则用 let (out)。

In American English, however, you **rent** all of these things, and the owner **rents** them **out**. This is now starting to be used in British English as well. 但在美国英语中, 租用所有物品都用 rent, 物主出租所有物品都用 rent out。英国英语也在开始采用这种用法。

In American English you **hire** people for any job, but in British English you only **hire** people for a particular purpose for a short time. Otherwise you **employ** them or **take them on** (or, more formally, **appoint** them). 在美国英语中, 雇人做任何工作都用 hire, 但在英国英语中, 只有短期雇用某人做某一特定工作才用 hire。如长期雇用则用 employ 或 take on (或者更正式一点, 用 appoint): *We hired a caterer for the wedding reception.* 我们为婚宴雇了一名酒席承办人。| *Business is good – we'll have to take on more workers.* 生意不错, 我们得再多雇些工人。

In both American English and British English groups, companies etc may **charter** buses, ships, or planes for a special purpose. 无论在美国或英国英语中, 集团、公司等为某一特定用途包租车辆、船只或飞机均可用 charter: *UNICEF has chartered a plane to carry supplies to the disaster area.* 联合国儿童基金会租了一架飞机将物资运往灾区。

hire² *n* [U] **1** *BrE* an arrangement by which you borrow something for a short time in exchange for money【英】〔短期〕租用; 出租: *a car hire company* 汽车出租公司 | **for hire** (=available to hire) 可供出租 *boats for hire* 可供出租的小船 | **on hire from** (=being hired) 从…处租用 *The crane is on hire from a construction company.* 吊车是从一家建筑公司租来的。**2** *old use* wages【旧】工资, 工钱 —see also 另见 **ply for hire** (PLY¹ (4))

hired hand /ˌ· ˈ· ·/ *n* [C] *AmE* someone who is employed to help on a farm【美】农场雇工

hire·ling /ˈhaɪrlɪŋ; ˈhaɪəlɪŋ/ *n* [C] someone who will work for anyone who is willing to pay 受雇后任人使唤者

hire pur·chase /ˌ· ˈ· ·/ *n* [U] *BrE* a way of buying expensive goods by regularly paying small amounts over a period of time【英】分期付款购买方式; INSTALLMENT PLAN *AmE*【美】

Hi·ro·hi·to /ˌhɪroˈhito; ˌhɪərəʊˈhiːtəʊ/ (1901-89) the EMPEROR of Japan from 1926 to 1989 裕仁天皇〔(1901-1989)，日本天皇, 1926 至 1989 年间在位〕

Hi·rosh·i·ma /hɪˈroʃɪmə; hɪˈrɒʃɪmə/ a city in Japan which was destroyed in 1945 during World War II, when a US NUCLEAR

bomb was dropped on it, killing very many people. It was rebuilt after the war, and is now a large industrial city again. 广岛〔日本一城市。1945年二战期间，美国在此投下原子弹，造成许多人死亡，该市遭到严重毁坏。战后进行了重建，现重新成为一座大型工业城市〕—see also 另见 NAGASAKI

Hirs·horn /ˋhɚʃ-hɔrn; ˈhɜːʃ-hɔːn/ also 又作 **the Hirshorn Museum and Sculpture Garden** a museum of modern art in Washington, D.C., which is part of the Smithsonian Institution 赫什霍恩博物馆及雕塑园〔位于华盛顿的一家现代艺术博物馆，属史密森学会〕

hir·sute /ˋhɚsut; ˈhɜːsjuːt/ *adj literary or humorous* having a lot of hair especially on your body and face【文或幽默】〔尤指身体和面部〕多毛的，毛茸茸的

his¹ /ɪz; ɪz; *strong* 强读 hɪz; hɪz/ *determiner* [possessive form of 'he' he的所有格] **1** used to talk about something that belongs to or is connected with someone who has already been mentioned or who the person you are talking to already knows about（属于）他的: *He broke his arm while playing football with his children.* 他与（他的）孩子们踢足球时摔断了胳膊。| *A man of his age shouldn't be running about like that.* 像他这种年纪的人不应该如此东奔西跑。**2** used especially after words like 'everyone', 'anyone', 'no one' etc when you mean 'their' 他的〔尤用于everyone, anyone, no one等词之后〕: *Who cares what everyone else is doing – each to his own, I say.* 谁会在意别人在干什么，我说呀，还是各管各的事吧。—compare 比较 THEIR

his² *pron* [possessive form of 'he' he的所有格] **1** used to talk about something that belongs to or is connected with someone who has already been mentioned or who the person you are talking to already knows about（属于）他的（东西）；同他有关的（人）: *That's not Philip's wife – his is a tall blonde woman.* 那不是菲利普的妻子，他的妻子是个高个子的金发女人。| **sb/sth of his** *That stupid brother of his ran into my car.* 他那个傻瓜兄弟撞了我的车。**2** used after words like 'everyone', 'anyone', 'no one' etc when you mean 'theirs'〔用在everyone, anyone, no one等词后〕他的: *Everyone only wants what is his by right.* 每个人都只想得到理应属于他的东西。—compare 比较 THEIRS

Hi·span·ic /hɪsˋpænɪk; hɪˈspænɪk/ *adj* from or connected with a country where Spanish or Portuguese is spoken 来自说西班牙语[葡萄牙语]国家的；与说西班牙语[葡萄牙语]国家有关的 —**Hispanic** *n* [C]

His·pan·i·o·la /ˌhɪspænɪˋolə; ˌhɪspæniˈəʊlə/ an island in the Caribbean Sea, formerly called Santo Domingo, and now divided into the countries of Haiti and the Dominican Republic 伊斯帕尼奥拉岛〔加勒比海一岛屿，旧称圣多明各。现分成海地和多米尼加共和国两个国家〕

hiss /hɪs; hɪs/ *v* **1** [I] to make a noise which sounds like 'ssss' 发出嘶嘶声: *The snake slowly uncoiled, making a loud hissing noise.* 那条蛇慢慢地伸直了身子，一边发出很响的嘶嘶声。**2** [I, T] to say something in a loud whisper 用嘘声说出: *"Be quiet," she hissed.* "别出声。"她嘘声道。**3** [T] to hiss at a performer or speaker that you do not like〔因不满而〕对〔表演者或发言人〕发出嘘声 —**hiss** *n* [C] —see picture on page A19 参见A19页图

Hiss, Al·ger /ˋældʒɚ; ˈældʒə/ (1904-96) a US government official who was put in prison from 1950 to 1954 for being a Communist SPY. Many people believed he was not guilty, and documents from the former Soviet Union seemed to prove this, when they were made public in 1992. 希斯〔(1904-1996)，美国一政府官员，1950至1954年间被认为是共产党间谍而入狱。许多人认为他是无辜的。前苏联于1992年公开的有关文件似乎也可证明这一点〕

hist /hɪst; hɪst/ *interjection old use* a sound used to get someone's attention or to ask someone to be quiet【旧】嘘！〔用于引起注意或要求肃静〕

his·ta·mine /ˋhɪstəmin; ˈhɪstəmiːn/ *n* [C] a chemical compound that can increase the flow of blood in your body 组胺〔一种能催进体内血液流动的化合物〕

his·to·gram /ˋhɪstəˌgræm; ˈhɪstəgræm/ *n* [C] a BAR CHART〔用于统计上的〕条形图（表）

his·to·ri·an /hɪsˋtɔriən; hɪˈstɔːriən/ *n* [C] someone who studies or writes about history 历史学家，史学工作者

his·tor·ic /hɪsˋtɔrɪk; hɪˈstɒrɪk/ *adj* **1** a historic event or place is important because it is, or will be, remembered as part of history 有重大历史意义的，历史性的: *an historic building* 一座有历史意义的建筑物 | *a historic meeting between two great leaders* 两位伟大领导人的历史性会晤 **2** historic times are the periods of time whose history has been recorded 有历史记载的 —compare 比较 PREHISTORIC

his·tor·i·cal /hɪsˋtɔrɪkl; hɪˈstɒrɪkəl/ *adj* **1** connected with the study of history（有关）历史的；历史学的: *historical research* 史学研究 **2** historical events, facts, people etc happened or existed in the past 历史上的，属于过去的: *Was King Arthur a real historical figure?* 亚瑟王是一位真实的历史人物吗？**3** describing or based on events in the past 反映历史事件的；基于史实的: *a historical novel* 历史小说 —**historically** /-klɪ; -kli/ *adv*

historic pres·ent /ˌ· ˌ·· ˈ··/ *n* [singular] the present tense, used in some languages to describe events in the past to make them seem more real 历史现在时〔在一些语言中，在叙述过去发生的事情时使用现在时以求生动〕

his·to·ry /ˋhɪstrɪ; ˈhɪstəri/ *n*

1 ►**PAST EVENTS** 过去的事件◄ [U] all the things that happened in the past, especially the political, social, or economic development of a nation 历史: *India has been invaded several times during its history.* 印度在历史上曾几次受到侵略。| *Throughout history the achievements of women have been largely ignored.* 在整个历史过程中妇女的成就在很大程度上都被人忽略了。| **change the course of history** *Those decisions made at the Yalta Conference changed the course of history.* 雅尔塔会议上所作的那些决定改变了历史的进程。

2 ►**SUBJECT OF STUDY** 学科◄ [U] the study of history, especially as a subject in school or university 历史学: *a degree in European history* 欧洲史学位

3 ►**DEVELOPMENT OF STH** 发展过程◄ [singular, U] the development of a subject, activity, institution etc since it started 发展史，沿革，发展过程: *the worst disaster in the history of space travel* 宇航史上最大的灾难

4 ►**BOOK** 书◄ [C] a book about past events 史书，史记: *a history of World War II* 第二次世界大战史记

5 ►**PAST LIFE** 过去的生活◄ **a history of** if someone has a history of illness, problems, or criminal activity, these things have happened to them or been done by them in the past 个人经历，履历〈如病史、犯罪记录等〉: *The defendant had a history of violent assaults against women.* 被告曾有强暴妇女的前科。

6 make history to do something important that will be recorded and remembered 创造历史，做出值得载入史册的重要事情: *Lindbergh made history when he flew across the Atlantic in 1927.* 林白于1927年飞越大西洋，写下了历史的新篇章。

7 will go down in history something that will go down in history is important enough to be remembered and recorded 将被载入史册: *This day will go down in history as the start of a new era in South Africa.* 南非踏入新纪元的这一天将被载入史册。

8 ...and the rest is history used to say that everyone knows the rest of a story you have been telling …接下来的就是尽人皆知的事了

9 that's past/ancient history *spoken* used to say that something is not important any more【口】那已是往事了〔表示某事已不再重要〕

10 history repeats itself used to say that things often happen in the same way as they happened before 历史在不断重演 —see also 另见 NATURAL HISTORY, CASE HISTORY

his·tri·on·ics /ˌhɪstrɪˋɑnɪks; ˌhɪstriˈɒnɪks/ *n* [plural] loud, extremely emotional behaviour that is intended to get people's sympathy and attention 矫揉造作，装腔作势 —**histrionic** *adj*

hit¹ /hɪt; hɪt/ *v past tense and past participle* **hit** *present participle* **hitting**

1 ►**TOUCH SB/STH HARD** 用劲碰某人/物◄ [T] to touch someone or something quickly and usually hard with your hand, a stick etc 打，击: **hit sth with** *Billy was hitting a tin can with a spoon.* 比利用匙子敲打着一个罐头。| **hit sb on the nose/in the stomach/over the head etc** *She hit him playfully over the head with her newspaper.* 她用报纸闹着玩，打了一下他的头。| **get hit** *Stand back you lot, or you'll get hit.* 你们全都往后站，否则会被击中的。—compare 比较 PUNCH¹ (1), SLAP¹ (1)

2 ►**HIT/CRASH INTO STH** 撞上某物◄ [T] to move into something quickly and hard 撞击，碰撞: *The football hit the trash can with a bang.* 足球砰的一声打在垃圾桶上。| *The driver was drunk and hit three stationary cars.* 司机酒后驾驶，撞上了三辆停着的车。

3 ►**ACCIDENTALLY** 意外地◄ [T] to move a part of your body quickly and hard against something so that it hurts you〔使身体某部位〕撞[碰]着: **hit sth on/against etc** *I fell and hit my head on the table.* 我摔倒了，头撞在桌子上。

4 ►**IN SPORT** 体育运动中◄ [T] **a)** to make something such as a ball move by hitting it with a bat, stick etc〔用球拍等〕击打〔球〕: *He hit the shuttlecock gently this time.* 他这次轻击了一下羽毛球。**b)** to get a point or some points by hitting a ball etc 击球得分: **hit two goals/a six etc** *The batter hit a home run.* 击球员打出了一个本垒打。

5 ►**WORK A MACHINE ETC 操作机器等**◄ [T] to press a part in a machine, car etc to make it work 按, 揿: *Hit the brakes!* 揿刹车!
6 ►**HURT SB 伤害某人**◄ [T] to deliberately move your hand, a stick etc against someone and hurt them〔用手、棍子等〕打(伤): *Mom, she keeps hitting me!* 妈妈, 她老是打我! | **hit sb with sth** *They used to hit the kids with a leather belt.* 他们过去常用皮带打孩子。| **hit sb over the head/in the stomach etc** *She hit him as hard as she could around his face.* 她用尽力气在他的脸上乱打一气。
7 ►**BULLETS/BOMBS ETC 子弹/炸弹等**◄ [T often passive 常用被动态] to wound someone or damage something with a bullet, bomb etc 击伤〔某人〕; 击毁〔某物〕: **hit sb/sth in/on etc** *A second shot hit her in the back.* 第二枪击中了她的背部。| **be badly hit** *Our ship was badly hit and sank within minutes.* 我们的船受到重击, 没过几分钟就沉没了。
8 ►**ATTACK 攻击**◄ [I,T usually passive 一般用被动态] to attack someone suddenly〔突然〕攻击: *The convoy was hit by Afghan government troops.* 车队遭到阿富汗政府军的攻击。
9 ►**HURT, BUT NOT PHYSICALLY 造成非肉体上的伤害**◄ [T] *informal* to do something that harms someone【非正式】伤害: **hit sb where it hurts** (=in the way you think will be most upsetting for them) 击中某人的要害, 触到某人的痛处 *You should hit your husband where it hurts most – in his wallet!* 你应该击中你丈夫的要害 —— 瞄准他的钱包! | **hit sb when they are down** (=harm someone even though they are already defeated or very weak) 乘人之危打击某人, 落井下石
10 ►**BAD LUCK ETC 噩运等**◄ [I,T] if something such as bad luck, illness, bad weather etc hits or hits someone, it suddenly affects them〔噩运、疾病、坏天气等〕突然袭击[影响]: *The storm finally hit.* 暴风雨终于来临了。| *The guilt hit him like a lead weight.* 内疚的感觉像铅块一样落在他的身上。| **be badly/severely/hard hit** *The company has been badly hit by the drop in prices.* 这家公司因价格下跌而受到重创。| **worst/hardest hit** *the areas of the country hardest hit by the recession* 该国受经济衰退影响最严重的地区
11 ►**REACH A LEVEL/NUMBER 达到某一水平/数量**◄ [T] to reach a particular level or number 达到〔某水平或数量〕: *Youth unemployment has hit the one million mark.* 年轻人的失业人数已达到一百万。| **hit rock-bottom/hit an all-time low** (=reach an extremely low level) 达到最低点 *World oil prices have hit rock-bottom.* 全球石油价格已跌至最低点。
12 ►**PROBLEM/TROUBLE 问题/麻烦**◄ [T] to experience trouble, a problem etc 碰到, 遇到〔困难、问题等〕: *I had hit a few snags in my work.* 我在工作上碰到了一些难题。| **hit a bad patch** *spoken* (=have a short period of difficulty)【口】遇到暂时的困难
13 ►**REALIZE 意识到**◄ [T] if a fact hits you, you suddenly realize its importance and feel surprised or shocked 使〔某人〕突然意识到: *The full meaning of the night's events hit me and I started crying.* 我突然意识到当晚发生的事情的全部意义, 开始哭了起来。| **it hits sb** *Suddenly it hit me. He was trying to ask me to marry him.* 我突然明白了, 他是在向我求婚。
14 **not know what hit you** *informal* to be so surprised or shocked by something that you cannot think clearly【非正式】因惊吓而无法正常思考; 大为惊讶
15 ►**ARRIVE 到达**◄ [T] *informal* to arrive or go somewhere【非正式】到达〔某地〕: *They hit the main road two kilometres further on.* 他们又前进了两公里后就到了大路。| **hit town** *especially AmE*【尤美】*I'll look for work as soon as I hit town.* 我一到镇上就去找工作。
16 **hit the road** *informal* to start on a journey【非正式】出发, 动身
17 ►**TELL SB STH 告诉某人某事**◄ [T] *informal* if you hit someone with some information or news, you tell them something surprising or entertaining【非正式】透露〔令人惊讶或有趣的消息〕: *Once you've hit the customer with the price you want to close the deal quickly.* 你一旦将价钱告诉顾客, 就想尽快做成买卖。
18 **hit it off (with sb)** *informal* if two people hit it off with each other, they like each other as soon as they meet【非正式】(与某人)一见如故, 合得来: *I knew you'd hit it off with Mike.* 我早就知道你与迈克会一见如故的。
19 **hit the big time** *informal* to suddenly become very famous, successful and rich【非正式】突然成名, 突然发迹
20 **hit the bottle** *informal* to start to drink a lot of alcohol【非正式】开始酗酒, 喝过量的酒
21 **hit the dirt/the deck** *informal* to fall to the ground because of danger【非正式】〔因遭遇危险而〕突然跌倒在地
22 **hit the ground running** to start doing something successfully without any delay 立刻着手顺利地做某事
23 **hit the jackpot a)** to win a lot of money 赢得大笔金钱, 中头彩 **b)** *informal* to have a big success【非正式】大获成功
24 **hit the nail on the head** *especially spoken* used to say that what someone has said is exactly right【尤口】正中要害, 一针见血, 说话中肯
25 **hit the roof/the ceiling** *spoken* to become extremely angry【口】大发雷霆, 暴跳如雷: *Dad hit the roof when I got home at 2 am.* 我凌晨两点才回到家, 爸爸生气极了。
26 **hit the sack** *informal* to go to bed【非正式】上床睡觉
27 **hit the spot** *informal* if food hits the spot, it stops you being hungry and tastes good【非正式】〔食物〕让人吃得饱而满意, 切合需要 —see also 另见 **the shit hit the fan** (SHIT¹ (12))

hit back *phr v* [I] to attack or criticize a person or group that has attacked or criticized you 回击, 反击: **hit back (at sb/sth)** *Stung by Maria's contempt, Philip hit back with a few well-chosen words.* 菲利普被玛丽亚的蔑视刺痛了, 便用两三句巧妙的话来进行反击。

hit on *phr v* [T] **1** [**hit on** sth] also 又作 **hit upon** to have a good idea after thinking about a problem for a long time〔经考虑后〕突然想出〔好主意〕: *He hit upon this ingenious method of freezing food.* 他突然灵机一动, 想出了这个巧妙的冷冻食品的办法。**2** [**hit on** sth] also 又作 **hit upon** to discover something by a lucky chance 偶然发现: *I think you may have hit upon the only error in the whole program.* 我想你可能无意中发现了整个程序中唯一的一处错误。**3** [**hit on** sb] *AmE informal* to talk to someone in a way that shows you are sexually attracted to them【美, 非正式】用语言挑逗: *Don spent the whole night hitting on anything that moved.* 唐整个晚上都在不择对象地挑逗别人。

hit out *phr v* [I] **1** to express strong disapproval of someone or something 严厉批评, 猛烈抨击: **[+at/against]** *The bishop has hit out at the government's policy on homeless people.* 主教就政府针对无家可归者的政策进行了猛烈的抨击。**2** to try to hit someone〔试图〕打某人: **[+at]** *He hit out at me without thinking.* 他想都没想就动手打我了。

hit sb **up for** sth *phr v* [T] *AmE spoken* to ask someone for something【美口】要求〔某人〕提供〔某物〕: *Can I hit you up for a loan till Thursday?* 你能否借我点钱, 我星期四还给你?

hit² *n* [C usually singular 一般用单数] **1** a quick, hard touch with your hand or something you are holding〔用手或手持之物的〕打, 击: *That was a hard hit!* 那真是一记重击! **2** an occasion when something that is aimed at something else touches it, reaches it, or damages it 命中, 击中: *I scored a hit with my first shot.* 我第一枪就命中了目标。| **a direct hit** *Our ship took a direct hit and sank.* 我们的船被直接击中下沉了。**3** something such as a piece of music, a film, or a play that is extremely popular 成功并风行一时的事物〈如音乐、电影、戏剧等〉: **a hit single/show etc** *the latest Broadway hit musical, "The Mask"* 火爆的百老汇最新音乐剧《面具》| **a big/smash hit** *Chris de Burgh had a smash hit with "Lady in Red".* 克里斯·德伯格的歌曲《红衣女郎》大受欢迎。**4 be/make a hit with sb** to be liked very much by someone 极受某人喜爱: *Your husband was a big hit with the kids.* 你的丈夫极受孩子们的喜爱。**5 a hit at sb** a remark that is intended to hurt someone 伤害某人的话 **6** *slang* the action of deliberately breathing in the smoke of an illegal drug【俚】吸毒 **7** *AmE slang* a murder【美俚】谋杀 —see also 另见 HIT MAN 3

hit-and-miss /ˌ· · ˈ·/ *adj* done in a way that is not planned or organized 碰运气的, 无周详计划的

hit-and-run /ˌ· · ˈ·◂/ *adj* [only before noun 仅用于名词前] **1** a hit-and-run accident is one in which the driver of a car hits a person or another car and then drives away without stopping to help〔交通事故〕撞了人[另一辆车]而逃逸的: **hit-and-run driver** (=one who does not stop after an accident) 肇事逃逸的司机 **2** a hit-and-run military attack is one in which the attackers arrive suddenly and unexpectedly and leave quickly〔军事行动中〕打了就跑的, 攻击后马上撤离的

hitch¹ /hɪtʃ; hɪtʃ/ *v* **1** [I,T] *informal* to ask for a free ride from the drivers of passing cars by putting your hand out with your thumb raised; HITCHHIKE【非正式】搭免费便车旅行, 搭顺风车: **[+across/around/to]** *They hitched all the way across Europe.* 他们搭顺风车穿越了整个欧洲。| **hitch a ride with sb** *We hitched a ride with a trucker from New York to Montreal.* 我们搭了一位卡车司机的便车从纽约到了蒙特利尔。**2 get hitched** *spoken informal* to get married【口, 非正式】结婚 **3** [T always+adv/prep] to fasten something such as a TRAILER (1) to the back of a car so that it can be pulled 将〔拖车等〕挂上钩 **4** [T always+adv/prep] to tie a horse to something 将〔马匹〕拴住, 套住

H

hitch sth ↔ **up** *phr v* [T] **1** to pull, especially a piece of clothing, upwards 将〔衣物〕向上拉: *He hitched up his trousers and started to work.* 他把裤子向上拉了拉，开始干活。**2 hitch up a horse/wagon/team etc** to tie a horse to something, so that the horse can pull it 把马/马车/几匹马套在…上: *He hitched up his wagon and headed west.* 他套上马车向西走了。

hitch² *n* [C] **1** a problem that delays something for a short time 〔短暂的〕故障，障碍: *Except for a few technical hitches the show went very well.* 除了一些小小的技术故障外，演出进行得非常顺利。| **without a hitch** *The Miss Universe pageant went off without a hitch.* 环球小姐选美大赛进行得非常成功。**2** a short, sudden pull upwards 向上急拉: *He gave his belt a hitch.* 他猛地将腰带向上提了提。

Hitch·cock /ˈhɪtʃkɑk; ˈhɪtʃkɒk/, **Sir Al·fred** /ˈælfrɪd; ˈælfrɨd/ (1899-1980) a British film DIRECTOR who made films in the UK and then in Hollywood for almost 50 years. He made THRILLERS (=films that tell exciting stories about crime and murder) such as *The Thirty-Nine Steps* (1935), *Psycho* (1960), and *The Birds* (1963). He is famous for his use of SUSPENSE (=a feeling of fear and excitement that you have when you expect that something bad is going to happen). People sometimes use the word 'Hitchcockian' to describe a story or situation in which there is a lot of suspense. 希区科克〔(1899-1980)，英国电影导演。他先在英国制作影片，然后去了好莱坞，从事导演工作将近50年。他制作的惊险影片有《三十九级台阶》(1935)、《精神病患者》(1960)和《鸟》(1963)等。他善于运用悬念，因而人们有时借用Hitchcockian(希区科克风格)一词来形容悬念迭起的故事或局势〕

hitchhike 搭免费便车旅行

hitch·hike /ˈhɪtʃˌhaɪk; ˈhɪtʃhaɪk/ also 又作 **hitch** *v* [I] to travel by asking drivers of passing cars for free rides 搭免费便车旅行，搭顺风车 —**hitchhiker** *n*

CULTURAL NOTE 文化注释

When someone is hitchhiking they stand at the side of the road and put out their thumb, or hold up a sign with the name of the place they want to go to written on it. Hitchhiking is less common in the US and the UK than it used to be, and many people think that it is dangerous because there have been cases of hitchhikers or the drivers who picked them up being attacked or killed. 搭便车时，人站在路边伸出大拇指，或举着写有目的地名称的牌子。搭便车在英美不如以往普遍，很多人认为这样做很危险，因为曾发生过搭便车的人或司机遇袭或被害的案件。

Hitch·hik·ers' Guide to the Gal·ax·y, The /ˌ··· ˈ···ˈ···/ a humorous British radio programme written by Douglas Adams, which later became a book and a television programme. It is a SCIENCE FICTION story about an Englishman called Arthur Dent who gets on a SPACESHIP just before the Earth is destroyed, and the adventures he has in space with the other characters on this spaceship.《银河系搭便车指南》〔英国一喜剧广播节目，由道格拉斯·亚当斯创作，之后改编成小说和电视节目。这是一个科幻故事，讲述一位名叫亚瑟·登特的英国人在地球毁灭之前登上太空船与飞船上的同伴一起漫游宇宙的冒险经历〕

hi-tech /ˌhaɪ ˈtɛk; ˌhaɪ ˈtek◂/ another spelling of HIGH-TECH high-tech 的另一种拼法

hith·er /ˈhɪðɚ; ˈhɪðə/ *adj old use* here【旧】这儿，这里: **hither and thither** (=in many directions) 这儿和那儿，到处 *A little girl was running hither and thither.* 一个小女孩正在四处奔跑。

hith·er·to /ˌhɪðɚˈtu; ˌhɪðəˈtuː◂/ *adv formal* up to this time【正式】到目前为止，迄今，至今: *The printing press made books available to people hitherto unable to afford them.* 印刷机使以前买不起书的人们能买得起书。

Hit·ler /ˈhɪtlɚ; ˈhɪtlə/, **Ad·olf** /ˈædɑlf; ˈædɒlf/ (1889-1945) the leader of the Nazi Party in Germany from 1921. He was born in Austria and was the 'Führer' (=leader) of Germany from the mid-1930s until his death. He allowed no opposition, and attempted to establish a pure race of German people through a policy of anti-Semitism, as a result of which millions of Jewish people were killed in CONCENTRATION CAMPS. He started World War II by ordering his armies to enter Poland in 1939, and killed himself in 1945, just before Germany lost the war. His name is now sometimes used to describe someone who uses their authority in a cruel or unfair way, or someone who wants to control everything. 希特勒〔(1889-1945)，德国纳粹党党魁，1921年起出任该职。他生于奥地利，20世纪30年代中期直至去世一直担任德国国家元首。他不容任何反对声音，执行反犹太主义政策，试图建立一个纯正的德意志民族，结果上百万名犹太人在集中营惨遭杀害。1939年，他派兵入侵波兰，发动了第二次世界大战。他于1945年德国战败前自杀。现在，人们有时借用他的名字来指称心狠手辣、滥用职权之人，或者企图控制一切之人〕

Hitler Youth /ˌ·· ˈ·/ an organization established by Adolf Hitler in 1933 to train German boys according to the ideas and principles of the Nazi Party 希特勒青年团〔希特勒于1933年建立的一组织，旨在根据纳粹党的思想和原则训练德国男青年〕

hit list /ˈ· ·/ *n* [C] *informal* the names of people, organizations etc who you plan to do bad things to【非正式】〔有计划地针对某些人或组织的〕打击名单，袭击名单: *The company has a hit list of factories it wants to close down.* 公司列出了一份拟关闭的工厂的名单。

hit man /ˈ· ·/ *n* [C] a criminal who is employed to kill someone 职业杀手

hit pa·rade, the /ˈ· ·ˌ·/ *n old-fashioned* a list of popular records, usually songs, showing which records have sold the most copies【过时】〔流行歌曲的〕唱片排行榜

HIV /ˌetʃ aɪ ˈvi; ˌeɪtʃ aɪ ˈviː◂/ *n* [U] a kind of VIRUS (=very small living thing that causes disease) that enters the body through blood or sexual activity, and can cause AIDS 人类免疫缺陷病毒，艾滋病病毒〔该病毒是通过受感染的血液和性接触传播的〕: **be HIV positive** (=have the HIV virus in your body) 艾滋病病毒呈阳性的

hive¹ /haɪv; haɪv/ *n* **1** [C] **a)** also 又作 **beehive** a small box where BEEs are kept 蜂箱 **b)** the group of bees who live together in a hive〔同一蜂箱内的〕蜂群 **2 a hive of industry/activity etc** *BrE* a place that is full of people who are very busy【英】人群繁忙的场所，熙熙攘攘的地方 **3 hives** [U] a skin disease in which a person's skin becomes red and painful 荨麻疹

hive² *v*

hive sth ↔ **off** *phr v* to separate one part of a business from the rest, usually by selling it〔常通过出售〕将〔部分业务〕分离出去

hi·ya /ˈhaɪjə; ˈhaɪjə/ *interjection spoken* used to say hello【口】你好!

Hiz·bol·lah /ˌhɪzbuˈlɑ; ˌhɪzbʊˈlɑː/ another spelling of HEZBOLLAH Hezbollah的另一拼法

HM *BrE*【英】the abbreviation for 缩写= His or Her Majesty 陛下

h'm, hmm /həm; m, hm/ *interjection* a sound that you make to express doubt, a pause, or disagreement 唔，嗯，哼，姆〔表示怀疑、停顿或不赞同的轻哼声〕

HMI /ˌetʃ ɛm ˈaɪ; ˌeɪtʃ em ˈaɪ/ *n* His/Her Majesty's Inspector; a British government official, employed by OFSTED whose job is to check the standards of education in schools in the UK. HMIs visit schools and watch lessons, then they make reports about the teachers, the lessons, and the general character of the school. 英国皇家督学〔在教育品质标准署供职的英国政府官员。其职责是检查英国学校的教育品质。他们视察学校、听课，然后就学校的师资状况、课堂教学以及总体特征作出汇报〕

HMS /ˈ· · ·/ His/Her Majesty's ship; a title for a ship in the British Navy, and for places on the land that are used by the navy 英国皇家海军舰艇; 英国海军舰艇陆上基地: *HMS Belfast* 皇家海军舰艇贝尔法斯特号

HMSO /ˌetʃ ɛm ɛs ˈo; ˌeɪtʃ em es ˈəʊ/ *n* His/Her Majesty's Stationery Office; a British government organization which prints government documents, books etc 英国文书局〔英国一政府机构，负责印刷政府文档、书籍等〕—compare 比较 the GPO

hoard¹ /hɔrd; hɔːd/ *n* [C] a collection of things that someone keeps hidden because they like them or consider them to be valuable 藏匿的宝物; 宝库: [**+of**] *He kept a little hoard of chocolates in his top drawer.* 他在最上面的抽屉里藏了一些巧克力糖。

hoard² *v* also 又作 **hoard up** [T] to collect and save large amounts of food, money etc 贮藏，囤积

hoard·er /ˈhɔrdɚ; ˈhɔːdə/ *n* [C] someone who likes to keep things 喜好贮藏东西的人

hoard·ing /ˈhɔrdɪŋ; ˈhɔːdɪŋ/ *n* [C] *BrE*【英】**1** a high fence around a piece of land where something is being built〔建筑工地四周的〕围栏, 围板 **2** a high fence or board on which large advertisements are stuck 广告牌[板]; BILLBOARD *AmE*【美】

hoar·frost /ˈhɔr,frɔst; ˈhɔːfrɒst/ *n* [U] FROST[1] (1) 白霜

hoarse /hɔrs; hɔːs/ *adj* **1** a hoarse voice sounds rough, as if the speaker has a sore throat〔嗓音〕沙哑的: *His voice was hoarse from laughing.* 他笑得嗓子都沙哑了。**2** a person who is hoarse has a hoarse voice〔人〕嗓音沙哑的 **—hoarsely** *adv* **—hoarseness** *n* [U]

hoar·y /ˈhɔrɪ; ˈhɔːri/ *adj old-fashioned*【过时】**1** very old 陈旧的: *a hoary old joke* 老掉牙的笑话 **2** hoary hair is grey or white〔头发〕灰白的, 花白的; 白的 **3** having grey or white hair 头发灰白[白]的 **—hoariness** *n* [U]

hoax[1] /hoks; həʊks/ *n* [C] **1** a false warning about something dangerous or bad 恶作剧, 假警告: *a bomb hoax* 虚报有炸弹的恶作剧 | **hoax call** (=a telephone call that gives false information) 恶作剧电话 **2** an attempt to make people believe something that is not true 骗局: *The Hitler Diaries were an elaborate hoax.*《希特勒日记》是一场精心编造的骗局。

hoax[2] *v* [T] to trick someone by means of a hoax 欺骗, 作弄 **—hoaxer** *n* [C]

hob /hab; hɒb/ *n* [C] *BrE*【英】**1** the flat top of a COOKER (1) that you cook on〔炉具上的〕炉盘 **2** *old use* a metal shelf next to a fire【旧】〔火堆旁的〕金属搁架

Hob·bes /habz; hɒbz/, **Thomas** (1588-1679) an English political PHILOSOPHER. In his book *Leviathan* he expressed the opinion that, since people think only of themselves and behave badly, it is best if they are ruled by one powerful authority. 霍布斯〔(1588-1679), 英国政治思想家。他在《利维坦》一书中阐述的观点是: 既然人是自私的, 而且行为不端, 那么最好由一个强权政府来统治〕

Hob·bit, The /ˈhabɪt; ˈhɒbɪt/ (1937) a very popular book by J.R.R. Tolkien. It describes the exciting and magical adventures of Bilbo Baggins, who is a hobbit, in a place called Middle Earth.《霍比特人》〔(1937), J.R.R.托尔金所著的一本畅销书。该书描述一霍比特人比尔博·巴金斯在"中土世界"激动人心的魔幻经历〕—see also 另见 The LORD OF THE RINGS

hob·ble /ˈhabl̩; ˈhɒbəl/ *v* **1** [I] to walk with difficulty, especially as a result of an injury to your legs or feet 跛行, 一瘸一拐地走: *an old man hobbling along the street* 在街上一瘸一拐地行走的老头 **2** [T] to loosely fasten two of an animal's legs together, to stop it from running away〔为防止动物跑掉而松松地〕捆缚〔动物的腿〕**3** [T] to deliberately make sure that a plan, system etc cannot work successfully 妨碍〔系统等的正常运作〕

hob·ble·de·hoy /ˈhabl̩dɪ,hɔɪ; ˈhɒbəldihɔɪ/ *n* [C] *old-fashioned* a rude young person【过时】粗鲁的年轻人

(S3) **hob·by** /ˈhabɪ; ˈhɒbi/ *n* [C] an activity that you enjoy doing in your free time 业余爱好, 嗜好: *One of her hobbies is horse-riding.* 她的业余爱好之一是骑马。

hob·by·horse /ˈhabɪ,hɔrs; ˈhɒbihɔːs/ *n* **1** [C] a child's toy like a horse's head on a stick, which the child pretends to ride on〔儿童放在胯下当马骑的〕竹马, 马头杆 **2 be on your hobbyhorse** to talk for a long time about a subject you think is very interesting 长时间地谈论喜爱的话题

hob·gob·lin /ˈhab,gablɪn; hɒbˈgɒblɪn/ *n* [C] a GOBLIN that plays tricks on people 好恶作剧的小妖精

hob·nail /ˈhab,nel; ˈhɒbneɪl/ *n* [C] a large nail with a big, flat top, used to make the bottom part of heavy boots and shoes stronger〔钉在笨重鞋子或靴子底部起加固作用的〕平头钉 **—hobnailed** *adj*

hob·nob /ˈhab,nab; ˈhɒbnɒb/ *v* [I] *informal* to spend time talking to people who are in a higher social position than you【非正式】〔与社会地位较高的人〕亲密交谈: [+with] *hobnobbing with the bosses at the sports club* 在体育俱乐部里与上司们亲密交谈

ho·bo /ˈhobo; ˈhəʊbəʊ/ *n* [C] *plural* **hobos** *AmE* someone, especially in the 1920s, who travelled from place to place because they had no home or job; TRAMP[1] (1)【美】〔尤指20世纪20年代的〕流浪汉, 无业游民

Hob·son's choice /ˈhabsənz ˈtʃɔɪs; ˌhɒbsənz ˈtʃɔɪs/ *n* [U] a situation in which there is only one thing you can do 无选择余地(的局面)

Ho Chi Minh /ˌho tʃi ˈmɪn; ˌhəʊ tʃiː ˈmɪn/ (1892-1969) the president of North Vietnam during the first part of the Vietnam War until his death. 胡志明〔(1892-1969), 越南战争初期担任北越主席直至去世〕

Ho Chi Minh Ci·ty /ˌ· · · ˈ· ·/ a city in the southern part of Vietnam. It was formerly known as Saigon, and was the capital of South Vietnam when the country was divided. 胡志明市〔越南南部一城市。旧称西贡, 为该国分裂时期南越首府〕

hock[1] /hak; hɒk/ *n* **1** [U] *especially BrE* a German white wine【尤英】霍克酒〔一种德国产的白葡萄酒〕**2** [C] the middle joint of an animal's back leg〔动物后腿上的〕跗关节 —see picture at 参见 HORSE[1] 图 **3 be in hock** *informal*【非正式】**a)** something that is in hock has been sold temporarily because you need money; pawned (PAWN[2]) 被典当, 被抵押 **b)** to be in debt 负债: *in hock to the big banks* 欠大银行的债 **4** [C] *especially AmE* a piece of meat from above the foot of an animal, especially a pig【尤美】〔尤指猪的〕腿肉: *pork hocks* 猪腿肉

hock[2] *v* [T] *informal* to sell something temporarily because you are poor and need the money; PAWN[2]【非正式】典当, 抵押

hock·ey /ˈhakɪ; ˈhɒki/ *n* [U] **1** *especially BrE* a game played on grass by two teams of 11 players each, with sticks and a ball【尤英】曲棍球; FIELD HOCKEY *AmE*【美】**2** *especially AmE* also 又作 **ice hockey** a team game similar to HOCKEY, but played on ice【尤美】冰球, 冰上曲棍球

ho·cus-po·cus /ˈhokəs ˈpokəs; ˌhəʊkəs ˈpəʊkəs/ *n* [U] a method or belief that you think is based on false ideas 花招, 把戏, 欺骗: *He thinks psychology is a load of hocus-pocus.* 他认为心理学完全是骗人的把戏。

hod /had; hɒd/ *n* [C] a container shaped like a box with a long handle, used for carrying bricks〔运砖用的带长柄的〕砖斗, 搬运斗

hodge·podge /ˈhadʒ ˌpadʒ; ˈhɒdʒ pɒdʒ/ *n* [singular] the American form of the word HOTCHPOTCH hotchpotch 的美语形式

hoe[1] /ho; həʊ/ *n* [C] a garden tool with a long handle used for breaking up the soil 锄头, (长柄)锄

hoe[2] *v* **hoed, hoeing** [I,T] to break up soil with a hoe 用锄头锄

Hof·fa /ˈhafə; ˈhɒfə/, **Jimmy** (1913?-1975) the president of the Teamsters, a powerful TRADE UNION in the US, who was put in prison in 1967 for financial crimes. He left prison in 1971, but disappeared in 1975 and many people believe that he was murdered, though his body was never found. 霍法〔(?1913-1975), 美国一实力工会(卡车司机、汽车司机、仓库工人和佣工国际工人兄弟会)的主席。1967年因经济犯罪入狱, 1971年出狱。他1975年失踪, 据说遭人暗杀, 但尸体一直没有找到〕

hog[1] /hag; hɒg/ *n* [C] **1** *especially AmE* a pig, especially a fat one for eating【尤美】猪〔尤指供食用的肥猪〕**2** a male pig that is kept for meat〔供食用的〕公猪 —compare 比较 BOAR, SOW[2] **3** *informal* a person who eats too much【非正式】贪吃的人: *You greedy hog!* 你贪吃得像头猪! **4 go the whole hog** to do something thoroughly 干到底, 全力以赴: *Why don't we go the whole hog and get wine?* 我们干吗不一不做二不休, 索性拿点葡萄酒来呢? **5 go hog wild** *AmE informal* to suddenly do a lot of some activity that you do not usually do【美, 非正式】尽情做某事〔指平常少做的事〕—see also 另见 ROAD HOG **—hoggish** *adj*

hog[2] *v* **hogged, hogging** [T] *informal* to keep or use all of something【非正式】攫取, 把…占为己有, 独占: *Keith's been hogging the bathroom all morning.* 基思整个上午都占用着浴室。| **hog the road** (=drive badly so that you take up too much space) 占着马路开车, 霸占路面

Ho·garth /ˈhogarθ; ˈhəʊgɑːθ/, **William** (1697-1764) a British artist who painted very detailed pictures showing the immoral pleasures of his time, such as *The Rake's Progress* and *Marriage à la Mode* 贺加斯〔(1697-1764), 英国艺术家。其作品以十分细腻的笔触描绘当时穷奢极欲的现象, 如《浪子生涯》和《时髦婚姻》〕

Hog·ma·nay /ˌhagməˈne; ˈhɒgməneɪ/ *n* [U] New Year's Eve and the parties that take place at that time in Scotland〔苏格兰的〕除夕(聚会)

CULTURAL NOTE 文化注释

In Scotland, Hogmanay is a very important celebration, and people often celebrate even more than they do at Christmas. Some Hogmanay traditions are also followed by people in other parts of the UK and in parts of the US. These include singing a song called *Auld Lang Syne* at midnight, and, in the UK, going FIRST-FOOTING, which means going to friends' houses after midnight to wish them a Happy New Year. It is thought to be lucky if the first person entering your home in the new year is a tall dark man carrying a piece of coal and some food. 除夕聚会是苏格兰一项很重要的庆祝活动, 人们对此的重视程度甚至超过圣诞节。在英国其他地方和美国某些地方的人也遵循

除夕夜聚会的一些传统，包括在午夜唱《友谊地久天长》。英国还有拜年的传统，即午夜过后去朋友家拜访，祝他们新年快乐。如果第一个来给你拜年的人是个又高又黑的男子，手里拿着一块煤和一些食物，就会被认为是好兆头。— see also Cultural Note at NEW YEAR 另见 NEW YEAR 文化注释

hogs·head /ˈhɑgzˌhɛd; ˈhɒgzhed/ *n* [C] a large container for holding beer, or the amount that it holds 装啤酒的大桶；一大桶之量

hog·wash /ˈhɑgˌwɑʃ; ˈhɒgwɒʃ/ *n* [U] stupid talk 蠢话，废话，胡言乱语：*That's a load of hogwash!* 那是一派胡言！

ho ho /ˌho ˋho; ˌhəʊ ˈhəʊ/ *interjection* used to represent the sound of laughter 呵呵〔表示笑声〕

ho-hum /ˌho ˋhʌm; ˌhəʊ ˈhʌm/ *adj informal* boring and ordinary【非正式】沉闷乏味的，无聊的，平淡无奇的：*It was a ho-hum sort of day.* 这一天过得真乏味。

hoick /hɔɪk; hɔɪk/ *v* [T] also 又作 **hoick up** *BrE informal* to lift or pull something up especially with a sudden movement【英，非正式】〔尤指猛然地〕向上提起：*She hoicked up her skirt and began to dance.* 她向上提了一下裙子，跳起舞来。

hoi pol·loi /ˌhɔɪ pəˋlɔɪ; ˌhɔɪ pəˈlɔɪ/ *n* **the hoi polloi** an insulting word for ordinary people 老百姓，乌合之众〔此词具侮辱性〕

hoist¹ /hɔɪst; hɔɪst/ also 又作 **hoist up** *v* [T] **1** to raise, lift, or pull up something, especially using ropes〔尤指用绳子〕吊起，升起，提起：*The sailors hoisted the cargo onto the deck.* 水手们把货物吊到甲板上。| *hoist the flag* 升旗 **2 be hoist with your own petard** to be harmed or embarassed by something that you planned yourself 搬起石头砸自己的脚，作茧自缚，害人反害己

hoist² *n* [C] **1** a piece of equipment for lifting heavy objects with ropes 吊升机械，起重机 **2** [usually singular 一般用单数] an upward pull 吊起，提起，升起

hoi·ty-toi·ty /ˋhɔɪtɪ ˋtɔɪtɪ; ˌhɔɪti ˈtɔɪti/ *adj old-fashioned* behaving in a proud way, as if you are important【过时】高傲的，爱摆架子的

ho·key /ˋhokɪ; ˈhəʊki/ *adj AmE* expressing emotions in a way that is too simple, old-fashioned, or silly【美】矫揉造作的；老掉牙的；愚蠢的：*a hokey song* 矫揉造作的歌曲

Hok·kai·do /hɑˋkaɪdo; hɒˈkaɪdəʊ/ the second largest of the main islands of Japan, in the north of the country 北海道〔日本第二大岛，位于该国北部〕

ho·kum /ˋhokəm; ˈhəʊkəm/ *n* [U] *slang especially AmE* stupid talk, especially talk used to deceive someone or make them admire you【俚，尤美】〔哄骗他人或博取他人称赞的〕空话，废话，胡扯；噱头：*All that talk about improving schools is just a bunch of hokum.* 所有那些改善学校条件的话只不过是一堆空话。

Ho·ku·sai /ˋhokʊˌsaɪ; ˈhəʊkʊsaɪ/, **Katsushika** (1760-1849) a Japanese artist famous for his prints 葛饰北斋〔(1760-1849)，日本画家，以版画作品著称〕

Hol·bein /ˋholbaɪn; ˈhəʊlbaɪn/, **Hans** /hæns; hæns/ also 又作 **Hans Holbein the Younger** (1497-1543) a German artist during the Renaissance, famous for his PORTRAITS, especially one of Henry VIII 霍尔拜因〔即小汉斯·霍尔拜因 (1497-1543)，文艺复兴时期德国画家，以肖像画、尤其是亨利八世的画像闻名〕

hold¹ /hold; həʊld/ *v past tense and past participle* **held** /hɛld; held/

① IN YOUR HANDS/ARMS 在手中/怀抱中
② HAVE/POSSESS 拥有/占有
③ KEEP/CONTROL 保持/控制
④ SAVE/STORE 保留/保存
⑤ KEEP STH IN A POSITION 使某物保持在某种位置上
⑥ SUPPORT/NOT BREAK 支撑/不断裂
⑦ NOT CHANGE/CONTINUE 不改变/保持
⑧ RESPONSIBILITY 责任
⑨ OPINION/BELIEF 观点/信念
⑩ STOP/DELAY STH 停止/拖延〔某事[物]〕
⑪ CONTAIN/INCLUDE 容纳/包含
⑫ OTHER MEANINGS 其他意思

① IN YOUR HANDS/ARMS 在手中/怀抱中

1 a) [T] to have something firmly in your hand or arms 握住，抓住；抱住：*He was holding a knife in one hand.* 他一只手里握着刀。| *Can you hold the groceries for me while I open the door?* 我开门时你能帮我拿着这些食品杂货吗？| *I held the baby in my arms.* 我把婴儿抱在怀里。| **hold hands** (=hold each other's hands) 手握着手 *The couple sat, holding hands under a tree.* 那一对夫妇手拉着手坐在树下。**b)** [T always+adv/prep] to move something that you have in your hands into a particular position 使〔手中之物〕处于某种位置：**hold sth out/up/towards etc** *Hold the negative up to the light so we can see.* 把底片对着光拿着，好让我们看清楚。

2 ►HOLD SB CLOSE 紧抱某人◄ [T] to put your arms around someone in order to comfort them, show you love them etc〔为表示安慰或爱〕紧抱〔某人〕：*She held him tightly, wiping away his tears.* 她紧紧地拥着他，为他擦去眼泪。

② HAVE/POSSESS 拥有/占有

3 hold a position/rank/job to have a particular job or position, especially an important or powerful one 拥有职务/级别/工作：*Most of the senior positions are held by men.* 大多数高级职位都由男性担任。

4 ►OWN STH 拥有某物◄ [T] to own or possess something, especially money or land 拥有〔尤指金钱或土地〕：*He holds a half share in the company.* 他拥有该公司一半的股份。

③ KEEP/CONTROL 保持/控制

5 ►ARMY 军队◄ [T] if an army holds a place, it either defends it from attack, or controls it by using force 防守，保卫；〔用武力〕占据：*The French army held the town for three days.* 法军在该镇守了三天。

6 ►KEEP SB SOMEWHERE 将某人关在某处◄ [T] to keep a person or animal somewhere, and not allow them to leave 关押，扣留：*Police are holding two men in connection with the jewel robbery.* 警方拘留了与抢劫珠宝案有关连的两名男子。| **hold sb prisoner/hostage/captive** (=to keep someone in a room, prison etc and not allow them to leave) 将某人作为囚犯/人质/俘虏扣押起来

④ SAVE/STORE 保留/保存

7 ►KEEP TO BE USED 保存待用◄ [T] to keep something to be used when it is needed 保存，保留〔以备后用〕：*Our computer holds all the records of births and deaths in Britain since 1950.* 我们的电脑存有1950年以来英国所有出生和死亡的记录。

8 hold a place/seat/room etc [T] to save a room, place etc for someone until they want to use it 保留地方/座位/房间等：*They're holding a table for us.* 他们为我们保留了一张桌子。

⑤ KEEP STH IN A POSITION 使某物保持在某种位置上

9 [T always+adv/prep] to make something stay in a particular position 使〔某物〕保持在某种位置上：**hold sth down/up/in place etc** *Ted held the ladder firmly in place.* 特德牢牢地扶住梯子不让它移动。| *Can you hold the lid down so I can lock the suitcase?* 你能不能把手提箱的盖子按住，让我把它锁上？| *It's only held on with a couple of screws.* 它只用几个螺钉固定着。| **hold sth open** *Mark held open the door as she came up behind him.* 她跟在马克后面走来时，马克用手扶住门，不让它关上。

10 ►ARM/LEG/BACK ETC 手臂/腿/背等◄ [T always+ adv/prep] to put or keep a part of your body in a particular position 使〔身体某个部位〕保持某种姿势：**hold sth up/out/straight etc** *Hold out your hand and I'll give you a present!* 伸出手来，我要送你一件礼物！

⑥ SUPPORT/NOT BREAK 支撑/不断裂

11 ►BE STRONG ENOUGH 够坚固◄ **a)** [T] to support the weight of something 承受，支撑〔重量〕：*Be careful, I don't think that branch will hold you.* 小心，我觉得那根树枝承受不了你的重量。**b)** [I] to continue to be able to support the weight of

something〔继续〕支撑住重量: *I don't think this shelf will hold if we put any more on it.* 我们如果再往搁架上放东西, 我怕它会承受不住。

⑦ NOT CHANGE/CONTINUE 不改变/保持

12 ▶AMOUNT/LEVEL 数量/水平◀ [T] to make something continue at a particular rate, level, or number 使保持〔某种速度、水平或数量〕: *hold spending to $10.2 billion* 将支出维持在102亿美元 | *Make sure you hold your speed at 30 mph in this area.* 在这个地区一定要将速度保持在每小时30英里。

13 hold sb's interest/attention to make someone continue being interested in something 使某人继续感兴趣, 吸引住…的注意: *Colourful pictures hold the students' interest.* 彩色图片能使学生保持兴趣。

14 ▶WEATHER/LUCK 天气/运气◀ also 又作 **hold out** [I] if good weather or good luck holds, it continues unchanged for a long time 保持不变, 持续: *If our luck holds we could reach the final.* 如果我们继续走运, 我们有望进入决赛。

15 ▶MUSIC 音乐◀ [T] to make a musical note continue for a long time 继续唱〔某音符〕, 保持〔长音〕

16 hold a course if an aircraft, ship etc holds a course, it continues to move in a particular direction〔飞机、船只等〕保持航向: *The ship held a northwesterly course.* 船一直往西北方向行驶。

17 [I] to still be true or continue to have an effect 继续有效: *What I said yesterday still holds.* 我昨天说的话仍然算数。

18 hold good/hold true to still be true in several different situations 继续适用[有效]: *This advice will hold good throughout your life.* 这个建议让你终生受用。

⑧ RESPONSIBILITY 责任

19 hold the fort to be responsible for looking after something while the person usually responsible is not there〔别人不在时〕代为处理事务: *She's holding the fort while the manager's on holiday.* 经理休假时由她负责处理业务。

20 be left holding the baby *BrE*【英】**/the bag** *AmE*【美】to become responsible for something that someone else has started 负责处理别人未办完的事情; 代人负起全责

21 hold sb responsible/accountable (for sth) to consider someone to be responsible for something, so that they will be blamed if anything bad happens 追究某人的责任, 唯…是问: *I'll hold you personally responsible if anything happens to the boy.* 如果男孩出了什么事, 我就唯你是问。

⑨ OPINION/BELIEF 观点/信念

22 [T not in progressive 不用进行时, usually passive 一般用被动态] *formal* to believe something to be true【正式】相信, 认为…是真的: [**+that**] *It is widely held that the council will decide to take military action.* 很多人相信委员会将会决定采取军事行动。| **hold sb/sth to be sth** *It is held to be his most important novel.* 这被认为是他最重要的一部小说。

23 ▶OPINIONS 观点◀ hold an opinion/view/belief etc to have a particular opinion about something 持有[怀有]观点/看法/信念: *She holds extreme political views.* 她持有极端的政治观点。| **commonly held belief** (=something that many people believe to be true) 普遍的看法

24 hold sth dear to think that something is very important 珍视某物: *a threat to everything that I hold dear* 对我所珍视的一切的威胁

25 hold fast to sth *formal* to keep believing in an idea or principles【正式】坚信: *They held fast to their faith in spite of their suffering.* 尽管受苦, 他们仍然坚持自己的信念。

⑩ STOP/DELAY STH 停止/拖延〔某事[物]〕

26 hold it! *spoken*【口】**a)** used to interrupt someone 等等!〔用来打断别人说话〕: *Hold it a minute! I've just had a really good idea.* 等等! 我刚刚想到了一个绝妙的主意。**b)** used to tell someone to wait or to stop what they are doing 停一下! 别动!

27 hold everything! *spoken* used to tell someone to immediately stop what they are doing【口】快停下!: *Hold everything! We have to change it all back again!* 快停下! 我们得全部改回原样!

28 hold your fire! a military order to tell soldiers to stop shooting 停止射击! 不要开火!〔军事命令〕

29 hold your horses! *spoken* used to tell someone to stop and think about something【口】停下来想想! 不要仓促行事!

⑪ CONTAIN/INCLUDE 容纳/包含

30 ▶HAVE SPACE FOR 有空间容纳◀ [T not in progressive 不用进行时] to have the space to contain a particular amount of something 能容纳: *This pan holds three gallons of water.* 这只锅能盛三加仑水。| *The movie theater holds 500 people.* 这家电影院能容纳500人。

31 [T] *formal* if the future or a future situation holds something, that may be part of it【正式】〔未来〕包含: *Who knows what the future holds?* 谁知道未来会如何?

⑫ OTHER MEANINGS 其他意思

32 hold a meeting/election/party etc [T] to arrange for an event, meeting, election, party etc to happen 举行会议/选举/晚会等: *The meeting will be held in the Town Hall.* 会议将在市政厅举行。

33 [I] also 又作 **hold the line** to wait until the person you have telephoned is ready to answer 不挂断电话 (等着): *Mr Stevenson's busy at the moment – would you like to hold?* 史蒂文森先生现在没空, 请你不要挂断, 等一下好吗?

34 ▶HAVE A QUALITY 具备某种特质◀ [T] *formal* to have a particular quality【正式】具备〔某种特质〕: *Such an emphasis on religion may hold little appeal for modern tastes.* 这种对宗教的注重对现代人来说可能没有多大吸引力。

35 hold a conversation to have a conversation 谈话, 和…交谈

36 not hold a candle to *informal* to be much worse than someone or something else【非正式】远比不上, 无法与…相比

37 hold all the cards to have a strong advantage in a situation 占绝对上风, 占极大优势

38 hold up your head to show pride or confidence in a difficult situation〔在困境中〕决不低头, 不垂头丧气: *I'll never be able to hold up my head in this town again.* 我再也无法在这个城镇里抬起头做人了。

39 hold your own to defend yourself, or to succeed, in a difficult situation〔在困境中〕坚守, 不退让: *Although he is the youngest competitor, he seems to be holding his own.* 虽然在众参赛者中他年纪最小, 但他看起来毫不示弱。

40 hold the road if a car holds the road well you can drive it quickly around bends without losing control〔指汽车急转弯时〕抓地性能良好

41 not hold water if an argument, statement etc does not hold water, it does not seem to be true or reasonable 站不住脚, 不可信: *His explanation of where the money came from just doesn't hold water.* 他对这笔钱的来源的解释根本站不住脚。

42 hold your drink/liquor/alcohol etc if someone can hold their drink, they are able to drink a lot of alcohol without becoming drunk 酒量很大

43 there's no holding sb *spoken* used when someone is so keen to do something you cannot prevent them from doing it【口】无法阻止某人〔做某事〕: *When he starts talking about football there's no holding him.* 他一谈起足球就没完没了。—see also 另见 **hold your breath** (BREATH (3)), **hold court** (COURT¹ (5)), **hold your tongue!** (TONGUE (16)), **hold your head high** (HIGH² (7))

hold sth **against** sb *phr v* [T] to allow something bad that someone has done to make you dislike them or want to harm them 对〔某人〕怀恨在心, 对〔某人〕有成见: *It all happened years ago. You can't still hold it against him, surely?* 这都是多年前的事了。你不能还对他怀恨在心, 是吧?

hold back *phr v* **1** [T **hold** sb/sth ↔ **back**] to make someone or something stop moving forward 阻挡, 抑制: *They had erected the barriers to hold back the flood.* 他们筑起屏障阻挡洪水。**2** [T **hold back** sth] to stop yourself from feeling or showing a particular emotion 控制〔情感〕: *We struggled to hold back our laughter.* 我们竭力忍住不笑。**3** [T **hold** sb ↔ **back**] to prevent someone from developing or improving 阻碍〔某人的发展〕: *Spending so much time playing sport is holding him back at school.* 他在体育运动上花的时间太多, 影响了学业。**4** [I] to be slow or unwilling to do something especially because you are being careful〔因谨慎而〕犹豫, 踌躇, 退缩: *The tone of his voice made Steven hold back.* 他说话的语气使史蒂文犹豫起来。**5** [I, T **hold** sth ↔ **back**] to keep something secret 隐瞒: *Tell me about it – don't hold anything back!* 把这事告诉我, 什么都别隐瞒!

hold sth/sb ↔ **down** *phr v* [T] **1** to prevent something such as prices from rising 抑制〔价格等〕的上升: *We shall hold down prices until the new year.* 我们会抑制价格上涨, 直至新的一年来临。| *the best way to hold down inflation* 抑制通货膨胀的最佳方法 **2** to keep people under control or limit their freedom 限制, 压制: *held down for centuries by their Ottoman conquerors* 许多个世纪以来受到奥斯曼征服者的压制 **3 hold down a job**

H

to succeed in keeping a job for a period of time 保住工作[职位]: *He's never held down a job for longer than a few weeks.* 他从未能把一份工作保住几周以上。

hold forth *phr v* [I] give your opinion on a subject, especially for a long time〔长篇大论地〕发表议论: [+on] *Archer was holding forth on the collapse of society.* 阿彻正在就社会解体大发议论。

hold off *phr v* **1** [I,T] to delay something 拖延, 推迟: *Buyers have been holding off until the price falls.* 买家们一直按兵不动, 等着价格下跌。| **hold off doing sth** *We will hold off making our decision until Monday.* 我们将推迟到星期一再作决定。**2** [T **hold** sb ↔ **off**] to prevent someone who is attacking you from coming any closer 抵挡, 使同…保持一定距离: *We managed to hold off the gang until the police arrived.* 我们设法挡住了那伙坏蛋, 直到警方赶到。**3** [I] if rain or snow holds off, none of it falls, although you thought it would〔雨、雪等〕延缓, 迟迟不来: *The rain held off until after the game.* 比赛结束后才下起雨来。

hold on *phr v* [I] **1 hold on!** *spoken*【口】**a)** used to tell someone to wait for a short time 等会儿!: *Hold on, I'll just get my coat.* 等一等, 我去拿外衣。**b)** used when you have just noticed something surprising 等等!〔表示发现令人惊讶的事〕: *Hold on! Isn't that your brother's car over there?* 等等! 那不是你兄弟的车吗? **2** to wait for a short period of time〔短时间〕等候: *I'll hold on for another few minutes if you like.* 如果你喜欢的话, 我就再等几分钟。| *It's coming soon, just hold on for it.* 马上就要来了, 再等一会儿吧。**3** to continue doing something when it is very difficult to do so 坚持下去: *They didn't know if they would be able to hold on until help arrived.* 他们不知道自己是否能够坚持到援兵到来。

hold on to sb/sth *phr v* [T] **1** to keep your hands or arms tightly around something so that it cannot move or you cannot fall 紧紧抓住[抱住]: *Hold on to the rail or you'll slip!* 抓住栏杆, 否则你会滑倒的! **2** to keep something by not losing it, selling it, or having it taken from you 守住, 保住: *Despite the attacks we held on to the bridge for three more days.* 尽管受到进攻, 我们仍然将大桥守了三天。| *I think I'll hold on to the records, but you can have the tapes.* 我想我会把唱片留着, 但你可以拿走磁带。

hold out *phr v* **1** [I] if something such as a supply of something holds out it has not all yet been finished or used〔供给品〕维持, 持续: *Will the water supply hold out through the summer?* 供水能持续整个夏天吗? **2** [I] to continue to defend a place that is being attacked 守住: *They'll have to surrender – they can't hold out forever.* 他们迟早得投降, 他们不可能永远守得住。**3 not hold out much hope/prospect of** to not think that something is possible or likely to have a good result 没有多大希望/前景: *Negotiators are no longer holding out much hope of a peaceful settlement.* 谈判人员对和平解决问题不再抱什么希望。

hold out for sth *phr v* [T] to not accept anything less than what you have asked for 坚持要求, 不肯让步: *The kidnappers are still holding out for the release of all political prisoners.* 绑架者仍坚持要求释放所有政治犯。

hold out on sb *phr v* [T] *informal* to refuse to give someone information or an answer that they need【非正式】拒绝提供〔资料或答案〕: *Why didn't you tell me straight away instead of holding out on me?* 你为什么对我隐瞒消息而不直接告诉我呢?

hold over *phr v* **1** [T **hold** sth **over**] to do or deal with something at a later date 推迟, 使延期: *The game was held over until the following week because of the bad weather.* 由于天气恶劣, 比赛被推迟到下一周了。—see also 另见 HOLDOVER **2** [**hold** sth **over** sb] to use knowledge about someone to threaten them 以…要挟: *He knows I've been in prison and is holding it over me.* 他知道我曾坐过牢, 并以此要挟我。**3 be held over** *AmE* if a play, film, concert etc is held over, it is shown for longer than planned, because it is very good【美】〔戏剧、电影、音乐会等因受欢迎〕公演时间被延长

hold sb **to** sth *phr v* [T] **1** to make someone do what they have promised 使〔某人〕恪守诺言: *"I'll ask him tomorrow." "All right, but I'm going to hold you to that."* "我明天跟他说。" "好吧, 不过你要说话算数。" **2** to prevent your opponent in a sports game from getting more than a particular number of points〔在体育比赛中〕不让对手超过〔某一得分〕: *We held them to 2-2.* 我们把与对方的比分保持在2比2。

hold together *phr v* **1** [I,T **hold** sth **together**] if a group or organization holds together or you hold it together it stays strong and does not break apart (使) 团结, (使) 不分开: *The party was held together by personal loyalty to the leader.* 该党凭借对领袖的忠诚团结在一起。**2** [I] to remain good enough to be used 保持完好: *I hope the washing machine holds together – I can't afford a new one.* 我希望洗衣机能正常运转, 我没钱买一台新的。

hold up *phr v* **1** [T **hold** sth ↔ **up**] to support something and prevent it from falling down 支撑: *The roof is held up by pillars.* 屋顶是用柱子支撑着的。**2** [**hold** sb/sth ↔ **up** often passive 常用被动态] to delay someone or something (使) 耽搁, 推迟, 阻延: *The building work has been held up by bad weather.* 由于天气不好, 建筑工程被耽搁下来了。| *Sorry we're late – we were held up at work.* 对不起我们来晚了, 我们在工作中给耽搁了一会儿。**3** [**hold up** sth] to rob or try to rob a place by using violence (试图) 抢劫: *His brother tried to hold up the drugstore and was sent to jail.* 他的兄弟企图抢劫药品杂货店, 因此被送进了监狱。—see also 另见 HOLD-UP **4** [I] to remain strong and not become weaker 保持强壮: *His physical condition held up remarkably well.* 他的身体状况保持得非常好。

hold sb/sth **up as** *phr v* [T] to use someone or something as an example 将…作为榜样: *The school is being held up as a model for other inner-city secondary schools.* 这所学校被树为其他旧城区中学学习的榜样。

hold with sth *phr v* [T usually in negatives 一般用于否定句] to approve of or agree with something 同意, 赞同: *We don't hold with physical violence in this school.* 我们这所学校内不允许有暴力行为。| **hold with doing sth** *I don't hold with letting people smoke in public places.* 我不赞成让人们在公共场所吸烟。

hold² *n*

1 ►**ACTION OF HOLDING STH 拿住某物**◄ [singular] the action of holding something tightly; GRIP¹ (1) 握, 抓, 拿: *She tightened her hold on the rope.* 她抓紧了绳子。| **have/keep hold of** *Make sure you keep hold of my hand when we cross the road.* 过马路时你一定要拉住我的手。

2 get/take/grab/seize hold of sth to take something and hold it with your hands 抓住, 拿住, 握住: *Grab hold of the rope and pull yourself up.* 抓住绳子爬上来。| *I took hold of her hand and gently led her away.* 我抓住她的手, 小心地带她离开。

3 get hold of a) to find or borrow something so that you can use it 找来使用: *I need to get hold of a car.* 我得找一辆车。**b)** to find someone for a particular reason〔出于某种原因要〕找到〔某人〕: *I must get hold of Vanessa to see if she can babysit for me.* 我必须找到瓦尼莎, 看看她能不能帮我照看一下孩子。

4 on hold waiting to speak or be spoken to on the telephone 等着通电话: **put sb on hold** *Do you mind if I put you on hold?* 你不介意等一会儿吧?

5 put sth on hold to delay doing or starting something 推迟, 使延期, 搁置

6 take hold to start to have an effect 开始起作用, 掌管: *The fever was beginning to take hold.* 发烧开始产生影响了。

7 ►**SPORT 体育**◄ [C] a particular position that you hold an opponent in, in a sport such as WRESTLING or JUDO〔摔跤或柔道运动中的〕擒拿技法

8 ►**CLIMBING 攀爬**◄ [C] somewhere you can put your hands or feet when you are climbing 供手攀或脚踩之处: *The cliff is steep and it's difficult to find a hold.* 那悬崖很陡, 很难找到攀踏的地方。

9 ►**SHIP 船只**◄ [C] the part of a ship below the DECK¹ (1) where goods are stored 底舱, 货舱

10 have a good hold of sth to understand something well 充分理解[掌握]

11 get hold of an idea/impression/story etc to learn or begin to believe something 得到[明白]某个想法/印象/说法等: *Where on earth did you get hold of that idea?* 你到底是从哪儿得来那个想法的?

12 have a hold over/on sb to have power or influence over someone 有左右某人的力量, 对某人有影响力: *Ever since he found out about her past, he's had a frightening hold on her.* 自从他发现了她的过去之后, 他对她的控制达到令人惧怕的地步。

13 no holds barred no rules or limits 无规则的, 无限制的, 不受约束的: *There are no holds barred when it comes to making a profit.* 赚取利润是无规则限制的。

hold·all /ˈhold͵ɔl; ˈhəʊld-ɔːl/ *n* [C] *BrE* a large bag for carrying clothes【英】〔装衣物的〕大旅行袋 —see picture at 参见 BAG 图

hold·er /ˈholdɚ; ˈhəʊldə/ *n* [C] **1** someone who possesses or has control of a place, land, tickets etc 拥有人, 持有人: *Season-ticket holders are furious at the rise in rail fares.* 季票持有人对

火车票价上涨极为愤怒。**2 candle/cigarette holder etc** a thing which is used to hold a CANDLE etc 烛台/香烟烟嘴

hold·ing /ˈholdɪŋ; ˈhəʊldɪŋ/ *n* [C] something which a person possesses, especially land or shares (SHARE² (5)) in a company 私人拥有的财产〔尤指地产或公司的股份〕—see also 另见 SMALLHOLDING

holding com·pa·ny /ˈ· · ,· · ·/ *n* [C] a company that holds a controlling number of the shares (SHARE² (5)) in other companies 控股公司

holding pat·tern /ˈ· · ,· ·/ *n* [C] the line of travel that an aircraft follows as it flies over a landing place while it is waiting for permission to land 待降[等待]航线〔指飞机待降时在着陆点上空的飞行航线〕

hold·o·ver /ˈhold,ovɚ; ˈhəʊld,əʊvə/ *n* [C] *especially AmE* an action, feeling, or idea that has continued from the past into the present; HANGOVER (2)【尤美】残余; 遗留物; 遗留影响: **[+from]** *Her fear of dogs is a holdover from her childhood.* 她怕狗的心理是从儿时遗留下来的。—see also 另见 **hold over** (HOLD¹)

hold-up 持枪抢劫

hold-up /ˈ· ·/ *n* [C] **1** a situation that stops something from happening for a short time; DELAY¹ (2) 延误, 耽搁: *An unexpected hold-up meant we had fallen 3 weeks behind schedule.* 由于一些意外的延误, 我们已经比原计划晚了三周。**2** a situation in which traffic stops or can only move very slowly 交通阻塞: *There was a hold-up on the highway this morning.* 今天上午公路上堵车了。**3** *informal* an attempt to rob someone by threatening them with a gun【非正式】持枪抢劫 —see also 另见 **hold up** (HOLD¹)

hole¹ /hol; həʊl/ *n* [C]

1 ▶SPACE IN STH SOLID 固体内的空间◀ an empty space in something solid 洞, 孔: **[+in]** *We'll just dig a big hole in the ground and bury the box in it.* 我们只要在地上挖个大坑把盒子埋进去就行了。

2 ▶SPACE STH CAN GO THROUGH 可穿过的空间◀ a space in something that allows things, light etc to get through to the other side; GAP (1)〔可穿过的〕洞, 裂口: **[+in]** *The dog got out of the yard through a hole in the fence.* 狗从院子篱笆上的一个窟窿里钻了出去。

3 ▶ANIMAL'S HOME 动物的巢穴◀ the home of a small animal〔小动物的〕窝, 洞穴: *a rabbit hole* 兔窟

4 ▶UNPLEASANT PLACE 不舒适的地方◀ *informal* an unpleasant place for living in, working in etc【非正式】令人不舒适的地方: *I've got to get out of this hole.* 我得离开这个破地方。

5 be in a hole to be in a difficult situation 处于困境

6 be full of holes an idea or plan that is full of holes can easily be proved wrong or has many faults〔想法、计划等〕漏洞[破绽]百出, 问题很多

7 ▶GOLF 高尔夫球◀ **a)** a hole in the ground that you try to get the ball into in the game of GOLF 球洞, 球穴 —see picture on page A23 参见 A23 页图 **b)** one part of a GOLF COURSE with this kind of hole at one end 球洞区〔一端有一球洞的击球区〕: *an 18 hole golf course* 有 18 个洞的高尔夫球场

8 hole in one an act of hitting the ball in GOLF from the starting place into the hole with only one hit〔高尔夫球运动中〕一杆进洞

9 make a hole in sth *informal* to use a large part of an amount of money, food etc【非正式】用去…的大部分, 大量消耗: *The cost of the house repairs made a big hole in my savings.* 修房子花掉了我一大笔积蓄。

10 need something like a hole in the head *spoken* used to say that you definitely do not need or want something【口】绝对不需要…

11 hole-and-corner secret or hidden, especially in a dishonest way 偷偷摸摸的, 鬼鬼祟祟的, 不光明正大的: *hole-and-corner meetings* 偷偷摸摸召开的会议 —see also 另见 BLACK HOLE, WATERING HOLE

hole² *v* [T] **1 be holed** if a ship or boat is holed, it has a hole in it〔船只〕出现破洞 **2** also 又作 **hole out** [I] to hit the ball into the hole in GOLF〔高尔夫球运动中〕击球入洞

hole up *phr v* [I always+adv/prep] *informal* to hide somewhere for a period of time【非正式】藏匿: **[+with/in]** *He escaped on his way to prison and holed up with his girlfriend.* 他在去监狱的路上逃走, 和他女朋友一同躲藏起来。

hole in the heart /,· · · ˈ·/ *n* [singular,U] a medical condition, where the two sides of someone's heart are not properly separated 心膜缺损

hole-in-the-wall /,· · · ˈ·/ *n* [C] **1** *BrE informal* CASH DISPENSER【英, 非正式】自动提款机 **2** *AmE* a small dark store or restaurant【美】狭小黑暗的店铺[餐馆]

hol·i·day¹ /ˈhɑlə,de; ˈhɒlɪdi/ *n* **1** *BrE* also 又作 **holidays** a time of rest from work, school etc【英】〔不用上班、上学的〕假期, 休假日; VACATION¹ (1) *AmE*【美】: *Everyone at work is ready for a holiday.* 每个上班的人都准备休假了。| *The school holidays start on Wednesday.* 学校假期从星期三开始。| **on (your) holiday** *Jackie's been on holiday for the last two weeks.* 杰基前两周一直在休假。**2** *BrE* also 又作 **holidays** a period of time when you travel to another place for pleasure【英】出外度假时期: *We're going to Spain for our holidays.* 我们将去西班牙度假。| **have a holiday** *I didn't have a proper holiday this year.* 我今年没有好好度过假。**3** a day fixed by law on which people do not have to go to work or school 法定假日, 公共假日: **public holiday** *Martin Luther King Day is now a public holiday in most states.* 马丁·路德·金纪念日现在在大多数州都是一个公共假日。| **national holiday** *The 4th of July is a national holiday in the US.* 7月4日是美国国庆节。| **bank holiday** *BrE*【英】*We're going to Devon for the bank holiday weekend.* 我们将去德文郡度过周末银行假日。

This graph shows how common the nouns **holiday** and **vacation** are in British and American English. 本图表所示为名词 holiday 和 vacation 在英国英语和美国英语中的使用频率。

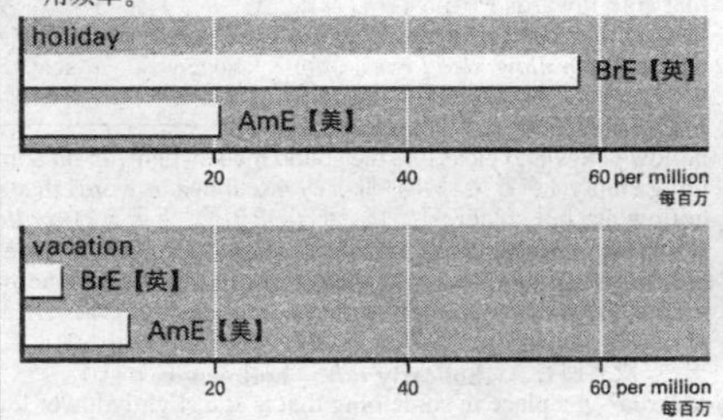

Based on the British National Corpus and the Longman Lancaster Corpus
据英国国家语料库和朗文兰开斯特语料库

In British English the word **holiday** is used to mean a time of rest from work, school etc, or a period of time when you travel to another place for pleasure. Americans use **vacation** for this meaning. In both American and British English **holiday** is used to mean a day fixed by law on which people do not have to go to work or school. In both American and British English **vacation** is used to mean one of the periods of time each year when universities are closed. 在英国英语中, 单词 holiday 是指不用去上班、上学等的休假日或假期, 也指外出度假的时期, 而美国英语则用 vacation 表示这些意思。holiday 在美国英语和英国英语中都用来指人们不用上班、上学的法定假日; vacation 在美国英语和英国英语中都用来指大学的假期。

holiday² *v* [I] *BrE* to spend your holiday in a place【英】度假; VACATION² *AmE*【美】: **[+in/at]** *They're holidaying in Majorca.* 他们正在马略卡岛上度假。

Holiday, Bil·lie /ˈbɪlɪ; ˈbɪli/ (1915-59) a US JAZZ and BLUES singer. She was one of the greatest jazz and blues singers ever, and was also called 'Lady Day'. 霍利戴〔(1915-1959), 美国爵士与布鲁斯歌手。她是有史以来最出色的爵士与布鲁斯歌手之一, 有"戴夫人"之称〕

holiday camp /ˈ· · · ,·/ *n* [C] *BrE* a place where people go for their holidays and where activities are organized for them【英】度假营

holiday home /ˈ· · · ,·/ *n* [C] *BrE* a house that someone owns where they go during their holidays【英】度假别墅, 度假屋

hol·i·day·mak·er /ˈhɑlədeˌmekɚ; ˈhɒlədiˌmeɪkə/ *n* [C] *BrE* someone who has travelled to another place for a holiday【英】到外地度假者; VACATIONER *AmE*【美】—**holidaymaking** *n* [U]

hol·i·er-than-thou /ˌ‥ ·ˈ·◂/ *adj* behaving in a way that shows that you think you are morally better than other people 自以为道德上高人一等的

hol·i·ness /ˈhəlɪnɪs; ˈhəʊlinɪ̣s/ *n* **1** [U] the quality of being pure and good in a religious way 神圣: *God's holiness* 上帝的神圣 **2 Your/His Holiness** used as a title for addressing or talking about the Pope 陛下, 圣座〔对教皇的尊称〕

ho·lis·tic /hoˋlɪstɪk; həʊˋlɪstɪk/ *adj* **1** based on the principle that a person or thing is more than just their many small parts added together 整体(论)的, 全面的: *a holistic approach to education* 教育的整体论方法 **2 holistic medicine** medical treatment based on the belief that the whole person must be treated, not just the part of their body that has a disease 整体医学 —**holistically** /-klɪ; -kli/ *adv*

Hol·land /ˈhɑlənd; ˈhɒlənd/ the usual English name for the Netherlands 荷兰〔该国的英语常用名〕—see also 另见 DUTCH

hol·ler /ˈhɑlɚ; ˈhɒlə/ *v* [I,T] *especially AmE informal* to shout loudly【尤美, 非正式】呼喊, 大叫: *The kid just kept hollering until she got her way.* 那孩子一直不停地叫喊, 直到得到她想要的东西。| **holler at sb** *Stop hollering at me! I'll be there in a second!* 别喊了! 我马上就来! —**holler** *n* [C]

Hol·li·day /ˈhɑlɪˌde; ˈhɒlɪdeɪ/, **John, "Doc"** (1849-87), a friend of the US MARSHAL Wyatt Earp. He fought on the side of Earp and his brothers in the GUNFIGHT at the OK Corral. He was a GAMBLER and DENTIST, and one of the most dangerous GUNFIGHTERS of the wild west. He died of TUBERCULOSIS. 霍利迪医生〔(1849-1887), 美国警长怀雅特·厄普的朋友。在OK镇畜栏大决斗中, 他和厄普及其兄弟们一起与人决斗。霍利迪是名牙医, 又是赌徒, 还是美国荒蛮西部最危险的枪手之一, 死于肺结核〕

hol·low¹ /ˈhɑlo; ˈhɒləʊ/ *adj* **1** having an empty space inside 空(心)的, 中空的: *The children hid in the hollow tree.* 孩子们躲在空心的树里。 **2 hollow face/eyes etc** eyes etc that sink inwards 凹陷的脸颊/双眼等: *I could feel her appraising me with those hollow, dead eyes.* 我可以感觉到她在用那双深陷的、毫无表情的眼睛打量我。 **3** a sound that is hollow is low and clear like the sound made when you hit something empty〔声音〕空洞的, 低沉的 **4** feelings or words that are hollow are not sincere〔感情、语言〕虚假的, 无诚意的: *hollow promises made by corrupt politicians* 腐败政客的空口诺言 **5 hollow laugh/voice etc** a hollow laugh or voice is one that makes a weak sound and is without emotion 干巴巴的笑声/声音等: *He gave a little hollow laugh and didn't reply.* 他干笑了一声, 没有回答。—**hollowly** *adv* —**hollowness** *n* [U]

hollow 中空的

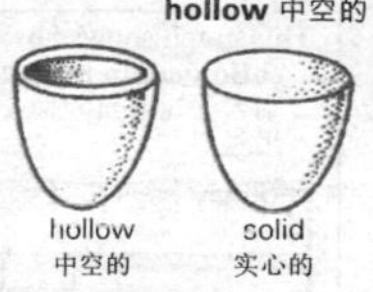

hollow² *n* a place in something that is at a slightly lower level than its surface 浅坑, 凹陷处: *The cat had tried to hide in a hollow in the ground.* 那只猫试图躲进地面上的一个浅坑里。

hollow³ *v*
hollow sth ↔ **out** *phr v* [T] to make a hole or empty space by removing the inside part of something 把…挖空[掏空], 使成中空

Hol·lo·way /ˈhɑləwe; ˈhɒləweɪ/ **1** an area of North London 霍洛韦〔北伦敦一地区〕 **2** a prison for women in North London 霍洛韦女子监狱〔位于北伦敦〕

hol·ly /ˈhɑlɪ; ˈhɒli/ *n* [U] a small tree with dark green sharp leaves and red berries (BERRY), or the leaves and berries of this tree used as a decoration at Christmas 冬青树; 〔常用作圣诞节装饰的〕冬青树叶及浆果

Holly, Buddy (1936-59) a US POP singer, GUITAR player, and songwriter who, with his band **The Crickets**, helped to make ROCK 'N' ROLL music popular in the 1950s. His songs include *That'll be the Day* and *Peggy Sue*. He was killed in a plane crash. 霍利〔(1936-1959), 美国流行歌手、吉他手和歌曲作家。20世纪50年代, 他与他的"蟋蟀"乐队推动了摇滚乐的流行。其歌曲包括《就在那一天》和《佩吉·苏》。他死于空难〕

Holly and the I·vy, The /ˌ‥ · ˈ‥/ a popular Christmas CAROL (=a traditional religious song)《冬青树和常春藤》〔一首流行圣诞颂歌〕

hol·ly·hock /ˈhɑlɪˌhɑk; ˈhɒlihɒk/ *n* [C] a tall thin garden plant with many flowers growing together 蜀葵(花)

Hol·ly·wood /ˈhɑlɪˌwʊd; ˈhɒliwʊd/ *n* [singular] a city in California where films are made and many famous actors live 好莱坞〔美国著名影城, 位于加利福尼亚州〕

Hollywood Bowl, the /ˌ‥ ˈ·/ a concert hall in Hollywood, California, which has a stage covered with a curved roof, and outdoor seats for people to watch and listen 好莱坞露天剧场〔加利福尼亚州好莱坞一音乐厅, 设有圆顶舞台和露天观众席〕

Holmes /homz; həʊmz/, **Mycroft** the elder brother of Sherlock Holmes, who appears in some of the stories written by Sir Arthur Conan Doyle. Mycroft, who is older than Sherlock, is cleverer than his younger brother but too lazy to be a DETECTIVE (=someone whose job is to solve crimes and catch criminals). 麦克罗夫特·福尔摩斯〔夏洛克·福尔摩斯的长兄, 出现在亚瑟·柯南道尔爵士的一些小说中。麦克罗夫特·福尔摩斯虽比弟弟年长、聪明, 但懒惰至极, 无法成为一名侦探〕

Holmes, Sher·lock /ˈʃɝlɑk; ˈʃɜːlɒk/ the main character in the stories by Sir Arthur Conan Doyle. He is a very clever DETECTIVE and he always notices very small details and then uses them to guess what has happened. 夏洛克·福尔摩斯〔亚瑟·柯南道尔爵士小说中的主人公。他是一位足智多谋的侦探, 总是明察秋毫, 并据此进行推断〕

Sherlock Holmes 夏洛克·福尔摩斯

hol·o·caust /ˈhɑləˌkɔst; ˈhɒləkɔːst/ *n* [C] **1** a situation in which there is great destruction and a lot of people die 大屠杀: *a nuclear holocaust* 核浩劫 **2 the Holocaust** the killing of millions of Jews by the Nazis in the 1930s and 1940s〔20世纪30和40年代纳粹党进行的〕对犹太人的大屠杀

hol·o·gram /ˈhɑləgræm; ˈhɒləgræm/ *n* [C] a kind of photograph made with a LASER that looks as if it is not flat when you look at it from an angle〔用激光制作的〕(立体)全息图

hols /hɑlz; hɒlz/ *n* [plural] *BrE old-fashioned spoken* holidays【英, 过时, 口】假期; 出外度假时期

Holst /holst; həʊlst/, **Gus·tav** /ˈgustɑv; ˈgʊstɑːv/ (1874-1934) a British COMPOSER whose most famous work is called *The Planets* 霍尔斯特〔(1874-1934), 英国作曲家。最有名的音乐作品是《行星》〕

Hol·stein /ˈholstaɪn; ˈhɒlstən/ *n* [C] *especially AmE* a black and white cow【尤美】霍斯坦种乳牛, 黑白花牛; FRIESIAN *BrE*【英】

hol·ster /ˈholstɚ; ˈhəʊlstə/ *n* [C] a leather object worn on a belt for carrying a small gun〔系在腰带上的〕手枪皮套

ho·ly /ˈholɪ; ˈhəʊli/ *adj* **1** connected with God and religion; SACRED (有关)上帝[宗教]的, 神圣的: *the holy city of Benares* 贝拿勒斯圣城 | *anointed with holy water* 涂了圣水的 **2** very religious 虔诚的: *a holy man* 虔诚的人 **3 holy cow/cats/shit/mackerel etc** *spoken especially AmE* used to express surprise, admiration, or fear【口, 尤美】天啊! 上帝呀! 〔表示惊讶、赞美或恐惧〕 **4 a holy terror** *informal* a child who causes trouble【非正式】捣蛋鬼, 顽皮的小孩 —see also 另见 **take (holy) orders** (ORDER¹ (20))

Holy Bi·ble /ˌ‥ ˈ‥/ *n* [singular] the BIBLE (1)《圣经》

Holy Com·mu·nion /ˌ‥ ·ˈ‥/ *n* [U] COMMUNION (2) 圣餐(仪式)

Holy Fam·i·ly /ˌ‥ ˈ‥/ *n* [singular] Jesus, his mother Mary, and her husband Joseph 圣家庭〔指耶稣、圣母马利亚以及马利亚的丈夫约瑟〕

Holy Fa·ther /ˌ‥ ˈ‥/ *n* [singular] used to address the Pope 罗马教皇

Holy Ghost /ˌ‥ ˈ·/ *n* [singular] the HOLY SPIRIT 圣灵

Holy Grail /ˌ‥ ˈ·/ *n* [singular] **1** something that you try very hard to get or achieve but never can 无法实现的梦想 **2** the cup believed to have been used by Christ before his death〔据信为耶稣死前用过的〕圣杯

Hol·y·head /ˈhɑlɪhɛd; ˈhɒlihed/ a town and port on Holy Island off the island of Anglesey, North Wales. Ships carrying passengers and cars sail from Holyhead to Ireland. 霍利黑德〔威尔士北部安格尔西岛附近的霍利岛上一城镇和港口。从霍利黑德到爱尔兰经常有运送乘客和车辆的渡轮〕

Holy Is·land /ˈ‥ ˌ‥/ **1** an island off the northeast coast of Northumberland, in northeast England. It is also known as **Lindisfarne**. 霍利岛〔英格兰东北部诺森伯兰东北海岸附近一岛, 又称林迪斯芳〕 **2** an island off the island of Anglesey, North Wales, whose main town is the port of Holyhead 霍利岛〔威尔士北部安格尔西岛附近一岛屿。其主要城镇是霍利黑德港〕

Holy Land /ˈ·· ·/ *n* [singular] the parts of the Middle East where most of the events mentioned in the Bible happened 圣地〔指中东的一些地区,《圣经》上记载的大部分事件发生于此〕

Holy Loch /ˌ·· ˈ·/ a narrow area of the Atlantic Ocean reaching into the land on the west coast of Scotland, northwest of Glasgow. The US Navy formerly had a base there for its NUCLEAR SUBMARINES. 霍利湾〔大西洋伸入苏格兰西岸陆地而形成的一狭长海域,位于格拉斯哥西北。美国海军曾在此拥有一个核潜艇基地〕

holy of ho·lies /ˌ·· · ˈ··/ *n* [singular] **1** *humorous* a room in a building where only important people are allowed to go【幽默】最神圣的地方〔指只许重要人物进入的房间〕 **2** the most holy part of a Jewish temple 犹太教会堂的内殿, 至圣所

Holy Ro·man Em·pire, the /ˌ·· ˌ·· ˈ··/ a group of European states which included parts of France, Germany, Austria, and Italy, and which were ruled by an EMPEROR. It was established by Charlemagne in 800, and continued until 1806. For most of the period from the 13th century to the 19th century, its ruling family were the Hapsburgs. 神圣罗马帝国〔包括法国部分地区、德国、奥地利和意大利等欧洲的一些君主制国家, 公元800年由查理曼建立, 直到1806年结束。从13世纪到19世纪, 罗马帝国多为哈布斯堡家族统治〕

Hol·y·rood Pal·ace /ˌhɑlɪrud ˈpælɪs; ˌhɒliruːd ˈpælʒs/ also 又作 **Holyrood House** a large building in Edinburgh, Scotland, owned by the British royal family. It was formerly the home of the Scottish royal family, and Mary Queen of Scots lived there in the 16th century. 霍利鲁德宫〔英国王室在苏格兰爱丁堡的一座大型宫殿, 原为苏格兰王宫。16世纪时, 苏格兰的玛丽女王曾在此居住〕

Holy See /ˌ·· ˈ·/ *n* [singular] *formal* the office of the Pope【正式】圣座, 宗座〔罗马教皇的圣职〕

Holy Spir·it /ˌ·· ˈ··/ *n* [singular] God in the form of a spirit according to the Christian religion 圣灵

holy war /ˈ·· ·/ *n* [C] a war that is fought to defend the beliefs of a religion 圣战〔维护宗教信仰而进行的战争〕

Holy Week /ˈ·· ·/ *n* [singular] the week before Easter in the Christian church〔基督教〕复活节前的一周, 受难周

Holy Writ /ˌ·· ˈ·/ *n* [U] **1** a piece of writing that people treat as if it were completely true in every detail 至高无上的权威著作; 箴言, 真言 **2** *old-fashioned* the Bible【过时】《圣经》

hom·age /ˈhɑmɪdʒ; ˈhɒmɪdʒ/ *n* [singular] *formal* something you do to show respect and honour for an important person【正式】崇敬, 致敬: **pay homage to sb** (=show respect and honour for someone) 向某人致敬 *The film pays homage to Woody Allen, using some of his best comic lines.* 该影片采用了伍迪·艾伦最精彩的喜剧台词表达对他的崇敬。

hom·burg /ˈhɑmbɝg; ˈhɒmbɜːg/ *n* [C] a soft hat for men, with a wide edge around it 霍姆堡毡帽〔一种男用的宽边软毡帽〕

[1] [1] **home¹** /hom; həʊm/ *n*

1 ▶PLACE WHERE YOU LIVE 居住的地方◀ [C,U] the house, apartment, or place where you live 家, 住家: *They have a comfortable home on the outskirts of the town.* 他们在城郊有一个舒适的家。| **at home** *Her daughter lives at college during the week and at home on the weekends.* 她的女儿平时住在大学校园里, 周末则住在家里。| **work from home** *BrE* (=do your work at home instead of at a company)【英】在家办公 | **make your home somewhere** *A family of swallows had made their home under the roof.* 一窝燕子在屋檐下安了家。

2 ▶WHERE YOU CAME FROM/BELONG 家, 家乡◀ [C,U] the place where you came from or where you usually live, especially when this is the place where you feel happy and comfortable〔使人感到亲切、愉快的〕家, 家乡, 故乡: **make somewhere your home** *She was born in Italy, but she's made Charleston her home.* 她在意大利出生, 但在查尔斯顿安家。| **back home** (=used to talk about the place where your family and friends live) 在家乡 *Sherri said she misses friends and family back home.* 雪莉说她很想念家乡的朋友和亲人。

3 be/feel at home a) to feel comfortable in a place or with a person 舒适自在, 不拘束: [+in] *I'm already feeling at home in the new apartment.* 我在新公寓里已感到习惯自如了。| [+with] *Penny is very much at home with Roger's family.* 彭尼与罗杰的家人相处时毫不拘束。 **b)** to feel happy or confident about doing or using something 驾轻就熟, 运用自如: [+with/in] *I've never felt particularly at home with computers.* 我对电脑一向不太在行。

4 ▶IN YOUR COUNTRY 在本国◀ at home in the country where you live, as opposed to foreign countries 在本国, 在国内: *improved sales of trucks both at home and abroad* 提高了的国内外市场上的货车销量 | *I miss the hot weather we have at home in India.* 我很怀念我的祖国印度那炎热的天气。

5 ▶FAMILY 家庭◀ [C,U] the place where a child and his or her family live 家, 家庭: **leave home** *He didn't leave home until he was 21.* 他直到21岁才离开家(自立)。| **come from a broken home** *old-fashioned* (=come from a family in which one parent has left the home)【过时】来自破碎的家庭〔指单亲家庭〕

6 ▶PROPERTY 财产◀ [C] a house, apartment etc considered as property which you can buy or sell〔作为财产的〕住宅, 住房: *Attractive, modern homes for sale.* 有漂亮的现代化住宅出售。

7 ▶FOR TAKING CARE OF SB 用于照料某人◀ [C] a place where people who are very old or sick, or children who have no family are looked after〔老人或病人的〕疗养所;〔儿童的〕养育院: *an old people's home* 养老院, 老人院 | *They had to put her mother in a home.* 他们不得不把她的母亲送进养老院。—see also 另见 REST HOME

8 dogs'/cats' home a place where animals with no owners are looked after (流浪)狗/猫的收容所

9 make yourself at home *spoken* used to tell someone who is visiting you that they should relax【口】请随便, 别拘礼〔招呼客人时说〕: *Make yourself at home while I get some coffee.* 随便坐吧, 我去倒杯咖啡。

10 make sb feel at home to make someone feel relaxed by being friendly towards them 使某人感到宾至如归: *I'd like to thank everyone again for making me feel so much at home.* 我要再次感谢大家, 让我感到像在自家一般。

11 find a home for *BrE* to find a place where something can be kept【英】找地方安置〔某物〕: *I'll have to find a home for the new wine glasses.* 我得找个地方放这些新酒杯。

12 the home of a) the place where something was first discovered, made, or developed 发祥地, 发源地: *America is the home of baseball.* 美国是棒球的发源地。 **b)** the place where a plant or animal grows or lives〔动物、植物的〕产地, 生长[栖息]地: *India is the home of elephants and tigers.* 印度是大象和老虎的生息地。

13 ▶SPORTS TEAM 运动队◀ at home if a sports team plays at home, they play at their own sports field〔球队〕在主场〔比赛〕

14 home from home *BrE*【英】, **home away from home** *AmE*【美】a place that you think is as pleasant and comfortable as your own house 像家一样舒适自在的地方

15 what's that when it's at home? *BrE spoken humorous* used to ask what someone means when they use a long or unusual word【英口, 幽默】说白了是什么意思?〔要求别人不要使用复杂难懂的词〕

16 home sweet home used to say how pleasant it is to be in your home 家真好啊!

17 ▶GAMES 体育比赛◀ [U] a place in some games or sports which a player must try to reach in order to win a point 终点; 目标; 本垒 —see also 另见 HOME PLATE, HOME RUN

home² *adv* **1** to or at the place where you live 到家, 回家; 在家: *Is Sue home from work yet?* 休下班回到家了吗? | *He stayed home for a week to finish writing his book.* 他在家待了一星期, 好把他的书写完。| **go home** *I'm going home now. See you tomorrow.* 我现在要回家了, 明天见。| **get home** (=arrive at your home) 回到家, 抵家 *By the time we got home the programme had finished.* 等我们回到家时, 节目已经结束了。| **return home** *After three months touring Europe they returned home to Boston.* 他们在欧洲游览了三个月后便回了老家波士顿。 **2 take home** to earn a certain amount of money after tax has been taken off 挣得〔税后收入〕: *The average store worker takes home around $300 a week.* 普通店员每周的税后净收入约为300美元。 **3 hit/drive/hammer etc sth home a)** to hit or push something firmly into the correct position 敲/推/锤击进合适的位置 **b)** to make sure that someone understands what you mean by saying it in an extremely direct and determined way 明确阐述〔使人充分理解〕: *a powerful film with imagery that really drives its message home* 一部通过形象描述将主题思想阐述清楚的具有巨大影响力的电影 **4 bring sth home to sb** to make you realize how serious, difficult or dangerous something is 使某人充分意识到某事〔的严重性、难度或危险性〕 **5 be home and dry** *informal especially BrE* to have succeeded in doing something【非正式, 尤英】大功告成, 达到目的 **6 be home free** *AmE informal* to have succeeded in doing the most difficult part of something【美, 非正式】成功完成某事最困难的部分: *Only one more page of the hard stuff and we're home free.* 只要再弄完一页, 我们就能完成最困难的部分了。—see also 另见 **close to home** (CLOSE² (20)) [1] [1]

home³ *adj* [only before noun 仅用于名词前] **1** connected with or belonging to your home or family 家的, 家庭的: **home address** *Make sure to give us your full home address.* 务必把你的

详细住宅地址告诉我们。| **home life** (=relationship with your family) 家庭生活 *The child has had an unhappy home life.* 这孩子在家里生活得并不愉快。**2** connected with a particular country, as opposed to foreign countries 本地的, 国内的: **home market** (=the country where something is made) 国内市场 *These cars are made mainly for the home market, not for export.* 这些汽车主要是为国内市场制造的, 不供出口。**3** done at home or intended for use in a home 在家做的; 家用的: *home cooking* 家常菜 | *a home computer* 家用电脑 **4** played or playing at a team's own sports field, rather than an opponent's field 在主场进行的; 主队的: *the home team* 主队 | *home games* 主场赛事 **5 home bird** *BrE* someone who prefers to stay at home rather than going to parties, travelling etc【英】喜欢留在家里的人 **6 home truths** facts about someone that are unpleasant for them to know but that are true 令人不快的事实: *It's time she was told a few home truths!* 到了该告诉她一些不中听的实话的时候了!

home⁴ *v*

home in on *phr v* [T] **1** to aim exactly at an object or place and move directly to it 对准〔某事物或地方〕: *The bat can home in on insects using a kind of 'radar'.* 蝙蝠能凭借某种"雷达"瞄准昆虫。**2** to direct your efforts or attention towards a particular fault or problem 将注意力集中于〔某个问题〕: *We homed in on the fault in the system and fixed it quickly.* 我们集中力量找出系统中的故障并迅速把它修好。

Home A·lone /,· ·'·/ (1990) a US humorous film in which a young boy is accidentally left at home alone when his parents go on holiday, and has to prevent two criminals from getting into his home and stealing things from it《小鬼当家》〔(1990), 美国一喜剧影片。故事中有一小男孩, 父母外出度假把他一人留在家里。他阻止了两个小偷入室行窃的阴谋〕

home base /'· ·/ *n* [U] [singular] *AmE* HOME PLATE【美】本垒板

home·bod·y /ˈhom,bɑdɪ; 'həʊm,bɒdi/ *n* [C] *informal* someone who enjoys being at home【非正式】喜欢留在家里的人

Home Box Of·fice /,· '· ,· ·/ *trademark* abbreviation 缩写为 **HBO** a US CABLE TELEVISION company that mostly shows films【商标】家庭影院〔美国一有线电视公司, 主要播放电影节目〕

home·boy /ˈhombɔɪ; 'həʊmbɔɪ/ *n* [C] *AmE slang* a friend or someone from the same area or GANG¹ (1) as you【美俚】老乡, 同乡; 同伙

home brew /,· '·/ *n* [U] beer made at home 家酿啤酒 — **home brewed** *adj*

home·com·ing /ˈhom,kʌmɪŋ; 'həʊm,kʌmɪŋ/ *n* [C] **1** an occasion when someone comes back to their home after a long absence〔长期在外后〕返乡, 回家 **2** *AmE* an occasion when former students return to their high school or college【美】校友返校的聚会, 校友返校日

> **CULTURAL NOTE 文化注释**
> Homecoming is held in the autumn, and is celebrated by students and former students. The school or university usually has a homecoming dance (=a social occasion when people dance), and many people go to parties before or after the homecoming game (=a game of football). In high school, students vote for a homecoming king and homecoming queen. They are usually chosen because they are popular and attractive, and the STEREOTYPE is that they are the best football player and a CHEERLEADER. 校友返校日一般在秋天举行, 在校学生和已经毕业的学生一起庆祝。学校一般举行校友返校日舞会。很多人会在返校日橄榄球友谊赛前后参加聚会。高中学生投票选出校友返校日国王和王后, 一般都是最佳橄榄球运动员和拉拉队长, 他们被选中通常是因为受众人欢迎、长相好看。

Home Coun·ties /,· '··/ *n* [plural] the counties (COUNTY¹) around London 伦敦周围各郡

> **CULTURAL NOTE 文化注释**
> People who live in the Home Counties are typically thought of as being MIDDLE CLASS and CONSERVATIVE and as having a comfortable life. 通常认为, 居住在伦敦周围各郡的人是保守的中产阶级, 生活优越。

home e·co·nom·ics /,· ··'··/ *n* [U] the study of cooking, SEWING, and other skills used at home, taught as a subject at school 家政学

home front /,· '·/ *n* [singular] the people who stay and work in their own country while others go abroad to fight in a war〔战时的〕大后方〔人民〕

home·grown /ˈhom`gron; ,həʊm'grəʊn◂/ *adj* **1** vegetables that are homegrown are grown in your own garden〔蔬菜〕自家园子里种植的 **2** made or produced in your own country, town etc 本国制造[出产]的; 本地制造[出产]的: *homegrown entertainment* 国产娱乐片

home help /,· '·/ *n* [C] *BrE* someone who helps ill or old people in their homes with cleaning, cooking etc【英】〔帮助病人或老人的〕家务助理

home·land /ˈhom,lænd; 'həʊmlænd/ *n* [C] **1** the country where someone was born 祖国, 家乡 **2** a large area of land in South Africa where part of the black population lived, under the APARTHEID system〔南非种族隔离制度下的〕"黑人家园"

home·less /ˈhomləs; 'həʊmləs/ *adj* **1** without a home 无家可归的: *homeless children* 无家可归的儿童 **2 the homeless** people who have nowhere to live, and who often live on the streets 无家可归者, 流浪街头者 —**homelessness** *n* [U]

> **CULTURAL NOTE 文化注释**
> In the UK, there are far more BEGGARS and homeless people on the streets of cities such as London and Brighton than in the past. Some people believe that one reason for this increase is the government's Care in the Community POLICY which closed many hospitals for people with mental problems and allowed them to return to the COMMUNITY. People have different opinions about beggars. Some people are willing to give them money, but other people think this just makes the problem worse and complain about beggars who behave AGGRESSIVELY. There are charities (CHARITY) such as Shelter which provide homeless people with advice and support. In the centres of British towns and cities, you will often see homeless people selling a magazine called **The Big Issue**. The aim of The Big Issue organization is to help homeless people help themselves, and the magazine sellers are allowed to keep a lot of the money they receive for selling the magazine. 在英国的伦敦和布赖顿等城市街头的乞丐和无家可归者远较过去为多, 有人认为原因之一是政府制定了"社区关爱"政策, 关闭了很多精神病院, 允许精神病人回到社区。人们对乞丐有不同看法。有人愿意给他们钱, 有人则认为这只会让问题恶化, 并抱怨乞丐的行为咄咄逼人。有收容所等慈善机构为无家可归者提供建议和帮助。英国城镇中心经常可见无家可归者卖一种名为《畅销》的杂志。《畅销》这一组织允许卖杂志的人留存大部分卖杂志的所得, 目的是帮助无家可归者自食其力。

home·ly /ˈhomlɪ; 'həʊmli/ *adj* **1** *BrE* simple and ordinary in a way that makes you feel comfortable【英】朴实无华的; 家常的: *The cottage had a warm, homely feel.* 那间小屋给人一种温馨的感觉。**2** *AmE* people or faces that are homely are unattractive or ugly【美】相貌平庸的; 丑陋的: *I've never seen such a homely dog in my life!* 我这辈子从未见过如此难看的狗!

home·made /ˈhom`med; ,həʊm'meɪd◂/ *adj* made at home and not bought from a shop 自制的, 家里做的: *homemade cake* 自制蛋糕

> **CULTURAL NOTE 文化注释**
> Homemade food is thought of as being better than PROCESSED FOOD because it is fresher and does not contain ADDITIVES and lots of sugar and salt. People also think that homemade food shows that you care more about both the food and about the people who are going to eat it, because of the time and effort needed to make it. Homemade clothes, decorations etc also seem to show that you care about the people you make them for, but they are not expected to be better than ones you can buy in a shop. 自制食品一般被看做优于加工食品, 因其更加新鲜, 不含添加剂, 盐和糖的含量也不是很多。因为自制食品做起来耗时费力, 所以做自制食品的人被认为既在乎食品的质量, 又关心是给谁享用。自制衣服、装饰等似乎也表明你更关爱使用这些物品的人, 但这些不一定比商店买来的东西更好。— see also 另见 CONVENIENCE FOOD, INSTANT¹ (2), TV DINNER

home·mak·er /ˈhom,mekə; 'həʊm,meɪkə/ *n* [C] *especially AmE* a woman who works at home cleaning and cooking etc and does not have another job; HOUSEWIFE【尤美】家庭主妇

home mov·ie /,· '··/ *n* [C] a film you make, often of a family occasion, that is intended to be shown at home, not in a cinema〔只供在家里放映的〕自制影片; 记录家庭活动的影片

Home Of·fice /ˈ· ,· ·/ *n* [singular] the British government department which deals with keeping order inside the country, controlling who enters the country etc〔英国的〕内政部

Home on the Range /,· · · ˈ· ·/ a popular US FOLK song, which many people think of as a typical song that COWBOYs would sing.《牧场之家》〔美国一流行民歌。一般认为这是牛仔常唱的一首歌曲〕:

O give me a home where the buffalo roam,
Where the deer and the antelope play;
Where seldom is heard a discouraging word,
And the skies are not cloudy all day.
噢，给我一个家，
那里有水牛漫步，
那里有小鹿和羚羊嬉戏;
那里没有令人沮丧的话语，
那里没有遮天蔽日的阴霾。

ho·me·o·path /ˈhomɪə,pæθ; ˈhəʊmiə,pæθ/ *n* [C] someone who treats diseases using homeopathy 用顺势疗法治病的医师

ho·me·op·a·thy /,homɪˈɑpəθɪ; ,həʊmiˈɒpəθi/ *n* [U] a system of medicine in which a disease is treated by giving extremely small amounts of a substance that has the same effect as the disease 顺势疗法 **—homeopathic** /,homɪəˈpæθɪk; ,həʊmiəˈpæθɪk◂/ *adj* **—homeopathically** /-klɪ; -kli/ *adv*

home·own·er /ˈhom,onə; ˈhəʊm,əʊnə/ *n* [C] someone who owns their home 房主，自己拥有住房者

home plate /ˈ· ˈ·/ *n* [singular] the place where you stand to hit the ball in BASEBALL and the last place the player who is running must touch in order to get a point〔棒球运动的〕本垒板 —see picture on page A22 参见 A22 页图

Hom·er /ˈhomə; ˈhəʊmə/ a Greek poet who probably lived around 800 to 700 years BC. His two EPIC poems, *The Iliad* and *The Odyssey*, which tell the stories of characters such as Achilles and Odysseus and the Greek war against Troy, have had great influence on European literature. 荷马〔希腊诗人，大约生活在公元前800至前700年之间。他的两部史诗《伊利亚特》和《奥德赛》讲述阿喀琉斯、奥德修斯等人的故事，还有希腊与特洛伊的战争，对欧洲文学产生了巨大影响〕**—Homeric** /hoˈmɛrɪk; həʊˈmerɪk/ *adj*

homer *n* [C] *AmE informal* a home run【美，非正式】〔棒球〕本垒打 **—homer** *v* [I]

Homer, Wins·low /ˈwɪnzlo; ˈwɪnzləʊ/ (1836-1910) a US ARTIST who painted many pictures of the sea and people connected with the sea 霍默〔(1836-1910)，美国画家。他的许多绘画作品是以大海以及与大海有关的人物为主题而创作的〕

home room /ˈ· ·/ *n* [C] *AmE* a classroom where students have to go at the beginning of every school day【美】〔学生每天到校后必须去的〕点到室，年级教室

home rule /,· ˈ·/ *n* [U] the right of the people in a country to control their own affairs, after previously being controlled by another country〔某国取得独立后实行的〕地方自治

home run /,· ˈ·/ *n* [C] a long hit in BASEBALL which allows the player who hits the ball to run around all the bases (BASE² (8)) and get a point〔棒球运动的〕本垒打，全垒打

Homes & Gar·dens /,· · ˈ· ·/ *trademark* a British magazine which contains articles and pictures about decorating your home, GARDENING, and cooking. In the US there is a similar magazine called *Better Homes and Gardens*.【商标】《住宅与花园》〔英国杂志，刊有家庭装潢、园艺及烹饪方面的文章和图片。美国也有一类似杂志，称《住宅与花园美化》〕

Home Sec·re·ta·ry /,· ˈ· · · ·/ *n* [C,U] the British Government minister who is in charge of the HOME OFFICE〔英国的〕内政大臣

home·sick /ˈhom,sɪk; ˈhəʊm,sɪk/ *adj* feeling unhappy because you are a long way from your home 想家的，思乡的 **—homesickness** *n* [U]

home·spun /ˈhom,spʌn; ˈhəʊmspʌn/ *adj* **1** homespun ideas are simple and ordinary〔想法〕简单的，朴实的，平凡的: *homespun philosophy* 朴素的哲学 **2** homespun cloth is woven at home〔布料〕家里纺的

home·stead¹ /ˈhom,stɛd; ˈhəʊmsted/ *n* [C] **1** a farm and the area of land around it〔包括四周土地的〕农庄，农家 **2** *AmE old use* a piece of land given by the government【美旧】政府分发的土地

homestead² *v* [I,T] *AmE old use* to live and work on a homestead【美旧】在农庄工作及生活 **—homesteader** *n* [C]

home stretch /,· ˈ·/ *n* [singular] **1** also 又作 **home straight** *BrE*【英】the last part of a race where there is a straight line to the finish〔赛跑中的〕最后一段直道[路程] **2** the last part of an activity or journey〔活动的〕最后一部分;〔行程的〕最后阶段

home time /ˈ· ·/ *n* [U] *BrE* the time at the end of the school day when you can go home【英】〔学校每天的〕放学时间

home town /,· ˈ·/ *n* [C] the place where you were born and spent your childhood 家乡，故乡

home·wards /ˈhomwədz; ˈhəʊmwədz/ also 又作 **homeward** *especially AmE*【尤美】— *adv* **1** towards home 向家; 向家乡: *The children were heading homewards.* 孩子们正在往家走。**2 homeward bound** *literary* going towards home【文】向家，朝着家 **—homeward** *adj*: *homeward journey* 归家的旅程 —opposite 反义词 OUTWARD (2)

home·work /ˈhom,wɜk; ˈhəʊmwɜːk/ *n* [U] **1** work that a student at school is asked to do at home〔学生的〕家庭作业，功课 —compare 比较 CLASSWORK **2** something you do to prepare for an important activity〔重要活动之前必要的〕准备工作: **sb has done their homework** (=someone has prepared something well) 某人准备工作做得好 *You could tell that she'd really done her homework.* 可以看得出，她的准备工作的确做得很好。 S2

home·work·er /ˈhom,wɜkə; ˈhəʊm,wɜːkə/ *n* [C] someone who works from their home 在家办公的人 **—homeworking** *n* [U]

hom·ey¹, homy /ˈhomɪ; ˈhəʊmi/ *adj AmE* pleasant, like home【美】像在家里一样的，舒适自在的: *Flora liked the homey atmosphere of Aunt Fran's farm.* 弗洛拉喜欢弗兰姑妈的农场中那种像家一样舒适的气氛。—compare 比较 HOMELY (1)

homey², homie *n* [singular] *AmE* a HOMEBOY【美】老乡，同乡; 同伙

hom·i·cid·al /,hɑməˈsaɪdl; ,hɒmɪ̈ˈsaɪdl◂/ *adj* likely to murder someone 嗜杀(成性)的: *a homicidal maniac* 杀人狂

hom·i·cide /ˈhɑmə,saɪd; ˈhɒmɪ̈saɪd/ *n* **1** [C,U] *especially AmE* murder【尤美】谋杀，杀人 **2** [U] *AmE* the police department that deals with murder【美】警方负责处理谋杀案件的部门，凶杀科

hom·i·ly /ˈhɑmɪlɪ; ˈhɒmɪ̈li/ *n* [C] *formal*【正式】**1** advice about how to behave that is often unwanted〔道德〕说教，陈词滥调 **2** *literary* a speech given as part of a Christian church ceremony【文】〔基督教的〕讲道，布道

hom·ing /ˈhomɪŋ; ˈhəʊmɪŋ/ *adj* a bird or animal that has a homing instinct has a special ability that helps it find its way home over long distances〔鸟、动物〕有返回原地之能力的

homing de·vice /ˈ· · ·,·/ *n* [C usually singular 一般用单数] a special part of a weapon that helps it to find the place that it is aimed at〔武器上的〕自动导向装置，寻的装置

homing pi·geon /ˈ· ·,· ·/ *n* [C] a PIGEON that is able to find its way home over long distances 信鸽

hom·i·ny /ˈhɑmənɪ; ˈhɒmɪ̈ni/ *n* [U] a food made from crushed SWEET CORN 甜玉米片粥

homo- /homo; həʊməʊ/ *prefix formal or technical* same【正式或术语】相同的，同(一)的: *homosexual* (=attracted to the same sex) 同性恋的 | *homographs* (=words spelt the same way) 同形异义词

ho·moe·o·path /ˈhomɪə,pæθ; ˈhəʊmiə,pæθ/ *n* [C] a British spelling of HOMEOPATH homeopath 的英式拼法

ho·moe·op·athy /,homɪˈɑpəθɪ; ,həʊmiˈɒpəθi/ *n* [U] a British spelling of HOMEOPATHY homeopathy 的英式拼法

ho·mo·ge·ne·ous /,homəˈdʒinɪəs; ,həʊməˈdʒiːniəs◂/ also 又作 **ho·mo·ge·nous** /həˈmɑdʒənəs; həˈmɒdʒɪ̈nəs/ *adj* consisting of people or things that are all of the same kind 由同种族人组成的; 由同类组成的: *a homogeneous community* 同种族人组成的社会 —compare 比较 HETEROGENEOUS **—homogeneously** *adv*

ho·mo·ge·nize also 又作 **-ise** *BrE*【英】/həˈmɑdʒə,naɪz; həˈmɒdʒənaɪz/ *v* [T] to change something so that its parts become similar or the same 使成均质; 使均匀，使纯一: *plans to homogenize the various school systems* 统一各类不同学制的计划

ho·mo·ge·nized /həˈmɑdʒə,naɪzd; həˈmɒdʒɪ̈naɪzd/ *adj* homogenized milk has had the cream on top mixed with the milk〔牛奶〕均质的

hom·o·graph /ˈhɑmə,græf; ˈhɒməgrɑːf/ *n* [C] a word that is spelt the same as another, but is different in meaning, origin, grammar, or pronunciation 同形异义词: *The noun 'record' and the verb 'record' are homographs of each other.* 名词 record 和动词 record 互为同形异义词。

hom·o·nym /ˈhɑmə,nɪm; ˈhɒmənɪm/ *n* [C] a word that is spelt the same and sounds the same as another, but is different in meaning or origin. The noun 'bear' and the verb 'bear' are homonyms 同音同形异义词〔如名词 bear 和动词 bear〕

ho·mo·pho·bia /,homəˈfobɪə; ,həʊməˈfəʊbiə/ *n* [U] hatred and fear of HOMOSEXUALs 对同性恋的憎恶和恐惧 **—homophobic** *adj*

H

hom·o·phone /ˈhɑmə,fon; ˈhɒməfəʊn/ *n* [C] a word that sounds the same as another but is different in spelling, meaning or origin 同音异形异义词: *'Knew' and 'new' are homophones.* knew 和 new 是同音异形异义词。

Ho·mo sa·pi·ens /,homo ˋsepɪɛnz; ,həʊməʊ ˈsæpienz/ *n* [U] the type of human being that exists now 智人〔现代人的学名〕

ho·mo·sex·u·al /,homəˋsɛkʃuəl; ,həʊməˈsekʃuəl◂/ *n* [C] someone, especially a man, who is sexually attracted to people of the same sex〔尤指男性〕同性恋者 —compare 比较 BISEXUAL[1] (1), HETEROSEXUAL —see also 另见 GAY[1] (1) —**homosexual** *adj* —**homosexuality** /,homə,sɛkʃuˋælətɪ; ,həʊməsekʃuˈælə̩ti/ *n* [U]

CULTURAL NOTE 文化注释

Until the 1960s, it was illegal in the UK for men to have sex with other men, and people were sometimes seriously punished for this. It is now legal in the UK for people over 18 who have agreed to have sex, although it is still illegal in the Isle of Man (=a small British island). In the US, some states still have laws against homosexual sex, but in most states these laws are never actually used. Although homosexuality is no longer a crime, many people still regard it as wrong or unacceptable, and because of this some homosexuals, especially well-known people, are unwilling to 'come out' (=tell people that they are homosexual). 20世纪60年代以前的英国，男性之间发生性行为仍是非法的，违者有时会受到严惩。现在在英国，年满18岁的男性相互自愿的性行为是合法的，但在马恩岛仍然属于违法。美国的一些州仍有禁止同性性行为的法律，但在大多数州这些法令从未真正实施。虽然同性恋不再是犯罪，很多人仍将其视为是错误和不可接受的，因此一些同性恋者，尤其是名人，不愿意公开宣布自己是同性恋。

There is still quite a lot of DISCRIMINATION against homosexuals (=they are treated unfairly), and people disagree about whether homosexual couples should have the same rights as married people or be allowed to ADOPT children. People who dislike homosexuals sometimes call them offensive names, but homosexuals themselves prefer the word 'gay' to describe homosexual people. 对同性恋的歧视仍然大量存在。同性恋伴侣是否应享有与已婚夫妇同等的权利，是否应被允许收养子女，这些问题都没有一致的看法。不喜欢同性恋者的人有时用一些难听的字眼叫他们，但同性恋者更愿意用 gay 一词指称自己。

Homosexuals in the army In the UK homosexuals are not allowed to serve in the army, navy etc, but in the US they are allowed to serve if they do not tell anyone that they are homosexual. The US government calls this policy 'don't ask, don't tell', meaning that the army does not ask about people's sexuality, and people serving in the army do not mention it. 军队中的同性恋者：英国不允许同性恋者参军。但在美国，如果同性恋者不告诉别人自己是同性恋，就可以参军。美国政府称这种政策为"不问不说"，意思是说军队不过问别人的性取向，军人对此也不提及。

Hon /ɑn; ɒn/ **1** the written abbreviation of 缩写= HONOURABLE (1), used in the titles of British NOBLES and Members of Parliament 尊敬的〔用于称呼英国贵族及议会议员〕: *the Hon Arthur Cobbett* 尊敬的阿瑟·科贝特 **2** the written abbreviation of 缩写= HONORARY (2) used in official job titles 名誉的〔用于官方职位中〕: *Hon Sec* (=honorary secretary) 名誉秘书

hon /hʌn; hʌn/ *pron AmE spoken* an abbreviation of 缩写= HONEY, used to address someone you love【美口】亲爱的，宝贝〔用于称呼心爱的人〕: *Come here, hon, let me tie your shoes.* 来，宝贝，让我给你系上鞋带。

hon·cho /ˈhɑntʃo; ˈhɒntʃəʊ/ *n* **the head honcho** *informal especially AmE* the person who is in charge【非正式，尤美】负责人，头儿

Hon·du·ras /hɑnˋdurəs; hɒnˈdjʊərəs/ a country in Central America between Guatemala and Nicaragua. Population: 6,406,000 (2001). Capital: Tegucigalpa. 洪都拉斯〔中美洲一国，位于危地马拉和尼加拉瓜之间。人口：6,406,000 (2001)，首都：特古西加尔巴〕 —**Honduran** *n, adj*

hone /hon; həʊn/ *v* [T] **1** to improve your skill at doing something, especially when you are already very good at it 磨练，训练；提高…的技艺: *He set about honing his skills as a draughtsman.* 他着手进一步提高自己的制图技艺。| **finely honed** (=extremely well-developed) 极度发达的 *finely honed intuition* 极度发达的直觉 **2** to make knives, swords etc sharp 把〔刀、剑等〕磨快[锋利]

hon·est /ˈɑnɪst; ˈɒnə̩st/ *adj*

1 ▶CHARACTER 人品◀ someone who is honest does not lie or steal etc 诚实的，正直的: *It was very honest of him to give them the money back.* 他真诚实，把钱还给了他们。| *an old woman with a plain, honest face you could trust* 长着一张平常、诚实可靠的面孔的老妇 | **scrupulously honest** (=always very honest) 极其诚实的 *She is scrupulously honest in all her business dealings.* 她在所有的买卖中都极其诚实。

2 ▶STATEMENT/ANSWER ETC 讲话/回答等◀ not hiding the truth or the facts about something 坦诚的，直率的，不隐瞒真相的: *an honest answer* 坦白的回答 | **let's be honest** *Let's be honest – the only reason she married him was for his money.* 说实话，她嫁给他就是为了他的钱。| **be honest with sb** *I'm not sure if Joe was being completely honest with me when he said he'd never met them before.* 乔说他以前从未见过他们，我不知道他是不是对我说了实话。| **be honest about sth** *At least he's been honest about it.* 起码在这件事上他是诚实的。

3 to be honest *spoken* used when you tell someone what you really think【口】说实话，老实说: *To be honest, I don't like him very much.* 老实说，我不太喜欢他。

4 honest! *spoken* used to try to make someone believe you【口】真的！不骗你！: *I didn't mean to hurt him, honest!* 我不是故意伤害他的，真的！

5 honest to God *spoken* used to emphasize that something you say is really true【口】确实，千真万确

6 ▶WORK 工作◀ honest work is done without cheating, using your own efforts 用正当手段的，努力认真的: *I bet he's never done an honest day's work in his life!* 我敢说他这辈子从未认认真真地工作过一天！| **earn an honest living** *young families struggling even to earn an honest living* 要想正正当当谋生都不容易的年轻人家庭

7 ▶ORDINARY/GOOD PEOPLE 普通的/好人◀ honest people are not famous or special, but behave in a good, socially acceptable way 诚实的；规矩的: *She came from a good, honest, working-class background.* 她出身于一个正派的工人阶级家庭。

8 make an honest woman (out) of *old-fashioned* to marry a woman because she is going to have a baby【过时】因…已怀孕而娶她为妻

hon·est·ly /ˈɑnɪstlɪ; ˈɒnə̩stli/ *adv* **1** in an honest way 诚实地，正直地: *"I don't know," she answered honestly.* 她诚实地回答："我不知道。" | *Did he come by the money honestly, or was it stolen?* 他的钱是正路来的，还是偷来的？ **2** used to say that you really think that something is true, especially when it seems surprising 真的，的确: *Does he honestly expect me to believe his story?* 他真的以为我会相信他说的话吗？ **3** *spoken* used when you are shocked or annoyed by something someone has said or done【口】真是的！真不像话！〔用以表示震惊或烦恼〕: *Honestly! Can't you think of something better to do with your time?* 真不像话！你难道没有更好的办法利用时间吗？ **4** *spoken* used to try to make someone believe that what you have just said is true【口】真的！不骗你！: *It wasn't me, honestly!* 那不是我，真的不是！

honest-to-good·ness /,‥ˈ‥/ *adj* [only before noun 仅用于名词前] simple and good 简单而美好的，普通的，平常的: *plain honest-to-goodness home cooking* 普通家常菜

hon·es·ty /ˈɑnɪstɪ; ˈɒnə̩sti/ *n* [U] **1** the quality of being honest 诚实，正直；坦诚: *a politician of rare honesty and courage* 具备少见的诚实品德及勇气的政治家 **2 in all honesty** *spoken* used when telling someone that what you are saying is what you really think【口】说实话: *I must add, in all honesty, that I think the task ahead of us will be difficult.* 我必须补充一句，说实话，我认为我们面临的任务是艰巨的。

hon·ey /ˈhʌnɪ; ˈhʌni/ *n* [U] **1** a sweet sticky substance produced by BEES, used as food 蜂蜜 **2** *especially AmE spoken* used to address someone you love【尤美，口】亲爱的，宝贝〔用于称呼心爱的人〕

hon·ey·bee /ˈhʌnɪ,bi; ˈhʌnibiː/ *n* [C] a BEE that makes honey 蜜蜂

hon·ey·comb /ˈhʌnɪ,kom; ˈhʌnikəʊm/ *n* [C] **1** a structure made by BEES, which consists of many six-sided cells in which honey is stored 蜂巢，蜂窝，蜂房 **2** something that is arranged or shaped in this pattern 蜂巢[窝]状物

hon·ey·combed /ˈhʌnɪ,komd; ˈhʌnikəʊmd/ *adj* [+with] filled with many holes, hollow passages etc 蜂巢[窝]状的

hon·ey·dew mel·on /,hʌnɪdju ˋmɛlən; ,hʌnidjuː ˈmelən/ *n* [C] a type of MELON 白兰瓜，蜜瓜，甜瓜 —see picture on page A8 参见 A8 页图

hon·eyed /ˈhʌnɪd; ˈhʌnid/ *adj literary* honeyed words or honeyed voices sound soft and pleasant, but are often insincere【文】

甜言蜜语的，阿谀的：*"How kind you are," Brett said in a honeyed voice.* "你真好！"布雷特甜言蜜语道。

hon·ey·moon¹ /ˈhʌnɪˌmun; ˈhʌnimuːn/ *n* [C] **1** a holiday taken by two people who have just got married 蜜月：**on your honeymoon** *We're going to Hawaii on our honeymoon.* 我们要去夏威夷度蜜月。**2** also 又作 **honeymoon period** the period of time when a new government, leader etc has just started and no one criticizes them〔新政府、新领导人上任初期的〕短暂的和谐时期，蜜月期

honeymoon² *v* [I always+adv/prep] to go somewhere for your honeymoon 去度蜜月 —**honeymooner** *n* [C]

hon·ey·pot /ˈhʌnɪˌpɑt; ˈhʌnipɒt/ *n* [C] something that is attractive to a lot of people 极有吸引力的事物

hon·ey·suck·le /ˈhʌnɪˌsʌk]; ˈhʌniˌsʌkəl/ *n* [C] a climbing plant with pleasant-smelling yellow or pink flowers 忍冬〔一种有香味的攀缘植物〕

Hong Kong /ˈhɑŋ ˌkɑŋ; ˌhɒŋ ˈkɒŋ◂/ an area on the south coast of China, consisting of Hong Kong Island, the Kowloon Peninsula, the New Territories and 235 outlying islands. Population: 6,720,000 (mid-2001). Hong Kong was occupied by the UK from 1842 to 1997, when it became the Hong Kong Special Administrative Region of China. Although it is part of China, it has its own government and financial system, and is an important financial and trade centre. 香港〔中国南部沿海一地区，由香港岛、九龙半岛、新界及235个离岛组成。人口：6,720,000（2001年中）。香港1842至1997年间为英国所侵占，1997年成为中国香港特别行政区。香港虽然是中国的一部分，但有自己的政府和金融体系，也是一个重要的金融和贸易中心〕

Hon·i soit qui mal y pense /ˌɑnɪ swɑ ki ˌmæl i ˈpɑns; ˌɒni swɑː kiː ˌmæl iː ˈpɒns/ *French* the MOTTO (=special saying) of the Order of the Garter. It is a French phrase which means 'Let anyone who thinks bad things about it be ashamed.'【法】凡对此心存歹念的人可耻〔铭于嘉德勋章上的法语格言〕

honk¹ /hɔŋk; hɒŋk/ *n* **1** a loud noise made by a car horn 汽车喇叭声 —see picture on page A19 参见A19页图 **2** a loud noise made by a GOOSE¹ (1) 鹅叫声

honk² *v* **1** [I,T] if a car horn or a GOOSE¹ (1) honks, it makes a loud noise〔汽车〕鸣（喇叭），按（喇叭）；〔鹅〕叫 **2** [I] also 又作 **honk up** *slang* to VOMIT¹【俚】呕吐

hon·ky, honkie /ˈhɑŋkɪ; ˈhɒŋki/ *n* [C] *AmE slang* an insulting word for a white person【美俚】白鬼子〔对白人的蔑称〕

hon·ky-tonk¹ /ˈhɑŋkɪ ˌtɑŋk; ˈhɒŋki tɒŋk/ *n* [C] *AmE* a cheap bar where COUNTRY MUSIC is played【美】演奏乡村音乐的低级酒吧

honky-tonk² *adj* [only before noun 仅用于名词前] **1 honky-tonk music/piano** a type of piano music which is played in a cheerful way 欢乐的乐曲/钢琴曲 **2** *AmE* cheap, brightly-coloured, and not good quality【美】低档俗艳的

Hon·o·lu·lu /ˌhɑnəˋlulu; ˌhɒnəˈluːluː/ the capital of Hawaii on the island of Oahu. It is a port and trade centre and is visited by many tourists. 火奴鲁鲁，又译檀香山〔夏威夷首府。位于瓦胡岛，为港口和贸易中心，也是旅游胜地〕

hon·or /ˈɑnə; ˈɒnə/ *n* [C,U] the American spelling of HONOUR honour 的美式拼法

hon·or·a·ble /ˈɑnərəb]; ˈɒnərəbəl/ *adj* the American spelling of HONOURABLE honourable 的美式拼法

hon·o·rar·i·um /ˌɑnəˋrɛrɪəm; ˌɒnəˈreəriəm/ *n* [C] *formal* a sum of money offered to someone for professional services【正式】〔提供专业服务的〕酬金，报酬

hon·or·ar·y /ˈɑnəˌrɛrɪ; ˈɒnərəri/ *adj* **1** an honorary title, rank, or university degree is given to someone as an honour〔称号、官阶、学位等〕作为一种荣誉授予的，荣誉的 **2** an honorary position in an organization is held without receiving any payment〔职位、职务〕名誉的，名义上的，无报酬的 **3** an honorary member of a group is treated like a member of that group but does not belong to it〔成员〕名誉的：*They regard her as a kind of honorary man.* 他们将她视作名誉成员。

hon·or·if·ic /ˌɑnəˋrɪfɪk; ˌɒnəˈrɪfɪk◂/ *n* [C] an expression or title that is used to show respect for the person you are speaking to 尊称，敬语〔用来表示尊敬的称号、用语〕

honor roll /ˈ‥ ·/ *n* [C] *AmE* a list of the best students in a school or college【美】成绩优异者名单；光荣榜

hon·ors /ˈɑnəz; ˈɒnəz/ *n* [plural] the American spelling of HONOURS honours 的美式拼法 —see also 另见 **with honours** (HONOUR¹ (12))

honor sys·tem /ˈ‥ ˌ‥/ *n* [C] *AmE*【美】**1** an agreement between members of a group to obey rules 信用制度〔指自觉遵守规章而不加监督的做法〕：*the school's honor system* 无监考考试制度，学校的信用制度 **2** a way of recording the fact that a student has achieved a high standard of work 优等生表彰制度

hon·our¹ *BrE*【英】, **honor** *AmE*【美】/ˈɑnə; ˈɒnə/ *n* 3

1 ▶RESPECT 尊敬◀ [U] the respect that you, your family, your country etc receive from other people, which makes you feel proud 荣誉；崇敬，敬重，敬意：*For the French team, winning tomorrow's game is a matter of national honour.* 对法国队来说，在明天的比赛中获胜事关国家荣誉。| **sb's honour is at stake** (=someone's honour could be badly affected if they do not succeed) 危及某人的声誉 *This can't get to the media. The company's honor is at stake here!* 不能让传媒知道这件事。这关系到公司的形象。

2 ▶STH THAT MAKES YOU PROUD 让人引以为荣的事◀ [singular] *formal* something that makes you feel very proud【正式】引以为荣的事，光荣：**it is an honour to do sth** (=used when saying politely that you are pleased to do something, especially at a formal occasion) 很荣幸做某事 | **have the honour of doing sth** *formal*【正式】*Earlier this year I had the honor of meeting the President and Mrs Bush.* 今年较早时候，我有幸见到了布什总统及他的夫人。| **do sb the honour of doing sth** (=make someone proud and happy by doing something for them) 为某人做某事使之感到荣幸，给面子为某人做某事 | **a rare honour** (=a very special honour) 殊荣

3 in honour of in order to show how much you admire and respect someone 为了表示对…的崇敬：*a memorial in honour of those who died for their country* 为纪念那些为国捐躯者而举行的仪式

4 ▶GIVEN BY A GOVERNMENT 由政府授予的◀ [C] something such as a special title or MEDAL given to someone to show how much people respect them for what they have achieved 荣誉称号；荣誉勋章：**highest honour** (=most important honour) 最高荣誉勋章[称号] *Churchill received many of his country's highest honours.* 丘吉尔曾获得很多由国家授予的最高荣誉勋章。

5 the place/seat of honour the place which is given to the most important guest 贵宾席，贵宾座

6 be an honour to to bring admiration and respect to your country, school, family etc because of your behaviour or achievements 为…增光：*a young man who was a great athlete and an honour to his college* 体育出色，为学院增光的年轻人

7 with full military honours if someone is buried with full military honours, there is a military ceremony at their funeral 以隆重的军葬礼下葬的

8 ▶MORAL PRINCIPLES 道德标准◀ [U] strong moral beliefs and standards of behaviour that make people respect and trust you 高尚品德，气节：**a matter/point/question of honour** (=something that you feel you must do because of your moral principles) 品德问题 *It is a point of honour with me to repay all my debts promptly.* 能否尽快偿还所有债务关系到我的名誉问题。| **man of honour** *old-fashioned* (=a man who always behaves in a way that is based on high moral standards)【过时】品德高尚的人

9 be/feel honour bound to feel that it is your moral duty to do something 在道义上有责任：*Don't tell Kit either, because she'd feel honour bound to do something about it.* 也别告诉姬特，因为她会觉得自己有责任为此做点什么。

10 on your honour a) if you swear on your honour to do something, you promise very seriously to do it 以名誉担保 **b)** *old-fashioned* if you are on your honour to do something, you are being trusted to do it【过时】得到信任的

11 do the honours *spoken* to pour the drinks, serve food etc at a social occasion【口】〔在社交场合上〕尽主人之谊〔指倒酒、上菜等〕

12 ▶UNIVERSITY 大学◀ *BrE*【英】**a) with honours** if you pass a university degree with honours, you pass it at a level that is higher than the most basic level 以优等成绩〔毕业、获得学位〕**b) First Class/Second Class Honours** the highest or second highest level of degree at a British university〔英国大学中的〕一级/二级荣誉学位[优等成绩]

13 Your Honour used when speaking to a judge 法官大人

14 ▶SEX 性◀ *old use* if a woman loses her honour, she has sex with a man she is not married to【旧】〔妇女的〕贞操，贞节 —see also 另见 **guest of honour** (GUEST¹ (6)), MAID OF HONOUR

honour² *BrE*【英】, **honor** *AmE*【美】— *v* [T] **1 be/feel honoured** to feel very proud and pleased 感到荣幸：**be/feel honoured to do sth** *I felt deeply honored to be playing against the former Wimbledon Champion.* 能与温布尔登网球赛的前冠军比赛，我深感荣幸。**2** to treat someone with special respect 礼待〔某人〕：*our honoured guests this evening* 今晚的贵宾 **3** *formal* to show publicly that someone is respected and admired,

H

especially by praising them or giving them a special title【正式】给…以荣誉, 表彰, 表扬 **4 honour a contract/agreement etc** to do what you have agreed to do in a contract etc 履行合同/协议 **5 honour a cheque/voucher etc** to accept a cheque etc as payment 接受[承兑]支票/代金券 **6 sb has decided to honour us with their presence** *humorous* used when someone arrives late, or to someone who rarely comes to a meeting, class etc【幽默】某人决定赏光出席了〔用于迟到的或不常参加会议或上课的人〕

Hon·our·a·ble /ˈɑnərəb]; ˈɒnərəbəl/ *written abbreviation* 缩写为 **Hon** *adj* **1** used in Britain in the titles of children whose father is a lord and in the titles of judges and members of parliament 尊敬的〔对英国贵族子女、法官和议员的尊称〕 **2 Honourable Member** used by British members of parliament when talking to or about each other in the House of Commons 尊敬的议员〔英国下议院议员相互之间的尊称〕—compare 比较 RIGHT HONOURABLE

honourable *BrE*【英】, **honorable** *AmE*【美】— *adj* **1** an honourable action or activity deserves respect and admiration〔行为或事件〕光荣的, 值得尊敬的: *My father doesn't think acting is an honorable profession.* 我父亲认为当演员不是受人尊敬的行业。**2** behaving in a way that is morally correct and shows you have high moral standards 品行高洁的, 品德高尚的: *a principled and honourable man* 一个讲求原则、品德高尚的人 **3** an honourable arrangement or agreement is fair to everyone who is involved in it〔安排或协议〕公平的, 公正的 **—honourably** *adv*

honourable men·tion *BrE*【英】, **honorable mention** *AmE*【美】/, ····ˈ··/ *n* [C] a special honour in a competition for work that was of high quality but did not get a prize〔给未获正式名次但有优异表现者颁发的〕荣誉奖

honours de·gree /ˈ·· ·,·/ *n* [C] a university degree that is above the basic level in one or two particular subjects at a British university〔英国大学的〕荣誉学位, 优等学位: *an honours degree in German* 德语荣誉学位 | **joint honours degree** (=a degree in two main subjects) 双主修荣誉学位, 联合荣誉学位

honours list /ˈ·· ,·/ *n* [singular] a list of important people in Britain to whom titles are given as a sign of respect〔英国的〕授勋者名册

CULTURAL NOTE 文化注释

The Honours System Twice a year, various honours are given to British people who have achieved something important or who have done something important for the nation which deserves a reward. The New Year's Honours list is announced at the end of December. Another similar list, the Birthday Honours list, is announced in the middle of June on the date of the Queen's official birthday. 授勋制度: 每年两次, 取得重大成就或为国家作出重要贡献、值得表彰的英国人可以获得各种勋位。12月底宣布"新年授勋名单"。还有一个类似的名单, 叫做"女王生日授勋名单", 于6月中旬女王的正式生日时宣布。

The honours which are given to people on these two occasions include LIFE PEERAGE*s*, KNIGHTHOOD*s*, and various less important titles such as a CBE, OBE, or MBE. Various MEDAL*s* and other DECORATION*s* are given to people, especially members of the police and the armed forces, for acts of BRAVERY. 每年两次授勋授予的称号包括终身贵族、骑士和其他相对次要的称号, 如英帝国二等勋位爵士、英帝国勋章获得者、帝国勋章获得者。获得荣誉者, 尤其是警察或军人因其英勇行为获得荣誉时, 会得到各种奖章、勋章。

The honours lists often cause a lot of discussion about whether a particular person really deserves an honour. Some people want to get rid of the honours system. They think it is unfair because honours are sometimes given for political reasons. Various famous people have refused to accept an honour or returned an honour, including David Bowie, Graham Greene, Harold Pinter, and John Lennon. 授勋名单常引起很多关于某人是否应得荣誉的争论。有人认为授勋制度不公平, 想将其取缔, 因为授勋有时是出于政治原因。很多名人拒绝接受荣誉或退回荣誉, 包括戴维·鲍伊、格雷厄姆·格林、哈罗德·品特和约翰·列侬。

Hon·shu /ˈhɑnʃu; ˈhɒnʃuː/ the largest of the four main islands of Japan. Most of Japan's largest cities are on Honshu. 本州〔日本四大岛中最大的一个岛。日本的多数大城市位于该岛〕

hooch, hootch /hutʃ; huːtʃ/ *n* [U] *especially AmE* strong alcoholic drink that has been made illegally【尤美】〔非法制造的〕烈酒

hood /hud; hʊd/ *n* [C] **1** a part of a coat that you can pull up to cover your head〔大衣上的〕风帽, 兜帽: *a fur-lined hood* 有毛皮衬里的风帽 **2** a cover fitted above a COOKER (1) to remove the smell of cooking〔炉灶上方的〕排风罩, 抽油烟罩 **3** *AmE* the metal covering over the engine on a car【美】汽车引擎盖: *Check under the hood and see what that noise is.* 打开引擎盖查查是什么声音。**4** *BrE* a folding cover on a car or PRAM, which gives protection from the rain【英】〔汽车或婴儿车上用于挡雨的〕折合式车篷; 篷盖 **5** a cover that someone puts over their head to prevent them from being recognized〔为了不让人认出而戴上的〕蒙脸罩 **6** *slang originally AmE* a hoodlum【俚, 原美】恶棍, 暴徒: *gangs of hoods roaming the streets* 成群结队在街上游荡的恶棍

-hood /hud; hʊd/ *suffix* [in nouns 构成名词] the state or time of being something …状态; …时期: *a happy childhood* 快乐的童年 | *growing to manhood* 长大成人 | *There's not much likelihood.* 那不太可能。

Hood, Robin —see 见 ROBIN HOOD

hood·ed /ˈhudɪd; ˈhʊdɨd/ *adj* having or wearing a hood 带风帽的; 戴着风帽的; 有罩的: *a hooded cape* 带风帽的斗篷

hood·lum /ˈhudləm; ˈhuːdləm/ *n* [C] *informal* a violent criminal【非正式】恶棍, 暴徒

hoo·doo /ˈhudu; ˈhuːduː/ *n* [U] a type of VOODOO 巫术, 魔法

hood·wink /ˈhud,wɪŋk; ˈhʊd,wɪŋk/ *v* [T+into] to trick someone in a clever way so that you can get an advantage for yourself 欺诈, 哄骗

hoo·ey /ˈhuɪ; ˈhuːi/ *n* [U] *AmE* stupid talk; nonsense【美】胡说八道, 瞎话

hoof¹ /huf; huːf/ *n* [C] *plural* **hoofs** *or* **hooves** /huvz; huːvz/ **1** the hard foot of an animal such as a horse, cow etc 蹄 —see picture at 参见 HORSE¹ 图 **2 on the hoof** *BrE* if you make decisions on the hoof, you make them while you are doing other things, without stopping to think【英】不假思索地〔作决定〕

hoof² *v* **hoof it** *slang* to run away quickly【俚】快速逃走

hoof·er /ˈhufɚ; ˈhuːfə/ *n* [C] *AmE slang* a dancer【美俚】舞蹈演员

hoo-ha /ˈhu ,hɑ; ˈhuː hɑː/ *n* [U] *BrE* noisy talk or excitement about something unimportant【英】吵闹, 叫嚷; 大惊小怪: *What's all the hoo-ha about?* 干什么这么吵闹呀?

hooks 钩子

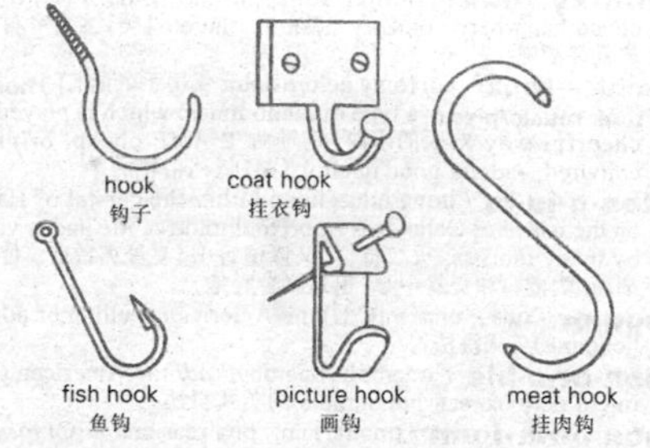

hook¹ /huk; hʊk/ *n* [C]

1 ►FOR HANGING THINGS ON 用来挂东西◄ a curved piece of metal or plastic that you use for hanging things on 挂钩, 吊钩: *Put your coat on the hook.* 把你的外套挂在钩上。

2 ►FOR CATCHING FISH 用来钓鱼◄ a curved piece of thin metal with a sharp point for catching fish 鱼钩, 钓钩: *a fish hook* 鱼钩

3 by hook or by crook if you are going to do something by hook or by crook, you are determined to do it 千方百计地, 下定决心地: *In the old days if you had a deadline, you met it by hook or by crook.* 过去, 如果规定了最后期限, 你就要用尽方法把工作按时完成。

4 let/get sb off the hook to allow someone or help someone to get out of a difficult situation 让/帮某人脱离困境: *We almost sued the magazine for libel, but in the end we let them off the hook.* 我们差点要控告这家杂志诽谤, 但最后还是饶了他们。

5 leave/take the phone off the hook to leave or take the telephone RECEIVER (=the part you speak into) off the part where it is usually placed so that no one can call you〔因不想接听电话而〕摘下电话听筒

6 ▶WAY OF HITTING SB 拳击方法◀ a way of hitting your opponent in BOXING, in which your elbow is bent〔拳击中的〕钩拳

7 hook, line, and sinker if someone believes something hook, line, and sinker, they believe a lie completely 完全地, 无保留地〔相信谎言〕: *She swallowed the whole story hook, line, and sinker.* 她完全相信了这整件事。

8 ▶A TUNE 曲调◀ a part of the tune in a song that makes it very easy to remember 曲调中易记的部分 —see also 另见 BOAT HOOK, **sling your hook** (SLING¹ (4))

hook² *v* [T]

1 ▶FISH 鱼◀ to catch a fish with a hook〔用钩〕钓鱼: *I hooked a 20 pound salmon last week.* 我上周钓了一条20磅重的鲑鱼。

2 ▶FASTEN 固定◀ [always+adv/prep] to fasten or hang something onto something else 吊, 挂; 把…固定住: **hook sth over/around/onto etc** *He managed to hook his leg over the branch.* 他终于设法把一条腿钩在树枝上。| **get hooked on/onto** *My jacket got hooked on a rosebush.* 我的上衣被玫瑰丛钩住了。

3 ▶BEND YOUR FINGER/ARM ETC 屈起手指/手臂等◀ [always+adv/prep] to bend your finger, arm, or leg, especially so that you can pull or hold something else 用〔手指、手臂或腿〕箍住; 钩住: **hook sth around/over etc** *Jack hooked his arm around the other man's neck.* 杰克用胳膊箍住另一个人的脖子。

4 ▶ATTRACT 吸引◀ *AmE informal* to succeed in attracting someone【美, 非正式】勾引; 吸引

hook sth ↔ **up** *phr v* [T] *especially AmE* to connect a piece of electronic equipment to another piece of equipment or to an electricity supply【尤美】〔电器〕连接, 接通: *Is the video hooked up to the TV?* 录像机和电视机连接上了吗?

hook up with *phr v* [T] *especially AmE*【尤美】**a)** to meet someone and become friendly with them 跟…结交: *I'll give you a few names of people to hook up with out there.* 我会告诉你一些人的名字, 你到那儿后可以和他们结交。**b)** to agree to work together with another organization for a particular purpose 挂钩〔指与某个组织合作〕

Hook, Captain —see 见 CAPTAIN HOOK

hook·ah /ˈhʊkə; ˈhʊkə/ *n* [C] a pipe for smoking drugs that consists of a long tube and a container of water 水烟筒

hook and eye /ˌ· · ˈ·/ *n* [U] a small metal hook and ring used for fastening clothes〔衣服上作纽扣用的〕钩和环, 钩眼扣 —see picture at 参见 FASTENER 图

hook and lad·der /ˌ· · ˈ··/ *n* [C] *AmE* a FIRE ENGINE with long LADDERS fixed to it【美】〔配备有长梯的〕云梯消防车

hooked /hʊkt; hʊkt/ *adj* **1** curved outwards or shaped like a hook 钩状的: *hooked claws* 钩爪 | *a hooked nose* 鹰钩鼻 **2** [not before noun 不用于名词前] *informal* if you are hooked on a drug, you feel a strong need for it and you cannot stop taking it; ADDICTED (1)【非正式】〔吸毒〕成瘾的 **3** [not before noun 不用于名词前] if you are hooked on something, you enjoy it very much and you want to do it as often as possible 对…上瘾的, 对…着迷的: *I got hooked on TV when I was sick.* 我生病期间对电视着了迷。**4** having one or more hooks 有钩的

hook·er /ˈhʊkɚ; ˈhʊkə/ *n* [C] *informal* a woman who has sex with men for money; PROSTITUTE【非正式】妓女

hook-nosed /ˈ· ,·/ *adj* having a large nose that curves outwards in the middle 长着鹰钩鼻的

hook-up /ˈ· ·/ *n* [C] a temporary connection between two pieces of equipment such as computers, or between a piece of equipment and an electricity supply〔仪器的〕临时连接: *a satellite hook-up* 卫星连接[联播]

hook·y, hookey /ˈhʊkɪ; ˈhʊki/ *n* **play hooky** *informal AmE* to stay away from school without permission【非正式, 美】逃学

hoo·li·gan /ˈhulɪgən; ˈhuːlɪgən/ *n* [C] a noisy violent person who causes trouble by fighting etc 流氓, 恶棍: *football hooligans* 足球流氓 —**hooliganism** *n* [U]

hoop /hup; huːp/ *n* [C] **1 jump/go through hoops** to have to do a lot of difficult things as a test of how suitable you are for something 经受考验[磨练] **2** one of the circular bands of metal or wood around a BARREL¹ (1)〔箍桶用的金属或木质〕箍 **3** a curved piece of wood or metal that is stuck into the ground and used in the game of CROQUET〔槌球戏中的〕拱门 **4** a large ring that CIRCUS (1) animals are made to jump through or that children used to play with in the past〔马戏团中供动物钻过的〕大圈;〔旧时儿童当玩具的〕环 —see also 另见 COCK-A-HOOP, HULA HOOP —**hoop** *v* [T]

hoop·la /ˈhup lɑ; ˈhuːp lɑː/ *n* [U] **1** *especially AmE* excitement about something which attracts a lot of public attention【尤美】喧闹, 大吹大擂: *all the hoopla that surrounded the trial* 对法庭的审判议论纷纷 **2** *BrE* a game in which prizes can be won by throwing a ring over an object from a distance【英】投环套物游戏

hoo·ray /hʊˈre; hʊˈreɪ/ *interjection* shouted when you are very glad about something〔表示高兴的呼喊声〕好哇! —see also 另见 **hip hip hooray** (HIP²) —**hooray** *n* [C]

hoose-gow /ˈhusgaʊ; ˈhuːsgaʊ/ *n* [C] *AmE old use* a prison【美旧】监狱

hoot¹ /hut; huːt/ *n* [C] **1** a shout or laugh that shows you think something is funny or stupid〔听到可笑或愚蠢的事时发出的〕嘘声; 嘲笑声: **hoots of laughter/derision** *a speech that was greeted with hoots of derision* 被报以阵阵嘲笑声的演讲 **2** a sound that an OWL makes 猫头鹰的叫声 **3** a short clear sound made by a vehicle or ship, as a warning〔汽车喇叭、船的汽笛的〕鸣响声〔以示警告〕**4 be a hoot** *spoken* to be very funny or amusing【口】很可笑, 很滑稽 **5 don't give a hoot/don't care two hoots** *spoken* used when saying that you do not care about something at all【口】一点也不在乎, 完全不放在心上: *I don't give a hoot for her opinion!* 我根本不在乎她的看法!

hoot² *v* **1** [I,T] if a vehicle or ship hoots, it makes a loud clear noise as a warning〔汽车〕鸣喇叭;〔船〕鸣笛〔以作警告〕: **[+at]** *The car behind was hooting at me.* 我身后的汽车冲着我鸣喇叭。**2** [I] if an OWL hoots, it makes a long 'oo' sound〔猫头鹰〕发出鸣叫声 **3** [I,T] to laugh loudly because you think something is funny or stupid 嘲弄地大笑: **[+with]** *hooting with laughter* 大声嘲笑

hoot·er /ˈhutɚ; ˈhuːtə/ *n* [C] **1** *BrE* a piece of equipment that makes a loud noise and is used on cars, ships, or in factories【英】〔汽车的〕喇叭;〔船、工厂的〕汽笛 **2** *BrE slang* your nose【英俚】鼻子 **3 hooters** [plural] *AmE* an offensive word for a woman's breasts【美】一对乳房〔具冒犯性的说法〕

hoo·ver¹ /ˈhuvɚ; ˈhuːvə/ *n* [C] *BrE trademark* VACUUM CLEANER【英, 商标】〔胡佛牌〕真空吸尘器

hoover² *v* [I,T] *BrE* to clean a floor, CARPET etc using a VACUUM CLEANER (=a machine that sucks up dirt)【英】用真空吸尘器清洁〔地板、地毯等〕—see picture at 参见 CLEAN² 图

Hoover, Herbert (1874-1964) a US politician in the Republican Party who was the President of the US from 1929 to 1933, during the first years of the Great Depression, when many US citizens did not have jobs 胡佛〔(1874-1964), 美国共和党政治家, 1929至1933年间任美国总统。当时正处于经济大萧条的最初几年, 许多美国公民找不到工作〕

Hoover, J. Ed·gar /ˌdʒeɪ ˈɛdgɚ; dʒeɪ ˈedgə/ (1895-1972) the most important DIRECTOR of the FBI, from 1924 until his death. He had very strong anti-Communist views, and he was later criticized for having too much power and for collecting information about people who were not criminals or enemies of the country. 胡佛〔(1895-1972), 美国联邦调查局最有影响力的局长, 1924年起任该职直至去世。他的反共观点颇为强硬。有人曾批评说, 他的权力过大。有些人既没犯罪, 也未与国家为敌, 他照样会搜集他们的资料〕

Hoover Dam /ˌ·· ˈ·/ a DAM on the Colorado River on the border between the US states of Arizona and Nevada. It supplies electricity and water to several states, and is one of the tallest dams in the world. It was formerly known as **Boulder Dam**. 胡佛大坝〔科罗拉多河上的一座大坝, 位于美国亚利桑那州和内华达州的边界。它为数个州供电送水, 为世界上最高的水坝之一。旧称博尔德水坝〕

hooves /huvz; huːvz/ the plural of HOOF

hop¹ /hɑp; hɒp/ *v* **hopped, hopping**

1 ▶JUMP 跳跃◀ [I] to move by jumping on one foot〔人〕单足蹦跳: *a child hopping up and down the stairs* 一个在楼梯上单足跳上跳下的孩子

2 [I] if a bird, an insect, or a small animal hops, it moves by making quick short jumps〔鸟、昆虫、小动物〕〔快速小步〕跳跃

3 [I always+adv/prep] *informal* to get into, onto, or out of something, especially a vehicle【非正式】跳上[跳下]〔车辆〕: **[+in/out/on etc]** *Hop in – I'll drive you to the bus stop.* 上车吧, 我送你去公共汽车站。

4 hop a plane/bus/train etc *AmE informal* to get on a plane, bus, train etc, especially after suddenly deciding to do so【美, 非正式】〔尤指突然决定〕搭乘〔飞机、公共汽车、火车等〕: *So we hopped a bus to Phoenix that night.* 因此我们那天晚上便坐上公共汽车到了凤凰城。

5 hop it! *BrE spoken* used to tell someone to go away【英口】走开! 滚开!

6 hopping mad *informal* very angry【非正式】非常生气, 暴跳如雷: *Mrs C's going to be hopping mad when she hears!* C太太听到这事会非常生气的!

H

hop² *n* [C]

1 keep sb on the hop *informal* to make someone very busy【非正式】让某人十分忙碌: *The children keep me on the hop all day.* 孩子们让我整天忙个不停。

2 catch sb on the hop to do something when someone is not expecting it and is not ready 使某人措手不及

3 ▶JUMP 跳跃◀ a short jump〔小步〕跳跃, 蹦跳

4 ▶PLANT 植物◀ [usually plural 一般用复数] part of a flower that is used for making beer, or the tall plant on which it grows 忽布(花), 啤酒花〔用来酿制啤酒〕

5 ▶FLIGHT 飞行◀ a single short journey by plane 短程飞行: *crossing Australia in a series of hops* 通过一连串短程飞行穿越澳大利亚

6 ▶DANCE 跳舞◀ a social event at which people dance 舞会

hop, step, and jump /,·,·'·/ *n* [singular] *informal* the TRIPLE JUMP【非正式】三级跳远

hope¹ /hop; həʊp/ *v* [I,T] **1** to want something to happen or be true, and to believe it is possible 希望, 期望, 指望: **hope (that)** *I hope you have a lovely birthday.* 我希望你能过一个快乐的生日。| *I hope I'm not disturbing you.* 希望我没有打扰你。| *Let's just hope we can find somewhere to park.* 但愿我们能找到停车的地方。| **hope to do sth** *Joan's hoping to study Law at Harvard.* 琼盼望能到哈佛大学念法律。| [+for] *We were hoping for good weather.* 我们在盼望好天气。| **hope for the best** (=hope that a situation will end well when there is a risk of things going wrong) 抱乐观的态度, 尽量往好处想 *All we can do is hope for the best and wait.* 我们唯一能做的就是抱着乐观的态度耐心等待。| **hope against hope** (=continue to hope for something even when it is unlikely to happen) 抱一线希望 *Daniel waited all day, hoping against hope that Annie would change her mind.* 丹尼尔等了一整天, 抱着一丝希望盼安妮会改变主意。

Frequencies of the verb **hope** in spoken and written English
动词 hope 在英语口语和书面语中的使用频率

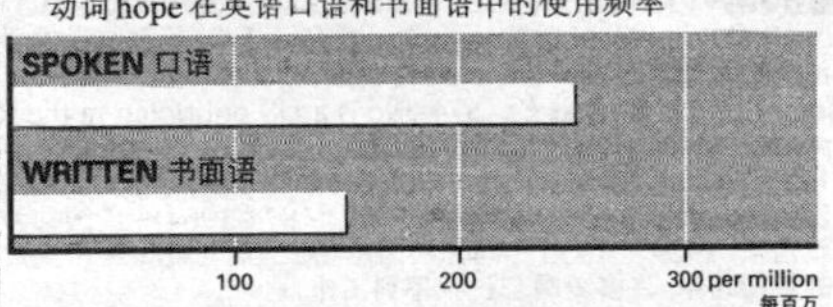

Based on the British National Corpus and the Longman Lancaster Corpus
据英国国家语料库和朗文兰开斯特语料库

This graph shows that the verb **hope** is much more common in spoken English than in written English. This is because it is used in a lot of common spoken phrases. 本图表显示, 动词 hope 在英语口语中的使用频率远远高于书面语, 因为口语中很多常用短语是由 hope 构成的。

hope (*v*) **SPOKEN PHRASES**
含 hope 的口语短语

2 I hope (that) used to say that you hope something will happen 我希望…: *I hope you're coming to the party.* 我希望你能来参加聚会。| **I do hope (that)** *BrE* (=a polite way of saying that you hope something will happen)【英】我真希望… *It was great to see you and I do hope that we'll meet up again soon.* 很高兴能见到你, 真希望我们不久能再次见面。**3 I hope so** used to say that you hope something that has been mentioned happens or is true 希望如此!: *"Do we get paid this week?" "I certainly hope so!"* "我们这星期能拿到工资吗?" "希望如此!" **4 I hope not** used to say that you hope something that has been mentioned does not happen or is not true 但愿不会!: *I don't think I'm busy that day, at least I hope not anyway.* 我想那天我不会很忙, 至少我是这样期望的。**5 I am hoping** used to say that you hope something will happen, especially because you are depending on it 我非常希望…: **I am hoping (that)** *I'm hoping he's going to do my car for me because I can't afford to take it to the garage.* 我真的希望他能帮我修修车, 因为我没钱把车送到修理厂去。| **I'm hoping to do sth** *Oh what a shame! We were hoping to see you today.* 噢, 真可惜! 我们本来以为今天能见到你的。**6 let's hope (that)** used to tell someone that you hope something will happen or will not happen 但愿…: *Let's just hope someone finds her bag and hands it in.* 但愿有人捡到她的手提包并把它交回来。**7 I should hope so (too)** *BrE* used to say that you feel very strongly that something should happen【英】我(也)希望如此!: *"Well, they should get their money back." "I should hope so too, after being treated like that."* "啊, 他们该把钱要回来。" "要是我受到如此对待, 我也会这么想。" **8 I hope to God (that)** used to say that you hope very much that something will happen or will not happen, because otherwise there will be serious problems 上帝啊! 但愿…〔表示非常希望某事发生或不发生, 否则就会有很大的麻烦〕: *I hope to God I haven't left the car window open.* 上帝啊! 但愿我没有忘了关车窗。

hope² *n* [U]

1 ▶FEELING 感觉◀ a feeling of wanting something to happen, and a belief that it is likely to happen 希望, 期望, 盼望: [+for] *The people are full of hope for the future.* 人们对未来充满了希望。| **give/offer hope to sb** (=make it possible for people to have hope) 给某人以希望 *This new treatment may offer hope to thousands of cancer patients.* 这种新的治疗方法可能会给成千上万的癌症患者带来希望。| **lose hope/give up hope** (=stop hoping) 失去/放弃希望 *Michael's parents had almost given up hope of ever seeing him again.* 迈克尔的父母几乎已经不指望能再见到他了。| **in the hope that** (=because you hope that something will happen) 对…怀有希望 *He showed me a picture of the missing girl in the hope that I might recognize her.* 他给我看了一张失踪女孩的照片, 希望我能认出她。| **glimmer/ray of hope** (=something that gives you a little hope) 一线希望 *The union's offer to negotiate offered a ray of hope.* 工会提出谈判, 这带来了一线希望。| **live in hope** (=keep hoping for something) 抱有希望 *We haven't had any success yet, but we live in hope.* 我们尚未取得成功, 但我们仍抱着希望。| **not hold out any hope** (=not give someone any reason to hope for something) 不抱希望 *I'm afraid the doctors didn't hold out much hope.* 恐怕医生们已经不抱多少希望了。

2 ▶STH YOU HOPE FOR 希望发生的事◀ [C] something that you hope will happen 希望发生的事: *She told me all her secret hopes and fears.* 她告诉了我她心里所有的期望和担忧。| [+of] *hopes of fame and fortune* 对名利的期望 | **have hopes of doing sth** (=hope to do it) 希望做某事 *At one time he had hopes of playing at Wimbledon.* 他曾经一度希望自己能参加温布尔登网球赛。| **my one hope is...** *My one hope was that I would see my family again.* 我的一个希望是能再次与家人团聚。| **have high hopes for** (=hope that someone or something will be successful) 对…抱有很高期望 *the high hopes parents have for their children* 父母对子女的厚望 | **hopes are fading** (=people are beginning to lose hope) 希望正在破灭 *The search for survivors continues, but hopes are fading fast.* 寻找生还者的工作仍在继续, 但希望越来越渺茫。| **pin your hopes on** (=hope that something will happen because all your plans depend on it) 将希望寄托于 *I can't pin my hopes on getting this job.* 我不指望能获得这份工作。—see 见 WISH¹ (USAGE)

3 raise/dash sb's hopes to make someone's hopes seem more likely, or make them seem impossible 使某人抱有希望/使某人的希望破灭: *Sally's hopes of meeting someone nice were dashed again.* 萨莉遇上好人的希望又一次破灭了。

4 get/build sb's hopes up to make someone's hopes seem more likely, or to feel that your hopes are more likely to happen 使某人抱有希望: *I don't want to get your hopes up, but I know you're a favorite for the part.* 我不想让你存有过高的期望, 但我知道你是最有希望担任这一角色的人选。

5 ▶CHANCE 机会◀ [C,U] a chance of succeeding or of something good happening 机会, 可能性: [+of] *There was no hope of escape.* 没有逃脱的希望了。| **hope that** *There is some hope that we'll find a solution to our problems.* 我们还有一点希望能找到解决问题的方法。| **not a hope!** *spoken* (=used to mean that there is no chance of something happening)【口】没希望! 不可能! *"Do you think they'll refund our money?" "Not a hope!"* "你认为他们会把钱退给我们吗?" "不可能!" | **not a hope in hell** *spoken* (=not even the smallest chance of success)【口】什么希望也没有! *They don't have a hope in hell of winning this game.* 他们压根儿没有希望打赢这场比赛。| **some hope/what a hope!** *BrE spoken humorous* (=used to say that there is no chance that something will happen)【英口, 幽默】没希望! 妄想! *"Your dad might lend you the car." "Some hope!"* "你父亲也许会把车借给你。" "不可能!"

6 there's hope for you yet! *spoken* used to say that someone could still be successful, often in a joking way【口】还有希望!

7 be sb's last/only hope to be someone's last or only chance of getting the result they want 是某人最后/唯一的希望: *For many people who couldn't find work, the colonies were the last hope.* 对很多找不到工作的人来说, 去殖民地是他们最后的希望。

8 be beyond hope if a situation is beyond hope it is so bad

H

that there is no chance of any improvement 没有好转的希望，无可救药：[+of] *Some of these patients are beyond hope of recovery.* 有些病人已经没有痊愈的希望了。

hope chest /ˈ· ·/ *n* [C] *AmE* things needed for starting a home that young women used to collect before getting married【美】〔女子结婚前准备的〕嫁妆；BOTTOM DRAWER *BrE*【英】

hope·ful[1] /ˈhopfəl; ˈhəʊpfəl/ *adj* **1** believing that what you hope for is likely to happen 抱有希望的，抱乐观态度的：[+about] *Everyone's feeling pretty hopeful about the future.* 人人都对未来充满希望。| **hopeful that** *We're hopeful that the team will be fit for next Saturday's game.* 我们有信心球队能以良好的状态参加下星期六的比赛。| **be hopeful of doing sth** *BrE*【英】 *The police are hopeful of finding more clues to the murder.* 警方有望找到更多有关这宗谋杀案的线索。**2** *informal* making you feel that what you hope for is likely to happen【非正式】给人以希望的：*Things might get better, but it doesn't look very hopeful right now.* 事情可能会好转，但目前看来希望不大。—**hopefulness** *n* [U]

hopeful[2] *n* [C] someone who is hoping to be successful, especially in acting, music etc〔尤指演艺、音乐界等〕希望获得成功的人：**young hopefuls** *hundreds of young hopefuls waiting to be auditioned* 几百个等候试演的希望成名的年轻人

S1 **hope·ful·ly** /ˈhopfəlɪ; ˈhəʊpfəli/ *adv* **1** [sentence adverb 句子副词] used when you are saying what you hope will happen 如果顺利的话，可望…：*Hopefully we can solve the problem.* 如果顺利的话，我们可望解决这个问题。**2** in a way that shows that you are hopeful 怀有希望地，充满希望地：*"Will there be any food left over?" he asked hopefully.* 他满怀希望地问道："会有剩下的食物吗？"

S3 **hope·less** /ˈhoplɪs; ˈhəʊpləs/ *adj* **1** a hopeless situation is so bad that there is no chance of success or improvement 没有希望（好转）的：**be in a hopeless mess/state/condition** *The economy is in a hopeless mess.* 经济已经无可救药了。**2** if something that you try to do is hopeless, there is no possibility of it being successful 没有成功可能的，无望的：**it is hopeless** *We tried to stop the flames from spreading, but we knew it was hopeless.* 我们试图阻止火势蔓延，但知道这是不可能的。| *a hopeless task* 不可能成功的任务 **3** *informal* very bad at doing something【非正式】糟透的，不行的，无能的：*a hopeless cook* 糟糕的厨师 | **be hopeless (at doing sth)** *I've always been hopeless at spelling.* 我的拼写一向很糟糕。| *Oh, Dan you forgot the potatoes – you're hopeless.* 哎呀，丹，你把马铃薯忘了。你真无可救药。**4** feeling no hope 绝望的：*hopeless looks on the faces of the refugees* 难民脸上的绝望表情 **5 hopeless case** *often humorous* someone who cannot be helped【常幽默】无药可救的人：*He had power to cure even hopeless cases.* 他甚至能治愈没有希望的病人。—**hopelessness** *n* [U]

hope·less·ly /ˈhoplɪslɪ; ˈhəʊpləsli/ *adv* **1** used when emphasizing how bad a situation is, and saying that it will not get better 没有希望地，无望地；完全地：*We found ourselves hopelessly outnumbered by the enemy.* 我们发现敌人的人数已经远远超过了我们。**2 be hopelessly in love** to have very strong feelings of love for someone 爱得不可自拔 **3** feeling that you have no hope 绝望地：*staring hopelessly into space* 两眼绝望地盯着空中

Hop·kins /ˈhɑpkɪnz; ˈhɒpkɪnz/ **, Ger·ard Man·ley** /ˈdʒɛrard ˈmænlɪ; ˈdʒerɑːəd ˈmænli/ (1844-89) a British poet who was also a Catholic priest, and whose poems are mostly about religious ideas and the beauty of nature 霍普金斯〔(1844-1889)，英国诗人，天主教神父。他的诗歌以表达宗教思想和赞颂自然之美为主〕

Hop o' My Thumb /ˌ· · · ˈ·/ also 又作 **Little Thumb** a French FAIRY TALE (=a children's story in which magical things happen). Hop o'My Thumb is the youngest of seven children, and he protects his brothers and sisters after their parents leave them in the forest because they have no money. He steals some magic boots from an OGRE, and uses them to make money which he gives to his parents.《小拇指》〔法国一童话故事。小拇指是七个孩子中最小的一个。父母因为没钱把他们遗弃在森林里，他担当起了保护哥哥姐姐的责任。他偷了吃人妖魔的魔靴，把用魔靴换来的钱交给父母〕

hopped-up /ˌ·ˈ·◂/ *adj AmE slang*【美俚】**1** happy and excited, especially because of the effects of drugs〔尤指因吸毒而〕兴奋的，亢奋的 **2** a hopped-up car, engine etc has been made much more powerful〔汽车、引擎等〕功率增大了的，马力更大的：*a hopped-up Mustang* 一辆功率增大了的野马汽车

hop·per /ˈhɑpə; ˈhɒpə/ *n* [C] a large FUNNEL[1] (1) 料斗，漏斗

Hopper, Edward (1882-1967) a US ARTIST who painted REALISTIC paintings of everyday life. His work influenced the development of POP ART. 霍珀〔(1882-1967)，美国画家。他创作有反映日常生活的现实主义作品，对大众艺术的发展产生了影响〕

hop·scotch /ˈhɑpˌskatʃ; ˈhɒpskɒtʃ/ *n* [U] a children's game using squares marked on the ground in which each child has to jump from one square to another 跳房子〔儿童游戏〕

Hor·ace /ˈhɑrɪs; ˈhɒrəs/ (65-8 BC) a Roman poet and writer of SATIRE (=literature making fun of stupid or evil people), whose work greatly influenced English poetry. His full Latin name was Quintus Horatius Flaccus. 贺拉斯〔(公元前65-前8)，罗马诗人、讽刺作家。其作品对英语诗歌产生了重要影响。他的拉丁语全名是昆图斯·贺拉斯·弗拉库斯〕

horde /hord; hɔːd/ *n* [C] a large crowd moving in a noisy uncontrolled way〔吵吵嚷嚷移动着的〕一大群：[+of] *hordes of people milling around the station* 在车站转来转去的人群

ho·ri·zon /həˈraɪzn̩; həˈraɪzən/ *n* **1 the horizon** the line far away where the land or sea seems to meet the sky 地平线：*We could see a ship on the horizon.* 我们能看见一艘船出现在地平线上。**2 horizons** [plural] the limit of your ideas, knowledge, experience〔思想、知识、经验的〕范围，界限；眼界：*narrow political horizons* 狭隘的政治见解 | **broaden/expand sb's horizons** *a course of study that will broaden your horizons* 一个能开阔眼界的课程 **3 be on the horizon** to seem likely to happen in the future 将要发生：*Business is good now, but there are a few problems on the horizon.* 目前生意很好，但有些问题已初露端倪了。

hor·i·zon·tal[1] /ˌhɑrəˈzɑntl; ˌhɒrəˈzɒntl◂/ *adj* flat and level 水平的：*a horizontal surface* 水平面 —**horizontally** *adv* —opposite 反义词 VERTICAL[1] —compare 比较 DIAGONAL —see picture at 参见 VERTICAL[1] 图

horizontal[2] *n* **1** [C] a horizontal line or surface 水平线；水平面 **2 the horizontal** a horizontal position 水平位置

hor·mone /ˈhɔrmon; ˈhɔːməʊn/ *n* [C] a chemical substance produced by your body that influences your body's growth, development and condition 激素，荷尔蒙 —**hormonal** /hɔrˈmonl; hɔːˈməʊnəl/ *adj*

hormone re·place·ment ther·a·py /ˌ· · ˈ· · · ˈ· · ·/ *n* [U] a treatment for women during or after the MENOPAUSE, that adds hormones to the body〔妇女更年期的〕激素[荷尔蒙]替代疗法

horn[1] /hɔrn; hɔːn/ *n*

1 ▶OF AN ANIMAL 动物的◀ [C] one of the pair of hard pointed parts that grow on the heads of cows, goats, and other animals〔牛、羊等头上的〕角

2 ▶SUBSTANCE 物质◀ [U] **a)** the substance that animals' horns are made of 角质：*a knife with a horn handle* 一把有角质柄的刀 **b)** [C] a part of an animal's head that stands out like a horn, for example on a SNAIL〔蜗牛等头上的〕触角

3 ▶ON A CAR 汽车上◀ [C] the thing in a vehicle that is used to make a loud sound as a signal or warning 喇叭：**blow/sound your horn** (=make a noise with your horn) 鸣喇叭，按喇叭 —see picture on page A2 参见 A2 页图

4 ▶MUSICAL INSTRUMENT 乐器◀ [C] **a)** one of several musical instruments that consist of a long metal tube, wide at one end, that you play by blowing〔乐器中的〕号 **b)** a musical instrument made from an animal's horn 号角 —see also 另见 ENGLISH HORN, FRENCH HORN, POST HORN

5 drinking horn/powder horn etc a container in the shape of an animal's horn, used in the past for drinking from, carrying GUNPOWDER etc 角制[形]酒杯/火药盒

6 draw/pull in your horns to reduce the amount of money you spend 减少开支

7 be on the horns of a dilemma to be in a situation in which you have to choose between two unpleasant or difficult situations 进退维谷，左右为难 —see also 另见 **blow your own trumpet/horn** (BLOW[1] (21))，**take the bull by the horns** (BULL[1] (3))，**lock horns with sb (over sth)** (LOCK[1] (6))

horn[2] *v AmE*【美】

horn in *phr v* [I] to interrupt or try to take part in something when you are not wanted 强行参加，闯入，侵入：[+on] *He horned in on my date.* 我跟别人约会时他硬插进来。

Horn, the —see 见 CAPE HORN

horn·bill /ˈhɔrnˌbɪl; ˈhɔːnˌbɪl/ *n* [C] a tropical bird with a very large beak 犀鸟

Horn·blow·er /ˈhɔrnˌbloə; ˈhɔːnbləʊə/**, Ho·ra·ti·o** /həˈreʃɪo; həˈreɪʃiəʊ/ the chief character in the *Hornblower* stories by C.S. Forester. He is an officer in the British navy. 霍恩布洛尔〔C.S.福里斯特创作的霍恩布洛尔系列故事中的主人公。他是一名英国海军军官〕

horned /hɔrnd; hɔːnd/ *adj* having horns or something that looks like horns 有角的; 有角状物的: *horned cattle* 有角的牛

hor·net /ˈhɔrnɪt; ˈhɔːnɪ̍t/ *n* [C] **1** a large black and yellow insect that can sting 大黄蜂 **2 stir up a hornet's nest** to cause a lot of trouble and quarrelling without intending to 捅马蜂窝, 惹大麻烦

Horn of Af·ri·ca, the /ˌ· · ˈ· · ·/ the part of East Africa that includes Somalia and some of Ethiopia 非洲之角〔指东非一部分, 包括索马里和埃塞俄比亚部分地区〕

horn of plen·ty /ˌ· · ˈ· ·/ *n* [C] a CORNUCOPIA (1)〔象征丰饶的〕角饰, 角状盛器; 丰饶角

horn·pipe /ˈhɔrnˌpaɪp; ˈhɔːnpaɪp/ *n* [C] a traditional dance performed by SAILORS or the music for this dance〔水手跳的〕角笛舞(曲)

horn-rimmed /ˌ· ˈ·◂/ *adj* horn-rimmed SPECTACLES have frames made of plastic that is made to look like horn〔眼镜〕仿角质框的

horn·y /ˈhɔrnɪ; ˈhɔːni/ *adj* **1** made of a hard substance, such as horn 角制的, 角质的, 硬质的 **2** skin that is horny is hard and rough〔皮肤〕粗硬的 **3** *informal* sexually excited【非正式】性兴奋的, 欲火中烧的: *feeling horny* 感到欲火中烧 **4** *informal* sexually attractive【非正式】性感的: *I think he's horny.* 我觉得他很性感。

hor·o·scope /ˈhɔrəˌskop; ˈhɒrəskəʊp/ *n* [C] a description of your character and the things that will happen to you, based on the position of the stars or PLANETS at the time of your birth 占星术

Hor·o·witz /ˈhɑrəvɪts; ˈhɒrəvɪts/**, Vlad·i·mir** /ˈvlædɪmɪə; ˈvlædʒ̍mɪə/ (1904-89) a US PIANIST, born in Russia, who played CLASSICAL music 霍洛维茨〔(1904-1989), 美国古典音乐钢琴演奏家, 生于俄国〕

hor·ren·dous /hɔˈrɛndəs; hɒˈrendəs/ *adj* **1** frightening and terrible 可怕的, 骇人的: *a horrendous experience* 可怕的经历 **2** *spoken* extremely unreasonable or unpleasant【口】极不像话的, 极讨厌的: *horrendous prices* 吓人的价格 **—horrendously** *adv*

2 **hor·ri·ble** /ˈhɔrəbḷ; ˈhɒrɪ̍bəl/ *adj* **1** very unpleasant and often frightening or upsetting 可怕的, 吓人的, 令人恐惧的: *a horrible murder* 恐怖的谋杀案 **2** *spoken* very bad or unpleasant【口】糟糕的, 令人不快的, 极讨厌的: *horrible weather* 糟糕的天气 | *I have a horrible feeling we're going to miss the plane.* 我有一个不祥的预感, 我们会赶不上这班飞机。**3** *spoken* rude and unfriendly【口】粗鲁的, 不友好的: *What a horrible man.* 多么粗鲁的男人! **—horribly** *adv*: *Her face was horribly scarred.* 她的脸上有难看的疤。

hor·rid /ˈhɔrɪd; ˈhɒrɪ̍d/ *adj informal especially BrE*【非正式, 尤英】**1** very unpleasant 令人非常不快的, 令人讨厌的: *a horrid smell* 极难闻的气味 **2** behaving in a nasty unkind way 极不友好的: *Don't be so horrid!* 别那么凶! **—horridly** *adv*

hor·rif·ic /hɔˈrɪfɪk; hɒˈrɪfɪk/ *adj* extremely bad, especially in a way that is frightening or upsetting 令人恐惧的, 可怕的, 恐怖的: *horrific accidents* 可怕的事故 **—horrifically** /-klɪ; -kli/ *adv*

hor·ri·fy /ˈhɔrəˌfaɪ; ˈhɒrɪ̍faɪ/ *v* [T] to make someone feel very shocked and upset or afraid 使震惊, 使害怕, 使毛骨悚然: **horrified to see/hear etc** *We were horrified to see children living in such terrible conditions.* 看到孩子们生活在如此恶劣的环境中, 我们都感到震惊。**—horrifying** *adj*: *horrifying news* 可怕的消息 **—horrifyingly** *adv*

hor·ror /ˈhɔrə; ˈhɒrə/ *n* **1** [U] a strong feeling of shock and fear 惊恐; 震惊: *The crowd gasped in horror as Senna's car crashed.* 森那的车撞毁时, 人群吓得屏住了呼吸。| **to sb's horror** (=making someone shocked or afraid) 使某人震惊地, 使某人恐惧地 *To her horror, Rachel realized her savings account had been cleaned out.* 雷切尔震惊地发现自己的存款已被提空。**2** [C] something that is very terrible, shocking, or frightening 令人惊恐的事: *the horrors of modern warfare* 现代战争的恐怖 **3 have a horror of** to be very frightened of something or dislike it very much 非常惧怕; 憎恶, 讨厌: *He has a horror of snakes.* 他非常怕蛇。**4 give sb the horrors** to make someone feel unreasonably frightened or nervous 令某人感到非常恐惧〔紧张〕**5 little horror** *especially BrE* a young child who behaves badly【尤英】淘气鬼, 讨厌鬼〔指小孩子〕**6** [C] something that is extremely ugly 极丑陋的东西 3

horror film /ˈ· · ˌ·/ *BrE*【英】, **horror mov·ie** /ˈ· · ˌ· ·/ *AmE*【美】*—n* [C] a film in which strange and frightening things happen, for example Dracula or Frankenstein 恐怖(影)片

horror sto·ry /ˈ· · ˌ· ·/ *n* [C] **1** *informal* a report about bad experiences, bad conditions etc【非正式】对可怕事件的报道: *horror stories about patients being given the wrong drugs* 有关给病人吃错药的可怕报道 **2** a story in which strange and frightening things happen 恐怖故事

horror-struck /ˈ· · ·/ also 又作 **horror-strick·en** /ˈ· · ˌ· ·/ *adj* suddenly very shocked and frightened 大吃一惊的; 惊恐万状的: *He stared horror-struck as the car moved towards the edge of the cliff.* 他眼睁睁看着汽车开向悬崖边, 吓得目瞪口呆。

hors de com·bat /ˌɔr də ˈkɑmbɑ; ˌɔː də ˈkɒmbɑː/ *adj French formal* unable to fight because you are wounded【法, 正式】〔因受伤而〕丧失战斗能力的

hors d'oeu·vre /ˌɔr ˈdɝv; ˌɔː ˈdɜːv/ *n plural* **hors d'oeuvres** /-ˈdɝvz; -ˈdɜːvz/ [C] food that is served in small amounts before the main part of the meal〔餐前的〕开胃小吃

horse[1] /hɔrs; hɔːs/ *n* **1** [C] a large strong animal that people ride on and use for pulling heavy things 马 **2 the horses** *informal* horse races【非正式】赛马 **3 straight from the horse's mouth** if you hear something straight from the horse's mouth,

horse 马

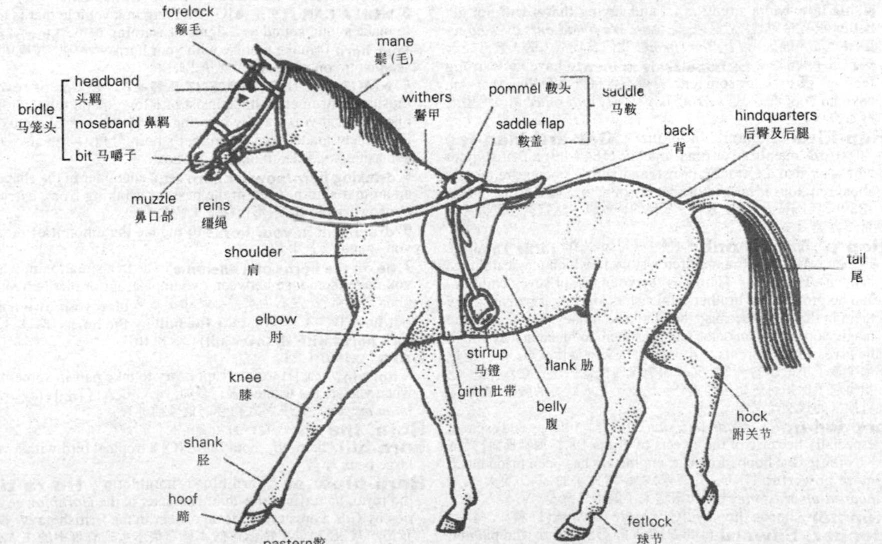

you are told it by someone who has direct knowledge of it〔消息〕第一手的, 直接得来的 **4** [C] a piece of sports equipment in a GYMNASIUM used for jumping over; VAULTING HORSE 跳马〔体操器械〕**5 horse sense** *old-fashioned* sensible judgement gained from experience; COMMON SENSE【过时】常识 **6** the process of trying to reach an agreement by offering each other things in exchange for other things 讨价还价 **7** [U] *old-fashioned slang* HEROIN【过时, 俚】海洛因 —see also 另见 **dark horse** (DARK[1] (9)), **never/don't look a gift horse in the mouth** (GIFT (6)), **be flogging a dead horse** (FLOG (3)), **hold your horses!** (HOLD[1] (29)), **put the cart before the horse** (CART[1] (4)), STALKING HORSE, WHITE HORSES

horse[2] *v*

horse around/about *phr v* [I] *informal* to play roughly【非正式】胡闹, 哄闹: *Stop horsing around, you'll break something!* 别胡闹了, 你会打破东西的!

horse·back /ˈhɔrsˌbæk; ˈhɔːsbæk/ *n* **on horseback** riding a horse 骑着马 —**horseback** *adj*

horse·box /ˈhɔrsˌbɑks; ˈhɔːsbɒks/ *n* [C] *BrE* a large vehicle for carrying horses, often pulled by another vehicle【英】运马拖车, 运马棚车; HORSE TRAILER *AmE*【美】

horse chest·nut /ˌ· ˈ· ·/ *n* [C] **1** a large tree which produces shiney brown nuts and has white and pink flowers 七叶树 **2** a nut from this tree 七叶树的坚果

horse-drawn /ˈ· ·/ *adj* [only before noun 仅用于名词前] pulled by a horse 用马拉的

horse·fly /ˈhɔrsˌflaɪ; ˈhɔːsflaɪ/ *n* [C] a large fly that bites horses and cattle〔叮咬牛马的〕虻, 马蝇

Horse Guards, the /ˈ· ·, ·/ —see 见 the ROYAL HORSE GUARDS

Horse Guards Pa·rade /ˌ· · · ˈ·/ a wide square in central London used for public ceremonies by the Blues and Royals and other British army REGIMENTS〔英国〕皇家骑兵卫队阅兵场〔伦敦市中心一宽阔广场, 是皇家蓝军骑兵团等陆军军团举行阅兵仪式的地方〕

horse·hair /ˈhɔrsˌhɛr; ˈhɔːsheə/ *n* [U] the hair from a horse's MANE and tail, sometimes used to fill the inside of furniture 马毛〔马鬃或马尾的毛〕

horse·man /ˈhɔrsmən; ˈhɔːsmən/ *n plural* **horsemen** /-mən; -mən/ [C] someone who rides horses 骑马者, 骑手

horse·man·ship /ˈhɔrsmənˌʃɪp; ˈhɔːsmənʃɪp/ *n* [U] the practice or skill of riding horses 骑术, 马术

Horse of the Year Show, the /ˌ· · · · ˈ· , ·/ a SHOW JUMPING competition held every year in London〔伦敦〕年度马术表演

horse·play /ˈhɔrsˌple; ˈhɔːspleɪ/ *n* [U] *old-fashioned* rough, noisy behaviour in which older children play by pushing or hitting each other for fun【过时】〔青少年之间的〕嬉戏, 打闹

horse·pow·er /ˈhɔrsˌpauə; ˈhɔːsˌpauə/ written abbreviation 缩写为 **hp** *n* [U] a unit for measuring the power of an engine 马力〔引擎的功率单位〕

horse rac·ing /ˈ· ,· ·/ *n* [U] a sport in which horses race against each other 赛马

horse·rad·ish /ˈhɔrsˌrædɪʃ; ˈhɔːsˌrædɪʃ/ *n* [C,U] a plant whose root has a very strong hot taste and is eaten with meat 辣根

horse·rid·ing /ˈ· · ·/ *n* [U] the activity of riding horses 骑马 —**horse-riding** *adj*

horse·shit /ˈhɔrsˌʃɪt; ˈhɔːsˌʃɪt/ *AmE taboo* nonsense; BULLSHIT【美讳】屁话, 废话: *That's total horseshit!* 那完全是废话!

horse·shoe /ˈhɔrsˌʃu; ˈhɔːʃ-ʃuː/ *n* [C] **1** a curved piece of iron that is nailed on to the bottom of a horse's foot 马蹄铁, 马掌 **2** a sign of good luck in the shape of a horseshoe 马掌形吉祥物〔符号〕

horse·shoes /ˈhɔrsˌʃuz; ˈhɔːʃ-ʃuːz/ *n* [U] an American outdoor game in which horseshoes are thrown at a post〔美国的〕掷马蹄铁套柱游戏

horse show /ˈ· ·/ *n* [C] a sports event in which people riding horses compete to show their skill in riding 马术比赛; 马匹展览会

horse trail·er /ˈ· ,· ·/ *n* [C] *AmE* a large vehicle for carrying horses, pulled by another vehicle【美】运马拖车, 运马棚车; HORSEBOX *BrE*【英】

horse·whip /ˈhɔrsˌhwɪp; ˈhɔːsˌwɪp/ *v* [T] to beat someone hard with a whip 鞭打〔某人〕

horse·wom·an /ˈhɔrsˌwumən; ˈhɔːsˌwumən/ *n* [C] *plural* **horsewomen** /-ˌwɪmɪn; -ˌwɪmɪn/ a woman who rides horses 女骑手

hors·ey, horsy /ˈhɔrsɪ; ˈhɔːsi/ *adj* **1** very interested in horses and fond of riding horses 爱马的, 爱骑马的 **2 horsey face/appearance/smell etc** a face etc that is like a horse's 像马的脸/外表/气味等

hor·ti·cul·ture /ˈhɔrtɪˌkʌltʃə; ˈhɔːtɪ̣ˌkʌltʃə/ *n* [U] the practice or science of growing flowers, fruit and vegetables 园艺(学) —**horticultural** /ˌhɔrtɪˈkʌltʃərəl; ˌhɔːtɪ̣ˈkʌltʃərəl◂/ *adj* —**horticulturalist** *n* [C] —compare 比较 AGRICULTURE

ho·san·na /hoˈzænə; həʊˈzænə/ *n* [C] *biblical* a shout of praise to God【圣经】和散拿〔赞美上帝用语〕—**hosanna** *interjection*

hose[1] /hoz; həʊz/ *n* [C,U] **1** *BrE* a long rubber or plastic tube which can be moved and bent to put water onto fires, gardens etc【英】软管, 胶管, 水龙带; HOSEPIPE *BrE*【英】**2** a word meaning TIGHTS, STOCKINGS (1), or socks, used especially in shops〔尤用于商店〕连裤袜; 长筒袜; 短筒袜 **3** tight-fitting trousers worn by men in past times〔旧时的〕男式紧身裤

hose[2] *v* [T] **1** to cover something with water using a hose 用软管浇水 **2** *AmE slang* to cheat or deceive someone【美俚】欺骗, 哄骗

hose sth/sb ↔ **down** *phr v* [T] to wash something or someone using a hose 用软管冲洗: *Would you hose down the car for me?* 你帮我冲洗一下汽车好吗?

hose·pipe /ˈhozˌpaɪp; ˈhəʊzpaɪp/ *n* [C] *BrE* a long hose【英】长软管, 长胶管, 水龙带

ho·sier /ˈhoʒə; ˈhəʊziə/ *n* [C] *old-fashioned* someone who sells socks and men's underwear【过时】出售袜子和男人内衣裤的零售商

ho·sier·y /ˈhoʒərɪ; ˈhəʊzjəri/ *n* [U] a general word for TIGHTS, STOCKINGS (1), or socks, used in shops and in the clothing industry 袜类〔用于商店及成衣业〕

hos·pice /ˈhɑspɪs; ˈhɒspɪ̣s/ *n* [C] **1** a special hospital where people who are dying are looked after〔晚期病人的〕安养院, 善终医院 **2** *old use* a house for people who are travelling to stay and rest in【旧】旅客招待所, 旅店

hos·pi·ta·ble /ˈhɑspɪtəbl; ˈhɒspɪtəbəl/ *adj* friendly, welcoming, and generous to visitors 好客的, 殷勤的, 热情友好的: *The local people were very kind and hospitable.* 当地人十分友善、好客。—**hospitably** *adv*

hos·pi·tal /ˈhɑspɪtl̩; ˈhɒspɪtl/ *n* [C,U] a large building where sick or injured people are looked after and receive medical treatment 医院: **in/to/from hospital** *BrE*【英】*He's in hospital, recovering from an operation.* 他手术后正在医院里康复。| **in/to/from the hospital** *AmE*【美】*After the accident Jane was rushed to the hospital.* 事故发生后简被紧急送往医院。| **be admitted to (the) hospital** (=be brought into a hospital for treatment) 被收进医院 *A man has been admitted to hospital with gunshot wounds.* 一个受枪伤的男人被收进了医院。| **hospital bed** (=a place in a hospital for a sick person) 病床 S2 W1

hos·pi·tal·i·ty /ˌhɑspɪˈtælətɪ; ˌhɒspɪ̣ˈtælɪ̣ti/ *n* [U] friendly behaviour towards visitors 好客, 殷勤: *Thanks for your hospitality over the past few weeks.* 感谢你们过去几星期的热情款待。—see also 另见 **corporate hospitality** (CORPORATE (4))

hos·pi·tal·ize also 又作 **-ise** *BrE*【英】/ˈhɑspɪtlˌaɪz; ˈhɒspɪtl-aɪz/ *v* [T] **be hospitalized** to be taken into a hospital for treatment 住院, 留医 —**hospitalization** /ˌhɑspɪtəlɪˈzeʃən; ˌhɒspɪtl-aɪˈzeɪʃən/ *n* [U]

host[1] /host; həʊst/ *n* [C] W3

1 ►AT A PARTY 在聚会上◄ someone at a party, meal etc who has invited the guests and who provides them with food, drink etc 东道主, 主人: *Our host brought in some more wine.* 主人又拿了一些酒进来。—see also 另见 HOSTESS (1)

2 ►ON TELEVISION 电视中◄ someone who introduces the guests on a television or radio programme; COMPÈRE 节目主持人: *a game show host* 游戏节目主持人 —see also 另见 HOSTESS (2)

3 ►COUNTRY/GOVERNMENT 国家/政府◄ a country, government or organization that provides the necessary space, equipment etc for a special event 主办者, 东道国[主]: **host country/government/city etc** *the host city for the next Olympic Games* 下届奥林匹克运动会的主办城市 | **play host (to)** (=provide the place, food etc for a special meeting or event) 主办 *Japan played host to the first World Championship Grand Prix.* 日本主办了第一届世界锦标大奖赛。

4 a (whole) host of a large number of 大量, 许多: *a host of possibilities* 许多可能性

5 ►IN CHURCH 在教堂里◄ the Host *technical* the bread that is used in the Christian ceremony of Communion【术语】〔圣餐仪式中的〕圣饼

6 ►ANIMAL/PLANT 动物/植物◄ *technical* an animal or plant on which a smaller animal or plant is living as a PARASITE【术语】寄主, 宿主〔寄生物所寄生的动物或植物〕

7 ►ARMY 军队◄ *old use* an army【旧】部队: *the approaching host* 逐渐逼近的军队

8 *old use* a man in charge of a hotel【旧】旅馆老板

host² *v* [T] **1** to provide the place and everything that is needed for an organized event 主办，作…的东道主: *Which country is going to host the next World Cup?* 哪个国家将主办下一届世界杯? **2** to be the host on a radio or television programme 做〔广播或电视〕的节目主持人: *a chat show hosted by Oprah Winfrey* 奥普拉·温弗里主持的清谈节目

hos·tage /ˈhɑstɪdʒ; ˈhɒstɪdʒ/ *n* [C] **1** someone who is kept as a prisoner by an enemy so that the other side will do what the enemy demands 人质: **hold sb hostage** (=keep someone as a hostage) 把某人扣作人质 *The group are holding three western tourists hostage.* 这伙人把三名西方游客挟持作人质。| **take sb hostage** (=seize someone and use them as a hostage) 抓走某人作人质 *the aid-worker who was taken hostage by a rebel militia* 被叛军抓去当人质的救护人员 **2 give hostages to fortune** to take a risk that may bring trouble in the future, especially by making promises〔尤指因作出许诺而〕承担风险

hos·tel /ˈhɑstl; ˈhɒstl/ *n* [C] **1** somewhere where people, especially people living away from home, can stay and eat fairly cheaply〔为外地人提供廉价食宿的〕旅舍，招待所 **2** a YOUTH HOSTEL 青年旅舍 **3** a place where people who have no homes can stay 无家可归者收容所

hos·tel·ler also 又作 **hosteler** *AmE*【美】/ˈhɑstlɚ; ˈhɒstələ/ *n* [C] someone travelling from one YOUTH HOSTEL to another 投宿青年旅舍的旅行者

hos·tel·ry /ˈhɑstlrɪ; ˈhɒstəlri/ *n* [C] **1** *old use* a hotel【旧】旅馆，旅店 **2** *BrE humorous* a PUB【英，幽默】酒馆，酒吧

host·ess /ˈhostɪs; ˈhəʊstɪ̣s/ *n* [C] **1** a woman at a party, meal etc who has invited all the guests and provides them with food, drink etc〔聚会的〕女主人 **2** a woman who introduces the guests on a television or radio show〔广播或电视节目的〕女主持人 **3** a woman who shows people to seats in a restaurant in the US〔美国饭馆里的〕女领座员；女侍应

hos·tile /ˈhɑstl; ˈhɒstaɪl/ *adj* **1** angry and deliberately unfriendly towards someone and ready to argue with them 怀有敌意的，敌对的，不友善的: *The President was given a hostile reception by a crowd of angry farmers.* 总统受到一群愤怒的农民很不友好的接待。**2** opposing a plan or idea very strongly 强烈反对的: [**+to/towards**] *Senator Lydon was openly hostile to our proposals.* 莱登参议员公开反对我们的建议。**3** belonging to an enemy 敌人的，敌方的: *hostile territory* 敌方领土 **4 hostile environment** conditions that are difficult to live in or exist in 逆境，艰苦的条件

hos·til·i·ty /hɑsˈtɪlətɪ; hɒˈstɪlɪ̣ti/ *n* **1** [U] a feeling or attitude that is extremely unfriendly 敌意，敌对态度: [**+towards/between**] *hostility towards foreigners* 对外国人的敌意 | **open hostility** (=hostility that is clearly shown) 公开的敌意 **2** [U] strong or angry opposition to a plan or idea 强烈的反对: *The reform program was greeted with hostility by conservatives.* 改革方案遭到保守派人士的强烈反对。**3 hostilities** [plural] *formal* acts of fighting【正式】战斗，战争: *a cessation of hostilities* 休战

hos·tler /ˈhɑslɚ; ˈɒslə/ *n* [C] the usual American spelling of OSTLER ostler 的一般美式拼法

hot¹ /hɑt; hɒt/ *adj* **hotter, hottest**

① HIGH TEMPERATURE 高温
② HOT TASTE 辣味
③ DIFFICULT TO DEAL WITH 棘手的
④ ANGRY 愤怒的
⑤ POPULAR 受欢迎的
⑥ FOLLOWING CLOSELY 紧随
⑦ OTHER MEANINGS 其他意思

hot 烫的

cold 冷 — hot 烫

- hot 烫的
- warm 温（热）的
- tepid/lukewarm 微温的
- cold 冷的

① HIGH TEMPERATURE 高温

1 ►WEATHER/FOOD/LIQUID ETC 天气/食物/液体等◄ having a high temperature 热的，烫的；炎热的: *It's too hot in here – shall I open a window?* 这里太热了，要开窗吗? | *a nice hot bath* 舒服的热水浴 | *How hot is the water?* 水有多热? | *the hottest summer I can remember* 我记忆中最炎热的一个夏天 | *hot countries* 炎热国家 | **red hot** (=used to describe an object or surface that is very hot)〔物体或表面〕炽热的，赤热的 | **white hot** (=used to describe metal that is extremely hot)〔金属〕白热的 | **boiling/broiling/scorching/baking/roasting hot** (=used to describe weather that is extremely hot)〔天气〕炎热的，火热的 *a scorching hot day in August* 8月里炙热的一天 | **boiling/scalding hot** (=used to describe liquid that is extremely hot)〔液体〕滚烫的 | **piping hot** (=used to describe food or water that is nice and hot)〔食物、水〕热腾腾的；滚烫的 *Pour the sauce over the pasta and serve piping hot.* 将酱汁浇在意大利面条上，趁热上桌。| **burning hot** (=used to describe the sun or a surface when it is extremely hot)〔太阳或表面〕炙热的，灼热的 *the burning hot sands of the desert* 沙漠中炙热的沙子 | **stifling/sweltering hot** *informal* (=used to describe weather or places that are uncomfortably hot)【非正式】〔天气或地方〕闷热的，热得令人发昏的 | **be hot as hell** *informal* (=used to describe a place that is extremely hot)【非正式】〔地方〕热死人的

2 ►FEELING HOT 感觉热◄ [not before noun 不用于名词前] feeling hot in a way that is uncomfortable〔感觉〕热的，热乎乎的: *I was hot and tired at the end of the day.* 一天结束时我觉得又热又累。—see 见 COLD¹ (USAGE)

② HOT TASTE 辣味

3 food that tastes hot contains pepper etc and has a burning taste〔食物〕辣的，辛辣的

③ DIFFICULT TO DEAL WITH 棘手的

4 hot issue/topic etc a subject that people disagree strongly about 有争议的热门话题: *Abortion is a hot issue on both sides of the Atlantic.* 人工流产在大西洋两岸都是一个具争议性的热门话题。

5 be too hot to handle if a problem or situation is too hot to handle it is impossible to deal with because it is causing too much trouble and anger〔问题〕太棘手: *The Watergate investigation eventually became too hot to handle.* 对水门事件的调查最终变得不可收拾。

6 be a hot potato *informal* if a subject or problem is a hot potato, it is difficult to deal with【非正式】是棘手的问题

7 ►DIFFICULT/UNPLEASANT SITUATION 困境◄ [not before noun 不用于名词前] *informal* if a situation or place becomes too hot for someone, it is because other people are angry with them【非正式】棘手的，难办的: *When things got too hot for him he sold up and left town.* 当问题变得十分难办时，他便卖掉全部家当离开了镇子。| **make it hot for** (=cause a lot of trouble for someone) 使〔某人〕难以应付；让〔某人〕日子不好过

8 get into hot water to get into a difficult situation by doing something wrong〔因做错事而〕陷入困境

④ ANGRY 愤怒的

9 hot temper someone who has a hot temper becomes angry very easily 火暴脾气，急脾气 —see also 另见 HOT-TEMPERED

10 get hot under the collar *spoken* to become angry and ready to quarrel【口】恼怒的，气冲冲的

⑤ POPULAR 受欢迎的

11 *informal* popular at a particular point in time【非正式】受欢迎的，红极一时的: *Bros was a really hot group a few years ago.* 布洛斯乐队几年前红极一时。| **hot property** (=an actor, singer etc that many theatre or film companies want) 当红明星 *Michael Jackson soon became the hottest property in show business.* 迈克尔·杰克逊很快便成了演艺界最抢手的明星。

12 be a hot ticket *AmE* to be a very popular and fashionable person whom everyone wants to see【美】成为红人: *Jodie Foster seems to be this year's hot ticket.* 朱迪·福斯特看来是今年当红的影星。

⑥ **FOLLOWING CLOSELY 紧随**
13 **in hot pursuit** following someone quickly, and closely because you want to catch them〔因想抓住某人而〕紧追其后, 穷追不舍: *The car sped away with the police in hot pursuit.* 汽车飞驰而去, 警察则在后面紧追不舍。
14 **be hot on sb's trail/track** to be close to and likely to catch someone you have been chasing 紧紧追踪某人, 快要逮住某人
15 **be hot on sb's heels** to be very close behind someone 紧随某人之后: *Jake came sprinting towards me with Mrs Bass's dog hot on his heels.* 杰克向我冲过来, 后面紧跟着巴斯太太的狗。
16 **come hot on the heels of** to happen very soon after another event 紧接…之后发生

⑦ **OTHER SENSES 其他意思**
17 **►GOOD AT STH 擅长于◄** *informal* very good at doing something【非正式】十分擅长于某事: *a hot new guitar player* 优秀的新吉他手
18 **be hot stuff** *spoken*【口】**a)** to be very good at a particular activity 是个能手: *You should see him on the tennis court – he's really hot stuff.* 你真该看看他在网球场上的表现, 他可真是名好手。**b)** to be sexually attractive 性感
19 **not so hot** *spoken* not very good【口】并不怎么样, 不很好的: *"How are you feeling?" "Not so hot; I'm really tired."* "你感觉怎么样?" "不太好, 我觉得很累。"
20 **be in the hot seat** to have the job of making difficult and sometimes unpleasant decisions 处于须解决难题、作出棘手决策的职位上
21 **be hot on sth** *informal*【非正式】**a)** to know a lot about something 通晓[熟知]某事: *I'm not very hot on European history.* 我对欧洲历史不大熟悉。**b)** to be very strict about something 对某事要求很严格: *They're really hot on punctuality here.* 他们这里对守时要求十分严格。
22 **be hot on sb** to be sexually attracted to someone 对某人表示出性欲, 迷恋某人
23 **be hot at sth** *informal* to be very good at doing something【非正式】做某事拿手, 擅长于某事: *I'm not too hot at basketball.* 我打篮球不太在行。
24 **►COMPETITION 比赛◄** competition that is hot is between people or companies that are trying very hard to win or succeed 激烈的, 紧张的: *Competition for the best jobs is getting hotter all the time.* 对好工作的竞争正日趋激烈。
25 **►NEWS 消息◄** hot news is about very recent events and therefore interesting or exciting 最近的; 炙手可热的: *a hot news item* 一条最新消息
26 **be hot off the press** if a newspaper, report etc is hot off the press, it has only just been printed 刚印好; 刚见报
27 **hot favourite** *BrE*【英】, **hot favorite** *AmE*【美】a competitor that most people expect to win a race or competition 最被看好的选手, 最热门的参赛者
28 **hot tip** a very good piece of advice about which horse is likely to win a race〔有关赌赛马的〕好建议
29 **hot air** if someone talks hot air, they make statements which sound impressive, but are really meaningless 大话, 空话: *It's all just hot air – he hasn't the money to pay for it.* 那全是空话, 他花不起这笔钱。
30 **hot spot a)** a place where there is likely to be trouble, fighting etc 可能发生动乱或战事的地区, 多事地区 **b)** an area that is popular for a particular activity or type of entertainment〔因某项活动而〕受到人们欢迎的地区, 热点
31 **go hot and cold a)** to suddenly feel very worried or frightened by something〔由于担忧或害怕而〕感到浑身一阵热一阵冷: *When I saw a police car outside, I went hot and cold all over.* 看到外边的警车, 我吓得浑身一阵热一阵冷。**b)** to experience sudden changes in the temperature of your body because you are ill〔因生病而〕感到浑身一阵热一阵冷 —see also 另见 **blow hot and cold** (BLOW[1] (15))
32 **be hot and bothered** *informal* to be so worried and confused by things going wrong that you cannot think clearly【非正式】烦躁不安的, 焦急的; 被搞糊涂的
33 **►STOLEN 偷来的◄** *slang* goods that are hot have been stolen【俚】偷来的: *He was caught trying to sell hot video recorders.* 他在企图出售偷窃来的录像机时被逮住。
34 **hot money** money that is frequently moved from one country to another in order to make a quick profit〔在各国间频繁流动以获利的〕游资; 寻求短期回报的流动资金; 热钱
35 **►MUSIC 音乐◄** having a strong exciting RHYTHM 节奏强劲的
36 **►SEXUALLY EXCITING 激起性欲的◄** a film, book etc that is hot is sexually exciting〔电影、书籍等〕情色的 —see also 另见 RED-HOT, HOTLY, HOTS

hot[2] *v* **hotted, hotting**
hot up *phr v* [I] *informal especially BrE* to become more exciting or dangerous with a lot more activity; INTENSIFY【非正式, 尤英】加剧, 变得激烈: *The election campaign is hotting up.* 竞选活动正在热烈起来。

hot-air bal·loon /ˌ· ˈ· ·ˌ·/ *n* [C] a large BALLOON filled with hot air used for carrying people up into the sky 热气球

hot·bed /ˈhɑtˌbɛd; ˈhɒtbed/ *n* **be a hotbed of** a place where a lot of a particular kind of activity, especially bad or violent activity, happens 是…的温床, 有利于〔坏事〕滋长的地方: *Bavaria was a hotbed of extremist politics in the 1920s and 1930s.* 巴伐利亚在20世纪20、30年代曾是极端主义政治的温床。

hot-blood·ed /ˌ· ˈ··◂/ *adj* having very strong emotions such as anger or love, that are difficult to control; PASSIONATE 热血沸腾的, 情感强烈的, 激昂的

hot cake /ˌ· ˈ·/ *n* [C] **be selling/going like hot cakes** *spoken* to be sold very quickly and in large amounts【口】非常抢手, 非常畅销

hot choc·o·late /ˌ· ˈ··/ *n* [C,U] a hot drink made with chocolate powder and milk or water 热巧克力奶

hotch·potch /ˈhɑtʃˌpɑtʃ; ˈhɒtʃpɒtʃ/ *especially BrE*【尤英】, usually 一般作 **hodgepodge** *AmE*【美】— *n* [singular] *informal* a number of things mixed up without any sensible order or arrangement; MISHMASH【非正式】杂乱的一大堆东西, 大杂烩

hot-cross bun /ˌ· · ˈ·/ *n* [C] a small round sweet cake, with a cross-shaped mark on top, that is eaten just before Easter〔受难节时吃的〕十字甜面包

hot dish /ˌ· ˈ·/ *n* [C,U] *AmE* hot food cooked and served in a deep covered dish【美】砂锅菜肴

hot dog[1] /ˌ· ˈ·/ *n* [C] a cooked SAUSAGE in a long round piece of bread 热狗〔用长面包夹住熟香肠〕

hot dog 热狗

hot dog[2] /ˌ· ˈ·/ *interjection AmE* used to express pleasure or surprise【美】太棒了, 好极了〔用以表示高兴或惊讶〕

hot dog[3] /ˈ· ·/ *v* [I] *AmE informal* to do a fast and exciting sport, especially skiing (SKI[2]), in a way that will attract a lot of attention and admiration【美, 非正式】〔尤指在滑雪运动中〕卖弄技巧: *skiers hot dogging down the slopes* 在斜坡上卖弄技巧的滑雪者

ho·tel /hoˈtɛl; həʊˈtel/ *n* [C] a building where people pay to stay and eat meals〔供住宿及用膳的〕饭店, 旅馆, 旅社, 酒店 

ho·tel·i·er /ˌhotəˈlɪr; həʊˈteliеɪ/ *n* [C] someone who owns or manages a hotel 旅馆老板; 旅馆经理

hot flush /ˌ· ˈ·/ *especially BrE*【尤英】, usually 一般作 **hot flash** *AmE*【美】— *n* [C] a sudden hot feeling, which women have during their MENOPAUSE〔妇女更年期时的〕潮热, 阵发性发热感, (热)潮红

hot·foot[1] /ˈhɑtˌfʊt; ˌhɒtˈfʊt◂/ *adv informal* moving fast and eagerly【非正式】火速地, 急匆匆地: *We ran hotfoot to the scene of the accident.* 我们火速赶往事故现场。

hotfoot[2] *v* **hotfoot it** *informal* to walk or run quickly【非正式】急行, 快跑

hot·head /ˈhɑtˌhɛd; ˈhɒthed/ *n* [C] someone who does things too quickly without thinking 性急的人 —**hotheaded** /ˈhɑtˈhɛdɪd; ˌhɒtˈhedɪd◂/ *adj* —**hotheadedly** *adv*

hot·house /ˈhɑtˌhaʊs; ˈhɒthaʊs/ *n* [C] **1** a heated building, usually made of glass, where flowers and delicate plants can grow 温室, 暖房 —compare 比较 GREENHOUSE **2** a place or situation where a lot of people are interested in particular ideas or activities 有利于…的地方[环境]; 温床: *Vienna was a hothouse of artistic activity.* 维也纳是艺术活动的温床。**3 hothouse atmosphere/environment etc** conditions in which strong attitudes and emotions develop among a group of people who are separated from ordinary people〔一群人的〕偏激气氛/环境等: *the hothouse atmosphere of a girls boarding school* 女子寄宿学校中的偏激气氛

hot line /ˈ· ·/ *n* [C] **1** a direct telephone line between government leaders in different countries, which is only used in serious situations〔政府首脑之间的〕直通电话, 热线: *the hot*

line between Washington and Moscow 华盛顿和莫斯科之间的热线 **2** a special telephone line for people to find out about or talk about something〔用于咨询服务或讨论的〕专线电话，热线: *Call our crime hot line today.* 今天就拨打我们的罪案举报热线电话。

hot·ly /ˈhɑtlɪ; ˈhɒtli/ *adv* **1 hotly debated/disputed/denied etc** discussed etc very angrily or with very strong feelings 受到激烈争论的/有激烈争议的/遭到强烈否认的等: *The rumor has been hotly denied.* 这个流言遭到强烈的否认。**2 hotly pursued** chased closely by someone 被紧紧追踪的: *The man ran out of the store hotly pursued by two security guards.* 那个人跑出商店，后面有两名保安人员紧追不放。

hot pants /ˈ· ·/ *n* [plural] very short tight women's shorts (SHORT[3] (2a)) 女式紧身超短裤，热裤

hot·plate /ˈhɑtˌplet; ˈhɒtpleɪt/ *n* [C] a metal surface, usually on a COOKER, that can be heated so that you can cook a pan of food on it〔电炉灶上的〕烤盘，加热板

hot·pot /ˈhɑtˌpɑt; ˈhɒtpɒt/ *n* [C,U] *BrE* a mixture of meat, potatoes and onions, cooked slowly together【英】罐焖（马铃薯）羊肉〔或其他肉类〕；火锅

hot rod /ˈ· ·/ *n* [C] *informal especially AmE* an old car that has been fitted with a more powerful engine to make it go very fast【非正式，尤美】由旧车改装成的高速汽车

hots /hɑts; hɒts/ *n* **have/get the hots for sb** *informal* to be sexually attracted to someone【非正式】对…具有强烈的情欲

hot·shot /ˈhɑtˌʃɑt; ˈhɒtʃɒt/ *n* [C] *informal* someone who is very successful and confident【非正式】艺高而自负的人；高手 —**hotshot** *adj*: *a hotshot lawyer* 一位信心十足的律师

hot spring /ˌ· ˈ·/ *n* [C] a place where hot water comes up naturally from the ground 温泉

hot-tem·pered /ˌ· ˈ··◂/ *adj* having a tendency to become angry easily 性情暴躁的，火暴脾气的

hot tub /ˌ· ˈ·/ *n* [C] a heated bath that several people can sit in〔供多人共浴的〕热水澡缸 —compare 比较 JACUZZI

hot-water bot·tle /ˌ· ˈ·· ˌ··/ *n* [C] a rubber container full of hot water used to make a bed warm 热水袋 —see picture at 参见 BOTTLE[1] 图

hot-wire /ˈ· ·/ *v* [T] *slang* to start the engine of a vehicle, by using the wires of the IGNITION system【俚】用点火装置电线短路的方法发动〔汽车〕

Hou·di·ni /huˈdinɪ; huːˈdiːni/, **Harry** (1874-1926) a US MAGICIAN (=an entertainer who performs magic tricks), who became famous for his great skill at escaping from chains, HANDCUFFS, and locked containers, even when he was under water 乌丹尼〔(1874-1926)，美国魔术师。他能从锁链、镣铐、上锁的容器中解脱出来，即使在水下也可以做到。他因具有如此非凡的本领而著名〕

hou·mous, houmus /ˈhuməs; ˈhuːməs/ *n* [U] other spellings of HUMMUS hummus（鹰嘴豆泥）的另一种拼法

hound[1] /haund; haʊnd/ *n* [C] **1** a dog used for hunting 猎狗: **ride to hounds** *BrE old-fashioned* (=go FOXHUNTING)【英，过时】去猎狐 **2** *informal* a dog【非正式】狗

hound[2] *v* [T] **1** to keep following someone and asking them questions in an annoying or threatening way; HARASS (1)（不断）骚扰，烦扰: *After the court case Lee was hounded relentlessly by the Press.* 案件庭审后，李不断受到新闻界的无情骚扰。**2 hound sb out (of)** to make things so unpleasant for someone that they are forced to leave 不断骚扰某人使之退出，逼使某人离开…

Hound of the Bas·ker·villes, The /ˌhaund əv ðə ˈbæskəˌvɪlz; ˌhaʊnd əv ðə ˈbæskəvɪlz/ (1902) a NOVEL by Sir Arthur Conan Doyle in which the DETECTIVE Sherlock Holmes tries to find out who is responsible for killing two people who seem to have been attacked by a large hunting dog, but who have really been murdered《巴斯克维尔的猎犬》〔(1902)，阿瑟·柯南道尔爵士创作的一部小说。夏洛克·福尔摩斯侦探力图查出杀害两名受害人的主谋。受害人看似被一条大猎犬攻击过，但实际上是被人杀害的〕

hour /aʊr; aʊə/ *n* [C]

1 ▶60 MINUTES 60分钟◀ a period of 60 minutes. There are 24 hours in a day 小时: *The flight to Moscow takes just over three hours.* 飞往莫斯科要花三小时多一点的时间。| *Karen is paid $10 an hour.* 卡伦的报酬是每小时10美元。| **in an hour/in an hour's time** (=an hour from now) 一小时内 *I'll be back in an hour.* 我一小时内回来。| **an hour's work/wait etc** *The system crashed and I lost three hours' work.* 系统突然瘫痪，我白干了三个小时。| **pay/charge by the hour** (=pay or charge someone according to the number of hours it takes to do something) 按小时付费/收费

2 ▶DISTANCE 距离◀ the distance you can travel in an hour 一小时行程: **be an hour from** *We're only an hour by car from New York.* 我们离纽约开车只需一小时。| **an hour's drive/walk etc** (=a distance that takes an hour to drive, walk etc) 开车/步行等一小时的路程 *It's only about an hour's drive from here, isn't it?* 从这儿开车只有一小时的路程，对吗？

3 ▶TIMES FOR BUSINESS/WORK ETC 营业/工作时间等◀ **hours** [plural] a fixed period of time in the day when a particular activity, business etc happens〔某一活动、业务的〕（固定）时间: *hours of business 9.00–5.00* 营业时间：9点－5点 | **office/opening hours** (=when an office or shop is working or open) 办公/营业时间 | **visiting hours** (=when you can visit someone in hospital)〔医院的〕探病时间 | **out of hours** *BrE* (=before or after the usual working or business hours)【英】在正常工作或营业时间之外 | **after hours** (=after the time when a business, especially a bar, is supposed to close) 办公[营业]时间之后；〔尤指酒吧〕关门后 | **lunch/dinner hour** (=the period in the middle of the day when people stop work for a meal) 午餐/晚餐时间 —see also 另见 RUSH HOUR, HAPPY HOUR

4 work long/regular etc hours if you work long, regular etc hours, the period that you work is longer than usual, always the same etc 工作时间长/固定: *the long hours worked by hospital doctors* 医院医生很长的工作时间 | **work unsocial hours** (=work in the evenings so that you cannot spend time with family or friends) 在晚间工作〔因而妨碍家庭或社交活动〕| **work all the hours that God sends** (=work all the time that you can) 利用一切可能的时间工作

5 ▶TIME OF DAY 一天里的时间◀ *often plural* a particular period or point of time during the day or night〔一天里的某个〕时刻，时间段: **the small hours** (=the period between midnight and two or three o'clock in the morning) 凌晨时分 *The celebrations went on into the small hours.* 庆祝活动一直持续到凌晨时分。| **the hours of darkness/daylight** *literary*【文】*Few people dared to venture out during the hours of darkness.* 很少有人敢在黑夜里冒险外出。| **at this hour** *spoken* (=used when you are surprised or annoyed by something happening too late at night or too early in the morning)【口】这种时候〔因某事发生在凌晨或深夜而表示惊讶或生气〕*Who can be calling at this late hour?* 谁会这么晚打电话来呢？| **unearthly/ungodly hour** *spoken* (=used when you are complaining about how early or late something is)【口】〔抱怨太早或太晚〕鬼时间/该死的时间，不适当的时间 *We had to get up at some ungodly hour to catch a plane.* 我们得一大早就起床去赶飞机。| **at all hours (of the day or night)** *spoken* (=at any time)【口】在任何时间，随时 *Our neighbours play loud music at all hours.* 我们的邻居一天到晚不停地在高声放音乐。| **till all hours** *spoken* (=until an unreasonably late time at night)【口】直至深夜 *She's up till all hours studying.* 她温习一直到深夜才睡。| **keep late/regular etc hours** (=go to bed and get up at late, regular etc times) 晚睡晚起/定时作息 —see also 另见 **waking hours/life/day etc** (WAKING)

6 ▶LONG TIME 长时间◀ a) hours [plural] *informal* a long time or a time that seems long【非正式】长时间: *We had to spend hours filling in forms.* 我们花了很长时间填表。| *I've been waiting here for hours.* 我已经在这儿等了大半天了。| **hours and hours** (=a very long time) 很长时间 *a really boring lecture – and it just went on for hours and hours* 十分枯燥，没完没了的讲课 **b) hour after hour** continuously for many hours 连续许多个小时地

7 within hours of only a few hours after doing something or after something happening〔某事发生〕几小时后: *Within hours of landing, troops had started to advance inland.* 部队登陆几小时后，就开始向内陆挺进。

8 ▶O'CLOCK 钟点◀ the time of the day when a new hour starts, for example one o'clock, two o'clock etc …点钟；钟点: **strike the hour** (=if a clock strikes the hour, it rings, to show that it is one o'clock, seven o'clock etc)〔时钟〕在整点报时 | **(every hour) on the hour** (=every hour at six o'clock, seven o'clock etc)（每小时的）整点 *There are flights to Boston every hour on the hour.* 每小时整点都有航班飞往波士顿。

9 1300/1530/1805 hours used to give the time in official or military reports and orders 13时/15时30分/18时05分〔官方或军队使用的24小时计时制〕

10 by the hour/from hour to hour if a situation is changing by the hour or from hour to hour, it is changing very quickly and very often〔变化〕快速不断地；每小时都有变化: *This financial crisis is growing more serious by the hour.* 这场金融危机正在快速加剧。

11 ▶POINT IN HISTORY OR SB'S LIFE 历史或人一生中的时刻◀ an important moment or period in history or in your life 重

要时刻[时期]: **finest hour** *This was our country's finest hour.* 这是我国最光辉的时刻。| **sb's hour of need/glory etc** (=a time when someone needs help, is very successful etc) 某人需要帮助的时刻/光荣时刻 *Don't desert me in my hour of need.* 别在我需要帮助的时候抛下我。
12 of the hour of a particular time, especially the present time 某一刻〔尤指目前〕: *one of the burning questions of the hour* 目前急需解决的问题之一 | **the hero/man of the hour** (=someone who does something very brave, is very successful etc at a particular time) 当时的英雄/成功人士 —see also 另见 **the eleventh hour** (ELEVENTH (2)), HOURLY, ZERO HOUR

hour·glass /ˈaʊr,glæs; ˈaʊəglɑːs/ *n* [C] **1** a glass container for measuring time in which sand moves slowly from the top half to the bottom in exactly one hour〔计时用的〕沙漏 **2 hourglass figure** a woman who has an hourglass figure has a narrow waist in comparison with her chest and HIPS〔女性的〕蜂腰体型

hour hand /ˈ· ,·/ *n* [C] the shorter of the two pieces on a clock or watch that show you what time it is〔钟表上的〕时针

hour·ly /ˈaʊrli; ˈaʊəli/ *adj* **1** happening or done every hour 每一小时的; 每小时一次的: *hourly news broadcasts* 每小时一次的新闻广播 **2 hourly pay/earnings/fees etc** the amount you earn or charge for every hour you work 按小时计的工资/收入/费用等 —**hourly** *adv*: *The database is updated hourly.* 数据库每一小时更新一次。

house[1] /haʊs; haʊs/ *plural* **houses** /ˈhaʊzɪz; ˈhaʊzɨz/ *n* [C]
1 ▶WHERE YOU LIVE 住处◀ a) a building that you live in, especially one that has more than one level and is intended to be used by one family 房屋, 房子; 住宅: *a four bedroom house* 一幢有四个卧室的房子 | *Why don't you all come over to our house for coffee?* 你们全都上我家去喝杯咖啡如何? | **set up house** (=start to live in a house, especially with another person)〔尤指和另外一个人一起〕开始有自己的家 | **move house** *BrE* (=leave your house and go to live in another one)【英】搬家, 迁居 —see picture on page A4 参见 A4 页图 **b)** all the people who live in a house〔住在一幢房子里的〕一家人: *He gets up at six and disturbs the whole house.* 他6点钟起床, 吵醒全家人。
2 keep house to do all the cooking, cleaning etc in a house 做家务, 料理家务
3 ▶LARGE BUILDING 大楼, 大厦◀ a) opera house/court house etc a large public building used for a particular purpose 歌剧院/法院等 **b) House** used in the names of office buildings〔地名中〕大楼, 大厦: *Longman House, Harlow, Essex* 埃塞克斯郡哈洛市朗文大厦
4 hen house/coach house/storehouse etc a building used for keeping animals, goods, equipment etc in 鸡舍/客车车库/仓库等
5 ▶COMPANY 公司◀ a company, especially one that produces books, lends money, or designs clothes 公司, 商号, 商行〔尤指出版社、银行、服装公司等〕: *America's oldest publishing house* 美国历史最悠久的出版社 | *the House of Dior*〔巴黎〕迪奥时装公司
6 in house if you work in house, you work at the offices of a company or organization, not at home 在办公室里〔工作〕
7 put/set your own house in order if someone should put or set their own house in order, they should improve the way they behave before criticizing other people〔在批评别人之前〕把自己的事管好
8 get on like a house on fire *informal* to quickly have a very friendly relationship with someone【非正式】〔和某人〕很快成为好朋友, 一见如故
9 ▶PARLIAMENT 议会◀ a group of people who make the laws of a country 议院(成员): *The President will address both houses of Congress.* 总统将向国会两院发表讲话。| **the house** (=the house of Commons or Lords in Britain, or the house of representatives in the US) 英国上、下议院; 美国众议院 —see also 另见 LOWER HOUSE, UPPER HOUSE
10 this house *formal* used to mean the people who are voting in a formal DEBATE when you are stating the proposal that is being discussed【正式】(辩论后)参加投票的议员
11 ▶IN A SCHOOL 学校里◀ a group of children of different ages at the same school which competes against other groups in the school, for example in sports competitions〔学校里为进行体育比赛等而分的〕组
12 ▶THEATRE 剧院◀ a) the part of a theatre, cinema etc where people sit 观众席: **full/packed/empty house** (=a large or small AUDIENCE) 满座/空场 *The show has been playing to packed houses since it opened.* 该演出自开演以来场场爆满。—see also 另见 HOUSE LIGHTS **b)** the people who have come to watch a performance; AUDIENCE 观众 **c)** a performance that is one of a series during the day 演出场次
13 be on the house if drinks or meals are on the house you do not have to pay for them because they are provided free by the owner of the bar, restaurant etc 由店家出钱, 免费招待
14 house wine ordinary wine that is provided by a restaurant to be drunk with meals〔餐馆里供应的〕佐餐用葡萄酒: *A glass of house red, please.* 请来一杯贵店提供的佐餐用红葡萄酒。
15 go all round the houses *BrE* to go through an unnecessarily complicated process in order to do something or answer something【英】兜圈子, 绕弯子
16 ▶ROYAL FAMILY 王室◀ an important family, especially a royal family〔尤指〕王室, 王朝, 皇族: *the House of Windsor* 温莎王室 —see also 另见 COUNCIL HOUSE, **eat sb out of house and home** (EAT (4)), OPEN HOUSE, PUBLIC HOUSE, **(as) safe as houses** (SAFE[1] (5))
17 bring the house down to make a lot of people laugh, especially when you are acting in a theatre〔尤指戏剧表演〕博得满堂喝彩

house[2] /haʊz; haʊz/ *v* [T] **1** to provide someone with a place to live 让…居住, 给…提供住房: *The refugees are being housed in temporary accommodation.* 难民被安置在临时住房里。**2** if a building houses something, it is kept there 收藏; 存放: *The library is currently housed in the British Museum.* 该图书馆现设在大英博物馆中。

house ar·rest /ˈ· ·,·/ *n* **be under house arrest** to be told that you must stay inside your house by the government (本宅)软禁

house·boat /ˈhaʊs,bot; ˈhaʊsbəʊt/ *n* [C] a boat that you can live in 船屋

house·bound /ˈhaʊs,baʊnd; ˈhaʊsbaʊnd/ *adj* unable to leave your house, especially because you are ill or old〔尤指因病或年老而〕出不了门的, 闭门不出的

house·boy /ˈhaʊs,bɔɪ; ˈhaʊsbɔɪ/ *n* [C] *old use* a word which is now considered offensive, meaning a man who is employed to do general work at someone's house【旧】男仆, 家童〔现被视为贬义〕

house·break·er /ˈhaʊs,brekə; ˈhaʊs,breɪkə/ *n* [C] a thief who enters someone else's house by breaking locks, windows etc; BURGLAR〔破门入室的〕窃贼 —**housebreaking** *n* [U]

house·bro·ken /ˈhaʊs,brokən; ˈhaʊs,brəʊkən/ *adj AmE* an animal that is housebroken has been trained not to make the house dirty with its URINE and FAECES【美】〔家养小动物〕训练后不在室内随地便溺的; HOUSE-TRAINED *BrE*【英】

house·coat /ˈhaʊs,kot; ˈhaʊs-kəʊt/ *n* [C] a long, loose coat worn at home to protect clothes while cleaning etc 家居便服,〔在家穿的〕宽松长袍

house·craft /ˈhaʊs,kræft; ˈhaʊs-krɑːft/ *n* [U] *BrE old-fashioned* DOMESTIC SCIENCE【英, 过时】家政学

house·fly /ˈhaʊs,flaɪ; ˈhaʊsflaɪ/ *n plural* **houseflies** [C] a common type of fly that lives in houses 家蝇, 苍蝇

house·ful /ˈhaʊsful; ˈhaʊsfʊl/ *n* **a houseful of** a large number of people or things in your house 一屋子, 满屋〔人或东西〕: *We had a houseful of guests last weekend.* 上周末我们家来了一屋子的客人。

house guest /ˈ· ,·/ *n* [C] a friend or relative who is staying in your house for a short time 暂住客人

house·hold[1] /ˈhaʊs,hold; ˈhaʊshəld/ *n* [C] *BrE* all the people who live together in one house【英】一家人; 同住一幢房子的人

household[2] *adj* [only before noun 仅用于名词前] **1** connected with looking after a house and the people in it; DOMESTIC 家庭的, 家用的, 家务的: **household goods/products/items** *washing powder and other household products* 洗衣粉及其他家用产品 | *household chores* 家务杂活 **2 be a household name/word** to be very well known 家喻户晓; 十分出名: *Coca Cola is a household name around the world.* 可口可乐是全世界都家喻户晓的品牌。

Household Cav·al·ry, the /,·· ˈ···/ a group of British soldiers on horses who are responsible for guarding the Queen or King and the royal PALACE. The Household Cavalry consists of two REGIMENTS, the Life Guards and the Blues and Royals.〔英国〕皇家近卫军骑兵旅〔由近卫骑兵团和皇家蓝军骑兵团组成, 负责守护女王或国王及皇宫〕

house·hold·er /ˈhaʊs,holdə; ˈhaʊs,həʊldə/ *n* [C] *formal* someone who owns or is in charge of a house【正式】房主; 户主; 家长

house hus·band /ˈ· ,··/ *n* [C] a husband who stays at home and does the cooking, cleaning etc 操持家务的丈夫

house·keep·er /ˈhaʊs,kipə; ˈhaʊs,kiːpə/ *n* [C] someone who is employed to manage the cleaning, cooking etc in a house or hotel 管家; 旅馆勤杂工人

house·keep·ing /ˈhaʊsˌkipɪŋ; ˈhaʊsˌkiːpɪŋ/ *n* [U] **1** the work and organization of things that need to be done in a house, for example cooking and buying food 家务管理, 料理家务 **2** also 又作 **housekeeping money** an amount of money that is kept and used to pay for food and other things needed in the home 家务开支, 家用钱 **3** jobs that need to be done to keep a system working properly〔维持某个系统正常运转的〕内务工作

house lights /ˈ· ·/ *n* [plural] the lights in the part of a cinema or theatre where people sit〔影剧院中〕观众席照明灯

house·maid /ˈhaʊsˌmed; ˈhaʊsmeɪd/ *n* [C] *old-fashioned* a female servant who cleans someone's house【过时】女佣, 女仆

house·man /ˈhaʊsˌmən; ˈhaʊsmən/ *n plural* **housemen** /-mən; -mən/ *BrE* [C] someone who has nearly finished training as a doctor and is working in a hospital【英】驻院实习医生; INTERN *AmE*【美】

house mar·tin /ˈ· ˌ··/ *n* [C] a small black and white European bird of the SWALLOW[2] (1) family 毛脚燕〔欧洲的一种鸟〕

house·mas·ter /ˈhaʊsˌmæstɚ; ˈhaʊsˌmɑːstə/ *n* [C] *especially BrE* a male teacher who is in charge of one of the houses (HOUSE[1] (11)) in a school【尤英】〔学校里负责体育比赛某一分组的〕男督导

house·mis·tress /ˈhaʊsˌmɪstrɪs; ˈhaʊsˌmɪstrɪ̣s/ *n* [C] *especially BrE* a female teacher who is in charge of one of the houses (HOUSE[1] (11)) in a school【尤英】〔学校里负责体育比赛某一分组的〕女督导

house mu·sic /ˈ· ˌ··/ *n* [U] a type of popular music 豪斯音乐〔电子乐器演奏的一种流行音乐〕

house of cards /ˌ· · ˈ·/ *n* [singular] **1** a plan that is so badly arranged that is likely to fail 筹划不周而可能失败的计划, 不可靠的计划 **2** an arrangement of PLAYING CARDS built carefully but easily knocked over 纸牌屋

House of Com·mons /ˌ· · ˈ··/ *n* [singular] the part of the British or Canadian parliament whose members are elected by the people〔英国或加拿大议会中的〕下议院

house of God /ˌ· · ˈ·/ *n* [singular] *literary* a church【文】教堂, 礼拜堂

House of Lords /ˌ· · ˈ·/ *n* [singular] the part of the British parliament whose members are not elected but have positions because of their rank or title〔英国议会中的〕上议院, 贵族院

House of Rep·re·sen·ta·tives /ˌ· · ˌ····ˈ···/ *n* [singular] the larger of the two parts of the US Congress or of the parliament of Australia or New Zealand〔美国、澳大利亚、新西兰国会中的〕众议院 —compare 比较 SENATE (1)

house of wor·ship /ˌ· · ˈ··/ *n* [C] *especially AmE* a church【尤美】教堂

house·par·ent /ˈhaʊsˌpɛrənt; ˈhaʊsˌpeərənt/ *n* [C] someone who looks after a group of children who live together in a special home because they have no families or need special care〔孤儿院等中的〕管理员, 舍监

house par·ty /ˈ· ˌ··/ *n* [C] a group of people who stay as guests in a large country house 在乡间别墅里留宿的客人

house·phone /ˈhaʊsˌfon; ˈhaʊsfəʊn/ *n* [C] a telephone that can only be used to make calls within a building, especially a hotel〔尤指旅馆里的〕内线电话

house·plant /ˈhaʊsˌplænt; ˈhaʊsplɑːnt/ *n* [C] a plant that you grow indoors for decoration 室内盆栽植物

house·proud /ˈhaʊsˌpraʊd; ˈhaʊspraʊd/ *adj* spending a lot of time on keeping your house clean and tidy 注重保持家居整洁的; 热衷于美化家庭环境的

house·room /ˈhaʊsˌrum; ˈhaʊsruːm/ *n* [U] *especially BrE*【尤英】**1 not give sth houseroom** to not like something and not want it 不要某物, 不留存某物 **2** space in a house for a person or thing〔房子中住人或摆放东西的〕房间

house-sit /ˈ· ·/ *v* [I] to look after someone's house while they are away〔房主外出时〕代为看管房屋

Houses of Par·lia·ment /ˌ· · ˈ···/ *n* [singular] the buildings where the British parliament meets, or the parliament itself〔英国的〕议会大厦; 议会

House that Jack Built, The /ˌ· · ˈ· ˌ·/ the title of a well-known NURSERY RHYME (=an old song or poem for children) which begins 'This is the house that Jack built'《杰克造的房子》〔一著名儿歌的歌名。首句为"这是杰克造的房子"〕

house-to-house /ˌ· · ˈ·◂/ *adj* **house-to-house inquiries/survey/search etc** inquiries etc that are made by visiting each house in a particular area 挨家挨户的询问/调查/搜查等: *The abduction sparked a house-to-house search in the Willenhall area.* 劫持案导致威伦霍尔地区进行了一次挨家挨户的大搜查。

house·tops /ˈhaʊsˌtɑps; ˈhaʊs-tɒps/ *n* **shout/broadcast/proclaim sth from the housetops** to say something publicly so that everyone will hear or know about it 公开喊叫/播出/声称

house-trained /ˈ· ·/ *adj BrE* a pet that is house-trained has been trained not to make the house dirty with its URINE and FAECES【英】〔家养宠物〕训练后不在室内随地便溺的; HOUSEBROKEN *AmE*【美】 —**housetrain** *v* [T]

House Un-A·mer·i·can Ac·tiv·i·ties Com·mit·tee, the /ˌ·ˌ····· ˈ···· ˌ·ˈ·/ the full name of HUAC HUAC 的全称

house·wares /ˈhaʊsˌwɛrz; ˈhaʊsweəz/ *n* [plural] *AmE* small things used in the home, for example plates, lamps etc, or the department of a large shop that sells these things【美】家用器皿;〔百货公司的〕家居用品部

house-warm·ing /ˈ· ˌ··/ *n* [C] a party that you give to celebrate moving into a new house〔迁入新居后举行的〕庆祝乔迁聚会: *Are you coming to Jo's house-warming on Friday?* 周五你去参加乔的乔迁庆祝聚会吗?

house·wife /ˈhaʊsˌwaɪf; ˈhaʊs-waɪf/ *n plural* **housewives** /-waɪvz; -waɪvz/ [C] a married woman who works at home doing the cooking, cleaning etc, but does not have a job outside the house; HOMEMAKER〔不在外工作的〕家庭妇女, 家庭主妇 —**housewifely** *adj*

> **CULTURAL NOTE 文化注释**
>
> In the past, the typical wife was a housewife. The STEREOTYPE of a good housewife was someone who was expected to clean her house regularly, take good care of her children, and have a meal prepared for her husband as soon as he returned home from work. She should be good at cooking and sewing, be kind and caring to her children and husband, and allow her husband to make all of the main decisions for the family. Many housewives did not work professionally because their husbands earned enough money to support the whole family. Today, very few women are housewives because most married women work and both the husband and the wife are responsible for cooking, cleaning, and taking care of the children. 在过去, 妻子一般都是家庭主妇。好主妇的典型形象是: 定期打扫屋子, 好好照顾孩子, 丈夫下班一回家就已备好饭菜, 精于烹饪和女工, 相夫教子, 体贴入微, 家里的重大决定由丈夫做主。很多家庭主妇不出门工作, 因为丈夫挣的钱已足够养家。现在, 很少有女性是家庭主妇, 因为已婚女性大多都有工作, 丈夫和妻子共同负责做饭、打扫和照料子女。—see Cultural Note at FAMILY 见 FAMILY 文化注释

house·work /ˈhaʊsˌwɝk; ˈhaʊswɜːk/ *n* [U] work that you do to take care of a house such as washing, cleaning etc 家务(劳动): *I spent all morning doing the housework.* 我整个上午都在做家务。

hous·ing /ˈhaʊzɪŋ; ˈhaʊzɪŋ/ *n* **1** [U] the houses or conditions that people live in 住房; 住房条件; 居住环境: *health problems caused by bad housing* 住房条件差引起的健康问题 **2** [U] the work of providing houses for people to live in 供给住房: *government housing policy* 政府的住房政策 **3** [C] a protective cover for a machine〔机器的〕外罩, 外壳, 护盖: *the engine housing* 发动机机壳

Housing and Ur·ban De·vel·op·ment /ˌ· · ˌ·· ·ˈ···/ the full name of HUD HUD 的全称

housing as·so·ci·a·tion /ˈ·· ··ˌ··ˈ··/ *n* [C] an association in Britain, formed by a group of people so that they can build homes for themselves, or can buy homes of their own〔英国的一种以建房或购房为目的的〕住房互助协会, 房屋协会

housing es·tate /ˈ·· ·ˌ·/ *BrE*【英】, **housing de·vel·op·ment** /ˈ·· ·ˈ···/ *AmE*【美】—*n* [C] a large number of houses that have been built together in a planned way〔经规划建造的〕住宅区

housing pro·ject /ˈ·· ˌ··/ *n* [C] *especially AmE* a group of houses or apartments, usually built with government money, for poor families【尤美】〔政府出资建造供低收入家庭居住的〕住房项目, 住宅区

Hous·ton /ˈhjustṇ; ˈhjuːstən/ **1** a city and port in the US state of Texas, where the US government space centre, NASA, is based 休斯顿〔美国得克萨斯州一城市和港口, 为美国国家航空航天局所在地〕**2 Houston, we have a problem** the words that one of the ASTRONAUTS on the unsuccessful Apollo 13 space MISSION, in order to say that he thought something was going wrong with the mission. People often use these words in a humorous way in other situations. 休斯顿, 我们遇到麻烦了〔一宇航员在执行失败的"阿波罗 13 号"宇航计划时说的话。意思是该计划出了问题。人们常在其他场合诙谐地引用这句话〕

Houston /ˈhustn̩; ˈhuːstən/, **Sam** /sæm; sæm/ (1793-1863) a US soldier and politician who fought to make Texas independent from Mexico. He was president of the Republic of Texas from 1836 until it became a state of the US in 1845. The city of Houston in Texas was named after him. 休斯顿〔(1793-1863),美国军人、政治家。他曾为得克萨斯脱离墨西哥实现独立而战斗。1836年起,他出任得克萨斯共和国总统,直至1845年得克萨斯成为美国的一个州。得克萨斯州的休斯顿市得名于他的姓氏〕

hove /hov; həʊv/ *v* [I] the past tense and past participle of HEAVE[1]

hov·el /ˈhʌvl̩; ˈhɒvəl/ *n* [C] a small dirty place where someone lives, especially a very poor person〔尤指穷人居住的〕简陋肮脏的住处

hov·er /ˈhʌvɚ; ˈhɒvə/ *v* [I] **1** if a bird, insect, or HELICOPTER hovers, it stays in one place in the air〔鸟、昆虫〕盘旋;〔直升机〕悬停 **2** to stay nervously in the same place especially because you are waiting for something or are uncertain what to do〔等待或拿不定主意时〕徘徊; 走来走去: **[+around/about]** *I noticed several reporters hovering around outside the courtroom.* 我注意到几名记者在法庭外徘徊。**3** [always+adv/prep] to be in an uncertain state 不确定, 摇摆不定: **[+around/between etc]** *The dollar has been hovering around the 110 yen level.* 美元一直在110日圆水平上下摆动。

hov·er·craft /ˈhʌvɚˌkræft; ˈhɒvəkrɑːft/ *n plural* **hovercraft** or **hovercrafts** [C] a vehicle that travels just above the surface of land or water by means of a strong current of air forced out beneath it 气垫船 —compare 比较 HYDROFOIL

hover mow·er /ˈ‥ ˌ‥/ *n* [C] a machine for cutting grass that moves just above the ground 气垫割草机

1 1 **how¹** /hau; haʊ/ *adv*

1 ►QUESTIONS 疑问◄ **a)** used to ask about what way or what method you should use to do something, find out about something, go somewhere etc 怎样, 如何: *How do you spell foyer?* "foyer"这个词怎么拼? | *How should I dress for this job interview?* 我该如何打扮去参加这次招聘面试? | *How on earth do you manage to afford so many holidays?* 你到底有什么办法负担得起这么多次度假呢? | *I want to know how you say 'good luck' in Japanese.* 我想知道日语怎样说"祝你好运"。**b)** used to ask about the amount, size, degree etc of something〔数量、大小、程度〕多少: *How big is the state of Louisiana compared to England?* 与英格兰相比, 路易斯安那州有多大? | *How many kids do they have now?* 他们现在有几个孩子? | *How long did you live in Manchester for?* 你在曼彻斯特住了多久? | **how much?** (=used to ask the price of something) 多少钱?〔询问价格〕*How much is that sweater, the blue one?* 那件毛衣多少钱, 那件蓝色的? **c)** used to ask about someone's health or about their feelings〔身心感觉〕怎么样, 如何: *How's your ankle this morning? Has the swelling gone down?* 你的脚踝今天上午感觉怎么样? 肿消下去了吗? **d)** used to ask about someone's opinion of something or about their experience of something〔看法、经历〕怎么样: *How did your exams go?* 你考试考得怎么样? | *How was the play?* 那出话剧怎么样? **e)** used to ask about the way something looks, behaves, or is expressed〔外表、行为、表达〕怎么样, 如何: *How does that speech of Macbeth's end, the one about 'a tale told by an idiot'?* 麦克白的那段话是怎么结尾的, 就是关于"傻瓜讲的故事"的那段话? | *How does that song go, anyway?* 好了, 那首歌是怎么唱的?

2 ►EMPHASIZE 强调◄ used before an adjective or adverb to emphasize the quality you are mentioning 多么, 何等〔加强语气〕: *He was impressed at how well she could read.* 他对她有这么高的阅读水准感到很钦佩。| *"John's been in an accident." "Oh, how awful!"* "约翰出事了。""哦, 太糟了!" | *It depends on how busy they are whether they'll be able to go or not.* 他们能不能去要看他们有多忙。

Frequencies of the word **how** in spoken and written English
单词how在英语口语和书面语中的使用频率

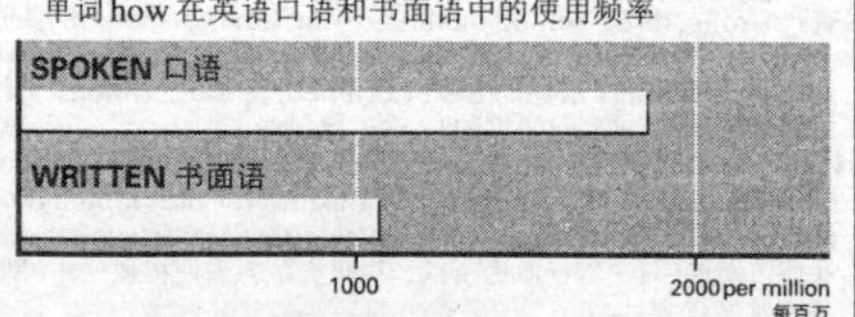

Based on the British National Corpus and the Longman Lancaster Corpus
据英国国家语料库和朗文兰开斯特语料库

This graph shows that the word **how** is much more common in spoken English than in written English. This is because it is used a lot to ask questions, is used to emphasize what you are saying, and is used in a lot of common spoken phrases. 本图表显示, 单词how在英语口语中的使用频率远远高于书面语, 因为该词经常用来提问, 或用于强调说话的语气, 而且口语中很多常用短语是由how构成的。

how (*adv*) SPOKEN PHRASES
含how的口语短语

3 how are you? used when you meet someone, to ask if they are well 你好吗?〔见面问候语〕: *"Hi Francie, how are you?" "Fine, thanks, how are you?"* "嗨, 弗朗西, 你好吗?" "很好, 谢谢, 你呢?"

4 how's it going?/how are you doing? a) used when you meet someone, to ask if they are well, happy etc 你最近好吗?/你过得好吗?: *"Hey, how's it going?" "OK."* "嗨, 你最近好吗?""还好。" **b)** used to ask if someone is happy with what they are doing 怎么样〔询问事情进行得是否顺利〕: *So how's it going at work these days? Still enjoying it?* 那么这几天工作怎么样? 仍然很开心吗?

5 how about...? a) used to make a suggestion about what to do …好吗? …行吗?〔征求意见〕: *No, I'm busy on Monday. How about Tuesday at seven?* 不行, 我星期一没空。星期二7点行吗? | **how about doing sth** *How about putting the sofa closer to the window?* 把沙发挪得离窗户近一些好吗? | **how's about** *informal especially AmE*【非正式, 尤美】*How's about going to the beach this afternoon?* 今天下午去海滩好吗? **b)** used to introduce a new idea, fact etc that has not yet been discussed …又怎么样呢?〔提及新的话题〕: *"Mary and Ken are still away." "And how about Billy?"* "玛丽和肯还没回来。""那比利呢?"

6 how about you? used to ask someone what they want or what their opinion is, after you have said what you want or what your opinion is 你呢?〔询问某人的需求或看法〕: *I can't stand opera, how about you?* "我受不了歌剧, 你呢?"

7 how do you mean? used to ask someone to explain something they have just said 你是什么意思?〔要求进一步解释〕: *"What's your family situation?" "How do you mean?" "Are you married?"* "你的家庭状况如何?""你是什么意思?""你结婚了吗?"

8 how's that? used to ask someone whether something is satisfactory 怎么样?〔询问是否满意〕: *How's that? Can you see now?* 怎么样? 你现在看见了吗?

9 how come? used to ask why something has happened or been said, especially when you are surprised by it 怎么会呢?〔尤表示惊讶〕: *How come Dave's home? Isn't he feeling well?* 戴夫怎么会在家呢? 他不舒服吗?

10 how do you do? a polite expression used when you meet someone for the first time 您好!〔初次见面时的问候语〕

11 how are things? used when you meet someone, to ask if they are well, happy etc 你好吗? 最近好吗?: *"Hello Peter, how are things?" "Oh, not too bad."* "你好, 彼得, 最近好吗?""哦, 还不错。"

12 how do you know? used to ask how someone found out about something or why they are sure about something 你怎么知道?: *"Better bring an umbrella. It's going to rain later." "How do you know?"* "最好带上一把雨伞, 一会儿要下雨。""你怎么知道?"

13 how can you/how could you...? used when you are very surprised by or disapprove strongly of something 你怎么能…?〔表示震惊或强烈反对〕: *William! How could you say such a thing!* 威廉! 你怎么能说这种话呢?

14 how about that!/how do you like that! used to ask what someone thinks of something that you think is surprising, rude, very good etc 你觉得怎么样?〔征求别人的意见〕: *He lost 15 pounds in a month! How about that!* 他一个月内体重减了15磅! 你说神奇不神奇?

15 how so? used to ask someone to explain an opinion they have given 为什么? 怎么会这样?〔要求解释原因〕: *"Rick's parents are a little strange, I think." "How so?"* "我觉得里克的父母有些怪。""为什么?"

16 and how! *AmE old-fashioned* an expression meaning 'yes, very much,' used to strongly emphasize your reply to a question【美, 过时】那还用说! 当然啦!: *"Was Matt drunk?" "And how!"* "马特醉了吗?""那还用说!"

how² *conjunction* **1** used at the beginning of a CLAUSE (2) in which you explain the method of doing something 怎样…, 如何…: *He has to understand that this is how we do things in this household, even if his mother does them differently.* 他必须明

白，尽管他母亲有不同的做法，但在我们家就是这么做的。| **how to do sth** *The class teaches students how to plan a budget.* 这堂课教学生怎样做预算。**2** used at the beginning of a CLAUSE (2) in which you introduce a fact or statement 关于…的事: *We were both travelling across Europe, and that's how we first met.* 我们俩都在环游欧洲，我们就是那样认识的。| *Okay, do you remember how we discussed yesterday the Roman rule of Britain?* 好，你还记得我们昨天谈到的有关古罗马人统治不列颠的事吗？**3** *spoken* in whatever way【口】无论用什么方法: *In your own house you can act how you want.* 在你自己家里你可以为所欲为。

How·ard League for Pe·nal Re·form, the /,· · · · ,· · ·ˈ·/ a British organization which is against physical punishment and the death sentence, and wants change in international attitudes to punishment and imprisonment 霍华德刑法改革联盟〔英国一组织，反对体罚和死刑，并希望国际社会改变对刑罚和监禁的态度〕

how·dah /ˈhaudə; ˈhaʊdə/ *n* [C] a covered seat used for riding an elephant 象轿〔一种架在象背上供人乘坐的有盖座位〕

how·dy /ˈhaudɪ; ˈhaʊdi/ *interjection AmE* used to say hello in an informal, usually humorous way【美】你好!〔一般为幽默用法的非正式招呼语〕

S2 W1 **how·ev·er**[1] /hauˋɛvɚ; haʊˈevə/ *adv* **1** used when you are adding a fact or piece of information that seems surprising, or seems to disagree with what you have just said 然而，不过，但是: *People like this are usually harmless. They can, however, be a nuisance.* 这类人通常是无恶意的。不过他们会讨人厌。| *This method has been widely adopted. However, it is not yet clear that it is the best method.* 这种方法一直被广泛使用，但还不能肯定这就是最好的方法。—see 见 BUT[1] (USAGE) **2 however hard/serious/long/carefully etc** it makes no difference how hard, serious, long, carefully etc 无论多难/严重/长/小心等: *You should report any incident, however serious or minor it is.* 有任何事你都应该报告，不管事情是大是小。| *We'll have to finish the job, however long it takes.* 无论要花多长时间，我们都得把这件工作做完。| **however much/many** (=it makes no difference, how much or how many) 无论多少 *I really want the car, however much it costs.* 不管那辆车多贵，我真的很想要。**3** used to mean how, when you want to show that you find something very surprising (到底) 如何?〔表示惊讶〕: *However did he get that job?* 他到底是怎样得到那份工作的呢?

however[2] *conjunction* in whatever way 不管怎样，无论如何: *You can do it however you like.* 你可以按自己的意思去做。| *If we win the match we'll be delighted however it happens.* 如果我们能赢这个比赛，不管怎么赢的我们都会高兴。

How Green was My Val·ley /·,· · · ·ˈ· ·/ (1939) a NOVEL by Richard Llewellyn about a MINER's family in South Wales《青山翠谷》〔(1939)，理查德·卢埃林创作的一部小说，讲述南威尔士一矿工家庭的故事〕

how·it·zer /ˈhauɪtsɚ; ˈhaʊɪtsə/ *n* [C] a heavy gun which fires shells (SHELL[1] (2)) high into the air so that they travel a short distance 榴弹炮〔一种能以大仰角射击近距离目标的重炮〕

howl[1] /haul; haʊl/ *v* **1** [I] if a dog, WOLF, or other animal howls, it makes a long loud sound〔狼、狗等〕嗥叫，长嚎: *The dogs howled all night.* 那几只狗整夜嗥叫。**2** [I] to make a long loud cry because you are unhappy, in pain, or angry〔因悲伤、痛苦、愤怒〕不停地嚎哭; 咆哮: *the constant howling from the baby upstairs* 楼上的婴儿不断的哭叫声 **3** [I,T] to shout or demand something angrily 怒吼，大声要求: **[+for]** *Right wing Republicans have been howling for military intervention.* 右翼共和党人一直在愤怒地要求进行军事干预。**4** [I] if the wind howls, it makes a loud high sound as it blows〔风〕怒号: *wind howling in the trees* 在林中怒号的风 **5 howl with laughter** to laugh very loudly 狂笑 **6 be a howling success** to be extremely successful 极其成功

howl sb/sth ↔ **down** *phr v* [T] to prevent someone or something from being heard by shouting loudly and angrily 大声怒叫以盖过…的声音

howl[2] *n* [C] **1** a long loud sound made by a dog, WOLF or other animal〔狗、狼等的〕嗥叫声，长嚎 **2** a loud cry of pain or anger〔痛苦、愤怒的〕嚎叫，咆哮 **3 howl of laughter** a very loud laugh 狂笑

howl·er /ˈhaulɚ; ˈhaʊlə/ *n* [C] *BrE informal* a stupid mistake that makes people laugh【英，非正式】可笑的错误

how·so·ev·er /,hausoˈɛvɚ; ,haʊsəʊˈevə/ *adv literary* HOWEVER【文】不管怎样，无论如何

how·zat /,hauˈzæt; ,haʊˈzæt/ *interjection* used in CRICKET when claiming that a player is OUT[1] (37)〔板球比赛中宣布球员〕出局

HP /,·ˈ·/ **1** an abbreviation of 缩写= HORSEPOWER **2** *BrE*【英】an abbreviation of 缩写= HIRE PURCHASE: **on HP** *We bought it on HP.* 我们分期付款买下了它。

HP sauce /,etʃ pi ˈsɔs; ,eɪtʃ piː ˈsɔːs/ *trademark* a type of thick, dark brown liquid made of vegetables, fruit, and SPICES, which is sold in a tall, thin bottle, and poured over food, especially fried (FRY) food such as eggs and SAUSAGES. It is popular in the UK.【商标】HP 酱〔英国流行的一种调味酱。呈深棕色浓稠状，主要成分为蔬菜、水果和香料，采用瓶装销售，瓶体细长。一般浇在食物上食用，尤其适于煎制的食物，如煎鸡蛋和煎香肠等〕

HQ /,etʃ ˋkju; ,eɪtʃ ˈkjuː/ an abbreviation of 缩写= HEADQUARTERS

hr *plural* **hrs** a written abbreviation of 缩写= HOUR

HRH an abbreviation of 缩写= His or Her Royal Highness 殿下

HRT /,etʃ ɑr ˋti; ,eɪtʃ ɑː ˈtiː/ *n* [U] an abbreviation of 缩写= HORMONE REPLACEMENT THERAPY

HSE, the /,etʃ ɛs ˋi; ,eɪtʃ es ˈiː/ the abbreviation of 缩写= the HEALTH AND SAFETY EXECUTIVE

ht the written abbreviation of 缩写= HEIGHT

HUAC, the /,hjuæk, ,etʃ ju e ˋsi; ˈhjuːæk, ,eɪtʃ juː eɪ ˈsiː/ the House Un-American Activities Committee; a group in the US House of Representatives which tried to find out whether US citizens were enemies of the government. It was especially active during the early 1950s as a result of McCarthyism. At this time, the Committee judged many cases involving politicians, military officers, and other well-known people who were believed to be Communists. It stopped operating in 1975. 众议院反美活动调查委员会〔美国众议院调查与美国政府为敌的美国公民的小组。该组织受麦卡锡主义的影响，20 世纪 50 年代尤为活跃。当时，该委员会审理了许多案件，涉及被认为是共产主义者的政治人物、军官和其他知名人士。1975 年，该委员会停止活动〕

hub /hʌb; hʌb/ *n* [C] **1** the central and most important part of an area, system etc, which all the other parts are connected to〔地域、系统的〕中心，枢纽: **[+of]** *York used to be the hub of a vast rail network.* 约克曾经是一个巨大铁路网的枢纽。**2** the central part of a wheel to which the AXLE is joined (轮) 毂 —see picture at 参见 BICYCLE[1] 图

Hub·bard /ˈhʌbɚd; ˈhʌbəd/, **L Ron** /rɑn; rɒn/ (1911-86) a US writer who started a new religion called the Church of Scientology. He also wrote many SCIENCE FICTION books. 哈伯德〔(1911-1986)，美国作家。他曾创立科学论派教会，而且写了不少科幻小说〕

Hub·ble Tel·e·scope, the /ˈhʌbḷ ,tɛləskop; ˈhʌbəl ,teləskəʊp/ a very powerful TELESCOPE (=a piece of equipment for making distant objects look larger and closer) which is attached to a SATELLITE in space, going around the Earth, and can see much further into space than telescopes on Earth 哈勃天文望远镜〔一种性能强大的望远镜，安装在环绕地球运行的卫星上，要比地球望远镜观测的距离更远〕

hub·bub /ˈhʌbʌb; ˈhʌbʌb/ *n* [singular,U] a mixture of loud noises, especially the noise of a lot of people talking at the same time〔人群的〕喧闹声，嘈杂声

hub·by /ˈhʌbɪ; ˈhʌbi/ *n* [C] *informal* husband【非正式】老公，丈夫

hub·cap /ˈhʌb,kæp; ˈhʌbkæp/ *n* [C] a metal cover for the centre of a wheel on a vehicle〔汽车的〕毂盖 —see picture on page A2 参见 A2 页图

hu·bris /ˈhjubrɪs; ˈhjuːbrɪs/ *n* [U] *literary* great and unreasonable pride【文】傲慢，自大，目中无人

huck·le·ber·ry /ˈhʌkḷ,bɛrɪ; ˈhʌkəlbəri/ *n* [C] a small dark-blue North American fruit that grows on a bush〔产于北美的〕美洲越橘

Huckleberry Finn /,hʌkḷbɛrɪ ˋfɪn; ˈhʌkəlbəri fɪn/ —see 见 Huckleberry FINN

huck·ster /ˈhʌkstɚ; ˈhʌkstə/ *n* [C] **1** *AmE* someone who uses very strong, direct selling methods, sometimes dishonestly【美】〔有时用欺骗手段的〕强行推销者 **2** *old-fashioned* someone who sells small things in the street or to people in their houses【过时】〔沿街叫卖或上门兜售的〕小贩; 推销员

HUD /hʌd; hʌd/ Housing and Urban Development; a US government department which is responsible for providing houses for people to live in, and for the way cities are developed 住房和城市发展部〔美国一政府部门。其职责是为人们提供住房，制定城市发展规划〕

hud·dle[1] /ˈhʌdḷ; ˈhʌdl/ *v* **huddled, huddling 1** [I,T] also 又作 **huddle together/up** if a group of people huddle together, they gather closely together in a group, especially because they are cold or frightened〔尤因寒冷或恐惧而〕挤作一团，聚成一堆: *A few diehard football fans huddled together in the rain waiting*

for tickets. 几个铁杆足球迷在雨中挤作一团等买票。**2** [I always+adv/prep] to lie or sit with your arms and legs close to your body because you are cold or frightened 蜷缩着身体: *I jumped in bed and huddled under the blankets.* 我跳上床,在毯子下蜷着身体。

huddle² *n* [C] **1** a group of people standing or sitting close together, or a group of things placed together in a confused way 紧紧聚在一起的一群人; 杂乱的一堆东西: **[+of]** *a huddle of straw huts* 杂乱的一片茅草屋 **2** a group of players in American football who gather around one player who tells them the plan for the next part of the game〔美式橄榄球运动续赛前〕聚在一起听取指示的一群队员 **3 get/go into a huddle** to form a small group away from other people in order to discuss something 私下集中商量,进行秘密商谈

Hud·dle·ston /ˈhʌdḷstən; ˈhʌdlstən/, **Tre·vor** /ˈtrɛvɚ; ˈtrevə/, **Bishop** (1913-98), a British priest who became famous for trying to end APARTHEID in South Africa. He worked in South Africa from 1943 until 1956. 赫德斯顿主教〔(1913-1998),英国牧师。1943至1956年,他曾在南非工作,因致力于结束南非的种族隔离政策而著名〕

Hud·son /ˈhʌdsn; ˈhʌdsən/, **Henry** (1565-1611) an English SAILOR and EXPLORER who made several attempts to find the Northeast Passage (=along the northern coast of Russia) and the Northwest Passage (=along the northern coast of Canada). He discovered Hudson Bay in 1610. 哈得孙〔(1565-1611),英国水手、探险家。他曾多次尝试找到东北通道和西北通道。1610年,他发现了哈得孙湾〕

Hudson, Rock (1922-85) a US film actor who was very good-looking. He made several humorous films with Doris Day, such as *Pillow Talk* (1959). He was one of the first famous people to die of AIDS. 赫德森〔(1922-1985),美国男演员。他十分英俊,曾与多丽斯·戴合演《枕边细语》(1959)等多部喜剧影片。他是最早死于艾滋病的名人之一〕

Hudson Bay /,‥ ˈ·/ a large area of sea in northern Canada which is frozen for most of the year 哈得孙湾〔加拿大北部一广阔海域,一年大部分时间处于结冰状态〕

Hudson Riv·er, the /,‥ ˈ‥/ a river in New York State in the US, which meets the Atlantic Ocean in New York City 哈得孙河〔美国纽约州一河流,在纽约市注入大西洋〕

Hudson River School, the /,‥ ˈ‥ ,·/ a group of US painters between 1820 and 1880, who painted LANDSCAPES (=paintings of areas of countryside) in a romantic style 哈得孙河画派〔1820至1880年的一批美国画家。他们的风景画具有浪漫主义风格〕

Hudson's Bay Com·pa·ny /,‥ˈ·, ‥·/ a British company, established in 1670, which exchanged goods for furs with the Native Americans and once owned large areas of land in Canada 哈得孙湾公司〔英国一公司,创立于1670年。该公司与印第安人从事毛皮交易,曾在加拿大拥有大片土地〕

hue /hju; hjuː/ *n* [C] *especially literary*【尤文】**1** a colour or kind of colour 颜色; 色调; 色度: *Her hair turned a deep golden hue in the light of the sun.* 她的头发在阳光下变成了一种深金黄色。**2** a type of opinion, belief etc 一种〔观点、看法等〕: **of every hue** (=of many kinds) 各种各样的,形形色色的 *Political opinions of every hue were represented at the conference.* 形形色色的政治见解在大会上提了出来。

hue and cry /,‥ ˈ·/ *n* [singular] angry protests about something 愤怒的抗议

huff¹ /hʌf; hʌf/ *v* [I] *informal*【非正式】**1 huff and puff** to breathe out noisily, especially because you are tired〔尤因疲倦而〕气喘吁吁: *By the time he got to the top he was huffing and puffing.* 他爬到顶时已经是气喘吁吁了。**2 huffing and puffing** behaviour that shows that someone disagrees strongly with something such as an official plan〔某人对某事物的〕强烈反对

huff² *n* **in a huff** feeling angry or bad-tempered, especially because someone has offended you〔尤指因受到冒犯而〕生气,气恼: **go off/walk off/leave in a huff** *I told her she was always late and now she's gone off in a huff.* 我说她老是迟到,她就大发脾气地走了。

huff·y /ˈhʌfɪ; ˈhʌfi/ *adj informal* in a bad temper【非正式】怒气冲冲的,气鼓鼓的: *It's no use getting all huffy about it.* 为此生这么大的气是没有用的。—**huffily** *adv*

hug¹ /hʌg; hʌg/ *v* **hugged, hugging** [T] **1** to put your arms around someone and hold them tightly to show love or friendship 热烈地拥抱〔某人〕: *Jane threw her arms around him and hugged him tight.* 简张开双臂紧紧地拥抱他。—see picture on page A21 参见A21页图 **2** to hold something in your arms close to your chest 抱住〔某物〕: *He was hugging a big pile of books.* 他抱着一大堆书。**3** to move along the side, edge, top etc of something, staying very close to it 靠近[紧挨]…走: *The boat hugged the coast.* 小船贴近海岸航行。**4 hug yourself with joy/delight etc** to feel very pleased with yourself 沾沾自喜

hug² *n* [C] the action of putting your arms around someone and holding them tightly to show love or friendship 拥抱,紧抱: **give sb a hug** *Paul gave me a big hug and smiled.* 保罗热情地拥抱了我,脸上充满微笑。—see also 另见 BEAR HUG

huge /hjudʒ; hjuːdʒ/ *adj* **1** extremely large 巨大的,庞大的: *huge sums of money* 大笔的钱 | *Your room's positively huge compared to mine.* 你的房间跟我的比确实很大。**2** to a very great degree 程度很大的: **a huge success/disappointment etc** *The play was a huge success.* 这部剧获得巨大的成功。—**hugely** *adv*: *hugely successful* 极其成功的 —**hugeness** *n* [U]

S2 W2

Hug·gies /ˈhʌgɪz; ˈhʌgiz/ *trademark* a type of NAPPY for babies, which is thrown away after being used, sold in the US and the UK【商标】好奇纸尿裤〔在美国和英国销售的一种一次性婴儿纸尿裤〕

Hughes /hjuz; hjuːz/, **Howard** (1905-76) a US businessman, aircraft designer, pilot, and film PRODUCER, famous for being very rich but also for being very unwilling to spend money. He was a RECLUSE (=someone who lives on their own and does not want to see other people) for the last 26 years of his life. 休斯〔(1905-1976),美国商人、飞机设计师、飞行员和电影制片人。他以非常富有但也非常吝啬而出名。他以隐居方式度过了一生中的最后26年〕

Hughes, Lang·ston /ˈlæŋstn̩; ˈlæŋstən/ (1902-67) a black US poet and writer, known for using African-American language and patterns of speech in his work 休斯〔(1902-1967),美国黑人诗人、作家。他以运用非裔美国黑人的英语和话语模式创作而著称〕

Hughes, Ted /tɛd; ted/ (1930-98) a British poet who wrote especially about the cruelty of animals and nature. He was married to the US poet Sylvia Plath. He became Poet Laureate (=the Queen's official poet) in 1984. 休斯〔(1930-1998),英国诗人。其作品主要反映动物和大自然的残酷性。他与美国诗人西尔维娅·普拉斯结婚,1984年获桂冠诗人称号〕

Hu·go /ˈhjugo; ˈhjuːgəʊ/, **Victor** (1802-85) a French writer of poems, plays, and NOVELS. Two of his most famous novels are *The Hunchback of Notre Dame* and *Les Misérables* 雨果〔(1802-1885),法国诗人、剧作家和小说家。他的两部最著名的小说是《巴黎圣母院》和《悲惨世界》〕

huh /hʌ; hʌh/ *interjection spoken*【口】**1** *especially AmE* used at the end of a question, often to ask for agreement【尤美】嗯,啊〔用于问句末尾常用作征求对方认同〕: *Not a bad little place, huh?* 这个小地方不错,嗯? **2** used to show that you have not heard or understood a question 嗯〔表示没听到或没听懂问题〕: *"Carly, are you listening to me?" "Huh?"* "卡莉,你在听我说话吗?""嗯?" **3** used to show disagreement or surprise, or to show that you do not find something impressive 嗯,哼〔表示异议、惊讶或对某事印象平平〕: *"She looks nice." "Huh! Too much make-up, if you ask me."* "她看起来挺漂亮。""哼!我倒觉得妆化得太浓了。"

hu·la /ˈhulə; ˈhuːlə/ *n* [singular] a Polynesian dance done by women using gentle movements of the HIPS〔波利尼西亚女子跳的〕呼拉舞,草裙舞 —**hula** *adj*: *hula skirts* 呼拉舞裙,草裙

hula hoop /ˈ‥ ·/ *n* [C] a large ring which you make swing around your waist by moving your HIPS 呼拉圈

hulk /hʌlk; hʌlk/ *n* [C] **1** a large heavy person or thing 身材高大的人; 庞然大物; 笨重的人[东西]: *a hulk of a man* 大汉,壮汉 **2** the main part of an old ship that is not used any more 废弃的旧船体

hulk·ing /ˈhʌlkɪŋ; ˈhʌlkɪŋ/ *adj* [only before noun 仅用于名词前] very big and often awkward 大而笨拙的: *a hulking great figure of a man* 男人笨重的身体

hull¹ /hʌl; hʌl/ *n* [C] the main part of a ship 船体,船身: **wooden-hulled/steel-hulled etc** (=having a wood, steel etc hull) 木质/钢质等船体 —see picture at 参见 YACHT 图

hull² *v* [T] to take off the outer part of vegetables, rice, grain etc 除去…外皮[荚、壳等]

hul·la·ba·loo /ˈhʌləbə,lu; ˌhʌləbəˈluː/ *n* [C usually singular 一般用单数] **1** excited talk, newspaper stories etc, especially when something surprising or shocking is happening; UPROAR〔尤指对使人震惊的事件的〕激烈评论,集中报道: *the huge hullabaloo over the film in the press* 新闻界对该影片的大肆报道 **2** a lot of noise, especially made by people shouting 吵闹声,喧嚣声

hul·lo /həˈlo; hʌˈləʊ/ *interjection especially BrE spoken*【尤英,口】another spelling of HELLO hello的另一种拼法

hum[1] /hʌm; hʌm/ *v* **hummed, humming 1** [I,T] to sing a tune by making a continuous sound with your lips closed 哼(曲子): *Carol hummed quietly to herself as she worked.* 卡萝尔一边工作一边轻声地哼着曲子。**2** [I] to make a low, continuous sound 发出嗡嗡声: *insects humming in the hot summer air* 炎热的夏日空中嗡嗡飞着的昆虫 **3** [I] to be very busy and full of activity 忙碌, 活跃: [+with] *Wall Street was humming with rumours.* 华尔街谣言满天飞。**4 hum and haw** *BrE* to take a long time to say something etc because you are not sure what to say【英】支吾其词, 吞吞吐吐 —see also 另见 **hem and haw** (HEM[2] (2))

hum[2] *n* [singular] a low continuous sound 嗡嗡声; 低而持续的嘈杂声: *the hum of bees* 蜜蜂的嗡嗡声 | *the distant hum of traffic* 远处嘈杂的车流声

1 **hu·man[1]** /ˈhjumən; ˈhjuːmən/ *adj* **1** belonging to or concerning people, especially as opposed to animals or machines 人的; 人类的: *theories of human behaviour* 人类行为理论 | *The cat's eyes looked almost human.* 那只猫的双眼看起来几乎像人的一样。**2** human weaknesses, emotions etc are typical of ordinary people 普通人(特有)的: *common human failings such as greed and envy* 贪婪和忌妒等普通人的常见弱点 **3 sb is only human** used to say that someone should not be blamed for what they have done 某人只是个普通人而已〔表示不应苛求〕 **4** someone who seems human shows that they have the same feelings and emotions as ordinary people 有人情味的, 有人性的: *He's really not so bad. When you get to know him he seems quite human.* 他实际上没那么坏。一旦你对他有所了解, 就会发现他是颇有人情味的。—opposite 反义词 INHUMAN **5 the human touch** someone, especially someone in authority, who has the human touch deals with people in a kind, friendly way 人情味, 人性: *Senior managers have been accused of lacking the human touch.* 高层管理人员被指责缺乏人情味。**6** mistakes made by a person, rather than by a machine〔错误〕人为的 **7** a quality that makes a story interesting because it is about people's feelings, relationships etc〔故事〕有关人的感情的, 有关人与人之间关系的 —see 见 MAN[1] (USAGE)

3 **human[2]** also 又作 **human be·ing** /ˌ·· ˈ··/ *n* [C] a man, woman, or child 人〔指男人、女人或小孩〕 —see also 另见 MAN[1] (3)

hu·mane /hjuˋmen; hjuːˈmeɪn/ *adj* treating people or animals in a way that is not cruel and causes them as little pain or suffering as possible 人道的, 仁慈的: *Farmers will be asked to consider more humane ways of transporting livestock.* 农民会被要求考虑用更人道的方法来运送家畜。—**humanely** *adv* —opposite 反义词 INHUMANE

Humane So·ci·e·ty, the /·ˈ· ·,··/ a US organization that takes care of unwanted pets, especially ones that were treated cruelly, and tries to find them new homes. It also encourages people to treat animals better. 动物保护协会〔美国一组织, 旨在保护被遗弃的宠物, 尤其是受虐待的宠物, 并试图为它们找到新家。该组织还鼓励人们善待动物〕

Human Ge·nome Proj·ect, the /,·ˈ·· ,·/ an international scientific project that started in 1988. Its aim was to find and describe every GENE in every CHROMOSOME in the human body, and to find out what each gene's purpose is, especially in order to discover which ones cause particular diseases. 人类基因组计划〔始于1988年的一项国际性科研项目。其目标是发现并描述人类染色体中的每个基因及其功能, 尤其是发现引起某些疾病的基因类型〕

hu·man·is·m /ˈhjumən,ɪzəm; ˈhjuːmənɪzəm/ *n* [U] **1** a system of beliefs concerned with the needs of people and not with religious ideas 人道主义; 人本主义 **2** the study in the Renaissance of the ideas of the ancient Greeks and Romans〔文艺复兴时期〕对古希腊、古罗马思想的研究; 人文主义 —**humanist** *n* [C] —**humanistic** /ˌhjumənˈɪstɪk; ˌhjuːməˈnɪstɪk◂/ *adj*

hu·man·i·tar·i·an /hju,mænəˋtɛrɪən; hjuː,mænɪ̯ˈteəriən/ *adj* concerned with improving bad living conditions and preventing unfair treatment of people 博爱的; 人道主义的: *humanitarian aid to the refugees* 向难民提供的人道主义援助 —**humanitarian** *n* [C] —**humanitarianism** *n* [U]

hu·man·i·ties /hjuˋmænətɪz; hjuːˈmænɪ̯tiz/ *n* **the humanities** subjects of study such as literature, history, PHILOSOPHY etc 人文学科〈如文学、历史、哲学等〉

hu·man·i·ty /hjuˋmænətɪ; hjuːˈmænɪ̯ti/ *n* [U] **1** people in general 人, 人类: *30% of humanity lives in conditions of terrible poverty.* 30%的人生活在极度贫困的条件下。**2** the state of being human and having qualities and rights that all people have 人性, 普通人具有的特性: *We must never forget our common humanity.* 我们永远不要忘记我们共有的人性。**3** kindness, respect, and sympathy towards other people 仁慈, 博爱, 同情心

hu·man·ize also 又作 **-ise** *BrE* /ˈhjumə,naɪz; ˈhjuːmənaɪz/ *v* [T] to make a system more pleasant or more suitable for people【英】使人性化; 使仁慈: *an attempt to humanize the huge governmental bureaucracy* 使庞大的政府官僚体系人性化的努力

hu·man·kind /ˈhjumən,kaɪnd; ˌhjuːmənˈkaɪnd/ *n* [U] people in general 人类

hu·man·ly /ˈhjumənlɪ; ˈhjuːmənli/ *adv* **be humanly possible a)** to do as much as anyone could possibly do 尽最大努力: *Doctors did everything humanly possible to save the child's life.* 医生们尽了最大努力去挽救那孩子的生命。**b)** if something is humanly possible, it can be done using a great deal of effort 在人力所及范围内, 人可以做到的: *I'm not sure it will be humanly possible to prevent the disease from spreading.* 我无法肯定人力是否可以阻止该疾病的扩散。

human na·ture /,·· ˈ··/ *n* [U] **1** the qualities or ways of behaving that are natural and common to most people 人性 **2 it's (only) human nature** used to say that a particular feeling or way of behaving is normal and natural〔感情或行为〕是正常的, 是人之常情

hu·man·oid /ˈhjumənɔɪd; ˈhjuːmənɔɪd/ *adj* something, especially a machine, that is humanoid has a human shape and qualities〔尤指机器〕具人的形状[特性]的, 类人的: *a humanoid robot* 人形的机器人 —**humanoid** *n* [C]

human race /,·· ˈ·/ *n* **the human race** all people, considered together as a single group 人类〔总称〕 —see also 另见 MAN[1] (3)

human re·sourc·es /,·· ·ˈ··/ *n* **1** [plural] the abilities and skills of people 人力资源 **2** the department in a company that deals with employing, training, and helping people; PERSONNEL (2)〔公司的〕人力资源部, 人事部

human rights /,·· ˈ·/ *n* [plural] the basic rights which every person has to be treated in a fair, equal way without cruelty, especially by their government 人权: *flagrant human rights violations* 对人权明目张胆的侵犯

Hum·ber·side /ˈhʌmbɚsaɪd; ˈhʌmbəsaɪd/ a former COUNTY in northeast England, which is now called East Yorkshire 亨伯赛德郡〔原英格兰东北部一郡, 现名东约克郡〕

hum·ble[1] /ˈhʌmbḷ; ˈhʌmbəl/ *adj* **1** having a low social class or position〔地位〕卑微的, 低下的: **humble background/origins etc** *Iacocca rose from humble beginnings to become boss of Ford.* 亚科卡出身卑微, 后来成了福特公司的总裁。| *a humble country parson* 地位低下的乡村牧师 **2** not considering yourself or your ideas to be as important as other people's 谦虚的, 谦卑的: *He thanked us again with a humble smile.* 他带着谦卑的微笑再次向我们表示感谢。—opposite 反义词 PROUD (2) **3 my humble apologies** *spoken* used to say you are sorry, but not in a very serious way【口】是我错〔一种不太认真的口气〕 **4 in my humble opinion** *spoken* used to give your opinion about something in a slightly humorous way【口】敝人以为, 依我愚见〔略带幽默的说法〕 **5** simple and not advanced, but useful or effective 简单而实用的: **the humble** *high-priced successor to the humble pocket calculator* 取代简单而实用的袖珍计算器的昂贵的下一代产品 **6 eat humble pie** to admit that you were wrong about something〔低声下气地〕承认错误; 赔礼道歉 **7 your humble servant** a formal way of ending a letter, used in the past 您卑微的仆人; 卑职; 愚〔旧时信末的自谦词〕—**humbly** *adv* —see also 另见 HUMILITY

humble[2] *v* **humbled, humbling 1 be humbled** if you are humbled, you realize that you are not as important, good, kind etc as you thought you were 使谦卑, 使感到自惭: *He felt humbled by their offer.* 他们的出价令他自惭形秽。**2** [T] to easily defeat someone who is much stronger than you are〔轻易〕击败〔强敌〕: *The mighty US army was humbled by a small South East Asian country.* 强大的美军竟被一个小小的东南亚国家轻易击败。**3 humble yourself** to show that you are not too proud to ask for something, admit you are wrong etc 作出谦恭的姿态; 不耻下问; 勇于认错 —**humbling** *adj*: *a humbling experience* 自尊心受挫的经历

hum·bug /ˈhʌm,bʌg; ˈhʌmbʌg/ *n* **1** [U] insincere words or behaviour, especially pretending to feel shocked or disapprove of something 诡计, 花招; 假道学 **2** [U] *old-fashioned* someone who pretends to be someone they are not, or to have qualities or opinions they do not have【过时】骗子, 假冒者 **3** [C] *BrE* a sweet made of hard boiled sugar, usually tasting of mint (MINT[1] (2))【英】薄荷硬糖

hum·ding·er /ˌhʌmˈdɪŋɚ; hʌmˈdɪŋə/ *n* [singular] *informal* a very exciting or impressive game, performance, or event【非正式】精彩的比赛[节目, 事件]: **a real humdinger** *Foreman's next match promises to be a real humdinger.* 福尔曼的下一场比赛肯定精彩绝伦。

hum·drum/ˈhʌmˌdrʌm; ˈhʌmdrʌm/ *adj* boring and ordinary, and having very little variety or interest 单调的，过于平凡的，乏味的: **a humdrum existence/job** *a humdrum office job* 单调乏味的办公室工作

Hume/hjum; hjuːm/, **David** (1711-76) a Scottish writer on PHILOSOPHY and history. His most famous works are *A Treatise of Human Nature* and *History of England*. He believed in EMPIRICISM, the idea that human knowledge comes only from what we see and feel, and his ideas had great influence on European philosophy. 休谟〔(1711-1776)，苏格兰哲学家、历史学家。他最著名的作品是《人性论》和《英国史》。他相信经验论，即人类的知识只能来自眼见身受。他的观点对欧洲哲学产生过重大影响〕

Hume, John (1939-) a politician from Northern Ireland, who was the leader of the SDLP (=Social Democratic Labour Party) from 1979 to 2001. John Hume has been active in trying to bring an end to violence in Northern Ireland, and trying to start peace talks between Catholics and Protestants. In 1998 he shared the Nobel Prize for peace with David Trimble. 休姆〔(1939-)，北爱尔兰政治家，1979至2001年间任社会民主工党领袖。他一直积极致力于结束北爱尔兰存在的暴力活动，开启天主教和新教之间的和平会谈。1998年，他与戴维·特林布尔一起分享诺贝尔和平奖〕

hu·mer·us/ˈhjumərəs; ˈhjuːmərəs/ [C] *n technical* the bone between your shoulder and elbow【术语】肱骨

hu·mid/ˈhjumɪd; ˈhjuːmɨd/ *adj* weather that is humid makes you feel uncomfortable because the air feels very hot and wet〔天气〕潮湿的: *Tokyo is extremely humid in mid-summer.* 仲夏的东京十分闷热潮湿。—compare 比较 DRY¹ (2)

hu·mid·i·fi·er/hjuˋmɪdəˌfaɪɚ; hjuːˈmɪdɨfaɪə/ *n* [C] a machine that makes the air in a room, container etc less dry 加湿器，增湿器

hu·mid·i·fy/hjuˋmɪdəˌfaɪ; hjuːˈmɪdɨfaɪ/ *v* [T] to add very small drops of water to the air in a room etc because the air is too dry 使湿润

hu·mid·i·ty /hjuˋmɪdətɪ; hjuːˈmɪdɨti/ *n* [U] **1** the amount of water contained in the air 湿度；湿气: *90% humidity* 90%湿度 **2** air or weather that is uncomfortably warm and wet 闷热潮湿的空气[天气]

hu·mil·i·ate/hjuˋmɪlɪˌet; hjuːˈmɪlieɪt/ *v* [T] to make someone feel ashamed and upset, especially by making them seem stupid or weak 使蒙羞，羞辱: *Her boss humiliated her in front of all her colleagues.* 她的老板在所有同事面前羞辱了她。—**humiliated** *adj*: *I've never felt so humiliated in all my life!* 我这辈子从未感到过如此丢人!

hu·mil·i·at·ing/hjuˌmɪlɪˋetɪŋ; hjuːˈmɪlieɪtɪŋ/ *adj* making you feel ashamed, embarrassed, and angry because you have been made to look weak or stupid 使蒙受耻辱的，丢脸的，不光彩的: *a humiliating defeat* 丢脸的失败

hu·mil·i·a·tion/hjuˌmɪlɪˋeʃən; hjuːˌmɪliˈeɪʃən/ *n* **1** [U] a feeling of shame and great embarrassment, because you have been made to look stupid or weak 羞辱，丢脸，蒙耻: *She would do anything rather than suffer the humiliation of asking her parents for money.* 她无论如何都不愿厚着脸皮去跟父母要钱。**2** [C usually singular 一般用单数] a situation that makes you feel humiliated 使人蒙羞的情形

hu·mil·i·ty/hjuˋmɪlətɪ; hjuːˈmɪlɨti/ *n* [U] the quality of not being too proud about yourself 谦逊，谦恭 —see also 另见 HUMBLE¹

humming bird/ˈ· · ·/ *n* [C] a very small brightly-coloured tropical bird whose wings move very quickly 蜂鸟

hum·mock/ˈhʌmək; ˈhʌmək/ *n* [C] a very small hill; HILLOCK 小山丘，冈

hum·mus, **humus**/ˈhuməs; ˈhuːməs/ *n* [U] a type of Greek food made from a soft mixture of CHICK PEAS, oil and GARLIC 鹰嘴豆泥〔用鹰嘴豆捣碎后加油、大蒜等制成的希腊食品〕

hu·mor·ist/ˈhjumərɪst; ˈhjuːmərɨst/ *n* [C] someone, especially a writer, who tells funny stories（谈吐）诙谐的人；〔尤指〕幽默作家

hu·mor·ous/ˈhjumərəs; ˈhjuːmərəs/ *adj* deliberately funny and entertaining, especially in a clever way 幽默的，诙谐的: *a humorous account of her travels in South America* 对她南美之行的幽默描述 —**humorously** *adv*

hu·mour¹ *BrE*【英】, **humor** *AmE*【美】/ˈhjumɚ; ˈhjuːmə/ *n* **1** [U] the quality in something that makes it funny 幽默，风趣: *Mr Thorne failed to see the humour in the situation.* 索恩先生看不到这种情景的幽默之处。**2** [U] the way that a particular person or group find certain things amusing〔某人或人群的〕幽默方式: *English humour* 英国式幽默 | **sense of humour** *Ackroyd's often bizarre sense of humor* 阿克罗伊德常有的奇特幽默感 **3** [U] the ability to understand and enjoy amusing situations or to laugh at things 幽默感，感受幽默的能力: *Paul radiated humour and charm.* 保罗全身散发着幽默感和魅力。| **sense of humour** *It's vital to have a sense of humor in this job.* 做这份工作必须具备幽默感。**4 good humour** the ability to remain cheerful, especially in situations that would make some people upset or angry〔尤指在不利形势中的〕良好情绪: *Danny reacted to these criticisms with his usual good humour.* 丹尼以他惯常的好情绪对待这些批评。**5 in a good humour/in a bad humour etc** in a good or bad temper 心情好/坏等 —see also 另见 GOOD-HUMOURED **6** [C] one of the four liquids that in the past were thought to be present in the body and to influence someone's character〔旧时认为存在于体内并会影响性格的〕四种体液之一 **7 out of humour** *old-fashioned* in a bad temper【过时】心情不好

humour² *BrE*【英】, **humor** *AmE*【美】 *v* [T] to agree with someone even though you know they are wrong 迁就，迎合: *I decided I'd better try and humour him, as I couldn't face another argument.* 我决定最好还是试着迎合他，因为我不想再和他争辩了。

hu·mour·less/ˈhjumɚlɪs; ˈhjuːmələs/ *adj* too serious and not able to laugh at things that other people think are amusing 缺乏幽默感的，一本正经的 —**humourlessly** *adv* —**humourlessness** *n* [U]

hump¹/hʌmp; hʌmp/ *n* **1** [C] a large round shape that rises above the surface of the ground or a surface 巨大鼓包，圆形隆起物: *I could just make out the hump of a hill in the distance.* 我只能依稀辨认出远处隆起的山丘。**2** [C] one of the two raised parts on the back of a CAMEL 驼峰 **3** [C] a raised part on someone's back that is caused by an unusually curved SPINE (1)〔人的〕驼背 **4 be over the hump** to have succeeded in doing the most difficult part of something 完成最困难的部分，渡过最困难的阶段 **5 give sb the hump/get the hump** *BrE spoken* to make someone feel angry or upset, or to feel angry or upset【英口】使…生气[烦恼]/生气: *He'll get the right hump when he finds out you've drunk all his Scotch.* 一旦他发现你喝光了他的苏格兰威士忌，他一定会发火的。

hump² *v* **1** [T always+adv/prep] *BrE informal* to carry something heavy somewhere, especially with difficulty【英，非正式】背，扛，搬运: **hump sth down/along/across etc** *I just about managed to hump the suitcases upstairs.* 我勉强将那些箱子搬上了楼。**2** [I,T] *slang* to have sex with someone【俚】与…性交

hump·back/ˈhʌmpˌbæk; ˈhʌmpbæk/ *n* [C] another form of HUNCHBACK hunchback 的另一种形式

hump-backed bridge/ˌ· · ˈ·/ also 又作 **hump-back bridge** *n* [C] *especially BrE* a short steep bridge【尤英】弓形桥，驼峰桥

humpback whale/ˌ· · ˈ·/ *n* [C] a large WHALE 座头鲸

humph/hʌmf; hʌmf/ *interjection* used to show that you do not believe something or do not approve of something 哼〔表示怀疑、异议〕

Hump·ty Dump·ty/ˌhʌmptɪ ˋdʌmptɪ; ˌhʌmpti ˈdʌmpti/ a character in a NURSERY RHYME (=an old song or poem for young children) and in the book *Through the Looking-Glass* by Lewis Carroll, who is like a large egg in shape. 矮胖子〔一首童谣中的人物，也是刘易斯·卡罗尔的童话《镜中世界》中的人物。他长得像一只大鸡蛋〕:

Humpty Dumpty sat on a wall,
Humpty Dumpty had a great fall.
All the King's horses and all the King's men
Couldn't put Humpty together again.
矮胖子坐墙头，
矮胖子栽斤斗。
国王的马，国王的兵，
无法还他原来的样。

hu·mus/ˈhjuməs; ˈhjuːməs/ *n* [U] soil made of decayed plants, leaves etc which is good for growing plants 腐殖质，腐质土（壤）

Hun, the/hʌn; hʌn/ *n slang* an insulting word for German people, used especially during the First and Second World Wars【俚】德国佬〔第一、二次世界大战中对德国人的蔑称〕

hunch¹/hʌntʃ; hʌntʃ/ *n* [C] a feeling that something is true or that something is happening, even though you have very little information about it 基于直觉的想法，预感: *"How did you know that Campbell was a murderer?" "Oh, it was just a hunch."* "你怎么知道坎贝尔是杀人凶手?" "噢，那只是直觉。" | **have a hunch (that)** *I had a hunch that something like this would happen.* 我早就预感到这种事会发生。

hunch² *v* **1** [I always+adv/prep] to bend down and forwards so that your back forms a curve 弓起背: [+over] *She hunched nervously over her drink.* 她弓着背紧张地喝着饮料。**2 hunch your shoulders** to raise your shoulders into a rounded shape, especially because you are cold, anxious etc〔尤因寒冷、紧张等〕耸起双肩 —**hunched** *adj*

hunch·back /ˈhʌntʃˌbæk; ˈhʌntʃbæk/ *n* [C] an offensive word for someone whose back has a large raised part on it because their SPINE (1) curves in an unusual way 驼背(的人), 驼子〔冒犯用语〕

Hunchback of Not·re Dame, The /ˌ· · ·, · · ˈ· ·/ (1831) a NOVEL by Victor Hugo about a kind but ugly HUNCHBACK (=someone whose back has a large raised part on it) called Quasimodo, who rings bells in the CATHEDRAL of Notre Dame in Paris in the 15th century. He secretly loves a beautiful woman called Esmeralda, and when she is wrongly punished for being a murderer, he tries to save her.《巴黎圣母院》〔(1831), 维克托·雨果创作的一部小说, 讲述15世纪巴黎圣母院的敲钟人卡西莫多的故事。卡西莫多是一个心地善良但形貌丑陋的驼背人。他偷偷地爱着美丽的女子艾丝美拉达。在她被冤枉杀了人受到惩罚时, 卡西莫多竭力营救她〕

hun·dred /ˈhʌndrəd; ˈhʌndrɪ̵d/ *number* **1** 100 百: *a hundred years* 一百年 | *two hundred miles* 两百英里 **2 a hundred times** many times 许多次: *I've told you a hundred times not to do that!* 我已经无数次警告过你不要那样干了! **3 a hundred per cent** *spoken*【口】**a)** completely 百分之百, 完全: *I agree with you a hundred per cent.* 我完全同意你的看法。**b)** well 健康的, 完全复原的: *I'm still not really feeling a hundred per cent.* 我觉得自己仍然没有完全康复。

> **USAGE NOTE 用法说明: HUNDRED**
> GRAMMAR 语法
> Singular and plural forms of the number words **dozen, hundred, thousand, million** and **billion** are all used in the same ways. 数词dozen、hundred、thousand、million和billion的单、复数形式用法均相同。
> When one of these words follows a word showing number or amount, it is not put in the plural and does not have *of* after it. 如出现在具体数字之后, 不必用复数形式, 后面也不加of: *a/three/several hundred years* 一/三/几百年 (NOT 不用 *three hundreds of years*) | *ten million people* 一千万人 | *a few dozen eggs* 几十只蛋 | *about fifty thousand miles* 约五万英里
> Where there is no other word showing a number or amount, the plural is used. 如不与具体数字相连, 则用复数形式: *He has hundreds of books.* (NOT 不用 *He has hundred of books.*) *It will cost thousands of dollars* (=I do not know how many thousand exactly). 他有几百本书。这要花费几千美元。

hundreds and thou·sands /ˌ· · · ˈ· ·/ *BrE n* [plural] small thin pieces of coloured sugar used to decorate cakes【英】〔蛋糕上作装饰用的〕彩色珠子糖

hun·dredth /ˈhʌndrədθ; ˈhʌndrɪ̵dθ/ *n* [C] **1** one of the hundred equal parts of something 百分之一 **2** 100th 第一百(个)

hun·dred·weight /ˈhʌndrədˌwet; ˈhʌndrɪ̵dweɪt/ written abbreviation 缩写为 **cwt** *n* [C] a unit for measuring weight equal to 112 pounds or 50.8 kilograms 英担〔相当于112磅或50.8公斤〕—see table on page C4 参见C4页附录

Hundred Years War, the /ˌ· · · ˈ· ·/ a series of wars between England and France from 1337-1453, when the English kings tried to keep control of land which they ruled in France. The French finally won, and forced the English to leave France. 百年战争〔指1337至1453年英法两国间的一系列战争。当时, 英格兰国王试图维系对法国土地的统治。最终, 法国取胜, 把英国人赶出了法国〕

hung /hʌŋ; hʌŋ/ past tense and past participle of HANG

Hun·gar·ian¹ /hʌŋˋgɛrɪən; hʌŋˈgeərɪən/ *n* **1** [U] the language of Hungary 匈牙利语 **2** [C] someone from Hungary 匈牙利人

Hungarian² *adj* from or connected with Hungary 匈牙利的

Hun·ga·ry /ˈhʌŋgrɪ; ˈhʌŋgəri/ a country in central Europe, east of Austria and west of Romania. Population: 10,106,000 (2001). Capital: Budapest. From 1945 to 1989, Hungary was one of the Communist countries of Eastern Europe. The people of Hungary are sometimes called **Magyars**. 匈牙利〔中欧一国, 位于奥地利以东, 罗马尼亚以西。人口: 10,106,000 (2001), 首都: 布达佩斯。1945至1989年间, 该国为东欧共产党执政的国家之一。匈牙利人有时也称马扎尔人〕—**Hungarian** /hʌŋˋgɛrɪən; hʌŋˈgeərɪən/ *n, adj*

hun·ger¹ /ˈhʌŋgɚ; ˈhʌŋgə/ *n* **1** [U] lack of food, especially for a long period of time, that can cause illness or death; STARVATION〔尤指长期的〕饥饿; 饥荒: *Thousands of people are dying from hunger every day.* 每天都有成千上万人因饥饿而死亡。**2** [U] the feeling that you need to eat 饥饿感: *Babies often cry from hunger.* 婴儿常常因饥饿而哭叫。| **hunger pangs** (=sudden feelings of being hungry) 突如其来的饥饿感 **3 hunger for** a strong need or desire for something 对…的渴求[渴望]: *the West's hunger for material wealth* 西方人对物质财富的渴求

hunger² *v* [I] *literary* to want something very much【文】渴望, 渴求: [+for/after] *a nation hungering for change* 渴望变革的国家

hunger strike /ˈ· · ˌ·/ *n* [C] a situation in which someone refuses to eat for a long time in order to protest about something 绝食抗议 —**hunger striker** *n* [C]

hung ju·ry /ˌ· ˈ· ·/ *n* [singular] a JURY (1) that cannot agree about whether someone is guilty of a crime〔因意见不一致而〕未能作出裁定的陪审团

hung·o·ver /hʌŋˋovɚ; hʌŋˈəʊvə/ *adj* feeling ill because you have drunk too much alcohol the previous evening 因宿醉而感到难受的, 宿醉的 —see also 另见 HANGOVER

hung par·lia·ment /ˌ· ˈ· · ·/ *n* [C] *BrE* a parliament in which no one political party has more elected representatives than the others added together【英】各党派势均力敌的议会

hun·gri·ly /ˈhʌŋgrɪlɪ; ˈhʌŋgrɪ̵li/ *adv* **1** in a way that shows you want to eat something very much 饥饿地: *J.D. ate hungrily, covering the french fries with layers of catsup.* J.D.在炸薯条上浇上厚厚的番茄酱, 狼吞虎咽地吃着。**2** in a way that shows you very much want something 充满渴望地: *Her gaze fell hungrily on my diamond ring.* 她的目光充满渴求地落在我的钻石戒指上。

hun·gry /ˈhʌŋgrɪ; ˈhʌŋgri/ *adj* **1** wanting to eat something 饥饿的: *There's tons of food – I hope you're all hungry!* 那儿有好多食物, 希望你们都已经饿了! | **get hungry** *If you get hungry between meals, have a piece of fruit.* 你如果在两顿饭之间感到饿, 就吃一块水果。**2** ill or weak as a result of not having enough to eat for a long time 挨饿的: *We can't justify wasting food when half the world is hungry.* 世界上有一半人在挨饿, 我们没有理由浪费食物。**3 the hungry** people who do not have enough food to eat 挨饿的人 **4 go hungry** to not have enough to eat 吃不饱, 挨饿: *Thousands of families go hungry every day in this country.* 这个国家里每天都有数以千计的家庭吃不饱肚子。**5 be hungry for** to want or need something very much 渴望得到…: *young people hungry for excitement and adventure* 渴望刺激和冒险的年轻人 **6 power-hungry/news-hungry etc** wanting power, news etc very much 渴求权力/消息等的

hung-up /ˌ· ˈ·/ *adj informal* very anxious and unhappy about a situation【非正式】焦虑的, 担心的: [+about] *She's really hung-up about her parents.* 她十分担心她的父母。

hunk /hʌŋk; hʌŋk/ *n* [C] **1** a thick piece of something, especially food, that has been cut or torn from a bigger piece〔切下或撕下的〕一大块, 一大片〔尤指食物〕: [+of] *a hunk of bread* 一大块面包 — see picture on page A7 参见A7页图 **2** [C] *informal* a man who is attractive because he is big and strong【非正式】高大健壮的男子

hun·ker /ˈhʌŋkɚ; ˈhʌŋkə/ *v* [I] *AmE* to sit on your heels with your knees bent up in front of you; SQUAT【美】蹲坐, 蹲: [+down] *They hunkered down by the fire.* 他们蹲坐在火边。

hunker down *phr v* [I,T often passive 常用被动态] *AmE* to work hard to completely prepare yourself for a difficult situation【美】认真准备〔以应付艰难的情况〕

hun·kers /ˈhʌŋkɚz; ˈhʌŋkəz/ *n* **on your hunkers** sitting on your heels with your knees bent up in front of you 蹲坐, 蹲: *The little boy was squatting on his hunkers, completely absorbed in his game.* 小男孩蹲着, 完全沉浸在游戏之中。

hunk·y /ˈhʌŋkɪ; ˈhʌŋki/ *adj* a man who is hunky is attractive and strong-looking〔男性〕高大健壮的

hun·ky-dor·y /ˌhʌŋkɪ ˋdorɪ; ˌhʌŋki ˈdɔːri/ *adj* [not before noun 不用于名词前] *informal* a situation that is hunky-dory is one in which everyone feels happy and there are no problems【非正式】〔情况〕令人十分满意的, 一切如意的

hunt¹ /hʌnt; hʌnt/ *v* **1** [I,T] to chase animals and birds in order to catch and kill them 追猎, 猎杀〔鸟兽〕: *At one time man had to hunt to survive.* 从前人类要以打猎为生。| **hunt sth** *hunting big game in Kenya* 在肯尼亚捕猎大型动物 **2** [I] to look hard for something you have lost 搜寻, 寻找: *We've been hunting for the car keys for the last half-hour.* 过去的半小时里, 我们一直在找汽车钥匙。**3** [I,T] *BrE* to hunt foxes (FOX¹ (1)) as a sport, riding on horses and using dogs【英】〔骑马用猎犬〕猎(狐) **4** [T] to search for and try to catch someone, especially a criminal

搜捕，追捕〔罪犯〕: *Police are hunting the killer.* 警方正在追捕杀人凶手。

hunt sb/sth ↔ **down** *phr v* [T] to catch someone in order to kill, hurt, or punish them, after chasing them or trying very hard to catch them〔几经艰苦下〕追捕到，捉住

hunt sb/sth ↔ **out** *phr v* [T] **1** to search for someone in order to catch or get rid of them 搜捕，追捕〔某人〕: *Military Police were ordered to hunt out subversives.* 宪兵队奉命搜捕颠覆分子。**2** to look for something that you have not used or seen for a long time 搜寻，寻找〔某物〕: *I must try and hunt out that old tennis racket.* 我必须尽力找到那只旧网球拍。

hunt² *n* **1** [C] an occasion when people chase animals in order to catch and kill them 打猎，狩猎: *a tiger hunt* 猎虎 **2** [singular] a search for someone or something that is difficult to find 搜索，搜寻: **the hunt for** *the hunt for the remains of the Titanic* 对"泰坦尼克号"残骸的搜索工作 | **the hunt is on** (=used to say that people have started looking for someone or something) 开始搜寻 | **have a hunt around for** *informal* (=look for something)【非正式】搜寻，寻找 *I'll have a hunt around for it in my desk.* 我会在书桌里找找它。**3** [C] an organized sporting event in Britain in which people riding on horses hunt foxes (FOX¹ (1)) using dogs 骑马〔用猎犬〕猎狐〔英国的一种体育项目〕 **4** [C] *BrE* a group of people who regularly hunt foxes (FOX¹ (1)) together【英】经常在一起猎狐的人

CULTURAL NOTE 文化注释

In the US hunting, especially for DEER or ducks, is a popular sport with some people, but other people think that it is cruel. Most hunters eat what they kill. In the UK, hunting is thought of as an UPPER CLASS sport, especially FOXHUNTING. Many people think foxhunting should not be allowed because they think it is cruel. 一些美国人喜欢打猎，尤其是猎鹿和猎野鸭，但也有人认为打猎是残忍的行为。多数猎人把猎物吃掉。打猎，尤其是猎狐，在英国被视为上流社会的运动。很多人认为猎狐太残忍，应取缔。—see Cultural Note at FOXHUNTING 见 FOXHUNTING 文化注释

Hunt, Wil·liam Hol·man /ˋwɪljəm ˋholmən; ˈwɪljəm ˈhəʊlmən/ (1827-1910) a British painter who, with Millais and Rossetti, started the Pre-Raphaelite Brotherhood in 1848 亨特〔(1827-1910)，英国画家。1848年，他同密莱司和罗塞蒂共同创立了拉斐尔前派兄弟会〕

hunt·er /ˋhʌntɚ; ˈhʌntə/ *n* **1** [C] a person or animal that hunts wild animals 猎人，捕猎野兽的人;〔猎食其他动物的〕猎兽 **2 souvenir/autograph/bargain etc hunter** someone who looks for or collects a particular type of thing 搜集纪念品/签名/便宜货的人等 **3** [C] a strong horse used in Britain for hunting foxes (FOX¹ (1))〔英国猎狐用的〕狩猎用马 —see also 另见 BOUNTY HUNTER, FORTUNE HUNTER

hunt·ing /ˋhʌntɪŋ; ˈhʌntɪŋ/ *n* [U] **1** the act of chasing and killing animals for food or for sport〔为猎食或作为运动的〕打猎，狩猎 **2** the sport of hunting foxes (FOX¹ (1)) in Britain〔英国的〕猎狐运动 **3 job-hunting/house-hunting etc** the activity of looking for a job, house etc 找工作/房子等 **4 go hunting** to hunt for animals, especially as a sport〔尤作为运动〕去打猎 —**hunting** *adj*: *a hunting rifle* 猎枪

hunting ground /ˈ·· ·/ *n* **1** [C] a place where animals are hunted 狩猎场 **2 a happy/good hunting ground for** a place where people who are interested in a particular thing can easily find what they want 能让人轻易找到自己感兴趣东西的地方;…爱好者的天堂

hunt·ress /ˋhʌntrɛs; ˈhʌntrɪ̈s/ *n* [C] *literary* a female hunter【文】女猎人，女狩猎者

hunt sab·o·teur /ˌ· ˈ···ˌ/ *n* [C] *BrE* member of a group that tries to stop people from hunting foxes (FOX¹ (1))【英】阻止猎狐者，反狩猎活动者

hunts·man /ˋhʌntsmən; ˈhʌntsmən/ *n* [C] *especially BrE*【尤英】**1** a man who hunts animals (男)猎人，狩猎者 **2** the person in charge of the dogs in FOXHUNTING〔猎狐时的〕猎犬管理员

hur·dle¹ /ˋhɝdl; ˈhɜːdl/ *n* **1** [C] a frame that a person or horse has to jump over during a race〔跨栏赛跑或马术表演中用的〕栏架: **clear a hurdle** (=successfully jump over a hurdle) 跨越栏架 **2** [C] a problem or difficulty that you must deal with before you can achieve something〔必须克服的〕障碍，困难: *Finding enough money was the first hurdle.* 首先需要克服的困难是筹措足够的资金。| **clear a hurdle** (=deal successfully with a problem) 克服困难 **3 the 100 metres/400 metres hurdles** a race in which the runners have to jump over hurdles 100米/400米跨栏赛跑 **4** [C] a moveable part of a temporary fence around animals or land〔用以围起动物或土地的〕临时活动围栏

hurdle² *v* **1** [T] to jump over something while you are running〔跑步过程中〕跨越: *Barrett hurdled the fence and ran off down the street.* 巴雷特跨过护栏沿着街逃走了。**2** [I] to run in hurdle races 进行跨栏赛跑 —**hurdler** *n* [C] —**hurdling** *n* [U]

hur·dy-gur·dy /ˋhɝdɪ ˌgɝdɪ; ˈhɜːdi ˌgɜːdi/ *n* [C] a small musical instrument that you operate by turning a handle 手摇风琴

hurl /hɝl; hɜːl/ *v* **1** [T always+adv/prep] to throw something violently and with a lot of force, especially because you are angry 猛投，(用力)投掷〔尤因生气〕: **hurl sth through/across/over etc** *Demonstrators were hurling bricks through the windows.* 示威者在向窗里掷砖头。**2 hurl abuse/insults/accusations etc at sb** to shout at someone in a loud and angry way 漫骂/辱骂/责骂某人等 **3 hurl yourself at/against** to throw yourself at someone or something with a lot of force 向…猛扑过去

hurl·ing /ˋhɝlɪŋ; ˈhɜːlɪŋ/ *n* [U] an Irish ball game played between two teams of 15 players 爱尔兰式曲棍球

hur·ly-bur·ly /ˋhɝlɪˌbɝlɪ; ˈhɜːliˌbɜːli/ *n* [U] a lot of busy, noisy activity 骚动，喧哗闹腾: *the hurly-burly of city life* 城市生活的喧嚣

Hu·ron /ˋhjurən; ˈhjʊərən/, **Lake** the second largest of the Great Lakes, on the border between the US and Canada 休伦湖〔五大湖中的第二大湖，位于美国和加拿大边境一带〕

hur·ray /həˋre; hʊˈreɪ/ also 又作 **hur·rah** /həˋrɑ; hʊˈrɑː/ *interjection old-fashioned* a shout that shows you are pleased【过时】好哇！加油！万岁！〔表示高兴的呼喊声〕—see also 另见 **hip, hip, hurray!** (HIP²)

hur·ri·cane /ˋhɝɪˌken; ˈhʌrɪ̈kən/ *n* [C] a violent storm, especially in the western Atlantic ocean〔尤指大西洋西部的〕飓风 —compare 比较 CYCLONE, TYPHOON, TORNADO —see picture on page A13 参见 A13 页图

Hurricane a type of British fighter aircraft which became famous in World War II for its success against enemy bombers and fighters 飓风式战斗机〔英国一种战斗机。二战期间因成功阻击敌军的轰炸机和战斗机出名〕

hurricane lamp /ˈ··· ·/ *n* [C] a lamp that has a strong cover to protect the flame inside from the wind 防风灯

hur·ried /ˋhɝɪd; ˈhʌrid/ *adj* [usually before noun 一般用于名词前] done very quickly, often too quickly, because you are in a hurry; RUSHED 匆忙完成的，赶出来的: *We just caught the plane after several hurried phone calls from the airport.* 我们从机场匆忙打了几个电话后，刚刚好赶上了飞机。—**hurriedly** *adv*

hur·ry¹ /ˋhɝɪ; ˈhʌri/ *v* **1** [I,T] to do something or go somewhere more quickly than usual, especially because there is not much time 赶紧，匆忙: *The movie begins as six – we'll have to hurry.* 电影6点开始，我们得赶快点。| **hurry through/along/down etc** *She hurried down the corridor as fast as she could.* 她以最快速度沿着走廊急匆匆地走了。| **hurry after sb** *John went hurrying off after his girlfriend.* 约翰急着去追他的女朋友了。| **hurry to do sth** *They were hurrying to catch their train.* 他们匆匆忙忙去赶火车。| **hurry sth** *I don't want to have to hurry my meal.* 我不想匆匆忙忙吃饭。**2** [T] to make someone do something more quickly 催促，使匆忙: *Don't hurry me; I'm working as fast as I can.* 别催我，我正在尽快干呢！**3 hurry up!** *spoken* used to tell someone to do something more quickly【口】快点！: *Hurry up, we're late!* 快点，我们迟到了！| **hurry up with** *Hurry up with the accounts – the boss is waiting for them.* 快把账做好，老板等着要呢！**4** [T always+adv/prep] to take someone or something quickly to a place 急送: **hurry sth to/through/across etc** *Emergency supplies have been hurried to the areas worst hit by the famine.* 应急物资已经被紧急运往饥荒最严重的地区。

hurry sb/sth **up** *phr v* [T] to make someone do something more quickly or to make something happen more quickly 催促，使加快

hurry² *n* **1 be in a hurry** to do something, go somewhere, need something etc more quickly than usual, often too quickly 匆匆忙忙，仓促，赶时间: *Sorry, I can't stop, I'm in a hurry.* 对不起，我不能停下，我有急事。| *You'll make mistakes if you do things in too much of a hurry.* 办事太匆促会出错的。| **be in a hurry to do sth** *Why are you in such a hurry to leave?* 你干嘛这么急着要走？**2 will not be doing sth (again) in a hurry** *spoken* used to say that you do not want to do something again【口】再也不愿干某事: *We won't be going back there again in a hurry, I can tell you.* 我可以告诉你，我们再也不愿回到那里去了。**3 in your hurry to do sth** while you are trying to do something too quickly 在匆忙做某事的时候: *In his hurry to leave the* S3

H

room he tripped over a chair. 他在匆匆忙忙离开房间时，被椅子绊了一下。**4 be in no hurry/not be in any hurry** to be able to wait because you have plenty of time in which to do something 不急于，不着急：*I'll wait till you've closed up – I'm not in any hurry.* 我等到你关门，我不着急。**5 be in no hurry to do sth/not be in any hurry to do sth** to be unwilling to do something or not want to do it soon 不急着做某事：*I'm in no particular hurry to leave.* 我不特别急着要走。**6 (there's) no hurry** *spoken* used to tell someone that they do not have to do something soon【口】不用着急！：*You can give me the money back next month. There's no great hurry.* 你可以下个月还钱给我，不用急。**7 what's (all) the hurry?/why (all) the hurry?** *spoken* used to say that someone is doing something too quickly【口】急什么？：*We've got plenty of time – what's all the hurry?* 我们有的是时间，急什么？

2 3 **hurt[1]** /hɝt; hɜːt/ *v past tense and past participle* **hurt 1** [I,T] if a part of your body hurts, you feel pain in it〔身体〕感到疼痛：*My back hurts.* 我的背痛。| **it hurts** *Where does it hurt?* 哪儿痛？| **hurt sb** *My shoulder's really hurting me.* 我的肩膀疼得厉害。| **hurt like hell** (=hurt very much) 痛死了 **2** [T] if you hurt part of your body you injure it or make it feel painful, especially in an accident〔尤指在意外中〕弄伤，弄痛〔身体某部位〕：*Several people were seriously hurt in the accident.* 好几个人在事故中受了重伤。| **hurt your arm/leg/nose etc** *I hurt my finger in the door.* 我的手指让门夹伤了。| **hurt yourself** (=injure yourself) 弄伤自己 *Careful you don't hurt yourself – it's very sharp.* 小心别伤了你自己，它很锋利。**3** [I,T] if something hurts part of your body, it makes it feel painful〔某物〕使〔身体某个部位〕感到疼痛；*The sun's hurting my eyes.* 阳光刺痛我的双眼。**4** [T] to cause physical pain to someone 弄痛〔某人〕：*Put that thing down – you might hurt someone with it.* 快放下它，你会伤着别人的。**5** [I,T] to make someone feel very upset, unhappy, sad etc 伤害〔感情〕，使伤心：**hurt sb's feelings** *I'm really sorry, I didn't mean to hurt your feelings.* 真对不起，我不是故意伤害你的感情的。| **what hurts is that** *What really hurts is that he never even said goodbye.* 真正令人伤心的是，他甚至没有和我道别。| **hurt sb** *The last thing I want to do is to hurt you.* 我最不愿伤害你。**6 be hurting yourself** to be making yourself feel even more unhappy, upset, sad etc 加重自己的痛苦 **7** [T] to have a bad effect on someone or something, especially by making them less successful or powerful 造成损害，产生不良影响：*Foreign competition has definitely hurt the firm's position in the market.* 来自国外的竞争的确已经对公司的市场地位造成损害。**8 be hurting a)** *AmE informal* to feel very upset, unhappy, sad etc【美，非正式】感到十分痛苦 **b)** if a group, organization etc is hurting, they do not have something important that they need, for example money〔团体、组织等〕急需；缺乏：[**+for**] *Our division in Salem is hurting for competent staff right now.* 我们的塞勒姆分部目前急需精兵强将。**9 it won't/doesn't hurt (sb) to do sth** *spoken* used to say that there is no reason why someone cannot or should not do something【口】做某事不会有坏处：*It won't hurt Julia to get up early for once.* 偶尔早起一次不会对朱莉娅造成什么不便。**10 one more won't hurt** *spoken* used to encourage someone to have another drink, piece of chocolate etc【口】再来一杯[块]不会有问题的！〔用于劝人喝酒或吃东西〕—compare 比较 HARM[2]

hurt[2] *adj* **1** [not usually before noun 一般不用于名词前] physically injured〔肉体〕受伤的：**badly/seriously hurt** *This man needs a doctor – he's badly hurt.* 这个人需要医生治疗，他伤得很重。**2** very upset or unhappy because someone has said or done something unkind, dishonest, or unfair〔感情上〕受伤害的，痛苦的：*a hurt expression* 痛苦的表情 | **deeply hurt** *I was feeling deeply hurt by what she had just said.* 她刚才说的话深深地伤害了我。

hurt[3] *n* [C,U] a feeling of great unhappiness because someone, especially someone you trust, has treated you unkindly or unfairly〔对感情造成的〕伤害，痛苦：*the hurt caused by the breakup of his marriage* 婚姻破裂对他造成的伤害 —compare 比较 HARM[1]

hurt·ful /ˋhɝtfəl; ˈhɜːtfəl/ *adj* making you feel very upset or offended〔感情上〕伤害人的，使人痛苦的：*a hurtful remark* 刻薄的话 —**hurtfully** *adv* —**hurtfulness** *n* [U]

hur·tle /ˋhɝtl̩; ˈhɜːtl/ *v* [I always+adv/prep] if something, especially something big or heavy, hurtles somewhere, it moves or falls very fast〔巨大物体〕飞速移动；快速落下，猛冲：**hurtle down/through/along etc** *Huge pieces of rock went hurtling down the mountainside.* 巨大的岩石块沿着山坡飞滚而下。

1 1 **hus·band[1]** /ˋhʌzbənd; ˈhʌzbənd/ *n* **1** [C] the man that a woman is married to 丈夫：*Have you met her husband?* 你见过她的丈夫吗？| **ex-husband** (=a man that a woman used to be married to) 前夫 —see picture at 参见 FAMILY 图 **2 husband and wife** a man and woman who are married 夫妻，夫妇

husband[2] *v* [T] *formal* to be very careful in the way you use your money, supplies etc and not waste any【正式】节约地使用：*carefully husbanded resources* 谨慎节约使用的资源

hus·band·man /ˋhʌzbəndmən; ˈhʌzbəndmən/ *n* [C] *old use* a farmer【旧】农夫，农民

hus·band·ry /ˋhʌzbəndrɪ; ˈhʌzbəndri/ *n* **1** [U] *technical* farming【术语】农业；饲养业；农牧业：*animal husbandry* 畜牧业 **2** [U] *old-fashioned* careful management of money and supplies【过时】〔对资金、物资的〕节约；管理

hush[1] /hʌʃ; hʌʃ/ *v* **1 hush!** *spoken* used to tell people to be quiet or to comfort a child who is crying or upset【口】嘘！〔叫人别出声〕：*Hush, now. Try to get to sleep.* 嘘，别出声了。睡吧。**2** [T] to make someone stop shouting, talking, crying etc 使安静（下来）**3** [I] to stop shouting, talking etc 安静（下来）

hush sth ↔ **up** *phr v* [T] to prevent the public from knowing about something dishonest or immoral 隐瞒，遮掩：*The whole affair has been hushed up by school officials.* 校方行政管理人员隐瞒了整个事件。

hush[2] *n* **1** [singular] a period of silence that comes after there has been a lot of noise, shouting etc, especially because people are expecting something to happen〔吵闹过后的〕寂静，安静：**a hush falls/descends** (=everyone becomes quiet) 一片寂静 *A sudden hush descended on the crowd.* 人群突然变得鸦雀无声。**2 can we have/ let's have a bit of hush** *BrE spoken* used to ask people, especially noisy children, to be quiet【英口】让我们安静一点

hushed /hʌʃt; hʌʃt/ *adj* [usually before noun 一般用于名词前] quiet because people are listening, waiting to hear something, or talking quietly 安静的，寂静的：*A hushed courtroom awaited the verdict.* 法庭上一片寂静，人们在等待裁决。| **hushed tones/voice/whispers etc** (=quiet speech) 轻声/低声/小声耳语等

hush-hush /,ˑ ˈ◂/ *adj informal* an official operation etc that is hush-hush is very secret【非正式】秘密的

hush mon·ey /ˈ·,··/ *n* [U] money that is paid to someone not to tell other people about something embarrassing〔不让丑事张扬出去的〕封嘴钱，封口费

Hush Pup·pies /ˈ·,··/ *trademark* a company that makes shoes, or the shoes that this company makes【商标】暇步士（鞋）〔一家制鞋公司的名称或该公司生产的鞋类产品〕

hush pup·py /ˈ·,··/ *n* [C] a small fried cake made of MAIZE flour eaten in the southern states of the US〔美国南部常吃的〕油炸玉米饼

husk[1] /hʌsk; hʌsk/ *n* [C,U] the dry outer part of grains, seeds etc and some types of nut〔谷粒、种子、某几类坚果的〕外皮；壳；荚

husk[2] *v* [T] to remove the husks from grains, seeds etc 去除外皮，剥壳

hus·ky[1] /ˋhʌskɪ; ˈhʌski/ *adj* **1** a husky voice is deep, quiet, and rough-sounding, often in an attractive way〔声音〕沙哑的，嘶哑的：*"Come quickly," she said in a husky whisper.* "快来！"她用沙哑的声音小声说。**2** *especially AmE* a man who is husky is big and strong【尤美】〔男子〕高大健壮的 —**huskily** *adv* —**huskiness** *n* [U]

husky[2] *n* [C] a dog with thick hair used in Canada and Alaska to pull SLEDGES over the snow 爱斯基摩犬

hus·sar /hʊˋzɑr; hʊˈzɑː/ *n* [C] a British CAVALRY (2) soldier〔英国军队中的〕轻骑兵

Hus·sein /hʊˋsen; hʊˈseɪn/**, King** (1935- 99) the king of Jordan from 1952 until his death in 1999. He was admired by many people for his attempts to encourage peace between Israel and the Arab countries that surround it. 侯赛因〔(1935-1999)，约旦国王，1952年即位直至1999年去世。他试图促使以色列和周边阿拉伯国家和平相处，因而颇受赞赏〕

Hussein, Sad·dam /sæˋdæm; sæˈdæm/ —see 见 SADDAM HUSSEIN

hus·sy /ˋhʌsɪ; ˈhʌsi/ *n* [C] *old-fashioned* a woman who is sexually immoral【过时】荡妇，淫妇：*The shameless hussy!* 这个不要脸的荡妇！

hus·tings /ˋhʌstɪŋz; ˈhʌstɪŋz/ *n* **the hustings** *BrE* the process of trying to persuade people to vote for you by making speeches etc【英】竞选活动〈如拉票、演说等〉：**be at/on the hustings** *All the candidates are out on the hustings.* 所有候选人都在外出进行竞选拉票活动。

hus·tle[1] /ˋhʌsl̩; ˈhʌsəl/ *v* **hustled, hustling 1** [T] to make someone move quickly, especially by pushing them roughly 推搡，硬挤；催促：**hustle sb out/into/through etc** *I was hustled out of the building by a couple of security men.* 我被几个保安人员推

出了大楼。| **hustle sb off somewhere** *She hustled the kids off to school.* 她催促孩子们去上学。**2** [I,T] *AmE* to sell or obtain things, especially unofficially or illegally【美】非法买卖: *small time thieves hustling stolen goods on the street* 在街上非法兜售赃物的小偷 **3** [I] *AmE* to do something with a lot of energy and determination【美】拼命干, 努力干: *C'mon kids, let's hustle!* 来吧, 孩子们, 我们加把劲! **4** [I] *AmE slang* to work as a PROSTITUTE【美俚】当妓女, 卖淫

hustle² *n* [U] **1** busy and noisy activity 忙碌; 喧闹: **hustle and bustle** *the hustle and bustle of the market place* 市场上的熙熙攘攘 **2** *AmE* dishonest and illegal ways of getting money【美】非法获利; 欺诈行为

hus·tler /ˋhʌslɚ; ˈhʌslə/ *n* **1** [C] *especially AmE* someone who tries to trick people into giving them money【尤美】骗子 **2** [C] *AmE* a PROSTITUTE【美】妓女

Hus·ton /ˋhjustn̩; ˈhjuːstən/, **John** (1906-87) a US film DIRECTOR and film writer and actor whose many films include *The Maltese Falcon* (1941), *The African Queen* (1951), and *Prizzi's Honor* (1984) 休斯顿〔(1906-1987), 美国电影导演、剧作家和演员。其影片包括《马尔他之鹰》(1941)、《非洲女皇号》(1951)和《普里奇家族的荣誉》(1984)〕

hut /hʌt; hʌt/ *n* [C] a small, simple building with only one or two rooms (简陋的) 小屋, 棚屋, 茅舍: *a wooden hut* 小木屋

hutch /hʌtʃ; hʌtʃ/ *n* [C] **1** a small wooden CAGE used for keeping small animals in, especially rabbits〔尤指关兔子等小动物用的〕小笼子, 小木箱 **2** [C] *AmE* a piece of furniture used for storing and showing dishes【美】碗碟柜, 餐具柜; WELSH DRESSER *BrE*【英】

Hux·ley /ˋhʌkslɪ; ˈhʌksli/, **Al·dous** /ˋɔldəs; ˈɔːldəs/ (1894-1963) a British writer whose most famous work is *Brave New World*, about a society of the future where people are completely controlled and have no freedom 赫胥黎〔(1894-1963), 英国作家。其最著名的作品是《美丽新世界》, 讲述一个人类被完全控制、没有丝毫自由的未来社会〕

hy·a·cinth /ˋhaɪə͵sɪnθ; ˈhaɪəsɪ̵nθ/ *n* [C] a garden plant with blue, pink, or white bell-shaped flowers and a sweet smell〔植物〕风信子

hy·ae·na /haɪˋinə; haɪˈiːnə/ another spelling of HYENA hyena 的另一种拼法

hy·brid /ˋhaɪbrɪd; ˈhaɪbrɪ̵d/ *n* **1** [C] an animal or plant produced from parents of different breeds or types 杂种动物; 杂交植物; 杂交生成的生物体: *Most modern roses are hybrids.* 现代的玫瑰多数是杂交品种。**2** [C] something that consists of or comes from a mixture of two or more other things〔两种或两种以上不同物质组成的〕混合体

Hyde Park /͵ · ˈ ◂/ **1** a large park in central London, which includes the Serpentine, a lake, and Speaker's Corner, a place where ordinary people can make speeches about anything that they have strong opinions about 海德公园〔伦敦市中心一大型公园, 包括蛇湖和演讲角。在演讲角, 人们可针对任何事情发表有力的观点〕**2** an area in the south part of Chicago, in the US state of Illinois, where the University of Chicago is based 海德公园〔美国伊利诺伊州芝加哥南部一地区, 为芝加哥大学所在地〕

hy·dra /ˋhaɪdrə; ˈhaɪdrə/ *n plural* **hydrae** /-drɪ; -dri/ [C] **1** a snake in ancient Greek stories with many heads that grow again when they are cut off〔古希腊神话中头被斩去后会立即复生的〕多头蛇 **2** something that is evil and very difficult to get rid of 难于根除的祸患

hy·drant /ˋhaɪdrənt; ˈhaɪdrənt/ *n* [C] a water pipe in a street where you can get water to put on fires that are burning 消防栓; 消防龙头

hy·drate /ˋhaɪdret; ˈhaɪdreɪt/ *n* [C] *technical* a chemical substance that contains water【术语】水合物

hy·draul·ic /haɪˋdrɔlɪk; haɪˈdrɒlɪk/ *adj* [usually before noun 一般用于名词前] moved or operated by the pressure of water or other liquid 水[液]力的, 水[液]压的: *a hydraulic pump* 水压泵, 液压泵 | *hydraulic brakes* 液压制动器 —**hydraulically** /-klɪ; -kli/ *adv*

hy·draul·ics /haɪˋdrɔlɪks; haɪˈdrɒlɪks/ *n* [plural] the scientific study of the use of moving liquids 水力学

hydro- /haɪdro; haɪdrəʊ/ *prefix* **1** concerning or using water 水的: *hydroelectricity* (=produced by water power) 水力发电; 水电 | *hydrotherapy* (=treatment of disease using water) 水疗法 **2** concerning or containing HYDROGEN 含氢的, 氢化的: *hydrocarbons* 烃, 碳氢化合物

hy·dro·car·bon /͵haɪdroˋkɑrbən; ͵haɪdrəˈkɑːbən/ *n* [C] *technical* a chemical compound that consists of HYDROGEN and CARBON (1), such as coal or gas【术语】烃, 碳氢化合物

hy·dro·chlor·ic ac·id /͵haɪdrəˋklorɪk ˋæsɪd; ͵haɪdrəklɒrɪk ˈæsɪ̵d/ *n* [U] a strong acid used especially in industry 氢氯酸, 盐酸

hy·dro·e·lec·tric /͵haɪdro·ɪˋlɛktrɪk; ͵haɪdrəʊ-ɪˈlektrɪk◂/ *adj* using water power to produce electricity 水力发电的: *a hydroelectric power station* 水 (力发) 电站 —**hydroelectrically** /-klɪ; -kli/ *adv* —**hydroelectricity** /͵haɪdroɪlɛkˋtrɪsətɪ; ͵haɪdrəʊɪlekˈtrɪsɪ̵ti/ *n* [U]

hy·dro·foil /ˋhaɪdrə͵fɔɪl; ˈhaɪdrəfɔɪl/ *n* [C] a large boat that raises itself above the surface of the water when it travels at high speeds 水翼船 —compare 比较 HOVERCRAFT

hy·dro·gen /ˋhaɪdrədʒən; ˈhaɪdrədʒən/ *n* [U] a simple chemical substance that is found in water, and also exists as a gas which is lighter than air 氢

hydrogen bomb /ˈ··· ͵ ·/ *n* [C] a very powerful NUCLEAR bomb 氢弹

hydrogen per·ox·ide /͵··· ·ˈ··/ *n* [U] a chemical liquid used for killing BACTERIA and making hair lighter; PEROXIDE 过氧化氢, 双氧水

hy·dro·pho·bi·a /͵haɪdrəˋfobɪə; ͵haɪdrəˈfəʊbiə/ *n* **1** [U] *technical* RABIES【术语】狂犬病 **2** fear of water 恐水, 畏水

hy·dro·plane¹ /ˋhaɪdrə͵plen; ˈhaɪdrəpleɪn/ *n* **1** [C] a HYDROFOIL 水翼船 **2** [C] *AmE* a plane that can take off from and land on water; SEAPLANE【美】水上飞机

hydroplane² *v* [I] **1** *AmE* if a car hydroplanes, it slides uncontrollably on a wet road【美】〔汽车〕湿路打滑; AQUAPLANE² (2) *BrE*【英】**2** if a boat hydroplanes, it travels very quickly just touching the surface of the water〔船〕水上滑行, 掠过水面

hy·e·na, hyaena /haɪˋinə; haɪˈiːnə/ *n* [C] a wild animal like a dog that feeds on the meat of dead animals 鬣狗〔形似狗, 食动物尸体〕

hy·giene /ˋhaɪdʒin; ˈhaɪdʒiːn/ *n* **1** [U] the study and practice of preventing illness or stopping it from spreading by keeping things clean 卫生 (学); 保健 (学): *public hygiene* 公共卫生 **2** [U] the practice of keeping your body clean 个人卫生

hy·gien·ic /͵haɪdʒɪˋɛnɪk; haɪˈdʒiːnɪk/ *adj* clean and likely to prevent bacteria, infections, or disease from spreading 卫生的; 清洁的: *food processed in hygienic conditions* 在卫生的条件下加工的食品 | *That's not very hygienic.* 那不太卫生。—**hygienically** /-klɪ; -kli/ *adv*

hy·gien·ist /ˋhaɪdʒɪənɪst; ˈhaɪdʒiːnɪ̵st/ *n* [C] *BrE* someone who helps a DENTIST by cleaning patients' teeth and giving advice about keeping teeth healthy【英】牙医助手; DENTAL HYGIENIST *AmE*【美】

hy·men /ˋhaɪmən; ˈhaɪmən/ *n* [C] a piece of skin that partly covers the entrance to the VAGINA of some girls or women who have not had sex 处女膜

hymn /hɪm; hɪm/ *n* [C] a song of praise to God 圣歌, 赞美诗: *a hymn book* 圣歌集

hymn book /ˈ· ·/ also 又作 **hym·nal** /ˋhɪmnəl; ˈhɪmnəl/ *technical n* [C] a book containing Christian songs of praise to God【术语】〔基督教〕圣歌集, 赞美诗集

Hymns An·cient and Mod·ern /͵· ·, ·· ˈ··/ a book of HYMNS (=songs of praise to God) which is often used in churches of the Church of England《古今圣诗集》〔英国国教会各教堂经常使用的圣歌集〕

hype¹ /haɪp; haɪp/ *n* [U] attempts to make the public interested in a product, film etc by saying how good it is on television, radio etc〔传媒的〕大肆宣传: **media hype** *Despite all the media hype, I found the film very disappointing.* 尽管媒体大肆宣传, 但我发觉这部影片十分让人失望。

hype² *v* [T] to try to get a lot of public attention for something by saying how good it is on television, radio etc〔通过媒体〕大肆宣传

hype sth ↔ **up** *phr v* [T] to make an event, thing, or person seem better or more important than it is 夸大地宣传, 鼓吹, 炒作

hyped up /͵· ˈ·/ *adj* [not before noun 不用于名词前] *informal* excited or nervous about something that is going to happen【非正式】〔对即将发生的事感到〕兴奋的, 激动的; 紧张的: [+**about**] *Jerry is really hyped up about his exams.* 杰里确实对考试感到很紧张。

hy·per /ˋhaɪpɚ; ˈhaɪpə/ *adj informal* extremely excited or nervous about something【非正式】非常兴奋的; 非常紧张的

hyper- /haɪpɚ; haɪpə/ *prefix* more than usual; especially too much 过分 (的), 过度 (的): *hypersensitive* (=too sensitive) 过度敏感的 | *hyperinflation* 极度通货膨胀

hy·per·ac·tive /͵haɪpɚˋæktɪv; ͵haɪpərˈæktɪv◂/ *adj technical* a hyperactive child is too active and can only keep still or quiet

H

for very short periods of time【术语】〔儿童〕过分活跃的, 多动的 —**hyperactivity** /ˌhaɪpɚækˈtɪvətɪ; ˌhaɪpəræk'tɪvɪ̈ti/ *n* [U]

hy·per·bo·le /haɪˋpɝbəˌlɪ; haɪ'pɜːbəli/ *n* [U] a way of describing something by saying it is much bigger, smaller, worse etc than it actually is 夸张(法)〔一种修辞法〕: *To say 'This chair weighs a ton' is an example of hyperbole.* "这张椅子有一吨重"是一种夸张的说法。—see also 另见 EXAGGERATE —**hyperbolic** /ˌhaɪpɚˋbɑlɪk; ˌhaɪpə'bɒlɪk◂/ *adj*

hy·per·crit·i·cal /ˌhaɪpɚˋkrɪtɪkḷ; ˌhaɪpə'krɪtɪkəl◂/ *adj* too eager to criticize other people and things, especially about small details 吹毛求疵的, 过分挑剔的, 苛求的 —**hypercritically** /-kḷɪ; -kli/ *adv*

hy·per·in·fla·tion /ˌhaɪpɚɪnˋfleʃən; ˌhaɪpərɪn'fleɪʃən/ *n* [U] a rapid rise in prices that seriously damages a country's economy 极度通货膨胀, 超通货膨胀

hy·per·mar·ket /ˋhaɪpɚˌmɑrkɪt; 'haɪpəˌmɑːkɪ̈t/ *n* [C] *BrE* a very large SUPERMARKET, usually built outside a town【英】巨型超级市场

hy·per·sen·si·tive /ˌhaɪpɚˋsɛnsətɪv; ˌhaɪpə'sensɪ̈tɪv◂/ *adj* **1** [+to] extremely sensitive to any change in conditions, to pain, to certain chemicals, drugs etc 过敏的 **2** too easily hurt or upset by unimportant things 感情脆弱的: **[+to/about]** *She's hypersensitive to any form of criticism.* 她经不起任何批评。—**hypersensitivity** /ˌhaɪpɚˌsɛnsəˋtɪvətɪ; ˌhaɪpəsensɪ̈'tɪvɪ̈ti/ *n* [U]

hy·per·ten·sion /ˌhaɪpɚˋtɛnʃən; ˌhaɪpə'tenʃən/ *n* [U] *technical* a medical condition in which your BLOOD PRESSURE is too high【术语】高血压

hy·phen /ˋhaɪfən; 'haɪfən/ *n* [C] a short written or printed line (-) that joins words or SYLLABLES 连字符, 连(字)号: *'Co-operate' can be written with or without a hyphen.* "co-operate"这个词书写中连字符可有可无。—compare 比较 DASH² (1)

hy·phen·ate /ˋhaɪfənˌet; 'haɪfəneɪt/ *v* [T] to join words or SYLLABLES with a HYPHEN 用连字符[号]连接 —**hyphenation** /ˌhaɪfəˋneʃən; ˌhaɪfə'neɪʃən/ *n* [U]

hy·phen·a·ted /ˋhaɪfənˌetɪd; 'haɪfəneɪtɪ̈d/ *adj* containing a hyphen 带有连字符[号]的

hyp·no·sis /hɪpˋnosɪs; hɪp'nəʊsɪ̈s/ *n* **1** [U] a sleep-like state of the brain in which someone's thoughts and actions can be influenced by the person who caused this state (受)催眠状态: **under hypnosis** (=in a state of hypnosis) 处于被催眠状态中 *describing details of your early childhood while under hypnosis* 在受催眠状态下描述你童年时代的细节 **2** [U] the act of hypnotizing (HYPNOTIZE) someone 催眠(术)

hyp·no·ther·a·py /ˌhɪpnoˋθɛrəpɪ; ˌhɪpnəʊ'θerəpi/ *n* [U] the use of hypnosis to treat emotional or physical problems 催眠疗法 —**hypnotherapist** *n* [C]

hyp·not·ic¹ /hɪpˋnɑtɪk; hɪp'nɒtɪk/ *adj* **1** making you feel tired or unable to think clearly, especially because of a regularly repeated sound or movement 催人入眠的, 使人昏昏欲睡的: *The steady ticking of the clock had a hypnotic effect.* 时钟发出的有规律的滴答声使人昏昏欲睡。**2** [only before noun 仅用于名词前] connected with HYPNOSIS 催眠(术)的: *a hypnotic trance* 催眠后的恍惚状态 —**hypnotically** /-kḷɪ; -kli/ *adv*

hypnotic² *n* [C] *technical* a drug that helps you to sleep; SLEEPING PILL【术语】安眠药

hyp·no·tise /ˋhɪpnəˌtaɪz; 'hɪpnətaɪz/ *v* [T] the British spelling of HYPNOTIZE hypnotize 的英式拼法

hyp·no·tis·m /ˋhɪpnəˌtɪzəm; 'hɪpnətɪzəm/ *n* [U] the practice of hypnotizing people 催眠(术)

hyp·no·tist /ˋhɪpnətɪst; 'hɪpnətɪ̈st/ *n* [C] someone who hypnotizes people, especially in public for entertainment〔尤在公共场所以娱乐他人为目的的〕施行催眠术的人, 催眠师

hyp·no·tize also 又作 **-ise** *BrE*【英】/ˋhɪpnəˌtaɪz; 'hɪpnətaɪz/ *v* [T] **1** to make someone be in a sleep-like state in which their thoughts and actions can be influenced by your suggestions 对…施行催眠术 **2 be hypnotized** to be so interested or excited when seeing or listening to something that you cannot think of anything else 沉醉于, 为…所陶醉: *We were completely hypnotized by Bylsma's performance of the Haydn.* 我们完全陶醉在比尔斯马所演奏的海顿作品之中。

hy·po /ˋhaɪpo; 'haɪpəʊ/ *n* [C] *informal* a HYPODERMIC【非正式】皮下注射器

hypo- /haɪpo; haɪpəʊ/ *prefix technical* less than usual, especially too little【术语】过少(的); 低于正常(的): *dying of hypothermia* (=too low body temperature) 死于体温过低

hy·po·chon·dri·a /ˌhaɪpəˋkɑndrɪə; ˌhaɪpə'kɒndriə/ *n* [U] a state in which you continuously worry that there is something wrong with your health, even when you are not ill 疑病症, 忧郁症

hy·po·chon·dri·ac /ˌhaɪpəˋkɑndrɪˌæk; ˌhaɪpə'kɒndriæk/ *n* [C] someone who always worries about their health, even when they are not ill 疑病症患者, 忧郁症患者 —**hypochondriac** *adj*

hy·poc·ri·sy /hɪˋpɑkrəsɪ; hɪ'pɒkrɪ̈si/ *n* [U] a way of behaving in which you pretend to have better moral principles than you actually do 伪善, 虚伪: **sheer hypocrisy** *It's sheer hypocrisy for politicians to preach about family values when so many of them are having affairs.* 政客们口口声声宣扬家庭的各种重要性是纯属虚伪, 他们中有很多人都有婚外恋情。

hyp·o·crite /ˋhɪpəˌkrɪt; 'hɪpəkrɪt/ *n* [C] someone who pretends to be morally good 伪君子, 伪善的人

hyp·o·crit·i·cal /ˌhɪpəˋkrɪtɪkḷ; ˌhɪpə'krɪtɪkəl◂/ *adj* behaving in a way that is intended to make people believe that you are morally better than you really are 伪善的, 虚伪的, 假惺惺的: *hypocritical concern for the less privileged members of society* 对社会中处于弱势地位者假惺惺的关心

hy·po·der·mic¹ /ˌhaɪpəˋdɝmɪk; ˌhaɪpə'dɜːmɪk◂/ *n* [C] an instrument with a very thin hollow needle used for putting drugs directly into the body through the skin; a SYRINGE 皮下注射器

hypodermic² *adj* used in an INJECTION (1) beneath the skin 用于皮下注射的: *a hypodermic needle* 皮下注射器针头 —**hypodermically** /-kḷɪ; -kli/ *adv*

hy·pot·e·nuse /haɪˋpɑtṇˌjus; haɪ'pɒtɪ̈njuːz/ *n* [C] *technical* the longest side of a TRIANGLE that has a RIGHT ANGLE【术语】〔直角三角形的〕斜边, 弦 —see picture at 参见 SHAPE¹ 图

hy·po·ther·mi·a /ˌhaɪpəˋθɝmɪə; ˌhaɪpəʊ'θɜːmiə/ *n* [U] a serious medical condition caused by extreme cold 体温过低

hy·poth·e·sis /haɪˋpɑθəsɪs; haɪ'pɒθɪ̈sɪ̈s/ *n plural* **hypotheses** /-ˌsiz; -siːz/ **1** [C] an idea that is suggested as a possible way of explaining a situation, proving an idea etc, which has not yet been shown to be true 假设, 假说: **put forward a hypothesis** (=suggest a hypothesis) 提出假设 *A number of hypotheses have been put forward concerning the possible origins of mankind.* 人们已经提出了一些关于人类起源的假设。**2** [U] ideas or guesses rather than facts 猜想: *All this is mere hypothesis.* 这一切纯属猜想。

hy·po·thet·i·cal /ˌhaɪpəˋθɛtɪkḷ; ˌhaɪpə'θetɪkəl◂/ *adj* based only on an idea or suggestion about what might happen or might be true and not on a real situation (基于)假设的, 假定的: *Let's consider a hypothetical case.* 让我们考虑一个假设的情况吧! | **purely hypothetical** (=completely hypothetical) 纯粹假设的 *The question is purely hypothetical.* 这个问题纯属假设。—compare 比较 IMAGINARY —**hypothetically** /-kḷɪ; -kli/ *adv*

hys·ter·ec·to·my /ˌhɪstəˋrɛktəmɪ; ˌhɪstə'rektəmi/ *n* [C,U] a medical operation to remove a woman's WOMB 子宫切除(术)

hys·te·ri·a /hɪsˋtɪrɪə; hɪ'stɪəriə/ *n* **1** [U] extreme excitement that makes people cry, laugh, shout etc uncontrollably 歇斯底里: *an outbreak of hysteria among the group's fans* 该组合的热心追随者中爆发的一阵歇斯底里 **2** [U] a situation in which a lot of people are affected by the same extreme emotion such as fear or anger which often makes them behave in an unreasonable way〔众人的〕狂热情绪的爆发: *anti-communist hysteria* 反共狂热情绪 | **mass hysteria** *Since the General's death, the population has been gripped by mass hysteria.* 自将军死后, 全国人民已陷入群众性激动情绪的状态。**3** *technical* a medical condition which upsets someone's emotions and makes them suddenly feel very nervous, excited, anxious etc【术语】癔症 —**hysteric** /hɪsˋtɛrɪk, hɪ'sterɪk/ *adj*

hys·ter·i·cal /hɪsˋtɛrɪkḷ; hɪ'sterɪkəl/ *adj* **1** behaving in a wild, uncontrollable way, especially by shouting or crying because you are extremely excited 歇斯底里的; 狂热的: *Hysterical fans tried to stop Madonna's car at the airport.* 狂热的歌迷企图在机场拦截麦当娜的汽车。**2** *spoken* extremely funny【口】极可笑的, 滑稽的 —**hysterically** /-kḷɪ; -kli/ *adv*

hys·ter·ics /hɪsˋtɛrɪks; hɪ'sterɪks/ *n spoken*【口】**1 have hysterics** to be extremely upset or angry 暴跳如雷的; 极度心烦的: *Mum'd have hysterics if she knew what you'd done.* 妈妈如果知道你干的好事, 肯定会暴跳如雷的。**2 be in hysterics/have sb in hysterics** to be laughing uncontrollably or to make someone laugh uncontrollably 狂笑不止/使某人狂笑不止

Hz *n* [C] the written abbreviation for 缩写= HERTZ

H

I,i

I, i[1] /aɪ; aɪ/ **1** *plural* **I's, i's** *n* [C] the ninth letter of the English alphabet 英语字母表的第九个字母 **2** the ROMAN NUMERAL representing the number one〔罗马数字的〕1

I[2] /aɪ; aɪ/ *pron* used as the subject of a verb when you are the person speaking 我〔用作主语〕: *I've just seen a strange man in your garden.* 我刚才看见你家园子里有个陌生男人。| *I'm not late again, am I?* 我不是又迟到了吧? —see 见 ME (USAGE)

I[3] *AmE* the abbreviation of 缩写= INTERSTATE (=an important road between states in the US)【美】州际公路: *the point where I95 meets I40* 95号与40号州际公路交会处

-i /ɪ; i/ *plural* **-is** *suffix* **1** [in nouns 构成名词] a person or the language of a particular place or country, especially in Asia〔尤指亚洲〕某地[某国]的人[语言]: *two Pakistanis* 两个巴基斯坦人 | *speakers of Nepali* 说尼泊尔语的人 **2** [in adjectives 构成形容词] of a particular place or country 某地的; 某国的: *Bengali food* 孟加拉食品 | *the Israeli army* 以色列军队

IA the written abbreviation of 缩写= IOWA

I·a·coc·ca /ˌaɪə`kokə; ˌaɪə'kəʊkə/, **Lee** (1924-) a US businessman who was president of the Ford car company and later greatly increased the profits made by the Chrysler car company after a period when it had not been very successful. He also wrote an AUTOBIOGRAPHY (=the story of his own life), which was very popular. 亚科卡〔(1924-), 美国实业家。他曾担任福特汽车公司总裁, 后来又使一度经营不佳的克莱斯勒汽车公司利润大增。他著有一部自传, 十分畅销〕

I·a·go /ɪ`ɑgo; i'ɑːgəʊ/ a character in the play *Othello* by William Shakespeare. Iago is an evil man who deliberately lies and tells Othello that Desdemona, Othello's wife, is having a sexual relationship with another man, and as a result Othello kills her. 伊阿古〔威廉·莎士比亚戏剧《奥赛罗》中的人物。他为人阴险, 故意向奥赛罗谎称奥氏之妻苔丝狄蒙娜与人有染, 结果奥赛罗杀死了自己的妻子〕

-ial /ɪəl; iəl/ *suffix* another form of the suffix -AL 后缀 -al 的另一种形式: *a managerial job* (=with the duties of a manager) 管理工作

i·amb /`aɪæmb; 'aɪæm/ also 又作 **i·am·bus** /aɪ`æmbəs; aɪ'æmbəs/ *n* [C] *technical* a unit of RHYTHM (1) in poetry, that has one short or weak beat followed by a long or strong beat, as in the word 'alive'【术语】抑扬格〔诗歌的音步单位, 即一个短或弱音节之后跟着一个长或强音节, 如alive〕—**iambic** /aɪ`æmbɪk; aɪ'æmbɪk/ *adj*

iambic pen·tam·e·ter /·,·· ·`···/ *n* [C,U] a common pattern of beats in English poetry, in which each line consists of five iambs 抑扬格五音步〔一种常见的英诗节拍模式, 每行有五个抑扬格〕

-ian /ɪən; iən/ *suffix* [in adjectives and nouns 构成形容词和名词] another form of the suffix -AN 后缀 -an 的另一种形式: *Dickensian characters* (=like those in Dickens' books) 与狄更斯作品中的人物相似者 | *a librarian* (=someone who works in a library) 图书馆馆员

-iana /ɪ`ɑnə; iɑːnə/ *suffix* also 又作 **-ana** [in nouns 构成名词] a collection of objects, papers, etc, connected with someone or something 一批与某人[某物]有关的物件[资料]: *Churchilliana* 丘吉尔文物总汇 | *Shakespeariana* 莎士比亚研究资料汇编

IATA /aɪ`ɑtə; aɪ'ɑːtə/ the International Air Transport Association; an international association of airlines which makes decisions about plane services, such as rules about safety or the price of plane tickets 国际航空运输协会〔该协会就航空服务进行决策, 如制定安全规则或确定机票价格〕

I·be·ri·a /aɪ`bɪrɪə; aɪ'bɪəriə/ the area of western Europe which consists of Spain and Portugal 伊比利亚〔西欧一地区, 包括西班牙和葡萄牙〕

I·be·ri·an /aɪ`bɪrɪən; aɪ'bɪəriən/ *adj* connected with Spain or Portugal 伊比利亚的; 与西班牙[葡萄牙]有关的: *the Iberian peninsula* 伊比利亚半岛

i·bex /`aɪbɛks; 'aɪbeks/ *plural* **ibexes** or **ibex** *n* [C] a wild goat that lives in the mountains of Europe, Asia, and North Africa 北山羊〔一种生活在欧洲、亚洲和北非等地山区的野山羊〕

IBF /ˌaɪ bi `ɛf; ˌaɪ biː 'ef/ International Boxing Federation; one of the organizations responsible for controlling professional BOXING. A BOXER who holds an IBF title is described as a world CHAMPION. 国际拳击联合会〔负责管理职业拳击运动的组织之一。国际拳联冠军即称世界冠军〕

ib·id /`ɪbɪd; 'ɪbɪd/ also 又作 **ib·i·dem** /ɪ`baɪdɛm; 'ɪbɪdem/ *adv Latin* from the same book, writer, or article as the one that has just been mentioned【拉丁】出处同前〔来自刚提过的同一本书、作者或文章〕

-ibility /əbɪlətɪ; ə̩bɪlə̩ti/ *suffix* [in nouns 构成名词] another form of the suffix -ABILITY 后缀 -ability 的另一种形式: *invincibility* 不可战胜

I·bi·za /ɪ`biθə; ɪ'biːθə/ a Spanish island southwest of Majorca, where a lot of European tourists go 伊维萨岛〔西班牙一岛屿。位于马略卡西南部, 大批欧洲游客前去观光〕

-ible /əbḷ; ə̩bəl/ *suffix* [in adjectives 构成形容词] another form of the suffix -ABLE 后缀 -able 的另一种形式: *irresistible* 不可抗拒的

IBM /ˌaɪ bi `ɛm; ˌaɪ biː 'em/ *trademark* International Business Machines; the world's largest computer company, based in the US, which produces both HARDWARE and SOFTWARE, especially for business users. IBM is sometimes informally called 'Big Blue'.【商标】国际商用机器公司〔世界上最大的电脑公司, 总部设在美国。该公司主要面向商业用户生产硬件和软件。人们有时非正式地称它为"巨蓝"〕

IBM-com·pat·i·ble /ˌaɪ bi ɛm kəm`pætəbḷ; ˌaɪ biː em kəm'pætə̩bəl/ *adj* an IBM-compatible computer is designed to work in the same way as a type of computer made by the IBM company, and can use the same computer PROGRAMS[1] (1) 与IBM兼容的〔指电脑与IBM公司生产的电脑有相同的操作模式, 并可使用相同的电脑程序〕—**IBM-compatible** *n* [C]

Ib·sen /`ɪbsn; 'ɪbsən/, **Hen·rik** /`hɛnrɪk; 'henrɪk/ (1828-1906) a Norwegian writer of plays who wrote especially about MIDDLE-CLASS society and criticized social attitudes and behaviour. His best-known plays include *Peer Gynt*, *A Dolls House*, *Hedda Gabler*, *An Enemy of the People*, and *Ghosts*. 易卜生〔(1828-1906), 挪威剧作家。作品以描写中产阶级社会为主, 批评社会心态和行为。最有名的剧本包括《彼尔·英特》、《玩偶之家》、《海达·加布勒》、《人民公敌》和《群鬼》〕

-ic /ɪk; ɪk/ *suffix* [in adjectives 构成形容词] **1** of, like, or connected with a particular thing …的, 像…的, 与…相关的: *photographic* (=of photography) 摄影的 | *an alcoholic drink* (=containing alcohol) 含酒精的饮料 | *polysyllabic* (=containing several SYLLABLES) 多音节的 | *pelvic* (=of the PELVIS) 骨盆的 | *Byronic* (=like or connected with the poet Byron) 拜伦(式)的 **2** [in nouns 构成名词] someone who is affected by a particular unusual condition, a mental illness for example 受〔某种异常状态, 如精神疾病〕困扰的人: *an alcoholic* (=someone who cannot stop drinking alcohol) 酗酒者 —**-ically** /ɪklɪ; ɪkli/ [in adverbs 构成副词] *photographically*〔像照片那样〕逼真地

ICA, the /ˌaɪ si `e; ˌaɪ siː 'eɪ/ the Institute of Contemporary Arts; a building in central London where modern paintings, films etc are shown 当代艺术协会〔伦敦中部展出现代画作和电影作品的一幢建筑〕

-ical /ɪkḷ; ɪkəl/ *suffix* [in adjectives 构成形容词] another form of the suffix -ic (1) 前缀 -ic (1) 的另一种形式: *historical* (=of history) (有关)历史的 | *satirical* 讽刺的 —**-ically** /ɪklɪ; ɪkli/ [in adverbs 构成副词]: *historically* 历史地

Icarus 伊卡洛斯

Ic·a·rus /`ɪkərəs; 'ɪkərəs/ in ancient Greek stories, the son of the inventor Daedalus, who made wings fastened together with WAX for himself and Icarus so that they could escape from the

island of Crete by flying. But Icarus flew too close to the sun, so that the wax melted, and he fell and died. 伊卡洛斯〔古希腊传说中发明家代达罗斯之子。代达罗斯为自己和儿子伊卡洛斯制作了用蜡黏合的羽翼，以便逃出克里特岛。但伊卡洛斯飞得过于靠近太阳，结果因蜡被熔化而坠落身亡〕

ICBM /ˌaɪ si bi ˋɛm; ˌaɪ siː biː ˈem/ *n* [C] Intercontinental Ballistic Missile; a MISSILE (1) that can travel very long distances 洲际弹道导弹

ICC, the /ˌaɪ si ˋsi; ˌaɪ siː ˈsiː/ the abbreviation of 缩写= the INTERSTATE COMMERCE COMMISSION

2 3 **ice**[1] /aɪs; aɪs/ *n* **1** [U] water that has frozen into a solid state 冰: *Would you like some ice in your drink?* 您的饮料中要放点儿冰吗? | *The wind blew the snow across the ice on the lake.* 风把雪花吹过结了冰的湖面。| *Her hands were as cold as ice.* 她双手冷冰冰的。**2 keep/put something on ice** to do nothing about a plan or suggestion for a period of time 〔将计划、建议〕搁置，冻结: *Opposition to Irish home rule was put on ice for the duration of the war.* 反对爱尔兰自治的建议因战争持续而被搁置起来。**3 be (skating) on thin ice** to be in a situation in which you are likely to upset someone or cause trouble 如履薄冰〔处于会惹人不高兴或招麻烦的情况〕: *Don't question him too closely about where he got the money – you'd be on very thin ice.* 不要追问他在哪儿弄到了钱，这样做只会自找麻烦。**4** [C] **a)** a cold sweet food like ICE CREAM, made with fruit juice instead of milk or cream; SORBET 〔像冰激凌，但不含牛奶或奶油，用果汁制成的〕冰冻甜食; 冰糕，雪糕 **b)** *old-fashioned, especially BrE* an ICE CREAM【过时，尤英】冰激凌 **5** [U] *AmE old-fashioned* diamonds【美，过时】钻石 —see also 另见 ICY, BLACK ICE, DRY ICE, **break the ice** (BREAK[1] (30)), **cut no ice** (CUT[1] (35))

ice 冰

ice[2] *v* [T] *especially BrE* to cover a cake with ICING (=a mixture made of liquid and powdery sugar)【尤英】〔在糕饼上〕覆盖糖衣 —compare 比较 FROST[2]

ice sth ↔ **down** *phr v* [T] *AmE* to cover an injury in ice to stop it from swelling【美】冰敷〔受伤处，阻止肿胀〕: *Make sure you ice that ankle down as soon as you get inside.* 你进屋后一定要立即把脚踝用冰敷上。

ice over/up also 又作 **be iced over/up** *phr v* [I] to become covered with ice 被冰覆盖，结冰: *The lake was iced over by morning.* 到了早晨，湖面已结了冰。| *The plane's engines had iced up.* 飞机的发动机被冻住了。

Ice Age /ˈ· ·/ *n* [C] one of the long periods of time, thousands of years ago, when ice covered many northern countries 冰川期，冰河时代

ice axe also 又作 **ice ax** *AmE*【美】/ˈ· ·/ *n* [C] a metal tool, used by mountain climbers to cut into ice 〔登山者使用的〕冰镐; 碎冰斧 —see also 另见 ICE PICK

ice·berg /ˋaɪsˌbɝg; ˈaɪsbɜːg/ *n* [C] a very large mass of ice floating in the sea, most of which is under the surface of the water 冰山 —see also 另见 **the tip of the iceberg** (TIP[1] (7))

iceberg 冰山

iceberg let·tuce /ˌ·· ˈ·· ·/ *n* [C,U] a firm round, pale green LETTUCE 卷心[球叶]莴苣

ice·bound /ˋaɪsˌbaund; ˈaɪsbaʊnd/ *adj* surrounded by ice, especially so that it is impossible to move 冰封的，被冰封住的: *The Russian Fleet was icebound.* 那支俄罗斯舰队遭遇了冰封。

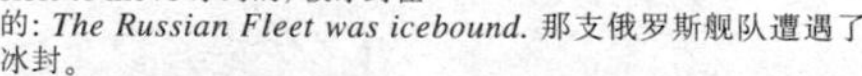

ice·box /ˋaɪsˌbɑks; ˈaɪsbɒks/ *n* [C] **1** *AmE old-fashioned* a REFRIGERATOR【美，过时】电冰箱 **2** a box where food is kept cold with blocks of ice 〔里面放冰块以冷藏食物的〕冰箱

ice·break·er /ˋaɪsˌbrekɚ; ˈaɪsˌbreɪkə/ *n* [C] **1** a ship that cuts a passage through floating ice 破冰船 **2** something that you say or do to make people less nervous when they first meet 〔第一次见面时〕消除拘谨的话语[举动]: *This game is an effective icebreaker at the beginning of a semester.* 这场比赛可以有效地消除开学初期的拘谨气氛。—see also 另见 **break the ice** (BREAK[1] (30))

ice buck·et /ˈ· ˌ·· / *n* [C] **1** a container filled with ice to keep bottles of wine cold 冰桶〔用于冰镇葡萄酒〕 **2** a container in which pieces of ice are kept for putting in drinks 冰桶〔用于盛放加入饮料中的小冰块〕

ice cap /ˈ· ·/ *n* [C] an area of ice that permanently covers land or sea, such as that on the North or South Poles 冰盖，冰冠〔常年被冰覆盖的陆地或海洋，诸如南北极地区〕

ice-cold /ˌ· ˈ·◂/ *adj* extremely cold 极冷的，冰冷的: *ice-cold drinks* 冰冷的饮料 | *Her hands were ice-cold.* 她两手冰凉。

ice cream /ˌ· ˈ·◂/ *n* **1** [U] a frozen sweet food made of milk or cream, sugar etc, with an added taste of fruit, nuts, chocolate etc 冰激凌，雪糕: *vanilla ice cream* 香草冰激凌 **2** [C] *BrE* a small amount of this food for one person【英】一人份的冰激凌: *"Mummy, can I have an ice cream?"* "妈，我能要一份冰激凌吗?" 2

ice-cream so·da /ˌ· ˈ· ˈ··/ *n* [C] a mixture of ice cream, sweet SYRUP, and SODA WATER, served in a tall glass 〔由冰激凌、糖浆、苏打水混合制成的〕冰激凌苏打水，雪糕苏打

ice cube /ˈ· ·/ *n* [C] a small block of ice used to make drinks cold 〔加入饮料中的〕小方冰块

iced cof·fee /ˌ· ˈ··/ *n* [C,U] cold coffee with ice and milk, or a glass of this drink 〔放了冰块和牛奶的〕冰咖啡; 一杯冰咖啡

iced tea /ˌ· ˈ·/ *n* [C,U] cold tea with ice, lemon, and sugar, or a glass of this drink 冰茶; 一杯冰茶

ice floe /ˈ· ·/ *n* [C] an area of ice floating in the sea, that has broken off from a larger mass 〔海洋上的〕浮冰，冰盘

ice hock·ey /ˈ· ˌ··/ *n* [U] a sport played on ice, in which players try to hit a hard flat round object into the other team's GOAL (3) with special sticks 冰球运动

Ice·land /ˋaɪslənd; ˈaɪslənd/ an island country in the Atlantic Ocean just south of the Arctic Circle. Population: 278,000 (2001). Capital: Reykjavik 冰岛〔紧靠北极圈南边的大西洋一岛国。人口: 278,000 (2001)，首都: 雷克雅未克〕

Ice·land·er /ˋaɪsləndɚ; ˈaɪsləndə/ *n* [C] someone from Iceland 冰岛人

Ice·lan·dic /aɪsˋlændɪk; aɪsˈlændɪk/ *adj* connected with Iceland, its people, or their language 冰岛的，冰岛人的; 冰岛语的

ice lol·ly /ˈ· ˌ··/ *plural* **ice lollies** *n* [C] *BrE* a piece of sweet tasting ice on a stick, that you suck【英】冰棍，冰棒，雪糕; POPSICLE *AmE*【美】

ice·man /ˋaɪsˌmæn; ˈaɪs-mæn/ *n plural* **icemen** /-ˌmɛn; -men/ [C] *AmE* a man who delivered ice to people's houses in the past, so that they could keep food cold【美】送冰人〔过去送冰上门供人们贮藏食物的人〕

ice pack /ˈ· ·/ *n* [C] **1** a bag containing ice, used to keep injured or painful parts of your body cold 冰袋〔用以冷敷受伤或疼痛处〕 **2** a large area of crushed ice floating in the sea 〔海上〕浮冰群，大片浮冰 —compare 比较 PACK ICE

ice pick /ˈ· ·/ *n* [C] a sharp tool used for cutting or breaking ice 碎冰锥

ice rink /ˈ· ·/ *n* [C] a specially prepared surface of ice where you can ICE-SKATE 溜冰场

ice sheet /ˈ· ·/ *n* [C] an ICE CAP 冰盖，冰冠

ice-skate /ˈ· ·/ *v* [I] to slide on ice wearing ice skates 溜冰，滑冰 —**ice-skater** *n* [C] —**ice-skating** *n* [U]

ice skate /ˈ· ·/ *n* [C usually plural 一般用复数] a special boot with thin metal blades on the bottom, that allows you to move quickly on ice 冰鞋，溜冰鞋 —compare 比较 ROLLER SKATE

ice wa·ter /ˈ· ˌ··/ *n* [C,U] very cold water with pieces of ice in it, or a glass of this 冰水; 一杯冰水

Ich·a·bod Crane /ˌɪkəbɑd ˋkren; ˌɪkəbɒd ˈkreɪn/ —see 见 Ichabod CRANE

I Ching, The /ˌi ˋdʒɪŋ; ˌiː ˈdʒɪŋ/ an ancient Chinese book, also known as the Book of Changes, which some people believe helps you to understand events happening in your life and tells you what will happen in the future. To use the *I Ching*, you throw a set of sticks or coins, and the patterns that they make are connected to specific parts of the book which explain the meaning of each pattern.《易经》〔中国一部古书。有些人认为该书可帮助人们理解人世浮沉，预知未来之事。使用《易经》时，要抛掷小棒或硬币，书中对形成的卦象都有相应的解析〕

ich·neu·mon fly /ɪkˋnjumən flaɪ; ɪkˈnjuːmən flaɪ/ *n* [C] an insect that lays eggs on or inside the LARVA of another insect 姬蜂〔一种将卵产于其他昆虫幼体表面或体内的昆虫〕

-ician /ɪʃən; ɪʃən/ *suffix* [in nouns 构成名词] a skilled worker who deals with a particular thing …能手，…(专)家: *a beautician* (=someone who gives beauty treatments) 美容师 | *a technician* 技术员

i·ci·cle /ˋaɪsɪkl; ˈaɪsɪkəl/ *n* [C] a long thin pointed piece of ice hanging from a roof or other surface 冰柱，垂冰〔自屋顶或其他表面垂下来的冰〕

-icide /ɪsaɪd; ɪsaɪd/ *suffix* also 又作 **-cide** [in nouns 构成名词] killer; killing 杀害者; 杀: *insecticide* (=chemical substance for

killing insects) 杀虫剂 | *suicide* (=act of killing oneself) 自杀 —**-icidal** /ɪsaɪdl/ [in adjectives 构成形容词]—**-icidally** /ɪsaɪdlɪ; ɪsaɪdl-i/ [in adverbs 构成副词]

i·ci·ly /ˋaɪsılı; ˈaɪsɨli/ *adv* if you say something icily or look at someone icily you do it in an angry or very unfriendly way 生气地, 冷淡地, 不友好地: *She started talking, but he glared at her icily.* 她开始说话, 他却对她冷眼而视。

ic·ing /ˋaɪsɪŋ; ˈaɪsɪŋ/ *n* [U] **1** a mixture made from powdery sugar and liquid, used to cover cakes〔覆在糕饼上的〕糖衣, 酥皮; FROSTING (1) *AmE*【美】**2 the icing on the cake** something that makes a very good experience perfect 锦上添花, 好上加好: *It was a great evening but meeting you here was just the icing on the cake!* 那是一个美好的夜晚, 而在这儿遇到你更是美妙至极!

icing sug·ar /ˊ· · ,· ·/ *n* [U] *BrE* powdery sugar that is mixed with liquid to make icing【英】〔制糖衣用的〕糖粉; CONFECTIONER'S SUGAR *AmE*【美】

ick·y /ˋɪkı; ˈɪki/ *adj informal* very unpleasant, especially to look at, taste, or feel【非正式】〔尤指在视觉、味觉、触觉上〕非常令人讨厌的: *Those dumplings look really icky!* 那些饺子看上去令人恶心!

I Claudius /ˌaɪ ˋklɔdɪəs; ˌaɪ ˈklɔːdiəs/ a NOVEL by Robert Graves, published in 1934, about Claudius, who became Roman EMPEROR after the death of his NEPHEW Caligula. Graves also wrote *Claudius the God*, which described the REIGN of Claudius.《我, 克劳狄》〔罗伯特·格雷夫斯1934年出版的一部小说, 讲述克劳狄在侄子卡里古拉死后继任罗马皇帝的故事。格雷夫斯还写过《天神克劳狄》, 描述克劳狄统治时期的故事〕

i·con /ˋaɪkɑn; ˈaɪkɒn/ *n* [C] **1** a small sign or picture on a computer SCREEN[1] (1) that is used to start a particular operation〔电脑屏幕上标示某一操作的〕图标: *To open a new file, click on the icon at the top of the screen.* 要打开新文件, 就点击屏幕上方的那个图标。**2** someone famous who is admired by many people and is thought to represent an important idea 偶像, 崇拜对象: *Anita Roddick has been feted as some kind of environmentally conscious feminist icon.* 安妮塔·罗迪克被赞誉为具有环保意识的女权主义偶像。**3** also 又作 **ikon** a picture or figure of a holy person that is used in worship in the Greek or Russian Orthodox Church〔希腊或俄罗斯东正教的〕圣像 —**iconic** /aɪˋkɑnɪk; aɪˈkɒnɪk/ *adj*

i·con·o·clast /aɪˋkɑnəˌklæst; aɪˈkɒnəklæst/ *n* [C] someone who attacks established ideas and customs 攻击传统观念和习俗的人

i·con·o·clas·tic /aɪˌkɑnəˋklæstɪk; aɪˌkɒnəˈklæstɪk◂/ *adj* iconoclastic ideas, opinions, writings etc attack established beliefs and customs〔思想、意见、著作等〕反对传统观念和习俗的: *Wolfe's theories were revolutionary and iconoclastic.* 沃尔夫的理论是革命性和反传统的。

i·co·nog·ra·phy /ˌaɪkəˋnɑgrəfı; ˌaɪkəˈnɒgrəfi/ *n* [U] the way that a particular people, religious or political group etc represent ideas in pictures or images〔特定民族、宗教或政治派别用来表达思想的〕图示法, 象征手法: *Crocodiles and hippopotami are both symbols of evil in the iconography of ancient Egypt.* 在古埃及的图示法中, 鳄鱼和河马都代表邪恶。

-ics /ɪks; ɪks/ *suffix* [in nouns 构成名词] **1** the scientific study or use of something …学, …研究: *linguistics* (=the study of language) 语言学 | *electronics* (=the study or making of electronic apparatus) 电子学 | *acoustics* 声学 **2** the actions typically done by a particular type of people〔由特定的人做的〕活动: *athletics* (=running, jumping, throwing, etc) 田径运动 | *acrobatics* 杂技 **3** qualities or events connected with something〔与某物有关的〕性质, 现象: *the acoustics* (=sound qualities) *of the hall* 大厅的音响效果

ic·y /ˋaɪsı; ˈaɪsi/ *adj* **1** extremely cold 极冷的: *An icy wind blew from the north.* 刺骨的寒风从北方吹来。| *The bath water was icy cold.* 洗澡水是冰冷的。**2** covered in ice 被冰覆盖的: *The roads will be icy tonight.* 道路今夜将结冰。**3** an icy comment, look etc shows that you feel annoyed with or unfriendly towards someone〔评语、目光等〕冷冷的, 不友好的: *Jo fixed the other woman with an icy stare.* 乔冷冷地盯着另一个女人。—see also 另见 ICILY—**iciness** *n* [U]

I'd /aɪd; aɪd/ **1** the short form of 缩略式= 'I had': *I wish I'd been there.* 真希望我当时在那里。**2** the short form of 缩略式= 'I would': *I'd leave now if I were you.* 我要是你的话, 现在就走。

ID[1] /ˌaɪ ˋdi; ˌaɪ ˈdiː/ *n* [C,U] a document that shows your name and date of birth, usually with a photograph 身份证明(文件): *Do you have any ID, sir?* 先生, 您有身份证明吗?

ID[2] the written abbreviation of 缩写= IDAHO

id /ɪd; ɪd/ *n* [U] *technical* according to Freudian PSYCHOLOGY (1), the part of your mind that is completely unconscious but has hidden needs and desires【术语】伊德, 本我〔据弗洛伊德心理学, 这是潜意识的最深一层, 隐藏了需要和欲望〕—compare 比较 EGO (3), SUPEREGO

I·da·ho /ˋaɪdəho; ˈaɪdəhəʊ/ abbreviation 缩写为 **ID** a state in the northwestern US, which is an important producer of food, especially potatoes 爱达荷州〔美国西北部一州, 为重要的粮食产区, 尤其出产土豆〕

ID card /ˌaɪ ˋdi kɑrd; ˌaɪ ˈdiː kɑːd/ *n* [C] an IDENTITY CARD 身份证

> **CULTURAL NOTE 文化注释**
>
> Most people in the US have either a driver's license or an official ID card. ID cards and DRIVER'S LICENSEs have your photograph, date of birth, height, weight, eye colour, hair colour, permanent address, and SIGNATURE printed on them. You are usually asked to show your ID when you are buying alcohol in order to prove your age, or when using a CHEQUE to pay for something. 美国大多数人有驾驶执照或身份证。这两种证件上印有照片、出生日期、身高、体重、眼睛颜色、头发颜色、永久住址和签名。买酒时常要出示身份证证明年龄, 使用支票付款时也要出示身份证。
>
> In the UK, people do not have official ID cards, and many people think that it is wrong for the police and government to force people to carry an ID with them all the time. When people in the UK need to prove who they are or how old they are, they show their DRIVING LICENCE, BIRTH CERTIFICATE, or PASSPORT. The UK government wants to introduce ID cards as a way of preventing crime and TERRORISM. 英国人没有身份证, 很多人认为警方和政府强迫人们随身携带身份证是不对的。在英国如果有人需要证明自己的身份或年龄, 他们会出示驾驶执照、出生证或护照。英国政府想引入身份证, 以此防范犯罪和恐怖主义。

-ide /aɪd; aɪd/ *suffix* [in nouns 构成名词] *technical* a chemical compound【术语】…化(合)物: *cyanide* 氰化物 | *sulphide* 硫化物

i·dea /aɪˋdɪə; aɪˈdɪə/ *n* S1 W1

1 ►PLAN/SUGGESTION 计划/建议◄ [C] a plan or suggestion for a possible course of action, especially one that you think of suddenly〔尤指突然想到的〕计划, 建议, 想法, 主意: [+for] *What gave you the idea for the book?* 是什么使你产生写这本书的想法? | [+of] *What do you think about John's idea of recruiting two new people?* 你认为约翰招收两个新人的主意怎么样? | **idea that** *What do you think of this idea that we should all wear uniforms?* 你认为大家都穿制服这个想法怎么样? | **it is sb's idea to do sth** *It was Mary's idea to hold the party outside.* 在室外举行聚会是玛丽的主意。| **good/great idea** *What a good idea!* 真是好主意! | **have an idea** (=think of an idea) 想到一个主意 *George has had a brilliant idea – let's hire the church hall.* 乔治想出一个绝妙的主意——租用教堂大厅。| **hit on/come up with an idea** (=to think of an idea) 想到一个主意 | **new idea** *These meetings are intended to pool knowledge and inspire new ideas.* 这些会议的目的是集思广益, 启发新想法。| **toy with the idea of doing sth** (=think about a plan or suggestion, but not very seriously)〔不很认真地〕考虑〔计划、建议等〕*We toyed with the idea of going to Paris.* 我们很随意地想到过是否去巴黎。| **entertain an idea** (=consider it as a possibility) *formal*【正式】考虑一个想法〔认为有可能〕: *There is evidence to show that she entertained the idea of suicide long before this.* 有证据显示她在此很久之前就考虑过自杀。| **bright idea** (=a very clever idea, often used jokingly to mean a very stupid idea or action) 好主意, 馊主意〔常用于开玩笑, 指非常愚蠢的想法或行为〕*Whose bright idea was it to turn the fridge off, then?* 那么把冰箱的电源关掉是谁的馊主意?

2 ►KNOWLEDGE 知道◄ [C,U] **a)** a general understanding of something, based on knowing something about it 概括的了解: *Before I undertake this work, I need an idea of the problems involved.* 在着手这项工作前, 我需要大致了解一下有关的问题。| **some idea** (=at least a little knowledge about something)〔对某事的〕一些了解 *You must have some idea of where they went.* 对他们的行踪你肯定略知一二。| **general/rough idea** (=a not very exact idea) 大致的想法 *Can you give me a rough idea of how much the repairs will cost?* 你能否告诉我修理费用大约是多少? **b)** to not know at all 根本不知道, 一无所知: **have no idea** *I've no idea where she's gone.* 我一点儿也不知道她去哪里了。| *"When are they arriving?" "No idea."* "他们什么时间到?" "不知道。" | **not have the faintest/slightest/foggiest idea** *spoken*【口】*I don't have the foggiest idea how much he earns.* 我一点儿也不知道他挣多少钱。

3 ►AIM/INTENTION 目的/意图◄ [C,U] the aim, intention, or purpose of doing something〔做某事的〕目的, 意图: *The idea was to buy a new dress, but we only got as far as the supermarket!* 我们原打算买一件新的连衣裙, 却只走到了超级市场! | [+of] *The idea of the game is get the ball past your opponent.* 这项运动的目的是不让对手把球拦截掉。| **big ideas** (=plans to become important, successful etc) 远大的抱负 *He was a man with big ideas – he even dreamed of becoming president.* 他抱负远大, 甚至梦想做总统。| **have other ideas** (=have different plans from the ones that someone else has for you) 另有打算 *They wanted Mike to go to law school, but he had other ideas.* 他们想让迈克上法学院, 但他另有打算。

4 ►IMAGE 印象◄ [C,U] an image in your mind of what something is like or should be like 概念, 想法: [+of] *Chefs differ in their idea of what makes a good dessert.* 好的餐后甜点应该是什么样子, 厨师们观点各异。| **not my idea of fun/a good time etc** *Walking up a mountain in the pouring rain isn't my idea of fun.* 在滂沱大雨中爬山, 在我看来毫无乐趣。

5 ►BELIEF 信念◄ [C usually plural 一般用复数] an opinion or belief 意见, 信念: *Jack has some pretty strange ideas.* 杰克有一些相当奇怪的想法。| [+about] *traditional ideas about women* 有关妇女的传统观念

6 **have an idea (that)** to be fairly sure that something is true, without being completely sure 猜想, 估计〔认为确有某事, 但无绝对把握〕: *I'm not certain where she is, but I've a pretty good idea.* 我不知道她在哪儿, 但大体上能猜出来。| *Benson? Yes, I have an idea he works in the library.* 本森? 对啦, 我想他在图书馆工作。

7 ►PRINCIPLE 原则◄ [C] a principle or belief about how something is or should be 原则, 信念: [+of] *The whole idea of democracy was something strange and new to most people.* 对于当时大部分人来说, 民主这个概念又奇怪又新鲜。| **idea that** *It's based on the idea that all people are created equal.* 它是基于人人生而平等这个信念的。

8 **it is a (good) idea to do sth** *spoken* used to give someone advice about what to do【口】做某事是个不错的主意〔用于提供建议〕: *It'd be a good idea to call and let them know you're coming.* 最好打电话让他们知道你要来。

9 **get the idea** *informal* to begin to understand something or be able to do something【非正式】开始明白或能做〔某事〕: *Just read through the instructions – you'll get the idea.* 把说明书读一遍, 你会明白的。

10 **get the wrong idea** to think that something is true when it is not 误解: *Don't get the wrong idea about Dan and Helen – they're just friends.* 不要误解丹和海伦, 他俩不过是朋友而已。

11 **have the right idea** to be using the right kind of method or general principle in something that you are trying to do〔做某事〕方法正确, 方向对头: *He still makes a few mistakes but I reckon he's got the right idea.* 他还犯一些错误, 但我认为他已经找到了窍门。

12 **where did you get that idea?** *spoken* used to say that what someone thinks is in fact completely wrong【口】你这想法是哪儿来的?〔指对方的想法完全错误〕: *No, I'm not seeing Jane. Where did you get that idea?* 不, 我不是去见简。你这想法是从哪儿来的?

13 **put ideas into sb's head** to make someone think of doing something that they had not thought of before, especially something stupid or impossible 使某人产生某种念头〔尤指愚蠢或不切实际的想法〕: *Nick tells me he wants a motorbike. Have you been putting ideas into his head?* 尼克对我说想要一辆摩托车。这个想法是不是你引起的?

14 **that's an idea!** *spoken* used to say that you like what someone has just suggested【口】好主意!〔用来表示赞同别人的建议〕: *"We could hire a car when we get there." "That's an idea!"* "到那儿之后我们可以租一辆车。""好主意!"

15 **that's the idea** *spoken* used to tell someone who is learning to do something that they are doing it the right way, in order to encourage them【口】对了, 就是这样〔用来鼓励正在学着做某事的人〕

16 **sb's idea of a joke** *informal* something that is intended to be a joke but makes you angry【非正式】某人意在开玩笑的做法〔结果却把人惹生气了〕: *I suppose hiding the car keys was his idea of a joke!* 我看他把车钥匙藏起来本是想开个玩笑!

17 **you have no idea** *spoken* used when you are telling someone that something is extremely good, bad etc【口】你简直想不到〔用于告诉某人某事好或坏到极端地步〕: *You have no idea how worried I was.* 你简直想不到我当时多么着急。

18 **the idea!** *old-fashioned* used to express surprise or disapproval when someone has said something stupid or strange【过时】什么话!〔用于对方说了愚蠢或奇怪的话时, 表示惊讶或不赞成〕—see also 另见 **buck your ideas up** (BUCK²)

This graph shows some of the words most commonly used with the noun **idea**. 本图表所示为含有名词idea的一些最常用词组。

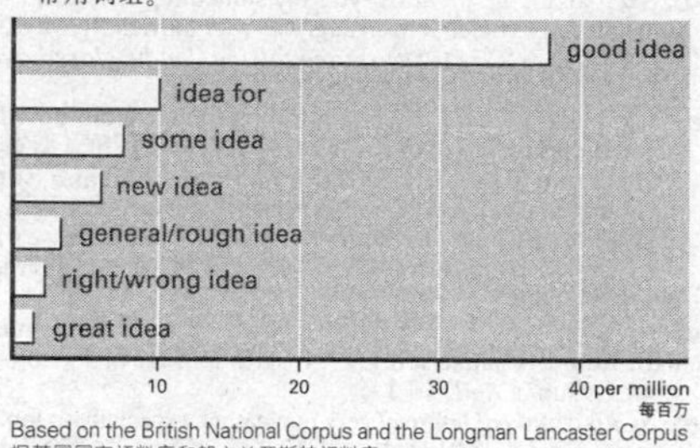

Based on the British National Corpus and the Longman Lancaster Corpus
据英国国家语料库和朗文兰开斯特语料库

i·deal¹ /ˌaɪˈdɪəl; ˌaɪˈdɪəl◂/ *adj* **1** the best that something could possibly be 理想的, 最好的: *advice on how to reach your ideal weight* 如何达到理想体重的建议 | *an ideal place for a picnic* 理想的野餐地点 **2** [only before noun 仅用于名词前] an ideal world, job, system etc is one that you imagine to be perfect, but that is not likely to really exist〔世界、职业、制度等〕想象的; 理想中的: *In an ideal world there would be no need for a police force.* 在理想的世界中不需要警察。

ideal² *n* [C] **1** a principle or perfect standard that you hope to achieve〔希望实现的〕理想: *Social justice and equality, like many ideals, are difficult to realise.* 社会正义和平等, 如许多理想那样, 是难以实现的。**2** an idea of what something would be like if it had no faults or problems 完美典型〔想象中完美的事物〕: [+of] *the democratic ideal of government* 民主政体的完美典型

Ideal Home /ˌ.. ˈ./ *trademark* a British magazine containing pictures of beautiful houses and articles about ways to decorate your own home【商标】《理想家居》〔英国一杂志, 刊登漂亮的住宅照片和有关家庭装潢的文章〕

Ideal Home Ex·hi·bi·tion, the /ˌ.. . .ˈ.. ./ an EXHIBITION of furniture and objects for the house, held every year in London 理想家居展览会〔一年一度在伦敦举办的家具和家庭用品展览〕

i·deal·ise /aɪˈdɪəlˌaɪz; aɪˈdɪəlaɪz/ *v* [T] a British spelling of IDEALIZE idealize 的英式拼法

i·deal·is·m /aɪˈdɪəlˌɪzəm; aɪˈdɪəlɪzəm/ *n* [U] **1** strong belief in principles or perfect standards, even when they are very difficult to achieve in real life 理想主义: *youthful idealism* 青年人的理想主义 | *The movement appealed to their idealism.* 这场运动投合他们的理想主义观点。**2** *technical* a way of using art to show the world as a perfect place, even though it is not【术语】理想主义〔指通过艺术来表现完美的世界, 尽管事实上世界并不完美〕—compare 比较 REALISM (2), NATURALISM

i·deal·ist /aɪˈdɪəlɪst; aɪˈdɪəlɪst/ *n* [C] someone who tries to live according to principles or perfect standards, especially in a way that is not practical or possible 理想主义者; 空想家

i·deal·is·tic /aɪˌdɪəlˈɪstɪk; aɪˌdɪəˈlɪstɪk◂/ *adj* believing in principles or perfect standards that cannot really be achieved 理想主义(者)的; 空想的: *We were young and idealistic and anything seemed possible.* 当时我们年轻, 充满幻想, 似乎什么事都有可能。—**idealistically** /-klɪ; -kli/ *adv*

i·deal·ize also 又作 **-ise** *BrE*【英】/aɪˈdɪəlˌaɪz; aɪˈdɪəlaɪz/ *v* [T] to imagine or represent something or someone as being perfect or better than they really are 把〔某人、某物〕理想化; 对〔某人、某物〕作理想化的描述: *Boys often idealize their fathers.* 男孩子常常把自己的父亲理想化。—**idealization** /aɪˌdɪələˈzeʃən; aɪˌdɪəlaɪˈzeɪʃən/ *n* [U]

i·deal·ly /aɪˈdɪəlɪ; aɪˈdɪəli/ *adv* **1** [sentence adverb 句子副词] used to describe the way you would like things to be, even though this may not be possible 理想地: *How many orders are you hoping for, ideally?* 在最理想的情况下, 你希望拿到多少订单? | *Ideally I'd like a job where I can work from home.* 最理想的是我能找到一份能在家里办公的工作。**2** **ideally suited/placed/qualified etc** having very suitable qualities etc for a particular situation 非常适合/位置理想/条件合适等: *He was ideally suited for the job.* 他做这个工作非常合适。

id·em /ˈaɪdɛm; ˈɪdem/ *Latin* from the same book, author etc as the one that has just been mentioned【拉丁】同前, 同上〔指来自刚提过的同一本书、作者等〕

i·den·ti·cal /aɪˋdɛntɪkḷ; aɪˈdentɪkəl/ *adj* exactly the same 完全相同的: *four identical houses* 四幢一模一样的房子 | [+to] *This system is identical to the one used in France.* 这个系统与法国所用的那个完全相同。—**identically** /-kḷɪ; -kli/ *adv*

identical twin /ˌ· ˌ···ˈ·/ *n* [C usually plural 一般用复数] one of a pair of brothers or sisters born at the same time, who look almost exactly alike 长相酷似的双胞胎之一, 同[单]卵双胞胎之一

i·den·ti·fi·a·ble /aɪˋdɛntəˌfaɪəbḷ; aɪˈdentɪ̣faɪəbəl/ *adj* someone or something that is identifiable can be recognized 可识别的, 可辨认出来的: *Only three people in the photograph are identifiable.* 照片上只有三个人可以辨认出来。

i·den·ti·fi·ca·tion /aɪˌdɛntəfəˋkeʃən; aɪˌdentɪ̣fɪ̣ˈkeɪʃən/ *n* [U] **1** official papers or cards, such as your PASSPORT, that prove who you are 身份证明(文件)〈如护照〉: *Do you have any identification?* 你有什么身份证明文件吗? | **means of identification** *My only means of identification was my driver's licence.* 我唯一的身份证明是驾驶执照。—see also 另见 ID[1] **2** your ability to say who someone is because you have seen them before 辨认〔某人的能力〕, 认出: *procedures for the identification of suspects* 辨认嫌疑犯的程序 **3** the act or process of recognizing something 确定〔某物〕: *Correct identification of needs is vital.* 正确判定需求十分关键。**4** a strong feeling of sympathy with someone that makes you able to share their feelings 情感相通, 认同: *identification with the heroine of the play* 对剧中女主角的认同

identification pa·rade /·ˌ···ˈ·· ·ˌ·/ *n* [C] *BrE* a process in which a WITNESS to a crime looks at a group of people to see if they can recognize the criminal【英】列队辨认〔指目击者在一群人中辨认嫌疑犯的过程〕; LINE-UP (4) *AmE*【美】

[1] **i·den·ti·fy** /aɪˋdɛntəˌfaɪ; aɪˈdentɪ̣faɪ/ *v* [T] **1** to recognize and correctly name someone or something 认出〔某人或某物〕, 识别: *I agreed to try and identify the body.* 我同意去辨认那具尸体。| **identify sb/sth** *The aircraft were identified as American.* 那些飞机被认出是美国的。**2** to recognize something or discover exactly what it is, what its nature or origin is, etc 确定; 发现: *The first task is to identify local crime problems.* 首要任务是搞清楚地方犯罪问题。| *Scientists have identified the gene that causes abnormal growth.* 科学家已发现了造成畸形发育的基因。**3** to make it clear to other people who someone is 表明[显示]身份: **identify sb as sb** *His accent identified him as a Frenchman.* 他的口音表明他是法国人。

identify with *phr v* [T] **1** [**identify with** sb] to feel able to share or understand the feelings of another person 与〔某人〕在感情上认同, 与〔某人〕有同感: *I didn't enjoy the movie because I couldn't identify with any of the characters.* 我不喜欢那部电影, 因为我对里面的任何人物都不能认同。**2 be identified with** to be closely connected or involved with something such as a political group 与〔政治派别等〕关系紧密: *She has always been identified with the radical left.* 她与激进的左翼派别一直联系密切。**3** [**identify** sth **with** sb/sth] to think that something is the same as, or closely connected with, something else 将〔某物〕等同于〔某物〕: *It is a mistake to identify art with life.* 将艺术等同于生活是错误的。

i·den·ti·kit /aɪˋdɛntɪˌkɪt; aɪˈdentɪˌkɪt/ *n* [C] *BrE*【英】**1** a method used by the police for producing a picture of a possible criminal from descriptions given by a WITNESS or witnesses 容貌拼具〔指警方根据证人的描述拼出嫌疑犯的头像的方法〕; COMPOSITE² (2) *AmE*【美】: *an identikit portrait* 容貌拼具拼出的肖像 **2 identikit houses/popstars etc** all exactly the same, and with no interesting or unusual features 千篇一律的房屋/流行歌手等

[2] **i·den·ti·ty** /aɪˋdɛntətɪ; aɪˈdentɪ̣ti/ *n* **1** [C,U] **sb's identity** who someone is; someone's name 某人的身份; 某人的姓名: *The identity of the killer is still unknown.* 凶手的身份仍未查明。| **mistaken identity** (=when someone is mistaken for someone else) 误认〔以为是另一个人〕 *He was chased and shot by the police in a case of mistaken identity.* 他因被误认而遭警察开枪追捕。**2** [U] the qualities and attitudes you have that make you feel you have your own character and are different from other people 个性; 个人特性: **sense of identity** *He has no sense of his own identity.* 他缺乏自我意识。| **cultural/ethnic/social identity** (=a strong feeling of belonging to a particular group, race etc) 文化/民族/社会认同 | **identity crisis** (=a feeling of uncertainty about who you really are and what your purpose in life is) 身份危机〔指对自己的身份和人生目标感到迷茫〕 **3** [U] *formal* exact SIMILARITY between two things【正式】〔两件事物〕相同, 一致

identity card /·ˈ··· ·ˌ·/ *n* [C] a card with your name, date of birth, photograph, and SIGNATURE on it, that proves who you are; ID CARD 身份证

id·e·o·gram /ˋɪdɪəˌgræm; ˈɪdiəgræm/ also 又作 **id·e·o·graph** /-græf; -grɑːf/ *n* [C] a written sign, for example in Chinese, that represents an idea rather than the sound of a word 表意文字〈如汉字〉; 表意符号

i·de·o·lo·gic·al /ˌaɪdɪəˋlɑdʒɪkḷ; ˌaɪdiəˈlɒdʒɪkəl◂/ *adj* based on strong beliefs or ideas, especially political or economic ideas, that may not be practical in real life 意识形态的, 观念的; 不现实的: *an ideological commitment to privatization* 意识形态上对私有化的坚持 —**ideologically** /-kḷɪ; -kli/ *adv*

i·de·ol·o·gy /ˌaɪdɪˋɑlədʒɪ; ˌaɪdiˈɒlədʒi/ *n* [C,U] **1** a set of ideas on which a political or economic system is based〔政治或经济的〕思想体系, 意识形态: *the ideologies of fascism and capitalism* 法西斯主义和资本主义的意识形态 **2** a set of ideas and attitudes that strongly influence the way people behave〔强烈影响人的行为的〕思想; 观念: *an ideology that views women as 'the weaker sex'* 认为妇女是"弱势性别"的思想 [3]

ides /aɪdz; aɪdz/ *n* [plural] a date or period of time around the middle of the month in the ancient Roman calendar 古罗马历法每月中间的一天[月中的一段时间/中旬]

Ides of March, the /ˌ· · ·ˈ·/ March 15th, famous for being the day on which Julius Caesar was killed by a group of his former friends because they thought he had too much power. Caesar is supposed to have been warned by a FORTUNE-TELLER to 'Beware the Ides of March'. 3月15日〔因尤利乌斯·凯撒在这一天遇刺而闻名。凯撒是被他的一些故友杀死的, 因为他们认为他权力过于集中。据说有一位算命者曾告诫过凯撒: "一定当心3月15日"〕

id·i·o·cy /ˋɪdɪəsɪ; ˈɪdiəsi/ *n* **1** [U] extreme stupidity or silliness 极度愚蠢: *the idiocy of our rulers* 统治者的极度愚蠢 **2** [C] a very stupid remark or action 极愚蠢的言论[行为]

id·i·o·lect /ˋɪdɪəlɛkt; ˈɪdiəlekt/ *n* [C,U] *technical* the way in which a particular person uses language【术语】个人言语方式, 个人语型 —compare 比较 DIALECT

id·i·om /ˋɪdɪəm; ˈɪdiəm/ *n* **1** [C] a group of words with a meaning of its own that is different from the meanings of each separate word put together 习语, 成语: *'Under the weather' is an idiom meaning 'ill'.* 习语 under the weather 意为"生病"。**2** [C, U] *literary* a style of expression in writing, speech, or music, that is typical of a particular group of people【文】〔某团体在写作、言语、音乐方面典型的〕风格, 特色

id·i·o·mat·ic /ˌɪdɪəˋmætɪk; ˌɪdiəˈmætɪk◂/ *adj* **1 idiomatic phrase/expression** an idiom 习惯用语/惯用表达法: *an idiomatic phrase* 习惯短语 **2** typical of the natural way in which someone using their own language speaks or writes〔说话或书写〕符合某一语言习惯的, 地道的: *After a year in Madrid, her Spanish was fluent and idiomatic.* 在马德里住了一年后, 她的西班牙语已很流利地道了。—**idiomatically** /-kḷɪ; -kli/ *adv*

id·i·o·syn·cra·sy /ˌɪdɪəˋsɪnkrəsɪ; ˌɪdiəˈsɪŋkrəsi/ *n* [C] **1** an unusual habit or way of behaving that someone has〔个人特有的〕习性, 癖好: *Her idiosyncrasies included talking to her plants.* 她的怪癖之一是对自己种植的草木说话。**2** an unusual or unexpected feature that something has〔某物的〕异质; 特点: *one of the many idiosyncrasies of English spelling* 英语拼写众多特点之一 —**idiosyncratic** /ˌɪdɪosɪnˋkrætɪk; ˌɪdiəsɪnˈkrætɪk◂/ *adj*

id·i·ot /ˋɪdɪət; ˈɪdiət/ *n* [C] **1** a stupid person or someone who has done something stupid 笨蛋, 蠢材: *Some idiot drove into the back of my car.* 有个笨蛋开车撞上了我汽车的尾部。**2** *old use* someone who is mentally ill or has a very low level of intelligence【旧】白痴 —**idiotic** /ˌɪdɪˋɑtɪk; ˌɪdiˈɒtɪk◂/ *adj* —**idiotically** /-kḷɪ; -kli/ *adv*

idle¹ /ˋaɪdḷ; ˈaɪdl/ *adj* **1** not working or producing anything 不工作的; 空闲的: **lie/stand idle** *We can't leave this expensive machinery lying idle.* 我们不能让这套昂贵的机器闲置着。| *The whole team stood idle, waiting for the mechanic.* 整队人干站着等技工来。**2** lazy 懒惰的: *a crowd of idle students* 一群懒散的学生 | *Come on, you idle lot!* 快点, 你们这群懒虫! **3** not serious, or not done with any definite intention 不认真的; 漫无目的的: *The doctor hated wasting time on idle chatter.* 这个医生讨厌把时间浪费在闲聊上。| *If you say 'no', mean it. Never make idle threats.* 说"不"就是"不", 别作无谓的威胁。**4 the idle rich** rich people who do not have to work 不用工作的富人

idle² *v* **idled, idling 1** [I always+adv/prep] to spend time doing nothing 虚度时间, 闲混, 无所事事: *Tom was idling at the corner when a well-dressed businessman came up to him.* 汤姆正在街角闲逛, 突然一位衣冠楚楚的商人朝他走来。**2** [I,T] if an engine idles or if you idle it, it runs slowly while it is not connected to the system that makes parts move (使)〔发动机低速

地)空转 **3** [T] to stop using a factory or stop providing work for your workers, especially temporarily〔尤指暂时〕使〔工厂〕闲置;使〔工人〕闲着

idle sth ↔**away** *phr v* [T] to spend time in a relaxed way, doing nothing 虚度〔光阴〕,消磨〔时间〕: *We were just idling away the time by the river.* 我们当时只是在河边闲逛。

id·ler /ˋaɪdlɚ; ˈaɪdlə/ *n* [C] *old-fashioned* someone who is lazy and does not work【过时】懒汉,游手好闲者

i·dol /ˋaɪdḷ; ˈaɪdl/ *n* [C] **1** someone or something that you love or admire very much 偶像: **be the idol of** *a football player who was the idol of the younger boys* 成为小男孩们偶像的足球球员 | **TV/pop idol** (=a famous actor or performer that many people admire) 电视/流行乐偶像 *the chance to meet your favorite TV idol* 与你最喜爱的电视偶像见面的机会 **2** a picture or STATUE that is worshipped as a god 神像

i·dol·a·ter /aɪˋdɑlətɚ; aɪˈdɒlətə/ *n* [C] *formal* someone who worships a picture or STATUE of a god【正式】〔神像的〕崇拜者

i·dol·a·tress /aɪˋdɑlətrɪs; aɪˈdɒlətrɨs/ *n* [C] *formal* a woman who worships a picture or STATUE as a god【正式】〔神像的〕女崇拜者

i·dol·a·try /aɪˋdɑlətrɪ; aɪˈdɒlətri/ *n* [U] **1** the practice of worshipping IDOLs 偶像崇拜 **2** too much admiration for someone or something〔对某人或某物的〕过分崇拜: *idolatry of power* 对权力的极度崇拜 —**idolatrous** *adj*

i·dol·ize also 又作 **-ise** *BrE*【英】/ˋaɪdḷˌaɪz; ˈaɪdəl-aɪz/ *v* [T] to admire and love someone so much that you think they are perfect 极度钦佩〔某人〕;喜爱: *They had one child, a girl whom they idolized.* 他们有一个女儿,他们对她宠爱备至。

id·yll /ˋaɪdḷ; ˈɪdəl/ *n* [singular] *literary* a place or experience in which everything is peaceful and everyone is perfectly happy【文】平静快乐的地方;安宁愉快的经历: *the rural idyll of peace and plenty* 恬静富庶的乡村生活

i·dyl·lic /aɪˋdɪlɪk; ɪˈdɪlɪk/ *adj* very happy and peaceful, with no problems or dangers 快乐祥和的: *an idyllic setting on the shores of a lake* 湖畔恬静宜人的环境 —**idyllically** /-kḷɪ; -kli/ *adv*: *idyllically happy* 悠然欢畅

i.e. /ˌaɪ ˋi; ˌaɪ ˈiː/ *Latin* used to explain the exact meaning of something that you have just said【拉丁】即;也就是〔用于对刚才所说作确切的说明〕: *The film is only open to adults, i.e. people over 18.* 该影片只限成年人观看,即18岁以上者。

-ie /ɪ; i/ *suffix* [in nouns 构成名词] *informal* another form of the suffix -y² (1)【非正式】后缀 -y² (1) 的另一种形式: *dearie* 亲爱的

If /ɪf; ɪf/ a famous poem by Rudyard Kipling which starts with the words "*If you can keep your head when all about you/Are losing theirs and blaming it on you...*". It describes the qualities of character that some people think of as typically English, such as the ability to remain calm in difficult situations.《假如》〔拉迪亚德·吉卜林的一首名诗。开头这样写道:"假如你能在别人失去理智并对你横加指责的时候,保持清醒的头脑…",描述人们心目中英国人的典型性格,如处乱不惊等〕

if¹ *conjunction* **1** used to talk about something that might happen 假若,倘若,如果: *What can you do if your child behaves badly in a public place?* 如果你的孩子在公共场所胡闹,你能怎么办? | *If you don't leave now I'm calling the police.* 你现在若不离开,我就报警。| *We can always get a taxi if there's a problem with the car.* 如果车子出了毛病,我们总可以叫一辆出租车。| **if by any chance** *If by any chance Peter should phone, can you tell him I'll talk to him later?* 万一彼得来电话,告诉他我待会儿跟他谈,好吗? | **if not** *I think there's a train at midday. If not you'll have to wait till 12.30.* 我想正午会有一班火车。要是没有,你只好等到12时30分了。**2** used when you are talking about something that always happens in a particular situation 无论何时;只要: *If I go to bed late I feel dreadful in the morning.* 我如果睡得晚,第二天早上就感到很不舒服。| *Plastic will melt if it gets too hot.* 塑料过热就会熔化。**3 even if** although something is true or something happens 即使;虽然: *Even if I did lose a stone, I still wouldn't look skinny.* 即使我的体重减轻一英石,看上去也不会皮包骨头。**4** used to mean 'though', when you are describing someone or something that you like 虽然〔用于描述所喜爱的人或物〕: *He's a pleasant child, if a little spoiled.* 他是个很讨人喜爱的孩子,只是有点儿给宠坏了。**5** used like 'whether' when asking or deciding whether something is true or will happen 是否〔询问或判断对错或事情是否会发生时,与whether的用法相似〕: *I rang them to see if I could cancel the appointment.* 我给他们打电话,看能不能取消预约。| *Ask him if he'll lend me some money.* 问问他能否借我一些钱。| *I wonder if John's home yet.* 我不知道约翰是否到家了。**6** used when saying that you are surprised, upset, angry etc that something has happened or is true〔用于表示由于某事发生或对某种情况惊讶、心烦、气恼等〕: *I'm sorry if you took it that way.* 你要是那样理解我很遗憾。| *I don't care if he is my brother. He's still an idiot.* 我不在乎他是不是我兄弟,他就是个笨蛋。**7 if I were you** used when giving advice and telling someone what you think they should do 我要是你的话〔用于给人忠告〕: *If I were you I'd jump at the chance of a job like that.* 我要是你,就会立即抓住那样好的工作机会。**8 it isn't as if.../it's not as if...** used when saying that you do not understand why someone is doing something 似乎并不〔用于对某人的做法表示不理解〕: *I can't think why they're being so mean. It's not as if they're short of money.* 我不明白他们怎么变得这么吝啬,他们似乎并不缺钱啊。

if² *n* **1 ifs and buts** *BrE*【英】/**ifs, ands, or buts** *AmE*【美】if you do not want any ifs and buts, you want someone to do something quickly without arguing〔为故意拖延而作的〕借口,托词: *No ifs and buts – just make sure the job is done by tomorrow!* 别找任何借口,一定要保证在明天把工作完成! **2 and it's a big if** used to say that something is not likely to happen 这是一大疑问〔用于表示某事不大可能发生〕: *We can do it if, and it's a big if, we get the money.* 这事我们有钱就能做,但能否找到钱是一大疑问。

if·fy /ˋɪfɪ; ˈɪfi/ *adj informal* full of uncertainty【非正式】不确定的,充满不确定性的: *The whole plan is beginning to look pretty iffy.* 整个计划开始让人觉得扑朔迷离。| *I'm a bit iffy about having a party here.* 是否在这里举行聚会,我还没有拿定主意。

-iform /ɪfɔrm; ɨfɔːm/ *suffix* [in adjectives 构成形容词] *technical* like or in the shape of something【术语】…样的,具有…形状的: *cruciform* (=cross-shaped) 十字形的

If·tar /ˋɪftɑ; ˈɪftɑː/ the first meal that Muslims eat when Ramadan finishes 开斋饭〔指穆斯林在斋月期间每天禁食结束后吃的第一餐〕

-ify /ɪfaɪ; ɨfaɪ/ *suffix* [in verbs 构成动词] also 又作 **-fy** **1** to affect something in a particular way, or become something (使)成为…,(使)…化: *to purify* (=make or become pure) 净化 | *to clarify the situation* (=make it clear) 澄清情况 **2** to fill someone with a particular feeling 使〔某人〕充满〔某种感情〕: *They terrify me.* (=fill me with terror) 他们使我充满恐惧。**3 a)** *informal* to do something in a silly or annoying way【非正式】愚蠢地〔令人讨厌地〕做某事: *to speechify* (=make speeches, use important sounding words) 高谈阔论;夸夸其谈 **b)** to make something or someone be like or typical of a person or group 使类似于〔某人或团体〕: *Frenchified* (=like the French) 法国化的

ig·loo /ˋɪglu; ˈɪgluː/ *n* [C] a house made from blocks of hard snow or ice〔用坚硬的雪或冰块筑成的〕小屋

Ig·nat·i·us of Loy·o·la /ɪgˌneʃəs əv lɔɪˋolə; ɪgˌneɪʃəs əv lɔɪˈəʊlə/, **St** also 又作 **St Ignatius Loyola** (1491-1556) a Spanish priest who started the Jesuit order (=a Roman Catholic group of missionary priests, which is also called the Society of Jesus) 罗耀拉的圣依纳爵〔(1491-1556),西班牙神甫,曾创立天主教耶稣会〕

ig·ne·ous /ˋɪgnɪəs; ˈɪgniəs/ *adj technical* igneous rocks are formed from LAVA (=hot liquid rock under the ground)【术语】〔岩石〕火成的

ig·nite /ɪgˋnaɪt; ɪgˈnaɪt/ *v* **1** [I,T] *formal* to start burning or to make something start burning【正式】点燃;使燃烧: *The fuel is ignited by a high voltage spark.* 这种燃料由高压火花点燃。**2 ignite controversy/resentment etc** to make people suddenly feel very angry or upset about something 激起争论/愤怒等

ig·ni·tion /ɪgˋnɪʃən; ɪgˈnɪʃən/ *n* **1** [singular] the electrical part of a vehicle's engine that makes it start working〔汽车发动机的〕点火装置,点火开关 —see picture on page A2 参见A2页图 **2** [U] *formal* the act of starting to burn, or making something do this【正式】着火,起火燃烧;点火

ig·no·ble /ɪgˋnobḷ; ɪgˈnəʊbəl/ *adj formal* ignoble thoughts, feelings, or actions are ones that you should feel ashamed or embarrassed about【正式】卑鄙的,可耻的,不光彩的 —**ignobly** *adv*

ig·no·min·i·ous /ˌɪgnəˋmɪnɪəs; ˌɪgnəˈmɪniəs/ *adj formal* making you feel ashamed, especially because you seem stupid, unimportant, or dishonest【正式】〔因显得愚蠢、渺小或奸诈而感到〕丢脸的,不光彩的: *an ignominious departure* 不光彩的离任 | *another ignominious failure* 又一次令人丢脸的失败 —**ignominiously** *adv*

ig·no·mi·ny /ˋɪgnəˌmɪnɪ; ˈɪgnəmɪni/ *n formal*【正式】**1** [C] an event or situation that makes you feel ashamed 难堪;耻辱〔指事件或处境〕: *He came last, an ignominy he could hardly bear.* 他得了最后一名,这是他难以忍受的耻辱。**2** [U] shame and public dishonour 耻辱;不名誉: *the ignominy of defeat* 失败的耻辱

ig·no·ra·mus /ˌɪgnəˋreməs; ˌɪgnəˈreɪməs/ *n* [C] *plural* **ignoramuses** someone who does not know about things that most people know about 无知的人, 愚人

ig·no·rance /ˋɪgnərəns; ˈɪgnərəns/ *n* [U] **1** lack of knowledge or information about something 无知, 愚昧: *My mistake was caused by ignorance, not malice.* 我的错误是无知所致, 并非出于恶意。| **keep sb in ignorance** (=not tell someone about something that they should know about) 不让某人知道〔他应知道的事〕*Adopted children shouldn't be kept in ignorance about their true origins.* 不应该瞒着领养的孩子他们的亲生父母是谁。**2 ignorance is bliss** used to say that if you do not know about a problem, you cannot worry about it 无知是福

ig·no·rant /ˋɪgnərənt; ˈɪgnərənt/ *adj* **1** not knowing facts or information that you ought to know 无知的, 没有学识的, 愚昧的: *an ignorant and uneducated man* 不学无术的人 | [**+of**] *They were ignorant of any events outside their own town.* 他们对镇外的事情一无所知。| [**+about**] *I'm very ignorant about politics.* 我对政治一窍不通。—see 见 IGNORE (USAGE) **2** caused by a lack of knowledge and understanding 因无知而产生的: *What an ignorant thing to say!* 这话太无知了! | *ignorant opinions* 无知的看法 **3** *BrE spoken* rude or impolite; ILL-MANNERED【英口】粗鲁的, 不礼貌的

2 2 **ig·nore** /ɪgˋnɔr; ɪgˈnɔː/ *v* [T] **1** to behave as if you had not heard or seen someone or something 不管; 忽视; 不理: *Either she didn't see me wave or she deliberately ignored me.* 要么她没看见我招手, 要么就是故意不理我。| *Sam rudely ignored the question.* 萨姆粗鲁地对这个问题不予理睬。**2** to deliberately pay no attention to something that you have been told or that you know about〔故意对知道的事〕置之不理: *As far as homelessness goes, the vast majority of people just sit back and ignore it.* 对于无家可归这个问题, 大多数人都袖手旁观, 熟视无睹。

USAGE NOTE 用法说明: IGNORE

WORD CHOICE 词语辨析: **ignore, be ignorant of**

If you **ignore** something, you know about it or have seen or heard it, but choose not to take notice of it. ignore是指视而不见、听而不闻或故意不予理睬: *Some drivers simply ignore speed limits.* 有些司机就是对速度限制视而不见。

If you are **ignorant of** something, you do not know about it. ignorant of指对某事不知道, 不了解: *No driver can pretend to be ignorant of speed limits.* 没有哪个司机能够佯装不知道速度限制。

i·gua·na /ɪˋgwɑnə; ɪˈgwɑːnə/ *n* [C] a large tropical American LIZARD 鬣蜥〔一种大型热带美洲蜥蜴〕

Ike —see 见 Dwight David EISENHOWER

i·kon /ˋaɪkɑn; ˈaɪkɒn/ *n* [C] another spelling of ICON (3) icon (3)的另一种拼法

IL the written abbreviation of 缩写= ILLINOIS

il- /ɪl; ɪl/ *prefix* the form used for IN- before l〔前缀 in- 用于 l 前的形式〕: *illogical* (=not logical) 不合逻辑的

i·lex /ˋaɪlɛks; ˈaɪleks/ *n* [C,U] **1** a type of OAK tree with leaves that are always green 圣栎〔一种常绿橡树〕**2** *technical* one of a family of trees and bushes including HOLLY【术语】冬青属植物

Il·i·ad, The /ˋɪlɪæd; ˈɪliæd/ an ancient Greek EPIC poem by Homer which tells the story of the Trojan War《伊利亚特》〔古希腊史诗, 由荷马所著, 讲述特洛伊战争的故事〕

Il·i·um /ˋɪlɪəm; ˈɪliəm/ a Latin name for the ancient city of Troy 伊利昂〔特洛伊古城的拉丁文名〕

ilk /ɪlk; ɪlk/ *n* **of that/his/their ilk** of that type, his type etc 与那个/他/他们同类的: *Irving Berlin and composers of his ilk* 欧文·伯林及其同类作曲家

I'll /aɪl; aɪl/ the short form of 缩略式= 'I will' or 'I shall'

3 3 **ill¹** /ɪl; ɪl/ *adj* **1** [not usually before noun 一般不用于名词前] *especially BrE* suffering from a disease or not feeling well; sick【尤英】有病的; 不适的: *Bridget can't come – she's ill.* 布丽奇特不能来了, 她生病了。| **feel ill** *I was feeling ill that day, and decided to stay at home.* 我那天不太舒服, 决定待在家里。| **be taken ill/fall ill** (=become ill) 患病; 病倒 *She was suddenly taken ill at school.* 她突然病倒在学校里。| **seriously ill** (=very ill) 病重 *seriously ill in hospital* 在医院里病得很重 | **mentally ill** (=with a disease of the mind) 患精神病的 | **terminally ill** (=with an illness that you will die from) 病入膏肓的 *a hospice for the terminally ill* 晚期病人的安养院 | **ill health** *He had to resign due to ill health.* 他由于身体欠佳只好辞职。—see also 另见 ILLNESS —see 见 SICK¹ (USAGE) **2** [not before noun 不用于名词前] *BrE* suffering from the effects of an injury【英】伤的, 受伤的: *The two policemen are still seriously ill with gunshot wounds.* 这两名警察的枪伤仍然十分严重。**3** [only before noun 仅用于名词前] bad or harmful 坏的, 有害的: *She seemed to have suffered no ill effects from her ordeal.* 她似乎未因这次苦难而受到不良影响。| *accusations of ill treatment by the police* 对警察虐待的指控 **4 ill at ease** nervous, uncomfortable, or embarrassed 紧张, 不自在, 窘迫: *He always felt shy and ill at ease at parties.* 他每次参加聚会都感到害羞和不自在。**5 it's an ill wind (that blows nobody any good)** *spoken* used to say that every problem brings an advantage for someone【口】只有恶风才会对一切人都不利〔即指任何麻烦总会使某些人获益〕—see also 另见 ILL FEELING, ILL WILL

This graph shows how common the adjectives **ill** and **sick** are in British and American English. 本图表所示形容词 ill 和 sick 在英国英语和美国英语中的使用频率。

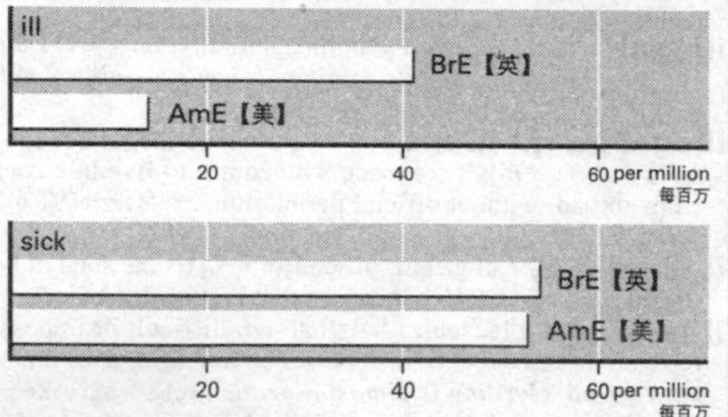

Based on the British National Corpus and the Longman Lancaster Corpus
据英国国家语料库和朗文兰开斯特语料库

In British English the word **ill** means not healthy. Americans usually use **sick** for this meaning. In British English **sick** can be used in this way, but is more commonly used in expressions such as **be sick** or **feel sick** meaning to VOMIT or feel that you are going to VOMIT. 英国英语用ill表示身体不健康, 而美国英语一般用sick表示这个意思。在英国英语里sick也可以这样用, 但更常见的是用在be sick或feel sick这样的短语中, 表示"呕吐"或"恶心"的意思。

ill² *adv* **1 be ill treated/ill used etc** to be treated badly, unpleasantly, or cruelly 受虐待: *Most of our clients have been ill-treated as children.* 我们的多数委托人在孩提时代都受过虐待。**2** not well or not enough; badly 不好, 不够; 恶劣地: *She was ill prepared for the ordeal ahead.* 她对未来的严峻考验准备不足。| *"I see one third of a nation ill-housed, ill-clad, ill-nourished." (F.D. Roosevelt)* "我看见一个国家有三分之一的人民屋不遮雨, 衣不蔽体, 食不果腹。"(F.D.罗斯福) **3 can ill afford (to do) sth** to be unable to do something without making the situation you are in very difficult 难以承担做某事的后果: *I was wasting time I could ill afford to lose.* 我当时是在浪费我浪费不起的时间。**4 think/speak ill of** *formal* to think or say unpleasant things about someone【正式】对〔某人〕抱有恶感; 说〔某人〕坏话: *She really believes you should never speak ill of the dead.* 她的确认为你不应该讲死者的坏话。

I

ill³ *n* **1** [plural] problems and difficulties 问题; 困难: *Free-market economics was seen as the cure for all our ills.* 自由市场经济曾被看作是医治我们一切弊病的良药。**2** [U] *formal* harm, evil, or bad luck【正式】伤害; 邪恶; 厄运: *She did not like Mathew but she would never wish him ill.* 她虽不喜欢马修, 但也不会希望他倒霉。

ill-ad·vised /ˌ· ·ˈ·◂/ *adj* not sensible or not wise and likely to cause problems in the future 不理智的〔日后可能惹麻烦〕; 不明智的: *an ill-advised response to the crisis* 对危机作出的不明智反应 | **you would be ill-advised to do sth** (=used to advise someone not to do something stupid) 你要是做某事就太不明智了〔用于忠告别人不要做蠢事〕*You would be ill-advised to lend him any money.* 你要是借钱给他就太不明智了。—**ill-advisedly** *adv*: *Scott ill-advisedly took matters into his own hands.* 斯科特揽下这些事情, 太不明智了。

ill-as·sort·ed /ˌ· ·ˈ··◂/ *adj* an ill-assorted group of people or things do not seem to belong together in a group〔一组人或事物〕不相配的; 拉杂的

ill-bred /ˌ·ˈ·◂/ *adj* rude or behaving badly, especially because your parents did not teach you to behave well 粗鲁的〔尤指没有家教〕; 无教养的: *an ill-bred upstart criticizing everyone else* 对所有人都横加指责的缺乏教养的暴发户

ill-con·sid·ered /ˌ· ·ˈ··◂/ *adj* decisions, actions, ideas etc that are ill-considered have not been carefully thought about 考虑不周的: *The program is ill-considered and a waste of everyone's time.* 该方案考虑欠周全, 浪费了大家的时间。

ill-de-fined /ˌ· ˈ·◂/ *adj* **1** not described clearly enough 不清楚的，不明确的：*The party's policies were often vague and ill-defined.* 该党的政策常常模糊不清，界定不明。**2** not clearly marked, or not having a clear shape; INDISTINCT 轮廓模糊不清的：*an ill-defined track between the two lakes* 两湖之间一条时宽时窄、若隐若现的小径

ill-dis-posed /ˌ· ·ˈ·/ *adj formal* unfriendly or unsympathetic【正式】不友好的；漠不关心的：**[+towards]** *I was feeling generally ill-disposed toward my fellow man.* 我当时对同伴一般都不友善。

il-le-gal¹ /ɪˈligl; ɪˈliːgəl/ *adj* not allowed by the law 违法的：*They were caught selling illegal drugs.* 他们在贩卖违禁药品时被捕。| **it is illegal to do sth** *It's illegal to drive without a licence.* 无照驾驶是违法的。—opposite 反义词 LEGAL (1) —**illegally** *adv*

illegal² *n* [C] *AmE spoken* an illegal immigrant【美口】非法移民：*We don't want illegals coming for welfare dollars!* 我们不想收容那些为福利金而来的非法移民！

illegal im-mi-grant /ˌ· ·· ˈ···/ also 又作 **illegal a-li-en** *AmE*【美】/ˌ· ·· ˈ···/ *n* [C] someone who comes to live in a country from abroad, without official permission〔来自国外的〕非法居留者，非法移民

il-le-gal-i-ty /ˌɪlɪˈgæləti; ˌɪlɪˈgælɪ̣ti/ *n* **1** [U] the state of being illegal 违法，非法 **2** [C] an action that is illegal 违法行为

il-le-gi-ble /ɪˈlɛdʒəbl; ɪˈledʒɪ̣bəl/ *adj* difficult or impossible to read〔字迹〕难以[不能]辨认的：*I'm not sure what this note says – Dad's writing is almost illegible!* 我搞不清这张便条上写了什么——爸爸的字几乎无法辨认！—opposite 反义词 LEGIBLE —**illegibly** *adv* —**illegibility** /ɪˌlɛdʒəˈbɪləti; ɪˌledʒɪ̣ˈbɪlɪ̣ti/ *n* [U]

il-le-git-i-mate /ˌɪlɪˈdʒɪtəmɪt; ˌɪlɪ̣ˈdʒɪtɪ̣mɪ̣t◂/ *adj* **1** born to parents who are not married 私生的 **2** not allowed or acceptable according to established rules or agreements 不合规则[约定]的：*illegitimate use of public funds* 滥用公款 —**illegitimately** *adv* —**illegitimacy** *n* [U]

ill-e-quipped /ˌ· ·ˈ·◂/ *adj* not having the necessary equipment or skills for a particular situation or activity 装备不足的；能力欠缺的：*They were ill-equipped for the journey.* 他们这次旅行的装备不够充足。| **ill-equipped to do sth** *an inexperienced teacher who was ill-equipped to deal with such children* 一位既缺乏经验又没有能力对付这样的孩子的教师

ill-fat-ed /ˌ· ˈ··◂/ *adj literary* unlucky and leading to serious problems or death【文】不幸的，倒霉的〔导致严重问题甚至死亡的〕：*One of the group was killed on the ill-fated expedition.* 队伍中有一人死于这场倒霉的远征。

ill-fa-voured *BrE*【英】，**ill-favored** *AmE*【美】/ˌ· ˈ··◂/ *adj literary or old-fashioned* having an unattractive face; ugly【文或过时】长相丑陋的，其貌不扬的

ill feel-ing /ˌ· ˈ··/ *n* [U] angry feelings towards someone 敌意，反感：*Whatever ill feeling there had been between them had vanished by now.* 他们之间以往的恩恩怨怨现在已烟消云散了。

ill-found-ed /ˌ· ˈ··/ *adj formal* not based on true facts【正式】缺乏根据的，凭空的：*Unfortunately her faith in British justice proved ill-founded.* 不幸的是，她对英国司法的信任原来毫无根据。

ill-got-ten /ˌ· ˈ··◂/ *adj* **ill-gotten gains/wealth etc** *especially humorous* money that was obtained in an unfair or dishonest way【尤幽默】来路不正的钱财：*They rushed home to gloat over their ill-gotten gains.* 他们赶紧回家，对来路不正之财沾沾自喜。

il-lib-e-ral /ɪˈlɪbərəl; ɪˈlɪbərəl/ *adj formal*【正式】**1** not supporting freedom of expression or of personal behaviour 不开明的，狭隘的，不容异说的：*illiberal and undemocratic policies* 专制、不民主的政策 **2** not generous 吝啬的，小气的 —**illiberally** *adv* —**illiberality** /ɪˌlɪbəˈræləti; ɪˌlɪbəˈrælɪ̣ti/ *n* [U]

il-li-cit /ɪˈlɪsɪt; ɪˈlɪsɪ̣t/ *adj* not allowed by laws or rules, or strongly disapproved of by society 非法的，违禁的，社会不容许的：*an illicit love affair* 有违世俗的爱情 | *illicit diamond trading* 非法钻石交易 —**illicitly** *adv*

Il-li-nois /ˌɪlɪˈnɔɪ; ˌɪlɪ̣ˈnɔɪ/ abbreviation 缩写为 **IL** a state in the Midwest of the US, famous for its farming and industry. Chicago is its largest city. 伊利诺伊州〔美国中西部一州，以工农业闻名。芝加哥是该州最大的城市〕

il-lit-e-rate /ɪˈlɪtərɪt; ɪˈlɪtərɪ̣t/ *adj* **1** someone who is illiterate has not learned to read or write 不识字的，文盲的 **2** badly written, in an uneducated way〔因未受教育而〕满纸别字的，病句连篇的：*It was an illiterate letter, full of mistakes.* 这封信文笔很差，错误连篇。**3 politically/scientifically etc illiterate** knowing very little about politics, science etc 对政治/科学知识等一窍不通 —**illiteracy** *n* [U]

ill-judged /ˌ· ˈ·◂/ *adj formal* an action that is ill-judged has not been thought about carefully enough【正式】判断不当的，轻率的：*an ill-judged decision* 轻率的决定

ill-man-nered /ˌ· ˈ··◂/ *adj formal* not polite; behaving badly in social situations【正式】粗鲁的；〔在社交场合〕不礼貌的 —opposite 反义词 WELL-MANNERED

ill-na-tured /ˌ· ˈ··◂/ *adj formal* unpleasant or unkind【正式】令人讨厌的，不友善的：*ill-natured gossip* 流言飞语

ill-ness /ˈɪlnɪs; ˈɪlnɪ̣s/ *n* [C,U] a disease of the body or mind 病，疾病：*She had all the normal childhood illnesses.* 儿童的常见病她小时候都患过。| *mental illness* 精神疾病 | **serious illness** *an insurance policy that guarantees an income in the event of serious illness* 保证身患重病时仍有收入的保险单 | **minor illness** (=one that is not very serious) 小病，微恙 *people who go to the doctor even for the most minor illnesses* 那些稍有不适就去找医生的人 —see also 另见 DISEASE

il-lo-gi-cal /ɪˈlɑdʒɪkl; ɪˈlɒdʒɪkəl/ *adj* **1** not sensible or reasonable 不合理的，悖理的：*erratic and illogical behaviour* 古怪、乖戾的行为 —opposite 反义词 LOGICAL (1) **2** not based on the principles of LOGIC 不合逻辑的：*an illogical conclusion* 荒谬的结论 —**illogically** /-klɪ; -kli/ *adv* —**illogicality** /ɪˌlɑdʒɪˈkæləti; ɪˌlɒdʒɪ̣ˈkælɪ̣ti/ *n* [U]

ill-o-mened /ˌ· ˈ··◂/ *adj literary* likely to bring a lot of problems or suffering in the future【文】不祥的，很可能导致问题[苦难]的：*an ill-omened business venture* 有不祥之兆的投资

ill-starred /ˌ· ˈ·◂/ *adj literary* unlucky and likely to cause or experience a lot of problems or unhappiness【文】倒霉的，不吉利的：*an ill-starred love affair* 苦命的爱情

ill-tem-pered /ˌ· ˈ··◂/ *adj formal*【正式】**1** easily made angry or impatient 易怒的，脾气暴躁的 **2** an ill-tempered meeting, argument etc is one in which people are angry and often rude to each other〔会议、争论等〕怒气冲冲的，粗鲁无礼的：*ill-tempered exchanges in the presidential debate* 总统竞选辩论中火药味十足的唇枪舌剑

ill-timed /ˌ· ˈ·◂/ *adj* happening, done, or said at the wrong time 不合时宜的：*His remarks are ill-timed and inappropriate.* 他那番话说得不是时候，内容也有失妥当。

ill-treat /ˌ· ˈ·/ *v* [T] to be cruel to someone, especially to a child or animal 虐待〔尤指对孩子或动物〕—**ill-treatment** *n* [U]

il-lu-mi-nate /ɪˈluməˌnet; ɪˈluːmɪ̣neɪt/ *v* [T] **1** to make a light shine on something, or fill a place with light 照射，照亮，照明：*The room was illuminated by the glow of the fire.* 房间被炉火照得通明。**2** *formal* to make something much clearer and easier to understand【正式】阐明〔某物〕，解释；使易懂：*His lecture illuminated and explained many scientific phenomena.* 他的讲演阐明并解释了许多科学现象。**3** to decorate buildings, streets, etc with lights for a special occasion〔节日时〕用灯装饰〔建筑物、街道等〕**4** *literary* to make someone look happy or excited【文】使〔某人〕面露喜色，容光焕发：*A sudden smile illuminated her face.* 突然她的脸上露出了笑容。

il-lu-mi-nat-ed /ɪˈluməˌnetɪd; ɪˈluːmɪ̣neɪtɪ̣d/ *adj* **1** lit up by lights〔用灯〕照亮的，发光的：*a big illuminated sign over the entrance* 入口处上方的大型灯标 **2 an illuminated book/bible/manuscript etc** a book of a type produced by hand in the Middle Ages, whose pages are decorated with gold paint and other bright colours 缀以颜色的书籍/圣经/手稿等〔指在中世纪以手工制作的一种书籍，页面上有金漆及其他亮丽色彩的装饰〕

il-lu-mi-nat-ing /ɪˈluməˌnetɪŋ; ɪˈluːmɪ̣neɪtɪŋ/ *adj* making things much clearer and easier to understand 使清楚的，容易理解的：*I didn't find his reply very illuminating.* 我觉得他的答复意思不太明确。

il-lu-mi-na-tion /ɪˌluməˈneʃən; ɪˌluːmɪ̣ˈneɪʃən/ *n* **1** [U] lighting provided by a lamp, light etc 光亮，照明：*An electric light bulb provided the only illumination.* 一只电灯泡提供唯一的照明。| *The illumination is too weak to show the detail of the painting.* 照明太差，显示不出这幅画的细节。**2** [C usually plural 一般用复数] a picture or pattern painted on a page of a book, especially in former times〔尤指旧时书籍中页面上的〕彩饰，图案装饰：*valuable manuscripts with many illuminations* 带有许多彩饰的珍贵手稿 **3 illuminations** *especially BrE* a show of coloured lights used to make a town bright and colourful【尤英】〔装饰城市的〕灯彩，灯饰：*the famous Blackpool illuminations* 著名的布莱克浦市灯饰 **4** [U] *formal* clear explanation of a particular subject【正式】阐明〔某主题〕：*illumination of a previously unexplored topic* 对以前从未涉及的话题的阐释

ill-use /ˌɪl ˈjuz; ˌɪl ˈjuːz/ *v* [T usually passive 一般用被动态] *formal* to treat someone badly or unfairly【正式】虐待〔某人〕；不公正对待〔某人〕：*She's been ill-used by her colleagues.* 她一直受到同事的苛待。—**ill-usage** /-ˈjusɪdʒ; -ˈjuːsɪdʒ/ *n* [U]

il·lu·sion /ɪˋluʒən; ɪˈluːʒən/ *n* [C] **1** an idea or opinion that is wrong, especially about yourself〔尤指对自己的〕幻觉, 幻想: **illusion that** *He cherished the illusion that she loved him.* 他幻想她爱他。| **be/labour under an illusion** (=believe something that is not true) 误以为, 有错觉 | **have no illusions about** (=realize the unpleasant truth about something) 对…不存幻想〔意识到使人不愉快的真相〕*He has no illusions about the harsh realities of the economic climate.* 他对经济局势的严峻现实不抱幻想。**2** something that seems to be different from the way it really is 假象, 错觉: *The mirrors in the room gave an illusion of greater space.* 房间里的镜子给人一种空间变大了的错觉。—see also 另见 OPTICAL ILLUSION

il·lu·sion·ist /ɪˋluʒənɪst; ɪˈluːʒənɪst/ *n* [C] someone who does surprising tricks that make things seem to appear or happen〔运用幻术使人感到某物突然出现或某事突然发生的〕魔术师

il·lu·so·ry /ɪˋlusərɪ; ɪˈluːsəri/ also 又作 **il·lu·sive** /ɪˋlusɪv; ɪˈluːsɪv/ *adj formal* false but seeming to be real or true【正式】虚假的, 貌似真实的: *the apparent but illusory successes of the last 15 years* 近 15 年来虚幻的成功表象

W2 **il·lus·trate** /ˋɪləstret; ˈɪləstreɪt/ *v* [T] **1** to make the meaning of something clearer by giving examples 举例说明〔某事物〕: *To illustrate the point, Dr Fisher told a story.* 费希尔博士讲了个故事来说明这一点。**2** to be an example which shows that something is true or that a fact exists 作为例证说明〔事实〕: *Nixon's downfall illustrates the immense power of the media.* 尼克松的倒台显示出媒体的巨大威力。**3** [usually passive 一般用被动态] to put pictures in a book, article etc〔给书籍、文章等〕作插图: *a beautifully illustrated book* 插图精美的书

il·lus·tra·tion /ˌɪləsˋtreʃən; ˌɪləˈstreɪʃən/ *n* **1** [C] a picture in a book, article etc, especially one that helps you to understand it〔书籍、文章中的〕插图; 图解: *Children like books with lots of illustrations.* 儿童喜欢看有大量插图的书。**2** [C,U] a story, event, action etc that shows the truth or existence of something very clearly 实例, 例证: **[+of]** *a striking illustration of 19th century attitudes to women* 19 世纪对待妇女的态度的明显例证 | **by way of illustration** (=as an example) 作为例子 *By way of illustration, I should like to mention a recent case.* 作为一个例子, 我想提一件最近发生的事。**3** [U] the act or process of illustrating something 说明; 图解, 图示

il·lus·tra·tive /ɪˋlʌstrətɪv; ˈɪləstreɪtɪv/ *adj* helping to explain the meaning of something 起辅助说明作用的: *an illustrative example* 起辅助说明作用的例子 —see also 另见 ILLUSTRATE (2)

il·lus·tra·tor /ˋɪləsˌtretɚ; ˈɪləstreɪtə/ *n* [C] someone who draws pictures, especially for books〔尤指图书的〕插图画家

il·lus·tri·ous /ɪˋlʌstrɪəs; ɪˈlʌstriəs/ *adj formal* famous and admired because of what you have achieved in the past【正式】著名的, 杰出的, 卓越的: *I would like to introduce our illustrious guest, Professor Brookes.* 我向大家介绍这位声誉卓著的嘉宾——布鲁克斯教授。

ill will /ˌ· ˈ·/ *n* [U] strong dislike; HOSTILITY 厌恶; 敌意: *At first there was a lot of suspicion and ill will among the team.* 起初, 队员互相猜忌, 充满敌意。| **bear sb no ill will** (=feel no dislike or anger towards someone) 对某人不怀敌意

ILO, the /ˌaɪ ɛl ˋo; ˌaɪ el ˈəʊ/ the abbreviation of 缩写= the INTERNATIONAL LABOUR ORGANIZATION

I'm /aɪm; aɪm/ the short form of 缩略式= 'I am' : *I'm a student.* 我是个学生。

im- /ɪm; ɪm/ *prefix* the form used for IN- before b, m, or p〔用在 b, m 或 p 前, 代替 in-〕: *immobilize* 使固定 | *impossible* 不可能的

S3 W1 **im·age** /ˋɪmɪdʒ; ˈɪmɪdʒ/ *n* [C]

1 ▶PUBLIC OPINION 公众舆论◀ the general opinion that most people have of a person, organization, product etc〔某人、组织、产品等的〕形象: *The party is seeking to improve its image with women voters.* 该党正力图改善它在女性选民心目中的形象。| **project an image** (=make an image) 树立形象 *The princess aimed to project an image of herself as serious and hardworking.* 公主想为自己塑造一个认真勤奋的形象。

2 ▶IDEA IN MIND 脑海中的想法◀ a picture that you have in your mind, especially about what someone or something is like or the way they look〔脑海中对某人或某物的〕印象, 形象: *She had a clear image of how she would look in twenty years' time.* 20年后她将是什么模样, 她心中有一个清楚的形象。| *He didn't really conform to the hard-drinking, hard-living image of the political journalist.* 他不太符合政治记者那种饮酒无度、生活艰苦的形象。

3 ▶PICTURE/WHAT YOU SEE 图像/所见的东西◀ a) a picture of an object in a mirror or in the LENS (2) of a camera〔镜子或照相机镜头中的〕映象: *She gazed at her image in the glass.* 她凝视着镜子中自己的映象。**b)** a picture on the SCREEN[1] (1,2) of a television, cinema, or computer〔电视机、电脑屏幕上或银幕上的〕图像: *The image on a computer screen is made up of thousands of pixels.* 电脑屏幕上的图像是由千万个像素组成的。**c)** a copy of the shape of a person or thing, especially cut in wood, stone etc 塑像, 雕像〔尤指用木头或石头雕刻成的人或物的形状〕: *carved images in the rocks* 刻于岩石上的图像

4 ▶DESCRIPTION 描绘◀ a phrase or word that describes something in a poetic way〔修辞中的〕比喻: *the image of man as a prisoner of the gods* 将人比喻为众神之囚

5 be the (very/living/spitting) image of to look exactly like someone or something else 酷似〔某人或某物〕: *He's the very image of his father.* 他长相酷似他的父亲。

6 in the image of *literary* in the same form or shape as someone or something else【文】与…同形: *According to the Bible, man was made in the image of God.* 据《圣经》说, 人是按照上帝的模样创造出来的。—see also 另见 MIRROR IMAGE

im·ag·e·ry /ˋɪmɪdʒrɪ; ˈɪmɪdʒəri/ *n* [U] **1** the use of poetic phrases and images to describe something in literature〔文学中的〕意象, 形象化描述; 比喻: *the symbolic imagery of Dylan Thomas* 迪伦·托马斯的象征性比喻 **2** the representation of ideas in paintings, films etc〔绘画、电影等中表达思想的〕意象, 形象化描述: *the romantic imagery of the Pre-Raphaelite painters* 前拉斐尔派画家创造的浪漫意象

i·ma·gi·na·ble /ɪˋmædʒɪnəbl; ɪˈmædʒɪnəbəl/ *adj* **the best/worst/kindest etc imaginable** used to emphasize that something is the best, worst etc example of something that it is possible to imagine 可想象到的最好/坏/善良等的〔用于强调〕: *He was defeated in the most humiliating circumstances imaginable.* 他在人们能够想象到的最屈辱的情况下被打败了。| **every imaginable** *Posters were plastered on every imaginable surface.* 只要是能想到的空白的表面都给张贴了海报。

i·ma·gi·na·ry /ɪˋmædʒəˌnɛrɪ; ɪˈmædʒɪnəri/ *adj* not real, but produced from pictures or ideas in your mind 想象的, 虚构的: *All the characters in this book are imaginary.* 本书人物纯属虚构。—compare 比较 IMAGINATIVE

i·ma·gi·na·tion /ɪˌmædʒəˋneʃən; ɪˌmædʒɪˈneɪʃən/ *n* **1** [C, U] the ability to form pictures or ideas in your mind 想象力: *Children often have very vivid imaginations.* 儿童常有生动的想象力。| *With a little imagination, he could visualize the old house as a luxury hotel.* 他稍加幻想, 便可以把这幢旧房子想象成豪华饭店。**2** [U] something that is caused only by your mind, and does not really exist or did not really happen 幻觉, 幻象; 空想: *Did you hear that noise, or was it my imagination?* 你听到那个声音了吗? 还是我的幻觉? **3 in your imagination** only existing or happening in your mind, not in real life 只存在于[发生于]脑海中的, 幻想的: *The difficulties are all in your imagination.* 这些困难全是你想象出来的。**4 capture/catch sb's imagination** to make people feel very interested and excited 使某人出神, 使某人入迷: *His music captured the imagination of a whole generation of young people.* 他的音乐吸引了整整一代年轻人。**5 leave sth to sb's imagination** to deliberately not describe something because you think someone can guess or imagine it 留给某人自己去想象〔因认为人们能够猜测或想象到, 故意不描述某事〕: *I'll leave the details of the affair to your imagination.* 事情的细节留给你去想象吧。**6 use your imagination!** *spoken* used to tell someone that they can easily guess the answer to a question, so you should not need to tell them【口】动动脑筋!〔用于告诉某人他能轻易猜到答案〕—see also 另见 **not by any stretch of the imagination** (STRETCH[2] (5)) S3 W3

i·ma·gi·na·tive /ɪˋmædʒəˌnetɪv; ɪˈmædʒɪnətɪv/ *adj* **1** someone who is imaginative is good at thinking of new, interesting ideas, and at forming pictures in their mind〔人〕想象力丰富的: *an imaginative child* 想象力丰富的孩子 **2** something that is imaginative contains new and interesting ideas used in a clever way〔某物〕富有想象力的: *imaginative writing* 富有想象力的文章 | *an imaginative solution to the problem* 富有想象力的解决方法 —compare 比较 IMAGINARY —**imaginatively** *adv*

i·ma·gine /ɪˋmædʒɪn; ɪˈmædʒɪn/ *v* [T] S2 W2

1 ▶MENTAL PICTURE 心中的图像◀ [not usually in progressive 一般不用进行时] to form a picture or idea in your mind about what something could be like 想象: **imagine (that)** *Try to imagine that you are a tourist arriving in London for the first time.* 试想象自己是第一次来伦敦的游客。| *Close your eyes and imagine a tropical island.* 闭上眼睛, 想象一个热带岛屿。| **imagine what/how/why etc** *I can just imagine what the place is going to look like in a few years' time.* 我能想象出这个地方几年之后会变成什么样子。| **imagine sb doing sth** *I can just imagine Sarah running her own business.* 我能想象出萨拉自己开

公司的情景。| **imagine doing sth** *It's hard to imagine working in a place like that.* 在那种地方工作，真是难以想象。| **imagine sb/sth as** *I never knew my grandmother but I always imagine her as a kind, gentle person.* 我从未见过祖母，但我总把她想象成一个心地善良、和蔼可亲的人。| **imagine sb in/with/without etc** *Somehow I can't imagine him without a beard.* 不知为什么，我就是想象不出他没有胡子的样子。

2 ▶WRONG IDEA 错误的想法◀to have a false or wrong idea about something 幻想，误以为：*She doesn't love him, he's just imagining it.* 她不爱他，他不过是在幻想。| *imagined dangers* 凭空臆想出来的危险 | **imagine (that)** *He imagines that people don't like him but they do.* 他误以为人们不喜欢他，但事实并非如此。| **imagine sb/sth to be sth** *I was surprised when I saw the farm. I had imagined it to be much bigger.* 看见这个农场时我大为惊讶——我原来想象它会大得多。

3 ▶THINK STH 猜想某事◀[not in progressive 不用进行时] to think that something is true, but without being sure or having proof〔不肯定或没有根据地〕猜想，猜测：*You must miss him, I imagine.* 我猜想你一定很想念他。| **imagine (that)** *I imagine she's home by now if you want to phone her.* 如果你要给她打电话，我想她现在已经到家了。

4 you can't imagine *BrE spoken* used to emphasize how good, bad etc something is【英口】你想象不到〔用于强调某物好、坏等的程度〕：*You can't imagine what a terrible week we had.* 你简直想象不出我们经历了多么可怕的一个星期。

5 ▶SURPRISED 感到惊讶◀ **(just) imagine!** *spoken old-fashioned* used to show surprise, shock, or disapproval【口，过时】真想不到！〔表示惊讶、震惊或反对〕：*He dyed his hair bright yellow! Just imagine!* 真没想到，他竟然把头发染成了鲜艳的黄色！| **imagine doing sth** *Imagine going all that way for nothing!* 真想不到走了那么远却毫无所获！

This graph shows how common the different grammar patterns of the verb **imagine** are. 本图表所示为动词 imagine 构成的不同语法模式的使用频率。

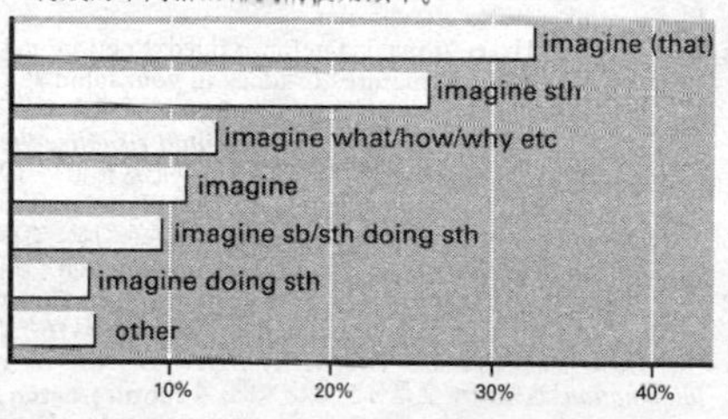

Based on the British National Corpus and the Longman Lancaster Corpus
据英国国家语料库和朗文兰开斯特语料库

i·ma·gin·ings /ɪˋmædʒɪnɪŋz; ɪˈmædʒɪnɪŋz/ *n* [plural] *literary* situations or ideas that you imagine, but which are not real or true【文】想象的情形[概念]〔实际上是虚妄的〕

im·am /ɪˋmɑm; ˈɪmɑːm/ *n* [C] a Muslim religious leader or priest 伊玛目〔伊斯兰教的宗教领袖或祭司〕

im·bal·ance /ɪmˋbæləns; ɪmˈbæləns/ *n* [C,U] a lack of a fair or correct balance between two things, which results in problems or unfairness 不平衡，失调：*a hormonal imbalance* 激素失衡 | **redress an imbalance** (=put it right) 恢复平衡 *an attempt to redress the imbalance between rich and poor* 平均财富的努力

im·be·cile /ˋɪmbəsḷ; ˈɪmbəsiːl/ *n* [C] **1** someone who is very stupid or behaves very stupidly 蠢人，笨蛋：*He looked at me as if I was a complete imbecile.* 他看着我，好像我是个大笨蛋。**2** *old-fashioned* a word meaning someone who is mentally ill, now considered offensive【过时】低能儿〔现代用法中为冒犯用词〕—**imbecilic** /ˌɪmbəˋsɪlɪk; ˌɪmbɪ̈ˈsɪlɪk◂/ *adj*

im·be·cil·i·ty /ˌɪmbəˋsɪlətɪ; ˌɪmbɪ̈ˈsɪlɪ̈ti/ *n* **1** [C,U] very stupid behaviour or an action that is very stupid 愚蠢的行为 **2** [U] the condition of being an imbecile 愚蠢；低能，弱智

im·bed /ɪmˋbɛd; ɪmˈbed/ *v* **imbedded, imbedding** [T] another spelling of EMBED embed 的另一种拼法

im·bibe /ɪmˋbaɪb; ɪmˈbaɪb/ *v* [I,T] *formal or humorous*【正式或幽默】**1** to drink something, especially alcohol 喝〔尤指酒〕，饮：*Having imbibed rather too freely, he fell forward against the table.* 由于酒喝得太多，他一头栽在桌子上。**2** to accept and be influenced by qualities, ideas, values etc 接受〔品质、观点、价值等〕并受到影响：*imbibing radical political ideas* 受激进的政治主张的影响

im·bro·gli·o /ɪmˋbroljo; ɪmˈbrəʊliəʊ/ *n plural* **imbroglios** [C] a difficult, embarrassing, or confusing situation, especially in politics or public life〔尤指政治或公务中出现的〕错综复杂的局面：*He found himself in the greatest imbroglio of his tenure at the UN.* 他发现自己陷入了在联合国任职期间最大的困境。

im·bue /ɪmˋbju; ɪmˈbjuː/ *v*

imbue sb with sth *phr v* [T usually passive 一般用被动态] to make someone feel an emotion very strongly 使〔某人〕充满〔强烈情感〕：*a people deeply imbued with national pride* 内心充满自豪感的民族

IMF, the /ˌaɪ ɛm ˋɛf; ˌaɪ em ˈef/ *n* the International Monetary Fund; an international organization that tries to encourage trade between countries and to help poorer countries develop economically 国际货币基金组织〔促进国际贸易，并协助贫穷国家发展经济的国际组织〕

im·i·tate /ˋɪməˌtet; ˈɪmɪ̈teɪt/ *v* [T] **1** to copy something because you think it is good〔认为是好的而〕仿效〔某物〕：*Do kids really imitate the violence they see on TV?* 孩子真会模仿在电视上看到的暴力吗？| *Our methods have been imitated all over the world.* 全世界都在效仿我们的办法。**2** to copy the way someone behaves, speaks, moves etc, especially in order to make people laugh 模仿〔某人的行为、说话、动作等，尤指引人发笑的模仿〕：*"Give that back!" she screeched, imitating Jess's high-pitched squeal.* "还给我！"她模仿着杰斯的尖嗓音高声喊道。—**imitator** *n* [C]

im·i·ta·tion /ˌɪməˋteʃən; ˌɪmɪ̈ˈteɪʃən◂/ *n* **1** [C,U] an attempt to imitate someone or something, or the act of doing this 模仿，仿效：*Bill can do a passable imitation of an American accent.* 比尔对美国腔调的模仿还真挺像。| *Children learn a lot by imitation.* 孩子通过模仿学到很多东西。| **a pale imitation** (=something that is much less good than the thing it imitates) 拙劣的仿制品 *The remake of 'Casablanca' was a pale imitation of the original movie.* 重拍的《卡萨布兰卡》与原版相比大为逊色。**2** [C] a copy of something 仿制品，赝品：*The table is a genuine antique not a cheap imitation.* 这张桌子是真品古董，不是便宜的仿制品。| **imitation leather/wood/ivory etc** (=something that looks like an expensive material but is a copy of it) 人造皮革／木材／象牙等

im·i·ta·tive /ˋɪməˌtetɪv; ˈɪmɪ̈tətɪv/ *adj formal* copying someone or something, especially in a way that shows you do not have any ideas of your own【正式】〔尤指缺乏个人的思想〕模仿的，仿效的 —**imitatively** *adv* —**imitativeness** *n* [U]

im·mac·u·late /ɪˋmækjəlɪt; ɪˈmækjɡ̈lɪ̈t/ *adj* **1** very clean and tidy 非常洁净整齐的：*Richard looked immaculate in a white silk dinner jacket.* 理查德穿着白色丝绸礼服上装，看上去干净利落。**2** exactly correct or perfect in every detail 精确的；完美的：*Your timing is immaculate!* 你时间把握得分秒不差！—**immaculately** *adv*

Immaculate Con·cep·tion /·ˌ··· ˈ··/ *n* the Christian belief that Christ's mother Mary was a VIRGIN (=someone who has never had sex) when Christ was born 圣母无原罪始胎〔此说认为圣母马利亚童贞怀孕生下耶稣〕

im·ma·nent /ˋɪmənənt; ˈɪmənənt/ *adj formal*【正式】**1** a quality that is immanent seems to be naturally present〔指特质〕内在的；天生的：*Hope seems immanent in human nature.* 抱有希望似乎是人类与生俱来的本性。**2** God or another spiritual power that is immanent is present everywhere〔上帝或另一种精神力量〕无所不在的 —compare 比较 EMINENT, IMMINENT —**immanence, immanency** *n* [U]

im·ma·te·ri·al /ˌɪməˋtɪrɪəl; ˌɪməˈtɪəriəl◂/ *adj* **1** not important in a particular situation; IRRELEVANT 无关紧要的；不相关的：*The causes of the problem are immaterial now – we need solutions.* 问题的原因现在已无关紧要，我们需要的是解决方法。**2** *formal* not having a real physical form【正式】非实体的，无形的

im·ma·ture /ˌɪməˋtjʊr; ˌɪməˈtʃʊə/ *adj* **1** someone who is immature behaves or thinks in a way that is typical of someone much younger〔行为、思想〕不成熟的：*I married much too young – I was very immature.* 我结婚时太年轻，当时还很不成熟。**2** not fully formed or developed 发育未全的：*The immature plants are susceptible to frost.* 幼小的植物易受霜冻侵袭。—**immaturity** *n* [U]

im·mea·su·ra·ble /ɪˋmɛʒərəbḷ; ɪˈmeʒərəbəl/ *adj* too big or too extreme to be measured 无法计量的：*This latest scandal has done immeasurable damage to his reputation.* 最近的丑闻给他的名誉造成了难以估计的伤害。—**immeasurably** *adv*: *The company's position has improved immeasurably since last year.* 去年以来，公司的地位得到极大提高。

im·me·di·a·cy /ɪˋmidɪəsɪ; ɪˈmiːdiəsi/ *n* [U] the quality of seeming to happen right now that makes something seem more

important or urgent to you 即时; 紧迫; 刻不容缓: *Television brings a new immediacy to world events.* 电视使世界大事更迅捷地呈现在众眼前。

2 2 **im·me·di·ate** /ɪˋmidɪɪt; ɪˈmiːdiət/ *adj*
1▶NO DELAY 立即, 不延误◀ happening or done at once and without delay 立刻的, 即时的: *The police response to the situation was forceful and immediate.* 警方对局面作出迅速有力的反应。| *seek immediate medical attention* 寻求即时医疗护理
2▶NOW 目前◀ [only before noun 仅用于名词前] existing now, and needing to be dealt with quickly 目前的〔要迅速处理的〕, 当下的: *Our immediate concern was to stop the fire from spreading.* 我们的当务之急是阻止火势蔓延。| *I have no immediate plans to leave.* 我目前没有离开的打算。
3▶AFTER/BEFORE 之后/之前◀ [only before noun 仅用于名词前] happening just before or just after someone or something else 最接近的, 紧接的: *My immediate predecessor went to work for a rival firm.* 我的上届前任去了一家与我们竞争的公司工作。| *the immediate future* 最近的将来
4▶NEAR 附近的◀ [only before noun 仅用于名词前] next to, or very near to, a particular place 〔地方〕邻近的; 紧邻的: *The immediate area was sealed off after the bombing.* 轰炸之后, 紧邻地区被封锁起来。
5 immediate family/kin people who are very closely related to you, such as your parents, children, brothers, and sisters 直系亲属〈如父母、儿女、兄弟姐妹等〉

2 1 **im·me·di·ate·ly¹** /ɪˋmidɪɪtlɪ; ɪˈmiːdiətli/ *adv* **1** without delay 即刻, 马上: *Cook the mixture for ten minutes and serve immediately.* 将混合物烹调10分钟后即刻上桌。| *As soon as I got their fax, I wrote back immediately.* 我一收到他们的传真, 就立刻写了回信。**2** [+adj/adv] very soon before or after something 〔某事之前或之后〕立即: *The baby was given up for adoption immediately after birth.* 那个婴儿刚出生就交给别人领养了。**3** [+adj/adv] very near to something 贴近地: *Charles lives in the apartment immediately above ours.* 查尔斯就住在紧靠我们家楼上的那个公寓套间。**4 immediately involved/concerned/affected etc** very closely involved etc in a particular situation 〔与某事〕有直接牵连/关系; 直接〔受某事〕影响: *All those immediately involved will be informed of the decision.* 这个决定将通知所有直接相关人员。

immediately² *conjunction BrE formal* as soon as【英, 正式】一…就…: *Make sure the property you are buying is insured immediately you exchange contracts.* 合同互换之后, 应立刻给所购房产买保险。

im·me·mo·ri·al /ˌɪməˋmorɪəl; ˌɪmɪ̈ˈmɔːriəl◂/ *adj* **1 since/from time immemorial** for longer than people can remember 自古以来: *The tribe had inhabited the area since time immemorial.* 自远古以来, 该部落就在这个地区居住。**2** *formal* starting longer ago than people can remember, or than written history shows【正式】年代久远没人记得的; 史前的: *an immemorial custom* 源远流长的风俗

im·mense /ɪˋmɛns; ɪˈmens/ *adj* extremely large 巨大的: *An immense amount of money and time has been put into finding a cure.* 为寻找治疗方法, 已投入了大量金钱和时间。

im·mense·ly /ɪˋmɛnslɪ; ɪˈmensli/ *adv* very much; extremely 非常; 极大地: *We enjoyed the play immensely.* 我们极为欣赏该剧。| *immensely popular* 非常流行的; 非常受欢迎的; 非常有声望的

im·men·si·ty /ɪˋmɛnsətɪ; ɪˈmensɪ̈ti/ *n* [U] **1** the great size and seriousness of something such as a problem you have to deal with or a job you have to do 〔指规模或困难程度的〕巨大: *the immensity of the task before us* 我们所面临的极为浩繁的任务 **2** also 又作 **immensities** [plural] the great size of something, especially something that cannot be measured 浩瀚无际: *the immensities of outer space* 浩瀚无际的外太空

im·merse /ɪˋmɝs; ɪˈmɜːs/ *v* [T] **1** *especially technical* to put someone or something deep into a liquid so that it is completely covered【尤术语】使浸没〔于液体中〕: **immerse sb/sth in** *Immerse your foot in ice cold water to reduce the swelling.* 把你的脚泡在冰凉的水中可以消肿。**2 immerse yourself in** to become completely involved in an activity 潜心于, 专心于: *Jane was determined to immerse herself in the African way of life.* 简决心潜心研究非洲人的生活方式。—**immersed** *adj*: *completely immersed in his job* 完全投入工作

im·mer·sion /ɪˋmɝʃən; ɪˈmɜːʃən/ *n* [U] **1** the fact of being completely involved in something you are doing 专心〔做某事〕, 投入: *He was well respected, despite his immersion in the murkier side of politics.* 他虽然与政治的黑暗面有很深的牵连, 但仍然很受尊敬。**2 a)** the action of immersing something in liquid, or the state of being immersed 沉浸, 浸没 **b)** BAPTISM (=a ceremony to introduce someone into a church) in which someone's whole body is put into water 〔全身入水的〕洗礼, 浸礼 **3** the language teaching method in which people are put in situations where they have to use the new language 〔将学生置于必须使用外语的环境的〕沉浸式语言教学法 **4** *BrE informal* an immersion heater【英, 非正式】浸入式热水器

immersion heat·er /ˈ·ˌ· ˌ··/ *n* [C] *BrE* an electric water heater that provides hot water for a house【英】浸入式热水器〔一种家用电热水器〕

im·mi·grant /ˋɪməgrənt; ˈɪmɪ̈grənt/ *n* [C] someone who comes from abroad to live permanently in another country 〔外来的〕移民 —compare 比较 EMIGRANT

CULTURAL NOTE 文化注释

Immigrants in the US The US has received large groups of immigrants from all over the world throughout its history. In the 19th century and early 20th century, large numbers of Europeans came to the US as immigrants. They left their home countries because they could not get work there, or because they were treated badly because of their religious or political beliefs. Many people came to live in the US because they saw it as the 'land of opportunity', a place where you could become rich and successful. Today most US immigrants come from Central and South America or Asia rather than Europe. 美国的移民: 美国历史上接纳了大批来自世界各地的移民。19世纪和20世纪初, 大量欧洲人在本国找不到工作, 或因宗教或政治信仰遭到迫害, 因而移民美国。很多人认为美国是一个"机遇之乡", 可以致富、成功, 因此去美国生活。今天, 美国的大多数移民来自中美洲、南美洲和亚洲, 而不是欧洲。— see also 另见 ELLIS ISLAND

Immigrants in the UK The UK has received large numbers of immigrants. Some were REFUGEE*s*, especially before and during World War II. In the 1950s and 1960s, many people went to the UK from the COMMONWEALTH especially from the Caribbean, India, and Pakistan. In the 1970s, a number of BOAT PEOPLE from Vietnam were allowed to live in the UK. 英国的移民: 英国也接纳了大量移民, 其中一些人是难民, 二战前和二战期间尤其如此。20世纪50、60年代, 很多人从英联邦国家, 尤其是加勒比地区、印度和巴基斯坦移民英国。20世纪70年代, 一些越南船民获准在英国居住。

Today there are strict rules preventing people from going to live in the US and the UK, and unless one of their parents is from there, they are married to a US or UK citizen, or they are bringing a large amount of money with them, it is very difficult for someone to live in either country permanently. Many illegal immigrants have come to live and work in the US, especially from Mexico and other Central American countries. Many of these immigrants do jobs that most Americans do not want to do, such as farm work, and the US has sometimes made special rules that allow some of these illegal immigrants to stay and become citizens. ASYLUM SEEKER*s* are allowed to live in the UK and the US until it is safe for them to return to their own country, and some are given permission to live in the UK or the US permanently. 现在, 移民美国和英国有严格限制, 想在两国永久居住很难, 除非父母或配偶是英国或美国公民, 或者自己带去一大笔钱。很多非法移民在美国生活和工作, 来自墨西哥和其他中美洲国家的尤其多, 其中很多人做一些大多数美国人不愿意做的工作, 如在农场打工。美国有时会制定特别条例, 允许一些非法移民居留并获得公民身份。政治避难者可以在英美居住, 直到能安全返回本国为止, 其中一些人获得在英国或美国永久居住的许可。— see Feature on page F18 见 F18 页文化特写

im·mi·grate /ˋɪməˌgret; ˈɪmɪ̈greɪt/ *v* [I] to come into a country in order to live there permanently 〔为定居而从外国〕移入 —see also 另见 EMIGRATE

im·mi·gra·tion /ˌɪməˋgreʃən; ˌɪmɪ̈ˈgreɪʃən/ *n* [U] **1** the process of entering another country in order to live there 移民入境: *normal immigration procedures* 正常的移民入境程序 **2** the total number of people who do this 移民人数: *Immigration fell in the 1980s.* 20世纪80年代移民人数下降。**3** also 又作 **immigration control** the place at an airport, sea port etc where officials check the documents of everyone entering the country 〔机场、港口等的〕入境检查处

Immigration and Nat·u·ral·i·za·tion Ser·vice, the /·.·. · ·.·..·. ·.·/ abbreviation 缩写为 **the INS** a US gov-

ernment organization which deals with IMMIGRATION, making sure that people from other countries obey official rules about who is allowed to live or work in the US. It also has the power to decide whether these people can become US citizens. 移民归化局〔美国一政府机构，负责移民问题，确保外来移民遵守有关居住或工作的法规。该机构还有权决定外来移民能否成为美国公民〕

im·mi·nent /ˈɪmənənt; ˈɪmɪ̥nənt/ *adj* an event that is imminent will happen very soon 即将发生的；逼近的：*A declaration of war now seemed imminent.* 现在宣战似乎已是箭在弦上。| *The company is now in imminent danger of collapse.* 该公司现在濒临倒闭。—compare 比较 IMMANENT —**imminence** *n* [U] —**imminently** *adv*

im·mo·bile /ɪˈmobl̩; ɪˈməʊbaɪl/ *adj* **1** not moving at all 不活动的，固定的：*A few soldiers were lounging around on two immobile tanks.* 几个士兵懒洋洋地倚在两辆停驶的坦克上。**2** unable to move or walk normally 不能正常走动的：*Kim's illness had rendered her completely immobile.* 金的病使她完全丧失了活动能力。—**immobility** /ˌɪmoˈbɪlətɪ; ˌɪməˈbɪlɪ̥ti/ *n* [U]

im·mo·bi·lize also 又作 **-ise** *BrE*【英】/ɪˈmobl̩ˌaɪz; ɪˈməʊbɪ̥laɪz/ *v* [T] **1** to prevent someone or something from moving 使〔人或物〕不能动，使固定：*The broken limb must be immobilized immediately.* 断肢必须立即加以固定。**2** to stop something from working 使〔某物〕停止运转：*The car's security device will immobilize the ignition system.* 这辆汽车的安全装置能使点火系统停止工作。—**immobilization** /ɪˌmoblaɪˈzeʃən; ɪˌməʊbɪ̥laɪˈzeɪʃən/ *n* [U]

im·mod·e·rate /ɪˈmɑdərɪt; ɪˈmɒdərɪ̥t/ *adj formal* not within reasonable and sensible limits; EXCESSIVE【正式】无节制的；过度的：*immoderate wage demands* 无理的工资要求 | *immoderate drinking* 酗酒，暴饮 —**immoderately** *adv*

im·mod·est /ɪˈmɑdɪst; ɪˈmɒdɪ̥st/ *adj* **1** having a very high opinion of yourself and your abilities, and not embarrassed about telling people how clever you are etc 骄傲的，不谦虚的 —opposite 反义词 MODEST (1) **2** *old-fashioned* behaviour or clothes that are immodest may embarrass or offend people because they do not follow the usual social rules concerning sexual behaviour【过时】〔行为或衣着〕不端庄的，不正派的，下流的，有伤风化的 —**immodestly** *adv* —**immodesty** *n* [U]

im·mo·late /ˈɪməˌlet; ˈɪməleɪt/ *v* [T] *formal* to kill someone or something by burning them【正式】烧死 —**immolation** /ˌɪməˈleʃən; ˌɪməˈleɪʃən/ *n* [U]

im·mor·al /ɪˈmɔrəl; ɪˈmɒrəl/ *adj* **1** morally wrong 不道德的，道德败坏的：*They condemned slavery as immoral.* 他们谴责奴隶制是不道德的。**2** not following accepted standards of sexual behaviour 放荡的，淫荡的；伤风败俗的 —compare 比较 AMORAL —**immorally** *adv*

im·mo·ral·i·ty /ˌɪməˈrælətɪ; ˌɪməˈrælɪ̥ti/ *n* [U] behaviour that is morally wrong 缺德，道德败坏；伤风败俗：*the immorality of bombing civilians* 轰炸平民的不道德行为

im·mor·tal /ɪˈmɔrtl̩; ɪˈmɔːtl/ *adj* **1** living or continuing forever 不死的；永存的：*Plato believed that the soul is immortal.* 柏拉图认为灵魂不灭。**2** an immortal line, play, song etc is so famous that it will never be forgotten〔诗句、戏剧、歌曲等〕不朽的，流传百世的：*Shakespeare's immortal lines* 莎士比亚的不朽诗句 —**immortal** *n* [C]

im·mor·tal·i·ty /ˌɪmɔrˈtælətɪ; ˌɪmɔːˈtælɪ̥ti/ *n* [U] the condition of living forever or being remembered forever 永生，长存，永恒，永垂不朽

im·mor·tal·ize also 又作 **-ise** *BrE*【英】/ɪˈmɔrtl̩ˌaɪz; ɪˈmɔːtəlaɪz/ *v* [T] to make someone or something famous for a long time, especially by writing about them, painting a picture of them etc〔通过著书、画像等〕使不朽，使名垂千古：*Dickens' father was immortalized as Mr Micawber in 'David Copperfield'.* 狄更斯的父亲作为麦考伯先生的原型出现在《大卫·科波菲尔》中，从而名留千古。

Immortal Mem·o·ry, The /ˌ·ˌ·· ˈ···/ especially in Scotland, the title of a TOAST (=when people drink a glass of alcohol to show respect for someone) to the poet Robert Burns, usually made at parties on **Burns Night** 不朽的记忆〔尤指苏格兰彭斯之夜聚会上致诗人罗伯特·彭斯的祝酒词〕

im·mov·a·ble /ɪˈmuvəbl̩; ɪˈmuːvəbəl/ *adj* **1** impossible to move 不可移动的，固定的：*Lock your bike to something immovable like a railing or lamp-post.* 把自行车锁到一个固定的地方，如栏杆或路灯柱上。**2** impossible to change or persuade 坚定不移的，不为所动的：*The president is immovable on this issue.* 在这个问题上，总统的立场坚定不移。—**immovably** *adv*

im·mune /ɪˈmjun; ɪˈmjuːn/ *adj* **1** someone who is immune to a particular disease cannot catch it〔对疾病〕有免疫力的 **2** not affected by something such as criticism, bad treatment etc 不受〔批评、虐待等〕影响的：[**+to**] *They're always so rude that I've almost become immune to it.* 他们总是如此粗暴无礼，我都几乎习以为常了。**3** specially protected from something unpleasant 豁免的；可免…的：[**+from**] *Peterson was told he would be immune from prosecution if he co-operated with the police.* 彼得森被告知，如果他与警方合作，就可免受起诉。

immune sys·tem /·ˈ· ˌ··/ *n* [C] the system by which your body protects itself against disease〔身体的〕免疫系统

im·mu·nise /ˈɪmjəˌnaɪz; ˈɪmjʊ̥naɪz/ *v* a British spelling of IMMUNIZE immunize 的英式拼法

im·mu·ni·ty /ɪˈmjunətɪ; ɪˈmjuːnɪ̥ti/ *n* [U] the fact of not being affected by a disease or harmed by something unpleasant 免疫；免除；豁免：[**+to**] *immunity to infection* 对传染病的免疫力 | [**+from**] *They were granted immunity from prosecution.* 他们获准免受起诉。

im·mu·nize also 又作 **-ise** *BrE*【英】/ˈɪmjəˌnaɪz; ˈɪmjʊ̥naɪz/ *v* [T] to protect someone from a particular illness, especially by putting a substance into their body by INJECTION (1)〔尤指通过注射而〕使〔人〕免疫：**immunize sb against sth** *All girls are routinely immunized against German measles.* 所有女孩都按常规接种德国麻疹疫苗。—compare 比较 VACCINATE —**immunization** /ˌɪmjunəˈzeʃən; ˌɪmjʊ̥naɪˈzeɪʃən/ *n* [C,U]

im·mu·no·de·fi·cien·cy /ˌɪmjunodɪˈfɪʃənsɪ; ˌɪmjʊ̥nəʊdɪˈfɪʃənsi/ *n* [C,U] a medical condition in which your body is unable to fight infection in the usual way 免疫缺陷（病）—**immunodeficient** *adj*

im·mu·nol·o·gy /ˌɪmjuˈnɑlədʒɪ; ˌɪmjʊ̥ˈnɒlədʒi/ *n* [U] the scientific study of the prevention of disease and how the body reacts to disease 免疫学

im·mure /ɪˈmjur; ɪˈmjʊə/ *v* [T] *formal or literary* to shut someone in somewhere so that they cannot get out【正式或文】监禁，禁闭

im·mu·ta·ble /ɪˈmjutəbl̩; ɪˈmjuːtəbəl/ *adj formal* never changing or impossible to change【正式】永恒的；不能改变的：*the immutable principles of liberty and justice* 永恒的自由与公正原则 —**immutably** *adv* —**immutability** /ɪˌmjutəˈbɪlətɪ; ɪˌmjuːtəˈbɪlɪ̥ti/ *n* [U]

imp /ɪmp; ɪmp/ *n* [C] **1** a small creature in stories who has magic powers and behaves very badly〔故事中有魔法爱作弄人的〕小魔鬼，小妖精 **2** a child who behaves badly, but in a way that amuses people rather than annoying them 顽童，小淘气 —see also 另见 IMPISH

im·pact¹ /ˈɪmpækt; ˈɪmpækt/ *n* [C] **1** the effect or influence that an event, situation etc has on someone or something 影响；作用：*the environmental impact of increased road traffic* 道路交通增加对环境的影响 | **have an impact (on)** *Warnings about the dangers of smoking seem to have little impact on this age group.* 吸烟有害的警告对这个年龄段的人似乎没有多大作用。**2** the force of one object hitting another 冲击力，撞击力：*The impact pushed the engine backwards and crushed my legs.* 冲击力把发动机向后推，压伤了我的双腿。**3 on impact** at the moment when one thing hits another〔与另一物体〕碰撞时：*a missile which explodes on impact* 一枚在撞击时爆炸的导弹

impact² /ɪmˈpækt; ɪmˈpækt/ *v* [I+on,T] *especially AmE* to have an important or noticeable effect on someone or something【尤美】产生〔重要或明显的〕影响：*How will this program impact on the local community?* 这项计划对当地社区会产生什么样的影响？

im·pact·ed /ɪmˈpæktɪd; ɪmˈpæktɪ̥d/ *adj* a tooth that is impacted is growing under another tooth so that it cannot develop properly〔牙齿〕阻生的

im·pair /ɪmˈpɛr; ɪmˈpeə/ *v* [T] to make something less good than it usually is or less good than it should be 削弱，损害，损伤〔某物〕：*Do not boil the sauce as this can impair the flavor.* 调味汁不要煮沸，否则影响味道。—**impairment** *n* [U]

im·paired /ɪmˈpɛrd; ɪmˈpeəd/ *adj* not as good as before or not as good as it should be 受损的；变差的：*a special device for viewers with impaired hearing.* 为听力受损的观众而设的特殊装置 | *TV reception may be impaired in some areas.* 某些地区电视的接收效果可能会受到影响。

im·pa·la /ɪmˈpɑlə; ɪmˈpɑːlə/ *n* [C] a large brown graceful African animal; ANTELOPE〔非洲的〕黑斑羚

im·pale /ɪmˈpel; ɪmˈpeɪl/ *v* [T often passive 常用被动态] to push a sharp pointed object through something or someone〔以尖物〕刺穿，插进：*Gregson fell to a horrible death, impaled on the railings below.* 格雷格森跌下去，身体被下面的栅栏刺穿，死得很惨。—**impalement** *n* [U]

im·pal·pa·ble /ɪmˈpælpəbl̩; ɪmˈpælpəbəl/ *adj formal*【正式】**1** impossible to touch or feel physically 触摸不着的，感觉不到

的 —opposite 反义词 PALPABLE (2) **2** very difficult to understand 难懂的

im·pan·el /ɪm`pænl; ɪm'pænl/ *v* [T] another spelling of EMPANEL empanel 的另一种拼法

im·part /ɪm`pɑrt; ɪm'pɑːt/ *v* [T] *formal*【正式】**1** to give information, knowledge, wisdom etc to someone〔向某人〕传授〔知识、智慧〕; 透露〔信息〕; 告知 **2** to give a particular quality to something 赋予〔某种品质〕, 给予: *Oregano imparts a delicious flavour to the stew.* 牛至给炖菜一种鲜美的味道。

im·par·tial /ɪm`pɑrʃəl; ɪm'pɑːʃəl/ *adj* not giving special favour or support to any one person or group; fair 不偏不倚的; 公正的: *We offer impartial advice on pensions and investments.* 我们对养老金和投资问题提供公正的建议。| *an impartial observer* 不带偏见的观察家 **—impartially** *adv* **—impartiality** /ˌɪmpɑrʃɪ`ælətɪ; ɪmˌpɑːʃi'æləti/ *n* [U]

im·pass·a·ble /ɪm`pæsəbl; ɪm'pɑːsəbəl/ *adj* a road, path, or area that is impassable is impossible to travel along or through 不能通行的, 无法通过的: *The road is impassable due to snow.* 道路因积雪而无法通行。

im·passe /`ɪmpæs; æm'pɑːs/ *n* [singular] a situation in which it is impossible to continue with a discussion or plan because the people involved cannot agree 僵局: **reach an impasse** *Negotiations seemed to have reached an impasse.* 谈判似乎陷入了僵局。

im·pas·sioned /ɪm`pæʃənd; ɪm'pæʃənd/ *adj* an impassioned speech, request, argument etc is full of strong feeling and emotion〔演说、要求、争辩等〕充满激情的, 激昂的: *She appeared on television to make an impassioned appeal to the kidnappers.* 她在电视上向绑架者发出激昂的呼吁。

im·pas·sive /ɪm`pæsɪv; ɪm'pæsɪv/ *adj* not showing any emotion or feeling 神情冷漠的; 木然的: *Oscar's face remained impassive throughout the trial.* 在整个审讯中, 奥斯卡都面无表情。**—impassively** *adv* **—impassivity** /ˌɪmpæ`sɪvətɪ; ˌɪmpæ'sɪvəti/ *n* [U]

im·pa·tience /ɪm`peʃəns; ɪm'peɪʃəns/ *n* [U] **1** annoyance at having to accept delays, other people's weaknesses etc 不耐烦, 无耐心: *Fiona's impatience with her slower students was beginning to show.* 菲奥娜对迟钝的学生的不耐烦开始显露出来。**2** great eagerness for something to happen, especially something that is going to happen soon〔尤指对即将发生的事〕渴望, 企盼

im·pa·tient /ɪm`peʃənt; ɪm'peɪʃənt/ *adj* **1** annoyed because of a situation you cannot control, especially when you have to wait for something 不耐烦的, 无耐心的; 急躁的: *After an hour's delay, passengers were becoming impatient.* 延误一小时后, 旅客开始焦躁起来。| *I'm coming – don't be so impatient!* 我这就来——别这么不耐烦! **2** very eager for something to happen and not wanting to wait 焦急的, 切盼的: **[+for]** *The woman stood there, impatient for me to be gone.* 那女人站在那儿, 焦急地等我离开。| **impatient to do sth** *Glen was clearly impatient to be off.* 格伦显然急着要走。**—impatiently** *adv*

im·peach /ɪm`pitʃ; ɪm'piːtʃ/ *v* [T] *law*【法律】**1** to charge a public official with a serious crime, especially in the US〔尤指在美国〕弹劾〔政府官员〕: *The House Judiciary Committee voted that President Nixon should be impeached.* 众议院司法委员会投票赞成弹劾尼克松总统。**2** to say that someone is guilty of a serious crime, especially a crime against the state 指控〔某人犯有严重罪行, 尤指危害国家罪〕; 检举 **—impeachment** *n* [U]

im·pec·ca·ble /ɪm`pɛkəbl; ɪm'pekəbəl/ *adj* completely perfect and without any mistakes 完美的; 无任何错误的: *Eliza had impeccable manners.* 伊丽莎的举止无懈可击。| *an impeccable performance* 完美的表演 **—impeccably** *adv*: *impeccably dressed* 穿着非常得体

im·pe·cu·ni·ous /ˌɪmpɪ`kjunɪəs; ˌɪmpɪ'kjuːniəs◂/ *adj formal or humorous* having very little money, especially over a long period【正式或幽默】〔尤指长期〕没钱的: a *gifted but impecunious painter* 一贫如洗的天才画家 **—impecuniously** *adv* **—impecuniousness** *n* [U]

im·ped·ance /ɪm`pidṇs; ɪm'piːdəns/ *n* [singular,U] *technical* a measure of the power of a piece of electrical equipment to stop the flow of an ALTERNATING CURRENT【术语】阻抗

im·pede /ɪm`pid; ɪm'piːd/ *v* [T] to prevent something from happening in the normal way, or make it happen more slowly 妨碍, 阻碍; 防止, 延缓: *Storms at sea impeded our progress.* 海上风暴阻碍了我们的行程。

im·ped·i·ment /ɪm`pɛdəmənt; ɪm'pedɨmənt/ *n* [C] *formal*【正式】**1** a physical or nervous problem that makes it difficult for someone to speak or move normally〔生理或神经疾病所致的〕言语[行动]不能自如: *a speech impediment* 口吃, 结巴 **2** a situation or event that makes it difficult or impossible for someone or something to succeed or make progress 阻碍, 障碍(物); 绊脚石: **[+to]** *The main impediment to development is the country's huge foreign debt.* 该国发展的主要障碍是巨额外债。

im·ped·i·men·ta /ˌɪmpɛdə`mɛntə; ɪmˌpedɨ'mentə/ *n* [plural] *often humorous* bags, animals, supplies etc that you take with you on a journey, and that may slow you down【常幽默】〔旅行中〕妨碍行进的重负〔如行李、动物、补给等〕

im·pel /ɪm`pɛl; ɪm'pel/ *v* [T] an idea, emotion etc that impels you to do something makes you feel very strongly that you must do it〔想法、情感等〕促使, 驱使: **impel sb to do sth** *Donnelly felt impelled to write and complain.* 唐纳利觉得非写信投诉不可。—compare 比较 COMPEL

im·pend·ing /ɪm`pɛndɪŋ; ɪm'pendɪŋ/ *adj* an impending event or situation, especially an unpleasant one, is going to happen very soon〔尤指不愉快的事情〕逼近的, 即将发生的: *I had a sense of impending doom.* 我有一种厄运即将降临的预感。| *an impending ecological crisis* 即将发生的生态危机

im·pen·e·tra·ble /ɪm`pɛnətrəbl; ɪm'penɨtrəbəl/ *adj* **1** impossible to get through, see through, or get into 不能通过的, 不能看透的, 无法进入的: *an impenetrable barrier of thorn bushes* 无法穿过的荆棘灌木丛 | *impenetrable darkness* 漆黑 **2** very difficult or impossible to understand 难以理解的, 费解的: *The document was written in impenetrable lawyer's jargon.* 文件是用晦涩的律师行话写成的。**—impenetrably** *adv* **—impenetrability** /ɪmˌpɛnətrə`bɪlətɪ; ɪmˌpenɨtrə'bɪlɨti/ *n* [U]

im·pen·i·tent /ɪm`pɛnətənt; ɪm'penɨtənt/ *adj formal* not feeling sorry for something bad or wrong that you have done【正式】不知悔悟的, 没有悔意的 **—impenitently** *adv* **—impenitence** *n* [U]

im·per·a·tive[1] /ɪm`pɛrətɪv; ɪm'perətɪv/ *adj* **1** extremely important and needing to be done or dealt with immediately 紧急的, 极为重要而必须立即处理的: **it is imperative (that)** *It is absolutely imperative that these safety measures are implemented immediately.* 这些安全措施必须立刻执行。| **it is imperative to do sth** *By now, it had become imperative to evacuate the area.* 撤离该地区已刻不容缓。**2** a voice, manner etc that is imperative is very firm and has a feeling of authority〔嗓音、态度等〕坚定的, 显示权威的 **3** *technical* an imperative verb is one that expresses a command【术语】〔动词〕祈使的 **—imperatively** *adv*

imperative[2] *n* [C] **1** something that must be done urgently 紧急的事: *Reducing unemployment has become an imperative for the government.* 减少失业已成为政府的当务之急。**2** *technical* the form of a verb that expresses a command【术语】祈使语气的动词形式: *In 'Come here!' the verb 'come' is in the imperative.* 在 Come here!(过来!) 中, come 是祈使语气。**3** *formal* an idea, belief, or emotion that strongly influences people to behave in a particular way【正式】强烈的欲望; 冲动: *the sexual imperative* 性欲

im·per·cep·ti·ble /ˌɪmpɚ`sɛptəbl; ˌɪmpə'septɨbəl/ *adj* an imperceptible change, movement etc is difficult to see or notice because it is very small〔变化、动作等由于极微小而〕难以察觉的: *an almost imperceptible change of speed* 难以察觉的变速 **—imperceptibly** *adv*: *The daylight faded almost imperceptibly into night.* 天色不知不觉地暗了下来。**—imperceptibility** /ˌɪmpɚˌsɛptə`bɪlətɪ; ˌɪmpəseptɨ'bɪlɨti/ *n* [U]

im·per·fect[1] /ɪm`pɝfɪkt; ɪm'pɜːfɪkt/ *adj* not completely correct or perfect 有缺点的, 不完美的: *an imperfect knowledge of German* 粗通德语 | *I got it cheap because it's slightly imperfect.* 这东西因为有点小毛病, 所以我很便宜就买到了。**—imperfectly** *adv* **—imperfection** /ˌɪmpɚ`fɛkʃən; ˌɪmpə'fekʃən/ *n* [C,U]

imperfect[2] also 又作 **imperfect tense** *n* [singular] *technical* the form of a verb that shows an incomplete action in the past【术语】〔动词的〕过去未完成时

im·pe·ri·al /ɪm`pɪrɪəl; ɪm'pɪəriəl/ *adj* **1** connected with an EMPIRE or with the person who rules it 帝国的; 皇帝的: *Britain's imperial expansion in the 19th century* 19 世纪英帝国的扩张 | *a major imperial power* 一个主要的帝国 **2** [only before noun 仅用于名词前] connected with the system of weights and measurements based on INCHES, miles etc〔以英寸、英里等为基本度量衡单位的制度〕英制的 —compare 比较 METRIC

Imperial Col·lege /ˌ···'··/ abbreviation 缩写为 **IC** one of the colleges of the University of London, which is famous for education and RESEARCH in science, computing, and engineering 帝国理工学院〔伦敦大学下设学院之一, 以自然科学、计算机技术和工程学的教学与研究著称〕

im·pe·ri·al·is·m /ɪm`pɪrɪəlˌɪzəm; ɪm'pɪəriəlɪzəm/ *n* [U] **1** a political system in which one country rules a lot of other coun-

tries, and tries to find more that it can defeat and govern 帝国主义 **2** methods by which a rich or powerful country can get political or trade advantages over poorer countries〔富国或强国对贫穷国家在政治或贸易上的〕掠取利益的手段 —compare 比较 COLONIALISM—**imperialist** *n*—**imperialist, imperialistic** /ɪm,pɪrɪəlˋɪstɪk; ɪm,pɪərɪəˈlɪstɪk◂/ *adj*

Imperial War Mu·se·um, the /ˌ·ˌ·· ˈ··ˌ·ˈ/ a military MUSEUM in London, where people can see EXHIBITs relating to wars that the UK has fought in. 帝国战争博物馆〔伦敦一军事博物馆, 陈列的展品都与英国参加过的战争有关〕

im·per·il /ɪmˋpɛrəl; ɪmˈperḷl/ *v formal*【正式】**imperilled** *BrE*【英】, **imperiled** *AmE*【美】[T] to put something in danger 危及: *The whole project was imperilled by a lack of funds.* 资金缺乏危及整个项目。

im·pe·ri·ous /ɪmˋpɪrɪəs; ɪmˈpɪəriəs/ *adj* giving orders and expecting to be obeyed, in a way that seems too proud 专横的; 飞扬跋扈的; 傲慢的: *She had an imperious domineering manner which Tim did not like.* 她那飞扬跋扈、作威作福的样子让蒂姆很反感。| *an imperious voice* 傲慢的口气—**imperiously** *adv* —**imperiousness** *n* [U]

im·per·ish·a·ble /ɪmˋpɛrɪʃəbḷ; ɪmˈperɪʃəbəl/ *adj formal* formed or made in a way that will exist for a long time or for ever【正式】坚固的; 永存的: *The manufacturers claim that the material is imperishable.* 制造商声称这种材料永不磨损。| *imperishable memories* 永不磨灭的记忆 —opposite 反义词 PERISHABLE

im·per·ma·nent /ɪmˋpɝmənənt; ɪmˈpɜːmənənt/ *adj formal* not staying the same forever; TEMPORARY【正式】非永久的, 临时的: *A row of precarious and impermanent wooden huts clung to the hillside.* 一排临时小木屋紧靠着山坡。—**impermanence** *n* [U]: *The impermanence of the situation worried him.* 局势动荡令他忧虑。

im·per·me·a·ble /ɪmˋpɝmɪəbḷ; ɪmˈpɜːmiəbəl/ *adj technical* not allowing liquids or gases to pass through【术语】不容〔液体或气体〕透过的, 不可渗透的: *an impermeable shell membrane* 不透水的蛋壳膜

im·per·mis·si·ble /ˌɪmpɝˋmɪsəbḷ; ˌɪmpɜːˈmɪsḷbəl/ *adj formal* something that is impermissible cannot be allowed【正式】不许可的, 不允许的: *an impermissible infringement of the rules* 不能容许的违规

im·per·son·al /ɪmˋpɝsṇḷ; ɪmˈpɜːsənəl/ *adj* **1** not showing any feelings of sympathy, friendliness etc 不表示同情[友善等]的; 冷漠的: *She left a short impersonal note, saying that she was leaving.* 她留下一张措辞冰冷的便条, 说她要走了。**2** a place or situation that is impersonal does not make people feel that they are important or valued〔地方或情况〕没有人情味的; 冷淡的: *a large impersonal city* 一座人情淡薄的大城市 | *Health care has become increasingly bureaucratic and impersonal.* 卫生保健〔制度〕越来越繁琐拖拉, 人情味越来越淡薄。**3** *technical* in grammar, an impersonal sentence or verb is one where the subject is represented by a word such as 'it', as in the sentence 'It rained all day'【术语】〔语法中〕非人称的, 无人称的〔指句子或动词的主语是 it 等词, 如 It rained all day〕—compare 比较 PERSONAL[1]—**impersonally** *adv*

im·per·so·nate /ɪmˋpɝsṇˌet; ɪmˈpɜːsəneɪt/ *v* [T] **1** to pretend to be someone else by copying their appearance, voice, and behaviour, especially in order to deceive people〔尤指为行骗而〕假扮〔他人〕, 假冒: *He gained access to the building by impersonating a police officer.* 他假扮警察而得以进入大楼。**2** to copy someone's voice and behaviour, especially in order to make people laugh〔尤指为逗人发笑而〕模仿〔某人的说话、动作〕: *Eddie was standing on the table, trying to impersonate John Wayne.* 埃迪站在桌子上, 模仿约翰·韦恩的模样。—**impersonation** /ɪmˌpɝsṇˋeʃən; ɪmˌpɜːsəˈneɪʃən/ *n* [C,U]: *On the club circuit, he's renowned for his Elvis impersonations.* 在夜总会的巡回演出中, 他以模仿埃尔维斯而见称。

im·per·so·nat·or /ɪmˋpɝsṇˌetɚ; ɪmˈpɜːsəneɪtə/ *n* [C] someone who copies the way that other people look, speak, and behave, as part of a performance〔在表演中模仿他人的〕模仿者

im·per·ti·nent /ɪmˋpɝtṇənt; ɪmˈpɜːtḷnənt/ *adj* rude and not respectful, especially to someone who is older or more important〔尤指对尊长〕不礼貌的; 莽撞无礼的: *The question about her age was very impertinent.* 询问她的年龄太失礼了。—**impertinently** *adv*—**impertinence** *n* [U]

im·per·tur·ba·ble /ˌɪmpɚˋtɝbəbḷ; ˌɪmpəˈtɜːbəbəl/ *adj* remaining calm and unworried in spite of problems or difficulties 从容镇定的, 沉着的, 冷静的: *His steady, imperturbable nature reassured me.* 他沉着镇定的性格让我感到放心。—**imperturbably** *adv*—**imperturbability** /ˌɪmpɚˌtɝbəˋbɪlətɪ; ˌɪmpətɜːbəˈbɪlḷti/ *n* [U]

im·per·vi·ous /ɪmˋpɝvɪəs; ɪmˈpɜːviəs/ *adj* **1** not affected or influenced by something and seeming not to notice it 不受影响的; 无动于衷的: [+to] *Janet carried on reading, impervious to the row going on around her.* 珍妮特不受周围的嘈杂声影响, 继续看书。| *He seems to be impervious to criticism.* 他好像对批评毫不在乎。**2** not allowing anything to enter or pass through〔任何东西都〕不能进入的; 不能穿过的: *impervious volcanic rock* 不透水不透气的火山岩

im·pe·ti·go /ˌɪmpɪˋtaɪgo; ˌɪmpḷˈtaɪgəʊ/ *n* [U] an infectious skin disease 脓疱病〔传染性皮肤病〕

im·pet·u·ous /ɪmˋpɛtʃʊəs; ɪmˈpetʃʊəs/ *adj* tending to do things very quickly, without thinking carefully first〔做事〕过快的, 鲁莽的: *It was an impetuous decision which she soon regretted.* 她作了仓促的决定, 不久就感到后悔。—**impetuously** *adv*—**impetuousness** *n* [U]—**impetuosity** /ɪmˌpɛtʃʊˋɑsətɪ; ɪmˌpetʃuˈɒsḷti/ *n* [U]

im·pe·tus /ˋɪmpətəs; ˈɪmpḷtəs/ *n* [U] **1** feeling an influence that makes people or helps something to develop or continue doing something 刺激; 推动(力); 促进: **gain/lose impetus** *The campaign is already gaining impetus.* 这场运动的气势正在增加。| *As a result of this failure, a lot of the initial impetus was lost.* 由于这次失败, 大大减弱了当初的冲劲。| [+for] *Einstein's work provided the impetus for a major shift in the study of physics.* 爱因斯坦的研究成果促使物理学研究发生了重大转变。**2** *technical* the force that makes an object start moving, or keeps it moving once it has started【术语】〔使物体移动的〕动量, 冲力

im·pi·e·ty /ɪmˋpaɪətɪ; ɪmˈpaɪḷti/ *n formal*【正式】**1** [U] lack of respect for religion or God〔对宗教或上帝〕不虔诚, 亵渎 **2** [C usually plural 一般用复数] an action that shows a lack of respect for religion or God〔对宗教或上帝的〕不敬的行为 —see also 另见 IMPIOUS

im·pinge /ɪmˋpɪndʒ; ɪmˈpɪndʒ/ *v*
impinge on/upon *phr v* [T] *formal* to have an effect on someone or something; influence【正式】对…起作用; 影响: *The change of government scarcely impinged on ordinary people's lives.* 政府的更迭对平民百姓的生活几乎没有影响。| *We were discussing the way welfare policies impinge on women.* 我们在讨论福利政策对妇女的影响。—**impingement** *n* [U]

im·pi·ous /ˋɪmpɪəs; ˈɪmpiəs/ *adj formal* lacking respect for religion or God【正式】〔对宗教或上帝〕不恭敬的, 不虔诚的 —**impiously** *adv*—**impiousness** *n* [U] —see also 另见 IMPIETY

imp·ish /ˋɪmpɪʃ; ˈɪmpɪʃ/ *adj* behaving badly and causing trouble, but in a way that is amusing rather than serious or annoying; MISCHIEVOUS 调皮捣蛋的, 淘气的—**impishly** *adv*: *Tony grinned impishly at her.* 托尼向她调皮地咧嘴一笑。—**impishness** *n* [U]

im·plac·a·ble /ɪmˋplækəbḷ; ɪmˈplækəbəl/ *adj* very determined to continue opposing someone or something 决意〔与…〕作对的; 〔对…〕毫不宽容的: *an implacable enemy* 死敌 | *The tabloid newspapers remained implacable in their opposition.* 那些小报执意坚持对立观点。—**implacably** *adv*: *A few organizations remain implacably opposed to Sunday trading.* 一些组织执意反对周日交易。—**implacability** /ɪmˌplækəˋbɪlətɪ; ɪmˌplækəˈbɪlḷti/ *n* [U]

im·plant[1] /ɪmˋplænt; ɪmˈplɑːnt/ *v* **1** [T] to strongly fix an idea, feeling, or way of behaving in someone's mind, so that it becomes part of their character 灌输〔思想、感情或行为方式〕: *a deep sense of patriotism that had been implanted in him by his father* 他父亲向他灌输了强烈的爱国主义情感 | *The phrase implanted itself in my memory.* 这句话深深地印在我的脑海里。**2** [T] to put something into someone's body by doing a medical operation 把〔某物〕植入〔体内〕; 移植: *Surgeons successfully implanted an artificial kneejoint.* 外科医生成功植入一个人造膝关节。—**implantation** /ˌɪmplænˋteʃən; ˌɪmplɑːnˈteɪʃən/ *n* [U]

im·plant[2] /ˋɪmplænt; ˈɪmplɑːnt/ *n* [C] something that has been implanted in someone's body in a medical operation〔通过手术被移植人体的〕植入物: *silicone implants* 硅酮植入片 —compare 比较 TRANSPLANT[2]

im·plau·si·ble /ɪmˋplɔzəbḷ; ɪmˈplɔːzḷbəl/ *adj* difficult to believe and therefore unlikely to be true 难以置信的; 不大可能真实的: *an implausible explanation* 让人难以相信的解释 | *His excuses were totally implausible.* 他的借口根本不合情理。—**implausibly** *adv*—**implausibility** /ɪmˌplɔzəˋbɪlətɪ; ɪmˌplɔːzḷˈbɪlḷti/ *n* [U]

im·ple·ment[1] /ˋɪmpləˌmɛnt; ˈɪmplḷment/ *v* [T] **implement a plan/policy/proposal etc** to take action or make changes that you have officially decided should happen〔正式地〕执行计划/

政策/建议等: *We have decided to implement the committee's suggestions in full.* 我们已决定全面实施委员会提出的建议。

im·ple·ment² /ˋɪmpləmənt; ˈɪmplɪ̣mənt/ *n* [C] a tool or instrument, especially a fairly large one with no motor〔尤指相当大、非马达驱动的〕工具, 用具, 器具: *ploughs, hoes, and other farming implements* 犁、锄和其他农具

im·ple·men·ta·tion /ˌɪmpləmɛnˋteʃən; ˌɪmplɪ̣menˈteɪʃən/ *n* [U] the act of implementing a plan, policy etc 实施, 贯彻, 执行: *implementation of the peace plan* 和平计划的实施

im·pli·cate /ˋɪmplɪˌket; ˈɪmplɪ̣keɪt/ *v* [T] **1** to show or seem to show that someone is involved in something wrong or criminal (仿佛) 表明〔某人〕与〔错误或罪行〕有牵连: **implicate sb in sth** *The letter seemed to implicate Mitchell in the robbery.* 这封信似乎表明米切尔与这件抢劫案有牵连。**2** to show or seem to show that something is the cause of something bad or harmful (仿佛) 表明〔某物〕导致〔不好或有害的事〕: *Tobacco has already been implicated as one of the causes of the disease.* 烟草已被认为是导致这种疾病的原因之一。

im·pli·ca·tion /ˌɪmplɪˋkeʃən; ˌɪmplɪ̣ˈkeɪʃən/ *n* **1** [C usually plural 一般用复数] a possible future effect or result of a plan, action, or event, which must be considered or discussed〔计划、行为或事件需要考虑或讨论的〕可能的影响, 可能的后果: **[+of]** *What are the implications of these proposals?* 这些提议会有什么后果? | **have implications for** *This could have serious implications for the company's future.* 这对公司的未来可能会产生严重影响。| *You can't just close reactors down – there are all sorts of safety implications.* 反应堆不是说关闭就能关闭的, 有各种各样的安全问题需要考虑。**2** [C,U] something that you do not say directly but that you seem to want people to believe 含意, 暗示: **[+that]** *I resent the implication that I would have lied to you.* 有人暗示我会对你说谎, 对此我感到很生气。| **by implication** *The law bans organized protests and, by implication, any form of opposition.* 这条法律禁止有组织的抗议, 言外之意是不许进行任何形式的反对。—see also 另见 IMPLY (1) **3** [U] a situation in which someone is shown to be involved in something wrong or criminal〔某人〕牵涉〔错误或罪行〕, 卷入: **[+of]** *the implication of the former Chief of Staff in a major scandal* 前任参谋长卷入一宗重大的丑闻 **4** something that you believe to be shown by a particular situation, action etc〔特定的情况、行动等〕显示[表明]的内容: **[+in]** *The implication in this case is that he's innocent.* 这个情况表明他是清白无辜的。—see also 另见 IMPLICATE

im·pli·cit /ɪmˋplɪsɪt; ɪmˈplɪsɪ̣t/ *adj* **1 implicit criticism/threat/approval** criticism etc that is suggested or understood without being stated directly 含蓄的批评/隐含的恫吓/默许: *Her words contained an implicit threat.* 她话里带着威胁。| *implicit criticism* 含蓄的批评 —compare 比较 EXPLICIT **2 be implicit in** *formal* to form a central part of something, but without being openly stated【正式】隐含其中的; 不明言的: *Confidentiality is implicit in your relationship with a counsellor.* 在你与律师的关系中, 他会为你保守秘密是不言而喻的。**3 implicit trust/faith** trust etc that is complete and contains no doubts 绝对的信任/信心: *They had an implicit faith in his powers.* 他们绝对相信他的才能。—**implicitly** *adv*: *We trusted Lopez implicitly.* 我们绝对信任洛佩斯。

im·plode /ɪmˋplod; ɪmˈpləʊd/ *v* [I] to explode inwards 向心聚爆; 内爆 —compare 比较 EXPLODE (1) —**implosion** /ɪmˋploʒən; ɪmˈpləʊʒən/ *n* [C,U]

im·plore /ɪmˋplɔr; ɪmˈplɔː/ *v* [T] *formal* to ask for something in an emotional way; PLEAD (1)【正式】恳求; 乞求; 哀求: *John, I implore you, stop now before it's too late.* 约翰, 我求你快停下, 不然就来不及了。| **implore sb to do sth** *She implored the soldiers to save her child.* 她乞求那些士兵救她的孩子。

im·ply /ɪmˋplaɪ; ɪmˈplaɪ/ *v* [T] **1** to suggest that something is true without saying this directly 暗示, 暗指: **imply (that)** *She managed to imply she'd contributed the money without actually saying so.* 她设法暗示了钱是她捐的, 而没有直接说出来。| *an implied threat* 隐含的威胁 —see 见 INFER (USAGE) **2** if a fact, event etc implies something, it shows that it is likely to be true 意味着〔某事可能是真的〕: *The high level of radiation in the rocks implies that they are volcanic in origin.* 岩石内的高辐射意味着它是火山作用形成的。**3** if a principle, action, idea etc implies something, it makes other actions or conditions necessary〔原则、行动、思想等〕必然包含…: *Democracy implies a respect for individual liberties.* 民主必然包含对个人自由的尊重。

im·po·lite /ˌɪmpəˋlaɪt; ˌɪmpəˈlaɪt◂/ *adj* not polite; rude 无礼的; 粗鲁的: *It was very impolite not to write and thank them.* 不写信向他们致谢是很不礼貌的。—**impolitely** *adv* —**impoliteness** *n* [C,U]

im·pol·i·tic /ɪmˋpɑlətɪk; ɪmˈpɒlɪ̣tɪk/ *adj formal* not sensible or not behaving in a way that is likely to bring you advantage【正式】不明智的; 失策的: *It was considered impolitic for him to spend too much time with the radicals in the party.* 他花太多时间与党内的激进分子在一起被认为是不明智的。

im·pon·de·ra·ble¹ /ɪmˋpɑndərəbl; ɪmˈpɒndərəbəl/ *adj formal* something that is imponderable cannot be exactly measured, judged, or calculated【正式】无法精确估量的, 难以判断的

imponderable² *n* [C usually plural 一般用复数] *formal* something that cannot be exactly measured, judged, or calculated【正式】无法准确估量的事物: *There are so many imponderables that it is impossible to make an accurate prediction.* 不可估量的情况太多, 所以难以作出准确预测。

im·port¹ /ˋɪmpɔrt; ˈɪmpɔːt/ *n* **1** [C] something that is brought into one country from another in order to be sold 进口商品: *cheap imports of grain* 廉价进口的谷物 **2** [U] the process or business of bringing goods into one country from another〔商品的〕进口, 输入: *The government eventually banned the import of all electrical goods.* 政府最后禁止所有电气产品的进口。—opposite 反义词 EXPORT¹ **3** [U] *formal* importance or meaning【正式】重要性; 含意: *a matter of no great import* 一件小事

im·port² /ɪmˋpɔrt; ɪmˈpɔːt/ *v* [T] **1** to bring something into a country from abroad in order to sell it 进口, 输入〔商品〕: *imported oil* 进口的石油 **2** *technical* to move information from one computer into another【术语】〔从一台电脑到另一台电脑〕输入〔信息〕—opposite 反义词 EXPORT²

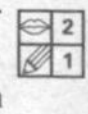

im·por·tance /ɪmˋpɔrtn̩s; ɪmˈpɔːtəns/ *n* [U] **1** the quality of being important 重要(性): *The doctor stressed the importance of regular exercise.* 医生强调了经常锻炼的重要性。| **attach importance to** (=treat something as if it is important) 给予重视 *Much greater importance is now attached to environmental concerns.* 环境问题越来越受到重视。| **of great/vital/crucial importance** (=very important) 极为重要 *This is an issue of great importance to all disabled people.* 这个问题对于残疾人士至关重要。**2** the reason why something is important 重要的原因: *The real importance of this law is the protection it gives to female workers.* 这项法律的真正重要意义在于它对女工所提供的保护。

Importance of Be·ing Ear·nest, The /·ˌ···ˋ··/ (1895) a play by Oscar Wilde in which a man pretends that his name is Ernest because he thinks this will give him an advantage with a woman he admires《认真的重要》〔(1895), 奥斯卡·王尔德创作的剧本。剧中有一名男子自称 Ernest (厄恩斯特, 意为"认真的"), 因为他认为这个名字有利于他接近自己欣赏的一位女人〕—see also 另见 Lady BRACKNELL

im·por·tant /ɪmˋpɔrtn̩t; ɪmˈpɔːtənt/ *adj* **1** an important event, decision, problem etc has a big effect or influence on people's lives or on events in the future 重要的, 重大的: *a very important meeting* 一次极为重要的会议 | *Listen everyone, I've got some important news!* 大家注意, 我有重要消息宣布。| **it is important to do sth** *It is important to explain to the patient what is happening.* 对病人说明病情是很重要的。| **it is important that** *It's vitally important that you understand the danger.* 了解危险所在是极为重要的。| **be important to sb/sth** *Money was the only thing that was important to Carson.* 对卡森来说, 钱是唯一重要的东西。**2** people who are important have a lot of power or influence〔人〕有势力的; 有影响的: *a very important customer* 一位大客户 | *an important client* 一位有影响的委托人

im·por·tant·ly /ɪmˋpɔrtn̩tlɪ; ɪmˈpɔːtəntli/ *adv* **1 more/equally/less importantly** [sentence adverb 句子副词] used to show that the next statement or question is more, equally etc important than what you said before it 更/同等/不太重要的是: *Most importantly, you must keep a record of everything you do.* 更重要的是, 你必须把你所做的事一一记录下来。**2** in a way that shows you think that what you are saying or doing is important 煞有介事地; 自以为了不起地: *"I've got to look after his books," the youngest boy said importantly.* "我得照管他这些书。"最小的男孩一本正经地说道。| *striding importantly into the room* 神气十足地大步走进房间

im·por·ta·tion /ˌɪmpɔrˋteʃən; ˌɪmpɔːˈteɪʃən/ *n* **1** [U] the business of buying goods from another country and having them sent to your country to be sold there 进口, 输入 **2 a)** [U] the act of bringing into a country something new or different such as a new plant, custom, or idea〔新鲜事物的〕引进 **b)** [C] something that is brought into a country in this way 舶来品, 从外国引进的事物 —compare 比较 IMPORT¹

import du·ty /ˋ·· ˌ··/ *n* [C,U] a tax on goods that are brought into one country from another country 进口关税

im·port·er /ɪm`pɔrtɚ; ɪm'pɔːtə/ *n* [C] a person, company, or country that buys goods from another country, to be sold or used in their own country 进口者; 进口商; 进口国, 输入国: *Japan is one of the world's largest importers of tropical timber.* 日本是全球热带木材进口大国之一。—opposite 反义词 EXPORTER

import li·cence /ˈ··, ··/ *n* [C] a document that gives permission for goods to be brought into one country from another 进口许可证

im·por·tu·nate /ɪm`pɔrtʃənɪt; ɪm'pɔːtʃʊnət/ *adj formal* always asking for things in an annoying or unreasonable way【正式】纠缠不休的, 无理的: *importunate demands* 蛮横无理的要求 —**importunately** *adv* —**importunity** /ˌɪmpɚ`tjunətɪ; ˌɪmpə'tjuːnəti/ *n* [U]

im·por·tune /ˌɪmpɚ`tjun; ˌɪmpə'tjuːn/ *v* [T] *formal* to ask someone for something repeatedly, especially in an annoying or unreasonable way; beg【正式】〔向某人〕再三要求〔尤指纠缠不休或不合理地〕; 乞求: **[+for]** *importuning passers-by for money* 缠着过路人讨钱

2 **im·pose** /ɪm`poz; ɪm'pəʊz/ *v* **1 impose a ban/tax/fine etc (on)** to officially order that something should be forbidden, restricted, taxed etc, or that someone should be punished〔正式〕实施禁令/征收税款/惩收罚款等: *The government imposed a ban on the sale of ivory.* 政府禁止买卖象牙。| *We have decided to impose sanctions on countries that break the agreement.* 我们决定对违约国加以制裁。**2 impose a burden/strain etc (on/upon)** to have a bad effect on something or someone by causing them problems 增加负担/压力等: *The President's health care proposals would not impose any great burden on the state's finances.* 总统提出的医疗保健计划不会给国家财政带来任何巨大的负担。**3** [T] to force someone to have the same ideas or beliefs as you〔将想法、信仰〕强加于〔某人〕: **impose sth on sb** *parents who impose their own moral values on their children* 把自己的道德价值观强加于孩子们的父母 **4** [I] to unreasonably expect or ask someone to do something for you when this is inconvenient for them 麻烦〔别人〕: **[+on/upon]** *We could ask them to let us stay the night, but I don't want to impose on them.* 我们可以请求他们让我们在这里过夜, 但我不想麻烦他们。

im·pos·ing /ɪm`pozɪŋ; ɪm'pəʊzɪŋ/ *adj* large, important-looking, and impressive 壮观的, 宏伟的; 气势雄伟的: *an imposing building* 气势宏伟的建筑

im·po·si·tion /ˌɪmpə`zɪʃən; ˌɪmpə'zɪʃən/ *n* **1** [C usually singular 一般用单数] something that someone unreasonably expects or asks you to do for them, which is inconvenient 无理要求: *I regarded his request for a loan as something of an imposition.* 我认为他的贷款要求有点强人所难。**2** [U] the introduction of something such as a rule, tax, or restriction〔规章、税种、限制等的〕实施; 征收: *the imposition of martial law* 实施军事管制

2 2 **im·pos·si·ble** /ɪm`pɑsəbl; ɪm'pɒsəbəl/ *adj*

1 ▶CAN'T BE DONE 不能完成◀ something that is impossible cannot happen or be done 不可能发生的; 办不到的: *Further research is impossible without more money.* 没有更多的资金, 进一步研究就不可能。| *This crossword's absolutely impossible!* 这个纵横填字谜游戏根本不可能做出来! | *Impossible! It can't be true.* 不可能! 不会是真的! | **find it impossible to do sth** *Members with young children often found it impossible to attend evening meetings.* 有小孩的会员经常无法参加晚间的会议。| **ask the impossible** (=ask for something that cannot be done) 要求不可能做到的事 *Expecting the project to be completed by October was really asking the impossible.* 指望10月前完成该项目是要人家做办不到的事。| **do the impossible** (=succeed in doing something that seems impossible) 实现不可能的事 *Somehow, Jen had done the impossible and got us all tickets.* 珍不知用什么方法, 办成了不可能做到的事, 给大家都买到了票。| **impossible demands/requests etc** (=demands etc for something that is impossible) 办不到的要求/请求等

2 ▶SITUATION 情形◀ a situation that is impossible is extremely difficult to deal with 极难对付的: *Helen's refusal to cooperate has put me in an impossible position.* 海伦拒绝合作, 使我进退两难。| *His bad temper is making life impossible for the rest of the family.* 他的坏脾气让全家人度日如年。

3 ▶PERSON 人◀ someone who is impossible behaves in a very unreasonable and annoying way〔行为〕不讲道理的, 令人讨厌的: *You're impossible! Yesterday you said you didn't like carrots, and today you won't eat potatoes!* 真拿你没办法! 昨天你说不喜欢胡萝卜, 今天又不吃马铃薯! —**impossibly** *adv*: *impossibly difficult* 极为困难的 | *They were asking an impossibly high price.* 他们要价高得难以接受。—**impossibility** /ɪmˌpɑsə`bɪlətɪ; ɪmˌpɒsə'bɪləti/ *n* [C,U] *To walk there would have been a virtual impossibility.* 步行去那里实际上是不可能的。

im·pos·tor also 又作 **imposter** *AmE*【美】/ɪm`pɑstɚ; ɪm'pɒstə/ *n* [C] someone who pretends to be someone else in order to trick people 冒充他人的骗子

im·pos·ture /ɪm`pɑstʃɚ; ɪm'pɒstʃə/ *n* [U] *formal* a situation in which someone tricks people by pretending to be someone else【正式】冒名行骗; 招摇撞骗

im·po·tent /`ɪmpətənt; 'ɪmpətənt/ *adj* **1** unable to take effective action because you do not have enough power, strength, or control 不能采取有效行动的, 无能为力的: *Emergency services seem almost impotent in the face of such a disaster.* 面对这种灾难, 急救服务似乎无能为力。| *impotent rage* 无奈的狂怒 **2** a man who is impotent is unable to have sex because he cannot get an ERECTION (1)〔指男子〕无性交能力的, 阳痿的 —**impotently** *adv* —**impotence** *n* [U]

im·pound /ɪm`paund; ɪm'paʊnd/ *v* [T] *law* if the police or law courts impound your possessions they take them and keep them until you claim them【法律】扣押〔某物直到物主认领〕: *Last time I went to Rome my car was impounded.* 我上次去罗马, 汽车被扣了。

im·pov·e·rish /ɪm`pɑvərɪʃ; ɪm'pɒvərɪʃ/ *v* [T] **1** [often passive 常用被动态] to make someone very poor 使贫困, 使赤贫: *Many peasants were impoverished by the land tax.* 土地税使许多农民一贫如洗。**2** to make something worse in quality 使质量降低: *Crop rotation has not impoverished the soil.* 农作物轮作没有使土壤贫瘠。—**impoverishment** *n* [U]

im·pov·e·rished /ɪm`pɑvərɪʃt; ɪm'pɒvərɪʃt/ *adj* **a)** very poor 赤贫的: *an impoverished student* 贫困的学生 **b)** worse in quality 质量下降的: *Our lives would be impoverished without music.* 没有音乐, 我们的生活就会变得更贫乏。

im·prac·ti·ca·ble /ɪm`præktɪkəbl; ɪm'præktɪkəbəl/ *adj* something that is impracticable cannot be done even though it seems a good idea 不现实的, 行不通的: *It was an appealing plan but quite impracticable.* 这个计划有吸引力, 但完全行不通。—**impracticably** *adv* —**impracticability** /ɪmˌpræktɪkə`bɪlətɪ; ɪmˌpræktɪkə'bɪləti/ *n* [U]

im·prac·ti·cal /ɪm`præktɪkl; ɪm'præktɪkəl/ *adj* **1** an idea, suggestion, or action that is impractical is not sensible because it would be too difficult, too expensive etc〔念头、建议、活动〕不切实际的, 不现实的, 过于昂贵的: *A 24-hour service would be impractical for a small organization like this.* 这样小的机构提供24小时服务是不切实际的。**2** someone who is impractical is not good at dealing with ordinary practical matters, such as making or repairing things〔人〕无实践能力的〈如维修物件〉; 动手能力差的: *a hopelessly impractical man, who couldn't even boil an egg* 一个连鸡蛋都不会煮的笨手笨脚的人 —**impractically** /-klɪ; -kli/ *adv* —**impracticality** /ɪmˌpræktɪ`kælətɪ; ɪmˌpræktɪ'kæləti/ *n* [U]: *the sheer impracticality of such a large scale screening program* 如此大规模甄别计划的不切实际性

im·pre·ca·tion /ˌɪmprɪ`keʃən; ˌɪmprɪ'keɪʃən/ *n* [C] *formal* an offensive word or phrase that you say when you are very angry; a CURSE² (2)【正式】骂人的话; 咒骂, 诅咒

im·pre·cise /ˌɪmprɪ`saɪs; ˌɪmprɪ'saɪs◂/ *adj* not exact; INACCURATE 不精确的, 不确切的: *a very imprecise method of measurement* 很不精确的测量方法 | *an imprecise term* 不确切的说法 —**imprecisely** *adv* —**imprecision** /-`sɪʒən; -'sɪʒən/ *n* [U]

im·preg·na·ble /ɪm`prɛgnəbl; ɪm'pregnəbəl/ *adj* **1** a building that is impregnable is so strong that no one can get into it by force〔建筑物〕攻不破的, 固若金汤的: *an impregnable fortress* 坚不可摧的堡垒 **2** *formal* attitudes, opinions etc that are impregnable cannot be changed or influenced【正式】〔态度、意见等〕无法改变的, 无法动摇的: *her impregnable obstinacy* 她那顽固不化的倔强 —**impregnably** *adv* —**impregnability** /ɪmˌprɛgnə`bɪlətɪ; ɪmˌpregnə'bɪləti/ *n* [U]

im·preg·nate /`ɪmprɛgnet; 'ɪmpregneɪt/ *v* [T] **1** to make a substance spread completely through something, or to spread completely through something 浸透, 浸渍; 使饱和: **[+with]** *The material has been impregnated with disinfectant.* 这种材料已用消毒剂浸渍过。**2** to make a woman or female animal PREGNANT 使怀孕, 使受精

im·pre·sa·ri·o /ˌɪmprɪ`sɑrɪˌo; ˌɪmprɪ'sɑːriəʊ/ *n* [C] someone who organizes performances in theatres, concert halls etc〔剧院、音乐厅的〕演出主办人; 演出经理

im·press¹ /ɪm`prɛs; ɪm'pres/ *v* [T] **1** [not in progressive 不用进行时] if something or someone impresses you, you admire them because you notice how good, clever, successful etc they are 令人称羡; 使留下深刻印象: *What impressed us most about the book was its vivid language.* 这本书给我们印象最深的是它生动的语言。| *Steve borrowed his dad's sports car to impress his girlfriend.* 史蒂夫借来他爸爸的跑车以便对女友炫耀。| **be**

impressed with/by *We're very impressed with the standard of the children's work.* 这些儿童作品水准之高，给我们留下了深刻印象。| **be favourably impressed** *I think the boss was favourably impressed by your presentation.* 我认为老板对你的报告相当满意。| **be suitably impressed** (=be impressed as you should be) 恰如其分地感到印象深刻 **2** to make the importance of something clear to someone 使〔某人〕了解〔某事〕的重要性: **impress sth on sb** *Father impressed on me the value of hard work.* 父亲向我强调努力工作的重要意义。**3** to press something into a soft surface so as to make a mark or pattern as a result of this pressure 把〔某物〕压入〔柔软的平面〕; 压印; 盖〔印〕于: **be impressed in/on** *patterns impressed in the clay* 压印在黏土上的图案

im·press² /ˈɪmprɛs; ˈimpres/ *n* [C] *formal or literary* a mark or pattern made by pressing something into a surface【正式或文】印记; 压痕

impression 压痕

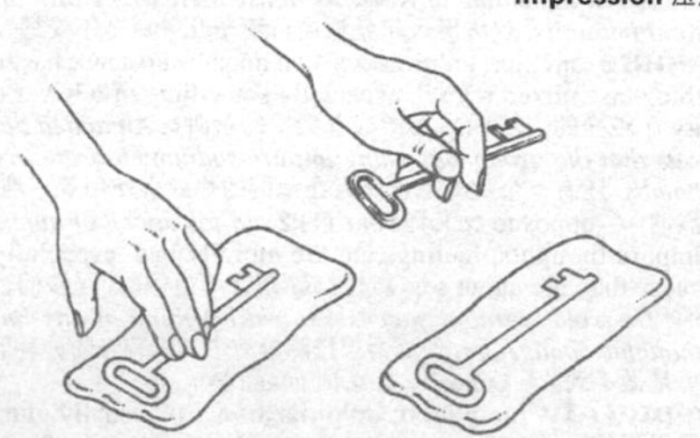

He took an impression of the key.
他压取了钥匙的模子。

3 2 **im·pres·sion** /ɪmˈprɛʃən; imˈpreʃən/ *n*

1 ►OPINION 想法◄ [C] the opinion or feeling you have about someone or something because of the way they seem〔对人、事的〕印象; 感想: [+of] *What's your impression of Frank as a boss?* 你对身为老板的弗兰克印象如何? | *Now I have a very different impression of England.* 如今我对英格兰的印象大不相同了。| **first impression** *First impressions can be deceptive.* 第一印象可能是靠不住的。| **create a good/bad impression** *Arriving late won't create a very favourable impression.* 迟到不会给人留下好印象。| **make an impression (on)** (=make someone admire you) 留下好印象 *It was their first meeting, and Richard was determined to make an impression.* 这是他们第一次见面，理查德决心给人留下好印象。| **have/get the impression (that)** (=think that something is a fact because of the way the situation seems) 觉得 *I get the distinct impression that we're not wanted here.* 我明显感到我们在这里是不受欢迎的。| **be under the impression (that)** (=wrongly believe that something is a fact because of the way the situation seems) 原以为, 误以为 *I'm sorry, I was under the impression that you were the manager.* 对不起, 我误以为你是经理呢。

2 ►COPYING SB 模仿某人◄ [C] the act of copying the speech or behaviour of a famous person in order to make people laugh〔对名人言行的〕滑稽模仿: **do an impression (of)** *Jean does a great impression of Tina Turner.* 琼模仿蒂娜·特纳真是惟妙惟肖!

3 ►MARK 印痕◄ [C] a mark left by pressing something into a soft surface 印记; 压痕: *An impression of a heel was left in the mud.* 泥地上留下了一个脚后跟的印记。

4 ►BOOK 书籍◄ [C] all the copies of a book printed at one time 印次〔一次印刷成的图书总数量〕—compare 比较 EDITION

im·pres·sion·a·ble /ɪmˈprɛʃənəbḷ; imˈpreʃənəbəl/ *adj* easy to influence, especially because you are young〔尤因年轻而〕易受影响的: **at an impressionable age** *It's damaging to criticize kids when they're at an impressionable age.* 指责年幼无知的孩子, 有害无益。—**impressionability** /ɪmˌprɛʃənəˈbɪlətɪ; imˌpreʃənəˈbilɪ̣ti/ *n* [U]

im·pres·sion·is·m /ɪmˈprɛʃənˌɪzəm; imˈpreʃənizəm/ *n* [U] **1** a style of painting used especially in France in the 19th century which uses colour instead of details of form to produce effects of light or feeling 印象主义, 印象派〔不拘泥于细节, 而以色彩来表达光线或感觉的绘画风格, 盛行于 19 世纪的法国〕**2** a style of music from the late 19th and early 20th centuries that produces feelings and images by the quality of sounds rather than by a pattern of notes 印象主义, 印象派〔以音色而不是旋律来产生效果的音乐风格, 盛行于19世纪末20世纪初〕—**impressionist** *adj*: *impressionist painters* 印象派画家

im·pres·sion·ist /ɪmˈprɛʃənɪst; imˈpreʃənɪ̣st/ *n* [C] **1** someone who uses impressionism in the paintings or music that they produce 印象派画家; 印象派作曲家 **2** someone who copies the speech or behaviour of famous people in order to entertain other people 模仿名人的滑稽演员

im·pres·sion·is·tic /ɪmˌprɛʃənˈɪstɪk; imˌpreʃəˈnɪstɪk◄/ *adj* based on a general feeling of what something is like, rather than on specific facts or details 仅凭一般印象的; 主观的: *an impressionistic account of what happened* 对所发生事情单凭印象的描述 —**impressionistically** /-kḷɪ; -kli/ *adv*

3 **im·pres·sive** /ɪmˈprɛsɪv; ɪmˈpresɪv/ *adj* something that is impressive seems very good, large, important etc so that you admire it 给人深刻印象的: *Among the guests was an impressive array of authors and critics.* 来宾中以作家和评论家为多, 引人注目。| *the remains of an impressive Roman villa* 一座令人赞叹的古罗马别墅遗迹 —**impressively** *adv* —**impressiveness** *n* [U]

im·pri·ma·tur /ˌɪmprɪˈmetɚ; ˌɪmprɪ̣ˈmeɪtə/ *n* [singular] **1** *usually humorous* approval of something, especially from an important person【一般幽默】〔尤指来自重要人物的〕批准, 认可, 同意 **2** official permission to print a book, especially when this is given by the Roman Catholic Church〔尤指天主教对书刊的〕印刷出版许可

im·print¹ /ˈɪmprɪnt; ˈɪmprɪnt/ *n* [C] **1** the mark left by an object being pressed into or onto something 印记; 压痕: [+of] *the imprint of her hand on the soft sand* 她留在细沙上的手印 **2** *technical* the name of a PUBLISHER as it appears on a book【术语】〔印在书籍上的〕出版者名称: *This dictionary is published under the Longman imprint.* 这本辞典的出版者是朗文。

im·print² /ɪmˈprɪnt; ɪmˈprɪnt/ *v* **1 be imprinted on your mind/memory** if something is imprinted on your mind or memory, you can never forget it 铭记在心/在脑海中: *The sight of her waving from the window was forever imprinted on my mind.* 她站在窗口挥手的情景永远留在我的脑海中。**2** [T] to print or press the mark of an object on something 在…上压印[盖印]: **be imprinted with** *notepaper imprinted with the Duke's monogram* 印有公爵姓名首字母图案的信笺

im·pris·on /ɪmˈprɪzṇ; ɪmˈprɪzən/ *v* [T] **1** to put someone in prison or to keep them somewhere and prevent them from leaving 监禁; 禁锢: *The government imprisoned or exiled all opposition leaders.* 政府不是把反对派领导人监禁就是流放。**2** if a situation or feeling imprisons people it restricts what they can do〔行为受到〕束缚, 限制: *Many elderly people felt imprisoned in their own homes.* 许多老年人感到自己有如被监禁在家里似的。

im·pris·on·ment /ɪmˈprɪzṇmənt; ɪmˈprɪzənmənt/ *n* [U] the state of being in prison, or the time someone spends there 囚禁; 服刑: *sentenced to a long term of imprisonment* 被判处长期监禁 | **life imprisonment** (=imprisonment for the rest of your life, or for a long time) 终身监禁, 无期徒刑 *life imprisonment for murder* 因杀人而被判处无期徒刑

im·prob·a·ble /ɪmˈprɑbəbḷ; ɪmˈprɒbəbəl/ *adj* **1** not likely to happen or to be true 不大可能发生的; 未必确实的: **it is improbable that** *It seems improbable that he could have driven home in less than an hour.* 他开车一小时之内就能到家, 这似乎不大可能。| **highly improbable** *a highly improbable explanation* 极不可信的解释 **2** surprising and slightly strange 不可思议的: *Theirs was an improbable partnership.* 他们的合伙关系让人不可思议。—**improbably** *adv* —**improbability** /ɪmˌprɑbəˈbɪlətɪ; ɪmˌprɒbəˈbɪlɪ̣ti/ *n* [C,U]

im·promp·tu /ɪmˈprɑmptu; ɪmˈprɒmptjuː/ *adj* done or said without any preparation or planning 无准备的; 即兴的; 即席的: *an impromptu party* 即兴聚会 —**impromptu** *adv*: *He insists he was speaking impromptu.* 他坚称自己刚才的是即席讲话。

im·prop·er /ɪmˈprɑpɚ; ɪmˈprɒpə/ *adj* **1** unacceptable according to the normal standards of moral, social, or professional behaviour 不适当的, 不合适的, 不妥当的: *It is quite improper for you to have an affair with one of your students.* 与自己的学生发生暧昧关系是很不合适的。| **an improper suggestion** (=about sex) 猥亵的话 **2** illegal or dishonest 不合法的; 不诚实的: *allegations of improper banking practices* 对银行违规经营的指控 **3** not correct according to a set of rules 不正确的; 不合乎规则的: *the improper use of a singular verb with a plural subject* 单数动词与复数主语的不正确搭配 —**improperly** *adv*: *If you are improperly dressed, you will not be admitted.* 你若衣着不当, 就会被拒入内。

improper frac·tion /ˌ· ˌ·· ˈ··/ *n* [C] *technical* a FRACTION (2) such as 107/8 in which the top number is larger than the bottom number【术语】假分数〔分子大于分母的分数, 如 107/8〕—compare 比较 PROPER FRACTION

im·pro·pri·e·ty /ˌɪmprəˋpraɪətɪ; ˌɪmprəˈpraɪəti/ *n formal* [C] behaviour or a particular action that is unacceptable according to moral, social, or professional standards【正式】不正当的行为[行动]; 不得体的举止: *Accusations of impropriety were made against the company's directors.* 对公司董事不正当的行为提出了指控。

im·prove /ɪmˋpruv; ɪmˈpruːv/ *v* **1** [T] to make something better 改善, 改进: *a course for students wishing to improve their English* 为想提高英语水平的学生开的一门课 | *Many dishes are greatly improved by adding fresh herbs.* 许多道菜的味道都因加入了新鲜香草而大有改善。**2** [I] become better 变得更好: *Let's hope the weather improves before Saturday.* 但愿星期六以前天气转好。| *Some wines improve with age.* 有些葡萄酒历久弥香。—see 见 RAISE[1] (USAGE)

improve on/upon sth *phr v* [T] to do something better than before or make it better than before 改进, 做得比…更好, 超过: *Bertorelli has scored 165 points, and I don't think anyone will improve on that.* 博托雷利得了165分, 我看没人能超出这个分数。

im·proved /ɪmˋpruvd; ɪmˈpruːvd/ *adj* better than before 已改善的: *improved performance throughout the company* 公司上下已改善的工作表现 | *New improved formula!* 新改进的配方!

im·prove·ment /ɪmˋpruvmənt; ɪmˈpruːvmənt/ *n* **1** [C,U] an act of improving or a state of being improved 改善, 改进; 提高: [+in] *There's certainly been an improvement in the children's behaviour.* 孩子们的行为举止确实有进步。| [+to] *We need to carry out some improvements to the computer system.* 我们需要对电脑系统进行一些改进。| **show an improvement** *This month's trading figures show some improvement.* 本月的贸易统计数字表明情况有所改善。| **room for improvement** (=the possibility of improving even more) 改进余地 *Your English is much better but there's still room for improvement.* 你的英语比以前好多了, 但仍有提升空间。**2** [C] a change or addition that improves something 改进之处: *Power steering is just one of the improvements to be found in the new 160cc model.* 动力转向装置只是新160立方厘米型号的其中一项改良。**3 be an improvement on** to be better than something similar that existed before 好于〔旧有的同类东西〕, 强于: *The new electronic controls are a big improvement on the old system.* 新型电子控制装置是对旧系统的一项很大的改进。

im·prov·i·dent /ɪmˋprɑvədənt; ɪmˈprɒvɪdənt/ *adj formal* too careless to save any money or to plan for the future【正式】挥霍的; 无远见的: *the generous but improvident welfare provision of the 1960s* 20世纪60年代慷慨但无远见的福利供应 —**improvidence** *n* [U]—**improvidently** *adv*

im·pro·vise /ˋɪmprəˌvaɪz; ˈɪmprəvaɪz/ *v* **1** [I] to do something without any preparation, because you are forced to do this by unexpected events〔事先无准备, 但因出乎意料的事而被迫〕临时做; 即兴作出: *I forgot to bring the notes for my speech, so I just had to improvise.* 我忘了带发言稿, 只好即席演讲。**2** [T] to make something by using whatever you can find because you do not have the equipment or materials that you need〔因缺乏所需用具或材料而〕临时拼凑: *We improvised a crude shelter using branches.* 我们用树枝临时搭了个简陋的蔽身之所。**3** [I] to perform music, DRAMA or COMEDY that comes straight from your imagination and has never been performed before 即兴演奏; 即兴表演: *You can't be a good jazz musician if you can't improvise.* 不会即兴演奏, 就不能成为一名优秀的爵士乐手。—**improvisation** /ˌɪmprəvaɪˋzeʃən; ˌɪmprəvaɪˈzeɪʃən/ *n* [C,U]

im·pru·dent /ɪmˋprudnt; ɪmˈpruːdənt/ *adj formal* not sensible or wise【正式】不明智的, 轻率的, 鲁莽的: *It would be rather imprudent to invest in an arms company at the moment.* 目前投资兵器公司是很不明智的。—**imprudently** *adv*—**imprudence** *n* [C,U]

im·pugn /ɪmˋpjun; ɪmˈpjuːn/ *v* [T] *formal* to express doubts about someone's honesty, courage, ability etc【正式】对〔某人的诚实、勇气、能力等〕表示怀疑: *The honour of our country has been grossly impugned!* 我们国家的荣誉受到了巨大挑战!

im·pulse /ˋɪmpʌls; ˈɪmpʌls/ *n* **1** [C,U] a sudden strong desire to do something before thinking whether it is a sensible thing to do 冲动; 突然的欲望: **impulse to do sth** *Gerry couldn't resist the impulse to skip work and go down to the beach.* 格里抵制不了放下工作去海边的冲动。| **on impulse** (=because of an impulse) 因一时冲动 *She had invited Joseph on a sudden impulse but was now regretting it.* 她当初一时冲动邀请了约瑟夫, 现在却后悔了。| **impulse buying** (=buying things without planning or choosing carefully) 未经计划或细心选择而购买 **2** [C] an aim or reason that causes a particular kind of activity or behaviour 推动; 动力: *The prime impulse of capitalism is the making of money.* 资本主义的首要推动力是赚钱。**3** [C] *technical* a single push or force moving for a short time in one direction along a nerve or electric wire【术语】神经冲动; (电)脉冲

im·pul·sion /ɪmˋpʌlʃən; ɪmˈpʌlʃən/ *n* [U] a sudden strong desire to do something 冲动; 强烈的欲望

im·pul·sive /ɪmˋpʌlsɪv; ɪmˈpʌlsɪv/ *adj* tending to do things as soon as you think of them, without considering the possible dangers or problems 冲动的; 草率的, 莽撞的: *Arthur Morel was a quick, careless, impulsive boy.* 阿瑟·莫雷尔是个性情急躁、粗心大意、容易冲动的男孩。| *In a burst of impulsive generosity I offered to pay.* 由于一时冲动, 我慷慨地提出付款。—**impulsively** *adv*—**impulsiveness** *n* [U]

im·pu·ni·ty /ɪmˋpjunətɪ; ɪmˈpjuːnəti/ *n* **do sth with impunity** if you do something wrong or immoral with impunity, there is no risk that you will be punished for it 做错事而免受惩处: *Men used to be able to violently abuse their wives with almost total impunity.* 过去男人粗暴地虐待妻子几乎完全不受惩罚。

im·pure /ɪmˋpjʊr; ɪmˈpjʊə/ *adj* **1** an impure substance has something else mixed with it, especially something of a lower quality 不纯净的; 掺杂的〔尤指掺有劣质的东西〕: *An added danger was that the group was using impure sodium chlorate in their bombs.* 还有一个危险是这伙人在他们的炸弹中使用了不纯的氯酸钠。—opposite 反义词 PURE (1) **2** *old-fashioned or humorous* impure thoughts, feelings etc are morally bad, especially because they are about sex【过时或幽默】不道德的, 淫秽的, 下流的: *He tried, without success, to rid his mind of any impure thoughts about Julia.* 他尽力想排除脑海中对朱莉娅的种种邪念, 可是做不到。—opposite 反义词 PURE (4)

im·pu·ri·ty /ɪmˋpjʊrətɪ; ɪmˈpjʊərəti/ *n* **1** [C usually plural 一般用复数] part of an almost pure substance that is of a lower quality 杂质: *All natural minerals contain impurities.* 一切天然矿物都含有杂质。**2** [U] the state of being impure 不纯; 掺杂

im·pu·ta·tion /ˌɪmpjʊˋteʃən; ˌɪmpjʊˈteɪʃən/ *n formal*【正式】**1** [C] a statement that someone is guilty of a crime or of doing something bad 罪名; 责难的话: *It was the first time she had confronted him with such direct imputations.* 她是第一次以如此直接的指责与他对质。**2** [U] [+of] the act of imputing something 归罪, 归咎

im·pute /ɪmˋpjut; ɪmˈpjuːt/ *v*

impute sth **to** sb/sth *phr v* [T] *formal* to say, often unfairly, that someone or something is responsible for something that has happened【正式】〔通常不公平地〕把〔某事〕归因于〔某人或某物〕: *The police were not guilty of the violence imputed to them.* 警方把归咎于他们的暴力罪行洗脱了。—**imputable** *adj* —**imputation** /ˌɪmpjʊˋteʃən; ˌɪmpjʊˈteɪʃən/ *n* [C,U]

IN the written abbreviation of 缩写 = INDIANA

in- /ɪn; ɪn/ *prefix* in some adjectives and nouns, shows a negative, an opposite, or a lack; not 不, 非, 无〔用在某些形容词和名词里表示否定、相反或缺乏之意〕: *insensitive* (=not sensitive) 不敏感的 | *inattention* (=lack of attention) 漫不经心 —compare 比较 UN-

-in /ɪn; ɪn/ *suffix* [in nouns 构成名词] an activity in which a group of people do something together for a purpose〔一群人为达到某目的而一起进行的〕活动: *a sit-in* (=where people sit in a place to prevent its usual activity) 静坐示威 | *a teach-in*〔大学师生共同参加的〕时事专题讨论会

in[1] /ɪn; ɪn/ *prep* **1** used with the name of a container, place, or area to say where someone or something is 在〔容器、地点或地区〕里, 在…内: *There's some sugar in the cupboard.* 碗橱里有一些糖。| *My mother was in the kitchen.* 母亲在厨房里。| *He spends a lot of time driving round in his car.* 他花费很多时间驾车到处转悠。| *She spent the day in bed.* 她在床上度过了那一天。| *He spent fifteen years in prison.* 他在狱中度过了15年。**2** used with the names of countries and towns to say where someone or something is 在某国家[某城镇]: *Mr Fisher is in Boston this week.* 费希尔先生本周在波士顿。| *The taxi man got lost in Manchester.* 出租车司机在曼彻斯特迷了路。| *My parents live in New Zealand now.* 我父母现在住在新西兰。**3** used with the names of months, years, seasons etc to say when something happens 在某月[某年、某季节等]: *He first visited Russia in 1937.* 他于1937年第一次访问苏联。| *These changes first started in the 1840s.* 这些变化最初发生在19世纪40年代。| *He retired in October.* 他已于10月份退休。**4** during a period of time 在…期间: *It was amazing how much we managed to do in a day.* 真想不到我们在一天之内做了这么多事情。**5** at the end of a period of time 在一段时间之后: *I'll be with you in a minute.* 我马上就到你那儿。| *I think he'll be a millionaire in a year or two.* 我看他一两年后就会成为百万富翁。**6** if you have not done some-

thing in several weeks, years etc you have not done it for that period of time 在…期间〔没做某事〕: *I haven't enjoyed myself so much in years.* 我已多年没有玩得这么开心了。**7** included as part of something 包含在…之内: *She said all this in her speech.* 所有这些她在演讲中都说了。| *You shouldn't believe everything you read in the newspapers.* 报纸上看到的东西不可全信。**8** working at a particular kind of job 从事某种工作: *She used to be a teacher, but she's in marketing now.* 她以前是教师，现在从事市场营销。| *He's been in politics for fifteen years.* 他从政已有15年了。**9** wearing something 穿着; 穿戴: *He looked very handsome in his uniform.* 他穿着制服，看上去很英俊。| *She was dressed in a blue linen suit.* 她身穿蓝色亚麻布套装。**10** using a particular way of talking or writing 以某种方式说[写]: *Her parents always talk to her in German.* 她的父母和她说话总是用德语。| *She shouted my name in a harsh voice.* 她高声厉喝我的名字。| *The children are only allowed to write in pencil.* 孩子们只许用铅笔写字。**11** arranged so as to form a particular shape or group 排列成某种形状[群体]: *The soldiers stood in a line and waited for orders.* 士兵们站成一列，等候命令。| *People were sitting in small groups chatting.* 人们三五成群地坐着闲聊。| *Arrange the words in alphabetical order.* 将单词按字母顺序排列。**12** used with numbers or amounts to show a proportion 每〔与数字或数量连用，表示比例〕: *One in every 10 children now suffers from asthma.* 现在每十个儿童中有一个患有哮喘。**13** used to show a connection between two things 〔用来表示两件事物之间的联系〕: *We need a further increase in investment.* 我们需要进一步增加投资。| *Milk is very rich in calcium.* 牛奶中含有丰富的钙质。| *She never showed any interest in music.* 她对音乐从未表现出什么兴趣。| *an expert in human biology* 人体生物学专家 **14** used to show the feelings you have when you do something 处于…中〔用来表示做某事时的感情〕: *She looked at me in horror.* 她惊恐地看着我。| *It was all done purely in fun.* 做这些事纯粹是为了好玩儿。**15** used to say how one person should consider another 〔用来表示一个人应如何看待另一人〕: *You've got a very good friend in Pat.* 你有个好朋友帕特。| *We have a very good candidate in Peter Dobrowski.* 彼德·杜勃罗夫斯基是我们一个很好的候选人。**16 in that** because 由于: *The situation is rather complicated in that we have two managing directors.* 由于我们有两位总经理，所以情况很复杂。**17 in all** used when giving a total amount 总共: *There were about 800 people in all.* 总共有800人左右。**18 in doing sth** when or by doing something 在做某事时; 借着做某事: *In raising money to support her work, Baker made contact with many organisations that were sympathetic to her ideas.* 贝克在筹款以支持她的工作时，接触过许多赞同她的想法的机构。

S1 W1 **in²** *adv* **1** so as to be contained inside something or surrounded by it 在…内，在里面: *She opened the cupboard and put the tins in.* 她打开碗橱，把几个罐头放进去。| *He picked up a glass and poured some water in.* 他拿起一个玻璃杯，向里面倒了一些水。**2** inside a building, especially the building where you live or work 在建筑物里〔尤指居住或工作的地方〕: *I'm afraid Mr Stewart won't be in until tomorrow morning.* 恐怕斯图尔特先生明天上午才能回来。| *She's never in when I call.* 我每次打电话，她都不在。| *We're staying in this evening.* 我们今晚不外出。**3** if a train, boat, or plane is in, it has arrived at a station, airport etc 〔车、船、飞机等〕已经到达: *Our train's not in yet.* 我们的火车还没到站。| *When's her flight due in?* 她乘坐的航班什么时候到？**4** if you send something in, you send it to an organization, where it will be dealt with 送至〔某机构〕; 递交: *All entries must be in by next week.* 所有参赛作品必须在下周之前提交。| *Letters have been pouring in from all over the country.* 信件从全国各地纷至沓来。**5** if you write, paint, or draw something in, you add it 填上; 着色; 加画: *Fill in your name and address on the form provided.* 在所提供的表格上填上姓名和地址。| *The information is typed in by trained keyboarders.* 信息由专业录入人员输入电脑。**6** if clothes, colours etc are in, they are fashionable 〔衣服、色彩等〕流行的，时髦的: *Stripes are definitely in this summer.* 条纹时装在今夏确实流行起来。**7** if a person or team is in, they are batting (BAT² (1)) in a game such as CRICKET (2) 〔板球等的〕击球: *Surrey have chosen to go in first.* 萨里选择先击球。**8** if a ball is in during a game, it is inside the area where the game is being played 〔球类比赛中，球〕在界内: *Her second serve was just in.* 她第二次发球刚好落在界内。**9 be in for sth** if someone is in for something unpleasant, it is going to happen to them 将要遭遇〔不愉快的事〕: *I'm afraid he's in for a bit of a disappointment.* 恐怕他要失望了。**10 be in for it** *informal* if someone is in for it, they are going to be punished 【非正式】将受到惩罚: *We're really in for it now.* 现在我们真要受到惩罚了。**11 be/get in on sth** to be involved in something that is happening 参与某事: *I think you ought to be in on this discussion, Ted.* 我看你应加入这场讨论，特德。**12 have (got) it in for sb** *informal* if someone has got it in for you, they do not like you and want to cause problems or difficulties for you 【非正式】刁难; 伺机报复: *I think the teacher's really got it in for me.* 我看这是老师有意刁难我。**13** if something falls or turns in, it falls or turns towards the centre 朝里，向中心: *The map had started to curl in at the edges.* 这张地图的边缘已开始向内弯曲了。**14** if a boat or the TIDE¹ (1) comes in, it comes towards the shore 〔船〕向岸边移动; 〔潮水〕上涨: *The tide was coming in.* 潮水正在上涨。| *The boat drifted in to the shore.* 小船向岸边漂去。**15 be in with sb** *informal* to be friendly with someone 【非正式】与某人友好相处: *She's in with the theatrical crowd.* 她与戏剧界的关系不错。**16 be in at sth** to be present when something happens 当时在场: *I was lucky enough to be in at the start of the research project.* 我很幸运在研究项目开始时便已参与。

in³ *adj* **1** *informal* clothes or colours that are in are fashionable 【非正式】〔服装、色彩等〕流行的: *Red is definitely the in colour this year.* 红色无疑是今年流行的颜色。| *Long skirts are in at the moment.* 时下流行穿长裙。**2** [only before a noun 仅用于名词前] an in joke is a private joke that is understood by only a small group of people 只为少数人听得懂的〔笑话〕，只限于小圈子的〔笑话〕

in·a·bil·i·ty /ˌɪnəˋbɪlətɪ; ˌɪnəˈbɪlɪ̥ti/ *n* [singular, U] the fact of being unable to do something 没办法，没能力: *the government's inability to control inflation* 政府无力控制通货膨胀

in·ac·ces·si·ble /ˌɪnəkˋsɛsəbḷ; ˌɪnəkˈsesɪ̥bəl◂/ *adj* **1** difficult or impossible to reach 难到达的; 不可及的: *These mountain villages are completely inaccessible in winter.* 这些山村到冬天就完全无法进入。**2** difficult or impossible to understand or afford 难懂的; 得不到的: *an inaccessible subject such as theoretical nuclear physics* 像理论核物理学这样难懂的学科 —**inaccessibly** *adv* —**inaccessibility** /ˌɪnəkˌsɛsəˋbɪlətɪ; ˌɪnəksesɪ̥ˈbɪlɪ̥ti/ *n* [U]

in·ac·cu·ra·cy /ɪnˋækjərəsɪ; ɪnˈækjɜ̥rəsi/ *n* **1** [C] a statement that is not completely correct 不准确的说法; 错误，差错: *I think your report contained various inaccuracies and half-truths.* 我认为你的报告里有各种各样的错误和半真半假的说法。**2** [U] a lack of correctness 不准确: *As a journalist you simply cannot tolerate inaccuracy.* 作为记者，决不能容忍报道失实。

in·ac·cu·rate /ɪnˋækjərɪt; ɪnˈækjɜ̥rɪ̥t/ *adj* not completely correct 不完全准确的: *an inaccurate translation of the French* 一份不完全正确的法语译文 —**inaccurately** *adv*

in·ac·tion /ɪnˋækʃən; ɪnˈækʃən/ *n* [U] the fact that someone is not doing anything 〔人〕无行动，没反应: *Several newspapers have criticized the President for his inaction.* 好几家报纸批评总统无所作为。

in·ac·tive /ɪnˋæktɪv; ɪnˈæktɪv/ *adj* not doing anything or not working 不活动的，不工作的; 懒散的 —**inactivity** /ˌɪnækˋtɪvətɪ; ˌɪnækˈtɪvɪ̥ti/ *n* [U]

in·ad·e·qua·cy /ɪnˋædəkwəsɪ; ɪnˈædɪ̥kwɪ̥si/ *n* [U] **1** a feeling that you are unable to deal with situations because you are not as good as other people 〔指人〕不够好，不胜任: *Unemployment can often cause feelings of inadequacy and low self-esteem.* 失业往往使人感到不够格和自卑。**2** [U] the fact of not being good enough in quality, ability, size etc for a particular purpose 〔质量、能力、大小等的〕不足，欠缺: [+of] *the inadequacy of local health care* 当地医疗保健制度的不健全 **3** [C] a fault or weakness in your character 〔性格上的〕缺点，不足之处: *I'm quite aware of my own inadequacies.* 我很清楚自身的不足之处。

in·ad·e·quate /ɪnˋædəkwɪt; ɪnˈædɪ̥kwɪ̥t/ *adj* **1** not good enough, big enough, skilled enough etc for a particular purpose 〔对某一特定目的而言〕不够好的，不足的，不强的: *An inadequate supply of vitamin A can lead to blindness.* 维生素A不足会导致失明。| [+for] *The parking facilities are inadequate for such a busy shopping centre.* 停车设施不足以应付这样热闹的购物中心。**2** someone who feels inadequate feels unable to deal with situations because they think they are not as good as other people 〔人自以为〕不胜任的; 不够好的; 能力不足的: *The teacher made us feel inadequate and stupid if we made mistakes.* 我们出错时，老师总是让我们觉得自己能力差，脑子笨。—**inadequately** *adv*

in·ad·mis·si·ble /ˌɪnədˋmɪsəbḷ; ˌɪnədˈmɪsɪ̥bəl◂/ *adj formal* 【正式】**inadmissible evidence** information that is not allowed to be used in a court of law 〔在法庭上〕不可接受的证据 —**inadmissibly** *adv* —**inadmissibility** /ˌɪnədmɪsəˋbɪlətɪ; ˌɪnədmɪsɪ̥ˈbɪlɪ̥ti/ *n* [U]

in·ad·vert·ent·ly /ˌɪnədˋvɝtn̩tlɪ; ˌɪnədˈvɜːtəntli/ *adv* without realizing what you are doing 粗心大意地; 非故意地: *I inad-*

vertently stepped on his toe. 我不留神踩了他的脚趾。—**inadvertent** *adj*: *the inadvertent disclosure of sensitive information* 无意中泄露敏感信息 —**inadvertence** *n* [C,U]

in·ad·vis·a·ble /ˌɪnədˋvaɪzəbḷ; ˌɪnədˈvaɪzəbəl◂/ *adj* an action that is inadvisable is not sensible; unwise〔行动〕不可取的，不明智的，失策的: *It is inadvisable to climb in these mountains on your own.* 独自一人爬这几座山是很不明智的。

in·a·li·en·a·ble /ɪnˋeljənəbḷ; ɪnˈeɪliənəbəl/ *adj formal* an inalienable right cannot be taken away from you【正式】〔权利〕不可剥夺的

i·nam·o·ra·ta /ɪnˌæməˋrɑtə; ɪˌnæməˈrɑːtə/ *n* [C] *literary or humorous* the woman that a man loves【文或幽默】情妇

i·nane /ɪnˋen; ɪˈneɪn/ *adj* extremely stupid or without much meaning 愚蠢至极的；无意义的；空洞的: *inane remarks* 空话 | *an inane conversation* 无聊的谈话 —**inanely** *adv* —**inanity** /ɪnˋænətɪ; ɪˈnænəti/ *n* [C,U]

in·an·i·mate /ɪnˋænəmɪt; ɪnˈænəmət/ *adj* not living 无生命的: *A rock is an inanimate object.* 岩石是没有生命的物体。

in·ap·pli·ca·ble /ɪnˋæplɪkəbḷ; ˌɪnəˈplɪkəbəl/ *adj* a description, question, or rule that is inapplicable to a particular subject cannot sensibly be used about it〔描述、问题或规则对特定主题〕不适用的: [+to] *These new regulations are inapplicable to us.* 这些新规定对我们不适用。—**inapplicability** /ɪnˌæplɪkəˋbɪlətɪ; ˌɪnəplɪkəˈbɪləti/ *n* [U]

in·ap·pro·pri·ate /ˌɪnəˋproprɪɪt; ˌɪnəˈprəʊpri-ət/ *adj* **1** not suitable for a particular purpose or situation〔对特定目的或情况〕不合适的，不恰当的: *I thought his comments were wholly inappropriate on such a solemn occasion.* 我认为他在如此庄严的场合说这样的话极不恰当。| [+for] *an inappropriate gift for a child* 不适合送给孩子的礼物 **2** not correct according to generally accepted rules of social, moral, or professional behaviour〔根据普遍接受的社会、道德或专业行为规则〕不适宜的，不恰当的: *It would be inappropriate for me to discuss her case at this meeting.* 让我在这个会上讨论她的事情是不恰当的。—**inappropriately** *adv*: *inappropriately dressed* 穿着不得体 —**inappropriateness** also 又作 **inappropriacy** *n* [U]

in·apt /ɪnˋæpt; ɪnˈæpt/ *adj formal* an inapt phrase, statement etc is not right for a particular situation【正式】〔措辞、陈述〕不恰当的，不适宜的: *a very inapt comment* 很不恰当的评论 —compare 比较 INEPT —**inaptly** *adv* —**inaptness** *n* [U]

in·ar·tic·u·late /ˌɪnɑrˋtɪkjəlɪt; ˌɪnɑːˈtɪkjələt◂/ *adj* **1** not able to express yourself clearly when you speak〔说话时〕词不达意的，口齿不清的 **2** speech that is inarticulate is not clearly expressed or pronounced〔话语〕表达不清楚的；发音不清的: *inarticulate mutterings* 含糊不清的咕哝 —**inarticulately** *adv* —**inarticulateness** also 又作 **inarticulacy** *n* [C,U]

in·as·much /ˌɪnəzˋmʌtʃ; ˌɪnəzˈmʌtʃ/ *adv formal*【正式】**inasmuch as** used to introduce an additional phrase that explains the rest of your sentence or says in what limited way it is true 鉴于，由于〔用于开端以说明接下来的说话〕: *Anne is also guilty, inasmuch as she knew what the others were planning.* 安妮知道他们的谋划，所以也是有罪的。

in·at·ten·tion /ˌɪnəˋtɛnʃən; ˌɪnəˈtenʃən/ *n* [U] lack of attention 不注意；疏忽，漫不经心: [+to] *inattention to detail* 对细节的疏忽

in·at·ten·tive /ˌɪnəˋtɛntɪv; ˌɪnəˈtentɪv◂/ *adj* not giving enough attention to someone or something 不够注意的；漫不经心的: *an inattentive student* 注意力不集中的学生 —**inattentively** *adv* —**inattentiveness** *n* [U]

in·au·di·ble /ɪnˋɔdəbḷ; ɪnˈɔːdəbəl/ *adj* too quiet to be heard〔声音小得〕听不见的: *inaudible muttering* 听不清的小声低语 —**inaudibly** *adv* —**inaudibility** /ˌɪnɔdəˋbɪlətɪ; ɪnˌɔːdəˈbɪləti/ *n* [U]

in·au·gu·ral /ɪnˋɔgjərəl; ɪˈnɔːgjərəl/ *adj* [only before noun 仅用于名词前] **1 inaugural speech/lecture** the first speech given by someone starting an important job, such as a president or a university PROFESSOR〔总统等的〕就职演说；〔大学教授的〕首次讲课 **2 inaugural meeting/concert etc** the first in a series of meetings, concerts etc 会议的开幕式；音乐会的首场演出

in·au·gu·rate /ɪnˋɔgjəˌret; ɪˈnɔːgjəreɪt/ *v* [T] **1** if an event inaugurates an important change or period of time, it comes at the beginning of it 开始〔一个重要变化〕；开创…时代: *The International Trade Agreement inaugurated a period of high economic growth.*《世界贸易协定》开创了一个经济高速发展的阶段。**2** to introduce a new person into an important job such as that of president, by holding a special ceremony 为〔新总统等〕举行就职典礼 **3** to open a building or service for the first time or to start a public event with a ceremony 举行〔新建筑物〕落成典礼；为〔公共活动〕举行开幕式 —**inauguration** /ɪnˌɔgjəˋreʃən; ɪˌnɔːgjəˈreɪʃən/ *n* [C,U] *Eight months after Hoover's inauguration came the Wall Street Crash.* 胡佛就任总统八个月后，就发生了华尔街股市暴跌。

Inauguration Day /·,··ˈ··/ the day an American President is INAUGURATEd, which is always on January 20. There is usually a PARADE and the new President makes a speech about what he plans for the US.〔美国〕总统就职日〔1月20日。此日通常有游行活动，新任总统就施政计划发表演说〕

in·aus·pi·cious /ˌɪnɔˋspɪʃəs; ˌɪnɔːˈspɪʃəs◂/ *adj formal* seeming to show that future success is unlikely【正式】不祥的，不吉利的，凶兆的: *an inauspicious start to the journey* 这次旅行不祥的开始 —**inauspiciously** *adv*

in-be·tween /ˌ··ˈ·◂/ *adj informal* in the middle between two points, sizes, periods of time etc【非正式】介于两者之间的: *Neither the 12 nor the 14 fits properly – I must be an in-between size.* 12码和14码都不合适，我的尺码肯定在两者之间。

in·board /ˋɪnˌbord; ˈɪnbɔːd/ *n* [C] a motor inside a boat 船内侧发动机 — compare 比较 OUTBOARD MOTOR

in·born /ɪnˋbɔrn; ˌɪnˈbɔːn◂/ *adj* an inborn quality or ability is one that you have had naturally since birth 天生的，与生俱来的: *Lincoln had an inborn sense of the truth.* 林肯天生诚实正直。

in·bound /ˋɪnˋbaund; ˈɪnbaʊnd/ *adj AmE* an inbound flight or train is coming towards the place where you are【美】〔班机或火车〕返航的，回程的

in·bounds /ˌ·ˈ·◂/ *adj AmE* if the ball is in-bounds in a sport, it is in the playing area【美】〔球赛中球〕在界内的

in·bred /ɪnˋbrɛd; ˌɪnˈbred◂/ *adj* **1** having developed as a natural part of your character 天生的: *an inbred responsiveness to music* 对音乐天生的敏感 **2** produced by INBREEDING 近亲繁殖的

in·breed·ing /ˋɪnˌbridɪŋ; ˈɪnbriːdɪŋ/ *n* [U] the producing of children, animals, or new plants from closely related members of the same family 近亲交配；近亲繁殖

in·built /ˋɪnˋbɪlt; ˈɪnbɪlt/ *adj especially BrE* an inbuilt quality, feature etc is part of the character of someone or something and cannot be removed【尤英】内在的；固有的: *an organization with an inbuilt tendency to expand* 一个有内在扩展趋势的组织

Inc /ɪŋk; ɪŋk/ the written abbreviation of 缩写= INCORPORATED; used in the US after the name of a company to show that it has become a CORPORATION (1) 股份有限的〔在美国用于公司名称后，表示已成为法人组织〕: *General Motors Inc* 通用汽车股份有限公司 —compare 比较 LTD, PLC

in·cal·cu·la·ble /ɪnˋkælkjələbḷ; ɪnˈkælkjələbəl/ *adj* too many or too great to be calculated 数不清的；不可估量的: *A scandal of this nature would do the school incalculable harm.* 这类丑闻将给学校造成不可估量的损害。—**incalculably** *adv*

in·can·des·cent /ˌɪnkənˋdɛsṇt; ˌɪnkænˈdesənt◂/ *adj* **1** giving a bright light when heated 炽热的，白炽的 **2 incandescent with rage** *BrE* extremely angry【英】怒不可遏的 —**incandescence** *n* [U]

in·can·ta·tion /ˌɪnkænˋteʃən; ˌɪnkænˈteɪʃən/ *n* [C,U] the set of special words that someone uses in magic, or the act of saying these words 咒语；念咒语

in·ca·pa·ble /ɪnˋkepəbḷ; ɪnˈkeɪpəbəl/ *adj* **1** [not before noun 不用于名词前] unable to do something or to feel a particular emotion 无能力〔做某事〕的；不能〔有某种感情〕的: [+of] *incapable of understanding even the simplest instructions* 甚至连最简单的说明都不懂 | *incapable of pity* 不会有怜悯之心 **2** weak and unable to care for yourself 体弱而不能照顾自己的 —**incapably** *adv* —**incapability** /ˌɪnkepəˋbɪlətɪ; ɪnˌkeɪpəˈbɪləti/ *n* [U]

in·ca·pa·ci·tate /ˌɪnkəˋpæsəˌtet; ˌɪnkəˈpæsəteɪt/ *v* [T often passive 常用被动态] if something such as an illness or accident incapacitates you, it makes you too ill or weak to live and work normally〔疾病或意外事故等〕使无能力〔正常生活和工作〕: *He was permanently incapacitated after the accident.* 这次事故使他终身残疾，不能正常生活和工作。—**incapacitation** /ˌɪnkəpæsəˋteʃən; ˌɪnkəpæsəˈteɪʃən/ *n* [U]

in·ca·pa·ci·ty /ˌɪnkəˋpæsətɪ; ˌɪnkəˈpæsəti/ *n* [singular, U] **1** the condition of being too ill or weak to live and work normally 无正常生活和工作的能力: *temporary incapacity through illness* 由于疾病而暂时不能正常生活和工作 **2** the inability to do something 无能力〔做某事〕: *the author's incapacity to convey his ideas* 作者无法表达自己的思想

in·car·ce·rate /ɪnˋkarsəˌret; ɪnˈkɑːsəreɪt/ *v* [T usually passive 一般用被动态] *formal* to keep someone in a place, especially a prison【正式】监禁，禁闭 —**incarceration** /ɪnˌkarsəˋreʃən; ɪnˌkɑːsəˈreɪʃən/ *n* [U]

in·car·nate[1] /ɪnˋkarnɪt; ɪnˈkɑːnət/ *adj* [only after noun 仅用于名词后] **evil/wisdom/the devil etc incarnate** someone who is considered to be the human form of evil, wisdom etc 邪恶/智慧/魔鬼等的化身

in·car·nate² /ɪn`kɑrnet; ˈɪnkɑːneɪt/ *v* [T] *formal*【正式】**1** to be the human form of a particular quality 成为…的化身 **2** to make something appear in a human form 使〔某物〕具有人形

in·car·na·tion /ˌɪnkɑr`neʃən; ˌɪnkɑːˈneɪʃən/ *n* **1** [C] the period of time, according to some religions, during which someone is alive in the form of a particular person or animal〔某些宗教中的〕前世, 上辈子: *She believed that in a previous incarnation she had been an Egyptian queen.* 她认为自己前世是一位埃及王后。**2 be the incarnation of goodness/evil/sweetness** to perfectly represent goodness etc in human form 是善良/邪恶/仁慈的化身: *She was the incarnation of perfect wisdom.* 她是完美智慧的化身。**3 the Incarnation** the act of God coming to Earth in the human form of Jesus Christ, according to the Christian religion〔基督教的〕道成肉身〔指上帝化身成基督来到人间〕

in·cau·tious /ɪn`kɔʃəs; ɪnˈkɔːʃəs/ *adj* done or said without thinking about the possible effects, and therefore causing problems 轻率的; 不谨慎的: *incautious remarks* 轻率的言论 —**incautiously** *adv*

in·cen·di·a·ry¹ /ɪn`sɛndɪˌɛrɪ; ɪnˈsendiəri/ *adj* [only before noun 仅用于名词前] **1 incendiary bomb/device/attack etc** designed to cause a fire 燃烧弹/燃烧装置/火攻等 **2** an incendiary speech or piece of writing is intended to make people angry and is likely to cause trouble〔演讲、文章〕煽动性的

incendiary² *n* [C] a bomb designed to cause a fire 燃烧弹

in·cense¹ /`ɪnsɛns; ˈɪnsens/ *n* [U] a substance which has a pleasant smell when you burn it, and which is used in religious ceremonies〔祭祀时焚烧用的〕香

in·cense² /ɪn`sɛns; ɪnˈsens/ *v* [T] to make someone extremely angry 使〔某人〕十分愤怒: *Spectators, incensed by the referee's decision, ran onto the field.* 观众对裁判的判罚极为愤怒, 冲进了球场。

in·censed /ɪn`sɛnst; ɪnˈsenst/ *adj* extremely angry 极为愤怒的: *When I reported the matter to Stalin, he became incensed.* 我把此事向斯大林汇报时, 他勃然大怒。

⊜3 **in·cen·tive** /ɪn`sɛntɪv; ɪnˈsentɪv/ *n* [C,U] something which encourages you to work harder, start new activities etc 刺激; 动力; 鼓励: *With prices so low there is little incentive for the farmers.* 价格太低, 因此农民并不积极。| **incentive to do sth** *The chance of a higher salary gives young people the incentive to work harder.* 由于有加薪的机会, 年轻人工作更卖力了。| **tax incentives** (=offers of reduced taxes) 减税优惠

in·cep·tion /ɪn`sɛpʃən; ɪnˈsepʃən/ *n* [singular] *formal* the start of an organization or institution【正式】〔组织、机构的〕开创, 开端: *a history of the Labour Party from its inception to the present day* 工党建党至今的历史

in·ces·sant /ɪn`sɛsn̩t; ɪnˈsesənt/ *adj* an incessant activity, noise etc continues without stopping, in an annoying way〔令人感到厌烦的活动、噪音等〕持续不断的, 没完没了的: *The child's incessant talking started to irritate her.* 孩子喋喋不休, 使她烦躁起来。—**incessantly** *adv*

in·cest /`ɪnsɛst; ˈɪnsest/ *n* [U] illegal sex between people who are closely related, for example between a brother and sister, or father and daughter 乱伦

in·ces·tu·ous /ɪn`sɛstʃuəs; ɪnˈsestʃuəs/ *adj* **1** an incestuous relationship is a sexual relationship between people who are closely related in a family 乱伦的 **2** an incestuous relationship is one in which a small group of people or organizations only help each other, in a way that is unfair to other people〔群体或组织〕排外的; 小圈子内的: *the incestuous relationship between sport and television* 体育界与电视媒体间的小集团关系 —**incestuously** *adv* —**incestuousness** *n* [U]

⊜2 ✎3 **inch¹** /ɪntʃ; ɪntʃ/ *n* [C] **1** a unit for measuring length, equal to 2.54 centimetres 英寸〔长度单位, 等于 2.54 厘米〕—see table on page C3 参见 C3 页附录 **2** a very small distance 很小的距离: *A bullet thudded into the wall only inches from where I was standing.* 一颗子弹砰的一声射进离我站的地方只有几英寸的墙内。| *The bus missed our car by inches.* (=almost hit it) 这辆公共汽车差一点就撞着我们的车。**3** enough rain or snow to cover an area an inch deep 一英寸的降水[降雪]: *Over five inches of rain has fallen in the last week.* 上周降雨量超过了五英寸。**4 every inch a)** completely or in every way 完全地; 不折不扣地: *He looked every inch a gentleman.* 他看上去像个地地道道的绅士。**b)** the whole of an area〔某地区的〕全部: **[+of]** *They're determined to defend every inch of their territory.* 他们决心保卫每一寸领土。**5 give sb an inch and they'll take a yard/mile** used to say that if you allow someone a little freedom or power, they'll try to take a lot more 得寸进尺 **6 inch by inch** moving very gradually and slowly〔移动〕一点一点地, 缓慢地: *Inch by inch the soldiers were driven back.* 这些士兵被逐渐击退了。**7 not give/budge an inch** to refuse to change your opinion even slightly about something in spite of attempts to persuade you 寸步不让: *Neither side is prepared to give an inch in the negotiations.* 谈判中双方都无意作丝毫让步。**8 beat/thrash sb within an inch of their life** to hit someone so hard and so many times that you almost kill them 几乎把某人打死

inch² *v* [I always+adv/prep, T always+adv/prep] to move very slowly in a particular direction, or make something do this (使) 缓慢移动: **[+along/towards/around etc]** *I started inching forward along the ledge towards the open window.* 我沿着窗台缓慢地挪向开着的窗子。| **inch sth along/towards etc** *He slowly inched the box forward, unable to lift it.* 由于无法把那只箱子提起来, 他一点一点地向前挪动它。

in·cho·ate /ɪn`ko ɪt; ɪnˈkəʊət/ *adj formal* inchoate ideas, plans, attitudes etc are only just starting to develop【正式】〔想法、计划、态度等〕刚开始形成的

in·ci·dence /`ɪnsədəns; ˈɪnsədəns/ *n* [singular] *formal* the number of times something bad happens, for example how many people have a particular illness or how many crimes there are【正式】〔疾病、罪行等坏事的〕发生率: *a survey to determine the incidence of heart defects among premature babies* 确定早产儿心脏发育不全比率的调查 | *the high incidence of alcoholism among the unemployed* 失业者中高比率的酗酒现象

in·ci·dent /`ɪnsədənt; ˈɪnsədənt/ *n* [C] **1** something that happens, especially something that is unusual〔尤指不平常的〕事件: *After the children had been punished, nobody mentioned the incident again.* 孩子受到惩罚后, 再没人提起这件事了。| **without incident** (=without anything unusual or unpleasant happening) 没有发生不寻常[不愉快]的事; 平安无事 *Despite my fears the meal passed without incident.* 尽管我有些担心, 但吃饭时并未发生什么事。**2** a serious or violent event that causes disagreement〔导致争论的〕严重[暴力]事件: *a major diplomatic incident* 重大外交事件 ✎2

in·ci·den·tal¹ /ˌɪnsə`dɛntl; ˌɪnsəˈdentl◂/ *adj* **1** happening or existing in connection with something else that is more important 附带的; 伴随的; 次要的: *minor incidental details* 附带的次要细节 | **incidental expenses** (=small expenses connected with a particular activity)〔与某特定活动相关的〕杂费: *Keep a record of any incidental expenses on your trip.* 把旅途中的杂费都记录下来。**2** [not before noun 不用于名词前] happening as a result of something in a way that can be expected〔意料之内〕由…引发的; 免不了的: **[+to]** *Drinking too much is almost incidental to bartending.* 从事酒吧服务几乎免不了过度饮酒。

incidental² *n* [C usually plural 一般用复数] something that you have to do, buy etc which you had not planned to do or buy 原来没打算要做的事[要买的东西]: *It's useful to carry extra cash for taxis, tips and other incidentals.* 有必要额外带些现金用来坐出租车、付小费和其他临时开支。

in·ci·den·tal·ly /ˌɪnsə`dɛntl̩ɪ; ˌɪnsəˈdentəli/ *adv* **1** [sentence adverb 句子副词] used when adding more information to what was said before, or when you want to talk about something else you have just thought of 顺便提一下〔用来补充说过的事情, 或提及刚想到的事〕: *a beautiful town which, incidentally, is where they filmed 'The French Lieutenant's Woman'* 真是个美丽的小镇, 顺便说一句, 电影《法国中尉的女人》就是在那儿拍摄的 | *Incidentally, this wine goes particularly well with cheese.* 顺便提一下, 这种葡萄酒配干酪特别好。**2** happening in a way that was not planned, but as a result of something else〔情况的发生〕偶然地: *Quite incidentally, I found out some very useful information at the party.* 我在聚会上非常偶然地发现了一些十分有用的信息。 ⊜3

incidental mu·sic /ˌ····`··/ *n* [U] music played during a play, film etc in order to give the right feeling〔戏剧、电影的〕配乐

in·cin·e·rate /ɪn`sɪnəˌret; ɪnˈsɪnəreɪt/ *v* [T usually passive 一般用被动态] to burn something completely in order to destroy it 将…烧成灰烬; 烧毁: *All the infected clothing was incinerated.* 所有沾染病菌的衣服都被焚毁了。—**incineration** /ɪnˌsɪnə`reʃən; ɪnˌsɪnəˈreɪʃən/ *n* [U]

in·cin·e·ra·tor /ɪn`sɪnəˌretə; ɪnˈsɪnəreɪtə/ *n* [C] a machine designed to burn things at a very high temperature in order to destroy them〔废物〕焚化炉

in·cip·i·ent /ɪn`sɪpɪənt; ɪnˈsɪpiənt/ *adj* [only before noun 仅用于名词前] *formal* starting to happen or exist【正式】刚开始的, 早期的: *those tiny yawns that are sure signs of incipient boredom* 那些轻微的哈欠肯定是开始感到厌倦的信号 —**incipiently** *adv*

in·cise/ɪn`saɪz; ɪn'saɪz/ *v technical*【术语】**1** [T +in/into] to cut a pattern or mark into a surface〔在表面〕雕刻〔图案或记号〕**2** [T] to cut carefully into something with a sharp knife〔用锋利的刀〕小心切入

in·ci·sion/ɪn`sɪʒən; ɪn'sɪʒən/ *n* [C,U] a cut into something, especially into someone's body using a special knife during a medical operation, or the act of making this kind of cut〔手术〕切口, 切痕; 切开, 切入: *The incision was carefully stitched and bandaged.* 切口被小心翼翼地缝合包扎起来。

in·ci·sive/ɪn`saɪsɪv; ɪn'saɪsɪv/ *adj* words, remarks etc that are incisive are very clear and direct and deal immediately with the most important part of a subject〔言语〕直截了当的, 切中要害的: *Her questions were well-formulated and incisive.* 她的问题提得很好, 个个切中要害。—**incisively** *adv* —**incisiveness** *n* [U]

in·ci·sor/ɪn`saɪzə; ɪn'saɪzə/ *n* [C] one of the teeth at the front of your mouth which have a sharp edge 门齿, 切牙 —compare 比较 CANINE TOOTH, MOLAR —see picture at 参见 TEETH 图

in·cite/ɪn`saɪt; ɪn'saɪt/ *v* [T] to deliberately encourage people to cause trouble, fight, argue etc 煽动, 鼓动, 激起: **incite sb to do sth** *He was charged with inciting the students to riot.* 他被指控煽动学生暴乱。| **incite sb to sth** *inflammatory articles that incited people to violence and hatred* 激起暴力和仇恨的煽动性文章 —**Incitement** *n* [U]

in·ci·vil·i·ty/ˌɪnsə`vɪlətɪ; ˌɪnsʒ'vɪlʒti/ *n* [U] *formal* impolite behaviour【正式】不文明行为, 无礼举动

in·clem·ent/ɪn`klɛmənt; ɪn'klemənt/ *adj formal* inclement weather is unpleasant because it is cold, rainy etc【正式】〔天气〕恶劣的, 寒冷的, 多雨的 —**inclemency** *n* [U]

in·cli·na·tion/ˌɪnklə`neʃən; ˌɪnklʒ'neɪʃən/ *n*

1 ▶DESIRE 欲望◀[C,U] a feeling that makes you want to do something 意向; 倾向: *You always follow your own inclinations instead of considering other people's feelings.* 你总是随心所欲, 不考虑别人的感受。| **inclination to do sth** *I have not the slightest inclination to take unnecessary risks.* 我丝毫不想冒不必要的风险。

2 ▶TENDENCY 趋势◀[C,U] tendency to think or behave in a particular way〔思想或行为的〕倾向: **inclination to do sth** *an inclination to see everything in political terms* 从政治角度看待一切事物的倾向

3 inclination of the head the movement of bending your neck so that your head is lowered 点头: *With a slight inclination of the head she showed her approval.* 她微微点了一下头表示认可。

4 ▶SLOPE 斜面◀[C,U] *formal* a slope or the angle at which something slopes【正式】斜坡; 斜度

in·cline¹/ɪn`klaɪn; ɪn'klaɪn/ *v* [not in progressive 不用进行时] *formal*【正式】

1 ▶TEND TO DO STH 倾向于做某事◀**a)** to think that a particular belief or opinion is most likely to be right 倾向于〔某个信念或意见〕: [+to/ towards] *He has always inclined to the belief that all men are capable of great evil.* 他一直倾向于认为人性本恶。| **incline to do sth** *I incline to accept the official version of events.* 我倾向于接受官方对这些事件的说法。**b)** to tend to behave in a particular way or to show a particular quality 趋向于〔以某种特定方式行事〕; 易于〔显示出某种习性或品格〕: [+to/towards] *The child has always inclined towards laziness.* 这孩子一直表现得懒散。

2 ▶INFLUENCE 影响◀[T] if a situation, fact etc inclines you to do or think something, it influences you towards a particular action or opinion 使去做〔某事〕; 使倾向于〔某观点〕: **incline sb to do sth** *I know that you acted hastily, but that does not incline me to forgive you.* 我知道你做得匆忙, 但我不能因此就原谅你。

3 incline your head to bend your neck so that your head is lowered 点头

4 ▶TO SLOPE 倾斜◀[I,T] to be sloping at a particular angle or to make something do this (使) 有斜度, (使) 倾斜

in·cline²/`ɪnklaɪn; 'ɪnklaɪn/ *n* [C] a slope 斜坡; 斜度: *a steep incline* 陡坡

3 **in·clined**/ɪn`klaɪnd; ɪn'klaɪnd/ *adj*

1 ▶TENDING TO DO STH 倾向于做某事◀[not before noun 不用于名词前] tending to behave in a particular way 有…意向的; 倾向于…的: **be inclined to do sth** *She's inclined to tell lies.* 她好说谎。

2 be inclined to agree/think/believe etc to have a particular opinion but not to hold it very strongly 倾向于赞同/认为/相信等: *Arthur has some strange ideas, but on this occasion I'm inclined to agree with him.* 阿瑟有一些奇怪的想法, 但这次我倒是倾向于同意他的观点。

3 ▶WISHING TO DO SOMETHING 希望做某事◀[not before noun 不用于名词前] wanting to do something 想要做…的: **inclined to do sth** *You can even swim in the lake – if you feel inclined to.* 你甚至可以在湖里游泳, 如果你想的话。

4 mathematically/linguistically/musically inclined naturally interested in or good at something such as mathematics or languages 有数学/语言/音乐天赋的: *We sent her to the Arts school because she's very musically inclined.* 我们送她去上艺术学校, 因为她很有音乐天赋。

5 ▶SLOPING 倾斜的◀sloping or leaning in a particular direction 倾斜的; 有坡度的

in·close/ɪn`kloz; ɪn'kləʊz/ *v* [T] another spelling of ENCLOSE enclose 的另一种拼法

in·clos·ure/ɪn`kloʒə; ɪn'kləʊʒə/ *n* [C,U] another spelling of ENCLOSURE enclosure 的另一种拼法

in·clude/ɪn`klud; ɪn'kluːd/ *v* [T] **1** [not in progressive 不用进行时] if a group or a set includes something or someone, it has that thing or person as one of its parts 包括; 含有: *Our tour party included several retired couples.* 我们这个旅游团有几对退休夫妇。| *The price includes postage charges.* 这价钱包括邮费。—see 见 COMPRISE (USAGE) **2** to make someone or something part of a larger group or set 使〔某物〕成为整体的一部分; 把〔某人〕算入: *The team is looking strong, especially now they have included Roscoe.* 球队看上去很强大, 特别是现在有罗斯科加入进来。| **include sth in/on etc** *Teachers must include attendance figures in their monthly reports.* 教师在每月的汇报中必须把出勤率包括进去。| *Is service included in the bill?* 账单里包括服务费吗? **3 include me out** *spoken* a humorous way of saying you do not want to be included in a group【口】把我包括在外〔一种幽默说法〕—opposite 反义词 EXCLUDE

in·clud·ed/ɪn`kludɪd; ɪn'kluːdʒd/ *adj* [only after noun 仅用于名词后] **myself/John etc included** including myself, John etc 包括我自己/约翰等在内: *Everyone has to go to the dentist's, you included.* 每个人都得去看牙医, 包括你在内。

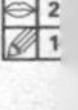

in·clud·ing/ɪn`kludɪŋ; ɪn'kluːdɪŋ/ *prep* used to introduce something or someone that is included in the larger group or amount you have just mentioned 包括〔用于表示某物或某人是刚才谈及的整体的一部分〕: *There were twelve of us, including me and Tom.* 共有12人, 包括我和汤姆。| *£25.50 including postage and packing* 一共25.5镑, 包括邮寄费和包装费 —opposite 反义词 EXCLUDING

in·clu·sion/ɪn`kluʒən; ɪn'kluːʒən/ *n* **1** [U] the act of including someone or something in a larger group or set, or the fact of being included in one 包含, 包括: *His inclusion in the team has caused a lot of controversy.* 他的入队, 引起了很多争议。**2** [C] someone or something that has been included in a larger group or set 包括在整体中的某人[某物]: *With the recent inclusions there will be 28 delegates in all.* 连同新近加入的, 总共有28位代表。

in·clu·sive/ɪn`klusɪv; ɪn'kluːsɪv/ *adj* **1** an inclusive price or cost includes everything〔价钱或费用〕包括一切的: *an all-inclusive charge* 包括一切费用在内的价格 | [+of] *The rent is £50 a week, inclusive of heating and lighting.* 房租每星期50英镑, 包括暖气费和照明费。**2 April to June inclusive/15 to 20 inclusive, etc** including April, June and all the months between them, 15 and 20 and all the numbers between them etc 从4月到6月 (包括4月和6月); 从15到20 (包括15和20)

USAGE NOTE 用法说明: INCLUSIVE
AmE-BrE DIFFERENCE 美－英用法差异
Where British English speakers might use **inclusive** in this way 英国英语会这样用 inclusive: *Monday to Friday inclusive* 周一到周五; American speakers may use **through** 美国英语则会用 through: *Monday through Friday* 周一到周五

in·cog·ni·to/ɪn`kɑgnɪˌto; ˌɪnkɒg'niːtəʊ/ *adv* if a famous person travels incognito, they travel without letting people know who they are 隐瞒身份地, 微服地〔诸如名人出游〕

in·co·her·ent/ˌɪnko`hɪrənt; ˌɪnkəʊ'hɪərənt◂/ *adj* **1** thoughts, ideas etc that are incoherent are very badly expressed or badly arranged and are difficult to understand〔思想、观点等〕条理不清的, 紊乱的: *At times the narrative is completely incoherent.* 有时候叙述完全是前言不搭后语。**2** speaking unclearly 言语不清的: *As the child's temperature soared she became incoherent.* 随着体温急剧升高, 女孩开始语无伦次。—**incoherently** *adv* —**incoherence** *n* [U]

in·come/`ɪnˌkʌm; 'ɪŋkʌm/ *n* [C,U] the money that you earn from your work or that you receive from INVESTMENTS〔工作的〕收入;〔投资的〕收益: *Most of my income goes on my rent.* 我的大部分收入都用来支付房租。| **be on a high/low income** *It's*

only reasonable that people on a high income should pay more tax. 高收入的人多纳税是合情合理的。| **live within your income** (=to not spend more than you earn) 量入为出 | **unearned income** (=income from property, INVESTMENTS etc) 非劳动收入, 非工资收入〔指来自财产、投资等的收入〕—compare 比较 EXPENDITURE (1) —see 见 PAY¹ (USAGE)

income tax /ˈ·· ·/ *n* [U] tax paid on the money that you earn (个人)所得税

in·com·ing /ˈɪnˌkʌmɪŋ; ˈɪnkʌmɪŋ/ *adj* [only before noun 仅用于名词前] **1** arriving or coming in 正到达的; 正进入的: *incoming flights* 正到达的航班 | *the incoming tide* 涨潮 **2** an incoming president, government etc has just been elected or chosen〔总统、政府等〕新当选的: *It is hoped that the incoming administration will inject some life into Capitol Hill.* 希望新一届政府能给国会注入一些活力。

in·com·mode /ˌɪnkəˋmod; ˌɪnkəˈməʊd/ *v* [T] *formal* to make a situation difficult for someone【正式】使〔某人〕不便; 妨碍

in·com·mo·di·ous /ˌɪnkəˋmodɪəs; ˌɪnkəˈməʊdiəs◂/ *adj formal* inconvenient, difficult, or uncomfortable【正式】不便的, 困难的, 不舒服的

in·com·mu·ni·ca·do /ˌɪnkəˌmjunɪˋkado; ˌɪnkəmju:nɪˈkɑ:dəʊ/ *adv* if you are kept incommunicado, you are kept in a place where you cannot see or talk to anyone else 不得与他人接触地: *The men were arrested and held incommunicado in prison camps.* 这些人被逮捕, 并被监禁在集中营, 不得与外界接触。

in·com·pa·ra·ble /ɪnˋkampərəbl̩; ɪnˈkɒmpərəbəl/ *adj* so good, beautiful etc that nothing else can even be compared to it 无可比拟的, 举世无双的: *a writer of incomparable prose* 举世无双的散文家 | *the incomparable view of San Marco* 圣马科美妙绝伦的景色—**incomparably** *adv*

in·com·pat·i·ble /ˌɪnkəmˋpætəbl̩; ˌɪnkəmˈpætɪ̈bəl◂/ *adj* **1** two people who are incompatible have completely different characters so that it is difficult for them to have a good relationship〔两个人〕不能和睦相处的, 合不来的: *God knows why they ever got married. They're totally incompatible!* 天知道他们为什么结为夫妻 —— 他们根本合不来! **2** two beliefs, statements, actions etc that are incompatible cannot exist or be accepted together because they are completely different〔观点、言论、行为等完全相左而〕不相容的, 不能共存的: [+**with**] *His business interests are incompatible with his presidential responsibilities.* 他的商业利益与他的总统职责是不相容的。**3** two things that are incompatible are of different types so that they cannot be used together 不相配的, 相互排斥的: *Their blood groups were incompatible.* 他们的血型不相配。—**incompatibly** *adv*—**incompatibility** /ˌɪnkəmˌpætəˋbɪlətɪ; ˌɪnkəmpætɪ̈ˈbɪlɪ̈ti/ *n* [U]

in·com·pe·tence /ɪnˋkampətəns; ɪnˈkɒmpɪ̈təns/ *n* [U] lack of the ability or skill to do your job properly 不胜任, 不称职: *The manager in charge was fired for incompetence.* 主管经理因不称职而被解雇。

in·com·pe·tent /ɪnˋkampətənt; ɪnˈkɒmpɪ̈tənt/ *adj* not having the ability or skill to do your job properly 不称职的, 不胜任的: *an incompetent teacher* 不称职的教师—**incompetent** *n* [C]—**incompetently** *adv*

in·com·plete /ˌɪnkəmˋplit; ˌɪnkəmˈpli:t◂/ *adj* **1** not having all its parts 不完全的, 不完整的: *Unfortunately I do not have the information because our records are incomplete.* 很遗憾, 由于我们的记录不完整, 我无法提供有关资料。**2** not completely finished 未完成的, 未结束的: *an incomplete process* 未完成的程序—**incompletely** *adv*—**incompleteness** *n* [U]

in·com·pre·hen·si·ble /ˌɪnkamprɪˋhɛnsəbl̩; ɪnˌkɒmprɪˈhensɪ̈bəl/ *adj* difficult or impossible to understand 难懂的, 不可理解的: *Legal documents are full of incomprehensible jargon.* 法律文书充满难懂的行话。| *I find your whole attitude quite incomprehensible.* 我觉得你的整个态度很难理解。—**incomprehensibly** *adv*—**incomprehensibility** /ˌɪnkamprɪˌhɛnsəˋbɪlətɪ; ɪnˌkɒmprɪhensɪ̈ˈbɪlɪ̈ti/ *n* [U]

in·com·pre·hen·sion /ˌɪnkamprɪˋhɛnʃən; ɪnˌkɒmprɪˈhenʃən/ *n* [U] the state of not being able to understand something 不理解, 不懂: *"Are you leaving me?" she cried, her face full of incomprehension and rage.* "你要离开我吗?" 她喊道, 一脸的迷惑和愤怒。

in·con·cei·va·ble /ˌɪnkənˋsivəbl̩; ˌɪnkənˈsi:vəbəl/ *adj* too strange or unusual to be thought real or possible 难以置信的, 不可思议的: *A few years ago a car fuelled by solar energy would have been inconceivable.* 几年前太阳能动力汽车是不可思议的。| **it is inconceivable that** *It seemed inconceivable that a man in such a powerful position could be so stupid.* 似乎难以想象一个身居要职的人竟会如此愚蠢。—**inconceivably** *adv*—**inconceivability** /ˌɪnkənˌsivəˋbɪlətɪ; ˌɪnkənsi:vəˈbɪlɪ̈ti/ *n* [U]

in·con·clu·sive /ˌɪnkənˋklusɪv; ˌɪnkənˈklu:sɪv◂/ *adj* not leading to a clear decision or result 非结论性的, 无确定结果的: *The evidence against the two men was inconclusive.* 针对两个人的不利证据并不令人信服。| *The talks were inconclusive and both parties agreed to further meetings.* 会谈没有取得结果, 双方同意继续会晤。—**inconclusively** *adv*—**inconclusiveness** *n* [U]

in·con·gru·i·ty /ˌɪnkaŋˋgruətɪ; ˌɪnkənˈgru:ɪ̈ti/ *n* **1** [U] strangeness, especially in being unsuitable, unusual, or unexpected in relation to the things around〔与环境〕不协调, 不合适, 不相称: *He was suddenly struck by the incongruity of drinking champagne out of plastic glasses.* 他突然感到用塑料杯喝香槟酒很不协调。**2** [C] an act or event which seems strange or unsuitable because it seems very different from what is happening around it〔与环境〕不相称; 不协调的行为[事件]

in·con·gru·ous /ɪnˋkaŋgruəs; ɪnˈkɒŋgruəs/ *adj* something that is incongruous seems strange and unsuitable because it is so unexpected in a particular situation and so different from everything around it 不协调的, 不相称的: *The modern building looked incongruous in such a quaint old village.* 这座现代化建筑与这个古老雅致的村庄显得格格不入。—**incongruously** *adv*—**incongruousness** *n* [U]

in·con·se·quen·tial /ˌɪnkansəˋkwɛnʃəl; ɪnˌkɒnsɪ̈ˈkwenʃəl◂/ *adj* not important; INSIGNIFICANT 不重要的; 微不足道的: *He made a few inconsequential remarks before moving on to the next guests.* 他寒暄了几句后便去招呼下一批客人。—**inconsequentially** *adv*

in·con·sid·e·ra·ble /ˌɪnkənˋsɪdərəbl̩; ˌɪnkənˈsɪdərəbəl◂/ *adj* **not inconsiderable** *formal* fairly large or important【正式】相当大的; 相当重要的: *He has built up a not inconsiderable business empire.* 他已建立起一个规模非同小可的商业帝国。

in·con·sid·er·ate /ˌɪnkənˋsɪdərɪt; ˌɪnkənˈsɪdərɪ̈t◂/ *adj* not caring about the feelings, needs or comfort of other people 不考虑他人的, 不为别人着想的: *It was inconsiderate of him to keep us waiting like that.* 让我们等这么久, 他太不体谅人了。—**inconsiderately** *adv*

in·con·sis·ten·cy /ˌɪnkənˋsɪstənsɪ; ˌɪnkənˈsɪstənsi◂/ *n* **1** [U] changes in someone's behaviour or reactions that make their ideas, wishes etc unclear〔行为或反应的〕反复无常, 出尔反尔: *Inconsistency in management creates unnecessary anxieties among the workforce.* 管理层的出尔反尔在员工中造成了不必要的忧虑。**2** [C usually plural 一般用复数] two statements that cannot both be true because they each state the facts differently〔两个说法〕不协调, 不一致, 前后矛盾: *There were several inconsistencies in his report.* 他的报告中有几处前后矛盾。

in·con·sis·tent /ˌɪnkənˋsɪstənt; ˌɪnkənˈsɪstənt◂/ *adj* **1** ideas or statements that are inconsistent cannot be accepted or believed together because they each state the facts differently〔指主意、说法〕不一致的, 前后矛盾的: *The accounts of the witnesses are inconsistent.* 几位目击者的说法并不一致。| [+**with**] *What the Government says now is inconsistent with its election promises.* 政府现在的说法与竞选时的许诺互相矛盾。**2** **be inconsistent with** behaviour that is inconsistent with a particular set of principles or standards is not right according to those principles etc〔行为〕与〔原则、标准〕相悖的, 不相称的: [+**with**] *conduct inconsistent with what is expected of a congressman* 与人们对议员的期望不相称的行为 **3** inconsistent behaviour, work etc changes too often from good to bad or from situation to situation〔行为、工作等〕时好时坏的, 变化无常的: *The team's performance has been highly inconsistent this season.* 该队在本赛季的发挥极不稳定。| *an inconsistent approach to discipline* 前后不一的处罚手段

in·con·so·la·ble /ˌɪnkənˋsoləbl̩; ˌɪnkənˈsəʊləbəl◂/ *adj* so sad that it is impossible for anyone to comfort you〔悲痛至极而〕无法安慰的, 伤心欲绝的: *The boy was inconsolable after the death of his dog.* 小狗死后, 那个男孩伤心不已。—**inconsolably** *adv*: *weeping inconsolably* 哭个不停

in·con·spic·u·ous /ˌɪnkənˋspɪkjuəs; ˌɪnkənˈspɪkjuəs◂/ *adj* not easily seen or noticed 不显眼的, 不引人注意的: *She put on an inconspicuous grey dress, hoping she wouldn't be seen in the crowd.* 她穿了一条不显眼的灰色连衣裙, 希望在人群中不会被发现。—**inconspicuously** *adv*—**inconspicuousness** *n* [U]

in·con·stant /ɪnˋkanstənt; ɪnˈkɒnstənt/ *adj formal* unfaithful in love or friendship【正式】〔对友谊或爱情〕不忠实的: *She was charming, but an inconstant and unreliable friend.* 她很可爱, 但她不是一个忠实可靠的朋友。—**inconstancy** *n* [U]

in·con·tes·ta·ble /ˌɪnkənˋtɛstəbl̩; ˌɪnkənˈtestəbəl◂/ *adj* clearly true and impossible to disagree with; INDISPUTABLE 无可

I

否认的；不可争辩的：*incontestable evidence of her innocence* 她无罪的铁证 —**incontestably** *adv* —**incontestability** /ˌɪnkən-ˌtɛstəˋbɪlətɪ; ˌɪnkəntestəˈbɪlɪ̥ti/ *n* [U]

in·con·ti·nent /ɪnˋkɑntənənt; ɪnˈkɒntɪ̥nənt/ *adj* **1** unable to control the passing of food waste from your body〔大小便〕失禁的 **2** *old use* unable to control your sexual urges【旧】〔性冲动〕不能控制的；荒淫的 —**incontinence** *n* [U]

in·con·tro·ver·ti·ble /ˌɪnkɑntrəˋvɝtəbl̩; ɪnˌkɒntrəˈvɜːtɪ̥bəl/ *adj* a fact that is incontrovertible is definitely true and no one can prove it to be false; INDISPUTABLE 不容置疑的；无可辩驳的：*The photograph provides incontrovertible evidence that Martin was at the scene of the crime.* 这张照片提供了案发时马丁在场的确凿证据。—**incontrovertibly** *adv* —**incontrovertability** /ɪnˌkɑntrəvɝtəˋbɪlətɪ; ɪnˌkɒntrəvɜːtəˈbɪlɪ̥ti/ *n* [U]

in·con·ve·ni·ence[1] /ˌɪnkənˋvinjəns; ˌɪnkənˈviːniəns/ *n* **1** [C] something that causes you problems or difficulty 不便之处；麻烦事：*Compared to the trouble we've had in the past, this is only a minor inconvenience.* 与我们过去遇到的困难相比，这不过是个小麻烦。**2** [U] the state of having problems or difficulty 麻烦；不便：*We hope the delay has not caused any inconvenience to our customers.* 希望这次延误没有给我们的顾客带来任何不便。

inconvenience[2] *v* [T] to cause someone problems or difficulty 给〔某人〕带来不便；添麻烦；打扰：*I hope it won't inconvenience you to drive me to the station.* 我希望你开车送我去车站不会给你添麻烦。

in·con·ve·ni·ent /ˌɪnkənˋvinjənt; ˌɪnkənˈviːnjənt◂/ *adj* causing problems or difficulty, often in a way that is annoying; not CONVENIENT 带来麻烦的；不方便的：*It's a bit inconvenient for me to get to the centre of town. Can we meet somewhere else?* 我去市中心有点不方便，我们能否换个地方会面？| *an inconvenient time* 不方便的时间 —**inconveniently** *adv*

in·cor·po·rate /ɪnˋkɔrpəˌret; ɪnˈkɔːpəreɪt/ *v* [T] to include something as part of a group, system, plan etc 把〔某物〕并入，包含；吸收：**incorporate sth into/in** *We've incorporated many environmentally-friendly features into the design of the building.* 我们在这座建筑的设计中加进了许多环保特点。| *Our original proposals were not incorporated in the new legislation.* 新立法没有包括我们当初的提议。—**incorporation** /ɪnˌkɔrpəˋreʃən; ɪnˌkɔːpəˈreɪʃən/ *n* [U]

in·cor·po·rat·ed /ɪnˋkɔrpəˌretɪd; ɪnˈkɔːpəreɪtɪ̥d/ written abbreviation 缩写为 **Inc** *adj* used after the name of a company in the US to show that it has become a CORPORATION (1) 股份有限的〔在美国用于公司名称后，表示成为法人组织〕

in·cor·po·re·al /ˌɪnkɔrˋpɔrɪəl; ˌɪnkɔːˈpɔːriəl/ *adj formal* not existing in any physical form but only as a spirit【正式】无形体的；非实体的，精神的 —**incorporeally** *adv*

in·cor·rect /ˌɪnkəˋrɛkt; ˌɪnkəˈrekt◂/ *adj* **1** not correct or true 不正确的；不真实的：*incorrect spelling* 错误的拼写 **2** not following the rules of polite behaviour〔行为〕不恰当的，不合礼节的 —**incorrectly** *adv* —**incorrectness** *n* [U]

in·cor·ri·gi·ble /ɪnˋkɔrɪdʒəbl̩; ɪnˈkɒrɪ̥dʒɪ̥bəl/ *adj often humorous* someone who is incorrigible is bad in a way that cannot be changed or improved【常幽默】〔人〕屡教不改的，无可救药的：**an incorrigible liar/gambler/rogue etc** *Peter, you are an incorrigible flirt!* 彼得，你总喜欢跟女人调情，真是无可救药！—**incorrigibly** *adv*

in·cor·rup·ti·ble /ˌɪnkəˋrʌptəbl̩; ˌɪnkəˈrʌptɪ̥bəl◂/ *adj* **1** too honest to be influenced by anything that is illegal or morally wrong 诚实正直的，刚正不阿的，廉洁的：*A good judge must be incorruptible.* 好法官必须廉洁。**2** *formal* material that is incorruptible will never decay and cannot be destroyed【正式】〔物质〕不腐蚀的，不会毁坏的：*Gold was precious because it was incorruptible.* 黄金不会腐蚀，所以珍贵。—**incorruptibly** *adv*: *incorruptibly honest* 廉洁正直的 —**incorruptibility** /ˌɪnkəˌrʌptəˋbɪlətɪ; ˌɪnkərʌptɪ̥ˈbɪlɪ̥ti/ *n* [U] —see also 另见 CORRUPT[1]

in·crease[1] /ɪnˋkris; ɪnˈkriːs/ *v* **1** [I] to become larger in amount, number, or degree 增加，增大，增强：*The population of London increased dramatically in the first half of the 20th century.* 20世纪上半叶，伦敦的人口大幅度地增长。| *The pain increased steadily until I could think of nothing else.* 疼痛越来越剧烈，弄得我只觉得痛，别的什么事情都想不了！| **increase in value/price/importance etc** *Investments are certain to increase in value.* 投资一定会增值。| **[+by]** *Food prices increased by 10% in less than a year.* 不到一年，食品价格就上涨了10%。—see 见 RAISE[1] (USAGE) **2** [T] to make something larger in amount, number, or degree 使增加；使增大，使增强：*Now they want to increase our rents!* 如今他们要提高我们的房租！| *political tensions that might increase the likelihood of a nuclear war* 可能引发核战争的紧张政局 —**increasing** *adj*: *There is increasing difficulty in finding trained staff.* 越来越难找到训练有素的职员了。—opposite 反义词 DECREASE[1] —compare 比较 REDUCE

in·crease[2] /ˋɪnkris; ˈɪnkriːs/ *n* [C,U] a rise in amount, number, or degree 增加，增强，增大：**[+in]** *an increase in the crime rate* 犯罪率的上升 | **pay/price/tax increase** *Recent tax increases have affected the poor more than the rich.* 新近提高的税收对穷人的影响比富人大。| **be on the increase** (=be increasing) 正在增加 *Diseases like TB and pneumonia are on the increase.* 像肺结核、肺炎这样的疾病正在增加。

in·creased /ɪnˋkrist; ɪnˈkriːst/ *adj* larger than before 增强的，增大的：*an increased awareness of the risks involved* 对相关风险已有所提高的警惕

in·creas·ing·ly /ɪnˋkrisɪŋlɪ; ɪnˈkriːsɪŋli/ *adv* more and more all the time [+adj/adv] 不断增加地，越来越多地：*The classes at the college have become increasingly full over the past five years.* 在过去的五年中，这所学院的各班级越来越满。| [sentence adverb 句子副词] *Increasingly, it is the industrial power of Japan and South East Asia that dominates world markets.* 主宰世界市场的是日本和东南亚的工业实力，这一情况日益明显。

in·cred·i·ble /ɪnˋkrɛdəbl̩; ɪnˈkredɪ̥bəl/ *adj* **1** too strange to be believed or very difficult to believe 不可相信的，难以置信的：*She told us the incredible story of her 134 days lost in the desert.* 她向我们讲述了在沙漠迷途了134天的惊人经历。| *It's incredible how much Tom has changed since he met Sally.* 汤姆自认识萨莉后，他的变化之大让人难以置信。**2** extremely good or extremely large 极好的；极大的：*Tony has an incredible singing voice.* 托尼唱歌嗓音好极了。| *They stock an incredible range of goods.* 他们进货的范围简直无所不包。—**incredibility** /ˌɪnkrɛdəˋbɪlətɪ; ɪnˌkredɪ̥ˈbɪlɪ̥ti/ *n* [U]

Incredible Hulk, the /·,··· ˈ·/ a character in a US COMIC (=a magazine with stories told in pictures), television programmes, and films. The Incredible Hulk is a man who changes into a very large green creature who has great strength, usually when he becomes angry about someone else's cruel or evil behaviour. 绿巨人浩克〔美国连环漫画杂志、电视节目和影片中的一个人物。对他人的残忍或邪恶行为感到愤怒时，他就会变成一个力大无比的绿色庞然大物〕

in·cred·i·bly /ɪnˋkrɛdəblɪ; ɪnˈkredɪ̥bli/ *adv* **1** [+adj/adv] extremely 极端地，非常地：*I'm sorry I haven't phoned. I've been incredibly busy this week.* 很对不起没有打电话，我这周简直忙得焦头烂额。**2** [sentence adverb 句子副词] in a way that is hard to believe 难以置信地：*Incredibly, even though the car was a write-off, he wasn't hurt at all.* 车都报废了，他却毫发未损，真不可思议。

in·cre·du·li·ty /ˌɪnkrəˋdjulətɪ; ˌɪnkrɪ̥ˈdjuːlɪ̥ti/ *n* [U] a feeling that you cannot believe something; DISBELIEF 不相信；怀疑：*Matt's comment brought a look of complete incredulity to Jill's face.* 马特的话使得吉尔满脸狐疑。

in·cred·u·lous /ɪnˋkrɛdʒələs; ɪnˈkredjɪ̥ləs/ *adj* unable or unwilling to believe something 不能相信的；不愿相信的：*He raised his eyebrows and gave me an incredulous look.* 他眉毛一扬，用怀疑的神色看了我一眼。—**incredulously** *adv*

in·cre·ment /ˋɪŋkrəmənt; ˈɪŋkrɪ̥mənt/ *n* [C] **1** an amount that is regularly added to the amount that someone is paid each year〔每年薪金定期的〕增加，增额：*The starting salary is £10,000, but with increments it can rise to £16,500.* 起薪1万英镑，通过年度加薪，可增加到1.65万英镑。**2** the amount by which a number, value, or amount increases〔数字、价值、数量的〕增加额 —**incremental** *adj*

in·crim·i·nate /ɪnˋkrɪməˌnet; ɪnˈkrɪmɪ̥neɪt/ *v* [T] to make someone seem guilty of a crime 使〔某人〕显得有罪；连累，牵连：*He refused to speak because he was worried that he would incriminate himself.* 他因担心自己受到牵连而拒绝讲话。| *incriminating evidence* 可显示有罪的证据 —**incrimination** /ɪnˌkrɪməˋneʃən; ɪnˌkrɪmɪ̥ˈneɪʃən/ *n* [U]

in·crim·i·na·to·ry /ɪnˋkrɪmənəˌtorɪ; ɪnˈkrɪmɪ̥nətəri/ *adj* making someone seem to be guilty 使〔某人〕显得有罪的

in-crowd, the /ˈ· ·/ *n* a small group of people who are admired by other people, for example because they are very fashionable, and who do not let many other people join them〔因时髦等受到羡慕但排外的〕小集团；小圈子：*I was never one of the in-crowd at school.* 我在学校从来没有参加过小圈子。

in·crus·ta·tion /ˌɪnkrʌsˋteʃən; ˌɪnkrʌsˈteɪʃən/ *n* [C] an amount of dirt, salt etc which forms a hard layer on a surface〔在表面形成的一层硬的〕凝结物；积垢，沉积物：**[+of]** *an incrustation of salt on the bottom of the boat* 船底部的盐垢

in·cu·bate /ˋɪŋkjəˌbet; ˈɪŋkjɪ̥beɪt/ *v* [I,T] **1** if a bird incubates its eggs or if they incubate, they are kept warm by the bird until

the young birds come out 孵〔蛋〕;〔蛋〕被孵化 **2** [I,T] *technical* if a disease incubates, or if you incubate it, it develops in your body until you show physical signs of it【术语】〔疾病在体内〕潜伏

in·cu·ba·tion /ˌɪnkjəˋbeʃən; ˌɪŋkjʊˈbeɪʃən/ *n* [U] the period between becoming infected with a disease and showing the first physical signs of it〔疾病的〕潜伏期

incubator 恒温箱

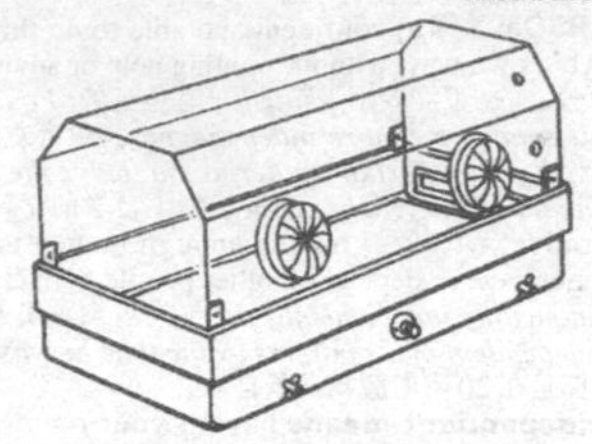

in·cu·ba·tor /ˋɪnkjəˌbetɚ; ˈɪŋkjʊbeɪtə/ *n* [C] **1** a heated container for keeping eggs warm until the young birds etc come out 孵化器, 孵化箱 **2** a piece of hospital equipment used for keeping very small or weak babies alive〔用于放置很小或体弱初生婴儿的〕恒温箱

in·cu·bus /ˋɪŋkjəbəs; ˈɪŋkjʊbəs/ *n* [C] **1** someone or something that causes a lot of worries 造成严重忧虑的人[事] **2** a male DEVIL that is supposed to have sex with a sleeping woman 梦淫妖〔传说与睡梦中的女人交合的妖怪〕—compare 比较 SUCCUBUS **3** *literary* a bad dream; NIGHTMARE (1)【文】噩梦, 梦魇

in·cul·cate /ɪnˋkʌlket; ˈɪŋkʌlkeɪt/ *v* [T] *formal* to fix ideas, principles etc in someone's mind【正式】灌输〔观念、原则等〕, 教诲: **inculcate sth in/into** *She tries very hard to inculcate traditional values into her students.* 她想方设法给学生灌输传统的价值观。| **inculcate sb with sth** *Schools inculcate children with patriotic ideas from an early age.* 学校从孩子年幼开始就向他们灌输爱国思想。—**inculcation** /ˌɪnkʌlˋkeʃən; ˌɪŋkʌlˈkeɪʃən/ *n* [U]

in·cul·pate /ɪnˋkʌlpet; ˈɪŋkʌlpeɪt/ *v* [T] *formal* to show that someone is guilty of a crime【正式】显示〔某人〕有罪

in·cum·ben·cy /ɪnˋkʌmbənsɪ; ɪnˈkʌmbənsi/ *n* [C] *formal* the period of time during which someone is an incumbent【正式】〔特指政治职位的〕任期

in·cum·bent[1] /ɪnˋkʌmbənt; ɪnˈkʌmbənt/ *n* [C] *formal*【正式】**1** someone in an official position, especially a political one 任职者, 现任者〔尤指政治职位〕: *Castillo was to be the new incumbent at the City Controller's office.* 卡斯蒂略当时即将就任城市审计办公室的新主管。**2** a priest who is in charge of a church〔掌管教堂的〕牧师

incumbent[2] *adj formal*【正式】**1 it is incumbent upon sb to do sth** if it is incumbent upon you to do something, it is your duty or responsibility to do it 做某事是某人的职务[责任]: *It is incumbent upon the teacher to maintain discipline.* 教师有责任维护纪律。**2 the incumbent president/priest/Senator etc** the president etc at the present time 现任的总统/牧师/参议员等

in·cur /ɪnˋkɝ; ɪnˈkɜː/ *v* **incurred, incurring** [T] **1** to put yourself in an unpleasant situation by your own actions, so that you lose something, get punished etc〔因自己的举动而〕招致〔不愉快的事〕; 招惹, 遭受: **incur losses/debts etc** *Milton incurred debts of over $300,000.* 米尔顿负债三十多万美元。| **incur sb's anger/disapproval etc** *We incurred her displeasure.* 我们把她惹得很不高兴。**2 incur expenses** to have to spend money on something 招致花费

in·cur·a·ble /ɪnˋkjurəbḷ; ɪnˈkjʊərəbəl/ *adj* **1** impossible to cure 无法治愈的, 不可救药的: *an incurable disease* 不治之症 **2** impossible to change 不可改变的: *My mother is an incurable optimist.* 我母亲是个不可动摇的乐天派。—**incurably** *adv*: *incurably romantic* 无可救药地浪漫 —**incurable** *n* [C]

in·cu·ri·ous /ɪnˋkjurɪəs; ɪnˈkjʊəriəs/ *adj formal* not naturally interested in finding out about the things around you【正式】〔对周围〕没有好奇心的, 不感兴趣的: *The child watched with an incurious gaze.* 那个小孩用漠然的眼神看着。

in·cur·sion /ɪnˋkɝʒən; ɪnˈkɜːʃən/ *n* [C] *formal*【正式】**1** a sudden attack into an area that belongs to other people 突袭; 侵入, 侵犯: *a British and French incursion into China in 1857* 1857 年英法联军侵入中国 **2** the unwanted arrival of something in a place where it does not belong〔不受欢迎的〕进入〔其他地方〕; 来到: *the incursion of tabloid-style reporting into such a famous newspaper* 小报式的报道对如此著名的一家报纸的入侵

in·debt·ed /ɪnˋdɛtɪd; ɪnˈdetɪ̣d/ *adj* **be indebted to** to be very grateful to someone for the help they have given you 对〔某人给予帮助而〕感激的: **greatly/deeply indebted** *I am indebted to my husband for helping me edit the book.* 我很感激我丈夫帮助我编辑这本书。—**indebtedness** *n* [U]

in·de·cen·cy /ɪnˋdisṇsɪ; ɪnˈdiːsənsi/ *n* [U] *law* behaviour that is sexually offensive, especially INDECENT EXPOSURE【法律】猥亵; 下流〔尤指猥亵的裸露〕: *gross indecency* 低级下流

in·de·cent /ɪnˋdisṇt; ɪnˈdiːsənt/ *adj* **1** indecent behaviour, movements, clothes etc are likely to shock or offend people, because they involve sex or because they show parts of the body that are usually covered〔行为、动作、衣着等〕下流的, 猥亵的: *You can't go to a dinner party in that dress – it's positively indecent!* 你不能穿那种衣服参加宴会, 太不雅观了! **2** not acceptable 不合适的, 不适当的: *The funeral formalities were performed with almost indecent haste.* 葬礼几乎是草率了事。—**indecently** *adv*: *indecently dressed* 穿着不体面的

indecent as·sault /ˌ· ·ˋ·/ *n* [C,U] *law* an attack on a person which includes sexual violence【法律】强暴猥亵行为

indecent ex·po·sure /ˌ· ·ˋ··/ *n* [U] *law* the criminal offence of deliberately showing your sex organs in a place where this is likely to offend people【法律】猥亵暴露, 露阴〔指故意裸露性器官〕—see also 另见 FLASHER

in·de·ci·pher·a·ble /ˌɪndɪˋsaɪfərəbḷ; ˌɪndɪˈsaɪfərəbəl◂/ *adj* impossible to read or understand 难以辨认的, 难以读懂的: *an indecipherable signature* 难以辨认的签名

in·de·ci·sion /ˌɪndɪˋsɪʒən; ˌɪndɪˈsɪʒən/ *n* [U] the state of being unable to decide what to do 犹豫不决; 无决断能力; 优柔寡断: *tortured by doubt and indecision* 饱受疑惑和优柔寡断的折磨

in·de·ci·sive /ˌɪndɪˋsaɪsɪv; ˌɪndɪˈsaɪsɪv◂/ *adj* **1** unable to make clear decisions or choices 不果断的, 犹豫不决的: *an indecisive leader* 优柔寡断的领导人 **2** having an unclear result; INCONCLUSIVE 结果不明确的; 非结论性的: *a confused indecisive battle* 不分胜负的一场混战 —**indecisively** *adv* —**indecisiveness** *n* [U]

in·dec·o·rous /ɪnˋdɛkərəs; ɪnˈdekərəs/ *adj formal* behaving in a way that is not polite or socially acceptable【正式】不礼貌的; 不得体的, 不雅的 —**indecorously** *adv*

in·deed /ɪnˋdid; ɪnˈdiːd/ *adv* **1** [sentence adverb 句子副词] used to emphasize a statement or answer 当然, 确实〔用于强调陈述或答案〕: *"Would it help if you had an assistant?" "It would, indeed."* "你要是有个助手, 会有帮助吗?""那是肯定的。"| *There are few, if indeed any, authors with such a gift for dialogue.* 写对话有如此天赋的作家, 即使真的有, 也十分少。**2** *formal* used to introduce additional information that emphasizes what you have just said【正式】甚至; 其实〔用来补充内容, 强调刚说过的话〕: *I didn't mind at all. Indeed, I was pleased.* 我一点也不介意, 事实上我非常高兴。**3** *especially BrE* used to emphasize the word 'very' in expressions such as 'very good indeed' and 'very much indeed'【尤英】确实, 实在〔在 very good indeed 和 very much indeed 这类的短语中用来强调 very〕: *I am very sorry indeed for my foolish behaviour.* 我对自己的愚蠢行为深感抱歉。| *Thank you very much indeed.* 万分感谢。**4** *especially BrE spoken* used to express disbelief, surprise, or annoyance at something you have been told【尤英, 口】真的, 真是〔表示对所听到消息的怀疑、惊讶、恼火等〕: *"He's taken a three hour lunch break." "Has he, indeed?"* "他午间休息了三个小时。""他真的这样做?" | *"Why would anyone say such a horrible thing?" "Why, indeed?"* "怎么会有人说这样恶劣的话?""是呀, 怎么会呢?"

in·de·fat·i·ga·ble /ˌɪndɪˋfætɪgəbḷ; ˌɪndɪˈfætɪgəbəl/ *adj formal* determined and never becoming tired【正式】坚定的, 坚持不懈的: *an indefatigable campaigner for human rights* 不屈不挠的人权运动者 —**indefatigably** *adv*

in·de·fen·si·ble /ˌɪndɪˋfɛnsəbḷ; ˌɪndɪˈfensɪ̣bəl◂/ *adj* **1** too bad to be excused or defended 不可原谅的; 无法辩解的: *indefensible behaviour* 不可原谅的行为 **2** impossible or very difficult to defend from military attack〔对武装攻击〕无法防御的, 无法保卫的 —**indefensibly** *adv*

in·de·fi·na·ble /ˌɪndɪˋfaɪnəbḷ; ˌɪndɪˈfaɪnəbəl◂/ *adj* an indefinable feeling, quality etc is difficult to describe or explain〔情感、品质等〕难以描述的, 难以解释的: *She felt a sudden indefinable sadness.* 她突然感到一种难以名状的悲伤。—**indefinably** *adv*

in·def·i·nite /ɪnˋdɛfənɪt; ɪnˈdefənɪ̣t/ *adj* **1** an indefinite action or period of time has no definite end arranged for it〔行动

或时间〕无限期的: *an indefinite ban on imports of gold* 无限期禁止黄金进口的禁令 **2** not clear or definite; VAGUE 不清楚的, 不明确的; 模糊的: *indefinite opinions* 模糊不清的意见 —**indefiniteness** *n* [U]

indefinite ar·ti·cle /ˌ... ˈ.../ *n* [C] the word 'a' or 'an' in the English language or a word in another language that is used like 'a' or 'an' 不定冠词〔如英语中的 a 或 an, 以及其他语言中与 a 或 an 功能相似的词语〕—compare 比较 DEFINITE ARTICLE —see also 另见 ARTICLE (4)

in·def·i·nite·ly /ɪnˋdɛfənɪtlɪ; ɪnˈdefənətli/ *adv* **1** for a period of time for which no definite end has been arranged 无限期地: *Negotiations have been suspended indefinitely.* 谈判已无限期中止。**2** without giving clear or exact details〔细节〕不清楚地; 模糊粗略地

in·del·i·ble /ɪnˋdɛləbḷ; ɪnˈdeləbəl/ *adj* **1** impossible to remove or forget; permanent 难以去掉的, 难以忘记的; 永恒的: *The teacher's words left an indelible impression on me for years to come.* 在后来的岁月里, 老师的话让我难以忘怀。**2 indelible ink/pencil/marker etc** ink etc that makes a permanent mark which cannot be removed 不退色墨水/铅笔/记号笔等 —**indelibly** *adv*: *a moment indelibly imprinted on my mind* 刻骨铭心的一刻

in·del·i·cate /ɪnˋdɛləkət; ɪnˈdeləkət/ *adj* likely to embarrass or shock people 令人窘迫的; 令人震惊的: *He made an indelicate remark at the dinner table.* 他在饭桌上说了一些很粗鄙的话。—**indelicately** *adv* —**indelicacy** *n* [U]

in·dem·ni·fi·ca·tion /ɪnˌdɛmnəfəˋkeʃən; ɪnˌdemnəfəˈkeɪʃən/ *n law*【法律】**1** [U+for/against] the act of paying, or promising to pay, someone for loss, injury, or damage〔对所受损失、损伤或损坏的〕赔偿; 赔偿承诺 **2** [C,U+for] a payment made to someone for loss, injury or damage 赔偿金, 赔款

in·dem·ni·fy /ɪnˋdɛmnəˌfaɪ; ɪnˈdemnəfaɪ/ *v* **indemnified, indemnifying** [T] *law*【法律】**1** [+against/for] to promise to pay someone if something they possess is damaged or lost 保证〔遇损坏或损失时〕赔偿 **2** [+for] to pay someone money because of loss, injury, or damage that they have suffered 赔偿〔损失、伤害、损毁等〕, 补偿

in·dem·ni·ty /ɪnˋdɛmnətɪ; ɪnˈdemnəti/ *n law*【法律】**1** [U] protection against loss or damage, especially in the form of a promise to pay for any losses or damage〔尤指以保证赔偿形式的〕保障, 保护 **2** [C] a payment for the loss of money, goods etc 赔偿金

in·dent¹ /ɪnˋdɛnt; ɪnˈdent/ *v* **1** [T] to start a line of writing further towards the middle of the page than other lines〔在书写的一行中〕缩格 **2** [I+for] *especially BrE* to order goods by writing on an official form【尤英】〔填写订单〕订购

in·dent² /ˋɪndɛnt; ˈɪndent/ *n* [C+for] *especially BrE*【尤英】**1** an order for goods to be sent abroad, or for supplies for an army 出口订货; 军需订货 **2** an official written order for goods 正式书面订货单

in·den·ta·tion /ˌɪndɛnˋteʃən; ˌɪndenˈteɪʃən/ *n* [C] **1** a cut into the surface or edge of something 凹口, 凹陷, 缺口: *The bite left deep indentations.* 这一咬留下了深深的齿痕。**2** a space at the beginning of a line of writing〔书写时的〕行首空格 **3** [C,U] the act of indenting 缩格, 缩排

in·dent·ed /ɪnˋdɛntɪd; ɪnˈdentəd/ *adj* an indented edge or surface has cuts or marks in it〔边缘或表面呈〕锯齿状的; 有凹痕的: *a deeply indented coastline* 蜿蜒曲折的海岸线

in·den·ture /ɪnˋdɛntʃɚ; ɪnˈdentʃə/ also 又作 **indentures** *plural* — *n* [C] a formal contract, especially in former times, between an APPRENTICE¹ and his master〔旧时的〕正式师徒契约

in·de·pen·dence /ˌɪndɪˋpɛndəns; ˌɪndəˈpendəns/ *n* [U] **1** political freedom from control by the government of another country 政治独立: [+from] *Nigeria gained independence from Britain in 1960.* 尼日利亚于 1960 年脱离英国独立。| *minority groups striving for political independence* 追求政治独立的少数民族 **2** the time when a country becomes politically independent 国家取得独立的时期: *The country has made great advances since independence.* 该国自独立以来发展迅速。**3** the freedom and ability to make your own decisions in life, without having to ask other people for permission, help, or money〔个人生活的〕独立, 自主: *financial independence* 经济独立 | *I was enjoying a new feeling of independence.* 我沉浸在一种独立自主的崭新感觉之中。

Independence Day /ˌ...ˌ. ˌ./ *n* [singular] the FOURTH OF JULY 美国独立纪念日〔7 月 4 日〕

Independence Hall /ˌ.... ˈ./ a building in Philadelphia, Pennsylvania, where the American *Declaration of Independence* was signed. Many tourists visit it. 独立厅〔宾夕法尼亚州费城一建筑。在此曾签署过美国《独立宣言》。有许多游客前往参观〕

in·de·pen·dent /ˌɪndɪˋpɛndənt; ˌɪndəˈpendənt◂/ *adj*

1 ►COUNTRY/ORGANIZATION 国家/机构◄ [no comparative 无比较级] not governed or controlled by another country or organization 独立的, 自主的: *India became independent in 1947.* 印度于 1947 年独立。| *The independent role of the Police Commission must never be compromised.* 警务委员会的独立身份绝对不能受到损害。| **independent school/broadcasting etc** *especially BrE* (=not owned or paid for by the government)【尤英】民办[私立]学校/独立广播等

2 ►PERSON 人◄ **a)** confident and able to do things by yourself in your own way, without wanting help or advice from other people 独立的, 不需要别人帮助的; 有主见的: *I quite like living alone, it's made me more independent.* 我很喜欢独居, 这样我能更加独立。| [+of] *study material that helps the student to be independent of the teacher* 有助于学生自学的学习材料 **b)** [no comparative 无比较级] having enough money to live so that you do not have to depend on other people 经济自立的, 自力谋生的: *financially independent* 经济自立的 | [+of] *Robert aimed to be independent of his parents by the time he was twenty.* 罗伯特的目标是在 20 岁时脱离父母自立。

3 of independent means having your own income from property, INVESTMENTS etc 靠财产、投资等获取个人收入的: *a woman of independent means* 自立谋生有自己收入的女人

4 independent inquiry/opinion/advice etc something that is done or given by people who are not involved in a particular situation and who can therefore be trusted to be fair in judging it 独立的调查/观点/建议等: *There have been demands for an independent inquiry into allegations of police misconduct.* 有人要求对警方涉嫌滥用职权的指控进行独立调查。

5 ►SEPARATE 分离的◄ existing separately and not connected with or influenced by any others 独立的; 不受别人影响的: *Three independent studies in three different countries all arrived at the same conclusion.* 在三个不同国家独立进行的三项研究得出了相同的结论。| [+of] *reports from two separate sources entirely independent of one another* 根据两个完全独立的信息来源所作的报道 —**independently** *adv*: *two systems that operate independently of each other* 两套独立运行的系统

Independent *n* [C] a politician who does not belong to a political party 无党派政治家

Independent, The *trademark* a serious British newspaper which generally supports liberal political ideas. The same company produces a similar paper on Sundays, called *The Independent on Sunday*.【商标】《独立报》〔英国支持自由党政治主张的严肃类日报。这家报社周末还出版同类报纸, 即《星期日独立报》〕

independent clause /ˌ.... ˈ./ *n* [C] *technical* a CLAUSE (2) which can make a sentence by itself, for example 'she went home' in the sentence 'She went home because she was tired.'; MAIN CLAUSE【术语】独立从句〔即能独立成句的从句, 如 She went home because she was tired. 中的 she went home; 也称主句〕

in-depth /ˋ. ./ *adj* [only before noun 仅用于名词前] **in-depth study/investigation/report etc** an examination or description of something that is thorough and complete so that all the details are considered 深入的研究/调查/报道等: *scientists doing an in-depth study of the causes of lung cancer* 正在对肺癌病因作深入研究的科学家

in·de·scri·ba·ble /ˌɪndɪˋskraɪbəbḷ; ˌɪndɪsˈkraɪbəbəl◂/ *adj* something that is indescribable is so terrible, so good, so strange etc that you cannot describe it, or it is too difficult to describe 难以名状的; 无法形容的: *a feeling of indescribable joy* 难以形容的喜悦 | *There was an indescribable tension in the room.* 房间内有一种难以名状的紧张气氛。—**indescribably** *adv*: *indescribably squalid conditions* 难以形容的肮脏环境

in·de·struc·ti·ble /ˌɪndɪˋstrʌktəbl; ˌɪndɪˈstrʌktəbəl◂/ *adj* too strong to be destroyed 不可摧毁的; 坚不可摧的: *indestructible optimism* 坚定不移的乐观精神 | *These toys are great because they're practically indestructible.* 这些玩具真不错, 几乎怎么玩都不坏。—**indestructibly** *adv* —**indestructibility** /ˌɪndɪˌstrʌktəˋbɪlətɪ; ˌɪndɪstrʌktəˈbɪləti/ *n* [U]

in·de·ter·mi·na·ble /ˌɪndɪˋtɝmɪnəbl; ˌɪndɪˈtɜːmənəbəl◂/ *adj* impossible to find out or calculate exactly 难以查明的; 无法准确计算的: *water of indeterminable depth* 深不可测的水域 —**indeterminably** *adv*

in·de·ter·mi·nate /ˌɪndɪˋtɝmənɪt; ˌɪndɪˈtɜːmənət◂/ *adj* impossible to know about definitely or exactly 难以肯定的, 无法确定的: *a girl of indeterminate age* 年龄难以确定的女孩 —**indeterminately** *adv* —**indeterminacy** *n* [U]

in·dex¹ /ˋɪndɛks; ˈɪndeks/ *n plural* **indices** /-dəˌsiz; -dəsiːz/ or **indexes** [C] **1** an alphabetical list of names, subjects etc at the

back of a book, with the numbers of the pages where they can be found〔书后人名、题目等的〕索引 **2** a set of cards, each with a name or piece of information on it, arranged in alphabetical order, as used in a library; CARD INDEX〔用于图书馆等处的〕卡片索引 **3** a sign by which the level of something can be judged or measured〔用于判断或量度水平的〕标志: *This may be taken as an index of economic growth.* 这可以视为经济增长的指标。 **4** *technical* a system by which prices, costs etc can be compared to those of a previous date【术语】〔用于比较今昔价格、费用等的〕指数

index² *v* [T] **1** to make an index for something 为〔某物〕编索引 **2** [+to] to arrange for the level of wages, PENSIONs etc to increase or decrease according to the level of prices 使〔工资、养老金等〕与物价指数挂钩 —**indexation** *n* [U,C]

index card /ˈ‥ ˌ/ *n* [C] one of the cards in an index 索引卡片

index fin·ger /ˈ‥ ˌ‥/ *n* [C] the finger next to your thumb; FOREFINGER 食指

index-linked /ˌ‥ ˈ◂/ *adj technical BrE* index-linked wages, PENSIONs etc, increase or decrease according to the rise or fall of prices【术语, 英】〔工资、养老金等〕与物价升降挂钩的

In·di·a /ˈɪndɪə; ˈɪndiə/ a large country in South Asia. Population: 1,030,000,000 (2001). Capital: New Delhi. India was ruled by the British from 1757 until 1947, and is now the largest democracy in the world. The official languages are Hindi and English, and most people belong to the Hindu religion, although there are also large populations of Muslims and Sikhs. 印度〔南亚一大国。人口: 1,030,000,000 (2001), 首都: 新德里。印度1757至1947年间处于英国统治之下, 现为世界上最大的民主政体国家。官方语言为印地语和英语。印度虽然有不少穆斯林和锡克教徒, 但多数人信奉印度教〕—**Indian** *n, adj*

In·di·a ink /ˈɪndɪə ˌɪŋk; ˈɪndiə ˌɪŋk/ *n* [U] black ink used especially for Chinese or Japanese writing with a brush〔中国或日本写毛笔字用的〕墨, 墨汁

In·di·an¹ /ˈɪndɪən; ˈɪndiən/ *n* **1** [C] someone from India 印度人 **2** [C] someone from one of the races that lived in North, South, and Central America before Europeans arrived〔美洲的〕印第安人

Indian² *adj* **1** from or connected with India 印度的 **2** connected with Indians 印度人的; 印第安人的

In·di·an·a /ˌɪndɪˈænə; ˌɪndiˈænə/ abbreviation 缩写为 **IN** a state in the Midwest of the US. It is an important farming state. 印第安纳州〔美国中西部一州, 以农业为主〕

In·di·a·nap·o·lis /ˌɪndiəˈnæpəlɪs; ˌɪndɪəˈnæpəlɪs/ the capital city of the US state of Indiana. An important car race called the **Indianapolis 500** takes place there every year. 印第安纳波利斯〔美国印第安纳州首府。一年一度的重大汽车赛事印第安纳波利斯500英里汽车赛在这里举行〕

Indian corn /ˌ‥ˈ‥ ˈ/ *n* [U] *old-fashioned, especially AmE* MAIZE【过时, 尤美】玉米

Indian file /ˈ‥‥ ˌ/ *n* [U] if people walk in Indian file, they walk one behind another; SINGLE FILE 单列纵队

Indian giv·er /ˌ‥‥ ˈ‥/ *n* [C] *AmE informal* an expression that is now considered offensive meaning someone who gives you something and then takes it back【美, 非正式】送礼物后又索回的人〔今认为具冒犯意思〕—**Indian giving** *n* [U]

Indian Guide /ˌɪndɪən ˈgaɪd; ˌɪndiən ˈgaɪd/ also 又作 **Y-Indian Guide** a member of a club for young boys and their fathers run by the YMCA in the US. The YWCA runs a similar programme for young girls and their mothers called **Indian Maidens**. 印第安向导〔指美国基督教青年会的父子俱乐部成员。基督教女青年会的母女俱乐部成员则取名"印第安少女"〕

Indian ink /ˌ‥‥ ˈ‥/ *n* [U] *BrE* black ink used especially for Chinese or Japanese writing with a brush【英】〔中国或日本写毛笔字用的〕墨, 墨汁

Indian Mu·ti·ny, the /ˌ‥ˈ‥‥/ violent action taken by Indian soldiers in 1857 against their British officers, which led to an attempt by the people of north and central India to take back power from the British. The MUTINY failed, and the British established control again in 1858. 印度兵变, 印军叛变事件〔指1857年印度士兵反抗英国军官的暴动。此举引发了印度中部和北部地方人民从英国人手中夺回主权的行动, 但暴动最终失败。英国于1858年重新确立了在印度的统治地位〕

Indian O·cean, the /ˌ‥ˈ‥‥/ the third largest ocean in the world, which lies between Africa and Australia 印度洋〔世界第三大洋, 位于非洲和澳大利亚之间〕

Indian sum·mer /ˌ‥‥ ˈ‥/ *n* [C] **1** a period of warm weather in the autumn 秋季的温暖天气; 小阳春 **2** a happy or successful time, especially near the end of your life or CAREER¹ (1) 幸福[成功]的时期〔尤指晚年或事业晚期〕

Indian Ter·ri·to·ry /ˌ‥ˈ‥‥/ an area of land west of the Mississippi River in the US, mainly in the state of Oklahoma, to which many Native Americans were forced to move in the middle of the 19th century. The land was later taken back from them by the US government. 印第安领地〔指美国密西西比河以西地区, 主要位于俄克拉何马州境内。19世纪中叶许多美洲土著被迫迁往该地, 后来被美国政府收回〕—see also 另见 the TRAIL OF TEARS

Indian Wars, the /ˌ‥‥ˈ/ the wars in the US between white Europeans and Native Americans in the 18th and 19th centuries. The fighting increased after 1830, when the government began to force Native American tribes to leave their land and live on RESERVATIONs (=special areas of land kept separate for Native Americans). By 1880, most of the fighting had ended. 印第安战争〔指18、19世纪欧洲血统的白人与美洲土著印第安人之间的战争。1830年, 美国政府强迫土著部落离开自己的家园到居留地居住。从此之后, 战争不断升级, 直到1880年才基本结束〕

Indian wrest·ling /ˌ‥‥ ˈ‥/ *n* [U] *AmE* a game in which you stand facing someone with your foot touching theirs, and try to push them over by pushing their hand【美】拽推比赛〔两人相向而立, 以一足相抵, 一掌互推, 身体失去平衡者为负〕

india rub·ber /ˌ‥ ˈ‥◂/ *n old-fashioned*【过时】**1** [U] rubber used for making toys, removing pencil marks etc〔制玩具或擦铅笔字迹用的〕橡皮: *an india rubber ball* 橡皮球 **2** [C] *BrE* a piece of rubber used for removing pencil marks; ERASER【英】〔擦铅笔字迹用的〕橡皮

in·di·cate /ˈɪndəˌket; ˈɪndɪkeɪt/ *v* ✍1

1 ▶FACTS 事实◀ [T] to show that a particular situation exists or that something is likely to be true 表明; 表示: *The survey results seem to indicate a connection between poor housing conditions and bad health.* 调查结果表明, 居住条件差与健康不佳之间似乎存在着关系。| **indicate that** *This indicates that rape is more widespread than people believe.* 这表明, 强奸案比人们认为的要普遍。

2 ▶POINT AT 指向◀ [T] to direct someone's attention to something, for example by pointing 指, 指着〔以引起注意〕: *"She's the one I was telling you about," whispered Toby, indicating a girl in a cheap cotton dress.* "她就是我跟你说过的那个人。"托比指着一位身穿廉价棉布衣服的女孩小声地说道。

3 ▶YOUR WISHES/INTENTIONS 希望/意愿◀ [T] to say or do something to make your wishes, intentions etc clear〔说或做某事〕表明〔意向等〕: *The Russians have already indicated their willingness to cooperate.* 俄国人已经表明了乐意合作的意向。| **indicate that** *Ralph patted the sofa to indicate that she should join him.* 拉尔夫拍拍沙发, 示意让她坐过来。

4 ▶A SIGN FOR 为…的标志◀ [T] to be a sign for something; REPRESENT 标志着; 代表: *The symbols indicate different groups of sounds.* 这些符号表示不同的音群。

5 ▶IN A CAR 在汽车里◀ [I,T] *BrE* to show the direction in which you intend to turn in a vehicle, using lights or your hands; signal【英】〔用指示车灯或手势〕指示〔转弯方向〕: *Don't forget to indicate before you pull out.* 驶离所在车道前别忘给出信号。—see picture on page A3 参见A3页图

6 ▶TREATMENT 治疗◀ be indicated *formal* if a particular kind of treatment is indicated, the need for it is shown【正式】显示有…的需要

Frequencies of **indicate** and **show** in spoken and written English 动词indicate 和 show在英语口语和书面语中的使用频率

SPOKEN 口语
indicate
show
WRITTEN 书面语
indicate
show
100 200 300 400 per million 每百万

Based on the British National Corpus and the Longman Lancaster Corpus
据英国国家语料库和朗文兰开斯特语料库

This graph shows that **show** is much more common than **indicate** in both spoken and written English. This is because **show** is much more general in meaning and is more commonly used in informal English than **indicate**. 本图表显示, show在英语口语和书面语中的使用频率都远远高于indicate。这是因为show的语义比较广泛, 在非正式场合中比indicate更常用。

3 **in·di·ca·tion** /ˌɪndəˋkeʃən; ˌɪndɪˈkeɪʃən/ *n* [C,U] a sign that something is probably happening or that something is probably true 迹象: **[+of]** *He gave no indication of his own feelings at all.* 他一点儿也没有显露自己的感情。| **[+that]** *a clear indication that they were in financial difficulty* 他们遭遇财政困难的明显迹象 | **every indication** (=very clear signs) 种种迹象 *The two leaders greeted each other with every indication of good feeling.* 两位领导人十分友好地互致问候。

in·dic·a·tive¹ /ɪnˋdɪkətɪv; ɪnˈdɪkətɪv/ *adj* **1 be indicative of** to be a clear sign that a particular situation exists or that something is likely to be true 显示出; 指明; 表明; 象征: *This behaviour is indicative of her whole attitude, I'm afraid.* 恐怕这种行为表明了她的整个态度。**2** *technical* an indicative verb form is used for making statements【术语】〔动词〕陈述语气的

indicative² *n* [C,U] *technical* the form of a verb that is used to make statements. For example, in the sentences 'Penny passed her test', and 'Michael likes cake', the verbs 'passed' and 'likes' are in the indicative.【术语】〔动词的〕陈述语气〈如 Penny passed her test 和 Michael likes cake 中的 passed 和 likes〉

in·di·ca·tor /ˋɪndəˌketə; ˈɪndɪkeɪtə/ *n* [C] **1** something that can be regarded as a sign which shows you in what way a situation is changing 指示者; 指示物: *All the main economic indicators suggest that trade is improving.* 所有的主要经济指标都表明贸易正在改善。**2** *BrE* one of the lights on a car that flash to show which way the car is turning【英】〔汽车上的〕转向指示灯; TURN SIGNAL *AmE*【美】**3** a POINTER (1) on a machine that shows the temperature, pressure, speed etc〔机器设备中表示温度、压力、速度等的〕指针 —see picture on page A2 参见 A2 页图

in·di·ces /ˋɪndəˌsiz; ˈɪndɪsiːz/ the plural of INDEX

in·dict /ɪnˋdaɪt; ɪnˈdaɪt/ *v* [I,T] *law especially AmE* to officially charge someone with a criminal offence【法律, 尤美】控告; 起诉〔某人〕: **indict sb for sth** *He was indicted for fraud before a grand jury.* 他在大陪审团前被指控犯有欺诈罪。—**indictment** *n* [C,U]

in·dict·a·ble /ɪnˋdaɪtəbḷ; ɪnˈdaɪtəbəl/ *adj law especially AmE* an indictable offence is one for which you can be indicted【法律, 尤美】〔罪行〕可被控告的

in·dict·ment /ɪnˋdaɪtmənt; ɪnˈdaɪtmənt/ *n* **1 be an indictment of** to be a very clear sign that a system, method etc is very bad or very wrong〔制度不善、方法错误等的〕明显象征: *The fact that these children cannot read is a damning indictment of our education system.* 这些孩子不能阅读, 分明显示出我们的教育制度有问题。**2** [C] *law especially AmE* an official written statement charging someone with a criminal offence【法律, 尤美】起诉书, 诉状 **3** [U] *law especially AmE* the act of officially charging someone with a criminal offence【法律, 尤美】起诉, 指控, 控告

in·die /ˋɪndɪ; ˈɪndi/ *n* [C] a small independent company, especially one that produces records of popular music or television programmes〔制作流行乐唱片或电视节目的〕小型独立公司

indie mu·sic /ˈ‥ ˌ‥/ *n* [U] records of popular music produced by a small independent company〔由小型独立公司出品的〕独立音乐唱片

in·dif·fer·ence /ɪnˋdɪfərəns; ɪnˈdɪfərəns/ *n* [U] lack of interest or concern 缺乏兴趣; 漠不关心: *He always treats Jane with complete indifference.* 他对简总是极其冷淡。| **be a matter of indifference to** (=be something that someone does not care about)〔对某人〕完全无所谓 *Whether you stay or leave is a matter of total indifference to me.* 你是留是走对我根本无所谓。

in·dif·fer·ent /ɪnˋdɪfərənt; ɪnˈdɪfərənt/ *adj* **1** not caring about what is happening, especially about other people's problems or feelings〔尤指对别人的困难或感情〕不关心, 不在乎: **[+to]** *Customs officials were indifferent to their plight.* 海关官员对他们的困境无动于衷。**2** not particularly good; MEDIOCRE 不太好的; 一般的; 平庸的: *an indifferent cook* 手艺平平的厨师 —**indifferently** *adv*

in·dig·e·nous /ɪnˋdɪdʒənəs; ɪnˈdɪdʒənəs/ *adj* indigenous animals, plants etc have always lived or grown naturally in the place where they are, as opposed to others that were brought there〔动、植物等〕土生土长的; 本地的: **[+to]** *There were no snakes indigenous to the islands.* 这些岛屿过去不产蛇。—**indigenously** *adv*

in·di·gent /ˋɪndədʒənt; ˈɪndɪdʒənt/ *adj formal* not having much money or many possessions; POOR (1)【正式】贫困的, 贫穷的 —**indigence** *n* [U] —**indigent** *n* [C]

in·di·ges·ti·ble /ˌɪndɪˋdʒɛstəbḷ; ˌɪndɪˈdʒestɪbəl◂/ *adj* **1** food that is indigestible cannot easily be broken down in the stomach into substances that the body can use〔食物〕难消化的 —opposite 反义词 DIGESTIBLE **2** facts that are indigestible are not easy to understand〔事实〕难懂的, 不好理解的: *indigestible statistics* 看不懂的统计数字 —**indigestibly** *adv*

in·di·ges·tion /ˌɪndəˋdʒɛstʃən; ˌɪndɪˈdʒestʃən◂/ *n* [U] pain that you get when your stomach cannot deal with food that you have eaten 消化不良(症): *You'll get indigestion eating that fast!* 你吃得那么快会消化不良的!

in·dig·nant /ɪnˋdɪgnənt; ɪnˈdɪgnənt/ *adj* expressing anger and surprise, because you feel insulted or unfairly treated〔由于受辱或受不公平待遇而表示〕气愤的, 愤慨的, 愤愤不平的: *Harriet was indignant at the suggestion that she might need help.* 哈丽雅特对有人暗示她可能需要帮助十分恼火。| *anger expressed by an indignant snort* 以气愤的哼声来表示的愤怒 —**indignantly** *adv*: *"Of course I didn't tell her!" Sasha said indignantly.* "我当然没有告诉她!"萨莎气愤地说。

in·dig·na·tion /ˌɪndɪgˋneʃən; ˌɪndɪgˈneɪʃən/ *n* [U] feelings of anger and surprise because you feel insulted or unfairly treated〔因受辱或受到不公平待遇而感到〕愤慨, 义愤, 愤怒: *Chamberlain found, to his great indignation, that he was not to be included in the team.* 张伯伦发现他将被排斥在小组之外, 因此感到十分气愤。| *anger fuelled by righteous indignation* 由于义愤而烧得更旺的怒火 | **[+at]** *Her indignation at such rough treatment was understandable.* 遭受如此粗暴的待遇, 她大为恼火是可以理解的。

in·dig·ni·ty /ɪnˋdɪgnətɪ; ɪnˈdɪgnɪti/ *n* [C,U] a situation that makes you feel very ashamed, unimportant, and not respected 侮辱; 轻蔑: *She suffered many such indignities during her years with their family.* 她与他们一家相处的几年里蒙受了许多屈辱。| **the indignity of** *At least the general was spared the indignity of a public trial.* 这位将军至少得以免受公审之辱。

in·di·go /ˋɪndɪˌgo; ˈɪndɪgəʊ/ *n* [U] a dark purplish blue colour 靛蓝色 —**indigo** *adj*

in·di·rect /ˌɪndəˋrɛkt; ˌɪndɪˈrekt◂/ *adj* **1** not by the fastest, easiest, or straightest way 迟缓的; 费力的; 迂回的: *They took an indirect route, avoiding the town centre.* 他们绕道而行, 避开了市中心。**2** not said in a clear direct way〔说话〕间接的, 不直截了当的: *It was an indirect way of asking me to leave.* 那是转弯抹角地要我离开的方法。**3** the indirect result of an action is not caused directly by it, but by something else which that action caused 间接引致的: *The accident was an indirect result of the bus being late.* 这次事故是公共汽车晚点间接造成的。—opposite 反义词 DIRECT¹ —**indirectly** *adv*: *Perhaps I was indirectly to blame for the misunderstanding.* 也许我应为这个误解承担间接责任。

indirect dis·course /ˌ‥‥ ˈ‥/ *n* [U] *AmE technical* INDIRECT SPEECH【美, 术语】间接引语

indirect ob·ject /ˌ‥‥ ˈ‥/ *n* [C] *technical* the second OBJECT¹ (6) of a verb in a sentence, which is the person or thing that the DIRECT OBJECT is given to, said to, made for etc. For example, in the sentence 'I asked him a question', the indirect object is 'him'.【术语】间接宾语〈如 I asked him a question 中的 him〉

indirect speech /ˌ‥‥ ˈ‥/ *BrE*【英】**indirect discourse** *AmE*【美】*n* [U] *technical* the style used to report what someone said without repeating their actual words. For example, in the sentence 'Julia said that she didn't want to go', the clause 'that she didn't want to go' is indirect speech. Her actual words were 'I don't want to go'.【术语】间接引语〔即不引用实际话语〕〈如 Julia said that she didn't want to go 中 that she didn't want to go 为间接引语。Julia 实际上说的是 I don't want to go.〉

indirect tax·a·tion /ˌ‥‥ ‥ˈ‥/ *n* [U] a system of collecting taxes by adding an amount to the price of goods and services that people buy 间接课税〔附加于商品或服务的税〕

in·dis·cer·ni·ble /ˌɪndɪˋsɝnəbḷ; ˌɪndɪˈsɜːnɪbəl◂/ *adj* very difficult to see, hear, or notice 难以看到的; 难以听见的; 难以察觉的: *The path was almost indiscernible in the mist.* 小路在浓雾之中几乎无法看清楚。

in·dis·ci·pline /ɪnˋdɪsəplɪn; ɪnˈdɪsɪplɪn/ *n* [U] a lack of control with the result that people behave badly 缺乏约束, 无纪律: *Indiscipline among the troops eventually led to a riot.* 军纪不严最终导致骚乱。—see also 另见 DISCIPLINE¹ (1)

in·dis·creet /ˌɪndɪˋskrit; ˌɪndɪˈskriːt◂/ *adj* careless about what you say or do, especially by talking about things which should be kept secret 言行失检的; 轻率的, 不慎重的〔尤指泄露机密〕: *It was very indiscreet of Colin to tell them about our plan.* 科林跟他们谈论我们的计划, 太不谨慎了。—**indiscreetly** *adv*

in·dis·cre·tion /ˌɪndɪˋskrɛʃən; ˌɪndɪˈskreʃən/ *n* **1** [U] a lack of careful thought or good judgment in the things that you say or do 轻率, 不谨慎〔说话或行为的〕: *the startling indiscretion*

of her statement to the press 她向媒体发表谈话时令人吃惊的轻率 **2** [C] an action or remark that shows a lack of careful thought or good judgment 鲁莽的言行, 轻率的言行 **3** [C] something you do that is morally or socially unacceptable 有失检点的行为: *The indiscretions of his youth were not entirely forgotten.* 他年轻时行为不检还没有被完全遗忘。

in·dis·crim·i·nate /ˌɪndɪˋskrɪmənɪt; ˌɪndɪˈskrɪmɪnɪt◂/ *adj* **1** indiscriminate killing, violence, damage etc is done without any thought about who is harmed or what is damaged〔杀戮、暴力、破坏等〕不加区别的, 盲目随意的, 不分青红皂白的: *the indiscriminate slaughter of innocent civilians* 滥杀无辜平民 **2** not thinking carefully before you make a choice〔选择〕任意的, 不假思索的 —**indiscriminately** *adv*

in·di·spen·sa·ble /ˌɪndɪˋspɛnsəbl; ˌɪndɪˈspensəbəl◂/ *adj* someone or something that is indispensable is so important or useful that it is impossible to manage without them 必需的, 不可或缺的: *a piece of equipment that modern divers regard as indispensable* 被现代潜水员视作不可或缺的一件装备 —**indispensably** *adv* —**indispensability** /ˌɪndɪˌspɛnsəˋbɪlətɪ; ˌɪndɪspensəˈbɪlɪti/ *n* [U]

in·dis·posed /ˌɪndɪˋspozd; ˌɪndɪˈspəʊzd/ *adj* [not before noun 不用于名词前] *formal*【正式】**1** ill and therefore unable to be present 有病而不能出席的: *Mrs Rawlins regrets that she is temporarily indisposed.* 罗林斯太太对自己临时身体不适而不能出席表示遗憾。**2 indisposed to do sth** not willing to do something 不愿意做某事

in·dis·po·si·tion /ˌɪndɪspəˋzɪʃən; ɪnˌdɪspəˈzɪʃən/ *n formal*【正式】**1** [C,U] a slight illness 小病, 微恙: *his wife's sudden indisposition* 他妻子突感不适 **2** [U] an unwilling attitude 不情愿, 不乐意

in·dis·pu·ta·ble /ˌɪndɪˋspjutəbl; ˌɪndɪˈspjuːtəbəl/ *adj* an indisputable fact is so certain that it must be true 无可争辩的, 不容置疑的: *The evidence was indisputable.* 这个证据不容置疑。—**indisputably** *adv*: *He was indisputably in the wrong.* 毫无疑问是他的错。

in·dis·so·lu·ble /ˌɪndɪˋsɑljəbl; ˌɪndɪˈsɒljʊbəl◂/ *adj formal* an indissoluble relationship cannot be destroyed【正式】〔关系〕牢不可破的: *an indissoluble union* 牢不可破的联盟 —**indissolubly** *adv* —**indissolubility** /ˌɪndɪˌsɑljəˋbɪlətɪ; ˌɪndɪsɒljʊˈbɪlɪti/ *n* [U]

in·dis·tinct /ˌɪndɪˋstɪŋkt; ˌɪndɪˈstɪŋkt◂/ *adj* an indistinct sound, image, or memory cannot be seen, heard, or remembered clearly〔声音、影像〕不清楚的;〔记忆〕模糊的: *She muttered something indistinct.* 她含含糊糊地嘟哝了什么。—**indistinctly** *adv* —**indistinctness** *n* [U]

in·dis·tin·guish·a·ble /ˌɪndɪsˋtɪŋgwɪʃəbl; ˌɪndɪˈstɪŋgwɪʃəbəl/ *adj* things that are indistinguishable are so similar that you cannot see any difference between them 难以分辨的, 难以区分的: **[+from]** *an artificial material that is almost indistinguishable from real silk* 与真丝几乎无法区分的人造材料 —**indistinguishably** *adv*

S3 W1 **in·di·vid·u·al¹** /ˌɪndəˋvɪdʒʊəl; ˌɪndɪˈvɪdʒuəl◂/ *adj* **1** [only before noun 仅用于名词前] considered separately from other people or things in the same group 单独的, 个别的: *Each individual leaf on the tree is different.* 树上每片叶子都不相同。| *the needs of the individual customer* 每位顾客的需求 **2** [only before noun 仅用于名词前] belonging to or intended for one person rather than a group 个人的, 供一个人的: *Everyone has their own individual opinions.* 每人都有各自的观点。| *The children get far more individual attention in these small classes.* 在这些小班里面, 孩子得到多得多的个别关注。| *individual portions of butter* 一人份的黄油 **3** an individual style, way of doing things etc is different from anyone else's; DISTINCTIVE〔风格、做事方式等〕独特的, 与众不同的: *a tennis player with a very individual style* 风格卓异的网球手 | *a very individual way of dressing* 非常个性化的着衣方式

W1 **individual²** *n* [C] **1** one person, considered separately from the rest of the group or society that they live in 个人, 个体: *the rights of the individual* 个人权利 | *It is important to know the HIV test can vary from individual to individual.* 对人体免疫缺陷病毒的检测可能因人而异, 了解这一点很重要。**2** a person with thoughts, feelings, and ideas of their own 有自己的思想、感情和观念的人: *With adequate support, any child will grow into a fully developed individual.* 有了适当的支持, 每个孩子都会充分成长为性格独立的人。**3** *informal* a person of a particular kind, especially one who is unusual in some way【非正式】有某种特点的人〔尤指在某些方面与众不同的人〕: *a strange-looking individual in a green jacket* 身穿绿色上衣、长相怪异的人

in·di·vid·u·al·is·m /ˌɪndəˋvɪdʒʊəlˌɪzəm; ˌɪndɪˈvɪdʒuəlɪzəm/ *n* [U] **1** the belief that the rights and freedom of individual people are the most important rights in a society 个人主义〔视个人权利和自由至上的信仰〕: *capitalism, which encouraged competition and individualism* 鼓励竞争、提倡个人主义的资本主义 **2** the behaviour or attitude of someone who does things in their own way without being influenced by other people 我行我素〔的行为或态度〕—**individualist** *adj*

in·di·vid·u·al·ist /ˌɪndəˋvɪdʒʊəlɪst; ˌɪndɪˈvɪdʒuəlɪst/ *n* [C] someone who does things in their own way and has different opinions from most other people 按自身意愿做事的人, 有自己独特性的人: *a rebel and an individualist* 叛逆、我行我素的人 —**individualistic** /ˌɪndəˌvɪdʒʊəlˋɪstɪk; ˌɪndɪvɪdʒuəˈlɪstɪk◂/ *adj* —**individualistically** /-klɪ; -kli/ *adv*

in·di·vid·u·al·i·ty /ˌɪndəˌvɪdʒʊˋælətɪ; ˌɪndɪvɪdʒuˈælɪti/ *n* [U] the quality that makes someone or something different from all other things or people 个性; 特性: *a strict regime, that left little room for individuality* 几乎不给个性留下任何空间的严厉政权

in·di·vid·u·al·ize also 又作 **-ise** *BrE*【英】/ˌɪndəˋvɪdʒʊəlˌaɪz; ˌɪndɪˈvɪdʒuəlaɪz/ *v* [T] to make something different so that it fits the special needs of a particular person or place 使有个性, 使有特色〔以适应特定的人或地方的特殊需要〕: *an individualized learner program* 个性化的学习课程

in·di·vid·u·al·ly /ˌɪndəˋvɪdʒʊəlɪ; ˌɪndɪˈvɪdʒuəli/ *adv* separately, not together in a group 分别地, 各自地: *The bridegroom thanked them all individually.* 新郎向大家一一道谢。| [sentence adverb 句子副词] *Individually, they're nice kids, but in a group they can be a nightmare!* 这些孩子个个都很乖, 但要是聚在一起, 他们就可能成为噩梦一般。

in·di·vid·u·ate /ˌɪndəˋvɪdʒʊˌet; ˌɪndɪˈvɪdʒueɪt/ *v* **1** [T] to make someone or something clearly different from others of the same kind 使有区别, 使区别开来: *The characters are beautifully individuated in the play.* 剧中人物各具个性, 处理得极为得体。**2** [I] *AmE* to have an idea of yourself as an independent person, separate from other people【美】自觉是独立的人, 个体化

in·di·vis·i·ble /ˌɪndəˋvɪzəbl; ˌɪndɪˈvɪzɪbəl◂/ *adj* something that is indivisible cannot be separated or divided into parts 分不开的, 不可分割的 —**indivisibly** *adv* —**indivisibility** /ˌɪndəˌvɪzəˋbɪlətɪ; ˌɪndɪvɪzɪˈbɪlɪti/ *n* [U]

Indo- /ɪndo; ɪndəʊ/ *prefix* **1** of India; Indian 印度的; 印度人的 **2** Indian and 印度和…的: *the Indo-Pakistani border* 印巴边界

In·do·chi·na /ˌɪndoˋtʃaɪnə; ˌɪndəʊˈtʃaɪnə/ a name given in the past to part of southeast Asia by Europeans. During the 19th century, Indochina included Vietnam, Cambodia, Myanmar, Thailand, Malaysia, and Laos, but in the 20th century Indochina came to mean the countries ruled by France: Vietnam, Cambodia, and Laos. These three countries were also called French Indochina. 印度支那〔欧洲人过去对东南亚部分地区的称呼。19 世纪, 该地区包括越南、柬埔寨、缅甸、泰国、马来西亚和老挝。到了 20 世纪, 该地区则指法国统治下的越南、柬埔寨和老挝, 又称法属印度支那〕

in·doc·tri·nate /ɪnˋdɑktrɪnˌet; ɪnˈdɒktrɪneɪt/ *v* [T] to train someone to accept a particular set of political or religious beliefs and not consider any others 向〔某人〕灌输〔政治或宗教思想, 使其排斥其他思想〕: *People were indoctrinated not to question their leaders.* 人们被灌输对领导人不得置疑的观念。—**indoctrination** /ɪnˌdɑktrɪˋneʃən; ɪnˌdɒktrɪˈneɪʃən/ *n* [U] *objective discussion, free from propaganda and indoctrination* 不受任何宣传和思想灌输影响的客观讨论

Indo-Eu·ro·pe·an /ˌ‥ ‥ˈ‥◂/ *adj* the Indo-European group of languages includes English, French, Hindi, Russian, and most of the languages of Europe and N India 印欧语系的〔印欧语系包括英语、法语、印地语、俄语和多数欧洲和印度北部的语言〕

in·do·lent /ˋɪndələnt; ˈɪndələnt/ *adj formal* lazy【正式】懒惰的 —**indolently** *adv* —**indolence** *n* [U] *a life of luxury and indolence* 奢侈懒散的生活

in·dom·i·ta·ble /ɪnˋdɑmətəbl; ɪnˈdɒmɪtəbəl/ *adj* **indomitable spirit/courage etc** determination or courage that can never be defeated 不屈不挠的精神/勇气等: *a woman of indomitable strength* 意志坚强的女人 —**indomitably** *adv*

In·do·ne·si·a /ˌɪndoˋniʒə; ˌɪndəʊˈniːziə/ a country in the southeast Indian Ocean consisting of more than 13,000 islands, the largest of which are Java, Sumatra, most of Borneo, Sulawesi, and Bali. Population: 228,438,000 (2001). Capital: Jakarta. In population, it is the fourth largest country in the world, and its official religion is Islam. 印度尼西亚, 印尼〔印度洋东南一国, 由 13,000 多个岛屿组成, 其中最大的岛屿是爪哇岛、苏门答腊岛、婆罗州(大部分)、苏拉威西岛和巴厘岛。人口: 228,438,000 (2001), 首都: 雅加达。该国人口居世界第四, 国教为伊斯兰教〕—**Indonesian** *n, adj*

in·door /ˈɪnˌdɔr; ˈɪndɔː/ *adj* [only before noun 仅用于名词前] used or happening inside a building 在室内使用的, 户内的: *an indoor swimming pool* 室内游泳池 | *indoor shoes* 室内穿的鞋 —opposite 反义词 OUTDOOR

in·doors /ˈɪnˈdɔrz; ˌɪnˈdɔːz◂/ *adv* into or inside a building 在室内; 往室内: *Let's go indoors and have something to eat.* 我们进屋吃点东西。| *It rained all afternoon, so we had to stay indoors.* 雨整整下了一个下午, 我们只好待在屋里。—opposite 反义词 OUTDOORS

in·dorse /ɪnˈdɔrs; ɪnˈdɔːs/ *v* another spelling of ENDORSE endorse 的另一种拼法

in·du·bi·ta·ble /ɪnˈdjubɪtəbl; ɪnˈdjuːbətəbəl/ *adj formal* definitely true without any possible doubt【正式】不容置疑的, 明确无误的 —**indubitably** *adv*: *"Are you sure we can rely on you?" "Indubitably."* "你肯定我们能依赖你吗?" "尽管放心好啦。"

in·duce /ɪnˈdjus; ɪnˈdjuːs/ *v* [T] **1** to make someone decide to do something, especially something that seems unwise 劝诱〔某人做某事, 尤指不好的事〕; 诱导: **induce sb to do sth** *Nothing would induce me to vote for him again.* 没有什么能诱使我再投他的票了。| *What could have induced you to do such a ridiculous thing?* 到底是什么诱使你做出这么荒谬可笑的事来? **2** to make a woman give birth to her baby, by giving her a special drug〔用药物〕为〔产妇〕引产: *She had to be induced because the baby was four weeks late.* 她的孩子晚了四星期仍未出生, 因此要给她引产。**3** *formal* to cause a particular physical condition【正式】诱发〔某种身体反应〕: *This drug may induce drowsiness.* 这种药可能会引起睡意。

in·duce·ment /ɪnˈdjusmənt; ɪnˈdjuːsmənt/ *n* [C,U] something such as money or a gift that you are offered to persuade you to do something 引诱物〔使某人做某事而赠送的金钱或礼物〕: **inducement to do sth** *They offered her a share in the business as an inducement to stay.* 他们提出为她配股, 诱使她留下来。

in·duct /ɪnˈdʌkt; ɪnˈdʌkt/ *v* [T often passive 常用被动态] *formal*【正式】**1** [+into] to officially place someone, especially a priest, in their new job, rank, position etc in a special ceremony〔举行仪式〕使〔牧师、神父等〕正式就职 **2** *AmE* to officially introduce someone into a group or organization, especially the army【美】正式吸收…为成员〔尤指入伍〕

in·duc·tee /ˌɪndʌkˈti; ˌɪndʌkˈtiː/ *n* [C] *AmE* someone who is being or has just been introduced into the army【美】刚应召入伍者

in·duc·tion /ɪnˈdʌkʃən; ɪnˈdʌkʃən/ *n* **1** [C,U] the introduction of someone into a new job, company, official position etc〔新工作、公司、官方职位等的〕入门: *an induction course* 入门课程 **2** [C] a ceremony in which someone is officially introduced into an official position or an organization 就职仪式; 入会仪式 **3** [C,U] the process of making a woman give birth to her baby by giving her a special drug〔药物〕引产(术) **4** [U] *technical* the production of electricity in one object by another that already has electrical or MAGNETIC power【术语】电磁感应 **5** [U] *technical* a process of thought that uses known facts to produce general rules or principles【术语】归纳(法) —compare 比较 DEDUCTION (1)

induction coil /-ˈ-- ˌ-/ *n* [C] *technical* a piece of electrical equipment that changes a low VOLTAGE to a higher one【术语】感应线圈〔用于增加电压〕

in·duc·tive /ɪnˈdʌktɪv; ɪnˈdʌktɪv/ *adj technical*【术语】**1** using known facts to produce general principles 归纳的, 归纳法的 **2** connected with electrical or MAGNETIC induction 电感的; 磁感的

in·due /ɪnˈdju; ɪnˈdjuː/ *v* [T] another spelling of ENDUE endue 的另一种拼法

in·dulge /ɪnˈdʌldʒ; ɪnˈdʌldʒ/ *v* **1** [I,T] to let yourself do or have something that you enjoy, especially something that is considered bad for you (使)〔自己〕沉溺于, 沉湎于: [+in] *Most of us were too busy to indulge in heavy lunchtime drinking.* 我们大多数人都忙得不能在午饭时尽情饮酒。| *Eva had never been one to indulge in self pity.* 伊娃从不是那种沉湎于自怜自哀的人。| **indulge yourself** *I haven't had strawberries and cream for a long time, so I'm really going to indulge myself* (=eat a lot). 我好久没吃奶油草莓了, 真要大吃一顿。| **indulge sth** *Ray has enough money to indulge his taste for expensive wines.* 雷有足够的钱来尽情享受昂贵的葡萄酒。**2** [T] to let someone have or do whatever they want, even if it is bad for them 放纵, 纵容, 迁就: **indulge sb's every whim** *His mother pampered and spoiled him, indulging his every whim.* 他母亲对他纵容娇惯, 千依百顺。

in·dul·gence /ɪnˈdʌldʒəns; ɪnˈdʌldʒəns/ *n* **1** [U] the habit of eating too much, drinking too much etc 放纵饮食 —see also 另见 SELF-INDULGENCE **2** [C] something that you do or have for pleasure, not because you need it 嗜好, 爱好: *An occasional glass of sherry was his only indulgence.* 偶尔喝一杯雪利酒是他唯一的嗜好。**3** [C,U] freedom from punishment by God, or a promise of this, which was sold by priests in the Middle Ages〔欧洲中世纪由神父出售的〕免罪, 赦免 **4** [U] *old use* permission【旧】允许, 许可

in·dul·gent /ɪnˈdʌldʒənt; ɪnˈdʌldʒənt/ *adj* willing to allow someone, especially a child, to do what they want, even if this is not good for them〔尤指对孩子〕溺爱的, 纵容的, 放纵的: *a camping trip paid for by their indulgent grandparents* 由溺爱孙辈的祖父母出资的野营旅行 —**indulgently** *adv*

in·dus·tri·al /ɪnˈdʌstrɪəl; ɪnˈdʌstriəl/ *adj* **1** connected with industry or the people working in it 工业的; 产业工人的: *industrial pollution* 工业污染 | *industrial output* 工业产量 | **industrial accident/injury** (=happening at work) 工业事故/工伤 **2** having many industries, or industries that are well developed 有很多工业的, 工业发达的: *an industrial nation* 工业国 **3** of the type used in industry 工业用的: *industrial detergents* 工业用洗涤剂 —compare 比较 INDUSTRIOUS —**industrially** *adv* W1

industrial ac·tion /-ˌ-- ˈ--/ *n* [U] *BrE* a protest such as a STRIKE (=stopping work) used by workers in a disagreement with their employer【英】工业行动〈如罢工〉

industrial ar·chae·ol·o·gy /-ˌ--- ˌ--ˈ---/ *n* [U] the study of the history of old factories, machines etc 工业考古学〔研究早期工厂、机器等的历史〕

industrial art /-ˌ--- ˈ-/ *AmE n* [U] a subject taught in school about how to use tools, machinery etc【美】〔学校中教授怎样使用工具、机器等的〕工艺课

industrial dis·pute /-ˌ--- -ˈ-/ *n* [C] a disagreement between a group of workers and their employer 劳资纠纷

CULTURAL NOTE 文化注释

In Britain, if an industrial dispute continues for a long time and agreement cannot be reached, the two sides may go to ACAS, an independent BODY (=organization) which tries to find agreement in industrial disputes. In the US, such a dispute may go to an arbitrator (ARBITRATE) who has been agreed upon by both sides. 在英国, 若劳资纠纷长期得不到解决, 双方可提请咨询调解仲裁处解决, 这是一个解决劳资纠纷的独立机构。在美国, 劳资纠纷可以提请劳资双方均认可的仲裁方来解决。

industrial es·pi·o·nage /-ˌ--- ˈ----/ *n* [U] attempts to steal secret information from another company in order to help your own company 企业谍报活动

industrial es·tate /-ˌ--- -ˈ-/ *BrE* a piece of land on the edge of a town planned as a place for factories and small businesses【英】〔圈划在城市边缘供建立工厂和小型企业用的〕工业区

in·dus·tri·al·is·m /ɪnˈdʌstrɪəlˌɪzəm; ɪnˈdʌstriəlɪzəm/ *n* [U] the system by which a society gets its wealth through industries and machinery 工业主义, 产业主义〔指主要依靠工业和机械获得财富的体制〕

in·dus·tri·al·ist /ɪnˈdʌstrɪəlɪst; ɪnˈdʌstriələst/ *n* [C] the owner or manager of a factory, industrial company etc 工业家, 实业家

in·dus·tri·al·ize also 又作 **-ise** *BrE*【英】/ɪnˈdʌstrɪəlˌaɪz; ɪnˈdʌstriəlaɪz/ *v* [I, T] if a country or place is industrialized or if it industrializes, it develops a lot of industry (使)工业化

in·dus·tri·a·lized /ɪnˈdʌstrɪəˌlaɪzd; ɪnˈdʌstriəlaɪzd/ *adj* having a lot of factories, mines, industrial companies etc (已实现)工业化的: *the industrialized nations of the West* 西方工业化国家

industrial re·la·tions /-ˌ--- -ˈ--/ *n* [plural] the relationship between workers and employers 劳资关系

industrial rev·o·lu·tion /-ˌ--- ˌ--ˈ--/ *n* [singular] the period, especially in the 18th and 19th centuries in Europe, when machines were invented and the first factories were established〔尤指欧洲在18、19世纪发明机器、建立第一批工厂的〕工业革命, 产业革命

industrial tri·bu·nal /-ˌ--- -ˈ--/ *n* [C] a type of court in Britain to which individual workers can make complaints against their employers〔英国的〕劳资关系审裁处, 行业纠纷审理委员会

in·dus·tri·ous /ɪnˈdʌstrɪəs; ɪnˈdʌstriəs/ *adj* tending to work hard 勤劳的, 勤奋的 —**industriously** *adv* —**industriousness** *n* [U] —compare 比较 INDUSTRIAL

in·dus·try /ˈɪndəstrɪ; ˈɪndəstri/ *n* **1** [U] the production of goods, especially in factories 工业; 制造业: *a decline in manufacturing industry* 制造业的衰退 | **heavy industry** (=the production S3 W1

of large goods such as aircraft, cars etc)〔生产飞机、汽车等大型产品的〕重工业 | **light industry** (=the production of small goods)〔生产小型产品的〕轻工业 **2** [singular] the people and organizations that work in industry〔工业的〕从业人员; 产业组织: *an agreement that will be welcomed by both sides of industry* (=employers and workers) 将受到劳资双方欢迎的协定 **3** [C] a particular type of industry, trade, or service〔某一工业、贸易或服务的〕行业: *the coal industry* 煤炭工业 | *Italy's thriving tourist industry* 蓬勃发展的意大利旅游业 | **service industries** (=businesses that provide services, such as hotels and banks) 服务业 **4** [singular] an area of work which is not really an industry but which has grown too large 产业〔比喻为产业, 指其规模过大〕: *another book from the Shakespeare industry* 莎士比亚研究的又一本专著

-ine /aɪn; aɪn/ *suffix formal or technical*【正式或术语】**1** of or concerning something 具有…属性的: *equine* (=of horses) 马的, 马科的 **2** made of or like something 由…制成的, …状的: *crystalline* 结晶状的

i·ne·bri·ate /ɪnˋibrɪɪt; ɪˈniːbriɨt/ *n* [C] *old-fashioned* someone who is often drunk【过时】酒鬼, 酗酒者 —**inebriate** *adj*

i·ne·bri·a·ted /ɪnˋibrɪˌetɪd; ɪˈniːbrieɪtɨd/ *adj formal*【正式】drunk 喝醉的 —**inebriation** /ɪnˌibrɪˋeʃən; ɪˌniːbriˈeɪʃən/ *n* [U]

in·ed·i·ble /ɪnˋɛdəbḷ; ɪnˈedɨbəl/ *adj* not suitable for eating 不宜食用的: *The food was so burnt as to be inedible.* 食物焦得太厉害, 不能吃了。

in·ed·u·ca·ble /ɪnˋɛdʒəkəbḷ; ɪnˈedjʊ̈kəbəl/ *adj formal* impossible or very difficult to educate【正式】难以教育的, 不可教育的

in·ef·fa·ble /ɪnˋɛfəbḷ; ɪnˈefəbəl/ *adj formal* too great or beautiful to be described in words【正式】〔好或美得〕难以名状的, 不可言喻的: *ineffable joy* 难以形容的喜悦 —**ineffably** *adv* —**ineffability** /ɪnˌɛfəˋbɪlətɪ; ɪnˌefəˈbɪlɨti/ *n* [U]

in·ef·fec·tive /ˌɪnəˋfɛktɪv; ˌɪnɨˈfektɪv◂/ *adj* something that is ineffective does not achieve what it is intended to achieve 无效果的, 不起作用的, 不奏效的: *The various treatments for AIDS have so far proved ineffective.* 艾滋病的种种疗法迄今都不见效果。—**ineffectively** *adv* —**ineffectiveness** *n* [U]

in·ef·fec·tu·al /ˌɪnəˋfɛktʃuəl; ˌɪnɨˈfektʃuəl◂/ *adj* not having the ability, confidence, or personal authority to get things done 无能力的, 无信心的, 无威望的: *an ineffectual leader* 无能的领导人 | *an ineffectual attempt* 无效的尝试 —**ineffectually** *adv*

in·ef·fi·cient /ˌɪnəˋfɪʃənt; ˌɪnɨˈfɪʃənt◂/ *adj* a worker, organization, or system that is inefficient does not work well and wastes time, money, or energy 效率差的; 不称职的: *an inefficient heating* system 效果差的供暖系统 | *Local government was inefficient and corrupt.* 地方政府效率低下, 腐败成风。—**inefficiently** *adv* —**inefficiency** *n* [C,U] *the inefficiency of the postal service* 邮政服务的低效率

in·el·e·gant /ɪnˋɛləgənt; ɪnˈelɪgənt/ *adj* not graceful 不雅的, 不精致的: *an inelegant belly-flop into the water*〔指跳水时〕胸腹先着水而入的不雅动作 —**inelegantly** *adv* —**inelegance** *n* [U]

in·el·i·gi·ble /ɪnˋɛlɪdʒəbḷ; ɪnˈelɨdʒɨbəl/ *adj* not being able to have or do something 无资格〔拥有或做某事〕的, 不合格的: [+for] *Temporary workers are ineligible for the staff discount scheme.* 临时工没有资格参加员工折扣计划。| **ineligible to do sth** *ineligible to vote in the election* 无资格参加选举投票 —**ineligibility** /ˌɪnɛlɪdʒəˋbɪlətɪ; ɪnˌelɨdʒɨˈbɪlɨti/ *n* [U]

in·e·luc·ta·ble /ˌɪnɪˋlʌktəbḷ; ˌɪnɪˈlʌktəbəl◂/ *adj literary* impossible to escape from; unavoidable【文】难以逃脱的, 不可避免的 —**ineluctably** *adv*

in·ept /ɪnˋɛpt; ɪˈnept/ *adj* having no skill 没有技能的: *an inept driver* 技术拙劣的司机 | *Blake was intellectually able but politically inept.* 布莱克很聪慧, 但对政治却一窍不通。| *He made some inept sexist comment.* 他说了一些不恰当的、带有性别歧视的话。—**ineptly** *adv* —**ineptitude, ineptness** *n* [U] —compare 比较 INAPT

in·e·qual·i·ty /ˌɪnɪˋkwɑlətɪ; ˌɪnɪˈkwɒlɨti/ *n plural* **inequalities** [C,U] an unfair situation, in which some groups in society have less money, influence, or opportunity than others〔社会上的〕不平等: *the inequalities still suffered by disabled people* 残疾人仍然遭受的不平等待遇

in·eq·ui·ta·ble /ɪnˋɛkwɪtəbḷ; ɪnˈekwɨtəbəl/ *adj formal* not equally fair to everyone; UNJUST【正式】不公平的, 不平等的: *an inequitable financial settlement after the divorce* 离婚后不公正的财产处理 —**inequitably** *adv*

in·eq·ui·ty /ɪnˋɛkwɪtɪ; ɪnˈekwɨti/ *n plural* **inequities** [C,U] *formal* unfairness, or something that is unfair【正式】不公正, 偏私; 不平之事: *gross inequities of income and wealth* 收入与财富的严重不公平

in·e·rad·i·ca·ble /ˌɪnɪˋrædɪkəbḷ; ˌɪnɪˈrædɪkəbəl◂/ *adj formal* an attitude or quality of character that is ineradicable can never be completely removed【正式】〔观点、性格等〕难以根除的, 根深蒂固的 —**ineradicably** *adv*

in·ert /ɪnˋɝt; ɪˈnɜːt/ *adj* **1** not having the strength or power to move 无力活动的: *an inert form lying on the bed* 躺在床上一动不动的人形 **2** very slow and unwilling to take any action 呆滞的, 迟缓的: *Congress remained inert and skeptical about the proposal.* 国会对这项提案仍然没有动作并持怀疑态度。**3** *technical* not producing a chemical reaction when combined with other substances【术语】惰性的, 不活泼的: *inert gases* 惰性气体 —**inertly** *adv* —**inertness** *n* [U]

in·er·tia /ɪˋnɝʃə; ɪˈnɜːʃə/ *n* [U] **1** a tendency for a situation to stay unchanged for a long time〔长期〕维持现状: *The government's wish to avoid conflict resulted in political inertia.* 政府意欲避免冲突, 结果导致政治上的迟钝。**2** lack of energy and a feeling that you do not want to do anything 懒惰, 惰性 **3** *technical* the force that keeps an object in the same position or state of movement until it is moved or stopped by another force【术语】惯性 —**inertial** *adj*

inertia reel seat-belt /·ˌ·· ˋ··/ *n* [C] a type of SEAT BELT that will unwind if it is pulled normally but not if it is pulled suddenly〔汽车的〕惯性卷筒式安全带〔突然受力时会自动绷紧〕

inertia sel·ling /·ˌ·· ˋ··/ *n* [U] *especially BrE* the practice of sending goods to people who have not asked for them, and then demanding payment if the goods are not returned【尤英】惯性销售〔指将商品送给没有要求购买的人, 若商品没有退还, 即要求付款〕

in·es·ca·pa·ble /ˌɪnəˋskepəbḷ; ˌɪnɪˈskeɪpəbəl◂/ *adj* impossible to avoid 不可避免的: *The inescapable conclusion is that Pamela stole the money.* 不可避免的结论是帕梅拉偷了钱。—**inescapably** *adv*

in·es·sen·tial /ˌɪnəˋsɛnʃəl; ˌɪnɨˈsenʃəl◂/ *adj formal* not needed; unnecessary【正式】不需要的, 非必需的: *He lived very simply with few inessential items in his apartment.* 他生活非常俭朴, 家里几乎没有多余的东西。—**inessentials** *n* [plural]

in·es·ti·ma·ble /ɪnˋɛstəməbḷ; ɪnˈestɨməbəl/ *adj formal* too much or too great to be calculated【正式】〔由于太多或太大而〕难以计算的, 无法估计的: *The legal case has done inestimable damage to his reputation.* 这桩案子给他的名誉造成了难以估量的损害。—**inestimably** *adv*

in·ev·i·ta·ble /ɪnˋɛvətəbḷ; ɪˈnevɨtəbəl/ *adj* **1** certain to happen and impossible to avoid 必然发生的, 难以避免的: *A further escalation of the crisis now seems inevitable.* 危机的进一步升级现在看来已不可避免。**2 the inevitable** a situation that is certain to happen 不可避免的事情: *One day the inevitable happened and I was caught sneaking in late.* 有一天, 不可避免的事情发生了: 我迟到了, 想偷偷溜进去时被人发现了。**3** [only before noun 仅用于名词前] happening so regularly that you know it will happen again 照例必有的: *the inevitable bouts of travel sickness on school trips* 学校旅行中必然出现的旅途恶心呕吐 —**inevitability** /ɪˌnɛvətəˋbɪlətɪ; ɪˌnevɨtəˈbɪlɨti/ *n* [U] 3

in·ev·i·ta·bly /ɪnˋɛvətəblɪ; ɪnˈevɨtəbli/ *adv* as was certain to happen and could not be prevented 必然地, 不可避免地: *Inevitably, we had overlooked a few points.* 不可避免地, 我们忽略了一些方面。 3

in·ex·act /ˌɪnɪgˋzækt; ˌɪnɪgˈzækt◂/ *adj* not exact 不精确的, 不准确的: *Sociology is an inexact science.* 社会学不是一门精确的科学。—**inexactness** *n* [U]

in·ex·cu·sa·ble /ˌɪnɪkˋskjuzəbḷ; ˌɪnɪkˈskjuːzəbəl◂/ *adj* inexcusable behaviour is too bad to be excused 不可原谅的, 不可宽恕的: *Such rudeness is inexcusable!* 如此莽撞无礼是不可原谅的! —**inexcusably** *adv*

in·ex·haus·ti·ble /ˌɪnɪgˋzɔstəbḷ; ˌɪnɪgˈzɔːstɨbəl◂/ *adj* existing in such large amounts that it can never be finished or used up 无穷无尽的, 用不完的: *a man of inexhaustible energy* 精力旺盛的人 | *an inexhaustible supply of firewood* 用之不竭的柴火 —**inexhaustibly** *adv*

in·ex·o·ra·ble /ɪnˋɛksərəbḷ; ɪnˈeksərəbəl/ *adj formal* an inexorable process cannot be stopped【正式】不可阻挡的, 不可更改的: *the inexorable decline of Britain's manufacturing industry* 英国制造业无可挽回的衰败 —**inexorably** *adv*: *The story moves inexorably towards its tragic conclusion.* 这个故事势必以悲剧结尾。—**inexorability** /ɪnˌɛksərəˋbɪlətɪ; ɪnˌeksərəˈbɪlɨti/ *n* [U]

in·ex·pe·di·ent /ˌɪnɪkˋspidɪənt; ˌɪnɪkˈspiːdiənt◂/ *adj formal* a plan or action that is inexpedient is not useful because it is not likely to achieve the result you want【正式】〔计划或行动〕不明智的〔因为不大可能奏效〕, 没用的 —**inexpedience, inexpediency** *n* [U]

in·ex·pen·sive /ˌɪnɪkˋspɛnsɪv; ˌɪnɪkˈspensɪv◂/ *adj* cheap and of good quality for the price you pay 价钱公道的，廉价的: *clean and inexpensive accommodation in the centre of town* 市中心整洁价廉的住房 —**inexpensively** *adv* —**inexpensiveness** *n* [U]

in·ex·pe·ri·ence /ˌɪnɪkˋspɪrɪəns; ˌɪnɪkˈspɪəriəns/ *n* [U] lack of experience 缺乏经验: *youthful inexperience* 少不更事

in·ex·pe·ri·enced /ˌɪnɪkˋspɪrɪənst; ˌɪnɪkˈspɪəriənst◂/ *adj* not having had much experience 经验不足的，不熟练的: *Lyn is still too young and inexperienced to go abroad on her own.* 林恩少不更事，不能一个人去国外。

in·ex·pert /ˌɪnɪksˋpɝt; ɪnˈekspɜːt/ *adj* not good at doing something〔对某事〕不熟练的，不内行的 —**inexpertly** *adv* —**inexpertness** *n* [U]

in·ex·plic·a·ble /ˌɪnˋɛksplɪkəbl̩; ˌɪnɪkˈsplɪkəbəl◂/ *adj* too unusual or strange to be explained or understood〔由于不寻常或太奇怪而〕无法解释的；费解的: *the inexplicable disappearance of a young woman* 一名年轻女子的离奇失踪 —**inexplicably** *adv* —**inexplicability** /ɪnˌɛksplɪkəˋbɪlətɪ; ˌɪnɪksplɪkəˈbɪlɨti/ *n* [U]

in·ex·pres·si·ble /ˌɪnɪkˋsprɛsəbl̩; ˌɪnɪkˈspresɨbəl◂/ *adj* **inexpressible joy/sorrow/relief etc** a feeling or condition that is too strong to be described in words 难以言传的喜悦/悲伤/欣慰等 —**inexpressibly** *adv*: *He looked inexpressibly sad.* 他看来有说不出的悲伤。

in·ex·press·ive /ˌɪnɪkˋsprɛsɪv; ˌɪnɪkˈspresɪv◂/ *adj* a face that is inexpressive shows no emotion at all 无表情的

in·ex·tin·guish·a·ble /ˌɪnɪkˋstɪŋgwɪʃəbl̩; ˌɪnɪkˈstɪŋgwɪʃəbəl◂/ *adj literary*【文】**inextinguishable hope/love/spirit etc** hope etc that is so strong that it cannot be destroyed 不可遏制的希望/爱情/精神等 —**inextinguishably** *adv*

in ex·tre·mis /ˌɪn ɪkˋstrimɪs; ˌɪn ɪkˈstriːmɪs/ *adv Latin formal*【拉丁，正式】**1** in a very difficult and urgent situation when very strong action is needed 在危急关头〔需要采取强烈行动〕**2** at the moment of death 在弥留之际

in·ex·tric·a·ble /ˌɪnˋɛkstrɪkəbl̩; ˌɪnɪkˈstrɪkəbəl◂/ *adj formal* two or more things that are inextricable cannot be separated from each other【正式】分不开的，解不开的: *Character development is an inextricable part of the novel.* 人物性格发展是这部小说不可分割的一部分。

in·ex·tric·a·bly /ˌɪnˋɛkstrɪkəblɪ; ˌɪnɪkˈstrɪkəbli/ *adv* **be inextricably linked/connected/mixed etc** if two or more things are inextricably linked etc, they are very closely connected and cannot be separated 紧密相连，密不可分: *Poor health and bad housing conditions are inextricably linked.* 健康不佳与住房条件恶劣有密切关系。

in·fal·li·ble /ɪnˋfæləbl̩; ɪnˈfælɨbəl/ *adj* **1** always right and never making mistakes 永远正确的，从不犯错误的: *I'm only human, I'm not infallible.* 我只是平常人，不可能不犯错误。| *an infallible memory* 绝对可靠的记忆 **2** something that is infallible always works or has the intended effect〔事物〕绝对有效的: *He had an infallible cure for a hangover.* 他有对付宿醉绝对灵验的良方。—**infallibly** *adv* —**infallibility** /ɪnˌfæləˋbɪlətɪ; ɪnˌfælɨˈbɪlɨti/ *n* [U]

in·fa·mous /ˋɪnfəməs; ˈɪnfəməs/ *adj* **1** well known for being bad or morally evil 声名狼藉的，臭名昭著的: *an infamous traitor* 臭名昭著的叛徒 | *plans to deal with Los Angeles' infamous smog* 治理恶名远播的洛杉矶烟雾的计划 —see 见 FAMOUS (USAGE) **2** *literary* evil【文】邪恶的: *infamous behaviour* 无耻的行为 —**infamously** *adv*

in·fa·my /ˋɪnfəmɪ; ˈɪnfəmi/ *n* **1** [U] the state of being evil or well known for evil things 臭名昭著，声名狼藉，丑恶 **2** [C usually plural 一般用复数] an evil action 丑行，恶行

in·fan·cy /ˋɪnfənsɪ; ˈɪnfənsi/ *n* [singular, U] **1** the period of a child's life before it can walk or talk 婴儿期: *She had five children, but four of them died in infancy.* 她生了五个孩子，但四个死于襁褓之中。**2** **in its infancy** something that is in its infancy is just starting to be developed 在初期，在早期: *Agricultural research is still in its infancy in parts of the Third World.* 农业研究在第三世界的一些地区才刚刚起步。

in·fant¹ /ˋɪnfənt; ˈɪnfənt/ *n* [C] **1** *literary or technical* a very young child or baby【文或术语】幼儿，婴儿: *The infant, cradled in Miriam's arms, began to cry.* 米丽娅姆抱在怀中的婴儿开始哭叫。—see picture at 参见 CHILD 图 **2** **infants** [plural] children in school in Britain between the ages of four and eight〔英国学校里四至八岁的〕学童 **3** **infant school/teacher/class etc** a school etc for children aged between four and eight in Britain〔英国为四至八岁儿童设立的〕儿童学校/教师/班级等

infant² *adj* [only before noun 仅用于名词前] an infant company, organization etc has just started to exist or be developed〔公司、组织等〕刚成立的，初创的: *The plan was designed to protect infant industries in Mexico.* 这个计划是为保护墨西哥的幼稚产业而设计的。

in·fan·ti·cide /ɪnˋfæntəˌsaɪd; ɪnˈfæntɨsaɪd/ *n* [U] *technical* the crime of killing a child【术语】杀婴罪

in·fan·tile /ˋɪnfənˌtaɪl; ˈɪnfəntaɪl/ *adj* **1** infantile behaviour seems silly in an adult because it is typical of a child 幼稚的，孩子气的: *I was sick of his infantile jokes.* 我很讨厌他那些幼稚的笑话。**2** *technical* affecting very young children【术语】婴幼儿患的: *infantile colic* 婴儿肠绞痛

infantile pa·ral·y·sis /ˌ··· ·ˈ···/ *n* [U] *old-fashioned* POLIO【过时】脊髓灰质炎，小儿麻痹症

infant mor·tal·i·ty rate /ˌ··ˈ··· ·/ written abbreviation 缩写为 **IMR** *n* [C] the number of deaths of babies under one year old, expressed as the number out of each 1,000 babies born alive in a year〔每年每1000名一岁以下婴儿的〕婴儿死亡率

infant prod·i·gy /ˌ·· ˈ···/ *n* [C] a child with an extremely high level of ability in music, art, mathematics etc〔极富音乐、艺术、数学等天赋的〕神童: *Mozart, the most famous infant prodigy of all* 名扬天下的神童莫扎特

in·fan·try /ˋɪnfəntrɪ; ˈɪnfəntri/ *n* [U] soldiers who fight on foot 步兵（部队）—compare 比较 CAVALRY

in·fan·try·man /ˋɪnfəntrɪmən; ˈɪnfəntrimən/ *n plural* **infantrymen** /-mən; -mən/ [C] a soldier who fights on foot 步兵

in·fat·u·at·ed /ɪnˋfætʃʊˌetɪd; ɪnˈfætʃueɪtɨd/ *adj* having unreasonably strong feelings of love, but only for a short time and especially for someone that you do not know very well〔尤指短时间，对不十分了解的人〕迷恋的，痴心的: **[+with]** *John had become infatuated with the French teacher.* 约翰迷恋上了法语老师。

in·fat·u·a·tion /ɪnˌfætʃʊˋeʃən; ɪnˌfætʃuˈeɪʃən/ *n* [C,U] unreasonably strong feelings of love that you only have for a short time, especially for someone that you do not know very well 迷恋，痴心〔尤指短时间、对不十分了解的人〕: *As I thought, it was another passing infatuation.* 正如我所料想的，那不过是另一次转瞬即逝的迷恋。

in·fect /ɪnˋfɛkt; ɪnˈfekt/ *v* [T] **1** to give someone a disease 传染〔疾病给人〕: *People with the virus may feel perfectly well, but they can still infect others.* 带有这种病毒的人可能毫无病征，却仍可能传染他人。**2** to put something that spreads disease into food, water, the air etc〔以病菌等〕污染〔食物、水、空气等〕**3** if your excitement, eagerness etc infects other people, it makes them begin to feel the same way〔情绪等〕感染〔别人〕，使〔人〕受影响: *Lucy's enthusiasm soon infected the rest of the class.* 露西的热情很快就感染了班里的其他人。

in·fect·ed /ɪnˋfɛktɪd; ɪnˈfektɨd/ *adj* **1** a part of your body or a wound that is infected, has harmful BACTERIA in it which prevent it from healing (HEAL (1))〔身体或伤口〕受到〔细菌〕感染的: *It was only a small cut, but it became infected.* 伤口虽然很小，但还是感染了。**2** food, water etc that is infected contains BACTERIA that spread disease〔食品、水等〕受到细菌污染的

in·fec·tion /ɪnˋfɛkʃən; ɪnˈfekʃən/ *n* [C,U] **1** a disease caused by BACTERIA or a VIRUS (1) that affects a particular part of your body〔由细菌或病毒造成对身体某部位的〕感染: *You ought to get some antibiotics for that ear infection.* 你的耳朵感染应该用些抗生素。**2** the act or result of infecting someone 传染；传染病: *Always sterilize the needle to prevent infection.* 注射用针每次都要消毒，以防传染。

in·fec·tious /ɪnˋfɛkʃəs; ɪnˈfekʃəs/ *adj* **1** an infectious illness can be passed from one person to another, especially through the air you breathe〔指疾病〕传染的〔尤指通过空气〕，传染性的: **highly infectious** *There seems to be a highly infectious type of flu going around.* 似乎有一种传染性极强的流感在流行。**2** someone who is infectious has an illness and could pass it to other people〔人〕患有传染病并能传染他人的 **3** infectious feelings or laughter spread quickly from person to another〔情感、笑声等〕极富感染力的: *Her giggles were infectious and soon we were all laughing.* 她咯咯的笑声极富感染力，我们很快都笑了起来。—**infectiously** *adv* —**infectiousness** *n* [U]

in·fer /ɪnˋfɝ; ɪnˈfɜː/ *v* **inferred, inferring** [T] to form an opinion that something is probably true because of other information that you already know〔根据其他资料〕推断，推定: **infer sth from** *facts that can be inferred from archaeological data* 可根据考古资料推断的事实 | **infer that** *It would be wrong to infer that people who are overweight are just greedy.* 根据身体肥胖就断定别人贪吃是错误的。

USAGE NOTE 用法说明: INFER
WORD CHOICE 词语辨析: **infer, imply**
In formal English the speaker or writer **implies** something, and the listener or reader **infers** it. 在正式英语中，讲话者或作者暗示某物用 imply，而听话人或读者进行推断则是 infer: *His report implied* (=suggested indirectly) *that the building was unsafe.* 他在报告中暗示这幢大楼不安全。*I inferred from his report that the building was unsafe* means that this is what I thought the report meant. 我从他的报告中推断出这幢大楼不安全，这表示我认为这就是他报告的本意。
Infer is now often used to mean **imply** but some people think that this is not correct. 现在 infer 常被用来表达 imply 的意思，但有人认为这种用法不正确: *Are you inferring I'm drunk?* (=are you trying to tell me I'm drunk?) 你是说我喝醉了？

in·fer·ence /ˋɪnfərəns; ˈɪnfərəns/ *n* **1** [C] something that you think is true, based on information that you already know 推论，推断的结果: **draw inferences** *What inferences have you drawn from this evidence?* 你从这个证据中得出了什么推论？**2** [U] the act of inferring something 推理，推断: **by inference** *measures directed against the enemies of National Socialism, including by inference all radicals and communists* 针对国家社会主义的敌人——包括类推的一切激进分子和共产党人——的措施 —**inferential** /ˌɪnfəˋrɛnʃəl; ˌɪnfəˈrenʃəl◂/ *adj*: *inferential evidence* 推论性证据 —**inferentially** *adv*

in·fe·ri·or¹ /ɪnˋfɪrɪɚ; ɪnˈfɪəriə/ *adj* **1** not good, or less good in quality, value, or skill than someone or something else〔质量、价值、技能等〕差的，次的: *I felt very inferior among all those academics.* 与那些大学教师在一起，我自惭形秽。| *Pay less, and you get an inferior product.* 便宜没好货。| **[+to]** *This machine is technically inferior to Western models.* 这台机器在技术上不如西方国家的产品。**2** *formal* lower in rank【正式】低级别的，下级的: *an inferior court of law* 初级法院；下级法院 —compare 比较 SUPERIOR¹ —**inferiority** /ɪnˌfɪrɪˋɑrətɪ; ɪnˌfɪəriˈɒrɪ̣ti/ *n* [U]

inferior² *n* [C] someone who has a lower position or rank than you in an organization 下级，下属，部下 —compare 比较 SUPERIOR²

inferiority com·plex /.ˋ.....ˌ../ *n* [C] a continuous worrying feeling that you are much less important, clever etc than other people 自卑情结；自卑感

in·fer·nal /ɪnˋfɝnl; ɪnˈfɜːnl/ *adj* **1** [only before noun 仅用于名词前] *old-fashioned* used to express anger or annoyance about something【过时】可恶的，恼人的〔用于表示愤怒或烦恼〕: *I wish the children would stop that infernal noise.* 我真希望孩子们别再瞎聒噪。**2** *literary* connected with HELL【文】阴间的；地狱的: *the infernal powers of darkness* 地狱中的魔鬼 —**infernally** *adv*

in·fer·no /ɪnˋfɝno; ɪnˈfɜːnəʊ/ *n* [C] *literary* an extremely large and dangerous fire【文】熊熊烈火，火海: **raging inferno** (=an extremely violent fire) 极端猛烈的大火 *Within minutes the oilrig had become a raging inferno.* 只几分钟工夫，石油钻塔便成了一片火海。

in·fer·tile /ɪnˋfɝtḷ; ɪnˈfɜːtaɪl/ *adj* **1** infertile land or soil is not good enough to grow plants in〔土地〕不肥沃的，贫瘠的，不毛的 **2** an infertile person or animal cannot have babies 不能生育的，无生育能力的 —**infertility** /ˌɪnfɚˋtɪlətɪ; ˌɪnfəˈtɪlɪ̣ti/ *n* [U]

in·fest /ɪnˋfɛst; ɪnˈfest/ *v* [T] if insects, rats etc infest a place, they appear in large numbers and usually cause damage〔昆虫、老鼠等〕成群侵扰〔通常造成破坏〕，横行: **[+with]** *hair infested with lice* 头发里生满虱子 | *shark-infested waters* 大批鲨鱼出没的水域 —**infestation** /ˌɪnfɛsˋteʃən; ˌɪnfeˈsteɪʃən/ *n* [C,U] *an infestation of cockroaches* 蟑螂横行

in·fi·del /ˋɪnfədḷ; ˈɪnfɪ̣dəl/ *n* [C] *old use* an insulting word for someone who does not believe what you consider to be the true religion【旧】异教徒，不信奉正统宗教者〔冒犯用词〕

in·fi·del·i·ty /ˌɪnfəˋdɛlətɪ; ˌɪnfɪ̣ˈdelɪ̣ti/ *n* [C,U] an act of being unfaithful to your wife, husband etc by having sex with someone else〔对丈夫或妻子的〕不贞行为: *Paul sometimes suspected her of infidelity.* 保罗有时怀疑她不贞。

in·field /ˋɪnˌfild; ˈɪnfiːld/ *n* [singular] **1** the part of a CRICKET (2) field nearest to the player who hits the ball〔板球场的〕内场 **2** the part of a BASEBALL field inside the four bases〔棒球场的〕内场，内野 —see picture on page A22 参见 A22 页图 **3** the group of players in the CRICKET (2) or BASEBALL infield〔板球的〕全体内场员，〔棒球的〕全体内野手 —compare 比较 OUTFIELD —**infielder** *n* [C]

in·fight·ing /ˋɪnˌfaɪtɪŋ; ˈɪnfaɪtɪŋ/ *n* [U] unfriendly competition and disagreement between members of the same group or organization 内部争斗，内讧: *political infighting* 政治内讧

in·fil·trate /ɪnˋfɪltret; ˈɪnfɪltreɪt/ *v* **1** [I always+adv/prep, T] to secretly join an organization or enter a place in order to find out information about them or harm them〔秘密地〕加入〔某组织〕，进入〔某地方，以刺探情报或进行破坏〕: *Police attempts to infiltrate neo-Nazi groups were largely unsuccessful.* 警方渗透入新纳粹集团的企图基本上不成功。| **[+into]** *Enemy forces have been infiltrating into our territory.* 敌军一直在偷偷向我国境内渗透。**2** **[+into]** to secretly introduce someone or something into an organization or place〔秘密地〕派人进入〔某组织或地方〕，使渗透: *plans to infiltrate sabotage agents into the UK* 派破坏分子渗入英国的计划 —**infiltrator** *n* [C] —**infiltration** /ˌɪnfɪlˋtreʃən; ˌɪnfɪlˈtreɪʃən/ *n* [U]

in·fi·nite /ˋɪnfənɪt; ˈɪnfɪ̣nɪ̣t/ *adj* **1** very great 极大的: *Hilary takes infinite care over her work.* 希拉丽对待工作极为谨慎。**2** without limits in space or time〔空间或时间〕无限的，无穷无尽的: *The universe is infinite.* 宇宙是无穷无尽的。—compare 比较 NON-FINITE (2)

in·fi·nite·ly /ˋɪnfənɪtlɪ; ˈɪnfɪ̣nɪ̣tli/ *adv* [+adj/adv] very much 极多地: *Living in the country is infinitely preferable to living in London.* 住在乡下比住在伦敦要好千百倍。

in·fin·i·tes·i·mal /ˌɪnfɪnəˋtɛsəml; ˌɪnfɪnɪ̣ˈtesɪ̣məl◂/ *adj* extremely small 极微小的: *infinitesimal changes in temperature* 极微小的气温变化 —**infinitesimally** *adv*

in·fin·i·tive /ɪnˋfɪnətɪv; ɪnˈfɪnɪ̣tɪv/ *n* [C] *technical* the basic form of a verb, such as 'be', 'make' or 'go', usually used with 'to' in the form 'to be', 'to make', 'to go' etc【术语】〔动词〕原形，不定式〈如 be, make 或 go，一般带 to，成为 to be, to make, to go 等〉—see also 另见 SPLIT INFINITIVE

in·fin·i·tude /ɪnˋfɪnəˌtjud; ɪnˈfɪnɪ̣tjuːd/ *n* [singular, U] *formal* a number or amount without limit; INFINITY【正式】〔数目或数量〕无限，无穷；无限大: *the vast infinitude of space* 广阔无垠的太空

in·fin·i·ty /ɪnˋfɪnətɪ; ɪnˈfɪnɪ̣ti/ *n* **1** [U] a space or distance without limits or an end 无垠的空间，无穷的距离: *The universe stretches away into infinity.* 宇宙无边无际。**2** [singular] a number that is too large to be calculated 无穷大: **an infinity of** *An infinity of interpretations have been put on the novel.* 对这部小说进行了无穷无尽的解释。

in·firm /ɪnˋfɝm; ɪnˈfɜːm/ *adj* **1** weak or ill, especially because you are old〔尤指由于年迈而〕体弱多病的: *Her grandmother is now old and infirm.* 她的祖母如今年迈体弱。**2** **the infirm** all the people who are weak or ill 体弱多病者

in·fir·ma·ry /ɪnˋfɝmərɪ; ɪnˈfɜːməri/ *n* [C] **1** a hospital 医院 **2** a room in a school or other institution where people can go if they are ill〔学校等的〕医务室

in·fir·mi·ty /ɪnˋfɝmətɪ; ɪnˈfɜːmɪ̣ti/ *n* [C,U] bad health or a particular illness 体弱，身体不佳；疾病: *She blamed her infirmity on the damp climate.* 她把身体不佳归咎于潮湿的气候。

in fla·gran·te de·lic·to /ɪn fləˌgræntɛ dɪˋlɪkto; ɪn fləˌgrænteɪ dɪˈlɪktəʊ/ *adv Latin, technical or humorous* in the act of having sex, especially with someone else's husband or wife【拉丁，术语或幽默】〔尤指与别人的丈夫或妻子〕做爱时

in·flame /ɪnˋflem; ɪnˈfleɪm/ *v* [T] *literary* to make someone's feelings of anger, excitement etc much stronger【文】加剧〔愤怒或兴奋等情绪〕，使火上浇油: *Seeing her again inflamed all his old desire.* 再次见到她，激起他所有往日的欲望。

in·flamed /ɪnˋflemd; ɪnˈfleɪmd/ *adj* a part of your body that is inflamed is red and swollen, because it is hurt or infected〔身体部位〕红肿的，发炎的

in·flam·ma·ble /ɪnˋflæməbḷ; ɪnˈflæməbəl/ *adj* **1** *BrE* inflammable materials or substances will start to burn very easily【英】易燃的: *Petrol is highly inflammable.* 汽油高度易燃。—opposite 反义词 NONFLAMMABLE **2** an inflammable temper easily becomes angry or violent 易怒的，性情暴躁的

in·flam·ma·tion /ˌɪnfləˋmeʃən; ˌɪnfləˈmeɪʃən/ *n* [C,U] swelling and soreness on or in part of your body, which is often red and hot to touch 发炎，炎症: *an inflammation of the eye* 眼睛发炎

in·flam·ma·to·ry /ɪnˋflæməˌtorɪ; ɪnˈflæmətəri/ *adj* **1** an inflammatory speech, piece of writing etc is likely to make people feel angry〔讲话、文字等〕使人激愤的，煽动性的: *His inflammatory remarks about the homeless were seized on by the press.* 他有关无家可归者的煽动性讲话立刻被媒体利用。**2** *technical* an inflammatory disease, condition etc causes inflammation【术语】〔疾病、环境等〕引发炎症的

in·fla·ta·ble[1] /ɪnˋfletəbḷ; ɪnˈfleɪtəbəl/ *adj* an inflatable object has to be filled with air before you can use it（需）充气的: *an inflatable mattress* 充气床垫

inflatable[2] *n* [C] a rubber boat filled with air 充气橡皮艇

inflate（使）充气

in·flate /ɪnˋflet; ɪnˈfleɪt/ *v* **1** [I,T] if you inflate something, or if it inflates, it fills with air or gas so that it becomes larger（使）充气: *It took us half an hour to inflate the dinghy.* 我们用了半小时给橡皮筏充气。| *Her life jacket failed to inflate.* 她的救生衣充不进气。**2** [T] to make something seem more important or impressive than it is 吹捧〔某物〕: *Our egos were already inflated by success.* 成功使我们自命不凡。**3** [T] *technical* to make prices increase【术语】使〔价格〕上涨: *The sudden influx of Westerners has inflated house prices out of all proportion.* 西方人突然涌入，把房价抬得离了谱。

in·flat·ed /ɪnˋfletɪd; ɪnˈfleɪtɪ̣d/ *adj* **1** inflated prices, sums etc are unreasonably high〔价格、数目等〕过高的: *These company directors are paid grossly inflated salaries.* 这些公司董事领的薪水过高。**2** inflated ideas, opinions etc about something make it seem more important than it really is〔想法、意见〕夸张的，言过其实的: *people with an inflated idea of their own importance* 自高自大的人 **3** filled with air or gas 充气的

2 2 **in·fla·tion** /ɪnˋfleʃən; ɪnˈfleɪʃən/ *n* [U] **1** a continuing increase in prices or the rate at which prices increase 物价上涨（率），通货膨胀（率）: *Inflation is now running at over 16%.* 通货膨胀率现已超过16%。**2** the process of filling something with air 充气 —compare 比较 DEFLATION

in·fla·tion·a·ry /ɪnˋfleʃənˌɛrɪ; ɪnˈfleɪʃənəri/ *adj* relating to or causing price increases 价格上涨的，〔引起〕通货膨胀的: *inflationary wage increases* 通货膨胀引起的工资增长 | **inflationary spiral** (=the continuing rise in wages and prices because an increase in one causes an increase in the other) 螺旋形通货膨胀〔指工资和物价交互影响而持续上涨〕

inflation-proof /ˈ·ˌ··ˌ·/ *adj* protected against price increases 不受通货膨胀影响的: *inflation-proof pensions* 不受通货膨胀影响的养老金

in·flect /ɪnˋflɛkt; ɪnˈflekt/ *v* **1** [I] if a word inflects, its form changes according to its meaning or use〔词形〕屈折变化 **2** [I,T] if your voice inflects or if you inflect it, the sound of it becomes higher or lower as you are speaking〔说话时〕变（音），转（调）

in·flect·ed /ɪnˋflɛktɪd; ɪnˈflektɪ̣d/ *adj* an inflected language contains many words which change their form according to their meaning or use〔语言〕屈折变化的: *German is an inflected language.* 德语是有屈折变化的语言。

in·flec·tion, inflexion /ɪnˋflɛkʃən; ɪnˈflekʃən/ *n* **1** [U] the way in which a word changes its form to show difference in its meaning or use〔单词的〕屈折变化 **2** [C] one of the forms of a word that changes in this way, or one of the parts that is added to it 屈折形式; 屈折成分 **3** [C,U] the way the sound of your voice goes up and down when you are speaking〔说话时声调的〕抑扬顿挫 —**inflectional** *adj*

in·flex·i·ble /ɪnˋflɛksəbḷ; ɪnˈfleksɪ̣bəl/ *adj* **1** inflexible rules, arrangements etc are impossible to change〔规则、协议等〕不可改变的，不容变更的 **2** unwilling to make even the slightest change in your attitudes or plans etc〔态度、计划等〕顽固的，僵化的: *an arrogant man with an inflexible will* 傲慢无礼、刚愎自用的人 **3** inflexible material is stiff and will not bend〔材料〕坚硬的，不能弯曲的 —**inflexibly** *adv* —**inflexibility** /ɪnˌflɛksəˋbɪlətɪ; ɪnˌfleksɪ̣ˈbɪlɪ̣ti/ *n* [U]

in·fle·xion /ɪnˋflɛkʃən; ɪnˈflekʃən/ *n* [C,U] another spelling of INFLECTION inflection 的另一种拼法

in·flict /ɪnˋflɪkt; ɪnˈflɪkt/ *v* **1** [T] to make someone suffer something unpleasant 使〔某人〕遭受〔不愉快的事〕，使承受: *The judge inflicted the severest possible penalty.* 法官判处了最严厉的惩罚。| **inflict sth on/upon sb** *He inflicted a great deal of suffering on his wife and children.* 他让妻子和孩子们吃了很多苦头。—see graph at 参见 PAIN[1] 图表 **2 inflict yourself on** *humorous* to visit or be with someone when they do not want you【幽默】不请自来: *Frank's in-laws are inflicting themselves on us for the weekend.* 弗兰克的姻亲不请自来，要在我们家度周末。—**infliction** /ɪnˋflɪkʃən; ɪnˈflɪkʃən/ *n* [U]

in-flight /ˈ· ·/ *adj* [only before a noun 仅用于名词前] provided during a plane journey 飞行途中提供的: *in-flight entertainment* 飞行旅程中提供的娱乐

in·flow /ˋɪnˌflo; ˈɪnfləʊ/ *n* **1** [C] the movement of people, money, goods etc into a place〔人、钱、商品等的〕流入，涌入: *the inflow of migrants* 移民的涌入 **2** [singular,U] the flow of water into a place〔水〕流入 —opposite 反义词 OUTFLOW

in·flu·ence[1] /ˋɪnfluəns; ˈɪnfluəns/ *n* **1** [C,U] power to have an effect on the way someone or something develops, behaves, or thinks without using direct force or commands 影响: [+with] *She used her influence with the chairman to get me the job.* 她利用对主席的影响力使我得到了这份工作。| **have an influence on** *Claude's work had a major influence on generations of musicians.* 克劳德的作品对几代音乐家都产生过重要影响。| **under the influence of** (=controlled by the influence of) 在…的影响下 *They had come under the influence of a strange religious sect.* 他们受到一个古怪教派的影响。**2** [C] someone or something that has an influence on other people or things 有影响的人[物]: **be a bad/good influence (on)** *Gaye's mother said I was a bad influence on her daughter.* 盖伊的母亲说我对她女儿产生了很坏的影响。| **outside influences** (=influences from beyond your own group) 外来的影响 *The tribe remains untouched by outside influences.* 这个部落仍然不受外界的影响。**3 under the influence** *informal* drunk【非正式】喝醉了 2 1

influence[2] *v* [T] to have an effect on the way someone or something develops, behaves, thinks etc without directly forcing or commanding them 影响，起作用: *Bruckner was much influenced by Wagner's orchestral music.* 布鲁克纳深受瓦格纳管弦乐作品的影响。| *Don't let me influence your decision.* 别让我影响你的决定。| **influence sb to do sth** *What influenced you to take the job?* 是什么影响你接受了这份工作? 2 2

in·flu·en·tial /ˌɪnfluˋɛnʃəl; ˌɪnfluˈenʃəl◂/ *adj* having a lot of influence and therefore changing the way people think and behave 有影响力的: *an influential politician* 一位有影响力的政治家 | **influential in doing sth** *Dewey was influential in shaping economic policy.* 杜威对制定经济政策颇有影响。| **highly influential** *a highly influential art magazine* 一本极有影响的艺术杂志

in·flu·en·za /ˌɪnfluˋɛnzə; ˌɪnfluˈenzə/ *n* [U] *technical* an infectious disease that is like a very bad cold; usually shortened to FLU【术语】流行性感冒〔一般简写为 flu〕

in·flux /ˋɪnˌflʌks; ˈɪnflʌks/ *n* [C] the arrival of large numbers of people or large amounts of money, goods etc especially suddenly〔人、钱、货物等突然的〕大量涌入: [+of] *Tourism has brought a huge influx of wealth into the region.* 旅游业使财富大量涌入该地区。

in·fo /ˋɪnfo; ˈɪnfəʊ/ *n* [U] *informal* information【非正式】信息，情报

in·fo·mer·cial /ˋɪnfomɝʃəl; ˈɪnfəʊmɜːʃəl/ *n* [C] *AmE* a long television advertisement that provides a lot of information and seems like a normal programme【美】商品信息[电视片，专题广告片]〔这类广告提供大量信息，看似普通的电视节目〕

in·form /ɪnˋfɔrm; ɪnˈfɔːm/ *v* [T] **1** to formally or officially tell someone about something or give them information〔正式〕通知〔某人〕，告知: *They thought it better to inform the police.* 他们认为最好告知警方。| **inform sb about/of** *Please inform us of any change of address as soon as possible.* 地址如有变更，请尽早通知我们。| **inform sb (that)** *We regret to inform you that your application has been rejected.* 我们很遗憾地通知你，你的申请未获接受。| **inform sb who/why/how etc** *Could you please inform us what books you have in stock?* 能否告知你们库存中有哪些书? **2** *formal* to influence someone's attitude or opinion【正式】影响: *Her experience as a refugee informs the content of her latest novel.* 她的难民经历对她最新推出的小说的内容有影响。 2 2

inform against/on sb *phr v* [T] to tell the police or an enemy information about someone that will harm them 告发，检举: *Treachery intervened when German sympathisers informed on them.* 出了叛徒，亲德分子告发了他们。

3 **in·for·mal** /ɪnˋfɔrml; ɪnˈfɔːməl/ *adj* **1** relaxed and friendly without being restricted by rules of correct behaviour 轻松的，友好的，不拘礼节的: *The atmosphere at work is fairly informal.* 工作气氛相当轻松。| *The two groups met for informal talks.* 两个小组会面举行非正式会谈。**2** an informal style of writing or speaking is suitable for ordinary conversations or letters to friends〔言谈或书信〕非正式的，日常使用的，适于朋友间的 **3** informal clothes are suitable for wearing at home or in ordinary situations〔衣服〕在家穿的，日常穿的: *Students and teachers shared a taste for informal dress.* 学生和老师都喜欢穿便服。—**informally** *adv* —**informality** /ˌɪnfɔrˋmælətɪ; ˌɪnfɔːˈmælɪ̣ti/ *n* [U]

in·for·mant /ɪnˋfɔrmənt; ɪnˈfɔːmənt/ *n* [C] **1** someone who gives secret information about someone else, especially to the police〔尤指向警方〕提供〔某人的〕秘密消息者，线人，告密者: *The FBI were warned about the spy ring by a paid informant.* 一名受雇的线人曾向联邦调查局报告过该间谍网的情况。—compare 比较 INFORMER **2** *technical* someone who gives information about their language, social customs etc to someone who is studying them【术语】〔为研究者提供语言、风俗等资料的〕资料提供人

1 1 **in·for·ma·tion** /ˌɪnfəˋmeʃən; ˌɪnfəˈmeɪʃən/ *n* **1** [U] facts or details that tell you something about a situation, person, event etc 情报，资料，消息: *For further information phone the number below.* 查询详情，请拨打下面的电话号码。| **information that** *We have received information that Grant may have left the country.* 我们得到消息，格兰特可能已经离开了这个国家。| **[+about/on]** *The book contains information about a wide variety of subjects.* 这本书内容广泛。| **provide information** *The guide will provide you with information about the area.* 导游将给你提供该地区的资料。| **additional/ further information** *For further information, please ask at Reception.* 详细情况请向服务台查询。| **gather/collect information** *The survey didn't collect any information about temporary workers.* 这次调查没有收集临时工的资料。| **relevant/necessary/useful information** *There is a severe lack of relevant information and research about this disease.* 这种疾病的相关资料和研究都极度缺乏。| **detailed information** *Readers requiring more detailed information should consult Herman and McCure.* 想得到更详细资料的读者可查阅赫尔曼和麦克里的著作。| **piece of information** *I've one or two useful pieces of information to pass on to you.* 我有一两条有用的消息告诉你。| **my/our information is** (=used when officially stating what you know about a situation) 我/我们得到的消息是〔用于发表正式谈话〕*Our information is that troops have already invaded the city.* 我们得到的消息是军队已侵入这座城市。**2 for your information** *spoken* used when you are telling someone that they are wrong about a particular fact【口】不妨告诉你一下〔用来纠正别人的错误〕: *For your information, I've worked as a journalist for six years.* 不妨告诉你一下，我做记者已有六年了。**3 for information only** written on copies of letters and documents that are sent to someone who needs to know about them but does not have to deal with them 仅供参考〔写在信件和文件的副本上，发给需要知道的人，但对方不用处理〕—see also 另见 **inside information** (INSIDE[4] (2)) **4** [U] *AmE* the telephone service which provides telephone numbers to people who ask for them【美】电话号码查询服务; DIRECTORY ENQUIRIES *BrE*【英】—**informational** *adj*

This graph shows some of the words most commonly used with the noun **information**. 本图表所示为含有名词 information 的一些最常用词组。

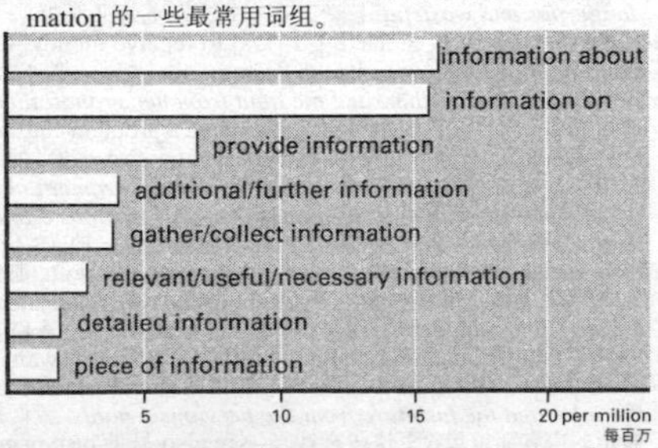

Collocation	Frequency (per million 每百万)
information about	~16
information on	~16
provide information	~7
additional/further information	~4
gather/collect information	~4
relevant/useful/necessary information	~3
detailed information	~2
piece of information	~2

Scale: 5, 10, 15, 20 per million 每百万

Based on the British National Corpus and the Longman Lancaster Corpus 据英国国家语料库和朗文兰开斯特语料库

information cen·tre /ˈ···, ˌ··ˈ··/ *n* [C] a place where you can get information about an area, event etc 信息[资讯]中心

information re·triev·al /ˈ········/ *n* [U] the process of finding stored information, especially on a computer 信息检索〔尤指从电脑存储的资料中查找〕; 资讯检索

information sci·ence /ˌ····ˈ··/ *n* [U] the science of collecting, arranging, storing, and sending out information 信息(科)学〔收集、整理、储存和发送资讯的科学〕; 情报(科)学

information su·per·high·way /ˌɪnfəˋmeʃən ˌsupəˋhaɪwe; ˌɪnfəmeɪʃən ˌsuːpəˈhaɪweɪ/ *n* [singular] the various systems that can be used to send or obtain information, pictures, films etc by electronic means, for example from a computer in one place to a computer in a different place 信息高速公路〔指用电子方法发送或取得信息、图画、影片等的各种系统，如通过电脑之间的互相传送〕

information tech·nol·o·gy /ˈ·····/ *n* [U] the study or use of electronic processes for storing information and making it available; IT 信息技术〔以电子方法储存和使用信息的科学及其应用〕

information the·o·ry /ˈ·····/ *n* [U] *technical* the mathematical principles related to sending and storing information【术语】信息论

in·for·ma·tive /ɪnˋfɔrmətɪv; ɪnˈfɔːmətɪv/ *adj* providing many useful facts or ideas 资料丰富的; 增进知识的: *She gave an informative talk on various aspects of child care.* 她就儿童保育的各方面作了一次内容丰富的讲话。—**informatively** *adv* —**informativeness** *n* [U]

in·formed /ɪnˋfɔrmd; ɪnˈfɔːmd/ *adj* **1** having a lot of knowledge or information about a particular subject or situation 了解情况的，见多识广的: *Informed sources have denied that the President was involved at all.* 消息灵通人士否认总统与此事有任何关系。**2 well-informed/ill-informed/badly-informed** knowing a lot or not knowing much about what is happening in the world 见多识广[消息灵通]的/信息闭塞的/信息不准确的: *She seemed to be fairly well-informed about the underlying economic issues.* 她对基础的经济问题似乎颇有了解。**3 informed guess/estimate/judgment etc** a guess etc that is based on knowledge of a subject or situation 有根据的猜测/估计/判断等 **4 keep sb informed** to give someone the latest news and details about a situation 不断给某人提供〔关于某事的〕最新消息: *Please keep me fully informed of any developments.* 事态如有发展，请向我提供详情。

in·form·er /ɪnˋfɔrmɚ; ɪnˈfɔːmə/ *n* [C] someone who is involved in an organization, especially a criminal organization, but who secretly tells the police, the army etc about its activities in return for money 告密者〔向警方、军方等告密，并收取金钱作回报的人，尤指犯罪团伙的成员〕—compare 比较 INFORMANT (1)

in·fo·tain·ment /ˋɪnfoˌtenmənt; ˈɪnfəʊˌteɪnmənt/ *n* [U] *AmE* television programmes that deal with important subjects in a way that people can enjoy【美】〔在电视中用轻松方式处理重要问题的〕信息娱乐节目

infra- /ɪnfrə; ɪnfrə/ *prefix technical* below something in a range; beyond【术语】在…之下，在…之外: *the infrared end of the spectrum* 光谱的红外线区 —compare 比较 ULTRA- (1)

in·frac·tion /ɪnˋfrækʃən; ɪnˈfrækʃən/ *n* [C,U+of] *formal* an act of breaking a rule or law【正式】违规行为，违法行为

infra dig /ˌɪnfrə ˋdɪg; ˌɪnfrə ˈdɪg/ *adj* [not before noun 不用于名词前] *informal BrE* below the standard of social behaviour that is suitable for a person of your class or rank【非正式，英】有失身份的: *It's a bit infra dig for her to wear jeans on such a formal occasion.* 她在如此正式的场合穿牛仔裤有点儿失身份。

infra-red /ˌɪnfrə ˋrɛd; ˌɪnfrə ˈred◂/ *adj* infra-red light gives out heat but cannot be seen 红外线的 —compare 比较 ULTRAVIOLET

in·fra·struc·ture /ˋɪnfrəˌstrʌktʃɚ; ˈɪnfrəˌstrʌktʃə/ *n* [C] the basic systems and structures that a country or organization needs in order to work properly, for example transport, communications, and banking systems 基础设施〈如运输、通讯、银行制度等〉; 基础结构: *the country's economic infrastructure* 国家的经济基础设施 —**infrastructural** *adj*

in·fre·quent /ɪnˋfrikwənt; ɪnˈfriːkwənt/ *adj* not happening often; rare 不经常发生的; 罕见的: *They would make infrequent visits to the house.* 他们偶尔去看一看那所房子。—**infrequently** *adv*: *We see them only very infrequently.* 我们只是偶然看到他们。—**infrequency** *n* [U] —see 见 RARE (USAGE)

in·fringe /ɪnˋfrɪndʒ; ɪnˈfrɪndʒ/ *v* [T] to do something that is against a law or someone's legal rights 违反〔法律〕，侵犯〔他人权利〕: *Increasing care must be taken not to infringe copyright.* 必须不断加强注意不要侵犯版权。—**infringement** *n* [C,U] *a minor infringement of the rules* 对规则的轻微违反

infringe on/upon sth *phr v* [T] to limit someone's freedom in some way〔在某方面〕限制〔某人的自由〕: *He found that all*

the media attention was infringing upon his private life. 他认为广泛的媒体关注侵犯了他的私生活。

in·fu·ri·ate /ɪn`fjʊrɪˌet; ɪn'fjʊərieɪt/ *v* [T] to make someone extremely angry 使〔某人〕大怒: *It infuriates me to think of all the money we've wasted.* 一想到我们浪费了那么多钱, 我就怒火中烧。

in·fu·ri·a·ting /ɪn`fjʊrɪˌetɪŋ; ɪn'fjʊərieɪtɪŋ/ *adj* very annoying 非常令人恼火的: *It was infuriating to be so close and yet unable to contact them.* 和他们近在咫尺却无法联系, 真叫人恼火。—**infuriatingly** *adv*

in·fuse /ɪn`fjuz; ɪn'fjuːz/ *v* **1** *formal* [T] to fill something or someone with a particular feeling or quality【正式】使充满〔某种感觉〕; 将〔某品质〕注入〔某物〕: **infuse sth/sb with** *She managed to infuse the situation with humour.* 她设法为紧张气氛注入一些幽默感。| **infuse sth into** *Hannah wanted desperately to infuse some vitality into their dull marriage.* 汉娜迫切地希望给他们平淡乏味的婚姻注入一些活力。**2** [I,T] if you infuse tea or HERBs or if they infuse, you leave them in very hot water while their taste passes into the water〔用热水〕泡〔茶或草药〕

in·fu·sion /ɪn`fjuʒən; ɪn'fjuːʒən/ *n* **1** [C,U] the act of putting a new feeling or quality into something〔新感觉或品质的〕注入, 灌输: *What the department needs is an infusion of new ideas.* 这个部门需要注入新思路。**2** [C] a drink made with HERBs in hot water that is usually taken as a medicine 草药泡剂; 花草茶

-ing /ɪŋ; ɪŋ/ *suffix* **1** forms the present participle of verbs〔构成动词的现在分词形式〕: *They're dancing.* 他们在跳舞。| *to go dancing* 去跳舞 | *a dancing bear* 一头摇摇晃晃行走的熊 **2** [in U nouns 构成不可数名词] the action or process of doing something 动作, 过程: *She hates swimming.* 她不喜欢游泳。| *No parking.* (=do not park here) 禁止停车。**3** [in U nouns 构成不可数名词] **a)** a case or example of doing something 做某事的实例: *to hold a meeting* 举行一次会议 **b)** a product or result of doing something〔动作的〕产物; 结果: *a beautiful painting* 一幅美丽的绘画 **4** [in nouns 构成名词] something used to do something or used for making something 做某事或制作某物的材料: *a silk lining* 丝质衬里 | *ten metres of shirting* (=cloth for shirts) 10米的衬衫布

in·ge·ni·ous /ɪn`dʒinjəs; ɪn'dʒiːniəs/ *adj* **1** an ingenious plan, idea, INVENTION etc is the result of clever thinking and new ideas, and works well〔计划、主意、发明等〕巧妙的, 精妙的: *an ingenious way of making money* 赚钱的妙法 | *an ingenious gadget* 巧妙的小玩意 **2** someone who is ingenious is very good at inventing things or thinking of new ideas〔人〕善于创造发明的, 足智多谋的 —**ingeniously** *adv*

in·gé·nue /`ændʒəˌnu; 'ænʒeɪnjuː/ *n* [C] *French* a young inexperienced girl, especially in a film or play【法】〔尤指电影或戏剧中〕涉世未深的少女

in·ge·nu·i·ty /ˌɪndʒə`nuətɪ; ˌɪndʒə'njuːɪ̵ti/ *n* [U] cleverness of inventing things and thinking of new ideas 心灵手巧, 善于创造发明; 足智多谋

in·gen·u·ous /ɪn`dʒɛnjuəs; ɪn'dʒenjuəs/ *adj* inexperienced, simple, trusting, and honest 阅历浅的, 纯朴的, 坦诚率直的 —**ingenuously** *adv* —**ingenuousness** *n* [U] —opposite 反义词 DISINGENUOUS

in·gest /ɪn`dʒɛst; ɪn'dʒest/ *v* [T] *technical* to take food into your body【术语】摄取〔食物〕; 咽下 —compare 比较 DIGEST[1] —**ingestion** /ɪn`dʒɛstʃən; ɪn'dʒestʃən/ *n* [U]

in·gle·nook /`ɪŋglˌnʊk; 'ɪŋgəlnʊk/ *n* [C] *especially BrE* a seat by the side of a large open fireplace, or the space that it is in【尤英】壁炉边的座位; 炉边

in·glo·ri·ous /ɪn`glorɪəs; ɪn'glɔːriəs/ *adj literary* causing shame and dishonour【文】不光彩的, 可耻的, 不名誉的: *an inglorious defeat* 可耻的失败 —**ingloriously** *adv*

in·got /`ɪŋgət; 'ɪŋgət/ *n* [C] a lump of pure metal in a regular shape, usually shaped like a brick〔纯金属的〕锭

in·grained /ɪn`grend; ɪn'greɪnd/ *adj* **1** ingrained attitudes or behaviour are firmly established and therefore difficult to change〔态度或行为〕根深蒂固的, 难以改变的: *an ingrained prejudice against all foreigners* 对一切外国人根深蒂固的偏见 **2** ingrained dirt is under the surface of something and very difficult to remove〔污物〕难以除掉的

in·grate /`ɪngret; ɪn'greɪt/ *n* [C] *formal* an ungrateful person【正式】忘恩负义者

in·gra·ti·ate /ɪn`greʃɪˌet; ɪn'greɪʃieɪt/ *v* **ingratiate yourself (with)** to try hard to get someone's approval, by doing things to please them, expressing admiration etc 使得到〔某人〕的欢心, 讨好〔某人〕: *The child glared so fiercely that I tried to ingratiate myself with her by offering candy.* 那个小女孩对我怒目而视, 我只好给她糖果来讨好她。

in·gra·ti·at·ing /ɪn`greʃɪˌetɪŋ; ɪn'greɪʃieɪtɪŋ/ *adj* trying too hard to get someone's approval 极力讨好奉承的: *I can't stand that ingratiating manner of his.* 我受不了他那副谄媚的样子。—**ingratiatingly** *adv*

in·grat·i·tude /ɪn`grætəˌtjud; ɪn'grætɪ̵tjuːd/ *n* [U] ungratefulness 忘恩负义: *I've never seen such ingratitude in all my life!* 我一辈子都未见过这样忘恩负义的!

in·gre·di·ent /ɪn`gridɪənt; ɪn'griːdiənt/ *n* [C] **1** one of the types of food you use to make a particular dish〔烹调用的〕原料, 材料, 成分: *Have we got all the ingredients for a casserole?* 做沙锅菜的原料都备齐了吗? **2** a quality you need to achieve something〔完成某事的〕要素, 因素: *Imagination and hard work are the ingredients of success.* 想象力与勤奋工作是成功的要素。

In·gres /`æŋgrə; 'æŋgrə/, **Jean Au·guste Dom·i·nique** /ˌʒɑn oʻgjust dɑmə`nik; ˌʒɒn 'əʊgjuːst 'dɒmɪ̵niːk/ (1780-1867) a French painter and leader of the NEOCLASSICAL school (=artists who copied the style of ancient Greece and Rome). He is famous for his PORTRAITS (=paintings of real people) and for his NUDES (=paintings of people, mostly women, without clothes) 安格尔〔(1780-1867), 法国画家、新古典主义画派的领袖, 以肖像画和裸体画闻名〕

in·gress /`ɪngrɛs; 'ɪngres/ *n* [U] *literary* the right to enter a place or the act of entering it【文】进入权; 进入

in-group /`· ·/ *n* [C] a small group of people in an organization or activity who like the same things and are friendly with each other, but do not want other people to join them; CLIQUE〔排他性的〕小集团, 小圈子 —**in-group** *adj*

in·grow·ing /ˌɪn`groɪŋ; ˌɪn'grəʊɪŋ◂/ *BrE*【英】, **in·grown** /ˌɪn`gron; ˌɪn'grəʊn◂/ *AmE*【美】—*adj* [no comparative 无比较级] an ingrowing TOENAIL grows inwards, cutting into the surrounding skin〔脚趾甲〕向内生长的, 长到肉里去的

in·hab·it /ɪn`hæbɪt; ɪn'hæbɪ̵t/ *v* [T] if animals or people inhabit an area or place, they live there〔动物或人〕居住于〔某地〕: *The island is mainly inhabited by sheep.* 这个岛屿主要栖居着绵羊。—**inhabitable** *adj*

in·hab·i·tant /ɪn`hæbətənt; ɪn'hæbɪ̵tənt/ *n* [C] one of the people who live in a particular place 居民: *a city of six million inhabitants* 有六百万居民的城市

in·ha·lant /ɪn`helənt; ɪn'heɪlənt/ *n* [C,U] a medicine or drug that you breathe in, for example when you have a cold 吸入药, 吸入剂

in·hale /ɪn`hel; ɪn'heɪl/ *v* [I,T] *especially technical* to breathe in air, smoke, or gas【尤术语】吸入〔空气、烟雾或气体〕: *It is dangerous to inhale ammonia fumes.* 吸入氨气是很危险的。| **inhale deeply** (=inhale a lot of air or smoke) 深深吸入 *Myra lit another cigarette and inhaled deeply.* 迈拉又点了一支烟, 深吸了一口。—opposite 反义词 EXHALE —**inhalation** /ˌɪnhə`leʃən; ˌɪnhə'leɪʃən/ *n* [C,U]

in·hal·er /ɪn`helə; ɪn'heɪlə/ *n* [C] a small plastic tube containing medicine that you breathe in in order to make breathing easier〔内含药品、用于使呼吸变得较顺畅的〕吸入器

in·here /ɪn`hɪr; ɪn'hɪə/ *v*

inhere in sth *phr v* [T] *technical* to be a natural part of something【术语】为〔某物〕固有的一部分

in·her·ent /ɪn`hɪrənt; ɪn'hɪərənt/ *adj* a quality that is inherent in something is a natural part of it and cannot be separated from it 内在的, 固有的: [**+in**] *I'm afraid the problems you mention are inherent in the system.* 你提及的这些问题恐怕本来就存在于这个体制中。—**inherently** *adv*: *Nuclear power is inherently dangerous and wasteful.* 核动力在本质上既危险又浪费。

in·her·it /ɪn`hɛrɪt; ɪn'herɪ̵t/ *v* **1** [I,T] to receive money, property etc from someone after they have died 继承〔遗产〕: **inherit sth from** *She inherited the land from her grandfather.* 她从祖父那里继承了这块土地。**2** [T] to have a problem caused by mistakes that other people have made in the past 承担〔他人过去错误造成的问题〕: **inherit sth from** *The government claims to have inherited all of its problems from the previous administration.* 政府声称所有问题都是前任政府遗留下来的。**3** [T] to have the same character or appearance as your parents 遗传得到〔父母的性格、外貌〕: **inherit sth from** *Gordon's inherited his father's bad temper.* 戈登的坏脾气得自父亲的遗传。**4** [T] *informal* to get something that someone else does not want any more【非正式】接收〔别人不再需要的东西〕: **inherit sth from** *We inherited the furniture from the previous tenants.* 我们从刚搬走的房客那里接收了这些家具。—see also 另见 DISINHERIT

in·her·i·tance /ɪn`hɛrətəns; ɪn'herɪ̵təns/ *n* **1** [C,U] money, property etc that you receive from someone who has died 继承的遗产: *She had squandered and gambled away her inheritance within a year.* 不出一年, 她就把她所继承的遗产挥霍赌博掉了。

2 [U] *formal* ideas, beliefs, skills, literature, music etc from the past that influence people in the present【正式】遗产〔指仍对人们有影响的思想、信念、技艺、文学、音乐等〕: *our literary inheritance* 我们的文学遗产

inheritance tax /ˈ· ··· ˌ·/ *n* [U] a tax on the money or property that you give to someone else after you die 遗产税, 继承税

in·her·i·tor /ɪnˋhɛrɪtɚ; ɪnˈherɪ̈tə/ *n* [C] someone who receives money, property etc from someone who has just died 遗产继承人

in·hib·it /ɪnˋhɪbɪt; ɪnˈhɪbɪ̈t/ *v* [T] **1** to prevent something from growing or developing as much as it might have done otherwise 抑制, 约束: *Failure to set up a good transport network inhibited the expansion of trade.* 未能建立良好的运输网络限制了贸易的发展。**2** to make someone feel embarrassed or less confident so that they cannot do or say what they want to 使羞于, 使怯于: **inhibit sb from doing sth** *Being too critical may inhibit a child from asking you things he needs to know.* 过分挑剔会使孩子不敢问你他想知道的事情。| *an inhibiting influence* 有约束作用的影响

in·hib·it·ed /ɪnˋhɪbɪtɪd; ɪnˈhɪbɪ̈tɪ̈d/ *adj* not confident or relaxed enough to do or say what you want to 拘谨的, 束手束脚的: **feel inhibited** *When discussing sexual matters many people feel very inhibited.* 谈到性的问题, 许多人都很不自在。—**inhibitedly** *adv*

in·hi·bi·tion /ˌɪnhɪˋbɪʃən; ˌɪnhɪ̈ˈbɪʃən/ *n* [C,U] a feeling of worry or embarrassment that stops you doing or saying what you really want to 〔忧虑、窘迫等造成的〕抑制, 顾虑, 拘谨: **lose your inhibitions** (=stop feeling worried etc) 无所顾忌 *That night she finally lost her inhibitions and told him how she felt.* 那天夜里, 她终于打消所有顾虑, 把自己的心思都告诉了他。

in·hos·pi·ta·ble /ɪnˋhɑspɪtəbḷ; ˌɪnhɒˈspɪtəbəl/ *adj* **1** an inhospitable place is difficult to live or stay in because of severe weather conditions or lack of shelter 〔地方〕荒凉的; 不适宜居住的〔由于天气恶劣或缺乏遮蔽处〕: *inhospitable desert regions* 荒凉的沙漠地区 **2** unfriendly to a visitor, especially by not welcoming them, offering them food etc 慢待〔尤指不欢迎, 不招待〕客人的, 不好客的

in-house /ˌ· ˈ·◂/ *adj, adv* within a company or organization rather than outside it 公司[组织]内部的; 在机构内部: *We have an in-house training unit.* 我们公司设有一个内部培训部。| *The keyboarding is done in-house.* 资料输入在公司内部完成。

in·hu·man /ɪnˋhjumən; ɪnˈhjuːmən/ *adj* **1** very cruel without any normal feelings of pity 残暴的, 无同情心的: *an inhuman tyrant* 野蛮的暴君 | *The slaves were subjected to inhuman discipline.* 奴隶受到残酷的管束。**2** lacking any human qualities in a way that seems strange or frightening 无人性的, 看似怪异[令人惊恐]的: *a fear of modern technology as something inhuman and threatening* 对现代科技的恐惧, 认为它缺乏人性、构成威胁 | *The interviewer had a cold, almost inhuman, manner.* 面试官态度冷峻, 几乎没什么人情味。—**inhumanly** *adv*

in·hu·mane /ˌɪnhjuˋmen; ˌɪnhjuːˈmeɪn/ *adj* causing too much suffering and therefore considered cruel and unacceptable 残忍的, 不人道的: **inhumane treatment/conditions/laws etc** *the inhumane treatment of political prisoners* 对政治犯的虐待 —**inhumanely** *adv*

in·hu·man·i·ty /ˌɪnhjuˋmænətɪ; ˌɪnhjuːˈmænɪ̈ti/ *n* [C usually plural 一般用复数,U] cruel behaviour or acts 残酷无情的行为[举止, 行动]: *The book focuses on the inhumanity of the labour camps.* 这本书着重描述劳改营的残酷情况。

in·im·i·cal /ɪnˋɪmɪkḷ; ɪˈnɪmɪkəl/ *adj formal* very unfavourable for something【正式】极为不利的: *a cold, inimical climate* 寒冷严酷的气候 | **[+to]** *conditions inimical to economic development* 对经济发展极为不利的条件 —**inimically** /-klɪ; -kli/ *adv*

in·im·i·ta·ble /ɪnˋɪmətəbḷ; ɪˈnɪmɪ̈təbəl/ *adj* too good or skilful for anyone else to copy with the same high standard 〔高超得〕难以模仿的, 无与伦比的: *the inimitable Billie Holliday* 盖世无双的比利·霍利迪 | *singing in his own inimitable style* 以其无与伦比的风格演唱 —**inimitably** *adv* —compare 比较 IMITATE

in·iq·ui·tous /ɪˋnɪkwətəs; ɪˈnɪkwɪ̈təs/ *adj formal* very unfair and morally wrong【正式】极不公正的, 邪恶的: *an iniquitous system of taxes that victimizes the poor* 损害穷人的极不公平的税收体制 —**iniquitously** *adv*

in·iq·ui·ty /ɪˋnɪkwətɪ; ɪˈnɪkwɪ̈ti/ *n* [C,U] *formal*【正式】**1** the quality of being very unfair or evil, or something that is very unfair 极不公正, 邪恶; 不公正的事 **2** **den of iniquity** *humorous* a place where there is a lot of immoral behaviour【幽默】罪恶的渊薮: *Our mother regarded the pub as a den of iniquity.* 我们的母亲认为那家酒吧是邪恶的场所。

i·ni·tial¹ /ɪˋnɪʃəl; ɪˈnɪʃəl/ *adj* [only before noun 仅用于名词前] happening at the beginning; first 开始的, 最初的: *She overcame her initial shyness and really enjoyed the evening.* 她克服了开始时的羞怯, 晚上玩得很高兴。| *an initial investment of £5000* 最初投资5000英镑 [2]

initial² *n* [C] **1** the first letter of someone's first name 名字的首字母: *"Can I have your initial, Mr Davies?!" "It's G, Mr G Davies."* "戴维斯先生, 您名字的首字母是什么?" "是G, G.戴维斯。" **2** **initials** [plural] the first letters of all your names in order 姓名的首字母: *His initials are DPH: they stand for David Perry Hallworth.* 他姓名的首字母是DPH, 代表戴维·佩里·霍尔沃思。

initial³ *v* **initialled, initialling** *BrE*【英】, **initialed, initialing** *AmE*【美】[T] to write your initials on a document to make it official or to show that you agree with something 在〔文件〕上签上姓名的首字母〔使其正式或表示同意〕: *You have to initial any corrections on a cheque.* 支票上任何更改之处都要签上你姓名的首字母。

i·ni·tial·ly /ɪˋnɪʃəlɪ; ɪˈnɪʃəli/ *adv* at the beginning 起初: *The president initially appeared to endorse the idea.* 总统起初好像赞同这个想法。 [3]

i·ni·ti·ate¹ /ɪˋnɪʃɪˌet; ɪˈnɪʃieɪt/ *v* [T] **1** *formal* to arrange for something important to start, such as an official process or a new plan【正式】开始实施〔重要的事, 如官方程序或新计划〕; 发起: *The plaintiffs initiated court proceedings in order to recover their debts.* 原告们开始法律诉讼以讨回债款。**2** to introduce someone to special knowledge or skills that they did not know about before 向〔某人〕传授专门知识[技巧]: *During that summer he was initiated into the mysteries of sex.* 那年夏天, 他对性的奥秘获得了初步了解。**3** to introduce someone into an organization, club, group etc, usually with a special ceremony 〔通过特殊仪式〕使〔某人〕加入〔组织、俱乐部、社团等〕: *In August Ivan was initiated into the Oakland chapter of the Hell's Angels.* 8月, 伊万被邀加入"地狱天使集团"的奥克兰分部。

initiate² *n* [C] someone who has been allowed to join a particular group and has been taught its secrets 被吸纳加入某组织并授以诀窍的人

i·ni·ti·a·tion /ɪˌnɪʃɪˋeʃən; ɪˌnɪʃiˈeɪʃən/ *n* [C,U] **1** the process of officially introducing someone into a club or group, or of introducing a young person to adult life, often with a special ceremony 〔正式加入俱乐部或社团的〕入会仪式; 〔青年男女的〕成年仪式: *The initiation ceremony involves elaborate dances.* 成年仪式包括各种复杂的舞蹈。**2** the act of starting something such as an official process, a new plan etc 〔新计划、官方方案等的〕发起, 实施

i·ni·tia·tive /ɪˋnɪʃɪˌetɪv; ɪˈnɪʃətɪv/ *n* [2]

1 ▶YOUR OWN DECISIONS 个人的决定◀ [U] the ability to make decisions and take action without waiting for someone to tell you what to do 自主决断行事的能力; 主动能力: *I wish my son would show a bit more initiative.* 我希望我的儿子能表现得再主动一些。| **use your (own) initiative** *Don't keep asking me for advice. Use your initiative.* 别总是要我给你出主意, 发挥你自己的决断能力吧。| **on your own initiative** (=without being told what to do) 主动地, 自主地: *Lieutenant Carlos was not obeying orders. He acted on his own initiative.* 卡洛斯中尉没有服从命令, 而是自己作主。

2 ▶PLAN 计划◀ [C] an important new plan or process that has been started in order to achieve a particular aim or to solve a particular problem 计划, 措施: *a government initiative to help exporters* 扶助出口商的政府计划

3 ▶ADVANTAGE 优势◀ **the initiative** the power to gain an advantage by taking actions that will influence events 〔能够影响事情发展的〕主动权: **seize/hold/lose the initiative** *Zhukov was quick to seize the initiative and launched a massive counter-attack.* 朱可夫迅速掌握主动, 发动大规模反攻。

4 take the initiative to be the first one to take action to improve a situation or relationship, especially when other people are waiting for someone else to do something 带头, 率先〔改善情况或关系, 尤指其他人都在等待某人先行动时〕: *Why don't you take the initiative and arrange a meeting?* 你为什么不带个头, 安排一次会议呢?

5 ▶TO CHANGE A LAW 修改法律◀ [C] *law* a process by which ordinary citizens can propose a change in the law by signing a PETITION¹ (1)【法律】公民〔签名提出修改法律的〕提案程序

in·ject /ɪnˋdʒɛkt; ɪnˈdʒekt/ *v* [T] **1** to put liquid, especially a drug, into someone's body by using a special needle 〔向体内〕注射〔液体, 尤指药液〕: **inject sth into** *The drug is injected directly into the base of the spine.* 药物被直接注射入脊椎底部。| **inject sb with** *The patient had been injected with a narcotic drug.* 病人已被注射了麻醉剂。**2** to improve something

by adding excitement, interest etc to it 增加〔气氛、兴趣等〕: *They hoped that the adoption of a child would inject new life into their marriage.* 他们希望收养一个孩子能给他们的婚姻增添生气。**3** [+into] to provide more money, equipment etc for something 投入〔更多的资金、设备等〕

3 **in·jec·tion** /ɪnˋdʒɛkʃən; ɪnˈdʒekʃən/ *n* **1** [C,U] an act of giving a drug by using a special needle 注射: **give sb an injection** *The nurse gave me a tetanus injection.* 护士给我注射了一剂破伤风预防针。**2** [C,U] the act of forcing a liquid into something〔液体的〕注入: *a fuel injection system* 燃油注入系统 **3** [C] an addition of money to something in order to improve it 资金注入〔为了改进某事〕: [+of] *a massive injection of public funds* 大量注入公用基金

in-joke /ˈ· ·/ *n* [C] a joke that is only understood by a particular group of people〔只有某圈子里的人才能听懂的〕内部笑话

in·ju·di·cious /ˌɪndʒuˋdɪʃəs; ˌɪndʒuːˈdɪʃəs/ *adj formal* an injudicious action, remark etc is not sensible and is likely to have bad results【正式】〔行为、言论等〕不明智的〔可能产生不良后果〕, 不谨慎的: *I thought his choice of words injudicious, to say the least.* 我认为他至少是措辞不当。—**injudiciously** *adv* —**injudiciousness** *n* [U]

In·jun /ˋɪndʒən; ˈɪndʒən/ *n* **honest Injun** *spoken especially AmE* used especially by children to make someone believe they are telling the truth【口, 尤美】是真的, 一点不假〔尤为儿语, 用于使人相信他们说的是真话〕

in·junc·tion /ɪnˋdʒʌŋkʃən; ɪnˈdʒʌŋkʃən/ *n* [C] **1** *law* an order given by a court which forbids someone to do something【法律】〔由法院发出的〕强制令: [+against] *The company is seeking an injunction against the strike.* 这家公司正要求法院下令禁止罢工。| **take out an injunction against** (=get an injunction from a court) 取得法院的禁令 *Johnson took out an injunction to prevent the publication going ahead.* 约翰逊取得禁令, 阻止这项出版继续进行。**2** *formal* a piece of advice or a command from someone in authority【正式】训谕, 忠告, 指令

in·jure /ˋɪndʒɚ; ˈɪndʒə/ *v* [T] **1** to cause physical harm to someone or to yourself, for example in an accident or an attack 受伤, 伤害: *One of the players injured his knee and had to be carried off.* 一个队员膝盖受伤被抬至场外。| **be badly/seriously/critically injured** *Two people have been critically injured in a road accident.* 在一次交通事故中, 有两人严重受伤。**2 injure sb's pride/self-esteem etc** to upset someone by damaging their confidence 伤害某人的自尊心等 —compare 比较 WOUND[3]

in·jured /ˋɪndʒɚd; ˈɪndʒəd/ *adj* **1** having an injury 受伤的: *He isn't injured – just shocked.* 他没有受伤, 只是受了惊吓。**2 the injured** injured people 伤者: *Firefighters had to cut open the wreckage in order to get the injured out.* 消防员必须割开残骸才能救出受伤者。**3 an injured look/expression etc** a look that shows you feel you have been treated unfairly 委屈的样子/表情等 **4 injured pride/feelings etc** a feeling of being upset or offended because you think you have been unfairly treated 受到伤害的自尊/情感等〔由于觉得受委屈〕 **5 the injured party** *formal* the person who has been unfairly treated in a particular situation【正式】受到不公正待遇的一方

in·ju·ri·ous /ɪnˋdʒurɪəs; ɪnˈdʒʊəriəs/ *adj formal* causing injury, harm, or damage【正式】有害的, 致伤的: *Smoking is injurious to health.* 吸烟危害健康。

2 **in·ju·ry** /ˋɪndʒərɪ; ˈɪndʒəri/ *n* **1** [C] a wound or damage to part of your body caused by an accident or attack〔对身体的〕伤害, 损害: **sustain injuries** *formal* (=be injured)【正式】受到伤害 *The driver of the lorry sustained only minor injuries to legs and arms.* 卡车司机只是四肢受了点轻伤。| **internal injuries** (=injuries inside your body) 内伤 **2** [U] physical harm that is caused by an accident or attack〔因事故或攻击造成的〕人身伤害: *insurance against injury at work* 工伤保险 **3 do yourself an injury** *BrE humorous* to accidentally hurt yourself【英, 幽默】〔意外地〕自我伤害: *Don't lift that tool-box – you'll do yourself an injury!* 别搬那只工具箱, 会砸着你的! —see also 另见 **add insult to injury** (ADD (8))

injury time /ˈ···, ·ˈ/ *n* [U] *BrE* playing time added on to a game such as football because of time lost when players are injured【英】补时〔足球赛中因球员受伤耽误而延长比赛时间〕

in·jus·tice /ɪnˋdʒʌstɪs; ɪnˈdʒʌstɪs/ *n* **1** [C,U] a situation in which people are treated very unfairly and not given their rights 不公正, 非正义: *the injustice of slavery* 奴隶制的非正义 | *innumerable injustices against the black population* 对黑人难以计数的不公正行为 **2 do sb an injustice** to judge someone's character unfairly 冤枉某人: *It would be doing Brett an injustice to say that he didn't care about other people.* 说布雷特不关心他人是冤枉他了。

ink[1] /ɪŋk; ɪŋk/ *n* **1** [C,U] coloured liquid used for writing, printing or drawing 墨水 **2** [U] the black liquid in sea creatures such as OCTOPUS and SQUID〔章鱼、乌贼等海洋生物分泌出的〕墨汁

ink[2] *v* [T] **1** to put ink on something 涂墨水于〔某物〕 **2** *AmE* to write something in ink, especially your SIGNATURE on a contract etc【美】用墨水书写〔尤指在合同上用墨水笔签名〕: *Just ink your name on the bottom line.* 请在底线上签名。

ink sth ↔ **in** *phr v* [T] to complete something done in pencil by drawing over it in ink 在〔铅笔底稿上〕用墨水加描

In·ka·tha /ɪnˋkɑtə; ɪnˈkɑːtə/ a political party in South Africa which represents the Zulu people. Its full name is **the Inkatha Freedom Party** 因卡塔〔南非一祖鲁人政党, 全称为因卡塔自由党〕

ink-jet print·er /ˋɪŋkdʒɛt ˌprɪntɚ; ˈɪŋkdʒet ˌprɪntə/ *n* [C] an electronic printer, usually connected to a small computer 喷墨打印机 —see picture on page A14 参见 A14 页图

ink·ling /ˋɪŋklɪŋ; ˈɪŋklɪŋ/ *n* **have an inkling** to have a slight idea about something 略知; 模糊的印象: *We had no inkling that he was leaving.* 我们根本不知道他要走。| *No one gave me the slightest inkling of what they were planning.* 他们在盘算什么, 没人给我透露半点消息。

ink pad /ˈ· ·/ *n* [C] a small box containing ink on a thick piece of cloth, used for putting ink onto a stamp (STAMP[1] (2)) that is pressed onto paper (打) 印台

ink·stand /ˋɪŋkˌstænd; ˈɪŋkstænd/ *n* [C] a container for pens and pots of ink, kept on a desk 墨水台

ink·well /ˋɪŋkˌwɛl; ˈɪŋk-wel/ *n* [C] a container for ink which fits into a hole in a desk〔嵌在桌上的〕墨水池

ink·y /ˋɪŋkɪ; ˈɪŋki/ *adj* **1** marked with ink 沾有墨水的: *inky fingers* 沾有墨水的手指 **2** *poetic* very dark【诗】漆黑的: *I stared out into the inky blackness of the night.* 我凝视着外面漆黑的夜色。—**inkiness** *n* [U]

INLA, the /ˌaɪ ɛn ɛl ˋe; ˌaɪ en el ˈeɪ/ the Irish National Liberation Army; a PARAMILITARY organization (=a group like an unofficial army) in Northern Ireland, which wants the two parts of Ireland to be united and uses violent methods to achieve its aims. Unlike the IRA, the INLA did not support the Northern Ireland peace talks of 1996-98 or the peace agreement of 1998. 爱尔兰民族解放军〔北爱尔兰一准军事组织, 旨在采取暴力手段实现爱尔兰统一。有别于爱尔兰共和军的是, 该组织不支持1996至1998年的北爱尔兰和平会谈及1998年的和平协议〕

in·laid /ˌɪnˋled; ˌɪnˈleɪd◂/ *adj* **1** an inlaid box, table, floor etc has a thin layer of another material set into its surface for decoration〔箱子、桌子、地板等〕镶嵌着…的: [+with] *a wooden jewellery box inlaid with ivory* 嵌有象牙的木制珠宝盒 **2** [+in/into] metal, stone etc that is inlaid into the surface of another material is set into its surface as decoration 镶入的, 嵌入的

in·land[1] /ˋɪnlənd; ˈɪnlənd/ *adj* [only before noun 仅用于名词前] an inland area, city etc is not near the coast 内陆的, 内地的

in·land[2] /ˋɪnˌlænd; ɪnˈlænd/ *adv* in a direction away from the coast and towards the centre of a country 向内陆, 在内地: *The mountains are five miles inland.* 这些山位于内陆五英里处。

Inland Rev·e·nue /ˌ·· ˈ···/ *n* [singular] the government department which collects national taxes in Britain〔英国的〕政府税收机关, 税务局

in-laws /ˈ· ·/ *n* [plural] *informal* your relatives by marriage, especially the father and mother of your husband or wife【非正式】姻亲〔尤指岳父母或公婆〕: *We have to spend Christmas with the in-laws.* 我们得和姻亲们一起过圣诞节。

in·lay /ˋɪnˌle; ˈɪnleɪ/ *n* **1** [C,U] a material which has been set into the surface of furniture, floors etc for decoration, or the pattern made by this 镶嵌物; 镶嵌图案: *a cedarwood casket with gold inlay* 镶金的雪松木小盒 **2** [C] a substance used by a DENTIST to fill a hole in a decayed tooth 补牙用的充填物

in·let /ˋɪnˌlɛt; ˈɪnlet/ *n* [C] **1** a narrow area of water reaching from the sea or a lake into the land or between islands 水湾〔海边、湖边或岛屿之间的狭长水域〕; 小港: *bays and sheltered inlets along the coast* 沿岸的海湾和可避风浪的小港 **2** the part of a machine through which liquid or gas flows in〔机器上液体或气体的〕入口, 进口: *a fuel inlet* 燃油注入口

in lo·co pa·ren·tis /ɪn ˋloko pəˋrɛntɪs; ɪn ˌləʊkəʊ pəˈrentɪs/ *adv Latin, formal or law* having the responsibilities of a parent for someone else's child【拉丁, 正式或法律】〔对别人的孩子〕代尽父母的责任: *As a teacher, you should regard yourself as being in loco parentis.* 作为教师, 你应知道自己有代尽父母的责任。

in·mate /ˋɪnmet; ˈɪnmeɪt/ *n* [C] someone who is kept in a prison or MENTAL HOSPITAL〔监狱中的〕囚犯; 〔精神病院的〕病人: *One of the inmates has escaped.* 有一名病人[犯人]逃跑了。

in me·mo·ri·am /ɪn məˋmɔrɪˏæm; ɪn mɪ̵ˈmɔːriəm/ *prep Latin* an expression meaning 'in memory of', used especially on the stone above a grave【拉丁】〔用在墓碑上表示〕为了纪念〔某人〕

in·most /ˋɪnˏmost; ˈɪnməʊst/ *adj* [only before noun 仅用于名词前] **1** your inmost feelings, desires etc are the ones you feel most strongly and keep private〔感情、欲望等〕内心深处的, 内心隐秘处的 **2** *formal* furthest inside【正式】最深处的: *She consigned the letter to the inmost recesses of her desk.* 她把那封信藏到书桌里面最隐秘的地方。—opposite 反义词 OUTERMOST

inn /ɪn; ɪn/ *n* [C] **1** *especially BrE* a small PUB or hotel, especially one in the countryside, built in an old-fashioned style【尤英】〔样式古老的〕小酒馆; 小旅馆 **2** a word used in the names of some PUBs and hotels …酒店〔用于某些酒馆、旅店的名称〕: *We're staying at the Holiday Inn.* 我们住在假日酒店。

in·nards /ˋɪnɚdz; ˈɪnədz/ *n* [plural] **1** *informal* the parts inside your body, especially your stomach【非正式】内脏〔尤指胃部〕 **2** the parts inside a machine 机器的内部

in·nate /ˌɪˋnet; ɪˈneɪt◂/ *adj* an innate quality has been part of your character since you were born〔素质〕天生的, 固有的: *Donna had an innate ability to sense when someone was unhappy.* 唐娜有一种天生的本领, 能觉察出谁心情不好。—**innately** *adv*: *the army's innately conservative values* 军队固有的保守价值观

[2] **in·ner** /ˋɪnɚ; ˈɪnə/ *adj* [only before noun 仅用于名词前] **1** on the inside or close to the centre of something 内部的, 靠近中心的: *an inner room* 内室 | *Dial 0171 for inner London.* 往伦敦中心区打电话要拨 0171。| *the inner ear* 内耳 —opposite 反义词 OUTER **2** connected with your soul or deepest feelings 心灵的, 内心的: *I really enjoy yoga – it gives me a sense of inner calm.* 我很喜欢瑜伽, 它使我感到内心平静。**3 inner meanings/thoughts etc** meanings or thoughts that are secret and not expressed 含蓄隐晦的意思/思想等: *Sarah suspected that his comment had an inner meaning.* 莎拉怀疑他的评论含有言外之意。**4 inner circle** the few people in an organization, political party etc who control it or share power with its leader〔组织、政党等的〕核心集团: *The invasion plans were only divulged to the President's inner circle.* 入侵计划只透露给总统的核心集团。**5 the inner man/woman a)** the soul 灵魂 **b)** *humorous* the desire for food; APPETITE (1)【幽默】食欲, 胃口

inner cit·y /ˌ‥ ˈ‥◂/ *n* [C] the part near the middle of a city where the buildings are in a bad condition and the people are poor 市中心贫民区: *the problem of deprivation in our inner cities* 旧城区的贫困问题 —**inner city** *adj*: *squalor in inner-city areas* 贫民区的肮脏穷困

Inner Heb·ri·des, the /ˌɪnɚ ˋhɛbrɪdiz; ˌɪnə ˈhebrɪ̵diːz/ a group of islands west of Scotland and east of the Outer Hebrides. The largest islands are Skye, Islay, and Mull, and many tourists go there in the summer. 内赫布里底群岛〔苏格兰以西、外赫布里底群岛以东的一群岛屿, 最大岛屿为斯凯岛、艾莱岛和马尔岛。夏季这一地区游客络绎不绝〕

Inner Mon·go·li·a /ˌɪnɚ mɑŋˋgoliə; ˌɪnə mɒŋˈgəʊliə/ an Autonomous Region in the north of China which has large areas of grasslands and desert 内蒙古〔中国北方一自治区, 有大片草原和沙漠〕

in·ner·most /ˋɪnɚˏmost; ˈɪnəməʊst/ *adj* [only before noun 仅用于名词前] **1** your innermost feelings, desires etc are the ones you feel most strongly about and do not talk about〔情感、欲望等〕隐秘的, 内心深处的 **2** *formal* furthest inside【正式】最里面的: *the innermost depths of the cave* 山洞的最深处

Inner Tem·ple, the /ˌ‥ ˈ‥/ a London organization of law students and BARRISTERs and the buildings they use, which is the oldest of the four Inns of Court 内殿律师学院〔伦敦四个律师学院中历史最悠久的一个学院〕

inner tube /ˈ‥ ˌ/ *n* [C] **1** the air-filled rubber tube inside a tyre〔轮胎的〕内胎 **2 go inner-tubing** *AmE* to ride on an inner tube either on water or down a snow-covered hill【美】用内胎冲浪[滑雪]

in·ning /ˋɪnɪŋ; ˈɪnɪŋ/ *n* [C] one of the nine playing periods in a game of BASEBALL or SOFTBALL〔棒球或垒球九局比赛的一〕局

in·nings /ˋɪnɪŋz; ˈɪnɪŋz/ *n plural* **innings 1** [C] the period of time when a cricket team or player bats (BAT² (1))〔板球球队或球员可以击球的〕局 **2 he/ she had a good innings** *BrE informal* used about someone who has died to say that they had a long life【英, 非正式】他/她享高寿〔指已逝世的人〕: *It's sad. Still, she was 89 – she had a good innings.* 真叫人伤心。不过, 她活了89岁, 很长寿了。

inn·keep·er /ˋɪnˏkipɚ; ˈɪnˏkiːpə/ *n* [C] *old use* someone who owns or manages an INN【旧】小旅馆老板; 客栈掌柜

in·no·cence /ˋɪnəsn̩s; ˈɪnəsəns/ *n* [U] **1** the fact of being not guilty of a crime 清白无罪: *Can you prove your innocence?* 你能证明自己无罪吗? | **protest your innocence** (=say repeatedly that you are not guilty) 再三申明无罪 *The prisoners continued to protest their innocence.* 犯人们一再申明他们无罪。**2** the state of not having much experience of life or knowledge about evil in the world, especially so that you are easily deceived 阅世不深, 天真, 单纯: *In our innocence we believed everything we were told.* 我们太幼稚, 他们所说的我们都信以为真。| *the innocence of childhood* 童年的天真单纯 **3 in all innocence** if you do or say something in all innocence, you have no intention of doing harm or of offending anyone 完全没有恶意

in·no·cent¹ /ˋɪnəsn̩t; ˈɪnəsənt/ *adj* **1** not guilty of a crime 无罪的: *Nobody would believe that I was innocent.* 没人肯相信我是无罪的。| [+of] *He's innocent of murder.* 他没犯杀人罪。**2 innocent victims/bystanders/ people etc** people who get hurt or killed in a war or as a result of a crime though they are not involved in it〔战争或犯罪行为〕无辜的受害者/旁观者/人们等: *innocent victims of ruthless terrorism* 残忍恐怖主义的无辜受害者 **3** done or said without intending to harm or offend anyone 不带恶意的: *He was startled by their angry reaction to his innocent remark.* 他们对他那并无恶意的话如此愤怒, 使他大为惊讶。**4** not having much experience of life, so that you are easily deceived; NAIVE 天真无邪的, 阅世不深的: *I was thirteen years old and very innocent.* 我那时13岁, 年幼无知。—**innocently** *adv*

innocent² *n* [C] someone who does not have much experience of life or knowledge about evil in the world 涉世不深的人

in·noc·u·ous /ɪˋnɑkjuəs; ɪˈnɒkjuəs/ *adj* not offensive, dangerous, or harmful 无意冒犯的, 不危险的, 无害的: *an innocuous remark* 无恶意的话语 | *Those innocuous-looking cases contain enough explosive to destroy this building.* 那些貌似无害的箱子里面装的炸药足以摧毁这幢大楼。—**innocuously** *adv* —**innocuousness** *n* [U]

in·no·vate /ˋɪnəˏvet; ˈɪnəveɪt/ *v* [I] to start to use new ideas, methods, or inventions 革新, 创新, 改革

in·no·va·tion /ˌɪnəˋveʃən; ˌɪnəˈveɪʃən/ *n* **1** [C] a new idea, [3] method, or invention 新观念, 新方法, 新发明: *recent technological innovations* 最近的技术发明 **2** [U] the introduction of new ideas or methods 革新; 创新: *We must encourage innovation if the company is to remain competitive.* 公司要想保持竞争力, 就必须鼓励革新。

in·nov·at·ive /ˋɪnəˏvetɪv; ˈɪnəˏveɪtɪv/ *adj* **1** an innovative process, method, plan etc is new, different, and better than those that existed before〔程序、方法、计划等〕新颖的, 有创新精神的 **2** using clever new ideas and methods 运用新观念和新方法的: *a young innovative company* 一家富有新意的新公司

in·no·vat·or /ˋɪnəˏvetɚ; ˈɪnəveɪtə/ *n* [C] someone who introduces changes and new ideas 革新者, 创新者

Inns of Court, the /ˌ· · ˈ·/ the four law societies and their buildings in London, for students and practising BARRISTERs, which an English barrister must belong to. The four societies are Lincoln's Inn, the Inner Temple, the Middle Temple, and Gray's Inn. 律师学院〔英国伦敦的四个培养律师的机构。它们分别是林肯律师学院、内殿律师学院、中殿律师学院和格雷律师学院。英格兰大律师必须是其中一个学院的成员〕

in·nu·en·do /ˌɪnjuˋɛndo; ˌɪnjuˈendəʊ/ *n plural* **innuendoes** or **innuendos 1** [C] an indirect remark about sex or about something bad that someone has done 影射〔性或某人所做的坏事〕的话, 暗讽的话: *lies and innuendoes* 谎言与暗讽 **2** [U] the act of making such unpleasant remarks 含沙射影; 暗讽: *a despicable smear campaign based on rumour, innuendo, and gossip* 以造谣、暗讽和流言飞语为内容, 为人所不齿的有组织的诽谤行动

In·nu·it /ˋɪnjuɪt; ˈɪnjuɪ̵t/ *n* [U], *adj* another spelling of INUIT Inuit 的另一种拼法

in·nu·me·ra·ble /ɪˋnjumərəbl̩; ɪˈnjuːmərəbəl/ *adj* very many, or too many to be counted 不可胜数的: *They received innumerable letters of complaint about the programme.* 他们收到了大量对该计划的投诉信。

in·nu·mer·ate /ɪˋnjumərɪt; ɪˈnjuːmərɪ̵t/ *adj* unable to do calculations or understand basic mathematics 不会计算的, 不会基础数学的 —**innumeracy** *n* [U]

i·noc·u·late /ɪnˋɑkjəˏlet; ɪˈnɒkjʊ̵leɪt/ *v* [T] to protect someone against a disease, usually by injecting (INJECT (1)) them with a weak form of it 给〔某人〕接种, 给〔某人〕作预防注射: [+against] *All the children had been inoculated against hepatitis.* 所有孩子都注射了肝炎预防针。—compare 比较 IMMUNIZE, VACCINATE —**inoculation** /ɪˌnɑkjəˋleʃən; ɪˌnɒkjʊ̵ˈleɪʃən/ *n* [C,U]

in·of·fen·sive /ˌɪnəˋfɛnsɪv; ˌɪnəˈfensɪv◂/ *adj* unlikely to offend anyone 不触犯人的，不会得罪人的：*Her husband was a small, inoffensive-looking man.* 她丈夫个子不高，看上去很随和。—**inoffensively** *adv* —**inoffensiveness** *n* [U]

in·op·e·ra·ble /ɪnˋɑpərəbḷ; ɪnˈɒpərəbəl/ *adj* **1** an inoperable illness or TUMOUR (=lump) cannot be treated or removed by a medical operation〔疾病、肿瘤〕无法用手术治疗的：*an inoperable spinal tumour* 不能用手术治疗的脊椎肿瘤 **2** an inoperable system or method is not practical and therefore cannot be used〔系统、方法〕不实际的，行不通的

in·op·e·ra·tive /ɪnˋɑpəˌrətɪv; ɪnˈɒpərətɪv/ *adj formal*【正式】**1** a machine that is inoperative is not working, or is not in working condition〔机器〕不运转的；不在工作状态的 **2** a system or a law that is inoperative is not working or cannot be made to work〔系统、法律〕不能实施的，无效的

in·op·por·tune /ˌɪnɑpəˋtjun; ɪnˈɒpətjuːn/ *adj formal*【正式】**1** an inopportune moment or time is not suitable or good for something〔时间等〕不合适的，不适宜的：*I'm afraid you've called at rather an inopportune moment.* 我恐怕你的电话打得有些不是时候。**2** happening at an unsuitable or bad time〔时间〕不凑巧的，不合时宜的：*an inopportune visit* 不合时宜的探访 —**inopportunely** *adv* —**inopportuneness** *n* [U]

in·or·di·nate /ɪnˋɔrdṇɪt; ɪˈnɔːdənɪ̈t/ *adj* far more than you would reasonably or normally expect 超出合理限度的，过分的：*Testing is taking up an inordinate amount of teachers' time.* 测试工作占去了教师们太多的时间。—**inordinately** *adv*: *She's inordinately fond of her parrot.* 她溺爱她那只鹦鹉。

in·or·gan·ic /ˌɪnɔrˋgænɪk; ˌɪnɔːˈgænɪk◂/ *adj* **1** not consisting of anything that is living 无机的，无生命的：*inorganic matter* 无机物质 **2** not produced or allowed to develop in a natural way 非自然长成[发展]的 —opposite 反义词 ORGANIC (1,5) —**inorganically** /-klɪ; -kli/ *adv*

inorganic chem·is·try /ˌ‥‥ˈ‥‥/ *n* [U] *technical* the part of chemistry concerning the study of substances that do not contain CARBON【术语】无机化学 —compare 比较 ORGANIC CHEMISTRY

in·pa·tient /ˋɪnˌpeʃənt; ˈɪnpeɪʃənt/ *n* [C] someone who stays in a hospital for treatment, rather than coming in for treatment from outside 住院病人 —compare 比较 OUTPATIENT

3 **in·put¹** /ˋɪnˌput; ˈɪnpʊt/ *n* [singular,U] **1** ideas, advice, money, or effort that you put into a job, meeting etc in order to help it succeed 投入(物)〔指向工作、会议等提供的意见、建议、资金、努力等〕：*The conference would not have been such a success without your valuable input.* 没有您的宝贵投入，会议不会开得如此成功。**2** *technical*【术语】**a)** electrical power that is put into a machine for it to use〔输入机器供其使用的〕电力 **b)** information that is put into a computer〔输入电脑的〕信息 —compare 比较 OUTPUT¹

input² *v past tense and participle* **inputted** or **input** [T] to put information into a computer〔向电脑〕输入〔信息〕

in·quest /ˋɪnkwɛst; ˈɪŋkwest/ *n* [C] **1** a legal process to find out the cause of someone's death〔调查死因的〕讯问，审理：**hold an inquest (into)** *An inquest will be held into the death of the actor, Tom Barnard.* 对于演员汤姆·巴纳德的死因将进行审讯。**2** an unofficial discussion about the reasons for someone's defeat or failure to do something〔对某人的失败进行的非正式的〕讨论

in·qui·e·tude /ɪnˋkwaɪəˌtjud; ɪnˈkwaɪɪ̈tjuːd/ *n* [U] *literary* anxiety【文】焦虑；不安

in·quire, enquire /ɪnˋkwaɪr; ɪnˈkwaɪə/ *v* [I,T] **1** to ask someone for information 询问，打听：*"Are you getting married?" the television interviewer inquired.* "你准备结婚了吗？"电视采访记者问道。| **[+about]** *I am writing to inquire about your advertisement in The Times.* 您在《泰晤士报》刊登广告，特此致函询问详情。| **inquire whether/why/how etc** *The waiter inquired whether we would like to sit near the window.* 侍者问我们是否想靠窗坐着。—see 见 ASK (USAGE) **2 inquire within** used on notices, especially in shop windows, to mean that you can find out more about something inside 详情请入内查询〔用于商店橱窗内的告示，意思是你若进入店内，可得知更多情况〕：*Vacancies – inquire within.* 招聘——有意者入内咨询。—**inquirer** *n* [C]

inquire after sb/sth *phr v* [T] to ask someone about someone else, about how they are and what they are doing 问候，问好：*He called me aside to inquire after my daughter.* 他把我叫到一旁，打听我女儿的情况。

inquire into sth *phr v* [T] to ask questions in order to get more information about something 查问，查究，调查：*The investigation will inquire into the exact circumstances of the sale.* 这次调查将查问这项销售的具体情况。

inquire sth **of** sb *phr v* [T] *formal* to ask someone a question about something【正式】向〔某人〕询问：*He nervously inquired of his host whether he could light a cigarette.* 他不好意思地问主人是否可以吸烟。

in·quir·ing, enquiring /ɪnˋkwaɪrɪŋ; ɪnˈkwaɪərɪŋ/ *adj* [only before noun 仅用于名词前] **1** an inquiring look or expression shows that you want to ask about something〔神色〕有疑问的 **2 an inquiring mind** someone who has an inquiring mind is very interested in finding out more about everything 好探索的精神：*As a child he had a lively inquiring mind.* 他小时候凡事都想问个明白。—**inquiringly** *adv*: *Victor raised an eyebrow inquiringly.* 维克托眉毛一扬，露出探询的神色。

in·quir·y, enquiry /ɪnˋkwaɪrɪ; ɪnˈkwaɪəri/ *n* **1** [C] a question you ask in order to get information 询问，打听：**[+about]** *We're getting a lot of inquiries from travel companies about our new London-Rio service.* 许多旅行社询问我们新开设的伦敦－里约热内卢旅行线路的情况。| **make inquiries** *I don't know who sent the gift, but I'll make discreet inquiries.* 我不知道礼物是谁送的，但我会小心地打听一下。| **be helping the police with their inquiries** *BrE* (=be answering questions about a crime)【英】协助警方调查〔罪案〕**2** [U] the act of asking questions in order to get information 查问：*On further inquiry, it emerged that Malcolm had not been involved in the campaign.* 进一步调查表明，马尔科姆与该运动无关。| **line of inquiry** (=method of inquiry) 查询方法 *No definite information yet – but we're following up a most promising line of inquiry.* 现在还没有确切情报，但我们正循着一个很可望成功的办法进行调查。**3 enquiries** the name of a service or office from which you can get information 询问处；咨询处 **4** [C] an official process, in the form of a series of meetings, intended to find out why something happened〔以一系列会议形式开展的〕官方调查程序：**[+into]** *Local residents are calling for a public inquiry into the accident.* 当地居民要求对这次事故进行公开调查。| **hold/conduct an inquiry** *complaints that the inquiry is being conducted behind closed doors* 对于非公开秘密调查的不满 **5 scientific inquiry** a process of trying to discover facts by scientific methods 用科学方法调查 3

inquiry a·gent /ˈ‥ ˌ‥/ *n* [C] *BrE old-fashioned* a PRIVATE DETECTIVE【英，过时】私人侦探

in·qui·si·tion /ˌɪnkwəˋzɪʃən; ˌɪŋkwɪ̈ˈzɪʃən/ *n* [singular] a series of questions that someone asks you in a threatening or unpleasant way〔带威胁、令人不快的〕盘问，查问：*When I got home I had to face a two-hour inquisition from my parents about where I'd been.* 我回家后遭受父母长达两小时的盘问，问我去了哪儿。

Inquisition, the an official Roman Catholic organization which tried to find and punish HERETICS (=people with unacceptable religious beliefs) during the Middle Ages, and used many cruel ways to TORTURE and kill people. The most famous part of the organization was the Spanish Inquisition, led in the 15th century by Tomas de Torquemada. 宗教法庭〔中世纪罗马天主教专门审讯和惩罚异教徒的一个机构。该法庭使用许多残酷手段进行刑讯和处决有罪之人。其中最有名的是15世纪以托马斯·德·托尔克马达为首的西班牙宗教法庭〕

in·quis·i·tive /ɪnˋkwɪzətɪv; ɪnˈkwɪzɪ̈tɪv/ *adj* **1** asking too many questions and trying to find out too many details about something or someone 过分好奇的，过分好问的，好追根究底的：*Don't be so inquisitive – it makes people uncomfortable.* 不要打听个没完，弄得人很不舒服。**2** interested in a lot of different things and wanting to find out more about them 好奇的，爱钻研的：*a cheerful, inquisitive little boy* 一个快乐、好奇的小男孩 —**inquisitively** *adv*: *He peeped inquisitively into the drawer.* 他好奇地往抽屉里窥视。—**inquisitiveness** *n* [U]

in·quis·i·tor /ɪnˋkwɪzətə; ɪnˈkwɪzɪ̈tə/ *n* [C] **1** someone who is asking you a lot of difficult questions and making you feel very uncomfortable〔提出很多难题，令人不舒服的〕盘问者，询问者 **2** an official of the INQUISITION 宗教法庭审判官 —**inquisitorial** /ɪnˌkwɪzəˋtɔrɪəl; ɪnˌkwɪzɪ̈ˈtɔːriəl◂/ *adj* —**inquisitorially** *adv*

in·quo·rate /ɪnˋkwɔrɪt; ɪnˈkwɔːrɪ̈t/ *adj formal* an inquorate meeting does not have enough people to make decisions or vote【正式】〔会议〕未达到法定出席人数的

in re /ɪn ˋri; ɪn ˈriː/ *prep* an expression used especially in business letters that means 'concerning' 关于〔尤用于商务信函〕

in·roads /ˋɪnˌrodz; ˈɪnrəʊdz/ also 又作 **inroad** *n* **make inroads into/on a)** to become more and more successful, powerful, or popular and so take away power, trade, votes etc from a competitor or enemy〔在力量、贸易、选票等方面〕进攻〔竞争者或敌方的领域〕，侵占：*Video is making huge inroads into attendance figures at movie theaters.* 录像带正在大量夺走电影院的观众。

b) to use more and more of something such as space, time, money, or energy so that there is less available〔空间、时间、金钱、精力等不断的〕消耗: *The administrative workload is making massive inroads into our working day.* 行政事务占去了我们大量的工作时间。

INS, the /ˌaɪ ɛn ˋɛs; ˌaɪ en ˈes/ the abbreviation of 缩写= the IMMIGRATION AND NATURALIZATION SERVICE

in·sa·lu·bri·ous /ˌɪnsəˋlubrɪəs; ˌɪnsəˈluːbriəs◂/ *adj formal* insalubrious conditions or places are unpleasant and bad for your health【正式】〔条件或地方〕不卫生的, 不利于健康的

ins and outs /ˌ. . ˈ. / *n* [plural] all the exact details of a complicated situation, problem, system etc〔复杂的局面、难题等的〕详情, 细节: *I don't really know all the ins and outs of the matter.* 我并不知道这件事的所有细节。

in·sane /ɪnˋsen; ɪnˈseɪn/ *adj* **1** *informal* completely stupid or crazy, often in a way that is dangerous【非正式】愚蠢的, 疯狂的: *I don't know what made Sarah marry him – she must have been totally insane.* 我不明白莎拉为什么要嫁给他, 她肯定是发疯了。| *The whole idea sounds absolutely insane to me.* 整个主意在我看来愚蠢至极。**2** *especially law* someone who is insane is permanently and seriously mentally ill so that they cannot live in normal society【尤法律】(患)精神病的, 精神失常的, 疯癫的: *The killer was declared criminally insane.* 这名杀人犯被定为精神失常犯罪。**3 drive sb insane** *informal* to make someone feel more and more annoyed or angry, usually over a long period of time【非正式】逼得某人发疯〔一般指经过长时间〕: *I had to give up teaching – it was driving me insane.* 我当时不得不放弃教书, 它都要把我逼疯了。—**insanely** *adv*: *insanely jealous* 发疯似地妒忌

in·san·i·ta·ry /ɪnˋsænəˌtɛrɪ; ɪnˈsænɪ̵təri/ *adj* insanitary conditions or places are very dirty and likely to cause disease 肮脏的, 不卫生的, 对健康不利的; UNSANITARY *especially AmE*【尤美】

in·san·i·ty /ɪnˋsænətɪ; ɪnˈsænɪ̵ti/ *n* [U] **1** very stupid actions that may cause you serious harm 极端愚蠢的行为: *It was sheer insanity to drive across the mountains in the dark.* 黑夜驾车翻山越岭, 简直荒唐透顶。**2** *especially law* the state of being seriously mentally ill, so that you cannot live normally in society【尤法律】精神错乱: *The court acquitted Campbell on the grounds of temporary insanity.* 法庭以坎贝尔一时精神错乱为由而将他无罪释放。

in·sa·tia·ble /ɪnˋseʃəbl̩; ɪnˈseɪʃəbəl/ *adj* always wanting more and more of something 贪得无厌的, 不能满足的: **insatiable appetite/desire/demand etc** *an insatiable demand for Western consumer goods* 对西方消费品越来越多的需求 —**insatiably** *adv*

in·scribe /ɪnˋskraɪb; ɪnˈskraɪb/ *v* [T] to carefully cut, print, or write words on something, especially on the surface of a stone or coin〔尤指在石头或硬币表面细致地〕雕刻, 印制, 题写: **inscribe sth in/on etc** *Inside the cover someone had inscribed the words 'To Thomas, with love'.* 在书的内封面上, 题写了"托马斯惠存"几个字。| **inscribe sth with** *The tomb was inscribed with a short epitaph.* 墓碑上刻有简短的墓志铭。

in·scrip·tion /ɪnˋskrɪpʃən; ɪnˈskrɪpʃən/ *n* [C] a piece of writing inscribed on a stone, in the front of a book etc 碑文, 题词

in·scru·ta·ble /ɪnˋskrutəbl̩; ɪnˈskruːtəbəl/ *adj* someone who is inscrutable shows no emotion or reaction in the expression on their face so that it is impossible to know what they are feeling or thinking〔因不露声色而〕难以理解的, 高深莫测的: *an inscrutable smile* 诡秘的微笑 —**inscrutably** *adv* —**inscrutability** /ɪnˌskrutəˋbɪlətɪ; ɪnˌskruːtəˈbɪlɪ̵ti/ *n* [U]

in·sect /ˋɪnsɛkt; ˈɪnsekt/ *n* [C] a small creature such as a fly or ANT, that has six legs, and sometimes wings 昆虫: *an insect bite* 昆虫叮咬的伤口 | *mosquitoes and other flying insects* 蚊子和其他飞虫

in·sec·ti·cide /ɪnˋsɛktəˌsaɪd; ɪnˈsektɪ̵saɪd/ *n* [U] a chemical substance used for killing insects 杀虫剂, 杀虫药 —compare 比较 PESTICIDE —**insecticidal** /ɪnˌsɛktəˋsaɪdl̩; ɪnˌsektɪ̵ˈsaɪdl◂/ *adj*

in·sec·ti·vore /ɪnˋsɛktəˌvɔr; ɪnˈsektɪ̵vɔː/ *n* [C] a creature that eats insects for food 食虫动物[植物] —**insectivorous** *adj*

in·se·cure /ˌɪnsɪˋkjʊr; ˌɪnsɪˈkjʊə◂/ *adj* **1** not feeling at all confident about yourself, your abilities, your relationships etc 无自信的, 没有把握的: *I'd only just started at university and I still felt very shy and insecure.* 当时我刚开始上大学, 还很腼腆而且不自信。**2** a job, INVESTMENT etc that is insecure does not give you a feeling of safety, because it is likely to be taken away or lost at any time〔工作、投资等〕无保障的, 无安全感的: *Running a small business is a very insecure occupation.* 做小买卖是一个没有什么保障的职业。**3** a building or structure that is insecure is not safe, because it is likely to fall down〔建筑、结构等〕不牢固的, 可能垮掉的 —**insecurity** *n* [U] *Student teachers often suffer from a great sense of insecurity.* 实习教师常为自信心不足而苦恼。—**insecurely** *adv*

in·sem·i·nate /ɪnˋsɛməˌnet; ɪnˈsemɪ̵neɪt/ *v* [T] to put SPERM into a female animal in order to make her have a baby 使怀孕, 使受精 —**insemination** /ɪnˌsɛməˋneʃən; ɪnˌsemɪ̵ˈneɪʃən/ *n* [U] —see also 另见 ARTIFICIAL INSEMINATION

in·sen·sate /ɪnˋsɛnset; ɪnˈsenseɪt/ *adj formal*【正式】**1** not able to feel things; INANIMATE 没感觉的, 无生命的 **2** unreasonable and crazy 无理智的, 疯狂的: *insensate rage* 失去理智的狂怒

in·sen·si·bil·i·ty /ˌɪnsɛnsəˋbɪlətɪ; ɪnˌsensɪ̵ˈbɪlɪ̵ti/ *n* [U] **1** *formal* the state of being unconscious【正式】无知觉 **2** *old use* inability to experience feelings such as love, sympathy, anger etc【旧】冷淡, 无感情

in·sen·si·ble /ɪnˋsɛnsəbl̩; ɪnˈsensɪ̵bəl/ *adj formal*【正式】**1** not knowing about something that could happen to you; UNAWARE 没意识到的, 没觉察到的: **[+of]** *She remained insensible of the dangers that lay ahead.* 她对即将出现的危险毫无察觉。**2** unable to feel something or be affected by it 无感觉的: **[+to/of]** *insensible to the cold* 感觉不到寒冷 **3** *old use* not conscious【旧】失去知觉的: *He fell to the ground, insensible.* 他跌倒在地, 失去了知觉。—**insensibly** *adv*

in·sen·si·tive /ɪnˋsɛnsətɪv; ɪnˈsensɪ̵tɪv/ *adj* **1** not noticing other people's feelings, and not realizing when they are upset or when something that you do will upset them 麻木不仁的, 缺乏同情心的: *One insensitive official insisted on seeing her husband's death certificate.* 一位不近人情的官员非要看看她丈夫的死亡证明不可。| **[+to]** *She's totally insensitive to Jack's feelings.* 她根本不理会杰克的感情。**2** not paying attention to what is happening or to what people are saying, and therefore not changing your behaviour because of it〔对发生的事或别人的话〕置之不理的, 不作反应的: **[+to]** *Companies that are insensitive to global changes will lose sales.* 对全球变化无动于衷的公司, 其销售额必会下降。| *Outwardly he seems insensitive to criticism.* 从表面上看, 他似乎对批评漠然置之。**3** not affected by physical effects or changes 身体无感觉的, 麻木的: **[+to]** *insensitive to pain* 无疼痛感 | *insensitive to light* 无光感 —**insensitively** *adv* —**insensitivity** /ɪnˌsɛnsəˋtɪvɪtɪ; ɪnˌsensɪ̵ˈtɪvɪ̵ti/ *n* [U]

in·sep·a·ra·ble /ɪnˋsɛpərəbl̩; ɪnˈsepərəbəl/ *adj* **1** people who are inseparable are always together and are very friendly with each other〔人〕常在一起的, 亲密无间的: *Jane and Sarah soon became inseparable companions.* 简与莎拉很快就形影不离了。**2** things that are inseparable cannot be separated or cannot be considered separately〔东西〕分不开的, 不可分离的: **[+from]** *In poetry meaning is inseparable from form.* 在诗歌中, 意义与形式不可分离。—**inseparably** *adv* —**inseparability** /ˌɪnsɛpərəˋbɪlətɪ; ɪnˌsepərəˈbɪlɪ̵ti/ *n* [U]

in·sert[1] /ɪnˋsɝt; ɪnˈsɜːt/ *v* [T] **1** to put something inside or into something else 插入, 放进: **insert sth in/into/ between** *He inserted a sheet of paper into the printer.* 他把一张纸放入打印机。| *Insert one 20p coin.* 投入一枚20便士的硬币。**2** to add something to the middle of a document or piece of writing〔在文件或文稿中〕加入, 加进: *The manager wanted to insert a clause giving him 30% of any future earnings.* 经理想加入一项条款, 规定他在未来的赢利中可以获得30%的分红。

insert 插入

in·sert[2] /ˋɪnsɝt; ˈɪnsɜːt/ *n* [C] **1** printed pages that are put inside a newspaper or magazine in order to advertise something〔夹在报刊中的〕插页广告: *a six-page insert on computer software* 六张关于电脑软件的插页广告 **2** something that is designed to be put inside something else 插入物: *He wore special inserts in his shoes to make him look taller.* 他在鞋里垫了一些东西, 以使他显得个子高一点儿。

in·ser·tion /ɪnˋsɝʃən; ɪnˈsɜːʃən/ *n* **1** [U] the act of putting something inside something else 放入, 插入 **2** [C] something that is added to the middle of a document or piece of writing〔文件或文稿中的〕插入物

in-ser·vice /ˌ. ˈ. .◂/ *adj* **in-service training/courses etc** training etc that you do while you are working in a job 在职培训/课程等

INSET /ˋɪnsɛt; ˈɪnset/ in-service education training; in the UK, training for teachers which takes place during the school year〔英国每学年进行的〕教师在职培训: *an INSET day* 教师培训日

in·set¹ /ˋɪnset; ˈɪnset/ *n* [C] a small picture, map etc in the corner of a page or larger picture etc, which shows more detail or information 嵌入物, 附加物〔尤指附加在大图片、大地图角位上, 以显示细部或提供更详尽资料的小图片或小地图〕: *See inset for a comparison of world grain exporters.* 要对全球粮食出口国进行比较, 请看附图。

in·set² /ɪnˋset; ɪnˈset/ *v past tense and past participle* **inset** *or* **insetted** [T] **1** to put something in as an inset on a printed page〔在一页印刷品中〕嵌入, 加入 **2 be inset with** if something is inset with decorations, jewels etc, it has them set in its surface 被嵌入〔饰品、珠宝等〕

in·shore /ˌɪnˋʃɔr; ˌɪnˈʃɔː◂/ *adv* near, towards, or to the shore 靠近海岸, 向海岸: *The fishing boats usually stay close inshore.* 渔船通常停留在近海海域。—**inshore** *adj*: *an inshore lifeboat* 海岸救生艇

S2 W2 **in·side¹** /ɪnˋsaɪd; ɪnˈsaɪd/ *prep*

1 ►CONTAINER 容器◄ in a container or other closed space so that it is completely covered or surrounded 在〔容器或其他封闭的空间〕里面: *I'll leave the keys inside an envelope.* 我会把钥匙放在一个信封里。| *The jewels were locked away inside the safe.* 珠宝都锁入了保险箱。

2 ►BUILDING/ROOM 建筑物/房间◄ in a room or building, especially when you are looking at it from the outside 在房间内, 在楼内〔尤指从外面看〕: *Mail was piled up just inside the doorway.* 入口处堆满了邮件。

3 ►COUNTRY 国家◄ a word meaning in a country or area, used when you want to emphasize that something is happening there and not outside it 在某国家[地区]内部〔强调某事只在那里发生〕: *Very little is known of events inside Albania.* 几乎没有人知道阿尔巴尼亚国内发生的事情。| *The guerrillas were said to be operating from bases inside the war zone.* 据说游击队员是从战区内部的基地进行活动的。

4 ►ORGANIZATION 组织◄ a word meaning in an organization or company, used when you want to emphasize that something is happening or known about there, but not outside it 在〔组织或公司的〕内部〔强调某事只在那里发生〕: *women's influence inside the Party* 妇女在党内的影响力 | *There have been rumours of bitter disputes inside the company.* 一直有谣传说公司内部常有激烈的争执。

5 ►FEELING 情感◄ if you have a feeling inside you, you feel it but do not express it or tell other people about it〔感情〕在心里: *It's no good bottling all the anger up inside you – you've got to let it out.* 把怒气憋在心里不好, 你应当发泄出来。

6 ►HEAD/MIND 头脑/心灵◄ if something happens inside you, or inside your head or mind, it is part of what you think and feel 在…脑海中, 在…心里: *Something inside of me told me not to trust him.* 我的直觉告诉我不能相信他。| *Steve's a strange guy – you never know what's going on inside his head.* 斯蒂夫是个怪人, 谁也不知道他脑子里在想什么。

7 ►BODY 身体◄ in your body 在…体内: *She could feel the baby kicking inside her.* 她感到胎儿在腹内踢蹬。| *You'll feel better once you've got a good meal inside you* (=after you have eaten something). 好好吃一顿, 你就会感觉好些的。

8 ►TIME 时间◄ *especially spoken* if you do something inside a particular amount of time, it takes you slightly less than that amount of time to do it【尤口】〔时间〕在…内, 少于…: *Jonson's time of 9.3 seconds was just inside the world record.* 琼森用了9.3秒, 刚好破了世界纪录。| **inside (of) two hours/inside (of) fifteen minutes etc** *We did the return trip to Birmingham in just inside three hours.* 我们返回伯明翰用了不到三个小时。

S2 W3 **in·side²** /ɪnˋsaɪd, ɪnˈsaɪd/ *adv* **1** in something 在〔某物〕里面: *The car was locked and the keys were inside.* 车已锁上, 钥匙却在车里。| *The purse had £50 inside.* 钱包里有50英镑。**2** in a house or other building 在〔房子或其他建筑物〕内: *It's raining. We'll have to go inside.* 下雨了, 我们进屋去吧。| *She could hear voices inside, but no-one came to the door.* 她听到里面有说话声, 但没有人来开门。**3** if you have a feeling inside, you have the feeling but do not show it to other people〔感觉〕在心里: *You just don't understand how I feel inside!* 你根本不懂我心里在想什么! **4** *informal* in prison【非正式】在监狱里, 坐牢: *My boyfriend's been inside for a year.* 我的男友在狱里已一年了。**5 inside of a)** within a particular period of time 在〔一定时间〕之内: *We should get it finished inside of a month.* 我们必须一个月内完成。**b)** *AmE* on the inside of something【美】在〔某物〕内: *There were now about a thousand people inside of the stadium.* 体育场里此时约有一千人。

in·side³ /ɪnˋsaɪd; ɪnˈsaɪd/ *n* **1 the inside a)** the inner part of something, which is surrounded or hidden by the outer part 里面, 内部: *The apple's rotten on the inside.* 这个苹果里面烂了。| *The door had been locked from the inside.* 门已从里面上锁。—opposite 反义词 OUTSIDE⁴ (1) **b)** the part of a road that is nearest to the edge on the side where you are driving〔道路的〕内侧: *He tried to overtake me on the inside.* 他试图从内侧超过我。**2 inside out** with the usual outside parts on the inside 里面朝外地: *You've got that jumper inside out.* 你把套头毛衣穿反了。| *Turn cushion covers inside out to wash them.* 把坐垫套子里外翻过来洗洗。**3 on the inside** someone who is on the inside is a member of a group or an organization〔团体或组织的〕内部人员: *Someone on the inside must have helped with the robbery.* 这桩抢劫案肯定有内应协助。**4 sb's inside/insides** *informal* someone's stomach【非正式】肠胃; 肚子: *My insides are beginning to complain about the lack of food.* 我开始感到肚子饿。**5 turn sth inside out** to search a place very thoroughly by moving everything that is in it 对某处进行彻底搜寻: *The drug squad turned the apartment inside out.* 缉毒组把公寓搜了个遍。**6 know sth inside out** to know something in great detail 知道得一清二楚: *She knows her subject inside out.* 她对她的课题了解得很透彻。

in·side⁴ /ˋɪnsaɪd; ˈɪnsaɪd/ *adj* **1** on or facing the inside of something 里面的, 内部的; 朝里的: *the inside pages of the newspaper* 报纸的里页 **2 inside information/the inside story etc** information that is available only to people who are part of a particular group or organization 内部消息; 内幕: *Police believe the robbers may have had inside information.* 警方认为抢劫犯可能得到了内部消息。

inside lane /ˌ·· ˈ·/ *n* [C] **1** the part of a road that is closest to the edge, usually used by slow vehicles〔靠近路边、多为慢速车辆行驶的〕内车道 —see picture on page A3 参见A3页图 **2** the part of a circular track for racing that is nearest to the centre of the circle and is therefore shorter〔比赛跑道的〕内圈

in·sid·er /ɪnˋsaɪdɚ; ɪnˈsaɪdə/ *n* [C] someone who has a special knowledge of a particular organization because they are part of it〔团体〕内部的人, 圈内人, 业内人士: *an insider's view of the way that a Japanese company works* 业内人士对日本公司运作方式的看法 —compare 比较 OUTSIDER (3)

insider trad·ing /·,·· ˈ··/ also 又作 **insider dealing** *n* [U] illegal buying and selling of a company's shares (SHARE² (5)) involving the use of secret information known only by people connected with the company〔股票的〕内幕交易, 内线交易〔指利用秘密的内幕消息来非法买卖一家公司的股票〕

inside track /ˌ·· ˈ·/ *n* [C] **1** the part of a circular track for racing that is nearest to the centre of the circle and is therefore shorter〔比赛的〕内圈跑道〔最接近圆心, 因此较短〕**2** *AmE* a position that gives someone an advantage over the people they are competing against【美】〔竞争中的〕有利地位, 有利形势: *the inside track to success in business* 企业成功的有利形势

in·sid·i·ous /ɪnˋsɪdɪəs; ɪnˈsɪdiəs/ *adj* an insidious danger or problem spreads gradually without being noticed, and causes serious harm〔危险或问题〕暗中为害的,〔祸害〕潜伏的: *an insidious trend towards censorship of the press* 实行新闻审查的逆流 —**insidiously** *adv* —**insidiousness** *n* [U]

in·sight /ˋɪnˌsaɪt; ˈɪnsaɪt/ *n* **1** [U] the ability to understand and realize what people or situations are really like 洞察力, 眼光: *a woman of great insight* 一位极有眼光的女子 **2** [C] a sudden clear understanding of something, especially something complicated〔尤指对复杂事情的〕顿悟, 猛省: [+into] *The article gives us a real insight into the causes of the present economic crisis.* 这篇文章分析目前经济危机的原因, 发人深省。

in·sig·ni·a /ɪnˋsɪgnɪə; ɪnˈsɪgniə/ *n plural* **insignia** [C] a BADGE (1) or sign that shows what official or military rank someone has, or which group or organization they belong to〔表示官衔、军阶的〕徽章,〔隶属某个组织或机构的〕标志: *the royal insignia* 王权的徽章 | *military insignia* 军阶标志

in·sig·nif·i·cant /ˌɪnsɪgˋnɪfəkənt; ˌɪnsɪgˈnɪfɪkənt◂/ *adj* too small or unimportant to consider or worry about 不重要的, 价值不大的, 无意义的: *Looking at the Earth from space makes you realize how small and insignificant we all are.* 从太空看地球, 会使你发现我们都是多么渺小。| *an insignificant difference* 微小的区别 —**insignificantly** *adv* —**insignificance** *n* [U]

in·sin·cere /ˌɪnsɪnˋsɪr; ˌɪnsɪnˈsɪə◂/ *adj* pretending to be pleased, sympathetic etc, especially by saying nice things, but not really meaning what you say 不诚恳的, 虚伪的: *insincere praise* 虚情假意的赞扬 | *an insincere smile* 虚伪的微笑; 谄笑 —**insincerely** *adv* —**insincerity** /ˌɪnsɪnˋsɛrətɪ; ˌɪnsɪnˈserɪ̈ti/ *n* [U]

in·sin·u·ate /ɪnˋsɪnjuˌet; ɪnˈsɪnjueɪt/ *v* [T] **1** to say something which seems to mean something unpleasant without saying it directly, for example saying indirectly that someone is being dishonest 暗示〔令人不快的内容〕; 含沙射影地说: **insinuate that**

Are you insinuating that the money was stolen? 你是在暗示钱被偷了吗？**2 insinuate yourself into** to gradually gain someone's love, trust etc by pretending to be friendly and sincere〔假装友善和真诚〕使自己取得〔某人的喜爱、信任等〕: *He managed to insinuate his way into her affections.* 他终于设法赢得了她的感情。

in·sin·u·a·tion /ɪn͵sɪnjʊ`eʃən; ɪn͵sɪnju'eɪʃən/ *n* **1** [C] something that someone insinuates 影射, 暗示: *the insinuation that they did not know how to run their own business* 关于他们经营无方的暗示 **2** [U] the act of insinuating something 暗示, 暗指

in·sip·id /ɪn`sɪpɪd; ɪn'sɪpɪ̈d/ *adj* **1** food or drink that is insipid does not have much taste〔饮食〕淡而无味的: *an insipid pasta dish* 一盘没有味道的面点 **2** not interesting, exciting, or attractive 枯燥无味的, 不吸引人的: *an insipid young man* 木讷的年轻人 **—insipidly** *adv* **—insipidness, insipidity** /͵ɪnsɪ`pɪdətɪ; ͵ɪnsɪ̈'pɪdɪ̈ti/ *n* [U]

S3 W2 **in·sist** /ɪn`sɪst; ɪn'sɪst/ *v* [I] **1** to say firmly and repeatedly that something is true, especially when other people think it may not be true 坚持宣称, 坚决认为: **insist that** *Mike insisted that he was right.* 迈克坚决认为自己是对的。| **[+on]** *She kept insisting on her innocence.* 她再三坚持自己无罪。**2** to demand that something should happen and refuse to let anyone say no 坚持主张, 坚决要求, 一定要: **[+on]** *Her parents insisted on speaking to the headmistress.* 她父母坚持要和女校长谈话。| *Stay for supper – I insist!* 你一定要留下来吃晚饭！| **insist that** *They insisted that everyone should come to the party.* 他们坚决要求每个人都来参加晚会。**3 if you insist** *spoken* used when agreeing to do something that you do not really want to do【口】如果你一定要这样〔用来对你并不真正想做的事表示同意〕: *"Why don't you call them up today?" "Oh, if you insist!"* "你何不今天就给他们打电话?""好吧, 如果你一定要我这样办的话。"

insist on sth *phr v* [T] **1** to think that something is very important, and demand that you have it 认为〔某事〕非常重要〔并坚持得到它〕: *We insist on the highest standards of cleanliness in the hotel.* 我们坚持要酒店的卫生水平达到最高标准。**2** to keep doing something, especially something that is inconvenient or annoying 坚持做〔尤指麻烦或令人讨厌的事〕: *She will insist on washing her hair just when I want to have a bath.* 正当我要洗澡的时候, 她偏要去洗头发。

in·sis·tence /ɪn`sɪstəns; ɪn'sɪstəns/ *n* [U] an act of demanding that something should happen and refusing to let anyone say no 坚决要求, 坚持: **insistence that** *his insistence that they discuss the problem* 他坚持要他们讨论这个问题 | **[+on]** *an insistence on punctuality* 坚决主张守时 | **at sb's insistence** (=because someone insisted) 由于某人的坚持 *At her father's insistence, she joined them for a drink.* 由于父亲的坚持, 她和他们一起喝了一杯酒。

in·sis·tent /ɪn`sɪstənt; ɪn'sɪstənt/ *adj* **1** demanding firmly and repeatedly that something should happen 坚持的, 坚决要求的: **insistent that** *She was insistent that they should all meet for dinner.* 她坚持要大家聚在一起吃晚饭。| **[+on]** *insistent on good manners* 坚持彬彬有礼 **2** making a continuous loud sound that is difficult to ignore〔响声〕持续不断的: *the insistent pounding of drums* 持续不断的击鼓声 **—insistently** *adv*

in si·tu /ɪn `saɪtju; ɪn 'sɪtjuː/ *adv Latin* if something remains in situ, it remains in its usual place【拉丁】在原地, 在原来位置

in·so·far /͵ɪnso`fɑr; ͵ɪnsə'fɑː/ *adv* —see 见 **in so far as/in as far as/insofar as** (FAR[1] (30))

in·sole /`ɪn͵sol; 'ɪnsəʊl/ *n* [C] a foot-shaped piece of cloth, leather etc that you put inside your shoe 鞋垫

in·so·lent /`ɪnsələnt; 'ɪnsələnt/ *adj* rude and not showing any respect 粗鲁无礼的, 傲慢的: *an insolent tone of voice* 傲慢的语气 | *You insolent child!* 你这个没礼貌的孩子！**—insolently** *adv* **—insolence** *n* [U]

in·sol·u·ble /ɪn`sɑljəbl̩; ɪn'sɒljʊ̈bəl/ *adj* **1** an insoluble problem is or seems impossible to solve〔问题〕(似乎)不能解决的: *insoluble conflicts within the department* 部门内难以调和的冲突 **2** an insoluble substance does not become a liquid when you put it into a liquid〔物质〕不能溶解的 —compare 比较 DISSOLVE (1)

in·sol·va·ble /ɪn`sɑlvəbl̩; ɪn'sɒlvəbəl/ *adj especially AmE* an insolvable problem is or seems impossible to solve; INSOLUBLE (1)【尤美】〔问题〕(似乎)不能解决的 **—insolvably** *adv*

in·sol·vent /ɪn`sɑlvənt; ɪn'sɒlvənt/ *adj* not having enough money to pay what you owe; BANKRUPT 无偿债能力的, 破产的: *insolvent private companies* 无偿债能力的私人公司 **—insolvency** *n* [U]

in·som·ni·a /ɪn`sɑmnɪə; ɪn'sɒmniə/ *n* [U] the condition of not being able to sleep 失眠

in·som·ni·ac /ɪn`sɑmnɪæk; ɪn'sɒmniæk/ *n* [C] someone who cannot sleep easily 失眠症患者 **—insomniac** *adj*

in·so·much /͵ɪnsə`mʌtʃ; ͵ɪnsəʊ'mʌtʃ/ *adv formal*【正式】**1 insomuch that** *especially AmE* to such a degree that【尤美】到…的程度(因此…) **2** another form of the word INASMUCH inasmuch 的另一种形式

in·sou·ci·ance /ɪn`susɪəns; ɪn'suːsiəns/ *n* [U] *formal* a cheerful feeling of not caring or worrying about anything【正式】无忧无虑: *He strolled through the house with an air of insouciance.* 他在这座房子里踱来踱去, 一副逍遥自在的样子。**—insouciant** *adj* **—insouciantly** *adv*

in·spect /ɪn`spɛkt; ɪn'spekt/ *v* [T] **1** to examine something carefully in order to find out more about it or that it is not satisfactory 仔细检查; 检验: *I got out of the car to inspect the damage.* 我下车检查损坏情况。| **inspect sth for cracks/faults etc** (=in order to check that there are no cracks etc) 检查某物有无裂缝/毛病等 *He carefully inspected the china for cracks.* 他仔细检查瓷器看有无裂纹。—see graph at 参见 EXAMINE 图表 **2** to make an official visit to a building, organization etc to check that everything is satisfactory and that rules are being obeyed 视察; 检阅: *The building is regularly inspected by the fire-safety officer.* 消防安全官定期视察这座大楼。| *General Allenby arrived to inspect the troops.* 艾伦比将军来此检阅部队。

in·spec·tion /ɪn`spɛkʃən; ɪn'spekʃən/ *n* [C,U] **1** an official visit to a building or organization to check that everything is satisfactory and that rules are being obeyed 视察; 检阅: **[+of]** *regular inspections of the prison* 定期视察监狱 | **carry out an inspection** *An inspection was carried out at the school.* 有人来学校视察了一遍。| **tour of inspection** (=an official journey or visit to inspect something) 巡察 **2** a careful examination of something to find out more about it 仔细检查: **on closer inspection** (=when looked at more closely) 再仔细一看 *On closer inspection, the scrap of paper turned out to be a £20 note.* 再仔细一看, 这张小纸片原来是一张面值 20 英镑的钞票。 S3

in·spec·tor /ɪn`spɛktɚ; ɪn'spektə/ *n* [C] **1** an official whose job is to check that something is satisfactory and that rules are being obeyed 检查员; 督察员: *ticket inspectors* 查票员 | *a Health and Safety inspector* 卫生与安全稽查员 **2** a police officer of middle rank 督察, 巡官〔中级警官〕: *Inspector Blake* 布莱克巡官 —see also 另见 CHIEF INSPECTOR **3** *BrE* someone whose job is to visit schools and judge the quality of the teaching【英】督学

in·spec·tor·ate /ɪn`spɛktərɪt; ɪn'spektərɪ̈t/ *n* [C] the group of INSPECTOR*s* who officially inspect schools, factories etc〔学校、工厂等的〕检查团, 督察队

Inspector Morse —see 见 Inspector MORSE

inspector of tax·es /·͵·· ·`··/ *n* [C] *BrE* a government official who calculates what tax each person should pay【英】税务稽查员

in·spi·ra·tion /͵ɪnspə`reʃən; ͵ɪnspɪ̈'reɪʃən/ *n* [C,U] **1** a sudden good idea about what you should do or say 灵感: *I haven't started writing the article yet – I'm still waiting for inspiration.* 我还没有开始写那篇文章, 我还在等待灵感。**2** the state of being given encouragement or good ideas about what you should do 鼓舞, 启示: **divine inspiration** (=inspiration from God or gods) 神的启示, 神灵感应 **3** a person, experience, place, etc that you get inspiration from 给人以灵感的人物[经历、地点等]: *The seascapes of Cape Cod were her inspiration.* 科德角的海景给了她灵感。**4 be an inspiration to sb** to make someone feel encouraged to be as good, successful etc as possible 给某人以鼓舞: *Maya, who bears her illness with such patience, is an inspiration to us all.* 马娅坚忍地对待疾病, 给我们很大的鼓舞。

in·spi·ra·tion·al /͵ɪnspə`reʃənl̩; ͵ɪnspɪ̈'reɪʃənəl◂/ *adj* providing inspiration 鼓舞人心的; 给予灵感的: *Jones proved an inspirational figure in Welsh rugby.* 事实证明, 琼斯是威尔士橄榄球运动中能鼓舞人心的人物。

in·spire /ɪn`spaɪr; ɪn'spaɪə/ *v* [T] **1** to encourage someone by making them feel confident and eager to achieve something great 鼓舞, 激励: *We need a new captain – someone who can inspire the team.* 我们需要一位能振奋士气的新队长。| **inspire sb to sth** *I hope this success will inspire you to greater efforts.* 希望这次成功能激励你更加努力。**2** to make someone have a particular feeling or react in a particular way 使〔某人〕产生〔某种感情或反应〕, 激起, 唤起: *Gandhi's quiet dignity inspired respect even among his enemies.* 甘地不怒自威, 连他的敌人都肃然起敬。| **not inspire confidence** (=make people feel anxious because they do not trust your ability) 难以让人信任: *His driving hardly inspires confidence.* 他的开车技术让人难以放心。**3** to give someone the idea for a story, painting, poem etc 给〔某人〕创作灵感: *The story was inspired by a chance meeting with*

an old Russian duke. 这个故事的创作灵感来自与一位俄国老公爵的不期而遇。**4** *technical* to breathe in【术语】吸气

in·spired /ɪnˈspaɪrd; ɪnˈspaɪəd/ *adj* **1** having very exciting special qualities that are better than anyone or anything else 卓越的, 激动人心的: *an inspired leader* 卓越的领导人 | *Wordsworth's most inspired poems* 华兹华斯极富灵感的诗 **2 inspired guess** a correct guess that is based on feelings rather than facts 凭灵感[直觉]的正确猜测 **3 politically inspired** started for political reasons 基于政治原因: *We suspect that the violence was politically inspired.* 我们认为这次暴力冲突由政治原因导致。

in·spir·ing /ɪnˈspaɪrɪŋ; ɪnˈspaɪərɪŋ/ *adj* giving people energy, a feeling of excitement, and a desire to do something great 鼓舞人心的; 启发灵感的: *inspiring music* 激励人心的音乐 | *King, 27 years old, was a great orator and an inspiring leader.* 27 岁的金是伟大的演说家和鼓舞人心的领袖。

inst /ɪnst; ɪnst/ *adj BrE formal old-fashioned* used after a date in business letters to mean 'of the present month'【英, 正式, 过时】本月〔用于商务信件中的日期后〕: *Thank you for your letter of the 21st inst.* 感谢你本月 21 日的来信。

in·sta·bil·i·ty /ˌɪnstəˈbɪləti; ˌɪnstəˈbɪlɨti/ *n* [U] **1** uncertainty in a situation that is caused by the possibility of sudden change〔形势的〕不稳定: *the instability of the market* 市场的变化无常 | *political instability* 政治上的动荡 **2** mental problems that are likely to cause sudden changes of behaviour〔可能导致行为突然失常的〕精神疾病: *nervous instability* 神经错乱

3 **in·stall, instal** /ɪnˈstɔl; ɪnˈstɔːl/ *v* [T] **1** to put a piece of equipment somewhere and connect it so that it is ready to be used 安装〔设备〕, 设置: *They've installed the new network at last.* 他们终于安装了新网络。**2** to put someone in an important job or position, especially with a ceremony〔尤指通过特别仪式〕正式任命, 使正式就职: *Churchill was installed as Chancellor of the university.* 丘吉尔被任命为那所大学的校长。**3 install yourself in/at etc** to settle somewhere as if you are going to stay for a long time 把自己安顿在〔某地逗留很长一段时间〕, 安置

in·stal·la·tion /ˌɪnstəˈleʃən; ˌɪnstəˈleɪʃən/ *n* **1** [C] a piece of equipment that has been fitted in its place 装置, 设备: *The whole computer installation was nearly new.* 整套电脑设备几乎是全新的。**2** [U] the act of fitting a piece of equipment somewhere 安装: *the installation of a new washing machine* 安装一台新洗衣机 **3** [C] a place where industrial or military equipment, machinery etc has been put〔工业或军事〕设施, 基地: *nuclear installations* 核设施 **4** [U] *formal* the ceremony of putting someone in an important job or position【正式】就职仪式: *the installation of the new bishop* 新主教的就职仪式

installment plan /·ˈ·· ·/ *n* [singular,U] *AmE* a system of paying for goods by a series of small regular payments【美】分期付款购物法; HIRE PURCHASE *BrE*【英】

in·stal·ment also 又作 **installment** *AmE*【美】/ɪnˈstɔlmənt; ɪnˈstɔːlmənt/ *n* [C] **1** one of a series of regular payments, that you make until you have paid all the money you owe〔分期付款中的〕每期付款额: *the second instalment of a loan* 一项贷款的第二期还款 | **pay by instalments** *They're letting me pay for the washing machine by instalments.* 他们允许我以分期付款方式买这台洗衣机。**2** one of the parts of a story that appears as a series of parts in a magazine, newspaper etc; EPISODE (2)〔在报刊上分期连载故事的〕一期

3 2 **in·stance**[1] /ˈɪnstəns; ˈɪnstəns/ *n* **1 for instance** for example 例如: *You can't rely on her. For instance, she arrived an hour late for an important meeting yesterday.* 她这个人靠不住, 比如说, 昨天有个重要会议, 她晚来了一小时。**2** [C] an example of a particular kind of situation〔特定情况的〕例子, 实例: [+of] *instances of injustice* 种种不公的事例 | **in this instance** *Hilary is right about most things, but in this instance I think she was mistaken.* 多数情况下希拉丽都是对的, 但这件事上我认为她弄错了。**3 at sb's instance** *formal* because of someone's wish or request【正式】应某人的请求 **4 in the first instance** at the beginning of a series of actions〔一连串行动的〕第一步, 首先: *Anyone wishing to join the society should apply in the first instance to the secretary.* 任何人加入协会都得先向秘书提出申请。

instance[2] *v* [T] *formal* to give something as an example【正式】举…为例: *She instanced the first chapter as proof of his skill in constructing scenes.* 她以第一章为例证明他构思情节的技巧。

3 **in·stant**[1] /ˈɪnstənt; ˈɪnstənt/ *adj* **1** happening or produced immediately 立刻的, 马上的: *The women took an instant dislike to one another.* 那些女人立即相互厌恶起来。| *a system that provides instant hot water* 即时热水供应系统 **2** [only before noun 仅用于名词前] instant food, coffee etc is in the form of powder and prepared by adding hot water〔食物、咖啡〕速溶的, 调制方便的: *instant coffee* 速溶咖啡

instant[2] *n* **1** [C usually singular 一般用单数] a moment 片刻, 顷刻: *She caught his eye for an instant.* 她在一瞬间与他的目光相遇。| **in an instant** (=immediately) *When the rain started, the crowd vanished in an instant.* 下雨了, 人群立刻散尽。**2 the instant (that)** as soon as something happens 一…(就…): *The instant I saw him, I knew he was the man the police were looking for.* 我一看到他就认出他正是警方要找的人。**3 this instant** *spoken* used when telling someone, especially a child, to do something immediately【口】立即, 此刻〔尤用于催促小孩〕: *Come here this instant!* 赶紧过来!

in·stan·ta·ne·ous /ˌɪnstənˈteniəs; ˌɪnstənˈteɪniəs◂/ *adj* happening immediately 即刻的: *The computer gives an instantaneous response.* 电脑瞬间作出反应。—**instantaneously** *adv* —**instantaneousness** *n* [U]

in·stant·ly /ˈɪnstəntli; ˈɪnstəntli/ *adv* immediately 立即, 马上: *They recognised him instantly.* 他们立刻认出了他。| *All four victims died instantly.* 四名受害人都当即死去。

instant re·play /ˌ·· ˈ··/ *n* [C] *AmE* an important moment in a sports game on television that is shown again immediately after it happens【美】〔电视体育比赛节目中重要镜头的〕即时重放; ACTION REPLAY *BrE*【英】

in·stead /ɪnˈstɛd; ɪnˈsted/ *adv* **1 instead of** in place of something or someone 代替; 而不是: *We should do something instead of just talking about it.* 我们不能只是谈论, 应当做点什么。| *You must have picked up my keys instead of yours.* 你肯定拿走了我的钥匙, 而不是你自己的。| *Could I have tuna instead of ham?* 我可否要金枪鱼来代替火腿? **2** in place of something that has just been mentioned 作为替代: *If Joe can't attend the meeting, I could go instead.* 如果乔不能去开会, 我可以代他去。| *We didn't have enough money for a movie, so we went to the park instead.* 我们的钱不够看电影, 于是去了公园。| [sentence adverb 句子副词] *Cardew did not join the navy. Instead, he decided to become an actor.* 卡迪尤没有参加海军, 而是决定当演员。 1 1

in·step /ˈɪnˌstɛp; ˈɪnstep/ *n* [C] **1** the raised part of your foot between your toes and your ANKLE 脚背 —see picture at 参见 FOOT[1] 图 **2** the part of a shoe or sock that covers this part 鞋面; 袜背 —see picture at 参见 SHOE[1] 图

in·sti·gate /ˈɪnstəˌget; ˈɪnstɨgeɪt/ *v* [T] **1** to start something such as a legal process or an official inquiry 开始〔法律程序、正式调查等〕; 发起: *Without evidence it would be impossible to instigate an official investigation.* 没有证据就不能进行正式调查。**2** to start trouble by persuading someone to do something bad 唆使; 煽动: *A foreign government was accused of having instigated the bloodshed.* 某外国政府被指控煽动了这次流血事件。—**instigator** *n* [C]

in·sti·ga·tion /ˌɪnstəˈgeʃən; ˌɪnstɪˈgeɪʃən/ *n* **1 at sb's instigation** *formal* because of someone's suggestion, request or demand【正式】在某人的建议[请求, 要求]下: *At Canham's instigation, a clerk brought in an electric fan.* 在坎汉的建议下, 办事员拿来一台电风扇。**2** [U] the act of starting something 发动; 发起

in·stil *BrE*【英】, **instill** *AmE*【美】/ɪnˈstɪl; ɪnˈstɪl/ *v* [T] to teach someone a way of thinking or behaving over a long period of time 逐渐灌输〔思想或行为方式〕: **instil sth in/into sb** *They instilled good manners into their children at an early age.* 他们从小就教育孩子要有礼貌。—**instillation** /ˌɪnstɪˈleʃən; ˌɪnstɪˈleɪʃən/ *n* [U]

in·stinct /ˈɪnstɪŋkt; ˈɪnstɪŋkt/ *n* [C,U] a natural tendency or ability to behave or react in a particular way without having to learn it or think about it 本能; 直觉; 天性: [+for] *an instinct for self-preservation* 自我保存的本能 | **instinct to do sth** *a lion's instinct to hunt* 狮子的猎食本能 | *My instinct would be to wait and see.* 我的本能反应是再等等看。—compare 比较 INTUITION

in·stinc·tive /ɪnˈstɪŋktɪv; ɪnˈstɪŋktɪv/ *adj* based on instinct (出于) 本能的; (出于) 天性的; (出于) 直觉的: *instinctive behaviour* 本能行为 | *an instinctive sympathy with the younger boys* 对小男孩的天生恻隐之心 —**instinctively** *adv*: *Instinctively, we dived for cover.* 我们本能地迅速躲藏起来。

In·sti·net /ˈɪnstənɛt; ˈɪnstənet/ an electronic network that allows people to buy and sell shares using a computer when a STOCK EXCHANGE is closed. Instinet is owned by Reuters. 机构网络公司〔供人们在证券交易所收市后进行证券交易的一个电子网络, 属路透社所有〕

in·sti·tute[1] /ˈɪnstəˌtjut; ˈɪnstɨtjuːt/ *n* [C] an organization that has a particular purpose such as scientific or educational work, or the building where this organization is based 学院; 研究院, 研究所: *The Institute for Contemporary Arts* 当代艺术学院 | *research institutes* 研究所

institute[2] *v* [T] *formal* to introduce or start a system, rule, legal process etc【正式】制定〔制度、规则等〕；提起〔诉讼〕：*institute divorce proceedings* 提出离婚诉讼

Institute of Economic Affairs /ˌ‥‥, ‥ˈ‥, ‥/ a British organization formed in 1957 to promote free market economics. Its ideas were popular with Margaret Thatcher, the Conservative Prime Minister from 1979 to 90. 经济事务研究所〔英国一组织，成立于1957年，旨在促进自由市场经济学的发展。其观点颇受1979至1990年间任英国首相的保守党领袖玛格丽特·撒切尔的青睐〕

1 **in·sti·tu·tion** /ˌɪnstəˈtjuʃən; ˌɪnstɪˈtjuːʃən/ *n* [C]
1 ▶FOR SCIENCE/BUSINESS 关于科学/企业◀ a large establishment or organization that has a particular kind of work or purpose 机构，团体：*the most advanced medical institution in the world* 全球最先进的医疗机构 | *a financial institution* 金融机构
2 ▶HOSPITAL ETC 医院等◀ **a)** a large building where old people or ORPHANS live and are looked after by an official organization 慈善机构；养老院；孤儿院：*The atmosphere of the institution was rather impersonal.* 这家养老院缺乏人情味。**b)** a word meaning a mental hospital, used when you want to avoid saying this directly 精神病院〔委婉语〕
3 ▶CUSTOM 习俗◀ an established system or custom in society 习俗，惯例，制度：*the institution of marriage* 婚姻制度
4 ▶STARTING STH 开始某事◀ the act of starting or introducing a system, rule etc 开创；制定：[+of] *They approved the institution of a new law.* 他们同意实施一部新法律。
5 ▶PERSON 人物◀ **be an institution** *humorous* to be so well known in a place that you seem to be a permanent part of it【幽默】在某地为人所熟知的人：*Bill Tucker has been the postman in our village for 40 years. He's become something of an institution.* 比尔·塔克在我们村里做邮递员已有40年，他已经成为我们村的知名人物。—**institutional** *adj*

in·sti·tu·tion·al·ize also 又作 **-ise** *BrE*【英】/ˌɪnstəˈtjuʃənlˌaɪz; ˌɪnstɪˈtjuːʃənəlaɪz/ *v* [T] *old-fashioned* to put someone in a mental hospital or institution for old people etc【过时】把〔某人〕送到精神病院[养老院]

in·sti·tu·tion·al·ized also 又作 **-ised** *BrE*【英】/ˌɪnstəˈtjuʃənlˌaɪzd; ˌɪnstɪˈtjuːʃənəlaɪzd/ *adj* **1 institutionalized violence/racism/corruption** violence etc that has happened for so long in an organization or society that it has become accepted as normal 习以为常的暴力行为/种族歧视/腐败 **2** *formal* someone who has become institutionalized has lived for a long time in a prison, mental hospital etc and now cannot easily live outside one【正式】长期坐牢[住精神病院]〔已不适应外界生活〕的

in-store /ˌ·ˈ·◂/ *adj* happening within a large shop or DEPARTMENT STORE 发生在大商店[百货公司]内的：*in-store sales demonstrations* 商店内的销售展示

in·struct /ɪnˈstrʌkt; ɪnˈstrʌkt/ *v* [T] **1** to officially tell someone what to do 命令；指示：**instruct sb to do sth** *Our staff have been instructed to offer you every assistance.* 我方工作人员已奉命为您提供一切帮助。| **as instructed** (=in the way that you have been instructed) 依照指示 *We returned the questionnaire as instructed.* 我们依照指示交回调查表。**2** to teach or show someone how to do something 教授，指导：**instruct sb in sth** *Mr. Andersen was instructing them in the art of screen printing.* 安德森先生在教他们丝网印刷法。—see 见 TEACH (USAGE) **3** [usually passive 一般用被动态] *formal* to officially inform someone about something【正式】通知：**instruct sb that** *We were instructed that the assembly would not vote until noon.* 我们得到通知，大会中午才投票。**4** *law* to employ a lawyer to deal with your case in court【法律】聘请〔律师〕出庭：*Once you have decided to proceed with a case, you should instruct a good solicitor.* 一旦你决定打官司，就应当聘请一位好律师。

3 2 **in·struc·tion** /ɪnˈstrʌkʃən; ɪnˈstrʌkʃən/ *n* **1 instructions** [plural] the printed information that tells you how to use a piece of equipment etc 操作指南；使用说明：*We forgot to read the instructions.* 我们忘了看使用说明书。| **follow the instructions** *Follow the instructions on the back of the box.* 按照盒子背面印的说明去做。**2** [C, usually plural 一般用复数] a statement telling someone what they must do 命令，指示：**instructions to do sth** *He had explicit instructions to check everyone's identity card at the door.* 他接到明确指示，在入口处检验每个人的身份证。| **instructions that** *Mrs Edwards left strict instructions that she was not to be disturbed.* 爱德华兹夫人留下严格指示，不许任何人打扰她。| **on sb's instructions** (=because you have been officially told to do it) 按照某人的吩咐 *On his instructions, the luggage had been sent on.* 按照他的吩咐，行李已先行送走。| **my instructions are** (=used to tell someone what you have been officially told to do) 我得到的命令是 *My instructions are to give the package to him personally.* 我得到的命令是把包裹当面交给他。**3** [U] *formal* teaching that you are given in a particular skill or subject【正式】讲授，教学；指导：*religious instruction* 宗教指导 | *driving instruction* 驾驶技术指导 | [+in] *You will receive basic instruction in navigation.* 你将接受有关航行的基础指导。| **under (sb's) instruction** (=while being taught by someone) 在某人的教导下 *Under Stewart's instruction, I slowly mastered the art of glass blowing.* 在斯图尔特的教导下，我逐渐学会了玻璃吹制技术。

in·struc·tion·al /ɪnˈstrʌkʃənl; ɪnˈstrʌkʃənəl/ *adj formal* providing instruction【正式】提供指导的；教学用的：*instructional materials* 教材

instruction ma·nu·al /·ˈ·· ,···/ *n* [C] a book that gives you instructions on how to use or look after a machine〔机器的〕使用[维修]手册

in·struc·tive /ɪnˈstrʌktɪv; ɪnˈstrʌktɪv/ *adj* providing a lot of useful information, explanations, and knowledge about something 有教育意义的；有启发性的；增长知识的：*an instructive book on photography* 增进摄影知识的书 | *a very instructive experience* 极富教育意义的经历 —**instructively** *adv*

in·struc·tor /ɪnˈstrʌktɚ; ɪnˈstrʌktə/ *n* [C] **1** someone who teaches a sport or practical skill〔运动或技艺的〕指导员；教练；教员：*a driving instructor* 驾驶教练 | *ski instructors* 滑雪教练 **2** *AmE* someone who teaches in an American college or university before they have finished being trained【美】大学讲师：*a social studies instructor* 社会科学讲师

in·stru·ment /ˈɪnstrəmənt; ˈɪnstrʊmənt/ *n* [C] 2
1 ▶TOOL 工具◀ a small tool used in work such as science or medicine where very careful movements are necessary〔指用来进行细致工作的〕器械，器具：*surgical instruments* 外科（手术）器械
2 ▶MUSIC 音乐◀ an object such as a piano, horn, VIOLIN etc, used for producing musical sounds; MUSICAL INSTRUMENT 乐器：*stringed instruments* 弦乐器
3 ▶FOR MEASURING 测量◀ a piece of equipment for measuring and showing distance, speed, temperature etc 仪器，仪表：*The pilot studied his instruments anxiously.* 飞行员焦虑地查看各种仪表。| **instrument flying/landing** (=flying or bringing down an aircraft using only instruments) 仪表飞行/着陆
4 ▶METHOD 方法◀ [usually singular 一般用单数] a system, method, or law that is used by people in power to get a particular result 制度；方法；法律：*Sometimes military force can become an instrument of government policy.* 军事力量有时会成为政府政策的工具。
5 ▶DOCUMENT 文件◀ *formal* a legal document【正式】法律文件
6 *literary*【文】**instrument of fate/God** someone or something that is used by an unseen power which is beyond our control 受命运/上帝摆布的人[物]
7 instrument of torture a piece of equipment used to make people suffer pain 刑具

in·stru·men·tal[1] /ˌɪnstrəˈmɛntl; ˌɪnstrʊˈmentl◂/ *adj* **1 be instrumental** *formal* to be important in making something possible【正式】对…重要的，有帮助的：*Wilson was instrumental in introducing new methods of production.* 在引进新的生产方法上，威尔逊起了很大作用。**2** instrumental music is for instruments, not for voices 器乐的；用乐器演奏的 —**instrumentally** *adv* —**instrumentality** /ˌɪnstrəmɛnˈtælətɪ; ˌɪnstrʊmenˈtælɪti/ *n* [U]

instrumental[2] *n* [C] a piece of music or a part of a piece of music where no voices are used, only instruments 器乐曲；乐曲中只有器乐演奏的部分

in·stru·men·tal·ist /ˌɪnstrəˈmɛntlɪst; ˌɪnstrʊˈmentəlɪst/ *n* [C] someone who plays a musical instrument 乐器演奏者 —compare 比较 VOCALIST

in·stru·men·ta·tion /ˌɪnstrəmɛnˈteʃən; ˌɪnstrʊmenˈteɪʃən/ *n* [U] **1** the way in which a piece of music is arranged to be played by several different instruments 器乐曲的谱写 **2** the set of instruments (INSTRUMENT (3)) used to help in controlling a machine〔用于控制某机器的全部〕仪表：*the complex instrumentation in an aircraft's cockpit* 飞机驾驶舱内复杂的仪表

instrument pan·el /ˈ···, ··/ *n* [C] the board in front of the pilot of an aircraft, where all the instruments (INSTRUMENT (3)) are〔飞机驾驶舱中的〕仪表板

in·sub·or·di·nate /ˌɪnsəˈbɔrdṇɪt; ˌɪnsəˈbɔːdənɪt◂/ *adj* refusing to obey someone who has a higher rank than you in the army, navy etc〔军队中〕下级不服从的，违抗命令的 —**insubordination** /ˌɪnsəˌbɔrdṇˈeʃən; ˌɪnsəbɔːdɪˈneɪʃən/ *n* [U]: *Howell*

was dismissed for gross insubordination. 豪厄尔因为严重违抗命令而被开除。

in·sub·stan·tial /ˌɪnsəbˈstænʃəl; ˌɪnsəbˈstænʃəl◂/ *adj* **1** *formal* something that is insubstantial is much too small or weak and does not look solid enough【正式】不坚固的; 脆弱的: *a slender rope bridge, terrifyingly insubstantial* 细长的索桥, 不牢固的样子令人害怕 **2** *literary* not existing as a real object or person【文】非实体的; 虚幻的: *Pale figures, like insubstantial ghosts, moved through the mist.* 影影绰绰的人影, 就像虚幻的幽灵, 在雾中穿行。—**insubstantiality** /ˌɪnsəbstænʃɪˋælətɪ; ˌɪnsəbstænʃiˈæləti/ *n* [U]

in·suf·fe·ra·ble /ɪnˋsʌfrəbl; ɪnˈsʌfərəbəl/ *adj* extremely annoying or unpleasant 令人极厌恶[不快]的: *the insufferable heat* 炽热难耐 | *Lou can be pretty insufferable at times.* 卢有时很令人讨厌。—**insufferably** *adv*: *insufferably arrogant* 傲慢得不能忍受

in·suf·fi·cient /ˌɪnsəˋfɪʃənt; ˌɪnsəˈfɪʃənt◂/ *adj* not enough 不足的, 不够的: *insufficient supplies* 供应不足 | **[+for]** *There were insufficient funds for a research project.* 资金不足以进行一个研究项目。| **insufficient to do sth** *The evidence is quite insufficient to convict him.* 证据不足以给他定罪。—**insufficiently** *adv* —**insufficiency** *n* [singular,U] *an insufficiency of capital* 资本不充足

in·su·lar /ˋɪnsələ; ˈɪnsjʊlə/ *adj* **1** not interested in anything except your own group, country, way of life etc 思想狭隘的; 保守的: *In today's small world, we must guard against an insular outlook.* 如今世界已变小, 我们必须防止眼光狭隘。**2** *formal* like or connected with an island【正式】岛屿般的; 岛屿的 —**insularity** /ˌɪnsəˋlærətɪ; ˌɪnsjʊˈlærɪti/ *n* [U] *the insularity of the British* 英国人的岛民特性

in·su·late /ˋɪnsəˌlet; ˈɪnsjʊleɪt/ *v* [T] **1** to cover or protect something so that electricity, sound, heat etc cannot get in or out 使绝缘; 使隔热; 使隔音: *insulated cables* 绝缘电缆 | **insulate sth from/against** *A bird fluffs up its feathers to insulate itself against the cold.* 鸟抖松羽毛以御寒。**2** to protect someone from unpleasant experiences or unwanted influences 把〔某人〕隔离, 使隔绝〔以免遭受不愉快的经历或不良影响〕: **insulate sb from sth** *students insulated from the experiences of real life* 受到隔绝而不懂人情世故的学生

insulating tape /ˈ····, ·ˈ/ *n* [U] narrow material used for wrapping around electric wires to insulate them 绝缘胶带

in·su·la·tion /ˌɪnsəˋleʃən; ˌɪnsjʊˈleɪʃən/ *n* [U] **1** material used to insulate something, especially a building〔尤指建筑物的〕绝缘材料 **2** the act of insulating something or the state of being insulated 隔绝: *Good insulation can save you lots of money on heating bills.* 好的隔热效果能节省很多取暖费。

in·su·la·tor /ˋɪnsəˌletə; ˈɪnsjʊleɪtə/ *n* [C] an object or material that insulates, especially one which does not allow electricity to pass through it〔尤指不导电的〕绝缘体; 隔音材料

in·su·lin /ˋɪnsəlɪn; ˈɪnsjʊlɪn/ *n* [U] a substance produced naturally by your body which allows sugar to be used for energy 胰岛素 —see also 另见 DIABETES

in·sult¹ /ɪnˋsʌlt; ɪnˈsʌlt/ *v* [T] to say or do something that is rude and offensive to someone 侮辱; 冒犯: *Nobody insults my family and gets away with it!* 谁也别想侮辱了我的家庭之后就不了了之! | *I hope Andy won't feel insulted if I turn down his invitation.* 要是我拒绝安迪的邀请, 希望他不要介意。| **insult sb by doing sth** *Please don't insult me by offering me money.* 请不要用给我钱的办法来侮辱我。

in·sult² /ˋɪnsʌlt; ˈɪnsʌlt/ *n* [C] **1** a rude or offensive remark or action 辱骂, 凌辱; 侮辱性的言行: *She was shouting insults at her boyfriend.* 她正在对她的男朋友破口大骂。| *$200 for all that work? It's an insult.* 干那么多工作才给 200 美元? 简直是对我的侮辱。| **take sth as an insult** *Carol will take it as an insult if you don't come to the party.* 你要是不来参加聚会, 卡萝尔会认为是对她的不敬。**2 be an insult to sb's intelligence** if something such as a book, lesson, or television programme is an insult to your intelligence, it offends you by being too simple or stupid 对某人智力的侮辱〔指书、课程或电视节目等过于幼稚、愚蠢〕—see also 另见 **add insult to injury** (ADD (8))

in·sult·ing /ɪnˋsʌltɪŋ; ɪnˈsʌltɪŋ/ *adj* very rude and offensive to someone〔对某人〕侮辱的, 无礼的: *insulting remarks* 侮辱性的言论

in·su·pe·ra·ble /ɪnˋsupərəbl; ɪnˈsjuːpərəbəl◂/ *adj formal* an insuperable difficulty or problem is impossible to deal with【正式】〔困难或问题〕不能克服的, 无法解决的: *Getting an agreement between the two leaders proved to be an insuperable obstacle.* 要想使两位领导人达成协议, 简直不太可能。—**insuperably** *adv*

in·sup·por·ta·ble /ˌɪnsəˋpɔrtəbl; ˌɪnsəˈpɔːtəbəl◂/ *adj formal* too unpleasant for you to bear【正式】〔极讨厌而〕难以忍受的, 不能容忍的: *insupportable behaviour* 难以容忍的行为 | *insupportable pain* 不堪忍受的痛苦

in·sur·ance /ɪnˋʃurəns; ɪnˈʃʊərəns/ *n* **1** [U] an arrangement with a company in which you pay them money each year and they pay the costs if anything bad happens to you, such as an illness or an accident 保险: *health insurance* 健康保险 | *life insurance* (=so that your family receive money if you die) 人寿保险 | **[+against]** *insurance against permanent disability* 终身残疾保险 | **[+on]** *Do you have insurance on your household contents?* 你买家庭财产保险了吗? | **claim for sth on your insurance** (=get an insurance company to pay for something)〔就某物〕提出保险索赔 *We can probably claim for the damage on the insurance.* 我们可以让保险公司赔偿损失。| **take out insurance** (=start paying for insurance protection) 买保险 **2** [U] the money that you pay regularly to an insurance company; INSURANCE PREMIUM 保险费: **[+on]** *Insurance on my house is very high.* 我家房子的保险费很高。**3** [U] the business of providing insurance 保险业: *He works in insurance.* 他从事保险业。**4** [singular,U] protection against something bad happening 保障; 预防措施: **[+against]** *I put an extra lock on the door as an added insurance against burglars.* 为了防盗, 我在门上又加了一把锁。—see also 另见 ASSURANCE (3), NATIONAL INSURANCE

insurance ad·just·er /ˈ·····, ··ˈ/ *n* [C] *AmE* someone who is employed by an insurance company to decide how much to pay people who have had an accident, had something stolen etc【美】〔保险公司雇请的〕险损估价人, 保险理算师; LOSS ADJUSTER *BrE*【英】

insurance bro·ker /ˈ·····, ··ˈ/ also 又作 **insurance agent** *n* [C] someone who arranges and sells insurance as their job 保险经纪人, 保险代理人

insurance pol·i·cy /ˈ·····, ···ˈ/ *n* [C] a written agreement with an insurance company 保险合同; 保险单

insurance pre·mi·um /ˈ·····, ···ˈ/ *n* [C] the money that you pay regularly to an insurance company〔定期交纳的〕保险费

in·sure /ɪnˋʃur; ɪnˈʃʊə/ *v* **1** [I,T] to buy insurance to protect yourself against something bad happening to you, your family, your possessions etc 给…保险, 为…投保: *Have you insured the contents of your home?* 你给家里的财产投保了吗? | **insure (sth/sb) against sth** *It would be wise to insure your property against storm damage.* 为防风暴带来的损失而给财产保险是明智之举。| **insure sth for £1000/$2000 etc** *I would advise you to insure the painting for at least £100,000.* 我建议你给这幅油画至少投保 100,000 英镑。**2** [T] to provide insurance for something or someone 为〔某物或某人〕提供保险: *Many companies won't insure young drivers.* 许多公司都不愿意为年轻司机提供保险。**3** an American spelling of ENSURE ensure 的美式拼法

insure against sth *phr v* [T] to protect yourself against the risk of something bad happening by planning or preparing 对…采取预防措施: *No matter what precautions you may take, you cannot insure against every eventuality.* 不管你采取什么样的预防措施, 都不能确保万无一失。

USAGE NOTE 用法说明: INSURE

WORD CHOICE 词语辨析: **assure, reassure, insure, ensure, make sure**

If you **assure** someone of something, you tell them that it is really true or will happen. assure 是向某人保证某事是真实的或将要发生: *The receptionist assured me that I would not have to wait long.* 接待人员向我保证说不会久等。| *Christianity assures us there is life after death.* 基督教使我们相信人死后可得永生。

You **reassure** someone who is worried by telling them that there is nothing to worry about. reassure用来向焦虑的人表示安慰, 请他们不必担心: *The doctor reassured me that there would be no pain.* 医生要我放心, 说不会疼痛的。

You may **insure** something against something bad happening to it by paying money to an insurance company. insure 意思是为防不测而向保险公司投保: *Is the house insured against fire?* 这所房子是否保了火险? | *Julia Roberts' legs are insured for a large amount of money.* 朱莉娅·罗伯茨为她的双腿投了大额保险。It is also possible to **insure** your life against death, though where something is certain to happen one day the technical British English word is **assure**. insure 也有为死亡而向保险公司投保的用法。然而, 英国英语中关于总有一天会发生的事情的术语是 assure。

If you **ensure** (usually **insure** in American English) that something happens, that means you make certain or **make sure** (more informal) it does happen. ensure〔美国英语中多用 insure〕意思是"确保某事发生", 义同 make sure〔较为不正式〕: *Please ensure that the lights are switched off before leaving the building.* 请确保离开大楼前关掉所有电灯。In some situation **assure** can be used in this meaning too where the object is reflexive or what is ensured is something such as success, safety, comfort etc. 如果宾语是反身代词, 或确保的对象为成功、安全、舒适等, 也可用 assure: *I assured myself of a seat at the front* (=I made sure I got one). 我确保自己在前排有个座位。| *The band's latest release has assured their success in the rock world* (=ensured that they will be successful). 这支乐队的最新唱片确保了它在摇滚乐坛的成功。

in·sured /ɪn`ʃʊrd; ɪn'ʃʊəd/ *adj* **1** having insurance 已保险的: *Mike's bike was stolen and it wasn't insured.* 迈克的自行车被偷了, 且车子没上险。| **insured to do sth** *You wouldn't be insured to drive Anne's car.* 你开安妮的车不享受保险。| [**+against**] *Is your house insured against fire?* 你的房子保火险了吗? **2 the insured** *law* the person or people who are insured【法律】被保险人, 保户, 受保人

in·sur·er /ɪn`ʃʊrɚ; ɪn'ʃʊərə/ *n* [C] a person or company that provides insurance 承保人; 保险公司: *The insurer will pay the full cost of storm damage.* 保险公司将全额偿付风暴造成的损失。

in·sur·gent /ɪn`sɝdʒənt; ɪn'sɜːdʒənt/ *n* [C often plural 常用复数] one of a group of people fighting against the government of their own country 起义者, 暴动者, 叛乱者 —**insurgency** *n* [U] —**insurgent** *adj*: *the insurgent forces* 叛军 —see also 另见 COUNTERINSURGENCY

in·sur·moun·ta·ble /ˌɪnsɚ`maʊntəbḷ; ˌɪnsə'maʊntəbəl◂/ *adj* a difficulty or problem that is insurmountable is too large or too difficult to deal with〔困难或问题〕不可逾越的; 难以克服的; 难以处理的: *The language barrier proved an insurmountable barrier to their relationship.* 语言障碍是他们关系中难以克服的障碍。

in·sur·rec·tion /ˌɪnsə`rɛkʃən; ˌɪnsə'rekʃən/ *n* [C,U] an attempt by a large group of people within a country to take control using force and violence 起义; 暴动; 造反; 叛乱: *an armed insurrection against the party in power* 反对执政党的武装暴乱 —**insurrectionist** *n*

in·tact /ɪn`tækt; ɪn'tækt/ *adj* [not before noun 不用于名词前] not broken, damaged, or spoiled, usually after something bad has happened 完好无损的; 未受损伤的: *The fireplace was the only thing that remained intact after the tornado.* 龙卷风过后, 只有壁炉完好无损。| *Somehow his reputation survived the scandal intact.* 这场丑闻过后, 不知为什么他的名声竟然丝毫未受影响。

in·ta·gli·o /ɪn`tæljo; ɪn'tɑːliəʊ/ *n* [C,U] the art of cutting patterns into a hard substance or the pattern that you get by doing this 凹雕艺术; 凹雕图案

in·take /`ɪnˌtek; 'ɪnteɪk/ *n* **1** [singular] the amount of food, drink etc that you take into your body〔食物、饮品等的〕纳入量: *Lower your intake of fat and alcohol to improve your health.* 为了增进健康, 减少脂肪和酒精的摄入量。**2** the number of people allowed to enter a school, profession etc〔学校、行业等的人员〕接收数量: *an increase in the intake of foreign students* 接收留学生人数的增加 **3** [C] a tube, pipe, etc through which air, gas, or liquid is taken in〔空气、可燃气体或液体注入的〕管道: *air intakes on a jet engine* 喷气式发动机的进气口 **4 an intake of breath** a sudden act of breathing in, showing that you are shocked etc 倒吸一口气〔表示吃惊〕

in·tan·gi·ble /ɪn`tændʒəbḷ; ɪn'tændʒɨbəl/ *adj* an intangible quality or feeling cannot be clearly felt or described, although you know it exists; INDEFINABLE〔性质或感受〕难以捉摸的; 无法形容的; 难以确认的: *The island of Iona has an intangible quality of holiness.* 艾奥纳岛有一种说不出的神圣感。| *Customer goodwill is an important and intangible asset of a business.* 商誉是企业重要的无形资产。—**intangibly** *adv* —**intangibility** /ɪnˌtændʒə`bɪlətɪ; ɪnˌtændʒɨ'bɪlɨti/ *n* [U]

in·te·ger /`ɪntədʒɚ; 'ɪntɨdʒə/ *n* [C] *technical* a whole number【术语】整数: *6 is an integer, but 6.4 is not.* 6 是整数, 而 6.4 不是。

in·te·gral /`ɪntəgrəl; 'ɪntɨgrəl/ *adj* forming a necessary part of something 构成整体所必需的, 不可缺少的: *Effective communication is an integral part of being a teacher.* 有效的沟通技巧是一名教师不可缺少的部分。| [**+to**] *Her talents are integral to the team's good performance.* 她的才华对于全队的良好表现是不可或缺的。—**integrally** *adv*

integral cal·cu·lus /ˌ··· `··/ *n* [U] *technical* a method of measuring the distance a moving object has moved at a particular moment, by using your knowledge of its speed until then【术语】积分(学)

in·te·grate /`ɪntəˌgret; 'ɪntɨgreɪt/ *v* **1** [I,T] to join in the life and customs of the group or society that you live in so that you are accepted by them, or to help someone do this (使)融入〔某群体或社会〕; (使)成为一体: [**+into/with**] *The child was only adopted a year ago, but she has completely integrated into the family's life.* 这个孩子虽然才领养了一年, 但她已完全融入了这个家庭的生活。| *Attempts to integrate the new immigrants have failed.* 同化新移民的努力已告失败。**2** [T] to combine things that work well together in order to make an effective system 使合并〔成为有效的系统〕, 使结合: *Train and bus services have been fully integrated.* 火车和公共汽车两种系统已完全结合了起来。| **integrate sth with sth** *The school integrates maths lessons with computer studies.* 学校把数学课与电脑课结合起来。**3** [I,T] to end the separation of races in a place or institution, usually by making separation illegal; DESEGREGATE (使)取消种族隔离: *Laws were passed in the US in order to integrate all schools.* 美国已通过法律, 在所有学校中取消种族隔离。—compare 比较 SEGREGATE

in·te·grat·ed /`ɪntəˌgretɪd; 'ɪntɨgreɪtɨd/ *adj* an integrated system, institution etc combines many different groups, ideas, or parts in a way that works well〔各组成部分〕相互协调的; 综合的: *an integrated public transport system* 综合公共交通体系 | *a fully integrated school with children from many races and classes* 兼收不同种族及不同社会阶层儿童的学校 —compare 比较 SEGREGATED

integrated cir·cuit /ˌ···· `··/ *n* [C] *technical* a very small set of electronic connections printed on a single piece of SEMICONDUCTOR material instead of being made from separate parts【术语】集成电路

in·te·gra·tion /ˌɪntə`greʃən; ˌɪntɨ'greɪʃən/ *n* [U] **1** the combining of two or more things so that they work together effectively 结合; 综合; 集成; 整合: *the closer integration of the countries' economies* 各国经济更密切的联合 **2** the acceptance of people in a group or society 同化; 融入: *complete integration of racial groups* 不同种族群体的完全融合 **3** the ending of laws that make people of different races live, work etc separately 种族隔离法规的废除 W3

in·teg·ri·ty /ɪn`tɛgrətɪ; ɪn'tegrɨti/ *n* [U] **1** the quality of being honest and of always having high moral principles 正直; 诚实: *a man of absolute integrity, with the highest moral standards* 刚正不阿、道德高尚的人 **2** *formal* the state of being united as one complete thing【正式】完整, 完全: *Removing the chapter destroys the integrity of the book.* 去掉这一章会破坏全书的完整。

in·teg·u·ment /ɪn`tɛgjəmənt; ɪn'tegjʊmənt/ *n* [C] *technical* something such as a shell which covers something else【术语】覆盖物; 外皮〈如甲壳〉

in·tel·lect /`ɪntḷˌɛkt; 'ɪntɨlekt/ *n* **1** [C,U] the ability to understand things and to think intelligently 智力; 理解能力; 思维能力: *new scientific ideas that are a challenge to the human intellect* 对人类智慧构成挑战的新科学观点 | *a woman of superior intellect* 聪颖过人的女子 **2** [C] someone who is very intelligent 才智出众者: *some of the greatest intellects in the world of science* 科学界中几位最伟大的智者

in·tel·lec·tual[1] /ˌɪntḷ`ɛktʃuəl; ˌɪntɨ'lektʃuəl◂/ *adj* **1** an intellectual activity, quality etc involves intelligent thinking in order to understand or enjoy something 智力的; 需用脑力的: *an intellectual film* 寓意深奥的影片 | *The student showed enormous intellectual ability.* 这个学生表现出极高的智力。**2** an intellectual person is well-educated and interested in serious ideas and subjects such as science, literature etc 有知识的, 受过良好教育的: *an intellectual family* 有知识的家庭 —**intellectually** *adv*: *intellectually stimulating* 给人以知识启迪的 —**intellectualize** *v* [I,T] W3

intellectual[2] *n* [C] an intelligent, well-educated person who spends a lot of their time thinking about complicated ideas and discussing them 知识分子: *He likes to think of himself as an intellectual.* 他喜欢把自己看成知识分子。—see 见 INTELLIGENT (USAGE)

intellectual prop·er·ty /ˌ····· `···/ *n* [U] *law* something which someone has invented or has the right to make or sell, especially something protected by a PATENT[1] (1), TRADEMARK, or COPYRIGHT【法律】知识产权

in·tel·li·gence /ɪn`tɛlədʒəns; ɪn'telɨdʒəns/ *n* [U] **1 a)** the ability to learn, understand, and think about things 智力; 理解 S3 W3

力: *a child of low intelligence* 智力低下的孩子 | *Don't act like such an idiot – use your intelligence!* 别干这种傻事, 动动脑筋! **b)** a high level of this ability 聪颖, 聪明: *a woman of beauty, charm, and intelligence* 美丽、迷人、聪慧的女子 **2 a)** information about the secret activities of foreign governments, the military plans of an enemy etc 情报, 谍报: *intelligence gathering* 情报收集 **b)** a group of people or an organization that gathers this information for their government 情报机构; 谍报人员: *He works for British Intelligence.* 他为英国情报机构工作。| *reports from Military Intelligence* 来自军事情报部门的报告

intelligence quo·tient /ˈ· · · ·, · ˈ· · · · ·/ *n* [C] IQ 智商

in·tel·li·gent /ɪnˈtɛlədʒənt; ɪnˈtelɪ̇dʒənt/ *adj* **1** having a high level of mental ability so that you are good at understanding ideas and thinking quickly and clearly 有智慧的; 聪明的; 悟性强的: *If you're reasonably intelligent the maths involved should present no problems.* 你如果智力还过得去, 这里所涉及的数学根本不成问题。**2** an intelligent animal is able to think and understand 〔动物〕有智能的: *Are there intelligent forms of life on other planets?* 在其他星球上是否有智能生命形式存在? —**intelligently** *adv*

> **USAGE NOTE 用法说明: INTELLIGENT**
> WORD CHOICE 词语辨析: **intelligent, intellectual**
> An **intelligent** person is someone with a quick and clever mind, but an **intellectual** person is someone who is well-educated and interested in subjects that need long periods of study. A small child, or even a dog, can be **intelligent** but cannot be called **intellectual**. intelligent 指人头脑敏捷, 智力聪颖; intellectual 则指人受过良好教育, 对需要长期研究的学科感兴趣。可以用 intelligent 来形容一个小孩, 甚至一条狗, 但不能用 intellectual。
> **Intelligent** and **intellectual** are both adjectives, but **intellectual** can also be a noun. intelligent 和 intellectual 都是形容词, 但 intellectual 还可作名词: *There are too many intellectuals in the government.* 政府中知识分子太多。

in·tel·li·gent·si·a /ɪn,tɛləˈdʒɛntsɪə; ɪn,telɪ̇ˈdʒentsiə/ *n* **the intelligentsia** the people in a society who are most highly educated and who are most interested in new ideas and developments, especially in art, literature, or politics 〔尤指艺术、文学和政界的〕知识分子; 知识阶层

in·tel·li·gi·ble /ɪnˈtɛlɪdʒəbl; ɪnˈtelɪ̇dʒɪ̇bəl/ *adj* intelligible speech, writing, or ideas can be easily understood 〔言语、文章、观点〕明白易懂的: *He was so drunk that his speech was barely intelligible.* 他醉得说话几乎让人听不懂。| [+to] *Newspapers must be intelligible to all levels of readers.* 报纸必须让各种水平的读者都看得懂。—**intelligibly** *adv* —**intelligibility** /ɪn,tɛlɪdʒəˈbɪlətɪ; ɪn,telɪ̇dʒɪ̇ˈbɪlɪ̇ti/ *n* [U] —opposite 反义词 UNINTELLIGIBLE

in·tem·per·ate /ɪnˈtɛmpərɪt; ɪnˈtempərɪ̇t/ *adj formal* 【正式】 **1** not having enough control over your feelings so that you behave in a way that is unacceptable to other people 〔行为〕无节制的; 过度的; 放纵的: *an intemperate outburst* 过度的感情发泄 **2** regularly drinking too much alcohol 纵酒的, 酗酒的 —**intemperately** *adv* —**intemperance** *n* [U]

in·tend /ɪnˈtɛnd; ɪnˈtend/ *v* [T] **1** to have something in your mind as a plan or purpose 计划, 打算, 想要: **intend to do sth** *I intend to get there as soon after 5 as I can.* 我打算在5点后尽快赶到那里。| **intend sb/sth to do sth** *I didn't intend her to see the painting until it was finished.* 我原本不想在画还没有完成时就让她看。| *He was insulted by my remark, but I hadn't intended it to be offensive.* 他感到我的话侮辱了他, 但我根本没有这个意思。| **it is intended that** *It is intended that all new employees will receive appropriate training.* 按计划所有新员工都要接受适当的培训。| **fully intend** (=definitely intend) 明确打算 *Kate had fully intended returning home on Sunday but she couldn't get a flight.* 凯特原来打定主意星期日回家, 可是她没有买到飞机票。—see 见 PROPOSE (USAGE) **2 be intended for sb/sth** to be provided or designed for a particular purpose or person 是为…而准备的; 专供…使用的: *a book intended for young children* 专供幼儿阅读的书 **3 intended target/victim/destination etc** the person, thing, result etc that an action is intended to affect or reach 预期的目标/被害人/目的地等: *It seems likely that General Rocha was the intended victim.* 罗卡将军很可能是袭击的目标。

in·tend·ed /ɪnˈtɛndɪd; ɪnˈtendɪ̇d/ *n* **sb's intended** *old-fashioned or humorous* the person that you are going to marry 【过时或幽默】未婚夫; 未婚妻: *Meet my intended, Miss Robinson.* 这是我的未婚妻鲁宾逊小姐。

in·tense /ɪnˈtɛns; ɪnˈtens/ *adj* **1** having a very strong effect or felt very strongly 强烈的, 剧烈的: *intense pain* 剧痛 | *The heat was intense.* 天气酷热。**2** there is intense activity, effort etc when people are working, trying, or thinking extremely hard 紧张的; 认真的: *a period of intense concentration and study* 全神贯注、力学不倦的时期 **3** having feelings or opinions that are extremely strong, serious etc 〔感情或意见〕极为强烈的, 极为严肃的: *She can be so intense, it makes me exhausted.* 她有时会过于严肃, 让我感到精疲力竭。| *an intense young man* 十分严肃认真的年轻人 —**intensely** *adv*: *intensely exciting* 极度兴奋 —**intensity** *n* [U]

in·ten·si·fi·er /ɪnˈtɛnsə,faɪr; ɪnˈtensɪ̇faɪə/ *n* [C] *technical* a word, usually an adverb, that is used to emphasize an adjective, adverb, or verb, for example the word 'absolutely' in the phrase 'that's absolutely wonderful' 【术语】〔一般是副词, 用以加强形容词、副词或动词词义的〕强调成分; 加强语〈如 that's absolutely wonderful 中的 absolutely〉

in·ten·si·fy /ɪnˈtɛnsə,faɪ; ɪnˈtensɪ̇faɪ/ *v* [I,T] if an activity, effort, feeling etc intensifies, or if you intensify it, it increases in degree or strength 加强, 增强: *Police have now intensified the search for the lost child.* 警方已加紧寻找那个失踪的孩子。—**intensification** /ɪn,tɛnsəfəˈkeʃən; ɪn,tensɪ̇fɪ̇ˈkeɪʃən/ *n* [U] *the intensification of the conflict in Bosnia* 波斯尼亚冲突的加剧

in·ten·sive /ɪnˈtɛnsɪv; ɪnˈtensɪv/ *adj* **1** involving a lot of activity, effort, or careful attention in a short period of time 加强的; 集中的: *a one-week intensive course in English* 为期一周的英语强化课程 | *a period of intensive fighting* 战斗激烈的时期 **2 intensive farming/agriculture** farming which produces a lot of food from a small area of land 精耕细作; 集约式农业: *Most of lowland Britain is intensively cultivated.* 大多数的英国低地都进行精耕细作。—**intensively** *adv* —see also 另见 LABOUR-INTENSIVE

intensive care /·,· · ˈ·/ *n* [U] a department in a hospital that gives special attention and treatment to people who are very seriously ill or badly injured 危重病人监护部, 特护部

in·tent[1] /ɪnˈtɛnt; ɪnˈtent/ *n* [U] **1 to all intents (and purposes)** *especially spoken* almost completely 【尤口】实际上; 几乎在一切方面: *To all intents and purposes, their marriage is over.* 他们的婚姻实际上已结束。**2** *formal* what you intend to do; intention 【正式】目的; 意图: *She behaved foolishly but with good intent.* 她虽然干了蠢事, 但意图是好的。**3** *law* the intention to do something illegal 【法律】〔犯罪〕意图: *arrested for loitering with intent* 因四处游荡伺机作案而被捕 | **intent to do sth** *Jefferson was charged with intent to damage property.* 杰斐逊被指控企图破坏财产。

intent[2] *adj* **1** giving careful attention to something so that you think about nothing else 专注的, 专心致志的: *watching the game with an intent stare* 目不转睛地观看比赛 | **[+on/upon]** *Intent upon her work, she ignored the cold.* 她专心于工作, 不顾寒冷。**2 be intent on (doing) sth** to be determined to do something or achieve something, especially something that may cause damage 执意〔某事〕〔尤指会造成破坏的事〕: *Pete seems intent on stirring up trouble.* 皮特好像故意要惹出乱子。—**intently** *adv*: *I noticed her gazing intently at one of the photographs.* 我发觉她全神贯注地看着其中一张照片。—**intentness** *n* [U]

in·ten·tion /ɪnˈtɛnʃən; ɪnˈtenʃən/ *n* [C,U] something that you intend to do 意图, 目的; 打算: **have no intention of doing sth** *I have no intention of helping him after what he said to me.* 听了他对我说的话, 我再也不想帮他了。| **with the intention of doing sth** *They went into town with the intention of visiting the library.* 他们进城的目的是去图书馆。| **Intention to do sth** *It is our intention to be the number one distributor of health products.* 我们的目标是成为保健产品第一大经销商。| **good intentions/the best intentions** (=intentions to do something good or kind especially when you do not succeed in doing) 一片好心/一片好意〔尤用于事情没做成时〕: *So much for all our good intentions!* 我们的一片好心到此为止吧! —see also 另见 WELL-INTENTIONED

in·ten·tion·al /ɪnˈtɛnʃənl; ɪnˈtenʃənəl/ *adj* done deliberately and usually intended to cause harm 故意的; 蓄意的: *I did trip him, but it wasn't intentional.* 我是把他绊倒了, 但不是故意的。—**intentionally** *adv*: *intentionally vague promises* 故意含糊其辞的允诺 —opposite 反义词 UNINTENTIONAL

in·ter /ɪnˈtɝ; ɪnˈtɜː/ *v* **interred, interring** [T] *formal* to bury a dead person 【正式】埋葬〔死者〕—opposite 反义词 DISINTER

inter- /ɪntə; ɪntə/ *prefix* between; among a group 在…之间: *intermarry* (=marry someone of another race, religion, etc) 〔不同种族、宗教之间〕通婚

in·ter·act /ˌɪntəˋækt; ˌɪntərˈækt/ *v* [I] **1** if people interact with each other, they talk to each other and understand each other 交流; 交往; 互相理解: **[+with]** *Vanessa interacts well with other children in the class.* 瓦妮莎和班里的其他孩子相处得很好。**2** if two or more things interact, they have an effect on each other and work together 相互作用, 相互影响: *social and economic factors interacting to produce a recession* 社会因素与经济因素相互作用造成经济衰退 | *hormones interacting in the body* 荷尔蒙在体内相互影响

3 **in·ter·ac·tion** /ˌɪntəˋækʃən; ˌɪntərˈækʃən/ *n* [C,U] **1** a process by which two or more things have an effect on each other and work together 相互作用, 相互影响: **[+of]** *the interaction of the tones of demand and supply* 供求消长趋势的相互作用 | **[+with/between]** *complex interaction between mind and body* 身心之间复杂的相互影响 **2** the activity of talking to other people and understanding them 交流: **[+with/between]** *the degree of interaction between teacher and student* 师生之间交流的程度

in·ter·act·ive /ˌɪntəˋæktɪv; ˌɪntərˈæktɪv◂/ *adj* **1** interactive teaching methods, processes etc involve people working together and discussing what they do 互动的; 相互影响的; 相互配合的 **2** **interactive programs** computing programs etc involving communication between a computer and the person using it〔人和电脑〕交互式[互动]程序: *interactive educational software* 交互式[互动]教育软件 —**interactively** *adv* —**interactivity** /ˌɪntərækˋtɪvɪtɪ; ˌɪntərækˈtɪvəti/ *n* [U]

in·ter a·li·a /ˌɪntə ˋelɪə; ˌɪntər ˈeɪliə/ *adv Latin formal* among other things【拉丁, 正式】除了别的事情之外: *The paper discussed, inter alia, political, economic, and judicial issues.* 除了其他方面之外, 这篇论文还讨论了政治、经济和司法问题。

in·ter·breed /ˌɪntəˋbrid; ˌɪntəˈbriːd/ *v past tense and past participle* **interbred** /-ˋbrɛd; -ˈbred/ [I+**with**,T] to produce young animals from parents of different breeds or groups (使)杂交繁殖 —compare 比较 CROSSBREED¹, INBREEDING

in·ter·cede /ˌɪntəˋsid; ˌɪntəˈsiːd/ *v* [I] to speak in support of someone, especially in order to try to prevent them from being punished 代为请求, 说情: **[+with]** *My good friend, Senator Bowie, interceded with the authorities on my behalf.* 我的好友鲍伊参议员为我向当局求情。—see also 另见 INTERCESSION

intercept 拦截

in·ter·cept /ˌɪntəˋsɛpt; ˌɪntəˈsept/ *v* [T] to stop or catch something or someone that is going from one place to another 拦截, 截住, 阻截: *We rely on the coastguard to intercept boats running drugs from the island.* 我们靠海岸警卫队拦截来自那个岛的毒品走私船。| *Harker's phone calls had been intercepted.* 哈克的电话被人窃听了。—**interception** /-ˋsɛpʃən; -ˈsepʃən/ *n* [C,U]

in·ter·cep·tor /ˌɪntəˋsɛptə; ˌɪntəˈseptə/ *n* [C] a light fast military aircraft 截击机

in·ter·ces·sion /ˌɪntəˋsɛʃən; ˌɪntəˈseʃən/ *n* **1** [U+**with**] an act of interceding 求情, 说情 **2** [C,U] a prayer asking for someone to be helped or cured〔请求救助某人的〕祈祷; 代祷

in·ter·change¹ /ˋɪntəˌtʃendʒ; ˈɪntətʃeɪndʒ/ *n* **1** [singular, U] an exchange, especially of ideas or thoughts〔观点、思想的〕交流: *the interchange of ideas between students and staff* 学生与教职工的意见交流 **2** [C] a point where a MOTORWAY and a main road join and are connected by several smaller roads〔高速公路的〕立体交叉道

in·ter·change² /ˌɪntəˋtʃendʒ; ˌɪntəˈtʃeɪndʒ/ *v* [I,T] to put each of two things in the place of the other or to be exchanged in this way (使)〔两者〕交换位置; 互换

in·ter·chan·gea·ble /ˌɪntəˋtʃendʒəbl; ˌɪntəˈtʃeɪndʒəbəl/ *adj* things that are interchangeable can be used instead of each other 可以互换的: *interchangeable parts* 可互换的部件 | *These two words are almost interchangeable.* 这两个单词几乎可以互换。—**interchangeably** *adv* —**interchangeability** /ˌɪntətʃendʒəˋbɪlətɪ; ˌɪntətʃeɪndʒəˈbɪlɪti/ *n* [U]

in·ter·cit·y /ˌɪntəˋsɪtɪ; ˌɪntəˈsɪti◂/ *adj* [only before noun 仅用于名词前] happening between two or more cities, or going from one city to another 城市之间的; 往来于城市之间的: *an intercity train service* 城际列车服务 | *intercity rivalry* 城市之间的竞争

in·ter·col·le·giate /ˌɪntəkəˋlidʒɪɪt; ˌɪntəkəˈliːdʒɪt/ *adj* intercollegiate competitions are between members of different colleges 学院之间的: *an intercollegiate football game* 校际足球赛

in·ter·com /ˋɪntəˌkɑm; ˈɪntəkɒm/ *n* [C] a communication system by which people in different parts of a building, aircraft etc speak to each other〔楼房、飞机等〕内部通话系统: *The pilot spoke to the passengers over the intercom.* 飞行员用内部通话设备向乘客讲话。

in·ter·com·mu·ni·cate /ˌɪntəkəˋmjunəˌket; ˌɪntəkəˈmjuːnɪkeɪt/ *v* [I+**with**] **1** *formal* to communicate with each other and exchange information【正式】互相联系; 互相通讯; 互通消息 **2** if two rooms intercommunicate, there is a door leading from one to the other〔两房之间〕相通 —**intercommunication** /ˌɪntəkəˌmjunəˋkeʃən; ˌɪntəkəmjuːnɪˈkeɪʃən/ *n* [U]

in·ter·con·nect /ˌɪntəkəˋnɛkt; ˌɪntəkəˈnekt/ *v* [I+**with**] if two systems interconnect, they are connected to each other〔两个系统〕相连: *a set of interconnecting pipes* 一套相连的管道 —**interconnected** *adj*

in·ter·con·ti·nen·tal /ˌɪntəˌkɑntəˋnɛntəl; ˌɪntəkɒntɪˈnentl◂/ *adj* happening between two CONTINENTS (=for example Africa and Asia) or going from one continent to another 跨洲的〈例如非洲和亚洲〉; 洲际的: *intercontinental trade* 洲际贸易 | *an intercontinental flight* 洲际飞行

in·ter·course /ˋɪntəˌkɔrs; ˈɪntəkɔːs/ *n* [U] *formal*【正式】**1** the act of having sex; SEXUAL INTERCOURSE 性交; 性行为 **2** an exchange of ideas, feelings etc which make people or groups understand each other better 交流; 沟通: *social intercourse* 社交

in·ter·de·nom·i·na·tio·nal /ˌɪntədɪˌnɑməˋneʃənl; ˌɪntədɪnɒmɪˈneɪʃənəl/ *adj* between or involving Christians from different groups〔基督教〕教派之间的; 涉及不同教派的

in·ter·de·part·men·tal /ˌɪntədɪˌpɑrtˋmɛntl; ˌɪntəˌdiːpɑːtˈmentl/ *adj* between or involving different departments of a company, government etc〔公司、政府等〕部门之间的; 牵涉不同部门的: *intense interdepartmental rivalry* 部门之间的激烈竞争

in·ter·de·pen·dence /ˌɪntədɪˋpɛndəns; ˌɪntədɪˈpendəns/ *n* [U] a situation in which people or things depend on each other 互相依赖

in·ter·de·pen·dent /ˌɪntədɪˋpɛndənt; ˌɪntədɪˈpendənt◂/ *adj* depending on or necessary to each other 互相依赖的, 互相需要的: *countries with interdependent economies* 经济上相互依赖的国家 —**interdependently** *adv*

in·ter·dict /ˋɪntəˌdɪkt; ˈɪntədɪkt/ *n* [C] **1** *law* an official order from a court telling someone not to do something【法律】〔法庭作出的〕禁令 **2** *technical* a punishment in the Roman Catholic Church, by which someone is not allowed to take part in church ceremonies【术语】〔罗马天主教禁止某人参加宗教仪式的〕禁令 —**interdict** /ˌɪntəˋdɪkt; ˌɪntəˈdɪkt/ *v* [T]

in·ter·dis·ci·plin·ary /ˌɪntəˋdɪsəplɪnɛrɪ; ˌɪntəˌdɪsɪˈplɪnəri/ *adj* an interdisciplinary course of study includes two or more subjects 跨学科的: *an interdisciplinary course* 跨学科的课程

in·terest¹ /ˋɪntərɪst; ˈɪntrɪst/ *n* S2 W1

1 ►FEELING 情感◄ [singular, U] a feeling that makes you want to pay attention to something or to find out more about it 兴趣: *Ruth listened with evident interest.* 露丝明显感兴趣地听着。| **[+in]** *They share an interest in poetry.* 他们都爱好诗歌。| **lose interest** (=stop being interested) 失去兴趣 *The older ones soon lost interest in the game.* 年纪大一些的人很快就失去对那个游戏的兴趣了。| **take an interest (in)** (=be interested in something) (对…) 产生兴趣: *Babies soon begin to take an interest in the world around them.* 婴儿很快就开始对周围的事物产生兴趣。| **show/express interest** (=say you are interested in something or want to buy it) 表现出/表达出兴趣 *Ben has shown an interest in learning French.* 本表示想学法语。| *Several football clubs have expressed an interest in Giggs.* 好几家足球俱乐部都已表示对吉格斯感兴趣。

I

口语 S 及书面语 W 中最常用的 1 000词, 2 000词, 3 000词

2 ▶**QUALITY** 性质◀ [U] a quality or feature of something that attracts your attention or makes you want to know more about it 引起关注或好奇心的性质; 趣味: *Add interest to your decor with a patterned border.* 用带图案的花边给你的装饰增加趣味。| **of interest** (=interesting) 有趣的; 能引起兴趣的 *Tourist information will give you a list of local places of interest.* 旅游信息中心将给你一份地方名胜目录。| **of general interest** (=that everyone wants to know about) 广为感兴趣的 *a subject of general interest* 普遍感兴趣的话题 | **of special/particular interest** *This book will be of particular interest to those studying British Politics since 1900.* 那些研究1900年以来英国政治的人会对这本书特别感兴趣。| **be of no interest (to)** (=not be interesting to someone) 丝毫不感兴趣 *Your private problems are of no interest to me.* 对你的私人问题我毫无兴趣。

3 ▶**ACTIVITY** 活动◀ [C] something that you enjoy doing or a subject that you enjoy studying when you are not working 兴趣; 爱好: *Her main interest in life is tennis.* 她生活中的主要爱好是网球。| *List your leisure time interests on the back of the form.* 在表格背面列出你的业余爱好。

4 ▶**MONEY** 钱◀ [U] **a)** a charge made for borrowing money 〔借贷的〕利息: *competitive rates of interest* 有竞争力的利率 | [+on] *The interest on the loan is 16.5% per year.* 贷款年利率为16.5%。**b)** money paid to you by a bank or financial institution when you keep money in an account there 存款利息 —see also 另见 COMPOUND INTEREST, SIMPLE INTEREST

5 ▶**ADVANTAGE** 优势◀ [C,U] the things that bring advantages to someone or something 利益, 好处: **be in your (best) interest(s)** (=be helpful for you) 对你(最)有利 *It would be in your interests to do as he says.* 按他说的去做, 对你有好处。| **look after/protect/safeguard your interests** *The company is endeavouring to protect its own interests.* 这家公司正竭力维护自身利益。| *the national interest* 国家利益 | **have sb's (best) interests at heart** (=care about someone and want to improve their situation) (极为)关心某人的利益 *Private employment agencies may not have your best interests at heart.* 私人职业介绍所可能并不关心你的利益。

6 **be in the public/national interest** be good or necessary for the safety or success of a country and its people 出于公众/国家利益: *The documents were kept secret 'in the public interest'.* 这些文件"出于公众利益"而被保密。

7 **in the interest(s) of justice/efficiency etc** in order to make a situation or system fair, efficient etc 出于公正/效率等的考虑: *In the interest of justice, I must speak the truth.* 为了维护正义, 我必须说实话。

8 **(just) out of interest/as a matter of interest** *spoken* used to say that you are asking a question only because you are interested and not because you need to know【口】(只是)出于兴趣〔提问时用〕: *Just out of interest, how much did they offer you?* 只是出于感兴趣问一下, 他们打算给你多少钱? | *As a matter of interest, where did you meet him?* 我只是感兴趣问一下, 你是在哪里遇见他的?

9 **have no interest in doing sth** not to want to do something 不想做某事: *I have no interest in continuing this conversation.* 我不想继续谈下去。

10 **declare an interest (in sth)** to state that you are connected with something or someone, and so cannot be completely fair and independent when making a decision involving them 宣布〔与某事〕有利害关系: *I must declare an interest here, the second candidate is a friend of mine.* 我必须在此宣布有关利害关系, 第二位候选人是我的朋友。

11 **human interest/love interest** the part of a story or film which is interesting because it is about people's lives or romantic relationships 〔小说或影片中的〕人们的生活/爱情情节

12 **pay sb back with interest** *informal* to harm or offend someone in an even worse way than they have harmed you【非正式】向某人加倍报复

13 ▶**SHARE IN COMPANY** 公司股份◀ [C] *technical* a share in a company, business etc【术语】权益; 股份: *She's sold all her interests in the company.* 她把她在这家公司的股份全部卖掉了。| **controlling interest** (=enough shares to control what decisions are taken) 控股权益 *Müller has a controlling interest in the factory.* 米勒有这家工厂的控股权。

14 ▶**POWERFUL GROUP** 强大团体◀ [C] *technical* a group of people in the same business who share aims or ideas【术语】利益集团; 利益相关者: *landed interests* 地产业主 | *shipping interests* 运输业主 —see also 另见 SELF-INTEREST, VESTED INTEREST

This graph shows some of the words most commonly used with the noun **interest**. 本图表所示为含有名词interest最常用的一些词组。

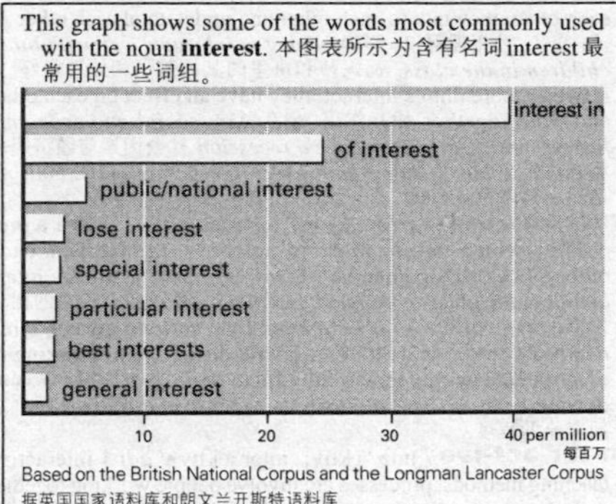

Based on the British National Corpus and the Longman Lancaster Corpus
据英国国家语料库和朗文兰开斯特语料库

interest² *v* [T] **1** to make someone feel interested 使〔某人〕感兴趣: *Here's an article which might interest you.* 这里有一篇文章, 也许你会感兴趣。| *What interests me is all the history of these places.* 使我感兴趣的是这些地方的历史。| **it may interest you to know** *spoken* (=used to introduce a fact which you think may surprise someone)【口】你听了可能会感兴趣 *It may interest you to know that she is now head of a major company.* 你听了可能会感兴趣: 她现在是一家大公司的老板。**2 could I interest you in a drink/a meal etc?** *spoken* used as a polite way of offering someone something【口】可否赏脸跟我喝一杯/吃顿饭等?

in·terest·ed /ˈɪntərɪstɪd; ˈɪntrɨstɨd/ *adj* **1** giving a lot of attention to something because you want to find out more about it 很感兴趣的, 关心的: [+in] *I'm not really interested in politics.* 我对政治不太感兴趣。| *Carrie's fourteen now, and all she's interested in is clothes.* 卡丽14岁了, 只对穿戴感兴趣。| **be interested to hear/know/see etc** *I'd be very interested to hear your opinion.* 我非常想听听你的意见。—opposite 反义词 UNINTERESTED **2** *informal* eager to do or have something【非正式】热切的: *I offered to help but they weren't interested.* 我主动帮忙, 他们却不着急。| **to be interested in doing sth** *Sheila's interested in starting her own business.* 希拉很想自己开一家公司。| [+in] *Would you be interested in a secondhand Volvo?* 您想不想买一辆二手的沃尔沃汽车? **3 interested party/group** a person or group that is directly or personally concerned with a situation and is likely to be affected by its results 当事人/团体: *All interested parties should write to the chairman of the inquiry.* 所有当事人都应给调查委员会主席写信。—**interestedly** *adv* —see also 另见 DISINTERESTED

interest-free /ˌ.. ˈ..◂/ *adj* an interest-free LOAN¹ (1) has no interest charged on it 〔贷款〕无息的: *interest-free credit* 免息信贷

interest group /ˈ.. ˌ./ *n* [C] a group of people who join together to try to influence the government in order to protect their own particular rights, advantages etc 〔试图左右政府决策以保护自身利益的〕利益集团

in·terest·ing /ˈɪntərɪstɪŋ; ˈɪntrɨstɪŋ/ *adj* unusual or exciting in a way that keeps your attention 有趣的, 令人关注的: *an interesting film* 有趣的影片 | *I found his talk very interesting.* 我觉得他的讲话很引人入胜。| **it is interesting to see/know etc** *It would be interesting to see figures supporting this argument.* 看看支持这个论点的一些数字会很有意思。| **it is interesting that** *It's interesting that no one remembers seeing the car.* 竟没人记得见过这辆车, 真是有趣。—see 见 BORED (USAGE)

in·terest·ing·ly /ˈɪntərɪstɪŋlɪ; ˈɪntrɨstɪŋli/ *adv* **1** [sentence adverb 句子副词] used to introduce a fact that you think is interesting 有趣的是: *Interestingly enough, Pearson made no attempt to deny the rumour.* 说来真有意思, 皮尔逊没有试图否认谣传。**2** in an interesting way 有趣地

interest rate /ˈ.. ˌ./ *n* [C] the PERCENTAGE amount charged by a bank etc when you borrow money or paid to you by a bank when you keep money in an account there 〔银行贷款或存款的〕利率: *The government intends to keep interest rates low.* 政府打算保持低利率。

in·ter·face¹ /ˈɪntəˌfes; ˈɪntəfeɪs/ *n* [C] **1** *technical* the part of a computer system through which two different machines are connected【术语】接口 **2** the way in which two subjects, events etc affect each other 相互作用, 相互影响 **3** *technical* the surface where two things touch each other【术语】〔两个物体接触的〕界面

interface² *v* [I, T+**with**] *technical* if you interface two parts of a computer system, or if they interface, you connect them【术语】(使)联系,(使)接合

in·ter·fere /ˌɪntə`fɪr; ˌɪntəˈfɪə/ *v* [I] to deliberately get involved in a situation that does not concern you, and try to influence what happens in a way that annoys people 介入; 干涉; 干预: *I wish you'd stop interfering – you've caused enough problems already.* 我希望你别再插手,你惹的麻烦已经够多了。| *the interfering old busybody* 多管闲事的老家伙 | [+**in**] *Some people believe it's not the church's job to interfere in politics.* 有人认为干预政治不是教会应做的事。

interfere with sth/sb *phr v* [T] **1** to prevent something from succeeding or from happening in the way that was planned 妨碍,阻止: *Anxiety can interfere with children's performance at school.* 忧虑紧张会影响孩子在学校的表现。**2** if something interferes with a radio or television broadcast, it spoils the sound or picture that you receive 干扰〔广播或电视播送〕**3** to touch a child sexually 对〔儿童〕性侵犯: *He was arrested for interfering with young boys.* 他因猥亵男童而被捕。

in·ter·fer·ence /ˌɪntə`fɪrəns; ˌɪntəˈfɪərəns/ *n* [U] **1** an act of interfering 干涉; 干预; 妨碍; 扰乱: *I resent his interference in my work.* 我讨厌他干预我的工作。| *Industrial relations should be free from state interference.* 劳资关系应不受政府干预。**2** unwanted noise on radio or television or on the telephone, or faults in the television picture〔收音机、电视机、电话等受到的〕干扰: *The bad weather's causing a lot of television interference.* 恶劣的天气给电视接收造成很大干扰。**3** *especially AmE* the act of blocking another player in ICE HOCKEY, American football etc by standing in front of them【尤美】〔冰上曲棍球、美式橄榄球等中的〕掩护阻挡; OBSTRUCTION (4) *BrE*【英】**4 run interference** *AmE*【美】**a)** the act of protecting a player who has the ball in American football by blocking players from the opposing team〔美式橄榄球比赛中为保护本方持球队员而〕掩护阻挡 **b)** the act of helping someone to achieve something by dealing with people or problems that might cause trouble〔为帮助某人成就某事而〕对付可能制造麻烦的人[事]

in·ter·fer·on /ˌɪntə`fɪrɑn; ˌɪntəˈfɪərɒn/ *n* [U] a chemical substance that is produced by your body to fight against VIRUSes that cause disease〔体内产生的抗病毒的〕干扰素

in·ter·ga·lac·tic /ˌɪntəgə`læktɪk; ˌɪntəgəˈlæktɪk◂/ *adj* between the large groups of stars in space 星系之间的: *intergalactic travel* 星系间旅行

in·ter·im¹ /`ɪntərɪm; ˈɪntərɪm/ *adj* [only before noun 仅用于名词前] an interim arrangement, report, payment etc is used or accepted temporarily, until a final or complete one is made; PROVISIONAL 过渡期间的; 临时的: *an interim report* 中期报告 | *He received an interim payment of £10,000.* 他收到暂时支付的10,000英镑。

interim² *n* **in the interim** in the period of time between two events; MEANWHILE 在此期间; 与此同时: *The child will be adopted but a relative is looking after him in the interim.* 这孩子将由人领养,但现在这段时间暂由一名亲属照管。

in·te·ri·or¹ /ɪn`tɪrɪə; ɪnˈtɪəriə/ *n* **1** [C usually singular 一般用单数] the inner part or inside of something 内部: *His new Porsche has red bodywork with a black leather interior.* 他新买的保时捷车身是红色的,内饰是黑色皮革。—opposite 反义词 EXTERIOR¹ (1) **2 the interior** the part of a country that is farthest away from the coast 内地,腹地: *The interior of the country is mainly desert.* 这个国家的内陆地带主要是沙漠。**3 Minister/Department of the Interior** the minister or department that deals with matters within a country rather than abroad 内政部长/内政部

interior² *adj* [only before noun 仅用于名词前] inside or indoors 内部的,里面的; 室内的: *The interior walls are all painted white.* 室内墙壁都漆成了白色。—opposite 反义词 EXTERIOR² (1)

interior de·co·ra·tor /ˌ·,··· ˈ···/ also 又作 **interior de·sign·er** /ˌ·,··· ·ˈ··/ *n* [C] someone whose job is to plan and choose the colours, materials, furniture etc for the inside of people's houses 室内设计师

in·ter·ject /ˌɪntə`dʒɛkt; ˌɪntəˈdʒekt/ *v* [I,T] to interrupt what someone else is saying with a sudden remark 突然插入(话): *"That's absolute rubbish!" he interjected.* "全是废话!"他突然插嘴道。

in·ter·jec·tion /ˌɪntə`dʒɛkʃən; ˌɪntəˈdʒekʃən/ *n* **1** [C] a word or phrase used to express a strong feeling such as shock, pain, or pleasure; EXCLAMATION 感叹语,感叹词 **2** [C,U] an INTERRUPTION or the act of interrupting 打断〔别人的话〕; 插嘴

in·ter·lace /ˌɪntə`les; ˌɪntəˈleɪs/ *v* [I,T] to join things together by weaving and twisting them over and under each other, or to be joined in this way (使)交织; (使)交错: *The threads were interlaced with strands of gold.* 这些线是夹杂着金丝编成的。

in·ter·lard /ˌɪntə`lɑrd; ˌɪntəˈlɑːd/ *v* [T+**with**] *literary* to add things that are not necessary to a speech or piece of writing, such as foreign phrases【文】〔在讲话或文章中〕夹杂〔不必要的内容,如外来词语等〕

In·ter·lin·gua /ˌɪntə`lɪŋgwə; ˌɪntəˈlɪŋgwə/ an international language developed in 1951 which has been used as the common language at medical and scientific meetings 国际语〔1951年创造的一门国际语言,常在医学和科学会议上使用〕

in·ter·link /ˌɪntə`lɪŋk; ˌɪntəˈlɪŋk/ *v* [I,T] to connect or be connected with something else (使)连结: *a chain of interlinking loops* 连结成链的套环

in·ter·lock¹ /ˌɪntə`lɑk; ˌɪntəˈlɒk/ *v* [I,T] if two or more things interlock or are interlocked, they fit firmly together (使)连锁; (使)相互扣住; (使)连结: *a puzzle with 500 fully interlocking pieces* 由500个紧密相连的图块组成的拼图

in·ter·lock² /`ɪntəlɑk; ˈɪntəlɒk/ *n* [C] *technical* a special part of a computer that prevents particular operations happening unless other operations have already happened【术语】联锁装置

in·ter·loc·u·tor /ˌɪntə`lɑkjətə; ˌɪntəˈlɒkjʊtə/ *n* [C] *formal* the person who is speaking to you【正式】对话者,参加谈话的人

in·ter·lop·er /ˌɪntə`lopə; ˈɪntələʊpə/ *n* [C] someone who enters a place or group where they should not be 擅自进入者,闯入者: *The village women stared at the interloper with curiosity.* 村里的女人们好奇地盯着这位不速之客。

in·ter·lude /`ɪntə,lud; ˈɪntəluːd/ *n* [C] **1** a period of time or an event that is different from what happens before and afterwards 间歇: *a brief interlude of peace before a return to the battlefield* 重返战场之前的短暂平静 **2** a short period of time between the parts of a play, concert etc〔戏剧、音乐会等的〕幕间休息 **3** a short piece of music, talk etc used to fill such a period〔幕间休息时的〕幕间音乐[讲话等]

in·ter·mar·riage /ˌɪntə`mærɪdʒ; ˌɪntəˈmærɪdʒ/ *n* [U] **1** marriage between members of different races, families, or social groups〔不同种族、家族、阶层间的〕通婚: *intermarriage between black and white* 黑人与白人通婚 **2** marriage within your own family or within a small group of relatives 近亲结婚: *intermarriage between cousins* 堂[表]兄弟姐妹间的通婚

in·ter·mar·ry /ˌɪntə`mærɪ; ˌɪntəˈmæri/ *v* [I+**with**] **1** if two groups or races intermarry, people from each group marry people from the other 不同家族[种族]之间通婚 **2** to marry someone within your own group or family 近亲结婚: *It is not unusual for royal cousins to intermarry.* 皇室成员近亲结婚并不少见。

in·ter·me·di·a·ry /ˌɪntə`midɪ,ɛrɪ; ˌɪntəˈmiːdiəri/ *n* [C] a person or organization that tries to help two other people or groups to agree with each other 调解人; 中间人: *Jackson acted as an intermediary between the two parties.* 杰克逊在双方之间充当调解人。—**intermediary** *adj*: *an intermediary role in the negotiations* 谈判中调解人的角色

in·ter·me·di·ate /ˌɪntə`midɪɪt; ˌɪntəˈmiːdiət◂/ *adj* **1** an intermediate stage in a process of development is between two other stages 中间的,居中的: *an intermediate stage during which the disease is dormant* 疾病处于潜伏状态的中期 **2** an intermediate class, course etc is at a level between the first level and advanced level 中级程度的,中等水平的

intermediate school /····ˌ·/ *n* [C] *AmE* a JUNIOR HIGH SCHOOL or MIDDLE SCHOOL【美】初级中学

intermediate tech·no·lo·gy /ˌ····· ·ˈ···/ *n* [C,U] a practical science which is suitable for use in developing countries because it is cheap and simple 中间技术〔适用于发展中国家的廉价而简单的实用科学技术〕

in·ter·ment /ɪn`tɝmənt; ɪnˈtɜːmənt/ *n* [C,U] *formal* the act of burying a dead body【正式】安葬; 埋葬

in·ter·mez·zo /ˌɪntə`mɛtso; ˌɪntəˈmetsəʊ/ *n* [C] a short piece of music, especially one that is played between the main parts of a concert, OPERA etc〔音乐会、歌剧等的〕间奏曲

in·ter·mi·na·ble /ɪn`tɝmɪnəbl; ɪnˈtɜːmɪnəbəl/ *adj* very long and boring 冗长乏味的: *interminable delays* 无休止的拖延 —**interminably** *adv*: *an interminably long speech* 喋喋不休的沉闷讲话

in·ter·min·gle /ˌɪntə`mɪŋgl; ˌɪntəˈmɪŋgəl/ *v* [I,T usually passive 一般用被动态] to mix together or mix something with something else (使)混合; (使)〔…与…〕混在一起: [+**with**] *reds and oranges intermingled with pink* 与粉红色混在一起的各种红色和橙色

in·ter·mis·sion /ˌɪntə`mɪʃən; ˌɪntəˈmɪʃən/ *n* [C] *especially AmE* a short period of time between the parts of a play, concert etc【尤美】〔歌剧、音乐会等的〕幕间休息; INTERVAL (5) *BrE*【英】

I

in·ter·mit·tent /ˌɪntə`mɪtn̩t; ˌɪntəˈmɪtənt◂/ *adj* happening repeatedly for short periods, but not regularly or continuously 间歇的; 断断续续的: *The weather forecast is for sun, with intermittent showers.* 天气预报为晴天，有间歇阵雨。—**intermittently** *adv*

in·ter·mix /ˌɪntə`mɪks; ˌɪntəˈmɪks/ *v* [I,T] to mix together, or mix things together (使)混合; (使)混杂

in·tern¹ /ɪn`tɝn; ɪnˈtɜːn/ *v* [T] to put someone in prison or limit their movements for political reasons or during a war, without charging them with a crime〔指战时或出于政治原因〕拘留，扣押: *Seven hundred men were interned in the camps.* 七百人被关押于集中营。

in·tern² /`ɪntɝn; ˈɪntɜːn/ *AmE* someone who has nearly finished training as a doctor and is working in a hospital【美】实习医师; HOUSEMAN *BrE*【英】

in·ter·nal /ɪn`tɝnl; ɪnˈtɜːnl/ *adj* **1** [only before noun 仅用于名词前] inside something rather than outside 内部的，里面的: *They've knocked down a couple of internal walls.* 他们已拆掉了几面内墙。| *the internal measurements of the car* 汽车内部空间的大小 **2** inside your body 体内的: *The X-rays showed there were no internal injuries.* X 光片显示没有内伤。| *an internal examination* 内科检查 **3** within an organization, place etc rather than outside it〔机构、地方等〕内部的: *There's to be an internal inquiry into the whole affair.* 对整个事件将进行内部调查。| *the internal mail* 内部邮件 **4** within a particular country 国内的: *internal trade* 国内贸易 | *Internal security became a priority after the bomb attack.* 炸弹袭击后，国内安全成为一项必须首先解决的问题。**5** existing in your mind 内心的: *internal doubts* 心里的疑虑 —**internally** *adv*: *The matter will be dealt with internally.* 这件事将在内部解决。| *This medicine must not be taken internally.* 此药不得内服。—opposite 反义词 EXTERNAL

internal com·bus·tion en·gine /·ˌ·· ·ˈ·· ˈ··/ *n* [C] an engine that produces power by burning petrol 内燃机

in·ter·nal·ize also 又作 -ise *BrE*【英】/ɪn`tɝnlˌaɪz; ɪnˈtɜːnəlaɪz/ *v* [T] if you internalize a particular belief, attitude, pattern of behaviour etc it becomes part of your character 使〔信仰、态度、行为模式等〕内在化〔成为性格的一部分〕—**internalization** /ɪnˌtɝnl̩ə`zeʃən; ɪnˌtɜːnəlaɪˈzeɪʃən/ *n* [U]

internal med·i·cine /·ˌ·· ˈ···/ *n* [U] *AmE* a type of medical work in which doctors say what is wrong with a person and treat illnesses but do not do operations【美】内科(学)

Internal Rev·e·nue Ser·vice /·ˌ·· ˈ···· ˌ··/ also 又作 **Internal Revenue** *n* [singular] the department that collects national taxes in the US〔美国〕国内税务局 — compare 比较 INLAND REVENUE

in·ter·na·tion·al¹ /ˌɪntə`næʃənl̩; ˌɪntəˈnæʃənəl◂/ *adj* connected with or involving more than one nation 国际的: *an international peace-keeping force* 国际维持和平部队 | *an international conference* 国际会议

international² *n* [C] **1** an international sports game 国际体育比赛 **2** *BrE* someone who plays for one of their country's sports teams【英】国际体育比赛选手

International Bri·gade, the —see 见 the SPANISH CIVIL WAR

International Court of Jus·tice, the /ˌ····ˌ··ˈ··/ the court of law of the United Nations, based in The Hague in the Netherlands. It judges international cases, for example those connected with WAR CRIMES.〔联合国〕国际法庭〔总部设在荷兰的海牙，负责审理战争罪等国际性案件〕

international date line /ˌ·····ˈ·ˌ·/ *n* [singular] an imaginary line that goes from the NORTH POLE to the SOUTH POLE, to the east of which the date is one day later than it is to the west 国际日期变更线，日界线

In·ter·na·tion·ale, the /ˌɪntənæʃə`nɑl; ˌɪntənæʃəˈnæl/ *n* the international SOCIALIST¹ (1) song 国际歌

International Her·ald Tri·bune, The /ˌ····ˌ ··ˈ··/ also 又作 **The Herald Tribune** an international daily newspaper, written in English and sold in many countries. Some of its articles are from the US, and it is often read by US citizens when they are abroad.《国际先驱者论坛报》〔在许多国家销售的一国际性英语日报。其中一些文章来自美国，美国公民出国期间经常阅读〕

in·ter·na·tion·al·is·m /ˌɪntə`næʃənl̩ˌɪzəm; ˌɪntəˈnæʃənəlɪzəm/ *n* [U] the belief that nations should work together and help each other 国际主义 —**internationalist** *n*

in·ter·na·tion·al·ize also 又作 -ise *BrE*【英】/ˌɪntə`næʃənl̩ˌaɪz; ˌɪntəˈnæʃənəlaɪz/ *v* [T] to make something international or bring it under international control 使国际化; 把…置入国际共管之下 —**internationalization** /ˌɪntəˌnæʃənl̩ə`zeʃən; ˌɪntənæʃənəlaɪˈzeɪʃən/ *n*

International La·bour Or·gan·i·za·tion, the /ˌ·····ˈ··· ,··/ abbreviation 缩写为 **the ILO** a UN organization based in Geneva, Switzerland, which helps workers around the world by making sure they are treated fairly, paid equally for the same jobs, not forced to work in dangerous conditions etc 国际劳工组织〔联合国一机构，总部设在瑞士日内瓦，旨在给世界各国受雇人员提供帮助，确保他们得到公平对待，同工同酬，不会被迫在危险条件下工作等等〕

in·ter·na·tion·al·ly /ˌɪntə`næʃənlɪ; ˌɪntəˈnæʃənəli/ *adv* in many different parts of the world 世界地，国际性地: *A recent investment boom should help firms to compete internationally.* 最近的投资景气应有助于各企业进行国际竞争。| **internationally famous/recognized/celebrated etc** *Callas quickly became internationally famous.* 卡拉斯很快就闻名世界。

International Mon·e·ta·ry Fund /ˌ····ˈ····ˌ/ *n* the IMF 国际货币基金组织

in·ter·ne·cine /ˌɪntə`nisɪn; ˌɪntəˈniːsaɪn◂/ *adj formal* internecine fighting, disputes etc happen between members of the same group or nation【正式】内部斗争的; 自相残杀的; 内讧的: *bitter internecine strife* 激烈的内部冲突

in·tern·ee /ˌɪntɝ`ni; ˌɪntɜːˈniː/ *n* [C] someone who is put into prison during a war or for political reasons, usually without a TRIAL¹ (1)〔战时或由于政治原因〕被拘留者，拘留犯: *a call for the release of all internees* 要求释放所有被拘留者的呼吁

In·ter·net, the /`ɪntəˌnɛt; ˈɪntənet/ *n* a computer system that allows millions of computer users around the world to exchange information 因特网

in·tern·ist /`ɪntɝnɪst; ˈɪntɜːnɪst/ *n* [C] *AmE* a doctor who has a general knowledge about all illnesses and medical conditions but who does not do operations【美】内科医师

in·tern·ment /ɪn`tɝnmənt; ɪnˈtɜːnmənt/ *n* **1** [U] the act of keeping people in prison or in special camps for political reasons, without charging them with a crime 拘留〔指由于政治原因关押于监狱或集中营〕**2** [C] the period of time during which someone is kept in this way 拘留期

in·ter·pen·e·trate /ˌɪntə`pɛnəˌtret; ˌɪntəˈpenɪtreɪt/ *v* [I, T] *formal* to spread through something or spread through each other【正式】贯穿; 渗透; 相互贯穿; 相互渗透 —**interpenetration** /ˌɪntəˌpɛnə`treʃən; ˌɪntəpenɪˈtreɪʃən/ *n* [C, U]

in·ter·per·son·al /ˌɪntə`pɝsənl; ˌɪntəˈpɜːsənəl◂/ *adj* involving relations between people 人与人之间的; 人际关系的: *interpersonal skills* 人际交往技巧

in·ter·plan·e·ta·ry /ˌɪntə`plænəˌtɛrɪ; ˌɪntəˈplænɪtəri◂/ *adj* [only before noun 仅用于名词前] between the PLANETS 行星间的: *interplanetary travel* 星际旅行

in·ter·play /`ɪntəˌple; ˈɪntəpleɪ/ *n* [U] the way in which two people or things react with one another or affect each other 相互作用; 相互影响

In·ter·pol /`ɪntəˌpol; ˈɪntəpɒl/ *n* [singular] an international police organization that helps national police forces to catch criminals 国际刑(事)警(察)组织

in·ter·po·late /ɪn`tɝpəˌlet; ɪnˈtɜːpəleɪt/ *v* [T] *formal*【正式】**1** to put additional words into a piece of text 在文本中插入〔字句〕**2** to interrupt someone by saying something 插〔话〕—**interpolation** /ɪnˌtɝpə`leʃən; ɪnˌtɜːpəˈleɪʃən/ *n* [C,U]

in·ter·pose /ˌɪntə`poz; ˌɪntəˈpəʊz/ *v* [T] *formal*【正式】**1** to put yourself or something else between two other things 使介入〔两者之间〕; 使插入: *Local activists interposed between party leaders and the people.* 地方政治活动分子插入了党派领袖和群众之间。**2** to introduce something between the parts of a conversation or argument 插〔话〕: *"That might be difficult," interposed Regina.* "那可能有困难。"雷吉娜插嘴说。

in·ter·pret /ɪn`tɝprɪt; ɪnˈtɜːprɪt/ *v* **1** [T] to believe that someone's actions or behaviour or an event as having a particular meaning 把〔某人的行为或某一事件〕理解为; 解释为: **interpret sth as** *The EC's refusal to intervene in Bosnia should not be interpreted as a sign of weakness.* 不可把欧共体拒绝干涉波斯尼亚的局势视为软弱的表现。**2** [I,T] to change words spoken in one language into another 口译: *They spoke good Spanish, and promised to interpret for me.* 他们西班牙语说得很好，而且答应为我当口译。—see also 另见 TRANSLATE (1) **3** [T] to explain the meaning of something 解释，阐释: *Freud's attempts to interpret the meaning of dreams* 弗洛伊德解释梦的含义的尝试 **4** [T] to perform a part in a play, a piece of music etc in a way that shows your feelings about it or what you think it means〔表演者根据自己对戏剧、音乐等的感受或理解来〕表演，演绎; 体现

in·ter·pre·ta·tion /ɪnˌtɝprɪ`teʃən; ɪnˌtɜːprɪˈteɪʃən/ *n* [C,U] **1** an attempt to explain the reason for an event, a result, someone's actions etc 解释，说明，阐明: *One possible interpretation*

is that they want you to resign. 一种可能的解释是，他们想要你辞职。| **put an interpretation on** (=explain something in a particular way) 对…作某种解释 *It's difficult to put an accurate interpretation on the survey results.* 对调查结果难以作出精确的解释。**2** the way in which someone performs a play, a piece of music etc and shows what they think and feel about it〔体现表演者对戏剧、音乐等的观点或感受的〕表演，演绎：*Laurence Olivier's brilliant interpretation of Henry V* 劳伦斯·奥利维尔扮演亨利五世的精彩演出

in·ter·pre·ta·tive /ɪnˋtɝprɪˌtetɪv; ɪnˈtɜːprɨtətɪv/ *adj* concerned with explaining the reasons for something or with the way someone performs a play, piece of music etc〔对某事原委〕解释的，阐释的；〔对表演或音乐〕艺术处理的：*an interpretative framework* 起解释作用的框架 | *interpretative skills* 艺术处理技巧

in·ter·pret·er /ɪnˋtɝprɪtɚ; ɪnˈtɜːprɨtə/ *n* [C] **1** someone who changes spoken words from one language into another, especially as their job 口译者，传译员 —see also 另见 TRANSLATOR **2** a computer PROGRAM[1] (1) that changes an instruction into a form that can be understood directly by the computer〔电脑的〕解释程序

in·ter·pre·tive /ɪnˋtɝprɪtɪv; ɪnˈtɜːprɨtɪv/ *adj* INTERPRETATIVE 解释的；艺术处理的

interpretive cen·ter /ˈ·····, ˌ·/ *n* [C] *AmE* a room or building where visitors and tourists can receive historical information about the place they are visiting【美】讲解中心〔给游客提供旅游点历史的询问处〕

in·ter·ra·cial /ˌɪntɚˋreʃəl; ˌɪntəˈreɪʃəl◂/ *adj* between different races of people 不同种族间的：*interracial harmony* 种族间的和睦 —**interracially** *adv*

Inter-Rail pass /ˈ···, ·/ *trademark* a special type of railway ticket that allows you to travel on trains all over Europe for a fixed period. These tickets are especially popular with students and other young people.【商标】欧洲铁路联票〔一种全欧通用但有时限的特种火车票，颇受学生等年轻人的喜爱〕

in·ter·reg·num /ˌɪntɚˋrɛgnəm; ˌɪntəˈregnəm/ *n plural* **interregnums** or **interregna** /-nə; -nə/ [C] **1** a period of time when a country has no king or queen, because the new ruler has not yet started to rule〔新王即位前的〕空位期 **2** a period of time when a company, organization etc has no leader, because the new leader has not started their job 空位过渡期〔由于新领导人尚未接任而使公司、机构等没有领导的一段时期〕

in·ter·re·late /ˌɪntɚrɪˋlet; ˌɪntərɪˈleɪt/ *v* [I,T] if two things interrelate or you interrelate them, they are connected and have an effect on each other（使）相互关联；（使）相互影响：*a model interrelating population, capital, and natural resources* 联系人口、资本与自然资源的模型

in·ter·re·lat·ed /ˌɪntɚrɪˋletɪd; ˌɪntərɪˈleɪtɨd◂/ *adj* things that are interrelated are connected and have an effect on each other 相互关联的；相互影响的：*Unemployment and inflation are interrelated.* 失业与通货膨胀是相互联系的。| *Many interrelated factors are at work here.* 这里许多相互关联的因素在起作用。

in·ter·re·la·tion·ship /ˌɪntɚrɪˋleʃənʃɪp; ˌɪntərɪˈleɪʃənʃɪp/ also 又作 **interrelation** /-rɪˋleʃən; -rɪˈleɪʃən/ *n* [C,U] a connection between two things that makes them affect each other 相互联系，相互关系

in·ter·ro·gate /ɪnˋtɛrəˌget; ɪnˈterəgeɪt/ *v* [T] **1** to ask someone a lot of questions for a long time in order to get information, sometimes using threats〔长时间地〕讯问；审问；盘问：*The police interrogated the suspect for several hours.* 警察盘问了这名嫌疑犯好几个小时。**2** *technical* to try to get information directly from a part of a computer【术语】〔在电脑上〕查询〔资料〕：*We're having trouble in interrogating the database.* 我们在查询电脑数据库时遇到了麻烦。—**interrogator** *n* [C]: *He refused to tell his interrogators anything.* 他拒绝向讯问者提供任何信息。—**interrogation** *n* [C,U]

in·ter·ro·ga·tion mark /·ˌ··ˈ··, ·/ *n* [C] *formal* a QUESTION MARK【正式】问号

in·ter·rog·a·tive[1] /ˌɪntəˋrɑgətɪv; ˌɪntəˈrɒgətɪv◂/ *adj technical* an interrogative sentence, PRONOUN etc, asks a question or has the form of a question【术语】〔句子、代词等〕疑问的：*'Who' and 'what' are interrogative pronouns.* who 和 what 都是疑问代词。—**interrogatively** *adv*

interrogative[2] *n technical*【术语】**1 the interrogative** the form of a sentence or verb that is used for asking questions〔句子或动词的〕疑问形式：*Put this statement into the interrogative.* 把这个陈述句改为疑问句。**2** [C] a word such as 'who', or 'what' that is used in asking questions 疑问词〈如 who, what〉

in·ter·rupt /ˌɪntəˋrʌpt; ˌɪntəˈrʌpt/ *v* **1** [I,T] to stop someone from continuing what they are saying or doing by suddenly speaking to them, making a noise etc 打断〔某人的〕讲话；中断〔某人的〕行动；打扰：*Don't interrupt –I haven't finished yet.* 别插嘴，我还没说完呢。| **interrupt sb** *She began to explain but I interrupted her.* 她开始解释，但我打断了她。**2** [T] to make a process or activity stop temporarily 使〔过程、活动〕暂时停止：*My studies were interrupted by the war.* 我的学业由于战争而暂时中止。**3** [T] *literary* if something interrupts a line, surface, view etc it stops it from being continuous【文】中断〔直线、平面、风景等的连续性〕—**interruption** /-ˋrʌpʃən; -ˈrʌpʃən/ *n* [C, U]: *Let's go somewhere where we can talk without interruption.* 我们去找个说话不受打扰的地方吧。

in·ter·sect /ˌɪntɚˋsɛkt; ˌɪntəˈsekt/ *v* **1** [I,T] if two lines or roads intersect, they meet or go across each other（和…）相交，（和…）交叉 **2** [T usually passive 一般用被动态] to divide an area with several lines, roads etc〔用线或路把一个区域〕分隔：*The plain is intersected by a network of canals.* 平原上运河网络纵横交错。

in·ter·sec·tion /ˌɪntɚˋsɛkʃən; ˌɪntəˈsekʃən/ *n* [C] **1** a place where roads, lines etc cross each other, especially where two roads meet〔尤指两条道路的〕交叉口，十字路口；〔线的〕交点 **2** [U] the act of intersecting something 横断；交叉

in·ter·sperse /ˌɪntɚˋspɝs; ˌɪntəˈspɜːs/ *v* [T usually passive 一般用被动态] **1 be interspersed with** if something is interspersed with a particular kind of thing, it has a lot of them in it〔大量〕点缀着，散布着：*sunny periods interspersed with occasional showers* 间或有阵雨的晴朗天气 **2 intersperse sth with** to put something in between pieces of speech or writing, parts of a film etc 在某物中夹杂

in·ter·state[1] /ˌɪntɚˋstet; ˌɪntəˈsteɪt◂/ *n* [C] *AmE* a very wide road for long distance travel【美】州际公路

interstate[2] *adj* [only before noun 仅用于名词前] involving different states, especially in the US〔尤指美国〕州际的：*interstate commerce* 州际贸易 —**interstate** *adv*: *travelling interstate on company business* 为公司业务从一个州去另一个州

Interstate Com·merce Com·mis·sion, the abbreviation 缩写为 **the ICC** the US government organization that deals with the way the US states buy, sell, and exchange goods with each other 州际商务委员会〔美国一政府机构，负责州际商品交易活动〕

in·ter·stel·lar /ˌɪntɚˋstɛlɚ; ˌɪntəˈstelə◂/ *adj* [only before noun 仅用于名词前] happening or existing between the stars 星际的；恒星之间的

in·ter·stice /ɪnˋtɝstɪs; ɪnˈtɜːstɨs/ *n* [C usually plural 一般用复数] *formal* a small space or crack between things placed close together【正式】裂缝；空隙；间隙：*small plants in the interstices of the rock* 岩石裂缝中长出的小草

in·ter·twine /ˌɪntɚˋtwaɪn; ˌɪntəˈtwaɪn/ *v* [I,T] **1** if two things intertwine or are intertwined, they are twisted together（使）缠绕；（使）交织在一起：*intertwining stems* 枝干盘结 **2 be (closely) intertwined** if two situations, ideas etc are intertwined, they are closely connected with each other〔局势、观点等〕（紧密）相关：*The problems of crime and unemployment are closely intertwined.* 犯罪问题与失业问题密切相关。

in·ter·val /ˋɪntɚvl; ˈɪntəvəl/ *n* [C] **1** the period of time between two events, activities etc〔两件事情、两种活动等之间的〕间隔，间歇：*He left the room, returning after a short interval with a message.* 他离开房间，隔了一会儿就回来报告一条消息。| **[+between]** *The interval between arrest and trial can be up to six months.* 从逮捕到审判之间的间隔可达六个月。**2 sunny/bright intervals** short periods of fine weather between cloudy, rainy weather etc〔阴雨天中的〕短暂晴朗 **3 at weekly/20 minute etc intervals** every week, 20 minutes etc 每周/每20分钟等：*The bell rang at half-hourly intervals.* 每半小时响铃一次。**4 at regular intervals a)** something that happens at regular intervals happens often 每隔一定时间：*The phone rang at regular intervals all afternoon.* 整个下午每隔一定时间电话铃就响一次。**b)** objects that are placed at regular intervals have all been placed at the same distance from each other〔物件〕按相同间距〔摆放〕：*Trees had been planted at regular intervals.* 树已按相同间距栽种。**5** *BrE* a short period of time between the parts of a play, concert etc【英】〔戏剧、音乐会等的〕幕间休息；INTERMISSION *especially AmE*【尤美】：*We can get some drinks in the interval.* 我们可以在幕间休息时喝点什么。**6** *technical* the amount of difference in PITCH[1] (6) between two musical notes【术语】音程

in·ter·vene /ˌɪntɚˋvin; ˌɪntəˈviːn/ *v* [I] **1** to do something to try and stop a quarrel, or a war, or to deal with a problem, especially one that you are not directly involved in〔尤指本身不直

接牵涉在内，但为了停止争吵、战争或解决问题而〕干涉，干预：[+in] *The police don't usually like to intervene in disputes between husbands and wives.* 警方通常不愿意干预夫妻之间的争吵。| *The Federal Reserve Bank had to intervene to protect the value of the dollar.* 联邦储备银行不得不干预以保护美元的币值。**2** if an event intervenes it happens in a way that prevents or interrupts something else〔某事发生对另一事件形成〕阻碍，使中断：*He was just establishing his career when the war intervened.* 他刚刚开始创建自己的事业，战争便爆发了。**3** if a period of time intervenes, it comes between two events〔时间〕介于两件事情之间

in·ter·ven·ing /ˌɪntɚˋvinɪŋ; ˌɪntəˈviːnɪŋ◂/ *adj* **the intervening years/months/decades etc** the amount of time between two events 两件事情之间的那些年/那些月/几十年等：*I hadn't seen him since 1980, and he had aged a lot in the intervening years.* 我自1980年以来就没见过他，这期间他老了不少。

in·ter·ven·tion /ˌɪntɚˋvɛnʃən; ˌɪntəˈvenʃən/ *n* [C,U] the act of intervening in something such as an argument or activity to influence what happens 干涉，干预；介入：*government intervention to regulate prices* 政府干预调控物价

in·ter·ven·tion·is·m /ˌɪntɚˋvɛnʃənˌɪzəm; ˌɪntəˈvenʃənɪzm/ *n* [U] **1** the belief that a government should try to influence trade by spending government money 干预主义〔认为应由政府出资干涉贸易的主张〕**2** the belief that a government should try to influence what happens in foreign countries 干涉主义〔主张干预其他国家的事务〕—**interventionist** *adj*

in·ter·view[1] /ˋɪntɚˌvju; ˈɪntəvjuː/ *n* **1** [C,U] a formal meeting at which someone is asked questions in order to find out whether they are suitable for a job, course of study etc〔求职、入学等的〕面试，面谈：**[+for]** *He has an interview next Thursday for a job on the Los Angeles Times.* 他下周四参加《洛杉矶时报》的求职面试。**2** [C] an occasion when a famous person is asked questions about their life, experiences, or ideas for a newspaper, magazine, TV programme etc〔报纸、杂志、电视的〕采访；访谈：**[+with]** *an interview with the President* 对总统的采访 | **give an interview** *Mellor gave an off-the-cuff interview to reporters outside his home.* 梅勒在家门口接受记者们的即席采访。**3** [C] an official meeting with someone who asks you questions〔与提问者的〕正式晤谈，接见，会见：*a police interview* 警察问讯

interview[2] *v* [T] **1** to ask someone questions, in order to find out if they are good enough for a job, course of study etc 对〔求职者、学校考生等〕进行面试：*We're interviewing six candidates this afternoon.* 我们今天下午要对六位候选人进行面试。**2** to ask a famous person questions about their life or ideas 采访〔名人〕**3** to ask someone questions officially 向〔某人〕正式提问

in·ter·view·ee /ˌɪntɚvjuˋi; ˌɪntəvjuːˈiː/ *n* [C] the person who answers the questions in an interview 接受面试者；被采访者

in·ter·view·er /ˋɪntɚˌvjuɚ; ˈɪntəvjuːə/ *n* [C] the person who asks the questions in an interview 采访者；〔对候选人〕进行面试的人

in·ter·war /ˌɪntɚˋwɔr; ˌɪntəˈwɔː◂/ *adj* happening or connected to the period between the First and the Second World Wars 在第一次与第二次世界大战之间的：*the interwar years* 两次世界大战之间的岁月

in·ter·weave /ˌɪntɚˋwiv; ˌɪntəˈwiːv/ *v past tense* **interwove** /-ˋwov; -ˈwəʊv/ *past participle* **interwoven** /-ˋwovən; -ˈwəʊvən/ **1 be interwoven** if two lives, problems etc are interwoven they are closely connected in a complicated way〔两个生命、问题等〕交织在一起：*The histories of our two families are closely interwoven.* 我们两个家族的历史紧密地连结在一起。**2** [T] to weave two or more things together 使交错编织：*silk interwoven with gold and silver threads* 金线和银线交错编织而成的丝制品 **3** [T] to mix together different styles or methods 使〔不同的风格、方法〕混合

in·tes·tate /ɪnˋtɛstet; ɪnˈtesteɪt/ *adj law*【法律】**die intestate** to die without having made a WILL (=an official statement about who you want to have your property after you die) 去世时没有立遗嘱

in·tes·tine /ɪnˋtɛstɪn; ɪnˈtestɪn/ *n* [C] the long tube that takes food from your stomach out of your body 肠 —**intestinal** *adj*: *intestinal bacteria* 肠道细菌 —see also 另见 LARGE INTESTINE, SMALL INTESTINE

In the Bleak Mid·Win·ter /ˌ· · ˌ· · ˈ· ˈ·/ a Christmas CAROL (=a traditional religious song) which is especially popular in the UK《阴冷的隆冬时节》〔尤为英国人喜爱的一首圣诞颂歌〕

in·thing /ˌ· ˈ·/ *n* **be the in-thing** *informal* to be very fashionable at the moment【非正式】是目前极时髦的

in·ti·ma·cy /ˋɪntəməsɪ; ˈɪntɪməsi/ *n* **1** [U] a state of having a close personal relationship with someone 亲密，亲近：*the intimacy and friendliness of family life* 家庭生活的亲密友好 | **[+between]** *a surprising lack of intimacy between parents and children* 父母与子女之间令人吃惊的疏远 **2 intimacies** *plural* remarks or actions of a type that happen only between people who know each other very well 亲昵的言语[行为]：*The women often met to exchange intimacies about their social life.* 妇女们常常见面，亲密地谈起她们的社交生活。**3** [U] a word meaning sex, used especially by lawyers and police when they want to avoid using the word 'sex' 性行为〔尤指律师和警方的委婉用语〕：*Intimacy took place on several occasions.* 曾发生过数次性行为。

in·ti·mate[1] /ˋɪntəmɪt; ˈɪntɪmɪt/ *adj*

1 ▶FRIENDS 朋友◀ having an extremely close relationship 亲密的：*intimate friends* 亲密的朋友 | **be on intimate terms with** *She's on intimate terms with important people in the government.* 她与政府要员关系密切。

2 ▶PRIVATE 私人的◀ connected with very private or personal matters 隐私的，个人的：*Valerie always tells me about the most intimate details of their relationship.* 瓦莱丽总是把他们之间的隐私细节告诉我。

3 an intimate knowledge of sth very detailed knowledge of something as a result of careful study or a lot of experience〔因细心研究或经验丰富而〕精通某事

4 ▶RESTAURANT/MEAL/PLACE 饭店/餐饮/地方◀ private and friendly so that you feel comfortable 幽静亲切的〔因此使人感觉舒服的〕：*The Wisteria café has a pleasant intimate atmosphere.* 紫藤咖啡馆的气氛亲切宜人。| *an intimate meal for two* 亲密幽静的两人用餐〔环境〕

5 ▶CONNECTION 关联◀ intimate link/connection etc a very close connection between two things〔两者间的〕密切联系

6 ▶SEXUAL 性的◀ a) connected with sex 与性有关的：**intimate relations/contact** *The virus can only be transmitted through intimate contact.* 这种病毒只能通过性接触来传播。**b) be intimate with** *formal* to have sex with someone【正式】与…发生性关系 —**intimately** *adv*

in·ti·mate[2] /ˋɪntəˌmet; ˈɪntɪmeɪt/ *v* [T] *formal* to make people understand what you mean without saying it directly【正式】暗示；提示：**intimate that** *He intimated, politely but firmly, that we were not welcome.* 他有礼貌但很坚决地暗示我们是不受欢迎的。

in·ti·mate[3] /ˋɪntəmɪt; ˈɪntɪmɪt/ *n* [C] a close personal friend 知己，密友，至交

in·ti·ma·tion /ˌɪntəˋmeʃən; ˌɪntɪˈmeɪʃən/ *n* [C,U] *formal* an indirect or unclear sign that something may happen【正式】先兆；预兆：*the first intimations of the approaching conflict* 冲突即将发生的最初预兆

in·tim·i·date /ɪnˋtɪməˌdet; ɪnˈtɪmɪdeɪt/ *v* [T] to frighten someone by behaving in a threatening way, especially in order to make them do what you want 恐吓，恫吓，威胁〔尤指强迫某人做某事〕：*Buildings were bombed in an attempt to intimidate the opposition.* 几幢大楼被炸，目的是威胁反对派。—**intimidation** *n* [U] *allegations of police intimidation* 对警察使用恐吓手段的指控

in·tim·i·dat·ed /ɪnˋtɪməˌdetɪd; ɪnˈtɪmɪdeɪtɪd/ *adj* [not before noun 不用于名词前] feeling worried and less confident, for example because you are in a difficult situation or other people seem better than you〔因陷于困境或自卑而〕胆怯的；畏缩的：*I was shy, and felt intimidated by the older students.* 我很腼腆，看见年纪比我大的学生就胆怯。

in·tim·i·dat·ing /ɪnˋtɪməˌdetɪŋ; ɪnˈtɪmɪdeɪtɪŋ/ *adj* making you feel worried and less confident 令人紧张不安的：*Some people find interview situations very intimidating.* 有些人认为面试的环境令人紧张不安。

in·to /ˋɪntə; ˈɪntə; *before vowels* 在元音前 ˋɪntu; ˈɪntʊ; *strong* 强读 ˋɪntu; ˈɪntuː/ *prep*

1 ▶INSIDE CONTAINER, PLACE, AREA 在容器、地点、区域之内◀ in order to be inside something or to be in a place or area 进入；到…里面：*I saw Jim this morning; he was going into the paper shop.* 我今天上午看见吉姆，当时他正走进一家报刊零售店。| *Sue got back into bed and pulled the quilt over her head.* 休回到床上，拉过被子蒙住头。| *I've got to go into town this morning and do some shopping.* 我今天上午得进城去买些东西。| *They decided to put £1000 into an investment account.* 他们决定将1000英镑存入投资账户。

2 ▶INVOLVED IN STH 卷入某事◀ becoming involved in a situation or activity 从事；卷入：*At the age of 16, I went into the printing trade as an apprentice.* 我16岁时进入印刷业当学徒。|

Sorry, I haven't time to go into all these details now. 对不起，我目前没有时间说明全部细节。| *She puts a lot of time and effort into her work.* 她把大量时间和精力投入到工作中。| *You'll get into trouble if you're not careful.* 你如果不细心就会遇到麻烦。
3 ►DIFFERENT APPEARANCE, SITUATION 不同的外观、情况◄ in a different situation or a different physical form 处于不同情况，具有不同外形: *They're going to move Ian into a different class.* 他们打算把伊恩转入另一个班。| *You'll have to eat your vegetables if you want to grow into a big strong boy.* 你如果想长成一个高大强壮的孩子，就得吃蔬菜。| *Put the car into reverse.* 挂上倒挡倒车。| *Cut the cake into pieces.* 把蛋糕切成小块。
4 ►HIT, TOUCH, MEET 碰撞，接触，遇见◄ coming near, or hitting someone or something in a sudden or violent way 靠近；〔突然或剧烈地〕撞击: *Fred bumped into her, knocking her over.* 弗雷德和她撞个满怀，把她撞倒了。| *He lost control of the car and it crashed into the wall.* 他对汽车失去控制，车子撞在墙上。| *I ran into Brad* (=met him) *at the Bluebird last night.* 我昨晚在"蓝鸟"遇见了布拉德。
5 be into sth *spoken* to like and be interested in something【口】对〔某物〕感兴趣；喜欢: *I've really got into French films lately.* 我近来对法国电影很着迷。
6 *spoken* used when you are dividing one number by another【口】除〔用一个数目除另一数目〕: *Eight into twenty four is three.* 8 除 24 等于 3。
7 ►TIME 时间◄ at or until a certain time 在[直到]〔某个时间〕: *Andy and I talked well into the night.* 安迪和我一直谈到深夜。| *John was well into his forties before he got married.* 约翰结婚时已经四十多岁了。
8 ►DIRECTION 方向◄ in a particular direction 朝…方向: *Sue stared straight into the camera.* 休盯着照相机的镜头。| *Make sure you're speaking directly into the microphone.* 说话时一定要对准话筒。

in·tol·e·ra·ble /ɪn`tɑlərəbl; ɪn'tɒlərəbəl/ *adj* too difficult, unpleasant, annoying etc for you to bear〔太困难、太讨厌、太烦人而〕难以忍受的: *The arms race was placing an intolerable strain on the Russian economy.* 军备竞赛给俄罗斯的经济带来难以承受的压力。—**intolerably** *adv*

in·tol·e·rant /ɪn`tɑlərənt; ɪn'tɒlərənt/ *adj* not willing to accept ways of thinking and behaving that are different from your own 不能包容的；不容异己的；心胸狭窄的: **[+of]** *intolerant of other people's political beliefs* 不能容忍他人的政治信仰 —**intolerantly** *adv* —**intolerance** *n* [U] *nationalistic rivalry and racial intolerance* 民族间的对抗和种族间的互不相容

in·to·na·tion /ˌɪnto`neʃən; ˌɪntə'neɪʃən/ *n* [C,U] **1** the way in which the level of your voice changes in order to add meaning to what you are saying, for example by going up at the end of a question 语调〈如疑问句的结尾是升调〉；音调 **2** [U] the act of intoning something 吟诵

in·tone /ɪn`ton; ɪn'təʊn/ *v* [T] say something slowly and clearly without making your voice rise and fall much as you speak〔以平直的音调缓慢清晰地〕吟诵: *The priest intoned the blessing.* 神父吟诵赐福词。

in to·to /ˌɪn `toto; ˌɪn 'təʊtəʊ/ *adv Latin* as a whole; totally【拉丁】全然；完全，全部: *They accepted the plan in toto.* 他们完全接受这个计划。

in·tox·i·cant /ɪn`tɑksəkənt; ɪn'tɒksɪ̯kənt/ *n* [C] *technical* something that makes you drunk, especially an alcoholic drink【术语】致醉物〔尤指酒精饮料〕

in·tox·i·cat·ed /ɪn`tɑksəˌketɪd; ɪn'tɒksɪ̯keɪtɪ̯d/ *adj* **1** drunk 喝醉的: *The driver was clearly intoxicated.* 司机显然喝醉了。**2** happy, excited, and unable to think clearly, especially as a result of love, success, power etc〔因爱情、成功、权力等而〕极为兴奋的；陶醉的: *intoxicated with the experience of freedom* 陶醉于自由的经历 —**intoxicate** *v* [T]

in·tox·i·cat·ing /ɪn`tɑksəˌketɪŋ; ɪn'tɒksɪ̯keɪtɪŋ/ *adj* **1** intoxicating drinks can make you drunk〔饮料〕致醉的 **2** making you feel happy, excited, and unable to think clearly 令人极兴奋的；令人陶醉的: *the intoxicating combination of her beauty, wit and charm* 让人陶醉的美貌、智慧与魅力在她身上的结合

in·tox·i·ca·tion /ɪnˌtɑksə`keʃən; ɪnˌtɒksɪ̯'keɪʃən/ *n* [U] the state of being drunk 醉酒

in·tra- /ɪntrə; ɪntrə/ *prefix formal or technical*【正式或术语】**1** inside; within 在…之内（的）: *intra-departmental* (=within a department) 部门内部的 | *intracranial pressure* (=inside the head) 颅内压力 **2** into 进入: *an intravenous injection* (=into a VEIN) 静脉注射

in·trac·ta·ble /ɪn`træktəbl; ɪn'træktəbəl/ *adj formal*【正式】**1** an intractable problem is very difficult to deal with or find an answer to 难解决的；难对付的: *the seemingly intractable problem of human greed* 人类的贪婪这个似乎难以解决的问题 **2** having a strong will and difficult to control 倔强的，难以管束的: *They found the islanders intractable, resisting their offers of gifts.* 他们发现岛民性格执拗，不愿接受他们赠送的礼物。—**intractably** *adv* —**intractability** /ɪnˌtræktə`bɪlətɪ; ɪnˌtræktɪ̯'bɪlɪ̯ti/ *n* [U]

in·tra·mu·ral /ˌɪntrə`mjurəl; ˌɪntrə'mjʊərəl◄/ *adj especially AmE* intramural courses, competitions etc happen within a school or college and are intended for the students of the school or college【尤美】〔课程、比赛等〕校内的 —opposite 反义词 EXTRAMURAL

in·tran·si·gent /ɪn`trænsɪdʒənt; ɪn'trænsɪ̯dʒənt/ *adj formal* unwilling to change your ideas or behaviour in a way that seems unreasonable【正式】〔执拗地〕不妥协的；不让步的: *an intransigent attitude* 不妥协的态度 —**intransigence** *n* [U] —**intransigently** *adv*

in·tran·si·tive /ɪn`trænsətɪv; ɪn'trænsɪ̯tɪv/ *adj technical* an intransitive verb has a subject but no object. For example, in the sentence 'my cup broke', 'break' is intransitive. Intransitive verbs are marked [I] in this dictionary.【术语】〔动词〕不及物的〔即有主语而无宾语的动词，如 my cup broke 中的 break。在本辞典中，不及物动词以 [I] 标明〕—**intransitive** *n* [C] —**intransitively** *adv* —opposite 反义词 TRANSITIVE

in·tra·state /ˌɪntrə`stet; ˌɪntrə'steɪt◄/ *adj AmE* within one state, especially in the US【美】〔美国〕州内的: *intrastate commerce* 州内贸易 —compare 比较 INTERSTATE[2]

in·tra·ve·nous /ˌɪntrə`vinəs; ˌɪntrə'viːnəs◄/ *adj* **1 intravenous injection** an INJECTION that is done into a VEIN (=tube in the body taking blood back to the heart) 静脉注射 **2 intravenous drugs/fluids etc** drugs etc that are put directly into a vein 静脉注射用的药物/液体等 —**intravenously** *adv*

in tray /ˈ· ·/ *n* [C] a container on your desk in which you keep work and letters that need to be dealt with〔存放待处理文件或信件的〕收文格 —compare 比较 OUT TRAY —see picture at 参见 TRAY 图

in·trench /ɪn`trɛntʃ; ɪn'trentʃ/ *v* [T] another spelling of ENTRENCH entrench 的另一种拼法

in·trep·id /ɪn`trɛpɪd; ɪn'trepɪ̯d/ *adj especially literary* willing to do dangerous things or go to dangerous places【尤文】无畏的，勇敢的: *intrepid explorers* 勇敢的探险家

in·tri·ca·cy /`ɪntrəkəsɪ; 'ɪntrɪkəsi/ *n* **1** [C usually plural 一般用复数] one of the small parts or details that together form a pattern, system, method etc〔构成一幅图案、一个系统或一种方法的〕细节: **the intricacies of** *I still haven't mastered the intricacies of the filing system.* 我还是没有掌握文件归档系统错综复杂的细节。**2** [U] the state of containing a large number of parts or details 错综复杂；盘根错节: *designs of amazing intricacy and sophistication* 极为复杂精妙的设计

in·tri·cate /`ɪntrəkɪt; 'ɪntrɪkɪ̯t/ *adj* containing many small parts or details that all work or fit together 错综复杂的: *intricate patterns* 花纹精致的图案

in·trigue[1] /ɪn`trig; ɪn'triːg/ *v* **1** [T] if something intrigues you, you are very interested by it, especially because it seems strange or mysterious〔尤指因某事奇特或神秘而〕激起兴趣；引起好奇心；迷住: *I was intrigued by his request.* 他的请求引起了我的好奇。**2** [I] *literary* to make secret plans to harm someone or make them lose their position of power【文】密谋；施诡计〔伤害某人或夺去其权势〕: *While King Richard was abroad, the barons had been intriguing against him.* 理查国王在国外时，贵族们一直在密谋反对他。

in·trigue[2] /`ɪntrig; 'ɪntriːg/ *n* **1** [U] the act or practice of secretly planning to harm someone or make them lose their position of power 阴谋；密谋；诡计: *It's an exciting story of political intrigue and murder.* 那是一个关于政治阴谋和谋杀的扣人心弦的故事。| *a web of intrigue* 一套阴谋诡计 **2** [C] a secret plan to harm someone or make them lose their position of power〔伤害某人或夺去其权势的〕阴谋

in·tri·guing /ɪn`trigɪŋ; ɪn'triːgɪŋ/ *adj* something that is intriguing is very interesting because it is strange, mysterious, or unexpected〔由于奇特、神秘或出人意料而〕引起好奇心的；令人感兴趣的: *an intriguing discovery* 令人感兴趣的发现 —**intriguingly** *adv*: *The book is intriguingly titled "The Revenge of the Goldfish"!* 这本书有一个引人入胜的书名，叫做《金鱼的复仇》！

in·trin·sic /ɪn`trɪnsɪk; ɪn'trɪnsɪk/ *adj* being part of the nature or character of someone or something 本质的，内在的，固有的: *The job is of little intrinsic interest.* 这份工作本身没什么乐趣。| *intrinsic goodness* 天生的善良 | **[+to]** *problems that are in-*

I

trinsic to the situation 这种局势必然带来的困难 —**intrinsically** /-klɪ; -kli/ *adv*

in·tro /ˈɪntro; ˈɪntrəʊ/ *n* [C] *informal* the introduction to a song, piece of writing etc【非正式】〔歌曲、文章等的〕引子

in·tro- /ɪntrə; ɪntrə/ *prefix* into, especially into the inside 向内: *introspection* (=examining your own feelings) 内省, 反省

in·tro·duce /ˌɪntrəˈdjus; ˌɪntrəˈdjuːs/ *v* [T]

1 ▶WHEN PEOPLE MEET 人们相遇时◀ if you introduce someone to another person, you formally tell them each other's names, for example at a party or meeting 介绍, 引见; 使相互认识: *"Have you two been introduced? Tom, this is Greg."* "有人给你们俩介绍了吗? 汤姆, 这位是格雷格。" | **introduce sb to sb** *I was introduced to Mrs Myers.* 我被引见给迈尔斯太太。| **introduce yourself** (=formally tell someone who you are)〔正式的〕自我介绍 *Let me introduce myself; my name is Melody Johnson.* 让我自我介绍一下, 我叫梅洛迪·约翰逊。

2 ▶MAKE STH HAPPEN/EXIST 使某事物发生/存在◀ to make a change, plan, system etc happen or exist for the first time 引进〔变革、计划、制度等〕, 实施; 推行: *plans to introduce a new system of welfare payments* 实施新的福利费支付系统的计划 | *The teachers' association wanted to introduce a new kind of test.* 教师协会想引进一种新型的测试方法。

3 ▶BRING TO A PLACE 带到某地◀ to take or bring something to a place for the first time from somewhere else 首次引入〔某物〕, 使传入: **introduce sth to/into** *The grey squirrel was introduced into Britain from North America.* 灰松鼠是由北美引入英国的。

4 ▶NEW EXPERIENCE 新经历◀ **introduce sb to sth** to show someone something or tell them about it for the first time 使某人初次尝试某物: *Malcolm introduced me to the joys of wine-tasting.* 马尔科姆让我初次尝到品酒的乐趣。

5 ▶TELEVISION/RADIO 电视/广播◀ to speak at the beginning of a TV or radio programme and say what is going to happen〔在电视或广播节目开始时为节目〕作开场白: *Tonight's programme will be introduced by James Adams.* 今晚的节目将由詹姆斯·亚当斯作开场白。

6 ▶BE THE START OF 为…的开始◀ if an event introduces a particular period or change, it is the beginning of it〔某事的发生〕作为[标志着]〔一个时期或变化〕的开始: *The death of Pericles in 429 BC introduced a darker period in Athenian history.* 公元前 429 年伯里克利之死标志着雅典历史上一段黑暗时期的开始。

7 ▶LAW 法律◀ to formally present a new law to be discussed and voted on, especially in the British parliament〔尤指在英国议会, 将一项新法律〕提交讨论

8 ▶PUT STH INTO 把某物放入◀ *technical* to put something carefully into something else【术语】小心地把〔某物〕放入〔另一物里〕: *Fuel was introduced into the jet pipe.* 将燃油注入喷管。

in·tro·duc·tion /ˌɪntrəˈdʌkʃən; ˌɪntrəˈdʌkʃən/ *n*

1 ▶START TO USE 开始使用◀ [U] the act of making something start to be used or exist for the first time〔初次〕采用: **[+of]** *the introduction of new working methods* 采用新的工作方法 | *Since their introduction, compact discs have taken over from records.* 激光唱片面世后, 已经取代了〔传统〕唱片。

2 ▶BRING STH TO A PLACE 把某物带到一个地方◀ **a)** [U] the act of bringing something to a place for the first time from somewhere else 初次引入, 带到: **[+of]** *the introduction of Buddhism to China nearly 2000 years ago* 约 2000 年前佛教引入中国 **b)** [C] something that is brought into a place for the first time from somewhere else 初次引入的东西: *The potato was a sixteenth century introduction.* 马铃薯是 16 世纪引进的。

3 ▶WHEN MEETING SB 见面时◀ [C often plural 常用复数] the act of formally telling two people each other's names when they first meet 介绍, 引见: *There isn't time for formal introductions.* 没时间作正式引见。

4 ▶BOOK/SPEECH 书/演讲◀ [C] a written or spoken explanation at the beginning of a book or speech 引言, 序言, 导言; 开场白: *In the introduction there's a brief account of Lawrence's life.* 序言里对劳伦斯的生平有一个简要的说明。

5 ▶EXPLANATION 解释◀ [C] something that provides a way of learning about something for the first time〔提供初学者学习途径的〕入门指导: **[+to]** *This little book is a very good introduction to geometry.* 这本小书是一本很好的几何学入门读物。

6 ▶LETTER 信◀ [C] an official letter that explains who you are, given to someone you have not met before 介绍信

7 ▶PUT STH INTO STH 把某物放入某物◀ [U] *technical* the act of putting something into something else【术语】放入: **[+of]** *the introduction of air into the heating system* 将空气注入暖气系统

in·tro·duc·to·ry /ˌɪntrəˈdʌktərɪ; ˌɪntrəˈdʌktəri◀/ *adj* **1 introductory remarks/paragraph etc** things that someone says or writes at the beginning of a book, speech etc in order to explain what it is about〔书、讲话等的〕开场白/导言段落等 **2 introductory course/ lesson etc** a course, lesson etc that is intended for people who have never done a particular activity before 基础教程/入门课等 **3 introductory offer** a special low price to encourage people to buy a new product〔推销新产品的〕特惠价格, 特价优惠: *Don't miss our introductory offer!* 不要错过我们的新产品特价优惠!

in·tro·spec·tion /ˌɪntrəˈspɛkʃən; ˌɪntrəˈspekʃən/ *n* [U] the process of thinking deeply about your own thoughts and feelings to find out their real meaning 内省, 反省: *He stopped his introspection to listen.* 他停止内省, 开始倾听。

in·tro·spec·tive /ˌɪntrəˈspɛktɪv; ˌɪntrəˈspektɪv/ *adj* tending to think deeply about your own thoughts, feelings etc (好) 内省的; (好) 反省的: *a shy and introspective person* 一个腼腆内向的人 —**introspectively** *adv*

in·tro·vert /ˈɪntrəˌvɝt; ˈɪntrəvɜːt/ *n* [C] someone who thinks mainly about their own thoughts and personal life and does not enjoy spending time with other people 性格内向的人 —opposite 反义词 EXTROVERT

in·tro·vert·ed /ˈɪntrəˈvɝtɪd; ˈɪntrəvɜːtɪ̵d/ *adj* someone who is introverted spends a lot of time thinking about their own problems and interests and finds it difficult to talk to other people 性格内向的; 不善交际的: *The young girl had become nervous and introverted.* 那个女孩变得神经质, 不爱与人交往。—opposite 反义词 EXTROVERTED —**introversion** /ˌɪntrəˈvɝʃən; ˌɪntrəˈvɜːʃən/ *n* [U]

in·trude /ɪnˈtrud; ɪnˈtruːd/ *v* **1** [I] to interrupt someone or become involved in their private affairs in an annoying and unwanted way, especially with the result that you upset or offend them 打扰〔别人的私事, 尤指令对方不快或感到受冒犯〕; 干涉; 侵扰: *Would I be intruding if I came with you?* 我要是和你一起去, 会不会打扰你? | **[+into/on/upon]** *It would be very insensitive to intrude on their private grief.* 干涉人家不愿公开的伤心事, 太不明事理了。**2** [I+on] to have an unwanted effect on a situation〔不受欢迎地〕强加于

in·trud·er /ɪnˈtrudɚ; ɪnˈtruːdə/ *n* [C] **1** someone who illegally enters a building or area, usually in order to steal something 非法闯入者〔常指小偷〕: *The police think the intruder got in through an unlocked window.* 警察认为闯入者是由未锁的窗子进来的。**2** someone who is in a place where they are not wanted 不请自来者: *They had always regarded me as an unwelcome intruder.* 他们一直把我看作不受欢迎的不速之客。

in·tru·sion /ɪnˈtruʒən; ɪnˈtruːʒən/ *n* [C,U] **1** an unwanted event or person in a situation that is private〔讨厌的事或人的〕干扰, 侵扰: *She considered Pam's presence in the kitchen an intrusion.* 她认为帕姆待在厨房是一种干扰。| **[+into/on/upon]** *I resented this intrusion into my domestic affairs.* 我讨厌这种对我家事的干涉。**2** something that has an unwanted effect on a situation, on people's lives etc〔对某种情况、别人生活等的〕侵袭; 打扰: *the intrusion of Western values on a culture that has existed for centuries* 西方价值观对一种已存在几百年的文化的侵袭

in·tru·sive /ɪnˈtrusɪv; ɪnˈtruːsɪv/ *adj* affecting someone's private life or interrupting them in an unwanted and annoying way 干涉的; 打扰的: *They found the television cameras too intrusive.* 他们认为电视摄像机太讨厌了。

in·trust /ɪnˈtrʌst; ɪnˈtrʌst/ *v* another spelling of ENTRUST entrust 的另一种拼法

in·tu·it /ɪnˈtjuɪt; ɪnˈtjuːɪ̵t/ *v* [I,T] *formal* to understand that something is true through your feelings rather than your thoughts【正式】凭直觉知道

in·tu·i·tion /ˌɪntjʊˈɪʃən; ˌɪntjuˈɪʃən/ *n* **1** [U] the ability to understand or know something by using your feelings rather than by carefully considering the facts 直觉 (力): *women's intuition* 女人的直觉 | *Imagination and intuition are vital to good science.* 想象力和直觉对于成功的科学研究是至关重要的。**2** [C] an idea about what is true in a particular situation based on strong feelings rather than facts 直觉感知, 直觉知识: *He had an intuition there was trouble brewing.* 他凭直觉感到麻烦就要发生。

in·tu·i·tive /ɪnˈtjuɪtɪv; ɪnˈtjuːɪ̵tɪv/ *adj* **1** an intuitive idea is based on feelings rather than on knowledge or facts〔想法〕凭直觉获知的: *He seemed to have an intuitive awareness of how I felt.* 他好像凭直觉就知道我的感受。**2** someone who is intuitive is able to understand situations using their feelings without being told or having any proof〔人〕有直觉的 —**intuitively** *adv* —**intuitiveness** *n* [U]

in·u·it /ˋɪnjuɪt; ˈinjuǀt/ *n* [C] a member of a race of people living in the very cold northern areas of North America 因纽特人〔居住在北美北部严寒地区〕—compare 比较 ESKIMO —**Inuit** *adj*

in·un·date /ˋɪnʌnˏdet; ˈɪnʌndeɪt/ *v* [T] **be inundated a)** to receive so much of something that you cannot easily deal with it all 收到太多而应接不暇: *After the broadcast, we were inundated with requests for more information.* 节目播出之后，不断收到提供详情的请求，使我们无法应付。**b)** *formal* to be covered with water【正式】被水淹没 —**inundation** /ˌɪnənˋdeʃən; ˌɪnənˈdeɪʃən/ *n* [C,U]

in·ure /ɪnˋjur; ɪˈnjʊə/ *v*

inure sb **to** sth *phr v* [T usually passive 一般用被动态] to make someone become used to something unpleasant, so that they are no longer upset by it 使习惯[适应]〔令人不愉快的事物〕: *Nurses soon became inured to the sight of suffering.* 护士们很快就习惯了那些病痛的场面。

in·vade /ɪnˋved; ɪnˈveɪd/ *v* **1** [I,T] to enter a country, town, or area using military force, in order to take control of it 武力入侵，侵略，侵占: *Hitler invaded Poland in 1939.* 希特勒在1939年入侵波兰。**2** [T] to go into a place in large numbers, especially when you are not wanted〔尤指不受欢迎地〕涌入；蜂拥而入: *Every summer the town is invaded by tourists.* 每年夏天，大量游客涌入小镇。| *Fans invaded the pitch at half-time.* 球迷在中场休息时涌入球场。**3** [T] to affect someone in an unwanted and annoying way 侵扰〔某人〕: *Her image invaded his mind with immense power.* 她的形象势不可挡地占据了他的头脑。| **invade sb's privacy** *Does that give you an excuse to invade my privacy?* 这就给了你借口来干涉我的私事吗？| **invade sb's territory** (=start to deal with things that they think they should deal with) 越权去做〔认为该做的事就去做〕—see also 另见 INVASION

in·vad·er /ɪnˋvedɚ; ɪnˈveɪdə/ *n* [C] someone in an army that enters a country or town by force in order to take control of it 侵略者: *Invaders from the south ransacked the town.* 来自南面的侵略军把小镇洗劫一空。

in·val·id[1] /ɪnˋvælɪd; ɪnˈvælǀd/ *adj* **1** a contract, ticket, claim etc that is invalid is not legally or officially acceptable〔合约、票、要求等〕无效的；作废的: *Without the right date stamped on it, your ticket will be invalid.* 票上若没有加盖正确的日期就是废票。**2** reasons, opinions etc that are invalid are not based on clear thoughts or accurate facts〔观点、理由等〕站不住脚的: *Their argument was manifestly invalid.* 他们的论点显然站不住脚。—opposite 反义词 VALID (1)

in·va·lid[2] /ˋɪnvəlɪd; ˈɪnvəliːd/ *n* [C] someone who cannot look after themselves because of illness, old age, or injury 病人；病弱者；年迈者；伤残者；残疾者: *I resented being treated as an invalid.* 我讨厌别人把我当病人看待。—**invalid** *adj*

in·va·lid[3] *v*

invalid sb **out** *phr v* **be invalided out** to have to leave the army, navy etc because you are ill or injured〔军人因病或伤而〕退役

in·val·i·date /ɪnˋvæləˏdet; ɪnˈvælǀdeɪt/ *v* [T] **1** to show that something such as a belief or explanation is wrong 证明〔信念或解释〕是错误的: *The theory was invalidated by later findings.* 这个理论被后来的发现推翻了。**2** to make a document, ticket, claim etc no longer legally or officially acceptable 使〔文件、票券、所有权等〕无效

invalid chair /ˈ···, ·/ *n* [C] *BrE old-fashioned* a WHEELCHAIR【英，过时】轮椅

in·va·lid·it·y /ˌɪnvəˋlɪdətɪ; ˌɪnvəˈlɪdǀti/ *n* [U] **1** the state of being too ill, old, or injured to work 伤残；年迈；病残: *invalidity benefit* 病残救济金 **2** the state of being not legally or officially acceptable〔法律或官方上〕无效: *How is the invalidity of an agreement to be decided?* 一项协议无效是如何决定的？

in·val·u·a·ble /ɪnˋvæljəbḷ; ɪnˈvæljuəbəl/ *adj* extremely useful 极有价值的: Your advice has been invaluable to us. 你的建议对我们非常宝贵。

in·var·i·a·ble /ɪnˋvɛrɪəbḷ; ɪnˈveəriəbəl/ *adj* **1** always happening in the same way, at the same time etc 恒定的，不变的；始终如一的: *His invariable answer was "Wait and see."* 他的回答总是那句话："等着瞧吧。" **2** *technical* never changing【术语】不变的；常数的: *Mass, unlike weight, is invariable.* 与重量不同，质量是不变的。

in·var·i·a·bly /ɪnˋvɛrɪəblɪ; ɪnˈveəriəbli/ *adv* if something invariably happens or is invariably true, it almost always happens or is true, so that you expect it 始终不变地；永远如此地；可预测地: *It invariably rains when I go there.* 我每次去那儿都肯定下雨。| *The security guards were invariably ex-servicemen.* 保安人员毫无例外地都是退伍军人。

in·va·sion /ɪnˋveʒən; ɪnˈveɪʒən/ *n* **1** [C,U] an occasion when one country's army enters another country by force, in order to take control of it 侵犯，入侵，侵略: *the invasion of Normandy* 对诺曼底的入侵 **2** [C] the arrival in a place of a lot of people or things, often where they are not wanted〔不受欢迎的人或物〕涌入；蜂拥而来: *the annual invasion of teenagers and hippies for the Glastonbury Pop Festival* 每年一度吸引大批青少年和嬉皮士的格拉斯顿伯里流行音乐节 **3 invasion of privacy** a situation in which someone tries to find out personal details about another person's private affairs in a way that is upsetting and often illegal 对隐私的侵犯

in·va·sive /ɪnˋvesɪv; ɪnˈveɪsɪv/ *adj* invasive medical treatment involves cutting into someone's body〔治疗〕需手术的: *invasive surgery* 有创外科手术

in·vec·tive /ɪnˋvɛktɪv; ɪnˈvektɪv/ *n* [U] *formal* rude and insulting words that someone says when they are very angry【正式】咒骂: *a stream of invective* 一连串咒骂

in·veigh /ɪnˋve; ɪnˈveɪ/ *v*

inveigh against sb/sth *phr v* [T] *formal* to criticize someone or something strongly【正式】猛烈抨击

in·vei·gle /ɪnˋvegḷ; ɪnˈveɪgəl/ *v*

inveigle sb **into** sth *phr v* [T] *formal* to persuade someone to do what you want, especially in a dishonest way【正式】诱骗〔某人〕做〔某事〕: *She had inveigled me into taking messages to her lover.* 她诱骗我给她的情人送信。

in·vent /ɪnˋvɛnt; ɪnˈvent/ *v* [T] **1** to make, design, or produce something new for the first time 发明；创造: *Alexander Bell invented the telephone in 1876.* 亚历山大·贝尔于1876年发明了电话。**2** to think of an idea, story etc that is not true, usually in order to deceive people 捏造，编造〔观点、故事等〕；虚构: *They invented a very convincing alibi.* 他们编造了很有说服力的不在犯罪现场的证据。

> **USAGE NOTE 用法说明: INVENT**
> WORD CHOICE 词语辨析: **invent, discover**
> You **invent** something that did not exist before, such as a machine or a method. invent 表示发明过去不存在的事物，如机器或方法: *Who invented the computer?* 谁发明了计算机？
> You **discover** something that existed before but was not known, such as a place, thing, or fact. discover 表示发现过去就存在但不为人知的事物，如地点、物体或事实等: *In the sixties, oil was discovered under the North Sea.* 20世纪60年代，在北海海底发现了石油。

in·ven·tion /ɪnˋvɛnʃən; ɪnˈvenʃən/ *n* **1** [C] a useful machine, tool, instrument etc that has been invented 发明物〈如机器、工具、仪器等〉: *The dishwasher is a wonderful invention.* 洗碗机是一项奇妙的发明。**2** [U] the act of inventing something 发明: *The invention of the computer has revolutionized the business world.* 电脑的发明使商界彻底发生了变革。**3** [C,U] a story, explanation etc that is not true 虚构的故事；编造的解释；假话: *They subsequently admitted that the story was pure invention.* 他们后来承认他们的说法纯属虚构。**4** [U] the ability to think of new and clever ideas 发明才能；创造力: *They accused the painter of a total lack of invention.* 他们指责这位画家毫无创造力。

in·ven·tive /ɪnˋvɛntɪv; ɪnˈventɪv/ *adj* able to think of new, different, or interesting ideas 善于发明创造的；有创造力的: *one of the most talented and inventive drummers in modern music* 现代音乐界最有才华、最有创造力的鼓手之一 —**inventively** *adv* —**inventiveness** *n* [U] *mechanical inventiveness* 机械发明能力

in·ven·tor /ɪnˋvɛntɚ; ɪnˈventə/ *n* [C] someone who has invented something, or whose job is to invent things 发明者；发明家: *the inventor of the vacuum cleaner* 真空吸尘器的发明者

in·ven·tory /ˋɪnvənˏtorɪ; ˈɪnvəntri/ *n* **1** [C] a list of all the things in a place〔一个地方所有东西的〕详细目录；清单: *We made a complete inventory of everything in the apartment.* 我们把这公寓套间里的所有东西开列了一份详细清单。**2** [U] *AmE* all the goods in a shop; STOCK[1](2)【美】存货；库存

In·ver·ness /ˌɪnvɚˋnɛs; ˌɪnvəˈnes◂/ a town in northern Scotland which many people consider to be the capital of the Highlands 因弗内斯〔苏格兰北部一镇。许多人视该地为苏格兰高地的首府〕

in·verse[1] /ɪnˋvɝs; ˌɪnˈvɜːs◂/ *adj* [only before noun 仅用于名词前] **1 in inverse proportion/relation to** getting bigger at the same rate as something else gets smaller, or getting smaller at the same rate as something else gets bigger 与…成反比: *Clearly, the amount of money people save increases in inverse proportion to the amount they spend.* 显然，人们的储蓄与他们

的花费成反比。**2** *technical* exactly opposite, especially in order or position【术语】〔尤指次序或位置〕相反的; 逆向的: *an inverse correlation* 逆向关联 —**inversely** *adv*

inverse² *n* [C] *technical* the complete opposite of something【术语】相反; 颠倒

in·ver·sion /ɪnˋvɜʃən; ɪnˈvɜːʃən/ *n* [C,U] **1** *formal* the changing of something so that it is the opposite of what it was before, or of turning something upside down【正式】反向; 倒置; 颠倒 **2** *technical* a kind of weather condition in which the air nearest the ground is cooler than the air above it【术语】逆温〔指越接近地面气温越低〕

in·vert /ɪnˋvɝt; ɪnˈvɜːt/ *v* [T] *formal* to put something in the opposite position to the one it was in before, especially by turning it upside down【正式】使反向; 使颠倒; 使倒置

in·ver·te·brate /ɪnˋvɝtəbrɪt; ɪnˈvɜːtɪ̈brɪ̈t/ *n* [C] a living creature that does not have a BACKBONE (1) 无脊椎动物 —compare 比较 VERTEBRATE —**invertebrate** *adj*

inverted com·ma /ˌ·.. ˈ··/ *n* [C usually plural 一般用复数] *BrE*【英】**1** one of a pair of marks (" ") or (' ') that are put at the beginning and end of a written word, sentence etc to show that someone said it or wrote it, or when writing the title of a book, song etc; QUOTATION MARK 引号 —see picture at 参见 PUNCTUATION MARK 图 **2** **in inverted commas** *spoken* used to show that a word you are using to describe something is only what it is usually called, and not what you think it really is【口】所谓的〔表示用来描述某物的词只是它通常的名称，而不是你所认为的意思〕: *Her friends, in inverted commas, all disappeared when she was in trouble.* 当陷入困境时，她那些所谓的"朋友"全都消失了。

inverted snob·ber·y /ˌ··· ˈ···/ *n* [U] *BrE* the idea that everything that is typical of the upper classes must be bad【英】倒转的势利观点〔认为属于上层社会的一切事物都必然是坏的观点〕

3 **in·vest** /ɪnˋvɛst; ɪnˈvest/ *v* **1** [I,T] to give money to a company, business, or bank, in order to get a profit 投资; 入股: **invest (sth) in sth** *Jones invested $7 million in an ultra-modern video studio.* 琼斯把700万美元投资于一个超现代的摄影棚。| **invest heavily** (=invest a lot of money) 投入巨资 *Maxwell had invested heavily in the bond market.* 马克斯维尔已在债券市场上投入巨资。**2** [T] to use a lot of time, effort etc in order to make something succeed 投入〔大量时间、精力等以成就某事〕: **invest sth in sth** *I've invested a lot of time and effort in this project, and I don't want it to fail.* 我在这个项目上投入了大量时间和精力，我不想它失败。

invest in sth *phr v* [T] **1** to buy something in order to sell it again when the value increases and so make a profit 买进〔以便高价卖出赚钱〕: *Oliver made a fortune by investing in antique furniture.* 奥利弗买卖古董家具发了财。**2** to buy something because it will be useful for you 买〔对自己有用的东西〕: *It's about time you invested in a new shirt!* 你该买件新衬衫了!

invest sb/sth **with** sth *phr v* [T often passive 常用被动态] *formal*【正式】**1** to officially give someone power to do something 授权给: *invested with the authority to enforce his recommendations* 被授权执行他的建议 **2** to make someone or something seem to have a particular quality or character 使似乎具有〔某种特性或品质〕: *Richard's heavy-rimmed glasses invested him with an air of dignity.* 理查德的厚边眼镜使他显得很威严。

2 **in·ves·ti·gate** /ɪnˋvɛstəˌget; ɪnˈvestɪ̈geɪt/ *v* **1** [I,T] to try to find out the truth about something such as a crime, accident, or scientific problem 查明〔犯罪、事故或科学问题等的真相〕; 调查; 审查: *The allegations were investigated, and found to be untrue.* 经过调查发现所有指控都不符合事实。| *I heard a noise and went downstairs to investigate.* 我听见响声，就下楼去看个究竟。**2** [T] to try to find out more about someone's character, actions etc, because you think they may have been involved in a crime〔由于可能牵涉犯罪而〕调查〔某人〕: *Penney was already being investigated by the police on suspicion of murder.* 彭尼因有杀人嫌疑而被警方调查过了。

2 **in·ves·ti·ga·tion** /ɪnˌvɛstəˋgeʃən; ɪnˌvestɪˈgeɪʃən/ *n* **1** [C] an official attempt to find out the reasons for something such as a crime, accident, or scientific problem〔针对犯罪、事故或科学问题而进行的正式〕调查, 探究: *a criminal investigation* 犯罪调查 | [+into] *The authorities are planning to launch a full-scale investigation into the crash which claimed over 200 lives.* 当局计划对这桩造成二百余人死亡的坠机事件展开全面调查。**2** [U] the act of investigating something 调查: *the investigation of computer fraud* 对利用电脑诈骗的调查 | **under investigation** (=being investigated) 正在调查中 *The whole issue is still under investigation.* 整个事件仍在调查之中。

in·ves·ti·ga·tive /ɪnˋvɛstəˌgetɪv; ɪnˈvestɪ̈gətɪv/ *adj* **investigative journalism/report/work** work or activities that involve investigating something 调查性新闻报道/报告/工作

in·ves·ti·gat·or /ɪnˋvɛstəˌgetɚ; ɪnˈvestɪ̈geɪtə/ *n* [C] someone who investigates things, especially crimes〔尤指针对犯罪的〕调查员, 侦察员: *Government investigators are going through the financial records.* 政府调查人员正在审查账目。

in·ves·ti·ga·to·ry /ɪnˋvɛstəgəˌtorɪ; ɪnˈvestɪ̈gətəri/ *adj* connected with investigating something 与调查有关的

in·ves·ti·ture /ɪnˋvɛstətʃɚ; ɪnˈvestɪ̈tʃə/ *n* [C] *formal* a ceremony at which someone is given an official title【正式】授衔仪式: *the investiture of the Prince of Wales* 册封威尔士亲王的仪式

in·vest·ment /ɪnˋvɛstmənt; ɪnˈvestmənt/ *n* **1** [C,U] the money that people or organizations have put into a company, business, or bank in order to get a profit, or to make a business activity successful 投资(的款项): [+in] *Wellings made a number of high-risk investments in the property market during the late 80s.* 80年代后期韦林斯在房地产市场进行了多项高风险投资。| *new measures aimed at attracting foreign investment into South Africa* 旨在吸引外国投资到南非的新措施 **2** something that you buy or do because it will be useful for later 投资: **a good/sound investment** *The lessons cost me over $500, but I consider them a good investment.* 这些课程花了我五百多美元，但我认为这是很好的投资。**3** [C,U] a large amount of time, energy, emotion etc that you spend on something〔大量时间、精力、情感等的〕花费: *a huge investment of time and effort* 时间和精力的大量投入 1

in·vest·or /ɪnˋvɛstɚ; ɪnˈvestə/ *n* [C] someone who gives money to a company, business, or bank in order to get a profit 投资者 3

in·vet·e·rate /ɪnˋvɛtərɪt; ɪnˈvetərɪ̈t/ *adj* [only before noun 仅用于名词前] **1** **inveterate liar/smoker/womanizer etc** someone who smokes a lot, lies a lot etc and cannot stop 惯于说谎的人/烟瘾很大的人/沉迷女色的人等: *a voracious reader and inveterate talker* 一个看起书来如饥似渴、说起话来喋喋不休的人 **2** **inveterate fondness/distrust/hatred etc** an attitude or feeling that you have had for a long time and cannot change 根深蒂固的喜爱/怀疑/仇恨等 —**inveterately** *adv*

in·vid·i·ous /ɪnˋvɪdɪəs; ɪnˈvɪdiəs/ *adj* unpleasant, especially because it is likely to offend people or make you unpopular 令人不快的; 惹人反感的: *an invidious task* 招人不满的任务 —**invidiously** *adv* —**invidiousness** *n* [U]

in·vi·gi·late /ɪnˋvɪdʒəˌlet; ɪnˈvɪdʒɪ̈leɪt/ *v* [I,T] *BrE* to watch the people who are taking an examination and make sure that they do not cheat【英】〔考试〕监考; PROCTOR² *AmE*【美】—**invigilator** *n* [C] —**invigilation** /ɪnˌvɪdʒəˋleʃən; ɪnˌvɪdʒɪ̈ˈleɪʃən/ *n* [U]

in·vig·o·rat·ed /ɪnˋvɪgəˌretɪd; ɪnˈvɪgəreɪtɪ̈d/ *adj* feeling healthier, stronger, and having more energy than you did before 感到〔比原来〕更健康[强壮, 精力充沛]的: *He felt invigorated after his day in the country.* 在乡下住了一天，他感到精力充沛多了。—**invigorate** *v* [T]

in·vig·o·ra·ting /ɪnˋvɪgəˌretɪŋ; ɪnˈvɪgəreɪtɪŋ/ *adj* making you feel more active, and healthy 使精力充沛的; 使健康强壮的: *an invigorating swim before breakfast* 早餐前的健身游泳 —**invigoratingly** *adv*

in·vin·ci·ble /ɪnˋvɪnsəbl; ɪnˈvɪnsɪ̈bəl/ *adj* **1** an invincible team, army etc is too strong to be destroyed or defeated〔队伍、军队等〕不可消灭的; 无敌的: *the once invincible East German athletics team* 曾经战无不胜的东德田径队 **2** an invincible belief, attitude etc is extremely strong and cannot be changed〔信念、态度等〕不屈不挠的; 坚定不移的: *her invincible determination* 她那坚定不移的决心 —**invincibly** *adv* —**invincibility** /ɪnˌvɪnsəˋbɪlətɪ; ɪnˌvɪnsɪ̈ˈbɪlɪ̈ti/ *n* [U]

in·vi·o·la·ble /ɪnˋvaɪələbl; ɪnˈvaɪələbəl/ *adj formal* an inviolable right, law, principle etc is extremely important and should not be got rid of【正式】〔权利、法律、原则等〕不可违背的; 不可侵犯的 —**inviolably** *adv* —**inviolability** /ɪnˌvaɪələˋbɪlətɪ; ɪnˌvaɪələˈbɪlɪ̈ti/ *n* [U]

in·vi·o·late /ɪnˋvaɪəlɪt; ɪnˈvaɪəlɪ̈t/ *adj formal* something that is inviolate cannot be attacked, changed, or destroyed【正式】不受打击[改变, 损毁]的

in·vis·i·ble /ɪnˋvɪzəbl; ɪnˈvɪzɪ̈bəl/ *adj* **1** something that is invisible cannot be seen 看不见的; 无形的: *The house was surrounded by trees and invisible from the road.* 这所房子树木环绕，从路上是看不见的。| [+to] *germs that are invisible to all but the most powerful microscopes* 只有用最大倍数的显微镜才可看见的细菌 **2** **invisible earnings/exports/trade etc** earnings etc that are connected with services rather than products 无形收

益/输出/贸易等: *Insurance is one of Britain's largest invisible exports.* 保险业是英国最大的无形输出之一。—**invisibly** *adv* —**invisibility** /ɪn͵vɪzəˋbɪlətɪ; ɪn͵vɪzʝˈbɪlʝti/ *n* [U]

invisible ink /͵· ˈ··· ˈ·/ *n* [U] secret ink that cannot be seen on paper until it is heated〔遇热才能看见的〕隐形墨水

Invisible Man /͵· ˈ··· ˈ·/ **1 The Invisible Man** (1897) a SCIENCE FICTION NOVEL by H. G. Wells about a scientist who discovers a way of making himself unable to be seen《隐形人》〔(1897), H.G.韦尔斯创作的一部科幻小说, 讲述一名科学家发现隐身术的故事〕 **2 Invisible Man** (1952) a novel by the US writer Ralph Ellison about the life of a young black man in New York City《隐形人》〔(1952), 美国作家拉尔夫·埃利森创作的一部小说, 讲述纽约市一名年轻黑人男子的故事〕

in·vi·ta·tion /͵ɪnvəˋteʃən; ͵ɪnvʝˈteɪʃən/ *n* **1** [C] a written or spoken request to someone, inviting them to go somewhere or do something〔书面或口头〕邀请: **[+to]** *Did you get an invitation to the party?* 你收到参加聚会的请柬了吗? | **invitation to do sth** *Shortly afterwards, Dawson received an invitation to speak at a scientific conference.* 不久之后, 道森受邀在一次科学会议中发言。| **accept an invitation** *President Yeltsin has accepted an invitation to visit the White House in June.* 叶利钦总统已接受了6月份访问白宫的邀请。| **decline an invitation** *formal* (=to not accept an invitation)【正式】谢绝邀请 | **by invitation only** (=only those people who have been invited can attend) 凭请柬参加〔即只让受到邀请的人参加〕 **2** [C] a card inviting someone to attend a party, wedding etc 请柬: *Have you sent out all the wedding invitations yet?* 婚礼请柬都发出了吗? **3 without invitation** without having been invited 并未受到邀请: *They were always dropping by to visit, usually without invitation.* 他们常来串门, 通常不请自来。**4** [singular, U] encouragement to do something 鼓动[激励]〔做某事〕: **take sth as an invitation to do sth** *He seemed to take my silence as an invitation to talk.* 他似乎把我的沉默理解为鼓励他讲话。**5 at sb's invitation** also 又作 **at the invitation of sb** if you go somewhere or do something at someone's invitation, you go there or do it because they have invited you to 应某人的邀请 **6 open/standing invitation** an invitation to do something, especially to visit someone, at any time you like 不受限制/长期有效的邀请〔尤指可随时探望某人〕: *My cousin Diana is living in China, and I have an open invitation to visit her.* 我的堂姐黛安娜现住在中国, 她邀请我随时去看她。**7 be an open invitation for/to sb** to make it very easy for someone to rob you or harm you 公开让人〔来抢劫或伤害〕: *Leaving the car unlocked like that is just an open invitation to thieves.* 离开汽车而不上锁等于摆明了让窃贼来偷。

in·vite¹ /ɪnˋvaɪt; ɪnˈvaɪt/ *v* [T] **1** to ask someone to come to a party, wedding, meal etc 邀请: **invite sb to sth** *Who should we invite to the party?* 我们应请谁来参加聚会? | **invite sb to do sth** *I'm thinking of inviting them to spend the summer with me in Italy.* 我正考虑邀请他们和我一起在意大利过夏天。| **invite sb for a drink/meal etc** *Why don't you invite her for a drink at the club one evening?* 你何不找一天晚上请她在夜总会喝酒? | **be invited** *I'm afraid I wasn't invited.* 恐怕我没有被邀请。**2** *formal* to politely ask someone to do something【正式】〔礼貌地〕请求〔某人做某事〕: **invite sb to do sth** *The interviewer invited Senator Axelmann to comment on recent events.* 采访记者请阿克塞尔曼参议员评论近来的事件。**3** to encourage something bad such as trouble or criticism to happen to you, especially without intending to〔尤指无意地〕招致〔麻烦或批评等不好的事〕; 引诱: *Any government that sells arms to these dictators is inviting trouble.* 任何卖武器给这些独裁者的政府都是自找麻烦。

invite sb **along** *phr v* [T] to ask someone if they would like to come with you when you are going somewhere〔去某地时〕邀请〔某人〕同往: *We were going to the beach and I decided to invite her along.* 我们正要去海滩, 我决定请她同去。

invite sb **back** *phr v* [T] to ask someone to come to your home, hotel etc after you have been out somewhere together〔在与某人一同外出之后〕再邀请他到自己的住处: *Richard often used to invite me back for coffee after the show.* 理查德常常在看完演出后请我到他家里喝咖啡。

invite sb **in** *phr v* [T] to ask someone to come into your home 邀请〔某人〕进屋: *Mr Vosset came to the door but didn't invite me in.* 沃塞特先生来到门口, 但并未请我进去。

invite sb **over** *phr v* [T] to ask someone to come to your home, usually for a drink or a meal 邀请〔某人〕来家里〔通常是请他喝酒或吃饭〕: *Max has invited me over for dinner.* 马克斯已经邀请了我去他家吃饭。

in·vite² /ˋɪnvaɪt; ˈɪnvaɪt/ *n* [C] *informal* an invitation to a party, meal etc【非正式】〔聚会、吃饭等的〕邀请

in·vit·ing /ɪnˋvaɪtɪŋ; ɪnˈvaɪtɪŋ/ *adj* an inviting sight, smell, offer etc is very attractive and makes you want to go somewhere or do something〔景象、气味、建议等〕诱人的; 吸引人的: *The log fire looked warm and inviting.* 篝火看上去温暖诱人。—**invitingly** *adv*: *She smiled invitingly.* 她很迷人地笑了笑。

in vi·tro fer·ti·li·za·tion /ɪn ͵vaɪtro fɝtələˋzeʃən; ɪn ͵viːtrəʊ fɜːtʝlaɪˈzeɪʃən/ *n* [U] *technical* a process in which a human egg is fertilized (FERTILIZE) outside a woman's body; IVF【术语】体外受精

in·vo·ca·tion /͵ɪnvəˋkeʃən; ͵ɪnvəˈkeɪʃən/ *n literary* [C,U] a request for help, especially from a god【文】〔尤指祈求神灵的〕救助: **[+to]** *an invocation to Zeus* 向宙斯的求助

in·voice¹ /ˋɪnvɔɪs; ˈɪnvɔɪs/ *n* [C] a list of goods that have been supplied or work that has been done, showing how much you owe for them 发票; 发货清单; 已完成工作的清单〔单上注明应支付的款项〕

invoice² *v* [T] **1** to send someone an invoice 寄送发票〔给某人〕 **2** to prepare an invoice for goods that have been supplied or work that has been done 开…的发票[发货清单]

in·voke /ɪnˋvok; ɪnˈvəʊk/ *v* [T] *formal*【正式】**1** to use a law, principle, or THEORY to support your views 援引〔法律、原则或理论以支持自己的论点〕: *Such legislation has frequently been invoked to silence political opposition.* 这类法规常常被援引以压制政治反对派的言论。**2** to make a particular idea, image or feeling appear in people's minds〔在脑海中〕唤起〔某个想法、形象或感受〕; 引起, 产生: *His earlier novels invoke a romanticized picture of life in the countryside.* 他早期的小说使人脑海中浮现一幅乡村生活的浪漫图画。**3** to ask for help from someone more powerful than you, especially a god 祈求〔有权力者, 尤指神灵〕帮助: *Isagoras invoked the aid of King Cleomenes.* 伊萨戈拉斯向克莱奥梅尼国王求助。**4** to make spirits appear by using magic〔用魔法〕使〔灵魂〕显现: *invoking the spirits of their dead ancestors* 为死去的先人招魂

in·vol·un·ta·ry /ɪnˋvɑlən͵tɛrɪ; ɪnˈvɒləntəri/ *adj* an involuntary movement, sound, reaction etc is one that you make suddenly and without intending to because you cannot control yourself〔动作、声音、反应等〕无意识做出的; 非故意的: *an involuntary cry of shock* 不由自主的惊叫 —**involuntarily** *adv* —**involuntariness** *n* [U]

in·volve /ɪnˋvɑlv; ɪnˈvɒlv/ *v* [T] **1** to include something as a necessary part or result 包含〔必要的部分或结果〕, 包括, 需要: *What will the job involve?* 这份工作包括什么? | *I didn't realize putting on a play involved so much work.* 我没有想到演出一场戏需要做这么多的工作。| **involve doing sth** *Every day each of us makes decisions that involve taking a chance.* 每天我们每个人做出的决定都包含碰运气的成分。**2** to include or affect someone or something 涉及; 影响: *These changes will involve everyone on the staff.* 这些变化将涉及每一位职员。| *an accident involving a coach and two cars* 涉及一辆长途汽车和两辆汽车的事故 | *charges involving accusations of widespread corruption* 涉及大规模贪污的控诉 **3** to ask or allow someone to take part in something〔邀请或允许某人〕参与: **involve sb in sth** *Try to involve as many children as possible in the game.* 尽量让更多的孩子参与游戏。| *We want to involve the workforce at all stages of the decision-making process.* 我们希望在决策过程中的各个阶段都有职工参与。**4 involve yourself** to take part actively in a particular activity 积极参与: **[+in]** *The US has so far been extremely unwilling to involve itself in the crisis in Bosnia.* 直到现在, 美国仍然极不愿意卷入波斯尼亚的危机中去。

in·volved /ɪnˋvɑlvd; ɪnˈvɒlvd/ *adj* **1 be involved** to take part in an activity or event, or be connected with it in some way 参与某活动[某事件]的; 与某活动[某事件]有关联的: **[+in]** *More than 30 software firms were involved in the project.* 三十多家软件公司参与了这项工程。| **deeply/heavily involved** (=be involved a lot) 大量参与 *At law school Hilary became heavily involved in student politics.* 在法学院, 希拉里积极参与学生政治活动。| **get involved in an argument/discussion/fight etc** *I don't want to get involved in some lengthy argument about who is to blame.* 我不想卷入谁该承担责任的冗长争论。| *The Mafia could well be involved.* 黑手党很可能与此事有牵连。**2 be involved in an accident/fight/crash etc** to be one of the people in an accident, crash etc 牵涉进一次事故/打斗/坠机等: *I'm afraid your son's been involved in an accident.* 恐怕你儿子牵涉进了一次事故。**3 work/effort etc involved in doing sth** [not before noun 不用于名词前] the work, money, effort, risk etc that is involved in doing something is the amount that is needed in order to succeed in doing it 为成就某事必须做的工作/付出的努力等: *Most people don't realize the amount of effort that is involved in writing a novel.* 大多数人都不明白写一

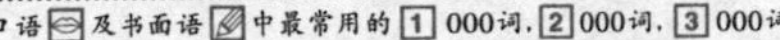
口语 及书面语 中最常用的 1 000词, 2 000词, 3 000词

本小说要花多少心血。| *I would never go climbing on my own – there's too much risk involved.* 我绝不会一个人去爬山，那样太冒险了。**4 be involved with sb** to be having a sexual relationship with someone, especially someone you should not have a relationship with 与〔某人〕有不正当的性关系: *Matt's involved with a married woman at work.* 玛特与同事中一名有夫之妇有染。**5** having so many different parts that it is difficult to understand; complicated 复杂难懂的: *The plot was so involved that very few people knew what was going on.* 情节太复杂，几乎没人知道是怎么回事。

3 **in·volve·ment** /ɪn`vɑlvmənt; ɪn'vɒlvmənt/ *n* [U] **1** the act of taking part in an activity or event, or the way in which you take part in it 卷入; 牵连: [+in] *President Clinton defended US involvement in Haiti's domestic affairs.* 克林顿总统为美国干预海地内政进行辩护。| *What exactly was his involvement in the murder?* 他与这起谋杀案到底有什么牵连? **2** the feeling of excitement and satisfaction that you get from an activity 满足; 兴奋: *a student's emotional involvement in the learning experience* 学生在学习过程中的情感满足

in·vul·ne·ra·ble /ɪn`vʌlnərəbl; ɪn'vʌlnərəbəl/ *adj* someone or something that is invulnerable cannot be harmed or damaged if you attack or criticize them 〔人或物〕无法伤害的; 攻不破的; 无懈可击的: *Gerry's confidence seemed to make him invulnerable.* 格里的自信使他似乎无懈可击。| [+to] *The castle was invulnerable to attack.* 这座城堡固若金汤。—**invulnerably** *adv* —**invulnerability** /ˌɪnvʌlnərə`bɪlətɪ; ɪnˌvʌlnərə'bɪlɪ̣ti/ *n* [U] —compare 比较 VULNERABLE

in·ward /`ɪnwɚd; 'ɪnwəd/ *adj* **1** [only before noun 仅用于名词前] felt or experienced in your own mind but not expressed to other people 内心的; 精神的: *a feeling of inward satisfaction* 内心的满足感 | *inward panic* 潜藏于心的惶恐 **2** moving towards the inside or centre of something 向内的; 朝向中心的 —**inwardly** *adv*: *I managed to smile, but inwardly I was furious.* 我勉强装笑，心里却气得很。—opposite 反义词 OUTWARD

inward-look·ing /'‥ˌ‥/ *adj* an inward-looking person or group is more interested in themselves than in other people 〔人或团体〕只关注自身的: *an inward-looking and isolated country community* 一个闭关自守、与世隔绝的乡间社区

in·wards /`ɪnwɚdz; 'ɪnwədz/ *especially BrE* 【尤英】, **inward** *especially AmE* 【尤美】 —*adv* towards the inside of something 向内: *A breeze blew the curtains inward for a moment.* 微风把窗帘向屋里吹了一会儿。—opposite 反义词 OUTWARDS

i·o·dine /`aɪəˌdaɪn; 'aɪədiːn/ *n* [U] a dark blue chemical substance used on wounds to prevent infection 碘

IOM the written abbreviation of 缩写= ISLE OF MAN

i·on /`aɪən; 'aɪən/ *n* [C] *technical* an atom which has been given a positive or negative force by adding or taking away an ELECTRON 【术语】离子

-ion /ən; ən/ *suffix* [in nouns 构成名词] the act, state, or result of doing something 行为, 状态; 〔行动的〕结果: *the completion* (=completing) *of the task* 任务的完成 | *his election* (=he was elected) *to the post* 他当选该职位 | *several volcanic eruptions* 数次火山爆发

I·o·na /aɪ`onə; aɪ'əʊnə/ an island off western Scotland, one of the Inner Hebrides, famous as the starting place in the 6th century of Scots Christianity, and the home of the **Iona Community**, an ECUMENICAL Christian group 艾奥纳岛〔与苏格兰西海岸隔海相望的一座岛屿，属于内赫布里底群岛。该岛是公元6世纪苏格兰基督教的发源地，也是支持基督教大联合的艾奥纳团的大本营〕

I·o·nes·co /ˌiə`nɛsko; ˌiːə'nɛskəʊ/, **Eu·gène** /ju`ʒin; juː'ʒiːn/ (1912-94) a French writer of plays, born in Romania, who wrote about the meaningless lives of human beings and their difficulty in communicating with each other. This type of play was known as the 'Theatre of the Absurd'. Ionesco's plays include *The Bald Prima Donna*, *Rhinoceros*, and *The Chairs*. 尤内斯库〔(1912-1994)，法国剧作家，生于罗马尼亚。他笔下的人类生活毫无意义，人际间交流困难。这种戏剧称"荒诞剧"。其代表剧作包括《秃头歌女》、《犀牛》和《椅子》〕

I·on·ic /aɪ`ɑnɪk; aɪ'ɒnɪk/ *adj* made in the simply decorated style of ancient Greek building 〔古希腊〕爱奥尼亚建筑风格的〔风格简单〕: *an Ionic column* 爱奥尼亚式柱子

i·on·ize also 又作 **-ise** *BrE* 【英】 /`aɪənˌaɪz; 'aɪənaɪz/ *v* [I,T] to form ions or make them form 〔使〕形成离子 —**ionization** /ˌaɪənə`zeʃən; ˌaɪənaɪ'zeɪʃən/ *n* [U]

i·on·i·zer also 又作 **-iser** *BrE* 【英】 /`aɪənaɪzɚ; 'aɪənaɪzə/ *n* [C] a machine used to make the air in a room more healthy by producing negative IONS 负离子发生器〔用于使室内空气清新〕

i·on·o·sphere /aɪ`ɑnəˌsfɪr; aɪ'ɒnəsfɪə/ *n* **the ionosphere** the part of the ATMOSPHERE (1) which is used to help send radio waves around the Earth 电离层

i·o·ta /aɪ`otə; aɪ'əʊtə/ *n* [singular] **1 not one iota** not even a small amount 一点也不: *It's no use talking to him – it won't make an iota of difference.* 跟他说没用，一点作用也没有。**2** the Greek letter 'I' 希腊字母 I

IOU /ˌaɪ o `ju; ˌaɪ əʊ 'juː/ *n* [C] *informal* a note that you sign to say that you owe someone some money 【非正式】借条, 借据

IOW the written abbreviation of 缩写= ISLE OF WIGHT

I·o·wa /`aɪəwə; 'aɪəwə/ abbreviation 缩写为 **IA** a state in the Midwest of the US. It produces mainly meat, MAIZE and SOYA BEANS. 艾奥瓦，又译衣阿华〔美国中西部一州，主要出产肉类、玉米和大豆〕—**Iowan** *n, adj*

IPA /ˌaɪ pi `e; ˌaɪ piː 'eɪ◂/ *n* [singular] the International Phonetic Alphabet; a system of special signs, used to represent the sounds made in speech 国际音标

ip·so fac·to /`ɪpso `fækto; ˌɪpsəʊ 'fæktəʊ/ *adv Latin formal* used to show that something is known from or proved by the facts 【拉丁, 正式】根据事实本身〔用来表示某事是根据事实得知或有事实依据〕

IQ /ˌaɪ `kju; ˌaɪ 'kjuː/ *n* [C] intelligence quotient; your level of intelligence, measured by a special test, with 100 being the average result 智力商数〔智力的水平, 用特殊测验测试, 以 100 为平均数〕: *an IQ of 130* 智商为 130

ir- /ɪ; ɪ/ *prefix* the form used for IN- before r; not 不; 否, 没有〔在 r 之前用来代替 in-〕: *irregular* (=not regular) 不规则的

IRA /ˌaɪ ɑr `e; ˌaɪ ɑːr 'eɪ/ *n* the Irish Republican Army; an organization that wants to unite Northern Ireland and the Republic of Ireland 爱尔兰共和军 —see also 另见 SINN FÉIN

I·ran /ɪ`rɑn; ɪ'rɑːn/ a country in southwest Asia, between Iraq and Afghanistan. Population: 66,129,000 (2001). Capital: Tehran. Iran was called **Persia** until 1935, and is an important oil-producing country. Iran is a democratic country in which Muslim religious leaders have had a lot of political power since the Shah was removed in 1979 and the Ayatollah Khomeini came to power. 伊朗〔亚洲西南部一国家, 位于伊拉克和阿富汗之间。人口: 66,129,000 (2001)，首都: 德黑兰。伊朗 1935 年以前称波斯，为重要的石油出产国。该国是一个民主国家。自 1979 年国王被废黜，阿亚图拉霍梅尼上台以来，穆斯林领导人一直拥有很大的政治权力〕—**Iranian** /ɪ`reniən; ɪ'reɪniən/ *n, adj*

I·ran·gate /ɪ`rɑnˌget; ɪ'rɑːngeɪt/ also 又作 **the Iran-Contra Affair** a political SCANDAL in 1987, when it was discovered that members of President Reagan's government had sold weapons to Iran in exchange for the return of US HOSTAGES (=people kept as prisoners by an enemy), and had then used the profits to support the Contras, an unofficial army that was fighting the government in Nicaragua 伊朗门事件〔1987 年的一件政治丑闻。据揭露，里根政府官员向伊朗出售武器以换回美国人质，并用所获利润支持尼加拉瓜反政府武装集团〕

Iran-Iraq War /ˌ‥ˌ‥ '‥/ a war between Iran and Iraq from 1980 to 1988 两伊战争〔1980 至 1988 年伊朗和伊拉克之间爆发的战争〕

I·raq /ɪ`ræk; ɪ'rɑːk/ a country in southwest Asia, between Iran and Saudi Arabia. Population: 23,332,000 (2001). Capital: Baghdad. It is an oil-producing country. Under its leader Saddam Hussein, Iraq was at war with Iran from 1980 to 1988, and its INVASION of Kuwait in 1990 led to the Gulf War. 伊拉克〔亚洲西南部一国家，位于伊朗和沙特阿拉伯之间。人口: 23,332,000 (2001)，首都: 巴格达，为石油出产国。在萨达姆·侯赛因的领导下，该国 1980 至 1988 年间与伊朗交战，并于 1990 年入侵科威特，导致海湾战争〕—**Iraqi** *n, adj*

i·ras·ci·ble /ɪ`ræsəbl; ɪ'ræsɪ̣bəl/ *adj formal* easily becoming angry 【正式】易怒的: *He was an irascible, energetic little man.* 他是个脾气暴躁、精力充沛的小个子男人。—**irascibly** *adv* —**irascibility** /ɪˌræsɪ`bɪlətɪ; ɪˌræsɪ̣'bɪlɪ̣ti/ *n* [U]

i·rate /aɪ`ret; ˌaɪ'reɪt◂/ *adj* extremely angry, especially because you think you have been treated unfairly 极愤怒的〔尤指认为受到不公平待遇时〕: *The company received several complaints from irate customers.* 公司收到几名怒气冲冲的顾客投诉。—**irately** *adv*

ire /aɪr; aɪə/ *n* [U] *literary* anger 【文】愤怒: *the ire of angry enemies* 愤怒的敌人的怒火

Ire·land /`aɪrlənd; 'aɪələnd/ a large island to the west of Great Britain, from which it is separated by the Irish Sea. It is divided politically into Northern Ireland and the Republic of Ireland. Northern Ireland is part of the UK, and many people there belong to the Protestant religion. The Republic of Ireland has been an independent state since 1921, and most people there belong

to the Roman Catholic religion. Ireland is famous for its beautiful green countryside, and is sometimes called the **Emerald Isle**. 爱尔兰〔大不列颠西面一座大岛，与大不列颠隔爱尔兰海相望。该岛在政治上分为北爱尔兰和爱尔兰共和国。北爱尔兰属于英国，许多居民为新教徒。爱尔兰共和国自1921年起独立，居民多为天主教徒。爱尔兰以美丽的绿色乡村著称，有时被称为"绿宝石岛"〕—see also 另见 the REPUBLIC OF IRELAND

ir·i·des·cent /ˌɪrəˋdɛsn̩t; ˌɪrɪ̇ˈdesənt◂/ *adj* showing colours that seem to change in different lights〔因光线不同而〕变色的: *The painting has a shimmering iridescent quality.* 这幅油画闪烁着微光，色彩随光线的变化而变化。—**iridescence** *n* [U]

i·rid·i·um /ɪˋrɪdɪəm; ɪˈrɪdiəm/ *n* [U] a rare metal used in medicine 铱

i·ris /ˋaɪrɪs; ˈaɪərɪ̇s/ *n* [C] **1** a tall plant with long, thin leaves and large purple, yellow, or white flowers 鸢尾属植物 **2** the round coloured part of your eye, that surrounds the black PUPIL (2)〔瞳孔周围的〕虹膜 —see picture at 参见 EYE[1] 图

I·rish[1] /ˋaɪrɪʃ; ˈaɪərɪʃ/ *n* **the Irish** people from Ireland 爱尔兰人

Irish[2] *adj* from or connected with Ireland 爱尔兰的

Irish cof·fee /ˌ‥ ˈ‥/ *n* [C,U] coffee with cream and WHISKY added 爱尔兰咖啡〔加奶油和威士忌酒的咖啡〕

Irish Guards, the /ˌ‥ ˈ·/ a REGIMENT (=a large group of soldiers) in the British army that is part of the Guards 爱尔兰近卫团

I·rish·man /ˋaɪrɪʃmən; ˈaɪərɪʃmən/ *n* [C] a man from Ireland 爱尔兰男人

Irish Na·tion·al Lib·e·ra·tion Ar·my, the /ˌ‥ ˌ‥‥ ‥ˈ‥ ˈ‥/ the full name of the INLA 爱尔兰民族解放军〔INLA 的全称〕

Irish Re·pub·lic, the /ˌ‥ ·ˈ‥/ the Republic of Ireland 爱尔兰共和国

Irish Re·pub·li·can Ar·my, the /ˌ‥ ·ˈ‥‥ ˈ‥/ the full name of the IRA 爱尔兰共和军〔IRA 的全称〕

Irish Sea, the /ˌ‥ ˈ·/ the sea between Great Britain and Ireland 爱尔兰海〔位于大不列颠和爱尔兰之间的海域〕

Irish Set·ter /ˌ‥ ˈ‥/ *n* [C] a type of large dog with long hair 爱尔兰塞特犬，爱尔兰雪达犬〔一种长毛大狗〕

Irish stew /ˌ‥ ˈ·/ *n* [C,U] a dish of meat, potatoes, and onions boiled together 马铃薯洋葱炖肉

I·rish·wom·an /ˋaɪrɪʃˌwʊmən; ˈaɪərɪʃˌwʊmən/ *n* [C] a woman from Ireland 爱尔兰女人

irk /ɝk; ɜːk/ *v* [T] if something irks you, it makes you feel annoyed, especially because you feel you cannot change the situation 使恼怒；使气愤〔尤指因对局势无能为力时〕: *Luna never told me what irked her that Sunday morning.* 卢娜从没告诉我那个星期日早上是什么把她惹恼了。

irk·some /ˋɝksəm; ˈɜːksəm/ *adj formal* annoying【正式】恼人的: *an irksome journey* 一次恼人的旅行

3 2 **i·ron[1]** /ˋaɪɚn; ˈaɪən/ *n*

1 ►METAL 金属◄ [U] a common hard metal that is used to make steel, is MAGNETIC and is found in very small quantities in food and blood 铁: *There were huge iron gates in front of the mansion.* 这宅第前面有两扇巨大的铁门。| *iron ore* 铁矿石 | *Spinach is full of iron.* 菠菜含丰富铁质。

2 ►FOR CLOTHES 用于衣物◄ [C] a thing that you use for making clothes smooth, which has a heated flat metal base 熨斗

3 have several irons in the fire to be involved in several different activities or have several plans 同时从事数种不同活动；同时有数项计划

4 ►SPORT 运动◄ [C] a GOLF CLUB (2) made of metal rather than wood〔高尔夫球〕铁头球杆 —see picture on page A23 参见 A23 页图

5 ►CHAINS 锁链◄ irons [plural] *especially literary* a chain used to prevent a prisoner from moving【尤文】镣铐: **clap sb in irons** *old use* (=put chains on them)【旧】给某人戴上镣铐

6 have a will of iron/an iron will to have an extremely strong and determined character 具有坚强的意志 —see also 另见 **pump iron** (PUMP[2] (8)), **rule sb/sth with a rod of iron** (RULE[2] (6)), **strike while the iron is hot** (STRIKE[1] (24))

3 **iron[2]** *v* [T] to make clothes smooth using an iron〔用熨斗〕熨平: *Have you ironed my shirt?* 你把我的衬衫熨过了吗？—see also 另见 IRONING

iron sth out *phr v* [T] **1** to solve or get rid of problems or difficulties, especially small ones 消除，解决〔尤指小问题或困难〕: *We need to iron out a few operating problems first.* 我们需要先解决几个操作上的问题。| **iron out the kinks** *AmE* (=deal with small problems so that you can succeed)【美】处理小问题 *You'll need to iron out the kinks in your routine before you go on stage.* 你在登台表演之前，有必要处理那套动作中的一些小毛病。**2** to remove folds from your clothes by ironing them 用熨斗熨平〔衣褶〕

iron[3] *adj* [only before noun 仅用于名词前] very firm and strong or determined 极坚强的；极坚定的: *iron discipline* 铁的纪律

Iron Age, the /ˈ‥ ·/ the period of time about 3,000 years ago when iron was first used for making tools, weapons etc〔约 3000 年前的〕铁器时代 —compare 比较 BRONZE AGE, STONE AGE

I·ron·bridge /ˋaɪrnbrɪdʒ; ˈaɪənbrɪdʒ/ a bridge over the River Severn in Shropshire, western England, or the area surrounding it . It was the first CAST IRON bridge ever built, in 1779, and the area around the bridge was a centre of the Industrial Revolution and is now a MUSEUM. 艾恩布里奇铁桥〔位于英格兰西部什罗普郡内塞文河上的一座大桥。该桥建于1779年，为有史以来第一座铸铁大桥。该名也指大桥附近地区，那里曾为工业革命的中心，现在是一座博物馆〕

Iron Cur·tain, the /ˌ‥ ˈ‥/ the name that was used for the border between the Communist countries of Eastern Europe and the rest of Europe 铁幕〔原指东欧共产党国家与其他欧洲国家的边界〕

Iron Duke, the /ˌ‥ ˈ·/ a name sometimes used for the Duke of Wellington 铁公爵〔指威灵顿公爵〕

iron-grey *BrE*【英】, **iron-gray** *AmE*【美】/ˌ‥ ˈ·◂/ *adj* iron-grey hair is a dark grey colour 铁灰色的

i·ron·ic /aɪˋrɑnɪk; aɪˈrɒnɪk/ also 又作 **i·ron·i·cal** /-ɪkl̩; -ɪkəl/ *adj* **1** using words that are the opposite of what you really mean, especially in a joking way, or to show that you are annoyed 具有讽刺意味的〔尤指出于开玩笑或表示不快〕，讽刺的: *As the rain lashed down, my mother's one ironic comment was: "An ideal day for a wedding."* 大雨倾盆而下时，妈妈说了一句带讽刺意味的话："真是结婚的理想日子。"—compare 比较 SARCASTIC **2** an ironic situation is one in which something strange and unexpected happens, especially in a way that seems amusing〔情况〕有讽刺意味的；出乎意料的；令人啼笑皆非的: *Your car was stolen at the police station! How ironic!* 你的车在警察局被偷，真让人哭笑不得！

i·ron·i·cal·ly /aɪˋrɑnɪklɪ; aɪˈrɒnɪkli/ *adv* **1** [sentence adverb 句子副词] used when talking about a situation that seems strange, unexpected, and often amusing 具有讽刺意味的是；出乎意料的是；让人哭笑不得的是: *Ironically, his cold got better on the last day of his holiday.* 具有讽刺意味的是，他的感冒竟在假期的最后一天好了。**2** in an ironic way 用讽刺的方式: *"Oh, no problem!" said Terry, ironically.* "啊，没问题！"特里说道，很有挖苦的味道。

i·ron·ing /ˋaɪɚnɪŋ; ˈaɪənɪŋ/ *n* [U] **1** the activity of making clothes smooth with an iron 熨衣服: **do the ironing** *I hate doing the ironing.* 我讨厌熨衣服。**2** clothes that are waiting to be ironed or have just been ironed 待熨[刚熨好]的衣物

ironing board /ˈ‥ ‥ ·/ *n* [C] a small narrow table used for making clothes smooth with an iron 熨衣板

Iron La·dy, the /ˌ‥ ˈ‥/ a name that was formerly used, especially in newspapers, for Margaret Thatcher when she was the British Prime Minister. She was called this because people thought of her as a strong leader who did not change her mind easily. 铁娘子〔英国前首相玛格丽特·撒切尔在任期间的别称，尤其见于报纸。她被认为态度强硬，故得此名〕

iron lung /ˌ‥ ˈ·/ *n* [C] a large machine with a metal case that fits round your body and helps you to breathe 铁肺；人工呼吸器

i·ron·mon·ger's /ˋaɪɚnˌmʌŋgɚz; ˈaɪənˌmʌŋgəz/ *n* [singular] *BrE old-fashioned* a shop that sells equipment and tools for your home and garden【英，过时】五金商店 —**ironmongery** *n* [U]

iron 熨〔衣服〕

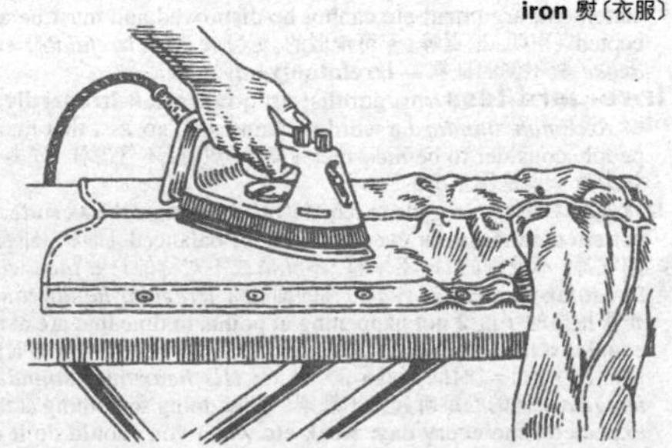

iron-on /ˈ· · ·/ *adj* labels that you can stick to your clothes using a hot iron〔标签〕可用熨烫法黏附于衣服上的

iron ra·tions /ˌ· · ˈ· ·/ *n* [plural] small amounts of high energy food, carried by soldiers, climbers etc〔士兵、登山运动员等随身携带的〕应急口粮〔即量小但能量高的食品〕

i·ron·stone /ˈaɪɚnˌston; ˈaɪənstəʊn/ *n* [U] a type of rock that contains a lot of iron 含铁矿石

i·ron·ware /ˈaɪɚnˌwɛr; ˈaɪənweə/ *n* [U] articles made of iron 铁器

i·ron·work /ˈaɪɚnˌwɝk; ˈaɪənwɜːk/ *n* [U] fences, gates and other parts of buildings made of iron bent into attractive shapes〔房屋的〕铁制构件〈如栅栏、大门等〉

i·ron·y /ˈaɪrənɪ; ˈaɪərəni/ *n* [U] **1** the use of words that are the opposite of what you really mean, in order to be amusing or to show that you are annoyed 反语: **heavy irony** (=a lot of irony) 强烈的反语 *"Of course Michael won't be late: you know how punctual he always is," she said with heavy irony.* "当然, 迈克尔不会迟到, 你知道他一贯守时。"她用强烈的讽刺口吻说道。—compare 比较 SARCASM **2** a situation that seems strange and unexpected or amusing, or the reason it is like this 具有讽刺意味[出乎意料, 令人啼笑皆非]的情况[原因]: *The tragic irony is that the drug was supposed to save lives.* 可悲的讽刺在于这药本来应该是用来挽救生命的。—see also 另见 DRAMATIC IRONY

ir·ra·di·ate /ɪˈredɪˌet; ɪˈreɪdieɪt/ *v* [T] **1** *technical* to treat someone or something with X-RAYS or similar beams【术语】用 X 射线或类似的射线来治疗[处理]: *The tomatoes are irradiated to make them stay fresh longer.* 番茄经 X 线照射后可延长保鲜期。**2** *literary* to make something look bright by shining light onto it【文】照耀; 使发光 —**irradiation** /ɪˌredɪˈeʃən; ɪˌreɪdiˈeɪʃən/ *n* [U]

ir·ra·tion·al /ɪˈræʃənḷ; ɪˈræʃənəl/ *adj* **1** irrational behaviour, feelings etc seem strange because they are not based on clear thought or reasons〔行为、感受等〕不合理的; 荒谬的: *My sister keeps telling me that my fear of flying is irrational.* 我妹妹不断对我讲害怕坐飞机是没道理的。**2** someone who is irrational tends to behave or do things without thinking clearly or without good reasons 无理性的; 失去理智的: *He's becoming increasingly irrational.* 他越来越没理智了。—**irrationally** *adv* —**irrationality** /ɪˌræʃəˈnælətɪ; ɪˌræʃəˈnæləti/ *n* [U]

ir·rec·on·cil·a·ble /ɪˈrɛkənˌsaɪləbḷ; ɪˌrekənˈsaɪləbəl◂/ *adj* irreconcilable opinions, positions etc are so strongly opposed to each other that it is not possible for them to reach an agreement〔观点、立场等〕不能一致的; 势不两立的; 不可调和的: *The differences between the Israelis and the Palestinians seemed completely irreconcilable.* 以色列人和巴勒斯坦人之间的分歧似乎完全不可调和。| **[+with]** *This belief was irreconcilable with the Church's doctrine of salvation.* 这种信仰与教会的救赎教义是不相容的。—**irreconcilably** *adv*

ir·re·cov·er·a·ble /ˌɪrɪˈkʌvərəbḷ; ˌɪrɪˈkʌvərəbəl◂/ *adj* something that is irrecoverable is lost or has gone and you cannot get it back 不能挽回的, 无法补救的: *irrecoverable costs* 无法挽回的损失 —**irrecoverably** *adv*

ir·re·deem·a·ble /ˌɪrɪˈdiməbḷ; ˌɪrɪˈdiːməbəl◂/ *adj* **1** *especially literary* too bad to be corrected or repaired【尤文】〔因太坏、太糟而〕无法补救的; 不可救药的 **2** *technical* irredeemable STOCK[1] (3) cannot be exchanged for money【术语】〔证券〕不能偿还的; 不可赎回的 —**irredeemably** *adv*: *irredeemably wicked* 邪恶透顶

ir·re·du·ci·ble /ˌɪrɪˈdjusəbḷ; ˌɪrɪˈdjuːsəbəl◂/ *adj* an irreducible sum, level etc cannot be made smaller or simpler〔金额、水平等〕不能缩减的; 不能简化的 —**irreducibly** *adv*

ir·re·fu·ta·ble /ˌɪrɪˈfjutəbḷ; ˌɪrɪˈfjuːtəbəl◂/ *adj* an irrefutable statement, argument etc cannot be disproved and must be accepted〔声明、论点等〕无可辩驳的; 必须接受的: *irrefutable evidence* 驳不倒的证据 —**irrefutably** *adv*

ir·re·gard·less /ˌɪrɪˈgardlɪs; ˌɪrɪˈgɑːdləs/ *adv* **irregardless of** *AmE non-standard* a word meaning REGARDLESS, that many people consider to be incorrect【美, 不规范】不管怎样〔许多人认为这个词是不正确的〕

ir·reg·u·lar[1] /ɪˈrɛgjələ·; ɪˈregjələ/ *adj* **1** having a shape, surface, pattern etc that is not even, smooth, or balanced〔形状、外表、图案等〕不规则的〔即不平整、不光滑或不对称的〕: *a face with irregular features* 五官不匀称的面孔 | *irregular handwriting* 歪歪扭扭的字迹 **2** not happening at points in time that are at an equal distance from each other 无规律的〔即不是按同样的时间间隔发生的〕,〔时间〕间隔不一致的: *His heartbeat sounded irregular.* 他的心跳听起来不规则。**3** not doing something at the expected time every day, week etc when you should do it or when something normally happens〔做事〕不按时的, 不定期的: *Jason's attendance at school has been somewhat irregular.* 贾森一直是不定期地上学。| *irregular meals* 吃饭不定时 **4** *formal* not obeying the usually accepted legal or moral rules【正式】不合法的; 不合道德规范的: **highly irregular** (=extremely irregular) 极不合常规的; 极不道德的 *It would be highly irregular for a minister to accept payments of this kind.* 身为部长接受这类报酬是极不合法的。**5 irregular word/verb/plural etc** a word etc that does not follow the usual pattern of grammar〔语法中〕不规则的词/动词/复数形式等: *'Go' is an irregular verb.* go 是不规则动词。**6** *AmE* a word meaning CONSTIPATED (=unable to pass food waste from your body) used when you want to avoid saying this directly【美】便秘的〔委婉的用法〕—**irregularly** *adv* —**irregularity** /ɪˌrɛgjəˈlærətɪ; ɪˌregjəˈlærəti/ *n* [C,U]: *He lived a life of complete irregularity.* 他的生活一点规律都没有。

irregular[2] *n* [C] a soldier who is not an official member of a country's army 非正规军人

ir·rel·e·vance /ɪˈrɛləvəns; ɪˈreləvəns/ also 又作 **ir·rel·evan·cy** /-vənsɪ; -vənsi/ *n* **1** [U] a lack of importance in a particular situation 不相干; 无关紧要: *The irrelevance of his remark irritated her.* 他那些不相干的话让她很恼火。**2** [C] someone or something that is not important in a particular situation 无关紧要的人[物]

ir·rel·e·vant /ɪˈrɛləvənt; ɪˈreləvənt/ *adj* **1** something that is irrelevant is not important because it is not connected with the situation or subject that you are dealing with, or it has no effect or influence on a situation 不重要的; 不相干的: *Age is irrelevant if he can do the job.* 如果他能做好这个工作, 年龄是无关紧要的。| **[+to]** *Her comments seemed irrelevant to the real issue.* 她的评论似乎与问题的实质没有关联。**2** having no real or useful purpose 没用的, 没意义的: *Students viewed Latin as boring and irrelevant.* 学生们认为拉丁语枯燥无用。—**irrelevantly** *adv*

ir·re·li·gious /ˌɪrɪˈlɪdʒəs; ˌɪrɪˈlɪdʒəs◂/ *adj formal* opposed to religion or not having any religious feeling【正式】反宗教的; 无宗教信仰的

ir·re·me·di·a·ble /ˌɪrɪˈmidɪəbḷ; ˌɪrɪˈmiːdiəbəl◂/ *adj formal* so bad that it is impossible to make it better【正式】不可救药的; 无法纠正的 —**irremediably** *adv*

ir·rep·a·ra·ble /ɪˈrɛpərəbḷ; ɪˈrepərəbəl/ *adj* irreparable damage, harm etc is so bad that it can never be repaired or made better〔破坏、伤害等〕不能修复的; 无法弥补的: *irreparable damage to his heart* 对他的心脏造成永久的伤害 —**irreparably** *adv*

ir·re·place·a·ble /ˌɪrɪˈplesəbḷ; ˌɪrɪˈpleɪsəbəl◂/ *adj* too special, valuable, or unusual to be replaced by anything else〔因特别或贵重而〕独一无二的; 不可代替的: *the loss of several great works of art, many of them irreplaceable* 几件伟大艺术品的丢失, 其中不少是举世无双的

ir·re·pres·si·ble /ˌɪrɪˈprɛsəbḷ; ˌɪrɪˈpresəbəl◂/ *adj* full of energy, confidence, and happiness so that you never seem unhappy〔精力、信心、快乐〕压抑不住的; 控制不了的: *an irrepressible optimist* 精力充沛的乐观主义者 —**irrepressibly** *adv*

ir·re·proach·a·ble /ˌɪrɪˈprotʃəbḷ; ˌɪrɪˈprəʊtʃəbəl◂/ *adj formal* something such as someone's behaviour that is irreproachable is so good that you cannot criticize it【正式】〔行为等〕无可指责的; 无可挑剔的 —**irreproachably** *adv*

ir·re·sis·ti·ble /ˌɪrɪˈzɪstəbḷ; ˌɪrɪˈzɪstəbəl◂/ *adj* **1** so attractive, desirable etc that you cannot prevent yourself from wanting it 无法抗拒的; 富有诱惑力的: *Chocolate is irresistible for a lot of people.* 巧克力的诱惑力对于许多人来说是无法抗拒的。| **find sb/sth irresistible** *Men find Natalie irresistible.* 男人们觉得无法抗拒纳塔莉的魅力。**2** too strong or powerful to be stopped or prevented〔力量太大而〕不可抗拒的; 不可避免的: *I had an irresistible urge to kiss him!* 我有一种抑制不住的欲望要亲吻他! —**irresistibly** *adv*

ir·res·o·lute /ɪˈrɛzəˌlut; ɪˈrezəluːt/ *adj formal* unable to decide what to do; uncertain【正式】没有决断力的; 犹豫不决的 —**irresolutely** *adv* —**irresolution** /ɪˌrɛzəˈluʃən; ɪˌrezəˈluːʃən/ *n* [U]

ir·re·spec·tive /ˌɪrɪˈspɛktɪv; ˌɪrɪˈspektɪv/ *adv* **irrespective of** used when saying that a particular fact such as someone's age or race, something's size etc has no effect on a situation and is not important 不顾…; 不考虑…; 不问…〔用来表示某事实, 如年龄、种族、某物的大小等, 对某事没有影响, 不重要〕: *The course is open to anyone irrespective of age.* 这门课没有年龄限制。

ir·re·spon·si·ble /ˌɪrɪˈspɑnsəbḷ; ˌɪrɪˈspɒnsəbəl◂/ *adj* doing careless things without thinking or worrying about the possible bad results 不负责任的: **be (highly) irresponsible of sb to do sth** *It was highly irresponsible of him to leave the children on*

their own in the pool. 他把孩子单独留在游泳池里，真是太不负责任了。—**irresponsibly** *adv* —**irresponsibility** /ˌɪrɪˌspɑnsəˋbɪlətɪ; ˌɪrɪspɒnsəˈbɪlɪti/ *n* [U]

ir·re·trie·va·ble /ˌɪrɪˋtrivəbl; ˌɪrɪˈtriːvəbəl◂/ *adj formal*【正式】**1** an irretrievable situation cannot be made right again 不能挽回的；无法复原的：*the irretrievable breakdown of their marriage* 他们无法挽救的婚姻 **2 irretrievable loss** the loss of something that you can never get back 不可弥补的损失 —**irretrievably** *adv*: *irretrievably lost* 永远的失去

ir·rev·e·rent /ɪˋrɛvərənt; ɪˈrevərənt/ *adj* having a lack of respect for organizations, customs, beliefs etc〔对组织、习俗、信仰等〕不尊敬的；不恭的：*an irreverent laugh* 无礼的一笑 —**irreverently** *adv* —**irreverence** *n* [U]

ir·re·ver·si·ble /ˌɪrɪˋvɝsəbl; ˌɪrɪˈvɜːsəbəl◂/ *adj* **irreversible damage/change/decline etc** damage, change etc that is so serious or so great that you cannot change something back to how it was before 不可挽回的损失／不可逆转的变化／不可逆转的衰退等 —**irreversibly** *adv*

ir·rev·o·ca·ble /ɪˋrɛvəkəbl; ɪˈrevəkəbəl/ *adj* an irrevocable decision, action etc cannot be changed or stopped〔决定、行动等〕不可更改的，不可取消的；不可撤回的 —**irrevocably** *adv*: *machines that irrevocably changed the pattern of rural life* 使农村生活模式发生不可逆转的变化的机器

ir·ri·gate /ˋɪrəˌget; ˈɪrəgeɪt/ *v* [T] **1** to supply land or crops with water 灌溉〔土地或庄稼〕**2** *technical* to wash a wound with a flow of liquid【术语】冲洗〔伤口〕—**irrigation** /ˌɪrəˋgeʃən; ˌɪrəˈgeɪʃən/ *n* [U]

ir·ri·ta·ble /ˋɪrətəbl; ˈɪrətəbəl/ *adj* **1** getting annoyed quickly or easily 易怒的：*Jo was tired, irritable, and depressed.* 乔疲惫、急躁而且情绪低落。**2** *technical* very sensitive and sore【术语】过敏的；红肿的；疼痛的：*irritable skin* 过敏的皮肤 —**irritably** *adv* —**irritability** /ˌɪrətəˋbɪlətɪ; ˌɪrətəˈbɪləti/ *n* [U]

ir·ri·tant /ˋɪrətənt; ˈɪrətənt/ *n* [C] **1** something that makes you feel annoyed over a period of time 使人〔在某段时间内〕烦躁的事物：*Low flying aircraft are a constant irritant in this area.* 低空飞行的飞机使这个地区终日不得安宁。**2** a substance that can make a part of your body painful and sore〔使身体某部分肿痛的〕刺激物

ir·ri·tate /ˋɪrəˌtet; ˈɪrəteɪt/ *v* [T] **1** to make someone feel annoyed or impatient over a long period, especially by repeatedly doing something〔尤指不断重复做某事而〕使〔人长期〕烦躁；激怒 **2** to make a part of your body painful and sore 使〔身体的一部分〕疼痛：*This cream may irritate sensitive skin.* 这种润肤霜对过敏性皮肤可能有刺激。

ir·ri·tat·ed /ˋɪrəˌtetɪd; ˈɪrəteɪtəd/ *adj* **1** feeling annoyed and impatient about something 恼火的；急躁的：**[+about/at/with/by]** *John was irritated by the necessity for polite conversation.* 约翰对于必须彬彬有礼地谈话很不耐烦。**2** painful and sore 疼痛的；发炎的

ir·ri·tat·ing /ˋɪrəˌtetɪŋ; ˈɪrəteɪtɪŋ/ *adj* an irritating habit, situation etc is annoying〔习惯、情况等〕烦人的；使人不快的：*She has an irritating habit of interrupting everything you say.* 她有一个很烦人的习惯：你说什么她都打断你。—**irritatingly** *adv*

ir·ri·ta·tion /ˌɪrəˋteʃən; ˌɪrəˈteɪʃən/ *n* **1** [U] the feeling of being annoyed about something, especially something annoying that happens repeatedly or for a long time 烦恼〔尤指反复发生或持续很长一段时间的事〕，不快：*Newspaper reports of yet more scandals are a constant source of irritation for the government.* 报纸上登载的丑闻接二连三，使政府的烦恼连续不断。**2** [C] something that makes you annoyed 令人气恼的事物：*The children are just an irritation for him when he's trying to work.* 他在工作，孩子们来捣乱。**3** [U] a painful, sore feeling on a part of your body〔身体某部位的〕疼痛：*irritation of the skin* 皮肤疼痛

ir·rup·tion /ɪˋrʌpʃən; ɪˈrʌpʃən/ *n* [C] *formal* a sudden rush of people into a place【正式】〔人〕突然涌入：*an irruption of the audience onto the stage* 观众突然拥到台上

Irvine, Andrew —see 见 George MALLORY

Ir·ving /ˋɝvɪŋ; ˈɜːvɪŋ/, **Washington** (1783-1859) a US writer known especially for his stories set in New York at the time when it was ruled by the Dutch. His two most famous stories are *Rip Van Winkle*, about a man who falls asleep for 20 years, and *The Legend of Sleepy Hollow*, about a teacher who meets a 'headless horseman'. 欧文〔(1783-1859)，美国作家。他创作的以荷兰人统治时期的纽约为背景的小说尤为有名。最著名的两部作品是《瑞普·范·温克尔》和《睡谷的传说》。前者讲述一名昏睡20年的男子的故事，后者讲述一名教师遇见"无头骑士"的故事〕

is /s, z; s, z *strong* 强读 ɪz; ɪz/ the third person singular of the present tense of BE 动词 be 的第三人称单数现在式

ISA *n* Individual Saving Account; a type of savings account in Britain on which you do not have to pay tax 个人储蓄账户〔英国的一种免税储蓄账户〕

I·saac /ˋaɪzək; ˈaɪzək/ in the Old Testament of the Bible, the son of Abraham and the father of Jacob and Esau 以撒〔《圣经·旧约》中亚伯拉罕之子，雅各和以扫之父〕

I·sai·ah /aɪˋzaɪə; aɪˈzaɪə/ (8th century BC) in the Jewish and Christian religions, a Hebrew PROPHET who said that God would send a MESSIAH to save the Jews. The *Book of Isaiah* in the Old Testament of the Bible contains his prophecies (PROPHECY). 以赛亚〔(公元前8世纪)，犹太教和基督教中的希伯来先知。他预言上帝将派救世主弥赛亚来拯救犹太人。《圣经·旧约·以赛亚书》中有他的预言〕

-i·sa·tion /əzeʃən; aɪzeɪʃən/ *suffix* a British spelling of -IZATION -ization 的英式拼法

ISBN /ˌaɪ ɛs bi ˋɛn; ˌaɪ es biː ˈen/ *n* a number that is given to every book 国际标准图书编号

Is·car·i·ot, Judas —see 见 JUDAS

-ise /aɪz; aɪz/ *suffix* [in verbs 构成动词] a British spelling of -IZE -ize 的英式拼法

-ish /ɪʃ; ɪʃ/ *suffix* **1** [in nouns 构成名词] the people or language of a particular country or place〔某国或某地的〕人[语言]：*Are the British unfriendly?* 英国人不友善吗？| *learning to speak Turkish* 学说土耳其语 | *She's Swedish.* 她是瑞典人。**2** [in adjectives 构成形容词] of a particular place 某地方的：*Spanish food* (=from Spain) 西班牙食品 **3** [in adjectives 构成形容词] typical of or like a particular type of person 属于[类似]某种类型的人的：*foolish behaviour* (=typical of a fool) 愚蠢的行为 | *Don't be so childish!* (=Don't behave like a child) 别这么孩子气！| *snobbish* 势利的 **4** [in adjectives 构成形容词] the ending of some adjectives that show disapproval〔作为一些形容词的后缀表示贬义〕：*selfish* 自私的 | *raffish* 粗俗的 **5** [in adjectives 构成形容词] rather; quite 相当：*youngish* (=not very young, but not old either) 还算年轻 | *tallish* 个子略高的 | *reddish hair* 浅红色的头发 **6** [in adjectives 构成形容词] *spoken* about; **approximately** (APPROXIMATE[1])【口】大约，大致：*We'll expect you eightish.* (=at about 8 o'clock) 我们希望你8点左右来。| *He's fortyish.* (=about 40 years old) 他大约40岁。

I·sis /ˋaɪsəs; ˈaɪsəs/ in ancient Egyptian MYTHOLOGY, the most important GODDESS. She was the goddess of nature and was also the wife and sister of Osiris. 伊希斯〔古埃及神话中地位最高的女神。她是大自然女神，也是俄赛里斯的妻子和妹妹〕

Is·lam /ˋɪsləm; ˈɪslɑːm/ *n* [U] **1** the Muslim religion, which was started by Muhammad and whose holy book is the Koran 伊斯兰教〔由穆罕默德创立，经典是《古兰经》〕**2** the people and countries that follow this religion 伊斯兰教徒；伊斯兰教国家 —**Islamist** *n* [C] —**Islamic** /ɪzˋlæmɪk; ɪzˈlæmɪk/ *adj*

Is·lam·a·bad /ɪzˋlɑməbæd; ɪzˈlɑːməbæd/ the capital city of Pakistan 伊斯兰堡〔巴基斯坦首都〕

Is·lam·ic Ji·had /ɪzˌlæmɪk dʒɪˋhɑd; ɪsˌlæmɪk dʒɪˈhæd/ an Islamic organization that supports Palestinian independence 伊斯兰圣战组织〔支持巴勒斯坦独立的一个伊斯兰组织〕

is·land /ˋaɪlənd; ˈaɪlənd/ *n* [C] [W2] **1** a piece of land completely surrounded by water 岛屿：*a small island in the middle of the lake* 湖中央的小岛 | *the Hawaiian Islands* 夏威夷群岛 —see also 另见 DESERT ISLAND **2** a place that is different in some way from the area that surrounds it〔与周围地区不尽相同的〕地方，处所：**an island of peace/calm etc** *The park is an island of peace in the noisy city.* 在这座喧嚣的城市中，这个公园是一块宁静的地方。

island 岛

is·land·er /ˋaɪləndɚ; ˈaɪləndə/ *n* [C] someone who lives on an island 岛民，岛上居民

Is·lay /ˋaɪlə; ˈaɪlə/ an island off the west coast of Scotland and one of the Inner Hebrides. It has many distilleries (DISTILLERY), where WHISKY is made. 艾莱岛〔与苏格兰西海岸隔海相望的一个岛屿，属于内赫布里底群岛。该地有不少威士忌酒厂〕

isle /aɪl; aɪl/ *n* [C] a word for an island, used in poetry or in names of islands 岛〔用于诗歌或岛名〕：*the Scilly Isles* 锡利群岛

Isle of Dogs, the /ˌ··ˈ·/ an area of East London, surrounded on three sides by the River Thames. It used to be a very WORKING-CLASS area, with a lot of industry and DOCKS (=places where ships are loaded). But it is now part of Docklands and there are a lot of new houses and offices there. 多格斯岛〔东伦敦一地区，三面临泰晤士河。这里曾是一个十足的工人阶级地区，有不少工厂和码头。现在属船坞区，新建有不少住宅和办公楼〕

Isle of Man, the /ˌ· ·ˈ·/ also 又作 **Man** an island in the Irish Sea. It is under British control, but has its own parliament, the Tynwald, and its own laws. Many rich British people live there or keep their money there because taxes are lower than in the UK. A well-known series of MOTOR-CYCLE races called the **TT** (Tourist Trophy) races is held in the Isle of Man every year. The adjective for describing people or things from the Isle of Man is **Manx**. 马恩岛〔爱尔兰海一岛, 属于英国, 但有独立的议会(即马恩岛议会)和法律。英国不少富人在此居住或把钱存在这里, 因为当地的税率比英国低。该岛每年举办著名的摩托车系列赛事"旅游杯赛"。描述该岛的人或事物的形容词为Manx〕

Isle of Wight abbreviation 缩写为 **IOW** an island off the coast of southern England and an English COUNTY. It is a popular place for English families to go to on holiday and for people who enjoy sailing. 怀特岛〔与英格兰南部海岸隔海相望的一个岛屿。该岛为英格兰一郡, 是英格兰人家庭出游和帆船运动爱好者的好去处〕

is·let /ˈaɪlɪt; ˈaɪlɪ̣t/ *n* [C] a very small island 小岛

Is·ling·ton /ˈɪzlɪŋtən; ˈɪzlɪŋtən/ a BOROUGH of northeast London, where many MIDDLE-CLASS people live 伊斯灵顿〔伦敦东北部一区。许多中产阶级在此居住〕

is·m /ˈɪzəm; ˈɪzəm/ *n* [C] *informal* used to describe a set of ideas or beliefs whose name ends in 'ism', especially when you think that they are not sensible or practical【非正式】主义, 学说〔用来称呼名称以 ism 结尾的思想或信仰, 尤指你认为这种理论不合理或不实际〕

-ism /ɪzəm; ɪzəm/ *suffix* [in nouns 构成名词] **1** a political belief or religion based on a particular principle or the teachings of a particular person 政治信仰; 宗教: *socialism* 社会主义 | *Buddhism* 佛教 **2** the action or process of doing something〔做某事的〕行为[过程]: *his criticism of my work* (=he CRITICIZES it) 他对我工作的批评 **3** an action or remark that has a particular quality 具有某种特征的行为[评论]: *her witticisms* (=funny or WITTY remarks) 她诙谐[俏皮]的评论 **4** the state of being like something or someone, or having a particular quality 像某物[某人]; 具有某种特征: *heroism* (=being a HERO; bravery) 英雄气概 | *magnetism* (=being MAGNETIC) 磁性 **5** illness caused by too much of something 由于某物过多而引起的疾病: *alcoholism* 酗酒 **6** the practice of treating people unfairly because of something 歧视: *sexism* (=making unfair differences between men and women) 性别歧视 | *racism* 种族歧视 | *heightism* (=against people who are very tall or short) 身高歧视

is·n't /ˈɪzṇt; ˈɪzənt/ the short form of 缩略式= 'is not'

ISO /ˌaɪ ɛs ˈo; ˌaɪ es ˈəʊ/ *trademark* International Standards Organization; an international organization which sets standards for the size, shape, and technical features of industrial goods, electrical products etc. ISO has members in more than 70 countries.【商标】国际标准化组织〔制定工业品、电器等产品的规格、形状和技术标准的一个国际组织, 其成员遍及70多个国家〕

iso- /aɪso; aɪsəʊ/ *prefix technical* the same all through or in every part; equal【术语】同; 等: *an isotherm* (=line joining places of equal temperature) 等温线

i·so·bar /ˈaɪsəˌbɑr; ˈaɪsəbɑː/ *n technical* a line on a weather map joining places where the air pressure is the same【术语】〔气象图上的〕等压线

i·so·late /ˈaɪsḷˌet; ˈaɪsəleɪt/ *v* [T] **1** to prevent a country, political group etc from getting support from other countries or groups etc, so that it becomes weaker 孤立〔国家或政治团体等〕: *The US has sought to isolate Cuba both economically and politically.* 美国一直想在经济和政治上孤立古巴。**2** *technical* to separate a substance, disease etc from other substances so that it can be studied【术语】分离〔物质、疾病等以作研究〕: **[+from]** *The hepatitis B virus has been isolated from breast milk.* 乙型肝炎病毒已从母乳中分离出来。**3** to separate an idea, word, problem etc so that it can be examined or dealt with by itself 分离〔观点、单词、问题等〕: **isolate sth from** *It is impossible to isolate political responsibility from moral responsibility.* 不可能把政治责任与道德责任分离开来。**4** to make someone feel separate from other people in a society or group, and make them feel lonely or unhappy〔在社会、团体中〕使〔某人〕孤立: **isolate sb from** *Presley's phenomenal early success isolated him from his friends.* 普雷斯利年纪轻轻便成就超群, 这使他在朋友圈中陷于孤立。**5** to make a place separate from other places so that people cannot enter it 使某地与其他地方隔离: *villages which have been isolated by recent flooding* 由于不久前的洪水而与外界隔绝的村庄 **6** to keep someone separate from other people, especially because they have a disease 把〔某人, 尤指病人〕与其他人隔离: **isolate sb from** *New-born babies must be isolated from possible contamination.* 新生儿必须隔离, 以免受感染。

i·so·lat·ed /ˈaɪsḷˌetɪd; ˈaɪsəleɪtɪ̣d/ *adj* **1** an isolated building, village etc is far away from any others〔建筑物、村庄等〕孤零零的; 偏僻的: *Not many people visit this isolated spot.* 没有多少人来这个偏僻的地方。**2** feeling alone and unable to meet or speak to other people〔人〕孤单的: *Young mothers often feel isolated and cut off from the rest of the world.* 年轻的母亲们常常感到孤独, 好像与外界失去了联系。**3** an isolated action, event, example etc happens only once, and is not likely to happen again〔行动、事件、例子等〕孤立的; 个别的: **an isolated incident/episode** *Police say that last week's protest was an isolated incident.* 警方说上周的抗议是个别的事件。

i·so·la·tion /ˌaɪsḷˈeʃən; ˌaɪsəˈleɪʃən/ *n* [U] **1** the state of being completely separate from any other place, group etc 隔离; 孤立; 分离: *Because of its geographical isolation, the area developed its own unique culture.* 由于地理位置的隔绝, 该地区发展了自己独特的文化。**2** a feeling of being lonely and unable to meet or speak to other people 孤独; 孤单: *Retirement can often cause feelings of isolation.* 退休生活常让人感到孤独。**3 in isolation** if something exists or is considered in isolation, it exists or is considered separately from other things that are connected with it 孤立地: *Taken in isolation, these events have no particular significance, but there is, in fact, an underlying pattern.* 孤立地看, 这些事件毫无特殊意义, 但事实上却有一个潜在的模式。**4** the act of deliberately separating one group, person, or thing from others〔故意把一个团体、人或物体〕隔离; 孤立: *isolation of political prisoners* 对政治犯的隔离

i·so·la·tion·is·m /ˌaɪsḷˈeʃənɪzəm; ˌaɪsəˈleɪʃənɪzəm/ *n* [U] a disapproving word for beliefs or actions that are based on the political principle that your country should not be involved in the affairs of other countries 孤立主义〔用于指信仰或行为的贬义词, 指一个国家不应卷入其他国家的事务〕—**isolationist** *n* [C] —**isolationist** *adj*

isolation pe·ri·od /·ˈ·· ˌ···/ *n* [C] the period of time that someone with an infectious illness needs to be kept apart from other people〔传染病患者的〕隔离期

I·sol·de /ɪˈzoldə; ɪˈzɒldə/ —see 见 TRISTAN AND ISOLDE

i·so·met·rics /ˌaɪsəˈmɛtrɪks; ˌaɪsəˈmetrɪks/ *n* [plural] exercises that make your muscles stronger by pushing against each other 等长收缩肌肉锻炼法〔一种以互推动作来增强肌肉的运动〕

i·sos·ce·les tri·an·gle /aɪˈsɑsḷˌiz ˈtraɪæŋgḷ; aɪˌsɒsəliːz ˈtraɪæŋgəl/ *n* [C] a three-sided shape in which two of the sides are the same length 等腰三角形 —compare 比较 EQUILATERAL TRIANGLE, SCALENE TRIANGLE —see picture at 参见 SHAPE[1] 图

i·so·therm /ˈaɪsəˌθɜm; ˈaɪsəθɜːm/ *n* [C] *technical* a line on a weather map joining places where the temperature is the same【术语】〔气象图上的〕等温线, 恒温线

i·so·tope /ˈaɪsəˌtop; ˈaɪsətəʊp/ *n* [C] *technical* one of the possible different forms of an atom of a particular ELEMENT (=simple chemical substance)【术语】同位素

Is·rael /ˈɪzrɪəl; ˈɪzreɪl/ a country on the eastern side of the Mediterranean Sea. It is situated at the connection of Asia, Africa and Europe. Population: 6,631,000 (2002). Israel was established in 1948 as a home for the Jewish people. It has no formal written constitution. The official languages are Hebrew and Arabic. Most of the people believe in Judaism. 以色列〔地中海东岸一国。位于亚、非、欧三大洲结合处。人口: 6,631,000 (2002)。1948年作为犹太人家园而建国。该国无正式成文宪法。希伯来语和阿拉伯语为官方语言。居民大多信奉犹太教〕

Is·rae·li /ɪzˈrelɪ; ɪzˈreɪli/ *n* [C] someone from Israel 以色列人

Is·rael·ite /ˈɪzrɪəlˌaɪt; ˈɪzrəlaɪt/ *n, adj* (in the Bible) (a person) of the ancient kingdom of Israel 古以色列人; 〔《圣经》中〕古以色列王国的

is·sue[1] /ˈɪʃu; ˈɪʃuː/ *n*

1 ►SUBJECT/PROBLEM 话题/问题◄ [C] a problem or subject that people discuss 问题; 议题: *Drugs testing of employees is a sensitive issue.* 对雇员进行毒品检测是个敏感问题。| *the immigration issue* 移民问题 | **raise the issue** (=say that a problem should be discussed) 提出问题〔表示该问题需要讨论〕 *We should raise the issue of discrimination with the council.* 我们应向委员会提出讨论歧视问题。| **sth is not the issue** *spoken* (=used to say that something is not the important part of what you are discussing)【口】某事不是谈论的主要问题 *Unemployment is not the issue – the real problem is the decline in public morality.* 失业不是主要问题, 真正的问题是公众道德水准的下降。| **not be an issue** (=not be a problem) 不是问题 *I just got a raise, so money's no longer an issue.* 我刚加了薪, 所以钱不再是问题了。| **avoid/dodge/duck/evade the issue** (=avoid discussing a problem or subject) 逃避讨论某问题[某话题] *When asked about the bill, the senator tried to duck the issue.* 当问及

这项议案时, 参议员试图回避这个问题。| **confuse/cloud the issue** (=make a problem or subject more difficult by talking about things that are not directly connected with it) 把问题搞乱, 把问题搞得模糊不清: *clouding the issue with uninformed judgements* 以缺乏根据的判断把问题弄得模糊不清 | **what's the big issue?** *spoken* (=used when you do not think that something is a problem and you cannot understand why people are worried or arguing)【口】有什么大不了的〔用于表示你认为某事不是问题, 不明白为什么其他人担心或争论〕

2 ▶MAGAZINE 杂志◀ [C] a magazine or newspaper printed for a particular day, week, or month〔杂志、报纸的〕期; 号: *the latest issue of Vogue* 最新一期的《时尚》

3 at issue the problem or subject at issue is the most important part of what you are discussing or considering 问题的焦点: *What is at issue is the extent to which exam results reflect a student's ability.* 问题的关键是, 考试成绩在多大程度上反映学生的能力。

4 take issue with to disagree or argue with someone about something〔向某人对某事〕提出异议: *It is difficult to take issue with his analysis.* 对他的分析很难有不同看法。

5 make an issue (out) of sth to argue about something, especially in a way that annoys other people because they do not think it is important 挑起争端〔尤指对方认为是小题大做〕: *I was upset by Eleanor's remarks, but decided not to make an issue of it.* 我对埃莉诺的话很恼火, 但还是决定不去理会她。

6 ▶SET OF THINGS FOR SALE 待售之物◀ [C] a new set of something such as shares (SHARE² (5)) or stamps, made available for people to buy〔新股票或邮票的〕发行: *a new issue of bonds* 新发行的债券

7 ▶ACT OF GIVING STH 给予某物◀ [singular] the act of officially giving people something to use〔正式〕发给; 分配: *the issue of identity cards to all non-residents* 向所有无定居身份的居民发放身份证

8 die without issue *old use and law* to die without having any children【旧和法律】死后无嗣

2 **issue²** *v* [T] **1** to officially make a statement, give an order, warning etc 发表〔声明〕; 颁布; 发出〔命令、警告等〕: *Silva issued a statement denying all knowledge of the affair.* 席尔瓦发表声明, 宣称对此事一无所知。| *a warning issued by the Surgeon General*〔美国〕卫生局局长发出的警告 **2** to provide something for each member of a group 分给〔团体中每个成员〕; 配发: **issue sb with** *All the workers were issued with protective clothing.* 所有工人都配发了防护服。**3** to officially produce something such as new stamps, coins, or shares (SHARE² (5)) and make them available for people to buy 正式发行〔新邮票、硬币、股票等〕

issue forth *phr v* [I] *literary* to go or come out of a place【文】〔从某处〕发出: *A low grunt issued forth from his throat.* 他喉咙里发出一阵低沉的咕哝声。

issue from *phr v* [T] *formal* if something, especially a sound or liquid, issues from somewhere, it comes out of it【正式】〔尤指声音或液体〕来自, 产生于: *Smoke issued from the factory chimneys.* 烟从工厂烟囱中冒出。

-ist /ɪst; ɪ̠st/ *suffix* **1** [in nouns 构成名词] someone who believes in a particular religion or set of principles or ideas〔某宗教、主义的〕信仰者: *a Buddhist* 佛教徒 | *a Scottish Nationalist* 苏格兰民族党党员 **2** [in adjectives 构成形容词] connected with or showing a particular political or religious belief 与某政治[宗教]信仰有关的; 显示某政治[宗教]信仰的: *her socialist views* 她的社会主义观点 | *He's very rightist.* (=supports the political RIGHT³ (4b)) 他是个极右派。**3** [in nouns 构成名词] someone who studies a particular subject, plays a particular instrument or does a particular type of work〔某学科的〕研究者;〔某乐器的〕演奏者;〔某工作的〕从事者: *a linguist* (=someone who studies or learns languages) 语言学家 | *a novelist* (=someone who writes NOVELS) 小说家 | *a guitarist* (=someone who plays the GUITAR) 吉他手 | *a machinist* (=someone who operates a machine) 机械师 —see also 另见 -OLOGIST **4** [in adjectives 构成形容词] treating people unfairly because of something 歧视的: *a very sexist remark* (=making unfair differences between men and women) 严重的性别歧视言论 **5** [in nouns 构成名词] someone who treats people unfairly because of something 歧视分子: *They're a bunch of racists.* 他们是一群种族歧视分子。

Is·tan·bul /ˌɪstæn'bʊl; ˌɪstæn'bʊl/ a large city and port in northwest Turkey, at the point where Europe joins Asia. From 330 AD to 1923 it was called Constantinople, and before that it was known as Byzantium. It is the largest city in Turkey, but it is not the capital city (which is Ankara). 伊斯坦布尔〔土耳其西北部一大城市, 港口, 位于欧亚交界处。公元330至1923年间称君士坦丁堡, 之前称拜占庭。它是土耳其最大的城市, 但并非首都(土耳其首都为安卡拉)〕

isth·mus /'ɪsməs; 'ɪsməs/ *n* [C] a narrow piece of land with water on both sides, that connects two larger areas of land 地峡: *the Isthmus of Panama* 巴拿马地峡

IT /ˌaɪ 'tiː; ˌaɪ 'tiː/ *n* [U] the study or use of electronic processes for storing information and making it available; INFORMATION TECHNOLOGY 信息技术

it /ɪt; ɪt/ *pron* [used as subject or object 用作主语或宾语] **1** used to talk about the thing, situation, idea etc that has already been mentioned or that the person you are talking to already knows about 它, 这, 那〔指已经提及或已为对方所知晓的事物、情况、想法等〕: *"What should I do with the key?" "Oh just leave it on the table."* "这把钥匙我怎么办?" "噢, 把它放在桌子上就可以了。" | *There were people crying, buildings on fire. It was terrible!* 有人在哭喊, 楼房在燃烧。太可怕了! | *She complained about the food so much that I was sorry I mentioned it in the end.* 她对食物如此不满, 因此我对自己最后提到食物感到十分抱歉。**2** the situation that someone is in now〔指某人目前所处的境况〕: *I can't stand it any longer. I'm resigning.* 我再也忍受不了了, 我要辞职。| *How's it going Bob? I haven't seen you for ages.* 鲍勃, 近况如何? 我们好久不见了。| *And the worst of it is the car isn't even paid for yet.* 最糟糕的是这辆车子还没有付钱。**3** used as the subject or object of a verb when the real subject or object is later in the sentence〔用作动词的主语或宾语, 而真正的主语或宾语置于句子的后部〕: *It makes me sick the way she thinks everyone's in love with her.* 她以为人人都喜欢她, 这真让我恶心。| *What's it like being a sailor?* 当水手是什么滋味? | *Apparently it's cheaper to fly than go by train.* 显然, 乘飞机比坐火车便宜。| *It's a pity you couldn't come.* 你来不了, 真遗憾。**4** used with the verb 'be' to make statements about the weather, the time, distances etc〔与动词be连用来构成句子, 表明天气、时间、距离等〕: *It's over 200 miles from London to Manchester.* 从伦敦到曼彻斯特有二百多英里。| *It was 4 o'clock and the mail still hadn't come.* 4点钟了, 邮件还没到。| *It had obviously been snowing but none of it stuck to the ground.* 显然曾经下过雪, 但地上并没有积雪。| *Can you believe she's forgotten it's my birthday today?* 你相信她忘了今天是我的生日吗? **5** used to emphasize that one piece of information in a sentence is more important than the rest〔用来强调句子里的某条信息比其他部分重要〕: *It was Jane who paid for the meal yesterday.* (=it was Jane and not another person) 昨天是简付饭钱的。| *It was the meal that Jane paid for yesterday.* (=it was a meal and not something else) 简昨天付的是饭钱。| *It was yesterday that Jane paid for the meal.* (=it was yesterday and not at another time) 简是昨天付饭钱的。**6** used as the subject of 'seem', 'appear', 'look' and 'happen'〔用作 seem, appear, look 和 happen 的主语〕: *It seems that no one really knows where he's gone.* 似乎没有人真正知道他去了哪里。| *Since it happened to be such a nice day they thought they'd go to the beach.* 既然碰巧赶上一个好天气, 他们觉得应当去海边。**7** used to talk about a child or an animal when you do not know what sex they are〔用来指性别不明的孩子或动物〕: *What will you call it if it's a boy?* 要是男孩的话, 你想给他取个什么名字? **8 a) it's me/John/a car etc** used to give the name of a person or thing when it is not already known 是我/约翰/一辆汽车等〔用来表明某人或某物的名字[名称]〕: *"Who was that at the door?" "It was a man selling house insurance."* "门口那个人是谁?" "是一个卖房屋保险的人。" | *"I can't quite make out what it's a photograph of." "Oh, it's our new boat."* "我看不出这张照片上是什么。" "啊, 是我们新买的一条船。" **b) it's me/John etc** used to say who is speaking on a telephone 是我/我是约翰等〔用来说明打电话的是谁〕: *Hello, it's Carmel here. Is Polly there, please?* 喂, 我是卡梅尔, 请问波莉在吗? **9 if it weren't for/ if it hadn't been for** if something had not happened 要不是; 要是没有: *We would have arrived much earlier if it hadn't been for the snow.* 要不是下雪, 我们早就到了。**10 a)** *informal* a particular ability or quality【非正式】〔表示某种能力或品质〕: *In a job like advertising, you've either got it or you haven't!* 像广告这种职业, 你要么有这份才能, 要么没有! **b)** *slang* SEXUAL INTERCOURSE【俚】性交: *Have you done it with him yet?* 你已经和他发生性关系了吗? **11 this is it!** *spoken* used to say that something you expected to happen is actually going to happen【口】就是它!〔表示你预计发生的事真要发生了〕**12 That's it!** *spoken*【口】**a)** used to say that a particular situation has finished 完了! 没有了!〔表示某个情况已结束〕*You can have one more cookie and then that's it!* 你可以再吃一块小甜饼, 吃完就没了! **b)** used to praise someone because they have done something correctly 做得对! 就是这样!〔用来称赞某人做对事情〕**13 think you're it** *informal* to think you are more important than you are【非正式】自以为了不起: *Just because he got a higher mark he really thinks he's it.* 他因为分数比别人高就自以为了不起。

I·tal·i·an¹ /ɪˋtæljən; ɪ'tæliən/ *n* [U] **1** the language of Italy 意大利语 **2** someone from Italy 意大利人

Italian² *adj* from or connected with Italy 意大利的

I·tal·i·a·nate /ɪˋtæljənˌet; ɪ'tæliəneɪt/ *adj literary* with an Italian style or appearance【文】意大利风格的; 意大利特色的

i·tal·i·cize also 又作 **-ise** *BrE*【英】/ɪˋtæləˌsaɪz; ɪ'tælɪsaɪz/ *v* [T] to put or print something in italics 把…排成斜体; 用斜体字印刷〔某物〕—**italicized** *adj*

i·tal·ics /ɪˋtælɪks; ɪ'tælɪks/ *n* [plural] a type of printed letters that lean to the right, often used to emphasize particular words 斜体字〔常用来表示强调〕: **in italics** *This example is written in italics.* 这个例句是用斜体排印的。—compare 比较 ROMAN —**italic** *adj*: *italic script* 斜体书法

Italo- /ɪtælo; ɪtæləʊ/ *prefix* Italian 意大利(人)的: *the Italo-Austrian border* 意(大利)奥(地利)边界

It·a·ly /ˋɪtlɪ; 'ɪtəli/ a country in southern Europe, surrounded on three sides by the Mediterranean Sea. Italy is a member of the EU. Population: 57,680,000 (2001). Capital: Rome. In ancient times, Italy was home of the Roman civilization, which has had a great influence on how people in Europe live and think. The Renaissance began in Italy in the 14th century. Italy has many beautiful paintings, SCULPTUREs, and buildings. 意大利〔欧洲南部一国，三面临地中海，为欧盟成员国。人口：57,680,000 (2001)，首都：罗马。意大利是古罗马文明的发祥地，罗马文明对欧洲人的生活和思维方式产生了巨大影响。文艺复兴 14 世纪始于意大利。该国有许多优秀的绘画作品、雕塑和建筑〕

ITC, the /ˌaɪ ti ˋsi; ˌaɪ tiː ˌsiː/ the Independent Television Commission; the organization which is responsible for controlling the operation of private television companies in the UK 独立电视委员会〔英国负责管理私人电视公司的专门机构〕

itch¹ /ɪtʃ; ɪtʃ/ *v* **1** [I,T] if part of your body or your clothes itch, you have an unpleasant feeling on your skin that makes you want to rub it with your nails (使)发痒: *My feet were itching terribly.* 我的脚痒得厉害。| **itch sb** *AmE*【美】: *The label on this shirt itches me.* 这件衬衫上的商标刺得我发痒。**2 be itching to do sth** *informal* to want to do something very much as soon as possible【非正式】急切地想做某事: *You could tell they were itching to leave.* 你能看出他们急着要离开。

itch² *n* [singular] **1** an uncomfortable feeling on your skin that makes you want to rub it with your nails 痒 **2** *informal* a strong desire to do or have something【非正式】〔想做某事、要某物的〕强烈愿望: **[+for]** *an itch for adventure* 进行探险的强烈愿望

itch·y /ˋɪtʃɪ; 'ɪtʃi/ *adj* **1** part of your body that is itchy has an unpleasant feeling that makes you want to rub it with your nails 发痒的: *My eyes sometimes get red and itchy in the summer.* 夏天我的眼睛有时会红肿发痒。**2** clothes that are itchy make you have this feeling on your skin〔衣服〕令人发痒的: *These tights are all itchy.* 这些紧身衣让人浑身发痒。**3** wanting to go somewhere new or do something different 渴望〔去新的地方、做不同的事情〕: *He's had that job now for about eight years, and he's starting to get itchy.* 他做那份工作约八年了，现在开始不安心了。**4 have itchy feet** *especially BrE informal* to want to travel or go somewhere new【尤英，非正式】脚痒〔想旅行或去新的地方〕: *I've only been back home for a few months and I've already got itchy feet.* 我回家不过才几个月，就又想出门了。**5 itchy fingers** *informal* someone with itchy fingers is likely to steal things【非正式】手痒〔想偷东西〕: *I tucked the bills deep into my pocket, away from itchy fingers.* 我把钞票藏在口袋深处，以防扒手偷走。**6 itchy palm** *informal* an official who has an itchy palm is willing to dishonestly accept money 手心痒，贪财〔指官员想接受贿赂〕—**itchiness** *n* [U]

it'd /ˋɪtəd; 'ɪtəd/ *usually spoken*【一般口】the short form of 缩略式= 'it would' or 'it had': *I'd do it if I thought it'd help.* 如果我认为这样做有用，我就会去做的。

-ite /aɪt; aɪt/ *suffix* **1** [in nouns 构成名词] a follower or supporter of a particular idea or person〔某个思想或人的〕支持者，追随者: *a group of Trotskyites* (=followers of Trotsky's political ideas) 一群托洛茨基分子 | *the Pre-Raphaelites* 前拉斐尔派画家 **2** [in adjectives 构成形容词] connected with a particular set of religious or political ideas, or with the ideas of a particular person 具有〔某宗教、政治或某人〕观点的: *his Reaganite opinions* 他的里根主义观点 **3** someone who lives in a particular place or belongs to a particular group 住在…的人; 属于…组织的人: *a Brooklynite* (=someone from Brooklyn) 布鲁克林区的人 | *the Israelites* (=in the Bible)〔《圣经》中的〕古以色列人

i·tem /ˋaɪtəm; 'aɪtəm/ *n* **1** [C] a single thing, especially part of a list, group, or set〔尤指清单上、一群或一组事物中的〕一项; 一件; 一条: *The professor wanted to see item 15, the Egyptian pot.* 教授想看第 15 件——那个埃及壶。| **[+of]** *an item of furniture* 一件家具 **2** [C] a single, usually short, piece of news in a newspaper or magazine, or on TV〔报纸、杂志、电视上的〕一条(短)消息: *He sat at the kitchen table with the paper reading each item aloud.* 他坐在厨房餐桌前，拿着报纸大声朗读每条新闻。**3 be an item** *informal* if two people are an item, they have a sexual relationship【非正式】有性关系: *They're not an item any more.* 他们不再有性关系了。

i·tem·ize also 又作 **-ise** *BrE*【英】/ˋaɪtəmˌaɪz; 'aɪtəmaɪz/ *v* [T] to make a list and give details about each thing on the list 分条列举; 详细列举 —**itemized** *adj*: *an itemized bill* 逐项开列的账单

Ith·a·ca /ˋɪθəkə; 'ɪθəkə/ in ancient Greek stories, an island off the east coast of Greece which was the home of Odysseus 伊萨基岛〔古希腊传说中与希腊东部海岸隔海相望的一座岛屿，为奥德修斯的家乡〕

i·tin·e·rant /aɪˋtɪnərənt; aɪ'tɪnərənt/ *adj* [only before noun 仅用于名词前] *formal* travelling from place to place, especially to work【正式】〔尤指工作上〕巡回的; 流动的: *itinerant labourers* 流动劳工

i·tin·e·ra·ry /aɪˋtɪnəˌrɛrɪ; aɪ'tɪnərəri/ *n* [C] a plan or list of the places you will visit on a journey 旅行计划; 预定行程: *His itinerary would take him from Bordeaux to Budapest.* 他的旅行计划是从波尔多到布达佩斯。

-itis /aɪtɪs; aɪtɪs/ *suffix* [in U nouns 构成不可数名词] **1** an illness or infection that affects a particular part of your body〔身体某部分的〕炎症: *tonsillitis* (=infection of the TONSILS) 扁桃体炎 **2** *humorous* the condition of having too much of something or liking something too much【幽默】…迷; …癖: *televisionitis* (=watching too much television) 电视癖

it'll /ˋɪtl; 'ɪtl/ *usually spoken*【一般口】the short form of 缩略式= 'it will': *It'll be dark before they get back.* 他们回来之前天就会黑了。

ITN /ˌaɪ ti ˋɛn; ˌaɪ tiː 'en◂/ *trademark* Independent Television News; a British news service which provides news for ITV, Channel 4, Channel 5, and independent radio stations in the UK【商标】独立电视新闻社〔英国一新闻机构，为独立电视台、第四频道、第五频道及独立广播电台提供新闻〕

it's /ɪts; ɪts/ **1** the short form of 缩略式= 'it is': *It's raining.* 正在下雨。**2** a short form of 缩略式= 'it has': *It's been cloudy all day.* 已经阴了一整天。

its /ɪts; ɪts/ *determiner* the possessive form of IT〔it 的所有格形式〕: *The baby had fallen out of its crib.* 婴儿从婴儿床上跌落下来。| *I must admit the plan does have its merits.* 我必须承认这项计划确有它的优点。

it·self /ɪtˋsɛlf; ɪt'self/ *pron* **1** the reflexive form of IT〔it 的反身形式〕: *The cat lay on the sofa, washing itself.* 猫躺在沙发上给自己舔干净。| *It is generally felt that the government has made an idiot of itself.* 人们普遍认为政府做了一件大蠢事。**2** used to emphasize the pronoun 'it'〔用来强调代词 it〕: *We've checked the wiring and the aerial so the problem may be the television itself.* 线路和天线我们都检查过了，所以问题也许在电视机本身。**3 in itself** considered without other related ideas or situation 就其本身而言: *There is a little infection in the lung which in itself is not important.* 肺部有些感染，但就其本身而言并没什么关系。**4 (all) by itself a)** alone 独自: *Will the dog be safe left in the car by itself?* 把狗独自留在车里安全吗? **b)** without help 无须外力地: *The door seemed to open all by itself.* 那扇门好像是自己打开的。**5 (all) to itself** if something has something else to itself, it does not have to share that thing with others 全部为自己所有; 非共用: *This idea deserves a chapter to itself.* 这个观点值得单独写一章。

it·sy-bit·sy /ˌɪtsɪ ˋbɪtsɪ; ˌɪtsi 'bɪtsi◂/ also 又作 **it·ty-bit·ty** /ˌɪtɪ ˋbɪtɪ; ˌɪti 'bɪti◂/ *adj* [only before noun 仅用于名词前] *spoken humorous* very small【口，幽默】极小的

-i·tude /ətjud; ɪtjuːd/ also 又作 **-tude** [in nouns 构成名词] *suffix formal* the state of having a particular quality【正式】有…特性: *certitude* (=being certain) 必然(性) | *exactitude* 精确(性)

ITV /ˌaɪ ti ˋvi; ˌaɪ tiː 'viː/ *trademark n* [U] Independent Television; a group of British television companies that are paid for by advertising【商标】〔英国〕独立电视公司〔由几家电视公司组成，靠广告收入维持〕: *Is there anything good on ITV tonight?* 独立电视台今晚有什么好节目吗?

-ity /ətɪ; ɪti/ also 又作 **-ty** *suffix* [in nouns 构成名词] the state of having a particular quality, or something that has that quality 具有某种特性的状态; 具有某种特性的事物: *with great regularity* (=regularly) 很有规律地 | *such stupidities* (=stupid actions or remarks) 如此荒谬的言行

IUD /ˌaɪ ju ˋdi; ˌaɪ juː 'diː/ *n* [C] a small plastic or metal object used inside a woman's UTERUS (=place where a baby develops) to prevent a baby being born; COIL² (4)〔妇女用〕子宫内避孕器

IV /ˌaɪ ˋvi; ˌaɪ 'viː/ *n* [C] *AmE* medical equipment that is used to put liquid directly into your blood【美】〔静脉〕滴注器; DRIP[2] (3) *BrE*【英】

I·van·hoe /ˋaɪvənho; 'aɪvənhəʊ/ the main character in the NOVEL *Ivanhoe* (1819) by Sir Walter Scott, set in England in the 12th century. Sir Wilfred of Ivanhoe is a brave KNIGHT who has many adventures. 伊凡赫〔沃尔特·司各特爵士创作的小说《伊凡赫》(1819) 中的主人公。小说以12世纪的英格兰为背景, 描写勇敢的骑士威尔弗雷德爵士的许多冒险经历〕

I·van the Ter·ri·ble /ˌaɪvən ðə ˋtɛrɪbl; ˌaɪvən ðə 'terəbəl/ (1530-84) the first Russian ruler to take the title Tsar. He was famous for his cruel and unfair leadership.〔伊凡〕雷帝〔(1530-1584), 首位称沙皇的俄国统治者。他以残暴和专制出名〕

I've /aɪv; aɪv/ *usually spoken*【一般口】the short form of 缩略式 = 'I have': *I've never been here before.* 我以前从未来过这儿。

-ive /ɪv; ɪv/ *suffix* [in nouns and adjectives 构成名词和形容词] someone or something that does something or can do something (能) 做某事的人[物]: *an explosive* (=substance that can explode) 炸药 | *a detective* (=someone who tries to discover facts about crimes) 侦探 | *the adoptive parents* (=who ADOPT a child) 养父养母

Ives /aɪvz; aɪvz/, **Charles** (1874-1954) an American COMPOSER who wrote modern music that later influenced many other composers, and who used FOLK MUSIC and familiar songs in his works. He is known for his symphonies (SYMPHONY) and for his *Concord Sonata*. 艾甫斯〔(1874-1954), 美国作曲家。他创作的现代音乐对许多作曲家产生了影响。他的音乐作品采用了民乐和民歌, 创作的交响乐和《康科德奏鸣曲》十分著名〕

IVF /ˌaɪ vi ˋɛf; ˌaɪ viː 'ef/ *technical* a process in which a human egg is fertilized (FERTILIZE (1)) outside the woman's body; IN VITRO FERTILIZATION【术语】体外受精

i·vied /ˋaɪvɪd; 'aɪvid/ *adj literary* covered with ivy【文】常春藤覆盖的

i·vo·ry /ˋaɪvərɪ; 'aɪvəri/ *n* **1** [U] the hard smooth yellowish-white substance from the TUSKs (=long teeth) of an ELEPHANT 象牙 (质): *an ivory chess set* 一副象牙国际象棋 **2** [U] a yellowish white colour 象牙色; 乳白色 **3** [C often plural 常用复数] something made of ivory, especially a small figure of a person or animal 象牙制品〔尤指小型人像或动物像〕: *a collection of Chinese ivories* 中国象牙制品藏品 **4 the ivories** [plural] *informal* the KEYs (=parts you press down) of a piano【非正式】钢琴键 —see also 另见 **tickle the ivories** (TICKLE[1] (5)) **5** *AmE humorous* someone's teeth【美, 幽默】〔某人的〕牙齿 **6 ivory tower** a place or situation where you are separated from the difficulties of ordinary life and so are unable to understand them 象牙塔〔脱离现实生活中困境的小天地〕: *ivory tower linguists* 象牙塔中的语言学家

Ivory Coast /ˌ‥‥ˈ‥/ the English name for Côte d'Ivoire, a country in West Africa 象牙海岸〔西非国家科特迪瓦的英语名〕

I Vow To Thee My Coun·try /ˌ‥ˌ‥ˈ‥/ a British PATRIOTIC song, the music for which was written by Gustav Holst, which is often played at school ceremonies and similar events in the UK《祖国, 我向你起誓》〔英国一爱国歌曲, 由古斯塔夫·霍尔斯特作曲, 常在学校庆典等类似活动中播放〕

i·vy /ˋaɪvɪ; 'aɪvi/ *n* [C, U] a climbing plant with dark green shiny leaves 常春藤 —see also 另见 POISON IVY

Ivy League, the /ˌ‥ˈ‥/ *n* a group of old and respected universities in the eastern part of the US 常春藤联盟〔由美国东部的某些历史悠久的名牌大学组成的一个联盟〕—**Ivy League** *adj*: *an Ivy League college* 常春藤联盟成员

> CULTURAL NOTE 文化注释
>
> Ivy League colleges are generally considered to be some of the most respected and impressive places to study in the US. They claim to offer a very high standard of education, and they tend to choose their students very carefully. Most of the students who are accepted at these colleges have earned very high grades in high school, have very impressive skills and talents in sports, music etc, have a parent or relative who went to the same college, or come from a rich and successful family. GRADUATEs from the Ivy League tend to become successful, powerful people in US society, especially in professions such as law, politics, and business. Ivy League colleges are also some of the oldest, most expensive, and most traditional institutions in the US. Because of this, they are sometimes considered to be too proud of their high social position. 常春藤联盟院校一般被看做美国最受尊重、最值得羡慕的读书圣地, 它们宣称能提供高水平的教育, 挑选学生往往也十分严格。这些院校接收的学生大多在高中阶段成绩优异, 技能突出, 在体育或音乐等方面有天赋, 有父母或亲属曾在该校就学, 或来自富有和成功的家庭。这些院校的毕业生一般都会成为美国社会中有影响的成功人士, 尤其在法律界、政界或商界更是如此。常春藤联盟也是美国最古老、最昂贵、最传统的一批院校, 因此有时人们认为它们对自己社会地位之高过于自傲。

I·wo Ji·ma /ˌiwə ˋdʒimə; ˌiːwə 'dʒiːmə/ an island in the Pacific Ocean belonging to Japan, where US forces won a very difficult battle in World War II. There is a STATUE in Washington D.C., of US MARINEs raising the US flag on Iwo Jima after they had won the battle. 硫黄岛〔太平洋一岛, 属于日本。二战期间, 美军在此打赢了一场艰苦的战役。华盛顿特区有一尊雕像, 展现美国海军在硫黄岛一役取胜后升起国旗的情景〕

-ization /əzeʃən; aɪzeɪʃən/ *suffix* makes nouns from verbs ending in -IZE〔加在以 -ize 结尾动词之后使之成为名词〕: *civilization* 文明 | *crystallization* 结晶

-ize also 又作 **-ise** *BrE*【英】/aɪz; aɪz/ *suffix* [in verbs 构成动词] **1** to make something have more of a particular quality 使某物更大程度地具有某种特点: *We need to modernize our procedures.* (=make them more modern) 我们要使我们的程序现代化。| *Americanized spelling* (=spelling made more American) 美式拼写 | *privatized transport systems* (=put back into private ownership) 私有化的运输系统 **2** to change something to something else, or be changed to something else 转变; 变成: *The liquid crystallized.* (=turned into CRYSTALs) 液体结晶了。**3** to speak in a particular way 以某种方式讲话: *to soliloquize* (=speak a SOLILOQUY, to yourself) 自言自语 | *I sat and listened to him sermonizing.* (=speaking solemnly, as if in a SERMON) 我坐着听他那布道式的讲话。**4** to put into a particular place 置于某处: *She was hospitalized after the accident.* 她在事故发生后被送往医院。

iz·zat·so /ɪˌzætˋso; ɪˌzæt'səʊ/ *interjection AmE* used to show that you do not believe something that someone has just said【美】真的吗?〔用来表示不相信某人刚刚说的话〕

I

J,j

J, j /dʒe; dʒeɪ/ *plural* **J's, j's** *n* [C] the tenth letter of the English alphabet 英语字母表的第十个字母

J the written abbreviation of 缩写= JOULE

J-17 /ˌdʒe sɛvənˈtin; ˌdʒeɪ sevənˈtiːn/ *trademark* a British magazine for TEENAGE girls, formerly called *Just Seventeen*, which contains pictures and articles about fashion, health, music, boys etc, and answers to readers' questions about personal problems. In the US there is a similar magazine called *Seventeen*.【商标】《豆蔻年华》〔英国一少女杂志，旧称 Just Seventeen（《刚满十七》）。该杂志刊登时尚、健康、音乐和男孩等方面的图片和文章，解答读者提出的个人问题。美国也有一类似杂志，称作 Seventeen（《十七岁》）〕

jab¹ /dʒæb; dʒæb/ *v* **jabbed, jabbing** [I,T] to push something into or towards something else with short quick movements 戳，刺，捅；猛击：**jab sb with sth** *Stop jabbing me with your elbow!* 别用胳膊肘捅我！｜[+at] *She jabbed at the elevator buttons.* 她迅速按了一下电梯按钮。

jab² *n* [C] **1** a sudden hard push, especially with a pointed object or your FIST (=closed hand)〔用尖物或拳头〕击，推，戳：**right/left jab** (=with your right or left hand) 用右手/左手击打 **2** *BrE informal* an INJECTION (1) given to prevent you from catching a disease; SHOT¹ (15)【英，非正式】预防针：*a typhoid jab* 伤寒预防针

jab·ber /ˈdʒæbɚ; ˈdʒæbə/ *v* [I,T] to talk quickly, excitedly, and not very clearly 急促、激动而含糊不清地说话 —**jabber** *n* [singular,U]

jack¹ /dʒæk; dʒæk/ *n* [C]

1 ►TOOL FOR LIFTING 起重工具◄ a piece of equipment used to lift a heavy weight off the ground, such as a car, and support it while it is in the air 起重器，千斤顶：*a hydraulic jack* 液压千斤顶

2 ►CARD GAMES 纸牌游戏◄ a card used in card games that has a man's picture on it and is worth less than a queen and more than a ten〔纸牌中介于王后和十之间的〕"J"牌，杰克：*a pair of jacks* 一对杰克

3 ►ELECTRICAL 电的◄ an electronic connection for a telephone or other electric machine 插座，插口

4 ►CHILDREN'S GAME 儿童游戏◄ **a) jacks** [plural] a children's game in which the players try to pick up small objects while bouncing (BOUNCE) and catching a ball 抛接子游戏〔一面拍球一面设法拾起小物件〕 **b)** a small metal or plastic object that has six points, used in this game〔抛接子游戏中用的〕带有六个尖端的金属[塑料]小物件

5 ►BALL 球◄ a small white ball at which players aim larger balls in the game of bowls (BOWL¹ (3a))〔滚木球戏中用作靶子的〕小白球

6 I'm all right, Jack *BrE usually spoken* someone with an I'm all right Jack attitude is happy with their life and does not care about other people【英，一般口】反正我过得挺好〔指自己生活得很快活，对别人却漠不关心〕

7 ►PERSON 人◄ **every man jack** *BrE old-fashioned* every single person; everyone【英，过时】每个人：*Every man jack of them is without a job.* 他们谁都没有工作。

8 jack shit/diddly *AmE spoken* an impolite expression meaning nothing at all【美口】一点都不〔不礼貌说法〕：*He knows jack shit about cars.* 他对汽车一窍不通。—see also 另见 JUMPING JACK, UNION JACK

jack² *v*

jack sb **around** *phr v* [T] *AmE slang* to waste someone's time by deliberately making things difficult for them【美俚】故意刁难〔某人〕以浪费其时间：*Stop jacking me around and make up your mind!* 别浪费我的时间了，拿定主意吧！

jack sth ↔ **in** *phr v* [T] *BrE informal* to stop doing something【英，非正式】停止做：*I'd love to jack in my job and go live in the Bahamas.* 我很愿意辞去工作，去巴哈马居住。

jack off *phr v* [I,T] *AmE taboo* to MASTURBATE【美讳】手淫

jack sb/sth ↔ **up** *phr v* [T] **1** to lift something heavy off the ground using a jack〔用起重器〕顶[托]起〔重物〕：*Jack the car up higher – I can't get the tire off.* 把车再托高些，不然车胎拿不下来。**2** *informal* to increase prices, sales etc by a large amount【非正式】大幅度提高〔价格、销量等〕：*jacking up their profit margins* 大幅度提高他们的盈利率 **3 be jacked up** *AmE informal* to be excited and nervous【美，非正式】又兴奋又紧张

jack·al /ˈdʒækəl; ˈdʒækɔːl/ *n* [C] a wild animal like a dog that lives in Asia and Africa and eats the remaining parts of dead animals〔亚洲和非洲的〕豺，胡狼

Jack and Jill /ˌdʒæk ənd ˈdʒɪl; ˌdʒæk ənd ˈdʒɪl/ two children in a NURSERY RHYME (=an old song or poem for young children) 杰克和吉尔〔一儿童歌谣中的两名孩童〕：*Jack and Jill went up the hill/To fetch a pail of water;/Jack fell down and broke his crown,/And Jill came tumbling after.* 杰克和吉尔，/上山抬水忙；/杰克摔破头，/吉尔栽跟头。

Jack and the Bean·stalk /ˌdʒæk ənd ðə ˈbinstɔk; ˌdʒæk ənd ðə ˈbiːnstɔːk/ also 又作 **Jack the Giant-killer** /ˌ· · ˈ· ·ˌ· ·/ a FAIRY TALE (=old story for children) about a boy called Jack who buys some magic beans that grow into a tall BEANSTALK (=the main stem of a bean plant). Jack climbs up it into the clouds, where he finds a GIANT's castle. He enters it and finds a magic HEN (=a female chicken) that produces golden eggs. Jack steals the hen, and goes back down the beanstalk. The giant tries to follow him, but when Jack arrives back on the ground he cuts down the beanstalk, the giant falls and dies, and Jack becomes rich as a result of the golden eggs.《杰克和仙豆茎》〔一童话故事。故事中，一个名叫杰克的男孩买了些后来长出高大豆茎的魔豆。他顺着豆茎爬上云霄，来到一个巨人的城堡。他走进去，看到一只能下金蛋的神母鸡。他偷了神母鸡，顺着豆茎逃离。巨人一路追踪，但杰克一着地就砍断豆茎，把巨人给摔死了。杰克得了金蛋，发了财〕

jack·ass /ˈdʒækˌæs; ˈdʒæk-æs/ *n* [C] **1** *BrE old-fashioned or AmE informal* an annoying stupid person【英，过时或美，非正式】傻瓜，蠢货 **2** a male ASS (=animal similar to a horse) 公驴

jack·boot /ˈdʒækˌbut; ˈdʒækbuːt/ *n* [C] a boot worn by soldiers that covers their leg up to the knee 长筒军靴 —**jack-booted** *adj*

jack·daw /ˈdʒækˌdɔ; ˈdʒækdɔː/ *n* [C] a black bird like a CROW¹ (1) that sometimes steals small, bright objects 寒鸦

jack·et /ˈdʒækɪt; ˈdʒækɪ̥t/ *n* [C] **1** a short, light coat 夹克，外套：*a denim jacket* 牛仔布夹克｜*Gene has to wear a jacket and tie to work.* 吉恩必须穿着外套打着领带去上班。—see also 另见 DINNER JACKET, LIFE JACKET —see picture on page A17 参见A17页图 **2** a stiff piece of folded paper that fits over the cover of a book to protect it; DUST JACKET〔书籍的〕护封；书套 **3** *AmE* a stiff paper cover that protects a record【美】唱片封套；SLEEVE (4) *BrE*【英】 **4** a cover that surrounds and protects some types of machines〔机器的〕外罩，保护罩

jacket po·ta·to /ˈ· · ˌ· ·/ *n* [C] *BrE* a potato baked with its skin on【英】带皮烤的马铃薯

Jack Frost /ˌ· ˈ·/ *n* [singular] a way of describing FROST¹ (1) as a person, used especially when talking to children〔拟人化的〕霜〔常用于与儿童说话时〕

jack·ham·mer /ˈdʒækˌhæmɚ; ˈdʒækˌhæmə/ *n* [C] *AmE* a large powerful tool used to break hard materials such as the surface of a road【美】风钻；凿岩机；PNEUMATIC DRILL *BrE*【英】

jack-in-the-box /ˈ· · · ˌ·/ *n* [C] a children's toy shaped like a box with a figure inside that springs out when the box is opened 玩偶匣〔内装小人，盒盖开启，小人即跳出〕

jack-knife¹ /ˈ· ·/ *n plural* **jack-knives** /-ˌnaɪvz; -naɪvz/ [C] **1** a knife with a blade that folds into its handle 折刀 **2** a DIVE² (1) in which you bend at the waist when you are in the air 屈体跳水

jack-knife² *v* **jack-knifing, jack-knifed** [I] if a large vehicle with two parts jack-knifes, the back part swings towards the front part〔前后铰接的车辆〕发生弯折：*The truck skidded and jack-knifed.* 那辆铰接卡车打滑后发生了弯折。

jack-of-all-trades /ˌ· · ˈ· ·/ *n* [singular] someone who can do many different types of work, but who often is not very skilled at any of them 博而不精的人

jack-o'-lan·tern /ˌdʒæk ə ˈlæntɚn; ˌdʒæk ə ˈlæntən/ *n* [C] a PUMPKIN (1) that has a face cut into it and a CANDLE put inside to shine through the holes 南瓜灯笼〔在南瓜上挖出人面形窟窿，内点蜡烛〕

jack·pot /ˈdʒækˌpɑt; ˈdʒækpɒt/ *n* [C] a large amount of money that you can win in a game that is decided by chance〔在靠运气

的游戏中可赢得的〕巨额奖金 —see also 另见 **hit the jackpot** (HIT[1] (23))

jack·rab·bit /ˈdʒæk͵ræbɪt; ˈdʒæk͵ræbɨt/ *n* [C] a large North American HARE (=animal like a large rabbit) with very long ears 〔北美洲的〕长耳大野兔

Jack Rob·in·son /͵dʒæk ˋrɑbɪnsn̩; ͵dʒæk ˈrɒbɨnsən/ *n* **before you can say Jack Robinson** *old-fashioned* very quickly or suddenly【过时】迅速地; 突然地

Jackson /ˈdʒæksn̩; ˈdʒæksən/ the capital city of the US state of Mississippi 杰克逊〔美国密西西比州首府〕

Jack·son, Andrew (1767-1845) a US soldier and politician in the Democratic Party who was the President of the US from 1829 to 1937. He became popular because of his success as a military leader in the battles against the Creek tribe in 1812 and against the British in 1815. His picture is printed on the US twenty-dollar bill. 杰克逊〔(1767-1845), 美国军人、民主党政治家, 1829 至 1837 年任美国总统。他 1812 年率军打败克里克部落, 1815 年战胜英军, 因此深受民众爱戴。20 美元的纸币上印有他的头像〕

Jackson, Mi·chael /ˈmaɪkl̩; ˈmaɪkəl/ (1958-2009) a very successful US POP singer, songwriter, and dancer. As a child, he was a member of The Jackson Five in the 1970s. He then worked on his own and became even more successful with the ALBUMS *Thriller* and *Bad*, and with his performances in concert. 杰克逊〔(1958-2009), 美国杰出的流行歌手、歌曲作家和舞蹈演员。20 世纪 70 年代, 他还是个小孩时就已经是杰克逊五兄弟组合的一员。之后, 他独自发展, 靠《颤栗》和《真棒》两张专辑和演唱会上的表演获得了更大成功〕

Jackson, Stonewall /͵stonˋwɔl; ͵stəʊnˈwɔːl/ (1824-63) a US GENERAL in the Confederate army during the American Civil War, whose real name was Thomas Jackson. He fought at the battle of Bull Run and helped to defeat the Union army there. 杰克逊〔(1824-1863), 美国南北战争期间南部邦联的将军, 真名托马斯·杰克逊。他在布尔溪一役中战胜了联邦军队〕

Jackson, the Reverend Jes·se /ˈdʒɛsɪ; ˈdʒesi/ (1941-) a US politician in the Democratic Party, who is also a minister in the Baptist Church and one of the leading black politicians in the US. He was active in the civil rights movement during the 1960s, and is a very effective public speaker who has always supported black people and other groups who have been unfairly treated in the past. 杰克逊〔(1941-), 美国民主党政治家、浸礼会牧师, 为美国主要的黑人政治家之一。20 世纪 60 年代, 他积极参与民权运动。他是个优秀的演说家, 一直支持黑人及其他未得到公平待遇的群体〕

Jack Sprat /͵·ˈ·/ a character in a NURSERY RHYME (=an old song or poem for children) 杰克·斯普拉特〔一儿童歌谣中的人物〕: *Jack Sprat would eat no fat,/His wife would eat no lean,/ And so between them both, you see,/They licked the platter clean.* 杰克不吃肥, /媳妇不吃瘦, /瞧他小两口儿, /盘子舔精光。

Jack the Lad /͵··ˈ·/ *n* [singular] *BrE spoken* a young man who enjoys drinking beer and going out with his male friends, and who thinks he is sexually attractive【英口】〔爱喝啤酒、常与男性伙伴外出、自以为很有性魅力的〕青年男子

Jack the Rip·per /͵··ˈ··/ the name given to a man who killed and cut up the bodies of several PROSTITUTES (=women who are paid to have sex) in the Whitechapel area of London in 1888. The police never caught him and never discovered who he was. The name 'the Ripper' is now sometimes used to describe criminals who murder people in a similar way. 开膛手杰克, 杀人狂杰克〔1888 年在伦敦怀特查普尔地区杀死数名妓女并将尸体肢解的一名男子。警方未能将其抓获, 也未能确定其身份。现在 the Ripper (杀人狂) 一词有时被用来形容以类似方式杀人的罪犯〕

Ja·cob /ˈdʒekəb; ˈdʒeɪkəb/ in the Old Testament of the Bible, the son of Isaac, and the brother of Esau. Jacob's 12 sons were the ANCESTORS of the 12 tribes of Israel. 雅各〔《圣经·旧约》中以撒之子, 以扫之弟。他的 12 个儿子是以色列 12 个支派的祖先〕

Jac·o·be·an /͵dʒækəˋbiən; ͵dʒækəˈbiːən◂/ *adj* belonging to or typical of the period between 1603 and 1625 in Britain, when James I was king of England 英王詹姆斯一世时期 (1603–1625) 的: *Jacobean drama* 詹姆斯一世时代的戏剧

Jac·o·bite /ˈdʒækə͵baɪt; ˈdʒækəbaɪt/ *n* [C] someone in the 17th or 18th centuries who supported King James II of England and wanted one of his DESCENDANTS to rule England 〔17 或 18 世纪〕拥护詹姆斯二世并主张由他的后裔来统治英国的人 —**Jacobite** *adj*

Jac·o·bite Ris·ing, the /͵···ˈ··/ also 又作 **the Jacobite Rebellion**/͵···ˈ··/ **1** the failed attempt in 1715-16 to make James Edward Stuart (the Old Pretender) king of England 詹姆斯党人叛乱〔1715 至 1716 年间, 詹姆斯党人试图拥立詹姆斯·爱德华·斯图亚特 (老僭王) 为英格兰国王, 但以失败告终〕 **2** the failed attempt in 1745-46 to make Bonnie Prince Charlie (Charles Edward Stuart) king of England, which ended all hope of making the Stuart family kings of England again. 詹姆斯党人叛乱〔1745 至 1746 年间, 詹姆斯党人试图拥立英俊的查理王子为英格兰国王, 但以失败告终, 斯图亚特王朝复辟的希望彻底破灭〕

Jacuzzi "爵士"浴缸

Ja·cuz·zi /dʒəˋkuzɪ; dʒəˈkuːzi/ *n* [C] *trademark* a large indoor bath that makes hot water move in strong currents around your body【商标】"爵士"浴缸 —compare 比较 HOT TUB, SPA (2)

jade /dʒed; dʒeɪd/ *n* **1** [U] a hard, usually green stone often used to make jewellery 碧玉, 翡翠 **2** [U] the light green colour of this stone 绿玉色, 翡翠绿 —see picture on page A5 参见 A5 页图 **3** [C] *old use* a woman, especially a rude or immoral woman【旧】〔尤指粗鲁或淫荡的〕妇女; 荡妇

ja·ded /ˈdʒedɪd; ˈdʒeɪdɨd/ *adj* someone who is jaded is no longer interested in or excited by life, especially because they have experienced too many things 〔尤因饱经世故而〕对世事冷漠: *magnificent meals to tempt the most jaded appetites* 可挑起最厌食之人胃口的美馔佳肴

Jaf·fa /ˈdʒæfə; ˈdʒæfə/ *n* [C] *BrE* a large orange, especially one that comes from Israel【英】〔尤指产于以色列的〕雅法橙

jag /dʒæg; dʒæg/ *n* [C] *informal*【非正式】**crying/shopping/talking etc jag** a short period of time when you suddenly cry etc without controlling how much you do it 〔不加控制的〕一阵大哭/狂买/喋喋不休等

jag·ged /ˈdʒægɪd; ˈdʒægɨd/ *adj* having a rough, uneven edge or surface, often with sharp points on it 锯齿状的; 凹凸不平的: *the jagged rocks of St. Saviour's Point* 圣基督角的锯齿状岩石 —**jaggedly** *adv*

Jag·ger /ˈdʒægɚ; ˈdʒægə/, **Mick** /mɪk; mɪk/ (1943-) a British singer and songwriter with the group The Rolling Stones. He is famous for his exciting stage performances. 贾格尔〔(1943-), 英国歌手、歌曲作家, 滚石乐队成员, 以激情的舞台表演闻名〕

Jag·u·ar /ˈdʒægwɑr; ˈdʒægjuə/ also 又作 **Jag** *informal trademark* a famous type of British car that is large and very comfortable【非正式, 商标】美洲豹〔英国制造的一种宽敞舒适的名牌汽车〕

jaguar *n* [C] a large South American wild cat with brown and yellow fur with black spots 〔产于南美的〕美洲豹

jai a·lai /ˈhaɪ əˋlaɪ; ͵haɪ əˈlaɪ/ *n* [U] a game played by two, four, or six people in which they use an object like a basket on a stick to throw a ball 回力球〔一种用一头有篮筐的棒抛球, 由二人、四人或六人参加的游戏〕

jail[1] also 又作 **gaol** *BrE*【英】/dʒel; dʒeɪl/ *n* [C,U] a place where criminals are kept as part of their punishment, or where people who have been charged with a crime are kept before they are judged in a law court; PRISON (1) 监狱

jail[2] also 又作 **gaol** *BrE*【英】—*v* [T] to put someone in jail 监禁; 拘留: *They ought to jail him for life.* 他们应把他终身监禁。

jail·bird also 又作 **gaolbird** *BrE*【英】/ˈdʒel͵bɝd; ˈdʒeɪlbɜːd/ *n* [C] *informal* someone who has spent a lot of time in prison【非正式】长期坐牢的人

jail·break also 又作 **gaolbreak** *BrE*【英】/ˈdʒel͵brek; ˈdʒeɪlbreɪk/ *n* [C] an escape or an attempt to escape from prison, especially by several people 〔尤指多人的〕越狱

jail·er also 又作 **gaoler** *BrE*【英】/ˈdʒelɚ; ˈdʒeɪlə/ *n* [C] *old-fashioned* someone who is in charge of guarding a prison or prisoners【过时】监狱看守, 狱卒

J

Jain /dʒaɪn; dʒaɪn/ *n* [C] someone whose religion is Jainism 耆那教教徒 —**Jain** *adj*

Jain·is·m /ˈdʒaɪnɪzəm; ˈdʒaɪnɪzəm/ *n* [C] a religion of India that is against violence towards any living things 耆那教〔印度的一种宗教，反对暴力和杀生〕

Ja·kar·ta /dʒəˋkɑrtə; dʒəˈkɑːtə/ the capital and largest city of Indonesia, on the island of Java, which is an important industrial city, port, and tourist centre, and one of the largest cities in southeast Asia 雅加达〔印尼首都和最大城市，位于爪哇岛，为该国重要的工业城市、港口和旅游中心，也是东南亚最大城市之一〕

jal·a·pe·ño /ˌhɑləˈpenjo; ˌhæləˈpeɪnjəʊ/ *n* [C] a small, very hot green PEPPER used especially in Mexican food 墨西哥青辣椒〔极辣，尤用于墨西哥食物〕

ja·lop·y /dʒəˋlɑpɪ; dʒəˈlɒpi/ *n* [C] *old-fashioned* a very old car in bad condition【过时】破旧的汽车 —see also 另见 BANGER (2)

jam¹ /dʒæm; dʒæm/ *n* **1** [C,U] a very thick sweet substance made from boiled fruit and sugar and eaten especially on bread; CONSERVE 果酱: *strawberry jam* 草莓酱 **2** [C] a situation in which it is difficult or impossible to move because there are so many people, things, cars etc close together 拥挤；堵塞: **traffic jam** *Sorry we're late. We got stuck in a traffic jam.* 对不起，我们来晚了，因为路上堵车。**3 be in a jam** *informal* to be in a difficult or uncomfortable situation【非正式】处于困境 **4 jams** [plural] *AmE* brightly coloured trousers that stop above your knee【美】〔长及膝盖以上的〕彩色短裤 **5 jam tomorrow** *BrE informal* good things that you are promised if you are patient enough to wait for them【英，非正式】许而不与的好东西〔指对耐心的人来说美好的事物总会到来〕

jam² *v*

1 ►PUSH HARD 用力推◄ [T] to push something somewhere using a lot of force, or to push too many things into a small place 用力推挤，塞进〔将许多物件塞进一个小处所〕: **jam sth into/under/on** *I'll never jam all my clothes into one suitcase.* 我不会把我的衣服都塞进一个箱子里。| **be jammed (up) against sth** (=pushed tightly against something) 与某物紧紧塞在一起

2 ►MACHINE 机器◄ also 又作 **jam up** [I,T] if a lock or a moving part of a machine jams, or if you jam it, it no longer works properly because something is preventing it from moving (使)卡住；(使) 发生故障: *The front roller has jammed on the photocopier.* 复印机的前滚筒卡住了。

3 ►BLOCK 堵塞◄ also 又作 **jam up** [T] if a lot of people or vehicles jam a place, they block it so that it is difficult to move 〔人、车〕堵塞〔某地〕: *Crowds jammed the entrance to the stadium.* 体育场入口处堵满了人。—see also 另见 JAMMED (2)

4 ►MUSIC 音乐◄ [I] to play music informally with others without practising first 未经练习的非正式演奏，即兴演奏 —see also 另见 JAM SESSION

5 jam on the brakes to slow down a car suddenly by putting your foot down hard on the BRAKE¹ (1) 猛踩刹车

6 jam the switchboard if telephone calls jam the switchboard, so many people are telephoning the same organization that its telephone system cannot work properly 使电话线路堵塞

7 ►RADIO 无线电◄ [T] to deliberately prevent broadcasts or other electronic signals from being received by sending out noise on the same WAVELENGTH 干扰〔无线电广播或其他电子信号〕

8 sb is jamming *AmE spoken* used to say that someone is doing something well【美口】某人干得好

JAMA /ˌdʒe e ɛm ˋe; ˌdʒeɪ eɪ em ˈeɪ/ *trademark* Journal of the American Medical Association; a highly-respected US magazine which provides reports on recent medical developments, new drugs and medical treatments etc【商标】《美国医学会杂志》〔美国一颇受推崇的杂志，报导医学进展、新药物以及最新疗法，等等〕—see also 另见 The LANCET

Ja·mai·ca /dʒəˋmekə; dʒəˈmeɪkə/ an island in the Caribbean Sea which is an independent state and a member of the British Commonwealth. Population: 2,666,000 (2001). Capital: Kingston. Many SLAVES were brought there from Africa from the 17th to the 19th centuries. Jamaica is the home of REGGAE music and the Rastafarian religion.牙买加〔加勒比海一岛国，为英联邦成员国。人口: 2,666,000 (2001)，首都: 金斯顿。17至19世纪，许多非洲奴隶被运到该岛。该国是雷盖音乐和拉斯塔法里宗教的发源地〕—**Jamaican** *n, adj*

jamb /dʒæm; dʒæm/ *n* [C] a side post of a door or window 〔门、窗的〕侧柱

jam·ba·la·ya /ˌdʒæmbəˋlaɪə; ˌdʒæmbəˈlaɪə/ *n* [U] a dish from the southern US containing rice, and SEAFOOD 什锦饭〔美国南部食品，由米饭和海鲜烹调而成〕

jam·bo·ree /ˌdʒæmbəˋri; ˌdʒæmbəˈriː/ *n* [C] **1** a big noisy party or celebration, usually outdoors 喧闹的大型聚会[庆祝]〔通常在露天举行〕**2** a large meeting of scouts (SCOUT¹ (1)) or guides (GUIDE¹ (4)) 童子军大会

James /dʒemz; dʒeɪmz/, **Henry** (1843-1916) a US writer of NOVELS, who lived for many years in Europe and is famous especially for writing about the effect that Europe had on Americans who travelled there. His many books include *Washington Square*, *The Portrait of a Lady*, and the GHOST story *The Turn of the Screw*. 詹姆斯〔(1843-1916)，美国小说家。他曾旅居欧洲多年，尤以描写欧洲对旅欧美国人的影响而著称。著作颇丰，包括《华盛顿广场》、《贵妇画像》以及鬼怪故事《螺丝在拧紧》〕—**Jamesian** *adj: a Jamesian plot* 詹姆斯风格的故事情节

James, Jes·se /ˋdʒɛsɪ; ˈdʒesi/ (1847-82) a US criminal who became famous for robbing banks and trains with his brother Frank. He was shot and killed by one of the members of his own GANG (=group of criminals). 詹姆斯〔(1847-1882)，美国臭名昭著的大盗。他伙同其兄弟弗兰克抢劫银行、火车，后被一同伙枪杀身亡〕

James I /ˌdʒemz ðə ˋfɝst; ˌdʒeɪmz ðə ˈfɜːst/, **King** (1566-1625) the king of England from 1603 until his death. Before he became king of England, he was already the king of Scotland (as James VI), and in 1603 the two KINGDOMS were united under one king. 詹姆斯一世〔(1566-1625)，英格兰国王，1603年即位直至去世。任英格兰国王之前，他已是苏格兰国王，称詹姆斯六世。1603年，两个王国合并，由同一国王统治〕

James II /ˌdʒemz ðə ˋsɛkənd; ˌdʒeɪmz ðə ˈsekənd/, **King** (1633-1704) the king of England from 1685 until 1688, when he was forced to give up his position because he had become a Catholic. In 1690 he tried to get back power from the new British king, William III, but he was defeated at the Battle of the Boyne in Ireland. 詹姆斯二世〔(1633-1704)，英格兰国王，1685至1688年在位，因信奉天主教而被迫退位。1690年，他试图从英王威廉三世手中夺回王权，但在爱尔兰博因河一役中战败〕

James·town /ˋdʒemztaun; ˈdʒeɪmztaʊn/ a town in Virginia which was the first town built by English people who went to live in North America. It was established in 1607, and is a popular place for tourists to visit. 詹姆士敦〔1607年来北美定居的英国人兴建的第一个城镇，位于弗吉尼亚州。现为旅游胜地〕

jammed /dʒæmd; dʒæmd/ *adj* **1** [not before noun 不用于名词前] impossible to move because of being stuck between two or more surfaces 夹住不能动的: *The child had got his finger jammed in the door.* 那孩子的一个手指被门夹住了。**2** *AmE* full of people or things; jam-packed【美】挤满人[物]的: *The place is jammed. We'll never get in.* 那地方太拥挤了，我们绝对进不去。

jam·mies /ˋdʒæmɪz; ˈdʒæmiz/ *n* [plural] *informal* PYJAMAS【非正式】睡衣裤

jam·my /ˋdʒæmɪ; ˈdʒæmi/ *adj BrE slang*【英俚】**1 jammy bastard/cow/bugger etc** an impolite expression meaning someone who has been very lucky 走运的家伙〔粗俗词语〕**2** very easy 非常容易的

jam-packed /ˌ· ˈ·◂/ *adj informal* full of people or things that are very close together【非正式】挤满人[物]的: **[+with]** *The square was jam-packed with revelers celebrating the New Year.* 广场上挤满了庆祝新年的狂欢者。

jam ses·sion /ˈ· ˌ··/ *n* [C] an occasion when JAZZ¹ (l) or ROCK¹ (2) musicians play music together informally 爵士乐[摇滚乐]非正式演奏会，即兴演奏会

Jan /dʒæn; dʒæn/ the written abbreviation of 缩写 - January

Jane /dʒen; dʒeɪn/ the main female character in the books and films about Tarzan 珍妮〔《人猿泰山》小说和影片中的女主人公〕

Jane Doe /ˌdʒen ˋdo; ˌdʒeɪn ˈdəʊ/ *n* [singular] *AmE* a woman whose name is not known, especially one who is involved in a law case【美】某甲，某女〔指不知姓名的妇女，尤指诉讼案件中的女当事人〕—compare 比较 JOHN DOE

Jane Eyre /ˌdʒen ˋɛr; ˌdʒeɪn ˈeə/ (1847) a book by Charlotte Brontë about a young woman called Jane Eyre who becomes a GOVERNESS and agrees to marry her employer,Mr Rochester, not knowing that he already has a wife who is mentally ill and kept locked in the ATTIC (=a room under the roof) of the house.《简·爱》〔(1847)，夏洛蒂·勃朗特的一部名著。小说讲述一位年轻家庭女教师简·爱的故事。其雇主罗切斯特先生的妻子因精神失常被关在阁楼里。简·爱在不知情的前提下愿与他共结良缘〕

jan·gle /ˋdʒæŋgl; ˈdʒæŋgəl/ *v* **1** [I,T] if metal objects or bells jangle or if you jangle them, they make a sharp sound when they hit each other (使)〔金属物件或铃铛〕发出尖锐的声音: *jangling bracelets* 叮当作响的手镯 **2** also 又作 **jangle on** [T usually passive 一般用被动态] to make someone feel nervous or

J

upset 使焦躁不安: *jangled nerves* 紧张不安的神经 —**jangle** *n* [singular]

jan·i·tor /ˋdʒænətɚ; ˈdʒænɪtə/ *n* [C] *AmE or ScotE* someone who looks after a school or other large building【美或苏格兰】〔学校或大楼的〕看门人, 门房; CARETAKER (1) *BrE*【英】

Jan·u·a·ry /ˋdʒænjuˏɛrɪ; ˈdʒænjuəri/ written abbreviation 缩写为 **Jan** *n* [C,U] the first month of the year, between December and February 一月: **in January** *Our new office is opening in January 2000.* 我们的新办事处定于2000年1月开始办公。| **last/next January** *I haven't heard from him since last January.* 从去年1月到现在, 我没有收到过他的信。| **on January 29th** (also 又作 **on 29th January** *BrE* 英) *Rosie's party was on January 29th.* 罗西的聚会是在1月29日。(spoken as 读作: *on January the twenty-ninth* or 或 *on the twenty-ninth of January* or 或 (*AmE* 美) *on January twenty-ninth*)

CULTURAL NOTE 文化注释

In the UK and northern US, when people think of January, they think of the New Year and cold weather. 在英国和美国北方, 1月常让人联想起新年和寒冷的天气。

Ja·nus /ˋdʒenəs; ˈdʒeɪnəs/ in Roman MYTHOLOGY, the god of gates and doorways and of new beginnings. Janus is usually shown in pictures with two faces, one of which looks back at the past while the other looks forward towards the future. 雅努斯, 贾奴斯〔罗马神话中的门神与新开端之神。图片中的雅努斯一般有两张面孔, 一面回顾过去, 一面展望未来〕

Japan a country in East Asia consisting of four large islands, Hokkaido, Honshu, Shikoku, and Kyushu, and many smaller ones. Population: 126,771,662 (2001). Capital: Tokyo. The main religions are Shinto and Buddhism. 日本〔东亚一国家, 包括北海道、本州、四国、九州四大岛及许多小岛。人口: 126,771,662 (2001), 首都: 东京。主要宗教为神道教和佛教〕

Japan, the Sea of also 又作 **the East Sea** the sea that separates Korea from Japan 日本海〔位于日本和朝鲜半岛之间的海域〕

Jap·a·nese[1] /ˏdʒæpəˋniz; ˌdʒæpəˈniːz◂/ *n* **1** [U] the language of Japan 日语 **2 the Japanese** people from Japan 日本人

Japanese[2] *adj* from or connected with Japan 来自日本的, 与日本有关的

Japanese lan·tern /ˏ‥ ˋ‥/ *n* [C] a paper decoration, usually with a light inside〔装饰用〕纸灯笼

jape /dʒep; dʒeɪp/ *n* [C] *old-fashioned* a trick or joke【过时】把戏; 玩笑

jar[1] /dʒɑr; dʒɑː/ *n* [C] **1** a round glass container with a wide lid, used for storing food such as JAM[1] (1) and HONEY (1)〔用来盛果酱、蜂蜜等的玻璃〕广口瓶 **2** the amount of food, drink, etc contained in a jar 一广口瓶所装之量: *half a jar of peanut butter* 半瓶花生酱 **3** [singular] the shock of two things hitting each other, or a sudden pain from something hitting you〔两物碰撞引起的〕震动; 突然的痛楚: *It must have been the jar of the impact that broke her ankle.* 肯定是由于碰撞的震动把她的脚踝折断了。**4** a round container made of clay, stone etc used especially in the past for keeping food or drink in〔过去用来盛食物或饮料、用黏土或石头等制成的〕坛, 罐 **5** *BrE informal* a glass of beer【英, 非正式】一杯啤酒: *We'd had a few jars down the pub.* 我们已在小酒馆喝了几杯啤酒。

jar[2] *v* **jarred, jarring** **1** [T] to slightly hurt a part of your body by hitting it against something 撞伤〔身体的一部分〕: *Alice landed badly, jarring her ankle.* 艾丽斯落地姿势不好, 扭伤了脚踝。**2** [I,T] if you jar something or if two things jar, they are suddenly shaken or hit (使)〔某物〕震动; 相撞: *Oops, sorry, did I jar your elbow?* 哎哟, 对不起, 我撞着你的肘部了吗? **3** [I,T] also 又作 **jar on** to make someone feel slightly annoyed or uncomfortable 令〔人〕略感不快[不舒服]: **jar on sb's nerves** *The baby's screaming was starting to jar on my nerves.* 那个婴儿的尖叫声开始使我心烦。**4** [I] to be different in style or appearance from something else and therefore look strange 不和谐, 不相配: **[+with]** *a modernistic lamp that jarred with the rest of the room* 与房间其他地方不相称的一盏非常时髦的灯 —**jarring** *adj*

jar·gon /ˋdʒɑrgən; ˈdʒɑːgən/ *n* [U] technical words and expressions that are used mainly by people who belong to the same professional group and are difficult to understand〔难懂的〕行话, 术语: *documents full of legal jargon* 全是法律术语的文件

Jarls·berg /ˋjɑrlzbɝg; ˈjɑːlzbɜːg/ *trademark* a type of hard, pale yellow cheese made in Norway, which has holes in it and a not very strong taste【商标】亚尔斯贝格干酪〔挪威出产的一种浅黄色有孔硬干酪, 口味清淡〕

Jar·man /ˋdʒɑrmən; ˈdʒɑːmən/, **Der·ek** /ˋdɛrɪk; ˈderɪk/ (1942-94) a British artist, writer, and film DIRECTOR whose unusual and original films, including *Sebastiane* (1975), *Caravaggio* (1986), and *Edward II* (1991), often contained HOMOSEXUAL characters 贾曼〔(1942-1994), 英国艺术家、作家和电影导演。其影片新颖独特, 常有同性恋人物。代表作包括《塞巴斯蒂安》(1975)、《卡拉瓦乔》(1986) 和《爱德华二世》(1991)〕

Jar·row /ˋdʒæro; ˈdʒærəʊ/ an industrial town in northeast England on the River Tyne, where ships were built and steel was made until 1930, when many people lost their jobs as a result of the Great Depression. In 1936 many unemployed people walked from Jarrow to London as a protest, in what was known as the Jarrow March. This was the most famous of the Hunger Marches of the 1920s and 1930s in the UK. 贾罗〔英格兰东北部一工业城镇, 临泰恩河。该镇曾以造船和炼钢为主, 直到1930年大萧条时期许多人失去了工作。在1936年的"贾罗游行"中, 许多失业者从贾罗步行到伦敦以示抗议。这是英国20世纪20、30年代最有名的一次反饥饿游行〕

jas·mine /ˋdʒæzmən; ˈdʒæzmɪn/ *n* [C,U] a climbing plant with sweet-smelling small white or yellow flowers 茉莉, 素馨

Ja·son /ˋdʒesn̩; ˈdʒeɪsən/ in ancient Greek stories, a HERO who sailed with a group of men called the Argonauts in the ship Argo to find the Golden Fleece. Together they had many exciting adventures. 伊阿宋〔古希腊传说中的英雄。他曾与阿耳戈群雄坐上"阿耳戈"号快船寻找金羊毛, 经历了许多激动人心的奇遇〕

jas·per /ˋdʒæspɚ; ˈdʒæspə/ *n* [U] a red, yellow, or brown stone that is not very valuable〔呈红、黄、棕等颜色不大值钱的〕碧玉

jaun·dice /ˋdʒɔndɪs; ˈdʒɔːndɪs/ *n* [U] a medical condition in which your skin and the white part of your eyes become yellow 黄疸(病)

jaun·diced /ˋdʒɔndɪst; ˈdʒɔːndɪst/ *adj* **1** tending to judge people and things unfavourably, often because you have had disappointing experiences yourself〔由于受过挫折而对世事〕有偏见的: *a jaundiced view of life* 有偏见的人生观 | **with a jaundiced eye** (=thinking of people and situations in a jaundiced way) 带着偏见的眼光 **2** suffering from jaundice 患黄疸病的

jaunt /dʒɔnt; dʒɔːnt/ *n* [C] a short journey for pleasure 短途旅游 —**jaunt** *v* [I]

jaun·ty /ˋdʒɔntɪ; ˈdʒɔːnti/ *adj* jaunty actions, clothes etc show that you are confident and cheerful〔动作、衣着等〕满怀信心的, 愉快的: **at a jaunty angle** *His hat was tilted at a jaunty angle.* 他歪戴着帽子, 显得轻松愉快。—**jauntily** *adv* —**jauntiness** *n* [U]

Ja·va[1] /ˋdʒɑvə; ˈdʒɑːvə/ an island which is part of Indonesia. It is not the largest of the Indonesian islands, but it includes the capital, Jakarta, and it has the highest population. 爪哇岛〔印尼一岛。虽然不是印度尼西亚群岛面积最大的岛屿, 但却是首都雅加达的所在地, 人口为诸岛之冠〕—**Javanese** /ˏdʒɑvəˋniz; ˌdʒɑːvəˈniːz◂/ *n, adj*

Ja·va[2] *trademark* a computer language, used especially to write PROGRAMS for the INTERNET【商标】Java 程序语言〔一种计算机语言, 尤用于编写适于互联网的程序〕

jav·e·lin /ˋdʒævlɪn; ˈdʒævəlɪn/ *n* [C] **1** a light SPEAR for throwing, now used mostly in sport〔现多用于体育运动的〕标枪 **2 the javelin** a sporting event in which competitors throw a javelin 掷标枪〔比赛项目〕

jaw[1] /dʒɔ; dʒɔː/ *n* **1** [C] the lower part of your face that moves when you eat 颌, 下颚: *Tyson punched his opponent on the jaw.* 泰森一拳狠狠打在对手的下颚上。—see picture at 参见 HEAD[1] 图 **2 sb's jaw dropped** used to say that someone looked surprised or shocked〔用来形容某人惊讶或震惊得〕张口结舌: *Her jaw dropped when I told her Jean had left her husband.* 我告诉她琼已与丈夫分手, 她惊讶得说不出话来。**3 jaws** [plural] **a)** the mouth of a person or animal, especially a dangerous animal〔尤指猛兽的〕嘴: *a crocodile snapping its jaws* 鳄鱼的嘴开合时劈啪作响 **b)** the two parts of a machine or tool that move together to hold something tightly〔工具或机器的〕夹住东西的部分, 钳口 **4** [C usually singular 一般用单数] the shape of someone's jaw, especially when it shows something about their character〔某人的〕下颚形状〔尤指显示其性格〕: *She's got a very determined jaw.* 她个性坚毅。**5 the jaws of death/defeat/despair** *literary* a situation in which you almost die, are almost defeated etc【文】生死关头/胜负关头/绝望边缘 **6 the jaws of a cave/tunnel etc** the entrance to a place which is dark and dangerous 黑暗而危险处的入口 **7 have a jaw** *old-fashioned* to have a conversation【过时】聊天

jaw[2] *v* [I] *informal* to talk【非正式】闲谈

jaw·bone /ˋdʒɔˏbon; ˈdʒɔːbəʊn/ *n* [C] one of the two big bones of the jaw, especially the lower jaw 颌骨〔尤指下颌骨〕; 颚骨 —see picture at 参见 SKELETON 图

jaw·break·er /ˈdʒɔˌbrekə; ˈdʒɔːˌbreɪkə/ *n* [C] *AmE* a round hard sweet【美】圆形硬糖; GOBSTOPPER *BrE*【英】

Jaws /dʒɔz; dʒɔːz/ (1975) an exciting and frightening US film made by Steven Spielberg, about a SHARK (=a large, dangerous fish) that kills people who go swimming in the sea and then tries to kill a group of men who go out in a boat to catch it《大白鲨》〔(1975), 史蒂文·斯皮尔伯格制作的一部美国惊险影片。故事中有一条鲨鱼咬死了在海里游泳的人, 后来还试图伤害前去捕捉它的一船人〕

jay /dʒe; dʒeɪ/ *n* [C] a noisy brightly-coloured European bird of the CROW[1] (1) family 樫鸟〔一种产于欧洲、羽毛艳丽的鸦属鸟〕—see also 另见 BLUEJAY

Jay, John (1745-1829) a US lawyer who became the first Chief Justice of the US Supreme Court in 1789. He helped to make peace with Britain after the American Revolutionary War, and in 1794 made an arrangement with Britain called *Jay's Treaty*, that included an agreement on trade 杰伊〔(1745-1829), 美国律师, 1789 年成为美国最高法院首席法官。美国革命战争后, 他参与了美英之间的和平谈判, 并于 1794 年与英国签署了《杰伊条约》, 其中包括一项贸易协定〕

Jay·cee /ˌdʒeˈsi; ˌdʒeɪˈsiː/ a member of an organization with branches in many towns and cities in the US. They are called the Jaycees from the letters JC, an abbreviation for Junior Chamber (of Commerce), and they encourage useful and interesting activities for local people.〔美国〕青年商会会员〔该商会在美国许多城镇设有分支机构。Jaycee (青商会员) 一词源自英文字母 JC 的读音, JC 为Junior Chamber (青年商会) 的缩写。该组织鼓励其成员通过实用性、趣味性活动为当地人服务〕

jay·walk·ing /ˈdʒeˌwɔkɪŋ; ˈdʒeɪˌwɔːkɪŋ/ *n* [U] the act of crossing streets with traffic in a careless and dangerous way 不遵守交通规则胡乱穿越马路 —**jaywalker** *n* [C]

jazz[1] /dʒæz; dʒæz/ *n* [U] **1** music originally played by black Americans with a strong beat and parts in which performers can play alone 爵士乐: *a jazz band* 爵士乐乐队 **2 and all that jazz** *spoken* and things like that【口】诸如此类的东西: *I'm fed up with rules, responsibilities and all that jazz.* 我对规则、责任等诸如此类的东西感到厌烦。

jazz[2] *v*

jazz sth ↔ **up** *phr v* [T] *informal* to make something more attractive or exciting【非正式】使更活泼; 使更诱人: *Jazz up your everyday meals with our new range of seasonings.* 用我们新系列的调味品使你的一日三餐更有味道。—**jazzed-up** *adj*

jazz·y /ˈdʒæzi; ˈdʒæzi/ *adj informal*【非正式】**1** bright, colourful or very modern in appearance〔外表〕炫丽的; 花哨的: *jazzy writing paper* 色彩鲜艳的信纸 **2** in the style of jazz music 爵士乐风格的

jct the written abbreviation of 缩写 = JUNCTION

jeal·ous /ˈdʒɛləs; ˈdʒeləs/ *adj* **1** feeling angry and unhappy because someone has something that you would like; ENVIOUS 嫉妒的, 妒忌的: [+of] *Why are you so jealous of his success?* 你为什么这么嫉妒他的成功? | **make sb jealous** *It makes me jealous, seeing all these women with babies.* 看见这些女人都有孩子, 真让我嫉妒。**2** feeling angry and unhappy because someone you like or love is showing interest in another person, or another person is showing interest in them 吃醋的: *She gets jealous if I even look at another woman.* 我即使只看别的女人一眼, 她也会醋意大发。| **jealous husband/wife/lover** *You're acting like a jealous husband.* 你的表现就像一个爱吃醋的丈夫。**3 jealous of** wanting to keep or protect something that you have because you are proud of it〔因对某物引以自豪而〕珍惜的; 小心守护的: *a country jealous of its heritage* 珍惜其文化遗产的国家 —**jealously** *adv*: *a jealously guarded secret* 小心守着的秘密

J

jeal·ous·y /ˈdʒɛləsɪ; ˈdʒeləsi/ *n* [C,U] a feeling of being jealous 妒忌; 嫉妒 (之情)

jeans /dʒinz; dʒiːnz/ *n* [plural] trousers made of DENIM (=a strong, usually blue cotton cloth) 粗斜纹蓝布裤, 牛仔裤

Jed·da /ˈdʒɛdə; ˈdʒedə/ also 又作 **Jiddah** /ˈdʒɪdə; ˈdʒɪdə/ the largest port of Saudi Arabia, on the Red Sea 吉达〔沙特阿拉伯最大港口, 濒临红海〕

jeep, Jeep *trademark*【商标】/dʒip; dʒiːp/ *n* [C] a type of car made for travelling over rough ground 吉普车

jeer /dʒɪr; dʒɪə/ *v* [I,T] to laugh unkindly at someone to show that you strongly disapprove of them 嘲笑; 嘲弄: [+at] *Of course they jeered at you – you lost the game, right?* 他们当然嘲笑你——你输了比赛, 对吧? —**jeer** *n* [C]: *hurtful jeers* 刻薄的嘲笑

jeer·ing /ˈdʒɪrɪŋ; ˈdʒɪərɪŋ/ *adj* a jeering remark or sound is unkind and shows disapproval〔说话、声音〕不友好的; 有恶意的: *jeering laughter* 嘲笑声 —**jeering** *n* [U] —**jeeringly** *adv*

Jeeves /dʒivz; dʒiːvz/ a character in many humorous stories by P. G. Wodehouse. Jeeves is the VALET (=male servant) of an UPPER-CLASS young man called Bertie Wooster, and is a very patient, sensible man. Wooster depends on him a lot and he always manages to solve Wooster's problems. 吉夫斯〔P.G.沃德豪斯创作的幽默小说中的人物, 为上层社会青年伯迪·伍斯特的男仆。吉夫斯是个耐心且明智的男人。伍斯特对他十分依赖, 而吉夫斯也总能为他排忧解难〕

jeez /dʒiz; dʒiːz/ *interjection AmE* used to strongly express feelings such as surprise, anger, etc【美】哎呀〔用来强烈地表示惊讶、气愤等〕

Jef·fer·son /ˈdʒɛfəsn̩; ˈdʒefəsən/, **Thomas** (1743-1826) the third President of the US, from 1801 to 1809. Jefferson was an important member of the Continental Congress and wrote most of *The Declaration of Independence*. When he was president, the US bought the Louisiana Purchase, and the SLAVE trade officially stopped being legal. 杰斐逊〔(1743-1826), 美国第三任总统, 1801 至 1809 年在任。他是大陆会议的重要成员之一, 撰写了《独立宣言》的大部分内容。在他担任总统期间, 美国买下了路易斯安那购置地, 并且从法律上正式禁止了买卖奴隶的行为〕

Jefferson City /ˌ··· ˈ··/ the capital city of the US state of Missouri 杰斐逊城〔美国密苏里州首府〕

Je·ho·vah /dʒɪˈhovə; dʒɪˈhəʊvə/ *n* a name given to God in the OLD TESTAMENT (=first part of the Bible) 耶和华〔《圣经·旧约》中对上帝的称呼〕

Jehovah's Wit·ness /·ˌ·· ˈ··/ *n* [C] a member of a religious organization that believes the end of the world will happen soon and sends its members to people's houses to try to make them join 耶和华见证人〔一个宗教教派的成员。该教派认为世界末日即将来临, 并派信徒上门传教, 试图劝人们加入〕

je·june /dʒɪˈdʒun; dʒɪˈdʒuːn/ *adj formal*【正式】**1** ideas that are jejune are too simple〔观点〕幼稚的: *jejune political opinions* 幼稚的政治观点 **2** writing or speech that is jejune is boring〔文章、讲话〕枯燥乏味的

Jek·yll and Hyde /ˌdʒɛkɪl ənd ˈhaɪd; ˌdʒekɪl ənd ˈhaɪd/ *n* [C] someone who is sometimes nice but at other times is unpleasant 具有善恶两重性格的人

jell /dʒɛl; dʒel/ *v* [I] **1** also 又作 **gel** *BrE*【英】if a thought, plan etc jells, it becomes clearer or more definite〔思想、计划等〕定形, 成形; 具体化: *Things were confused before, but they are really starting to jell now.* 情况曾经很混乱, 但现在确实开始清楚明朗了。**2** also 又作 **gel** if a liquid jells it becomes firmer, or thicker〔液体〕凝成胶状

jel·lied /ˈdʒɛlɪd; ˈdʒelid/ *adj* [only before noun 仅用于名词前] *especially BrE* cooked or served in jelly【尤英】煮成胶冻状的: *jellied eels* 鳝鱼冻

Jell-o, jello /ˈdʒɛlo; ˈdʒeləʊ/ *n* [U] *AmE trademark* JELLY (1)【美, 商标】果冻

jel·ly /ˈdʒɛlɪ; ˈdʒeli/ *n* **1** [C,U] *BrE* a soft solid substance made with sweetened fruit juice and GELATINE【英】果冻 (甜食); JELLO *AmE*【美】: *raspberry jelly* 山莓果冻 **2** [U] *AmE* a very thick sweet substance made from boiled fruit and sugar with no pieces of fruit in it; clear JAM[1] (1)【美】〔不含水果碎粒的〕果酱; 清果酱: *a peanut butter and jelly sandwich* 花生酱果酱三明治 **3** [U] *especially BrE* a soft solid substance made from meat juices and GELATINE; ASPIC【尤英】肉冻 **4** [U] substance that is solid but very soft, and moves easily when you touch it 胶冻, 胶冻状物: *frogs' eggs floating in a protective jelly* 在有保护作用的胶冻状物内漂浮的青蛙卵 **5 feel like/turn to jelly** if your legs, knees etc feel like jelly, they start to shake because you are frightened or nervous〔腿、膝盖等由于恐惧或紧张而〕开始颤抖

jelly ba·by /ˈ·· ˌ··/ *n* [C] *BrE trademark* a small soft sweet made in the shape of a baby in a variety of colours【英, 商标】胶糖娃娃〔一种做成娃娃形状、有各种颜色的软糖〕

jelly bean /ˈ·· ·/ *n* [C] a small soft sweet with different tastes and colours that is shaped like a bean 软心豆粒糖〔有不同颜色和味道〕

CULTURAL NOTE 文化注释

Jelly beans are popular in the US, especially at Easter, when they are put in EASTER BASKETS. 软心豆粒糖在美国很流行, 尤其是复活节时常放在复活节篮子里。

jel·ly·fish /ˈdʒɛlɪˌfɪʃ; ˈdʒelifɪʃ/ *n* [C] a round transparent sea animal that sometimes stings people 水母; 海蜇

jelly roll /ˈ·· ˌ·/ *n* [C] *AmE* a long thin cake that is rolled up with JAM[1] (1) or cream inside【美】〔夹有果酱或奶油的〕蛋糕卷, 瑞士卷; SWISS ROLL *BrE*【英】

jem·my /ˈdʒɛmɪ; ˈdʒemi/ *BrE*【英】, **jimmy** *AmE*【美】*n* [C] a metal bar used especially by thieves to break open locked doors, windows etc〔窃贼用来撬开门窗等的〕金属撬棍 —**jemmy** *v* [T+open]

je ne sais quoi /ˌʒɛ nə ˌse ˈkwɑ; ˌʒə nə seɪ ˈkwɑː/ *n French, often humorous*【法, 常幽默】**a certain je ne sais quoi** a good quality that you cannot easily describe 难以形容的好品质: *The place looks pretty old and crumbly, but it does have a certain je ne sais quoi.* 这地方看上去相当破旧, 但确实有一种难以形容的美。

Jen·ner /ˈdʒɛnɚ; ˈdʒenə/, **Edward** (1749-1823) a British doctor who developed the principle of VACCINATION. He discovered that putting a small amount of COWPOX (=a disease that affects cows and people, but that is less serious than smallpox) into people's bodies protected them from SMALLPOX, a related disease that had killed many people until then. 詹纳〔(1749-1823), 英国医生、接种疫苗原理的创立者。他发现给人体接种少量牛痘可预防天花。在此之前, 天花曾夺去了许多人的生命〕

jen·ny /ˈdʒɛnɪ; ˈdʒeni/ *n* [C] a SPINNING JENNY 珍妮多轴纺纱机

jeop·ar·dize also 又作 **-ise** *BrE*【英】/ˈdʒɛpɚdˌaɪz; ˈdʒepədaɪz/ *v* [T] to risk losing or spoiling something important or valuable 使〔重要或珍贵事物〕处于危险之中; 危害

jeop·ar·dy /ˈdʒɛpɚdɪ; ˈdʒepədi/ *n* **in jeopardy** in danger of being lost or harmed 在危险中〔会失去或受到危害〕: **put/place sth in jeopardy** *The killings could put the whole peace process in jeopardy.* 这些杀人事件会危及整个和平进程。

Jer·e·mi·ah /ˌdʒɛrəˈmaɪə; ˌdʒerɪ̈ˈmaɪə◂/ (6th century BC) in the Jewish and Christian religions, a Hebrew PROPHET who said that Jerusalem would be defeated and that God would become angry with the Jews and punish them. *The Book of Jeremiah* in the Old Testament of the Bible contains his prophecies (PROPHECY). A PESSIMISTIC person, who always says that bad things are going to happen, is sometimes called a Jeremiah. 耶利米〔(公元前6世纪), 犹太教和基督教的希伯来先知。他曾预言耶路撒冷将被打败, 上帝将对犹太人动怒并惩罚他们。这一预言可见于《圣经·旧约·耶利米书》。"耶利米"一名有时也可用来指称凡事总往坏处想的悲观主义者〕

Jer·i·cho /ˈdʒɛrɪko; ˈdʒerɪkəʊ/ a city in the Middle East, north of the Dead Sea. It is the oldest city in the world. According to the Old Testament of the Bible, it was attacked by Joshua , the leader of the ISRAELITES, and his army shouted and blew their TRUMPETS so loudly that the walls of the city fell down. 杰里科〔中东地区一城市, 位于死海以北, 是世界上最古老的城市。据《圣经·旧约》记载, 以色列首领约书亚曾率军攻打该城, 士兵的呐喊声和号角声惊天动地, 把城墙都给震塌了〕

jerk¹ /dʒɝk; dʒɜːk/ *v* **1** [I,T] to pull something suddenly and roughly 急拉; 猛拉: [+at/on] *Don't keep jerking at the drawer, it won't open.* 不要不停地猛拉那个抽屉, 打不开的。**2** [I,T] to move or make something move in short, sudden movements (使) 颠簸行进: **jerk to a stop/halt** *Suddenly the train jerked to a halt.* 火车猛然刹车, 停了下来。

jerk sb **around** *phr v* [T] *AmE informal* to waste someone's time or deliberately make things difficult for them【美, 非正式】浪费〔某人〕时间; 故意刁难〔某人〕

jerk off *phr v* [I,T] *taboo especially AmE* to MASTURBATE【讳, 尤美】手淫

jerk out *phr v* [I,T] to say something quickly and nervously 快速而紧张地说: *I jerked out some stupid remark.* 我情急之下说了一些蠢话。

jerk² *n* **1** [C] a sudden quick movement 猛的一动: **with a jerk** *The train moved off with a jerk.* 火车猛地一颠开动了。| **give sth a jerk** (=pull something suddenly) 猛地一拉某物 —see also 另见 PHYSICAL JERKS **2** [C] *informal* a stupid man who does not care about the effects of his actions【非正式】〔不顾行为后果的〕蠢人; 笨蛋: *Tim's such a jerk! He always says the wrong thing.* 蒂姆是个笨蛋! 他总是说错话。

jer·kin /ˈdʒɝkɪn; ˈdʒɜːkɪ̈n/ *n* [C] a short jacket that covers your body but not your arms 无袖外套

jerk·wa·ter /ˈdʒɝkˌwɔtɚ; ˈdʒɜːkwɔːtə/ *adj* [only before noun 仅用于名词前] *AmE spoken* a jerkwater place, organization etc is small and uninteresting【美口】〔地方、组织等〕无足轻重的; 小而乏味的

jerk·y¹ /ˈdʒɝkɪ; dʒɜːki/ *adj* movements that are jerky are rough, with many starts and stops〔在行进中〕不平稳的; 颠簸的: *The bus came to a jerky halt.* 公共汽车颠簸着停下来。—**jerkily** *adv* —**jerkiness** *n* [U]

jerky² *n* [U] *AmE* meat that has been cut into thin pieces and dried in the sun or with smoke【美】〔切成薄片, 晒过或熏过的〕肉干

jer·o·bo·am /ˌdʒɛrəˈboəm; ˌdʒerəˈbəʊəm/ *n* [C] a very large wine bottle 大酒瓶

Jer·ome /dʒɪˈrom; dʒɪ̈ˈrəʊm/, **Jerome K.** (1859-1927) a British writer of humorous NOVELs, best known for his book *Three Men in a Boat* 杰罗姆〔(1859-1927), 英国幽默小说作家, 以《三人同舟》最为有名〕

Jer·ry /ˈdʒɛrɪ; ˈdʒeri/ *n plural* **Jerries** [C] *especially BrE* an insulting word meaning a German【尤英】德国佬〔侮辱的称呼〕

jer·ry-built /ˈdʒɛrɪˌbɪlt; ˈdʒeribɪlt/ *adj* built cheaply, quickly, and badly 匆促草率建成的, 偷工减料盖成的

Jer·sey¹ /ˈdʒɝzɪ; ˈdʒɜːzi/ *n* **1** the largest of the Channel Islands, between England and France, which belongs to the UK. Jersey is famous for its cream and new potatoes, and is popular with tourists. 泽西岛〔海峡群岛中最大的岛屿, 位于英法之间。该岛属于英国, 以出产奶油和新马铃薯著称, 为旅游胜地〕**2** *AmE* an informal name for the US state of New Jersey【美】泽西州〔新泽西州别名〕

Jersey² *n* [C] a light brown cow 泽西种乳牛

jersey *n* **1** [C] a shirt made of soft material worn by players of sports such as football and RUGBY〔足球、橄榄球等运动员穿的〕紧身运动套衫 **2** [C] a piece of clothing made of wool that covers the upper part of your body and your arms; SWEATER 毛衣, 套头毛衣 **3** [U] a soft material made of cotton or wool 棉[毛]质的柔软衣料

Je·ru·sa·lem¹ /dʒəˈrusələm; dʒɪ̈ˈruːsələm/ a city in Israel, which is of great historical importance to Jews, Christians, and Muslims. It has many important places for all these religions, such as the Wailing Wall, the Mount of Olives, and the Dome of the Rock, an ancient and very holy Muslim building. 耶路撒冷〔以色列一城市。对犹太教徒、基督徒和穆斯林来说, 该市具有重要的历史地位。耶路撒冷有不少宗教圣地, 诸如哭墙、橄榄山、神圣的穆斯林古建筑岩顶圣殿〕

Jerusalem² a HYMN (=a song of praise to God) based on a poem by William Blake, which English people sometimes sing on PATRIOTIC occasions.《耶路撒冷》〔根据威廉·布莱克的一首诗改编而成的赞美诗。英国人常在举行爱国活动时演唱〕

Je·ru·sa·lem ar·ti·choke /dʒəˌrusələm ˈɑrtɪtʃok; dʒəˌruːsələm ˈɑːtɪ̈tʃəʊk/ *n* [C] an ARTICHOKE (2) 菊芋 —see picture on page A9 参见A9页图

Jerusalem Bi·ble, the /ˌ.... ˈ../ an English translation of the Bible made by Roman Catholic SCHOLARs in the 1960s《耶路撒冷圣经》〔20世纪60年代由天主教学者翻译的英文版《圣经》〕

jest¹ /dʒɛst; dʒest/ *n* **1** **in jest** something you say in jest is intended to be funny, not serious〔说话〕开玩笑地 **2** [C] *old-fashioned* something that you say or do to amuse people; joke【过时】笑话; 玩笑

jest² *v* [I+about] *old use* to say things that you do not really mean in order to amuse people【旧】说笑话; 开玩笑: **I jest!** *spoken* (=used to say that you are joking)【口】我是说着玩的! —**jestingly** *adv*

jest·er /ˈdʒɛstɚ; ˈdʒestə/ *n* [C] a man employed in the past by a king or ruler to entertain people with jokes, stories etc〔昔时为国王或统治者说笑逗乐的〕弄臣

Je·su·it /ˈdʒɛʒuɪt; ˈdʒezjuɪ̈t/ *n* [C] a man who is a member of the Roman Catholic religious Society of Jesus 天主教耶稣会会士

Je·sus¹ /ˈdʒizəs; ˈdʒiːzəs/ also 又作 **Jesus Christ** /ˌ.. ˈ./ *n* the person who Christians believe was the son of God, and whose life and teachings Christianity is based on 耶稣〔基督徒认为他是上帝的儿子, 他的生平和传教活动是基督教信仰的基础〕

Jesus² *interjection slang* used to express anger or surprise【俚】天啊〔用来表示愤怒或惊讶〕: *Oh Jesus! What are we going to do?* 哦, 天啊! 我们该怎么办?

USAGE NOTE 用法说明: JESUS

FORMALITY AND POLITENESS 正式与礼貌程度

Jesus!, **Christ!** and **Jesus Christ!** are all used in a non-religious way in very informal spoken English. They have the same uses as **God!**, but are even stronger. Jesus!, Christ! 和 Jesus Christ! 都以非宗教意义用于非正式的口语中, 用法与 God! 相同, 但语气更强: *Jesus, that hurts.* 哎呀, 太痛了。| *Jesus! What are you going to live on?* 天啊! 你打算靠什么生活?

Some people, especially those who believe in the Christian religion, are offended by these uses of these words. 有些人, 特别是信仰基督教的人, 对这些词用作感叹词感到反感。

jet¹ /dʒɛt; dʒet/ *n* **1** [C] an aircraft with a jet engine 喷气式飞机: **jet fighter/aircraft** *British jet fighters have joined the UN forces.* 英国的喷气式战斗机已加入联合国部队。**2** [C] a narrow stream of liquid or gas that comes quickly out of a small hole, or the hole itself〔液体、气体的〕喷射流: *a water jet* 水柱 **3** [U] a hard black stone that is used for making jewellery 煤玉, 黑玉

jet² *v* **jetted, jetting** [I always+adv/prep] **1** *informal* to travel by plane, especially when you go to many different places【非正式】坐飞机旅行〔尤指去很多不同的地方〕: *business executives jetting around the world* 坐飞机周游世界的企业行政人员 **2** if a liquid or gas jets out from somewhere, it comes quickly out of a small hole〔液体、气体〕喷射, 喷出

jet-black /ˌ· ˈ·◂/ *adj* very dark black 乌黑的: *jet-black hair* 乌黑的头发

jet en·gine /ˌ· ˈ··/ *n* [C] an engine that pushes out a stream of hot air and gases behind it, used in aircraft 喷气发动机 —see picture at 参见 AIRCRAFT 图

jet foil /ˈ· ·/ *n* [C] a boat that rises out of the water on structures that look like legs when it is travelling fast 喷流水翼船

jet lag /ˈ· ·/ *n* [U] the tired and confused feeling that you can get after flying a very long distance 飞行时差综合征 —**jet-lagged** *adj*

jet-pro·pelled /ˌ· ·ˈ·◂/ *adj* using a jet engine for power 喷气发动机推进的

jet pro·pul·sion /ˌ· ·ˈ··/ *n* [U] the use of a JET ENGINE for power 喷气推进

jet·sam /ˈdʒɛtsəm; ˈdʒetsəm/ *n* [U] things that are thrown from a ship and float on the sea towards the shore〔漂浮至岸边的〕从船上投进海里的物品 —see also 另见 **flotsam and jetsam** (FLOTSAM (2))

jet set /ˈ· ·/ *n* **the jet set** *old-fashioned* rich and fashionable people who travel a lot【过时】常乘飞机旅行又时髦的有钱阶层 —**jet-setter** *n* [C]

jet-ski /ˈ· ·/ *n* [C] a small fast boat that one or two people can ride on for fun〔供一人或两人乘坐游玩的〕喷气式滑水橇

jet stream /ˈ· ·/ *n* [singular,U] a current of very strong winds high above the Earth's surface〔地球高空上的〕急流

jet·ti·son /ˈdʒɛtəsn̩; ˈdʒetɪsən/ *v* [T] **1** to get rid of methods, ideas, or ways of doing things 除掉, 摆脱〔做事的方法、想法或方式〕: *The new President quickly jettisoned most of the previous economic policies.* 新上任的总统很快便废除了大部分旧有的经济政策。**2** to throw things away, especially from a moving plane or ship〔尤指从正在行进中的飞机或船上〕抛出〔物品〕, 丢弃

jet·ty /ˈdʒɛtɪ; ˈdʒeti/ *n* [C] a wide wall or flat area built out into the water, used for getting on and off ships 突堤; 码头 —compare 比较 PIER (1) —see picture on page A12 参见 A12 页图

Jew /dʒu; dʒuː/ *n* [C] a member of the group of people whose religion is Judaism, who lived in ancient times in the land of Israel, some of whom now live in the modern state of Israel and others in various countries throughout the world 犹太人; 犹太教徒〔古时犹太人居住在以色列地, 现在他们中有的住在现代的以色列国, 还有许多人散居在世界各地〕—**Jewish** *adj*: *the Jewish religion* 犹太教 | *My husband is Jewish.* 我丈夫是犹太人。

J

jew·el /ˈdʒuəl; ˈdʒuːəl/ *n* [C] **1** a small valuable stone, such as a diamond 宝石 **2 jewels** [plural] jewellery or decorative objects made with valuable stones 宝石饰物; 首饰 **3** a very small stone used in the machinery of a watch〔钟表内的〕宝石轴承; 钻 **4** *informal* someone who is very important to you, or the best things in a group of things【非正式】宝贵的人[物品]; 珍宝: *The Matisse was the jewel of her art collection.* 马蒂斯的画是她的艺术收藏品中的珍品。**5 the jewel in the crown** the best or most valuable part of something 皇冠上的珠宝〔指某物最好或最有价值的部分〕—see also 另见 CROWN JEWELS

jew·elled *BrE*【英】, **jeweled** *AmE*【美】/ˈdʒuəld; ˈdʒuːəld/ *adj* decorated with jewels 镶有宝石的: *the famous jewelled eggs of Fabergé* 著名的镶有宝石的法贝热复活节彩蛋

jew·el·ler *BrE*【英】, **jeweler** *AmE*【美】/ˈdʒuələ˞; ˈdʒuːələ/ *n* [C] **1** someone who owns or works in a shop that sells jewellery 珠宝商; 宝石商 **2** someone who makes or repairs jewellery 宝石匠

W3 **jew·el·lery** *BrE*【英】, **jewelry** *AmE*【美】/ˈdʒuəlrɪ; ˈdʒuːəlri/ *n* [U] small things that you wear for decoration, such as rings or NECKLACES 珠宝, 首饰: *a piece of jewellery* 一件首饰 —see also 另见 COSTUME JEWELLERY

Jew·ess /ˈdʒuɪs; ˈdʒuːɪ̥s/ *n* [C] *old-fashioned* a word meaning a Jewish woman, now usually considered offensive【过时】犹太女人〔此词现在一般视为具有冒犯性〕

Jew·ry /ˈdʒurɪ; ˈdʒuːri/ *n* [U] *old use* the Jewish people【旧】犹太人

Jez·e·bel /ˈdʒɛzəbl̩; ˈdʒezəbəl/ *n* [C] *old use* a sexually immoral woman【旧】荡妇

JFK /ˌdʒe ɛf ˈke; ˌdʒeɪ ef ˈkeɪ/ **1** John Fitzgerald Kennedy 约翰·菲茨杰拉德·肯尼迪 **2** one of the main airports in New York City 肯尼迪国际机场〔纽约市一主要机场〕

jib¹ /dʒɪb; dʒɪb/ *n* [C] **1** a small sail 艏三角帆, 小帆 —compare 比较 MAINSAIL —see picture at 参见 YACHT 图 **2** the long part of a CRANE¹ (1)〔起重机的〕悬臂

jib² *v* **jibbed, jibbing** [I] if a horse jibs, it stops suddenly and will not move〔马〕突然停步, 不肯走动

jib at sth *phr v* [T] *especially BrE informal* to become suddenly unwilling to do or accept something【尤英, 非正式】突然不肯做[接受]〔某事〕: *If he jibbed at five hundred pounds, he'll hardly pay four thousand!* 他如果连五百英镑都不肯付, 就更别说4000英镑了!

jibe¹, gibe /dʒaɪb; dʒaɪb/ *n* [C] an unkind remark intended to make someone seem silly 嘲讽的话: *She was tired of his constant jibes.* 她受够了他没完没了的挖苦。

jibe² *v* [I+with] *AmE* if two statements, reports etc jibe, the information in them matches【美】〔两个陈述、报告等〕相一致, 符合

jibe at sb/sth *phr v* [T] to say something that is intended to make someone seem silly 嘲讽, 挖苦

jif·fy /ˈdʒɪfɪ; ˈdʒɪfi/ also 又作 **jiff** /dʒɪf; dʒɪf/ *n* [singular] *spoken*【口】**in a jiffy** very soon 很快; 一会儿: *I'll be with you in a jiffy.* 我很快就来你这儿。

Jiffy bag /ˈ·· ·/ *n* [C] *BrE trademark* a thick soft envelope, used for posting things that might break【英, 商标】〔供邮寄易碎物品用的〕有衬垫的大封套

jig¹ /dʒɪg; dʒɪg/ *n* [C] a type of quick dance, or a piece of music for this dance 吉格舞(曲)〔一种轻快的舞蹈或为这种舞蹈伴奏的乐曲〕

jig² *v* **jigged, jigging 1** [I] to dance a jig 跳吉格舞 **2** [I always+adv/prep] to move up and down with quick short movements 上下急动; 蹦跳

jig·ger /ˈdʒɪgə˞; ˈdʒɪgə/ *n* [C] a small amount of alcoholic drink, or the cup this is measured with 少量的酒; 量酒的小杯

jig·gered /ˈdʒɪgə˞d; ˈdʒɪgəd/ *adj* [not before noun 不用于名词前] *BrE old-fashioned*【英, 过时】**I'll be jiggered!** used when you are very surprised 我感到吃惊!〔表示非常惊奇〕

jewellery 珠宝, 首饰

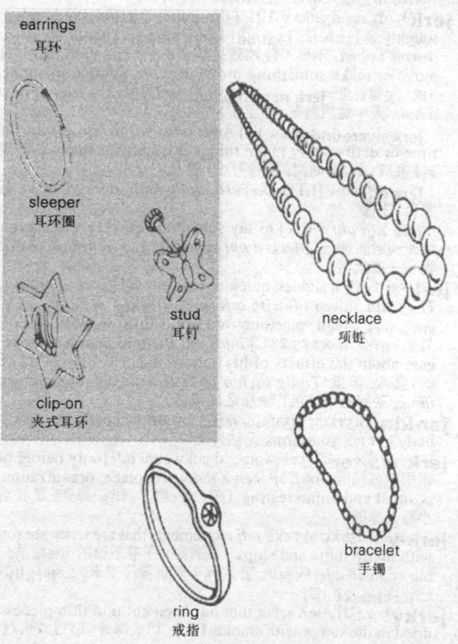

jig·ger·y-po·ker·y /ˌdʒɪgərɪ ˋpokərɪ; ˌdʒɪgəri ˈpəʊkəri/ *n* [U] *BrE informal* secret dishonest activity to make something seem what it is not【英, 非正式】诈骗; 骗局: *social jiggery-pokery behind the scenes* 幕后的卑鄙社交勾当

jig·gle /ˈdʒɪgl; ˈdʒɪgəl/ *v* **jiggled, jiggling** [I,T] to move or make something move from side to side with short quick movements (使) 急速地左右摆动

jigsaw 拼图玩具

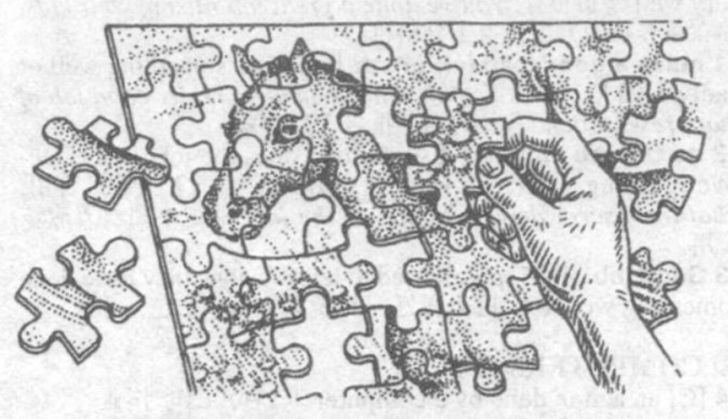

jig·saw /ˈdʒɪg,sɔ; ˈdʒɪgsɔː/ *n* [C] **1** also 又作 **jigsaw puz·zle** /ˈ‥, ·ˈ/ a picture cut up into many pieces that you try to fit together 拼图玩具 **2** a special SAW (=cutting tool) for cutting out shapes in thin pieces of wood 线锯, 镂花锯 —see picture at 参见 TOOL[1] 图

ji·had /dʒɪˋhɑd; dʒɪˈhɑːd/ *n* [C] a holy war fought by Muslims 〔伊斯兰教的〕圣战

jilt /dʒɪlt; dʒɪlt/ *v* [T] to end a relationship with someone 抛弃〔情人〕, 和…分手

Jim Crow /ˌdʒɪm ˋkro; ˌdʒɪm ˈkrəʊ/ *n AmE* a system of laws and practices in the US that separated black and white people【美】〔美国的〕歧视黑人的法律[做法]

jim·my /ˈdʒɪmɪ; ˈdʒɪmi/ *n* [C] the American form of the word JEMMY jemmy 的美式拼写 —**jimmy** *v* [T]

jin·gle[1] /ˈdʒɪŋgl; ˈdʒɪŋgəl/ *v* **jingled, jingling** [I,T] to shake metal things together so that they make a sound like small bells 使〔金属物件〕发出叮当声: *Stop jingling those coins in your pocket.* 别把口袋里的硬币弄得叮当作响。

jingle[2] *n* **1** [C] a short song used in advertisements 〔广告中的〕短歌 **2** [singular] the sound of small metal objects being shaken together 〔小金属物件撞击发出的〕叮当声 —see picture on page A19 参见 A19 页图

Jingle Bells /ˈ‥, ·/ the title and first words of a popular Christmas song.《铃儿响叮当》〔一流行圣诞歌曲名及歌词首句〕: *Jingle bells, jingle bells, / Jingle all the way. /Oh, what fun it is to ride / In a one-horse open sleigh.* 叮叮当, 叮叮当, /铃儿响叮当。/哦, 我们滑雪多快乐, /我们坐在雪橇上。

jin·go·is·m /ˈdʒɪŋgoɪzəm; ˈdʒɪŋgəʊɪzəm/ *n* [U] a strong belief that your own country is better than others 沙文主义; 极端爱国主义: *a mood of warlike jingoism* 好战的沙文主义情绪 —**jingoistic** /ˌdʒɪŋgoˋɪstɪk; ˌdʒɪŋgəʊˈɪstɪk◂/ *adj*

jinks /dʒɪŋks; dʒɪŋks/ *n* —see 见 HIGH JINKS

jinn /dʒɪn; dʒɪn/ *n* [C] a GENIE 妖魔, 精灵

Jin·nah /ˈdʒɪnə; ˈdʒɪnə/, **Mo·ham·med Al·i** /moˋhæmɪd ˋɑlɪ; məʊˈhæmɪ̈d ˈæli/ (1876-1948) the first governor-general of Pakistan, from 1947 until his death. Jinnah was for many years the leader of the Muslim League in India, an organization that wanted a separate country for India's Muslims. He was mainly responsible for establishing the state of Pakistan in 1947. 真纳〔(1876-1948), 1947年任巴基斯坦首任总督直至去世, 曾多年担任印度穆斯林联盟领袖。该组织主张建立一个独立的印度穆斯林国家。真纳为1947年巴基斯坦建国作出了重要贡献〕

jinx /dʒɪŋks; dʒɪŋks/ *n* [singular] a strange power that brings bad luck 不祥之物: **[+on]** *So many things have gone wrong, we're beginning to think there's a jinx on the whole wedding.* 那么多事情不对头, 我们开始认为整个婚礼交了噩运。

jinxed /dʒɪŋkst; dʒɪŋkst/ *adj* often having bad luck, or making people have bad luck 倒霉的; 带来噩运的

jit·ter·bug /ˈdʒɪtɚ,bʌg; ˈdʒɪtəbʌg/ *n* [singular] a popular fast JAZZ dance in the 1940s 吉特巴舞〔一种20世纪40年代流行的快节奏爵士舞〕

jit·ters /ˈdʒɪtɚz; ˈdʒɪtəz/ *n* **get the jitters** *informal* to feel anxious, especially before an important event or before something difficult【非正式】〔尤指在重大或困难事件发生之前〕感到紧张[恐慌]: *It's my driving test next week, and I've got the jitters already.* 下周我要参加驾驶考试, 我现在已经感到很紧张了。

jit·ter·y /ˈdʒɪtərɪ; ˈdʒɪtəri/ *adj informal* anxious or nervous【非正式】焦虑的; 紧张的

jive[1] /dʒaɪv; dʒaɪv/ *n* [C] **1** a very fast dance, popular especially in the 1930s and 40s, performed to SWING[2] (5) music 〔尤其流行于20世纪30和40年代, 伴随摇摆乐跳的快节奏〕摇摆舞 **2** [U] *AmE informal* statements that you do not believe are true【美, 非正式】假话; 花言巧语: *Don't give me any of that jive!* 别对我花言巧语!

jive[2] *v* **1** [I] to dance a jive 跳摇摆舞 **2** [T] *AmE informal* to try to make someone believe something that is not true, as a joke【美, 非正式】胡扯; 开玩笑, 愚弄

Jnr *adj BrE*【英】the written abbreviation of 缩写= JUNIOR

Joad family, the /ˈdʒod ˌfæməlɪ; ˈdʒəʊd ˌfæməli/ the main characters in the book *The Grapes of Wrath* (1939) by John Steinbeck 乔德一家〔约翰·斯坦贝克作品《愤怒的葡萄》(1939)中的主人公一家〕

Joan of Arc 圣女贞德

Joan of Arc /ˌdʒon əv ˋɑrk; ˌdʒəʊn əv ˈɑːk/ also 又作 **St Joan** (1412-31) the PATRON SAINT of France. As a young girl, she believed that she heard holy voices telling her to fight the English and force their army to leave France. Dressed as a man, she led a French army which defeated the English at Orléans, and became known as the 'Maid of Orléans'. Later she was made a prisoner, and a court found her guilty of being a WITCH (=a woman with evil magic powers), and she was punished by being burned to death. 圣女贞德〔(1412-1431), 法国的主保圣人。她小的时候认为自己听到了上帝的声音, 叫她与英军作战, 把他们赶出法国。她女扮男装, 率领法军在奥尔良打败英军, 人称"奥尔良少女"。后来, 她被捕入狱, 法庭给她冠以女巫的罪名, 并对她处以火刑〕

Job /dʒɑb; dʒɒb/ *n* **1** in the Old Testament of the Bible, a man who continued to have faith in God even though God destroyed his property and his family 约伯〔《圣经·旧约》中财产和家庭被上帝毁掉却仍信仰上帝的一个人物〕 **2 Job's comforter** someone who tries to make you feel more cheerful, but actually makes you feel worse 反让人更难过的安慰者; 好心安慰别人却适得其反的人 **3 have the patience of Job** to be extremely patient 极其有耐心

J

S1 W1

job /dʒɑb; dʒɒb/ *n*

① WORK 工作
② STH YOU MUST DO 责任, 义务
③ DO STH WELL/BADLY 干得好/干得差
④ COMPUTERS 电脑
⑤ CRIME 罪行
⑥ OTHER MEANINGS 其他意思

① WORK 工作

1 [C] the regular paid work that you do for an employer 工作; 职位; 职业: **get/find a job (as sth)** *Eventually, Mary got a job as a waitress.* 玛丽终于找到了一份服务员的工作。| **take a job** (=accept a job that is offered to you) 接受一份工作 *I was so desperate that I took the first job that came along.* 我求职心切, 第一份出现的工作就接受了。| **lose a job** *At least there's no danger of you losing your job.* 你至少没有失业的危险。|

temporary/permanent job *It's a temporary job, but I'm hoping it'll be made permanent.* 那是份临时工作，但我希望能成为固定的。| **offer (sb) a job** *Well, Ms Taylor, we'd like to offer you the job.* 嗯，泰勒女士，我们想聘请你。| **part-time/full-time job** (=a job you do for only part of the day or week, or all of the day or week) 兼职/全职工作 | **apply for a job** (=try to get a job) 申请工作 *I've applied for a job at the university.* 我申请了一份在大学里的工作。| **job satisfaction** (=the enjoyment that you get from doing your job) 工作满足感 | **leave/quit a job** *Oh Rick, you didn't quit your job, did you?* 里克，你没把工作辞掉吧？| **change jobs** (=get a different job) 转换工作 | **hold down a job** (=keep a job) 保住工作 | **job security** (=how permanent your job is likely to be) 就业保障〔指职位的固定性〕| **Saturday/summer/holiday job** (=a job that you only do on Saturdays etc) 在星期六/暑期/假日做的工作 | **steady job** (=a job that is likely to continue) 稳定的工作 | **be out of a job** (=not have a job) 失业 *If the project fails we'll all be out of a job.* 如果计划失败，我们都将失业。| **know your job** (=be very experienced at the work you do) 对自己的工作很内行 | **job losses** *Four hundred more job losses were announced this week.* 本周又宣布有四百多人失业。—see also 另见 JOB DESCRIPTION

2 on the job a) as part of a particular job 作为工作的一部分: *Most clerical training is done on the job.* 大部分文书培训都是在职进行的。**b)** doing a particular job 从事某种工作: *We'll put our best people on the job.* 我们会安排最优秀的人做这项工作。**c)** *BrE spoken* having sex【英口】在性交时

3 I'm only doing my job *spoken* used to say that it is not your fault if you have to do something in your work that other people do not like【口】我只是在做我的工作〔用来表示你所做的事情虽然有人不喜欢，但那属于你的职责范围，并非你的过错〕

4 it's more than my job's worth *BrE spoken* used to tell someone that you cannot do what they want because it is against your company's rules【英口】我的职位会保不住〔用于告诉某人你不能按照他们的意愿做事，因为那违反了公司的规章〕

5 jobs for the boys *BrE* work that someone in power has given to their friends, especially work that is not necessary【英】〔当权者〕给自己人安排的职位〔尤指没有必要的职位〕

② STH YOU MUST DO 责任，义务

6 [C] something that you have to do which involves working or making an effort 费劲的事: *Fixing the roof is going to be the biggest job.* 修缮屋顶将是一件最大的工作。| **odd jobs** (=small things that need to be done, especially in the house or garden) 〔尤指房子或花园里的〕杂活 | **get on with a job** (=continue doing a job) 继续工作 | **the job in hand** (=the work that you are doing now) 手头的工作

7 ►DUTY 责任◄ [singular] if it is your job to do something, it is your duty to do it 职责；责任: *Leave the dishes – that's my job.* 盘碟留给我，那是我的工作。| **it is sb's job (to do sth)** *It's my job to make sure that the work's finished on time.* 确保工作按时完成是我的责任。

8 fall down on the job to fail to do something you were supposed to do 未能完成该做的事

9 a job of work *BrE old-fashioned* something that you have to do, whether you enjoy it or not【英，过时】〔无论是否喜欢〕非做不可的事

③ DO STH WELL/BADLY 干得好/干得差

10 do a good/great/marvellous job (with) to do something very well 干得很好: *You've done a great job raising your kids.* 你在培养孩子方面做得十分出色。

11 make a good/bad job of sth *BrE* to do something well or badly【英】把某事做好/做坏: *Sarah made a really good job of that presentation.* 莎拉的那个报告真是精彩。

12 do the job *informal* if something does the job, it is effective in doing what you want it to do【非正式】〔某物〕管用: *That little screwdriver should do the job.* 那把小螺丝刀应该管用。

13 Good job! *AmE spoken* used to tell someone they have done something well【美口】干得好！〔称赞某人做事出色〕

④ COMPUTERS 电脑

14 [C] an action done by a computer（一件）工作，作业

⑤ CRIME 罪行

15 [C] *informal* a crime in which money is stolen from a bank, company etc【非正式】〔从银行、公司等〕盗窃: *a bank job* 抢劫银行 | **an inside job** (=one done by a member of the organization in which it happens) 内贼作案；监守自盗

⑥ OTHER MEANINGS 其他意思

16 it's a good job *BrE spoken* used to say that it is lucky that something happened【英口】真幸运〔用来表示幸亏做了某事〕: *It's a good job you had your safety belt on.* 幸好你系了安全带。

17 have a job doing/to do sth *BrE spoken* to have difficulty doing something【英口】做某事很困难: *I had an awful job getting that stain out.* 我费了好大劲才把那污渍去掉。

18 make the best of a bad job *especially BrE* to do the best that you can in a situation that you do not like but cannot change【尤英】〔在不喜欢但无法改变的情况下〕尽力而为

19 give sth up as a bad job *BrE* to accept that something is not going to succeed and stop trying to do it【英】因感到无望而放弃做某事

20 just the job *BrE spoken* exactly what is needed for a particular situation【英口】正是需要的东西: *That table you gave us was just the job!* 你给我们的那张桌子，我们正需要！

21 ►KIND OF THING 某种东西◄ *spoken* used to say that something is of a particular type【口】〔用来说明某物属于某类型〕: *Jack's got a new car – a red two-seater job.* 杰克买了一辆新车，是红色双座的那种。

22 a job lot *BrE* a mixed group of things that are sold together【英】混合出售的一批物品: *a job lot of furniture* 混杂出售的一批家具 – see also 另见 BLOW JOB, HAND JOB, NOSE JOB

J

USAGE NOTE 用法说明: JOB

WORD CHOICE 词语辨析: **job, work, post, position, line of work/business, do, occupation, trade, profession, vocation, career**

What you do to earn your living is your **job** [C], especially if you work for someone else. job〔可数名词〕指谋生的工作，尤指为他人所雇: *I need a part-time job.* 我需要一份兼职工作。| *a boring job delivering pizzas* 外送比萨饼的乏味工作

Work [U] is something you are paid for doing, especially regularly. work〔不可数名词〕指有报酬的工作，尤指固定工作: *She wants to return to work after having the baby.* 她想生完孩子后继续工作。But it can also be used where there is no payment or you are not working for someone else. 但也可指无报酬的工作，或不为他人雇用: *voluntary work* 志愿工作 | *housework* 家务 | *her work as a self-employed trainer* 她当自雇教练

Post and **position** are more formal words for a particular job in a company etc. post 和 position 是较为正式的用语，指在公司等机构里某个专门的职位: *He was appointed to the post/position of professor of English at Stanford University.* 他被聘任为斯坦福大学的英语教授。

In spoken English, the kind of work or job someone does may be called their **line of work/business**, or the verb **do** is often used, especially in questions. 口语中，某人从事的行业可称为 line of work/business。动词 do 也很常用，尤其用于问句: *What do you do?* 你是做什么工作的？| *I'd like to get into that line of work!* 我想从事那种职业！

More formally, your kind of work or job is your **occupation** [C]. occupation〔可数名词〕表示所从事的职业，是更正式的用语。On a form you might see 在申请表中可能看到: *Please state your name and occupation.* 请填写你的姓名和职业。

A **trade** is a skilled kind of work in which you make or do things with your hands. trade 指有专门技术的手工行业: *She's an electrician by trade.* 她的职业是电工。

A **profession** is a kind of work such as that of a doctor or lawyer, for which you need special training and a good education. Some **professions**, such as teaching and nursing, are also called **vocations**, which suggests that people do them in order to help others rather than to earn a lot of money. profession 指需要受过特殊训练和良好教育的工作，如医生和律师。一些旨在帮助他人，而不是为了挣钱的职业，如教书和护理，也可称作 vocation。

A **career** is a type of work that you do or hope to do for most of your life. career 指终生从事的事业: *Her political career began 20 years ago.* 她的政治生涯始于20年前。

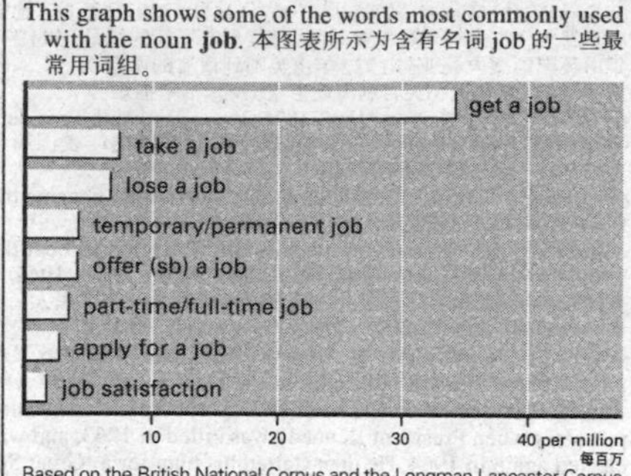

job·ber /ˈdʒɑbɚ; ˈdʒɒbə/ *n* [C] *especially BrE* someone whose job is buying and selling stocks (STOCK[1] (3)) and shares (SHARE[2] (5))【尤英】证券[股票]经纪人

job·bing /ˈdʒɑbɪŋ; ˈdʒɒbɪŋ/ *adj BrE*【英】**jobbing gardener/painter etc** someone who does small pieces of work for different people 打零工的园丁/漆匠等

job cen·tre /ˈ·,··/ *n* [C] a British government service where jobs are advertised and training courses are provided for people who are looking for work〔英国政府的〕就业服务中心

job de·scrip·tion /ˈ··,··/ *n* [C] an official list of the work and responsibilities that you have in your job〔正式的〕工作职责说明

job·less /ˈdʒɑblɪs; ˈdʒɒbləs/ *adj* without a job; UNEMPLOYED[1] 无业的; 失业的

job-shar·ing /ˈ·,··/ *n* [U] an arrangement by which two people both work PART-TIME doing the same job 职位共享〔两人分担一份全职工作〕—**job-share** *n* [C]

jobs·worth /ˈdʒɑbzwɝθ; ˈdʒɒbzwɜːθ/ *n* [C] *BrE informal* someone who follows the rules of their job too exactly without using any imagination【英, 非正式】工作中墨守成规的人, 工作死板的人

Jo'burg, the /ˈdʒobɝg; ˈdʒəʊbɜːg/ informal name for Johannesburg 约翰内斯堡〔该城市的非正式名称〕

jock /dʒɑk; dʒɒk/ *n* [C] **1** *BrE informal* an insulting word for someone from Scotland【英, 非正式】苏格兰佬〔侮辱的称呼〕**2** *AmE informal* an insulting word for someone who does a lot of sport【美, 非正式】运动员〔对酷爱运动的人的侮辱性称呼〕

jock·ey[1] /ˈdʒɑkɪ; ˈdʒɒki/ *n* [C] someone who rides horses in races 赛马骑师

jockey[2] *v* **1 jockey for position** to try to get into the best position or situation 争取最有利的位置: *businessmen jockeying for position at the bar* 在酒吧抢位子的商人 **2** [T] to gradually persuade someone to do something 逐渐说服〔某人做某事〕; 诱使: **jockey sb into doing sth** *Do you think you can jockey them into accepting our offer?* 你觉得你能说服他们接受我们的提议吗?

Jockey Club, the /ˈ·· ·/ the organization in charge of horse racing in the UK. Some other countries also have a Jockey Club.〔英国〕赛马总会〔英国管理赛马的组织。其他一些国家也有赛马总会〕

jockey shorts /ˈ·· ·/ *n* [plural] *trademark* a type of men's cotton underwear that fits very tightly【商标】乔基裤〔一种男式棉质紧身内裤〕

jock·strap /ˈdʒɑk,stræp; ˈdʒɒkstræp/ *n* [C] a piece of men's underwear that supports their sex organs during sport〔男人运动时用的〕下体护身

jo·cose /dʒoˈkos; dʒəˈkəʊs/ *adj literary* joking【文】开玩笑的 —**jocosely** *adv* —**jocoseness, jocosity** /dʒoˈkɑsətɪ; dʒəˈkɒsɪ̣ti/ *n* [U]

joc·u·lar /ˈdʒɑkjələ; ˈdʒɒkjʊ̈lə/ *adj formal* joking or humorous【正式】开玩笑的; 幽默的: *jocular remarks* 诙谐的话 —**jocularly** *adv* —**jocularity** /,dʒɑkjəˈlærətɪ; ,dʒɒkjʊ̈ˈlærɪ̣ti/ *n* [U]

joc·und /ˈdʒɑkənd; ˈdʒɒkənd/ *adj literary* cheerful and happy【文】愉快的, 欢乐的 —**jocundly** *adv* —**jocundity** /dʒoˈkʌndətɪ; dʒəʊˈkʌndɪ̣ti/ *n* [U]

jodh·purs /ˈdʒɑdpɚz; ˈdʒɒdpəz/ *n* [plural] a special type of trousers that you wear when riding horses 马裤

Jod·rell Bank /,dʒɑdrəl ˈbæŋk; ,dʒɒdrəl ˈbæŋk/ an OBSERVATORY (=place from which scientists study the stars, etc) in Cheshire, northwest England 乔德雷尔班克天文台〔位于英格兰西北部柴郡的一座天文台〕

Joe Bloggs /,dʒo ˈblɑgz; ,dʒəʊ ˈblɒgz/ *BrE*【英】, **Joe Blow/Schmo** /-ˈblo, -ˈʃmo; -ˈbləʊ, -ˈʃməʊ/ *AmE*【美】*n* [singular] *spoken* the ordinary average person【口】普通人, 常人

Joffrey /ˈdʒɔfrɪ; ˈdʒɔːfri/, **Robert** (1930-88) an American BALLET dancer and CHOREOGRAPHER (=someone who arranges how dancers will move). He started the American Ballet Centre, a school for dancers, in 1953, and a ballet group in 1956. His ballet group later became the Joffrey Ballet, one of the most important ballet groups in the US. 乔夫里〔(1930-1988), 美国芭蕾舞演员、舞蹈编导。他于1953年创办了一所舞蹈学校, 名为美国芭蕾中心, 1956年成立芭蕾舞团, 后更名为乔夫里芭蕾舞团, 是美国最重要的芭蕾舞团之一〕

jog[1] /dʒɑg; dʒɒg/ *v* **jogged, jogging 1** [I] to run slowly and steadily, especially as a way of exercising〔尤指为锻炼身体而〕慢跑: *two figures jogging along the beach* 沿海滩慢跑的两个人 **2** [T] to knock or push something lightly by mistake〔非故意〕轻碰, 轻推: *You jogged my elbow.* 你碰了一下我的肘部。**3 jog sb's memory** to make someone remember something 使某人记起某事: *Perhaps this photo will help to jog your memory.* 也许这张照片能帮助你回忆。

jog along *phr v* [I] *informal* to continue in the same way as usual【非正式】如常进行, 照旧继续

jog[2] *n* [singular] **1** a slow steady run, especially done as a way of exercising〔尤指为锻炼身体而进行的〕慢跑: **go for a jog** *Mike goes for a two-mile jog every morning.* 迈克每天早上慢跑两英里。**2** a light knock or push done by accident〔意外地〕轻碰, 轻推

jog·ger /ˈdʒɑgɚ; ˈdʒɒgə/ *n* [C] someone who runs slowly and steadily as a way of exercising〔健身锻炼的〕慢跑者

jog·ging /ˈdʒɑgɪŋ; ˈdʒɒgɪŋ/ *n* [U] the activity of running slowly and steadily as a way of exercising〔作为健身锻炼的〕慢跑

jogging suit /ˈ·· ·/ *n* [C] loose thick cotton clothes that you wear when you are running for exercise〔宽松厚身的棉质〕慢跑运动服

jog·gle /ˈdʒɑgḷ; ˈdʒɒgəl/ *v* [I,T] *informal* to shake or move up and down slightly【非正式】轻微摇晃

jog trot /ˈ· ·/ *n* [singular] a slow steady run 小跑; 慢跑 —**jog-trot** *v* [I]

Jo·han·nes·burg /dʒoˈhænɪsbɝg; dʒəʊˈhænɪ̣sbɜːg/ also 又作 **Jo'burg** *informal*【非正式】the largest city in South Africa, and a centre for business and industry. Before the end of APARTHEID, black people were not allowed to live there, and had to live in TOWNSHIPS outside the city, especially in Soweto. 约翰内斯堡〔南非最大城市和工商业中心。种族隔离制度废除之前, 黑人不许在该市居住, 只能住在城外的城镇, 尤其是索韦托〕

john /dʒɑn; dʒɒn/ *n* [C] *AmE*【美】**1** *informal* a toilet【非正式】卫生间, 厕所 **2** *slang* the customer of a PROSTITUTE【俚】嫖客

John, El·ton /ˈɛltṇ; ˈeltən/ (1947-) a British POP singer and songwriter, now officially called Sir Elton John, who was especially successful in the 1970s. One of his best-known songs, *Candle in the Wind*, was recorded again in 1997 with new words, to remember Princess Diana after she was killed in a car crash. 约翰〔(1947-), 英国流行歌手、歌曲作家, 现在正式称埃尔顿·约翰爵士。20世纪70年代, 他的音乐生涯达到巅峰。其最著名的歌曲之一《风中之烛》于1997年重新填词灌制, 以纪念死于车祸的英国王妃戴安娜〕

John, King (1167-1216) the king of England from 1199 until his death. He signed the *Magna Carta* in 1215, by which he agreed to accept limits on his power as king. These events are described in a play by William Shakespeare called *King John*. 约翰王〔(1167-1216), 英格兰国王, 1199年即位直至去世。他于1215年签署了限制王权的《大宪章》。他的生平逸事可见于莎士比亚的剧作《约翰王》〕

John, Saint one of Jesus Christ's DISCIPLES (=his close friends and followers), who wrote several of the books of the New Testament of the Bible: *The Gospel according to St John*, which describes the life and teaching of Jesus, the three *Epistles of John*, and *The Book of Revelation*. He is sometimes called St John the Evangelist or St John the Divine. 圣约翰〔耶稣基督的门徒之一。《圣经·新约》中的《约翰福音》、《约翰一书》、《约翰二书》、《约翰三书》和《启示录》为其所作, 其中《约翰福音》主要记述耶稣生平和教诲。有时人们亦称他为福音书作者圣约翰和圣徒圣约翰〕

John Bar·ley·corn /,dʒɑn ˈbɑrlɪkɔrn; ,dʒɒn ˈbɑːlikɔːn/ *literary* or *old-fashioned* the PERSONIFICATION (=the representation of a thing as a person, in literature or art) of alcoholic drink, especially strong drinks such as WHISKY【文或过时】大麦约翰〔含酒精饮料的拟人化名称, 尤指威士忌一类的烈性酒〕

John Birch So·ci·e·ty, the /,· '· ·, ·· ·/ a very RIGHT-WING organization started in the US during the 1950s to fight Communism 约翰·伯奇协会〔20世纪50年代于美国建立的一极右反共组织〕

John Brown's Bod·y /,· · '· ·/ a US FOLK song about John Brown, a man who fought against SLAVERY in the US.《约翰·布朗的遗体》〔歌颂废奴主义者约翰·布朗的一首美国民歌〕: *John Brown's body lies a-mouldering in the grave,/But his soul goes marching on...* 约翰·布朗的遗体在坟墓中腐化，/但他的精神常驻不衰…

John Bull 英国佬

John Bull /,· '·/ *n old-fashioned*【过时】**1** [U] England or the English people 英国; 英国人 **2** [C] an insulting word for an Englishman, especially one who does not like foreigners〔尤指不喜欢外国人的〕英国佬〔侮辱性称呼〕

John Doe /,· '·/ *n* [singular] *AmE* a man whose name is not known, especially one who is involved in a law case【美】某甲, 某男〔尤指诉讼程序中对不知真实姓名的男当事人的称呼〕— compare 比较 JANE DOE

John Han·cock /,dʒɑn 'hænkɑk; ,dʒɒn 'hænkɒk/ *n* [C] *AmE informal* your signature【美, 非正式】亲笔签名

john·ny /'dʒɑnɪ; 'dʒɒni/ *n* [C] **1** *BrE slang* a CONDOM【英俚】避孕套 **2** *old-fashioned* a man【过时】男人 **3** *AmE slang* a PENIS【美俚】阴茎

Johnny-on-the-spot /,· · · '·/ *n* [singular] *AmE informal* someone who immediately offers to help, takes an opportunity etc【美, 非正式】随时提供帮忙的人; 随时利用机会的人

John of Gaunt /,· · '·/ (1340-99) an English politician, son of Edward III, who acted as head of government until Richard II was old enough to rule 冈特的约翰〔(1340-1399), 英格兰政治家, 爱德华三世之子, 曾代理查二世主政, 直至其长大成人〕

John O' Groats /,dʒɑn ə 'grots; ,dʒɒn ə 'grəʊts/ a place in northeast Scotland, which people think of as the most northern part of the UK, although in fact it is not. It is used especially in the phrase 'from Land's End to John O'Groats', which means right across the UK. 约翰奥格罗茨〔苏格兰东北部一地, 被视为英国的最北端, 虽然事实并非如此。该名词尤用于 *from Land's End to John O'Groats* (从兰兹角[天涯海角]到约翰奥格罗茨) 这一短语, 意指"贯穿英国"〕

John Paul I /,dʒɑn pɔl 'fɝst; ,dʒɒn pɔːl; 'fɜːst/, **Pope** (1912-78) an Italian priest who was POPE (=the leader of the Roman Catholic religion) for only 34 days before his death 约翰·保罗一世〔(1912-1978), 意大利神父, 任教皇仅34天即与世长辞〕

John Paul II /,dʒɑn pɔl ðə 'sɛkənd; ,dʒɒn pɔːl ðə 'sekənd/, **Pope** (1920-2005) a Polish priest, who became the first Polish POPE (=the leader of the Roman Catholic religion) in 1978. He has travelled more than any Pope before, visiting countries all over the world. He has often spoken about his opposition to birth control and to the idea of women becoming priests. 约翰·保罗二世〔(1920-2005), 波兰神父, 1978年成为首位波兰籍教皇。他比以前的教皇更频繁地出访多个国家, 并多次表明自己对节育和女性担任神职持反对态度〕

johns /dʒɑnz; dʒɒnz/ *n* [plural] —see 见 LONG JOHNS

Johns, Jasper /'dʒæspɚ; 'dʒæspə/ (1930-) a US painter who is important in the development of Pop Art 琼斯〔(1930-), 美国画家, 在波普艺术的发展中起到重要作用〕

John·son /'dʒɑnsn̩; 'dʒɒnsən/, **A·my** /'emɪ; 'eɪmi/ (1903-41) a British pilot who flew alone in several famous flights in which she broke new records, for example from England to Australia in 1930, and from England to South Africa in 1932. She died when her plane disappeared over the English Channel during World War II. 约翰逊〔(1903-1941), 英国飞行员。她曾独自驾驶飞机进行过数次著名的飞行, 创造了新的纪录, 如1930年由英国到澳大利亚与1932年由英国到南非的两次飞行。二战期间, 她驾驶飞机在英吉利海峡上空失踪, 不幸罹难〕

Johnson, Andrew (1808-1875) the seventeenth President of the US, from 1865 to 1869 约翰逊〔(1808-1875), 美国第十七任总统, 1865至1869年在任〕

Johnson, Jack (1878-1946), a US BOXER who became the first black American to win the world HEAVYWEIGHT CHAMPIONSHIP. Johnson was a very skilful boxer who beat the world CHAMPION Tommy Burns in 1908. 约翰逊〔(1878-1946), 美国拳击手, 获世界重量级拳击比赛冠军的第一位美国黑人。他拳技十分娴熟, 于1908年击败前世界冠军汤米·伯恩斯〕

Johnson, Lyn·don B. /'lɪndən 'bi; 'lɪndən 'biː/ also 又作 **LBJ** (1908-73) a US politician in the Democratic Party who was the President of the US from 1963 to 1969. He first became president when President Kennedy was killed in 1963, and was elected again in 1964. He then started his plan for a 'Great Society' by introducing laws that helped poor people, improved medical care and education, and gave CIVIL RIGHTS to all US citizens whatever their race. When the US became more involved in the Vietnam War, however, he became unpopular. 约翰逊〔(1908-1973), 美国民主党政治家, 1963至1969年任美国总统。1963年肯尼迪总统遭暗杀后, 他首次出任美国总统, 1964年再度当选。于是, 他开始通过推出一系列法律实施他的"伟大社会"计划, 这些法律旨在帮助穷人, 完善医疗保健和教育制度, 不分种族赋予美国人平等的公民权利。然而, 随着美国逐渐卷入越南战争, 他失去了民心〕

Johnson, Sam·u·el /'sæmjuəl; 'sæmjʊəl/ (1709-84), known as **Dr Johnson**, a British CRITIC and dictionary writer, famous for his *Dictionary of the English Language* (1755). He was well-known in London society in the 18th century, and considered to be an excellent CONVERSATIONALIST (=his conversation was intelligent, amusing, and interesting). 约翰逊〔(1709-1784), 即约翰逊博士, 英国评论家、词典编纂家, 以《英语词典》(1755) 著称。他在18世纪的伦敦上流社会中享有盛名, 被认为是一位十分健谈的人〕

Johnson, Virginia Eshelman /vɚ'dʒɪnjə 'ɛʃəlmən; və'dʒɪniə 'eʃəlmən/ —see 见 MASTERS AND JOHNSON

John the Bap·tist, Saint /,· · '· ·/ (?12 BC-?28 AD) in the New Testament of the Bible, a religious teacher who told people that Jesus Christ was coming, and who BAPTIZED Jesus in the River Jordan 施洗约翰〔(公元前?12-公元?28),《圣经·新约》中的一名传道士。他曾告诉人们耶稣基督将要降临, 后来又在约旦河为耶稣施洗〕

John XXIII /,dʒɑn ðə twɛntɪ 'sɛkənd; ,dʒɒn ðə twenti 'sekənd/ (1881-1963) an Italian priest who became POPE (=the leader of the Roman Catholic religion) in 1958 约翰二十三世〔(1881-1963), 意大利神父, 1958年成为教皇〕

john thom·as /,dʒɑn 'tɑməs; ,dʒɒn 'tɒməs/ *n* [C] *slang* a PENIS【俚】阴茎

joie de viv·re /,ʒwɑ də 'vivr; ,ʒwɑː də 'viːvrə/ *n* [U] *French* a feeling of pleasure and excitement because you are alive【法】〔由于活着而产生的〕快乐兴奋

join¹ /dʒɔɪn; dʒɔɪn/ *v*

1 ►CONNECT 连接◄ a) [T] to connect or fasten things together 连接, 接合; 连结: *Join the two pieces of wood with strong glue.* 用强力胶水把两块木头黏合起来。| *The hip bone is joined to the thigh bone.* 髋骨和股骨相连。**b)** [I,T] to come together and become connected 汇合, 聚合: *Where does the river join the sea?* 这条河在什么地方入海?

2 ►GROUP/ORGANIZATION 群体/组织◄ [T] to become a member of an organization, society, or group 成为…的一员, 加入, 加盟: *When did you join the Labour Party?* 你何时加入工党的? | *Woods joined the Daily Dispatch as a reporter in 1960.* 伍兹于1960年进入《每日快讯报》当记者。

3 ►ACTIVITY 活动◄ [T] to begin to take part in an activity that other people are involved in 参加〔活动〕: **join a course/class/scheme etc** *I joined the class halfway through the second term.* 我在第二个学期中途插入这个班。| *Church leaders have joined the campaign to end foxhunting.* 教会领袖参加了禁止猎狐的运动。

4 join a queue/line/row etc to go and stand at the end of a line of people 排队: *Meanwhile, Carl joined the queue for tickets.* 同时, 卡尔排队买票。

5 join sb (for sth) to meet someone in order to do something together 与某人作伴(做某事): *I'm going to the theatre tonight. Would you care to join me?* 我今晚去剧院, 你愿意一起去吗?

6 join sb in doing sth to do or say something together with someone else 与某人一起说[做]某事: *I'm sure you'll all join me in thanking today's speaker.* 我相信你们都会和我一起感谢今天的演讲者。

7 join hands if people join hands, they hold each other's hands 携手

8 join the club! *spoken* used to say that you and a lot of other people are in the same situation【口】大家都一样!〔指你和其他许多人的境况一样〕: *"I can't find a job at all." "Yeah? Join the club!"* "我根本找不到工作。""是吗? 我们都一样!"

9 join battle *formal* to begin fighting【正式】开始交战

10 be joined in marriage/holy matrimony *formal* to be married【正式】结婚, 结成夫妇 —see also 另见 **join/combine forces** (FORCE[1] (7)), **if you can't beat 'em, join 'em** (BEAT[1] (20))

join in *phr v* [I,T] to take part in an activity as one of a group of people 参加〔活动〕; 加入进来: *Come on, Ian, join in! You can sing!* 伊恩, 你也来! 你会唱歌! | **join in the fun/party** *We couldn't wait to join in the fun.* 我们迫不及待地参加进去一起玩。

join up *phr v* [I] to become a member of the army, navy, or airforce 从军

join up with sb/sth *phr v* [T] *informal* to combine with other people in order to do something【非正式】与〔某人〕结伙〔干某事〕: *We joined up with a couple from Derbyshire to make a quiz team.* 我们和德比郡的一对夫妇组成一个问答比赛小组。

join with sb *phr v* [T] *formal* to do or say something together, as a group【正式】与…一同做[说]: **join with sb in doing sth** *Please join with me in praying for Sarah's recovery.* 请和我一起祈祷萨拉早日康复。

USAGE NOTE 用法说明: JOIN

WORD CHOICE 词语辨析: **join, enrol(l) in/at, enlist in, go to, come to, attend, join in, participate in**

If you go to be with someone, you **join** them. join 指和某人在一起: *He was looking forward to joining his wife/family in Detroit* (NOT 不用 *joining with them*). 他盼望着在底特律与妻子/家人团聚。

You may also **join** (=become a member of) many kinds of groups of people, such as a club, a team, a political party, a tour group, a company, a church, or a congregation (NOT 不用 *join in*). A country may **join** the EU, the UN, or another international organization. join 还可指加入各种各样的团体, 如俱乐部、团队、政党、旅游团、公司、教会、教堂会众等。一个国家可以加入欧盟、联合国或其他国际组织。

You may **join** the army, navy etc or more formally **enlist in** it. You **go to** war (NOT 不用 *join* it). 可以用 join 指参加军队〔陆军、海军等〕, 更正式的说法是 enlist in。"参军打仗"是 go to war。

You may **join** a class, course, or university at the beginning, but the more official word is **enrol in/at** (*AmE* **enroll**). join 可表示在开学时加入一个班、修读一个课程或入读大学, 但更正式的用语是 enrol in/at〔美 enroll〕: *I want to enrol in/join the linguistics class* (NOT 不用 *join to*). 我想上语言学的课。| *Diane has enrolled at the University of Essex.* 黛安娜入读了埃塞克斯大学。When you **go** regularly **to** a class, school etc, you formally **attend** it (NOT 不用 *attend to* it). 经常地听课或上学等, 是 attend〔出席〕。

You usually **go/come to** or more formally **attend** an event such as a meeting, football game, wedding, church service or official dinner (NOT 不用 *join*). 参加一项活动, 如会议、足球比赛、婚礼、教堂礼拜或正式宴会, 通常用 go/come to, 较正式的用语是 attend: *Are you coming to my birthday party?* 你打算来参加我的生日聚会吗?

If you actively take part in something that a group is doing, you **join in** or more formally **participate in** what it does. join in 或更正式的用语 participate in 是指积极参加一群人正在做的某事: *I hope you will participate in all our club activities.* 我希望你能参加我们俱乐部的所有活动。| *Chris joined in the class discussion enthusiastically.* 克里斯积极地参与课堂讨论。

You **go to, attend**, or more actively **participate in** a conference. "参加会议"可用 go to 或 attend, 而 participate in 表示更积极地参加。

join² *n* [C] a place where two parts of an object are connected or fastened together〔两个物体的〕连接处: **you can hardly see the join** *It's been glued back together so well, you can hardly see the join.* 这东西粘回原样, 粘得很好, 几乎看不出其中的接口。

join·er /ˈdʒɔɪnɚ; ˈdʒɔɪnə/ *n* [C] someone who makes wooden doors, window frames etc〔制造木门、窗框等的〕细木工人 —compare 比较 CARPENTER

join·er·y /ˈdʒɔɪnəri; ˈdʒɔɪnəri/ *n* [U] the trade and work of a joiner 细木工行业[手艺] —compare 比较 CARPENTRY

joint¹ /dʒɔɪnt; dʒɔɪnt/ *adj* [only before noun 仅用于名词前] **1** [W2]
shared, owned by, or involving two or more people or groups 共享的; 共有的; 共同的: *a joint bank account* 共有的银行账户 | *joint first prize* 共同获得的头奖 | *joint army and airforce operations* 陆军与空军的联合行动 **2 joint effort** a situation in which two or more people work together 共同努力: *"Who cooked the meal?" "Well it was a joint effort really."* "这顿饭是谁做的?" "这是我们共同努力的成果。" **3 joint venture** a business activity begun by two or more people or companies working together 合资经营项目; 合资企业 **4 joint resolution** *law* a decision or law agreed by both houses of the US Congress and signed by the President【法律】〔由美国国会众议院和参议院两院同意并经总统签署的〕共同决议 —**jointly** *adv*: *tenants who are jointly responsible for their rent* 共同分担房租的房客

joint² *n* [C] **1** a part of your body where two bones meet 骨关节: *knee joint* 膝关节 **2** *BrE* a large piece of meat for cooking, usually containing a bone【英】〔供烹调的〕一大块肉〔一般带有骨头〕: *a joint of beef* 一大块牛肉 **3** a place where two things or parts of an object are joined together〔两个物体或部分的〕接合处; 汇合处: *Rain penetrates the joints between the concrete panels.* 雨水渗过水泥板的接合处。**4 out of joint a)** if a bone in your body is out of joint, it has been pushed out of its correct position〔骨〕脱臼, 脱节 **b)** if a system, group etc is out of joint, it is not working properly〔系统、组织〕混乱, 不协调: *Something is out of joint in our society.* 我们的组织出了毛病。—see also 另见 **put sb's nose out of joint** (NOSE[1] (18)) **5** *informal* a cheap bar, club, or restaurant【非正式】廉价酒馆[俱乐部、餐厅]: *a hamburger joint* 廉价汉堡包店 —see also 另见 CLIP JOINT **6** *slang* a cigarette containing CANNABIS【俚】〔含有大麻的〕香烟 —see also 另见 **case the joint** (CASE[2] (2))

joint³ *v* [T] to cut meat into joints (JOINT[2] (2)) 把〔肉〕切成大块

Joint Chiefs of Staff, the /,· · · · ˈ·/ the leaders of the four main parts of the US military forces, the Army, the Navy, the Airforce, and the Marines. Their job is to advise the US President on important military matters. 参谋长联席会议〔由美国陆军、海军、空军和海军陆战队四大军种的高级将领组成的一个机构。其职责是就重大军事问题向美国总统提出建议〕

joint·ed /ˈdʒɔɪntɪd; ˈdʒɔɪntɨd/ *adj* having joints and able to move and bend 有活动关节的: *a jointed puppet* 关节能活动的木偶

joint hon·ours /,· ˈ··/ *n* [U] a university degree course in Britain in which two main subjects are studied〔英国大学的〕联合学位课程〔即攻读两门主要学科〕—compare 比较 SINGLE HONOURS

joint-stock com·pa·ny /,· ˈ· ,···/ *n* [C] *AmE technical* a company that is owned by all the people with shares (SHARE[2] (5)) in it【美, 术语】股份公司

joist /dʒɔɪst; dʒɔɪst/ *n* [C] one of the beams that support a floor or ceiling〔支撑地板或天花板的〕托梁

joke¹ /dʒok; dʒəʊk/ *n* [C] [S2]
1 ►STH FUNNY 有趣的事◄ something that you say or do to [W3]
make people laugh, especially a funny story or trick 笑话, 玩笑: *Do you know any good jokes?* 你知道什么好玩的笑话吗? | *Don't get mad – it was only a joke!* 别发火, 那不过是个玩笑! | **crack/make a joke** (=say something funny) 开玩笑 | **tell a joke** (=tell a short funny story) 讲一个笑话 | **get the joke** *informal* (=understand why a joke is funny)【非正式】明白笑话〔为什么好笑〕| **play a joke on sb** (=trick them) 戏弄某人 | **dirty joke** (=about sex) 猥亵的笑话 | **sick joke** (=about something unpleasant) 令人不悦的笑话 | **have a joke** (=not mean something seriously) 开个玩笑〔表示不要当真〕*I was only having a joke!* 我不过是开个玩笑!

2 ►STH ANNOYING 讨厌的事◄ *informal* a situation which is so silly or unreasonable that it makes you angry【非正式】荒唐可笑的事: *The whole meeting was a complete joke.* 整个会议完全是一场闹剧。

3 go/get beyond a joke a situation that gets beyond a joke has become serious and worrying〔情况〕不是闹着玩的; 严肃的: *I haven't heard from them for three weeks now – it's gone beyond a joke.* 我至今已有三周没有收到他们的信, 这不是闹着玩的事了。

4 be no joke used to emphasize that a situation is serious or that someone really means what they say 并非开玩笑〔用来强调情况严重或某人的说话是认真的〕: *These rail strikes every week are no joke.* 铁路罢工每周都有, 绝不是开玩笑的事。| **it's**

no joke *It's no joke, I think she really means to kill herself.* 我认为她的确想自杀，绝不是闹着玩的。

5 take a joke to be able to laugh at a joke about yourself 经得起开玩笑: *Your problem is you just can't take a joke!* 你的问题是你经不起开玩笑!

6 make a joke of to treat something serious as if it was intended to be funny 拿〔严肃的事〕开玩笑: *Sure, he made a joke of it but he was clearly hurt.* 不错，他确实拿它开玩笑，但他明显地受到伤害。

7 not get the joke to not understand why someone thinks a situation is funny 不明白有什么好笑: *"Is that a proposition?" I asked, but she didn't get the joke.* "你是想勾引我吗?"我问道，但她却没悟到这是个玩笑。

8 sb's idea of a joke *spoken* a situation that someone else thinks is funny but you do not【口】某人的鬼主意，某人开玩笑的方式: *I suppose hiding the car key was his idea of a joke.* 我想他大概认为把别人的车钥匙藏起来很好玩。

9 the joke's on you/her etc used to say that the person who was trying to make other people seem silly now seems silly themselves〔想开别人的玩笑反而〕把玩笑开到自己身上了; 被戏弄的反面是自己 —see also 另见 IN-JOKE, PRACTICAL JOKE, **standing joke** (STANDING¹ (4))

joke² *v* [I] **1** to say things that are intended to be funny 开玩笑，说笑话: [**+about/with**] *It's serious, Donny, don't joke about it!* 事情很严重，唐尼，别开玩笑了! **2 you're joking!/you must be joking!** *spoken* used to tell someone that what they are suggesting is so strange or silly that you cannot believe that they are serious【口】你(一定)是在开玩笑吧!〔用来表示某人说的话很奇怪或愚蠢，你无法相信他们是认真的〕: *What! Buy a house on my salary? You must be joking!* 什么? 用我的薪水买房子? 你一定是在开玩笑吧? **3 only joking** *BrE spoken* used to say that you did not really mean what you just said【英口】只是说着玩的，开个玩笑而已〔用来表示刚才所说并不是认真的〕: *Only joking, darling – I love you really!* 亲爱的，只不过开个玩笑，我真的很爱你! **4 joking apart/aside** *BrE* used before you say something serious after you have been joking【英】说正经的〔用来表示停止开玩笑，开始说严肃的事〕: *Joking apart, she is a very talented painter.* 说正经的，她真是一位很有才华的画家。—**jokingly** *adv*

jok·er /ˈdʒokɚ; ˈdʒəʊkə/ *n* [C] **1** *informal* someone who behaves in a way you think is stupid【非正式】傻瓜，蠢人: *Some joker had nailed it to the floor.* 不知哪个笨蛋把它钉在地板上了。**2** a PLAYING CARD that has no fixed value and is only used in some card games〔某些纸牌游戏中可充作任何点数的〕百搭牌 **3** someone who makes a lot of jokes 爱开玩笑的人 **4 the joker in the pack** something or someone whose effect on future events cannot be known 难以预料的事; 难以捉摸的人

jok·ey, joky /ˈdʒokɪ; ˈdʒəʊki/ *adj BrE* not serious and tending to make people laugh【英】滑稽的，令人发笑的: *Her jokey manner put us at ease.* 她诙谐的态度让我们放松下来。—**jokily** *adv* —**jokiness** *n* [U]

Jolli·et /ʒolˈje; ˈʒɒlieɪ/, **Lou·is** /ˈluɪ; ˈluːi/ (1645-1700) a French-Canadian EXPLORER who, with Jacques Marquette, discovered the upper Mississippi River in 1673 若利埃〔(1645-1700)，法裔加拿大探险家，1673年曾与雅克·马奎特一起发现了密西西比河上游〕

jol·li·fi·ca·tion /ˌdʒɑləfəˈkeʃən; ˌdʒɒlɪfɪˈkeɪʃən/ *n* [C,U] *old-fashioned* fun and enjoyment【过时】欢乐，欢闹

jol·ly¹ /ˈdʒɑlɪ; ˈdʒɒli/ *adj* **jollier, jolliest** *especially BrE*【尤英】**1** happy and cheerful 快乐的，愉快的: *Everybody was in a very relaxed and jolly mood.* 大家的心情都很轻松愉快。**2** *old-fashioned* very pleasant and enjoyable【过时】令人愉快的: *a very jolly occasion* 令人非常愉快的时刻

jolly² *adv BrE old-fashioned*【英，过时】**1** very 很，非常: *Sounds like a jolly good idea to me.* 在我听起来，这个主意很好。**2 jolly well** used to emphasize that you are annoyed 真是〔用于强调自己很不耐烦〕: *I wish he'd jolly well hurry up.* 但愿他真能快一些。**3 jolly good!** *spoken* used to say that you are pleased by what someone has just said【口】说得好!〔用来表示你对某人刚刚所说的话感到满意〕

jolly³ *v* [T] **jolly sb into doing sth** *BrE informal* to gently persuade someone to do something【英，非正式】哄某人做某事

jolly sb **along** *phr v* [T] *BrE* to try to make someone do something faster by encouraging them【英】鼓励〔某人加快行动〕: *You'll have to jolly people along if you want to get this work finished.* 如果你想把这件事完成，就要鼓励一下人们。

jolly sth ↔ **up** *v* [T] *BrE* to make a place brighter and more cheerful【英】使〔某地方〕更明亮宜人

jolly⁴ *n* [C] **1 get your jollies** *AmE spoken* to get pleasure from a particular experience or activity【美口】〔从某经历或活动中〕得到快乐 **2** *BrE old-fashioned* an informal event at which people have fun and enjoy themselves【英，过时】寻欢作乐的活动

Jolly Ro·ger /ˌ.. ˈ../ *n* a black flag with a picture of bones on it, used in former times by PIRATES; SKULL AND CROSSBONES (1)〔昔日海盗使用的〕骷髅旗

Jol·son /ˈdʒolsn̩; ˈdʒəʊlsən/, **Al** /æl; æl/ (1886-1950) a white US singer who wore black MAKE-UP to look like a black person, and sang songs associated with black people. He is famous for his emotional performances, and for appearing in the first film with sound, *The Jazz Singer*, in 1927, in which he said the famous phrase "You ain't heard nothin' yet!" His songs include *Mammy* and *Swanee*. Today, if white actors and singers wore make-up to look like black people, it would be regarded as very offensive. 乔尔森〔(1886-1950)，美国白人歌手。他化装成黑人模样演唱与黑人有关的歌曲，以动情的表演和1927年出演首部有声电影《爵士乐歌星》闻名。他在影片中有一句著名台词"你还什么都没听见呢!"他的歌曲包括《妈咪》和《斯旺尼河》。今天，如果白人演员或歌手再扮成黑人模样，那么就是极为冒犯的行为〕

jolt¹ /dʒolt; dʒəʊlt/ *v* **1** [I,T] to move suddenly and roughly, or to make someone or something move in this way (使)突然移动[颠簸]: *The car jolted and Rachel was thrown backwards.* 汽车猛地摇晃，使雷切尔向后摔去。**2** [T] to give someone a sudden shock 使〔某人〕震惊

jolt² *n* [C] **1** a sudden rough shaking movement〔突然的〕震动，摇晃: *I felt every jolt of the bus.* 公共汽车的每一次摇晃我都感觉得到。**2** a sudden shock 震惊: **with a jolt** *I realized with a jolt that they must have gone without me.* 我惊讶地意识到他们一定是扔下我走了。

Jo·nah /ˈdʒonə; ˈdʒəʊnə/ **1** someone who seems to bring bad luck 带来厄运的人 **2** in the Old Testament of the Bible, a man who disobeyed God and tried to escape from him by getting on a ship. God caused a storm, and the other sailors threw Jonah into the sea. He was then swallowed by a WHALE, and spent three days in its stomach before escaping onto land. 约拿〔《圣经·旧约》述及的一个男子。他违背上帝旨意，并试图乘船逃跑。于是，上帝降下风暴，其他水手便把他扔进海里，被一条鲸鱼吞掉。他在鲸鱼腹中待了三天才逃上岸〕

Jones /dʒonz; dʒəʊnz/, **Brid·get** /ˈbrɪdʒɪt; ˈbrɪdʒɪt/ the main character in the popular NOVEL *Bridget Jones' Diary* (1996) by British writer Helen Fielding, about an unmarried woman in her 30s and the problems she has in her busy life, such as trying to avoid smoking and eating too much. 琼斯〔英国作家海伦·菲尔丁的畅销小说《BJ单身日记》(1996)中的主人公。该书讲述一位30多岁的未婚女性及其在忙碌的生活中遇到的问题，如戒烟和节食等等〕

Jones, Ca·sey /ˈkesɪ; ˈkeɪsi/ (1863-1900) an American train driver and FOLK HERO who saved the lives of passengers in a train crash, but was killed himself 琼斯〔(1863-1900)，美国火车司机，也是民间传颂的英雄。他在一次火车撞车事故中营救了不少旅客，但他本人却不幸遇难〕

Jones, Indiana /ˌɪndɪˈænə; ˌɪndiˈænə/ a character played by Harrison Ford in a series of films by Steven Spielberg, including *Raiders of the Lost Ark*. Indiana Jones is an ARCHAEOLOGIST who tries to find valuable ancient objects and has many exciting adventures. 琼斯〔史蒂文·斯皮尔伯格制作的系列影片(其中包括《夺宝奇兵》)中的人物，由哈里森·福特饰演。印第安纳·琼斯是位考古学家，致力于寻找有价值的古文物，经历了种种惊险奇遇〕

Jones, In·i·go /ˈɪnɪgo; ˈɪnɪgəʊ/ (1573-1652) an English ARCHITECT who designed many important buildings, especially in London. He was the first person to introduce the Italian Palladian style of building into the UK. He also designed SCENERY for the theatre. 琼斯〔(1573-1652)，英国建筑师，曾设计了许多重要的建筑，尤其是在伦敦地区。他首次将意大利的帕拉第奥式建筑风格引入英国，还设计过剧场舞台布景〕

Jones, Jim —see 见 JONESTOWN

Jones·es /ˈdʒonzɪz; ˈdʒəʊnzɪz/ *n* —see 见 **keep up with the Joneses** (KEEP¹)

Jones·town /ˈdʒonztaun; ˈdʒəʊnztaʊn/ a place in Guyana where people who followed the religious leader Jim Jones lived. In 1974, they all killed themselves with poison as part of a ceremony, which became known as the **Jonestown Massacre**. 琼斯敦〔圭亚那一地区，为宗教领袖吉姆·琼斯的信徒的居住地。1974年，在一次宗教仪式上全体信徒服毒自杀。这就是"琼斯敦惨案"〕

Jon·son /ˈdʒɑnsn̩; ˈdʒɒnsən/, **Ben** (1572-1637) an English writer of plays, poetry, and criticism. His most famous plays are *Volpone*, *The Alchemist*, and *Bartholomew Fair*. 琼森〔(1572-1637)，英国剧作家、诗人和评论家。他的代表剧作有《狐狸》、《炼金术士》和《巴托罗缪集市》〕

Jop·lin /ˈdʒɑplɪn; ˈdʒɒplɨn/, **Jan·is** /ˈdʒænɪs; ˈdʒænɨs/ (1943-70) a US singer, popular in the 1960s, who was known for her low, rough singing voice, and for her exciting performances on stage. She died as a result of taking drugs. 乔普林〔(1943-1970), 20世纪60年代美国著名女歌手, 以低沉沙哑的嗓音与动人的舞台表演闻名, 后死于吸毒〕

Joplin, Scott (1868-1917) a US piano player and COMPOSER famous especially for his RAGTIME music, such as *Maple Leaf Rag* and *The Entertainer* 乔普林〔(1868-1917), 美国钢琴演奏家、作曲家, 尤以《枫叶雷格》和《演艺人》等雷格泰姆音乐闻名〕

Jor·dan /ˈdʒɔrdn̩; ˈdʒɔːdən/ an Arab country in the Middle East, which is surrounded by Israel, Syria, Iraq, and Saudi Arabia. Population: 5,153,000 (2001). Capital: Amman. 约旦〔中东一阿拉伯国家, 与以色列、叙利亚、伊拉克和沙特阿拉伯接壤。人口: 5,153,000 (2001), 首都: 安曼〕 —**Jordanian** /dʒɔrˈdenɪən; dʒɔːˈdeɪniən/ *n, adj* —see 见 WEST BANK

Jordan, the also 又作 **the Jordan River** a river in Israel and Jordan, which flows into the Dead Sea. It is often mentioned in the Bible, and was the river in which John the Baptist BAPTIZE*d* Jesus. 约旦河〔流经以色列和约旦注入死海的一条河流。《圣经》中常提及该河, 施洗约翰曾在此为耶稣施行洗礼〕

Joseph[1] /ˈdʒozəf; ˈdʒəʊzɨf/ in the Old Testament of the Bible, the favourite son of Jacob. Joseph was given a 'coat of many colours' by his father, and this made his brothers JEALOUS of him. They sold him as a slave to some Egyptians, but Joseph later became powerful by becoming an adviser to the Egyptian king, and brought his people to live in Egypt. 约瑟〔《圣经·旧约》中雅各最宠爱的一个儿子。他因得到父亲所赠的"彩衣"而引起兄弟的嫉妒, 被卖给埃及人为奴。后来, 他当上了埃及国王的顾问, 大权在握, 将族人接到埃及居住〕

Joseph[2] in the New Testament of the Bible, the husband of Mary, the mother of Jesus. Joseph was a CARPENTER in Nazareth. 约瑟〔《圣经·新约》中耶稣之母马利亚的丈夫。他是拿撒勒的一名木匠〕

Jo·seph, Chief (?1840-1904) the chief of a Native American tribe who fought against the US army in 1870. He was not successful, and his tribe was forced to leave their land and move to a RESERVATION. 约瑟夫酋长〔(?1840-1904), 北美印第安人部落首领。他于1870年率领族人抵抗美军, 但没有成功。于是, 他的部落被迫离开家园, 迁居到保留地〕

Jo·se·phine /ˈdʒosəfin; ˈdʒəʊsɨfiːn/ (1763-1814) the EMPRESS of France from 1804 to 1809. She married Napoleon in 1796, but he got a DIVORCE in 1809 because they had not produced any children together. 约瑟芬〔(1763-1814), 1804至1809年的法国皇后。她于1796年与拿破仑结婚, 但因婚后无子于1809年离婚〕

Joseph of Ar·i·ma·the·a /ˌdʒozəf əv ˌærɪməˈθiə; ˌdʒəʊzɨf əv ˌærɨməˈθiːə/, **Saint** in the New Testament of the Bible, a rich follower of Jesus who asked to be given Jesus's dead body so that he could bury it in the TOMB that he had built for himself. There is also an old story that he brought the Holy Grail (=the cup used by Jesus at the Last Supper) to England and built the first Christian church in England at Glastonbury. (亚利马太的)圣约瑟〔据《圣经·新约》所述, 他是耶稣的一位富有的门徒, 曾要求领回耶稣的遗体, 好安葬在他为自己修建的墓穴里。还有传说称他曾把圣杯带到了英格兰, 并在格拉斯顿伯里修建了英格兰首座基督教教堂〕

josh /dʒɑʃ; dʒɒʃ/ *v AmE old-fashioned* 【美, 过时】 **1** [I+with] to talk to someone in a joking way〔用开玩笑的口吻〕与〔某人〕说话 **2** [T] to laugh at someone in a friendly way〔无恶意地〕嘲弄: *The guys josh him and call him an egghead.* 那些人逗他, 叫他书呆子。

Josh·u·a /ˈdʒɑʃʊə; ˈdʒɒʃjuːə/ in the Old Testament of the Bible, a man who led the Jews to the 'Promised Land' of Canaan. When Joshua and his army attacked the city of Jericho they blew their TRUMPET*s* so loudly that the walls of the city fell down and they were able to take control of it. The *Book of Joshua* describes how the Jews took control of Canaan. 约书亚〔《圣经·旧约》中率领犹太人前往"应许之地"迦南的男子。约书亚及其军队攻打杰里科城时猛吹号角, 居然把城墙给震塌了, 从而夺取了该城。《约书亚记》描述了犹太人夺取迦南的经过〕

joss stick /ˈdʒɑs ˌstɪk; ˈdʒɒs ˌstɪk/ *n* [C] a stick of INCENSE[1]〔祭供时用的〕线香

jos·tle /ˈdʒɑsl̩; ˈdʒɒsəl/ *v* [I,T] to push or knock against someone in a crowd, especially so that you can get somewhere or do something before other people〔在人群中〕推, 撞〔尤指让自己前往某处或比其他人早做某事〕: *The couple were shoved and jostled by reporters as they left the courtroom.* 这对夫妇离开法庭时受到记者们的推搡。

jot[1] /dʒɑt; dʒɒt/ *v* **jotted, jotting**
jot sth ↔ down *phr v* [T] to write something quickly 匆匆记下: *Let me jot down your number and I'll call you tomorrow.* 让我记下你的号码, 明天给你回电话。

jot[2] *n* **not a jot** *BrE old-fashioned* not at all or none at all 【英, 过时】一点也不; 一点也没有: *It doesn't make a jot of difference.* 一点儿影响都没有。

jot·ter /ˈdʒɑtɚ; ˈdʒɒtə/ *n* [C] *BrE* a small book for writing notes in 【英】便条本, 便笺簿

jot·tings /ˈdʒɑtɪŋz; ˈdʒɒtɪŋz/ *n* [plural] *informal* short notes, usually written to remind yourself about something 【非正式】〔为提醒自己而写的〕简短记事

joule /dʒul; dʒuːl/ *n* [C] *technical* a measure of energy or work 【术语】焦耳〔能或功的单位〕

jour·nal /ˈdʒɝnl̩; ˈdʒɜːnl/ *n* [C] **1** a serious magazine produced for professional people or those with a particular interest〔供专业人士或具有某种兴趣的人读的〕期刊, 杂志: *the British Medical Journal*《英国医学杂志》 **2** *literary* a written record that you make of the things that happen to you each day; DIARY (1) 【文】日记; 日志

jour·nal·ese /ˌdʒɝnl̩ˈiz; ˌdʒɜːnəlˈiːz/ *n* [U] language that is typical of newspapers 新闻用语

jour·nal·is·m /ˈdʒɝnl̩ˌɪzəm; ˈdʒɜːnəl-ɪzəm/ *n* [U] the job or activity of writing news reports for newspapers, magazines, television or radio 新闻业; 新闻工作

jour·nal·ist /ˈdʒɝnl̩ɪst; ˈdʒɜːnəl-ɨst/ *n* [C] someone who writes news reports for newspapers, magazines, television, or radio 新闻工作者; 新闻记者 —compare 比较 REPORTER (W3)

jour·ney[1] /ˈdʒɝni; ˈdʒɜːni/ *n* [C] **1** *especially BrE* a trip from one place to another, especially over a long distance 【尤英】〔尤指长途的〕旅行, 旅程: *a train journey across Europe* 横跨欧洲的长途火车旅行 | *I have a 25-minute journey to work.* 我上班路上要用25分钟。| **break your journey** (=stop somewhere for a time to rest) 中途停留休息 **2** *literary* the process by which something gradually changes and develops 【文】历程, 过程: *our journey through life* 我们的人生历程 —see 见 TRAVEL (USAGE) (S3, W2)

journey[2] *v* [I always+adv/prep] *literary* to travel 【文】旅行

jour·ney·man /ˈdʒɝnɪmən; ˈdʒɜːnimən/ *n* [C] *old-fashioned* 【过时】 **1** a trained worker who works for someone else〔为他人雇用的〕熟练工人 **2** an experienced worker whose work is reasonable but not excellent〔技术合格但并不出色的〕熟手

jour·no /ˈdʒɝno; ˈdʒɜːnəʊ/ *n* [C] *informal* a JOURNALIST 【非正式】新闻工作者; 新闻记者

joust /dʒaust; dʒaʊst/ *v* [I] to fight with LANCE*s* (=long sticks) while riding a horse 骑着马用长矛比武 —**joust** *n* [C]

Jove /dʒov; dʒəʊv/ *n* **by Jove!** *BrE old-fashioned* used to express surprise or to emphasize something 【英, 过时】哎呀!〔用来表示惊讶或强调某事〕: *By Jove, you're right!* 哎呀, 你说得对!

jo·vi·al /ˈdʒovɪəl; ˈdʒəʊviəl/ *adj* friendly and cheerful 友好的; 高兴的: *a jovial smile* 友善的微笑 —**jovially** *adv* —**joviality** /ˌdʒovɪˈælətɪ; ˌdʒəʊviˈælɨti/ *n* [U]

jowl /dʒaul; dʒaʊl/ *n* [C] **1** [usually plural 一般用复数] the skin that covers your lower jaw on either side of your face 下颌垂肉 **2 heavy-jowled** having large jowls that hang down slightly 有下颌垂肉的, 双下巴的 —see also 另见 **cheek by jowl** (CHEEK[1] (4))

joy[1] /dʒɔɪ; dʒɔɪ/ *n* **1** [U] great happiness and pleasure 欢欣, 愉快, 喜悦: **to sb's joy** *To Beth's surprise and joy, she was awarded first prize.* 贝丝得了头奖, 使她又惊又喜。| **jump for joy** (=be very pleased) 高兴得跳起来 **2** [C] something or someone that gives you happiness and pleasure 使人高兴的事物[人]: *the joys and sorrows of bringing up a family* 养育子女的苦与乐 | **be a joy to use/drive etc** (=be very pleasant to use/drive etc) 使用〔某物〕/驾驶〔某车〕是件乐事 *The new Merc's a joy to drive.* 驾驶这辆新的梅塞德斯汽车真是件乐事。 **3** [U only in questions or negatives 仅用于疑问句或否定句] *BrE spoken* success in doing what you are trying to do 【英口】成功: *You could ask the library to trace the book, but I doubt you'll get any joy.* 你可以请图书馆查找这本书, 但我看不会有什么结果。 (W3)

joy[2] *v*
joy in sth *phr v* [T] *literary* to be happy because of something 【文】由于…而高兴

Joyce /dʒɔɪs; dʒɔɪs/, **James** (1882-1941) an Irish writer of NOVEL*s*. Joyce greatly influenced the way English novels were written, with his use of unusual and invented words, and different styles of writing such as stream of consciousness (=expressing thoughts and feelings as they pass through the mind). His most famous novels are *Portrait of the Artist as a Young Man*, *Ulysses*, and *Finnegans Wake*. 乔伊斯〔(1882-

1941)，爱尔兰小说家。他采用生僻和自造词汇以及意识流等不同写作风格，极大地影响了英语小说的创作方式。其代表作有《青年艺术家的肖像》、《尤利西斯》和《为芬尼根守灵》〕

joy·ful /ˈdʒɔɪfəl; ˈdʒɔɪfəl/ *adj* very happy, or likely to make people very happy 欢乐的; 令人高兴的: *the joyful news* 令人高兴的消息 —**joyfully** *adv* —**joyfulness** *n* [U]

joy·less /ˈdʒɔɪlɪs; ˈdʒɔɪləs/ *adj* without any happiness at all 不高兴的, 不快乐的: *a joyless marriage* 毫不幸福的婚姻 —**joylessly** *adv* —**joylessness** *n* [U]

Joy of Cook·ing, The /, · · ˈ· ·/ a very popular cookbook in the US, which has instructions on how to cook many standard US and foreign dishes《烹饪乐》〔美国一畅销烹饪书籍, 介绍美国及国外许多家常菜的做法〕

joy·ous /ˈdʒɔɪəs; ˈdʒɔɪəs/ *adj literary* very happy, or likely to make people very happy【文】欢乐的; 令人愉快的: *a joyous occasion* 欢乐的场合 —**joyously** *adv* —**joyousness** *n* [U]

joy·rid·ing /ˈdʒɔɪˌraɪdɪŋ; ˈdʒɔɪˌraɪdɪŋ/ *n* [U] the crime of stealing a car and driving it in a fast and dangerous way for fun 偷盗汽车并开快车兜风[罪] —**joyride** *v* [I] —**joyrider** *n* [C]

joy·stick /ˈdʒɔɪˌstɪk; ˈdʒɔɪˌstɪk/ *n* [C] an upright handle that you use to change the direction in which something such as a plane moves〔飞机等的〕操纵杆

JP /ˌdʒe ˈpi; ˌdʒeɪ ˈpiː/ *n* [C] a JUSTICE OF THE PEACE; a MAGISTRATE in Britain〔英国〕治安法官; 地方官

Jr *AmE* the written abbreviation of 缩写= JUNIOR; used after the name of a man who has the same name as his father【美】小〔置于与父亲同名的男子姓名后〕: *Alan Parks, Jr.* 小阿伦·帕克斯

JSA /ˌdʒe si ˈe; ˌdʒeɪ siː ˈeɪ/ *n* Jobseeker's Allowance; money paid by the British government to help people who have no work, and are trying to find work 择业津贴〔英国政府为正在找工作的失业者发放的补助金〕

jub·i·lant /ˈdʒubḷənt; ˈdʒuːbḷənt/ *adj* extremely happy and pleased because you have been successful, or full of people who feel this way〔因成功而〕欢腾的; 兴高采烈的: *jubilant celebrations* 欢庆活动 —**jubilantly** *adv*

ju·bi·la·tion /ˌdʒubḷˈeʃən; ˌdʒuːbḷˈleɪʃən/ *n* [U] *formal* happiness and pleasure because you have been successful【正式】〔因成功而〕欢欣, 愉快: *shouts of jubilation from the crowd* 人群发出的欢呼声

ju·bi·lee /ˈdʒubḷˌi; ˈdʒuːbḷiː/ *n* [C] a date that is celebrated because it is exactly 25 years, 50 years etc after an important event〔重要事件25年、50年等的〕周年纪念 —see also 另见 DIAMOND JUBILEE, GOLDEN JUBILEE, SILVER JUBILEE

Ju·dah /ˈdʒudə; ˈdʒuːdə/ in the Old Testament of the Bible, one of Jacob's sons 犹大〔《圣经·旧约》中雅各之子〕

Ju·da·is·m /ˈdʒudɪˌɪzəm; ˈdʒuːdeɪ-ɪzəm/ *n* [U] the Jewish religion based on the Old Testament of the Bible, the Talmud, and the later teachings of the RABBIS 犹太教 —**Judaic** /dʒuˈde·ɪk; dʒuːˈdeɪ-ɪk/ *adj*

Ju·das /ˈdʒudəs; ˈdʒuːdəs/ **1 Judas Iscariot** in the New Testament of the Bible, one of Jesus's DISCIPLES (=his close friends and followers). He received 'thirty pieces of silver' from the Jewish authorities as payment for BETRAY*ing* Jesus. He later felt guilty about what he had done, and hanged himself. 加略人犹大〔《圣经·新约》中耶稣的门徒之一。他收了犹太当局的30个银币, 将耶稣出卖, 后感到罪孽深重自缢而死〕 **2** [C] someone who is not loyal to a friend; TRAITOR 出卖朋友的人; 叛徒

jud·der /ˈdʒʌdə; ˈdʒʌdə/ *v* [I] if a vehicle or machine judders, it shakes violently〔车辆或机器〕剧烈震动: *The engine juddered to life.* 引擎剧烈震动着发动起来。—**judder** *n* [C]

2 **judge**[1] /dʒʌdʒ; dʒʌdʒ/ *n* [C] **1** the official in control of a court who decides how criminals should be punished 法官; 审判官: **federal judge/high court judge** (=a judge in a particular court) 联邦法官/高等法院法官

> **CULTURAL NOTE 文化注释**
>
> In the US, Supreme Court judges are chosen by the President and must be approved by the Senate. Many judges in the lower courts are elected by people living in the area. 美国最高法院的法官由总统确定人选, 须经参议院批准。很多下级法院的法官由当地居民选举产生。
>
> In the UK, judges of the High Court are chosen by the Lord Chancellor from BARRISTERS. SOLICITORS who have more than thirteen years' experience can be appointed as judges in the Crown Court and the County Court. 英国高等法院的法官由大法官从出庭律师中选出。具有13年以上从业经验的事务律师可获选担任刑事法庭和郡法院的法官。— see also 另见 MAGISTRATE

2 someone who decides on the result of a competition〔比赛的〕裁判员, 评判: *The panel of judges included several well-known writers.* 评判小组中包括几位著名作家。**3 be no judge** *informal* to not have enough skill or knowledge to be able to give an opinion on a particular subject【非正式】并非…的鉴定人〔指没有足够的技能或知识来评价某事〕: *I don't like this wine – not that I'm any judge of these things.* 我不喜欢这种酒, 但我不是这玩意儿的鉴赏家。**4 a good/bad judge of** someone whose opinion on something is usually right or wrong 对…判断力很好/很差的人: *Sandra's a very good judge of character.* 桑德拉很善于鉴别人的性格。**5 let me be the judge of that** *spoken* used to tell someone angrily that you do not need their advice【口】由我来决定〔愤怒地向某人表示你不需要他的劝告〕 —see also 另见 **as sober as a judge** (SOBER[1] (l))

judge[2] *v* **judged, judging**  2 3

1 ►OPINION 看法◄ [I,T] to form or give an opinion about someone or something after thinking carefully about all the information you know about them〔认真考虑后〕认为; 判断; 断定; 评价: *It seems a good idea, but without all the facts it's hard to judge.* 这看来是个好主意, 但在所有事实都不清楚的情况下, 难以作出决断。| **judge sb/sth by sth** *Teachers tend to be judged by their students' exam grades.* 人们常以学生的考试成绩来判断教师的优劣。| **judge sb/sth on sth** *Why can't they judge me on my brains, not my looks?* 他们为什么不能凭我的智力而不是我的相貌来评价我呢? | **judge that** *I judged that Williams was a spy.* 据我判断, 威廉斯是个间谍。| **judge sb/sth (to be) sth** *Their reunion was judged to be a great success.* 他们的重新统一被认为是极成功的。| **judge who/what/how etc** *Well, Sam, can you judge where they might go next?* 好吧, 萨姆, 你能断定他们下一步可能去哪儿吗? | **judge sth/sb (to be) good/bad/fair etc** *The headmaster was judged incompetent by school inspectors.* 校长被督学评定为不称职。| **judge it unwise/expedient/ inappropriate etc to do sth** *At that point we judged it wise to leave them alone.* 在那种情况下, 我们认为不去打扰他们是明智的。

2 ►GUESS 猜测◄ [I,T] to guess an amount, distance, height, weight etc; ESTIMATE 猜测, 估计: *"How long will it take?" "It's impossible to judge."* "要花多长时间?" "无法估计。" | **judge sb/sth to be sth** *Trevor judged the distance to be about 30 yards.* 特雷弗估计距离大约为30码。| **judge how far/long/wide etc sth is** *In this fog, we can't judge how far it is to the other side of the river.* 在这样的大雾天气, 我们很难估计离河对岸有多远。

3 judging by/from used to say that you are making a guess based on what you have just seen, heard or learned 依据〔所见、所闻、所听〕来判断: *Judging by the look on Adam's face, the news must have been terrible.* 从亚当的表情来看, 那肯定是可怕的消息。

4 ►COMPETITION 竞赛◄ [I,T] to decide on the result of a competition 裁判, 评判: *Who's judging the talent contest?* 这次智力比赛谁是评判? | **judge sb on sth** *Competitors will be judged on speed and accuracy.* 根据速度和准确性来评判参赛者。

5 ►CRITICIZE 批评◄ [I,T] to form an opinion about someone, especially in an unfair or criticizing way〔尤指不公正或批判地〕(对…)作出评价: *What right have you to judge the way they live?* 你有什么权利对他们的生活方式说三道四?

6 ►LAW 法律◄ [T] to decide whether someone is guilty of a crime in court〔在法庭上〕审判, 审理

7 It's not for me to judge *spoken* used to say that you do not think you have the right to give your opinion about something【口】轮不到我来判断〔指你认为自己没有权利对某事发表意见〕

8 as far as I can judge used to say that you think what you are saying is true, but you are not sure 据我判断〔用来说明你相信自己说的话没错, 但没有十足把握〕

9 don't judge a book by its cover used to say that you should not form an opinion based only on the way something looks 不要以封面来评定一本书; 不要以貌取人〔指不可凭事物的外表作出判断〕

judg·ment also 又作 **judgement** *BrE*【英】/ˈdʒʌdʒmənt; ˈdʒʌdʒmənt/ *n* 2

1 ►OPINION 看法◄ [C,U] an opinion that you form after thinking carefully about something〔认真思考后的〕意见; 看法; 评价: **in sb's judgment** *In my judgment, we should accept his offer.* 依我看, 我们应接受他的建议。| **pass judgment** (=give your opinion or criticism) 作出评论[批评] | **reserve judgment** (=refuse to decide before you have all the facts)〔在掌握全部事实之前〕拒绝作出判断

2 ►ABILITY TO DECIDE 决断力◄ [U] the ability to make decisions about situations or people 判断力: *The minister's remarks*

show a lack of political judgement. 部长的谈话显示他缺乏政治判断力。| **sound judgment** (=good judgment) 良好的判断力 *sound editorial judgment* 良好的编辑判断力

3 ▶LAW 法律◀ [C,U] an official decision given by a judge or a court of law〔法官或法庭的〕审判, 判决: *a judgment delivered by the European court* 欧洲法庭作出的判决

4 against your better judgment if you do something against your better judgment, you do it even though you do not think it is the right thing to do〔做某事〕违心的; 明知是不对的: *In the end I agreed to lend her the money, but it was against my better judgment.* 我最后还是同意把钱借给她, 但这样做违背我的心愿。

5 a judgment something unpleasant that happens which seems like a punishment for the things you have done wrong 报应; 天谴

6 sit in judgment over sb to criticize someone's behaviour, especially unfairly 对某人的行为进行批评〔尤指不公正的批评〕

7 judgment call *AmE* a decision you have to make yourself because there are no fixed rules in a situation【美】裁判员的判决〔指由于没有固定的规章可循而必须自行作出的决定〕—see also 另见 LAST JUDGMENT, VALUE JUDGMENT

judg·ment·al also 又作 **judgemental** *BrE*【英】/dʒʌdʒˋmɛntl; dʒʌdʒˈmentl/ *adj* too quick and willing to criticize people 轻率批评人的

judgment day /ˈ· · ·/ also 又作 **day of judgment** *n* [singular, not with *the* 不与 the 连用] the time after death when everyone is judged by God for what they have done in life, according to Christianity and some other religions〔基督教等的〕最后审判日〔指人死后, 上帝按各人所行的进行审判〕

ju·di·ca·ture, the /ˋdʒudɪkətʃɚ; ˈdʒuːdɪkətʃə/ *n formal* judges and the organization, power etc of the law【正式】司法系统; 司法权

ju·di·cial /dʒuˋdɪʃəl; dʒuːˈdɪʃəl/ *adj* **1** connected with a court of law, judges, or their decisions 法庭的; 法官的; 裁决的: *the judicial system* 司法系统 —compare 比较 EXECUTIVE[2] (1), LEGISLATIVE (2) **2** behaviour that is judicial is sensible and shows good judgment〔行为〕明智的, 有判断力的 —**judicially** *adv*

ju·di·cia·ry, the /dʒuˋdɪʃɪˌɛrɪ; dʒuːˈdɪʃəri/ *n formal* all the judges in a country who, as a group, form part of the system of government【正式】司法部; 司法系统[部门]

ju·di·cious /dʒuˋdɪʃəs; dʒuːˈdɪʃəs/ *adj formal* done in a sensible and careful way【正式】明智的; 审慎的: *a judicious choice* 明智的选择 —**judiciously** *adv* —**judiciousness** *n* [U]

ju·do /ˋdʒudo; ˈdʒuːdəʊ/ *n* [U] a sport from the Far East, in which you try to throw your opponent onto the ground 柔道

Ju·dy —see 见 PUNCH AND JUDY SHOW

jugs 罐, 壶

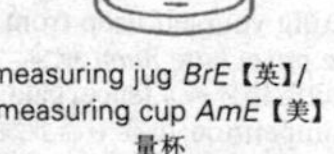

measuring jug *BrE*【英】/ measuring cup *AmE*【美】 量杯

jug *BrE*【英】/ pitcher *AmE*【美】〔有柄带嘴的〕壶, 罐

jug /dʒʌg; dʒʌg/ *n* [C] **1** *BrE* a container for liquids with a handle and a SPOUT (=for pouring)【英】〔有柄带嘴的〕壶, 罐; PITCHER (1) *AmE*【美】 **2** also 又作 **jug·ful** /ˋdʒʌgful; ˈdʒʌgfʊl/ the amount of liquid that a jug will hold 一壶的容量: *a jug of milk* 一壶牛奶 **3 in (the) jug** *BrE old-fashioned* in prison【英, 过时】坐牢

jug-eared /ˋdʒʌg ˌɪrd; ˈdʒʌg ˌɪəd/ *adj* having large ears that stick out 长着一对招风耳的

jugged hare /ˌ· ˈ·/ *n* [U] *BrE* a dish made of HARE that has been cooked in liquid【英】清炖野兔肉, 罐焖野兔

jug·ger·naut /ˋdʒʌgɚˌnɔt; ˈdʒʌgənɔːt/ *n* [C] **1** *BrE* a very large vehicle, that carries goods over long distances【英】〔长途运输用的〕重型货车; SEMI (3) *AmE*【美】 **2** something large and powerful that destroys everything it meets 有强大毁灭力量的物体; 强大的摧毁力

jug·gle /ˋdʒʌgl; ˈdʒʌgəl/ *v* **1** [I,T] to keep three or more objects moving through the air by throwing and catching them very quickly (用…)玩杂耍〔同时抛接数件物品〕: **[+with]** *juggling with plates* 抛耍盘子 **2** [I,T] if you juggle two or more jobs, activities etc, you try to fit all of them into your life 试图应付〔两个或更多的职务、活动等〕: *juggling the needs of your family with the demands of the job* 尝试应付家庭的需要与工作的要求 **3** [T] to arrange numbers, information etc in the way that you want 篡改〔数字、资料等〕: *No amount of financial juggling could hide the fraud.* 假账造得再多也掩盖不了这欺诈行为。—**juggler** *n* [C] —see also 另见 **juggling act** (ACT[1] (12))

juggle 玩杂耍

jug·u·lar /ˋdʒʌgjələ˞; ˈdʒʌgjələ/ *n* [C] **1** a jugular vein 颈静脉 **2 go for the jugular** *informal* to criticize or attack someone very strongly, especially in order to harm them【非正式】强烈批评[攻击]〔某人, 尤指为了要伤害对方〕

jugular vein /ˌ· · · ˈ·/ *n* [C usually singular 一般用单数] the large VEIN (=tube) in your neck that takes blood from your head back to your heart 颈静脉

juice[1] /dʒus; dʒuːs/ *n* **1** [C,U] the liquid that comes from fruit and vegetables, or a drink that is made from this〔水果、蔬菜的〕汁; 水果[蔬菜]汁饮料: *a carton of orange juice* 一纸盒橙汁 **2** [U] the liquid that comes out of meat when it is cooked 肉汁 **3 gastric/digestive juice(s)** the liquid inside your stomach that helps you to DIGEST[1] (1) food 胃液, 消化液 **4** [U] *informal* something that produces power, such as petrol or electricity【非正式】能源〈如汽油或电力〉—see also 另见 **stew in your own juice** (STEW[2] (2))

juice[2] *v* [T] to get the juice out of fruit or vegetables; SQUEEZE[1] (2) 榨〔水果或蔬菜〕的汁

juice sth ↔ **up** *phr v* [T] *AmE informal* to make something more interesting or exciting【美, 非正式】使有生气, 使活跃

juiced /dʒust; dʒuːst/ *adj AmE old-fashioned* drunk【美, 过时】喝醉了的

juic·er /ˋdʒusɚ; ˈdʒuːsə/ *n* [C] **a)** *AmE* a small kitchen tool used for getting juice out of fruit【美】〔厨房用的小型〕榨果汁器; LEMON SQUEEZER *BrE*【英】 **b)** an electric machine for doing this 电动榨果汁机

juic·y /ˋdʒusɪ; ˈdʒuːsi/ *adj* **1** containing a lot of juice 多汁的, 多液的: *a juicy steak* 多汁的牛排 **2 juicy stories/gossip/details** *informal* stories etc that contain interesting or shocking information, especially about people's sexual behaviour【非正式】有趣[绘声绘色]的故事/流言/细节〔尤与人们的性行为有关〕 **3** *informal* involving a lot of money【非正式】大笔钱款的: *a big fat juicy cheque* 一张很大额的支票 **4** *informal* giving you work to do that will lead to a feeling of satisfaction【非正式】〔工作〕给人以满足感的: *a juicy part in 'Moby Dick'*《白鲸》中一个可有充分发挥的角色 —**juiciness** *n* [U]

ju·jit·su /dʒuˋdʒɪtsu; ˌdʒuːˈdʒɪtsuː/ *n* [U] a type of fighting from Japan, in which you hold, throw, and hit your opponent 柔术, 柔道

ju·ju /ˋdʒudʒu; ˈdʒuːdʒuː/ *n* [C,U] a type of West African magic involving objects with special powers, or one of these objects〔使用带有魔力的物件的〕非洲西部巫术

juke·box /ˋdʒuk ˌbɑks; ˈdʒuːk bɒks/ *n* [C] a machine in public bars that plays music when you put money in〔酒吧内的〕投币式自动唱机

ju·lep /ˋdʒulɪp; ˈdʒuːlɪp/ *n* —see 见 MINT JULEP

Ju·li·an cal·en·dar, the /ˋdʒulɪən ˋkæləndɚ; ˈdʒuːliən ˈkæləndə/ the calendar introduced by Julius Caesar in Rome in 46 BC, that fixed the normal year at 365 days. The Gregorian calendar, the usual calendar used in Western countries in modern times, is based on the Julian calendar. 儒略历〔公元前46年尤利乌斯·凯撒在罗马开始采用的历法, 将一年定为365天。现在西方国家使用的公历就是基于此而发展的〕

Ju·li·et /ˋdʒulɪət; ˈdʒuːliət/ the main female character in the play *Romeo and Juliet* by William Shakespeare 朱丽叶〔威廉·莎士比亚的剧作《罗密欧与朱丽叶》中的女主角〕—see also 另见 the CAPULETS AND MONTAGUES

Ju·li·us Cae·sar /ˌdʒulɪəs ˋsizɚ; ˌdʒuːliəs ˈsiːzə/ a play by William Shakespeare about the murder of the Roman leader Julius Caesar, and about his friend Brutus, who thinks Caesar is

taking too much power and so joins his murderers. After Julius Caesar's death his friend Mark Antony makes a famous speech to the crowd beginning with the words "Friends, Romans, countrymen, lend me your ears".《尤利乌斯·凯撒》〔威廉·莎士比亚创作的剧本。主要剧情是，罗马人的领袖尤利乌斯·凯撒遭人谋杀，他的朋友布鲁图认为他专权而也成了凯撒的谋杀者之一。尤利乌斯·凯撒死后，他的朋友马克·安东尼发表了一则著名演讲，开头一句是"各位朋友，各位罗马同胞们！请听在下陈述"〕

Ju·ly /dʒuˈlaɪ; dʒʊˈlaɪ/ written abbreviation 缩写为 **Jul** *n* [C,U] the seventh month of the year, between June and August 七月: **in July** *a society founded in July 1890* 成立于1890年7月的学会 | **last/next July** *Anne's starting work next July.* 安妮将于明年七月开始工作。| **on July 12th** (also 又作 **on 12th July** *BrE* 英) *"When's the concert?" "On 12th July."* "音乐会什么时候举行？""7月12日。" (spoken as 读作: *on the twelfth of July* or 或 *on July the twelfth* or 或 (*AmE* 美) *on July twelfth*)

CULTURAL NOTE 文化注释

In the UK and the US, when people think of July, they think of warm weather and the start of summer holidays. In the US Independence day is on the Fourth of July. 英国人和美国人想到7月，会想到温暖的天气和暑假的开始。7月4日是美国独立日。

jum·ble[1] /ˈdʒʌmbl; ˈdʒʌmbəl/ *n* **1** [singular] an untidy mixture of things〔东西〕混乱，杂乱的一堆: **[+of]** *a jumble of thoughts and feelings* 杂乱的想法与情感 **2** [U] *BrE* things to be sold at a jumble sale【英】供义卖的旧杂货; RUMMAGE[2] (2) *AmE*【美】

jumble[2] also 又作 **jumble up** *v* [T often passive 常用被动态] to mix things together so that they are not in a neat order 使混乱，使杂乱: *In his excitement Ben's words became jumbled.* 本兴奋得语无伦次。

jumble sale /ˈ··· ·/ *n* [C] *BrE* a sale of used clothes, books etc in order to get money to help a local church, school etc; RUMMAGE SALE【英】旧杂货的义卖〔以据助本地教会、学校等〕

jum·bo /ˈdʒʌmbo; ˈdʒʌmbəʊ/ *adj* [only before noun 仅用于名词前] *informal* larger than other things of the same type【非正式】〔同类中〕特大的，巨大的: *jumbo-sized hot dogs* 巨无霸热狗

jumbo jet /ˈ·· ·/ also 又作 **jumbo** *n* [C] a very large aircraft for carrying passengers 巨型喷气式客机，珍宝客机

jump[1] /dʒʌmp; dʒʌmp/ *v*

1 ►UPWARDS 向上◄ **a)** [I] to push yourself suddenly up in the air using your legs 跳，跃: **[+over/across/onto etc]** *He jumped over the wall and ran off.* 他跳墙而逃。| **jump up and down** *The kids love jumping up and down on their beds.* 孩子喜欢在床上跳上跳下。| **jump clear** (=jump out of danger) 跳离危险 *We managed to jump clear of the car before it hit the wall.* 在汽车撞到墙前，我们及时跳了出来。**b)** [T] to go over or across something by jumping 跳过〔某物〕，跃过: *They jumped the barriers to avoid paying for tickets.* 他们为了逃票而跳过栅栏。

2 ►DOWNWARDS 向下◄ [I] to let yourself drop from a place that is above the ground 跳下，跃下: **[+out/down etc]** *Three people saved themselves by jumping from the window.* 三人从窗户跳下得以捡回性命。

3 ►MOVE FAST 快速移动◄ [I always+adv/prep] to move quickly or suddenly in a particular direction〔朝某方向〕快速[突然]移动: **[+out/away/up etc]** *Matt jumped up to fetch the TV guide.* 马特突然起身去取电视节目指南。

4 ►IN FEAR/SURPRISE 由于恐惧/惊讶◄ [I] to make a quick sudden movement because you are surprised or frightened〔因惊讶或受惊而〕突然一跳: *Sorry, I didn't mean to make you jump.* 对不起，我不是有意吓你一跳的。| **jump out of your skin** (=move suddenly because you are very surprised) 吓了一大跳

5 ►MACHINE 机器◄ [I] if a machine jumps, it makes a wrong movement 错误地跳动: *The typewriter jumps every time you press 'a'.* 每次按a，打字机都跳键。

6 ►KEEP CHANGING 不断变化◄ [I] to change quickly from one place, position, idea etc to another, often missing something that comes in between〔地方、位置、思想等〕突然转换〔常漏掉中间连接部分〕: **jump from sth to sth** *Cathy's conversation jumped wildly from one topic to another.* 卡茜谈话时胡乱地从一个话题突然转到另一个话题。| **jump ahead** *I can't resist jumping ahead when I read crime novels.* 我看侦探小说时，总是忍不住跳过一些章节。

7 ►INCREASE 增加◄ [I] to increase suddenly and by a large amount〔数量〕突然上升，暴涨: **[+to]** *ICA's profits jumped to £20 million last year.* 国际合作署的利润去年猛增到2000万英镑。

8 ►ATTACK 攻击◄ [T] *informal* to attack someone suddenly【非正式】突然袭击〔某人〕: *Somebody jumped him in the park last night.* 他昨天晚上在公园里遭人袭击。

9 jump down sb's throat *informal* to suddenly speak angrily to someone【非正式】突然训斥某人: *You don't have to jump down my throat! I was only asking how you were.* 你用不着对我这么生气！我只是问候你而已。

10 jump to conclusions to form an opinion about something before you have all the facts〔在掌握全部事实之前〕仓促作出结论: *Don't jump to conclusions – he may just want to be friends.* 别急着下结论，他也许只想交个朋友。

11 jump the gun to start doing something too soon, especially without thinking about it properly〔没有认真考虑而〕过早地做某事

12 jump for joy to be extremely happy and pleased 高兴至极: *You don't have to jump for joy, but at least smile!* 你不必高兴得跳起来，但至少要笑一笑！

13 (go) jump in a lake! *spoken* used to tell someone rudely to go away【口】滚开！〔粗鲁地叫别人离开〕

14 jump to it! *spoken* used to order someone to do something immediately【口】赶快！〔命令某人立即做某事〕

15 jump bail to leave a town, city, or country where a court of law has ordered you to stay until your TRIAL[1] (1) 弃保潜逃

16 jump rope *AmE* to jump over a rope as you pass it over your head and under your feet as a game【美】跳绳; SKIP *BrE*【英】—see also 另见 JUMP ROPE

17 jump the queue *BrE*【英】, **jump in line** *AmE*【美】to join a line of people in front of others who were already waiting 不按次序排队，插队; cut in line (CUT[1] (17)) *AmE*【美】—see also 另见 QUEUE-JUMP

18 jump a light to drive past red TRAFFIC LIGHTS 闯红灯

19 jump a claim *AmE old-fashioned* to claim someone else's land as your own【美，过时】强占他人的土地

20 jump a train *especially AmE* to travel on a train, especially a goods train, without paying【尤美】不买票乘火车〔尤指运货火车〕

21 jump ship to leave a ship on which you are working as a sailor, without permission〔水手〕擅自离船

22 ►SEX 性◄ [I,T] *AmE taboo* to have sex with someone【美讳】〔与…〕性交

23 ►CAR 汽车◄ [T] *AmE* to start a car in which the BATTERY[1] (1) has lost power by connecting it to the BATTERY of another car; JUMP-START (1)【美】用跨接法启动〔汽车〕

jump at sth *phr v* [T] to eagerly accept the chance to do something 马上接受〔机会〕: *Yvonne jumped at the chance of a trip to Asia.* 伊冯娜欣然接受了这次到亚洲旅行的机会。

jump in *phr v* [I] to interrupt someone or suddenly join a conversation 打断某人的话; 突然插话

jump on sb *phr v* [T] *informal* to criticize or punish someone, especially unfairly【非正式】〔尤指不公正地〕批评; 惩罚: **[+for]** *Ryder used to jump on me for every little mistake.* 赖德以前常常对我犯的每一个小错误都严加斥责。

jump out at sb *phr v* [T] if something jumps out at you, it is extremely easy to notice〔某物〕在…面前明摆着

jump[2] *n* [C]

1 ►UP 向上◄ an act of pushing yourself suddenly up into the air using your legs 跳，跃: *That was his best jump of the competition.* 那是他在比赛中最好的一跳。

2 ►DOWN 向下◄ an act of letting yourself drop from a place that is above the ground 跳下: *a parachute jump* 跳伞

3 ►STH YOU JUMP OVER 跳过的物体◄ a fence, gate, or wall for jumping over in a race or competition 比赛中需要跳过的障碍物〈如栅栏或墙〉: *Her horse cleared all the jumps in the first round.* 她的马在第一轮比赛中跃过了所有的障碍物。

4 ►INCREASE 增加◄ a sudden large increase in an amount or value〔数量或价值的〕激增: **[+in]** *a jump in inflation rates* 通货膨胀率的剧增

5 ►PROGRESS 进展◄ a large or sudden change, especially when it improves things 巨大[突然]的变化〔尤指改善〕: *a great jump forward for human rights* 人权的极大改善

6 stay one jump ahead of sb *informal* to keep your advantage over the people you are competing with by always being the first to do something new or better【非正式】保持领先优势〔常常率先改善或创新〕

7 have the jump on sb *informal especially AmE* to have an advantage because you started doing what was necessary before your competitor【非正式，尤美】〔由于比竞争对手先开始做必须做的事而〕占有优势，抢在某人之前 —see also 另见 HIGH JUMP, LONG JUMP, RUNNING JUMP

jump ball /'· ·/ *n* [C] the act of throwing the ball up in a game of BASKETBALL, so that one player from each team can try to gain control of it〔篮球比赛中的〕跳球，争球 —see picture on page A22 参见 A22 页图

jumped-up /,· '·◂/ *adj* [only before noun 仅用于名词前] *BrE* believing that you are more important than you really are, because you have improved your social position【英】〔刚发迹而〕自命不凡的: *some jumped-up little bureaucrat* 某个暴发的小官僚

S3 **jump·er** /'dʒʌmpɚ; 'dʒʌmpə/ *n* [C] **1** *BrE* a piece of clothing made of wool that covers the upper part of your body and arms; SWEATER【英】套头毛衣 **2** *AmE* a dress without SLEEVES usually worn over a shirt【美】〔通常穿在衬衣外面的〕无袖连衣裙; PINAFORE *BrE*【英】 **3** a person or animal that jumps 跳跃的人〔动物〕

jump·er ca·bles /'·· ,··/ *n* [plural] *AmE* JUMP LEADS【美】跳线，跨接线

jump·ing jack /,·· '·/ *n* [C] a jump that is done from a standing position with your arms and legs pointing out to the side; STAR JUMP 跳跃运动〔两腿分开、两臂举起原地跳跃〕

jumping-off point /,·· '·, ·/ *n* [C] a place to start from, especially at the beginning of a journey〔旅程的〕起点，出发地点

jump jet /'· ·/ *n* [C] *especially BrE* an aircraft that can take off and land by going straight up and down【尤英】垂直起降喷气机

jump-leads /'dʒʌmp lidz; 'dʒʌmp li:dz/ *n* [plural] *BrE* thick wires used to connect the batteries (BATTERY¹ (1)) of two cars in order to start one that has lost power【英】〔用以连接两辆汽车的电瓶以发动其中一辆的〕跳线，跨接线

jump rope /'· ·/ *n* [C] *AmE* a long piece of rope that children use for jumping over【美】〔跳绳游戏用的〕绳子，跳绳; SKIPPING ROPE *BrE*【英】

jump shot /'· ·/ *n* [C] the action in BASKETBALL in which you throw the ball towards the basket as you jump in the air〔篮球的〕跳起投篮 —see picture on page A22 参见 A22 页图

jump-start /,· '·/ *v* [T] **1** to start a car whose BATTERY¹ (1) has lost power by connecting it to the battery of another car 用跨接法起动〔汽车〕 **2** to help a process or activity start or become more successful 推动〔过程或活动〕，促进: *lowering taxes to jump-start the economy* 降低税收以推动经济发展 —**jump start** *n* [C]

jump·suit /'dʒʌmpsut; 'dʒʌmpsu:t/ *n* [C] a piece of clothing like a shirt and a pair of trousers joined together, worn by women 女式连衫裤

jump·y /'dʒʌmpɪ; 'dʒʌmpi/ *adj* worried or excited especially because you are expecting something bad to happen〔尤指因预计将发生不祥之事而〕心惊肉跳的 —**jumpily** *adv* —**jumpiness** *n* [U]

junc·tion /'dʒʌŋkʃən; 'dʒʌŋkʃən/ *n* [C] a place where one road, track etc joins another〔公路、铁轨等的〕联接点，汇合处，交叉口: *the junction of Abbot's Road and Church Street* 阿伯特路与教堂街的交叉口

junc·ture /'dʒʌŋktʃɚ; 'dʒʌŋktʃə/ *n* **at this juncture** *spoken formal* at this point in an activity or period of time【口，正式】值此之际: *At this juncture I'd like to suggest we take a short break.* 在这个时刻，我建议大家休息一下。

June /dʒun; dʒu:n/ written abbreviation 缩写为 **Jun** *n* [C,U] the sixth month of the year, between May and July 六月: **in June** *My birthday is in June.* 我的生日在6月。| **last/next June** *I finished school last June.* 我去年6月完成了学业。| **on June 1st** (also 又作 **on 1st June** *BrE* 英) *We met on June 1st.* 我们在6月1日见过面。(spoken as 读作: *on June the first* or 或 *on the first of June* or 或 (*AmE* 美) *on June first*)

> **CULTURAL NOTE 文化注释**
>
> In the UK and the northern US, when people think of June, they think of the beginning of summer and good weather. In the UK, it is the time when students at school and university sit important exams. British people also think of events such as Wimbledon and Royal Ascot. 在英国和美国北部，人们想到6月，会想到夏天宜人天气的开始。在英国，这是学生参加重要考试的月份。英国人还会联想起温布尔登网球赛和皇家阿斯科特赛马等盛事。

Juneau /'dʒu,no; 'dʒu:nəʊ/ the capital city of the US state of Alaska 朱诺〔美国阿拉斯加州首府〕

Jung /juŋ; jʊŋ/, **Carl Gus·tav** /karl 'gʌstav; kɑ:l 'gʊstɑ:v/ (1875-1961) a Swiss PSYCHIATRIST who studied the importance of dreams and religion in problems of the mind, and divided people into two groups, INTROVERTS and EXTROVERTS. Jung developed the idea of the collective unconscious, the belief that people's feelings and reactions are often based on deep memories of human experience in the past. He worked with Sigmund Freud until they had a serious disagreement. 荣格〔(1875-1961)，瑞士精神病学家，曾研究精神障碍中梦和宗教的重要性，并把人分为内向型与外向型两类。他提出了集体无意识的概念，即人的感情和反应都是以人类过去经历的深层记忆为基础的。他曾与西格蒙德·弗洛伊德合作，后因严重分歧而分道扬镳〕—**Jungian** *adj*: *Jungian analysis* 荣格精神分析法

jun·gle /'dʒʌŋgl; 'dʒʌŋgəl/ *n* **1** [C,U] a thick tropical forest with many large plants growing very close together 热带丛林 **2** [singular] a place that is very untidy and where a lot of things have been placed close together〔堆满东西的〕杂乱的地方: *This place is turning into a jungle already.* 这个地方已变得一片凌乱。**3** [singular] a situation in which it is difficult to become successful or get what you want, especially because a lot of people are competing with each other〔尤因竞争者众多〕难以成功的局面: *You've got to be tough – it's a jungle out there.* 你必须坚强一些，那个地方竞争激烈。—see also 另见 CONCRETE JUNGLE, **law of the jungle** (LAW (10))

Jungle Book, The /'·· ,·/ a book of stories by Rudyard Kipling about a young boy called Mowgli who grows up in the JUNGLE in India and is cared for by animals, such as Baloo the bear and Bagheera the PANTHER. It was made into a very popular CARTOON film by Walt Disney in 1967.《丛林故事》〔拉迪亚德·吉卜林创作的故事集，讲述一位名叫莫格利的小男孩在印度的丛林中由大熊巴鲁和黑豹巴赫拉等动物照顾而长大成人的故事。1967年，该书被沃尔特·迪斯尼公司改编成一部广受欢迎的卡通影片〕

jungle gym /'·· ,·/ *n* [C] *AmE* a large frame made of metal bars for children to climb on【美】〔儿童玩的〕攀登架; CLIMBING FRAME *BrE*【英】

Ju·ni·or /'dʒunjɚ; 'dʒu:niə/ written abbreviation 缩写为 **Jr** *AmE* W3
【美】, **Jnr** *BrE*【英】[only after noun 仅用于名词后] used after the name of a man who has the same name as his father 小〔置于与父亲同名的男子姓名之后〕: *John J. Wallace, Jr.* 小约翰·J. 华莱士

junior¹ *adj* **1** [only before noun 仅用于名词前] having a low rank in an organization or profession〔在组织或行业中〕级别[职位]低的: *a junior doctor* 初级医生 —opposite 反义词 SENIOR¹ **2 be junior to sb** to have a lower rank than someone〔级别〕低于某人 —see also 另见 SENIOR¹

junior² *n* **1 be two/five/ten etc years sb's junior** to be two, five, ten etc years younger than someone 比某人小两岁/五岁/十岁等: *She married a man seven years her junior.* 她嫁给一个比她小七岁的男人。**2** [C] *especially BrE* someone who has a low rank in an organization or profession【尤英】低级职位的人: *an office junior* 低级职员 **3** [C] *BrE* a pupil in a JUNIOR SCHOOL【英】小学生 **4** [C] *AmE* a student in the year before the final year of HIGH SCHOOL or university【美】〔四年制大学或高中的〕三年级学生 —compare 比较 FRESHMAN; SENIOR² (2); SOPHOMORE **5** [singular] *AmE especially humorous* a way of speaking to or about your son【美，尤幽默】〔指自己的〕儿子: *What are we going to do about junior if we go out tonight?* 我们今晚如果外出，儿子怎么办? —see also 另见 SENIOR²

junior col·lege /,··· '··/ *n* [C,U] a college in the US or Canada where students take a course of study that continues for two years; COMMUNITY COLLEGE〔美国或加拿大的〕两年制专科学院

junior high school /,··· '· ·/ also 又作 **junior high** *n* [C,U] a school in the US and other countries for children aged 12 to 13 or 14 初级中学〔美国等国家12至13或14岁的孩子上的学校〕—compare 比较 MIDDLE SCHOOL, SENIOR HIGH SCHOOL

Junior Mints /'···, ·/ *trademark* a type of small, soft, circle-shaped MINT that is covered with chocolate【商标】臭小子薄荷糖〔一种外裹巧克力的圈状薄荷小软糖〕

junior school /'···, ·/ *n* [C,U] a school in Britain for children aged 7 to 11 小学〔英国7至11岁的孩子上的学校〕

junior var·si·ty /,··· '···/ *n* [C,U] *AmE* a team of younger or less experienced sports players who represent a school or college【美】〔学校或学院的〕体育代表队二队，乙级队 —compare 比较 VARSITY (1)

ju·ni·per /'dʒunəpɚ; 'dʒu:nɪpə/ *n* [C,U] a small bush that produces berries (BERRY) and has leaves that are green all year 桧，刺柏

junk¹ /dʒʌŋk; dʒʌŋk/ *n* **1** [U] old or unwanted objects that have no use or value 废旧杂物: *I must get rid of all this junk.* 我必须把这些废旧杂物都丢掉。**2** [C] a Chinese sailing boat 中国平底

帆船 **3** [U] *slang* a dangerous drug, especially HEROIN【俚】毒品〔尤指海洛因〕 **4** *spoken* JUNK FOOD【口】〔多热量、少营养的〕劣质[垃圾]食物

junk² *v* [T] to get rid of something because it is old or useless 丢掉〔废旧物品〕

junk bond /ˈ· ·/ *n* [C] a BOND[1] (1) which has a high risk and is often sold to pay for a TAKEOVER 低档债券, 风险债券, 垃圾债券

Jun·kers /ˈjuŋkəz; ˈjʊŋkəz/ *n* a type of German military aircraft designed by Hugo Junkers (1859-1935) and used by the German air force in World War I and World War II 容克式飞机〔雨果·容克(1859-1935)设计的一种德式军用飞机。两次世界大战期间, 德国空军曾使用这种飞机〕

jun·ket /ˈdʒʌŋkɪt; ˈdʒʌŋkɨt/ *n* **1** [U] a sweet dish made from thickened milk 乳冻甜食 **2** [C] *informal especially AmE* a free trip that is paid for by government money【非正式, 尤美】公款旅行, 公费旅游

junk food /ˈ· ·/ *n* [U] *informal* food that is not healthy because it contains a lot of fat, sugar, or CARBOHYDRATE【非正式】〔高脂肪、高糖分、高碳水化合物的〕不利健康的劣质食品, 垃圾食品

junk·ie, junky /ˈdʒʌŋkɪ; ˈdʒʌŋki/ *n* [C] *slang*【俚】**1** someone who takes dangerous drugs and is dependent on them 有毒瘾者 **2 television/soap opera etc junkie** *humorous* someone who likes something so much that they seem to be dependent on it【幽默】看电视/肥皂剧等上瘾的人, 电视/肥皂剧迷: *a television junkie* 电视迷

junk mail /ˈ· ·/ *n* [U] letters that advertisers send to people 垃圾邮件〔指商家寄给消费者的广告信件〕

junk shop /ˈ· ·/ *n* [C] a shop that buys and sells old things〔收售旧货的〕旧货商店

junk·y /ˈdʒʌŋkɪ; ˈdʒʌŋki/ *n* [C] another spelling of JUNKIE junkie 的另一种拼法

junk yard /ˈ· ·/ *n* [C] *AmE* a place where old or unwanted things can be left, bought, and sold【美】废品旧货栈 —compare 比较 DUMP² (1), TIP¹ (4)

Ju·no /ˈdʒuno; ˈdʒuːnəʊ/ in Roman MYTHOLOGY, the goddess of women and marriage. She was the wife of Jupiter. In Greek mythology her name is Hera. 朱诺〔罗马神话中司女性和婚姻的女神, 朱庇特之妻。希腊神话中称赫拉〕

jun·ta /ˈdʒʌntə; ˈdʒʌntə/ *n* [C] a military government that has gained power by using force〔靠武力取得政权的〕军政府

Ju·pi·ter /ˈdʒupətə; ˈdʒuːpɨtə/ *n* [singular] a large PLANET that moves around the sun 木星 —see picture at 参见 SOLAR SYSTEM 图

Jur·as·sic Park /dʒʊˌræsɪk ˈpɑrk; dʒʊˌræsɪk ˈpɑːk/ (1993) an exciting and frightening US film made by Steven Spielberg, about DINOSAURS (=very large animals that lived on the Earth millions of years ago) that have been made by scientists and put in a special park where people can go and see them. The dinosaurs escape and try to kill people.《侏罗纪公园》〔(1993), 美国惊险影片, 由史蒂文·斯皮尔伯格导演。影片中, 科学家造出恐龙, 并把恐龙关在公园里供人观赏。结果, 恐龙逃了出来, 试图伤害人类〕

ju·rid·i·cal /dʒʊˈrɪdɪkḷ; dʒʊˈrɪdɪkəl/ *adj formal* connected with judges or the law【正式】司法上的, 法律上的

jur·is·dic·tion /ˌdʒurɪsˈdɪkʃən; ˌdʒʊərɨsˈdɪkʃən/ *n* [U] the right to use an official power to make legal decisions 司法权; 审判权; 管辖权: *That area is not within the State Police's jurisdiction.* 那个地区不在州警察局的管辖范围之内。

ju·ris·pru·dence /ˌdʒurɪsˈprudṇs; ˌdʒʊərɨsˈpruːdəns/ *n* [U] *formal* the science or study of law【正式】法学, 法律学

ju·rist /ˈdʒurɪst; ˈdʒʊərɨst/ *n* [C] *formal* someone who has a very detailed knowledge of law【正式】法学家, 法律学者

ju·ror /ˈdʒurə; ˈdʒʊərə/ *n* [C] a member of a JURY 陪审员; 评判员

ju·ry /ˈdʒurɪ; ˈdʒʊəri/ *n* [C] **1** a group of 12 ordinary people who listen to details of a case in court and decide whether someone is guilty or not〔由12位公民组成的〕陪审团: *The jury finds the defendant not guilty.* 陪审团认为被告无罪。| **sit on a jury** (=be part of a jury) 担任陪审员 **2** a group of people chosen to judge a competition〔竞赛的〕评判委员会 **3 the jury is out on sth** used to say that something is still not yet certain 陪审团仍在商议中〔指某事仍然没有定论〕: *The jury is still out as to the overall impact of the programme.* 关于该计划的整体影响, 评委会仍在进行商议。—see also 另见 GRAND JURY

jury box /ˈ·· ·/ *n* [C usually singular 一般用单数] the place where the jury sits in a court 陪审团席

jury du·ty /ˈ·· ˌ··/ *n* [U] *AmE* a period of time during which you must be part of a jury【美】〔一段时间内〕担任陪审员的义务; JURY SERVICE *BrE*【英】

ju·ry·man /ˈdʒurɪmən; ˈdʒʊərimən/ *n* [C] a male member of a jury 男陪审员

jury serv·ice /ˈ·· ˌ··/ *n* [U] *BrE* a period of time during which you must be part of a jury【英】担任陪审员的义务; JURY DUTY *AmE*【美】

CULTURAL NOTE 文化注释

In the US, anyone who is allowed to vote can be called to serve on a jury or GRAND JURY. In Britain, anyone between the ages of 18 and 65 who has lived in Britain for at least five years since the age of 13 can be called for jury service. Some people, such as priests and judges, are not called for jury service, and neither are people living in Northern Ireland. In both the US and in Britain, jury service usually continues for two weeks, unless you are chosen to be a jury member during a long trial, when you must be on the jury until it ends. 在美国, 凡是合法选民都可担任陪审团或大陪审团的陪审员。在英国, 年龄在18岁至65岁之间, 13岁以后在英国居住满5年的人都可担任陪审团的陪审员, 但牧师、法官和北爱尔兰的居民除外。在英美两国, 担任陪审员一般为期两周。不过, 若获选成为陪审员参加较长的审判时, 就必须坚持到审判结束。

jur·y·wom·an /ˈdʒurɪˌwumən; ˈdʒʊəriˌwʊmən/ *n* [C] a female member of a jury 女陪审员

just¹ /dʒəst; dʒəst; *strong* 强读 dʒʌst; dʒʌst/ *adv* **1** exactly 正好, 恰好: *Thank you. That's just what I need.* 谢谢, 那正是我需要的。| *The house was large and roomy; just right for us.* 那幢房子大而宽敞, 正适合我们。| *She looks just like her mother.* 她看上去就像她妈妈。**2** only 仅仅, 只是: *He's not a thief, just a little boy who likes biscuits.* 他不是贼, 只是个爱吃饼干的小男孩。| *It'll just take a few minutes.* 只需花几分钟。**3** if something has just happened, it happened only a short time ago 刚刚〔发生〕, 方才: *John's just told me that he's getting married.* 约翰刚刚告诉我他要结婚了。| *I've just been out shopping.* 我刚才出去买东西了。**4** if you are just doing something, or just about to do something you are starting to do it or going to do it soon 刚要〔做某事〕, 正准备: *He was just leaving when the phone rang.* 他正准备离开时, 电话铃响了。| *I'll just change my clothes, if you don't mind waiting a minute.* 如果你不介意等一下, 我这就去换一下衣服。**5** used to emphasize something you are saying〔用于加强语气〕: *I needed some fresh air, so work would just have to wait.* 我需要透透气, 只好等一下再工作。| *He just got in his car and drove off.* 他径直钻进汽车, 开车走了。**6 just before/after/over etc** only a short time before, after etc 稍前/稍后/刚刚超过等: *We moved here just after our son was born.* 儿子出生不久我们就搬到这儿来了。| *I saw her just before she died.* 就在她去世前不久, 我见过她。| *It's just under three centimeters long.* 差一点儿才够三厘米长。**7 (only) just** if something just happens or is just possible, it does happen or is possible, but it almost did not happen or was not possible 勉强地, 不太可能地: *He just managed to get home before dark.* 他勉强赶在天黑前到家。| *Those pants only just fit you now.* 那几条裤子你现在穿勉强合身。**8 just about** almost 几乎, 差不多: *The plums are just about ripe now.* 李子差不多都熟了。| *Just about everybody will be affected by the tax increases.* 几乎每个人都将受到加税的影响。**9 just as** equally as 和…一样: *Brad is just as good as the others.* 布拉德和其他人完全一样。**10 just then** at exactly that moment 正在那时: *Just then there was a sound in the hall.* 正在那时, 大厅里传来响声。**11 just the thing** *informal* exactly the right thing【非正式】正合适的东西: *This soup is just the thing for a cold winter's day.* 寒冷的冬日里喝这种汤正合适。**12** *informal* completely【非正式】完全地: *She was just horrified at my choice of husband.* 她对于我选择的丈夫大感吃惊。—see also 另见 **just my luck** (LUCK¹ (7))

Frequencies of the adverb **just** in spoken and written English 副词 just 在英语口语和书面语中的使用频率

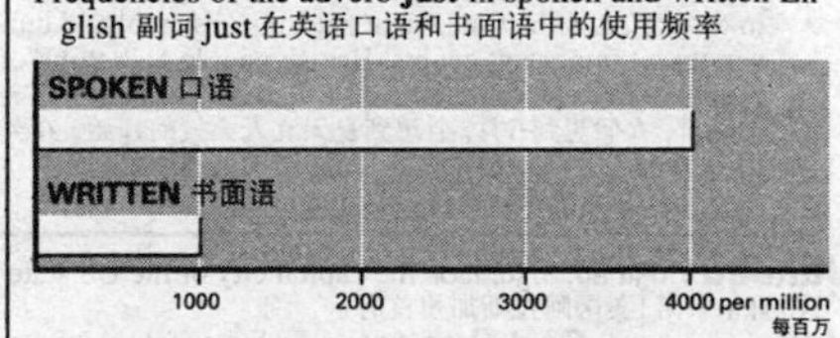

Based on the British National Corpus and the Longman Lancaster Corpus
据英国国家语料库和朗文兰开斯特语料库

This graph shows that the adverb **just** is much more common in spoken English than in written English. This is because it is very commonly used in spoken English to mean 'exactly' or to mean 'a short time before or after'. It also has special uses in spoken English and is used in a lot of common spoken phrases. 本图表显示，副词just在英语口语中的使用频率远远高于书面语，因为它在口语中常常用来表示“正好”或“稍前/稍后”的意思。它在口语中还有许多特殊用法，而且口语中有很多常用短语都是由just构成的。

just (*adv*) SPOKEN USES AND PHRASES
含just的口语用法及短语

13 just a) used to pause while you think what to say next or think how to describe something〔用于短暂停顿，以便思考接着说什么或如何描述某事等〕: *When I told him the news he just ... he just sat there and didn't say a word.* 我告诉他这个消息时，他嗯…坐在那儿一言不发。| *It wasn't an argument, it was just, it was more like a discussion.* 那不是争论，那是嗯…倒更像是讨论。**b)** used when politely asking something or telling someone to do something〔用于礼貌地要求某事或请某人做某事〕: *Could I just say a few words before we start?* 我们开始前，能否让我先说几句话? **c)** used when firmly telling someone to do something〔用于严厉地命令某人做某事〕: *Look, just shut up for a minute!* 喂，把你的嘴闭一会儿! **14 just a minute/second/moment a)** used to ask someone to wait for a short time while you do something 请稍等一下〔当你做某事时请别人等一等〕: *Just a minute, I'll see if I can find it for you.* 稍等一下，我看看能否给你找到它。**b)** used to interrupt someone in order to ask them something, disagree with them etc 请等一下〔用于打断别人的话，以询问某事或表示不同意等〕: *Just a minute, I'm not sure I agree with your last point.* 请等一下，我不同意你说的最后一点。**15 just now a)** a moment ago or a very short time ago 刚才: *Where have my glasses gone? I had them just now.* 我的眼镜哪里去了? 我刚才还戴着呢。**b)** *especially BrE* at the moment【尤英】现在，眼下: *We're busy just now, can you come back later?* 我们现在很忙，你过一会再来好吗? **16 would just as soon** if you would just as soon do something, you would prefer to do it 宁愿，宁可: *I'd just as soon not be here when she comes.* 她来的时候，我宁可不在这里。**17 may just/might just** might possibly 也许，有可能: *You could try Renee; she might just know where they live now.* 你不妨问问勒妮，她也许知道他们现在住在哪儿。**18 not just yet** not quite yet 还不能: *I can't leave just yet. I've still got a couple of letters to write.* 我现在还不能离开，还有几封信要写。**19 it's just that** used when explaining the reason for something, especially when someone thinks there is a different reason 只是〔用来说明原因，尤其在有人认为另有原因时使用〕: *No, I do like Chinese food, it's just that I'm not hungry.* 不，我的确喜欢中国菜，只是我现在不饿。**20 just think/look/listen** used to tell someone to imagine, look at or listen to the same thing that you are imagining, looking at, or listening to 且想想/看看/听听〔自己想象、看见或听见的事物〕: *Just think – in a week we'll be lying on a beach in the sun!* 你想想——一星期后我们将躺在沙滩上晒太阳! **21 be just looking** to be looking at things in a shop without intending to buy anything〔在商店里〕随便逛逛〔不准备购物〕: *"Can I help you?" "No thanks, I'm just looking."* “你要什么?”“不，谢谢。我只是随便看看。” **22 just because ... doesn't mean** used to say that although one thing is true, another thing is not necessarily true 尽管…但不表示…: *Just because you're older than me doesn't mean you can tell me what to do.* 尽管你年纪比我大，但不表示你有权命令我。**23 it's/that's just as well** used to say that it is lucky that something happens because otherwise there would be problems 幸亏，幸而: *It's just as well Kathy didn't come to the film. She'd have hated it.* 幸亏凯茜没来看这部电影，她会讨厌这电影的。**24 might just as well** if you might just as well do something, it would be sensible, or a good idea to do it 还不如…〔用来表示做某事是明智或恰当的〕: *There's no point in waiting here. We might just as well go home.* 在这儿等没有意义，我们还不如回家。**25 just the same** used to say that your opinion is the same about something, although someone has said something to try to change your opinion 尽管那样〔表示不管别人怎样说，你对某物的看法仍然一样〕: *"The new model is a lot better." "Just the same, I'd rather have the old one I'm used to."* “新型号好得多。”“尽管如此，我仍然喜欢我熟悉的旧型号。” **26 isn't she just/aren't they just** *old-fashioned* used to strongly agree with something someone has said about a person or thing【过时】没错，的确〔对某人的话表示强烈赞同〕: *"He's a selfish, rude, ignorant man!" "Isn't he just!"* “他是个自私、粗鲁又无知的家伙!”“可不是嘛!” **27 just testing a)** used to tell someone that you only asked them something to check if they knew the answer 只是问问/考考你〔用来表示之所以发问是想看某人是否知道答案〕: *"What's the capital of France?" "Paris, of course!" "Just testing."* “法国的首都是哪里?”“当然是巴黎!”“只是想考考你。” **b)** used when you have made a mistake, to pretend that you only did it to see if someone would notice 只是试验〔做错事时，用来假装你做此事只是为了试验别人有没有注意到〕: *"That isn't how you spell 'receive'!" "I know, just testing!"* “receive这个词不是这样拼的!”“我知道，只是试试你能不能看出来!” **28 just on** *BrE* almost exactly【英】差不多，将近: *It's just on three o'clock.* 快到三点了。**29 just so a)** with everything arranged neatly and tidily 井然有序，有条不紊: *Her house always has to be just so.* 她的家总是收拾得井井有条。**b)** *old-fashioned* used to say yes or agree with something【过时】对; 是这样; 正是如此

USAGE NOTE 用法说明: JUST

AmE-BrE DIFFERENCE 美国英语与英国英语的区别

Time adverbs **just, already**, and **yet** are often used with the simple past tense in American English. 美国英语中，时间副词just, already和yet常与一般过去时连用: *The bell just rang* (=it rang a short time ago). 铃刚响过。| *I already saw him.* 我已经见过他。| *Did you eat yet?* 你吃过饭了吗?

This use is also fairly common now in British English, but it is still considered more correct to say 这种用法现在在英国英语中也相当普遍，但人们仍然认为更准确的说法是: *The bell has just rung.* 铃刚响过。| *I've already seen him.* 我已经见过他。| *Have you eaten yet?* 你吃过饭了吗?

just² /dʒʌst; dʒʌst/ *adj* **1** morally right and fair 正义的，公正的，公平的: *A medal of honour was his just reward.* 一枚荣誉奖章是对他的公正奖赏。| *I think this is a just punishment bearing in mind the seriousness of the crime.* 考虑到罪行的严重性，我认为这是很公正的惩罚。**2 get your just deserts** to be punished or suffer in a way that other people think you deserve 得到应有的惩罚，罪有应得: *I hope that he's caught and gets his just deserts.* 我希望他被抓住并得到应有的惩罚。—**justly** *adv*: *These men are criminals, but they must be dealt with justly.* 这些人虽然是罪犯，但也应公正对待。 S3 W3

jus·tice /ˈdʒʌstɪs; ˈdʒʌstɪs/ *n* **1** [U] fairness in the way people are treated 正义; 公正; 合理: *Sometimes I wonder if there's any justice in this world.* 我有时候怀疑世上还有没有公义。—opposite 反义词 INJUSTICE —see also 另见 POETIC JUSTICE W2

CULTURAL NOTE 文化注释

Justice is often represented by a woman who has her eyes covered, and has SCALES in one hand and a sword in the other. This represents the idea that justice should treat everyone equally, examine (or 'weigh') all the EVIDENCE, decide whether it shows that the person is guilty or not, and punish those who are guilty. In London there is a famous STATUE of Justice on the Old Bailey, the main court for criminal cases in London. 正义的象征通常是一个蒙着眼睛的女子，一手持天平，一手持剑，表示正义是平等待人，核查(或“衡量”)所有证据，判定某人有罪或无罪，并惩罚罪犯。伦敦老贝利法庭(中央刑事法庭)是审判刑事案件的主要法庭，屋顶上有一尊著名的正义女神塑像。

2 [U] the system by which people are judged in courts of law and criminals are punished 司法制度; 审判; 法律制裁: *This has restored my faith in British justice.* 这件事使我恢复了对英国司法制度的信心。| **escape justice** (=avoid being punished for a crime)〔犯罪后〕逃避法律制裁 **3 bring sb to justice** to catch someone who you think is guilty of a crime and arrange for them to go to court 将犯人缉拿归案: *We will not rest until her killer is brought to justice.* 不把杀害她的凶手绳之以法，我们决不罢休。**4 justice has been done/served** used to say that someone has been treated fairly or has been given a punishment they deserve 正义得以伸张 **5 do justice to sb/sth** also 又作 **do sb/sth justice** to treat or represent someone or something in a way that is fair and shows their best qualities 公平对待某人/某物; 充分展现某人/某物的最佳素质: *The photo doesn't do her jus-*

tice – she was really beautiful. 这张照片没有把她拍好——她其实很美。| *It's impossible to do justice to Mahler's music without a full orchestra.* 没有完整的管弦乐队，马勒的音乐就不可能得到充分展现。**6 do yourself justice** to do something such as a test well enough to show your real ability〔在考试等中〕充分发挥自己的能力: *Sara panicked in the exam and didn't do herself justice.* 萨拉在考试中由于紧张未能充分发挥自己的水准。**7** also 又作 **Justice a)** [C] *AmE* a judge in a law court【美】法官 **b)** [C] *BrE* the title of a judge in the High Court【英】〔高等法院的〕法官的头衔 **8** [U] the quality of being right and deserving fair treatment 正确; 公正: *No one doubts the justice of our cause.* 没有人怀疑我们的动机的合理性。—see also 另见 **rough justice** (ROUGH[1] (14))

Justice of the Peace /ˌ· · · · ˈ·/ abbreviation 缩写为 **JP** *n* [C] someone who judges less serious cases in small law courts and, in the US, can perform marriage ceremonies 地方官; 治安法官〔在美国还有证婚权〕

jus·ti·fi·a·ble /ˈdʒʌstəˌfaɪəbl̩; ˈdʒʌstɪ̥faɪəbəl/ *adj* actions, reactions, decisions etc that are justifiable are done for good reasons〔行为、反应、决定等〕有道理的: *justifiable anger* 情有可原的愤怒 —**justifiably** *adv*

justifiable hom·i·cide /ˌ· · · · · ˈ· · ·/ *n* [U] *law* a situation in which you are not punished for killing someone, usually because you did it to defend yourself【法律】正当杀人〔一般指因自卫而杀人，因此不受惩罚〕

jus·ti·fi·ca·tion /ˌdʒʌstəfəˈkeʃən; ˌdʒʌstɪ̥fɪ̥ˈkeɪʃən/ *n* [C,U] **1** a good and acceptable reason for doing something 正当的理由, 可接受的理由: *The committee could see no justification for a pay rise.* 委员会找不出提高工资的恰当理由。**2 in justification (of)** to explain why an idea or action is right 为…辩解〔解释为何某想法或行动是正确的〕

jus·ti·fied /ˈdʒʌstəˌfaɪd; ˈdʒʌstɪ̥faɪd/ *adj* **1** having an acceptable explanation or reason 有正当理由的, 有合理解释的: *I think your conclusions were fully justified.* 我认为你的结论完全合理。| **be justified in doing sth** *Under the circumstances, the principal was justified in expelling this student.* 在这种情况下，校长完全有理由开除这名学生。**2 right/left justified** *technical* printed material that is right or left justified has a straight edge where all the words line up on the left or right of a page【术语】〔印刷品中的文字在页面〕右侧/左侧对齐的

jus·ti·fy /ˈdʒʌstəˌfaɪ; ˈdʒʌstɪ̥faɪ/ *v* [T] **1** to give an acceptable explanation for something that other people think is unreasonable 证明〔别人认为不合理的事〕有道理; 为…辩护: *How can you justify the expense?* 你怎样对这笔开支作合理的解释呢？| **justify doing sth** *It's hard to justify making everyone wait for so long.* 让大家等这么久对此很难作出合理的解释。**2 justify yourself (to sb)** to prove that what you are doing is reasonable（向某人）为自己辩护: *I'm in charge here; I don't have to justify myself to you.* 这里由我负责，我没有必要为我的行为向你解释。**3** to be a good and acceptable reason for something 是…的正当理由: *Nothing justifies murdering another human being.* 没有任何正当的理由可以为杀人这种罪行辩解。

Just Sev·en·teen /ˌ· ˈ· · ·/ —see 见 J-17

Just Wil·liam books, the /ˌ· ˈ· · · ·/ a series of humorous British books for children by Richmal Crompton, the first of which was called *Just William* (1922), about an English schoolboy called William Brown who likes to play tricks on adults and who always gets into trouble.《威廉的故事》〔英国一儿童幽默小说集，由里奇马尔·克朗普顿所著。第一部为《公正的威廉》（1922），讲述一名爱捉弄大人并常惹事端的英格兰学生威廉·布朗的故事〕

jut /dʒʌt; dʒʌt/ *v* **jutted, jutting** [I always+adv/prep] also 又作 **jut out** something that juts up or out sticks up or out further than the other things around it 突出, 伸出: *Tall jagged rocks jutted out over the beach.* 高耸嶙峋的岩石在海滩上延伸出来。

jute /dʒut; dʒuːt/ *n* [U] a natural substance that is used for making rope and rough cloth〔用于制绳子和粗布的〕黄麻纤维

Jut·land /ˈdʒʌtlənd; ˈdʒʌtlənd/ a PENINSULA (=a long, thin area of land with sea on three sides) in northern Europe belonging partly to Denmark and partly to Germany. The **Battle of Jutland** was fought between the British navy and German navy off the coast of Jutland in World War I. 日德兰半岛〔北欧一半岛，分属丹麦和德国。第一次世界大战期间，英德海军在该岛海岸附近交战，史称日德兰海战〕

ju·ve·nile /ˈdʒuvənl̩; ˈdʒuːvənaɪl/ *adj* **1** [only before noun 仅用于名词前] *especially law* connected with young people who are not yet adults【尤法律】少年的: *juvenile crime* 少年罪行 **2** silly and typical of a child rather than an adult 幼稚的, 年幼无知的: *a very juvenile sense of humour* 很幼稚的幽默感 —**juvenile** *n* [C]

juvenile de·lin·quent /ˌ· · · ·ˈ· ·/ *n* [C] a child or young person who behaves in a criminal way 少年罪犯 —**juvenile delinquency** *n* [U]

Ju·ven·tus /juˈvɛntəs; juːˈventəs/ an Italian football team, based in Turin 尤文图斯队〔意大利一足球队，在都灵〕

jux·ta·pose /ˌdʒʌkstəˈpoz; ˌdʒʌkstəˈpəʊz/ *v* [T] *formal* to put things together, especially things that are not normally together, in order to compare them or to make something new【正式】把…并列[并置]〔以作比较或制作新东西〕—**juxtaposition** /ˌdʒʌkstəpəˈzɪʃən; ˌdʒʌkstəpəˈzɪʃən/ *n* [C,U]

K,k

K, k /ke; keɪ/ *plural* **K's, k's** *n* [C] the eleventh letter of the English alphabet 英语字母表的第十一个字母

K, k **1** *informal*【非正式】an abbreviation of 缩写= one thousand 一千: *salary of £30k a year* 年薪三万英镑 **2** an abbreviation of 缩写= KILOBYTE (=a measurement of computer information) 千字节〔电脑的信息单位〕

K2 /ˌke ˋtu; ˌkeɪ ˈtuː/ also 又作 **Mount Godwin Austen** the second highest mountain in the world after Mount Everest, on the border between Kashmir and China 乔戈里峰, 戈德温奥斯丁峰〔世界第二高峰, 仅次于珠穆朗玛峰, 位于克什米尔地区与中国边境〕

ka·bob /kəˋbɑb; kəˈbɑːb/ *n* [C] an American spelling of KEBAB kebab 的美式拼法

Ka·bul /ˋkɑbʊl; ˈkɑːbʊl/ the capital city of Afghanistan 喀布尔〔阿富汗首都〕

Kaczynski, Theodore —see 见 UNABOMBER

kaf·fee·klatch /ˋkæfeˌklætʃ; ˈkæfeɪklætʃ/ *n* [C] *AmE* an informal social situation when people drink coffee and talk【美】咖啡叙谈会

kaf·fir /ˋkæfɚ; ˈkæfə/ *n* [C] *SAfrE taboo* an offensive word for a black African, used only by white people【南非, 讳】非洲黑鬼〔白人对非洲黑人的冒犯用语〕

Kaf·ka /ˋkɑfkə; ˈkæfkə/, **Franz** /frɑnts; frænts/ (1883-1924) a Czech writer who wrote in German, famous for his NOVELS such as *The Trial* and *The Castle*, and his short stories such as *Metamorphosis*, in which a man turns into a large and ugly insect. His stories deal with the struggle of ordinary people on their own against the state or large organizations. The word **Kafkaesque** is used to describe this type of experience, in which you feel that no one understands you and there is no way of escaping from an unpleasant situation. 卡夫卡〔(1883-1924), 捷克德语作家, 以《审判》、《城堡》等小说和《变形记》等短篇故事闻名。《变形记》讲述一男子变成又大又丑的昆虫的故事。他的故事一般以普通百姓独自与国家或庞大组织相抗争为主题。Kafkaesque (卡夫卡风格的) 一词常用来描述这样一种情形: 一个人觉得自己得不到别人理解, 却又找不到摆脱困境的出路〕

kaf·tan /ˋkæftən; ˈkæftæn/ *n* [C] another spelling of CAFTAN caftan 的另一种拼法

Kahlo /ˋkɑlo; ˈkɑːləʊ/, **Frida** /ˋfridə; ˈfriːdə/ (1907-54) a Mexican painter in the style of SURREALISM, who was the wife of the painter Diego Rivera 卡洛〔(1907-1954), 墨西哥超现实主义画家, 画家迭戈·里维拉之妻〕

Kai·ser, the /ˋkaɪzɚ; ˈkaɪzə/ Wilhelm II, the King of Germany from 1888 to 1918. He was given the NICKNAME 'Kaiser Bill' by the British in World War I. 德国皇帝〔即威廉二世, 1888至1918年在位。一战期间, 英国人送给他一个绰号, 叫他"比尔皇帝"〕

Kal·a·ha·ri Des·ert, the /ˌkæləhɑrɪ ˋdɛzɚt; ˌkæləhɑːri ˈdezət/ also 又作 **the Kalahari** a large desert in southern Africa 卡拉哈里沙漠〔非洲南部一大沙漠〕

Ka·lash·ni·kov /kəˋlæʃnɪkɑf; kəˈlæʃnɪkɒf/ *n* [C] a type of RIFLE (=long gun) that can fire very quickly 卡拉什尼科夫步枪, AK-47步枪

kale /kel; keɪl/ *n* [C,U] a dark green CABBAGE (=type of vegetable) 羽衣甘蓝

ka·lei·do·scope /kəˋlaɪdəˌskop; kəˈlaɪdəskəʊp/ *n* [C] **1** a pattern, situation, or scene that is always changing and has many details or bright colours 千变万化的图案[情况, 景致]: [+of] *the kaleidoscope of American ethnic groups* 五光十色的美国各民族 **2** a tube with mirrors and pieces of coloured glass at one end, that shows coloured patterns when you turn it 万花筒

ka·lei·do·scop·ic /kəˌlaɪdəˋskɑpɪk; kəˌlaɪdəˈskɒpɪk◂/ *adj* kaleidoscopic scenes, colours, or patterns change often and quickly〔景致、色彩或图案〕千变万化的 —**kaleidoscopically** /-klɪ; -kli/ *adv*

Ka·li /ˋkɑlɪ; ˈkɑːli/ in Hindu MYTHOLOGY, a GODDESS of death and destruction 迦利, 又译时母〔印度神话中的死亡和破坏女神〕

Ka·ma Su·tra, the /ˌkɑmə ˋsutrə; ˌkɑːmə ˈsuːtrə/ an ancient Hindu book about sex and love, famous for the many positions it describes for sexual acts《爱经》, 又译《性爱圣典》〔古印度性爱书籍, 尤以描写多种性交姿势闻名〕

kam·i·ka·ze /ˌkæmɪˋkɑzɪ; ˌkæmɪˈkɑːzi◂/ *adj* **1 kamikaze pilot** a pilot who deliberately crashes his plane on enemy camps, ships, etc knowing he will be killed 神风队飞行员 **2 kamikaze attitude/behaviour** willingness to take risks, without caring about your safety 敢于冒险不计自身安危的态度/行为: *kamikaze lorry drivers* 不顾生命危险的卡车司机

Kam·pa·la /kɑmˋpɑlə; kæmˈpɑːlə/ the capital city of Uganda, on Lake Victoria 坎帕拉〔乌干达首都, 濒临维多利亚湖〕

Kam·pu·che·a /ˌkæmpuˋtʃiə; ˌkæmpʊˈtʃiːə/ a former name of Cambodia, a country in southeast Asia 柬埔寨〔东南亚一国家, 该国的旧称〕

Kan·chen·jun·ga /ˌkɑntʃənˋdʒʊŋgə; ˌkæntʃənˈdʒʊŋgə/ one of the world's highest mountains, on the border between India and Nepal 干城章嘉峰〔世界最高峰之一, 位于印度和尼泊尔边境〕

Kandinsky /kænˋdɪnskɪ; kænˈdɪnski/, **Wassily** /vɑˋsɪlɪ; vɑːˈsiːli/ (1866-1944) a Russian painter of ABSTRACT art 康定斯基〔(1866-1944), 俄国抽象派画家〕

Kane /ken; keɪn/, **Bob** (1915-98) a US COMIC book artist, who was the creator of Batman in 1939. Batman was so successful that by 1940 he had his own comic. 凯恩〔(1915-1998), 美国连环漫画艺术家。1939年, 他创作了"蝙蝠侠", 并产生了很大反响。1940年, 他开始有了自己的连环漫画杂志〕

kan·ga /ˋkæŋgə; ˈkæŋgə/ *n* [C] a woman's dress from Africa, consisting of a long piece of cloth wound around the body 肯加衣裙〔源于非洲妇女的衣着, 用一条长布包缠身躯而成〕

kan·ga·roo /ˌkæŋgəˋru; ˌkæŋgəˈruː◂/ *n* [C] an Australian animal that moves by jumping and carries its babies in a POUCH (=a special pocket of skin) 袋鼠

kangaroo court /ˌ‥ˈ·/ *n* [C] an unofficial court that punishes people unfairly "袋鼠法庭"〔私设的判案不公的法庭〕

Kan·sas /ˋkænzəs; ˈkænzəs/ **1** abbreviation 缩写为 **KS** a state in the Great Plains area of the central US, which produces large amounts of wheat 堪萨斯州〔位于美国中部大平原的一个州, 盛产小麦〕 **2 we're not in Kansas any more** *AmE* a line from the film *The Wizard of Oz*, which people sometimes use humorously when they are in a strange or difficult situation.【美】我们已不在堪萨斯州了〔电影《绿野仙踪》中的一句台词。遇到奇境或困境时, 人们有时会借用这句话以示幽默〕

Kansas Cit·y /ˌ‥ˈ‥/ **1** abbreviation 缩写为 **KC** a city and port in west Missouri, USA 堪萨斯城〔美国密苏里州西部一港口城市 **2** a city and port in northeast Kansas, USA 堪萨斯城〔美国堪萨斯州东北部一港口城市〕

CULTURAL NOTE 文化注释

When people in the US mention Kansas City, they usually mean the city in Missouri. 美国人提到堪萨斯城时, 他们通常指的是密苏里州的堪萨斯城。

Kant /kɑnt; kænt/, **Im·man·u·el** /ɪˋmænjuəl; ɪˈmænjuəl/ (1724-1804) a German PHILOSOPHER who believed that moral decisions must be based on reason, and whose most important book is the *Critique of Pure Reason*. His works had great influence on 19th century philosophy. 康德〔(1724-1804), 德国哲学家。他认为判断道德是非必须以理性为基础。其最重要的著作是《纯粹理性批判》。他的著作对19世纪的哲学产生过巨大影响〕

ka·o·lin /ˋkeəlɪn; ˈkeɪələn/ *n* [U] a type of white clay used for making cups, plates etc, and also in medicine 高岭土, 瓷土

Kap·i·tal, Das /kæpɪˋtɑl, dæs; kæpɪˈtɑːl, dæs/ (1867) a book by Karl Marx in which Marx explains his ideas about the class struggle and about the way that capitalism works. It had a great influence on the development of Communism.《资本论》〔(1867), 卡尔·马克思的著作。他在书中阐述了自己的阶级斗争观及资本主义的运行机制。该书对共产主义的发展产生过重大影响〕

ka·pok /ˋkepɑk; ˈkeɪpɒk/ *n* [U] a very light material like cotton used for filling soft things like cushions (CUSHION[1] (1)) 木棉

K

ka·put /kəˋpʊt; kəˈpʊt/ *adj* [not before noun 不用于名词前] *spoken* broken【口】坏了的; 不能使用的: **go kaput** (=become broken) 坏了; 不能用了

Ka·ra·chi /kəˋrɑtʃɪ; kəˈrɑːtʃi/ a city in southern Pakistan, formerly the capital and still the main port and industrial centre 卡拉奇〔巴基斯坦南部一城市, 曾为该国首都, 现为该国主要港口和工业中心〕

kar·a·o·ke /ˏkɑrəˋokɪ; ˌkæriˈəʊki/ *n* **1** [U] the activity of singing to recorded music for entertainment 卡拉 OK〔以录好的音乐作伴奏跟着唱〕 **2** [C] a machine that plays recorded music which people can sing to 卡拉 OK 伴唱机

kar·at /ˋkærət; ˈkærət/ *n* [C] an American spelling of CARAT carat 的美式拼法

ka·ra·te /kɑˋrɑtɪ; kəˈrɑːti/ *n* [U] a style of fighting from the Far East, in which you kick and hit with your hands 空手道〔源自远东的一种徒手搏击术〕

Ka·ri·ba Dam, the /kəˏribə ˋdæm; kəˌriːbə ˈdæm/ one of the world's biggest DAMS (=a large wall built across a river or lake), built across the Zambezi river in southern Africa 卡里巴水坝〔世界上最大的水坝之一, 横跨非洲南部的赞比西河〕

Kar·loff /ˋkɑlɔf; ˈkɑːlɒf/, **Bor·is** /ˋbɔrɪs; ˈbɒrɪs/ (1887-1969) a British actor who worked in US HORROR FILMS (=films that are intended to make you feel frightened), and who is especially famous for appearing as the MONSTER in the film *Frankenstein* (1931) 卡洛夫〔(1887-1969), 英国演员。他曾出演过美国的恐怖影片, 尤其以在《科学怪人》(1931) 中饰演怪物而名声大噪〕

kar·ma /ˋkɑrmə; ˈkɑːmə/ *n* [U] **1** the force that is produced by the things you do in your life and that will influence you in the future, according to the Hindu and Buddhist religions〔印度教、佛教中的〕羯磨; 业〔指现世活动将影响来世报应〕 **2** *informal* luck resulting from your actions; FATE【非正式】命运; 因果报应 —**karmic** *adj*

Kar·nak /ˋkɑrnæk; ˈkɑːnæk/ a village in Egypt where many TEMPLES (=holy buildings) of the Pharaohs have been found, especially a very large and impressive temple built for the god Amon 凯尔奈克〔埃及一村落。此处已发现法老的许多神殿, 尤其是供奉阿蒙神的那座高大宏伟的神殿〕

Kash·mir /ˏkæʃˋmɪr; ˌkæʃˈmɪə◂/ an area of northwest India and northeast Pakistan. After India became independent in 1947, Kashmir was divided so that part of it now belongs to India, and part to Pakistan. 克什米尔〔印度西北部和巴基斯坦东北部一地区。1947年印度独立后, 该地区一分为二, 分别归印度和巴基斯坦所有〕 —**Kashmiri** *n, adj*

Kath·e·rine of Ar·a·gon /ˏkæθərɪn əv ˋærəgɑn; ˌkæθərɪn əv ˈærəgən/ — see 见 CATHERINE OF ARAGON

Kath·man·du /ˏkætmænˋdu; ˌkætmænˈduː◂/ also 又作 **Katmandu** the capital city of Nepal, in the Himalayas 加德满都〔尼泊尔首都, 位于喜马拉雅山〕

ka·ty·did /ˋketɪˏdɪd; ˈkeɪtidɪd/ *n* [C] *AmE* a type of large GRASSHOPPER that makes a noise like the sound of the words 'katy did'【美】螽斯〔一种大型蚱蜢〕

kay·ak /ˋkaɪæk; ˈkaɪæk/ *n* [C] a type of light CANOE[1] 小皮艇, 轻型独木舟

Ka·zakh·stan /ˏkæzækˋstɑn; ˌkæzækˈstɑːn/ a country in central Asia, between Russia and China, which was part of the former Soviet Union, and is now an independent country. Population: 16,731,000 (2001). Capital: Almaty. 哈萨克斯坦〔中亚一国家, 位于俄罗斯和中国之间, 原属于前苏联, 现为一独立国家。人口: 16,731,000 (2001), 首都: 阿拉木图〕

ka·zoo /kəˋzu; kəˈzuː/ *n* [C] a simple musical instrument that you play by holding it to your lips and making sounds into it 卡祖笛

Kb an abbreviation of 缩写= KILOBYTE

KC /ˏke ˋsi; ˌkeɪ ˈsiː/ *n BrE* King's Counsel; the highest level of BARRISTER (=lawyer who speaks in court) when the ruler is a king【英】王室法律顾问; 大律师 —compare 比较 QC

Kea·ton /ˋkitn; ˈkiːtn/, **Buster** /ˋbʌstɚ; ˈbʌstə/ (1896-1966) a US film actor who made many humorous SILENT FILMS (=films made with no sound). He is famous for appearing as a character with a serious, sad face, who never smiles. 基顿〔(1896-1966), 美国电影演员。他曾拍摄过许多无声喜剧影片, 以扮演神情忧郁、面容严肃的角色闻名〕

Keats /kits; kiːts/, **John** (1795-1821) a British poet and a leading figure in the Romantic Movement. His most famous poems include ODES (=long poems expressing his feelings about a particular person or thing) such as *To a Nightingale*, *On a Grecian Urn*, and *To Autumn*. He died very young from TUBERCULOSIS. 济慈〔(1795-1821), 英国诗人, 浪漫主义运动的杰出代表。其最著名的诗歌包括《夜莺》、《希腊古瓮》和《秋颂》等颂诗。他因肺结核而英年早逝〕

ke·bab /kɪˋbæb; kɪˈbæb/ also 又作 **kabob** *AmE*【美】*n* [C] small pieces of meat and vegetables cooked on a stick 烤肉串

> **CULTURAL NOTE 文化注释**
>
> In Britain, kebabs are sold in TAKEAWAY shops and kebab VANS parked by the side of the road. These places are open until late at night, and some people like to have a kebab after they have been to the PUB, but this is known for often causing STOMACH UPSETS. 在英国, 能买到烤肉串的地方有外卖餐馆和停在街边的烤肉串货摊车。这些地方营业到很晚, 有些从酒馆出来的人喜欢买个烤肉串吃, 但人们也知道吃过之后肚子常常会不舒服。

kedg·e·ree /ˋkɛdʒəˏri; ˈkedʒəriː/ *n* [U] a cooked dish of fish, rice, and eggs mixed together 鱼蛋烩饭

keel¹ /kil; kiːl/ *n* **1** a bar along the bottom of a boat that keeps it steady in the water〔船的〕龙骨 —see picture at 参见 YACHT 图 **2 on an even keel** steady without any sudden changes 平稳的; 稳定的: *Now that the crisis is over, we must try to get things back on an even keel.* 既然危机已结束, 我们就应设法使情况恢复稳定。

keel² *v*

keel over *phr v* [I] to fall over sideways 翻倒, 倾覆: *Several soldiers keeled over in the hot sun.* 几名士兵在烈日下晕倒了。

keel·haul /ˋkilˏhɔl; ˈkiːlhɔːl/ *v* [T] **1** *usually humorous* to punish someone severely【一般幽默】严惩〔某人〕 **2** to pull someone under the keel of a ship with a rope as a punishment 对…施以拖刑〔用绳子将人拖过船底〕

keen¹ /kin; kiːn/ *adj*

1 ▶INTERESTED/EAGER 感兴趣的/渴望的◀ *especially BrE* someone who is keen is very interested in something or is eager to do it【尤英】热衷的, 渴望的, 热切的: *a keen photographer* 热衷于摄影的人 | **[+on]** *Daniel's very keen on tennis.* 丹尼尔非常喜爱打网球。| **keen to do something** *She's out of hospital and keen to get back to work.* 她已经出院, 并急于重返工作岗位。

2 ▶ATTRACTED 着迷的◀ *especially BrE*【尤英】**be keen on sb** to be very attracted to someone 对某人十分着迷: *He must be pretty keen on her – they've been dancing all night.* 他肯定迷上她了——他俩整晚都在跳舞。

3 ▶CLEVER 聪明的◀ someone with a keen mind is quick to understand things 头脑敏捷的

4 ▶COMPETITION 竞争◀ keen competition a situation in which people compete strongly 激烈的竞争: *We won the contest in the face of keen competition.* 在激烈的竞争中我们赢得了比赛。

5 ▶SIGHT/SMELL/HEARING 视觉/嗅觉/听觉◀ a keen sense of smell or keen sight or hearing is an extremely good ability to smell etc 灵敏的, 敏锐的: *Dogs have a very keen sense of smell.* 狗的嗅觉十分灵敏。

6 ▶SHARP 锋利的◀ *literary* a keen knife or blade is extremely sharp【文】〔刀、刃〕锋利的

7 ▶WIND 风◀ *old-fashioned* a keen wind is cold and strong【过时】〔风〕刺骨的

8 keen as mustard *BrE informal*【英, 非正式】**a)** extremely eager 极其渴望的 **b)** very quick to understand things 非常聪颖的 —**keenly** *adv* —**keenness** *n* [U]

keen² *v* [I] *old use* to sing a loud, sad song for someone who has died【旧】哀歌, 唱挽歌

keep¹ /kip; kiːp/ *v past tense and past participle* **kept** /kɛpt; kept/ 

1 ▶NOT GIVE BACK 不归还◀ [T] to have something and not need to give it back 保留; 保存; 留下: *You can keep it. I don't need it.* 你留着吧, 我不需要了。| *Try it for a week and we guarantee you'll want to keep it.* 试用一周, 我们保证你会想把它留下的。

2 ▶NOT LOSE 不丢失◀ [T] to continue to have something and not lose it or get rid of it 保管, 保藏: *No, we're going to keep the house in Vermont and rent it out.* 不, 我们打算留下弗蒙特州的房子, 把它租出去。| *It's not getting a job that's the problem – it's keeping it!* 找个工作不是难事, 问题是怎样保住它!

3 ▶NOT CHANGE/MOVE 不变/不动◀ [I, linking verb 连系动词] to continue to be in a particular state, condition, or place and not change or move 保持〔某种状态〕; 保持不动[不变]: *I'm trying to cut his hair but he won't keep still.* 我在为他剪头发,

但他动个不停。| **keep warm/safe/dry etc** *With this wind it's so difficult to keep warm!* 风这么大,很难保暖呢! | **keep left/right** (=stay to the left or right of a path or road as you move) 靠左侧/右侧〔行走〕

4 ▶MAKE SB/STH NOT CHANGE/MOVE 使某人/某物不变/不动◀ [T] **a)** to make someone stay in a place 使〔某人〕停留于某处: *How long are they going to keep her in the hospital?* 他们想让她在医院里住多久? **b)** to make someone or something continue being in a particular state or situation 使〔某人或某物〕保持〔某种状态〕: **keep sb warm/safe etc** *Take my overcoat. It'll keep you warm.* 拿上我的大衣,可以给你保暖。| *some toys to keep the kids busy* 能让孩子们忙碌一阵子的玩具 | **keep sth clean/open etc** *We try to keep the major roads open right through winter.* 我们设法使主要道路整个冬天畅通无阻。| **keep sb/sth doing sth** *I'll try not to keep you waiting.* 我会尽量不让你久等。| *Keep the engine running.* 别让发动机熄火。| **keep sb in suspense** (=keep someone waiting anxiously to know a result) 使某人焦急等待〔结果〕 *How much longer are you going to keep us in suspense?* 你还想再让我们等多久才告诉我们结果? | **keep on the right side of sb** (=not do anything to annoy them) 尽量别惹恼某人 *Keep on the right side of Mrs Salazar, she's very strict.* 别去惹恼萨拉查夫人,她可是很严厉的。

5 ▶DO STH REPEATEDLY 反复做某事◀ [I,T] to continue doing an activity or repeat the same action several times 继续[重复]做: **keep (on) doing sth** *I keep forgetting to mail this letter.* 我老是忘记把这封信寄出。| *Daddy! Melanie keeps on hitting me!* 爸爸!梅拉妮老是打我!

6 ▶DELAY SB 使某人耽搁◀ [T] to delay someone 阻止;拖延: *He should be here by now. What's keeping him?* 他现在本该到这儿了,什么事把他耽搁了?

7 ▶STORE STH 存放某物◀ [T always+adv/prep] to leave something in one particular place so that you can find it easily 存放: **keep sth in/on/under etc** *I always keep a first aid box in the car, in case we have an accident.* 我总是在车里放一个急救箱,以备不时之需。

8 keep a record/account/diary etc to regularly record written information somewhere 定期记录/记账/写日记等

9 keep your promise/word etc to do what you have promised to do 履行诺言: *How do I know you'll keep your word?* 我怎么知道你会履行诺言?

10 keep a secret to not tell anyone about a secret that you know 保守秘密: *Can I trust all of you to keep a secret?* 我能相信你们所有人都会保守秘密吗?

11 keep to yourself also 又作 **keep yourself to yourself** *BrE* to live a very quiet private life and not do many things that involve other people【英】深居简出,不与人交往;不理会别人的事

12 keep guard/watch to guard a place or watch around you all the time 守卫;防守;看守

13 ▶FOOD 食物◀ [I] if food keeps, it stays fresh enough to still be eaten 保鲜: *Eat the salmon because it won't keep till tomorrow.* 把这条鲑鱼吃了吧,明天就不新鲜了。

14 keep your head to stay calm in a difficult situation or an EMERGENCY 〔在困境或紧急情况中〕保持冷静: *Just keep your head and try to steer in the direction of the skid.* 保持冷静,朝侧滑的方向打方向盘。

15 ▶ANIMALS 动物◀ [T] to own and look after animals 饲养: *We keep chickens and a couple of pigs.* 我们养了一些鸡和几头猪。

16 ▶SHOP 商店◀ [T] *BrE old-fashioned* to own a small business and work in it【英,过时】经营〔小店铺〕: *Frank used to keep a butcher's on Park Road.* 弗兰克曾在帕克路开过一家肉铺。

17 ▶LOOK AFTER 照料◀ [T] to take care of someone, providing them with money, food etc 照顾;供养: **keep sb in sth** *There's enough money there to keep you in silk stockings for a year!* 那里有足够的钱供你丰衣足食一年之久!

18 ▶PROTECT 保护◀ [T] *formal* to guard or protect someone【正式】保护,保卫: **keep sb (from harm)** *The Lord bless you and keep you.* 上帝赐福于你并保佑你。

19 ▶CELEBRATE STH 庆祝某事◀ [T] *old-fashioned* to do the things that are traditionally done to celebrate something such as Christmas【过时】庆祝〔节日〕: *People don't keep Christmas the way they used to do.* 人们如今过圣诞节的方式与过去不同。—see also 另见 **keep in touch** (TOUCH[2] (6)), **home/keep your eye on sb** (EYE[1] (3)), **keep house** (HOUSE[1] (2)), **keep pace with** (PACE[1] (5)), **keep sb company** (COMPANY (2)), **keep the peace** (PEACE (5)), **keep time** (TIME[1]), **keep your hand in** (HAND[1] (11)), **keep/lose track of** (TRACK[1] (8))

Frequencies of the verb **keep** in spoken and written English
动词 keep 在英语口语和书面语中的使用频率

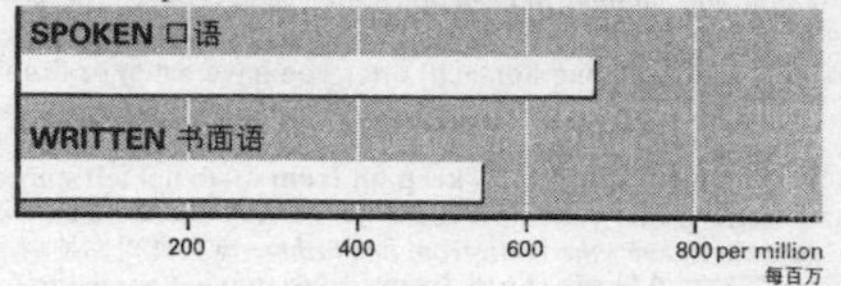

Based on the British National Corpus and the Longman Lancaster Corpus
据英国国家语料库和朗文兰开斯特语料库

This graph shows that the verb **keep** is more common in spoken English than in written English. This is because the expression **keep doing sth** is very commonly used in spoken English to mean 'continue to do something' or 'do something repeatedly'. **Keep** is also used in a lot of common spoken phrases. 本图表显示动词 keep 在英语口语中的使用频率高于书面语,因为 keep doing sth 在英语口语中使用十分普遍,表示"持续做某事"或"重复做某事"。keep 还用于许多常见的口语短语中。

keep (*v*) **SPOKEN PHRASES**
含 keep 的口语短语

20 keep going used to encourage someone who is doing something and to tell them to continue 继续做下去〔用于鼓励〕: *"Well done, that's it, keep going!"* "干得不错,就是那样,继续做下去!"

21 keep it used to tell someone that they can keep something you have given them or lent them 你留着吧: *Keep it. I've got plenty more at home.* 你留着吧,我家里还有很多呢。

22 keep quiet used to tell someone not to say anything or make any noise 安静点,小点声: *Keep quiet! I'm trying to watch the game.* 安静一点!我要看比赛。

23 keep away/back! used to tell someone not to go near something or to move away from something 离远一点!不要靠近!: *Keep back everyone – this is dangerous!* 大家离远一点,这里危险!

24 keep down! used to tell someone to keep near the ground so they cannot be seen, shot etc 趴下!

25 keep it down used to tell someone to be quieter 安静一点: *Keep it down, will you. We're trying to sleep.* 请小点声,我们要睡觉了。

26 how are you keeping? used to ask if someone is well 你身体好吗?: *"Hi, Mark! How are you keeping?" "Oh, not so bad."* "你好,马克,近来身体怎么样?""还可以。"

27 keep the change used when paying someone, to tell them they can keep the extra money you have given them 不用找钱: *"That's $18." "Here's $20. Keep the change."* "这要 18 美元。""这是 20 美元,不用找零了。"

28 keep your hair/shirt on! used to tell someone to be more calm, patient etc 保持冷静!;耐心点!: *Keep your hair on! We've got plenty of time.* 耐心点!我们有的是时间。

29 it'll keep used to say that you can tell someone something or do something later 以后告诉你;以后再做: *"I'd love to hear about it but I've got to go." "Don't worry, it'll keep."* "我很想听听,但现在就得走。""别担心,我以后再告诉你。"

30 that'll keep you going used to tell someone that what you are giving them will last for some time 够你用一段时间: *Here's £50 – that'll keep you going for a while.* 这是 50 英镑,够你用一阵子的。

keep at *phr v* [T] **1** [**keep** sb **at** sth] to force someone to continue to work hard 逼迫〔某人〕继续苦干: *She kept us at it until eight o'clock!* 她竟要我们一直干到 8 点! **2** [**keep at** sth] to continue working hard at something 坚持苦干: *Let's just keep at it until we're finished.* 让我们坚持下去,直到干完为止。

keep away *phr v* [I,T **keep** sb/sth **away**] to avoid going somewhere or seeing someone, or to make someone or something do this (使)远离: *You keep away from my daughter!* 你离我女儿远点儿!

keep back *phr v* **1** [T **keep** sth ↔ **back**] to not tell someone something that you know 隐瞒〔某事〕: *I got the feeling he was keeping something back.* 我感到他有什么事隐瞒着。**2** [T **keep** sth ↔ **back**] *especially BrE* to not give or pay something that you were going to give【尤英】留下,扣除: *They kept back some of his wages to pay for the damage.* 他们扣下他的一部分工资以赔偿损失。

K

keep sb/sth ↔ **down** *phr v* [T] **1** to control something and prevent it from increasing 控制, 抑制〔某物以防止其增长〕: *You can use herbicides to keep down the weeds.* 你可以用除草剂控制杂草的生长。**2** to be able to not VOMIT something (=pass it back up from your stomach) after you have eaten or drunk it 〔在吃喝之后〕阻止…呕[吐]出: *I could hardly keep anything down for about three days.* 这三天我几乎吃什么吐什么。

keep from *phr v* [T] **1** [**keep** sth **from** sb] to not tell someone something that you know 隐瞒, 不把…告诉〔某人〕: *You won't be able to keep the truth from her father.* 事实真相你是瞒不了她父亲的。**2** [**keep** sb/sth **from** sth] to prevent someone from doing something or prevent something happening 阻止; 避免: **keep sb from doing sth** *Mulligan was the only person who kept us from running amok completely.* 马利根是唯一阻止我们的人, 使我们没有完全任性胡为。| **keep (yourself) from doing sth** *I could hardly keep from laughing, it was so funny.* 太滑稽了, 我简直忍不住笑起来。| **keep sth from doing sth** *You put the potatoes in salted water to keep them from turning black.* 把马铃薯放到盐水里以防变黑。

keep sb **in** *phr v* [T] *BrE* to force someone to stay inside, especially as a punishment in school【英】使〔某人〕留在里面; 罚…课后留校〔尤作为学校中的一种惩罚〕

keep in with sb *phr v* [T] *BrE* to try to stay friendly with someone, especially because this helps you【英】与〔某人〕友好相处〔尤因这样做对自己有利〕; 获得…的欢心: *You should try to keep in with Benson – he has a lot of influence around here.* 你应想办法讨好本森, 他在这一带很有影响力。

keep off *phr v* **1** [T **keep** sth ↔ **off**] to prevent something affecting something else 防止; 避开; 使免受〔某物〕的影响: *They have these transparent covers to keep the dust off.* 他们用这些透明盖子来遮挡灰尘。**2** [I] if rain keeps off, it does not fall 〔雨〕不下

keep on *phr v* **1 keep on doing sth** to continue doing something 继续做某事: *I've told him to stop but he keeps on scratching it!* 我叫他停下来, 他还是刮个不停! **2** [T **keep** sb **on**] to continue to employ someone 继续雇用: *If you're good they might keep you on after Christmas.* 你如果表现不错, 圣诞节后他们或许会继续用你。**3** [I] *informal* to talk continuously in an annoying way【非正式】喋喋不休地说: [+**at/about**] *Do you have to keep on about your medical problems the whole time?* 你有必要没完没了地谈你的病情吗?

keep out *phr v* **1 keep out!** used on signs to tell people to stay away from a place or not enter it 切勿接近! 闲人免进!〔用于警示牌〕**2** [T **keep** sth ↔ **out**] to prevent someone or something getting into a place 阻止〔某人或某物〕进入: *Take this. It should at least keep the rain out.* 拿上这个, 至少可以挡挡雨。

keep out of sth *phr v* [T] to try not to become involved in something 不卷入; 避开: *We've always tried to keep out of local politics.* 我们总是尽可能不卷入地方政治中。

keep to *phr v* [T] **1** [**keep to** sth] to stay on a particular road, course, piece of ground etc 不离开〔某一道路、方向、地方等〕: *It's best to keep to the paved roads.* 最好不要偏离铺过的道路。**2** [**keep to** sth] to do what you have promised or agreed to do 履行, 实施: *Keep strictly to the terms of the contract.* 严格执行合同条款。**3 keep sth to yourself** to keep something secret 保守秘密: *It's official. We're leaving, but do me a favour and keep it to yourself will you.* 这是公事。我们即将启程, 但请帮忙保密, 你自己知道就行了。**4 keep to the point/subject etc** to talk or write only about the subject you are supposed to be talking about 紧扣要点/主题等 **5** [**keep** sth **to** sth] to prevent an amount, degree, or level from going higher than it should 防止〔数量, 程度或水平〕高于应有的限度: *Can you please keep costs to a minimum?* 请你把成本保持在最低水平行吗? **6 keep to your room/bed** to stay in your room or bed because you are ill or upset〔因有病或心烦而〕不出门/不下床

keep up *phr v* **1** [T **keep** sth ↔ **up**] to prevent something from falling or going to a lower level 使不掉下来; 使不下降: *The shortage of supplies is keeping the price up.* 供应不足使价格保持坚挺。**2** [I,T **keep** sth ↔ **up**] to continue doing something, or to make something continue (使) 继续: *Keep up the good work!* 继续好好干! | *I don't think I can keep this up any longer.* 我认为这事我再也坚持不下去了。**3** [I] to manage to go or learn as fast as someone〔进展、学习等〕跟上〔某人〕, 不落后: *Slow down, Davey can't keep up.* 放慢速度, 戴维跟不上了。| [+**with**] *I'm having trouble keeping up with the rest of the class.* 跟上全班的学习我有困难。**4** [I] to continue to read and learn about a particular subject 跟上〔某学科〕: [+**with**] *It's hard to keep up with the changes in computer technology.* 要跟上电脑技术的变化是很难的。**5 keep your spirits/strength/morale etc up** to try to stay happy, strong, confident etc 保持愉快心境/体力/士气等: *We sang as we marched, to keep our spirits up.* 我们一面行进一面唱歌, 以保持高昂的情绪。**6** [T **keep** sb **up**] *informal* to prevent someone from going to bed【非正式】不让〔某人〕上床睡觉: *I hope I'm not keeping you up.* 我希望我没有耽误你上床休息。**7 keep up appearances** to pretend that everything in your life is normal and happy even though you are in trouble, especially financial trouble 装面子; 摆阔气〔尽管遇到钱财方面的麻烦〕**8 keep up with the Joneses** to try to have all the possessions that your friends have because you want people to think that you are as good as them 与朋友比阔气

keep² *n* **1** [U] all the things such as food, clothing etc that you need to keep you alive, or the cost of providing this 生活必需品〈如食物、衣服等〉; 生活费: **earn your keep** (=do things in return for the things that are provided for you) 自谋生活 *It's time you got a job and started earning your keep.* 是你找工作养活自己的时候了。**2 for keeps** *informal* for ever【非正式】永远; 永久: *I'm going to settle this argument for keeps!* 我要一劳永逸地解决这场争论! | *Marriage ought to be for keeps.* 婚姻应当是永久性的。**3** [C] a large strong tower, usually in the centre of a castle〔城堡的〕主楼

Keep A·mer·i·ca Beau·ti·ful /ˌ· ·ˌ··· ˈ···/ a phrase used by a group of people who want to encourage American people not to drop LITTER in the streets 让美国永远美丽〔美国一社会团体使用的口号, 旨在宣导人们不要在街头乱扔垃圾〕

keep·a·way /ˈ· · ·/ *n* [U] *AmE* a children's game in which you try to catch a ball that is being thrown between two other people【美】〔儿童的〕传球游戏〔截住另外两人之间抛接的球〕; **piggy in the middle** (PIGGY¹ (2)) *BrE*【英】

Keep Brit·ain Ti·dy /ˌ· ˌ·· ˈ··/ a phrase used by a group of people who want to encourage British people not to drop LITTER in the streets 让英国永远整洁〔英国一社会团体使用的口号, 旨在宣导人们不要在街头乱扔垃圾〕

keep·er /ˈkipɚ; ˈkiːpə/ *n* [C] **1** someone whose job is to look after a particular place 看守人, 管理员: *a lighthouse keeper* 灯塔管理员 | **shopkeeper/storekeeper** (=who owns and works in a shop) 店主 **2** someone who cares for or protects animals 动物园管理员; 猎场管理员: **zookeeper/gamekeeper** *The zoo keeper ordered the public away from the lion house.* 动物园管理员嘱咐公众远离狮舍。—see also 另见 GAMEKEEPER **3** also 又作 **goalkeeper** someone who guards the GOAL (3) in a sport〔体育运动的〕守门员

keep fit /ˌ· ˈ·◂/ *n* [U] *BrE* a class in which you do exercises to keep yourself healthy【英】健身(课) —**keep-fit** *adj*

keep·ing /ˈkipɪŋ; ˈkiːpɪŋ/ *n* [U] **1 in sb's keeping** being looked after or guarded by someone 由某人照顾[保管] **2 in safe keeping** being carefully guarded somewhere 被安全保管 **3 in keeping/out of keeping (with sth)** suitable or not suitable for a particular occasion or purpose (与某物) 协调[一致]/不协调[不一致]: *Please ensure your remarks are in keeping with the seriousness of the occasion.* 你要确保自己的言谈与该场合的严肃性相协调。

keep·sake /ˈkipˌsek; ˈkiːpseɪk/ *n* [C] a small object that reminds you of someone 小纪念品

keg /kɛg; keg/ *n* [C] a round wooden container with a flat top and bottom, used especially for storing beer; BARREL¹ (1)〔尤指盛啤酒用的〕圆木桶: **keg beer/bitter** (=beer etc served from a keg) 桶装啤酒/苦啤酒

keg·ger /ˈkɛgɚ; ˈkegə/ *n* [C] *AmE slang* a big party, usually outside, where beer is served from KEGS【美俚】大型露天啤酒会

keis·ter /ˈkistɚ; ˈkaɪstə/ *n* [C] *AmE old-fashioned* BUTTOCKS (=part of your body that you sit on)【美, 过时】臀部

Kel·ler /ˈkɛlɚ; ˈkelə/, **Hel·en** /ˈhɛlən; ˈhelən/ (1880-1968) a US writer who is famous for the way she learned to speak and write after becoming BLIND (=unable to see) and DEAF (=unable to hear) as a baby. She greatly helped blind and deaf people by collecting money, making speeches, and trying to change people's attitudes. She was the subject of a famous book and film about her life called *The Miracle Worker.* 凯勒〔(1880-1968), 美国作家。她尤以在婴儿时期失聪失明后学会说话和书写闻名。她通过募捐、演讲以及努力改变人们的态度等方式大力帮助盲人和聋人。《创奇者》及同名影片即取材于她, 讲述她的生平故事〕

Kel·logg Pact, the /ˈkɛlɔg pækt; ˈkelɒg pækt/ also 又作 **the Kellogg-Briand Pact** an agreement, signed by 15 nations in 1928, to deal with arguments between countries peacefully, without war or weapons. It was suggested by Aristide Briand, the French Foreign Minister, to Frank B. Kellogg, the US Secretary of State. 《凯洛格(一白里安)公约》〔1928 年 15 国共同签

K

署的一项协定，旨在不通过战争或使用武器和平解决国际争端。该公约是法国外长阿里斯蒂德·白里安向美国国务卿弗兰克·B.凯洛格提议的〕

Kells /kɛlz; kelz/, **The Book of** an ILLUMINATED (=with the pages decorated with gold paint and other bright colours) copy of the four Christian Gospels, produced during the 8th century at a MONASTERY in the town of Kells in the Republic of Ireland《凯尔斯书》〔饰本福音书，成书于公元8世纪爱尔兰共和国凯尔斯镇的一所隐修院〕

Kel·ly /ˈkɛlɪ; ˈkeli/, **Gene** /dʒɪn; dʒiːn/ (1912-96) a US dancer, singer, actor, and DIRECTOR who appeared in many musical films in the 1940s and 1950s, especially as a dancer. His most famous film was *Singin' in the Rain*, in which he sings and dances to a song with the same name. 金·凯利〔(1912-1996)，美国舞蹈演员、歌手、演员和导演。20世纪40、50年代，他以舞蹈演员的身份出演了不少音乐片。最著名的影片为《雨中曲》。他曾在影片中演唱同名歌曲并和着节拍跳舞〕

Kelly, Grace (1928-82) a US film actress who was famous for her beauty, and who appeared in such films as *High Noon* (1952) and *High Society* (1956). She became Princess Grace of Monaco when she married Prince Rainier in 1956. 格雷斯·凯利〔(1928-1982)，美国女电影演员，以美貌著称。她曾演过《正午》(1952) 和《上流社会》(1956) 等影片。1956年，她与摩纳哥王子兰尼埃结婚，成为摩纳哥格雷斯王妃〕

Kelly, Ned /nɛd; ned/ (1855-80) an Australian bank robber who was in a GANG (=group of criminals) with his brother Dan. They became very famous, and some people considered Ned to be a HERO. He was caught by the police and hanged in 1880. 凯利〔(1855-1880)，澳大利亚一银行劫匪，曾与其兄弟丹伙同作案。他们颇有名气，有人把凯利视为英雄。1880年，他被警方抓获并处以绞刑〕

kelp /kɛlp; kelp/ *n* [U] a type of large brown SEAWEED 巨藻，大型褐藻

kel·vin /ˈkɛlvɪn; kelvən/ *n* [C] a unit for measuring temperature 开〔开尔文温标的计量单位〕

Kem·pis /ˈkɛmpɪs; ˈkempɪs/, **Thom·as à** /ˈtɑməs ə; ˈtɒməs ə/ (1380-1471) a German MONK (=a member of a religious group of Christian men who live apart from other people) who is believed to have written *The Imitation of Christ* (坎普腾的) 托马斯〔(1380-1471)，德国天主教修士。人们认为他就是《效法基督》的作者〕

ken[1] /kɛn; ken/ *n* **beyond your ken** outside your knowledge or understanding 超出…的知识范围[理解程度]

ken[2] *v* [I,T] *ScotE* to know【苏格兰】知道；认识：*D'ye ken John Peel?* 你认识约翰·皮尔吗？

Kennedy /ˈkɛnədɪ; ˈkenədi/, **Jack·ie** /ˈdʒækɪ; ˈdʒæki/ also 又作 **Jackie Kennedy Onassis** (1929-94) the wife of John F. Kennedy, who became very popular when she was the First Lady of the US from 1961 to 1963 because she was considered very beautiful and fashionable. In 1968, five years after Kennedy's death, she married Aristotle Onassis. 杰奎琳〔(1929-1994)，约翰·F.肯尼迪之妻，1961至1963年间为美国第一夫人。她貌美时尚，深受人民喜爱。1968年，即肯尼迪去世5年后，她嫁给了亚里士多德·奥纳西斯〕

Kennedy, John Fitzgerald /ˌdʒɑn fɪtsˈdʒɛrəld; ˌdʒɒn fɪtsˈdʒerəld/ (1917-63) a US politician in the Democratic Party, also known as **Jack Kennedy** and **JFK**, who was President of the US from 1961 to 1963. He was an extremely popular president, and he planned to improve education, the system of medical care, and CIVIL RIGHTS in the US, although it was Lyndon B. Johnson who achieved most of these plans after Kennedy's death. In 1961 Kennedy ordered the INVASION of the Bay of Pigs in Cuba, and he was strongly criticized for this. Two years later he was shot in Dallas, Texas, and Lee Harvey Oswald was ACCUSED*d* of killing him. 约翰·肯尼迪〔(1917-1963)，美国民主党政治家，又称杰克·肯尼迪和JFK，1961至1963年间任美国总统。他是一位很有声望的总统，曾计划改善美国的教育体制、医疗体系和民权状况，但大部分计划是在他去世后由林登·B.约翰逊实现的。1961年，肯尼迪下令入侵古巴猪湾，因此受到强烈谴责。两年后，他在得克萨斯州达拉斯遇刺身亡，李·哈维·奥斯瓦尔德被指控为凶手〕

Kennedy, Rob·ert Fran·cis /ˈrɑbɚt ˈfrænsɪs; ˈrɒbət ˈfrɑːnsəs/ also 又作 **Kennedy, Bobby** (1925-68) a US politician in the Democratic Party who was the brother of John F. Kennedy. He became a SENATOR for New York in 1965. In 1968, when he was trying to become elected President of the US, he was shot. 罗伯特·肯尼迪〔(1925-1968)，美国民主党政治家，约翰·F.肯尼迪的弟弟，1965年成为纽约州参议员，1968年竞选美国总统时遇刺身亡〕

Kennedy Cen·ter, the /ˈ⋯ˌ⋯/ also 又作 **the John F. Kennedy Center for the Performing Arts** a theatre built as the official MEMORIAL to President Kennedy, in Washington, D.C., where there are OPERA, BALLET, and musical performances. Every year there is a special ceremony there, where prizes are given to singers, actors, dancers, musicians etc. 肯尼迪中心〔华盛顿特区一剧院，为纪念肯尼迪总统而建。该剧院经常表演歌剧、芭蕾舞和音乐节目，每年举行一次特别庆典活动，给歌手、演员、舞蹈演员和音乐人士等颁奖〕

Kennedy Space Cen·ter, the /ˌ⋯ˈ⋯ˌ⋯/ a place in Florida where US SPACECRAFT are built and sent into space 肯尼迪宇航中心〔位于佛罗里达州，美国的宇宙飞船在此建造并发射升空〕

ken·nel /ˈkɛnl; ˈkenl/ *n* [C] **1** a small HUT where a dog sleeps 狗舍，狗窝 **2** also 又作 **kennels** *BrE* a place where dogs are bred (BREED[1] (1,2)) or can stay while their owners are away【英】养狗场；狗房；狗繁殖场

Kennel Club, the /ˈ⋯ˌ/ abbreviation 缩写为 **KC** a British organization for people who breed dogs, which decides what physical features each type of dog should have. The Kennel Club also organizes dog shows, including Cruft's, and it keeps records of the PEDIGREE*s* of all PUREBRED dogs in the UK. 养狗人俱乐部〔英国一育犬人组织，负责确定每种狗的体形特征，同时还举办包括克拉夫特在内的狗展，记录英国所有纯种狗的系谱〕

Ken·sing·ton /ˈkɛnzɪŋtən; ˈkenzɪŋtən/ also 又作 **Kensington and Chelsea** /ˌ⋯ˈ⋯/ an expensive and fashionable BOROUGH in West London just north of the River Thames 肯辛顿〔西伦敦一自治区，位于泰晤士河北岸。该区现代时尚，物价颇高〕

Kensington Gar·dens /ˌ⋯ˈ⋯/ a park in central London that has a statue of Peter Pan 肯辛顿花园〔伦敦市中心一公园，园中有彼特·潘的一尊雕像〕

Kensington Pal·ace /ˌ⋯ˈ⋯/ an official royal house in central London 肯辛顿宫〔伦敦市中心的一座皇宫〕

Kent /kɛnt; kent/ a COUNTY in southeast England, sometimes called the 'Garden of England' because of the fruit and vegetables it produces. 肯特郡〔英格兰东南一郡。因出产水果和蔬菜，故有时被称为"英格兰花园"〕

Kent, Clark /klɑrk; klɑːk/ a character in US COMIC*s* (=magazines with stories told in pictures), films, and television programmes about Superman. Clark Kent seems like a very ordinary, quiet man, but secretly he is Superman. 肯特〔美国漫画、杂志、影片和电视剧中的人物。他看似普通、内敛，实际上他就是超人〕

Kent State /ˌ⋅ˈ/ an event in 1970 when soldiers from the National Guard killed four students who were part of a large PROTEST MARCH against the Vietnam War at **Kent State University** in Ohio 肯特州立大学枪击事件〔1970年，有四名学生在俄亥俄州肯特州立大学参加大规模反越战示威游行时遭到国家警卫队士兵枪杀〕

Ken·tuck·y /kənˈtʌkɪ; kenˈtʌki/ abbreviation 缩写为 **KY** a state in the south of the US, known as the Bluegrass State. It is one of the poorest states in the US, and is famous for its country and western music, and for its WHISKEY. 肯塔基州〔美国南部一州。该州有"蓝色牧草州"之称，是美国最贫困的州之一，以乡村与西部音乐和威士忌酒闻名〕

Kentucky Der·by, the /ˌ⋅⋯ˈ⋯/ a famous race for three-year-old horses held each year on the first Saturday in May in Louisville, Kentucky 肯塔基赛马会〔著名的3龄马比赛，每年5月份的第一个星期六在肯塔基州的路易斯维尔举行〕

Ken·ya /ˈkɛnjə; ˈkenjə/ a country in East Africa which became independent from Britain in 1963, and is a member of the British Commonwealth. Population: 30,766,000 (2001). Capital: Nairobi. Kenya produces coffee and tea, and is popular with tourists who go to see the wild animals in the SAFARI PARK*s* there. 肯尼亚〔东非一国家，1963年脱离英国独立，为英联邦成员国。人口: 30,766,000 (2001)，首都: 内罗毕。该国出产咖啡和茶叶。参观当地野生动物园的游客络绎不绝〕 —**Kenyan** *n, adj*

Kenya, Mount a mountain that is an inactive VOLCANO in central Kenya 肯尼亚火山〔肯尼亚中部一休眠火山〕

Ken·yat·ta /kɛnˈjɑtə; kenˈjætə/, **Jo·mo** /ˈdʒomo; ˈdʒəʊməʊ/ (?1893-1978) a Kenyan politician who was President from 1964 until his death. He was one of the leaders of Kenya's fight for independence from the UK, and he was put in prison in the 1950s for his connection with the Mau Mau organization. 肯雅塔〔(?1893-1978)，肯尼亚政治家，1964年出任总统直至去世，是肯尼亚脱离英国独立运动领导人之一。20世纪50年代，他因与茅茅恐怖组织有牵连而入狱〕

Ke·ogh Plan /ˈkio plæn; ˈkiːəʊ plæn/ in the US, a personal PENSION plan for self-employed people 基奥计划〔美国自由职业者的个人退休金计划〕

K

Kep·ler /ˋkɛplɚ; ˈkeplə/, **Jo·han·nes** /ˋjohɑn; ˈjəʊhæn/ (1571-1630) a German ASTRONOMER (=a scientist who studies the stars) who discovered how the PLANETS move around the sun. These principles are known as **Kepler's Laws**, and they greatly influenced the work of Sir Isaac Newton. 开普勒〔(1571-1630)，德国天文学家。他曾发现行星围绕太阳运行的规律，称开普勒定律，对牛顿的研究产生了极大影响〕

kept the past tense and past participle of KEEP[1]

kept wom·an /ˌ· ˈ· ·/ *n* [C] *old-fashioned* a woman who is given a place to live, money and clothes by a man who visits her regularly for sex【过时】〔受供养的〕情妇，姘妇

kerb *BrE*【英】, **curb** *AmE*【美】/kɝb; kɜːb/ *n* [C] the edge of the PAVEMENT (=raised path) at the side of a street〔街道的〕路缘 —see picture on page A4 参见 A4 页图

kerb craw·ler *BrE*【英】, **curb crawler** *AmE*【美】/ˈ· ˌ· ·/ *n* [C] a man who drives his car slowly along the road looking for a PROSTITUTE (=woman who has sex for money) 沿路慢驶召妓者 —**kerb crawling** *n* [U]

ker·chief /ˋkɝtʃɪf; ˈkɜːtʃɪ̈f/ *n* [C] **1** a square piece of cloth, worn especially by women in former times around their head or neck〔旧时妇女用的〕方头巾；围巾，披肩 **2** *old-fashioned* a handkerchief【过时】手帕

ker·fuf·fle /kəˋfʌfl; kəˈfʌfəl/ *n* [C,U] *BrE informal* unnecessary noise and activity; FUSS[1] (2)【英，非正式】吵闹，喧哗；混乱

Ker·mit /ˋkɝmɪt; ˈkɜːmɪt/ also 又作 **Kermit the Frog** a PUPPET in the form of a green FROG, who is one of the main characters in the television programmes *The Muppets* and *Sesame Street* 克米特〔又称青蛙克米特，为一只蛙形木偶，是电视剧《木偶剧场》和《芝麻街》中的主人公之一〕

Kern /kɝn; kɜːn/, **Je·rome** /dʒəˋrom; dʒəˈrəʊm/ (1885-1945) a US COMPOSER and songwriter who wrote many MUSICALS (=films or plays that use singing and dancing to tell a story), such as *Showboat* (1927), which contains the famous song *Ol' Man River* 克恩〔(1885-1945)，美国作曲家、词作家。他曾创作过许多音乐剧，如《演艺船》(1927) 等，其中有一首著名的歌曲《老人河》〕

ker·nel /ˋkɝnl; ˈkɜːnl/ *n* [C] **1** the centre part of a nut or seed, usually the part you can eat〔坚果或种子的〕核，仁 **2** something that forms the most important part of a statement, idea, plan etc 核心，要点，要素: *There may be a kernel of truth in what he says.* 他说的话也可能有真实的成分。

ker·o·sene, kerosine /ˋkɛrəˌsin; ˈkerəsiːn/ *n* [U] *AmE, AustrE, NzE* an oil that is burnt for heat and used in lamps for lighting【美，澳，新西兰】〔供取暖和照明用的〕煤油；PARAFFIN (1) *BrE*【英】

Ker·ou·ac /ˋkɛruæk; ˈkeruæk/, **Jack** (1922-69) a US writer who was a leading figure of the 1950s Beat Generation. His most famous NOVEL is *On the Road*, which describes the adventures of two friends as they travel across the US. 凯鲁亚克〔(1922-1969)，美国作家，20 世纪 50 年代"垮掉的一代"的代表人物。最有名的小说《在路上》描述两个朋友游历美国时的种种奇遇〕

Ker·ry /ˋkɛrɪ; ˈkeri/ a COUNTY in the southwest of the Republic of Ireland, popular with tourists because of its beautiful mountains and countryside 凯里郡〔爱尔兰共和国西南部一郡。该郡山色乡野秀美，深受游客喜爱〕

kes·trel /ˋkɛstrəl; ˈkestrəl/ *n* [C] a type of small FALCON 茶隼，红隼

ketch /kɛtʃ; ketʃ/ *n* [C] a small sailing ship with two masts (MAST (1)) 双桅小帆船

ketch·up /ˋkɛtʃəp, ˈketʃəp/ also 又作 **catsup** *especially AmE*【尤美】*n* [U] a thick red liquid made from tomatoes (TOMATO) that you eat with food 番茄酱

ket·tle /ˋkɛtl; ˈketl/ *n* [C] **1** a metal or plastic container with a lid, a handle, and a SPOUT (=for pouring), used to boil water〔煮开水用的〕水壶 —see picture on page A10 参见 A10 页图 **2 put the kettle on** to boil water in a kettle 用水壶煮水: *I'll put the kettle on for tea.* 我要煮水沏茶。**3 another/a different kettle of fish** *informal* used to say that a situation that is very different from one that you have just mentioned【非正式】完全不同的两回事: *She enjoys public speaking but being on TV is a different kettle of fish.* 她喜欢当众演讲，但上电视就完全是另一回事了。**4 a fine/pretty kettle of fish** a situation that will cause you problems 困境；尴尬的局面

ket·tle·drum /ˋkɛtḷˌdrʌm; ˈketldrʌm/ *n* [C] a large metal drum with a round bottom, used in an ORCHESTRA 定音鼓；铜鼓 —see also 另见 TIMPANI

Kew Gar·dens /ˌkju ˋgardṇz; ˌkjuː ˈgɑːdnz/ the UK's largest and most important BOTANICAL garden, in West London, which contains plants and trees from all over the world 基尤植物园〔英国最大、最重要的植物园，位于西伦敦，有来自世界各地的植物和树种〕

kew·pie doll /ˋkjupɪ ˌdɑl; ˈkjuːpi dɒl/ also 又作 **kewpie** *n* [C] a type of American plastic DOLL[1] (1) with a fat body and a curl of hair on its head 丘比特娃娃〔身体肥胖、头有鬈发的塑料娃娃〕

key[1] /ki; kiː/ *adj* very important and necessary for success or to understand something 极为重要的，关键的: *Put your most experienced players in the key positions.* 把最有经验的选手放在关键位置上。| **key points/questions/issues etc** (=most important) 要点/关键问题等 *You can summarize the key points of his speech in a few lines.* 你可以用几句话来总结他的讲话要点。| **key mover/player** (=most important person in achieving a result, change etc) 关键人物 S2 W1

key[2] *n* [C] S2 W3

1 ►LOCK 锁◄ a small specially shaped piece of metal which you put into a lock and turn in order to lock or unlock a door, start a car etc 钥匙

2 ►IMPORTANT PART 重要部分◄ the key the part of a plan, action, etc, that everything else depends on〔计划、行动等的〕关键（部分）: [+to] *Concentration is the key to effective study.* 集中精力是有效学习的关键。

3 ►MACHINE/MUSICAL INSTRUMENT 机器/乐器◄ the part of a machine, computer, or musical instrument that you press with your fingers to make it work 键: *Press the ESCAPE key to exit.* 按 ESCAPE 键退出。| *She ran her fingers over the piano keys.* 她用手指在钢琴键上扫过。

4 ►MUSICAL NOTES 音调◄ a set of musical notes with a particular base note, and the quality of sound that they have〔音乐的〕调，主音: *a tune played in the key of C* 用 C 调演奏的曲子

5 ►MAP/DRAWING 地图/图纸◄ the part of a map, technical drawing etc that explains the signs etc on it 图例，符号说明

6 ►ISLAND 岛◄ a small flat island, especially one near the coast of Florida〔尤指靠近佛罗里达海岸的〕低岛，小岛；礁: *the Florida Keys* 佛罗里达群岛

7 ►TEST ANSWERS 测试答案◄ the printed answers to a test or to the questions in a TEXTBOOK[1] that are used to check your work〔教科书中附有的测验或问题的〕答案，题解 —see also 另见 LOW-KEY

key[3] *v* [T] *especially BrE* to prepare a surface so that a covering such as paint will stick to it【尤英】〔为涂油漆等〕处理好〔表面〕

key sth ↔ **in** *phr v* [T] to put information into a computer by using a KEYBOARD[1] (1)〔用键盘〕把〔信息〕输入电脑 —see also 另见 KEYED UP

key sth **to** sth *phr v* [T usually passive 一般用被动态] *especially AmE* to slightly change a system, plan etc so that it works well with something else【尤美】〔对体系、计划等略加改动〕使适合于〔另一事物〕: **be keyed to the needs of** (=match the needs of) 适于…的需要 *The daycare hours are keyed to the needs of working parents.* 日托时间是根据在职家长的需要制定的。

Key, Francis Scott (1779-1843) a US poet, who wrote the words of *The Star-Spangled Banner*, the national ANTHEM (=official song) of the US 法朗西斯·斯科特·基〔(1779-1843)，美国诗人，美国国歌《星条旗之歌》的词作者〕

key·board[1] /ˋkiˌbɔrd; ˈkiːbɔːd/ *n* [C] **1** a row or several rows of keys (KEY[2] (3)) on a musical instrument like a piano or a machine like a computer〔乐器或机器上的〕键盘: *a computer keyboard* 电脑键盘 —see picture on page A14 参见 A14 页图 **2** also 又作 **keyboards** [plural] a musical instrument with a keyboard that can sound like a piano, drums etc 键盘乐器

keyboard[2] *v* **1** [I] to use the KEYBOARD[1] (1) of a computer, printing machine etc 操作〔电脑、打印机等的〕键盘 **2** [T] to put information into a computer by using a KEYBOARD[1] (1) 用键盘将〔资料〕输入电脑 —**keyboarder** *n* [C]

key card /ˈ· ·/ *n* [C] a special plastic card that you put in an electronic lock to open a door etc〔电子门锁的〕钥匙卡，卡式钥匙

keyed up /ˌ· ˈ·/ *adj* [not before noun 不用于名词前] worried or excited 紧张的；兴奋的: [+about] *Don't get all keyed up about the exam.* 对这次考试不要过于紧张。

key·hole /ˋkiˌhol; ˈkiːhəʊl/ *n* [C] the hole containing a lock that you use a key in 锁眼，钥匙孔

keyhole sur·ge·ry /ˌ·· ˈ··· / *n* [U] a medical operation that is done through a very small hole in the body 微创外科手术，栓孔手术〔只在身体上切一小口进行的手术〕

Keynes /kenz; keɪnz/, **John May·nard** /dʒɑn ˋmenɑrd; dʒɒn ˈmeɪnɑːd/ (1883-1946) a British economist whose ideas

greatly influenced economic thinking in the 20th century. Keynes believed that governments should use public money to control the level of employment, for example by spending money on public works (=buildings, roads etc built by the government) in order to provide more jobs in periods of high unemployment. 凯恩斯〔(1883-1946),英国经济学家。其观点对20世纪的经济思想有重大影响。他认为政府应当使用公共资金来控制就业水平,例如,在失业率高时可投资基础设施建设以增加就业机会等〕 —**Keynesian** *adj*: *Keynesian economics* 凯恩斯经济学

key·note /ˈkiˌnot; ˈkiːnəʊt/ *n* [C] **1** the main point in a piece of writing, system of beliefs, activity etc, that influences everything else; THEME (1) 主旨,要旨;基调: **[+of]** *Stability was the keynote of the reign of Queen Mary I.* 稳定是女王玛丽一世统治时期的基调。**2 keynote address/speech** a speech that introduces a formal meeting〔正式会议的〕基调演说/主题发言 **3** the note on which a musical key is based〔音乐的〕基调;主音

key·pad /ˈkiˌpæd; ˈkiːpæd/ *n* [C] **1** a small KEYBOARD[1] (1) which you hold in your hand, such as the REMOTE CONTROL for a television〔电视遥控器等能拿在手上操作的〕小型键盘 **2** the part of a computer KEYBOARD[1] (1) that has the number and command keys on it〔电脑键盘的〕扩充键盘,辅助键盘〔数字键和命令键部分〕

key ring /ˈ· ·/ *n* [C] a metal ring that you keep keys on 钥匙圈

key sig·na·ture /ˈ· ˌ···/ *n* [C] a set of marks at the beginning of a line of written music to show which KEY[2] (4) it is in〔乐谱上的〕调号

key·stone /ˈkiˌston; ˈkiːstəʊn/ *n* [C usually singular 一般用单数] **1** the large central stone in an ARCH[1] (1) that keeps the other stones in position 拱顶石 —see picture at 参见 ARCH[1] 图 **2** the most important part of an idea, belief etc 主旨,基础;基本原则: **[+of]** *Social justice is the keystone of our policies.* 社会正义是我们政策的基石。

Keystone Kops, the /ˌ·· ˈ·/ a group of characters in humorous US SILENT FILMS (=old films made with no sound). They are police officers who are very stupid and are always making silly mistakes. 基斯东警察,闹剧警察〔美国无声喜剧影片中的角色。他们是一群傻里傻气、老犯愚蠢错误的警察〕

key·stroke /ˈkiˌstrok; ˈkiːstrəʊk/ *n* [C] the action of pressing a key on a TYPEWRITER or computer KEYBOARD[1] (1)〔对打字机或电脑键盘的〕按键,击键

Key West /ˌ· ˈ·/ an island off the coast of Florida, one of the Florida Keys, which is popular with tourists because of its warm weather and interesting buildings 基韦斯特〔佛罗里达州沿海一岛屿,属佛罗里达群岛。当地气候温暖,建筑别致,吸引着大量游客〕

kg the written abbreviation of 缩写= KILOGRAM or KILOGRAMS

KGB, the /ˌke dʒi ˈbi; ˌkeɪ dʒiː ˈbiː/ *n* the secret police of the former USSR 克格勃,国家安全委员会〔前苏联的秘密警察机关〕

kha·ki /ˈkɑkɪ; ˈkɑːki/ *n* [U] **1** a dull green-brown or yellow-brown colour 土黄色,卡其黄,黄褐色 —see picture on page A5 参见A5页图 **2** cloth of this colour, especially when worn by soldiers 卡其布〔尤指士兵穿的军服用料〕 —**khaki** *adj*

kha·kis /ˈkɑkɪz; ˈkɑːkiz/ *n* [plural] *AmE* trousers made of KHAKI (2) cloth【美】卡其裤

kha·lif /ˈkelɪf; ˈkeɪlɪ̵f/ *n* [C] another spelling of CALIPH caliph 的另一种拼法

kha·li·fate /ˈkeləˌfet; ˈkeɪlɪ̵feɪt/ *n* [C] another spelling of CALIPHATE caliphate 的另一种拼法

Khamenei, Ayatollah Ali (1939-) the religious leader of Iran who succeeded Ayatollah Khomeini in 1989. He is regarded by Iranians as God's representative on earth and has the highest position of power in the country. 哈梅内伊〔(1939-),伊朗宗教领袖。1989年,他接替宗教领袖霍梅尼之位,被伊朗人视为真主在凡间的代表,掌握着国家最高权力〕

khan /kɑn; kɑːn/ *n* [C] a ruler or official in Asia, or their title 可汗,汗〔亚洲一些国家统治者或官员的尊称〕

Khar·toum /kɑrˈtum; kɑːˈtuːm/ the capital city of Sudan 喀土穆〔苏丹首都〕

Khmer Re·pub·lic, the /kəˌmɛr rɪˈpʌblɪk; ˌkmeə rɪˈpʌblɪk/ a former name of Cambodia, from 1975 to 1979 高棉共和国〔1975至1979年间柬埔寨国名〕

Khmer Rouge, the /kəˌmɛr ˈruʒ; ˌkmeə ˈruːʒ/ a very left-wing military organization which took control of the government of Cambodia in 1975, under its leader Pol Pot. Around 3 million Cambodians are believed to have been killed under Khmer Rouge rule, which continued until 1979. 红色高棉〔1975年在波尔布特领导下夺取柬埔寨政权的一极左军事组织。据信,1975至1979年红色高棉统治期间,该国300万人遭杀害〕

Kho·mei·ni /koˈmenɪ; kɒˈmeɪni/**, Ayatollah** (1900-89) a religious and political leader in Iran, who was the head of its Islamic government from 1979 until his death. Khomeini demanded the exact following of Islamic laws. 霍梅尼〔(1900-1989),伊朗宗教和政治领袖。1979年起,他出任伊朗伊斯兰政府首脑直至去世。他要求人们严格遵守伊斯兰教律法〕

Khrush·chev /ˈkrʌstʃɛf; ˈkrʊstʃef/**, Ni·ki·ta** /nɪˈkitə; nɪˈkiːtə/ (1894-1971) a Russian politician who was leader of the Soviet Union from 1953 to 1964. He publicly criticized Stalin and his policies (POLICY) after Stalin's death in 1953. 赫鲁晓夫〔(1894-1971),苏联政治家,1953至1964年间为苏联领导人。1953年斯大林去世后,他公开对斯大林及其政策进行批评〕

Khy·ber Pass, the /ˌkaɪbɚ ˈpæs; ˌkaɪbə ˈpɑːs/ a steep road that goes through mountains and joins Pakistan and Afghanistan. For centuries it was the main road to India from the West. 开伯尔山口〔巴基斯坦与阿富汗之间的陡峭山口。数个世纪以来,该山口一直是从西方进入印度的主要通道〕

kHz the written abbreviation of 缩写= KILOHERTZ

kib·ble[1] /ˈkɪbl; ˈkɪbəl/ *n* [U] *especially AmE* small round pieces of dry dog food【尤美】〔圆形小块〕干狗食

kibble[2] *v* [T] *especially BrE* to crush grain into small pieces【尤英】把〔谷物〕磨成粗粒

kib·butz /kɪˈbuts; kɪˈbʊts/ *n* [C] a type of farm in Israel where many people live and work together〔以色列的〕合作农庄,居民点,基布兹

kib·itz /ˈkɪbɪts; ˈkɪbɪts/ *v* [I] *AmE* to make unhelpful comments while someone is doing something【美】〔在某人正在做某事时〕妄加评论 —**kibitzer** *n* [C]

ki·bosh /ˈkaɪbɑʃ; ˈkaɪbɒʃ/ *n* **put the kibosh on sth** *old-fashioned informal* to stop a plan, idea etc from developing; RUIN[2]【过时,非正式】阻止〔某计划、想法等〕;使…破灭

kick[1] /kɪk; kɪk/ *v* (S2 W3)

1 ►HIT WITH YOUR FOOT 用脚碰撞◄ [I,T] to hit something with your foot 踢: *She kicked me under the table.* 她在桌子下踢了我一下。| *Joe, stop kicking!* 乔,别踢了!| **kick sth down/over etc** *The police kicked the door down.* 警察把门踢倒了。| **kick sth around/towards etc** *Billy was kicking a ball around the yard.* 比利绕着院子踢球。| **kick sb in the head/face/stomach etc** *I got kicked in the face playing rugby.* 我打橄榄球时脸被踢了一下。

2 ►MOVE YOUR LEGS 移动双腿◄ [I,T] to move your legs as if you were kicking something 蹬,踩: *The cow may kick a bit when you milk her.* 挤奶时,奶牛可能会有一点踢蹬。| **kick your legs** *They danced and sang and kicked their legs high in the air.* 他们边跳边唱,把腿踢得很高。

3 ►KICK A GOAL 踢进球门◄ [T] to SCORE[2] (1) by kicking 踢入〔球门〕得分: **kick a goal** *He kicked two penalty goals in the last ten minutes.* 在最后十分钟,他踢进了两个罚球。

4 kick a habit to stop doing something that is a harmful habit 戒除恶习: *Some smokers find it surprisingly easy to kick the habit.* 有些吸烟者发现戒除这一恶习原来出奇地容易。

5 be kicking yourself/will kick yourself/could have kicked yourself *spoken* used to say that someone is annoyed with themselves because they realize that they have made a mistake or missed a chance【口】懊悔,自责: *I could have kicked myself for getting her name wrong.* 我弄错了她的名字,真该自责。| *You'll kick yourself when I tell you the answer.* 我把答案告诉你时,你会懊悔的。| *I bet they are kicking themselves now.* 我敢说他们正后悔不已。

6 kick sb when they are down to criticize or attack someone who is already in a weak position or having difficulties 落井下石: *The newspapers cannot resist kicking a man when he is down.* 报纸总忍不住要干落井下石的事。

7 kick sb in the teeth *informal* to disappoint or DISCOURAGE someone very much, especially when they need support or hope【非正式】使某人大失所望[大为泄气]〔尤指在其需要帮助或鼓励之时〕: *Why is it that whenever I ask you for help you kick me in the teeth?* 为什么我每次求你帮忙你都让我失望?

8 kick (sb's) ass *AmE slang*【美俚】**a)** to punish or defeat someone 惩罚;打败: *We really kicked their ass today, didn't we?* 我们今天好好教训了他们一顿,对吧? **b)** to have fun in a noisy violent way 热闹一下: *Come on, let's kick some ass!* 来啊,我们一起热闹一下!

9 kick over the traces *BrE* to free yourself from control and start to behave as if there are no moral restrictions【英】摆脱约束;放任,放纵: *Haven't you ever felt you must go out and kick over the traces?* 你是否曾经觉得你必须到外面去放纵一下自己?

10 kick sb upstairs to move someone to a job that seems to be more important than their present one but actually means that they have less influence 使明升暗降

11 kick your heels to waste time waiting for something 无聊地等: *We were sitting around kicking our heels for half the day.* 我们坐在那儿无聊地等了半天。
12 kick the bucket *humorous informal* to die【幽默，非正式】死，蹬腿儿

kick about/around *phr v* **1 be kicking about/ around (sth) a)** to be lying somewhere untidily, especially when forgotten 被随意放着: *You should find a copy of the report kicking around somewhere.* 你应该能在什么地方找到那份报告的副本，它只是被随意搁在某处罢了。| *Goodness knows how many bottles he has kicking about his flat.* 天知道有多少瓶子被他随意丢在公寓里。**b)** to be travelling around a place with no fixed plan 漫无目的地到处旅行: *He's been kicking around Australia for eight months.* 他在澳大利亚周游了八个月。**2** [T] **kick sth ↔ about/ around** to discuss an idea with a group of people in order to decide whether it is good or not 商量，讨论，谈论: *Perhaps we could kick one or two of these ideas around for a while.* 也许我们可以在这些观点中挑一两个来花点时间讨论一下。**3** [T] **kick sb about/around** to treat someone badly and unfairly 虐待，欺凌: *She was tired of being kicked around by her boss.* 她腻透了老板对她的欺凌。

kick (out) against *phr v* [T] to react strongly against something 反对；反抗: *She has kicked out against authority all her life.* 她一生都在反抗权威。

kick in *phr v* **1** [I] *informal* to begin to have an effect or come into operation【非正式】开始产生效果；开始运作: *I could feel the painkillers kick in.* 我能感到止痛药开始起效了。| *Other benefits kick in at a certain level of income.* 在收入处于某一水平时享有其他津贴。**2** [I,T] *AmE* to join with others in giving money or help; CONTRIBUTE【美】凑份子；捐助: *He doesn't really want to kick in and help.* 他并不真正愿意捐助。| *We're going to buy Bob a present – do you want to kick in something?* 我们打算给鲍勃买份礼物，你也算一份吗？**3 kick sb's face/sb's head in** to severely wound someone by kicking them 严重踢伤某人: *He threatened to kick my head in.* 他威胁说要踢死我。**4** [T] to kick a door so hard that it breaks open 把〔门〕踢开，踢坏: *We had to get the police to kick the door in.* 我们只好让警察把门踹开。

kick off *phr v* **1** [I] when a game of football kicks off, it starts〔足球比赛〕开球: *The match kicks off at 3 o'clock.* 比赛3点开始。**2** [I,T] if you kick off a meeting, event etc, or if it kicks off, it starts〔会议、事情等〕开始: *The meeting kicked off at 11.00.* 会议于11点开始。| *Right, who would like to kick off?* 好吧，谁先发言？| **kick sth ↔ off (with)** *I'm going to kick off today's proceedings with a few remarks about next year's budget.* 我先讲几句下一年的预算，以此来开始今天的议程。**3** [T] **kick your shoes ↔ off** to remove your shoes by shaking them off your feet 抖落掉脚上穿的鞋: *I slumped into the armchair and kicked off my shoes.* 我一屁股坐到沙发上，抖落掉脚上的鞋子。

kick sb **↔ out** *phr v* [T] to make someone leave or dismiss them 撵走；开除〔某人〕: *Bernard's wife had kicked him out.* 伯纳德的太太把他撵了出去。| [+of] *He's been kicked out of the golf club.* 他被开除出该高尔夫俱乐部。

kick up sth **↔** *phr v* [T] **1 kick up a fuss/row** to loudly complain and show you are annoyed about something〔因不满而〕大吵大闹: *He was kicking up an awful fuss about his cold meal.* 他因那道菜凉了而大吵大闹。**2** to make something, especially dust, go up into the air while you are walking〔走路时〕扬起〔尘土〕: *As they marched, the soldiers kicked up clouds of dust.* 士兵行进时，扬起一团团尘土。

kick² *n* **1** [C] an act of hitting something with your foot 踢；蹬: *Brazil scored with the last kick of the match.* 巴西队在比赛中最后一脚射门得分。| **give sb/sth a good kick** (=to kick them hard) 用力踢某人/某物 *If the outer door won't open just give it a good kick.* 外门如果打不开，就使劲踢开它。**2** [C] an opportunity, allowed by the referee, for one team in a game of football or RUGBY to kick the ball without being stopped by the other team〔足球或橄榄球中的〕任意球: *a free kick* 任意球 | **take a kick** *Pearce came forward to take the kick.* 皮尔斯跑到前面去踢这个任意球。**3 a kick up the arse/backside etc** *informal* severe criticism or punishment for something you have done wrong【非正式】严厉批评；严惩: *Phil needs a good kick up the arse.* 得好好教训一下菲尔。**4 be a kick in the teeth** *informal* to be very disappointing or discouraging, especially when you need support or hope【非正式】令人大失所望，令人大为泄气〔尤指在需要帮助或鼓励时〕: *Her refusal to see me was a real kick in the teeth.* 她拒绝见我，让我大为失望。**5 get a kick out of sth/ get a kick from sth** to really enjoy doing something 从做某事中得到乐趣: *Alan gets a real kick out of his job.* 艾伦从他的工作中得到真正的乐趣。**6 give sb a kick** to give someone a strong feeling of pleasure 给某人以极大乐趣: *It gives her a kick to get you into trouble.* 给你制造麻烦使她得到极大的乐趣。**7 do sth for kicks/get your kicks from sth** *informal* to do something, especially something dangerous or harmful, in order to get a feeling of excitment【非正式】为寻求刺激而干某事〔尤指危险或有害的事〕: *Apparently she steals from supermarkets just for kicks.* 显然，她在超市偷东西只是为了寻找刺激。**8 have a kick (to it)** *informal* to have a strong effect or taste, especially alcohol【非正式】〔尤指烈性酒〕有劲；有浓烈的味道 **9 be on a health/decorating/Italian food etc kick** *informal* to have a strong new interest【非正式】热衷于保健/装饰/意大利式食物等: *I'm on a health kick at the moment.* 目前我正热衷于保健。

kick-ass /ˈ· ·/ *adj AmE slang* strong, powerful, and sometimes violent【美俚】强壮的；粗暴的: *a kick-ass attitude that will get him into trouble* 会给他招惹麻烦的蛮横态度

kick·back /ˈkɪkˌbæk; ˈkɪkbæk/ *n* [C,U] *slang* money that you pay secretly or dishonestly for someone's help; BRIBE【俚】佣金，回扣；贿赂

kick·ball /ˈkɪkˌbɔl; ˈkɪkbɔːl/ *n* [U] an American children's game, similar to BASEBALL, in which you kick the ball rather than hit it〔按棒球规则进行的美国〕儿童足球游戏

kick·box·ing /ˈkɪkˌbɑksɪŋ; ˈkɪkˌbɒksɪŋ/ *n* [U] a form of BOXING in which you kick as well as PUNCH (=hit) 跆拳道

kick·off /ˈkɪkˌɔf; ˈkɪk-ɒf/ *n* [C usually singular 一般用单数] **1** the time when a game of football starts, or the first kick〔足球比赛的〕开球；比赛开始: *Kickoff is at 3.00.* 足球比赛3点开始。**2** *informal* the beginning of a new activity【非正式】〔新活动的〕开始，序幕

kick·stand /ˈkɪkˌstænd; ˈkɪkstænd/ *n* [C] a thing that supports a bicycle or MOTORCYCLE when it is not moving, and keeps it in an upright position〔脚踏车或摩托车的〕撑脚架，支架

kick-start¹ /ˈ· ·/ *v* [T] **1** to do something to help a process or activity start or develop more quickly 启动；促进: *lowering interest rates to kick-start the economy* 通过降低利率来促进经济 **2** to start a MOTORCYCLE using your foot 用脚发动〔摩托车〕

kick-start² also 又作 **kick-start·er** /ˈ· ,··/ *n* [C] the part of a MOTORCYCLE that you press with your foot to start it〔摩托车的〕脚踏起动器

kid¹ /kɪd; kɪd/ *n* **1** [C] *informal* a child【非正式】小孩，儿童: **the kids** (=children that you are responsible for)〔由某人负责照管的〕孩子们 *I'm taking the kids to the zoo today.* 我今天要带孩子们去动物园。—see 见 CHILD (USAGE) **2** [C] *informal* a young person【非正式】年轻人: *college kids* 大学生 **3** [C] *informal* a son or daughter【非正式】孩子；儿子；女儿 **4 kid's stuff** *BrE*【英】**/kid stuff** *AmE*【美】something that is very easy or boring 非常容易[乏味]的事情 **5** [C,U] a young goat, or the leather made from its skin 小山羊；小山羊皮革 **6 treat/ handle someone with kid gloves** to treat someone very carefully because they easily become upset 小心谨慎地对待某人〔尤指易生气的人〕 

kid² *v* **kidded, kidding** *informal*【非正式】**1** [I,T] to say something that is not true, especially as a joke〔尤指作为玩笑〕戏弄；嘲笑；欺骗: **just/only kidding** *spoken*【口】*Don't get mad, I was only kidding.* 别生气，我刚才不过是开个玩笑。| **you're kidding (me)** *spoken*【口】*You won $5,000? You're kidding!* 你赢了5000美元？骗人！**2** [T] to make yourself believe something untrue or unlikely 欺骗，哄骗〔自己〕: **not kid yourself (that)** *Don't kid yourself he'll ever change.* 别欺骗自己以为他会改的。**3 no kidding a)** *spoken* used when you do not completely believe someone, or are surprised by what they say【口】不是开玩笑吧: *Carlotta's 39? No kidding?* 卡洛塔39岁了？不是开玩笑吧？**b)** used to warn someone that you mean what you say 说真的；不骗你 **4 I kid you not** *spoken* used to emphasize that you are telling the truth【口】跟你说正经的，骗你不是人 —**kidder** *n* [C] *AmE*【美】

kid around *phr v* [I] to behave in a silly way 胡闹: *Stop kidding around and listen to me.* 别胡闹了，听我说。—**kidding** *n* [U]

kid³ *adj informal especially AmE*【非正式，尤美】**kid sister/ brother** your kid sister or brother is younger than you are 小妹妹/弟弟

kid·die, kiddy /ˈkɪdɪ; ˈkɪdi/ *n* [C] *especially BrE informal* a young child【尤英，非正式】小孩 —**kiddie** *adj*: *a kiddie seat* 儿童座位

kid·do /ˈkɪdo; ˈkɪdəʊ/ *n* [C usually singular 一般用单数] *especially AmE spoken* a way of addressing someone you know, usually a young person【尤美口】年轻人，小伙子〔对认识的人，一般对年轻人的一种称呼〕: *Come on kiddo, let's go.* 喂，小伙子，我们走吧。

K

kid·nap /ˋkɪdnæp; ˈkɪdnæp/ *v* **kidnapped, kidnapping** also 又作 **kidnaped, kidnaping** *AmE*【美】[T] to take someone away illegally, usually by force, in order to get money for returning them 绑架; 诱拐; 劫持 —**kidnapper** *n* [C]

Kid·napped /ˋkɪdnæpt; ˈkɪdnæpt/ (1886) an adventure story by Robert Louis Stevenson about a young man called David Balfour who is kidnapped, but escapes. He and his friend Alan Breck see a man being killed, and people think that they did it, so they run away and travel across the Highlands of Scotland. 《绑架》〔(1886), 罗伯特·路易斯·史蒂文森创作的一部冒险小说, 讲述名叫戴维·鲍尔弗的年轻人遭绑架后死里逃生的故事。他和朋友艾伦·布雷克目击到一名男子被人杀害, 因此有人认为是他们干的。于是, 他们穿越苏格兰高地一路逃命〕

kid·nap·ping /ˋkɪdnæpɪŋ; ˈkɪdnæpɪŋ/ also 又作 **kidnap** *especially BrE*【尤英】—*n* [C,U] the crime of kidnapping someone 绑架; 诱拐; 劫持: *the recent series of kidnappings* 近来发生的一连串绑架事件 | *a kidnap attempt* 绑架企图

S3 **kid·ney** /ˋkɪdnɪ; ˈkɪdni/ *n* **1** [C] one of the two organs in your lower back that separate waste liquid from your blood and make URINE 肾, 肾脏 **2** [C,U] one or more of these organs from an animal, used as food 腰子〔指供食用的动物肾脏〕: *steak and kidney pie* 牛排和腰子馅饼

kidney bean /ˋ‥ ·/ *n* [C] a dark red bean that is shaped like a KIDNEY 菜豆, 四季豆 —see picture on page A9 参见 A9 页图

Kier·ke·gaard /ˋkɪrkəgɑrd; ˈkɪəkəgɑːd/, **Sö·ren Aa·bye** /ˋsɜrən ˋɑbɪ; ˈsɜːrən ˈɑːbi/ (1813-55) a Danish PHILOSOPHER whose ideas had an important influence on EXISTENTIALISM 克尔恺郭尔〔(1813-1855), 丹麦哲学家。其理论对存在主义哲学产生过重要影响〕

Ki·ev /ˋkiɛf; ˈkiːef/ the capital city of Ukraine, an industrial centre and important port 基辅〔乌克兰首都、工业中心和重要港口〕

Kigali /kɪˋgɑlɪ; kɪˈgɑːli/ the capital city of Rwanda 基加利〔卢旺达首都〕

Kil·dare /kɪlˋdɛr; kɪlˈdeə/ a COUNTY in the east of the Republic of Ireland 基尔代尔郡〔爱尔兰共和国东部一郡〕

Kil·i·man·ja·ro /ˌkɪləmənˋdʒɑro; ˌkɪl̩mənˈdʒɑːrəʊ/ also 又作 **Mount Kilimanjaro** a mountain in Tanzania that is the highest mountain in Africa 乞力马扎罗山〔位于坦桑尼亚境内, 为非洲最高山峰〕

Kil·ken·ny /kɪlˋkɛnɪ; kɪlˈkeni/ a COUNTY in the southeast of the Republic of Ireland 基尔肯尼郡〔爱尔兰共和国东南部一郡〕

S1 W1 **kill**[1] /kɪl; kɪl/ *v*

1 ▶MAKE SB/STH DIE 使某人/某物死亡◀ [I,T] to make a living thing die 弄死; 杀死: *His parents were killed in a plane crash.* 他的父母死于飞机失事。| *What's the best way to kill weeds?* 什么是除草的最好办法? | *Drug abuse can kill.* 滥用药物可以致命。| **kill yourself** *You're going to kill yourself on that motorcycle.* 你骑那辆摩托车会送命的。| *The jury returned a verdict that he killed himself with an overdose.* 陪审团作出裁决, 认定他因过量服药而丧命。

2 ▶MAKE STH STOP/FAIL 使某物停止/失败◀ [T] to make something stop or fail, or turn off the power to something 使停止; 使失败; 使关闭: *Nothing that the doctor gives me kills the pain.* 医生给我的药都不止痛。| *Quick! Kill the lights.* 快! 关灯! | *You've got to kill that story before it gets printed* (=prevent it being printed). 你得在刊印之前删掉这篇报道。| **kill the conversation** (=stop people talking) 使谈话中止 | **kill a beer/bottle of wine etc** *AmE spoken* (=finish drinking)【美口】喝光一杯啤酒/一瓶葡萄酒等 *Let's kill these beers and go.* 我们把这几杯啤酒喝光再走吧。| **kill the ball** (=completely stop a fast moving ball) 截球, 停球 | **kill your speed** (=drive slowly) 减速行驶

3 ▶BE ANGRY WITH SB 对某人生气◀ [T] *informal* to be very angry with someone【非正式】对〔某人〕大发雷霆: *Maria will kill me if I'm late again.* 如果我再迟到, 玛丽亚一定会对我大发雷霆。

4 ▶MAKE SB TIRED/SAD 令某人疲倦/难过◀ [T] to make someone feel extremely tired, unhappy etc 使极度疲倦[难过等]: **it kills me/her/them** *It kills me to see him working so hard for nothing.* 看见他工作如此艰辛而没有任何回报, 真让我难过。

5 the suspense is killing me *spoken* used to say you are impatient to know the result of something【口】这样悬而不决真让我受不了

6 my head is/feet are etc killing me *spoken* used to say that a part of your body is hurting a lot【口】我的头/脚等痛得要命: *I've walked miles and my feet are killing me.* 我步行了好几英里路, 脚痛得要命。

7 ▶MAKE SB LAUGH 令某人大笑◀ [T] to make someone laugh a lot at something 使发笑: *You really killed them tonight, Frenchie!* 弗兰奇, 你今晚可真让他们笑死了! | **kill yourself laughing** (=laugh a lot) 让自己笑个半死

8 it won't kill sb (to do something) *spoken* used when saying that someone could easily do something, and ought to do it【口】(做某事) 对某人来说十分容易〔因此应该去做〕: *It wouldn't kill you to give me a bit of help.* 帮我一点小忙不会要你的命的。

9 kill time to do something that is not very useful or interesting while you are waiting for something to happen 消磨时光, 打发时间

10 kill two birds with one stone to achieve two things with one action 一石二鸟, 一举两得, 一箭双雕

11 kill someone with kindness to be too kind to someone 对待某人好得过分, 宠坏某人

12 ▶SPOIL STH'S APPEARANCE 破坏某物的外表◀ [T] if something kills the way something else looks, the two things look wrong together 破坏; 搞糟: *That hat kills her whole outfit.* 那顶帽子令她全身的衣着打扮失色不少。

13 it will kill or cure used to say that what you plan to do will either work very well or fail completely 不是一举成功, 就是一败涂地; 成败在此一举

14 kill the fatted calf to welcome someone home with a big meal etc after they have been away for a long time 盛宴款待〔长期离家归来的人〕—see also 另见 **dressed to kill** (DRESSED (4)), **kill the goose that lays the golden egg** (GOOSE[1] (4))

kill sth ↔ **off** *phr v* [T] to cause the death of a lot of living things 使〔生物〕大量死亡; 使灭绝: *Pollution is rapidly killing off plant life.* 污染使大量植物迅速死亡。

USAGE NOTE 用法说明: KILL

WORD CHOICE 词语辨析: **kill, murder, execute, put to death, kill oneself, commit suicide, slaughter, assassinate, massacre**

Kill is the general word meaning to make someone or something die. kill 是表示"使人或物死亡"的普通用词: *My uncle was killed in a plane crash.* 我叔叔死于飞机失事。| *A sharp frost can kill young plants.* 一场突降的霜冻能冻死幼苗。

Murder means to kill someone deliberately and illegally. murder 指蓄意、非法地杀害某人: *Davies is accused of murdering his wife and their three young children.* 戴维斯被指控谋杀妻子和三个年幼的孩子。

If someone is killed legally as a punishment for a crime, they are **executed** or **put to death**. 如果某人因犯罪而被依法处决, 他就是被 executed 或 put to death: *Should serial killers be executed?* 连环杀手应当被处死吗? | *Thousands of revolutionaries were put to death after the coup.* 成千上万的革命者在政变后被处死。

If someone **kills himself or herself**, they **commit suicide**. kill himself or herself 意为"自杀" (commit suicide)。

Slaughter is the technical word for killing animals for food, leather etc but it is also used to describe the violent and unnecessary killing of a large number of people. slaughter 是屠宰动物〔供食用或制革〕的术语, 但也指使用暴力杀害大批无辜者: *Thousands of people are slaughtered every year in road accidents.* 每年都有成千上万的人死于交通事故。

To **assassinate** someone means to murder an important, famous, and usually powerful person for political reasons. assassinate 指为了政治原因刺杀一名重要而著名的, 而且通常是有权势的人物: *Who really assassinated President Kennedy?* 到底是谁刺杀了肯尼迪总统?

To **massacre** means to kill large numbers of ordinary people, especially people who cannot defend themselves. massacre 指大量屠杀平民, 尤其是没有自卫能力的人: *Hundreds of men, women, and children were massacred in the attack.* 在这次袭击中, 有数百个男女和儿童遭到屠杀。

kill[2] *n* **1** the act of killing a hunted animal 捕杀: *The hawk's talons grip tight as it makes its kill.* 老鹰捕杀猎物时双爪紧紧收拢。**2 move in/close in for the kill** to come nearer to something and prepare to kill, defeat, or destroy 逐渐靠近以伺机杀死[击败, 摧毁]: *Enemy submarines were moving in for the kill.* 敌人的潜艇正靠近目标准备攻击。| **be in at the kill** (=watch something being killed, someone being defeated etc) 目击某物被毁[某人被击败等] **3** [singular] an animal killed by another animal, especially for food〔尤指作食物而被杀死的〕猎获物

kill·er /ˋkɪlɚ; ˈkɪlə/ *n* [C] **1** a person, animal, or thing that kills 杀手; 杀生的人[动物, 事物]: *Heart disease is America's number one killer.* 心脏病是美国的头号杀手。—see also 另见 SERIAL KILLER **2** *AmE slang* something or someone that is very attractive or very good【美俚】极有吸引力的人[物]; 极好的人

K

[物]: *a killer movie* 一部绝好的电影 —see also 另见 LADY-KILLER **3 a/the killer instinct** a desire to succeed that is so strong that you are willing to harm other people 嗜杀的本性 —**killer** *adj*: *a killer disease* 致命的疾病

killer whale /ˈ· · ˌ·/ *n* [C] a black and white WHALE that eats meat 逆戟鲸, 虎鲸, 杀人鲸

kill·ing[1] /ˈkɪlɪŋ; ˈkɪlɪŋ/ *n* [C] **1** a murder 谋杀: *a series of gangland killings* 一系列的黑社会谋杀案 **2 make a killing** *informal* to make a lot of money in a short time【非正式】发横财

killing[2] *adj informal*【非正式】**1** extremely tiring 令人精疲力竭的: *a killing workload* 令人疲惫不堪的工作负担 **2** *old-fashioned* very funny【过时】滑稽的, 好笑的 —**killingly** *adv*

Killing Fields, The /ˈ· · ˌ·/ (1984) a British film about the events in Cambodia in 1975-79, when Pol Pot and the Khmer Rouge were in power and killed millions of people《战火屠城》, 又译《杀戮战场》〔(1984), 英国影片。该片讲述1975至1979年在柬埔寨发生的一系列事件。当时, 波尔布特及其领导的红色高棉执政, 杀害了数百万人〕

kill·joy /ˈkɪlˌdʒɔɪ; ˈkɪldʒɔɪ/ *n* [C] someone who spoils other people's pleasure 令人扫兴的人

kiln /kɪln; kɪln/ *n* [C] a special OVEN for baking clay pots, bricks etc〔烧制陶器、砖头等的〕窑

ki·lo /ˈkilo; ˈkiːləʊ/ *n plural* **kilos** [C] an informal word for KILOGRAM kilogram的非正式用词: *The box weighs 6 kilos.* 这个箱子重6公斤。

kilo- /kɪlə; kɪlə/ *prefix* 1,000 times a particular unit 千; 一千倍: *a kilogram* (=1,000 grams) 一千克 —see table on page C4 参见C4页附录

kil·o·byte /ˈkɪləˌbaɪt; ˈkɪləbaɪt/ also 又作 **K** *n* [C] a unit for measuring computer information equal to 1,024 BYTES〔电脑信息单位〕千字节〔相等于1,024个字节〕

kil·o·gram /ˈkɪləˌgræm; ˈkɪləgræm/ *n* [C] a unit for measuring weight equal to 1,000 grams 千克, 公斤 —see table on page C3 参见C3页附录

kil·o·hertz /ˈkɪləˌhɜts; ˈkɪləhɜːts/ written abbreviation 缩写为 **kHz** *n* [C] a unit for measuring wave lengths, especially of radio signals, equal to 1,000 HERTZ 千赫(兹)

3 **kil·o·me·tre** *BrE*【英】, **kilometer** *AmE*【美】/ˈkɪləˌmitɚ; ˈkɪləˌmiːtə/ *n* [C] a unit for measuring length, equal to 1,000 metres 千米, 公里 —see table on page C3 参见C3页附录

kil·o·watt /ˈkɪləˌwɑt; ˈkɪləwɒt/ *n* [C] a unit for measuring electrical power equal to 1,000 WATTS 千瓦

kilowatt hour /ˌ· · · ˈ·/ *n* [C] the amount of ENERGY produced by a KILOWATT in one hour 千瓦时

kilt /kɪlt; kɪlt/ *n* [C] a type of thick skirt, traditionally worn by Scottish men 褶裥短裙〔苏格兰男子的传统服饰〕—**kilted** *adj*

CULTURAL NOTE 文化注释

People often make jokes about the fact that Scotsmen are believed to wear nothing under their kilts. 人们常常开玩笑说苏格兰男人的褶裥短裙下面什么都不穿。

kil·ter /ˈkɪltɚ; ˈkɪltə/ *n* **out of kilter** not working as well as usual 失常, 失调: *Things in my life seem all out of kilter lately.* 近来我的生活中似乎一切都不正常。

Kimberley /ˈkɪmbɚlɪ; ˈkɪmbəli/ a city which is the centre of a DIAMOND mining area in northern Cape Province, South Africa. 金伯利〔南非好望角省北部一城市, 为钻石矿区的中心〕

ki·mo·no /kəˈmonə; kɪˈməʊnəʊ/ *n* [C] **1** a traditional piece of Japanese clothing like a long coat, that is worn at special ceremonies〔日本的〕和服 **2** *especially AmE* a long, loose piece of clothing worn informally indoors, especially by women【尤美】〔尤指妇女在家中穿的〕宽松晨衣

kin /kɪn; kɪn/ *n* [plural] **1** *informal* also 又作 **kinfolk** your family【非正式】家人, 家属; 亲属 **2 next of kin** *formal* your most closely related family【正式】最近的亲属: *We'll have to notify the next of kin of his death.* 我们得把他去世的消息告知他最近的亲属。—compare 比较 KINDRED[1] (1) —see also 另见 KITH AND KIN

-kin /kɪn; kɪn/ also 又作 **-kins** /kɪnz; kɪnz/ *suffix* [in nouns 构成名词] a word meaning something small, used especially to children 小…〔尤用于对儿童说话时〕: *a lambkin* 小羔羊

1 1 **kind[1]** /kaɪnd; kaɪnd/ *n* **1** [C] a type or sort or person or thing 种; 类: [+of] *What kind of fish is this?* 这是哪一种鱼? | *Are you in some kind of trouble?* 你遇到什么麻烦了吗? | *victimization of the worst kind* 最恶劣的一种迫害 | **all kinds of** *They sell all kinds of different things.* 他们出售各种各样的东西。| **of this kind** *Operations of this kind always carry risks.* 这种手术总是有风险的。| **of its kind** *the best wine of its kind* 同类酒中最好的 **2 kind of** also 又作 **kinda** *AmE spoken*【美口】**a)** slightly or in some ways 有点; 有几分: *I'm kind of glad I didn't win.* 我倒是有点高兴我没有赢。**b)** used when you are explaining something and want to avoid giving the details 大致是这样: *I kind of made it look like the post office had lost his letter.* 总之, 我把它弄得看起来好像是邮局把他的信丢了。**3 a kind of (a)** *especially spoken* used to say that your description of something is not exact【尤口】稍稍, 几分: *a kind of a reddish-brown* 略呈红的棕色 **4 something of the/that kind** *spoken* something similar to what has been mentioned【口】类似所提及的某事物: *"Are you sure he was wearing jeans?" "Well, something of the kind."* "你肯定他穿的是牛仔裤吗?" "唔, 类似那种裤子。" **5 nothing/anything of the kind** used to emphasize what you are saying when you disagree with someone 完全不是那样: *I never said anything of the kind!* 我从来没说过那种话! **6** [U] people or things that are similar in some way or belong to the same group 相似的人[事物]; 同一类的人[事物]: **sb's (own) kind** *Grace only made friends among her own kind.* 格雷丝只与跟自己同一类的人交朋友。**7 be the kind** to be a person of a particular type 属于某种类型的人: *She may not be the marrying kind.* 她可能不是那种想结婚的人。| **be the kind to do sth** *He's not the kind to get excited about money.* 他不是那种见钱就心动的人。**8 two/three etc of a kind** two or three people or things that are of the same type 属于同一类的两/三个人[事物]等: *You and your brother are two of a kind.* 你和你弟弟两人属于同一类型。**9 one of a kind** the only one of a particular type of something; UNIQUE 唯一的, 独一无二的: *Each plate is handpainted and one of a kind.* 每只盘子都是手工绘制, 因此也是独一无二的。**10 of a kind** used to say that something is not as good as it should be 名不符实的: *Elections of a kind are held, but there is only one party to vote for.* 有些所谓的选举进行了, 但只有一个党派参加竞选。**11 payment in kind** a method of paying someone with goods or services instead of money 以实物[服务]〔而非钱款〕支付, 以货代款 **12 respond/retaliate etc in kind** to react by doing the same thing as someone else has just done 以同样方式回应/反击等: *If other papers cut their prices, we'll have to respond in kind.* 如果其他报纸降价, 我们也只好用降价回应。

USAGE NOTE 用法说明: KIND

FORMALITY 正式程度

Remember that **would you be kind enough to/would you be so kind as to...?** are formally polite. When you are speaking or writing informally they may sound unfriendly and it would be better to say, for example 要记住 would you be kind enough to/would you be so kind as to...? 是正式场合下的礼貌说法, 而在非正式的口语或书面语中, 这种说法则可能听起来并不友善, 因此用其他说法会更好, 例如: **Please could you.../Could you possibly...?**

On the other hand, **kind of** and **sort of** meaning that something is uncertain or partly true (mainly before adjectives and verbs) are used only in informal contexts. 另外, 表示某事不确定或只是部分真实的 kind of 和 sort of〔主要用于形容词和副词前〕只用于非正式场合中: *I kinda like that color.* 我有点喜欢那种颜色。| *"Did he help you?" "Well, kind of."* (=not as much as I hoped) "他帮你忙了吗?" "嗯, 可以说帮了一点。"〔意指不如我希望的那样〕In very informal speech you sometimes use **kind of** and **sort of** to make a serious statement sound weaker or amusing. 在很不正式的口语中, 有时用 kind of 和 sort of 来减弱话语的严肃性或使其滑稽有趣: *He sort of came up to me and pushed me. So I kind of hit him in the face.* 他凑到我面前推我, 于是我就那么给了他一记耳光。Some people do not consider this to be good English. 有些人认为这种用法不是规范的英语。

GRAMMAR 语法

Kind(s) of or **sort(s) of** is regularly used in the singular or plural before singular and uncountable nouns. 在单数名词和不可数名词前可用单数的 kind of 或 sort of, 也可以用复数的 kinds of 或 sorts of: *one kind of flower/person/bread* 一种花/人/面包 | *many kinds of car/person/cheese/attraction* 许多种类的车/人/乳酪/吸引 | *several sorts of paint* 几种油漆

The plural **kinds of/sorts of** is also used before plural nouns in more informal English. 在较为非正式的英语里, 复数名词前也用 kinds of/sorts of: *these/many kinds of flowers/programs/people* 这些/许多种类的花/程序/人 (but NOT 但不用 *this kind/sort of programs*, though you can more formally say 不过可用更正式的说法 *programs of this kind/sort*)。

Remember that whether **kind** or **sort** itself is singular or plural also relates to the word used just before. 要记住kind或sort用单数还是复数取决于用在其前面的词语: *this/one/each/every kind of...* 这/一/每一/各种… | *another sort of cheese* 另一种乳酪 but you say 但说 *these/ten/many/all/a few kinds of...* 这些/十个/许多/所有/少数种类的… | *in other kinds of school* 在其他类别的学校 | *shops of all sorts* 各种各样的商店。In informal spoken English people do say things like 在非正式的口语中，人们确实也用如下的说法: *Those kind/sort of questions are very difficult* 那种题目非常难, but some people think this is incorrect. 但有些人认为这种用法不正确。

3 **kind²** *adj* **1** saying or doing things that show that you care about other people and want to help them or make them happy 体贴的; 亲切的; 和蔼的: *It's really kind of you to let us use your pool.* 感谢你让我们使用你的游泳池。| *Ms Jarvis is unable to accept your kind invitation.* 贾维斯女士不能接受你的友好邀请。| **[+to]** *He's been very kind to me.* 他对我一直很友善。—see 见 KINDLY² (USAGE) **2** not causing harm or suffering 关照的, 厚待的: *Life has been very kind to me.* 我的生活一向不错。| *I need a soap that's kinder to my skin.* 我需要一种对皮肤较为柔和的肥皂。**3 would you be kind enough to do sth/be so kind as to do sth** *formal* used to make a polite request【正式】劳驾, 请您…好吗: *Would you be kind enough to close the door, please?* 劳驾，请您关上门好吗? —opposite 反义词 UNKIND —see also 另见 KINDLY², KINDNESS

kin·der·gar·ten /ˈkɪndɚˌgɑrtṇ; ˈkɪndəgɑːtn/ *n* [C,U] **1** *AmE* a school or class for young children, usually aged five, that prepares them for normal school【美】〔通常为五岁儿童开设的〕幼儿园, 学前班 **2** *BrE* a school for children aged two to five【英】〔为二岁至五岁儿童开办的〕幼儿园 —compare 比较 NURSERY

kind-heart·ed /ˌ· ˈ··◂/ *adj* kind and generous 乐善好施的 —**kind-heartedly** *adv* —**kind-heartedness** *n* [U]

kin·dle /ˈkɪndḷ; ˈkɪndl/ *v* [I,T] **1** to start burning, or to make something start burning 点燃; (使) 燃烧起来: **kindle a fire** (=make a fire using small pieces of wood etc) 点火; 生火 **2 kindle excitement/interest etc** to make someone interested, excited etc 引起兴奋/兴趣等: *The love of poetry was kindled in him by her teaching.* 她的教学引发了他对诗歌的兴趣。

kin·dling /ˈkɪndlɪŋ; ˈkɪndlɪŋ/ *n* [U] small pieces of dry wood, leaves etc that you use for starting a fire 引火物〈如干的木柴、树叶等〉

kind·ly¹ /ˈkaɪndlɪ; ˈkaɪndli/ *adv* **1** in a kind way; generously 友善地; 亲切地: *Mr Nunn has kindly agreed to let us use his barn for the dance.* 纳恩先生很友好地同意我们用他的谷仓举行舞会。**2** *spoken formal* a word meaning 'please', which is often used when you are annoyed【口, 正式】请〔常用来表示不快〕: *Will you kindly put that book back?* 请你把那本书放回去好吗? **3 not take kindly to** to be unwilling to accept a situation because it annoys you 不愿意接受: *Eddie would not take kindly to her working.* 埃迪不会接受她去工作。**4 look kindly on** to approve of someone or something 赞成, 同意: *He hoped the committee would look kindly on his request.* 他希望委员会能同意他的请求。**5 think kindly of** to have fond thoughts about someone 怀念, 想念: *Think kindly of me when I'm gone.* 我走后希望还能记着我。

kindly² *adj* kind and caring for other people 友善的; 亲切的; 和蔼的; 体贴的: *Mrs Gardiner was a kindly old soul.* 加德纳夫人是个和蔼可亲的老人。—**kindliness** *n* [C]

USAGE NOTE 用法说明: KINDLY

FORMALITY 正式程度

A request like **would you kindly...?** or **kindly shut the door!** is formally polite. In informal contexts it sounds as though you are annoyed and **could you possibly...?** would be more usual. 像 Would you kindly...? 或 Kindly shut the door! 这样的请求是正式而客气的。但在非正式场合下，这种说法显得说话人好像不耐烦，比较常用的说法是 Could you possibly...?

WORD CHOICE 词语辨析: **kindly, kind**

Kindly is either the adverb of **kind** kindly 既是 kind 的副词形式: *He kindly opened the door for me* 他体贴地为我开门, or an adjective with a slightly different meaning from **kind** which is much less common 同时又是形容词, 但意思与 kind 略有不同, 而且也不很常见: *She is a kindly person.* 她是个和蔼可亲的人。

The adjective **kindly** describes a person's general character. **Kind** may also do this, but often describes someone's behaviour at one particular moment. 形容词 kindly 用于描写一个人的总体性格。kind 也有这个用法, 但常描写某人在某特定时刻的行为: *It was kind of you to help me.* 谢谢你友好的帮忙。| *She's often kind to me* (NOT 不用 *kindly*). 她常友善待我。

kind·ness /ˈkaɪndnɪs; ˈkaɪndnɪ̵s/ *n* **1** [U] kind behaviour towards someone 仁慈; 和蔼; 好意; 体贴: *I can't thank you enough for your kindness.* 我对你的好意感激不尽。**2** [C] a kind action 友好的行为: **do sb a kindness** *It would be doing him a kindness to tell him the truth.* 把实情告诉他对他是件好事。—see also 另见 **kill someone with kindness** (KILL¹ (11))

kin·dred¹ /ˈkɪndrɪd; ˈkɪndrɪ̵d/ *n* [U] **1** *old use* your family【旧】家人; 亲属 —compare 比较 KIN **2 [+with]** *formal* a family relationship; KINSHIP【正式】亲属关系, 血缘关系

kindred² *adj* [only before noun 仅用于名词前] **1 a kindred spirit** someone who thinks and feels the way you do 志趣相投的人 **2** *formal* belonging to the same group or family【正式】同宗的; 同类的; 同源的

ki·net·ic /kɪˈnɛtɪk; kɪˈnetɪk/ *adj technical* connected with movement【术语】运动的; 动力的

kinetic art /·ˌ·· ˈ·/ *n* [U] art, such as SCULPTURE, that has moving parts 动态艺术〈如动态雕塑〉

kinetic en·er·gy /·ˌ·· ˈ···/ *n* [U] *technical* the power of something moving, such as running water【术语】动能〈如流水的能量〉

ki·net·ics /kɪˈnɛtɪks; kɪˈnetɪks/ *n* [U] *technical* the science that studies the action or force of movement【术语】动力学

kin·folk /ˈkɪnˌfok; ˈkɪnfəʊk/ *n* [plural] an American form of KINSFOLK kinsfolk 的美语形式

king /kɪŋ; kɪŋ/ *n* [C] 

1 ▶RULER 统治者◀ a man who is ruler of a country because he is from a royal family 国王: *He became king on the death of his father.* 他在父亲死后成为国王。| **[+of]** *Henry VIII, King of England* 英格兰国王亨利八世

2 ▶THE BEST 最好者◀ a) someone that you think does a particular thing the best 最优秀的人: **[+of]** *the King of Rock 'n' Roll* 摇滚乐之王 **b)** something that is the best of its type〔同类事物中的〕最优秀者: **[+of]** *the king of Swiss cheeses* 瑞士乳酪中的极品

3 ▶CHESS 国际象棋◀ the most important piece in a game of CHESS 王〔国际象棋中最重要的棋子〕

4 ▶CARDS 纸牌◀ a playing card with a picture of a king on it 老K〔绘有国王图像的纸牌〕

5 ▶IMPORTANT 重要的◀ be king if something is king at a particular time, it has a big influence on people 极具影响: *back in the days when jazz was king* 在往昔爵士乐极为盛行的年代

6 king of the jungle/of beasts the most important male animal 丛林之王/百兽之王: *The lion is king of the jungle.* 狮子是丛林之王。

7 a king's ransom an extremely large amount of money 一笔巨款

8 live like a king to have a very good quality of life 养尊处优 —see also 另见 QUEEN¹

King, Martin Luther /ˈmɑrtɪn ˈluθɚ; ˈmɑːtɪ̵n ˈluːθə/ (1929-68) a black US religious leader who became the most important leader of the civil rights movement and worked hard to achieve social changes for black people. He was a great public speaker, and many people remember his famous speech that starts with the words "I have a dream". He encouraged people to try to achieve changes without using violence, and in 1964 he won the Nobel Peace Prize. In 1968 he was shot and killed in Memphis, Tennessee. In the US there is a national holiday in January to celebrate his birthday. 马丁·路德·金〔(1929-1968), 美国黑人宗教领袖, 民权运动最为重要的领导人。他曾竭力为黑人实现社会变革。他是一位出色的演说家, 不少人对他的著名演讲"我有一个梦想"记忆犹新。他鼓励人们用非暴力手段去实现社会变革。1964年, 他荣获诺贝尔和平奖, 1968年在田纳西州的孟菲斯市遭枪杀。在美国, 每年1月有一天国定假日庆祝他的生日〕

King, Rod·ney /ˈrɑdnɪ; ˈrɒdni/ (1966-) a black US man who was violently attacked by a group of white police officers in Los Angeles in 1991. By chance an ordinary citizen filmed the attack, and this film was later shown on US television. When the police officers were judged in a court of law in 1992, the JURY decided that they were not guilty of being too violent, and this led to the Los Angeles RIOTS (=violent public protests). Many people in the US thought that this event proved that black people were still not being treated fairly by the legal system. 罗德尼·

K

金〔(1966-)，美国黑人。1991年，他在洛杉矶遭一伙白人警察殴打，一名普通市民碰巧拍下了打人过程，后来在电视上播出。1992年参与行凶的警察被带上法庭受审，但陪审团却作出无罪裁定，从而引发了洛杉矶骚乱。不少美国人认为这起事件证明黑人仍然得不到司法体系的公平对待〕

King, The an informal name still used for the famous singer Elvis Presley, used especially by people who love his music 猫王〔埃尔维斯·普雷斯利的别称，至今尤为其歌迷所使用〕

3 **king·dom** /ˈkɪŋdəm; ˈkɪŋdəm/ *n* [C] **1** a country governed by a king or queen 王国: *the kingdom of Thailand* 泰王国 **2 the kingdom of** an imaginary place where a particular thing or quality has the greatest influence〔以某物或某品质为主宰的〕领域: *the kingdom of love* 爱情王国 **3 the animal/plant/mineral kingdom** one of the three parts into which the natural world is divided 动物界/植物界/矿物界〔大自然三界〕 **4 the kingdom of heaven/God** heaven 天国 **5 blow sb/sth to kingdom come** *informal* to completely destroy someone or something【非正式】把〔某人〕送上西天；彻底摧毁〔某物〕 **6 wait till kingdom come** to wait for ever 永远等待

king·fish·er /ˈkɪŋˌfɪʃɚ; ˈkɪŋˌfɪʃə/ *n* [C] a small brightly-coloured bird with a blue body that eats fish in rivers 翠鸟〔一种食河鱼的鸟〕

King James Bi·ble, the /ˌ· ˌ ˈ· ·/ also 又作 **the King James Version** an English translation of the Bible produced for King James I of England in 1611, which is also known in Britain as the **Authorized Version**. For hundreds of years this was the main type of Bible used in both the US and the UK, and many well-known SAYINGS from the Bible come from this translation. It is now used much less often and has been replaced by more modern translations. 钦定本英文《圣经》〔又名英王詹姆士一世钦定《圣经》英译本，成书于1611年。数百年来一直是美英使用的主要《圣经》版本。许多《圣经》名言来自该译本。现已较少使用，为现代译本所取代〕

King Kong /ˌkɪŋ ˈkɑŋ; ˌkɪŋ ˈkɒŋ/ a very large GORILLA who is the main character in the film *King Kong* (1933). He is taken to New York City, but he escapes and destroys buildings and hurts or kills many people. 金刚〔电影《金刚》(1933)的主角。它是一只大猩猩，被运到了纽约市，逃脱后开始破坏房屋，并伤害了许多人〕

King Lear /ˌkɪŋ ˈlɪr; ˌkɪŋ ˈlɪə/ a play by William Shakespeare about an old king who decides to divide his KINGDOM among his three daughters according to how much each of them says she loves him. Two daughters, Goneril and Regan, pretend to love him very much, and he divides the kingdom between them. The third daughter, Cordelia, is the only one who really loves him, but she receives nothing because she says that she loves him no more and no less than she should. As a result there are many sad and terrible events, including the deaths of Lear and his three daughters. 《李尔王》〔威廉·莎士比亚创作的剧本，讲述一位老国王决定按三个女儿说爱他的程度来分割王国。大女儿高纳里尔和二女儿里根装出十分爱他的样子，国王据此把王国分给了她们。其实，唯有三女儿考狄利娅真正爱他，但因为她的表白很实在，所以什么也没有得到。结果导致了一系列的悲剧，李尔王和他的三个女儿全部丧生〕

king·ly /ˈkɪŋlɪ; ˈkɪŋli/ *adj* good enough for a king, or typical of a king 国王的；配得上国王身份的；有皇家气派的: *a kingly feast* 豪华盛宴

king·mak·er /ˈkɪŋˌmekɚ; ˈkɪŋˌmeɪkə/ *n* [C] someone who influences the choice of people for important jobs 对任命要职人员有影响力的人

King of Loving, A /ˌ· · ˈ· ·/ a book by Stan Barstow that tells the story of a young WORKING-CLASS man who marries a woman he does not love after she becomes pregnant. The book was made into a film and was one of several British books of the 1960s that told the stories of ordinary people in a realistic way. 《一种爱情》〔斯坦·巴斯托创作的小说，讲述一名年轻的工薪阶层男子让一个他不爱的女子怀了孕而与其奉子成婚的故事。该小说被改编成电影，是20世纪60年代以现实主义方式讲述普通人生活的英国小说之一〕

King of the Jews /ˌ· · · ˈ·/ in the New Testament of the Bible, another name for Jesus 犹太人之王〔《圣经·新约》中耶稣的别称〕

king·pin /ˈkɪŋˌpɪn; ˈkɪŋˌpɪn/ *n* [C usually singular 一般用单数] **1** the most important person or thing in a group〔在某群体中〕最重要的人[事物]；领袖 **2** *technical* a thin strong piece of metal used in hinges (HINGE[1])【术语】〔铰链的〕中心轴，转向立轴

King's Bench, the /ˌ· ˈ·/ also 又作 **the King's Bench Division** /ˌ· ˈ· ˌ· ·/ part of the High Court of Justice in England and Wales. This name is used during the times when Britain is ruled by a king. 王座法庭〔英格兰和威尔士高等法院的组成部分。该名称用于英国国王执政时期〕— compare 比较 the QUEEN'S BENCH

King's Col·lege Chap·el /ˌ· ˌ· · ˈ· ·/ a beautiful old church which is part of King's College, one of the colleges of the University of Cambridge, in eastern England 国王学院礼拜堂〔英格兰东部剑桥大学国王学院的一座美丽而古老的教堂〕

King's Coun·sel /ˌ· ˈ· ·/ *n* a KC 王室法律顾问

King's Cross /ˌ· ˈ·◂/ an area in north central London that has two important railway stations, King's Cross and St Pancras, from which trains go to Scotland and northeast England 国王十字区〔伦敦中北部一地区，建有两座重要火车站，即国王十字火车站和圣潘克拉斯火车站。火车由此驶往苏格兰和英格兰东北部〕

King's Eng·lish, the /ˌ· ˈ· ·/ *n* *old-fashioned* correct English, as it is spoken in Britain【过时】标准[规范]英语 —see also 另见 QUEEN'S ENGLISH

king's ev·i·dence /ˌ· ˈ· · ·/ *n* **turn King's evidence** *BrE* to give information about other criminals in order to get a less severe punishment【英】〔罪犯为减刑〕提供对同案犯不利的证据，〔罪犯〕作为污点证人指控同党; STATE'S EVIDENCE *AmE*【美】—see also 另见 QUEEN'S EVIDENCE

king·ship /ˈkɪŋʃɪp; ˈkɪŋʃɪp/ *n* [U] the official position or condition of being a king 王权，王位: *the responsibilities of kingship* 王权的责任

king-size /ˈ· ·/ also 又作 **king-sized** *adj* **1** very large, and usually the largest size of something 大号的；特大号的: *a king-size bed* 特大的床 **2** *informal* very big or strong【非正式】极大的；极强烈的: *a king-size thirst* 极强的渴望

Kings·ley /ˈkɪŋzlɪ; ˈkɪŋzli/, **Charles** (1819-75) a British writer of historical NOVELS such as *Westward Ho!* and *Hereward the Wake*, who also wrote the children's story *The Water Babies*. 金斯利〔(1819-1875)，英国历史小说作家。他创作了《向西方!》和《觉醒者赫里沃德》等小说，还著有儿童读物《水孩儿》〕

Kings Road, the /ˌ· ˈ·/ a fashionable, expensive shopping street in London which was a very famous place for young people to spend time and buy clothes in the 1960s 国王大道〔伦敦一新潮高档购物街。20世纪60年代，这里曾是年轻人休闲或购买时装的著名商业街〕

Kings·ton /ˈkɪŋstn; ˈkɪŋstən/ the capital city of Jamaica and the island's business centre, main port, and largest town 金斯顿〔牙买加首都，是该国商业中心、主要港口和最大城市〕

King Tut /kɪŋ ˈtut; kɪŋ ˈtʊt/ —see 见 TUTANKHAMEN

kink[1] /kɪŋk; kɪŋk/ *n* [C] **1** a twist in something that is normally straight 扭结；绞缠: [**+in**] *The water hose had a kink in it.* 水龙软管有一处扭结。**2** something strange or dangerous in your character〔某人性格中〕奇特[危险]的成分；怪癖

kink[2] *v* [I,T] to get or give something a kink (使)扭结；(使)绞缠

kink·y /ˈkɪŋkɪ; ˈkɪŋki/ *adj* **1** *informal* someone who is kinky, or does kinky things, has strange ways of getting sexual excitement【非正式】〔性行为〕变态的 **2** kinky hair has a lot of small curves〔头发〕鬈曲的 —**kinkiness** *n* [U] —**kinkily** *adv*

Kin·sey /ˈkɪnzɪ; ˈkɪnzi/, **Al·fred Charles** /ˈælfrɪd tʃɑrlz; ˈælfrɪd tʃɑːlz/ (1894-1956) a US scientist who studied human sexual behaviour. His two books, *Sexual Behavior in the Human Male* (1948) and *Sexual Behavior in the Human Female* (1953), usually called the *Kinsey Reports*, showed that people's sexual practices were very different from what most people had thought. 金赛〔(1894-1956)，美国科学家。他曾致力于人类性行为的研究，著有《男性性行为》(1948)和《女性性行为》(1953)(也称《金赛报告》)，表明人类的性行为与多数人已有的观点大相径庭〕

kins·folk /ˈkɪnzˌfok; ˈkɪnzfəʊk/ also 又作 **kinfolk** *AmE*【美】*n* [plural] *old-fashioned* your family【过时】家人；亲属

Kinshasa /kɪnˈʃɑsə; kɪnˈʃɑːsə/ the capital city of the Democratic Republic of Congo, on the River Congo, formerly called Leopoldville 金沙萨〔刚果民主共和国首都，濒临刚果河，旧称利奥波德维尔〕

kin·ship /ˈkɪnʃɪp; ˈkɪnʃɪp/ *n* **1** [U+**with**] *literary* a family relationship【文】亲属关系: *the ties of kinship* 亲属关系 **2** [singular, U] a strong connection between people 紧密联系: [**+with/between**] *Poe shows his kinship with his literary ancestors.* 坡显示出他和他的文学先辈之间的密切联系。

kins·man /ˈkɪnzmən; ˈkɪnzmən/ *n* [C] *old use* a male relative【旧】男性亲戚

kin·swom·an /ˈkɪnzˌwumən; ˈkɪnzˌwʊmən/ *n* [C] *old use* a female relative【旧】女性亲戚

ki·osk /kɪˈɑsk; ˈkiːɒsk/ *n* [C] **1** a small building in the street where newspapers, sweets etc are sold〔街上出售报纸、糖果等

的）小亭 **2** *BrE old-fashioned* a public telephone box【英，过时】公用电话亭

kip[1] /kɪp; kɪp/ *n* [singular,U] *BrE informal* a period of sleep【英，非正式】一段睡眠时间：**have a kip** (=sleep for a short time) 睡一觉 | **get some kip** *I'm going to lie down and try to get some kip.* 我想躺下睡一会儿。

kip[2] *v* **kipped, kipping** [I] *BrE informal*【英，非正式】**1** to sleep 睡觉 **2** to lie down in order to sleep 躺下睡觉：**[+down]** *kipping down for the night* 晚间上床睡觉

Kip·ling /ˈkɪplɪŋ; ˈkɪplɪŋ/, **Rud·yard** /ˈrʌdjɚd; ˈrʌdjəd/ (1865-1936) a British writer born in India. He is famous for his NOVELs, poems, and short stories set in that country, especially his popular children's story *The Jungle Book*, and for poems such as *Gunga Din* and *If*. He won the Nobel Prize for Literature in 1907. He is sometimes criticized now as being a strong supporter of the British Empire and British Imperialism. 吉卜林〔1865-1936〕，英国作家。他生于印度，他的以印度为背景的小说、诗歌和短篇故事很有名，尤其是流行儿童读物《丛林故事》及诗歌《贡格·丁》和《如果》。1907年，他荣获诺贝尔文学奖。现在，人们有时对他提出批评，说他是大英帝国和英帝国主义的坚定支持者〕

kip·per /ˈkɪpɚ; ˈkɪpə/ *n* [C] a type of fish that has been preserved using smoke and salt 腌熏鲱鱼 —**kippered** *adj*: *kippered herring* 熏鲱鱼

Kir·ghiz·i·a /kɪrˈgɪzɪə; kɜːˈgɪziə/ another name for KYRGYZSTAN 吉尔吉斯斯坦〔Kyrgyzstan 的别称〕

Kir·i·bat·i /ˌkɪrɪˈbɑtɪ; ˌkɪrɪˈbɑːti/ a country in the Pacific Ocean, consisting of 33 islands. Population 94,149 (2001). Capital: Bairiki. It was formerly ruled by the UK and called the Gilbert Islands, but has been independent since 1979. 基里巴斯〔太平洋一岛国，由33座岛屿组成。人口：94,149（2001），首都：拜里基。该国原为英国统治，称吉伯特群岛，1979年独立〕

kirk /kɝk; kɜːk/ *n ScotE*【苏格兰】**1** [C] a church 教堂 **2 the Kirk** the Church of Scotland 苏格兰教会

Kirk /kɝk; kɜːk/, **Captain** one of the main characters in the television programme *Star Trek*, whose full name is **Captain James T. Kirk**. Captain Kirk is a brave, determined man who is in charge of the Starship Enterprise. 柯克〔电视剧《星际旅行》的主人公，全名为詹姆斯·T.柯克船长。他勇敢无畏、意志坚定，负责管理"创业"号星际飞船〕

Kirk·wall /ˈkɝkwɔl; ˈkɜːkwɔːl/ a town on the largest island of the Orkney islands, where the local government for the islands is based 柯克沃尔〔奥克尼群岛最大岛屿上的一座城镇，为当地政府所在地〕

kirsch /kɪrʃ; kɪəʃ/ *n* [U] a strong alcoholic drink made from CHERRY (1) juice 樱桃酒〔一种烈性酒〕

kis·met /ˈkɪzmɛt; ˈkɪzmet/ *n* [U] *literary* the things that will happen to you in your life; FATE (1)【文】命运，天命

3 3 **kiss**[1] /kɪs; kɪs/ *v* **1** [I,T] to touch someone with your lips as a greeting or to show them love 吻：*They kissed again, passionately.* 他们再一次热烈地亲吻。| **kiss sb on** *Did he kiss you on the cheek or on the mouth?* 他吻了你的脸还是嘴？| **kiss sb goodbye/goodnight etc** *Kiss Daddy goodnight.* 亲亲爸爸说晚安。**2** [T] to touch something with your lips as a sign of respect 用唇接触〔以示敬意〕：*She raised the crucifix to her lips and kissed it.* 她把十字架举到嘴边亲吻了一下。**3 sb can kiss goodbye to sth/kiss sth goodbye** *informal* used when you think it is certain that someone will lose their chance of getting or doing something【非正式】〔某人〕肯定会失去…的机会：*If you don't work harder you can kiss goodbye to your chances of going to university.* 如果你不加把劲学习，你上大学的机会肯定十分渺茫。**4 kiss sth away/ better** *spoken* an expression meaning to take away the pain of something by kissing someone, used especially with children【口】亲亲就不痛了；吻掉〔尤用于对孩子说话〕：*Here, let Mommy kiss it better.* 来，让妈妈亲亲就不那么痛了。**5 kiss my ass** *AmE taboo slang* an insulting expression used to show that you do not respect someone【美，讳，俚】去你的〔侮辱性用语〕**6 kiss (sb's) ass** *AmE taboo slang* to be too nice to someone who can give you something you want【美，讳，俚】拍马屁，巴结〔某人〕—compare 比较 KISS-ASS **7** [T] *literary* if the wind, sun etc kisses something, it gently moves or touches it【文】〔风、阳光等〕轻拂；轻触

CULTURAL NOTE 文化注释

People usually only kiss someone on the mouth if they are having a romantic relationship. Parents and children will also kiss each other on the cheek or FOREHEAD. People also sometimes kiss each other on the cheek in order to greet each other or say goodbye. Sometimes, especially in the UK, people kiss hello or goodbye on both cheeks. It is fairly common for people, when they are kissing someone on the cheek, to not actually kiss them, but instead to make a kissing movement next to their cheek. In both the US and the UK, it is unusual for men to kiss each other unless they are GAY. 通常只有恋爱的人才亲吻嘴唇。父母和子女相互之间会亲吻面颊和前额。人们在问候和道别时有时也会互相亲吻脸颊。有时人们会在左右两边的脸颊上各亲一下，这在英国尤其常见。通常人们在靠近对方的脸颊时并不真的会亲一下，而是仅仅做出亲的动作。在美国和英国，除了同性恋之外，男人们是不会相互亲吻的。— see also 另见 HUG

kiss up to sb *phr v* [T] *AmE informal* to try to please someone in order to get them to do something for you【美，非正式】〔为了让某人做某事而〕奉承：*That guy got his promotion by kissing up to the boss.* 那家伙对老板阿谀奉承才得到了提升。

kiss[2] *n* [C] **1** an act of kissing 吻，接吻：*Do you remember your first kiss?* 你记得你的初吻吗？| **give sb a kiss** *Come and give your old Grandma a kiss.* 过来吻一下你年迈的奶奶。**2 the kiss of death** *informal* something that spoils or ruins a plan, activity etc【非正式】损害[破坏]计划[活动等]的事 —see also 另见 FRENCH KISS, KISS OF LIFE, **blow sb a kiss** (BLOW[1] (16))

kiss·a·gram *n* [C] another spelling of KISSOGRAM kissogram 的另一种拼法

kiss-ass /ˈ· ·/ *adj* [only before noun 仅用于名词前] *AmE slang* a very impolite word used to describe the behaviour of someone who tries too hard to please other people【美俚】拍马屁的〔粗俗用语〕

kiss·ing cous·in /ˌ·· ˈ··/ *n* [C] *AmE old-fashioned* someone you are not closely related to, but whom you know well【美，过时】关系亲密的人

Kis·sin·ger /ˈkɪsɪndʒɚ; ˈkɪsɪndʒə/, **Henry** (1923-) a US politician and university teacher, who was born in Germany and who was the US Secretary of State from 1973 to 1977. He won the Nobel Peace Prize in 1973 for helping to achieve the agreement that ended the Vietnam War. 基辛格〔（1923- ），美国政治家、大学教师。他出生于德国，1973至1977年任美国国务卿，1973年因促成越战停战协议而获得诺贝尔和平奖〕

kiss of life /ˌ· · ˈ·/ *n* **1 give sb the kiss of life** *especially BrE* to make someone start breathing again by blowing air into their lungs when they have almost DROWNED etc【尤英】对某人进行人工呼吸 **2** something that helps you continue an activity that you thought would fail 使…起死回生的事物：*a grant that was a kiss of life to the project* 使这项工程起死回生的拨款

kiss·o·gram, kissagram /ˈkɪsəˌgræm; ˈkɪsəgræm/ *n* [C] a humorous greeting for your BIRTHDAY etc that is delivered by someone in a special COSTUME, or the person who delivers it and kisses you 亲吻电报〔一种幽默的祝贺生日等的方式，由穿着特殊服装的人转达祝辞并亲吻被祝贺者〕；送亲吻电报的人

kit[1] /kɪt; kɪt/ *n* **1 shaving/sewing/repair kit** [C] a set of tools, equipment etc that you use for a particular purpose or activity 剃须/缝纫/修理等用的成套工具 **2** [C] something such as furniture that you buy in parts and put together yourself 成套的组合部件〈如家具〉：*He made the model from a kit.* 他用一套元件组装成模型。**3** *BrE* [U] a set of clothes and equipment that you use when playing a sport【英】〔运动用的〕成套服装和用品：*football kit* 成套足球用品 **4** [U] a set of clothes and equipment used by soldiers, SAILORs etc〔士兵、水手等的〕成套服装和设备：*survival kit* 一套救生用品 **5 the whole kit and caboodle** *old-fashioned* everything【过时】全部，一切 —see also 另见 FIRST AID KIT, TOOL KIT

kit[2] *v* **kitting, kitted** *especially BrE*【尤英】

kit sb **out** *phr v* [T] **1** to provide someone with the clothes and equipment they need for an activity 向〔某人〕提供〔进行某种活动〕所必需的服装和设备 **2 be kitted out/up** to have the correct clothes and equipment to do a particular activity 配备必需的装备：*all kitted out in waterproof clothes* 配齐了防水服装

kit bag, kitbag /ˈkɪt bæg; ˈkɪt bæg/ *n* [C] *especially BrE* a long narrow bag used by soldiers, SAILORs etc, for carrying their clothes and other possessions【尤英】〔士兵、水手等使用的长而窄的〕背包；行李袋

kitch·en /ˈkɪtʃɪn; ˈkɪtʃɪn/ *n* [C] **1** the room where you prepare and cook food 厨房：*Can you help me carry these dishes into the kitchen?* 你能帮我把这些碟子拿到厨房去吗？| *the kitchen table* 厨房用桌 **2 everything but the kitchen sink** *humorous* used when someone has brought too many things with them【幽默】能带来的都带了〔用于表示某人带来过多的东西〕 1 2

kitchen cab·i·net /ˌ·· ˈ···/ *n* [C] an informal group of people who advise the leader of the government〔政府首脑的〕私人顾问团, 智囊团, 厨房内阁

Kitch·en·er /ˈkɪtʃɪnə; ˈkɪtʃnə/, **Ho·ra·ti·o** /həˈreʃɪo; həˈreɪʃiəʊ/ (1850-1916) a British army officer, also known as **Lord Kitchener**, who fought successfully in the Boer War. During World War I he was responsible for building up the British army, and his picture appeared on a famous POSTER with the words 'Your country wants YOU, Join your country's army, God save the King'. 基钦纳〔(1850-1916), 英国陆军军官, 又称基钦纳勋爵, 曾在布尔战争中大获全胜。一战期间, 他负责组建英国陆军, 他的画像印在一张著名的海报上, 上面写着"祖国需要你, 请加入祖国的军队。天佑吾王"〕

kitchen gar·den /ˌ·· ˈ··/ *n* [C] a part of a garden where you grow your own fruit and vegetables 家庭菜园

kitchen roll /ˈ·· ·/ *BrE*【英】also 又作 **kitchen tow·el** /ˈ·· ˌ··/ *n* [U] thick paper used for cleaning up small amounts of liquid, food etc 厨房洁纸

kitchen sink dra·ma /ˌ·· ˈ· ˌ··/ *n* [C] *BrE* a serious play or film about problems that families have at home【英】厨房水槽剧〔描写家庭问题的严肃剧或电影〕

kite[1] /kaɪt; kaɪt/ *n* [C] **1** a light frame covered in coloured paper or plastic that you let fly in the air on the end of one or two long strings 风筝 **2** a type of HAWK (=bird that eats small animals) 鸢〔鹰的一种, 以小动物为食〕**3** *AmE informal* an illegal cheque【美, 非正式】空头支票; 假支票 **4 fly a kite** to make a suggestion to see what people will think of it 试探舆论 —see also 另见 **go fly a kite** (FLY[1] (21)), **high as a kite** (HIGH[1] (14))

kite[2] *v* **kited, kiting** [I,T] *AmE informal*【美, 非正式】**1** also 又作 **kite up** to raise the cost of something 提高〔费用〕; *Soaring medical costs keep kiting up insurance premiums.* 迅速增加的医疗费用使得保险费猛升。**2** to obtain money using an illegal cheque 开〔空头支票〕; 使用假支票骗钱

kite-fly·ing /ˈ· ˌ··/ *n* [U] **1** the game or sport of flying a kite 放风筝 **2** the act of telling people about an idea, plan etc in order to get their opinion 试探风声[反应]

kith and kin /ˌkɪθ ən ˈkɪn; ˌkɪθ ən ˈkɪn/ *n* [plural] *old-fashioned* family and friends【过时】家人和朋友, 亲友

kitsch /kɪtʃ; kɪtʃ/ *n* [U] kitsch decorations, films etc that are made without much serious thought and are SENTIMENTAL and often amuse people because of this 俗气的装饰; 庸俗的文艺作品 —**kitsch** *adj*

kit·ten /ˈkɪtn̩; ˈkɪtn/ *n* [C] **1** a young cat 小猫 **2 have kittens** *informal* to be very anxious or upset about something【非正式】焦虑; 烦躁

kit·ten·ish /ˈkɪtnɪʃ; ˈkɪtn-ɪʃ/ *adj old-fashioned* a kittenish woman behaves in a silly way in order to attract men【过时】〔女人〕卖弄风情的, 搔首弄姿的

kit·ty /ˈkɪtɪ; ˈkɪti/ *n* **1** [C usually singular 一般用单数] the money that people have collected for a particular purpose〔为某目的〕凑集起来的钱款: *How much money is there left in the kitty?* 公共储金还剩下多少钱? **2** [C usually singular 一般用单数] the money that the winner of a game of cards receives〔纸牌戏中的〕全部赌注 **3** [C] a word for a cat, used especially by children 小猫, 猫咪〔尤为儿语〕

kitty-cor·ner /ˌ·· ˈ··/ *adv AmE informal* on the opposite corner of a street from a particular place【美, 非正式】在街道斜对面; 成对角线地: [**+from/to**] *The drugstore is kitty-corner from the bank.* 药店在银行的斜对面。

Kitty Hawk /ˈ·· ˌ·/ the place in North Carolina, in the US, where the Wright brothers made the world's first successful flight in a plane in 1903 基蒂霍克〔美国北卡罗来纳州一地名。1903 年, 莱特兄弟在此进行了世界上第一次载人飞行, 并获得成功〕

Ki·wa·nis, the /kɪˈwanɪz; kɪˈwɑːniz/ a US organization whose members work together to support their local areas, especially by doing CHARITY work. The Kiwanis have clubs all over the US, especially in small towns. A member of the club is called a **Kiwani**. 基瓦尼斯〔美国一组织。其成员主要通过慈善活动共同为所在地区服务。基瓦尼斯会所遍及全美国, 特别是小城镇。该组织成员称 Kiwani〕

ki·wi /ˈkiwɪ; ˈkiːwiː/ *n* [C] **1** a New Zealand bird that has very short wings and cannot fly 鹬鸵, 几维〔新西兰的一种短翅不会飞翔的鸟〕**2** *informal* someone from New Zealand【非正式】新西兰人

kiwi fruit /ˈ·· ·/ *n* [C] a small sweet fruit with a brown skin, which is green inside 猕猴桃, 奇异果 —see picture on page A8 参见 A8 页图

KKK /ˌke ke ˈke; ˌkeɪ keɪ ˈkeɪ/ *n* the abbreviation of 缩写= KU KLUX KLAN

klans·man /ˈklænzmən; ˈklænzmən/ *n* [C] *AmE* a member of the Ku Klux Klan【美】三 K 党成员

klax·on /ˈklæksn; ˈklæksən/ *n* [C] a loud horn that was fixed onto police cars and other official vehicles in the past〔旧时安装在警车及其他官方车辆上的〕高音喇叭, 警报器

Klee /kle; kleɪ/, **Paul** (1879-1940) a Swiss painter of ABSTRACT art 克利〔(1879-1940), 瑞士抽象派画家〕

Kleen·ex /ˈklinɛks; ˈkliːneks/ *n* [C,U] *trademark* a TISSUE (1)【商标】舒洁纸巾; 纸巾

klep·to·ma·ni·a /ˌklɛptəˈmenɪə; ˌkleptəˈmeɪniə/ *n* [U] a mental illness in which you have a desire to steal things 盗窃癖, 偷窃狂

klep·to·ma·ni·ac /ˌklɛptəˈmenɪæk; ˌkleptəˈmeɪniæk/ also 又作 **klep·to** /ˈklɛpto; ˈkleptəʊ/ *informal*【非正式】*n* [C] someone suffering from kleptomania 有盗窃癖的人, 偷窃狂者

Klimt /klɪmt, klɪmt/, **Gustav** /ˈgʊstɑf; ˈgʊstɑːf/ (1862-1918) an Austrian artist who was the founder of the Vienna Secession, the Austrian art nouveau movement. 克里木特〔(1862-1918), 奥地利画家, 奥地利新艺术运动"维也纳分离派"创始人〕

Klin·gon /ˈklɪŋgɑn; ˈklɪŋgɒn/ an imaginary race of AGGRESSIVE people from another planet, who appeared in the television series *Star Trek*. 克林贡人〔电视连续剧《星际旅行》中一假想的具有攻击力的外星人〕

Klon·dike, the /ˈklɑndaɪk; ˈklɒndaɪk/ an area in northwest Canada, in the Yukon. Gold was discovered there in the 1890s, and this caused a Gold Rush (=when many people go to an area to look for gold). 克朗代克〔位于加拿大西北部育空地区, 19 世纪 90 年代曾发现金矿, 从而引起一阵淘金热〕

klutz, clutz /klʌts; klʌts/ *n* [C] *AmE* someone who drops things and falls easily【美】笨手笨脚的人 —**klutzy** *adj*

km *n* the written abbreviation of 缩写= KILOMETRE

knack /næk; næk/ *n informal*【非正式】**1** [singular] a special skill or ability that you usually gain by practice 窍门, 技能, 本领: *There's a knack to starting our lawn mower.* 发动我们那台刈草机有个窍门。**2 have a knack of doing sth** to have a tendency to do something 有做某事的习惯: *He has a knack of saying the wrong thing.* 他总爱说一些不合时宜的话。

knack·er /ˈnækə; ˈnækə/ also 又作 **knacker out** *v* [T] *BrE spoken*【英口】**1** to become extremely tired 使精疲力竭: **knacker yourself out** *Slow down – you'll knacker yourself out!* 放慢点儿, 你这样会累坏的! **2 knacker your elbow/hand etc** to hurt your elbow etc so that you cannot use it 使胳膊肘/手等受伤致残

knack·ered /ˈnækəd; ˈnækəd/ *adj BrE spoken*【英口】**1** extremely tired 极累的, 精疲力竭的 **2** too old or broken to use 旧[破]得不能用的: *a knackered old bike* 旧得不能骑的自行车

knackers' yard /ˈ·· ˌ·/ also 又作 **knacker's** *n* [C] *BrE*【英】**1** a place where horses are killed 宰马场 **2 ready for the knacker's yard** too old to be useful or work properly 旧得不能用

knap·sack /ˈnæpˌsæk; ˈnæpsæk/ *n* [C] a bag that you carry on your shoulders 背包

knave /nev; neɪv/ *n* [C] **1** *BrE* the playing card with a value between the ten and queen; JACK[1] (2)【英】杰克〔纸牌中介于十点与王后之间的一张牌〕—see also 另见 **cards** (CARD[1] (7)) **2** *old-fashioned* a dishonest boy or man【过时】狡诈的男孩[男人] —**knavish** *adj* —**knavishly** *adv*

knav·e·ry /ˈnevərɪ; ˈneɪvəri/ *n* [C,U] *old use* dishonest behaviour【旧】无赖行为, 不诚实的行为

knead /nid; niːd/ *v* [T] **1** to press a mixture of flour and water many times with your hands 揉, 捏〔湿面粉〕: *Knead the dough for three minutes.* 将面团揉三分钟。—see picture on page A11 参见 A11 页图 **2** to press someone's muscles many times in order to help cure pain 按摩, 推揉

knee[1] /ni; niː/ *n* [C] **1** the joint that bends in the middle of your leg 膝, 膝盖: *Lift using your knees, not your back.* 举的时候膝盖用力, 而不是背部用力。—see picture at 参见 BODY 图 **2** the part of your clothes that covers your knee〔裤子的〕膝部: *holes in both knees* 裤子膝部的破口子 **3 on sb's knee** on the top part of your legs when you are sitting down 在某人膝上: *Daddy, can I sit on your knee?* 爸爸, 我能坐你的腿上吗? **4 with your knees knocking (together)** feeling very afraid or very cold 怕[冷]得双膝颤抖 **5 on your knees** in a way that shows you have no power or are very sorry 跪下〔表示没有能力或悲伤〕: *He begged me, on his knees, to forgive him.* 他双膝跪下乞求我原谅他。**6 bring sb/sth to their knees a)** to defeat a country or group of people in a war〔在战争中〕打败〔某一国家或一队人马〕**b)** to have such a bad effect on an organization, activity etc that it cannot continue 使〔组织、活动等〕难以继续: *The recession has brought many companies to their knees.* 经济衰退使许

多公司难以维持。**7 put sb over your knee** *old-fashioned* to punish a child by hitting them【过时】打孩子〔以示惩罚〕**8 on bended knee(s)** *old-fashioned* in a way that shows great respect for someone【过时】跪着〔表示对某人极大的敬意〕: *worshipping on bended knee* 跪拜 —see also 另见 **knee/elbow pad** (PAD¹ (1)), **learn/be taught sth at your mother's knee** (MOTHER¹ (5)), **the bee's knees** (BEE (4)), **weak at the knees** (WEAK (11))

knee² *v* [T+in] to hit someone with your knee 用膝盖碰撞: *I kneed him in the groin.* 我用膝盖撞击他的阴部。

knee breech·es /ˈ· ˌ·/ *n* [plural] tight trousers that end at your knee, worn especially in the past〔尤指旧时人们穿的〕齐膝紧身短裤

knee cap /ˈ· ·/ *n* [C] the bone at the front of your knee 髌骨, 膝盖骨 —see picture at 参见 SKELETON 图

knee·cap /ˈniˌkæp; ˈniːkæp/ *v* **kneecapped, kneecapping** [T] to shoot someone's kneecaps as an unofficial punishment 枪击〔某人〕的膝盖骨〔作为一种非法的报复手段〕

knee-deep /ˌ· ˈ·◂/ *adj* **1** deep enough to reach your knees 齐膝深的: **[+in]** *knee-deep in mud* 陷入齐膝深的烂泥 **2** *informal* having a lot of something【非正式】非常多的: **[+in]** *knee-deep in work* 工作繁多

knee-high¹ /ˌ· ˈ·◂/ *adj* **1** tall enough to reach your knees 齐膝高的, 没膝的: *knee-high grass* 齐膝高的草 **2 knee-high to a grasshopper** *old-fashioned* used when talking about the past to say that someone was a very small child then【过时】〔某人〕还是很小的孩子时

knee-high² *n* [C] a sock that ends just below your knee〔高及膝盖下的〕长筒袜

knee-jerk /ˈ· ·/ *adj* a knee-jerk reaction, opinion etc is what you feel or say about a situation from habit, without thinking about it 本能[自动]反应的

kneel 跪

kneel /nil; niːl/ also 又作 **kneel down** *v past tense and past participle* **knelt** /nɛlt; nelt/ also 又作 **kneeled** *AmE*【美】[I] to be in or move into a position where your body is resting on your knees 跪, 跪着, 跪下: *a statue of a kneeling figure* 一尊下跪者的塑像 | **[+on]** *We knelt on the floor to have a good look at the map.* 我们跪在地板上仔细查看地图。

knee-length /ˈ· ·/ *adj* long or tall enough to reach your knees 长[高]及膝部的: *a knee-length skirt* 长及膝部的裙子

knees-up /ˈ· ·/ *n* [C] *BrE informal* a noisy party【英, 非正式】喧闹的集会: *After the wedding there was a bit of a knees-up.* 婚礼之后是一小阵子喧闹的庆祝活动。

knell /nɛl; nel/ *n* [C] *literary* the sound of a bell being rung slowly because someone has died【文】丧钟 —see also 另见 DEATH KNELL

Knes·set, the /ˈknɛsɛt; ˈkneset/ the Israeli parliament 克拉赛〔以色列议会〕

knew /nju; njuː/ *v* the past tense of KNOW¹

knick·er·bock·ers /ˈnɪkɚˌbɑkɚz; ˈnɪkəˌbɒkəz/ *n* [plural] short loose trousers that fit tightly at your knees, worn especially in the past〔尤指旧时穿的膝部扎紧的〕灯笼裤

knick·ers /ˈnɪkɚz; ˈnɪkəz/ *n* [plural] *BrE informal*【英, 非正式】**1** a piece of women's underwear worn between your waist and the top of your legs; PANTIES 女用短衬裤: *a pair of frilly knickers* 一条镶褶边的女用短衬裤 —see picture at 参见 UNDERWEAR 图 **2** *AmE* KNICKERBOCKERS【美】〔膝部扎紧的〕灯笼裤 **3 get your knickers in a twist** *BrE spoken* to get upset【英口】感到不快, 恼火

knick-knack /ˈnɪkˌnæk; ˈnɪk næk/ *n* [C] a small object used as a decoration 小装饰品, 小摆设: *They had various knick-knacks on the top of the bookcase.* 他们的书柜顶上放有各种小摆设。

knives 刀

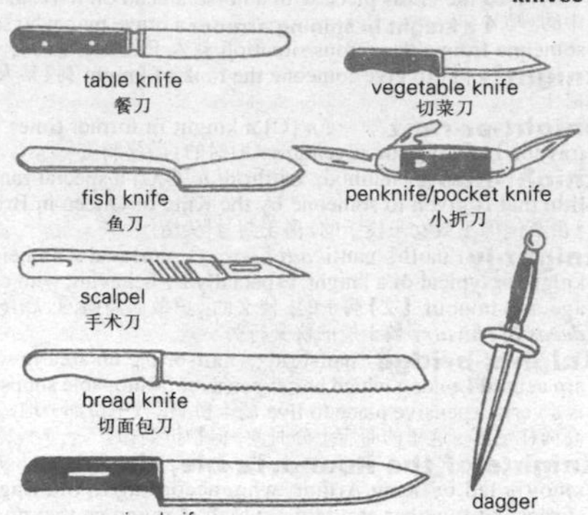

knife¹ /naɪf; naɪf/ *n plural* **knives** /naɪvz; naɪvz/ [C] **1** a metal blade fixed into a handle, used for cutting or as a weapon〔有柄的〕刀: *knife and fork* 刀叉 | *He had been stabbed with a knife.* 他被刀扎伤了。| **kitchen/bread/vegetable etc knife** (=knife used in the kitchen, for cutting bread etc) 厨房用刀/面包刀/菜刀等 —see picture on page A11 参见 A11 页图 **2 the knives are out** *informal* used to say that people are being extremely unfriendly to each other【非正式】剑拔弩张 **3 have/get your knife into someone** *informal* to dislike someone and be very unfriendly towards them【非正式】讨厌[敌视]某人 **4 twist/turn the knife** to say something that makes someone more upset about a subject they are already unhappy about 火上浇油 **5 under the knife** *humorous* having a medical operation【幽默】在手术刀下, 做手术 **6 you could cut the atmosphere/air with a knife** used to say that you felt the people in a room were angry with each other〔屋内人之间的紧张气氛〕使人透不过气 —see also 另见 PAPER KNIFE

knife² *v* [T+in] to put a knife into someone's body; STAB¹ (1) 用刀扎〔某人〕

knife-edge /ˈ· ·/ *n* **1 be on a knife-edge a)** to be in a situation in which the result is extremely uncertain 对结果毫无把握: *Success or failure is balanced on a knife-edge.* 是成功还是失败仍是未知数。**b)** very anxious about the future result of something 急于知道结果, 对结果焦虑不安: *She is on a knife-edge about her promotion.* 她急于想知道自己晋升的情况。**2** [singular] something that is narrow or sharp 窄长[锋利]的东西: *The cliff narrowed down to a knife-edge.* 悬崖逐渐变窄, 形似刀刃。

knight 骑士, 武士

knight¹ /naɪt; naɪt/ *n* [C] **1** a man with a high rank in former times who was trained to fight while riding a horse 骑士, 武士: *knights in armour* 披盔戴甲的骑士 —see also 另见 WHITE KNIGHT **2** a man who has received a knighthood and has the title 'SIR'

(4) before his name 爵士〔受封为爵士的人，其名前冠有 Sir 这一头衔〕**3** the CHESS piece with a horse's head on it〔国际象棋中的〕马 **4 a knight in shining armour** a brave man who saves someone from a dangerous situation 救人于危难之中的勇士

knight² *v* [T] to give someone the rank of knight 封〔某人〕为爵士

knight-er·rant /ˌ· ˈ· ·/ *n* [C] a knight in former times who travelled looking for adventure〔旧时的〕游侠骑士

knight·hood /ˈnaɪthʊd; ˈnaɪthʊd/ *n* [C,U] a special rank or title that is given to someone by the King or Queen in Britain〔由英国国王或女王授予的〕爵士封号[头衔]

knight·ly /ˈnaɪtlɪ; ˈnaɪtli/ *adj literary* connected with being a knight or typical of a knight, especially by behaving with courage and honour【文】骑士的；侠义的；勇敢而高尚的：*knightly deeds of chivalry* 骑士般的侠义行为

Knights·bridge /ˈnaɪtsbrɪdʒ; ˈnaɪtsbrɪdʒ/ an area in western central London which has expensive, fashionable shops and is a very expensive place to live 骑士桥〔伦敦中西部一地区，为高尚住宅区。这里的商店十分时尚，但物价高昂〕

Knights of the Round Ta·ble, the /ˌ· · · ·, · ˈ· ·/ the KNIGHTS led by King Arthur, who, according to old English stories, sit together at a table, which is round so that no one should seem to be more important than any of the others 圆桌骑士〔亚瑟王麾下的骑士。据英格兰传说故事所述，亚瑟王的骑士围圆桌而坐，无尊卑之分〕

Knights Tem·plars, the /ˌnaɪts ˈtɛmpləːz; ˌnaɪts ˈtempləz/ also 又作 **the Knights of the Temple of Solomon** a military and Christian religious group of KNIGHTS during the Middle Ages, who protected people travelling in and to the Holy Land during the Crusades 圣殿骑士团〔中世纪一基督教军事组织。十字军东征时期，该组织曾保护前往圣地的朝圣者〕

knit /nɪt; nɪt/ *v past tense and past participle* **knitted** *or* **knitting** [I,T] **1** also 又作 **knit up** to make clothing out of wool using two KNITTING NEEDLES〔用毛线和两根编织针〕编织，针织：**knit sb sth** *She's knitting me a sweater.* 她在给我织毛衣。—compare 比较 CROCHET **2** *technical* to use a PLAIN (=basic) knitting stitch【术语】织平针：*Knit one, purl one.* 平织一针，反织一针。**3** to join people, things or ideas more closely, or to be closely connected 使〔人、物或想法〕紧密结合：**[+together]** *Wherever they live, the Jewish people are knit together by a common faith.* 犹太人无论住在哪里，共同的信仰都把他们紧紧连在一起。| **well/closely/tightly etc knit** (=with all the parts joined closely) 紧密结合的 *a closely knit community* 紧密团结的社区 **4** **[+together]** a bone that knits after being broken grows into one piece again〔折骨〕愈合 **5 knit your brows** to show you are worried, thinking hard etc by moving your EYEBROWS together 紧皱眉头〔表示忧虑、思索等〕—**knitter** *n* [C] —see also 另见 CLOSE-KNIT

knit·ting /ˈnɪtɪŋ; ˈnɪtɪŋ/ *n* [U] something that is being knitted 编织物

knitting nee·dle /ˈ· · ˌ· ·/ *n* [C] one of the two long sticks with round ends that you use to knit something 编织针 —see picture at 参见 NEEDLE¹ 图

knit·wear /ˈnɪtˌwɛr; ˈnɪt-weə/ *n* [U] knitted (KNIT (1)) clothing 针织品，编织的衣物：*a knitwear shop* 针织品商店

knives /naɪvz; naɪvz/ *n* the plural of KNIFE¹

knob /nɑb; nɒb/ *n* [C] **1** a round handle or thing that you turn to open a door, turn on a radio etc 球形把手；旋钮 **2 a knob of** a small piece of something 一小块：*Melt a knob of butter in the pan.* 用平底锅融化一小块黄油。**3** *BrE taboo slang* a PENIS【英，讳，俚】阴茎 **4 with (brass) knobs on** *BrE old-fashioned* used especially by children to reply to an insult【英，过时】〔尤为小孩反唇相讥时用语〕更是那样："*Idiot!*" "*Same to you, with knobs on!*" "你是白痴！" "你才是呢，你是个大白痴！"

knob·bly /ˈnɑblɪ; ˈnɒbli/ also 又作 **knob·by** /ˈnɑbɪ; ˈnɒbi/ *AmE*【美】*adj* with hard parts that stick out from under the surface of something 带有似球形突出物的；多结节的：*knobbly knees* 突出的膝盖骨

knock¹ /nɑk; nɒk/ *v*

1 ▶DOOR/WINDOW 门/窗◀ [I] to hit a door or window with your closed hand to attract the attention of the people inside 敲门[窗]：*Why don't you knock before you come in?* 你进来前为什么不敲门？| **[+at/on]** *I turned to see Jane knocking frantically on the taxi window.* 我转过身看见简发疯似地敲着出租车的车窗。

2 ▶HIT/MAKE STH MOVE 碰撞/使某物移动◀ [I always+adv/prep, T] to hit someone or something with a short quick action, so that it moves, falls down etc 碰撞；碰倒，撞倒：*Don't knock the camera, the picture will be blurry.* 别碰相机，不然照片就模糊了。| **knock sth ↔ down/off/over etc** *The dog managed to knock over a table.* 那条狗竟然弄翻了桌子。| **knock sth ↔ against/into/in** *I need a hammer to knock these tent pegs in.* 我需要一把锤子把这些帐篷桩敲进去。| **knock sb/sth flying** *BrE informal* (=hit something or someone so that they move a long distance)【英，非正式】把某人/某物撞得很远 *Holly ran through the crowd, knocking people flying.* 霍莉冲过人群，把周围的人撞得四散。| **knock a hole in** (=make a hole in something) 在…上撞出一个洞

3 ▶HIT SB HARD 用力撞击某人◀ a) knock sb flat/knock sb to the ground to hit someone so hard that they fall down 撞倒某人：*His assailant knocked him to the ground and ran off with his briefcase.* 袭击者把他撞倒在地上，抢了他的公文包跑了。**b) knock sb unconscious/senseless** to hit someone so hard that they fall unconscious 击昏某人：*The blast from the explosion knocked him unconscious.* 他被爆炸的冲击波击昏了。**c) knock the living daylights out of/hell out of** *informal* to hit someone many times or very hard【非正式】多次猛击〔某人〕

4 I'll knock your block off *spoken* used when threatening to hit someone very hard【口】我会把你痛打一顿：*If you touch her, I'll knock your block off!* 你要是碰她一下，我就会狠狠揍你一顿！

5 knock it off *spoken* used to tell someone to stop doing something, because it is annoying you【口】〔因受干扰而叫某人〕停下来："*Hey, knock it off!*" *Jesse shouted furiously.* "喂，给我停下来！" 杰西愤怒地吼道。

6 ▶CRITICIZE 批评◀ [T] to criticize someone or their work, especially in an unfair or annoying way 指责，责难；批评：*Some movie reviewers seem to knock every picture they see.* 有些电影评论家似乎对他们所观看的每一部影片都加以批评。| **don't knock it** *spoken* (=used to tell someone not to criticize something)【口】别指责 "*Bungee jumping! You must be crazy!*" "*Don't knock it till you've tried it.*" "蹦极？你疯了吧？" "你没试过就先别瞎说。"

7 knock sb/sth into shape *informal* to make changes to something in order to make it good enough【非正式】使人/事物更完善：*We've only got until Thursday to knock this play into shape.* 我们必须在星期四之前把剧本修改好。

8 ▶MAKE A NOISE 发出噪音◀ [I] if an engine or pipes etc knock, they make a noise like something hard being hit, usually because something is wrong with them〔发动机、管道等因出毛病而〕发出爆震[碰撞]声

9 ▶BALL 球◀ [T always+adv/prep] to kick or hit a ball somewhere 踢〔球〕；击〔球〕：**knock sth about/past/back etc** *We were just knocking a ball about in the yard.* 我们只是在院子里踢球。

10 knock the stuffing out of *informal* to make someone lose their confidence【非正式】使某人气馁：*Getting such low grades this semester seems to have knocked the stuffing out of him.* 这学期得这么低的分数，似乎使他信心全无了。

11 knock sb's socks off also 又作 **knock 'em dead** *spoken* to surprise and please someone by being very impressive【口】令某人又惊又喜：*Go out there and knock 'em dead, kid.* 孩子，出去给他们一个惊喜。

12 knock some sense into sb/into sb's head *informal* to make someone learn to behave in a more sensible way【非正式】让某人得个教训/懂事一些：*Who knows. Maybe getting arrested will knock some sense into him.* 谁知道，也许被抓起来能让他以后懂事一些。

13 knock spots off *BrE spoken* to be much better than someone or something【英口】比〔某人或某物〕强得多；远远胜过：*Our new computer system knocks spots off the old one.* 我们的新电脑系统比旧的强多了。

14 knock sth on the head *BrE informal* to prevent you from doing something you have planned【英，非正式】阻止某人做某事；破坏〔计划〕：*I wanted to go for a picnic, but the rain's knocked that on the head.* 我本想去野餐，可这场雨使计划泡了汤。

15 knock (sb's) heads together *informal* to talk angrily to people who are quarrelling or behaving stupidly【非正式】强制令某人停止〔争吵或胡闹〕：*If you kids don't settle down I'm going to come up and knock your heads together!* 如果你们这帮孩子再不安静下来，我就要来教训你们了！

16 you could have knocked me down with a feather *old-fashioned* used to emphasize how surprised you were by something【过时】令我惊讶不已：*When I heard I'd won, you could have knocked me down with a feather.* 听说我赢了，这使我大为惊讶。

17 knock the bottom out of *informal* to make something, such as a price much lower or weaker【非正式】使〔价格等〕大跌[疲软]：*A rise in interest rates would completely knock the bottom out of the property market.* 提升利率可能使房地产市场价格大

跌。—see also 另见 **with your knees knocking (together)** (KNEE[1] (4))

knock around also 又作 **knock about** *BrE*【英】*phr v informal*【非正式】

1 ▶**HIT SB** 打某人◀ [T **knock** sb **about/around**] to hit someone several times 多次打〔某人〕: *My father used to knock me and my brother around a lot.* 父亲以前常打我和弟弟。

2 ▶**RELAX** 放松◀ [I,T] to spend time in a relaxing way, without doing anything very important 悠闲地度过: **knock around town/the house etc** *We spent the weekend just knocking around the house.* 我们就在家里悠哉地过了个周末。

3 ▶**TRAVEL** 旅行◀ [I,T **knock around** sth] to travel to different places 到各处旅行; 漫游; 流浪: *I've knocked around a few places in my life.* 我这辈子去过一些地方。

4 ▶**IDEAS** 主意◀ [T **knock** sth ↔ **around**] to discuss and think about an idea, plan etc with other people 讨论, 商讨: *We've been knocking around a few ideas.* 我们一直在讨论一些想法。

5 ▶**BALL** 球◀ [T **knock** sth **about**] *BrE* to play a game with a ball, but not in a serious way【英】玩〔球〕, 打〔球〕

6 ▶**BE SOMEWHERE** 在某处◀ [I] *BrE* if something or someone is knocking around a place, it is somewhere in that place but you are not sure exactly where【英】在什么地方, 在某处: *Is there a screwdriver knocking about anywhere?* 能在什么地方找到一把螺丝刀吗?

knock back *phr v* [T] *informal*【非正式】**1** [**knock** sth ↔ **back**] to quickly drink large quantities of an alcoholic drink 狂饮, 豪饮: **knock it/them back** *spoken*【口】*Steve can really knock it back – he's drunk five pints already.* 史蒂夫真能喝, 已经喝了五品脱啤酒了。**2** [**knock** sb **back** sth] to cost you a lot of money 使花费〔大笔钱〕: *Our summer holiday knocked us back £600 this year.* 我们今年度暑假花费了600英镑。**3** [**knock** sb **back**] *BrE* to surprise or shock someone【英】使吃惊; 使震惊: *The news of her death really knocked him back.* 她去世的消息着实使他大吃一惊。

knock down *phr v* [T]

1 ▶**DRIVING A CAR** 驾车◀ [**knock** sb **down**] to hit someone with a car while you are driving, so that they are hurt or killed 〔驾车〕把〔某人〕撞倒: *He was knocked down by a drunk driver.* 他被一名醉汉开车撞倒。| **get knocked down** *Someone said a kid got knocked down by a truck.* 有人说一个小孩被卡车撞倒了。

2 ▶**DESTROY** 摧毁◀ [**knock** sth ↔ **down**] to destroy a building or part of a building 摧毁, 拆毁〔建筑物或其部分〕: *We knocked down one of the walls to make a bigger kitchen.* 我们拆掉了一面墙把厨房改大。

3 ▶**REDUCE PRICE** 减价◀ [**knock** sth ↔ **down**] *informal* to reduce the price of something by a large amount【非正式】使大幅降价: *The new stove we bought was knocked down from $800 to $550.* 我们新买的炉子的价钱从800美元降到了550美元。—see also 另见 KNOCKDOWN

4 ▶**ASK SB TO REDUCE PRICE** 讨价还价◀ [**knock** sb **down to**] *informal* to persuade someone to reduce the price of something they are selling you【非正式】使降价, 杀〔某人〕的价: *I tried to knock him down to £50.* 我试图把他的要价压到50英镑。

5 ▶**DRINK** 饮酒◀ [**knock** sth ↔ **down**] *AmE informal* to quickly drink large quantities of an alcoholic drink【美, 非正式】狂饮, 豪饮

6 ▶**PROVE STH WRONG** 证明某事错误◀ [**knock** sth ↔ **down**] *BrE informal* to prove that an idea, plan etc is not good or right【英, 非正式】证明〔某主意、计划等〕不妥[不对]: *They knocked the proposal down on the grounds that it was impractical.* 他们以不切实际为由否定了这个建议。

knock sth **into** sth *phr v* [T] to make two rooms into one room by taking away the wall that divides them 拆掉…的隔墙〔把两间房变为一间房〕: *We knocked the sitting room and the dining room into one.* 我们拆掉了客厅与饭厅之间的隔墙, 使两室合二为一。

knock off *phr v informal*【非正式】

1 ▶**STOP WORK** 停止工作◀ [I] to stop working at the end of the day, before lunch etc 停止工作; 下班: *What time do you knock off for lunch?* 你们什么时候歇工吃午饭? | **knock off early** *Is it okay if I knock off a little early today?* 我今天早点下班行不行?! | **knock off work** *Alex usually knocks off work about 5:30.* 亚历克斯通常约5点半下班。| **knock off for the day** *We knocked off for the day at eight.* 我们8点钟收工。

2 ▶**REDUCE A PRICE** 减价◀ [T **knock** sth ↔ **off**] to reduce the price of something by a particular amount 从价钱中减去: *He said he'd knock off a couple of pounds if I bought two.* 他说我如果买两个就可以少收几英镑。

3 ▶**REDUCE AMOUNT** 减量◀ [T **knock** sth ↔ **off**] to take a particular amount away from a total〔从总量中〕去掉: *We're knocking off one mark for each mistake.* 每出一个错我们就减掉一分。

4 ▶**PRODUCE** 制造◀ [T **knock** sth ↔ **off**] to produce something quickly and easily〔快速轻松地〕做出; 做完: *Roland makes huge amounts of money knocking off copies of famous paintings.* 罗兰靠快速仿制名画, 赚取大笔大笔的钱。

5 ▶**MURDER** 谋杀◀ [T **knock** sb **off**] to murder someone 杀害〔某人〕

6 ▶**STEAL** 偷◀ [T **knock** sth ↔ **off**] *BrE* to steal something, especially easily【英】〔尤指不费力地〕偷盗

7 ▶**SEX** 性◀ [T **knock** sb **off**] *BrE slang* to have sex with someone【英俚】与…性交

knock out *phr v* [T]

1 ▶**UNCONSCIOUS** 无知觉的◀ [**knock** sb/sth **out**] to make someone become unconscious 使失去知觉, 把…击昏: *Tyson knocked out his opponent in Round 5.* 泰森在第五回合将对手击昏。| *The shock from an electric eel is powerful enough to knock a man out.* 一条电鳗的电击足以把一个人击昏。—see also 另见 KNOCKOUT[1] (2)

2 ▶**DEFEAT** 击败◀ [**knock** sb/sth **out**] to defeat a person or team in a competition so that they can no longer take part 击败, 淘汰: **knock sb out of** *Indiana knocked Purdue out of the semifinals.* 印第安纳队将珀杜队淘汰出半决赛。—see also 另见 KNOCKOUT[1] (4)

3 ▶**ADMIRE** 钦佩◀ [**knock** sb **out**] *informal* to make you feel surprised and full of admiration【非正式】令人惊叹; 使极其钦佩: *The music was just brilliant – it really knocked me out.* 这音乐太美妙了, 真让我着迷。

4 ▶**SHOCK** 震惊◀ [**knock** sb **out**] *informal* to shock someone so much that they do not know what to say or do【非正式】使惊得目瞪口呆: *When she told me the real truth it just totally knocked me out.* 她把真相告诉我后, 我简直惊呆了。

5 ▶**PRODUCE WITH DIFFICULTY** 费力地做出◀ [**knock** sth ↔ **out**] *BrE informal* to produce something, especially when you find this difficult【英, 非正式】〔尤指吃力地〕做成: *It took him several years to knock out a book on the subject.* 他花了好几年才就这个主题写出了一本书。| **knock sth ↔ out of** *Let's see if we can knock a decent sound out of this old piano.* 我们来试试看能不能让这架旧钢琴发出像样的声音吧。

6 ▶**PRODUCE EASILY** 轻易地做出◀ [**knock** sth ↔ **out**] *AmE informal* to produce something easily and quickly, especially so that it is not of very good quality【美, 非正式】草草弄成, 匆匆弄出;〔轻易地〕完成: *We can knock out about 50 dresses in a day.* 我们一天能做出大约50件连衣裙。

7 **knock yourself out** *informal* to work very hard in order to do something well【非正式】〔为做好某事而〕苦干: *The Nelsons really knocked themselves out to give Amy a nice wedding.* 为了把艾米的婚礼办得圆满, 纳尔逊一家人真是竭尽全力。

knock over *phr v* [T] **1** [**knock** sb **over**] to hit someone with a car while you are driving, so that they are hurt or killed〔开车〕撞伤; 撞死: *Beth was knocked over by a motorcyclist when she was crossing the street.* 贝丝横过马路时被摩托车撞伤。**2** [**knock** sth ↔ **over**] *AmE informal* to rob a place such as a shop or bank and threaten or attack the people who work there【美, 非正式】抢劫〔商店、银行等〕

knock sth ↔ **together** *phr v* [T] *informal* to make something quickly, using whatever you have available【非正式】〔以现有材料〕迅速拼凑: *We should be able to knock something together with what's in the fridge.* 就冰箱里有的东西, 我们应该能拼凑出一点什么。

knock up *phr v* [T] **1** [**knock** sth ↔ **up**] *informal* to make something quickly and without using much effort【非正式】仓促制成; 赶做: *A local carpenter knocked up some kitchen units for us out of old pine.* 一位本地木匠用旧松木给我们赶制了几件厨房用具。**2** [**knock** sb ↔ **up**] *BrE informal* to wake someone up by knocking on their door【英, 非正式】敲门把〔某人〕唤醒: *What time do you want me to knock you up in the morning?* 你想我早上几点敲门把你叫醒? **3** [**knock** sb **up**] *informal* to make a woman PREGNANT【非正式】使〔女子〕怀孕

knock² *n* **1** [C] the sound of something hard hitting a hard surface 敲击声: *a loud knock at the door* 很响的敲门声 | *a knock in the engine* 发动机的爆震声 **2** [C] the action of something hard hitting your body 撞击: *He got a knock on the head when he fell.* 他跌倒时头被撞了一下。**3** **take a knock** *informal* to have some bad luck or trouble【非正式】倒霉, 遇到麻烦: *Clive's taken quite a few hard knocks lately.* 克莱夫近来受到不少挫折。

K

knock·a·bout /ˈnakə͵baut; ˈnɒkəbaʊt/ *adj BrE* knockabout entertainers make people laugh with their silly behaviour, for example by falling over things and pushing each other around 【英】〔演员〕以喧闹笨拙的表演引人发笑的

knock·down /ˈnak͵daun; ˈnɒkdaʊn/ *adj* [only before noun 仅用于名词前] a knockdown price is very cheap〔价格〕很低的 —see also 另见 **knock down** (KNOCK[1])

knock-down-drag-out /ˈ· · , · ·/ *adj AmE* using the most extreme methods to win【美】不惜一切手段的: *a knock-down-drag-out political campaign* 不择手段的政治运动

knock·er /ˈnakə; ˈnɒkə/ *n* **1** [C] a piece of metal on an outside door that you use to knock loudly〔门上供敲门用的〕门环 **2 knockers** [plural] *slang* an offensive word meaning a woman's breasts【俚】〔女人的〕乳房, 奶子〔冒犯用语〕**3** [C] someone who is always criticizing 爱挑剔的人

knock-kneed /, · ˈ·◂/ *adj* having knees that point inwards slightly 膝外翻的

knock-off /ˈnak͵ɔf; ˈnɒkɒf/ *n* [C] *AmE informal* a cheap copy of something expensive【美, 非正式】〔贵重物品的〕廉价仿制品

knock-on /ˈ· ·/ *adj* **have a knock-on effect** to start a process in which each part is directly influenced by the one before it 引起连锁反应: *These price rises will have a knock-on effect throughout the economy.* 这些价格的上涨将给整个经济带来连锁反应。

knock·out[1] /ˈnak͵aut; ˈnɒk-aʊt/ *n* [C] **1** an act of knocking your opponent down in BOXING so that he cannot get up again〔拳击中〕击倒对手: *The fight ended in a knockout.* 这场比赛以一方被击倒而结束。**2 knockout punch/blow a)** a hard hit that knocks someone down so that they cannot get up again 把对手打倒的一击 —see also 另见 **knock out** (KNOCK[1]) **b)** an action or event that causes defeat or failure 导致失败的行为[事件]: *High interest rates have been a knockout blow to the business.* 高利率一直是该企业的致命伤。**3** *informal* someone or something that is very attractive or successful【非正式】极有魅力的人[物]; 非常成功的人[物]: *Baby, you're a knockout.* 宝贝, 你太迷人了。**4** *BrE* a competition in which winning players or teams continue playing until there is only one winner【英】淘汰赛

knockout[2] *adj informal* making someone unconscious【非正式】使人昏迷的: *knockout pills* 麻醉药 | *the knockout punch* 把对手击昏的一拳

knock-up /ˈ· ·/ *n* [C] *BrE* a short time before a game when the players practise, especially in tennis【英】〔尤指网球的〕赛前练习

knoll /nol; nəʊl/ *n* [C] a small round hill 土墩, 小圆丘

knot[1] /nat; nɒt/ *n* [C]

1 ▶TIED STRING 绑好的绳◀ a join made by tying together two ends of rope, cloth, string etc〔绳索、布条、线等两端打成的〕结: *Here, let me fix the knot in your tie.* 来, 我替你把领带上的结整理一下。| *Can you help me undo this knot?* 你能帮我解开这个结吗?

2 ▶HAIR 毛发◀ **a)** a mass of hairs, threads etc accidentally twisted together 绞成一团的头发[线等]: *I can't get the knots out of my hair.* 我分不开缠结在一起的头发。**b)** a way of arranging your hair into a tight round shape at the back of your head 发髻, 圆髻

3 ▶SHIP'S SPEED 船速◀ written abbreviation 缩写为 KT, a measure of speed used for ships and aircraft that is about 1,853 metres per hour 节〔即 1853 米/小时, 船和飞机的速度单位〕

4 ▶PEOPLE 人◀ a small group of people standing close together〔站在一起的〕一小群人

5 ▶HARD MASS 硬结◀ a hard mass that is formed by a lot of things that are close together 硬结, 隆起(物): *a knot of muscles* 肌肉块

6 ▶WOOD 木头◀ a hard round place in a piece of wood where a branch once joined the tree〔木材上枝与干分离处的〕节, 节疤

7 a knot in your stomach/throat etc a hard uncomfortable feeling in your stomach etc caused by a strong emotion such as fear or anger〔恐惧或愤怒等强烈情绪导致的〕心窝揪紧/喉咙哽住等 —see also 另见 GORDIAN KNOT, **at a rate of knots** (RATE[1] (7)), **tie the knot** (TIE[1] (4)), **tie yourself (up) in knots** (TIE[1] (5))

knot[2] *v* **knotted, knotting 1** [T] to tie together two ends of rope, cloth, string etc 使打结, 使缠结 **2** [I,T] **a)** if hair or threads knot they become twisted together (使)〔头发、线〕绞缠 **b) knot your hair** to arrange and fasten your hair into a tight round shape at the back of your head 把头发盘成一个圆髻 **3** [I,T] if a muscle or other part of your body knots, or is knotted it feels hard and uncomfortable (使)〔肌肉〕暴突, (使)〔身体某部分〕紧揪: *Fear and anxiety knotted her stomach.* 恐惧和焦虑使她胃部紧揪。

knot·ted /ˈnatɪd; ˈnɒtɪ̣d/ *adj*

1 ▶FULL OF KNOTS 多结的◀ [only before noun 仅用于名词前] containing a lot of knots 多结的: *pieces of knotted string* 几根打有许多结的绳子

2 ▶MUSCLE 肌肉◀ if a muscle or other part of your body is knotted, it feels hard and uncomfortable 暴突的, 揪紧的: *knotted shoulder muscles* 肩膀暴突的肌肉

3 Get knotted! *BrE spoken* used to tell someone rudely to go away or that you do not agree with them【英口】滚开! 见鬼去!

4 ▶HANDS 手◀ knotted hands or fingers are twisted because of old age or too much work〔手或手指因年老或过度劳累形成的〕骨节突出弯曲的

knot·ty /ˈnatɪ; ˈnɒti/ *adj* **1** difficult to solve 难以解决的: *a knotty problem* 棘手的问题 **2** knotty wood contains a lot of KNOTS (=hard round places)〔木材〕多节(疤)的

knot 结; 节疤

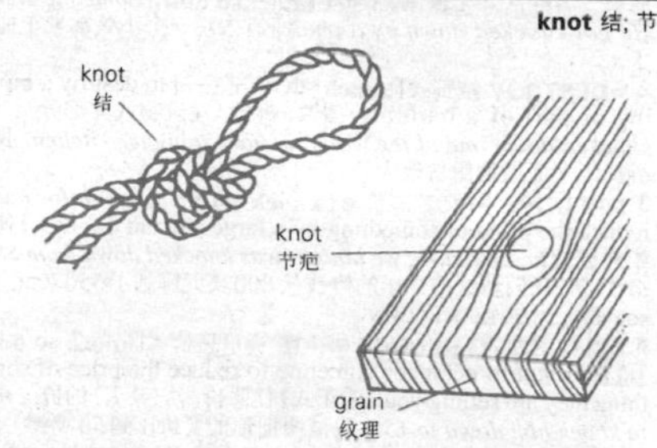

know[1] /no; nəʊ/ *v past tense* **knew** /nju; njuː/ *past participle* **known** /non; nəʊn/

① INFORMATION 信息
② I KNOW 我知道
③ I DON'T KNOW 我不知道
④ YOU KNOW 你知道
⑤ BE CERTAIN 有把握
⑥ SKILL/EXPERIENCE 技术/经验
⑦ PERSON/PLACE 人/地点
⑧ LANGUAGE/MUSIC ETC 语言/音乐等
⑨ REALIZE 意识到
⑩ RECOGNIZE 认出
⑪ EXPERIENCE 体验
⑫ SPOKEN PHRASES 口语短语
⑬ OTHER MEANINGS 其他意思

① INFORMATION 信息

1 [I,T not in progressive 不用进行式] to have information about something 知道; 了解: *Who knows the answer?* 谁知道答案? | *Do you happen to know the time?* 你知道现在几点钟吗? | *When are they arriving? Maybe Mrs. Mott knows.* 他们什么时候到达? 也许莫特太太知道。| *instructions telling you everything you need to know* 写明所有须知事项的说明书 | *Marriage cancels a will, didn't you know that?* 婚前遗嘱无

效，这一点你竟然不知道？| *I had spoken without knowing all the facts.* 我当时是在并不了解全部事实的情况下说的。| **know what/where/when etc** *Do you know what I'm supposed to be doing?* 你知道我现在该做什么吗？| *I don't know where to go.* 我不知道应该到哪里去。| **know about** *The council has known about the leak for six months.* 委员会获悉消息泄露的情况已六个月了。| **know all about** *spoken*【口】*We know all about David and what he's been up to!* 我们对于戴维以及他一直在搞些什么都十分了解！| **know (that)** *She knew that her father was sick, but not how serious it was.* 她知道父亲病了，但不知病情严重到什么程度。| **knowing that** (=because you know) 了解到 *I went to bed early knowing that I had to get up at six a.m.* 我知道早晨6点就得起床，所以早早就睡了。| **want to know** (=want to be told) 想知道 *I want to know what happened.* 我想知道发生了什么事。| *I thought you'd want to know immediately.* 我以为你立刻就想知道呢。| *"When do I start?" Carlos wanted to know.* "我什么时候开始？"卡洛斯问道。| **I'm dying to know** *spoken* (=I am very eager to find out)【口】我急切地想知道 *I'm dying to know who won!* 我极想知道谁赢了！| **without sb knowing** (=secretly, privately, or without someone being told) 秘密地，私下地 *You can't do anything without the whole town knowing.* 你干任何事都不可能瞒得了全镇的人。| **know to do sth** (=know that you should do it) 知道该做什么 *She knows not to tell anyone about it.* 她知道不可以把这件事告诉任何人。| **know sth/sb to be sth** (=know that something is true about them) 知道某物/某人确是某种情况 *a story which he knew to be true* 他知道确有其事的一个故事 | *I know him to be a good worker.* 我知道他做起事来确实很卖力。| **how do you know?** *spoken* (=how did you find out or what makes you think that?)【口】你是怎么知道的？你为什么这样认为？*How did he know our names?* 他是怎么知道我们的名字的？| *"Jason won't want to be involved." "How do you know?"* "贾森不想被牵连进去。""你为什么这样认为？" | **as you/we know** *spoken*【口】*As you know, there's been a tremendous revival of interest in the project.* 你知道，人们对这个计划重新又有了极大的兴趣。| **as/so far as I know** (=I believe that it is true, but I am not certain) 据我所知 *No other athlete, so far as I know, has won so many medals.* 据我所知，还没有其他运动员得过这么多奖牌。| **know for certain/sure** *I think she's going but I don't know for sure.* 我想她会去，但我不敢肯定。| **know from experience** *I know from experience that he's got a foul temper.* 根据我的经验判断，他是个脾气暴躁的人。| **I wouldn't know** *spoken* (=I do not know, and I am not the person you should ask)【口】我不知道〔你不应该问我〕*"When is he coming back?" "I wouldn't know."* "他什么时候回来？""我不知道。" | **know the way** (=know how to get to a place) 知道路 *Does he know the way to your house?* 他知道去你家的路吗？

2 let sb know to tell someone about something 让某人知道，将某事告诉某人：*When it stops, let me know.* 停下来的时候，告诉我一声。| *Give him this medicine, and let us know if he's not better in two days.* 给他服这种药，两天后要是他没有好转，请告诉我们。| *Thank you for your application; we'll let you know.* (=we will tell you soon whether you have been successful) 谢谢你的申请，我们会把结果通知你。| **let it be known (that)** (=let other people know what your opinions or intentions are) 让人知道〔自己的意见或意图〕*The Prince has let it be known that he does not approve of his son's behaviour.* 亲王已让大家知道他不认同儿子的行为。

3 know sth inside out also 又作 **know sth backwards** to know something extremely well 熟知某事：*We expect you to know these codes inside out, men.* 我们指望你们能对这些密码倒背如流，伙计们。

② I KNOW 我知道

4 I know *spoken*【口】**a)** used to say that you have suddenly had an idea, thought of a solution to a problem, etc 我知道了〔表示灵机一触〕：*"What should we do?" "I know, we could ask Anne to help."* "我们该怎么办？""我知道，可以请安妮帮忙。" **b)** used to agree with someone or to say that you feel the same way 我知道〔表示赞同或有同感〕：*"I'm so worn out!" "Yeah, I know."* "我累坏了。""嗯，我知道。" **c)** used to prevent someone from objecting to what you say by saying the objection first 我知道〔用来抢先提出反对意见，以阻止某人反对你的说法〕：*It sounds silly, I know, but try it anyway.* 我知道这听起来很愚蠢，但无论如何试一试吧。| *I know, I know, I should have had the car checked out before now.* 我知道，我知道，我早应该把车开去检查一下的。

③ I DON'T KNOW 我不知道

5 I don't know *spoken*【口】**a)** used to say that you do not have the answer to a question 我不知道〔表示不知道某问题的答案〕：*"When did they arrive?" "I don't know."* "他们什么时候到的？""不知道。" | *"Why did you do that?" "I don't know."* "你为什么那样做？""我不知道。" **b)** used to show that you disagree slightly with what has just been said 我不清楚〔表示略有异议〕：*"I couldn't live there." "Oh, I don't know. It might not be so bad."* "我不能住那儿。""是吗？我不大了解，也许没那么糟吧。" **c)** used when you are not sure about something 我拿不准〔表示没有把握〕：*Oh, I don't know, sixty, seventy?* 我也说不准，六十，七十？| [+if/whether/that] *I don't know if I would want to teach.* 我拿不准是否想去教书。**d)** used to show that you are slightly annoyed 我不知道〔表示有点不耐烦〕：*Oh, I don't know! You're hopeless!* 噢，我不知道！你真令人失望！

6 I don't know how/why etc used to criticize someone 我不明白怎么会/为什么等〔用于批评某人〕：*I don't know how people could treat a child like that.* 我真不明白人们怎么会那样对待一个孩子。

7 I don't know whether you want to...? *spoken* used to ask someone politely to do something【口】能否请你…？〔用于有礼貌地请人做某事〕：*I don't know whether you want to respond to that?* 能否请你对此作出回应？

8 I don't know about you but... *spoken* used to give an opinion, suggestion, or decision of your own which might be different from that of the person listening【口】我不知道你怎么想，但…；我不敢苟同〔表示异议〕：*I don't know about you, but I'm going home.* 你怎么想我不知道，但我可要回家了。

9 I don't know how to thank you/repay you *spoken formal* used to thank someone【口，正式】真不知该怎样感谢你/报答你〔用于表示感谢〕

④ YOU KNOW 你知道

10 you know *spoken*【口】**a)** used to emphasize a statement 你知道〔用于强调〕：*There'll be trouble, you know.* 会有麻烦的，真的。| *I don't like to brag but, you know, I did do pretty well.* 我不喜欢自吹自擂，不过你知道，我的确干得很出色。**b)** used when you need to keep someone's attention, but cannot think of what to say next 你知道〔用于要保持对方的注意力但又想不出下面说什么时〕：*I was just, you know, looking through my slides before you came.* 刚才，你知道，你来之前我是在看我的这些幻灯片呢。**c)** used when you are explaining or describing something and want to give more information 你知道的〔用于在解释或描述某事时希望提供更多的信息〕：*That padding that you put on the car, you know, that stuff on the doors.* 你安装在车里的那种衬垫，你知道，就是车门上的那种材料。

11 you know/do you know *spoken* used to start talking about something, or make someone listen【口】你知道/你知道吗〔用于开始谈及某事或使人注意听你讲话〕：*You know your cousin? You'll never guess what she did!* 你知道你表妹吗？你绝对猜不到她干了些什么！| *You know, it's a sad thing about this guy.* 你知道，这个人真是够惨的。| *Do you know, when I went out this morning that man was still there.* 你知道吗？我今天早晨出去时，那个人还在那里。| **(do) you know what/something?** *But do you know what? He got fired.* 你知道吗？他被解雇了。

⑤ BE CERTAIN 有把握

12 [I,T not in progressive 不用进行式] to be sure about something〔对某事〕确信：*I just know I won't get the job.* 我就知道我不会得到这份工作。| *I knew you'd say that.* 我早知道你会这么说。| *The boy stared at him uncertainly, not knowing whether to believe him.* 那个男孩疑惑地盯着他，不知道该不该相信他的话。| **how do you know?** (=what makes you feel certain?) 你怎么知道？*How do you know he won't do it again?* 你怎么知道他不会再做这样的事？

⑥ SKILL/EXPERIENCE 技术/经验

13 [T not in progressive 不用进行式] to have learned a lot about something or be skilful and experienced at doing something 精通，熟悉；懂得：*I don't know enough history to make a comparison.* 我对历史了解不多，不能加以比较。| *I taught him everything he knows.* 他现在通晓的东西都是我教给他的。| **know how to** *Do you know how to change a fuse?* 你知道怎么换保险丝吗？| **know about** *I have a friend who knows about antiques.* 我有一个朋友对古董很在行。| **know all about** *Politicians know all about the power of language.* 政治家们十分了解语言的力量。| **know what you are doing** (=have enough skill and experience to deal with something properly) 有足够

的技术和经验做好某事 | **know what you are talking about** *You listen to Aunt Kate, she knows what she's talking about.* 你听听凯特姨妈的话，她在这方面很在行。| **know your job/subject** also 又作 **know your stuff** (=be good at and know all you should know about a job or subject) 对某项工作/话题非常了解[很在行]

14 think you know everything/think you know all the answers to behave in a way that is too confident, always trying to give people advice 过于自信，自以为什么都知道

15 know a thing or two *informal* to have a lot of useful information gained from experience【非正式】富有经验，见多识广

⑦ PERSON/PLACE 人/地点

16 [T] to be familiar with a person, place, etc 熟悉〔某人、某地等〕: *I've known her for twenty years.* 我认识她有20年了。| *Are you really thinking of leaving Kevin for a guy you barely know?* 你真打算为一个你刚刚认识的人而离开凯文？| *Anyone who knows his work and who knows Wales will see the connection.* 任何熟悉他的作品又熟悉威尔士的人，都会看出两者之间的联系。| *Do you know the Boy's Club in Claremont?* 你熟悉克莱尔蒙特的男孩俱乐部吗？| **know sb well** *We did not know each other well enough to talk freely.* 我们之间当时还没有熟悉到可以随意交谈的地步。| **get to know** *I'm getting to know the neighbors.* 我开始跟邻居混熟了。| *You need time to get to know a new instrument.* 你需要一段时间才能熟悉一件新工具。| **as we know it** (=in the form that we are familiar with) 我们所熟知的 *That will mean an end to the Tory Party as we know it.* 那将意味着我们所熟知的英国保守党的终结。| **know sb/sth inside out** (=be very familiar with them) 对某人/某事物十分熟悉 *We need someone who knows the area inside out.* 我们需要一个对此地十分熟悉的人。| *That's the thing about Mom, she knows me inside out.* 妈妈的问题就在这里，她对我太了解了。| **know sb by sight** (=often see them, but not know them well) 与某人面熟 *I know her by sight, but I don't think I've ever spoken to her.* 我只是和她面熟，但我想我从来没有和她说过话。| **knowing him/if I know him** (=I know what he is like and expect him to do a particular thing) 我了解他 *Knowing Sumi, my note's probably still in her pocket.* 我了解苏米，我的字条可能还在她的衣袋里呢。| *He'll be chatting up the women, if I know Ron!* 我了解罗恩这个人，他可能还在和那些女人聊得起劲哩！

⑧ LANGUAGE/MUSIC ETC 语言/音乐等

17 know a language to be able to speak, read, and understand a foreign language 懂一门语言: *I know some French.* 我懂一点儿法语。

18 know a song/a tune/a poem etc to be able to sing a song, play a tune, say a poem etc because you have learned it 能唱某首歌/演奏某支曲子/朗诵某首诗等: *Do you know all the words to 'As Time Goes By'?* 你知道《随时光流逝》的全部歌词吗？| **know sth (off) by heart** (=to have learned it and be able to repeat it from memory) 能把…背诵出来

⑨ REALIZE 意识到

19 [I,T] to realize, find out about, or understand something 意识到；发现；了解: *Miss Brown knew as soon as she came in that something was wrong.* 布朗小姐一进来就发觉有点不对头。| *Hardly knowing what he was doing, Nick pulled out a cigarette.* 尼克下意识地拿出一支烟。| *I know I have been avoiding the issue.* 我知道自己一直在回避这个问题。| **(do/if) you know what I mean?** *spoken* (=used to ask if someone has understood you)【口】你明白我的意思吗？*It's nice to have a change sometimes. Know what I mean?* 间或改变一下是件好事。明白我的意思吗？| **I/she etc should have known** *spoken* (=used to say that someone ought to have realized something)【口】我/她等本该意识到 *I should have known it would take this long.* 我早就应该知道需要这么长的时间。| **I might have known** *BrE spoken* (=I should not be surprised that something has happened, but I am annoyed)【英口】我就知道 *I might have known you'd be mixed up in this mess!* 我就知道你会牵涉到这种乱七八糟的事情里去！| **know exactly/precisely** *I know exactly how you feel.* 我完全清楚你目前是什么心情。| **know perfectly well/full well/only too well** *You know perfectly well what I mean.* 你完全明白我的意思。| **sb will never know/no one will ever know** (=no one will realize that something has happened) 谁也不会知道 *Just take it, no one will ever know.* 你拿着吧，不会有人知道的。| **and you know it** *spoken*【口】*This has nothing to do with gratitude and you know it.* 这与感激不感激没关系，这你

知道。| **if I had known/if I'd have known** *If I had known they were in trouble, I'd have gone to help.* 我当时要是知道他们有麻烦，我是会去帮忙的。| **little did she know** *literary*【文】*As she closed the door, she little knew that this was the last time she would leave this house.* 她关上门的时候，一点也不知道这是她最后一次离开这所房子。

⑩ RECOGNIZE 认出

20 [T] to be able to recognize someone or something 认出: *Honestly, it had been so long, I hardly knew her.* 说实话，隔了这么长时间，我几乎认不出她了。| [+by] *He looked very different, but I knew him by his voice.* 他外表变化很大，但我凭他的嗓音认出了他。

21 know sth from sth to understand the difference between one thing and another 分辨，区分出来: *Lloyd doesn't even know his right from his left.* 劳埃德甚至分不出自己的左边和右边。| *She knows right from wrong: she can't claim she was insane.* 她分得清好歹，她不能声称自己曾经有过精神错乱。

22 not know sb from Adam *informal* to not know who someone is at all【非正式】完全不认识某人

⑪ EXPERIENCE 体验

23 [T] to live through an experience 经历；体验: [+about] *I know all about being poor, so don't think I don't.* 我知道贫穷是什么滋味，所以别以为我不明白。

24 I've never known used to say that you have never heard of or experienced something as surprising as the thing you are describing 我从不知道: *This weather is amazing. I've never known anything like it!* 这种天气真令人吃惊，我从未经历过这样的天气！

25 I've never known sb to do sth used to say that someone never does something 从来不知道某人会做某事: *I've never known him to iron anything.* 我从来没有见到过他熨衣服。

26 sb/sth is not known to be sth also 又作 **sb/sth has never been known to do sth** used to say that there is no information that says that a person or animal behaves in a particular way 据知某人.某事物不是某痰情况[不会做某事]: *This species is not known to be vicious.* 据知这个物种并不凶猛。

27 I've known sb to do sth also 又作 **sb has been known to do sth** used to say that someone does something sometimes, even if it is unusual 我听说过某人做某事: *Watch it. He's been known to eat a whole pizza himself!* 注意看。据说他可以吃下一整块意大利薄饼！

⑫ SPOKEN PHRASES 口语短语

28 you never know used to say that it is possible that something good may happen 也许；很难说: *I might be able to catch the earlier train, you never know.* 我也许能赶上早一点的那班火车，这很难说。

29 how should I know?/how am I to know?/how do I know? used to say that it is not reasonable to expect that you should know something 我怎么会知道？: *"What's it like?" "I haven't seen it, so how should I know?"* "它是什么样子的？" "我没见过，怎么会知道？"

30 how was I to know?/how did I know? used as an excuse or to say that you are sorry（当时）我怎么会知道？: *It's not my fault – how was I to know it would rain!* 这不能怪我，我怎么知道会下雨？

31 I ought to know used to emphasize that you know about something because you made it, experienced it etc 我最清楚了: *"Are you sure there's no sugar in it?" "Of course. I ought to know, I made it!"* "你肯定这里面没放糖吗？" "当然。我最清楚了，因为是我亲手做的！"

32 not that I know of used when answering a question to say that you believe that the answer is 'no', but there may be facts that you do not know about 据我所知没有: *"Andrew didn't phone today, did he?" "Not that I know of."* "安德鲁今天没有来电话，是吗？" "据我所知没有。"

33 if you must know used when you are annoyed at having to give information to someone 如果你一定要知道〔表示不耐烦〕: *"Where is it?" "In an envelope, if you must know," said James impatiently.* "它在哪儿？" "在一个信封里，如果你一定要知道的话。" 詹姆斯不耐烦地说。

34 for all I know used to say that you do not know about something and it does not really matter because you are not involved or affected 说不定: *It cost millions. It could be billions for all I know.* 它花费了数百万，可能花了几十亿也说不定呢。

35 there's no knowing it is impossible to know 不可能知道:

There is no knowing what she will do next. 没法知道她下一步要干什么。

36 (I'm/I'll be) damned if I know! used to emphasize that you do not know something, and are annoyed or think something is hopeless 鬼才知道!: *"Whatever are we going to do?" "Damned if I know."* "我们到底要干什么?" "鬼才知道。"

37 Heaven/God/who/goodness knows! a) used to say that you do not have any idea what an answer might be, and do not expect to know 天知道!〔表示对某事一无所知, 也不想知道〕: *"Where do you think he's disappeared to this time?" "God knows!"* "你认为他这次又跑到哪里去了?" "天知道!" **b)** used to emphasize a statement 天晓得!〔用于加强语气〕: *I haven't seen her for goodness knows how long.* 天晓得我有多长时间没有见到她了。| *It might make us more efficient, which heaven knows we need.* 它也许能让我们更有效率, 老天爷知道这是我们需要的。

38 not want to know *informal* to refuse to listen to a complaint or a problem【非正式】不想知道; 不想听: *We phoned the council about the damage, but they just didn't want to know.* 我们打电话向委员会报告损毁情况, 但他们根本不想听。

39 knowing my luck used to say that you expect something bad will happen because you are usually unlucky 知道不走运〔表示自己可能要倒霉, 因为运气通常不佳〕: *Knowing his luck, he'll get hit with a golf ball or something.* 他知道自己运气不好, 也许会被高尔夫球打中或出点别的什么毛病。

40 (well,) what do you know! used to express surprise 真想不到!: *Well, what do you know – look who's arrived!* 啊, 真想不到, 你看谁来了?

41 the next thing you know used to say that something happens suddenly and unexpectedly 突然又: *One minute everybody's laughing and the next thing you know, they're all arguing!* 他们一会儿哈哈大笑, 一会儿又突然争吵起来!

42 I will (want to) know the reason why an expression meaning you will want an explanation, used in a threatening way 我倒想知道原因何在〔有威胁之意〕: *It had better be right this time, or I'll know the reason why.* 这回最好不要出错, 否则我就要你作出解释。

43 if you know what's good for you used to tell someone that they should do something, or you will harm them in some way 如果你知道好歹: *You'll just keep your mouth shut about this if you know what's good for you!* 如果你不想吃苦头的话, 对这件事你就闭上嘴吧!

44 you know who/what used to talk about someone or something without mentioning their name 你知道的那人[物]〔用来谈论某人或某物而不必指名道姓〕: *I saw you know who yesterday.* 我昨天看见了你知道的那个人。

⑬ OTHER MEANINGS 其他意思

45 be known as to also be called something 被称为: *Chicago is known as 'the windy city'.* 芝加哥被称为'风城'。

46 know better a) to be wise or experienced enough to avoid making mistakes 有头脑, 明事理(而不至于): **know better than to...** *She ought to know better than to expect any help from Roger.* 她应该明白不能指望罗杰帮忙。**b)** to know or think you know more than someone else (自认为) 知道得比某人多: *They said it was gold, but Sharon knew better.* 他们说那是金子, 但莎伦知道并非如此。

47 know best used to say that someone should be obeyed or that their way of doing things should be accepted because they are experienced〔表示由于某人经验丰富而〕最具权威: *I think I know best how to deal with my own staff!* 我认为如何对待我手下的职员, 我最清楚。| **Mother/Father etc knows best** *Don't argue. Daddy knows best!* 不要争辩了, 爸爸比你懂!

48 know your own mind to be confident and have firm ideas about what you want and like 有自信心; 有自己的想法

49 you will be delighted/pleased to know that *formal* used before you give someone information that they will be pleased to hear【正式】你会很高兴/乐意知道: *You will be pleased to know that we have accepted your offer.* 你一定乐意知道, 我们已接受了你的提议。— see also 另见 **know no bounds** (BOUND[4] (6)), **know the ropes** (ROPE[1] (2)), **know the score** (SCORE[1] (5)), **know your place** (PLACE[1] (30)), **not know what hit you** (HIT[1] (14))

know of sb/sth *phr v* [T] to have been told or to have read that something exists, but not know much about it 听说(但所知不多), 知道有…: *I know of one company that makes these things.* 我听说有一家公司生产这类物品。

USAGE NOTE 用法说明: KNOW

WORD CHOICE 词语辨析: **know, find out, hear/read about, get to know, learn, study**

If you **know** a fact, person, or place, or how to speak a language, drive a car etc, you have information about it in your mind, or the skills to do it. 知道 (know) 某一事实、某个人或某个地方, 或者能讲某种语言、会开车等等, 就意味着拥有相关的信息或相关的技术。

Often you **know** something only after you have **heard or read about** it, or if you have **found it out** (especially deliberately) or **got to know** about it (especially by chance). 知道 (know) 某事常常是在听说到 (hear about) 或从书里读到 (read about) 这件事之后, 或者是由于有意识地发现 (find out) 或偶然得知 (get to know) 这件事: *When he heard about the affair he became extremely angry.* 他听说这件事后极为愤怒。| *I use my dictionary to find out the correct pronunciation* (NOT 不用 *know*). 我用词典查找正确的读音。| *During the visit we got to know something about the American way of life.* 访问期间我们了解到某些美国的生活方式。You also **get to know** a person. get to know 也指结识一个人。

If you **learn** something, that may mean that you **find it out**, but this is a formal use of the word. learn 可以指发现某事 (find it out), 但这是该词的正式用法: *He learnt the news/that he had won a prize.* 他已得知这个消息/他得了奖。Usually to **learn** means to make an effort to remember something you have found out or been taught, or to practise a skill, so that you then **know** it. 通常 learn 指努力记住所发现或别人所教的某种东西, 或努力练习一种技能, 这样才会懂得 (know): *I'm trying to learn the names of all the students in my class* (NOT 不用 *know*). 我正在努力记住我班上所有学生的名字。| *She is learning English/learning to drive.* 她在学习英语/学习开车。

If you spend time learning about something, especially in a school, university etc you **study** it. study 指花时间学习 (learn about) 某物, 尤指在学校、大学等地方学习: *Gina is studying engineering at London University.* 吉娜正在伦敦大学攻读工程学。

know² *n* **in the know** *informal* having more information about something than most people【非正式】知情, 熟知内情: *People in the know say that interest rates will have to rise again soon.* 知道内情的人说, 利率将很快再次上升。

know-all /ˈ· ·/ *n* [C] *BrE informal* someone who behaves as if they know everything【英, 非正式】自以为无所不知的人; KNOW-IT-ALL *AmE*【美】

know-how /ˈ· ·/ *n* [U] *informal* practical ability or skill【非正式】实用本领; 技能; 知识; 窍门: *Jeff needs more technical know-how to do his new job.* 要做好这项新的工作, 杰夫需要更多的技能。

Frequencies of the verb **know** in spoken and written English 英语口语和书面语中动词 know 的使用频率

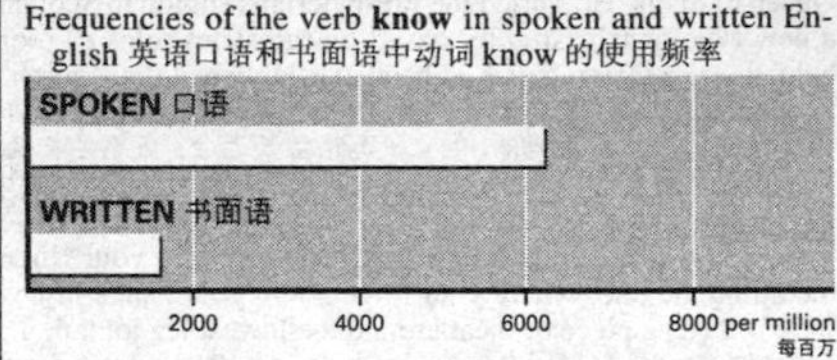

Based on the British National Corpus and the Longman Lancaster Corpus
据英国国家语料库和朗文兰开斯特语料库

This graph shows that the verb **know** is much more common in spoken English than in written English. This is because it is used in a lot of common spoken phrases. These are marked *spoken* in the entry. 本图表显示动词 know 在英语口语中的使用频率远远高于书面语, 因为该词用于许多常用的口语短语中。在词条中这些短语都有 *spoken*【口】标记。

know·ing /ˈnoɪŋ; ˈnəʊɪŋ/ *adj* showing that you know all about something 会意的, 心照不宣的: *He said nothing but gave us a knowing look.* 他一言不发, 只是会意地看了我们一眼。

know·ing·ly /ˈnoɪŋlɪ; ˈnəʊɪŋli/ *adv* **1** in a way that shows you know about something secret or embarrassing 会意地: *She smiled knowingly at us.* 她会意地对我们一笑。**2** deliberately 故意地, 有意地: *He would never knowingly upset people.* 他从来不故意让别人生气。

K

know-it-all /ˈ· · ˌ·/ *n* [C] *informal especially AmE* someone who behaves as if they know everything【非正式, 尤美】自以为无所不知的人; KNOW-ALL *BrE*【英】

2 1 **knowl·edge** /ˈnɑlɪdʒ; ˈnɒlɪdʒ/ *n* [U] **1** the facts, skills, and understanding that you have gained through learning or experience 知识; 学问: *You need specialist knowledge to do this job.* 做这项工作要有专门知识。| **[+of]** *His knowledge of ancient civilizations is unrivalled.* 他在古代文明方面的学问无人能比。| **[+about]** *We now have greater knowledge about the risks of using these chemicals.* 我们现在对于使用这些化学品的危险性已有了更多的认识。**2 in the knowledge that** knowing that something has happened or is true 已知道, 了解到: *Kay smiled, secure in the knowledge that she was right.* 凯笑了, 她很有把握知道自己是对的。**3 not to your knowledge** *spoken* used to say that something is not true, based on what you know【口】据…所知某事并不确实: *"Is it true that she's leaving the company?" "Not to my knowledge."* "她要离开这家公司, 这是真的吗?" "据我所知不是这样。" **4** information that you have about a particular situation, event etc 消息, 信息: **in full knowledge of** (=knowing all the details of a situation) 充分了解… *He acted in full knowledge of the possible consequences.* 他这么做时完全明白所有可能的后果。| **deny all knowledge of sth** (=say that you do not know anything about it) 否认知道某事 *Evans denied all knowledge of the robbery.* 伊文斯说对这桩抢劫案一概不知。| **come to sb's knowledge** *formal* (=become known about)【正式】被某人获悉[知道] *The incident first came to our knowledge about a fortnight ago.* 我们是大约两周前第一次听说这次事故的。| **bring sth to sb's knowledge** *formal* (=give someone information they did not know)【正式】将某事告诉某人 **5 to the best of your knowledge** used to say that you think something is true, although you may not have all the facts 就某人所知: *To the best of my knowledge the new project will be starting in June.* 据我所知, 新项目将于6月开始进行。**6 without your knowledge** without knowing what is happening 在某人不知情的情况下: *He was annoyed to find the contract had been signed without his knowledge.* 他发现合同已在他不知情的情况下签署, 这使他很恼火。—see also 另见 GENERAL KNOWLEDGE, **common knowledge** (COMMON[1] (3)), **working knowledge** (WORKING[1] (5))

knowl·edge·a·ble /ˈnɑlɪdʒəbl; ˈnɒlɪdʒəbəl/ *adj* knowing a lot 有知识的; 博学的: **[+about]** *Graham's very knowledgeable about wines.* 格雷厄姆对酒很在行。—**knowledgeably** *adv*

known¹ /non; nəʊn/ the past participle of KNOW[1]

3 **known²** *adj* [only before noun 仅用于名词前] known about, especially by many people 知名的, 众所周知的: *a known crack dealer* 出了名的精明商人 | *Yes, yes, it's a known problem.* 对, 对, 这是一个大家都知道的问题。| **be known for** (=be famous for) 以…知名 *The Saumur region is known for its sparkling wines.* 索米尔地区以出产香槟酒而闻名。—see also 另见 **little known** (LITTLE[3] (2)), **well-known**

Knox /nɑks; nɒks/, **John** (?1505-72) a Scottish Protestant religious leader, who opposed Scotland's Catholic queen, Mary Queen of Scots. He started the Presbyterian religion in Scotland, a new type of Christianity based on the strict rules of moral behaviour of Calvinism, and he also established the Church of Scotland. 诺克斯〔(?1505-1572), 苏格兰新教领袖。他反对信仰天主教的苏格兰女王玛丽, 创立了苏格兰长老会。苏格兰长老会是一个新型基督教团体, 尊崇加尔文主义宣导的严格的道德行为准则〕

knuck·le¹ /ˈnʌkl; ˈnʌkəl/ *n* **1** [C] the joints in your fingers including the ones where your fingers join your hands 指节; 掌指关节 **2** [C] a piece of meat around the lowest leg joint 肘子: *a knuckle of pork* 猪肘子 **3 near the knuckle** *BrE informal* rude, or likely to give offence【英, 非正式】粗鲁的; 近乎下流的: *Some of his jokes are a bit near the knuckle.* 他的一些笑话近乎下流。—see also 另见 **a rap on/over the knuckles** (RAP[2] (5))

knuckle² *v*

knuckle down *phr v* [I] *informal* to suddenly start working or studying hard【非正式】〔突然〕开始努力工作[学习]: *If he doesn't knuckle down soon, he'll never get through those exams.* 他如果不立即开始用功, 就绝不会通过那些考试。

knuckle under *phr v* [I] *informal* to accept someone's authority or orders without wanting to【非正式】屈服; 认输

knuckle-dust·er /ˈ· ·, · ·ˌ·/ *n* [C] a metal covering for the backs of the fingers, used as a weapon 指节铜套〔一种武器〕

knuck·le·head /ˈnʌklˌhɛd; ˈnʌkəlhed/ *n* [C] *AmE spoken* used to address someone who you like who has done something stupid【美口】小傻瓜〔用来称呼自己喜爱但又做了蠢事的人〕: *You knucklehead, you can't go around saying things like that!* 你这个小傻瓜, 不可以到处去讲那种话!

ko·a·la /kəˈɑlə; kəʊˈɑːlə/ also 又作 **koala bear** /·ˌ· · ˈ·/ *n* [C] an Australian animal like a small bear with no tail that climbs trees 树袋熊, 考拉〔产于澳大利亚似熊的一种无尾树栖动物〕

kohl /kol; kəʊl/ *n* [U] a black pencil used around women's eyes to make them more attractive 眼线笔〔女性化妆用品〕

Kon-Ti-ki ex·pe·di·tion, the /kɑn ˈtikɪ ɛkspɪˌdɪʃən; kɒn ˈtiːki ekspəˌdɪʃən/ a journey made in 1947 by the Norwegian EXPLORER, Thor Heyerdahl, and five other people. They sailed a RAFT, called the **Kon-Tiki**, from Callao in Peru to Tuamoto Island in the South Pacific Ocean in order to show that the Polynesians had done this in earlier times. "康-提基"号探险〔1947年挪威探险家托尔·海尔达尔等六人的远征探险。他们乘坐"康-提基"号木筏从秘鲁的卡亚俄出发到达南太平洋的土阿莫土岛, 以证明波利尼西亚人早期也进行过类似航行〕

kook /kuk; kuːk/ *n* [C] *AmE informal* someone who is silly or crazy【美, 非正式】傻瓜; 狂人 —**kooky** *adj*

kook·a·bur·ra /ˈkukəˌbʌrə; ˈkʊkəbʌrə/ *n* [C] an Australian bird whose song sounds like laughter 笑翠鸟〔产于澳大利亚、叫声似笑声的一种鸟〕

Kool-Aid /ˈkuled; ˈkuːleɪd/ *trademark* a type of powder that you mix with water and sugar to make a cold drink. Kool-Aid is sold in the US, and is drunk especially by children【商标】酷爱果粉〔一种在美国出售的加糖加水可制成冷饮的果粉, 在美国销售, 多为小孩饮用〕: *grape Kool-Aid* 酷爱葡萄果粉

Ko·ran, the /kəˈræn; kɔːˈrɑːn/ *n* also 又作 **the Qur'an** the holy book of the Muslims《古兰经》,《可兰经》〔伊斯兰教的经典〕—**Koranic** *adj*

Ko·re·a /koˈriə; kəˈriːə/ a country in East Asia which, in 1948, was divided into two countries, North Korea and South Korea 朝鲜〔东亚一国家, 1948年分成朝鲜和韩国两个国家〕

Ko·re·an War, the /kəˌriən ˈwɔr; kəˌriːən ˈwɔː/ a war between China and North Korean forces on one side and US and South Korean forces on the other. The war began in 1950 and ended in 1953. 朝鲜战争〔战争一方为中国和朝鲜, 另一方为美国和韩国。这场战争于1950年爆发, 1953年结束〕

Ko·resh /kəˈrɛʃ; kəˈreʃ/, **David** (1959-93) the leader of a small religious group called the Branch Davidians, who lived together in Waco, Texas, in the US. In 1993 the FBI came to arrest him for illegally having guns, and Koresh and 86 members of his group were killed. 考雷什〔(1959-1993), 宗教小团体大卫教派教主。其教众住在美国得克萨斯州的韦科。1993年, 联邦调查局因考雷什非法持有枪支逮捕他, 考雷什及其86名教徒丧生〕

kor·ma /ˈkɔrmə; ˈkɔːmə/ *n* [U] an Indian dish made with meat and cream 考莫〔一种用肉和奶油做成的印度菜肴〕: *chicken korma* 鸡肉考莫

ko·sher /ˈkoʃɚ; ˈkəʊʃə/ *adj* **1 a)** kosher food is prepared according to Jewish law〔食品〕按犹太教规制成的 **b)** kosher restaurants or shops sell food prepared in this way〔餐馆或商店〕供应符合犹太教规食物的 **2** *informal* honest or lawful; actually being what is claimed【非正式】诚实可靠的; 合法的; 真正的: *Are you sure this offer is kosher?* 你确实认为这个建议可靠吗?

Ko·so·vo /ˈkɑsəvo; ˈkɒsəvəʊ/ an area in southern Serbia, where people of Albanian origin wanted independence. Many Albanians were killed in Kosovo in fights with Serb forces in the 1990s. 科索沃〔塞尔维亚南部一地区。该地区的阿尔巴尼亚族人想要独立。20世纪90年代, 不少阿尔巴尼亚族人在科索沃与塞尔维亚族军队发生冲突并遭杀害〕

Ko·tex /ˈkotɛks; ˈkəʊteks/ *trademark* a type of SANITARY TOWEL【商标】"高洁丝"卫生巾

kow·tow /kaʊˈtaʊ; ˌkaʊˈtaʊ/ *v* [I **+to**] *informal* to be too eager to obey or be polite to someone in authority【非正式】顺从, 巴结, 唯命是从

KP /ˌkeˈpi; ˌkeɪ ˈpiː/ *n* [U] *AmE* work that soldiers or children at a camp have to do in a kitchen【美】炊事值勤, 帮厨

kph the written abbreviation of 缩写= kilometres per hour 千米〔公里〕/小时

kraal /krɑl; krɑːl/ *n* [C] **1** a village in South Africa with a fence around it〔用栅栏围起来的〕(南非) 栅栏村庄 **2** *SAfrE* an enclosed piece of ground in which cows, sheep, etc are kept at night【南非】牲畜栏

Krakatoa /ˌkrækəˈtoə; ˌkrɑːkəˈtəʊə/ also 又作 **Krakatua** a mountain that is an active VOLCANO in the Sunda Strait near Indonesia. In 1883 it ERUPT*ed* and caused the deaths of 36,000 people. 喀拉喀托〔位于印尼附近巽他海峡一活火山。1883年, 该火山爆发, 造成36,000人死亡〕

Kra·ken /ˈkrɑkən; ˈkrɑːkən/ in Norse MYTHOLOGY, a very large frightening sea-animal 北海巨妖〔古斯堪的那维亚神话中一可怕的巨型海怪〕

kraut /kraut; kraʊt/ *n* [C] *slang* an insulting word for someone from Germany【俚】德国佬〔侮辱性用语〕

Krem·lin, the /ˋkrɛmlɪn; ˈkremlɪ̣n/ *n* **a)** the government of Russia and the former USSR 俄罗斯政府；前苏联政府 **b)** the government buildings of Russia and the former USSR in Moscow 克里姆林宫〔位于莫斯科的俄罗斯和前苏联政府大楼〕

krill /krɪl; krɪl/ *n* [U] small SHELLFISH 磷虾（群）

Krish·na /ˋkrɪʃnə; ˈkrɪʃnə/ in Hindu MYTHOLOGY, the most important AVATAR (=a god in human form) of the god Vishnu. He is often shown in art as a beautiful young man, often with blue skin and sometimes playing a FLUTE. 克里希那，黑天〔印度教神话中毗湿奴神最重要的化身。在画中，他是一名蓝皮肤的英俊青年，有时吹奏长笛〕

Kriss Krin·gle /ˏkrɪs ˋkrɪŋgḷ; ˌkrɪs ˈkrɪŋgəl/ *n* [singular] *AmE* another name for SANTA CLAUS【美】圣诞老人〔Santa Claus 的另一叫法〕

kro·na /ˋkronə; ˈkrəʊnə/ *n plural* **kronor** /-nɔr; -nɔː/ or **kronur** /-nɚ; -nə/ the standard unit of money in Sweden and Iceland 克朗〔瑞典和冰岛的标准货币单位〕

kro·ne /ˋkronɛ; ˈkrəʊnə/ *n plural* **kroner** /-nɛr; -nə/ [C] the standard unit of money in Denmark and Norway 克朗〔丹麦和挪威的货币单位〕

Kruger /ˋkrugɚ; ˈkruːgə/**, Freddy** /ˋfrɛdɪ; ˈfredi/ a frightening character in the film *Nightmare on Elm Street* (1984). He is a serial killer who has knives instead of fingernails. 克鲁格〔电影《猛鬼街》(1984) 中的恐怖人物。他是个指尖带有利刃的连环杀手〕

Kru·ger·rand /ˋkrugəˏrænd; ˈkruːgəˌrænd/ *n* [C] a South African gold coin〔南非的〕克鲁格[富格林]金币

kryp·ton[1] /ˋkrɪptɑn; ˈkrɪptɒn/ *n* [U] a gas that is an ELEMENT (=basic substance), found in the air 氪（气）

Krypton[2] the imaginary PLANET where the character Superman was born 氪星，克里普顿星〔虚构的行星，超人的出生地〕

Kryp·ton·ite /ˋkrɪptənaɪt; ˈkrɪptənaɪt/ *n* [U] a type of rock that comes from the PLANET Krypton in the Superman stories. It is harmful to Superman. 氪星石〔超人故事中来自氪星的一种岩石，对超人有害〕

KS the written abbreviation of 缩写= KANSAS

Kt the written abbreviation of 缩写= KNIGHT

kt the written abbreviation of 缩写= KNOT[1] (3)

K through 12 in the US, the period of schooling from KINDERGARTEN through to grade 12 – the final year of high school（美国）幼儿园到高中毕业教育阶段

Kua·la Lum·pur /ˏkwɑlə lʊmˋpʊr; ˌkwɑːlə ˈlʊmpʊə/ the capital and largest city of Malaysia, established in the 19th century and an important business and industrial centre 吉隆坡〔马来西亚首都和最大城市，建于19世纪，为重要的工商业中心〕

Kub·lai Khan /ˏkublə ˋkɑn; ˌkuːblə ˈkɑːn/ (1216-94) a Mongol EMPEROR of China from 1259 until his death, whose grandfather was Genghis Khan. He moved the capital of China to Peking. There is a famous English poem about him called *Kubla Khan*, by Samuel Taylor Coleridge. 忽必烈〔(1216-1294)，中国的蒙古皇帝，1259年即位直至去世，祖父为成吉思汗。他把首都迁至北京。塞缪尔·泰勒·柯尔律治的著名英语诗《忽必烈汗》讲述的就是他的故事〕

Ku·brick /ˋkubrɪk; ˈkuːbrɪk/**, Stanley** /ˋstænlɪ; ˈstænli/ (1928-99), a US film DIRECTOR, producer, and writer, whose films include *2001: A Space Odyssey* (1968), *A Clockwork Orange* (1971), and *The Shining* (1980) 库布里克〔(1928-1999)，美国电影导演、制片人和作家。其影片包括《2001太空漫游》(1968)、《发条橘》(1971) 和《闪灵》(1980)〕

ku·dos /ˋkjudɑs; ˈkjuːdɒs/ *n* [U] admiration and respect that you get for being important or doing something important 荣誉，光荣；名声；威信

Ku Klux Klan, the /ˏku klʌks ˋklæn; ˌkuː klʌks ˈklæn/ *n* a secret American political organization of Protestant white men who oppose people of other races or religions 三K党〔反对其他种族或宗教的美国白种男性新教徒的秘密政治组织〕

kum·quat /ˋkʌmkwɑt; ˈkʌmkwɒt/ *n* [C] the American spelling of CUMQUAT cumquat的美式拼法

kung fu /ˏkʌŋ ˋfu; ˌkʌŋ ˈfuː/ *n* [U] an ancient Chinese fighting art in which you attack people with your hands and feet 中国功夫[拳术]

Kupang the capital of Timor, Indonesia 古邦〔位于印度尼西亚帝汶岛的省会〕

Kurd /kɝd; kɜːd/ *n* [C] a member of a people living in countries such as Iran, Iraq, and Turkey 库尔德人〔居住在伊朗、伊拉克和土耳其等国〕

Kurd·is·tan /ˏkɝdɪˋstɑn; ˌkɜːdɪˈstɑːn/ an area of land which consists of parts of Turkey, Iran, Iraq, Syria, and Armenia where the Kurds live, but which is not a separate country 库尔德斯坦〔指库尔德人分布区，包括土耳其、伊朗、伊拉克、叙利亚和亚美尼亚等国的部分地区，但不是一个独立的国家〕

Ku·ro·sa·wa /ˏkurəˋsɑwə; ˌkʊərəˈsɑːwə/**, A·ki·ra** /əˋkɪrə; əˈkɪərə/ (1910-98) one of Japan's greatest film DIRECTORs, who is famous for films such as *The Seven Samurai* (1954) and *Kagemusha* (1980) 黑泽明〔(1910-1998)，日本最杰出的电影导演之一，以《七武士》(1954) 和《影子武士》(1980) 闻名〕

Kurtz /kɝts; kɜːts/ a character in the NOVEL *Heart of Darkness* by Joseph Conrad. Kurtz is an educated white man in central Africa, who has stopped accepting Western values and has become the violent, powerful ruler of an African community. 库尔兹〔约瑟夫·康拉德的小说《黑暗的心》中的人物。他是非洲中部一名有文化的白人，但却不再接受西方价值观而成为非洲某一社会的首领，性情残暴，不可一世〕

Ku·wait /kuˋwaɪt; kʊˈweɪt/ a country in the Middle East, north of Saudi Arabia and south of Iraq. Population: 2,042,000 (2001). Capital: Kuwait City. It is an oil-producing country. Iraq attacked it in 1990, causing the Gulf War. 科威特〔中东一产油国，位于沙特阿拉伯以北，伊拉克以南。人口：2,042,000 (2001)，首都：科威特城。1990年伊拉克侵占该国，引发了海湾战争〕—**Kuwaiti** *n, adj*

kvetch /kvɛtʃ; kvetʃ/ *v* [I] *AmE informal* to continually complain about something【美，非正式】〔对某事〕不断抱怨 —**kvetch** *n* [C]

kw the written abbreviation of 缩写= KILOWATT

kwe·la /ˋkwelə; ˈkweɪlə/ *n* [U] a kind of dance music popular among black South African people 基维拉舞曲〔南非黑人喜爱的一种舞曲〕

kwh the written abbreviation of 缩写= KILOWATT HOUR

KY the written abbreviation of 缩写= KENTUCKY

Kyr·gy·zstan /ˏkɪrgɪˋstæn; ˌkɪəgɪˈstɑːn/ also 又作 **kirghizia** /kɪrˋgɪzɪə; kɪəˈgɪziə/ a country in central Asia between China and Uzbekistan, which used to be part of the former Soviet Union. Population: 4,753,000 (2001). Capital: Bishkek. 吉尔吉斯斯坦〔中亚一国家，位于中国和乌兹别克斯坦之间，过去曾为前苏联的一部分。人口：4,753,000 (2001)，首都：比什凯克〕

Ky·u·shu /kɪˋuʃu; kiˈuːʃuː/ the most southern and the third largest of the main islands of Japan, whose main cities are Fukuoka and Nagasaki 九州〔日本第三大岛，是日本四大岛屿中最南端的一座，主要城市有福冈和长崎〕

K

L,l

L, l /ɛl; el/ *n plural* **L's, l's** [C] **1** the 12th letter of the English alphabet 英语字母表的第十二个字母 **2** the number 50 in the system of ROMAN NUMERALS 罗马数字 50

l 1 the written abbreviation of 缩写= LITRE **2** the written abbreviation of 缩写= line **3** also 又作 **L** the written abbreviation of 缩写= lake

LA¹ /ˌɛl ˋe; ˌel ˈeɪ◂/ the abbreviation of 缩写= LOS ANGELES

LA² the written abbreviation of 缩写= LOUISIANA

la /lɑ; lɑː/ *n* [singular] the sixth note in a musical SCALE¹ (8), according to the SOL-FA system 全音阶第六音

Lab the written abbreviation of 缩写= LABOUR PARTY

lab /læb; læb/ *n* [C] *informal* a LABORATORY【非正式】实验室

3 **la·bel¹** /ˋlebl; ˈleɪbəl/ *n* [C] **1** a piece of paper or other material that is stuck onto something and gives information about it 标签, 标记: *a luggage label* 行李标签 **2** the name of a record company 唱片公司名: *their new release on the Ace Sounds label* 由Ace Sounds唱片公司给他们灌制的新唱片 **3** a word or phrase which is used to describe a person, group, or thing, but which is unfair or not correct〔用以描述人、组织或事物的〕称号, 外号, 绰号;〔以不公平或不正确的称号将人扣上的〕帽子: *Men tend to accept these arrangements in order to avoid attracting the 'sexist' label.* 男人往往愿意接受这些安排, 以免被扣上"性歧视"的大帽子。

label² *v* **labelled, labelling** *BrE*【英】, **labeled, labeling** *AmE*【美】[T] **1** to fix a label onto something or write information on something 贴标签于; 用标签标明: *Label the diagram as shown.* 按所示在图表上标明。| **label sth poison/secret etc** *The file was labelled 'Top Secret'.* 该文件被标为"绝密"。**2** to use a word or phrase to describe someone or something, but often unfairly or incorrectly〔用称号、外号、绰号〕描述〔某人或某物〕; 给…扣帽子: **label sb/sth (as) sth** *The newspapers had unjustly labelled him a troublemaker.* 报界都不公正地给他扣上闹事者的帽子。

la·bi·a /ˋlebɪə; ˈleɪbiə/ *n* [plural] the outer folds of the female sex organ 阴唇

la·bi·al /ˋlebɪəl; ˈleɪbiəl/ *n* [C] *technical* a speech sound made using one or both lips【术语】唇音 —**labial** *adj* —see also 另见 BILABIAL

La Bo·hème /lɑ boˋɛm; lɑː bəʊˈem/ (1896) an OPERA by Puccini about a young woman called Mimi who has a relationship with a poet called Rodolfo, but later becomes very ill and dies《绣花女》, 又译《波西米亚人》〔(1896), 普契尼创作的一部歌剧。剧中有个名叫咪咪的年轻姑娘与诗人鲁道夫产生了感情, 但后来咪咪得重病去世〕

la·bor /ˋlebɚ; ˈleɪbə/ *n* [U] the American spelling of LABOUR labour 的美式拼法

la·bor·a·tory /ˋlæbrəˌtorɪ; ləˈbɒrətri/ *n* [C] a special room or building in which a scientist tests and prepares substances 实验室: *a research laboratory* 研究实验室 | **laboratory experiments/animals etc** *tests on laboratory animals* 在实验室动物身上做的试验 —see also 另见 LANGUAGE LABORATORY 3

Labor Day /ˋ‥ ˌ‥/ *n AmE* a public holiday in the US on the first Monday in September【美】劳工节〔9月的第一个星期一, 为美国的公众假日〕

> **CULTURAL NOTE 文化注释**
>
> Labor Day was originally established to honour workers, but now most people think of it as the last day of summer and celebrate it with PICNICS and BARBECUES over **Labor Day Weekend**. 劳工节本是为工人设立, 以示敬重, 但是现在多数人把这一天看成是夏季的最后一天, 并在劳工节周末举行野餐和烧烤来庆祝。

la·bored /ˋlebɚd; ˈleɪbəd/ *adj* the American spelling of LABOURED laboured 的美式拼法

laboratory 实验室

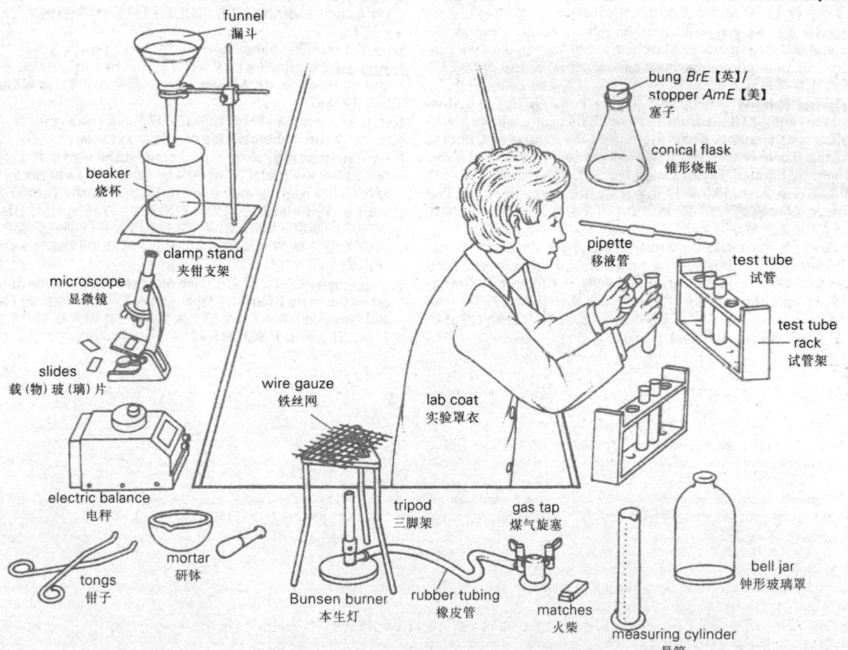

la·bor·er /ˈlebərə; ˈleɪbərə/ *n* [C] the American spelling of LABOURER labourer的美式拼法

labor-in·ten·sive /ˌ‥ˈ‥◂/ *adj* the American spelling of LABOUR-INTENSIVE labour-intensive 的美式拼法

la·bo·ri·ous /ləˈbɔriəs; ləˈbɔːriəs/ *adj* **1 laborious task/process/method etc** a job or piece of work that is difficult and needs a lot of effort 费劲的工作/过程/方法等: *the laborious task of collating all the evidence* 核对所有证据的艰苦工作 **2** seeming to be done slowly and with difficulty 缓慢而吃力的: *laborious progress through the work* 工作的进展缓慢而吃力 —**laboriously** *adv*: *Selina was laboriously copying out her homework.* 塞利娜当时在吃力地抄写作业。—**laboriousness** *n* [U]

labor-sav·ing /ˈ‥ ,‥/ *adj* the American spelling of LABOUR-SAVING labour-saving 的美式拼法

labor u·nion /ˈ‥ ,‥/ *n* [C] *AmE* an organization that represents the ordinary workers in a particular trade or profession, especially in meetings with employers【美】〔尤指在某一行业中代表普通工人与雇主交涉的〕工会; TRADE UNION *BrE*【英】

la·bour¹ *BrE*【英】, **labor** *AmE*【美】/ˈlebə; ˈleɪbə/ *n*
1 ►WORK 工作◄ [U] effort or work, especially physical work 努力; 工作〔尤指体力劳动〕: *The garage charges £30 an hour for labour.* 汽车修理厂每小时收取30英镑的工钱。| **manual labour** (=work with tools you hold in your hands) 体力劳动 *Building still involves a lot of manual labour.* 建筑仍然包含许多体力劳动。| **withdraw your labour** (=protest by stopping work) 停工〔抗议〕*Workers withdrew their labour for twenty-four hours.* 工人停工24小时。—see also 另见 HARD LABOUR
2 ►WORKERS 劳动者◄ [U] all the people who work for a company or in a country 员工, 工人: *Organized labour banded together to fight the anti-union laws.* 有组织的工人联合起来反对反工会法。| **skilled/unskilled labour** *a shortage of skilled labour* 缺乏熟练工人 | **cheap labour** (=people who are paid very low wages) 廉价劳工 | **labour costs/shortages etc** *Immigrants may help to solve labour shortages.* 移民可以有助于解决劳动力短缺的问题。—see also 另见 LABOUR FORCE
3 ►BABY 婴儿◄ [singular,U] the process in which a baby is born by being pushed from its mother's body, or the period of time during which this happens 分娩; 产程: **be in labour** *Meg was in labour for 6 hours.* 梅格分娩了六个小时。| **go into labour** *Diane went into labour at 2 o'clock.* 黛安娜2点钟开始分娩。| **labour pains/ward/room** *No men were allowed in the labour room.* 产房禁止男士进入。
4 a labour of love something that is hard work but that you do because you want to 心甘情愿所做的苦工
5 my/your labours *formal* a period of hard work【正式】我/你的一段时间的辛勤工作: *We sat down to rest after our labours.* 苦干了一阵子后, 我们坐下来休息。

labour² *BrE*【英】, **labor** *AmE*【美】*v* **1** [I,T] to try very hard to do something; struggle 努力做〔某事〕; 奋争: **[+over]** *I've been labouring over this report all morning.* 整个早上我都忙于做这份报告。| **labour to do sth** *Ray had little talent but laboured to acquire the skills of a writer.* 雷没有什么才能, 但努力学习写作技巧。**2** [I] to work hard 辛勤工作: *Marina had laboured late into the night to finish her essay.* 为完成文章, 玛丽娜工作到深夜。**3 labour under a delusion/misconception/misapprehension etc** to believe something that is not true 错觉, 误解 **4 labour the point** to describe or explain something in too much detail or when people have already understood it 过于详细地讲述某事 **5** [I] if an engine labours it turns too slowly and with difficulty〔引擎〕缓慢而困难地运转

Labour³ *n* [U,not with *the* 不与the连用] the British LABOUR PARTY〔英国〕工党: *We all vote Labour in this house.* 在本院中我们都投工党的票。

Labour⁴ *adj* supporting or connected with the British LABOUR PARTY 支持工党的; 与工党有关的: *a Labour MP* 工党下议院议员 | *Labour policies* 工党的方针政策

labour camp *BrE*【英】, **labor camp** *AmE*【美】/ˈ‥ ‥/ *n* [C] a prison camp where prisoners have to do hard physical work 劳动营, 劳改营

la·boured *BbE*【英】, **labored** *AmE*【美】/ˈlebəd; ˈdeɪbəd/ *adj* showing signs of effort and difficulty 吃力的, 费劲的: *laboured breathing* 费力的呼吸

la·bour·er *BrE*【英】, **laborer** *AmE*【纥】/ˈlebərə; ˈleɪbərə/ *n* [C] someone whose wkrk needs strength rather than skill, especially someone who works outdoors 体力劳动者; 工人〔尤指户外劳动者〕: *a farm labourer* 农场工人

labour ex·change /ˈ‥ ,‥/ *n* [C] a former British government office where people went to find jobs 职业介绍所〔旧时英国的政府机构〕—compare 比较 JOB CENTRE

labour force *BrE*【英】, **labor force** *AmE*【美】/ˈ‥ ‥/ *n* **the labour force** all the people who work for a company or in a country 劳动力

labour-in·ten·sive *BrE*【英】, **labor-intensive** *AmE*【美】/ˌ‥ˈ‥◂/ *adj* an industry or type of work that is labour-intensive needs a lot of workers 劳动密集型的: *labour-intensive farming methods* 劳动密集型的耕作法 —see also 另见 CAPITAL INTENSIVE

labour mar·ket *BrE*【英】, **labor market** *AmE*【美】/ˈ‥ ,‥/ *n* **the labour market** the combination of workers available and jobs available in one place at one time 劳工市场, 劳动力市场: *married women reentering the labour market* 重新进入劳动力市场的已婚妇女

labour move·ment *BrE*【英】, **labor movement** *AmE*【美】/ˈ‥ ,‥/ *n* **the labour movement** the political parties representing working people, and all other organizations which have the same beliefs and aims 工人运动

Labour Par·ty, the /ˈ‥ ,‥/ *n* a political party in Britain and some other countries that aims to improve social conditions for ordinary working people and poorer people〔英国和其他一些国家的〕工党, 劳工党

CULTURAL NOTE 文化注释

The Labour Party is one of the two main political parties in the UK. It was traditionally a SOCIALIST party that was closely connected with the TRADE UNIONS, but during the 1980s and 1990s it changed and moved towards the political centre, especially after Tony Blair became party leader in 1994. Since then the party has also been known as New Labour. The Labour Party lost power to the Conservative Party in 1979, but won power from the Conservatives in 1997 and won the election again in 2001.工党是英国的两大主要政党之一。传统上的工党曾是一个与工会有着密切联系的社会党。但是20世纪80、90年代, 特别是托尼·布莱尔1994年成为党首之后, 工党发生了变化, 其政治立场渐向政治中间地带靠近。从那时起, 该党亦被看做新工党。1979年工党败给了保守党, 但是1997年又从后者手中赢回了权柄, 其后在2001年的选举中再次获胜。—compare 比较 CONSERVATIVE PARTY

labour re·la·tions *BrE*【英】, **labor relations** *AmE*【美】/ˈ‥ ,‥/ *n* [plural] the relationship between employers and workers 劳资关系: *a company with good labour relations* 劳资关系和谐的公司

labour-sav·ing *BrE*【英】, **labor-saving** *AmE*【美】/ˈ‥ ,‥/ *adj* [only before noun 仅用于名词前] **labour-saving device/gadget/equipment etc** something that makes it easier for you to do a particular job 节省劳力的装置/器具/设备等

Lab·ra·dor /ˈlæbrəˌdɔr; ˈlæbrədɔː/ *n* [C] a large dog with fairly short black or yellow hair 拉布拉多猎犬, 纽芬兰拾猿—see picture at 参见 DOG¹ 图

la·bur·num /ləˈbɝnəm; ləˈbɜːnəm/ *n* [C,U] a small tree with long hanging stems of yellow flowers and poisonous seeds 金链花; 金链花属植物

lab·y·rinth /ˈlæbəˌrɪnθ; ˈlæbərɪnθ/ *n* [C] **1** a large network of paths or passages which cross each other, making it very difficult to find your way; MAZE (3) 迷宫; 曲径: **[+of]** *a labyrinth of long corridors* 迷宫似的长廊 **2** something that is very complicated and difficult to understand 复杂难懂的事物: **[+of]** *a labyrinth of EC directives* 错综复杂的欧共体的指示 —**labyrinthine** /ˌlæbəˈrɪnθɪn; ˌlæbəˈrɪnθaɪn◂/ *adj*: *the labyrinthine complexity of bureaucracy* 官僚主义的繁文缛节

lace¹ /les; leɪs/ *n* **1** [U] a fine cloth made with patterns of many very small holes 网眼织物, 花边: *a handkerchief trimmed with lace* 饰有花边的手绢 | *lace curtains* 网眼纱帘 —see also 另见 LACY —see picture on page A16 参见A16页图 **2** [C] a string that is pulled through special holes in shoes or clothing to pull the edges together and fasten them 鞋带; 系带 —see picture at 参见 SHOE¹ 图

lace² *v* [T] **1** also 又作 **lace up** to pull something together or fasten something by tying a LACE¹ (2) 系〔(鞋)带〕, 用带子将…系紧: *Lace up your shoes or you'll trip over.* 把鞋带系好, 否则你会绊倒。| **lace sth to** *The canvas was laced to a steel frame.* 油画布被固定在钢制的画框内。**2** to pass a string or LACE¹(2) through holes in something such as a pair of shoes 将线[绳, 带]穿过〔鞋子等〕的孔眼 **3** to add a small amount of alcohol or a drug to a drink 给〔饮料〕掺酒[药物]: **lace sth with** *coffee laced with Irish whiskey* 掺有爱尔兰威士忌的咖啡 **4 be laced with** if a book, lesson, speech etc is laced with something, it has a lot

of a particular quality all through it〔书、课文、演讲等中〕掺有…: *The novel is laced with sexual imagery.* 这本小说掺杂着大量的性描述。**5** *literary* to weave or twist something together【文】把〔某物〕交织在一起: *Hannah laced her fingers together.* 汉娜把手指扣在一起。

la·ce·rate /ˈlæsəˌret; ˈlæsəreɪt/ *v* [T] to tear skin or flesh with something sharp〔用锐器〕撕裂, 划破, 割伤〔皮肤或肉体〕: *badly lacerated by bomb fragments* 被炸弹碎片严重割伤

la·ce·ra·tion /ˌlæsəˈreʃən; ˌlæsəˈreɪʃən/ *n* [C,U] *technical* serious cuts in your skin or flesh【术语】〔皮肤或肉体的〕严重划破, 撕裂, 割伤: [**+to**] *multiple lacerations to the upper arms* 上臂的多处割伤

lace-up /ˈ· ·/ *n* [C usually plural 一般用复数] *especially BrE* shoes fastened with laces (LACE[1] (2))【尤英】系带的鞋 —**lace-up** *adj*: *shiny black lace-up shoes* 光亮的黑色系带鞋

lach·ry·mal /ˈlækrəml; ˈlækrɪməl/ *adj technical* connected with tears【术语】眼泪的: *lachrymal glands* 泪腺

lach·ry·mose /ˈlækrəˌmos; ˈlækrɪməʊs/ *adj formal*【正式】**1** often crying; TEARFUL 爱哭的; 泪汪汪的: *Avril was feeling tired and lachrymose.* 埃夫里尔累得想哭。**2** making you feel sad 使人伤感的: *lachrymose drama* 催人泪下的戏剧

S2 W2 **lack[1]** /læk; læk/ *n* [singular, U] the state of not having something, or of not having enough of it 没有; 不足; 缺乏: [**+of**] *Lack of vitamin B can produce a variety of symptoms.* 缺少维生素 B 会引发多种症状。| **a complete/distinct/marked/total lack of** *Rosie was showing a marked lack of interest in her school work.* 罗西明显表露出对学业缺乏兴趣。| **for/through lack of** (=because there is a lack of) 因缺乏…: *new mums, exhausted through lack of sleep* 由于缺乏睡眠而疲惫不堪的新妈妈们 | **no lack of** (=used when there is a lot of something) 不缺 *There was no lack of willing helpers.* 不乏自愿帮助者。

W3 **lack[2]** *v* **1** [T] to not have something that you need, or not have enough of it 没有; 缺乏: *Alex's real problem is that he lacks confidence.* 亚历克斯的真正问题是缺乏信心。**2 lack for nothing** *formal* to have everything that you need【正式】应有尽有: *Russell's parents made sure that he lacked for nothing.* 拉塞尔的父母设法确保他什么都不缺。

lack·a·dai·si·cal /ˌlækəˈdezɪkl; ˌlækəˈdeɪzɪkəl◂/ *adj* not showing enough interest in something or not putting enough effort into it 无精打采的; 懒散的: *David has a rather lackadaisical approach to his work.* 戴维对工作的态度相当懒散。—**lackadaisically** /-klɪ; -kli/ *adv*

lack·ey /ˈlækɪ; ˈlæki/ *n* [C] someone who behaves like a servant by always doing what someone else tells them to 走卒, 唯命是从者

lack·ing /ˈlækɪŋ; ˈlækɪŋ/ *adj* [not before noun 不用于名词前] **1 be lacking in** to not have enough of something such as a quality or skill 缺乏〔某种品质或技能〕: *She seems to be sadly lacking in tact.* 她似乎太不够老练了。**2** if something that you need is lacking, you do not have it 缺少的, 没有的: *Financial backing for the project is still lacking.* 这个项目仍然缺少财政支持。**3** *old fashioned* not very intelligent【过时】智力欠缺的: *The poor lad's a bit lacking.* 这个可怜的小伙子智力有点欠缺。

lack·lus·tre *BrE*【英】, **lackluster** *AmE*【美】/ˈlækˌlʌstɚ; ˈlækˌlʌstə/ *adj* not very exciting, impressive etc; dull 毫无生气的; 无光泽的; 乏味的: *a lacklustre performance* 不精彩的演出 | *lacklustre hair* 干枯的头发

la·con·ic /ləˈkɑnɪk; ləˈkɒnɪk/ *adj* using only a few words to say something〔语言〕简短的 —**laconically** /-klɪ; -kli/ *adv*

lac·quer[1] /ˈlækɚ; ˈlækə/ *n* [U] **1** a liquid painted onto metal or wood to form a hard shiny surface〔涂在金属、木材上的〕漆 **2** *old-fashioned* a transparent liquid that you put on your hair so that it keeps its shape【过时】〔用于固定发型的〕发胶

lacquer[2] *v* [T] **1** to cover something with LACQUER[1] (1) 用漆涂盖: *a black lacquered box* 涂了黑漆的箱子 **2** to use LACQUER[1] (2) on your hair 给〔头发〕喷定型发胶

la·crosse /ləˈkrɔs; ləˈkrɒs/ *n* [U] a game played on a field by two teams of ten players, in which each player has a long stick with a net on the end of it and uses this to throw, catch and carry a small ball 兜网球, 长曲棍球〔用带网的曲棍来掷球、捕球、持球的队际运动〕

> **CULTURAL NOTE 文化注释**
> In Britain many people think of lacrosse as being played only by girls at private schools. 在英国, 很多人认为兜网球只是私立学校的女学生玩的运动。

lac·tate /ˈlækˌtet; lækˈteɪt/ *v* [I] *technical* to produce milk in your breasts【术语】泌乳

lac·ta·tion /lækˈteʃən; lækˈteɪʃən/ *n* [U] *technical* the production of milk in a mother's breasts for her baby, or the period during which this milk is produced【术语】泌乳; 泌乳期

lac·tic /ˈlæktɪk; ˈlæktɪk/ *adj technical* connected with milk【术语】乳汁的

lactic a·cid /ˌ·· ˈ··/ *n* [U] an acid found in sour milk and used to help keep food fresh 乳酸

lac·tose /ˈlæktos; ˈlæktəʊs/ *n* [U] a type of sugar found in milk, sometimes used as a food for babies and sick people 乳糖

la·cu·na /ləˈkjunə; ləˈkjuːnə/ *n plural* **lacunae** /-ni; -niː/ or **lacunas** [C] *formal* an empty space in a piece of writing, where something is missing【正式】〔文章中的〕脱漏

lac·y /ˈlesɪ; ˈleɪsi/ *adj* made of LACE[1] (1) or looking like lace 网眼织物的; 网眼状的; 有花边的; (似) 带子的: *lacy underwear* 网眼织物做的内衣 | *a plant with delicate, lacy leaves* 长着精巧网状叶子的植物

lad /læd; læd/ *n* [C] *old-fashioned or literary*【过时或文】**1** a boy or young man 男孩; 少年, 男青年, 小伙子: *Things were different when I was a lad.* 我年轻的时候, 情况不大相同。**2 the lads** *BrE spoken* a group of men you know and work with or spend your free time with【英口】伙伴: *a night out with the lads* 和伙伴们外出的一个通宵 | **one of the lads** (=a member of your group of friends) 伙伴之一 **3** a boy or man who works with horses; STABLE BOY 马倌, 马夫 **4 a bit of a lad** *BrE spoken* a man that people like even though he behaves rather badly【英口】放荡不羁的人: *That Charlie's a bit of a lad, isn't he?* 那个查利是个放荡鬼, 对不对? —compare 比较 LASS —see also 另见 JACK THE LAD S3 W3

lad·der[1] /ˈlædɚ; ˈlædə/ *n* [C] **1** a piece of equipment for climbing a wall, the side of a building etc, consisting of two long pieces of wood, metal, or rope, joined to each other by RUNGS (=steps) 梯子 —see also 另见 ROPE LADDER, STEPLADDER 

> **CULTURAL NOTE 文化注释**
> Some people believe the old SUPERSTITION that it is unlucky to walk under a ladder that is leaning against a wall. 有人相信一个古老的迷信说法, 即从斜靠着墙的梯子下走过会带来噩运。

2 a series of jobs by which you gradually become more important within an organization〔在机构内逐渐晋升的〕阶梯, 途径: *clerical workers on the bottom rung of the ladder* 在晋升阶梯底层的办事员 **3** *BrE* a long thin hole in knitted (KNIT (1)) clothing, STOCKINGS or TIGHTS where stitches have broken【英】〔织物的〕抽丝, 脱针, 脱线; RUN[2] (19) *AmE*【美】**4** a list of players of a game such as SQUASH or tennis who play each other regularly in order to decide who is the best〔壁球或网球等运动中的〕名次排列表 —see also 另见 SNAKES AND LADDERS

ladder[2] *v* [I,T] *BrE* if a STOCKING (1) or a pair of TIGHTS ladders or is laddered, a long thin hole is made in them【英】(使)〔裤袜等〕抽丝; RUN[2](19) *AmE*【美】

lad·die, laddy /ˈlædɪ; ˈlædi/ *n* [C] *informal especially BrE* a boy【非正式, 尤英】男孩, 少年, 小伙子

la·den /ˈledn; ˈleɪdn/ *adj literary*【文】**1** heavily loaded with something 装满的, 满载的: [**+with**] *a Christmas tree laden with presents* 挂满了礼物的圣诞树 | **fully/ heavily laden** *The lorry was fully laden.* 这货车满载了。**2 laden with troubles/problems etc** full of troubles etc 充满忧虑/问题等: *Antonia was laden with doubts about the affair.* 关于此事安东尼娅满腹疑虑。

ladies' man /ˈ·· ·/ *n* [C] a man who likes to spend time with women and thinks they enjoy being with him 喜欢与女人厮混的男人

ladies' room /ˈ·· ·/ *n* [C] *AmE* a women's toilet【美】女厕所, 女洗手间; the ladies *BrE*【英】

la·ding /ˈledɪŋ; ˈleɪdɪŋ/ *n* [C,U] —see 见 BILL OF LADING

la·dle[1] /ˈledl; ˈleɪdl/ *n* [C] a large deep spoon with a long handle, used for lifting liquid out of a container 长柄勺: *a soup ladle* 汤勺 —see picture at 参见 SPOON[1] 图

ladle[2] *v* [T] to serve soup or other food onto plates or bowls, especially using a ladle〔尤指用长柄勺〕舀, 盛

ladle sth ↔ out *phr v* [T] to give someone too much of something such as advice or praise, without thinking carefully about it〔不假思索地〕大量给予〔建议或称赞〕; 随便滥给: *ladling out compliments* 大肆恭维

la·dy /ˈledɪ; ˈleɪdi/ *n plural* **ladies** [C] 

1 ►WOMAN 妇女◄ **a)** a word meaning woman, used because people think it is a more polite word 女士; 夫人; 小姐〔礼貌用语〕: *Give your coat to the lady over there.* 把你的外衣交给那位女士。| *The young lady at reception sent me up here.* 接待处

的小姐让我来这里的。| *the ladies' darts team* 女子掷镖队 | **tea lady/cleaning lady etc** (=a woman who does a particular job) 端茶小姐/清洁女工等 | **lady doctor/councillor etc** (=a polite word, which many women find offensive, for a woman doctor, councillor, etc) 女医生/女议员等〔礼貌用语，很多妇女认为这类词具冒犯性〕—see also 另见 DINNER LADY **b)** *approving especially AmE* a woman, especially one with a strong character【褒，尤美】女士，夫人；小姐〔尤指个性很强的女性〕: *She's a real smart lady.* 她是位很时髦的女性。

2 ►POLITE WOMAN 文雅的女性◄ a woman who is always polite and behaves very well 举止文雅的女人，淑女: *Sheila always tries to be a lady.* 希拉总是尽力做个淑女。

3 ►WOMAN OF HIGH CLASS 贵妇◄ a woman born into a high social class in Britain〔英国的〕贵妇人，贵族小姐: *a lady of noble birth* 贵族出身的小姐

4 ►WIFE/GIRLFRIEND 妻子/女友◄ *old-fashioned or literary* a man's wife or female friend【过时或文】妻子；女友: *the captain and his lady* 船长和他的妻子

5 ►WHEN SPEAKING TO A WOMAN 称呼妇女时◄ *AmE* a way of addressing a woman, which many women consider to be offensive【美】太太，女士，小姐〔称呼妇女的一种方式，很多女性认为具冒犯性〕: *Hey, lady, watch where you're going!* 嘿，女士，走路瞧着点！

6 the ladies *BrE* a women's toilet【英】女厕所，女洗手间；LADIES ROOM *AmE*【美】—compare 比较 **the gents** (GENT (2))

7 Lady a) used as the title of the wife or daughter of a British NOBLEMAN or the wife of a KNIGHT[1] (2) 太太，夫人，小姐〔用作对英国贵族女眷或爵士妻子的称呼〕: *Lady Diana* 戴安娜小姐 **b)** *BrE* used in the title of women with a high official position【英】职位高的女人〔用在其称呼之前〕: *Lady President* 女总统

8 the lady of the house *old-fashioned* the most important woman in a house, usually the mother of a family【过时】女主人

9 lady of leisure *often humorous* a woman who does not work and has a lot of free time【常幽默】休闲夫人: *So you're a lady of leisure now that the kids are at school?* 孩子们都上学去了，你当起休闲夫人啦？

10 lady friend *often humorous* a man's female friend; GIRLFRIEND【常幽默】女性朋友；女友: *I saw him with his new lady friend.* 我看见他与新的女友在一起。—see also 另见 BAG LADY, FIRST LADY, OLD LADY, OUR LADY

Lady, The a rather old-fashioned British magazine for women, typically read by older, UPPER-CLASS women. It also contains advertisements for servants and nannies (NANNY).《淑女》〔英国出版的一种十分传统的女性杂志。主要读者为年长的上流社会女士。杂志上还刊有征聘用人和保姆的广告〕

Lady and the Tramp /ˌ· · · ˈ·/ (1955) a CARTOON made by Walt Disney, about two dogs who meet and have a romantic relationship. **Lady** is a PEDIGREE dog (=a special type of dog), and she is very well cared for, but **Tramp** is a MONGREL (=a mixture of different types of dogs) who lives on the street.《小姐与流氓》〔(1955) 沃尔特·迪斯尼公司制作的一部卡通片，讲述两条狗相识相恋的故事。片中的"小姐"是条纯种狗，并得到精心照料，而"流氓"则是条流落街头的杂种狗〕

la·dy·bird /ˈledɪˌbɝd; ˈleɪdibɜːd/ *BrE*【英】, **la·dy·bug** /ˈledɪˌbʌg; ˈleɪdibʌg/ *n* [C] *AmE* a small round BEETLE (=a type of insect) that is usually red with black spots【美】瓢虫

Lady Chat·ter·ley's Lov·er /ˌledɪ ˌtʃætəlɪz ˈlʌvɚ; ˌleɪdi ˌtʃætəliz ˈlʌvə/ a NOVEL by D. H. Lawrence which was written in 1928, but could not legally be sold in the UK until 1960 because the story contained a lot of descriptions of sex and was considered to be very shocking. It is about Lady Chatterley, a married woman from a high social class, who has a sexual relationship with her GAMEKEEPER (=someone whose job is to take care of wild birds that are bred to be shot for sport).《查特莱夫人的情人》〔D.H.劳伦斯 1928 年创作的一部长篇小说。该书到 1960 年才在英国合法销售，因为书中有不少性爱内容，这在当时令人十分震惊。该书讲的是上流社会已婚妇女查特莱夫人的故事，其与家中猎场看守人之间保持着性关系〕

CULTURAL NOTE 文化注释

At a famous court case in 1960, sometimes called the 'Lady Chatterley Trial', the JURY decided that the book should be allowed to be sold, and people sometimes connect this decision with the general change in attitudes towards sex in the 1960s. 在1960年的一次著名诉讼案，即有时被称为"查特莱夫人审判案"中，陪审团裁定该书可以销售。人们有时将这一裁定与20世纪60年代性观念的普遍转变联系起来。

Lady Day /ˈ· · ·/ 25 March, the day of the Annunciation, on which, according to Christian belief, the news was given to Mary by the Angel Gabriel that she would become the mother of Jesus Christ. Formerly, Lady Day was officially regarded as the first day of the legal year in the UK. 圣母报领节〔3月25日，据基督教教义，这天天使加百列向童贞女马利亚传报，说她将成为耶稣基督之母。圣母报领节这一天曾一度被英国官方确认为法定年历上的第一天〕

la·dy·fin·ger /ˈledɪˌfɪŋgɚ; ˈleɪdiˌfɪŋgə/ *n* [C] *AmE* a small cake shaped like a finger, used to make DESSERTS【美】手指饼干〔用于制作甜品〕

lady-in-wait·ing /ˌ· · ˈ· ·/ *n* [C] a woman who looks after and serves a queen or PRINCESS〔女王或公主的〕女侍臣，女官，宫廷女侍

lady-kill·er /ˈ· · ˌ· ·/ *n* [C] *informal* a man who is very attractive to women but treats them badly【非正式】使女人倾心但对女人不好的男人〔玩弄女性的情场杀手〕: *Matt thinks he's such a lady-killer.* 马特自认为是一位情场杀手。

la·dy·like /ˈledɪˌlaɪk; ˈleɪdilaɪk/ *adj old-fashioned* behaving in the polite, quiet way that was once supposed to be typical of or suitable for women【过时】贵妇人似的，举止似大家闺秀的: *scratching herself in a way that was certainly not ladylike* 她搔痒的样子肯定有失大家闺秀的风度

Lady Macbeth —see 见 Lady MACBETH

Lady Muck /ˌ· · ˈ·/ *n* [C] *humorous* a woman who has a very high opinion of her own importance【幽默】自命不凡的女人: *Look at Lady Muck over there with her parasol.* 瞧那边那个打着太阳伞的神气女人。

Lady of the Lake, the /ˌ· · · · ˈ·/ a mysterious woman in old stories about King Arthur. When Arthur is dying, his sword, Excalibur, is thrown into a lake, and the Lady of the Lake's hand appears from under the water and catches it. She is also one of the three queens who take Arthur by boat to Avalon to die. 湖夫人〔亚瑟王传说中的一位神秘女子。亚瑟王生命垂危之际把神剑掷入湖中，湖夫人之手从水中伸出将其接住。她也是用舟将亚瑟王载至阿瓦隆安逝的三位女王之一〕

Lady of the Lamp, the /ˌ· · · · ˈ·/ —see 见 Florence NIGHTINGALE

la·dy's fin·gers /ˈ· · ˌ· ·/ *n* [plural] OKRA 秋葵，疗伤绒毛花

la·dy·ship /ˈledɪˌʃɪp; ˈleɪdiʃɪp/ *n* **1 your ladyship/her ladyship** used as a way of speaking to or talking about a woman with the title of Lady 夫人，小姐〔对有 Lady 头衔女子的尊称〕: *Her ladyship is waiting for you in the drawing-room.* 夫人正在客厅等你。**2** *BrE spoken* a humorous way of talking about a woman who thinks she is very important【英口】贵夫人，娇小姐〔对自负女人的幽默称谓〕: *Do you think her ladyship will be joining us?* 你认为夫人她会加入我们吗？

lag[1] /læg; læg/ **lagged, lagging** *v* **1** [I] to move or develop more slowly than others 落后，拖后: *Britain was still lagging in the space race.* 在太空竞赛方面英国仍落在后面。| **[+behind]** *Jessica always lags behind, looking in shop windows.* 杰茜卡总是落在后面看各种商店橱窗。**2** [T] *BrE* to cover water pipes etc with a special material to prevent heat from being lost【英】给〔水管等〕加上外罩保暖: *We've had the hot-water tank lagged.* 我们已给热水箱加上了保暖外罩。

lag[2] *n* [C] a delay or period of waiting between one event and a second event; TIME LAG〔两起事件之间的〕延迟，间歇；时差 —see also 另见 JET LAG, OLD LAG

la·ger /ˈlɑgɚ; ˈlɑːgə/ *n BrE*【英】**1** [C,U] a light-coloured beer or a glass of that beer〔一杯〕淡啤酒: *Two halves of lager, please.* 请来两杯半品脱淡啤酒。**2 lager lout** a young man who drinks too much and then behaves violently or rudely〔酒醉后有暴力行为或举止粗鲁的〕年轻酒徒 S3

lag·gard /ˈlægɚd; ˈlægəd/ *n* [C] *old-fashioned* someone or something that is very slow or late【过时】迟缓[落后]的人[物] —**laggardly** *adj*

lag·ging /ˈlægɪŋ; ˈlægɪŋ/ *n* [U] the material used to protect a water pipe or container from heat or cold〔覆盖水管或容器的〕隔热[保温]材料

la·goon /ləˈgun; ləˈguːn/ *n* [C] **1** a lake of sea water partly or completely separated from the sea by sand, rock etc 潟湖，咸水湖，环礁湖: *a tropical lagoon* 热带潟湖 —see picture on page A12 参见 A12 页图 **2** *AmE* a small lake which is not very deep, near a larger lake or river【美】〔大湖或江河附近的〕小而浅的淡水湖

La·gos /ˈlegɑs; ˈleɪgɒs/ the largest city and port in Nigeria and the former capital of the country 拉各斯〔尼日利亚最大城市和港口，曾是该国首都〕

La Guardia /lə ˈgwɑrdɪə; lə ˈgwɑːdiə/ one of the main airports in New York City 拉瓜迪亚机场〔纽约主要机场之一〕

lah-di-dah /ˌlɑ dɪ ˋdɑ; ˌlɑː diː ˈdɑː/ *adj spoken* talking and behaving as if you think you are better or from a higher class than you really are【口】装腔作势的, 故作斯文的

laid /led; leɪd/ past tense and past participle of LAY²

laid-back /ˌ· ˈ·◂/ *adj* relaxed and seeming not to be worried about anything 自在的, 不在乎的: *I don't know how you can be so laid-back about your exams.* 我弄不懂你对考试怎么会如此不在乎。

lain /len; leɪn/ the past participle of LIE¹

lair /lɛr; leə/ *n* [C] **1** the place where a wild animal hides and sleeps 兽穴[窟]; 野兽躲藏处 **2** a place where you go to hide or to be alone 藏身处; 独处的地方: *The police tracked the rapist to his lair.* 警察跟踪找到了强奸犯的藏身处。

laird /lɛrd; leəd/ *n* [C] a Scottish landowner 苏格兰地主 —compare 比较 SQUIRE(1)

lais·sez-faire, laisser-faire /ˌlɛse ˋfɛr; ˌleseɪ ˈfeə/ *n* [U] *French* the principle of allowing private businesses to develop without any state control【法】自由放任主义〔国家对私营企业发展不作任何限制〕: *laissez-faire policies* 自由放任政策

la·i·ty, the /ˈleətɪ; ˈleɪəti/ *n* all the members of a religious group apart from the priests 一般信徒, 俗人

lake /lek; leɪk/ *n* **1** [C] a large area of water surrounded by land 湖: *boating on the lake* 在湖上划船 | *Lake Michigan* 密歇根[密执安]湖 **2 wine lake/milk lake etc** a very large amount of wine, milk etc that is not needed or used 酒池/奶池等〔指生产过量的葡萄酒/牛奶等〕—see also 另见 MOUNTAIN (3)

Lake Dis·trict, the /ˈ· ˌ··/ an area in northwest England famous for its beautiful lakes and mountains and visited by many tourists. The highest mountain in England, Scafell Pike, is in the Lake District, and the area is connected in people's minds with many writers and poets who lived there, especially William Wordsworth and his sister Dorothy. 湖区〔位于英格兰西北部, 以秀美的湖光山色而闻名遐迩, 吸引来大批游客。英格兰最高峰斯科费尔峰即位于湖区。人们提到湖区, 自然会联想到曾在那里居住过的许多作家与诗人, 尤其是威廉·华兹华斯及他的妹妹多萝西〕

lake·side /ˈlekˌsaɪd; ˈleɪksaɪd/ *adj* beside a lake 湖边的, 湖滨的: *a lakeside restaurant* 湖滨饭店 —**lakeside** *n* [singular]

Lake Wo·be·gon /lek ˋwobɪgɒn; leɪk ˈwəʊbɪgɒn/ an imaginary town in stories written by Garrison Keillor, which is typical of a small US town in Minnesota 沃伯根湖镇〔加里森·基勒创作的故事中一虚构小镇, 是美国明尼苏达州的典型小镇〕

lakh /læk; læk/ *number IndE & PakE* a hundred thousand【印和巴】十万

La-la Land /ˈ· · ˌ·/ *n AmE informal*【美, 非正式】**1** another name for Los Angeles, used to mean that the people who live there are slightly crazy拉拉之地〔洛杉矶别称, 用来意指当地人稍有些疯癫〕**2 in La-la Land** if you say that someone is in La-la Land, you mean that they are slightly crazy 疯疯癫癫

La·lique /læˋlik; læˈliːk/, **Re·né** /rəˋne; ˈreneɪ/ (1860-1945) a French designer of jewellery and GLASSWARE (=objects made of glass) in the art nouveau style 拉里克〔(1860-1945), 法国设计大师, 以设计具有新艺术风格的珠宝和玻璃器皿见长〕

lam¹ /læm; læm/ *v*

lam into sb *phr v* [T] *BrE informal* to hit someone or speak angrily to them【英, 非正式】狠击; 怒斥

lam² *n* **on the lam** *AmE informal* escaping from someone, especially the police【美, 非正式】在潜逃中: *Sykes was recaptured after three weeks on the lam.* 赛克斯潜逃三个星期后又被抓获了。

la·ma /ˈlɑmə; ˈlɑːmə/ *n* [C] a Tibetan or Mongolian Buddhist priest 喇嘛〔蒙、藏佛教僧侣〕

La·ma·is·m /ˈlɑməɪzəm; ˈlɑːmə-ɪzəm/ *n* [U] a type of the Buddhism practiced in China's Tibet, Inner Mongolia etc 藏传佛教

La Manche /lɑ ˋmɑnʃ; læ ˈmɒnʃ/ the French name for the English Channel 拉芒什海峡〔英吉利海峡的法语名〕

lamb¹ /læm; læm/ *n* **1** [C] a young sheep 羔羊, 小羊 **2** [U] the meat of a young sheep 羔羊肉: *roast lamb with mint sauce* 薄荷汁烤羊肉 **3** [C] *spoken* someone gentle and loveable, especially a child【口】温柔可爱的人〔尤指小孩〕: *Benny's asleep now, the little lamb.* 本尼, 这个可爱的小宝贝正在睡觉。**4 like a lamb** quietly and without any argument 似羔羊般顺从地: *Suzie went off to school like a lamb today.* 苏齐今天乖乖地去上学了。**5 like a lamb to the slaughter** used when someone is going to do something dangerous but do not realize it 像送去屠宰的羔羊〔指将有危险而未觉察〕

lamb² *v* [I] *technical* to give birth to lambs【术语】生产羊羔: *The ewes are lambing this week.* 本周母羊将要产羊羔。

Lamb, Charles (1775-1834) a British writer of essays, who worked with his sister **Mary Lamb** (1764-1847) on *Tales from Shakespeare*, a book for children that tells the stories of Shakespeare's plays in simple language 兰姆〔(1775-1834) 英国散文家, 与姐姐玛丽·兰姆 (1764-1847) 合著了《莎士比亚戏剧故事集》。该书以少年儿童为读者对象, 用简单易懂的语言讲述莎士比亚的戏剧故事〕

lam·ba·da /læmˋbɑdə; læmˈbɑːdə/ *n* [singular, U] a sexy DISCO dance from Brazil 朗巴达舞〔巴西的一种色情迪斯科舞〕

lam·baste /læmˋbest; læmˈbeɪst/ also 又作 **lam·bast** /-ˋbæst; -ˈbæst/ *v* [T] to attack or criticize someone very strongly 猛烈攻击; 抨击: *Her new play was really lambasted by the critics.* 她的新剧本着实遭到了评论家的猛烈抨击。

lam·bent /ˈlæmbənt; ˈlæmbənt/ *adj literary*【文】**1** clever in a gentle and amusing way 伶俐的, 巧妙的, 诙谐的: *lambent wit* 隽智 **2** a lambent light or flame shines softly and pleasantly〔光或火焰〕闪烁的, 柔和的

Lam·beth Con·fe·rence, the /ˌlæmbəθ ˋkɑnfərəns; ˌlæmbəθ ˈkɒnfərəns/ a formal meeting of all the BISHOPS (=high-ranking priests) of the Church of England from all over the world, which takes place every 10 years 兰贝斯会议〔世界各地的英格兰国教会主教每 10 年举行的一次正式会议〕

Lambeth Pal·ace /ˌ·· ˈ··/ a large very old building that is the official home in London of the Archbishop of Canterbury. The name Lambeth Palace is sometimes used in news reports to mean the people who are in charge of the Church of England. 兰贝斯宫〔坎特伯雷大主教的一幢宏大古老的官邸, 位于伦敦。新闻界有时用该词来指称掌管英格兰国教会的高级神职人员〕: *Lambeth Palace has condemned government policies on the inner city.* 兰贝斯宫谴责政府对内城区所实行的政策。

Lambeth Walk, The /ˌ·· ˈ·/ a dance which was especially popular in the UK in the 1930s and 1940s, in which dancers form a long line, usually in the street. It was danced to a popular song, also called *The Lambeth Walk.* 兰贝斯慢步舞〔20 世纪 30、40 年代英国特别流行的一种集体舞。跳舞的人通常在大街上排成一长行, 舞曲是一首流行歌曲, 名叫《兰贝斯漫步》〕

Lamb of God, the /ˌ· · ˈ·/ another name for Jesus 上帝的羔羊〔耶稣的别名〕

lamb·skin /ˈlæmˌskɪn; ˈlæmˌskɪn/ *n* **1** [C,U] the skin of a lamb, with the wool still on it〔带羊毛的〕羔羊皮: *lambskin gloves* 羔羊皮手套 **2** [U] leather made from the skin of lambs 羔羊皮, 羔皮革

la·mé /lɑˋme; ˈlɑːmeɪ/ *n* [U] cloth containing gold or silver threads 有金[银]线的织物, 金[银]锦缎: *a gold lamé evening skirt* 有金线的晚装女裙

lame¹ /lem; leɪm/ *adj* **1** unable to walk properly because your leg or foot is injured or weak 瘸的, 跛的: **go lame** (=become lame) 变成瘸子 **2** a lame explanation or excuse does not sound very believable〔解释或借口〕无说服力的, 站不住脚的: *Nancy came out with some lame excuse about missing the bus again.* 南希又一次搬出未赶上公共汽车这种牵强的借口。—see also 另见 LAMELY **3 lame duck** a person, business etc that is experiencing difficulties and needs to be helped 跛足鸭〔遭遇困难需要帮助的人或企业等〕**4 lame duck president/administration etc** *especially AmE informal* a president, government etc whose period in office will soon end【尤美, 非正式】任期即将结束的总统/政府等 —**lameness** *n* [U]

lame² *v* [T usually passive 一般用被动态] to make a person or animal unable to walk properly 使〔人或动物〕跛[瘸]; 使残废

lame·brain /ˈlembren; ˈleɪmbreɪn/ *n* [C] *AmE informal* a stupid person【美, 非正式】笨蛋, 蠢货: *Don't do it that way, lamebrain; you'll break it.* 别那样弄, 笨蛋; 你会把它弄坏的。

lame·ly /ˈlemlɪ; ˈleɪmli/ *adv* if you say something lamely, you do not sound confident and other people find it difficult to believe you〔说话〕不自信地, 令人难以相信地: *"But I still love you," he added rather lamely.* "但我还是爱你的。"他很不自信地补充道。

la·ment¹ /ləˋmɛnt; ləˈment/ *v* **1** [I,T] to express feelings of great sadness about something (为…) 悲痛, 哀悼; 痛惜; 悲叹: *The nation lamented the death of its great war leader.* 全国为战时的伟大领袖之死而悲痛。| **[+over]** *lamenting over her luck in love* 为她恋爱的不幸而悲叹 **2** [T] to express annoyance or disappointment about something you think is unsatisfactory or unfair 抱怨: *another article lamenting the decline of popular television* 又一篇抱怨大众化电视走下坡路的文章

lament² *n* [C] a song, piece of music, or something that you say, that expresses a feeling of sadness 挽歌, 哀乐, 悼词: *A lone piper played a lament.* 孤单的风笛手吹奏了一首哀乐。

lam·en·ta·ble /ˈlæməntəbl; ˈlæməntəbəl/ *adj formal* very unsatisfactory or disappointing【正式】可叹的, 令人惋惜的; 让人失望的: *Riley showed a lamentable lack of tact.* 赖利显得特别不够圆通, 令人失望。—**lamentably** *adv*

lam·en·ta·tion /ˌlæmənˈteʃən; ˌlæmənˈteɪʃən/ *n* [C, U] *formal* deep sadness or something that expresses it【正式】悲痛, 悲恸, 哀悼: *There was lamentation throughout the land at the news of the defeat.* 听到战败的消息, 举国为之悲恸。

lam·i·nar flow /ˌlæmɪnɚ ˈflo; ˌlæmɪnə ˈfləʊ/ *n* [U] *technical* a smooth flow of liquid or gas over a solid surface【术语】层流

lam·i·nate /ˈlæməˌnɪt; ˈlæmɪnɪt/ *n* [C,U] laminated material 层压板材

lam·i·nated /ˈlæməˌnetɪd; ˈlæmɪneɪtɪd/ *adj* **1** laminated material has several thin sheets joined on top of each other 由薄片叠成的; 层压的: *laminated glass* 层压玻璃 **2** covered with a layer of thin plastic or metal 由塑料[金属]薄片覆盖的: *wood laminated with plastic* 由塑料贴面覆盖的木制品 —**laminate** *v* [T]

S3 **lamp** /læmp; læmp/ *n* [C] **1** an object that produces light by using electricity, oil, or gas 灯: *a table lamp* 台灯 —see also 另见 HEADLAMP, STANDARD LAMP, STREETLAMP, SAFETY LAMP —see picture at 参见 LIGHT¹ 图 **2** a piece of electrical equipment used to provide a special kind of heat, especially as medical treatment〔尤指治疗用的〕发热灯;〔发出热射线等的〕照射器: *an infrared lamp* 红外线灯 —see also 另见 SUNLAMP, BLOW-LAMP

lamp-black /ˈ· ·/ *n* [U] a fine black colouring material made from SOOT (=the black powder produced by smoke) 灯黑〔由灯上煤炱制成的黑色颜料〕

lamp·light /ˈlæmpˌlaɪt; ˈlæmp-laɪt/ *n* [U] the soft light produced by a lamp 灯光: *Her eyes shone in the lamplight.* 她的眼睛在灯光下闪闪发亮。

lamp·light·er /ˈlæmpˌlaɪtɚ; ˈlæmpˌlaɪtə/ *n* [C] someone whose job was to light lamps in the street in the past 灯夫〔旧时点街灯者〕

lam·poon /læmˈpun; læmˈpuːn/ *v* [T] to write about someone, especially a politician, in a way that makes them seem stupid 用文章讽刺[挖苦]〔政客等〕—**lampoon** *n* [C]

lamp-post /ˈ· ·/ *n* [C] **1** *especially BrE* a tall pole supporting a lamp that lights a street or public area【尤英】路灯柱, 灯杆 —see picture on page A4 参见 A4 页图 **2** *AmE* a pole supporting an old-fashioned type of lamp【美】〔旧式灯的〕灯杆

lamp·shade /ˈlæmpˌʃed; ˈlæmpʃeɪd/ *n* [C] a decorative cover fixed over a lamp to reduce or direct its light 灯罩 —see picture at 参见 LIGHT¹ 图

LAN /læn; læn/ *n* [C] *technical* local area network; a system for communicating by computer in a large place such as an office building【术语】局域网〈如办公楼内的电脑通讯系统〉

Lan·ark·shire /ˈlænəkʃɚ; ˈlænəkʃə/ an area in south central Scotland, which includes the counties (COUNTY) of South and North Lanarkshire 拉纳克郡〔苏格兰中南部一地区, 包括南拉纳克郡和北拉纳克郡〕

Lan·ca·shire /ˈlæŋkəʃɚ; ˈlæŋkəʃə/ abbreviation 缩写为 **Lancs.** a COUNTY in northwest England, which was once the centre of the cotton industry in the UK and had many factories that produced cloth. The large cities of Liverpool and Manchester were formerly part of Lancashire, but now form their own local government areas. 兰开夏郡〔英格兰西北部一郡, 曾经是英国的棉纺工业中心, 建有许多纺织厂。利物浦和曼彻斯特两个大城市原属于该郡, 但现在已成为由各自地方政府管理的地区〕

Lan·cas·ter Gate often used in British newspapers to mean the English Football Association (FA). Lancaster Gate is a road in West London, where the FA building is. 兰开斯特门〔英国报纸常借以指称英国足球协会。它是西伦敦的一条大道, 英国足球协会大楼就坐落于此〕

lance¹ /læns; lɑːns/ *n* [C] a long thin pointed weapon that was used in the past by soldiers on horses〔昔日骑兵用的〕长矛

lance² *v* [T] to cut a small hole in someone's flesh with a sharp instrument to let out PUS (=yellow liquid produced by infection)〔用锋利的刀子〕切开〔放脓〕: *to lance a boil* 切开疖子

lance cor·po·ral /ˌ· ˈ···/ *n* [C] a low level rank in the Marines or the British army, or someone who has this rank〔美国海军陆战队或英国陆军中的〕一等兵 —see table on page C6 参见 C6 页附录

Lan·ce·lot, Sir /ˈlænsəlɑt; ˈlɑːnsəlɒt/ the most famous of King Arthur's KNIGHTs in old stories. Lancelot has a romantic relationship with Arthur's wife, Guinevere, and is the father of Sir Galahad. 朗斯洛〔传说中亚瑟王麾下最出名的骑士。他与亚瑟王之妻圭尼维尔有染, 是加拉哈爵士的父亲〕

lanc·er /ˈlænsɚ; ˈlɑːnsə/ *n* [C] a soldier belonging to a REGIMENT (=part of the army) that used to be armed with lances 长矛轻骑兵, 枪骑兵

lan·cet /ˈlænsɪt; ˈlɑːnsɪt/ *n* [C] **1** a small very sharp pointed knife with two cutting edges, used by doctors to cut flesh〔医疗用的〕手术刀, 柳叶刀 **2 lancet arch/window** *technical* a tall narrow ARCH¹ (1) or window that is pointed at the top【术语】尖拱/尖窗

Lancet, The a British magazine for doctors and other people in the medical profession, produced by the British Medical Association. *The Lancet* provides reports on recent developments, new drugs and medical treatments etc.《柳叶刀》〔英国一杂志, 由英国医学协会出版, 供医学界人士阅读, 报导最新医学发展动态、新研发的药物以及新型治疗方法等等〕—see also 另见 JAMA, the NEW ENGLAND JOURNAL OF MEDICINE

Lancs. the written abbreviation of 缩写= LANCASHIRE

land¹ /lænd; lænd/ *n* S1 W1

1 ▶NOT SEA 非海洋◀ [U] the solid dry part of the Earth's surface 陆地: *After 21 days at sea we sighted land.* 经过 21 天的海上航行, 我们见到了陆地。| **by land** *It's quicker by land than sea.* 走陆路要比走海路快捷。| **on land** *The crocodile lays its eggs on land.* 鳄鱼在陆地上产卵。

2 ▶GROUND 土地◀ [U] ground, especially when used for farming or building on 土地〔尤指耕作或建筑用地〕: *the use and management of land* 土地的使用和管理 | *fertile land* 肥沃的土地 | *high land prices* 昂贵的地价

3 ▶COUNTRY 国土◀ [C] *especially literary* a country【尤文】国土, 国家: *people of many lands* 很多国家的人们 | **native land** (=the land where you were born) 祖国 *She returned at last to her native land.* 最终她回到了自己的祖国。

4 ▶NOT CITY 非城市◀ **the land** the countryside thought of as a place that is quiet and peaceful, or as a place where people grow food 乡村, 农村; 田地: *We want to leave London and get back to the land.* 我们要离开伦敦回到乡村。| **live off the land** (=grow or catch all the food you need) 靠土地生活

5 ▶PROPERTY 财产◀ [U] also 又作 **lands** *plural* the area of land that someone owns 地产, 田产: *Get off my land!* 从我的土地上滚开! | *The Duke's lands lay south of the mountains.* 公爵的地产在山南。

6 see/find out how the land lies to try to discover what the situation really is before you make a decision〔作出决定前〕了解情况, 摸清现状[形势]

7 in the land of the living *spoken humorous* awake【口, 幽默】醒着: *Now you're back in the land of the living you can put the kettle on.* 既然你醒了, 你可以把水壶放上去了。

8 land of milk and honey an imaginary place where life is easy and pleasant〔虚构中的〕乳蜜之乡, 富饶之地

9 the land of nod *old-fashioned* an expression meaning sleep, used especially when talking to children【过时】睡梦之乡〔尤用于和孩子说话时〕—see also 另见 **be/live in cloud-cuckoo-land** (CLOUD¹ (6)), DRY LAND, **the lie of the land** (LIE³ (3))

USAGE NOTE 用法说明: LAND

WORD CHOICE 词语辨析: **world, earth, land, ground, floor, soil, country**

When you are talking about **the world** as a whole, compared with other planets, you often call it **the Earth** (or **the earth**). 与其他行星相对时, the world 作为整体提及时常叫作 the Earth (或 the earth): *From space, the earth looks like a shining blue ball.* 从太空中看, 地球像是一个发光的蓝球。But in some phrases *the* is not usually used. 但在某些短语中通常不用 the: *Billions of people live on earth* (NOT usually 一般不用 *on the earth* and definitely NOT 一定不用 *in the earth*). 地球上住着数十亿的人。

The hard surface of the world, when it is compared with the area covered by sea, is called **land** [U], but when you are comparing it with the air you say **the ground** or, on a larger scale, **(the) earth**. 当与海域相对时, 地球的硬表层叫作 land〔不可数〕, 但当与太空相对时, 则叫作 the ground, 规模更大的叫作 (the) earth: *After a week adrift at sea, we spotted land.* 经过一星期的海上漂浮, 我们见到了陆地。| *The horse fell to the ground.* 马倒在地上。| *I won't relax until we're safely back on the ground.* 要到我们安全返回地面时我才会松口气。| *Once a meteor from outer space fell to earth here.* 曾经有一颗流星从外太空掉落到了这里的地面上。| *The earth shook and huge cracks appeared.* 大地震动, 巨大的裂缝出现了。

Inside a building the surface you walk on is usually called **the floor** (but it is called **the ground** outside). 室内供行

L

走的地面称为 the floor〔而室外则称作 the ground〕: *The dishes crashed to the kitchen floor.* 盘子掉到厨房的地板上碎了。| *The ground's too wet for camping.* 地面太湿了, 不能扎营。

An area thought of as property is a piece of **land** [U]. land〔不可数〕指当作财产的一块地: *the high price of land in Tokyo* 东京昂贵的地价 | *He owns a lot of land in New Mexico* (NOT 不用 **earth** or 或 **ground** or 或 **big land**). 他在新墨西哥州拥有很多地产。Also when you are talking about large areas, especially when it is used for a particular purpose, you say **land**. 大面积的地, 特别是用于特定的用途的, 也称作 land: *The land isn't much good for raising corn.* 这块地不大适合种植玉米。| *Much of the land here is used for industry.* 这里的大部分土地用于工业。

A smaller area is likely to be called a piece of **ground** [U]. 小块地可称作 a piece of ground〔不可数〕: *a small piece of ground where I could plant potatoes* 一小块我可以种马铃薯的地 | *a patch of waste ground behind the house* 屋后的一块荒地

The substance that plants grow in is **soil** [U] or **earth** [U] or (*AmE*) **dirt** [U]. 生长植物的土为 soil〔不可数〕或 earth〔不可数〕或 dirt〔美, 不可数〕: *The soil/earth is pretty good here.* 这里的土壤很好。| *The kids were playing on a mound of dirt in the yard.* 小孩在院内的土堆上玩耍。But when you are talking about its quality, type, or condition, you usually use **soil**. 但当谈论土质、土壤类型或状况的时候, 通常用 soil 一词: *soil erosion* 土壤的侵蚀 | *To improve clay soil, dig in as much sand as you can.* 要改良黏土, 尽量多掺入点沙。

Land that is not covered in buildings is **the country**, often compared with the town or city. 通常, 与城镇相对而言, 没有楼群覆盖的地方为 the country: *Why don't we take a trip to the country and get some fresh air?* (NOT 不用 *land*). 我们为何不到郊外旅行呼吸点新鲜空气?

You call a country a **land** [C] only if you want to communicate a particular meaning. 只有在传达特殊的意义时, 才可称国土为 land〔可数〕。In a story, perhaps, or to show your feelings about a country you might say 或许, 在一个故事中或要表达对一个国家的感情时, 可以说: *My homeland/native land is India* (=that is the country I feel I belong to). 我的祖国是印度〔=我认为我属于那个国度〕。| *He visited many foreign lands* (=strange and mysterious countries). 他去过了很多充满异域风情的国度〔=陌生和神秘的国家〕。Compare this with the following which is a report of simple facts. 将这和下面的例句相比较, 下面的例句是简单事实的记述: *I come from India.* 我来自印度。| *He visited many foreign countries.* 他去过了许多国家。

land² *v*

1 ►**PLANE** 飞机◄ [I,T] if an aircraft lands or if a pilot lands it, it moves down onto the ground (使) 着陆, (使) 降落: *We are due to land at Heathrow at 12:50.* 我们〔的航班〕定于 12 点 50 分在希思罗机场降落。

2 ►**ARRIVE BY BOAT/PLANE** 乘船/乘飞机抵达◄ [I] to arrive somewhere in an aircraft, boat etc〔乘飞机、船等〕到达: *1969, when the first men landed on the moon* 1969 年人类首次登上月球时

3 ►**GOODS/PEOPLE** 货物/乘客◄ [T] to put something or someone on land from an aircraft or boat〔从飞机或船上〕卸下〔货物〕; 使〔乘客〕下飞机[船]: *Troops were landed by helicopter.* 军队乘直升机降落。| *Trawlers were landing their catch at the harbour.* 拖网渔船正在港口卸渔获。

4 ►**FALL/COME DOWN** 掉下/落下◄ [I always+adv/prep] to come down through the air onto something 从空中落到〔某物上〕: **[+in/on/under etc]** *Louis fell out of the tree and landed in a holly bush.* 路易斯从树上掉下来落到冬青树丛中。| *I felt a few drops of rain landing on my head.* 我觉得头上落了几滴雨。

5 ►**PROBLEMS** 问题◄ [I always+adv/prep] to be given to someone unexpectedly, and cause problems that they will have to deal with 不期而至〔引发需要解决的问题〕: **[+in/on/under etc]** *Just when I thought my problems were over, this letter landed on my desk.* 正当我认为所有问题都解决了时, 这封信送到了我的桌上。

6 ►**JOB/CONTRACT ETC** 工作/合同等◄ [T] *informal* to succeed in getting a job, contract etc that was difficult to get【非正式】谋取〔一份难得的工作、合同等〕: *Fay landed a plum job with the BBC.* 费伊从英国广播公司谋得一份好差事。| **land yourself sth** *Bill's just landed himself a part in a Broadway show.* 比尔刚在百老汇演出中谋到了一个角色。

7 ►**FISH** 鱼◄ [T] to catch a large fish 捕到〔大鱼〕

8 **land a punch/blow** to succeed in hitting someone 击中〔某人〕—see also 另见 **fall/land on your feet** (FOOT¹ (18))

land sb **in** sth *phr v* [T] **1 land sb in trouble/hospital/court etc** to cause serious problems for someone 使某人陷入困境/得病住院/卷入诉讼之中: *We all knew his drinking would land him in court one day.* 我们都认为他总有一天会因酗酒被送上法庭。 **2 land sb in it** *spoken* to get someone into trouble by saying that they did something wrong【口】使某人陷入困扰之中: *Micky landed me in it by saying I was the last one to use the photocopier.* 米基说我是最后一个使用复印机的人, 这使我陷入了麻烦中。

land on sb *phr v* [T] *AmE informal* to speak angrily to someone【美, 非正式】痛斥〔某人〕: *Dale landed on him for forgetting the documents.* 戴尔因他忘了文件而痛斥了他一顿。

land up *phr v* [I always+adv/prep] *informal* to finally get into a particular place, situation, or position after a lot of things have happened to you【非正式】〔历经许多事后〕最终落到〔某一处境〕: **land up in/on etc** *We landed up in a bar at 3 am.* 凌晨 3 点钟我们终于到达了一家酒吧。| *Be careful that you don't land up in serious debt.* 当心, 切勿债台高筑。

land sb **with** sth *phr v* [T usually passive 一般用被动态] *informal* to give someone something unpleasant to do, because no one else wants to do it【非正式】让某人做〔无人愿做的事〕: *Maria's been landed with all the tidying up as usual.* 像往常一样, 所有的收拾工作都留给了玛丽亚。

Land, Ed·win Her·bert /ˈɛdwɪn ˈhɝbət; ˈedwɪn ˈhɜːbət/ (1909-91) a US scientist who invented POLAROID (=a special substance that is put on glass to make the sun seem less bright), which is used on SUNGLASSES and car windows. He also invented the Polaroid camera, which uses a special film to produce photographs as soon as they have been taken. 兰德〔(1909-1991) 美国科学家。他发明了用于太阳镜和汽车挡风玻璃的偏振片, 还有宝丽来相机。该相机使用一种特制胶卷, 可一次成像〕

land a·gent /ˈ· ,··/ *n* [C] someone who looks after land, cattle, farms etc that belong to someone else〔包括看管农田、牲畜等在内的〕地产管理人

lan·dau /ˈlændɔ; ˈlændɔː/ *n* [C] a four-wheeled carriage that is pulled by horses and has two seats and a top that folds back in two parts 活顶双座四轮马车

land·ed /ˈlændɪd; ˈlændɪd/ *adj* [only before noun 仅用于名词前] **1 landed gentry/family/nobility** a family or group that has owned a lot of land for a long time 拥有大量土地的乡绅/家族/贵族 **2** including a lot of land 包括大量土地的: *landed estates*〔包含大量土地的〕地产

land·fall /ˈlænd,fɔl; ˈlændfɔːl/ *n* [C usually singular 一般用单数] the first land that you see or arrive at after a long journey by sea or air〔长时间飞行或航行后的〕初见陆地; 首次登上陆地: *We made our landfall just south of Stornoway.* 我们恰好在斯托诺韦的南面首次登陆。

land·fill /ˈlænd,fɪl; ˈlændfɪl/ *n* **1** [U] the practice of burying waste under the soil, or the waste buried in this way 废弃物的填埋; 填埋的废弃物 **2** [C] a place where this waste is buried 废弃物填埋场

land·ing /ˈlændɪŋ; ˈlændɪŋ/ *n* [C] **1** the floor at the top of a set of stairs or between two sets of stairs 楼梯〔过渡〕平台, 楼梯过道 —see picture on page A4 参见 A4 页图 **2** an act of arriving on land or of bringing something onto land from the sea or air 登陆, 着陆; 降落: *troop landings in Normandy in 1944* 1944 年部队在诺曼底的登陆 | **crash landing/emergency landing** (=an aircraft's sudden landing because of trouble with the engine etc) 强行[摔机]着陆/紧急着陆

landing charge /ˈ·· ,·/ *n* [C] *technical* money that you have to pay when goods are unloaded at a port【术语】卸货费, 上岸费, 着陆费

landing craft /ˈ·· ,·/ *n* [C] a flat-bottomed boat that opens at one end to allow soldiers and equipment to land directly onto a shore 登陆艇

landing field /ˈ·· ,·/ *n* [C] a LANDING STRIP 机场跑道

landing gear /ˈ·· ,·/ *n* [U] an aircraft's wheels and wheel supports〔飞机等的〕起落架, 起落装置 —see picture at 参见 AIRCRAFT 图

landing net /ˈ·· ,·/ *n* [C] a net on a long handle used for lifting a fish out of the water after you have caught it 抄网〔用以捞取上了钩的较大的鱼〕

landing stage /ˈ·· ,·/ *n* [C] a wooden structure onto which passengers and goods are landed from boats 浮码头, 趸船

landing strip /ˈ·· ,·/ *n* [C] a level piece of ground that has been prepared for aircraft to use; AIRSTRIP 机场跑道

land·la·dy /ˈlænd,ledɪ; ˈlænd,leɪdi/ *n* [C] **1** the woman that you rent a room, building, or piece of land from 女房东, 女地主 **2** a woman who owns or is in charge of a PUB〔酒店、酒馆等的〕女店主

land·less /ˈlændlɪs; ˈlændləs/ *adj* owning no land 不拥有土地的, 没有土地的

land·locked /ˈlænd,lɑkt; ˈlændlɒkt/ *adj* a landlocked country is surrounded by other countries and has no coast 陆围的, 内陆的

W3 **land·lord** /ˈlænd,lɔrd; ˈlændlɔːd/ *n* [C] **1** the man that you rent a room, building, or piece of land from 房东, 地主 **2** a man who owns or is in charge of a PUB〔酒店、酒馆等的〕店主

land·lub·ber /ˈlænd,lʌbɚ; ˈlænd,lʌbə/ *n* [C] *old-fashioned* someone who does not have much experience of the sea or ships【过时】旱鸭子〔不谙航海的人或蹩脚水手〕

land·mark /ˈlænd,mɑrk; ˈlændmɑːk/ *n* [C] **1** an event, idea, or discovery that marks an important part of someone's life, of the development of knowledge etc〔个人生活或认识发展等中的〕里程碑; 重大转折: *The discovery of penicillin was a landmark in the history of medicine.* 青霉素的发现是医药史上的里程碑。| **landmark discovery/decision etc** *the landmark decision to join NATO* 加入北大西洋公约组织的重大决定 **2** something that is easy to recognize, such as a tall tree or building, and will help you know where you are 地标, 陆标

land·mass /ˈlænd,mæs; ˈlændmæs/ *n* [C] *technical* a large area of land【术语】地块, 大陆(块)

land·mine /ˈlændmaɪn; ˈlændmaɪn/ *n* [C] a kind of bomb hidden in the ground that explodes when someone walks or drives over it 地雷

land of·fice /ˈ· ,··/ *n* [C] a government office in the US that records the sales of all public land〔美国〕土地管理局

Land of Hope and Glo·ry /,· · · , · ˈ··/ a song, based on the music from Elgar's *Pomp and Circumstance*, which praises Britain and is often sung on PATRIOTIC occasions《希望和荣耀的土地》〔这首歌曲的旋律取自埃尔加创作的《威仪堂堂进行曲》, 歌颂英国, 常在充满爱国主义气氛的场合演唱〕

> **CULTURAL NOTE 文化注释**
>
> *Land of Hope and Glory* is always sung at the Last Night of the Proms and at large meetings of the British Conservative Party. Some people regard it as too JINGOISTIC (=expressing the idea that your country is better than all others). Its first words are: 'Land of Hope and Glory, Mother of the Free, How shall we extol thee, who are born of thee?'《希望和荣耀的土地》总会在逍遥音乐会的最后夜场和英国保守党的大型集会上唱起。有人认为这首歌充斥着大国沙文主义色彩。这首歌的前几句歌词是:"希望和荣耀的土地, 自由的母亲。我们这些您孕育的孩子, 要怎样颂扬您?"

Land of My Fa·thers /,· · · ˈ··/ the English name of the national ANTHEM (=official national song) of Wales《我先辈的土地》〔威尔士国歌的英文名〕

land·own·er /ˈlænd,onɚ; ˈlænd,əʊnə/ *n* [C] someone who owns a large amount of land 土地拥有者, 地主 —**landowning** *adj*: *the landowning aristocracy* 拥有大批土地的贵族 —**landownership** *n* [U]

land re·form /ˈ· ·,·/ *n* [C,U] the political principle of sharing farm land so that more people own some of it 土地改革

land re·gis·try /ˈ· ,···/ *n* [C] a government office in Britain that keeps records about the sales and ownership of land〔英〕土地管理局; 土地登记处

Land Rov·er /ˈ· ,··/ *n* [C] *BrE trademark* a type of strong car made for travelling over rough ground【英, 商标】路虎汽车

W3 **land·scape¹** /ˈlændskep; ˈlændskeɪp/ *n* **1** [C] an area of countryside or land, considered in terms of how attractive it is to look at〔陆上的〕风景, 景致, 景色: *the beauty of the New England landscape in autumn* 美丽的新英格兰秋色 | *a desolate urban landscape* 城市荒凉的景色 **2** [C] a picture showing an area of countryside or land 风景照, 风景画: *Cézanne's landscapes* 塞尚的风景画 **3** [U] the painting or drawing of landscapes in art 风景绘画, 山水绘画 **4 the political/intellectual etc landscape** the general situation in which a particular activity takes place 政治/知识界的概貌: *She dominated the intellectual landscape of Paris.* 她掌控着巴黎知识界的整体情况。**5** [U] *technical* LANDSCAPE MODE【术语】横向格式 —see also 另见 **a blot on the landscape** (BLOT² (2))

landscape² *v* [T often passive 常用被动态] to make a park, garden etc look attractive and interesting by planting trees and bushes, making different levels etc 用园艺美化〔公园、花园等〕

landscape ar·chi·tec·ture /,··ˈ····/ *n* [U] the profession or art of planning the way an area of land looks, including roads, buildings, and planted areas 园林建筑业, 园林建筑术 —**landscape architect** *n* [C]

landscape gar·den·ing /,··ˈ···/ *n* [U] the profession or art of arranging gardens and parks so that they look attractive and interesting 园艺业, 园艺学 —**landscape gardener** *n* [C]

landscape mode /ˈ·· ,·/ *n* [C] *technical* a piece of paper, picture, etc that has its longer edge at the top and bottom【术语】横向格式 —opposite 反义词 PORTRAIT MODE

land·scap·er /ˈlændskepɚ; ˈlændskeɪpə/ *n* [C] *AmE* someone whose job is to arrange plants, paths etc in gardens and parks【美】园艺师

Land's End /,· ˈ·/ a place on the southwest coast of England, which most people think of as the furthest point in the southwest of the UK. It is used especially in the phrase 'from Land's End to John O'Groats', because people think of John O'Groats as the furthest point in the northeast of the UK. 兰兹角〔英格兰西南海岸一地。多数人认为这是英国最西南端的一个地方。该词尤用于 from Land's End to John O'Groats (从兰兹角到约翰·奥格罗兹; 从英国的一端到另一端) 这一短语。约翰·奥格罗兹被认为是英国最东北端的一个地方〕

land·slide /ˈlænd,slaɪd; ˈlændslaɪd/ *n* [C] **1** a sudden fall of a lot of earth or rocks down a hill, cliff etc 山崩; 滑坡; 塌方 **2** a victory in an election in which one person or party gets a lot more votes than all the others 一边倒的胜利,〔竞选中〕一方选票占压倒性多数: **by a landslide** *The SNP candidate won by a landslide.* 苏格兰民族党候选人以压倒性多数获胜。| *a landslide victory* 一边倒的胜利

land·slip /ˈlænd,slɪp; ˈlændslɪp/ *n* [C] a small landslide〔小规模的〕山崩; 滑坡; 塌方; 山泥倾泻

land·ward /ˈlændwɚd; ˈlændwəd/ *adj* facing towards the land and away from the sea 朝岸的, 向陆地的: *the landward side of the hill* 朝向陆地的山坡 —**land·wards** /ˈlændwɚdz; ˈlændwədz/ *adv*

lane /len; leɪn/ *n* [C] **1** a narrow road between fields or houses, especially in the countryside〔尤指乡间〕小道; 小巷; 胡同; 里弄: *a dusty lane leading to some cottages* 通向几座乡间村舍的小土路 **2** the two or three parallel areas on a main road which are divided by painted lines to keep fast and slow traffic apart 车道, 行车线: **the inside/outside lane** *Use the outside lane for overtaking only.* 只能使用外车道超车。| **the fast lane** (=the lane for going past other vehicles) 快车道 **3** used in the names of roads …巷〔用于路名〕: *a hotel in Park Lane* 园林巷上的酒店 **4** one of the narrow parallel areas marked for each competitor in a running or swimming race 跑道; 泳道: *The champion is running in lane five.* 上届冠军正在第五跑道上跑。**5** a line or course along which ships or aircraft regularly travel between ports or airports〔船舶或飞机的〕航线, 航道: *busy shipping lanes* 繁忙的海运航道 —see also 另见 **life in the fast lane** (FAST LANE (2)) S3 W3

Lane, Lo·is /ˈlo·ɪs; ˈləʊɪs/ in the stories about Superman, a female reporter who works for the *The Daily Planet*, and has a romantic relationship with Superman 莱恩〔超人故事中与超人相恋的《每日星球报》女记者〕

Lang /læŋ; læŋ/, **Fritz** /frɪts; frɪts/ (1890-1976) an Austrian film DIRECTOR, who worked in Germany and the US and had an important influence on the development of the cinema. His films include *Metropolis* (1926), *Fury* (1936), and *The Big Heat* (1953). 朗〔(1890-1976) 奥地利电影导演。他曾在德国和美国拍摄影片, 对电影艺术的发展产生过重要影响。导演的影片包括《大都市》(1926)、《狂怒》(1936) 和《巨变》(1953)〕

lan·guage /ˈlæŋgwɪdʒ; ˈlæŋgwɪdʒ/ *n* S2 W1

1 ►ENGLISH/FRENCH/ARABIC ETC 英语/法语/阿拉伯语等◄ [C,U] a system of communication by written or spoken words, which is used by the people of a particular country or area〔某国家或地区的书面或口头的〕语言(文字): *the Japanese language* 日语 | *How many languages do you speak?* 你能说几种语言? | **native language** (=the first language you learned) 母语 *Andrea's native language is German.* 安德烈亚的母语是德语。| **modern language** (=a language that is still spoken today) 当代语言 | **dead language** (=a language that is no longer spoken) 过时语言 | **the language barrier** (=the difficulty of communicating with people who speak a different language) 语言上的障碍

2 ►COMMUNICATION 沟通◄ [U] the use of written or spoken words to communicate〔书面或口头的〕语言(文字): *the origins of language* 语言的起源

3 ►COMPUTERS 电脑◄ [C,U] *technical* a system of instructions and commands for operating a computer【术语】电脑语

L

言: *a programming language such as BASIC or Pascal* 程序语言, 如BASIC语言〔初学者通用符号指令码〕或帕斯卡语言
4 ▶STYLE/TYPE OF WORDS 词语的风格/类型◀ [U] the kind of words and style used in one kind of writing or by people in a particular job or activity 行话, 专门用语, 术语: *medical language* 医学用语 | *poetic language* 诗词用语
5 ▶SOUNDS/SIGNS/ACTIONS 声音/手势/动作◀ [U] a way of expressing meaning or giving information through sounds, signs, movements etc〔使用声音、手势、动作等的〕表达方式: *the language of music* 音乐语汇
6 ▶SWEARING 谩骂◀ [U] *informal* words that most people think are offensive【非正式】粗话, 骂人话: *You never heard such language! It was disgusting.* 你从未听过如此粗鲁的语言!真恶心! | **mind/watch your language** (=stop swearing) 你说话别太脏
7 strong language a) angry words used to tell people exactly what you mean 措辞强硬的话, 激烈的言辞 **b)** words that most people think are offensive; swearing 粗话, 骂人话
8 speak the same language if two people speak the same language, they have similar attitudes and opinions 有共同语言〔表示两个人看法和观点一致〕—see also 另见 BODY LANGUAGE, SIGN LANGUAGE

language la·bor·a·tory /ˈ· · ·, · · ·/ *n* [C] a room in a school or college where you can learn to speak a foreign language by listening to TAPES and recording your own voice 语言实验室

lan·guid /ˈlæŋgwɪd; ˈlæŋgwɪd/ *adj* **1** moving slowly and making very little effort, but in an attractive way 悠然的, 慵懒的, 缓缓的: *Sebastian left with a languid wave of the hand.* 塞巴斯蒂安缓缓地挥了挥手就离开了。**2** lazily slow and peaceful 懒洋洋的, 悠闲的: *a languid afternoon by the river* 在河边悠闲度过的下午 —**languidly** *adv*

lan·guish /ˈlæŋgwɪʃ; ˈlæŋgwɪʃ/ *v* [I] **1** to be forced to stay somewhere where you are unhappy 受煎熬: *Shaw languished in a Mexican jail for fifteen years.* 肖在墨西哥监牢里受了15年的煎熬。**2** to become weaker or less successful 变得(越来越)衰弱: *Local food production languished through lack of government support.* 得不到政府的支持, 地方的食品生产渐渐萎缩。| *The conversation was languishing.* 越谈越不合拍。**3** [+for] to become ill and unhappy because you want someone or something very much〔因渴望得到某人或某物而〕变得憔悴, 闷闷不乐

lan·guor /ˈlæŋgɚ; ˈlæŋgə/ *n especially literary*【尤文】**1** [C, U] a pleasant feeling of tiredness or lack of strength 倦怠 **2** [U] pleasant or heavy stillness of the air〔空气的〕平静, 凝滞: *the languor of a hot afternoon* 炎热午后的沉闷 **3** [C] a feeling of sadness because you want someone or something very much 愁闷 —**languorous** *adj* —**languorously** *adv*

lank /læŋk; læŋk/ *adj* lank hair is thin, straight and unattractive〔头发〕稀疏的, 平直而难看的 —**lankly** *adv* —**lankness** *n* [U] —see picture on page A6 参见A6页图

lank·y /ˈlæŋkɪ; ˈlæŋki/ *adj* unattractively tall and thin 瘦高难看的: *long lanky legs* 又瘦又长的细腿 —**lankiness** *n* [U]

lan·o·lin /ˈlænəlɪn; ˈlænəl-ɪn/ *n* [U] an oil that is in sheep's wool and is used in skin creams 羊毛脂

lan·tern /ˈlæntɚn; ˈlæntən/ *n* [C] **1** a lamp that you can carry consisting of a metal or glass container surrounding a flame or light 灯笼, 提灯—see picture at 参见 LIGHT[1] 图 **2** *technical* a structure at the top of a tower or LIGHTHOUSE, that has windows on all sides【术语】〔灯塔上的〕灯室 —see also 另见 CHINESE LANTERN, MAGIC LANTERN

lantern-jawed /ˌ· · ˈ·◂/ *adj* having a long narrow jaw and cheeks that sink inwards 下巴窄长且双颊深陷的

lan·yard /ˈlænjɚd; ˈlænjəd/ *n* [C] **1** a short piece of rope, used on a ship to tie things〔船上系物的〕短绳 **2** a thick string with a knife or whistle on it, that sailors wear around their necks〔水手用以系小刀或哨子等的〕颈带, 项带

Lanza /ˈlænzə; ˈlænzɑ/, **Mario** /ˈmærɪo; ˈmærɪo/ (1921-59) an American singer with a good TENOR voice. He sang in OPERA and made several musical films, including *The Great Caruso* (1951). 兰扎〔(1921-1959), 美国男高音歌唱家。他音质优美, 演唱歌剧并制作了几部音乐片, 其中包括《歌王卡罗索》(1951)〕

Laos /lauz; laʊs/ a country in southeast Asia between China and Cambodia. Population: 5,636,000 (2001). Capital: Vientiane. 老挝〔亚洲东南部一国家, 位于中国和柬埔寨之间。人口: 5,636,000 (2001), 首都: 万象〕—**Laotian** *n, adj*

Lao-Tsu /ˈlauˈdzʌ; ˈlaʊˈdzʌ/ also 又作 **Lao-Tse** /ˈlauˈdz; ˈlaʊˈdz/ (6th century BC) a Chinese PHILOSOPHER who is considered to be the person who began Taoism, and who wrote the *Tao Te Ching*. 老子〔(公元前6世纪), 中国哲学家, 被认为是道家的创始人, 著书《道德经》〕

lap[1] /læp; læp/ *n*
1 ▶LEGS 腿◀ [C] the upper part of your legs when you are sitting down〔人坐着时腰以下到膝为止的〕大腿部: *Come and sit on my lap, Ginny.* 金尼, 过来坐在我的腿上。
2 ▶RACE 赛跑◀ [C] one journey around or along a running track, race course etc〔跑道等的〕一圈; 一次往返: *Hill finished a lap ahead of his team-mate.* 希尔领先队友一圈跑完全程。| **do/run/swim a lap** *Come on, let's do a few laps in the pool.* 快来, 让我们在游泳池内游几个来回。| **lap of honour** *BrE*【英】, **victory lap** *AmE*【美】(=a lap that you do after winning)〔优胜者的〕绕场一周
3 ▶PART OF JOURNEY 部分旅程◀ [singular] a part of a long journey 长途旅行中的一段: *The last lap of their journey was by ship.* 他们最后的一段旅程是坐船。
4 in the lap of luxury having an easy, comfortable life with plenty of money, possessions etc 处在优裕、舒适的生活环境中
5 in the lap of the gods if the result of something is in the lap of the gods, you do not know what will happen 听天由命, 难以预料
6 drop/dump sth in sb's lap *spoken* to make someone responsible for dealing with something difficult【口】把难事推给某人去做: *Ben just dumped all this work in my lap and told me to get on with it.* 本就把这工作全部往我身上一推, 让我来完成。

lap[2] *v*
1 ▶SEA/LAKE/RIVER 海/湖/河◀ [I,T] if water laps something or laps against something such as the shore or a boat, it moves against it or hits it in small waves〔波浪〕轻轻拍打, 冲刷: [+against] *The water of the lake lapped gently against the rocks.* 湖水轻轻地拍打岩石。
2 ▶DRINK 饮, 喝◀ [I, T] if an animal laps something, it drinks it by making small tongue movements〔动物〕舔饮
3 ▶IN A RACE 在比赛中◀ **a)** [T] to pass a competitor in a race after having completed a whole lap more than they have 领先〔另一竞赛者〕一圈: *Casey gave up after being lapped twice.* 凯西在被人超过了两圈之后放弃了比赛。**b)** [I] to make a single journey around a track, race course etc in a particular time〔在特定时间内〕跑完一圈
4 ▶PARTLY COVER 部分重叠◀ [I,T] *technical* if one thing laps another, a part of one covers part of the other; OVERLAP[1]【术语】(使)部分重叠; 叠盖
5 ▶FOLD/WRAP 折叠/包住◀ [T always+adv/prep] *literary* to fold or wrap something around something else【文】包住; 包围; 裹住 —**lapping** *n* [U]

lap ↔ sth **up** *phr v* [T] **1** to get a lot of pleasure and enjoyment from something, without worrying about whether it is good, true etc〔不分良莠地〕欣然接受: *She seems to be lapping up all the attention she's getting.* 她似乎只要得到注意就高兴。| *They sat listening to his story, spellbound, lapping it up.* 他们坐下来听他的故事, 全都入了迷, 被吸引住了。**2** to drink all of something eagerly 畅饮

lap·a·ro·scope /ˈlæpərəskop; ˈlæpərəskəʊp/ *n* [C] *technical* a piece of equipment with a lighted tube that a doctor uses to look inside someone's body【术语】腹腔镜

lap·a·ros·co·py /ˌlæpəˈrɑskəpɪ; ˌlæpəˈrɒskəpi/ *n* [C, U] *technical* an examination or medical operation on the inside of someone's body, using a laparoscope【术语】腹腔镜检查[手术]

La Paz /lɑˈpɑz; lɑːˈpæz/ the capital and largest city of Bolivia, in the Andes Mountains on the La Paz River. It is the highest capital in the world. 拉巴斯〔玻利维亚首都和最大城市, 位于安第斯山区, 拉巴斯河畔, 是世界上海拔最高的首都〕

lap belt /ˈ· ·/ *n* [C] a type of safety belt that fits across your waist when you are sitting in the back of a car〔汽车后座上的〕安全带

lap·dog /ˈlæpˌdɔg; ˈlæpdɒg/ *n* [C] **1** a small pet dog 小宠物狗, 叭儿狗 **2** someone who is completely under the control of someone else and will do anything they say 趋炎附势[仰人鼻息]的人

la·pel /ləˈpɛl; ləˈpel/ *n* [C] the part of the front of a coat or JACKET (1) that is joined to the collar and folded back on each side〔西服上衣或夹克的〕翻领

lap·i·da·ry[1] /ˈlæpəˌdɛrɪ; ˈlæpɪdəri/ *adj* [only before noun 仅用于名词前] *technical* connected with the cutting or polishing of valuable stones or jewels【术语】宝石雕刻[加工]的

lapidary[2] *n* [C] someone who is skilled in cutting and polishing jewels and valuable stones 玉石匠, 宝石匠

lap·is laz·u·li /ˈlæpɪs ˈlæzjəlɪ; ˌlæpɪs ˈlæzjʊli/ *n* **1** [C,U] a valuable bright blue stone 天青石, 青金石 **2** [U] a bright blue colour 天青石色, 青金石色

Lap·land /ˈlæpˌlænd; ˈlæplænd/ an area of northern Europe consisting of parts of Norway, Sweden, Finland, and Russia. The people who live there are called Saami, though the old English name for them was Lapps. 拉普兰〔北欧一地区，由挪威、瑞典、芬兰和俄罗斯等国的部分地区组成，居民为撒米人，古英语中称其为拉普人〕—**Laplander** *n*

lap robe /ˈ· ·/ *n* [C] *AmE* a small thick BLANKET[1] (1) used to cover your legs when your are travelling【美】〔用来盖腿的〕毛毯，膝毯

lapse[1] /læps; læps/ *n* [C] **1** a short time when someone is careless or forgetful〔短暂的〕疏忽；健忘: [+in] *There haven't been any lapses in security recently.* 近来在保安方面没有出现过疏忽大意。| [+of] *A single lapse of concentration cost Becker the game.* 一时的分心使得贝克尔输掉了比赛。| **a memory lapse** (=when you cannot remember something for a short time) 一时想不起 **2** [C] a failure to do something you should do, especially to behave correctly〔尤指举止〕疏忽，过失，过错: *He didn't offer Darren a drink and Marie did not appear to notice the lapse.* 他没有给达伦饮料，玛丽看来也没有发现这一疏忽。**3** [C usually singular 一般用单数] a period of time between two events〔两事件中的〕时间间隔: *The usual time lapse between request and delivery is two days.* 从要求订购到交货一般要两天。| [+of] *a lapse of about ten seconds* 约10秒钟的间隔

lapse[2] *v* [I] **1** to gradually come to an end or to stop for a period of time 慢慢地结束；中止: *I let the conversation lapse and Kelly finally spoke up.* 我让谈话慢慢中止，凯莉最终发言了。**2** if a contract, agreement, legal right etc lapses, it comes to an end, for example because an agreed time limit has passed〔合同、协议、合法权利等如因期限已过而〕终止，失效

lapse into sth *phr v* [T] **1lapse into silence/sleep/a daydream etc** to go into a quiet or less active state 陷入沉默/进入睡眠/做起白日梦等: *The girl lapsed into a sulky silence.* 那女孩生起了闷气。| *He lapsed into a coma and died two days later.* 他陷入了昏迷，两天后就死了。**2** to start behaving or speaking in a different and usually less good or acceptable way 陷入，进入〔一般指背离正道〕: *Following his death, the Empire lapsed into chaos.* 他死后，帝国就陷入了混乱之中。| *She would sometimes deliberately lapse into another dialect.* 她有时会故意用另一种方言说话。

lapsed /læpst; læpst/ *adj* [only before noun 仅用于名词前] **1** no longer having the beliefs you had, especially religious beliefs 背弃的，背教的: *a lapsed Catholic* 离经叛道的天主教徒 **2** *law* not used any more【法律】不再使用的，过时的，失效的

lap·top /ˈ· ·/ *n* [C] a small computer that you can carry with you 笔记本电脑；手提电脑: *executives with their laptops* 配备有手提电脑的行政主管—**lap·top** *adj*

lap·wing /ˈlæpˌwɪŋ; ˈlæpˌwɪŋ/ *n* [C] a small black and white European bird with raised feathers on its head; PEEWIT 田凫（鸟）；麦鸡

lar·board /ˈlɑrbɚd; ˈlɑːbəd/ *n* [U] *old-fashioned* the left side of a ship; PORT (4)【过时】左舷

lar·ce·nist /ˈlɑrsṇɪst; ˈlɑːsənɪst/ *n* [C] *law* a thief【法律】窃贼

lar·ce·ny /ˈlɑrsṇi; ˈlɑːsəni/ *n* [C, U] *law* the act or crime of stealing【法律】偷窃罪 —see also 另见 PETTY LARCENY

larch /lɑrtʃ; lɑːtʃ/ *n* [C,U] a tree that looks like a PINE tree but drops its leaves in winter 落叶松

lard[1] /lɑrd; lɑːd/ *n* [U] white fat from pigs that is used in cooking 猪油

lard[2] *v* [T] **1be larded with sth** if a speech, piece of writing etc is larded with particular types of words or phrases, there are a lot of them in it〔讲话和文章等〕大量使用[穿插]某类词语: *a speech larded with Biblical quotations* 穿插很多圣经引文的讲话 **2** to put small pieces of BACON onto meat before cooking it〔烹调前〕把小块腌肉片铺在〔其他〕肉上

lard-ass /ˈ· ·/ *n* [C] *AmE spoken* an insulting word for someone who is fat【美口】肥猪〔侮辱性词语〕

lar·der /ˈlɑrdɚ; ˈlɑːdə/ *n* [C] a small room or large cupboard for storing food in a house〔家中的〕食品贮藏室；食品贮藏柜

1 1 **large** /lɑrdʒ; lɑːdʒ/ *adj*

1▶BIG 大的◀ bigger or more than usual in number, amount, or size 大量的；巨大的: *Los Angeles is the second largest city in the US.* 洛杉矶是美国第二大城市。| *The T-shirt comes in Small, Medium and Large.* 这种T恤有小号、中号和大号的货。| *This could create a large number of new jobs.* 这可以创造一大批新的就业机会。| *The town has a large population of elderly people.* 该镇的老年人口众多。—see 见 WIDE (USAGE), BIG (USAGE)

2▶PERSON 人◀ a large person is very tall and wide 身材高大的: *A large man with a shotgun blocked our path.* 一个身材高大、手持猎枪的人挡住了我们的去路。—see 见 FAT[1] (USAGE)

3be at large if a dangerous person or animal is at large, they have escaped from somewhere and may cause harm or damage〔危险人物或动物〕在逃的；不受控制的: *Two of the escaped prisoners are still at large.* 两名逃犯仍逍遥法外。

4the world/country/public at large people in general 全世界/全国/全体民众: *The organization provides information on health issues to the public at large.* 这个组织向全体民众提供关于健康问题的资料。

5▶MORE GENERAL 更加普遍的◀ the larger issues/view/picture the important general facts and questions about a situation, problem etc 更重大的问题/更主要的观点/更大的局面: *a useful book about the conflict, which helps to explain the larger picture* 一本关于这场冲突的有用书籍，有助于解释更广泛的局势

6(as) large as life *spoken* used when someone has appeared or is present in a place where you did not expect to see them【口】确确实实（就在眼前）〔用于表示没有料到某人的出现〕: *I turned a corner and there was Joe, as large as life.* 我在拐角处转了个弯，那不是乔吗，确确实实是他。

7larger than life someone who is larger than life attracts a lot of attention because they are more amusing, attractive, or exciting than most people〔比多数人〕更有趣更具吸引力的，与众不同的，极不平常的

8in large part/measure *formal* mostly【正式】大部分，基本上 —see also 另见 **by and large** (BY[2] (5)), **loom large** (LOOM[2] (3)), **writ large** (WRIT[2])—**largeness** *n* [U]

large in·tes·tine /ˌ· ·ˈ· ·/ *n* [C] the lower part of your BOWELS, where food is changed into solid waste matter 大肠 —compare 比较 SMALL INTESTINE

large·ly /ˈlɑrdʒli; ˈlɑːdʒli/ *adv* mostly or mainly 大半地，主要地: *The state of Nevada is largely desert.* 内华达州大部分是沙漠。| *Kevin's success is largely due to sheer hard work.* 凯文的成功主要靠踏踏实实的苦干。 S3 W2

large-scale /ˌ· ˈ·◂/ *adj* [only before noun 仅用于名词前] **1** using or involving a lot of effort, people, supplies etc 大规模的: *a large-scale rescue operation* 大规模的营救行动 **2** a large-scale map, model etc is drawn or made bigger than usual, so that more details can be shown〔地图、模型等〕大型的，用大比例尺制作的

lar·gesse, largess /ˈlɑrdʒɪs; lɑːˈʒes/ *n* [U] *formal* the quality or act of being generous and giving money or gifts to people who have less than you, or the money or gifts that you give【正式】慷慨的赠与；赏金；赠送之物

larg·ish /ˈlɑrdʒɪʃ; ˈlɑːdʒɪʃ/ *adj informal* fairly big【非正式】相当大的

lar·go[1] /ˈlɑrgo; ˈlɑːgəʊ/ *adj, adv technical* played or sung slowly and seriously【术语】演奏[唱]缓慢庄严的[地]

largo[2] *n* [C] *technical* a piece of music played or sung slowly and seriously【术语】缓慢而庄严的乐章，广板

lar·i·at /ˈlærɪət; ˈlæriət/ *n* [C] *AmE* a LASSO[1]【美】套索

lark[1] /lɑrk; lɑːk/ *n* [C] **1** a small brown singing bird with long pointed wings; SKYLARK 百灵科鸟；云雀 **2** *informal* something that you do to amuse yourself or as a joke, especially something bad【非正式】玩笑，玩乐〔尤指恶作剧〕: **do sth for a lark** *They hid her passport for a lark.* 他们把她的护照藏起来，以此取乐。**3blow/sod etc that for a lark** *BrE spoken* used when you stop doing something or refuse to do something because it needs too much effort【英口】开玩笑〔某事太费精力而不想干时的用语〕: *Paint the whole room? Sod that for a lark!* 油漆整个房间？简直是开玩笑！**4this dieting/exercise/gardening lark** *BrE spoken* used to describe an activity that you think is silly or unpleasant【英口】节食/锻炼/栽培花木这种无聊的事〔用于自认为愚蠢或使人不快的活动〕: *Salad again? How long are you going to keep up this healthy eating lark?* 又是沙拉？这种所谓的健康食物你还要吃多久？**5be up with the lark** to get up very early 很早起床 —see also 另见 **happy as a lark** (HAPPY (8))

lark[2] *v*

lark about/around *phr v* [I] *BrE informal* to have fun by behaving in a silly way【英，非正式】胡闹，闹着玩: *A group of kids was larking about near the shops.* 一群小孩正在商店附近嬉闹。

Lar·kin /ˈlɑrkɪn; ˈlɑːkɪn/, **Philip** (1922-85) a British poet. He often wrote about death and loneliness and his poems are sometimes very sad, but people like them because they are written in plain and simple language. His most famous poems are *Aubade*, *High Windows*, and *Whitsun Weddings*. 拉金〔(1922-1985)，英国诗人。其作品常以死亡和孤独为题材，他的诗歌有时颇令人伤感，但语言简洁易懂，为广大读者所喜爱。最著名的诗歌有《晨曲》、《高窗》和《降临节婚礼》〕

lar·va /ˈlɑrvə; ˈlɑːvə/ *n plural* **larvae**/-vi; -viː/ [C] a creature like a fat WORM that is a young insect which has left the egg and has not yet changed into an insect with wings〔昆虫的〕幼虫，幼体 —**larval***adj*

lar·yn·gi·tis /ˌlærɪnˋdʒaɪtɪs; ˌlærɨnˈdʒaɪtɨs/ *n* [U] an illness which makes talking difficult because your larynx and throat are swollen 喉炎

lar·ynx /ˋlærɪŋks; ˈlærɪŋks/ *n plural* **larynges**/ləˋrɪndʒiz; ləˈrɪndʒiːz/ or **larynxes**[C] *technical* the hollow box-like part in your throat where you make voice sounds【术语】喉 —see picture at 参见 RESPIRATORY 图

la·sa·gne *BrE*【英】, **lasagna***AmE*【美】/ləˋzɑnjə; ləˈsænjə/ *n* [C,U] a type of Italian food made with flat pieces of PASTA, meat or vegetables, cheese and a SAUCE made with milk〔一种意大利〕卤汁宽面条

La Salle /lə ˋsæl; lə ˈsæl/ **, Ren·é Ro·bert** /rəˋne rɑˋbɛr; ˈreneɪ ˈrɒbeə/ **, Sieur de**/ˋsjɚ də; ˈsjɜː də/ (1643-87) a French EXPLORER who travelled through North America, down the Mississippi River, and claimed a large area of the southern part of North America for France, naming it Louisiana. He was killed by his followers when another EXPEDITION he was leading was unsuccessful and they got lost. 拉萨尔〔(1643-1687)，法国探险家。他曾游历北美，沿密西西比河一路南下，使法国获得北美南部大片土地，称之为路易斯安那。他率领的另一次远征未能成功，所有人陷入迷途，他被自己的随从杀害〕

La Sca·la /lɑ ˋskɑlə; læ ˈskɑːlə/ a theatre in Milan, in northern Italy, where OPERAs are performed. It is one of the greatest opera houses in the world. 拉斯卡拉歌剧院〔意大利北部米兰市一歌剧院，被认为是世界上最大的歌剧院之一〕

Las·caux /læˋsko; læˈskəʊ/ a cave in southwest France that has PREHISTORIC paintings of animals and hunters on its walls, which were painted about 17,500 years ago 拉斯科洞穴〔位于法国西南部一洞穴。洞壁上有史前的狩猎图，成画约在17,500年之前〕

las·civ·i·ous /ləˋsɪvɪəs; ləˈsɪviəs/ *adj* showing strong sexual desire 好色的，淫荡的；猥亵的：*Mandy gave him a lascivious wink.* 曼迪挑逗地瞟了他一眼。—**lasciviously** *adv* —**lasciviousness***n* [U]

la·ser /ˋlezɚ; ˈleɪzə/ *n* [C] a piece of equipment that produces a powerful narrow beam of light that can be used in medical operations, to cut metals, or to make patterns of light for entertainment 激光（器），雷射（装置）：*laser surgery* 激光（外科）手术

laser disk /ˋ·· ,·/ *n* [C] a computer DISK that can be read by laser light 激光影碟，雷射光碟[盘]

laser print·er /ˋ·· ,··/ *n* [C] a machine connected to a computer system that prints by using laser light 激光[雷射]打印机 —see picture on page A14 参见 A14 页图

lash[1] /læʃ; læʃ/ *v*

1 ►TIE 捆扎◄[T always+adv/prep] to tie something tightly to something else with a rope, or tie two things together〔用绳〕把…与…捆在一起，把…捆在一起：**lash sth to/onto etc** *The oars were lashed to the sides of the boat.* 桨拴在船的两侧。

2 ►WIND/RAIN ETC 风/雨等◄[I always+adv/prep, T] to hit against something with violent force 猛击：*The rain lashed her face.* 雨点击打着她的脸。| *waves lashing the shore* 波浪猛烈地拍击岸边 | [**+against/down/ across**] *The wind lashed violently against the door.* 风猛烈地撞击着大门。

3 ►HIT 击打◄[I,T] to hit someone very hard with a whip, stick etc 鞭打，抽打：*The guards would lash any of the prisoners who fell behind.* 卫兵总会鞭打落在后面的犯人。

4 ►TAIL 尾巴◄[I,T] if an animal lashes its tail or its tail lashes, it moves it from side to side quickly and strongly, especially because it is angry〔尤指动物生气时〕摆动（尾巴），（尾巴）摆动

5 ►CRITICIZE 批评◄[T] a word meaning to criticize someone angrily, used especially in newspapers 抨击：*Judge lashes drug-dealers.* 法官猛烈抨击毒品贩子。

6 lash sb into a fury/rage/frenzy etcto deliberately make a group of people have strong violent feelings 煽动〔群众〕：*The crowd was being lashed into a frenzy by the speaker.* 人群的愤怒情绪正被演讲者煽动起来。

lash out*phr v* [I] **1** to suddenly speak angrily to someone 猛烈抨击，痛斥：[**+at**] *I used to lash out at my children for no reason.* 过去我经常无缘无故地训斥我的孩子。**2** to try to hit someone, with a series of violent, uncontrolled movements 疯狂地攻击：*In its panic, the bear started to lash out.* 熊在惊慌之中开始猛击。

lash[2] *n* [C] **1** a hit with a whip, especially as a punishment 鞭打：*They were each given fifty lashes.* 他们每人挨了50鞭。**2** [usually plural 一般用复数] one of the hairs that grow around the edge of your eyes; EYELASH 睫毛 **3** a sudden or violent movement like that of a whip 突然猛烈的一甩：*With a lash of its tail, the lion sprang at its prey.* 狮子猛地甩了一下尾巴就向它的猎物扑了过去。**4** the thin piece of leather at the end of a whip 鞭梢

lash·ing /ˋlæʃɪŋ; ˈlæʃɪŋ/ *n* [C] **1 lashings of***BrE old-fashioned* a large amount of food or drink【英，过时】大量的〔食品或饮料〕：*apple pie with lashings of cream* 涂有大量奶油的苹果馅饼 **2** a punishment of hitting someone with a whip 鞭笞 **3** a rope that fastens something tightly to something else〔捆绑用的〕绳索，系索

lash-up /ˋ· ·/ *n* [C] *BrE informal* an arrangement of things, for example electrical equipment or wires, put together quickly to be used for only a short time【英，非正式】应急办法，应急之物，临时凑合的东西

Las Pal·mas/lɑs ˋpɑlməs; læs ˈpælməs/ a town on the island of Gran Canaria in the Canary Islands, which is very popular with British tourists 拉斯帕尔玛斯〔加那利群岛大加纳利岛上的一座城镇，颇受英国游人喜爱〕

lass /læs; læs/ also 又作 **las·sie**/ˋlæsɪ; ˈlæsi/ *n* [C] *ScotE & NEngE*【苏格兰和英格兰北部】**1** a girl or young woman 女孩，少女 **2** a girlfriend 女友 —compare 比较 LAD

Las·sie/ˋlæsɪ; ˈlæsi/ a dog who was the main character in seven films made between 1943 and 1951 and later in television programmes. Lassie is very brave and clever, and she often saves people from danger, especially members of the family that she belongs to. 拉西〔在1943至1951年间拍摄的七部影片以及后来的电视节目中充当主角的一条狗。拉西勇敢机敏，经常救人，尤其是其主人家的人〕

las·si·tude /ˋlæsə,tjud; ˈlæsɨtjuːd/ *n* [U] *formal*【正式】**1** tiredness and lack of energy 疲倦，疲乏 **2** laziness or lack of interest 懒惰，厌倦：*Cheam was accused of moral lassitude.* 奇姆被指责为不仁不义。

las·so[1] /ˋlæsu; ləˈsuː/ *n* [C] a rope with one end tied in a circle, used to catch cattle and horses, especially in the western US〔尤指美国西部套捕牛、马等用的〕套索

lasso[2] *v* [T] to catch an animal using a lasso〔用套索〕套捕

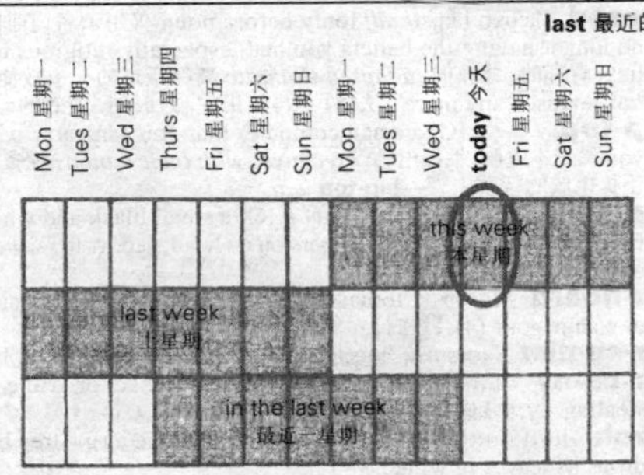

last[1] /læst; lɑːst/ *determiner* **1** most recent; the nearest one to the present time 最近的，最近一段时间的，最近一次的：*I haven't seen you since the last meeting.* 自从上次会面后，我再没有见到你。| **last night/week/year etc***Did you watch the game on TV last night?* 昨晚你在电视上看比赛了没有？| *Fashion has changed in the last twenty years.* 在过去的20年中时装潮流发生了变化。| **(the) last time**(=the most recent occasion) 上一次 | *The last time I spoke to Bob he seemed happy enough.* 上次我跟鲍勃说话的时候，他显得够高兴的。—compare 比较 NEXT[1] (2) **2** happening or existing at the end, with no others after 最后的：*I didn't read the last chapter of the book.* 我还没有读这本书的最后一章。| *Anna was the last person to see him alive.* 安娜是最后一个见到他活着的人。**3** remaining after all others have gone, been used etc 最后剩下的：*Is this your last cigarette?* 这是你最后一支烟吗？| *These are the last four birds of their kind still in existence.* 这些鸟是这种鸟中仅存的四只。**4 the last person/thing a)** one that you did not expect at all 最未料到的人/事：*She's the last person I'd expect to meet in a disco.* 我怎么也想不到会在迪斯科舞厅中见到她。**b)** one that you do not want at all, that is most unsuitable etc 最不想要的人/事；最不合适的人/事：*The last thing we wanted was for the newspapers to find out what was going on.* 我们最不希望报界发现所发生的

事。**5 last thing (at night)** at the very end of the day 在一天的末了: *Take a couple of these pills last thing at night to help you get to sleep.* 晚上睡前吃两颗药丸以帮助入睡。**6 on your last legs** *informal*【非正式】**a)** very tired 很疲倦的: *Sarah looks as if she's on her last legs.* 萨拉看上去似乎很疲惫。**b)** very ill and likely to die soon 病危的 **7 on its last legs** *informal* old or in bad condition, and likely to stop working soon【非正式】老化的, 糟透的: *We'll have to get a new lawn mower this year – the old one is really on its last legs.* 今年我们得买一台新的割草机——原来那台真的不好用了。**8 have the last word a)** to make the last statement in an argument, which gives you an advantage〔在争论中〕作最后的陈述〔具有一定优势〕**b)** to be the person who makes the final decision on something 作最终的裁定者, 为最后的决定者: *The finance committee always has the last word on expenditure.* 在开支上财政委员会总是最后的决定者。**9 be the last word in** to be the best, most modern, or most comfortable example of something 在…方面是最好[现代, 舒适]的: *It's the last word in luxury holidays.* 这是最舒服的豪华假期。

S1 W1 **last²** *adv* **1** most recently before now 最近, 上次: *When I last saw her, she was working in New York.* 我上次见到她时, 她正在纽约工作。**2** after everything or everyone else 最后: *They told me I'd be interviewed last.* 他们告诉我, 我最后一个接受面试。| *Mix together flour, butter, and sugar, and add the eggs last.* 把面粉、牛油和砂糖混在一起, 最后加上鸡蛋。| **last of all** (=used when giving a final point or piece of information) 最后 (一点[一条]) *Last of all, I'd like to thank the catering staff for a splendid meal.* 最后我要感谢提供美餐的员工们。**3 last but not least** used when mentioning the last person or thing in a list, to emphasize that they are still important 最后但并非最不重要的 (一点): *Last but not least, let me introduce Jane, our new secretary.* 最后但同样重要的是, 让我来介绍简, 我们新来的秘书。

S1 W1 **last³** *n, pron* **1 the last** the person or thing that comes after all the others 最后的人[事物]: *He was the first to arrive and the last to leave.* 他是最早到又最晚走的一个人。| *I think this box is the last.* 我想这个盒子是最后一个。**2 at (long) last** if something happens at last, it happens after you have waited a long time 最终, 终于: *I'm so pleased that Jane's managed to get a job at last.* 简终于找到工作了, 我真为此感到高兴。—see 见 LASTLY (USAGE) **3 the day/week/year etc before last** the day, week etc before the one that has just finished 前天/上上周/前年等: *I sent the letter off the week before last.* 上上周我把信寄出了。**4 the last of** the remaining parts of something 最后剩下的…: *Joan took the last of the meat from the dish and passed it to her mother.* 琼拿起了盘中最后剩下的肉递给她母亲。**5 haven't heard the last of** if you have not heard the last of a problem, it has not yet finished and it may cause problems for you in the future …还未了结: *I have a nasty feeling we haven't heard the last of this.* 我有一种不好的感觉, 这件事还没有了结。**6 the last I heard** *spoken* used to tell someone the most recent news that you know about a person or situation【口】最近听到的消息〔告诉别人知道的最新消息时的用语〕: *The last I heard, she was going back to college to study law.* 最近听说, 她正打算回校去学习法律。**7 to the last** *formal* until the end of an event or the end of someone's life【正式】直到终了; 至死: *He died in 1987, insisting to the last he was innocent.* 他死于1987年, 至死仍坚称自己是清白的。

S1 S2 **last⁴** *v* **1** [I always+adv/prep, linking verb 连系动词] to continue for a particular length of time 持续: [+**for/until/ through etc**] *The hot weather lasted for the whole month of June.* 炎热的天气在6月份持续整整一个月。| **last an hour/ten minutes etc** *Each lesson lasts an hour.* 每堂课持续一小时。| *The ceasefire didn't last long.* 停火时间不长。**2** [I] to continue to exist or remain in good condition for a long time 继续存在, 保持良好状态: *This good weather won't last.* 这种好天气不会持续很久。| *We wondered whether all this concern about the environment would really last.* 我们对于所有这种对环境的关心是否会真的保持下去感到怀疑。**3** [I+adv/prep] to manage to remain in the same situation, even when this is difficult 尽力维持原状: *They won't be able to last much longer without fresh supplies.* 没有新的供应, 他们就不能维持多久了。| *The new manager is very inexperienced – I doubt if he'll last long.* 新经理很没有经验——我怀疑他是否能继续待下去。**4** [linking verb 连系动词] to be enough for someone to use 足够〔某人〕使用 **last (sb) two days/three weeks etc** 让 (某人) 够用两天/三周等: *The water supply should last another 48 hours.* 供水可以再用48小时。| *We only had $50 to last us the rest of the month.* 我们只有50美元来度过这个月余下的日子。

last⁵ *n* [C] a piece of wood or metal shaped like a human foot, used by a shoemaker 鞋楦

La Stampa an Italian newspaper《新闻报》〔意大利一报纸〕

last call /,· '·/ *n* [C] *AmE* the words used by the person who is in charge of a bar when it is going to close and people can order just one more drink【美】最后一杯〔酒吧负责人在酒吧快打烊时的用语〕; LAST ORDERS *BrE*【英】

last-ditch /,· '·◂/ *adj* **a last-ditch attempt/effort etc** a final attempt to achieve something before it is too late 最后的图谋/努力等: *The negotiators made a last-ditch effort to reach an agreement.* 谈判者为达成协议尽了最后的努力。

last hur·rah /,· ·'·/ *n* [C usually singular 一般用单数] *AmE* a final effort, event etc at the end of a long period of work etc【美】最后的努力[一搏]

last·ing /'læstɪŋ; 'lɑːstɪŋ/ *adj* strong enough, well enough planned etc to last for a very long time 持久的, 耐久的: *The reforms will bring lasting benefits.* 改革将带来长远的利益。| *a lasting peace settlement* 持久的和平协议 | **leave a lasting impression** *Our first meeting left a lasting impression on me.* 我们的第一次见面给我留下了不可磨灭的印象。

last judg·ment /,· '··/ *n* **the last judgment** the time after death when everyone is judged by God for what they have done in life, according to Christianity and some other religions; JUDGMENT DAY〔基督教及其他一些宗教所称的上帝对人类的〕末日审判; 最终审判 (日)

last·ly /'læstlɪ; 'lɑːstli/ *adv* [sentence adverb 句子副词] used when you want to say one more thing at the end of a list 最后 (一点): *Lastly, could I ask all of you to keep this information secret.* 最后, 我请求各位对这一消息严守秘密。

USAGE NOTE 用法说明: LASTLY

WORD CHOICE 词语辨析: **lastly, last of all, finally, in the end, at last**

Lastly, last of all and **finally** are often used to end a set of points where time is not involved. lastly、last of all 和 finally 都常用以结束不考虑时间因素的一系列要点: *There are three reasons why I hate him: first(ly) he's rude, second(ly) he's a liar, and lastly/last of all/finally he owes me money* (NOT 不用 *at last*). 我讨厌他有三个原因: 第一, 他很粗鲁; 第二, 他撒谎; 最后一点是他欠我钱。

Last (of all) and **finally** also end a set of actions, often at points of time. last (of all) 和 finally 亦用来结束一系列动作, 经常按照时间的顺序排列: *First I get dressed, next I bring in the paper, then I feed the cat, and last/finally I fix my breakfast* (NOT 不用 *at last*). 首先我穿好衣服, 然后把报纸拿进来, 接着喂猫, 最后准备早餐。

Finally is also used, like **in the end**, just to mark something as happening after a long period of time. finally 和 in the end 一样, 仅用来表示很长时间后发生的事: *I tried hard and finally/in the end I managed it.* 我尽了很大努力, 最终我成功了。| *He fell ill and finally died/in the end he died.* 他病倒了, 最终撒手人寰。

At last has a similar use, but only when something good happens after a period of time. at last 用法相仿, 区别在于经过一段时间后所发生的是好事: *I tried and at last I managed it.* 我尽了努力, 终于完成了。| *At last I have a good dictionary!* (=I have waited a long time to find one) 我终于有了一本好词典〔=我等了好长时间才找到它〕。

last-minu·te /,· '··◂/ *adj* [only before noun 仅用于名词前] happening or done as late as possible within a process, event, or activity 最后一分钟的, 紧要关头的: *last-minute changes to the script* 剧本最后一刻的改动

last name /,· '·/ *n* [C] *especially AmE* a SURNAME【尤美】姓

Last Night of the Proms, the /,· · · · '·/ the last concert of the Proms (=a series of concerts held each summer in the Albert Hall in London). The second part of the concert always consists of the same TUNES and songs, and the people who go to the concert join the singing. 逍遥音乐会终场之夜〔每年夏天在伦敦艾伯特音乐厅举行的系列音乐会的最后一场。该场音乐会的下半场总是演奏固定曲目, 观众也常一起歌唱〕

Last of the Mo·hi·cans, The /,· · · · '·/ (1826) a NOVEL by James Fenimore Cooper about the lives of Native Americans and the adventures of PIONEERS (=the first Europeans) in North America《最后的莫希干人》〔(1826) 詹姆斯·费尼莫尔·库珀创作的一部小说。书中描写北美印第安人的生活及拓荒者的冒险经历〕

last or·ders /,· '·/ *n* [plural] *BrE* the words used by the person who is in charge of a bar or PUB when it is going to close

and people can order just one more drink【英】最后一杯〔酒吧负责人在酒吧快打烊时的用语〕; LAST CALL *AmE*【美】

last post, the /, · ' ·/ *n* the tune played on a BUGLE at British military funerals, or to call soldiers back to camp for the night〔英国〕军人葬礼号;〔军人的〕夜间回营号

last rites /, · ' ·/ *n* [plural] the ceremony performed in some religions, especially the Catholic religion, for people who are dying〔尤指天主教〕为临终者举行的圣礼

Last Sup·per, the /, · ' · ·/ **1** in the New Testament of the Bible, the meal eaten by Jesus and his twelve DISCIPLES on the evening before he was crucified (CRUCIFY). Jesus gave everyone bread and wine, and the Christian ceremony of the Eucharist is based on this meal. 最后的晚餐〔《圣经·新约》中, 耶稣被钉上十字架之前与12个门徒吃的最后一顿晚餐。耶稣把面包与酒分给众人, 基督教的圣餐仪式盖源于此〕**2** a painting of this event, especially the one painted by Leonardo da Vinci from 1495 to 1497, on the wall of a MONASTERY in Milan《最后的晚餐》〔根据这一事件创作的绘画作品, 尤指列奥纳多·达·芬奇1495至1497年在米兰一修道院的墙上所作的壁画〕

Last Tan·go in Pa·ris /, · , · · · ' · ·/ (1972) a US film in which Marlon Brando appears as a man living in Paris who has a sexual relationship with a young woman. Some people found it shocking when it was first shown because it contained a lot of sex scenes.《巴黎最后探戈》〔(1972), 美国电影。马龙·白兰度饰演的男子居住在巴黎, 同一名年轻女子有性关系。该片中有大量性爱镜头, 初次上映时令一些人感到十分震惊〕

Las Ve·gas /lɑs ˋvegəs; læs 'veɪgəs/ also 又作 **Vegas** *informal*【非正式】a city in the desert in the US state of Nevada, famous for its CASINOS. Las Vegas also has many Chapels where people can get married immediately, and is a popular place for people to spend their HONEYMOON. 拉斯维加斯〔美国内华达州沙漠中一城市, 以赌场闻名。拉斯维加斯有许多小教堂, 情侣们可随时在此结婚。拉斯维加斯还是新婚蜜月的好去处〕

lat the written abbreviation of 缩写= LATITUDE

latch¹ /lætʃ; lætʃ/ *n* [C] **1** a small metal bar that drops into a U-shaped object to keep doors, gates, windows etc closed〔门或窗的〕闩: *Gwen lifted the latch and opened the gate.* 格温提起门闩开门。**2** *especially BrE* a kind of lock for a door that you can open from the inside by turning a handle but that you need a key to open from the outside【尤英】碰锁, 碰簧锁: **on the latch** (=shut but not locked) 闩上〔关上但没有锁上〕*Ray went out, leaving the door on the latch.* 雷走出去, 把门闩上了。

latch² *v* [T] to fasten a door, window etc with a latch 用碰〔簧〕锁锁上〔门窗等〕

latch on *phr v* [I] *BrE informal* to understand【英, 非正式】理解: *He's so thick it took him ages to latch on.* 他这么笨, 花了很长时间才能理解。

latch onto sb/sth *phr v* [T] *informal*【非正式】**1** to follow someone and keep trying to talk to them, get their attention etc, especially when they would prefer to be left alone 缠住…不放: *He latched onto Sandy at the party and wouldn't go away.* 在聚会上他缠住桑迪不放。**2** get very interested in something so that you spend a lot of time thinking about it or discussing it 对〔某事〕深感兴趣: *It's the kind of issue that the media really latch onto.* 媒体真正感兴趣的是这类问题。

latch·key /ˋlætʃ,ki; 'lætʃki:/ *n* [C] **1** a key that opens a lock on an outside door of a house or apartment〔住所大门的〕碰〔簧〕锁的钥匙; 公寓门上的钥匙 **2 latchkey kid** *old fashioned* a child whose parents both work and who spends time alone in the house after school【过时】挂钥匙的儿童〔父母都外出上班的孩子, 放学后独自待在家中〕

late¹ /let; leɪt/ *adj*

1 ▶AFTER EXPECTED TIME 晚于预期时间◀ arriving, happening, or done after the time that was expected, agreed, or arranged 晚的, 迟的; 迟到的: *Sorry I'm late – I overslept.* 对不起, 来晚了 — 我睡过头了。| *The train was late.* 火车晚点了。| *We apologize for the late departure of flight AZ709.* 我们为AZ709航班的延误起飞表示道歉。| *Are we too late to get tickets?* 我们是不是太晚了而拿不到门票了? | [**+for**] *Cheryl overslept and was late for school.* 谢里尔睡过了头, 上学迟到了。

2 ▶AFTER USUAL TIME 晚于通常时间◀ happening or done after the usual or normal time 晚的: *a late breakfast* 晚早餐 | *The harvest was rather late this year.* 今年的收获季节来得相当晚。

3 ▶NEAR THE END 将近末尾◀ [only before noun 仅用于名词前] near to the end of a period of time 晚期的, 后期的: *the late eighteenth century* 18世纪末期 | *Paul's in his late forties.* 保罗快50岁了。

4 as late as used to express surprise that something considered old-fashioned was still happening so recently〔过时的东西〕到…如此晚的时候仍然在发生〔表示惊讶〕: *Capital punishment was still used in Britain as late as the 1950s.* 直到20世纪50年代英国还在沿用死刑。

5 ▶PAYMENTS ETC 支付等◀ a) paid, given back etc after the agreed date 迟付的, 迟还回的: *There are strict penalties if repayments on the loan are late.* 若不能按时偿还贷款会有严厉的处罚。**b) be late with** to pay something, bring something back etc after the agreed date 迟交款的, 迟还回的: *We try never to be late with the rent.* 我们尽量不拖欠租金。

6 ▶EVENING 晚上◀ [only before noun 仅用于名词前] near the end of the day 临近一天之末的: *the late movie* 夜场电影 | *We stopped by for a late drink.* 我们夜里顺便拜访来喝一杯。

7 her late husband/the late president etc used to talk about someone who has died 她的先夫/已故总统等

8 a late developer a child whose physical size or character develops slowly 发育晚的孩子

9 it's (a little) late in the day used to show disapproval because someone has done something too late for it to be effective 已〔有点〕晚了〔抱怨做事太晚而失去效用〕: *It's a little late in the day to say you're sorry!* 说对不起已有点晚了!

10 late of *formal* having lived in a place until fairly recently【正式】不久前住在〔某地〕的: *Billy Hicks, late of this parish* 不久前住在这一教区的比利·希克斯

late² *adv* **1** after or later than the usual time 晚于〔通常时间〕: *The stores are open late on Thursdays.* 这些商店星期四开门晚。| *Ellen has to work late tonight.* 艾伦今晚得工作到很晚。**2** after the arranged or expected time 迟, 晚; 迟于安排[预期]的时间: *The bus came ten minutes late.* 公共汽车晚到了10分钟。**3** near to the end of a period of time or an event〔时期或事件〕临近末尾: **late in August/the evening/1995** *The wedding took place late in May.* 婚礼在5月底举行。**4 of late** *formal* recently【正式】最近: *Maureen hasn't been feeling too well of late.* 莫琳最近一直感到不太舒服。**5 late in life** if you do something late in life, you do it at an older age than most people do it 比一般人年岁大一点〔干某事〕**6 better late than never** used to say that you are glad someone has done something, or that they should do something, although they are late 迟做总比不做好 —see also 另见 **be running late** (RUN¹ (48))

late-break·ing /' · · ·/ *adj* late-breaking news concerns events that happen just before a news broadcast or just before a newspaper is printed〔消息〕刚得到的;〔事件〕刚发生的

late·com·er /ˋlet,kʌmɚ; 'leɪt,kʌmə/ *n* [C] someone who arrives late 迟到者, 后来者; 新进者

late·ly /ˋletlɪ; 'leɪtli/ *adv* recently 近来, 最近: *I've been feeling ill just lately.* 最近我感到不适。

late-night /' · · ·/ *adj* [only before noun 仅用于名词前] happening late at night 深夜的,〔后〕半夜的: *late-night television* 午夜的电视节目 | *late-night shopping* 晚间购物

la·tent /ˋletn̩t; 'leɪtənt/ *adj* something that is latent is present but hidden, and may develop or become more noticeable in the future 潜在的, 潜伏的: *The virus remains latent in the body for many years.* 该病毒在体内潜伏了许多年。| *latent aggression* 潜在的侵略 —**latency** *n* [U]

latent heat /, · · ' ·/ *n* [U] *technical* the additional heat necessary to change a solid into a liquid, or a liquid into a gas【术语】潜热

lat·er¹ /ˋletɚ; 'leɪtə/ *adv* **1** after the time you are talking about or after the present time 后来, 此时以后: *I'm going out for a bit – I'll see you later.* 我出去一会儿 — 回头见。| **two years later/three weeks later etc** *He became Senator two years later.* 两年后他成了参议员。| **later that day/ morning/week** *The baby died later that night.* 婴儿在那晚的后半夜夭折。| **later in the day/week/year** *The dentist could fit you in later in the week.* 牙医可以在后半周给你补牙。—see 见 LASTLY (USAGE) **2 later on** at some time later or in the future 过后, 以后, 将来: *I can't eat all of this – I'll finish it later on.* 我吃不下所有的东西 — 我过后再吃完它。**3 not later than** used when saying that something must be done by a particular time in the future 不得晚于, 须早于: *Completed entry forms should arrive not later than 31st July.* 填写好的参加表格不得晚于7月31日送达。

later² *adj* [only before noun 仅用于名词前] **1** coming in the future or after something else 较晚时候的, 以后的: *The role of marketing is dealt with in a later chapter.* 市场销售的作用会在稍后的一章中述及。| *The launch was postponed to a later date.* 发射延期了。**2** more recent 更新近的: *The engine has been greatly improved in later models.* 在新近的型号中发动机作了很大的改进。**3 in later years/life** when someone is older 在晚

年: *Using a sunscreen when you are young helps you to have healthy skin in later years.* 年轻的时候使用防晒油会使你在年老时拥有健康的皮肤。

lat·e·ral[1] /ˈlætərəl; ˈlætərəl/ *adj technical* connected with the sides of something, or movement to the side【术语】侧面的; 横(向)的: *The wall is weak and requires lateral support.* 墙体不坚固, 需要侧面的支撑。 —**laterally** *adv*

lateral[2] *n* [C] *technical* something that is at the side or comes from the side【术语】在侧面的东西; 横向伸出的东西

lateral think·ing /,···ˈ··/ *n* [U] a way of thinking in which you use your imagination to make connections between things that are not normally thought of together 横向思考(法)

lat·est[1] /ˈletɪst; ˈleɪtɨst/ *adj* [only before noun 仅用于名词前] the most recent or the newest 最近的; 最新的: *all the latest gossip* 最近所有的流言飞语 | *Metallica's latest album* 重金属乐队的最新专辑

latest[2] *n* **1 the latest** *informal* the most recent news, fashion, or technical improvement【非正式】最新消息[款式, 技术改进]: *the latest in computer software* 最新的电脑软件 **2 at the latest** no later than the time mentioned 最迟, 最晚: *I should be back by 11 o'clock at the latest.* 我最迟 11 点会回来。

Late Sum·mer Hol·i·day, the /·,··ˈ···/ —see 见 AUGUST BANK HOLIDAY

la·tex /ˈletɛks; ˈleɪteks/ *n* [U] **1** a thick whitish liquid produced by some plants, especially the rubber tree 胶乳; 〔尤指橡胶树的〕橡浆 **2** an artificial substance similar to this, used in making paint, glue etc〔人工的〕胶乳

lath /læθ; lɑːθ/ *n* [C] *plural* **laths** /læθs; lɑːðz/ a long flat narrow piece of wood used in building to support PLASTER (=material used to cover walls) (木)板条

lathe /leð; leɪð/ *n* [C] a machine that shapes wood or metal, by turning it round and round against a sharp tool 车床

la·ther[1] /ˈlæðɚ; ˈlɑːðə/ *n* [singular, U] **1** a white mass of BUBBLES produced by mixing soap in water〔肥皂水等的〕泡沫 **2** a white mass that forms on a horse's skin when it has been sweating (SWEAT[1] (1))〔马的〕汗沫 **3 in a lather** *BrE informal* very anxious, especially because you do not have enough time【英, 非正式】〔尤指因时间不足而〕紧张不安, 着急, 焦躁 —**lathery** *adj*

lather[2] *v* **1** [I] to produce a lather 起泡沫: *This soap lathers really well.* 这种肥皂真的易起泡沫。**2** [T] to cover something with lather〔用泡沫〕覆盖〔某物〕**3** [T] *informal* to hit someone violently【非正式】狠击〔某人〕

Lat·i·mer /ˈlætəmɚ; ˈlætɨmə/**, Bishop Hugh** /hju; hjuː/ (1485-1555) an English BISHOP (=a Christian priest of high rank) who was one of the leaders of the Reformation in England (=the time when many Christians left the Catholic religion and started the Protestant religion). When Mary I, who was a Catholic, became queen of England, she ordered him to be officially killed by being burned. 拉蒂默〔(1485-1555), 英格兰主教, 英格兰宗教改革领袖之一。信仰天主教的玛丽一世即位后下令将他处以火刑〕

Lat·in[1] /ˈlætn; ˈlætɪn/ *n* **1** [U] the language of the ancient Romans 拉丁语; 拉丁系语言 **2** [C] someone who comes from Southern Europe 拉丁人〔指欧洲南部的人〕

Latin[2] *adj* **1** written in Latin 用拉丁语写成的: *a Latin text* 拉丁文版本 **2** connected with a nation that speaks a language such as Italian, Spanish, or Portuguese that developed from Latin 拉丁语系各民族的〈如意大利人、西班牙人, 或葡萄牙人〉

Latin A·mer·i·ca /,··ˈ···/ the countries of South America and Central America, where Spanish and Portuguese are spoken 拉丁美洲〔指讲西班牙语或葡萄牙语的南美洲和中美洲国家〕

Latin A·mer·i·can /,··ˈ···◂/ *adj* connected with South or Central America 拉丁美洲的

La·ti·no /læˈtino; læˈtiːnəʊ/ *n* [C] *AmE* someone living in the US whose family came from a Central or South American country【美】〔居住在美国的〕拉丁美洲人 —**Latino** *adj*: *Latino culture* 拉丁美洲文化

Latin Quar·ter, the /ˈ··,··/ a part of Paris on the Left Bank of the River Seine, which is traditionally an area where many students, writers, and artists live, but is now a popular place for tourists to visit 拉丁区〔巴黎塞纳河左岸一地区, 历来是大学生、作家和艺术家居住之地, 现为旅游胜地〕

lat·i·tude /ˈlætə,tjud; ˈlætɨtjuːd/ *n* **1** [C,U] *technical* the distance north or south of the EQUATOR (=the imaginary line around the middle of the world) measured in degrees【术语】纬度 —compare 比较 LONGITUDE —see picture at 参见 EARTH[1] 图 **2 latitudes** [plural] an area at a particular latitude 特指的纬度区域: *At these latitudes you often get strong winds.* 在这些纬度地区经常有大风。**3** [U] *formal* freedom to choose what you do or say【正式】自由度, 选择的余地: *Pupils enjoy considerable latitude in deciding what they want to study.* 小学生们想学什么有相当大的选择余地。 —**latitudinal** /,lætəˈtjudənl; ,lætɨˈtjuːdɨnəl/ *adj*

lat·i·tu·di·na·ri·an /,lætə,tudn̩ˈɛrɪən; ,lætɨtjuːdɨˈneəriən/ *n* [C] *formal* someone who is willing to accept other people's beliefs and behaviour【正式】乐于接纳他人信仰和行为的人 —**latitudinarian** *adj*

lat·ke /ˈlɑtkə; ˈlɑːtkə/ *n* [C] a Jewish food like a round flat PANCAKE made from raw potato 马铃薯烙饼〔犹太食品〕

la·trine /ləˈtrin; ləˈtriːn/ *n* [C] a toilet that is outdoors in a camp or military area〔营地或军营的〕户外厕所

lat·ter[1] /ˈlætɚ; ˈlætə/ *n* **the latter** *formal* the second of two people or things just mentioned【正式】〔刚提及的两个人或物中的〕后者: *The system brings both financial and environmental benefits, the latter being especially welcome.* 该制度对财政和环境都有益处, 后者特别受欢迎。—opposite 反义词 FORMER[2] (1) 2

latter[2] *adj* [only before noun 仅用于名词前] *formal*【正式】**1** being the second of two people or things, or the last in a list just mentioned〔两者之中〕后者的;〔刚提到的列表之中〕最后者的: *In the latter case, buyers pay a 15% commission.* 在后一种的情况下, 购买者付 15% 的佣金。**2** the latter part of a period of time is nearest to the end of it 末期的, 后期的: *Celebrations are planned for the latter part of November.* 庆祝计划在 11 月下旬举行。

latter-day /ˈ···/ *adj* [only before noun 仅用于名词前] **a latter-day Versailles/Tsar/Robin Hood etc** something or someone that exists now but is like a famous thing or person that existed in the past 当今的凡尔赛/沙皇/罗宾汉等: *ruling his business empire like a latter-day Tsar* 像当代的沙皇一样统治着他的商业帝国

Latter-Day Saints /,···ˈ·/ *n* [plural] the MORMONS 末世圣徒, 摩门教教徒

lat·ter·ly /ˈlætɚlɪ; ˈlætəli/ *adv formal*【正式】**1** recently 近来, 最近: *Jim's behaviour has been a little strange latterly.* 吉姆的举止近来一直有点古怪。**2** towards the end of a period of time〔一段时间的〕末期: *O'Rourke retired after a 15-year career with Bisons, latterly as chief executive.* 奥罗克在比森斯公司工作了 15 年, 后来以总裁身份退休。—compare 比较 FORMERLY

lat·tice /ˈlætɪs; ˈlætɨs/ *n* [C] **1** also 又作 **lat·tice·work** /ˈlætɪs,wɝk; ˈlætɨswɜːk/ a pattern or structure made of long flat narrow pieces of wood, plastic etc that are arranged so that they cross each other and the spaces between them are shaped like diamonds (DIAMOND (2)) 格子图案[结构] **2 lattice window** a type of window made of a pattern of many small pieces of glass shaped like diamonds (DIAMOND (2)) 格子窗 **3** *technical* a regular arrangement of objects over an area or in space【术语】晶格; 格构

Lat·vi·a /ˈlætvɪə; ˈlætviə/ a country in northeast Europe on the Baltic Sea, between Estonia and Lithuania, which used to be part of the former Soviet Union. Population: 2,385,000 (2001). Capital: Riga. 拉脱维亚〔欧洲东北部一国家, 濒临波罗的海, 位于爱沙尼亚和立陶宛之间, 原属前苏联。人口: 2,385,000 (2001), 首都: 里加〕 —**Latvian** *n, adj*

laud /lɔd; lɔːd/ *v* [T] *formal* to praise someone or something【正式】称赞, 赞美

lau·da·ble /ˈlɔdəbl̩; ˈlɔːdəbəl/ *adj formal* deserving praise or admiration, even if not completely successful【正式】值得称赞[赞美]的: *a laudable attempt* 值得称赞的尝试 —**laudably** *adv*

lau·da·num /ˈlɔdənəm; ˈlɔːdənəm/ *n* [U] a substance containing the drug OPIUM, used in the past to control pain and help people to sleep 鸦片酊[酒]

lau·da·to·ry /ˈlɔdə,torɪ; ˈlɔːdətəri/ *adj formal* expressing praise or admiration【正式】表达称颂[赞美]的: *a laudatory biography* 颂扬性的传记

laugh[1] /læf; lɑːf/ *v*

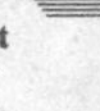

1 ▶MAKE SOUND 发出声音◀ [I] to make the sounds and movements of the face that people make when they think something is funny 发出笑声, 笑: *Jonathan kept pulling funny faces at me, and I couldn't stop laughing.* 乔纳森一直朝我扮鬼脸, 我禁不住大笑。| [**+at/about**] *I couldn't understand why they were all laughing at me.* 我不明白他们为什么都在笑我。| **burst out laughing** (=suddenly start laughing) 突然放声大笑 *When we saw what had happened to the cake we burst out laughing.* 当我们见到蛋糕变成的模样时, 我们爆发出一阵大笑。| **laugh your head off** (=laugh loudly and a lot) 大笑不止 | **laugh out loud** (=suddenly laugh loudly) 突然放声大笑

2 ▶SPEAK 说话◀ [T] to say something in a voice that shows you are amused 笑着说: *"You look ridiculous!" Nick laughed.* "你看起来很可笑!" 尼克笑着说。

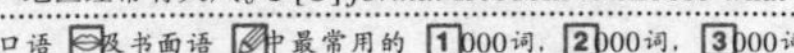

3 be laughing *spoken* to be happy or in a good situation, for example because something has had a successful result for you【口】正高兴; 处于佳境中: *Well they paid me, didn't they, so I'm laughing.* 啱, 他们付钱给我了, 是不是, 所以我正高兴呢。

4 don't make me laugh *spoken* used when someone has just told you something that is completely untrue, asked for something impossible etc【口】别逗了: *"Do you think we'll finish this today?" "Don't make me laugh."* "你认为我们今天会完成吗?" "别逗了。"

5 no laughing matter *informal* something serious that should not be joked about【非正式】严肃的事, 不是闹着玩的事: *Losing your job is no laughing matter.* 把工作丢了, 这可不是闹着玩的事。

6 be laughing all the way to the bank *informal* to be in a good situation because you have made a lot of money without making much effort【非正式】一路笑着去银行〔因赚钱容易而境况良好〕

7 be laughed out of court *especially BrE* if a person or idea is laughed out of court, the idea is not accepted because people think it is completely stupid【尤英】对…一笑了之; 不予考虑: *We can't propose that! We'd be laughed out of court!* 我们不能提那建议!我们会被瞧不起的!

8 sb will be laughing on the other side of their face *spoken* used unkindly to mean that although someone is happy or confident now, they will be in trouble or in difficulty later【口】有…哭的时候

9 laughing stock someone who has done something so stupid that everyone laughs at them 笑柄, 笑料: *He was the laughing stock of the school!* 他是全校的笑料!

10 not know whether to laugh or cry to feel upset or annoyed by something bad or unlucky that has happened 哭笑不得: *And when I couldn't find the passports – honestly, I didn't know whether to laugh or cry!* 而当我找不到护照的时候——说真的, 我不知道该哭还是笑!

11 you have to laugh *spoken* used to say that, even though a situation is annoying or disappointing, you can also see that there is something funny about it【口】〔尽管情况令人心烦或失望, 但还是觉得滑稽而〕不由得好笑

12 laugh in sb's face to behave towards someone in a way that shows that you do not respect them or care about what they think 当面嘲笑[取笑]: *I asked them not to park in front of my garage, but they just laughed in my face.* 我请他们别在我的车库前停车, 他们却当面嘲笑我。

13 laugh up your sleeve to be secretly happy, especially because you have played a trick on someone or criticized them without them knowing 暗笑, 窃笑, 偷笑

laugh at sb/sth *phr v* [T] **1** to treat someone or something as if they are stupid, by laughing or making funny and unkind remarks about them 嘲笑, 取笑: *I can't go to school wearing that – everyone'll laugh at me.* 我不能穿着它去上学——大家会取笑我的。**2** to seem not to care about something that most people would worry about 不在乎, 不当一回事: *Young offenders just laugh at this sort of sentence.* 年轻的冒失鬼们对这种判决根本不在乎。

laugh sth ↔ **off** *phr v* [T] to pretend that something is less serious than it really is by laughing or joking about it 用笑摆脱; 用笑话来排除; 对…一笑了之: *I tried to tell him he was drinking too much but he just laughed it off.* 我告诉他, 他喝得太多了, 可是他只是一笑了之。

laugh² *n* [C] **1** the sound you make when you laugh 笑声: *a nervous laugh* 神经质的一笑 | **give a laugh** *She gave a little laugh and squeezed my arm.* 她轻轻笑一声, 并捏我的手臂。**2 have a (good) laugh** *BrE*【英】**a)** *informal* to have fun and enjoy yourself【非正式】尽情地笑; 玩得很痛快: *We always have a good laugh when Kevin comes to stay.* 每当凯文来的时候, 我们总是玩得很痛快。**b)** to laugh about something in a happy way with other people 把…当笑话: *It was a nightmare at the time, but afterwards we all had a good laugh about it.* 那时候这事极可怕, 但是后来我们都把它当成笑话。**3 be a (good) laugh** *BrE informal*【英, 非正式】**a)** to be amusing and fun to be with 和…一起很愉快: *I hope Sarah comes – she's a real laugh.* 我希望萨拉会来——她真是个有趣的人。**b)** if an occasion, activity etc is a good laugh, you enjoy yourself and have fun 是件开心痛快的事: *We all went to the beach last night – it was a really good laugh.* 昨晚我们都去沙滩了——那真是件开心痛快的事。**4 do sth for a laugh** *BrE informal* to do something because you think it will be fun, not for a serious reason【英, 非正式】做某事只是为了取乐 **5 have the last laugh** to be successful, win an argument etc in the end, after other people have criticized you, defeated you etc earlier〔经历非议、失败等〕最终获胜[成功] **6 be a laugh a minute** *informal* to be very funny, cheerful, and amusing; sometimes used humorously to mean the opposite【非正式】有趣, 快乐, 令人好笑; 〔有时幽默地指〕无趣, 不快

laugh·a·ble /ˈlæfəbl; ˈlɑːfəbəl/ *adj* so bad, silly, or unbelievable that it makes you want to laugh 可笑的, 荒唐的: *The profit figures are laughable!* 这些利润数字是荒唐的! —**laughably** *adv*

Laughing Cav·a·lier, The /,· · ·ˈ·/ a painting by the 17th century artist Frans Hals, which shows a wealthy man with a large MOUSTACHE who is slightly smiling in a proud way《微笑的骑士》〔17世纪画家弗朗斯·哈尔斯的作品。画中是一位留着大胡子的有钱人, 面带微笑, 神情得意〕

laugh·ing gas /ˈ· · ·/ *n* [U] *informal* a gas that is sometimes used to stop you feeling pain during an operation【非正式】〔手术中止痛的〕笑气, 一氧化二氮

laughing jack·ass /,· · ˈ· ·/ *n* [C] *informal* a KOOKABURRA【非正式】笑翠鸟

laugh·ing·ly /ˈlæfɪŋli; ˈlɑːfɪŋli/ *adv* **1** if something is laughingly called something or described in a particular way, you think it is so bad that the name or description seems stupid 开玩笑地: *This room is laughingly referred to as the 'Quality Control Centre'.* 这个房间被戏称为"质量控制中心"。**2** if you do something laughingly, you are laughing while you do it 带笑地〔做〕

laugh lines /ˈ· ·/ *n* [plural] the American form of LAUGHTER LINES laughter lines 的美语形式

laugh·ter /ˈlæftə; ˈlɑːftə/ *n* [U] the act of laughing or sound of people laughing 笑; 笑声: *We could hear riotous laughter from next door.* 我们能够听到隔壁房间狂欢的笑声。| **roar/howl/shriek with laughter** (=laugh very loudly) 发出哄笑/狂笑/尖笑声 | **dissolve into laughter** (=start to laugh when you have been trying not to) 情不自禁地大笑

laughter lines /ˈ· · ·/ *n* [plural] *BrE* lines on your skin around your eyes which can be seen when you laugh【英】〔眼睛周围的〕笑纹; LAUGH LINES *AmE*【美】

launch¹ /lɔntʃ; lɔːntʃ/ *v* [T]

1 ►START STH 开始做某事◄ to start something, especially an official, public, or military activity that has been carefully planned 发动, 发起, 开始进行: **launch a campaign/appeal/inquiry** *Police have launched a murder enquiry following the discovery of a woman's body.* 发现女尸后, 警方开始进行谋杀案的调查。| **launch an attack/assault/offensive** *The press launched a vicious attack on the President.* 新闻界对总统发起了恶意的攻击。

2 ►PRODUCT 产品◄ to make a new product, book etc available for sale for the first time 把〔新产品、新书等〕投放市场, 出版, 发行: *It was a party to launch her new novel.* 就发行她的新小说而举行了招待会。

3 ►BOAT 船◄ to put a boat or ship into the water 将〔船或舰〕下水

4 ►SKY/SPACE 天空/太空◄ to send a weapon or SPACECRAFT into the sky or into space 发射〔武器或太空船〕: *A test satellite was launched from Cape Canaveral.* 实验人造卫星从卡纳维拉尔角发射升空。

5 launch yourself forwards/up/from etc to jump up and forwards into the air with a lot of energy〔用力〕扑向前/跃起/从…扑过去等

launch into sth *phr v* [T] to suddenly start a description or story, or suddenly start criticizing something 突然开始〔描述、叙述、抨击〕: *The preacher launched into an attack on adultery.* 传教士突然开始抨击通奸。

launch out *phr v* [I always+adv/prep] to start something new, especially something that involves risk 开始, 着手〔新事情, 尤指有风险的事〕: **[+into]** *Dickson left his father's firm and launched out into business on his own.* 迪克森离开了他父亲的公司, 开创自己的事业。

launch² *n* [C] **1** an occasion at which a new product, book etc is made available or made known〔新产品的〕投放市场, 〔新书的〕发行: *the launch of our new hatchback* 掀背式后背的新款小汽车的推出 **2** a large boat with a motor 游艇, 汽艇

launch·er /ˈlɔntʃə; ˈlɔːntʃə/ *n* [C] a structure from which a weapon, ROCKET, or SPACECRAFT is sent into the sky 发射架, 发射装置

launch pad /ˈ· ·/ also 又作 **launching pad** /ˈ· · ·/ *n* [C] a base from which a ROCKET or MISSILE is sent up into the sky〔火箭、导弹的〕发射台, 发射坪

laun·der /ˈlɔndə; ˈlɔːndə/ *v* [T] **1** to put money which has been obtained illegally into legal businesses and bank accounts, so that you can hide it or use it 洗〔黑钱〕〔即把非法得来的钱注入合法

的生意中或存入银行, 以便隐藏或使用) **2** *formal* to wash and IRON[2] clothes, sheets etc【正式】洗熨〔衣服等〕 —**laundered** *adj*

laun·der·ette /ˌlɔndəˋrɛt; ˌlɔːndəˈret/ also 又作 **laundrette** /lɔnˋdrɛt; lɔːnˈdret/ *BrE n* [C] a place where you can go to wash your clothes in machines that work when you put coins in them【英】〔装有投币洗衣机的〕自助洗衣店

laun·dry /ˋlɔndrɪ; ˈlɔːndri/ *n* **1** [C] a place or business where clothes etc are washed and ironed (IRON[2]) 洗熨衣服的地方, 洗衣房; 洗衣店 **2** [U] clothes, sheets etc that need to be washed or have just been washed 待洗[洗过]的衣物

laundry bas·ket /ˋ· · , · ·/ *n* [C] **1** *BrE* a large basket that you put dirty clothes in until you wash them【英】〔放置待洗脏衣服的〕洗衣筐; HAMPER[2] (2) *AmE*【美】—see picture at 参见 BASKET 图 **2** a basket used for carrying wet clothes that have been washed〔装已洗湿衣的〕篮子

laundry list /ˋ· · ·/ *n* [C] *AmE* a list you write to remind you of things you have to do or buy【美】〔提醒〕要做之事[购物]的清单

Lau·ra·sia /lɔˋreʒə; lɔːˈreɪʃə/ the very large area of land that existed about 200 million years ago, before it broke apart to form North America, Europe, Asia, and Greenland 劳亚古大陆〔2亿年前一块广袤的陆地, 后出现断裂, 形成北美洲、欧洲、亚洲和格陵兰〕—see also 另见 GONDWANALAND, PANGAEA

laur·e·ate /ˋlɔrɪɪt; ˈlɔːriət/ *n* [C] someone who has won an important prize, especially the NOBEL PRIZE 重要奖项〔尤指诺贝尔奖〕获得者: *Nigeria's Nobel laureate, Wole Soyinka* 尼日利亚的诺贝尔奖获得者, 沃雷·索因卡 —see also 另见 POET LAUREATE

laur·el /ˋlɔrəl; ˈlɒrəl/ *n* **1** [C,U] a small tree with smooth shiny dark green leaves that do not fall in winter 月桂树 **2 rest/sit on your laurels** to be satisfied with what you have achieved and therefore stop trying to achieve anything new 满足于已有成绩, 不求上进 **3 look to your laurels** to work hard in order not to lose the success that you have achieved 尽力保住已获得的成功

Laurel and Har·dy /ˌ· · · ˋ· ·/ two US COMEDIANS, **Stan Laurel** (1890-1965), who was born in the UK, and **Oliver Hardy** (1892-1957), who made many humorous and popular films together from the 1920s to the 1950s. Laurel is famous for being a thin stupid character, who is easily upset, and Hardy is famous for being a fat character with a small MOUSTACHE, who often gets angry with Laurel and says to him, "That's another fine mess you've gotten me into!" 劳莱和哈代〔美国一对喜剧搭档, 即斯坦·劳莱 (1890-1965, 生于英国) 和奥利弗·哈代 (1892-1957)。20世纪20年代至50年代, 他们合演了许多妙趣横生的影片, 颇受观众喜爱。劳莱扮演一个形销骨立、愚笨不堪, 动辄怄气的角色。哈代饰演一个留有小胡子的大胖子, 经常和劳莱过不去, 总会冲着他喊道: "瞧你干的好事, 又把我给折腾进去了!" 他们因扮演这两个角色而闻名〕

lav /læv; læv/ *n* [C] *BrE spoken* a lavatory【英口】厕所, 洗手间

la·va /ˋlɑvə; ˈlɑːvə/ *n* [U] **1** hot liquid rock that flows from a VOLCANO〔火山喷出的〕岩浆, 熔岩 **2** this rock when it has become cold and solid 火山岩

lav·a·to·ri·al /ˌlævəˋtɔrɪəl; ˌlævəˈtɔːriəl◂/ *adj* lavatorial humour or jokes are about going to the toilet or about sex〔有关上厕所或性方面的幽默或笑话〕低级粗俗的

lav·a·to·ry /ˋlævəˌtɔrɪ; ˈlævətəri/ *n* [C] *formal* a toilet or the room a toilet is in【正式】厕所, 洗手间

lav·en·der /ˋlævəndə; ˈlævɪ̣ndə/ *n* **1** [C,U] a plant that has purple flowers with a strong pleasant smell 薰衣草 **2** [U] the dried flowers of this plant, often used to make things smell nice 晾干的薰衣草花 **3** [U] a pale purple colour 浅紫色

lavender bag /ˋ· · · , ·/ *n* [C] a small bag containing dried lavender that you put in a drawer to make your clothes smell nice 存放干薰衣草花的袋子

lavender wa·ter /ˋ· · · , · ·/ *n* [U] a PERFUME[1] (1) made from lavender oil and alcohol 薰衣草香水

la·ver /ˋlɑvə; ˈlɑːvə/ *n* [U] a type of sea plant that you can eat 紫菜

laver bread /ˋ· · ·/ *n* [U] a dish made from laver that is boiled and then cooked in butter 紫菜面包〔由紫菜和黄油制的食品〕

CULTURAL NOTE 文化注释

Laver bread is a favourite Welsh dish usually eaten at breakfast. The laver is cut up and boiled then fried (FRY) in butter. Although it is called 'bread', it is more liquid than solid and feels slippery. 紫菜面包是受人喜爱的威尔士菜肴, 常作早餐食用。紫菜剁碎后先煮一下, 然后用黄油炸。尽管叫做"面包", 紫菜面包并不是固态的, 而更像是一种流质食物, 口感滑爽。

lav·ish[1] /ˋlævɪʃ; ˈlævɪʃ/ *adj* **1** lavish gifts, meals etc are large and generous, and look as if they have cost a lot of money 过分多的, 过分铺张的, 过分丰盛的: *They would organize lavish dinners for potential customers.* 他们会设下铺张的宴会招待潜在客户。| *a lavish production of 'Tosca', with fine costumes and elaborate stage sets* 采用华丽服装和精美舞台布景巨资打造的《托斯卡》 **2 be lavish with** to give something very generously 过分慷慨地给与, 过于大方地出手: *He's never very lavish with his praises.* 他从不随便夸奖。—**lavishly** *adv*: *lavishly decorated with fruit and flowers* 装点着大量水果和花朵 —**lavishness** *n* [U]

lavish[2] *v*

lavish sth **on/upon** sb *phr v* [T] to give someone a lot of something such as expensive presents, love, or praise〔过分〕慷慨地给予〔某人〕〈如贵重礼物、爱或夸奖〉: *Roberta lavished attention on the children.* 罗伯塔对孩子们关怀备至。

law /lɔ; lɔː/ *n* (S1) (W1)

1 ►SYSTEM OF RULES 规则体系◄ [singular, U] the whole system of rules that citizens of a country or place must obey 法律 (体系), 法规: **against the law** (=illegal) 违法的 *Sex discrimination is against the law.* 性别歧视是违法的。| **break the law** (=do something illegal) 犯法 *There were easy profits for businessmen who were prepared to break the law.* 对于存心以身试法的商人而言盈利是容易的。| **against the law (for sb) to do sth** *It is against the law for children to work before they are fifteen.* 儿童在15岁以前工作是违法的。| **become law** (=be officially made a law) 立法, 成为法律 *The Criminal Justice Bill became law amidst much controversy.*《刑事审判法案》在一片争议声中成为了法律。| **by law** (=according to the law) 依照法律 *Seatbelts must, by law, be worn by all passengers.* 依照法律, 乘客必须系上安全带。| **keep/stay/remain/operate within the law** (=make sure that what you do is legal) 在法律许可范围之内进行 *They make tough business deals, but are always careful to operate within the law.* 他们做一些棘手的买卖, 但总会小心翼翼地在法律许可的范围内进行。| **tax law/divorce law/libel law etc** (=all the laws relating to tax etc) 税法/离婚法/诽谤法等 *a specialist in company law* 公司法专家 | *She's a partner in a major New York law firm.* 她是纽约一家大律师事务所的合伙人。—see also 另见 CRIMINAL LAW, LAW FIRM

2 ►A RULE 规则◄ [C] a rule that people in a particular country, city or local area must obey 法则, 法令: *Under the new law, any gathering of over 10 people is considered a crime.* 按照新的法律, 任何超过10人的集会均被视为犯罪。| **[+on]** *European laws on equal opportunities* 欧洲的均等机会法 | **[+against]** *There ought to be a law against cutting down trees.* 应该制定一项禁止伐树的法律。

3 there's no law against (it) *spoken* used to tell someone who is criticizing you that you are not doing anything wrong【口】没有法律规定说不可以 (这样)

4 ►POLICE 警察◄ the law the police 警方, 警察: *I think she may be in trouble with the law.* 我想她会和警察惹上麻烦。| **I'll have the law on you** *spoken* (=used to threaten someone that you will call the police)【口】我要叫警察了 *Get away from my car or I'll have the law on you!* 离开我的车, 否则我要叫警察了!

5 law and order a situation in which people respect the law, and crime is controlled by the police, the prison system etc 法律和秩序, 法治: *The soldiers were brought in to restore law and order after the riots.* 骚乱发生后士兵被派来维持治安。

6 have the law on your side to be legally right in what you are doing〔做事〕合法

7 ►SPORT 体育运动◄ [C] one of the rules that say how a sport should be played 运动规则: *the laws of football* 足球规则

8 ►BUSINESS/ART 商业/艺术◄ [C] a way in which things happen in an activity such as business or art, which is thought of as a rule because it seems impossible to change 规则: *the law of supply and demand* 供需规律 | *the law of perspective* 透视法

9 ►NATURAL LAW 自然规律◄ [C] a statement that describes and explains how nature works 法则, 定律: *the laws of nature* 自然法则 | *the Second Law of Thermodynamics* 热力学第二定律 | *the law of gravity* 万有引力定律

10 the law of the jungle a) the idea that people should only look after themselves and not care about other people, if they want to succeed 想要成就, 莫顾他人 **b)** the principle that only the strongest creatures will stay alive 丛林法则; 弱肉强食法则; 强者生存原则

11 the law of averages the PROBABILITY that one result will happen as often as another if you try something often enough 平均律, 均值定理, 概率: *By the law of averages you'll have to throw a six eventually.* 根据概率你最后必会掷出六点。

L

12 be a law unto himself/herself etc to behave in an independent way and not worry about the usual rules of behaviour or what other people do or think 我行我素，独断专行

13 take the law into your own hands to do something illegal in order to put right something that you think is unjust, for example by violently punishing someone instead of informing the police 不通过法律擅自处理；用私刑处罚：*vigilantes who take the law into their own hands* 擅自执法的治安会成员

14 go to law to go to court in order to settle a problem 提起诉讼，打官司 —see also 另见 CIVIL LAW, COMMON LAW, **lay down the law** (LAY[2]), POOR LAW, ROMAN LAW, SOD'S LAW, **unwritten law** (UNWRITTEN)

law-a·bid·ing /ˈ· ·,· ·/ *adj* **law-abiding citizens/people/neighbours etc** people who respect and obey the law 守法的公民/人民/邻居等

law·break·er /ˈ· ,· ·/ *n* [C] someone who does something illegal 犯法的人，违法的人—**law-breaking** *n* [U]

law·court /ˈlɔ,kɔrt; ˈlɔːkɔːt/ *n* [C] a room or building where legal cases are judged 法庭，法院

law en·force·ment /ˈ· ·,· ·/ *n* [U] the job of making sure that the law is obeyed 执法

law enforcement a·gent /ˈ· ·,· ·,· ·/ *n* [C] *AmE* a policeman or policewoman【美】警察

law firm /ˈ· ·/ *n* [C] *especially AmE* a company that provides legal services and employs many lawyers【尤美】律师事务所

law·ful /ˈlɔfəl; ˈlɔːfəl/ *adj formal or law*【正式或法律】**1** considered by the government or law courts to be legal and correct 合法的；依法的；法定的：*a lawful marriage* 合法婚姻 **2** allowed by law 法律许可的：*doubts as to whether these dealings were lawful* 对这些交易是否合法的怀疑 | *lawful forms of protest* 法律许可的抗议形式—**lawfully** *adv*—**lawfulness** *n* [U]

law·less /ˈlɔlɪs; ˈlɔːləs/ *adj* not obeying the law, or not controlled by the law 不守法的；不受法律控制的：*lawless terrorists* 无法无天的恐怖分子 | *a lawless frontier town* 不受法律控制的边境城镇—**lawlessly** *adv*—**lawlessness** *n* [U]

Law Lords /ˈ· ·/ *n* **the Law Lords** the members of the British House of Lords holding high positions in the legal profession, and who form the highest court in the British legal system 英国上议院中拥有高级司法职位的议员；上议院高级法官

law·mak·er /ˈlɔ,mekɚ; ˈlɔːmeɪkə/ *n* [C] *especially AmE* any elected official responsible for making laws【尤美】立法者，立法官员

law·man /ˈlɔmæn; ˈlɔːmæn/ *n plural* **lawmen** /-mɛn; -men/ [C] *AmE* any professional officer who is responsible for making sure that the law is obeyed【美】执法者，执法官员

lawn /lɔn; lɔːn/ *n* **1** [C] an area of ground in a garden or park that is covered with short grass〔草修剪得很短的〕草坪，草地；**mow the lawn** (=cut the grass) 修剪草坪 **2** [U] a fine cloth made from cotton or LINEN 上等细棉布；上等细麻布

lawn bowl·ing /ˈ· ,· ·/ *n* [U] *AmE* a game played on grass in which you try to roll a big ball as near as possible to a smaller ball called the JACK[1] (5)【美】草坪滚木球戏；BOWLS *BrE*【英】

lawn chair /ˈ· ·/ *n* [C] *AmE* a light chair like a folding bed, that you can sit or lie on outside when the sun is shining【美】草地躺椅；SUN LOUNGER *BrE*【英】—see picture at 参见 CHAIR[1] 图

lawn mow·er /ˈ· ,· ·/ *n* [C] a machine that you use to cut grass 刈草机，割草机

lawn par·ty /ˈ· ,· ·/ *n* [C] *AmE* a formal party held outside in the afternoon, especially in a large garden【美】〔尤指在大花园里举行的正式〕草坪招待会；GARDEN PARTY *BrE*【英】

lawn sign /ˈ· ·/ *n* [C] *AmE* a sign that you put in front of your house before an election to say which person or political party you support【美】〔选举前贴在屋前的〕草坪告示〔写上所支持的人或政党〕

lawn ten·nis /,· ˈ· ·/ *n* [U] *formal* TENNIS【正式】网球，草地网球

Law of Mo·ses, the /,· · ˈ· ·/ —see 见 MOSAIC LAW

Law·rence /ˈlɔrəns; ˈlɒrəns/, **D. H.** (1885-1930) a British writer who wrote stories of life in industrial society, in which his characters show strong emotion and sexual desire. His books include *Sons and Lovers, Women in Love*, and *Lady Chatterley's Lover*. 劳伦斯〔(1885-1930)，英国作家。其作品以工业社会的生活为题材，笔下的人物均表现出强烈的激情与性欲。作品有《儿子与情人》、《恋爱中的女人》和《查特莱夫人的情人》〕

Lawrence, Stephen (1974-93) a young black man who was murdered in Eltham, south London, in 1993 by a group of young white men. Five men were arrested, but the Crown Prosecution Service decided there was not enough evidence to bring them to TRIAL. In 1996 Stephen's parents brought a private PROSECUTION for murder against the five men, but they were found not guilty. Mr and Mrs Lawrence also complained that the police had not carried out a proper investigation into the murder because Stephen was black. An inquiry was held and in 1999 its chairman Sir William Macpherson criticized the police in his report. He said there was institutional RACISM in the Metropolitan Police Force. 劳伦斯〔(1974-1993)，一名黑人青年，1993年在伦敦南部的埃尔特姆被一伙白人青年杀害。凶手中有五人被逮捕，但刑事检察院却认定犯罪证据不足，不能付诸庭审。1996年，劳伦斯·斯蒂芬的父母自诉这五人犯有谋杀罪，但他们却被判无罪。劳伦斯夫妇同时诉说，警察之所以没有对案件进行必要的调查，就是因为斯蒂芬是黑人。1999年，威廉·麦卡弗森爵士主持案件的调查工作，并在其报告中批评了都市警察局，说其存在制度性种族主义〕

Lawrence, T. E. (1888-1935) a British soldier and writer, also known as **Lawrence of Arabia**. Lawrence helped the Arabs in their fight against the Turks (1914-18), and was strongly in favour of Arab independence. He wrote *The Seven Pillars of Wisdom* about his adventures in the desert. 劳伦斯〔(1888-1935)，英国军人、作家，又称"阿拉伯的劳伦斯"。劳伦斯曾帮助阿拉伯人抗击土耳其人(1914-1918)，并坚决支持阿拉伯独立。他根据自己在沙漠中的冒险经历，撰写了《七根智慧之柱》一书〕

law school /ˈ· ·/ *n* [C,U] a school in the US where you study to become a lawyer after your BACHELOR'S DEGREE〔美国已获学士学位的学生为取得律师资格就读的〕法学院

Law So·ci·e·ty, the /ˈ· ·,· · ·/ an organization for members of the legal profession in the UK. The Law Society is in charge of the education and training of lawyers, and is responsible for making sure that they do their jobs in a professional and honest way. 律师公会〔英国法学界专业人员组成的一个组织，负责培养和培训律师，并确保他们遵守职业道德，秉公执事〕

law·suit /ˈlɔ,sut; ˈlɔːsuːt/ *n* [C] a charge, claim, or complaint against someone that is made in a court of law by a private person or company, not by the police or state; SUIT[1] (4) 诉讼〔非刑事案件〕：**file a lawsuit** *Local people filed a private lawsuit against the oil company over water contamination.* 当地百姓对石油公司造成水污染提起了私人诉讼。

law·yer /ˈlɔjɚ; ˈlɔːjə/ *n* [C] someone whose job is to advise people about laws, write formal agreements, or represent people in court 律师 —see also 另见 ADVOCATE[2], ATTORNEY, BARRISTER, SOLICITOR

CULTURAL NOTE 文化注释

'Lawyer' is the most general word for talking about someone who either represents people in a court of law or advises people about legal problems. Lawyers sometimes do legal work that is related to only one particular area of the law, such as medical cases, or company law, or they can do general work for many different types of legal cases. 无论是在法庭上代别人打官司，还是为人提供法律咨询，这些人都可以用lawyer这一最普通的词来表示。律师有时只做一个特定领域的法律工作，例如医疗案件或公司法，当然他们也可以涉足很多不同类型的法律案件。

USAGE NOTE 用法说明：LAWYER

WORD CHOICE 词语辨析：**lawyer, counsellor/counselor, attorney, barrister, solicitor**

In American English a **lawyer** is often called a **counsellor** (also spelt 又拼作 **counselor**) or, especially if he or she speaks in court, an **attorney**. 在美国英语中，lawyer 常被称作 counsellor，若在法庭上辩护尤称 attorney。

In British English a **lawyer** who speaks in court is called a **barrister**, while a **solicitor** works mainly from an office, but may also appear in the less formal and important courts. 在英国英语中，在法庭上作辩护的 lawyer 被称作 barrister，而 solicitor 主要从事事务性的工作，但也可在不太正式和次重要的法庭上出庭。

lax /læks; læks/ *adj* **1** not strict or careful enough about standards of behaviour, work, safety etc; SLACK[1] (1) 不严格的；疏忽的；松散的：*lax security* 不严格的保安措施 **2** muscles or arms or legs that are lax are not firm or strong and therefore tend to hang loosely〔肌肉、臂或腿〕松弛的—**laxly** *adv*—**laxity** *n* [U] —**laxness** *n* [U]

lax·a·tive /ˈlæksətɪv; ˈlæksətɪv/ *n* [C] a medicine or something that you eat which makes your BOWELS empty easily 通便药，轻泻剂—**laxative** *adj*

lay¹ /le; leɪ/ *v* the past tense of LIE¹

lay 平放

lay² *v past tense and past participle* **laid**/led; leɪd/
1 ▶**PUT SB/STH DOWN** 把某人/某物放下◀[T always+adv/prep] to put someone or something down carefully into a flat position 把〔某人/某物〕平放: **lay sth in/on/under etc** *Laying my coat carefully on the bed, I crept towards the door.* 我把外套小心地放在床上，然后悄悄地向门走去。| *The bodies were laid under the trees to await burial.* 尸体被放在树下准备埋葬。| *Sharon laid her hand on my arm.* 莎伦把手放在我胳膊上。
2 **lay bricks/carpet/concrete/cables etc** to put or fix bricks, a carpet etc in the correct place, especially on the ground or floor 砌砖/铺地毯/铺水泥/铺设电缆等: *The man's coming to lay the carpet on Saturday.* 星期六有人会来铺地毯。| *laying an oil pipeline across the desert* 铺设一条横贯沙漠的输油管道
3 ▶**EGGS** 蛋◀[I,T] if a bird, insect etc lays eggs, it produces them from its body 下（蛋）；产（卵）: *The flies lay their eggs on decaying meat.* 苍蝇在变腐的肉上产卵。
4 ▶**RISK MONEY** 赌钱◀[T] to risk an amount of money on the result of a race, sports game etc; BET² (1) 押〔赌注〕；用…打赌: **lay £5/$10 etc on** *She laid £5 on the favourite, Golden Boy.* 她把五英镑押在呼声最高的赛马"金童"身上。
5 **lay the blame on** to blame someone for something that has happened 责怪，责备: *Then both sides start trying to lay the blame on each other!* 然后双方开始设法互相指责！
6 **lay a charge/proposal etc** *formal* to make a statement, suggestion etc in an official or public way【正式】〔正式或公开地〕提出控告/建议等: *Your employer has laid a serious charge against you.* 你的雇主已对你提出了严重指控。| *Several proposals have been laid before the committee.* 几项建议已提交给委员会。
7 **lay sth open/bare** to remove what covers, hides, or shelters something 使某物暴露
8 **lay sth ↔ waste** to destroy or damage everything in a place, especially in a war〔尤指战争中〕把某物彻底摧毁，夷为平地
9 **lay stress/emphasis on** to emphasize something because you regard it as very important 强调: *a political philosophy that lays great stress on individual responsibility* 着重强调个人责任的政治哲学
10 **lay plans/a trap etc** to carefully prepare something, especially something that will harm someone else 制订计划/设圈套等
11 **lay the table** to put the cloth, plates, knives, forks etc on a table, ready for a meal 摆好餐桌〔准备开饭〕
12 ▶**HAVE SEX** 发生性行为◀[T] *slang* to have sex with someone【俚】与…性交: **get laid** (=find someone to have sex with) 寻找机会发生性关系
13 **lay sb/sth flat** to hit someone or something and knock them down 击倒某人/某物: *Laid him flat with a single punch!* 只一拳就将他击倒在地！
14 **lay yourself open to blame/criticism/ridicule etc** to do something that makes it possible that you will be blamed, criticized etc 使自己受到责备/批评/奚落等: *I don't want to lay myself open to charges of nepotism.* 我不想别人指责我任人唯亲。
15 **lay sth on the line** a) to state something, especially a threat, demand, or criticism, in a very clear way 非常明确地提出〔尤指威胁、要求或批评〕 b) to risk losing your life, your job etc, especially in order to help someone〔尤指为了帮助别人而〕冒〔牺牲、失业等〕危险
16 **lay sb low** a) [usually passive 一般用被动态] if an illness lays someone low, they are unable to do their normal activities for a period of time 使某人病倒: *She's been laid low with flu for a week.* 她因患流感病（倒）了一星期。b) *literary* to knock someone down or injure them seriously【文】把某人击倒；使某人重伤
17 **lay the ghost (of)** to finally get rid of something from your past that has been worrying you 摆脱（某事）—see also 另见 **lay your hands on**(HAND¹ (30)), **lay/provide the foundation(s) for**(FOUNDATION (5)), **not lay a finger on sb**(FINGER¹ (5)), **put/lay your cards on the table**(CARD¹ (12))

lay about sb *phr v* [T] *literary or old-fashioned* to attack someone violently【文或过时】猛烈攻击〔某人〕: *He laid about his attackers with his stick.* 他用棍子狠揍攻击他的人。

lay sth ↔ **aside** *phr v* [T] **1** to store something to use in the future 储存〔某物〕待用[备用]: *She'd managed to lay aside a few pounds each week from her wages.* 她设法每周从薪水中存上几个英镑。**2** to stop using, doing, or preparing something, for a short time 暂时把〔某事〕搁在一边: *The building plans may have to be laid aside till things improve.* 在情况得到改善前，建筑规划可能只得搁置起来。

lay sth ↔ **down** *phr v*
1 ▶**TOOLS/WEAPONS** 工具/武器◀[T] to put down your tools, weapons etc as a sign that you will stop using them 放下: *Lay down your weapons and walk slowly towards the door!* 放下武器，慢慢走到门边去！
2 ▶**OFFICIALLY STATE** 正式阐述◀[usually passive 一般用被动态] to officially state rules that must be obeyed, systems that must be used etc or state something officially or firmly〔正式或坚决地〕阐述；声明: *The regulations lay down a rigid procedure for checking safety equipment.* 该条例明确规定了检验安全设备的严格程序。| **lay down that** *It is laid down in the regulations that all members must carry their membership cards at all times.* 根据规定，所有会员必须随时带着会员证。
3 **lay down your life** *formal* to lose your life, for example in a war, in order to help other people【正式】牺牲生命: *prepared to lay down his life for his comrades* 准备为同志们牺牲他自己的生命
4 **lay down the law** to tell other people what to do, how they should think etc, in an unpleasant or rude way〔用严厉或粗鲁的方式〕发号施令
5 ▶**START** 开始◀ to start building or making something by doing the first part of the work 开始建造；开始做: *Crick and Watson laid down the foundations of modern genetic research.* 克里克和沃森为现代遗传学研究奠定了基础。
6 ▶**WINE ETC** 酒等◀ to store something, especially wine, to use in the future 储存〔尤指酒〕

lay sth ↔ **in** *phr v* [T] to obtain and store a large supply of something to use in the future 储存〔某物〕

lay into sb *phr v* [T] to attack someone physically or with words 痛打；抨击: *You should have heard her laying into Tommy!* 你一定听到了她痛斥汤米！

lay off *phr v* **1** [T **lay** sb ↔ **off**] to stop employing a worker, especially for a period in which there is not much work to do〔尤指在生意萧条期临时性地〕解雇〔雇员〕: *Harry was laid off for six months during the recession.* 在营业衰退时期，哈里被解雇了六个月。**2** [I,T **lay off** sth] *informal* to stop doing, having, or using something【非正式】停止，中止: *I think you'd better lay off alcohol for a while.* 我想你最好一段时间内不要饮酒。| **lay off doing sth** *Just lay off hassling me, would you!* 你就别和我争了，行不行！

lay on *phr v* [T] **1** [**lay** sth ↔ **on**] to provide food, entertainment etc in a very generous way〔慷慨〕提供〔食物等〕；款待；安排: *The organizers have laid on a huge meal for us.* 组织者款待了我们一顿丰盛的饭菜。| *It's great! – transportation, hotel, food, it's all laid on.* 太好了！——交通、旅馆、食物，一切都安排妥当了。**2** [**lay** sth **on** sb] to give someone something such as a responsibility or problem that is hard to deal with 把〔责任或困难等〕推给〔某人〕: *Sorry to lay this on you, but we need someone to go to Italy next week.* 很抱歉把此事交给你，但是我们下周需要有人去意大利。**3** **lay it on (a bit thick)** *informal*【非正式】a) to praise or admire someone or something too much, especially in order to please someone 拍马奉承〔尤指刻意取悦某人〕 b) to state or describe something in a way that goes beyond the truth; EXAGGERATE 过分吹嘘[渲染]

lay sb/sth **out** *phr v* [T]
1 ▶**SPREAD** 铺展◀ to spread something out 铺开，展开: *Lay out the map on the table and let's have a look.* 把地图铺在桌上，让我们看一下。
2 ▶**ARRANGE** 布置◀ to arrange or plan a building, town, garden etc 布置；设计〔建筑、城镇、花园等〕: *The garden is laid out in a formal pattern.* 这花园设计得井然有序。

3▶SPEND 花费◀ *informal* to spend money, especially a lot of money【非正式】花费〔尤指大笔钱〕: **lay out sth on** *We've just laid out £500 on car repairs.* 我们刚花了 500 英镑修车。—see also 另见 OUTLAY

4▶HIT 击打◀ to knock someone down, especially hard enough to make them unconscious 击倒, 打昏〔某人〕: *One of the guards had been laid out and the other was missing.* 一个卫兵被打昏, 另一个卫兵则不知去向。

5▶BODY 尸体◀ to prepare a dead body so that it can be buried 给…做殡葬准备

lay over *phr v* [I] *AmE* to stay somewhere for a short time before continuing your journey【美】途中停留

lay to *phr v* [I,T **lay** sth **to**] *technical* if a ship lays to or if you lay it to, it stops moving【术语】(使)〔船〕停驶

lay sb/sth ↔ **up** *phr v* [T] **1 be laid up (with)** to have to stay in bed because you are ill or injured〔因患病或受伤〕卧床不起: *laid up for a week with flu* 因流感卧床一周 **2 lay up problems/difficulties etc** to do something that will cause problems in the future〔做某事〕自讨苦吃, 自找麻烦: *I tell you, she's just laying up trouble for herself, she really is.* 我说, 她就是自讨苦吃, 她就是这样。**3** *old-fashioned* to collect and store something to use in the future【过时】储存〔某物〕备用: *laying up firewood for the winter* 为冬季储存柴火

> **USAGE NOTE 用法说明: LAY**
>
> GRAMMAR 语法
>
> You **lay** [T] something somewhere, but you **lie** [I] somewhere. 把某物放在某处用 lay〔及物动词〕, 但是躺在某处用 lie〔不及物动词〕: *He laid his things on the bed* 他把东西放在床上 but 但用 *He lay on the bed* (NOT 不用 *lied*) 他躺在床上。In spoken British English you will also sometimes hear things like 在英国口语中有时也会听到: *I want to lay down* (instead of 而不是 *I want to lie down*) 我想躺下 but some people consider this to be incorrect. 但是有人认为这种用法不正确。
>
> A third verb **lie** [I] **(lying, lied, lied)** means 'to tell a lie'. **Lied** should not be confused with **lived**. 第三个动词 lie〔不及物动词〕的意思是"说谎"。切勿将 lied 与 lived 相混淆: *She lied when she said she lived in Beverley Hills.* 她说自己住在贝弗利山是说谎。

lay³ *n* [C] **1 the lay of the land** *especially AmE*【尤美】**a)** the situation that exists at a particular time〔特定时候的〕形势, 情况: *I'll go in and get the lay of the land – see if Pam's in a better mood.* 我进去了解情况, 看看帕姆的心情好点没有。**b)** the appearance of an area of land, the way it slopes etc 地形; 地貌 **2 be a great/good lay** *slang* to be good to have sex with【俚】是够骚的娘们〔骚货, 性交对象〕**3** *literary* a poem or song【文】诗; 歌

lay⁴ *adj* [only before noun 仅用于名词前] **a)** not trained or knowing much about a particular profession or subject 非专业的; 外行的: *To the lay observer, these technical terms are incomprehensible.* 对于外行人来说, 这些专业术语不易理解。**b)** not in an official position in the church 非神职的: *a lay preacher* 非神职传教士

lay·a·bout /ˈleə,baut; ˈleɪəbaut/ *n* [C] *BrE informal* a lazy person who avoids work, responsibility etc【英, 非正式】游手好闲之徒; 躲避工作[责任]的人; 不务正业的人

lay·a·way /ˈleə,we; ˈleɪəweɪ/ *n* [U] *AmE* a method of buying goods in which the goods are kept by the seller for a small amount of money until the full price is paid【美】分期累积预付购货法〔指预付定金留货, 付足货款后再交货的方式〕: *I've put the dress on layaway.* 我已付定金预购了服装。—**layaway** *adj*: *a layaway plan* 预购计划

lay-by /ˈ· ·/ *n* [C] *BrE* a space next to a road where vehicles can stop【英】路侧停车带

lay·er¹ /ˈleə; ˈleɪə/ *n* [C] **1** an amount of a substance that covers all of a surface〔覆盖〕层: [+of] *A thick layer of dust lay on the furniture.* 家具上蒙了一层厚厚的灰尘。**2** one of several levels of substances lying one on top of another〔物质〕层: [+of] *a thin layer of coal between two layers of rock* 两层岩石间薄薄的一层煤 | *He pulled off layer upon layer of clothing.* 他把衣服一件件地脱掉。—see also 另见 OZONE LAYER **3** one of several different levels in a complicated organization, system, set of ideas etc〔组织、系统、思想等的〕层次: [+of] *There are many layers of meaning to be discovered in the poem.* 在这首诗中有许多层含义有待解读。| *major changes that have eliminated two layers of management* 消除双层管理的重大变动 **4 multi-layered/single-layered etc** having a lot of layers, one layer etc 多层/单层等的

layer² *v* [T] **1** to make a layer of something or put something down in layers 铺一层…; 把…堆成层: *potatoes layered with cheese* 夹有几层乳酪的马铃薯 **2** to cut someone's hair in layers rather than all to the same length 把〔头发〕分层剪短

lay·ette /leˋɛt; leɪˈet/ *n* [C] a complete set of clothing and other things a new baby needs 全套新生儿用品

lay fig·ure /ˈ· ,· ·/ *n* [C] a model of the human body used in painting or drawing〔供绘画用的〕人体模型

lay·man /ˈlemən; ˈleɪmən/ *n plural* **laymen** /-mən; -mən/ [C] **1** someone who is not trained in a particular subject or type of work, especially when they are being compared with someone who is 门外汉, 外行人: **the layman** (=laymen in general)〔泛指〕外行人 *technical terms not easily understood by the layman* 门外汉不易理解的专业术语 | **in layman's terms** (=used when explaining something in simple language) 用外行的话说 *the GNP or, in layman's terms, the amount of goods produced by a country* 国民生产总值, 或是用外行的话说, 一个国家所生产货物的总量 **2** someone who is not a priest but is a member of a church 非神职教徒, 平信徒, 普通信徒

lay-off /ˈ· ·/ *n* [C] the act of stopping a worker's employment because there is not enough work〔因工作清淡而导致的〕临时解雇, 下岗: *more lay-offs in the car industry* 在汽车制造业较多暂遭解雇的工人 —see also 另见 **lay off** (LAY²)

lay·out /ˈle,aut; ˈleɪaʊt/ *n* [C] **1** the way in which something such as a town, garden, or building is arranged〔城镇、花园或建筑物等的〕布局, 设计 **2** the way in which writing and pictures are arranged on a page〔文章和画的〕版面编排, 版面设计 —see also 另见 **lay sb/sth out** (LAY²)

lay·o·ver /ˈle,ovɚ; ˈleɪəʊvə/ *n* [C] *AmE* a short stay between parts of a journey, especially a long plane journey【美】〔尤指长途飞行的〕中途停留; STOPOVER *BrE*【英】

lay·per·son /ˈle,pɝsn̩; ˈleɪ,pɜːsən/ *n plural* **laypersons** [C] a word for a LAYMAN used when the person could be a woman or a man 外行, 门外汉; 普通信徒

lay read·er /,· ˈ· ·/ *n* [C] someone in Christian churches who is not a priest but who has been given authority to lead a religious service and PREACH (1)〔基督教堂里被授权在仪式中领读经文的〕平信徒读经员

lay-up /ˈ· ·/ *n* [C] a throw in BASKETBALL made from very close to the basket or from under it〔篮球的〕上篮

lay·wom·an /ˈle,wumən; ˈleɪ,wʊmən/ *n plural* **laywomen** /-,wɪmɪn; -,wɪmɪn/ [C] **1** a woman not trained in a particular subject or type of work, especially when she is being compared with someone who is〔女性〕外行人 **2** a woman who is not a priest but is a member of a church〔女性〕非神职教徒, 平信徒, 普通信徒

Laz·a·rus /ˈlæzərəs; ˈlæzərəs/ a friend of Jesus whose story is told in the Bible. When he died, Jesus brought him back to life. 拉撒路〔耶稣的一位友人, 其故事可见于《圣经》。他死后, 耶稣使他复活〕

laze /lez; leɪz/ *v* [I always+adv/prep] to relax and enjoy yourself in a lazy way 懒散度日, 混日子: *Warren spent the afternoon lazing in the sun.* 沃伦懒懒地晒太阳消磨了整个下午。| **laze about/around** *lazing around when they should have been working* 他们该工作的时候却吊儿郎当 —**laze** *n* [singular]

la·zy /ˈlezɪ; ˈleɪzi/ *adj* **1** disliking work and physical activity, and never making any effort 懒惰的; 不努力的: *the laziest boy in the class* 班上最懒的男孩 | *I was feeling lazy so I called a taxi.* 我懒得走, 所以叫了出租车。**2** a lazy period of time is spent doing nothing except relaxing〔时段〕懒洋洋度过的: *a lazy Sunday* 懒洋洋的星期日 **3** moving slowly 慢吞吞的; 缓慢的: *a lazy river* 水流缓慢的河 —**lazily** *adv* —**laziness** *n* [U]

layer〔覆盖〕层

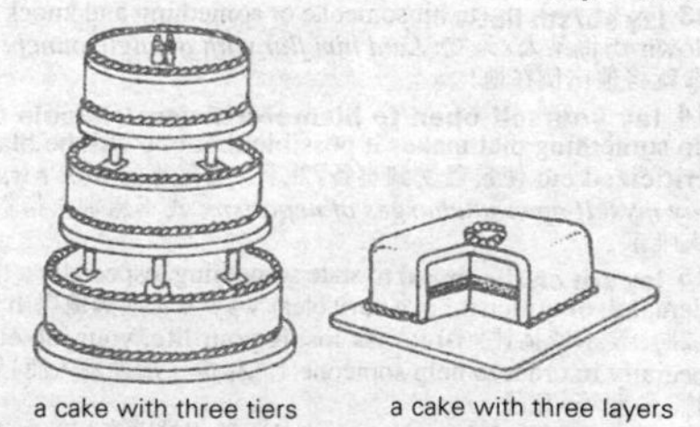

a cake with three tiers 一个三层蛋糕 a cake with three layers 一块三层蛋糕

la·zy·bones /ˈlezɪˌbonz; ˈleɪzibəʊnz/ *n* [C] *informal* a word for a lazy person, often used in a friendly way to someone you like 【非正式】懒鬼，懒骨头〔通常表示友好〕: *Come on, lazybones! Get out of bed.* 快起来，懒鬼！该起床了。

lb *plural* **lbs** the written abbreviation of 缩写= pound, a unit of weight equal to 0.454 kilograms 磅〔重量单位，等于0.454千克〕: *a 3lb bag of flour* 一袋三磅重的面粉

LBJ /ˌɛl bi ˋdʒe; ˌel biː ˈdʒeɪ/ —see 见 Lyndon B. JOHNSON

lbw /ˌɛl bi ˋdʌblju; ˌel biː ˈdʌbəljuː/ *adv* leg before wicket; a way in which your INNINGS can end in CRICKET (2), when the ball hits your leg that is in front of your WICKET〔板球中的〕(击球员) 腿碰球 (犯规) 出局

LCD /ˌɛl si ˋdi; ˌel siː ˈdiː/ *n* [C] **1** liquid crystal display; the part of a watch, CALCULATOR, or small computer where numbers and letters are shown by means of an electric current that is passed through a special liquid 液晶显示 —see picture on page A14 参见A14页图 **2** the written abbreviation of 缩写= LOWEST COMMON DENOMINATOR

LCM the written abbreviation of 缩写= LOWEST COMMON MULTIPLE

LDS the written abbreviation of 缩写= LATTER-DAY SAINTS —see 见 MORMON

lea /li; liː/ *n* [C] *poetical* an area of land with grass【诗】草地，草原

leach /litʃ; liːtʃ/ also 又作 **leach out** *v* [I,T] *technical* if a substance leaches or is leached from a larger mass such as the soil, it is removed from it by water passing through the larger mass【术语】(使) 滤掉；(使) 流失: *Nitrates from agricultural fertilizers leached into the rivers.* 农业肥料中的硝酸盐流失到河中。

S1 W1

lead¹ /lid; liːd/ *v past tense and past participle* **led** /lɛd; led/

① GO SOMEWHERE 去某地
② CONTROL 控制
③ WIN 赢
④ CAUSE STH 引发某事
⑤ LIVE 过生活
⑥ BE BEST/FIRST 最好/领先
⑦ OTHER MEANINGS 其他意思

① GO SOMEWHERE 去某地

1 ▶GO IN FRONT 走在前面◀ [I,T] to go in front of a group of people or vehicles〔走在前面〕(给…) 带头；(为…) 开路: *You lead and we'll follow.* 你带路，我们跟着。| *A truck with a jazz band on it was leading the parade.* 一辆载着爵士乐队的卡车在游行队伍前开道。| *a procession led by a man on a horse* 由一名骑士引领的游行队伍 | **lead the way** (=go in front and show the way) 领路，引路

2 ▶GUIDE SB 引导某人◀ **a)** [T always+adv/prep] to take someone to a place by going with them 为〔某人〕带[引]路: **lead sb through/to/along etc** *An official led me along the corridor to a large office.* 一位官员领我沿着走廊走到一间大的办公室。**b)** [T] to take a person or animal somewhere while holding the person's arm or pulling a rope tied to the animal 引导〔人〕；牵引〔动物〕: **lead sb up/down/through etc sth** *The hostages were blindfolded and led to a waiting car.* 人质被蒙上眼睛，带到一辆正在等候的汽车上。| *A groom was leading a racehorse out of the stable.* 马夫牵着一匹赛马走出马厩。

3 ▶ROAD/WIRE 道路/电线◀ [I] if something such as a path, pipe, or wire leads somewhere or leads in a particular direction, it goes there or goes in that direction 通到；通往，通向: [**+down/into/towards etc**] *a flight of steps leading down to the beach* 一段通往下面沙滩的台阶 | *animal tracks that led into the woods* 通向森林的野兽脚印 | *The thieves cut the wires leading to the surveillance cameras.* 小偷切断了连接监视摄影机的电线。| *Where does this road lead?* 这条路通到哪里？

4 ▶DOOR 门◀ [I] if a door or passage leads to a particular room or place, you can get there by going through it 进入: [**+to/into**] *a door leading to the conference room* 进入会议室的门

② CONTROL 控制

5 ▶BE IN CHARGE 负责◀ [T] to be in charge of something such as an important activity, a group of people, or an organization, especially a political party 领导，率领，带领: *a communist-led strike* 共产党领导的罢工 | *Major will lead the Conservative Party at the next election.* 在下届选举中梅杰将领导保守党。| *Inspector Roberts is leading the investigation into Susan Carr's murder.* 罗伯茨警官在负责苏珊·卡尔谋杀案的调查。

6 lead sb astray to encourage someone to do bad or immoral things that they would not normally do 把某人引入歧途: *We think Harry was led astray by some of the older boys.* 我们认为哈里是被一些大孩子引入歧途的。

7 ▶CONVERSATION 谈话◀ [I,T] to direct a conversation or discussion, especially so that it develops in the way you want 引导〔谈话或讨论〕: *Mary led the conversation around to the topic of salaries.* 玛丽把谈话引到了薪资话题上。

8 lead sb by the nose *informal* to make someone do anything you want them to【非正式】牵着某人的鼻子走，使某人完全听命于自己

③ WIN 赢

9 [I,T] to be winning a game or competition〔游戏或竞赛中〕胜过，领先: **lead by ten points/two sets/four frames etc** *Agassi was leading by two sets when rain stopped play.* 当下雨中止比赛时，阿加西领先两局。| **lead sb/sth** *Brazil led Germany 1-0.* 巴西以1:0领先德国。| *Schumacher led the race from start to finish.* 舒马赫自始至终领先。| *With two minutes to play the Lakers are still leading.* 还有最后两分钟，湖人队仍然领先。

④ CAUSE STH 引发某事

10 [T] to be the thing that makes someone decide to do something 使得，引导〔某人做某事〕: **lead sb to do sth** *What led you to take up acting as a career?* 什么让你开始从事演艺事业的？| *Ian's death led me to rethink what I wanted out of life.* 伊恩的死让我重新思考生活中自己追求什么。

11 lead sb to believe/expect/understand *formal* to make someone think something is true, especially when it is not【正式】使某人相信/期望/理解〔尤指不真实的情况〕: *We were led to believe that all the money from the concert was going to charity.* 我们误以为所有音乐会所得的钱都要捐给慈善事业。

⑤ LIVE 过生活

12 lead a normal/exciting/dull etc life to have a particular kind of life 过正常/刺激/枯燥乏味等的生活: *We lead a very quiet life since Ralph retired.* 自从拉尔夫退休后，我们过着非常平静的生活。

⑥ BE BEST/FIRST 最好/领先

13 [I,T] to be more successful than other people, companies, or countries in a particular activity or area of business or study〔在某项活动或领域中〕领先: *US companies lead the world in biotechnology.* 美国公司在生物科技领域上领先于世界。| *Asian-American students under 12 lead in literacy and numeracy.* 12岁以下的亚裔美国学生在识字认数上占优势。| **lead the field** (=be the most successful person etc in a particular area of business or study) 在某领域中领先 *a company that leads the field in software applications* 在软件应用方面领先的公司

14 lead the way to be the first to do something, especially something good or successful, which is likely to encourage others to do the same thing 带头，先行: *The Japanese led the way in using industrial robots.* 日本在工业机器人应用方面处于领先地位。

⑦ OTHER MEANINGS 其他意思

15 market-led/demand-led/service-led etc in which the market, demand etc is the most important influence on the way something happens 由市场/需求/服务等推动的: *a demand-led recovery* 由需求推动的经济复苏

16 this leads me to... *spoken* used in a speech or discussion to introduce a new subject and connect it with what you have just said【口】这使我联想到…: *This leads me to our sales targets for next year.* 这使我联想到明年的销售目标。

L

17 **lead sb a dance** *informal* to make someone feel worried and confused, especially because they do not know what you are going to do next【非正式】使人感到忧虑[不知所措]: *Once they were married, Gwen led her poor husband a hell of a dance.* 他们结婚后，格温让她可怜的丈夫感觉非常迷茫。

18 **lead sb up the garden path** *informal* to deceive someone【非正式】欺瞒某人

19 [I **+with**, T] to play a particular card as your first card in one part of a game of cards 率先出〔牌〕: *He led with the eight of hearts.* 他先出了一张红桃八。

20 **lead with your left/right** to hit someone mainly with your left or right hand in BOXING〔拳击中主要〕用左拳/右拳出击

lead into sth *phr v* [T not in passive 不用被动态] if one subject, discussion etc leads into another, the second one follows naturally from the first because there is a clear connection between them 引发，引起: *Fox mentioned the Korean deal, which led into a general discussion on our prospects in Asia.* 福克斯提到了对韩国的政策，从而引发了关于我们在亚洲发展前景的广泛讨论。

lead off *phr v* 1 [I,T] to start something such as a meeting, discussion, or performance by saying or doing something〔以说或做某事〕作为开头: *I'd like to lead off by thanking Rick Jones for finding the time to be with us today.* 我首先要感谢里克·琼斯今日的到来。| **lead off with** *John, would you lead off with your views on the merger?* 约翰，请你先谈谈对合并的看法好吗？| **lead sth ↔off** *Hal led off the evening with some folk songs.* 哈尔唱了几首民歌来作为晚会的开始。2 [I,T] if a road, room etc leads off a place, it connects directly with that place〔路、房间等〕(与…)相连接，通向: **lead off from sth** *Go on for about 100 yards and you'll see a path leading off from the main road.* 再走大约100码，你就能见到从主道岔出的一条路。| **lead off sth** *a dining room leading off the hall corridor* 与大厅走廊相连接的饭厅 3 [I] *AmE* to be the first player to try to hit the ball in an INNING (=period of play) in a game of BASEBALL【美】〔棒球比赛在一局中〕率先击球

lead to sth *phr v* [T not in passive 不用被动态] to make something happen or exist as a result 导致…: *an investment program that will lead to the creation of hundreds of new jobs* 会创造数百个新职位的投资项目 | *The bank has offered a reward for any information leading to the arrest of the men.* 银行对能使这些人被绳之以法的任何情报悬赏。

lead up to sth *phr v* [T not in passive 不用被动态] 1 if events lead up to something important that happens, they come before it, and often cause it 作为…的先导；引起: *The book describes the trial and the events leading up to it.* 本书叙述该次审判以及导致其发生的一系列事件。2 to gradually introduce a subject into a conversation, especially a subject that may be embarrassing or upsetting for you or the person you are talking to 渐渐引入〔话题，尤指可能使说者或听者尴尬或不舒服的话题〕: *I suppose all this talk about "business opportunities" is leading up to a request for money?* 我想这关于"商业机会"的所有谈话是不是开口要钱的头一步？

USAGE NOTE 用法说明: LEAD

WORD CHOICE 词语辨析: **lead, show the way, take, bring, guide, see, direct, tell the way**

To **lead** is to **show the way** by going first. to lead 指在前面领路 (show the way): *You lead and we'll follow.* 你带路，我们跟着。| *She led them down the mountain.* 她把他们领下山。

More usually to show someone the way you just **take or bring** them somewhere. 给人带路更通常的用法是把某人take或bring到某处: *Please pick him up and take him to the hotel/bring him to my house* (NOT usually 一般不用 *lead*). 请接他去旅馆/把他带到我家里。

Roads, tunnels, corridors etc. may **lead** to places, but cars, planes etc usually **take** you there. 道路、隧道和走廊等通向某地可用lead，但是汽车、飞机等载人去某地通常用take: *This road leads to/takes you to Chicago* 这条路通往芝加哥 but 但是 *The train took me to Grand Central Station* 火车把我送到大中央车站 (NOT 不用 *led*, unless you were following behind the train! 除非你跟在火车后面!)

If someone needs a lot of help you **guide** them somewhere in order to show them the way and explain things. 某人若需要很多帮助，用 guide 表示给他带路并沿途讲解: *We'll need someone to guide us through the hills.* 我们需要有人带我们参观这山区。| *He guides tourists around the castle.* 他带领游客参观城堡。

See someone somewhere may be used especially if you go with someone to a place because there may be some danger rather than because they do not know the way. 如果和某人去某地不是因为对方不认识路，而是怕有危险，可用 see someone somewhere: *It's very late – Do you want me to see you home?* 很晚了 — 你要我送你回家吗？

To **direct** (slightly formal) is to explain to someone how to get to a place, but not to go with them. To direct〔稍正式的用法〕指告诉某人如何去某地，但并没有一同去: *Could you direct me to the station, please?* 可以告诉我去车站的路吗？Less formally you **tell** someone **the way**. 给某人指路略为不正式的说法是tell someone the way: *Can you tell me the way to the station, please?* 能不能告诉我去车站的路？

GRAMMAR 语法

Remember the past tense and past participle of **lead** are both **led**. 记住 lead 的过去式和过去分词都是 led: *She's led an interesting life* (NOT 不用 *lead*). 她过着有趣的生活。

lead² *n*

1 ▶**RACES ETC** 比赛等◀ **the lead** the position in front of everyone else in a race or competition 领先的地位: **be in the lead** *Le Mond was in the lead after the third lap.* 利·蒙德在第三圈后处于领先的地位。

2 **take the lead** a) to go ahead of the other competitors in a race or competition 居领先地位: *South Korea has taken the lead in ship-building.* 韩国在造船业中已居领先地位。b) to take the responsibility for organizing something 负责〔组织某事〕: *It's up to the older members to take the lead and explain things to the newcomers.* 该由老会员负责给新会员作讲解。c) to be the first to do something, hoping that others will copy you 带头: *The Americans have taken the lead in banning nuclear tests.* 美国人已带头禁止核试验。

3 ▶**WINNING AMOUNT** 赢的数量◀ [singular] the distance, number of points etc by which one competitor is ahead of another〔距离、得分等的〕超前量，领先程度: [**+over**] *The Bulls had a 17 point lead over the Celtics by halftime.* 公牛队上半场结束时领先凯尔特人队17分。| [**+of**] *The latest polls give the Republicans a lead of 32%.* 最近的选举中共和党获32%的优势。

4 ▶**EXAMPLE** 榜样◀ [C] a suggestion or example for people to copy 引导；典范，榜样: **give (sb) a lead** *It's up to you to give a moral lead.* 你得树立一个道德的榜样。| **follow sb's lead** *You say what you think is best. I'll follow your lead.* 你说怎么做最好，我会听你的。

5 ▶**INFORMATION** 消息◀ [C] a piece of information that may help you to make a discovery or help find the answer to a problem; CLUE¹ (1) 线索: *The police have several leads as to the location of the stolen goods.* 警察掌握了几条被偷物资位置的线索。

6 ▶**PERFORMER** 表演者◀ a) [C] the main acting part in a play, film etc 主角: *playing the lead in an amateur production of 'Hamlet'* 在业余爱好者制作的《哈姆雷特》一剧中扮演主角 b) **lead singer/guitarist etc** the main singer, GUITAR player etc in a musical group 主唱/首席吉他手等

7 ▶**FOR DOG** 狗用的◀ [C] *BrE* a piece of rope, leather etc fastened to a dog's collar in order to control it; LEASH¹ (1)【英】〔牵狗的〕绳子，皮带

lead 领先(地位)

Number 4 is in the lead. 4号领先。

8▶**ELECTRIC WIRE** 电线◀ [C] *BrE* an electric wire used to connect a piece of electrical equipment to the power supply【英】导线, 引线, 连接线; CORD[1](3) *AmE*【美】

9**be your lead** if it is your lead in a game of cards, you have the right to play your card first〔某人〕先出牌

lead³ /lɛd; led/ *n* **1** [U] a soft heavy easily melted greyish-blue metal, used for water pipes, covering roofs etc 铅: *lead piping* 铅管 **2** [C,U] the central part of a pencil 铅笔芯 **3go down like a lead balloon** if a suggestion or joke goes down like a lead balloon, people do not like it at all〔建议或笑话〕无人感兴趣 **4** [U] *AmE old-fashioned* bullets【美, 过时】子弹: *They filled him full of lead.* 他们朝他狂射子弹。**5leads** [plural] **a)** sheets of lead used for covering a roof〔盖屋顶用的〕铅片 **b)** narrow pieces of lead used for holding small pieces of glass together to form a window〔固定窗玻璃的〕铅框 —see also 另见 BLACK LEAD, WHITE LEAD

lead·ed gas /ˌlɛdɪd ˋgæs; ˌledɪd ˈgæs/ *n* also 又作 **leaded gasoline** /ˌ‥ˋ‥/ [U] *AmE* petrol containing lead【美】含铅汽油; LEADED PETROL *BrE*【英】

leaded lights /ˌlɛdɪd ˋlaɪts; ˌledɪd ˈlaɪts/ *n* [plural] *BrE* windows with thin narrow pieces of lead (LEAD³ (1)) separating small pieces of glass shaped like squares or diamonds (DIAMOND (2))【英】铅框玻璃窗

leaded pet·rol /ˌlɛdɪd ˋpɛtrəl; ˌledɪd ˈpetrəl/ *n* [U] *BrE* petrol containing lead (LEAD³ (1))【英】含铅汽油; LEADED GAS *AmE*【美】

leaded win·dows /ˌlɛdɪd ˋwɪndoz; ˌledɪd ˈwɪndəʊz/ *n* [plural] LEADED LIGHTS 铅框玻璃窗

lead·en /ˋlɛdn; ˈledn/ *adj* **1** *literary* dark grey【文】深灰色的: *a leaden sky* 灰暗的天空 **2** without happiness, excitement, or energy 阴郁的; 死气沉沉的, 沉闷的: *a leaden performance* 沉闷的演出

S3 W1 **lead·er** /ˋlidə; ˈliːdə/ *n* [C]

1▶**IN CONTROL** 控制者◀ the person who directs or controls a team, organization, country etc 领导者; 领袖; 首领, 首长: *The prize was awarded to President de Klerk and the ANC leader Nelson Mandela.* 这个奖授给了德克勒克总统和非洲国民大会领导人纳尔逊·曼德拉。| *a born leader* 天生的领袖 | [+of] *the leader of the local black community* 当地黑人社区的领袖

2▶**RACE** 比赛◀ the person, organization etc that is in front of all the others in a race or competition 领先者: *Schumacher was now catching up and challenging the leaders.* 舒马赫正追上来, 直逼领先者。| [+in] *leaders in the field of information technology* 信息技术领域的领先者 —see also 另见 MARKET LEADER

3▶**NEWSPAPER** 报纸◀ *BrE* a piece of writing in a newspaper giving the paper's opinion on a subject; EDITORIAL【英】社论

4▶**MUSICIAN** 音乐家◀ *BrE* the main VIOLIN player in an ORCHESTRA【英】首席小提琴手; CONCERTMASTER *AmE*【美】

5▶**MUSICAL DIRECTOR** 音乐指挥◀ *AmE* someone who directs the playing of a musical group; CONDUCTOR (1)【美】乐团指挥

6▶**TAPE** 磁带◀ *technical* the part at the beginning of a film or recording tape which has nothing on it【术语】〔胶卷、磁带等前端的〕空白段

7▶**BRANCH** 枝条◀ *technical* a long thin branch that grows from the stem of a bush or tree beyond other branches【术语】〔树干或枝上的〕顶枝

8▶**FISHING** 钓鱼◀ *technical* a short piece of a special string used to tie the hook onto the end of a fishing line (LINE¹ (16))【术语】〔钓鱼线末端上的〕接钩绳

Leader of the House, the /ˌ‥‥ˋ‥/ a member of the UK government who is responsible for organizing the work of the British Parliament. There are two Leaders of the House, one for the House of Commons and one for the House of Lords. 议长〔负责组织英国议会工作的英国政府官员。上下两院共有两名议长, 即下议院议长和上议院议长〕

Leader of the Op·po·si·tion, the /ˌ‥‥‥ˋ‥/ the leader of the main party opposing the government in the British parliament〔英国议会中的〕反对党领袖

S3 W2 **lead·er·ship** /ˋlidəʃɪp; ˈliːdəʃɪp/ *n* **1** [U] the position of being the leader of a team, organization etc 领导地位; 领导权: *Burns took over the leadership of the party.* 伯恩斯夺取了政党领导权。**under sb's leadership** (=while a particular person is leader) 在某人的领导下 **2** [U] the quality of being good at leading a team, organization, country etc 领导才能; 领导素质: *someone with vision and leadership* 既有洞察力又有领导才能的人 **3** [C] all the people who lead a group, organization etc [also+plural verb *BrE* 英] 领导人员; 领导层: *The party leadership are in agreement on this matter.* 党的全体领导层在此问题上取得一致。**4** [U] the position of being in front of others in a competition 领先地位: *the company's leadership in robot technology* 公司在机器人技术上的领先地位

lead-free /ˌlɛd ˋfri; ˌled ˈfriː◂/ *adj* lead-free petrol contains no LEAD³ (1); UNLEADED〔汽油〕无铅的

lead-in /ˋlid ˌɪn; ˈliːd ɪn/ *n* [C] remarks made by someone to introduce a radio or television show〔介绍广播或电视节目的〕开场白

W2 **lead·ing¹** /ˋlidɪŋ; ˈliːdɪŋ/ *adj* [only before noun 仅用于名词前]

1▶**MOST IMPORTANT/BEST** 最重要的/最佳的◀ best, most important, or most successful 最好的; 最重要的; 最成功的: *the leading software provider in the domestic PC markets* 国内个人电脑市场的最佳软件供应商 | *a leading heart specialist* 最好的心脏病专家

2**leading edge** **a)** *technical* the front edge of something【术语】〔物体的〕前缘 **b)** the area of an activity where the most modern and advanced equipment and methods are used 前沿领域: *working at the leading edge of genetic engineering* 工作在遗传工程学的前沿 —see also 另见 LEADING-EDGE

3**leading light** a respected person who leads a group or organization, or is important in a particular area of knowledge or activity 受人尊敬的领导人物; 有影响的重要人物

4**leading question** a question that deliberately tricks someone into giving the answer you want 诱导性问题

5**leading lady/man** the woman or man who acts the most important female or male part in a film, play etc 扮女/男主角的演员 —see also 另见 LEADING ARTICLE

lead·ing² /ˋlɛdɪŋ; ˈledɪŋ/ *n* [U] *technical*【术语】**1** lead (LEAD³ (1)) used for covering roofs, for window frames etc〔盖屋顶用的〕铅片;〔固定窗玻璃的〕铅框 **2** the space left between lines of print on a page〔印刷品的〕行间隔

leading ar·ti·cle /ˌlidɪŋ ˋɑrtɪkḷ; ˌliːdɪŋ ˈɑːtɪkəl/ *n* [C] *BrE* a piece of writing in a newspaper giving the paper's opinion on a subject; EDITORIAL【英】〔报纸的〕评论文章; 社论

leading-edge /ˌlidɪŋ ˋɛdʒ; ˌliːdɪŋ ˈedʒ/ *adj* [only before noun 仅用于名词前] leading-edge machines, systems etc are the most modern and advanced ones that exist〔机器、系统等〕最现代的, 最先进的: *It uses leading-edge voice-recognition software.* 它运用最先进的语音识别软件。

lead-off /ˋlid ɔf; ˈliːd ɒf/ *adj AmE* happening or going first or before others【美】最先发生的; 开头的

S2 W2 **leaf¹** /lif; liːf/ *n plural* **leaves** /livz; liːvz/

1▶**PLANT** 植物◀ [C] one of the flat green parts of a plant that are joined to its stem or branches 树叶; 叶子: *a flowering bush with large shiny leaves* 长着光亮大叶子的开花灌木 | **be in leaf/come into leaf** *The forest was just coming into leaf.* 森林里的树刚开始长叶。

2**take a leaf out of sb's book** to copy the way someone else behaves because you admire them 学某人的样; 以某人为榜样

3**turn over a new leaf** to decide you will change the way you behave and become a better person 翻开新的一页; 改过自新; 重新做人

4▶**PAPER** 纸◀ [C] *technical* a thin sheet of paper, especially a page in a book【术语】纸页,〔尤指书的〕一页 —see also 另见 LOOSE-LEAF, OVERLEAF

5▶**OF TABLE** 桌子的◀ [C] a part of the top of a table that can be taken out to make the table smaller 活动桌面板

6▶**METAL** 金属◀ [U] metal, especially gold or silver, in a very thin sheet; GOLD LEAF 金属箔〔尤指金、银箔〕—see also 另见 **shake like a leaf** (SHAKE¹ (1))

leaf² *v*

leaf through sth *phr v* [T] to turn the pages of a book quickly, without reading it properly 匆匆翻阅: *I was leafing through an old school magazine when I came across your photo.* 当我匆匆翻阅一本学校的旧杂志时, 我发现了你的相片。

leaf·age /ˋlifɪdʒ; ˈliːfɪdʒ/ *n* [U] the leaves on a tree or plant; FOLIAGE 叶子〔总称〕

leaf·let¹ /ˋliflɪt; ˈliːflɪt/ *n* [C] a small piece of printed paper giving information or advertising 散页印刷品; 传单; 广告单张: *a leaflet on skin cancer* 有关皮肤癌的传单

leaflet² *v* [I,T] to give out leaflets in a particular area (向…)散发传单: *He's leafleting the neighborhood.* 他正在居民区散发传单。

leaf mould *BrE*【英】, **leaf mold** *AmE*【美】/ˋ· ·/ *n* [U] dead decaying leaves that form a rich surface on soil 腐叶土

leaf·y /ˋlifɪ; ˈliːfi/ *adj* **1** having a lot of leaves 多叶的: *leafy green vegetables such as spinach* 菠菜之类的多叶绿色蔬菜 **2** having a lot of trees and plants 多树木的, 茂密的: *a leafy suburb* 树木茂密的郊外

league¹ /lig; liːg/ *n* [C] **1** a group of sports teams or players who play games against each other to see who is best〔体育运动〕联合会，联赛: *Spurs finished fourth in the league this season.* 本赛季热刺队在联赛中获第四名。—compare 比较 CONFERENCE (3) **2 be in a different league from/not be in the same league as** to be much better, or much worse, than someone or something else 和…在不同的档次上/不在同一等级上: *They're not in the same league as the French at making wine.* 他们酿葡萄酒的水准比不上法国人。**3 be in league** to be working together secretly, especially for a bad purpose 暗中合谋，私下勾结: [+with] *Union leaders were accused of being in league with the Mafia.* 工会领袖被指控与黑手党勾结。**4** a group of people or countries who have joined together because they have similar aims, political beliefs etc 联盟，同盟: *the Young Communist League* 共青团 **5** an old unit for measuring, equal to about five kilometres 里格〔旧时长度单位，约5公里〕

league² *v* [I, T] *formal* to join together with other people, especially in order to fight for or against something【正式】(与…)联合，(与…)结成同盟

League a·gainst Cru·el Sports, the /,· · ·, ·· '·/ a UK organization which wants to make killing animals for sport illegal. It is especially opposed to the sport of hunting foxes.〔英国的〕反残酷运动联盟〔英国一组织，旨在使狩杀动物的运动非法化，尤其反对猎狐运动〕

League of Na·tions, the /,· · '· ·/ an international organization that was established after World War I to encourage countries to work together and achieve international peace. It was replaced in 1946 by the United Nations. 国际联盟〔第一次世界大战之后成立的一个国际组织，旨在促进国际合作，争取世界和平。1946年，该组织被联合国所取代〕

League of Wom·en Vot·ers, the /,· · ·, ·· '· ·/ a US organization that encourages women to vote, and makes sure that laws or policies (POLICY) that affect women are properly discussed and thought about 妇女投票者联盟，女选民联盟〔美国一组织，鼓励妇女参加投票，并确保政府在讨论和制订涉及妇女利益的法律与政策时能做到公正与平等〕

league ta·ble /'· ,· ·/ *n* [C] *especially BrE* a list that shows the positions of people, teams, or organizations that are competing against each other【尤英】比赛名次表

> **CULTURAL NOTE 文化注释**
> The UK government prints league tables of schools which put the schools in order according to their examination results. Some people think that this helps parents to choose the best school for their children, but other people think that they are unhelpful and are not a good way of judging how successful a school is. 根据学校考试成绩的优劣，英国政府会印发学校的名次表。有人认为这有助于父母为子女选择最好的学校，但也有人认为这个参考价值不大，同时也不是衡量学校优劣的好方法。

leak¹ /lik; liːk/ *v* **1** [I,T] if a container, pipe, roof etc leaks, or if it leaks gas, liquid etc, there is a small hole or crack in it that lets the gas or liquid flow out or flow through (使)漏; (使)渗: *The roof always leaks when it rains.* 一下雨，屋顶总是漏水。| **leak sth** *My car seems to be leaking oil.* 我的汽车好像正在漏油。**2** [I] if a gas or liquid leaks, it gets in or through a hole in something〔气体、液体〕漏出: [+into/through/out of etc] *Gas was leaking out of the pipes.* 煤气从管子里漏出来了。**3** [T] to deliberately give secret information to a newspaper, television company etc 泄露〔秘密给报纸、电视台等〕: **leak sth to** *Details of his business dealings were leaked to the press.* 他的商务来往的详情已被泄露给新闻界了。**4 leak like a sieve** to leak very badly 漏得很厉害

leak out *phr v* [I] if secret information leaks out, a lot of people find out about it 泄露: *News of his dismissal soon leaked out.* 他被免去职务的消息不久便泄露出去。

leak² *n* [C] **1** a small hole that lets liquid or gas flow into or out of something 漏洞; 裂缝: *There's a leak in the car radiator.* 汽车的散热器上有条裂缝。**2 a gas/oil/water leak** an escape of gas or liquid through a hole in something 煤气/油/水的泄漏 **3** a situation in which secret information is deliberately given to a newspaper, television company etc〔向报纸、电视台等〕透露秘密: *a leak suggesting that the hospital is to be closed* 透露医院要关闭的消息 **4 take/have a leak** *slang* to pass water from your body; URINATE【俚】小便，撒尿 —see also 另见 **spring a leak** (SPRING² (9))

leak·age /'likɪdʒ; 'liːkɪdʒ/ *n* [C,U] **1** an example of gas, water etc leaking, or the amount of gas or liquid that has leaked 漏出; 渗出; 漏出量 **2** the deliberate spreading of information that should be kept secret〔秘密的〕泄露，透露

Lea·key /'likɪ; 'liːki/ a family of British scientists working in the area of PALEONTOLOGY (=the study of ancient animals and plants that have been preserved in rock). The family includes **Mary Leakey** (1913-96), her husband **Louis Leakey** (1903-72), and their son **Richard Leakey** (1944-), all of whom discovered many FOSSILs and human bones in Tanzania, which have provided important information about how humans first developed. 利基〔从事古生物学研究的一个英国科学家家庭。该家庭中妻子玛丽·利基(1913-1996)，丈夫路易士·利基(1903-1972)以及他们的儿子理查·利基(1944-)在坦桑尼亚发现了大量古人类化石，为研究人类早期的进化历史提供了重要的资料〕

leak·y /'likɪ; 'liːki/ *adj* having a hole or other fault so that liquid or gas passes through a container, roof, pipe etc 漏的; 有漏洞的; 有裂缝的: *the constant dripping of a leaky tap* 漏水的水龙头不断的滴漏 —**leakiness** *n* [U] —see picture on page A18 参见A18页图

lean¹ /lin; liːn/ *v past tense and past participle* **leaned** or **leant** /lɛnt; lent/ *especially BrE*【尤英】**1** [I always+adv/prep] to move or bend your body in a particular direction 屈身: [+forward/back etc] *Robert was leaning forward, talking to the people in front.* 罗伯特正向前弯着身和前面的人说话。| *They were leaning over her, trying to wake her up.* 他们弯下身去想把她弄醒。**2** [I] to slope or bend from an upright position 倾斜; 弯曲: *trees leaning in the wind* 在风中倾斜的树木 **3** [I always+adv/prep] to support yourself or be supported in a sloping position against a wall or other surface 倚，斜靠: [+on/against] *He was leaning on the bar with a drink in his hand.* 他手上拿着一杯酒，正靠在酒吧的柜台上。| *There was a ladder leaning against the wall.* 墙上斜靠着一部梯子。**4** [T always+adv/prep] to put something in a sloping position where it is supported 把〔某物〕斜靠着放: **lean sth on/against sth** *Gail leant her head on his shoulder.* 盖尔把头靠在他的肩上。

lean on sb/sth *phr v* [T] **1** to depend on someone or something for support and encouragement, especially at a difficult time 依靠，倚赖〔尤指在困难时刻〕: *It's good to know you've got friends to lean on.* 很高兴知道你有可以依靠的朋友。**2** *informal* to try to influence someone, especially by threatening them【非正式】对〔某人〕施加压力〔尤指通过恐吓〕: **lean on sb to do sth** *Lean on them to pay up.* 威胁他们把钱付清。

lean towards sth *phr v* [T] to tend to support, or begin to support, a particular set of opinions, beliefs etc 倾向于支持，开始支持: *My wife is voting Democrat but I'm leaning towards the Republicans.* 我妻子准备投民主党的票，但是我倾向支持共和党。

lean² *adj* **1** thin in a healthy and attractive way 苗条的; 健美的: *lean and athletic looking* 外表健美强壮的 —see 见 THIN (USAGE) **2** lean meat does not have much fat on it〔肉〕瘦的，脂肪少的 **3** a lean organization, company etc uses only as much money and as many people as it needs, so that nothing is wasted〔机构、公司等〕节俭的，精简的 **4** a lean period is a very difficult time because there is not enough money, business etc 不景气的: *a lean year for business* 生意不景气的一年 —**leanness** *n* [U]

lean³ *n* [U] the fleshy part of meat and not the bone or fat 瘦肉

Lean, Sir David (1908-91) a British film DIRECTOR who made many well-known films, such as *Brief Encounter* (1945), *The Bridge on the River Kwai* (1957), *Lawrence of Arabia* (1962), *Dr Zhivago* (1965), and *A Passage to India* (1984) 利恩〔(1908-1991)，英国电影导演，摄制了许多著名影片，如《相见恨晚》(1945)、《桂河大桥》(1957)、《阿拉伯的劳伦斯》(1962)、《日瓦戈医生》(1965)和《印度之旅》(1984)〕

lean·ing /'linɪŋ; 'liːnɪŋ/ *n* [C] a tendency to prefer or agree with a particular set of beliefs, opinions etc; INCLINATION (2) 倾向，偏爱: *Fran has Conservative leanings.* 弗兰有亲保守党的倾向。| [+towards] *a leaning towards the Right* 右翼倾向

Leaning Tow·er of Pi·sa, the /,linɪŋ ,tauə əv 'pizə; ,liːnɪŋ ,taʊə əv 'piːzə/ a tall round tower in Pisa, Italy, which does not stand straight, but leans to one side. It was built in the 12th century and is popular with tourists. 比萨斜塔〔位于意大利比萨城的一座圆形高塔，塔身不正，向一边倾斜。该塔建于12世纪，是著名旅游景点〕

leant /lɛnt; lent/ the past tense and past participle of LEAN¹

lean-to /'· ·/ *n* [C] a small roughly made building that rests against the side of a larger building 靠着大屋所建的单坡屋顶小屋，披屋

leap¹ /lip; liːp/ *v past tense and past participle* **leapt** /lɛpt; lept/ *especially BrE*【尤英】, **leaped** *especially AmE*【尤美】

1 ▶JUMP 跳◀ **a)** [I always+adv/prep] to jump high into the air or to jump in order to land in a different place 跳, 跳跃: *Jen leapt across the stream.* 珍跳过了小溪。**b)** [T] *literary* to jump over something【文】跳过, 跃过〔某物〕: *Brenda leaped the gate and ran across the field.* 布伦达跃出大门跑过田野。

2 ▶MOVE FAST 快速移动◀ [I always+adv/prep] to move very quickly and with a lot of energy 敏捷地移动; 迅速地反应: [+up/out/into etc] *I leapt up the stairs three at a time.* 我一步三级地跃上楼梯。| **leap to your feet** *Morgan leapt to his feet and started shouting.* 摩根立刻跳起来开始大叫大嚷。| **leap to sb's assistance/defence etc** *Wendi leaped to his assistance.* 温迪赶紧去援助他。

3 ▶INCREASE 增加◀ [I] to increase quickly and by a large amount 迅速大幅增加: *The price of gas leapt 15% overnight.* 煤气价格一夜之间就上涨了 15%。

4 leap at the chance/opportunity/offer to accept a chance, opportunity, or offer very eagerly 抓住机会; 急忙接受: *They were offering a free holiday in the Algarve, so naturally I leapt at the chance.* 他们正在提供去阿尔加维的免费度假, 我自然赶紧抓住这个机会。

5 leap out at you if something you are looking at leaps out at you, it is very easy for you to notice because it is unusual or unexpected〔非同寻常或意料之外的事〕特别引人注目, 很容易注意到

6 ▶HEART 心脏◀ [I] *especially literary* if your heart leaps, you feel a sudden surprise, happiness, or excitement【尤文】突然感到惊奇[幸福; 激动]: *My heart leaped when I saw Paul at the airport.* 当我在机场看到保罗的时候, 我感到惊喜万分。—see also 另见 **look before you leap** (LOOK¹ (10))

leap² *n* [C] **1** a big jump 跨跃: *Bill cleared the ditch with a single leap.* 比尔一跃就跳过了水沟。**2 by/in leaps and bounds** if someone or something increases, develops, grows etc by leaps and bounds, they increase etc very quickly 迅速地; 突飞猛进地: *Andrew's German is improving by leaps and bounds.* 安德鲁的德语突飞猛进。**3** a sudden large increase in the number or amount of something 数量的激增: [+in] *a leap in prices* 物价猛涨 **4** a mental process that is needed to understand something difficult or see the connection between two very different ideas 思维的发挥: **a leap of imagination** *It takes a great leap of imagination to see John as a teacher.* 要发挥丰富的想象力才能看得出约翰是一位老师。**5 a leap in the dark** something you do, or a risk that you take, without knowing what will happen as a result 冒险举动, 轻举妄动; 瞎闯

leap·frog¹ /ˈlip,frɑg; ˈliːpfrɒg/ *n* [U] a children's game in which someone bends over and someone else jumps over them 跳背游戏

leapfrog 跳背游戏

leapfrog² *v* [I,T] to achieve something more quickly than usual by missing some of the usual stages 越过; 超越; 越级: *Nigel leapfrogged two ranks and was made a colonel.* 奈杰尔越了两级升为上校。

leapt /lɛpt; lept/ the past tense and past participle of LEAP¹

leap year /ˈ· ·/ *n* [C] a year, which happens every fourth year, when February has 29 days instead of 28 闰年〔每四年一次, 二月份有 29 天而不是 28 天〕

Lear /lɪr; lɪə/, **Edward** (1812-88) a British artist and poet, who wrote the *Book of Nonsense*, a collection of humorous poems 李尔〔(1812-1888), 英国艺术家、诗人, 著有幽默诗集《无理书》〕

Lear, King —see 见 KING LEAR

learn /lɝn; lɜːn/ *v past tense and past participle* **learned** or **learnt** /lɝnt; lɜːnt/ *especially BrE*【尤英】 1 1

1 ▶SUBJECT/SKILL 科目/技艺◀ [I,T] to gain knowledge of a subject, or skill in an activity, by experience, by studying it, or by being taught 学习; 学到; 学会: *What's the best way to learn a language?* 学习语言的最佳方法是什么? | *Children are usually very quick at learning.* 小孩通常学得很快。| [+about] *I am very keen to learn about the town's history.* 我很想了解该城镇的历史。| **learn (how) to do sth** *I learnt to drive when I was 17.* 我 17 岁那年学会了开车。| **learn how/what/who etc** *In the first lesson we'll learn how to format a text file.* 第一课我们将学习如何安排文本文件的版式。—compare 比较 TEACH, see 见 KNOW¹ (USAGE)

2 ▶FIND OUT 发现◀ [I,T] *formal* to find out information, news etc by hearing it from someone else【正式】获悉, 得知, 听到: [+of/about] *We were all saddened to learn of her death.* 得知她的死讯, 我们都很难过。| **learn sth** *Where did you learn the news?* 你在哪里听到这个消息的? | **learn (that)** *May was pleased to learn that he had arrived safely.* 知道他安全抵达, 梅很高兴。| **learn who/what/whether etc** *We have yet to learn who will be the new manager.* 我们还未听说谁将是新的经理。

3 ▶REMEMBER 记住◀ [T] to get to know something so well that you can easily remember it; MEMORIZE 背诵; 记住: *The actor was busy learning his lines.* 那名男演员正在忙于背台词。

4 ▶CHANGE YOUR BEHAVIOUR 改变行为◀ [T] to gradually understand a situation and start behaving in the way that people expect you to behave〔渐渐〕懂得,〔慢慢〕领悟: **learn (that)** *They have to learn that they can't just do whatever they like.* 他们得明白他们不能随心所欲地做事。| **learn to do sth** *gamblers who had learned to modify their behaviour* 学会改正行为的赌徒

5 learn from your mistakes to improve the way you do things because of mistakes you have made 从错误中学习

6 learn (sth) the hard way to understand a situation or develop a skill by learning from your mistakes and bad experiences〔从错误和教训中〕学会〔某事〕

7 learn your lesson to suffer so much because you did something wrong or stupid, that you will not do it again 得到教训: *I really learned my lesson when I got sunburned last year on vacation.* 当我去年度假晒伤了皮肤时, 我真的得到了教训。—see also 另见 **live and learn** (LIVE¹ (27))

This graph shows how common the different grammar patterns of the verb **learn** are. 本图所示为动词 learn 构成的不同语法模式的使用频率。

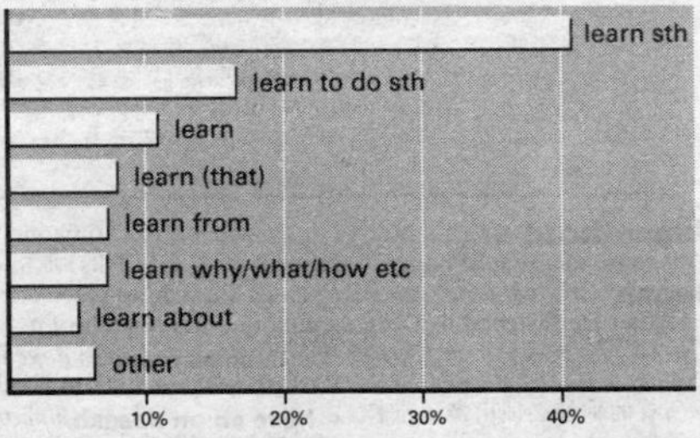

learn sth
learn to do sth
learn
learn (that)
learn from
learn why/what/how etc
learn about
other
10% 20% 30% 40%

Based on the British National Corpus and the Longman Lancaster Corpus
据英国国家语料库和朗文兰开斯特语料库

learn·ed /ˈlɝnɪd; ˈlɜːnɪd/ *adj formal*【正式】**1** having a lot of knowledge because you have read and studied a lot 有学问的; 博学的 **2 learned books/works etc** books etc to be used by advanced students 学术性书籍/著作等 —**learnedly** *adv*

learn·er /ˈlɝnə; ˈlɜːnə/ *n* [C] **1** someone who is learning to do something 学习者; 初学者: *Jill's a very quick learner.* 吉尔是一位善于学习的人。| [+of] *a grammar book for learners of English* 英语初学者的语法书 **2** also 又作 **learner driver** *BrE* someone who is learning to drive a car【英】实习司机, 见习司机

learner's per·mit /ˈ· · ,· ·/ *n* [C] *AmE* an official document that gives you permission to learn to drive【美】驾驶学习证; PROVISIONAL LICENCE *BrE*【英】

learn·ing /ˈlɝnɪŋ; ˈlɜːnɪŋ/ *n* [U] knowledge gained through reading and study 知识, 学问: *a man of great learning* 学问渊博的人 3 2

learning curve /ˈ· · ,·/ *n* [C] the rate at which you learn a new skill 学习曲线

learning dis·a·bil·i·ty /ˈ· · ·, · ·/ *n* [C] a mental problem that affects a child's ability to learn things 学习障碍, 学习能力缺陷

learnt /lɝnt; lɜːnt/ the past tense and past participle of LEARN

lease¹ /lis; liːs/ *n* [C] **1** a legal agreement which allows you to use a car, building etc for a period of time, in return for rent 租约, 租契: **take out a lease** (=sign a lease so that you can rent something) 签租约 *We've taken out a lease on an office building.* 我们已经签了一幢办公楼的租约。**2 a new lease of life** *especially BrE*【尤英】, **a new lease on life** *AmE*【美】**a)** if someone has a new lease of life, they become healthy, active, or happy again after being weak, ill, or tired 重新恢复生气: *The vacation has given me a new lease of life.* 假期使我重新恢复了精力。**b)** 3

if something has a new lease of life, improvements are made that mean it will last longer 延长使用寿命: *Give dirty rugs a new lease of life with our super steam cleaner!* 使用我们的高效能蒸汽除垢器能延长脏地毯的使用寿命!

lease² *v* [T] **1** also 又作 **lease out** to use or let someone use buildings, property etc on a lease 出租: **lease sb sth/lease sth to sb** *They decided to lease the building to another company.* 他们决定把楼租给另外一家公司。**2** to pay to use expensive machinery or equipment for a long period, instead of buying it 长期租用〔某物〕: *We lease all our computers.* 我们长期租用所有的电脑。

lease·back /ˈlisˌbæk; ˈliːsbæk/ *n* [C,U] *technical* an arrangement in which you sell or give something to someone, but continue to use it by paying them rent【术语】售后回租〔租用已出售的财产〕

lease·hold /ˈlisˌhold; ˈliːshəʊld/ *adj especially BrE* leasehold property is owned only for as long as is stated in a lease【尤英】根据地契年期而拥有的; 租赁的 —compare 比较 FREEHOLD —**leasehold** *adv*: *Buying leasehold is cheaper.* 按地契年期购买要便宜些。

CULTURAL NOTE 文化注释

In England, Ireland, and Wales, many apartments and some houses are **leasehold**, especially in London. If you buy a leasehold property, you own it for a fixed amount of time which is stated in the **lease**, and typically you pay **ground rent** to the owner of the **freehold** (=the right to own a property permanently). A lease can last for a very long time, sometimes hundreds of years. If you buy a leasehold property, you can often buy the freehold to it. In Scotland, almost all property is freehold. 在英格兰、爱尔兰和威尔士, 尤其是在伦敦, 许多公寓和住宅都是有地契年期的。如果购买了一处有地契年期的房产, 通常你只是在地契中规定的固定年限内拥有其所有权, 并且要向该房产的终身保有者支付地租。地契的有效期很长, 有些长达几百年。买下一处有地契年期的房产, 你通常也可以花钱买下它的终身保有权。在苏格兰, 几乎所有的房产都是有终身保有权的。

lease·hold·er /ˈlisˌholdɚ; ˈliːshəʊldə/ *n* [C] someone who lives in a leasehold house, apartment etc〔房屋等的〕承租人

leash¹ /liʃ; liːʃ/ *n* [C] *especially AmE*【尤美】**1** a piece of rope, leather etc fastened to a dog's collar in order to control it〔牵狗的〕绳子, 皮带; LEAD² (7) *BrE*【英】: **be on leash** *All dogs must be on a leash by order of the Parks Department.* 园林部门规定所有的狗都必须用带子牵着。**2** **have sb on a leash** *humorous* to be able to control someone【幽默】能控制某人: *Jerry's wife has him on a tight leash.* 杰里的老婆牢牢地控制着他。

leash² *v* [T] *AmE* to put a leash on a dog【美】〔用牵狗绳〕系住〔狗〕

1 1 **least¹** /list; liːst/ *determiner, pron* **1 at least a)** not less than a particular number or amount 至少, 起码〔就数量而言〕: *It will take you at least 20 minutes to get there.* 到那里至少要花掉你 20 分钟。| *He had been dead for at least a fortnight.* 他死了至少有两星期。| **at the very least** (=not less than and probably much more than) 最起码 *It would cost $1 million at the very least.* 最起码要付 100 万美元。**b)** even if nothing else is true, or even if nothing else happens 不管怎样, 无论如何: *I think you should at least consider his offer.* 我认为你至少应考虑他的建议。| *Well, at least I don't spend all my money on drink like some people.* 好了, 不管怎样, 我不会像有些人那样把所有的钱都花在喝酒上。**c)** used when you are mentioning an advantage that makes certain problems or disadvantages seem less serious 至少, 起码〔用于指出某些问题或不利条件的优点〕: *At least he was safe now.* 至少他当时是安全的。| *The film wasn't very interesting, but at least it filled the time.* 该电影没有多少意思, 但起码打发了时间。**d)** used when you are correcting or changing something that you have just said 至少, 起码〔用于纠正刚说过的话〕: *Mary was depressed all evening. Or at least it seemed that way.* 玛丽整夜情绪都很低落。至少看起来如此。| *She has no plans to return to England yet, at least as far as I know.* 她还没有回英国的计划, 至少据我所知是这样。**2** the smallest in number, amount, or importance〔数量、重要性〕最小, 最少: *It's not always wise to buy the one that costs the least.* 买最便宜的货并非总是明智之举。| *Those with the least money pay the least in taxes.* 收入最少的人纳税也最少。**3 not the least/not in the least/not the least bit** none at all, or not at all 一点也不: *It doesn't matter in the least if you're a bit late.* 如果你迟来些, 一点也没有关系。| *She didn't seem the least bit worried.* 她似乎一点也不担忧。| *He came up without the least hesitation and asked me what I was doing there.* 他毫不犹豫地走过来问我在那儿干什么。**4 the least sb could do** used when saying what you think someone should or could do to help someone else 起码能〔为别人〕做的事: *The least he could do is give them some money towards the rent.* 他起码能给他们一些钱付房租。**5 to say the least** used to show that something is worse or more serious than you are actually saying 退一步讲, 至少可以说: *He was rather offended, to say the least.* 说得轻点, 他相当恼火。**6 the least of your worries** something you are not worried about because there are other more important problems 最不担心的事: *Deciding what to wear for the trial is the least of my worries.* 穿什么衣服参加预赛是我最不担心的。

least² *adv* **1** less than anything or anyone else 最少; 最小: *It happened when we least expected it.* 此事在我们最没有料想到的时候发生了。| *He was the least experienced of the teachers.* 他是教师中经验最少的。| *The tax hits those who can least afford it.* 税收使那些最交不起税的人受到打击。**2 least of all** especially not a particular person〔在多者中〕最不的: *No one knew where he was, least of all his family.* 没有人知道他在哪里, 更不用说他的家人了。**3 not least** *formal* especially【正式】尤其; 特别: *The president's speeches were alarming, not least to the country's allies.* 总统的演讲令人恐慌, 对那些盟国尤其如此。

least com·mon mul·ti·ple /ˌ· ·· ˈ···/ LOWEST COMMON MULTIPLE 最小公倍数

least·wise /ˈlistˌwaɪz; ˈliːstwaɪz/ also 又作 **least·ways** /-wez; -weɪz/ *adv AmE informal* at least; anyway【美, 非正式】至少; 无论如何: *He was there a minute ago, leastwise that's what Sue said.* 刚才他还在那儿, 至少休是那么说的。

leath·er¹ /ˈlɛðɚ; ˈleðə/ *n* [U] **1** animal skin that has been treated to preserve it, and is used for making shoes, bags etc〔动物的〕皮, 皮革: *a book bound in leather* 皮面装帧的书 —see picture on page A16 参见 A16 页图 **2 leathers** [plural] special leather clothes worn for protection by someone riding a MOTORCYCLE〔骑摩托车穿的〕皮革防护衣 —see also 另见 **run/go hell for leather** (HELL¹ (24)) 3

leather² *adj* made of leather 皮制的: *a leather jacket* 皮夹克

leath·er·ette /ˌlɛðəˈrɛt; ˌleðəˈret/ *n* [U] a cheap material made to look like leather 人造革, 人造皮; NAUGAHYDE *AmE*【美】

leath·er·y /ˈlɛðərɪ; ˈleðəri/ *adj* hard and stiff like leather rather than soft or smooth 似皮革的; 坚韧的: *leathery skin* 粗糙的皮肤

1 1 **leave¹** /liv; liːv/ *v past tense and past participle* **left** /lɛft; left/

① LEAVE A PLACE, VEHICLE 离开某地、某交通工具	④ REMAIN 剩下
② LEAVE YOUR JOB, HOME, WIFE ETC 离职, 离开家/妻子等	⑤ NOT DO STH 不做某事
③ LEAVE STH SOMEWHERE 留某物于某处	⑥ STATE/POSITION 状态/位置
	⑦ DECIDE/CHOOSE 决定/选择
	⑧ DEATH 死亡
	⑨ OTHER MEANINGS 其他意思

① LEAVE A PLACE, VEHICLE 离开某地、某交通工具

1 ►LEAVE 离开◄ [I,T] to go away from a place or a person 离开; 前往, 出发: *What time did you leave the office?* 你什么时候离开办公室的? | *They were so noisy that the manager asked them to leave.* 他们吵闹得以至于经理请他们离开。| **[+for]** *They're leaving for Rome in the morning.* 他们打算早晨动身去

L

罗马。| **leave to do sth** *Franca left early to meet her mother.* 弗兰卡很早出门去接她母亲。| **leave sb doing sth** *Ann left Keith dozing in the chair.* 安由着基思在椅子上打瞌睡。

2 ►TRAIN/SHIP ETC 火车/船等◄[T] to get off a train, ship etc 下〔火车、船等〕: *Make sure to check the overhead luggage compartments before you leave the plane.* 下飞机前别忘了检查头顶上的行李厢。

3 leave sb to sth to go away and let someone continue what they are doing 离开后让某人继续做某事: *I'll leave you to your work.* 我走了，你接着干吧。

4 leave him to himself/leave her to herself etc to go away from someone so that they are alone 让他/她等独自待着

② LEAVE YOUR JOB, HOME, WIFE ETC 离职，离开家/妻子等

5 ►HOME/SCHOOL ETC 家/学校等◄[I,T] to stop living at your parents' home, stop going to school etc 离(家); 离(校): *Zoe wants to be a hairdresser when she leaves school.* 佐伊离校后想当一位美发师。| *Tom wants to leave home.* 汤姆想离开家。

6 ►HUSBAND/WIFE ETC 丈夫/妻子等◄[I,T] to stop living with someone you had a close relationship with 离开(亲密的人): **leave sb for sb** (=leave in order to live with someone else) 离开某人与另一人同居 *Jan's husband's left her for another woman.* 简的丈夫离开她要和另一个女人同居。

7 ►COUNTRY/PLACE 国家/地方◄[I,T] to stop living in a country, town etc and go somewhere else 迁离: *They're leaving Minneapolis to live in Santa Fe.* 他们即将离开明尼阿波利斯去圣菲居住。

8 ►JOB/COMPANY 工作/公司◄[I,T] to stop working for a particular organization or being a member of a group 离职; 脱离(某团体): *Bill's leaving the company after 25 years' service.* 比尔在工作了25年后要离开公司了。| *We are concerned about the number of young people leaving the church.* 我们关心年轻人离教的人数。| *a leaving present* (=for someone who is leaving) 临别礼品

9 leave sb alone to stop annoying or upsetting someone 不去打扰某人，让某人独自待着: *Why can't you just leave her alone?* 你为什么不能让她一个人待会儿?

10 leave sth alone to stop touching something 别碰某物: *Will you leave that piano alone?* 你别碰那架钢琴好吗? | **leave it/this alone** *Leave it alone or you'll break it!* 别碰它，否则你会把它弄坏的!

11 leave go of/leave hold of *BrE* to stop holding something【英】放开，松手; 放掉: *Leave go of me!* 放开我!

12 leave it at that used to say that you have said or done enough about something 就到此为止; 别再争论下去了: *Let's leave it at that for today.* 我们今天就到此为止。

③ LEAVE STH SOMEWHERE 留某物于某处

13 ►LET STH REMAIN 使某物仍处于某种状态◄[T always+adv/prep] to let something or someone stay where they are when you go away 把〔某物或某人〕留在原处: **leave sth in/on etc** *Someone's left their car in the middle of the driveway.* 有人把车留在车道中间。| *If you leave that on the floor, it'll get trodden on and broken.* 如果你把这留在地板上，它会被踩碎的。| *I've left the kids with Sandra.* 我把孩子们留给桑德拉照顾了。

14 ►FORGET STH 忘记某物◄[T always+adv/prep] to forget to take something with you when you leave a place 丢下; 遗忘: **leave sth behind/in/on etc** *Oh no! I've left the paperwork in my office.* 哎呀不好! 我把全部文件忘在办公室了。

15 ►FOR SB TO FIND 让某人找到◄[T] to put something in a place where someone else can find it 留，留下〔把某物放在某人找得到的地方〕: *Miriam always leaves a spare key under the plant.* 米里亚姆总是把一把备用钥匙留在那株植物下。| *I'll leave you some milk in the fridge.* 我会在冰箱里给你留些牛奶。

16 ►LETTER/MESSAGE 信件/口信◄[T] to leave a letter, package, message etc somewhere for someone 给〔某人〕留下〔信件、包裹、口信等〕: *If you'd care to leave your name and number, he'll call you right back.* 如果你愿意留下姓名和电话号码，他一回来就会给你打电话。| **leave sth for sb/leave sb sth** *Lucy left a note for you.* 露茜给你留了一张便条。| *Who left me this message?* 谁给我留了这个口信? | **leave word with sb** (=leave a message with someone) 给某人留下口信 *Could you leave word with my secretary if you can't make it?* 如果你办不成的话，能否给我的秘书留一个口信?

④ REMAIN 剩下

17 ►BE LEFT 被剩下◄[T] to remain after everything else has been taken away or used 剩下，剩余; 留下来: *I'll have another brandy if there's any left.* 如果还有剩余的话，我就再喝一杯白兰地。| *By 5 o'clock there was hardly anyone left in the office.* 到5点的时候，办公室里几乎走得没有人了。| **have sth left** *How much time do we have left to finish this?* 我们还剩多少时间完成这个? | **be left over** (=remain after you have used or spent all the rest) 余下，用后剩下 *If there's any money left over, you can keep it for yourself.* 如果钱还有剩余，就归你了。

⑤ NOT DO STH 不做某事

18 ►DELAY 推迟◄[T] to not do something until later 留待; 留到: *Let's leave the dishes for tomorrow.* 我们把盘子留到明天洗吧。| *Leave it another week, then tell him he'll have to decide.* 把此事再往后放一周，到时告诉他必须作出决定。| *Leave the batter to stand for 15 minutes.* 让面糊搁置15分钟。| **leave sth for now** *Leave the filing for now. You can do it later.* 文档整理现在暂时搁一下，你可以稍后再做。

19 ►NOT DO STH 不做某事◄[T] to not do something that you ought to do 留下，不去做〔该做的事〕: *I couldn't face the ironing so I just left it.* 我怕熨烫衣服，所以我就没有去做。

20 ►NOT EAT/DRINK 不吃/喝◄[T] if you leave food or drink, you do not eat it because you do not like it or you have had enough〔因不喜欢或已吃饱而〕把〔食物或饮料〕留下来不吃[不喝]: *If you don't like the stew, just leave it.* 如果你不喜欢炖菜，那就别吃。

21 leave sb/sth be to not disturb or annoy someone, or not touch or move something 不要去打扰，不去管某人; 别动某物: *Just leave Jenny be and she'll sort things out for herself.* 别打扰珍妮，她自己会把事情处理好的。

22 leave well (enough) alone to not try to change a situation in case you make it worse than it was before 不要弄巧成拙; 不如维持现状为好: *If I were you I would leave well alone.* 我要是你，我会维持原状，免得弄巧成拙。

23 leave sb to their own devices to not tell someone what to do or offer them help, but let them do what they decide to do 听某人自便; 不要支配[帮助]某人

⑥ STATE/POSITION 状态/位置

24 [T] **a)** to make something stay, or let something stay in a particular state or position 使〔某物〕留下[处于]〔某种状态或位置〕: *How did you leave things after the meeting?* 会议后你把事情处理得怎样? | **leave sth open/empty/untidy etc** *I wish you'd stop leaving the door open.* 我希望你别老开着门。| *The trial left a lot of questions unanswered.* 试验留下了许多问题没有解答。| **leave sth on/off/out etc** *Leave the television on, will you?* 让电视开着，好吗? | **leave sth doing sth** *I'll just leave the engine running while I pop in.* 我顺便到里面去一下的时候，会让发动机继续开着。**b)** if something leaves you in a particular condition, you are in that condition as a result of it 使〔某人〕落到某种地步: *Paying for the repairs left Jim without a cent.* 付了修理费后吉姆已身无分文。| *Frankly, their rudeness left me speechless.* 坦率地讲，他们的粗鲁使我无话可说。| **leave sb doing sth** *Carla's narrow escape left her shaking with terror.* 卡拉死里逃生，吓得浑身发抖。

⑦ DECIDE/CHOOSE 决定/选择

25 ►LET SB DECIDE/TAKE RESPONSIBILITY 让某人决定/负责◄[T] to let someone decide something or take responsibility for something 把…留交〔某人决定或负责〕; 委托; 交由: **leave sth with sb** *Leave it with me and I'll fix it for you.* 把它留给我，我会帮你修好的。| **leave sth to sb** (=let someone choose or decide) 把某事交由某人〔选择或决定〕*I've always left financial decisions to my wife.* 我总是把财务大权交给妻子负责。| **leave doing sth to sb** *I'll leave buying the tickets to you.* 我把买票的事交给你去办。| **leave sb to do sth** *BrE*【英】*I'll leave you to choose which film we see.* 我让你来选择我们看哪部电影。| **leave it to me** (=I'll take responsibility for it) 我来负责 *Leave it to me. I'll make sure it gets posted.* 把它交给我吧，我保证把它寄出去。| **leave it (up) to sb to do sth** *We left it to Dad to get the packing done.* 我们把打包的事交给爸爸负责。| *I'll leave it up to you to decide.* 我把这件事交给你决定。| **leave sth to chance** (=take no action and just wait and see what happens) 听天由命; 顺其自然

26 leave sb with no choice/option to force someone to do something because there is nothing else they can do 让某人别无选择: *You leave me with no option but to resign.* 你让我别无选择，只有辞职。

⑧ **DEATH** 死亡

27 ▶WHEN YOU DIE 临死时◀ [T] **a)** to give something to someone after you die 遗赠; 遗留: *The old lady left $5 million.* 老妇人遗留下了500万美元。| **leave sth to sb/sth** *He had left all his money to charity.* 他把所有的钱都遗赠给了慈善事业。| **leave sb sth** *Hugo left me his mother's ring.* 雨果把他母亲的戒指遗赠给了我。**b)** to have members of your family still alive when you die〔去世后〕遗下: *Collins leaves a wife and three children.* 柯林斯遗下了妻子和三个孩子。

⑨ **OTHER MEANINGS** 其他意思

28 leave a space/gap etc to deliberately make a space etc when you are doing something 留有余地[空间等]: *Leave a 10 centimetre gap between the young plants.* 秧苗之间留下10厘米的空间。| **leave room** *Drivers should always leave plenty of room for cyclists.* 司机总是应该给骑车人留出足够的空间。

29 leave a mark/stain/scar etc to make a mark etc that remains afterwards 留下记号/污迹/疤痕等: *The cut was deep and left a terrible scar.* 刀口很深，留下了可怕的伤疤。| *William had left a trail of muddy footprints across the floor.* 威廉在地板上留下了一串泥脚印。

30 leave sb cold to not interest or excite someone at all 丝毫引不起某人的兴趣: *Modern Jazz leaves me cold, I'm afraid.* 现代爵士乐恐怕引不起我一点儿兴趣。

31 leave sb/sth standing *informal* to be much better, quicker etc than someone or something else【非正式】远远胜过某人/某物: *Anna leaves all her classmates standing.* 安娜远远超过了她所有的同班同学。

32 leave a lot to be desired to be very unsatisfactory 令人极不满意; 有很大的改进余地: *Your conduct this term has left a lot to be desired.* 这学期你的品行有很多地方仍有待改进。

33 leave a bad taste in your mouth if an experience leaves a bad taste in your mouth, remembering it upsets you or makes you feel uncomfortable 留下了坏的感觉[印象]: *The things she said really left a nasty taste in my mouth.* 她说的事情确实给我留下了恶劣的印象。

34 leave no stone unturned to do everything that you can in order to find something or solve a problem 千方百计, 竭尽全力: *Jarvis left no stone unturned in his search for the manuscript.* 贾维斯竭尽全力寻找手稿。

35 leave sth aside/leave sth to one side to not think about or consider something for a time, so that you can think about something else〔暂时〕把某事搁置起来: **leaving aside** (=used to say that you do not want to consider something for a time) 暂不考虑 *Leaving aside the question of expense, what's your opinion?* 暂不考虑费用问题, 你的意见如何? —see also 另见 **take it or leave it** (TAKE[1] (18a))

leave sb/sth **behind** *phr v* [T] **1** to forget to take something with you when you leave a place 忘了带; 遗忘: *I think I left my credit card behind at the restaurant.* 我想我把信用卡遗忘在餐厅里了。**2** to move far ahead of someone who cannot run, walk, or drive as fast as you can 将〔某人〕抛在后面: **leave sb far behind** *BrE*【英】/**leave sb way behind** *especially AmE*【尤美】*I was soon left far behind.* 很快我就被远远地抛在了后面。**3** to let something or someone stay in a place when you go away, especially permanently〔尤指永久地〕离开〔某物或某人〕: *Sooner or later we have to leave our parents behind.* 迟早我们都得离开父母。**4 be/get left behind** to not work as well or as quickly as someone else, so that you make less progress than they do 落后: *You'll have to put in some extra work at night if you don't want to get left behind.* 如果你不希望落后的话, 就得晚上加些班。

leave off *phr v* [I,T] *informal* to stop doing something【非正式】停止: *I wish the rain would leave off for five minutes.* 我希望雨能停五分钟。| *Let's start again from where we left off.* 让我们从中断处重新开始。| **leave off (doing) sth** *BrE*【英】: *Leave off shouting! I can't hear myself think in here.* 别喊了! 我在这儿没法思考了。

leave sb/sth **out** *phr v* [T] **1** to not include someone or something in a group, list, activity etc 遗漏, 漏掉: *You've left out a zero in this phone number.* 你在这电话号码中漏掉了一个零。| **leave sb/sth out of sth** *Kidd has been left out of the team.* 基德被球队除了名。**2 be/feel left out** to feel as if you are not accepted or welcome in a social group 被忽视[冷落]; 觉得被忽视[冷落]: *All the others seemed to know each other and I began to feel left out.* 其他所有人似乎都彼此互相认识, 我开始感到被冷落了。**3 leave it out!** *BrE spoken* used to tell someone to stop lying, pretending, or being annoying【英口】〔用于告知某人〕别撒谎[装蒜, 烦人]了!

leave² *n*

1 ▶HOLIDAY 假期◀ [U] time that you are allowed to spend away from your work, especially in the armed forces 假期, 假日;〔尤指军人的〕休假: *I've applied for three days' leave.* 我已经请了三天假。| **be on leave** *I'm in command while Farringdon is on leave.* 法林顿休假期间我负责指挥。

2 sick/maternity/compassionate leave time that you are allowed to spend away from work because you are ill, because you have had a baby, or because of a personal problem such as the death of a relative 病假/产假/丧假

3 leave of absence a period of time that you are allowed to spend away from work for a particular purpose 准假: *She's been given leave of absence to attend a computer course.* 她获准休假参加电脑课程培训。

4 take leave of your senses to become crazy and behave in a strange way 发疯: *You want to marry him? Have you taken leave of your senses?* 你要嫁给他? 你是不是疯了?

5 ▶PERMISSION 许可◀ [U] *formal* permission to do something, especially something you would not normally be allowed to do【正式】许可, 准许: *All this was done entirely without my leave.* 所有这些都是在根本没有得到我许可的情况下进行的。| **leave to do sth** *Julia had special leave to do her exams at home.* 朱莉娅获得特许在家完成考试。| **ask leave** *He asked leave to speak to her in private.* 他请求允许私下和她谈话。

6 without so much as a by your leave *old-fashioned* without asking permission, in a way that seems very rude【过时】未经许可, 擅自: *How dare you come marching into my office without so much as a by your leave?* 你怎敢未经许可擅自闯入我的办公室?

7 take leave of sb/take your leave *formal* to say goodbye to someone【正式】向某人告别/离开

8 by your leave *old use* used when asking permission to do something【旧】请允许我〔用于征求许可做某事〕; 对不起; 请原谅 —see also 另见 **take French leave** (FRENCH[2] (3))

leav·en¹ /ˈlɛvən; ˈlevən/ also 又作 **leav·en·ing** /ˈlɛvənɪŋ; ˈlevənɪŋ/ *n* **1** [U] a substance, especially YEAST, that is added to a mixture of flour and water so that it will swell and can be baked into bread 酵母, 面肥 **2** [C,U] *literary* a small amount of a quality that makes an event or situation less boring and more interesting or cheerful【文】使事件[情景]变得有趣[生动]的东西

leaven² *v* [T] **1** *formal* to make something less boring and more interesting or cheerful【正式】使〔某物〕变得有趣[生动, 高兴] **2** *old-fashioned* to add leaven to a mixture of flour and water【过时】加发酵剂[酵母]于〔面粉和水的混合物〕; 使发酵; 使发松 —see also 另见 UNLEAVENED

Leav·en·worth /ˈlɛvənˌwɝθ; ˈlevənwɜːθ/ a town in the American state of Kansas, famous for its prison 莱文沃思〔美国堪萨斯州一镇, 以其监狱闻名〕: *He's serving time at Leavenworth.* 他在莱文沃思服刑。

leaves /livz; liːvz/ the plural of LEAF

Leaves of Grass /ˌ· · ˈ·/ (1855) a collection of poems by Walt Whitman, written in FREE VERSE (=poetry without regular patterns), which strongly express his love of nature and his respect for freedom. These poems are important because they made free verse more acceptable and influenced later US writers.《草叶集》〔(1855), 沃尔特·惠特曼创作的诗集, 以自由诗的形式呈现。这些诗歌激情洋溢地抒发了作者对大自然的热爱和对自由的尊崇。其重要性在于, 他的诗歌提高了自由诗的可接受度, 也对后来的美国作家产生了很大影响〕

leave-tak·ing /ˈ· ·ˌ·/ *n* [C] *literary* an act of saying goodbye when you go away【文】告别, 辞别

leav·ings /ˈlivɪŋz; ˈliːvɪŋz/ *n* [plural] *old-fashioned* things that are left because they are not wanted, especially food【过时】〔尤指食物的〕剩余物, 残余 —compare 比较 **leftovers** (LEFTOVER[2] (1))

Leb·a·non /ˈlɛbənən; ˈlebənən/ also 又作 **the Lebanon** a country in the Middle East on the Mediterranean Sea, between Israel, Palestine and Syria. Population: 3,628,000 (2001). Capital: Beirut. There was a long civil war in the 1970s and 1980s which did a lot of damage to the country. The economic and political situation improved during the 1990s. 黎巴嫩〔中东地区地中海沿岸一国家, 位于以色列、巴勒斯坦和叙利亚之间。人口: 3,628,000 (2001), 首都: 贝鲁特。20世纪70、80年代, 这里发生长期内战, 给该国造成严重破坏。20世纪90年代, 黎巴嫩的经济、政治形势有所改善〕—**lebanese** /ˌlɛbəˈniz; ˌlebəˈniːz/ *n, adj*

lech¹, letch /lɛtʃ; letʃ/ *n* [C] *BrE informal* a lecher【英, 非正式】淫荡的人, 好色之徒

lech², letch *v*

lech after/over sb *phr v* [T] *BrE informal* to show sexual desire for a woman in a way that is unpleasant or annoying【英, 非正式】对〔某女人〕抱有性欲: *a middle-aged man leching after young girls* 对年轻女子抱有性欲的中年男子

lech·er /ˈlɛtʃɚ; ˈletʃə/ *n* [C] an insulting word for a man who is always thinking about sex or trying to get sexual pleasure 淫荡的人, 好色之徒〔侮辱性词语〕

lech·er·ous /ˈlɛtʃərəs; ˈletʃərəs/ *adj* a lecherous man is always thinking about sex or trying to get sexual pleasure〔男人〕纵欲的; 淫荡的, 好色的 —**lecherously** *adv*

lech·er·y /ˈlɛtʃərɪ; ˈletʃəri/ *n* [U] too much interest in or desire for sex 好色, 色欲, 淫荡

Le Cor·bu·si·er /lə ˌkɔrbuzˋje; lə kɔːˈbjuːziei/ (1887-1965) a French ARCHITECT (=someone who designs buildings) who was born in Switzerland. He believed that buildings should look modern, be made of modern materials such as CONCRETE and glass, and that they should be FUNCTIONAL (=simple and practical, without unnecessary decoration). He built many important buildings, and planned the city of Chandigarh in India. 勒科比西埃〔(1887-1965), 法国建筑师, 生于瑞士。他主张建筑应具有现代气息, 应采用混凝土和玻璃等现代材料, 并强调建筑物的功能性。他设计了许多著名的建筑, 并亲自规划了印度的昌迪加尔市〕

Lecter, Dr Hannibal /ˈhænəbl; ˈhænɪbəl/ the main character in the book and film *Silence of the Lambs*, written by the US NOVELIST Thomas Harris. Dr Lecter is a very intelligent, evil, and dangerous serial killer who eats people. 莱克特〔《沉默的羔羊》一书及电影中的主要人物。该书作者是美国小说家托马斯·哈里斯。莱克特博士既聪明机智又阴险邪恶, 是个危险的连环杀手和食人恶魔〕

lec·tern /ˈlɛktɚn; ˈlektən/ *n* [C] a high, sloping surface for putting an open book or notes on while you are giving a lecture, SERMON etc〔桌面倾斜的〕书桌; 读经台

lec·ture¹ /ˈlɛktʃɚ; ˈlektʃə/ *n* [C] **1** a long talk given to a group of people on a particular subject, especially as a method of teaching in universities〔尤指大学中的〕讲座; 讲课; 演讲: [**+on/about**] *a lecture on medieval art* 关于中世纪艺术的讲座 | **give a lecture** *She's giving a series of lectures on molecular biology.* 她正在作分子生物学的系列讲座。**2** an act of criticizing someone or warning them about something in a long, serious talk, in a way that they think is unfair or unnecessary〔冗长、严肃、但其对象认为不公平或不必要的〕教训, 告诫, 训斥: [**+on/about**] *My aunt gave me a long lecture about the dangers of drink.* 姨妈长篇大论地告诫我酗酒的种种危害。

lecture² *v* **1** [T] to talk angrily or seriously to someone in order to criticize or warn them, in a way that they think is unfair or unnecessary 教训, 告诫; 训斥: *I wish you'd stop lecturing me!* 我希望你不要再教训我! | **lecture sb about/on** *Mrs Reed was continually lecturing her children about their behaviour.* 里德太太不断批评自己孩子的行为。**2** [I] to talk to a group of people on a particular subject, especially as a method of teaching at a university 讲授; 讲课; 作讲座; 演讲

lec·tur·er /ˈlɛktʃərɚ; ˈlektʃərə/ *n* [C] **1** someone who gives a lecture (LECTURE¹ (1)) 讲课者; 讲授者; 演讲者: *a brilliant lecturer* 才华横溢的演讲者 **2** someone who has the lowest teaching rank at a British university or college〔英国大学或学院中的〕讲师 —see 见 PROFESSOR (USAGE) **3** *AmE* someone who makes speeches in different places on a subject they know well【美】〔就自己熟知的某一主题在不同地方演讲的〕演讲者

lec·ture·ship /ˈlɛktʃɚˌʃɪp; ˈlektʃəʃɪp/ *n* [C] the lowest teaching rank at a British university or college 讲师职位〔英国大学或学院中最低的教学级别〕: [**+in**] *a lectureship in mathematics* 数学讲师职位

LED /ˌɛl i ˋdi; ˌel iː ˈdiː/ *n* [C] *technical* light emitting diode; a small piece of equipment on a watch, computer screen etc that produces light when electricity passes through it【术语】发光二极管

led /lɛd; led/ the past tense and past participle of LEAD¹

-led /lɛd; led/ *suffix* [in adjectives 构成形容词] having a particular thing as the most important or effective cause, influence etc 以…为先导的; 以…为重点的: *an export-led economic recovery* 以出口为先导的经济复苏

Le·da /ˈlidə; ˈliːdə/ in Greek MYTHOLOGY, the wife of the king of Sparta , who had a sexual relationship with the god Zeus, when he changed himself into a SWAN (=a large white bird) to visit her secretly 勒达〔希腊神话中斯巴达国王之妻, 宙斯化作天鹅偷偷与其交媾〕

ledge /lɛdʒ; ledʒ/ *n* [C] **1** a narrow flat surface of rock that is parallel to the ground 岩架; 岩礁 **2** a narrow flat shelf or surface, fixed to a wall〔固定于墙上的〕窄平的架子[表面]; 壁架: **window ledge** (=narrow shelf below a window) 窗台

led·ger /ˈlɛdʒɚ; ˈledʒə/ *n* [C] **1** a book recording the money received and spent by a business, bank etc 总账, 分类账 **2** a ledger line〔五线谱的〕加线

ledger line /ˈ· · ˌ·/ *n* [C] a line on which you write musical notes that are too high or low to be recorded on a STAVE¹ (1)〔五线谱的〕加线

lee /li; liː/ *n* [singular] **1 the lee of a wall/hedge etc** the part of a wall etc that provides shelter from the wind 墙/篱等的背风[避风]处 **2** the side of something, especially a ship, that is away from the wind〔尤指船的〕背风面, 下风面 **3 the lees** the thick substance that collects at the bottom of a bottle of wine; SEDIMENT〔酒瓶中的〕沉淀物, 沉渣 —compare 比较 DREGS —see also 另见 LEE SHORE

Lee, Bruce (1941-73) a Chinese actor, born in the US, who was famous for his skill at KUNG FU (=an ancient Chinese style of fighting), and who appeared in films such as *Enter the Dragon* (1973) 李小龙〔(1941-1973), 生于美国的华裔演员, 以功夫高强闻名, 出演过《龙争虎斗》(1973) 等影片〕

Lee, General Rob·ert E. /ˈrɑbɚt i; ˈrɒbət iː/ (1807-70) a US soldier who was the commander of the Confederate army during the American Civil War. Many people consider him the best military leader in that war. 李〔(1807-1870), 美国南北战争期间南部邦联军队总司令, 被公认为南北战争中最杰出的军事将领〕

Lee, Laur·ie (1914-97) a British writer and poet, who wrote *Cider with Rosie*, which describes English country life when he was a child 李〔(1914-1997), 英国作家、诗人, 著有小说《同罗茜共饮苹果汁》, 描写他孩提时代的英格兰乡村生活〕

Lee, Spike (1957-) a black US film DIRECTOR who makes films about the lives of black people in the US, including *She's Gotta Have It* (1986), *Do the Right Thing* (1989), and *Malcolm X* (1992) 李〔(1957-), 美国黑人电影导演, 所摄制的影片大都反映美国黑人的生活, 包括《她罪有应得》(1986), 《要做好事》(1989), 《马尔科姆·X》(1992)〕

leech /litʃ; liːtʃ/ *n* [C] **1** a small soft creature that fixes itself to the skin of animals in order to drink their blood 蚂蟥, 水蛭 **2** someone who takes advantage of other people, usually by taking their money, food etc 吸血鬼, 占他人便宜者〔通常榨取钱财、食物等〕 **3** *old use* a doctor【旧】医生

Leeds /lidz; liːdz/ a city in West Yorkshire, in the north of England, which is an important industrial and business centre 利兹〔英格兰北部西约克郡一城市, 是重要的工商业中心〕

Leeds U·ni·ted /ˌ· ·ˈ· ·/ an English football team based in Leeds, northern England 利兹联队〔英格兰一足球队, 在英格兰北部的利兹〕

Lee-En·field /li ˋɛnfild; liː ˈenfiːld/ *trademark* a type of RIFLE (=long gun) used by the British army in World Wars I and II【商标】李·恩菲尔德式步枪〔第一、二次世界大战期间英国军队使用的一种步枪〕

leek /lik; liːk/ *n* [C] a vegetable with a long white stem and long flat green leaves, which tastes a little like an onion 韭葱 —see picture on page A9 参见 A9 页图

leer /lɪr; lɪə/ *v* [I] to look at someone in an unpleasant way that shows that you find them sexually attractive〔色迷迷地〕斜眼瞅[瞟, 瞥]: [**+at**] *Stop leering at those girls!* 别色迷迷地瞅那些女孩子! —**leer** *n* [C]: *a disgusting leer* 令人厌恶的色迷迷的眼神

leer·y /ˈlɪrɪ; ˈlɪəri/ *adj informal* careful in the way that you deal with something or someone because you do not trust them; WARY【非正式】怀有戒心的; 不信任的: [**+of**] *I was very leery of him after I found out he had lied to Jennifer.* 我发现他对珍妮弗说谎后, 我对他很留神。

lee shore /ˌ· ˈ·/ *n* [singular] *technical* a shore which the wind from the sea is blowing onto【术语】背风岸, 下风岸

lee·ward /ˈliwɚd; ˈliːwəd/ *adj technical*【术语】**1** the leeward side of something is the side that is sheltered from the wind 背风的, 下风的 **2** a leeward direction is the same direction as the wind is blowing 向下风方向的, 顺风的: **to leeward** *The ship cruised slowly to leeward.* 船顺风缓慢航行。—**leeward** *adv* —opposite 反义词 WINDWARD¹

Lee·ward Is·lands, the /ˈliwɚd ˌaɪləndz; ˈliːwəd ˌaɪləndz/ a group of islands in the Caribbean Sea, between Puerto Rico and Martinique, which includes the islands of Antigua, Montserrat, and Guadeloupe, and the Virgin Islands 背风群岛〔加勒比海一群岛, 位于波多黎各和马提尼克之间, 由安提瓜岛、蒙特塞拉特岛、瓜德罗普岛以及维尔京群岛组成〕

lee·way /ˈliˌwe; ˈliːweɪ/ *n* [U] **1** freedom to do things in the way you want to〔按个人意愿做事的〕余地；灵活性：*Our reporters have a lot of leeway in what they write.* 我们的记者写报道有很大的灵活性。**2** *BrE* time that you have lost that means you are at a disadvantage【英】时间的损失；落后：*Janet's got a lot of leeway to make up in her studies after her illness.* 珍妮特病好以后有许多落后的学业要补上。**3** *technical* the sideways movement of a ship caused by strong wind【术语】〔航船因强风而引起的〕偏航

Le Figaro a French newspaper《费加罗报》〔法国报纸〕

left¹ /lɛft; left/ *adj* [only before noun 仅用于名词前] **1** on the side of your body that contains your heart〔身体〕左侧的：*She held out her left hand.* 她伸出左手。—opposite 反义词 RIGHT¹ (4a) **2** on, by, or in the direction of your left side 左边的，左面的，左方的：*Hank had scribbled notes in the left margin.* 汉克在左边的空白处草草地做了笔记。| *Take a left turn at the crossroads.* 在十字路口向左拐。**3 have two left feet** *informal* to be very awkward in the way you move; be CLUMSY (1)【非正式】行动非常笨拙 **4 the left hand doesn't know what the right hand is doing** used to say that one part of a group or organization does not know what the other parts are doing 互不沟通〔指某一集团或组织的一部分不知道其他部分在做什么〕—opposite 反义词 RIGHT¹ —see also 另见 LEFT-OF-CENTRE, LEFT-WING¹

left² *adv* towards the left side 向左地，朝左地：*Turn left after the gas station.* 过了加油站向左转。—opposite 反义词 RIGHT² (4)

left³ *n* **1** [singular] the left side or direction 左侧，左方，左面：*Take the next road on the left.* 下一条路左转。| *On your left you can see the Houses of Parliament.* 在左边你可以看到议会大厦。| *Our house is just to the left of the school.* 我家就在学校的左边。**2 the left/the Left** political parties or groups, such as Socialists and Communists, that want money and property to be divided equally, and generally support workers rather than employers 左派政党[组织] **3** [C] a hit made with your left hand 左手的一击，左手拳：*I caught him on the chin with a straight left.* 我用一记左直拳击中他的下巴。

left⁴ the past tense and past participle of LEAVE¹

Left Bank, the /ˌ·ˈ·◂/ an area of Paris on the south bank of the River Seine, famous from the 1890s for being popular with artists, writers, and students〔巴黎的〕左岸〔塞纳河南岸一带。自19世纪90年代起，该区为艺术家、作家和学生所喜爱，并因此出名〕

left field /ˈ· ·/ *n* [singular] **1** a position in BASEBALL in the left side of the OUTFIELD〔棒球运动中的〕左外场 **2 (way) out in left field** *AmE informal* strange or unusual【美，非正式】奇怪的，怪诞的；不常见的：*Some of his ideas are way out in left field.* 他的有些想法很古怪。**3 come from out in left field** *AmE informal* to be very surprising or unexpected【美，非正式】令人惊讶，出乎意料：*His comment about Kia's hair came from out in left field.* 他对基亚头发的评价非常令人惊讶。

left field·er /ˈ· ˌ··/ *n* [C] someone who plays on the left side of a BASEBALL field〔棒球运动中的〕左外场球员，左外野手

left-hand /ˌ·ˈ·◂/ *adj* [only before noun 仅用于名词前] **1** on the left side of something 左手的，左边的：*We live about halfway down the street on the left-hand side.* 我们住在这条街的左边，大约往下走半条街。**2** curving to the left 向左转弯的：*a left-hand bend* 一个左转弯 **3** always using your left hand to do a particular thing 惯用左手的，左撇子的：*David was a left-hand bowler.* 戴维是左手投球手。—opposite 反义词 RIGHT-HAND

left-hand drive /ˌ· · ˈ·/ *adj* a left-hand drive vehicle has the STEERING WHEEL on the left side〔方向盘在左边的〕左座驾驶的，左御的—**left-hand drive** *n* [singular]

left-hand·ed /ˌ·ˈ··◂/ *adj* **1** someone who is left-handed uses their left hand for most things, especially writing〔尤指写字〕惯用左手的，左撇子的 **2** done with the left hand 用左手做的，左手操作的：*a left-handed shot* 左手射击 **3** made to be used by left-handed people 为惯用左手的人做的：*left-handed scissors* 左手用的剪刀 **4 left-handed compliment** *AmE* a statement that seems to express admiration or praise, but at the same time is insulting【美】〔含有侮辱意味的〕虚情假意的恭维—**left-handed** *adv*—**left-handedness** *n* [U] —opposite 反义词 RIGHT-HANDED

left-hand·er /ˌ·ˈ··/ *n* [C] **1** someone who uses their left hand, especially for throwing a ball 左撇子，惯用左手的人〔尤指左撇子投手〕**2** a hit made with your left hand 左手的一击，左手拳 —opposite 反义词 RIGHT-HANDER

left·ie /ˈlɛftɪ; ˈlefti/ another spelling of LEFTY lefty 的另一种拼法

left·ist /ˈlɛftɪst; ˈleftɪ̣st/ *adj* supporting LEFT-WING politics, groups, or ideas 左派的；左翼的：*leftist views* 左翼观点 | *a prominent leftist student group* 著名的左派学生团体—**leftism** *n* [U] —**leftist** *n* [C]

left lug·gage of·fice /ˌ·ˈ·· ˌ··/ *n* [C] *BrE* a place in a station, airport etc where you can pay to leave your bags and get them later【英】〔车站、机场等的〕行李寄存处

left-of-cen·tre *BrE*【英】, **left-of-center** *AmE*【美】/ˌ· · ˈ··◂/ *adj* having ideas or opinions that agree more with the LEFT³ (2) in politics than with the RIGHT³ (4b) 倾向于左派的，中间偏左的

left·o·ver¹ /ˈlɛftˌovə; ˈleftəʊvə/ *adj* [only before noun 仅用于名词前] remaining after all the rest has been used, eaten etc 剩余的，未用完的；未吃完的：*Any leftover vegetables can be used to make a soup.* 任何剩下的蔬菜都可以用来做汤。

leftover² *n* **1 leftovers** [plural] food that has not been eaten at the end of a meal 剩饭菜：*Give the leftovers to the dog.* 把吃剩的饭菜喂狗。**2** [singular] an object, habit, method etc that remains from an earlier time, even though you would expect it to have gone 遗留物〔过去留下的东西、习惯、方法等〕：*They still slept with the lights on, a leftover from more dangerous times.* 他们还是亮着灯睡觉，这是从前危险时期养成的习惯。

left·ward /ˈlɛftwəd; ˈleftwəd/ *adj* on or towards the left 在左边的，向左边的：*a leftward bend* 向左的转弯 —opposite 反义词 RIGHTWARD—**leftward/leftwards** *adv*

left-wing¹ /ˌ·ˈ·◂/ *adj* supporting the political aims of groups such as Socialists and Communists, such as the idea that money and property should be divided more fairly 左翼的，激进（派）的：*She's very left-wing.* 她很激进。| *a left-wing newspaper* 左翼报纸 —opposite 反义词 RIGHT-WING—**left-winger** *n* [C]

left wing² /ˌ·ˈ·/ *n* [singular] the group of people, within a larger political group, whose ideas are more left-wing than those of other members of the group 左翼，左派（人士）：*He's on the left wing of the Conservative Party.* 他是保守党中的左派。| *The party has a small but powerful left wing.* 党内有一小股强有力的左翼势力。

left·y, leftie /ˈlɛftɪ; ˈlefti/ *n* [C] **1** *informal especially BrE* a humorous or slightly insulting way of talking about someone who has left-wing political ideas【非正式，尤英】左派分子〔幽默或稍带贬损〕**2** *informal especially AmE* someone who uses their left hand to write, throw etc【非正式，尤美】左撇子—**lefty** *adj*: *My lefty friends keep telling me I'm a fascist.* 我的左派朋友们老说我是个法西斯分子。

leg¹ /lɛg; leg/ *n*

1 ▶BODY PART 身体部位◀ [C] either of the two long parts of your body that your feet are joined to, or a similar part on an animal or insect 腿：*Angie broke her leg skiing.* 安吉滑雪时摔断了腿。| *A spider has 8 legs.* 蜘蛛有八条腿。| *She's got long skinny legs.* 她的腿又瘦又长。—see picture at 参见 BODY 图

2 ▶FOOD 食物◀ [C,U] the leg of an animal when eaten as food 腿肉：*roast leg of lamb* 烤羊腿

3 ▶FURNITURE 家具◀ [C] one of the upright parts that supports a piece of furniture 腿脚，支架：*a chair leg* 椅子腿

4 ▶CLOTHING 衣服◀ [C] the part of your trousers that covers your leg 裤腿：*The legs of my jeans were covered in mud.* 我的牛仔裤裤腿上沾满了泥。

5 ▶JOURNEY/RACE 旅程/比赛◀ [C] a part of a long journey, race, process etc that is done one part at a time〔旅程、赛程、过程等的〕一段，一站：*the final leg of the Tour de France* 环法自行车赛赛程的最后一段

6 four-legged/two-legged etc having four legs, two legs etc 四条腿的/两条腿的等：*four-legged animals* 四条腿的动物 —see also 另见 CROSS-LEGGED, BOW-LEGGED

left-handed（惯）用左手的

Dad is left-handed. 爸爸是左撇子。

She caught the ball left-handed. 她用左手接球。

L

7 leg room space in which to put your legs comfortably when you are sitting in a car, theatre etc〔汽车、戏院等座位前的〕供伸腿的空间, 腿部活动空间

8 not have a leg to stand on *informal* to be in a situation where you cannot prove or legally support what you say【非正式】〔论点等〕没有根据, 站不住脚: *If you didn't sign a contract, you won't have a leg to stand on.* 如果你不签合同, 你就没有法律上的支撑。

9 pull sb's leg *informal* to make a joke by telling someone something that is not actually true【非正式】愚弄某人, 开某人的玩笑

10 be on its last legs *informal* to be in very bad condition and about to stop working【非正式】糟糕(的); 即将停止运作(的): *The Chevy really is on its last legs now.* 现在这辆雪佛兰汽车快要不行了。

11 get your leg over *BrE slang* to have sex with someone【英俚】与〔某人〕性交

12 ▶SPORT 运动◀ [C] *BrE* one of the parts of a special football competition that is played in two parts【英】〔足球赛的〕半场

13 have legs *informal especially AmE* if a piece of news has legs, people continue to be interested in it and talk about it【非正式, 尤美】〔新闻〕继续受人关注, 继续被人谈论: *These allegations don't have legs – they'll be forgotten by next week.* 这些说法没人会继续感兴趣的 —— 到下周就会被忘得一干二净。—see also 另见 **break a leg** (BREAK[1] (46)), LEG-PULL, LEG-UP, PEG LEG, SEA LEGS, **shake a leg** (SHAKE[1] (11)), **show a leg** (SHOW[1] (22)), **stretch your legs** (STRETCH[1] (12))

leg² v **leg it** *BrE informal* to run in order to escape from someone or something【英, 非正式】跑; 逃脱: *We saw him coming, and legged it out of the house.* 我们见他来了, 就从屋里逃了出来。

leg·a·cy /ˈlɛgəsɪ; ˈlegəsi/ *n* [C] **1** a situation that exists as a result of things that happened at an earlier time 遗留下来的状况; 遗留问题; 后遗症: [+of] *The civil wars in the region are largely a legacy of apartheid.* 这个地区的内战在很大程度上是种族隔离的后遗症。**2** money or property that you receive from someone after they die 遗产, 遗赠物: *a legacy from her aunt* 她姨妈留下的一份遗产

3 1 **le·gal** /ˈligḷ; ˈliːgəl/ *adj* **1** allowed, ordered, or approved by law 法律允许的, 合法的, 法定的: *He had twice the legal limit of alcohol in his bloodstream.* 他血液中的酒精含量是法定限度的两倍。| *plans to make the carrying of identity cards a legal requirement* 使携带身份证成为法定要求的计划 | **the legal age for** *the legal age for voting* 选举的法定年龄 **2** [only before noun 仅用于名词前] concerned with or connected with the law (有关)法律的: *free legal advice* 免费法律咨询 | *a costly legal dispute* 代价高昂的法律纠纷 **3 take legal action/proceedings** to use the legal system to settle an argument, put right an unfair situation etc 采取法律行动/提起法律诉讼: *Unless the money is paid immediately we shall be forced to take legal action.* 如不立刻付款, 我们将被迫采取法律行动。—opposite 反义词 ILLEGAL[1] —see also 另见 LEGALLY

le·gal·ese /ˌligḷˈiz; ˌliːgəlˈiːz/ *n* [U] *informal* language used by lawyers that is difficult for most people to understand【非正式】法律行话, 法律术语〔大多数人难以理解的律师用语〕

le·gal·ise /ˈligḷˌaɪz; ˈliːgəlaɪz/ *v* [T] a British spelling of LEGALIZE legalize 的英式拼法

le·gal·ist·ic /ˌligḷˈɪstɪk; ˌliːgəˈlɪstɪk◂/ *adj* too concerned about small legal details, and not concerned enough about what is really important 拘泥于法规[条文]的 —**legalistically** /-klɪ; -kli/ *adv* —**legalism** /ˈligḷɪzəm; ˈliːgəlɪzəm/ *n* [U]

le·gal·i·ty /lɪˈgælətɪ; lɪˈgælə̇ti/ *n* [U] the fact of being allowed by law 合法性, 法律性: *Some people questioned the legality of the US's attack on Baghdad.* 有人对美国攻击巴格达的合法性提出了质疑。

le·gal·ize also 又作 **-ise** *BrE*【英】/ˈligḷˌaɪz; ˈliːgəlaɪz/ *v* [T] to make a law that allows people to do something that was not allowed before 使合法化, 使得到法律认可: *the campaign to legalize cannabis* 使大麻合法化的运动 —**legalization** /ˌligḷəˈzeʃən; ˌliːgəlaɪˈzeɪʃən/ *n* [U]

le·gal·ly /ˈligḷɪ; ˈliːgəli/ *adv* **1** according to the law 依据法律, 法律上: *Legally he's still my husband.* 法律上他还是我的丈夫。| *The ship was legally authorized to carry 200 passengers.* 这艘船依照法律规定可载 200 名乘客。| *Which of them is legally responsible for the accident?* 他们之中谁负这次事故的法律责任? **2 legally binding** an agreement or document that is legally binding must be obeyed by law〔协议或文件〕具有法律约束力的

legal pad /ˈ· · ·/ *n* [C] a PAD[1] (2) of yellow writing paper with lines, of a type sold in the US 标准拍纸簿

legal pro·fes·sion, the /ˈ· · ·,· ·/ *n* lawyers, judges, and other people who work in courts of law or advise people about legal problems 法律行业, 法律界〔律师、法官、法庭工作人员、法律顾问等〕

legal-size /ˈ· · ·/ *adj AmE* legal-size paper is 14 inches (INCH[1] (1)) long and 8 inches wide【美】〔纸张〕大小适合于法律文件的〔14 英寸长 8 英寸宽〕; 法定尺寸的

legal sys·tem /ˈ· ·, · ·/ *n* [C] the laws and the way they work in a particular country 法律体制, 法制

legal ten·der /ˌ· · ˈ· ·/ *n* [U] coins or bank notes that are officially allowed to be used as money 法定货币

leg·ate /ˈlɛgɪt; ˈlegə̇t/ *n* [C] an important official representative 使节

leg·a·tee /ˌlɛgəˈti; ˌlegəˈtiː/ *n* [C] *law* someone who is given money or property after another person dies【法律】遗产承受人, 受遗赠人

le·ga·tion /lɪˈgeʃən; lɪˈgeɪʃən/ *n* [C] **1** an office that represents a government in a foreign country but is lower in rank than an EMBASSY 公使馆: *the Cuban legation* 古巴公使馆 **2** the people who work in this office 公使馆全体人员

le·ga·to /lɪˈgɑto; lɪˈgɑːtəʊ/ *adj, adv technical* played or sung so that each note connects to the next one without pauses between them【术语】〔音乐中〕连奏的[地], 连音的[地]

le·gend /ˈlɛdʒənd; ˈledʒənd/ *n* **1** [C] an old, well-known story, often about brave people, adventures, or magical events 传说, 传奇(故事): *the legend of Rip Van Winkle who slept for 100 years* 瑞普·凡·温克尔昏睡百年的传说 **2** [U] all stories of this kind 民间传说: *Celtic legend* 凯尔特人的民间传说 **3** [C] someone who is famous and admired for being extremely good at doing something〔某领域中的〕传奇式人物: *Pelè, Maradona, and other footballing legends* 贝利、马拉多纳以及其他足球传奇人物 —see also 另见 LIVING LEGEND **4** [C usually singular 一般用单数] **a)** *literary* words that have been written somewhere, for example on a sign【文】〔牌匾等上的〕镌刻文字, 铭文: *A sign above the door bore the legend 'patience is a virtue'.* 门上方的匾上题写着"忍耐即美德"。**b)** *old-fashioned* the words that explain a picture, map etc【过时】〔图片、地图等的〕文字说明, 图例

le·gen·da·ry /ˈlɛdʒəndˌɛrɪ; ˈledʒəndəri/ *adj* **1** famous and admired 非常有名的, 大名鼎鼎的; 传奇式的: *the legendary Babe Ruth, one of the greatest baseball players of all time* 传奇式人物贝布·鲁思, 历史上最伟大的棒球运动员之一 **2** talked or read about in legends 传说(中)的: *legendary sea monsters* 传说中的海怪

Legend of Sleep·y Hol·low, The /ˌ· · · ·, · · ˈ· ·/ (1820) a popular story by Washington Irving in which the main character, Ichabod Crane, rides quickly through a frightening place called Sleepy Hollow because he thinks he is being chased by a Headless Horseman《睡谷的传说》〔(1820), 华盛顿·欧文创作的一部畅销小说。故事的主人公伊卡博德·克莱恩感觉有一名无头骑士在追他, 因此策马急速穿过一个名为"睡谷"的恐怖地方〕

Léger, Fernand (1881-1955) a French painter and one of the most important painters of the Cubist style 莱热〔(1881-1955), 法国画家, 立体派最重要的画家之一〕

le·ger·de·main /ˌlɛdʒɚdɪˈmen; ˌledʒədəˈmeɪn/ *n* [U] *old-fashioned* skilful use of your hands when performing tricks【过时】魔术, 戏法

-legged /lɛgɪd; legə̇d/ *suffix* [in adjectives 构成形容词] having legs of a particular type or number 有…腿的: *four-legged animals* 四条腿的动物 | *a long-legged runner* 长腿跑步者

leg·gings /ˈlɛgɪŋz; ˈlegɪŋz/ *n* [plural] **1** women's tight trousers without a ZIP[1] (1), which stretch to fit the shape of your body 女式紧身裤 **2** trousers worn to protect your legs 绑腿, 裹腿; 护腿

leg·gy /ˈlɛgɪ; ˈlegi/ *adj* a woman or child who is leggy has long legs〔女人或小孩〕腿细长的: *a leggy blonde* 双腿修长的金发美女 —**legginess** *n* [U]

le·gi·ble /ˈlɛdʒəbḷ; ˈledʒə̇bəl/ *adj* written or printed clearly enough for you to read〔字迹〕可以辨认的, 易读的: *Her handwriting was so tiny it was barely legible.* 她的字写得这么小, 简直都看不清楚。—**legibly** *adv* —**legibility** /ˌlɛdʒəˈbɪlətɪ; ˌledʒə̇ˈbɪlə̇ti/ *n* [U] —opposite 反义词 ILLEGIBLE

le·gion¹ /ˈlidʒən; ˈliːdʒən/ *n* [C] **1** a large group of soldiers, especially in ancient Rome〔尤指古罗马的〕军团 **2** *literary* a large number of people【文】〔人的〕众多, 大批, 无数

legion² *adj* [not before noun 不用于名词前] *literary* very many; NUMEROUS【文】众多的, 大批的: *The stories of her adventures were legion.* 她的历险故事多极了。

le·gion·a·ry /ˋlidʒən,ɛrɪ; ˈliːdʒənəri/ *n* [C] a member of a legion（古罗马）军团士兵

le·gion·naire /,lidʒənˋɛr; ,liːdʒəˈneə/ *n* [C] a member of a legion, especially the French Foreign Legion〔尤指法国外籍军团的〕士兵

legionnaire's dis·ease /,·· ˈ· ·,·/ *n* [U] a serious lung disease 军团病，退伍军人协会会员病〔一种严重的肺部疾病〕

leg i·rons /ˈ· ··/ *n* [plural] metal circles or chains that are put around a prisoner's legs 脚镣

le·gis·late /ˋlɛdʒɪs,let; ˈledʒɪsleɪt/ *v* [I] to make a law about something 制定法律，立法: **[+against/for/on]** *There are plans to legislate against computer-related crime.* 已经有打击电脑犯罪的立法计划了。

2 **le·gis·la·tion** /,lɛdʒɪsˋleʃən; ,ledʒɪ̇ˈsleɪʃən/ *n* [U] **1** a law or set of laws 法规，法律: *an important piece of human rights legislation* 人权法规中的重要部分 | *legislation governing minimum wage rates* 规定最低工资的法规 **2** the act of making laws 法律制定，立法

le·gis·la·tive /ˋlɛdʒɪs,letɪv; ˈledʒɪ̇slətɪv/ *adj* **1** a legislative institution has the power to make laws 有立法权的: *a legislative assembly* 立法议会 **2** concerned with laws or with making laws 法律的，立法的: *new legislative measures to stem the flow of drugs into the US* 阻止毒品流入美国的新法律措施 —compare 比较 EXECUTIVE[2] (1), JUDICIAL (1)

le·gis·la·tor /ˋlɛdʒɪs,letɚ; ˈledʒɪ̇sleɪtə/ *n* [C] someone who has the power to make laws or belongs to an institution that makes laws 立法者，立法委员

le·gis·la·ture /ˋlɛdʒɪs,letʃɚ; ˈledʒɪ̇sleɪtʃə/ *n* [C] an institution that has the power to make or change laws 立法机关: *the Iowa state legislature* 艾奥瓦[衣阿华]州立法机关 —compare 比较 EXECUTIVE[1] (2), JUDICIARY

le·git /ləˋdʒɪt; lɪ̇ˈdʒɪt/ *adj* [not before noun 不用于名词前] *spoken*【口】**1** legal or following official rules; LEGITIMATE[1] (1) 合法的；守规则的: *Don't worry, the deal's strictly legit.* 不用担忧，这项交易是完全合法的。**2** honest and not trying to deceive people 诚实不欺人的: *Are you sure he's legit?* 你敢肯定他没有骗人？

le·git·i·mate¹ /lɪˋdʒɪtəmɪt; lɪˈdʒɪtɪ̇mɪ̇t/ *adj* **1** correct, allowable, or operating according to the law 合法的，法律许可的，依法的: *The Mafia uses legitimate business operations as a front.* 黑手党利用合法经营作掩护。**2** fair, correct, or reasonable according to accepted standards of behaviour 公正的，正当的，合理的: *Is this a legitimate use of taxpayers' money?* 这是正当使用纳税人的钱吗？| *I think that's a perfectly legitimate question.* 我认为那是一个完全正当的问题。**3** legitimate children are born to parents who are legally married to each other 合法婚姻所生的，婚生的 —**legitimately** *adv* —**legitimacy** *n* [U]

le·git·i·mate² /lɪˋdʒɪtə,met; lɪˈdʒɪtɪ̇meɪt/ *v* [T] the usual American form of LEGITIMIZE legitimize 的一般美语形式

le·git·i·mize also 又作 **-ise** *BrE*【英】/lɪˋdʒɪtə,maɪz; lɪˈdʒɪtɪ̇maɪz/ *v* [T] **1** to make something that is unfair or morally wrong seem acceptable and right 使〔某种不公平或不道德的事〕被接受；使显得正当: *Mussolini's use of symbols from ancient Rome to try to legitimize Fascist policies* 墨索里尼使用古罗马的象征符号企图使法西斯政策正当化 **2** to make something official or legal that had not been before 使〔某事〕得到公开承认；使〔某事〕合法化 **3** to make a child LEGITIMATE[1] (3) 使〔某小孩〕被认定为婚生子

leg·less /ˋlɛglɪs; ˈlegləs/ *adj BrE informal* drunk【英，非正式】烂醉如泥的

leg·o /ˋlɛgo; ˈlegəʊ/ *n* [U] *trademark* a toy consisting of plastic pieces of various sizes that can be fitted together to build things【商标】乐高玩具〔由各种大小的塑料模块组成〕

leg-pull /ˈ· ·/ *n* [C usually singular 一般用单数] *BrE* a joke in which you make someone believe something that is not true【英】愚弄人 —see also 另见 **pull sb's leg** (LEG[1] (9))

leg room /ˈ· ·/ *n* [U] space for your legs in front of the seats in a car, theatre etc〔汽车、戏院等的座位下〕供伸腿的空间，腿的活动余地

leg·ume /ˋlɛgjum; ˈlegjuːm/ *n* [C] **1** a plant of the bean family that has seeds in a POD (=a long thin case) 豆科植物 **2** *especially AmE* a bean, PEA, LENTIL etc, used as food【尤美】食用豆类 —**leguminous** /lɪˋgjumənəs; lɪˈgjuːmɪ̇nəs/ *adj*

leg-up /ˈ· ·/ *n* **give sb a leg-up** *informal*【非正式】**a)** to help someone to get up to a high place by joining your hands together so they can use them as a step〔双手交叉〕让某人踩着登高 **b)** *especially BrE* to help someone to succeed in their job【尤英】助某人一臂之力

leg-warm·er /ˈ· ,··/ *n* [C] a piece of clothing made from wool, which covers the lower part of your leg 暖腿套

leg·work /ˋlɛg,wɝk; ˈlegwɜːk/ *n* [U] *informal* the hard boring work that has to be done in order to achieve something【非正式】跑腿活，跑外工作

Le Ha·vre /lə ˋɑvrə; lə ˈɑːvrə/ a city and port in northwest France where the River Seine flows into the English Channel. Ferries (FERRY) from the south of England take cars and passengers to Le Havre. 勒阿弗尔〔法国西北部一城市和港口，塞纳河在此注入英吉利海峡。渡轮可将小汽车与乘客从英格兰南部载往勒阿弗尔〕

lei /le; leɪ/ *n* [C] a circle made of flowers you put around someone's neck as a greeting, especially in Hawaii〔尤指在夏威夷迎客时套在客人颈上的〕花环

Leib·niz /ˋlaɪbnɪts; ˈlaɪbnɪts/, **Gottf·ried Wil·helm** /ˋgɑtfrid ˋvɪlhɛlm; ˈgɒtfriːd ˈvɪlhelm◂/, **Baron von** (1646-1716) a German PHILOSOPHER and MATHEMATICIAN who invented CALCULUS at the same time as Newton 莱布尼兹〔(1646-1716)，德国哲学家、数学家，与牛顿同时创立了微积分的概念〕

Leices·ter·shire /ˋlɛstɚʃɚ; ˈlestəʃə/ abbreviation 缩写为 **Leics.** a county in central England 莱斯特郡〔英格兰中部一郡〕

Leices·ter Square /,lɛstɚ ˋskwɛr; ,lestə ˈskweə/ a square in central London which has several cinemas, restaurants, shops, and AMUSEMENT ARCADEs. It is a popular place for tourists and young people. 莱斯特广场〔位于伦敦市中心，有数家电影院、饭店、商场及游乐场，深受游客和年轻人喜欢〕

Leigh /li; liː/, **Viv·i·en** /ˋvɪvɪən; ˈvɪviən/ (1913-67) a British actress, famous for her beauty and for appearing as the characters Scarlett O'Hara in the film *Gone with the Wind* (1939) and Blanche Dubois in the film *A Streetcar Named Desire* (1951). She was married to Laurence Olivier for many years. 费雯·丽〔(1913-1967)，英国女演员，以美貌著称，并因饰演电影《乱世佳人》(1939) 中的郝思嘉和《欲望号街车》(1951) 中的布朗希·迪布瓦而享有盛名。她与劳伦斯·奥利弗的婚姻持续了许多年〕

Lein·ster /ˋlɛnstɚ; ˈlenstə/ a province in the Republic of Ireland which includes 12 counties (COUNTY) and the city of Dublin 伦斯特〔爱尔兰共和国一省，包括12个郡以及都柏林市〕

Leip·zig /ˋlaɪpsɪg; ˈlaɪpsɪg/ a city in eastern central Germany, which has a famous university and is an important centre for business 莱比锡〔德国中东部一城市，有一所著名大学，是重要的商业中心〕

lei·sure /ˋliʒɚ; ˈleʒə/ *n* [U] **1** time when you are not working or studying and can relax and do things you enjoy 空闲，闲暇，业余时间: *gardening, sailing, and other leisure pursuits* 园艺、帆船运动和其他业余爱好 | **leisure time** *In her leisure time she visits museums and galleries.* 在空闲的时候，她去参观博物馆和美术馆。| **the leisure industry** (=the business of providing leisure activities) 休闲娱乐行业，提供业余活动的行业 **2 at your leisure** as slowly as you want and when you want 有空时；方便时: *Take the leaflets home and read them at your leisure.* 把这些传单拿回家，闲暇时阅读。**3 gentleman/lady of leisure** *humorous* someone who does not have to work【幽默】〔无须工作的〕有闲先生/女士 3

leisure cen·tre /ˈ·· ,··/ *n* [C] *BrE* a place where you can do many different sports activities, exercise classes etc【英】休闲中心，娱乐中心；健身中心

lei·sured /ˋliʒɚd; ˈleʒəd/ *adj* **1** having no regular work and a lot of leisure time, especially because you are rich〔尤因富有而〕有空闲的，悠闲自在的 **2** leisurely 从容的，不慌不忙的

lei·sure·ly /ˋliʒɚlɪ; ˈleʒəli/ *adj* moving or done in a relaxed way, without hurrying 从容的，不慌不忙的: *a leisurely stroll* 悠闲的散步 | *working at a leisurely pace* 不慌不忙地干活 —**leisurely** *adv*: *The great ship sailed leisurely across the bay.* 这艘巨轮缓缓地横渡海湾。—**leisureliness** *n* [U]

leisure suit /ˈ·· ·/ *n* [C] *AmE* an informal suit popular during the 1970s, consisting of a shirt-like JACKET and trousers made of the same material【美】〔20世纪70年代流行的〕休闲套装

lei·sure·wear /ˋliʒɚ,wɛr; ˈleʒəweə/ *n* [U] a word meaning clothes that are made to be worn when relaxing or playing sport, used especially by shops or by the companies that make these clothes 休闲服，运动服，便服

leit·mo·tif, leitmotiv /ˋlaɪtmo,tif; ˈlaɪtməʊ,tiːf/ *n* [C] **1** a musical phrase that is played at various times during an OPERA or similar musical work to represent a particular character or idea〔音乐用语〕主导主题；主旋律 —compare 比较 MOTIF (3) **2** a feature that appears often in something such as a book, a speech, or an artist's work〔书、演说、艺术作品等中的〕主题，主旨

Lei·trim /ˋlitrɪm; ˈliːtrɪ̇m/ a COUNTY in the north of the Republic of Ireland 利特里姆郡〔爱尔兰共和国北部一郡〕

Le Mans /lə ˋmɑn; lə ˈmɒn/ a city in northwest France where a famous car race takes place every year. The race continues

without stopping for 24 hours, and the winner is the car that has driven the most times around the track in that time. 勒芒〔法国西北部一城市。每年在此举行的汽车赛十分有名，比赛连续进行24小时，绕车道行驶圈数最多的赛车为获胜者〕

lem·ming /ˈlɛmɪŋ; ˈlemɪŋ/ *n* [C] **1** a small rat-like animal that is known for killing itself by following other lemmings and jumping into the sea in large numbers 旅鼠 **2** someone who copies other people's actions and ideas without thinking about it 盲目仿效者

lem·on /ˈlɛmən; ˈlemən/ *n* **1** [C, U] a fruit with a hard yellow skin and sour juice 柠檬: *fish served with slices of lemon* 配上柠檬片的鱼 —see picture on page A8 参见 A8 页图 **2** [U] *BrE* a drink made from this fruit【英】柠檬汁 **3** [U] a pale yellow colour 淡黄色 —see picture on page A5 参见 A5 页图 **4** [C] *AmE informal* something that is useless because it fails to work or work properly【美，非正式】无用之物，易出故障之物: *He has an old Dodge that's a real lemon.* 他有一辆旧道奇车，那真是辆烂车。**5** [C] *BrE informal* a silly person【英，非正式】傻瓜，笨蛋: *I felt such a lemon when I realized I'd gone on the wrong day.* 当我意识到去错了日子，我感到自己真是个傻瓜。

3 **lem·on·ade** /ˌlɛmənˈed; ˌleməˈneɪd◂/ *n* [U] **1** a drink made from lemons, sugar, and water 柠檬水 **2** *BrE* a sweet colourless FIZZY drink【英】柠檬汽水

lemon curd /ˌ·· ˈ·/ *n* [U] *BrE* a sweet food made of eggs, butter, and lemon juice, eaten on bread【英】柠檬酪〔由蛋、黄油、柠檬汁制成〕

lemon sole /ˌ·· ˈ·/ *n* [C] a flat fish used as food 檬鲽〔可食用的一种扁鱼〕

lemon squeez·er /ˈ·· ˌ··/ *n* [C] a small kitchen tool for getting the juice out of a lemon 柠檬榨汁器〔厨房用具〕

lend 借出，借给

I borrowed $20. 我借了 20 美元。 My friend lent me $20. 我的朋友借给我 20 美元。

I paid her back the next day. 第二天我把钱还给了她。

3 3 **lend** /lɛnd; lend/ *v past tense and past participle* **lent** /lɛnt; lent/ **1 ▶MONEY/CAR/BOOK ETC** 钱/汽车/书籍等◀ **a)** [T] to let someone borrow money from you or use something that you own, which they will give you back later 借给〔某人钱或东西〕；借出: **lend sb sth** *I wish I'd never lent him my car.* 但愿我从未把汽车借给过他。| *Can you lend me $20 till Friday?* 你能不能借我 20 美元，到星期五还给你？| **lend sth to sb** *Reluctantly, I agreed to lend it to her.* 我勉强同意把它借给她。**b)** [I,T] if a bank or financial institution lends money, it lets someone borrow it on condition that they pay it back, often gradually, with an additional amount as interest〔银行或金融机构〕贷(款)；贷出: *We aim to lend money at reasonable rates of interest.* 我们力求以合理的利率贷出款项。| **lend sth to sb** *US banks lent billions of dollars to Third World countries in the 1970s.* 20世纪70年代美国的银行贷给第三世界数十亿美元的款项。—see 见 BORROW (USAGE)

2 lend (sb) a hand to help someone do something, especially something that needs physical effort 帮助(某人)做事〔尤指需要体力的事〕

3 lend an ear to listen to someone, especially in a sympathetic way 听，〔尤指同情地〕倾听

4 lend itself to to be suitable for being used in a particular way 适用于: *None of her books really lends itself to being made into a film.* 她的书没有一本真正适合于拍成电影。

5 ▶GIVE A QUALITY 增添某种特性◀ [T] *formal* to give a situation, event etc a particular quality【正式】给予；增添〔某种特性〕: *The Duke's presence lent the occasion a certain air of dignity.* 公爵的光临使场面增添了几分庄严感。| **lend sth to sth** *His soft accent lends a kind of warmth to his words.* 他柔和的声调给他的话注入了一点温情。

6 lend support/assistance to support or help someone 提供支持/帮助

7 lend weight to to make an opinion, belief etc seem more likely to be correct 使〔意见、看法等〕更可信: *The new evidence lends weight to the theory that the killer was a man.* 新证据使得凶手是一名男性的推测变得更可信。

8 lend your name/voice to to announce publicly that you support something someone is trying to do 公开支持，声援 —**lender** *n* [C]

lend·ing li·bra·ry /ˈ·· ˌ···/ *n* [C] a library that lends books, records etc for people to use at home〔可外借书籍、唱片等的〕图书馆 —compare 比较 REFERENCE LIBRARY

lending rate /ˈ·· ·/ *n* [C] the rate of INTEREST[1] (4) that you have to pay to a bank or other financial institution when you borrow money from them; INTEREST RATE 借贷利率，贷款利率

length /lɛŋθ; leŋθ/ *n* 2 2

length 长度

height 高度
length 长度
width 宽度

1 ▶SIZE 尺寸◀ [C,U] the measurement of something from one end to the other 长；长度: [+of] *The fish can grow to a length of four feet.* 这种鱼可长到 4 英尺长。| **2 feet in length/10 metres in length etc** *Vehicles of over 3 metres in length pay an additional toll.* 汽车超过3米长要付额外的通行费。| *pieces of string of different lengths* 不同长度的绳子 —compare 比较 BREADTH, WIDTH

2 ▶TIME 时间◀ [C,U] the amount of time that you spend doing something or that something continues for 时间长度: *reducing the average length of stay in hospital* 降低平均住院时间 | **not for any length of time** (=not for very long) 一刻也不 *I didn't want to be left alone with him for any length of time.* 我一刻也不愿和他单独在一起了。

3 ▶BOOKS/FILMS ETC 书/电影等◀ [C, U] the amount of writing in a book, or the amount of time that a film, play etc continues for〔书的〕字数[页数]；〔电影、戏剧等的〕长度: *We had to cut the length of the book by two-thirds.* 我们得削减此书三分之二的页数。| *Films of this length are pretty unusual.* 这样长度的电影很少见。

4 go to any lengths/great lengths to do sth to be willing to use any methods to achieve something that you are very determined to achieve 千方百计/竭尽全力做某事: *Gerald is prepared to go to any lengths to get his daughter back.* 杰拉尔德准备竭尽全力去把他的女儿要回来。

5 at length a) if you talk at length about something, you talk about it for a long time 长时间地: *We've already discussed the subject at great length in previous meetings.* 在以前的会议上，我们已经用了很长时间讨论这一题目。**b)** *literary* after a long time【文】长时间后，最后，最终: *"How have you been?" she said at length.* "你最近过得怎样？"她最终问了一句。

6 the length and breadth of in or through every part of a large area 各处，四面八方

7 walk/travel/drive the length of walk, travel etc the whole distance along something 沿着…走完/驶完全程: *They walked the length of the pier.* 他们沿着长堤走到头。

8 ▶PIECE 根◀ [C] a piece of something long and thin 细长的物件: [+of] *a length of steel tubing* 一根钢管

9 ▶IN RACES 在比赛中◀ [C] the measurement from one end of a horse, boat etc to the other, used when saying how far one is ahead of another〔马、船等在比赛中超出的〕自身长度: *The horse won by three lengths.* 这匹马以领先三个马身而获胜。

10 ▶SWIMMING 游泳◀ [C] the distance from one end of a swimming pool to the other〔游泳池的〕长度: *I was really bad at swimming – I could barely do a length.* 我真的游不好——游泳池的一个长度我几乎都游不了。—see also 另见 **at arm's length** (ARM[1] (9)), FULL-LENGTH, **measure your length** (MEASURE[2] (5)), SHOULDER-LENGTH

length·en /ˈlɛŋθən; ˈleŋθən/ *v* [I,T] to make something longer or to become longer (使)延长；(使)加长: *Can you lengthen this skirt for me?* 你能不能为我加长这条裙子？| *The days lengthened as summer approached.* 随着夏季临近，白日延长了。—opposite 反义词 SHORTEN

length·ways /ˈlɛŋθˌwez; ˈleŋθweɪz/ also 又作 **length·wise** /-waɪz; -waɪz/ *adv* in the direction or position of the longest side 纵长地; 纵向地; LONGWAYS *AmE*【美】: *Lay the bricks lengthways.* 纵向地砌砖。

length·y /ˈlɛŋθɪ; ˈleŋθi/ *adj* **1** continuing for a long time, often too long 长时间的; 过长的: *a lengthy court trial* 漫长的庭审 **2** a speech, piece of writing etc that is lengthy is long and often contains too many details〔讲话、文章等〕冗长的, 过于详尽的 —**lengthiness** *n* [U] —**lengthily** *adv*

le·ni·ent /ˈliniənt; ˈliːniənt/ *adj* not strict in the way you punish someone or control their behaviour 宽大的, 仁慈的: *Judges have been accused of being far too lenient in rape cases.* 法官被指责在审理强奸案件中过分宽容。| *a very lenient sentence* 极为宽大的判决 —**leniently** *adv* —**leniency** also 又作 **lenience** *n* [U]

Len·in /ˈlɛnɪn; ˈlenɪn/, **Vlad·i·mir Il·yich** /ˈvlædɪmɪr ˈɪlɪtʃ; ˈvlædʒmɪə ˈɪlɪtʃ/ (1870-1924) a Russian Marxist revolutionary and writer who was leader of the Bolshevik party and first leader of the Soviet Union (1918-24) 列宁〔(1870-1924), 俄国马克思主义革命家、作家, 曾任布尔什维克党领袖和苏联第一任领导人(1918-1924)〕

Len·in·grad /ˈlɛnɪnˌgræd; ˈlenɪngræd/ the name of the Russian city of St Petersburg during the time when Russia was part of the former Soviet Union. It was named after Lenin, the first leader of the Soviet Union. 列宁格勒〔俄罗斯城市圣彼德堡在苏联时期的名称, 以苏联第一位领导人列宁的名字命名〕

Len·in·is·m /ˈlɛnɪnɪzəm; ˈlenɪnɪzəm/ the teachings of Lenin, based on those of Karl Marx, regarding political, economic, and social matters; MARXISM-LENINISM (马克思)列宁主义

Len·non /ˈlɛnən; ˈlenən/, **John** (1940-80) a British singer and songwriter, who was a member of The Beatles, and wrote most of their songs with Paul McCartney. After The Beatles separated, he continued to write and sing songs, especially about peace and love, including *Give Peace a Chance* and *Imagine*. He was married to the artist Yoko Ono. He was shot and killed outside his home in New York City. 列侬〔(1940-1980), 英国歌手、词曲作家, 甲壳虫乐队成员之一。乐队的大部分歌曲是由他和保罗·麦卡特尼一起写成的。乐队解散后, 他继续创作, 并演唱以爱与和平为主题的歌曲, 其中包括《给和平一次机会》和《想象》。他与艺术家小野洋子结婚, 后来在纽约的家门口遭人枪杀〕

lens /lɛnz; lenz/ *n* [C] **1** a piece of curved glass or plastic which makes things look bigger or smaller, for example in a pair of GLASSes or in a TELESCOPE[1] 凸透镜; 凹透镜; 透镜; 镜片: *Jan wears glasses with thick lenses.* 简戴着镜片很厚的眼镜。—see picture at 参见 GLASS[1] 图 **2** the part of a camera through which the light travels before it hits the film〔照相机、摄影机的〕镜头: *a standard 50mm lens* 50毫米标准镜头 —see picture at 参见 CAMERA 图 **3** the clear part inside your eye that focuses (FOCUS[1] (3)) so you can see things clearly〔眼球的〕晶状体 —see picture at 参见 EYE[1] 图 **4** one of a pair of small curved pieces of plastic that fit closely to your eyes to help you see better; CONTACT LENS 隐形眼镜

Lent /lɛnt; lent/ *n* [U] the period before Easter during which Christians traditionally eat less food or stop doing something that they enjoy〔基督教的〕大斋期, 四旬斋 —**Lenten** *adj*

lent the past tense and past participle of LEND

len·til /ˈlɛntḷ; ˈlentl/ *n* [C] a small round seed like a bean, dried and used for food 小扁豆

len·to /ˈlɛnto; ˈlentəʊ/ *adj, adv technical* music that is played lento is played slowly【术语】〔音乐〕缓慢的[地]

Le·o /ˈlio; ˈliːəʊ/ *n* **1** [singular] the sign of the ZODIAC represented by a lion and believed to affect the character and life of people born between 23 July and 22 August 狮子宫[座] **2** [C] someone who was born between 23 July and 22 August 狮子宫[座]时段〔7月23日至8月22日〕出生的人

Le·o·nar·do da Vin·ci /lioˌnardo də ˋvɪntʃɪ; liːəˌnɑːdəʊ də ˈvɪntʃi/ (1452-1519) an Italian painter, inventor, and scientist of the Renaissance period, who is one of the greatest artists and GENIUSes who ever lived. His most famous paintings are 'The Mona Lisa' and 'The Last Supper'. As a scientist and engineer, he made many important discoveries and designed and invented many machines, including one that looks similar to a modern HELICOPTER. 列奥纳多·达·芬奇〔(1452-1519), 意大利文艺复兴时期的画家、发明家和科学家, 被公认为有史以来最伟大的画家与天才之一。他最为著名的画作是《蒙娜丽莎》和《最后的晚餐》。作为一名科学家和工程师, 他曾有许多重要的发现, 还设计发明了许多机械装置, 其中一项发明看起来像现代直升机〕

Le·o·ne /liˈonɪ; liˈəʊni/, **Ser·gi·o** /ˈsɝdʒɪo; ˈsɜːdʒiəʊ/ (1921-89) an Italian film DIRECTOR famous for his SPAGHETTI WESTERNs (=films about the American West in the 19th century, made in Europe by Italian directors), such as *A Fistful of Dollars* (1964) and *The Good, the Bad and the Ugly* (1966) 里昂列〔(1921-1989), 意大利电影导演, 以拍摄意大利风格的美国西部影片著称。这类影片有《为了几美元》(1964)和《好人、坏蛋和丑八怪》(1966)等〕

le·o·nine /ˈliəˌnaɪn; ˈliːənaɪn/ *adj* connected with lions, or like a lion in character or appearance 狮子的; 狮子般勇猛的; 狮子般雄壮的

leop·ard /ˈlɛpɚd; ˈlepəd/ *n* [C] **1** a large animal of the cat family, with yellow fur and black spots, which lives in Africa and South Asia 豹 **2 a leopard can't change its spots** used to say that people cannot change their character 本性难移

le·o·tard /ˈliətɑrd; ˈliːətɑːd/ *n* [C] a tight-fitting piece of women's clothing that covers your whole body from your neck to the top of your legs and is worn for exercise or dancing〔运动或跳舞穿的〕女式紧身连衣裤 —see picture at 参见 UNDERWEAR 图

lep·er /ˈlɛpɚ; ˈlepə/ *n* [C] **1** someone who suffers from the disease of leprosy 麻风病人 **2** someone that people avoid because they have done something that people disapprove of〔因做了不为人赞许的事〕别人避之唯恐不及的人: *They treated me as if I was some kind of leper.* 他们把我当作某种让人避之唯恐不及的人。

lep·re·chaun /ˈlɛprəˌkɔn; ˈleprəkɔːn/ *n* [C] an imaginary creature in the form of a little old man, in old Irish stories〔爱尔兰古代民间传说中的〕矮妖精

lep·ro·sy /ˈlɛprəsɪ; ˈleprəsi/ *n* [U] a very serious infectious disease in which the flesh and nerves are gradually destroyed 麻风病 —**leprous** *adj*

ler·gy /ˈlɝgɪ; ˈlɜːgi/ *n* [C] another spelling of LURGY lurgy 的另一种拼法

Ler·wick /ˈlɝwɪk; ˈlɜːwɪk/ a town and port which is the capital of the Shetland Islands. Lerwick is on Mainland island and is a centre of the fishing industry. 勒威克〔设得兰群岛首府, 为一城镇和港口。该镇位于梅恩兰岛, 为渔业中心〕

les·bi·an /ˈlɛzbɪən; ˈlezbiən/ *n* [C] a woman who is sexually attracted to other women 女同性恋者 —**lesbian** *adj*: *lesbian writers* 女同性恋作家 —**lesbianism** *n* [U]

lese-ma·jes·ty /ˈliz ˋmædʒɪstɪ; ˌliːz ˈmædʒɪsti/ *n* [U] **1** *humorous* behaviour that shows a lack of respect towards an important person【幽默】犯上行为 **2** *law* a crime against a king or government【法律】冒犯君主罪, 叛逆罪

Le Shut·tle /lɛ ˋʃʌtḷ; le ˈʃʌtl/ *trademark* a type of train which goes from Folkestone in the south of England to Calais in the north of France using the Channel Tunnel, and which carries cars and goods vehicles【商标】隧道快列, 乐谢拖〔一列由英格兰南部的福克斯通启程经由英吉利海峡隧道抵达法国北部加莱的火车。车上可运载小汽车及货车〕: *Take a day-trip to France on Le Shuttle.* 乘隧道快列去法国一日游。—compare 比较 EUROSTAR

le·sion /ˈliʒən; ˈliːʒən/ *n* [C] *technical*【术语】**1** a wound 伤口; 损伤: *multiple lesions to the skin* 皮肤上的多处伤口 **2** a dangerous change in part of someone's body such as their lungs or brain, caused by injury or illness〔因伤、病而致的〕损伤, 损害; 病变: *cerebral lesions* 大脑损伤

Les Mis·é·rables /le ˌmɪzəˋrɑbḷ; leɪ ˌmɪzəˈruːbəl/ *informal*【非正式】a MUSICAL (=a play that uses song and dance to tell a story) which is one of the most popular stage shows ever and has been performed all over the world. It is based on a NOVEL by Victor Hugo, and tells the story of a failed revolution in 19th century France. 《悲惨世界》〔有史以来最受欢迎的音乐剧之一, 曾在世界各地上演。该剧根据维克多·雨果的同名小说改编而成, 反映了19世纪以失败告终的法国大革命〕

Le·so·tho /ləˈsutu; ləˈsuːtuː/ a country in South Africa that has a lot of mountains, and is completely surrounded by the Republic of South Africa. It is a member of the British Commonwealth. Population: 2,177,000 (2001). Capital: Maseru. 莱索托〔非洲南部一山地国家, 位于南非共和国境内, 为英联邦成员国。人口: 2,177,000 (2001), 首都: 马塞卢〕

-less /lɪs; ləs/ *suffix* [in adjectives 构成形容词] **1** without something 无…的: *a childless couple* (=who have no children) 无子女的夫妇 | *It's quite harmless.* (=will not harm you) 这没什么害处。| *He was hatless.* (=wore no hat) 他没戴帽子。| *endless complaints* (=that never end) 没完没了的抱怨 **2** never doing something 永不…的: *a tireless helper* (=who never gets tired) 永不知疲倦的助人为乐者 **3** unable to be treated in a particular way 不能…的: *on countless occasions* (=too many to be counted) 在无数场合中

less[1] /lɛs; les/ *adv* **1** not so much; to a smaller degree 不那么多; 更[较]少地; 至更[较]小程度: *I found the second half of the play less interesting than the first.* 我发现剧本的下半部分没有上半部分那么有趣。| *We go to Paris less frequently now.* 现在我们较不常去巴黎了。| *You ought to smoke less.* 你应该少吸点烟

了。—opposite 反义词 MORE¹ (1) **2less and less** gradually becoming smaller in amount or degree 越来越少[小]: *Our trips became less and less frequent.* 我们外出的次数越来越少了。**3 much/still less** *formal* certainly not【正式】更不用说, 更何况: *They did not intend even to tell the authorities about the experiments, still less seek their approval.* 他们甚至不打算告诉当局有关试验的事, 更不用说寻求当局的批准了。

less² *determiner, pron* **1 a)** not as much 不那么多, 更[较]少: *You ought to eat less salt.* 你应该少吃点盐。| *Most of the workers were paid £5 per day, but some received even less.* 大多数工人每天得五英镑工资, 但有些工人得到的甚至更少。| *Give him less of the medicine if it seems to upset him.* 如果用药看来使他不舒服的话, 就给他少一点。| *a distance of less than 100 metres* 不足 100 米的距离 **b)** used to mean fewer or not as many, but often considered incorrect in this meaning 为数更少, 为数不那么多〔此用法常被认为不正确〕: *There were less people there than we expected.* 那里的人比我们预料的要少。**2no less than** used when you are giving a number, to emphasize that it is surprisingly large 不少于, 多达: *The book has been translated into no less than 40 languages.* 此书已翻译成多达 40 种语言。**3less than helpful/perfect etc** not at all helpful, perfect etc 一点也没有帮助/不完善等: *Doctors have been less than successful in treating this condition.* 在治疗这种病上, 医生一直没有获得成功。**4in less than no time** very quickly or very soon 很快地, 很迅速地: *The debts increased alarmingly, and in less than no time they found that they owed over $10,000.* 负债增长惊人, 很快他们发现已经欠了 1 万多美元。**5nothing less than** used to emphasize how important or serious something really is 简直是: *His appearance in the show was nothing less than a sensation.* 他在演出中的亮相简直是轰动一时的事件。**6no less** used to emphasize that the person or thing you are talking about is very important 正是〔强调谈及的人、物很重要〕: *The building was opened by no less a person than the Prince of Wales.* 为大楼主持揭幕典礼的正是威尔士亲王。| *His case is supported by the Police Complaints Committee no less.* 他的案子正是由警察投诉委员会支持的。**7less of** *spoken* used to tell someone, usually a child, to stop doing something【口】不要做…〔通常对小孩说的话〕: *Less of that noise, please!* 请不要吵! **8not ... any the less** just as much 不减少; 仍然不变; 还是那么多: *I know he's done a dreadful thing, but I don't love him any the less.* 我知道他做了件很不好的事, 但我仍然一样爱他。

less³ *prep* taking away or not counting a particular amount 减去; 不计: *What is 121 less 36?* 121 减去 36 是多少? | *He gave us our money back less the $2 service charge.* 他把钱还给我们, 但扣除了两美元服务费。

les·see /lɛˈsi; leˈsiː/ *n* [C] *law* someone who is legally allowed to use a house, building, land etc by agreement for a fixed period of time in return for payment to the owner【法律】承租人, 租户 —compare 比较 LESSOR

less·en /ˈlɛsn̩; ˈlesən/ *v* [I,T] to become smaller in size, importance, or value, or make something do this (使) 降低; (使) 减少: *Garlic is supposed to lessen the risk of heart disease.* 大蒜被认为可以降低心脏病的发病率。| *International tensions lessened after the end of the Cold War.* 冷战结束后国际紧张局势缓和了。

less·er /ˈlɛsə; ˈlesə/ *adj* [only before noun 仅用于名词前] **1** *formal* not as large, as important, or as much as something else【正式】更小的; 次要的; 更少的: *They originally asked for $5 million, but finally settled for a lesser sum.* 他们原先要求 500 万美元, 但最后同意较少的金额。| **to a lesser extent/degree** *the growing influence of Tokyo, and to a lesser extent Frankfurt, as financial centers* 作为金融中心, 东京的影响正在提高, 其次是法兰克福 —see also 另见 **lesser/ordinary/mere mortals** (MORTAL² (1)) **2the lesser of two evils** the less unpleasant or harmful of two unpleasant choices 两害之较轻者 **3lesser known** not well known or not as well known as others 比较鲜为人知的, 知名度较小的: *a lesser known French poet* 比较鲜为人知的法国诗人 **4** used in the names of some types of animal, bird, or plant that are slightly smaller than the main type〔用于鸟兽、植物的名字中, 表示比主要品种〕略小的

Les·sing /ˈlɛsɪŋ; ˈlesɪŋ/, **Dor·is** /ˈdɔrɪs; ˈdɒrɪs/ (1919-) a British writer of NOVELS and short stories, born in Rhodesia (now Zimbabwe). She wrote *The Grass Is Singing, The Golden Notebook*, and a set of five novels, *The Children of Violence*, concerning politics and feminism. 莱辛〔(1919-), 英国小说家, 著有长篇及短篇小说多种, 出生于罗得西亚 (今津巴布韦)。她的作品有《草原在歌唱》、《金色笔记》及五本一套的长篇系列小说《狂暴的孩子们》, 作品反映出她对政治及女权主义的看法〕

les·son /ˈlɛsn̩; ˈlesən/ *n* [C]

1▶LEARNING A SKILL 学习技能◀ a period of time in which someone is taught a particular skill, for example how to play a musical instrument or drive a car 课; 课程: *piano lessons* 钢琴课 | **take lessons** *She's started taking driving lessons.* 她已开始上驾驶课。| [+on/in] *lessons in social etiquette* 社交礼仪课

2▶IN SCHOOL 在学校◀ *BrE* a period of time in which students in a school are taught a particular subject【英】一堂课; CLASS¹ (3) *AmE*【美】: *What did you do last lesson?* 上一堂课你们干什么了? | *boring Maths lessons* 乏味的数学课 | [+in/on] *lessons on eight different subjects every week* 每周八个不同科目的课

3▶WARNING 警告◀ an experience, especially an unpleasant one, that makes you more careful in the future 经验; 〔尤指〕教训: *Pearl Harbor was a painful lesson for the US.* 珍珠港事件对美国是一次惨痛的教训。

4let that be a lesson to you *spoken* used to warn someone that they must be more careful in order to avoid the same bad experience happening to them again【口】引以为诫

5▶BOOK 书◀ a part of a book that is used for learning a particular subject, especially in school〔课本中的〕课: *Turn to lesson 25.* 翻到第 25 课。

6▶CHURCH 礼拜◀ a short piece that is read from the Bible during a religious ceremony〔宗教仪式中选读的《圣经》里的〕经文 —see also 另见 **learn your lesson** (LEARN (7)), **teach sb a lesson** (TEACH (6))

les·sor /ˈlɛsɔr; leˈsɔː/ *n* [C] *law* someone who allows someone else to use their house, building, land etc for a period of time for payment【法律】出租人 —compare 比较 LESSEE

lest /lɛst; lest/ *conjunction formal*【正式】**1** in order to make sure that something will not happen 免得, 以免, 唯恐: *She pulled away from the window lest anyone see them.* 她从窗口躲开了, 免得有人见到她们。**2** used to show that someone is afraid or worried that a particular thing might happen〔与表示害怕或担心的词连用〕: *The child watched them, nervous lest they hurt themselves.* 小孩看着它们, 怕它们自己伤了自己。| *He paused, afraid lest he say too much.* 他停顿下来, 唯恐说得太多。

-let /lɪt; lɪ̥t/ *suffix* [in nouns 构成名词] **1** a small kind of something 小: *a booklet* (=small paper-covered book) 小册子 | *a piglet* (=young pig) 小猪 **2** a band worn on a particular part of your body 佩戴的环形物: *an anklet* (=worn on the ankle) 脚镯

let¹ /lɛt; let/ *v past tense and past participle* **let** *present participle* **letting**

1▶ALLOW 允许◀ [T not in passive 不用被动态] **a)** to allow someone to do something 让, 允许: *I wanted to go out but my Dad wouldn't let me.* 我要出去, 但爸爸不允许。| **let sb do sth** *She won't let her children play by the river.* 她不许她的孩子在河边玩。| *Don't let your boss hear you say that.* 别让你的老板听到你那么说。| **let sb have sth** (=give something to someone) 给某人某物 *I can let you have a copy of the report.* 我可以给你一份这篇报告的副本。—see graph at 参见 PERMIT¹ 图表 —see graph at 参见 FORBID 图表 **b)** to allow something to happen 使〔某事发生〕: **let sth do sth** *Max let the door swing open.* 马克斯使门大开。| *She didn't let her anger show.* 她压住怒火。| *It'll drive you crazy if you let it.* 如果你放任它, 它会把你逼疯。—see 见 CAN (USAGE) —see graph at 参见 PERMIT¹ 图表

2let go to stop holding something 放手; 松开: *Let go! You're hurting me.* 松开手! 你把我弄痛了。| **let go of** *She wouldn't let go of the rope.* 她不会松开绳子的。

3let sb go a) to allow a person or animal to leave a place where they have been kept 放掉某人, 放走某人: *They said they wouldn't let her go until her family paid the ransom.* 他们说她家付赎金后才会放她走。**b)** a phrase meaning to dismiss someone from their job, used to avoid saying this directly 解雇某人〔委婉说法〕: *I'm afraid we're going to have to let you go.* 恐怕我们得让你走人了。

4let yourself go a) to allow yourself to relax completely in a social situation, and not worry about what other people think 放松自己; 放纵自己 **b)** to take less care of your appearance than usual 不修边幅, 不注意外表: *She's really let herself go since her husband died.* 自从她丈夫死后, 她就很不注意打扮了。

5let sth go for £2/$150 etc *informal* to sell something for a low price【非正式】以 2 英镑/150 美元等贱卖

6let sb know to tell someone something 让某人知道, 告诉某人: *I'd appreciate it if you'd let me know as soon as possible.* 如蒙尽快赐告, 本人不胜感激。| **let sb know if/whether** *Let us know if you need any more information.* 如果你需要更多的信息, 请告诉我们。

7let alone used to say that because one thing does not happen or is not true etc, another thing cannot possibly happen or be true 更不用说, 更谈不上: *The baby can't even crawl yet, let alone walk!* 这孩子连爬都不会, 更不用说走了!

8 ►WISH 愿望◄ *literary* used to express a wish that something will happen or will not happen【文】让〔用来表达愿望〕: **(not) let sb/sth do sth** *Don't let him be the one who died, she prayed.* 但愿死的不是他，她祈求说。| **let there be** *Let there be roses and sparkling champagne.* 要是有玫瑰和起泡沫的香槟酒该多好。

9 let yourself be bullied/imposed on etc to allow other people to treat you badly 容忍被别人欺负/被强加于〔某事〕等: *Don't let yourself be pushed around.* 别让人摆布你。

10 never let a day/week go by without... to do something every day or every week 每天/每周都〔做某事〕: *I never let a day go by without phoning my mother.* 我没有一天不给妈妈打电话。

11 ►ROOM/BUILDING 房间/大楼◄ [T] to allow someone to use a room or building in return for money every week or month; LEASE[2] (1) 出租: *Interhome has over 20,000 houses to let across Europe.* 英特霍姆地产公司在全欧洲有两万多幢房屋出租。| **let sth to sb** *I've let my spare room to a Japanese student.* 我把空余的房间租给了一个日本学生。| **To Let** *BrE*【英】/**For Let** *AmE*【美】(=words on a sign outside a building to show that it is empty and can be rented)〔空屋〕出[招]租 —compare 比较 HIRE[1] (1), RENT[1] (3)

12 ►IMAGINE 想象◄ *formal*【正式】**a) let us suppose/say/imagine** used to ask a reader or listener to imagine that something is true, as a way of helping them understand what you are talking about 假设/假如说/设想: *Let us suppose that interest rates go up again. What effect will this have on the property market?* 假设利率再次上升，这对房地产市场会有什么影响? **b) let sth be/equal/represent** used in mathematics or science to mean that one thing can be imagined as representing another 假设某物为/等于/代表: *Let angle A be 45°.* 设角 A 为 45°。

13 let sb alone also 又作 **let sb be** to stop annoying someone, or asking them things 不打扰某人: *Your mother's tired – let her alone!* 你妈妈累了 —— 别打扰她!

14 let sth drop/rest to stop discussing something or trying to deal with something that has been annoying you or worrying you 停止谈论某事; 别去管某事: *He's apologized, so I think you should let it drop now.* 他已经道歉，所以我想你现在应该不要再提这件事情。

15 let sth go/pass to decide not to react to something bad or annoying that someone has done or said 对某事不计较: *I know you didn't mean to offend her, so we'll let it pass this time.* 我知道你不是有意伤害她，所以这次我们对此事就不计较了。

16 let sth ride a) if you let a situation ride, you let it continue for a time before deciding whether to take any action〔作决定前〕放任某情况持续一段时间 **b)** if you let a remark that has annoyed you ride, you do not say anything about it 对恼人的话不理睬

17 let drop/fall to say a piece of information as though by accident, although really you want someone to know about it 似不经意地脱口而出: *She decided that she would casually let drop the news about having the baby.* 她决定似不经意地把怀了孩子的事说出来。

18 let slip to accidentally say a piece of information that you did not want someone to know 走漏〔秘密〕

19 let yourself in for *informal* to do something that will cause you a lot of trouble【非正式】给自己招来〔麻烦〕: *I don't think Carol realizes what she's letting herself in for.* 我认为卡萝尔并没有意识到她在给自己招来什么麻烦。

20 let sb have it *informal*【非正式】**a)** to shout at someone because you are angry with them 大声训斥某人: *Mrs Bates really let him have it for leaving the classroom early.* 由于他早早地离开了教室，贝茨女士大声训斥他。**b)** to hit or shoot someone 打击某人; 向某人射击 —see also 另见 **let fly** (FLY[1] (20)), **let your hair down** (HAIR (5)), **let it all hang out** (HANG[1]), **live and let live** (LIVE[1] (28)), **let sth rip** (RIP[1] (5))

Frequencies of the verb **let** in spoken and written English
动词 let 在英语口语和书面语中的使用频率

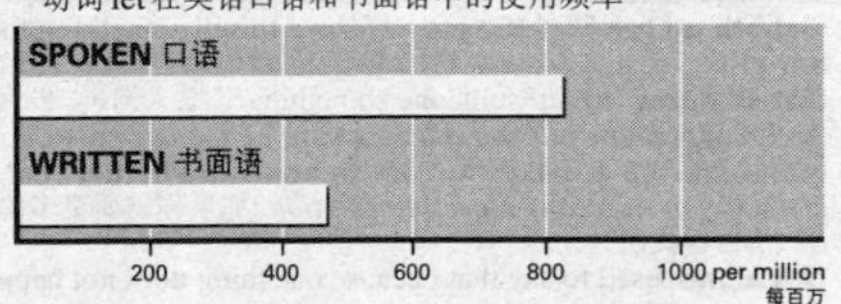

Based on the British National Corpus and the Longman Lancaster Corpus
据英国国家语料库和朗文兰开斯特语料库

This graph shows that the verb **let** is much more common in spoken English than in written English. This is because it is more commonly used in spoken English than **allow**, which is more formal and is more common in written English. **Let** is also used in a lot of common spoken phrases. 本图表显示，动词 let 在英语口语中的使用频率远远高于书面语，因为它在英语口语中比 allow 使用得更加普遍，而 allow 较为正式，在书面语中使用得较普遍。let 也用于许多常用口语短语中。

let (*v*) **SPOKEN PHRASES**
含 let 的口语短语

21 let's used to suggest to someone that you and they should do something together 让我们〔一起〕; 咱们，大家: *Come on, let's dance!* 来吧，让我们一起跳舞! | *Right, let's get these plates washed.* 对，让我们把这些盘子洗了吧。| *Let's move on to the report itself: any comments?* 让我们继续来看报告本身，有意见吗? | **let's not** *Let's not talk about work now.* 咱们现在别谈工作。| **don't let's** *BrE*【英】*Don't let's quarrel.* 大家不要吵了! —see 见 PROPOSE (USAGE)

22 let's see a) used to say that you are going to try to do something 让我们试试看: **let's see if/whether** *Let's see if I can get the car to start.* 让我试试看我能否把车起动。**b)** used when pausing to remember something or find a piece of information 让我们想一下，让我们找一找: *Now, let's see...here it is: "Video recorder, good condition, £75".* 好吧，咱们瞧一瞧…在这里:"录像机，性能良好，75英镑。" | *Let's see, oh, I wanted to ask what you are doing next Wednesday.* 让我想一下，哦，我想问下星期三你打算干什么。**c)** used to ask someone to show you something 让我们看一下: *"Come on, let's see." "No, it's a secret!"* "得了吧，让我们看一下。""不，这是秘密!" | *Let's see your new dress.* 让我们看一下你的新衣服。| *Right, let's see what you can do with that guitar!* 对，让我们瞧瞧你能用那吉他演奏些什么曲子!

23 let me see/think used when pausing to think of some information or think what to do next 让我想一想: *You sent it to, um, let me see, ... Mike Toghill.* 你把它寄给，嗯，让我想一想，…迈克·托格希尔。

24 let me do sth a) used to politely offer to do something for someone 让我〔为你〕做某事: *Here, let me help you with those bags.* 喂，让我帮你拿那些袋子。**b)** used to tell someone what you are going to do next 让我做某事，我要做某事: *Let me just take your blood pressure.* 我要量一下你的血压。| *Let me finish this typing then I'll make us some coffee.* 让我打完这些字，然后给大家煮些咖啡。

25 let's say used to ask someone to imagine something in order to discuss it or understand it better 譬如说: *OK, you buy an object – let's say a bicycle – for $100. How much interest would you have to pay?* 好吧，你买一样东西 —— 譬如说是一辆自行车 —— 要 100 美元。你需要付多少利息? | **let's say (that)** *Let's say you did fail your exams, you could retake them, couldn't you?* 假如说你的确没有通过考试，你可以再考一次，不是吗?

26 let's just say used to say that you are not going to tell someone all the details about something 知道…就够了〔用于不打算告诉某人所有细节时〕: *"So who did it?" "Let's just say it wasn't anyone in this family."* "那么是谁干的呢?" "知道不是这个家庭里的人就够了。"

27 let him/them etc a) used to say that you do not care whether someone does something or not 随他/他们等去: *Let her tell everyone, then – I don't care.* 那么让她去告诉大家好了 —— 我不在乎。| *Well, if he wants to go and kill himself, let him!* 哦，如果他要去自杀，那就让他去好了! **b)** used to say that someone else should do something instead of you 让他/他们等去〔做某事〕: *Let them clear up the mess, it's their fault.* 让他们去打扫这乱糟糟的东西，这是他们的过失。

28 let's hope used to say that you hope something will happen, so that there will not be problems 我们希望〔某事会发生〕: *Let's just hope he got your letter in time.* 我们只希望他及时收到你的信。

29 let's face it/let's be honest used to say that you must accept an unpleasant fact 我们认了吧: *Let's face it, Ben, no one's going to lend us any more money.* 我们认了吧，本，没有人会再借钱给我们了。

30 let well (enough) alone to not try to change a situation, because you may make it worse 维持现状; 不画蛇添足: *He's happier now – I'd let well enough alone if I were you.* 他现在比过去开心 —— 我要是你，我不会去改变目前的状况。

31 let me tell you! used to emphasize that a feeling you had was very strong 告诉你吧!: *I was pretty surprised, let me tell you!* 我感到很吃惊,告诉你吧!
32 I'll/we'll let it go at that used to tell someone that you will not punish or criticize them any more for something bad they have done 我/我们不再惩罚[批评]〔某人〕: *Well you've missed your favorite program so we'll let it go at that.* 算了,你已经错失了你所喜爱的节目,所以我们就不再批评你了。

let sb/sth ↔ **down** *phr v* [T] **1** to make someone feel disappointed because you have not behaved well or not done what you said you would do 让〔某人〕失望,失信于〔某人〕: *I'm counting on you to support me – don't let me down!* 我指望你支持我呢 — 别让我失望! | **let sb down badly** *She felt badly let down by her friends.* 她觉得她的朋友们太让她失望了。**2 a)** to give something to someone who is in a lower place than you are 把〔某物〕放下来: *Let down a rope so that I can climb up.* 把绳子放下来,我好爬上去。**b)** to move something that is on a string, rope etc downwards 把〔系在绳子等上的某物〕向下放: *Let the basket down gently.* 把篮子轻轻地往下放。**3 let your hair down** *informal* to relax and enjoy yourself, especially after working hard【非正式】〔尤指辛劳后〕使某人放松: *The Christmas party gives everyone a chance to let their hair down.* 圣诞晚会给了大家轻松一下的机会。**4** *BrE* to allow the air to escape from something so that it loses its shape and firmness【英】使〔某物中的气〕跑掉: *Someone's let my tyres down!* 有人把我轮胎的气放掉了! **5 let the side down** *BrE informal* to cause embarrassment or disappointment to your friends, family, team etc, for example by not behaving as they expect you to behave【英,非正式】让〔亲友、团队等〕丢脸;辜负了〔亲友、团队等〕**6 let sb down lightly** to give someone bad news in a way that will not upset them too much 委婉地把坏消息告知某人 **7** to make a piece of clothing longer 使〔衣服〕加长: *I'm going to let down this old dress for my daughter.* 我打算把这件旧衣服加长,让女儿穿。

let sb/sth ↔ **in** *phr v* [T] **1** to open the door of a room, building etc so that someone can come in 让〔某人〕进来: *I unlocked the door and let him in.* 我开门让他进来。| *My mother let herself in.* 我妈自己进来了。**2** to allow light, water, air etc to enter a place 让〔光线、水、空气等〕进入: *The windows don't let in much light.* 这些窗户采光不足。**3 let sb in on** to tell someone about a secret plan, idea etc, and trust them not to tell other people 让某人知道并让其严守〔秘密计划、想法等〕

let sb/sth **into** sth *phr v* [T] **1** to allow someone to come into a room or building 让〔某人〕进入: *Who let you into my office?* 谁让你进我的办公室? **2 let sb into a secret** to tell someone something secret or private 告诉某人秘密 **3 be let into** *technical* if something such as a window or a decoration is let into a wall, brick etc, it is placed so that it is level with the surface it is in【术语】镶入,嵌入

let sb/sth **off** *phr v* [T] **1** to not make someone do a piece of work which they should be doing 免除〔某人应做之事〕: *Since you practiced the piano yesterday, I'll let you off today.* 既然你昨天练习了钢琴,今天我就让你免了。| **let sb off sth** *She let her son off his chores.* 她免了她儿子的家务。**2** to not punish someone 免处罚〔某人〕: *I'll let you off this time, but don't do it again.* 这次我就饶了你,但是不要再这么做了。| **let sb off with sth** *The judge let two of the three prisoners off with only a reprimand.* 法官对三名犯人中的两名只训斥了一顿,免于处罚。| **let sb off lightly** (=give someone a less serious punishment than they deserve) 轻罚某人 **3 a)** to fire a gun 开〔枪〕**b)** to make a bomb or FIREWORK explode 引爆〔炸弹〕;放〔烟火〕—see also 另见 **let/get sb off the hook** (HOOK[1] (4)), **let off steam** (STEAM[1] (4))

let on *phr v* [I,T] *informal* to tell someone something that was meant to be a secret【非正式】泄露,透露(秘密): *I think he knows more about it than he's letting on.* 我认为关于此事,他知道的比他透露给我们的要多。| **let on (that)** *Don't let on that I told you.* 不要告诉别人是我对你说的。| **let on who/why/how etc** *You mustn't let on who gave it to us.* 你千万别说出去谁把它给我们的。

let out *phr v* **1** [T **let** sb ↔ **out**] to allow someone to leave a room, building etc 放…出去;释放: *Let the dog out, will you?* 让狗出去,行吗? | *He was in a high-security jail and would probably never be let out.* 他关在戒备森严的监狱里,可能永远也不会被释放出来。| **let sb out of sth** *Quietly, I let myself out of her apartment.* 我悄悄走出了她的公寓。**2** [T **let** sth ↔ **out**] to allow light, water, air etc to leave a place 让〔光线、水、空气等〕跑掉: *Close the door, you're letting all the heat out.* 关上门,你把暖气都放跑了。**3 let out a scream/cry/roar etc** to make a sound, especially a loud sound 发出尖叫声/叫喊声/吼叫声等: *She let out a sudden scream.* 她突然尖叫起来。**4** [T **let** sth ↔ **out**] to make a piece of clothing wider or looser, especially because the person it belongs to has become fatter 加宽,加大〔衣服〕**5** [T **let** sth ↔ **out**] *especially BrE* to allow someone to use a room, building etc in exchange for money【尤英】出租〔房间、大楼等〕—see 见 HIRE[1] (USAGE) **6** [I] *AmE* if a school, film etc lets out, it ends, so that the people attending it can leave【美】放学;散场: *What time does the play let out?* 戏什么时候散场? —see also 另见 **let the cat out of the bag** (CAT (2))

let up *phr v* [I] **1** if something, such as bad weather or an unpleasant situation, lets up, it stops or becomes less serious 停止,结束;缓和: *When do you think this rain will let up?* 你认为这场雨什么时候会停? **2 not let up** if someone does something without letting up, they do it continuously, especially in an annoying way〔尤指恼人地〕不停〔做某事〕: *I wish you'd stop nagging! You just never let up, do you?* 我希望你停止唠叨!你就是没完没了,是不是?

let² *n* **1** [C] *BrE*【英】**a)** a period during which a house or flat is rented to someone; RENT[1] (1)〔房屋或公寓的〕出租期: *a long let* 长期出租 **b)** a house or flat that can be rented 出租的房屋[公寓] **2 without let or hindrance** *law* happening freely without being prevented in any way【法律】毫无障碍地

letch /lɛtʃ; letʃ/ another spelling of LECH lech 的另一种拼法

let·down /ˈlɛtˌdaʊn; ˈletdaʊn/ *n* [singular] *informal* an event, performance etc that is not as good as you expected it to be; disappointment【非正式】失望;令人失望的事: *The ending of the book was a real letdown.* 这本书的结尾确实是败笔。—see also 另见 **let down** (LET[1])

le·thal /ˈliθəl; ˈliːθəl/ *adj* **1** causing death, or having the power to cause death 致命的,致死的;具杀伤力的: *a lethal dose of a drug* 药品的致死剂量 **2** *often humorous* likely to be dangerous or dangerously effective【常幽默】危险的,危害的: *That cocktail looks pretty lethal.* 那鸡尾酒看起来相当浓烈。**3 a lethal combination** a very bad or dangerous combination of two or more things 恶劣[危险]的组合: *Alcohol and tranquillizers are a lethal combination.* 烈性酒和镇静剂搭配在一起极为危险。

le·thar·gic /lɪˈθɑrdʒɪk; lɪ̍ˈθɑːdʒɪk/ *adj* feeling as if you have no energy and no interest in doing anything 无精打采的,懒洋洋的: *The hot weather was making us all lethargic.* 炎热的天气使我们昏昏欲睡。—**lethargically** /-klɪ; -kli/ *adv*

leth·ar·gy /ˈlɛθɚdʒɪ; ˈleθədʒi/ *n* [U] the feeling of being lethargic 无精打采,懒洋洋: *New mothers often complain of tiredness, lethargy and mild depression.* 刚当上妈妈的人经常诉说疲倦、乏力和轻微的抑郁。

Le·the /ˈliθɪ; ˈliːθi/ in ancient Greek MYTHOLOGY, a river in Hades (=the place under the ground where the spirits of dead people are supposed to live). When people who have died drink its water, they forget everything that happened when they were alive. 忘川,忘河〔古希腊神话中冥府中的一条河,死去的人喝了忘川水之后,就会忘却生前的一切〕

let's /lɛts; lets/ the short form of 缩略式= 'let us': *C'mon, let's go!* 来吧,我们一起走吧! —see 见 PROPOSE (USAGE)

let·ter¹ /ˈlɛtɚ; ˈletə/ *n* [C] **1** a written or printed message that is usually put in an envelope and sent by mail 信,书信: *Bart's writing a letter to his parents.* 巴特正在给他父母写信。| *I got a long letter from Melanie today.* 今天我收到梅拉妮的一封长信。| **mail a letter** *AmE*【美】*Can you mail this letter for me on your way out?* 你在出去时能顺道替我寄这封信吗? | **post a letter** *BrE*【英】*I'm just going to post a letter.* 我正要去寄信。**2** any of the signs in writing or printing that represent a speech sound 字母: *'B' is a capital letter, 'b' is a small letter.* B是大写字母,b是小写字母。**3 do sth to the letter** to pay exact attention to the details of an agreement, rule, set of instructions etc 严格按照字面意思做某事;不折不扣做某事: *He kept his promise to the letter.* 他不折不扣地遵守诺言。| *I followed all the instructions to the letter, but it still wouldn't work.* 我严格地执行所有指令,但仍行不通。**4 the letter of the law** the exact words of a law or agreement rather than the intended or general meaning〔法律或协议的〕字面含义: *various methods of avoiding taxes while adhering to the letter of the law* 既按法律字面含义遵守法规、又可避免纳税的各种办法 **5** *AmE* a large cloth letter to put on to clothes, given as a reward for playing in a school or college sports team【美】校队队衣上的大写字母〔作为对优秀运动员的奖励〕: *She got her letter in track.* 在赛跑中她获得了校队字母的奖励。**6 English/American/German letters** [plural] *formal* the study of the literature of a particular country or language【正式】英国/美国/德国文学[语言]: *a major figure in English letters at the turn of the century* 世纪交替时期的一位英国文学

大师 —see also 另见 CHAIN LETTER, DEAD LETTER, DEAR JOHN LETTER, LETTER OF CREDIT, MAN OF LETTERS, OPEN LETTER

letter[2] *v* [I] *AmE* to earn a LETTER[1] (5) in a sport【美】赢得运动项目的校队字母奖励: [**+in**] *He lettered in basketball at Brandeis.* 他在布兰迪斯举行的篮球赛中获得校名首字母奖励荣誉。

letter[3] *adj AmE* LETTER-SIZE【美】信纸尺寸的

letter bomb /ˈ‥ ˌ/ *n* [C] a small bomb hidden in a package and sent to someone in order to kill or harm them 邮件炸弹

let·ter·box /ˈlɛtɚˌbɑks; ˈletəbɒks/ *n* [C] **1** a narrow hole in a door, or a special box where letters, packages etc are delivered〔收方设的〕信箱 **2** *BrE* a box in a post office or street, in which letters can be posted【英】〔邮局设的〕邮箱, 邮筒; MAILBOX *AmE*【美】

CULTURAL NOTE 文化注释

Letterboxes are much more common in the UK than in the US, where most people have a MAILBOX instead. 指信箱时, letterbox 在英国用得更为普遍; 而在美国, 大多数人用 mailbox。— see Cultural Note at MAILBOX 见 MAILBOX 文化注释

let·tered /ˈlɛtɚd; ˈletəd/ *adj formal*【正式】**1** well educated 有学问的 **2 badly lettered/carefully lettered** with badly drawn, beautifully drawn etc letters or words 字写得差的/字写得工整的: *a brightly lettered sign on the boy's door* 男孩门上写有亮闪闪字迹的牌子

let·ter·head /ˈlɛtɚˌhɛd; ˈletəhed/ *n* [C] the name and address printed at the top of a sheet of writing paper 信笺抬头, 信头〔印于信笺上端的名称和地址〕

let·ter·ing /ˈlɛtərɪŋ; ˈletərɪŋ/ *n* [U] **1** written or drawn letters, especially of a particular type, size, colour etc 字体: *a yellow board with black lettering* 上有黑字的黄色牌子 **2** the art of writing or drawing letters or words 字母图案绘制术; 印字; 刻字; 烫印

letter of cred·it /ˌ‥ ˈ‥ ˌ/ *n* [C] an official letter from a bank allowing a particular person to take money from another bank〔银行开出的〕信用证

letter-per·fect /ˌ‥ ˈ‥◂/ *adj AmE* correct in every detail【美】正确无误的, 一字不差的: *The District Attorney's case was letter-perfect.* 地方检察官的案情陈述完全正确。

letter-qual·i·ty /ˈ‥ ˌ‥/ *adj* a letter-quality PRINTER (1) produces print that is good enough to be used for business letters, reports etc 打印质量佳的

letter-size /ˈ‥ ˌ/ also 又作 **letter** *adj AmE* paper that is letter-size is $8^1/_2$ inches (INCH[1] (1)) wide and 11 inches long【美】信纸大小的〔宽 $8^1/_2$ 英寸, 长 11 英寸〕

let·ting /ˈlɛtɪŋ; ˈletɪŋ/ *n* [C] *BrE* a house or apartment that can be rented【英】可租用的房屋[公寓]: *a holiday letting* 假日出租公寓

let·tuce /ˈlɛtɪs; ˈletɪs/ *n* [C,U] a round vegetable with thin green leaves used in SALADS 生菜, 莴苣 —see picture on page A9 参见 A9 页图

let·up /ˈlɛtˌʌp; ˈletʌp/ *n* [singular, U] a pause or a reduction in a difficult, dangerous, or tiring activity 中止, 暂停; 减弱: *There is no sign of a letup in the fighting.* 战斗无停息的迹象。| *We were working seven days a week with no letup.* 我们一星期连续不停地工作了七天。—see also 另见 **let up** (LET[1])

leu·co·cyte /ˈljukəˌsaɪt; ˈluːkəsaɪt/ *n* [C] *technical* another spelling of LEUKOCYTE【术语】leukocyte 的另一种拼法

leu·cot·o·my /luˈkɑtəmɪ; luːˈkɒtəmi/ *n* [C] *BrE* a LOBOTOMY【英】叶切断(术), 脑白质切断(术)

leu·ke·mi·a also 又作 **leukaemia** *BrE*【英】/ljuˈkimɪə; luːˈkiːmiə/ *n* [U] a type of CANCER in which the blood contains too many WHITE BLOOD CELLS, causing weakness and sometimes death 白血病

leu·ko·cyte /ˈljukəˌsaɪt; ˈluːkəsaɪt/ *n* [C] *technical* one of the cells in your blood which fights against infection; WHITE BLOOD CELL【术语】白血球, 白细胞

Le·vant, the /ləˈvænt; ləˈvænt/ an old name for the area of land at the eastern end of the Mediterranean Sea, including Syria, Palestine, Lebanon, Israel, and parts of Turkey 黎凡特〔地中海东岸地区旧称, 包括叙利亚、巴勒斯坦、黎巴嫩、以色列和土耳其部分地区〕 —**Levantine** /ˈlɛvəntaɪn; ˈlevəntain/ *n, adj*

lev·ee[1] /ˈlɛvɪ; ˈlevi/ *n* [C] a special wall built to stop a river flooding (防洪)堤, 堤岸

lev·ee[2] /ˈlɛvɪ; ˈlevi/ *n* [C] *old use* a meeting in which a king receives visits from important people【旧】〔国王的〕召见, 接见

lev·el[1] /ˈlɛvl̩; ˈlevəl/ *n* [C]

1 ▶AMOUNT 数量◀ a) the measured amount of something that exists at a particular time or in a particular place〔测得的〕数量, 数值: *Inflation had dropped to its lowest level in 30 years.* 通货膨胀降到了 30 年来的最低值。| [**+of**] *concern about the level of carbon monoxide in the air* 对空气中一氧化碳的含量的关注 | **high/low levels** *High levels of radiation were found in the sea.* 在海洋中探测到高能级辐射。**b)** the amount of a quality that someone has or that exists in a situation 水平, 水准, 程度: *a very high level of commitment among the workforce* 工人们的极度投入 | *These simple exercises can dramatically reduce stress levels.* 这些简单的运动能迅速减轻紧张的程度。

2 ▶HEIGHT 高度◀ the height of something in relation to the ground or to another object 水平高度; 相对高度: *Hold out your arm at the same level as your shoulder.* 伸出你的手臂与肩同高。| **at eye level** (=at the same height as your eyes) 与眼睛相同高度

3 ▶LIQUID 液体◀ the height of the surface of a liquid from the ground or from the bottom of a container 液体的高度: *Check the water level in the car radiator.* 检查一下汽车散热器内水的高度。—see also 另见 SEA LEVEL, WATER LEVEL

4 ▶STANDARD 标准◀ a particular standard of skill or ability, for example in education or sport 标准, 水平, 水准, 级别: *Students at this level tend to have a lot of problems with grammar.* 这一水平的学生在语法上会有很多问题。| *By 21, she was regularly playing at international level.* 她 21 岁就经常在国际级的比赛中演奏。| *an advanced level coursebook* 高级程度课本

5 ▶FLOOR/GROUND 地板/地面◀ a floor or piece of ground, especially when considered in relation to another floor or piece of ground that is higher or lower〔高低不同的〕楼层, 地层, 层面: *The town is built on different levels.* 这个城镇建在高低不同的地面上。| *The medical center should be on one level for the convenience of patients.* 为了方便病人, 医疗中心应该设在同一层楼上。

6 ▶RANK OF JOB 工作的级别◀ all the people or jobs within an organization, industry etc that have similar amounts of importance and responsibility 等级, 级别: *Training was offered at each level in the department.* 部门内各级人员都要进行培训。| *Decisions like this can only be made at board level.* 这种决定只能由董事会作出。

7 at local level/at national level happening within a small area or the whole area of a country 地方级的/国家级的: *Decisions are made at local and not national level.* 决定是由地方而不是由国家作出的。

8 on/at one level ... on/at another level used when you are considering something in one way and then in another way 一方面…另一方面: *At one level I really enjoy the work, but at another level I feel I should be doing something more challenging.* 一方面我确实喜欢这工作, 但是另一方面我感到应该做些更具挑战性的事。

9 on a practical level/on a personal level etc used to talk about something, considering it in a practical, personal etc way 从实际的角度/从个人的角度等: *On a more practical level, we should consider how we are going to find the money.* 从比较实际的角度, 我们应该考虑怎样找到这笔钱。

10 be on the level *informal* to be honest【非正式】老实的, 诚实的, 真诚的: *I'd like to buy that bloke's car, but I'm not sure he's on the level.* 我想买那个家伙的车子, 但我不知道他是否诚实。

11 ▶TOOL 工具◀ *especially AmE* a tool used for checking that a surface is flat; SPIRIT-LEVEL【尤美】水准仪, 水准器

level[2] *adj* **1** a surface, piece of land etc that is level is flat and does not slope in any direction 平的, 平坦的, 水平的: *Make sure the ground is completely level before you lay the turf.* 铺草皮前要确定地面完全平整。**2 be level a)** two things that are level are at the same height as each other 同等高度: [**+with**] *The top of the tree was level with the roof of the house.* 树顶和屋顶一样高。**b)** *BrE* two sports teams, competitors etc that are level have the same number of points【英】同等比分: **draw level** (=get enough points to be level) 拉平比分 *Faldo has drawn level with Ballesteros on twelve under par.* 福尔多拉平了与巴列斯特罗斯的比分, 都负 12 杆。| **finish level** *The two teams finished level, with 10 points each.* 两队终局比分拉平, 各得 10 分。—see also 另见 LEVEL-PEGGING **3 do your level best** to try as hard as possible to do something 尽力〔去做某事〕: *I'll do my level best to help you.* 我会尽力帮助你。**4 a level voice/look/gaze** a steady voice, look etc, that shows you are calm or determined 平静[坚定]的声音/神色/目光 **5 level spoon(ful)/cup** an amount of a substance, that is just enough to fill a spoon or cup, used as a measure in cooking 一平匙/杯(之量)

level[3] *v* **levelled, levelling** *BrE*【英】, **leveled, leveling** *AmE*【美】[T] **1** to make something flat and even 使平坦, 使平整; 把…弄平: *Pat levelled the wet concrete with a piece of wood.*

帕特用一块木片抹平湿混凝土。**2** to knock down or destroy a building or area completely 推倒，夷平: *The bombing raid levelled a large part of the town.* 空袭把这城镇的一大部分地区夷为了平地。**3 level the score** *BrE* to make the score in a game or competition equal【英】使比分拉平，使比分相同

level sth **at** *phr v* [T] **1** to aim something such as a weapon at someone or something 用〔某物〕瞄准，对准 **2 level a charge/accusation/criticism at** to publicly criticize someone or say they are responsible for a crime, mistake etc 将指控/指责/批评针对〔某人〕: *Outrageous accusations were levelled against some of Hollywood's most famous stars.* 粗暴的指责是针对好莱坞某些著名的影星。

level off/out *phr v* **1** [I] to stop climbing or falling, and continue at a fixed height 作水平飞行，平飞: *After climbing steeply through woodland the path levelled off.* 小路穿过陡峭的林地后变得平坦。| *The plane levelled out at 30,000 feet.* 飞机在3万英尺的高空作水平飞行。**2** [I] to become steady in development or growth 变得平稳: *Inflation has begun to level off.* 通胀开始趋于平稳。**3** [T **level** sth ↔ **off/out**] to make something flat and smooth 使〔某物〕平坦[平整]

level with sb *phr v* [T] *informal* to speak honestly to someone, not hiding any unpleasant facts from them【非正式】直言相告: *He asked Ron to level with him about what people were saying about him.* 他要求罗恩直言不讳地告诉他人们对他的议论。—see also 另见 **be on the level** (LEVEL[1] (10))

level cross·ing /ˌ·· ˈ··/ *n* [C] *BrE* a place where a road and railway cross each other, usually protected by gates【英】〔公路与铁路的〕平面交叉点，平交道口

level-head·ed /ˌ·· ˈ··◂/ *adj* calm and sensible in making judgments or decisions 头脑清醒的; 稳健的

lev·el·ler *BrE*【英】, **leveler** *AmE*【美】/ˈlɛvl̩ɚ; ˈlevələ/ *n* [C] something, especially death or illness, that makes people of all classes and ranks seem equal 使人平等的事物〔尤指死亡或疾病〕

Lev·el·lers, the /ˈlɛvl̩ɚz; ˈlevələz/ a religious and political group in England in the 17th century, which began during the English Civil War, and demanded equal political rights and freedom of religion for everyone 平均派〔英格兰17世纪一政治和宗教组织，创立于英格兰内战时期。该组织要求人人享有平等的政治权利和宗教信仰自由〕

level-peg·ging /ˌ·· ˈ··/ *n* **be level-pegging** *BrE* if competitors in a race, election etc are level-pegging, they are equal and it is difficult to know who will win【英】势均力敌，不分高低

level play·ing-field /ˌ·· ˈ··, ·/ *n* [singular] a situation in which different companies, countries etc can all compete fairly with each other because no one has special advantages 公平的竞争基础: *It's not really a level playing-field when one country is subsidizing its car industry with massive government grants.* 当一国给予其汽车工业大量的政府补贴，这就不是一个真正的公平竞争。

le·ver[1] /ˈlɛvɚ; ˈliːvə/ *n* [C] **1** a long thin piece of metal that you use to lift something heavy by putting one end under the object and pushing the other end down 杠杆 **2** a stick or handle fixed to a machine, that you move to make the machine work〔机器的〕操纵杆，控制杆 —see also 另见 GEAR LEVER **3** something you use to influence a situation to get the result that you want〔影响局势的〕方法，手段

lever[2] *v* [T] **1** to move something with a lever〔用杠杆〕撬动: **lever sth off/up/out etc** *Marc grunted as he levered the stone into place.* 马克一边嘟哝一边用杠杆把石头撬正。**2** to make someone leave a particular job, situation etc 挤走〔某人〕: [+**out**] *They're trying to lever him out of his job as CEO.* 他们正试图把他从首席执行官的职位上挤走。

le·ver·age[1] /ˈlɛvərɪdʒ; ˈliːvərɪdʒ/ *n* [U] **1** influence that you can use to make people do what you want 影响力: *Diplomatic leverage by the US persuaded several governments to cooperate.* 美国施加外交影响说服一些国家进行合作。**2** the action, power, or use of a lever 杠杆作用，杠杆力量

leverage[2] *v* [T] *AmE technical* to make money available, using a particular method【美，术语】举债经营，借贷经营: *using public funds to leverage private investment* 借用公共基金经营私人投资

lev·e·ret /ˈlɛvərɪt; ˈlevərɪt/ *n* [C] a young HARE[1] (1) 小野兔

le·vi·a·than /lɪˈvaɪəθən; lɪˈvaɪəθən/ *n* [C] **1** something very large and strong 庞然大物: *a leviathan of a ship* 庞大的巨轮 **2** a very large and frightening sea animal 海中巨兽

Le·vis /ˈlivaɪz; ˈliːvaɪz/ *trademark* a popular and fashionable type of JEANS【商标】李维斯牛仔裤: *a pair of Levis* 一条李维斯牛仔裤

lev·i·tate /ˈlɛvəˌtet; ˈlevɪteɪt/ *v* [I] to rise and float in the air by magic〔靠魔力〕浮在空中，飘浮 —**levitation** /ˌlɛvəˈteʃən; ˌlevɪˈteɪʃən/ *n* [U]

lev·i·ty /ˈlɛvətɪ; ˈlevɪti/ *n* [U] *formal* lack of respect or seriousness when you are dealing with something serious【正式】轻浮，轻率

lev·y[1] /ˈlɛvɪ; ˈlevi/ *v* [T] **levy a tax/charge etc** to officially make someone pay a tax etc 征税/征费等: [+**on**] *A new tax has just been levied on all electrical goods.* 一种新税已刚开始对所有电器商品进行征收。

levy[2] *n* [C] an additional sum of money, usually paid as a tax 征收额; 税款

lewd /lud; luːd/ *adj* using rude words or movements that make you think of sex 好色的，下流的，淫荡的: *lewd comments* 下流的评论 —**lewdly** *adv* —**lewdness** *n* [U]

Lew·is, C. S. (1898-1963) a British writer and university teacher. He wrote literary and religious works but is famous for his children's stories *The Chronicles of Narnia*, which include the well-known NOVEL *The Lion, the Witch and the Wardrobe.* 刘易斯〔（1898-1963），英国作家、大学教师。他曾创作文学和宗教作品，但以儿童故事集《纳尼亚传奇》而闻名，其中包括广受欢迎的小说《狮子、女巫和魔衣橱》〕

Lewis /ˈluɪs; ˈluːɪs/**, Meriwether** —see 见 LEWIS AND CLARK

Lewis, Sinclair /ˈsɪŋklɛr; ˈsɪŋkleə/ (1885-1951) a US writer of NOVELs, including *Main Street*, *Babbitt*, and *Elmer Gantry*, in which he makes fun of life in small US towns. He won the Nobel Prize for Literature in 1930. 刘易斯〔（1885-1951），美国小说家。其作品包括《大街》、《巴比特》和《埃尔默·甘特利》，讽刺美国的小镇生活。1930年获诺贝尔文学奖〕

Lewis and Clark /ˌ·· · ˈ·/ two EXPLORERs, **Meriwether Lewis** (1774-1809) and **William Clark** (1770-1838), who travelled across North America from 1804 to 1806, going up the Missouri River and over the Rocky Mountains to the Pacific coast. They drew maps and gathered information about the Native American people who lived there. 刘易斯与克拉克〔即梅里韦瑟·刘易斯（1774-1809）与威廉·克拉克（1770-1838）两位探险家。1804年至1806年，他们沿密苏里河而上，翻越落基山脉后抵达太平洋沿岸，旅程横贯北美。他们沿途绘制地图，并收集了有关当地美洲土著居民的信息〕

lex·i·cal /ˈlɛksɪkl̩; ˈleksɪkəl/ *adj technical* dealing with words, or related to words【术语】词汇的

lex·i·cog·ra·phy /ˌlɛksəˈkɑgrəfɪ; ˌleksɪˈkɒgrəfi/ *n* [U] the skill, practice, or profession of writing dictionaries 词典编纂学; 词典编纂; 词典编纂业 —**lexicographer** *n* [C] —**lexicographical** /ˌlɛksəkoˈgræfɪkl̩; ˌleksɪkəˈgræfɪkəl/ *adj*

lex·i·col·o·gy /ˌlɛksɪˈkɑlədʒɪ; ˌleksɪˈkɒlədʒi/ *n* [U] *technical* the study of the meaning and uses of words【术语】词汇学

lex·i·con /ˈlɛksɪkɑn; ˈleksɪkən/ *n* **1 the lexicon** *technical* all the words and phrases used in a language or that a particular person knows【术语】〔某种语言或某人知晓的〕全部词汇 **2** [C] a book containing an alphabetical list of words with their meanings 词典; 字典

Lex·ing·ton /ˈlɛksɪŋtən; ˈleksɪŋtən/ a city in north Kentucky in the US, where many THOROUGHBRED horses are produced for horse-racing 列克星敦〔美国肯塔基州北部一城市，专产供赛马用的大批纯种良马〕

lex·is /ˈlɛksəs; ˈleksɪs/ *n* [U] *technical* all the words in a language【术语】〔某种语言的〕全部词汇

Lex·us /ˈlɛksəs; ˈleksəs/ *trademark* a type of large comfortable car made by Toyota【商标】雷克萨斯，又译凌志〔丰田公司制造的一种宽敞舒适型汽车〕

ley line /ˈle ˌlaɪn; ˈleɪ laɪn/ *n* [C] an imaginary line connecting old buildings, places etc that is believed to follow an ancient track that has special power〔史前地貌的〕假想线

li·a·bil·i·ty /ˌlaɪəˈbɪlətɪ; ˌlaɪəˈbɪlɪti/ *n* **1** [U] legal responsibility for something, especially for paying money that is owed, or for damage or injury 责任，义务: [+**for**] *Tenants have legal liability for any damage they cause.* 承租人对于他们造成的任何损坏负有法律责任。**2 liabilities** *technical* the amount of debt that must be paid【术语】负债，债务 **3** [singular] someone or something that is likely to cause problems for someone 惹麻烦的人[事]: *A kid like Tom would be a liability in any classroom.* 像汤姆这样的孩子放到任何班上都是个累赘。**4 liability to sth** the amount that something is likely to be affected by a particular kind of problem, illness etc 易有〔某种〕倾向: *The patient may suffer greater liability to bacterial diseases.* 这病人可能更易患细菌性疾病。—see also 另见 LIMITED LIABILITY

li·a·ble /ˈlaɪəbl̩; ˈlaɪəbəl/ *adj* **1 be liable to do sth** to be likely to do or say something or to behave in a particular way, espe-

cially because of a fault or natural tendency 易于做某事, 倾向于…: *The car is liable to overheat on long trips.* 这辆汽车跑长途容易过热。**2** [not before noun 不用于名词前] legally responsible for the cost of something 有赔偿责任的: [+for] *Manufacturers are liable for any defects in the equipment.* 制造商对设备的任何缺陷都负有赔偿责任。**3** likely to be affected by a particular kind of problem, illness etc 易出问题的; 易得病的: [+to] *You're more liable to injury when you don't get regular exercise.* 要是你不经常锻炼, 会更易受伤。**4** *law* likely to be legally punished or forced to do something by law【法律】可能受处罚的; 可能承担法律义务的: [+to] *Anyone found trespassing is liable to a maximum fine of $100.* 任何人擅自闯入, 一经发现, 最高可被罚款 100 美元。| [+for] *All males between 18 and 60 are liable for military service.* 所有 18 岁到 60 岁的男性公民都有服兵役的义务。

li·aise /lɪˋez; liˈeɪz/ *v* [I+with] to exchange information with someone who works in another organization or department so that you can both be more effective 联络, 联系: *Part of Anne's job as a librarian is to liaise with local schools.* 作为图书馆管理员, 安妮的部分工作是联络当地的学校。

li·ai·son /ˋlɪəˌzɑn; liˈeɪzən/ *n* **1** [singular, U] the regular exchange of information between groups of people, especially at work, so that each group knows what the other is doing 联络, 联系: [+between] *close liaison between army and police* 军方和警方的密切联系 | **in liaison with** *The project has been set up in liaison with the art department.* 该项目已经与艺术部门建立了联系。**2** [C] a word meaning a sexual relationship between a man and a woman who are not married to each other, used to avoid saying this directly〔男女间的〕私通〔委婉语〕

liaison of·fi·cer /ˈ···ˌ···/ *n* [C] someone whose job is to talk to different departments or groups and to tell each of them about what the others are doing 联络官

li·ar /ˋlaɪɚ; ˈlaɪə/ *n* [C] someone who tells lies 说谎者

Lib *BrE*【英】the written abbreviation of 缩写= LIBERAL[3] —**Lib** *adj*

lib /lɪb; lɪb/ *n* —see 见 AD-LIB, WOMEN'S LIB

li·ba·tion /laɪˋbeʃən; laɪˈbeɪʃən/ *n* [C] a gift of wine to a god〔对神的〕祭酒, 奠酒

lib·ber /ˋlɪbɚ; ˈlɪbə/ *n* **women's libber** —see 见 WOMEN'S LIB

Lib Dem /ˌlɪb ˋdɛm; ˌlɪb ˈdem◂/ *n* [C] *BrE* LIBERAL DEMOCRAT【英】自由民主党 —**Lib Dem** *adj*

li·bel[1] /ˋlaɪbl; ˈlaɪbəl/ *n* [C,U] an act of writing or printing untrue statements about someone so that other people are likely to have a bad opinion of them 诽谤; 诽谤性文字: *Holt sued the newspaper for libel.* 霍尔特控告该报社诽谤。| *a libel action* (=a court case against someone for libel) 诽谤诉讼案 —compare 比较 SLANDER[1] (2)

libel[2] *v* **libelled, libelling** *BrE*【英】, **libeled, libeling** *AmE*【美】[T] to write or print a libel against someone 诽谤〔某人〕

li·bel·lous *BrE*【英】, **libelous** *AmE*【美】/ˋlaɪbələs; ˈlaɪbələs/ *adj* containing untrue written statements about someone which could make other people have a bad opinion of them 诽谤的, 中伤的: *libellous gossip* 诽谤性的流言

Lib·e·ra·ce /ˌlɪbəˋrɑtʃɪ; ˌlɪbəˈrɑːtʃi/ (1919-87) a US piano player and entertainer, who played well-known CLASSICAL piano music on stage and on his own television programme. He was known for wearing clothes that were amusing because they looked so expensive and there were so many decorations on them, and there was always a decorated CANDLE holder on his piano. 利伯拉奇〔(1919-1987), 美国钢琴演奏家、表演艺术家。他常在舞台上和自己主持的电视节目中弹奏经典钢琴曲。他因穿着华贵、装饰繁冗、滑稽可笑而尽人皆知。他弹奏的钢琴上总是摆放着一盏装饰过的烛台〕

lib·e·ral[1] /ˋlɪbərəl; ˈlɪbərəl/ *adj* **1** willing to understand and respect other people's ideas, opinions, and feelings〔对别人的想法、意见、感情〕宽宏大度的, 开明的: *Young people nowadays take a more liberal attitude towards sexuality.* 当今的年轻人对性行为采取更加开明的态度。**2** supporting or allowing gradual political and social changes〔思想〕自由的, 开放的; 支持变革的: *a more liberal policy on issues of crime and punishment* 对待犯罪及量刑问题更加开明的政策 **3** given in large amounts 丰富的, 充足的: *a liberal supply of drinks* 饮料的充足供应 **4** generous with your money 慷慨大方的 **5** not exact 不拘一格的; 不拘泥于字面的: *a liberal interpretation of the original play* 对原剧的灵活诠释 **6 liberal education** a kind of education which encourages you to develop a large range of interests and knowledge and respect for other people's opinions 通才教育

liberal[2] *n* [C] someone with liberal opinions or principles 开明人士: *a society dominated by white bourgeois liberals* 白人资产阶级开明人士主导的社会

Liberal[3] *n* [C] someone who supports or belongs to the former LIBERAL PARTY or the LIBERAL DEMOCRATS in Britain〔旧时英国的〕自由党支持者[党员]; 自由民主党支持者[党员] —**Liberal** *adj*

liberal arts /ˌ···ˈ·/ *n* [plural] the areas of learning which develop someone's ability to think and increase their general knowledge, rather than developing technical skills 文科

Liberal Dem·o·crats /ˌ···ˈ···/ *n* [plural] a British political party of the centre〔英国的〕自由民主党 —**Liberal Democrat** *adj*

lib·e·ral·is·m /ˋlɪbərəlˌɪzəm; ˈlɪbərəlɪzəm/ *n* [U] liberal opinions and principles, especially on social and political subjects 自由主义

lib·e·ral·i·ty /ˌlɪbəˋrælətɪ; ˌlɪbəˈræləti/ *n* [U] *formal*【正式】**1** understanding of, and respect for, other people's opinions 宽宏大度, 开明: *a spirit of liberality and fairness* 开明公平的精神 **2** the quality of being generous 慷慨大方

lib·e·ral·ize also 又作 **-ise** *BrE*【英】/ˋlɪbərəlˌaɪz; ˈlɪbərəlaɪz/ *v* [T] to make a system, laws, or moral attitudes less strict 使自由化; 放松对…的限制 —**liberalization** /ˌlɪbərələˋzeʃən; ˌlɪbərəlaɪˈzeɪʃən/ *n* [U]

Liberal Par·ty /ˈ···ˌ··/ *n* [singular] a former British political party of the centre 自由党〔旧时英国的一个温和派政党〕

liberal stud·ies /ˌ···ˈ··/ *n* [plural] *especially BrE* subjects that are taught in order to increase students' general knowledge and their ability to write, speak, and study more effectively【尤英】文科科目 —compare 比较 LIBERAL ARTS

lib·e·rate /ˋlɪbəˌret; ˈlɪbəreɪt/ *v* [T] **1** to free someone from feelings or conditions that make their life unhappy or difficult 使解脱, 使解放: [+from] *liberated from shame* 从羞愧中解脱出来 | *the liberating power of education* 教育的解放力量 **2** to free prisoners, a city, a country etc from someone's control 释放〔囚犯〕; 解放〔城市、国家等〕—**liberator** *n* [C] —**liberation** /ˌlɪbəˋreʃən; ˌlɪbəˈreɪʃən/ *n* [U]

lib·e·rat·ed /ˋlɪbəˌretɪd; ˈlɪbəreɪtɪd/ *adj* free to behave in the way you want, and not restricted by old rules of social and sexual behaviour〔在社交和男女关系上〕不受约束的, 思想解放的: *the magazine for the liberated woman* 面向思想解放的妇女的杂志

Li·be·ri·a /laɪˋbɪrɪə; laɪˈbɪəriə/ a country in West Africa on the Atlantic Ocean, next to Sierra Leone. Population: 3,226,000 (2001). Capital: Monrovia. The modern country of Liberia was established in 1822 as a place for black slaves from the southern US to go and live after they had been made free. 利比里亚〔西非一国家, 濒临大西洋。人口: 3,226,000 (2001), 首都: 蒙罗维亚。现代利比里亚创建于 1822 年, 当时是美国南方黑奴获得解放后的投奔之地〕—**Liberian** *n, adj*: *a Liberian-registered oil tanker* 一艘在利比里亚注册的油轮

lib·er·tar·i·an /ˌlɪbɚˋtɛrɪən; ˌlɪbəˈteəriən/ *n* [C] someone who believes strongly that people should be free to do and think what they want to 自由论者 —**libertarian** *adj*

lib·er·tine /ˋlɪbɚˌtin; ˈlɪbətiːn/ *n* [C] someone who leads an immoral life and always looks for pleasure, especially sexual pleasure 放荡不羁的人; 淫荡的人 —**libertine** *adj*

Liberty a short form of the name **the National Council for Civil Liberties**, which is an independent British organization which aims to defend and increase the rights of ordinary citizens 全国公民自由理事会〔英国一独立组织, 旨在维护和扩大普通公民的权利〕

lib·er·ty /ˋlɪbɚtɪ; ˈlɪbəti/ *n*

1 ▶FREEDOM 自由◀ [U] the freedom and the right to do whatever you want without asking permission or being afraid of authority 自由; 自由权: *People will resent these restrictions on their liberty.* 人们会憎恨这些对他们自由的限制措施。

2 ▶LEGAL RIGHT 合法权利◀ [C usually plural 一般用复数] a particular legal right〔某种〕合法权利: *liberties such as freedom of speech that we take for granted* 合法权利, 诸如我们认为理所当然的言论自由

3 ▶WITHOUT PERMISSION 未经许可◀ [singular] something you do without asking permission, which may offend or upset someone else 擅自的行为; 冒犯的举动; 放肆的行为: *What a diabolical liberty!* 多么放肆的举动! | **take the liberty of doing sth** *I took the liberty of cancelling the reservation for you.* 我擅自取消了你的预订。

4 be at liberty to do sth *formal* to have the right or permission to do something【正式】有权做某事; 获许可做某事: *I'm afraid that I am not at liberty to discuss these matters.* 恐怕我无权讨论这些问题。

5 take liberties with sb/sth a) to make unreasonable changes in something such as a piece of writing〔对写作等〕随便地改动: *The film-makers took too many liberties with the original*

novel. 制片人对原著改动太多了。**b)** *old-fashioned* to treat someone without respect by being too friendly too quickly, especially in a sexual way【过时】与某人相处时太放肆，太随便对待某人〔尤指性行为上〕: *He's been taking liberties with our female staff.* 他对待我们的女职员太随便了。

6 at liberty if a prisoner or an animal is at liberty, they are no longer in prison or enclosed in a small place〔犯人或动物〕不受拘禁的，获得自由的

Liberty Bell, the /ˈ···, ·/ a bell, kept in Philadelphia, in the US state of Pennsylvania, which was rung on July 8th, 1776, during the American Revolutionary War to tell people of the Declaration of Independence from Britain. Because of this, the bell became a symbol of liberty for the US. In 1846 it cracked when it was rung to celebrate the birthday of George WASHINGTON, and it could not be repaired. 自由钟〔保存在美国宾夕法尼亚州费城的一口钟。1776年7月8日，美国独立战争期间曾敲响此钟，向人民宣布脱离英国的《独立宣言》。因此，该钟成为美国自由精神的象征。1846年，纪念乔治·华盛顿诞辰时，该钟被撞裂，无法修补〕

Liberty Is·land /ˈ···, ··/ the small island in New York Harbor where the Statue of Liberty stands 自由岛〔纽约港一小岛，自由女神像耸立于此〕

li·bi·do /lɪˋbido; lɪˈbiːdəʊ/ *n* [C,U] *technical* someone's desire to have sex【术语】性欲 —**libidinous** /lɪˋbɪdn̩əs; lɪˈbɪdɪnəs/ *adj*

Li·bra /ˋlibrə; ˈliːbrə/ *n* **1** [singular] the seventh sign of the ZODIAC, represented by a pair of SCALES, and believed to affect the character and life of people born between September 23rd and October 23rd 天秤宫；天秤（星）座 **2** [C] someone who was born between September 23rd and October 23rd 天秤座时段〔9月23日至10月23日〕出生的人

li·brar·i·an /laɪˋbrɛrɪən; laɪˈbreəriən/ *n* [C] someone who works in a library 图书馆管理员 —**librarianship** *n* [U]

S2 W1 **li·bra·ry** /ˋlaɪˌbrɛrɪ; ˈlaɪbrəri/ *n* [C] **1** a room or building containing books that can be looked at or borrowed 图书馆，图书室: *a public library* 公共图书馆 | *the college library* 大学[学院]图书馆 | *a library book* 图书馆的书 —compare 比较 BOOKSHOP **2** a group of books, records etc, collected by one person 私人收藏的书籍[唱片等] **3** a set of books, records etc that are produced by the same company and have the same general appearance 文库，书库〔指同一公司出版、外观相同的丛书或唱片集等〕: *a library of modern classics* 现代经典文库

Library of Con·gress, the /, ····ˈ··/ the largest library in the US, in Washington, D.C. It is one of the largest libraries in the world. Publishers have to give a copy of every book, magazine etc that is produced in the US to the Library. 国会图书馆〔美国最大的图书馆，位于华盛顿特区，是世界上最大的图书馆之一。出版商在美国出版任何一本书籍或杂志，都要给国会图书馆赠送一个样本供收藏之用〕

library pic·tures /ˈ···, ··/ *n* [plural] *BrE* pictures shown in a television programme that were made at a previous time【英】〔电视节目中放映的〕资料图片

li·bret·tist /lɪˋbrɛtɪst; lɪˈbretɪst/ *n* [C] someone who writes librettos〔歌剧的〕歌词作者

li·bret·to /lɪˋbrɛto; lɪˈbretəʊ/ *plural* **librettos** *n* [C] the words of an OPERA or musical play〔歌剧、音乐剧的〕歌词[脚本]

Li·bre·ville /ˋlibrəˌvɪl; ˌliːbrəˈvil/ the capital city of Gabon 利伯维尔〔加蓬首都〕

Lib·y·a /ˋlɪbɪə; ˈlɪbiə/ an oil-producing country in North Africa on the Mediterranean Sea. Population: 5,241,000 (2001). Capital: Tripoli. 利比亚〔北非一石油生产国，濒临地中海。人口: 5,241,000 (2001)，首都: 的黎波里〕 —**Libyan** *n, adj*

lice /laɪs; laɪs/ *n* the plural of LOUSE[1] (1)

S3 W2 **li·cence** *BrE*【英】, **license** *AmE*【美】/ˋlaɪsn̩s; ˈlaɪsəns/ *n*

1 ►DOCUMENT 文件◄[C] an official document giving you permission to own or do something for a period of time 许可证，执照；证书: *a firearms license* 枪支许可证 | *How much is the licence fee?* 许可证的费用是多少？| **lose your licence** (=have your driving licence taken by the police as punishment) 被扣留驾驶执照

2 ►FREEDOM 自由◄[U] **a)** freedom to do or say what you think is best〔行动、言论的〕自由，不受拘束: *Headteachers should be allowed greater licence in the exercise of their power.* 应允许校长在行使权力中有更大的自由。**b)** freedom to behave in a way that is sexually immoral 放纵；淫荡

3 artistic/poetic licence the way in which a writer or painter changes the facts of the real world to make their story, description, or picture of events more interesting or more beautiful 艺术/诗的自由发挥

4 ►RIGHT TO DO STH 做某事的权利◄[C] official permission to do something, which seems to give someone the right to do something that is wrong 许可，特许: [+for] *Church groups see the new laws as a licence for promiscuity.* 各教派视新的法律为对男女滥交的认同。| **licence to print money** (=an officially approved plan in which there is no control over how much money is spent) 滥印钞票的许可权〔指获得正式批准但对开销不加以控制的计划〕

5 under licence if something is sold, made etc under licence it is sold etc with the permission of a company or organization 获得许可〔出售、生产等〕

li·cense also 又作 **licence** *BrE*【英】/ˋlaɪsn̩s; ˈlaɪsəns/ *v* [T usually passive 一般用被动态] to give official permission for someone to do something or for an activity to take place 批准，许可: **be licensed to do sth** *The restaurant is now licensed to sell alcohol.* 这家餐厅现在获准售酒。

li·censed also 又作 **licenced** /ˋlaɪsn̩st; ˈlaɪsənst/ *adj* **1** *BrE* having a licence to sell alcoholic drinks【英】获准售酒的，许可售酒的: *a licensed restaurant* 许可售酒的餐馆 **2** a car, gun etc that is licensed is one that someone has official permission to own or use 领有执照的；正式许可拥有[使用]的 **3** having been given official permission to do a particular job 获准执业的: *a licensed private investigator* 获准执业的私人侦探

licensed vict·ual·ler /, ··ˈ···/ *n* [C] *BrE technical* an owner of a shop or PUB who is allowed to sell alcoholic drink【英，术语】特许出售酒类店铺[酒吧]的老板

li·cen·see /ˌlaɪsn̩ˋsi; ˌlaɪsənˈsiː/ *n* [C] someone who has official permission to do something 执照持有人；许可证持有人

license plate /ˈ·· ·/ *n* [C] *AmE* one of the signs with numbers on it at the front and back of a car【美】〔汽车的〕牌照，车牌，号码牌; NUMBER PLATE *BrE*【英】—see picture on page A2 参见A2页图

CULTURAL NOTE 文化注释

In the US, each state makes its own license plates. If you move from one state to live in another state, you are expected to change your car's plates. In some states, license plates belong to the car owner, so that if the owner sells their car, they can keep the plates and use them on a different car. 在美国，每个州发放自己的汽车号牌。从一州移居另一州通常要更换汽车号牌。在有些州，汽车号牌归车主所有，因此车主卖掉汽车后仍可以保留号牌并把它用到另一辆车上。

In the UK, NUMBER PLATES (=license plates) usually belong to a particular car, and you do not change them if you move to another part of the UK or buy another car. British number plates contain letters which show the area where the car was bought and numbers which show how old the car is. 在英国，汽车号牌通常归属于特定的汽车，迁到另一个地区并不需要更换号牌，也不能把号牌取下用在新车上。英国的汽车号牌上有显示汽车购买地的字母以及汽车年代的数字。

Some people in both the US and the UK **buy personalized license plates** with letters that spell out part of their name. In the US, these are fairly common and not too expensive, but in the UK they are very expensive, and are usually only bought by people who want to show that they are rich. 在英美两国，均有人购买个性化的汽车号牌，他们姓名的一部分能从号牌上的字母拼出。个性化号牌在美国比较普遍，价钱也不是很高；但在英国非常昂贵，通常也只有那些想炫耀自己财富的人才会购买。

licens·ing hours /ˈ···, ·/ *n* [plural] the hours during which it is legal to sell alcohol in Britain〔英国的〕合法售酒时间，许可售酒时间

licensing laws /ˈ···, ·/ *n* [plural] *BrE* the laws that say when and where you can sell alcohol【英】售酒法〔规定酒类的销售时间和地点〕

li·cen·ti·ate /laɪˋsɛnʃɪɪt; laɪˈsenʃiət/ *n* [C] someone who has been given official permission to practise a particular art or profession 有从事某种专业资格的人，持有专业证书者: *a licentiate of the Royal College of Music* 皇家音乐学院证书持有者

li·cen·tious /laɪˋsɛnʃəs; laɪˈsenʃəs/ *adj formal* behaving in a sexually immoral or uncontrolled way【正式】淫荡的；放荡的 —**licentiously** *adv* —**licentiousness** *n* [U]

li·chee /ˋlaɪtʃi; ˈlaɪtʃiː/ *n* [C] another spelling of LYCHEE lychee 的另一种拼法

li·chen /ˋlaɪkən; ˈlaɪkən/ *n* [U] a grey, green, or yellow plant that spreads over the surface of stones and trees 地衣 —compare 比较 MOSS

Lichtenstein, Roy (1923-97) a US painter who was important in the development of POP ART. He is famous for his paintings that look like COMIC STRIPS. 利希滕斯坦〔美国画家，是推动波普艺术发展的一位重要人物。他的绘画作品看上去像连环漫画，他也因此而著称〕

lick¹ /lɪk; lɪk/ *v*

1▶TONGUE 舌头◀ [T] to move your tongue across the surface of something in order to eat it, clean it etc 舔；舔吃: *The dog jumped up and licked her face.* 狗跳起来舔她的脸。

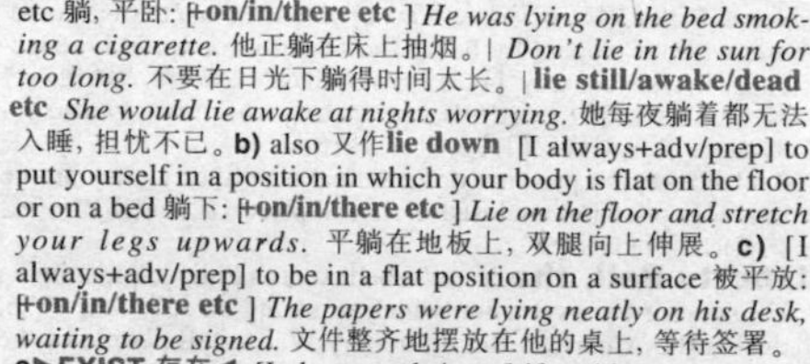

lick 舔

2▶SPORT 体育运动◀ [T] *informal* to defeat an opponent【非正式】击败〔对手〕: *I reckon we could lick the best teams in Georgia.* 我估计我们能击败乔治亚州最强的队。

3▶FLAMES/WAVES 火焰/波浪◀ [I, T] *literary* if flames or waves lick something, they touch it again and again with quick movements【文】〔火焰〕吞噬；〔波浪〕拍击: [**+at/against**] *Soon the flames were licking at the curtains.* 很快火焰便吞噬着窗帘。

4have (got) sth licked *informal* to have succeeded in dealing with a difficult problem【非正式】使〔难题〕得到解决

5lick your lips to feel eager and excited because you are expecting to get something good 舔唇向往，热切期盼

6lick your wounds to quietly think about the defeat or disappointment you have just suffered 舔愈伤口，重整旗鼓

7lick sb's boots to obey someone completely because you fear them or want to please them 巴结[奉承]某人 —see also 另见 BOOTLICKING, **knock/lick sb into shape** (SHAPE¹ (7))

lick sth **↔up** *phr v* [T] to drink or eat something by licking it 舔饮；舔吃

lick² *n* **1** [C usually singular 一般用单数] an act of licking something with your tongue 舔: *Can I have a lick of your ice cream?* 我可以舔一下你的冰激凌吗? **2a lick of paint/colour etc** a small amount of paint etc put onto the surface of something to improve its appearance 少量油漆/颜料等 **3give sth a lick and a promise a)** *BrE* to wash or clean something quickly and carelessly【英】马虎地清洗[清扫]某物 **b)** *AmE* to do a job quickly and carelessly【美】草率地做某事 **4at a great lick/at a hell of a lick** *informal especially BrE* very fast【非正式，尤英】迅速地 **5** [C] *informal* an act of hitting someone【非正式】一击

lick·e·ty-split /ˌlɪkətɪ ˈsplɪt; ˌlɪkəti ˈsplɪt/ *adv AmE old-fashioned* very quickly【美，过时】快速地，迅速地

lick·ing /ˈlɪkɪŋ; ˈlɪkɪŋ/ *n* [singular] *informal*【非正式】**1** a defeat in a sports competition or match〔体育竞赛或比赛的〕失败，挫折: *We got a real licking in the final.* 在决赛中我们被打得惨败。**2** a severe beating as a punishment 狠揍，痛打〔作为惩罚〕

lic·o·rice /ˈlɪkərɪʃ; ˈlɪkərɪs/ *n* [U] the American spelling of LIQUORICE liquorice 的美式拼法

lid /lɪd; lɪd/ *n*

1▶COVER 盖子◀ [C] a cover for the open part of a pot, box, or other container〔容器的〕盖子: *Can you get the lid off this jar for me?* 你能帮我打开这个罐子的盖吗? | *a dustbin lid* 垃圾桶盖

2keep the lid on to control a situation so that it does not become worse 控制…的局势: *keeping the lid on inflation* 控制住通货膨胀的势头 | *She was trying to keep the lid on her simmering anger.* 她尽力按捺住难以控制的怒火。

3▶EYE 眼睛◀ [C] an EYELID 眼睑

4put the lid on *informal* to do something that finally ruins or ends someone's plans or hopes【非正式】毁灭〔希望〕；结束〔计划〕

5take the lid off sth/lift the lid on sth to let people know the true facts about a bad or shocking situation 揭露〔真相〕；披露〔丑闻〕: *Their latest documentary takes the lid off the world of organized crime.* 他们最新的纪录片揭露了集团犯罪的真相。

lid·ded /ˈlɪdɪd; ˈlɪdɪd/ *adj* **1heavy-lidded eyes** eyes with large EYELIDS 眼皮重垂的眼睛 **2** a lidded container, pot etc has a lid〔容器〕带盖子的

li·do /ˈlido; ˈliːdəʊ/ *n* [C] *especially BrE* an outdoor public area, often at a beach, lake etc, for swimming and lying in the sun【尤英】〔沙滩或湖边的〕浴场；露天游泳池

lie¹ /laɪ; laɪ/ *v present participle* **lying** *past tense* **lay** /le; leɪ/ *past participle* **lain** /len; leɪn/

1▶FLAT POSITION 放平的位置◀ a) [I always+adv/prep] to be in a position in which your body is flat on the floor, on a bed etc 躺，平卧: [**+on/in/there etc**] *He was lying on the bed smoking a cigarette.* 他正躺在床上抽烟。| *Don't lie in the sun for too long.* 不要在日光下躺得时间太长。| **lie still/awake/dead etc** *She would lie awake at nights worrying.* 她每夜躺着都无法入睡，担忧不已。**b)** also 又作 **lie down** [I always+adv/prep] to put yourself in a position in which your body is flat on the floor or on a bed 躺下: [**+on/in/there etc**] *Lie on the floor and stretch your legs upwards.* 平躺在地板上，双腿向上伸展。**c)** [I always+adv/prep] to be in a flat position on a surface 被平放: [**+on/in/there etc**] *The papers were lying neatly on his desk, waiting to be signed.* 文件整齐地摆放在他的桌上，等待签署。

2▶EXIST 存在◀ [I always+adv/prep] if an idea or a quality lies in a particular action, person etc, it exists or is expressed in that action, person, etc 存在，在于: [**+in/with/outside etc**] *The answer must lie in finding alternative sources of power.* 答案必定在于找到替代的能源。| **the future lies in** (=something will be very important in the future) 未来取决于… *The future lies in multimedia.* 未来取决于多媒体。

3▶BE IN A PLACE 在某个地方◀ [I always+adv/prep] if a town, village, etc lies in a particular place, it is in that place 位于: [**+in/on/below**] *The town lies in a small wooded valley.* 该城镇坐落于一个林木茂盛的小山谷中。

4lie ahead/lie before you/lie in store if something lies ahead of you etc, it is going to happen to you in the future 将要发生: *How will we cope with the difficulties that lie ahead?* 我们将如何处理以后出现的困难呢? | *I was wondering what lay in store for us.* 我正想知道我们以后会遇到什么事情。

5lie open/empty/undisturbed etc to be open etc 处于打开/空/未扰乱的状态等: *The book lay open on the table.* 那本书在桌子上翻开着。| *The town now lay in ruins.* 该城镇现已成为一片废墟。

6lie in wait (for) a) to remain hidden in a place and wait for someone so that you can attack them 埋伏着等待: [**+for**] *a giant crocodile lying in wait for its prey* 埋伏着等待猎物的巨鳄 **b)** if something unpleasant lies in wait for you, it is going to happen to you〔不愉快的事〕将会发生

7lie low to remain hidden because someone is trying to find you or catch you 躲藏: *We'll have to lie low until tonight.* 我们得躲藏至今晚。

8lie at the heart of *formal* to be the most important part of something【正式】处在…中最重要的地位: *the issue that lies at the heart of the present conflict* 在目前冲突中至关重要的那个问题

9lie heavy on *formal* if something lies heavy on you, it makes you feel unhappy【正式】沉重地压在…；使…感到不安: *The feelings of guilt lay heavy on him.* 犯罪感使他感到不安。

10lie second/third/fourth etc *BrE* to be in second, third etc position in a competition【英】〔在竞赛中〕名列第二/第三/第四等: *Liverpool are lying third in the football championship.* 利物浦队在足球锦标赛中名列第三。

11▶DEAD PERSON 死者◀ [I always+adv/prep] if someone lies in a particular place, they are buried there 被埋葬 · **here lies ...** (=written on a gravestone) …被埋葬于此〔写于墓碑上〕 *Here lies Percival Smythe.* 珀西瓦尔·斯迈思长眠于此。

12lie in state if an important person who has died lies in state, their body is put in a public place so that people can go and show their respect for them〔遗体〕停放于某处供瞻仰

13▶STAY 停留◀ [I always+adv/prep] *old use* to spend the night somewhere【旧】〔在某处〕过夜: *He was to lie that night at a neighbour's.* 他那晚要在邻居家过夜。—see also 另见 **let sleeping dogs lie** (SLEEP¹ (6))

lie about/around *phr v* **1** [I,T] if something is lying around, it has been left somewhere untidily, rather than being in its proper place 零乱地摆放着: *If you leave your shoes lying around like that, you'll trip over them.* 如果你把鞋子这样到处乱放，你会被它们绊倒的。| **lie around/about sth** *Papers and books lay around the room in complete chaos.* 房间内到处放着报纸和书，简直乱七八糟。**2** [I] if you lie around, you spend time lying down and not doing anything 无所事事地闲躺着混日子: *I felt so lazy just lying around on the beach all day.* 我整天只是在海滨躺着，感到太懒散了。

lie behind sth *phr v* [T] if something lies behind an action, it is the real reason for the action even though it may be hidden 是〔某行为〕的原因: *I knew that something else lay behind his sudden interest in football.* 我知道他突然对足球感兴趣是另有原因的。

lie down *phr v* **1** [I] to put yourself in a position in which your body is flat on the floor or on a bed 躺下: *You must lie down and rest.* 你必须躺下休息。**2take sth lying down** *informal* to accept bad treatment without complaining【非正式】

屈从, 逆来顺受: *I'm not going to take this lying down! You'll be hearing from my lawyer.* 我不会就此屈服！你等着我的律师找你。

lie in *phr v BrE* [I] to remain in bed in the morning for longer than usual【英】迟起, 睡懒觉: *I can't wait to be able to lie in this weekend!* 要到本周末才能睡个懒觉, 我可等不了！

lie with sb *phr v* [T] **1** if a power, duty etc lies with someone, they have that power etc 是某人的〔权力、职责等〕; 决定于某人: *The responsibility for this problem lies firmly within the government.* 这个问题的责任完全在于政府。**2** *old use* to have sex with someone【旧】和〔某人〕性交

3 **lie[2]** *v past tense* **lied** *present participle* **lying** **1** [I] to deliberately tell someone something that is not true 说谎, 撒谎: *I could tell from her face that she was lying.* 我可以从她的表情上看出她在说谎。| **lie to sb** *I would never lie to you.* 我再也不会向你说谎了。| **lie through your teeth** (=say something that is completely untrue) 撒弥天大谎 **2** [I] if a picture, account etc lies, it does not show the true facts or the true situation 造成假象; 欺骗: *Statistics can often lie.* 统计资料往往会给人假象。| *The camera never lies.* 照相机从不骗人。

lie[3] *n* **1** [C] something that you say or write that you know is untrue 谎言, 假话: *There's no truth in her story. It's all lies!* 她的话没有一句是真的, 全是谎言！| **tell a lie** *I always know when he's telling lies.* 我总是知道什么时候他在说谎。| **tell sb a lie** *Of course it's true. I wouldn't tell you a lie.* 当然这是真的, 我不会对你说谎的。| **pack of lies** (=a story or set of statements that is completely untrue) 一派胡言, 一堆谎话 *Their whole account of the event was a pack of lies.* 他们对事件的描述全是一派胡言。| **barefaced lie** (=a shocking lie) 无耻的谎言 | **white lie** (=a lie that is not serious, or one that is told to avoid upsetting someone) 无关紧要的谎言, 善意的谎言 **2 give the lie to** *formal* to show that something is untrue【正式】揭穿…的谎言: *This report gives the lie to the company's claim that there has been no pollution.* 这份报告揭穿了这家公司声称没有污染的谎言。**3 the lie of the land/the way the land lies** the way that a situation is developing at a particular time 〔某一时期〕形势的发展, 情况的变化: *I want to see how the land lies before I decide whether or not to take the job.* 在决定是否接受这份工作以前, 我先要观察一下形势的发展。**4 (I) tell a lie** *BrE spoken* used when you realize that something you have just said is not correct【英口】说错了〔用于意识到自己刚说的话不对时〕: *It was £25, no, tell a lie, £35.* 是25英镑, 不, 说错了, 是35英镑。

Lieb·frau·milch /ˈlibfraʊmɪlʃ; ˈliːbfraʊmɪlʃ/ a sweet white wine from Germany 莱茵白葡萄酒〔德国出产的一种口感甜润的白葡萄酒〕

Liech·ten·stein /ˈlɪktənˌstaɪn; ˈlɪktənstaɪn/ a very small country between Austria and Switzerland. Population: 32,528 (2001). Capital: Vaduz. Many foreign companies have their main offices there because taxes are low and the banks keep information about companies secret. 列支敦士登〔位于奥地利和瑞士之间的一小国。人口: 32,528 (2001), 首都: 瓦杜兹。该国税率较低, 银行保密性强, 所以不少外国公司都把总部设在这里〕— **Liechtensteiner** *n, adj*

lie de·tec·tor /ˈ· ·,··/ *n* [C] a piece of equipment used especially by the police to check whether someone is lying, by measuring sudden changes in their heart rate 测谎仪, 测谎器

lie down /ˈlaɪˌdaʊn; ˈlaɪdaʊn/ *n* [singular] *BrE* a short rest, usually on a bed【英】〔一般躺在床上的〕小睡, 小憩: *I'm going upstairs to have a lie down.* 我要上楼去躺着休息一下。

lief /lif; liːf/ *adv old use* willingly or gladly【旧】乐意地, 高兴地

liege /lidʒ; liːdʒ/ *n* [C] **1** also 又作 **liege lord** a lord who was served and obeyed in the Middle Ages〔中世纪的〕君主; 王侯 **2** also 又作 **leigeman** someone who had to serve and obey a lord in the Middle Ages〔中世纪的〕臣民

lie-in /ˈ· ·/ *n* [singular] *BrE* an occasion when you stay in bed longer than usual in the morning【英】睡懒觉

li·en /ˈliən; ˈliːən/ *n* [C+**on**] *law* the legal right to keep something that belongs to someone who owes you money, until the debt has been paid【法律】扣押权, 留置权

lieu /lu; ljuː/ *n* **in lieu (of)** instead of 代替: *extra time off in lieu of payment* 用额外的休假来代替付款

Lieut the written abbreviation of 缩写= LIEUTENANT

lieu·ten·ant /luˈtɛnənt; lefˈtenənt/ *n* **1 a)** [C] a fairly low rank of an officer in the army, navy, or air force, or a fairly high rank in the US police 陆军中尉; 海军上尉; 空军上尉; 〔美警察部队的〕中尉, 少尉 **b)** an officer who has this rank 拥有上尉[中尉, 少尉]头衔的官员 **2 lieutenant colonel/general/Governor etc** an officer or official with the rank below COLONEL, GENERAL[2], GOVERNOR etc 中校/中将/副州长等 **3** [C] someone who does work for, or in place of, someone in a higher position; DEPUTY (1) 代理官员; 副职官员 —see table on page C6 参见 C6 页附录

Life /laɪf; laɪf/ *trademark* a US magazine that is known for having many photographs【商标】《生活》〔美国一杂志, 以刊登很多照片而闻名〕

1 1 **life** *n plural* **lives** /laɪvz; laɪvz/

① PERIOD OF LIVING 一生
② HUMAN EXPERIENCES 人的经历
③ LIFE AND DEATH 生和死
④ LIVING THINGS 生物
⑤ REAL/TRUE 真的/真实的
⑥ HOW LONG STH CONTINUES 某事物的持续时间
⑦ ACTIVITY/EXCITEMENT 活动/兴奋
⑧ OTHER MEANINGS 其他意思

① PERIOD OF LIVING 一生

1 [C,U] the period between a person's birth and death during which they are alive 一生; 寿命: *Learning goes on throughout life.* 学习是一生的事。| *You have your whole life ahead of you.* 你前面还有漫长的一生呢。| **in your life** *I'd never seen the woman before in my life.* 我以前从未见过这个女人。| **spend your life** *She spent her life moving from one town to another.* 她的一生在从一个城镇搬到另一个城镇的颠簸之中度过。| **all your life** (=for the whole of your life) 整个一生 *I've lived in Mayo all my life.* 我一辈子都住在梅奥。| **early life** (=the part of your life when you were young) 早年, 青年时期的生活 *We don't know much about the poet's early life.* 我们对这位诗人的早年生活知道得不多。| **in later life** (=in the later part of your life) 在晚年〔生活中〕*My grandfather was troubled with illness in later life.* 我祖父晚年时受到疾病的折磨。| **late in life** (=when you are older than the usual age) 晚于一般年龄 *She had her children late in life.* 她晚年得子。| **for life** (=not changing for the rest of your life) 终生 (不变) *As far as I'm concerned, when you get married it's for life.* 对我而言, 一旦结了婚, 那是终身的事。| **working life** (=the part of your life when you are working) 工作生活, 工作生涯 *Norman had started his working life in the shipyards.* 诺曼在船厂开始了他的工作生涯。

② HUMAN EXPERIENCES 人的经历

2 ►A PERSON'S EXPERIENCES 个人经历◄ [C usually singular 一般用单数] the kind of experience that someone has during their life 经历; 生活: *a life spent at sea* 海上的经历 | **lead a happy/exciting/normal etc life** *Maria led a full and happy life.* 玛莉亚过着充实而幸福的生活。| **a hard life** (=a life full of difficulty and trouble) 艰难的生活 **live a life of crime/sacrifice etc** *Marc dreamed of getting rich and living a life of luxury.* 马克梦想致富并过着豪华的生活。—see also 另见 LIFE STORY

3 ►TYPICAL EXPERIENCES 独特的经历◄ [C,U] all the experiences and activities that are typical of a particular way of living〔特定的〕生活 (方式); 〔某种〕生活经历: **army/city/country etc life** *Isobel was bored with country life and longed for London.* 伊索贝尔厌倦了乡村生活, 渴望去伦敦。| **the life of a soldier/film star etc** *According to his book, the life of a rock star is not a happy one.* 据他的书所称, 摇滚乐明星的生活并不幸福。| **married life** *after 25 years of married life* 25年的婚姻生活之后

4 private/social/sex etc life activities in your life that are private, done with friends, concerned with sex etc 私/社交/性生活: *She enjoys a very active social life.* 她喜欢活跃的社交生活。

L

5 ▶ALL HUMAN EXPERIENCE 所有的人生经验◀ [U] all human existence considered as a variety of activities and experiences 世事; 处事经验: *My Aunt Julia had very little experience of life.* 我姨妈朱莉娅的生活经验很少。| *life's rich pattern* 人生经历的丰富模式 | *Life was hard in the mining communities.* 矿工的生活很艰辛。
6 **way of life** the way someone chooses to live their life 生活方式: *a traditional way of life* 传统的生活方式 | *the American way of life* 美国的生活方式
7 **quality of life** the level of health, comfort, and pleasure in someone's life 生活质量
8 **be sb's (whole) life** to be the most important thing or person in someone's life 是某人的(全部)生活; 是某人的生活寄托: *Music is Laura's whole life.* 音乐是劳拉全部生活的寄托。
9 **start/make a new life** to completely change your life, for example by moving to another place 开始新生活〈如去异地谋生〉: *They emigrated to Australia to start a new life there.* 他们移民到澳大利亚, 在那里开始新生活。

③ LIFE AND DEATH 生和死

10 ▶ALIVE NOT DEAD 活着的◀ [C,U] the state of being alive 生; 生存: *Miss Byatt thinks her life is in danger.* 拜厄特小姐认为她的生命有危险。| *Smoke detectors protect life and property.* 烟雾警报器使生命和财产得到保障。| **save sb's life** *A seatbelt could save your life.* 座椅安全带可以救命。| **risk your life** *Two fire fighters risked their lives to rescue the children.* 两名消防员冒着生命危险营救孩子们。| **risk life and limb** (=do something that is very dangerous) 出生入死 | **lose your life** (=die) 丧生 *Thousands lost their lives in the earthquake.* 成千上万的人在地震中罹难。| **take your own life** (=deliberately kill yourself) 自杀 | **give your life/lay down your life** (=die in order to save other people or because of a strong belief) 捐躯 | **take sb's life** (=kill someone) 杀死某人 | **take your life in your (own) hands** (=put yourself in danger of death) 冒生命危险 *Every time you cross these busy roads you take your life in your hands.* 人们每次穿过这几条繁忙的道路都冒着生命危险。
11 **a matter of life and death** a serious situation in which someone might die 生死攸关的事

④ LIVING THINGS 生物

12 [U] **a)** the quality that animals and plants have and that rocks, machines, and dead bodies do not have 生命, 性命: *the seeds of life* 生命的萌芽 | **bring sth to life** (=make something live) 赋予某物以生命 *In the story the artist brings the statue to life.* 在小说中, 艺术家赋予塑像以生命。**b)** living things, such as people, animals, or plants 生物, 有生命之物〈如人、动物、植物等〉: *Is there life on other planets?* 其他行星上有生物吗? | **animal/plant/bird life** *The island is rich in bird life.* 该岛鸟类繁多。

⑤ REAL/TRUE 真的/真实的

13 **real life** what really happens as opposed to what happens in people's imaginations or in stories 真实生活: *a real life drama* 取自真实生活的戏剧 | **in real life** *In real life crimes are never solved by amateur detectives.* 在现实生活中犯罪案件从未被业余侦探侦破过。
14 **paint/draw from life** to paint or draw something real, not from another picture 写生
15 **be true to life** to represent life as it really is 真实反映生活: *I prefer stories that are true to life.* 我喜欢真实反映生活的故事。

⑥ HOW LONG STH CONTINUES 某事物的持续时间

16 [singular] **a)** the period of time during which something takes place or exists 〔某事物的〕存在期: [+of] *during the life of the present parliament* 本届国会的任职期间 **b)** the period of time during which something is still good enough to use or fresh enough to eat 使用期; 有效期; 保鲜期: [+of] *What's the average life of a passenger aircraft?* 客机的平均服役期是多久? —see also 另见 SHELF LIFE

⑦ ACTIVITY/EXCITEMENT 活动/兴奋

17 [U] activity or movement 活动; 动静: **sign of life** *The door was open but there was no sign of life.* 门开着却没有动静。
18 **come to life** to start to become exciting or interesting 变得令人兴奋[有趣]: *The game really came to life in the second half.* 下半场, 比赛变得令人兴奋起来。
19 **bring sth to life** to make something more exciting or interesting 使某事物更令人振奋[有趣]: *Her songs bring our history to life again.* 她的歌曲又一次使我们的历史活现了。
20 **full of life** very cheerful and active 充满活力: *Katie seemed young and full of life.* 凯蒂看上去很年轻, 充满了活力。
21 **come to life/roar into life/splutter into life etc** to suddenly start working 突然开始运作[工作]: *Finally the car spluttered into life.* 最后小轿车突然噼啪几声发动起来了。
22 **be the life and soul of the party** to be the person who brings fun and excitement to a social group or occasion 在社会团体或社交场合中最活跃的人

⑧ OTHER MEANINGS 其他意思

23 **get a life!** *spoken* used to tell someone you think they are boring【口】别无聊!
24 **that's life** *spoken* used when you are disappointed or upset that something has happened but realize that you must accept it【口】生活就是这样〔表示无奈地接受令人失望或生气之事〕: *Oh well, that's life!* 算了, 生活就是这样!
25 **have the time of your life** to have a very enjoyable time 玩得很高兴: *The kids had the time of their lives at the waterslide.* 这些孩子玩水上滑梯玩得很高兴。
26 **make life difficult/easier etc** to make it difficult, easier etc to do something 使〔做某事〕变得困难/较容易等: *This constant complaining isn't going to make life any easier!* 这种不停的埋怨于事无补!
27 **for dear life** with the greatest possible effort and strength, especially in order to avoid harm 拼命地, 竭尽全力地〔尤指为避免伤害〕: *Vera was clinging onto the branch for dear life.* 薇拉拼命抱住那根树枝。
28 **cannot for the life of me** *spoken* used to say that you cannot remember or understand something even when you try hard【口】无论如何不能, 无法: *I cannot for the life of me see why you are so annoyed.* 我怎么也无法理解你为什么如此烦恼。
29 **not on your life** *spoken* used to say that you definitely will not do something【口】绝不〔做某事〕
30 ▶PRISON 监狱◀ [U] also 又作 **life imprisonment** the punishment of being put in prison for the rest of your life 终身监禁: *He was sentenced to life imprisonment for the murder.* 他因谋杀罪被判终身监禁。—see also 另见 LIFE SENTENCE
31 **the race/game/fright etc of your life** the best race you have ever run, the best game you have ever played 生平最出色的赛跑/最佳的比赛/最大的惊吓等
32 **be the life and soul of the party** to make people feel happy by talking a lot, telling jokes etc 成为聚会上的活宝
33 ▶BOOK/FILM 书/电影◀ [U] the story of someone's life; BIOGRAPHY 人物故事; 传记: *Boswell's Life of Johnson* 鲍斯韦尔所著的《约翰逊传记》
34 **the next life/the life to come** a continued existence that is expected after death 下辈子/来生
35 **the woman/man in your life** the woman or man with whom you have a sexual or romantic relationship 生活中的女人/男人〔指性生活的对象或情人〕—see also 另见 HIGH LIFE, LOW LIFE, CHANGE OF LIFE, **(as) large as life** (LARGE (6)), **a new lease of life** (LEASE[1] (2))

USAGE NOTE 用法说明: LIFE

WORD CHOICE 词语辨析: **life, living**

In general, the word **life** relates to the whole experience of living while the word **living** is more about the physical needs of living, for example, how much money you need, etc. 一般来说, life一词与整个人生经历有关, 而living一词则较多关于生活上的物质需要, 例如: 你需要多少钱, 等等: *He had a good life* (他生活得很好) means that he had a lot of good experiences and enjoyed it but 这句话的意思是他有许多美好的生活经历并且感到快乐, 但 *They have a pretty good living* (他们日子过得很好) means they have enough food, money etc. 这句话的意思是他们有足够的食物和钱等。

If you **make or earn a living** doing something, the work you do means you can provide yourself with the things that are necessary for life. 如果以做某事来 make or earn a living, 指所干的工作能供给生活所需的物品: *Joanne earns a living as a dancer in a nightclub.* 乔安妮在夜总会当舞女, 以此谋生。

If you **make a life** for yourself somewhere, you go there and find work, establish a home etc. 去异地 make a life 指去那里找到了工作并且建立家庭等: *thousands of refugees,*

making a new life across the border 成千上万的难民，越过边境去寻求新的生活。

The way in which someone or a group of people generally lives is their **way of life**, or less often their **way of living**. 某人或一群人平常的生活方式即是说他们的 way of life，或较少使用的 way of living。

If you are thinking more of the sort of rooms people live in, whether they have things like water, heating etc, you talk about their **living** conditions (NOT 不用 *life conditions*). 如果考虑较多人们居住空间之类的事，像他们是否有水、暖气等，那么谈论的是他们的 living conditions（生活条件）: *the appalling living conditions of millions of old people* 无数老人恶劣的生活条件

If you are thinking of the level of comfort of someone's life, and how much money they have to spend on things that are not necessary, you talk about their **standard of living**. 如果考虑某人的生活舒适度，在非必需品上得花多少钱，那么谈论的是他们的 standard of living（生活水平）: *Most Americans have a higher standard of living than Europeans.* 大多数美国人的生活水平比欧洲人高。

The **cost of living** is how much people need to spend in order to buy necessary things. cost of living 指基本的生活费用: *The cost of living keeps rising, but my salary stays the same* (NOT 不用 *the cost of life*). 基本的生活费用不断上涨，而我的工资却原封未动。

If you are thinking more of the type of food that someone enjoys eating, the exercise they take, and what they do when they are not working, you talk about their **lifestyle**. 如果考虑多一点某人爱吃的食物种类、运动的类型及工作之余做什么，那么谈论的是他们的 lifestyle（生活方式）: *The typical lifestyle of a 60s rock star included lots of alcohol, sex and drugs.* 20世纪60年代摇滚乐明星的典型生活方式包括了大量的酒精、性生活和毒品。

If you are talking about how enjoyable someone's life is, you call it their **quality of life**. 如果谈论的是某人的生活如何愉快，那么指的是他们的 quality of life（生活质量）: *Having a decent washing machine would improve the quality of my life no end!* 有一台好的洗衣机会大大改善我的生活质量！

GRAMMAR 语法

When talking about **life** [U] in general, you never use *the*. 泛指生活时不用冠词 the: *Life is hard* (NOT 不用 *The life...*). 生活很艰难。| *She loves life in the city.* 她热爱城市生活。

life as·sur·ance /ˈ· ·,· ·/ *n* [U] *BrE* LIFE INSURANCE【英】人寿保险

life belt /ˈ· ·/ *n* [C] **1** *BrE* a LIFE BUOY【英】救生圈 **2** *AmE* a special belt you wear in the water to prevent you from sinking【美】救生带

life-blood /ˈ· ·/ *n* [U] **1** the most important thing needed by an organization, relationship etc to continue to exist or develop successfully 生命线；命脉: *Communication is the life-blood of a good marriage.* 沟通是良好婚姻的命脉。**2** *literary* your blood【文】人的血液

life·boat /ˈlaɪf,bot; ˈlaɪfbəʊt/ *n* [C] **1** a boat that is sent out to help people who are in danger at sea（海上）救生艇[船] **2** a small boat carried by ships in order to save people if the ship sinks〔船上备用的〕救生艇

CULTURAL NOTE 文化注释

The Royal National Lifeboat Institution (RNLI) is the British organization that provides lifeboats to save people who are in trouble at sea. It is a CHARITY organization, and it collects money from the public in order to pay for its boats and equipment. All the people who work in the lifeboats are VOLUNTEERS (=they work for no money). 皇家全国救生艇协会是英国的一个组织，负责提供救生艇去救助遭遇海难的人。这是一个慈善组织，从公众那里募集资金用以添置和养护救生艇及救生设备。所有参与救生的人员都是志愿者。

In the US, however, lifeboat services are provided by the COASTGUARD, which is one of the government's military forces. 在美国，救生艇服务由海岸警卫队提供。海岸警卫队是美国军队的一个组成部分。

life buoy /ˈ· ·/ *n* [C] a large ring made out of material that floats, which you throw to someone who has fallen in the water, to prevent them from drowning 救生圈

life cy·cle /ˈ· ,· ·/ *n* [C] all the different levels of development that an animal or plant goes through during its life〔生物的〕生命周期，生命环

life ex·pec·tan·cy /ˌ· ·ˈ· · ·/ *n* [C] **1** the length of time that a person or animal is expected to live〔人或动物的〕预期寿命；平均（期望）寿命 **2** the length of time that something is expected to continue to work, be useful etc〔某物的〕平均有效期，预期使用寿命

life form /ˈ· ·/ *n* [C] a living thing such as a plant or animal 生物: *life forms on other planets* 其他行星上的生物

life guard 救生员

life guard /ˈ· ·/ *n* [C] someone who works at a beach or swimming pool to help swimmers who are in danger〔海滨或游泳池的〕救生员

Life Guards, the /ˈ· ,·/ a REGIMENT (=large group of soldiers) in the British army which is part of the Household Cavalry 近卫骑兵团〔英国军队一军团，属皇家骑兵〕

life his·to·ry /ˌ· ˈ· · ·/ *n* [C] all the events and changes that happen during the life of a living thing 生活史

life in·sur·ance /ˈ· ·,· ·/ *n* [U] a type of insurance that someone makes regular payments into so that when they die their family will receive money 人寿保险

life jack·et /ˈ· ,· ·/ *n* [C] a piece of clothing that can be filled with air and worn around your upper body to stop you from sinking in the water 救生衣

life·less /ˈlaɪflɪs; ˈlaɪfləs/ *adj* **1** *especially literary* dead or appearing to be dead【尤文】死的；看似无生命的 **2** lacking the positive qualities that make something or someone interesting, exciting, or active 单调的；无生气的，无活力的: *The actors' performances were lifeless.* 演员们的表演单调乏味。**3** not living, or not having living things on it 无生机的，没有生物的: *The surface of the moon is arid and lifeless.* 月球表面干旱没有生命。—**lifelessly** *adv*—**lifelessness** *n* [U]

life·like /ˈlaɪf,laɪk; ˈlaɪflaɪk/ *adj* a lifelike picture, model etc looks exactly like a real person or thing〔图画、模型等〕生动的，逼真的: *a very lifelike statue* 栩栩如生的塑像

life·line /ˈlaɪflaɪn; ˈlaɪflaɪn/ *n* [C] **1** something which someone depends on completely 生命线；命脉: *The telephone is her lifeline to the rest of the world.* 电话是她与外界联系的命脉。**2** a rope used for saving people in danger, especially at sea〔尤指用于海上的〕救生索

life·long /ˈlaɪfˈlɔŋ; ˈlaɪflɒŋ/ *adj* [only before noun 仅用于名词前] continuing or existing all through your life 终身的，毕生的: *a lifelong friend* 终身的朋友

life peer /ˌ· ˈ·/ *n* [C] someone who has the rank of a British PEER[1] (2) but who cannot pass it on to their children〔不可世袭的〕终身贵族

CULTURAL NOTE 文化注释

There are two types of peer in the House of Lords: life peers and HEREDITARY PEERS. The Government chooses people to become life peers, based on their special legal, political, or social experience. 上议院中有终身贵族和世袭贵族两类贵族。法律、政治或社会方面的特殊经历是政府挑选谁当终身贵族的依据。— see also Cultural Note at ARISTOCRACY 见 ARISTOCRACY 文化注释

life peer·ess /ˌ· ˈ· ·/ *n* [C] a woman who has the rank of a British PEER but cannot pass it on to her children〔不可世袭的〕终身女贵族

life pre·serv·er /ˈ· ·,· ·/ *n* [C] *AmE* something such as a LIFE BELT or LIFE JACKET that can be worn in the water to prevent you from sinking【美】救生用品；救生带；救生衣

lif·er /ˈlaɪfə; ˈlaɪfə/ *n* [C] *informal* someone who has been sent to prison for life【非正式】无期徒刑犯人

life raft /ˈ· ·/ *n* [C] a small rubber boat that can be filled with air and used by passengers on a sinking ship 救生筏

Life Sav·ers /ˈ· ,··/ *trademark* a type of small hard round sweet with a hole in the middle, which is produced in many different FLAVOURS. It is sold in the US.【商标】"救生圈"糖〔美国销售的一种圆形小硬糖，中间有孔，有多种口味〕

life·sav·er /ˈlaɪf,sevə; ˈlaɪfseɪvə/ *n* [C] **1** someone or something that helps you avoid a difficult or unpleasant situation 帮助解决困难的人[物]，救星: *Thanks for all your help, Carrie, you've been a real lifesaver!* 谢谢你的帮助，卡丽，你真是位救星！**2** a LIFE GUARD 救生员

life·sav·ing /ˈlaɪf,sevɪŋ; ˈlaɪfseɪvɪŋ/ *n* [U] the skills necessary to save a person from drowning〔救溺水者的〕救生术: *She has a bronze medal in lifesaving.* 她有一枚救生铜章。

life sci·en·ces /, ˈ···/ *n* [plural] subjects such as BIOLOGY that are concerned with the study of humans, plants and animals 生命科学〈如生物学〉

life sen·tence /, ˈ··/ *n* [C] the punishment of sending someone to prison for life 无期徒刑

life-size /ˈ· ·/ also 又作 **life-sized** *adj* a picture or model of something or someone that is life-size is the same size as they are in real life 与实物[真人]大小一样的: *a life-sized statue of the president* 与真人大小一样的总统雕像

3 **life·span** /ˈlaɪfspæn; ˈlaɪfspæn/ *n* [C] the average length of time that someone will live or that something will continue to work〔人的〕平均寿命；〔物的〕使用期: *Men have a shorter lifespan than women.* 男人的平均寿命比女人短。—compare 比较 LIFETIME

life story /ˈ· ,··/ *n* [C] the story of someone's whole life 传记，生平故事: *For some reason, she insisted on telling me her whole life story.* 由于某种原因，她坚持要给我讲述她一生的经历。

life·style /ˈlaɪf,staɪl; ˈlaɪfstaɪl/ *n* [C] the way someone lives, including the place they live in, the things they own, the kind of job they do, and the activities they enjoy 生活方式: *a luxurious lifestyle* 奢侈的生活方式

life sup·port sys·tem /ˈ· ··, ,··/ *n* [C] **1** a piece of equipment that keeps someone alive when they are extremely ill〔病重时使用的〕生命维持系统 **2** a piece of equipment that keeps people alive in conditions where they would not normally be able to live, such as in space〔宇航员的〕生命保障系统 **3** a natural system that is necessary for life to continue, for example the process that produces oxygen for people to breathe〔维持生命所必需的〕自然的维生系统

life·time /ˈlaɪf,taɪm; ˈlaɪftaɪm/ *n* [C usually singular 一般用单数] **1** the period of time during which someone is alive or something exists 一生，终身；生存期: *During her lifetime she had witnessed two world wars.* 她一生经历了两次世界大战。**2 the chance/experience etc of a lifetime** the best opportunity, experience etc that you will ever have 千载难逢的机遇/经历等 —compare 比较 LIFESPAN

life vest /ˈ· ·/ *n* [C] *AmE* a LIFE JACKET【美】救生衣

Liffe the London International Financial Futures and Options Exchange; an organization for buying and selling business shares 伦敦国际金融期货和期权交易所

Lif·fey, the /ˈlɪfɪ; ˈlɪfi/ a river in the Republic of Ireland which flows through Dublin 利菲河〔爱尔兰共和国一河流，流经都柏林〕

2 2 **lift¹** /lɪft; lɪft/ *v*

1 ▶MOVE STH WITH YOUR HANDS 用手搬某物◀ [T] to take something in your hands and raise it, move it, or carry it somewhere 举起，抬起，抱起: *He tried to lift the sleeping girl, but she was too heavy.* 他试图抱起正在睡觉的女孩，但是她太重了。| **lift sth onto/out of/off etc** *I lifted down my suitcase and opened it.* 我放下旅行箱，把它打开。—see 见 RAISE¹ (USAGE)

2 ▶RAISE 升起◀ also 又作 **lift up** [I,T] to move something upwards, into the air, or to move upwards into the air 抬起〔某物〕；向上升: *He lifted both hands in a gesture of despair.* 他举起双手，一副绝望的样子。| *At high speeds the front of the boat would lift out of the water.* 在高速行驶中，船的头部会抬离水面。

3 ▶HEAD/EYES 头/眼睛◀ [T] to move your head or eyes upwards so that you can look at someone or something 抬〔头或眼看事物〕: *Brig lifted his head as the others came into the room.* 当其他人进来的时候，布里格抬起头来。| *She lifted her gaze from her book for a minute.* 她把目光从书本上抬起来停了一会儿。

4 ▶CONTROLS/LAWS 控制措施/法律◀ [T] to remove a rule or a law that says that something is not allowed 解除，撤销〔限制〕: *the lifting of sanctions* 撤销制裁

5 ▶CLOUDS/MIST 云/雾◀ [I] if cloud or mist lifts, it disappears〔云或雾〕消散

6 ▶BY PLANE 用飞机◀ [T] to take people or things to or from a place by aircraft 空运〔人或物〕: *More troops are being lifted into the area as the fighting spreads.* 随着战争的扩大，更多的军队正被空运到这个地区。

7 not lift a finger *informal* to do nothing to help【非正式】一点都不帮忙

8 lift sb's spirits to make someone feel more cheerful and hopeful 使某人心情较开朗

9 ▶SAD FEELINGS 悲伤的情绪◀ [I] if feelings of sadness lift, they disappear〔悲伤〕消失: *Jan's depression seemed to be lifting at last.* 简的沮丧情绪看来终于逐渐消失了。

10 ▶USE SB'S IDEAS/WORDS 使用某人的观点/话语◀ [T] to copy words, ideas, music etc that someone else has written 剽窃，抄袭: *The words were lifted from an article in a medical journal.* 这段文字是从某医学杂志上的一篇文章中抄来的。

11 ▶STEAL 偷◀ [T] *informal* to steal something【非正式】偷〔某物〕

12 ▶VOICE 嗓音◀ also 又作 **lift up** [T] *literary* if you lift your voice, you speak, shout, or sing more loudly【文】提高〔嗓音〕

13 ▶INCREASE 增加◀ [T] to increase the amount or level of something 增加〔某物〕的量；提高〔某物〕的水平: *This policy lifted Canadian exports of wheat and flour.* 这个政策增加了加拿大小麦和面粉的出口量。

14 ▶VEGETABLES 蔬菜◀ [T] to dig up vegetables that grow under the ground 掘出〔长在地下的蔬菜〕: *lifting potatoes* 挖马铃薯

lift off *phr v* [T] if an aircraft or space vehicle lifts off, it leaves the ground and rises into the air〔飞机〕起飞；〔宇宙飞船〕升空

lift² *n* 3 3

1 ▶IN A BUILDING 在建筑物内◀ [C] *BrE* a machine that you can ride in, that moves up and down between the floors in a tall building【英】电梯；升降机；ELEVATOR (1) *AmE*【美】: *She pressed the button to call the lift.* 她按键叫电梯。| **take the lift** *They took the lift down to the bar.* 他们乘电梯去楼下的酒吧。

2 ▶IN A CAR 在车上◀ [C] *BrE* if you give someone a lift, you take them somewhere in your car【英】〔让某人〕搭便车；RIDE² (1) *AmE*【美】: *Do you want a lift into town?* 你要搭便车进城吗？| **give sb a lift** *I'll give you a lift back to London.* 我让你搭便车回伦敦。

3 ▶MAKE SB HAPPIER 使某人较高兴◀ **give sb a lift** to make someone feel more cheerful and more hopeful 使某人精神振奋

4 ▶LIFTING MOVEMENT 提升的运动◀ a movement in which something is lifted or raised up 被抬起[被举起]的运动: *the gentle lift and sway of the dinghy* 小艇轻微的起伏摇晃

5 ▶WIND/AIRCRAFT 风/飞机◀ [U] the pressure of air that keeps something up in the air or lifts it higher 升力，浮力 —see also 另见 CHAIRLIFT, SKI LIFT

lift-off /ˈ· ·/ *n* [C,U] the moment when a vehicle that is about to travel in space leaves the ground〔宇宙飞船的〕发射: *Ten seconds to lift-off!* 离发射还有10秒！—compare 比较 TAKE-OFF (1)

lig·a·ment /ˈlɪgəmənt; ˈlɪgəmənt/ *n* [C] a band of strong material in your body, similar to muscle, that joins bones or holds an organ in its place 韧带

lig·a·ture /ˈlɪgətʃə; ˈlɪgətʃə/ *n* [C] *technical* something such as a thread used for tying a BLOOD VESSEL to stop someone bleeding【术语】〔绑着血管、止血用的〕结扎线，缚线

light¹ /laɪt; laɪt/ *n*

1 ▶NATURAL/ARTIFICIAL LIGHT 自然光/人造光◀ **a)** [U] the energy from the sun, a flame, a lamp etc that allows you to see things 光，光线: *the morning light streaming in through the windows* 透过窗户照进来的晨光 | *We could see a tiny glimmer of light in the distance.* 我们可以看到远处有一点微微闪烁的光。| **good/strong/bright light** *The light isn't good enough to take a photograph.* 光线亮度不够，没法拍照。| **poor/dim/fading light** *In the fading light she could just make out the shape of a tractor.* 光线渐渐暗下来，她只能看清拖拉机的轮廓。| **by/in the light of** (=using the light produced by something) 利用…的光 *She was trying to read by the light of a flickering candle.* 她想办法利用摇曳的烛光看书。| **in/into the light** (=out of the shadows where there is light) 在亮处/走进亮处 *Come into the light where I can see you.* 走到亮的地方来，好让我可以看清楚你。| **soft/warm**

light *The valley was bathed in the soft light of dawn.* 山谷沐浴在黎明的柔光中。| **cold/harsh light** *the cold blue light of the Arctic* 北极的蓝色冷光 | **blinding/dazzling light** (=extremely bright light) 耀眼的光 *a sudden flash of blinding light* 耀眼的光突然一闪 | **a beam/ray of light** (=a thin line of light) 光柱/光束 *the beam of light from her flashlight* 从她的手电筒射出的光柱 **b)** [C] a particular type of light, with its own particular colour, level of brightness etc〔有某种光色、亮度的〕光: *Monet painted a series of river views in different lights.* 莫奈用不同的光色画了一系列的河上风景。—see also 另见 NORTHERN LIGHTS, **a trick of the light** (TRICK[1] (10))

2 the light the light produced by the sun during the day 日光: *We worked for as long as the light lasted.* 我们一直干到天黑。

3 first light *literary* the first light that appears in the morning sky; DAWN[1] (l)【文】曙光, 黎明: **at first light** *The search continued at first light next morning.* 第二天黎明搜查继续进行。

4 ►LAMP/ELECTRIC LIGHT ETC 灯/电灯等◄ [C] **a)** an electric light 电灯: *the neon lights of the city* 城市的霓虹灯 | *lights from the hotel shining on the wet sidewalk* 照在潮湿的人行道上的旅馆灯光 | **turn/switch/put on ↔ the light** *Please turn the light on.* 请开灯。| **turn/switch/put off ↔ the light** also 又作 **turn etc the light out** *Alan switched the overhead light off.* 艾伦关掉了头顶上的灯。| **the light is/comes/goes/on** *The street lights are coming on now.* 现在街灯亮了。| **the light goes off/out** *Suddenly all the lights in the house went out.* 突然屋内所有的灯都熄灭了。| **turn the lights down/dim the lights** (=make lights less bright) 把灯光调暗 *Sarah turned the lights down low to add a touch of romance.* 萨拉把灯光调暗来增加一点浪漫的氛围。| **the house lights** (=the lights in a cinema, theatre etc) 影院[剧场等]的灯光 —see also 另见 **the bright lights** (BRIGHT (13)) **b)** something such as a lamp or a TORCH[1] (1) 灯; 手电筒: *Shine a light over here, will you?* 请把灯往这边照一照, 好吗?

5 ►TRAFFIC CONTROL 交通控制◄ [C usually plural 一般用复数] one of a set of red, green and yellow lights used for controlling traffic; TRAFFIC LIGHTS 交通信号灯: *We waited for the lights to change.* 我们等待交通信号灯变换。| *The driver had failed to stop at a red light.* 红灯亮起时司机没有停车。—see also 另见 GREEN LIGHT, RED LIGHT DISTRICT, **jump a light** (JUMP[1] (18))

lights 灯

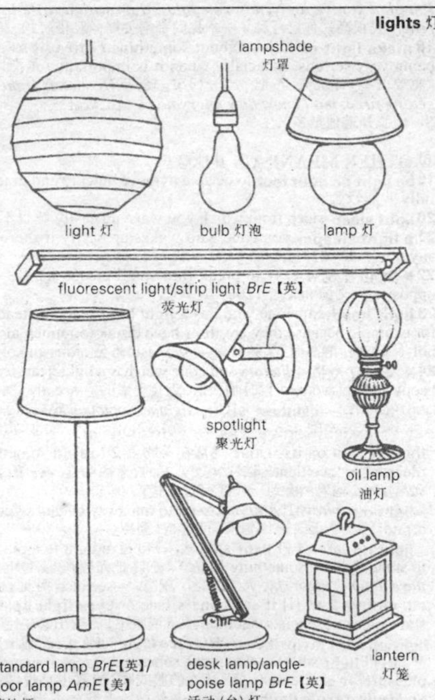

6 ►ON A VEHICLE 在车上◄ [C, usually plural 一般用复数] one of the lights on a car, bicycle etc, especially a HEADLIGHT〔汽车、自行车等的〕车灯〔尤指前灯〕: *You've left your lights on.* 你忘了关车灯。—see also 另见 BRAKE LIGHT, PARKING LIGHT

7 be/stand in sb's light to prevent someone from getting all the light they need to see or do something 挡住某人的光线: *Could you move to the left a little – you're standing in my light.* 你能靠左一点吗 —— 你挡住了我的光线。

8 ►FOR A CIGARETTE 用于香烟◄ **a light** a match or CIGARETTE LIGHTER to light a cigarette 火柴; 打火机: **have you got a light?** *BrE*【英】**/do you have a light?** *AmE*【美】你有火吗?

9 set light to to make something start burning 给〔某物〕点火: *The candle fell over and set light to the barn.* 蜡烛倒了, 把谷仓点着了。

10 in a new/different/bad etc light if someone or something is seen or shown in a new, different etc light, you begin to understand them in a particular way or make someone else do this 从新的/不同的/坏的等角度看: *There was Brian, pushing the pram, and I suddenly saw him in a new light.* 布赖恩就在那里, 推着婴儿车, 我突然对他有新的看法。| *an incident that presented the company in the worst possible light* 使公司形象严重受损的事件

11 in the light of *BrE*【英】**/in light of** *AmE*【美】if you do or decide something in the light of something else, you do it after considering that thing 考虑到〔某事物〕; 根据; 鉴于: *In light of the tragic news about our chairman, we have cancelled the 4th of July celebrations.* 鉴于主席的不幸消息, 我们已经取消了7月4日的庆祝活动。| **in (the) light of experience** (=as a result of your experience of something) 根据经验

12 come to light/be brought to light if new information comes to light, it becomes known〔新情况〕为人所知/被披露出来

13 throw/shed/cast light on to provide new information that makes a difficult subject or problem easier to understand 使〔难题等〕更容易理解: *These discoveries may throw some new light on the origins of the universe.* 这些发现可能会使人们进一步了解宇宙的起源。

14 see the light a) to suddenly understand something 忽然理解, 顿悟 **b)** to begin to believe in a religion very strongly 开始虔诚地信仰某宗教

15 see the light (of day) a) if an object sees the light of day, it is taken from the place where it has been hidden, and becomes publicly known 公开, 问世, 发表: *Some of the Pentagon papers will never see the light of day.* 五角大楼的有些文件永远也不会公开。**b)** if a law, decision etc sees the light of day, it comes into existence for the first time〔法律、决定等〕出台, 颁布

16 ►IN YOUR EYES 在某人眼中◄ [singular, U] *literary* an expression in your eyes that shows an emotion or intention【文】眼神: *There was a murderous light in his eyes.* 在他的眼中有一股杀气。

17 light and shade brightness and darkness in a painting〔画中的〕亮部与暗部

18 light at the end of the tunnel something that gives you hope for the future after a long and difficult period 经历长期磨难后终于看到希望: *It's been a hard few months, but we're finally beginning to see the light at the end of the tunnel.* 这几个月一直很艰难, 但是我们终于开始见到曙光了。

19 have your name in lights *informal* to be successful and famous in theatre or films【非正式】在舞台上[电影中]成名, 在演艺界成名

20 go/be out like a light *informal* to go to sleep very quickly because you are very tired【非正式】〔因很疲倦而〕很快入睡

21 a leading light in/of *informal* someone who is important in a particular group【非正式】〔某组织中的〕权威人士, 重要人物: *She's one of the leading lights of the local dramatic society.* 她是当地戏剧界的权威人士。

22 according to your own lights *formal* according to your own personal opinions or ideas of right and wrong【正式】根据个人的是非[道德]观

23 ►WINDOW 窗◄ [C] *technical* a window or other opening in a roof or wall that allows light into a room【术语】窗; 天窗; 采光口

24 ►FOOD 食品◄ **lights** [plural] *old-fashioned* the lungs of sheep, pigs etc used as food【过时】〔供食用的羊、猪等的〕肺 —see also 另见 **in the cold light of day** (COLD[1] (14)), **hide your light under a bushel** (HIDE[1] (7)), **be all sweetness and light** (SWEETNESS (2))

light² *adj*

① NOT DARK 浅色的
② NOT HEAVY 不重的
③ WITHOUT MUCH FORCE 不强烈的
④ NOT DIFFICULT/SEVERE 不难的/不严厉的
⑤ SMALL AMOUNT 少量
⑥ FOOD AND DRINK 食品和饮料
⑦ NOT VERY SERIOUS 不很严肃的
⑧ OTHER MEANINGS 其他意思

① NOT DARK 浅色的

1 ▶COLOUR 颜色◀ a light colour or light skin is pale and not dark〔颜色或皮肤〕淡色的, 浅色的: *the lightest shade of blue* 最浅的蓝色色调 | **light orange/grey etc** *light green curtains* 淡绿色的窗帘 —compare 比较 DARK[1] (2); DEEP[1] (7)

2 ▶DAYLIGHT 白昼◀ **it is light** if it is light, there is the natural light of day 天亮, 天明: **it gets light** (=it becomes light) 天亮, 天明 *It gets light at about 4:00 in the summer.* 夏天大约4点钟天就亮了。

3 ▶ROOM 房间◀ a room that is light has plenty of light in it, especially from the sun 明亮的〔尤指阳光充足〕: *The studio was light and spacious.* 这间工作室明亮宽敞。—opposite 反义词 DARK[1] (1)

② NOT HEAVY 不重的

4 not weighing very much, or weighing less than you expect 轻的; 比预计轻的: *You can carry this bag – it's fairly light.* 你可以拿这个袋子 — 它相当轻。| **as light as air/as light as a feather** (=extremely light) 分量极轻/轻如羽毛 —opposite 反义词 HEAVY[1] (1) —see also 另见 LIGHTEN, LIGHTWEIGHT

5 be a kilo/pound etc (too) light if something is a kilo etc light, it weighs that amount less than it should weigh 少了一公斤/磅等〔指比应有的重量更轻〕

6 light clothes are thin and not very warm〔衣服〕薄的, 不温暖的: *She took a light sweater in case the evening was cool.* 她带了一件薄毛衣, 以防晚上天气凉。—opposite 反义词 THICK[1] (1)

③ WITHOUT MUCH FORCE 不强烈的

7 ▶WIND 风◀ blowing without much force 微弱的: *a light breeze* 微风 —opposite 反义词 STRONG (17)

8 ▶SOUND 声音◀ very quiet 很轻的: *There was a light tap at the door.* 有轻轻的敲门声。—opposite 反义词 LOUD[1] (1)

9 ▶TOUCH 接触◀ very gentle and soft 轻柔的: *She gave him a light kiss on the cheek.* 她在他的脸颊上轻柔地吻了一下。—see also 另见 LIGHTLY (1)

④ NOT DIFFICULT/SEVERE 不难的/不严厉的

10 ▶WORK/EXERCISE 工作/锻炼◀ not very tiring 不累的, 轻松的: *She only has a few light duties around the house.* 她只负责房子里这儿那儿的一些轻松工作。

11 ▶PUNISHMENT 惩罚◀ not very severe 不严厉的: *I thought the sentence was too light.* 我认为这判决太轻。—opposite 反义词 HARSH (3)

12 make light work of to finish a job quickly and easily 轻而易举地完成〔某事〕

⑤ SMALL AMOUNT 少量

13 small in amount, or less than you expected 少量的; 比预计少的: *The traffic seems very light today.* 今天的交通似乎并不拥挤。| **a light meal/lunch etc** (=a meal in which you only eat a small amount) 吃得不多的一顿饭/午餐等

14 a light smoker/drinker/eater etc someone who does not smoke etc very much 抽烟/饮酒/吃饭等少的人

⑥ FOOD AND DRINK 食品和饮料

15 a) food or alcoholic drink that is light either does not have a strong flavour or is easy to DIGEST[1] (1) 清淡的; 浓度低的; 易消化的: *a light white wine* 低度白葡萄酒 | *a light dessert* 清淡的甜食 —compare 比较 FULL-BODIED, HEAVY[1] (19) **b)** not containing much fat 低脂肪的: *a new light cheese spread with only half the fat* 只含一半脂肪的新低脂肪干酪酱

⑦ NOT VERY SERIOUS 不很严肃的

16 not serious in meaning, style, or manner, and only intended for entertainment〔意义、风格或方式〕不严肃的; 供消遣的: *an evening of light music* 轻音乐晚会 | **light reading** *Christie bought a woman's magazine for a little light reading.* 克里丝蒂买了一本女性杂志作消遣性读物。| **a light touch** (=a relaxed and pleasant style) 轻松愉快的风格 *Your writing style is very formal; you should aim for a lighter touch.* 你的写作风格很拘谨; 你应该追求较轻快的风格。| **on a lighter note/in a lighter vein** (=used when you are introducing a joke, funny story etc after you have been speaking about something serious) 说点轻松的话题〔用于在严肃话题结束后引入笑话等〕—see also 另见 LIGHTLY (4)

17 light relief something that is pleasant and amusing after something sad or serious〔悲伤或严肃的事情后的〕轻松调剂: *I'm glad you've arrived – we could all do with a little light relief!* 我很高兴你已经到了 — 我们都需要略微轻松轻松。

18 make light of to joke about something or treat it as not being very serious, especially when it is important〔尤指〕拿〔重要的事〕开玩笑, 不把…当一回事, 轻视: *He makes light of getting fired, but I know how angry he is.* 他把被解雇不当一回事, 但我知道他是多么生气。

⑧ OTHER MEANINGS 其他意思

19 be light on your feet to be able to move quickly and gracefully 步履轻盈

20 light sleep sleep from which you wake up easily 睡得不沉

21 a light sleeper someone who wakes up easily if there is any noise etc 睡觉易醒的人

22 ▶SOIL 土壤◀ easy to break into small pieces 松软的 —opposite 反义词 HEAVY[1] (20a)

23 light head someone who has a light head feels unsteady, for example because they are ill or have drunk too much alcohol〔因生病、醉酒而〕头脑眩晕 —see also 另见 LIGHT-HEADED

24 ▶HEART 心情◀ *literary* someone who has a light heart feels happy and not worried【文】愉快的, 无忧无虑的 —see also 另见 LIGHT-HEARTED —**lightness** *n* [U]: *a lightness of touch* 轻松的手法

light³ *v past tense and past participle* **lit** /lɪt; lɪt/ or **lighted** **1** [T] to deliberately make something start to burn 使〔某物〕燃烧, 点燃: *I lit another cigarette.* 我又点了一支香烟。| **put a lighted match/candle to sth** *Martin put a lighted match to the papers.* 马丁用一根点燃的火柴点燃文件。—see also 另见 FIRE (USAGE) **2** [I] to start to burn 开始燃烧: *The fire won't light.* 火点不着。**3** [T usually passive 一般用被动态] to give light to something 照亮〔某物〕: *His bedroom was lit by a bare electric bulb.* 他的卧室用没有灯罩的电灯泡照明。| **well/poorly etc lit** also 又作 **well/poorly etc lighted** *The room was brightly lit.* 这房间灯火通明。—see also 另见 LIGHTEN **4 light sb into/along etc** also 又作 **light sb's way** *old-fashioned* to provide light for someone while they are going somewhere【过时】用灯给某人照路; 拿灯引路

light on/upon sth *phr v* [T] *literary*【文】**1** to fly to something and sit on it; ALIGHT 飞落在某物上 **2** to find something pleasant by accident 偶然发现〔美好的〕东西: *His eye lit on a ruby ring.* 他偶然看到一枚红宝石戒指。

light out *phr v* [I] *AmE informal* to run away because you are afraid【美, 非正式】〔因惊慌而〕逃走, 溜掉

light up *phr v* **1** [T **light** sth ↔ **up**] to give light to a place or to shine light on something 照亮〔某处〕; 把光照在〔某物〕上: *A flare lit up th night sky.* 火焰照亮了夜空。—see also 另见 LIGHTING UP TIME **2 a)** [I] if someone's face or eyes light up, they show pleasure, excitement etc〔脸上或眼中〕流露出喜悦[兴奋]: **light up with joy/pride etc** *His face lit up with glee.* 他一脸高兴。**b)** [T **light** sth ↔ **up**] to make someone's face or eyes show pleasure or excitement 使〔某人的脸或眼〕流露出喜悦[兴奋]: *Suddenly a smile lit up her face.* 忽然她脸上绽放出笑容。**3** [I] to become bright with light or colour 变得明亮: *As the screen*

lit up, he typed in a code. 当荧光屏变亮时，他输入密码。**4** [I] *informal* to light a cigarette【非正式】点香烟

light[4] *adv* **travel light** to travel without much luggage 轻装地旅行

light air·craft /ˌ· ˈ··/ *n* [C] a small plane 轻型飞机

light ale /ˌ· ˈ·/ *n* [U] a type of fairly weak pale beer 淡啤酒

Light Brigade, the —see 见 the CHARGE OF THE LIGHT BRIGADE

light bulb /ˈ· ·/ *n* [C] the glass object inside a lamp that produces light and has to be replaced regularly 灯泡

light·en /ˈlaɪtn; ˈlaɪtn/ *v* **1** [T] to reduce the amount of work, worry, debt etc that someone has 使〔工作、担忧、负债等〕减轻，减少，缓和: *Maybe we should hire another secretary to lighten Barbara's workload.* 或许我们应该再雇一位秘书以减轻芭芭拉的工作负担。**2** [I] if someone's face or expression lightens, they begin to look more cheerful〔脸或表情〕变得高兴: *His whole face would lighten when anyone mentioned Nancy.* 当别人一提起南希，他就满脸喜悦。**3** [I,T] to become brighter or less dark, or to make something brighter etc (使) 变亮，(使) 明亮: *As the sky lightened we were able to see where we were.* 天亮了，我们能看清自己在什么地方。—compare 比较 DARKEN **4** [I,T] to reduce the weight of something or become less heavy (使) 变轻 **5 lighten up!** *AmE spoken* used to tell someone not to be so serious about something【美口】别认真！别当真！: *It was a joke, Kath – lighten up!* 这是一个玩笑，凯瑟 —— 别当真！

light·er /ˈlaɪtɚ; ˈlaɪtə/ *n* [C] **1** a small object that produces a flame for lighting cigarettes etc 打火机；点火器 **2** a large, open, low boat used for loading and unloading ships〔用于装卸货物的〕驳船

light·er·age /ˈlaɪtərɪdʒ; ˈlaɪtərɪdʒ/ *n* [U] the service of moving goods on a lighter, or the charge made for this service 驳运；驳运费

light-fin·gered /ˌ· ˈ··◂/ *adj* **1** likely to steal things 惯于偷窃的 **2** able to move your fingers easily and quickly, especially when you play a musical instrument〔尤指演奏乐器〕手指灵巧的

light-foot·ed /ˌ· ˈ··◂/ *adj* able to move quickly and gracefully 步履轻盈的

light-head·ed /ˌ· ˈ··◂/ *adj* unable to think clearly or move steadily, for example during a fever or after drinking alcohol; DIZZY (1)〔发热或饮酒后〕神志不清的；脚步不稳的；眩晕的: *The sun and the wine had made him a little light-headed.* 阳光和酒使他有些头晕。—**light-headedness** *n* [U]

light-heart·ed /ˌ· ˈ··◂/ *adj* **1** not intended to be serious 非严肃的，轻松的: *a light-hearted comedy* 轻松的喜剧 **2** cheerful and not worried about anything 轻松愉快的；无忧无虑的: *I found her in a light-hearted mood.* 我觉得她心情轻松愉快。—**light-heartedly** *adv* —**light-heartedness** *n* [U]

light heav·y·weight /ˌ· ˈ···/ *n* [C] a BOXER (1) who weighs between 72.5 and 79.5 kilograms〔体重在 72.5 到 79.5 公斤之间的〕轻[次]重量级拳击手 —**light heavyweight** *adj*

light·house /ˈlaɪtˌhaʊs; ˈlaɪthaʊs/ *n* [C] a tower with a powerful flashing light that guides ships away from danger 灯塔

light in·dus·try /ˌ· ˈ···/ *n* [U] the part of industry which produces small goods, such as things used in the house 轻工业

3 **light·ing** /ˈlaɪtɪŋ; ˈlaɪtɪŋ/ *n* [U] the lights that light a room, building, or street, or the quality of the light produced 照明；照明设备: *Better street lighting might help to reduce crime.* 改善街道的照明可能有助于减少犯罪。

lighting up time /ˌ·· ˈ· ˌ·/ *n* [U] *BrE* the time of the evening when the street lights come on and you must put your car lights on【英】〔车辆的〕规定开灯时间

light·ly /ˈlaɪtli; ˈlaɪtli/ *adv* **1** with only a small amount of weight or force; gently 轻轻地，轻微地: *Martin kissed his bride lightly on the cheek.* 马丁轻轻地吻了吻他新娘的脸颊。**2** using or having only a small amount of something 少许，少量: *Rub a casserole lightly with olive oil.* 用少许橄榄油擦砂锅。| *lightly armed soldiers* 轻武装士兵 **3** without worrying, or without appearing to be worried 轻松地；无忧无虑地: *Ma chuckled lightly and went back upstairs.* 妈妈轻松地笑了笑，转身上了楼。**4** done without serious thought 轻率地，不慎重地: **take sth lightly** *Divorce is not a matter you can afford to take lightly.* 离婚不是一桩能草率对待的事。**5 escape/get off lightly** to be punished in a way that is less severe than you deserve 逃脱重罚

light me·ter /ˈ· ˌ··/ *n* [C] an instrument used by a photographer to measure how much light there is〔摄影用的〕曝光表

light·ning[1] /ˈlaɪtnɪŋ; ˈlaɪtnɪŋ/ *n* [U] **1** a powerful flash of light in the sky caused by electricity and usually followed by thunder 闪电: **be struck by lightning** (=be hit by lightning) 被闪电击中 —see picture on page A13 参见 A13 页图 **2 like lightning** extremely quickly 迅如闪电: *The horse streaked like lightning down the track.* 马在跑道上闪电般飞奔。

lightning[2] *adj* very fast, and often without warning 很快的〔往往没有任何预兆〕: *a lightning attack* 闪电般的袭击 | **at/with lightning speed** (=extremely quickly) 以闪电般的速度

lightning bug /ˈ·· ·/ *n* [C] *AmE* an insect with a tail that shines in the dark; FIREFLY【美】萤火虫

lightning con·duc·tor /ˈ·· ·ˌ··/ *BrE*【英】, **lightning rod** /ˈ·· ·/ *AmE*【美】—*n* [C] a metal wire or bar connecting the highest point of a building to the ground to protect the building from lightning 避雷器，避雷针

lightning strike /ˌ·· ˈ·/ *n* [C] *BrE* a STRIKE (=act of stopping work) without any warning【英】〔事先没有警告的〕闪电式罢工

light pen /ˈ· ·/ *n* [C] a piece of equipment like a pen used to draw lines on a computer screen〔用于在电脑荧光屏上画线的〕光笔

light rail·way /ˌ· ˈ··/ *BrE*【英】, **light rail** /ˌ· ˈ·/ *AmE*【美】— *n* [C] an electric railway system that uses light trains and usually carries only passengers, not goods〔载客用的〕轻便铁路，轻轨

light·ship /ˈlaɪtˌʃɪp; ˈlaɪtˌʃɪp/ *n* [C] a small ship that stays near a dangerous place at sea and guides other ships using a powerful flashing light〔导航用的〕灯船

light show /ˈ· ·/ *n* [C] a series of moving coloured lights, especially at a POP concert〔尤指流行音乐会上的〕灯光表演

lights-out /ˌ· ˈ·/ *n* [U] the time at night when a group of people who are in a school, the army etc must put the lights out and go to sleep〔学校、军队等〕熄灯 (就寝) 时间

light·weight[1] /ˈlaɪtˌwet; ˈlaɪt-weɪt/ *n* [C] **1** someone who has no importance or influence, or who does not have the ability to think deeply 微不足道的人，无足轻重的人；思想浅薄的人: *an intellectual lightweight* 智力平庸的人 **2** a BOXER (1) who weighs between 59 and 61 kilograms〔体重为 59 至 61 公斤的〕轻量级拳击手 **3** someone or something of less than average weight 重量低于平均的人[物]

lightweight[2] *adj* **1** weighing less than average 比平均重量轻的: *special lightweight fabric* 特别轻的织物 **2** showing a lack of serious thought 思想浮浅的，浅薄的: *She's written nothing but lightweight novels.* 她只写了一些浅薄的小说。

light year /ˈ· ·/ *n* [C] **1** the distance that light travels in one year, about 9,500,000,000,000 kilometres, used for measuring distances between stars 光年 **2** also 又作 **light years** *plural informal* a very long time【非正式】很长的时间: *It all seems light years ago now.* 这一切现在看来都是很久以前的事了。

lig·ne·ous /ˈlɪgnɪəs; ˈlɪgniəs/ *adj technical* like wood【术语】木的，木质的；木头似的

lig·nite /ˈlɪgnaɪt; ˈlɪgnaɪt/ *n* [U] a soft substance like coal, used as FUEL[1] (1) 褐煤

lik·a·ble, likeable /ˈlaɪkəbl; ˈlaɪkəbəl/ *adj* likable people are nice and easy to like〔人〕可爱的，讨人喜欢的: *a friendly likeable little boy* 友善可爱的小男孩

like[1] /laɪk; laɪk/ *prep* **1** similar in some way to something else 像，相似: *My mother has a car like yours.* 我妈妈有一辆车与你的相似。| *He crawled out of the hut on his belly, like a snake.* 他像蛇一样匍匐着爬出了小屋。| **very like** *He's very like his brother.* 他很像他的哥哥。| **look/sound/feel/taste/seem like** *The building looked like a church.* 这座建筑物看上去像教堂。| *At last he felt like a real soldier.* 他终于感到像一名真正的战士了。| **just like** (=exactly like) 完全像 *She was just like all the other girls.* 她跟所有其他女孩完全一样。| **like new** (=in perfect condition) 像新的 *The carpet just needs a good clean and it'll be like new.* 地毯只需好好地清洗一下，就会像新的一样。**2 nothing like/anything like** used to say that something is not at all similar to something else, or to ask whether it is similar 一点也不像/是否像〔用于指某物不像另一物或询问是否相似〕: *The course was nothing like what I'd expected.* 这门课程一点也不像我期望的那样。| *Was the film anything like the book?* 这部电影拍得是否和原著相似？**3 like this/like so** *spoken* used when you are showing someone how to do something【口】就像这样〔用于教人做事时〕: *You have to fold the corners back, like so.* 你得把角往回折叠，就像这样。**4** typical of a particular person 符合〔某人〕的特点: *It's not like Steven to be late.* 史蒂文一向不迟到的。**5 what is sb/sth like?** used when asking someone to describe or give their opinion of a person or thing 某人/某物怎样[如何]？〔用于叫某人形容某人[物]或发表意见〕: *Have you met the new boss? What's he like?* 你见到新老板没有？他这个人怎样？**6** for example 例如，像: *far-off countries like Australia and China* 遥远的国家，如澳大利亚和中国 | *nutritious foods like eggs and fish* 营养食品，如鸡蛋和鱼 **7 something like** not much more or less than a particular amount; about 大概，大约: *The machinery alone will*

cost something like thirty thousand pounds. 单是机器就要花费大约3万英镑。**8 more like** used when giving an amount or number that you think is more accurate than one that has been mentioned 更可能像(是)〔提供更准确的数量或数字〕: *The builders say they'll be finished in three months, but I think it'll be more like six.* 建筑商说他们会在三个月内完工, 但是我认为更可能会是六个月。**9 there's nothing like** *spoken* used to say that a particular thing is the best【口】没有什么比得上〔用于指某事物是最好的〕: *There's nothing like a nice cup of tea!* 没有什么比喝杯好茶更好的了! **10 that's more like it** *spoken* used to tell someone that what they are doing or suggesting is more satisfactory than what they did or suggested before【口】这比较像样, 这还差不多〔用于告诉某人他现在的行为或建议比以前好〕

like² *v* [T not usually in progressive 一般不用进行时] **1** to enjoy something or think that it is nice 喜欢, 喜爱; 爱好: *I like your new dress.* 我喜欢你的新裙子。| *Bill doesn't like Chinese food.* 比尔不喜欢中国菜。| **like sth best** (=prefer it) 最喜欢某物 *Which of these colours do you like best?* 这几种颜色你最喜爱哪种? | **like doing sth** *I like swimming, playing tennis, and things like that.* 我爱好游泳、打网球及诸如此类的运动。| **like to do sth** *I like to see the children enjoying themselves.* 我喜欢看到孩子玩得开心。| **like sth about sth/sb** *What I like about this job is the flexibility.* 这工作我喜欢的是它的灵活性。| **like it** *I don't like it when you look at me like that!* 我不喜欢你那样看着我! | *It was a great place for a vacation. You'd have liked it there.* 那是度假的好地方, 要是你到那里会喜欢它的。| **like the idea/thought of (doing) sth** *Sandra didn't like the idea of being so far from home.* 桑德拉不想离家那么远。| **like the look/sound of** *I don't like the look of that black cloud over there. We'd better go in.* 我看那边的那块乌云不太妙, 我们最好进屋里去。| **get to like sth** *informal* (=begin to like it)【非正式】开始喜欢某物 *I don't think I'll ever get to like modern art.* 我不认为我还会喜欢现代艺术。**2** to think that someone is nice or enjoy being with them 喜欢〔某人〕: *I don't think he likes me – he never talks to me.* 我不认为他喜欢我 —— 他从来没有跟我说过话。**3** to prefer that something is done in one particular way or at one particular time rather than another 想要〔某事以特定的方式或在某时间做〕; 希望: **like sth** *"How do you like your coffee?" "Black, please."* "你喜欢喝什么样的咖啡?" "不加牛奶的, 谢谢。" | *I like films with action in them. None of this boring romantic stuff.* 我喜欢动作片, 不喜欢这种乏味的言情片。**4** to think that it is good to do something, so that you do it regularly or want other people to do it regularly 喜好〔认为做某事有益, 于是定期做或想其他人也定期做〕: **like to do sth** *I always like to get up early in the summer.* 夏天我总是喜欢早起。| **like sb to do sth** *We like our students to take a full part in college social and sports activities.* 我们希望学生全面参与学院的社交和体育活动。**5 not like to do sth/not like doing sth** *especially BrE* to not want to do something because you do not feel it is polite, fair, nice etc【尤英】不愿意做某事〔因认为是无礼、不公平、不友善等〕: *I don't like bothering him when he's busy.* 他忙的时候, 我不愿意打扰他。**6** to approve of something or have a good opinion of it 赞成, 同意〔某事〕: *I really didn't like the way he avoided giving us direct answers.* 我确实不赞成他回避正面答复我们的做法。| **like sb doing sth** *Claus doesn't like anyone arguing with him.* 克劳斯讨厌任何人和他争论。| **like sb to do sth** *I'd like you to be honest with me.* 我要你对我诚实。

Frequencies of the verb **like** in spoken and written English
动词like在英语口语和书面语中的使用频率

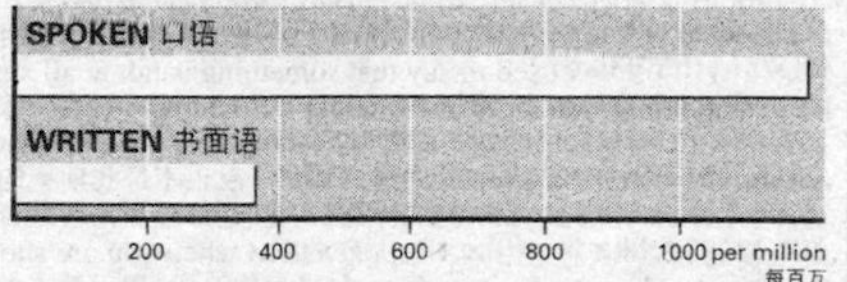

Based on the British National Corpus and the Longman Lancaster Corpus
据英国国家语料库和朗文兰开斯特语料库

This graph shows that the verb **like** is much more common in spoken English than in written English. This is because it is used in a lot of common spoken phrases. 本图表显示, 动词like在英语口语中的使用频率远远高于书面语, 因为口语中很多常用短语是由like构成的。

like (*v*) **SPOKEN PHRASES**
含like的口语短语

7 I'd like used to say what you want 我想要: **I'd like sth** *I'd like a cheeseburger.* 我想要干酪汉堡包。| **I'd like you/John etc to do sth** *I'd like her to be at tomorrow's meeting.* 我想要她出席明天的会议。**8 would you like ...? a)** used to ask someone if they want something 你想要…吗?〔用于问某人是否要某物〕: **would you like sth** *Would you like some more cake?* 你还想要些蛋糕吗? | **would you like to do sth?** *Well, would you like to come shopping with me?* 那么, 你愿意和我一起去购物吗? | **would you like me/her etc to do sth?** *Would you like me to pick you up in the morning?* 你要我早晨来接你吗? **b)** also 又作 **How would you like ...?** used to offer someone something that someone does not expect, but that you know they will like 你觉得…如何?〔用于征求某人对某建议的意见, 对方没料想有此一问, 但估计会同意〕: **(How) would you like to do sth?** *How would you like to go to the camp in the mountains this summer?* 今年夏天去山里的营地你觉得怎么样? **9 would like** used to express politely what you want to happen or do 想要〔用于礼貌地表达愿望〕: *We'd really like a holiday in Italy, but it's so expensive.* 我们真想去意大利度假, 但是太贵了。| **would like to do** *I'd just like to comment on a few things that were said.* 我想就说过的几件事发表一下意见。| **would like sb to do** *We'd like you to come in for a second interview on Monday, if possible.* 若可能的话, 请你星期一来做第二次面试。| **would like (to have) sth done** *I'd like to have the report finished by tomorrow.* 我想这份报告明天就得完成。**10 if you like** *especially BrE*【尤英】**a)** used to suggest or offer something 如果你愿意〔用于提出建议〕: *If you like, I could go with you to the doctor's.* 如果你愿意, 我可以陪你去看医生。**b)** used to agree to something, even if it is not what you want yourself 要是你喜欢〔用于表示赞同, 即使并非自己所愿〕: *"Can we have spaghetti tonight?" "If you like."* "今晚我们吃意大利面条好吗?" "你喜欢就行。" **c)** used to suggest one possible way of describing something or someone 可以说是〔用于提出形容某物或人的可行方法〕: *This experience was, if you like, a door that opened up a whole new world.* 这次经历, 可以说, 是开启整个新天地的门户。**11 whatever/anything etc you like** *especially BrE* whatever you want【尤英】你想要怎样就怎样: *"Which play shall we go to see?" "Oh, whichever you like."* "我们去看哪部话剧?" "哦, 你想看哪部就看哪部吧。" | *Come and stay with us for as long as you like.* 来我家住, 你愿待多久就待多久。**12 I like that! a)** used to say that you like what someone has said, shown you etc 我喜欢!〔用于表示赞同他人所言、所示等〕: *"That's a great story!" he said, roaring with laughter, "I really like that!"* "这故事太棒了!" 他大声地笑着说, "我真的喜欢极了!" **b)** *especially BrE* used to say that what someone has said or done is rude and unfair【尤英】亏你说得出口[干得出来]!〔用于表示对粗鲁和不公正言行的反感〕: *"I thought you were older than her." "Well, I like that!"* "我以为你的年纪比她大。" "嘿, 亏你说得出口!" **13 how would you like...? a)** used to ask someone if they want something, especially when you already know they want it 你想要…吗?〔用于问某人是否要某物, 尤用于已知道他想要时〕: **how would you like sth?** *How would you like a cup of coffee?* 给你来杯咖啡好吗? | **how would you like to do sth?** *Say, how would you like to go to Italy next summer?* 你说, 明年夏天去意大利怎么样? **b)** used to ask someone to imagine how they would feel if something bad happened to them instead of to you or someone else 你会怎么想〔用于叫某人想象自己遇到坏事时会有什么感觉〕: **how would you like it if?** *How would you like it if you got home to find you'd been burgled?* 如果你回到家里发现被盗, 你会怎么想? | **How would you like sb doing sth?** *How would you like your boss calling you an idiot?* 老板叫你白痴, 你会感觉如何? **14 how do you like? a)** used to ask someone for their opinion of something 你觉得怎样?〔用于征询意见〕: *How do you like my new jacket?* 你觉得我的新短上衣怎样? **b) how do you like that?** used to ask someone what they think after you have done something or told them something surprising, unpleasant etc 你对这事有何想法?〔做了某事, 或告诉了对方令人惊讶、讨厌的事情后, 问他们的想法〕 **15 (whether you) like it or not** used to emphasize that something unpleasant is true or will happen and cannot be changed 不管[无论]你喜不喜欢〔强调令人讨厌的事是真的或即将发生, 并且无法改变〕: *You're coming to your grandparents' today whether you like it or not!* 不管你喜不喜欢, 今天你都要去祖父母家! **16 I'd like to see you/him do sth** used to say that you do not believe someone can do some-

thing 我倒要看看你/他做某事〔表示不相信某人能做某事〕: *I'd like to see you run as fast as that!* 我倒要看看你跑那么快! **17 I'd like to think/believe (that) a)** used to say that you wish or hope something is true, when you are not sure that it is 我但愿[希望]…〔用于表示希望某事是真的, 但不肯定〕: *I'd like to believe that one day he'll be well enough to lead a normal life.* 我但愿他有一天会康复到能过正常人的生活。**b)** used to say that you think you do something well, especially when you do not want to make yourself seem better than other people 我倒认为…〔表示认为自己做得好, 尤用于不想自夸时〕: *I'd like to think that my work is as good as anybody's here.* 我倒认为我的工作和这里任何一个人的都一样好。

like³ *n* **1 sb's likes and dislikes** all the things you like and do not like 某人的好恶[爱憎]: *All the children have their likes and dislikes when it comes to food.* 在吃的方面, 所有孩子都有他们的好恶。**2 and the like** and similar things 诸如此类, 等等: *He was interested in natural disasters, such as volcanoes, earthquakes and the like.* 他对自然灾害很感兴趣, 如火山、地震等等。**3 the like of sb/sth** also 又作 **sb's/sth's like** something similar to someone or a particular person or thing, or of equal importance or value 像某人[物]一样〔重要或有价值〕的〔人/物〕: *He gave a superb performance, the like of which has never been seen since.* 他的表演精彩绝伦, 前无古人。| *The man was a genius. We shall not see his like again.* 那人是位天才, 我们不会再见到这样的人物。**4 the likes of** *spoken*【口】**a)** used to talk about someone you do not like 类似…的人〔用于谈论不喜欢的人〕: *I'd never vote for the likes of him!* 我决不会投他那种人的票! **b)** used to talk about people of a particular type or social class …的一类人〔用以谈论某种人〕: *Those expensive restaurants with fancy food aren't for the likes of us.* 那些饭菜讲究、收费昂贵的餐厅不是为我们这种人开的。

S1 W3 **like⁴** *adj* [only before noun 仅用于名词前] *formal*【正式】**1** similar in some way 相似的, 相像的: *They understand each other because they are of like mind.* 他们彼此理解, 因为他们志趣相投。**2 be like to do sth** *old use* to be likely to do something【旧】有可能做某事

S1 **like⁵** *conjunction especially spoken*【尤口】**1** in the same way as 像…一样的方式: *Don't talk to me like you talk to a child.* 不要像跟孩子说话一样跟我说话。**2 like I say/said** used when you are repeating something that you have already said 正如我说的/说过的那样: *Like I said, I don't mind helping out on the day.* 正如我说过的, 那天去帮忙我没意见。**3** as if 好像, 似乎: *I acted like I couldn't see them.* 我装得好像看不见他们一样。

S1 **like⁶** *adv spoken*【口】**1** used in speech to fill a pause while you are thinking what to say next 嗯〔用在说话中垫补思考下文时出现的停顿〕: *This bloke will look at it for me, like, and he'll tell me what it needs.* 这家伙会替我查看它, 嗯, 他会告诉我需要些什么。**2 as like as not/like enough** probably 很可能: *The car will be written off as like as not.* 这辆汽车很可能报废。

-like *n* /laɪk; laɪk/ *suffix* [in adjectives 构成形容词] typical of, or suitable to something 像…似的; 有…特征的; 适于…的: *a jelly-like substance* 胶冻状的物质 | *childlike simplicity* 孩子般的单纯 | *ladylike behaviour* 贵妇人似的举止

like·a·ble /ˈlaɪkəbl; ˈlaɪkəbəl/ *adj* another spelling of LIKABLE likable的另一种拼法

like·li·hood /ˈlaɪklɪˌhʊd; ˈlaɪklihʊd/ *n* [singular, U] **1** the degree to which something can reasonably be expected to happen; PROBABILITY 可能(性): **[+of]** *taking steps to reduce the likelihood of disease* 采取措施减少染病的可能性 | **[+(that)]** *a greater likelihood that you will make a profit* 你将获利的更大可能性 **2 in all likelihood** almost certainly 几乎肯定地; 极可能地: *If I refused, it would in all likelihood mean I'd lose my job.* 如果我拒绝, 那就极可能意味着我会丢掉工作。

S1 W1 **like·ly¹** /ˈlaɪklɪ; ˈlaɪkli/ *adj* **likelier, likeliest** **1** something that is likely will probably happen or is probably true 可能的; 可能发生的; 可能是真的: *Snow showers are likely in the next 24 hours.* 未来24小时内可能有阵雪。| *the likely cost of the operation* 手术可能的费用 | *the likeliest outcome of the talks* 会谈最有可能的成果 | **likely to do sth** *remarks that are likely to offend some war veterans* 可能会冒犯某些退伍军人的话语 | **more than likely (that)** (=almost certain) 几乎肯定的; 极可能的 *Ian had been sick too, so it's more than likely you caught it from him.* 伊恩也生过病, 所以几乎可以肯定你是从他那儿传染的。**2** [only before noun 仅用于名词前] as suitable or almost certain to produce good results 很合适的; 很可能成功的: *a likely candidate* 可能当选的候选人 | *Search all the most likely places first – maybe he's hiding in the cellar.* 首先搜索所有最有可能躲藏的地方——可能他正躲在地窖中。| **likely-looking** (=seeming likely to produce results) 可能产生结果的 **3 a likely story** *spoken* used to tell someone you do not believe what they have just said【口】说得像真的似的〔告诉某人你不相信他刚说过的话〕

likely² *adv* **1** probably 大概, 很可能: *I'd very likely have done the same thing in your situation.* 在你那种情况下, 我很可能做同样的事。| **likely as not** *spoken* (=probably)【口】很可能 *Likely as not, we'll never be told what really happened.* 很可能, 我们永远也不会被告知到底发生了什么事。**2 not likely!** *spoken especially BrE* used to disagree strongly, or to say that something will not happen【口, 尤英】才不呢! 绝不可能!〔表示强烈反对或某事不会发生〕: *"He said you'd be giving them a lift." "Not likely!"* "他说你会让他们搭便车。" "绝不可能!"

like-mind·ed /ˌ· ˈ··◂/ *adj* having similar interests and opinions 趣味相投的; 想法一致的 —**like-mindedness** *n* [U]

lik·en /ˈlaɪkən; ˈlaɪkən/ *v*

liken sb/sth **to** sb/sth *phr v* [T usually passive 一般用被动态] *formal* to describe something or someone as being similar to another person or thing【正式】将〔某人或某物〕比作〔另一人或物〕: *Critics have likened the new theater to a supermarket.* 评论家将新剧院比作超级市场。

like·ness /ˈlaɪknɪs; ˈlaɪknɪ̆s/ *n* **1** [C,U] similarity in appearance between people; RESEMBLANCE〔人的外表〕相似, 相像: **[+to]** *Hugh's uncanny likeness to his father* 休和他父亲出奇的相像 **2** [C] a painting or photograph of a person, especially one that looks very like the person; PORTRAIT¹ (1)〔尤指酷似本人的〕画像, 肖像; 相片: *That's a remarkable likeness of Julia.* 那是朱莉娅一张非常出众的肖像。

like·wise /ˈlaɪkˌwaɪz; ˈlaɪk-waɪz/ *adv* **1** *formal* in the same way; similarly【正式】同样地; 相似地: *I was up at dawn, and my host likewise.* 我天一亮就起床, 主人也是这个时候起床。| **do likewise** *Nanny put on a shawl and told the girls to do likewise.* 南妮披上披肩, 并且告诉女孩们也这样做。| [sentence adverb 句子副词] *There has been an upsurge of interest in chamber music. Likewise opera is receiving a boost from increased record sales.* 人们对室内乐的兴趣大增, 同样地, 歌剧因唱片销量的增长而受到了推动。**2 likewise** *spoken* used to return someone's greeting or polite comment【口】也, 同样〔用于回答问候或客气的评论〕: *"You're always welcome at our house." "Likewise."* "欢迎你随时来我家作客。" "彼此彼此。"

lik·ing /ˈlaɪkɪŋ; ˈlaɪkɪŋ/ *n* **1 have a liking for sth** *formal* to like something【正式】喜欢某物: *a liking for chocolate* 喜欢吃巧克力 **2 take a liking to sb** to like someone you have just met〔刚见面便〕喜欢上某人 **3 to your liking** *formal* being just what you wanted【正式】对你的胃口, 合你的心意: *I hope everything in the suite was to your liking, Sir.* 先生, 我希望套房内的一切都合你的心意。

Li·kud, the /lɪˈkud; lɪˈkʊd/ one of the main political parties in Israel. It is a RIGHT WING party. 利库德集团, 自由党, 联合党〔以色列的主要政党之一, 是一支右翼党派〕

li·lac /ˈlaɪlək; ˈlaɪlək/ *n* **1** [C] a small tree with pale purple or white flowers 丁香 **2** [U] a pale purple colour 淡紫色 —**lilac** *adj*: *a lilac dress* 淡紫色的连衣裙 —see picture on page A5 参见A5页图

Lil·ith /ˈlɪlɪθ; ˈlɪlɪ̆θ/ a female DEVIL (=an evil spirit), who, according to an ancient Jewish tradition, was the first wife of Adam, and was also a VAMPIRE (=an evil spirit that sucks people's blood) 夜妖, 女魔鬼〔据古犹太传说, 她是亚当的第一任妻子, 是个吸血鬼〕

Lil·li·bur·le·ro /ˌlɪlɪbəˈlɛro; ˌlɪlibəˈleərəʊ/ a song which is a SATIRE on Irish Roman Catholics and the appointment of General Talbot as Lord Lieutenant of Ireland in 1687《利利布雷洛》〔一首讽刺爱尔兰天主教和1687年任命塔尔博特将军为爱尔兰总督一事的歌曲〕

Lil·li·put /ˈlɪlɪpʌt; ˈlɪlɪ̆pʌt/ an imaginary country in the book *Gulliver's Travels* by Jonathan Swift, where all the people, animals, and buildings are very small 小人国〔乔纳森·斯威夫特创作的《格列佛游记》(又名《大人国与小人国》) 中一个虚构的国家。该国国民、动物和建筑都格外地小〕

lil·li·pu·tian /ˌlɪlɪˈpjuʃən; ˌlɪlɪ̆ˈpjuːʃən◂/ *adj* extremely small compared to the normal size of things〔同正常物体比较〕极小的

Li·lo /ˈlaɪlo; ˈlaɪləʊ/ *n* [C] *BrE trademark* a rubber MATTRESS filled with air and used as a bed or for floating on water【英, 商标】充气垫〔用作床或用于水上漂浮〕

lilt /lɪlt; lɪlt/ *n* [singular] a pleasant pattern of rising and falling sound in someone's voice or in music 抑扬顿挫的声音; 优美的旋律 —**lilting** *adj*: *a lilting melody* 优美的曲调

li·ly /ˈlɪlɪ; ˈlɪli/ *n* [C] one of several types of plant with large bell-shaped flowers of various colours, especially white 百合(花) —see also 另见 **gild the lily** (GILD (3)), WATER LILY

lily-liv·ered /ˌ··ˈ··◂/ *adj old-fashioned* lacking courage【过时】胆小的，懦弱的

lily of the val·ley /ˌ·····ˈ··/ *n* [C] a plant with several small white bell-shaped flowers 铃兰

lily pad /ˈ··ˌ·/ *n* [C] the leaf of the WATER LILY that floats on the surface of the water 睡莲的漂浮叶

lily-white /ˌ··ˈ·◂/ *adj* **1** *literary* pure white【文】纯白的: *lily-white skin* 白皙的皮肤 **2** *informal* morally perfect【非正式】道德高尚的: *You're not so lily-white yourself!* 你本人也并非如此品格端正!

Li·ma /ˈlimə; ˈliːmə/ the capital city of Peru, which is an important industrial centre and has a 16th century university 利马〔秘鲁首都，为该国重要工业中心。该市有一所16世纪创立的大学〕

li·ma bean /ˈlaɪmə bin; ˈliːmə biːn/ *n* [C] a flat bean that grows in tropical America, or the plant that produces it 利马豆

limb /lɪm; lɪm/ *n* [C] **1** **out on a limb** alone and without help or support 孤立无援: *All the other EU governments have signed the agreement, leaving Britain out on a limb.* 所有其他欧盟国家的政府都签署了协议，这使英国孤立无援。| **go out on a limb** (=take a risk) 冒险 **2** an arm or leg 肢; 手臂; 腿 **3** a large branch of a tree 大树枝 **4** **strong-limbed/long-limbed etc** having strong, long etc arms and legs 四肢强壮的/四肢长的等 —see also 另见 **tear sb limb from limb** (TEAR² (10))

lim·ber¹ /ˈlɪmbɚ; ˈlɪmbə/ *v*

limber up *phr v* [I] to do gentle exercises in order to make your muscles stretch and move easily, especially when preparing for a race, competition etc〔尤指在赛跑、比赛等前〕做热身运动

limber² *adj* able to move and bend easily; SUPPLE 易弯曲的; 柔软灵活的

lim·bo /ˈlɪmbo; ˈlɪmbəʊ/ *n* **1** **be in limbo** to be in an uncertain situation in which it is difficult to know what to do 处于不确定的状态: *I'm in limbo now until I know whether I've got the job.* 我现在心中没有着落，要一直到我知道是否得到那份工作。**2** **the limbo** a West Indian dance in which the dancer leans backwards and goes under a stick that is lowered gradually〔西印度群岛的〕林波舞〔舞者向后弯腰通过逐步降低的横杆〕

lime¹ /laɪm; laɪm/ *n* **1** [C] a small juicy green fruit with a sour taste, or the tree this grows on 酸橙(树) —see picture on page A8 参见A8页图 **2** [C] a tree with pleasant-smelling yellow flowers; LINDEN 椴树 **3** [U] a white substance obtained by burning LIMESTONE, used for making cement, marking sports fields etc; QUICKLIME 石灰; 生石灰 —see also 另见 BIRDLIME

lime² *v* [T] *technical* to add lime to soil to control acid【术语】撒石灰于〔土壤中以控制酸性〕

lime·ade /ˌlaɪmˈed; ˌlaɪmˈeɪd/ *n* [U] a drink made from the juice of limes 酸橙饮料

lime green /ˌ·ˈ·◂/ *n* [U] a light yellowish green colour 浅黄绿色, 酸橙绿色 —**lime-green** *adj* —see picture on page A5 参见A5页图

lime·light /ˈlaɪmˌlaɪt; ˈlaɪmlaɪt/ *n* [singular] a situation in which someone receives a lot of attention, especially from newspapers, television etc 公众关注的中心: **be in the limelight** *Tad loves being in the limelight.* 塔德喜欢成为公众关注的焦点。| **steal the limelight** *She's afraid this new actor will steal the limelight from her.* 她害怕这位新演员会抢去她的风头。

Lim·e·rick /ˈlɪmərɪk; ˈlɪmərɪk/ **1** a COUNTY in the southwest of the Republic of Ireland 利默里克郡〔爱尔兰共和国西南部一郡〕 **2** the main town of this county 利默里克〔利默里克郡主要城镇〕

limerick *n* [C] a humorous short poem, with three long lines and two short ones 五行打油诗〔三句长, 两句短〕

lime·scale /ˈlaɪmˌskel; ˈlaɪmskeɪl/ *n* [U] a hard white or grey substance that forms on the inside of pipes, TAPS and water containers 水碱

lime·stone /ˈlaɪmˌston; ˈlaɪmstəʊn/ *n* [U] a type of rock that contains CALCIUM 石灰岩

li·mey /ˈlaɪmɪ; ˈlaɪmi/ *n* [C] *AmE old-fashioned* a slightly insulting word for a British person【美, 过时】英国佬〔略带冒犯〕

lim·it¹ /ˈlɪmɪt; ˈlɪmɪt/ *n*

1 ▶**GREATEST AMOUNT ALLOWED** 最大的限量◀ [C] the greatest amount, number, speed etc that is allowed 限度; 极限: *a 55 mph speed limit* 55英里的时速限制 | [+to/on] *Is there any limit to the amount of time we have?* 我们的时间有没有限制? | **set a limit (on)** *attempts to set limits on consumer waste* 试图设定生活垃圾的限量 | **lower/upper limit** (=lowest or highest point something is allowed to reach) 最低/最高限度 *an upper limit for pollution levels* 污染水平的上限

2 ▶**GREATEST AMOUNT POSSIBLE** 可能的最大量◀ also 又作 **limits** [C] the greatest possible amount of something that can exist or be obtained〔现有的或可获取的〕最大量[限度]; [+of] *the limits of human knowledge* 人类知识的限度 | **to the limit** *Our finances are already stretched to the limit.* 我们的财力已经用到了极限。| **there is no limit (to)** *There's no limit to what you can do if you try.* 如果你努力, 成就无可限量。

3 ▶**PLACE** 地方◀ [C] the furthest point or edge of a place, that must not be passed〔不可以通过的〕界限, 边界: *The public is not allowed within a 2-mile limit of the missile site.* 公众禁止进入导弹发射场两英里以内的范围。

4 **within limits** within the time, level, amount etc considered acceptable 在合理限度内: *You can come and go when you want – within limits.* 你可以来去自由, 但要有分寸。

5 **know your limits** *informal* to know what you are good at doing and what you are not good at【非正式】知道长处和短处: *I know my limits. I'm not an administrator.* 我有自知之明。我不是搞行政管理的料。

6 **have your limits** *informal* to have a set of ideas about what is reasonable to do, and to not accept behaviour that does not follow those ideas【非正式】有〔行为的〕准则: *You cannot smoke pot in this house. Even I have my limits!* 你不可以在这屋内抽大麻, 甚至连我都有原则!

7 **there are limits!** *spoken* used to express shock or disapproval of someone's behaviour【口】要有个分寸!〔对某人的行为表示震惊或不赞成〕—see also 另见 **the sky's the limit** (SKY (3))

8 **be the limit** *spoken* to be so annoying that you upset someone【口】令人无法容忍; 太过分: *Have you lost your glasses again? You really are the limit!* 你又把眼镜弄丢了? 你真是太过分了!

9 **be over the limit** to have drunk more alcohol than is legal or safe for driving〔驾驶〕饮酒过量

10 **off limits** *especially AmE* beyond the area where someone is allowed to go【尤美】禁止入内: *That area of beach was off limits to us 'city kids'.* 我们"城市孩子"禁止进入沙滩的那个范围。

limit² *v* **1** [T] to stop an amount or number from increasing beyond a particular point〔在量或数上〕限制, 限定: *a decision to limit imports of foreign cars* 限制外国汽车进口的决定 | **limit sth to** *Seating is limited to 500.* 限定500个座位。**2** [T] to stop someone from using as much of something as they want or from behaving in the way they want〔使用或行为上〕限制: *Obviously I'm limited by my pension situation.* 显然, 我受到养老金状况的限制。| **limit yourself to sth** *We must limit ourselves to one gallon of water per day.* 我们必须限定自己每天最多使用一加仑水。**3** **be limited to** to exist or happen only in a particular place, group, or area of activity 局限于〔某地方、团体或活动范围〕: *Her traveling has been limited to a few French resorts.* 她的旅行局限于几处法国旅游胜地。

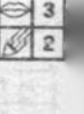

lim·i·ta·tion /ˌlɪməˈteʃən; ˌlɪmɪˈteɪʃən/ *n* **1** [U] the act of limiting something 限制: [+of] *the limitation of armaments* 军备限制 —see also 另见 **damage limitation** (DAMAGE¹ (7)) **2** [C usually plural 一般用复数] a limit on how good someone or something can be, what they are able to do etc〔某人或物的〕局限, 不足之处: **have your limitations** *It's a good little car, but it has its limitations.* 这是一辆很好的小汽车, 但是有它的不足之处。

lim·it·ed /ˈlɪmɪtɪd; ˈlɪmɪtɪd/ *adj* **1** not very great in amount, number, ability etc, and impossible to improve or increase 有限的〔不可能改善或增加〕: *My time is more limited now that I have a baby.* 由于我有了孩子, 我的时间就更有限了。| *families on limited incomes* 收入有限的家庭 | *a student of limited intelligence* 智力平平的学生 **2** **Limited** written abbreviation 缩写为 **Ltd** used after the name of British business companies that have LIMITED LIABILITY 有限责任的〔置于英国有限责任公司名称之后〕—compare 比较 INCORPORATED

limited com·pa·ny /ˌ····ˈ···/ *n* [C] a company whose owners only have to pay a limited amount if the company gets into debt (股份)有限公司 —compare 比较 PUBLIC LIMITED COMPANY

limited e·di·tion /ˌ····ˈ··/ *n* [C] a fixed number of copies of a book, picture etc produced at one time〔书画等的〕特定版, 限量版

limited li·a·bil·i·ty /ˌ······ˈ··/ *n* [U] *technical* the legal position of being responsible for paying only a limited amount of debt if something bad happens to yourself or your company【术语】有限责任

limited liability com·pa·ny /ˌ······ˈ··, ···/ *n* [C] *technical* a LIMITED COMPANY【术语】(股份)有限(责任)公司

lim·it·ing /ˈlɪmətɪŋ; ˈlɪmɪtɪŋ/ *adj* **1** preventing any improvement or increase in something 限制性的: **limiting factor** *A limiting factor in health care is the way resources are distributed.* 资源的分配方式是医疗保健的一个限制性因素。**2** *informal* preventing someone from developing and doing what they are interested in【非正式】有局限的〔阻止某人发展或做有兴趣的事〕: *The job's OK, but it's sort of limiting.* 这工作不错, 但有点束缚。

lim·it·less /ˈlɪmɪtlɪs; ˈlɪmɪtləs/ *adj* without a limit or end 无限的: *limitless possibilities* 无限的可能 —**limitlessly** *adv* —**limitlessness** *n* [U]

lim·o /ˈlɪmo; ˈlɪməʊ/ *n* [C] *informal* a limousine【非正式】大型豪华轿车; 中型客车

Li·moges /lɪˈmoʒ; lɪˈməʊʒ/ a city in west central France, where fine PORCELAIN cups, plates etc are made 利摩日〔法国中西部一城市, 出产精细瓷杯、瓷盘等〕

lim·ou·sine /ˈlɪməˌzin; ˈlɪməziːn/ *n* [C] **1** a big expensive comfortable car 大型豪华轿车 **2** a small comfortable bus that people take to and from airports in the US〔美国往返机场的〕中型客车

limp¹ /lɪmp; lɪmp/ *adj* not firm or strong 软的; 不强壮的: *a limp handshake* 无力的握手 | *His limp body collapsed forward.* 他软弱的身体向前瘫倒了。—**limply** *adv* —**limpness** *n* [U]

limp² *v* [I] **1** to walk slowly and with difficulty because one leg is hurt or injured〔因受伤而〕跛行, 一瘸一拐地走 —see picture on page A24 参见 A24 页图 **2** if a ship or aircraft limps somewhere, it goes there slowly, because it has been damaged〔船或飞机因损坏而〕缓慢地前进

limp³ *n* [C] the way someone walks when they are limping 跛行: *Young walked with a slight limp.* 扬走路有一点跛。

lim·pet /ˈlɪmpɪt; ˈlɪmpɪt/ *n* [C] a small sea animal with a shell, which holds tightly onto the rock where it lives 蝛, 帽贝 —see picture at 参见 SHELL¹ 图

lim·pid /ˈlɪmpɪd; ˈlɪmpɪd/ *adj literary* clear or transparent【文】清澈的, 透明的: *limpid blue eyes* 清澈的蓝眼睛 —**limpidly** *adv* —**limpidness** *n* [U] —**limpidity** /lɪmˈpɪdətɪ; lɪmˈpɪdɪti/ *n* [U]

Lim·po·po, the /lɪmˈpopo; lɪmˈpəʊpəʊ/ a river in southern Africa, which flows from South Africa and through Mozambique to the Indian Ocean 林波波河〔非洲南部一河流, 从南非流经莫桑比克, 最后注入印度洋〕

limp-wrist·ed /ˌ· ˈ··◂/ *adj* a man who is limp-wristed is considered to lack strong, traditionally male qualities〔男子〕缺乏阳刚气的

lim·y /ˈlaɪmɪ; ˈlaɪmi/ *adj* containing or covered in LIME¹ (3) 含有石灰的, 石灰质的: *limy particles* 石灰微粒

linch·pin, lynchpin /ˈlɪntʃˌpɪn; ˈlɪntʃˌpɪn/ *n* **the linchpin of** the person or thing in a group, system etc that is most important, because everything depends on them〔团体、制度等中的〕关键人物, 关键东西

Lin·coln¹ /ˈlɪŋkən; ˈlɪŋkən/ the capital city of the US state of Nebraska 林肯〔美国内布拉斯加州首府〕

Lincoln² *trademark* a type of large US car made by the Ford company. The **Lincoln Continental** is one of the best-known LUXURY cars in the US.【商标】林肯〔美国福特汽车公司生产的一种大型汽车。"林肯-大陆"车是美国最为知名的豪华轿车之一〕

Lincoln, Abraham (1809-65) a US politician in the Republican Party who was President of the US from 1861 to 1865. He won political support in the Northern US states because of his speeches against SLAVERY, but this made him unpopular in the Southern states, where slaves did most of the farm work. The American Civil War started soon after he became President, when the Southern states decided to leave the US. In 1863 he announced *The Emancipation Proclamation*, by which all slaves in the US became free people. He also gave a famous speech known as *The Gettysburg Address* in 1863. A few days after the war ended, he was shot and killed in a theatre by an actor called John Wilkes Booth. Lincoln is one of the most important US presidents, and was sometimes called 'Honest Abe' because everyone admired his honesty. 林肯〔(1809-1865), 美国共和党政治家, 1861-1865 年间任美国总统。他发表了许多反对黑奴制的演说, 从而获得美国北方各州的支持, 却也因此遭到南方诸州的反对, 因为南方大部分农活都是由黑奴完成的。他当选总统不久, 南方诸州决定脱离美利坚合众国, 从而引发了一场内战。1863 年, 他颁布了《解放宣言》, 宣布全美国的黑奴都为自由人。同年, 他又发表了著名的《葛底斯堡演说》。内战结束后仅数天, 他在一家剧院被一名叫约翰·威尔克斯·布思的男演员枪杀。林肯被认为是最有名望的美国总统之一, 并因众所公认的诚实品德被冠以"诚实的阿贝"的美名〕

Lincoln Cen·ter /ˈ·· ˌ··/ also 又作 **the Lincoln Center for the Performing Arts** an important CULTURAL centre in New York City, consisting of several buildings where plays, concerts, and OPERAs are performed. It includes the Metropolitan Opera House and the New York City Ballet. 林肯中心, 林肯表演艺术中心〔纽约市一重要文化中心, 由好几幢建筑组成, 上演话剧、音乐会和歌剧。大都会歌剧院和纽约市芭蕾舞团也在林肯艺术中心内〕

Lincoln Me·mo·ri·al, the /ˌ·· ·ˈ···/ a MARBLE building in Washington, D.C., which has a large STATUE (=carved stone figure) of Abraham Lincoln 林肯纪念堂〔位于华盛顿特区的一幢大理石建筑, 内有一尊巨型林肯雕像〕

Lincoln's Birth·day /ˌ·· ˈ··/ the birthday of Abraham Lincoln, February 12th, which is a legal holiday in many US states 林肯诞辰日〔即2月12日。这一天是美国许多州的法定假日〕—see also 另见 PRESIDENTS' DAY

Lin·coln·shire /ˈlɪŋkənʃɚ; ˈlɪŋkənʃə/ abbreviation 缩写为 **Lincs.** a COUNTY in eastern England, on the North Sea coast 林肯郡〔英格兰东部一郡, 濒临北海〕

Lincoln's Inn /ˌ·· ˈ·/ one of the Inns of Court in London 林肯律师学院〔伦敦四所律师学院之一〕

Lincoln Tun·nel, the /ˌ·· ˈ··/ a TUNNEL for traffic under the Hudson River in New York City, which connects Manhattan with New Jersey 林肯隧道〔纽约市哈得孙河一隧道, 连接曼哈顿区和新泽西州〕

Lincs. the written abbreviation of 缩写= LINCOLNSHIRE

linc·tus /ˈlɪŋktəs; ˈlɪŋktəs/ *n* [U] *BrE* a liquid medicine used for curing coughs【英】止咳糖浆

lin·dane /ˈlɪnden; ˈlɪndeɪn/ *n* [U] a chemical for killing insects, that is dangerous to people 林丹〔杀虫剂, 对人体有害〕

Lind·bergh /ˈlɪndbɜg; ˈlɪndbɜːg/, **Charles** (1902-74) a US pilot who in 1927 became the first person to fly alone across the Atlantic Ocean without stopping. He flew from New York to Paris in his plane called The Spirit of Saint Louis. 林德伯格〔(1902-1974), 美国飞行员。1927 年, 他成为第一位独自完成横越大西洋不着陆飞行的飞行员。当时, 他驾驶着"圣路易斯精神"号飞机从纽约飞抵巴黎〕

lin·den /ˈlɪndən; ˈlɪndən/ *n* [C] *AmE or poetic* a LIME¹ (2) tree【美或诗】椴树

Lin·dis·farne /ˈlɪndɪsfɑrn; ˈlɪndɪsfɑːn/ another name for Holy Island 林迪斯芳岛〔霍利岛的别称〕

Lin·dis·farne Gos·pels, the /ˌ··· ˈ··/ an ILLUMINATED (=with the pages decorated with gold paint and other bright colours) copy of the four Christian Gospels, produced at the end of the 7th century on the island of Lindisfarne and now kept in the British Museum 林迪斯芳福音书〔一本烫金的福音书, 7 世纪末于林迪斯芳岛完成, 现收藏于大英博物馆〕

S1 W1

line¹ /laɪn; laɪn/ *n*

① LONG THIN MARK 线条	⑨ LIES/EXCUSES 谎言/借口
② SHAPE/EDGE 轮廓/边缘	⑩ RAILWAY LINE 铁路线
③ OPINION/ATTITUDE 看法/态度	⑪ DIRECTION 方向
④ WAY/METHOD 方式/方法	⑫ WORK/INTEREST 工作/兴趣
⑤ TELEPHONE LINE 电话线	⑬ OBEY 服从
⑥ STRING 绳子	⑭ WAR 战争
⑦ WRITING/WORDS 写作/词句	⑮ DO THE SAME 做同样的事
⑧ ROW OF PEOPLE/THINGS 人/物的排	⑯ OTHER MEANINGS 其他意思

① **LONG THIN MARK 线条**

1 [C] a long thin, usually continuous mark on a surface 线; 线条: *A wiggly line showed where the river was.* 一条弯弯曲曲的线标示着河流的位置。| **straight line** *Can you draw a straight*

line? 你能画一条直线吗？| **dotted line** (=a broken straight line drawn or printed on paper) 虚线 *Sign your name on the dotted line.* 在虚线处签上你的名字。

2 [C] a long thin mark used to show a limit or border 界线；边界线：*a broken white line in the middle of the road* 道路中间的白色虚线 | *If the ball goes over the line, it's out of play.* 如果球出了界，就成了死球。

3 [C] an imaginary line, for example one that shows the limits of an area of land 设想的线，想象的线〈如边界线〉：*the line that divides northern and southern Ireland* 北爱尔兰和南爱尔兰的分界线 | *lines of longitude* 经线

4 county line/state line *AmE* a border between two counties, states etc【美】县界/州界

5 ►ON SB'S FACE 在某人的脸上◄ [C] a line on the skin of someone's face or skin; WRINKLE¹ (1)〔皮肤上的〕纹路，皱纹：*a forehead etched with deep lines* 刻着深深皱纹的前额

6 the line *technical* the EQUATOR【术语】赤道

② SHAPE/EDGE 轮廓/边缘

7 [C usually plural 一般用复数] the outer shape of something long or tall〔长或高的物件的〕轮廓，外形：*a dress that follows the lines of the body* 合身的连衣裙 | *I admired the ship's clean elegant lines.* 我欣赏这艘船简洁优雅的轮廓。

③ OPINION/ATTITUDE 看法/态度

8 [C usually singular 一般用单数] an attitude or belief, especially one that is stated publicly〔尤指公开发表的〕态度，看法：[+on] *What's the candidate's line on abortion?* 候选人对人工流产是什么态度？| **the party line** (=the official opinion of a political party) 政党的路线[方针] *By supporting Robertson, she's going directly against the party line.* 她支持罗伯逊，直接反对党的方针。

9 take a firm/hard/strict etc line on to have a very strict attitude towards something〔对某事〕采取坚定的/强硬的/严格的态度等：*a judge notorious for taking a tough line on drug users* 以对吸毒者采取严厉态度而著称的法官

④ WAY/METHOD 方式/方法

10 line of action/thought/reasoning etc a way or method of doing something or thinking about something 行为/思维/推理等的方式[方法]：**line of inquiry** (=a way of trying to find out about something) 询问[查问，调查]方式 *Police are following several lines of inquiry.* 警察正在使用几种方式进行调查。| **line of argument** (=a way of persuading someone about something) 游说方法 *Which line of argument is Clarke likely to take?* 克拉克可能会采用哪种游说方法？

11 along those/similar/different etc lines done or doing something in that way, a similar way etc 用那些/相似的/不同的等方法：*We've both been thinking along the same lines.* 我们两人一直都以同样的方法在思考。| **something along those lines** (=something like that) 诸如此类的事 *They're organizing a trip to the beach or something along those lines.* 他们正在组织去海滨的旅游或诸如此类的事。| **along the lines of** (=in a particular way) 以某种方式 *We'll probably end up doing something along the lines of what you're suggesting.* 我们很可能最终会按照你所建议的方式做点什么。

12 on the right lines done or doing something in the right kind of way 正确的，对的：*These new proposals are certainly on the right lines.* 这些新建议肯定是正确的。

⑤ TELEPHONE LINE 电话线

13 [C usually singular 一般用单数] a telephone wire or connection 电话线(路)：*We rent the line from British Telecom.* 我们租用英国电信公司的电话线。| **on the line** *There's a fault on the line.* 电话线路出现故障。| **bad line** (=a line that is not working properly so that you cannot easily hear the other person talking) 线路不良〔听不清楚对方说话〕

14 hold the line *spoken* used to politely ask the person who is on the telephone to wait for a short time【口】请别挂断电话：*Hold the line, please. I'll put you through to Mr Bork.* 请不要挂断电话。我给你接通博克先生。

⑥ STRING 绳子

15 ►DRYING CLOTHES 晾衣服◄ [C] a piece of string or rope that you hang wet clothes etc on in order to dry them; CLOTHESLINE, WASHING LINE 晾衣绳：**the line** *You'd better get your washing off the line – it's raining.* 你最好把晾在绳子上的衣服收下来——下雨了。

16 ►FISHING 钓鱼◄ [C] a strong thin string with a hook on the end, used for catching fish 钓鱼线

⑦ WRITING/WORDS 写作/词句

17 [C] a line of words on a page, for example in a poem or a report〔诗或报告中的〕一行字：*a few lines from Shakespeare* 选自莎士比亚作品的几行诗

18 ►ACTOR'S SPEECH 演员的台词◄ [plural] the words of a play or performance that an actor learns 台词：*After 30 years on the stage, I still forget my lines.* 当了30年演员，我仍记不住台词。

19 ►PUNISHMENT 处罚◄ **lines** [plural] *BrE* a punishment given to school children that consists of writing the same thing a lot of times【英】罚写〔对小学生的处罚〕：*Take a hundred lines!* 罚写一百遍！

20 drop sb a line *informal* to write a short letter to someone【非正式】给某人写短信[便条]：*Drop me a line and let me know how you're getting on.* 给我写一封短信，告诉我你过得怎么样。

⑧ ROW OF PEOPLE/THINGS 人/物的排

21 [C] a row of people or things next to each other 排，列，行：[+of] *a line of poplar trees beside the road* 路旁的一排杨树 | **in a line** *four little boys standing in a line* 站成一行的四个小男孩

22 [C] *AmE* a row of people standing one behind the other while waiting for something【美】〔人在等候时排的〕队；QUEUE¹ (1) *BrE*【英】：*I was talking with Karen in the lunch line.* 排队等候午餐时我和卡伦聊天。—see picture at 参见 PUSH¹ 图

⑨ LIES/EXCUSES 谎言/借口

23 shoot a line/spin (sb) a line to tell someone things that are not true in order to persuade them or to make them admire you 吹牛/编造谎言〔以说服某人或博取欢心〕

24 don't give me that line *spoken* used to tell someone that you do not believe their excuse【口】别跟我来那一套〔表示不相信对方的借口〕：*"We just haven't had enough time to..." "Oh, don't give me that line."* "我们实在没有足够的时间…" "哦，别跟我来那一套。"

⑩ RAILWAY LINE 铁路线

25 a track that a train travels along 铁路(线)；路轨：**the line** *A train had broken down further along the line.* 一列火车在前面的铁路线上出故障了。| **railway line** *a bridge over the railway line* 架在铁路线上方的桥 | **the Brighton/ Manchester/Cambridge etc line** (=a line that goes to Brighton etc) 布赖顿/曼彻斯特/剑桥等铁路线 | **Piccadilly/Victoria/Central etc line** (=a line on London's UNDERGROUND system)〔伦敦的〕皮卡迪利/维多利亚/中央等地铁路线

⑪ DIRECTION 方向

26 [C usually singular 一般用单数] the direction or imaginary line along which something travels between two points in space〔某物行进的〕方向：**in a straight line** *Light travels in a straight line.* 光沿直线传播。| **line of fire/attack/movement etc** (=the direction in which someone shoots, attacks, moves etc) 射击/进攻/运动等的方向 *I was directly in the animal's line of attack.* 野兽扑过来，我首当其冲。| **line of vision** (=the direction in which you are looking) 视线的方向

⑫ WORK/INTEREST 工作/兴趣

27 ►JOB 工作◄ [C usually singular 一般用单数] the kind of work someone does 专业，行业：**line of business** *What line of business is he in?* 他是干哪一行的？| **be in the building/retail etc line** 从事建筑业/零售业等 —see 见 JOB (USAGE)

28 in the line of duty if you do something in the line of duty, you do it as part of your job〔做某事是〕应尽的职责：*Don't thank me, madam – it's all in the line of duty.* 不用谢，夫人，这都是我的分内事。

29 be in sb's line to be the type of thing that someone is interested in or good at 是某人感兴趣的事；是某人的专长：*I'm afraid cookery isn't really in my line.* 恐怕烹饪不是我真正的专长。

⑬ OBEY 服从

30 fall into line *informal* to start to do something in the way that a company, organization etc wants you to【非正式】〔做事与公司、机构等〕取得一致：*Don't worry, I'm sure he'll soon fall into line and sign with the rest of us.* 不用担心，我敢肯定他很快会同意并和我们其余的人签订合同。

L

31 bring sb into line *informal* to make someone behave the way you want them to【非正式】使某人行动一致: *The right wing of the party has got to be brought into line.* 必须使这个政党的右翼采取一致的行动。

32 be out of line *AmE* if someone's behaviour is out of line, it is unacceptable【美】〔行为〕出格, 不可接受

⑭ WAR 战争

33 ▶WAR 战争◀ [C often plural 常用复数] a row of military defences in front of the area that an army controls during a war 防线: **behind the line(s)** (=in the area where your enemy is) 在敌区 *Parachutists dropped behind the lines.* 伞兵降落在敌区。| **enemy lines** *The base was stationed 100 miles inside enemy lines.* 基地驻扎在敌军防线内100英里处。

34 [C] the line of positions that an army has when it is fighting a battle 前线: *the line of battle* 战线

⑮ DO THE SAME 做同样的事

35 in line with if something changes in line with something else, it changes in the same way and at the same rate 与…一致; 符合〔某物〕: *Pensions will be increased in line with inflation.* 退休金将随着通货膨胀而相应提高。

36 bring sth into line with to make something work or happen according to a particular system or set of rules 使某物与〔制度或规则〕一致: *British law will have to be changed to bring it into line with the latest European ruling.* 英国的法律将要修改, 以使它符合欧洲最新的规定。

37 along religious/party/ethnic lines if people divide along religious, party etc lines they divide according to which religion, political party, or other group they belong to 按照宗教/政党/民族路线〔划分〕

⑯ OTHER MEANINGS 其他意思

38 a thin/fine line between only a slight difference between two things, one of which is something bad〔两事〕之间的细小差别〔其中之一是坏事〕: *There's a very fine line between tax evasion and fraud.* 逃税和诈骗之间只有一线之差。

39 be in line for sth to be very likely to get or be given something 很有可能获得某物: *Ted's in line for the chairmanship .* 特德很有可能当主席。| **first/second etc in line for** *She's about second in line for the management job.* 她大概是第二个有望争取到这份管理工作的人选。

40 be on the line *informal* if your job, position etc is on the line, there is a possibility you might lose it【非正式】〔工作、职位等〕有失去的可能: *From now on, all our jobs are on the line.* 从现在起, 我们都有失业的危险。

41 somewhere along the line *informal* during the time that you are involved in an activity or process【非正式】在活动[过程]中的某段时间: *Somewhere along the line, Errol seemed to have lost interest in their marriage.* 有段时间, 埃罗尔似乎对他俩的婚姻失去了兴趣。

42 ▶PRODUCT 产品◀ [C] a type of goods for sale in a shop〔货物的〕种类, 类型: *this season's new lines from Paris* 来自巴黎的本季度的新款式 | **discontinue a line** (=stop selling a type of goods) 停止销售某种商品

43 on line communicating with or by means of a computer 与〔电脑〕连接着: [+to] *The system is on line to the bank's mainframe computer.* 这系统与银行的电脑主机连接着。| *We need to bring the network back on line.* 我们需要使网络恢复连接状态。—see also 另见 ONLINE

44 ▶COMPANY 公司◀ [C usually singular 一般用单数] a company that provides a system for moving goods by sea, air, road etc 运输公司: *a shipping line* 海运公司 | *the Cunard line* 丘纳德轮船公司

45 be in the firing line/in the line of fire **a)** to be one of the people who could be criticized or blamed for something 成为批评[指责]的对象: *As one of the President's chief advisers, he's bound to be in the firing line.* 作为总统的主要顾问之一, 他势必成为批评的对象。**b)** to be in a place where a bullet etc might hit you 可能遭到枪击

46 ▶SPORT 运动◀ [C] a row of players in a game such as American football or RUGBY that is formed when they move into position before play starts again〔美式或英式橄榄球等比赛中球员的〕对阵开球队员

47 get a line on *informal* to get information about someone or something【非正式】获得〔某人或事〕的消息: *Have we got any kind of line on that guy Marston?* 有没有得到任何关于马斯顿那家伙的消息?

48 ▶DRUG 毒品◀ [C] *informal* an amount of an illegal drug in powder form, arranged in a line before it is taken【非正式】〔粉末状毒品在吸食前排成的〕一行: [+of] *a line of coke* 一行可卡因

49 ▶FAMILY 家族◀ [singular] the people that came or existed before you in your family〔家庭中的〕长辈, 先辈: *She comes from a long line of actors.* 她出身演员世家。| **be of sb's line** (=be their GRANDCHILD, GREAT-GRANDCHILD etc) 某人的孙辈[曾孙辈等] *There was no-one directly of James's line to succeed to the throne.* 詹姆斯家族没有直系孙辈继承王位。—see also 另见 **draw the line (at sth)** (DRAW[1] (35)), **hard lines** (HARD[1] (21)), **hook, line, and sinker** (HOOK[1] (7)), **lay sth on the line** (LAY[2] (15)), **picket line** (PICKET[1] (1)), **the poverty line/level** (POVERTY (2)), **read between the lines** (READ[1] (11)), **spin a story/yarn/line** (SPIN[1] (6))

line² *v* [T] **1** to cover the inside of a piece of material with another material 给〔某物〕加衬里: *Are those curtains lined?* 那些窗帘加衬里了吗? | **line sth with** *a coat lined with silk* 有丝绸衬里的外衣 **2** to form a layer over the inner surface of something 形成内衬: *the mucus that lines the stomach* 胃内壁的黏液 | **line sth with** *The bird lined its nest with feathers.* 鸟在窝内垫上羽毛。**3** [usually passive 一般用被动态] to form rows along something 沿〔某物〕排列成行: *tree-lined avenues* 林荫大道 | *Crowds lined the route to the palace.* 人群在通往皇宫的路上夹道排列。**4 line your own pockets** to make yourself richer, especially by doing something dishonest 捞一把; 中饱私囊

line up *phr v* **1** [I,T] to form a row or arrange people or things in a row (使) 排成行: *Line up, everybody!* 大家排好队! | **line sb/sth ↔up** *The men were being lined up for an inspection.* 男人们正在排队接受检查。**2** [T] to make arrangements so that something will happen or that someone will be available for an event 安排〔某事〕; 安排〔某人〕出席: **line sb/sth up** *Sue's lined up some excellent speakers for tonight.* 休为今晚邀请了几位出色的演讲者。—see also 另见 LINE-UP

lin·e·age /ˈlɪnɪɪdʒ; ˈlɪni-ɪdʒ/ *n* [C,U] *formal* the way in which members of a family are descended (DESCEND) from other members【正式】血统, 世系, 家系: *a family of ancient lineage* 古老世家

lin·e·al /ˈlɪnɪəl; ˈlɪniəl/ *adj* **1** *formal* related directly to someone who lived a long time before you【正式】直系的, 嫡系的: *lineal descendants* 直系后代 **2** another form of LINEAR linear 的另一种拼法—**lineally** *adv*

lin·e·a·ment /ˈlɪnɪəmənt; ˈlɪniəmənt/ *n* [C usually plural 一般用复数] *formal*【正式】**1** a feature of your face 容貌; 面部轮廓 **2** a typical quality 特征

lin·e·ar /ˈlɪnɪə; ˈlɪniə/ *adj* **1** consisting of lines, or in the form of a straight line 线的; 直线的: *a linear diagram* 线条图 **2** [only before noun 仅用于名词前] concerning length 长度的: *linear measurements* 长度测量 **3** involving a series of directly connected events, ideas etc 涉及一连串直接相关事物的; 线性的: *linear thinking* 线性思维 —compare 比较 LATERAL THINKING—**linearly** *adv*—**linearity** /ˌlɪnɪˈærətɪ; ˌlɪniˈærʒti/ *n* [U]

linear ac·cel·e·ra·tor /ˌ··· ˈ····/ *n* [C] *technical* a piece of equipment that makes PARTICLES (=small pieces of atoms) travel in a straight line at increasing speed【术语】直线加速器〔使粒子沿着直线加速运动的装置〕

linear per·spec·tive /ˌ··· ·ˈ··/ *n* [U] a way of drawing and painting that gives the appearance of distance or depth 直线透视法〔表现距离或深度的画法〕

line·back·er /ˈlaɪnˌbækə; ˈlaɪnˌbækə/ *n* [C] a player in American football who tries to TACKLE[1] (3) members of the other team〔美式橄榄球的〕中后卫, 线后卫

lined /laɪnd; laɪnd/ *adj* **1** a coat, skirt etc that is lined has a piece of thin material covering the inside〔外衣、裙子等〕有衬里的: *a fleece-lined jacket* 有羊毛衬里的夹克 **2** paper that is lined has straight lines printed or drawn across it〔纸〕印[画]有直线的 **3** skin that is lined has WRINKLES on it〔皮肤〕有皱纹的

line draw·ing /ˈ· ˌ··/ *n* [C] a DRAWING consisting only of lines 线条画

line drive /ˈ· ·/ *n* [C] a BASEBALL hit with great force in a straight line fairly near the ground〔棒球中击出的〕平直球

line·man /ˈlaɪnmən; ˈlaɪnmən/ *n plural* **linemen** /-mən; -mən/ [C] **1** *especially AmE* someone whose job is to take care of railway lines or telephone wires【尤美】〔铁路的〕养路工人;〔电话线的〕线务员; LINESMAN (2) *especially BrE*【尤英】**2** *AmE* a player in the front line of a sports team【美】进攻线卫; 防守线卫

line man·age·ment /ˈ· ,···/ *n* [U] **1** the system of passing information and instructions in an organization by which each person tells the one immediately higher or lower than them in rank 分级管理，直线管理〔指组织内部直属上下级之间传送信息〕 **2** the group of managers in a company who are responsible for its main activities, such as production and sales〔公司负责生产、销售等主要活动的〕分级管理层

line man·a·ger /ˈ· ,···/ *n* [C] **1** a manager in a company who is responsible for the main activities of production, sales etc〔公司负责生产、销售等主要活动的〕分级经理，部门经理 **2 sb's line manager** someone who is one level higher in rank than you in a company and is in charge of your work 某人的顶头上司

lin·en /ˈlɪnɪn; ˈlɪnɪn/ *n* [U] **1** sheets, TABLECLOTHs etc 家庭日用织品: *bed linen* 床单 | *table linen* 桌布 **2** cloth made from the FLAX plant, used to make high quality clothes, home decorations etc 亚麻布〔用于制作优质衣服、家庭装饰等〕: *a linen jacket* 亚麻布制的短外衣 **3** *old use* underwear【旧】内衣裤

linen bas·ket /ˈ·· ,··/ *n* [C] a LAUNDRY BASKET 待洗衣物筐 —see picture at 参见 BASKET 图

linen cup·board /ˈ·· ,··/ *n* [C] a special cupboard in which sheets, TOWELs etc are kept〔床单、毛巾等的〕家庭日用织品储存柜

line of scrim·mage /,· · ˈ··/ *n* [C] a line in American football where the ball is placed at the beginning of a particular PLAY[2] (3)〔美式橄榄球的〕争球线

line-out /ˈ· ·/ *n* [C] the way of starting play again in a RUGBY UNION game, when the ball has gone off the field 界外球〔英式联合会橄榄球出界后继续比赛的方式〕

line print·er /ˈ· ,··/ *n* [C] a machine that prints information from a computer at a very high speed〔电脑的〕行式打印机 —**line printing** *n* [U]

lin·er /ˈlaɪnə; ˈlaɪnə/ *n* **1** [C] a piece of material used inside something in order to protect it〔起保护作用的〕衬里，衬垫: *a trash can liner* 垃圾筒的衬垫 | *nappy liners* 尿布衬垫 **2** [C] a large passenger ship, especially one of several owned by a company〔轮船公司的〕邮轮，大客轮: *an ocean liner* 远洋邮轮 —see also 另见 AIRLINER, CRUISE LINER **3** [C,U] *informal* EYELINER【非正式】眼线笔

liner notes /ˈ·· ,·/ *n* [plural] *AmE* printed information about a record that appears on its cover【美】〔唱片封套上的〕说明文字

lines·man /ˈlaɪnzmən; ˈlaɪnzmən/ *n plural* **linesmen** /-mən; -mən/ [C] **1** an official in a sport who decides when a ball has gone out of the playing area〔球类运动中〕边线裁判；巡边员；司线员 —see picture on page A23 参见 A23 页图 **2** *especially BrE* someone whose job is to take care of railway lines and telephone wires【尤英】〔铁路的〕养路工人；〔电话线的〕线务员；LINEMAN (1) *especially AmE*【尤美】

line-up /ˈ· ·/ *n* [C usually singular 一般用单数] **1** a group of people, especially performers, who have agreed to be involved in an event 全体参与人员〔尤指演员〕: *Tonight's line up includes Suzanne Vega.* 今晚的演出阵容包括苏珊妮·维加。**2** the players in a sports team who play in a particular game〔出赛的〕运动员阵容: **starting line-up** (=the first ones to play in a game) 开场阵容 **3** a set of events or programmes arranged to follow each other 一系列项目[节目]: *the best line-up of radio entertainment in the world* 世界上最佳的广播娱乐节目系列 **4** *especially AmE* a row of people examined by a WITNESS to a crime in order to try to recognize a criminal【尤美】〔待目击者辨认的〕排嫌疑犯；IDENTIFICATION PARADE *BrE*【英】

ling /lɪŋ; lɪŋ/ *n* [U] a plant very like HEATHER 帚石楠〔一种植物〕

-ling /lɪŋ; lɪŋ/ *suffix* [in nouns 构成名词] a small, young, or unimportant kind of something 小，幼；不重要: *a duckling* (=young duck) 小鸭 | *minor Prussian princelings* (=unimportant princes) 次要的普鲁士小王公

lin·ger /ˈlɪŋgə; ˈlɪŋgə/ *v* [I] **1** to stay somewhere a little longer, especially because you do not want to leave〔尤指因不愿意离开而〕逗留，徘徊: [**+over/on etc**] *They lingered over coffee and missed the last bus.* 他们慢吞吞地喝咖啡，没有赶上末班车。**2** [always+adv/prep] to continue looking at or dealing with something for longer than is usual 盯着〔某物〕；拖延〔某事〕: [**+on/over etc**] *Mike couldn't help letting his eyes linger on her face.* 迈克的双眼不由自主地盯着她的脸。**3** also 又作 **linger on** to be slow to disappear 缓慢消失: *The taste lingers in your mouth.* 这味道在你嘴里很久不会消失。**4** also 又作 **linger on** to be dying slowly so that you stay alive for a long time although you are extremely weak 苟延残喘: *Horribly wounded he lingered on to die two years later.* 他伤势严重，但是拖了两年才死。—**lingerer** *n* [C]

lin·ge·rie /,lɑnʒəˈre; ˈlænʒəri/ *n* [U] women's underwear 女式内衣裤

lin·ger·ing /ˈlɪŋgərɪŋ; ˈlɪŋgərɪŋ/ *adj* slow to finish or disappear 拖延的，久缠不去的: *lingering doubts about the need for reform* 对于是否需要改革持续不断的疑问 | **a lingering death** (=slow and often painful) 漫长〔痛苦〕的死亡 —**lingeringly** *adv*

lin·go /ˈlɪŋgo; ˈlɪŋgəʊ/ *n* [C usually singular 一般用单数] *informal*【非正式】**1** a language, especially a foreign one 语言〔尤指外语〕: *I'd like to go to Greece, but I don't speak the lingo.* 我想去希腊，可是不会说希腊语。**2** words used only by a group of people who do a particular job or activity 行话，术语: *the estate agent's baffling lingo* 难懂的房地产经纪人行话

lin·gua fran·ca /,lɪŋgwə ˈfræŋkə; ,lɪŋgwə ˈfræŋkə/ *n* [C] a language used between people whose main languages are different〔母语不同的人之间使用的〕通用语: *English serves as a lingua franca in many countries.* 英语是很多国家的通用语。

lin·gual /ˈlɪŋgwəl; ˈlɪŋgwəl/ *adj* **1** related to the tongue 舌的 **2** a lingual sound is made by the movement of the tongue 舌音的 —see also 另见 BILINGUAL

lin·gui·ni /lɪŋˈgwinɪ; lɪŋˈgwiːni/ *n* [plural] long thin flat pieces of PASTA〔意大利〕扁面条

lin·guist /ˈlɪŋgwɪst; ˈlɪŋgwɪst/ *n* [C] **1** someone who studies and is good at foreign languages 通晓几种外语的人 **2** someone who studies or teaches linguistics 语言学家

lin·guis·tic /lɪŋˈgwɪstɪk; lɪŋˈgwɪstɪk/ *adj* related to language, words, or linguistics 语言的；语言学的: *a child's linguistic development* 儿童的语言发展 —**linguistically** /-klɪ; -kli/ *adv* 3

lin·guis·ti·cian /,lɪŋgwɪsˈtɪʃən; ,lɪŋgwɪˈstɪʃən/ *n* [C] a LINGUIST (2) 语言学家

lin·guis·tics /lɪŋˈgwɪstɪks; lɪŋˈgwɪstɪks/ *n* [U] the study of language in general and of particular languages, their structure, grammar, and history 语言学 —compare 比较 PHILOLOGY

lin·i·ment /ˈlɪnəmənt; ˈlɪnɪmənt/ *n* [U] a liquid containing oil that you rub on your skin to cure soreness and stiffness 皮肤擦剂〔用以消除疼痛和僵硬〕

lin·ing /ˈlaɪnɪŋ; ˈlaɪnɪŋ/ *n* [C,U] a piece of material covering the inside of a box, piece of clothing etc〔盒子、衣服等的〕衬里，里子: *The coat has a silk lining.* 这件外衣有丝绸衬里。| *brake linings* 制动装置衬面 —see picture at 参见 SHOE[1] 图

Link /lɪŋk; lɪŋk/ *trademark* in the UK, a system by which people can get money from their bank or Building Society accounts by using a special plastic card (a **Link card**) in a cash machine【商标】联通〔英国一自动取款服务网络。客户可在自动提款机上使用联通卡从自己的银行账户或购房互助协会账户中提取现金〕

link[1] *v* **1 be linked** if people or events are linked, they are connected in some way 有联系，有关联: *Police think the murders are linked.* 警方认为这些谋杀案有关连。| [**+with/to**] *They believe that this illness is linked to the use of chemical pesticides.* 他们相信这种病和使用化学杀虫剂有关系。**2** [T] to connect computers, broadcast systems etc, so that electronic messages can be sent between them 联系，连接〔电脑、广播系统等，使电子信息能在它们之间传递〕: **link sth to** *You can link your TV to your stereo for better sound.* 你可以把电视机连接到立体声设备上，以获得更好的音响效果。| **link sth with** *We'll link your PC with our network via modem.* 我们将通过调制解调器把你的个人电脑和我们的网络连接。**3** [T] to connect two or more things together 把〔两个或以上的事物〕联系在一起. *These traditional stories link the past and the present.* 这些传统故事把过去和现在联系在一起。**4** [T] to believe that one fact or situation is connected with or caused by another〔某事或情况〕和…有联系；由…引起: **link sth to/with** *There are compelling reasons for linking crimes like burglary and car theft with poverty.* 有令人信服的理由认为入室行窃和偷车等罪行是由贫穷引起的。**5** [T] to join one place to another 连接〔另一处〕: *the coastal highway linking Saigon and Hanoi* 连接西贡和河内的海滨公路 **6 link arms** to bend your arm and put it through someone else's bent arm 挽着手臂 2

link up *phr v* [I] to make a connection with something 连接；联系: [**+with**] *The train links up with the ferry at Holyhead.* 这趟列车连接霍利黑德渡口。| *My work links up with previous research.* 我的工作和以前的研究相联系。—see also 另见 LINKUP

link 链，环

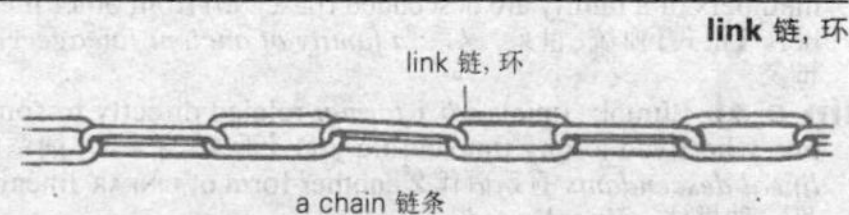

link[2] *n* [C] **1** a relationship between two things or ideas, in which one is caused or affected by the other〔两种事物或思想 3 2

的因果〕关联：[+between] *the link between smoking and cancer* 抽烟和癌症之间的关联 **2** a relationship between two or more people, countries, organizations etc〔人、国家、组织等之间的〕联系，关系：[+with/between] *They have severed all political links with the Left.* 他们已经同左翼断绝了所有政治上的联系。**3** one of the rings in a chain〔链的〕一环 **4 rail/road/telephone link** something that joins two places and allows you to travel or communicate between them 铁路/公路/电话线连接：*a transatlantic conference via satellite link* 通过卫星连接的横越大西洋的会议 **5 link in the chain** one of the steps involved in a process 过程中的一环 **6 weak link** the weakest part of a plan or the weakest member of a team〔计划中的〕薄弱环节；〔一队中的〕最弱队员 —see also 另见 CUFF LINK, LINKS, MISSING LINK

link·age /ˈlɪŋkɪdʒ; ˈlɪŋkɪdʒ/ *n* **1** [singular, U] a condition in a political or business agreement, by which one country or company agrees to do something, only if the other promises to do something in return 关联原则〔政治或商业协议中，一方同意做某事，以换取对方做某事的条件〕**2** [singular,U] a LINK[2] (1) 因果关联 **3** [C] a system of links or connections 连接，接合

link·man /ˈlɪŋkmən; ˈlɪŋkmæn/ *n* [C] a man whose job is to introduce all the separate parts of a radio or television broadcast〔广播或电视节目的〕男主持人

links /lɪŋks; lɪŋks/ *plural* **links** *n* a piece of ground near the sea on which GOLF is played〔海滨的〕高尔夫球场

link·up /ˈlɪŋk,ʌp; ˈlɪŋk-ʌp/ *n* [C] a connection between computers, broadcasting systems etc that sends electronic messages between them〔电脑、广播系统等的〕连接

link·wom·an /ˈlɪŋk,wʊmən; ˈlɪŋk,wʊmən/ *n* [C] a woman whose job is to introduce all the separate parts of a radio or television broadcast〔广播或电视节目的〕女主持人

Lin·nae·us, Ca·ro·lus /lɪˈniəs; lɪˈniːəs/, /kæˈroləs; kæˈrəʊləs/ (1707-78) a Swedish BOTANIST (=a scientist who studies plants) who invented the system, called the **Linnaean System**, by which plants and animals are put into groups according to their GENUS (=general type) and SPECIES (=particular type) 林尼厄斯〔(1707-1778)，瑞典植物学家，创立“林氏双名法”，即将植物和动物按种、属进行分类的方法〕

lin·net /ˈlɪnɪt; ˈlɪnɪ̈t/ *n* [C] a small brown singing bird 朱顶雀

li·no /ˈlaɪno; ˈlaɪnəʊ/ *n* [U] *BrE informal* linoleum【英，非正式】油毡

li·no·cut /ˈlaɪno,kʌt; ˈlaɪnəʊkʌt/ *n* **1** [U] the art of cutting a pattern on a block of linoleum 油毡浮雕艺术 **2** [C] a picture printed from such a block 油毡浮雕版画

li·no·le·um /lɪˈnolɪəm; lɪ̈ˈnəʊliəm/ *n* [U] smooth shiny material in flat sheets used to cover a floor〔铺地用的〕油毡

Li·no·type /ˈlaɪno,taɪp; ˈlaɪnəʊtaɪp/ *n* [U] *trademark* a system for arranging TYPE[1] (3) in the form of solid metal lines【商标】莱诺铸排机〔用于印刷的排字系统〕

lin·seed /ˈlɪn,sid; ˈlɪnsiːd/ *n* [U] the seed of the FLAX (1) plant 亚麻籽

linseed oil /,.. ˈ./ *n* [U] the oil from linseed used in some paints, inks etc 亚麻籽油〔用于某些油漆、墨水中〕

lint /lɪnt; lɪnt/ *n* [U] **1** *especially AmE* soft light pieces of thread or wool that come off cotton, wool, or other material【尤美】绒屑，飞花；FLUFF *BrE*【英】**2** *BrE* soft material used for protecting wounds【英】〔裹伤口的〕软敷料

lin·tel /ˈlɪntḷ; ˈlɪntl/ *n* [C] a piece of stone or wood across the top of a window or door, forming part of the frame〔门、窗上的〕过梁

Li·nus /ˈlaɪnəs; ˈlaɪnəs/ a character in a US CARTOON STRIP called *Peanuts*. He is a boy who takes his BLANKET (=a cover for a bed) with him everywhere, because he would not feel happy or confident without it. 莱纳斯〔美国连环漫画《花生》中的人物。这个小男孩无论到哪里都随身带着一块毯子，否则他就会感到不开心或缺乏信心〕

li·on /ˈlaɪən; ˈlaɪən/ *n* [C] **1** a large yellowish-brown animal of the cat family that eats meat, and lives in Africa and parts of Southern Asia 狮子：*the lion's roar* 狮子的吼声 —see also 另见 LIONESS **2** *especially literary* someone who is very important, powerful, or famous【尤文】要人；名人 **3 the lion's share (of)** the largest part of something〔某物〕最大的一份：*The Department of Defense will take the lion's share of the federal budget.* 国防部将占去联邦预算的最大份额。**4 in the lion's den** among people who are your enemies 身处敌穴 **5 be thrown/ tossed to the lions** to be put in a dangerous or unpleasant situation 被送到危险[难堪]的境地

CULTURAL NOTE 文化注释

People often think about lions as strong, brave, and frightening animals. The lion is sometimes called 'the king of the JUNGLE'. In the UK, the lion is often used on flags and signs to represent the country. 人们通常认为狮子是强壮、勇猛、吓人的动物。狮子有时被称为“丛林之王”。在英国，狮子常被用在旗帜和标牌上，是国家的象征。

li·on·ess /ˈlaɪənɪs; ˈlaɪənes/ *n* [C] a female lion 母狮

lion-heart·ed /,.. ˈ..◂/ *adj literary* very brave【文】非常勇敢的

li·on·ize also 又作 **-ise** *BrE*【英】/ˈlaɪən,aɪz; ˈlaɪənaɪz/ *v* [T] to treat someone as being important or famous 视〔某人〕为要人[名人] —**lionization** /,laɪənəˈzeʃən; ,laɪənaɪˈzeɪʃən/ *n* [U]

Lions, the /ˈlaɪənz; ˈlaɪənz/ —see 见 the BRITISH LIONS

Lions Club /ˈ.. ,./ an international organization whose members work together to help their local areas by doing CHARITY work 国际狮子会〔一国际性组织。其会员通过慈善活动共同帮助所在地区〕

Lion, the Witch and the War·drobe, The /,.. .. ,. ˈ../ (1950) a children's book by C. S. Lewis, in which four children enter the imaginary land of Narnia by walking through a WARDROBE, and have many adventures there. It is the first of the series of books called *The Chronicles of Narnia*. 《狮子、女巫和魔衣橱》〔(1950)，C.S.刘易斯创作的儿童故事。故事讲述四个孩子通过一个衣橱来到了虚构的纳尼亚国，经历了种种冒险活动。这是系列丛书《纳尼亚传奇》的第一部〕

lip /lɪp; lɪp/ *n* **1** [C] one of the two edges of your mouth where your skin is redder or darker 嘴唇：*Marty kissed me right on the lips!* 马蒂就吻在我的嘴唇上！—see picture at 参见 HEAD[1] 图 **2** [U] *informal* a word meaning rude, angry talk, used especially by adults to children【非正式】无礼[唐突]的话〔此词尤在成年人对儿童的话中使用〕：**give sb lip** *Don't give me any of your lip!* 不许对我无礼！**3 thin-lipped/full-lipped etc** with lips that are thin, round etc 薄嘴唇的/厚嘴唇等的 **4** [C usually singular 一般用单数] the edge of something you use to pour liquid from〔容器的〕嘴，开口：*There's a crack in the lip of that jug.* 那个水壶的壶嘴上有一条裂缝。**5** [C] the edge of a hollow or deep place in the land, usually one made out of rock〔通常由岩石形成的洞或深凹地势的〕边缘：*the lip of the canyon* 峡谷的边缘 **6 my lips are sealed** *spoken* used to say that you will keep a secret【口】我会保密 **7 sth will not pass my lips** used to say that you will not talk about something that is secret 我不会说出某事〔指秘密的事〕：*Don't worry, not a word of this shall pass my lips!* 放心，关于此事一个字也不会从我嘴里说出去！**8 on everyone's lips** being talked about by everyone 大家正在谈论的：*a name that will soon be on everyone's lips* 很快就会成为大家谈论的一个名字 **9** [C] *BrE spoken* an angry expression【英口】怒容：*Look at the lip on her!* 瞧她那气愤的样子！—see also 另见 **lick your lips** (LICK[1] (5)), **read sb's lips** (READ[1] (15)), **keep a stiff upper lip** (STIFF[1] (9)) W2

lip balm /ˈ. ./ *n* [C,U] *AmE* a substance used to protect dry lips【美】〔防干燥的〕润唇膏

lip gloss /ˈ. ./ *n* [C,U] a substance used to make lips look very shiny 亮唇膏，唇彩

lip·id /ˈlaɪpɪd; ˈlɪpɪ̈d/ *n* [C] *technical* one of several types of FATTY substances in living things, such as fat, oil, or WAX[1] (1)【术语】脂质〈如脂肪、油或蜡〉

lip·o·suc·tion /ˈlɪpo,sʌkʃən; ˈlɪpəʊ,sʌkʃən/ *n* [U] a way of removing fat from someone's body using SUCTION 抽脂肪，脂肪抽吸法

lip·py /ˈlɪpɪ; ˈlɪpi/ *adj BrE informal* not showing respect in the way that you speak to someone【英，非正式】〔与某人说话时〕出言不逊的

lip-read /ˈlɪp,rid; ˈlɪp riːd/ *v* [I,T] to understand what someone is saying by watching the way their lips move, especially because you cannot hear〔尤因失聪而〕唇读，观察唇形以理解〔语义〕—**lip-reading** *n* [U]

lip salve /ˈ. ./ *n* [C,U] *especially BrE* a substance used to make sore lips feel better【尤英】〔舒缓疼痛的〕护唇油膏

lip ser·vice /ˈ. ,../ *n* **pay lip service to** to say that you support or agree with something without doing anything to prove your support 空口答应，口惠而实不至：*They're only paying lip service to women's rights.* 他们只是口头上支持妇女的权利。

lip·stick /ˈlɪp,stɪk; ˈlɪp,stɪk/ *n* [C,U] a piece of a substance shaped like a small stick, used for adding colour to your lips 唇膏，口红 —see picture at 参见 MAKE-UP 图

lip synch /ˈlɪp sɪŋk; ˈlɪp sɪŋk/ *n* [U] the action of moving your lips at the same time as a recording is being played, to give the appearance that you are singing〔放录音时的〕对口型假唱 — **lip-synch** *v* [I]

liq·ue·fac·tion /ˌlɪkwɪˈfækʃən; ˌlɪkwɪ̈ˈfækʃən/ *n* [U] *technical* the act of making something a liquid or of becoming a liquid【术语】液化（作用）

liq·ue·fy /ˈlɪkwəˌfaɪ; ˈlɪkwɪ̈faɪ/ *v* [I,T] *formal* to become liquid, or make something become liquid【正式】（使）液化: *Some gases liquefy at cold temperatures.* 有些气体在寒冷的温度下会成为液体。

li·ques·cent /lɪˈkwɛsn̩t; lɪˈkwesənt/ *adj technical* becoming or tending to become liquid【术语】液化性的; 易融化的

li·queur /lɪˈkɝ; lɪˈkjʊə/ *n* [C,U] a sweet and very strong alcoholic drink, drunk in small quantities after a meal〔饭后浅酌的〕利口酒, 甜酒 —compare 比较 LIQUOR

liq·uid[1] /ˈlɪkwɪd; ˈlɪkwɪ̈d/ *n* **1** [C,U] a substance that is not a solid or a gas, which flows, is wet, and has no fixed shape 液体, 液态物: *Water is a liquid.* 水是液体。**2** [C] *technical* either of the CONSONANT sounds /l/ and /r/【术语】流音〔指 /l/ 和 /r/〕—see also 另见 WASHING-UP LIQUID

liquid[2] *adj* **1 liquid oxygen/soap etc** oxygen etc in the form of a liquid, instead of its usual gas or solid form 液态氧/肥皂液等 **2** clear and shiny, like water 清澈的, 明亮的: *liquid green eyes* 清澈明亮的绿眼睛 **3** *literary* liquid sounds are clear and pure【文】〔声音〕清脆的 **4** easily exchanged or sold to pay debts 易变为现金的: *liquid funds* 流动资金 —see also 另见 LIQUID ASSETS **5 liquid refreshment** *humorous* drink, especially alcoholic drink【幽默】饮料〔尤指酒类〕

liquid as·sets /ˌ.. ˈ../ *n* [plural] *technical* the money that a company or person has, and the property they can easily exchange for money【术语】〔公司或个人拥有的〕流动资产

liq·ui·date /ˈlɪkwɪˌdet; ˈlɪkwɪ̈deɪt/ *v* **1** [I,T] to close a business or company in order to pay its debts 停业清盘, 清算〔公司, 以偿还债务〕**2** [T] *technical* to pay a debt【术语】偿还, 清偿〔债务〕: *The stock will be sold to liquidate the loan.* 将出售股票以偿还贷款。**3** [T] *informal* to kill someone【非正式】杀死〔某人〕

liq·ui·da·tion /ˌlɪkwɪˈdeʃən; ˌlɪkwɪ̈ˈdeɪʃən/ *n* [C,U] **1** the act of closing down a company in order to pay its debts by selling its assets (ASSET (1)) 停业清盘, 清算〔指公司停业, 出售资产以还债〕: **go into liquidation** *land being sold off because the builder has gone into liquidation* 由于建筑商已经停业清盘而正在削价变卖的土地 **2** the act of paying a debt〔债务的〕清偿

liq·ui·da·tor /ˈlɪkwɪˌdetɚ; ˈlɪkwɪ̈deɪtə/ *n* [C] an official who ends the trade of a company, so that its debts can be paid〔公司资产的〕清算人, 清盘人

liquid gas /ˌ.. ˈ./ *n* [U] gas changed to liquid by extreme cold〔气体遇上极冷而凝结成的〕液态气体

li·quid·i·ty /lɪˈkwɪdətɪ; lɪˈkwɪdɪ̈ti/ *n* [U] *technical*【术语】**1** a situation in which you have money or goods that can be sold to pay debts 拥有流动资产 **2** the state of being LIQUID[1] (1) 液态

liq·uid·ize also 又作 **-ise** *BrE*【英】/ˈlɪkwəˌdaɪz; ˈlɪkwɪ̈daɪz/ *v* [T] to crush fruit or vegetables into a thick liquid 把〔水果或蔬菜〕榨出浓汁

liq·uid·iz·er also 又作 **-iser** *BrE*【英】/ˈlɪkwəˌdaɪzɚ; ˈlɪkwɪ̈daɪzə/ *n* [C] *BrE* a small electric machine that makes solid foods into liquids; BLENDER【英】榨汁机

liquid lunch /ˌ.. ˈ./ *n* [C] *humorous* a LUNCH in which you mainly have alcoholic drinks rather than eating food【幽默】〔以酒为主的〕液态午餐

liq·uor /ˈlɪkɚ, ˈlɪkə/ *n* [U] **1** *AmE* a strong alcoholic drink, such as WHISKY【美】烈酒〈如威士忌〉—compare 比较 LIQUEUR **2** *BrE technical* alcoholic drink【英, 术语】酒精类饮料

liq·uo·rice *BrE*【英】, **licorice** *especially AmE*【尤美】/ˈlɪkərɪs; ˈlɪkərɪs/ *n* **1** [U] a black substance produced from the root of a plant, used in medicine and sweets〔药用、制糖果的〕甘草根浸出物 **2** [C,U] a sweet or sweets made from this substance 甘草糖

liquorice all·sorts /ˌlɪkərɪs ˈɔlsɔrts; ˌlɪkərɪs ˈɔːlsɔːts/ *n* [plural] *BrE* a mixture of differently shaped brightly coloured sweets containing liquorice【英】什锦甘草糖果

liquor store /ˈ.. ./ *n* [C] *AmE* a shop where alcohol is sold【美】卖酒的商店; OFF-LICENCE *BrE*【英】

lir·a /ˈlɪrə; ˈlɪərə/ *n plural* **lire** /-re; -reɪ/ *or* **liras** [C] the standard unit of money in Malta and Turkey, and used in Italy before the euro 里拉〔马尔他和土耳其的标准货币单位, 也是意大利在使用欧元前的货币单位〕

Lis·bon /ˈlɪzbən; ˈlɪzbən/ the capital city and main port of Portugal 里斯本〔葡萄牙首都和主要港口〕

lisle /laɪl; laɪl/ *n* [U] cotton material, used in the past for GLOVES and STOCKINGS 莱尔线〔旧时用来织手套和长袜〕

lisp[1] /lɪsp; lɪsp/ *v* [I,T] to speak, pronouncing 's' sounds as 'th' 咬舌（说话）; 口齿不清地说话〔把 s 发成 th 音〕

lisp[2] *n* [singular] if someone has a lisp, they lisp when they speak 说话时咬舌[口齿不清]: *She speaks with a slight lisp.* 她说话有点口齿不清。

lis·som, lissome /ˈlɪsəm; ˈlɪsəm/ *adj literary* a body that is lissom is thin and graceful【文】〔身材〕清瘦优雅的: *her slender lissom figure* 她修长优美的身材

list[1] /lɪst; lɪst/ *n* [C] **1** a set of words, numbers etc written one below the other, for example so that you can remember them 名单; 清单; 目录: *a shopping list* 购物清单 | *an alphabetical list* 按字母顺序列出的名单 | [+of] *Make a list of the things you have to do.* 把必须做的事情列成清单。| **at the top/bottom of the list** (=regarded as most or least important) 最紧要的/最不紧要的 **2 enter the lists** *BrE* to become involved in an argument, competition, etc【英】卷入〔争论、竞争等中〕—see also 另见 CIVIL LIST, **be on the danger list** (DANGER (4)), HIT LIST, MAILING LIST, SHORT LIST, WAITING LIST

list[2] *v* **1** [T] to write a list, or mention things one after the other 列出清单; 列举: *The guidebook lists 1,000 hotels and restaurants.* 这本导游书列出了 1000 家旅馆和餐厅。**2** [I] if a ship lists, it leans to one side〔船〕倾斜 **3** [I] *old use* to listen【旧】听, 闻

list·ed build·ing /ˌ.. ˈ../ *n* [C] a building of historical interest in Britain, that is protected by a government order〔英国登录入册的〕文物保护建筑物

lis·ten[1] /ˈlɪsn̩; ˈlɪsən/ *v* [I] **1** to pay attention to what someone is saying or to a sound that you can hear〔注意地〕听: *listening to music* 听音乐 | *Listen! There's a strange noise in the engine.* 听! 发动机内有一种奇怪的杂音。| [+to] *I like listening to the radio.* 我喜欢听收音机。| **listen hard** (=try to hear something that is very quiet) 尽力去听〔很轻的声音〕| **listen intently** (=very carefully and with interest) 留意听, 留神听 **2** *spoken* used to tell someone to pay attention to what you are about to say【口】听着, 听好〔用于告诉某人留意你要说的话〕: *Listen, I'm sure we can work this out, if everybody calms down.* 听着! 如果大家冷静下来, 我肯定我们能解决这件事。**3** to consider carefully what someone says to you 听从, 听信: *I told him not to go, but he just wouldn't listen.* 我告诉他不要去, 可是他就是不听。| [+to] *I wish I'd listened to your advice.* 我要是当初听你的劝告就好了。

listen for sth/sb *phr v* [T] to pay attention so that you are sure you will hear a sound 留心听: *Listen for the moment when the music changes.* 留心听音乐变化的那一瞬间。

listen in *phr v* [I] **1** to listen to a broadcast on the radio 收听〔电台广播〕: [+to] *I must remember to listen in to the news at noon.* 我一定要记住听午间新闻。—see also 另见 **tune in** (TUNE[2]) **2** to listen to someone's conversation without them knowing it 偷听, 窃听: [+on] *It sounded like someone was listening in on the extension.* 听起来好像有人在分机上偷听。

listen out *phr v* [I] *BrE informal* to listen carefully, especially for an unexpected sound【英, 非正式】注意听, 留心听〔尤指突如其来的声音〕: **listen out for** *Listen out for the baby in case she wakes up.* 注意听宝宝有没有醒来。

listen up *phr v* [I] *especially AmE spoken* used to get people's attention so they can hear what you are going to say【尤美, 口】注意, 听着〔用于吸引别人的注意, 使他们能听见你将要说的话〕: *Hey everybody, listen up!* 喂, 各位, 注意听!

USAGE NOTE 用法说明: LISTEN
Grammar 语法
Remember you can only **listen to** (or sometimes **for**) something. 别忘记, 听某事只能用 listen to〔有时用 for〕: *He's listening to music* (NOT 不用 *He's listening music*). 他正在听音乐。

listen[2] *n* [singular] *BrE informal* an act of listening【英, 非正式】听: *Have a listen to this new album!* 听一听这张新唱片!

lis·ten·a·ble /ˈlɪsn̩əbl; ˈlɪsənəbəl/ *adj informal* pleasant to hear【非正式】悦耳动听的

lis·ten·er /ˈlɪsn̩ɚ; ˈlɪsənə/ *n* [C] **1** someone who listens, especially to the radio〔尤指电台广播的〕收听者, 听众: *Some of our regular listeners have complained about the new program schedule.* 有些长期听众对我们新节目的时间安排有怨言。—compare 比较 VIEWER (1) **2 a good listener** someone who listens patiently and sympathetically to other people 耐心听别人说话的人

lis·ten·ing de·vice /ˈ··· ·ˌ·/ *n* [C] a piece of equipment that allows you to listen secretly to other people's conversations; a BUG[1] (5) 窃听器 —compare 比较 HEARING AID

Lis·ter /ˈlɪstə; ˈlɪstə/, **Joseph** (1827-1912) a British SURGEON (=a doctor who does operations on the body) who was the first person to use ANTISEPTICS (=chemicals that prevent wounds from becoming infected) during operations 利斯特〔(1827-1912),英国外科医生。他最先在外科手术中使用消毒剂〕

lis·te·ri·a /lɪˋstɪrɪə; lɪˈstɪəriə/ *n* [U] a type of BACTERIA that makes you sick 利斯特菌, 利氏杆菌

list·ing /ˈlɪstɪŋ; ˈlɪstɪŋ/ *n* **1** [C] something that is on a list〔清单中的〕列项 **2 listings** [plural] lists of films, plays, and other events with the times and places at which they will happen〔电影、戏剧等的〕节目表

list·less /ˈlɪstlɪs; ˈlɪstləs/ *adj* feeling tired and not interested in things 倦怠的, 无精打采的, 懒洋洋的: *The heat was making me listless.* 炎热的天气使我懒洋洋的。—**listlessly** *adv* —**listlessness** *n* [U]

list price /ˈ· ·/ *n* [C] a price that is suggested for a product by the people who make it〔厂商的〕定价

Liszt /lɪst; lɪst/, **Franz** /frɑnts; frænts/ (1811-86) a Hungarian COMPOSER and PIANIST who many people considered to be the greatest pianist of the 19th century. He is famous especially for writing piano music in the romantic style. 李斯特〔(1811-1886),匈牙利作曲家、钢琴家,被认为是19世纪最伟大的钢琴家,尤以浪漫主义手法创作钢琴曲而闻名〕

lit[1] /lɪt; lɪt/ the past tense and past participle of LIGHT[2]

lit[2] an abbreviation of 缩写= LITERATURE or LITERARY

lit·a·ny /ˈlɪtṇɪ; ˈlɪtəni/ *n* [C] **1** a long prayer in the Christian church in which the priest says a sentence and the people reply 连祷, 应答祈祷 **2** something that takes a long time to say that repeats phrases, or sounds like a list 冗长乏味的陈述; 反复的赘述: *a long litany of complaints* 絮絮叨叨的抱怨

li·tchi /ˈlitʃi; ˈlaɪtʃiː/ *n* [C] another spelling of LYCHEE lychee 的另一种拼法

lite beer /ˌlaɪt ˋbɪr; ˌlaɪt ˈbɪə/ *n* [U] *AmE* beer that has fewer CALORIES than normal beer【美】莱特啤酒, 淡啤酒〔热量比一般的啤酒低〕

li·ter /ˈlitə; ˈliːtə/ *n* [C] the American spelling of LITRE litre 的美式拼法

lit·e·ra·cy /ˈlɪtərəsɪ; ˈlɪtərəsi/ *n* [U] **1** the state of being able to read and write 有读写能力, 有文化: *a new adult literacy campaign* 新的成年人识字运动 **2 computer literacy** the ability to understand and use computers 使用电脑的能力

lit·e·ral[1] /ˈlɪtərəl; ˈlɪtərəl/ *adj* **1** the literal meaning of a word or expression is its basic or original meaning〔词〕本义的, 原义的, 字面意思的: **literal meaning/sense/interpretation etc** *A trade war is not a war in the literal sense.* 贸易战不是字面意义上的战争。—compare 比较 FIGURATIVE (1) **2 literal translation** a translation that gives a single word for each original word instead of giving the meaning of the whole sentence in a natural way 直译, 逐字翻译 **3 literal-minded** not showing much imagination; PROSAIC 缺乏想象力的; 乏味的 —**literalness** *n* [U]

literal[2] *n* [C] *BrE technical* a printing mistake, especially in the spelling of a word; TYPO【英, 术语】印刷错误〔尤指拼写错误〕

lit·e·ral·ly /ˈlɪtərəlɪ; ˈlɪtərəli/ *adv* **1** according to the most basic or original meaning of a word or expression 按照原义, 根据字面意思: *'Inspire' literally meant 'to breathe into'.* inspire 的原义是"吸入"。| **mean sth literally** (=mean exactly what you say) 意思和字面所说的一样 *I know I said I felt like quitting, but I didn't mean it literally!* 我知道我说过想退出, 可我实际上不是这个意思。**2 take sb/sth literally** to only understand the most basic meaning of words, phrases etc, often with the result that you do not understand what someone really means 仅仅从字面上理解某人/某事物: *Christians who take the Bible literally* 只从字面上理解《圣经》的基督徒 **3** used to emphasize that something is actually true 的确, 确实〔用于加强语气〕: *The Olympic Games were watched by literally billions of people.* 奥林匹克运动会确实有几十亿人观看。**4** *spoken* used to emphasize something you say that is already expressed strongly【口】简直〔用于加强本已强烈的语气〕: *Dad was literally blazing with anger.* 爸爸简直是火冒三丈。

lit·e·ra·ry /ˈlɪtəˌrɛrɪ; ˈlɪtərəri/ *adj* **1** connected with LITERATURE 文学的: *a literary prize* 文学奖 | *literary criticism* 文学评论 **2** typical of the style of writing used in literature rather than in ordinary writing and talking〔文风〕常见于文学的〔有别于一般书面语和口语〕; 典雅的: *a very literary style of writing* 非常典雅的文体 **3** liking literature very much, and studying or producing it 爱好文学的, 从事文学研究〔创作〕的: *a literary woman* 女文人 —**literariness** *n* [U]

lit·e·rate /ˈlɪtərɪt; ˈlɪtərʒt/ *adj* **1** able to read and write 能读会写的, 识字的 —compare 比较 NUMERATE **2 computer literate/musically literate etc** having enough knowledge to use a computer, play a musical instrument etc 会使用电脑的/会演奏乐器的等 **3** well educated 受过良好教育的 —opposite 反义词 ILLITERATE (1) —see also 另见 LITERACY —**literately** *adv* —**literateness** *n* [U]

lit·e·ra·ti /ˌlɪtəˋretaɪ; ˌlɪtəˈrɑːti/ *n* **the literati** *formal* a small group of people in a society who know a lot about literature【正式】文学家, 文人学士

lit·e·ra·ture /ˈlɪtərəˌtʃʊr; ˈlɪtərətʃə/ *n* [U] **1** books, plays, poems etc that people think have value 文学〔作品〕: *one of the great works of English literature* 英国文学中的伟大作品之一 **2** works such as these that are studied as a subject〔作为学科研究的〕文学: *a course in modern African literature* 非洲现代文学课程 **3** all the books, articles, etc on a particular subject〔某一学科的〕著述, 文献资料: *literature on the history of science* 科学史方面的文献资料 **4** printed information produced by organizations that want to sell something or tell people about something〔促销商品或提供信息的〕印刷材料, 宣传材料: *Do you have any sales literature available?* 你们有没有现成的关于销售方面的印刷材料?

lithe /laɪð; laɪð/ *adj* having a body that moves easily and gracefully〔动作〕灵活优美的: *the dancer's lithe long-limbed body* 舞蹈表演者优美修长的身材 —**lithely** *adv*

lith·i·um /ˈlɪθɪəm; ˈlɪθiəm/ *n* [U] a soft silvery ELEMENT (=simple substance) that is the lightest known metal 锂〔已知的最轻的金属〕

lith·o·graph[1] /ˈlɪθəˌgræf; ˈlɪθəgrɑːf/ *n* [C] a printed picture made by lithography 平版印刷画, 石版画

lithograph[2] *v* [T] to print a picture by lithography 用平版印刷术印刷

li·thog·ra·phy /lɪˋθɑgrəfɪ; lɪˈθɒgrəfi/ *n* [U] a process for printing patterns, pictures, etc from something that has been cut into a piece of stone or metal〔石板、金属板的〕平版印刷术 —**lithographic** /ˌlɪθəˋgræfɪk; ˌlɪθəˈgræfɪk◂/ *adj*

Lith·u·a·ni·a /ˌlɪθuˋenɪə; ˌlɪθjuˈeɪniə/ a country in northeast Europe on the Baltic Sea, between Latvia and Poland, which used to be part of the former Soviet Union. Population: 3,611,000 (2001). Capital: Vilnius. 立陶宛〔欧洲东北部一国家, 濒临波罗的海, 位于拉脱维亚和波兰之间, 曾为前苏联的一部分。人口: 3,611,000 (2001), 首都: 维尔纽斯〕—**Lithuanian** *n, adj*

lit·i·gant /ˈlɪtəgənt; ˈlɪtʒgənt/ *n* [C] *law* someone who is making a claim against someone or defending themselves against a claim in a court of law【法律】诉讼当事人

lit·i·gate /ˈlɪtəˌget; ˈlɪtʒgeɪt/ *v* [I,T] *law* to take a claim or complaint against someone to a court of law【法律】提出诉讼; 起诉〔某人〕

lit·i·ga·tion /ˌlɪtəˋgeʃən; ˌlɪtʒˈgeɪʃən/ *n* [U] *law* the process of taking claims to a court of law, in a non-criminal case【法律】〔民事案件的〕诉讼, 讼争

li·ti·gious /lɪˋtɪdʒɪəs; lɪˈtɪdʒəs/ *adj formal* too willing to take any disagreements to a court of law【正式】好讼争的, 好打官司的 —**litigiousness** *n* [U]

lit·mus /ˈlɪtməs; ˈlɪtməs/ *n* [U] a chemical that turns red when touched by acid, and blue when touched by an ALKALI 石蕊〔遇酸变红, 遇碱变蓝〕

litmus pa·per /ˈ·· ˌ··/ *n* [U] paper containing litmus used to test whether a chemical is an acid or an ALKALI 石蕊试纸

litmus test /ˈ·· ·/ *n* [singular] **1** something that makes it clear what someone's attitude, intentions etc are〔某人的态度、意图等的〕检验办法, 试金石: *The election will be an interesting litmus test on the 'greening' of politics.* 选举将是检验"环保"政治的有趣的试金石。**2** a test using litmus paper 石蕊试验

li·to·tes /ˈlaɪtoˌtiz; ˈlaɪtətiːz/ *n* [U] *technical* a way of expressing your meaning by using a word that has the opposite meaning with a negative word such as 'not', for example by saying 'not bad' when you mean 'good'【术语】反语法, 反叙法〈如以"不坏"表示"好"〉

li·tre *BrE*【英】, **liter** *AmE*【美】/ˈlitə; ˈliːtə/ *n* [C] **1** the basic unit for measuring an amount of liquid, in the METRIC system 升〔公制容量单位〕—see table on page C3 参见 C3 页附录 **2 1.3/2.4 etc litre engine** a measurement that shows the size and power of a vehicle's engine 1.3/2.4升等的发动机〔汽车引擎的大小和功率的测量〕

lit·ter[1] /ˈlɪtə; ˈlɪtə/ *n* **1** [U] bits of waste paper, containers etc that people have thrown away and left on the ground in a public

place〔扔在公共场所的〕垃圾，废弃物: *Please take your litter away with you.* 请把垃圾随身带走。—compare 比较 GARBAGE, RUBBISH, TRASH **2** [C] a group of baby animals such as dogs or cats which one mother gives birth to at the same time 一窝〔小狗、小猫等〕 **3** **cat/kitty litter** [U] small grains of a special substance that you put in a container where your cat gets rid of its solid and liquid waste 猫砂〔特殊物质的颗粒，放在容器中供猫便溺用〕: *a litter tray* 猫砂盘 **4** [U] STRAW (1) that a farm animal sleeps on〔家畜睡觉用的〕褥草 **5** **a litter of** a group of things arranged in a very untidy way 杂乱的一堆: *a litter of notes, papers and textbooks* 乱糟糟的一堆笔记、试卷和课本 **6** [C] a very low bed for carrying important people on, used in former times〔旧时载重要人物的〕轿，舆

litter² *v* **1** also 又作 **litter up** [T] if things litter an area there are a lot of them in that place, scattered in an untidy way〔在某处〕乱丢东西; 把〔某处〕弄乱: *Clothes littered the floor.* 地板上到处都是乱丢的衣服。| **be littered with** *The road was littered with debris.* 路上遍地瓦砾。**2** **be littered with** if something is littered with things, there are a lot of those things in it 充满〔某物〕: *History is littered with examples of failed colonialism.* 历史上有许多殖民主义失败的例子。**3** [I,T] to leave bits of waste paper etc on the ground in a public place〔在公共场所〕乱扔〔废弃物〕 **4** [I] *technical* if an animal such as a dog or cat litters, it gives birth to babies【术语】〔狗、猫等动物〕产仔

lit·te·ra·teur /ˌlɪtərəˈtɜː; ˌlɪtərəˈtɜː/ *n* [C] someone who is interested in literature, especially a writer whose work is not considered to be very good 文人〔尤指作品水平一般的作家〕

litter bin /ˈ· · ·/ also 又作 **litter bas·ket** /ˈ· · ˌ· ·/ *BrE*【英】*n* [C] a container in a public place for people to put things in that they are throwing away, such as papers or cans〔公共场所的〕垃圾箱

lit·ter·bug /ˈlɪtəbʌg; ˈlɪtəbʌg/ also 又作 **litter lout** *BrE*【英】*n* [C] someone who leaves waste on the ground in public places〔在公共场所〕乱扔废物者，垃圾虫

lit·tle¹ /ˈlɪtl; ˈlɪtl/ *adj*

1 ▶**SIZE** 尺寸◀ small in size 小的: *a little house* 小屋 | *their little group of supporters* 他们为数不多的支持者 | **a little bit of** *especially BrE* (=a small piece of something)【尤英】一小片〔块，段等〕的 *little bits of paper all over the floor* 地板上到处都是小纸片 | **little tiny** *spoken* (=extremely small)【口】极小的 *a little tiny puppy* 极小的狗 | **a little something** *informal* (=a small present)【非正式】小礼物 *I promised the kids a little something if they ate all their dinner.* 我答应孩子，如果他们把晚餐全部吃完的话，我会送给他们小礼品。

2 used about something or someone that is small to show that you like or dislike them, or that you feel sorry for them 小的〔用于小的人或物，表示喜欢、厌恶或同情〕: **nice little/clever little etc** *a nice little house* 漂亮的小屋 | *a clever little gadget* 灵巧的小装置 | *It wasn't a bad little car.* 那是一辆不错的小汽车。| **nasty little/silly little etc** *another of her silly little jokes* 她的另一个愚蠢的玩笑 | *a boring little man* 无聊的小个子男人 | **poor little/pathetic little** (=used when you feel sympathetic) 可怜的小…〔表示同情〕 *her sad little face looking up at me* 她痛苦的小脸仰起来看着我 | *a poor little bird with a broken wing* 断了一只翅膀的可怜的小鸟

3 done in a way that is not very strong or noticeable; slight 微弱的; 不明显的; 轻微的: *a wry little smile* 微微的苦笑

4 ▶**TIME/DISTANCE** 时间/距离◀ short in time or distance 短的: *I can have a nice little nap in the car.* 在汽车内我可以舒服地小睡片刻。| *You'll find it a little way along this path.* 沿着这条小路走不远你就会找到它。| **a little while** (=a short period of time) 一会儿 *He arrived a little while ago.* 他刚到一会儿。| *We sat there for a little while longer.* 我们在那里多坐了一会儿。

5 ▶**YOUNG** 年轻的◀ young and small 年轻的; 幼小的: *a cute little puppy* 可爱的小狗 | *We didn't have toys like this when I was little.* 在我小时候，我们没有这样的玩具。| **a little boy/girl** *two little boys playing in the street* 两个在街上玩的小男孩 | **your little girl/boy** (=your son or daughter who is still a child) 你的小女儿/儿子〔意指仍然是儿童〕 *Mum, I'm 17 – I'm not your little girl any longer.* 妈，我17岁了——我不再是你的小女儿了。| **little brother/sister** (=a younger brother or sister who is still a child) 小弟弟/小妹妹

6 ▶**UNIMPORTANT** 不重要的◀ **a)** not important 不重要的: *I'm too busy to worry about little things like broken windows.* 我无暇顾及窗户破了之类的小事。**b)** used jokingly when you really think that something is important 微不足道的〔用于开玩笑，实指某事很重要〕: *There's just that little matter of the £5,000 you owe me.* 就是你欠我5000英镑这件小事情。

7 **a little bird told me** *humorous spoken* used to say that someone who you are not going to name has told you something about another person【幽默，口】有人告诉我〔某人的事，不愿意透露消息来源时使用〕: *A little bird told me you're getting married soon.* 有人告诉我你快要结婚了。

8 **the little woman** *spoken* an expression meaning someone's wife, often considered offensive especially by women【口】老婆，婆娘〔指某人的妻子，常被认为是冒犯用语，尤其是妇女〕

Frequencies of **a little** and **a bit** in spoken and written English a little 和 a bit 在英语口语和书面语中的使用频率

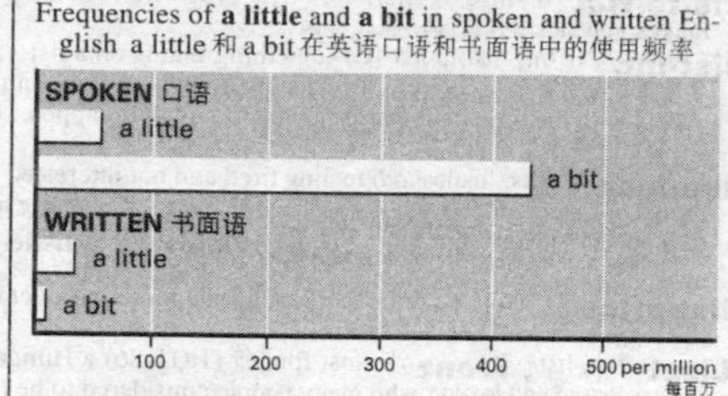

Based on the British National Corpus and the Longman Lancaster Corpus 据英国国家语料库和朗文兰开斯特语料库

This graph shows that **a bit** is much more common in spoken English than **a little**. This is because **a bit** is informal and is therefore more commonly used in ordinary conversation. However, in written English **a little** is more common than **a bit**. 本图表显示，a bit 在英语口语中的使用频率远远高于 a little。因为 a bit 是非正式用语，所以在日常对话中用得较为普遍。但 a little 在书面语中的使用频率远远高于 a bit。

USAGE NOTE 用法说明: LITTLE

Word choice 词语辨析: **little, small**

Little often suggests that you are talking about someone or something small that you are fond of or feel sympathetic towards. little 通常表示谈到的人或东西既小又令你喜欢或同情: *What a sweet little dog!* 多么可爱的小狗! | *A little old lady lived in the house opposite.* 一个矮小的老太太住在对面的房子里。

Small simply describes the size of something. small 只描述某物的大小: *My daughter's room is smaller than mine.* 我女儿的房间比我的小。| *He packed his things into a small bag.* 他把自己的东西装进一个小包内。You also use **small** when you are giving information and facts. 当提供信息和事实时也可以用 small: *There has been a small increase in production.* 产量稍有增长。

Little can also suggest that someone or something is unimportant. little 也可以表示人或物是不重要的: *What a silly little man!* 多么无足轻重的蠢家伙! When you are speaking it often sounds more friendly or polite to say something is **little** rather than **small**. 说话时谈到某物，用 little 比 small 友善或有礼貌: *I have a little problem, can you help me?* 我有个小问题，你能帮我吗? makes the problem sound less serious or urgent than 使问题的严重或紧急程度小于: *I have a small problem* and 而 *We're going to have a little test* 我们要做一个小测试 sounds a little less frightening than 则不及以下这句骇人: *We're going to have a small test.*

little² *quantifier*

1 only a small amount or hardly any of something 一点儿; 少得几乎没有: *Little is known about these areas of the moon.* 月球上这些地区鲜为人知。| *There's little to be gained from an official complaint.* 从正式投诉中得不到什么。| *I paid little attention to what the others were saying.* 我不大注意别人在说什么。| **very little** *During that period I ate very little and slept even less.* 那期间我吃得不多，睡得更少。| *There's very little money left.* 没剩下多少钱了。| *There seems very little point in continuing this discussion.* 看来继续进行这场讨论已没有多少意义。| **little or no** *peasants who have little or no land* 少地或无地的农民 | **little of** *Little of their wealth now remains.* 现在他们的财富已所剩无几。| **do little to help/benefit etc** *The new filing system has done little to improve efficiency.* 新的归档系统没有提高多少效率。| **as little as possible** (=the smallest amount that you can have or do) 尽可能少的 *He always writes as little as possible.* 他总是尽可能少写。| **little real effect/importance etc** (=used to emphasize that there is hardly any effect etc) 很少实

际效果/极不重要等〔用于强调〕*The laboratory tests are of little real value.* 这些实验室里的实验没有多少真正的价值。| **precious little** (=very little) 很少 *There's precious little good news.* 现在好消息少得可怜。—see 见 FEW (USAGE)
2 a little also 又作 **a little bit** a small amount 少量的: *I told him a little bit about it.* 关于此事我告诉了他一点点情况。| *Fortunately I had a little time to spare.* 很幸运, 我有一点空闲时间。| *She speaks a little French.* 她会说一些法语。| *A little over half the class can swim.* 班上有一半多一点的人会游泳。| **a little more/less** *He poured me out a little more wine.* 他又给我倒了一点酒。| *"Would you like some more coffee?" "Just a little, thanks."* "你还要来点咖啡吗?" "一点点就够了, 谢谢。" | **a little of** *The city is regaining a little of its former splendour.* 这座城市正在恢复一些昔日的辉煌。
3 ▶TIME/DISTANCE 时间/距离◀ a short time or distance 短时间; 短距离: *a little over 60 years ago* 六十多年前 | *We walked on a little and then turned back.* 我们走了一会儿, 然后就折返。
4 what little the small amount that there is, that is possible etc 仅有的一点; 尽可能的一点: *We did what little we could to help.* 我们尽了绵薄之力去相助。| *The firemen recovered what little remained of the bodies.* 消防员发现了尸体仅剩的一点残骸。

S1 W1 **little³** *adv* **1 a little** also 又作 **a little bit** to a small degree 稍许, 一点儿: *She trembled a little as she spoke.* 她说话时有些颤抖。| *I was a little bit disappointed with my test results.* 我的测验成绩令我有点沮丧。| **a little more/better/ further etc** *We shall have to wait a little longer to see what happens.* 我们得再等一会儿才能看到会发生什么事情。**2** not much or only slightly 很少, 略微: *The pattern of life here has changed little since I was a boy.* 从我小时候至今, 这里的生活模式几无改变。| **little known/understood etc** (=not known etc by many people) 鲜为人知 *a little known corner of the world* 世上鲜为人知的角落 | **little more/better etc (than)** *His voice was little more than a whisper.* 他的声音和耳语差不了多少。| **very little** *The situation has improved very little, in spite of all our efforts.* 虽然我们全力以赴, 但情况仍无多大改观。| **as little as possible** *I try to disturb her as little as possible when she's working.* 在她工作的时候, 我尽可能不去打扰她。**3 little did sb think/realize** also 又作 **sb little thought/realized** used to mean that someone did not think or realize that something was true 某人没有想到/认识到〔某事是真的〕: *Little did he realize that we were watching his every move.* 他没有意识到我们正在观察他的一举一动。**4 little by little** gradually 逐渐地: *Little by little things returned to normal.* 情况逐渐恢复正常。**5 more than a little/not a little** *formal* extremely【正式】极度地; 极端地: *Graham was more than a little frightened by what he had seen.* 格雷厄姆被自己所看到的事吓了一大跳。**6 (just) that little bit extra/harder/better etc** more, harder etc by a small amount that will have an important effect 更多一点的/更努力一点的/更好一点的等〔会有重要的影响〕: *people who work just that little bit harder than anyone else* 工作比别人更尽力一点的人

Little Bear /ˌ‥ ˈ‥/ *especially BrE*【尤英】, **Little Dip·per** /ˌ‥ ˈ‥/ *especially AmE*【尤美】— *n* **the Little Bear** a group of stars 小熊星座

Little Big·horn, the /ˌlɪtl̩ ˋbɪghɔrn; ˌlɪtl ˈbɪghɔːn/ a river in the US state of Montana, where General Custer fought against and was killed by Native Americans led by Sitting Bull and Crazy Horse in the Battle of Little Bighorn in 1876 小比格霍恩河〔美国蒙大拿州一河流。1876年, 卡斯特将军在小比格霍恩河战役中与"坐牛"和"疯马"率领的印第安人作战, 并在此丧生〕

Little Bo Peep /ˌlɪtl̩ bo ˋpip; ˌlɪtl bəʊ ˈpiːp/ also 又作 **Bo Peep** a character in a NURSERY RHYME (=old song or poem for young children). She is a young girl who loses the sheep that she is supposed to be taking care of. 小波比〔一首童谣中的人物。小女孩波比把自己应该照管好的羊儿给弄丢了〕: *Little Bo Peep has lost her sheep/And doesn't know where to find them;/Leave them alone, and they'll come home,/Bringing their tails behind them.* 小小波比丢了羊, /一筹莫展费思量。/不找也罢随它去, /羊儿摆尾识归途。

Little Boy Blue /ˌ‥ ˈ‥/ a character in a NURSERY RHYME (=an old song or poem for young children). He is a young boy who is dressed in blue and goes to sleep instead of taking care of the cows and sheep. 蓝衫小牧童〔一首童谣中的人物。这个身着蓝衫的小牧童不管牛羊, 只顾蒙头大睡〕: *Little Boy Blue, come blow your horn,/The sheep's in the meadow, the cow's in the corn;/But where is the boy that looks after the sheep?/He's under a haycock, fast asleep.* 蓝衫小牧童, 螺号快吹起; /羊儿进草地, 牛儿吃玉米; /牧童不见归, 牛羊谁来追? / 卧在干草堆, 蒙头酣然睡。

Little Dip·per, the /ˌ‥ ˈ‥/ *AmE* another name for Ursa Minor, a group of bright stars【美】小熊星座〔Ursa Minor 的别称〕

little fin·ger /ˌ‥ ˈ‥/ *n* [C] the smallest finger on your hand 小指

CULTURAL NOTE 文化注释

It used to be considered polite to keep the little finger straight when holding something like a cup, but people now think this is AFFECTED (=not real, natural, or sincere) and make fun of people who do it. 用手拿杯子等东西时伸直小指曾被认为是一种礼貌, 但是现在人们认为这是一种做作的行为, 并且会拿这样做的人开玩笑。

Little House on the Prai·rie /ˌ‥ ‥ ‥ ˈ‥/ a book for children by the US writer Laura Ingalls Wilder, which describes her life as a child in the Midwest in the 19th century, when her family were among the first white people to live there. It is also the name of a popular US television programme of the 1970s, which was based on Wilder's books.《草原小屋》〔美国作家劳拉·英戈尔斯·怀尔德创作的一部儿童小说。该书描写她自己的童年生活。当时正值19世纪, 她家是首批迁居美国中西部的白人。20世纪70年代, 美国有一档家喻户晓的同名电视节目, 该节目取材于怀尔德创作的几部作品〕

Little Jack Hor·ner /ˌlɪtl̩ dʒæk ˋhɔrnɚ; ˌlɪtl dʒæk ˈhɔːnə/ a character from a NURSERY RHYME (=an old song or poem for young children) 小杰克·霍纳〔一首童谣中的人物〕: *Little Jack Horner sat in a corner, /Eating his Christmas pie; /He put in his thumb, and pulled out a plum, /And said "What a good boy am I".* 小杰克, 坐里角, / 过圣诞, 吃果派; / 弯拇指, 抠梅子, / 自诩道: "乖宝宝"。

Little John /ˌ‥ ˈ‥/ one of Robin Hood's followers, in old English stories. He is called Little John as a joke because he is so big and strong. 小约翰〔英国古老传说中罗宾汉的一个追随者。他长得又高大又强壮, 被戏称为"小约翰"〕

Little League /ˈ‥ ˌ‥/ *n* a BASEBALL LEAGUE for children in the US〔美国〕少年棒球联合会

Little Lord Faunt·le·roy /ˌlɪtl̩ lɔrd ˋfɔntlərɔɪ; ˌlɪtl lɔːd ˈfɔːntlərɔɪ/ the main character in the 19th century children's book *Little Lord Fauntleroy* (1886) by Frances Hodgson Burnett. He is an American boy who becomes an English lord when his father dies, and has long BLOND curly hair, neat clothes, and behaves well and politely. 方特勒罗伊小爵爷〔弗朗西丝·霍奇森·伯内特19世纪创作的一部儿童文学作品《方特勒罗伊小爵爷》(1886) 中的主人公。他是一个美国少年, 父亲去世后承袭为英国勋爵。他留着长长的金黄色卷发, 衣着整洁, 品行良好〕

Little Mer·maid, The /ˌ‥ ˈ‥/ a FAIRY TALE by Hans Christian Andersen in which a MERMAID (=a woman with a fish's tail who lives in the sea) changes her fish's tail for legs, even though this is very painful, because she loves a human prince. But the prince marries a human princess instead, and the little mermaid dies.There is a STATUE of the Little Mermaid at the entrance to the HARBOUR in Copenhagen, the capital city of Denmark.《美人鱼》〔汉斯·克利斯蒂安·安徒生创作的一则童话, 讲述一条美人鱼爱上了人间的一个王子, 因而宁愿忍着剧痛把自己的鱼尾变成双脚。然而, 那位王子娶了一位公主, 美人鱼则牺牲了自己的生命。丹麦首都哥本哈根的港口入口处有一尊美人鱼塑像〕

Little Miss Muf·fet /ˌlɪtl̩ mɪs ˋmʌfɪt; ˌlɪtl mɪs ˈmʌfɪt/ a character from a NURSERY RHYME (=an old song or poem for young children). She is a young girl who is frightened by a SPIDER and runs away. 小玛菲特小姐〔一首童谣中的人物, 被一只蜘蛛给吓得跑了〕: *Little Miss Muffet/Sat on a tuffet,/Eating her curds and whey;/There came a great spider,/Who sat down beside her,/And frightened Miss Muffet away.* 小小玛菲特, / 矮凳上面坐, / 吃了乳清吃酥酪; / 一只大蜘蛛, / 小姐身旁驻, / 吓跑小姐直发怵。

Little Nell /ˌlɪtl̩ ˋnɛl; ˌlɪtl ˈnel/ a character in the book *The Old Curiosity Shop* (1841) by Charles Dickens. Many people think of the death of Little Nell as one of the saddest stories in English literature, although some people think it is so sad that it seems silly and emotional. 小耐儿〔查尔斯·狄更斯的小说《老古玩店》(1841) 中的人物。许多人认为小耐儿的死是英国文学中最催人泪下的故事之一, 但有些人却认为这个故事过于伤感, 近乎荒唐和煽情〕

Little Or·phan An·nie /ˌlɪtl̩ ˌɔrfən ˋænɪ; ˌlɪtl ˌɔːfən ˈæni/ a character in the US CARTOON STRIP *Little Orphan Annie*. She is an ORPHAN (=a child whose parents have died) who gets into a lot of trouble, especially when the man who takes care of her, Daddy Warbucks, is away. 小孤女安妮〔美国卡通连环漫画《小孤女安妮》中的角色。她是一个孤儿, 常常遇到麻烦, 尤其当照顾她的那位沃巴克斯老爹不在家时更是如此〕

L

little peo·ple /ˈ··,··ˈ/ *n* [plural] **1** all the people in a country or organization who have no power 老百姓，平民：*It's the little people who bear the brunt of taxation.* 承担税收的主力是平民百姓。**2 the little people** fairies (FAIRY (1)), especially Irish LEPRECHAUNS 小仙子；〔尤指爱尔兰传说中的〕矮妖精

Little Red Book, The /,·· ˈ·ˈ/ a small book with a red cover, printed in China and containing many sayings from the speeches and writings of the Chinese leader Mao Zedong. It was read especially during the Cultural Revolution of the late 1960s, and at public meetings large crowds of people used to wave their copies of the Little Red Book. 红宝书，《毛主席语录》〔中国出版的一种红色封面的小开本书，收录了中国前领导人毛泽东的许多演讲及著作片段。该书在20世纪60年代的"文化大革命"期间有众多读者。在当时的许多公众聚会上，大批群众常常挥舞着手中的"红宝书"〕

Little Red Ridding Hood 小红帽

Little Red Rid·ing Hood /ˌlɪtl̩ rɛd ˋraɪdɪŋ hʊd; ˌlɪtl red ˈraɪdɪŋ hʊd/ also 又作 **Red Ridinghood** a character in the old children's story *Little Red Riding Hood*, who is a young girl. In the story the Big Bad Wolf eats Little Red Riding Hood's grandmother and puts on her clothes. When Little Red Riding Hood goes to visit her grandmother she is surprised by her appearance and says, "Oh, Grandma, what big teeth you have!", and the wolf replies, "All the better to eat you with" and swallows Little Red Riding Hood. A WOODCUTTER (=someone whose job is to cut down trees) kills the wolf, cuts open its stomach, and saves Little Red Riding Hood and her grandmother. 小红帽〔早年童话故事《小红帽》中的小女孩。故事中，大灰狼把小红帽的外婆吃掉后穿上她的衣服。小红帽去探望外婆，见到那副相貌后大惊失色地问道："哎呀，外婆，你的牙齿怎么这样大呀？"大灰狼答道："牙齿大好把你来吃呀"，说着就把小红帽吞下去了。后来，一个樵夫杀了大灰狼，切开它的肚子，救出了小红帽和她的外婆〕

Little Rock /ˈ·· ·ˈ/ the capital of the US state of Arkansas. In 1957 the US President had to send US government soldiers to a school, because the state governor was using Arkansas state soldiers to prevent nine black children from going to a school where all the children were white. 小石城〔美国阿肯色州首府。1957年，阿肯色州州长曾派该州军队前去阻止九名黑人子弟到一所白人学校上学，由此引发美国政府军出动前去维持秩序〕

Little Wo·men /,·· ˈ·ˈ/ (1868) a book for girls written by Louisa May Alcott which describes the family life of four sisters in New England, whose names are Jo, Meg, Beth, and Amy《小妇人》〔(1868)，露易莎·梅·奥尔科特为女孩子创作的一部小说，描述新英格兰四姐妹的家庭生活。她们分别为乔、梅格、贝丝和埃米〕

lit·to·ral /ˈlɪtərəl; ˈlɪtərəl/ *n* [C] *technical* an area of land near the coast【术语】沿海地区，海岸地区 —**littoral** *adj*

li·tur·gi·cal /lɪˋtɜ·dʒɪkl̩; lɪˈtɜːdʒɪkəl/ *adj* [only before noun 仅用于名词前] related to church services and ceremonies 教堂仪式的，礼拜仪式的 —**liturgically** /-kl̩ɪ; -kli/ *adv*

lit·ur·gy /ˈlɪtə·dʒɪ; ˈlɪtədʒi/ *n* **1** [C,U] a way of praying in a religious service using a fixed order of words, prayers etc 礼拜仪式 **2 the Liturgy** the written form of these services 礼拜公祷文，祈祷书

liv·a·ble, liveable /ˈlɪvəbl̩; ˈlɪvəbəl/ *adj* **1** also 又作 **livable in** *BrE* a place that is livable in is suitable to live in; HABITABLE【英】适宜居住的 **2** if your life is livable, you can bear it; ENDURABLE〔生活〕能忍受的

live¹ /lɪv; lɪv/ *v*

① IN A PLACE/TIME 在某处/某时
② LIVE IN A PARTICULAR WAY 以某种方式生活
③ BE ALIVE 活着
④ SEXUAL RELATIONSHIP 性关系
⑤ LIVE FOR A REASON 为某种理由而活
⑥ IN YOUR MIND 在心中
⑦ OTHER MEANINGS 其他意思

① IN A PLACE/TIME 在某处/某时

1 ▶IN A PLACE/HOME 在某处/某家◀ [I always+adv/prep] to have your home in a particular place〔在某处〕居住：**live in/at/with/near etc** *Where do you live?* 你住在哪里？| *We used to live in Bakersfield.* 我们过去住在贝克斯菲尔德。| *They have one daughter who still lives with them.* 他们有一个女儿还和他们住在一起。| **live at home** (=live with your parents) 住在家里〔和父母住在一块〕| **look for a place to live** (=look for a house to live in) 找住处 | **live rough** *BrE* (=have no home and sleep outdoors)【英】无家可归，风餐露宿

2 ▶PLANT/ANIMAL 植物/动物◀ [I always+adv/prep] a plant or animal that lives in a particular place grows there or has its home there〔在某处〕生长[栖息]：**live in/on/near etc** *The birds live only on this island.* 这种鸟只栖息在这个岛上。

3 ▶AT A PARTICULAR TIME 在某时◀ [I always+adv/prep] to be alive at a particular time or when particular events happen〔在某时或某事发生时〕生存，活着：[**+before/in/at**] *Pythagoras lived a century before Socrates.* 毕达哥拉斯生活在苏格拉底之前一个世纪。| *He lived during the time of the plague.* 在瘟疫流行期间他还活着。

4 ▶TO BE KEPT SOMEWHERE 被置于某处◀ [I always+adv/prep] *informal especially BrE* to be kept in a particular place【非正式，尤英】被放置在某处：**live in/on etc** *Where does this dish live?* 这盘子放在哪里？

② LIVE IN A PARTICULAR WAY 以某种方式生活

5 [I always+adv/prep,T] to have a particular type of life, or live in a particular way 过…生活；以〔某种方式〕生活：**live in/under/like etc** *These people are living in appalling conditions.* 这些人生活在极其恶劣的环境之中。| *He lived like a king.* 他过着国王一样的生活。| **live well** (=have plenty of money, food etc) 生活过得很富裕 | **live a quiet/active/healthy life** *Ben has to live a quiet life.* 本不得不过着一种平静的生活。| **live the life of** *She lived the life of an aristocrat.* 她过着贵族的生活。| **live a life of crime/luxury** *a movie star living a life of luxury* 过着奢华生活的电影明星 | **live in fear (of)** *Colin lives in fear of having a heart attack.* 科林生活在恐惧中，怕心脏病发作。| **live from day to day** (=deal with each day as it comes without making plans) 日复一日地得过且过 | **be living on the breadline** (=be very poor) 生活贫困 | **live out of a suitcase** (=travel a lot, especially as part of your work) 经常奔走旅行〔尤指是工作的一部分〕

6 ▶LIVE BY DOING STH 靠做某事生活◀ [I] to keep yourself alive by working, eating etc 靠〔工作，吃某食物等〕为生：*They earn barely enough to live.* 他们赚的钱刚够糊口。| **live by doing sth** *They live by hunting and killing deer.* 他们靠捕杀鹿为生。| **live on beans/potatoes/grass etc** (=eat only a particular type of food) 以豆/马铃薯/草等维持生命 *living on a diet of bread and cheese* 靠吃面包和干酪维持生命 | **live out of tins/cans** (=eat mainly food from cans, not fresh food) 主要吃罐头食品 | **live on benefit/welfare/£40 a week etc** (=have only a small amount of money with which to buy food, pay bills etc) 靠抚恤金/福利救济/每周40英镑等过日子 *I challenge anyone to try to live on the state pension.* 我倒要看看谁能靠政府养老金生活。

7 live it up *informal* to do things that you enjoy and spend a lot

L

of money【非正式】享乐，过花天酒地的生活：*living it up at the Hotel California* 在加利福尼亚酒店享乐一番
8 ▶LIVE BY A PRINCIPLE/RULE ETC 按照某种原则/规则等生活◀ [I] to always behave according to a particular set of rules or ideas 总是按…的规定[观念]行事：*people who live by the Bible* 以《圣经》为行事准则的人
9 live by your wits to get money by being clever or dishonest, and not by doing an ordinary job 靠耍小聪明[不诚实手段]赚钱
10 live a lie to pretend all the time that you feel or believe something when actually you do not 过虚伪的生活：*I had to divorce him, I couldn't go on living a lie.* 我得和他离婚，我不能继续过着虚伪的生活。
11 ▶EXCITING LIFE 令人兴奋的生活◀ [I] to have an exciting life 过令人兴奋的生活：*We're beginning to live at last!* 我们终于开始好好地过日子了！

③ BE ALIVE 活着
12 ▶BE/STAY ALIVE 活着，生存◀ [I] to be alive or be able to stay alive 活着；生存：*Without light, plants couldn't live.* 没有阳光，植物就无法生存。| *He is extremely ill and not expected to live.* 他病得很重，看来活不成了。| *The baby only lived a few hours.* 婴儿只活了几个小时。| *Females live longer on average than males.* 女人一般来说比男人寿命长。| **give sb six months/a year etc to live** (=expect someone who is ill to only live for six months etc) 预期某病人只能活六个月/一年等 | **live to see/witness sth** (=live long enough to see it) 活着见到某事 *I'm glad she did not live to witness the break-up of her daughter's marriage.* 我很欣慰，她活着时没有看到女儿婚姻破裂。
13 the best/greatest/worst... that ever lived someone who was better, greater etc at doing something than anyone else in the past or present 迄今为止最好的/最伟大的/最差的〔做某事的人〕：*I think Jimi Hendrix was definitely the greatest guitarist that ever lived.* 我认为吉米·亨德里克斯肯定是迄今为止最伟大的吉他演奏家。
14 be living on borrowed time to be still alive after the time that you were expected to die 比预期活得更久

④ SEXUAL RELATIONSHIP 性关系
15 live with/together [I] if two people live together, they live with each other in a sexual relationship without getting married 和…(未婚)同居：*We wanted to live together and have a child.* 我们想同居并生个小孩。| *the man she's been living with for the last four years* 这个最近四年与她同居的男人
16 live in sin *old-fashioned* to live together and have a sexual relationship without being married【过时】同居；姘居

⑤ LIVE FOR A REASON 为某种理由而活
17 live for sb/sth if you live for someone or something, they are so important to you that they seem to be your main reason for living 为某人/某事物而活：*He lived for his art.* 他为自己的艺术而活着。| *All through the football season, I lived for Saturdays.* 在整个足球赛季，我为星期六而活着。
18 live and breathe sth to enjoy doing something so much that you spend most of your time on it 投身于某事：*Politics is the stuff I live and breathe.* 我投身于政治活动，如鱼得水。
19 live for the day when to want something to happen very much 盼望有一天〔某事发生〕：*She lives for the day when she can have an apartment of her own.* 她盼望有一天能有自己的公寓。

⑥ IN YOUR MIND 在心中
20 live in a world of your own/live in a dream world to have strange ideas about life that are not like those of other people 活在自己想象的世界里/活在梦幻的世界里
21 live in the past to have old-fashioned ideas and attitudes 生活在过去之中〔观点和态度过时〕：*You can't go on living in the past.* 你不能继续生活在过去之中。
22 live in sb's memory/live with sb to continue to exist in someone's memory 活在某人的记忆中：*The expression of terror on my son's face lived with me for years.* 儿子脸上的惊恐表情在我的记忆中留存了好多年。
23 ▶IMAGINE STH 想象某事物◀ [I always+adv/prep] to imagine that you are experiencing something 想象正在经历某事：[+in/through etc] *an old actress living in her past glory* 沉醉在昔日光辉中的年迈女演员

⑦ OTHER MEANINGS 其他意思
24 ▶STILL HAVE INFLUENCE 仍有影响◀ [I] if someone's idea or work lives, it continues to influence people〔某人的观念和作品〕继续影响人们：*Shakespeare's words live with us still.* 莎士比亚的话仍然影响着我们。
25 as long as I live used to emphasize that you will always do or feel something 只要我还活着〔用于强调〕：*I'll never forget it as long as I live.* 只要我还活着，我永远也不会忘记它。
26 not live sth down if you cannot live down something bad that you have done, people do not forget about it 无法使人忘记〔自己做过的坏事〕：*I was tempted to admit defeat, but I would never have lived it down.* 我很想承认失败，但是我永远无法让人忘记它。
27 you live and learn used to say that you have just heard or learnt something surprising 真是活到老学到老〔用于表示刚得知令人惊讶的事〕
28 live and let live used to say that you should accept other people's behaviour, even if it seems strange 自己活也得让别人活〔表示对他人奇怪行为的宽容〕
29 you haven't lived used to say that someone's life will be boring if they do not have a particular experience 你白活了〔用于表示某人的生活因未有某种经历而枯燥乏味〕：*You haven't lived until you've tasted champagne.* 没有尝过香槟酒的话，你就算白活了。
30 sb will live to regret it used to say that someone will wish that they had not done something 某人将会对所做的事感到懊悔：*If you marry him, you'll live to regret it.* 如果你和他结婚，你早晚会后悔的。
31 if I live to be 100/1,000 etc used to say that you will never understand something 即使我活到100岁/1000岁等〔用于表示永远也不能理解某事〕：*If I live to be a thousand years old, I'll never see why she does these things!* 即使我活到一千岁，我也无法明白她为什么做这些事！
32 live to fight/see another day to continue to live or work after a failure or after you have dealt with a difficult situation〔经历失败或困难处境后〕继续生存[工作]下去：*A lot of stores like ours have closed down, but we'll live to see another day.* 像我们这样的商店很多都倒闭了，但我们继续经营下去。
33 long live the King/Queen! etc *spoken* used as an expression of loyal support【口】国王/女王万岁！
34 long live democracy/America/the people etc used to show support for an idea, principle, or nation 民主/美国/人民等万岁〔对某思想、原则或国家表示支持〕

live in *phr v* [I] if someone who does paid work in a place lives in, they live at that place 住宿在办公地点 —see also 另见 LIVE-IN

live off sth/sb *phr v* [T] to get your income or food from a supply of money or from another person 靠〔某经济来源或某人〕过活：*Mom used to live off the interest from her savings.* 妈妈过去靠存款的利息过日子。| *Rick disapproves of people who are living off the welfare.* 里克不赞同靠福利救济过日子的人。| **live off the land** (=get food from growing vegetables, hunting etc) 靠土地〔种植蔬菜、打猎等〕生存

live on *phr v* [I] to continue to exist 继续存在着：*Alice's memory will live on.* 大家会怀念艾丽斯的。—see also 另见 LIVE¹ (24)

live out *phr v* **1** [I] when someone who does paid work in a place lives out, they do not live in that place 不住在办公地点 **2** [T] **live out sth** to experience or do something that you have planned or hoped for 实现某事〔已计划或想做的事〕：*The money enabled them to live out their dreams.* 这笔钱可以使他们实现自己的梦想。**3 live out your life in/on/along etc** to continue to live in a particular way or place until you die 以〔某种方式〕/在〔某地方〕终老：*He lived out his life in solitude.* 他在孤独中度过余生。

live through sth *phr v* [T] to experience difficult or dangerous conditions 经历〔艰难或险境〕：*It was hard to describe the nightmare she had lived through.* 她所经历的恐惧难以描述。

live up to sth *phr v* [T] if something or someone lives up to a standard, reputation, or promise, they do as well as they were expected to, do what they promised etc 符合〔标准〕；不负〔盛名〕；履行〔诺言〕：*The bank is insolvent and will be unable to live up to its obligations.* 银行已经破产，将无力履行其义务。| **live up to your expectations** *The book certainly lived up to his expectations.* 这本书无疑符合他的期望。

live with sth *phr v* [T] to accept a difficult situation that is likely to continue for a long time 忍受，承受〔可能会为时长久的困难局面〕：*You have to learn to live with stress.* 你得学会承受压力。

L

live² /laɪv; laɪv/ *adj*
1 ►LIVING 活的◄ [only before noun 仅用于名词前] not dead or artificial; living 活的〔非死的或人造的〕; 有生命的: *They are campaigning against experiments on live animals.* 他们正在开展反对用活的动物做实验的运动。—compare 比较 DEAD¹ (1)
2 live broadcast/programme etc a programme that is seen or heard on television or radio at the same time as it is being made 〔电视或广播的〕现场直播[实况转播]/现场直播的节目等
3 live performance/act/music etc a performance in which the entertainer performs for people who are watching rather than for a film, record etc〔为观众所作的〕现场表演/节目/音乐(会)等: *Did the introduction of CDs affect the interest in live music?* 激光唱片流行以后, 有没有影响大众对现场音乐表演的兴趣? | *Madonna live in concert* 麦当娜现场演唱会 | **live recording** (=a recording made of a live performance) 实况录制 | **live audience** (=the people who watch a live performance) 现场观众 *It's always different singing in front of a live audience.* 在现场观众面前演唱总是不一样的。
4 ►ELECTRIC 带电的◄ a wire or equipment that is live has electricity flowing through it〔电线、设备〕通电的, 带电的 —see also 另见 LIVE WIRE (2)
5 ►BULLETS/BOMBS 子弹/炸弹◄ a live bullet, bomb etc still has the power to explode because it has not been used 会爆炸的: *live ammunition* 会爆炸的弹药
6 live match a match that has not yet been used to produce a flame 未用过的火柴
7 live coals pieces of coal that are burning 正在燃烧的煤
8 live issue/concern an issue that still interests or worries people 当前大家关注的问题
9 ►COMPUTER 电脑◄ when a computer system is put into live use, it is used in a real situation by ordinary people instead of just being tested by the people who designed it〔电脑系统〕已投入使用的
10 live yoghurt yoghurt containing BACTERIA that are still alive 含活菌的酸乳酪
11 a real live ... *spoken* an expression used to emphasize that something surprising has been seen or exists, used especially to or by children【口】活生生的, 真的〔用于强调, 指看到或存在的事物令人惊讶, 尤为儿语〕: *We saw a real live elephant!* 我们看到一头真的大象!

live³ *adv* **1 broadcast a programme/show/speech etc live** to broadcast something at the same time as it actually happens 现场直播节目/演出/讲话等: *We will be broadcasting the program live from Austin.* 我们将从奥斯汀现场直播这个节目。**2 perform live** to perform in front of people who have come to watch, rather than for a film, record etc〔在观众面前〕现场演出[表演]

live·a·ble /ˈlɪvəbl; ˈlɪvəbəl/ *adj* another spelling of LIVABLE livable 的另一种拼法

Live Aid /ˈlaɪv ed; ˈlaɪv eɪd/ two popular music concerts held in London and Philadelphia on the same day in 1985, which were organized by the musician Bob Geldof to collect money to help people dying of hunger in Ethiopia. Live Aid led to other similar events, such as Comic Relief 现场赈灾音乐会〔1985年伦敦和费城两地在同一天举行的流行音乐会。该音乐会的发起人是音乐家鲍勃·格尔多夫, 目的是为挣扎在死亡线上的埃塞俄比亚饥民筹集救济款。此项义举还引发了其他类似救灾活动, 如喜剧演员济贫会的演出等〕—see also 另见 BAND-AID

-lived /lɪvd; lɪvd/ *suffix* [in adjectives 构成形容词] lasting or living for a particular length of time 寿命…的, 生活…的: *Her enthusiasm was short-lived.* (=did not last long) 她的热情很短暂。| *to come from a long-lived family* 出生于一个长寿的家族

lived-in /ˈ· ·/ *adj* a place that looks lived-in has been used often by people so that it does not seem too new〔某地方看上去像〕有人住过的: **have a lived-in look** *often humorous*【常幽默】*Jared's apartment has that lived-in look.* 贾里德的房子看上去曾经有人住过。

live-in /ˈlɪv ɪn; ˈlɪv ɪn/ *adj* [only before noun 仅用于名词前] **1 live-in maid/nanny etc** a worker who lives in the house where they work 住在雇主家的女佣/保姆等 **2 live-in lover/boyfriend etc** a phrase meaning someone who lives with their sexual partner without being married to them, used especially by people who do not approve of this (未婚)同居的情人/男朋友等〔尤为不赞成同居的人使用〕

live·li·hood /ˈlaɪvlɪˌhʊd; ˈlaɪvlihʊd/ *n* [C,U] the way you earn money in order to live 生计: *New fishing regulations will threaten our livelihood.* 新的捕鱼条例将威胁到我们的生计。

live·long /ˈlɪvˌlɔŋ; ˈlɪvlɒŋ/ *adj AmE old-fashioned*【美, 过时】**all the livelong day** a phrase meaning all day, used when this seems like a long time to you 整整一天〔用于似乎时间很漫长时〕

live·ly /ˈlaɪvlɪ; ˈlaɪvli/ *adj*
1 ►FULL OF ENERGY 充满活力的◄ someone who is lively has a lot of energy and is very active 充满活力的, 精力充沛的, 活泼的: *He'd always been a bright and lively child.* 他向来是个聪明活泼的孩子。
2 ►FULL OF INTEREST 充满兴趣的◄ something that is lively is exciting and involves quick, intelligent thinking〔某事〕激烈的〔包含敏锐的思考〕, 热烈的: *That was a pretty lively debate!* 那是一场相当热烈的辩论! | **a lively interest** (=strong interest) 浓厚的兴趣 *Eric has a lively interest in Eastern cuisine.* 埃里克对东方烹饪有着浓厚的兴趣。
3 ►EXCITING 让人激动的◄ a place or situation that is lively is exciting because a lot of things are happening〔地方或情况〕激动人心的〔因发生了很多事情〕: *Not exactly a lively vacation, was it?* 假期不很刺激, 是吗?
4 ►COLOUR 颜色◄ very bright 鲜艳的: *a dress of lively reds and yellows* 鲜艳的红黄色连衣裙
5 lively imagination someone with a lively imagination tends to invent stories, descriptions etc that are not true 生动的想象力
6 make things lively (for sb) to make a situation more exciting or more difficult for someone (使某人)感到更激动[困难]: *Our trainer was threatening to make life lively for us if we didn't improve.* 教练威胁我们, 如果我们没有改进就有我们好受的。
7 Look/step lively! *spoken* used to tell someone to hurry【口】赶快! 走快点! —**liveliness** *n* [U]

liv·en /ˈlaɪvən; ˈlaɪvən/ *v*
liven up *phr v* **1** [I,T] to become more exciting, or to make an event become more exciting (使)活跃起来: *The party really livened up when Mattie arrived.* 马蒂来到后, 聚会真的热闹了起来。| **liven sth ↔ up** *Why don't we play some games? That'll liven things up!* 我们为什么不玩些游戏? 那样会使气氛活跃起来! **2** [T] to make something look, taste etc more interesting or colourful 使〔某物〕更好看[更有趣味]: **liven sth ↔ up** *Why not liven up the room with some flowers?* 为什么不用一些花把房间点缀得更漂亮呢? **3** [I,T] to become more interested or excited, or to make someone feel like this (使)变得更有兴趣[兴奋]: *I'm sure she'll liven up when she sees Malcolm.* 我确信她见到马尔科姆后会高兴的。

liv·er /ˈlɪvɚ; ˈlɪvə/ *n* **1** [C] a large organ in your body which produces BILE (1) and cleans your blood〔人体的〕肝脏 —see picture at 参见 DIGESTIVE SYSTEM 图 **2** [U] the livers of animals used as food〔供食用的〕动物肝脏 **3 a clean/fast etc liver** someone who lives their life in a morally good, exciting etc way 洁身自好/生活放荡等的人

Li·ver Buil·ding, the /ˈlaɪvɚ ˌbɪldɪŋ; ˈlaɪvə ˌbɪldɪŋ/ a well-known building in Liverpool, on the River Mersey. On it are two figures of the Liver Bird, an imaginary bird which is the symbol of Liverpool. 利物大厦〔利物浦一著名大厦, 濒临默西河。大厦上有两只象征利物浦的"利物鸟"〕

Liv·er·pool /ˈlɪvɚpul; ˈlɪvəpu:l/ a city in the northwest of England, on the River Mersey. 利物浦〔英国西北部一城市, 濒临默西河〕

CULTURAL NOTE 文化注释

Liverpool is still a big port, but it is much less important than it was in the 19th and early 20th centuries. Much of the city's industry has also closed down, bringing high unemployment to the area. In the 1960s, Liverpool became famous and very fashionable as the place where the Beatles and several other bands started playing music. Football is very popular in Liverpool, and the city has two well-known teams: Liverpool and Everton. 利物浦虽然仍是一个大的港口, 但是现在它已经不像19世纪和20世纪早期那么重要了。工厂大量倒闭导致了很高的失业率。20世纪60年代, 因为有甲壳虫等几个乐队在此兴起, 利物浦声名鹊起, 成了时尚之都。足球在利物浦很受追捧, 这里有两支著名的足球队: 利物浦队和埃弗顿队。

Well-known places in Liverpool include the Albert Dock, the two Cathedrals, the Royal Liver Building, the Tate Liverpool ART GALLERY, the Walker Art Gallery, and the Cavern Club (the club where the Beatles first started playing). 利物浦的名胜有艾伯特码头、两座大教堂、皇家利物大厦、泰特利物浦美术馆、沃克美术馆和深洞俱乐部(此俱乐部为甲壳虫乐队首次献唱的地方)。

Liverpool was chosen to be the European City of Culture for 2008, and in 2004 it became a World Heritage Site. 2008年利物浦被选为"欧洲文化之都", 而早在2004年它就成了世界文化遗产保护地。

The STEREOTYPE of a person from Liverpool is someone who is WORKING CLASS, has SOCIALIST political beliefs, and is good at telling jokes and making people laugh. People who come from Liverpool are called **Liverpudlians** or, informally, **Scousers**. The Liverpool ACCENT (=way of pronouncing words) is very easy to recognize, and is informally called a **Scouse** accent. 利物浦人的典型形象是出身工人阶级，有社会主义政治信仰，善于讲笑话逗人哈哈大笑。人们把利物浦人叫做Liverpudlians，非正式场合叫做Scousers。利物浦口音很容易辨识，非正式场合称Scouse accent。

Famous people from Liverpool include Beryl Bainbridge (a NOVELIST), Cilla Black (a singer and television PERSONALITY), Ricky Tomlinson (an actor), the poets Adrian Henri and Roger McGough, and the COMEDIANS Ken Dodd and Jimmy Tarbuck. 利物浦的名人有小说家贝丽尔·班布里奇、歌手和电视名人卡拉·布莱克、演员里基·汤姆林森、诗人阿德里安·亨利和罗杰·麦高夫，还有喜剧演员肯·多德和吉米·塔巴克。

live rail /ˌlaɪv ˋrel; ˌlaɪv ˈreɪl/ *n* [C] a thick metal bar along a railway track that supplies electricity to trains〔铁道上向火车供电的〕电轨

liv·e·ried /ˈlɪvərid; ˈlɪvərid/ *adj* wearing LIVERY (1) 穿制服的: *a liveried servant* 穿制服的仆人

liv·er·ish /ˈlɪvərɪʃ; ˈlɪvərɪʃ/ *adj BrE informal* slightly ill, especially after eating or drinking too much【英，非正式】患病的〔尤指暴饮暴食之后〕

liver saus·age /ˈ··,··/ *n* [U] *BrE* a type of cooked soft SAUSAGE made mainly of LIVER (2)【英】肝泥香肠; liverwurst *AmE*【美】

liv·er·wort /ˈlɪvɚˌwɝt; ˈlɪvəwɜːt/ *n* [C,U] a small flat green plant without flowers that grows in wet places 叶苔

liv·er·wurst /ˈlɪvɚˌwɝst; ˈlɪvəwɜːst/ *n* [U] *AmE* a type of cooked soft SAUSAGE made mainly of LIVER (2)【美】肝泥香肠; liver sausage *BrE*【英】

liv·e·ry /ˈlɪvərɪ; ˈlɪvəri/ *n* **1** [C,U] a type of old-fashioned, expensive-looking uniform for servants〔样子昂贵的旧式〕仆人制服 **2** [U] *poetic* natural bright colours that cover something【诗】〔覆盖物体的〕鲜艳的自然色彩 **3** [C,U] *BrE* a set of colours and designs used by a company on its property and vehicles【英】〔公司财产或汽车上的〕标志性的色调[图案] —see also 另见 LIVERIED

livery com·pa·ny /ˈ···,··/ *n* [C] one of the GUILDs (=ancient trade associations) of London〔伦敦的〕同业公会

liv·e·ry·man /ˈlɪvərɪmən; ˈlɪvərimən/ *n plural* **liverymen** /-mən; -mən/ [C] someone who works in a LIVERY COMPANY〔伦敦的〕同业公会会员

livery sta·ble /ˈ···,··/ *n* [C] a place where people pay to have their horses kept, fed etc or where horses can be hired〔付钱寄养马匹的〕代养马房; 马匹出租处

lives /laɪvz; laɪvz/ the plural of LIFE

live·stock /ˈlaɪvˌstɑk; ˈlaɪvstɒk/ *n* [plural, U] the animals that are kept on a farm 牲畜, 家畜

live wire /ˌlaɪv ˋwaɪr; ˌlaɪv ˈwaɪə/ *n* [C] **1** *informal* someone who is very active and has a lot of energy【非正式】活跃分子; 精力充沛的人 **2** a wire that has electricity passing through it 载电线, 火线

liv·id /ˈlɪvɪd; ˈlɪvɪ̈d/ *adj* **1** extremely angry; FURIOUS 非常愤怒的, 暴怒的: *Mom will be livid if she finds out.* 妈妈要是发现了, 会非常生气的。**2** a mark on your skin that is livid is dark blue and grey〔皮肤伤痕呈现〕乌青色的: *livid bruises* 乌青色的淤伤 **3** *literary* a face that is livid is very pale【文】〔脸色〕苍白的 —**lividly** *adv*

liv·ing[1] /ˈlɪvɪŋ; ˈlɪvɪŋ/ *adj* **1** alive now 活(着)的: *one of the greatest living composers* 当今最伟大的作曲家之一 **2 living proof** if someone is living proof of a particular fact, they are a good example of how true it is 活证据: *I'm living proof that you don't need a college degree to be successful.* 没有大学学位也能获得成功, 我就是活证据。**3 in living memory** for as long as anyone can remember 在人们的记忆里: *the worst storm in living memory* 人们记忆中最厉害的风暴 **4 in/within living memory** a long time ago but within the lives of people who are still alive〔很久以前, 但仍然〕在今人的记忆中: *the worst recession in living memory* 人们的记忆中最严重的经济衰退 **5 living things** anything that lives, such as plants, animals or people 生物 **6 living language** a language that is still spoken today 现在仍使用的语言, 活语言

2 **living**[2] *n* **1** [C usually singular 一般用单数] the way that you earn money or the money that you earn 生计; 收入: *It's not a great job, but it's a living.* 这不是一份了不起的工作, 而是生计。| **do sth for a living** (=as your job) 做某事以维持生计 *So what do you do for a living?* 那你是靠做什么谋生的? | **earn/make a living** *It's hard to make a decent living as a musician.* 想靠当音乐家过上好的生活是很难的。| **scrape/scratch a living** (=get just enough to eat or live) 勉强为生 —see 见 LIFE (USAGE) **2 the living** all the people who are alive as opposed to dead people 活着的人 **3** [U] the way in which someone lives their life 生活方式: *the stresses of city living* 城市生活的压力 **4** [C] the position or income of a PARISH priest; BENEFICE 教区牧师的圣职[圣俸] —see also 另见 **cost of living** (COST[1] (1)), **in the land of the living** (LAND[1] (7)), STANDARD OF LIVING

living death /ˌ··ˈ·/ *n* [singular] a life that is so unpleasant, it would seem better to be dead 生不如死的生活

living fos·sil /ˌ··ˈ··/ *n* [C] *technical* an animal or plant of a very ancient type, that has not changed and still exists【术语】活化石

living hell /ˌ··ˈ·/ *n* [singular] a situation that causes you a lot of suffering for a long time 活地狱〔使人长期受苦的处境〕: *Walter made my life a living hell.* 沃尔特使我受尽了折磨。

living le·gend /ˌ··ˈ··/ *n* [C] someone who is famous for being extremely good at something〔某方面极为擅长的〕活着的传奇人物: *John Lee Hooker isn't just a great blues player – he's a living legend.* 约翰·李·胡克不只是伟大的布鲁斯音乐演奏家—他是活着的传奇人物。

living quar·ters /ˈ··,··/ *n* [plural] the part of an army or industrial camp etc where the soldiers or workers live and sleep〔军营或工业区内的〕生活区

living room /ˈ·· ·/ *n* [C] the main room in a house where people relax, watch television etc 起居室, 客厅 —compare 比较 DRAWING ROOM, FRONT ROOM, LOUNGE[1] (3), PARLOUR (2)

living stan·dard /ˈ··,··/ *n* [C usually plural 一般用复数] the level of comfort and wealth that people have; STANDARD OF LIVING 生活水平[水准]: *a decline in the country's living standards* 该国生活水平的下降

Liv·ing·stone /ˈlɪvɪŋstən; ˈlɪvɪŋstən/, **Dr David** (1813-73) a Scottish MISSIONARY (=someone who goes to a foreign country to teach people about Christianity) and EXPLORER of Africa. He was the first European to see the Zambezi River and the Victoria Falls. A journalist called Henry Morton Stanley, who did not know Livingstone, went to look for him. When they met he said, "Dr Livingstone, I presume". People sometimes say this as a joke when they meet someone. 利文斯通〔(1813-1873)，苏格兰传教士、非洲探险家。他是第一个见到赞比西河与维多利亚大瀑布的欧洲人。有一位名叫亨利·莫顿·斯坦利的记者不认识利文斯通，但却要前去找他。他们谋面时，他便问道："我想你就是利文斯通博士吧。"后来，人们遇到陌生人有时会借用这句话开玩笑〕

living wage /ˌ··ˈ·/ *n* [singular] wages high enough to allow you to buy the things that you need to live 基本生活工资

living will /ˌ··ˈ·/ *n* [C] *AmE* a document explaining what medical or legal decisions should be made if you become so ill that you cannot make those decisions yourself【美】活遗嘱, 生前嘱咐〔一种文件, 说明当事人病危无法作决定时, 应采取哪种医疗或法律决定〕

Liv·y /ˈlɪvɪ; ˈlɪvi/ (59 BC-AD 17) a Roman historian known for his very large history of Rome, which greatly influenced historical writing. His Latin name was Titus Livius. 李维〔(公元前59年-公元17年)，罗马历史学家，以撰写的罗马历史巨著闻名。其著作对后人书写历史产生了很大影响。他的拉丁名是Titus Livius〕

liz·ard /ˈlɪzɚd; ˈlɪzəd/ *n* [C] a type of REPTILE that has four legs, and a long tail 蜥蜴

lizard 蜥蜴

Lizard, the an area of land going out into the sea in the south-west of England, which is the part of the UK that is furthest to the south 利泽得〔英格兰西南部伸入海中的一块陆地，为英国最南端〕

Ljub·lja·na /ˈljubljɑnə; luːbˈljɑːnə/ the capital of Slovenia 卢布尔雅那〔斯洛文尼亚首都〕

ll the written abbreviation of 缩写 = 'lines', used in books〔书中的〕行

lla·ma /ˈlɑmə; ˈlɑːmə/ *n* [C] a South American animal with thick woolly hair, rather like a camel without a hump 美洲驼, 亚美利加驼

Llan·dud·no /lænˋdɪdno; lænˈdɪdnəʊ/ a town on the coast of North Wales that is popular with tourists 兰迪德诺〔威尔士北部一沿海城镇，深受游客喜欢〕

Llan·fair·pwll·gwyn·gyll·go·ger·y·chwyrn·dro·bwll·llan·ty·si·lio·go·go·goch /hlæn,vaɪrpuhl-

ˌgwɪŋgɪhlgɑˌgɛrəxwɪrnˌdrɑbuhlˌhlæntɪˌsɪljɑˌgɑgɑˈgɑx; hlæn-ˌvaɪrpʊhlˌgwɪŋgɪhlgɒˌgerəxwɪrnˌdrɒbuhlˌhlæntɪˌsɪljɒˌgɒgɒˈgɒx/ also 又作 **Llanfair PG** /ˌlænfɛr pi ˋdʒi; ˌlænfeə piː ˈdʒiː/ a small village on Anglesey in North Wales, famous for being the place with the longest name in the UK 兰韦尔普〔威尔士北部安格尔西郡一小村庄，以拥有英国最长的地名而闻名〕

LLB *n* [C] Bachelor of Laws; a first university degree in law 法学士

LLD *n* [C] Doctor of Laws; a DOCTORATE in law 法学博士

LLM *n* [C] Master of Laws; a MASTER's degree in law 法学硕士

Lloyd George /ˌ·ˈ·/, **David** (1863-1945) a Liberal politician who was British Prime Minister from 1916 to 1922. He was against increasing the British Empire and in favour of political change. He introduced PENSIONS and National Insurance. 劳合·乔治〔(1863-1945)，自由党政治家。1916年至1922年间任英国首相。他反对大英帝国不断扩张，支持政治改革，推行养老金制度和国民保险制度〕

Lloyd's /lɔɪdz; lɔɪdz/ also 又作 **Lloyd's of London** an organization based in London, which provides all types of insurance, including insurance for ships and aircraft. People with a lot of money can become members of Lloyd's (who are called 'names'), and can make more money by sharing in its profits. But they can also lose a lot of money if Lloyd's loses money. 劳埃德保险公司〔伦敦一金融机构。该机构开展各种保险业务，其中包括船舶和飞机保险。有钱人士可成为劳埃德保险公司的成员(称为 names〔名士〕)，靠利润分成获得收益。不过，一旦公司出现亏损，他们也会蒙受损失〕

Lloyd's Re·gis·ter /ˌ·ˈ···/ also 又作 **Lloyd's Register of Shipping** a list, produced every year, which puts all non-military ships into groups according to their type and size and gives other information about them《劳氏船舶年鉴》〔每年出版一次。该年鉴对所有非军用船只按用途和大小进行分级，并收录其他相关信息〕

Lloyd Web·ber /ˌlɔɪd ˋwɛbɚ; ˌlɔɪd ˈwebə/, **Andrew** (1948-) a British COMPOSER, now officially called Lord Lloyd-Webber, who has written many very successful MUSICALS (=plays that use singing and dancing to tell a story), including *Jesus Christ Superstar*, *Evita*, and *Cats*. Some of his musicals were written with Tim Rice. 劳埃德·韦伯〔(1948-)，英国作曲家，现正式称劳埃德·韦伯勋爵。他创作了多部优秀音乐剧，包括《万世巨星》、《艾薇塔》和《猫》。有些作品是与蒂姆·莱斯合写的〕

lo /lo; ləʊ/ *interjection old use* look; used to tell someone to pay attention to something that is surprising【旧】看哪，瞧〔用于叫人注意出乎意料的事〕—see also 另见 LO AND BEHOLD

load¹ /lod; ləʊd/ *n* [C]

1 ▶**AMOUNT OF STH** 某物的量◀ a large quantity of something that is carried by a vehicle, person etc〔车辆、人等的〕负载物: *Take this load of wood over to the barn.* 把这批木头搬到仓库里去。—see also 另见 **shed its load** (SHED² (8))

2 **a load/loads (of sth)** *informal especially BrE* a lot of something【非正式，尤英】很多，大量: *We got a load of complaints about the loud music.* 我们收到对吵闹的音乐声的很多投诉。| *Don't worry, there's loads of time.* 不用担心，时间很充裕。| **loads to do/see/eat etc** *There was loads to eat at the party.* 聚会上有很多吃的。

3 **truckload/carload etc** the biggest amount or number of something that a vehicle can carry 满满一卡车/一辆汽车等: *a busload of tourists* 满满一辆公共汽车的游客

4 **a load of crap/rubbish/bull etc** *spoken especially BrE* used to say that something is complete nonsense or stupid【口，尤英】十足的废话[蠢话]: *I never heard such a load of crap in all my life!* 我一生中从未听到过这种十足的胡言乱语！

5 ▶**WORK** 工作◀ the amount of work that a person or machine has to do〔一个人或一台机器的〕工作量，负荷: *The computer couldn't handle the load and crashed.* 电脑应付不了负荷而死机。| **a light/heavy load** (=not much work, or a lot of work) 轻松的/繁重的工作 *Hans has a heavy teaching load this semester.* 这学期汉斯的教学负担很重。| **work load** *My work load has doubled since Mandy left.* 自从曼迪走后，我的工作量加倍了。

6 **a heavy/difficult load to bear** a responsibility or worry that is difficult to deal with 沉重的/难以承受的负担: *Coping with her mother's long illness was a heavy load to bear.* 应付她母亲的长期疾病是个难以承受的重担。—see also 另见 **be a load/weight off your mind** (MIND¹ (15))

7 ▶**WASHING** 洗涤◀ a quantity of clothes etc that are washed together in a washing machine〔洗衣机的一次〕洗衣量: *Do all the whites in one load.* 把所有的白色衣物用洗衣机洗一次。

8 **get a load of** *spoken* used to tell someone to look at or listen to something surprising or funny【口】看，听〔令人惊奇或可笑的事，用于叫人注意〕: *Get a load of that weird hairdo!* 瞧那稀奇古怪的发型！

9 ▶**WEIGHT** 重量◀ the amount of weight that the frame of a building or structure can support〔建筑物或结构的〕承重量: *a load-bearing wall* 承重墙

10 ▶**ELECTRICITY** 电◀ an amount of electrical power 电荷

load² *v* **1** also 又作 **load up** [I,T] to put a load of something on or into a vehicle (把…)装上[装进]〔运输工具〕: *Have you finished loading up?* 你装完货了吗？| [+with] *The boat called at Lerwick to load up with fresh vegetables.* 船停靠在勒威克装新鲜蔬菜。| **load sth** *It took an hour to load the van.* 把货物装进运货车花了一小时。| **load sth into/onto** *Be careful loading that piano into the truck!* 把钢琴装上货车要小心！**2** [T] to put bullets into a gun, a film into a camera etc 给〔枪〕上子弹；给〔相机〕装入胶卷: **load sth with** *Did you load it with 200 or 400 film?* 你装了200还是400的胶卷？| **load sth into** *Can you load the CD into the player, please?* 请你把激光唱片放入唱机中好吗？**3** [T] to put a PROGRAM¹ (1) into a computer 把(程序)输入电脑: **load sth into/from** *You have to load it from the A drive.* 你得从A驱动器装载程序。**4** **load sb with** to give someone a lot of things to carry 让某人拿[搬运]〔很多东西〕: *Em always loaded the kids with groceries to carry.* 埃姆总是让孩子们提杂货。

load sb/sth **down** *phr v* [T usually passive 一般用被动态] **1** to give someone more responsibility, work etc than they can deal with 给〔某人〕过重的负担: *Jane felt loaded down with money worries.* 简被金钱的烦恼压得透不过气来。**2** to make someone carry too many things 使〔某人〕携带太多东西: *She staggered home loaded down with shopping bags.* 她拿着大包小包的购物袋，摇摇晃晃地往家走。

load·ed /ˈlodɪd; ˈləʊdʒd/ *adj*

1 ▶**VEHICLE** 运载工具◀ carrying a load of something 有负载的，装着货的: *a loaded truck* 装了货的货车

2 ▶**GUN/CAMERA** 枪/相机◀ containing bullets, film etc 装了子弹的；装上胶卷的: *a loaded pistol* 上了子弹的手枪

3 ▶**RICH** 富有的◀ [not before noun 不用于名词前] *informal* very rich【非正式】富有的，很有钱的: *Giles can afford it – he's loaded.* 贾尔斯花得起这笔钱 —— 他有的是钱。

4 ▶**FULL** 充满的◀ **be loaded with** *informal* to be full of a particular quality, attitude etc, or contain a lot of something, especially something bad【非正式】充斥着〔某素质、态度等〕；充满…〔尤指不好的东西〕: *Your paper's loaded with spelling mistakes.* 你的试卷全是拼写错误。| *a voice loaded with menace* 充满威胁的声音

5 ▶**WORD/STATEMENT** 词/陈述◀ a loaded word, statement etc has more meaning, especially a negative meaning, than you first think〔单词、陈述等〕有暗含意义的〔尤指负面意思〕: *He 'deserved' it? That's a loaded word.* 这是他"应得"的吗？那是话中有话的词。

6 **loaded question** a question that is unfair because it makes you answer in a particular way 不公正的问题，有偏袒的问题〔诱导人以某种方式去回答〕—compare 比较 **leading question** (LEADING¹ (4))

7 ▶**DRUNK** (酒)醉的◀ *informal* very drunk【非正式】酩酊大醉

8 **the dice/odds are loaded against sb/sth** used to say that someone or something is not likely to succeed or win 败局已定〔用于表示某人/某事不会成功〕

9 **loaded dice** DICE¹ (1) that have weights in them so that they always fall with the same side on top 灌铅色子，做了手脚的色子〔总是掷出某一面〕

load·ing /ˈlodɪŋ; ˈləʊdɪŋ/ *n* [U] an amount added to the cost of an insurance agreement because of special risks, profits etc〔保险协议的〕附加费

load·sa /ˈlodzə; ˈləʊdzə/ *adj spoken* a lot of【口】很多的，许多的: *He gets to shoot loadsa bad guys and snog the girlies.* 他枪杀许许多多坏蛋，并赢得妞儿们欢心。

load·star /ˈlodˌstar; ˈləʊdstɑː/ *n* [C] another spelling of LODESTAR lodestar的另一种拼法

load·stone /ˈlodˌston; ˈləʊdstəʊn/ *n* [C] another spelling of LODESTONE lodestone的另一种拼法

loaf¹ /lof; ləʊf/ *n plural* **loaves** /lovz; ləʊvz/ [C] **1** bread that is shaped and baked in one piece and can be cut into SLICES〔面包的〕一条: *a loaf of bread* 一条面包 **2** **meat/nut loaf** meat or nuts that have been cut very finely, pressed together, and baked〔切得很细、压在一起，然后焙烤的〕肉/果仁糕 **3** **use your loaf** *BrE old-fashioned* used to tell someone to be more sensible or think harder【英，过时】〔告诉某人〕机灵点，动动脑筋

loaf² *v* [I] *informal* to waste time in a lazy way when you should be working【非正式】虚度光阴; 闲荡: **loaf around/about** *They spend all day loafing around on street corners.* 他们整天在街角闲荡。

loaf·er /ˈlofə; ˈləʊfə/ *n* [C] **1** a flat leather shoe that does not need to be fastened onto your foot 平跟船鞋; 懒汉鞋 —see picture at 参见 SHOE¹ 图 **2** someone who loafs around 游手好闲者

loam /lom; ləʊm/ *n* [U] good quality soil consisting of sand, clay, and decayed plants 沃土, 壤土 —**loamy** *adj*

S2 W2 **loan¹** /lon; ləʊn/ *n* **1** [C] an amount of money that your borrow from a bank etc〔银行等的〕借款: **take out a loan** (=borrow money) 借款 | **repay a loan** *We're repaying the loan over a three-year period.* 我们以三年期偿还贷款。| **bank loan** (=money lent by a bank) 银行贷款 | **student loan** (=money lent to students) 学生贷款 **2** [singular] the act of lending something 借出: **[+of]** *Thanks for the loan of your camera.* 谢谢你借相机给我。| **give sb the loan of sth** (=lend someone something) 借某物给某人 **3 on loan** if something such as a painting or book is on loan, someone is borrowing it〔画或书等〕暂借(的): *The book I wanted was out on loan.* 我要的书借出去了。| *pictures on loan from the Louvre* 从卢浮宫借来的画

loan² *v* [T] **1** *especially AmE* to lend someone something, especially money【尤美】借给〔某人某物〕〔尤指钱〕: **loan sb sth/loan sth to sb** *Can you loan me $5?* 你能借我5美元吗? **2** *BrE* to lend something valuable, such as a painting, to an organization【英】把〔贵重物品〕出借〔某机构〕: *The family loaned their collection of paintings for the exhibition.* 这家族把收藏的画借给了展览会。—see 见 BORROW (USAGE)

loan cap·i·tal /ˈ· ,···/ *n* [U] the part of a company's money that was borrowed to help start it〔帮助公司成立的〕借入资本

lo and be·hold /, · · ˈ·/ *interjection humorous* used to make someone pay attention when you are going to mention something surprising that has happened【幽默】瞧, 真怪呀〔用于使人注意将提及的令人惊讶的事〕

loan shark /ˈ· ·/ *n* [C] someone who lends money at very high rates of INTEREST¹ (4) and will often use threats or violence to get the money back 放高利贷者

loan·word /ˈlon,wɜd; ˈləʊnwɜːd/ *n* [C] a word taken into one language from another 外来语, 借词 —see also 另见 BORROWING (1)

loath /loθ; ləʊθ/ *adj* **be loath to do sth** *formal* to be unwilling to do something【正式】不愿意做某事: *Sarah was loath to tell her mother all that had happened.* 萨拉不愿意告诉妈妈所发生的一切。

loathe /loð; ləʊð/ *v* [T not in progressive 不用进行时] to hate someone or something very much 厌恶, 憎恨: *Lucinda loathes spiders.* 露辛达讨厌蜘蛛。| **loathe doing sth** *I absolutely loathe travelling.* 我极其憎恶旅行。

loath·ing /ˈloðɪŋ; ˈləʊðɪŋ/ *n* [singular, U] a very strong feeling of hatred 强烈的厌恶[憎恨]: **[+for]** *The more he called me 'Sugar', the more my loathing for him increased.* 他越叫我"宝贝", 我越讨厌他。

loath·some /ˈloðsəm; ˈləʊðsəm/ *adj* very unpleasant or cruel; DISGUSTING 令人厌恶[憎恨]的: *How I detest you, you loathsome creature!* 我实在讨厌你, 你这可恨的家伙! —**loathsomeness** *n* [U]

loaves /lovz; ləʊvz/ the plural of LOAF

lob /lɑb; lɒb/ *v* **lobbed, lobbing** [T] **1** *informal* to throw something somewhere, especially over a wall, fence etc【非正式】扔〔尤指越过墙、篱笆等〕: **lob sth into/at/over etc** *The kids were lobbing pine cones into the neighbor's yard.* 孩子们把松果扔进邻居的院子中。**2** to throw or hit a ball in a slow high curve, especially in a game of tennis or CRICKET (2)〔打网球或板球时〕将〔球〕挑高: *Martinez lobbed the ball high over Graf's head.* 马丁内斯将球挑过格拉夫的头顶。—**lob** *n* [C] —see picture on page A22 参见 A22 页图

lob·by¹ /ˈlɑbɪ; ˈlɒbi/ *n* [C] **1** a wide passage or large hall just inside the entrance to a public building〔公共场所入口处的〕门廊, 大厅: *a hotel lobby* 旅馆大堂 —compare 比较 FOYER (1) **2** a group of people who try to persuade a government that a particular law or situation should be changed〔游说政府更改某项法律或改变某种局面的〕群众团体: *The tobacco lobby is trying to change the no smoking laws.* 烟草游说团正企图更改禁烟法。—see also 另见 LOBBY² **3** an attempt to persuade a government to change a law, make a new law etc〔试图说服政府更改法律、制定新法律的〕游说: **[+of]** *a mass lobby of Parliament by women's organizations* 妇女团体对议会的大量游说 —see also 另见 LOBBY² **4 a)** a hall in the British Parliament where members of parliament and the public meet〔英国议院中的〕民众接待厅 **b)** one of the two passages in the British Parliament where members go to vote for or against a BILL¹ (2)〔英国议院中的〕投票走廊〔其一供投赞成票, 另一供投反对票〕

lobby² *v* [I,T] to try to persuade the government or someone with political power that a law or situation should be changed 游说〔政府或政治上的掌权者更改法律或改变局面〕: **[+for/against]** *The group is lobbying for a reduction in defense spending.* 该团体正在游说, 以期削减国防开支。| **lobby sb to do sth** *We've been lobbying our State Representative to support the new health plan.* 我们一直在劝说我们的州议员支持新的保健计划。—**lobbyist** *n* [C]

lobby sth **through** *phr v* [T] to get a law officially approved by the government by lobbying〔通过游说使政府〕通过〔某法律〕: *After months of debate the bill was finally lobbied through Parliament.* 经过数月的辩论, 议会最终通过了这项法案。

lobe /lob; ləʊb/ *n* [C] **1** the soft piece of flesh at the bottom of your ear; EARLOBE 耳垂 **2** *technical* a round part of an organ in your body, especially in your brain or lungs【术语】〔尤指脑、肺等的〕叶 —**lobed** *adj*

lo·bot·o·my /loˈbɑtəmɪ; ləʊˈbɒtəmi/ *n* [C] a medical operation to remove part of someone's brain in order to make them less violent, rarely done now 叶切断(术), 脑白质切断(术)〔过去用来减少暴力行为的手术, 现已罕用〕; LEUCOTOMY *BrE*【英】—**lobotomize** also 又作 **-ise** *BrE*【英】*v* [T]

lob·ster /ˈlɑbstə; ˈlɒbstə/ *n* **1** [C] a sea animal with eight legs, a shell, and two large CLAWs 龙虾 **2** [U] the meat of this animal used for food 龙虾肉

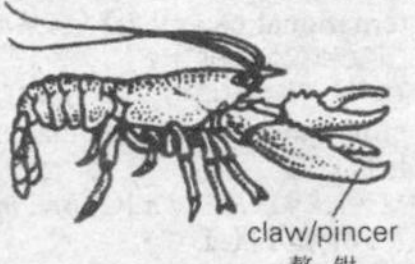

lob·ster·pot /ˈlɑbstəpɑt; ˈlɒbstəpɒt/ *n* [C] a trap shaped like a basket in which lobsters are caught (诱捕)龙虾笼

S1 W1 **lo·cal¹** /ˈlokl; ˈləʊkəl/ *adj* **1** connected with a particular place or area, especially the place you live in 地方性的, 当[本]地的〔尤指居住地的〕: *the local hospital* 当地医院 | *members of the local community* 本地社区的成员 **2** *technical* affecting or limited to one part of your body【术语】〔身体上〕局部的: *a local infection* 局部感染 | **local anaesthetic** *The tooth was removed under local anaesthetic.* 在局部麻醉下把牙拔掉。

S3 **local²** *n* [C] **1** [often plural 常用复数] someone who lives in the place where you are or the place that you are talking about 本地人, 当地居民: *We asked one of the locals to recommend a hotel.* 我们请一位当地人介绍一家旅馆。**2** *BrE* a pub near where you live, especially one where you often drink【英】〔尤指经常光顾的〕住处附近的小酒馆: *I usually have a pint or two at my local on Friday nights.* 星期五晚上我通常在邻近的小酒馆里喝上一两品脱。**3** *AmE* a bus, train etc that stops at all regular stopping places【美】〔每站都停的〕普通公共汽车[列车] **4** *AmE* a branch of a TRADE UNION【美】〔工会的〕地方分会

lo-cal /,lo ˈkæl; ,ləʊ ˈkæl◂/ *adj* another spelling of LOW-CAL low-cal 的另一种拼法

local ar·e·a net·work /,··, ··ˈ··/ *n* [C] *technical* LAN【术语】〔电脑〕局域网

local au·thor·i·ty /,·· ·ˈ···/ *n* [C] *BrE* the group of people elected or paid to be the government of a particular area, town, or city in Britain【英】〔英国市、镇等的〕地方当局: *The local authority are considering his grant application.* 地方当局正在考虑他的补助金申请。

local call /ˈ·· ,·/ *n* [C] a telephone call to a place near you that does not cost much money 市内通话

local col·our *BrE*【英】, **local color** *AmE*【美】/,·· ˈ··/ *n* [U] additional details in a story or picture that give you a better idea of what a place is really like〔小说或图画中使场面逼真的〕地方色彩, 乡土气息: *His description of the smells from the market added a touch of local colour.* 他对菜市场的种种气味的描述, 使作品添加了一点地方色彩。

local coun·cil /,·· ˈ··/ *n* [C] the group of people responsible for providing houses, schools, parks etc in a small area such as a town or DISTRICT〔负责镇或行政区的住房、学校、公园等的〕地方议会

lo·cale /loˈkæl; ləʊˈkɑːl/ *n* [C] the place where something happens or where the action takes place in a book or a film〔书或电影中某事发生的〕地点, 现场: *We need a tropical locale for this scene.* 我们需要一个热带的地方作这一幕的场景。

local gov·ern·ment /,·· ˈ···/ *n* [C,U] the government of cities, towns etc by elected representatives of the people living in them〔市、镇等经选举产生的〕地方政府

local his·to·ry /ˌ‥ˈ‥‥/ *n* [U] the history of a particular area 地方史、地方志 —**local historian** /ˌ‥ˈ‥‥/ *n* [C]

lo·cal·i·ty /loˋkælətɪ; ləʊˈkælɪ̣ti/ *n* [C] a small area of a country, city etc 地区; **in the locality** (=near to the place you are talking about) 在这个地区, 在附近 *What kind of leisure facilities are there in the locality?* 附近有哪些休闲设施?

lo·cal·ize also 又作 **-ise** *BrE*【英】/ˋlokḷˌaɪz; ˈləʊkəlaɪz/ *v* [T] *formal*【正式】**1** to find out exactly where something is 找出…的确切位置: *A mechanic is trying to localize the fault.* 技师正在寻找故障所在。**2** to limit the effect that something has, or the size of area it covers 使〔某物的影响〕限于局部, 限制…的范围 —**localization** /ˌlokḷəˋzeʃən; ˌləʊkəlaɪˈzeɪʃən/ *n* [U]

lo·cal·ized also 又作 **-ised** *BrE*【英】/ˋlokḷˌaɪzd; ˈləʊkəlaɪzd/ *adj formal* a word meaning within one small area, used especially to talk about something unpleasant or unwanted【正式】局部的, 小范围的〔尤指令人不快或讨厌的事物〕: *localized flooding* 局部的洪水泛滥 | *a localized infection* 局部感染

2 **lo·cal·ly** /ˋlokəlɪ; ˈləʊkəli/ *adv* **1** near the area where you are or the area you are talking about 在本地, 在当地: *I live locally, so it's easy to get to the office.* 我住在本地, 所以上班很方便。**2** in particular small areas 局部地: *Most of the country will be dry, but there will be some rain locally.* 全国大部分地区天气干燥, 但局部地区有雨。

local pa·per /ˌ‥ˈ‥/ *n* [C] **1** a newspaper that gives mainly local news〔以刊载当地新闻为主的〕地方报纸 **2** *AmE* a newspaper printed in a town which contains local, national, and international news【美】〔在某城市发行的〕地方报纸〔包括本地、国家和国际新闻〕

local ra·di·o /ˌ‥ˈ‥‥/ *n* [U] a radio service that broadcasts programmes for a particular area of the country 地方广播电台, 地区广播

local rag /ˌ‥ˈ/ *n* [C] *BrE informal* a local newspaper【英, 非正式】地方报纸

local time /ˈ‥ˌ/ *n* [U] the time of day in a particular part of the world 当地时间: *We'll arrive in Boston at 4:00 local time.* 我们将于当地时间四点到达波士顿。

3 3 **lo·cate** /ˋloket; ləʊˈkeɪt/ *v* **1** [T] to find the exact position of something 找出〔某物〕的准确位置: *We couldn't locate the source of the radio signal.* 我们无法确定无线电信号的来源。**2** **be located in/by/near etc** to be in a particular position 位于[坐落在]…/…边上/…附近等: *The business is located right in the center of town.* 商店正好位于市中心。**3** [I always+adv/prep] *AmE* to come to a place and start a business, company etc there【美】将〔公司等〕设立〔在某处〕: [+in/at etc] *We are offering incentives for companies to locate in our city.* 我们正在鼓励企业来本市设立公司。

3 2 **lo·ca·tion** /loˋkeʃən; ləʊˈkeɪʃən/ *n* **1** [C] a particular place or position, especially in relation to other areas, buildings etc〔尤指与其他地区、建筑物等有关的〕地点, 位置: *Could you give me your precise location?* 你能给我你的精确位置吗? —see 见 POSITION[1] (USAGE) **2** [C,U] a place outside or away from a film STUDIO where scenes are filmed〔电影的〕外景拍摄地: *It was hard to find a suitable location for the desert scenes.* 要找到拍摄沙漠镜头的合适外景地很困难。| **on location** *Most of the movie was shot on location in Africa.* 这部影片大部分是在非洲的外景地拍摄的。**3** [U] the act of finding the position of something〔某物的〕定位: *The main problem for engineers was the location of underground rivers in the area.* 工程师的主要问题是定位该地区的地下河流。

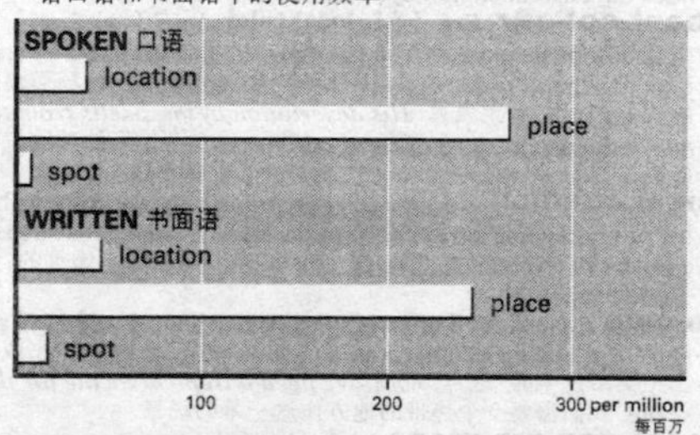

Frequencies of the nouns **location, place** and **spot** in spoken and written English 名词 location, place 和 spot 在英语口语和书面语中的使用频率

Based on the British National Corpus and the Longman Lancaster Corpus
据英国国家语料库和朗文兰开斯特语料库

This graph shows that **place** is much more common than **location** or **spot** in both spoken and written English. This is because **place** is the most general of the three words. **Location** is used to mean a particular place or position, especially in relation to other buildings, areas etc. **Spot** is used to mean a pleasant place or area where you spend time or do something.
本图表显示, 在英语口语和书面语中 place 的使用频率远远高于 location 或 spot, 因为 place 在这三个词中是最普通的。location 用于表示某一特定地点或位置, 尤其是和其他建筑物和地区等有关。spot 用于表示某人愉快地度日或做事的地方或地区。

loch /lɑk; lɒx/ *n* [C] *ScotE* a lake or a part of the sea partly enclosed by land【苏格兰】湖;〔部分伸入陆地的〕海湾: *Loch Ness* 尼斯湖

Loch Lo·mond /ˌlɑk ˋlomənd; ˌlɒx ˈləʊmənd/ a lake in western Scotland near Glasgow, popular with tourists. There is a well-known old song about Loch Lomond. 洛蒙德湖〔位于苏格兰西部格拉斯哥附近, 深受游客喜爱。当地有一首著名的老歌就是以洛蒙德湖为主题的〕

the Loch Ness Monster 尼斯湖水怪

Loch Ness Mon·ster, the /ˌlɑk nɛs ˋmɑnstɚ; ˌlɒx nes ˈmɒnstə/ a very large animal which is supposed to live in **Loch Ness**, a large very deep lake in northern Scotland. 尼斯湖水怪〔据说是生活在苏格兰北部又大又深的尼斯湖里的一种庞大动物〕

CULTURAL NOTE 文化注释

Although some people say that they have seen the monster, its existence has never been proved, and for most people it is just a story. It is often shown in pictures as a creature like a long black or green DINOSAUR, and it is informally called **Nessie**. 尽管有人声称自己看到过尼斯湖水怪, 但它的存在并未得到证实; 对多数人来说, 尼斯湖水怪只是一种传闻。图画中把尼斯湖水怪画成类似恐龙的动物, 身体很长, 呈黑色或绿色, 非正式称作 Nessie。

lo·ci /ˋlosaɪ; ˈləʊsaɪ/ the plural of LOCUS

lock[1] /lɑk; lɒk/ *v* 2 3

1 ▶**FASTEN SOMETHING** 拴住某物◀ [I,T] to fasten something with a lock or be fastened with a lock 锁住〔某物〕; *Did you lock the car?* 你把车锁好了吗? | *I can't get the door to lock.* 我没法把门锁上。

2 ▶**PUT STH IN A SAFE PLACE** 把某物放在安全的地方◀ [T always+adv/ prep] to put something in a safe place and lock the door, lid etc 把〔某物〕锁藏起来: **lock sth up/away/in etc** *Joe locked the money in the safe.* 乔把钱锁藏在保险箱内。

3 **be locked together/in an embrace** if two people are locked together or locked in an embrace, they are holding each other very tightly〔两个人〕紧紧搂[抱]住: *The fighters were locked together.* 拳击手搂抱在一起。| *lovers locked in a deep embrace* 紧紧拥抱在一起的情人

4 **lock arms** to join your arms tightly together with someone else 臂挽着臂: *The police locked arms to form a barrier against the protesters.* 警察们臂挽着臂组成一道阻挡抗议者的壁垒。

5 **be locked in battle/combat/dispute etc** to be involved in a serious argument, fight etc with someone 卷入斗争/战斗/争论等之中: *We found ourselves locked in a costly legal battle.* 我们发现卷进了一场代价高昂的诉讼之中。

6 **lock horns with sb (over sth)** to argue or fight with someone (为某事)与某人争吵[打架]

7 ▶**WHEEL/PART OF A MACHINE** 轮子/机器的部件◀ [I] to become fixed in one position and impossible to move 卡住〔不能运转〕: *The wheels suddenly locked.* 轮子突然卡住不动了。—**lockable** *adj*

lock sb/sth **away** *phr v* [T] **1** to put something in a safe place and lock the door, lid etc 把…锁藏起来: *We locked all our valuables away before we went on vacation.* 我们外出度假之前把所有贵重物品都锁藏起来了。**2** to put someone in prison 把〔某人〕关进监狱

lock sb **in** *phr v* [T] to prevent someone from leaving a room or building by locking the door 把〔某人〕锁在〔房间或建筑物〕里面: *Help me, somebody – I'm locked in.* 来人哪，救救我！我被锁在里面了。

lock onto sth *phr v* [T] if a MISSILE locks onto a TARGET, it finds it and follows it closely 〔导弹〕锁定〔目标〕

lock sb **out** *phr v* [T] **1** to keep someone out of a place by locking the door 把〔某人〕锁[关]在门外: *Oh no, I've locked myself out!* 啊，糟糕，我把自己关在门外啦！**2** if employers lock workers out, they do not let them enter their place of work until they accept the employers' conditions for settling a disagreement 不让〔工人〕进厂〔直到争执按雇主的条件解决时为止〕—see also 另见 LOCKOUT

lock up *phr v* **1** [I,T] to make a building safe by locking the doors, especially at night 〔尤指在夜间〕锁好〔建筑物的〕门: **lock sth up** *Don't forget to lock up the warehouse.* 别忘了锁仓库。**2** [T **lock** sth **up**] to put something in a safe place and lock its door, lid etc 把〔某物〕锁藏起来 **3** [T **lock** sb **up**] *informal*【非正式】**a)** to put someone in prison 把〔某人〕关进监狱: *Rapists should be locked up.* 应把强奸犯关进监狱。**b)** *often humorous* to put someone in a hospital for people who are mentally ill【常幽默】把〔某人〕关进精神病院 **4 be locked up (in sth)** if your money is locked up, you have put it into a business, INVESTMENT etc and cannot easily move it or change it into CASH[1] 把〔钱〕搁死〔在不易兑成现金的地方〕

lock[2] *n* [S2]

1 ▶ON A DOOR 在门上◀ [C] a thing for fastening a door, drawer etc, that you can only open with a key 锁: *The rear doors are fitted with childproof locks.* 后门都装上了儿童安全锁。| **pick a lock** (=use something like a pin to open a lock, especially for an illegal purpose) 撬开锁〔尤指用于非法目的〕

2 under lock and key a) kept safely in a box, cupboard etc that is locked 安全地锁藏着: *Dad keeps all his liquor under lock and key.* 爸爸把他所有的藏酒都锁起来了。**b)** kept in a place such as a prison 被关押着

3 lock, stock, and barrel including every part of something 全部，完全: *He moved the whole company, lock, stock, and barrel, to Mexico.* 他把整家公司都搬到了墨西哥。

4 ▶HAIR 头发◀ a) [C] a small BUNCH of the hair on your head 一绺头发: *a stray lock of hair* 一绺散乱的头发 **b) locks** [plural] *poetic* your hair【诗】头发: *long flowing locks* 飘逸的长发

5 ▶ON A RIVER ETC 在河上等◀ [C] a part of a CANAL (1) or river that is closed off by gates so that the water level can be raised or lowered to move boats up or down a slope 〔运河、河流的〕水闸，船闸

6 ▶IN A FIGHT 在搏斗中◀ [C] a HOLD[2] (7) which WRESTLERS use to prevent their opponent from moving 〔摔跤中的〕抱，夹: *a head lock* 夹头

7 ▶VEHICLE 运载工具◀ [C, U] *especially BrE* the degree to which a vehicle's STEERING WHEEL can be turned in order to turn the vehicle【尤英】〔汽车方向盘的〕转动程度: **on full lock** (=turned as far as possible) 最大的转动程度

8 ▶MACHINE 机器◀ [U] the state of a machine when it is stopped in such a way that it cannot be operated 锁定状态: *in the lock position* 处在锁定位置

Locke /lɑk; lɒk/, **John** (1632-1704) an English PHILOSOPHER who developed the idea of EMPIRICISM in his *Essay Concerning Human Understanding*. In his *Two Treatises on Civil Government* he wrote that a king or government received the right to rule from the people and not from God, and that the people should be able to change their government if they were not satisfied with it. These ideas influenced *The Declaration of Independence* in the US. 洛克〔(1632-1704)，英格兰哲学家。他在《人类理解论》一书中提出"经验论"思想。他在《政府论》中写道：国王与政府的统治权是人民给予的，而非上帝赋予。假如人民对自己的政府不满意，就理应有权推翻它。这些思想对美国的《独立宣言》产生了一定影响〕

lock·er /ˈlɑkɚ; ˈlɒkə/ *n* [C] **1** a small cupboard where you leave your outdoor clothes, bags etc while you work or play sports 〔工作或运动时供存放衣物等的〕锁柜，寄物柜 **2** *AmE* a very cold room used for storing food in a restaurant or factory【美】〔餐馆或工厂用于储存食物的〕冷藏室: *a meat locker* 肉类冷藏室

Lock·er·bie /ˈlɑkɚbɪ; ˈlɒkəbi/ a town in southwest Scotland. Lockerbie became famous when a US plane, known as Pan Am Flight 103, crashed onto the town in 1988, killing 270 people. A Libyan man called Abdelbaset Ali Mohmed Al Megrahi, was found guilty of the killing and was sentenced to life in prison. 洛克比〔苏格兰西南部一镇。1988年，泛美航空公司的103号航班在此坠毁，造成270人死亡，此镇因此闻名。一个叫阿卜杜勒·巴塞特·阿里·迈格拉希的利比亚人被证明有罪，并被判处终身监禁〕

locker room /ˈ· · ˌ·/ *n* [C] a room in a sports building, school etc where people change their clothes and leave them in lockers 〔体育馆、学校等的〕衣物间；更衣室

lock·et /ˈlɑkɪt; ˈlɒkɪ̈t/ *n* [C] a piece of jewellery that you wear around your neck on a chain, with a small metal case in which you can put a picture, a piece of hair etc 纪念品饰盒〔悬在项链上，可以存放照片、头发等的金属小盒〕

lock·jaw /ˈlɑkˌdʒɔ; ˈlɒkdʒɔː/ *n* [U] *non technical* TETANUS【非术语】破伤风

lock keep·er /ˈ· ˌ· ·/ *n* [C] someone whose job is to open and close the gates of a LOCK[2] (5) or a CANAL (1) 水闸[闸门]管理员

lock·out /ˈlɑkˌaʊt; ˈlɒk-aʊt/ *n* [C] a period of time when a company does not allow workers to go back to work, especially in a factory, until they accept its working conditions 闭厂〔公司在工人接受工作条件前不让其返回工作场所的一段时间〕—see also 另见 **lock out** (LOCK[1]), compare 比较 STRIKE[2] (1)

lock·smith /ˈlɑkˌsmɪθ; ˈlɒkˌsmɪθ/ *n* [C] someone who makes and repairs locks 锁匠

lock·step /ˈlɑkˌstɛp; ˈlɒkstep/ *n* **in lockstep** *especially AmE* following rules and accepted ideas without thinking【尤美】因循守旧

lock·up /ˈlɑkˌʌp; ˈlɒk-ʌp/ *n* [C] a small prison where a criminal can be kept for a short time, often in a village or small town 〔尤指乡镇上的〕临时拘留所，监牢

lock-up gar·age /ˌ· · ˈ· ·/ *n* [C] *BrE* a garage that you can rent to keep cars, goods etc in【英】可租用的车库

lo·co /ˈloko; ˈləʊkəʊ/ *adj AmE informal* crazy【美，非正式】发疯的: **go loco** *That guy's going loco!* 那家伙在发疯！—see also 另见 IN LOCO PARENTIS

lo·co·mo·tion /ˌlokəˈmoʃən; ˌləʊkəˈməʊʃən/ *n* [U] *formal or technical* movement or the ability to move【正式或术语】运动(能力)；移动(能力)

lo·co·mo·tive[1] /ˌlokəˈmotɪv; ˌləʊkəˈməʊtɪv/ *n* [C] *technical or AmE* a railway engine【术语或美】机车；火车头

locomotive[2] *adj technical* connected with movement【术语】与运动有关的

lo·co·weed /ˈlokoˌwid; ˈləʊkəʊwiːd/ *n* [C] a plant that grows in America and makes animals ill if they eat it 疯草〔生长于美洲，动物食后会得病〕

lo·cum /ˈlokəm; ˈləʊkəm/ *n* [C] *BrE* a doctor or priest who does another doctor's or priest's work while they are on holiday, ill etc【英】〔医生或牧师的〕临时代理人

lo·cus /ˈlokəs; ˈləʊkəs/ *n plural* **loci** /ˈlosaɪ; ˈləʊsaɪ/ [C] **1 locus of** *formal* a place or position where something is particularly known to exist or happen【正式】〔某事存在或发生的〕地点，场所: *areas identified as the locus of poverty and deprivation* 被认为是贫穷和匮乏的地区 **2** *technical* the set of all points given by a particular rule in mathematics【术语】〔数学上的〕轨迹

lo·cust /ˈlokəst; ˈləʊkəst/ *n* [C] an insect that lives mainly in Asia and Africa and flies in a very large group, eating and destroying crops 蝗虫: *a swarm of locusts* 一大群蝗虫

lo·cu·tion /loˈkjuʃən; ləʊˈkjuːʃən/ *n technical*【术语】**1** [U] a style of speaking 讲话的风格 **2** [C] a phrase, especially one used in a particular area or by a particular group of people 〔某地区或阶层使用的〕惯用语；行话

lode /lod; ləʊd/ *n* [C usually singular 一般用单数] an amount of ORE (=metal in its natural form) 矿藏 —see also 另见 MOTHER LODE

lode·star, loadstar /ˈlodˌstɑr; ˈləʊdstɑː/ *n especially literary*【尤文】**1** [singular] a principle or fact that guides someone 准则，指导原则: *the economic lodestar for achieving low interest rates* 实现低利率的经济准则 **2** the POLE STAR, used as a guide by sailors 北极星

lode·stone, loadstone /ˈlodˌston; ˈləʊdstəʊn/ *n* [C,U] *old use* iron, or a piece of iron that acts as a MAGNET (1)【旧】天然磁石

lodge[1] /lɑdʒ; lɒdʒ/ *v*

1 ▶STAY SOMEWHERE 暂住在某处◀ [I always+adv/prep] to pay someone rent so you can live in a room in their house 租住，寄宿，寄住: [+at/with etc] *Paul lodged with a family in Bristol when he first started work.* 保罗刚开始工作时寄住在布里斯托尔的一户人家里。

2 lodge a complaint/protest/appeal etc *BrE* to make a formal or official complaint, protest etc【英】提出控告/抗议/上诉等: *They lodged a complaint against the doctor for negligence.* 他们控告医生疏忽。

3 ▶BE STUCK 卡住◀ [I always+adv/prep,T usually passive 一般用被动态] to become firmly stuck somewhere, or make something become stuck（使）卡住,（使）固定在…里: [+in/down etc] *The fishbone lodged in her throat.* 鱼刺卡在她的喉咙内。| **be lodged in/down etc** *The bullet was lodged in his spine.* 那颗子弹嵌在他的脊椎骨里。

4 ▶PUT SB SOMEWHERE 安排某人住在某处◀ [T] to give or find someone a place to stay for a short time, usually for payment 供…寄住; 给…找寄住处〔通常要付钱〕: *a building used to lodge prisoners of war* 一座关押战俘的建筑物 | **lodge sb in/at etc** *The refugees were lodged in old army barracks.* 难民被安置在旧兵营中。

5 ▶IN A SAFE PLACE 在安全的地方◀ [T] *formal* to put something in an official place so that it is safe【正式】把〔某物〕存放〔在正规的地方〕: **lodge sth with sb** *Be sure to lodge a copy of the contract with your solicitor.* 一定要在你的律师那儿留一份合同副本。

lodge² *n* [C] **1** a small house built on the land of a large country house〔乡村大宅院中的〕小屋, 侧屋 **2** a room for someone whose job is to see who enters a building or around a building〔建筑物的〕门房, 管理员室: *the porter's lodge* 传达室 **3** a small house in country or mountain areas, used by hunters, skiers (SKI²) etc〔乡村或山间供猎人、滑雪者等使用的〕小屋, 小舍 **4 a)** an organisation of FREEMASONs 共济会的分会: *a Masonic lodge* 共济会的分会 **b)** the building where this group meets 共济会分会集会处 **5** a BEAVER's home〔河狸的〕洞穴 **6** *AmE* a hotel in the mountains【美】山区旅馆 **7** *AmE* a WIGWAM【美】〔印第安人居住的〕棚屋

lodg·er /ˈlɑdʒɚ; ˈlɒdʒə/ *n* [C] *especially BrE* someone who pays rent to live in a house with its owner【尤英】房客; ROOMER *AmE*【美】: **take in a lodger** (=start having a paying guest in your home) 收房客

lodg·ing /ˈlɑdʒɪŋ; ˈlɒdʒɪŋ/ *n* [singular, U] **1** a place to stay 寄宿处: **board and lodging** *BrE*【英】: *It's £70 a week for board and lodging.* 食宿费每周70英镑。—compare 比较 BOARD¹ (9), ROOM AND BOARD **2 lodgings** *plural* a house where you pay rent to the owner so you can live in one of their rooms〔出租房间的〕公寓

lodging house /ˈ· · · ˌ·/ *n* [C] *BrE* a building where rooms can be rented for a few days or weeks【英】〔按日或星期出租房间的〕公寓; ROOMING HOUSE *AmE*【美】

loft¹ /lɔft; lɒft/ *n*

1 ▶ON A FARM 在农场里◀ [C] a raised area in a BARN used for keeping HAY (1) or other crops〔谷仓内贮放干草或其他作物的〕厩楼: *a hayloft* 贮放干草的厩楼

2 ▶UNDER A ROOF 在屋顶下面◀ [C] *BrE* a room or space under the roof of a building; ATTIC【英】顶楼; 阁楼

3 ▶TYPE OF ROOM/BUILDING 房间/建筑物的样式◀ [C] *especially AmE*【尤美】**a)** a room that is on a raised level within another room〔房间里的〕阁楼房间 **b)** a building that has this feature 有阁楼的建筑物: *a loft apartment* 阁楼式公寓

4 ▶FOR BIRDS 供鸟用的◀ [C] a set of CAGEs used to keep PIGEONs in 鸽舍

5 ▶IN A CHURCH 在教堂里◀ the place where a church ORGAN (2) is〔教堂的〕风琴楼: *the organ loft* 风琴楼

loft² *v* [T] to hit a ball very high in GOLF or CRICKET〔高尔夫球或板球中将球〕击高[吊高]

loft·y /ˈlɔftɪ; ˈlɒfti/ *adj* **1** seeming to think you are better than other people 高傲的, 傲慢的: *a lofty manner* 傲慢的举止 **2** lofty ideas, beliefs, attitudes etc are of an unusually high moral quality〔理想、信仰、态度等〕高尚的, 崇高的: *lofty ideals of equality and social justice* 平等和社会正义的崇高理想 **3** *literary* lofty mountains, buildings etc are very high【文】〔山、建筑物等〕巍峨的, 高耸的 —**loftily** *adv* —**loftiness** *n* [U]

3 **log¹** /lɔg; lɒg/ *n* [C] **1** a thick piece of wood cut from a tree〔树上砍下的〕大木头; 原木, 圆材 **2** an official record or written record of something, especially a journey in a ship or plane 航海日志; 飞行日志; 航行记录 **3** a LOGARITHM 对数 —see also 另见 **it's as easy as falling off a log** (FALL¹ (29)), **sleep like a log/top** (SLEEP¹ (1))

log² *v* **logged, logging 1** [T] to make an official record of events, facts etc 正式记录〔事件、事实等〕**2** [T] to travel a particular distance or for a particular length of time, especially in a plane or ship 飞行[航行]〔若干距离或小时〕: *The pilot has logged 1,200 flying hours.* 飞行员已经飞行了1200小时。**3** [I,T] to cut down trees 砍伐（树木）

log in/on *phr v* [I] to do the necessary actions on a computer system that will allow you to begin using it 登录计算机系统

log off/out *phr v* [I] to do the actions that are necessary when you finish using a computer system 退出计算机系统

Lo·gan /ˈlogən; ˈləʊgən/, **Mount** the highest mountain in Canada, in the southwest Yukon 洛根山〔加拿大最高峰, 位于育空地区西南部〕

lo·gan·ber·ry /ˈlogənˌbɛrɪ; ˈləʊgənbəri/ *n* [C] a soft dark red fruit similar to a RASPBERRY 罗甘莓〔似悬钩子的深红色果子〕—see picture on page A8 参见 A8 页图

log·a·rith·m /ˈlɔgəˌrɪðəm; ˈlɒgərɪðəm/ *n* [C] *technical* a number representing another number in a mathematical system so that complicated multiplying may be done as simple addition; LOG¹ (3)【术语】〔数学中的〕对数

log cabin（原木）小木屋

log book /ˈ· ·/ *n* [C] **1** *BrE* an official document containing details about a vehicle and the name of its owner【英】车辆登记证 **2** a LOG¹ (2) 航海[飞行]日志

log cab·in /ˌ· ˈ· ·/ *n* [C] a small house made of logs (LOG¹ (1))（原木）小木屋

CULTURAL NOTE 文化注释

Abraham Lincoln, one of the greatest US Presidents, was born in a log cabin. Most children learn this fact in school because it is supposed to show that you do not have to come from a rich powerful family in order to become President. The idea that any US citizen who was born in the US can become President is an important part of the way Americans think of their country. 美国最伟人的总统之一亚伯拉罕·林肯就出生在一个小木屋中。很多孩子在学校都学过这个, 故事旨在表明当上总统并不需要出身于权贵家庭。在美国出生的任何公民都有可能当上总统, 这是美国人看待自己国家的一个重要观念。

loge /loʒ; ləʊʒ/ *n* [C] *AmE* a set of seats at the side of the lower BALCONY in a theatre or concert hall【美】〔剧院或音乐厅的〕楼上前座

log·ger /ˈlɔgɚ; ˈlɒgə/ *n* [C] someone whose job is to cut down trees; LUMBERJACK 伐木工人

log·ger·heads /ˈlɔgɚˌhɛdz; ˈlɒgəhedz/ *n* **be at loggerheads (with sb)** if two people or groups are at loggerheads, they disagree very strongly（与某人）不和, 争吵: *Clare's at loggerheads with her boss over the new working hours.* 克莱尔在新定的工作时间上和老板争吵起来。

log·ging /ˈlɔgɪŋ; ˈlɒgɪŋ/ *n* [U] the work of cutting down trees in a forest 伐木: *the logging industry* 伐木业

lo·gic /ˈlɑdʒɪk; ˈlɒdʒɪk/ *n* **1** [U] the science or study of careful reasoning using formal methods 逻辑学 **2** [U] a set of reasons someone uses in order to reach an opinion 推理方法: *I couldn't follow Pete's logic.* 我不能理解皮特的逻辑。**3** [singular, U] sensible reasons or reasonable thinking 合乎逻辑的道理; 合理的想法: **there is a (certain) logic in/to** *There is a certain logic in bringing Simon with us because he does know the area.* 我们带西蒙来是有道理的, 因为他确实熟悉这地方。| **logic behind an idea/statement etc** *I fail to see the logic behind that idea.* 我不理解这想法背后的道理。**4** [U] *technical* a set of choices that a computer uses to solve a problem【术语】〔电脑的〕逻辑

lo·gic·al /ˈlɑdʒɪkḷ; ˈlɒdʒɪkəl/ *adj* **1** seeming reasonable and sensible 合情合理的: *It's a logical site for a new supermarket, with the housing development nearby.* 随着附近住房的发展, 在这里开设新超级市场是合情合理的。| *a logical conclusion* 合理的结论 —opposite 反义词 ILLOGICAL (1) **2** based on a series of facts, reasons, and ideas that are connected in a correct and intelligent way 合乎逻辑的: *The detective has to discover the murderer by logical deduction.* 侦探必须通过逻辑推理来找出凶手。—**logically** /-klɪ; -kli/ *adv* —**logicality** /ˌlɑdʒɪˈkæləti; ˌlɒdʒɪˈkælɪti/ *n* [U] 3

lo·gi·cian /ləˈdʒɪʃən; ləˈdʒɪʃən/ *n* [C] someone who studies or is skilled in logic 逻辑学家

-logist /lədʒɪst; lədʒɪst/ *suffix* [in nouns 构成名词] another form of the suffix -OLOGIST 后缀 -ologist 的另一种拼法

lo·gis·tics /ləˈdʒɪstɪks; ləˈdʒɪstɪks/ *n* **1 the logistics of** the practical arrangements that are needed in order to make a plan

or activity successful〔使计划或活动成功的〕统筹安排, 后勤〔工作〕: *the complex logistics of supplying food to the famine areas* 给饥荒地区提供食品的复杂后勤工作 **2** [U] the study or skill of moving soldiers, supplying them with food etc 后勤学; 物流学; 〔军队和食物供给等的〕调度技巧 **—logistic** also 又作 **logistical** *adj* **—logistically** /-klɪ; -kli/ *adv*

log·jam /ˈlɔg,dʒæm; ˈlɒgdʒæm/ *n* [C] **1** a problem or difficult situation that must be dealt with〔必须处理的〕僵局, 困难局面: *There's a logjam of bills before Congress.* 国会面临处理议案的僵局。**2** a tightly packed mass of floating LOGS on a river〔河道中输送木材时的〕木材堵塞

LOGO /ˈlogo; ˈləʊgəʊ/ *n* [U] an easy computer language that is often used in schools〔电脑的〕Logo 语言〔常用于学校〕

lo·go /ˈlogo; ˈləʊgəʊ/ *n plural* **logos** [C] a small design that is the official sign of a company or organization〔公司或组织的〕标识, 标志

log·roll·ing /ˈlɔg,rolɪŋ; ˈlɒg,rəʊlɪŋ/ *n* [U] **1** *AmE informal* the practice in the US Congress of helping a member to pass a bill, so that they will do the same for you later【美, 非正式】〔美国国会议员的〕互相赞成票〔以通过彼此支持的法案〕**2** *AmE* the practice of praising or helping someone, so that they will do the same for you later【美】相互吹捧[帮忙] **3** a sport in which two people stand on and roll a log floating on water, each person trying to make the other fall off 水上踩滚木游戏〔两人同站在一根漂浮在水面的圆木上, 设法使对手落水〕

-logue also 又作 **-log** *AmE*【美】/lɔg; lɒg/ *suffix* [in nouns 构成名词] something spoken; talk 言语; 谈话: *a monologue* (=speech by one person) 独白

-logy /lədʒɪ; lədʒi/ *suffix* [in nouns 构成名词] another form of the suffix -OLOGY 后缀-ology的另一种拼法: *genealogy* 系谱(学)

loin /lɔɪn; lɔɪn/ *n* **1** [C,U] a piece of meat from the lower part of an animal's back〔动物的一块〕腰肉 **2 loins** [plural] *especially literary*【尤文】**a)** the part of your body below your waist and above your legs 腰部 **b)** the area directly around your sexual organs 下身, 下部 **3 the fruit of your loins** *biblical or humorous* your children【圣经或幽默】儿女 —see also 另见 **gird (up) your loins** (GIRD (1))

loin·cloth /ˈlɔɪn,klɔθ; ˈlɔɪnklɒθ/ *n* [C] a piece of cloth that men in some hot countries wear around their loins〔热带国家男人用以蔽体的〕(缠)腰布

Loire, the /lwar; lwɑː/ a river in central France which is famous for the many beautiful castles called chateaux (CHATEAU) along its banks and for the wine which is made in the area 卢瓦尔河〔法国中部一河流, 以两岸美丽的城堡和出产的葡萄酒闻名〕

loi·ter /ˈlɔɪtə; ˈlɔɪtə/ *v* [I] **1** to stand or wait somewhere, especially in a public place, without any clear reason〔尤指在公共场所〕闲逛; 游荡: *Watch out for any strangers loitering in residential streets.* 要当心任何在住宅区街上徘徊的陌生人。**2** to move or travel slowly, or to keep stopping when you should keep moving 磨蹭; 走走停停: *Don't loiter on the way home, there's heavy snow forecast.* 别在回家的路上磨蹭, 天气预报有大雪。**—loiterer** *n* [C]

loi·ter·ing /ˈlɔɪtərɪŋ; ˈlɔɪtərɪŋ/ *AmE*【美】, **loitering with in·tent** /,‥‥ ˈ‥/ *BrE*【英】*n* [U] *law* the offence of staying in a place for a long time without having any reason to be there, so that it seems as if you are going to do something illegal【法律】伺机作案

Lo·ki /ˈlokɪ; ˈləʊki/ in Norse MYTHOLOGY, the god of evil and destruction 洛基〔北欧神话中的邪恶和破坏之神〕

Lo·li·ta /ləˋlitə; ləˈliːtə/ *noun* **1** a character in the NOVEL *Lolita* (1955) by Vladimir Nabokov. It is the story of a MIDDLE-AGED man who has very strong sexual feelings for a young girl. 洛丽塔〔弗拉基米尔·纳博科夫的小说《洛丽塔》(1955)中的人物。小说讲述一中年男子对一位少女怀有强烈情欲的故事〕**2** a girl who is too young to have sex legally, but who behaves in a sexually attractive way 洛丽塔式的少女, 早熟的性感姑娘

loll /lal; lɒl/ *v* **1** [I always+adv/prep] to sit or lie in a very lazy and relaxed way 懒洋洋地坐[躺]: [+**around/about/beside etc**] *We spent our vacation lolling around beside the pool.* 我们懒洋洋地在游泳池边上度假。**2** [I,T] if your head or tongue lolls or if you loll your head, you allow it to hang in a relaxed uncontrolled way (使)〔头或舌〕垂下

lol·li·pop also 又作 **lollypop** *AmE*【美】/ˈlalɪ,pap; ˈlɒlipɒp/ *n* [C] **1** *BrE* frozen juice or ICE CREAM on a stick【英】冰棍, 冰棒; POPSICLE *AmE*【美】**2** a hard sweet made of boiled sugar on a stick 棒棒糖

lollipop la·dy /ˈ‥‥, ‥/ *n* [C] *BrE* a woman whose job is to help school children cross a road safely【英】〔帮助学生安全地过马路的〕女交通纠察

lollipop man /ˈ‥‥, ‥/ *n* [C] *BrE* a man whose job is to help school children cross a road safely【英】〔帮助学生安全地过马路的〕男交通纠察

lol·lop /ˈlaləp; ˈlɒləp/ *v* [I +**around/across/about**] *informal* to run with long awkward steps【非正式】笨拙地大步跑: *Simon's dog came lolloping up the beach.* 西蒙的狗笨拙地沿着海滩跑。

lol·ly /ˈlalɪ; ˈlɒli/ *n BrE informal*【英, 非正式】**1** [C] **a)** frozen juice or ICE CREAM on a stick; LOLLIPOP (1) 冰棍 **b)** a hard sweet made of boiled sugar on a stick; LOLLIPOP (2) 棒棒糖 **2** [U] *old-fashioned* money【过时】钱

lol·ly·pop /ˈlalɪ,pap; ˈlɒlipɒp/ *n* [C] an American spelling of LOLLIPOP lollipop的美式拼法

Lom·bard Street /ˈlambəd strit; ˈlɒmbəd striːt/ a street in the City of London, where there are many banks and financial institutions 伦巴第大街〔伦敦市一街道, 街上有许多银行和金融机构〕

Lomé /,loˋme; ləʊˋmeɪ/ the capital, largest city, and main port of Togo 洛美〔多哥首都、最大城市和主要港口〕

Lon·don /ˈlʌndən; ˈlʌndən/ the capital city of the UK, in south-east England on the River Thames, which is also an important port and centre for tourists. Population: about 7,000,000. 伦敦〔英国首都, 位于英格兰东南部, 濒临泰晤士河, 也是重要港口和旅游中心。人口: 约 7,000,000〕**—Londoner** *n*

London, Jack (1876-1916) a US writer of adventure NOVELS, including *The Call of the Wild* and *White Fang* 杰克·伦敦〔(1876-1916), 美国冒险小说作家, 代表作有《荒野的呼唤》和《白牙》〕

London Assembly, the a group of 25 people who are elected every four years, and who are responsible for checking the performance of the Mayor of London 伦敦议会〔由 25 人组成, 每四年选举一次, 负责检查伦敦市长的工作〕

London Bank·ers' Clear·ing House, the /,‥,‥ ˈ‥/ in the UK, an organization owned by the large banks which deals with all the payments made every day using cheques, SWITCH etc, in order to find out how much each bank owes other banks 伦敦银行票据交换所, 伦敦银行清算所〔英国一家由各大银行拥有的金融机构, 处理日常的支票兑现及转账等业务, 以清算银行间的借贷款项〕

London Blitz, the /,‥ ˈ/ —see 见 the BLITZ

London Bridge /,‥ ˈ/ a bridge over the River Thames in London, famous because of a NURSERY RHYME (=an old song or poem for children) called 'London Bridge is Falling Down'. In 1965, it was sold and taken to the US state of Arizona, where many tourists go to see it, and a new bridge over the Thames was built to replace it. 伦敦桥〔伦敦泰晤士河上的一座桥, 因一首名为《伦敦桥要倒了》的童谣而闻名。1965 年, 该桥被收购并运至美国亚利桑那州, 吸引了许多游客前去观赏。泰晤士河上另建造了一座新桥〕

London Cen·tral Mosque /,‥,‥ ˈ/ a large MOSQUE (=building in which Muslims worship) in Regent's Park in London 伦敦中央清真寺〔位于摄政公园的一座大型清真寺〕

London Col·i·se·um, the /,lʌndən kalɪˋsiəm; ,lʌndən kɒlɪˈsiːəm/ a large theatre in London, where the English National Opera is based 伦敦大剧院〔位于伦敦市内, 为英国国家歌剧团总部所在地〕

Lon·don·der·ry /ˈlʌndəndɛrɪ; ˈlʌndənderi/ the second largest city in Northern Ireland. It is usually called Derry by its Roman Catholic population, especially by people who want Northern Ireland to leave the UK. 伦敦德里〔北爱尔兰第二大城市。当地的天主教居民通常称之为"德里", 在要求北爱尔兰独立的人群当中尤为多用〕

London Eye, the a Ferris wheel in London that is 450 feet tall and which gives people who ride in it very good views of the city 伦敦眼〔伦敦一座高达450英尺的巨型摩天轮。游人坐在摩天轮里, 市内景色尽收眼底〕

London Mar·a·thon, the /,‥ ˈ‥/ a MARATHON (=a running race of about 42 kilometres/26 miles) that takes place in London every year. Over 25,000 runners take part in the race. Some of these are professional runners, but most are ordinary people, many of whom do the marathon in order to collect money for CHARITY organizations. 伦敦马拉松比赛〔每年在伦敦举行的马拉松比赛。参加者有 25,000 多人, 其中有职业选手, 但大部分为普通人。许多人参赛是为了给慈善机构募集资金〕

London Pal·la·di·um, the /,lʌndən pəˈledɪəm; ,lʌndən pəˈleɪdiəm/ a theatre in central London, famous especially for MUSICALS (=shows that use singing and dancing to tell a story) and for VARIETY SHOWS (=shows with many different short performances, by singers, dancers, people telling jokes etc) 伦敦帕拉狄昂剧院〔伦敦市中心一著名剧院, 尤以上演音乐剧和综艺表演而知名〕

London Phil·har·mon·ic Or·ches·tra, the /,·· ··'··,··/ abbreviaton 缩写为 **the LPO** one of the leading orchestras (=large group of musicians playing together) in the UK 伦敦爱乐管弦乐团〔英国最主要的乐团之一〕

London School of E·co·nom·ics, the /,··,·· ··'··/ abbreviaton 缩写为 **the LSE** one of the colleges of London University, which is famous for teaching politics and economics 伦敦经济学院〔伦敦大学下属学院之一，以政治学和经济学专业闻名〕

London Sea·son, the /,·· '··/ also 又作 **the Season** a series of social events held every year in or near London and attended by people from the highest social class. In the past, this was an important part of life for the British UPPER CLASS, and it is often mentioned in literature, but it is much less important now. It includes parties for DEBUTANTES, and several well-known sports events, including Royal Ascot, and the Henley Regatta. 伦敦社交活动节〔每年在伦敦或伦敦近郊举行的一系列社交活动，参加者来自上层社会。过去，这是英国上流社会生活的一项重要内容，文学作品也常有描述，但现在已大不如往昔。活动内容包括为初入社交界的年轻女子举办的聚会和几项著名体育赛事，如皇家阿斯科特赛马会、亨利赛船会等〕

London Sym·pho·ny Or·ches·tra, the /,·· '···,··/ abbreviation 缩写为 **the LSO** one of the leading orchestras (=large group of musicians playing together) in the UK, based at the Barbican in central London 伦敦交响乐团〔英国最主要的乐团之一，总部设在伦敦市中心的巴比肯艺术中心〕

London U·ni·ver·si·ty /,·· ··'···/ also 又作 **the University of London** the third oldest university in England, which consists of several different colleges in London, including Imperial College, University College, King's College, and the London School of Economics. 伦敦大学〔英国第三位的老牌大学，由伦敦的几所学院组成，其中包括帝国理工学院、大学学院、国王学院以及伦敦经济学院〕

London Zoo /,·· '·/ a large old zoo in north central London, which was established in the early 19th century 伦敦动物园〔位于伦敦市中北部一大型动物园，建于19世纪初〕

lone /lon; ləʊn/ *adj* [only before noun 仅用于名词前] *especially literary*【尤文】**1** completely alone, and sometimes seeming sad 孤独的，孤单的；孤寂的：*a lone figure standing at the bus stop* 站在公交车站的孤单身影 —see 见 ALONE (USAGE) **2 lone mother/father/parent** someone who is looking after their children on their own 单身母亲/单身父亲/单亲

lone·ly /ˈlonlɪ; ˈləʊnli/ *adj* **1** unhappy because you are alone and feel that you do not have anyone to talk to 孤单的，寂寞的：*Don't you get lonely being on your own all day?* 你整天独自一人不感到寂寞吗？**2** *especially literary* a place that is lonely is a long way from where people live and very few people go there【尤文】荒凉的，荒无人烟的：*a lonely beach* 荒凉的海滩 —see also 另见 LONESOME, ALONE (USAGE) —**loneliness** *n* [U]

lonely hearts /,·· '·/ *n* **lonely hearts club/page/column** a club or an advertisement page of a newspaper that is used by people who want to meet a friend or a lover 征婚俱乐部/专版/专栏

lon·er /ˈlonɚ; ˈləʊnə/ *n* [C] someone who prefers to be alone or someone who has no friends 喜欢独处的人；孤独的人：*Ken's always been a bit of a loner, even at school.* 肯总是有点孤僻，甚至上学时也是那样。

lone·some /ˈlonsəm; ˈləʊnsəm/ *adj especially AmE*【尤美】**1** feeling very unhappy because you are alone or have no friends 孤寂的；孤单的，孤独的：*Beth is lonesome without the children.* 孩子们不在身边，贝丝感到寂寞。**2** a lonesome place is one that is a long way from where people live and very few people go there 荒僻的，荒无人烟的：*a lonesome spot near the canyon* 靠近峡谷人烟稀少的地方 **3 on/by your lonesome (self)** *informal* alone【非正式】单独，独自：*What are you doing sitting there all on your lonesome?* 你独自一人坐在那里干什么？

lone wolf /,· '·/ *n* [C] a loner 喜欢独处的人；孤独的人

long[1] /lɔŋ; lɒŋ/ *adj*

1 ▶OBJECT/LINE 物体/线◀ measuring a great length or a greater length than usual from one end to the other 长的：*Cher used to have really long hair.* 谢尔以前头发非常长。| *The line to get into the movie was so long we gave up.* 看电影的队伍排得那么长，我们不看了。| *The Aleutian Islands form the longest archipelago in the world.* 阿留申群岛形成了世界上最长的群岛。—opposite 反义词 SHORT[1] (1) —see picture on page A6 参见A6页图

2 ▶TIME 时间◀ continuing for a large amount of time 长时间的，长久的：*I thought the play was a little too long.* 我觉得这个剧有点儿太长了。| *recovering from a long illness* 久病康复 | *People who exercise regularly generally live longer, healthier lives.* 经常运动的人一般更长寿，更健康。| **a long time** *They've been married a long time.* 他们已经结婚很长时间了。| **get longer** *The days are beginning to get longer.* 白天开始变长。| **for the longest time** *AmE spoken* (=for a very long time)【美口】在很长的时间里 *I thought for the longest time that his name was Don, but it's really Ron.* 很久以来，我都以为他的名字叫唐，但实际上他叫罗恩。—opposite 反义词 SHORT[1] (4)

3 ▶DISTANCE 距离◀ continuing or travelling a great distance from one place to another 长距离的：*a long distance runner* 长跑运动员 | **long walk/flight/drive** *It's a long walk to the shops from here.* 从这里去商店要走很远。| **a long way** *We're still a long way from Aberdeen.* 我们到阿伯丁还有很长一段路。—opposite 反义词 SHORT[1] (4)

4 ▶HOW LONG 多长；多久◀ [usually after noun 一般用于名词后] having a particular length or continuing for a particular amount of time〔距离或时间〕长的；长久的：*How long is the concert going to be?* 音乐会要开多久？| **an hour/two metres/three pages etc long** *The room is about 10 metres long and 5 metres wide.* 这房间大约10米长，5米宽。| *The article should be about 1,500 words long.* 这篇文章应该在1500字左右。

5 ▶BOOKS/NAMES/LISTS ETC 书/名字/清单等◀ books, lists etc that are long contain a lot of pages, details etc 页数多的；详细的：*War and Peace is one of the longest novels I've ever read.*《战争与和平》是我读过的最长的小说之一。| *He has a long, unpronounceable last name.* 他的姓很长，很难念。—opposite 反义词 SHORT[1] (16)

6 ▶CLOTHING 衣服◀ long dresses, trousers, sleeves etc cover your body to the ANKLES or wrists〔衣服、裤子、袖子等〕长的：*a long ballgown* 长礼服

7 all day/year/summer etc long during all of the day etc 整个一天/一年/夏天等

8 ▶SEEMING TOO LONG 似乎过长的◀ *spoken* seeming to continue for a longer time or distance than is usual, especially because you are bored, tired etc【口】〔因不耐烦、疲倦等而觉得时间或距离〕显得过长的：*It's been a long week and all I want to do is go home.* 过了漫长的一个星期，我想做的事就是回家。

9 ▶WORK 工作◀ if you work long hours or a long day, you work for more time than is usual 工作时间特别长的：*Doctors often work long hours.* 医生经常长时间工作。

10 go a long way/have come a long way to be likely to be successful and achieve things, or to have been successful and achieved things 可望成功/大有进展：*Genetic research has come a long way in the last few years.* 基因研究在最近几年里大有进展。

11 go a long way towards doing sth to help greatly in achieving something 对做某事大有帮助：*Your contributions will go a long way towards helping children in need.* 你的捐助对有困难的孩子们大有帮助。

12 a little of sth goes a long way *spoken* used to say you do not need much of something【口】有一些就够了：*A little ketchup goes a long way.* 有一点番茄酱就美味极了。

13 at long last after a long period of time; finally〔长时间以后〕最终；终于：*The house sold, at long last, in September.* 那房子终于在九月份卖掉了。

14 long time no see *spoken* used to say hello when you have not seen someone for a long time【口】很久不见〔用于打招呼〕

15 the long and the short of it *spoken* used when you are trying to tell someone something complicated in only a few words【口】长话短说，总而言之：*Well, the long and the short of it is that we missed the train.* 好吧，总而言之，我们错过了火车。

16 not by a long chalk/shot *informal* not at all or not nearly【非正式】绝对没有，远远没有：*Oh, I've not finished yet – no, not by a long chalk.* 哦，我还没有完成——不，还差得很远。

17 how long is a piece of string? *BrE spoken* used when you think there is no certain answer to a question【英口】很难说：*"How long will it take to finish?" "How long is a piece of string?"* "要花多长时间才能完成？""很难说。"

18 a long memory an ability to remember things that happened a long time ago 好记性：*Those of you with long memories may recall Cooper's fight with Muhammad Ali.* 你们之中记性好的人可能还记得库珀和穆罕默德·阿里的那场拳赛。

19 ▶VOWEL 元音◀ a long vowel in a word is pronounced for a longer time than a short vowel with the same sound〔元音〕长的

20 long odds if there are long odds against something happening, it is very unlikely that it will happen 可能性不大

21 long drink a) a large cold drink, containing little or no alcohol, served in a tall glass〔用深口杯盛，无酒精或低酒精的〕

大杯冷饮 **b)** if you take a long drink, you drink a large amount of liquid at one time 痛饮

22 long in the tooth *informal* too old【非正式】太旧了: *Some of our vehicles are getting a bit long in the tooth.* 我们有些汽车有点旧了。—see also 另见 **as long as your arm** (ARM[1] (11)), **a long face** (FACE[1] (2)), **long/slow haul** (HAUL[2] (2)), **in the long run** (RUN[2] (4)), **a long shot** (SHOT[1] (12)), **it's a long story** (STORY (8)), **cut a long story short** (STORY (11)), **in the long/short/medium term** (TERM[1] (10)), **take the long view (of)** (VIEW[1] (10))

S1 W1 **long[2]** *adv* **1** for a long time 长久地, 长期地: *Have you been waiting long?* 你是否等了很长时间? | *It took me longer than I thought it would to paint the kitchen.* 油漆厨房所花的时间比我所想的要长。| *How long have you lived in New Jersey?* 你在新泽西州住了多久? **2** at a time that is a long time before or after a particular time 很久以前; 很久以后: **long before/after** *This all happened long before you were born.* 这些都发生在你出生前很久的时候。| **long ago/since** *If they'd stayed out of the war it would have been over long ago.* 如果他们不插手的话, 这场战争早就结束了。| **sth won't be long** *especially spoken* (=used when something is going to happen soon)【尤口】某事很快会发生 *Dinner won't be long – only five minutes.* 晚餐很快就好了 — 只需五分钟。| **sb won't be long** *spoken* (=used to say that someone will be ready, back etc soon)【口】某人马上就准备好[回来等] *Wait here, I won't be long.* 在这里等, 我马上就回来。| **it wasn't long before** (=used when something happens very soon after a particular event) 很快[不久]就… *It wasn't long before we realized Dan had left.* 我们不久便意识到丹走了。**3 no longer/not any longer** used when something used to happen in the past but does not happen now 不再: *The extra workers won't be needed any longer.* 不再需要额外的工人。**4 for long** [usually in questions and negatives 一般用于疑问句和否定句] for a long time 长久地, 长期地: *I haven't known them for very long.* 我已经很久没有听到他们的消息了。**5 before long** soon 很快, 不久: *It looks like it's going to rain before long.* 看来马上就要下雨了。**6 as/so long as** used to say that one thing can happen or be true only if another thing happens or is true 只要, 假如: *You can go out to play as long as you stay in the back yard.* 只要不出后院, 你可以出去玩。**7 so long** *spoken especially AmE* goodbye【口, 尤美】再见

long[3] *v* [I] to want something very much, especially when it seems unlikely to happen soon 渴望, 盼望: **long to do/have sth** *I long to see her again.* 我盼望再见到她。| **long for sth** *Patsy longed for some excitement, something new.* 帕齐渴望一些刺激, 一些新东西。| **long for sb to do sth** *I was longing for him to go.* 我渴望他走。| **longed-for** *the birth of a longed-for daughter* 盼望已久的女儿的出生 —see also 另见 LONGING

long[4] the written abbreviation of 缩写= LONGITUDE

Long. the written abbreviation of 缩写= LONGFORD

Long, Hu·ey Pierce /ˈhjuɪ pɪrs; ˈhjuːi pɪəs/ (1893-1935) a US politician in the Democratic Party who was GOVERNOR of Louisiana from 1928-31, and a US SENATOR from 1930. He was called the 'Kingfish' and was popular especially with poorer people because of his plans for social and economic changes that would help the poor. But he used his position to keep complete political control in Louisiana, and he was shot and killed in 1935. 朗〔(1893-1935), 美国民主党政治家, 1928-1931年间任路易斯安那州州长, 1930年起任美国参议员。有"龙头"之称的朗由于实行有利于穷人的社会与经济改革计划而受到穷人的拥护。但他利用职权对路易斯安那州实行政治垄断, 1935 年被人枪杀〕

long-a·wait·ed /ˌ· ·ˈ··◂/ *adj* [only before noun 仅用于名词前] a long-awaited event, moment etc is one that you have been expecting for a long time 期待的: *We finally got our long-awaited pay rise.* 我们终于得到了久久盼望的加薪。

Long Beach /ˌ· ˈ·/ a city in southwest California which is named after its long wide beach. It is an important shipping and industrial city, with many oil wells. 长滩〔加利福尼亚州西南部一城市, 因其海滩宽阔绵长而得名。该市是一个重要的航运和工业城市, 有许多油井〕

long·boat /ˈlɔŋˌbot; ˈlɒŋbəʊt/ *n* [C] a type of big rowing boat used especially for travelling on the sea〔尤用于航海的〕大划艇

long·bow /ˈlɔŋˌbo; ˈlɒŋbəʊ/ *n* [C] a large BOW[3] (1) made from a long thin curved piece of wood, used in former times for hunting or fighting〔旧时用于打猎或打仗的〕长弓, 大弓

long-dis·tance /ˌ· ˈ··◂/ *adj* [only before noun 仅用于名词前] **1 long-distance runner/driver etc** someone who runs, travels etc a long distance 长跑运动员/长途司机等 **2 long-distance call** a telephone call to a place that is far away 长途电话 —**long-distance** *adv*

long di·vi·sion /ˌ· ·ˈ··/ *n* [C,U] a method of dividing one large number by another〔算术的〕长除法

long-drawn-out /ˌ· · ˈ·◂/ *adj* continuing for a longer time than necessary〔时间〕拖长了的, 冗长的: *The official enquiry was a long-drawn-out process.* 官方调查的程序冗长缓慢。

Long·fel·low /ˈlɔŋfɛlo; ˈlɒŋfeləʊ/, **Hen·ry Wads·worth** /ˈhɛnri ˈwɑdzwɚθ; ˈhenri ˈwɒdzwəθ/ (1807-82) a popular US poet who wrote long poems about US LEGENDS (=old and popular stories of brave people, great events or adventures etc). His most famous poems are *The Song of Hiawatha, The Courtship of Miles Standish, Paul Revere's Ride,* and *The Wreck of the Hesperus.* 朗费罗〔(1807-1882), 大众喜爱的美国诗人, 以有关美国传奇故事的长诗见长。最著名的作品包括《海华沙之歌》、《迈尔斯·斯坦狄什的求婚》、《保罗·里维尔的夜奔》以及《金星号遇难》〕

lon·gev·i·ty /lɑnˈdʒɛvətɪ; lɒnˈdʒevɪ̊ti/ *n* [U] **1** *formal* long life【正式】长寿: *The inhabitants enjoy good health and longevity.* 此地的居民健康长寿。**2** *technical* the length of a person or animal's life【术语】〔人或动物的〕寿命

Long·ford /ˈlɔŋfɚd; ˈlɒŋfəd/ abbreviation 缩写为 **Long.** a COUNTY in the Republic of Ireland 朗福德郡〔爱尔兰共和国一郡〕

long·hand /ˈlɔŋˌhænd; ˈlɒŋhænd/ *n* [U] ordinary writing by hand, as opposed to SHORTHAND, TYPING etc 普通书写〔与速记、打字等相对〕

long-haul /ˈ· ·/ *adj* a long-haul aircraft or flight goes a very long distance without stopping〔飞机〕长途运输的; 长途飞行的 —compare 比较 SHORT-HAUL —see also 另见 **long/slow haul** (HAUL[2] (2))

long·horn /ˈlɔŋhɔrn; ˈlɒŋhɔːn/ *n* [C] a cow with long horns, kept for meat〔供食用的〕长角牛

long·house /ˈlɔŋhaus; ˈlɒŋhaʊs/ *n* [C] a kind of house, about a hundred feet long, that was used by some NATIVE AMERICAN tribes 长屋〔一些印第安部落的房子, 约 100 英尺长〕

long·ing[1] /ˈlɔŋɪŋ; ˈlɒŋɪŋ/ *n* [singular,U] a strong feeling of wanting something or someone; YEARNING 渴望, 盼望: *an expression of heartfelt longing* 殷切期待的表情 | [+for] *a longing for peace* 对和平的渴望

longing[2] *adj* [only before noun 仅用于名词前] wanting something very much 渴望的, 盼望的: *a longing glance* 渴望的一瞥 —**longingly** *adv*: *Inez was gazing longingly at him.* 伊内兹以渴望的目光凝视着他。

long·ish /ˈlɔŋɪʃ; ˈlɒŋɪʃ/ *adj informal* fairly long【非正式】略长的; 相当长的

Long Is·land /ˌ· ˈ··/ an island in the US that contains the New York City BOROUGHs of Queens and Brooklyn. Further east it has many other towns and cities, some of which are by the sea and popular in summer. 长岛〔美国一岛屿, 包括纽约市的昆斯和布鲁克林两个行政区。往东有很多城镇, 其中一些地处海滨, 是消夏的好去处〕

lon·gi·tude /ˈlɑndʒəˌtud; ˈlɒndʒɪ̊tjuːd/ *n* [C,U] a position on the Earth that is measured in degrees east or west of a MERIDIAN (=an imaginary line drawn from the top point of the Earth to the bottom)〔地球的〕经度: *The town is at longitude 21° east.* 这个镇位于东经 21 度。—compare 比较 LATITUDE (1) —see picture at 参见 EARTH[1] 图

lon·gi·tu·di·nal /ˌlɑndʒəˈtudn̩l; lɒndʒɪ̊ˈtjuːdɪ̊nəl◂/ *adj* **1** going from top to bottom, not across 纵长的, 纵向的: *longitudinal muscles* 纵行肌 **2** *formal* related to the development of something over a period of time【正式】历时性的: *longitudinal research on populations* 对人口的纵观研究 **3** *technical* measured according to longitude【术语】经度的 —**longitudinally** *adv*

long johns /ˈlɔŋ dʒɑnz; ˈlɒŋ dʒɒnz/ *n* [plural] warm underwear with long legs 长内裤

Long John Sil·ver /ˌ· · ˈ··/ a character from the adventure story *Treasure Island* (1883) by Robert Louis Stevenson. Long John Silver is a cruel and frightening PIRATE (=someone who sails on the sea, attacking other ships and stealing from them), who has part of one leg missing and a PARROT that sits on his shoulder. 朗·约翰·西尔弗〔罗伯特·路易士·史蒂文森创作的儿童冒险故事《金银岛》(1883) 中的一个人

Long John Silver
朗·约翰·西尔弗

物。他是一个性情残忍，相貌恐怖的独腿海盗，肩上常栖有一只鹦鹉〕

long jump /ˈ· ·/ *n* **the long jump** a sport in which each competitor tries to jump further than anyone else 跳远 —**long jumper** *n* [C]

long-last·ing /ˌ· ˈ··◂/ *adj* continuing for a long time 持久的：*long-lasting effects* 持久的效果

Long·leat /ˈlɔŋlit; ˈlɒŋliːt/ a large house in Wiltshire owned by the Marquess of Bath, which has a SAFARI PARK, where there are many lions 朗利特宅邸〔巴思侯爵的一幢大宅，位于维尔特郡，内有一游猎园，里面有不少狮子〕

long-life /ˌ· ˈ·◂/ *adj BrE* long-life milk, batteries etc are treated so that they stay fresh or continue working for a long time【英】〔经过处理的牛奶、电池等〕保鲜期[使用期]长的，经久耐用的

long-lived /ˌlɔŋ ˈlaɪvd; ˌlɒŋ ˈlɪvd◂/ *adj* living or existing a long time 长寿的；长期存在的：*He comes from a long-lived family.* 他生在长寿家庭。| *long-lived discontent* 长期存在的不满 —compare 比较 SHORT-LIVED

long-lost /ˌ· ˈ·◂/ *adj* [only before noun 仅用于名词前] lost or not seen for a long time 丢失很久的；长久未见的：*long-lost treasures* 丢失很久的珍宝 | **long-lost relative/uncle/friend etc** *a long-lost cousin* 久未见面的表弟

Long March, the /ˌ· ˈ·/ a long journey across China made in 1934-35 by Mao Zedong and his Communist army in order to reach a new base in northwest China. It was a dangerous journey because the marchers were often attacked by their enemies in the Nationalist army, and many of them died. Many of the people who took part in the Long March later became important members of the Communist government, including Deng Xiaoping. Only one third of the people were alive at the end. 长征〔为了到达位于西北的新根据地，毛泽东及其率领的共产党军队1934-1935年间进行的一次纵贯中国的远征。由于经常遭到国民党军队的袭击，长征路上充满艰险，许多人牺牲。许多参加过长征的人后来都成了共产党政府的重要成员，其中包括邓小平等。长征结束时只有三分之一的人活了下来〕

long-play·ing rec·ord /ˌ· ˌ·· ˈ··/ also 又作 **long-play·er** /ˌ· ˈ··/ *n* [C] an LP 密纹[慢转]唱片

long-range /ˌ· ˈ·◂/ *adj* [only before noun 仅用于名词前] **1** a long-range decision, plan etc is about a period far in the future〔决定、计划等〕长远的，长期的：*long-range weather forecast* 远期天气预报 **2** a long-range missile, bomb etc is able to hit something that is a long way away〔导弹、炸弹等〕远程的，远距离的

long-run·ning /ˌ· ˈ··◂/ *adj* [only before noun 仅用于名词前] a long-running battle, show etc has been happening for a long time〔战斗、表演等〕持续长时间的：*the long-running dispute over farm subsidies* 对农业津贴旷日持久的争论

long·ship /ˈlɔŋʃɪp; ˈlɒŋˌʃɪp/ *n* [C] a long narrow open ship used by the Vikings〔北欧海盗使用的〕狭长无盖战船

long·shore·man /ˈlɔŋʃɔrmən; ˈlɒŋʃɔːmən/ *n* [C] someone whose job is to load and unload ships at a DOCK[1] (1) 码头工人；DOCKER *BrE*【英】

long·sight·ed /ˌlɔŋˈsaɪtɪd; ˌlɒŋˈsaɪtɪd◂/ *adj especially BrE* able to see objects or read things clearly only when they are far from your eyes【尤英】远视的；FAR-SIGHTED (2) *AmE*【美】—opposite 反义词 SHORT-SIGHTED (1)

long-stand·ing /ˌ· ˈ··◂/ *adj* having continued or existed for a long time 持续长久的；长期存在的：**long-standing argument/debate etc** *a long-standing feud between the two families* 两家的世仇 | **long-standing arrangement/offer/relationship etc** *We have a long-standing tradition of hunting every fall.* 我们有一个长期沿袭的传统，每年秋季都去打猎。

long·suf·fer·ing /ˌlɔŋˈsʌfərɪŋ; ˌlɒŋˈsʌfərɪŋ◂/ *adj* patient in spite of problems and other people's annoying behaviour〔长期〕耐心忍受的：*Tom goes out drinking every night, leaving his longsuffering wife to look after the children.* 汤姆每晚都出去喝酒，让含辛茹苦的妻子照顾孩子。

3 **long-term** /ˌ· ˈ·◂/ *adj* continuing for a long period of time into the future, or connected with what will happen in the distant future 长期的；有长期打算的：*long-term loans* 长期贷款 | *the long-term implications of the crisis* 这场危机造成的长期影响 —see also 另见 **in the long/short/ medium term** (TERM[1] (10))

long-time /ˌ· ˈ·◂/ *adj* [only before noun 仅用于名词前] having existed or continued to be a particular thing for a long time 长时间的：*a long-time supporter of civil rights* 始终不渝的民权支持者

long ton /ˌ· ˈ·/ *n technical* a British unit of weight equal to 2,240 pounds【术语】吨，长吨〔英制重量单位，等于2240磅〕

lon·gueur /lɔŋˈgɜ; lɒŋˈgɜː◂/ *n* [C usually plural 一般用复数] *literary* a very boring part of a book or period of time【文】〔书〕乏味的部分；乏味的时期

long va·ca·tion /ˌ· ·ˈ··/ also 又作 **long vac** /ˌ· ˈ·/ *informal*【非正式】—*n* [C] *BrE* the period of three months in the summer when university students have holidays【英】〔大学的〕暑假〔三个月〕；SUMMER VACATION *AmE*【美】

long wave /ˌ· ˈ·◂/ written abbreviation 缩写为 **LW** *n* [U] radio broadcasting or receiving on waves of 1,000 metres or more in length 长波 —compare 比较 MEDIUM WAVE, SHORT WAVE

long·ways /ˈlɔŋˌwez; ˈlɒŋweɪz/ also 又作 **long·wise** /-waɪz; -waɪz/ *AmE*【美】*adv* in the direction of the longest side; LENGTHWAYS 纵向[长]地

long·wear·ing /ˌlɔŋˈwɛrɪŋ; ˌlɒŋˈweərɪŋ◂/ *adj AmE* longwearing clothes, shoes etc remain in good condition for a long time even when they are used a lot【美】〔衣服、鞋子等〕耐用的，耐穿的；HARD-WEARING *BrE*【英】

long·wind·ed /ˈlɔŋˈwɪndɪd; ˌlɒŋˈwɪndɪd◂/ *adj* continuing for too long or using too many words in a way that is boring 冗长乏味的，絮絮叨叨的：*Bray's explanation was unnecessarily long-winded.* 布雷的解释不必那么絮叨。—**longwindedly** *adv* —**longwindedness** *n* [U]

long·wise /ˈlɔŋˌwaɪz; ˈlɒŋwaɪz/ *adv* the usual American form of LONGWAYS; LENGTHWAYS 纵向[长]地〔longways的一般美式拼法〕

Lons·dale Belt, the /ˌlɑnzdel ˈbɛlt; ˌlɒnzdeɪl ˈbelt/ the most important prize in British professional boxing, which is a decorated belt which is given to a champion and is kept by him if he wins it four times 朗斯代尔奖带〔英国职业拳击赛最高奖项。奖品是一条装饰精美的奖带，授予拳击冠军。若四次夺冠，则可终生拥有〕

loo /lu; luː/ *n plural* **loos** [C] *BrE informal* a toilet【英，非正式】卫生间，洗手间，厕所

loo·fah, loofa /ˈlufɑ; ˈluːfə/ *n* [C] a rough kind of SPONGE[1] (1), made from the dried inner part of a tropical fruit 丝瓜络

look[1] /lʊk; lʊk/ *v*

1 ►SEE 看◄ [I] to turn your eyes towards something, so that you can see it 看，瞧，望：*Sorry, I didn't see – I wasn't looking.* 对不起，我没看见 —— 我没看。| *If you look carefully you can see that the painting represents a naked man.* 如果你仔细看，你会看出这幅画画的是一个裸体男子。| **[+at]** *"It's time we left," Ian said, looking at his watch.* "我们该走了。"伊恩看了看表说。| *Look at me when I'm talking to you!* 我和你说话时，要看着我！| **[+away/over/down etc]** *Dad looked up from his paper and smiled.* 爸爸从报纸上抬起头来笑了笑。| *I saw you, I was looking through the window.* 我看到你了，我正向窗外望呢。—see 见 GAZE[1] (USAGE)

2 ►SEARCH 寻找◄ [I] to try and find something using your eyes〔用眼睛〕寻找：*We looked everywhere but we couldn't find it.* 我们到处都找遍了，但没有找到。| **look in/under/between etc** *Try looking under the bed.* 试着在床底下找一找。

3 ►SEEM 看似◄ [linking verb 连系动词] to seem to be something, especially by having a particular appearance 看上去，看起来：*How do I look in this dress?* 我穿这件连衣裙看起来怎样？| **look like** *The intruder was holding what looked like a shotgun.* 闯入者手里握着看似猎枪一样的东西。| **look as if** *You look as if you haven't slept all night.* 你看上去似乎整夜没有睡觉。| **it looks as if** (=seems likely) 好像是 *The cause of death seems clear – it looks as if he was poisoned.* 死因似乎很清楚 —— 他好像是中毒。| **look good/impressive etc** *The plan looks good at the moment, but none of the details have been thought of.* 计划此刻看来很好，但细节问题都没有考虑过。| **look happy/pale/tired etc** *I thought Reg was looking very tired.* 我觉得雷吉看上去很疲惫。

4 be looking to do sth *informal* to be planning or expecting to do something【非正式】正打算[期待]做某事：*We're looking to buy a new car early next year.* 我们正打算明年初买一辆新轿车。

5 look daggers at *informal* to look at someone with a very angry expression on your face【非正式】怒视〔某人〕

6 look sb up and down to look at someone examining them carefully from their head to their feet, as if you are judging their appearance 上下打量某人

7 look sb in the eye/face to look directly at someone when you are speaking to them, especially to show that you are not afraid of them or that you are telling the truth 正眼看某人〔尤表示无畏或真诚〕：*Owen was burning with humiliation. He dared not look his father in the eye.* 欧文羞愧得无地自容，不敢正眼看父亲。

8 look down your nose at *informal* to behave as if you think that someone or something is not good enough for you【非正式】看不起, 轻视, 对…不屑一顾: *He looks down his nose at anyone or anything foreign.* 他看不起外国人或洋东西。 **9 ▶FACE A DIRECTION** 朝着某方向◀ if a building looks in a particular direction, it faces that direction〔建筑物〕面向, 朝向: *The cabin looks east, so we get the sun first thing in the morning.* 小屋朝东, 所以我们早上第一眼看到的是太阳。 **10 look before you leap** used to say that it is wise to think about possible dangers or difficulties before doing something 三思而后行

Frequencies of the verb **look** in spoken and written English
动词look在英语口语和书面语中的使用频率

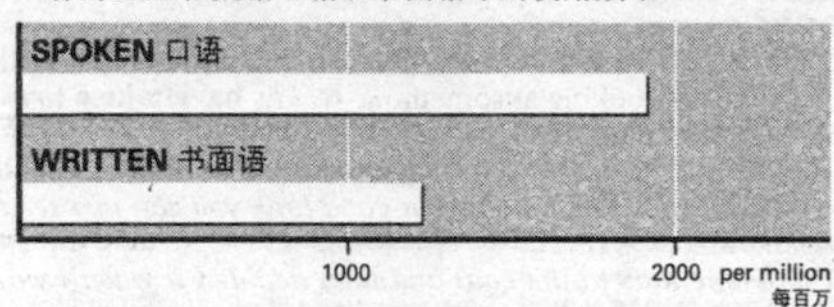

Based on the British National Corpus and the Longman Lancaster Corpus
据英国国家语料库和朗文兰开斯特语料库

This graph shows that the verb **look** is much more common in spoken English than in written English. This is because it has special uses in spoken English and is used in a lot of common spoken phrases. 本图表显示, 动词look在英语口语中的使用频率远远高于书面语, 因为它在口语中有特殊的用法并用于许多常见的口语短语中。

look (*v*) **SPOKEN USES AND PHRASES**
含look的口语用法和短语

11 look a) used to tell someone to look at something that you think is interesting, surprising etc 瞧, 当心, 注意, 留神〔用于让某人注意有趣、惊讶的事等〕: *Look! There's a fox!* 瞧! 有一只狐狸! **b)** used to get someone's attention so that you can tell them something 瞧, 注意〔用于让人注意接着要说的事〕: *Look. Why don't you think about it and give me your answer tomorrow?* 瞧, 你为什么不考虑一下此事, 明天给我答复呢? | *Look, I've had enough of this. I'm going home.* 瞧, 这我已经受够了, 我要回家了。 **12 it looks like/it looks as if** used to say that something seems to be likely or true 看起来好像: *There are no buses so it looks like we'll be walking home.* 没有公共汽车了, 看来我们要走路回家了。 **13 look out!** used to warn someone that they are in danger 注意! 当心!: *Look out! There's a car coming.* 当心! 一辆汽车开过来了。 **14 Look at that!** used to tell someone to look at something that you think is interesting, bad etc 瞧瞧那!: *Look at that! What a horrible mess!* 瞧瞧! 简直是一团糟! **15 Look who's here!** used when someone arrives unexpectedly 看谁来了!: *Well, look who's here! It's Jill and Paul!* 哎, 看谁来了! 是吉尔和保罗! **16 don't look now** used when you see someone you want to avoid 别看他: *Oh no! Don't look now but here comes Tony.* 糟糕! 真是冤家路窄, 托尼来了。 **17 look what you're doing/look where you're going etc** used to tell someone to be careful 瞧你在干什么/瞧你往哪儿走〔用于告诉某人要小心〕: *Look where you're putting your feet, there's mud all over the carpet.* 瞧你脚踩过的地方, 弄得地毯上到处都是泥巴。 **18 not be looking yourself** to appear tired, unhappy, ill etc, when you are not usually 看上去不是某人平时的状态〔显得疲倦、不快、满面病容等〕: *She should take a break – she hasn't been looking herself lately.* 她应该休息一下 —— 最近她看上去不像平时那样健康。 **19 look what you've done!** used to angrily tell someone to look at the result of a mistake they have made or something bad they have done 瞧你干了些什么!: *Look what you've done – my jacket's ruined!* 瞧你干的事 —— 我的夹克给毁了! **20 look here** *old-fashioned* used to get someone's attention in order to tell them something, especially when you are annoyed with them【过时】听着〔尤用于生某人气时, 让人注意要说的话〕: *Look here, you can't say things like that to me!* 听着, 你不能这样跟我说话! **21 (I'm) just looking** used when you are in a shop, to say that you are only looking at things, but do not intend to buy anything now (我) 只是看看〔不打算现在就买〕: *"Can I help you?" "No, thank you. I'm just looking."* "你要买什么吗?" "不, 谢谢。我只是看看。"

look after sb/sth *phr v* [T] *especially BrE*【尤英】**1** to take care of someone by helping them, giving them what they need, or keeping them safe 照顾, 照料: *Don't worry, I'll look after the kids tomorrow.* 不用担心, 明天我会照看这些孩子。| *Susan looked after us very well, she's an excellent cook.* 苏珊把我们照顾得很好, 她是出色的厨师。| **be well looked after** *You could tell just by looking at the horse that it had been well looked after.* 你只要看一下这匹马就会知道它被照料得很好。**2** to be responsible for dealing with something 负责处理: *I'm leaving you here to look after the business until I get back.* 在我回来之前, 由你料理生意。**3 look after yourself** *spoken especially BrE* used when you are saying goodbye to someone in a friendly way【口, 尤英】好好照顾自己〔友好的离别用语〕**4 be able to look after yourself** to not need anyone else to take care of you 能照顾好自己: *Don't worry about Maisie – she can look after herself.* 不用担心梅茜, 她能照顾好自己。

look ahead *phr v* [I] to plan future situations, events etc, or to think about the future 向前看, 作未来的打算, 考虑将来: *Looking ahead, we must expect radical changes to be made in our system of government.* 展望未来, 我们确信政体将作彻底改革。

look around/round *BrE*【英】*phr v* **1** [I] to search 寻找: [+for] *Jason's going to start looking around for a new job.* 贾森正打算开始找新的工作。**2** [I,T] to look at what is in a place such as a building, shop, town etc, especially when you are walking 参观, 边走边看: *Do we have to pay to look around the castle?* 我们参观城堡要付钱吗? | *Let's look round the shops.* 我们一道去逛逛商店吧。

look at sb/sth *phr v* [T] **1** to turn your eyes towards something, so that you can see it 看〔某物或某人〕: *The twins looked at each other and smiled.* 这对双胞胎相视而笑。**2** to read something quickly, but not thoroughly, in order to form an opinion of it 泛泛地阅读: *I really can't comment on the report – you see, I've not had time to look at it yet.* 我真的无法评论这报告 —— 你瞧, 我还没有时间看一下呢。**3** if someone with a special skill, such as a doctor, looks at something that is damaged or broken, they examine it and try to find out what is wrong with it〔医生等〕检查, 察看: *You should get the doctor to look at that cut.* 你应该找医生检查一下伤口。| *Can you look at my car? There's a strange noise coming from the front wheel.* 你能检查一下我的汽车吗? 前轮发出怪怪的声音。**4** to study and consider something, especially in order to decide what to do 仔细地研究[考虑]〔尤指要决定做什么〕: *We need to look very carefully at ways of improving our efficiency.* 我们需要仔细研究提升效率的方法。**5 look at ...!** *spoken* used when you are talking about something as an example of a situation【口】看看…!〔用于指视某物为榜样或引以为戒〕: *Look at Mrs Godfrey, smoking killed her!* 瞧瞧戈弗雷夫人, 抽烟把她的命都送掉了! **6** to think about something in a particular way〔以某种方法〕思考: *I'd like to be friends again, but Richard doesn't look at it that way.* 我愿意重新成为朋友, 可是理查德不这么想。**7 not much to look at** *informal* if someone is not much to look at, they are not attractive【非正式】相貌不好看[不吸引人]

look back *phr v* [I] **1** to think about something that happened in the past 回忆起, 回顾: [+on/to] *When I look back on those days I realize I was desperately unhappy.* 回想起那些日子, 我感觉痛苦透顶。| **looking back on it** *informal*【非正式】*Looking back on it, I still can't figure out what went wrong.* 回顾过去的事, 我仍找不到什么地方出错了。**2 never look back** to become more and more successful, especially after a particular event〔尤指在某事之后〕越来越成功: *After winning the scholarship he never looked back.* 赢得奖学金以后, 他便一帆风顺。

look down on sb/sth *phr v* [T] to think that you are better than someone else, for example because you are more successful, or of a higher social class than they are 轻视, 瞧不起: *Mr Garcia looks down on anyone who hasn't had a college education.* 加西亚先生看不起任何未受过大学教育的人。

look for sb/sth *phr v* [T] **1** to try to find something that you have lost, or someone who is not where they should be 寻找: *I'm looking for Steve – have you seen him?* 我在找史蒂夫 —— 你见过他吗? | *Detectives are still looking for the prisoner who escaped three days ago.* 侦探们仍在找三天前越狱的犯人。—— see graph at 参见 SEARCH² 图表 **2 be looking for** to be trying to find a particular kind of thing or person that you need or want 正设法寻找〔所需的某物或某人〕: *I'm sorry, we're really looking for someone with no family commitments.* 对不起, 我们其实需要没有家庭拖累的人。| **be what/who you are looking for** *Salubrious! That's just the word I was looking for.* 有益健康的! 那正是我在找的字眼。**3 be looking for trouble** *informal* to be behaving in a way that makes it likely that problems will happen

【非正式】在自找麻烦: *You're looking for trouble if you say things like that to me!* 你要是那样对我说话，你是在自找麻烦！

look forward to *phr v* [T] to be excited and pleased about something that is going to happen〔兴奋地〕期待，盼望: *I'm really looking forward to our vacation.* 我热切期待着假期的到来。| **look forward to doing sth** *My mother says she's looking forward to meeting you.* 我母亲说她盼着与你见面。—see 见 WAIT (USAGE)

look in *phr v* [I] *informal* to make a short visit to someone, while you are going somewhere else, especially if they are ill or need help【非正式】探望，作短暂访问〔尤在某人生病或需要帮助时〕: **[+on]** *I promised to look in on Dad and see if he's feeling any better.* 我答应去探望爸爸，看他是否好一点了。

look into sth *phr v* [T] to try to find out the truth about a problem, crime etc in order to solve it 调查〔问题、罪行等〕: *Police are looking into the disappearance of two children.* 警察正在调查两个孩子失踪的事。

look on *phr v* **1** [I] to watch something happening, without being involved in it or trying to stop it 旁观: *Only one man tried to help us, the rest just looked on in silence.* 只有一个人设法帮助我们，其余的人都只是袖手旁观。**2** also 又作 **look upon** [T **look on** sb/sth] to consider something in a particular way, or as a particular thing 看作，视为: **[+as]** *I look on him as a good friend.* 我视他为好朋友。| **[+with]** *I look upon all my nephews and nieces with equal affection.* 我对我的侄儿侄女都一样疼爱。

look sth ↔ **out** *phr v* [T] to search for and find a particular thing amongst your possessions〔从自己的东西中〕找出: *I'll look out some of my old books for you to read.* 我将从我的旧书中找几本给你看。

look out for sth *phr v* [T] **1** to pay attention to what is happening around you, so that you will notice a particular person or thing if you see them 注意察看〔周围情况，以便找到〕: **[+for]** *Look out for your Aunt while you're at the station.* 你在车站的时候，留神寻找你的姨妈。| *He's looking out for a nice apartment downtown.* 他正在留意寻找一套位于市中心的舒适公寓。**2** **look out for yourself/for number one** to think only about what will bring you an advantage, and not think about other people 只从个人利益考虑〔不管他人〕

look sth/sb ↔ **over** *phr v* [T] to examine something quickly, without paying much attention to detail 迅速地检查，浏览: *Do you have a few minutes to look these samples over?* 你有没有几分钟的时间很快地看看这些样品？—see also 另见 OVERLOOK

look round *phr v* [I,T] *especially BrE* to LOOK AROUND【尤英】到处看看

look through sb/sth *phr v* [T] **1** to look for something among a pile of papers, in a drawer, in someone's pockets etc 翻阅，翻找: *I've looked through all my papers but I still can't find the contract.* 我翻阅了所有文件，但依然没有找到那份合同。**2** to not notice or pretend not to notice someone you know, even though you see them（假装）没有注意到: **look straight/right through sb** *I saw Fiona in the street yesterday and she looked straight through me.* 昨天我在街上看到菲奥娜，而她装作没有看到我。

look to sb/sth *phr v* [T] **1** to depend on someone to provide help, advice etc 指望，依靠: **[+for]** *We look to you for support.* 我们指望得到你的支持。| **look to sb to do sth** *They're looking to the new manager to make the company profitable.* 他们指望新经理使公司赢利。**2** to pay attention to something, especially in order to improve it 注意〔改进等〕: *We must look to ways of encouraging new ideas.* 我们必须想方设法鼓励新思维。

look up 查找，查阅

He looked up the word in his dictionary. 他翻辞典查这个词。

look up *phr v* **1** [I] if a situation is looking up, it is improving〔形势〕好转，改善: **things are looking up** *Now the summer's here things are looking up!* 夏天到了，情况正在好转！**2** [T **look** sth ↔ **up**] if you look up information in a book, on a computer etc, you try to find a particular bit of information there〔在书、电脑中〕查找，查阅: *Look up the word in the dictionary.* 翻翻辞典查一下这个词。| *I'll just look up the train times.* 我将查一下火车时刻表。**3** [T **look** sb ↔ **up**] to visit someone you know, especially when you are in the place where they live for a different reason 看望，拜访: *Don't forget to look me up when you come to Atlanta.* 你来亚特兰大时，别忘了来看看我。

look up to sb *phr v* [T] to admire or respect someone 仰慕；尊敬〔某人〕: *I've always looked up to Bill for his courage and determination.* 我一直很敬重比尔，他既勇敢又果断。

look² *n*

1 ►LOOKING AT STH 看某物◄ [C usually singular 一般用单数] an act of looking at something 看，瞧: **have/take a look at** *Let me have a look at that – I think it's mine.* 让我看一下那个东西——我想它是我的。| **have a good/close look** (=look carefully) 仔细地看，细心看 *If you have a good look you can just see the lighthouse.* 如果你仔细看，刚好能看得见灯塔。| **take one look** *I took one look at the coat and then decided it wasn't worth £50.* 我看了看那件外套，断定它不值50英镑。—see 见 GLANCE¹ (USAGE) | **have/take a look around** also 又作 **have/take a look round** *BrE* (=look at all the things in a particular place)【英】〔在某处〕四下察看 *I have a special interest in old houses. Do you mind if I take a look around?* 我对老房子特别感兴趣，你介意我四下看看吗？

2 ►EXPRESSION 表情◄ [C] an expression that you make with your eyes or face, especially to show someone that you are angry, or that you do not like them 眼色；神色，面部表情〔尤指向某人表示愤怒或厌恶〕: **give sb a look** *Mike gave him such a severe look he didn't dare argue.* 迈克以如此严厉的眼光看他，他不敢争论了。| **dirty look** (=unfriendly look) 不友好的表情 *Why has Jake been giving me dirty looks all morning?* 为什么杰克整个早上都没有给我好脸色看？

3 ►APPEARANCE 外表◄ [C usually singular 一般用单数] the appearance of something or someone 外观，外表: *The whole area has a very seedy look to it.* 整个地区看上去很破旧。| *Mr Flynn had a tired, ill look in his eyes.* 弗林先生的眼中显出倦意和病态。| **by the look(s) of it/him** (=it seems that) 从外表看，看样子 *The doctor's back from holiday by the looks of it.* 看样子医生是度假回来了。| **not like the look of** (=think that something bad has happened or will happen because of something's appearance) 看来已[会]出问题 *We should turn back now, it's getting dark and I don't like the look of those rain clouds.* 我们现在应该回去，天越来越黑，雨云密布，看来要下雨。

4 ►SB'S BEAUTY 某人的美貌◄ looks [plural] someone's physical attractiveness 吸引人的外貌: *Fiona's got everything – looks, money and youth.* 菲奥娜什么都有了——美貌、金钱和青春。| **lose your looks** (=become less attractive) 容颜衰老 *When she lost her looks she found it difficult to get an acting part.* 当她容颜衰老后，她觉得很难找到演戏的角色。| **good looks** (=attractive appearance) 美貌 *You get your good looks from your mother.* 你的美貌是你妈妈遗传给你的。

5 ►FASHION 时尚◄ [singular] a fashionable style in clothes, hair, furniture etc〔服装、头发、家具等的〕时髦样式[款式，风格]: *The hippy look is back again.* 嬉皮士风格复苏了。

look·a·like /ˈlʊkəˌlaɪk; ˈlʊkəlaɪk/ *n* [C] *informal* someone who looks very similar to someone who is famous【非正式】长相极像名人的人: *a Marilyn Monroe lookalike* 一个长得酷似玛丽莲·梦露的人

Look Back in An·ger /ˌ· ·ˌ · ˈ· ·/ (1956) a play by John Osborne about a young WORKING CLASS man called Jimmy Porter, who continually argues with his wife, criticizing her and her family because they represent a traditional society he does not respect. The play influenced many British writers in the 1950s.《愤怒的回顾》(1965)，约翰·奥斯本创作的一部剧本。剧中有一位名叫吉米·波特的工薪阶层年轻人没完没了地同妻子争吵，批评她及其家人，因为她的家庭是传统社会的代表，而波特对此却不屑一顾。这部戏剧对20世纪50年代的许多英国作家产生了一定影响

look·er /ˈlʊkə; ˈlʊkə/ *n* [singular] *informal* someone who is attractive, usually a woman【非正式】美貌迷人者〔通常指女人〕: *She's a real looker!* 她真是个美人！

looker-on /ˌ· · ˈ·/ *n plural* **lookers-on** [C] someone who watches something happening without taking part in it; ONLOOKER 旁观者

look-in /ˈ· ·/ *n* [singular] *informal*【非正式】**1 get/have a look-in** to have a chance to take part in or succeed in something 有参与[成功]的机会: *Their team was so good that we barely got a look-in.* 他们队那么棒, 我们简直毫无希望。**2** a short visit 短暂的探访 —see also 另见 **look in** (LOOK¹)

look·ing glass /ˈ· · ·/ *n* [C] *old-fashioned* a MIRROR¹ (1)【过时】镜子

look·out /ˈlukˌaut; ˈlʊk-aʊt/ *n*

1 be on the lookout for to watch a place or situation continuously in order to find something you want or to be ready for problems or opportunities 监视, 留神观察: *Police were on the lookout for anyone behaving suspiciously.* 警察随时注意可疑的人。| *We're always on the lookout for new business opportunities.* 我们随时留意新的商机。

2 keep a lookout to keep watching carefully for something or someone, especially for danger 密切注视〔尤指危险〕: **keep a sharp/special lookout** *When you're driving keep a sharp lookout for cyclists.* 驾车时要特别注意骑自行车的人。

3 ▶PERSON 人◀ [C] someone whose duty is to watch carefully for something, especially danger 监视者, 守望者: *A lookout reported an enemy plane approaching.* 监视哨报告说一架敌机正在飞近。

4 ▶PLACE 地方◀ [C] a place for a lookout to watch from 哨所, 瞭望台: *a coastguard lookout on the clifftop* 海边悬崖顶上的哨所

5 it's your/their own lookout *BrE spoken* used to say that what someone has chosen to do is their own problem or risk, and no one else's【英口】那是你们/他们自己的事〔与别人不相干〕: *If he wants to ruin his health with all these drugs, that's his own lookout.* 如果他要用这些毒品毁掉自己的健康, 那是他自己的事。

6 be a poor/bad lookout for sb *BrE spoken* used to say that something bad or unsatisfactory is likely to happen【英口】对某人不是件好事, 事情不妙: *It'll be a poor lookout for James if she finds that letter.* 如果她发现那封信, 詹姆斯就惨了。

look-see /ˌ· ˈ·/ *n* [C] *AmE informal* a quick look at something【美, 非正式】一瞥: **have a look-see** *Can you wait a minute? I just want to have a look-see.* 你能否等一下? 我只想去看一眼。

loom¹ /lum; luːm/ *n* [C] a frame or machine on which thread is woven into cloth 织布机

loom² *v* [I] **1** [always+adv/prep] to appear as a large, unclear shape, especially in a threatening way〔尤指阴森森地〕隐约出现[耸现]: **[+up/out/ahead etc]** *A tall figure loomed up out of the mist.* 一个高大的人影从雾中隐隐出现。**2** if a problem or difficulty looms, it is likely to happen very soon〔问题或困难〕逼近, 临近: *I must start revising – final exams are looming.* 我必须开始温习功课了 —— 期末考试正逐渐逼近。**3 loom large** to seem important, worrying, and difficult to avoid 显得重要[令人担忧, 无法回避]: *Fear of failure loomed large in his mind.* 失败的恐惧沉重地压在他的心头。

loon /lun; luːn/ *n* [C] **1** a large North American bird that eats fish and that makes a long wild sound〔北美〕潜鸟 **2** a silly or strange person 傻子; 怪人 —see also 另见 **crazy as a loon** (CRAZY¹ (7))

loon·y /ˈlunɪ; ˈluːni/ *n* [C] *informal* someone who is crazy or strange【非正式】疯子; 怪人: *Her brother's a complete loony.* 她的弟弟是个十足的疯子。—**loony** *adj*: *loony ideas* 疯狂的念头

loony bin /ˈ· · ·/ *n* [C] *humorous* a hospital for people who are mentally ill【幽默】疯人院, 精神病院

loony tune /ˈ· · ·/ *n* [C] *AmE* a loony【美】疯子; 怪人

loop¹ /lup; luːp/ *n* [C]

1 ▶SHAPE OR LINE 形状或线条◀ a shape like a curve or a circle made by a line curving back towards itself 圈, 环: *The road formed a loop around the peninsula.* 道路绕着半岛形成一个圆环。

2 ▶TO FASTEN STH 扣住某物◀ something that has this curved shape, especially when used as a handle or to hold something in place 拎环, 襻〔尤用作把手或扣住某物〕: *a belt loop* 皮带环 | *The best bicycle locks are made of a loop of solid metal.* 最好的自行车锁是用坚固的金属做成的环形锁。

3 ▶IN WOMAN'S BODY 在妇女体内◀ a curved metal or plastic object that is put inside a woman's UTERUS (=place where a baby develops) to prevent her from becoming PREGNANT〔一种置入子宫内的〕避孕环

4 ▶COMPUTER 电脑◀ a set of commands in a computer PROGRAM¹ (1) that are intended to be followed repeatedly〔电脑程序中的〕循环, 回路

5 ▶PLANE 飞机◀ a pattern like a circle made by a plane flying upwards, backwards, and then downwards〔飞机〕翻跟斗; 翻圈飞行

6 ▶FILM/TAPE 胶片/磁带◀ a film or TAPE¹ (1a) loop contains images or sounds that are repeated again and again 环形胶片; 环形磁带〔可循环播放〕

7 ▶RAILWAY 铁路◀ a railway line that leaves the main track and then joins it again further on〔铁路的〕会车线

8 in the loop/out of the loop *AmE informal* part of a group of people who make decisions about important subjects, or not part of this group【美, 非正式】在〔决策〕圈内/圈外: *White House officials insist the Secretary of State is still in the loop.* 白宫官员坚持说国务卿仍然在决策圈内。

9 knock/throw sb for a loop *AmE informal* to surprise and upset someone【美, 非正式】使某人惊慌[烦恼]: *Yeah, the news really knocked me for a loop.* 是, 这消息确实令我惊慌失措。

loop² *v* **1** [T always+adv/prep] to fasten or join something with a loop〔用环〕扣[套]住: **loop sth over/around/together etc** *Loop the wire over the gate to keep it shut.* 用铁丝绕在门上把它关住。**2** [I,T] to make a loop or make something into a loop (使)成圈[环]; (把…)绕成圈: *a rug with looped threads* 用绳圈做成的小地毯 **3** [I] to move in a circular direction that forms the shape of a loop 绕转成圈: *little streams that loop through the valley* 环绕山谷的小溪 **4 loop the loop** to fly a plane in a loop 翻跟斗飞行

Loop, the the central business area of Chicago. The name comes from an ELEVATED RAILWAY that forms a large circle or LOOP around the area. 卢普区〔芝加哥的商业中心区, 周围是一圈 (loop) 高架铁路, 故名〕

loop·hole /ˈlupˌhol; ˈluːphəʊl/ *n* [C] a small mistake in a law that makes it possible to avoid doing something that the law is supposed to make you do〔法律中的〕漏洞, 空子: *tax loopholes* 税收上的漏洞

loop·y /ˈlupɪ; ˈluːpi/ *adj informal*【非正式】**1** crazy or strange 发疯的, 疯狂的; 奇怪的 **2 go loopy** *spoken*【口】**a)** *BrE* to become extremely angry【英】变得狂怒 **b)** to become mentally ill 变得精神失常

loose¹ /lus; luːs/ *adj* S3 W3

1 ▶NOT FIXED 未固定的◀ not firmly fixed in place 松的, 松动的: *One of my buttons is loose.* 我的一颗纽扣松了。| *a loose floorboard* 松动的地板 | **come/work loose** (=become loose) 变得松动 *A piece of stair carpet had come loose.* 楼梯上的一块地毯松了。

2 ▶ROPE/CHAIN ETC 绳/链等◀ a rope, chain etc that is loose is not fastened as firmly or pulled as tight as it should be 松开的, 未系牢的

3 ▶CLOTHES 衣服◀ clothes that are loose are big and do not fit your body tightly 宽大的, 不合身的: *a loose sweatshirt* 宽松的运动衫

4 ▶FREE 自由的◀ an animal or person that is loose is free to move around and not tied to anything or shut in anywhere.〔动物或人〕自由的, 无束缚的, 没有系[关]住: **break/get loose** (=get free) 挣脱束缚 *Somehow the horses had broken loose during the night.* 不知怎的马在夜间挣脱了束缚。| **turn/let sth loose** (=let something go free) 让某物自由 *Don't let your dog loose if there are any sheep around.* 如果周围有羊, 不要放开你的狗。

5 ▶NOT TOGETHER 不在一起◀ not tied together, fastened to anything else, or put together in one package 未系[包]在一起的; 散装的: *Do they sell these olives loose?* 这些橄榄零卖吗? | *Do you like loose tea, or teabags?* 你要茶叶还是茶包? | *Her hair fell loose around her shoulders.* 她的头发松散地披在肩上。

6 ▶CLOTH/A KNOT ETC 布/绳结等◀ tied or woven in a way that is not tight 疏松的, 没系牢的: *a loose knot* 没系牢的结 | *a loose weave* 松织法

7 ▶NOT EXACT 不严谨的◀ [usually before noun 一般用于名词前] not exact or thoroughly done 不严谨的; 不精确的: **loose translation/interpretation etc** *This is only a loose translation of the original paper.* 这只是原文的一篇不精确的译文。

8 ▶NOT CONTROLLED 没有控制的◀ not strictly controlled or organized 控制[组织]不严的: *a loose, informal trading system* 组织不严的、非正规的贸易制度

9 ▶IMMORAL 道德败坏的◀ *old-fashioned* behaving in a way that is considered to be sexually immoral【过时】放荡的, 淫荡的: *a loose woman* 荡妇

10 ▶TALK 谈话◀ *old-fashioned* not careful about what you say or who is listening【过时】说话随便[轻率]的: *There's been a bit of loose talk about it.* 对这件事有些不负责任的话。

11 ▶BODY WASTE 身体排泄物◀ *not technical* having a problem in which the waste from your BOWELS has too much liquid in it【非术语】稀薄的: *loose motions* 稀湿的大便 | *He's a bit loose in the mornings.* 他早上都有点腹泻。

L

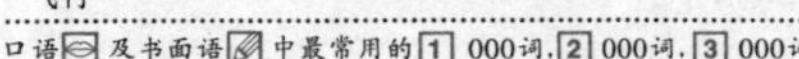

12 cut loose a) to free yourself from the influence of someone or something 去掉[摆脱]影响: *Anna had finally managed to cut loose from her father's domineering influence.* 安娜终于摆脱了专横的父亲对她的影响。**b)** *AmE informal* to start enjoying yourself in a happy, noisy way after a period of controlled behaviour【美，非正式】〔压抑过后的〕放任，发泄: *After the exams we'll really have a chance to cut loose.* 考试过后，我们就真的有机会轻松轻松了。
13 let sb loose on sth to allow someone to deal with something in the way they want to 让某人随意做某事: *Whatever you do, don't let Derek loose on the garden!* 不管你做什么，千万别让德里克在花园里任意胡为！
14 be at a loose end also 又作 **be at loose ends** *AmE*【美】to have nothing to do 无所事事，闲着: *I was at a loose end so I decided to go see an old movie.* 我闲着没事，所以决定去看一部老电影。
15 loose ends parts of something that have not been completed or properly done 未完成[做好]的部分: **tie up the loose ends** (=complete something, or deal with any remaining problems) 完成某事；收拾残局 *It's a good report but there are still a few loose ends to be tied up.* 这是一份很好的报告，但仍有少量没有说清楚的部分有待完善。
16 loose change coins that you have in your bag or pocket 零钱: *I've got twenty quid and a bit of loose change as well.* 我有20英镑和一些零钱。
17 hang/stay loose *AmE spoken* used to tell someone to stay calm, or not to worry about something【美口】保持镇定，别紧张 —**loosely** *adv*: *Just tie it loosely.* 只要大致捆一捆就行。| *Loosely translated it means 'watch out'.* 大致上可把它译成"当心"。—**looseness** *n* [U]

loose² *v* [T] **1** to untie someone or something, especially an animal 放开〔尤指动物〕；释放 **2** *literary* to fire an ARROW (1), a shot from a gun etc【文】射〔箭〕；放〔枪〕**3** to make something unpleasant begin 使不愉快的事情出现: *The recent court case has loosed a spate of racist attacks.* 法院最近处理的案件引发了大量种族攻击事件。

loose sth **on/upon** *phr v* [T] to allow something dangerous or destructive to begin to affect a situation or other people 使〔有危险或有害的事〕开始影响[侵袭]〔某局面或其他人〕: *A potentially lethal drug has been loosed upon unsuspecting kids looking for a quick high.* 一种可能致命的毒品已经开始侵扰毫无戒备之心又急于追求快感的年轻人。

loose³ *adv* loosely 很松地；不严密地，不严谨地 —see also 另见 **play fast and loose with** (FAST² (10))

loose⁴ *n* **be on the loose** if a criminal or dangerous animal is on the loose, they have escaped from prison or from their cage 〔罪犯或危险动物〕在逃

loose-fit·ting /,. '..◂/ *adj* loose-fitting clothes are loose on your body, so that they are comfortable 〔衣服〕宽松的: *wearing jeans and a loose-fitting jacket* 身着牛仔裤和宽松的夹克

loose-leaf /,. '.◂/ *adj* having pages that can be put in and removed easily 活页的: *a loose-leaf binder* 活页夹

loos·en /ˈlusn; ˈluːsən/ *v* **1** [I,T] to make something less tight or less firmly fixed, or to become less tight or less firmly fixed (使) 变松；松开: *You'll need a spanner to loosen that bolt.* 你需要扳子来拧松这个螺栓。| *Check the plug – there may be a loosened connection.* 检查一下插头 — 可能接触不良。**2** [T] to unfasten something, especially something you are wearing 解开〔尤指穿着的衣物〕: *Harry loosened his tie.* 哈利解开他的领带。**3** [T] to make laws, rules etc less strict 使〔法律、规定等〕放宽: *It was time to loosen economic constraints.* 该是放宽经济限制的时候了。**4 loosen your grip/hold a)** to reduce the control or power you have over someone or something 放松对…的控制[操纵]: *as communism began to loosen its hold on eastern Europe* 正当共产主义开始放松对东欧的控制 **b)** to start holding someone less tightly than you were before 放松[松开]抓着〔某人〕的手: [**+on**] *The policeman loosened his grip on my arm.* 警察松开了抓着我手臂的手。**5 loosen sb's tongue** to make someone talk more freely than usual, for example by making them drunk 使某人说话不那么拘束〈如将其灌醉等〉

loosen up *phr v* **1** [I, T **loosen** sth ↔ **up**] to exercise your muscles and joints to make them work more easily, especially before playing a sport or running; WARM-UP (1)〔尤指运动或跑步前〕活动肌肉和关节；热身 **2** [I] to stop worrying and become more relaxed 无拘无束，放松: *Try and loosen up a bit!* 尽量放松一点！

Loot /lut; luːt/ *trademark* a magazine, sold in the UK, which only contains advertisements by people who want to sell their cars or old furniture, rent their homes, buy a house etc.【商标】《露透》〔英国一杂志，内容全部为出售汽车或家具、出租或购置房屋等广告〕

loot¹ *n* [U] **1** *informal old-fashioned* goods or money that have been stolen【非正式，过时】〔偷来的〕赃物 **2** goods taken by soldiers from a place where they have won a battle 战利品，掠夺物 **3** *AmE informal humorous* things that you have bought or been given in large amounts【美，非正式，幽默】大量购买[赠送]之物: *Jodie came home from the mall with sacks of loot.* 乔迪从购物中心满载而归。

loot² *v* [I, T] to steal things, especially from shops or homes that have been damaged in a war or RIOT²〔尤指在战争或暴乱中〕抢劫，洗劫，掠夺: *Shops were looted and burned down.* 商店遭抢劫并被烧毁。—**looting** *n* [U] —**looter** *n* [C]

lop /lɑp; lɒp/ *v* **lopped, lopping** [T] to cut branches from a tree, especially with a single strong movement 砍掉〔树枝，尤指猛地一下砍掉〕

lop sth **off** *phr v* [T] **1** to cut a part of something off, especially a branch of a tree 砍掉〔某物的部分，尤指树枝〕**2** to remove a particular amount from a price or charge〔从价钱中〕削减: *They lopped $15 off the price.* 他们削价15美元。

lope /lop; ləʊp/ *v* [I always+adv/prep] to run easily with long steps 轻松地跑: [**+along/across/up etc**] *Brad loped across the field towards home.* 布拉德蹦跳着穿过田地跑回家。—**lope** *n* [singular]

lop-eared /,. '.◂/ *adj* a lop-eared animal such as a rabbit has long ears that hang down〔兔子等动物〕耳朵长而垂下的

lop·sid·ed /,. '..◂/ *adj* **1** having one side that is lower or heavier than the other 歪斜的: *a lopsided grin* 歪斜着嘴笑 **2** unequal or uneven in a way that seems unfair 不平等[平衡，公正]的: *a lopsided ratio of men to women* 男女的比例失衡

lo·qua·cious /loˈkweʃəs; ləʊˈkweɪʃəs/ *adj formal* liking to talk a lot, sometimes too much【正式】话多的；饶舌的 —**loquaciously** *adv* —**loquacity** /loˈkwæsətɪ; ləʊˈkwæsəti/ *n* [U]

lo·quat /ˈlokwɑt; ˈləʊkwɒt/ *n* [C] the small yellowish fruit of a tree that grows mostly in China and Japan 枇杷

Lorca —see 见 Federico GARCÍA LORCA

Lord /lɔrd; lɔːd/ *n* [singular] **1** also 又作 **the Lord** a title of God or Jesus Christ 上帝；耶稣: *Thank you, Lord, for your blessings.* 感谢上帝的恩赐。**2 the Lords a)** the members of the British House of Lords considered as a group 英国上议院全体议员 **b)** the House of Lords 上议院 **3 Lord (only) knows** *spoken* used when you do not know the answer to something【口】(只有) 天知道〔用于不知道答案时〕: *Lord knows where I left that bag.* 天晓得我把那袋子丢在哪里了。**4 (good) Lord!/Oh Lord!** *spoken* used when you are suddenly surprised, annoyed or worried about something【口】天哪！主啊！〔表示惊讶、恼怒或忧虑〕: *Good Lord! Is that the time?* 天哪！到时候了吗？**5 Lord willing** *spoken* used to say that you hope nothing will prevent something from happening【口】按上帝的旨意，按上帝的安排: *We'll finally be able to take that trip this year, Lord willing.* 我们今年终于能够去那里旅行，但愿这是上帝的旨意。**6 the Lord's Day** Sunday, considered as the holy day of the Christian religion 星期天〔基督教的礼拜日〕**7** *BrE* the title of someone who has a particular type of official job【英】大人，阁下〔对某些官员的尊称〕: *Lord Mayor of London* 伦敦市长大人

lord¹ *n* **1** [C] a man who has a rank in the ARISTOCRACY, especially in Britain, or his title〔尤指英国的〕贵族 (头衔): *Lord Hailsham* 黑尔什姆勋爵 —compare 比较 LADY (7) **2** [C] a man in medieval Europe who was very powerful and owned a lot of land〔中世纪欧洲的〕领主；庄园主: *the feudal lords* 封建领主 **3 my lord** used to address a judge or BISHOP (1) in Britain, and in the past to address a lord 大人，阁下〔对英国的法官、主教的尊称，旧时也用来称呼贵族〕**4 your lord and master** *humorous* someone who must be obeyed because they have power over you【幽默】主人；上司〔指要服从的人〕

lord² *v* **lord it over sb** to behave in a way that shows you think you are better or more powerful than someone else 对某人作威作福，在某人面前摆架子: *the outer office where Carol lorded it over her assistants* 外面办公室里卡萝尔对她的助手发号施令

Lord Ad·vo·cate, the /,. '.../ the most important official in Scotland's legal system. The Lord Advocate chooses new judges, suggests new laws, and decides whether or not a law needs to be changed. 检察总长〔苏格兰司法系统的最高级官员。其职责是挑选新法官，提议新法规，决定是否有必要修订某一法律〕

Lord Cham·ber·lain, the /,. '.../ in the UK, the person in charge of managing the ROYAL HOUSEHOLD (=the people who live with and work for the King or Queen) 宫务大臣〔英国管理王室事务的官员〕

Lord Chan·cel·lor, the/ˌ· ˈ···/ the most important official in the legal system of England and Wales. The Lord Chancellor gives legal advice to the King or Queen, chooses new judges, and decides whether or not a law needs to be changed. He is also the speaker of the House of Lords and an important member of the UK government. 大法官〔英格兰和威尔士司法系统的最高级官员。其职责是向国王或女王就法律事务提出建议、挑选新法官, 决定是否有必要修订某一法律。同时, 他还是上议院议长, 为英国政府重要官员〕

Lord Chancellor's De·part·ment, the/ˌ· ˈ····ˌ··/ a British government department, headed by the Lord Chancellor, which is in charge of the legal system and the courts in England and Wales, and is responsible for choosing judges. There is a similar department in the US called the Department of Justice. 司法部〔英国一政府部门, 以大法官为首, 主要负责英格兰和威尔士的司法系统和法庭事务, 并负责挑选法官。美国也有一类似部门, 称 Department of Justice〕

Lord Chief Jus·tice, the/ˌ· · ˈ··/ a judge who is second in importance to the Lord Chancellor in the legal system of England and Wales. The Lord Chief Justice is the judge in charge of cases which are judged at a Court of Appeal. 首席法官, 王座庭庭长〔在英格兰和威尔士司法系统中地位仅次于大法官, 负责审理上诉法院的案件〕

Lord is my Shep·herd, The/ˌ· · · ·ˈ··/ the title and first words of the *Twenty-Third Psalm*, one of the most famous Christian HYMNS (=religious songs) 《耶和华是我的牧者》〔《圣经·诗篇》第23首的标题和首句, 最著名的基督教赞美诗之一〕

Lord Lieu·ten·ant, the/ˌ· ·ˈ··/ *n plural* **Lords Lieutenant** in the UK, an official who represents the King or Queen in a county. The Lord Lieutenant has no real power, but performs ceremonial duties. 郡治安长官; 总督, 宫廷特派员〔英国的郡治安长官在一郡内代表国王或王后行使职权。他没有实权, 仅行使礼仪性职责〕

lord·ly /ˈlɔrdlɪ; ˈlɔːdli/ *adj* **1** behaving in a way that shows you think you are better or more important than other people 傲慢的, 高傲的: *Sebastian has a lordly disdain for such everyday affairs.* 塞巴斯蒂安对这类日常事务摆出高傲轻蔑的样子。**2** very grand or impressive 富丽堂皇的; 贵族气派的: *a lordly feast* 盛大的筵席 —**lordliness** *n* [U]

Lord Mayor's Ban·quet, the/ˌ· · · ˈ··/ a BANQUET (=formal dinner) held in the Guildhall, London, every year after the new Lord Mayor of London has been elected. Many important people are invited to this banquet, including the Prime Minister, who makes a speech to mark the occasion. 伦敦市长宴会〔伦敦新任市长就任后的一年会在伦敦市政厅举行的正式宴会。许多重要人物都应邀参加, 其中包括首相。首相还要发表讲话以示祝贺〕

Lord Mayor's Show, the/ˌ· ·ˈ·· ˌ·/ a street PARADE in which the new Lord Mayor of London travels in a golden carriage through the streets of London 市长就职巡游〔伦敦新任市长乘坐金色马车巡游本市主要大街的仪式〕

Lord of Mis·rule, the/ˌ· · · ·ˈ·/ the name given to the person who was put in charge of the Christmas games and fun in England in the 15th and 16th centuries〔英格兰15、16世纪圣诞节〕节庆司仪, 狂欢司仪

Lord of the Flies/ˌ· · · ·ˈ·/ (1954) a NOVEL by William Golding about a group of boys living on a DESERT ISLAND (=a small island with no people living on it) after a plane accident. At first they work together and help each other, but soon they become cruel and violent towards each other. 《蝇王》〔(1954), 威廉·戈尔丁所著的一部小说, 讲述一群男孩在飞机失事后生活在荒岛上的故事。起初, 他们一起干活, 互相帮助, 但不久便开始自相残杀〕

Lord of the Rings, The/ˌ· · · ·ˈ·/ (1954-55) a NOVEL by J. R. R. Tolkien, which continues the story of *The Hobbit*. It takes place in a land called Middle-Earth, and has many strange magical characters in it, including the wizard Gandalf and a Hobbit called Frodo, who has to save the world from great evil. 《指环王》, 又译《魔戒》〔(1954-1955), J.R.R.托尔金所著的一部小说, 是《霍比特人》的续集。故事发生在一个叫"中土世界"的地方, 里面有不少使用法术的古怪人物, 如男巫师甘道夫和一个名叫弗罗多的霍比特人。弗罗多受命拯救世界于邪恶之中〕

Lord Priv·y Seal, the/ˌ· · · ·ˈ·/ an important member of the British CABINET who is not responsible for a particular government department 掌玺大臣〔英国内阁一重要成员, 但并不负责某一具体的政府部门〕

Lord Pro·tect·or/ˌ· ·ˈ··/ the title used by Oliver Cromwell and later by his son Richard Cromwell when they were in charge of the government of Britain at the time when it was a REPUBLIC (1649-59) 护国公〔奥利弗·克伦威尔及其儿子理查·克伦威尔在英国共和政体时期(1649-1659)的头衔〕

Lords, the the House of Lords, or its members considered as a group 上议院; 上议院全体议员

lord·ship /ˈlɔrdʃɪp; ˈlɔːdʃɪp/ *n* [C] **1 your/his lordship** used when talking to or talking about a LORD[1] (1), or when addressing a British judge or BISHOP (1) 爵爷; 大人; 阁下〔用于称呼或提及贵族或尊称英国的法官或主教时〕 **2 his lordship** *BrE spoken* a humorous way of talking about a man who thinks he is very important【英口】大人, 老爷〔谈论自命不凡者的幽默方式〕: *So when will his lordship be back?* 那么, 老爷什么时候回来? **3** [U+ **over**] the power of a lord or the period of time when he rules〔贵族的〕权力; 统治时期 —compare 比较 LADYSHIP (1)

Lord's Prayer /ˌ· ˈ·/ *n* **the Lord's Prayer** the most important prayer of the Christian religion〔基督教的〕主祷文, 天主经

Lords Spir·i·tu·al, the/ˌ· ˈ····/ the BISHOPS and ARCHBISHOPS (=priests of high rank) in the Church of England who are members of the House of Lords 神职议员〔上议院中身份为英国国教会主教或大主教的议员〕—see 见 the LORDS TEMPORAL

Lord's Sup·per, the/ˌ· ˈ··/ another name for the EUCHARIST 圣餐〔Eucharist 的别名〕

Lords Tem·po·ral, the/ˌ· ˈ···/ the members of the House of Lords who are not BISHOPS or ARCHBISHOPS (=priests of high rank) in the Church of England 世俗议员〔上议院中非英国国教会主教或大主教的议员〕—see also 另见 the LORDS SPIRITUAL

lore /lɔr; lɔː/ *n* [U] knowledge or information about a subject, for example nature or magic, that is not written down but is passed from person to person〔口头流传的关于某一主题的〕知识; 传说: *This story has become part of the county lore of Ayrshire.* 这个故事已经成为艾尔郡传说的一部分。

lor·gnette /lɔrnˈjɛt; lɔːˈnjet/ *n* [C] a pair of GLASSES with a long handle at the side that you hold in front of your eyes 长柄眼镜

lorn /lɔrn; lɔːn/ *adj poetical* sad and lonely; FORLORN【诗】凄凉的, 孤苦伶仃的 —see also 另见 LOVELORN

Lor·na Doone/ˌlɔrnə ˈdun; ˌlɔːnə ˈduːn/ (1869) a book by R. D. Blackmore about the romantic relationship between Lorna Doone, a young woman from a family of criminals, and John Ridd, a young man whose father was killed by Lorna Doone's father. The story takes place in the 17th century on Exmoor, in southwest England. 《洛纳·杜恩》〔(1869), R.D.布莱克莫尔创作的一部小说, 讲述出身罪犯家庭的姑娘洛纳·杜恩与小伙子约翰·里德的爱情故事。约翰·里德的父亲当年被洛纳·杜恩的父亲杀死。故事发生在17世纪英格兰西南部的埃克斯穆尔〕

lor·ry /ˈlɔrɪ; ˈlɒri/ *n* [C] *BrE*【英】**1** a large vehicle for carrying heavy goods; TRUCK[1](1) 大卡车, 运货汽车 **2 it fell off the back of a lorry** *spoken humorous* used to say that something was probably stolen【口, 幽默】多半是偷来之物 S3

Los Al·a·mos/lɔs ˈæləmos; lɒs ˈæləmɒs/ a town in New Mexico, in the southwestern US, where the first ATOM BOMB and HYDROGEN BOMB were developed 洛斯阿拉莫斯〔美国西南部新墨西哥州一城镇。第一颗原子弹和氢弹均在此地研制成功〕—see also 另见 the MANHATTAN PROJECT

Los An·ge·les/lɔs ˈændʒələs; lɒs ˈændʒəliːz/ abbreviation 缩写为 **LA** the second largest city in the US, in California on the Pacific coast. 洛杉矶〔美国第二大城市, 濒临太平洋, 位于加利福尼亚州境内〕

CULTURAL NOTE 文化注释

Los Angeles is famous for being the centre of the American film industry, (in Hollywood,) and for having a lot of rich, famous, and beautiful people. Some people move to LA because they like the excitement and the very warm sunny weather. Other people think that the city is full of strange and crazy people, and call it 'La-La Land'. Los Angeles is one of the biggest cities in the US, and there are people there from very many different countries. In recent years, the population of Los Angeles has changed, so that there are now more Latin American and African-American people in the city than white people. Some parts of Los Angeles are thought of as being violent and dangerous because there are a lot of GANGS (=people involved in crime and violence, who fight against other gangs) and problems with RACISM and drugs. 洛杉矶以作为美国电影业的中心(在好莱坞)而闻名, 那里还有很多富豪名流、俊男靓女。很多人是冲着刺激的生活和温暖的阳光而移居洛杉矶的。有人认为这个城市满是怪人和疯子, 因此把它叫做"拉拉之都"。洛杉矶是美国最大的城市之一, 有来自世界各地的人。近些年来, 洛杉矶的人口有了变化, 现在拉美人和非

洲裔美国人的数量超过了白人。洛杉矶的一些地区被认为充满暴力和危险，因为有很多的黑帮在此活动，还有种族和毒品问题。

There are a lot of FREEWAYs in Los Angeles and the public TRANSPORTATION system is not very good, so most people go everywhere by car. This sometimes causes a serious problem with SMOG (=an unhealthy brown mist) caused by waste gas from cars, though this is not as bad as it was in the past. 洛杉矶有不少免费高速公路，公共交通系统却不怎么好，因此大多数人出门都要驾车。汽车尾气形成的烟雾有时会带来严重问题，尽管近年的情况不像过去那样糟糕。— see also Cultural Note at CALIFORNIA 另见 CALIFORNIA 文化注释; see also 另见 BEVERLY HILLS

Los Angeles Sym·pho·ny Or·ches·tra, the /·,···'···,··/ a US ORCHESTRA (=large group of musicians playing together) based in Los Angeles 洛杉矶交响乐团

Los Angeles Times, The /·,···'·/ *trademark* a serious daily newspaper produced in Los Angeles and also sold in other parts of the US【商标】《洛杉矶时报》〔在洛杉矶出版的严肃日报，美国其他地区也有售〕

lose /luz; luːz/ *v past tense and past participle* **lost** /lɔst; lɒst/

1 ►NOT HAVE ANY MORE 不再拥有◄ [T] to stop having something that is important to you or that you need 丧失，失去〔重要或需要的东西〕: *I can't afford to lose my job, I have a family to support.* 我可不能失去工作，我要养家糊口。| *I lost a lot of money on that deal.* 我在那桩交易上赔了很多钱。| *We're going to lose five teachers when the schools are merged.* 学校合并时，我们会失去五位教师。| **lose everything** *If they're lucky they'll make a fortune, if they're unlucky they stand to lose everything.* 如果运气好，他们会发大财；如果运气不好，他们就会一无所有。

2 ►NOT WIN 未赢◄ [I,T] to not win a game, argument, war etc 输掉〔比赛、辩论、战争等〕: *I'm not playing tennis with her any more – I always lose.* 我再也不和她打网球了——我总是输。| **lose to/against** *Cuba lost to Canada in the world volleyball championships.* 古巴在世界排球锦标赛中输给了加拿大。| **lose a game/fight/election etc** *Are they in danger of losing this battle?* 他们是不是有输掉这场战争的危险？| **lose by 1 goal/10 votes/20 points etc** *Smithson lost by 7,008 votes.* 史密森输了7008票。| **lose sb sth** (=be the reason why someone does not win something) 是某人失败的原因 *Allegations of corruption lost him the election.* 贪污的传言使他在这次选举中落败。—opposite 反义词 WIN[1] (1)

3 ►CANNOT FIND 找不着◄ [T] to be unable to find someone or something 丢失，找不到: *Whatever you do, don't lose those keys.* 无论怎么样，千万别把钥匙丢了。| *Make sure you don't lose each other in the crowd.* 你们务必注意别在人群中走散了。

4 lose your memory/sight/voice etc to stop having a particular ability or sense 失去记忆／视力／嗓音等: *She lost her sight in a car accident.* 她在一次车祸中失明了。| **lose your voice** (=temporarily not be able to speak) 失去嗓音〔暂时不能说话〕 *A few days before our first concert I got a cold and lost my voice.* 我们第一次开音乐会的前几天，我得了感冒，嗓子哑了。

5 lose an arm/leg etc to have an arm, leg etc cut off after injury in an accident or in war〔因受伤而〕失掉手臂／腿等: *He lost his right arm in a motorbike accident.* 他在摩托车事故中失去了右臂。

6 lose your temper/head/nerve/rag etc to become angry, nervous etc 发怒／失去理智／感到胆怯等: *It is vital that you do not lose your head* (=that you manage to stay calm) *even in the most serious crisis.* 关键是你不要失去理智，即使在最紧要的危急关头。| *I really wanted to do the jump, but lost my nerve* (=stopped feeling brave and confident) *at the last minute.* 我真想跳过去，但最后却胆怯了。

7 lose your way/bearings to not know where you are or which direction you should go 迷路／迷失方向: *It's very easy to lose your way in the forest.* 在森林中很容易迷路。

8 lose your balance/footing to become unsteady or fall 失去平衡／失足: *Sam lost his footing on the snowy bank.* 萨姆在积雪的堤岸上失足摔倒。

9 lose interest/hope/heart etc to stop being interested in something, having hope etc 失去兴趣／希望／勇气等: *Don't lose heart – there are plenty of other jobs you could apply for.* 不要灰心，有很多别的工作你可以申请。

10 lose your mother/father/wife etc used to say that someone's mother etc has died 丧母／父／妻等: *Paul's been very depressed since losing his mother.* 自从母亲去世后，保罗的情绪一直很低落。| **lose the baby** (=used when a woman's baby dies before it is born) 流产

11 lose weight to become thinner 体重减轻: *Kay's lost a lot of weight.* 凯体重轻了不少。| **lose 20lbs/3st/5kg** *I'd like to lose at least 7 pounds before I go on vacation.* 我希望在度假前至少能减去7磅。

12 lose your mind to become crazy or to stop behaving sensibly 发疯；失去理智: *Have you lost your mind? It's really dangerous to go climbing there without a guide.* 你是不是疯了？没有向导去那里爬山真的很危险。

13 lose your life to die 丧命: *His grandfather lost his life in a mining accident.* 他的祖父在一次矿难中丧生。

14 ►TIME 时间◄ [T] to waste time because of delays, INTERRUPTIONs etc〔因耽搁、打扰等〕浪费，失去〔时间〕: **lose time/2days/3hours etc** *We lost a lot of valuable time waiting for the others to arrive.* 为了等其他人到来，我们浪费了许多宝贵的时间。| **there's no time to lose** (=it is neccessary to hurry) 抓紧时间 *Hurry, there's no time to lose.* 赶快，没有时间磨蹭了。| **lose no time in doing sth** (=do something immediately) 马上做某事 *George could see how serious it was and lost no time in calling the doctor.* 乔治看到情况十分严重，立刻就去叫医生。—opposite 反义词 GAIN[1] (8)

15 ►CLOCK/WATCH 钟/表◄ [T] if a clock or watch loses time, it works too slowly 走慢: **lose time/5 minutes/1 hour** *This old watch loses about 2 minutes in every hour.* 这只旧表每小时大约慢两分钟。—opposite 反义词 GAIN[1] (9)

16 ►CONFUSE 混淆◄ to confuse someone when you are trying to explain something to them〔试图解释时〕把〔某人〕搞糊涂: *I'm sorry, you've lost me now – could you start again?* 抱歉，你已经把我搞糊涂了——可不可以重新来一遍？

17 ►ESCAPE FROM 摆脱◄ to escape from someone who is chasing or following you 甩掉〔追赶着的人〕: *His car was much faster but I eventually managed to lose him.* 他的汽车比我的快多了，但最后我还是甩掉了他。

18 lose yourself in sth to be so involved in something that you do not notice anything else 全神贯注于某事: *It's easy to lose yourself in the magic of this film.* 你很容易被这部电影的魅力所吸引。

19 have nothing to lose to be in a situation in which you should attempt to do something, because you may be successful, and it will not make things worse if you are not〔应该尝试做某事，因为有可能成功，即使不成功也〕不会损失什么: *You might as well apply for the job – you've got nothing to lose.* 你不妨申请这份工作——不成也没什么损失。

20 have a lot to lose/have too much to lose to be in a situation in which you will suffer very much if you do not succeed in doing something〔如果不成功〕损失会很大

21 lose sight of a) to stop being able to see someone or something 看不见…: *Soon we had lost sight of the boat as it sailed off downstream.* 船向下游驶去，我们很快就看不见它了。**b)** to forget to consider something important 忘记考虑〔重要事情〕: *She was enjoying herself so much, she'd almost lost sight of the purpose of her visit.* 她玩得这么高兴，几乎忘了此行的目的。

22 lose touch (with) a) to not speak to, write to, or see someone for a long time, so that you do not know where they are (和…) 失去联系: *I've lost touch with all my old school friends.* 我已经和所有老校友失去了联系。**b)** to not know the most recent information about something and therefore be unable to understand it properly〔不知某事的近况而〕(对…) 不明白: *When you're living abroad it's so easy to lose touch with what's happening back home.* 当你在国外生活时，很难了解国内发生的事。

23 lose it *spoken*【口】**a)** to become crazy 发疯: *I reckon Jack's losing it – he was walking the dog in his pyjamas.* 我想杰克疯了——他穿着睡衣在遛狗。**b)** be unable to stop yourself laughing, crying, shouting etc 情不自禁地笑[哭，喊等]: *Then she started doing this funny little dance and I just lost it completely.* 然后她开始跳这个滑稽的小舞蹈，我就情不自禁地笑个不停。

24 lose face to do something that makes people not trust or respect you any more, especially in a public situation 丢面子，出丑〔尤指在公共场合〕

25 lose height if an aircraft loses height it falls to a lower height in the sky〔飞机〕降低高度

lose out *phr v* [I] to not get something such as a job, business contract, or profit because someone else gets it instead 失利，输掉: *On this occasion both the dealer and the client lost out.* 在这件事上买卖双方都输了。| **lose out to sb** *We lost out to a French company as they could do the job more cheaply.* 我们输给了一家法国公司，因为他们能以更低的价格做这工作。| **lose out on sth** *Why is it that women always seem to lose out on career opportunities?* 为什么在就业机会上妇女似乎总是输家？

los·er /ˈluzə; ˈluːzə/ *n* [C] **1** someone who has lost a competition or game〔竞争或比赛中的〕失败者，输家: *The losers walked dejectedly off the field.* 输掉比赛的运动员沮丧地离开运动场。| **good/bad loser** (=someone who behaves well or badly after losing) 输得起/输不起的人 **2** someone who is in a worse situation than they were, because of something that has happened 不幸者，倒霉的人: *The real losers if Bailey died would be his kids.* 如果贝利死了，真正不幸的人会是他的孩子。**3** someone who is never successful in life, work, or relationships〔在生活、工作或关系方面〕总是输的人，老是失败的人: **a born loser** *I swear Joe's a born loser.* 我肯定乔是个天生的失败者。

2 1 **loss** /lɔs; lɒs/ *n*

1 ►NO LONGER HAVING STH 不再拥有某物◄ [C,U] the fact of no longer having something you used to have 失去，丧失: *Job losses were common in the 1980s.* 在20世纪80年代，失业是很普遍的。| [+of] *a temporary loss of memory* 暂时失去记忆 | **weight/blood etc loss** *rapid hair loss* 迅速掉发

2 ►MONEY 钱◄ [C,U] money that has been lost by a business, person, government etc 亏损，损失: *losses amounting to £12,000* 总共达12,000英镑的亏损 | *profit and loss* 盈亏 | **make a loss** *The company made a loss of $250,000 in its first year.* 公司在第一年亏损了25万美元。| **sell/operate sth at a loss** (=sell something or do something with the result that you have less money than you had in the beginning) 亏本销售/经营某物

3 ►LIFE 生命◄ [C,U] the death of someone 死亡: *My sympathy for your loss.* (=of someone you love) 我为你亲人的去世致哀。| **suffer heavy losses** *The US forces withdrew after suffering heavy losses.* 美军在遭到重大伤亡后撤退了。| **loss of life** *formal*【正式】*The blaze was overcome without loss of life.* 大火被扑灭了，没有造成人员伤亡。

4 be at a loss to be confused and uncertain about what to do or say 困惑，不知所措: *I was at a complete loss as to how to find the money in time.* 我完全不知道怎样能及时弄到这笔钱。| **be at a loss for words** (=be unable to think what to say) 不知说什么才好

5 ►FEELING 感受◄ [U] a feeling of being sad or lonely because someone or something is not there any more 伤感，孤独感: **sense of loss** *I still feel an aching sense of loss, even though Allen died four years ago.* 尽管艾伦已经去世四年，我仍然有一种痛楚的失落感。

6 ►PROBLEM 问题◄ [singular] a disadvantage caused by someone or something leaving or being removed〔因某人或某物的离去或挪移而造成的〕损失: **a great loss** *We see your going as a great loss to the company.* 我们把你的离去视为公司的重大损失。

7 that's your/their loss *spoken* used to say that something will affect someone in a much worse way than it will affect you【口】那是你的/他们的损失: *Well, if he doesn't want to come it's his loss.* 好吧，如果他不愿意来，那是他的损失。

8 ►GAME 比赛◄ [C] an occasion on which a competition or game is lost; DEFEAT[1] 输，失败: [+to] *The loss to the Lions meant we were out of the playoffs.* 输给雄狮队意味着我们不能进入季后赛。—see also 另见 **cut your losses** (CUT[1] (31)), **be a dead loss** (DEAD[1] (13))

loss ad·just·er /ˈ· ·,··/ *n* [C] *BrE* someone who is employed by an insurance company to decide how much should be paid to people who make CLAIMS on their insurance【英】〔保险公司雇用的〕险损估价人; INSURANCE ADJUSTER *AmE*【美】

loss lead·er /ˈ· ,··/ *n* [C] something that is sold at a very low price to make people go into a shop 亏本促销商品

2 3 **lost**[1] /lɔst; lɒst/ *adj*

1 ►CANNOT BE FOUND 找不到◄ something that is lost is something you had but cannot now find; MISSING 找不到的，遗失的: *The lost file eventually turned up among Branson's papers.* 丢失的档案结果出现在布兰森的文件堆中。

2 ►CANNOT FIND YOUR WAY 迷路◄ unable to find your way or not knowing where you are 迷路的: *Police are generally happy to give directions to lost tourists.* 警察一般都乐于为迷路的游客指路。| **get lost** (=become lost) 迷路 *I got thoroughly lost on the way here.* 我在来这里的路上完全迷了路。

3 ►WASTED 浪费的◄ [only before noun 仅用于名词前] not used properly; wasted 用得不恰当的; 浪费的，错过的: *It'll be impossible to make up the lost time.* 不可能把浪费的时间补回来。| **lost opportunities/chances etc** *lost market opportunities* 错过的市场机遇

4 feel/be lost (in the crowd) to not feel confident about what to do or how to behave, especially among people you do not know 感到陌生〔尤指在陌生人中胆怯〕: *Will your child feel lost at a nursery?* 你的孩子在托儿所怕生吗?

5 Get lost! *spoken* used to tell someone rudely to go away【口】〔粗鲁地叫别人〕走开! 滚开!

6 ►IN THOUGHT ETC 在思考中等◄ [not before noun 不用于名词前] thinking so hard about something or being so interested in something that you do not notice what is happening around you 想得出神; 沉浸于: [+in] *I was lost in the beauty of the scenery.* 我被这美丽的景色迷住了。| **lost in thought** *Poirot remained lost in thought.* 普瓦罗仍陷入沉思。| **lost to the world** *Alex sat reading, lost to the world.* 亚历克斯坐着看书，沉醉在书中的世界里。

7 get lost (in sth) to be forgotten or not noticed in a complicated process or busy time〔在复杂的过程或繁忙时间中〕被遗忘[忽略]: *It's easy for your main points to get lost in a long speech.* 在长篇演讲中，主要观点很容易被忽略。

8 ►NOT UNDERSTAND 不理解◄ **be lost** to be completely confused by a complicated explanation〔被复杂的解释〕弄糊涂: *"Did you understand the instructions?" "No, I'm totally lost."* "你看得懂这些使用说明吗?""不，我被彻底弄糊涂了。"

9 be lost on sb if something is lost on someone, they do not understand or want to accept it 为某人所不理解[接受]: *All my warnings were completely lost on Beth.* 我所有的警告贝丝根本听不进去。

10 be lost for words to be unable to say anything because you are very surprised, upset etc〔因非常惊讶、烦恼等而〕说不出话来: *It's not often Glenda's lost for words.* 格伦达说不出话来不是常有的事。

11 ►NOT EXISTING 不存在的◄ not existing or owned any more 不复存在的，不再拥有的: *the lost dreams of her youth* 她那些逝去的青春梦想

12 ►DESTROYED/KILLED 毁坏的/被杀的◄ destroyed, ruined, or killed 毁灭的; 遭难的; 被杀死的: **lost at sea/lost in battle etc** *The whole crew was lost at sea.* 全体船员葬身大海。

13 a lost cause something that has no chance of succeeding 注定失败的事: *Trying to interest my son in classical music is a lost cause.* 我试图让儿子对古典音乐感兴趣是注定无法成功的。

14 lost soul *often humorous* someone who does not seem to know where they are or what to do【常幽默】失魂落魄者; 茫然若失的人 —see also 另见 **give sb up for dead/lost etc** (GIVE[1]), **make up for lost time** (MAKE[1]), **there is no love lost between** (LOVE[2] (11))

lost[2] the past tense and past participle of LOSE

lost-and-found /, · ˈ·/ *n* **the lost-and-found** a place where things that are lost are kept until someone comes to claim them 失物招领处; LOST PROPERTY *BrE*【英】

Lost Gen·e·ra·tion, the /, · ·ˈ··/ **1** the young men who were killed in World War I, who could have been successful in art, science, literature etc 失去的一代〔指在一战中牺牲的年轻人，他们原本可在艺术、科学、文学等领域有所成就〕**2** all the people who became adults during or just after World War I, and who suffered great social and emotional disadvantages as a result 垮掉的一代〔一战期间或稍后时期走向成年的人群，他们饱受战争引起的社会问题与情感危机之苦〕**3** a group of US writers who grew up during World War I, such as Ernest Hemingway and F. Scott Fitzgerald, and who went to live in Paris in the 1920s 迷惘的一代〔一战期间成长起来的一批美国作家，如欧内斯特·海明威和F.斯科特·菲茨杰拉德等。20世纪20年代，他们去巴黎生活〕

lost prop·er·ty /, ˈ· ··/ *n BrE*【英】**1** [U] things that have been found in public places because people have lost or forgotten them 待领失物 **2** [C] also 又作 **lost property office** *BrE* a place where these things are kept until someone comes to claim them; LOST-AND-FOUND【英】失物招领处

lot /lɑt; lɒt/ *n* 1 1

1 ►LARGE AMOUNT 大量◄ **a lot** also 又作 **lots** *informal*【非正式】a large quantity or number 大量，许多: *The stereo cost a lot, but it was worth it.* 这台立体声音响很贵，但物有所值。| *"How much ice cream do you want?" "Lots, please."* "你要多少冰激凌?""多要点儿，谢谢。"| [+of] *There were lots of people at the party.* 聚会上来了很多人。| **a lot to do/see/eat etc** *There's a lot to do before the wedding.* 婚礼前有许多事情要做。| **an awful lot** (=a very large amount) 很多，极多

2 ►MUCH 许多◄ [+comparative] if something is a lot or lots better, easier etc, it is much better, easier etc …得多〔用于比较〕: *Benny can run lots faster than me.* 本尼跑得比我快得多。| *Andrea always had a lot more money than I had.* 安德烈亚的钱总是比我多得多。

3 have a lot on *BrE*【英】**/have a lot going on** *AmE*【美】to be very busy, with a lot of things to do in a short time 很忙，要赶做很多事情

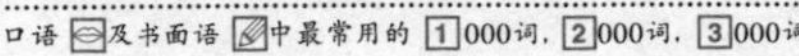

4 have a lot on your mind to have a lot of problems that you are worried about 有很多操心的事, 心事重重
5 thanks a lot *spoken*【口】**a)** thank you very much 非常感谢 **b)** used when you are annoyed about something and do not really mean thank you at all 谢谢〔反语, 用于生气时〕: *"I forgot to bring your money." "Well, thanks a lot!"* "我忘记把你的钱带来。""哦, 还得谢谢你!"
6 ▶TO BE SOLD 待售◀ [C] something that is sold, especially at an AUCTION[1]〔尤指拍卖的〕物品, 拍卖品: *Lot fifteen was a box of old books.* 第十五号拍卖品是一箱旧书。
7 have a lot to answer for to be responsible for a bad situation〔坏情况〕要对负责: *Jerry's got a lot to answer for. If it weren't for him, Ann would never have left Denver.* 杰里得负责任, 若不是他, 安决不会离开丹佛。
8 the lot *especially BrE* the whole quantity or number【尤英】全部[全数]: *I can't believe you ate the whole lot!* 我无法相信你竟然全吃下去了!
9 ▶FILM 电影◀ [C] a building and the land surrounding it where films are made; a film STUDIO (2) 电影摄制场: *the Universal Studios lot* 环球影片公司的摄制场
10 ▶SB'S LOT 某人的命运◀ *sometimes humorous* the work, responsibilities, social position etc that you have, especially when they could be better【有时幽默】〔尤指不好的〕命运, 运气: *She seems happy enough with her lot in life.* 她似乎对自己的命运感到满意。
11 ▶PEOPLE 人们◀ [singular] *BrE informal* a group of people, especially one you do not completely approve of【英, 非正式】〔尤指某人不完全赞同的〕一群人, 一批人: *Come on you lot, hurry up!* 加油, 你们大家, 赶快! | **the lot of you/them etc** (=all of you, them etc) 你们/他们等所有的人 *Outside, the lot of you!* 出去, 你们这些人!
12 ▶GROUP OF THINGS 一批东西◀ *BrE informal* a group of things【英, 非正式】一批[组]东西: *Let's drop this lot off and go home.* 我们送走这批东西, 然后回家。
13 ▶OF LAND 土地的◀ [C] *especially AmE* an area of land used for building on or for another particular purpose【尤美】一块地〔用于建屋或其他用途〕: *We could turn that vacant lot into a playground.* 我们可以把那块空地改成游戏场。| *a used-car lot* 旧车场 —see also 另见 PARKING LOT
14 have a lot on your plate *informal especially BrE* to have a lot of difficult problems to deal with【非正式, 尤英】有很多难题要处理: *Leave Mum alone – she's got a lot on her plate at the moment.* 别打扰妈妈, 现在她有许多难事要处理。
15 draw lots to decide on someone or something by choosing one piece of paper, object etc from among many〔用以作决定的〕抽签, 抓阄: *They drew lots to see who would go first.* 他们抽签看谁先走。
16 throw in/cast your lot with sb to join or support someone, so that what happens to you depends on what happens to them 与某人共命运〔加入或支持对方〕: *They threw their lot in with the allies.* 他们与盟友共命运。
17 by lot by drawing lots 用抽签[抓阄]的方法: *In Athens at that time, judges were chosen by lot.* 在那时候的雅典, 法官是通过抽签来选定的。—see also 另见 **bad egg/lot/sort/type** (BAD[1] (16)), **fall to sb's lot** (FALL[1]), **a fat lot of good/use** (FAT[1] (5))

loth /loθ; ləʊθ/ *adj* [not before noun 不用于名词前] another spelling of LOATH loath的另一种拼法

Lo·thi·an /ˈloðɪən; ˈləʊðiən/ a REGION in southeast Scotland, which contains the city of Edinburgh 洛锡安区〔苏格兰东南部一行政区, 包括爱丁堡市〕

lo·tion /ˈloʃən; ˈləʊʃən/ *n* [C,U] a liquid mixture that you put on your skin or hair to clean or protect it〔抹在皮肤或头发上起清理或保护作用的〕洁肤液; 润肤乳; 护肤液: *suntan lotion* 防晒霜

lot·sa /ˈlɑtsə; ˈlɒtsə/ *quantifier spoken*【口】a short form of 缩略式= lots of

Lot's wife /ˌ· ˈ·/ in the Old Testament of the Bible, a woman who was turned into a PILLAR (=a tall upright block) of salt by God, because she disobeyed his command not to look back when she and her family were escaping from Sodom, the city that God was going to destroy 罗得之妻〔《圣经·旧约》中被上帝变成盐柱的女子。当时, 上帝要灭所多玛城, 罗得的妻子与家人一起出逃时, 违背了上帝不许他们回头望的禁令而受如此惩罚〕

lot·te·ry /ˈlɑtərɪ; ˈlɒtəri/ *n* **1** [C] a system of raising money for the state or a CHARITY (2), in which people buy numbered tickets and some people win prizes 抽彩票给奖法: *a lottery ticket* 彩票 —compare 比较 RAFFLE[1], DRAW[2] (2) **2** [singular] an uncertain or risky situation 碰运气[冒险]的事: *The legal system is nothing but a lottery these days.* 法律制度如今全是碰运气。

lo·tus /ˈlotəs; ˈləʊtəs/ *n* [C] **1** a white or pink flower that grows on the surface of lakes in Asia 莲花, 荷花: *lotus blossom* 莲花丛 **2** the shape of this flower used in decorative patterns, especially in ancient Egyptian art〔尤指古埃及艺术中的〕莲[荷]花装饰图案 **3** a fruit that gives you a pleasant dreamy feeling after you eat it, according to Ancient Greek stories 落拓枣, 忘忧果〔据古希腊传说, 食后会有一种愉快的、如梦如幻的感觉〕

lotus-eat·er /ˈ· ·, ·ˈ/ *n* [C] someone who has a lazy, pleasant life and is not interested in other things 生活懒散、图安逸不问世事的人

loud[1] /laud; laʊd/ *adj* **1** making a lot of noise 大声的, 喧闹的: *a loud bang* 响亮的撞击声 | *That music's too loud.* 那音乐声太吵了。**2** someone who is loud talks too loudly and confidently〔人〕说话过于大声自信的: *The more Tom drank, the louder he became.* 汤姆喝得越多, 说话声音越大。**3** loud clothes are unpleasantly bright〔衣服〕花哨的, 刺眼的: *Butch was wearing a loud checked suit.* 巴奇穿着扎眼的格子套装。**4 be loud in your praise/opposition etc** to express your approval or disapproval very strongly 竭力赞同/反对等—**loudly** *adv* —**loudness** *n* [U]

loud[2] *adv* **1** loudly 响亮地, 大声地: *Could you speak a little louder?* 你能不能大声点? | *You've got the telly on too loud.* 你把电视机开得太响了。**2 loud and clear** in a way that is very easily understood 容易理解: *Sally got her message across loud and clear.* 萨莉把她的信息表达得很清楚, 容易理解。**3 out loud** in such a way that people can hear you; ALOUD 大声地: *Read it out loud, so we can all hear.* 大声念出来, 这样我们都能听到。| *If you've got anything to say, say it out loud.* 如果你有话要说, 就大声地说出来。| **laugh out loud** *Leo laughed out loud at her suggestion.* 利奥大声嘲笑她的建议。—see also 另见 **actions speak louder than words** (ACTION (15)), **for crying out loud** (CRY[1] (8))

loud·hail·er /ˌlaudˈhelɚ; ˌlaʊdˈheɪlə/ *n* [C] *especially BrE* a thing shaped like a tube that is wide at one end, that you speak through to make your voice louder; MEGAPHONE【尤英】喇叭筒, 扩音器

loud·mouth /ˈlaudˌmauθ; ˈlaʊdmaʊθ/ *n* [C] someone who talks too much and says offensive or stupid things 多嘴饶舌的人; 总说不中听的话的人 —**loudmouthed** /ˈlaudˌmauðd; ˈlaʊdmaʊðd/ *adj*

loud·speak·er /ˈlaudˈspikɚ; ˌlaʊdˈspiːkə/ *n* [C] **1** a SPEAKER (3) 扬声器 **2** a piece of equipment used to make sounds louder 扩音器, 喇叭: *Music blared from a loudspeaker.* 响亮的音乐从扩音器中传出。

lough /lɑk; lɒk/ *n* [C] *IrE* a lake or a part of the sea almost surrounded by land【爱尔兰】湖; 〔几乎为陆地所环绕的〕海湾: *Lough Neagh* 内伊湖

Lough Neagh /ˌlɑk ˈne; ˌlɒx ˈneɪ/ a lake in Northern Ireland west of Belfast, the largest lake in the UK 内伊湖〔位于北爱尔兰贝尔法斯特以西, 是英国最大湖泊〕

Lou·is /ˈluɪs; ˈluːɪs/, **Joe** /dʒo; dʒəʊ/ (1914-81) a US boxer, known as 'the Brown Bomber', who was world HEAVYWEIGHT CHAMPION from 1937 to 1949, which is the longest time that any boxer has held this title 路易士〔(1914-1981), 美国拳击手, 被誉为"棕色轰炸机"。1937-1949 年间, 他蝉联世界重量级拳击冠军, 成为拥有这一称号历时最久的拳击手〕

Louise /luˈiz; luːˈiːz/, **Lake** a lake in the Rocky Mountains near Banff, Alberta, Canada, which is a popular place for tourists because of its beautiful blue-green colour and the surrounding mountains 路易士湖〔加拿大落基山脉一湖泊, 位于艾伯塔省班夫附近。湖面呈青绿色, 十分漂亮, 群山环绕, 是大众喜爱的旅游胜地〕

Lou·i·si·a·na /luˌizɪˈænə; luːˌiːziˈænə/ abbreviation 缩写为 **LA** a state in the southern US whose largest city is New Orleans 路易斯安那州〔美国南部一州, 最大城市为新奥尔良〕

Louisiana Pur·chase, the /ˌ· ···· ˈ··/ the area of land which the US bought from France in 1803. It covered the land between the Mississippi River and the Rocky Mountains and between Canada and the Gulf of Mexico. The Louisiana Purchase more than doubled the size of the US. 路易斯安那购置地〔指 1803 年美国从法国购得的土地, 包括密西西比河、落基山脉、加拿大和墨西哥湾之间的土地。路易斯安那购置地的归入使美国的国土面积扩大了一倍以上〕

Lou·is·ville /ˈluiˌvɪl; ˈluːɪvɪl/ a city in North Kentucky on the Ohio River. The Kentucky Derby, an important horse race, is held there each year and Fort Knox, the building which holds the US Government's gold store, is nearby. 路易斯维尔〔俄亥俄河上肯塔基州北部一城市。该市每年都会举办肯塔基赛马会这一重要赛事。该市附近的诺克斯堡是美国政府的黄金储备库〕

Louis XIV /ˌluɪ ðə forˋtinθ; ˌluːi ðə fɔːˈtiːnθ/ (1638-1715) the King of France from 1643 to 1715. He was the called the 'Sun King' and his court at Versailles was very beautiful and expensively decorated. He supported important artists and writers, and people think of the time when he was King as a great period in French history. 路易十四〔(1638-1715)，法国国王，1643-1715年在位，被誉为"太阳王"。他在凡尔赛的王宫十分漂亮，装饰奢华。他曾资助过一批杰出的画家和作家。人们认为路易十四时期是法国历史上的一个鼎盛时期〕

Louis XVI /ˌluɪ ðə sɪksˋtinθ; ˌluːi ðə sɪksˈtiːnθ/ (1754-93) the King of France from 1774 to 1792. He and his wife Marie Antoinette were put in prison during the French Revolution, and were killed by having their heads cut off by the GUILLOTINE. 路易十六〔(1754-1793)，法国国王，1774-1792年在位。法国大革命期间，他与妻子玛丽·安托瓦内特被关入监狱，并一起被送上断头台〕

lounge[1] /laundʒ; laʊndʒ/ *n* [C] **1** a small comfortable public room in a hotel or other building used by many people〔旅馆等中的〕休息室: *the television lounge* 电视室 **2** a WAITING ROOM at an airport〔机场的〕等候室: *the departure lounge* 候机室 **3** *especially BrE* a comfortable room where you relax in your home【尤英】〔住所中的〕起居室 **4** *BrE* a lounge bar【英】酒吧雅座 —see also 另见 COCKTAIL LOUNGE, SUN LOUNGE

lounge[2] *v* [I] **1** [always+adv/prep] to stand or sit in a lazy way 懒洋洋地站[坐]着: [**+in/on etc**] *young lads lounging in doorways* 懒洋洋地站在门口的小伙子 **2 lounge around/about** *BrE* to spend time doing nothing【英】闲逛，百无聊赖地消磨[打发]时间: *He was just lounging around all day.* 他整天无所事事。

lounge bar /ˈ· ·/ *n* [C] *BrE* a room with comfortable furniture in a PUB; SALOON BAR【英】〔小酒馆中的〕雅座酒吧

loung·er /ˋlaundʒɚ; ˈlaʊndʒə/ *n* [C] **1** someone who is lazy and does no work 游手好闲的人 **2** a piece of garden furniture like a light narrow bed, used for lying in the sun〔花园中晒太阳用的〕躺椅; SUN LOUNGER *AmE*【美】

lounge suit /ˈ· ·/ *n* [C] *BrE old-fashioned* a suit that a man wears during the day, especially to work in an office【英，过时】〔尤指日常在办公室上班时穿的〕西装; BUSINESS SUIT *AmE*【美】

CULTURAL NOTE 文化注释

In Britain and the US many men who work in a bank, office etc have to wear a lounge suit when they go to work, even when the weather is very hot or very cold. It is usually in a dark colour such as grey or black and is usually worn with a shirt and tie. 在英美，不管天气是炎热还是寒冷，很多在银行、写字楼等地方上班的男士都要在上班时间穿西装。西装通常为深色，如灰色或黑色，而且通常要穿衬衫、打领带。

lour /laur; ˈlaʊə/ *v* [I] a British spelling of LOWER[3] lower[3]的英式拼法

Lourdes /lurd; lʊəd/ a small town in southwest France where Roman Catholics believe that Saint Bernadette saw the Virgin Mary appear. They consider Lourdes to be a holy place, and many sick people go there because they believe that the water there is holy and has the power to cure them. 卢尔德〔法国西南部一小镇。天主教徒相信圣贝尔娜黛特在此亲眼目睹童贞女马利亚现身，并且把卢尔德视为圣地。许多患病的人都前往该镇，因为他们相信那里的圣水能治病〕

louse[1] /laus; laʊs/ *n* [C] **1** *plural* **lice** a small wingless insect that lives on people's or animals' skin and hair 虱子 **2** *plural* **louses** *informal* someone who is nasty and unpleasant【非正式】卑鄙小人: *"You louse!" she yelled.* "你这个卑鄙小人！"她叫骂道。

louse[2] *v*

louse up *phr v AmE informal*【美，非正式】**1** [T **louse** sth **up**] to make something worse rather than better, or to spoil something 把…弄乱[搞糟，搞坏]: *I don't want to louse up your life.* 我不想破坏你的生活。**2** [I] to do something badly〔做事〕差，不好: [**+on**] *Chris really loused up on his exams.* 克里斯真的考得很糟。

lou·sy /ˋlauzɪ; ˈlaʊzi/ *adj* **lousier, lousiest 1** *especially spoken* very bad, unpleasant etc【尤口】非常糟糕的; 令人作呕的: *What lousy weather!* 多么糟糕的天气！| *I feel lousy.* 我感觉很难受。**2** *spoken* small, useless, or unimportant【口】不起眼的; 不起作用的; 微不足道的: *Harry wouldn't lend me ten lousy quid!* 哈里连区区十英镑都不借给我！**3 lousy with sth** *AmE spoken*【美口】**a)** a place that is lousy with people of a particular kind is too full of them〔某处〕满是〔某种人〕: *The town was lousy with tourists.* 镇上挤满了游客。**b)** someone who is lousy with money has a lot more of it than they need〔某人〕有大量的钱 **4** covered with lice (LOUSE[1] (1)) 布满虱子的

lout /laut; laʊt/ *n* [C] a rude, violent man 举止粗野的人: *Get up, you lazy lout!* 起来，你这又懒惰又粗鲁的家伙！—see also 另见 **lager lout** (LAGER (2)), —**loutish** *adj* —**loutishly** *adv* —**loutishness** *n* [U]

Louth /lauð; laʊð/ the smallest COUNTY in the Republic of Ireland, on the northeast coast 劳斯〔爱尔兰共和国最小一郡，位于东北部沿海地区〕

lou·vre *BrE*【英】, **louver** *AmE*【美】/ˋluvɚ; ˈluːvə/ *n* [C] **1** a narrow piece of wood, glass etc, in a door or window, sloping outwards to let some light in and keep rain or strong sun out〔窗或门上的〕叶板〔用来挡雨或强光〕**2 louvre window/door** a door or window made of these pieces of wood, glass etc 百叶窗/门 —**louvred** *adj*: *louvred shutters* 百叶窗

Louvre, the /ˋluvrə; ˈluːvrə/ the most famous French MUSEUM, which is in Paris and has many important paintings, including the 'Mona Lisa', and STATUEs, including 'Nike' or the 'Winged Victory' 卢浮宫〔法国最著名的博物馆，位于巴黎，藏有《蒙娜丽莎》等许多重要的绘画作品及《胜利女神奈基》等雕塑〕

lov·a·ble, loveable /ˋlʌvəbl; ˈlʌvəbəl/ *adj* friendly and attractive 友善可爱的，讨人喜欢的: *a lovable kitten* 可爱的小猫 | *not a very lovable child* 不十分讨人喜欢的孩子

love[1] /lʌv; lʌv/ *v* S1 W1

1 ▶ROMANTIC ATTRACTION 爱情的吸引力◀ [T not in progressive 不用进行时] to have a strong feeling of caring for and liking someone, combined with sexual attraction 爱情，恋爱，性爱: *I love you, really. Do you love me?* 我真的爱你，你爱我吗？| *He was the only man she had ever loved.* 他是她唯一爱过的男人。

2 ▶CARE ABOUT 关心◀ [T not in progressive 不用进行式] to care very much about someone, especially a member of your family or a close friend〔尤指家庭成员、亲密朋友的〕关心，钟爱: *Children need to feel loved.* 孩子需要感到有人关爱。| **much-loved/greatly-loved/well-loved** *one of America's best-loved TV personalities* 美国观众最喜爱的电视名人之一 | **loved ones** (=people you love) 钟爱的人 *women caring for loved ones who had been injured in the war* 照料在战争中受伤的亲人的妇女

3 ▶LIKE/ENJOY 喜欢/喜爱◀ [T not in passive 不用被动态] to like something very much or enjoy doing something very much 喜欢〔某物〕; 喜爱〔做某事〕: **love doing sth** *Max found that he really loved teaching.* 马克斯发现他很喜欢教书。| **love sth** *I love carrots.* 我喜欢吃胡萝卜。| *She loves anything to do with figures.* 她喜欢一切和数字有关的事。| **love to do sth** *We all love to talk about ourselves.* 我们都喜欢谈论自己。| *I love the way she sings that.* 我喜欢她那种唱歌方式。| **I'd love to** *spoken* (=used to say you would really like to do something)【口】我确实愿意〔做某事〕: *"Would you like to come swimming with us?" "I'd love to."* "你愿意和我们一起去游泳吗？""我很愿意。" | *I'd have loved to have stayed till the end.* 我很想一直逗留到结束。| *I'd love to know just why they did that.* 我真想知道他们到底为什么那样做。

4 I must love you and leave you *spoken* used to tell someone that you have to go, especially when you wish you could stay longer【口】我得走了〔尤用于希望逗留的时间能长些〕

5 ▶LOYALTY 忠诚◀ [T not in progressive 不用进行时] to have a strong feeling of loyalty to your country, an institution etc 热爱〔国家、组织等〕: *He really loved the police force.* 他非常热爱警队。

6 I love it! *spoken* used when you are amused by something, especially by someone else's mistake or bad luck【口】好玩！太有趣了！〔尤用于被他人的差错或坏运逗乐的时候〕: *"Henry was telling the prof all about relativity." "I love it! I love it!"* "亨利向教授大谈相对论。""太有趣了！太有趣了！"

7 she's going to love you/he's going to love this etc *spoken*【口】**a)** used to say that someone will enjoy something 某人会喜欢你[某事等]: *Listen guys, you're going to love this.* 大家听着，你们会喜欢听的。**b)** used jokingly to say that someone will not be pleased about something〔用于开玩笑地表示〕某人不会喜欢某事: *I'm going to love telling him we've changed our minds again.* 我不会高兴地告诉他我们又改变主意了。—see also 另见 LOVER

love[2] *n* S1 W1

1 ▶FOR FAMILY/FRIENDS 对家人/朋友◀ [U] a strong feeling of caring about someone, especially a member of your family or a close friend〔尤指对家人、亲密朋友的〕爱，关心，关爱: *What these kids need is love and support.* 这些孩子需要的是关心和支持。| [**+for**] *a mother's love for her child* 母亲对孩子的爱 —opposite 反义词 HATE[2], HATRED

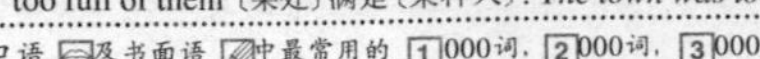

2 ►ROMANTIC 浪漫的◄ [U] a strong feeling of liking and caring about someone, especially combined with sexual attraction 恋爱, 爱情, 性爱: *She's seen him every day this week – it must be love!* 这个星期她每天都见他——那肯定是恋爱! | *a love song* 情歌 | **be/fall in love (with)** *I think I'm falling in love with your brother.* 我想我爱上了你的哥哥。| **madly in love/very much in love/head over heels in love** *It was obvious that they were very much in love.* 很明显他们在热恋之中。| **love at first sight** (=when you love someone the first time you see them) 一见钟情 | **true love** (=strong romantic love that remains for ever) 不变的真爱

CULTURAL NOTE 文化注释

Love is usually represented by a red heart or by Cupid. 通常用红心或爱神丘比特来象征爱情。— see Cultural Note at VALENTINE'S DAY 见 VALENTINE'S DAY 文化注释

3 ►PERSON YOU LOVE 钟爱的人◄ [C] someone that you feel a strong romantic and sexual attraction to 所爱的人: *He was her first love.* 他是她的初恋。| **the love of your life** (=the person that you have loved most of your life) 一生中最心爱的人

4 ►PLEASURE/ENJOYMENT 快乐/乐趣◄ **a)** [singular,U] a strong feeling of pleasure and enjoyment that something gives you 热爱: **love of/for** *a love of nature* 对大自然的热爱 **b)** [C] something that gives you a lot of pleasure and enjoyment 爱好, 喜爱: *Sailing was her great love.* 帆船运动是她最大的爱好。

5 make love a) to have sex with someone that you love 做爱, 性交: **make love to/with** *"I want to make love with you," she breathed.* "我想和你做爱。"她小声地说。**b)** *old use* to say loving things to someone, to kiss them etc【旧】〔向某人〕示爱

6 send your love (to) to ask someone to give your loving greetings to someone else when they see them, write to them etc 〔向某人〕致意[问候]: *Aunt Mary sends her love to you.* 玛丽姑妈向你问好。

7 give my love to *spoken* used to ask someone to give your loving greetings to someone else【口】转达我对〔某人〕的问候: *"Bye! Give my love to Jackie."* "再见! 请转达我对杰基的问候。"

8 love (from)/lots of love/all my love expressions used at the end of a letter to a friend, a member of your family, or someone you love 爱你的…/深爱你的/全心爱你的〔用于写给朋友、家人或所爱之人的信的末尾〕: *See you soon. Lots of love, Clare.* 希望很快能见到你。深爱你的, 克莱尔。

9 (my) love *spoken*【口】**a)** *especially BrE* a word used when you are talking to someone you love【尤英】亲爱的〔用于对所爱的人说话时〕: *Hurry up, love!* 赶快, 亲爱的! **b)** *BrE* a friendly way of talking to someone who you do not know, especially to a woman【英】亲爱的〔对陌生人说话的友好方式, 尤其是对妇女〕: *Are you OK, love?* 你没事吧, 亲爱的?

10 be a love and.../... there's a love *spoken, especially BrE* expressions used when you are asking someone to do something, used especially to children and members of your family【口, 尤英】乖乖的〔用于要孩子和家人做某事〕: *Say hello to your auntie, there's a love.* 乖乖的, 向阿姨问好。

11 there is no love lost between if there is no love lost between two people, they dislike each other〔两人之间〕没有好感, 互相厌恶: *There's never been any love lost between Paul and Geoff.* 保罗和杰夫两人彼此憎恨。

12 ►TENNIS 网球◄ [U] an expression meaning no points, used in the game of tennis〔网球比赛中的〕零分

13 not for love or/nor money *informal* if you cannot get something or do something for love or money, it is impossible to obtain or to do【非正式】无论怎样也不, 绝不: *I can't get hold of that book for love nor money.* 我无论如何也找不到那本书。

14 for the love of God/Mike etc *old-fashioned spoken* used to show that you are extremely angry, disappointed etc【过时, 口】看在上帝的分上〔用于表示怒不可遏、沮丧等〕

15 love nest *humorous* a place where two people who are having a romantic relationship live or meet each other【幽默】爱巢〔情人同居或幽会的地方〕—see also 另见 **a labour of love** (LABOUR[1] (4))

love af·fair /ˈ· ·ˌ·/ *n* [C] **1** a romantic sexual relationship, usually between two people who are not married to each other〔尤指非夫妻间的〕性关系; 风流韵事: *a passionate love affair* 火热的性关系 —see also 另见 AFFAIR (3) **2** a strong enjoyment of something〔对某物的〕强烈兴趣, 热爱, 酷爱: *the great American love affair with the automobile* 美国人对汽车的酷爱

love·bird /ˈlʌvˌbɝd; ˈlʌvbɜːd/ *n* [C] **1** a small brightly coloured PARROT[1] (1) 情侣鹦鹉 **2 lovebirds** *humorous* two people who show by their behaviour that they love each other very much【幽默】一对情侣

love bite /ˈ· ·/ *n* [C] *especially BrE* a red mark on someone's skin caused by someone else sucking it as a sexual act【尤英】爱的吮痕〔男女亲热时被对方在皮肤上吮出的红印痕〕; HICKEY *AmE*【美】

love·child /ˈlʌvtʃaɪld; ˈlʌvtʃaɪld/ *n* [C] a word used especially in newspapers meaning a child whose parents are not married 私生子〔报纸用语〕

love·less /ˈlʌvlɪs; ˈlʌvləs/ *adj* without love 没有爱的: *a loveless marriage* 没有爱情的婚姻

love let·ter /ˈ· ˌ··/ *n* [C] a letter that someone writes to tell someone else how much they love them 情书

love life /ˈ· ·/ *n* [C,U] the part of your life that involves your love relationships, especially sexual ones 爱情生活〔尤指性生活〕

love·lorn /ˈlʌvˌlɔrn; ˈlʌvlɔːn/ *adj literary* sad because the person you love does not love you【文】失恋的, 因失恋而憔悴的

love·ly¹ /ˈlʌvlɪ; ˈlʌvli/ *comparative* 比较级 **lovelier** *superlative* 最高级 **loveliest** *adj* **1** *especially BrE* beautiful or attractive【尤英】美丽的; 可爱的: *What a lovely baby!* 多么可爱的婴儿! | *Her hair's a lovely shade of red.* 她的头发是漂亮的红色。| **look lovely** *You look lovely in blue.* 你穿蓝衣服看上去很漂亮。**2** *informal especially BrE* friendly and pleasant【非正式, 尤英】亲切的, 令人愉快的: *Richard's a lovely person.* 理查德是一个讨人喜欢的人。**3** *BrE spoken* used to say that something is not at all enjoyable, or good【英口】令人败兴的; 糟透了的: *"The cat threw up all over the carpet!" "Lovely!"* "猫吐得地毯上到处都是!" "太糟糕了!" | *You've made a lovely mess in here.* 你把这里弄得乱糟糟的。**4** *spoken especially BrE* very pleasant, enjoyable, or good【口, 尤英】令人愉快[高兴]的; 美好的: *That was a lovely cup of tea.* 这是一杯上好的茶。| *Thank you for a lovely evening.* 谢谢你让我们度过了一个美好的夜晚。**5 lovely and warm/cold etc** *BrE spoken* used to emphasize how good something is【英口】非常暖和/寒冷等〔用于强调〕: *This bread's lovely and fresh.* 这面包新鲜极了。**6** *BrE spoken* used to show that you are pleased with something【英口】好极了〔用于表示对某事满意〕: *Push it right across. That's it, lovely.* 把它直接推过去。对, 棒极了。—**loveliness** *n* [U]

lovely² *n* [C] *old-fashioned* an attractive woman【过时】美人, 美女: *Samantha, a nineteen year old Liverpool lovely* 萨曼莎, 19岁的利物浦美女

love·mak·ing /ˈlʌvˌmekɪŋ; ˈlʌvˌmeɪkɪŋ/ *n* [U] sexual activity, especially the act of having sex 做爱, 性交 —see also 另见 **make love** (LOVE² (5))

lov·er /ˈlʌvɚ; ˈlʌvə/ *n* [C] **1** a sexual partner 性伙伴[伴侣]: *a jealous lover* 爱吃醋的性伴侣 **2** someone who has a sexual relationship for a long time with someone they are not married to〔长期保持性关系的〕情人: *Arabella had had many lovers.* 阿拉贝拉有过很多情人。—compare 比较 MISTRESS (1) **3** someone who enjoys doing a particular thing very much or is very interested in it〔…的〕爱好者: *music lovers* 音乐爱好者

love·seat /ˈlʌvˌsit; ˈlʌvsiːt/ *n* [C] **1** a seat in the shape of an S for two people, designed so that they can face each other 情人座〔面对面的S形双人座〕**2** *AmE* a small SOFA for two people【美】双人小沙发

love·sick /ˈlʌvˌsɪk; ˈlʌvˌsɪk/ *adj* spending all your time thinking about someone you love, especially someone who does not love you 单恋的, 害相思病的: *You're acting like a lovesick teenager!* 你像一个害相思病的少年!

Love's La·bour's Lost /ˌ· ·ˈ· ˈ·/ a humorous play by William Shakespeare in which a king and three of his friends promise to study and not become involved with women. However, they meet a PRINCESS and her friends, and fall in love with them, so that they are unable to do what they intended.《爱的徒劳》〔威廉·莎士比亚创作的一部喜剧。剧中有一位国王和他的三个朋友约定要开始学习, 不再沾染女人之事。可是, 当他们遇到一位公主和她的朋友, 就情难自禁, 再也无法做想做的事了〕

lov·ey /ˈlʌvɪ; ˈlʌvi/ *n* [C] *BrE spoken* a word used to address a woman or child, that many women think is offensive【英口】亲爱的, 宝贝〔对女人或孩子的称呼, 很多妇女认为是冒犯语〕—see also 另见 LUVVIE

lovey-dov·ey /ˌlʌvɪ ˈdʌvɪ; ˌlʌvi ˈdʌvi◄/ *adj informal* behaviour that is lovey-dovey is too romantic; SENTIMENTAL【非正式】情意绵绵的; 过分多情的: *Josh went all lovey-dovey when I said I was pregnant.* 当我说我怀孕了, 乔希就变得温柔多情起来。

lov·ing /ˈlʌvɪŋ; ˈlʌvɪŋ/ *adj* **1** [only before noun 仅用于名词前] behaving in a way that shows you love someone 钟爱的, 表示爱意的: *in memory of my loving wife* 悼念我的爱妻 | *What that*

child needs is plenty of loving care and attention. 那孩子所需要的是很多充满爱的关心和照顾。**2 peace-loving/home-loving etc** thinking that peace, your home etc is very important 热爱和平的/爱家的: *a peace-loving nation* 热爱和平的国家 | *Molly's a real home-loving type.* 莫莉是一个非常爱家的人。—**lovingly** *adv*: *Anna stroked the baby's cheek lovingly.* 安娜慈爱地抚摸婴孩的脸颊。

loving cup /ˈ· · ˌ·/ *n* [C] a very large cup with two handles that was passed around at formal meals in former times 爱杯〔旧时正式宴会上供宾客传饮的双柄大酒杯〕

loving kind·ness /ˌ·· ˈ··/ *n* [U] *especially literary* gentle and sincere friendship or love【尤文】慈爱, 仁爱; 温厚诚挚的友谊

low 低矮的

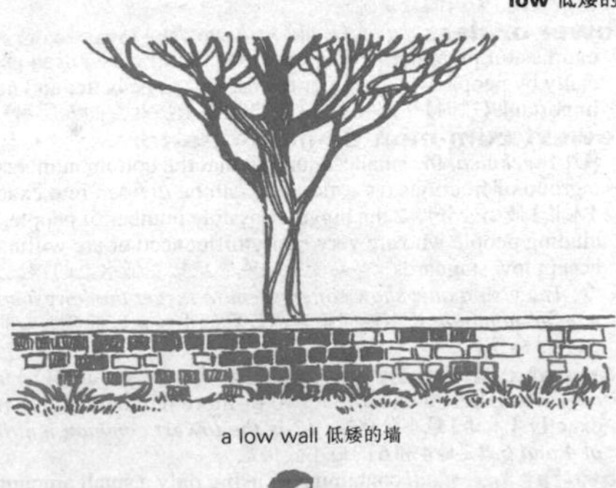

a low wall 低矮的墙

shallow water 浅水区

[1] [1] **low¹** /lo; ləʊ/ *adj*

1 ▶NOT HIGH 不高的◀ **a)** having a top that is not far above the ground 矮的: *He jumped over the low wall.* 他跳过了那堵矮墙。| *a long low building* 一栋长长的矮房子 **b)** at a point that is not far above the ground 低的, 下面的: *low clouds* 低垂的云 | *Put the books on the lowest shelf.* 把书放在最下面的书架上。**c)** below the usual height 低于一般高度的: *a low bridge* 矮桥 | *The river is low for this time of year.* 每年这个时候, 河水比较低。

2 ▶SMALL AMOUNT 少量◀ **a)** small, or smaller than usual, in amount, value etc〔数量、价值等〕少的: *The price of oil is at its lowest for 10 years.* 石油的价格是10年来最低的。| *families existing on very low incomes* 低收入家庭 | **low-cost/low-budget etc** *There's a desperate need for good low-cost housing.* 对价廉物美的住房有急迫的需求。**b) low in** having less than the usual amount of a substance or chemical〔某种物质或化学品等〕含量低的: *food that is low in calories* 低热量食品 | **low-fat/low-salt etc** *I only smoke low-tar cigarettes.* 我只抽焦油含量低的香烟。| *low-alcohol beer* 低酒精度啤酒 **c) in the low 20s/50s etc** a number, temperature etc in the low 20s etc is around 21, 22, or 23, but no higher〔数字、温度等〕20多一点〔21–23〕/50多一点〔51–53〕等: *Daytime temperature will be in the low 30s.* 白天温度将在31度至33度之间。

3 ▶BELOW USUAL LEVEL 低于一般水平◀ small, or smaller than usual, in level or degree〔水平或程度〕低的; 小于平常的: *In this sort of investment, the risks are fairly low.* 在这种投资中, 风险相当小。| *Morale has been low since the latest round of job-cuts.* 自最近一轮裁员以来, 士气一直很低落。| **low-risk/low-priority etc** *a low-security prison* 警戒不严的监狱, 低度设防监狱

4 ▶STANDARDS/QUALITY 标准/质量◀ below an acceptable or usual level or quality〔水平或质量〕低于可接受[平常]程度的: *Their safety standards seem to be pretty low.* 他们的安全标准似乎相当低。| *Cost-cutting has led to a lower quality of service.* 削减成本导致了服务质量的降低。

5 ▶SUPPLY 供应◀ a supply of something that is low is nearly finished 短缺的, 将耗尽的: **be/get/run low (on)** *We're running low on coffee.* 我们的咖啡不多了。| *Stocks are getting low.* 库存快耗尽了。

6 ▶SOUND 声音◀ a low voice, sound etc is quiet or deep 低声的, 轻声的: *I heard a low moaning noise.* 我听到低沉的呻吟声。| *The volume is too low – turn it up.* 音量太低了, 开响一点。| *a low whisper* 低声耳语

7 ▶LIGHT 光线◀ a light that is low is not bright 暗淡的: *low romantic lighting in a restaurant* 餐馆里具有浪漫色彩的暗淡灯光

8 ▶HEAT 热度◀ if you cook something on a low heat or in a low OVEN, you cook it using only a small amount of heat〔烹调时〕低温的, 低热度的

9 ▶BATTERY 电池◀ a BATTERY that is low does not have much power left in it〔电力〕不足的

10 ▶CLOTHES 衣服◀ a low dress, BLOUSE etc does not cover your neck and the top of your chest〔衣服〕领口低的, 低胸的

11 ▶UNHAPPY 不高兴的◀ [not before noun 不用于名词前] unhappy and without much hope for the future 不高兴的, 情绪低落的: *She's still feeling pretty low about failing that exam.* 她考试不及格, 情绪仍很低落。| **in low spirits** *Terry seems to be in rather low spirits today.* 特里今天似乎情绪相当低落。

12 ▶DISHONEST 不诚实的◀ *old-fashioned or humorous* behaviour that is low is not fair or honest【过时或幽默】卑鄙的, 卑劣的: *a low trick* 卑鄙的诡计

13 of low birth/breeding *old-fashioned* not from a high social class【过时】出身低微的 —see also 另见 **be at a low ebb** (EBB¹ (2)), —**lowness** *n* [U]

low² *adv* **1** in or to a low position or level 低; 低水平地: *He bent low over the engine.* 他俯身查看引擎。| *Turn the heating down low.* 把暖气关小。**2** near the ground 高出地面不多地, 不高地: *Watch out for low-flying aircraft.* 当心低空飞行的飞机。**3** if you play or sing musical notes low, you play or sing them with quiet deep notes〔弹奏或唱歌时〕用低音调, 低沉地: *Sing those bars an octave lower.* 这几小节用低八度唱。**4 search/look high and low** *informal* to look everywhere in order to find something【非正式】到处寻找 **5 lie low a)** to hide from people who are trying to catch you 躲藏, 隐匿 **b)** to wait and try not to be noticed by anyone 避免引人注目, 等候机会: *Just lie low for a while.* 别出头露面, 等一会儿。**6 lay sb low** to knock someone down onto the ground or to make someone feel very weak 击倒某人; 使某人身体虚弱: *laid low by flu* 因流感而病倒 **7 be brought low** *old-fashioned* to become much less rich or important【过时】变得远不如原来富有[重要] —see also 另见 LOWLY

low³ *n* **1** [C] a low price or level 低价; 低水平: **fall to a new low/ hit a new low** (=be worth less than ever before) 降到新低点/达到新低点 *The pound has fallen to a new low against the dollar.* 英镑对美元的汇价降到了新低。| **all-time low** (=much lower or worse than ever before) 前所未有的低[差] *Profits hit an all-time low this month.* 这个月的利润降到了历史最低点。**2** [C] a bad situation in someone's personal life〔某人生活中的〕低潮: **all-time low** (=a worse situation than ever before) 最差的境况 *1963 marked an all-time low in his family life.* 1963年是他家庭生活最糟的一年。| **highs and lows** (=good times and bad times) 好与差的时期 *the highs and lows in their marriage* 他们婚姻生活的高潮和低潮 **3** [C usually singular 一般用单数] **a)** an area of low pressure in the air 低气压区: *a low moving in over the Pacific* 从太平洋上空移入的低气压区 **b)** a low temperature 低温: *The overnight low will be 8°C.* 晚间低温为8摄氏度。**4 the lowest of the low a)** *informal* someone you think is completely unfair, cruel, immoral etc【非正式】最不公正[残忍, 不道德等]的人: *Property barons are among the lowest of the low.* 房地产巨头是最卑劣之徒。**b)** *often humorous* someone from a low social class【常幽默】社会地位低微的人

low⁴ *v* [I] *especially literary* if cattle low, they make a deep sound【尤文】〔牛〕哞哞叫

low beam /ˌ· ˈ·/ *n* **be on low beam** if the lights at the front of a car are on low beam, they light only a short distance of the road ahead and are not very bright〔汽车前灯的〕近距离光

low-born /ˌloˈbɔrn; ˌləʊˈbɔːn◂/ *adj old-fashioned* coming from a low social class【过时】出身低微的

low-brow /ˈloˌbrau; ˈləʊbraʊ/ *adj* not interested in or connected with literature, art etc 对文学、艺术等不感兴趣的; 与文学、艺术等无关的, 庸俗的: *lowbrow television shows* 庸俗的电视节目 —compare 比较 HIGHBROW

low-cal, lo-cal /ˌloˋkæl; ˌləʊˈkæl◂/ *adj informal* low-cal food or drink does not contain many CALORIES【非正式】〔食物或饮料〕低热量的

Low Church /ˌ·ˈ·◂/ *n* [U] the part of the Church of England that believes in the importance of faith and studying the BIBLE rather than in religious ceremonies〔英国〕低教会派〔认为信仰及对《圣经》的研习比宗教仪式重要〕—compare 比较 HIGH CHURCH

low-class /ˌ·ˈ·◂/ *adj* **1** *old-fashioned* WORKING CLASS【过时】工人阶级, 劳工阶级: *a low-class bar* 工人酒吧 **2** not good quality 质量低劣的

Low Coun·tries, the /ˈ· ˌ··/ another name for the Netherlands, a country in northwestern Europe, bordered by Belgium, Germany and the North Sea. It is called the Low Countries because the land is mostly flat, and some parts are below sea level. 低地国家〔荷兰的别称, 位于欧洲西北部, 与比利时和德国接壤, 濒临北海。该国大部分地区地势平坦, 有些地区甚至低于海平面, 故名〕

low-cut /ˌ·ˈ·◂/ *adj* a low-cut dress is shaped so that it shows your neck and the top of your chest〔连衣裙〕低胸的

low-down /ˈloˋdaʊn; ˈləʊdaʊn/ *n* **the lowdown (on)** *informal* the most important facts about something or someone【非正式】〔关于某事物或某人的〕最重要情况: *Give me all the lowdown on what happened at the meeting.* 告诉我会议的所有重点。

low-down /ˈ··/ *adj* [only before noun 仅用于名词前] *informal* dishonest and unkind【非正式】卑劣的, 卑鄙的: *What a low-down, dirty trick.* 多么卑劣肮脏的勾当!

Low·ell /ˈloəl; ˈləʊəl/, **Rob·ert** /ˈrɑbɚt; ˈrɒbət/ (1917-77) a US poet and writer of plays, who was also concerned about social questions and opposed to the Vietnam War. Two of his most famous poems are *The Quaker Graveyard in Nantucket* and *Colloquy in Black Rock.* 洛威尔〔(1917-1977), 美国诗人、剧作家。他同时关注社会问题, 反对越南战争。最著名的两首诗是《南塔凯特贵格会教徒墓地》和《黑岩上的谈话》〕

3 **low·er¹** /ˈloɚ; ˈləʊə/ *adj* **1** [only before noun 仅用于名词前] below something else, especially beneath something of the same type〔尤指在同类中处于〕较下的, 下层的: *Nina chewed her lower lip anxiously.* 尼娜焦虑不安地咬着下唇。| *the lower limbs* (=legs) 下肢 **2** [only before noun 仅用于名词前] at or near the bottom of something 在底部的; 接近底部的: *the lower slopes of the mountain* 山脚 **3** smaller in number or amount〔数字或数量〕较小的: *Temperatures will be lower over the weekend.* 周末气温会下降。**4** [only before noun 仅用于名词前] less important than something else of the same type〔同类中〕次重要的, 较低级的: *the lower levels of management* 较低级的管理层

lower² *v*

1 ▶REDUCE 减少◀ [I,T] to reduce something in amount, degree, strength etc, or to become less 减少, 降低: *After 20 minutes lower the temperature to 325°.* 20分钟后, 将温度降到325度。| *drugs to lower blood pressure* 降血压的药 | **lower your voice** (=make it quieter) 压低嗓音 *Helen lowered her voice as they approached.* 当他们走近时, 海伦压低了嗓音。

2 ▶MOVE DOWN 降下◀ [T] to move something down from higher up 把〔某物〕移低, 降下: *The flags were lowered to half-mast.* 降了半旗。| **lower sth down/into/between etc** *They lowered the coffin into the grave.* 他们把棺材放到墓穴中。

3 lower yourself [usually in negatives 一般用于否定句] to behave in a way that makes people respect you less 降低〔自己的〕身份: *I wouldn't lower myself to speak to her after what she's done.* 她做了那样的事以后, 我不会自降身份和她说话。

4 lower the tone *often humorous* to make a conversation, a social situation etc less polite, for example by telling rude jokes【常幽默】败坏〔谈话、社交场合等〕的格调: *They thought an influx of students would lower the tone of the neighborhood.* 他们认为学生的涌入会使这一带的风气变差。

5 lower your eyes to look down 向下看: *Katrina lowered her eyes demurely.* 卡特里娜含羞地垂下眼睛。—**lowered** *adj*: *Zoe watched through lowered eyelashes.* 佐伊透过垂下的眼睫毛向外观察。

low·er³ also 又作 **lour** *BrE*【英】/ˈlaʊɚ; ˈlaʊə/ *v* [I] **1** when the sky or the weather lowers, it becomes dark because there is going to be a storm〔暴风雨前的天〕变昏暗;〔天气〕变险恶: *lowering clouds* 阴沉沉的云 **2** *literary* to look threatening or annoyed; FROWN¹【文】露愠色; 皱眉: *lowering at us across the table* 隔着桌子生气地看着我们

lower case /ˌ··ˈ·◂/ *n* [U] letters in their small forms, such as a, b, c etc 小写字体〈如 a, b, c 等〉—compare 比较 CAPITAL¹ (3) —opposite 反义词 UPPER CASE—**lower case** *adj*: *lower case letters* 小写字母

lower class /ˌ··ˈ·◂/ also 又作 **lower classes** *n* [C] *old-fashioned* the social class that has less money, power, or education than anyone else【过时】下层阶级, 劳工阶级 —see also 另见 WORKING CLASS—**lower-class** *adj*

Lower East Side, the /ˌ·· ˈ· ˌ·/ also 又作 **the East Side** the southeastern part of Manhattan in New York City, which used to be a poor part of the city, but is now a fashionable place for artists and writers to live 下东河区〔指纽约市曼哈顿东南部地区, 曾经是该市的贫民区之一, 但现已成为艺术家和作家聚居的时尚之地〕

Lower House /ˌ··ˈ·/ also 又作 **Lower Cham·ber** /ˌ··ˈ··/ *n* [singular] a group of elected representatives who make laws in a country, for example the HOUSE OF COMMONS in Britain or the HOUSE OF REPRESENTATIVES in the US〔某国议会的〕下院〈如英国的下议院、美国的众议院〉

lower or·ders /ˌ··ˈ··/ *n old-fashioned* **the lower orders** an expression meaning people of a low social class, used especially by people who consider themselves to be better and more important【过时】下层社会〔尤为自视为上层社会的人所用〕

lowest com·mon de·nom·i·na·tor /ˌ··ˌ··ˈ····/ *n* [U] **1** *technical* the smallest number that the bottom numbers of a group of fractions (FRACTION (2)) can be divided into exactly【术语】最小公分母 **2** the biggest possible number of people, including people who are very easily influenced or are willing to accept low standards〔容易受影响或愿意接受低水准的〕社会大众: *Television quiz shows often seem to target the lowest common de-nominator.* 电视问答竞赛节目似乎经常以迎合大众的趣味为目标。

lowest com·mon mul·ti·ple /ˌ··ˌ··ˈ···/ *n* [C] *technical* the smallest number that two or more numbers divide into exactly【术语】最小公倍数: *12 is the lowest common multiple of 4 and 6.* 12是4和6的最小公倍数。

low-fat /ˌ·ˈ·◂/ *adj* containing or using only a small amount of fat 含脂肪少的; 低脂肪的: *a low-fat, high-fibre diet* 低脂肪高纤维膳食

low-fly·ing /ˌ·ˈ··◂/ *adj* flying close to the ground 低空飞行的

low gear /ˌ·ˈ·/ *n* [C,U] one of a vehicle's GEARs that you use when you are driving at a slow speed〔车辆的〕低速档, 低速齿轮传动装置

low-key /ˌ·ˈ·◂/ *adj* not intended to attract a lot of attention to an event, subject, or thing 低调的: *The reception was a low-key affair.* 那个招待会是一次低调的活动。| *a low-key approach to establishing women's rights* 确立妇女权利的低调处理方法

low·lands /ˈlolǝndz; ˈlǝʊlǝndz/ *n* [plural] an area of land that is lower than the land around it 低地: *the Scottish lowlands* 苏格兰低地—**lowland** *adj* [only before noun 仅用于名词前]: *lowland farming* 低地耕作—**lowlander** *n* [C] —compare 比较 HIGHLANDS

Low·lands, the /ˈlolǝndz; ˈlǝʊlǝndz/ the central part of Scotland which is lower than the land surrounding it 低地〔苏格兰中部, 海拔低于四周的土地〕—compare 比较 HIGHLANDS

low-lev·el /ˌ·ˈ··/ *adj* a low-level computer language is used to give instructions to a computer and is similar to the language that the computer operates in〔电脑语言〕低阶的, 低级的〔类似于电脑作业指令的〕—compare 比较 HIGH-LEVEL (4)

low life /ˈ· ·/ *n* **1** [U] the life and behaviour of people from a low social class, especially those who are involved in criminal activities 下层社会的生活〔尤指犯罪活动〕: *a novel about low life in Chicago in the 1930s* 描写20世纪30年代芝加哥下层社会生活的小说 **2** also 又作 **lowlife** [C] *AmE informal* someone who is involved in crime or who is bad【美, 非正式】罪犯; 恶棍: *Pete turned out to be a real lowlife.* 皮特原来是个十足的恶棍。—**low-life** *adj AmE informal*【美, 非正式】: *some low-life hooker Joe's taken up with* 某个和乔相好的低级妓女

low·lights /ˈloˌlaɪts; ˈlǝʊlaɪts/ *n* [plural] a dark colour that can be added to change the natural colour of some of your hair 深色染发剂 —compare 比较 **highlights** (HIGHLIGHT² (2))

low·ly /ˈloli; ˈlǝʊli/ *adj sometimes humorous* low in rank, importance, or social class; HUMBLE¹ (1)【有时幽默】〔等级、重要性或社会地位等〕低下的, 低级的; 卑微的: *He had left his lowly origins far behind.* 他已经彻底摆脱了低微的出身。| *Don't ask me, I'm just a lowly cleaner.* 别问我, 我只不过是一个普通的清洁工人。—**lowliness** *n* [U]

low-ly·ing /ˌ·ˈ··◂/ *adj* **1** low-lying land is not far above the level of the sea〔土地〕高出海面不多的 **2** below the usual level 低于一般水平的: *low-lying mist* 低层的雾

low-paid /ˌ·ˈ·◂/ *adj* providing or earning only a small amount of money 薪水低的: *low-paid jobs in catering* 饮食行业的低薪工作

low-pitched /ˌ·ˈ·◂/ *adj* **1** a low-pitched musical note or sound is deep〔音符〕低音的;〔声音〕低沉的: *the low-pitched hum of the generator* 发电机低沉的嗡嗡声 **2** a low-pitched roof is not steep〔屋顶〕不陡的, 缓坡的

low point /ˈ· ·/ *n* [C usually singular 一般用单数] the worst moment of a situation or activity〔情况或活动〕最糟的时刻: *For him, the low point came with a phone call from the police.* 对他来说, 最糟糕的时刻是警察打来电话那一刻。

low-pressure /ˌ·ˈ··/ *n* [U] a condition of the air over a large area that affects the weather 低气压

low pro-file /ˌ·ˈ··/ *n* **keep a low profile** to be careful not to attract attention to yourself or your actions 保持低姿态: *We'd better keep a low profile until the whole thing blows over.* 我们最好保持低调直到整件事情过去。—**low-profile** *adj*: *a low-profile campaign* 低姿态的〔竞选〕活动

low-rid-er /ˋloraɪdɚ; ˈləʊraɪdə/ *n* [C] *AmE* a big car that has its bottom very close to the ground, or a young man who drives this type of car【美】低底盘轿车; 年轻的低底盘轿车驾驶者

low-rise /ˈ· ·/ *adj* [only before noun 仅用于名词前] a low-rise building does not have many STOREYs〔建筑物〕层数少的 —compare 比较 HIGH-RISE

low-risk /ˌ·ˈ·◂/ *adj* [only before noun 仅用于名词前] likely to be safe or without difficulties 低风险的: *a low-risk investment* 低风险投资

Low·ry /ˋlaʊrɪ; ˈlaʊri/, **L. S.** (1887-1976) a British painter known for his scenes from the industrial North of England showing factories and crowds of small thin people (called matchstick men) rushing about. He used a very simple style of painting, and he especially combined the use of white and grey. 劳里〔(1887-1976), 英国画家。其作品以反映英格兰北部工业区的场景而著称, 画中有工厂及身材瘦小、到处奔波的"火柴棒式"人物。他的绘画风格十分简洁, 多用灰白混合色〕

low sea·son /ˈ· ˌ··/ *n BrE* the time of year when there is the least business for hotels, shops etc; OFF-SEASON【英】〔旅馆、商店等的营业〕淡季 —compare 比较 HIGH SEASON

low-spir·it·ed /ˌ·ˈ···◂/ *adj* unhappy; DEPRESSED (1) 闷闷不乐的, 没精打采的, 情绪消沉的: *He was a dull, low-spirited companion.* 他是一个乏味而无精打采的伙伴。

Low Sun-day /ˌ·ˈ··/ the Sunday following Easter 复活节后的第一个星期日

low-tech /ˌ·ˈ·◂/ *adj* not using the most modern machines or methods in business or industry〔商业或工业〕低技术的, 技术简单的 —opposite 反义词 HIGH-TECH

low tide /ˌ·ˈ·/ *n* [C,U] the time when sea water is at its lowest level〔海水的〕低潮(时间): *You can walk across to the island at low tide.* 在低潮时你可以走到对面的岛上。—opposite 反义词 HIGH TIDE (1)

low wa·ter /ˌ·ˈ··/ *n* [U] the time when the water in a river or the sea is at its lowest level because of the TIDE[1] (1)〔河、海的〕低水位, 低潮

low water mark /ˌ·ˈ·· ˌ·/ *n* [C] **1** a mark showing the lowest level reached by a river or other area of water 低潮线, 低水位线 **2** the worst time in someone's life, job etc〔某人生活或工作等中〕最不顺利的时期, 最低点: *Our fortunes had reached their low water mark.* 我们的时运到了最倒霉的时候。

lox /lɑks; lɒks/ *n* [U] *especially AmE* SALMON that has been treated with smoke in order to preserve it【尤美】熏鲑鱼, 熏大麻哈鱼

loy·al /ˋlɔɪəl; ˈlɔɪəl/ *adj* always supporting your friends, principles, country etc〔对…〕忠贞的, 忠实的, 忠诚的: [+to] *Dennis will always be loyal to this government, whatever it does.* 无论这届政府做什么, 丹尼斯都对它忠贞不渝。| *a loyal supporter of the team* 球队的忠实支持者—**loyally** *adv*

Loyalist *n* [C] **1** a Protestant in Northern Ireland who believes that it should remain part of the UK. The people who want Northern Ireland to become part of the Republic of Ireland are called 'Republicans' or 'Nationalists'. 效忠派〔指不赞成北爱尔兰脱离英国的北爱尔兰新教徒。主张北爱尔兰归属爱尔兰共和国者称"共和派"或"民族派"〕 **2** someone who was loyal to the royal family during the English Civil War〔英国内战时期〕效忠于王室的人 **3** someone who supported the elected government during the Spanish Civil War〔西班牙内战时期〕忠于共和政府的人 **4** someone who fought with the British during the American Revolutionary War〔美国独立战争期间〕亲英分子 **5** someone who supported the Union during the American Civil War〔美国独立战争期间〕支持联邦政府的人—**Loyalist** *adj*: *the Loyalist flag* 效忠派的旗帜

loy·al·ist /ˋlɔɪəlɪst; ˈlɔɪəlɪst/ *n* [C] someone who continues to support a government or country, when a lot of people want to change it〔支持某政府或国家的〕忠诚分子—**loyalist** *adj*

loy·al·ty /ˋlɔɪəltɪ; ˈlɔɪəlti/ *n* **1** [U] the quality of remaining faithful to your friends, principles, country etc 忠诚, 忠贞: [+to/towards] *These people feel a lot of loyalty to the company.* 这些人都对公司忠心耿耿。**2** [C usually plural 一般用复数] a feeling of support for someone or something 忠心, 忠于…的感情: *Don't let political loyalties affect your judgment.* 不要让政治倾向影响你的判断。| **divided loyalties** (=two strong feelings of loyalty that you must choose between) 相互抵触的忠诚 *the agony of divided loyalties for the children in a divorce* 离婚中孩子左右为难的痛苦

Loyola, St Ignatius (of) —see 见 ST IGNATIUS OF LOYOLA

loz·enge /ˋlɑzɪndʒ; ˈlɒzɪndʒ/ *n* [C] **1** a small flat sweet, especially one that contains medicine〔含有药物的〕小块扁糖, 糖锭, 药糖: *a cough lozenge* 止咳糖 **2** a shape similar to a square, with two angles of less than 90° opposite each other and two angles of more than 90° opposite each other 菱形

LP /ˌɛl ˋpi; ˌel ˈpiː/ *n* [C] long playing record; a record that turns 33 times per minute, and usually plays for between 20 and 25 minutes on each side 慢转[密纹]唱片

L-plate /ˋɛl plet; ˈel pleɪt/ *n* [C] a flat white square with a red letter L on it, that must be fixed to the back and front of a car being driven by a learner in Britain L字车牌, 学车牌〔在英国挂在学习驾驶者车辆的前后〕

LPO, the /ˌɛl pi ˋo; ˌel piː ˈəʊ/ the abbreviation of 缩写= the LONDON PHILHARMONIC ORCHESTRA

LRV /ˌɛl ɑr ˋvi; ˌel ɑː ˈviː/ *n* [C] Light Rail Vehicle; a type of train whose tracks run in or between streets, used especially in cities in the US〔尤指在美国城市中行走的〕轻轨火车

LSAT /ˌɛl ɛs e ˋti; ˌel es eɪ ˈtiː/ *n* Law School Admissions Test; an examination which must be passed by all students who want to attend a law school in the US 法律院校入学考试〔凡打算进入美国法律院校学习的学生必须通过的一种考试〕

LSD /ˌɛl ɛs ˋdi; ˌel es ˈdiː/ *n* [U] an illegal drug that makes you see things as more beautiful, strange, frightening etc than usual, or see things that do not exist; ACID[1] (2) 麦角酰二乙胺〔一种迷幻药〕

CULTURAL NOTE 文化注释

Drugs like LSD are sometimes called PSYCHEDELIC drugs, and are especially connected in people's minds with the HIPPIE period of the 1960s and 1970s. 麦角酰二乙胺之类的药物有时被称为迷幻药, 人们从这些药尤其会联想到20世纪60、70年代的嬉皮士时代。

Lsd, £sd /ˌɛl ɛs ˋdi; ˌel es ˈdiː/ *n* [U] *BrE old-fashioned*【英, 过时】**1** the abbreviation of 缩写= pounds, SHILLINGs, and pence, the system of money used in Britain before 1971 英镑, 先令和便士〔1971年前英国使用的货币体系〕**2** money 钱

LSE, the /ˌɛl ɛs ˋi; ˌel es ˈiː/ the abbreviation of 缩写= the LONDON SCHOOL OF ECONOMICS

LSO, the /ˌɛl ɛs ˋo; ˌel es ˈəʊ/ the abbreviation of 缩写= the LONDON SYMPHONY ORCHESTRA

Lt. the written abbreviation of 缩写= LIEUTENANT

Ltd the written abbreviation of 缩写= LIMITED (2), used in the names of companies or businesses 有限(责任)公司〔用于公司或企业名称〕: *M. Dixon & Son Ltd* 狄克逊父子有限公司 —compare 比较 INC, PLC

Luanda /luˋændə; luːˈændə/ the capital city of Angola 罗安达〔安哥拉首都〕

lu·bri·cant /ˋlubrɪkənt; ˈluːbrɪkənt/ *n* [C,U] a substance such as oil that you put on surfaces that rub together, especially parts of a machine, in order to make them move smoothly and easily 润滑剂[油]

lu·bri·cate /ˋlubrɪˌket; ˈluːbrɪkeɪt/ *v* [T] to put a lubricant on something in order to make it move more smoothly 使润滑, 给…加润滑剂[油]: *Lubricate all moving parts with grease.* 给所有活动部件加润滑油。—**lubrication** /ˌlubrɪˋkeʃən; ˌluːbrɪˈkeɪʃən/ *n* [U]

lu·bri·cious /luˋbrɪʃəs; luːˈbrɪʃəs/ *adj formal* too interested in sex, in a way that seems unpleasant or unacceptable【正式】淫荡的, 猥亵的—**lubriciously** *adv*

Luc·as /ˋlukəs; ˈluːkəs/, **George** (1944-) a US film DIRECTOR, PRODUCER, and film writer, who is most famous for making the Star Wars films. He also worked with Steven Spielberg to make *Raiders of the Lost Ark* (1981) and two other films about the character Indiana Jones. 卢卡斯〔(1944-), 美国电影导演、制片人和编剧, 以导演的《星球大战》系列影片闻名。他还与史蒂文·斯皮尔伯格合作拍摄了《夺宝奇兵》(1981) 和以印第安纳·琼斯为主角的另外两部影片〕

lu·cid /ˈlusɪd; ˈluːsɨ̣d/ *adj* **1** expressed in a way that is clear and easy to understand 表达清楚的，易于理解的：*a lucid and accurate account of the day's events* 对当日事件清楚而精确的描述 **2** a word meaning able to understand and think clearly, used especially about someone who is not always able to do this〔尤指总是迷迷糊糊的人〕神志还清醒的，头脑还清楚的：*In her more lucid moments the old lady would talk about her past.* 在头脑较清醒的时候，老太太会谈起她过去的事。—**lucidly** *adv* —**lucidity** /luˈsɪdətɪ; luːˈsɪdɨ̣ti/ *n* [U]

Lu·ci·fer /ˈlusəfə; ˈluːsɨ̣fə/ *n* the devil 魔王

luck¹ /lʌk; lʌk/ *n* [U]

1 ▶**GOOD FORTUNE** 好运◀ something good that happens by chance 好运，幸运：**have luck (with sth)** *Did you have any luck with the job application?* 你申请这份工作有什么进展吗？| *You're not having much luck today, are you?* 你今天运气欠佳，是不是？| **Good luck!/Best of luck!** *Good luck tomorrow in the exam!* 祝明天考试好运！| **wish sb luck** *Tom wished me luck in the race and left.* 汤姆祝我在比赛中好运，然后离开了。

2 ▶**CHANCE** 机会◀ the way in which good or bad things happen to people by chance 运气：*There's no skill in roulette, it's all a matter of luck.* 轮盘赌博没有什么技巧，完全是碰运气的事。| **good/bad luck** *We seem to have had a lot of bad luck lately.* 我们近来似乎噩运连连。| **sheer/pure luck** *It was sheer luck you were there to help.* 真是好运气，有你帮忙。

3 any luck? *spoken* used to ask someone if they have succeeded in doing something【口】做好了吗？成功了吗？：*"I phoned them about the car." "Any luck?" "Yes, it'll be ready on Tuesday."* "我给他们打电话讲汽车的事。""能弄好吗？""能，星期二就能弄好了。"

4 do sth for luck to do something because you think it might bring you good luck 为带来好运而做某事：*John always carried a rabbit's foot for luck.* 约翰总是带着一只兔脚，认为会带来好运。

5 be in luck to be able to do or get something, especially when you did not expect to〔出乎意料的〕走运：*We're in luck – the train hasn't gone yet.* 我们运气好——火车还没有开走。

6 be out of luck to be prevented from getting or doing something by bad luck 不走运：*I'm sorry, you're out of luck! I sold the last one this morning.* 对不起，你运气不好！最后一个我今天早上卖掉了。

7 just my luck! *spoken* used to say that you are not surprised something bad has happened to you, because you are usually unlucky【口】我总是运气不好！我总是不走运！：*He's married, is he? Just my luck!* 他已经结婚了，是不是？我总是不走运！

8 no such luck! *spoken* used to say you are disappointed, because something good that could have happened did not happen【口】没这样的运气！〔表示失望〕：*"Did you get a rise then?" "No such luck!"* "那么你得到加薪了吗？""没这样的运气！"

9 with (any) luck/with a bit of luck *spoken* if things happen in the way that you want; HOPEFULLY【口】要是走运的话；但愿：*With any luck, there'll be some food left.* 运气好的话，会有些食物剩下来。

10 better luck next time! used to say that you hope someone will be more successful the next time they try to do something〔祝某人〕下次好运些！

11 good luck to sb *spoken* used to say that you do not mind what someone does, because it does not affect you and may help them【口】祝某人好运〔用于表示不介意某人做的事，因不会受到影响，但对他有帮助〕：*Well if she wants to go on her own, good luck to her, but I'm staying here.* 好吧，如果她自己要去，祝她好运，但我会留在这里。

12 luck is on sb's side if luck is on someone's side, things go well for them 某人走运[交好运]：*Luck was on my side; all the traffic lights were green.* 我很走运，一路全是绿灯。

13 as luck would have it used to say that something happened by chance 碰巧：*As luck would have it, the bar was shut when we got there.* 真不巧，我们到的时候，酒吧已经关门了。

14 be down on your luck to have no money because you have had a lot of bad luck over a period of time〔因不走运而〕穷困潦倒：*You really find out who your friends are when you're down on your luck!* 在你穷困潦倒的时候，你才能发现谁是你的朋友！

15 the luck of the draw the result of chance rather than something you can control 碰运气的事：*You can't be sure of getting a ticket – it's all in the luck of the draw.* 你不可能保证买到票——这都是碰运气的事。

16 stroke of luck something very fortunate, happening by chance 真巧，真幸运：*What a stroke of luck, bumping into David in the street like that!* 真巧，就在街上碰到了戴维！

17 some people have all the luck! *spoken* used when someone else has got something that you would like【口】有些人运气就是好！〔用于别人得到你所喜爱的东西时〕：*Rich parents as well? Some people have all the luck!* 还有富有的父母？有些人真是运气好！

18 a run of bad luck a period of time when a lot of bad things happen to you 一段倒霉的日子

19 try/chance your luck to do something because you hope you will be successful, even though you know you may not be 碰碰运气：*The Hotel Europa was full, so we decided to try our luck elsewhere.* 欧罗巴酒店已经客满，所以我们决定到别处去碰碰运气。

20 bad/hard/tough luck! *spoken especially BrE* used to express sympathy when something unpleasant has happened to someone【口，尤英】真不幸！〔用于表示同情〕：*Oh bad luck! I'm sure you'll pass next time.* 哦，真不幸！我相信下次你会及格的。—compare 比较 **tough luck** (TOUGH¹ (7))

21 worse luck! *BrE spoken* unfortunately【英口】真倒霉！：*I've got to work this Saturday, worse luck!* 这个星期六我得工作，真倒霉！

22 (one) for luck *spoken* used when you take or add something for no particular reason【口】(取或加一个) 祈求好运〔用于无缘无故拿去或添加某物时〕

23 trust to luck to hope that things will happen in the way that you want, even though you cannot control them 靠运气〔希望得偿所愿〕：*I decided to just apply for the job and trust to luck for the rest.* 我决定去申请一下这份工作，剩下的事情就全靠运气了。—see also 另见 **hard-luck story** (HARD¹ (23)), **push your luck** (PUSH¹ (10))

luck² *v*

luck out *phr v* [I] *AmE informal* to be lucky【美，非正式】走运：*Yeah, we really lucked out, got a parking space right in front.* 是，我们真走运，正好前面有一个停车位。

luck·i·ly /ˈlʌkɪlɪ; ˈlʌkɨ̣li/ *adv* as a result of good luck 幸运地：*Luckily she can take a joke.* 幸而她经得起开玩笑。| **luckily for sb** *Luckily for us, the rain held off all day.* 我们真幸运，一整天没有下雨。

luck·less /ˈlʌklɪs; ˈlʌkləs/ *adj literary* having no luck in something you are trying to do【文】〔做某事而〕运气不好的，不幸的：*He died in the desert like so many other luckless explorers.* 他像许多不幸的探险者一样死在沙漠中。

luck·y /ˈlʌkɪ; ˈlʌki/ *adj* **1** having good luck; fortunate 运气好的；幸运的：**be lucky (enough) to do/be** *You were lucky to catch him in.* 你真幸运能在他家里碰见他。| *John was lucky enough to be selected for the team.* 约翰真幸运，能被选入球队。| **lucky (that)** *He's lucky he didn't break his neck.* 他幸好脖子没有断。| [+with] *We've been very lucky with the weather.* 我们很幸运，天气一直很好。| **think/count yourself lucky** *You can count yourself lucky he didn't hear you.* 算你幸运，他没听到你说什么。**2** resulting from good luck 由好运产生的：*I didn't really know your name – it was just a lucky guess.* 我真的不知道你的名字——只是碰运气猜中的。| *a lucky escape* 侥幸的逃脱 **3** bringing good luck 带来好运的，吉祥的：*a lucky charm* 吉祥饰物 **4 I/you should be so lucky!** *spoken* used to say that someone wants something that is unreasonable and not likely to happen【口】我/你没有那种福气！〔用于表示某人的要求不合理及不大可能实现〕：*You want a transfer to the London office? You should be so lucky!* 你想调到伦敦的办事处去工作？你没这运气！**5 lucky you/me etc!** *spoken* used to say that someone is fortunate to be able to do something【口】你/我等真幸运！〔指某人有幸能做某事〕：*"I'm going out tonight." "Lucky you."* "今晚我会外出！""你真幸运。" —see also 另见 **thank your lucky stars** (THANK (6)), **third time lucky** (THIRD¹)

> **CULTURAL NOTE 文化注释**
>
> Some people think it is lucky to find a FOUR-LEAVED CLOVER or to pick up a penny that you have found on the ground. Other people hang a horseshoe above the door to bring good luck. In the UK, people say that it is lucky if a black cat walks across your path, but in the US this is considered unlucky. 找到一片四叶苜蓿或从地上捡到一便士的硬币都会被有些人看作是好运的征兆。有人把一个马蹄铁悬挂在门上以祈求好运。在英国，如果有只黑猫从身前的路上穿过就会被人们说成会交好运，而这在美国则被认为是背运的事。— see also the Cultural Notes at SUPERSTITION, UNLUCKY 另见 SUPERSTITION, UNLUCKY 文化注释

lucky dip /ˌ··ˈ·/ *n BrE*【英】**1** [C] a game in which you put your hand into a container filled with small objects, and choose

one without looking 摸彩袋，运气袋; GRAB BAG (1) *AmE*【美】**2** [singular] a situation in which what happens depends on chance 由运气[机遇]来决定的事

Lucky Jim /ˌlʌkɪ ˋdʒɪm; ˌlʌki ˈdʒɪm/ (1954) a humorous NOVEL by Kingsley Amis about a young college LECTURER, Jim Dixon, who has modern political and social ideas, and has a lot of problems with the rather old-fashioned people that he works with《幸运的吉姆》〔(1954)，金斯利·艾米斯所著的一部幽默小说，描写一位大学讲师吉姆·狄克逊的故事。吉姆的政治观点和社会观念比较现代，遂与周围思想守旧的同事有种种摩擦〕

Lu·co·zade /ˈlukəzed; ˈluːkəzeɪd/ *trademark* a type of drink which contains GLUCOSE and is said to give people energy when they have been playing sports or when they have been ill【商标】葡萄适〔一种含葡萄糖的饮料。据说运动或生病期间喝此饮料可补充能量〕

lu·cra·tive /ˈlukrətɪv; ˈluːkrətɪv/ *adj* a job or activity that is lucrative lets you earn a lot of money; PROFITABLE〔职业或活动〕可赚大钱的; 盈利的: *Flynn had a lucrative contract at Warners.* 弗林在华纳公司有一份很赚钱的合同。

lu·cre /ˈlukɚ; ˈluːkə/ *n* **filthy lucre** money or wealth, used to show disapproval 肮脏钱，不义之财

Lu·cre·tius /luˈkriʃəs; luːˈkriːʃəs/ (?99-55 BC) a Roman PHILOSOPHER and poet, whose long poem *De rerum natura* (On the nature of things) discusses the nature of the universe 卢克莱修〔(公元前99年?-前55年)，罗马哲学家、诗人，以长诗《物性论》著称，诗中论及宇宙的本质〕

Lud·dite /ˈlʌdaɪt; ˈlʌdaɪt/ *n* [C] someone who is strongly opposed to using modern machines and methods 坚决反对使用现代机器、现代方法的人

lu·di·crous /ˈludɪkrəs; ˈluːdʒkrəs/ *adj* completely unreasonable, stupid, or unsuitable; RIDICULOUS 荒唐的，愚蠢荒谬的，可笑的: *She turned up wearing a ludicrous flowery hat.* 她戴着一顶可笑的花帽出现了。—**ludicrously** *adv*: *The test was ludicrously easy.* 这次测验是意想不到的容易。—**ludicrousness** *n* [U]

lu·do /ˈludo; ˈluːdəʊ/ *n* [U] *BrE trademark* a game played with COUNTERS (=small flat round objects) on a board【英，商标】鲁多〔一种用小的筹码在纸板上玩的游戏〕; PARCHEESI *AmE*【美】

Luft·waf·fe, the /ˈluftvɑfə; ˈlʊftwæfə/ the German Airforce, during World Wars I and II〔两次世界大战时期的〕德国空军

lug¹ /lʌg; lʌg/ **lugged, lugging** *v* [T] to pull or carry something heavy with difficulty 吃力地拖[拉]〔重物〕: **lug sth up/down/around etc** *I lugged my suitcase up the stairs and rang the bell.* 我费劲地拖着箱子上楼梯，按门铃。

lug² *n* [C] **1** a part of something that sticks out and can be used as a handle or a support〔用作柄、把手等的〕耳状物 **2** *BrE humorous* an ear; LUGHOLE【英，幽默】耳朵 **3** a LUGWORM 沙蠋 **4** *AmE old-fashioned* a rough, stupid, or awkward person【美，过时】笨拙的粗人: *You big lug!* 你这个大笨蛋!

luge /luʒ; luːʒ/ *n* [C] a vehicle with blades instead of wheels on which you slide down a track made of ice 仰卧滑行用的小雪橇

lug·gage /ˈlʌgɪdʒ; ˈlʌgɪdʒ/ *n* [U] the cases, bags etc carried by someone who is travelling 行李 —see also 另见 HAND LUGGAGE

luggage rack /ˈ· · ·/ *n* [C] a shelf in a train, bus etc for putting luggage on〔火车、公共汽车等内的〕行李架 —see picture at 参见 RACK¹ 图

luggage van /ˈ· · ·/ *n* [C] *BrE* the part of a train that boxes, cases etc are carried in【英】〔火车的〕行李车

lug·ger /ˈlʌgɚ; ˈlʌgə/ *n* [C] a small boat with one or more lugsails 有斜桁四角帆的小船

lug·hole /ˈlʌghol; ˈlʌghəʊl/ *n* [C] *BrE humorous* an ear【英，幽默】耳朵

Lu·go·si /luˈgosɪ; luˈgəʊsi/, **Bel·la** /ˈbɛlə; ˈbelə/ (1882-1956) a Hungarian born US actor, who became famous on Broadway for his role in *Dracula* (1927), which was made into a film in 1931. He had a heavy accent and often appeared in frightening films. 卢戈希〔(1882-1956)，生于匈牙利的美国演员，因出演《德拉库拉》(又译《吸血鬼》)(1927)而走红百老汇。该剧于1931年被搬上银幕。他说话口音很重，经常出演恐怖影片〕

lug·sail /ˈlʌgˌsel; ˈlʌgseɪl/ *n* [C] a four-sided sail that hangs down from a pole attached to the MAST (1) 斜桁四角帆

lu·gu·bri·ous /luˈgjubrɪəs; lʊˈguːbriəs/ *adj literary or humorous* very sad and serious【文或幽默】悲伤的，忧郁的: *a lugubrious voice* 悲哀的嗓音 —**lugubriously** *adv* —**lugubriousness** *n* [U]

lug·worm /ˈlʌgˌwɝm; ˈlʌgwɜːm/ *n* [C] a small WORM that lives in sand by the sea, often used to catch fish〔常用作钓饵的〕沙蠋

Luke /luk; luːk/, **Saint** one of Jesus Christ's DISCIPLES (=his close friends and followers). According to Bible stories, he was a doctor who wrote *The Gospel according to St Luke*, which describes the life and teaching of Jesus. 路加〔耶稣基督的门徒之一。据《圣经》故事记载，他曾当过医生，是《路加福音》的作者。《路加福音》记述耶稣的生平故事和传道历程〕

luke·warm /ˌlukˈwɔrm; ˌluːkˈwɔːm◂/ *adj* **1** food, liquid etc that is lukewarm is slightly warm and often not as hot or cold as it should be; TEPID〔食物、液体等〕微温的; 温热的: *Why do British people like lukewarm beer?* 为什么英国人喜欢喝温热的啤酒? —see picture at 参见 HOT¹ 图 **2** not showing much interest or excitement 不热心的，冷淡的: *His plan got only a lukewarm response from the committee.* 他的计划只得到委员会冷淡的反应。

lull¹ /lʌl; lʌl/ *v* [T] **1** to make someone feel calm or sleepy 使平静下来; 使昏昏欲睡: *The movement of the train gradually lulled me to sleep.* 火车的晃动渐渐使我入睡。**2** to make someone feel safe and confident so that they are completely surprised when you attack or cheat them 哄骗，使放松警惕: **lull sb into (doing) sth** *Felix's charm lulled me into believing he loved me.* 费利克斯的魅力骗得我相信他是爱我的。| **lull sb into a false sense of security** (=make someone think they are safe when they are not) 骗某人产生一种虚假的安全感

lull² *n* [C] **1** a short period of time when there is less activity or less noise than usual〔活动或吵声的〕暂停期，暂时平静期: **[+in]** *a brief lull in the conversation* 谈话短暂的停止 | *a lull in the fighting* 战斗的间歇期 **2 the lull before the storm** a short period of time when things are calm that is followed by a lot of activity, noise, or trouble 暴风雨到来前短暂的平静

lul·la·by /ˈlʌləˌbaɪ; ˈlʌləbaɪ/ *n* [C] a slow, quiet song sung to children to make them go to sleep 催眠曲，摇篮曲

lu·lu /ˈlulu; ˈluːluː/ *n* [C] *AmE informal*【美，非正式】**1** something very good or exciting 出众之物，令人兴奋的事: *The roller coaster at Magic Mountain is a real lulu.* 魔山的过山车真是妙极了。**2** something extremely silly, bad, embarrassing etc 极傻[糟糕，尴尬]的事: *She's said some stupid things in her life, but that one was a real lulu!* 她一生中说了不少傻话，而那一回真是傻透了!

lum·ba·go /lʌmˋbego; lʌmˈbeɪgəʊ/ *n* [U] pain in the lower part of the back 腰痛

lum·bar /ˈlʌmbɚ; ˈlʌmbə/ *adj technical* related to the lower part of the back【术语】腰部的: *pain in the lumbar region* 腰部疼痛

lum·ber¹ /ˈlʌmbɚ; ˈlʌmbə/ *v* **1** [I always+adv/prep] to move in a slow, awkward way 慢而笨拙地移动: **[+after/into/along etc]** *Mrs Moffat lumbered over to us, complaining about her arthritis.* 莫法特太太艰难地走过来，跟我们诉说得关节炎的痛苦。**2** [T] *informal* to give someone a job or responsibility that they do not want【非正式】让〔某人〕做不愿意做的事[接受不愿要的责任]: **get/be lumbered with** *As usual, Joe got lumbered with the babysitting.* 照例，乔被迫接受照料小孩的工作。**3** [I] *AmE* to cut down trees to make TIMBER (1)【美】伐木制材

lumber² *n* [U] **1** *BrE informal* large objects that are no longer useful or wanted【英，非正式】废旧的笨重物品 **2** trees that have been cut down to be used as wood; TIMBER (1) 木材，木料

lumberjack 伐木工人

lum·ber·jack /ˈlʌmbɚˌdʒæk; ˈlʌmbədʒæk/ *n* [C] someone whose job is cutting down trees for wood 伐木工人

lumber jack·et /ˈ· ·ˌ· ·/ *n* [C] a thick wool jacket, often with a CHECK² (5) pattern〔常有方格图案的〕厚毛夹克

lum·ber·man /ˈlʌmbɚmən; ˈlʌmbəmən/ *n* [C] someone whose job is cutting down trees or selling wood 伐木工人; 木材商

lum·ber·mill /ˈlʌmbɚmɪl; ˈlʌmbəmɪl/ *n* [C] *AmE* a building where trees are cut up to make wood【美】木材厂，锯木厂；SAWMILL *BrE*【英】

lumber room /ˈ··· ·/ *n* [C] *BrE* a room where old furniture, broken machines etc are kept【英】废旧物品堆藏室

lum·ber·yard /ˈlʌmbɚˌjɑrd; ˈlʌmbəjɑːd/ *n* [C] *AmE* a place where wood is kept before it is sold【美】〔售前堆放木料的〕木材场

Lu·mi·ère Broth·ers, the /ˌlumɪˈɛr ˌbrʌðɚz; ˈluːmieə ˌbrʌðəz/ two French brothers, **Auguste Lumière** (1862-1954) and **Louis Lumière** (1864-1948) who, in 1895, produced the first camera that was also a PROJECTOR, and made the first cinema film, *Workers Leaving the Lumière Factory*. 吕米埃兄弟〔指奥古斯塔·吕米埃(1862-1954)和路易·吕米埃(1864-1948)这一对法国兄弟。他们于1895年研制出世界上首台兼有投影仪功能的摄像机，拍摄了有史以来第一部电影，名为《工人们离开吕米埃工厂》〕

lu·mi·na·ry /ˈluməˌnɛrɪ; ˈluːmɪ̇nəri/ *n* [C] someone who is very famous or highly respected for their skill at, or knowledge of, a particular subject 名人，杰出人物：*luminaries of the women's movement* 妇女运动的杰出人物

lu·mi·nous /ˈlumənəs; ˈluːmɪ̇nəs/ *adj* **1** made of a substance or material that shines in the dark 发光的；夜明的：*luminous paint* 发光涂料 | *luminous road signs* 发光路标 **2** very brightly coloured, especially in green, pink, or yellow 色彩鲜艳的〔尤指绿色、粉红色或黄色〕：*luminous socks* 色彩鲜艳的短袜 —**luminously** *adv* —**luminosity** /ˌluməˈnɑsətɪ; ˌluːmɪ̇ˈnɒsɪ̇ti/ *n* [U]

lum·me /ˈlʌmɪ; ˈlʌmi/ *interjection BrE old-fashioned* used to express surprise【英，过时】哎呀，啊〔表示惊讶〕

2 **lump**[1] /lʌmp; lʌmp/ *n* [C] **1** a small piece of something solid, without a particular shape〔不定形的〕块：*There were lumps in the sauce.* 酱汁中有粒状的东西。| [+of] *a lump of coal* 一块煤 —see picture on page A7 参见A7页图 **2** something small that sticks out from someone's skin or grows in their body, usually because of an illness〔一般因患病而在皮肤上凸起或在身体内长出的〕肿块：*Check monthly for lumps on your breasts.* 每月检查你乳房有没有肿块。**3** a small square block of sugar 小方块糖：*One lump or two?* 要一块还是两块方糖？**4** **bring a lump to sb's throat** to make someone feel as if they want to cry 使某人哽结欲泣：*The scene where Laddie dies brought a lump to my throat.* 拉迪死亡的场面使我哽结欲泣。**5** **take your lumps** *AmE informal* to accept the bad things that happen to you and not let them affect you【美，非正式】认倒霉：*Forget about it, Rob, you have to take your lumps and go on.* 忘了它吧，罗布，你只有认倒霉并继续干。**6** *BrE spoken* someone who is stupid, or CLUMSY (1)【英口】愚蠢的人，笨拙的人：*You stupid great lump!* 你这个大笨蛋！

lump[2] *v* **lump it** *informal* to accept a situation or decision you do not like because you cannot change it【非正式】无奈地接受，勉强同意：**like it or lump it** *I'm going to that party! Like it or lump it!* 我打算去参加那个聚会！不管喜欢还是不喜欢！

lump sth **together** *phr v* [T] to consider two or more different things as a single type or group, rather than individually or separately 把…合在一起考虑：*Pacifists, atheists and journalists were all lumped together as 'troublemakers'.* 和平主义者、无神论者和记者都被归为"惹是生非者"。

lump·ec·to·my /lʌmpˈɛktəmɪ; lʌmpˈektəmi/ *n* [C] an operation in which a TUMOUR is removed from someone's body, especially from a woman's breast〔尤指乳房〕肿瘤切除术

lump·ish /ˈlʌmpɪʃ; ˈlʌmpɪʃ/ *adj* awkward or stupid 笨拙的；愚钝的

lump sum /ˌ· ˈ·/ *n* [C] an amount of money given in a single payment 一次付款总额：*When you retire you'll get a lump sum of £80,000.* 当你退休时，你将得到一次总付80,000英镑。

lump·y /ˈlʌmpɪ; ˈlʌmpi/ *adj* covered with or containing small solid pieces 布满团块的；有团块的：*a lumpy mattress* 不平整的床垫

Lu·mum·ba /luˈmumbə; lʊˈmʊmbə/, **Pa·trice** /pəˈtris; pəˈtriːs/ (1925-61) a Congolese politician from the Democratic Republic of Congo (formerly Zaïre), who was his country's first Prime Minister after it became independent (1960). He was murdered by a political opponent. 卢蒙巴〔(1925-1961)，刚果民主共和国(旧称扎伊尔)政治家。1960年该国独立后，他成为首任总理，后被政敌谋杀〕

lu·na·cy /ˈlunəsɪ; ˈluːnəsi/ *n* [U] **1** a situation or behaviour that is completely crazy 疯狂的状态[行为]：**complete/sheer/pure lunacy** *It would be sheer lunacy to turn down an offer like that.* 拒绝那样的提议简直是发疯。**2** *old-fashioned* mental illness【过时】精神病，精神失常：*the cause of Hamlet's lunacy* 哈姆雷特精神失常的原因 —see also 另见 LUNATIC

lu·nar /ˈlunɚ; ˈluːnə/ *adj* connected with the moon or with travel to the moon 月球的；与前往月球有关的：*a lunar eclipse* 月食

lunar month /ˌ·· ˈ·/ *n* [C] a period of 28 or 29 days between one NEW MOON and the next 太阴月；阴历一个月

lu·na·tic /ˈlunəˌtɪk; ˈluːnətɪk/ *n* [C] **1** someone who behaves in a crazy or very stupid way 疯狂的人；愚笨的人：*You lunatic – you nearly drove straight into me!* 你这个蠢货——你差点(用车)撞我个正着！**2** *old-fashioned* someone who is mentally ill【过时】精神错乱的人，疯子：*a dangerous lunatic* 可能伤害他人的精神病人 **3** **the lunatic fringe** *BrE* the people in a political group or organization who have the most extreme opinions or ideas【英】〔政治团体或组织中的〕极端分子 —**lunatic** *adj*: *lunatic behaviour* 疯狂的行为

lunatic a·sy·lum /ˈ··· ·ˌ··/ *n* [C] *old-fashioned* a hospital where people who are mentally ill are cared for【过时】精神病院

lunch[1] /lʌntʃ; lʌntʃ/ *n* [C,U] **1** a meal eaten in the middle of the day 午餐：**at lunch** *Anna said something at lunch about leaving.* 安娜吃午餐时说了她要走的事。| **have lunch** *When do you usually have lunch?* 你通常什么时候吃午饭？| **have some lunch** *I'm starved. Let's have some lunch.* 我饿极了，我们吃点午餐吧。| **have sth for lunch** *All I had for lunch was a salad sandwich.* 我午餐只吃了一份沙拉三明治。| **take sb out to lunch** *He decided to take her out to lunch.* 他决定请她吃午饭。| **go to lunch** (=go somewhere to eat lunch) 去吃午餐 *Rory went to lunch in a small Italian restaurant.* 罗里到一家意大利小饭馆去吃午餐。| **a working lunch** (=when you discuss business and eat) 工作午餐 | **packed lunch** *BrE*【英】/**bag lunch** *AmE*【美】(=food, usually SANDWICHes, that you take with you to work, school etc)〔上班、上学等带的〕盒装午餐〔通常是三明治〕**2** **out to lunch** *informal* behaving in a strange and confused way【非正式】举止有点失常 1 2

lunch[2] *v formal*【正式】**1** [I] to eat lunch 吃午饭，用午餐 **2** [T] to buy someone lunch 给…买午餐

lunch·box /ˈlʌntʃˌbɑks; ˈlʌntʃbɒks/ *n* [C] a box in which food is carried to school, work etc〔带上学、上班等的〕午餐盒，便当

lunch break /ˈ· ·/ *n* [C] LUNCH HOUR 午餐时间

lunch·eon /ˈlʌntʃən; ˈlʌntʃən/ *n* [C,U] *formal* lunch【正式】午餐，午宴

luncheon meat /ˈ·· ·/ *n* [U] meat that has been cooked, then pressed down, and is often sold in a can 午餐肉

> **CULTURAL NOTE 文化注释**
>
> Luncheon meat was popular in the UK after World War II, but it is no longer considered to be a fashionable food. 在二战后的英国，午餐肉很受欢迎，但是现在它已经不再是流行食品。

luncheon vou·cher /ˈ·· ˌ··/ *n* [C] a special ticket sometimes given to people in Britain by their employers, that can be used to buy meals or food 餐券，膳食券〔英国一些雇主发给员工的特殊餐券，可用于用餐或购买食物〕

> **CULTURAL NOTE 文化注释**
>
> Luncheon vouchers are given to people such as office workers. Although useful, people do not consider them to be a desirable PERK (=something that you get legally from your work in addition to your wages). 餐券一般发给公司职员一类的人。尽管能用，但它并不是人们特别想要的补贴。

lunch hour /ˈ· ·/ *n* [C] the period of time in the middle of the day when people stop working in order to eat 午餐时间

lunch·room /ˈlʌntʃrum; ˈlʌntʃruːm/ *n* [C] *AmE* a large room in a school or office where people can eat【美】〔学校或办公室的〕餐厅，食堂 —compare 比较 CAFETERIA

lunch·time /ˈlʌntʃˌtaɪm; ˈlʌntʃtaɪm/ *n* [C,U] the time in the middle of the day when people usually eat their LUNCH 午餐时间：*a lunchtime drink* 午餐饮料 3

Lun·dy /ˈlʌndɪ; ˈlʌndi/ **1** a small island in the Bristol Channel in southwest England, which has many wild flowers and birds, especially PUFFINS 兰迪岛〔布里斯托尔海峡一小岛，位于英格兰西南部，岛上多野花和鸟类，尤其是海鹦〕**2** in shipping forecasts, an area of water which includes the Bristol Channel and the eastern part of the Atlantic Ocean between the Republic of Ireland and southwest England 兰迪〔海运天气预报中所指的一个海域，包括布里斯托尔海峡、爱尔兰共和国和英格兰西南部之间的大西洋东部海域〕

lung /lʌŋ; lʌŋ/ *n* [C] one of the two organs in your body that you breathe with 肺：*Smoking can cause lung cancer.* 吸烟会引起肺癌。—see also 另见 IRON LUNG —see picture at 参见 RESPIRATORY 图

lunge /lʌndʒ; lʌndʒ/ *v* [I] to make a sudden strong movement towards someone or something, especially using your arm and to attack them 突然向前冲[扑等]〔尤指袭击某人或某物〕: [**+forwards/at/towards**] *They both lunged forwards to catch the ball.* 他们俩都冲上去抓球。 —**lunge** *n* [C]: *Brad made a lunge towards his opponent, but missed.* 布拉德扑向对手, 但没有打着。

lunk·head /ˈlʌŋk,hɛd; ˈlʌŋkhed/ *n* [C] *AmE informal* someone who is very stupid【美, 非正式】笨蛋, 傻瓜

lu·pin *BrE*【英】, **lupine** *AmE*【美】/ˈlupɪn; ˈluːpɪn/ *n* [C] a plant with a tall stem and many small flowers 羽扇豆

lurch¹ /lɝtʃ; lɜːtʃ/ *v* [I] **1** to move suddenly forwards or sideways, usually because you cannot control your movements 蹒跚而行, 东倒西歪地走: [**+across/into/along etc**] *Frank lurched back to his seat.* 弗兰克踉踉跄跄地走回自己的座位。| *The car lurched forward across the grass.* 汽车东歪西扭地穿过了草地。**2 your heart/stomach lurches** used to say that your heart or stomach seems to move as you suddenly feel shocked, frightened etc〔因震惊、惊恐等而〕感到心跳/胃里翻腾 **3 lurch from one crisis to the next/lurch from one extreme to the other etc** to seem to have no plan and no control over what you are doing 感到束手无策, 无法控制局面

lurch² *n* [C] **1** a sudden movement forwards or sideways, usually made because you cannot control your body or a machine〔身体或机器〕突然的晃动: *The train gave a violent lurch.* 火车突然剧烈地晃了一下。**2 leave sb in the lurch** to leave someone at a time when you should stay and help them; DESERT² (1) 临危舍弃某人, 置某人于困难之中(而不顾)

lure¹ /lʊr; lʊə/ *v* [T] to persuade someone to do something, especially something wrong, by promising them something they want; TEMPT 引诱, 诱惑: **lure sb into/to/away etc** *I think he's trying to lure you away from Jerry.* 我认为他在试图诱骗你离开杰里。| *prospectors lured to Alaska by the promise of gold* 被黄金诱惑到阿拉斯加的淘金者

lure² *n* **1** [C usually singular 一般用单数] something that you think is attractive, or the power that something has to attract you 诱惑力, 吸引力: [**+of**] *Settlers were drawn to the West by the lure of free land.* 移民在自由土地的吸引下来到西部。**2** [C] a piece of equipment, such as a plastic bird or fish, used to attract animals or fish so that they can be caught; DECOY (2) 诱捕动物或鱼用的假鸟[假鱼]; 诱饵

Lu·rex /ˈlurɛks; ˈljʊəreks/ *n* [U] *trademark* a type of thread that looks like metal, usually gold or silver, used in material for making clothes【商标】卢勒克斯(金银纱)〔用于做衣服〕: *a gold Lurex top* 金纱织成的上装

lur·gy /ˈlɝgɪ; ˈlɜːgi/ *n* [singular] *BrE humorous* an illness, especially one that is infectious but not serious【英, 幽默】疾病〔尤指不严重的传染病〕: *Anne's got the dreaded lurgy.* 安妮得了那种可怕的疾病。

lu·rid /ˈlurɪd; ˈlʊərɪd/ *adj* **1** a description, story etc that is lurid is deliberately shocking and involves sex or violence 耸人听闻的, 可怕的〔指描述、故事等内容包括性或暴力〕: *lurid headlines* 骇人听闻的标题 | *He told me in lurid detail what would happen to me.* 他把将要发生在我身上的事告诉了我, 细节之处耸人听闻。**2** too brightly coloured; GAUDY 色彩耀眼的, 俗气的: *a lurid orange dress* 一件俗气的橘黄色连衣裙 —**luridly** *adv* —**luridness** *n* [U]

lurk /lɝk; lɜːk/ *v* [I always+adv/prep] **1** to wait somewhere quietly and secretly, usually because you are going to do something wrong 潜伏, 埋伏: [**+around/in/beneath etc**] *A man was lurking around outside the shop.* 一个男人潜伏在商店外面。**2** to exist almost without being seen or known about 暗藏, 潜藏: *childish fears that lurk in all our hearts* 藏在我们所有人心中的幼稚的恐惧

Lu·sa·ka /luˈsakə; luːˈsɑːkə/ the capital city of Zambia 卢萨卡〔赞比亚首都〕

lus·cious /ˈlʌʃəs; ˈlʌʃəs/ *adj* **1** extremely good to eat 甘甜的, 美味的: *a luscious peach* 甘甜的桃子 **2** *informal* a word meaning very sexually attractive, used especially by men【非正式】十分性感的〔尤为男士用语〕: *a luscious young starlet* 性感的年轻女明星

lush¹ /lʌʃ; lʌʃ/ *adj* **1** plants that are lush grow many leaves and look healthy and strong〔植物〕茂盛的, 繁茂的, 郁郁葱葱的: *lush tropical vegetation* 茂盛的热带草木 **2** very beautiful, comfortable, and expensive 华丽的, 舒适的, 昂贵的: *lush carpets* 华丽的地毯

lush² *n* [C] *AmE informal* an ALCOHOLIC【美, 非正式】酒鬼, 醉汉

Lu·si·ta·ni·a, the /,lusɪˈtenɪə; ,luːsɪˈteɪniə/ a British passenger ship that was sunk off the Irish coast in 1915 by the German navy during World War I. Some of the 1195 people who were killed were Americans, and this made many Americans feel that the US should enter the war against Germany. 卢西塔尼亚号〔英国一客轮。该轮船于1915年一战期间在爱尔兰近海被德国海军击沉, 1195人遇难, 其中部分是美国乘客。这一事件使许多美国人感到美国应参战抵抗德国〕

lust¹ /lʌst; lʌst/ *n* **1** [C,U] very strong sexual desire, especially when it does not include liking or love 强烈的性欲; 淫欲: *What Len felt for her was pure lust.* 莱恩对她只有肉欲而已。**2** [U +for] a very strong desire to have something, usually power or money 强烈的欲望〔通常指对权力或金钱的欲望〕: *hard-faced men driven by a lust for gain* 利欲熏心、麻木不仁的人

lust² *v*

lust after sb/sth *phr v* [T] *often humorous*【常幽默】**1** to be strongly sexually attracted to someone, and think about having sex with them 对〔某人〕有强烈的性欲: *He thinks I'm only lusting after his body!* 他以为我仅仅渴望与他发生肉体关系! **2** to want something very much, especially something that you do not really need 对〔某物〕有强烈欲望, 贪恋〔尤指并不真正需要的东西〕: *This is the shop for those of you lusting after designer clothes.* 这家店是为那些追求名牌服装的人而开的。

lus·ter /ˈlʌstɚ; ˈlʌstə/ *n* [singular, U] the American spelling of LUSTRE lustre 的美式拼法

lust·ful /ˈlʌstfəl; ˈlʌstfəl/ *adj* feeling or showing strong sexual desire 色欲的, 好色的: *a jealous, lustful man* 妒忌心强的好色男子 —**lustfully** *adv*: *Max stared at her lustfully.* 马克斯色迷迷地盯着她看。

lus·tre *BrE*【英】, **luster** *AmE*【美】/ˈlʌstɚ; ˈlʌstə/ *n* [singular, U] **1** an attractive shiny appearance 光泽, 光亮: **add/give lustre to** *A little conditioner will give lustre to your hair.* 用一点护发素会给你的头发带来光泽。**2** the quality that makes something interesting or exciting 出色, 光彩: **add/give luster to** *Arnold's singing will add lustre to the affair.* 阿诺德的演唱将会给这个活动增添光彩。

lus·trous /ˈlʌstrəs; ˈlʌstrəs/ *adj* shining in a soft, gentle way 有光泽的, 光亮的: *lustrous black hair* 光亮的黑发

lust·y /ˈlʌstɪ; ˈlʌsti/ *adj* strong and healthy; powerful 健壮的; 强有力的: *The baby gave a lusty cry.* 婴儿发出洪亮的哭声。| *lusty young men* 强壮的小伙子 —**lustily** *adv*: *cheering lustily* 纵情欢呼 —**lustiness** *n* [U]

lute /lut; luːt/ *n* **1** [C] a musical instrument similar to a GUITAR with a round body, played especially in former times 鲁特琴〔旧时的一种类似吉他的圆形拔弦乐器, 琴身圆形〕 **2** [U] *technical* a type of clay or CEMENT used to fill holes or cracks【术语】封泥〔封堵洞穴或裂缝的黏土或水泥〕

Lu·ther /ˈluθɚ; ˈluːθə/, **Martin** (1483-1546) a German religious leader whose ideas have had great influence on religion in Europe. In 1517, he started the Reformation (=the time when many Christians in Europe left the Catholic religion and started the Protestant religion) by writing his *95 Theses*, in which he criticized the Catholic religion. He also translated the Bible from Latin into German. 路德〔(1483-1546), 德国宗教领袖。他的思想对欧洲宗教产生了重要的影响。1517年, 他写成《九十五条论纲》, 对天主教进行了抨击, 引发宗教改革运动。他还把拉丁文《圣经》翻译成德文〕

Lu·ther·an /ˈluθərən; ˈluːθərən/ *n* [C] a member of the church that follows the teachings and ideas of Martin Luther 路德会教徒 —**Lutheran** *adj*

Lu·ther·an·is·m /ˈluθrənɪzəm; ˈluːθərənɪzəm/ *n* [U] the beliefs or practice of that branch of the Protestant church which is based on the teachings of Martin Luther, especially the belief that SALVATION can be gained by faith alone 路德主义〔基于马丁·路德学说的新教派思想和宗教形式, 尤其相信得救的唯一途径就是信仰〕

luv /lʌv; lʌv/ *n BrE informal* an informal way of spelling LOVE when it is used to address someone【英, 非正式】〔love 的非正式拼法, 用于称呼某人〕: *Come on, luv, don't cry.* 得啦, 亲爱的, 别哭了。

luv·vie /ˈlʌvɪ; ˈlʌvi/ *n BrE*【英】**1** another spelling of LOVEY lovey 的另一种拼法 **2** [C] *informal* an actor or actress who behaves to other people in a very friendly way that is not sincere【非正式】〔假装友善的〕演员

Lux·em·bourg, Luxemburg /ˈlʌksəm,bɝg; ˈlʌksəmbɜːg/ a small country in western Europe, surrounded by Belgium, Germany, and France. Capital: Luxembourg-Ville. Population: 442,972 (2001). Luxembourg is a member of the EU, and its official name is the **Grand Duchy of Luxembourg** The EU's main law court, the European Court of Justice, is in Luxembourg. 卢森堡〔西欧一小国, 与比利时、德国和法国接壤。首都: 卢森堡

市，人口：442,972（2001）。该国是欧盟成员国，正式国名为卢森堡大公国。欧盟的主要法庭——欧洲法庭就设在卢森堡〕—**Luxembourger** *n*

Lux·em·burg /ˈlʌksəmˌbɝg; ˈlʌksəmbɜːg/, **Ro·sa** /ˈrozə; ˈrəʊzə/ (1871-1919) a German socialist leader, born in Poland. In 1892 she helped to start the Polish Socialist Party, and later the **Spartacus League**, a political group which became the German Communist Party. She was killed by soldiers during a protest organized by the Spartacus League. 卢森堡〔（1871-1919），德国社会党领袖，生于波兰。1892年，她协助创建了波兰社会民主党。后来，她又组建了斯巴达克斯联盟，即德国共产党的前身。她在斯巴达克斯联盟组织的一次抗议活动中遭士兵杀害〕

Lux·or /ˈlʌksɔr; ˈlʌksɔː/ a city in Egypt on the east bank of the River Nile, famous for its ancient TEMPLES (=holy buildings) 卢克索〔埃及一城市，位于尼罗河东岸，以古庙宇闻名〕

lux·u·ri·ant /lʌgˋʒʊrɪənt; lʌgˈzjʊəriənt/ *adj* **1** growing strongly and thickly 茂盛的，浓密的：*a luxuriant black beard* 浓密的黑胡子 | *luxuriant vegetation* 茂盛的草木 **2** giving a rich effect 华丽的：*luxuriant prose* 词藻华丽的散文 —**luxuriantly** *adv* —**luxuriance** *n* [U]

lux·u·ri·ate /lʌgˋʒʊrɪˌet; lʌgˈzjʊərieɪt/ *v*
luxuriate in sth *phr v* [T] to relax and consciously enjoy something 尽情享受：*Melanie was luxuriating in the sunshine when they arrived.* 当他们来到的时候，梅拉妮正在尽情享受阳光。

lux·u·ri·ous /lʌgˋʒʊrɪəs; lʌgˈzjʊəriəs/ *adj* very expensive, beautiful, and comfortable 奢华的，华丽的，舒适的：*The bathroom was luxurious, with gold taps and a thick carpet.* 浴室很奢华，配有金水龙头和厚地毯。—**luxuriously** *adv* —**luxuriousness** *n* [C]

lux·u·ry /ˈlʌkʃərɪ; ˈlʌkʃəri/ *n* **1** [U] very great comfort and pleasure, such as you get from expensive food, beautiful houses, cars etc 奢华，奢侈：*Caviar for breakfast! I was not used to such luxury.* 早餐吃鱼子酱！我不习惯这种奢侈！| **a life of luxury** *They led a life of luxury, in a huge house in the countryside.* 他们在乡村的大宅子里过着奢华的生活。| **luxury apartment/flat/car etc** (=expensive and large) 豪华的房间/套房/汽车等 **2** [C] something expensive that you do not need, but you buy for pleasure and enjoyment 奢侈品：*We can't afford luxuries like piano lessons any more.* 我们再也负担不起像上钢琴课这样奢侈的事。—see also 另见 **in the lap of luxury** (LAP[1] (4)) —compare 比较 NECESSITY (1)

LW the written abbreviation of 缩写＝ LONG WAVE

-ly /lɪ; li/ *suffix* **1** [in adverbs 构成副词] in a particular way 以某种方式：*He did it very cleverly.* (=in a clever way) 这件事他做得很聪明。| *walking slowly* 缓慢地走 **2** [in adverbs 构成副词] considered in a particular way 从某方面来考虑的：*Politically speaking it was a rather unwise remark.* 从政治上来讲，这是相当愚蠢的评论。| *a financially sound proposal* 财务上可行的建议 **3** [in adjectives and adverbs 构成形容词和副词] happening at regular periods of time 定期发生的：*an hourly check* (=done every hour) 每小时一次的检查 | *They visit monthly.* (=once a month) 他们每个月探望一次。**4** [in adjectives 构成形容词] like a particular thing in manner, nature, or appearance 举止像…的；有…态度[外貌]的：*with queenly grace* 有女王般的优雅风度 | *a motherly woman* (=showing the love, kindness etc of a mother) 慈母般的妇女

ly·ce·um /laɪˋsiəm; laɪˈsiːəm/ *n* [C] *AmE old-fashioned* a building used for public meetings, concerts, speeches etc【美，过时】〔举行公众会议、音乐会或演讲等的〕演讲厅，音乐厅，会堂

ly·chee, litchi /ˈlitʃi; ˈlaɪtʃiː/ *n* [C] a small round fruit with a rough pink-brown shell outside and sweet white flesh inside 荔枝 —see picture on page A8 参见A8页图

lych·gate, lichgate /ˈlɪtʃˌget; ˈlɪtʃgeɪt/ *n* [C] a gate with a roof leading into the area surrounding a church 通向教堂周围庭院的有顶的门道

Ly·cra /ˈlaɪkrə; ˈlaɪkrə/ *n* [U] *trademark* a material that stretches, used especially for making tight-fitting sports clothes【商标】莱卡〔弹性织物，尤用于制造紧身运动服〕

ly·ing /ˈlaɪɪŋ; ˈlaɪ-ɪŋ/ the present participle of LIE[1]

lying-in /ˌ·· ˈ·/ *n* [singular] *old-fashioned* the period of time during which a woman stays in bed before and after the birth of a child; CONFINEMENT (2)【过时】产褥期，产期

lying in state /ˌ··· ˈ·/ *n* [singular] the period of time when people can come and see the body of someone such as a president or king who has died, to show their respect〔总统或国王等死后的〕遗容瞻仰期

Lyme dis·ease /ˈlaɪm dɪˌziz; ˈlaɪm dɪˌziːz/ *n* [U] a serious illness that is caused by a bite from a TICK[1] (2) 莱姆病〔由蜱叮咬引起的一种严重疾病〕

Lyme Re·gis /ˌlaɪm ˋridʒəs; ˌlaɪm ˈriːdʒɪs/ a town in Dorset on the south coast of England, where there are many FOSSILS (=ancient plants and animals preserved in rock). It was a fashionable place for people to visit in the 19th century. 莱姆里杰斯〔英格兰南部沿海多塞特郡一城镇，以古化石而知名。19世纪时，该镇曾是旅游胜地〕

lymph /lɪmf; lɪmf/ *n* [U] a clear liquid that is formed in your body and passes into your blood system 淋巴 —**lymphatic** /lɪmˋfætɪk; lɪmˈfætɪk/ *adj*

lymph gland /ˈ· ·/ *n* [C] a lymph node 淋巴结，淋巴腺

lymph node /ˈ· ·/ *n* [C] a small rounded SWELLING in your body through which lymph passes to be made pure before entering your blood system 淋巴结

lynch /lɪntʃ; lɪntʃ/ *v* [T] if a crowd of people lynches someone, they HANG[1] (3) them as a punishment, without using the usual legal process〔一伙人〕用私刑绞死〔某人作为惩罚〕：*At that time you could be lynched for being black.* 那时候你可能会因为是黑人而被私刑绞死。—**lynching** *n* [C]

CULTURAL NOTE 文化注释

Many people think of lynching in the context of the American Wild West and with the illegal killing of African Americans in the South by the Ku Klux Klan or a MOB. 很多人想到用私刑将人绞死，就会联想到美国的荒蛮西部以及南方的三K党和暴徒非法杀害黑人的往事。

Lynch /lɪntʃ; lɪntʃ/, **David** (1946-), a US film DIRECTOR famous for making unusual and violent films such as *Blue Velvet* (1986). His other films include *The Elephant Man* (1980) and *Wild at Heart* (1990). He also made the CULT television programme *Twin Peaks*. 林奇〔（1946-），美国电影导演，以导演的《蓝丝绒》（1986）等诡异和暴力影片闻名。他导演的其他影片包括《象人》（1980）、《我心狂野》（1990）等。他还导演了风靡一时的电视连续剧《双峰》〕

lynch mob /ˈ· ·/ *n* [singular] a group of people that kills someone by hanging (HANG[1] (3)) them, without a legal TRIAL[1] (1) 实施私刑的暴民

lynchpin /ˈlɪntʃˌpɪn; ˈlɪntʃpɪn/ *n* [C] another spelling of LINCHPIN linchpin的另一种拼法

lynx /lɪŋks; lɪŋks/ *n* [C] a large wild cat that has no tail and lives in forests 猞猁；BOBCAT *AmE*【美】

Ly·ons /liˋɑn; ˈliːɒŋ/ the capital city of the department of the Rhône in east central France. Its correct French name is **Lyon**. 里昂〔法国中东部罗纳省省会，法文的正确拼法为Lyon〕

lyre /laɪr; laɪə/ *n* [C] a musical instrument with strings across a U-shaped frame, used especially in ancient Greece 里拉琴〔古希腊的一种弦乐器，琴身为U形〕

lyre·bird /ˈlaɪrˌbɝd; ˈlaɪəbɜːd/ *n* [C] a bird with a long U-shaped tail, that lives in Australia 琴鸟〔产于澳大利亚，有U形长尾〕

lyr·ic[1] /ˈlɪrɪk; ˈlɪrɪk/ *adj* [only before noun 仅用于名词前] expressing strong personal emotions such as love, in a way that is similar to music in its sounds and RHYTHM (1) 抒情的：*Wordsworth was one of the greatest lyric poets of his time.* 华兹华斯是他那个时代最伟大的抒情诗人之一。

lyric[2] *n* **1 lyrics** [plural] the words of a song, especially a modern popular song〔尤指现代流行歌曲的〕歌词：*music and lyrics by the Gershwin brothers* 格什温兄弟创作的歌曲和歌词 **2** [C] *technical* a poem, usually a short one, written in a lyric style【术语】抒情诗〔通常为短诗〕

lyr·i·cal /ˈlɪrɪkl; ˈlɪrɪkəl/ *adj* **1** beautifully expressed in words, poetry, or music 像诗歌[音乐]般抒情的：*Lawrence's lyrical descriptions of the natural world* 劳伦斯对自然界抒情诗般的描写 **2 wax lyrical** to talk about and praise something in a very eager way 热情地谈论[赞美]：*Simon waxed lyrical on the joys of hill-walking.* 西蒙兴高采烈地谈论爬山的乐趣。—**lyrically** /-klɪ; -kli/ *adv*

lyr·i·cis·m /ˈlɪrəˌsɪzəm; ˈlɪrɪsɪzəm/ *n* [U] the romantic or song-like expression of something in writing or music〔写作或音乐的〕抒情风格，抒情性

lyr·i·cist /ˈlɪrəsɪst; ˈlɪrɪsɪst/ *n* [C] someone who writes the words for songs, especially modern popular songs〔尤指现代流行歌曲的〕歌词作者

Ly·sis·trat·a /ˌlɪsəˋstrɑtə; laɪˈsɪstrətə/ the main character in the humorous ancient Greek play *Lysistrata* by Aristophanes. Lysistrata and the other women in Athens are angry because their husbands are fighting in a long war. Lysistrata organizes a protest, and the women refuse to have sex with their husbands until there is peace. 吕西斯忒拉忒〔阿里斯托芬创作的古希腊喜剧《吕西斯忒拉忒》中的主人公。她和雅典的其他妇女一样因丈夫参加一场旷日持久的战争而恼怒。于是，她组织妇女进行抗议，拒绝与丈夫同床，直至赢得和平〕

L

M,m

M, m /ɛm; em/ *plural* **M's, m's** *n* [C] **1** the 13th letter of the English alphabet 英语字母表的第十三个字母 **2** the number 1000 in the system of ROMAN NUMERALs〔罗马数字系统中的〕1000

M *BrE*【英】the abbreviation of 缩写= MOTORWAY: *M25* 25号高速公路 | *M1* 1号高速公路

m the written abbreviation of 缩写= **a)** metre **b)** mile **c)** million **d)** male **e)** married **f)** medium

M1 /ˌɛm ˋwʌn; ˌem ˈwʌn◂/ a British MOTORWAY (=large, fast road) that goes from London to Leeds in the north of England 1号高速公路〔英国一高速公路, 连接伦敦和英格兰北部的利兹〕

M25 /ˌɛm twɛntɪˋfaɪv; ˌem twentiˈfaɪv◂/ a British MOTORWAY (=large, fast road) that goes all around London, which is also called the London Orbital on signs 25号高速公路〔英国伦敦一环城高速公路。路标上也称London Orbital (伦敦外环路)〕

CULTURAL NOTE 文化注释

People sometimes make jokes about the M25 because there are so many cars etc on it that the traffic often moves very slowly. 人们有时会拿25号高速公路来开玩笑, 因为路上车辆太多导致交通并不"高速"。

MA¹ /ˌɛm ˋe; ˌem ˈeɪ/ *n* [C] Master of Arts; a university degree in an arts subject (ART¹ (5)) that you get after studying for a year or two longer after your first degree 文学硕士: *an MA in English literature* 英国文学硕士 | *Vanessa Clark, MA* 瓦妮莎·克拉克, 文学硕士 —compare 比较 MSC

MA² the written abbreviation of 缩写= MASSACHUSETTS

Ma, ma /mɑ; mɑː/ *n* [C] *informal*【非正式】**1** mother 妈, 妈妈: *What's for dinner, Ma?* 妈, 午餐吃什么? **2** a word meaning 'Mrs', used in some country areas of the US 夫人, 太太〔用于美国一些乡村地区〕: *old Ma Harris* 老哈里斯夫人

ma'am /mæm; mæm/ *n* **1** *AmE spoken* a polite way of addressing a woman【美口】夫人〔对妇女的礼貌称呼〕: *May I help you, ma'am?* 夫人, 要我帮忙吗? **2** *BrE spoken* a way of addressing the Queen, some women in authority, and, especially in the past, women of high social class【英口】夫人; 女士〔对女王、某些有权势的妇女的尊称, 尤其过去用于称呼上流社会的妇女〕

Maa·stricht /ˋmɑstrɪkt; ˈmɑːstrɪkt/ a city in the Netherlands. In 1991, the leaders of the countries in the EU (=European Union) met there and made an agreement to become more politically and economically united. This agreement, called the **Maastricht Treaty**, was signed in 1992. The main aim of the Treaty is to establish the principle of closer economic union in the EU and a single CURRENCY (=system of money), and it also includes the Social Chapter, which deals mainly with the rights of workers. 马斯特里赫特〔荷兰一城市。1991年, 欧盟各国领导人在该市会晤, 就进一步加强政治与经济联盟关系达成一项协议, 即《马斯特里赫特条约》。该条约于1992年签署, 主要目标是确立欧盟各国加强经济联盟的原则, 实行单一货币。该条约也包括关乎劳动者权利的《社会宪章》〕

Mab·i·nog·i·on, The /ˌmæbɪˋnogɪən; ˌmæbɪˈnɒgiɒn/ a collection of old Welsh stories about imaginary and magical people and places. It was written from the 11th to the 13th centuries, and some of the stories deal with Arthurian Legend.《马比诺吉昂》〔威尔士古代传说故事集, 讲述虚构的有魔力的人物和地方。这些故事写于公元11-13世纪, 其中有些与亚瑟王传奇有关〕

mac /mæk; mæk/ *n* [C] *BrE* a coat worn to keep out the rain; MACKINTOSH【英】雨衣

Mac *n AmE informal* used to address a man whose name you do not know【美, 非正式】老兄, 老弟〔用以称呼你不知其姓名的男子〕

ma·ca·bre /məˋkɑbrə; məˈkɑːbrə/ *adj* very strange and unpleasant and connected with death, serious accidents etc 恐怖的, 可怕的, 骇人的; 与死亡〔严重事故等〕有关的: *a macabre tale* 令人毛骨悚然的故事 | *a macabre sense of humour* 使人悚然的幽默感

Ma·cao, Macau /məˋkau; məˈkaʊ/ a small area in south China, which was occupied (OCCUPY) by Portugal from 1557-1999, when it became the Macau Special Administrative Region in China. It is a popular place for tourists. Population: 437,000 (2001). 澳门〔位于中国南部的一小块地域。1557至1999年曾为葡萄牙所侵占, 1999年回归中国后称为"澳门特别行政区"。澳门是一个旅游胜地。人口: 437,000 (2001)〕

ma·cad·am /məˋkædəm; məˈkædəm/ *n* [U] a road surface made of a mixture of broken stones and TAR¹ (1) or ASPHALT 柏油碎石路面; TARMAC¹ (1) *BrE*【英】

mac·a·ro·ni /ˌmækəˋronɪ; ˌmækəˈrəʊni◂/ *n* [U] a type of PASTA in the shape of small tubes, which is cooked in boiling water 通心粉, 通心面: *a plate of macaroni* 一盘通心粉 | **macaroni cheese** (=macaroni with a cheese sauce) 干酪通心面 —see picture at 参见 PASTA 图

mac·a·roon /ˌmækəˋrun; ˌmækəˈruːn/ *n* [C] a small round cake made of sugar, eggs, and crushed ALMONDs or COCONUT 蛋白杏仁饼; 蛋白椰子饼

Mac·Ar·thur /məˋkɑrθɚ; məˈkɑːθə/, **General Douglas** (1880-1964) a US military leader. During World War II he was in charge of all the armies of the Allies fighting in the areas around the Pacific Ocean. He commanded the US armies in Japan after the war ended, and he was also the leader of the United Nations forces in Korea in 1950-51 during the Korean War. 麦克阿瑟〔(1880-1964), 美国军事将领。第二次世界大战期间, 他率领盟军在太平洋地区作战, 战后任驻日美军总司令。1950-1951年朝鲜战争期间, 他任联合国驻朝部队的总司令〕

ma·caw /məˋkɔ; məˈkɔː/ *n* [C] a large brightly coloured bird like a PARROT¹ (1), with a long tail 鹦鹉, 金刚鹦鹉

Mac·beth /məkˋbɛθ; məkˈbeθ/ **1** (c.1005-57) the king of Scotland from 1040 to 1057, who killed the previous king, Duncan, in battle and was himself later killed by Duncan's son, Malcolm 麦克佩斯〔(约1005-1057), 1040-1057年间任苏格兰国王。他在战场上杀害了前国王邓肯, 后来自己又被邓肯之子马尔科姆所杀〕**2** a character in the play *Macbeth* by William Shakespeare. Macbeth is told by three WITCHes that he will become king. To do so, he murders the present king Duncan, who is visiting him in his castle. Although he feels very guilty about this, he kills several other people to keep his power until he is finally killed by Macduff. 麦克白〔威廉·莎士比亚的剧作《麦克白》中的人物。麦克白从三个女巫口中得知自己将成为国王。为了达到此目的, 他谋害了当时正在自己城堡中做客的国王邓肯。尽管他对此非常愧疚, 但为了保住自己的权力他又杀害了几个人。后来, 他被麦克达夫所杀〕

Macbeth, Lady a character in the play *Macbeth* by William Shakespeare. She encourages her husband, Macbeth, to kill Duncan, the king of Scotland, so that he can become king instead, and she is a stronger, more evil person than Macbeth himself. After the murder, however, she feels very guilty, and starts to walk in her sleep, trying to clean the imaginary blood of the dead king off her hands. 麦克白夫人〔威廉·莎士比亚的剧作《麦克白》中的人物。为了让丈夫成为国王, 她怂恿丈夫杀害苏格兰国王邓肯。她比起麦克白本人更为顽固、邪恶。然而, 谋杀事件发生之后, 她心中万分愧疚, 开始梦游, 总感觉手上有死去国王的血, 总想把它洗掉〕

Mac·don·ald /məkˋdɑnḷd; məkˈdɒnəld/, **Flo·ra** /ˋflɔrə; ˈflɔːrə/ (1722-90) a Scottish woman who helped Bonnie Prince Charlie to escape from Scotland after the Battle of Culloden by making him dress in women's clothes and pretend to be her 麦克唐纳〔(1722-1790), 苏格兰女子。卡洛登战役之后, 她让英俊的查理王子穿上女装, 装扮成她自己的样子逃离了苏格兰〕

Macdonald /məkˋdɑnḷd məkˈdɒnəld/, **Ram·sey** /ˋræmzɪ; ˈræmzi/ (1866-1937) a British politician in the Labour Party, who became the first Labour Prime Minister in 1924. He was later Prime Minister of a 'National Government' (=a government formed from members of all the political parties) during the period of economic difficulty and high unemployment of the 1930s. 麦克唐纳〔(1866-1937), 英国工党政治家, 1924年成为首位工党首相。他在20世纪30年代经济困难和高失业率时期任"国民政府"首相〕

Mac·duff /məkˋdʌf; məkˈdʌf/ **1** a character in the play *Macbeth* by William Shakespeare, who kills Macbeth at the end of the play 麦克达夫〔威廉·莎士比亚的剧作《麦克白》中的人物。全剧以他杀死麦克白而告终〕**2 lead on, Macduff** a slightly incor-

rect quotation from the play *Macbeth*, where the actual words are "lay on, Macduff". These words are now often used humorously when asking someone to lead you to a place.麦克达夫，带路吧〔引自剧作《麦克白》，与原文稍有出入。原话为"lay on, Macduff"（动手吧，麦克达夫）。现在，当请别人带路时，人们通常借用此说法，以示幽默〕

mace /mes; meɪs/ *n* **1** [U] powder made from the dried shell of a NUTMEG, used to give food a special taste〔调味用的〕肉豆蔻干皮（粉） **2** [C] a heavy ball with sharp points on a short metal stick, used in the past as a weapon〔旧时用作武器的〕狼牙棒，钉头锤 **3** [C] a decorated stick that is carried by an official in some ceremonies as a sign of power〔作为权力象征的〕权杖 **4 Mace** [U] *trademark* a chemical which makes your eyes and skin sting painfully, which some women carry to defend themselves【商标】〔妇女自卫用的〕梅斯催泪气体

Ma·ce·do·ni·a /ˌmæsɪˋdonɪə; ˌmæsəˈdəʊniə/ **1** a country in southeast Europe, north of Greece and south of Serbia. Population: 2,046,000 (2001). Capital: Skopje. It was formerly part of Yugoslavia, but became an independent country in 1991. The country's official name is the Former Yugoslav Republic of Macedonia (FYROM). 马其顿〔东南欧一国家，位于希腊以北，塞尔维亚以南。人口: 2,046,000 (2001)，首都: 斯科普里。该国曾是南斯拉夫的一部分，1991年独立，正式国名为"前南斯拉夫马其顿共和国"，缩写为 FYROM〕 **2** a province of northern Greece which is part of the ancient country of Macedonia. Its capital city is Thessaloniki, and the highest mountain in Greece, Mount Olympus, is on its southern border. 马其顿省〔希腊北部一省份，原为古马其顿王国的一部分，首府为塞萨洛尼基。其南部边境一带耸立着希腊最高山峰奥林匹斯山〕 **3** also 又作 **Macedon** /ˋmæsɪdən; ˈmæsɪdən/ an ancient country in the northern part of ancient Greece, whose most famous king was Alexander the Great 马其顿王国〔古希腊北部一古国。最著名的君王是亚历山大大帝〕—**Macedonian** *n, adj*

ma·cer·ate /ˋmæsəˌret; ˈmæsəreɪt/ *v* [I,T] *technical* to make something soft by leaving it in water, or to become soft in this way【术语】泡软，（把…）浸软 —**maceration** /ˌmæsəˋreʃən; ˌmæsəˈreɪʃən/ *n* [U]

Mac·heath /məkˋhiθ; məkˈhiːθ/, **Captain** a character in *The Beggar's Opera* (1728) by John Gay who is a HIGHWAYMAN (=a man who robbed travellers) 麦克希思上尉〔约翰·盖伊的剧作《乞丐的歌剧》(1728) 中的人物。他是个公路响马〕

ma·chet·e /məˋʃɛtɪ; məˈʃeti/ *n* [C] a large knife with a broad heavy blade, used as a weapon or a tool〔作武器或工具用的〕宽刃刀，大砍刀

Mach·i·a·vel·li /ˌmækɪəˋvɛlɪ; ˌmækiəˈveli/, **Nic·co·lò** /ˋnɪkəlo; ˈnɪkələʊ/ (1469-1527) an Italian political philosopher who is famous for his book *The Prince*, in which he explains how political leaders can cleverly use other people in order to gain power and keep it 马基雅弗利〔(1469-1527)，意大利政治思想家。其著作《君主论》最为著名。书中阐述了政治领袖应如何巧妙利用他人以谋取和维护个人权力〕

Mach·i·a·vel·li·an /ˌmækɪəˋvɛlɪən; ˌmækiəˈveliən◂/ *adj* using clever but immoral methods to get what you want 诡计多端的，狡诈的; 为达目的而不择手段的

mach·i·na·tions /ˌmækəˋneʃənz, ˌmæʃə-; ˌmækəˈneɪʃənz/ *n* [plural] secret and clever plans 密谋，诡计

1 1 **ma·chine**[1] /məˋʃin; məˈʃiːn/ *n* [C] **1** a piece of equipment that uses power such as electricity to do a particular job 机器: *a machine that fills the bottles* 装瓶机 | *Could you get me a Coke from the machine?* 给我从自动售卖机里买一罐可乐好吗? | **sewing/washing machine etc** (=a machine that can sew, wash clothes etc) 缝纫机/洗衣机等 | **by machine** *The letters are sorted by machine.* 信件都是由机器分拣的。**2** a computer 电脑: *a powerful machine that is ideal for software development* 一台对于软件开发来说很理想的功能强大的电脑 **3** a group of people that controls an organization, especially a political party〔控制某组织，尤指政党的〕核心人物; 领导核心: *the party machine* 政党的核心人物 | *the government's propaganda machine* 政府的宣传机器 **4 like a well-oiled machine** working very smoothly and effectively 像上足了油的机器一样;〔工作〕非常顺利有效: *The office runs like a well-oiled machine.* 那个办公室像上足了润滑油的机器一样运转顺利。**5** *informal* a vehicle【非正式】汽车: *That's an impressive-looking machine you've got there.* 你那辆车看上去真神气。**6** someone who works without stopping, or who seems to have no feelings or independent thoughts 机器〔指无休止工作或似乎没有感觉或独立思维的人〕: *He was a running machine, born to do nothing but win medals.* 他是一台赛跑机器，生来就是为了赢得奖牌。—see also 另见 CASH MACHINE, FRUIT MACHINE, TIME MACHINE

USAGE NOTE 用法说明: MACHINE

WORD CHOICE 词语辨析: **machine, device, thing, appliance, gadget**

You do not usually work a **machine** directly by hand, and it may be large. Often the word is used with another word before it that describes its purpose. machine 通常不是直接用手操纵的机器，而且它可能很庞大。这个词常与位于它前面、描述其用途的另外一个词连用: *The coffee machine has broken down.* 那台咖啡机已经坏了。

Device is more formal. A device may be worked by hand, or be electrical. device 这个词更正式一些，它可以是手动的也可以是电动的: *a device for opening bottles* 开瓶器。In spoken English people say **thing**. 在英语口语中人们用 thing 这个词: *a thing to open bottles with* 一个用来开瓶子的器具。**Device** is used especially for something that is used to measure or protect something else. device 特别用来指测量或保护其他物件的装置: *a device to find faults in plastic* 检测塑料瑕疵的仪器 | *a contraceptive device* 避孕用具

An **appliance** is a machine used for a particular purpose in the home, and is called this especially by the people who produce and sell them. appliance 是用于某一具体用途的家用机器，这种叫法尤为生产和销售这类机器的人所使用: *a household appliance such as a dishwasher* 家用电器如洗碗机 | *domestic appliances* 家用电器

A **gadget** is a cleverly designed small machine, often one that does a complicated action, and is usually modern. gadget 指设计巧妙、常用来做复杂的工作的小机器，而且通常是现代化的: *My latest gadget is a breadmaker.* 我最近购得的一台小机器是面包机。

SPOKEN-WRITTEN 口语－书面语

When the word before it describes what the machine is for, people sometimes leave out the word **machine**. 当 machine 前面的词描述其用途时，人们有时会省去 machine 这个词: *Can I use your fax (machine)?* 我可以用一下你的传真机吗?

When the word before **machine** ends in *-ing*, you can sometimes use the same word ending in *-er* on its own. 当 machine 前面是一个以 -ing 结尾的词，有时可单独使用该词以 -er 结尾的形式: *Lianne is in charge of the photocopier.* (formal 正式 **photocopying machine**) 利安负责管理那台复印机。

Often you do not use the word **machine** at all to talk about a particular machine. For example, you say **dishwasher**, not **dishwashing machine** and **tumble-drier** not **tumble-drying machine**. 人们通常不用 machine 这个词来谈论一台具体的机器，如人们说 dishwasher 而不说 dishwashing machine，说 tumble-drier 而不说 tumble-drying machine。

machine[2] *v* [T] **1** to fasten pieces of cloth together using a SEWING MACHINE 用缝纫机缝 **2** to make or shape something using a machine 用机器制造[加工]

machine code /ˌ·ˈ· ˌ·/ *n* [C,U] *technical* instructions in the form of numbers which are understood by a computer【术语】机器（代）码

machine gun /ˌ·ˈ· ˌ·/ *n* [C] a gun that fires a lot of bullets very quickly 机关枪—**machinegun** *v* [T]

machine lan·guage /ˌ·ˈ· ˌ··/ *n* [C,U] instructions in a form such as numbers that can be used by a computer 机器语言

machine-made /ˌ·ˈ· ˌ·/ *adj* made using a machine 机器制造的 —compare 比较 HANDMADE

machine-read·a·ble /ˌ·ˌ· ˈ···◂/ *adj* in a form that can be understood and used by a computer 机器可读的，电脑可读的: *information stored in machine-readable form* 以机读形式储存的信息

ma·chin·e·ry /məˋʃinərɪ; məˈʃiːnəri/ *n* [U] **1** machines, especially large ones 机器，机械〔尤指大型机械〕: *agricultural machinery* 农业机械 | *an expensive piece of machinery* 一台昂贵的机器 **2** the parts inside a machine that make it work〔使机器运转的〕部件: *Jack keeps tinkering with the machinery, but the car still won't go.* 杰克一直在摆弄机器，但汽车还是开不动。**3** system or set of processes for doing something 体系; 机构: *the machinery of government* 政府机构 3

machine tool /ˌ·ˈ· ˌ·/ *n* [C] a tool used for cutting and shaping metal, wood etc, usually run by electricity 机床

machine trans·la·tion /ˌ·ˈ· ˌ·ˈ··/ *n* [U] translation done by a computer 机器翻译，电脑翻译

ma·chin·ist /məˋʃinɪst; məˈʃiːnɪst/ *n* [C] someone who operates a machine, especially in a factory 机工, 机械师

ma·chis·mo /mɑˋtʃizmo; məˈtʃɪzməʊ/ *n* [U] traditional male behaviour that emphasizes how brave, strong, and sexually attractive a man is 大男子气概

mach·o /ˋmɑtʃo; ˈmætʃəʊ/ *adj informal* macho behaviour emphasizes a man's physical strength, lack of sensitive feelings, and other qualities considered to be typical of men【非正式】富有男子汉气概的: *Jim likes to pretend he's macho but he's actually quite a vulnerable guy.* 吉姆喜欢装出一副男子汉气概, 但他实际上是一个极为脆弱的家伙。| *He's so concerned with his macho image.* 他非常在意自己的男子汉形象。

CULTURAL NOTE 文化注释

A man who is macho or has macho attitudes wants to be thought of as strong, brave, and not easily upset, and macho men often think of women as weaker, less important people whose job is to serve men. But these attitudes are becoming less common in the US and UK. 有男子汉气概或态度举止显出男子汉气概的男人想给人一种强壮、勇敢并且不易心烦的感觉。有男子汉气概的男人常把女人看成无足轻重的弱者, 认为她们的主要职责是伺候男人。但在英美两国, 现在持这种态度的人已经不再普遍。— see also 另见 NEW MAN

macho man /ˈ‥ ·/ *n* [C] a man who is always trying to show that he is strong, brave etc 经常着意显示自己阳刚气概的人

Ma·chu Pic·chu /ˌmɑtʃu ˋpiktʃu; ˌmɑːtʃuː ˈpiːktʃuː/ an ancient ruined South American city high up in the Andes mountains in Peru. It was built by the Incas, a Native American people of South America, in about 1500 AD, and has a TEMPLE (=religious building) of the Sun and many other buildings. It is a popular place for tourists to visit. 马丘比丘〔南美洲一古城遗址, 位于秘鲁境内安第斯山上。该城是南美土著居民印加人在大约公元1500年建立的, 内有太阳神庙等诸多建筑, 现为一旅游胜地〕

mack /mæk; mæk/ *n* [C] *BrE*【英】another spelling of MAC mac的另一种拼法

Mac·ken·zie Moun·tains, the /məˌkɛnzi ˋmaʊntn̩z; məˌkenzi ˈmaʊntɪnz/ a range of mountains in the Canadian Rockies 马更些山脉〔加拿大境内落基山脉中的一段〕

Mackenzie Riv·er, the /·ˌ‥ ˈ‥/ a river in northwest Canada which is the longest river in Canada 马更些河〔加拿大西北部一河流, 是加拿大第一大河〕

mack·e·rel /ˋmækərəl; ˈmækərəl/ *n plural* **mackerel** [C] a sea fish that has oily flesh and a strong taste 鲭鱼〔一种海鱼〕

mack·in·tosh /ˋmækɪnˌtɑʃ; ˈmækɪntɒʃ/ *n* [C] *old-fashioned especially BrE* a coat worn to keep out the rain; MAC【过时, 尤英】雨衣

Mackintosh, Charles Ren·nie /tʃɑrlz ˋrɛnɪ; tʃɑːlz ˈreni/ (1868-1928) a Scottish architect, artist, and designer of furniture and glass. His work is considered to be among the best examples of the Art Nouveau style, and he designed many buildings in and around Glasgow in Scotland. 麦金托什〔(1868-1928), 苏格兰建筑师、画家、家具和玻璃器皿设计师。他的作品被认为是新艺术风格的典型代表。苏格兰格拉斯哥的许多建筑都是他设计的〕

Mac·Lean /məˋklen; məˈkleɪn/, **Don·ald** /ˋdɑnl̩d; ˈdɒnəld/ (1913-83) a British man who had an important job in the Foreign Office, but was at the same time secretly working as a SPY for the former Soviet Union. In 1951 he escaped to the Soviet Union with another British spy, Guy Burgess, and the names 'Burgess and Maclean' are often remembered together. 麦克莱恩〔(1913-1983), 英国外交部要员、前苏联间谍。1951年, 他与另一名英国间谍盖伊·伯吉斯一起逃往苏联。在人们的记忆中, "伯吉斯与麦克莱恩"这两个名字总是连在一起〕

Mac·mil·lan /məkˋmɪlən; məkˈmɪlən/, **Harold** (1894-1986) a British politician in the Conservative Party, who was Prime Minister from 1957 to 1963, during a period of great economic improvement. He made two expressions popular in the UK, when he told the British people "You've never had it so good" (meaning that most people had more money and a better life than they ever had before), and when he talked about "the winds of change" blowing through Africa (meaning that many African countries were becoming independent at that time). He later became **Lord Stockton**. 麦克米伦〔(1894-1986), 英国保守党政治家, 1957至1963年经济振兴期间任首相。他说过的两句话在英国广为流传。他曾对国民说道: "现在的日子真是好。"他还说过非洲大陆正在刮起"变革之风"。后来, 他被册封为"斯托克顿伯爵"〕

ma·cra·mé /ˋmækrəˌme; məˈkrɑːmi/ *n* [U] the art of knotting string together in patterns for decoration 流苏花边编结法, 装饰结编结技艺, 花带结艺术

mac·ro /ˋmækro; ˈmækrəʊ/ *n plural* **macros** [C] a set of instructions for a computer, stored and used as a unit〔电脑〕宏指令

macro- /ˋmækro; ˈmækrəʊ/ *prefix technical* large, especially concerning a whole system rather than particular parts of it【术语】大的; 巨型的; 宏观的: *macroeconomics* 宏观经济学 | *macromolecular structures* 高分子结构 —compare 比较 MICRO-

mac·ro·bi·ot·ic /ˌmækrobaɪˋɑtɪk; ˌmækrəʊbaɪˈɒtɪk/ *adj* macrobiotic food consists mainly of grains and vegetables, with no added chemicals 摄生饮食的〔指食物主要由谷物和蔬菜构成, 无化学添加剂〕

mac·ro·cos·m /ˋmækrəˌkɑzəm; ˈmækrəʊkɒzəm/ *n* [C] a large, complicated system such as the whole universe or a society, considered as a single unit〔视为单一体系的〕大而复杂的系统; 整个宇宙; 宏观世界 —compare 比较 MICROCOSM

mac·ro·ec·o·nom·ics /ˌmækroikəˋnɑmɪks; ˌmækrəʊekəˈnɒmɪks/ *n* [U] the study of large economic systems such as those of a whole country or area of the world 宏观经济学 — **macroeconomic** *adj*

Mac the Knife /ˌ· · ˈ·/ a character in *The Threepenny Opera* (1928), written by Bertolt Brecht with music by Kurt Weill, based on the character of Captain Macheath. 快刀麦克〔贝托尔特·布莱希特创作、库尔特·韦尔作曲的《三便士歌剧》中的角色, 以麦克希思上尉为原型〕

mad /mæd; mæd/ *adj* **madder, maddest** S2 W3

1 ▶ANGRY 生气的◀ [not before noun 不用于名词前] *informal especially AmE* angry【非正式, 尤美】生气的: *You make me so mad!* 你真把我气坏了! | *Stay clear of Tucker – he's mad as hell and looking for a fight.* 离塔克远一点 — 他在气头上, 正想找人打架呢。| **mad at sb** *AmE*【美】*Don't get mad at me, I'm just telling you what Ray said.* 别对我发火, 我只是在告诉你雷所说的话。| **mad with sb** *BrE*【英】*Mum's really mad with Peter since he borrowed her car.* 妈妈确实很生彼得的气, 因为他借走了她的汽车。| **go mad** *BrE informal* (=become extremely angry)【英, 非正式】变得极为愤怒, 变得狂怒 *Joe will go mad when he finds out how much I paid for that dress.* 乔要是知道了我买那件衣服花了多少钱, 他会气得火冒三丈。| **hopping mad** (=very angry) 怒不可遏; 气得暴跳如雷 | **as mad as a wet hen** *AmE* (=very angry)【美】非常生气

2 ▶CRAZY 疯狂的◀ *BrE* very silly or unwise; crazy【英】极愚蠢[不明智]的; 疯狂的: *Surely no one would be mad enough to fly in this weather?* 肯定没有人会傻到在这样的天气乘飞机吧? | *You've agreed to marry him! Are you mad?* 你已经同意跟他结婚了! 你疯了吗? | **stark raving mad** (=completely crazy) 完全疯了的; 傻透顶的 *My friends all think I'm stark raving mad.* 我的朋友都认为我傻透了。| **barking mad** (=completely crazy, with very strange ideas) 完全疯了的; 想法古怪的

3 ▶MENTALLY ILL 疯癫的, 患精神病的◀ *old-fashioned, not technical* mentally ill; INSANE (1)【过时, 非术语】疯癫的; 患精神病的; 精神错乱的: *Mr Rochester's mad wife* 罗切斯特先生的疯妻子 | *There was a mad gleam in his bloodshot eyes.* 他充血的双眼中有一丝疯癫的神色。

4 ▶WILD/UNCONTROLLED 狂暴的/失控的◀ *especially BrE* behaving in a wild, uncontrolled way, without thinking about what you are doing【尤英】举止狂暴的; 失控的: **a mad dash/rush etc** *We all made a mad dash for the door.* 我们所有人都发疯似地向门口冲去。| **be mad with rage/grief etc** *She was mad with grief when she heard about her son's death.* 当她听到儿子的死讯时, 悲伤得几乎发疯了。

5 go mad a) *not technical* to become mentally ill【非术语】变得精神失常, 患精神病, 发疯 **b)** *especially BrE* to start behaving in an excited or uncontrolled way【尤英】变得极度激动; 变得失去控制: *When Italy scored, the crowd went mad.* 意大利队得分后人群变得失去了控制。| *We went a bit mad and ordered a bottle of champagne.* 我们有些激动, 要了一瓶香槟酒。**c)** *BrE* to start feeling crazy because you are very bored, annoyed, or anxious【英】〔因十分无聊、烦躁或忧虑而感到要〕发疯: *Sometimes I thought I'd go mad with loneliness.* 有时我想我会因孤独而发疯。| *I'll go mad if I have to spend another day in that place.* 要是必须再在那个地方待上一天的话, 我会发疯的。**d)** *BrE informal* to become very angry【英, 非正式】大怒, 极为生气: *Mum will go mad when she finds out what I paid for this dress.* 要是妈妈知道我买这件衣服花了多少钱, 她会气疯的。

6 don't go mad *BrE spoken* used to tell someone not to work too hard or to get too excited【英口】别不要命地干; 别太激动: *I know you've got a lot to do before tomorrow morning but don't go mad.* 我知道你明天上午之前有许多事情要做, 但也别不要命地干。

M

7 you/she etc must be mad (to do sth) *BrE spoken* used when you think someone is very silly or stupid to do something【英口】某人（做某事）太愚蠢: *You've given up your job? You must be mad!* 你辞职了？你真是傻到家啦！

8 be mad about/on sb *BrE informal* to love someone in a strong, uncontrolled way【英，非正式】对某人爱得如醉如痴: *I was totally mad about him.* 我疯狂地爱上了他。

9 be mad about/on sth *informal BrE* to be very interested in an activity and spend a lot of time on it【非正式，英】痴迷于某事: *He's completely mad about computer games.* 他对电脑游戏完全着了迷。

10 be mad keen on *BrE informal* to be very interested in something or like it very much【英，非正式】对…极感兴趣; 非常喜欢: *Giles was mad keen on planes from an early age.* 贾尔斯从早年起就对飞机极感兴趣。

11 run/work etc like mad *BrE informal* to run, work etc as quickly as you can【英，非正式】拼命地奔跑/工作等: *She ran like mad to catch the bus.* 她拼命地跑去赶公共汽车。| *We've been working like mad to get the job finished.* 我们一直在拼命完成这项工作。

12 drive sb mad *BrE* to make someone so bored, annoyed, or anxious that they feel as if they are going crazy【英】逼得某人发疯: *I wish you'd stop making that noise, it's driving me mad!* 我希望你别再发出那种声音了，都快把我吵疯了。

13 power-mad/money-mad/sex-mad etc only interested in power, money etc 只对权/钱/性等感兴趣的: *a power-mad dictator* 权迷心窍的独裁者

14 as mad as a hatter *informal* behaving in a way that is very silly or strange, but unlikely to do any harm【非正式】〔举止〕疯狂怪诞的

Mad·a·gas·car /ˌmædəˋgæskɚ; ˌmædəˈgæskə/ a country that is an island in the Indian Ocean off the southeast coast of Africa. Population: 15,983,000 (2001). Capital: Antananarivo. Some types of animal live there that do not exist anywhere else in the world, such as the lemur. 马达加斯加〔印度洋一岛国，与非洲东南海岸隔海相望。人口: 15,983,000 (2001)，首都: 安塔那那利弗。生活在该国的狐猴等属该国独有的动物〕— **Madagascan** *n, adj*

mad·am /ˋmædəm; ˈmædəm/ *n* **1** a polite way of addressing a woman, especially a customer in a shop 女士〔对妇女，尤其对商店女顾客的礼貌称呼〕: *Are you being served, Madam?* 女士，有人接待您吗？ **2 Dear Madam** used at the beginning of a business letter to a woman 亲爱的女士〔用于写给妇女的商业信函开头〕 **3 Madam President/Ambassador etc** a way of addressing a woman who has an important official position 总统/大使阁下〔对身居要职的妇女的称呼〕 **4** [C] a woman who is in charge of a BROTHEL (=place where women are paid to have sex with men) 鸨母 **5 a (proper) little madam** *BrE informal* a young girl who expects other people to do what she wants【英，非正式】指望他人听其使唤的小女孩

Mad·ame /ˋmædəm; ˈmædəm/ *n plural* **Mesdames** /meˋdɑm; meɪˈdæm/ a title used to address a French-speaking woman, especially a married one; MRS 夫人，太太; 女士〔对讲法语，特别是已婚妇女的称呼〕: *Madame Lefevre* 勒菲弗夫人

Madame Bovary /ˌmædəm ˋbovərɪ; ˌmædəm ˈbəʊvəri/ a NOVEL by Gustave Flaubert, published in 1856, which tells the story of a doctor's wife, Emma Bovary, who, unhappy in her marriage, commits ADULTERY, falls into debt, and finally kills herself《包法利夫人》〔古斯塔夫·福楼拜的一部小说，发表于1856年。小说描述一位医生的妻子埃玛·包法利的故事。她婚姻不幸福，后与人通奸，又欠了债，最后自杀身亡〕

Madame But·ter·fly /ˌmædəm ˋbʌtɚflaɪ; ˌmædəm ˈbʌtəflaɪ/ **1** (1904) an OPERA by Puccini in which a Japanese woman marries an officer in the US navy called Lieutenant Pinkerton, who later leaves her in Japan and marries another woman in the US. When he returns to Japan with his American wife, his Japanese wife kills herself because she is so unhappy.《蝴蝶夫人》〔(1904)，普契尼创作的一部歌剧。剧中有一日本姑娘嫁给了一位名叫平克顿的美国海军上尉。后来，平克顿把姑娘留在日本，自己回到美国与另一女子结婚。当他带着美国妻子再次来到日本时，他的日本妻子因悲伤过度而自杀〕 **2** the main female character of *Madame Butterfly* 蝴蝶夫人〔《蝴蝶夫人》中的女主角〕

Madame Tus·saud's /ˌmædəm tuˋsoz; ˌmædəm təˈsɔːdz/ a MUSEUM in London that contains models of famous people, both living and dead, made of WAX 图索德夫人蜡像馆〔伦敦市内一博物馆，藏有现世名人和已故名人的蜡像〕

mad·cap /ˋmædˌkæp; ˈmædkæp/ *adj* a madcap idea seems crazy and unlikely to succeed〔想法〕疯狂的; 鲁莽的

mad cow dis·ease /ˌ·ˈ··ˌ·/ *n* [U] *not technical* BSE【非术语】牛海绵状脑病，疯牛病

MADD /mæd; mæd/ Mothers Against Drunk Driving; a US organization, started by a woman whose daughter was killed by a driver who was drunk. It has been successful in bringing the problem of drunk driving to people's attention in the US, and in encouraging the government to make stronger laws against it. 反对酒后驾车母亲协会〔美国一组织，发起者为一女士，其女儿死于酒后驾车者之手。该组织已卓有成效地使美国公众对酒后驾车问题予以关注，并敦促政府针对酒后驾车行为制定更为严厉的法律〕

mad·den /ˋmædn; ˈmædn/ *v* [T usually passive 一般用被动态] to make someone extremely angry or annoyed 使狂怒; 使极为恼火

mad·den·ing /ˋmædnɪŋ; ˈmædənɪŋ/ *adj* extremely annoying 使人极其恼火的: *maddening delays* 令人十分气恼的拖延 — **maddeningly** *adv*

made /med; meɪd/ **1** the past tense and past participle of MAKE[1] **2 be made for each other** *informal* to be completely suitable for each other, especially as husband and wife【非正式】〔尤指作为夫妻〕十分合适，完全般配: *Jacinta and Dermot were made for each other.* 贾欣塔和德莫特真是天生的一对。 **3 have (got) it made** *informal* to have everything that you need for a happy life【非正式】具备幸福生活所需的一切: *Nice house, good job, lovely family – you've got it made!* 漂亮的房子，称心的工作，美满的家庭 —— 你可是一应俱全啦！ **4 see what sb is (really) made of** *informal* to find out how strong, brave etc someone is【非正式】认识某人的真才实学[真本领] **5 I'm not made of money** *spoken* used to say that you cannot afford something【口】买不起〔某物〕: *I can't buy you shoes as well – I'm not made of money!* 我不能也给你买鞋 —— 我可不是钱堆的！ **6 be made (for life)** *informal* to be so rich that you will never have to work again【非正式】富有得一辈子用不着再干活: *If the deal is successful I'll be made for life.* 如果这笔交易能成功的话，我就可受用一辈子了。 **7 I wasn't made for** *BrE spoken* used to say that you are not enjoying a job or activity【英口】我不喜欢〔某工作或某活动〕: *I wasn't made for housework.* 我不喜欢做家务。

Ma·dei·ra /məˋdɪrə; məˈdɪərə/ *n* [U] a strong sweet wine 马德拉葡萄酒〔一种烈性甜酒〕

Madeira cake /·ˈ·· ˌ·/ *n* [U] a kind of plain yellow cake 马德拉蛋糕

Mad·e·moi·selle /ˌmædəmwəˋzɛl; ˌmædəmwəˈzel/ *n plural* **Mesdemoiselles** /ˌmedəmwəˋzɛl, ˌmeɪdəmwəˈzel/ a title used to address a young unmarried French-speaking woman; MISS[2] (1) 小姐〔对讲法语的年轻未婚妇女的称呼〕: *Mademoiselle Dubois* 迪布瓦小姐

made-to-mea·sure /ˌ·ˌ·ˈ··◂/ *adj* made-to-measure clothes are specially made to fit you〔衣服〕量体定做的

made-to-or·der /ˌ·ˌ·ˈ··◂/ *adj AmE* made-to-order clothing, furniture etc is made for one particular customer【美】〔服装、家具等〕定制的

made-up /ˌ·ˈ·◂/ *adj* **1** a story that is made-up is not true〔故事〕虚构的，不真实的: *This tale of hers is totally made-up.* 她讲的这个故事完全是虚构的。—see also 另见 **make up** (MAKE[1]) **2** wearing MAKE-UP (1) on your face 化了妆的: *She was heavily made-up.* 她浓妆艳抹。

Mad Hat·ter, the /ˌ·ˈ··/ a character in the book *Alice's Adventures in Wonderland* (1865) by Lewis Carroll. Alice goes to the Mad Hatter's tea party where no one eats or drinks anything, the Mad Hatter and the March Hare talk nonsense, and the Dormouse keeps falling asleep. 疯帽匠〔刘易斯·卡罗尔所著的《艾丽丝漫游奇境记》(1865) 中的人物。艾丽丝前去参加疯帽匠举办的茶会，但在茶会上大家既不吃也不喝。疯帽匠与三月兔只顾胡言乱语，睡鼠则不停打瞌睡〕—see also 另见 ALICE IN WONDERLAND

mad·house /ˋmædˌhaus; ˈmædhaʊs/ *n* [C] **1** a place with a lot of people, noise, and activity 人多嘈杂而混乱的场所: *This office is like a madhouse.* 这个办公室吵吵闹闹，乱糟糟的。 **2** *old use* a MENTAL HOSPITAL【旧】疯人院，精神病院

Mad·i·son /ˋmædɪsn; ˈmædɪsən/ the capital city of the US state of Wisconsin 麦迪逊〔美国威斯康星州首府〕

Madison, James (1751-1836) the President of the US from 1809 to 1817. He is sometimes called the 'Father of the Constitution' because of his work at the Constitutional Convention in 1787. He also helped to write *The Bill of Rights*. He started the War of 1812 against Great Britain, and it was called 'Mr Madison's War'. 麦迪逊〔(1751-1836)，美国总统，1809-1817年间在任，有时被称作"宪法之父"。他参加了1787年制宪会议的宪法起草工作，后来还协助起草了《人权法案》。1812年，他发动了一场抗英战争，故该次战争也称为"麦迪逊先生之战"〕

Madison Av·en·ue /ˌ··· ˈ···/ a street in New York City that is famous as the centre of the advertising business. Its name is sometimes used to mean the US advertising business in general. 麦迪逊大街〔纽约市一街道，以广告业中心而闻名。"麦迪逊大街"一词有时用以指称美国的广告业〕

Madison Square Gar·den /ˌ··· · ˈ··/ a place in New York City where concerts or sports events, especially boxing matches, are held, which very large crowds of people attend 麦迪逊广场花园〔纽约市一地名。该地经常举办音乐会或体育赛事，尤其是拳击比赛，吸引了许多观众〕

Madison Square Park /ˌ··· · ˈ·/ a small park in New York City between Madison Avenue, Broadway, and 23rd Street 麦迪逊广场公园〔纽约市一小型公园，位于麦迪逊大街、百老汇和第 23 大街之间〕

mad·ly /ˋmædlɪ; ˈmædli/ *adv* **1** in a wild, uncontrolled way 疯狂地，发疯似地: *She was beating madly on the door with her fists.* 她发疯似地用双拳捶打着门。**2 madly in love** very much in love 疯狂地爱着

Mad Mag·a·zine /ˈ· ···ˌ/ *trademark* a humorous US monthly magazine read especially by teenagers, which is famous for its parodies (PARODY) of recent events, films, famous people etc 【商标】《狂人杂志》〔美国一幽默月刊，读者主要为青少年。该刊物以嘲弄时事、电影和名人而著称〕

mad·man /ˋmædmən; ˈmædmən/ *n plural* **madmen** /-mən; -mən/ [C] **1 like a madman** in a wild, uncontrolled way 疯子似地: *He went racing off like a madman!* 他疯子般飞快地跑掉了。**2** *not technical* a man who is mentally ill 【非术语】疯子，神经错乱的人

mad·ness /ˋmædnɪs; ˈmædnɨs/ *n* [U] **1** *especially BrE* very stupid behaviour that could be dangerous 【尤英】非常愚蠢并可能有危险的行为: **it is/would be madness to do sth** *It would be sheer madness to try to cross the desert on your own.* 你试图独自穿越沙漠，简直是疯了。**2** *not technical* serious mental illness 【非术语】严重精神错乱 —see also 另见 **there's method in sb's madness** (METHOD (3))

Ma·don·na¹ /məˋdɑnə; məˈdɒnə/ *n* **1 the Madonna** Mary, the mother of Jesus, in the Christian religion 圣母马利亚〔基督教中耶稣的母亲〕 **2** [C] a picture or figure of Mary 圣母画像[雕像]

Madonna² (1958-) a US singer and film actress, one of the most successful pop musicians of the 1980s and 1990s. She is famous for dressing and performing in her concerts in a way that is sometimes shocking. Her songs include *Like a Virgin* and *Material Girl*, and her films include *Desperately Seeking Susan*, *Body of Evidence*, and *Evita*. 麦当娜〔(1958-)，美国歌手、电影演员，20 世纪 80、90 年代最优秀的流行音乐人之一。她在音乐会上的穿着和表演有时令人咋舌。她演唱的歌曲有《像个处女》、《拜金女郎》等。她演出的影片包括《寻找苏珊》、《肉体证据》和《贝隆夫人》〕

Ma·dras /məˋdrɑs; məˈdrɑːs/ a city and port in southeast India, the capital of Tamil Nadu state. Its official name is now Chennai. 马德拉斯〔印度东南部一城市和港口，为泰米尔纳德邦首府。现正式名为钦奈〕

madras *n* **1** [C,U] a kind of CURRY (=hot-tasting Indian dish) usually made with meat 马德拉斯〔一种印度辣味咖喱菜肴，通常加肉烹调〕 **2** [U] a kind of cotton cloth with stripes 马德拉斯条纹棉布

Ma·drid /məˋdrɪd; məˈdrɪd/ the capital city of Spain, in the centre of the country 马德里〔西班牙首都，位于该国中部〕

mad·ri·gal /ˋmædrɪgḷ; ˈmædrɪgəl/ *n* [C] a song for several singers without musical instruments, popular in the 16th and 17th centuries 无伴奏合唱曲〔流行于 16 与 17 世纪〕

mad·wom·an /ˋmædˌwʊmən; ˈmædwʊmən/ *n plural* **madwomen** /-ˌwɪmɪn; -wɪmɪn/ [C] *not technical* a woman who is mentally ill 【非术语】女疯子，疯女人

mael·strom /ˋmelstrəm; ˈmeɪlstrəm/ *n* [C] **1** a situation full of uncontrollable events or strong emotions that make people feel weak or frightened 极度混乱状态；失控状态: *a maelstrom of conflicting emotions* 矛盾情感的旋涡 **2** a violent storm 暴风雨

maes·tro /ˋmaɪstro; ˈmaɪstrəʊ/ *n* [C] someone who can do something very well, especially a musician 大师〔尤指音乐大师〕

Maf·e·king /ˋmæfɪkɪŋ; ˈmæfɨkɪŋ/ the old name of a town in the northern part of South Africa, now called **Mafikeng**. It is famous in British history because of the **Siege of Mafeking** in 1899-1900, when British soldiers defended the town against the Boers during the Boer War. The **Relief of Mafeking** took place after 217 days when more British forces arrived, and the news of this event caused great celebrations in the UK. 马弗京〔南非北部一城镇旧名，现名为Mafikeng (梅富根)。该镇在英国历史上以 1899-1900 年的"马弗京之围"著称。布尔战争期间，英国士兵守在马弗京，以抵御布尔人的进攻。217 天后，英军增援部队抵达该镇，才有了"马弗京解围"之说。消息传回英国，举国上下隆重庆祝〕

MAFF /mæf; mæf/ the abbreviation of 缩写= MINISTRY OF AGRICULTURE, FISHERIES AND FOOD

maf·i·a /ˋmɑfɪˌɑ; ˈmɑːfiə/ *n* [singular] **1 the Mafia** a large organised group of criminals who control many illegal activities especially in Italy and the US〔尤指意大利和美国的〕黑手党 **2** a powerful group of people within an organization or profession who support and protect each other〔某组织或行业内部相互支持并相互保护的〕势力集团: *the medical mafia* 医务界的势力集团

maf·i·o·so /ˌmæfiˋoso; ˌmɑːfiˈəʊsəʊ/ *n plural* **mafiosi** /-si; -siː/ [C] a member of the Mafia 黑手党成员

mag /mæg; mæg/ *n* [C] *informal* a magazine 【非正式】杂志

mag·a·zine /ˌmægəˋzin; ˌmægəˈziːn/ *n* [C] **1** a large thin book with a paper cover that contains news stories, articles, photographs etc, and is sold weekly or monthly 杂志，期刊: *a glossy fashion magazine* 用有光纸印刷的时装杂志 | *a literary magazine* 文学杂志 **2** the part of a gun that holds the bullets〔枪的〕弹夹，弹匣，弹仓 —see picture at 参见 GUN¹ 图 **3** the container that holds the film in a camera or PROJECTOR〔照相机或电影放映机的〕胶卷盒，底片盒 **4** a room or building for storing weapons, explosives etc 弹药室；军火库

Mag·da·len Bridge /ˌmægdəlɪn ˋbrɪdʒ; ˌmægdəlɪn ˈbrɪdʒ/ a bridge over the River Cherwell at Oxford, England. Every May Day a CHOIR sings from a tower near the bridge, and university students traditionally jump from the bridge into the river. 麦格达林大桥〔英格兰牛津查韦尔河上的一座大桥。每年 5 月 1 日，唱诗班会在大桥附近的塔楼上唱歌，也有大学生从桥上跳入河中的传统〕

Ma·gel·lan /məˋdʒɛlən; məˈgelən/**, Fer·di·nand** /ˋfɝdɪnænd; ˈfɜːdɪnænd/ (?1480-1521) a Portuguese sailor who most people consider to be the first person to sail all around the world. The Strait of Magellan at the bottom of South America was named after him. 麦哲伦〔(?1480-1521)，葡萄牙航海家。多数人认为他是环球航行第一人。南美洲南端的麦哲伦海峡以他的名字命名〕

ma·gen·ta /məˋdʒɛntə; məˈdʒentə/ *n* [U] a bright pink colour 品红色，洋红色 —**magenta** *adj* —see picture on page A5 参见 A5 页图

mag·got /ˋmægət; ˈmægət/ *n* [C] a small creature like a WORM that is the young form of a FLY and lives in decaying food, flesh etc 蛆

Ma·ghreb, the /ˋmɑgrɛb; ˈmɑːgreb/ the area of northwest Africa which includes the countries of Morocco, Algeria, Tunisia, and Libya. The people who live there are mainly Arab and Berber. 马格里布〔指包括摩洛哥、阿尔及利亚、突尼斯和利比亚在内的西北非地区。居民主要为阿拉伯人和柏柏尔人〕

Ma·gi, the /ˋmedʒaɪ; ˈmeɪdʒaɪ/ *n* [plural] the three wise men who brought gifts to the baby Jesus, according to the Christian religion〔根据基督教的说法，送礼物给刚刚降生的耶稣的〕三博士，东方三贤

ma·gic¹ /ˋmædʒɪk; ˈmædʒɪk/ *n* [U] **1** a secret power used to control events or do impossible things, by saying special words or performing special actions 魔法，法术；巫术: *Do you believe in magic?* 你相信魔法吗？| **work/do magic** *tales of wizards who could work magic* 关于会施法术的男巫的故事 —see also 另见 BLACK MAGIC, WHITE MAGIC **2** a special, attractive or exciting quality 魅力，魔力: *These old stories still retain their magic.* 这些老故事仍然保持着吸引力。**3** the skill of doing tricks that look like magic, used by a MAGICIAN, or the tricks a magician does 魔术，戏法；巫术 **4 like magic/as if by magic** in a surprising way that seems impossible to explain 像变魔术似地: *The bottle had disappeared as if by magic.* 瓶子像变魔术似地突然消失了。| **work like magic** (=be very effective) 非常有效

CULTURAL NOTE 文化注释

Very few people in Western countries believe in magic, but people enjoy watching entertainers perform magic tricks. 在西方国家，相信魔术的人寥寥无几，但是人们还是很陶醉于观看魔术表演。— see Cultural Note at MAGICIAN 见 MAGICIAN 文化注释

magic² *adj* **1** [only before noun 仅用于名词前] having special powers that are not normal or natural, so that you can do impos-

sible things 有魔力的；神奇的：*There is no magic formula for instant success.* 没有快速成功的神方妙法。| **magic spell/charm etc** *a magic hat that makes her invisible* 使她隐身的魔法帽子 | **magic trick**(=a trick in which something happens in a way that seems impossible to explain) 魔术戏法 *His best magic trick is sawing a lady in half.* 他最拿手的魔术戏法是把一位女士锯成两半。**2 magic number/word** a number or word that is very important or that has a powerful effect on people 神秘数字/词汇〔指非常重要或对人们有强烈影响的数字或词汇〕**3 have a magic touch** to have a special ability to make things work well or to make people happy 有使事情运行良好[使人高兴]的特殊才能：*The baby's always quiet for Gary – he has a magic touch.* 这个婴儿只要和加里在一起就不哭不闹 —— 加里有一种魔力。**4** [not before noun 不用于名词前] *BrE spoken* very good or very enjoyable【英口】非常好的；令人十分愉快的：*"Did you have a good time?" "Yeah, it was magic!"* "玩得痛快吗？""是的，痛快极了！" **5 magic bullet** *informal* a quick, painless cure for illness, or something that solves a difficult problem in an easy way【非正式】魔弹〔指快速而无痛苦的疾病疗法或能轻松解决难题之物〕

magic³ *v* **magicked, magicking** *BrE*【英】

magic sth/sb **away** *phr v* [T] to make someone or something disappear by using magic 用魔法使…消失：*I wish I could magic us away to a warm beach.* 我希望我能够施展魔法把我们大家送到一处温暖的海滩上去。

magic sth ↔ **up** *phr v* [T] to make something appear suddenly and unexpectedly 使…突然[出人意料]地出现

ma·gic·al /ˈmædʒɪkl; ˈmædʒɪkəl/ *adj* **1** very enjoyable, exciting or romantic, in a strange or special way 奇异的，瑰丽的；迷人的：*that magical evening we spent together* 我们一起度过的那个迷人的夜晚 **2** containing magic, or done using magic 有魔力的；用魔法做成的：*magical powers* 神奇的力量 —**magically** /-kḷɪ; -kli/ *adv*

magic car·pet /ˌ‥ ˈ‥/ *n* [C] a CARPET¹ (1) that people use to travel through the air in children's stories〔童话故事中人们用以在空中飞行的〕魔毯

magic eye /ˌ‥ ˈ/ *n* [C] *informal* a PHOTOELECTRIC CELL【非正式】电眼〔光电管的俗名〕

ma·gi·cian /məˈdʒɪʃən; məˈdʒɪʃən/ *n* [C] **1** someone in stories who can use magic; WIZARD (1)〔故事中的〕巫师，术士 **2** an entertainer who performs magic tricks; CONJURER 魔术师，变戏法的人

> **CULTURAL NOTE 文化注释**
>
> The STEREOTYPE of a magician is a man wearing a black CLOAK. He waves a MAGIC WAND and says magic words, for example 'ABRACADABRA', when he is performing magic tricks. Traditional tricks include making things appear and disappear, especially making a rabbit appear from a TOP HAT (=a tall black hat), and SAW*ing* a woman in half. The magician puts a woman in a box, then cuts through the middle of the box and appears to cut the woman in half. 魔术师的典型形象是一个身披黑色斗篷的男人。魔术师表演魔术时挥动魔棒口念诸如 abracadabra 的咒语。传统的魔术包括把一个东西变出来和变没有，特别是那种从黑色高顶大礼帽中变出一只兔子的魔术。另外还有，魔术师让一个女人进入箱子里，然后把箱子从中间锯开，给人的感觉是他将里面的女人锯成了两半。

magic lan·tern /ˌ‥ ˈ‥/ *n* [C] a piece of equipment used in the past to make pictures shine onto a white wall or surface〔旧时的〕幻灯

magic mush·room /ˌ‥ ˈ‥/ *n* [C] a type of MUSHROOM that has an effect like some drugs, and makes you see things that are not really there 神奇蘑菇，致幻蘑菇〔一种食用后像某些药物一样使人产生幻觉的蘑菇〕

Magic Real·is·m /ˌ‥ ˈ‥‥/ *n* [U] a style of imaginative NOVEL writing connected especially with 20th century writers from Latin America, such as Jorge Luis Borges, Gabriel García Marquez, and Isabel Allende, in which impossible events are described as if they are real 魔幻现实主义〔一种充满幻想的小说创作风格，尤为 20 世纪拉美作家豪尔赫·路易斯·博尔赫斯、加布里埃尔·加西亚·马尔克斯和伊莎贝尔·阿连德所推崇。其特征是把不可能发生的事件描写成真人真事〕

M

magic wand /ˌ‥ ˈ/ *n* [C] **1** a small stick used by a MAGICIAN 魔杖 **2 wave a magic wand** *humorous* to solve problems or difficulties immediately【幽默】挥舞魔杖〔立刻解决问题或困难〕：*I can't just wave my magic wand and make your problems disappear!* 我不可能只靠挥舞魔杖便使你的问题消失！

Ma·gi·not Line, the /ˈmæʒɪno ˌlaɪn; ˈmæʒɪ̈nəʊ ˌlaɪn/ a line of FORTS (=very strong buildings for use by an army) built before World War II to defend the eastern border of France against the Germans. It was not effective, because the German army avoided it by going through Belgium. 马其诺防线〔第二次世界大战之前法国修筑的一排堡垒，以防止德军从法国东部边境攻入。然而，德军取道比利时，绕过马其诺防线，使其未能发挥作用〕

ma·gis·te·ri·al /ˌmædʒɪsˈtɪrɪəl; ˌmædʒɪ̈ˈstɪəriəl◂/ *adj* **1** a magisterial way of behaving or speaking shows that you think you have authority〔行为或说话方式〕自以为权威的：*his magisterial voice* 他那盛气凌人的语调 **2** a magisterial book is written by someone who has very great knowledge about a subject 具有学术权威性的：*his magisterial study of the First World War* 他对第一次世界大战的权威性研究 **3** connected with or done by a magistrate 与地方法官有关的；由地方法官经办的：*magisterial district* 地方法官的管辖区 —**magisterially** *adv*

ma·gis·tra·cy /ˈmædʒɪstrəsɪ; ˈmædʒɪ̈strəsi/ *n* [U] **1** the official position of a magistrate, or the time during which someone has this position 地方法官的职位[任期]；治安法官的职位[任期] **2 the magistracy** magistrates considered together as a group〔总称〕地方法官；治安法官

ma·gis·trate /ˈmædʒɪsˌtret; ˈmædʒɪ̈streɪt/ *n* [C] someone who judges less serious crimes in a court of law 地方法官；治安法官

> **CULTURAL NOTE 文化注释**
>
> In England and Wales, a magistrate is also called a Justice of the Peace or JP. Magistrates in the UK do not have any special training in law, and they are not paid for their work. If they need information about the law, magistrates are advised by a clerk, who is either a SOLICITOR OR A BARRISTER. But the decision about whether someone is guilty or not is made by the magistrate. Being a magistrate is considered to be a very responsible position in society. 在英格兰和威尔士，治安法官也叫做 Justice of the Peace 或 JP。英国的治安法官并未接受过任何特殊的法律训练，同时他们从事此项工作也没有报酬。在需要法律帮助的时候，治安法官可以从事务律师或出庭律师那里获取建议。但最终判不判某人有罪还是由治安法官说了算。坐在治安法官的位子上被认为要担起很大的社会责任。

Magistrates' Court /ˈ‥‥, ˌ/ *n* [C] the lowest court of law in England and Wales, which deals with less serious crimes〔英格兰和威尔士审理轻罪案件的〕地方法庭

mag·ma /ˈmægmə; ˈmægmə/ *n* [U] *technical* hot melted rock below the surface of the Earth【术语】岩浆

Mag·na Car·ta /ˌmægnə ˈkartə; ˌmægnə ˈkɑːtə/ an important document in British history which King John of England signed in 1215 at Runnymede in the south of England. By doing this he agreed that limits could be set on royal powers. Later, especially in the 17th century, the document was seen as a statement of basic civil rights.《大宪章》〔英国历史上一重要文件，1215 年由英格兰国王约翰在英格兰南部的兰尼米德签署。此举表明国王同意对王室权力设限。之后，该文件被视为基本民权的一份声明，到 17 世纪尤为如此〕

mag·na cum lau·de /ˌmægnə kum ˈlɔdɪ; ˌmægnə kʌm ˈlɔːdi/ *adj, adv Latin* at the second of the three highest levels of achievement that American students can reach when they finish their college studies【拉丁】优等成绩的；以优等成绩〔美国大学生毕业时取得的三个最高等级成绩中的第二等〕—compare 比较 CUM LAUDE, SUMMA CUM LAUDE

mag·nan·i·mous /mægˈnænəməs; mægˈnænɪ̈məs/ *adj* kind and generous, especially to someone that you have defeated in some way 宽宏大量的，慷慨的〔尤指对被自己击败的人〕：*a magnanimous gesture* 宽宏大量的姿态 —**magnanimously** *adv* —**magnanimity** /ˌmægnəˈnɪmətɪ; ˌmægnəˈnɪmɪ̈ti/ *n* [U]

mag·nate /ˈmægnet; ˈmægneɪt/ *n* [C] **steel/oil/shipping magnate** a rich and powerful person in a particular industry 钢铁/石油/船运业大亨

mag·ne·sia /mægˈniʃə; mægˈniːʃə/ *n* [U] a light, white powder used in medicine and in industry 镁氧；氧化镁 —see also 另见 MILK OF MAGNESIA

mag·ne·si·um /mægˈniʃɪəm; mægˈniːziəm/ *n* [U] a common silver-white metal that burns with a bright yellow light 镁

mag·net /ˈmægnɪt; ˈmægnɪ̈t/ *n* [C] **1** a piece of iron or steel that can make other metal objects move towards it 磁铁；磁石，吸铁石 **2** a person or place that attracts many other people or things 有吸引力的人[地方]：*The region has become a magnet for small businesses.* 那里已变成一个吸引小企业的地区。

mag·net·ic /mæg`nɛtɪk; mæg'netɪk/ *adj* **1** connected with or produced by MAGNETISM 磁的; 磁性的: *magnetic forces* 磁力 | *a magnetic disk* 磁盘 **2 magnetic personality/charm etc** a personality etc that makes other people feel strongly attracted towards you 具有吸引力的个性/特点等 **3** having the power of a magnet 有磁力[磁性]的: *a magnetic bulletin board* 磁性公告板 —**magnetically** /-kl̩ɪ; -kli/ *adv*

magnetic field /·,··'·/ *n* [U] an area around an object that has magnetic power 磁场

magnetic head /·,··'·/ *n* [C] **1** the part of a TAPE RECORDER that records sound〔录音机的录音〕磁头 **2** the part of a computer that reads and writes DATA〔电脑读写数据的〕磁头

magnetic me·di·a /·,··'···/ *n* [plural,U] magnetic methods of storing information for computers, for example FLOPPY DISKs or MAGNETIC TAPE 磁介质〔为电脑储存信息的介质, 如软盘或磁带〕

magnetic north /·,··'·/ *n* [U] the northern direction shown by the needle on a COMPASS (1) 磁北 —compare 比较 TRUE NORTH

magnetic pole /·,··'·/ *n* [C] **1** one of the two points that are not firmly fixed but are near the North and South Poles of the Earth, towards which the needle on a COMPASS (1) points〔地球的〕磁极 **2** a POLE[1] (5a)〔磁铁的〕磁极

magnetic tape /·,··'·/ *n* [U] TAPE[1] (1a) on which sound, pictures, or computer information can be recorded using magnetism〔录音、录像或电脑储存信息用的〕磁带; 录音带; 录像带

mag·net·is·m /`mægnə,tɪzəm; 'mægnl̩tɪzəm/ *n* [U] **1** the physical force by which a MAGNET (1) attracts metal, or which is produced when an electric current is passed through iron or steel 磁力; 磁性 **2** a quality that makes other people feel attracted to you 魅力, 吸引力: *his extraordinary personal magnetism* 他那非凡的个人魅力

mag·net·ize also 又作 **-ise** *BrE*【英】/`mægnə,taɪz; 'mægnl̩taɪz/ *v* [T] **1** to make iron or steel able to attract other pieces of metal 使有磁性; 使磁化 **2** to have a powerful effect on people so that they feel strongly attracted to you 强烈吸引, 迷住: *His dark flashing eyes magnetized those around him.* 他那双炯炯有神的黑眼睛吸引住了周围的人。

mag·ne·to /mæg`nito; mæg'ni:təʊ/ *n* [C] a piece of equipment containing one or more magnets that is used for producing electricity, especially in the engine of a car〔尤指用于汽车引擎的〕磁电机, 永磁发电机

magnet school /'··,·/ *n* [C] *AmE* a school that has more classes in a particular subject than usual, and so attracts students from a wide area【美】磁铁学校, 特别才艺学校〔这种学校在某一学科上开设的课时比一般学校多, 所以学生来源的地域范围广〕

Mag·nif·i·cat /mæg`nɪfɪkæt; mæg'nɪfl̩kæt/ a song in praise of God which is used in some Christian church services. Its words are the words said by Mary in the New Testament of the Bible, after she discovers that she is going to be the mother of Jesus.《尊主颂》〔基督教某些礼拜仪式上赞美上帝的一首颂歌。歌词据《圣经·新约》记载是马利亚得知自己将成为圣母之后所说的话〕

mag·ni·fi·ca·tion /,mægnəfə`keʃən; ,mægnl̩fl̩'keɪʃən/ *n* **1** [U] the act of magnifying 放大: *The fingerprints showed up clearly under magnification.* 放大后指纹清晰地显示了出来。**2** [C] the degree to which something is able to magnify things 放大率, 放大倍数: *binoculars with a magnification of x12* 放大倍数为12倍的双筒望远镜

mag·nif·i·cent /mæg`nɪfəsn̩t; mæg'nɪfl̩sənt/ *adj* extremely impressive because of being very big, beautiful etc 宏伟的, 壮丽的; 华丽的, 富丽堂皇的: *The view from the summit was magnificent.* 从山顶望去, 景色壮观动人。| *a magnificent collection of Mexican art* 一批精美的墨西哥艺术收藏品 | *her magnificent mane of red hair* 她又长又密的漂亮红发 —**magnificently** *adv* —**magnificence** *n* [U]

mag·ni·fy /`mægnə,faɪ; 'mægnl̩faɪ/ *v* [T] **1** to make something look bigger than it is 放大: *The photo shows a human embryo, magnified 150 times.* 这张照片上是一个放大了150倍的人类胚胎。**2** to make something seem more important than it really is 夸张, 夸大: *This report tends to magnify the risks involved.* 这个报告有夸大所涉风险的倾向。**3** *formal* to make a problem much worst or more serious【正式】使〔问题〕加重: *The results of economic mismanagement were magnified by a series of natural disasters.* 经济管理不善造成的后果因一连串自然灾害而变得更加严重。**4** *biblical* to praise God【圣经】赞美〔上帝〕—**magnifier** *n* [C]

magnifying glass /'····,·/ *n* [C] a round piece of glass with a handle, used to make objects or print look bigger 放大镜 —see picture at 参见 MAGNIFY 图

mag·ni·tude /`mægnə,tjud; 'mægnl̩tju:d/ *n* **1** [U] greatness of size or importance 巨大, 庞大; 重要性: *They didn't seem to appreciate the magnitude of the problem.* 他们似乎没有意识到这个问题的重要性。**2** [C] *technical* the degree of brightness of a star【术语】〔恒星的〕光度, 星等

mag·no·li·a /mæg`nolɪə; mæg'nəʊliə/ *n* **1** [C] a tree with large white, pink, yellow, or purple flowers that smell sweet 木兰 **2** [U] a very pale pinkish-white colour 淡桃红色

mag·num /`mægnəm; 'mægnəm/ *n* [C] **1** a large bottle containing about 1.5 litres of wine, CHAMPAGNE etc〔约装1.5公升葡萄酒或香槟酒等的〕大酒瓶 **2** a type of large PISTOL 大口径手枪: *a 44 magnum* 口径0.44英寸的大口径手枪

magnum o·pus /,··'··/ *n* [singular] *Latin* the most important piece of work by a writer or artist【拉丁】〔作家或艺术家的〕最重要的作品, 代表作

mag·pie /`mæg,paɪ; 'mægpaɪ/ *n* [C] **1** a bird with black and white feathers and a long tail 喜鹊 **2** *informal* someone who likes collecting things【非正式】爱收集东西的人

Ma·gritte /mæ`grit; mæ'gri:t/, **Re·né** /rə`ne; 'reneɪ/ (1898-1967) a Belgian SURREALIST painter who combined in his pictures familiar objects that do not usually belong together 马格里特〔(1898-1967), 比利时超现实主义画家, 常把不相干的常见物体画在一起〕

mag tape /'··/ *n* [U] *BrE informal* MAGNETIC TAPE【英, 非正式】磁带

ma·ha·ra·jah, maharaja /,mahə`radʒə; ,ma:hə'ra:dʒə/ *n* [C] an Indian prince or king〔印度的〕王子; 国王; 王公; 土邦主

ma·ha·ra·ni, maharanee /mahə`rani; ,ma:hə'ra:ni:/ *n* [C] an Indian PRINCESS or queen〔印度的〕公主; 王妃; 土邦主之妻

ma·ha·rish·i /mə`harəʃi; ,ma:hə'ri:ʃi/ *n* [C] a HINDU holy teacher〔印度教的〕宗教教师

ma·hat·ma /mə`hætmə; mə'hætmə/ *n* a title used for a wise and holy man in India 圣雄, 圣人〔印度对智者、圣贤的称呼〕

Ma·ha·ya·na /,mahə`janə; ,ma:hə'ja:nə/ *adj* of the form of Buddhism practised in Tibet and other parts of China, based on developments of the original teachings of the Buddha starting in the first century 大乘的〔大乘是佛教的一种形式, 主要流行于中国西藏和其他地区, 由创立于一世纪的佛陀最初教义发展而来〕

Mah·di, the /`madɪ; 'ma:di/ in Islam, the name given to a holy leader who, according to Muslims, will be sent by God and will make all people in the world follow Islam. Many Muslim leaders have claimed to be the Mahdi. 马赫迪〔伊斯兰教对救世主的称呼。据伊斯兰教义, 真主将派马赫迪前来人间, 让世上所有的人都皈依伊斯兰教。曾有不少穆斯林领袖自称马赫迪〕

mah·jong, mahjongg /ma`dʒaŋ; ,ma:'dʒɒŋ/ *n* [U] a Chinese game played with small pieces of wood or bone 麻将〔中国的一种牌戏〕

Mah·ler /`malɚ; 'ma:lə/, **Gus·tav** /`gʌstav; 'gʊsta:v/ (1860-1911) an Austrian COMPOSER whose work is typical of the romantic style. His most famous works are his symphonies (SYMPHONY) and his sets of songs, *Das Lied von der Erde* and *Kindertotenlieder*. 马勒〔(1860-1911), 奥地利作曲家。其作品具有典型的浪漫主义风格, 以交响曲和组歌套曲最为有名, 如《大地之歌》和《亡儿悼歌》〕

ma·hog·a·ny /mə`hagənɪ; mə'hɒgəni/ *n* **1** [C,U] a type of hard reddish brown wood used for making furniture, or the tree that produces this wood〔制家具用的〕桃花心木, 红木; 桃花心木科的树 **2** [U] a dark, reddish brown colour 深赤褐色 —**mahogany** *adj*

magnify 放大

M

ma·hout /mə`haʊt; mɑːˈhuːt/ *n* [C] *IndE* someone who rides and trains elephants【印】象夫，御象者，赶象人，管象人

maid /med; meɪd/ *n* [C] **1** a female servant, especially in a large house〔尤指大户人家的〕女仆: *a kitchen maid* 厨房女用人 **2** *old use* a woman or girl who is not married【旧】未婚女子；姑娘，少女 —see also 另见 OLD MAID

maid·en¹ /`medn̩; ˈmeɪdn/ *n* [C] *literary* a girl who is not married【文】少女；姑娘

maiden² *adj* **1 maiden flight/voyage** the first journey that a plane or ship makes〔飞机或船的〕首次飞行/航行 **2 maiden speech** *BrE* the first speech that someone makes in parliament【英】〔在议会中的〕首次演说

maiden aunt /ˌ‥ ˈ·/ *n* [C] an AUNT who has never married〔从未结婚的〕姑；姨

mai·den·hair /`medn̩ˌhɛr; ˈmeɪdnheə/ *n* [U] a kind of FERN 掌叶铁线蕨，孔雀草

maid·en·head /`medn̩ˌhɛd; ˈmeɪdnhed/ *n old use*【旧】**1** [U] the state of being a female VIRGIN 童贞；处女时期 **2** [C] a HYMEN 处女膜

maid·en·ly /`medn̩lɪ; ˈmeɪdnli/ *adj old use* typical of a girl or young woman【旧】少女[年轻女子]所特有的: *maidenly modesty* 少女特有的谦逊

maiden name /ˈ‥ ˌ·/ *n* [C] the family name that a woman had before she got married 妇女的娘家姓

CULTURAL NOTE 文化注释

In both the US and the UK, women traditionally used to take their husband's last name when they got married, and stopped using their own last name. Now, however, many women decide to keep using their maiden name after they get married, especially if they have become known in their profession by that name. Other women, especially in the US, now use both their own and their husband's last name, often joined together with a hyphen. 在英美两国，传统上妇女结婚后使用丈夫的姓氏，而不再使用自己娘家的姓氏。可是现在很多已婚妇女决定仍使用娘家姓，特别是娘家姓在其职业上已经广为人知的妇女。还有些妇女，特别是在美国，现在既不放弃娘家姓又采用夫家的姓，通常在两个姓中间添一个连字符。— see also Cultural Note at MR 见 MR 文化注释

Maid Mar·i·an /ˌmed `mærɪən; ˌmeɪd ˈmæriən/ a woman who, in old English stories, has a romantic relationship with Robin Hood 玛丽安小姐〔英国古老传奇故事中罗宾汉的情人〕

maid of hon·our /ˌ‥ ˈ‥/ *n* [C] **1** the chief BRIDESMAID at a wedding 首席女傧相，主要伴娘 **2** an unmarried lady who serves a queen or a PRINCESS 女王[王后，公主]的未婚侍女 **3** *BrE* a type of small cake【英】牛奶蛋糊[杏仁]小馅饼

Maid of Or·le·ans, the /ˌmed əv `ɔrlɪənz; ˌmeɪd əv ɔːˈliːənz/ —see 见 JOAN OF ARC

maid·ser·vant /`medˌsɝvənt; ˈmeɪdˌsɜːvənt/ *n* [C] *old use* a female servant【旧】女用人，女仆 —compare 比较 MANSERVANT

Mai·gret /me`gre; ˈmeɪgreɪ/ a character who appears in many NOVELs by Georges Simenon. Maigret is a DETECTIVE (=a police officer whose job is to solve crimes) in Paris. 梅格雷〔乔治斯·西默农多部小说中的主人公。他是巴黎的一名侦探〕

3 3 **mail¹** /mel; meɪl/ *n* **1 the mail** *especially AmE* the system of collecting and delivering letters, packages etc; POST¹ (1)【尤美】邮政，邮递系统: *The mail here's really slow and unreliable.* 这里的邮递系统确实是既慢又不可靠。| **in the mail** *Your photos are in the mail.* 你的照片在邮寄途中。| *I'll put the check in the mail.* 我将把支票邮寄过去。| **by mail** *Did you send it by mail?* 你是把它邮寄过去的吗？—see also 另见 ELECTRONIC MAIL, SNAIL MAIL **2** [U] the letters, packages etc that are delivered to a particular person or at a particular time 邮件；邮包: *Did we get any mail this morning?* 我们上午收到什么邮件吗？| **in the mail** *Anything interesting in the mail?* 邮件中有什么有趣的东西吗？—see also 另见 JUNK MAIL **3** [U] armour made of metal worn in the Middle Ages〔中世纪穿的〕铠甲，锁子甲

3 **mail²** *v* [T] *especially AmE* to send a letter, package etc to someone【尤美】邮寄〔信件、包裹等〕; POST² (1) *BrE*【英】: **mail sth to sb** *I'll mail it to you tomorrow.* 我明天把它寄给你。

Mail, The another name for *The Daily Mail*《每日邮报》〔The Daily Mail 的别称〕

mail·bag /`melˌbæg; ˈmeɪlbæg/ *n* [C] **1** a large, strong bag used for carrying mail on trains etc〔火车等运送邮件的〕邮件袋 **2** *AmE* a bag used to deliver letters to people's houses【美】〔邮递员向住户递送邮件的〕邮袋; POSTBAG *BrE*【英】

mail·box /`melˌbɑks; ˈmeɪlbɒks/ *n* [C] *AmE*【美】**1** a box, usually outside a house, where someone's letters are delivered or collected〔通常置于住宅外的〕信箱 —compare 比较 LETTERBOX **2** a container where you post letters 邮箱，邮筒; POSTBOX *BrE*【英】

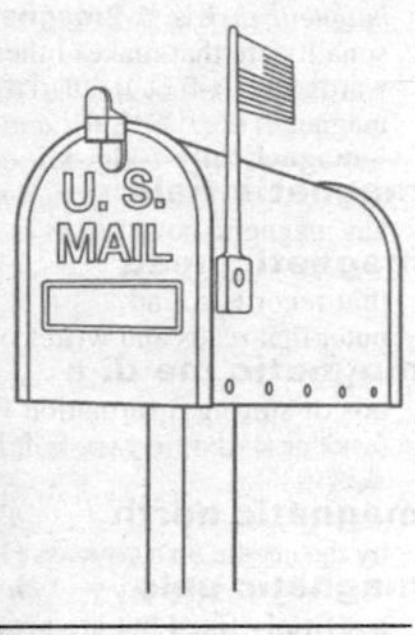

mailbox 信箱

CULTURAL NOTE 文化注释

In the US, most people have mailboxes, either next to their front door or in front of their house, near the street. Some mailboxes have a small flag on it that can be raised, and people can send mail from their home by putting a stamp on a letter and then putting it in their mailbox and raising the flag. 大多数美国人都有信箱，要么设在大门旁边，要么设在门前面的临街处。有些信箱上面有一个可以升起的小旗，人们只要将信贴上邮票，投入信箱，然后升起小旗，这样信就可以从家中寄出了。

mail car·ri·er /ˈ· ˌ‥/ *n* [C] *AmE old-fashioned* someone who delivers mail to people's houses【美，过时】邮递员

mail drop /ˈ· ·/ *n* [C] *AmE*【美】**1** an address where someone's mail is delivered, which is not where they live 通信地址〔非收件人居住地址〕**2** a box in a post office where your mail can be left〔设在邮局内的〕邮箱

mail·er /`melɚ; ˈmeɪlə/ *n* [C] *especially AmE* a container or envelope used for sending something small by mail【尤美】包装小邮件用的容器[信封]

Mailer, Norman (1923-2007) a US writer and journalist, who writes about social and political subjects and criticizes US society. His NOVELs often contain a lot of sex and violence, and many of them are based on real events. They include *The Naked and the Dead*, *The American Dream*, *The Armies of the Night*, and *The Executioner's Song*. 梅勒〔(1923-2007)，美国作家和记者。作品常涉及社会和政治题材，借以抨击美国社会。其小说不乏对性和暴力的描写，并多取材于真人真事。代表作有《裸者和死者》、《美国梦》、《黑夜的军队》和《刽子手之歌》

mailing list /ˈ‥ ˌ·/ *n* [C] a list of names and addresses kept by an organization, so that it can send information or advertising material by mail〔供寄送资料或广告材料用的〕邮寄名单

mail·man /`melˌmæn; ˈmeɪlmæn/ *n plural* **mailmen** /-ˌmɛn; -men/ [C] *AmE* a man who delivers mail to people's houses【美】邮递员; POSTMAN *BrE*【英】

Mail on Sun·day, The /ˌ· · ˈ‥/ a British TABLOID newspaper produced every Sunday by the same company that produces *The Daily Mail*《星期日邮报》〔英国一种周日发行的小报，与《每日邮报》同属一家报业公司〕

mail or·der /ˌ· ˈ‥◂/ *n* [U] a method of buying and selling in which the buyer chooses goods at home and orders them from a company which sends them by mail 邮购

mail·shot /`melʃɑt; ˈmeɪlʃɒt/ *n* [C] advertisements or information sent to many people at one time by mail〔大量发送的〕邮寄资料，邮寄广告

mail train /ˈ· ·/ *n* [C] a train that carries mail 邮政列车

maim /mem; meɪm/ *v* [T] to wound or injure someone very seriously and often permanently 使受重伤，使残疾: *landmines that kill or maim people in the rural areas* 乡村地区炸死或炸伤人的地雷 | **maimed for life** *Rod was maimed for life in a car smash.* 罗德在一次撞车事故中受重伤，终身残疾。

main¹ /men; meɪn/ *adj* [only before noun 仅用于名词前] **1** bigger or more important than all other things, ideas, influences etc of the same kind〔同类中〕主要的，最重要的；最大的: *I noted down the main points of her speech.* 我把她讲话的要点记了下来。| *The main bedroom is at the back of the house.* 主卧室在房子的后部。| *Lack of confidence was the main reason behind the team's defeat.* 缺乏信心是球队失败的主要原因。| *Our main concern is that the children are safe.* 我们最关心的是孩子们的安全。| *the main female character in the movie* 电影中的女主人公 **2 the main thing** *spoken* used to say what is the most important thing in a situation【口】最重要的事: *As long as you're not hurt, that's the main thing.* 只要你不受到伤害 — 这才是最重要的。| *The main thing is not to panic.* 最重要的是不要惊慌。  1 1

—see also 另见 **with an eye to the main chance** (EYE[1] (36)), **the main drag** (DRAG[2] (7))

main² *n* **1** [C] a large pipe or wire carrying the public supply of water, electricity or gas〔供水、供电、供煤气的〕总管道; 干线电缆: *a burst water main in the street* 街上爆裂的自来水总管道 **2 the mains** *BrE*【英】**a)** the place on a wall you can connect something to a supply of electricity 电源插座: *You can run it off batteries or plug it into the mains.* 你可以用电池或者把它插到电源插座上使用。| **at the mains** *Make sure that the television is turned off at the mains.* 一定要把电视机的电源关上。**b) mains gas/electricity/water** the public supply of gas etc through large pipes or wires 由总管道[干线]输送的煤气/电/水: *The heater will run off mains gas or bottled gas.* 加热器用管道煤气或罐装煤气均可。**3 in the main** mostly 大体上, 基本上: *Her fellow students were in the main from wealthy backgrounds.* 她的同学大都来自富有的家庭。—see also 另见 **with might and main** (MIGHT² (1))

main clause /, · ˈ·/ *n* [C] *technical* a CLAUSE that can form a sentence on its own【术语】主句〔能独立构成句子的分句〕

main course /ˈ· ·/ *n* [C] the main part of a meal 主菜

main drag, the /, · ˈ·/ *n AmE informal* the main street in a town or city where big shops and businesses are【美, 非正式】〔城镇的〕主要街道, 大街: *cruising along the main drag in Las Vegas* 沿着拉斯维加斯的主要大街慢驶

Maine /men; meɪn/ abbreviation 缩写为 **ME** a state in the northeast of the US, next to the Atlantic coast and the border with Canada. Maine is the largest state in New England, and is famous for its beautiful forests, mountains, and coast. 缅因州〔美国东北部一州, 濒临大西洋, 与加拿大接壤。该州是新英格兰最大的一个州, 以森林、山色和海岸之秀美而著称〕

main·frame /ˈmen͵frem; ˈmeɪnfreɪm/ *n* [C] a large computer that can work very fast and that a lot of people can use at the same time 主〔计算〕机

main·land, the /ˈmen͵lænd; ˈmeɪnlənd/ *n* the main area of land that forms a country, as compared to islands near it that are also part of that country 大陆, 本土〔与和它一起构成一个国家领土的邻近岛屿相对而言〕: *a ferry service between the islands and the mainland* 往返各岛屿与大陆之间的轮渡服务 —**mainland** *adj*: *mainland Britain* 英国本土

main line /, · ˈ·◂/ *n* [C] an important railway that connects two cities〔连接两座城市的〕铁路干线: *the main line to Moscow* 通往莫斯科的铁路干线 —**mainline** *adj*: *a mainline station* 铁路干线车站

main·line /ˈmen͵laɪn; ˈmeɪnlaɪn/ *v* [I,T] *slang* to INJECT illegal drugs into your blood【俚】向自己的血液中注射〔毒品〕: *By that time he was mainlining heroin.* 当时他正在注射海洛因。

main·ly /ˈmenlɪ; ˈmeɪnli/ *adv* as the largest or most important reason, thing, part of something etc 主要地; 大部分地: *Her illness was caused mainly by worry and stress.* 她的病主要是由焦虑和精神压力引起的。| *The workforce is mainly made up of women.* 劳动力主要是由妇女构成的。| *the mainly Zulu Inkatha Freedom Party* 主要由祖鲁人组成的因卡塔自由党 | [sentence adverb 句子副词] *"What did you do all evening?" "Well, we just talked mainly."* "你们整个晚上干什么了?" "噢, 我们主要是聊天而已。" | **mainly because** *I don't go out much, mainly because I have to look after the kids.* 我不大出去, 主要是因为我必须照看孩子们。| **mainly due to** (=caused to a great degree by) 主要由…引起 *Increased sales during the summer were mainly due to tourism.* 夏季销售额增加主要是由旅游业带动的。| **mainly why/what/how** *spoken*【口】*Boredom was mainly why I decided to quit.* 工作枯燥乏味是我决定辞职的主要原因。

main·mast /ˈmen͵mæst; ˈmeɪnmɑːst/ *n* [C] the largest or most important of the MASTS that hold up the sails on a ship〔船的〕主桅, 大桅

main road /, · ˈ·/ *n* [C] a large and important road 大路

main·sail /ˈmen͵sl; ˈmeɪnsəl; *not tech* 非术语 -sel; -seɪl/ *n* [C] the largest and most important sail on a ship〔船的〕主帆 —see picture at 参见 YACHT 图

main·spring /ˈmen͵sprɪŋ; ˈmeɪnsprɪŋ/ *n* [C] **1 the mainspring of/for** the most important reason or influence that makes something happen …的主要原因: *Romantic love had been the mainspring of Augustini's poetry.* 浪漫的爱情造就了奥古斯丁尼的诗歌。**2** the most important spring in a watch or clock〔钟表的〕主发条

main·stay /ˈmen͵ste; ˈmeɪnsteɪ/ *n* **the mainstay of a)** an important part of something that makes it possible for it to work properly or continue to exist …的主要依靠[支柱]: *Agriculture is still the mainstay of the country's economy.* 农业仍然是这个国家经济的主要支柱。**b)** someone who does most of the important work for a group or organization …的挑大梁的人物[台柱子, 骨干]: *She was the mainstay of the team.* 她是这个小组的骨干。

main·stream¹ /ˈmen͵strim; ˈmeɪnstriːm/ *n* **1 the mainstream of** the most usual way of thinking about something or doing something〔思想或行为〕的主流: *Environmental ideas have been absorbed into the mainstream of European politics.* 环境意识已被纳入欧洲政治的主流。**2 the mainstream** the people whose ideas about a subject are shared by most people and regarded as normal 主流派人物: *Genet started as a rebel, but soon became part of the literary mainstream.* 吉尼特开始是一位叛逆者, 但不久就成为文学主流派中的一员。—**mainstream** *adj*: *mainstream economic theory* 主流经济理论

mainstream² *v* [T] *AmE* to include a child with physical or mental problems in an ordinary class【美】把〔生理或心理上有问题的儿童〕安排到普通班级中

Main Street /ˈ· ·/ *n* **1** [C] the most important street, with many shops and businesses on it, in many small towns in the US〔美国许多小城镇的〕大街, 主街 —compare 比较 HIGH STREET **2** [U] *AmE* ordinary people who believe in traditional American values【美】〔信仰美国传统价值观的〕普通民众, 老百姓: *The President's new tax hikes won't go down too well on Main Street.* 总统再次提高税收, 这不会受到普通老百姓的欢迎。

> **CULTURAL NOTE 文化注释**
> Sinclair Lewis wrote a novel called *Main Street* about life in a small town in the MIDWEST in which the characters have traditional, conservative beliefs and are unwilling to accept or understand new ideas. 辛克莱·刘易斯的小说《大街》讲述美国中西部一个小镇的生活, 那里的人们思想传统而保守, 不愿意接受和理解新观念。

main·tain /menˈten; meɪnˈteɪn/ *v* [T]
1 ▶MAKE STH CONTINUE 使某事继续◀ to make something continue in the same way or at the same high standard as before 保持; 维持: *Britain wants to maintain its position as a world power.* 英国想保持其世界强国的地位。| *our commitment to maintaining a high-quality service* 我们保持高质量服务的承诺
2 ▶LEVEL/RATE 水平/速度◀ to make a level or rate of activity, movement etc stay the same 保持〔水平或速度〕: *It is important to maintain a constant temperature inside the greenhouse.* 使温室内的温度保持恒定是很重要的。
3 ▶MACHINE/BUILDING 机器/建筑物◀ to keep a machine, building etc in good condition by looking after it 维修; 保养〔机器、建筑物等〕: *The report found that safety equipment had been very poorly maintained.* 报告说安全设备保养得很糟糕。
4 maintain your silence/opposition etc to continue to be silent, to oppose something etc 保持沉默/坚持反对意见等: *Evans has always maintained his allegiance to the trade union movement.* 埃文斯一贯拥护工会运动。
5 ▶SAY 说◀ to strongly express your belief that something is true 断言〔某事〕属实; 坚持说…: **maintain (that)** *Critics maintain that these reforms will lead to a decline in educational standards.* 批评者坚称这些改革会导致教育水平下降。| **maintain your innocence** (=continue to say that you are not guilty of something) 坚称自己无罪
6 ▶MONEY/FOOD 金钱/食物◀ to provide someone with the things they need, such as money or food 供养; 赡养: *How can you maintain a family on $900 a month?* 你每月900美元怎么能维持一家人的生活呢?
7 maintain life to provide animals, plants etc with the things they need in order to exist 维持〔动植物等的〕生命

main·te·nance /ˈmentənəns; ˈmeɪntənəns/ *n* [U] **1** the repairs, painting etc that are necessary to keep something in good condition 维修; 养护, 保养: **[+of]** *The caretaker is responsible for the maintenance of the school buildings.* 管理员负责保养维修学校的各栋楼房。| **car/building etc maintenance** *evening classes in car maintenance* 汽车维修夜校课程 | **maintenance man** (=a man who looks after buildings and equipment for a school or company)〔为学校或公司看楼或看管设备的〕管理员 **2** *BrE* money paid by someone who is DIVORCED to their former wife or husband【英】〔付给前妻或前夫的〕赡养费; CHILD SUPPORT *AmE*【美】**3** the act of making a state or situation continue 保持; 维持: *the maintenance of good relations between the two countries* 两国间友好关系的保持

mai·son·ette /͵mezəˈnɛt; ͵meɪzəˈnet/ *n* [C] *BrE* an apartment, usually on two floors, that is part of a larger house【英】〔通常占有两层楼的〕公寓套房

mai·tre d' /͵metrə ˈdi; ͵metrə ˈdiː/ also 又作 **maître d'hôtel** /͵mɛtrə doˈtɛl; ͵metrə dəʊˈtel/ *n* [C] *French* someone who is in

charge of a restaurant, and who welcomes guests, gives orders to the waiters etc【法】餐馆经理; 餐馆服务员领班 —see picture on page A15 参见 A15 页图

maize /mez; meɪz/ *n* [U] *BrE* a type of tall plant with large yellow seeds which are used for food【英】玉蜀黍, 玉米; CORN (2a) *AmE*【美】

Maj. the written abbreviation of 缩写= MAJOR² (1)

ma·jes·tic /məˋdʒɛstɪk; məˈdʒestɪk/ *adj* very big and impressive 雄伟壮丽的; 威严的: *the majestic temples of Bangkok* 曼谷雄伟的寺庙 —**majestically** /-klɪ; -kli/ *adv*

ma·jes·ty /ˋmædʒɪstɪ; ˈmædʒɪsti/ *n* [U] **1 Your/Her/His Majesty** used when talking to or about a king or queen 陛下〔对国王或女王的称呼〕: *The Prime Minister is here to see you, Your Majesty.* 首相前来拜谒, 陛下。| *His Majesty the King* 国王陛下 **2** the quality of being impressive and powerful that something big has 雄伟, 壮丽; 庄严; 崇高: *the awesome majesty of the snow-capped Rocky Mountains* 白雪覆顶的落基山脉令人惊叹的壮丽

ma·jor¹ /ˋmedʒɚ; ˈmeɪdʒə/ *adj* **1** [usually before noun 一般用于名词前] very large or important, when compared to other things or people of a similar kind 较大的; 较重要的; 主要的: *There are two major political parties in the US.* 美国有两大政党。| *Mahler's music was a major influence on the young composer.* 马勒的音乐极大地影响了那位年轻的作曲家。| *one of the major causes of cancer* 癌症的主要病因之一 —opposite 反义词 MINOR¹ (1) **2** [usually before noun 一般用于名词前] having very serious or worrying results 后果十分严重的; 后果非常令人担忧的: *The loss of Cantona through injury was a major setback for the team.* 简东拿因伤缺阵使该队遭受了严重的损失。| **major problem** *This could create major traffic problems.* 这会产生严重的交通问题。**3** [not before noun 不用于名词前] *AmE spoken* very important【美口】非常重要的: *This is major? You got me out of bed for this?* 这就叫做重要? 你把我从床上弄起来就是为了这个? **4** a major key (KEY² (4)) is based on a musical SCALE in which there are SEMITONES between the third and fourth and the seventh and eighth notes〔音乐〕大音阶的, 大调的: *a symphony in D major* D大调交响乐 —compare 比较 MINOR¹ (2)

major² *n* [C] **1** an officer of middle rank in the British or US army or MARINES, or in the US airforce〔英国〕陆军[海军陆战队]少校; 〔美国〕陆军[空军、海军陆战队]少校 —see table on page C6 参见 C6 页附录 —see also 另见 DRUM MAJOR **2** *especially AmE* the main subject that a student studies at college or university【尤美】〔大学的〕主修科目, 专业: *Her major is history.* 她的主修科目是历史。—compare 比较 MINOR² (2) **3** *AmE* someone studying a particular subject as their main subject at college or university【美】〔大学中〕主修某科目的学生, 某专业的学生: *She's a history major.* 她是历史专业的学生。**4 the majors** [plural] the MAJOR LEAGUES〔美〕职业棒球大联盟, 职业棒球联合总会 —compare 比较 MINOR LEAGUE

major³ *v*

major in sth *phr v* [T] *especially AmE* to study something as your main subject at college or university【尤美】〔在大学〕主修: *He's majoring in Political Science.* 他主修政治学。

Major, John (1943-) a British politician in the Conservative Party, who became Prime Minister when Margaret Thatcher was forced to leave this position in 1990, and was then elected in 1992. He was defeated in the election of 1997. 梅杰〔(1943-), 英国保守党政治家。1990 年, 玛格丽特·撒切尔被迫下台后, 他继任首相, 1992 年再度当选, 在 1997 年大选中落败〕

Ma·jor·ca /məˋjɔrkə; məˈjɔːkə/, **Mallorca** /mɑˋjɔrkɑ; mɑːˈjɔːkə/ a Spanish island in the west Mediterranean Sea, the largest of the Balearic Islands, which is very popular with tourists 马略卡岛〔西班牙一岛屿, 位于地中海西部, 是巴利阿里群岛中最大的岛屿, 深受游客喜爱〕

ma·jor·do·mo /ˏmedʒɚˋdomo; ˌmeɪdʒəˈdəʊməʊ/ *n* [C] *old-fashioned* someone in charge of the servants in a large house【过时】大管家, 总管

ma·jor·ette /ˏmedʒəˋrɛt; ˌmeɪdʒəˈret/ *n* [C] a girl who spins a BATON while marching with a band〔乐队行进时手中转动着指挥棒的〕女指挥, 女领队

major gen·e·ral /ˌ‥ ˈ‥◂/ *n* [C] an officer of high rank in the British or US army or the US airforce〔英〕陆军少将;〔美〕陆军[空军]少将 —see table on page C6 参见 C6 页附录

ma·jor·i·ty /məˋdʒɔrətɪ; məˈdʒɒrɪti/ *n* **1** [singular] most of the people or things in a particular group 多数, 大多数〔人或物〕: [+of] *The majority of lone parents are divorced or separated women.* 单身父母中大多数是离婚或分居的妇女。| [also+plural verb *BrE* 英] *Among trade union leaders, a majority still believe in public ownership.* 工会领导人中多数仍然相信公有制。| **the great/vast majority** (=almost all of a group) 绝大多数, 几乎全体 *In the vast majority of cases the disease proves fatal.* 在绝大多数的病例中, 这种疾病结果都是致命的。| **a majority decision** (=a decision made by more people voting for it than against it) 多数人投票赞成的决定 **2 be in the majority** to form the largest part of a group 构成多数, 占多数: *Young people were in the majority at the meeting.* 这次会议年轻人占了多数。**3** [C] the difference between the number of votes gained by the winning party or person in an election and the number of votes gained by other parties or people 超过的票数〔选举中获胜党或个人所得票数与其他政党或候选人所得票数之间的差额〕: *Their majority in the House was reduced by 20.* 他们在议会中的多数议席减少了 20 席。| **overall majority** (=a situation in which one party wins more votes in an election than all the other parties)〔选举中一政党所获票数超过所有其他政党所获票数之和的〕总和多数票 | **by/with a majority** *He won by a majority of 500.* 他以 500 票的多数获胜。**4** [U] *law* the age when someone legally becomes a responsible adult【法律】成年; 法定年龄 —opposite 反义词 MINORITY

majority lead·er /ˌ·ˈ‥ ˌ‥/ *n* [C] the person who organizes the members of the political party that has the most people elected, in either the House of Representatives or the US Senate〔美国参议院或众议院中〕多数党领袖 —compare 比较 MINORITY LEADER

major-league /ˌ‥ ˈ·/ *adj* [usually before noun 一般用于名词前] **1** connected with the Major Leagues〔美国〕职业棒球大联盟的, 职业棒球联合总会的: *playing major-league baseball* 打联合会职业棒球赛 **2** *especially AmE* important or influential【尤美】重要的; 有影响的: *a major-league player in California politics* 在加州政坛上有影响力的人物

Major Leagues /ˌ‥ ˈ·/ *n* [plural] the group of teams that make up American professional baseball〔美国〕职业棒球大联盟, 职业棒球联合总会

make¹ /mek; meɪk/ *v past tense and past participle* made /med; meɪd/

① PRODUCE STH 制作某物	⑧ PRETEND 假装
② DO STH 做某事	⑨ MAKE IT 做成某事
③ CAUSE A STATE/SITUATION 导致某种状况/情况	⑩ CALCULATE 计算
	⑪ MANAGE 勉强应付
④ FORCE SB TO DO STH 迫使某人做某事	⑫ MAKE WAY 让路
⑤ MONEY 金钱	⑬ ARRIVE 到达
⑥ BE ADDED TOGETHER 加起来	⑭ BE GOOD/IMPORTANT 好/重要
⑦ BE SUITABLE 适合于	⑮ OTHER MEANINGS 其他意思

① PRODUCE STH 制作某物

1 [T] to produce something by working 做, 制作, 制造; 建造: *I'm going to make a cake for Sam's birthday.* 我打算为萨姆的生日做一个蛋糕。| *Did you make that dress yourself?* 那件衣服是你自己做的吗? | *a car made in Japan* 一辆日本制造的汽车 | *They're making a documentary about the Civil War.* 他们

正在拍一部有关南北战争的纪录片。| **make sth out of** *You could make some cushion covers out of those old curtains.* 你可以用那些旧窗帘做一些坐垫罩。| **make sth from** *We made a shelter from leaves and branches.* 我们用树叶和树枝搭了一个棚子。| **make sb sth** *Shall I make you a cup of coffee?* 我为你冲杯咖啡好吗? | **made (out) of** *a blouse made of silk* 丝绸做的女式衬衫

2 to produce something by doing something, often by accident 〔常指意外地〕使出现; 使形成: **make a hole/dent etc** *Make a hole in the paper.* 在纸上戳一个洞。| **make a mark/scratch etc** *Who made those marks on the wall?* 墙上那些污迹是谁留下的?

② DO STH 做某事

3 [T] **a)** used with some nouns to mean that someone performs the action of the noun 进行; 作出〔与某些名词连用, 表示某人完成一个由该名词表达的行为〕: **make a decision/mistake etc** *It's time to make a decision.* (=to decide) 该是作决定的时候了。| *Come on, you guys – make an effort!* 来吧, 哥们儿——努力干吧! | *The company was about to make a major purchase.* 公司当时正打算进行一项大宗的购货。**b)** used with some nouns of speaking, to mean that someone says something 作出〔与某些与说话有关的名词连用, 表示某人说某事〕: **make a suggestion/comment/observation etc** *May I make a suggestion?* 我可以提个建议吗? | *Jackson made a short statement to the press, denying all the charges.* 杰克逊向新闻界作了一个简短的声明, 否认所有的指控。

4 make an appointment/arrangement/date etc to arrange to do something, meet someone etc 进行预约/作出安排/进行约会等

5 make a contribution/donation/charge etc to give or ask for money for a particular purpose 捐献/捐款/收费等: *We have to make a small charge for use of the facilities.* 我们不得不收取少量设施使用费。

6 make an appearance/entrance etc to suddenly appear somewhere or enter a room 突然在某处出现/进入房间等

7 make a start to begin doing something 开始做〔某事〕: [+on/with] *I'd better make a start on the ironing.* 我最好开始熨衣服。

③ CAUSE A STATE/SITUATION 导致某种状况/情况

8 [T] to cause a particular state or situation, or make something happen 引起, 导致; 使〔某事〕发生: **make sb/sth do sth** *That tune makes me want to dance.* 那支曲子使我想跳舞。| *This lever here makes the heating come on.* 这里的这根控制杆控制暖气开启。| *I like him because he makes me laugh.* 我喜欢他因为他逗我笑。| **make sb/sth** *You could make this a really nice room if you got a new carpet.* 如果你买一块新地毯, 就能把这个房间变得十分漂亮。| *the movie that made him a star* 那部使他成为明星的电影 | **make sb ill/happy/popular etc** *The decision made her very unpopular with the staff.* 这一决定使她很不受员工们的欢迎。| *It makes me so angry to see children being treated like that.* 看到孩子们受那样的对待我非常气愤。| **make sb feel good/guilty/sick etc** *Jo's reassuring comments made me feel better.* 乔所说的那些安慰话使我感觉好多了。| **make sb look old/thin etc** *This photo makes her look much older than she really is.* 这张照片使她看起来比实际年龄大得多。| *I like the dress Jan, it makes you look really slim.* 简, 我喜欢那件连衣裙, 它让你看起来很苗条。| **make yourself heard/understood etc** *I had to shout to make myself heard above the music.* 我不得不大声喊叫以盖过音乐声使人们听到我的话。| **make it clear (that)** *I want to make it clear that I don't agree with this policy.* 我想讲清楚, 我不同意这个政策。| **make it known (that)** *He made it known that he would not be running for reelection.* 他公开宣布不打算竞选连任。

9 make trouble/a noise/a mess etc to do something that causes trouble, noise etc 制造麻烦/发出响声/弄脏[弄乱]等: *The kids had made a terrible mess.* 孩子们搞得到处又脏又乱。| *Do you have to make such a row?* 难道你们必须这样大吵大闹吗?

10 make sb captain/leader etc to give someone a new job or position in a group, organization etc 任命某人为船长/队长等: *She's now been made a full partner.* 她现在已成为一名正式股东。

11 make sth the best/worst/most expensive etc to result in something being the best, worst etc of a particular type 使某事成为最好/最差/最昂贵等: *These findings make Britain the country with the worst record on pollution.* 这些调查结果使英国成为污染记录最糟糕的国家。

④ FORCE SB TO DO STH 迫使某人做某事

12 [T] to force someone to do something, or force something to happen 强迫〔某人做某事〕; 迫使〔某事发生〕: **make sb do sth** *They made us write it out again ten times.* 他们强迫我们再把它写十遍。| *Marcia made the poor girl cry.* 马西娅把那个可怜的小姑娘弄哭了。| **be made to do sth** *I was made to wait two hours for an appointment.* 一个约会让我等了两个小时。

⑤ MONEY 金钱

13 [T] to earn or get money 挣得; 获得〔金钱〕: *She makes about £25,000 a year.* 她每年大约挣25,000英镑。| *We made $10,000 out of selling the house.* 我们卖掉那座房子赚了10,000美元。| **make money** *Dunson's one aim in life was to make money.* 邓森生活中的一个目的就是赚钱。

14 make a living (doing sth) to earn the money that you need (做某事) 谋生: *He makes a living repairing secondhand cars.* 他靠修理二手汽车谋生。

15 make a profit/loss to get or lose money in a trade or business 获利/赔钱: *The company has made a big loss this year.* 那家公司今年赔了不少钱。—see 见 GAIN[1] (USAGE)

⑥ BE ADDED TOGETHER 加起来

16 [linking verb 连系动词] to be a particular number or amount when added together 合计为, 总计: *Two and two make four.* 二加二等于四。| *So if Jan comes that makes four of us.* 这样, 如果简来的话我们就有四个人了。

⑦ BE SUITABLE 适合于

17 [linking verb 连系动词] to have the qualities, character etc necessary for a particular job, use, or purpose 宜用作; 具备…的素质: *I'm sure Penny will make a very good teacher.* 我相信彭尼会成为一名很好的教师。| *The hall would make an excellent theatre.* 这座大厅可以改装成一家一流的剧院。| *An old cardboard box makes a comfortable bed for a kitten.* 旧纸箱给小猫当床是很舒服的。

⑧ PRETEND 假装

18 make believe to pretend that something is true, especially as a game 假装〔尤指作为游戏〕; 假扮: *We made believe we were on a secret island.* 我们假装在一个人迹罕至的海岛上。—see also 另见 MAKE-BELIEVE

19 make like *AmE spoken* to behave in a way that you hope will give people a particular opinion of you【美口】假装; 装扮作: *He makes like he's got it all figured out.* 他装出一副什么都明白了的样子。

20 make as if to do sth to move in a way that makes it seem that you are going to do something 比画着好像要做某事: *Fred, still grinning, made as if to hit me.* 弗雷德仍然咧嘴笑着, 却比画着好像要打我。

⑨ MAKE IT 做成某事

21 make it *informal*【非正式】**a)** to arrive somewhere in time for something 及时到达, 赶上: *If we run, we should make it.* 如果跑着去的话, 我们应该还能赶得上。| [+to] *I just made it to the bathroom before throwing up.* 我忍住呕吐, 及时冲进了卫生间。**b)** to be successful in a particular activity or profession 取得成功: *I never thought Clare would make it as an actress.* 我从来没想到克莱尔会成为一名成功的女演员。| **make it big** *AmE* (=be very successful)【美】取得极大成功 *They've made it big in show business.* 他们在演艺界取得极大成功。**c)** *spoken* to be able to go to an event, meeting etc that has been arranged【口】能参加, 能出席〔已安排好的活动、会议等〕: *I'm really sorry, but I won't be able to make it on Sunday after all.* 非常抱歉, 我星期天还是不能出席。| *We didn't make it to the party in the end.* 我们最终还是没能参加那个聚会。**d)** to live through an illness or after an accident, or manage to deal with a very difficult experience 〔在生病或事故之后〕活下来;〔在一次困难的经历中〕挺了过来: *Frank was very ill, and the doctors didn't think he'd make it.* 弗兰克当时病得很厉害, 医生们认为他挺不过来了。| [+through] *I don't know how I'm going to make it through the day.* 我不知道如何熬过这一天。

22 make it up *BrE* to become friendly with someone again after you have had an argument【英】和解, 和好: *Have you made it up with your sister yet?* 你与你姐姐已经和好了吗?

23 make it up to to do something good for someone because you feel responsible for something bad that happened to them 弥补, 补偿: *I'll make it up to you one day, I promise.* 我总有一天会给你补偿的, 我保证做到。

M

24 make it quick/snappy *spoken* used to tell someone to do something as quickly as possible【口】赶快: *Two coffees please, and make it snappy.* 请来两杯咖啡，越快越好。
25 make it 6 o'clock/4.30 etc *BrE spoken* to think that it is a particular time, according to your watch【英口】〔按自己的表〕时间为六点/四点半等: *"What time do you make it?" "I make it half past two."* "你的表现在几点钟了?" "我的表两点半了。"
26 make it with *AmE* to have sex with someone【美】与〔某人〕做爱

⑩ CALCULATE 计算

27 [T] to decide that something is a particular amount or total by calculating 计算为，算出: *I make that $150 altogether.* 我算出总共为150美元。

⑪ MANAGE 勉强应付

28 make do (with/without) to manage with or without something, even though this is not completely satisfactory (在目前有/没有某物的情况下) 勉强应付: *New clothes are expensive, so you'll just have to make do with what you've got.* 新衣服很贵，所以你就只能有什么穿什么了。

⑫ MAKE WAY 让路

29 make way a) to move to one side so that someone or something can pass〔给某人或某物〕让路: **[+for]** *The crowd stepped aside, making way for the riders.* 人群走到一旁，给骑手们让路。**b)** to be removed so that something newer or better can be used or made instead 腾出地方: **[+for]** *Several houses were demolished to make way for an office development.* 好几栋房子被拆除以腾出地方来建一座办公楼。
30 make your way a) to move towards something, especially slowly or with difficulty〔尤指缓慢或艰难地〕前进: *We made our way down the hill towards the town.* 我们下了小山，朝镇上走去。**b)** to slowly become successful in a particular job, activity, or profession 缓慢获得成功: *Gradually, Henderson began to make his way in politics.* 慢慢地，亨德森开始在政坛上崭露头角。

⑬ ARRIVE 到达

31 [T] *informal* to arrive at or get to a particular place【非正式】到达: *I don't think we're going to make the town before nightfall.* 我认为黄昏之前我们到不了那个城镇。| *We didn't make the 6:30 train.* 我们没有赶上六点半的火车。
32 make the meeting/the party/Tuesday etc *spoken* to be able to go to something that has been arranged for a particular date or time【口】能够参加会议/晚会/星期二的活动等: *I'm sorry, I can't make Friday after all.* 对不起，星期五我还是来不了。| *Will you be able to make the next meeting?* 你能来参加下一次会议吗?
33 make a deadline/target/rate to succeed in doing something by a particular time, producing a particular amount etc 在限期内完成/实现目标/达到级别

⑭ BE GOOD/IMPORTANT 好/重要

34 make the papers/headlines/front page etc to be interesting or important enough to be printed in the papers etc 登上报纸/成为头条新闻/成为头版新闻等: *News of their divorce made the headlines.* 他们离婚的消息成了头条新闻。
35 make the team/squad etc to be good enough to be chosen to play in a sports team 被选进运动队等: *He'll never make the football team.* 他永远也进不了足球队。

⑮ OTHER MEANINGS 其他意思

36 make a difference to cause a change, especially an improvement, in a situation 引起变化〔尤指促进改进〕: *Their help has made a big difference to the team's success.* 他们的帮助对该团队的成功起了重要的作用。| *I tried to reason with him, but it made no difference.* 我设法劝导他，但不起作用。| **make all the difference** *That one extra day off made all the difference.* 那额外的一天假起了关键作用。
37 make a (phone) call to speak to someone using a telephone 打电话: *I have to make a few calls.* 我有几个电话得打。
38 make time to find enough time to do something, even though you are busy 抽出时间: *Somehow, she always makes enough time to take the kids out.* 不知怎的，她总是能腾出时间带孩子们出去。
39 make the bed to pull the sheets and covers over a bed so that it is tidy after someone has slept in it 整理床铺，铺床
40 make or break to cause either great success or complete failure 使大为成功或彻底失败，或成之或毁之: *Critics can make or break a young performer.* 评论家既能够捧红也能够毁掉一名年轻的演员。
41 it makes a change *spoken especially BrE* used to say that something is pleasantly different from normal【口，尤英】有所变化〔用以表示某事与平常不同而令人愉快〕: *It makes a change to get something other than bills in the post!* 从邮件中收到账单以外的东西，会使人分外高兴!
42 that makes two of us *spoken* used to agree with someone's opinion or to say that something that happened to them has also happened to you【口】对我来说也是如此，对我同样适用: *"I think I've had enough of this party." "That makes two of us."* "我想我对这个聚会已经感到厌烦了。" "我也有同感。"
43 make to do sth *old use* to seem to be starting to do something【旧】似乎正要做某事: *Greg made to speak, but I stopped him.* 格雷格好像要讲话，但我阻止了他。
44 ►MAKE STH PERFECT 使某物完美◄ [T] *informal* to provide the qualities that make something complete or successful【非正式】使完美: *The hat really makes the outfit.* 这顶帽子确实给整套服装锦上添花。—see also 另见 MADE, **make sb's day** (DAY¹ (35)), **make friends** (FRIEND (2)), **make good** (GOOD¹ (44)), **make sense** (SENSE¹ (9))

make away with sb/sth *phr v* [T] **1** *informal* to steal something【非正式】偷窃〔某物〕: *Thieves made away with thousands of dollars worth of jewelry.* 窃贼偷走了价值数千美元的珠宝。**2** *old-fashioned* to kill someone【过时】杀死〔某人〕

make for sth *phr v* [T] **1** to move towards something, or move in a particular direction 朝…走去; 朝…前进: *We made for St. Louis as fast as possible.* 我们以最快的速度向圣路易斯赶去。**2** to be likely to have a particular result or make something possible 有利于; 倾向于; 使可能: *The larger print makes for easier reading.* 大号字体会更方便阅读。| *Such statements don't exactly make for racial harmony.* 这样的声明不利于种族和睦。—see also 另见 **be made for each other** (MADE (2))

make sb/sth **into** sth *phr v* [T] **1** to change something so that it has a different form or purpose 将…制成[变成]: *We can make your room into a study.* 我们可以把你的房间改成一个书房。**2** [T] to change someone's character, job, or position in society 使转变为〔指改变某人的性格、工作或社会地位〕: *a film which made her into a star overnight* 使她一夜成名的一部电影

make sth **of** sb/sth *phr v* [T] **1** to understand something in a particular way, or have a particular opinion about something 了解，理解; 看待: *I don't know what to make of Kristin's recent behaviour at all.* 我一点也不知道该如何解释克里斯丁最近的行为。| *What do you make of this latest idea?* 你对这个最新的主意有何看法? **2** to use the chances, opportunities etc you have in a way that achieves a particular result〔利用机遇〕有所成就; 塑造: *Your college career is whatever you make of it.* 你的大学生活，你把它弄成什么样，它就是什么样。| *I want to make something of my life.* 我想这辈子有所成就。| **make the most of** (=use an opportunity as successfully or usefully as possible) 充分利用 *We only have one day in Paris, so we'd better make the most of it.* 我们在巴黎只待一天，因此我们最好充分利用这一天时间。**3 make a go of sth** *BrE informal* to make something as successful as possible by trying hard or working hard【英，非正式】尽力以使某事成功: *She's determined to make a go of the business this time.* 她下决心这次要把生意做得十分成功。**4 make too much of** to treat something as if it is more important than it really is 过分重视: *The press made too much of what was only meant as a joke.* 媒体对那件不过是儿戏的事情重视过头了。**5 make a day/night/evening of it** *informal* to decide to spend a whole day, night etc doing something【非正式】花整天/整夜/整个晚上的时间做某事: *Why don't we go for a meal after the movie and really make an evening of it.* 看完电影后我们何不去吃顿饭，玩它整整一个晚上呢。**6 do you want to make sth (out) of it?** *spoken* used to say that you are willing to have a fight or argument with someone【口】你想弄个明白吗?〔用来表示愿意跟某人打斗或争论〕—see also 另见 **see what sb is (really) made of** (MADE (4))

make off *phr v* [I] to leave quickly, especially in order to escape〔尤指为了逃跑〕匆忙离开; 溜掉

make off with sth *phr v* [T] *informal* to take something that does not belong to you【非正式】拿走〔他人之物〕; 抢走: *Two young men attacked him and made off with his wallet.* 两个年轻男子袭击了他并抢走了他的钱包。

make out *phr v* **1** [T **make** sth ↔ **out**] to be only just able to hear, see, or understand something〔勉强〕听出; 看出，辨认出:

I can scarcely make out his writing. 我难以看清他的字迹。| **make out who/how/when etc** *We couldn't make out what they were talking about.* 我们听不清楚他们正在谈论什么。**2** [T **make sb ↔ out**] *informal* to understand someone's character, or what they think, feel, want etc【非正式】了解〔某人的性格或想法、感觉、需要等〕: *Stuart's a strange guy – I can't make him out at all.* 斯图尔特是个怪人 —— 我一点都搞不懂他。**3 make out a cheque/bill etc** to write a cheque, bill etc 开支票/账单等: *Make the cheque out to 'Spencer Cross Ltd'.* 把支票开给"斯潘塞·克罗斯有限公司"。**4** [T] *informal* to claim or pretend that something is true when it is not【非正式】假称; 声称; 假装; 把…说成: **make out (that)** *She always makes out she's the only one who does any work.* 她总是声称她是唯一干了点活的人。| **make sb out to be sth** *Oh, Sean's not as bad as he's made out to be.* 哎呀, 肖恩并没有人们说的那么坏。**5 make out a case (for)** to find good enough reasons to prove something or explain why you need something 找到充分理由证明[解释]〔某事〕: *I'm sure we can make out a case for hiring another assistant.* 我确信我们可以找到充分理由再雇用一位助手。**6** [I] *especially AmE* to succeed or progress in a particular way【尤美】〔在某方面〕取得成功; 取得进展: *How did you make out at the interview?* 你面试情况怎样? **7** [I] *informal, especially AmE* to kiss and touch someone in a sexual way【非正式, 尤美】亲吻爱抚: *making out in the back seats of cars* 在汽车后座亲吻抚摸 **8 make out like a bandit** *AmE informal* to get a lot of money or gifts, win a lot etc【美, 非正式】获得大量金钱[礼物]; 赢得大量钱财: *Those kids make out like bandits every Christmas.* 那些孩子每年圣诞节都会得到不少的礼物。

make sth ↔ **over** *phr v* [T] **1** to officially and legally give money or property to someone else〔正式依法〕转让〔钱财〕: *He made over the whole estate to his son.* 他把全部财产转让给自己的儿子。**2** *AmE* to change something so that it looks different or has a different use【美】改造: *I've made that old blue dress over into a skirt.* 我把那件旧的蓝色连衣裙改成了一条裙子。—see also 另见 MAKEOVER

make towards sth *phr v* [T] to start moving towards something 朝〔某物〕移动, 移向…: *She made towards the door.* 她朝门走去。

make up *phr v*

1 ►EXCUSE/EXPLANATION 借口/解释◄ [T **make** sth ↔ **up**] to invent a story, explanation etc in order to deceive someone 编造〔说法、解释等〕: *I think they're making the whole thing up.* 我认为整件事情都是他们编造出来的。—see also 另见 MADE-UP

2 ►SONG/POEM 歌/诗◄ [T **make** sth ↔ **up**] to invent the words or music for a new song, story, poem etc 编〔歌词、曲子、故事、诗歌等〕: *We even made up a rude song about it.* 我们甚至写了一首关于此事的粗俗的歌曲。

3 ►SB'S FACE 某人的脸◄ [I,T **make** sb ↔ **up**] to put special paint, colour etc on someone's face in order to change the way they look 给〔某人〕化妆[化装]: *They made him up as an old man for the last act of the play.* 在这出戏的最后一幕, 他们把他化装成一个老头子。—see also 另见 MADE-UP, MAKE-UP

4 ►PREPARE/ARRANGE 准备/布置◄ [T **make** sth ↔ **up**] to prepare or arrange something by putting things together 准备; 布置: *I could make up a bed for you on the couch.* 我可以给你在长沙发上准备铺盖。| *Get the chemist to make up this prescription for you.* 让药剂师给你配好这个处方。

5 ►FORM/BE 形成/成为◄ [T **make up** sth] to combine together to form a particular system, group, result etc; CONSTITUTE 形成, 组成, 构成: *Women make up only 30% of the workforce.* 妇女仅占劳动力的30%。| **be made up of** *The committee is made up of representatives from every state.* 该委员会由来自每个州的代表组成。—see 见 COMPRISE (USAGE)

6 ►NUMBER/AMOUNT 数目/金额◄ [T **make up** sth] *especially BrE* to complete an amount or number to the level that is needed【尤英】凑足, 补齐: *I saved as much as I could, and my mum made up the rest of the money.* 我尽力攒了一些钱, 不足的部分由我妈妈凑齐。| *Do you want to make up a four for tennis?* 你们想凑足四个人打网球吗?

7 ►TIME/WORK 时间/工作◄ [T **make** sth ↔ **up**] to work at times when you do not usually work, so that you do all the work that you should have done 补上, 补回: *I'm trying to make up the time I lost while I was sick.* 我正在设法补回我生病期间耽误的时间。| *Is it OK if I make the work up next week?* 我下星期再补做这些工作可以吗?

8 ►FROM CLOTH 用布料◄ [T **make** sth ↔ **up**] to produce something from cloth by cutting and sewing 裁制; 缝制: **[+into]** *I plan on making that material up into a dress.* 我计划把那块衣料做成一件连衣裙。

9 ►FRIENDS 朋友◄ [I] *informal* to become friendly with someone again after you have had an argument【非正式】和好, 和解: **[+with]** *Have you made up with Patty yet?* 你与帕蒂和好了吗? | **kiss and make up** *When are you two going to kiss and make up?* 你们两个什么时候和好如初呀? —see also 另见 **make up your mind** (MIND¹ (4))

make up for sth *phr v* [T] **1** to make a bad or unpleasant situation seem better, by providing something pleasant 补偿: *That one weekend made up for all the disappointments I'd had.* 那一个周末补偿了我曾有过的一切失望。**2** to have so much of one quality that it does not matter that you do not have enough of something else 弥补: **make up for sth in/with** *What Jay lacked in experience, he made up for in enthusiasm.* 经验方面的不足, 杰伊用热情弥补上了。**3 make up for lost time a)** to work more quickly, or at times when you do not usually work, because something has prevented you from working before 补偿失去的时间: *We rehearsed all day Saturday, to make up for lost time.* 我们星期六排练了一整天, 以补回失去的排练时间。**b)** to become involved in an activity very eagerly, because you wish you could have done it earlier in your life 补偿早年应做而未做的事: *After all those years apart, we're making up for lost time getting to know each other!* 在分离了那么多年之后, 我俩正在相互了解, 以补偿失去的时间。

make up to sb *phr v* [T] to try to get someone's attention or approval by being friendly or praising them, especially in order to get an advantage for yourself 讨好, 奉承, 巴结〔尤指为了本人的利益〕—see also 另见 **make it up to** (MAKE¹ (23))

USAGE NOTE 用法说明: MAKE

COLLOCATION 搭配

There is no simple rule for when to use **make** or **do**. Generally you **make** something that did not exist before. 没有简单的规则规定何时用make, 何时用do。通常, make表示制造出以前不存在的东西: you *make lunch/trouble/peace/a noise/a plan/a joke/a mistake/ a speech/a promise* 做午饭/制造麻烦/讲和/发出声音/制订计划/开玩笑/犯错误/发表演讲/作出许诺 But other verbs are used in phrases like these 但是在下列短语中应当用其他动词: *I asked a question.* 我问了一个问题。| *He gave an answer.* 他给予了答复。| *We nearly had an accident.* 我们差点出了事故。

Make is also used when someone or something is changed in some way. make也用于表示某人或某物在某些方面发生了变化: *She made him comfortable.* 她使他觉得很舒服。| *He made a success of it.* 他把它做成了。| *They made friends.* 他们交上了朋友。| *How much money did Shane make?* 沙恩赚了多少钱? But 但说 *They did a lot of harm/damage.* 他们造成了很大的伤害/破坏。

When travel is involved, it is safer to use **go**. 当涉及旅行的时候, 用go更稳妥: *They went shopping/for a picnic/on vacation/on a trip.* 他们外出购物/野餐/度假/旅行去了。But you can also say 但也可以说: *They did the shopping* (他们去买了东西), and 及 *They made a trip to Boston.* (他们去了一趟波士顿)。

You **do** other actions. do用来表示其他的活动: *They did some exercises/some research/a test/the TOEFL exam.* 他们做了一些练习/做了一些研究/参加了一次测验/参加了托福考试。| *Would you do me a favour?* 你能帮我一个忙吗? But you 但说 *make fun of someone* (取笑某人), *make use of something* (使用某物), and 及 *make an effort/attempt/start.* (作一次努力/作一次尝试/开始)。Sometimes you would use **take** instead. 有时会用take代替: *take a class/take a look at something/take a ride on something* 上课/看某物一眼/乘坐某交通工具

Do is especially frequent with words that describe work and activities, often ending in *-ing*. do特别常与表示工作和活动的词连用, 这类词常以-ing结尾: *Her husband does all the shopping and cooking.* 购物和做饭全由她丈夫做。

GRAMMAR 语法

Apart from in certain fixed phrases, you do not use an adjective immediately after **make**. 除了在某些固定短语中之外, make后面不直接接形容词: *She always makes her classes interesting* (NOT 不用 *She always makes interesting her classes*). 她总是使自己的课生动有趣。

M

> You **make** someone do something. 用 make 表示让某人做某事: *The police officer made them empty their pockets* (NOT 不用 *The police officer made them to empty their pockets*). 那个警察要他们把口袋掏空。
> However, you do use **to** for the second verb when you are writing or speaking in the passive tense. 然而, 当用被动语态写或说时, 第二个动词前一定要用to: *They were made to empty their pockets.* 他们被要求掏空口袋。

make² *n* **1** a particular type of product, made by one company 〔由一家公司生产的〕产品样式; 品牌: *What make is your car?* 你的车是什么牌子的? | **[+of]** *a different make of computer* 不同品牌的电脑 **2 be on the make** *informal* 【非正式】 **a)** to be always trying to get an advantage for yourself 总是设法为自己谋求利益 **b)** to be trying to have a sexual relationship with someone 试图与某人发生性关系

Make-A-Wish Foun·da·tion, the /ˌ· · ˈ· · ˌ· ·/ a US CHARITY organization that helps children who are extremely ill get something that they want very much 喜愿基金会〔美国一慈善组织, 专门帮助病危儿童实现其愿望〕

make-be·lieve /ˈ· · ˌ·/ *n* [U] a state of imagining or pretending that something is real 假想; 假装: *She told me her parents are millionaires, but it's all just make-believe.* 她告诉我她父母是百万富翁, 但这纯属子虚乌有。

make·o·ver /ˋmekovɚ; ˈmeɪkəʊvə/ *n* [C] a process of improving your own or someone else's appearance with new clothes, a new haircut, MAKE-UP (1) etc 〔以新衣服、新发型、化妆品等〕装扮

mak·er /ˋmekɚ; ˈmeɪkə/ *n* [C] **1 mapmaker/watchmaker etc** someone who makes or produces maps etc 地图绘制员[生产商]/钟表制造商等 **2 decision maker/peacemaker etc** someone who is good at or responsible for making decisions, stopping arguments etc 决策者/调解人等: *She was the peacemaker in a family that was always quarreling.* 在一个争吵不休的家庭里她是个和事佬。—see also 另见 TROUBLEMAKER **3** also 又作 **makers** [plural] *especially BrE* 【尤英】—a firm that makes or produces something 制造商; 制造厂: *There's something wrong with my camera; I'm sending it back to the makers.* 我的照相机出毛病了, 我要把它寄回生产厂家。**4 meet your maker** *humorous* to die 【幽默】去见上帝, 死

make·shift /ˋmekˌʃɪft; ˈmeɪkʃɪft/ *adj* made for temporary use when you need something and there is nothing better available 权宜的; 临时(代用)的: *a makeshift sofa of crates and cushions* 用木箱和坐垫拼成的临时沙发

make-up 化妆品

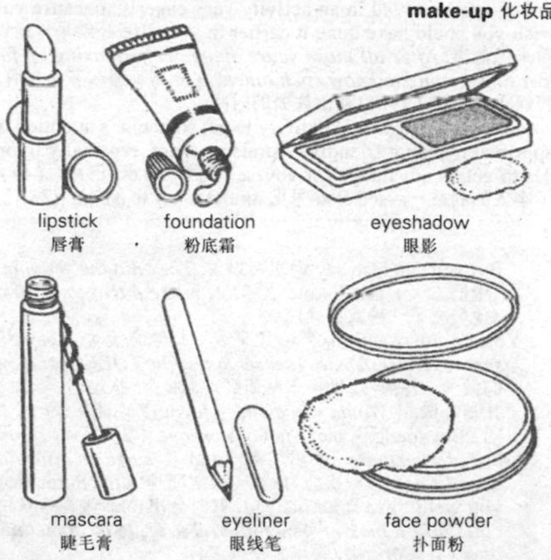

make-up /ˈ· ·/ *n* **1** [U] substances such as powder, creams, and LIPSTICK that some women and also actors put on their faces to improve or change their appearance 化妆品; 化装用品: *eye make-up* 眼部化妆品 —see also 另见 **make up** (MAKE¹) **2** [singular] a particular combination of people or things that form a group or whole 〔人或物的〕组成, 构成: *The make-up of the team should include both young and experienced players.* 这支队伍应包括年轻队员又应包括经验丰富的队员。**3 sb's make-up** the qualities, attitudes etc in someone's character 某人的性格: *It's in Bill's make-up to keep on fighting till the end.* 坚持战斗到底, 这是比尔的性格。**4** [C] *AmE* a test taken in school because you were not able to take a previous test 【美】补考

make-weight /ˈ· ·/ *n* [C] someone or something that is added only to make a necessary number or quantity 用来凑足数目的人[物], 充数的人[物]

make-work /ˈ· ·/ *n* [U] *AmE* work that is not important but is given to people to keep them busy 【美】〔为使人们有事干而提供的〕不重要的工作

mak·ing /ˋmekɪŋ; ˈmeɪkɪŋ/ *n* **1** [U] the process or business of making or producing something 制造, 制作, 生产: **the making of** *an interesting programme about the making of 'Jurassic Park'* 一个关于电影《侏罗纪公园》制作过程的有趣节目 | *involved in the making of policy* 参与政策的制定 | **dress making/decision making etc** *a region famous for cheese making* 一个以制作干酪而闻名的地区 **2 be the making of sb** to make someone a much better or more successful person 使某人更优秀[更加成功]: *It's a tough course, but I'm sure it will be the making of him.* 这是个艰难的过程, 但我敢肯定这会使他更加成功。**3 have the makings of** to have the qualities or skills needed to become a certain kind of person or thing 具有成为〔某种人或物〕的素质[技能]: *Giggs has the makings of a world-class footballer.* 吉格斯具有成为一名世界级足球运动员的素质。**4 in the making** in the process of being made or produced 在制造[制作]中: *His book was 20 years in the making.* 他的书写了20年的时间。**5 of your own making** problems or difficulties that are of your own making have been caused by you and no-one else 〔问题或困难〕由自己造成的

mal- /mæl; mæl/ *prefix* bad or badly 坏, 不良: *a malformed limb* (=wrongly shaped) 畸形的肢体 | *She maltreats her children.* (=treats them cruelly) 她虐待自己的孩子。

Mal·a·bar Coast, the /ˌmæləbɑr ˋkost; ˌmæləbɑː ˈkəʊst/ the southwest coast of India, which produces COCONUTS, rice, and SPICES 马拉巴尔海岸〔印度西南海岸, 出产椰子、大米和香料〕

mal·ad·just·ed /ˌmæləˋdʒʌstɪd; ˌmæləˈdʒʌstɪ̣d◂/ *adj* unable to form good relationships with people because of problems in your character and attitudes 不适应生活环境的; 心理失调的 —**maladjustment** *n* [U]

mal·ad·min·i·stra·tion /ˌmælədˌmɪnəˋstreʃən; ˌmælədmɪnɪ̣ˈstreɪʃən/ *n* [U] *formal* careless or dishonest management 【正式】管理不善; 弊政

mal·a·droit /ˌmæləˋdrɔɪt; ˌmæləˈdrɔɪt◂/ *adj formal* not good at dealing with people or problems 【正式】不善于与人打交道的, 不圆滑的; 不老练的 —**maladroitly** *adv* —**maladroitness** *n* [U]

mal·a·dy /ˋmælədɪ; ˈmælədi/ *n* [C] **1** *formal* something that is wrong with a system or organization 【正式】〔制度或机构的〕弊病, 弊端: *Public education suffers from the same malady as many other government programs.* 公共教育与其他许多政府项目一样受困于同一弊病。**2** *old use* an illness 【旧】疾病

Mal·a·ga /ˋmæləgə; ˈmæləgə/ a city and port in the south of Spain on the Mediterranean coast. It is a popular place for tourists, and the area around Malaga, the Costa de Sol, is also a popular place for older British people to go and live after they have finished working. 马拉加〔西班牙南部一城市和港口, 位于地中海沿岸。该市是旅游胜地, 附近的太阳海岸是上了年纪的英国人旅游或退休后安度晚年的好去处〕

ma·laise /mæˋlez; məˈleɪz/ *n* [singular,U] **1** a feeling of anxiety, dissatisfaction, and lack of confidence within a group of people that is not clearly expressed or understood 〔一群人中潜在的〕焦躁[不满, 缺乏信心的]情绪: *We detected a certain malaise among the staff.* 我们觉察到职员中有种莫名的不满情绪。**2** a feeling of being slightly ill that usually does not last very long 〔短期的〕不适, 不舒服

Mal·a·mud /ˋmæləmud; ˈmæləmʊd/, **Ber·nard** /bɚˋnɑrd; ˈbɜːnəd/ (1914-86) a US writer who often wrote about Jewish life and customs 马拉默德〔(1914-1986), 美国作家。其作品常以犹太人的生活和习俗为题材〕

Mal·a·prop /ˋmæləprɑp; ˈmæləprɒp/, **Mrs** a character in the 18th century play *The Rivals* by Richard Sheridan. She wrongly uses words in a funny way, saying a word that sounds similar to the one she intended to use, but means something completely different. This type of mistake is known as a malapropism because of her. 马拉普洛普夫人〔18 世纪作家理查·谢里丹所著的剧本《情敌》中的人物。她以妙趣横生的错误用词而出名, 即所用之词与想用之词读音相似, 但意思迥然不同。此类用词错误就是以她的名字定名的, 称作 malapropism〕

mal·a·prop·is·m /ˋmæləprɑpˌɪzəm; ˈmæləprɒpɪzəm/ *n* [C] an amusing mistake made by using a word that sounds similar to the word you intended to say but means something completely

different 令人发笑的词语误用〔指误用发音近似而意义完全不同的词语〕

ma·lar·i·a /mə`lɛrɪə; mə'leəriə/ *n* [U] a disease common in hot countries that is caused when an infected MOSQUITO bites you 疟疾 —**malarial** *adj*: *malarial fever* 疟疾

ma·lar·key /mə`lɑrkɪ; mə'lɑːki/ *n* [U] *informal* talk that is meant to impress or deceive you but does not mean anything; NONSENSE【非正式】胡言乱语; 废话; 蠢话: *All that stuff was a load of malarky!* 那些都是一派胡言!

Ma·la·wi /mə`lɑwi; mə'lɑːwi/ a country in East Africa, surrounded by Zambia, Tanzania, and Mozambique. Population: 10,548,000 (2001). Capital: Lilongwe. 马拉维〔东非一国家, 与赞比亚、坦桑尼亚和莫桑比克接壤。人口: 10,548,000 (2001), 首都: 利隆圭〕—**Malawian** *n, adj*

Ma·lay[1] /mə`le; mə'leɪ/ *n* **1** [C] someone from the largest population group in Malaysia 马来人 **2** [U] the language of these people 马来语

Malay[2] *adj* from or connected with Malaysia 马来西亚的

Ma·lay·a /mə`leə; mə'leɪə/ the former name of the Malay PENINSULA or West Malaysia, now a part of Malaysia 马来亚〔马来半岛或西马来西亚旧称, 现属马来西亚〕

Ma·lay·si·a /mə`leʒə; mə'leɪziə/ a country in southeast Asia made up of 13 states. Eleven of these are on the Malay peninsula and the other two, Sabah and Sarawak, are on the island of Borneo. Population: 22,229,000 (2001). Capital: Kuala Lumpur. Malaysia is an important producer of rubber, and it has also developed many other industries, including clothes, cars, and electrical goods. It is a member of the British Commonwealth. 马来西亚〔东南亚一国家, 由13个州组成, 其中11个州位于马来半岛, 其他两个州(沙巴和沙捞越)位于婆罗洲。人口: 22,229,000 (2001), 首都: 吉隆坡。马来西亚是重要的橡胶出产国, 也发展许多其他产业, 其中有服装、汽车和电器。该国属英联邦成员国〕—**Malaysian** *n, adj*

Mal·colm X /ˌmælkəm `ɛks; ˌmælkəm 'eks/ (1925-65) a black leader in the US who worked to improve the social and economic position of black people. He became a member of the Black Muslims in 1952, and spoke publicly about the need for black people in the US to live separately from white people, and he encouraged them to use violence to protect themselves. In 1964, he left the Black Muslims and established the Organization of Afro-American Unity. He was murdered in 1965 while making a speech in Harlem, New York City. 马尔科姆·艾克斯〔(1925-1965), 美国黑人领袖, 致力于提高黑人的社会与经济地位。1952年, 他成为黑人穆斯林组织成员, 在演讲中公开主张美国黑人在日常生活中与白种人划清界限, 鼓励黑人用暴力保护自己。1964年, 他脱离黑人穆斯林组织, 成立了非洲裔美国人联合会。1965年, 他在纽约市的哈莱姆区演讲时被谋杀〕

mal·con·tent /`mælkənˌtɛnt; 'mælkəntent/ *n* [C] *formal* someone who is likely to cause trouble because they are dissatisfied【正式】不满者, 反叛者

Mal·dives, the /`mɔldivz; 'mɔːldiːvz/ a country made up of a group of small islands in the Indian Ocean southwest of Sri Lanka, which are famous for their beautiful beaches. Population: 310,764 (2001). Capital: Malé. The Maldives are threatened by global warming, because if the sea level rises much, the islands could disappear. 马尔代夫〔印度洋一岛国, 位于斯里兰卡西南, 由一些小岛组成, 以景色美丽的沙滩闻名。人口: 310,764 (2001), 首都: 马累。马尔代夫受到全球气候变暖的威胁, 因为一旦海平面上升过高, 这些岛屿就会消失〕—**Maldivian** /mɔl`dɪvɪən; mɔːl'dɪviən/ *n, adj*

S3 W2 **male**[1] /mel; meɪl/ *adj* **1** belonging to the sex that cannot have babies 男的, 雄的, 公的: *a male lion* 雄狮 | *Women teachers often earn less than their male colleagues.* 女教师挣的钱常常比她们的男同事要少。**2** typical of or connected with this sex 男性特有的; 男性的, 男子的: *male aggression* 男人特有的攻击性 | *traditional male values* 传统的男性价值观 | *differences between male and female longevity* 男女两性寿命的差异 **3 male plant/flower etc** a plant etc that cannot produce fruit 雄性植物/花朵等 **4** *technical* a male PLUG[1] (1) fits into a hole or SOCKET (1)【术语】〔插头等〕阳的, 凸形的, 插入式的 **5 male bonding** the forming of strong friendships between men 男子间的牢固友谊之形成 —opposite 反义词 FEMALE[1] —**maleness** *n* [U]

W3 **male**[2] *n* [C] **1** a male animal 雄性动物: *The male is usually bigger and more brightly coloured than the female.* 雄性动物通常比雌性动物体型大, 颜色也更鲜艳。**2** a man, especially a typical man 男人, 男子: *She wouldn't appeal to your average male.* 她对普通男人不会有什么吸引力。| *Police described her attacker as a white male aged about 25.* 警察把袭击她的人描述为一个大约25岁的白人男子。

Malé /`mɑle; 'mɑːleɪ/ also 又作 **Daviyani** the capital city and main port of Maldives, on Male Island in the Indian Ocean 马累〔马尔代夫首都和主要港口, 位于印度洋的马累岛〕

male chau·vin·ist /ˌ· '···◂/ *n* [C] a man who believes that men are better than women and who has fixed, traditional ideas about the way men and women should behave 大男子主义者: *Bill was very much the male chauvinist, and wouldn't let his wife go out to work.* 比尔是个十足的大男子主义者, 不愿让妻子出去工作。| **male chauvinist pig** (=an insulting name for a male chauvinist) 奉行大男子主义的蠢猪

mal·e·dic·tion /ˌmælə`dɪkʃən; ˌmælɪ'dɪkʃən/ *n* [C] *formal* a wish or prayer that something bad should happen to someone; CURSE[2] (2)【正式】诅咒, 咒骂

mal·e·fac·tor /`mæləˌfæktɚ; 'mælɪfæktə/ *n* [C] *formal* someone who does evil things【正式】作恶的人, 坏人

ma·lef·i·cent /mə`lɛfəsn̩t; mə'lefɪsənt/ *adj formal* doing or able to do evil things【正式】作恶的, 犯罪的, 有害的 —**maleficence** *n* [U]

male men·o·pause /ˌ· '···/ *n* [singular] *humorous* a period in the middle of a man's life when he feels anxious and unhappy【幽默】男性更年期

male-voice choir /ˌ· · '·/ *n* [C] a large group of male singers 男声合唱团

ma·lev·o·lent /mə`lɛvələnt; mə'levələnt/ *adj* showing a desire to harm other people 有恶意的; 恶毒的 —**malevolence** *n* [U] —**malevolently** *adv*

mal·feas·ance /ˌmæl`fizn̩s; mæl'fiːzəns/ *n* [U] *law* illegal activity, especially by a government official【法律】〔尤指政府官员的〕违法行为; 渎职

mal·for·ma·tion /ˌmælfɔr`meʃən; ˌmælfɔː'meɪʃən/ *n* **1** [C] a part of the body that is badly formed〔身体的〕畸形: *congenital malformations in young children* 幼儿先天的身体畸形 **2** [U] the state of being badly formed 畸形: *bone malformation* 骨骼畸形

mal·formed /mæl`fɔrmd; ˌmæl'fɔːmd◂/ *adj* badly formed 畸形的, 变形的

mal·func·tion /mæl`fʌŋkʃən; mæl'fʌŋkʃən/ *n* [C] a fault in the way a machine or computer operates〔机器或电脑的〕故障, 失灵 —**malfunction** *v* [I]

Ma·li /`mɑlɪ; 'mɑːli/ one of the largest countries in West Africa. It contains a large area of the southern Sahara Desert. Population: 11,009,000 (2001). Capital: Bamako. 马里〔西非面积最大的国家之一, 包括撒哈拉大沙漠南部的广大地区。人口: 11,009,000 (2001), 首都: 巴马科〕—**Malian** *n, adj*

Mal·i·bu /`mælibu; 'mælɪbuː/ a beach in California, in the US, famous for SURFING. Many rich and famous people, especially film stars, live there. 马利布海滩〔美国加利福尼亚州一海滩, 以冲浪运动而著名。此处居住着不少富人和名人, 尤其是电影明星〕

mal·ice /`mælɪs; 'mælɪs/ *n* [U] **1** the desire or intention to deliberately harm someone 恶意, 害人之心: *There was no need for Jane to tell them – she did it out of sheer malice.* 简没有必要告诉他们 —— 她这么做纯粹出于恶意。| **bear sb no malice** (=not want to harm someone although they have behaved badly to you) 对某人无怀恨之心 **2 with malice aforethought** *law* a criminal act that is done with malice aforethought is done in a carefully planned and deliberate way【法律】精心策划的预谋犯罪

ma·li·cious /mə`lɪʃəs; mə'lɪʃəs/ *adj* showing a desire to harm or hurt someone 恶意的, 恶毒的: *malicious gossip* 恶意的闲话 —**maliciously** *adv* —**maliciousness** *n* [U]

ma·lign[1] /mə`laɪn; mə'laɪn/ *v* [T usually passive 一般用被动态] to say or write unpleasant things about someone that are untrue 诽谤, 诬蔑, 中伤: *She had seen herself repeatedly maligned in the newspapers.* 她已遭受报纸的多次诽谤。| **much maligned** (=criticized by a lot of people, often unfairly)〔常指不公正地〕受到众人猛烈批评的 *a much-maligned and controversial film* 一部受到猛烈抨击的有争议的电影

malign[2] *adj formal* harmful【正式】有害的: *a malign influence* 有害的影响 —**malignly** *adv* —**malignity** /mə`lɪgnətɪ; mə'lɪgnɪti/ *n* [U]

ma·lig·nan·cy /mə`lɪgnənsɪ; mə'lɪgnənsi/ *n* **1** [C] *technical* a TUMOUR【术语】恶性肿瘤 **2** [U] *formal* feelings of great hatred【正式】极度憎恨(的情绪)

ma·lig·nant /mə`lɪgnənt; mə'lɪgnənt/ *adj* **1** *technical* a malignant TUMOUR, disease etc is one that develops uncontrollably and is likely to cause death【术语】〔肿瘤、疾病等〕恶性的; 致命的 —compare 比较 BENIGN (2) **2** *formal* showing hatred and a strong desire to harm someone【正式】恶毒的, 恶意的; 立意害人的: *He advanced towards them with a malignant look.* 他朝他们走去, 满脸凶相。—**malignantly** *adv*

M

ma·lin·ger /mə`lɪŋgə; mə'lɪŋgə/ *v* [I] to avoid work by pretending to be ill 装病以逃避工作 —**malingerer** *n* [C]

Mal·i·now·ski /ˌmælə`nɑfskɪ; ˌmæl$\dot{ı}$'nɒfski/, **Bron·i·slaw** /`brɑnɪslæf; 'brɒnɪslæf/ (1884-1942) a British ANTHROPOLOGIST (=a scientist who studies people and their societies, and the way that their customs develop), born in Poland, who established the first university department of anthropology in Britain and wrote several important books on the subject 马林诺夫斯基〔(1884-1942)，英国人类学家，生于波兰。他在英国大学里首次开设了人类学系，著有多部重要的人类学著作〕

mall /mɔl; mɔːl/ *n* [C] *especially AmE* a large area where there are a lot of shops, usually a covered area where cars are not allowed【尤美】购物中心，商场

Mall, the 1 a straight road in central London that connects Buckingham Palace and Trafalgar Square. Whenever there is a royal wedding, funeral, or similar occasion, the royal family travels slowly along it, and many people come to watch 林荫大道〔伦敦市中心连接白金汉宫和特拉法尔加广场的一条直道。每当王室有婚庆葬礼，王室成员就沿林荫道缓缓而行，引来众多围观者〕 **2** a park in Washington, D.C., which is surrounded by the Washington Monument and several famous MUSEUMs, including the Smithsonian Institution. It is used for PICNICs, games, and concerts. 草地广场〔华盛顿市内一公园。周围有华盛顿纪念碑和一些著名的博物馆，包括史密森学会在内。广场上可进行野餐、运动和举办音乐会〕 —see 见 PALL MALL

mal·lard /`mæləd; 'mælɑːd/ *n* [C] a kind of wild duck 绿头鸭〔一种野鸭〕

mal·le·a·ble /`mælɪəbl; 'mæliəbəl/ *adj* **1** something that is malleable is easy to press or pull into a new shape 有延展性的；可锻[压，拉]的：*malleable steel* 展性钢 **2** someone who is malleable is easily influenced, changed, or trained 〔人〕易受影响的；易改变的；易训练的 —**malleability** /ˌmælɪə`bɪlətɪ; ˌmæliə'bɪl$\dot{ə}$ti/ *n* [U]

mal·let /`mælɪt; 'mæl$\dot{ı}$t/ *n* [C] **1** a wooden hammer with a large end 木槌 —see picture at 参见 TOOL[1] 图 **2** a wooden hammer with a long handle used when playing CROQUET and POLO〔打槌球、马球用的〕长柄球棍

Mal·lor·ca /mɑ`jɔrkɑ; mɑː'jɔːkə/ another spelling of Majorca 马略卡岛〔Majorca 的另一拼法〕

Mallory /`mælərɪ, 'mæləri/, **George** (1887-1924) a British mountain climber, who died while attempting to climb Mount Everest. In 1999 his body was found 2000 feet from the top of the mountain. Some people believe that he and another climber, Andrew Irvine, were the first people to reach the top of Everest, but died on the way down. 马洛里〔(1887-1924)，英国一登山者，攀登珠穆朗玛峰期间遇难。1999 年在距离山顶 2000 英尺的地方发现了他的尸体。有些人认为他与另一位登山者安德鲁·欧文是最早到达珠穆朗玛峰顶峰的两个人，但在下山途中遇难〕

mal·low /`mælo; 'mæləʊ/ *n* [C,U] a plant with pink or purple flowers and long stems 锦葵 —see also 另见 MARSHMALLOW (2)

mal·nour·ished /mæl`nɝɪʃt; ˌmæl'nʌrɪʃt◂/ *adj* ill or weak because of not having enough food to eat, or because of not eating good food 营养不良的

mal·nu·tri·tion /ˌmælnju`trɪʃən; ˌmælnjʊ'trɪʃən/ *n* [U] illness or weakness caused by not having enough food to eat, or by not eating good food 营养不良

mal·o·dor·ous /mæl`odərəs; ˌmæl'əʊdərəs/ *adj literary* smelling unpleasant【文】难闻的，恶臭的

Mal·o·ry /`mælərɪ; 'mæləri/, **Sir Thomas** (c.1410-71) an English writer who wrote *Le Morte d'Arthur* which tells the story of King Arthur 马洛礼〔(约1410-1471)，英国作家。其作品《亚瑟王之死》讲述亚瑟王的生平故事〕

mal·prac·tice /mæl`præktɪs; ˌmæl'prækt$\dot{ı}$s/ *n* [C,U] the act of failing to do a professional duty properly, or of making a mistake while doing it 玩忽职守，渎职：*She sued her doctor for malpractice.* 她以医疗失当罪起诉她的医生。

malt[1] /mɔlt; mɔːlt/ *n* **1** [U] grain, usually BARLEY, that has been kept in water for a time and then dried, used for making beer, WHISKY etc 麦芽 **2** [C] *AmE* a drink made from milk treated with malt, with ICE CREAM and something else such as chocolate added【美】麦乳精，麦乳精饮料：*Two strawberry malts, please.* 请来两杯草莓麦乳精饮料。**3** [C,U] also 又作 **malt whisky** —a type of high quality WHISKY from Scotland 麦芽威士忌〔一种苏格兰产的优质威士忌〕

malt[2] *v* [T] to make grain into malt 把…制成麦芽

Mal·ta /`mɔltə; 'mɔːltə/ a group of small islands in the Mediterranean Sea, and an independent republic and member of the British Commonwealth since 1964. It consists of three main islands, Malta, Gozo, and Comino. Population: 394,583 (2001). Capital: Valletta. 马耳他〔地中海一群岛。自1964年起成为独立共和国和英联邦成员国。该国由三大岛组成，即马耳他岛、戈佐岛和科米诺岛。人口：394,583 (2001)，首都：瓦莱塔〕 —**Maltese** /ˌmɔl`tiz; ˌmɔːl'tiːz◂/ *n, adj*

malt·ed /`mɔltɪd; 'mɔːlt$\dot{ı}$d/ *n* [C] *AmE* a MALT[1] (2)【美】麦乳精，麦乳精饮料

Mal·tese /mɔl`tiz; ˌmɔːl'tiːz◂/ *adj* from or connected with Malta 马耳他人的；马耳他语的；马耳他的

Maltese Cross /ˌ·· '·/ *n* [C] a cross with four pieces that become wider as they go out from the centre 马耳他十字〔十字四部分从中心向外渐宽〕

Mal·thus /`mælθəs; 'mælθəs/, **Thomas** (1766-1834) a British economist who studied population growth. He is famous for his opinion that, if the world's population was not controlled by disease, wars, or by sexual restraint, it would grow faster than the world's food supply. 马尔萨斯〔(1766-1834)，研究人口增长问题的英国经济学家。他的著名观点是，如果没有疾病、战争或节育来控制世界人口，那么其增长速度就会超过全世界粮食供应能力〕 —**Malthusian** /mæl`θuzɪən; mæl'θjuːzjən/ *adj*

malt liq·uor /ˌ· '··/ *n* [U] *AmE* a type of beer【美】麦芽啤酒

mal·treat /mæl`trit; mæl'triːt/ *v* [T] to treat a person or animal cruelly 虐待，残暴地对待 —**maltreatment** *n* [U]

Mal·vern /`mɔlvən; 'mɔːlvən/ a town in western central England, in the Malvern Hills. A theatre and music FESTIVAL is held there every year. 莫尔文〔英格兰中西部一城镇，位于莫尔文丘陵地带。这里每年举办戏剧音乐节〕

Malvern Hills, the /ˌ·· '·/ also 又作 **the Malverns** a group of hills in central England, where MINERAL WATER called **Malvern Water** is produced 莫尔文丘陵〔英格兰中部一丘陵地区，出产莫尔文矿泉水〕

Mal·vo·li·o /mæl`volɪo; mæl'vəʊliəʊ/ a character in the play *Twelfth Night* by William Shakepeare. Malvolio is one of Olivia's servants, and the people in Olivia's house play a trick on him by telling him that Olivia loves him. He then tries to begin a romantic relationship with her, but behaves so strangely that people think he is crazy and put him in prison. 马伏里奥〔威廉·莎士比亚的剧作《第十二夜》中的人物，为奥利维亚的仆人。奥利维亚府上的一些人有意捉弄他，骗他说奥利维亚对他有意思。于是，他想方设法向她求爱，但由于举止十分怪异，大家都以为他神经错乱，把他打入了监牢〕

mam /mæm; mæm/ *n* [C] *informal ScotE & NEngE* a mother【非正式，苏格兰及英格兰北部】母亲

ma·ma[1], **mamma** /`mɑmə; 'mɑːmə/ also 又作 **momma** *n* [C] *AmE informal* a word meaning mother, used by or to children【美，非正式】妈妈〔儿语〕

ma·ma[2] /`mɑmɑ; mə'mɑː/ *n* [C] *BrE old-fashioned* a mother【英，过时】妈妈

mama's boy /`mɑməz ˌbɔɪ; 'mɑːməz ˌbɔɪ/ *n* [C] *AmE* a boy or man who lets his mother look after him and protect him too much, so that people think he is weak【美】娇生惯养的男孩，过分依恋母亲的男孩；缺乏男子气的男人；MUMMY'S BOY *BrE*【英】

mam·ba /`mɑmbə; 'mæmbə/ *n* [C] a poisonous African snake that is black or green 曼巴〔非洲的一种黑色或绿色毒蛇〕

mam·ma /`mɑmə; 'mɑːmə/ *n* [C] another spelling of MAMA[1] mama[1] 的另一种拼法

mam·mal /`mæml; 'mæməl/ *n* [C] one of the class of animals that drinks milk from its mother's body when it is young 哺乳动物 —**mammalian** /mæ`melɪən; mæ'meɪliən/ *adj*

mam·ma·ry /`mæmərɪ; 'mæməri/ *adj technical* [only before noun 仅用于名词前] connected with or relating to the breasts【术语】乳房的

mammary gland /'··· ˌ·/ *n* [C] *technical* the part of a woman's breast that produces milk, or a similar part of a female animal【术语】乳腺

mam·mo·gra·phy /mæ`mɑgrəfɪ; mæ'mɒgrəfi/ *n* [U] examination of the breasts using X-RAYs to check for signs of CANCER 乳房 X 线照相术；乳房造影术

mam·mon /`mæmən; 'mæmən/ *n* [U] money, wealth, and profit, regarded as something that people want or think about too much〔人们过分想要或过分考虑的〕金钱，财富，利润

mam·moth[1] /`mæməθ; 'mæməθ/ *adj* [only before noun 仅用于名词前] extremely large 巨大的，庞大的：*a mammoth task* 巨大的任务 | *a mammoth corporation* 庞大的公司

mammoth[2] *n* [C] a large hairy ELEPHANT that lived on Earth thousands of years ago〔数千年前生活于地球上的〕猛犸，毛象

mam·my /`mæmɪ; 'mæmi/ *n* [C] *especially IrE* a mother【尤爱尔兰】母亲

man[1] /mæn; mæn/ *n plural* **men** /mɛn; men/ [C]

1 ►MALE PERSON 男人◄ [C] an adult male human 成年男子：

There were two men and a woman in the car. 车上有两男一女。| *He's a very kind man.* 他是个非常和蔼的人。| *a man's watch* 男式手表 | *Don't keep him waiting – he's a busy man.* 别让他老等着，他可是个大忙人。

2 ▶STRONG/BRAVE MAN 强壮/勇敢的男子◀ [C usually singular 一般用单数] a man who has the qualities that people think a man should have, such as being brave, strong etc 男子汉，大丈夫: **be a man** *Go on, be a man. Tell him he has to pay you more.* 坚持下去，拿出点男子汉气概来，告诉他必须给你加钱。| **be man enough to do sth** (=be strong or brave enough) 有足够的力量[勇气]去做某事 | **make a man (out) of** (=make a boy or young man start behaving in a confident way) 使一个男孩[年轻男人]树立信心 *Running his own business has really made a man out of Terry.* 经营他自己的企业使特里真正树立了信心。

3 ▶HUMAN BEING 人◀ **a)** [C] *old-fashioned* a person, either male or female【过时】人: *All men are equal in the eyes of the law.* 法律面前人人平等。**b)** [U] people as a group 人类: *This is one of the worst diseases known to man.* 这是人类已知的最厉害的疾病之一。| *the evolution of man* 人类的进化 | **prehistoric/stone-age man** (=the types of people who lived in the early stages of human development) 史前/石器时期的人类

4 ▶WORKER 工人◀ [C] **a)** [usually plural 一般用复数] a man who works for an employer 男雇员: *Bad conditions and low wages were making the men restless.* 恶劣的条件和很低的工资使工人们焦躁不安。**b)** a man who comes to your house to do a job for you, especially to repair something〔上门服务的〕修理工: *Has the man been to fix the TV?* 那个工人来修过电视吗？| **the gas man/rent man etc** *I waited in all day for the man to come and connect the heater.* 我一整天都在等工人来接通暖气。

5 ▶PARTICULAR KIND OF MAN 特定类别的人◀ **a ... man a)** a man who belongs to a particular organization, comes from a particular place, does a particular type of work etc〔属于某个组织、来自某个地方、从事某种工作等的〕人: *Bernard was a typical Foreign Office Man.* 伯纳德是个典型的外交部官员。| *I got it from the vegetable man in the market.* 我从市场上卖菜的那儿买到的。| *I think she married a Belfast man.* 我想她与一位贝尔法斯特男子结了婚。| **an Oxford/Yale/Cambridge man** (=one who has been to a particular university) 牛津/耶鲁/剑桥大学毕业生 **b)** a man who likes, or likes doing, a particular thing 喜欢某物[做某事]的人: *I'm more of a jazz man myself.* 我本人更喜欢爵士乐。| *Are you a betting man?* 你喜欢打赌吗？

6 Man! *spoken*【口】**a)** used for addressing an adult male, especially when you are excited, angry etc 老兄！老弟！〔用于称呼成年男子，尤其当说话人兴奋、生气时〕: *Stop talking nonsense, man!* 别胡说八道了，老兄！**b)** *especially AmE, CarE* used for addressing someone, especially an adult male【尤美，加勒比】老兄！老弟！〔尤用于称呼成年男子〕: *This party's really great, man!* 这个聚会真是棒极了，老兄！

7 ▶SOLDIER 士兵，战士◀ [C usually plural 一般用复数] a soldier or SAILOR who is under the authority of an officer 士兵；水兵: *The Captain ordered his men to fire.* 上校命令水兵们开火。

8 ▶HUSBAND 丈夫◀ [C] *informal* a woman's husband or sexual partner【非正式】丈夫；情人: *She spent five years waiting for her man to come out of prison.* 她花了五年的时间等她的丈夫出狱。

9 the man *spoken*【口】**a)** used to talk about a man you dislike, a man who has done something stupid etc 家伙，小子〔用于谈论你不喜欢或做了蠢事的某男子〕: *I don't know why she married him – I can't stand the man myself.* 我不懂她为什么与他结婚——我可受不了这个家伙。| *Don't listen to him the man's a complete idiot.* 别听他的，那家伙是个十足的白痴。**b)** *AmE* someone who has authority over you, especially a white man or police officer【美】头儿，上司〔用来指有权管你的某人，特别是白种人或警官〕

10 a man *old-fashioned spoken* used by a man to mean himself【过时，口】我〔男子用以指自己〕: *Can't a man read his paper in peace?* 难道就不能让我安静地读读报纸吗？

11 he's your/our man *spoken* used to say that a man is the best person for a particular job, situation etc【口】他是最合适的人: *If you need repairs done in the house, Brian's your man.* 如果你家里有什么修理的活儿，让布赖恩来干最合适。

12 a man of his word a man you can trust, who will do what he has promised to do 守信用的人，靠得住的人

13 a man of few words a man who does not talk very much 沉默寡言的人

14 be your own man to behave and think independently without worrying about what other people think 独立自主

15 it's every man for himself *spoken* used to say that people will not help each other【口】自顾自，不愿互相帮忙: *In journalism it's every man for himself.* 在新闻界大家都是自顾自。

16 the man in the street the average man or the average person 老百姓；普通人，常人: *This kind of music doesn't appeal to the man on the street.* 这种音乐不会引起一般人的兴趣。

17 a man of the people a man who understands and expresses the views and opinions of ordinary people 了解民意的人；为民众代言的人

18 a man's man a man who enjoys being with other men and doing male activities, and is popular with men rather than women〔喜欢与其他男人在一起，从事男人喜欢干的事的〕讨男人欢迎的男人

19 ladies' man a man who is popular with women and who likes to go out with a lot of different women〔喜欢在女人中间厮混的〕女人欢心的男人

20 man and boy if a man has done something man and boy, he has done it all his life 一辈子，从小到大: *I've worked on that farm man and boy.* 我在那个农场工作了一辈子。

21 be man and wife to be married 结为夫妇

22 live as man and wife to behave as though you are married, although you may not be 像夫妻般生活

23 as one man *especially literary* if a group of people do something as one man, they do it together【尤文】全体一致地: *The audience rose as one man to applaud the singers.* 观众全体起立为歌手们鼓掌。

24 to a man/to the last man *especially literary* used to say that all the men in a group do something or have a particular quality【尤文】所有人；无一例外地: *a disreputable crew, robbers and cutthroats to a man* 一个臭名昭著的团伙，全部都是强盗和杀手

25 man-about-town a rich man who spends a lot of time at parties, clubs, theatres etc〔经常出没于娱乐场所的〕纨绔子弟；花花公子

26 man of God a religious man, especially a priest 神职人员；〔尤指〕牧师，神甫

27 my (good) man *BrE old-fashioned spoken* used when talking to someone of a lower social class【英，过时，口】老兄，老弟〔对社会阶层较低的人说话时的用语〕

28 my man *spoken* used by some black British and American men to greet a friend【口】朋友〔某些英美黑人男子向朋友打招呼的用语〕

29 your man *IrE spoken* used to mean a particular man【爱尔兰口】那个人〔指某一特定的人〕: *I think your man over there's organizing the music.* 我想那边那个人正在安排音乐。

30 ▶SERVANT 仆人◀ [C] *old-fashioned* a male servant【过时】男仆: *My man will drive you to the station.* 我的仆人将开车送你去车站。

31 ▶GAME 游戏◀ [C] one of the pieces you use in a game such as CHESS 棋子

32 every man jack *old-fashioned* each person in a group【过时】〔某一群体中的〕每一个人

33 kick/hit a man when he's down to treat someone badly when you know that they already have problems 落井下石

34 man's best friend a dog 人类最好的朋友〔指狗〕

35 the man on the Clapham omnibus *BrE* someone who is supposed to represent the attitudes of ordinary people【英】普通人 —see also 另见 BEST MAN, MAN-TO-MAN, NEW MAN, OLD MAN, **be a man/woman of the world** (WORLD¹ (26))

USAGE NOTE 用法说明: MAN

POLITENESS 礼貌程度

Many people no longer use **man** to mean 'men and women in general' because it gives the impression that women are not included. They prefer to use **humans** or **human beings**. 许多人不再用 man 来统称"男人和女人"，因为这种用法给人的印象是妇女未被包括在内。他们更喜欢用 humans 或 human beings: *abilities found in humans* (rather than 而不用 *in man*) 人类的各种能力。Also you might see 此外还会看到: *every disease known to human kind*（人类已知的各种疾病）rather than 而不是 *every disease known to man/mankind*。

Generally you use the word **person** when it is not important to say whether you are talking about a man or a woman. 一般情况下，当没有必要说明是在谈论一个男人或女人时，可用 person 一词: *Sandy's a really nice person.* 桑迪真是个好人。| *unemployed people* 失业的人们。

It is also advisable not to use words that contain **man** in the names of jobs, because this seems to mean that only men

do that job or that the person is a man. So say that someone is a **chairperson**, rather than a **chairman**, especially when it is a woman. Similarly it is better to say **spokesperson, business-people**, or **salesperson**. 在职务名称中如果含有man, 最好也不要使用, 因为这种名称似乎意味着只有男人才能担任这种职务, 或者担任该职务的是一个男人。所以要说某人是个chairperson（主席）, 而不用chairman这个词, 当这个人是位女性时更应如此。同样, 最好说spokesperson（发言人）, business-people（商人）, 或salesperson（推销员）。

Sometimes you do not need to use **-man, -woman**, or **-person** in the names of jobs at all. For example, people are more likely to say **firefighter** than **fireman, police officer** rather than **policeman**, and in British English, **headteacher** or **head** instead of **headmaster** or **headmistress**. 有时职务名称中没有必要使用 -man, -woman 或 -person。例如, 人们更常用的是 firefighter（消防员）而不是 fireman, police officer（警察）而不是 policeman; 而在英国英语中人们则会用 headteacher（校长）或 head 来代替 headmaster 或 headmistress。

man² *v* **manned, manning** [T] to work at, use, or operate a system, piece of equipment etc 在〔某系统、设备等上〕工作; 使用, 操纵〔某系统、设备等〕: *The information desk is manned 24 hours a day.* 问讯处每天24小时有人值班。| *the first manned spacecraft* 第一艘载人宇宙飞船

man³ *interjection especially AmE* used to emphasize what you are saying【尤美】喂; 嘿; 啊呀〔用于强调正在说的话〕: *Man, that was a lucky escape!* 哎呀, 那真是死里逃生啊!

Man, the Isle of—see 见 ISLE OF MAN

man·a·cle /ˈmænəkl; ˈmænəkəl/ *n* [C usually plural 一般用复数] an iron ring on a chain that is put around the hands or feet of prisoners 镣铐, 手铐, 脚镣 —**manacled** *adj*

man·age /ˈmænɪdʒ; ˈmænɪdʒ/ *v*

1 ▶**DO STH DIFFICULT** 做困难之事◀[I,T] to succeed in doing something difficult, especially after trying very hard 设法做成（困难的事）; 努力完成: **manage to do sth** *Jenny managed to pass her driving test on the fifth attempt.* 珍妮考了五次才最终通过了驾驶考试。| *How do you manage to stay so slim?* 你是如何把身材保持得这么苗条的? | *We eventually managed to track down the elusive Ms Lewis.* 我们终于找到了那位难找的刘易斯女士。| **manage sth** *He tried to walk, but managed only a few shaky steps.* 他试图行走, 但只是颤巍巍地走了几步。| **manage it** *I said we'd be there by seven, do you think we'll manage it?* 我说我们将在7点钟之前到那儿, 你认为我们能做到吗?

2 ▶**DEAL WITH PROBLEMS** 处理问题◀[I] *especially spoken* to succeed in dealing with problems, living in a difficult situation etc【尤口】成功应付难题, 〔在困境等中〕得以对付过去: *Frankly, I don't know how single parents manage.* 坦率地说, 我不知道单身父母日子是怎么过的。| [**+without**] *How on earth do you manage without a washing machine?* 没有洗衣机你究竟是怎么生活的? | **manage with** (=use something even though it is not the best or most suitable thing) 凑合, 将就 *I can't afford to get you a new coat – you'll have to manage with the one you've got.* 我没有钱给你买新外套 —— 你只能凑合着穿你现有的那一件。

3 ▶**LIVE WITHOUT MUCH MONEY** 靠不多的钱生活◀[I] to succeed in buying the things you need to live even though you do not have very much money〔靠不多的钱〕生活下去, 勉强维持: *I honestly don't know how we'll manage now Keith's lost his job.* 基思失业了, 我确实不知道我们将如何生活下去。| [**+on**] *People like Jim have to manage on as little as $75 a week.* 像吉姆那样的人们不得不靠每周75美元的微薄收入来勉强过日子。

4 ▶**NOT NEED HELP** 无须帮忙◀[I,T] *especially spoken* to be able to do something or carry something without help【尤口】〔无须帮忙〕能干（某事）; 能搬（某物）: *"Do you want a hand with those bags?" "No, it's OK, I can manage."* "要我帮忙搬那些行李吗?" "不用, 没问题, 我应付得来。" | **manage sth** *You'll never manage that heavy suitcase; let me take it.* 那只笨重的箱子你是提不动的, 让我来吧。

5 ▶**CAUSE PROBLEMS** 引起问题◀[T] *especially spoken* used jokingly to mean to do something that causes problems【尤口】竟搞得, 竟做出〔用于开玩笑地表示做出成问题的事情〕: **manage to do sth** *The kids had managed to spill paint all over the carpet.* 孩子们竟然把颜料洒了整整一地毯。| *I don't know how I managed to arrive so late.* 我不知道自己怎么竟然会到得这么迟。

6 ▶**BUSINESS** 生意◀[T] to direct or control a business and the people who work in it; to be the manager of 经营, 管理; 当〔某企业〕的经理: *Managing four restaurants is extremely hard work.* 经营四家饭店是极其辛苦的工作。| *He used to manage a famous rock band.* 他过去曾当过一支著名摇滚乐队的经理。| *The company had been very badly managed.* 那家公司当时一直管理不善。

7 ▶**TIME/MONEY** 时间/金钱◀[T] to use your time or money effectively, without wasting them 有效使用〔时间或金钱〕: *Helena's never been very good at managing her money.* 海伦娜从来就不太善于理财。

8 ▶**KEEP TIDY** 保持整洁◀[T] to succeed in keeping something neat and tidy 把〔某物〕保持得井井有条: *He'll never manage such a big garden on his own.* 他单靠自己是无法料理这么大的一个花园。| *Silkesse conditioner makes hair easier to manage.* 西尔克西护发素能使头发更易于梳理。

9 ▶**CONTROL** 控制◀[T] to control the behaviour of a person or animal, so that they do what you want 驾驭, 控制〔人或动物的行为〕: *Audrey has the knack for managing difficult children.* 奥德丽有本事管住调皮的孩子。

10 ▶**BE STRONG ENOUGH** 足够强壮◀[T] to be able to do something because you are strong enough or healthy enough 强壮[健康]得能做〔某事〕: *Grandad can't manage the stairs any more.* 爷爷再也爬不动楼梯了。| *I can only manage three situps.* 我只能做三个仰卧起坐。

11 ▶**EAT/DRINK** 吃/喝◀[T] to be able to eat or drink something 能吃[喝]〔某物〕: *I think I could manage another glass of wine.* 我想我能再喝一杯酒。

12 **manage a smile/a few words etc** to make yourself say or do something when you do not really want to 勉强笑一笑/说几句等: *Tina managed a reluctant smile for the camera.* 蒂娜对着镜头勉强笑了笑。

13 ▶**HAVE TIME FOR** 有时间做◀ **manage Wednesday/7:30/lunch etc** to agree to meet someone or do something with them, even though you are busy 安排星期三/7点30分等〔见某人或做某事〕; 安排〔与某人〕吃午饭: *We should meet soon, can you manage Wednesday evening?* 我们应该早点会面, 你星期三晚上行吗?

man·age·a·ble /ˈmænɪdʒəbl; ˈmænɪdʒəbəl/ *adj* easy to control or deal with 易控制的; 易管理的; 易处理的: *My hair's more manageable since I had it cut.* 我的头发剪短后好梳理多了。—opposite 反义词 UNMANAGEABLE —**manageability** /ˌmænɪdʒəˈbɪləti; ˌmænɪdʒəˈbɪlɪ̣ti/ *n* [U]

man·age·ment /ˈmænɪdʒmənt; ˈmænɪdʒmənt/ *n* **1** [U] the act or skill of directing and organizing the work of a company or organization 经营; 管理: *He left the management of the firm to his son.* 他把公司的经营事宜交给了他的儿子。| *They sent me on one of those management training courses.* 他们派我去学那些管理培训课程中的一门。| **good/bad management** *The company's failure was mainly due to bad management.* 这家公司破产主要是由于经营不善。**2** [singular, U] the people who are in charge of a company or organization〔公司或组织的〕管理层: *Targets were agreed in consultation between management and staff.* 指标是由管理层和员工协商达成的。| [also+plural verb *BrE* 英] *The management are blaming the workers for the dispute.* 管理层将纠纷归咎于工人。| *a management decision* 管理层的决定 | **senior/junior management** *talks with senior management* 与高层管理人员的谈判 | **middle management** (=in charge of small groups within an organization) 中层管理人员 **3** [U] the act or skill of dealing with a situation that needs to be controlled in some way 管理; 管理技巧: *traffic management* 交通管理 | *better management of the Earth's natural resources* 对地球自然资源更有效的管理

management buy·out /ˌ···ˈ··/ *n* [C] the buying of shares (SHARE² (5)) of a company by the management so that they control the company 管理层收购

management con·sult·ant /ˈ·····ˌ··/ *n* [C] someone who is paid to advise the management of a company how to improve their organization and working methods 管理顾问, 业务顾问

man·ag·er /ˈmænɪdʒə; ˈmænɪdʒə/ *n* [C] **1** someone whose job is to manage part or all of a company or other organization〔公司或其他机构的〕经理: *a bank manager* 银行经理 | *the General Manager of Chevrolet* 雪佛兰公司总经理 | *one of our regional managers* 我们的一位地区经理 | *Can I speak to the manager?* 我能跟经理谈谈吗? **2** someone who is in charge of the business affairs of a singer, an actor etc〔歌手、演员等的〕经纪人 **3** someone who is in charge of training and organizing a sports team〔运动队的〕管理人, 经理: *Jack Charlton, the Ireland manager* 爱尔兰队的领队杰克·查尔顿 —see also 另见 LINE MANAGER

man·ag·er·ess /ˋmænɪdʒərɪs; ˌmænɪdʒəˈres/ *n* [C] *old-fashioned* a woman who is in charge of a business, especially a shop or restaurant【过时】〔尤指商店或饭店的〕女经理，女管理人

man·a·ge·ri·al /ˌmænəˋdʒɪrɪəl; ˌmænɪˈdʒɪəriəl/ *adj* connected with the job of a manager 经理的；管理的；经营的：*a managerial post* 经理职位

managing di·rec·tor /ˌ‥ ·ˋ‥/ *n* [C] *BrE* someone who is in charge of a large company or organization【英】〔大公司或机构的〕总经理，总裁

Ma·nag·ua /məˋnægwə; məˈnægwə/ the capital city of Nicaragua 马那瓜〔尼加拉瓜首都〕

ma·ña·na /mənˋjɑnə; mænˈjɑːnə/ *adv, adj, n Spanish* a word meaning tomorrow, used when talking about someone who seems too relaxed and always delays doing things【西】明天〔用于谈论某个过于散漫、做事拖拉的人〕：*a mañana attitude* 一种明日复明日的态度

man-at-arms /ˌ‥ ·ˋ/ *n* [C] *old use* a soldier【旧】士兵

Manche, La—see 见 LA MANCHE

Man·ches·ter /ˋmæntʃəstə; ˈmæntʃɪstə/ a large city in the northwest of England, which was formerly important for its wool and cotton industries, but is now the financial and business centre for the area. Many POP and ROCK bands come from Manchester, which is famous for its music industry, its many NIGHTCLUBS and its two football teams, Manchester United and Manchester City. People who come from Manchester are called Mancunians. 曼彻斯特〔英格兰西北部一大城市。历史上曾为棉、毛纺织业重镇，现已成为该地区的商务金融中心。曼彻斯特有很多流行乐队和摇滚乐队，故该市又以其音乐产业、众多夜总会和两支足球队（曼彻斯特联队和曼特斯特城市队）著称。曼彻斯特人称作 Mancunians〕

Manchester Ship Ca·nal, the /ˌ‥ · ·ˋ/ a long, narrow area of water in northwest England which goes from Manchester to the sea. It was built to help the cotton factories to move their goods in the 19th century. 曼彻斯特通海运河〔英格兰西北部一狭长运河，从曼彻斯特流向海洋。该运河开凿于 19 世纪，主要用于棉纺织厂运送货物〕

Manchester U·ni·ted /ˌ‥ ·ˋ‥/ also 又作 **Man United** *informal*【非正式】a very successful and popular English football team from Manchester. In 1999 they became the first team to win the European Cup, the FA Cup, and the Premiership competition in one season. 曼彻斯特联队，曼联队〔曼彻斯特市一战绩卓越、众人皆知的足球队。1999 年，该队成为第一支在同一赛季赢得欧冠、足总杯和英超联赛冠军的球队〕

Man·cu·ni·an /mænˋkjunɪən; mænˈkjuːniən/ *n* [C] someone who lives in or comes from Manchester 曼彻斯特人 —**Mancunian** *adj*

man·da·la /ˋmændələ; ˈmændələ/ *n* [C] a picture of a circle around a square, that represents the universe in Hindu and Buddhist religions 曼荼罗〔印度教和佛教中象征宇宙的内方外圆图案〕

Man·da·lay /ˌmændəˋle; ˌmændəˈleɪ/ a city in Myanmar 曼德勒〔缅甸一城市〕

Man·da·rin /ˋmændərɪn; ˈmændərɪn/ *n* [U] the official language of China, spoken by most educated Chinese people〔中国〕普通话，国语，官话

mandarin *n* [C] **1** a kind of small orange with skin that is easy to remove 橘子，柑橘 **2** *BrE* an important official in the Civil Service, especially one who is regarded as having too much influence【英】内务要员，达官贵人：*the mandarins of Whitehall* 白厅的高官们 **3** an important government official in the former Chinese EMPIRE (1)〔旧时中国帝制时代的〕高级官吏

mandarin or·ange /ˌ‥ ˋ‥/ *n* [C] a MANDARIN (1) 橘子，柑橘

man·date[1] /ˋmændet; ˈmændeɪt/ *n* **1** [C] the right and power to carry out certain policies, which is given to a government or elected official by the people who voted for them〔选民对政府或选出的官员执行某些政策的〕授权：**mandate to do sth** *The President was elected with a clear mandate to tackle violent crime.* 总统当选时获得了解决暴力犯罪问题的明确授权。| **seek a mandate** *They are seeking a mandate for tax reforms.* 他们正在寻求授权以进行税制改革。**2** [C] an official command given to a person or organization to do something〔对某人或某机构的〕命令；训令：*an envoy carrying out the Archbishop's mandate* 执行大主教命令的使节 **3** [C,U] the power given to one country to govern another country 委任统治权，托管权

man·date[2] /ˋmændet; mænˈdeɪt/ *v* [T] **1** *especially AmE* to give an official command that something must be done【尤美】命令，指示：*Austerity measures were mandated by the International Monetary Fund.* 国际货币基金组织指示采取紧缩措施。**2** [often passive 常用被动态] to give someone the right or power to do something 授权于〔某人〕，委任

man·dat·ed /ˋmændetɪd; mænˈdeɪtɪd/ *adj* a mandated country has been placed under the control of another country〔国家〕被托管的：*mandated territories* 托管地

man·da·to·ry /ˋmændəˌtorɪ; ˈmændətəri/ *adj* something that is mandatory must be done because the law says it must be done; COMPULSORY, OBLIGATORY 依法必须做的；强制性的；义务的：*Inspection of imported meat is mandatory.* 对进口肉类的检查是强制性的。| *Drug smuggling carried a mandatory death penalty.* 毒品走私必然会被判死刑。

Man·del·a /ˌmænˋdɛlə; ˌmænˈdelə/**, Nelson** (1918-) the leader of South Africa's ANC party since 1994, and the first black President of South Africa. Mandela was in prison from 1964 to 1990 for his opposition to the country's white government. In 1993 he shared the Nobel Prize for Peace with President F. W. de Klerk after they had worked together to end the system of APARTHEID. 曼德拉〔(1918-)，南非非洲人国民大会党 1994 年以来的领导人，南非第一位黑人总统。1964 至 1990 年期间，曼德拉因反对南非白人政府而被关入监狱。他曾与德克勒克总统共同努力以结束种族隔离制度，并于 1993 年共同获得诺贝尔和平奖〕

man·di·ble /ˋmændəbḷ; ˈmændɪbəl/ *n* [C] *technical*【术语】**1** the jaw of an animal or fish, especially the lower jaw〔动物或鱼的〕颌〔尤指下颌〕**2** the upper or lower part of a bird's beak 鸟喙的上[下]部 **3** a part like a jaw at the front of an insect's mouth 昆虫的大颚，上颚

man·do·lin /ˋmændḷˌɪn; ˌmændəˈlɪn/ *n* [C] a musical instrument with eight metal strings and a round back 曼陀林〔一种八根金属弦、圆形琴身的乐器〕

man·drake /ˋmændrek; ˈmændreɪk/ *n* [C] a plant from which drugs can be made which help people to sleep, and which was once thought to have magic powers 茄参〔一种可制安眠药的植物，旧时被认为有魔力〕

man·drill /ˋmændrɪl; ˈmændrɪl/ *n* [C] a large monkey like a BABOON with a brightly coloured face 山魈〔与狒狒相似，脸上有鲜明色彩〕

mane /men; meɪn/ *n* [C] **1** the long hair on the back of a horse's neck, or around the face and neck of a lion〔马、狮颈上的〕鬃毛 —see picture at 参见 HORSE[1] 图 **2** *informal* a person's long thick hair【非正式】又长又密的头发

man-eat·er /ˋ· ‥/ *n* [C] **1** an animal that eats human flesh 食人兽 **2** *humorous* a woman who has many sexual partners【幽默】放荡的女人 —**man-eating** *adj*: *a man-eating tiger* 食人虎

Man·et /mæˋne; ˈmæneɪ/**, Éd·ouard** /ˋɛdwərd; ˈedwəd/ (1832-83) a French painter who greatly influenced the Impressionists 马奈〔(1823-1883)，法国画家，曾对印象派画家产生过重大影响〕

ma·neu·ver /məˋnuvə; məˈnuːvə/ *n, v* the American spelling of MANOEUVRE manoeuvre 的美式拼法

ma·neu·ve·ra·ble /məˋnuvərəbḷ; məˈnuːvərəbəl/ *adj* the American spelling of MANOEUVRABLE manoeuvrable 的美式拼法

ma·neu·ve·ring /məˋnuvərɪŋ; məˈnuːvərɪŋ/ *n* [C,U] the American spelling of MANOEUVRING manoeuvring 的美式拼法

Man for All Sea·sons, A /ˌ· · · ·ˋ·/ (1960) a play by Robert Bolt about the life of Sir Thomas More, which was later made into a film《生死之交》〔(1960)，罗伯特·博尔特创作的剧本，描述托马斯·莫尔爵士的生平事迹。该剧后来被改编成电影〕

Man Fri·day /ˌ· ˋ‥/ **1** a character in the book *Robinson Crusoe* by Daniel Defoe. He is a black man who becomes Crusoe's servant and friend after Crusoe saves him from being killed by CANNIBALS (=people who eat other people). Crusoe calls him Man Friday because he meets him on a Friday. 星期五〔丹尼尔·笛福所著的小说《鲁宾逊漂流记》中的人物。他是个黑人。鲁宾逊·克鲁索把他从食人族那里救出来之后，他就成了克鲁索的仆人和朋友。克鲁索是在一个星期五遇见他的，所以就叫他"星期五"〕**2** a loyal and trusted male servant or helper 忠实可信的男仆[助手]

man·ful·ly /ˋmænfəlɪ; ˈmænfəli/ *adv* in a brave, determined way 勇敢地；果断地：*They struggled manfully on through the wind and rain.* 他们冒着风雨勇敢而艰难地前进。—**manful** *adj*

man·ga·nese /ˋmæŋgəˌniz; ˈmæŋgəniːz/ *n* [U] a greyish-white metal used for making glass, steel etc 锰

mange /mendʒ; meɪndʒ/ *n* [U] a skin disease of animals that makes them lose small areas of fur 兽疥癣，家畜疥

man·ger /ˋmendʒə; ˈmeɪndʒə/ *n* [C] a long open container that horses, cattle etc eat from〔马、牛等的〕食槽 —see also 另见 **dog in the manger** (DOG[1] (10))

M

CULTURAL NOTE 文化注释

According to the Bible, Jesus was born in a STABLE and laid in a manger as a bed, because there were no empty rooms in the town his parents had travelled to. Most people in the US and UK know the CAROL (=Christmas song) about this, which starts: *Away in a manger, no crib for a bed / The little Lord Jesus laid down his sweet head.* 据《圣经》所述，耶稣在马厩中出生，并把马槽当作睡觉的床，因为他父母所到的城镇那时已没有空房。在英美，大多数人都知道讲述此事的颂歌，前几句是：远处马槽里，无枕也无床/主啊小耶稣埋头睡，睡得甜蜜又安详。— see also 另见 CHRISTMAS, NATIVITY

mange·tout /ˌmɑnʒˈtu; ˌmɒnʒˈtuː/ *n* [C] *BrE* a kind of flat PEA whose outer part is eaten as well as the seeds【英】糖荚豌豆〔一种荚和豆均可吃的豌豆〕; SNOW PEA *AmE*【美】

man·gle¹ /ˈmæŋgḷ; ˈmæŋgəl/ *v* [T] **1** [often passive 常用被动态] to damage or injure something badly by crushing or twisting it 压坏; 扭伤: *The trap closed round her leg, badly mangling her ankle.* 夹子夹住了她的腿，重伤了她的脚踝。**2** to put clothes through a mangle 用轧液机轧压〔衣服〕

mangle² *n* [C] a machine with two rollers (ROLLER (1)), used to remove water from washed clothes 轧液机〔用于压去已洗净衣服的水分〕

man·go /ˈmæŋgo; ˈmæŋgəʊ/ *n* [C] a tropical fruit with a thin skin and sweet yellow flesh 芒果 —see picture on page A8 参见 A8 页图

man·grove /ˈmæŋgrov; ˈmæŋgrəʊv/ *n* [C] a tropical tree that grows in or near water and grows new roots from its branches 红树〔一种热带树木，生于水中或水边，并从树枝上长出新根〕: *a mangrove swamp* 生长红树的沼泽地

mang·y /ˈmendʒɪ; ˈmeɪndʒi/ *adj* **1** suffering from MANGE〔兽、畜〕患疥癣的: *emaciated mangy dogs* 瘦骨嶙峋的癞皮狗 **2** *informal* dirty and in bad condition【非正式】脏而破的，破旧的: *a mangy-looking rug* 看起来又脏又破的旧地毯

man·han·dle /ˈmænˌhændḷ; ˈmænhændl/ *v* [T] **1** to push or handle someone roughly 粗暴地推搡: **manhandle sb into/through etc** *The police manhandled him into the car.* 警察粗暴地把他推进汽车。**2** to move a heavy object using force 用力搬动〔重物〕: **manhandle sth up/into etc** *We managed to manhandle the piano up the stairs.* 我们费力地将钢琴搬上楼梯。

Man·hat·tan /mænˈhætṇ; mænˈhætn/ an island and BOROUGH of New York City in New York Bay, between the Hudson River and the East River 曼哈顿〔纽约市所属岛屿和行政区，濒临纽约湾，位于哈得孙河和东河之间〕

CULTURAL NOTE 文化注释

Manhattan is the business and CULTURAL centre of New York City. The business area is mainly on **Wall Street** at the southern end of Manhattan, where the **New York Stock Exchange** is, and where the **World Trade Center** used to be before it was destroyed by TERRORISTs on 11 September, 2001. **Fifth Avenue**, in the centre of Manhattan, is known for having many expensive shops and DEPARTMENT STOREs. There are many theatres on or near **Broadway**, and Manhattan has several important MUSEUMs. The **Metropolitan Museum of Art** is on the edge of **Central Park**, a very large park in the middle of Manhattan Island. Some parts of **Harlem**, which is north of Central Park, are poor with cheap houses and apartments, but the rest of Manhattan is very expensive to live in. 曼哈顿是纽约城的商业和文化中心。商业区主要位于曼哈顿南端的华尔街，也就是纽约证券交易所的所在地，同时也是2001年9月11日被恐怖主义分子摧毁的世贸中心的所在地。位于曼哈顿中心的第五大道以高档商场和百货商店众多著称。百老汇大街及其附近有很多剧院。此外曼哈顿还有数个重要的博物馆。大都会艺术博物馆位于中央公园的旁边，而中央公园是曼哈顿中央的一个很大的公园。中央公园的北侧是哈勒姆的部分地区，这里是有很多廉价房屋和公寓的穷人区，纽约除此之外的其他地方居住成本都很高。

When people say that they have visited New York, they often mean that they have been to Manhattan. The Manhattan SKYLINE (=the way that the city's many tall buildings look from a distance) is world-famous. Manhattan's famous SKYSCRAPERs (=tall buildings) include the **Empire State Building**, the **Chrysler Building**, and the **United Nations Headquarters**. The **Twin Towers** were two of Manhattan's most famous skyscrapers, but they were destroyed in the terrorist attack on the World Trade Center on 11 September, 2001. 那些说自己去过纽约的人通常指他们已经去曼哈顿看过。曼哈顿的空中轮廓线（即从远处看到的一个城市的众多高楼）世界知名。曼哈顿著名的摩天大楼有帝国大厦、克莱斯勒大厦和联合国总部。双子大厦也是曼哈顿过去非常著名的摩天大楼，但是它们毁于2001年9月11日恐怖主义分子对世贸中心的袭击。— see also 另见 GREENWICH VILLAGE, NEW YORK CITY, TIMES SQUARE

Manhattan Pro·ject, the /·ˌ··ˈ··/ the secret US scientific plan, which was started in 1942, to develop an ATOM BOMB 曼哈顿计划〔美国于1942年开始实施的一项研制原子弹的秘密科学计划〕—see also 另见 LOS ALAMOS

man·hole /ˈmænˌhol; ˈmænhəʊl/ *n* [C] a hole on the surface of a road covered by a lid, used to examine pipes, wires etc 人孔，检修孔〔路面上的有盖洞口，用于检修管道、电线等〕

man·hood /ˈmænhud; ˈmænhʊd/ *n* **1** [U] qualities such as strength, courage, and especially sexual power, that people think a man should have; VIRILITY 男子气概[气质]〈如力量、勇气，尤指性能力〉: *He took this remark as an insult to his manhood.* 他把这句话看成是对他的男子气概的污辱。**2** [U] the state of being a man and no longer a boy〔男子的〕成年，成人: *He had barely reached manhood when he married.* 他刚刚成年便结了婚。**3** [singular] *especially literary* a word meaning PENIS, used in order to avoid saying this directly【尤文】阳物，阴茎〔委婉语〕**4** [U] *literary* all the men of a particular nation【文】〔一个国家的〕全体男子: *America's manhood* 美国全国的男子 —compare 比较 WOMANHOOD

man-hour /ˌ·ˈ·/ *n* [C] the amount of work done by one person in one hour 人时，工时〔一人一小时完成的工作量〕

man·hunt /ˈmænˌhʌnt; ˈmænhʌnt/ *n* [C] an organized search, especially for a criminal or a prisoner who has escaped〔尤指对罪犯或逃犯的〕搜捕，追捕

ma·ni·a /ˈmenɪə; ˈmeɪniə/ *n* [C,U] **1** a very strong desire for something or interest in something, especially one that affects a lot of people at the same time 狂热，热衷; 癖好: **[+for]** *A mania for a game called Nibs ran through the school.* 一种名叫尼布斯的游戏掀起的狂热风潮席卷了全校。| **religious/football/disco etc mania** *The whole country is in the grip of football mania.* 整个国家都沉浸在对足球的狂热中。**2** *technical* a serious mental illness【术语】躁狂症

ma·ni·ac /ˈmenɪˌæk; ˈmeɪniæk/ *n* [C] **1** *informal* someone who behaves in a stupid or dangerous way【非正式】举止愚蠢[危险]的人，疯子: *Some maniac overtook us on a bend.* 一个疯子在拐弯处超过了我们。**2 a religious maniac/sex maniac etc** *informal* someone who thinks about religion, sex etc all the time【非正式】宗教迷/性欲狂等: *The woman's a sex maniac if you ask me.* 在我看来，那个女人是个性欲狂。**3** *old-fashioned* someone who is mentally ill【过时】狂躁者; 疯子，精神病患者

ma·ni·a·cal /məˈnaɪəkḷ; məˈnaɪəkəl/ *adj* behaving as if you are crazy 疯狂的; 狂躁的: *maniacal laughter* 疯狂的笑声 —**maniacally** /-kḷɪ; -kli/ *adv*

man·ic /ˈmænɪk; ˈmænɪk/ *adj* **1** *informal* behaving in a very anxious or excited way【非正式】急切的，激动的: *She seemed slightly manic.* 她好像有点激动。**2** *technical* connected with a feeling of great happiness and excitement that is part of a mental illness【术语】躁狂的

manic de·pres·sion /ˌ·· ·ˈ··/ *n* [U] a mental illness that makes people sometimes feel extremely happy and excited and sometimes extremely sad and hopeless 躁狂抑郁症

manic de·pres·sive /ˌ·· ·ˈ··/ *n* [C] someone who suffers from manic depression 狂躁抑郁症患者 —**manic-depressive** *adj*

man·i·cure /ˈmænɪˌkjʊr; ˈmænɪ̣kjʊə/ *n* [C,U] a treatment for the hands and nails that includes cutting and polishing the nails 修指甲 —**manicure** *v* [T]

man·i·cured /ˈmænɪˌkjʊrd; ˈmænɪ̣kjʊəd/ *adj* **1** manicured hands have nails that are neatly cut and polished〔指甲〕修剪整洁的 **2** manicured gardens or LAWNs are very neat and tidy〔花园或草坪〕修剪整齐的 —**manicurist** *n*

man·i·fest¹ /ˈmænəˌfɛst; ˈmænɪ̣fest/ *v* [T] *formal*【正式】**1** to show a feeling, attitude etc 显示，表明，表露〔感情、态度等〕: *They have so far manifested a total indifference to our concerns.* 到目前为止，他们对我们所关注的事情一直摆出一副漠不关心的态度。**2 manifest itself** to appear or to become easy to see 显现，显露: *Food allergies manifest themselves in a variety of ways.* 食物过敏症状会以多种方式表现出来。

M

manifest² *adj formal* plain and easy to see; OBVIOUS【正式】显而易见的，明显的：*a manifest error of judgment* 明显的判断错误 | **be made manifest** (=be clearly shown) 显示，显露 *Their devotion to God is made manifest in ritual prayer.* 他们对上帝的虔诚在宗教仪式的祷告中明白地显示出来。—**manifestly** *adv*: *manifestly untrue* 显然不真实

man·i·fes·ta·tion /ˌmænəfɛsˋteʃən; ˌmænɨfeˈsteɪʃən/ *n formal*【正式】**1** [C] a very clear sign that a particular situation or feeling exists 明显迹象；表现：[**+of**] *These latest riots are a clear manifestation of growing discontent.* 这些最近发生的骚乱是不满情绪日益增长的明显迹象。**2** [U] the act of appearing or becoming clear 显现；显示，表明：*Manifestation of the disease often doesn't occur until middleage.* 这种疾病的症状通常到中年才表现出来。**3** [C] the appearance of a GHOST or a sign of its presence〔鬼魂的〕显灵

Manifest Des·ti·ny /ˌ‥ ˈ‥‥/ the belief that the US people had the right and the duty to take land in North America from other people, because this was God's plan. This phrase was used by journalists and politicians in the 19th century when US citizens moved west across North America and the US gained Texas, California, Oregon, and Alaska. 上帝所命，天定命运（论）〔即相信美国人有权利和义务从其他民族手中夺取北美土地，因为这是上帝的旨意。19世纪，美国人向北美西部迁移，从而取得得克萨斯、加利福尼亚、俄勒冈以及阿拉斯加各州〕

man·i·fes·to /ˌmænəˋfɛsto; ˌmænɨˈfestəʊ/ *n* [C] a written statement by an organized group, especially a political party, saying what they believe in and what they intend to do 宣言

CULTURAL NOTE 文化注释

In the UK, the main political parties each produce a manifesto before a GENERAL ELECTION, which says what the party will do if it is elected. 在英国，主要政党每逢大选之前都要拟出一份宣言，阐述自己当选后的执政思路。

man·i·fold¹ /ˋmænəˌfold; ˈmænɨfəʊld/ *adj formal* many and of different kinds【正式】繁多的，多种多样的；多方面的：*manifold cultural differences* 多方面的文化差异

manifold² *n* [C] *technical* an arrangement of pipes through which gases enter or leave a car engine【术语】〔汽车发动机的〕歧管：*an exhaust manifold* 排气歧管 —see picture at 参见 ENGINE 图

man·i·kin, mannikin /ˋmænəkɪn; ˈmænɪkɨn/ *n* [C] **1** a model of the human body, used in art classes or for teaching medical students〔艺术或医学课用的〕人体模型 **2** *old use* a little man; DWARF¹【旧】矮子，侏儒

Ma·nil·a /məˋnɪlə; məˈnɪlə/ a city and port, the capital of the Philippines 马尼拉〔菲律宾一城市和港口，菲律宾首都〕

manila, manilla *n* [U] *old use* strong brown paper used for making envelopes【旧】〔做信封用的〕马尼拉纸

Man in the I·ron Mask, the /ˌ‥‥ ˈ‥‥/ a man who was kept as a prisoner in the Bastille, a prison in Paris, who died there in 1703. His face was always kept hidden by a MASK, and some people believe that he was the brother of the French king Louis XIV, but this is probably not true. 铁面人〔关押在巴黎巴士底狱一犯人，死于1703年。他脸上一直戴着面具，有些人认为他是法国国王路易十四的兄弟，但这一猜测可能有误〕

ma·nip·u·late /məˋnɪpjəˌlet; məˈnɪpjɡleɪt/ *v* [T] **1** to make someone think and behave exactly as you want them to, by skilfully deceiving them or influencing them〔通过巧妙地欺骗或影响而〕操纵，控制：*I don't like the way she manipulates people.* 我不喜欢她摆布别人的做法。| *It was a shameless attempt to manipulate public opinion.* 那是一种无耻的图谋，企图操纵舆论。**2** to work skilfully with information, systems etc to achieve the result that you want〔熟练地〕操作，使用〔信息、系统等〕：*Researchers can manipulate the data in a variety of ways.* 研究员们能以多种方式使用这些数据。**3** *technical* to skilfully move and press a joint or bone into the correct position【术语】推拿正〔骨〕**4** to use skill in moving or handling something 巧妙地移动〔某物〕；巧妙地处理〔某事〕—**manipulation** /məˌnɪpjuˋleʃən; məˌnɪpjɡˈleɪʃən/ *n* [U]

ma·nip·u·la·tive /məˋnɪpjəˌletɪv; məˈnɪpjɡlətɪv/ *adj* **1** clever at controlling or deceiving people to get what you want 善于控制[欺骗]他人的：*She has a very manipulative side to her character.* 她性格中有爱摆布人的一面。**2** *technical* connected with the skill of moving bones and joints into the correct position【术语】推拿正骨法的：*manipulative treatment* 推拿法治疗 **3** *technical* connected with the ability to handle objects in a skilful way【术语】操作的：*manipulative techniques* 操作技术

ma·nip·u·la·tor /məˋnɪpjuˌletɚ; məˈnɪpjɡleɪtə/ *n* [C] someone who is good at getting what they want by cleverly controlling or deceiving other people 善于摆布[欺骗]他人者，操控者

Man·i·to·ba /ˌmænɪˋtobə; ˌmænɨˈtəʊbə/ a PROVINCE in central Canada 马尼托巴省〔加拿大中部一省份〕

Man·i·tou·lin /ˌmænɪˋtulɪn; ˌmænɨˈtuːlɪn/ a large island in Lake Huron, Canada, which is the largest island in the world that is surrounded by fresh (=not containing salt) water 马尼图林岛〔加拿大休伦湖一大岛，是世界上最大的淡水湖岛屿〕

man·kind /mænˋkaɪnd; ˌmænˈkaɪnd/ *n* [U] all humans considered as a group 人类：*a great step forward for mankind* 人类迈进的一大步 —compare 比较 WOMANKIND —see 见 MAN¹ (USAGE)

man·ky /ˋmæŋkɪ; ˈmæŋki/ *adj BrE informal* looking dirty and unattractive【英，非正式】肮脏难看的：*a manky old sweater* 又脏又旧的毛衣

man·ly /ˋmænlɪ; ˈmænli/ *adj* having qualities that people expect and admire in a man, such as being brave and strong 有男子气概的；勇敢而强壮的：*a deep manly voice* 低沉雄浑的嗓音 —**manliness** *n* [U]

man-made /ˌ‥ˈ‥◂/ *adj* produced by people; not natural 人造的，人工的：*a man-made lake* 人工湖 | *man-made fibres* 人造纤维 —compare 比较 ARTIFICIAL, NATURAL¹

Mann /mæn; mæn/, **Thomas** (1875-1955) a German writer whose books include *Death in Venice*, *The Magic Mountain*, and *Doctor Faustus*. He won the Nobel Prize for Literature in 1929. 曼〔(1875-1955)，德国作家。其作品有《威尼斯之死》、《魔山》和《浮士德博士》等，1929年获诺贝尔文学奖〕

man·na /ˋmænə; ˈmænə/ *n* **1 manna from heaven** something that you need, which you suddenly or unexpectedly get or are given 天赐之物；意外收获 **2** [U] the food which, according to the Bible, was provided by God for the Israelites in the desert after their escape from Egypt 吗哪〔《圣经》中以色列人逃离埃及后在荒漠中获得的神赐食物〕

man·ne·quin /ˋmænəkɪn; ˈmænɪkɨn/ *n* [C] **1** a model of the human body used for showing clothes in shop windows〔商店橱窗中用以展示服装的〕人体模型 **2** *old-fashioned* a woman whose job is to wear fashionable clothes and show them to people; MODEL¹ (2)【过时】女时装模特

man·ner /ˋmænɚ; ˈmænə/ *n* S3 W2

1 ►WAY 方式◄ [singular] *formal* the way in which something is done or happens【正式】方式，方法：**manner of doing sth** *This seems rather an odd manner of deciding things.* 这似乎是一种十分古怪的决定事情的方法。| **in a … manner** *I felt stupid for reacting in such an impulsive manner.* 我以那样一种冲动的方式作出反应，自己都感到愚蠢。| *The matter should be submitted to the accounts committee in the usual manner.* 此事应按通常的方式提交财务委员会解决。

2 ►WAY OF SPEAKING/BEHAVING 说话/行事的方式◄ [singular] the way in which someone behaves towards or talks to other people 态度；举止：*She has a calm relaxed manner.* 她举止镇定而从容。| *I thought I noticed a certain coldness in his manner.* 我想我注意到他的态度有些冷淡。

3 manners [plural] **a)** polite ways of behaving in social situations 礼貌，礼仪：**good/bad manners** *She has such good manners.* 她是那样彬彬有礼。| **it's good/bad manners (to do sth)** *spoken* (=used to tell a child how to behave)【口】(做某事)是有/没有礼貌的 *It's bad manners to point at people.* 对人指指点点是不礼貌的。| **she/he has no manners** *spoken*【口】"*Vic and Lesley just got up and left.*" "*Some people have no manners.*" "维克和莱斯利站起来就走了。" "有些人就是没礼貌。" | **where are your manners?** *spoken* (=used to tell someone, especially a child, that they are behaving impolitely)【口】你的礼貌哪儿去了？| **table manners** (=the way that you behave at meals) 餐桌礼仪 **b)** *formal* the customs of a particular group of people【正式】习俗，风俗：*a book on the life and manners of Victorian London* 一本关于维多利亚时期伦敦的生活和风俗的书

4 in a manner of speaking in some ways though not exactly 在某种意义上：*I suppose you could call us refugees in a manner of speaking.* 我想在某种意义上你可以称我们为难民。

5 in the manner of in the style that is typical of a particular person or thing 体现…所特有的风格：*a painting in the manner of the early Impressionists* 一幅体现早期印象派风格的绘画

6 all manner of *formal* many different kinds of things or people【正式】各种各样的，形形色色的：*We would discuss all manner of subjects.* 我们常常讨论各种各样的话题。

7 not by any manner of means *BrE spoken* not at all【英口】一点也不，决不：*It's not over yet, by any manner of means.* 事情还没有结束，远远没结束。

M

8 what manner of...? *literary* what kind of【文】什么样的…?: *What manner of son would treat his mother in such a way?* 什么样的儿子会这样对待自己的母亲?

9 (as) to the manner born in a natural confident way doing something, as if you have done it many times before 熟练得仿佛是与生俱来的 —see also 另见 COMEDY OF MANNERS

man·nered /ˋmænəd; ˈmænəd/ *adj* **1 well-mannered/ bad-mannered/mild-mannered etc** polite, impolite etc in the way you behave in social situations 有礼貌的/没礼貌的/态度谦和的等 **2** behaving or speaking in an unnatural way, because you want to impress people 做作的, 不自然的: *He gave a very mannered performance in the lead role.* 他演那个主角演得太矫揉造作。

man·ner·is·m /ˋmænəˌrɪzəm; ˈmænərɪzəm/ *n* **1** [C,U] a way of speaking or moving that is typical of a particular person〔某人所特有的说话或动作的〕习性, 习气: *He has the same mannerisms as his father.* 他的小动作跟他父亲的一样。**2** [U] the use of a style in art that does not look natural〔艺术的〕矫饰风格

man·ni·kin /ˋmænɪkɪn; ˈmænɪkən/ *n* [C] a MANIKIN 人体模型; 侏儒

man·nish /ˋmænɪʃ; ˈmænɪʃ/ *adj* a woman who is mannish looks or behaves like a man, especially in a way that is considered unattractive〔女人长相或举止〕像男人的, 男人气的, 男子般的〔尤指被视为不美的〕: *She had strong, almost mannish features.* 她相貌粗犷, 几乎像男人。—**mannishly** *adv*

ma·noeu·vra·ble *BrE*【英】, **maneuverable** *AmE*【美】/məˋnuvərəbl; məˈnuːvərəbəl/ *adj* easy to move or turn within small spaces 容易移动的, 转动灵活的: *an easily manoeuvrable car* 容易操纵的汽车 —**manoeuvrability** /məˌnuvərəˋbɪlətɪ; məˌnuːvərəˈbɪləti/ *n* [U]

ma·noeu·vre¹ *BrE*【英】, **maneuver** *AmE*【美】/məˋnuvə; məˈnuːvə/ *n* **1** [C] a skilful or careful movement that you make, for example in order to avoid something or go through a narrow space 熟练[谨慎]的动作: *basic skiing manoeuvres* 滑雪的基本动作 **2** [C,U] a skilful or carefully planned action intended to deceive someone or achieve something 策略, 巧计, 花招: *They tried by diplomatic maneuvers to obtain an agreement.* 他们试图利用外交策略达成协议。**3 manoeuvres** [singular] a military exercise like a battle done to train soldiers 军事演习: **on manoeuvres** (=practising military exercises) 在演习中 *The regiment is abroad on manoeuvres.* 该团正在国外进行演习。**4 room for manoeuvre/freedom of manoeuvre** the possibility of changing your plans or decisions 回旋的余地: *They haven't left us much freedom of manoeuvre.* 他们没给我们留下多少回旋的余地。

manoeuvre² *BrE*【英】, **maneuver** *AmE*【美】*v* **1** [I always+adv/prep,T always+adv/prep] to move or turn skilfully or to move or turn something skilfully, especially something large and heavy 巧妙地移动[转动]〔大而沉重的物件〕: *She managed to manoeuvre expertly into the parking space.* 她熟练地将车了驶进了停车位置。| **manoeuvre sth along/into/out etc** *Josh manoeuvred himself out of bed and hobbled to the door.* 乔希从床上爬起来, 一瘸一拐地朝门口走去。**2** [I,T] to use cleverly planned and often dishonest methods to get the result that you want 策划; 诱使: **manoeuvre sb into/out of sth** *It was a well-organized plan to maneuvre the President out of office.* 那是一个精心安排的计划, 旨在使总统下台。

ma·noeu·vring *BrE*【英】, **maneuvering** *AmE*【美】/məˋnuvərɪŋ; məˈnuːvərɪŋ/ *n* [C,U] the use of clever and sometimes dishonest methods to get what you want 策略, 花招: *diplomatic manoeuvrings* 外交手段

man of let·ters /ˌ· · ˈ· ·/ *n* [C] a male writer, especially one who writes NOVELS or writes about literature 男作家〔尤指小说家或文学评论家〕

man-of-war /ˌ· · ˈ·/ also 又作 **man-o'-war** *n* [C] *old use* a fighting ship in the navy【旧】战舰

man·or /ˋmænə; ˈmænə/ *n* [C] **1** a big old house with a large area of land around it 庄园大宅 **2** the land that belonged to an important man, under the FEUDAL system〔封建领主的〕采邑, 领地; 庄园 **3** *BrE slang* an area that a particular POLICE STATION is responsible for【英俚】警察局的管辖区 —**manorial** /məˋnɔrɪəl; məˈnɔːriəl/ *adj*

manor house /ˈ· · ·/ *n* [C] a big old house in the countryside with a large area of land around it 庄园大宅

man·pow·er /ˋmænˌpaʊə; ˈmænˌpaʊə/ *n* [U] all the workers available for a particular kind of work 劳动力; 人力: *a lack of trained manpower* 缺乏训练有素的劳动力

man·qué /mɑnˋke; ˈmɒŋkeɪ/ *adj French*【法】**artist/actor/teacher manqué** someone who could have been successful as an artist etc, but never became one 本来可以成为艺术家/演员/教师却并未如愿以偿的人

man·sard /ˋmænsɑrd; ˈmænsɑːd/ also 又作 **mansard roof** /ˈ· · ·/ *n* [C] a roof whose lower part slopes more steeply than its upper part 复斜屋顶〔下半部比上半部陡〕

manse /mæns; mæns/ *n* [C] a house that is lived in by a priest, in certain Christian churches〔某些基督教会中的〕牧师住宅

man·ser·vant /ˋmænˌsɜvənt; ˈmænˌsɜːvənt/ *n* [C] *old-fashioned* a male servant, especially a man's personal servant【过时】男仆〔尤指某男子的贴身仆人〕

Mans·field /ˋmænsfild; ˈmænsfiːld/, **Kath·e·rine** /ˋkæθrɪn; ˈkæθərɪn/ (1888-1923) a writer who was born in New Zealand but who lived in England. Her best-known collection of stories is *The Garden Party.* 曼斯菲尔德〔(1888-1923), 生于新西兰的英国女作家。最著名的短篇小说集为《园会》〕

-manship /ˋmənʃɪp; ˈmənʃɪp/ *suffix* [in U nouns 构成不可数名词] the art or skill of a particular type of person〔某类人的〕技艺, 技能, 技术: *seamanship* (=sailing skill) 航海技术 | *statesmanship* 政治家才能 | *horsemanship* (=skill at horse-riding) 骑术, 马术

man·sion /ˋmænʃən; ˈmænʃən/ *n* [C] a large impressive-looking house 富丽堂皇的房子; 大厦; 宅第; 公馆

Mansion House /ˌ· · ˈ·/ a large house in London, the official home of the Lord Mayor of London, where official dinners are held 伦敦市长官邸〔常在此举行官方宴会〕

man-sized /ˈ· ·/ also 又作 **man-size** *adj* [only before noun 仅用于名词前] large and considered suitable for a man 适于成年男子使用的, 成年男人尺寸的: *That's a man-sized breakfast!* 那顿早餐足够一个成年男子食用! | *man-sized paper handkerchiefs* 男用纸手巾

man·slaugh·ter /ˋmænˌslɔtə; ˈmænˌslɔːtə/ *n* [U] *law* the crime of killing someone illegally but not deliberately【法律】过失杀人; 误杀 —compare 比较 MURDER¹ (1)

Man·son /ˋmænsn; ˈmænsən/, **Charles** (1934-) an American who had a group of followers that he called his 'family', who took drugs with him and regarded him as their religious leader. Under Manson's influence, his 'family' violently killed seven people in Los Angeles in 1969, including the actress Sharon Tate. 曼森〔(1934-), 美国人, 有一批追随者, 他称之为"家人"。其追随者跟他一起吸毒, 并把他奉为宗教领袖。在曼森的指使下, 其"家人"于1969年在洛杉矶残杀七人, 其中包括女演员莎朗·泰特〕

man·tel /ˋmæntl; ˈmæntl/ *n* [C] *especially AmE* a mantelpiece【尤美】壁炉架; 壁炉台; 壁炉面饰

man·tel·piece /ˋmæntlˌpis; ˈmæntlpiːs/ *n* [C] a frame surrounding a FIREPLACE, especially the top part that can be used as a shelf 壁炉架; 壁炉台; 壁炉面饰

man·tel·shelf /ˋmæntlˌʃɛlf; ˈmæntlʃelf/ *n* [C] *BrE* the top part of a mantelpiece that can be used as a shelf【英】壁炉台; 壁炉架

man·til·la /mænˋtɪlə; mænˈtɪlə/ *n* [C] a decorative piece of thin material that covers the head and shoulders, traditionally worn by Spanish women 连披肩的头巾〔西班牙妇女的传统服饰〕

man·tis /ˋmæntɪs; ˈmæntəs/ *n* [C] a PRAYING MANTIS 螳螂

man·tle¹ /ˋmæntl; ˈmæntl/ *n* **1 take on/assume/wear the mantle of** *formal* to accept or have a particular duty or responsibility【正式】承担/负有…的责任[义务]: *It is up to Europe to take on the mantle of leadership in environmental issues.* 在解决环境问题方面应由欧洲担当起领导责任。**2 a mantle of snow/darkness etc** *literary* something such as snow or darkness that covers a surface or area【文】一层雪/一片黑暗等: *A mantle of snow lay on the trees.* 树上覆盖着一层雪。**3** [C] a loose piece of outer clothing without SLEEVES, worn in former times〔旧时穿的〕披风, 斗篷 **4** [C] a cover put over the flame of a gas or oil lamp to make it shine more brightly〔煤气灯或油灯的〕白炽罩 **5** [C] *technical* the part of the Earth around the central CORE¹ (6)【术语】地幔

mantle² *v* [T] *literary* to cover the surface of something【文】覆盖

man-to-man /ˌ· · ˈ·◂/ *adv informal* if two men talk about something man-to-man, they discuss it in an honest, direct way【非正式】坦诚地, 开诚布公地: *You two need to discuss this man-to-man.* 你们两个人需要坦率地讨论一下这个问题。—**man-to-man** *adj*: *a man-to-man discussion* 坦诚的讨论

man·tra /ˋmæntrə; ˈmæntrə/ *n* [C] **1** a piece of holy writing in the Hindu religion 曼特罗, 真言〔印度教中的一段经文〕**2** a word or sound that is repeated as a prayer or to help people MEDITATE in the Hindu and Buddhist religions 曼特罗〔印度教和佛教中的祷文或咒语〕

man·u·al[1] /ˈmænjuəl; ˈmænjuəl/ *adj* **1** involving the use of the hands 手的; 手工的: *manual work* 手工[体力]活 | *manual skills* 手工技术 **2** operated or done by hand or without the help of electricity, computers etc 用手操作的; 手动的; 靠人工的: *a manual typewriter* 手动打字机 | *It would take too long to do a manual search of all the data.* 手工搜寻所有资料会花太多的时间。—**manually** *adv*

manual[2] *n* [C] **1** a book that gives instructions about how to use a machine〔机器的〕说明书, 使用手册: *an instruction manual* 说明手册 **2 on manual** if a machine is on manual it can only be operated by using your hands and not by AUTOMATIC means〔机器〕手工操作的, 手动的

manual la·bour *BrE*【英】, **manual labor** *AmE*【美】/ˌ··· ˈ··/ *n* [U] work done with your hands that does not need much thought or skill 体力劳动 —**manual labourer** *n* [C]

manual work·er /ˈ··· ˌ··/ *n* [C] someone whose work involves using their hands rather than their mind 体力劳动者 —**manual work** *n* [U]

man·u·fac·ture[1] /ˌmænjəˈfæktʃə; ˌmænjəˈfæktʃə/ *v* [T] **1** to make or produce large quantities of goods to be sold, using machinery〔用机器大量〕制造, 生产: *the company that manufactured the drug* 生产这种药的公司 | *manufactured goods* 工业品, 制成品 **2** *technical* if your body manufactures a particular substance, it produces it【术语】〔人体〕生成: *Bile is manufactured by the liver.* 胆汁是由肝脏生成的。**3** to invent an untrue story, excuse etc 编造〔虚假情况、借口等〕

manufacture[2] *n* **1** [U] *formal* the process of making or producing large quantities of goods to be sold【正式】〔大量的商品〕制造: *Cost will determine the methods of manufacture.* 成本将决定制造方法。**2 manufactures** [plural] *technical* goods that are produced in large quantities using machinery【术语】〔用机器大批量制造的〕商品

man·u·fac·tur·er /ˌmænjəˈfæktʃərə; ˌmænjəˈfæktʃərə/ *n* [C] also 又作 **manufacturers** [plural] a company or industry that makes large quantities of goods 制造商; 制造公司, 制造厂: *Read the manufacturer's instructions before using your new dishwasher.* 使用新洗碗机之前请先阅读厂家的说明书。| *The fridge was sent back to the manufacturers.* 那台冰箱被退给厂家了。

man·u·fac·tur·ing /ˌmænjəˈfæktʃərɪŋ; ˌmænjəˈfæktʃərɪŋ/ *n* [U] the process or business of producing goods in factories 制造; 制造业: *Thousands of jobs had been lost in manufacturing.* 制造业中已失去了数千个工作岗位。

Man U·nit·ed /ˌ· ·ˈ··/ an informal name for Manchester United football team 曼联队〔曼彻斯特联队的俗称〕

ma·nure /məˈnjʊr; məˈnjʊə/ *n* [U] waste matter from animals that is mixed with chemicals and put onto soil to produce better crops 粪肥 —**manure** *v* [T]

man·u·script /ˈmænjəˌskrɪpt; ˈmænjəskrɪpt/ *n* [C] **1** a book or piece of writing before it is printed 手稿; 底稿: *I read his novel in manuscript.* 我读过他小说的手稿。**2** a book or document written by hand before printing was invented 手抄本, 手写本

Man With No Name, The the main character in three WESTERNS, *A Fistful of Dollars* (1964), *For a Few Dollars More* (1965) and *The Good, the Bad and the Ugly* (1966). The Man With No Name is a BOUNTY hunter who kills many bad men. The actor Clint Eastwood played the part in all three films. 无名氏〔三部西部片中的主要人物, 由克林特·伊斯特伍德扮演。这几部影片是《荒野大镖客》(1964)、《黄昏双镖客》(1965)和《善、恶、丑》(1966)。无名氏是个赏金猎人, 杀了许多坏人〕

Manx /mæŋks; mæŋks/ *adj* from or connected with the Isle of Man 马恩岛的

man·y /ˈmɛnɪ; ˈmeni/ *quantifier* **1** [used especially in formal English, or in ordinary written or spoken English when in questions and negative sentences 尤用于正式英语, 或在普通书面语或口语中用于疑问句和否定句] a large number of people or things 许多: **many people/things/places etc** *Many people find this kind of movie unpleasant.* 许多人觉得这类影片令人讨厌。| *Rain has been forecast in many areas of the country.* 据预报那个国家许多地区有雨。| *Does she have many friends?* 她有许多朋友吗? | **many of** *Many of our staff are actually part time workers.* 我们的许多职员实际上都是兼职人员。| *Thousands of soldiers were sent into battle, many of them killed outright.* 成千上万的士兵被送上了战场, 其中有许多当场战死了。| **for many** *For many, the entrance exam proved too difficult.* 对许多人来说, 入学考试太难了。| **how many...?** *How many brothers and sisters do you have?* 你有几个兄弟姐妹? | **not many** (=only a few) 不多 *There weren't many people at the party.* 那个聚会上人不多。| **the many people/things/places etc** *The committee would like to thank the many visitors who gave money so generously.* 委员会谨向慷慨解囊的众多参观者表示感谢。| **many a person/thing/place etc** *Through many a crisis it was his family that helped him survive.* 在很多危急关头是他的家人帮他挺了过来。—compare 比较 LOT (1) **2 as many** the same number as another particular number 一样多, 同样数目: *Those cookies were great. I could eat as many again.* (=the same number again) 那些饼干太好吃了, 我还能再吃那么多。| **as many as** *Grandfather claimed to have as many medals as the general himself.* 祖父声称他拥有和将军一样多的勋章。| **in as many days/weeks etc** *A great trip! We visited five countries in as many days.* 一次多了不起的旅行啊! 我们五天里参观了五个国家。| **twice/three times etc as many** *The company now employs four times as many women as men.* 公司现在雇用的女工是男工的四倍。| **one/two etc too many** (=one more than necessary)〔比所需〕多出一个/两个等 *You've bought one too many. There are only three of us who need tickets.* 你多买了一张, 我们只有三个人需要票。**3 a) many a time** *old-fashioned* often【过时】时常, 常常: *I've sat here many a time and wondered what became of her.* 我时常坐在这儿, 想知道她后来怎样了。**b) many's the time/day (that/when)** used to say that a particular thing happens often (有)许多次/天〔用以表示某事经常发生〕: *Many's the time we've had to borrow money in order to get through the month.* 有许多次我们不得不借钱以撑到月底。**4 a good many** a fairly large number of people or things 相当多的: *Stop complaining! A good many people would be happy to have work.* 别发牢骚了! 很多人有工作做就感到满足了。**5 a great many** a very large number of people or things 很多很多, 极多: *Most of the young men went off to the war, and a great many never came back.* 大多数年轻人走上了战场, 好多人再也没有回来。**6 have had one too many** *informal* to be drunk【非正式】喝醉了: *Don't pay any attention to him – he's had one too many.* 别理他, 他喝醉了。**7 the many** *formal* a very large group of people, especially the public in general【正式】一大群人〔尤指公众〕: *This war is another example of the few sacrificing so much for the many.* 这场战争是少数人为多数人作出巨大牺牲的又一个例证。**8 be one too many for** *BrE old-fashioned* to be so clever that someone cannot gain advantage over you【英, 过时】胜过, 非〔某人〕能敌 —opposite 反义词 FEW —compare 比较 MORE, MOST —see also 另见 MUCH, **in as many words** (WORD[1] (19))

many-sid·ed /ˌ·· ˈ··◂/ *adj* consisting of many different qualities or features〔性质或特征等〕多方面的, 多样的: *a complex many-sided personality* 复杂的多重性格

Manzanar a large place in central California where people whose families originally came from Japan were forced to live during World War II. Many of these people lost their homes and businesses because of being forced to move. 曼萨纳尔〔加利福尼亚中部一地区。当地人的祖辈来自日本, 二战期间被迫在此安顿下来, 许多人由于被迫迁移而失去了家园和生意〕

Mao·is·m /ˈmauɪzəm; ˈmaʊɪzəm/ a form of Communism based on the ideas of Mao Zedong, who emphasized the importance of poor farm workers, rather than industrial workers, in the process of achieving a revolution 毛(泽东)主义〔指毛泽东思想, 即以毛泽东思想为基础的共产主义思想。他强调贫苦农民在争取革命胜利过程中的重要性〕—**Maoist** *n, adj*

Mao·ri /ˈmaurɪ; ˈmaʊri/ *n* **1** [C] someone who belongs to the race who first lived in New Zealand and who now form only a small part of the population 毛利人〔新西兰土著〕**2** [U] the language of the Maori people 毛利语 —**Maori** *adj*: *a Maori tradition* 毛利人的传统

map[1] /mæp; mæp/ *n* [C] **1** a drawing of an area of country showing rivers, roads, mountains, towns etc, or of a whole country or several countries 地图: *According to the map we should turn left.* 根据地图, 我们应该向左拐。| **[+of]** *a map of the world* 世界地图 | **a street/ road map** *a street map of Istanbul* 伊斯坦布尔市街道图 | **read a map** (=understand the information it gives) 看地图 **2 put sth on the map** to make a place famous, so that everyone knows it and talks about it 使某地出名: *It was the Olympic Games that really put Seoul on the map.* 真正使首尔出名的是那次奥运会。**3 off the map** *informal* a long way from towns or places where many people go【非正式】非常偏远的 —see also 另见 **wipe sth off the map** (WIPE[1] (8))

map[2] *v* **mapped, mapping** [T] **1** to make a map of a particular area 绘制〔某地区〕的地图: *Scientists have mapped the surface of the moon.* 科学家们已经绘制出了月球表面图。**2** to discover or show the shape and arrangement of something 发现; 显示〔某物的形状和排列形式〕: *to map the part of the brain responsible for perception* 显示大脑负责感知的部分

map sth ↔ **out** *phr v* [T] to plan something carefully 仔细计划, 筹划: *They had mapped out a demanding schedule for us.* 他们为我们精心制订了一个需费心费力才能完成的计划。

ma·ple /ˈmepl; ˈmeɪpəl/ *n* **1** [C] a tree with pointed leaves that grows in northern countries such as Canada〔生长在加拿大等北方国家的〕槭树, 枫树 **2** [U] the wood from a maple 槭木, 枫木

maple syr·up /ˌ‥ ˈ‥/ *n* [U] a sweet sticky liquid, obtained from some kinds of maple tree 槭糖浆, 槭树汁

map·ping /ˈmæpɪŋ; ˈmæpɪŋ/ *n* [C] *technical* a relationship between two mathematical sets in which a member of the first set is exactly matched by a member of the second【术语】〔数学中的〕函数, 映射

map-read·ing /ˈ‥ ˌ‥/ *n* [U] the practice of using a map to find which way you should go 地图阅读, 察看地图 —**map-reader** *n* [C]

Ma·pu·to /məˋputo; məˈpuːtəʊ/ a port on the Indian Ocean in southeast Africa, the capital city of Mozambique 马普多〔非洲东南面印度洋一港口, 为莫桑比克首都〕

Mar the written abbreviation of 缩写= MARCH

mar /mɑr; mɑː/ *v* **marred, marring** [T often passive 常用被动态] to make something less attractive or enjoyable; spoil 玷污; 损坏, 毁坏: *His appearance was marred by a scar on his left cheek.* 左颊上的一块疤痕破坏了他的外貌。

mar·a·bou, marabout /ˈmærəˌbu; ˈmærəbuː/ *n* [C] a large African STORK (=a long-legged bird) 秃鹳〔非洲的一种大鹳〕

ma·ra·cas /məˋrɑkəz; məˈrækəz/ *n* [plural] a pair of hollow balls, filled with small objects such as stones, that are shaken and used as a musical instrument 沙球, 响葫芦〔一种乐器〕

mar·a·schi·no /ˌmærəˋskino; ˌmærəˈskiːnəʊ/ *n* **1** [U] a sweet alcoholic drink made from a type of black CHERRY 黑樱桃酒 **2** [C] a CHERRY that has been kept in maraschino and is used for decorating cakes, drinks etc〔浸泡于黑樱桃酒中用以装饰糕点、饮料等的〕酒浸樱桃

mar·a·thon[1] /ˈmærəˌθɑn; ˈmærəθən/ *n* [C] **1** a long race of about 26 miles or 42 kilometres 马拉松赛跑〔全程约 26 英里或 42 公里〕: *the Boston Marathon* 波士顿马拉松赛跑 | **run a/the marathon** *Garcia ran the marathon in just under three hours.* 加西亚只用了不到三个小时就跑完了马拉松。**2** an activity that lasts a long time and needs a lot of energy, patience, or determination〔需要很大精力、耐心或决心的〕持久活动, 马拉松式的活动: *We finished the job but it was quite a marathon.* 我们完成了那项工作, 但它确实是费时耗力的活。

> **CULTURAL NOTE 文化注释**
> Many big cities have their own marathons every year. Some marathons, for example London, Boston, and New York, are very famous. Thousands of people enter, including many ordinary people as well as professional runners. The marathon is also an event in the Olympic Games. 很多大城市每年都举办自己的马拉松赛。有些城市的马拉松赛非常出名, 像伦敦、波士顿和纽约等。成千上万的人参加赛跑, 其中既有职业赛跑运动员, 也有很多普通百姓。马拉松赛跑也是奥运会的一个比赛项目。— see also 另见 LONDON MARATHON

marathon[2] *adj* [only before noun 仅用于名词前] a marathon event lasts a long time and needs a lot of energy, patience, or determination 马拉松式的, 持久的, 需要很大精力[耐力, 决心]的. *After a marathon round of negotiations, the two leaders reached an agreement.* 在经过一轮马拉松式的谈判之后, 两位领导人达成了一项协议。

ma·raud·ing /məˋrɔdɪŋ; məˈrɔːdɪŋ/ *adj* [only before noun 仅用于名词前] a marauding person or animal moves around looking for something to destroy or kill〔人或动物〕四处破坏[杀戮]的: *Local residents live in fear of marauding street-gangs.* 当地居民生活在街头流氓四处抢劫的恐惧之中。—**marauder** *n* [C]

Mar·bel·la /mɑrˋbeə; mɑːˈbeɪə/ a port and holiday RESORT on the Costa del Sol, on the southern coast of Spain 马贝亚〔西班牙南部沿海太阳海岸一港口和度假胜地〕

mar·ble /ˈmɑrbl; ˈmɑːbəl/ *n* **1** [U] a type of hard white rock that becomes smooth when polished, and is used for making buildings, STATUEs etc 大理石: *The columns were of white marble.* 柱子是白色的大理石制成的。| *a marble statue* 大理石雕像 **2** [C] a very small, coloured glass ball that children roll along the ground as part of a game 玻璃弹子[弹珠] **3 marbles** [U] a children's game played with marbles〔儿童玩的〕弹子游戏 **4 lose your marbles** *informal* to start behaving in a crazy way【非正式】举止开始失常 **5** [C] *technical* a STATUE or SCULPTURE made of marble【术语】大理石雕像; 大理石雕刻品

Marble Arch /ˌ‥ ˈ‥/ a large white stone ARCH in central London, where several big roads meet, including Oxford Street and Park Lane. It was built to celebrate the military victories of Nelson. 大理石拱门〔位于伦敦市中心的一座大型白色石拱门, 是牛津街和公园街等数条大街的交汇点。最初建造此拱门是为了庆祝纳尔逊取得的军事胜利〕: *Turn left at Marble Arch and go up Edgware Road.* 在大理石拱门处向左转, 然后沿艾奇韦尔路往前走。

mar·bled /ˈmɑrbḷd; ˈmɑːbəld/ *adj* having an irregular pattern of lines and colours 有大理石花纹的: *a marbled book cover* 有大理石花纹的书皮

march[1] /mɑrtʃ; mɑːtʃ/ *v* **1** [I] to walk quickly and with firm, regular steps like a soldier 快速齐步行进: *Wellington's army marched until nightfall.* 威灵顿的部队一直行军到黄昏。| [+across/along/through] *They had to march across the desert.* 他们不得不行军穿越沙漠。| **march 20km/40 miles etc** *We marched 50km across the foothills.* 我们行进 50 公里穿越了那片丘陵地带。**2** [I always+adv/prep] to walk somewhere quickly and with determination, often because you are angry〔常指因生气快速而毅然地〕走, 行走: [+down/off etc] *Brett marched out of the office, slamming the door behind him.* 布雷特快步走出办公室, 砰的一声摔上了门。**3** [I always+adv/prep] to walk somewhere slowly and in a large group to protest about something 游行抗议, 游行示威: *Hundreds of demonstrators are expected to march on the Council offices.* 预计数百名示威者将游行到市政会办公楼进行示威。**4** [T always+adv/prep] to force someone to walk somewhere with you, often pushing or pulling them roughly 迫使〔某人〕走〔常伴有推拽动作〕: **march sb to/along/into etc** *Mr Carter marched us to the principal's office.* 卡特先生将我们带进校长办公室。**5 be given/get your marching orders** *BrE informal* to be ordered to leave a particular place【英, 非正式】被命令离开某地 —**marcher** *n* [C]

march[2] *n* [C] **1** the act of walking with firm regular steps like a soldier 行进; 行军: *The soldiers did a march around the parade ground.* 士兵们绕阅兵场齐步走了一圈。**2** an organized event in which many people walk together to protest about something 示威游行, 抗议游行: *a massive Civil Rights march in Washington* 在华盛顿举行的一次大规模民权示威游行 | **go on a march** *I went on a lot of peace marches when I was a student.* 学生时期我参加了多次和平示威游行。**3** a piece of music with a regular beat for soldiers to march to 进行曲 **4 a day's march/two weeks' march etc** the amount of time it takes to march somewhere 一天/两周等的行军路程: *Lake Van was still three days' march away.* 离凡湖还有三天的路程。**5 marches** [plural] the area around the border of England and Wales or of England and Scotland 英格兰与威尔士[苏格兰]的交界地区 **6 on the march a)** an army that is on the march is marching somewhere〔军队〕在行军中, 在行进中 **b)** a belief, idea etc that is on the march is becoming stronger and more popular〔信仰、观念等〕越来越强烈, 越来越普遍: *Fascism is on the march again in some parts of Europe.* 在欧洲一些地区, 法西斯主义正在死灰复燃。**7 the march of time/history/events etc** *formal* the progress of time and of things happening that cannot be stopped【正式】时间的推移/历史的发展/事件的进展等 —see also 另见 **steal a march on** (STEAL[1] (8))

March written abbreviation 缩写为 **Mar** *n* [C,U] the third month of the year, between February and April 三月: **in March** *The theatre opened in March 1991.* 这家剧院 1991 年3月开业。| **last/next March** *She started work here last March.* 她去年3月开始在这儿工作。| **on March 6th/on 6th March** *The meeting will be on March 6th.* (spoken as 读作: *on the sixth of March* or 或 *on March the sixth* (*BrE* 英) or 或 *on March sixth* (*AmE* 美)) 会议将于三月六日召开。

> **CULTURAL NOTE 文化注释**
> In the UK and northern US, March is thought of as the first month of spring, when flowers, especially DAFFODILs, begin to appear. There is an old saying that "March comes in like a lion and goes out like a lamb", meaning that March begins with cold windy weather and ends with warmer weather. 在英国和美国北部, 3 月被认为是春季的第一个月。此时花儿, 尤其是水仙开始绽放。有一个古老的谚语说: "3月来像狮子, 3月走像羊羔。" 意思是说3月初还是寒风凛冽, 而月末就变得暖意融融了。

March Hare, the /ˌ‥ ˈ‥/ a character in the book *Alice's Adventures in Wonderland* (1865) by Lewis Carroll. He is a crazy hare who talks nonsense. 三月兔〔刘易斯·卡罗尔的小说《艾丽丝漫游奇境记》(1895) 中的角色, 为一只胡话连篇的疯兔〕—see also 另见 ALICE IN WONDERLAND

M

marching band /ˈ· ·, ·ˈ/ *n* [C] a group of people who play musical instruments while they march 行进乐队, 步操乐团

mar·chio·ness /ˈmɑrʃənɪs; ˌmɑːʃəˈnes/ *n* [C] **1** the wife of a MARQUIS 侯爵夫人 **2** a woman who has the rank of MARQUIS 女侯爵

March of Dimes, the /ˌ· · ˈ·/ a US CHARITY organization that collects money for children, especially those with serious mental or physical disabilities 小钱募集运动, 十美分游行会〔美国一慈善组织, 专为儿童, 尤其是患有严重精神或生理残疾的儿童募集资金〕

march-past /ˈ· ·/ *n* [C] the march of soldiers past an important person during a ceremony〔受阅部队从检阅者前通过时的〕分列式

Mar·ci·a·no /ˌmɑrsɪˈæno; ˌmɑːsiˈɑːnəʊ/, **Rocky** (1923-69) a US BOXER who was world HEAVYWEIGHT CHAMPION from 1952 to 1956. He gave up boxing in 1956, and is the only world heavyweight champion who was never defeated. 马西亚诺〔(1923-1969), 美国拳击手, 1952-1956年世界重量级拳击冠军。1956年退出拳坛, 是唯一未被击败的世界重量级拳击冠军〕

Mar·co·ni /mɑrˋkonɪ; mɑːˈkəʊni/, **Gu·gliel·mo** /gulˋjɛlmo; gʊlˈjelməʊ/ (1874-1937) an Italian electrical engineer who most people think of as the inventor of radio. He invented the method of sending radio signals called 'wireless telegraphy'. Before this, it had only been possible to send messages along wires. He won the Nobel Prize for physics in 1909. 马可尼〔(1874-1937), 意大利电气工程师。多数人认为他是无线电的发明人。他发明了发送无线电信号的方法, 称"无线电通信术", 在此之前信息只能通过电线发送。1909年, 他荣获诺贝尔物理学奖〕

Marco Polo —see 见 Marco POLO

Mar·cu·se /mɑrˋkuzə; mɑːˈkuːzə/, **Herbert** (1898-1979) a US PHILOSOPHER and writer on politics, born in Germany, who was especially popular in the 1960s. He wrote about the bad effects on people of modern economic ideas, industry, and science. 马尔库塞〔(1898-1979), 美国哲学家、政论作家, 生于德国, 20世纪60年代尤为著名。他著书立作抨击现代经济观念、现代工业和科学给人们带来的不良影响〕

Mar·di Gras /ˈmɑrdɪ ˋgrɑ; ˌmɑːdi ˈgrɑː/ *n* [singular] the day before Lent, or the music, dancing etc that celebrate this day in some countries〔基督教〕大斋期的前一日; 忏悔节,〔庆祝大斋期前一日的〕狂欢活动

> **CULTURAL NOTE 文化注释**
>
> In the US, the city of New Orleans, Louisiana, holds a famous Mardi Gras celebration which many people travel to see. 在美国路易斯安那州的新奥尔良, 有著名的肥美星期二庆祝活动, 很多人都慕名前去观看。— see colour photo on page F22 见 F22 页彩图

mare /mɛr; meə/ *n* [C] **1** a female horse or DONKEY 母马; 母驴 —compare 比较 STALLION **2** **mare's nest** **a)** a discovery that seems important but is actually of no value 似乎重要但实际上无价值的发现 **b)** a confused situation or a very untidy place 混乱的局势; 乱糟糟的地方

Mar·garet /ˈmɑrgrət; ˈmɑːgrət/, **Princess** (1930-2002) a British princess, the younger sister of Queen Elizabeth II 玛格丽特〔(1930-2002), 英国公主, 女王伊丽莎白二世的妹妹〕

mar·ga·rine /ˈmɑrdʒəˌrɪn; ˌmɑːdʒəˈriːn/ *n* [U] a yellow substance that is similar to butter but is not made from milk, which you eat with bread or use for cooking 麦淇淋, 人造黄油

mar·ga·ri·ta /ˌmɑrgəˋritə; ˌmɑːgəˈriːtə/ *n* [C] an alcoholic drink made with TEQUILA and LEMON or LIME juice 玛格丽塔鸡尾酒〔用龙舌兰酒和柠檬汁或酸橙汁调成〕

Mar·gate /ˈmɑrget; ˈmɑːgeɪt/ a town with a large beach on the northern coast of Kent in southeast England. People used to think of it as a typical place where working class people went for their holidays. 马盖特〔英格兰东南部肯特郡北部沿海一镇。该镇海滩宽阔, 过去曾被认为是工薪阶层度假的常往之地〕

marge /mɑrdʒ; mɑːdʒ/ *n* [U] *BrE spoken* margarine【英口】麦淇淋, 人造黄油

S3 W3 **mar·gin** /ˈmɑrdʒɪn; ˈmɑːdʒɪn/ *n* [C] **1** the empty space that goes down the side of a page 页边的空白, 页边, 白边: **in the margin** *She scribbled some notes in the margin.* 她在页边上草草写了一些评注。**2** the number of votes, or the amount of time or distance, by which an election or competition is won or lost〔选举或竞赛中胜方或负方在选票、时间或距离上的〕差数: **by a (wide/narrow) margin** *The election was won by a margin of only 200 votes.* 胜方仅以200票的优势赢得选举。**3** the difference between what a business pays for something and what they sell it for〔成本与售价间的〕差额, 利润, 赚头 —see also 另见 PROFIT MARGIN **4** **on the margin(s)** not belonging to the main or central part of a society, group, or activity 处于〔社会、集团或活动〕的边缘: *unemployed youths living on the margins of society* 生活在社会边缘的失业青年 **5** **margin of error** the degree to which a calculation can be wrong without affecting the final results 误差幅度, 误差值 **6** *literary* the edge of a forest, island, or other area【文】〔森林、岛屿或其他区域的〕边缘

mar·gin·al /ˈmɑrdʒɪnl; ˈmɑːdʒɨnəl/ *adj* **1** too small to make a difference 微不足道的: *a marginal increase in the unemployment figures* 失业人数的略微增加 **2** **marginal seat/constituency** *BrE* a SEAT[1] (5) in a parliament or similar institution, which can be won or lost by a small number of votes【英】〔议会或类似机构中〕以很小的票差就能赢得或失去的边缘席位/选区 **3** **marginal land** land that cannot produce good crops 贫瘠的土地 **4** written in a margin 写在页边的: *marginal notes* 边注, 旁注 —see also 另见 MARGINALLY

mar·gin·al·ize also 又作 **-ise** *BrE*【英】/ˈmɑrdʒɪnḷˌaɪz; ˈmɑːdʒɨnəlaɪz/ *v* [T] to make a group of people unimportant and powerless 使〔某群体〕不重要并处于无权势的地位; 使…边缘化: *The decline of these industries marginalized the unions.* 这些行业的衰退把工会推向边缘地位。

mar·gin·al·ly /ˈmɑrdʒɪnḷɪ; ˈmɑːdʒɨnəl-i/ *adv* not enough to make an important difference 稍微, 略微: *Gina's grades have improved marginally since last term.* 从上学期开始吉娜的成绩略有提高。| [+adj/adv] *The new system is only marginally more efficient than the old one.* 新系统的效率比旧系统仅仅略高一点。

ma·ri·a·chi /ˌmɑrɪˋɑtʃɪ; ˌmɑːriˈɑːtʃi/ *n* [U] a kind of Mexican dance music 街头音乐〔一种墨西哥舞曲〕

Mariana Trench, the /mærɪˌænə ˋtʃɛntʃ; mæriˌɑːnə ˈtʃentʃ/ the deepest part of the Earth's surface, which is near the Mariana Islands in the northwest Pacific Ocean 马里亚纳海沟〔地球表面最深的地方, 位于太平洋西北部的马里亚纳群岛附近〕

Mar·ie An·toi·nette /məˌri æntwəˋnɛt; ˌmæri æntwəˈnet/ (1755-93) the Queen of France from 1774 to 1792 and the wife of Louis XVI. She became unpopular because she did not seem to care about the poor citizens of France, and when she was told that they did not have enough bread to eat, she is supposed to have said, "Let them eat cake". She and Louis XVI were put in prison during the French Revolution, and were killed by having their heads cut off by the GUILLOTINE. 玛丽·安托瓦内特〔(1755-1793), 1774-1792年间的法国王后, 路易十六之妻。她对贫苦大众漠不关心而不得民心。据传有人曾告诉她穷人的面包不够吃时, 她居然说: "那就叫他们吃蛋糕吧。"法国大革命期间, 她和路易十六被关入监狱, 后来被一起推上了断头台〕

Marie Ce·leste, the /məˌri sɪˋlɛst; ˌmæri sɪˈlest/ a sailing ship that was found in the Atlantic Ocean in 1872, with no one on it. The ship was undamaged, and a table was prepared for a meal. No one knows why the sailors left the ship, or what happened to them. "玛丽·西莱斯特"号〔1872年在大西洋上发现的一艘帆船。船上空无一人, 船体完好无损, 有一张餐桌上还摆放着饭菜。水手为何弃船而去, 当时究竟发生了什么事, 都不得而知〕

Marie Claire /məˌri ˋklɛə; ˌmæri ˈkleə/ *trademark* a British monthly magazine for young women which contains articles on fashion, health etc【商标】《嘉人》〔一种以年轻女性为对象的英国月刊, 文章内容多涉及时尚、健康等〕

mar·i·gold /ˈmærəˌgold; ˈmærɨgəʊld/ *n* [C] a plant with golden-yellow flowers 万寿菊(花); 金盏花

mar·i·jua·na, marihuana /ˌmærəˋwɑnə; ˌmærɨˈwɑːnə/ *n* [U] an illegal drug smoked like a cigarette, made from the dried leaves of the HEMP plant 大麻烟; 大麻毒品

> **CULTURAL NOTE 文化注释**
>
> In the US and the UK, the possession or use of marijuana is illegal. Some people think that marijuana should be made legal because it is considered much less harmful than **hard drugs** such as COCAINE or HEROIN. Some doctors think that people with certain medical conditions should be allowed to use it because it can reduce pain. Smoking marijuana became popular in the 1960s among young people in the US and UK. Politicians are sometimes asked if they have tried it, and Bill Clinton said he had smoked it once but 'did not INHALE' (=did not suck the smoke into his LUNGS). 在英美两国, 拥有或者使用大麻都是违法的。有人认为不应把大麻列为违禁品, 因为较之可卡因和海洛因那样的硬毒品, 大麻的危害要小得多。有些医生认为, 应该允许患某些病症的病人使用大麻, 因为它能够止痛。20世纪60年代, 大麻开始在英美的年轻人中流行。政治家有时会被问到是否尝试吸食过大麻, 比尔·克林顿的回答是曾经抽过一次但"没有咽到肺里"。

M

> There are now some very strong STRAINS (=types) of marijuana, usually referred to as SKUNK in the UK and CHRONIC in the US. They first became popular in Holland, where the laws against smoking and growing marijuana are less severe than in the UK and the US, and are known especially for their very strong smell. 现在有一些强性大麻，在英国通常称为 skunk，在美国称为 chronic。它们首先在荷兰流行开来，因为那里的法律对待吸食和种植大麻不像英美那样严厉。这些大麻尤其以气味强烈著称。— see also Cultural Note at DRUG 另见 DRUG 文化注释

ma·rim·ba /mə`rɪmbə; mə'rɪmbə/ *n* [C] a musical instrument like a XYLOPHONE 马林巴琴〔类似木琴的一种乐器〕

ma·ri·na /mə`rinə; mə'ri:nə/ *n* [C] a small port or area of water where people keep boats that are used for pleasure〔供游艇停泊的〕小港湾

mar·i·nade /ˌmærə`ned; ˌmærɨ`neɪd/ *n* [C,U] a mixture of oil, wine and SPICES in which meat or fish is put for a time before cooking 混合调味汁〔用油、酒和香料混合调制而成，供肉或鱼烹饪前浸泡调味用〕

mar·i·nate /`mærəˌnet; 'mærɨneɪt/ also 又作 **marinade** *v* [I,T] to put meat or fish in a marinade, or to be left in a marinade for some time 将〔肉或鱼〕浸泡入调味汁中；浸渍〔于调味汁中〕

Ma·rin Coun·ty /məˌrɪn `kauntɪ; məˌrɪn 'kaʊnti/ an area to the north of San Francisco, California, where many wealthy people live 马林县〔加利福尼亚州旧金山以北的一个地区，住有许多富人〕

Ma·rine /mə`rin; mə'ri:n/ *n* [C] **1** a soldier who serves on a ship, especially a member of the Royal Marines or the Marine Corps 水兵；英国皇家海军陆战队士兵；美国海军陆战队士兵 —see also 另见 MERCHANT NAVY —see table on page C7 参见 C7 页附录 **2 the Marines a)** the Marine Corps 美国海军陆战队 **b)** the Royal Marines 英国皇家海军陆战队 **3 tell that to the Marines!** *spoken* used to say that you do not believe what someone has told you【口】鬼听了才会相信!〔用以表示不相信某人对你讲的话〕

marine *adj* [only before noun 仅用于名词前] **1** connected with the sea and the creatures that live there 海洋的: *marine biology* 海洋生物学 **2** connected with ships or the navy 船舶的；海军的

Marine Corps /·'· ·/ *n* [singular] one of the main parts of the US armed forces, consisting of soldiers who serve on ships 美国海军陆战队

mar·i·ner /`mærənə; 'mærɨnə/ *n* [C] *literary* a SAILOR【文】水手，海员

mar·i·o·nette /ˌmærɪə`nɛt; ˌmæriə'net/ *n* [C] a PUPPET whose arms and legs are moved by pulling strings 牵线木偶

Mar·is /`mærɪs; 'mærɨs/, **Roger** (1934-85) a US BASEBALL player who played for the New York Yankees team and is famous for hitting 61 home runs in 1961, which broke the record of Babe Ruth. 马里斯〔(1934-1985)，美国棒球运动员。他曾效力于纽约扬基队，1961 年打出 61 记本垒打，打破了巴布·鲁斯的纪录〕

mar·i·tal /`mærətl̩; 'mærɨtl/ *adj* connected with marriage 婚姻的: *marital difficulties* 婚姻上的难题 | **marital bliss** *humorous* (=the state of being very happily married)【幽默】美满婚姻 | **marital status** (=an expression used on official forms to ask if someone is married) 婚姻状况〔正式表格中用语〕

mar·i·time /`mærəˌtaɪm; 'mærɨtaɪm/ *adj* **1** connected with the sea or ships 海上的，海事的；与船舶有关的 **2** near the sea 近海的，沿海的: *the Canadian maritime provinces* 加拿大各沿海省份

mar·jo·ram /`mardʒərəm; 'mɑ:dʒərəm/ *n* [U] a HERB that smells sweet and is used in cooking 墨角兰，马郁兰〔草本植物，味香，用于食品调味〕

S3 W2 **mark**[1] /mark; mɑ:k/ *v*

1 ▶MAKE A MARK 留下痕迹◀ [I,T] to make a mark on something in a way that spoils its appearance, or to become spoiled in this way 留痕迹于，弄污；留下痕迹: *We were careful not to mark the paintwork.* 我们很小心，避免在漆面上留下印迹。| *The disease had marked her face for life.* 这种病已在她脸上留下了一辈子去不掉的疤痕。| *It's a beautiful table, but it marks very easily.* 这是一张漂亮的桌子，但桌面很容易留下印痕。

2 ▶SHOW POSITION 显示位置◀ [T] to show where something is 标示〔某物的位置〕: *A simple wooden cross marked her grave.* 一个简单的木十字架标出了她坟墓的位置。| *He had marked the route in red.* 他已用红色标出了路线。| **mark your place** (=put something in a book to show the page you had reached) 在书中夹上某物标明已读到那一页

3 ▶CELEBRATE 庆祝◀ [T] to celebrate an important event 庆祝，纪念〔重要事件〕: *a festival to mark the town's 200th anniversary* 庆祝该城市建立 200 周年的节日

4 ▶SHOW A CHANGE 显示变化◀ [T] to be a sign of an important change or an important stage in the development of something 标志〔重要变化或发展阶段〕: *His third film marks a major advance in cinematic techniques.* 他的第三部电影标志着电影技术的巨大进步。

5 be marked by to have a particular quality that is very typical of the way in which someone does something 具有…特征: *Her writing is marked by a subtle irony.* 她的写作特点是一种微妙的讥讽。

6 ▶STUDENT'S WORK 学生作业◀ [T] *especially BrE* to read a piece of written work and put a number or letter on it to show what standard it is【尤英】给〔学生作业〕打分数[评等级]; GRADE[2] (2) *AmE*【美】: *I've got a pile of exam papers to mark.* 我有一堆试卷要评阅打分。

7 ▶WRITE ON STH 在某物上写◀ [T] to write or draw on something, so that someone will notice what you have written 写[画]…做记号，在…上做记号: *I've marked the pages you need to look at.* 我已经在你需要阅读的那几页上做了记号。| *a document marked 'private and confidential'* 标有"私人档案，不得公开"字样的一份文件

8 ▶SPORT 体育运动◀ [T] *BrE* to stay close to a player of the opposite team during a game【英】〔比赛中〕盯住〔对方的队员〕

9 (you) mark my words! *old-fashioned spoken* used to tell someone that they should pay attention to what you are saying【过时，口】留心听我的话!: *There'll be trouble, you mark my words.* 就要有麻烦了，你留心我的话吧。

10 mark you *old-fashioned spoken* used to emphasize something you say【过时，口】你听着〔用于强调所说的某事〕: *Her uncle's just given her a car – given, mark you, not lent.* 她叔叔刚刚送给她一辆汽车。你听好了，是送给她，不是借给她。

11 mark time a) *informal* to spend time not doing very much except waiting for something else to happen【非正式】混时间，消磨时间；等待时机: *I was just marking time until a better job came up.* 我只是在混时间，直到有个更好的工作。**b)** if soldiers mark time, they move their legs as if they were marching, but remain in the same place〔士兵〕原地踏步

12 mark sb present/absent to write on an official list that someone is there or not there, especially in school〔尤指学校中〕记下某人出席/缺席 —see also 另见 MARKED

mark sb/sth ↔ **down** *phr v* [T] **1** to write something down, especially in order to keep a record 记下〔某事〕: *Mark down everything you eat on your daily chart.* 在你的日常记事表上记下你吃的每样东西。| **mark sb down as absent/present** *The teacher marked him down as absent.* 教师将他登记为缺席。**2** to reduce the price of items that are being sold 降低〔正在出售商品〕的价格: *Winter coats have been marked down from $80 to $50.* 冬用大衣的价格已从 80 美元降到 50 美元。**3** to form an opinion about someone when you first meet them 对〔某人〕形成第一印象: **mark sb down as sth** *When I first saw Gilbert play I marked him down as a future England player.* 当第一次看到吉尔伯特踢球时，我就认为他是未来的英格兰队球员。**4** to give someone a lower result in a test or exam because of something they have done wrong〔测验或考试中〕给〔某人〕打较低的分数: *Write neatly as you can be marked down if your paper looks messy.* 写得整齐些。如果考卷看起来乱糟糟的，你就要被扣分。

mark sb/sth ↔ **off** *phr v* [T] **1** to make an area separate by drawing a line around it, putting a rope around it etc 画线分隔出，用绳子等隔开: *The competitors' arena had been marked off with cones.* 比赛场地已经用圆锥筒分隔出来了。**2** to make a person, period of time etc seem different from others 使某人[某段时间]看起来不同: *Sara's natural flair for languages marked her off from the other students.* 萨拉的语言天赋使得她在学生中非常突出。**3** to make a mark on a list to show that something has been done or completed〔在单子上〕标出…已经做完: *I've marked off all the places we've already tried.* 我已经标出了我们已试过的所有地方。

mark sb/sth ↔ **out** *phr v* [T] **1** to show the shape or position of something by drawing lines around it 画线标出〔某物的形状或位置〕: *A volleyball court had been marked out on the grass.* 排球场已经在草坪上画了出来。**2** to make someone or something seem very different from or much better than other people or things 使…看上去非常不同于[大大地好于]…: **mark sb out as sth** *His efficient manner marked him out as a professional.* 他办事的麻利劲头使他看起来一派内行模样。| **mark sb out for sth** *She seemed marked out for success.* 看样子她肯定会成功。

mark sb/sth ↔ **up** *phr v* [T] **1** to increase the price of something, so that you sell it for more than you paid for it 给〔某物的进价〕加价: *Compact disks may be marked up as much as 80%.* 光盘的标价可能比进价高80%。—see also 另见 MARK-UP **2** to write notes or instructions on a piece of writing, music etc 在〔文章或乐谱〕上写评注[说明]: *Someone had already marked up the alto part.* 有人已经给男最高音部写了评注。

mark² *n*

1 ▶DIRT 污物◀ [C] a spot or small area on a surface, piece of clothing etc which is darker or dirtier than the rest and spoils its appearance 污迹; 污点: *I can't get these marks out of my T-shirt.* 我无法把我T恤衫上这些污迹去掉。| *His feet left dirty marks all over the floor.* 地板上全是他的脏脚印。| **finger marks** *There were finger marks smeared on the window.* 窗子上沾着一些手指印。

2 ▶DAMAGE 损坏◀ [C] a cut, hole, or other small sign of damage〔划破、小洞等毁损的〕痕迹: *a burn mark on the kitchen table* 厨房餐桌上的一块烧痕 | **bite mark/scratch mark etc** *Her teeth left bite marks in the apple.* 她的牙齿在苹果上留下了一些咬痕。

3 ▶COLOURED AREA 带颜色的地方◀ [C] a small area of darker or lighter colour on a plain surface such as a person's skin or an animal's fur〔人皮肤或动物皮毛等上的〕斑点, 色斑; 胎记: *The kitten is mainly white with black marks on her back.* 那只小猫主要是白色的, 背上有黑色斑点。—see also 另见 BIRTH-MARK

4 ▶SIGN 符号◀ [C] a shape or sign that is written or printed 符号; 记号; 标记: *What do those strange marks at the top mean?* 上面那些奇怪的符号表示什么意思? | **question mark/punctuation mark etc** *Her letter was full of exclamation marks.* 她的信满是感叹号。

5 ▶STUDENT'S WORK 学生作业◀ [C] *especially BrE* a letter or number given by a teacher to show what standard a piece of work is【尤英】〔老师给学生的〕分数, 成绩; GRADE¹ (5) *AmE*【美】: *The highest mark was a B+.* 最高分是B+。| *Her marks have been a lot lower this term.* 她这学期的成绩一落千丈。| **pass mark** (=the mark you needed in order to pass an exam)〔考试的〕及格分数 *The pass mark was 50%.* 及格分数是〔百分制〕50分。| **full marks** (=the highest possible mark) 满分

6 full marks for effort/trying etc *BrE* used to praise someone for trying hard to do something, even though they did not succeed【英】因努力尝试等而给的满分〔用于表扬某人已尽力做某事, 尽管没有成功〕

7 mark 2/6 etc a) a particular type of a car, machine etc 2型/6型等〔指汽车、机器等的型号〕: *The Mark 4 gun is much more powerful than the old Mark 3.* 4型枪比旧式3型枪威力大得多。**b)** *BrE* a measurement of the temperature of a gas OVEN【英】〔煤气烤箱的温度〕挡: *Cook for 40 minutes at gas mark 6.* 将煤气开到6挡加热40分钟。

8 ▶MONEY 货币◀ [C] the former standard unit of money in Germany 马克〔德国原标准货币单位〕

9 a mark of a sign that something is true or exists〔某物真实或存在的〕迹象; 标志; 表示: *She was carrying bags full of toys and clothes – the mark of a mother on the run.* 她手里拿着一些装满玩具和衣服的袋子 —— 一个忙碌不停的母亲模样。| **a mark of respect** *There was a 2-minute silence as a mark of respect for the dead.* 向死者默哀两分钟。

10 hit/miss the mark a) to hit or miss the thing that you were shooting at 击中/未中目标 **b)** to succeed or fail to have the effect you wanted 达到/未达到想要的效果: *His jibe had evidently hit the mark, for she laughed a little awkwardly.* 他的嘲讽显然达到了他要的效果, 因为她笑起来有些不自然。

11 off the mark/wide of the mark not correct; INACCURATE 不正确; 不准确: *Our cost estimate was way off the mark.* 我们对成本的估计太离谱了。

12 make your mark to become successful or famous 成功; 成名: *Wilkins was quick to make his mark, scoring the touchdown.* 威尔金斯很快就取得先机, 达阵得分。| [+ **on**] *Margaret Thatcher made an unforgettable mark on British politics.* 玛格丽特·撒切尔在英国政坛上取得的成功令人难忘。

13 leave its/their mark on to have an effect on someone or something that changes them in a permanent or very noticeable way 对〔某人〕产生持久[显著]的影响: *The years of hardship and poverty had left their mark on her.* 那些艰难困苦的岁月给她留下了难以抹去的影响。

14 not up to the mark *BrE*【英】**a)** not good enough 不够好; 不符合标准[要求]: *Her work just isn't up to the mark.* 她的工作根本不够好。**b)** *old-fashioned* not well and healthy【过时】身体不适: *I'm not feeling quite up to the mark today.* 我今天感到不太舒服。

15 be quick/slow off the mark *informal* to be quick or slow to understand things or react to situations【非正式】对事情理解快/慢; 对局势反应敏捷/迟钝

16 reach the 60 second/two-mile/£20 etc mark to reach a particular time, distance, or amount 达到60秒/两英里/20英镑等: *Membership is approaching the two million mark.* 会员人数正接近200万。

17 the halfway mark the point in a race, journey, or event that is halfway between the start and the finish〔赛跑、旅程或事件的〕中间点

18 on your marks, get set, go! *spoken* used to start a race【口】各就各位, 预备, 跑!〔用于开始赛跑〕

19 ▶SIGNATURE 签名◀ [C] *old use* a sign in the form of a cross, used by someone who is not able to write their name【旧】〔不会写自己名字者用来代替签名的〕十字画押

20 ▶CRIME 犯罪◀ [C] *AmE* someone that a criminal has decided to steal from or trick【美】被偷窃[欺骗]的对象 —see also 另见 EXCLAMATION MARK, **overstep the mark** (OVERSTEP (2)), PUNCTUATION MARK, QUESTION MARK, QUOTATION MARK, SPEECH MARKS

Mark, Saint one of Jesus Christ's DISCIPLES (=his close friends and followers). According to Bible stories, he wrote *The Gospel according to St Mark*, which describes the life and teaching of Jesus. 圣马可〔耶稣基督的门徒之一。据圣经故事记载, 他是《马可福音》的作者。《马可福音》记述耶稣的生平及教义〕

Mark Antony —see 见 Mark ANTONY

mark·down /ˈmɑrkˌdaʊn; ˈmɑːkdaʊn/ *n* [C] a reduction in the price of something 减价, 削价: *a markdown of $10* 减价10美元

marked /mɑrkt; mɑːkt/ *adj* **1** very clear and easy to notice 显著的, 明显的, 易见的: *He showed a marked lack of interest.* 他显然缺乏兴趣。| *a marked improvement in the patient's condition* 病人病情明显的好转 | **in marked contrast** *Sara wore red, in marked contrast to her sister's sombre colours.* 萨拉穿的是红色衣服, 与她姐姐所穿的暗色衣服形成鲜明的对比。**2 a marked man** a man who is in danger because an enemy wants to harm him 因仇敌打算报复而处于险境的人 —**markedly** /ˈmɑrkɪdlɪ; ˈmɑːkɪ̥dli/ *adv*: *They have a markedly different approach to the problem.* 对于这个问题他们有明显不同的处理方法。

mark·er /ˈmɑrkɚ; ˈmɑːkə/ *n* [C] **1** an object, sign etc that shows the position of something 标志; 标示物 **2** a pen with a thick point made of FELT, used for marking or drawing things 记号笔〔做记号或绘画用的粗毡头笔〕—see picture at 参见 PEN¹ 图 **3 put down a marker** to say or do something that makes your future intentions clear 显示自己未来的意图

marker pen /ˈ· · ·/ *n* [C] *BrE* a pen with a thick point made of FELT【英】记号笔

mar·ket¹ /ˈmɑrkɪt; ˈmɑːkɪ̥t/ *n*

1 ▶PLACE TO BUY THINGS 购物场所◀ [C] **a)** a place where people buy and sell goods, especially in an open area or a large building 集市; 市场: *There's a good antiques market here on Sundays.* 每逢周日这里都会有一个不错的古董集市。| *I usually buy all my vegetables at the market.* 我所需要的蔬菜通常都是在菜市场里购买。| **street market** (=with a lot of different people selling things from tables, STALLs etc in the street)〔各色人等在街上摆桌子或摆摊售货的〕街市 **b)** *AmE* a shop that sells food and things for the home【美】食品杂货店

2 the market a) the STOCK MARKET 证券市场: *Most analysts are forecasting a further downturn in the market.* 大多数分析家预测证券市场将会进一步下挫。| **play the market** (=risk money on the stock market) 在证券市场做风险投资; 在证券市场投机牟利 | **the markets** (=stock markets around the world) 全球证券市场 *The markets are nervous at the moment.* 全球证券市场眼下人心惶惶。**b)** the total amount of trade in a particular kind of goods〔某种货物的〕市场总额; 总销售量: *Honda is trying to increase its share of the market.* 本田公司正设法提高其市场总占有率。| **the art/diamond/bond etc market** *The art market is rather depressed.* 艺术品市场非常不景气。| **the market in** *the world market in aluminum* 全球铝市场 **c)** the system in which all prices and wages depend on what goods people want to buy, how many they buy etc 市场机制; 市场情况: *a naive belief in leaving everything to the market* 将一切都交给市场的天真想法

3 on the market available for people to buy 在出售, 可买到: *There are thousands of different computer games on the market.* 在市场上可买到成千上万种不同的电脑游戏。| **put a house/business etc on the market** (=offer it for sale) 将房屋/企业等投放市场出售 *We put our house on the market at the wrong time.* 我们在一个错误的时候将自己的房子投放到市场上出售。|

come onto the market (=become available for people to buy) 上市, 在市场上销售 *a revolutionary new drug that has just come onto the market* 刚刚上市的一种全新药物 | **on the open market** (=generally available for people to buy without any official restrictions) 在公开出售 *In some areas, handguns were freely available on the open market.* 在某些地区, 手枪曾可以随意公开出售。

4 ▶COUNTRY/AREA 国家/地区◀ [C] a particular country or area where a company sells its goods or where a particular type of goods is sold 商品销售国家[地区]: *Our main overseas market is Japan.* 我们的主要海外市场是日本。| *cars intended for the domestic market* 供国内市场销售的汽车 | **[+for]** *The main market for computer software is still in the US.* 电脑软件的主要销售市场仍然在美国。

5 ▶PEOPLE WHO BUY 购买者◀ [singular] the number of people who want to buy something, or the kind of people who want to buy it 欲购买某物的人数; 欲购买某物的群体; 销路: **[+for]** *The market for specialist academic books is pretty small.* 专业学术著作的市场非常小。| **there is a market for** (=people want to buy a product) 〔某商品〕有销路 *There isn't much of a market for second-hand mainframe computers.* 二手主机电脑没有多大的销路。

6 be in the market for to be interested in buying something 有意购买…: *Several terrorist groups were believed to be in the market for nuclear technology.* 据信有几个恐怖组织想购买核技术。

7 the job market/the labour market the number of jobs that are available 就业市场/劳务市场: *The job market has been badly hit by the recession.* 就业市场受到了经济衰退的沉重打击。

8 a buyer's/seller's market a time that is better for buyers because prices are low, or better for sellers because prices are high 买方/卖方市场 —see also 另见 BLACK MARKET, FLEA MARKET, **corner the market** (CORNER² (3)), **price yourself out of the market** (PRICE² (4))

market² *v* [T] **1** to try to persuade people to buy a product by advertising it in a particular way, using attractive packages etc 推销: *The success of any beauty product depends on the way it is marketed.* 美容产品成功与否, 取决于它的推销方式。**2** to make a product available in shops 〔在店铺〕出售: *The turkeys are marketed ready-to-cook.* 火鸡是以即可烹调的形式销售的。

mar·ket·a·ble /ˈmɑrkɪtəbl; ˈmɑːkḭtəbəl/ *adj* marketable goods, skills etc can be sold easily because people want them 有销路的, 畅销的: *It's a very marketable qualification* 这是一种非常符合市场需求的资历。—**marketability** /ˌmɑrkɪtəˈbɪlətɪ; ˌmɑːkḭtəˈbɪlḭti/ *n* [U]

market day /ˈ‥ ˌ/ *n* [C] *especially BrE* the day in the week when there is a market in a particular town【尤英】〔一周中〕有集市的日子, 集日

market-driv·en /ˌ‥ˈ‥◂/ *adj* MARKET LED 以市场 (需求) 为导向的

market e·con·o·my /ˌ‥ ˈ‥‥/ *n* [C] a system of producing wealth based on the free operation of business and trade without government controls 市场经济

mar·ket·eer /ˌmɑrkɪˈtɪr; ˌmɑːkḭˈtɪə/ *n* [C] **anti-Marketeer/pro-Marketeer** *old-fashioned* someone who is against/in favour of Britain being a member of the European Union【过时】反对/支持英国成为欧盟成员的人 —see also 另见 BLACK MARKETEER, FREE MARKETEER

market forc·es /ˌ‥ ˈ‥/ *n* [plural] the free operation of business and trade without any government controls, which decides the level of prices and wages at a particular time 市场力量; 市场自由运作

market gar·den /ˌ‥ ˈ‥/ *n* [C] *BrE* an area of land where vegetables and fruit are grown so that they can be sold【英】〔种植蔬菜和水果供出售的〕商品果蔬园; TRUCK FARM *AmE*【美】—**market gardener** *n* [C]

3 3 **mar·ket·ing** /ˈmɑrkɪtɪŋ; ˈmɑːkḭtɪŋ/ *n* [U] **1** the activity of trying to sell a company's products by advertising, using attractive packages etc 〔借助对产品做广告宣传、漂亮包装等进行的〕市场营销: *a marketing executive* 营销经理 | *a clever marketing ploy* 聪明的营销策略 **2 do the marketing/go marketing** *AmE old-fashioned* to go to the shops to buy things, especially food【美, 过时】去商店购物〔尤指食品〕

market lead·er /ˌ‥ ˈ‥/ *n* [C] the company that sells the most of a particular kind of product, or the product that is the most successful one of its kind 市场领导者〔占有某产品最大市场份额的公司〕; 市场领导产品〔占有最大市场份额的产品〕: *Kodak is still the market leader.* 柯达公司仍然处于市场的领导地位。

market-led /ˌ‥ ˈ◂/ *adj* market-led products, developments etc are a result of public demand for a particular product, service, or skill 以市场为导向的〔指根据公众对产品、服务或技术的需求而提供产品、开发等〕

market mak·er /ˈ‥ ˌ‥/ *n* [C] *technical* someone who works on the STOCK MARKET buying and selling stocks (STOCK¹ (3)) and shares (SHARE² (5))【术语】〔证券市场上的〕做市商; 市场经营者; 庄家

mar·ket·place /ˈmɑrkɪtˌples; ˈmɑːkḭtpleɪs/ *n* [C] **1 the marketplace** the part of business activity which is concerned with selling goods 市场〔指涉及营销的种种活动〕: *his uncanny ability to see new opportunities in the marketplace* 他那能在市场中看到新机会的神奇本领 **2** an open area in a town where a market is held 集市, 露天市场

market price /ˌ‥ ˈ/ *n* [singular] the price that people will actually pay for something at a particular time 市场价格, 市价, 时价

market re·search /ˌ‥ ˈ‥/ *n* [U] a business activity which involves collecting information about what goods people buy and why 市场调查

market town /ˈ‥ ˌ/ *n* [C] *BrE* a town where there is an outdoor market, usually once or twice a week【英】〔通常每周有一次或两次露天集市交易的〕集市城镇

market val·ue /ˌ‥ ˈ‥/ *n* [singular] the value of a product, building etc based on the price that people are willing to pay for it rather than the cost of producing it or building it 〔产品、建筑物等的〕市场价值〔即以人们愿意支付的价格而不以成本厘定的价值〕

mark·ing /ˈmɑrkɪŋ; ˈmɑːkɪŋ/ *n* **1** [C usually plural 一般用复数, U] the coloured patterns and shapes on an animal's fur, on leaves etc 〔动物皮毛、树叶等上的〕斑纹, 斑点: *The leopard has beautiful markings.* 豹子身上有美丽的斑纹。**2** [C usually plural 一般用复数, U] colours and shapes painted on aircraft, army vehicles etc 〔刷在飞机、军车等上的〕彩色装饰和图形 **3** [U] *especially BrE* the activity of checking students' written work【尤英】批改学生作业: *I have to do a lot of marking tonight.* 今晚我有许多作业要批改。

marks·man /ˈmɑrksmən; ˈmɑːksmən/ *plural* **marksmen** /-mən; -mən/ *n* [C] someone who can shoot very well 神枪手, 神射手

marks·man·ship /ˈmɑrksmənʃɪp; ˈmɑːksmənʃɪp/ *n* [U] the ability to shoot very well 射击术; 枪法

mark-up /ˈ‥ ˌ/ *n* [C] an increase in the price of something, especially from the price a shop pays for something to the price it sells it for 提价幅度〔尤指商店从进货价到售出价的增加幅度〕: *The retailer's mark-up is 50%.* 零售商的提价幅度是 50%。

Marl·bo·rough /ˈmɑrlbəro; ˈmɑːlbərə/ a town in Wiltshire, southwest England, where there is a famous PUBLIC SCHOOL (=a school that is paid for by the parents and not by the government), **Marlborough College**. 莫尔伯勒〔英格兰西南威尔特郡一城镇。著名的莫尔伯勒公学就位于此镇〕

Mar·ley /ˈmɑrlɪ; ˈmɑːli/, **Bob** (1945-81) a Jamaican singer and songwriter who, with his group **The Wailers**, helped to make REGGAE music popular. He was a RASTAFARIAN, and wore his hair in DREADLOCKS. His songs, which include *No Woman, No Cry* and *Redemption Song*, often have a political message. 马利〔(1945-1981), 牙买加歌手、词作家。他与其"哭泣者"乐队一起使雷盖音乐日渐流行。他是一个拉斯塔法里教徒, 喜欢把头发扎成"骇人"长发绺。其著名歌曲有《没有女人就没有哭泣》和《救赎曲》, 常含有一定政治色彩〕

Marley's Ghost /ˌ‥ ˈ/ the spirit of **Jacob Marley**, who is the dead business partner of Scrooge in the book *A Christmas Carol* (1843) by Charles Dickens. He appears to Scrooge on Christmas Eve, and tells him that he will be visited by three spirits. 马利的鬼魂〔查尔斯·狄更斯的小说《圣诞颂歌》(1843) 中斯克鲁奇死去的生意搭档。圣诞前夜, 他来到斯克鲁奇面前, 告诉他将有三个精灵造访〕

mar·lin /ˈmɑrlɪn; ˈmɑːlḭn/ *n* [C] a large sea fish with a long sharp nose, which people hunt for sport 马林鱼, 枪鱼

Mar·lowe /ˈmɑrlo; ˈmɑːləʊ/, **Chris·to·pher** /ˈkrɪstəfɚ; ˈkrɪstəfə/ (1564-93) an English poet and writer of plays, whose most famous plays are *Dr Faustus*, *Edward II*, and *Tamburlaine the Great*. Many people think he influenced the work of Shakespeare. He was killed in a fight in a TAVERN. 马洛〔(1564-1593), 英国诗人、剧作家, 最著名的作品有《浮士德博士》、《爱德华二世》和《帖木儿大帝》。许多人认为他对莎士比亚的创作产生过影响。他是在一个小酒馆里与人斗殴致死的〕

Marlowe, Philip a PRIVATE DETECTIVE (=someone who is employed to look for information or missing people) in stories

written by the US writer Raymond Chandler. Marlowe is a tough and determined character who does not often show his feelings, but he is honest and believes in justice. 马洛〔雷蒙德·钱德勒小说中的一名美国私家侦探。他性格顽强坚定，不轻易流露感情，但为人诚实，崇尚正义〕

mar·ma·lade /ˈmɑrmḷˌed; ˈmɑːməleɪd/ *n* [U] a JAM made from fruit such as oranges, LEMONs or GRAPEFRUIT, usually eaten at breakfast〔用橘子、柠檬或葡萄柚等制成的〕柑橘酱

Marmara —see 见 the SEA OF MARMARA

Mar·mite /ˈmɑrmaɪt; ˈmɑːmaɪt/ *trademark* a type of soft, dark brown substance with a strong salty taste, which is a YEAST EXTRACT. It is usually spread on bread in small quantities, but it can also be used to give taste to soups. It is a typically British food, sold in a round brown glass container. There is a similar product sold in Australia called Vegemite.【商标】马麦脱〔一种口味偏咸的深褐色软质酸酵母，通常可在面包上涂抹少许，也可加入羹汤调味。该产品是典型的英国食品，装在咖啡色的玻璃圆罐中出售。澳大利亚也有一种类似产品，名为 Vegemite（维吉麦特）〕

mar·mo·re·al /mɑrˈmɔrɪəl; mɑːˈmɔːriəl/ *adj literary* like MARBLE【文】大理石似的

mar·mo·set /ˈmɑrməˌzɛt; ˈmɑːməzet/ *n* [C] a type of small monkey with long hair and large eyes that lives in Central and South America 狨猴〔一种生活在中南美洲的长毛大眼小猴〕

Mar·on·ite /ˈmærənaɪt; ˈmærənaɪt/ *n* [C] a member of a Christian religious group, connected with the Roman Catholic Church, who live mainly in Lebanon 马龙派信徒〔与罗马天主教会有关联的一基督教宗教团体的信徒，主要居住在黎巴嫩〕

ma·roon[1] /məˈrun; məˈruːn/ *n* [U] a very dark red-brown colour 栗色，褐紫红色 —**maroon** *adj* —see picture on page A5 参见 A5 页图

maroon[2] *v* **be marooned** to be left in a place where there are no other people and where you cannot escape 被困于荒无人烟且无法脱身的地方: *The car broke down leaving us marooned in the middle of nowhere.* 汽车坏了，我们被困在茫茫荒野中。

maroon[3] *n* [C] a small ROCKET used as a signal by ships〔船舶用作信号的〕烟火；鞭炮

Mar·ple /ˈmɑrpḷ; ˈmɑːpəl/**, Miss Jane** a character in crime NOVELs by Agatha Christie. Miss Marple is a very nice polite old English lady who is also clever at discovering criminals, especially murderers. 马普尔小姐〔阿加莎·克里斯蒂的侦探小说中的一个人物。马普尔小姐是一位温文尔雅的英国老妇人，思维敏捷，善于查找罪犯，尤其是杀人凶手〕

marque /mɑrk; mɑːk/ *n* [C] the well-known name of a type of car or other product, especially an expensive one〔汽车或其他产品，尤指名贵产品的〕牌子，商标: *the prestigious Ferrari marque* 久负盛名的法拉利牌汽车

mar·quee /mɑrˈki; mɑːˈkiː/ *n* [C] **1** a large tent at an outdoor event or celebration, used especially for eating or drinking in〔大型户外活动或庆祝活动时，尤用作进餐或饮酒场所的〕大帐篷 **2** *AmE* a sign above the door of a theatre or cinema which gives the name of the play or film【美】〔戏院或电影院大门上方〕公布剧名[影片名]的招牌

mar·quess /ˈmɑrkwɪs; ˈmɑːkwɨs/ *n* [C] *BrE* a MARQUIS【英】侯爵

mar·quet·ry /ˈmɑrkətrɪ; ˈmɑːkɨtri/ *n* [U] a pattern made of coloured pieces of wood fastened together, or the art of making these patterns〔用着色木片嵌接而成的〕镶嵌图案；镶嵌工艺

Mar·quette /mɑrˈkɛt; mɑːˈket/**, Jacques** /ʒɑk; ʒæk/ (1637-75) a French MISSIONARY (=someone who goes to a foreign country to teach people about Christianity) and explorer in North America. He and Louis Joliet were the first Europeans to discover the Mississippi River. 马奎特〔(1637-1675)，法国传教士、北美探险家。他和路易斯·若利埃是最早发现密西西比河的两个欧洲人〕

Marquez —see 见 Gabriel GARCIA MARQUEZ

mar·quis /ˈmɑrkwɪs; ˈmɑːkwɨs/ *n* [C] a man who, in the British system of NOBLE titles, has a rank between DUKE and EARL〔英国的〕侯爵: *the Marquis of Bath* 巴思侯爵

Mar·ra·kesh, Marrakech /mærəˈkɛʃ; mærəˈkeʃ/ a city in western Morocco that is popular with tourists and famous for producing CARPETs and leather goods. 马拉喀什〔摩洛哥西部一城市。该市是一个旅游胜地，而且还以出产地毯和皮货闻名〕

mar·riage /ˈmærɪdʒ; ˈmærɪdʒ/ *n* **1** [C] the relationship between two people who are married 婚姻: *They have a very happy marriage.* 他们的婚姻非常美满。| *One in three marriages ends in divorce.* 三桩婚姻中就有一桩以离婚而告终。**2** [U] the state of being married 结婚: *My parents disapprove of sex before marriage.* 我父母不赞成婚前性行为。**3** [C] the ceremony in which two people get married; WEDDING 结婚仪式，婚礼: *The marriage took place at St Bartholomew's church.* 婚礼是在圣巴托罗缪教堂举行的。**4 by marriage** if you are related to someone by marriage, they are married to someone in your family 通过姻亲关系，由于婚姻

CULTURAL NOTE 文化注释

In the US and the UK, it is now common for people to live together without ever getting married or to live together for a period of time before deciding to get married. Some couples live together and then get married when they have children. 在美国和英国，同居现在是很寻常的事情。有些人根本就没打算结婚，有些是决定结婚前先共同生活一段时间。有些伴侣是同居后有了孩子然后结婚的。— see also Cultural Notes at DIVORCE and see also ONE-PARENT FAMILY 另见 DIVORCE 文化注释并见 ONE-PARENT FAMILY

mar·riage·a·ble /ˈmærɪdʒəbḷ; ˈmærɪdʒəbəl/ *adj old-fashioned* suitable for marriage【过时】适合结婚的: *a young woman of marriageable age* 达到结婚年龄的年轻女子 —**marriageability** /ˌmærɪdʒəˈbɪlətɪ; ˌmærɪdʒəˈbɪlɨti/ *n* [U]

marriage bu·reau /ˈ·· ˌ··/ *n* [C] an organization that helps people find partners to marry 婚姻介绍所

marriage cer·tif·i·cate /ˈ·· ·ˌ···/ *n* [C] an official document that proves that two people are married 结婚证书

marriage guid·ance /ˌ·· ˈ··/ *n* [U] advice given to people who are having difficulties in their marriage 婚姻指导[咨询]

marriage li·cence /ˈ·· ˌ··/ *n* [C] an official written document saying that two people are allowed to marry 结婚许可证

marriage lines /ˈ·· ·/ *n* [plural] *old-fashioned BrE* a MARRIAGE CERTIFICATE【过时，英】结婚证书

marriage of con·ve·ni·ence /ˌ·· · ·ˈ···/ *n* [C] a marriage for political or economic reasons, not for love 基于政治[经济]原因〔而非基于爱情〕的婚姻，权宜婚姻

Marriage of Fi·ga·ro, The /ˌmærɪdʒ əv ˈfɪgəro; ˌmærɪdʒ əv ˈfɪgərəʊ/ (1786) a humorous OPERA by Mozart with words by Lorenzo Da Ponte, which is based on the play *The Marriage of Figaro* by the French writer Beaumarchais《费加罗的婚礼》〔(1786)，莫扎特创作的一部幽默歌剧，由洛伦佐·达·蓬特作词，根据法国作家博马舍的同名剧本改编而成〕

marriage vows /ˈ·· ·/ *n* [plural] the promises that you make during the marriage ceremony 结婚誓约，婚誓

mar·ried /ˈmærɪd; ˈmærid/ *adj* **1** having a husband or a wife 已婚的，有配偶的: *Are you married or single?* 你是已婚还是单身？| *They've been married for 28 years.* 他们已经结婚 28 年了。| *More and more married women were returning to the workplace.* 越来越多的已婚妇女开始重新就业。| **[+to]** *She's married to my brother.* 她嫁给了我哥哥。| **get married** *We're getting married next month.* 我们下个月结婚。| **married life** (=your life when you are married) 婚后生活；婚姻生活 *How are you enjoying married life?* 你婚后过得怎么样？**2 be married to sth** to give most of your time and attention to a job or activity 专心致志于某事 —see also 另见 MARRY, YOUNG MARRIEDS

mar·row /ˈmæro; ˈmærəʊ/ *n* **1** [U] the soft fatty substance in the hollow centre of bones; BONE MARROW 骨髓: *a bone marrow transplant* 骨髓移植 **2** [C,U] a large long dark green vegetable that grows along the ground 西葫芦，食用葫芦 —compare 比较 SQUASH[2] (3) —see picture on page A9 参见 A9 页图 **3 chilled/frozen/shocked to the marrow** very cold or shocked 冷得刺骨；毛骨悚然: *She had walked all the way home, frozen to the marrow.* 她一路走着回了家，感到全身寒冷刺骨。

marrow bone /ˈ·· ·/ *n* [C,U] a large bone that contains a lot of MARROW (1) 多髓的大骨，髓骨

mar·ry /ˈmærɪ; ˈmæri/ *v* **marries, married, marrying 1** [I,T] to become someone's husband or wife 结婚；娶；嫁: **get married (to)** *I got married when I was 18.* 我 18 岁就结婚了。| *Billy got married to the first girl he went out with.* 比利和自己的初恋女友结了婚。| **marry sb** *one of those romances about a rich tycoon who marries his secretary* 大亨娶了女秘书为妻的那种浪漫故事中的一个 | **marry money** (=marry someone who is rich) 和有钱人结婚 **2** [T] to perform the ceremony at which two people get married 为…主持婚礼: *The priest who married us was really nice.* 为我们主持婚礼的那个牧师非常和蔼可亲。**3** [T] to find a husband or wife for one of your children 为自己的孩子找〔配偶〕: **marry sb to sb** *She's determined to marry all her daughters to rich men.* 她决心把她所有的女儿都嫁给有钱人。**4** [T] *formal* to combine two quite different ideas, designs, tastes etc together【正式】将〔两个差别很大的想法、设计、品味等〕结合在一起: **marry sth with sth** *The design marries tradi-*

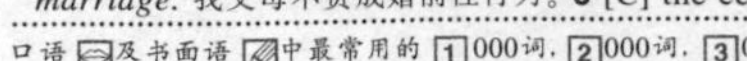

口语 及书面语 中最常用的 1 000词，2 000词，3 000词

tional styles with modern materials. 这个设计把传统风格和现代材料结合在一起。**5 not the marrying kind** not the kind of person who wants to get married 不是那种想结婚的人

marry into sth *phr v* [T] to join a family or social group by marrying someone who belongs to it 通过婚姻而加入〔配偶所属的家庭或社会团体〕: *She married into a very wealthy family.* 她嫁进了一个非常富有的人家。

marry sb ↔ **off** *phr v* [T] to find a husband or wife for someone 为〔某人〕寻得配偶: [+to] *They married her off to the first young man who came along.* 他们把她嫁给了第一个出现的年轻人。

USAGE NOTE 用法说明: MARRY

GRAMMAR 语法

You *marry someone* or *get/are married to someone,* not *with* them. But you can be *married with four children.* 表示"与某人结婚", 要说 marry someone 或 get/are married to someone, 而不用 with。但可以说 married with four children (已婚, 有四个孩子)。

SPOKEN-WRITTEN 口语—书面语

Get married is more informal and more common in spoken English than **marry**. 在英语口语中, get married 比 marry 更通俗随便, 更为常用: *Marti is getting married to Jeff next week.* 马蒂下周和杰夫结婚。(compare 比较 *Marti is marrying Jeff next week.*)

In spoken English, speakers often avoid *to* with **married** by saying, for example 在口语中, 人们常常避免在 married 后面用 to, 例如: *Jeff and Marti got married/are married.* 杰夫和马蒂结婚了。

Mars /marz; mɑːz/ *n* [singular] the PLANET that is fourth in order from the sun, is nearest to the Earth, and it shines with a red colour 火星〔距离太阳第四位的行星, 离地球最近, 发红色光〕—see picture at 参见 SOLAR SYSTEM 图

Mar·sa·la /marˋsɑlə; mɑːˈsɑːlə/ a sweet strong wine from Marsala in the island of Sicily 马沙拉葡萄酒〔产于意大利西西里岛马沙拉的一种高度甜葡萄酒〕

Mar·seil·laise /ˌmarslˋez; ˌmɑːsəˈleɪz/ *n* [singular] the national song of France 马赛曲〔法国国歌〕

Mar·seilles /marˋse; mɑːˈseɪ/ the second largest city in France, in the south of the country on the Mediterranean coast. It is an important port and industrial centre. Its correct French name is Marseille. 马赛〔法国第二大城市, 位于法国南部, 濒临地中海。该市是法国重要港口和工业中心。法语的正确拼法为 Marseille〕

marsh /marʃ; mɑːʃ/ *n* [C,U] an area of low flat land that is always wet and soft 沼泽, 湿地 —compare 比较 SWAMP[1], BOG[1] (1) —**marshy** *adj*: *marshy ground* 沼泽地

mar·shal[1] /ˋmarʃəl; ˈmɑːʃəl/ *n* [C] **1** an officer of the highest rank in an army or airforce〔陆军或空军〕元帅: *Marshal Zhukov* 朱可夫元帅 —see table on page C6 参见 C6 页附录 **2** *especially BrE* an official in charge of an important public event or ceremony【尤英】司礼官, 典礼官, 司仪〔主持重要公众活动或典礼的官员〕**3** an official in charge of a race or sports event〔体育竞赛等的〕主事官员 **4** *AmE* an official in a court of law; SHERIFF【美】执法官; 治安官; **5** *AmE* the officer in charge of a city's police force or fire-fighting department【美】警察局长; 消防队长

marshal[2] *v* **marshalled, marshalling** *BrE*【英】, **marshaled, marshaling** *AmE*【美】[T] **1 marshal your arguments/ideas/facts etc** to organize your arguments, ideas etc so that they are effective or easy to understand 整理论据/想法/事实等: *Briggs paused for a moment as if to marshal his thoughts.* 布里格斯停顿了一会儿, 好像要整理一下思路。**2** to control or organize a large group 控制; 组织; 引领: *Extra stewards had to be employed to marshal the huge crowds.* 必须聘请额外的服务员来安顿这大群大群的人。**3 marshal your forces** to organize all the people and things that you need in order to be ready for a battle, election etc 组织力量, 集结力量

Mar·shall /ˋmarʃəl; ˈmɑːʃəl/, **Thur·good** /ˋθɝgud; ˈθɜːgʊd/ (1908-93) a US lawyer who became the first black member of the Supreme Court in 1967. When he was a lawyer he won many important legal cases to help black US citizens get equal rights, such as the case of Brown v. Board of Education of Topeka. 马歇尔〔(1908-1993), 美国律师, 1967 年成为美国最高法院的首位黑人法官。他任律师期间打赢了许多重要的官司, 帮助美国黑人公民争取平等权利, 如"布朗诉托皮卡教育局"一案〕

Marshall aid /ˈ‥ˌ‥/ the economic help that was given to Europe by the US government under the Marshall Plan after World War II 马歇尔援助〔二战后美国政府根据马歇尔计划给欧洲提供的经济援助〕

marshalling yard /ˈ‥‥ˌ/ *n* [C] *BrE* a place where railway WAGONs are brought together to form trains【英】〔铁路上的〕调车场, 编组场

Marshall Islands /ˈ‥ˌ‥/ a country consisting of two 800-mile-long chains of CORAL ATOLLs in the central Pacific Ocean. Population: 70,822 (2001). Capital: Majuro. 马绍尔群岛〔太平洋中部一国家, 由两列长达 800 英里的环状珊瑚礁群组成。人口: 70,822 (2001), 首都: 马朱罗〕

Marshall Plan, the /ˈ‥ˌ‥/ a programme established by the US government in 1947 to give economic help to Europe after World War II. It was named after George C. Marshall, who was the US Secretary of State. Thousands of millions of dollars were provided for rebuilding cities, roads, industries etc. 马歇尔计划〔美国政府1947年制订的一项计划, 旨在对二战后的欧洲提供经济援助。该计划以美国国务卿乔治·C.马歇尔的名字命名。美国给欧洲提供了数十亿美元的援助, 用于城市、道路、工业重建〕

Marshal of the Roy·al Air·force /ˌ‥‥ˌ‥ˈ‥/ *n* [C] an officer of high rank in the British airforce〔英国〕皇家空军元帅

Mar·shal·sea, the /ˋmarʃəlsi; ˈmɑːʃəlsiː/ a prison in London in the past, where people were sent when they could not pay their debts. Part of the NOVEL *Little Dorrit* by Charles Dickens is set in this prison. 马夏尔西监狱〔伦敦过去的一座监狱, 专门关押拖欠债务者。查尔斯·狄更斯的小说《小杜丽》中部分背景取自该监狱〕

marsh gas /ˈ‥ ˌ/ *n* [U] gas formed from decaying plants under water in a MARSH; METHANE 沼气, 甲烷

marsh·land /ˋmarʃlænd; ˈmɑːʃlænd/ *n* [U] an area of land where there is a lot of MARSH 沼泽地

marsh·mal·low /ˋmarʃˌmælo; ˌmɑːʃˈmæləʊ/ *n* [C,U] **1** a very soft light sweet that is white or pink 棉花糖 **2** a tall wild plant with pink flowers 沼泽蜀葵, 药用蜀葵

Mar·ston Moor /ˌmarstn̩ ˋmuə; ˌmɑːstən ˈmʊə/, **Battle of** an important battle near York in 1644 during the English Civil War, which gave Cromwell control of the north of England 马斯顿荒原战役〔1644 年英国内战期间在约克附近进行的一场重要战役, 从而使克伦威尔控制了英格兰北部〕

mar·su·pi·al /marˋsjupɪəl; mɑːˈsuːpiəl/ *n* [C] an animal such as a KANGAROO which carries its babies in a pocket of skin on its body 有袋动物〈如袋鼠〉

mart /mart; mɑːt/ *n* [C] a market 市场: *the biggest cattle mart in the region* 该地区最大的牲畜市场

mar·ten /ˋmartɪn; ˈmɑːtɪn/ *n* [C] a small flesh-eating animal that lives mainly in trees 貂

Mar·tha /ˋmarθə; ˈmɑːθə/ in the New Testament of the Bible, a woman who lived with her sister, Mary. When Jesus visited them, Martha went and prepared food for Jesus and his DISCIPLES, and did not remain with Mary to listen to what he was saying. As a result Martha often represents the type of Christian who works hard to help other people. 马大〔《圣经·新约》中与妹妹马利亚同住的女子。耶稣探望她们时, 马大没有和妹妹一起听他讲道, 而是出去给耶稣及其门徒准备饭菜。鉴于此, 人们经常借用"马大"指称乐于助人的基督徒〕

Martha's Vine·yard /ˌ‥ˈ‥/ an island off the coast of the state of Massachusetts in the northeast of the US, south of Cape Cod. It is popular with writers and artists, and with tourists in the summer. 马撒葡萄园岛〔美国东北部与马萨诸塞州海岸隔海相望的 个岛屿, 位于科德角以南。该岛颇为作家和艺术家喜爱, 也是夏日旅游的好去处〕

mar·tial /ˋmarʃəl; ˈmɑːʃəl/ *adj* [only before noun 仅用于名词前] connected with war and fighting 军事的; 战争的: *martial music* 军乐

martial art /ˌ‥ ˈ/ *n* [C usually plural 一般用复数] a sport such as JUDO or KARATE, in which you fight with your hands and feet, and which was developed in Eastern countries〔东方国家的〕武术〈如柔道、空手道等〉

martial law /ˌ‥ ˈ/ *n* [U] a situation in which the army controls an area instead of the police, especially because of fighting against the government 军事管制, 戒严: *Fighting in the capital led to the imposition of martial law.* 首都发生的战斗导致了戒严的实施。

Mar·tian /ˋmarʃən; ˈmɑːʃən/ *n* [C] an imaginary creature from the PLANET Mars〔假想的〕火星人, 火星生物 —**Martian** *adj*

mar·tin /ˋmartɪn; ˈmɑːtɪn/ *n* [C] a small bird like a SWALLOW[2] (1) 岩燕

mar·ti·net /ˌmartn̩ˋet; ˌmɑːtɪˈnet/ *n* [C] *formal* someone who is very strict and makes people obey rules exactly【正式】严格遵守纪律的人

M

mar·ti·ni /mɑrˈtini; mɑːˈtiːni/ *n trademark* [C,U] an alcoholic drink made by mixing GIN or VODKA with VERMOUTH【商标】马蒂尼酒〔用杜松子酒或伏特加酒与苦艾酒混合而成的鸡尾酒〕

Mar·ti·nique /ˌmɑrtn̩ˈik; ˌmɑːtɪˈniːk/ a mountainous island in the Caribbean Sea, which is a DEPENDENCY of France. Population: 400,000 (1995). Capital: Fort-de-France. 马提尼克岛〔加勒比海一多山岛屿, 法国属地。人口: 400,000 (1995), 首府: 法兰西堡〕

Martin Luther King Day an American holiday on the third Monday in January to remember the day that Martin Luther King Jr. was born 马丁·路德·金日〔美国节日, 时间为每年一月的第三个星期一, 为马丁·路德·金诞辰纪念日〕

mar·tyr¹ /ˈmɑrtɚ; ˈmɑːtə/ *n* [C] **1** someone who is killed or punished because of their religious or political beliefs 殉道者; 烈士 **2** someone who tries to get other people's sympathy by complaining about how hard their life is 诉说自己生活如何艰苦以博取他人同情者: *She's such a martyr!* 她就是这样一个靠诉苦博取同情的人! **3 be a martyr to** *old-fashioned* to suffer a lot because of an illness【过时】〔因疾病〕受折磨, 受痛苦: *She's a martyr to her arthritis.* 她深受关节炎的折磨。

martyr² *v* **be martyred** to be killed or punished because of your religious beliefs〔因宗教信仰〕被处死; 受惩罚

mar·tyr·dom /ˈmɑrtɚdəm; ˈmɑːtədəm/ *n* [U] the death or suffering of a martyr 殉难; 殉道, 殉教; 受苦

mar·tyred /ˈmɑrtɚd; ˈmɑːtəd/ *adj* [only before noun 仅用于名词前] a martyred look or expression is an unhappy one, as if you want to make other people feel sorry for you〔好像为博取他人同情而显现的神色或表情〕痛苦的, 伤心的: *I wish you'd stop giving me those martyred looks.* 我希望你别再这么伤心地看着我。

mar·vel¹ /ˈmɑrvl̩; ˈmɑːvəl/ *v* **marvelled, marvelling** *BrE*【英】, **marveled, marveling** *AmE*【美】[I,T] to feel great surprise or admiration for something, especially someone's behaviour〔尤指对某人的行为〕感到惊讶, 钦佩: [+at] *I marvelled at my mother's ability to remain calm in a crisis.* 我佩服我母亲处事不惊的本领。| **marvel that** *I marvelled that anyone could be so stupid.* 我感到惊讶的是竟会有人如此愚蠢。

marvel² *n* [C] something or someone surprisingly useful or skilful, that you like and admire very much 十分有用[灵巧]的物[人]: *the marvels of modern science* 现代科学的奇迹 | *an electronic marvel* 奇妙的电子器件 | *I don't know how he did it – he's a bloody marvel!* 我不知道他是怎么成功的 —— 他真是个非常了不起的人物!

S2 **mar·vel·lous** *BrE*【英】, **marvelous** *AmE*【美】/ˈmɑrvl̩əs; ˈmɑːvələs/ *adj* extremely good, enjoyable, or impressive etc 极好的; 绝妙的; 了不起的: *"How was your holiday?" "Marvellous!"* "假期过得好吗?" "好极了!" | *It sounds like a marvellous idea.* 这个主意听起来很不错。| *It's marvelous what they can do with plastic surgery these days.* 如今他们能用整容手术做的事真是妙极了。—**marvellously** *adv*

Marx /mɑrks; mɑːks/, **Karl** /kɑrl; kɑːl/ (1818-83) a German writer and political PHILOSOPHER whose ideas have had an important influence on politics in the 20th century. He established the principles of communism in *The Communist Manifesto*, which he wrote with Friedrich Engels in 1848. He wrote his most important book *Das Kapital* in London. 马克思〔(1818-1883), 德国作家、政治思想家。其观点对20世纪的政治产生了重要影响。1848年, 他与弗里德里希·恩格斯合著的《共产党宣言》确定了共产主义的原理。他在伦敦完成了其最重要的著作《资本论》〕

Marx Broth·ers, the /ˈ· ,··/ a US family of actors known for their crazy humour and jokes. Together, they made many humorous films, which are still very popular. The most important members of the family were **Groucho** (1890-1977), **Harpo** (1888-1964), who never spoke and played the HARP, and **Chico** (1888-1964), who played the piano. Groucho, who was the most famous, had glasses, a large MOUSTACHE, and a strange way of walking, and he always carried a thick CIGAR. The Marx Brothers' films include *Horse Feathers* (1932), *Duck Soup* (1933), and *A Night at the Opera* (1935). 马克斯兄弟〔美国一演员之家, 以近乎荒唐的幽默搞笑闻名。他们合演了许多幽默影片, 至今仍广为流传。最重要的成员有葛劳丘(1890-1977)、从不说话只弹竖琴的哈泼(1888-1964)以及弹钢琴的奇科(1888-1964)。其中葛劳丘最为有名, 他戴着一副眼镜, 留着满脸胡须, 走路的样子有点古怪, 嘴里老是叼着一支粗大的雪茄。马克斯兄弟演过的电影有《趾高气扬》(1932)、《鸭汤》(1933)和《歌剧院之夜》(1935)〕

Marx·is·m /ˈmɑrksɪzəm; ˈmɑːksɪzəm/ *n* [U] the system of political thinking invented by Karl Marx, which explains changes in history as the result of a struggle between social classes 马克思主义 —**Marxist** *n* [C]

Marxism-Len·in·is·m /,··ˈ···/ *n* [U] the ideas of Marxism as explained and added to by the Russian leader Lenin, who believed in the 'dictatorship of the proletariat' (=when government is controlled by a combination of industrial workers and poor farm workers) as part of the process of achieving revolution 马克思列宁主义 —**Marxist-Leninist** *n, adj*

Ma·ry¹ /ˈmɛrɪ; ˈmeəri/ also 又作 **the Virgin Mary, Our Lady** in the Christian religion, the mother of Jesus Christ, and the most important of all the SAINTS. She was the wife of Joseph, but Christians believe she was a VIRGIN (=someone who has never had sex), at the time of Jesus's birth, because the father of Jesus is not a human being, but God. Christians, especially Roman Catholics often pray to her to ask for help. 童贞女马利亚〔基督教中的耶稣基督之母, 最重要的圣人。她是约瑟之妻, 但基督徒认为她孕育耶稣时仍是童贞女, 理由是基督之父并非凡人而是上帝。基督教徒, 尤其是天主教徒常向马利亚祷告祈助〕

Mary² in the New Testament of the Bible, a woman who lived with her sister, Martha. When Jesus visited them, Mary remained to listen to what he was saying while Martha went and prepared food for him and his DISCIPLES. As a result Mary often represents the type of Christian who spends their life thinking deeply about religious matters. 马利亚〔《圣经·新约》中与姐姐马大同住的女子。耶稣探望她们时, 马利亚留下来听他讲道, 马大出去给耶稣及其门徒准备饭菜。鉴于此, 人们经常借用"马利亚"指称终生深思宗教问题的基督徒〕

Mary, Mary, Quite Con·tra·ry /,··,··,··ˈ···/ a NURSERY RHYME (=an old song or poem for young children). The rhyme goes: *Mary, Mary, quite contrary, /How does your garden grow?/With silver bells and cockle shells,/And pretty maids all in a row.* 《玛丽, 玛丽, 别树一格》〔一首儿歌〕歌词如下: 玛丽小姑娘, 做事真不凡, /园中栽什么? /栽银钟种贝壳, /鲜花如少女, 朵朵排成行。

Mary had a Lit·tle Lamb /,····,··ˈ·/ a NURSERY RHYME (=an old song or poem for young children). The rhyme begins: *Mary had a little lamb,/Its fleece was white as snow;/And everywhere that Mary went/The lamb was sure to go.* 《玛丽有只小羔羊》〔一首儿歌〕歌词开头为: 玛丽有只小羔羊, /羊毛洁白如冬雪。/玛丽无论到何处, /羔羊一定随她去。

Mary I /ˌmɛrɪ ðə ˈfɝst; ˌmeəri ðə ˈfɜːst/, **Queen** also 又作 **Mary Tudor** (1516-58) the queen of England from 1553 until her death. She was the daughter of Henry VIII and Catherine of Aragon, and she married the king of Spain, Philip II. Mary tried to make England return to the Catholic religion, and many Protestants who refused to become Catholics were killed by being burned. For this reason, she was sometimes called **Bloody Mary**. 玛丽一世〔(1516-1558), 英格兰女王, 1553年即位直至去世。玛丽是亨利八世与阿拉贡的凯瑟琳之女, 后与西班牙国王腓力二世结婚。玛丽试图使英格兰重新信奉天主教, 结果许多不愿皈依天主教的新教徒被处以火刑。鉴于此, 人们有时称她"血腥玛丽"〕

Mary II /ˌmɛrɪ ðə ˈsɛkənd; ˌmeəri ðə ˈsekənd/ —see 见 King WILLIAM OF ORANGE

Ma·ry·land /ˈmɛrɪlənd; ˈmeərilənd/ abbreviation 缩写为 **MD** a state on the east coast of the US, and one of the 13 original states of the US. Its largest city is Baltimore, which is a busy port. 马里兰州〔美国东海岸一州, 为美国最早的13个州之一。最大城市是巴尔的摩, 为一繁忙港口〕

Mary Mag·da·le·ne /ˌmɛrɪ mægdəˈlinɪ; ˌmeəri mægdəˈliːni/, **Saint** in the New Testament of the Bible, a woman who Jesus cured. She attended Jesus's CRUCIFIXION and was the first person to see him when he returned to life after his death. She is usually thought to be the same woman as the PROSTITUTE who washed Jesus' feet, but who is not named in the Bible. (抹大拉的)马利亚〔《圣经·新约》中耶稣救治过的一名女子。她亲眼看到耶稣被钉上了十字架, 也是见证耶稣复活的第一人。人们通常认为她和给耶稣洗脚的那个妓女是同一个人, 只不过《圣经》中未提到而已〕

Mary Pop·pins /ˌmɛrɪ ˈpɑpənz; ˌmeəri ˈpɒpɪnz/ (1964) a US film in which Julie Andrews appears as a NANNY (=a woman who is employed to take care of the children in a family) called Mary Poppins, who has magical powers and can fly 《欢乐满人间》〔(1964)美国一影片。朱莉·安德鲁斯在剧中饰演一位保姆, 名叫玛丽·波平斯。她掌握魔法, 具有空中飞翔的本领〕

Mary Queen of Scots /,··,··ˈ·/ also 又作 **Mary Stuart** (1542-87) the daughter of the Scottish King James V. She became Queen of Scotland when she was one week old, but in 1568 she was forced to give up her position, and she escaped to England. Instead of helping her, the English queen, Elizabeth I

M

(who was her COUSIN) put her in prison. Many Catholics believed Mary should have been Queen of England instead of Elizabeth, who was a Protestant. Elizabeth later ordered Mary to be killed, because she believed Mary was involved in a secret plan to kill her. After Elizabeth's death, Mary's son James, who was the King of Scotland, also became the King of England (as James I). Mary had three husbands, and many stories and books have been written about her. (苏格兰女王)玛丽〔(1542-1587),苏格兰国王詹姆斯五世之女。她出生仅一星期就成为苏格兰女王,但于1568年被迫退位,逃往英格兰。英格兰女王伊丽莎白一世非但不帮助她,反而将她关进监狱。许多天主教徒认为英格兰女王本应是玛丽,而不应是身为新教徒的伊丽莎白。后来,伊丽莎白认为玛丽密谋暗杀自己,遂下令将她处死。伊丽莎白死后,时任苏格兰国王的玛丽之子詹姆斯也成了英格兰国王(史称詹姆斯一世)。玛丽先后嫁过三个丈夫,后世写有不少关于玛丽生平的故事和书籍〕

Mary Rose, The /ˌ· ˈ·/ a British WARSHIP which sank in the sea off the south coast of England on its first journey in 1545. It was brought to the surface in 1982, and can now be seen in Portsmouth. "玛丽·罗斯"号〔英国一艘战舰,1545年首航时在英格兰南部海岸不远的海域沉没。1982年被打捞出水,现陈列在朴茨茅斯〕

mar·zi·pan /ˈmɑrzəˌpæn; ˈmɑːzɪpæn/ *n* [U] a sweet food made from ALMONDs, sugar, and eggs, used to make sweets and for covering cakes 杏仁蛋白糖浆〔一种用杏仁、糖和蛋白混合而成的糖浆,用于做糖果或浇在糕饼上〕

masc the written abbreviation of 缩写= MASCULINE

mas·ca·ra /mæsˈkærə; mæˈskɑːrə/ *n* [U] a dark substance used by women to colour their EYELASH*es* and make them look thicker 睫毛膏,睫毛油 —see picture at 参见 MAKE-UP 图

mas·cot /ˈmæskɑt; ˈmæskət/ *n* [C] an animal, toy etc that represents a team or organization, and is thought to bring them good luck 吉祥物: *The team mascot is a grizzly bear.* 这支运动队的吉祥物是大灰熊。

mas·cu·line /ˈmæskjəlɪn; ˈmæskjʊlɪn/ *adj* **1** belonging to men, done by men, or considered to be typical of men 属于男性的; 男人做的; 男子气概的: *a masculine approach to the problem* 男人解决这一问题的方法 | *traditionally masculine subjects such as physics* 传统上属于男性的学科,如物理学 | *a dark, masculine face* 一张黝黑的男子汉的脸 **2** if a woman's appearance or voice is masculine, it is like a man's〔女子外貌或嗓音〕像男人的 **3** belonging to the class of words for males〔词〕阳性的〔此词指雄性生物〕: *'Drake' is the masculine word for 'duck'.* drake (公鸭)是 duck (鸭子)的阳性词。**4** a masculine noun, PRONOUN etc belongs to a class of words that have different INFLECTIONS from FEMININE or NEUTER words〔名词、代词等〕阳性的〔此词的词形变化与语法中阴性或中性的词不同〕: *The word for 'book' is masculine in French.* "书"这个词在法语里是阳性的。

mas·cu·lin·i·ty /ˌmæskjəˈlɪnətɪ; ˌmæskjʊˈlɪnɪti/ *n* [U] the characteristics and qualities considered to be typical of men 男性; 阳性; 男子气: *Children's ideas of masculinity tend to come from their fathers.* 孩子们对于何谓男子气的观念往往来自他们的父亲。

Mase·field /ˈmesfild; ˈmeɪsfiːld/**, John** (1878-1967) a British writer and sailor who wrote poems about the sea, such as *Sea Fever* and *Cargoes*. He became POET LAUREATE (=the Queen's official poet) in 1930. 梅斯菲尔德〔(1878-1967),英国作家、海员。他写有咏海洋的诗篇,如《海之恋》和《货物》,1930年获桂冠诗人称号〕

ma·ser /ˈmezɚ; ˈmeɪzə/ *n* [C] a piece of equipment that produces a very powerful electric force〔能产生极强电能的〕微波激射器 —compare 比较 LASER

Mas·e·ra·ti /ˌmɑsˈrɑtɪ; ˌmæzəˈrɑːti/ *trademark* a type of Italian sports car, famous for its speed and style【商标】玛莎拉蒂〔一种意大利高级跑车,以速度和款式著称〕

M·A·S·H /mæʃ; mæʃ/ a very popular US television programme (1972-82), based on Robert Altman's film of the same name (1970) about a US army medical camp during the Korean War. Although it treated the subject in a humorous way, it also showed the serious effects that war had on people. The letters stand for 'Mobile Army Surgical Hospital'.《陆军野战外科医院》〔美国一流行电视剧(1972-1982),根据罗伯特·奥尔特曼的同名影片(1970)改编,讲述的是朝鲜战争期间美国一家陆军医院发生的事。影片处理主题的笔调幽默风趣,但也反映了战争给人民造成的严重影响。MASH 即 Mobile Army Surgical Hospital 的缩写〕

M

mash[1] also 又作 **mash up** *v* [T] to crush something, especially a food that has been cooked, until it is soft and smooth 把〔某物,尤指已做熟的食物〕捣成泥状,捣烂: *Mash the banana and add it to the batter.* 把香蕉捣成泥状,然后掺到面糊里。—**masher** *n* [C] —see picture on page A11 参见 A11 页图

mash[2] *n* [U] **1** *BrE informal* potatoes that have been boiled and then crushed until they are smooth; MASHED POTATO【英,非正式】马铃薯泥,土豆泥: *bangers and mash* 香肠和土豆泥 **2** a mixture of grain cooked with water to make a food for animals〔不同谷物混合煮成的〕糊状饲料 **3** a mixture of MALT[1] (1) or crushed grain and hot water, used to make beer or WHISKY〔酿制啤酒或威士忌酒的〕麦芽浆

mashed po·ta·to /ˌ· ·ˈ··/ also 又作 **mashed potatoes** *n* [U] potatoes that have been boiled and then crushed until they are smooth 马铃薯泥,土豆泥

masks 面具; 口罩

gas mask
防毒面具

surgeon's mask
外科口罩

mask[1] /mæsk; mɑːsk/ *n* [C] **1** something that covers all or part of your face, to protect or to hide it 面具; 面罩; 口罩: *a surgical face mask* 外科手术口罩 **2** something that covers your face, and has another face painted on it 假面具,假面: *special masks used in Kabuki theater* 日本歌舞伎戏剧中专用的假面具 **3** [usually singular 一般用单数] an expression or way of behaving that hides your real emotions or character 伪装; 掩饰: *Her sarcasm is only a mask for her insecurity.* 她说挖苦话只是为了掩饰她的焦虑不安。—see also 另见 DEATH MASK, GAS MASK

mask[2] *v* [T] **1** to cover something so that it cannot be properly seen 遮盖,遮住: *an ugly concrete wall partially masked by straggling ivy* 一堵难看的水泥墙,其中一部分被蔓生的常春藤所掩盖 **2** a smell, taste, sound etc that is masked by a stronger one cannot be noticed because of it 盖住〔气味、味道、声音等〕**3** to hide the truth about a situation, about how you feel etc 掩饰,隐瞒,掩盖: *His clownishness masks his loneliness.* 他滑稽的举止掩盖着他内心的孤寂。| *so-called democratic institutions that mask the reality of power in Britain* 掩盖英国权力真相的所谓民主制度

masked /mæskt; mɑːskt/ *adj* wearing a mask 戴面具的; 戴面罩的; 戴口罩的

masked ball /ˌ· ˈ·/ *n* [C] a formal dance at which everyone wears masks 假面舞会; 化装舞会

masking tape /ˈ·· ˌ·/ *n* [U] long narrow paper that is sticky on one side, used especially to protect the edge of an area which you are painting〔绘画或喷漆时用的〕遮蔽胶带

mas·o·chis·m /ˈmæzəˌkɪzəm; ˈmæsəkɪzəm/ *n* [U] **1** enjoyment of being hurt or punished 受虐狂 **2** sexual behaviour in which you gain pleasure from being hurt 性受虐狂 —**masochist** *n* [C] —**masochistic** /ˌmæsəˈkɪstɪk; ˌmæsəˈkɪstɪk◂/ *adj*: *masochistic behavior* 受虐狂行为 —compare 比较 SADISM

ma·son /ˈmesn̩; ˈmeɪsən/ *n* [C] **1** a STONEMASON 石匠,石工 **2** a FREEMASON 共济会会员

Mason, Perry the main character in the books of Erle Stanley Gardner and in the US television programme *Perry Mason* (1957-66), about a defence lawyer who always finds out who the criminals are in the legal cases he has to defend 梅森〔厄尔·斯坦利·加德纳的小说和美国电视剧《佩里·梅森》(1957-1966)中的主人公。故事的主人公是一位辩护律师,每每能找出自己辩护的案件中真正的罪犯〕

Mason-Dix·on Line, the /ˌmesn̩ ˈdɪksn̩ laɪn; ˌmeɪsən ˈdɪksən laɪn/ *n* [singular] the border between the states of Maryland and Pennsylvania in the US. It divided the states of the South, where it was legal to own SLAVE*s*, from the states of the North, where it was illegal, until the end of the American Civil War. Some people still consider it to be a dividing line between the North and South of the US. 梅森-狄克森线〔美国马里兰州和宾夕法尼亚州的分界线。南北战争结束之前,这里曾是南方诸州和北方诸州的分界线。在这条线以南拥有黑奴是合法的。现在,有些人仍把它视为美国的南北分界线〕

Ma·son·ic /mə`sɑnɪk; mə'sɒnɪk/ *adj* involved or connected with Freemasons 共济会会员的: *a Masonic lodge* 共济会地方分会集会处

Mason jar /'·· ·/ *n* [C] *AmE* a glass pot with a tight lid used for preserving fruit and vegetables【美】梅森食品瓶〔一种带密封盖的玻璃瓶, 用于保存水果和蔬菜〕

ma·son·ry /`mesn̩rɪ; 'meɪsənri/ *n* [U] **1** the stones and MORTAR (=material which holds stones together) from which a building, wall etc is made〔盖房屋、砌墙等用的〕石料和砂浆: *Several people had been buried under falling masonry.* 好几个人被埋在坠落的砖石下面。**2** the skill of building with stone 砌石技艺 **3** FREEMASONRY 共济会的制度; 共济会仪式

Ma·so·ra, the /mə`sɔrə; mə'sɔːrə/ also 又作 **the Masorah** a set of notes about the Hebrew Bible, written by Jewish SCHOLARS between the sixth and the tenth centuries AD《圣经》马所拉本〔希伯来文《圣经》的系列评注, 公元6至10世纪期间由犹太学者写成〕

masque /mæsk; mɑːsk/ *n* [C] a play written in the 16th and 17th centuries that was written in poetry and included music, dancing, and songs 假面剧〔16、17世纪以诗歌形式写成的戏剧, 有音乐和歌舞〕

mas·que·rade¹ /,mæskə`red; ,mæskə'reɪd/ *n* **1** [C] a formal dance where people wear MASKs and unusual clothes 假面舞会, 化装舞会 **2** [C,U] a way of behaving or speaking that hides your true thoughts or feelings 伪装; 掩饰: *She didn't really love him, but she kept up the masquerade for years.* 她并不真正爱他, 但她却一直伪装了许多年。**3** [C] *AmE old-fashioned* a party at which people wear unusual clothes【美, 过时】穿奇装异服参加的聚会

masquerade² *v* [I] to pretend to be something or someone different 假装; 伪装; 假扮: [+as] *secret police officers masquerading as demonstrators* 伪装成示威者的秘密警察

Mass /mæs; mæs/ *n* **1** [C,U] the main ceremony in some Christian churches, especially the Roman Catholic Church 弥撒: **say/celebrate Mass** (=perform this ceremony as a priest) 做/主持弥撒 **2** [C] a piece of music written to be played at this ceremony 弥撒曲: *Mozart's Mass in C Minor* 莫扎特的《C小调弥撒曲》

2 **mass¹** *n*

1 ▶LARGE AMOUNT 大量◀ a) [C] a large amount of a substance, liquid, or gas, that does not have a clear shape 团, 块, 堆: *The food had all congealed into a sticky mass.* 食物全都凝结成了黏糊糊的一团。| [+of] *A mass of almost pure white cloud lay below us.* 一团近乎纯白的云朵飘浮在我们下面。**b) a mass of** a large amount or quantity of something 大量, 大宗: *a huge mass of data* 大量资料 | *The yard was just a mass of weeds.* 院子里简直是杂草丛生。**c) masses of** *BrE informal* a large amount of something, or a lot of people or things【英, 非正式】许多的, 大量的〔人或物〕: *Masses of books covered every surface in the room.* 大量的书籍摊满了整个房间。| *We still had masses of time to spare.* 我们仍然可以抽出许多时间。

2 ▶CROWD 人群◀ [singular] a large crowd 一大群人: [+of] *There was a mass of people around the club entrance.* 俱乐部门口聚集着一大群人。| **a solid mass** *The road was blocked by a solid mass of protesters.* 道路被密密麻麻的抗议者阻塞了。

3 the masses all the ordinary people in society who do not have power or influence, and are thought of as not being very educated 群众, 平民

4 the mass of people/workers/the population etc most of the people in a group or society; the MAJORITY 人民/工人/人口等的大多数: *The mass of black children there have fewer educational opportunities than their white counterparts.* 那里的大多数黑人孩子受教育的机会比当地的白人孩子都要少。

5 ▶SCIENCE 科学◀ [U] *technical* in science, mass is the amount of material in something【术语】质量: *the mass of a star* 恒星的质量

3 **mass²** *adj* [only before noun 仅用于名词前] **1** involving or intended for a very large number of people 民众的, 群众的; 大量的: *Radio can reach mass audiences.* 无线广播能够覆盖大量的听众。| *a mass protest* 群众抗议 **2 mass murderer** someone who has murdered a lot of people 杀了很多人的凶手

mass³ *v* [I,T] to come together, or make people or things come together, in a large group 聚集, 集结, 集中: *grey clouds massing behind the mountains* 灰色云团在群山之后积聚 | *The country massed several divisions of troops along its border.* 该国沿其边境地区集结了好几个师的军队。

Mas·sa·chu·setts /,mæsə`tʃusəts; ,mæsə'tʃuːsɪ̆ts/ abbreviation 缩写为 **MA** a state in the northeast of the US which has Boston as its capital city, and was the place where the Pilgrim Fathers first landed in America. It was one of the 13 original states of the US, and is famous for its universities, especially Harvard and MIT, and for its coast, which is popular with tourists in the summer. 马萨诸塞州〔美国东北部一州, 首府波士顿, 曾是清教徒先辈移民首次登陆美洲的地方。该州是美国最初成立的13个州之一, 以哈佛大学和麻省理工学院等名牌大学闻名。该州是夏季旅游的好去处〕

mas·sa·cre¹ /`mæsəkɚ; 'mæsəkə/ *v* [T] **1** to kill a lot of people, especially people who cannot defend themselves 大规模屠杀: *The army massacred 642 French civilians.* 那支军队屠杀了642个法国平民。—see 见 KILL¹ (USAGE) **2** *informal* to defeat someone very badly in a game or competition【非正式】〔在比赛或竞争中〕彻底击败

massacre² *n* **1** [C,U] the killing of a lot of people, especially people who cannot defend themselves 大屠杀: *One man, the only survivor of the massacre, lived to tell the gruesome story.* 一个男人 —— 那次大屠杀的唯一幸存者 —— 活了下来讲述当时发生的令人毛骨悚然的事。**2** [C] *informal* a very bad defeat in a game or competition【非正式】〔比赛或竞争中的〕惨败: *United lost in a 9-0 massacre.* 联队以零比九惨败。

Massacre of the In·no·ents, the /,·· · · ·'··/ a story in the New Testament of the Bible in which King Herod hears about the birth of the Messiah in Bethlehem. He orders all male babies in the town to be killed so that the Messiah will not live, but Jesus and his family escape before this happens. 屠杀男婴〔《圣经·新约》中的一则故事。希律王听说弥赛亚在伯利恒出生, 便下令将全城男婴杀死, 以灭除弥赛亚。耶稣一家在大屠杀之前逃出了伯利恒〕

mas·sage¹ /mə`sɑʒ; 'mæsɑːʒ/ *n* [C,U] the action of pressing and rubbing someone's body with your hands, to help them relax or to reduce pain in their muscles 按摩; 推拿: *Massage helps ease the pain.* 按摩有助于缓解疼痛。| **give/have a massage** *She gave me a relaxing massage.* 她给我做了一次按摩, 让我放松下来。

massage² *v* [T] **1** to press and rub someone's body with your hands, to help them relax or to reduce pain in their muscles 为…做按摩, 给…推拿: *Alex massaged Helena's aching back.* 亚历克斯给海伦娜疼痛的脊背做了推拿。—see picture on page A20 参见A20页图 **2** to change official numbers or information in order to make them seem better than they are 篡改〔官方数字或资料〕: *massaging the unemployment statistics* 篡改失业统计数据 **3 massage sb's ego** to try to make someone feel that they are important, attractive, intelligent etc 对某人讨好奉承, 拍某人的马屁: *secretaries who are expected to drop everything to get coffee or massage their boss's ego* 被指望放下一切事情为老板端来咖啡或对其讨好奉承的秘书们

massage par·lour *BrE*【英】, **massage parlor** *AmE*【美】/'·· ,··/ *n* [C] **1** a word meaning a BROTHEL (=place where people pay to have sex), used to pretend that it is not a brothel〔打着按摩院旗号以掩人耳目的〕妓院 **2** a place where you pay to have a MASSAGE 按摩院

masse —see 见 EN MASSE

massed /mæst; mæst/ *adj* **massed bands/choirs etc** a large number of musical groups playing together as one very large group 联合大乐队/大合唱团等

mas·seur /mæ`sɝ; mæ'sɜː/ *n* [C] someone who gives MASSAGEs 按摩师

mas·seuse /mæ`sɝz; mæ'sɜːz/ *n* [C] a woman who gives MASSAGEs 女按摩师

mas·sif /mæ`sif; 'mæsiːf/ *n* [C] *technical* a group of mountains forming one large solid shape【术语】山峦, 山岳

mas·sive /`mæsɪv; 'mæsɪv/ *adj* **1** very large, solid, and heavy 大而重的, 厚重的: *The bell is massive, weighing over 40 tons.* 那口钟非常大, 重量超过40吨。| *the castle's massive walls* 城堡的高大围墙 **2** unusually large, powerful, or damaging 巨大的; 强大的, 强烈的; 极具破坏力的: *a massive tax bill* 一张巨额税单 | *I had a massive argument with Vicky yesterday.* 我昨天同维基进行了一场十分激烈的辩论。| **a massive stroke/heart attack etc** *He suffered a massive haemorrhage.* 他遭受了一次大出血。 S2 W3

mass me·di·a, the /,· '···/ *n* all the people and organizations that provide information and news for the public, including television, radio, and newspapers 大众传播媒介〔包括电视、广播和报刊〕

mass-pro·duced /,· ·'·◂/ *adj* produced in large numbers using machinery, so that each object is the same and can be sold cheaply〔用机器〕大规模生产的, 大批量生产的: *mass-produced furniture* 大批量生产的家具 **—mass-produce** *v* [T] **—mass production** *n* [U]

M

mast /mæst; mɑːst/ *n* [C] **1** a tall pole on which the sails or flags on a ship are hung 船桅: **two/three masted** (=having two or three masts) 二/三桅的 —see picture at 参见 YACHT 图 **2** *BrE* a tall metal tower that sends out radio and television signals【英】〔发射无线电和电视信号的〕发射塔, 天线塔 **3** a tall pole on which a flag is hung 旗杆 —see also 另见 HALF-MAST

mas·tec·to·my /mæsˋtɛktəmɪ; mæˈstektəmi/ *n* [C] *technical* a medical operation to remove a breast【术语】乳房切除手术

Mas·ter /ˈmæstə; ˈmɑːstə/ *n* [C] **1** *old-fashioned* a way of addressing or referring to young boys【过时】少爷〔对小男孩的称呼或用于指小男孩〕: *How's young Master Toby today?* 托比小少爷今天好吗? **2** a religious leader in some religions 宗教领袖: *a Sufi Master* 一位〔伊斯兰教〕苏非派领袖 **3** the person who is in charge of some British university colleges〔英国某些大学学院的〕院长: *the Master of Trinity College, Cambridge* 剑桥大学三一学院院长

master¹ *n* [C]

1▶OWNER/LEADER 主人/领导◀ *old-fashioned* a man who has control or authority over other people, for example servants or workers【过时】主人; 雇主: *His staff were always very loyal to their master.* 他的所有雇员总是对雇主忠心耿耿。| **be your own master** (=control your own work or life) 自己当老板, 自己作主 *I started this business because I wanted to be my own master.* 我开这家公司是因为我想自己当老板。—compare 比较 MISTRESS

2 be master of to be in complete control of a situation 完全控制, 掌握: *Without these changes, Africa cannot be master of its own economic destiny.* 没有这些变化, 非洲就不能掌握自己的经济命运。

3▶SKILLED 有技能的◀ someone who is very skilled at something 大师; 能手; 手工艺灵巧的人: *Runyon was a master of the short story.* 鲁尼恩是一位短篇小说大师。| *learning from an acknowledged master* 向公认的大师学习

4 be a past master to be very good at doing something because you have done it a lot 擅长于, 善于, 精于: [+at/in/of] *He's a past master at getting free drinks out of people.* 他十分善于让人家请他喝酒。

5▶ORIGINAL 原物◀ a document, record etc from which copies are made 原件; 原版; 母(磁)带: *I gave him the master to copy.* 我把原件给他复制。

6▶TEACHER 教师◀ *BrE old-fashioned* a male teacher【英, 过时】男教师: *the maths master* 男数学教师 —see also 另见 HEADMASTER

7▶DOG OWNER 狗的主人◀ the male owner of a dog 狗的男主人: *a dog and its master* 狗和它的男主人

8▶SHIP 船◀ someone who commands a ship 船长 —see also 另见 GRAND MASTER, OLD MASTER, QUIZ-MASTER

master² *v* [T] **1** to learn a skill or a language so well that you understand it completely and have no difficulty with it 掌握, 精通: *that well-known difficulty of mastering the Chinese writing system* 掌握汉语书写系统那个众所周知的难题 **2 master your fear/weakness etc** to manage to control a strong emotion 控制住你的恐惧/软弱等

master³ *adj* [only before noun 仅用于名词前] **1 master copy/list/tape etc** the original thing from which copies are made 原始拷贝/清单/磁带等: *the master list of telephone numbers* 电话号码表的原件 **2** most important or main 最重要的; 主要的: *the master control center at NASA*〔美国〕国家航空和航天局的主要控制中心 **3 master craftsman/chef/plumber etc** someone who is very skilled at a particular job, especially a job that involves working with your hands 一流工匠/主厨/熟练水管工等

master-at-arms /ˌ··ˈ·/ *n* [C] an officer with police duties on a ship 船上的警卫官

master bed·room /ˈ··, ··/ *n* [C] the largest bedroom in a house or apartment, often with its own bathroom 主卧室

Mas·ter·Card /ˈmæstəˌkard; ˈmɑːstəkɑːd/ *trademark*【商标】**1** a large international credit card system operated by a group of banks 万事达国际信用卡系统 **2** a credit card belonging to the MasterCard system, used for obtaining goods and services which the user pays for later 万事达信用卡: *Do you take MasterCard?* 你们这儿可不可以用万事达信用卡?

master class /ˈ·· ·/ *n* [C] a lesson, especially in music, given to very skilful students by someone famous 高级音乐讲习班〔由名家给优秀生讲授的课, 尤指音乐课〕

mas·ter·ful /ˈmæstəfəl; ˈmɑːstəfəl/ *adj* **1** controlling people or situations in a skilful and confident way 善于控制人[局势]的: *We allowed him to take charge in his masterful way.* 我们让他以他那把握十足的方式负责把事情抓起来。**2** done with great skill and understanding 老练高明的: *a masterful analysis of the text* 对课文透彻的分析 —**masterfully** *adv*

master key /ˈ··, ·/ *n* [C] a key that will open all the door locks in a building 万能钥匙

mas·ter·ly /ˈmæstəlɪ; ˈmɑːstəli/ *adj* done or made very skilfully 熟练的; 巧妙的; 高明的: *a masterly analysis of the situation* 对局势高明的分析

mas·ter·mind¹ /ˈmæstəˌmaɪnd; ˈmɑːstəmaɪnd/ *n* [singular] someone who plans and organizes a complicated operation, especially a criminal operation〔尤指犯罪活动的〕出谋划策者: *the mastermind of an ingenious financial swindle* 一桩狡猾的金融诈骗案的谋划者

mastermind² *v* [T] to think of, plan, and organize a large, important, and difficult operation 策划, 组织〔重大而艰难的行动〕: *The election campaign was masterminded by Peter Walters.* 那次竞选运动是由彼得·沃尔特斯策划组织的。

Master of Arts /ˌ···ˈ·/ *n* [C] an MA 文学硕士; 文学硕士学位

master of ce·re·mo·nies /ˌ···ˈ····/ *n* [C] someone who introduces speakers or performers at a social or public occasion 司仪; 典礼官; EMCEE *AmE*【美】: *the master of ceremonies for the Miss World Pageant* 世界小姐选美大赛的司仪

Master of Sci·ence /ˌ···ˈ··/ *n* [C] an MSc 理学硕士; 理学硕士学位

Master of the Rolls /ˌ····ˈ·/ the most important judge in the Court of Appeal in England and Wales. Part of his job is to choose the judges who judge cases in this court. 主事官〔英格兰和威尔士法庭的最高法官。其职责之一是选用本庭审案的法官〕

mas·ter·piece /ˈmæstəˌpis; ˈmɑːstəpiːs/ *n* [C] a work of art, piece of writing or music etc that is of very high quality or that is the best that a particular artist, writer etc has produced 杰作; 名作; 最佳作; 代表作: *Mary Shelley was just 18 when she wrote the horror masterpiece 'Frankenstein'.* 玛丽·雪莱18岁时就写出了恐怖小说名作《弗兰肯斯坦》。| **a masterpiece of** (=a very good example of) 极好的例证 *His speech was a masterpiece of ambiguity.* 他的讲话是含糊其辞的典范。

master plan /ˈ·· ·/ *n* [C usually singular 一般用单数] a detailed plan for controlling everything that happens in a complicated situation 总体规划: *an irrigation master plan* 灌溉总体规划

Masters, William Howell —see 见 MASTERS AND JOHNSON

Masters and John·son /ˌ···ˈ·/ two American scientists, **William Howell Masters** (1915-2001) and **Virginia Eshelman Johnson** (1925-), who have studied human sexual behaviour, and written several books on the subject, including *Human Sexual Response*. 马斯特斯和约翰逊〔美国科学家, 即威廉·豪厄尔·马斯特斯(1915-2001)和弗吉尼亚·埃什尔曼·约翰逊(1925-)。他们研究人类的性行为, 写有多部专著, 其中包括《人类性反应》〕

Masters Tour·na·ment, the /ˈ··, ··/ also 又作 **US Masters Tournament, US Masters** a GOLF competition held once each year in the US 优秀选手赛, 名人赛, 大师赛〔一年一度在美国举行的一种高尔夫球比赛〕

mas·ter's /ˈmæstəz; ˈmɑːstəz/ *n* [C] *informal* a MASTER'S DEGREE【非正式】硕士学位

master's de·gree /ˈ··, ·/ *n* [C] a university degree such as an MA or an MSc, which you get by studying for one or two years after your first degree〔大学授予的文学或理学等〕硕士学位

mas·ter·stroke /ˈmæstəˌstrok; ˈmɑːstəstrəʊk/ *n* [C] a very clever, skilful, and often unexpected action that is completely successful 绝招, 高招; 妙举: *a masterstroke of diplomacy* 高明的外交手腕

master switch /ˈ··, ·/ *n* [C] the SWITCH that controls the supply of electricity to the whole of a building or area〔电源的〕主控开关, 总开关

mas·ter·work /ˈmæstəˌwɝk; ˈmɑːstəwɜːk/ *n* [C] a painting, SCULPTURE, piece of music etc that is the best that someone has done; MASTERPIECE〔油画、雕塑、音乐作品等的〕杰作; 名作; 最佳作; 代表作

mas·ter·y /ˈmæstərɪ; ˈmɑːstəri/ *n* [U] **1** complete control or power over someone or something 完全控制; 控制权: [+of/over] *man's mastery over his environment* 人类对环境的控制 **2** thorough understanding or great skill 熟练; 精通: [+of/over] *She combines technical mastery of her instrument with great flair and originality.* 她把熟练的乐器演奏技巧与巨大的天赋和创造力结合在一起。

mast·head /ˈmæstˌhɛd; ˈmɑːsthed/ *n* [C] **1** the name of a newspaper, magazine etc printed in a special design at the top

of the first page〔以特别设计印在首页上方的〕报刊[杂志]名称, 刊头 **2** the top of a MAST on a ship〔船只的〕桅顶

mas·tic /ˈmæstɪk; ˈmæstɪk/ *n* [U] a type of glue that does not crack or break when it is bent 玛琋脂; 胶黏剂, 胶合铺料

mas·ti·cate /ˈmæstəˌket; ˈmæstɪkeɪt/ *v* [I,T] *technical* to CHEW (=crush food between the teeth)【术语】咀嚼 —**mastication** /ˌmæstəˈkeʃən; ˌmæstɪˈkeɪʃən/ *n* [U]

mas·tiff /ˈmæstɪf; ˈmæstɪf/ *n* [C] a large, strong dog often used to guard houses〔常用于看家的〕獒, 大驯犬

Mas·troi·an·ni Mar·cel·lo /ˌmæstrɔɪˈjɑnɪ; ˌmæstrɔɪˈjɑːni/ /mɑrˈtʃɛlo; mɑːˈtʃeləʊ/ (1924-97) one of the greatest Italian film actors, famous especially for the film *La Dolce Vita* (1960) 马斯特罗亚尼〔(1924-1997), 意大利最出色的电影演员之一, 尤以影片《甜蜜生活》(1960) 而闻名〕

mas·tur·bate /ˈmæstɚˌbet; ˈmæstəbeɪt/ *v* [I] to make yourself sexually excited by touching or rubbing your sexual organs 手淫, 自渎, 自慰 —**masturbation** /ˌmæstɚˈbeʃən; ˌmæstəˈbeɪʃən/ *n* [U]

mat¹ /mæt; mæt/ *n* [C] **1** a small piece of thick rough material which covers part of a floor 地垫; 地席; 小地毯: *Wipe your feet on the mat.* 在地垫上蹭蹭你的脚。**2** a small flat piece of wood, cloth etc which protects a surface, especially on a table〔尤指用以保护桌面的木质或布质〕小垫子 **3** a piece of thick soft material used in some sports for people to fall onto〔某些体育运动中用的〕厚软垫 **4** **a mat of hair/fur/grass etc** a thick mass of pieces of hair etc which are stuck together〔绞在一起的〕一簇头发/兽毛/草等 —see also 另见 MATTING

mat² *adj* another spelling of MATT matt 的另一种拼法

mat·a·dor /ˈmætəˌdɔr; ˈmætədɔː/ *n* [C] a man who fights and kills BULLs during a BULLFIGHT 斗牛士

matador 斗牛士

Ma·ta Ha·ri /ˌmɑtə ˈhɑrɪ; ˌmɑːtə ˈhɑːri/ (1876-1917) a Dutch dancer and member of the German secret service in Paris during World War I, who obtained military secrets from Allied army officers of high rank. She was tried in court and shot by the French. Her name is sometimes used to represent an attractive woman that men want to please. 玛塔〔(1876-1917), 荷兰舞蹈演员, 一战期间德国驻巴黎秘密情报机构成员。她从协约国高级军官口中套取军事秘密, 后在法国受审并被执行枪决。她的名字有时用于指称男人欲想取悦的美貌女子〕

match¹ /mætʃ; mætʃ/ *n*

1 ▶FIRE 火◀ [C] a small wooden or paper stick, used to light a fire, cigarette etc 火柴: *a box of matches* 一盒火柴 | **strike a match** (=rub a match against a surface to produce a flame) 划火柴 | **put a match to** (=make something burn by using a match) 用火柴点燃 *I tore up the letter and put a match to it.* 我把信撕碎, 然后用火柴把它点着了。—see picture at 参见 LABORATORY 图

2 ▶GAME 比赛◀ [C] *especially BrE* an organized sports event between two teams or people【尤英】比赛, 竞赛: *a violent incident during Chelsea's match against Liverpool* 在切尔西队对利物浦队的比赛中发生的暴力事件 | *a cricket match* 板球比赛

3 ▶COLOURS/PATTERNS 颜色/图案◀ [singular] something that is the same colour or pattern as something else, or looks attractive with it〔颜色或图案上的〕相似[相配]之物: [+for] *That shirt's a perfect match for your blue skirt.* 那件衬衫和你的蓝裙子完全相配。

4 be more than a match for to be much stronger, cleverer etc than an opponent 比…强[聪明]得多, 远胜过

5 be no match for to be much less strong, clever etc than an opponent 根本不是…的对手: *Carlos was no match for the champion.* 卡洛斯远远不是那位冠军的对手。

6 a slanging/shouting match a loud angry argument in which two people insult each other 相互高声谩骂

7 be a perfect match if two people who love each other are a perfect match, they are very suitable for each other 是天作之合, 是非常般配的一对

8 make a good match *old-fashioned* to marry a suitable person【过时】结成良缘

9 ▶SUITABILITY 适宜◀ [singular] a situation in which something is suitable for something else, so that the two things work together successfully 适合, 适应; 匹配: [+between] *We need to establish a match between students' needs and teaching methods.* 我们有必要使教学方法适应学生的需要。—see also 另见 **meet your match** (MEET¹ (16)), **mix and match** (MIX¹ (7))

match² *v*

1 ▶LOOK GOOD TOGETHER 互相匹配, 相称◀ [I,T] if one thing matches another, or if two things match, they look attractive together because they have a similar colour, pattern etc (与…)相配, 相称: *The towels match the color of the bathroom tiles.* 这些毛巾和浴室瓷砖的色调很匹配。| **sth to match** (=something which matches) 相配之物 *a dining table with four chairs to match* 餐桌和与之相配的四把椅子 —see also 另见 MATCHING —see 见 FIT¹ (USAGE)

2 ▶LOOK THE SAME 看起来相同◀ [I,T] if one thing matches another or if two things match, they look the same (与…)成对: *Your socks don't match.* 你那两只袜子不是一双。

3 ▶SEEM THE SAME 好像一样, 相似◀ [I,T] if two reports or pieces of information match, or if one matches the other, there is no important difference between them (和…)相似, (和…)基本一致: *The witnesses' stories just didn't match.* 证人的证词不能相互印证。| *Traces of blood on the knife matched the suspect's blood-type.* 刀上的血迹与嫌疑犯的血型一致。

4 ▶PROVIDE WHAT IS NEEDED 提供所需之物◀ [T] to provide something that is suitable for a situation or enough for the people who need it 适应, 满足: *creating sufficient employment to match the rising population* 创造足够的就业机会以适应日益增长的人口的需要 | *teaching materials that match the individual needs of students* 适应学生各自所需的教材

5 ▶FIND STH/SB SIMILAR 找到相似的物/人◀ [T] to find something that is similar to or suitable for something else 找到与…相似[相配]之物: **match sth/sb to** *We get the children to match the animal pictures to the correct sounds.* 我们让孩子们把动物图片与正确的声音相配对。

6 ▶BE AS GOOD AS 与…一样好◀ [T] to be as skilful, intelligent etc as something or someone else 敌得过; 比得上: *No one can match Holden when it comes to winning an argument.* 说到在争论中获胜没有人比得上霍尔登。| *I've never seen a goal to match that one.* 我从未见过哪一次进球堪与那次相媲美。

7 well-matched/ill-matched very suitable/very unsuitable for each other 很相配的/很不相配的: *a well-matched pair* 十分相配的一对

8 evenly matched if two competitors are evenly matched they are equal in strength, skill, speed etc 旗鼓相当的, 势均力敌的

9 ▶GIVE MONEY 提供资金◀ [T] to give a sum of money equal to a sum given by someone else 提供〔同等数额的资金〕: *The government has promised to match any private donations to the earthquake fund.* 政府已经承诺给防震基金提供与个人捐款等额的资金。

10 ▶MAKE EQUAL 使相等◀ [T] to make something equal to or suitable for something else 使相等; 使相适应: **match sth to sth** *Match your spending to your income.* 你应该量入为出。

11 be matched with/against to be competing against someone else in a game or competition〔在体育运动或竞赛中〕与…相较量: *Agassi will be matched against Sampras in the men's final.* 阿加西在男子决赛中将与桑普拉斯对阵。

match up *phr v* **1** [I] if two reports or pieces of information match up, they seem the same〔两则报道或消息〕相似 **2** [**match** sth **up to** sth] to find something that is similar to or suitable for something else 把…和…配对起来 **3 match up to your hopes/expectations/ideals etc** to be as good as you expected, hoped etc 和所希望/期待/想象等的同样好

match·book /ˈmætʃbʊk; ˈmætʃbʊk/ *n* [C] a small folded piece of thick paper containing paper matches 纸夹火柴

match·box /ˈmætʃˌbɑks; ˈmætʃbɒks/ *n* [C] a small box containing matches 火柴盒

match·ing /ˈmætʃɪŋ; ˈmætʃɪŋ/ *adj* having the same colour, style, or pattern as something else〔与某物颜色、风格或式样〕相同的, 相配的: *pink cushions and a matching bedspread* 粉色的垫子和与之相配的床罩

match·less /ˈmætʃlɪs; ˈmætʃləs/ *adj literary* more intelligent, beautiful etc than anyone or anything else【文】无可匹敌的, 无双的: *the matchless beauty of the Parthenon* 帕台农神殿那无与伦比的美

match·mak·er /ˈmætʃˌmekɚ; ˈmætʃˌmeɪkə/ *n* [C] someone who tries to find a suitable partner for someone else to marry 媒人 —**matchmaking** *n* [U]

match point /ˌ· ˈ·/ *n* **1** [U] a situation in tennis when the person who wins the next point will win the match〔网球赛中再赢得一分即能胜出的〕决胜时刻 **2** [C] the point that a player

must win in order to win the match 赛点, 决胜分 —compare 比较 GAME POINT

match·stick /ˈmætʃˌstɪk; ˈmætʃˌstɪk/ *n* [C] **1** a wooden MATCH[1] (1) 火柴杆, 火柴棍 **2 matchstick men/figures** people drawn with thin lines to represent their arms, legs, and bodies, as if by a child〔似小孩所画的〕火柴棍人 / 人形

match·wood /ˈmætʃˌwʊd; ˈmætʃwʊd/ *n* **break/splinter etc into matchwood** to be broken into very small pieces of wood 裂成碎木片: *Their boat hit the rocks and splintered into matchwood.* 他们的小船撞在岩石上, 裂成了碎片。

3 **mate¹** /met; meɪt/ *n*

1 schoolmate/roommate/workmate etc someone you study with, live with etc 同学 / 同屋 / 同事等: *My flatmate and I aren't getting on very well!* 与我同住一套公寓的那个人跟我不大合得来! —see also 另见 RUNNING MATE, SOUL MATE

2 ▶FRIEND 朋友◀ a) [C] *BrE informal* a friend【英, 非正式】朋友, 伙伴: *I'm going out with my mates tonight.* 今天晚上我要跟伙伴们出去。**b)** *BrE and AustrE informal* used by men as a friendly way to address a man【英和澳, 非正式】老兄〔男人对男人友好的称呼〕: *What's the time, mate?* 老兄, 几点了?

3 ▶ANIMAL 动物◀ [C] the sexual partner of an animal〔动物的〕配偶

4 ▶HUSBAND/WIFE 夫/妻◀ *especially AmE* a word meaning your husband or wife, used especially in magazines【尤美】丈夫; 妻子; 配偶〔尤用于杂志中〕: *Does your mate snore?* 你爱人打呼噜吗?

5 ▶PAIR OF OBJECTS 物体的一对◀ [C] *especially AmE* one of a pair of objects【尤美】一对中的一个, 配对物: *I can't find the mate to my glove.* 我找不到我的另一只手套了。

6 ▶SAILOR 海员◀ [C] a ship's officer who is one rank below the captain〔船上的〕大副

7 ▶NAVY OFFICER 海军军官◀ [C] a US Navy PETTY OFFICER〔美国海军的〕军士

8 builder's mate/plumber's mate etc *BrE* someone who works with and helps a skilled worker; ASSISTANT【英】建筑工 / 管子工等的助手

9 ▶GAME 比赛◀ [C,U] CHECKMATE in the game of CHESS〔国际象棋比赛中王棋的〕将死

mate² *v* **1** [I+with] if animals mate, they have sex to produce babies〔动物〕交配 **2** [T] to put animals together so that they will have sex and produce babies 使〔动物〕交配 **3** [T] to achieve the CHECKMATE of your opponent in CHESS〔国际象棋中〕将死

ma·ter /ˈmetɚ; ˈmeɪtə/ *n* [C] *BrE old-fashioned or humorous* mother【英, 过时或幽默】母亲, 妈妈 —compare 比较 PATER

1 1 **ma·te·ri·al¹** /məˈtɪrɪəl; məˈtɪəriəl/ *n* **1** [C,U] cloth used for making clothes, curtains etc; FABRIC (1) 料子, 衣料, 布料: *curtain material* 窗帘布 —see picture at 参见 CLOTHES 图 **2** [C,U] a solid substance such as wood, plastic, or metal from which things can be made 材料, 原料〈如木材、塑料、金属等〉: *building materials* 建筑材料 **3** [U] also 又作 **materials** [plural] the things that are used for making or doing something 材料: *Videos often make good teaching material.* 录像带常常可用作很好的教学材料。| *artists' materials* 艺术家使用的材料 **4** [U] information or ideas used in books, films etc〔用于书本、电影等中的〕素材: *His act contains a lot of new material.* 他的表演中包含着许多新的素材。| [+for] *Anita is collecting material for her new novel.* 安妮塔正在为她的新小说收集素材。**5 officer material/executive material etc** someone who is good enough for a particular job or position 当军官 / 管理人员等的材料: *He's a good soldier, but not really officer material.* 他是个好士兵, 但不是当军官的料。

3 **material²** *adj* [usually before noun 一般用于名词前] **1** connected with people's money, possessions, living conditions etc, rather than the needs of their mind or soul 物质上的, 非精神上的: **material comforts/needs/well-being etc** *Improvements in health were linked to increasing material prosperity.* 健康水平的提高是与物质上的日益繁荣联系在一起的。**2** connected with the real world and physical objects 物质的, 实体的, 有形的: *material existence* 物质存在 **3** *law* important and needing to be considered when making a decision【法律】重要的, 需予以考虑的: *material evidence* 重要证据 | [+to] *facts material to the investigation* 对调查很重要的事实 **4** important and having a noticeable effect 重大并有显著影响的: *material changes* 重大的变化 —see also 另见 MATERIALLY, RAW MATERIALS

ma·te·ri·al·is·m /məˈtɪrɪəlˌɪzəm; məˈtɪəriəlɪzəm/ *n* [U] **1** the belief that money and possessions are more important than art, religion, moral goodness etc 实利主义, 物质主义〔认为钱财比艺术、宗教、道德等更为重要的信仰〕 **2** *technical* the belief that only physical things really exist【术语】唯物主义, 唯物论 —**materialist** *adj, n* [C]

ma·te·ri·a·lis·tic /məˌtɪrɪəlˈɪstɪk; məˌtɪəriəˈlɪstɪk◂/ *adj* caring only about money and possessions rather than things of the mind such as art or religion 实利主义的, 物质主义的: *People nowadays are so materialistic.* 现在的人太实利主义了。—**materialistically** /-klɪ; -kli/ *adv*

ma·te·ri·al·ize also 又作 **-ise** *BrE*【英】/məˈtɪrɪəlˌaɪz; məˈtɪəriəlaɪz/ *v* [I] **1** to happen or appear in the way that you planned or expected 成为现实, 实现;〔像计划或预期的那样〕发生, 出现: *The money we had been promised failed to materialize.* 答应给我们的钱并没有兑现。**2** to appear in an unexpected and strange way 突然出现: *The figure of a man suddenly materialized in the shadows.* 在阴暗的地方突然出现了一个人影。—**materialization** /məˌtɪrɪələˈzeʃən; məˌtɪəriəlaɪˈzeɪʃən/ *n* [U]

ma·te·ri·al·ly /məˈtɪrɪəlɪ; məˈtɪəriəli/ *adv* **1** in a big enough or strong enough way to change a situation 极大地; 强有力地; 实质性地: *This would materially affect US security.* 这将会严重影响美国的安全。| *This improvement is not materially significant.* 这一改进在实质上并不重要。**2** in a way that concerns possessions and money, rather than the needs of a person's mind or soul 物质上: *Materially we are better off than ever before.* 在物质上我们比以前任何时候都好。

ma·té·ri·el /məˌtɪrɪˈɛl; məˌtɪəriˈel/ *n* [U] supplies of weapons used by an army〔供军队使用的〕武器装备

ma·ter·nal /məˈtɝnḷ; məˈtɜːnl/ *adj* **1** typical of the way a good mother behaves or feels 母性的; 慈母似的: *I'm not maternal enough to have kids.* 我母性不够, 不能要孩子。| *She kept a maternal eye on them all.* 她像母亲似地照管着他们所有人。| **maternal instincts** (=the desire to have babies and take care of them) 母亲的天性, 母性 **2** [only before noun 仅用于名词前] of a mother or connected with being a mother 母亲的; 与做母亲有关的: *the relationship between maternal age and infant mortality* 生育年龄与婴儿死亡率之间的关系 **3 maternal grandfather/aunt etc** your mother's father, sister etc 外祖父 / 姨母等〔母方的亲戚〕—compare 比较 PATERNAL —**maternally** *adv*

ma·ter·ni·ty¹ /məˈtɝnətɪ; məˈtɜːnəti/ *adj* [only before noun 仅用于名词前] **1 maternity clothes/dress etc** clothes etc used by women who are PREGNANT (=going to have a baby) 孕妇装 / 裙等 **2 maternity benefits/pay/allowance** the money that a woman is given by an employer or a government when she has a baby〔由雇主或政府支付的〕产妇津贴

maternity² *n* [U] the state of being a mother 母性; 母亲身份

maternity leave /ˈ· ··· ˌ·/ *n* [U] time that a mother is allowed to spend away from work when she has a baby 产假

CULTURAL NOTE 文化注释

Maternity leave is taken with permission from the employer and usually with part or full pay. In Britain, the law says that women who have worked for an employer for more than six months must be given maternity leave with some pay by the employer. In the US, maternity leave is decided by the employer, but many employers do not allow very much. 休产假须征得雇主的同意, 一般能领取部分或全额薪酬。在英国, 法律规定妇女被雇用超过六个月的, 雇主必须准予产假并给予一定薪酬。在美国产假由雇主决定, 但很多雇主并不会给太长时间的产假。

maternity ward /ˈ· ··· ˌ·/ *n* [C] a department in a hospital where women who are having babies are cared for 产科病房

mat·ey¹ /ˈmetɪ; ˈmeɪti/ *adj BrE informal* behaving as if you were someone's friend【英, 非正式】友好的; 亲近的; 亲热的: *She's been very matey with the boss recently.* 她近来跟老板很亲近。

matey² *n BrE* used by men as a very informal or disrespectful way of addressing other men【英】伙计〔男子之间十分随便或不讲礼貌的称呼〕

math /mæθ; mæθ/ *n* [U] *AmE* mathematics【美】数学 2

math·e·mat·i·cal /ˌmæθəˈmætɪkḷ; ˌmæθəˈmætɪkəl◂/ *adj* **1** connected with or using mathematics 数学的: *a mathematical equation* 数学方程 | *mathematical analysis* 数学分析 **2** calculating things in a careful, exact way 仔细而准确计算的: *The whole trip was planned with mathematical precision.* 整个旅行计划得十分周密。**3 a mathematical certainty** something that is completely certain to happen 肯定会发生的事, 确定无疑的事 **4 a mathematical chance (of)** a very small chance that something will happen 极小的可能性 —**mathematically** /-klɪ; -kli/ *adv*

math·e·ma·ti·cian /ˌmæθəməˈtɪʃən; ˌmæθəməˈtɪʃən/ *n* [C] someone who studies or teaches mathematics, or is a specialist in mathematics 数学家; 数学教师

math·e·mat·ics /ˌmæθəˋmætɪks; ˌmæθɪ̵ˈmætɪks/ *n* [U] the science of numbers and of shapes, including ALGEBRA, GEOMETRY, and ARITHMETIC 数学

mathematical notations
数学符号

= is equal to 等号
≠ is not equal to 不等号
> is greater than 大于号
< is less than 小于号
≥ is greater than or equal to 大于等于号
≤ is less than or equal to 小于等于号
+ add 加号
– subtract 减号
÷ divide 除号
× multiply 乘号

Math·er /ˋmæðɚ; ˈmæðə/, **Cotton** (1663-1728) a US Christian leader who was a Puritan. He supported the Salem Witch Trials in 1692, when a court in Salem, Massachusetts, decided that 20 people were guilty of WITCHCRAFT (=using magic for evil purposes) and killed them as punishment. 马瑟〔(1663-1728)，美国基督教会领袖，为清教徒。他支持1692年的"赛勒姆女巫审判案"。当时，马萨诸塞州赛勒姆的一个法庭裁定有20个人犯有玩弄巫术罪，并给他们判了死刑〕

2 **maths** /mæθs; mæθs/ *n* [U] *BrE informal* mathematics【英，非正式】数学

mat·i·née /ˌmætn̩ˋe; ˈmætɪ̵neɪ/ *n* [C] a performance of a play or film in the afternoon〔戏剧或电影的〕下午场，午后的演出[放映]

matinée i·dol /ˋ···, ···/ *n* [C] *old-fashioned* an actor who is very popular with women【过时】受女观众欢迎的男演员，女人的男偶像

matinée jack·et /ˋ···, ···/ *n* [C] *old-fashioned BrE* a short coat for a baby【过时，英】婴儿短外套

mat·ing /ˋmetɪŋ; ˈmeɪtɪŋ/ *n* [U] sex between animals〔动物的〕交配，交尾：*the mating season* 交配季节

mat·ins, mattins /ˋmætɪnz; ˈmætɪ̵nz/ *n* [U] the first prayers of the day in the Christian religion; MORNING PRAYER〔基督教的〕晨祷

Ma·tisse /mæˋtis; mæˈtiːs/, **Hen·ri** /ˋɑnrɪ; ˈɒnri/ (1869-1954) a French painter and SCULPTOR who helped to develop FAUVISM as a style of painting. His paintings are mostly of ordinary places and objects, but they use pure bright colours and black lines. 马蒂斯〔(1869-1954)，法国画家、雕塑家，曾促进发展了野兽派绘画风格。他的作品大多描绘普通地方和物体，但采用了鲜艳色彩和黑色线条〕

matri- /ˋmetrɪ; ˈmeɪtrɪ/ *prefix* **1** concerning mothers 母亲的：*matricide* (=killing one's own mother) 弑母 **2** concerning women 妇女的：*a matriarchal society* (=controlled by women) 女性统治的社会；母系社会 —compare 比较 PATRI-

ma·tri·arch /ˋmetrɪˌɑrk; ˈmeɪtriɑːk/ *n* [C] a woman, especially an older woman, who controls a family or a social group 女家长；女族长；〔社会团体的〕女统治者 —compare 比较 PATRIARCH (1)

ma·tri·ar·chal /ˌmetrɪˋɑrkl; ˌmeɪtriˈɑːkəl◂/ *adj* **1** ruled or controlled by women 妇女统治[控制]的：*a matriarchal society* 女权制社会；母系社会 **2** connected with or typical of a matriarch 女家长的；女族长的

ma·tri·ar·chy /ˋmetrɪˌɑrkɪ; ˈmeɪtriɑːki/ *n* [C,U] **1** a social system in which the oldest woman controls a family and its possessions 母权制，母系制 **2** a society in which women hold all the power 女权制社会；母系社会 —compare 比较 PATRIARCHY

mat·ri·cide /ˋmetrəˌsaɪd; ˈmætrɪ̵saɪd/ *n* [U] the crime of murdering your own mother 弑母罪 —compare 比较 PARRICIDE (1), PATRICIDE

ma·tric·u·late /məˋtrɪkjəˌlet; məˈtrɪkjɪ̵leɪt/ *v* [I] to officially start a course as a student at a university〔在大学〕注册入学 —**matriculation** /məˌtrɪkjəˋleʃən; məˌtrɪkjɪ̵ˈleɪʃən/ *n* [U]

mat·ri·mo·ny /ˋmætrəˌmonɪ; ˈmætrɪ̵məni/ *n* [U] *formal* the state of being married【正式】婚姻；婚姻生活 —**matrimonial** /ˌmætrəˋmonɪəl; ˌmætrɪ̵ˈməʊniəl/ *adj*

ma·trix /ˋmetrɪks; ˈmeɪtrɪks/ *n plural* **matrices** /-trɪˌsiz; -trɪ̵siːz/ *or* **matrixes** [C] *technical*【术语】**1** an arrangement of numbers, letters, or signs on a GRID (=a background of regular lines) used in mathematics, science etc〔数学等的〕矩阵 **2** a situation from which a person or society can grow and develop〔人或社会的〕发源地，摇篮：*the cultural matrix* 文化发源地 **3** a living part in which something is formed or developed, such as the substance out of which the FINGERNAILs grow 基质；床〈如指甲床〉 **4** a MOULD (=a hollow container) into which melted metal, plastic, etc is poured to form a shape 铸模，模子 **5** the rock in which hard stones or jewels have formed〔形成硬石或宝石的〕母岩，脉岩 —see also 另见 DOT-MATRIX PRINTER

ma·tron /ˋmetrən; ˈmeɪtrən/ *n* [C] **1** *BrE* a woman who works as a nurse in a school【英】〔学校的〕女护士，女总管 **2** *especially AmE* a woman who is in charge of women and children, for example in a prison【尤美】〔监狱等的〕女看守 **3** *BrE old-fashioned* a nurse who is in charge of the other nurses in a hospital【英，过时】护士长 **4** *especially literary* an older married woman【尤文】较年长的已婚妇女

ma·tron·ly /ˋmetrənlɪ; ˈmeɪtrənli/ *adj* a word to describe a woman who is fairly fat and no longer young, used to avoid saying this directly 发福的〔委婉语，用于较年长的女性〕

matron of hon·our *BrE*【英】, **matron of honor** *AmE*【美】/ˌ··ˋ··/ *n* [C] a married woman who helps the bride on her wedding day〔已婚的〕女傧相，伴娘 —compare 比较 BRIDESMAID

matt, mat, matte /mæt; mæt/ *adj* matt paint, colour, or photographs have a dull surface; not shiny〔油漆、颜色或照片〕表面无光泽的，暗淡的：*matt black* 无光黑色 — compare 比较 GLOSS[1] (4)

mat·ted /ˋmætɪd; ˈmætɪ̵d/ *adj* twisted or stuck together in a thick mass 缠结在一起的；乱成一团的：*matted fur* 缠结的乱毛 | *His hair was dirty and matted.* 他的头发很脏，而且乱蓬蓬的。

1 1
mat·ter[1] /ˋmætɚ; ˈmætə/ *n*

① SUBJECT/SITUATION 事情/事态
② STH WRONG WITH …出了问题
③ NO MATTER 无论
④ AS A MATTER OF 作为…的事
⑤ IT'S A MATTER OF 是…的问题
⑥ SMALL AMOUNT 少量
⑦ BOOKS/NEWSPAPERS 书籍/报纸
⑧ SUBSTANCE 物质
⑨ OTHER MEANINGS 其他意思

① SUBJECT/SITUATION 事情/事态

1 [C] a subject or situation that you have to think about or deal with 事情，情况：*You do realize this is a serious matter, don't you?* 你确实意识到这是一件严肃的事情，对吧？| *He wasn't particularly interested in financial matters.* 他对财务上的事不是特别感兴趣。| **a matter of importance/concern/regret etc** (=a subject that is important, that people worry about etc) 重要/人们关注/令人遗憾等的事情 *Wilson always consulted Landers on matters of importance.* 在重要问题上威尔逊总是和兰德斯商量。| *The King's mental state was becoming a matter of concern.* 国王的精神状况正成为一件人们关注的事。| **be a matter for** (=be something that a particular person or group should deal with) 是〔某人或团体〕应该处理的事 *If he was murdered, it's a matter for the police.* 如果他是被谋杀的，那么就该由警察来管了。| **the heart/crux of the matter** (=the most important part of a situation) 问题的核心 *The report didn't get to the heart of the matter.* 报告没有触及问题的核心。| **raise the matter with** (=discuss a subject with someone) 与〔某人〕讨论问题；向〔某人〕提出问题 *Have you raised the matter with your union representative?* 你与你们的工会代表讨论过这个问题吗？| **let the matter rest/drop** (=decide to stop worrying about something) 不再操心某事 *I'm prepared to let the whole matter drop if he apologizes.* 如果他道歉的话，我准备让整个事情到此为止。| **the matter at/in hand** (=the thing that you should be dealing with now) 目前需办理的事情 *Could we please concentrate on the matter in hand?* 我们可以集中精力处理手头上的事吗？

2 subject matter the subject that is discussed or shown in a book, film, article etc〔书、电影、文章等的〕主题，内容，素材：*Because of its adult subject matter, the film is not suitable for*

M

under-16s. 这部电影是成人题材的，所以不适合16岁以下的少年儿童观看。

3 it's no small/laughing matter used to say that something must be treated seriously 绝不是小事/开玩笑的事〔用以表示某事必须严肃对待〕: *He ended up with a broken pelvis, which is no laughing matter, I can tell you.* 他最后弄得骨盆断裂了，我可以告诉你，这不是闹着玩的事情。

4 that's the end of the matter/let that be an end to the matter *spoken* used to tell someone that you do not want to talk about something any more【口】此事到此为止〔用以表示不想再谈论某事〕: *We will not let you date until you're 16, and that's the end of the matter.* 你16岁之前我们不会让你约会的，这事不要再谈了。

5 be a different matter also 又作 **be quite another matter** *especially BrE* used to say that one situation or problem is much more serious than another【尤英】不是一回事，完全是另一码事〔用以表示某个情况或问题比另一个严重得多〕: *Having the occasional drink is one thing, but being drunk every night is quite another matter.* 偶尔喝点酒是一回事，但每晚都喝醉就完全是另一码事了。

6 matters *plural* a situation that you are in or have been describing 事态；谈到的情况: *Maybe some of these suggestions will help to improve matters.* 也许这些建议中有些将有助于事态的好转。| **not help matters** *spoken* (=make a situation worse)【口】使情况更糟 *I had a headache when I took the test, which didn't help matters.* 测验的时候我头疼起来，这使情况变得更糟了。

7 to make matters worse making a bad situation even worse 使不好的情况更糟: *The car had broken down, and to make matters worse, it was beginning to rain.* 车子坏了，更糟糕的是，天下起雨来了。

8 take matters into your own hands to deal with a problem yourself because other people have failed to deal with it〔因别人不能处理而〕把事情接过来亲自处理: *Local people took matters into their own hands and hired their own security guards.* 当地人自己动手来解决问题，雇用了他们自己的保安人员。

② STH WRONG WITH …出了问题

9 what's the matter?/is anything the matter? *spoken* used when someone seems upset, unhappy, or ill and you are asking them why【口】怎么了？/有什么麻烦吗？〔用以询问某人生气、不高兴或生病的原因〕: *What's the matter, Mary? Have you been crying?* 怎么啦，玛丽？你一直在哭吗？

10 what's the matter with *spoken* used to ask why something is not working normally, someone seems upset or ill, or something looks wrong【口】…怎么啦，…出什么毛病了: *What's the matter with Bill?* 比尔怎么了？| *"The television had to go back to the store." "Why, what's the matter with it?"* "那台电视机不得不退回了商店。""为什么，它出什么毛病了？"

11 there's something the matter with/something's the matter with *spoken* used to say that something is not working normally, someone is upset or ill, or something looks wrong【口】〔某物〕运行不正常[有问题]；〔某人〕生气[生病]: *There's something the matter with the washing machine – it keeps leaking.* 洗衣机有毛病了，它漏水漏个不停。

12 there's nothing the matter with *spoken* used to say that someone is not ill or upset, or that something is working properly or looks good【口】〔某人〕没生病[牛气]；〔某物〕一切正常，看起来不错: *There was nothing the matter with it when I lent it to him.* 我借给他的时候它并没有什么毛病。| *There's nothing the matter with your haircut – I really like it!* 你的发型不错，我很喜欢！

③ NO MATTER 无论

13 no matter how/where/what etc used to say that something is always the same whatever happens, or in spite of someone's efforts to change it 不管怎样/哪里/什么等: *No matter how hard he tried, he couldn't get her to change her mind.* 不管他怎样努力劝说，也没能使她改变主意。| *My parents always waited up for me, no matter what time I got home.* 无论我什么时候回家，父母总是等着我。

14 no matter what (happens) *spoken* used to say that you will definitely do something【口】不管（发生）什么事；无论如何: *I'll call you tonight no matter what.* 我今晚无论如何都会给你打电话。

15 no matter *spoken* used to say that something you have asked about is not important【口】不要紧，无关紧要: *"She's not in her office." "No matter, I'll try and call her at home."* "她不在办公室里。""没关系，我给她家里打电话试试看。"

④ AS A MATTER OF 作为…的事

16 as a matter of fact *especially spoken*【尤口】**a)** used when saying something, especially something surprising, that is connected with what you are talking about 事实上，其实: *I knew him when we were in college – as a matter of fact we were on the same course.* 我们在大学的时候我就认识他 —— 事实上我们那时在学同样的课程。**b)** used when you do not agree with what someone has just said 事实恰恰相反〔表示不同意某人刚说过的话〕: *No, I wasn't annoyed. As a matter of fact I was very glad to see them.* 不，我并不生气。恰恰相反，见到他们我非常高兴。

17 as a matter of interest *BrE spoken* used when you want to ask or tell someone something that is not really necessary【英口】出于兴趣: *Just as a matter of interest, Tony, how much did you pay for your house?* 托尼，我只是好奇，你买这栋房子花了多少钱？

18 as a matter of course/routine as the correct and usual thing to do in a particular situation 作为理所当然的事/常规: *We will contact your former employer as a matter of course.* 我们当然会与你以前的雇主联系。

19 as a matter of principle/belief/policy etc because of your personal beliefs about what you should do 由于原则/信念/政策等的缘故: *They're supporting him as a matter of principle.* 基于原则他们支持他。

20 as a matter of urgency/priority *formal* done as quickly as possible because it is very important【正式】作为紧急/优先之事〔来处理〕: *I want a full safety check as a matter of urgency.* 我要求进行一次全面的紧急安全检查。

⑤ IT'S A MATTER OF 是…的问题

21 it's/that's a matter of opinion used to say that people have different opinions about a subject 这是看法因人而异的问题: *Personally I can't stand rock music, but I suppose it's all a matter of opinion.* 就个人来说我受不了摇滚乐，但我认为这完全是个见仁见智的问题。

22 it's only/just a matter of time used to say that something will definitely happen eventually 只是时间的问题〔用于说明某事终究会发生〕: *It's only a matter of time before somebody gets hurt.* 有人会受到伤害，这只是迟早的事。

23 it's a matter of life and death used to say that a situation is extremely serious or dangerous and something must be done immediately 这是关乎生死的问题〔用于说明情况十分危急〕: *We wouldn't usually operate on a pregnant woman, unless it's a matter of life and death.* 我们通常不会给一位孕妇做手术，除非情况十分危急。

24 it's (just) a matter of (doing) sth *spoken* used to say that you only have to do a particular thing, or do something in a particular way, in order to be successful【口】(只）是个（做）某事的问题: *Anyone can take good photographs – it's just a matter of being in the right place at the right time.* 任何人都能拍出好照片，问题只是你是否在合适的时间和合适的地点。

25 it's a matter of taste/cost/luck etc used to say that what happens or what you decide depends on your judgment, how much something costs, how lucky you are etc 这是个人爱好/成本/运气等的问题: *I can't say which wine is best – it's a matter of personal taste.* 我说不上哪种酒最好 —— 这是个人口味的问题。

26 the fact/truth of the matter (is) used to say what you think is really true 事实/事情真相（是）: *The sad fact of the matter is that Alice is just not good enough for the job.* 令人遗憾的事实是艾丽斯做这个工作就是不够资格。| *He doesn't love her any more – that's the truth of the matter.* 他不再爱她了，这就是事情的真相。

⑥ SMALL AMOUNT 少量

27 a matter of seconds/months/metres etc only a few seconds, metres etc 仅仅数秒/几个月/几米等: *The ambulance was there in a matter of minutes.* 仅仅几分钟后救护车就到那里了。| *In 1914 everyone expected the war to be over in a matter of months.* 1914年，每个人都以为战争会在几个月内结束。

⑦ BOOKS/NEWSPAPERS 书籍/报纸

28 reading/printed etc matter things that are written for people to read 阅读材料/印刷品等

⑧ SUBSTANCE 物质

29 waste/solid/organic/vegetable etc matter a substance that consists of waste material, solid material etc 废弃物/固体物质/有机物/植物性物质等

30 [U] *technical* the material that everything in the universe is made of, including solids, liquids, and gases【术语】〔构成宇宙万物的〕物质〔包括固体、液体和气体〕
31 [U] a yellow or white substance that is found in wounds or next to your eye〔伤口里的〕脓; 眼屎

⑨ **OTHER MEANINGS 其他意思**
32 or ... for that matter *spoken* used to say that what you are saying about one thing is also true about something else【口】对…同样如此: *Ben never touched beer, or any kind of alcohol for that matter.* 本从来不沾啤酒, 其实他是滴酒不沾。
33 there's the little matter of *spoken* used jokingly to remind someone about something important that they may have forgotten【口】还有这么一件小事〔以开玩笑的方式提醒某人他可能已忘记的要事〕: *OK, that's settled – but there's still the little matter of my fee to discuss.* 好, 这事就解决了, 但还有我的服务费这点小事要讨论。—see also 另见 GREY MATTER, **not mince matters** (MINCE[1] (3)), **mind over matter** (MIND[1] (50))

S1 W3 **matter²** *v* [I] **1** to be important, especially to be important to you personally or to have a big effect on what happens〔尤指对某人自己或对发生之事〕重要, 要紧, 有关系: **it doesn't matter/it won't matter etc** *"We've missed the train!" "It doesn't matter, there's another one in 10 minutes."* "我们已经误了火车了!" "没关系, 10分钟以后还有一班。" | **matter if** *Will it matter if I'm a little late?* 我晚来一会儿不要紧吧? | **matter about** *It won't matter about the mess – I'll clear it up later.* 脏乱没关系, 我过一会儿就收拾。| **matter who/why/what etc** *It doesn't matter what you wear, as long as you look neat and tidy.* 只要看起来干净整洁, 你穿什么都可以。| *Does it matter who goes first?* 谁先去有关系吗? | **matter to sb** ***It doesn't*** *really matter to me if we don't see the film – I've seen it already anyway.* 我们不看那部电影对我确实无所谓, 反正我已经看过了。| **it matters a lot/a great deal** (=it is very important) …非常重要 *It mattered a great deal to her what other people thought of her.* 其他人怎么看她对她来说极为重要。| **all that matters/the only thing that matters** (=the only thing that is important) 唯一要紧的 *All that matters is that you're safe.* 最要紧的是你平安无事。| *Money was the only thing that mattered to these people.* 对这些人来说金钱是唯一重要的东西。| **what matters is** *I don't care what it looks like – what matters is that it works.* 我不在乎它好看不好看——要紧的是它要好用。| **nothing else matters** *He wanted to win the championship – nothing else really mattered to him.* 他想获得冠军——除此之外没有什么对他来说是重要的了。**2 it doesn't matter** *spoken*【口】**a)** used to tell someone that you are not angry or upset about something, especially something that they have done 没关系〔表示你并不生气或介意〕: *"I've spilled some coffee on the carpet." "It doesn't matter."* "我把咖啡洒在地毯上了。" "没关系。" **b)** used to say that you do not mind which one of two things you have 没关系〔表示两者中要哪个你都不会介意〕: *"Red or white wine?" "Oh, either. It doesn't matter."* "你要红葡萄酒还是白葡萄酒?" "噢, 哪一种都行。没有关系。" **3 what does it matter (if)** *spoken* used to say that something is not very important【口】(即使)又何妨〔表示某事不很重要〕: *What does it matter if he drinks a little, at least he's happy.* 即使喝一点酒又有什么关系, 至少他高兴啊。

Frequencies of the verb **matter** in spoken and written English 动词matter在英语口语和书面语中的使用频率

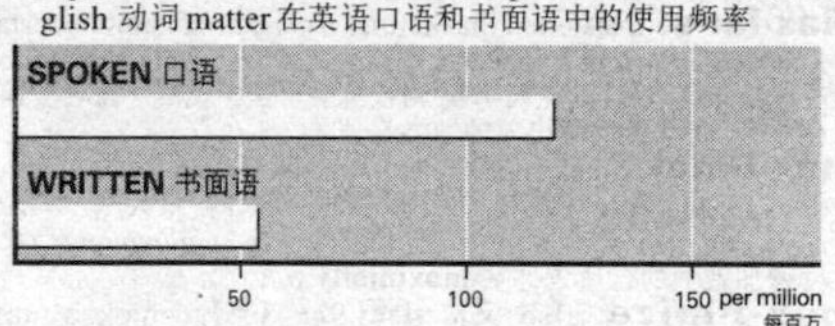

Based on the British National Corpus and the Longman Lancaster Corpus 据英国国家语料库和朗文兰开斯特语料库

This graph shows that the verb **matter** is much more common in spoken English than in written English. This is because it is used in a lot of common spoken phrases. 本图表显示, 动词matter在英语口语中的使用频率远远高于书面语, 因为它用于很多常见的口语短语中。

Mat·ter·horn, the /ˈmætəhɔrn; ˈmætəhɔːn/ a high mountain in the Alps near the border between Italy and Switzerland. It is popular with climbers, and is shaped like a PYRAMID. 马特峰〔阿尔卑斯山一山峰, 形似金字塔, 位于意大利和瑞士边境, 吸引了众多登山者〕

matter-of-fact /ˌ· · · ˈ·◂/ *adj* showing no emotion when you are talking about something exciting, frightening, upsetting etc 就事论事的; 不带感情的; 实事求是的: *Jan was surprisingly matter-of-fact about her divorce.* 简对待她的离婚出奇地淡然。—**matter-of-factly** *adv* —**matter-of-factness** *n* [U]

Mat·thew /ˈmæθju; ˈmæθjuː/**, Saint** one of Jesus Christ's DISCIPLES (=his close friends and followers). According to Bible stories, he was a tax collector and wrote *The Gospel according to St Matthew*, which describes the life and teachings of Jesus. 马太〔耶稣基督的门徒之一。据圣经故事记载, 他原为税吏, 是《马太福音》的作者。《马太福音》记述耶稣的生平和教义〕

Mat·thews /ˈmæθjuz; ˈmæθjuːz/**, Sir Stanley** (1915-2000) a British football player, one of the greatest English players ever, who played 54 times for the English national team. He played professional football for 33 years, until he was over 50. 马修斯〔(1915-2000), 英国足球运动员, 被认为是英格兰最出色的足球运动员之一。他曾54次代表英格兰国家队出战, 从事职业足球生涯长达33年之久, 直到50岁才挂靴〕

mat·ting /ˈmætɪŋ; ˈmætɪŋ/ *n* [U] strong rough material, used for making mats (MAT[1] (1))〔编席子用的〕编织材料: *straw matting* 编垫子用的麦秸[稻草]

mat·tins /ˈmætn̩z; ˈmætɪ̣nz/ *n* [U] another spelling of MATINS matins的另一种拼法

mat·tock /ˈmætək; ˈmætək/ *n* [C] a tool used for digging, with a long handle and a metal blade 鹤嘴锄

mat·tress /ˈmætrɪs; ˈmætrɪ̣s/ *n* [C] the soft part of a bed that you lie on 床垫, 褥垫: *an old, lumpy mattress* 凹凸不平的旧床垫

ma·tu·ra·tion /ˌmætʃʊˈreʃən; ˌmætʃʊ̣ˈreɪʃən/ *n* [U] *formal* the period during which something grows and develops【正式】成熟期, 成熟阶段

ma·ture¹ /məˈtjʊr; məˈtʃʊə/ *adj*
1 ▶SENSIBLE 理智的◀ a child or young person who is mature behaves in a sensible and reasonable way, as you would expect an older person to behave〔小孩或年轻人举止〕成熟的, 理智的, 明白事理的: *She's very mature for her age.* 就她这个年龄来说她算是很成熟的。| *John has always shown a mature attitude to his work.* 约翰对工作总是表现出一种老成持重的态度。—opposite 反义词 IMMATURE
2 ▶FULLY GROWN 成年的◀ fully grown and developed 成年的; 成熟的: *The mature eagle has a wingspan of over six feet.* 成年的鹰翼展超过六英尺。
3 ▶WINE/CHEESE ETC 酒/干酪等◀ mature cheese, wine etc has a good strong flavour which has developed during a long period of time 制成的; 已酿成的: *mature cheddar* 发酵成熟的切达干酪
4 ▶OLDER 较老的◀ a polite or humorous way of describing someone who is no longer young; MIDDLE-AGED 不再年轻的; 中年的〔礼貌或幽默的说法〕: *We design clothes for the maturer woman.* 我们为中年妇女设计服装。| **of mature years** *a respectable gentleman of mature years* 一位已届中年的体面绅士
5 ▶NOVEL/PAINTING ETC 小说/油画等◀ a mature piece of work by a writer or an artist shows a high level of understanding or skill 成熟的; 技巧娴熟的; 老练的
6 on mature reflection/consideration *formal* after thinking about something carefully【正式】经过仔细考虑: *On mature reflection we have decided to decline their offer.* 经过慎重考虑, 我们已决定谢绝他们的建议。
7 ▶FINANCIAL 金融的◀ *technical* a mature BOND[1] (1) or POLICY (2) is ready to be paid【术语】〔债券或保单〕到期应付的 —**maturely** *adv*

mature² *v* **matured, maturing 1** [I] to become fully grown or developed 变成熟; 完全长成: *A kitten matures when it is about a year old.* 小猫一岁左右就发育成熟了。**2** [I] to become sensible and start to behave like an adult 变理智;〔举止〕变成熟: *He has matured a lot since he left home.* 自从离家之后他成熟多了。**3** [I,T] if a cheese, wine, WHISKY etc matures or is matured, it develops a good strong flavour over a period of time (使)〔干酪、葡萄酒、威士忌酒等〕制成, (使)酿成; (使)成熟 **4** [I] *technical* if a financial arrangement such as a BOND[1] (1) or POLICY (2) matures, it becomes ready to be paid【术语】〔债券或保单〕到期

mature stu·dent /ˌ· ˈ· ·/ *n* [C] *BrE* a student at a university or college who is over 25 years old【英】大龄学生〔年龄超过25岁的大学生〕

M

CULTURAL NOTE 文化注释

It has become fairly common for people to go to university or college after having worked for some years or after their children have grown up. Most universities and colleges encourage them and some run special courses to help them learn to study. 越来越多的人工作几年后或者等儿女长大成人后再去读大学, 这是相当平常的事。多数大学或学院鼓励他们, 并为他们开设专门的课程以帮助他们学习。

ma·tu·ri·ty /məˈtjurətɪ; məˈtʃʊərə̩ti/ *n* [U] **1** the quality of behaving in a sensible way like an adult 成熟: *Beth remained calm, showing a maturity way beyond her 16 years.* 贝丝镇定自若, 表现出一种超出她 16 岁年龄的成熟。**2** the time when a person, animal, or plant is fully grown or developed〔人、动物或植物的〕成熟期: **reach maturity** *These insects reach maturity after a few weeks.* 这些昆虫几周后就达到成熟期。**3** *technical* the time when a financial arrangement such as a BOND[1] (1) or POLICY (2) becomes ready to be paid【术语】〔债券或保单的〕到期时间, 到期日

mat·zo /ˈmɑtsə; ˈmɒtsə/ *n* [C] a type of flat bread eaten especially by Jewish people during PASSOVER 无酵饼〔尤指犹太人在逾越节期间吃的一种薄面饼〕

maud·lin /ˈmɔdlɪn; ˈmɔːdlɪn/ *adj* talking or behaving in a sad, silly way, because you are drunk〔因醉酒〕言谈[举止]伤感的, 可笑的

Maugham /mɔm; mɔːm/, **Somerset** (1874-1965) a British writer of NOVELs and short stories. Many people consider him to be one of the best short story writers in English. His novels include *Of Human Bondage* and *The Moon and Sixpence*. 毛姆〔(1874-1965), 英国小说及短篇小说家; 被认为是最优秀的英语短篇小说家之一。最著名的小说包括《人性的枷锁》和《月亮和六便士》〕

maul /mɔl; mɔːl/ *v* [T] **1** to injure someone badly by tearing their flesh 撕裂…的皮肉, 抓裂: *The woman had been mauled by a panther.* 那个妇女被一只豹撕裂了皮肉。**2** to write very unfavourable comments about a new book, play etc 抨击〔新书、新戏剧等〕: *Her latest book was absolutely mauled by the critics.* 她的新书被评论家们批得体无完肤。**3** to touch someone in a rough sexual way which they think is unpleasant 对〔某人〕粗野地动手动脚: *Some guy came over and started mauling Jane.* 有个家伙走了过来, 开始对简粗野地动手动脚。

Mau Mau, the /ˈmau mau; ˈmaʊ maʊ/ a secret political organization which was started in Kenya in 1952 by the Kikuyu people, and which wanted Kenya to become independent from the UK. It used violence against Europeans whom it wanted to leave Kenya and against Africans who supported the British. 茅茅〔1952 年由吉库尤人在肯尼亚成立的一秘密政治组织, 目的是使肯尼亚摆脱英国统治并实现独立。该组织使用暴力手段逐出在肯尼亚的欧洲人, 并对付支持英国的非洲人〕

Mauna Loa /ˌmaunə ˈloə; ˌmaʊnə ˈləʊə/ a very large mountain that is an active VOLCANO in the south central part of the island of Hawaii. 冒纳罗亚〔位于夏威夷群岛中南部一巨大活火山〕

maun·der /ˈmɔndə; ˈmɔːndə/ *v* [I+on] *especially BrE* to talk or complain about something for a long time in a boring way【尤英】喋喋不休地说, 唠叨: *What are you maundering on about, Sid?* 锡德, 你在唠叨些什么?

Maun·dy mon·ey /ˈmɔndɪ ˌmʌnɪ; ˈmɔːndi ˌmʌni/ *n* [U] specially made coins given each year to poor people by the British queen or king in a traditional ceremony on **Maundy Thursday**, which is the Thursday before Easter 濯足节硬币〔一种特制硬币, 每年在复活节前的星期四, 即濯足节这一传统庆典上由英国女王或国王赐予穷人〕

Maun·dy Thurs·day /ˌmɔndɪ ˈθɜzdɪ; ˌmɔːndi ˈθɜːzdi/ *n* [U] the Thursday before Easter 濯足节〔复活节前的星期四〕, 圣星期四

Mau·pas·sant /ˌmopəˈsɑn; ˈməʊpæsɒn/, **Guy de** (1850-93) a French writer who wrote hundreds of short stories. He is one of the best short story writers ever. 莫泊桑〔(1850-1893), 法国作家, 创作了数百篇短篇小说, 是有史以来最优秀的短篇小说家之一〕

Mau·ri·ac /mɔrɪˈæk; ˈmɔːriˌæk/, **Fran·çois** /frɑnˈswɑ; ˈfrɒnswɑː/ (1885-1970) a French writer of NOVELs who won the Nobel Prize for Literature in 1952. 莫里亚克〔(1885-1970), 法国小说家, 1952 年获诺贝尔文学奖〕

Mau·ri·ta·ni·a /ˌmɔrɪˈtenɪə; ˌmɒrə̩ˈteɪniə/ a country in northwest Africa on the Atlantic coast. Population: 2,747,000 (2001). Capital: Nouakchott. 毛里塔尼亚〔非洲西北部一国家, 濒临大西洋。人口: 2,747,000 (2001), 首都: 努瓦克肖特〕—**Mauritanian** *n, adj*

Mau·ri·tius /mɔˈrɪʃɪəs; məˈrɪʃəs/ an island and country in the Indian Ocean, which is a member of the British Commonwealth. Population: 1,190,000 (2001). Capital: Port Louis. It is a popular place for tourists. 毛里求斯〔印度洋一岛国, 为英联邦成员国。人口: 1,190,000 (2001), 首都: 路易斯港。该国是游客喜欢的一个目的地〕—**Mauritian** *n, adj*

mau·so·le·um /ˌmɔsəˈliəm; ˌmɔːsəˈliːəm/ *n* [C] a large stone building containing many graves or built over a grave 陵墓

mauve /mov; məʊv/ *n* [U] a pale purple colour 淡紫色 —**mauve** *adj* —see picture on page A5 参见 A5 页图

ma·ven /ˈmevən; ˈmeɪvən/ *n* [C] *AmE* someone who knows a lot about a particular subject【美】专家, 内行: *The café is a hangout for the cultural mavens.* 那家咖啡馆是文化人常去的地方。

mav·e·rick /ˈmævrɪk; ˈmævərɪk/ *n* [C] an unusual person who has different ideas and ways of behaving from other people, and is often very successful 持不同意见者; 特立独行者: *Charles was always a bit of a maverick, even at school.* 查尔斯总是有点特立独行, 甚至在学校时也是如此。—**maverick** *adj*: *maverick tendencies* 特立独行的倾向

maw /mɔ; mɔː/ *n* [C] **1** *formal* something which seems to swallow things completely【正式】似能吞噬他物的东西; 无底洞: *Millions of dollars were poured into the maw of defense spending.* 数百万美元被投进了国防开支这个无底洞。**2** *literary* an animal's mouth or throat【文】动物的嘴[咽喉]

mawk·ish /ˈmɔkɪʃ; ˈmɔːkɪʃ/ *adj* showing too much emotion in a way that is embarrassing; SENTIMENTAL 情感过于外露的; 多愁善感的: *a mawkish love story* 感情浅露的爱情故事 —**mawkishly** *adv* —**mawkishness** *n* [U]

max[1] /mæks; mæks/ *n* [U] **1** an abbreviation of 缩写= MAXIMUM **2** *informal* at the most【非正式】最大量; 最大值; 最大限度: *It'll cost about ten dollars max.* 它的价钱至多 10 美元左右。**3 to the max** *AmE slang*【美俚】**a)** an expression meaning extremely, used to emphasize how good, bad etc something is 极其, 极端〔用以强调好、坏等的程度〕: *"He's gorgeous, isn't he?" "To the max!"* "他很帅, 是吧?" "帅极了!" **b)** if you push yourself to the max, you try as hard as you can to succeed 最大程度地〔努力以取得成功〕

max[2] *v*

max out *phr v* [I] *AmE slang*【美俚】**1** to do something with as much effort and determination as you can 全力以赴, 竭尽全力: *Hilary maxed out on the campaign.* 希拉里在那次竞选活动中使出了浑身解数。**2** to do too much, eat too much etc〔做、吃等〕过多: **[+on]** *"Want a beer?" "Nah, I maxed out on booze this weekend."* "要来杯啤酒吗?" "不要了, 我这个周末喝多了。" —**maxed out** *adj*

max·im /ˈmæksɪm; ˈmæksə̩m/ *n* [C] a well-known phrase or saying, especially one that gives a rule for sensible behaviour 箴言, 格言

Max·im's /ˈmæksɪmz; ˈmæksə̩mz/ *trademark* a famous restaurant and NIGHTCLUB in Paris, France, where rich and famous people go【商标】马克西姆餐厅[夜总会]〔法国巴黎一著名餐馆和夜总会, 是名流富豪出入的地方〕

max·i·mal /ˈmæksəməl; ˈmæksə̩məl/ *adj technical* as much or as large as possible【术语】最多的; 最大的; 最大限度的: *the right conditions for a maximal increase in employment* 最大限度增加就业的合适条件 —**maximally** *adv*

max·i·mize also 又作 **-ise** *BrE*【英】/ˈmæksəˌmaɪz; ˈmæksə̩maɪz/ *v* [T] to increase something such as profit or income as much as possible 使增加到最大限度: *The company's main function is to maximize profit.* 该公司的主要职能是最大限度地增加利润。—compare 比较 MINIMIZE —**maximization** /ˌmæksəməˈzeʃən; ˌmæksə̩maɪˈzeɪʃən/ *n* [U]

max·i·mum[1] /ˈmæksəməm; ˈmæksə̩məm/ *adj* [only before noun 仅用于名词前] the maximum amount, quantity, speed etc is the largest that is possible or allowed 最大量的, 最大限度的, 最大值的: *The car has a maximum speed of 120 mph.* 这辆汽车的最大速度为每小时 120 英里。| *The maximum number of students in each class is thirty.* 每个班学生人数的最高限额是 30 名。| *We must make maximum use of the resources available.* 我们必须最大限度地利用可得到的资源。| **for maximum effect** (=to get the best possible results) 为得到最佳效果 *Display it under a strong light for maximum effect.* 把它放在强光下以产生最佳效果。—compare 比较 MINIMUM[1]

maximum[2] *n plural* **maxima** /-mə; -mə/ *or* **maximums** [C] the largest number or amount that is possible or is allowed〔可能或可允许的〕最大量, 最大值: **[+of]** *Temperatures will reach*

M

a maximum of 45°C. 气温最高将达到45摄氏度。| **the maximum** *40 students per class is the absolute maximum.* 每班40名学生是绝对的最高限额。

Max·well /ˈmækswɛl; ˈmækswel/, **James Clerk** (1831-79) a British scientist who made important discoveries in ELECTROMAGNETISM, which made possible the development of radio and telephone 麦克斯韦〔(1831-1879), 英国科学家。他在电磁学领域有过重大发现, 促进了无线电和电话的发展〕

May /me; meɪ/ *n* [C,U] the fifth month of the year, between April and June 五月: **in May** *The theatre opened in May 1991.* 那家剧院开业于1991年5月。| **last/next May** *She started work here last May.* 她去年5月开始在这儿工作。| **on 6th May/on May 6th** *The meeting will be on 6th May.* (spoken as 读作: *on the sixth of May* or 或 *on May sixth* (*AmE* 美) or 或 *on May the sixth* (*BrE* 英)) 会议将于5月6日召开。

CULTURAL NOTE 文化注释

In the UK and northern US, when people think of May, they think of spring flowers in full BLOOM (=with the flowers fully open), warmer weather, and longer days. 在英国和美国北部, 人们想到5月, 就会联想到春花争奇斗艳, 温暖的天气和更长的白昼。

may[1] *modal verb negative short form* 否定缩略式为 **mayn't** *old-fashioned BrE*【过时, 英】

1 ►POSSIBILITY 可能性◄ if something may happen or may be true, there is a possibility that it will happen or be true but this is not certain 可能, 也许: *I may be late so start without me.* 我也许会晚来, 所以你们按时开始, 不要等我。| *Who knows what will happen. You may even have married by then.* 谁知道会发生什么呢? 到那时你甚至可能已经结婚了。| *It is feared that many workers may lose their jobs this winter.* 人们担心这个冬天有许多工人会失业。| *£50 may not be enough.* 50英镑可能不够。| *Ian may be able to help.* 伊恩也许能帮忙。—compare 比较 MIGHT[1]

2 ►PERMISSION 允许◄ **may I a)** *spoken* used to ask politely if you can do something【口】可以〔用以客气地问是否可做某事〕: *May I speak to you for a moment in private, please?* 请问我可以跟您私下里说几句话吗? | *I'd like to open a window, if I may.* 如果可以的话, 我想打开一扇窗子。**b)** *formal* used to say that someone is allowed to do something【正式】可以〔用以表示某人被允许做某事〕: *Thank you, you may go now.* 谢谢, 你现在可以走了。| *You may start writing now – the examination will finish in three hours.* 你们现在可以开始答题, 考试将在三小时后结束。| *Firearms may be used in an emergency.* 在紧急情况下可以开枪。**c) may I say/ask/suggest etc** *formal* used to say, ask, or suggest something politely【正式】我想(可否)说/询问/建议等〔礼貌说法〕: *May I just add that Oliver was a pleasure to work with and will be missed by everyone in the team.* 我想补充一句: 和奥利弗一块工作很愉快, 队里的每个人都会想念他。—compare 比较 CAN[1], MIGHT[1]

3 may you/he/they etc do sth *formal* used to say that you hope that a particular thing will happen to someone【正式】祝你/他/他们等…〔用以表示希望、祝愿〕: *May both the bride and groom have long and happy lives.* 祝新娘新郎幸福长寿。

4 may ... but ... used to say that although one thing is true, something else which seems very different is also true 尽管…但是…〔用以表示尽管某事是真实的, 但其他似乎与之非常不同的事也是真实的〕: *He may be lazy, but he can work very hard when he feels like it.* 他尽管懒惰, 但要是他愿意的话, 也能很勤奋地工作。| *You may think you're smart but you don't understand this kind of work at all.* 你也许自认为很聪明, 但你对这种工作一点也不懂。—compare 比较 MIGHT[1]

5 may well if something may well happen or may well be true, it is fairly likely to happen or be true 很可能, 极有可能: *These are excellent photographs and we may well be able to use them in our magazine.* 这些照片好极了, 我们很有可能把它们用在我们的杂志上。—compare 比较 **might well** (MIGHT[1] (7))

6 may as well *spoken* used to say that you will do something that you do not really want to do, because you cannot think of anything better【口】还是…的好, 倒不如〔表示你要做你并不真正想做的事, 因为想不出更好的办法〕: *I may as well go out tonight. There's nothing on television.* 我今晚还是出去的好, 电视上没有什么好看的。| *If you're not going to eat that pizza I may as well throw it out.* 如果你不打算吃那块比萨饼, 我还是把它扔掉的好。

7 ►PURPOSE 目的◄ *formal* used like 'can' after 'so that', to say that someone does something in order to make something else possible【正式】(以便) 能够, (使) 可以〔与 can 一样, 用于 so that 之后〕: *He gave up his life so that we may all live in a free and fair world.* 他献出了自己的生命, 为了使我们所有的人能够生活在一个自由、公平的世界上。—compare 比较 MIGHT[1]

8 ►POSSIBLE TO DO STH 有可能做某事◄ if something may be done, completed etc in a particular way, that is how it is possible to do it 有可能〔做到〕: *The problem may be solved in a number of ways, but there is only one correct answer.* 这道题可以用多种方法来解, 但正确答案只有一个。—see 见 CAN (USAGE)

may[2] *n* [U] HAWTHORN flowers 山楂花

May Ball /ˌ· ˈ·/ *n* [C] a formal dance held at the universities of Oxford and Cambridge every year in June. Students dress formally for a May Ball, and it is expensive to go to one. 通宵舞会〔牛津大学和剑桥大学每年6月份举行的一场正式舞会。舞会上学生穿着正式。参加这种舞会花费不小〕

may·be /ˈmebɪ; ˈmeɪbi/ *adv* [sentence adverb 句子副词] **1** used like 'perhaps' to say that something may happen or may be true but you are not certain 也许, 大概, 可能〔和 perhaps 一样用于表示某事可能发生或可能真实, 但不肯定〕: *"Do you think he'll come back?" "Maybe."* "你认为他会回来吗?" "也许会吧。" | *Maybe I was wrong about Karen; I don't know.* 或许我错怪了卡伦; 我不知道。| *He said he'd finish the work soon – maybe tomorrow.* 他说他很快就会完成那个工作 —— 也许是在明天。**2** used to show that you are not sure of an amount or number 也许〔表示对某一数额或数目不能确定〕: *There were three, maybe four hundred people at the concert.* 音乐会上有三百人, 也许四百人。**3** used to make a suggestion you are not quite sure about 或许〔用以作出不十分确定的建议〕: *We thought maybe we should lower the price we were asking for our house.* 我们想或许应该降低对我们那幢房子的要价。**4** used when politely asking someone to do something or offering to help them 也许〔用于客气地请某人做某事或表示愿意帮助他们〕: *Maybe you could help me tidy the livingroom.* 也许你能帮我收拾一下客厅。**5** *spoken* used to reply to a suggestion or idea when either you are not sure if you agree with it, or you do not want to say 'yes' or 'no'【口】也许〔用于不明确自己是否同意某建议或想法, 或不愿意明确表示同意与否之时〕: *"I think Sheila would be an excellent managing director." "Maybe."* "我想希拉会是一位优秀的总经理。" "也许是吧。" | *"Well, are you going to take the job or not?" "Maybe..."* "我说, 这份工作你到底要不要?" "也许啦…"

6 maybe ... but *spoken* used to agree with someone but say that there are also other facts to be considered【口】也许…不过〔用于表示同意某人的看法, 但说明同时也有其他因素要考虑〕: *"Mike should rent his own apartment and get away from home." "Maybe, but where would he get the money from?"* "迈克应该去租一套公寓房, 离开家人自己生活。" "也许是该这样, 但是他从哪里弄这笔钱呢?"

USAGE NOTE 用法说明: MAYBE

FORMALITY 正式程度

Maybe and **perhaps** mean the same thing, but **maybe** is more informal. maybe 和 perhaps 意思相同, 但 maybe 更为随便。To a friend you might say or write 对朋友可以这样说或写: *I'll maybe see you in August.* 我也许会在8月份见到你。To someone you do not know well you might say 而对一个不太熟悉的人你可以说: *Perhaps we could meet next week.* 或许我们能在下周见面。When you write a report or story you might put 写报告或故事时可以说: *New York is perhaps the most interesting city in the US.* 纽约也许是美国最有趣的城市。In a speech you might say 在演讲中, 可能会说: *Perhaps in closing I could just thank everyone for coming.* 也许在结束我的讲话时, 我可以对各位的光临表示感谢。but it would be less formal to say 但如果说 *Maybe...* 就不那么正式了。

SPELLING 拼法

Maybe is always spelt as one word when it means 'perhaps'. maybe 的意思如果是"也许", 总是拼写成一个词: *Maybe it'll be fun.* 也许它会很有趣。Compare 比较 *It may be fun.*

may·bug /ˈmebʌg; ˈmeɪbʌg/ *n* [C] a COCKCHAFER 金龟子

May Day /ˈ· ·/ *n* [C,U] the first day of May, when LEFT-WING political parties have celebrations, and when people traditionally used to celebrate the arrival of spring 五一劳动节; 五朔节〔过去传统上人们在这一天庆祝春天的到来〕

may·day /ˈmeˌde; ˈmeɪdeɪ/ *n* [singular] a radio signal used to ask for help when a ship or plane is in serious danger〔船只或飞机遇险时用的〕无线电求救信号 —compare 比较 SOS

may·est /ˈmeəst; ˈmeɪəst/ *v* **thou mayest** *old use*【旧】= you may

May·fair /ˋmefɛr; ˈmeɪfeə/ the most expensive part of London, in the area directly east of Hyde Park. Mayfair has many large and well-known hotels, and it was once a very fashionable place to live, but many of the houses have now been made into offices. 梅费尔区〔伦敦最奢华的一个地段，位于海德公园正东面。梅费尔区有许多著名大酒店。这里曾是非常时尚的居住区，如今许多住房已改为办公场所〕

May·flow·er, the /ˋmeflauə; ˈmeɪflaʊə/ the ship that took the Pilgrim Fathers to Plymouth, Massachusetts in the US in 1620. They were Puritans, who left England because they wanted to start a new society where they would be free to practise their religion. In the US people sometimes say, either seriously or jokingly, that someone's family "came over on the Mayflower", when they mean that someone's family originally arrived in the US a very long time ago. 五月花号〔1620年将清教徒先辈移民运往美国马萨诸塞州普利茅斯的船只。这批清教徒远离英国，目的是为了重建一个新社会，从而自由地信仰他们的宗教。美国人有时会认真或诙谐地说某人的家族是"乘坐五月花号来的"，意思是说其祖辈很早以前就来到了美国〕

may·fly /ˋmeflaɪ; ˈmeɪflaɪ/ *n plural* **mayflies** [C] a small insect that lives near water, and only lives for a short time 蜉蝣

may·hem /ˋmehɛm; ˈmeɪhem/ *n* [U] an extremely confused situation in which people are very frightened or excited; CHAOS 极端混乱的局面，大混乱: *There was complete mayhem after the explosion.* 爆炸后到处一片混乱。

may·n't /ˋment; ˈmeɪənt/ *old-fashioned BrE*【过时，英】the short form of 缩略式= 'may not'

May·o /ˋmeo; ˈmeɪəʊ/ a county in the west of the Republic of Ireland, on the Atlantic coast 梅奥〔爱尔兰共和国西部一郡，濒临大西洋〕

mayo *n* [U] *AmE informal* mayonnaise【美，非正式】蛋黄酱

Mayo Clin·ic, the /ˋ‥,‥/ a medical institution and hospital in Rochester, Minnesota, famous in the US for its modern equipment and successful treatment 梅奥诊所〔明尼苏达州罗切斯特一所医疗机构和医院，以现代化的设备和成功的治疗闻名美国〕

may·on·naise /ˋmeə,nez; ˌmeɪəˈneɪz/ *n* [U] a thick white SAUCE eaten with cold SALADS, on CHIPS etc 蛋黄酱

mayor /ˋmeə; meə/ *n* [C] **1** someone who is chosen or elected each year in Britain to represent a town or city at official public ceremonies〔英国的〕市长 **2** the person who has been elected to lead the government of a town or city in the US〔美国的〕市长 —**mayoral** *adj*: *mayoral duties* 市长的职责

mayor·al·ty /ˋmeərəltɪ; ˈmeərəlti/ *n* [U] *formal* the position of mayor, or the period when someone is mayor【正式】市长的职位; 市长的任期

mayor·ess /ˋmeərɪs; ˈmeərɪs/ *n* [C] *BrE* the wife of a mayor, or a woman who shares the work of a mayor【英】市长夫人; 女市长

maypole 五朔节花柱

may·pole /ˋme,pol; ˈmeɪpəʊl/ *n* [C] a tall pole around which people danced on May Day in England in the past 五朔节花柱〔过去英格兰人在五朔节围绕着这种柱子跳舞〕

May Queen /ˋ· ,·/ *n* [C] a young woman chosen as queen as part of the May Day celebrations. She wears a crown of flowers on her head, and she is also called **Queen of the May**. 五朔节王后〔五朔节时选出的一名美丽的年轻女子。她头戴花冠，亦称"五月王后"〕

Mays /mez; meɪz/, **Willie** (1931-) a US BASEBALL player who was one of the greatest ever. He joined the New York Giants in 1951 and played for them for many years. In 1964 he became the first black player to be made captain of a team in the Major Leagues. He was also the first National League player to hit more than 600 HOME RUNS. 梅斯〔(1931-)，美国棒球运动员，被认为是有史以来最杰出的棒球选手之一。1951年，他加入纽约巨人队，并效力多年。1964年，他成为职业棒球大联盟第一位黑人队长。他也是美国全国棒球联盟首位击出600多个本垒打的球员〕

mayst /mest; meɪst/ *v* **thou mayst** *old use*【旧】= you may

may've /ˋmeəv; ˈmeɪəv/ the short form of 缩略式= 'may have': *You may've heard this story before.* 你以前也许听过这个故事。

Maz·a·rin Bi·ble, the /ˌmæzərɪn ˋbaɪbl; ˌmæzərɪn ˈbaɪbəl/ another name for the Gutenberg Bible. It was called this because the first copy of it was found in the library of Cardinal Mazarin in Paris in 1760.《马萨林圣经》〔《古登堡圣经》别称。这个版本的《圣经》是1760年在巴黎马萨林红衣主教的藏书室里首次发现的，故名〕

maze /mez; meɪz/ *n* [C] **1 a maze of streets/paths/wires etc** a complicated and confusing arrangement of streets etc 迷宫似的街道/小路/电线等: *the maze of tiny streets in the old part of the city* 旧城区迷宫般的小街道 **2 a maze of rules/regulations/details etc** a large number of rules etc which are complicated and difficult to understand 一大堆复杂难懂的规则/规章/细节等 **3** a specially designed system of paths, often in a park or public garden, which is difficult to find your way through〔尤指公园中的〕迷宫，迷魂阵: *We got completely lost in the maze.* 我们在迷宫中彻底迷了路。**4** a children's game in which you draw a line through a complicated group of lines without crossing any of them 迷宫〔儿童画线游戏〕

Maze Pris·on, the /, ˋ ·‥/ also 又作 **the Maze** a prison in Northern Ireland where many prisoners, both Protestant and Roman Catholic, are kept 梅兹监狱〔北爱尔兰一监狱，关押着许多新教或罗马天主教囚犯〕

MB /ˌɛm ˋbi; ˌem ˈbiː/ the abbreviation of 缩写= Bachelor of Medicine 医学士

MBA /ˌɛm bi ˋe; ˌem biː ˈeɪ/ *n* [C] Master of Business Administration; a university degree in the skills needed to be in charge of a business 工商管理学硕士

Mba·ba·ne /ˌɛmbəˋbɑn; əmbɑːˈbɑːni/ a town and business centre which is the capital of Swaziland 姆巴巴纳〔斯威士兰首府，为一城镇和商业中心〕

MBE /ˌɛm bi ˋi; ˌem biː ˈiː/ *n* [C] Member of the Order of the British Empire; a special honour given to some British people for things they have done for their country〔英帝国〕五等爵士

MBSc /ˌɛm bi ɛs ˋsi; ˌem biː es ˈsiː/ the abbreviation of 缩写= Master of Business Science 工商学硕士

MC /ˌɛm ˋsi; ˌem ˈsiː/ *n* [C] **1** the abbreviation of 缩写= MASTER OF CEREMONIES —see also 另见 EMCEE **2** Military Cross; a MEDAL given to British army officers for bravery 军功十字勋章〔授予表现勇敢的英军军官〕 **3** *AmE*【美】the written abbreviation of 缩写= Member of Congress〔美国〕国会议员

MCAT /ˋɛm kæt; ˈem kæt/ Medical College Admissions Test; an examination which must be taken by anyone who wants to attend medical school in the US 医学院入学考试〔打算在美国读医科的人必须通过的一项考试〕

MCC, the /ˌɛm si ˋsi; ˌem siː ˈsiː/ The Marylebone Cricket Club; a famous CRICKET club that was established in 1787 and is based at Lord's cricket ground in North London. Although it is a private club, the MCC was until the 1960s in charge of the organization of cricket all over the world, and it is still responsible for the rules of the game. 玛丽勒本板球俱乐部〔一著名板球俱乐部，成立于1787年。本部设在北伦敦的贵族板球场。虽然是一个私人俱乐部，但20世纪60年代以前一直管理着世界各地的板球组织，至今仍负责有关比赛规则的事宜〕

Mc·Calls /məˋkɔlz; məˈkɔːlz/ a US magazine for women, especially popular with older women who have families《美开乐》〔美国一本女性杂志，颇受有家庭的中老年妇女喜爱〕

Mc·Car·thy /məˋkɑrθɪ; məˈkɑːθi/, **Joseph** (1909-57) a US politician in the Republican Party. He became famous in the early 1950s by saying publicly that many famous people, important politicians, and military officers were communists, and therefore enemies of the US. He influenced the development of strongly anti-Communist ideas in the US, and anyone who was called a Communist was treated extremely unfairly. In 1954, however, the US Senate formally criticized his actions,

and he lost most of his political support and power. 麦卡锡〔(1909-1957)，美国共和党政客。20世纪50年代早期，他公开宣称许多名人、重要政治家和军官是共产党人和美国的敌人，并因此而出名。在他的影响下，美国产生了强烈的反共思想，谁被称作共产党人，谁都会受到极不公正的待遇。1954年，美国参议院正式谴责了他的行为，他失去了政治上的大部分支持和权力〕

Mc·Car·thy·is·m/məˋkɑrθɪ͵ɪzəm; məˈkɑːθi-ɪzəm/ *n* [U] in the US in the 1950s, McCarthyism consisted of searching for and removing from public employment anybody who people thought might be a Communist. Senator Joseph McCarthy was responsible for this process. Many of the people accused were BLACKLIST*ed* (=not allowed to work) or imprisoned. People were encouraged to give the names of their friends and people they worked with to protect themselves. McCarthyism is sometimes used to mean any accusation of disloyalty to your country that is made without proof. 麦卡锡主义〔20世纪50年代美国参议员约瑟夫·麦卡锡掀起的一场政治运动。美国政府部门中被怀疑是共产党的任何人都会遭到查处和革职。许多人被列入黑名单或被关进监狱。他们采取诱供方式让当事人说出自己的朋友或同事以求自保。现在，麦卡锡主义有时指没有证据指控他人出卖国家的做法〕—see 见 the HUAC

Mc·Cart·ney/məˋkɑrtnɪ; məˈkɑːtni/**, Paul**(1942-) a British singer and songwriter, now **Sir Paul McCartney**, who was a member of The Beatles, and who wrote most of their songs with John Lennon. He led a new band called **Wings**in the 1970s, and has continued writing and performing music. His wife, **Linda McCartney**(1941-98), was a photographer who formed a company that sold ready-made VEGETARIAN food. 麦卡特尼〔(1942-)，英国歌手、歌曲作家，现称保罗·麦卡特尼爵士。他曾是甲壳虫乐队成员，与约翰·列侬合写了大部分歌曲。20世纪70年代，他领导一个名为"飞翼"的新乐队，继续写歌和表演。他的妻子琳达·麦卡特尼(1941-1998)是一位摄影师，成立了一家成品素食公司〕

Mc·Clel·lan/məˋklɛlən; məˈklelən/**, George**(1826-85) a US GENERAL (=military leader) in the Union army in the American Civil War 麦克莱伦〔(1826-1885)，美国内战时期联邦军队的一名将军〕

Mc·Coy/məˋkɔɪ; məˈkɔɪ/ *n* **the real McCoy** *informal* something that is real and is not a copy, especially something valuable【非正式】真货〔非复制品，尤指贵重物品〕: *"Is it a Rolex?" "Yes, it's the real McCoy."* "是一只劳力士牌手表吗?""不错，是真货。"

Mc·Crae/məˋkre; məˈkreɪ/**, John**(1872-1918) a Canadian poet who wrote the famous war poem *In Flanders Fields* 麦克雷〔(1872-1918)，加拿大诗人。其成名作是战争诗歌《弗兰德斯战场》〕

Mc·Cul·lers/məˋkʌlɚz; məˈkʌləz/**, Car·son** /ˋkɑrsən; ˈkɑːsən/ (1917-67) a US writer whose NOVEL*s* include *The Heart is a Lonely Hunter* and *Reflections in a Golden Eye*. Her best-known short stories are included in the collection *The Ballad of the Sad Café*. She often wrote about loneliness, and many of her characters are people who do not fit into ordinary society. 麦卡勒斯〔(1917-1967)，美国小说家。其作品包括《心是孤独的猎手》和《黄金眼睛的映像》。短篇小说集《伤心咖啡馆之歌》汇集了她最著名的短篇小说。她经常以孤独为主题创作，笔下的许多人物与普通社会格格不入〕

Mc·Gill U·ni·ver·si·ty/mə͵gɪl junəˋvɝsətɪ; mə͵gɪl juːnɪ̩ˋvɜːsɪ̩ti/ a well-known university in Montreal, in Canada 麦吉尔大学〔位于加拿大蒙特利尔的一所知名大学〕

Mc·Gwire/məˋgwaɪɚ; məˈgwaɪə/**, Mark**(1963-) US BASEBALL player. In 1998, he was the first player in history to hit 62 HOME RUN*s* in one SEASON (=set of games played during one year). 麦圭尔〔(1963-)，美国棒球运动员。1998年，他创造了一个赛季62个本垒打的世界纪录〕

Mc·Kin·ley/məˋkɪnlɪ; məˈkɪnli/**, Mount**—see 见 DENALI

Mc·Kin·ley, William (1843-1901) a US politician in the Republican Party who was President from 1897 to 1901. He greatly increased TARIFF*s* (=taxes on goods coming into the country) so that US companies would become stronger and more successful. He was shot and killed in Buffalo, New York. 麦金利〔(1843-1901)，美国共和党政治家，1897至1901年间任总统。他大幅度提高关税以增强美国公司的实力和绩效。他在纽约布法罗遭枪击身亡〕

Mc·Lu·han/məˋkluən; məˈkluːən/**, Mar·shall**/ˋmɑrʃəl; ˈmɑːʃəl/ (1911-80) a Canadian writer who was interested in the MEDIA (=newspapers, radio, and television), and is known for inventing the phrase 'the medium is the message', by which he meant that the way in which people receive information has more influence on what they think than the information itself. He also said that the world was becoming a 'global village', meaning that TELECOMMUNICATIONS were making the world seem smaller and that the countries of the world were becoming more dependent on one another. 麦克卢汉〔(1911-1980)，加拿大作家，对媒体感兴趣。他最早提出"媒介即信息"这一名言，意即获得信息的途径对个人意识的影响要大于信息本身。他还说过世界正在成为一个"地球村"，意指电信使世界日益变小，国际间的相互依赖越来越强〕

Mc·Naugh·ten Rules, the/məkˋnɔtn̩ ͵rulz; məkˈnɔːtn ͵ruːlz/ 又作 **the M'Naghten Rules**the rules in English law which say that, if it can be proved that someone did not know what they were doing when they carried out a crime or did not know that it was wrong, then they can plead insanity (=give madness as an excuse for their actions). The rules were established as a result of the case of Regina v. McNaughten in 1843. "南顿"规则〔英国法律条文。该条文指出如果当事人在犯罪时不知道自己在做什么或者不知道自己的行为是错误的，那么就可以以精神失常为由替自己辩护。该规则源自1843年的"里贾纳诉南顿案"〕

Mc·Pher·son /məkˋfɝsn̩; məkˈfɜːsən/**, Ai·mee Sem·ple**/ˋemɪ ˋsɛmpl̩; ˈeɪmi ˈsempəl/ (1890-1944) a US EVANGELIST, who travelled all around the US in the 1920s teaching the Christian religion. She became extremely popular and had her own radio station and a very large church in Los Angeles. She was officially charged with tricking people into giving her money, but a court of law decided she was not guilty. 麦克弗森〔(1890-1944)，美国一福音传道人。她曾于20世纪20年代环游美国传播基督教。后来，她名噪一时，在洛杉矶有了自己的电台和一座大教堂。她曾被正式起诉犯有诈骗钱财罪，但法庭最终裁定她无罪〕

Mc·Veigh/məkˋve; məkˈveɪ/**, Tim·o·thy**/ˋtɪməθɪ; ˈtɪməθi/ (1968-2001) a US man who was accused of exploding a bomb in front of a government building in Oklahoma City in 1996. More than 160 people were killed by the explosion. A court found him guilty of this crime in 1997, and sentenced him to death. He was killed in 2001. 麦克维〔(1968-2001)，美国一男子。他因1996年在俄克拉何马城的一幢政府大楼前引爆炸弹而被指控。此次爆炸造成160多人死亡。1997年，法庭裁定他有罪，并判处死刑，2001年被处死〕

MD[1]/͵ɛm ˋdi; ͵em ˈdiː/ *n* [C] **1** the written abbreviation of 缩写 = Doctor of Medicine 医学博士 **2** *especially spoken* the MANAGING DIRECTOR of a company【尤口】总经理; 董事总经理

MD[2] the written abbreviation of 缩写= MARYLAND

ME[1]/͵ɛm ˋi; ͵em ˈiː/ *n* [U] *BrE* myalgic encephalomyelitis; an illness that makes you feel very tired and weak and can last for a long time【英】肌痛性脑脊髓炎, ME综合征; EPSTEIN-BARR VIRUS *AmE*【美】

ME[2]the written abbreviation of 缩写= MAINE

me/mɪ; mi; *strong* 强读 mi; miː/ *pron* the object form of I 我〔I的宾格〕: *It fell off and hit me on the head.* 它掉下来砸在我的头上。| *He bought me a drink.* 他给我买了一杯酒。| *Give that book to me.* 把那本书给我。| *She's two years older than me.* 她比我大两岁。| *That's me, standing on the left of the bride.* 那是我，站在新娘子的左边。 S1 W1

USAGE NOTE 用法说明: ME

FORMALITY 正式程度: **me, her, him, us, we, they, them**

When you are speaking you usually use **me, her, him, us,** and **them** after **as, than,** and the verb **to be,** and with **and** and **or** in a phrase that is the subject of a clause. 口语中在as, than和动词to be之后，或者在由and或or连接、在句中作主语的词组中通常用me, her, him, us和them: *I'm not as pretty as her.* 我不如她漂亮。| *She's older than him.* 她比他年龄大。| *It's them.* 是他们。| *Tanya and me are off to Acapulco* (塔尼娅和我要去阿卡普尔科), or even 甚至可以说 *Me and Tanya are off to Acapulco.*

In very formal or old-fashioned writing you may see **I, she, he, we** and **they** used instead. 在非常正式或过时的书面语中，则会使用I, she, he, we 和 they: *None was as rich as he.* 没有人像他那样富有。You may also hear this in spoken English, but it often sounds much too formal or pompous. 在英语口语中你也会听到这种用法，但它常常听起来过于正式或傲慢: *It was they.* 是他们。| *My husband and I are going to the opera.* 我丈夫和我要去听歌剧。

You can avoid using either by rephrasing your sentence. 可以通过改变句子措辞来避免上述两种用法: *No one was as rich as he was.* 没有人像他那样富有。| *They were the ones.* 就是他们。| *I am going to the opera with my husband.* 我要和我丈夫一起去听歌剧。

M

me·a cul·pa /ˌmeə ˋkulpə; ˌmeɪə ˈkʊlpə/ *interjection Latin humorous* used to admit that something is your fault【拉丁，幽默】是我的过失，是我不好

mead /mid; miːd/ *n* **1** [U] an alcoholic drink made from HONEY 蜂蜜酒 **2** [C] *poetical* a meadow【诗】草地

Mead, Lake the largest RESERVOIR (=a lake where water is stored before it is supplied to people's houses) in the US, on the Colorado River behind the Hoover Dam 米德湖〔美国最大的水库，由科罗拉多河上的胡佛水坝拦蓄而成〕

Mead, Margaret (1901-78) a US ANTHROPOLOGIST, who studied the ways in which parents on the islands of Samoa, Bali, and New Guinea taught their children. She also tried to discover whether males and females are born with the differences in behaviour that they show, or whether they learn to behave differently as they grow up in their particular societies. Her best-known book is *Coming of Age in Samoa*. 米德〔（1901-1978），美国人类学家。她曾研究过萨摩亚、巴厘和新几内亚诸岛父母教育子女的不同方式，并试图发现男女在行为方式上的差异是与生俱来的，还是在特定社会环境下成长的过程中获得的。她最著名的著作是《萨摩亚人的成年》〕

mead·ow /ˈmɛdo; ˈmedəʊ/ *n* [C] a field with wild grass and flowers 草地 —see also 另见 WATER MEADOW

mead·ow·lark /ˆmɛdolɑrk; ˈmedəʊlɑːk/ *n* [C] a brown North American bird with a yellow front 草地鹨〔产于北美〕

mea·gre *BrE*【英】, **meager** *AmE*【美】/ˆmigɚ; ˈmiːgə/ *adj* a meagre amount of food, money etc is too small and is much less than you need〔食物、金钱等〕不足的，贫乏的: *meagre wages* 微薄的工资 | *a meager diet* 简单的饭食 —**meagrely** *adv* —**meagreness** *n* [U]

S2 W2 **meal** /mil; miːl/ *n* **1** [C] an occasion when you eat food, for example breakfast or lunch 餐，饭: *Dinner is the main meal of the day for most people.* 对多数人来说晚饭是一天中的主餐。| *What time are you having your meal?* 你们什么时间吃饭? | **go (out) for a meal** *After the movie we went for a meal in a Chinese restaurant.* 看完电影后我们去一家中国餐馆吃了一顿。| **take/ask sb out for a meal** *Why don't you ask her out for a meal?* 你为什么不请她出去吃顿饭? **2** [C] the food that you eat on a particular occasion 一餐吃的食物: *Michel cooked us a lovely French meal.* 米歇尔为我们做了一顿可口的法国餐。| *a five-course meal* 一顿五道菜的饭 —see also 另见 **a square meal** (SQUARE[1] (7)) **3** [U] grain that has been crushed into a powder, for making flour or animal food〔谷类的〕粗磨粉 —see also 另见 BONE MEAL **4 make a meal of** *informal* to spend too much time or effort doing something【非正式】花费过多的时间[精力]〔做某事〕，小题大做: *He made a real meal out of parking the car.* 他为了把车子停放好真肯花时间。

mea·lie /ˆmilɪ; ˈmiːli/ *n* [C,U] *SAfrE* MAIZE, or a piece of maize【南非】玉米，玉蜀黍；玉米穗

meal tick·et /ˈ· ,··/ *n* [C] **1** *informal* something or someone that you depend on to give you money or food【非正式】赖以为生的物[人] **2** a card that gives you the right to have free or cheaper meals at school or work in the US〔美国学校或工作场所的〕饭票，餐券

meal·time /ˆmiltaɪm; ˈmiːltaɪm/ *n* [C] a time during the day when you have a meal 进餐[开饭]时间: *The only time I see them is at mealtimes.* 我只有在吃饭时间才见得到他们。

meal·y /ˆmilɪ; ˈmiːli/ *adj* **1** fruit or vegetables that are mealy are dry and do not taste good〔水果或蔬菜〕干燥难吃的，面的: *mealy potatoes* 干巴巴不好吃的马铃薯 **2** containing MEAL (3) 含粉的，粉质的

mealy-mouthed /ˌ·· ˈ·◂/ *adj* not brave enough or honest enough to say clearly and directly what you really think 说话转弯抹角的；说话不真诚坦率的

S1 W1 **mean[1]** /min; miːn/ *v* [T] *past tense and past participle* **meant** /mɛnt; ment/

1 ►HAVE A PARTICULAR MEANING 有某种意思◄ [not in progressive 不用进行时] to have or represent a particular meaning 意思是，表示…的意思: *"What does 'Konbanwa' mean in English?" "It means 'Good Evening'."* "Konbanwa 译成英语是什么意思?" "它的意思是 Good Evening (晚上好)。" | *The red light means 'Stop'.* 红灯表示"停"。| **what is meant by** (=what something means) …是什么意思，…的意思是什么 *What is meant by the term 'random access'?* "随机存取"这个术语是什么意思? | **mean (that)** *This signal means your message has been received.* 这个信号表示你发送的信息已经收到了。

2 ►INTEND TO SAY STH 打算说某事◄ [not in progressive 不用进行式] to intend a particular meaning when you say something 意谓，意思是说: **mean (that)** *I meant we'd have to leave early – that's all.* 我的意思是说我们必须早点离开——没有别的。| **what you mean/what she means etc** *So what he means is that we'll have to start the whole thing again.* 喏，他的意思是说我们必须一切重新开始。

3 I mean *spoken*【口】**a)** used when explaining or giving an example of something, or when pausing to think about what you are going to say next 我的意思是〔用于进行解释或举例，或停下来考虑下面说什么时〕: *He's really very rude – I mean he never even says 'Good Morning'.* 他确实很无礼——我的意思是他甚至从来不说"早上好"。| *It's just not right. I mean it's unfair isn't it?* 这就不对。我是说这不公平，你说呢? **b)** used to quickly correct something you have just said 我是说〔用以快速纠正刚说过的话〕: *She plays the violin, I mean the viola, really well.* 她的小提琴——我是说中提琴——拉得确实好。

4 do you know what I mean?/if you know what I mean *spoken* used when checking that someone has understood what you are saying【口】你明白我的意思吗?/如果你明白我的意思〔用于核实某人是否已明白你正在说的话〕: *This year I want to buy her something really special. Do you know what I mean?* 今年我想给她买一件真正特殊的东西。你明白我的意思吗?

5 (do) you mean ...? *spoken* used when checking that you have understood what someone has said【口】你意思是说…?〔用于核实你确实听懂了某人所说的话〕: *You mean we're supposed to tell you if we want to leave early?* 你意思是说如果我们想早些离开就该告诉你吗?

6 I know what you mean *spoken* used to tell someone that you understand what they are talking about, because you have had the same experience yourself【口】我明白你的意思〔用以告诉某人你明白他所说的话，因为你有过同样的经历〕: *Oh, I know exactly what you mean. Things like that drive me crazy too.* 噢，我完全理解你的意思，那样的事情也会使我发疯的。

7 I see what you mean *spoken* used to tell someone that you now understand what they have been saying【口】我明白你的意思〔用以告诉某人，对他讲的话你现在已经听懂了〕: *Yes, I see what you mean. That would be the best way to do it.* 是的，我明白你的意思。那将是做这件事的最好办法。

8 see what I mean? *spoken* used when checking that someone has understood something you have said, often by showing them an example of it【口】懂我的意思吗?〔用于核实某人是否已听懂你说的话，常通过举例来说明〕: *See what I mean? Every time she calls me up she wants me to do something for her.* 懂我的意思吗? 她每次给我打电话都是要我给她办事。

9 that's what I mean *spoken* used when someone is saying the same thing that you were trying to say earlier【口】我就是这个意思〔用于表示某人说的话正是你刚才想说的〕: *"We might not have enough money." "That's what I mean, so we'd better find out the price first."* "我们也许钱不够。" "我就是这个意思，所以我们最好先弄清楚价钱。"

10 how do you mean? *spoken* used to ask someone to explain what they have just said or tell you more about it【口】你是什么意思?〔用以要求某人解释刚说过的话或提供更多与之相关的信息〕: *"He says he finds it difficult at times." "How do you mean?"* "他说他有时觉得挺难的。" "你是什么意思?"

11 what do you mean ...? *spoken*【口】**a)** used when you do not understand what someone is trying to say …是什么意思?〔用于表示没有听懂某人正在说的话〕**b)** used when you are very surprised or annoyed by what someone has just said 你是什么意思?〔用以表示对某人刚说过的话感到非常吃惊或不快〕: *What do you mean, you've cancelled the holiday?* 你说你取消了度假，是什么意思? | *What do you mean by that?* 你那么说是什么意思?

12 I mean to say *spoken* used when adding a reason or explanation for something you have just said, especially something you feel strongly about【口】我意思是说〔用以对自己刚刚说的话补充理由或解释，尤指你对之抱有强烈感情的某事〕: *Of course she wants to see the children, I mean to say, it's only natural isn't it?* 她当然想见到孩子们，我的意思是说，这不过是人之常情，对吧?

13 ►SAY WHICH PERSON/THING 说的是哪个人/物◄ **I mean sb/sth** *usually spoken* used to say that a particular person or thing is the one that you are talking about, pointing to etc【一般口】我指的是某人/某物: *"Hey you!" "Do you mean me?"* "嗨，你!" "你说的是我吗?" | *I didn't mean that one, I meant this one.* 我说的不是那一个，我指的是这一个。

14 ►INTEND (SB) TO DO (STH) 打算（让某人）做（某事）◄ *especially spoken* to intend to do something or intend that someone else should do something【尤口】意欲，打算: **mean to do sth** *I've been meaning to phone you all week.* 整整一星期以来我一直打算给你打电话。| *I didn't mean to interrupt your meal.* 我不是有意想打断你们吃饭。| **mean sb to do sth** *Oh no! I never*

meant her to read those comments. 真不应该！我从来没打算让她看那些评论。| **mean for sb to do sth** *especially AmE*【尤美】*I didn't mean for her to get hurt.* 我并没有让她受到伤害的意思。—see also 另见 **mean no harm** (HARM[1] (3))

15 mean business to be determined to do something even if it involves hurting someone, or be very serious about something 决心做某事〔即使会伤害他人〕;〔对某事〕是非常认真的: *We've got to show these gangsters we mean business.* 我们必须向这些歹徒表明我们是认真的。| *Get upstairs now! I mean business!* 现在就上楼去！我可不是说着玩的！

16 he/she means well *spoken* used to say that someone intends to be helpful or kind, but often makes a situation worse【口】他/她用心是好的: *He may sound a bit rude at times, but he means well.* 他讲话有时比较粗鲁，但他的用意是好的。—see also 另见 WELL-MEANING, WELL-MEANT

17 I/he etc meant it for the best *especially spoken* used to say that someone wanted to do something helpful, but their actions had the wrong effect【尤口】我/他本是出于好心: *I wasn't criticizing you, I really meant it for the best.* 我刚才并不是批评你，我真的是出于好意。

18 mean mischief/trouble to intend to cause trouble 有意找麻烦: *I could tell from the look on his face that he meant mischief.* 从他的面部表情上我能看出他是存心捣乱。

19 what do you mean by doing sth? *spoken* used to tell someone that you are very annoyed because of what they have done【口】你怎么竟然做某事?〔用以表示对某人做的事十分恼火〕: *What do you mean by calling me at this time of night?* 你怎么竟然这么晚还给我打电话?

20 ►SAY STH SERIOUSLY 严肃地说某事◄ [not in progressive 不用进行式] to have a serious purpose in something you say or write 当真，说到做到: **mean it** *We've heard these threats before, but I think he means it this time.* 这些威胁我们以前也听到过，但我认为这次他会来真的。| **mean what you say** *She meant what she said – you'll have to watch out.* 她是会说到做到的，你必须提高警惕。| **really mean** *You don't really mean that, do you?* 你并不当真是那个意思，对吧?

21 I didn't mean it *spoken* used to say that you did not intend to upset or hurt someone【口】我不是有意的: *I'm sorry, I didn't mean it – it was just a stupid thing to say.* 对不起，我不是有意的——我刚才说的确实是一句蠢话。| *I'm sure she didn't mean it, really.* 我敢肯定她不是有意的，真的。

22 ►RESULT IN STH 导致某事◄ [not in progressive 不用进行时] to have a particular result 引起，导致，造成: *The pit closures will mean a large rise in unemployment.* 关闭矿井将导致失业人数的大量增加。| **mean (that)** *His injury meant that he could no longer continue work.* 他的受伤意味着他不能再继续工作了。

23 that doesn't mean used to say that something is not definitely true, or is not definitely going to happen, even though it may seem to be true because of something else you have mentioned 那并不意味着: *Just because he's been in prison that doesn't mean he's some kind of violent criminal.* 仅仅因为他坐过牢并不意味着他就是某种残暴的罪犯。

24 ►INVOLVE DOING STH 包括做某事◄ [not in progressive 不用进行式] to involve having to do a particular thing 意味着: **mean doing sth** *I'm determined to solve this mystery even if it means travelling to New York myself.* 我决心解开这个秘密，即使这意味着我要亲自到纽约去一趟。

25 ►SHOW STH IS TRUE/WILL HAPPEN 表明某事真实/要发生◄ [not in progressive 不用进行式] to be a sign that something is true or will happen 表示；预示着: *When the boss sends for me it usually means trouble.* 要是老板派人叫我去见他，这通常就是说我要有麻烦了。| **mean (that)** *If the sky is red in the evening, it usually means it'll be fine the next day.* 如果傍晚天空发红，这通常预示着第二天是个晴天。

26 sth means a lot to sb used to say something is very important to someone 某事对某人很重要: *Her job means a lot to her.* 她的工作对她来说十分重要。| **sth means everything/the world to sb** *Their grandchildren mean everything to them.* 对他们来说，孙子孙女就是他们的一切。

27 mean nothing to sb a) to be unfamiliar to someone or impossible for them to understand 对某人完全陌生；不可能为某人所理解: *"Who's that message for?" "No idea. It means nothing to me."* "那张便条是给谁的?" "不知道，我完全看不懂。" **b)** to not be important to someone 对某人不重要: *Public honours mean nothing to her.* 荣誉对她来说是无所谓的。

28 mean something/anything to sb a) to be familiar to someone 为某人所熟悉: *Does the name 'Kanafani' mean anything to you?* 你熟悉Kanafani这个名字吗? **b)** to be important to someone 对某人重要: *I spent years believing that I actually meant something to him.* 有许多年，我以为自己对他来说还有一点什么重要性。

29 be meant to do sth a) if you are meant to do something, you should do it, especially because someone has told you to or because it is your responsibility〔尤因某人的吩咐或根据职责〕应该[必须]做某事: *We're meant to write our names at the top of the paper.* 按照规定我们应该把姓名写在考卷上方。| *I thought the police were meant to protect people.* 我以为警察的职责就是保护人民。**b)** to be intended to do something 意在做某事: *The diagram is meant to show the different stages of the process.* 这个图表意在显示整个过程的各个不同阶段。

30 be meant for to be intended for a particular person or purpose 为〔某人或某目的〕而准备的: *These chairs are meant for guests.* 这些椅子是为客人们准备的。

31 sb was never meant for sth/to be sth used to say that someone is not at all suitable for a particular job or activity 某人从来不是从事某种工作[活动等]的料: *I was never meant for the army.* 我从来就不是当兵的料。

32 be meant for each other if two people are meant for each other, they are very suitable as partners for each other 彼此很合得来，是天生的一对: *Monique and Didier were meant for each other.* 莫妮克和迪迪尔真是天生的一对。

33 sth was meant to be used to say that you think a situation was certain to happen and that no one had any power to prevent it 某事注定要发生: *They met in August, and were married within a month, so I guess it was just meant to be.* 他们在8月相遇，一个月不到就结婚了，所以我认为这完全是天意。

34 know/understand what it means to be sth to have experienced a particular situation, so that you know what it is like 知道/理解处于某种境况中意味着什么: *I understand your problems because I know what it means to be poor.* 我理解你的难处，因为我知道贫穷意味着什么。

Frequencies of the verb **mean** in spoken and written English 动词mean在英语口语和书面语中的使用频率

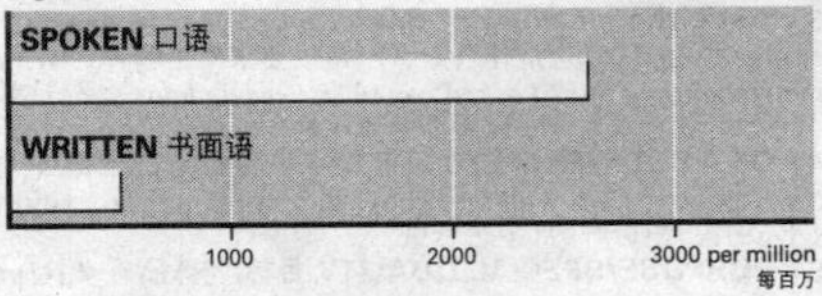

SPOKEN 口语

WRITTEN 书面语

1000 2000 3000 per million 每百万

Based on the British National Corpus and the Longman Lancaster Corpus 据英国国家语料库和朗文兰开斯特语料库

This graph shows that the verb **mean** is much more common in spoken English than in written English. This is because it is used in a lot of common spoken phrases. 本图表显示，动词mean在英语口语中的使用频率远远高于书面语，因为口语中很多常用短语是由mean构成的。

mean[2] *adj* **1** unkind or nasty 不善良的；卑鄙的；刻薄的: *That was a mean thing to do.* 那是一件很卑鄙的事情。| **[+to]** *Don't be so mean to her!* 不要对她如此刻薄！**2** *BrE* unwilling to spend any money or share what you have with other people; CHEAP[1] (6), STINGY【英】吝啬的，小气的: **[+with]** *He's always been mean with his money.* 他对钱总是很吝啬。**3** *especially AmE* cruel and bad-tempered【尤美】凶恶的，残忍的；脾气暴躁的: *That's a mean dog. Be careful it doesn't bite you.* 那是条恶狗，小心别让它咬着你。**4 no mean achievement/feat/task etc** something that is very difficult to do, so that someone who does it deserves to be admired 值得称道的成就/业绩/任务等: *Winning that competition was no mean feat.* 赢得那场竞争是了不起的成绩。**5 be no mean performer/player etc** to be very good at doing something 是一位了不起的演员/运动员等: *He was no mean batsman in those days.* 在那时他是一位优秀的板球击球手。**6** *AmE informal* very good and skilful【美，非正式】很好的；娴熟的: *She's one mean tennis-player.* 她是一位技艺精湛的网球选手。| *Brock plays a mean game of poker.* 布罗克玩扑克牌很老道。**7** [only before noun 仅用于名词前] *technical* average【术语】平均的: *the mean rate of consumption* 平均消耗速度 **8** [only before noun 仅用于名词前] *literary* poor or looking poor【文】简陋的，难看的，破旧的: *these mean streets* 这些简陋的街道 **9** [only before noun 仅用于名词前] *old use* belonging to a low social class【旧】〔社会地位〕低微的，卑微的: *a man of mean birth* 出身低微的人 —**meanly** *adv* —**meanness** *n* [U]

mean[3] *n* **1 the mean** *technical* the average amount, figure, or value【术语】平均数，平均值: *The mean of 7, 9 and 14 is 10.* 7,

M

9和14的平均数为10。**2 the/a mean between sth and sth** a method or way of doing something which is between two very different methods, and better than either of them 中庸之道，折中办法〔介于两种不同办法之间而比两者都好的做某事的一种办法〕: *It's a case of finding the mean between firmness and compassion.* 这是一个在坚决和同情之间找出折中办法的问题。—see also 另见 MEANS

me·an·der /mɪˈændə; miˈændə/ *v* [I] **1** if a river or stream meanders, it turns a lot as it flows〔河流〕蜿蜒流动: *a flat plain of meandering rivers* 河流蜿蜒其上的平原 **2** [always+adv/prep] to walk in a slow, relaxed way, not in any particular direction 漫步，闲逛: **[+along/through etc]** *We meandered aimlessly along the lanes.* 我们沿着小巷漫无目的地闲逛着。**3** also 又作 **meander on** to talk for a long time in a way that is unclear or boring 唠叨，东拉西扯地讲话: *Will meandered on for hours.* 威尔东拉西扯地谈了好几个小时。—**meanderings** *n* [plural] —**meander** *n* [C]

mean·ie, meany /ˈminɪ; ˈmiːni/ *n* [C] *spoken* a word meaning an unkind person, used especially by children【口】卑鄙的家伙；刻薄鬼〔尤作儿语〕: *Don't be such a meanie!* 别那么刻薄！

mean·ing[1] /ˈminɪŋ; ˈmiːnɪŋ/ *n*

1 ▶OF A WORD/SIGN ETC 关于词/符号等的◀ [C,U] the thing or idea that a word, expression, or sign represents 意义，意思；含义: **[+of]** *Can you explain the meaning of this word?* 你能解释一下这个词的意思吗？| *The expression has two very different meanings in English.* 这个短语在英语中有两个非常不同的含义。

2 ▶OF WHAT SB SAYS 某人所说的话的含义◀ [U] the things or ideas that someone wants you to understand from what they say〔某人的话的〕意思: **[+of]** *We couldn't work out the meaning of this last remark.* 我们搞不懂这最后一句话的意思。| **get/catch/understand sb's meaning** (=understand what they are trying to tell you) 明白某人的意思 *Barry could make things pretty unpleasant for us, if you get my meaning.* 巴里会给我们把事情搞得很糟糕的，你明白我的意思吗？

3 what's the meaning of this? *spoken* used to demand an explanation【口】这是什么意思？〔用以要求作出解释〕: *What's the meaning of this? I asked you to be here an hour ago!* 这是什么意思？我要求你一小时之前就要在这儿的！

4 ▶OF A BOOK/FILM ETC 关于书/电影等◀ [U] the ideas that a writer, artist etc wants to show in a book, picture, film etc〔书、图画、电影等的〕主题思想

5 ▶PURPOSE/SPECIAL QUALITY 目标/特殊品质◀ [U] the quality that makes something seem important and makes people feel that their life, work etc has a purpose and value 目标；价值: **lose its meaning** *Life seemed to have lost its meaning since Janet's death.* 珍妮特去世以后生活似乎失去了意义。| **have meaning** *Her studies no longer seemed to have any meaning.* 她的研究似乎不再有任何意义了。

6 ▶TRUE NATURE 本质◀ [U] the true nature and importance of something 本质；重要性: **[+of]** *I was starting to realize the full meaning of the night's events.* 我开始认识到晚上所发生事件的全部意义了。

7 (not) know the meaning of to (not) have experience and understanding of a particular situation or feeling 对…（没）有体验和了解，（不）知道…的含义: *Living in that area, they knew the meaning of fear.* 生活在那个地区，他们知道什么叫恐惧。| *"Guilty, she doesn't know the meaning of the word!"* "愧疚，她不知道这个词的含义！"

meaning[2] *adj* **a meaning look/expression** a look that expresses a particular feeling strongly 意味深长的眼神/表情

mean·ing·ful /ˈminɪŋfl; ˈmiːnɪŋfəl/ *adj* **1** having a meaning that is easy to understand and makes sense 有意义的；浅显易懂的: *The statistics are not very meaningful when taken out of context.* 这些统计数据离开了上下文就看不太明白了。| *Standards must be specified in meaningful terms.* 标准必须用浅显易懂的措辞写清楚。**2 a meaningful look/glance/smile etc** a look that clearly expresses the way someone feels, even though nothing is said 意味深长的眼神/一瞥/微笑等: *John gave us a meaningful look as if to say 'I told you so'.* 约翰意味深长地看了我们一眼，好像在说"我告诉过你们会是这个样子"。**3 a meaningful relationship/experience/argument etc** a relationship etc that is serious, important, or useful 严肃[重要，有用]的关系/经历/辩论等 —**meaningfully** *adv*

M

mean·ing·less /ˈminɪŋlɪs; ˈmiːnɪŋləs/ *adj* **1** something that is meaningless has no purpose or importance and does not seem worth doing or having; FUTILE 无意义的；无目的的；无价值的；不重要的: *a meaningless existence* 无意义的生活 **2** not having a meaning that you can understand or explain〔意义〕不可理解的，无法解释的: *To me the marks on the page were just meaningless symbols.* 对我来说这一页上的标记仅仅是一些没有意义的符号。—**meaninglessness** *n* [U]

means /minz; miːnz/ *n plural* **means**

1 ▶METHOD 方法◀ [C] a method, system, object etc that you use as a way of achieving a result 手段，方法；工具: **[+of]** *What would be the most effective means of advertising our product?* 宣传我们产品的最有效手段是什么呢？| **means of transport** *BrE*【英】**/transportation** *AmE*【美】*We had no means of transport except for two bicycles.* 除了两辆自行车以外，我们没有其他交通工具了。| **by honest/fair etc means** *The money was acquired by dishonest means.* 这些钱是用不正当手段获得的。| **means of identification** (=something that shows your name and address) 身份证明文件

2 by means of using a particular method or system 以…方法[装置]: *The blocks are raised by means of pulleys.* 那些大块物件是用滑轮吊起来的。

3 by all means *spoken* used to mean 'of course' when politely allowing someone to do something or agreeing with a suggestion【口】当然可以: *"Can I bring Alan to the party?" "By all means!"* "我能带艾伦来参加聚会吗？""当然可以！" | *By all means try the jacket on, but I think it will be too big for you.* 当然可以试穿一下这件上衣，但我觉得你穿太大了。

4 by no means/not by any means not at all 决不，一点都不: *It is by no means certain that the game will take place.* 比赛是否会举行完全不能肯定。| *She's not a bad kid, by any means.* 她不是个坏孩子，绝对不是。

5 a means to an end something that you do only to achieve a result, not because you want to do it 达到目的的手段: *For Geoff, the job was simply a means to an end.* 对杰夫来说，那份工作仅仅是达到目的的手段。

6 ▶MONEY 钱◀ [plural] the money or income that you have 钱；收入: **have the means to do sth** *I don't have the means to support a family.* 我没有钱养活一家人。| **according to your means** *Each member contributes according to his or her means.* 每个成员根据自己的财力捐款。| **beyond your means** (=costing more than you can afford) 超出自己的财力，负担不起 *These medical costs are beyond the means of most working people.* 这些医疗费用大多数劳工阶层都支付不起。| **within your means** (=not costing more than you can afford) 负担[支付]得起 *The cost should be well within the means of the average family.* 费用应该完全不超出一般家庭的支付能力。

7 man/woman of means *literary* someone who is rich【文】富翁/富婆

8 the means of production *technical* the material, tools, and equipment that are used in the production of goods【术语】生产资料: *public ownership of the means of production* 生产资料公有制 —see also 另见 **by fair means or foul** (FAIR[1] (13)), **ways and means** (WAY[1] (3))

mean-spir·it·ed /ˌ· ˈ···◂/ *adj* not generous or sympathetic 小气的，吝啬的；小心眼的；无同情心的: *a mean-spirited, jealous man* 心胸狭窄、嫉妒心强的男子

means test /ˈ· ·/ *n* [C] an official check in order to find out whether someone is poor enough to need money from the state 经济状况调查〔用以确定某人是否很贫穷而需要国家救济〕—**means-tested** *adj*: *means-tested benefits* 按经济状况调查结果而享受的补助

meant /mɛnt; ment/ *v* the past tense and past participle of MEAN[1]

mean·time /ˈminˌtaɪm; ˈmiːntaɪm/ *adv* **1 in the meantime** in the period of time between now and a future event, or between two events in the past 在此期间；与此同时: *The doctor will be here soon. In the meantime, try and relax.* 医生很快就来，你现在先设法放松一下。| *I didn't see her for another five years, and in the meantime she had got married and had a couple of kids.* 我又有五年没见到她，在此期间她结了婚并生了两个孩子。**2 for the meantime** for the present time, until something happens 目前，眼下: *The power supply should be back soon – for the meantime we'll have to use candles.* 应该很快就会恢复供电——眼下我们只好点蜡烛。**3** [sentence adverb 句子副词] *spoken* in the present period, before something else happens【口】在目前这段时间里: *Dinner will be at 7. Meantime, just make yourselves at home.* 七点钟开饭。开饭前，大家随便些，就像在自己家里一样。

mean·while /ˈminˌhwaɪl; ˈmiːnwaɪl/ *adv* [sentence adverb 句子副词] **1** in the period of time between two events 在此期间: *The flight will be announced soon. Meanwhile, please remain seated.* 航班很快就要宣布登机。宣布之前请继续坐在座位上。| **in the meanwhile** *I knew I wouldn't get my exam results for several weeks, and I wasn't sure what to do in the meanwhile.*

我知道我要数周以后才会得到自己的考试成绩，在此期间我拿不准该做点什么。**2** while something else is happening 与此同时：*Jim went to answer the phone. Meanwhile Pete started to prepare lunch.* 吉姆去接电话。皮特这时开始准备午饭。**3** used to compare two things that are happening at the same time 在这期间，与此同时〔用以比较同时发生的两件事〕：*The incomes of male professionals went up by almost 80%. Meanwhile, part-time women workers saw their earnings fall.* 男性职业人士的收入几乎增加了80%，而与此同时兼职女性的收入却下降了。

mean·y /ˈmiːnɪ; ˈmiːni/ *n* [C] another way of spelling MEANIE meanie 的另一种拼法

mea·sles /ˈmizḷz; ˈmiːzəlz/ *n* [U] also 又作 **the measles** an infectious illness in which you have a fever and small red spots on your face and body 麻疹 —see also 另见 GERMAN MEASLES

meas·ly /ˈmizlɪ; ˈmiːzli/ *adj informal* very small and disappointing in size, quantity, or value【非正式】〔大小、数量或价值〕微不足道的，小[少]得令人失望的：*All I got was a measly £5.* 我得到的只是区区五英镑。

mea·su·ra·ble /ˈmɛʒrəbḷ; ˈmeʒərəbəl/ *adj* **1** large or important enough to have a definite effect 重大的，重要的：*The tax will not have any measurable impact on the lives of most people.* 这种税收将不会对大多数人的生活产生重大的影响。**2** able to be measured 可测量的，可度量的：*measurable results* 可衡量的结果 —**measurably** *adv*: *His mood had improved measurably.* 他的情绪已经大大好转了。

3 **mea·sure¹** /ˈmɛʒɚ; ˈmeʒə/ *n*

1 ▶OFFICIAL ACTION 正式行动◀ [C] an official action that is intended to deal with a particular problem 措施，办法：*Stronger measures are needed to combat crime.* 需要采取更强有力的措施来与犯罪作斗争。

2 half measures things done to deal with a difficult situation that are not effective or firm enough 〔处理困难情况效果不佳或不够坚决的〕折中办法：*This was no time for half measures and compromises.* 这不是搞折中和妥协的时候。

3 ▶A CERTAIN AMOUNT 一定的量◀ **a measure of success/agreement/freedom etc** a certain amount of a good or useful quality 一定程度的成功/同意/自由等：*new legislation giving women a measure of economic independence* 给予妇女一定程度经济独立的新立法

4 ▶UNIT OF MEASUREMENT 度量单位◀ [C] an amount or unit in a measuring system 计量[度量]单位：*A centimetre is a measure of length.* 厘米是长度计量单位。| *a table of weights and measures* 度量衡表

5 a measure of alcohol/whisky etc a standard amount of an alcoholic drink 标准量的一杯酒/威士忌等

6 ▶SIGN/PROOF 标志/证明◀ **be a measure of sth** *formal* to be a sign of the importance, strength etc of something【正式】是某事的标志[证明]：*It is a measure of his popularity that he was able to travel around without a bodyguard.* 他能不带保镖到处旅行是他深得民心的证明。

7 ▶WAY OF JUDGING STH 判断某事的方法◀ **a measure of** a way of testing or judging something 测试[判断、评价]…的方法：*Exams are not necessarily the best measure of students' abilities.* 考试未必就是测试学生能力的最好方法。

8 beyond measure *formal* very great or very much【正式】非常大；非常多；极其：*The pride he felt was beyond measure.* 他感到无比的自豪。| *Her work has improved beyond measure.* 她的工作已大有进步。

9 for good measure in addition to what you have already done or given 〔在已做好或已给出的某物之外〕再增加；外加：*She tasted the mixture and added another glass of brandy for good measure.* 她尝了尝兑好的酒，然后又加进去一杯白兰地。

10 in large measure/in some measure to a great degree or to some degree 在很大/某种程度上：*The improvements are due in large measure to his leadership.* 这些改进在很大程度上是由于他领导有方。

11 in full measure if someone gives something back in full measure, they give back as much as they received 全部地〔回报所受之物〕：*They returned our hospitality in full measure.* 他们对我们报以同样的热情。

12 the full measure of *formal* the whole of something【正式】…的全部：*Ralph received the full measure of his mother's devotion.* 拉尔夫得到了母亲全部的关爱。

13 get the measure of sb/take sb's measure to form a judgment of someone's abilities or character, so that you are able to deal with them or defeat them 估量某人的能力[性格]，掂某人的分量：*She soon got the measure of her opponent.* 她很快就掂出了对手的分量。

14 ▶THING USED FOR MEASURING 计量之物◀ [C] something such as a piece of wood or a container used for measuring 量具，量器 —see also 另见 TAPE MEASURE

15 ▶SYSTEM FOR MEASURING 计量制◀ [U] a system for measuring amount, size, or weight 计量制，度量法：*liquid measure* 液体量度，液量

16 ▶MUSIC 音乐◀ [C] *AmE* one of a group of notes and rests (REST¹ (12)), separated by VERTICAL lines, into which a line of written music is divided【美】小节 —see also 另见 MADE-TO-MEASURE, **give sb short measure** (SHORT¹ (14))

measure 量，测量

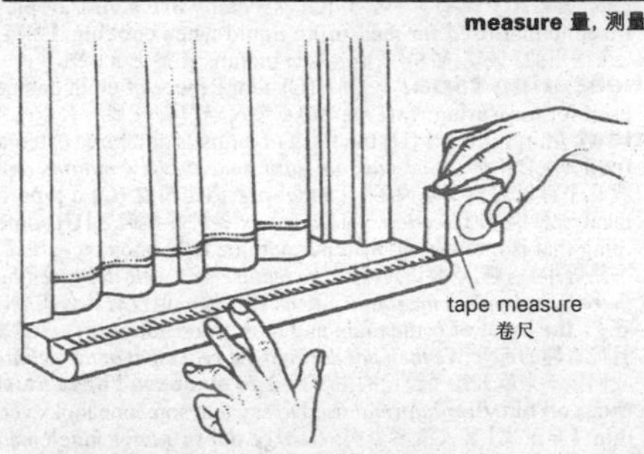

measure² *v* **1** [T] to find the size, length, or amount of something using standard units 量，测量；计量：*Could you measure the height of the wall for me?* 你能为我量一下墙的高度吗？| 2
The rainfall was measured over a three-month period. 对三个月内的降雨量进行了测量。| **measure sb for sth** (=measure someone in order to make clothes for them) 给某人量体裁衣 *She was being measured for her wedding dress.* 正在给她量尺寸做结婚礼服。**2** [T] to judge the importance, value, or true nature of something 估量，衡量〔某物的重要性、价值或真正性质〕：*What criteria can we use to measure women's progress in the workforce?* 我们能用什么标准来衡量妇女在劳动大军中的进步呢？| **measure sth by sth** *Education shouldn't be measured purely by examination results.* 教育不应该纯粹用考试成绩来衡量。**3** [linking verb 连系动词] to be a particular size, length, or amount 〔某物的〕体积[长度，数额]为…：*That old tree must measure at least 30 metres from top to bottom.* 那棵古树从树梢到地面至少有30米。| *an earthquake measuring 6.5 on the Richter scale* 里氏6.5级的地震 **4** [T] to show or record a particular kind of measurement 显示，记录〔长度、高度、大小等〕：*an instrument for measuring tiny amounts of electrical current* 测微量电流的仪器 **5 measure your length** *old use* to fall down flat on the ground【旧】跌倒在地，躺在地上

measure sb/sth **against** *phr v* [T] to judge someone or something by comparing them with another person or thing 〔用与他人或他物相比较的方法〕评判：*When measured against the work of a professional, her efforts look unimpressive.* 当和专业人员的工作相比时，她所作的努力看起来就不怎么起眼了。

measure sth ↔ **off** *phr v* [T] to measure a length of material and cut it from a larger piece 量出并裁下：*The assistant measured off enough fabric for three dresses.* 助手量出并剪裁下足够缝制三条连衣裙的衣料。

measure sth ↔ **out** *phr v* [T] to take a certain amount of liquid, powder etc from a larger amount 量出，量取：*Measure out 100 grams of flour.* 量出100克面粉。

measure up *phr v* **1** [I] to be good enough to do a particular job or to reach a particular standard 合格；达到标准：[+to] *How will the Secretary General measure up to his new responsibilities?* 秘书长将如何才能胜任他的新职责呢？| *We'll give you a week's trial in the job to see how you measure up.* 我们将让你在这个工作岗位试做一个星期，看你是否合格。**2** [I,T] to measure something 计量(某物)：*I'd better measure up before I start laying the carpet.* 在开始铺地毯之前我最好量一量。

mea·sured /ˈmɛʒɚd; ˈmeʒəd/ *adj* careful and slow or steady 慎重而缓慢的；平稳的：*a calm measured voice* 平缓的声音 | *a measured response* 慎重的答复

mea·sure·less /ˈmɛʒɚlɪs; ˈmeʒələs/ *adj literary* too big to be measured【文】大得无法测量的，无边无际的：*falling through the measureless ocean* 在茫茫大海中下坠

mea·sure·ment /ˈmɛʒɚmənt; ˈmeʒəmənt/ *n* **1** [C usually plural 一般用复数] the length, height etc of something 〔某物的〕长度；高度；大小：**waist/chest etc measurement** *What's your waist measurement?* 你的腰围有多大？| **make/take measure-** 3

ments (=measure something) 量尺寸, 测量 *The builders made careful measurements.* 建筑人员仔细地进行了测量。| **take sb's measurements** (=measure someone in order to make or find clothes for them) 〔为缝制或购买衣服〕给某人量尺寸 **2** [U] the act of measuring something 测量, 计量, 衡量: *the measurement of performance* 性能测试

measuring cup /'⋯, ·/ *n* [C] *especially AmE* a cup used for measuring food or liquid when cooking【尤美】〔烹饪用的〕量杯

measuring jug /'⋯, ·/ *n* [C] *especially BrE* a glass or plastic container used for measuring liquid when cooking【尤英】〔烹饪用的〕玻璃[塑料]量壶 —see picture at 参见 JUG 图

measuring tape /'⋯, ·/ *n* [C] a long piece of cloth or steel used for measuring; TAPE MEASURE 卷尺, 软尺, 皮尺

S2 W3 **meat** /mit; miːt/ *n* **1** [U] the flesh of animals and birds eaten as food〔供食用的〕肉: *I gave up eating meat a few months ago.* 我几个月以前就不吃肉了。| *meat pie* 肉馅饼 **2** [C] a type of meat 一种肉: *a selection of cold meats* 各种冷盘肉 **3** [U] something that is interesting or important in a talk, book etc〔谈话、书籍等中〕有趣[重要]的内容: *The lecture was well-delivered but there wasn't much meat in it.* 演讲讲得很好, 但没有什么实质内容。| **the meat of** (=the main and most interesting part) ⋯主要且最有趣的部分 *We then got down to the real meat of the debate.* 我们接下来就开始了辩论的主要部分。**4 sb doesn't have much meat on him/her** *informal* used to say that someone looks very thin【非正式】某人没多少肉: *George doesn't have much meat on him, does he?* 乔治身上没有几两肉, 是吧? **5 easy meat** *informal* someone who it is easy to deceive or hurt【非正式】易上当受骗的人; 易受伤害的人 **6 meat and drink to sb** something that someone enjoys doing or finds very easy to do 某人喜欢做的事; 某人认为很容易做的事: *The first five questions were on basketball, which was meat and drink to Larry.* 前五个问题是关于篮球的, 这对拉里来说轻而易举。| *Repairing cars is meat and drink to him.* 修车是他喜欢做的事。**7 be the meat in the sandwich** *BrE informal* to be friendly with two people or groups who are quarrelling【英, 非正式】跟争吵的双方都友好 **8 one man's meat is another man's poison** used to say that something that one person likes may not be liked by someone else 甲之熊掌, 乙之砒霜; 一个人喜欢的另一个人未必喜欢 **9 the meat and potatoes** *AmE informal* the most important part of a discussion【美, 非正式】〔讨论中〕最重要的部分: *Let's get down to the meat and potatoes; how much are you going to pay me for this?* 我们来讨论最关键的问题: 你打算为此付我多少钱?

meat·ball /'mit,bɔl; 'miːtbɔːl/ *n* [C] a small round ball made from thin pieces of meat pressed together 肉丸子

meat grind·er /'· ,··/ *n* [C] *AmE* a machine that cuts meat into very small pieces by forcing it through small holes【美】绞肉机; MINCER *BrE*【英】

Meath /mið, miːð/ a COUNTY in the northeast of the Republic of Ireland, an important area of good farming land 米斯郡〔爱尔兰共和国东北部一郡, 是该国重要的良田区〕

meat·loaf /'mit,lof; 'miːtləʊf/ *n* [C,U] a type of food made from meat and other foods which are mixed together in the shape of a LOAF and baked 肉糕〔一种用肉和其他食物搅拌在一起做成面包形状烤制而成的食物〕

meat-pack·ing /'·,··/ *n* [U] *AmE* the preparation of dead animals so that they can be sold as meat【美】肉类加工: *the meat packing industry* 肉类加工业 —**meat-packer** *n* [C]

meat·y /'mitɪ; 'miːti/ *adj* **1** containing a lot of meat or tasting strongly of meat 多肉的; 肉味浓的: *a delicious meaty gravy* 味美肉多的肉汁 **2** *informal* big and fat, with a lot of flesh【非正式】大而肥胖的: *a tall guy with meaty shoulders* 身材高大、双肩肥厚的男子 **3** *informal* containing a lot of interesting ideas or information【非正式】内容丰富的: *The lecture wasn't very meaty.* 这个讲座内容不是很丰富。

Mec·ca /'mɛkə; 'mekə/ a city in Saudi Arabia where the Prophet Muhammad was born. It is the holiest city of Islam. People who are not Muslims are not allowed to go there, but every Muslim must try to make a pilgrimage (=religious journey) to Mecca once in their lifetime. 麦加〔沙特阿拉伯一城市, 先知穆罕默德的诞生地、伊斯兰教最神圣的城市。非穆斯林人士不得进入麦加。每个穆斯林在有生之年都必须争取前往麦加朝圣一次〕—see 见 HAJ; MEDINA

mecca *n* [singular] **1** a place that many people want to visit for a particular reason 众人想去参观的地方, 众人向往之胜地: [+for] *Florence is a mecca for students of Art History.* 佛罗伦萨是修艺术史的学生们向往的胜地。**2 Mecca** a city in Saudi Arabia which is the holiest city of Islam 麦加〔沙特阿拉伯城市, 伊斯兰教的圣地〕

Mec·ca·no /mɪ'kɑno; mɪ'kɑːnəʊ/ *trademark* a type of toy used for building machines, vehicles, bridges, and other things. It consists of metal or plastic pieces in different shapes and sizes, which you connect with nuts and BOLTS. Meccano has been popular with children in the UK for over 50 years. There is a similar type of toy in the US called an Erector Set.【商标】麦卡诺〔一种玩具, 由各种形状和大小的金属或塑料部件组成, 可用螺帽螺栓连接拼装成机器、车辆、桥梁等。50余年来, 它一直是英国儿童喜欢的一种玩具。美国也有一类似产品, 名叫伊雷克特组合〕

me·chan·ic /mə'kænɪk; mɪ'kænɪk/ *n* **1** [C] someone who is skilled at repairing motor vehicles and machinery 技工; 机械工; 机修工 **2 mechanics** [U] the science that deals with the effects of forces on objects 力学; 机械学 —see also 另见 QUANTUM MECHANICS **3 the mechanics of (doing) sth** the way in which something works or is done (做)某事的方法[技巧, 技术细节]: *I still don't understand the mechanics of transferring computer files onto a different machine.* 我仍然不懂怎样把电脑文件转到另一台电脑上去。

me·chan·i·cal /mə'kænɪkl; mɪ'kænɪkəl/ *adj* **1** using power from an engine to do a particular kind of work 机械操纵的: *a mechanical digger* 挖掘机 **2** affecting or involving a machine 机械方面的: *The pump shut off as a result of a mechanical failure.* 由于机械故障, 泵停住了。**3** a mechanical action, reply etc is done without thinking, and has been done many times before〔动作、回答等〕机械的, 不加思考的: *He was asked the same question so many times that the answer became mechanical.* 他被多次问到同样的问题, 所以他的回答都变得机械起来。**4** *informal* someone who is mechanical understands how machines work【非正式】有机械方面知识的 **5** *technical* connected with or produced by physical forces【术语】物理的; 物理产生的: *the mechanical properties of solids* 固体的物理特性 —**mechanically** /-klɪ; -kli/ *adv*

mechanical en·gi·neer·ing /·,⋯ ·'·/ *n* [U] the study of the design and production of machines and tools 机械工程(学) —**mechanical engineer** *n* [C]

mechanically mind·ed /·,⋯ '··◂/ *adj* good at understanding how machines work and repairing them 精通机械的; 擅长机械修理的

mechanical pen·cil /·,⋯ '··/ *n* [C] *AmE* a pencil made of metal or plastic, with a thin piece of LEAD (=the part that you write with) inside【美】活动铅笔, 自动铅笔; PROPELLING PENCIL *BrE*【英】

mech·a·nis·m /'mɛkə,nɪzəm; 'mekənɪzəm/ *n* [C] **1** part of a machine that does a particular job 机械装置, 机件, 工作部件: *the brake mechanism* 刹车装置 **2** a system that is intended to achieve something or deal with a problem 机构; 结构; 机制; 体制: *mechanisms to stop the spread of nuclear weapons* 阻止核武器扩散的机制 | *The market system is an imperfect mechanism for achieving full employment.* 市场机制不是实现充分就业的最佳体制。**3** the way that something works 工作方式, 运行机制: *the mechanism of the brain* 大脑的运行机制 **4 defence/survival/escape mechanism** a way of behaving that helps you to avoid or deal with something that is difficult or dangerous 防卫/生存/逃避机制[手段]: *His aggression is actually a defence mechanism against rejection.* 他的好斗其实是出于自卫, 以免被人排斥。

mech·a·nis·tic /,mɛkə'nɪstɪk; ,mekə'nɪstɪk◂/ *adj* tending to explain the actions and behaviour of living things as if they were machines 机械论的: *a mechanistic view of the universe* 对宇宙的机械论观点 —**mechanistically** /-klɪ; -kli/ *adv*

mech·a·nize also 又作 **-ise** *BrE*【英】/'mɛkə,naɪz; 'mekənaɪz/ *v* [I,T] to change the way that something is made or done, so that the work is done by machines instead of people or animals (使)机械化: *Almost the entire process of car manufacturing has been mechanized.* 整个汽车制造过程已经几乎完全机械化了。—**mechanized** *adj*: *mechanized farming* 机械化耕作 —**mechanization** /,mɛkənə'zeʃən; ,mekənaɪ'zeɪʃən/ *n* [U]

M Econ *n BrE* Master of Economics; a university higher degree in ECONOMICS that you get after your first degree【英】经济学硕士; 经济学硕士学位

M Ed /,ɛm 'ɛd; ,em 'ed/ *n* Master of Education; a university higher degree in teaching that you get after your first degree 教育学硕士; 教育学硕士学位

Med, the /mɛd; med/ *n BrE informal* the area surrounding the Mediterranean Sea【英, 非正式】地中海沿岸地区

med·al /'mɛdl; 'medl/ *n* [C] a round flat piece of metal given to someone who has won a competition or who has done something brave 奖牌; 奖章; 勋章: *an Olympic gold medal* 奥运会金牌 —see also 另见 **deserve a medal** (DESERVE (3))

med·al·ist /ˈmɛdl̩ɪst; ˈmedl-ɨst/ *n* [C] the American spelling of MEDALLIST medallist的美式拼法

me·dal·li·on /mɪˈdæljən; mɨˈdæliən/ *n* [C] a piece of metal shaped like a large coin, worn as jewellery on a chain around the neck 圆形徽章〔形似大钱币, 用链子戴于颈部的金属饰物〕

med·al·list /ˈmɛdl̩ɪst; ˈmedl-ɨst/ *n* [C] *BrE* someone who has won a medal in a competition【英】奖牌获得者: *the Olympic silver medallist* 奥运会银牌得主

Medal of Hon·our /ˌ‥ ˈ‥/ *n* [C] the highest award given by Congress to a soldier, sailor etc who has done something extremely brave〔美国〕荣誉勋章〔由美国国会授予士兵、水兵等的最高军功勋章〕

Med·a·war /ˈmɛdəwɚ; ˈmedəwə/, **Sir Peter** (1915-87) a British ZOOLOGIST (=a scientist who studies animals and their behaviour), who made important discoveries about the IMMUNE SYSTEM (=the system that your body uses to protect itself from disease). He won a Nobel Prize for medicine. 梅达沃〔(1915-1987), 英国动物学家。他曾在免疫系统研究方面有过重大发现, 并获诺贝尔医学奖〕

med·dle /ˈmɛdl̩; ˈmedl/ *v* [I] **1** to deliberately become involved in a situation that does not concern you, or that you do not understand 干预, 干涉; 管闲事: **[+in/with]** *I wish you wouldn't meddle in my affairs.* 我希望你不要干涉我的事。**2** to touch something carelessly in a way that might break it 胡乱摆弄: **[+with]** *The kids are always meddling with the ornaments.* 孩子们总是乱动那些装饰品。—**meddler** *n* [C]

med·dle·some /ˈmɛdl̩səm; ˈmedlsəm/ *adj* tending to become involved in situations that do not concern you, in a way that annoys people 好干预的; 爱管闲事的: *that meddlesome old woman* 那个爱管闲事的老太太

Me·dea /məˈdiə; məˈdɪə/ in ancient Greek stories, a PRINCESS who could do magic, and who helped Jason to get the Golden Fleece. She later killed the children she and Jason had together when he decided to marry another woman. 美狄亚〔古希腊神话中一位公主。她懂魔法, 曾帮助伊阿宋找到了金羊毛。当伊阿宋决定娶另一个女人为妻时, 美狄亚就杀掉了自己和伊阿宋所生的孩子〕

Mé·de·cins sans Fron·tières /ˌmedəsæn sɑn frɑnˈtjɛr; ˌmeɪdəsæn sɑːn frɒnˈtjeə/ an international organization, similar to the Red Cross, that provides medical help to people who are suffering as a result of war or natural disasters. Its French name means 'Doctors without Borders'.【法语】无国界医生组织〔一个国际组织, 与红十字会类似。该组织为遭遇战争和自然灾害的人们提供医疗援助。名称为法语, 英文译名为"Doctors without Borders"〕

Me·del·lin /ˌmɛdl̩ˈin; ˌmedelˈiːn/ a city in the northwest of Colombia, which is an important industrial centre. People think of Medellin as a centre of the illegal trade in the drug COCAINE. 麦德林〔哥伦比亚西北部一城市, 是该国重要的工业中心。人们心目中的麦德林是一个可卡因非法交易中心〕

S2 W2 **me·di·a** /ˈmidiə; ˈmiːdiə/ *n* **1 the media** all the organizations, such as television, radio, and the newspapers, that provide information for the public 新闻媒体, 传媒, 大众传播媒介〈如电视、广播、报纸等〉: *The letter was leaked to the media by a White House official.* 这封信被一名白宫官员透露给了新闻媒体。| [also+plural verb *BrE* 英] *The media have launched a bitter attack on the Health Minister.* 大众传媒向卫生部长发起了猛烈攻击。| **media coverage** (=the amount of time or space given to an event by the media)〔新闻〕媒体报道量 *The war got massive media coverage.* 那次战争受到大众传媒的广泛报道。| **media event** (=an event that the media give a lot of attention to) 传媒瞩目的事件 | **media hype** (=a lot of attention given to an event by the media, making it seem much more important than it really is) 传媒宣传[渲染] **2** the plural of MEDIUM —see also 另见 MASS MEDIA

med·i·ae·val /ˌmidɪˈivl̩; ˌmediˈiːvəl◂/ *adj* another spelling of MEDIEVAL medieval的另一种拼法

me·di·an¹ /ˈmidɪən; ˈmiːdiən/ *n* **1** [C] *AmE* a thin area of land running down the middle of a road to keep traffic travelling in different directions apart【美】〔道路的〕中央分隔带, 中央分道区, 中间安全区; CENTRAL RESERVATION *BrE*【英】**2** [C] the middle measurement in a set of measurements that are arranged in order 中位数 **3** [C] *technical* a line passing from one of the points of a TRIANGLE to the opposite side【术语】〔三角形的〕中线

median² *adj* [only before noun 仅用于名词前] *technical*【术语】**1** in or passing through the middle 中间的; 穿过中点的 **2** *technical* related to a line passing from one of the points of a TRIANGLE to the opposite side【术语】〔三角形〕中线的

median strip /ˈ‥ ˌ/ *n* [C] *AmE* MEDIAN¹ (1)【美】〔道路的〕中央分隔带, 中央分道区, 中间安全区 —see picture on page A3 参见A3页图

media stud·ies /ˈ‥ ˌ‥/ *n* [U] *BrE* the study of newspapers, radio and television【英】媒体研究

me·di·ate /ˈmidɪˌet; ˈmiːdieɪt/ *v* **1** [I,T] to try to end a quarrel between two people or groups 调停, 调解, 斡旋: **[+between]** *The U.N. attempted to mediate between the warring factions.* 联合国试图在两个交战派别之间进行斡旋。| **mediate sth** *The court was set up to mediate civil disputes.* 该法庭是为调解民事纠纷而成立的。**2** [T] to find an agreement or solution by talking to two people or groups who are quarrelling 通过调解促成〔协议等〕: *They've succeeded in mediating a ceasefire.* 他们通过斡旋成功地促成了停火。**3** [T usually passive 一般用被动态] *formal or technical* if the effect of something is mediated by another thing, it changes because of that other thing【正式或术语】使变化; 使受影响: *Child mortality is mediated by economic factors.* 儿童死亡率受经济因素的影响。—**mediator** *n* [C] —**mediation** /ˌmidɪˈeʃən; ˌmiːdiˈeɪʃən/ *n* [U]

med·ic /ˈmɛdɪk; ˈmedɪk/ *n* [C] **1** *informal* a medical doctor【非正式】医生 **2** *BrE* a medical student【英】医科学生 **3** *AmE* someone in the army who gives medical treatment【美】随军卫生员

Med·i·caid /ˈmɛdɪˌked; ˈmedɪkeɪd/ *n* [U] a system in the US by which the government helps to pay the cost of medical treatment for poor people〔美国为穷人设立的〕医疗补助制度 —compare 比较 MEDICARE

med·i·cal¹ /ˈmɛdɪkl̩; ˈmedɪkəl/ *adj* connected with medicine and the treatment of disease or injury 医学的; 医术的; 医疗的: *The injury required urgent medical attention.* 那处伤口需要紧急治疗。| *medical college* 医学院 | *Poor people can only afford the most basic medical treatment.* 穷人只负担得起最基本的医疗。| **the medical profession** (=doctors, nurses, and other people who treat people who are ill) 医学界 —**medically** /-kl̩ɪ; -kli/ *adv* S2 W2

medical² *n* [C] *BrE* an examination of your body by a doctor to see if you are healthy【英】体格检查; PHYSICAL² *AmE*【美】: *You'll need to have a medical before starting the new job.* 在开始这项新工作以前你要进行体格检查。

medical cer·tif·i·cate /ˈ‥ ˌ‥‥/ *n* [C] an official piece of paper signed by a doctor saying that you are too ill to work or that you are completely healthy〔证明病重不能工作的〕诊断书; 健康证明

medical prac·ti·tion·er /ˌ‥ ˈ‥‥/ *n* [C] *BrE formal* a doctor【英, 正式】医生

Medical Re·search Coun·cil, the /ˌ‥ ˈ‥ ˌ‥/ a British organization that gives government money to hospitals, universities, and other institutions so that they can do medical research 医学研究委员会〔英国一组织, 专门为医院、大学等机构开展医学研究提供资助〕

medical school /ˈ‥ ˌ/ *n* [C,U] a college or university where people study to become doctors 医学院; 医科大学

me·dic·a·ment /məˈdɪkəmənt; mɪˈdɪkəmənt/ *n* [C] *formal* a substance used on or in the body to treat a disease【正式】药物, 药剂

Med·i·care /ˈmɛdɪˌkɛr; ˈmedɪkeə/ *n* [U] a system by which the US government helps to pay for the medical treatment of old people〔美国由政府设立的〕老年人医疗保健制度 —compare 比较 MEDICAID

med·i·cat·ed /ˈmɛdɪˌketɪd; ˈmedɨkeɪtɨd/ *adj* medicated soap or SHAMPOO contains a substance to help small medical problems of your skin or hair〔香皂或洗发剂〕含药物成分的

med·i·ca·tion /ˌmɛdɪˈkeʃən; ˌmedɨˈkeɪʃən/ *n* [C,U] medicine or drugs given to people who are ill 药物, 药剂: **be on medication** *She's on medication for her heart.* 她正在服药治疗心脏病。

Med·i·ci, the /ˈmɛdɪtʃi; ˈmedɨtʃiː/ a rich and powerful Italian family of bankers who ruled Florence from the 15th to the 18th centuries, and spent much of their money on art and on providing financial support to artists 美第奇家族〔意大利一有钱有势的银行世家。该家族15至18世纪统治着佛罗伦萨, 曾花费大量资金购买艺术品, 为艺术家提供财力支持〕

me·di·ci·nal /məˈdɪsn̩l; mɨˈdɪsənəl/ *adj* **1** a medicinal substance can cure illness or disease（医）药的; 药用的; 有疗效的: **medicinal properties** *Evening primrose oil is thought to have medicinal properties.* 夜来香油被认为有药物效用。**2 for medicinal purposes** *humorous* used to say jokingly that you drink alcohol because it is good for your health【幽默】为了医疗目的, 为了治病〔用以开玩笑地说因对健康有益而饮酒〕: *I keep a*

bottle of brandy handy – purely for medicinal purposes. 我手头经常准备着一瓶白兰地 —— 纯粹是为了治病。—compare 比较 MEDICAL[1] —**medicinally** *adv*

med·i·cine /ˋmɛdəsn̩; ˈmedsən/ *n* **1** [C,U] a substance used for treating illness, especially a liquid you drink 药, 药物〔尤指口服的药水〕: **take medicine** *Have you taken your medicine?* 你服过药了吗? **2** [U] the treatment and study of illnesses and injuries 医术; 医学: *He studied medicine at Yale.* 他曾经在耶鲁大学学医。| *homeopathic medicine* 顺势疗法 **3 the best medicine** the best way of making you feel better when you are sad 最好的药〔忧伤时使你心情好一些的最佳办法〕: *Laughter is the best medicine.* 大笑是最好的药。**4 give someone a dose/taste of their own medicine** to treat someone as badly as they have treated you 以其人之道, 还治其人之身: *I love 'em and leave 'em, she said. I do it to give men a taste of their own medicine.* 我爱他们, 但不会跟他们长相厮守, 她说。我这样对男人是以其人之道还治其人之身。**5 take your medicine (like a man)** to accept an unpleasant situation that you have caused, or a punishment, without complaining (像男子汉那样) 认罚, 没有怨言地忍受自己引起的不愉快的事情 —see also 另见 ALTERNATIVE MEDICINE

medicine chest /ˈ· · ·/ *n* [C] a small cupboard used to store medicines 药柜

medicine man /ˈ· · ·/ or **medicine wom·an** /ˈ· · ,· ·/ *n* [C] a person in a Native American tribe who is considered to have the ability to cure illness and disease 巫医〔美洲印第安人部落中被认为具有治病能力的人〕

med·i·co /ˋmɛdɪ,ko; ˈmedɪkəʊ/ *n* [C] *informal* a MEDIC【非正式】医生; 医科学生; 随军卫生员

med·i·e·val, mediaeval /,midɪˋivl; ,mediˈiːvəl◂/ *adj* **1** connected with the Middle Ages (=the period between about AD 1100 and 1500) 中世纪的, 中古时期的: *medieval literature* 中世纪文学 | *medieval Europe* 中世纪的欧洲 **2** *humorous* very old or old-fashioned【幽默】古老的; 旧式的; 过时的: *The plumbing in this house is positively medieval!* 这个房子里的水管实在太陈旧了!

Me·di·gap /ˋmɛdɪ,gæp; ˈmedi,gæp/ a system in the US by which people who have Medicaid pay money to a company so that they can receive additional medical care and services that they need 差额医疗险〔美国的一种医疗保险制度。享有医疗补贴者给保险公司缴纳一定费用以享受额外医疗保健和服务〕: *My mom has to pay high premiums every month for Medigap to cover prescription drugs.* 我妈妈每个月必须先缴不少差额医疗险才付得起处方药费。

Me·di·na /mɛˋdinə; meˈdiːnə/ a city in Saudi Arabia where Muhammad is buried. It is the most holy place in Islam except for Mecca, and people who are not Muslims are not allowed to go there. 麦地那〔沙特阿拉伯一城市, 穆罕默德陵墓所在地。该城市在伊斯兰教中的地位仅次于麦加, 非穆斯林人士不得进入〕

me·di·o·cre /ˋmidɪ,okɚ; ,miːdiˈəʊkə◂/ *adj* not very good 不太好的; 平凡的, 平庸的: *I thought the film was pretty mediocre.* 我认为这部电影非常一般。| *a mediocre student* 普通学生 —**mediocrity** /,midɪˋɑkrətɪ; ,miːdiˈɒkrʒti/ *n* [U]

med·i·tate /ˋmɛdə,tet; ˈmedʒteɪt/ *v* **1** [I] to empty your mind of thoughts and feelings, in order to relax completely or for religious purposes 默念, 默想; 冥想, 打坐: *I try to meditate for half an hour every evening.* 我每天晚上尽量默想半小时。**2** [I] to think seriously and deeply about something 思考, 沉思, 深思: **[+on/upon]** *She sat quietly, meditating on the day's events.* 她静静地坐着, 思考当天发生的事。**3** [T] to plan to do something, usually something unpleasant 策划, 计划〔不好的事〕: *Silently she meditated revenge.* 她默默地计划复仇。

med·i·ta·tion /,mɛdəˋteʃən; ,medʒˈteɪʃən/ *n* **1** [U] the practice of emptying your mind of thoughts and feelings, in order to relax completely or for religious reasons 默念, 默想; 冥想; 打坐: *Try to set aside an hour each day for meditation.* 每天设法抽出一个小时来打坐冥想。**2** [C usually plural 一般用复数, U] the act of thinking deeply and seriously about something 沉思, 深思, 思考: *He stood gazing into the water, lost in meditation.* 他站在那儿凝望着水面, 陷入了沉思。| *Rob interrupted his father's meditations.* 罗布打断了他父亲的思考。**3** [C usually plural 一般用复数] serious thoughts about a particular subject〔关于某主题的〕感想; 沉思: **[+on]** *meditations on death and loss* 对于死亡和损失的沉思

med·i·ta·tive /ˋmɛdə,tetɪv; ˈmedʒtətɪv/ *adj* thinking deeply and seriously about something 深思的, 沉思的, 思考的: *Dr Wijk contemplated the picture in meditative silence.* 威克医生凝视着那幅画, 默默地沉思。—**meditatively** *adv*

Med·i·ter·ra·ne·an[1] /,mɛdətəˋrenɪən; ,medʒtəˈreɪniən◂/ *n* **the Mediterranean** the sea that is surrounded by the countries of southern Europe, North Africa, and the Middle East 地中海

Mediterranean[2] *adj* from or connected with the Mediterranean Sea, or typical of the area of Southern Europe around it 地中海的; 地中海地区的; 南欧环地中海地区特有的: *the Mediterranean way of life* 地中海地区的生活方式

me·di·um[1] /ˋmidɪəm; ˈmiːdiəm/ *adj* **1** of middle size between large and small, of middle height between tall and short etc〔大小、高矮等〕中等的; 中号的: *What size do you want – large, medium, or small?* 你想要多大尺寸的 —— 大号、中号, 还是小号? | **medium sized/medium size** *a medium-sized onion* 中等大小的洋葱 | **of medium height/length/build etc** *She's of medium height.* 她中等身材。| *The man is of medium build and is in his late 20s.* 那个男子中等身材, 年近30。| *hair of medium length* 中等长短的头发 | **medium to large** *medium to large companies* 大中型公司 | **medium heat/oven** (=at a temperature that is warm but not too high or low) 中等的热度/温度中等的烤炉 *Bake in a medium oven for 25 minutes.* 在温度中等的烤炉里烤25分钟。**2 medium brown/blue etc** a colour which is neither light nor dark 中等色调的褐色/蓝色等: *His jacket's a medium brown colour.* 他的夹克衫是中等色调的褐色。

medium[2] *n plural* **media** /-dɪə; -diə/ or **mediums** [C] **1** a way of communicating information and news to people, such as newspapers, television etc 传播媒介〈如报纸、电视等〉: *Politicians prefer to use the medium of television.* 政治家们喜欢使用电视媒介。—see also 另见 MEDIA **2** a way of expressing your ideas, especially as a writer or an artist〔尤指作家或艺术家表达思想的〕方法, 手段; 艺术形式: **[+for]** *the novel as a medium for satire* 作为一种讽刺手段的小说 | *the visual media* 视觉媒介 **3 medium of instruction** a language that is used for teaching 教学语言: *English is still the main medium of instruction in Nigeria.* 在尼日利亚英语仍然是主要的教学语言。**4 medium of exchange** money or other ways of paying for things 交换媒介〔指金钱或其他的支付方法〕**5** *technical* a substance or material in which things grow or exist【术语】培养基 **6** *technical* a substance through which a force travels【术语】媒质, 媒介物; 传导体 —see also 另见 MAGNETIC MEDIA, **happy medium** (HAPPY (7))

medium[3] *n plural* **mediums** [C] someone who claims to have the power to receive messages from the spirits of the dead 灵媒, 巫师, 招魂者

medium term /ˈ· · ·, ·/ *n* [singular] the period of time a few weeks or months ahead of the present 中期: **in the medium term** *The company's prospects look good in the medium term.* 就中期而言, 公司的前景看好。| *medium term investments* 中期投资 —compare 比较 SHORT-TERM, LONG-TERM

medium wave /ˈ· · · ·/ *written abbreviation* 缩写为 **MW** *n* [U] a system of radio broadcasting using radio waves (WAVE[1] (3)) that are between 100 and 1000 metres in length〔无线电广播的〕中波

med·ley /ˋmɛdlɪ; ˈmedli/ *n* [C] **1** a group of songs or tunes sung or played one after the other as a single piece of music 集成曲, 组合曲; 一组联唱[联奏]的歌曲[乐曲]: *a medley of Eighties hits* 20世纪80年代走红歌曲汇成的组合曲 **2** a swimming race in which the competitors swim using four different strokes (STROKE[1] (2b))〔游泳的〕混合泳比赛, 混合泳接力比赛 **3** [usually singular 一般用单数] a mixture of different kinds of the same thing which produces an interesting or unusual effect 混合物; 大杂烩: *a medley of architectural styles* 各种不同建筑风格的大杂烩

Me·du·sa /mɪˋdjusə; mɪˈdjuːzə/ in ancient Greek MYTHOLOGY, a woman who had snakes instead of hair and turned everyone who looked at her into stone. She was killed by Perseus, who used his shiny SHIELD (=a metal object carried by soldiers to protect themselves) as a mirror so that he did not have to look at her directly, and cut off her head. 美杜莎〔古希腊神话中一蛇发女妖。谁看她, 她就把谁变成石头。她是珀尔修斯杀死的。珀尔修斯用一块闪亮的盾牌当作镜子, 这样眼睛就不用直接看她, 然后把她的脑袋砍下〕

Med·way, the /ˋmɛdwe; ˈmedweɪ/ a river in Kent in southeast England which flows through the **Medway Towns** (Rochester, Gillingham, and Chatham) and joins the River Thames near the sea 梅德韦河〔英格兰东南部肯特郡一河流, 流经罗切斯特、吉灵厄姆和查塔姆, 在沿海附近流入泰晤士河〕

meek /mik; miːk/ *adj* very quiet and gentle and unwilling to argue or express an opinion 温顺的, 驯服的: *a meek and obedient child* 一个温顺听话的孩子 | **meek and mild** (=extremely quiet and gentle) 极其温顺的 *She'd never stand up for herself, she's too meek and mild.* 她从来不替自己争辩, 她太温顺了。—**meekly** *adv*: *She smiled meekly.* 她温顺地笑了笑。—**meekness** *n* [U]

meet¹ /miːt; miːt/ *v past tense and past participle* **met** /mɛt; met/
1 ▶BE IN THE SAME PLACE 在同一地点◀ [I,T not in passive 不用被动态] **a)** to be in the same place as someone else because you have arranged to do this〔事先约好在某处〕会面，碰头: *Meet me at 8.00.* 8点钟和我会面。| *We agreed to meet in front of the theatre.* 我们约好在剧院前碰头。| *Why don't we meet for lunch on Friday?* 我们何不星期五一块吃午饭? **b)** to see someone by chance and talk to them 偶然遇见，碰到: *James and Tim met in the park.* 詹姆斯和蒂姆在公园相遇。| *You'll never guess who I met yesterday – my old teacher!* 你绝对猜不到我昨天遇见谁了——我过去的老师!
2 ▶SEE SB FOR THE FIRST TIME 第一次见到某人◀ [I,T not in passive 不用被动态] to see and talk to someone for the first time, or be introduced to them 认识，结识: *Diego and Susan met on vacation and were married six months later.* 迪哥和苏珊度假时相识，六个月后就结婚了。| *Jane, come and meet Alan and Dave.* 简，过来认识一下艾伦和戴夫。| *I met my husband at University.* 我在大学认识了我丈夫。
3 nice/pleased/glad to meet you *spoken especially BrE*【口，尤英】also 又作 **nice meeting you** *AmE spoken*【美口】used when meeting someone for the first time, especially when another person has introduced you to each other 认识你很高兴〔第一次见面时用，尤指有人介绍时〕: *"Farrah, this is Jean-Paul." "Nice to meet you."* "法拉，这是让-保罗。""幸会!"
4 ▶AT AN AIRPORT/STATION ETC 在机场/车站等◀ [T] to meet someone who has arrived at an airport, station etc 迎接: *Rob came to meet us at the airport.* 罗布来机场迎接我们。
5 ▶COMMITTEE, GROUP ETC 委员会，团体等◀ [I] to be together in the same place, usually in order to discuss something〔尤为商讨某事而〕聚集开会: *The committee meets once a month.* 委员会每月开一次会。
6 ▶OPPONENT 对手◀ [I,T not in passive 不用被动态] to play against another person or team in a competition, or to fight another army in a war〔在比赛中〕与对手交锋;〔在战争中〕与敌军交战; 迎战: *Manchester United will meet Blackburn Rovers in the sixth round of the Cup.* 曼彻斯特联队将在足总杯的第六轮中与布莱克本流浪队交锋。
7 ▶RIVERS/ROADS/LINES ETC 河流/道路/线条等◀ [I,T not in passive 不用被动态] to join together at a particular place 相接; 相交，交汇，会合: *The two roads meet just north of Flagstaff.* 这两条路就在弗拉格斯塔夫以北不远处会合。| **meet sth** *You can see on the map where the land meets the sea.* 你可以在地图上看到陆地和海洋的交汇处。
8 ▶PROBLEM/ATTITUDE/SITUATION 问题/态度/情况◀ [T] to experience a particular kind of problem, attitude, or situation; ENCOUNTER¹ 经历，遭遇，遭受: *I've never met this kind of problem before.* 我以前从来没碰到过这类问题。
9 meet a demand/need/requirement to satisfy a demand etc 满足需求/需要/要求: *The company is unable to meet these wage claims.* 该公司不能满足这些增加工资的要求。
10 meet an aim/goal/target etc to achieve an aim etc 达到目的/目标/指标等: *It's virtually impossible to meet the weekly sales targets.* 要达到每周的销售指标几乎是不可能的。
11 meet debts/costs/expenses etc to pay debts etc 偿付债务/支付费用/支付开销等: *The firm has found itself unable to meet its debts.* 公司发现自己无力偿债。
12 there's more to sb/sth than meets the eye used to say that someone or something is more interesting, intelligent etc than they seem to be 某人/某物比表面所看到的更为有趣[聪明等]
13 our/their eyes meet if two people's eyes meet they look at each other, because they are attracted to each other or because they are thinking the same thing 我们/他们的目光相遇: *Their eyes met across the crowded room.* 他们的目光越过拥挤的房间相遇了。
14 meet sb's eye/gaze/glance etc to look directly at someone who is looking at you 迎着[直视]某人的目光: *Martin met his father's accusing glance defiantly.* 马丁不服气地直视父亲责备的目光。
15 meet your eye/ear to be heard or seen 被看见/听见: *At the top of the mountain a scene of extraordinary beauty met our eyes.* 山顶上，异常美丽的景色映入了我们的眼帘。
16 meet your match to have an opponent who is stronger or more skilful than you are 遇到对手: *I think he's finally met his match.* 我想他终于遇到对手了。
17 meet sb halfway to do some of the things that someone wants, in order to reach an agreement with them 与某人妥协，迁就某人: *They won't pay all our expenses but they might be prepared to meet us halfway.* 他们不会支付我们的全部开销，但他们也许愿意支付一部分。
18 ▶TOUCH/HIT 接触/碰撞◀ [I,T] to touch or hit another object〔与另一物体〕接触，碰撞: *Their hands met under the table.* 他们的手在桌子下面碰了一下。
19 meet (sth) head-on a) if two vehicles or people that are moving quickly towards each other meet head-on, they hit each other suddenly and violently〔车辆或人〕迎头撞上(某物) **b)** if you meet a problem head-on, you deal with it directly without trying to avoid it 不回避地直接处理〔某一问题〕
20 meet your death/end to die in a particular way〔以某种方式〕死去: *The general met a violent end at the hands of a paid assassin.* 将军被一个雇佣杀手残暴地杀害了。
21 meet your maker *informal humorous* to die【非正式，幽默】去见上帝，死
22 sb has met their Waterloo used to say that someone will be defeated 某人已[将]被击败，某人遭遇了滑铁卢 —see also 另见 **make (both) ends meet** (END¹ (17))

meet up *phr v* [I] **1** to meet someone in order to do something together 碰头，相聚: *We often meet up after work and go for a drink.* 下班后我们常常一块去喝一杯。| [+with] *Pete met up with us after the game.* 看完比赛后皮特和我们聚在一起。**2** if roads, paths etc meet up they join together at a particular place〔道路等〕相互连接，相交，交会: [+with] *The path eventually meets up with the main road.* 这条小路最终与大路交会。

meet with sb/sth *phr v* [T] **1** to have a meeting with someone 会见，会晤: *Representatives of EC countries will meet with senior American politicians.* 欧共体国家的代表们将会晤美国高级政治人物。**2** to get a particular reaction or result 遭到，遭受; 获得: **meet with approval/disapproval/opposition** *The senator's suggestions met with widespread disapproval.* 参议员的建议遭到普遍反对。| **meet with success/failure** (=succeed or fail) 获得成功/遭到失败 *Our attempts at negotiation finally met with some success.* 我们谈判中的努力最终获得了一些成功。**3 meet with an accident/danger/death** *formal* to experience something by chance, often something unpleasant【正式】遭遇事故/危险/死亡: *Rizzio met with a fatal accident at Hollyrood Palace.* 里奇奥在荷里路德宫遭遇意外事故身亡。

meet² *n* [C] **1 track/sports meet** *especially AmE* a sports competition, especially a competition between people running races【尤美】田径/体育运动会 **2** *BrE* an occasion when a group of people riding horses go out to hunt foxes (FOX¹ (1))【英】集体骑马猎狐

meet³ *adj old use* right or suitable【旧】对的; 适合的

meet·ing /ˈmitɪŋ; ˈmiːtɪŋ/ *n* **1** [C] an event at which people meet to talk and decide things 会议; 集会: **attend a meeting** *Over a hundred people attended the meeting.* 一百多人参加了会议。| **be in/at a meeting** *Mrs Lavelle is in a meeting at the moment.* 拉韦尔夫人眼下正在开会。| **hold a meeting** *A meeting will be held in the City Hall on Thursday at 2pm.* 周四下午两点钟将在市政厅开会。**2 the meeting** *formal* all the people who attend a meeting【正式】所有参加会议的人，全体与会者: *I'd like to put a few ideas before the meeting.* 我想向与会者提出几点想法。**3** [usually singular 一般用单数] a situation of two or more people meeting each other by chance or because they have arranged to do this 会面，会见: *I had felt drawn to Alice ever since our first meeting.* 自从第一次见面后我就被艾丽斯吸引住了。**4** [C] a sports competition or a set of races for horses 运动会; 赛马会 **5 meeting of minds** a situation in which two people have very similar ideas and understand each other very well 彼此意见一致; 彼此非常理解: *There was a real meeting of minds between the composer and his young pupil.* 作曲家和他的年轻学生之间有一种真正的默契。**6** an event at which a group of Quakers (=a Christian religious group) worship together〔基督教贵格会教徒的〕宗教聚会，祈祷会

meeting-house /ˈ· · ·/ *n* [C] a building where Quakers worship〔基督教贵格会的〕聚会所

meg·a /ˈmɛgə; ˈmegə/ *adj slang* very big and impressive or enjoyable【俚】非常大的; 给人深刻印象的; 十分令人愉快的: *a really mega party* 令人非常愉快的聚会 —**mega** *adv*: *a mega big rock star* 摇滚乐天王巨星

mega- /ˈmɛgə; ˈmegə/ *prefix* **1** a million times a particular unit of something 百万倍: *a 100-megaton bomb* 一颗百万吨级的炸弹 —see table on page C4 参见 C4 页附录 **2** *informal* much larger than usual in amount, importance, or size【非正式】〔数量、重要性或尺寸〕大得异乎寻常的: *Hollywood megastars* 好莱坞巨星 | *Frank told me her new boyfriend is megarich.* 弗兰克告诉我她的新男友是一位巨富。

M

meg·a·bit /ˋmɛgəbɪt; ˈmegəbɪt/ *n* [C] *technical* a million bits (BIT[1](12))【术语】兆位, 兆比特

meg·a·bucks /ˋmɛgəbʌks; ˈmegəbʌks/ *n* [plural] *informal* a large amount of money【非正式】大量的钱: *She's earning megabucks now.* 她目前正在赚大钱。

meg·a·byte /ˋmɛgəbaɪt; ˈmegəbaɪt/ *n* [C] a million BYTE*s* 兆字节

meg·a·death /ˋmɛgədɛθ; ˈmegədeθ/ *n* [U] a word meaning one million deaths, used when talking about a NUCLEAR WAR 一百万人的死亡〔用于谈论核战争〕

meg·a·hertz /ˋmɛgəhɝts; ˈmegəhɜːts/ written abbreviation 缩写为 **MHz** *n* a million HERTZ 兆赫

meg·a·lith /ˋmɛgəˌlɪθ; ˈmegəlɪθ/ *n* [C] a large tall stone put in an open place by people in ancient times, possibly as a religious sign〔古代人们可能作为宗教标志竖立在空旷地上的〕巨石 —**megalithic** /ˌmɛgəˋlɪθɪk; ˌmegəˈlɪθɪk◂/ *adj*: *a megalithic monument* 巨石碑

meg·a·lo·ma·ni·a /ˌmɛgələˋmenɪə; ˌmegələʊˈmeɪniə/ *n* [U] the belief that you are extremely important and powerful, which makes you want to control other people's lives, and is often a kind of mental illness 夸大狂; 妄自尊大, 自高自大

meg·a·lo·ma·ni·ac /ˌmɛgələˋmenɪˌæk; ˌmegələʊˈmeɪniæk/ *n* [C] someone who believes they are extremely important or powerful and tries to control other people's lives 患夸大狂的人; 妄自尊大的人 —**megalomaniac** *adj*

Megan's law /ˋmɛgənz ˌlɔ; ˈmegənz ˌlɔː/ a US law that says people must be told when a person who has commited a sexual crime moves into their area to live.《梅根法》〔美国一法律。该法规定当有性犯罪前科者搬到一地居住时必须要告知当地居民〕

meg·a·phone /ˋmɛgəˌfon; ˈmegəfəʊn/ *n* [C] a piece of equipment like a large horn which you talk through to make your voice sound louder, when speaking to a crowd 扩音器, 喇叭筒

meg·a·star /ˋmɛgəstɑr; ˈmegəstɑː/ *n* [C] *informal* a very famous singer or actor【非正式】巨星, 超级明星〔指非常有名的歌手或演员〕: *rock megastar David Bowie* 摇滚巨星戴维·鲍伊

meg·a·ton /ˋmɛgəˌtʌn; ˈmegətʌn/ *n* [C] a measure of the power of an explosive that is equal to that of a million TON*s* of TNT (=a powerful explosive) 百万吨级〔相当于一百万吨黄色炸药的爆炸威力〕: *a five megaton atomic bomb* 五百万吨级的原子弹

Mein Kampf /ˌmaɪn ˋkæmpf; ˌmaɪn ˈkæmpf/ a book written by Adolf Hitler while he was in prison in 1923. It describes his political ideas and his plan for gaining power over the whole world.《我的奋斗》〔阿道夫·希特勒1923年在狱中写的一本书。书中阐述了他的政治观点和统治全球的计划〕

Me·ir /meˋɪr; meɪˈɪə/, **Gol·da** /ˋgoldə; ˈgəʊldə/ (1898-1978) an Israeli politician who was Israel's first woman Prime Minister, from 1969 to 1974 梅厄〔(1898-1978), 以色列政治家, 1969-1974年任以色列总理, 是以色列首位女总理〕

Me·kong, the /ˌmeˋkɔŋ; ˌmiːˈkɒŋ◂/ a river in southeast Asia, which flows from China through Cambodia and Laos to Vietnam. The **Mekong Delta** is one of the most important areas in Asia for growing rice, and there was also a lot of fighting in this area during the Vietnam War. 湄公河〔东南亚一河流, 源自中国, 流经柬埔寨、老挝至越南。湄公河三角洲是亚洲重要的稻米产区之一。越南战争期间, 这一带曾有过不少战事〕

mel·a·mine /ˋmɛləmin; ˈmeləmiːn/ *n* [U] a material like plastic used to make hard smooth surfaces on tables and shelves 密胺树脂

mel·an·cho·li·a /ˌmɛlənˋkolɪə; ˌmelənˈkəʊliə/ *n* [U] *technical* a feeling of great sadness and lack of energy, often caused by mental illness; DEPRESSION (1)【术语】〔常由精神疾病所导致的〕忧郁症, 抑郁症

mel·an·chol·ic /ˌmɛlənˋkɑlɪk; ˌmelənˈkɒlɪk◂/ *adj formal* feeling or tending to be very sad, often because you are mentally ill【正式】忧郁的, 忧郁症的: *the cause of Emilia's melancholic condition* 埃米莉亚所患抑郁症的原因

mel·an·chol·y[1] /ˋmɛlənˌkɑlɪ; ˈmelənkəli/ *adj* sad or making you feel sad 忧郁的; 令人伤感的: *a melancholy expression* 忧郁的表情 | *the seagulls' melancholy cry* 海鸥凄婉的叫声

melancholy[2] *n* [U] *formal* a feeling of sadness for no particular reason【正式】忧郁, 无名的伤感: *They sank into a mood of deep melancholy.* 他们陷入了深深的忧郁之中。| *the lingering melancholy of "Gloomy Sunday"*《黑色星期日》那挥之不去的抑郁之感

Mel·a·ne·si·a /ˌmɛləˋniʃə; ˌmeləˈniːziə/ a group of islands in the Pacific Ocean, northeast of Australia, including Vanuatu, the Solomon Islands, and Fiji 美拉尼西亚〔太平洋一群岛屿, 位于澳大利亚东北, 包括瓦努阿图、所罗门群岛和斐济〕

me·lange /meˋlɑnʒ; meɪˈlɑːnʒ/ *n* [singular] *French* a mixture of different things【法】混合物; 大杂烩: *a melange of sounds and smells* 各种声音和气味的混杂

mel·a·nin /ˋmɛlənɪn; ˈmelənɪn/ *n* [U] a natural dark brown colour in human skin, hair, and eyes〔人的皮肤、毛发和眼睛的〕黑(色)素

mel·a·no·ma /ˌmɛləˋnomə; ˌmeləˈnəʊmə/ *n* [C] *technical* a TUMOUR on the skin which causes CANCER【术语】〔致癌的〕黑瘤, 黑素瘤

Mel·ba toast /ˌmɛlbə ˋtost; ˌmelbə ˈtəʊst/ *n* [U] a kind of thin toast which breaks easily into small bits 梅尔巴吐司〔一种易碎的薄片烤面包〕

> **CULTURAL NOTE 文化注释**
>
> In the US Melba toast is often given to people who are ill or to babies when they are getting new teeth. In the UK it is often served with soup or PÂTÉ in restaurants. 在美国, 人们常把梅尔巴吐司给身体有恙的人或长牙的婴儿吃。在英国, 人们常在餐馆中就着汤或肝酱来吃这种吐司。

Mel·bourne /ˋmɛlbɚn; ˈmelbən/ the second largest city in Australia, which is the capital of the state of Victoria in the southeast of the country. It is an important business, industrial, and cultural centre. 墨尔本〔澳大利亚第二大城市, 澳大利亚东南部维多利亚州首府, 是重要的贸易、工业和文化中心〕

mel·ée /meˋle; ˈmeleɪ/ *n* [usually singular 一般用单数] a situation in which people rush around in a confused way〔人们四处乱窜的〕混乱局面: *Richard was thrown from his horse in the melée.* 在混乱中, 理查德从马上被甩了下来。

mel·li·flu·ous /məˋlɪfluəs; məˈlɪfluəs/ *adj formal* having a pleasant musical sound【正式】声音甜美的; 悦耳的, 动听的: *a mellifluous voice* 悦耳的嗓音 —**mellifluously** *adv*

Mel·lors /ˋmɛlɚz; ˈmeləz/ a character in the book *Lady Chatterley's Lover* by D. H. Lawrence. He is a GAMEKEEPER (=someone whose job is to take care of wild birds that are bred to be hunted), who has a sexual relationship with his employer's wife, Lady Chatterley, a woman from a high social class. 梅勒斯〔D.H.劳伦斯的小说《查泰莱夫人的情人》中的一个人物。梅勒斯是个猎场看守人, 与雇主的妻子查泰莱夫人这样一位上层社会女人有染〕

mel·low[1] /ˋmɛlo; ˈmeləʊ/ *adj* **1** a mellow colour or light looks soft, warm, and not too bright〔颜色或光线〕柔和的; 温暖的; 不耀眼的: *the mellow, golden light of early evening* 傍晚时分柔和的金色光线 | *mellow shades of brown and orange* 棕色和橘黄色相间的柔和色调 **2** a mellow sound is pleasant and smooth〔声音〕圆润的, 悦耳的, 流畅的: *the mellow sound of a trombone* 长号悦耳的声音 | *a friendly, mellow voice* 友善悦耳的声音 **3** mellow wine or fruit has a smooth, ripe taste〔水果〕成熟香甜的; 〔酒〕芳醇的: *a mellow red wine* 香醇的红葡萄酒 **4** gentle, calm, and sympathetic because of age or experience〔因年龄或阅历而〕温和的, 平静的, 有同情心的: *Tina's become more mellow since having children of her own.* 自从有了孩子之后, 蒂娜变得更加温和了。**5** feeling calm and relaxed, especially after drinking alcohol〔尤指饮酒后〕感觉平和轻松的: *They were feeling pleasantly mellow.* 他们感到轻松愉快。—**mellowness** *n* [U]

mellow[2] *v* [I,T] **1** if colours mellow or are mellowed, they begin to look warm and soft (使)〔颜色〕变得温馨而柔和 **2** if someone mellows or is mellowed, they become gentler and more sympathetic (使) 变得平和而有同情心: *Paul's certainly mellowed over the years.* 这些年来保罗的确变得平和了。**3** if wine mellows or is mellowed it gets a smooth taste (使)〔酒〕变得芳醇

mellow out *phr v* [I,T] *AmE informal* to become relaxed and calm, or make someone relaxed and calm【美, 非正式】(使) 变得轻松平静: *Mellow out, OK? It's no big deal!* 放松一点, 好吗? 没什么大不了的!

me·lod·ic /məˋlɑdɪk; məˈlɒdɪk/ *adj* **1** *technical* concerned with the main tune in a piece of music【术语】旋律的: *the melodic structure of Beethoven's symphonies* 贝多芬交响乐的旋律结构 **2** having a pleasant tune or a pleasant sound like music 旋律优美的; 声音悦耳的: *a sweet melodic voice* 甜美动听的嗓音

me·lo·di·ous /məˋlodɪəs; məˈləʊdiəs/ *adj formal* having a pleasant tune or a pleasant sound like music【正式】旋律优美的; 声音悦耳的, 动听的: *The piece was melodious and simple.* 这支曲子旋律优美纯朴。—**melodiously** *adv* —**melodiousness** *n* [U]

mel·o·dra·ma /ˋmɛləˌdrɑmə; ˈmelədrɑːmə/ *n* [C,U] **1** a story or play with many sudden exciting events, and very good or bad characters, who show feelings that are too strong or simple

to seem real 情节剧 **2** a situation in which people behave with too much emotion and excitement 人们过于兴奋和感情用事的局面: *Let's not make a melodrama out of this little problem.* 我们不要把这个小小的问题弄成一出闹剧。

mel·o·dra·mat·ic /ˌmɛlədrəˋmætɪk; ˌmelədrəˈmætɪk◂/ *adj* behaving or talking in an excited way with strong emotion 又哭又闹的，胡闹的；夸张的；感情用事的：*Stop being so melodramatic!* 别再这么胡闹了！—**melodramatically** /-klɪ; -kli/ *adv*

mel·o·dy /ˋmɛlədɪ; ˈmelədi/ *n* **1** [C,U] a song or tune 歌曲，曲调：*a haunting melody* 难以忘怀的曲子 **2** [C] the main tune in a complicated piece of music〔音乐的〕主旋律，主调：*variations on the original melody* 以主旋律为依据的变奏曲 **3** [U] the arrangement of musical notes in a way that is pleasant to listen to 悦耳的音调，美妙的音乐

mel·on /ˋmɛlən; ˈmelən/ *n* [C,U] a large round fruit with yellow, green, or red sweet juicy flesh 甜瓜，香瓜 —see picture on page A8 参见 A8 页图

melt /mɛlt; melt/ *v* **1** [I,T] if something solid melts or if heat melts it, it becomes liquid（使）融化；（使）熔化：*The snow was melting in the early morning sun.* 雪在清晨的阳光下渐渐融化。| **melt sth** *Melt the butter and mix it with the eggs.* 把黄油化开，然后和这些鸡蛋混合搅拌。—compare 比较 FREEZE¹ (1), THAW¹ (1) **2** also 又作 **melt away** [I] to gradually disappear 逐渐消失：*Julie's anger slowly melted away.* 朱莉的怒气渐渐地消了下去。| **melt into a crowd** *The man melted into the crowd and I lost sight of him.* 那个男子消失在人群中，我看不见他了。**3** [I,T] to become or make someone become more gentle and sympathetic than before（使）变得心软：**your heart melts** (=you suddenly feel very sympathetic) 心软下来 *He shouted at the little girl, but his heart melted when he saw her crying.* 他冲着那个小女孩大喊大叫，但看到她哭时，他的心软了。**4 melt into** if one sound, colour, or feeling melts into another one, it gradually becomes part of it until there is no difference between them〔声音、颜色或情感〕逐渐融入：*The sound of the trumpet melted into the strains of the orchestra.* 小号的声音逐渐融入了管弦乐队演奏的旋律中。**5 melt in your mouth** if food melts in your mouth, it is soft and delicious〔食物〕入口即化；松软可口 —see also 另见 **butter wouldn't melt in sb's mouth** (BUTTER¹ (2))

melt 融化

melt sth ↔ **down** *phr v* [T] to heat a metal object until it becomes a liquid, especially so that you can use the metal again 熔化〔金属物件〕：*People were melting down coins to make earrings and ornaments.* 人们把硬币熔化掉做成耳环和装饰品。

melt·down /ˋmɛltdaʊn; ˈmeltdaʊn/ *n* [C,U] a very dangerous situation in which the material in a NUCLEAR REACTOR melts and burns through its container, allowing RADIOACTIVITY to escape〔造成放射性物质逸出的〕核反应堆堆芯熔毁

melt·ing /ˋmɛltɪŋ; ˈmeltɪŋ/ *adj* [usually before noun 一般用于名词前] a melting look, voice, or expression makes you feel strong feelings of pity, love, or sympathy〔眼神、嗓音或表情〕令人爱怜的；让人同情的 —**meltingly** *adv*

melting point /ˈ‥ ˌ/ *n* [singular] the temperature at which a solid substance becomes a liquid 熔点

melting pot /ˈ‥ ˌ/ *n* [C usually singular 一般用单数] **1** a place where people from different races, countries, or social classes come to live together 大熔炉〔来自不同种族、国家或社会阶层的人生活在一起的地方〕：*America has been a melting pot since the beginning of European immigration.* 从欧洲人向美洲移民时起美国就是一个融合不同种族的大熔炉。**2** a situation or place in which many different ideas are discussed 多种不同思想在一起讨论的场面[地方] **3 in the melting pot** *BrE* still changing and not yet in a final state【英】仍在变化的，尚未最后定型的

Mel·ville /ˋmɛlvɪl; ˈmelvɪl/**, Her·man** /ˋhɝmən; ˈhɜːmən/ (1819-91) a US writer who wrote about his experiences as a sailor. He wrote *Moby-Dick*, one of the most famous American NOVELS. He also wrote *Billy Budd*, a story which Benjamin Britten used in his OPERA of the same name. 梅尔维尔〔(1819-1891)，美国作家。作品多取材于自己的航海经历。他创作的小说《白鲸》是最著名的美国小说之一。他还写了另外一部小说，名为《比利·巴德》，本杰明·布里顿据此创作了一部同名歌剧〕

1 1 **mem·ber** /ˋmɛmbɚ; ˈmembə/ *n* [C] **1** someone who has joined a particular club, group, or organization 会员，成员：*I'm a member of the local tennis club.* 我是本地网球俱乐部的会员。| **club/union/party etc members** *The strike was approved by a majority of union members.* 罢工得到了大多数工会会员的赞成。| **member states/countries/organizations etc** (=the states etc that have joined a particular group) 会员国/组织等 *UN member states* 联合国会员国 | **full member** (=a member in the most complete way) 正式成员 *Turkey wanted to become a full member of the EC.* 土耳其想成为欧共体的正式成员。**2** one of a particular group of people or things〔某一群人或物中的〕一员：*Dogs and wolves are both members of the same species.* 狗和狼属同一物种。| **member of a family** *The other members of his family were against the marriage.* 他家的其他成员反对这桩婚姻。| **member of staff** (=a worker at a particular company) 公司职员 *All members of staff must wear uniform.* 所有职员都必须穿制服。**3** *BrE* a Member of Parliament【英】下议院议员：*the member for Truro* 特鲁罗地区的下议院议员 **4** *technical or humorous* the male sex organ; PENIS【术语或幽默】男性性器官；阴茎 **5** *old use* a part of the body, especially an arm or leg【旧】身体的一部分〔尤指胳膊或腿〕

Member of Par·lia·ment /ˌ‥ ˈ‥‥/ *n* [C] an MP (1) 下议院议员

mem·ber·ship /ˋmɛmbɚˌʃɪp; ˈmembəʃɪp/ *n* **1** [U] the state of being a member of a club, group, organization, or system, and receiving the advantages of belonging to that group 会员身份[资格]：**[+of]** *Only full-time employees can apply for membership of the company pension plan.* 只有全职雇员才有资格申请成为该公司退休金计划的会员。| [also+**in** *AmE* 美] *I forgot to renew my membership in the sailing club.* 我忘了重续我的航海俱乐部会员资格。| **membership card** (=a card that shows you are a member) 会员证 **2** [singular] all the members of a club, group, or organization 全体会员：*The membership voted to change the rules.* 全体会员投票赞成修改规章。**3** [U] the number of people who belong to a club, group, or organization 会员人数：*We're trying to increase our membership.* 我们正在努力增加我们的会员人数。 2 2

mem·brane /ˋmɛmbren; ˈmembreɪn/ *n* [C,U] **1** a very thin piece of skin that covers or connects parts of the body〔覆盖或连接身体某些部分的〕膜，薄膜：*a vibrating membrane in the ear which conveys sound* 耳朵中传送声音的振动膜 **2** a very thin piece of material that covers or connects something〔覆盖或连接某物的〕膜状物 —**membranous** /ˋmɛmbrənəs; ˈmembrənəs/ *adj*

me·men·to /mɪˋmɛnto; məˈmentəʊ/ *n plural* **mementos** [C] a small thing that you keep to remind you of someone or something 小纪念物，小纪念品：**[+of]** *a memento of her time in Spain* 让她回想起在西班牙那段时光的小纪念品

mem·o /ˋmɛmo; ˈmeməʊ/ *n plural* **memos** [C] a short official note to another person in the same company or organization〔致同一个公司或组织内部另一人的〕公务便条：*She dictated an urgent internal memo.* 她口授了一份紧急内部通知。 3

mem·oir /ˋmɛmwɑr; ˈmemwɑː/ *n* **1 memoirs** [plural] an account written by someone, especially a famous person, about their life and experiences〔尤指名人〕回忆录：*Lady Thatcher had just published her memoirs.* 撒切尔夫人刚刚出版了她的回忆录。**2** [C] *formal* a short piece of writing about someone or something that you know well【正式】传略，实录

mem·o·ra·bil·i·a /ˌmɛmərəˋbɪlɪə; ˌmemərəˈbɪliə/ *n* [plural] things that you keep or collect because they are connected with a famous person, event, or time〔与某著名人物、事件或时代有关的〕纪念品，收藏品：*Elvis Presley memorabilia* 有关埃尔维斯·普雷斯利的纪念品

mem·o·ra·ble /ˋmɛmərəbl; ˈmemərəbəl/ *adj* very good, enjoyable, or unusual, and worth remembering 极好的，难忘的，值得纪念的：*a truly memorable performance* 真正令人难忘的演出 | **[+for]** *The play was memorable for its beautiful costumes.* 那出戏剧因其漂亮的戏装而令人难忘。—**memorably** *adv*

mem·o·ran·dum /ˌmɛməˋrændəm; ˌmeməˈrændəm/ *n plural* **memoranda** *or* **memorandums** [C] **1** *formal* a MEMO【正式】公务便条 **2** *law* a short legal document recording the conditions of an agreement【法律】协议备忘录

me·mo·ri·al¹ /məˋmorɪəl; məˈmɔːriəl/ *adj* [only before noun 仅用于名词前] made, held, or done in order to remind people of someone who has died 纪念的，追悼的：**memorial service/ceremony** *A memorial service will be held at 7 pm on Saturday.* 周六晚上7时将举行一个追悼仪式。| **memorial prize/scholarship/fund etc** *the John Kobal memorial prize for best young photographer* 约翰·科贝尔最佳青年摄影师纪念奖

memorial² *n* **1** [C] something, especially a stone with writing on it, to remind people of someone who has died 纪念碑：

the Albert memorial 艾伯特纪念碑 | [+to] *a memorial to the men who died in the war* 为在战争中牺牲的士兵而立的纪念碑
2 [singular] an achievement that reminds people of someone who has died〔对死者成就的〕纪念: *The college is his true memorial.* 这所学院就是对他真正的纪念。—see also 另见 WAR MEMORIAL

Memorial Day /·ˈ··· ·/ a US legal holiday, the last Monday in May, when people remember those killed in wars 阵亡将士纪念日，国殇日，悼念日〔美国一法定节日，每年5月的最后一个星期一纪念阵亡将士〕: *Memorial Day weekend* 阵亡将士纪念日周末

mem·o·rize also 又作 **-ise** *BrE*【英】/ˈmɛməˌraɪz; ˈmeməraɪz/ *v* [T] to learn words, music etc 记住，熟记

mem·o·ry /ˈmɛmərɪ; ˈmeməri/ *n*
1 ►ABILITY TO REMEMBER 记忆力◄ [C,U] the ability to remember things, places, experiences etc 记忆力，记性: *Grandpa was getting old and his memory wasn't so good.* 爷爷上年纪了，记性不太好。| **have a good/bad memory for sth** (=be good or bad at remembering things of a particular kind) 对某事记忆力好/差 *I have a terrible memory for names.* 我特别不善于记名字。| **have a short/long memory** (=remember something for a short time or for a long time) 记性不好/好 | **do sth from memory** (=do something such as say a poem or play a piece of music by remembering it) 凭记忆做某事 *The cellist played the whole piece through from memory.* 大提琴手凭记忆从头到尾演奏了那支曲子。
2 ►STH YOU REMEMBER 记得的某事◄ [C usually plural 一般用复数] something that you remember from the past about a person, place, or experience 记忆，回忆: [+of] *memories of the war* 对那场战争的回忆 | **happy/good/bad etc memories** *He has lots of happy memories of his stay in Japan.* 他对在日本逗留的那一段时光有许多美好的回忆。| **childhood memories** (=memories of the time when you were a child) 童年的记忆 *One of my earliest childhood memories is of my mother reading stories to me by the fire.* 我最早的童年记忆之一就是母亲在炉火边给我念故事。| **bring back memories** (=to remind you of pleasant events) 引起对美好往事的回忆 *Those old songs bring back memories.* 那些老歌使人回想起美好的往事。
3 a) [C] the part of a computer in which information can be stored〔电脑的〕存储器 **b)** [U] the amount of space that can be used for storing information on a computer〔电脑存储器的〕存储量: *30 megabytes of memory* 30兆字节的存储量
4 if my memory serves me (well/correctly) used when you are almost sure that you have remembered something correctly 如果我没有记错的话: *We first moved here in 1962, if my memory serves me correctly.* 如果我没有记错的话，我们最初搬到这里是在1962年。
5 speaking from memory *spoken* used to say that you are telling someone what you remember about something【口】凭记忆; 就记忆所及
6 have a memory like a sieve *spoken* to be very bad at remembering things【口】记忆力极差
7 sb's memory is playing tricks on them *spoken* used to say that someone is remembering things incorrectly【口】某人的记性在和他开玩笑，某人的记忆不准确: *My memory must be playing tricks on me; I'm sure I put that book on the desk.* 肯定是我的记忆出了问题，我明明记得把那本书放在书桌上了。
8 take a walk/trip down memory lane spend some time remembering the past 追忆往事
9 in living memory since the earliest time that people now alive can remember 在活着的人的记忆中: *the hottest summer in living memory* 在世的人们记忆中最炎热的夏天
10 within sb's memory during the time that someone can remember 就某人记忆所及: *There have been two world wars within the memory of my grandfather.* 两次世界大战都在我祖父脑海中留下记忆。
11 in memory of also 又作 **to the memory of** for the purpose of remembering someone and reminding other people of them after they have died 为了纪念〔已经故去的某人〕: *She set up a charitable fund in memory of her father.* 她设立了一项慈善基金以纪念她的父亲。
12 sb's memory lives on used to say that people still remember someone after they have died or gone away 某人〔去世或离开后〕仍然留在人们的记忆中

13 sb's memory the way you think about someone who has died who you knew very well 对〔熟悉的〕亡故者的纪念[怀念]: *a rose garden dedicated to his memory* 为缅怀他而建的玫瑰花园 —see also 另见 **commit sth to memory** (COMMIT (6)), **jog sb's memory** (JOG[1] (3)), **lose your memory** (LOSE (4)), **photographic memory** (PHOTOGRAPHIC (2)), **refresh sb's memory** (REFRESH (2))

This graph shows some of the words most commonly used with the noun **memory**. 本图表所示为含有名词 memory 的一些最常用短语。

memory of
from memory
memory for
good memory
living memory
5 10 15 per million 每百万

Based on the British National Corpus and the Longman Lancaster Corpus
据英国国家语料库和朗文兰开斯特语料库

memory bank /ˈ··· ˌ·/ *n* [C] the part of a big computer system that stores information〔大型电脑系统的〕存储体，数据总库

Mem·phis /ˈmɛmfəs; ˈmemfɪs/ the largest city in the state of Tennessee, US, on the Mississippi River, which is a port and industrial centre and is also famous for being the home of Elvis Presley 孟菲斯〔美国田纳西州最大城市，濒临密西西比河。该市是一港口和工业中心，以埃尔维斯·普雷斯利的故乡而闻名〕

mem·sahib /ˈmɛmˌsɑ·ɪb; ˈmemˌsɑːɪb/ *n* [C] *IndE, PakE old-fashioned* a European woman【印，巴，过时】欧洲妇女

men /mɛn; men/ *n* the plural of MAN

men·ace[1] /ˈmɛnɪs; ˈmenɪs/ *n* **1** [C] something or someone that is dangerous 危险的事物[人]: [+to] *hazardous chemicals that are a menace to public safety* 危害公共安全的危险化学品 | *That man's a menace to society!* 那个男子对社会是一个祸害! **2** [U] a threatening quality or manner 威胁，恐吓: *There was menace in her eyes as she spoke.* 她说话的时候目光中带着恫吓。**3** [C] a person, especially a child that is annoying or causes trouble; NUISANCE 讨厌的人，制造麻烦的人〔尤指小孩〕

menace[2] *v* [T] *formal* to threaten【正式】威胁，恐吓

men·ac·ing /ˈmɛnəsɪŋ; ˈmenɪsɪŋ/ *adj* making you expect something unpleasant; THREATENING 威胁的，不祥的，凶兆的: *dark, menacing clouds* 预示着暴风雨的乌云 | *a low, menacing laugh* 充满恐吓的一声轻笑 —**menacingly** *adv*

mé·nage /meˈnɑʒ; ˈmeɪnɑːʒ/ *n* [C] *formal or humorous* all the people who live in a particular house; HOUSEHOLD[1]【正式或幽默】家庭

ménage à trois /meˈnɑʒ ɑ ˈtrwɑ; ˌmeɪnɑːʒ ɑː ˈtrwɑː/ *n* [singular] *French* a sexual relationship involving three people who live together【法】三角家庭，三角性关系〔指居住在一起的三个人之间的性关系〕

me·na·ge·rie /məˈnædʒərɪ; mɪˈnædʒəri/ *n* [C] a collection of wild animals kept privately or for the public to see 私人豢养或向公众展览的野生动物

Men·ai Straits, the /ˌmɛnaɪ ˈstrets; ˌmenaɪ ˈstreɪts/ a narrow area of sea in North Wales, between the Welsh coast and the island of Anglesey 梅奈海峡〔威尔士北部一狭长海域，位于威尔士海岸与安格尔西岛之间〕

MENCAP /ˈmɛnkæp; ˈmenkæp/ the Royal Society for Mentally Handicapped Children and Adults; a British CHARITY organization that gives advice and practical help to people who have learning difficulties, and supports changes in the law that will help these people 皇家智障人士协会〔英国一慈善组织，给有学习障碍者提供建议和实际帮助，并支持有利于这类人群的法律修订工作〕

mend[1] /mɛnd; mend/ *v*
1 ►REPAIR 修理◄ [T] **a)** to repair a tear or hole in a piece of clothing 修补，缝补〔布料上的裂口或破洞〕: *My father used to mend our shoes.* 我父亲过去常为我们修补鞋子。**b)** *BrE* to repair something that is broken or not working; FIX[1] (1)【英】修理〔破损或有毛病的物件〕: *When are you going to mend that light in the hall?* 你什么时候修理一下厅里的那盏灯?
2 ►BECOME HEALTHY 变得健康◄ [I] **a)** *informal* if a broken bone mends, it becomes whole again【非正式】〔断骨〕愈合 **b)** [I] *old-fashioned* to become healthy again after being ill【过时】〔病后〕恢复健康，痊愈
3 mend your ways to improve the way you behave after behaving badly for a long time 改正不良行为
4 mend (your) fences to talk to someone you have offended or argued with, and try to persuade them to be friendly with you again 消释前嫌，重修旧好

5 ►**END A QUARREL** 结束争吵◄ [T] to end a quarrel or difficult situation by dealing with the problem that is causing it 结束〔争吵或困境〕: *I've tried to mend matters between us, but she's still very angry.* 我尽力去消除我们之间的不和，但她仍然很生气。 —**mender** *n* [C] *BrE*【英】

mend² *n* [C] **1 be on the mend** to be getting better after an illness or after a difficult period〔病后或困难时期过后〕正在好转: *He's had flu, but he's on the mend.* 他得了流感，但正在痊愈。| *signs that the economy is on the mend* 经济在好转的迹象 **2** a place in something where it has been repaired 修补过的地方

men·da·cious /mɛn`deʃəs; men'deɪʃəs/ *adj formal* not truthful【正式】不真实的，虚假的: *mendacious propaganda* 不真实的宣传 —**mendaciously** *adv*

men·da·ci·ty /mɛn`dæsətɪ; men'dæsəti/ *n* [U] *formal* the quality of being untruthful【正式】不真实，虚假

Men·del /`mɛndəl; 'mendəl/, **Greg·or Jo·hann** /`grɛgɔr `johan; 'gregɔː 'jəʊhæn/ (1822-84) an Austrian MONK (=a member of a group of Christian men who live apart from other people) who studied the PEA plant in order to find out how qualities are passed from parent plants to their children. Many years later his discoveries were used by scientists who were developing the new science of GENETICS. 孟德尔〔(1822-1884)，奥地利修道士。他研究豆类植物如何将基因遗传给下一代。许多年后，一些科学家采用他的发现成果，逐步创立了“遗传学”这一新兴学科〕

Men·de·ley·ev /,mɛndə`leɛv; ,mendə'leɪev/, **Dmi·tri I·van·o·vitch** /də`mitrɪ ɪ`vanəvɪtʃ; də'miːtri ɪ'vɑːnəvɪtʃ/ (1834-1907) a Russian scientist who invented the PERIODIC TABLE, which is a list of all the ELEMENTS (=basic chemical substances) arranged according to their atomic number 门捷列夫〔(1834-1907)，俄国科学家，元素周期表发明者。该表按照原子量大小对所有元素进行排列〕

Men·dels·sohn /`mɛndlsn; 'mendəlsən/, **Fe·lix** /`filɪks; 'fiːlɪks/ (1809-47) a German COMPOSER (writer of music), who wrote five symphonies (SYMPHONY) and the OVERTURE *Fingal's Cave*. The *Wedding March* from his *Incidental Music to a Midsummer Night's Dream* is often played at church weddings as the newly married man and woman leave the church. 门德尔松〔(1809-1847)，德国作曲家，创作了五首交响曲和《芬戈尔洞》序曲。《婚礼进行曲》源于他的《仲夏夜之梦序曲》，常在教堂举行婚礼中新郎新娘离开教堂时播放〕

men·di·cant /`mɛndɪkənt; 'mendɪkənt/ *n* [C] *formal* someone who begs for money in order to live, usually for religious reasons【正式】〔常因宗教原因〕以乞讨为生的人 —**mendicant** *adj*: *a mendicant monks' order such as the Franciscans* 化缘修士会，如圣方济各会

mend·ing /`mɛndɪŋ; 'mendɪŋ/ *n* [U] clothes that need to be mended 需缝补的衣服

Men·dip Hills, the /,mɛndɪp `hɪlz; ,mendɪp 'hɪlz/ also 又作 **the Mendips** a range of hills in southwest England, in the county of Somerset 门迪普丘陵〔英格兰西南部一丘陵，位于萨默塞特郡〕

Men·e·la·us /,mɛnə`leəs; ,menɪ'leɪəs/ in ancient Greek stories, the king of Sparta, the brother of Agamemmnon, and the husband of Helen of Troy 墨涅拉俄斯〔古希腊传说中的斯巴达国王。他是阿伽门农的兄弟，特洛伊的海伦之夫〕 —see also 另见 The ILIAD, the TROJAN WAR

men·folk /`mɛn,fok; 'menfəʊk/ *n* [plural] *old-fashioned* a word used by women meaning men, especially their male relatives【过时】男人们〔妇女指男人的用语，尤指男性亲属〕: *Round up the menfolk for dinner, please.* 把男人们都请来吃饭吧。

Mengele, Josef (1911-79) a doctor who did experiments on prisoners at the Auschwitz CONCENTRATION CAMP 门格勒〔(1911-1979)，在奥斯维辛集中营将罪犯作为实验对象的一名医生〕

me·ni·al¹ /`minɪəl; 'miːniəl/ *adj* menial work is boring, needs no skill, and is not important〔工作〕枯燥的; 无需技术的; 卑下的 —**menially** *adv*

menial² *n* [C] someone who does menial work, especially a servant in a house 干粗活的人〔尤指家仆〕

men·in·gi·tis /,mɛnɪn`dʒaɪtɪs; ,menɪn'dʒaɪtɪs/ *n* [U] a serious illness in which the outer part of the brain becomes swollen 脑(脊)膜炎

Men·no·nite /`mɛnənaɪt; 'menənaɪt/ *n* [C] a member of a Protestant religious group that refuses to join the armed forces or to hold official public positions, and does not BAPTIZE its children. There are several different Mennonite groups, including the Amish, and they live mostly in the US. 门诺派教徒〔一新教团体之教徒。他们拒绝参军，拒绝担任公职，也不对婴儿施洗礼。门诺派有多个派别，其中包括阿曼门诺派。门诺派教徒大多生活在美国〕 —**Mennonite** *adj*

Men of Har·lech /,mɛn əv `harlɪk; ,men əv 'hɑːlɪk/ the English title of a traditional PATRIOTIC Welsh song《哈勒赫士兵进行曲》〔威尔士一传统爱国歌曲的英文名〕

men·o·pause /`mɛnə,pɔz; 'menəpɔːz/ *n* [U] the time when a woman stops menstruating (MENSTRUATE), which usually occurs around age 50〔妇女的〕绝经期，更年期 —**menopausal** /,mɛno`pɔzəl; ,menəʊ'pɔːzəl◄/ *adj*

me·no·rah /mə`norə; mə'nɔːrə/ *n* [C] a Jewish CANDLESTICK that holds seven CANDLES〔犹太人用的〕七扦枝大烛台

Me·nor·ca /mə`nɔrkə; me'nɔːkə/ —see 见 MINORCA

MENSA /`mɛnsə; 'mensə/ an international organization for people who are very intelligent. People take a test and are accepted into the organization if they are among the top two percent in their country. 门萨国际〔国际高智商者组织。通过智商测试、成绩居本国前 2% 的人士方可入会〕

mensch /mɛnʃ; menʃ/ *n* [C] *AmE spoken* someone that you like and admire, especially because they have done something good for you【美口】让人喜欢的人，令人钦佩者〔尤因曾受过其恩惠〕: *You've been a real mensch.* 你是一个真正受爱戴的人。

men·ses /`mɛnsiz; 'mensiːz/ *n* [plural] *technical* the blood that flows out of a woman's body each month【术语】月经

men's room /`· ·/ *n* [C] *especially AmE* the men's toilet【尤美】男厕所，男盥洗室; gents (GENT (2)) *BrE*【英】

men·stru·al /`mɛnstruəl; 'menstruəl/ *adj* connected with the time each month when a woman menstruates 月经的，行经期的

menstrual pe·ri·od /`···, ···/ *n* [C] *formal* the time each month when a woman menstruates; PERIOD¹ (4)【正式】月经期，行经期

men·stru·ate /`mɛnstru,et; 'menstrueɪt/ *v* [I] *technical* when a woman menstruates, blood flows from her body every month【术语】行经，来月经 —**menstruation** /,mɛnstru`eʃən; ,menstru'eɪʃən/ *n* [C,U]

mens·wear /`mɛnzwɛr; 'menzweə/ *n* [U] clothing for men 男士服装: *a menswear shop* 男式服装店

-ment /mənt; mənt/ *suffix* [in nouns 构成名词] **1** the act, cause, means, or result of doing something〔表示做某事的〕动作; 原因; 手段; 结果: *the need for strong government* (=strong governing) 严格统治的必要性 | *the replacement* (=replacing) *of obsolete machinery* 陈旧机器的更换 | *some interesting new developments* 一些有趣的新进展 **2** the condition of being treated in a particular way〔表示遭受某种待遇的〕境况: *his confinement* (=being shut up) *in prison* 他被囚禁的境况 —**-mental** *suffix* [in adjectives 构成形容词]: *governmental* 政府的

men·tal /`mɛntl; 'mentl/ *adj*

1 ►**MIND** 精神◄ affecting the mind or happening in the mind 精神的; 智力的; 内心的: *mental health* 精神健康 | *a child's mental development* 儿童的智力发展 | **mental picture/image** (=a picture that you form in your mind) 在头脑中勾画出的形象: *I tried to get a mental picture of him from her description.* 我设法根据她的描述勾画出他的形象。

2 ►**MENTAL ILLNESS** 精神病◄ [only before noun 仅用于名词前] concerned with illnesses of the mind, or with treating illnesses of the mind 精神病的; 与精神病治疗有关的: *Mental patients have to be kept under strict supervision.* 精神病人必须置于严格的监管之下。| *a mental institution* 精神病院 —see also 另见 MENTAL HOME, MENTAL HOSPITAL

3 mental block a difficulty in remembering something or in understanding something 心理阻隔; 记忆阻隔; 思维阻隔: *I got a complete mental block as soon as the interviewer asked me a question.* 考官刚问了我一个问题，我的思维就完全阻断了。| *Julie has a mental block when it comes to math.* 只要涉及数学，朱莉就会产生心理阻隔。

4 make a mental note to make a special effort to remember something 记在脑子里

5 ►**CRAZY** 发疯的◄ [not before noun 不用于名词前] *BrE slang* thinking or behaving in a way that seems crazy or strange【英俚】〔思维或行为〕疯癫的，不正常的: *He must be mental!* 他一定是疯了!

6 go mental *BrE slang spoken*【英俚，口】**a)** to get very angry 非常生气: *She'll go mental if she finds out.* 她如果发现了会很气愤的。**b)** to start behaving in a crazy way 行为失常，发疯: *I can't understand why she's doing this – has she gone mental or something?* 我无法理解她为什么做这种事——她是疯了还是怎么的? —**mentally** *adv*: *mentally ill* 精神上有病的，患精神病的

mental age /`·· ,·/ *n* [C] a measure of someone's ability to think, obtained by comparing their ability with the average ability of children at various ages 智力年龄，心理年龄: *a 25-year-*

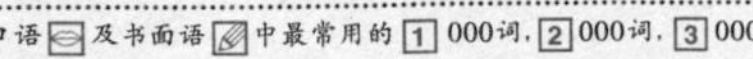

old man with a mental age of seven 一个智力年龄为7岁的25岁男子

mental a·rith·me·tic /,‥'‥·/ *n* [U] the act of adding numbers together, multiplying them etc in your mind, without writing them down 心算

mental home /'‥·/ *n* [C] *BrE old-fashioned* a mental hospital【英，过时】精神病院

mental hos·pi·tal /'‥,‥/ *n* [C] a hospital where people with mental illnesses are treated; PSYCHIATRIC HOSPITAL 精神病院

men·tal·i·ty /mɛn`tæləti; men'tæl¦ti/ *n* [C] a particular kind of attitude or way of thinking, especially one that you think is wrong or stupid〔尤指被视为错误或愚蠢的〕心态: *a get-rich-quick mentality* 快速致富的心态

mentally han·di·capped /,‥'‥·/ *adj* **1** a mentally handicapped person has a problem with their brain that affects their ability to think or control their body movements, usually from birth 弱智的 **2** [plural] **the mentally handicapped** people who are mentally handicapped 弱智者

men·thol /`mɛnθɑl; 'menθɒl/ *n* [U] a substance that smells and tastes of MINT to give cigarettes and sweets a special taste 薄荷脑，薄荷醇

men·tho·la·ted /`mɛnθə,letɪd; 'menθəleɪt¦d/ *adj* containing menthol 含薄荷醇的

men·tion¹ /`mɛnʃən; 'menʃən/ *v* [T] **1** to talk about something or someone in a conversation, piece of writing etc, especially without saying very much or giving details 提到，说起，谈到: *As I mentioned earlier, this has been a very successful year for our company.* 正如我刚才提到的，这是我们公司非常成功的一年。| *Jill mentioned something about a party on Saturday.* 吉尔提到了星期六举行的一个聚会的事。| *Was my name mentioned at all?* 我的名字被提到过吗？| **mention sth to sb** *I mentioned the idea to Joan, and she seemed to like it.* 我向琼说起过这个想法，她似乎很喜欢。| **mention (that)** *He mentioned that he was having problems, but he didn't explain.* 他说起过他碰到一些问题，但没作说明。| **it is worth mentioning that** (=this is a useful or important piece of information) 值得一提的是… *It's worth mentioning that the new regulations don't actually come into force until next year.* 值得一提的是新的规章制度要到明年才真正生效。**2 don't mention it** *spoken* used to say politely that there is no need for someone to thank you for helping them【口】不用谢：*"Thanks for the ride home!" "Don't mention it."* "谢谢你开车送我回家！""不用客气。" **3 not to mention** used to introduce an additional thing that makes a situation even more difficult, surprising, interesting etc 更不用说: *They already take pension and social security payments off my pay, not to mention state taxes.* 他们已经从我的工资里扣除了养老金和社会保障金，更不用说州税了。**4 mention sth in passing** to mention something quickly without paying much attention to it 顺便提到，附带说起: *Sue mentioned the party in passing, but I couldn't go.* 休顺便提到那个聚会，但我去不了。**5 above mentioned/mentioned above** mentioned earlier in a piece of writing 上述〔指在一篇文章前面提到过的〕**6 mentioned in dispatches** *BrE* honoured for being brave in a battle by being mentioned on an official list【英】〔因作战勇敢而〕在正式通报上受到表扬

mention² *n* [C usually singular 一般用单数，U] the act of mentioning something or someone in a conversation, piece of writing etc 提及，说起: *Just the mention of her name still upsets him.* 只要提起她的名字，他现在还是会不高兴。| **there's no mention** (=something is not mentioned) 没有提到 *There was no mention of any trip to Holland in his diaries.* 他的日记中没有提到过他曾经去过荷兰。| **get a mention** (=be mentioned when someone is talking or writing about something)〔在口头或文字中〕被提及，被谈到 *I didn't even get a mention in the list of contributors.* 我在捐赠者名单上甚至没有被提到。| **make no mention** (=not say anything about) 没提及，没说起 *He made no mention of his wife's illness to me.* 他没有向我提起他妻子生病的事。—see also 另见 HONOURABLE MENTION

men·tor /`mɛntɚ; 'mentɔː/ *n* [C] an experienced person who advises and helps a less experienced person 导师，指导者

men·tor·ing /`mɛntorɪŋ; 'mentɔːrɪŋ/ *n* [U] a system of using people with a lot of experience, knowledge etc to advise other people at work, or in their professional life 职业辅导制度: *Support for you in your new job will be provided by a system of mentoring.* 职业辅导制度将在你新的工作中为你提供支持。

men·u /`mɛnju; 'menjuː/ *n* [C] **1** a list of all the kinds of food that are available for a meal, especially in a restaurant〔尤指餐馆的〕菜单: *Is there any fish on the menu?* 菜单上有鱼吗？| *Could we have the menu, please?* 请把菜单给我们拿来，好吗？—see picture on page A15 参见A15页图 **2** a list of things that you can choose from or ask a computer to do, that is shown on the SCREEN of the computer〔电脑显示器上显示的〕功能选择单，选项单，菜单: **menu-driven** (=operated by using a menu) 由菜单驱动的

Men·uh·in /`mɛnjuɪn; 'menju¦n/, **Sir Ye·hu·di** /jɪ`hudɪ; jɪ'huːdi/ (1916-99) a US VIOLIN player, who became a British citizen in 1985. He lived in the UK, where he started a music school for children with special abilities and was given the official title **Lord Menuhin**. As well as playing CLASSICAL music, he played JAZZ with the violin player Stephane Grappelli. 梅纽因〔(1916-1999)，美国小提琴家，1985加入英国籍。他居住在英国，创办了一所培养音乐天才的学校，被册封为梅纽因勋爵。他不仅演奏古典音乐，而且还与小提琴家斯蒂芬尼·格拉佩利一起演奏爵士音乐〕

me·ow /mɪ`aʊ; mi'aʊ/ *v* [I] the usual American spelling of MIAOW miaow的一般美式拼法 —**meow** *n* [C]

MEP /`ɛm i `pi; ,em iː 'piː/ *n* [C] Member of the European Parliament; someone who has been elected as a member of the Parliament of the European Union 欧洲议会议员

Meph·i·stoph·e·les /,mɛfə`stɑfə,liz; ,mef¦'stɒf¦liːz/ *n* the Devil, especially in the story of Faust 魔鬼〔尤指关于浮士德的传说中的魔鬼〕，靡菲斯特 —**Mephistophelean** /,mɛfɪstə`filɪən; ,mefɪstə'fiːliən◂/ *adj*

Merc /mɝk; mɜːk/ *n* **1** especially British English an informal name for a Mercedes-Benz car【英】默克〔梅赛德斯-奔驰轿车别称〕**2** *AmE* an informal name for a car called the Mercury, made by Ford【美】墨克〔福特公司生产的墨丘利（水星）轿车的别称〕

mer·can·tile /`mɝkən,til; 'mɜːkəntaɪl/ *adj* [only before noun 仅用于名词前] *formal* concerned with trade; COMMERCIAL¹ (1)【正式】贸易的，商业的: *mercantile law* 商法

mercantile ma·rine /,‥·'·/ *n* [singular] *BrE* the MERCHANT NAVY【英】〔一个国家的〕全部商船，商船队；〔一个国家的〕全体商船船员

Mer·ca·tor pro·jec·tion /mɝ,ketɚ prə`dʒɛkʃən; mə,keɪtə prə'dʒekʃən/ also 又作 **Mercator's projection** *n* [U] a way of drawing a map of the world so that it can be divided into regular squares, instead of getting thinner at the northern or southern edges 墨卡托投影（法）〔绘制世界地图的一种方法〕

Mer·ce·des /mɚ`sedɪz; mɜː'seɪdiz/ also 又作 **Mercedes Benz** *trademark* a type of car made by the German company Daimler-Benz. Mercedes cars are bought especially by rich people, successful business people, and political leaders. In the UK, a Mercedes is informally called a 'Merc', and in the US it is informally called a 'Benz'.【商标】梅赛德斯-奔驰〔德国戴姆勒-奔驰公司生产的一种小汽车，购买者多为有钱人、成功商人和政治领袖。英国别称"默克"，美国别称"奔驰"〕

mer·ce·na·ry¹ /`mɝsn,ɛrɪ; 'mɜːsənəri/ *n* [C] a soldier who fights for any country or group that is willing to pay him 雇佣兵: *The Emperor hired an army of Saxon mercenaries.* 皇帝雇用了一支由撒克逊雇佣兵组成的军队。

mercenary² *adj* only interested in money, and not caring about whether your actions are right or wrong or about the effect of your actions on other people 只对钱感兴趣的，唯利是图的: *It's a purely mercenary relationship, not a friendship.* 它纯粹是一种金钱关系，而不是友谊。

mer·cer·ized cot·ton /,mɝsəraɪzd `kɑtn; ,mɜːsəraɪzd 'kɒtn/ *n* [U] cotton that has been treated with chemicals to make it shiny and strong 丝光棉〔经过化学处理的棉花〕

mer·chan·dise¹ /`mɝtʃən,daɪz; 'mɜːtʃəndaɪz/ *n* [U] goods that are produced in order to be sold, especially goods that are shown in a shop for people to buy 商品〔尤指在商店陈列供出售的货物〕

merchandise² *v* [T] to try to sell goods or services using methods such as advertising〔用广告等方式〕推销〔商品或服务〕: *If the product is properly merchandised, it should sell very well.* 这种产品如果推销得当，应该会卖得很好。

mer·chan·dis·ing /`mɝtʃəndaɪzɪŋ; 'mɜːtʃəndaɪzɪŋ/ *n* [U] toys, clothes, and other products based on a popular film, TV show etc and sold to make additional profits 文化衍生品〔指根据流行电影、电视节目等制作并销售以获取额外利润的玩具、服装及其他产品〕

mer·chant /`mɝtʃənt; 'mɜːtʃənt/ *n* [C] **1** someone who buys and sells goods in large quantities 商人；〔大宗货物〕批发商: *He's a wine merchant.* 他是个酒商。**2 con merchant/speed merchant etc** *BrE informal* someone who is involved in a particular activity, such as tricking people or driving very fast【英，非正式】骗子/开快车者等

merchant bank /ˌ‥ ˈ·/ *n* [C] a bank that provides banking services for business 商业银行〔指为企业提供服务的银行〕

Merchant-I·vo·ry /ˌ‥ ˈ‥·/ *trademark* a respected British film company started by the PRODUCER Ismail Merchant (1936-2005) and the DIRECTOR James Ivory (1928-). Many of their films, such as *A Room with a View* (1983), *Howards End* (1991), and *The Remains of the Day* (1992), are based on well-known works of English literature, and they are often about the lives of UPPER CLASS English people in the early 20th century, and about the English class system and its effects on people's behaviour.【商标】麦钱特-艾弗里制片公司〔英国一家颇有名望的电影制片公司，由制片人伊斯梅尔·麦钱特（1936-2005）和导演詹姆斯·艾弗里（1928- ）共同创建，拍摄了《看得见风景的房间》（1983）、《霍华德庄园》（1991）和《告别有情天》（1992）等多部影片。这些影片根据英国文学名著改编而成，往往反映20世纪初英国上层社会的生活，同时也关涉英国的等级制度及其对人的行为方式的影响〕

mer·chant·man /ˈmɝtʃəntmən; ˈmɜːtʃəntmən/ *n* [C] *old-fashioned* a ship used for carrying goods【过时】商船

merchant na·vy /ˌ‥ ˈ‥/ *BrE*【英】, **merchant ma·rine** *AmE*【美】/ˌ‥ ‥ˈ·/ *n* [singular] all of a country's ships that are used for trade, not war, and the people who work on these ships〔一个国家的〕全部商船，商船队；〔一个国家的〕全体商船船员：*John worked as a chef in the merchant navy.* 约翰在商船队里当厨师。

Merchant of Ve·nice, The /ˌ‥ ‥ ˈ‥/ a play by William Shakespeare about a man called Antonio who borrows money from Shylock . When Antonio cannot pay back the money, Shylock demands the right to cut out a 'pound of flesh' from Antonio's body. A famous speech from the play, made by the main female character, Portia, begins with the words, "The quality of mercy is not strained", by which Portia tells Shylock that he cannot be forced to show MERCY (=forgiveness), but that this would be a morally good thing to do.《威尼斯商人》〔威廉·莎士比亚的一部剧本。剧中有一个名叫安东尼奥的男子从高利贷商人夏洛克那里借了债。当他无力偿还债务时，夏洛克则要求履行从安东尼奥身上割下"一磅肉"的权利。剧中女主人公鲍西亚说过的一段话十分有名，第一句是："慈悲不是出于勉强。"鲍西亚借此想告诉夏洛克的是：谁都强迫不了他对别人表示同情，但表示仁慈却是一种善行〕

merchant sea·man /ˌ‥ ˈ‥/ *n* [C] a sailor in the merchant navy 商船船员

mer·ci·ful /ˈmɝsɪfəl; ˈmɜːsɪfəl/ *adj* **1 merciful death/end/release** a death that seems fortunate because it ends someone's suffering or difficulty 幸运的死亡/结束/解脱〔指结束了某人的痛苦或困境〕：*The final whistle came as a merciful relief.* 最后的哨声成了幸运的解脱。**2** being kind to people and forgiving them rather than punishing them or being cruel 宽大的，慈悲的，仁慈的：*Merciful God, save us.* 仁慈的上帝，救救我们吧。

mer·ci·ful·ly /ˈmɝsɪfəlɪ; ˈmɜːsɪfəli/ *adv* fortunately or luckily, because a situation could have been much worse 幸运地，幸而，幸亏〔指情况本来可能更糟〕：*Mercifully, I managed to stop the car just in time.* 幸运的是我及时刹住了车。

mer·ci·less /ˈmɝsɪlɪs; ˈmɜːsɪləs/ *adj* cruel and showing no kindness or forgiveness 冷酷无情的，残忍的：*a merciless attack on a defenceless village* 对没有防卫能力的村庄进行的残酷进攻 —**mercilessly** *adv* —**mercilessness** *n* [U]

Mer·co·sur /ˈmɝkosuə; ˈmɜːkəʊsuːə/ a trade association (=group of countries that have trade agreements with each other) consisting of Argentina, Brazil, Paraguay, and Uruguay, which was started in 1991 in order to encourage trade and reduce import taxes between these countries 南锥体共同市场，南方共同市场〔一贸易协会，成员有阿根廷、巴西、巴拉圭和乌拉圭等国。该协会成立于1991年，旨在促进区域贸易和降低进口关税〕

mer·cu·ri·al /mɝˈkjʊrɪəl; mɜːˈkjʊəriəl/ *adj* **1** *literary* changing mood suddenly and unexpectedly【文】〔情绪〕变化无常的，多变的：*an actor noted for his mercurial temperament* 以性情变化无常而著名的男演员 **2** *literary* quick and lively【文】敏捷的，聪敏的；活泼的：*her mercurial wit* 她的机智 **3** *technical* containing mercury【术语】含汞的，含水银的

Mer·cu·ry /ˈmɝkjərɪ; ˈmɜːkjʊri/ *n* [singular] the PLANET that is nearest the sun 水星 —see picture at 参见 SOLAR SYSTEM 图

mercury *n* [U] a heavy silver-white metal that is liquid at ordinary temperatures, and is used in THERMOMETERS 汞，水银〔在常温下呈液态的银白色重金属，用于温度计〕

Mercury pro·gram, the /ˈ‥ ˌ‥/ (1961-63) a US government space programme designed to put human beings in ORBIT around the Earth. In its first successful flight, John Glenn made three orbits of the Earth in 1962. 水星计划〔（1961-1963），美国政府的一项太空计划，目的是将人送入绕地球的轨道中去。约翰·格伦1962年绕地球轨道飞行了三圈，首次飞行取得圆满成功〕

mer·cy /ˈmɝsɪ; ˈmɜːsi/ *n* **1** [U] kindness, pity, and a willingness to forgive, which you show towards someone that you have power over〔对自己有权力支配的人所表示的〕仁慈，宽容，怜悯：**show no mercy** *The terrorists showed no mercy to the hostages.* 恐怖分子对人质残酷无情。| **have mercy (on)** *Oh Lord, have mercy on us sinners.* 主啊，对我们这些罪人发发慈悲吧。**2 it's a mercy** *spoken* used to say that it is lucky that a worse situation was avoided【口】幸运的是，幸亏〔用于表示更糟的情况得以避免总算是幸运〕：*It's a mercy the accident happened so near the hospital.* 幸亏事故发生在离医院很近的地方。**3 at the mercy of** unable to do anything to protect yourself from someone or something 任凭…的摆布〔而无力保护自己〕：*They were lost at sea, at the mercy of wind and weather.* 他们在海上迷失了方向，任凭风和天气的摆布。| *a housing policy that leaves people at the mercy of unscrupulous landlords* 使人们完全受肆无忌惮的房东摆布的住房政策 **4 leave sb to sb's (tender) mercies** *often humorous* to let someone be dealt with by another person, who may treat them very badly or strictly【常幽默】任凭某人受他人折磨[摆布] **5 be thankful/grateful for small mercies** to be pleased that a bad situation is not even worse 庆幸一种坏的情况还没有到更糟糕的地步 **6 mercy flight/mission etc** a journey taken to bring help to people 救援飞行/任务等：*a mercy dash to rescue stranded tourists* 快速救援被困游客 **7 throw yourself on sb's mercy** to BEG someone to help you or not to punish you 恳求某人帮忙[宽恕]

mercy kill·ing /ˈ‥ ˌ‥/ *n* [C,U] the act of killing someone who is very ill or old so that they do not have to suffer any more; EUTHANASIA 安乐死(术)

mere[1] /mɪr; mɪə/ *adj* [only before noun 仅用于名词前，no comparative 无比较级] **1** used to emphasize how small or unimportant something or someone is 仅仅，只不过〔用于强调某事或某人小或微不足道〕：*She lost the election by a mere 20 votes.* 她以仅仅20票之差落选。| *He's a mere child.* 他只不过是个孩子。**2** also 又作 **the merest** used when something small or unimportant has a big effect 极小的，极不重要的〔用于表示某物虽小或微不足道，却有很大的影响〕：*The merest little noise makes him nervous.* 一丁点儿声音也会使他紧张。| *The mere presence of a police officer made him feel guilty.* 仅仅是有警察在场就会使他感觉有罪。 W3

mere[2] *n* [C] *literary* a lake【文】湖

Mer·e·dith /ˈmɛrɪdɪθ; ˈmerɪ̈dɪθ/, **George** (1828-1909) a British writer whose works include the NOVEL *The Egoist* and *Poems and Lyrics of the Joy of Earth* 梅瑞狄斯〔（1828-1909），英国小说家、诗人，著有小说《利己主义者》和诗作《大地欢歌》〕

mere·ly /ˈmɪrlɪ; ˈmɪəli/ *adv* **1** used to emphasize that something or someone is very small or unimportant, especially when compared with something else; ONLY 仅仅，只不过：*It is an issue of merely local importance.* 它只不过是一个在本地有重要性的问题。| *This is merely the latest example of government interference.* 这仅仅是政府干预的最新例证。**2** *spoken* used to emphasize that you are doing something only for the reason you say【口】只是，仅仅是：*I'm not trying to criticize you, I'm merely trying to find out how the accident happened.* 我不是在批评你，我只是想弄清楚事故是如何发生的。 S2 W2

mer·e·tri·cious /ˌmɛrəˈtrɪʃəs; ˌmerɪ̈ˈtrɪʃəs◂/ *adj formal* seeming attractive but having no real value or not based on the truth【正式】华而不实的，徒有其表的，花哨的：*a meretricious argument* 华而不实的论据 —**meretriciously** *adv* —**meretriciousness** *n* [U]

merge /mɝdʒ; mɜːdʒ/ *v* **1** [I,T] to combine or join together to form one thing 合并；融合：**[+with]** *Rover is to merge with BMW, the German car manufacturer.* 罗孚汽车公司要和德国汽车制造商宝马公司合并。| **merge sth** *The company plans to merge its subsidiaries in the US.* 该公司计划合并其在美国的几家子公司。| **[+together]** *The sounds of the wind and the water merged together.* 风声和水声融合在一起。**2 merge into sth** to seem to disappear into something and become part of it 慢慢融入某物；逐渐消失在某物中：*As night fell, their outlines merged into the landscape.* 随着夜幕降临，它们的轮廓慢慢消失在景色之中。**3 merge into the background** *BrE informal* to behave very quietly in social situations, so that people do not notice you【英，非正式】社交场合中不显露头角；隐入幕后

merg·er /ˈmɝdʒɚ; ˈmɜːdʒə/ *n* [C] the act of joining together two or more companies or organizations to form one larger one 公司[组织]的合并：*job losses as a result of the merger*（公司）合并导致的失业

M

me·rid·i·an /məˋrɪdɪən; məˈrɪdiən/ *n* **1** [C] an imaginary line drawn from the NORTH POLE to the SOUTH POLE over the surface of the Earth, used to show the position of places on a map 子午线，经线 **2 the meridian** *technical* the highest point reached by the sun or another star, when seen from a point on the Earth's surface【术语】〔从地球表面某一点观测到的太阳或其他星体达到的〕最高点

me·ringue /məˋræŋ; məˈræŋ/ *n* [C,U] a light sweet food made by baking a mixture of sugar and the white part of eggs 蛋白酥〔糕饼〕

me·ri·no /məˋrino; məˈriːnəʊ/ *n* [U] a kind of sheep with long wool, or cloth made from this wool 美利奴绵羊；美利奴羊毛织物

mer·it[1] /ˋmɛrɪt; ˈmerɨt/ *n* **1** [C usually plural 一般用复数] one of the good features of something such as a plan or system 长处，优点：*The committee will look at the relative merits of the two proposals.* 委员会将会考虑这两个提案相比之下各自的优点。—opposite 反义词 DEMERIT (1) **2** [U] *formal* a good quality that makes something deserve praise or admiration【正式】〔使某物受赞扬或赞美的〕优秀品质：**have merit/be of merit** (=be good) 有可称道之处 *The arguments for legalizing marijuana have considerable merit.* 赞成大麻合法化的论据人有可取之处。| **artistic/literary merit** *a film lacking any kind of artistic merit* 一部毫无艺术价值的电影 **3 judge sth on its (own) merits** to judge something only by how good it is, without considering anything else 就某物（自身）的品质对其作出判断〔不考虑其他因素〕

merit[2] *v* [T not in progressive forms 不用进行式] *formal* to deserve something【正式】应得到，值得：*Your suggestion merits serious consideration.* 你的建议值得认真考虑。

mer·i·toc·ra·cy /ˌmɛrəˋtɑkrəsɪ; ˌmerɨˈtɒkrəsi/ *n especially BrE*【尤英】**1** [C] a social system that gives the greatest power and highest social positions to people with the most ability 精英管理（制度），贤能统治〔一种让能者居高位、掌大权的社会制度〕 **2** [singular] the people who have power in this kind of system 精英管理阶层，贤能统治者

mer·i·to·ri·ous /ˌmɛrəˋtɔrɪəs; ˌmerɨˈtɔːriəs◂/ *adj formal* very good and deserving praise【正式】极好而值得称赞的 —**meritoriously** *adv*

Mer·lin /ˋmɝlɪn; ˈmɜːlɨn/ a MAGICIAN (=someone who has magic powers) in old stories about King Arthur. 墨林〔亚瑟王传奇故事中的一名术士〕

mer·maid /ˋmɝˌmed; ˈmɜːmeɪd/ *n* [C] a woman in stories who has a fish's tail instead of legs〔传说中的〕美人鱼

mermaid 美人鱼

mer·ri·ment /ˋmɛrɪmənt; ˈmerɪmənt/ *n* [U] *formal* laughter, fun, and enjoyment【正式】欢笑；欢乐，兴高采烈：*His new hairstyle was the cause of much merriment.* 他的新发型引来一片笑声。

mer·ry /ˋmɛrɪ; ˈmeri/ *adj* **1 Merry Christmas!** used to say that you hope someone will have a happy time at Christmas 圣诞快乐！**2** cheerful and happy 欢快的：*He marched off, whistling a merry tune.* 他吹着欢快的口哨大步走了出去。**3 the more the merrier** *spoken* used to tell someone that you will be happy if they join you in something you are doing【口】〔人〕越多越好：*"Do you guys mind if I come with you?" "Sure – the more the merrier".* "如果我一块去你们大家不介意吧？""当然不会，人越多越热闹嘛。" **4** [not before noun 不用于名词前] *BrE informal* slightly drunk【英，非正式】微醉的：*We were all quite merry at the party last night.* 在昨晚的聚会上我们都有些喝醉了。**5 make merry** *literary* to enjoy yourself by drinking, singing etc【文】饮酒唱歌，寻欢作乐 **6** *old use* pleasant【旧】令人愉快的：*the merry month of June* 令人愉快的6月 —**merrily** *adv* —**merriness** *n* [U]

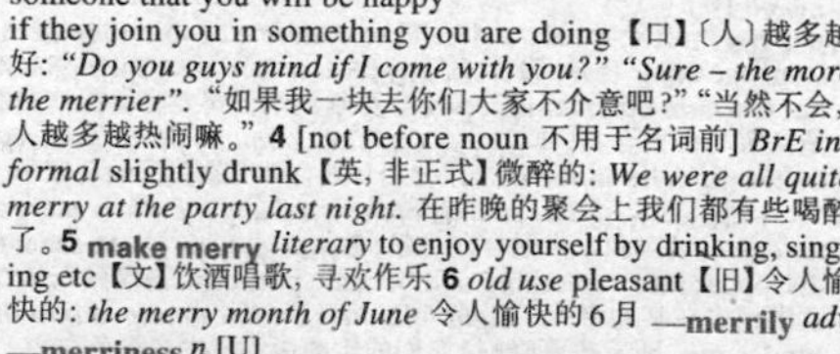

Merry En·gland /ˌmɛrɪ ˋɪŋglənd; ˌmeri ˈɪŋglənd/ also 又作 **Merrie England** England in the past, before the period when industry developed and large cities grew up. People sometimes imagine that life at that time was pleasant and simple, with lots of singing, dancing, and enjoyment. 快活的英格兰〔指早期的英格兰，工业尚未兴起，也没有出现很大的城市。在人们的想象中，当时的生活美好淳朴，一派歌舞升平的景象〕

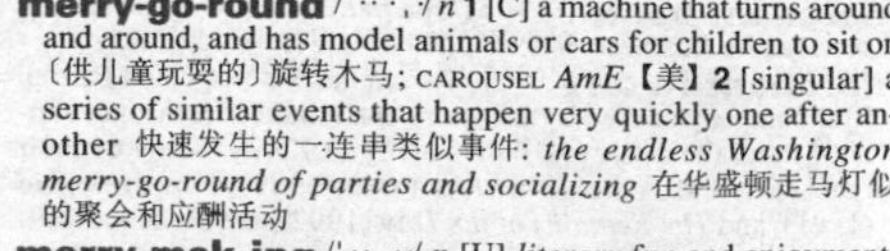

merry-go-round /ˋ· · ·, ˌ/ *n* **1** [C] a machine that turns around and around, and has model animals or cars for children to sit on〔供儿童玩耍的〕旋转木马；CAROUSEL *AmE*【美】**2** [singular] a series of similar events that happen very quickly one after another 快速发生的一连串类似事件：*the endless Washington merry-go-round of parties and socializing* 在华盛顿走马灯似的聚会和应酬活动

merry-mak·ing /ˋ· · ˌ· ·/ *n* [U] *literary* fun and enjoyment, especially drinking, dancing, and singing【文】寻欢作乐〔尤指喝酒、跳舞、唱歌〕—**merry-makers** *n* [C]

Merry Men /ˌ· · ˋ·/ the followers of Robin Hood, in old English stories 绿林好汉〔英国传说中跟随罗宾汉的好汉们〕：*Robin Hood and his Merry Men* 罗宾汉和他的绿林好汉

Merry Mon·arch, the /ˌ· · ˋ· ·/ a NICKNAME for the British King Charles II who was famous for enjoying himself and having many lovers 快乐君主〔英王查理二世的绰号，以享乐和风流闻名〕

Merry Wives of Wind·sor, The /ˌ· · ˌ· · ˋ· ·/ a humorous play by William Shakespeare in which the character Falstaff appears《温莎的风流娘儿们》〔莎士比亚一喜剧作品。剧中有一人物，名叫福斯塔夫〕

Mer·sey, the /ˋmɝzɪ; ˈmɜːzi/ a river in northwest England, which flows through Cheshire, Greater Manchester, and Merseyside into the Irish Sea 默西河〔位于英格兰西北部，流经柴郡、大曼彻斯特市和默西赛德郡，注入爱尔兰海〕

> **CULTURAL NOTE 文化注释**
>
> For British people, the Mersey is usually connected with Liverpool, and the music of the Beatles and other POP groups from Liverpool in the 1960s was known as the **Mersey sound** or the **Mersey beat**. 英国人常从默西河联想到利物浦以及甲壳虫等流行乐队的音乐。这些音乐是20世纪60年代从利物浦发端，也被称作"默西之音"或"默西节拍"。

Mer·sey·side /ˋmɝzɪsaɪd; ˈmɜːzisaɪd/ a COUNTY in the northwest of England, which includes Liverpool. It used to be an important industrial centre with many DOCKS (=places where ships are loaded and unloaded). 默西赛德郡〔英格兰西北部一郡，包括利物浦。该郡过去曾是重要的工业中心，建有许多码头〕

me·sa /ˋmesə; ˈmeɪsə/ *n* [C] a hill with a flat top and steep sides, in the southwestern USA 方山，平顶峭壁的山〔见于美国西南部地区〕

mes·ca·lin, mescaline /ˋmɛskəlɪn; ˈmeskəliːn/ *n* [U] a drug made from a CACTUS plant that makes people imagine that they can see things that do not really exist 墨斯卡灵，仙人球毒碱〔一种致幻剂〕

mesh[1] /mɛʃ; meʃ/ *n* [C,U] **1** a piece of material made of threads or wires that have been woven together like a net〔用线或金属丝编织的〕网状物：*Wire mesh covered all the windows to keep out flies.* 所有窗子都覆盖有铁丝纱网以防苍蝇飞入。**2** a complicated situation that makes you feel confused and trapped〔令人感到困惑及无能为力的〕错综复杂的局面；罗网：[+of] *He was caught in the mesh of emotions between the mother and her daughter.* 他陷入了那对母女间的感情纠葛之中。

mesh[2] *v* [I] **1** if two ideas or qualities mesh, they go well together and are suitable for each other〔想法或品性〕相合；相配；相互协调：*music in which classical harmonics mesh with the hypnotic rhythms of jazz* 古典和音与爵士音乐带催眠作用的节奏融为一体的音乐 **2** *technical* if two parts of an engine or machine mesh, they fit closely together and connect with each other【术语】〔引擎或机器部件〕啮合

mes·mer·ize also 又作 **-ise** *BrE*【英】/ˋmɛzməˌraɪz; ˈmezməraɪz/ *v* [T often passive 常用被动态] to make someone feel that they must watch or listen to something or someone, because they are so interested in it or attracted by it 使着迷，使迷住：*He was mesmerized by her charm and beauty.* 他被她的魅力和美貌迷住了。—**mesmerizing** *adj*

Mes·o·po·ta·mi·a /ˌmɛsəpəˋtemɪə; ˌmesəpəˈteɪmiə/ an area in western Asia around the River Tigris and the River Euphrates in Iraq, where, in ancient times, the world's first cities were built and several important ancient CIVILIZATIONS developed 美索不达米亚〔亚洲西部一地区，指伊拉克境内的底格里斯河和幼发拉底河流域。古时，这里建有世界上最早的城市，也是一些重要的古代文明的发祥地〕—see 见 the FERTILE CRESCENT

mess[1] /mɛs; mes/ *n*

1 ▶**DIRTY/UNTIDY** 脏的/凌乱的◀ [singular,U] a situation in which a place looks very untidy or dirty, with things spread all around 凌乱状态，脏乱情形：*Clean up this mess!* 把这脏乱的样

子收拾好！| *The house was an awful mess after the party.* 聚会之后屋里一片狼藉。| **make a mess** *You can make cookies if you promise not to make a mess in the kitchen.* 如果你答应不把厨房搞得乱七八糟，你就可以去做甜饼。

2 ►PROBLEMS/DIFFICULTIES 问题/困难◄ [singular] *informal* a situation in which there are a lot of problems and difficulties, especially as a result of mistakes or carelessness【非正式】〔尤指因错误或疏忽所造成的〕困难的局面：*We have to sort this problem out – the whole thing's a mess.* 我们必须解决这个问题——一切都乱套了。| *You got us into this mess, Terry. You can get us out of it.* 特里，你使我们陷入了这一困境，你把我们解脱出来吧。

3 be in a mess to be very untidy or dirty, very disorganized or full of problems 脏乱不堪；杂乱无章；问题成堆：*The previous chairman had left the company in a terrible mess.* 前任董事长使公司成了一个烂摊子。| *My life was in a real mess and I didn't know what to do.* 我当时的境况狼狈不堪，我也不知道该怎么办。

4 make a mess of *informal* to do something badly and make a lot of mistakes【非正式】把…搞得一塌糊涂：*I made a complete mess of that test.* 那次测验我考得一团糟。| *They've made such a mess of the economy.* 他们把经济搞得如此糟糕。

5 a mess of *AmE informal* a lot of【美，非正式】许多：*The dress had a high neck with a mess of buttons coming down the back.* 那件连衣裙是高领的，背部自上而下有许多纽扣。

6 ►ARMY/NAVY 陆军/海军◄ [C] a room in which members of the army, navy etc eat and drink together 军人食堂

7 ►WASTE MATTER 排泄物◄ [C,U] *informal especially BrE* solid waste material from a baby or animal【非正式，尤英】〔婴儿或动物的〕粪便：*The dog's made a mess on the carpet!* 狗把屎拉在地毯上啦！

mess² *v* [I] to have meals in a room where members of the army, navy etc eat together 在军人食堂就餐

mess around also 又作 **mess about** *BrE*【英】*phr v informal*【非正式】**1** [I] to spend time lazily, doing things slowly and in a way that is not planned 无所事事，漫无目的地度日：*He spent his vacation messing around on the farm.* 他在农场里东游西荡，无所事事地度过了假期。**2** [I] to behave in a silly way when you should be working or paying attention 游手好闲，不务正业：*Stop messing around and help me move this furniture.* 不要游手好闲了，来帮我搬搬这些家具吧。**3** [T **mess** sb **around/about**] to cause a lot of problems for someone, especially by changing your mind often or preventing them from getting what they want 对〔某人〕造成很多麻烦〔尤指不断改变自己的主意或阻止他人得到他所要的东西〕：*Don't mess me about – I want the money you promised me.* 别摆弄我——我要你答应过我的那笔钱。

mess around with also 又作 **mess about with** *BrE*【英】*phr v* [T] *informal*【非正式】**1** to have a sexual relationship with someone that you should not have a sexual relationship with 与…有不正当的性关系：*She'd been messing around with another man.* 她一直在和另一个男人勾搭着。**2** to spend time playing with something, repairing it etc 摆弄；修理：*Dave likes messing around with old cars.* 戴夫喜欢摆弄旧汽车。

mess up *phr v informal*【非正式】**1** [T **mess** sth ↔ **up**] to spoil or ruin something, especially something important or something that has been carefully planned 弄坏，毁掉〔尤指重要物品或精心策划的事情〕：*It took me ages to get this right – I don't want some idiot to mess it up.* 我花了好长时间才把这东西弄好，我不想让某个白痴把它毁掉。| *She felt she'd messed up her whole life.* 她感到她把自己整个生活都弄得一团糟。**2** [T **mess** sth ↔ **up**] to make something dirty or untidy 弄脏，弄乱：*Who messed up the kitchen?* 谁把厨房弄得又脏又乱？**3** [I,T **mess** sth ↔ **up**] to make a mistake and do something badly 出错；搞砸：*It doesn't matter if you mess it up, you can always try again.* 要是搞砸了也没关系，你总是可以再来一次的。| [+**on**] *I think I messed up on the last question.* 我想最后一个问题我答坏了。—see also 另见 MESSED UP, MESS-UP

mess with *phr v* [I,T] **don't mess with** *spoken*【口】**a)** used to warn someone not to annoy or argue with someone 别去招惹，不要和…争论：*Don't mess with me, buddy.* 喂，你不要惹我。**b)** used to warn someone not to get involved with something that is dangerous or harmful 不要沾染〔危险或有害之物〕：*Don't mess with illegal drugs. Just say no!* 不要去沾染非法毒品，要对它们说不！

mes·sage /ˈmɛsɪdʒ; ˈmesɪdʒ/ *n* [C] **1** a spoken or written piece of information that you send to another person 消息；口信；信息：*Did you get my message?* 你收到我发给你的信息了吗？| **leave a message** *He left a message saying he would probably be a little late.* 他留下口信说他可能会晚一会儿。| **can I take a message?** *spoken* (=used on the telephone when offering to give a message to someone)【口】我可以为你传个话吗？〔打电话时用〕*I'm sorry, she's out right now, can I take a message?* 对不起，她这会儿出去了，我可以传个话吗？**2** [singular] the main or most important idea that someone is trying to tell people about in a film, book, speech etc〔电影、书籍、讲话等的〕要旨，主题思想；寓意：*The message of the film is that good always triumphs over evil.* 这部电影的寓意是善良终会战胜邪恶。**3 get the message** *informal* to understand what someone means or what they want you to do【非正式】领会含意，明白：*OK, I get the message – I'm going!* 好吧，我明白了——我这就去！

messed up /ˌ· ˈ·◂/ *adj informal* someone who is messed up is very unhappy and has mental problems because of something that has happened to them【非正式】极不愉快的；精神有毛病的：*He's been really messed up since his wife left him.* 自从妻子离开他以后，他一直郁郁寡欢。

mes·sen·ger /ˈmɛsn̩dʒɚ; ˈmesɪndʒə/ *n* [C] **1** someone who takes messages to people 送信者，信使；通信员 **2 blame/shoot the messenger** to be angry with someone for telling you about something bad that has happened 责备/枪杀信使〔指迁怒于传递消息者〕

Mes·ser·schmitt /ˈmɛsɚˌʃmɪt; ˈmesəʃmɪt/ a type of military aircraft used by Germany in World War II and designed by **Willy Messerschmitt** (1898-1978), a German engineer 梅塞施米特战斗机〔第二次世界大战期间使用的一种军用飞机，由德国工程师威利·梅塞施米特 (1898-1978) 设计〕

mess hall /ˈ· ·/ *n* [C] a large room where soldiers eat 军人餐厅，部队食堂

mes·si·ah /məˈsaɪə; mɪ̍ˈsaɪə/ *n* [singular] **1 the Messiah a)** Jesus Christ, who is believed by Christians to be sent by God to save the world 救世主耶稣基督〔基督教徒认为上帝派他来拯救世界〕**b)** a great religious leader who, according to Jewish belief, will be sent by God to save the world 弥赛亚〔在犹太人的信仰中，指将被上帝派来拯救世界的一位伟大的宗教领袖〕**2** someone who people believe will save them from great social or economic problems〔社会或经济方面的〕救星：*He was seen as an economic messiah.* 他被视为经济方面的救星。

mes·si·an·ic /ˌmɛsɪˈænɪk; ˌmesiˈænɪk◂/ *adj formal*【正式】**1** someone who has messianic beliefs or feelings wants to make very big social or political changes connected with the belief that the world should be completely changed 有救世的信仰[情感]的；救世主似的：*messianic zeal* 救世主似的热情 **2** connected with the Messiah 救世主耶稣的；〔犹太人期待的救世主〕弥赛亚的

Mes·srs *BrE*【英】, **Messrs.** *AmE*【美】/ˈmɛsɚz; ˈmesəz/ the plural of MR, used especially in the names of companies 先生〔Mr 的复数，尤用于公司名称中〕：*Messrs Ford and Dobson* 福特和多布森先生

mess-up /ˈ· ·/ *n* [C] *informal* a situation in which someone has done something badly or made a lot of mistakes【非正式】混乱；一团糟的局面：*The whole thing had been a mess-up from start to finish.* 这件事从始至终都是乱糟糟的。

mess·y /ˈmɛsɪ; ˈmesi/ *adj* **1** dirty or untidy 脏的；不整洁的；凌乱的：*messy saucepans* 脏兮兮的平底锅 | *Sorry the place is so messy, I haven't had time to clear up.* 对不起，我这个地方又脏又乱，我一直没时间整理。**2** *informal* a messy situation is complicated and unpleasant to deal with【非正式】棘手的；难办的：*He's just been through a particularly messy divorce.* 他刚刚办完了离婚手续，过程十分曲折。—**messily** *adv* —**messiness** *n* [U]

mes·ti·zo /mɛsˈtizo; meˈstiːzəʊ/ *n plural* **mestizos** [C] someone who has one Spanish parent and one Native American parent 梅斯蒂索混血儿〔父母一方为西班牙人，一方为美洲土著人〕

Met, the /mɛt; met/ *n informal*【非正式】**a)** the Metropolitan Opera Company; the main OPERA company in New York 大都会歌剧团〔纽约的主要歌剧团〕**b)** the Metropolitan Police; the police force in London 都市警察局〔伦敦的警察部队〕

met the past tense and past participle of MEET[1]

meta- /mɛtə; metə/ *prefix technical* beyond the ordinary or usual【术语】超越，超出〔一般或通常情况〕：*metaphysical* (=beyond ordinary physical things) 形而上学的

me·tab·o·lis·m /məˈtæbl̩ˌɪzəm; mɪ̍ˈtæbəlɪzəm/ *n* [C,U] the chemical activity in your body that uses food to produce the energy you need to work and grow 新陈代谢 —**metabolic** /ˌmɛtəˈbɑlɪk; ˌmetəˈbɒlɪk◂/ *adj*: *An animal's lifespan is linked to its metabolic rate.* 动物的寿命与其新陈代谢速度是相联系的。

me·ta·bol·ize also 又作 **-ise** *BrE*【英】/məˈtæbl̩ˌaɪz; mɪ̍ˈtæbəlaɪz/ *v* [T] to break down food in the body by chemical activity and use it to produce energy 使发生新陈代谢

met·al /ˈmɛtl; ˈmetl/ *n* [C,U] a hard, usually shiny substance such as iron, gold, or steel 金属〈如铁、金或钢〉: *The frame is made of metal.* 这框架是用金属做的。| *a metal box* 金属盒子 | **precious metal** (=expensive metal used for making jewellery) 〔用以制作首饰的〕贵金属 —see also 另见 HEAVY METAL, METALLIC

met·a·lan·guage /ˈmɛtə,læŋgwɪdʒ; ˈmetə,læŋgwɪdʒ/ *n* [C,U] words used for talking about or describing language 〔用以论述或描写语言的〕元语言, 纯理语言

metal de·tect·or /ˈ‥ ‥,‥/ *n* [C] **1** a machine used to find pieces of metal that are buried under the ground 金属探测器 **2** a special frame that you walk through at an airport, used to check for weapons made of metal 金属探测框〔机场中供旅客穿行的特制门框, 用以探测金属制武器〕

metal fa·tigue /ˈ‥ ‥,‥/ *n* [U] a weakness in metal that makes it likely to break, caused for example by frequent shaking over a long period 金属疲劳

me·tal·lic /məˈtælɪk; mɪ̱ˈtælɪk/ *adj* **1** like metal in colour, appearance, or taste 〔颜色、外观或味道〕像金属的, 金属般的: *The sea was a dull metallic grey.* 大海呈现出昏暗的金属灰色。**2** a metallic noise sounds like pieces of metal hitting each other 〔声音〕似金属物件互相撞击的: *The pans made a metallic clatter as they crashed to the floor.* 那些锅当啷一声摔落在地板上。**3** made of or containing metal 金属制的; 含金属的: *metallic elements* 金属元素

met·al·lur·gy /ˈmɛtl̩,ɝdʒɪ; mɪ̱ˈtælədʒi/ *n* [U] the scientific study of metals and their uses 冶金学 —**metallurgist** *n* [C] —**metallurgical** /,mɛtl̩ˈɝdʒɪkl̩; ,metəˈlɜːdʒɪkəl◂/ *adj*

met·al·work /ˈmɛtl̩,wɝk; ˈmetlwɜːk/ *n* [U] **1** the activity or skill of making metal objects 金属加工; 金属加工术; 金工: *metalwork classes* 金工课 **2** objects made by shaping metal 金属制品 —**metalworker** *n* [C]

met·a·mor·pho·sis /,mɛtəˈmɔrfəsɪs; ,metəˈmɔːfəsɪ̱s/ *n plural* **metamorphoses** [C,U] **1** *formal* a process in which something changes completely into something very different 【正式】变化〔指由一物完全转变成另一物〕: *the metamorphosis of China under Deng's economic reforms* 在邓小平的经济改革政策下中国的彻底变化 **2** a process in which a young insect, frog etc changes into another stage in its development 〔幼虫、幼蛙等的〕变态 —**metamorphose** /,mɛtəˈmɔrfoz; ,metəˈmɔːfəʊz/ *v* [I,T]

met·a·phor /ˈmɛtəfɚ; ˈmetəfə/ *n* [C,U] **1** a way of describing something by comparing it to something else that has similar qualities, without using the words 'like' or 'as' 隐喻, 暗喻〔将一物比喻为具有相似品质的另一物, 而不用"像"、"如"等字眼〕: *'The sunshine of her smile' is a metaphor.* "她微笑中的阳光"是一个隐喻。| *His poetry is brought alive by his masterful use of metaphor.* 他的诗歌由于对隐喻的巧妙运用而显得生气勃勃。—compare 比较 SIMILE **2** **mixed metaphor** the use of two different metaphors at the same time to describe something, especially in a way that seems silly or funny 混杂隐喻〔指同时运用两个不同的隐喻描写某物, 尤指显得笨拙或滑稽〕 **3** [C,U] something in a book, painting, film etc that is intended to represent a more general idea or quality; SYMBOL 〔书、画、电影等中的〕象征: **[+for]** *Their relationship is a metaphor for the failure of communication in the modern world.* 他们之间的关系是现代世界中沟通失败的象征。

met·a·phor·i·cal /,mɛtəˈfɔrɪkl̩; ,metəˈfɒrɪkəl◂/ *adj* using words to mean something different from their ordinary meaning when describing something in order to achieve an effect 隐喻的; 含有隐喻的 —**metaphorically** /-klɪ; -kli/ *adv*: *He's got a big head – metaphorically speaking of course!* 他有一个大脑袋——这当然是比喻的说法!

met·a·phys·i·cal /,mɛtəˈfɪzɪkl̩; ,metəˈfɪzɪkəl◂/ *adj* **1** concerned with the study of metaphysics 形而上学的, 玄学的 **2** *spoken* used to describe a complicated arrangement of words and ideas 【口】难理解的, 深奥的; 抽象的 —**metaphysically** /-klɪ; -kli/ *adv*

met·a·phys·ics /,mɛtəˈfɪzɪks; ,metəˈfɪzɪks/ *n* [U] the part of the study of PHILOSOPHY that is concerned with trying to understand and describe the nature of reality 形而上学, 玄学

mete /mit; miːt/ *v*

mete sth ↔ **out** *phr v* [T] *formal* to give someone a punishment 【正式】给予〔惩罚〕: *Judges are meting out increasingly harsh sentences for car theft.* 法官们对汽车盗窃罪给予越来越严厉的刑罚。

me·te·or /ˈmitɪɚ; ˈmiːtiə/ *n* [C] a piece of rock or metal that floats in space, and makes a bright line in the night sky when it falls through the Earth's ATMOSPHERE (1) 流星

me·te·or·ic /,mitɪˈɔrɪk; ,miːtiˈɒrɪk◂/ *adj* **1** happening very suddenly and quickly 突然而迅疾发生的: **meteoric rise/career** *her meteoric rise to fame* 她的迅速成名 **2** from a METEOR 流星的: *meteoric stones* 陨石 —**meteorically** /-klɪ; -kli/ *adv*

me·te·o·rite /ˈmitɪər,aɪt; ˈmiːtiəraɪt/ *n* [C] a piece of rock or metal that has come from space and has landed on Earth 陨星; 陨石; 陨铁

Meteorological Of·fice, the the full name of the MET OFFICE 〔英国〕气象局〔Met Office的全称〕

me·te·o·rol·o·gy /,mitɪəˈrɑlədʒɪ; ,miːtiəˈrɒlədʒi/ *n* [U] the scientific study of weather conditions 气象学 —**meteorologist** *n* [C] —**meteorological** /,mitɪərəˈlɑdʒɪkl̩; ,miːtiərəˈlɒdʒɪkəl◂/ *adj*

-meter[1] /mitɚ; miːtə/ *suffix* [in nouns 构成名词] an instrument for measuring 测量仪器: *an altimeter* (=for measuring the height at which an aircraft is flying) 〔飞机的〕高度计, 高度表

-meter[2] *suffix* the American spelling of -METRE -metre的美式拼法

me·ter[1] /ˈmitɚ; ˈmiːtə/ *n* **1** [C] a machine that measures and shows the amount of something you have used or the amount of money that you must pay 计量器; 计价器: *The taxi driver turned off his meter.* 出租车司机关上了计价器。**2** [C,U] the American spelling of METRE metre的美式拼法 —see also 另见 PARKING METER

meter[2] *v* [T] to measure something with a meter, or supply gas, electricity etc through a meter 用仪表计量[测量]; 通过计量器供应〔煤气、电力等〕

meter maid /ˈ‥ ‥/ *n* [C] *AmE* a woman whose job is to make sure that cars are not parked in the wrong place or for longer than is allowed 【美】〔监督汽车在允许的地点和时间内停放的〕女交通督导员; TRAFFIC WARDEN *BrE* 【英】

meth·a·done /ˈmɛθədon; ˈmeθədəʊn/ *n* [U] a drug that is often given to people who are trying to stop taking HEROIN 美沙酮, 美散痛〔常供试图戒除海洛因者使用〕

me·thane /ˈmɛθen; ˈmiːθeɪn/ *n* [U] a colourless gas with no smell that can be burned to give heat 甲烷, 沼气

meth·a·nol /ˈmɛθənɔl; ˈmeθənɒl/ *n* [U] a poisonous alcohol that can be made from wood 甲醇

me·thinks /mɪˈθɪŋks; mɪˈθɪŋks/ *v past tense* **methought** /-ˈθɔt; -ˈθɔːt/ *old use or humorous* I think 【旧或幽默】我想, 据我看来: *a holiday somewhere nice, Florida methinks* 在某个好地方休假——我想是在佛罗里达

meth·od /ˈmɛθəd; ˈmeθəd/ *n* **1** [C] a planned way of doing something, especially one that a lot of people know about and use 方法, 办法: *traditional teaching methods* 传统教学法 | *I think we should try again using a different method.* 我想我们应该用不同的方法再试一次。| **[+of]** *There are several possible methods of payment.* 有好几种可以使用的付款办法。| **[+for]** *a new method for the early detection of cancer* 癌症早期诊断的新方法 **2** [U] *formal* proper planning of the way that something is done 【正式】条理, 秩序: *There's no method in the way they do their accounts.* 他们记账的方式没有条理。**3** **there's method in sb's madness** used to say that even though someone seems to be behaving strangely, there is a sensible reason for what they are doing 某人看起来举止怪异, 但行事合乎情理

me·thod·i·cal /məˈθɑdɪkl̩; mɪ̱ˈθɒdɪkəl/ *adj* **1** done in a careful and well organized way 有条理的; 井然的: *a methodical piece of work* 一项井井有条的工作 **2** always doing things carefully, using an ordered system 做事有条不紊的, 办事有条理的: *She's a very methodical person.* 她是个办事很有条理的人。—**methodically** /-klɪ; -kli/ *adv*: *The detective went through the papers methodically, one by one.* 侦探有条不紊地、一份一份地检查了那些文件。

Meth·o·dist /ˈmɛθədɪst; ˈmeθədɪ̱st/ *n* [C] someone who belongs to a Christian religious group that follows the teachings of John Wesley 〔遵循约翰·卫斯理教义的〕循道公会教徒 —**Methodist** *adj* —**Methodism** *n* [U]

meth·o·dol·o·gy /,mɛθədˈɑlədʒɪ; ,meθəˈdɒlədʒi/ *n* [C,U] the set of methods and principles that are used when studying a particular subject or doing a particular kind of work 方法论; 方法学; 〔某一学科的〕一套方法和原则: *teaching methodology* 教学法 —**methodological** /,mɛθədəˈlɑdʒɪkl̩; ,meθədəˈlɒdʒɪkəl◂/ *adj* —**methodologically** /-klɪ; -kli/ *adv*

me·thought /mɪˈθɔt; mɪˈθɔːt/ the past tense of METHINKS

meths /mɛθs; meθs/ *n* [U] *BrE informal* METHYLATED SPIRITS 【英, 非正式】甲基化酒精

Me·thus·e·lah /məˈθjuzələ; məˈθjuːzɪ̱lə/ *n* **as old as Methuselah** very old 年纪非常大的

meth·yl al·co·hol /,mɛθəl ˈælkə,hɔl; ,meθɪ̱l ˈælkəhɒl/ *n* [U] a poisonous alcohol that can be made from wood; METHANOL 甲醇 —compare 比较 ETHYL ALCOHOL

meth·yl·at·ed spir·its /ˌmɛθəˌletɪd ˈspɪrɪts; ˌmeθəleɪtəd ˈspɪrəts/ *n* [U] a kind of alcohol that is burned in lamps, heaters etc〔灯盏、加热器等用的〕甲基化酒精

me·tic·u·lous /məˈtɪkjələs; məˈtɪkjələs/ *adj* **1** very careful about small details, and always making sure that everything is done correctly 对细节十分注意的，一丝不苟的: *He kept meticulous accounts.* 他记账非常详细准确。| *She pasted the cuttings into the scrapbook with meticulous care.* 她小心翼翼地把剪下的资料粘贴到剪贴簿上。**2** if you are meticulous about doing something, you are very careful to always do it 总是非常注意做到的: **[+in/about]** *He's meticulous about replying to correspondence.* 他非常注意做到有信必复。—**meticulously** *adv* —**meticulousness** *n* [U]

met·i·er /meˈtje; ˈmetieɪ/ *n* [C usually singular 一般用单数] *formal* a kind of work or activity that you enjoy doing because you have a natural ability to do it well【正式】专长，特长，得心应手的工作: **not be sb's metier** *Modern music is not his metier.* 现代音乐不是他的专长。

Met Of·fice, the /ˌ·ˈ··/ also 又作 **the Meteorological Office** the national organization that collects information about the weather in the UK, and provides weather reports for newspapers, radio, and TV, and also for farmers, scientists, airports etc. There is a similar organization in the US called the National Weather Service.〔英国〕气象局〔英国一国家机构，专事收集气象信息，为报纸、电台、电视台、机场以及农民和科学家等提供气象预报。美国也有一类似机构，称 the National Weather Service（国家气象局）〕

-metre /mitɚ; miːtə/ *BrE*【英】, **-meter** *AmE*【美】*suffix* [in nouns 构成名词] part of a metre, or a number of metres 一米的一部分；若干米: *a millimetre* 一毫米 | *a kilometre* 一千米，一公里

S2 W3 **me·tre** *BrE*【英】, **meter** *AmE*【美】/ˈmitɚ; ˈmiːtə/ *n* **1** [C] the basic unit for measuring length in the METRIC SYSTEM 米，公尺〔公制长度的基本公制单位〕—see table on page C3 参见 C3 页附录 **2** [C,U] the arrangement of sounds in poetry into patterns of strong and weak beats〔诗的〕格律，韵律 —compare 比较 RHYTHM (1)

met·ric /ˈmɛtrɪk; ˈmetrɪk/ *adj* **1** using or connected with the metric system of weights and measures 公制的，米制的，十进制的: *the metric tonne* 公吨 | *metric sizes* 公制尺码 **2** metrical 用诗体写的，格律诗的 —compare 比较 IMPERIAL (2)

CULTURAL NOTE 文化注释

Children in the US are taught about the metric system, but it is not used very much in the US except by scientists. In the UK, however, the metric system is now the standard system of measurement. Children are taught the metric system in school, and no longer learn about the former system of measurement, known as the IMPERIAL system, which measures weights in STONES and POUNDS, liquids in GALLONS and PINTS, lengths in feet (FOOT) and INCHES, and distances in miles. In the UK, food and other products are sold in kilograms and litres. Beer, however, is still sold in pints in bars, and distances are still usually given in miles. Young people will often know their weight in kilograms, but both young and older people still measure their weight in stones and pounds. Young people also usually know their height in centimetres, but both young and older people still also measure their height in feet and inches. 在美国，从儿童时期就开始教授公制计量单位，但除了科学家之外一般人不怎么使用公制单位；而在英国，公制单位现在是标准的计量单位。孩子们在学校中学习使用公制单位，过去的那一套被称为"英制单位"的计量制度已不再教授。英制单位中的重量单位有英石和英磅，液量单位有加仑和品脱，长度单位是英尺和英寸，距离用英里计量。在英国，食品等产品以公斤和升出售。可是酒吧中卖的啤酒仍以品脱来度量，另外距离也常用英里来表示。年轻人一般知道自己有多少公斤重，但人们无论老幼仍在用英石和英磅计算自己的体重。年轻人通常也知道自己身高是多少厘米，但是人们无论老幼还是会用英尺和英寸来计量身高。— see also Cultural Note at CELSIUS 另见 CELSIUS 文化注释

met·ri·cal /ˈmɛtrɪkḷ; ˈmetrɪkəl/ *adj technical* written in the form of poetry, with regular beats【术语】用诗体写的，格律诗的 —**metrically** /-kḷɪ; -kli/ *adv*

met·ri·ca·tion /ˌmɛtrɪˈkeʃən; ˌmetrɪˈkeɪʃən/ *n* [U] the change to using the metric system of weights and measures〔度量衡的〕公制化

metric sys·tem /ˈ·· ˌ··/ *n* [singular] the system of weights and measures that is based on the metre and the kilogram 公制，米制

metric ton /ˌ·· ˈ·/ *n* [C] a unit for measuring weight equal to 1,000 kilograms 公吨，米制吨〔重量计量单位，等于 1000 公斤〕

met·ro /ˈmɛtro; ˈmetrəʊ/ *n* [C] a railway system that runs under the ground below a city 地下铁道系统，地（下）铁（道）: *the Paris Metro* 巴黎地下铁道系统

Metro-Gold·wyn-May·er /ˌmɛtro ˌgoldwɪn ˈmeɚ; ˌmetrəʊ ˌgəʊldwən ˈmeɪə/ —see 见 MGM

met·ro·nome /ˈmɛtrəˌnom; ˈmetrənəʊm/ *n* [C] a piece of equipment that shows the speed at which music should be played, by making a regular noise 节拍器〔显示音乐应以什么速度演奏的设备〕

me·trop·o·lis /məˈtrɑplɪs; məˈtrɒpələs/ *n* [C] a very large city that is the most important city in a country or area〔一国或一地区的〕首要城市；大都会

met·ro·pol·i·tan /ˌmɛtrəˈpɑlətn; ˌmetrəˈpɒlətən◂/ *adj* **1** connected with or belonging to a very large city 大城市的，大都会的: *the Los Angeles metropolitan area* 洛杉矶都市区 **2** *technical* connected with France, rather than its colonies (COLONY (1))【术语】法国本土〔而非其殖民地〕的: *metropolitan France* 法国本土

Metropolitan Mu·se·um of Art, the /·,······ ·/ also 又作 **the Met** *informal*【非正式】the most important art museum in the US, in New York City 大都会艺术博物馆〔美国最重要的艺术博物馆，位于纽约市〕

Metropolitan Op·e·ra, the /·,····ˈ···/ also 又作 **the Met** *informal*【非正式】a US OPERA company based at the Lincoln Center for the Performing Arts in New York City. Its performances are often broadcast on the radio. 大都会歌剧团〔美国一歌剧团。设在纽约市的林肯表演艺术中心内，其演出经常在电台上播出〕

Metropolitan Po·lice /·,····ˈ·/ *n* [singular] the police force that is responsible for London 都市警察局〔负责伦敦地区的警察部队〕

met·tle /ˈmɛtḷ; ˈmetl/ *n* [U] **1** courage and determination to do something even when it is very difficult 勇气，奋斗精神: *a man of mettle* 有奋斗精神的人 | **show/prove your mettle** (=show that you can do something well, in spite of difficulties) 显示出/证明你的勇气[决心，毅力] *It'll be a hard game, but it should give the team a chance to show their mettle.* 这将是一场艰苦的比赛，但它会给队员们一个显示自己毅力的机会。**2 be on your mettle** to be ready to try as hard as possible because your abilities are being tested 准备尽最大努力: *You'll have to be on your mettle in the oral exam.* 口试中你必须全力以赴。

met·tle·some /ˈmɛtḷsəm; ˈmetlsəm/ *adj literary* full of energy and determination【文】精力充沛的；刚毅的

mew /mju; mjuː/ *v* [I] to make the soft high crying sound that a cat makes 作猫叫声 —**mew** *n*

mews /mjuz; mjuːz/ *n plural BrE* a small street or yard surrounded by houses in a city, where horses used to be kept【英】〔城市中为房屋环绕、过去用作马厩的〕小街，小院

Mex·i·can[1] /ˈmɛksɪkən; ˈmeksəkən/ *adj* from or connected with Mexico 墨西哥的

Mexican[2] *n* [C] someone from Mexico 墨西哥人

Mexican War, the /ˌ···ˈ·/ also 又作 **the Mexican-American War** (1846-48) a war between the US and Mexico, which began when Texas, which had recently become independent from Mexico, became part of the US. Mexico and the US disagreed over the Texas-Mexico border. The US also wanted to buy California and New Mexico, but Mexico did not want to sell them. Led by Zachary Taylor, the US won the war, and bought a very large area of land, which included California, Nevada, Utah, and parts of several other states. 墨西哥战争〔(1846-1848)，美国与墨西哥之间的一场战争。当时，得克萨斯刚脱离墨西哥获得独立便并入美国的版图。墨西哥和美国在得克萨斯-墨西哥边境问题上产生了争议。同时，美国还想买下加利福尼亚和新墨西哥，而墨西哥却不愿出让，因而爆发战争。美国军队在扎卡里·泰勒的指挥下打赢了这场战争，并买下了包括加利福尼亚、内华达、犹他以及其他几个州部分地区在内的大片土地〕

Mexican wave /ˌ···ˈ·/ *n* [singular] *BrE* the effect that is made when all the people watching a game of football, BASEBALL etc stand up, move their arms up and down, and sit down again one after the other in a continuous movement【英】墨西哥人浪〔观看足球、棒球等比赛时所有人依次站起上下挥动双臂而后又坐下所形成的人浪〕

Mex·i·co /ˈmɛksɪˌko; ˈmeksəkəʊ/ a country to the south of the US and to the north of Guatemala. Population: 101,879,000 (2001). Capital: Mexico City. Before the arrival of Europeans, there were several important Native American Civilizations in Mexico, including the Aztecs and the Maya. The country was ruled by Spain from the 16th century, and became independent

in 1821. 墨西哥〔位于美国以南、危地马拉以北一国家。人口: 101,879,000 (2001), 首都: 墨西哥城。欧洲移民到达美洲之前, 墨西哥曾拥有一些重要的美洲土著文明, 其中包括阿兹特克文明与马雅文明。墨西哥自16世纪起由西班牙人统治, 1821年独立〕

Mexico City the capital city of Mexico, built on the RUINS of an ancient Aztec city 墨西哥城〔墨西哥首都, 建于古阿兹特克城废墟之上〕

mez·za·nine /ˋmɛzə͵nin; ˈmezəniːn/ *n* [C] **1** a small floor that is built between two other floors in a building〔两层楼之间的〕夹层楼面, 夹楼 **2** *AmE* the lowest BALCONY in a theatre, or the first few rows of seats in that balcony【美】〔剧院的〕最底层楼厅; 最底层楼厅的前几排座位

mez·zo[1] /ˋmɛtso; ˈmetsəʊ/ *adv* **mezzo forte/piano etc** *technical* a word meaning quite or not very loud, softly etc, used in instructions for performing music【术语】中强/中弱等〔演奏音乐中用作说明的词语〕

mezzo[2] *n* [C] a mezzo-soprano voice 女中音

mezzo-so·pra·no /͵‥ ·ˋ·/ *n* [C] **1** a voice that is lower than a SOPRANO'*s* but higher than an ALTO'*s* 女中音 **2** a woman who sings with this kind of voice 女中音歌手

mez·zo·tint /ˋmɛtsə͵tɪnt; ˈmetsəʊ͵tɪnt/ *n* [C,U] a picture printed from a metal plate that is polished in places to produce areas of light and shade 镂刻金属版印刷品

MFA /͵ɛm ɛf ˋe; ͵em ef ˈeɪ/ *n* [C] *AmE* Master of Fine Arts; a university degree in a subject such as painting or SCULPTURE【美】美术硕士; 美术硕士学位

MG /͵ɛm ˋdʒi; ͵em ˈdʒiː/ *trademark* a type of British sports car【商标】名爵跑车〔一种英国跑车〕

mg the written abbreviation of 缩写= MILLIGRAM

M Glam the written abbreviation of 缩写= MID GLAMORGAN

MGM /͵ɛm dʒi ˋɛm; ͵em dʒiː ˈem/ *trademark* Metro-Goldwyn-Mayer; a US film company based in Hollywood which has made many famous films and CARTOONS【商标】米高梅电影制片公司〔美国好莱坞一电影制片公司, 已拍摄了许多著名电影和卡通片〕

MHz the written abbreviation of 缩写= MEGAHERTZ

MI the written abbreviation of 缩写= MICHIGAN

mi /mi; miː/ *n* [singular] the third note in a musical SCALE[1] (8) according to the SOL-FA system 视唱法音阶中的第三音

MI5 /͵ɛm aɪ ˋfaɪv; ͵em aɪ ˈfaɪv/ *n* [not with *the* 不与 the 连用] a secret British government organization whose job it is to keep Britain safe from attack by enemies inside the country, such as foreign spies (SPY[1]) or TERRORISTS MI5局, 军情五处〔英国秘密政府机构, 负责保卫英国不受国家内部敌人, 如外国间谍或恐怖分子的破坏〕

MI6 /͵ɛm aɪ ˋsɪks; ͵em aɪ ˈsɪks/ *n* [not with *the* 不与 the 连用] a secret British government organization that sends people to foreign countries to try and **find out secret political and military information** MI6局, 军情六处〔英国秘密政府机构, 专门向外国派遣人员以搜集秘密的政治和军事情报〕

MIA /͵ɛm aɪ ˋe; ͵em aɪ ˈeɪ/ *n* [C] *AmE* missing in action; a soldier who has disappeared in a battle and who may still be alive【美】战斗中失踪人员

Mi·am·i /maɪˋæmɪ; maɪˈæmi/ a city in the southeast of Florida in the US, which is popular with tourists. It has a large Hispanic and Cuban population. 迈阿密〔美国佛罗里达州东南部一城市, 深受旅游人士喜爱。该市拉美裔和古巴裔人口居多〕

mi·aow, meow /mɪˋaʊ; miˈaʊ/ *v* [I] to make the crying sound that a cat makes 作猫叫声 —**miaow** *n* [C]

mi·as·ma /maɪˋæzmə; miˈæzmə/ *n* [singular,U] *literary*【文】**1** a thick, unhealthy, unpleasant mist 瘴气: *A foul miasma lay over the town.* 一阵难闻的瘴气笼罩在城市上空。**2** an evil influence or feeling 有害的影响; 不良的感觉: *The miasma of defeat hung over them.* 失败的气氛弥漫在他们中间。

mi·ca /ˋmaɪkə; ˈmaɪkə/ *n* [U] a mineral that consists of small flat transparent pieces of rock, which is used to make electrical instruments 云母

Mi·caw·ber /mɪˋkɔbɚ; mɪˈkɔːbə/, **Mr** a character in the book *David Copperfield* (1849-50) by Charles Dickens. Many people think that he is based on Dickens's own father. He is put in prison because he owes money and cannot pay it, but he is always happy and spends any money he gets on himself, confident that "something will turn up" to end his problems. 麦考伯〔查尔斯·狄更斯的小说《大卫·科波菲尔》(1849-1850) 中的一个人物。不少人认为该人物的原型是狄更斯的父亲。他因无力偿还债务而入狱, 可始终保持乐观, 手头一有钱就花个精光, 因为他相信总会时来运转, 困难会自行解决〕

mice /maɪs; maɪs/ the plural of MOUSE

Mi·chael /ˋmaɪkl; ˈmaɪkəl/ in the Old Testament of the Bible, an ARCHANGEL (=a good spirit of the highest rank who lives with God in Heaven) 米迦勒〔《圣经·旧约》中的一位天使长〕

Mich·ael·mas /ˋmɪkl̩məs; ˈmɪkəlməs/ *n* [C,U] 29th September, a Christian holy day in honour of Saint Michael 米迦勒节〔9月29日基督教纪念圣米迦勒的节日〕

Mi·chel·an·ge·lo /͵maɪkl̩ˋændʒəlo; ͵maɪkəlˈændʒələʊ/ (1475-1564) an Italian PAINTER, sculptor, and ARCHITECT (=someone who designs buildings) of the Renaissance period. One of the greatest artists who ever lived, he is famous especially for his statue of David (an ancient king of Israel) and for painting the ceiling of the Sistine Chapel in Rome with scenes from the Old Testament of the Bible, including the *Creation of Adam*. 米开朗琪罗〔(1475-1564), 意大利文艺复兴时期画家、雕塑家和建筑师, 被认为是有史以来最伟大的艺术家之一。其作品尤以大卫的雕像及罗马西斯廷教堂的天顶画闻名。这些作品取材于《圣经·旧约》, 其中包括《创造亚当》〕

Mich·e·lin Guide /ˋmɪtʃəlɪn ͵gaɪd; ˈmɪtʃəlɪn ͵gaɪd/ also 又作**Michelin** *trademark* a type of guidebook produced by the French company Michelin, which contains information for tourists visiting places in Europe and the US. The **green guides** contain maps and information about interesting places to visit, especially in Europe and the US, and the **red guides** contain lists of restaurants and hotels in Europe, which are given one, two, or three stars, according to a system for judging their quality. A restaurant with three Michelin stars is regarded as extremely good, and very few restaurants achieve this.【商标】《米其林指南》〔法国米其林公司出版的一种旅游指南, 为前往欧洲和美国的旅游人士提供各种信息。绿色指南部分的主要内容为欧美旅游名胜地图和简介。红色指南部分列有欧洲一、二、三星级餐厅和酒店。列入《米其林指南》的三星级餐厅被认为是最高级的餐厅, 获此殊荣的餐厅为数不多〕

Mich·i·gan /ˋmɪʃɪgən; ˈmɪʃɪgən/ **1** abbreviation 缩写为 **MI** a state in north central US, which is an industrial area and an important centre for producing cars 密歇根州〔美国中北部一州, 尤以汽车工业区闻名〕 **2 Lake Michigan** a large lake in north central US, one of the Great Lakes 密歇根湖〔美国中北部一大湖, 为五大湖之一〕

mick /mɪk; mɪk/ *n* [C] *BrE* an insulting word for someone from Ireland【英】爱尔兰人〔侮辱性词语〕

mick·ey /ˋmɪkɪ; ˈmɪki/ *n* **1 take the mickey (out of sb)** *informal especially BrE* to make someone look silly often in a friendly way, for example by copying them or by pretending something is true when it is not【非正式, 尤英】戏弄〔指善意地捉弄某人, 如模仿他的动作、哄骗他等〕: *Why are people always taking the mickey out of Nigel?* 人们为什么总是捉弄奈杰尔? **2** also 又作 **Mickey Finn** [C] a type of drug that you give to someone to make them unconscious 麻醉药; 蒙汗药

Mic·key Mouse[1] /͵‥ ˈ·/ *n trademark* a CARTOON character invented by Walt Disney. He is the most famous of all Disney's characters and is often used as a symbol of the Disney organization.【商标】米老鼠〔沃尔特·迪斯尼公司塑造的一卡通形象, 是迪斯尼所有动画形象中最有名的一个, 常用作迪斯尼公司的象征〕

Mickey Mouse[2] /͵‥ ˈ·◂/ *adj* **a Mickey Mouse operation/organization/outfit** a company or organization that is very small and unimportant, and not very good 无足轻重的企业/组织/机构

mi·cro /ˋmaɪkro; ˈmaɪkrəʊ/ *n* [C] *old-fashioned* a small computer; a PC[1]【过时】微型电脑; 个人电脑

micro- /ˋmaɪkro; ˈmaɪkrəʊ/ *prefix technical* extremely small【术语】极小的, 微小的: *a microcomputer* 微型电脑 | *microelectronics* 微电子学 —see table on page C4 参见 C4 页附录 —compare 比较 MACRO-, MINI-

mi·crobe /ˋmaɪkrob; ˈmaɪkrəʊb/ *n* [C] a living thing which is so small that it cannot be seen without a microscope, and which can sometimes cause disease 微生物; 病原体

mi·cro·bi·ol·o·gy /͵maɪkrobaɪˋɑlədʒɪ; ͵maɪkrəʊbaɪˈɒlədʒi/ *n* [U] the scientific study of very small living things such as BACTERIA 微生物学 —**microbiologist** *n* [C] —**microbiological** /͵maɪkrobaɪəˋlɑdʒɪkl̩; ͵maɪkrəʊbaɪəˈlɒdʒɪkəl/ *adj*

mi·cro·chip /ˋmaɪkrotʃɪp; ˈmaɪkrəʊ͵tʃɪp/ *n* [C] a very small piece of SILICON containing a set of electronic parts which is used in computers and other machines; a CHIP[1] (4a) 微型集成电路片, 微晶片, 芯片

mi·cro·com·put·er /͵maɪkrokəmˋpjutɚ; ͵maɪkrəʊkəmˈpjuːtə/ *n* [C] *old-fashioned* a small computer; a PC[1]【过时】微型电脑; 个人电脑

mi·cro·cos·m /ˋmaɪkrə͵kɑzəm; ˈmaɪkrəʊkɒzəm/ *n* [C] a small group, society, or place that has the same qualities as a much larger one 微观世界; 缩影; 小天地, 小宇宙 —compare 比较 MACROCOSM —**microcosmic** /͵maɪkrəˋkɑzmɪk; ͵maɪkrəʊˈkɒzmɪk◂/ *adj*

M

mi·cro·dot /ˈmaɪkrodɑt; ˈmaɪkrəʊdɒt/ *n* [C] a secret photograph of something such as a document, that is reduced to the size of a DOT so that it can easily be hidden 微粒照片〔指为便于藏匿而将文件等的机密照片缩小至微粒大小〕

mi·cro·e·lec·tron·ics /ˌmaɪkroɪlɛkˈtrɑnɪks; ˌmaɪkrəʊɪlekˈtrɒnɪks/ *n* [U] the practice or study of designing very small PRINTED CIRCUITs that are used in computers 微电子学 —**microelectronic** *adj*

mi·cro·fiche /ˈmaɪkrofiʃ; ˈmaɪkrəʊfiːʃ/ *n* [C,U] a sheet of film on which written information is stored in a very small form, and which can only be read using a special machine 〔存储文字资料的〕缩微胶片

mi·cro·film /ˈmaɪkrəˌfɪlm; ˈmaɪkrəʊfɪlm/ *n* [C,U] very small film for photographing maps, documents etc so that they can be easily stored 〔供拍摄地图、文件等以便存储用的〕缩微胶卷 —**microfilm** *v* [T]

mi·cro·light /ˈmaɪkrəlaɪt; ˈmaɪkrəʊlaɪt/ *n* [C] a very light small aircraft for one or two people 〔载一两人的〕微型飞机

mi·crom·e·ter /maɪˈkrɑmətə; maɪˈkrɒmɪtə/ *n* [C] an instrument for measuring very small distances 测微计, 千分尺

mi·cron /ˈmaɪkrɑn; ˈmaɪkrɒn/ *n* [C] one millionth of a metre 微米〔百万分之一米〕

Mi·cro·ne·si·a /ˌmaɪkroˈniʒə; ˌmaɪkrəʊˈniːziə/ a group of more than 2,000 small islands in the west Pacific Ocean, including the Caroline Islands, the Marshall Islands, and Kiribati. Population: 107,000 (1995) 密克罗尼西亚〔太平洋西部一群岛, 由2000多座小岛组成, 其中包括加罗林群岛、马绍尔群岛和基里巴群岛。人口: 107,000 (1995)〕—**Micronesian** *n, adj*

mi·cro·or·gan·is·m /ˌmaɪkroˈɔrgənˌɪzəm; ˌmaɪkrəʊˈɔːgənɪzəm/ *n* [C] a living thing which is so small that it cannot be seen without a microscope 微生物

mi·cro·phone /ˈmaɪkrəˌfon; ˈmaɪkrəfəʊn/ *n* [C] a piece of equipment that you speak into to record your voice or make it louder when you are speaking or performing in public 麦克风, 话筒, 传声器, 扩音器

mi·cro·pro·ces·sor /ˈmaɪkroˈprɑsɛsə; ˈmaɪkrəʊˌprəʊsesə/ *n* [C] the central CHIP[1] (4a) in a computer, which controls most of its operations 〔电脑的〕微处理器, 微处理机

mi·cro·scope /ˈmaɪkrəˌskop; ˈmaɪkrəskəʊp/ *n* [C] **1** a scientific instrument that makes extremely small things look larger 显微镜 —see picture at 参见 LABORATORY 图 **2 put sth under the microscope** to examine a situation very closely and carefully 认真仔细地检查某物

mi·cro·scop·ic /ˌmaɪkrəˈskɑpɪk; ˌmaɪkrəˈskɒpɪk◂/ *adj* **1** extremely small and therefore very difficult to see 极小的, 微小的, 小得难以看清的: *His handwriting is microscopic!* 他的字写得极小! | *The insect's legs are covered with microscopic hairs.* 昆虫的腿上覆有难以看到的细毛。**2** [only before noun 仅用于名词前] using a microscope 用显微镜的: *The cells were identified through microscopic analysis.* 那些细胞通过显微镜分析被识别出来。—**microscopically** /-kḷɪ; -kli/ *adv*

mi·cro·sec·ond /ˌmaɪkroˈsɛkənd; ˌmaɪkrəʊˈsekənd/ *n* [C] one millionth of a second 微秒〔百万分之一秒〕

mi·cro·wave[1] /ˈmaɪkrəˌwev; ˈmaɪkrəweɪv/ *n* [C] **1** also 又作 **microwave ov·en** /ˌ···ˈ··/ a type of OVEN that cooks food very quickly using very short electric waves instead of heat 微波炉 —see picture on page A10 参见 A10 页图 **2** a very short electric wave that is used in cooking food, sending messages by radio, and in RADAR 微波

microwave[2] *v* [T] to cook something in a microwave oven 用微波炉烹调 —**microwaveable, microwavable** *adj*

mid /mɪd; mɪd/ *prep poetic* among or in the middle of【诗】在…中间

mid- /mɪd; mɪd/ *prefix* middle 中部, 中间, 当中: *She's in her mid-20s.* (=is about 25 years old) 她25岁左右。| *in mid-July* 在7月中旬 | *a cold midwinter night* 寒冷的仲冬之夜

mid·air /ˌmɪdˈɛr; ˌmɪdˈeə◂/ *n* **in midair** in the air or the sky, away from the ground 在空中, 在半空中: *The planes collided in midair.* 飞机在半空中相撞。—**midair** *adj*: *a midair collision* 空中相撞

Mi·das /ˈmaɪdəs; ˈmaɪdəs/, **King** in ancient Greek stories, a king who was given the power to change everything he touched into gold. He soon realized this would not bring him happiness, when he found that even his food and drink changed into gold as soon as he touched them. 迈达斯〔古希腊神话中一国王。他被赋予点物成金的能力, 但不久他便发现这种能力并不能给自己带来幸福, 因为他要吃的食物和饮料经他一碰也全都变成了黄金〕

mid At·lan·tic /ˌ·ˈ··◂/ *adj* **mid Atlantic accent** a way of speaking that uses a mixture of American and British English sounds and words 中大西洋口音〔在发音和用词上混合使用美国英语和英国英语〕

mid·day /ˈmɪdˌde; ˌmɪdˈdeɪ◂/ *n* [U] the middle of the day; twelve o'clock 中午, 正午: **at midday** *I'm meeting him at midday.* 我中午要见他。| **midday meal/sun etc** *the full heat of the midday sun* 正午的炎炎烈日 —compare 比较 MIDNIGHT (1)

mid·den /ˈmɪdn̩; ˈmɪdn/ *n* [C] *old use* a pile of something such as animal waste or rubbish【旧】粪堆; 垃圾堆

mid·dle[1] /ˈmɪdḷ; ˈmɪdl/ *n* **1 the middle a)** the part that is furthest from the sides, edges, or ends 中间, 中央, 中部, 当中: *a seat in the middle of the front row* 前排中间的一个座位 | *Here's a photo of us on holiday – that's me in the middle.* 这是我们度假时拍的一张照片 —— 中间的那个是我。| **right in the middle/right down the middle etc** *The other car was driving right in the middle of the road.* 另一辆汽车行驶在路的正中间。| *Going through the middle of Tokyo in the rushhour can be a nightmare.* 在交通高峰期穿越东京市中心会是一场噩梦。**b)** the part that is between the beginning and the end of an event, story, period etc 〔事件、故事、阶段等的〕中间部分: *Why don't we meet sometime in the middle of the week?* 我们何不在这个星期中间的某个时候碰头呢? | *She started to feel sick in the middle of the exam.* 考试考到一半她开始感到身体不适。| *I arrived in Athens in the middle of a heatwave.* 我到达雅典时正逢酷暑。**c)** the position or rank that is between the highest and the lowest position in a list of people or things 中等, 中游: *Janine graduated top of the class and I finished somewhere around the middle.* 贾宁以全班第一名的成绩毕业而我却成绩中等。**d)** the inside part of an object such as a ball, or piece of fruit 〔球、水果等物体的〕内部, 里边: *Urgh! There's a maggot in the middle of this apple!* 哎呀! 这个苹果里头有一条蛆! **2 be in the middle of (doing sth)** to be busy doing something 正忙于(做某事): *Can I call you back – I'm in the middle of a meeting.* 我过一会儿给你回电话好吗 —— 我正在开会。| *She was just in the middle of getting the dinner ready.* 她恰好正忙着准备晚饭。**3** [C usually singular 一般用单数] *informal* the waist and the part of the body around the stomach【非正式】腰; 腹部: *Nick seems to be getting a bit fat round his middle.* 尼克的腰部好像有点发胖了。**4 in the middle of nowhere** a long way from the nearest town or from any interesting places 在偏远之地; 在茫茫蛮荒中: *So there we were, in the middle of nowhere, and out of gas.* 就这样我们困在了茫茫荒野中, 而且汽油也用光了。**5 divide/split sth down the middle** to divide something into equal halves or groups 沿中间分开/劈开某物: *The votes are divided right down the middle on this issue.* 有关这一问题的赞成票数和反对票数恰好相等。—see also 另见 **piggy in the middle** (PIGGY[1] (2))

middle[2] *adj* [only before noun 仅用于名词前] **1** nearest the centre, especially of a row, list, or group of things or people 居中的, 中央的, 中间的: *the middle house in a row of five* 一排五幢房子居中的那幢 | *Two of his middle front teeth were missing.* 他中间门牙有两颗掉了。| *the middle drawer of the filing cabinet* 档案柜中间的抽屉 **2** halfway through an event or period of time 〔事件或时间段〕中间部分的: *They spent the middle part of their vacation in Florida.* 假期的中期他们是在佛罗里达州度过的。**3 in your middle twenties/thirties etc** about 25, 35 etc years old 25/35岁等左右 **4 middle brother/child/daughter etc** the brother etc who is between the oldest and the youngest 排行中间的兄弟/孩子/女儿等 **5 middle course/way etc** a way of dealing with something that is between two opposite and often extreme ways 中庸之道, 中间路线: *The administration is trying to follow a middle course on health care reform.* 在医疗改革方面政府正在极力采取折中的办法。**6 Middle English/French etc** an old form of English, French etc, used in the Middle Ages (=between 1100 and 1500 AD) 中古英语/法语等〔使用于公元1100年至1500年之间〕—see also 另见 MIDDLE FINGER, MIDDLE NAME

middle age /ˌ··ˈ◂/ *n* [U] the period of your life when you are no longer young but are not yet old 中年: *The new technique allows women to have children well into middle age.* 那项新技术使妇女一直到中年都可以生育。

CULTURAL NOTE 文化注释

Middle age is usually considered to be from around age 40 to around age 60. Many people in their 30s do not want to become middle-aged, because when you are 40 you are no longer considered to be young, and middle-aged people are often thought of by younger people as being boring

and old-fashioned in their attitudes and way of life. 通常认为中年是从40岁左右到60岁左右的这段时间。很多30多岁的人不愿变成中年人,因为到了40岁就会被认为不再年轻。此外,中年人也会被年轻人认为在态度和生活方式上既乏味又守旧。

middle-aged /ˌ‥ˈ‥◂/ *adj* **1** no longer young but not yet old 中年的: *a middle-aged businessman* 中年商人 **2** middle-aged attitudes or ways of behaving are rather boring or old-fashioned 〔态度或行为方式〕有中年人特点的; 枯燥的; 过时的: *a middle-aged outlook on life* 中年人的人生观 **3 middle-aged spread** an area of fat that many people develop around their waist as they grow older 中年发福

Middle Ag·es, the /ˌ‥ˈ‥‥/ *n* the period in European history between about 1100 and 1500 AD 〔欧洲历史上的〕中世纪〔约公元1100年至1500年〕

CULTURAL NOTE 文化注释

In Western Europe, the Middle Ages were a time when Christianity was very important and the Roman Catholic Church had great influence on people's lives and on the way society was organized. It was also the period when most of the great CATHEDRALs (=large important churches) were built. The only people who could read and write were rich and powerful people, and MONKs. Society was organized in a FEUDAL system. The Middle Ages were also a time of many PLAGUEs (=serious infectious illnesses that killed many people), especially the Black Death. 在西欧,中世纪是基督教占据重要地位的世纪,罗马天主教会对人们的生活和社会的组织方式发挥巨大影响。也就是在这一时期很多大教堂建立起来。有钱有权的人和僧侣才会识字,社会结构是建立在封建制度之上的。中世纪也是很多瘟疫肆虐的一个时期,尤以黑死病为甚。— see also 另见 The CRUSADES, DARK AGES, FEUDALISM

Middle A·mer·i·ca /ˌ‥ ‥ˈ‥‥/ *n* [U] **1** the mid-western part of the United States 美国中西部 **2** Americans who are neither very rich nor very poor and who usually have traditional ideas about morality, education etc 美国中产阶级

mid·dle·brow /ˈmɪdlˌbrau; ˈmɪdlbraʊ/ *adj* middlebrow books, television programmes etc are not very difficult to understand 〔书籍、电视节目等〕易读的, 不难懂的 —compare 比较 HIGHBROW, LOWBROW

middle C /ˌmɪdl ˈsi; ˌmɪdl ˈsiː/ *n* [singular] the musical note C which is at the middle point of a piano KEYBOARD 中央C(音)

middle class, the /ˌ‥ˈ‥◂/ *n* also 又作 **the middle classes** the social class that includes professional people such as teachers or managers, but does not include people who are very rich or people who work mainly with their hands 中产阶级 —compare 比较 LOWER CLASS, UPPER CLASS, WORKING CLASS

middle-class *adj* **1** belonging to or typical of the middle class 中产阶级的: *a middle-class suburb* 中产阶级居住的郊区 | *She comes from a middle-class background.* 她来自中产阶级家庭。**2** middle-class attitudes, values etc are typical of middle-class people and are often concerned with work, education, and possessions 〔态度、价值观等〕中产阶级特有的

middle dis·tance, the /ˌ‥ˈ‥‥/ *n* the part of a picture or a view that is between the nearest part and the part that is farthest away 〔图画或景色前景和背景之间的〕中景

middle-dis·tance /ˈ‥ ‥‥/ *adj* [only before noun 仅用于名词前] a middle-distance race is neither very short nor very long, for example 800 or 1500 metres 〔赛跑〕中距离的〈如800米或1500米〉

middle ear /ˌ‥ˈ‥/ *n* [singular] the central part of the ear, between the outside part and the EARDRUM 中耳

Middle East, the /ˌ‥ˈ‥◂/ *n* the area including Iran and Egypt and the countries which are between them 中东 —compare 比较 FAR EAST —**Middle Eastern** *adj*

middle fin·ger /ˌ‥ˈ‥‥/ *n* [C] the longest finger, which is the middle one of the five fingers on your hand 中指

middle ground /ˌ‥ˈ‥/ *n* [U] something that two opposing groups can both agree about 中间观点; 中间立场; 折中办法: *The negotiators could find no middle ground.* 谈判人员找不到双方都能接受的立场。

mid·dle·man /ˈmɪdlˌmæn; ˈmɪdlmæn/ *plural* **middlemen** /-ˌmɛn; -men/ *n* [C] someone who buys things in order to sell them to someone else, or who helps to arrange business deals for other people 经纪人; 掮客; 中间人: *He acts as a middleman for British companies seeking contracts in the Gulf.* 他给在海湾地区寻找商机的英国公司当中间人。| **cut out the middleman** (=avoid having to use a middleman) 避开中间商 *Buy direct from the manufacturer and cut out the middleman.* 从厂家直接进货,绕开中间商。

middle man·age·ment /ˌ‥ˈ‥‥/ *n* [U] managers who are in charge of small groups of people but do not take the most important decisions 中层管理人员; 中级管理层 —**middle manager** *n* [C]

Mid·dle·march /ˈmɪdlˌmɑrtʃ; ˈmɪdlmɑːtʃ/ (1871) a NOVEL by George Eliot about the people who live in an imaginary town in central England called Middlemarch during a time of social and economic change. Many people consider it to be one of the greatest novels in English literature. 《米德尔马奇》(1871), 乔治·艾略特创作的一部小说, 描写了英格兰中部一虚拟小镇米德尔马奇的居民及其经历的社会和经济变迁。该小说被认为是英国文学中最伟大的作品之一

middle name /ˌ‥ˈ‥/ *n* [C] **1** the name that is between your first name and your family name 中名〔名和姓之间的名字〕 **2 sth is sb's middle name** *informal* used to say that someone has a lot of a particular personal quality【非正式】某人在某方面有突出个性: *Generosity's her middle name.* 慷慨是她显著的个性特征。

CULTURAL NOTE 文化注释

It is common in both the US and the UK for people to have one or more middle names, though they usually do not use these names. Some people give their children middle names that are the same as the first name of someone else in the family, for example a grandparent. Some people have more than one middle name. In the US, people often include the first letter of their middle name as part of their name, for example Michael J. Fox, especially in their SIGNATURE or on official forms or lists. 在美国和英国,人们有一个或多个中名的情况很普遍,尽管他们通常用不到这些中名。有人为子女起的中名和家族中的某个成员(如祖父母)的首名相同。有些人有多个中名。在美国,人们常把中名的首字母用作全名的一部分,例如迈克尔·J. 福克斯,尤其会在签名和正式的表格或名单中这样写。

middle-of-the-road /ˌ‥‥ˈ‥◂/ *adj* middle-of-the-road ideas, opinions etc are not extreme, and are similar to the ideas that most people have 〔思想、看法等〕中间路线的, 中间派的; 温和(路线)的: *Her political views are fairly middle-of-the-road.* 她的政治观点非常温和。

middle school /ˈ‥ ‥/ *n* **1** [C,U] a school in Britain for children between the ages of 8 and 12 中间学校〔英国8岁至12岁学生就读的学校〕 **2** [C,U] a school in the US for children between the ages of 11 and 14 初中〔美国11岁至14岁学生就读的学校〕

middle-sized /ˌ‥ˈ◂/ *adj* neither very large nor very small 中等大小的, 中号的: *a middle-sized house* 中等大小的房子

Middle Tem·ple, the /ˌ‥ˈ‥/ a London organization of law students and BARRISTERs and the buildings they use, which is one of the four Inns of Court 中殿律师学院〔伦敦一法学院,是四所法学院之一〕

Mid·dle·ton /ˈmɪdl-tən; ˈmɪdl-tən/, **Thomas** (1580-1627) an English writer of plays who wrote SATIRICAL comedies (COMEDY) and tragedies (TRAGDY), including *Women Beware Women* 米德尔顿(1580-1627), 英国剧作家, 擅长创作讽刺喜剧和悲剧作品, 代表作有《女人相互提防》等

mid·dle·weight /ˈmɪdlˌwet; ˈmɪdlweɪt/ *n* [C] a BOXER who is lighter than a LIGHT HEAVYWEIGHT and heavier than a WELTERWEIGHT 中量级拳击手

Middle West, the /ˌ‥ˈ‥/ *n* another form of the MIDWEST midwest 的另一种形式

mid·dling /ˈmɪdlɪŋ; ˈmɪdəlɪŋ/ *adj informal* not very good or bad, not very big or small etc; average【非正式】中等的, 一般的, 普通的: **fair to middling** (=about average) 过得去, 还算好 *"How are you?" "Oh, fair to middling."* "你好吗?" "哦,还好。"

mid·field /ˈmɪdˌfild; ˈmɪdfiːld/ *n* [U] **1** the middle part of the area where a game such as football or BASEBALL is played 〔足球场或棒球场等的〕中场: *a midfield player* 中场球员 **2** the members of a football team who play in this area 〔足球队的〕中场球员

mid·field·er /ˈmɪdˌfildɚ; ˈmɪdfiːldə/ *n* [C] a player who usually plays in the midfield 中场队员

midge /mɪdʒ; mɪdʒ/ *n* [C] a small flying insect that bites people 蠓; 摇蚊

midg·et¹ /ˋmɪdʒɪt; ˈmɪdʒɨt/ *n* [C] **1** a very small person who will never grow tall because there is something wrong with their body 侏儒，矮人 **2** *BrE informal* someone who is not very tall 【英，非正式】个子不很高的人

midget² *adj* **midget car/camera etc** a very small CAR etc 小型汽车/袖珍照相机等

Mid Gla·mor·gan /ˌmɪd gləˋmɒgən; ˌmɪd gləˈmɔːgən/ abbreviation 缩写为 **M Glam** a former COUNTY in southeast Wales, which used to have many coal mines 中格拉摩根郡〔威尔士东南部一郡，曾拥有许多煤矿〕

Mi·di /miˋdi; miːˈdiː/ the southern part of France 米迪〔法国南部地区的别称〕: *a holiday cottage in the Midi* 法国南部的一幢度假别墅

Mid·lands, the /ˋmɪdləndz; ˈmɪdləndz/ *n plural* the central part of England 英格兰中部地区 —**Midland** *adj* —**Midlander** *n* [C]

mid·life cri·sis /ˌmɪdlaɪf ˋkraɪsɪs; ˌmɪdlaɪf ˈkraɪsɨs/ *n* [C] feelings of worry and lack of confidence, when you are between 40 and 50 years old 中年危机，中年期心理危机〔指 40 岁至 50 岁的中年人所感受到的焦虑和缺乏自信〕

mid·night /ˋmɪdˌnaɪt; ˈmɪdnaɪt/ *n* [U] **1** 12 o'clock at night 半夜 12 点，子夜，午夜: *We close at midnight.* 我们晚上 12 点关门。| *the midnight train to Glasgow* 开往格拉斯哥的午夜火车 —compare 比较 MIDDAY **2 midnight feast** a secret meal eaten late at night, especially by children〔尤指孩子们偷偷举行的〕午夜餐 —see also 另见 **burn the midnight oil** (BURN¹ (24))

Midnight Mass /ˌ‥ ˈ‧/ *n* [C,U] a special Christian religious service held at midnight on Christmas Eve, to celebrate Christmas and the birth of Christ 子夜弥撒〔圣诞节前夕午夜时分基督徒为纪念圣诞而举行的一个特殊宗教仪式〕

midnight sun /ˌ‥ ˈ‧/ *n* **the midnight sun** the sun seen in the middle of the night in summer in the far north or south of the world〔极地夏季见到的〕子夜太阳，夜半太阳

mid·point /ˋmɪdˌpɔɪnt; ˈmɪdpɔɪnt/ *n* [C usually singular 一般用单数] a point that is halfway through or along something 中点;〔时间、事件等进程的〕一半: [+of] *We are now at the midpoint of this government's term of office.* 我们这届政府任期现在已经过半。

mid·riff /ˋmɪdrɪf; ˈmɪdrɪf/ *n* [C] the part of the body between your chest and your waist 腹部

mid·ship·man /ˋmɪdˌʃɪpmən; ˈmɪdʃɪpmən/ *n* [C] the rank of someone who is training to become an officer in the British Navy〔英国海军〕候补少尉 —see table on page C6 参见 C6 页附录

midst¹ /mɪdst; mɪdst/ *n* **1 in the midst of a)** in the middle of a period, situation, or event 在…的中期; 正值…的时候: *in the midst of the Cold War* 在冷战中期 **b)** in the middle of a place or a group of things 在〔某地〕中部; 在〔一堆事物〕中间 **2 in our/their midst** *formal* in a particular group 【正式】在我们/他们当中: *We have a traitor in our midst.* 我们当中有个叛徒。

midst² *prep old use* in the middle of or among 【旧】在…中间，在…之中

mid·sum·mer /ˋmɪdˋsʌmɚ; ˌmɪdˈsʌmə◂/ *n* [U] the middle of summer 仲夏: *one bright midsummer afternoon* 仲夏一个晴朗的下午

Midsummer Day /ˌ‥‥ ˈ‧/ also 又作 **Midsummer's Day** *n* [singular] *BrE* the 24th of June 【英】仲夏节; 施洗约翰节〔6 月 24 日〕

Midsummer Night's Dream, A /ˌ‥‥ ˌ‥ ˈ‧/ a humorous play by William Shakespeare in which Oberon, the king of the fairies, puts a magic spell on Titania, his queen, while she is sleeping, so that she falls in love with the first creature she sees when she awakes. This is Bottom, a weaver who has been given the head of a DONKEY by Oberon's servant, Puck, who has magic powers. It is one of Shakespeare's most popular plays, and it is often performed outdoors in the summer.《仲夏夜之梦》〔威廉·莎士比亚创作的一部喜剧。剧中仙王奥布朗给睡梦中的仙后提泰妮娅施了魔咒，使她爱上醒来后看到的第一个生物。结果她遇到的第一个人是纺织工波顿，奥布朗的仆人有魔力的派克给他套上了驴头。该剧是莎士比亚最有名的剧作之一，夏天时常在户外上演〕

mid·term¹ /ˌmɪdˋtɝm; ˌmɪdˈtɜːm◂/ *n* **1** [U] the middle period of an elected government's time in power〔政府任期的〕中期: *Nixon was the first president to resign in midterm.* 尼克松是第一位在任期中期辞职的总统。**2** [C] *AmE* an examination in the middle of one of the main periods in the year at university 【美】〔大学的〕期中考试

mid·term² /ˋmɪdˌtɝm; ˈmɪdtɜːm/ *adj* [only before noun 仅用于名词前] during or in the middle of one of the main periods in the school year, or in the middle of an elected government's time in power〔学期〕期中的;〔政府任期〕中期的: *midterm tests* 期中测验 —compare 比较 HALF-TERM

Mid·town /ˋmɪdtaʊn; ˈmɪdtaʊn/ a central area of a city, especially the part of Manhattan in New York City which is south of Central Park【美】市中心区〔尤指纽约市中央公园以南曼哈顿一带〕

midtown /ˌmɪdˋtaʊn; ˌmɪdˈtaʊn◂/ *adj, adv AmE* in the area of a city that is near the centre but is not the main business area 【美】靠近市中心区〔但不是主要商业区〕(的); 在市中心附近(的) —compare 比较 DOWNTOWN, UPTOWN —**midtown** *n* [U]

Mid·way /ˋmɪdwe; ˈmɪdweɪ/ two small islands in the Pacific Ocean northwest of Honolulu, used as a US military base. There was an important sea and air battle there in 1942 called the **Battle of Midway**. 中途岛〔太平洋两个小岛，位于火奴鲁鲁西北，被美国用作军事基地。1942 年，此处爆发过一场海空大战，名为中途岛战役〕

mid·way /ˋmɪdˋwe; ˌmɪdˈweɪ◂/ *adj, adv* **1** halfway between two places or along a line 在中途(的)，在半路(的); 在中间(的): [+between/along] *midway between Madagascar and the coast of Tanzania* 从马达加斯加到坦桑尼亚海岸的半路上 **2** halfway through a period of time〔指一段时间〕在中间(的); 到一半(的): *Tyson knocked out his opponent midway through the third round.* 泰森在第三个回合进行了一半时就击倒了对手。

mid·week /ˌmɪdˋwik; ˌmɪdˈwiːk◂/ *adj, adv* on one of the middle days of the week 一周中间(的)，在周中(的): *a midweek match against Liverpool* 周中与利物浦队的比赛 | *I don't go out much midweek anymore.* 我周中不再经常出去了。

Mid·west, the /ˋmɪdˋwɛst; ˌmɪdˈwest/ *n* the central area of the United States〔美国的〕中西部 —**Midwestern** *adj*

> **CULTURAL NOTE 文化注释**
>
> When people in the US think about the Midwest, they usually think about farms because these states are where most of the country's crops are grown. The STEREOTYPE of a farmer from the Midwest is someone who wears OVERALLS, drives a PICK-UP TRUCK, and has traditional beliefs about the family, sex etc. 美国人想起中西部，通常就会想到农场，因为美国大部分的粮食都产自中西部的这些州。中西部农场主的典型形象是穿工装裤，开小卡车，在家庭、性等方面的观念很传统。— see also 另见 MIDDLE AMERICA

mid·wife /ˋmɪdˌwaɪf; ˈmɪdwaɪf/ *n plural* **midwives** /-ˌwaɪvz; -waɪvz/ [C] a specially trained nurse, usually a woman, whose job is to help women when they are having a baby 助产士，接生员，产婆

mid·wif·e·ry /ˋmɪdˌwaɪfərɪ; ˈmɪdˌwɪfəri/ *n* [U] the skill or work of a midwife 助产(术)

mid·win·ter /ˋmɪdˋwɪntɚ; ˌmɪdˈwɪntə◂/ *n* [U] the middle of winter 仲冬: *They crossed the Great Smoky Mountains in midwinter.* 他们在仲冬翻越了大雾山。

mien /min; miːn/ *n* [singular] *literary* someone's typical expression or way of behaving 【文】仪表，神态，风度，样子: *a thoughtful and solemn mien* 沉思而又严肃的神态

Mies van der Ro·he /ˌmiz væn dɚ ˋroə; ˌmiːz væn də ˈrəʊə/, **Lud·wig** /ˋlʊdwɪg; ˈlʊdwɪg/ (1886-1969) a US ARCHITECT, born in Germany, who many people consider to be one of the most important architects of the 20th century. He designed many steel and glass SKYSCRAPERS such as the Seagram Building in New York City. He was a teacher in the Bauhaus in Germany, and his buildings are very plain, practical, and without decoration. 密斯〔(1886-1969)，生于德国的美国建筑师，20 世纪最杰出的建筑师之一。最著名的作品是纽约市西格拉姆大厦等钢铁和玻璃结构的摩天大楼。他曾在德国的包豪斯设计学校任教。他设计的建筑简洁实用，没有装饰〕

miffed /mɪft; mɪft/ *adj spoken* slightly annoyed or upset 【口】略微生气的，恼火的: *I was a bit miffed that you'd left without me.* 我有点生气的是你不带上我就离开了。

might¹ /maɪt; maɪt/ *modal verb negative short form* 否定缩略式为 **mightn't** **1** if something might happen or might be true, there is a possibility that it may happen or be true but you are not certain 也许，可能，大概: *Who knows – England might win the next World Cup!* 谁知道呢——英格兰队也许会赢得下一届世界杯! | *"Are you going to write her a letter?" "I might, I might not."* "你打算给她写封信吗?" "也许会，也许不会。" | *You might not have noticed but I've put up a 'no smoking' sign in here.* 你大概还没注意到，我已在这儿竖起了"禁止吸烟"的告示牌。| *Did you see the way he was driving? I might have been killed.* 你看见他是怎么开车的吗? 我差点丧了命。**2** the past tense

of may 也许, 可能; 可以〔may 的过去式〕: *Thinking it might rain, I decided to go in the car.* 我当时以为会下雨, 所以决定开车去。| *She asked if she might open a window.* 她问是否可以打开窗子。**3** used to give advice or make a suggestion 可以〔用于提建议〕: *If the police can't help, you might try the Citizens Advice Bureau.* 如果警察帮不了忙, 你可以试一试市民咨询局。| *I thought we might spend the lesson studying irregular verbs.* 我想我们可以用这节课学习不规则动词。**4 a)** *spoken old-fashioned* used to ask politely if you can do something【口, 过时】可以〔用于礼貌地请求允许做某事〕: *Might I come in?* 我可以进来吗? **b) might I say/ask/add etc** *spoken* used to politely give more information, ask a question, interrupt etc【口】我可否说/问/补充等〔用于礼貌地提供更多信息、问问题、插话等〕: *Might I just add that Miriam has been a pleasure to work with and we wish her every success in the future.* 请允许我补充一句: 与米丽亚姆一起工作是一种乐趣, 我们祝愿她将来事事成功。**5** used when you are angry or surprised when someone has not done something that you think they should do 应该, 本该〔表示说话人因某人还没做某事而生气或惊奇〕: *You might have cleaned up before you left!* 离开之前你为什么不收拾一下! | *Don't you think he might at least say thank you?* 你不认为他至少应该说声谢谢吗? **6 I might have known/guessed etc** *spoken* used to say that you are not surprised at a situation【口】我早该知道/猜到等〔表示对某种情况不感到吃惊〕: *Jake Thompson! I might have known you'd be behind all this!* 杰克·汤普森! 我早该料到所有这一切都是你在幕后操纵! **7 might well** if something might well happen or might well be true you think it is fairly likely to happen or be true 很可能, 极有可能: *You might well find that you'll need more by the weekend.* 到周末你很可能会发现你需要更多的东西。**8 might (just) as well** *usually spoken* used to suggest doing something that you do not really want to do, because you have no better ideas【一般口】最好还是…, 还是…为好, 倒不如…: *It's no good waiting for the bus. We might as well walk.* 等公共汽车来没用, 我们还不如步行呢。**9 might...but...** used to tell someone that although what they said is true, something else which seemed very different is also a fact 也许…但是…〔表示尽管某人所说是事实, 但与其似乎非常不同的事也真实〕: *You might be a strong swimmer but that doesn't mean you can win a triathlon.* 你也许在游泳上很有实力, 但这并不意味着你可以在铁人三项中获胜。**10** *formal* used to say why something happens or the reason why someone does something【正式】能, 会〔以表示原因〕: *Samuel left his children a letter, so that his family might understand why he had to go away.* 塞缪尔给孩子们留下了一封信, 以便家人能明白他为什么不得不离开。**11** *old-fashioned humorous* used to politely ask for information【过时, 幽默】〔用于客气地询问〕: *And who might you be, young man?* 你又是谁呢, 年轻人? —compare 比较 MAY[1]

might² *n* [U] **1** great strength and power 力量; 威力; 权力: *the full might of the Russian army* 俄罗斯军队的全部军力 | **with all your might** (=using all your strength and a lot of effort) 尽全力; 全力以赴 *He swung the ax with all his might.* 他用尽全身力气抡起斧头。| **with might and main** *literary* (=with a lot of strength)【文】竭尽全力地, 拼命地 **2 might is right** *BrE*【英】, **might makes right** *AmE*【美】used to say that powerful people and countries can do whatever they want 强权就是公理

might-have-beens /ˈ· · ,·/ *n* [plural] things that you wish had happened in the past but which never did 未遂心愿的事, 本应发生的事

might·i·ly /ˈmaɪtɪlɪ; ˈmaɪtɪli/ *adv especially literary*【尤文】**1** very 非常: *She seemed mightily impressed by his story.* 她好像被他的故事深深地打动了。**2** using great strength 用力地; 猛烈地: *Fred swung mightily at the ball.* 弗雷德使劲地挥棒击球。

might·n't /ˈmaɪtn̩t; ˈmaɪtənt/ *informal, especially BrE*【非正式, 尤英】the short form of 缩略式= 'might not'

might·y¹ /ˈmaɪtɪ; ˈmaɪti/ *adj especially literary* very strong and powerful, or very big and impressive【尤文】强有力的, 强大的; 巨大的, 雄伟的: *the mighty Mississippi river* 浩渺的密西西比河 | *a mighty king* 权力很大的国王 —see also 另见 **high and mighty** (HIGH[1] (19))

mighty² *adv* [+adj/adv] *AmE informal* very【美, 非正式】非常, 很: *It's mighty good to see you.* 见到你太好了。

mi·graine /ˈmaɪgren; ˈmiːgreɪn/ *n* [C] an extremely bad headache, during which you feel sick and have pain behind your eyes 偏头痛

mi·grant /ˈmaɪgrənt; ˈmaɪgrənt/ *n* [C] **1** someone who goes to another area or country, especially in order to find work〔尤指为了寻找工作而迁移的〕移民; 移居者: **migrant worker/labour/groups** *migrant workers in the depression of the 1930s* 20世纪30年代经济萧条时期的流动工人 | **economic migrant** (=someone who goes to another country because living conditions are better there) 经济移民 **2** a bird or animal that travels from one part of the world to another, especially in the autumn and spring 候鸟; 迁徙动物 —compare 比较 EMIGRANT, IMMIGRANT

mi·grate /ˈmaɪgret; maɪˈgreɪt/ *v* [I+from/to] **1** if birds or animals migrate, they travel from one part of the world to another, especially in the autumn and spring〔鸟或兽〕迁徙, 移栖 **2** to go to another area or country, especially in order to find work〔尤指为找工作〕移居; 迁移 —compare 比较 EMIGRATE, IMMIGRATE

mi·gra·tion /maɪˈgreʃən; maɪˈgreɪʃən/ *n* [C] the movement from one place to another of a large group of people, birds, animals etc〔一大群人的〕移居, 迁移;〔大量鸟、兽等的〕迁徙, 移栖: *the great migrations to America of the 19th century* 19世纪涌向美国的移民潮 2

Mikado, The (1885) a comic OPERA by Gilbert and Sullivan which is set in Japan and contains the well-known songs *The Flowers that Bloom in the Spring, Tra La* and *Three Little Maids from School*. The name 'Mikado' is a former title for the emperor of Japan.《日本天皇》〔(1885), 吉尔伯特和沙利文共同创作的一部喜歌剧。该剧以日本为背景, 剧中有几首著名歌曲, 如《春天花儿开, 特啦啦》和《三个女学童》等。剧名取自日本皇帝的旧称〕

mike¹ /maɪk; maɪk/ *n* [C] *informal* a MICROPHONE【非正式】麦克风, 话筒, 传声器, 扩音器 —see also 另见 OPEN MIKE, **for the love of Mike** (LOVE[2] (14))

mike² *v*

mike sb **up** *phr v* [T] *informal* to put a MICROPHONE on someone so that their voice can be recorded or made louder【非正式】给〔某人〕安麦克风

mi·la·dy /mɪˈledɪ; mɪˈleɪdi/ *n* [singular] another spelling of M'LADY m'lady 的另一种拼法

Mi·lan /mɪˈlæn; mɪˈlæn/ a city in northern Italy, an important financial and industrial centre, which is also a centre of the fashion industry and has a large CATHEDRAL and a famous OPERA house, La Scala 米兰〔意大利北部一城市, 该国重要的金融和工业中心以及时装业中心, 建有一座大教堂和著名的斯卡拉歌剧院〕

milch cow /ˈmɪltʃ kau; ˈmɪltʃ kaʊ/ *n* [C] another spelling of MILK COW milk cow 的另一种拼法

mild¹ /maɪld; maɪld/ *adj*

1 ▶WEATHER 天气◀ not too cold or wet, and sometimes pleasantly warm 温和的, 暖和的: *We had an exceptionally mild winter last year.* 去年我们过了一个异常暖和的冬天。

2 ▶ILLNESS 疾病◀ a mild illness or health problem is not serious 不严重的, 轻微的: *It's nothing – just a mild throat infection.* 没什么, 只是轻微的喉部感染。

3 ▶FOOD/TASTE 食物/味道◀ not very strong or hot-tasting 不浓烈的, 淡的; 不辣的: *a mild curry* 淡味咖喱

4 ▶PUNISHMENT/CRITICISM 惩罚/批评◀ not severe or strict 不严厉的; 婉转的: *a mild rebuke* 温和的指责

5 ▶SMALL EFFECT 小的影响◀ not serious enough to cause much suffering 不厉害的, 弱的, 轻的: *The recession in Germany has been comparatively mild.* 德国的衰退相对而言要轻一些。| *a mild earthquake* 轻微的地震

6 ▶CHARACTER/MANNER 性格/举止◀ having a gentle character and not easily getting angry 温和的, 温厚的: *Joe was a mild man who rarely raised his voice.* 乔是个性情温和的人, 极少大嗓门说话。

7 ▶SOAP ETC 肥皂等◀ soft and gentle to your skin 软性的; 柔性的: *a mild washing-up liquid* 柔性洗涤液 —see also 另见 MILDLY

mild² *n* [U] *BrE* dark beer with a mild taste【英】淡啤酒 —compare 比较 BITTER[2] (1)

mil·dew /ˈmɪl,dju; ˈmɪldjuː/ *n* [U] a white or grey substance that grows on leaves, walls, or other surfaces in wet, slightly warm conditions 霉; 霉菌 —**mildewed** *adj*

mild·ly /ˈmaɪldlɪ; ˈmaɪldli/ *adv* **1** [+adj] slightly 轻微地, 稍微: *The drug is only mildly addictive.* 这种药物只会使人略微有点上瘾。**2 to put it mildly** *spoken* used when saying that you could use much stronger words to describe something【口】说得婉转些: *The manager wasn't very happy, to put it mildly, when you came in two hours late for the meeting.* 说得婉转些, 你开会迟到两小时, 经理不太高兴。**3** in a gentle way without being angry 温和地, 和善地: *"Of course I don't mind," she answered mildly.* 她和善地答道: "我当然不介意。"

mild-man·nered /,· ˈ· ·◂/ *adj* gentle and polite 举止温柔的; 有礼貌的: *She had always struck me as being mild-mannered and quiet.* 她给我的印象一直是温柔而文静。

M

mile /maɪl; maɪl/ *n* [C] **1** a unit for measuring distance or length, equal to 1609 metres 英里〔距离或长度的计量单位, 等于 1609 米〕 —see table on page C3 参见 C3 页附录 **2 the mile** a race that is a mile in length 一英里赛跑: *the world record holder in the mile* 一英里赛跑的世界记录保持者 **3 miles** *informal* a very long distance【非正式】很长的距离: *We were miles from home, and very tired.* 我们离家很远, 而且很疲劳了。| **for miles** (=for a very long distance) 很远 *You can see for miles from the top of the hill.* 你从那座小山顶上能看很远。| **miles from anywhere/nowhere** (=a long way from the nearest town or city) 离最近的镇[城]很远; 在荒僻之地 *They lived in a little cottage miles from nowhere.* 他们住在茫茫荒野中的一间小屋里。**4 go the extra mile** to try a little harder in order to achieve something, after you have already used a lot of effort 再加把劲〔以完成某事〕: *Neither of the negotiating teams seems willing to go the extra mile.* 谈判双方似乎都不愿意再努力前进一步。**5 sth sticks out/stands out a mile** also 又作 **you can tell sth a mile away/off** *informal* used to say that something is very clear from someone's appearance or behaviour【非正式】某事物显而易见, 某事物一目了然: *It's obvious she's English – you can tell it a mile away.* 她显然是英格兰人——这一眼就能看出来。**6 talk a mile a minute** to speak very quickly without stopping 快而不停地说话, 连珠炮般地说话 **7 be miles away** *spoken* to not be paying attention to anything that is happening around you【口】心不在焉: *"Kate!" "Sorry, I was miles away!"* "凯特!" "对不起, 我走神了!" **8 miles older/ better/too difficult etc** *BrE informal* very much older, better, too difficult etc【英, 非正式】老很多/好很多/实在太难等: *You're going out with John? But he's miles older than you!* 你在和约翰恋爱吗? 他年龄可比你大好多呢! **9 miles out** *BrE informal* a measurement, guess, or calculation that is miles out is completely wrong【英, 非正式】〔测量、猜测或计算〕差远了 —see also 另见 NAUTICAL MILE, **run a mile** (RUN[1] (47)), **a miss is as good as a mile** (MISS[2] (8))

mile·age /ˈmaɪlɪdʒ; ˈmaɪlɪdʒ/ *n* **1** [C usually singular 一般用单数, U] the number of miles a vehicle has travelled since it was made〔车辆自出厂后的〕行驶里程: *For sale Red Ford Escort. Low Mileage.* 出售红色福特"护卫舰"牌汽车。行驶里程少。**2** [C usually singular 一般用单数, U] the number of miles a vehicle can travel using one GALLON or litre of fuel〔耗油一加仑或一升所行驶的〕英里数 **3** [U] the amount of use or advantage you get from something 利益, 好处; 用处: *The newspapers have had a lot of mileage out of the Royal divorce story.* 各家报纸已从王室离婚报道中赚了一大笔。**4** [C usually singular 一般用单数, U] also 又作 **mileage allowance** an amount of money paid for each mile that is travelled by someone using a car for work〔按英里支付的〕交通补贴 **5** [U] a distance in miles that is covered by a country's roads or railways〔一国公路或铁路的〕总英里里程

mile·om·e·ter, milometer /maɪˈlɑmətɚ; maɪˈlɒmɪtə/ *n* [C] *BrE* an instrument in a car that shows how many miles it has travelled【英】〔汽车的〕里程表, 里程记录器; ODOMETER *AmE*【美】—see picture on page A2 参见 A2 页图

mile·post /ˈmaɪlpost; ˈmaɪlpəʊst/ *n* [C] *especially AmE* a post next to a road or railway that shows the distance in miles to the next town【尤美】〔公路或铁路旁用英里显示下一城镇距离的〕里程标

mil·er /ˈmaɪlɚ; ˈmaɪlə/ *n* [C] a person or horse that competes in one-mile races 参加一英里赛跑的选手[马]

mile·stone /ˈmaɪl,ston; ˈmaɪlstəʊn/ *n* [C] **1** [usually singular 一般用单数] a very important event in the development of something 重大事件, 里程碑: [+in] *The agreement was a milestone in the history of US-Soviet relations.* 该协议是美苏关系史上的转折点。**2** a stone next to a road that shows the distance in miles to the next town〔路边的〕里程标

mi·lieu /miˈlju; ˈmiːljɜː/ *n plural* **milieux** /-ˈljuz; -ljɜːz/ *or* **milieus** [C,U] *French formal* the things and people that surround you and influence the way you live and think【法, 正式】出身背景, 周围环境: *Proust wrote exclusively about his own social and cultural milieu.* 普鲁斯特专门描写自己的社会和文化环境。

mil·i·tant /ˈmɪlətənt; ˈmɪlɪtənt/ *adj* a militant organization or person is willing to use strong or violent action in order to achieve political or social change 好斗的; 使用暴力的; 激进的: *militant trade unionists* 激进的工联主义者 | *After the assassination of Martin Luther King, black leaders became more militant.* 马丁·路德·金遇刺后, 黑人领袖变得更激进了。—**militant** *n* [C] —**militancy** *n* [U] —**militantly** *adv*

mil·i·ta·ris·m /ˈmɪlətə,rɪzəm; ˈmɪlɪtərɪzəm/ *n* [U] the belief that a country should build up its military forces and use them to get what it wants 军国主义; 穷兵黩武主义 —**militarist** *n* [C] —**militaristic** /,mɪlətəˈrɪstɪk; ,mɪlɪtəˈrɪstɪk◂/ *adj*

mil·i·ta·rized also 又作 **-ised** *BrE*【英】/ˈmɪlətə,raɪzd; ˈmɪlɪtəraɪzd/ *adj* a militarized area is one that has a lot of soldiers and weapons in it〔地区〕军事化的

mil·i·ta·ry[1] /ˈmɪlə,tɛrɪ; ˈmɪlɪtəri/ *adj* used by or connected with war or the army, navy, or airforce 军用的; 军事的; 军队的: *a military helicopter* 军用直升机 | *the use of military power* 使用军事力量 | *the supreme US military commander in Europe* 美国驻欧洲最高军事指挥官 —**militarily** *adv*

military[2] *n* **the military** the military forces of a country〔一国的〕武装力量, 军队: [also+plural verb *BrE* 英] *The military have taken control of the government.* 军方已控制了政府。| **in the military** *AmE* (=in the army, navy etc)【美】在部队服役 *My brother is in the military.* 我兄弟在部队服役。

Military A·cad·e·my /,····ˈ···/ *n* [C] **1** a national college where people are trained to be officers in the military forces 军事学院 **2** a private school in the US that gives students military training〔美国〕私立准军事学校

Military Cross /,····ˈ·/ *n* [C] a MEDAL given to British army officers for being brave in battle〔授予英国陆军军官的〕英勇十字勋章

military po·lice /,····ˈ·/ *n* [singular] a special police force whose job is to deal with members of the army etc who break the rules 宪兵队 —see also 另见 MP (2)

military ser·vice /,····ˈ··/ *n* [U] the system in which every adult man in a country has to be in the army, navy, or airforce, for a period of time 兵役（制）—compare 比较 DRAFT[1] (2)

mil·i·tate /ˈmɪlə,tet; ˈmɪlɪteɪt/ *v*

militate against *phr v* [T] *formal* to prevent something or make it less likely to happen【正式】阻止; 妨碍: *Environmental factors militate against building the power station in this area.* 环境因素不利于在这一地区建设发电站。

mi·li·tia /məˈlɪʃə; mɪˈlɪʃə/ *n* [C] a group of people trained as soldiers, who are not part of the permanent army 民兵队伍, 国民自卫队

mi·li·tia·man /məˈlɪʃəmən; mɪˈlɪʃəmən/ *n* [C] a member of a militia 民兵

milk[1] /mɪlk; mɪlk/ *n* [U] **1** a white liquid produced by cows or goats that is drunk by people 奶, 乳; 牛奶; 羊奶: *a bottle of milk* 一瓶牛奶 | *Would you like some milk in your tea?* 你的茶里要加点牛奶吗? **2** a white liquid produced by female animals and women for feeding their babies 奶汁, 母乳 **3** a liquid or juice produced by certain plants, especially the COCONUT (1)〔植物, 尤指椰树产出的〕汁液 **4 the milk of human kindness** *literary* ordinary kindness and sympathy for other people【文】人类的善良天性; 恻隐之心 —see also 另见 EVAPORATED MILK, SKIMMED MILK, **cry over spilt milk** (CRY[1] (5)), **land of milk and honey** (LAND[1] (8))

milk[2] *v* [T] **1** to take milk from a cow or goat 挤〔牛或羊〕的奶 **2** *informal* to get as much money or as many advantages as you can from a situation, in a very determined and sometimes dishonest way【非正式】榨取, 勒索: **milk sb for sth** *Their landlord regularly milks them for extra money by claiming for damage to his property.* 他们的房东经常声称房产被损坏向他们榨取额外的钱财。| **milk sth for all it is worth** *Reporters were milking Nixon's resignation for all it was worth.* 记者们利用尼克松辞职这件事大做文章。**3** to take the poison from a snake 取〔蛇〕的毒液

milk choco·late /,·ˈ··◂/ *n* [U] chocolate made with milk and sugar 牛奶巧克力 —see also 另见 PLAIN CHOCOLATE

milk churn /ˈ··/ *n* [C] *BrE* a large metal container with a lid used to carry milk from farms【英】〔有盖的金属〕牛奶罐

milk cow /ˈ··/ also 又作 **milking cow** /ˈ···/ *n* [C] a cow kept to give milk rather than for meat 奶牛

milk float /ˈ··/ *n* [C] *BrE* a vehicle used for delivering milk to people's houses, which is usually powered by electricity【英】送奶车

milking ma·chine /ˈ··,·/ *n* [C] a machine used for taking milk from cows 挤奶机, 挤奶器

milking par·lour *BrE*【英】, **milking parlor** *AmE*【美】/ˈ··,·/ *n* [C] a building on a farm where milk is taken from the cows 挤奶房

milk loaf /ˈ··/ *n plural* **milk loaves** [C] *BrE* a LOAF of white bread made with milk【英】牛奶面包

milk·maid /ˈmɪlk,med; ˈmɪlkmeɪd/ *n* [C] *old use* a woman who gets milk from cows on a farm【旧】挤奶女工

milk·man /ˈmɪlk,mæn; ˈmɪlkmən/ *n plural* **milkmen** /-,mɛn; -mən/ [C] someone who delivers milk to houses each morning 送奶工

CULTURAL NOTE 文化注释

In the UK, milkmen deliver milk in bottles to some people's houses early in the morning. Milkmen drive a special truck called a MILK FLOAT which usually has an engine powered by an electric BATTERY rather than by petrol, and is very slow. Many people now buy milk from SUPERMARKETS instead of having it delivered by a milkman. 在英国，一大早送奶工就将瓶装牛奶送到订户家中。送奶人开的送奶车是一种特殊的卡车，通常靠电池而不是靠汽油驱动，车速也非常慢。现在很多人从超市采购牛奶，已经不再需要送奶工了。

In the past, people often joked about milkmen having sex with women who stayed at home while their husbands were at work. If a child did not look very much like other members of his family, people would joke that the father was really the milkman. 过去人们常好开这种玩笑，说送奶工趁着主妇的丈夫外出工作而与她们瞎搞。如果一个孩子的相貌不像家族中的其他成员，人们便会取笑说孩子的父亲实际上是送奶工。

milk of mag·ne·sia /ˌ· · ·ˈ· ·/ *n* [U] a thick white liquid medicine used for stomach problems and CONSTIPATION 镁乳，氧化镁乳剂〔用于医治胃病和便秘的一种药，为白色浓稠液体〕

milk pud·ding /ˌ·ˈ· ·/ *n* [C] *BrE* a sweet food made of rice, TAPIOCA, or SAGO, baked in milk【英】牛奶布丁

milk round /ˈ· ·/ *n BrE*【英】**1** [C] the regular journey a milkman makes every day to deliver milk〔固定的〕送奶路线 **2 the milk round** *BrE* a series of visits to universities made each year by large companies to find people they may want to employ【英】〔大公司每年在各大学进行的〕巡回招聘

milk run /ˈ· ·/ *n* [C] **1** *BrE informal* a familiar, easy journey that you do regularly【英，非正式】例行的轻松差事 **2** *AmE informal* a train journey or regular plane flight that stops in many places【美，非正式】〔在多处停留的〕火车线路；定期航班

milk shake /ˌ·ˈ·/ *n* [C] **1** *BrE* a drink made of milk mixed with fruit or chocolate【英】奶昔〔牛奶与水果或巧克力混合的饮料〕**2** *AmE* a drink made of milk, ICE CREAM, and fruit or chocolate【美】泡沫牛奶〔牛奶与冰淇淋、水果或巧克力混合的饮料〕

milk·sop /ˈmɪlkˌsɑp; ˈmɪlksɒp/ *n* [C] *old-fashioned* a boy or man who is too gentle and weak, and who is afraid to do anything dangerous【过时】胆小懦弱的男孩[男人]；懦夫

milk·toast /ˈmɪlkˌtost; ˈmɪlktəʊst/ *n* [C] another spelling of MILQUETOAST milquetoast 的另一种拼法

milk tooth /ˈ· ·/ *n plural* **milk teeth** [C] *BrE* one of the first set of teeth developed by young children; BABY TOOTH【英】乳牙，乳齿

milk·weed /ˈmɪlkˌwid; ˈmɪlkwiːd/ *n* [U] a common North American plant that produces a bitter white substance when its stem is broken 马利筋〔一种北美洲常见的植物〕

milk·y /ˈmɪlkɪ; ˈmɪlki/ *adj* **1** a drink that is milky contains a lot of milk〔饮料〕掺奶的，多乳的：*milky coffee* 牛奶咖啡 **2** water or other liquids that are milky are not clear and look like milk〔水或其他液体〕不清的，混浊的；乳状的 **3** milky skin is white and smooth〔皮肤〕白而滑的，乳白色的 **—milkiness** *n* [U]

Milky Way, the /ˌ· ·ˈ· ·/ *n* the pale white band of stars that can be seen across the sky at night 银河（系）

3 **mill**[1] /mɪl; mɪl/ *n* [C] **1** a building containing a large machine for crushing grain into flour, or the machine itself 磨坊，磨粉厂；磨粉机：*an old mill with a ruined water-wheel* 水轮已坏的老磨坊 **2** a factory that produces materials such as cotton, cloth, steel〔生产布匹、钢铁等的〕工厂，制造厂：*a woollen mill* 毛纺厂 **3 coffee/pepper mill** a small machine for crushing coffee or pepper 咖啡/胡椒研磨机 **4 go through the mill** to go through a time when you experience a lot of difficulties and problems 历尽艰辛；经受磨练：*Go easy on him – he's been through the mill lately.* 对他温和些——他近来饱尝了辛酸。**5 put sb through the mill** to make someone answer a lot of difficult questions or do a lot of difficult things in order to test them 使某人经历严格的考查 **6** *AmE* a unit of money equal to 1/10 of a cent, used in setting taxes and for other financial purposes【美】密尔，厘〔等于1/10美分，用于定税或其他金融用途〕—see also 另见 RUN-OF-THE-MILL, **(all) grist to the mill** (GRIST)

mill[2] *v* [T] **1** to produce flour by crushing grain in a mill 将〔谷物〕碾碎，把…磨细 **2** to press, roll, or shape metal in a machine〔用机器〕碾[轧，铣]〔金属〕 **3** to mark the edge of a coin with regular lines 在〔硬币的边缘〕轧齿边，轧凸缘

mill around/about *phr v* [I] *informal* if a lot of people mill around, they move around a place in different directions without any particular purpose【非正式】〔许多人〕无目的地乱转，乱兜圈子：*Crowds of students were milling around in the street.* 一群群的学生在街上转来转去。

Mill, John Stuart (1806-73) a British PHILOSOPHER and economist who influenced modern ideas about politics and economics. He helped to develop the idea of UTILITARIANISM (=the principle that actions are good if they generally bring happiness, and bad if they do not), and in his book *On Liberty*, he said that people should be free to do what they want so long as they did not harm other people. 穆勒〔(1806-1873)，英国哲学家、经济学家，对现代政治学和经济学思想产生了一定影响。他对实利主义思想的发展起了促动作用。在《论自由》一书中，他说只要不伤害他人，人们应当有权去做任何想做的事情〕

Mil·lais /ˈmɪle; ˈmɪleɪ/**, Sir John Ev·e·rett** /dʒɑn ˈɛvərɪt; dʒɒn ˈevərɪ̈t/ (1829-96) a British painter who helped to establish the Pre-Raphaelite group of artists 密莱司〔(1829-1896)，英国画家，拉斐尔前派的创始人〕

mil·len·ni·um /məˈlɛnɪəm; mɪˈleniəm/ *n plural* **millennia** /-nɪə; -niə/ **1** [C] a period of 1000 years 1000年，千年期 **2** [C] the time when a new 1000-year period begins 新千年开始的时刻，新千年开始之际：*plans for celebrating the millennium, in the year 2000* 在2000年庆祝新千年开始的计划 **3 the millennium** the time in the future when Jesus Christ will return and rule on Earth for 1000 years 千禧年，千年王国〔指耶稣基督将复临并统治世界的1000年〕**—millennial** *adj*

Millennium Bridge, the a bridge that crosses the Thames River in London, built to celebrate the Millennium. People can walk over it, but no cars or buses are allowed. When it was first built it shook too much when people walked on it, and it had to be closed and strengthened. 千禧大桥〔位于伦敦泰晤士河上的一座桥，为庆祝新千年而建造。此桥允许行人通过，但禁止车辆通行。刚建成时，行人走在桥上，晃动剧烈，所以不得不关闭，重新予以加固〕

Millennium Dome /ˈ· · · ·, ˈ/ a very large temporary building in the shape of a DOME in Greenwich, London, built by the UK government to contain a big public exhibition celebrating the start of the new millennium in the year 2000 千禧圆顶纪念馆〔英国政府建造的一大型临时圆顶建筑，位于伦敦的格林尼治，内有一大型展览，庆祝2000千禧年的开始〕

mil·le·pede /ˈmɪləˌpid; ˈmɪlɪ̈piːd/ another spelling of MILLIPEDE millipede 的另一种拼法

mill·er /ˈmɪlɚ; ˈmɪlə/ *n* [C] someone who owns or operates a mill which makes flour 磨坊主；面粉厂厂主

Miller, Arthur (1915-2005) a US writer of plays that deal with political or moral problems. His most famous plays include *The Crucible*, about the Salem Witchcraft Trials in 17th century America, and *Death of a Salesman*. He is also famous for having been married to Marilyn Monroe. 米勒〔(1915-2005)，美国剧作家。作品常以政治或道德问题为题材，代表作有《炼狱》和《推销员之死》，其中《炼狱》取材于17世纪美国赛勒姆市的巫术审讯案。他亦以曾与玛丽莲·梦露结婚而知名〕

Miller, Glenn (1904-44) a US musician, band leader, and COMPOSER, whose SWING music was very popular during World War II. His most famous pieces of music are *In the Mood* and *Moonlight Serenade*. 米勒〔(1904-1944)，美国音乐家、乐队领队和作曲家。他的摇摆乐在二战期间十分流行。最有名的曲目是《心事重重》和《月光小夜曲》〕

Miller, Henry (1891-1980) a US writer whose NOVELS include *Tropic of Cancer* and *Tropic of Capricorn* 米勒〔(1891-1980)，美国作家，代表作有小说《北回归线》和《南回归线》〕

mil·let /ˈmɪlɪt; ˈmɪlɪ̈t/ *n* [U] the small seeds of a plant similar to grass, used as food 粟，小米

milli- /ˈmɪlɪ; ˈmɪlɪ̈/ *prefix* a 1000th part of a particular unit of something 千分之一：*a millilitre* (=0.001 litres) 1毫升 —see table on page C4 参见C4页附录

mil·li·bar /ˈmɪlɪˌbɑr; ˈmɪlɪ̈bɑː/ *n* [C] *technical* a unit for measuring the pressure of air【术语】毫巴〔气压单位〕

mil·li·gram /ˈmɪləˌɡræm; ˈmɪlɪ̈ɡræm/ written abbreviation 缩写为 **mg** *n* [C] a unit for measuring weight. There are 1000 milligrams in one gram. 毫克〔重量单位〕—see table on page C3 参见C3页附录

mil·li·li·tre *BrE*【英】, **milliliter** *AmE*【美】/ˈmɪləˌlitɚ; ˈmɪlɪ̈ˌliːtə/ written abbreviation 缩写为 **ml** *n* [C] a unit for measuring the amount of a liquid. There are 1000 millilitres in one litre. 毫升〔液体容量单位〕—see table on page C3 参见C3页附录

mil·li·me·tre *BrE*【英】, **millimeter** *AmE*【美】/ˈmɪləˌmitɚ; ˈmɪlɪ̈ˌmiːtə/ written abbreviation 缩写为 **mm** *n* [C] a unit for measuring length. There are 1000 millimetres in one metre. 毫米〔长度单位〕—see table on page C3 参见C3页附录

mil·li·ner /ˈmɪlənə; ˈmɪlɪnə/ *n* [C] *old-fashioned* someone who makes and sells women's hats【过时】制作和销售女帽的人, 女帽商

mil·li·ne·ry /ˈmɪləˌnɛrɪ; ˈmɪlɪnəri/ *n* [U] **1** a word meaning hats, used in shops and in the fashion industry 女帽〔总称〕 **2** the activity of making women's hats 女帽制作

mil·lion /ˈmɪljən; ˈmɪljən/ *plural* **million** or **millions** *number, quantifier* **1** 1,000,000 百万: *three million dollars* 300万美元 | *a population of 12 million people* 1200万的人口 **2** also 又作 **millions** an extremely large number of people or things 极其庞大的数目; 许多, 无数: *Millions of people will see that film.* 数以百万计的人将观看那部电影。| *He made millions* (=a lot of money) *on that deal.* 他在那次交易中大赚了一笔。| *I've heard that excuse a million times.* 那个借口我已听过无数次了。**3 not/never in a million years** *spoken* used to emphasize that something is impossible or very unlikely to happen【口】一百万年以后也不, 永远也不: *I'd never marry him – not in a million years.* 我决不嫁给他 —— 永远不会。**4 feel/look like a million dollars/bucks** *informal especially AmE* to feel or look very well or very attractive【非正式, 尤美】感觉很精神/看起来有吸引力: *Wow! You look like a million dollars tonight!* 哇! 你今晚精神极了! **5 one in a million** also 又作 **a wife/teacher/writer etc in a million** *informal* one of the best possible wives, teachers etc【非正式】万里挑一的好妻子/好教师/好作家等 —**millionth** *determiner, n, pron, adv*

mil·lion·aire /ˌmɪljənˈɛr; ˌmɪljəˈneə/ *n* [C] someone who is very rich and has at least a million pounds or dollars 富豪, 百万富翁

mil·lion·air·ess /ˌmɪljənˈɛrɪs; ˌmɪljəˈneərɪs/ *n* [C] *old-fashioned* a woman who is very rich and has at least a million pounds or dollars【过时】女富豪, 女百万富翁

mil·li·pede /ˈmɪləˌpid; ˈmɪlɪpiːd/ *n* [C] a long thin insect with a lot of legs 马陆, 千足虫

Mill on the Floss, The /ˌ· · · ˈ·/ (1860) a NOVEL by George Eliot about Maggie Tulliver, the daughter of a MILLER, and her brother, Tom《弗洛斯河上的磨坊》〔(1860), 乔治·艾略特创作的一部小说。书中描写磨坊主女儿麦琪·塔利弗和她哥哥汤姆的故事〕

mill·pond /ˈmɪlˌpɑnd; ˈmɪlpɒnd/ *n* [C] a very small lake that supplies water to turn the wheel of a WATERMILL 磨坊水池

Mills and Boon /ˌ· · ˈ·/ *trademark* a British publisher that produces very popular romantic NOVELs, bought especially by women. The typical Mills and Boon story is about the romance between a young, beautiful woman and a good-looking man, who usually get married after many difficulties.【商标】米尔斯-布恩出版公司〔英国一出版商。专门出版通俗爱情小说, 读者大多为妇女。典型的米尔斯-布恩风格的小说总是描写一对俊男靓女几经波折终成眷属的故事〕: *Tall, rich, and handsome, Garth was just like the hero of a Mills and Boon book.* 加思长的高高的, 又有钱又英俊, 正像米尔斯-布恩出版公司的爱情小说中的男主人公。

mill·stone /ˈmɪlˌston; ˈmɪlstəʊn/ *n* [C] **1** one of the two large circular stones that crush grain into flour in a MILL[1] (1) 磨石, 磨盘 **2 a millstone around your neck** something that causes you a lot of problems and prevents you from doing what you would like to do 某人的沉重负担[累赘, 包袱]: *His fame, so pleasant at first, became a millstone around his neck.* 他的名气开始是那样令人惬意, 后来却成了他的一个包袱。

mill·wheel /ˈmɪlhwil; ˈmɪlwiːl/ *n* [C] *especially BrE* a large wheel that is turned by water flowing past it to provide power to the machinery in a MILL[1] (1)【尤英】〔磨坊的〕水车轮

Milne /mɪln; mɪln/, **A. A.** (1882-1956) a British writer, famous for his books for children such as *Winnie the Pooh* and his collection of poems *When We Were Very Young* 米尔恩〔(1882-1956), 英国作家。以创作儿童读物著名, 作品有《小熊维尼》和诗集《当我们年轻时》〕

mil·om·e·ter /maɪˈlɑmətə; maɪˈlɒmɪtə/ *n* [C] another spelling of MILEOMETER mileometer的另一种拼法

milque·toast, milktoast /ˈmɪlktost; ˈmɪlktəʊst/ *n* [C] *AmE old-fashioned* a weak, quiet man with no courage; WIMP[1] (1)【美, 过时】胆小鬼, 懦夫

Mil·ton /ˈmɪltn; ˈmɪltən/, **John** (1608-74) an English poet who many people consider to be one of the most important writers in English literature. He wrote the EPIC poems *Paradise Lost* and *Paradise Regained* after he had gone blind. Before this, he was active in politics as a strong supporter of religious freedom and of Oliver Cromwell. 弥尔顿〔(1608-1674), 英国诗人, 英国文学史上最重要的作家之一。他在失明后创作了史诗《失乐园》和《复乐园》。此前, 他活跃在政坛上, 坚决支持宗教信仰自由和奥利弗·克伦威尔〕

Milton Keynes /ˌmɪltn̩ ˈkinz; ˌmɪltən ˈkiːnz/ a town in central southern England that was developed in 1967 as a new town. The Open University is based there. 米尔顿-凯恩斯〔英格兰中南部一城镇, 为1967年建成的新市镇。开放大学的总部设在该城〕

Mil·wau·kee /mɪlˈwɔki; mɪlˈwɔːki/ the largest city in the US state of Wisconsin, which is a port on Lake Michigan and an important centre of the beer-making industry 密尔沃基〔美国威斯康星州最大城市, 为密歇根湖一港口, 还是重要的啤酒酿造业中心〕

mime[1] /maɪm; maɪm/ *n* **1** [C,U] the use of actions or movements to express what you want to say without using words〔不用语言的〕比手画脚, 做手势 **2** [C] a simple play performed without using words 哑剧: *a mime artist* 哑剧艺术家 **3** [C] an actor who performs without using words 哑剧演员

mime[2] *v* [I,T] to act something using actions and movements without any words 以哑剧形式表演, 比手画脚地表演: *The children mimed the whole story for the rest of the class.* 孩子们以哑剧形式为班上其他同学表演了整个故事。

mi·met·ic /mɪˈmɛtɪk; mɪˈmetɪk/ *adj technical* copying the movements or appearance of someone or something else【术语】模仿的, 模拟的; 拟态的

mim·ic[1] /ˈmɪmɪk; ˈmɪmɪk/ *v past tense and past participle* **mimicked** [T] **1** to copy the way someone speaks or behaves, especially in order to make people laugh 模仿〔某人的言行, 尤指为了逗乐〕, 学…的样子: *Sally used to keep us entertained by mimicking the teacher.* 萨莉过去常常模仿老师逗我们乐。**2** to behave or operate in exactly the same way as something or someone else 学…的样子; 模拟: *Will computers ever be able to mimic the way humans think?* 将来电脑能模拟人类思维吗? **3** if an animal mimics something it tries to look or sound like something in order to protect itself〔动物为保护自己〕伪装成〔另一事物〕: *an insect that mimics the appearance of a wasp* 拟态为黄蜂的昆虫 —**mimicry** *n* [U]

mimic[2] *n* [C] **1** an entertainer who copies the way famous people speak or behave〔模仿名人言行的〕喜剧演员, 小丑 **2** a person or animal that is good at copying the movements, sound, or appearance of someone or something else 善于模仿的人[动物]

mimic[3] *adj* [only before noun 仅用于名词前] **1** *technical* providing protection by looking exactly like something else【术语】拟态的 **2** imitating behaviour or movements 模仿的, 模拟的: *the mimic marching of the children playing soldiers* 扮演士兵的孩子们模仿行军

mi·mo·sa /mɪˈmosə; mɪˈməʊzə/ *n* [C,U] a small tree that grows in hot countries and has small yellow flowers 含羞草

min 1 the written abbreviation of 缩写= MINIMUM **2** the written abbreviation of 缩写= minute or 或 minutes

min·a·ret /ˌmɪnəˈrɛt; ˌmɪnəˈret/ *n* [C] a tall thin tower on a MOSQUE from which Muslims are called to prayer〔清真寺旁的〕宣礼塔, 尖塔

min·a·to·ry /ˈmɪnəˌtɔrɪ; ˈmɪnətəri/ *adj formal* threatening【正式】威胁性的, 恐吓性的

mince[1] /mɪns; mɪns/ *v* **1** [T] to cut food, especially meat, into very small pieces, usually in a machine 切碎, 剁碎, 绞碎〔食物, 尤指肉〕: *minced lamb* 碎羔羊肉 **2** [I always+adv/prep] to walk in an unnatural way, taking short steps and moving your hips〔迈着碎步、摆着臀部〕扭扭捏捏地走: [+across/down/along etc] *She minced across the hall to her desk.* 她扭扭捏捏地迈着小步穿过大厅走到自己的办公桌旁。**3 not mince matters/your words** to say exactly what you think even if this may offend people 直言不讳地说, 毫不遮掩地说: *He's a brash New Yorker who doesn't mince his words.* 他是个傲慢的纽约人, 说话直来直去。

mince[2] *n* [U] *BrE* meat, especially BEEF, that has been cut into very small pieces using a special machine【英】切[剁, 绞]碎的肉〔尤指牛肉〕, 肉末; GROUND BEEF *AmE*【美】

mince·meat /ˈmɪnsˌmit; ˈmɪns-miːt/ *n* [U] **1** a mixture of apples, RAISINs, SUET, and SPICEs, but no meat, put inside PASTRY (1) and baked (百)果馅〔苹果、葡萄干、板油、香料混合而成的果饼馅, 不含肉〕 **2 make mincemeat of** *informal* to completely defeat someone in an argument, fight, or game【非正式】〔在辩论、战斗或比赛中〕彻底击败, 驳倒〔某人〕: *They made mincemeat of the opposition's arguments.* 他们把反方的论点驳得体无完肤。

mince pie /ˌ· ˈ·/ *n* [C] **1** a small PIE filled with mincemeat that is eaten especially at Christmas〔尤指在圣诞节食用的〕百果馅饼 **2** *AmE* a large PIE filled with mincemeat【美】大百果馅饼

minc·er /ˈmɪnsə; ˈmɪnsə/ *n* [C] *BrE* a machine that cuts meat into very small pieces by forcing it through small holes【英】绞肉机; MEAT GRINDER *AmE*【美】

minc·ing·ly /ˈmɪnsɪŋlɪ; ˈmɪnsɪŋli/ *adv* with little short steps 迈着小碎步地

MIND /maɪnd; maɪnd/ a British CHARITY organization which gives advice and practical help to people who are mentally ill and to their families, and which tries to make people in general understand more about mental illness 精神健康协会〔英国一慈善组织，为精神病患者及其家人提供指导和帮助，以期人们更加了解精神疾病〕

mind¹ /maɪnd; maɪnd/ *n*

① BRAIN/THINKING PROCESS 头脑/思维过程
② DECIDE 决定
③ THINKING ABOUT STH 思考某事
④ WORRY/STOP WORRYING 担心/停止担心
⑤ CRAZY/MENTALLY ILL 发疯的/有精神病的
⑥ FORGET 忘记
⑦ REMEMBER 记得
⑧ OPINION 看法
⑨ STRONG/DETERMINED 坚强的/坚决的
⑩ ATTENTION 注意(力)
⑪ IMAGINE 想象
⑫ INTEND/WANT 打算/想要
⑬ INTELLIGENCE 智力
⑭ OTHER MEANINGS 其他意思

① BRAIN/THINKING PROCESS 头脑/思维过程

1 [C,U] the part of a person, usually considered to be their brain, that they use to think and imagine things 头脑: *I have a picture of him in my mind – tall, blond and handsome.* 我心里记着他的样子——高个子，金发，很帅气。| *I don't know what's going on in her mind.* 我不知道她脑子里在想什么。

2 get sb/sth out of your mind to stop yourself thinking about someone or something 不再去想某人/某事: *I just can't seem to get her out of my mind.* 我就是无法不去想她。

3 go over sth/turn sth over in your mind to keep thinking about something because you are trying to understand it or solve a problem 反复思考某事: *I kept turning the conversation over in my mind.* 我脑子里一直思忖着那次谈话。

② DECIDE 决定

4 make up your mind a) to decide which of two or more choices you want, especially after thinking for a long time 作出决定；拿定主意: *I just couldn't make up my mind, so in the end I bought both.* 我就是拿不定主意，最后两个都买了。| *I wish you'd make your mind up whether you're coming or not.* 我希望你作出决定，到底来不来。**b)** to become very determined to do something, so that you will not change your decision 下定决心，决意: *I'm sorry but my mind's made up – I'm leaving.* 对不起，我决心已下——我要走了。| **make up your mind to do sth** *He's made his mind up to resign, and that's final.* 他已下决心辞职，不会改变主意了。| **make up your mind that** *They made up their mind that they would buy a new house once Larry changed jobs.* 他们下定决心，一旦拉里换了工作他们就买一座新房子。

5 change your mind to change your opinion or decision about something 改变主意[决定]: *I've changed my mind – I'll have a beer instead.* 我改变主意了——给我来一杯啤酒。| [+about] *Try and get her to change her mind about coming with us.* 设法让她改变主意，不要和我们一起去。

6 be in two minds about *informal* to be unable to make a decision about something【非正式】三心二意，拿不定主意，犹豫不决: *We're in two minds about whether to sell the house or not.* 我们对该不该卖掉房子拿不定主意。

7 set your mind on (doing) sth to decide that you want to do something very much 决心要做某事: *Tom had set his mind on a trip to the Seychelles.* 汤姆已决定去塞舌尔群岛旅行。

③ THINKING ABOUT STH 思考某事

8 be the last thing on sb's mind to be the thing that someone is least likely to be thinking about 是某人最不可能在考虑着的事: *One thing was for sure, marriage was the last thing on Nick's mind.* 有一件事是肯定的——结婚是尼克最不愿意想的事。

9 come/spring to mind [not in progressive 不用进行式] if something comes to mind or springs to mind you suddenly think of it 突然想到，猛然想起: *We needed someone to look after the kids, and your name sprang to mind.* 我们需要有个人照看孩子，于是一下子就想到了你。

10 cross/enter your mind (that) [not in progressive 不用进行时] if something crosses or enters your mind, you have a particular thought or idea, especially for a short time 掠过/进入脑海: *It never crossed my mind that Lisa might be lying.* 我从来没想过莉萨也许是在撒谎。

11 turn your mind to to begin to think about a subject after you have been thinking about something else 转而开始考虑…，把心思转向…: *Let's now turn our minds to tomorrow's meeting.* 现在让我们来考虑一下明天的会议。

④ WORRY/STOP WORRYING 担心/停止担心

12 take your mind off sth to make yourself stop thinking about something that is worrying you 不再想某事: *I decided to clean the car to take my mind off the events of the day.* 我决定去清洗一下汽车，好让自己不再去想那天发生的事。

13 set/put sb's mind at rest to make someone feel less worried or anxious 使某人放心，使某人安心: *Call your mom and tell her you've arrived safely, just to set her mind at rest.* 给你妈打个电话，告诉她你已经安全到达，好让她放心。

14 be out of your mind with grief/worry etc to be extremely worried, sad etc 极其悲伤/忧虑等: *Since her son was reported missing she's been out of her mind with worry.* 自从儿子被报失踪以后，她一直非常担心。

15 be a load/weight off your mind *informal* to be something that you no longer need to worry about【非正式】不再需要忧虑；心上的石头落地: *The police said the accident wasn't my fault. Boy, was that a load off my mind.* 警察说那次事故不是我的错。嘿，我这才放下心上的大石头。

16 on your mind if something is on your mind, you keep thinking about it and worrying about it 担心: *You look worried, Sarah. Is there something on your mind?* 萨拉，你看起来很焦虑。有什么心事吗？| **have a lot on your mind** (=have a lot of problems to worry about) 有许多忧心事 *With Jim losing his job and her mother being sick, Michelle has had a lot on her mind lately.* 米歇尔近来有许多烦心事，吉姆失业了，而母亲又在生病。

⑤ CRAZY/MENTALLY ILL 发疯的/有精神病的

17 be out of your mind/not be in your right mind *informal* to behave in a way that is crazy or stupid【非正式】发狂，发疯；犯傻. *Nobody in their right mind would go out on a night like this.* 精神正常的人不会在这样的夜晚出去。| *She must be out of her mind to marry him.* 她要是嫁给他，那准是疯了。

18 go out of your mind/lose your mind *informal* to start to become mentally ill or behave in a strange way【非正式】精神失常；失去理智: *I have so much to do – I feel like I'm going out of my mind.* 我有那么多事情要做，我觉得自己都要疯了。

19 be of sound mind *law* to have the ability to think clearly and be responsible for your actions【法律】心智健全

⑥ FORGET 忘记

20 your mind goes blank *informal* if your mind goes blank, you suddenly cannot remember something【非正式】脑子里突然一片空白，突然什么也想不起来: *My mind went blank as soon as I went into the exam room.* 我一走进考场就突然大脑一片空白。

21 out of sight, out of mind used to say that if you cannot see someone or something, you stop thinking about them and forget about them 眼不见，心不念

22 put sth out of your mind to deliberately try to forget about something unpleasant 把某事置于[抛诸]脑后: *Put the whole*

experience out of your mind and try to sleep. 忘掉这一切，试着睡觉吧。
23 go (right) out of your mind/slip your mind if something goes out of your mind, you forget it, especially because you are too busy doing other things〔通常指由于忙于做其他事情〕(完全)忘记，忘得干干净净：*Her birthday had gone right out of Jerry's mind.* 杰里把她的生日忘得一干二净。| **slip sb's mind that** *It slipped my mind that I'd agreed to meet him.* 我忘了自己已同意见他。

⑦ **REMEMBER 记得**
24 bring/call sth to mind a) to make yourself remember a name, fact etc 回想起某事：*I couldn't quite call his name to mind.* 我一时想不起他的名字了。**b)** to remind you of something 使回想起某事：*These violent scenes bring to mind the riots of last year.* 这些暴力场面使人想起去年的骚乱。
25 keep sth in mind to remember a fact or piece of information because it will be useful to you in the future 记住某事〔指将来对你有用的情况或信息〕：*It's a good idea – I'll keep it in mind.* 这是个好主意，我要记在心里。
26 bear sth in mind to remember a useful or important piece of information 记住某事〔指有用或重要的信息〕：*You should bear in mind that these exams affect your final result.* 你应该记住，这些考试会影响到你的最后成绩。
27 stick in your mind if a name, fact etc sticks in your mind, you remember it for a long time 对〔名字、事实等〕经久不忘：*For some reason the name really stuck in Joe's mind.* 由于某种原因，那个名字深深地印在了乔的脑子里。
28 at/in the back of your mind if something is at the back of your mind, you keep remembering it or feeling it, but you do not think about it directly 在内心深处：*At the back of his mind, Matt had been hoping that Beth would stay.* 在心底里，马特一直希望贝丝留下来。
29 put you in mind of [not in progressive 不用进行式] *old-fashioned* to remind you of a person or thing from your past【过时】使想起〔过去的人或事〕：*Seeing the movie put me in mind of my army days.* 这部电影让我想起了自己当兵的日子。

⑧ **OPINION 看法**
30 to my mind *BrE spoken* used when you are giving your opinion about something【英口】照我的意见，在我看来：*To my mind this is the finest building in Paris.* 依我看，这是巴黎最漂亮的建筑。
31 speak your mind to say exactly what you think about something, even when this might offend people 直言不讳
32 keep/have an open mind (about) to be willing to think about and accept new ideas or ways of doing things 思想开放，能接受新事物：*My parents have a very open mind about sex before marriage.* 我父母对婚前性行为态度很开明。
33 have a closed mind (about) to refuse to think about or accept new ideas or ways of doing things 不易接受新事物，守旧
34 be of one mind/of the same mind/of like mind to agree with someone about something 意见一致，看法相似：*It's not often that I meet people who are of like mind in politics.* 我并不是经常会碰到政治观点一致的人。| **[+on/about]** *We're all of the same mind on this issue.* 在这个问题上我们的看法都一致。

⑨ **STRONG/DETERMINED 坚强的/坚决的**
35 have a mind of your own to decide on your opinions and make your own decisions 有主见，能自作决定：*Even at the age of two, Joey had a mind of his own.* 乔伊早在两岁的时候，就自己拿主意了。
36 know your own mind to be very clear about what your opinions or beliefs are and not be influenced by what other people think 有自己明确的见解[信念]；有决断
37 put your mind to to decide to do something or achieve something by thinking and working very hard at it 专心于：*It won't take long to sort it out once you put your mind to it.* 一旦你专心做，用不了多长时间就能把它弄清楚。

⑩ **ATTENTION 注意(力)**
38 sb's mind is not on sth to not be thinking about what you are doing, because you are thinking or worrying about something else 某人的心思不在某事上：*Steve's mind just doesn't seem to be on the job these days. Is something wrong at home?* 史蒂夫这些天好像没心思工作，家里出什么事了吗？
39 keep your mind on to keep paying attention to something even if it is boring or if you want to think about something else 专心于，把注意力集中于：*It was difficult to keep our minds on the job with all the talk of war.* 关于战争的议论那么多，我们难以专心工作。
40 pay sb/sth no mind *AmE* to not pay any attention to someone or something or not care about what they are saying or doing【美】不把某人/某事放在心上
41 your mind wanders if your mind WANDERS, you no longer pay attention to something, especially because you are bored〔尤因无聊而〕心不在焉，走神

⑪ **IMAGINE 想象**
42 it's all in your mind used to tell someone that they have imagined something and it does not really exist 都是你自己想象出来的：*one of those doctors who say you're not really sick and it's all in your mind* 说你实际上没病、病都是你自己想出来的那些医生中的一个
43 in your mind's eye if you see something in your mind's eye, you can imagine what it looks like because you remember it 可以想象出，在脑海中浮现：*She could see in her mind's eye the whitewashed cottage of her childhood.* 她儿时住的那座用石灰水粉刷过的小屋仍浮现在她脑海中。

⑫ **INTEND/WANT 打算/想要**
44 have sth/sb in mind to be thinking about or considering a particular person, plan etc for a particular purpose 考虑到某物/某人：*It's a nice house, but it wasn't quite what we had in mind.* 这是座不错的房子，但和我们心目中想要的不完全一样。
45 have it in mind to do sth to intend to do something 打算做某事：*Once she had it in mind to win that trophy, nothing would have stopped her.* 一旦她想去赢得那座奖杯，什么事也阻挡不了她。
46 have a good mind/half a mind to do sth a) used as a not very serious threat when you want to show your disapproval of what someone has done 很想/有点想做某事〔用来随意吓唬以示对某人的行为不赞同〕：*I've a good mind to phone him up and tell him exactly what I think.* 我很想给他打个电话，告诉他我的确切想法。**b)** used when you are considering doing something but are not sure you will 很想/有点想做某事〔表示正在考虑做某事但拿不准是否会做〕：*I have half a mind just to take a cab home.* 我有点想坐出租车回家。

⑬ **INTELLIGENCE 智力**
47 [C usually singular 一般用单数] intelligence and ability to think rather than emotions; INTELLECT 思维能力；智能，心智：*Paul says he's doing the course to improve his mind.* 保罗说他正在学习那门课以提高思维能力。| *a bright child with an enquiring mind* 有求知欲的聪明孩子
48 [C] someone who is very intelligent, especially in a particular area of study or activity〔尤指在某一研究或活动领域〕有才智的人：*She is one of the finest political minds in the country.* 她是该国最具才华的政治家之一。
49 great minds think alike *spoken* used to say jokingly that you and someone else must be very intelligent because you both agree about something【口】智者所见略同
50 mind over matter an expression used when someone uses their intelligence to control a difficult situation 精神胜过物质〔指用智力控制物质世界的困难局面〕

⑭ **OTHER MEANINGS 其他意思**
51 frame/state of mind the way someone is thinking and feeling at a particular time 心情：*I'm not going to argue with you while you're in this frame of mind.* 你情绪这个样子，我不和你争论了。
52 give sb a piece of your mind *informal* to tell someone how angry you are with them【非正式】责备某人；向某人直陈不满
53 bored out of your mind *informal* extremely bored【非正式】厌烦之至的
54 stoned/drunk etc out of your mind affected by drugs or alcohol so that you do not really know what you are doing 因吸毒/喝酒等而神志不清的
55 time out of mind more often than you can remember 无数次地：*I've told you time out of mind to close that door when you leave the room.* 我不知跟你讲过多少次，离开房间时要关上那道门。

M

56 ►CHARACTER 性格, 性情◄ [C] a particular way of thinking that is part of someone's character〔作为性格一部分的〕思维方式: *If you ask me O'Rourke has a very devious mind.* 在我看来, 奥罗克很狡猾。—see also 另见 ONE-TRACK MIND, **blow your mind** (BLOW[1] (17)), **the mind boggles** (BOGGLE (1)), **meeting of minds** (MEETING (5)), **peace of mind** (PEACE (4)), PRESENCE OF MIND, **read sb's mind** (READ[1] (12))

mind² *v*

1 ►FEEL ANNOYED 感到恼火◄ [I,T not in progressive or passive 不用进行时或被动态, usually in questions and negatives 一般用于疑问句和否定句] to feel annoyed or upset about something 介意, 反对: *We'll have to leave early. Do you mind?* 我们很早就得离开, 你介意吗? | *I wouldn't have minded so much if he'd apologized.* 如果他道歉的话我就不会那么在意了。| **mind sth** *He didn't mind the lie she'd told him, it was the fact that she'd made him look stupid.* 他并不在意她对他撒的谎, 他在意的是她使他看上去像个傻瓜。| **mind sb doing sth** *I hope you don't mind me bringing the dog with me.* 希望你不要介意我把狗带在身边。| **mind that** *She didn't mind that he was late as long as he got there.* 他既然赶到了那儿, 她就没有计较他的迟到。

2 not mind doing sth to be willing to do something 愿意做某事: *I don't mind driving if you're tired.* 如果你累了, 我愿意开车。

3 ►NOT CARE WHICH ONE 不在乎哪一个◄ **not mind** [I,T not in progressive or passive 不用进行时或被动态] *especially BrE* to not care what is decided because you are equally happy with whatever is decided【尤英】不在乎, 无所谓: *I don't mind whether we see the film or not.* 我们看不看这个电影, 我都无所谓。

4 ►TAKE CARE OF 照看, 照料◄ [T] *BrE*【英】**a)** to be responsible for something for a short time; WATCH[1] (3)〔短期地〕看管, 照看〔某物〕: *Will you mind my bag while I buy my ticket?* 我买票的时候你照看一下我的包好吗? **b)** to take care of a child while their parents are not there; WATCH[1] (3) 照料, 照看〔孩子〕: *My sister minds the baby so I can go to my yoga class.* 我姐姐照料婴儿, 所以我可以去上瑜伽课。

5 mind your own business to not get involved in or ask questions about other people's lives or personal details 管你自己的事, 别管闲事: *Why don't you just mind your own business and leave me in peace?* 你为什么就不能别管闲事, 让我清静一下呢?

6 mind the store *AmE informal* to be in charge of something, especially while the person who is usually in charge is not there【美, 非正式】料理事务〔尤指负责人不在时〕: *If the president didn't know about the arms sales to Iran, who is really minding the store?* 如果总统不知道向伊朗出售武器一事, 那么究竟谁在管事呢?

7 mind your manners/language/p's and q's to be careful about what you say or how you behave so that you do not offend anyone 注意你的举止/语言/礼貌

8 ►OBEY 服从◄ [T not in progressive 不用进行时] *AmE* to obey someone's instructions or advice【美】听从, 服从: *Mind what your mother says, Anthony.* 安东尼, 要听你妈妈的话。

Frequencies of the verb **mind** in spoken and written English 动词 mind 在英语口语和书面语中的使用频率

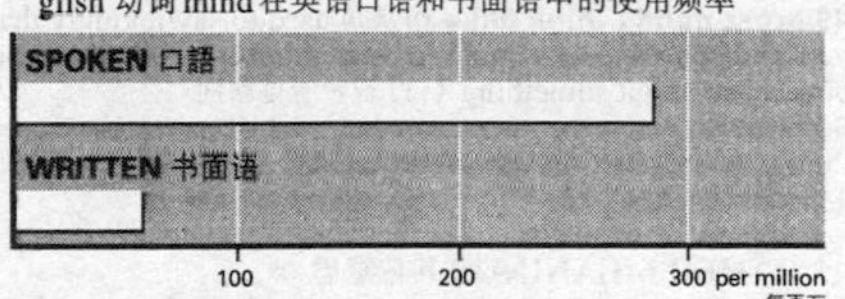

Based on the British National Corpus and the Longman Lancaster Corpus
据英国国家语料库和朗文兰开斯特语料库

This graph shows that the verb **mind** is much more common in spoken English than in written English. This is because it is used in a lot of common spoken phrases. 本图表显示, 动词 mind 在英语口语中的使用频率远远高于书面语, 因为口语中很多常用短语是由 mind 构成的。

mind (*v*) **SPOKEN PHRASES**
含 mind 的口语短语

9 never mind a) used to say that something is not important or serious, especially when someone seems worried or is saying sorry to you 不要紧, 没关系: *"I'm afraid I've broken the chair." "Never mind, I can easily get it fixed."* "恐怕我把椅子弄坏了。" "没关系, 我可以轻而易举地把它修好。" **b)** used to emphasize that something is impossible, because even something that should be easier is also impossible 更不用说, 更谈不上: *I can't even explain the problem to my colleagues, never mind anyone else.* 我对同事也无法把这个问题解释清楚, 更不用说对其他人解释了。**c)** used to emphasize that something else is also true, apart from the thing you have just mentioned 这还不算, 这还没有把…考虑在内: *Cars kill thousands of people each year, never mind the damage they do to the environment.* 汽车每年要造成数千人死亡, 这还没算上给环境造成的破坏。**d)** used to tell someone not to do something now, because it is less important than something else, or because you will do it later yourself 别管, 不用管: **never mind sth** *Never mind the dishes – I'll do them later.* 别管那些盘子 —— 我过一会儿会洗的。| **never mind doing something** *Never mind looking at the boys, we're supposed to be playing tennis.* 别看着那些男孩子了, 我们应该专心打网球。**e)** used to say that you do not really care about something because it is much less important than something else 不用担心, 不必在乎: *I want the best, never mind the cost!* 我要最好的, 不计较费用! | **[+about]** *Let's get the economy right, never mind about the unemployed.* 让我们先把经济整顿好, 先不要为失业的人担心。

10 never you mind *especially BrE* used to tell someone that you are not going to tell them something because it is private or secret【尤英】不关你的事: *"What's that you were saying to dad?" "Never you mind."* "你刚才跟爸爸说什么?" "不关你的事。"

11 mind you *BrE* used to say something that is the opposite of what you have just said, or that emphasizes it【英】尽管如此; 请注意, 听着: *The photos look very old. Mind you, she did take them over 20 years ago.* 这些照片看起来很旧。要知道, 这是她在二十多年前拍摄的。

12 would/do you mind used to ask someone something politely 请你…好吗, 倘若…你不介意吧: **would/do you mind doing sth** *Would you mind opening the window please?* 请你打开窗子好吗? | **would/do you mind if** *Do you mind if I smoke?* 我抽烟你不介意吧?

13 I wouldn't mind used to politely ask for something 我想, 我愿意〔用于客气地索要某物〕: *I wouldn't mind a drink if you have one.* 如果你有酒的话我想喝一杯。

14 do you mind! used when you are annoyed at something that someone has done 不要这样好不好! 你太冒失了!〔表示恼怒〕: *Do you mind! I just washed that floor!* 请不要这样不小心! 我刚刚冲洗过地板!

15 if you don't mind a) used when checking that someone is willing to do something or let you do something 如果你不介意的话: *I'll come along if you don't mind.* 如果你不介意我就一起去。**b)** used, sometimes rudely, when you do not want to do something that someone has suggested 不用你操心: *I can handle this myself, if you don't mind!* 我自己能处理这件事, 不用你操心!

16 if you don't mind my saying so used when you want to give advice or an opinion that you think might offend someone 如果我这么说你不见怪的话: *I don't think you should ever hit a child, if you don't mind my saying so.* 如果你不介意我这么说的话, 我认为你不应该打孩子。

17 mind! *BrE* used to warn someone to be careful because something bad or dangerous might happen【英】当心! 小心!: *Mind! That's my foot you're standing on.* 当心! 你踩在我脚上了。| **mind sth** *Mind the window! It's only just been repaired.* 小心窗子! 刚修好的呢。| **mind sb/sth doesn't do sth** *Mind you don't fall off the chair.* 小心别从椅子上掉下来。| **mind how/where/who etc** *Mind where you're walking. The floor's a bit slippery.* 注意脚下。地板有点滑。| **mind your head/back/fingers etc** *Mind your head. The ceiling's very low in here.* 小心别碰着头。这个地方天花板很低。

18 mind out! *BrE*【英】**a)** used to warn someone that they are in danger 当心! 注意!: *Mind out! There's a car coming!* 当心! 有辆汽车开过来了! **b)** used to ask someone to move so that you can pass them 让开! 闪开!: *Mind out! You're*

M

sitting right in front of the door. 让让！你刚好坐在门前面。
19 don't mind me used to tell someone not to pay any attention to you 别管我：*Just get on with your work, don't mind us!* 你干你的活，别管我们！
20 I don't mind if I do *humorous* used when politely accepting something such as food or drink that has been offered to you【幽默】好的〔用于客气地接受餐饮等〕："*Would you like a cigar?" "I don't mind if I do, thank you.*" "来支雪茄吗？" "好的，谢谢。"

mind-bend·ing /ˈ· ,··/ *adj informal* difficult to understand【非正式】令人费解的：*Filing letters is not exactly a mind-bending task.* 把信件存档并不是一件费脑筋的工作。

mind-blow·ing /ˈ· ,··/ *adj informal* very exciting, shocking, or strange【非正式】令人极度兴奋[震惊]的；非常奇怪的：*The astronauts had mind-blowing views of planet Earth.* 宇航员们看到了美妙的地球景观。| *a mind-blowing experience* 令人极度兴奋的经历 —see also 另见 **blow your mind** (BLOW[1] (17))

mind-bog·gling /ˈ· ,··/ *adj informal* difficult to imagine and very big, strange, or complicated【非正式】〔巨大、奇怪或复杂得〕令人难以想象的：*He's made a mind-boggling profit with his investments.* 他通过投资获得了惊人的巨额利润。

mind·ed /ˈmaɪndɪd; ˈmaɪndɨd/ *adj* **1 serious-minded/evil-minded etc** having a particular attitude or way of thinking 性格严肃的/心术不正的等：*a very serious-minded girl who studies hard* 一个学习用功、不苟言笑的女孩 **2 safety-minded/efficiency-minded etc** believing in the importance of safety etc 注重安全/效率等的：*People need to be more safety-minded in the home.* 人们在家里需要有更强的安全意识。**3 be minded to do sth** *formal* to want or intend to do something【正式】想要[有意]做某事：*He has enough money to travel, if he were minded to do so.* 只要他想，他有足够的钱去旅游。

mind·er /ˈmaɪndə; ˈmaɪndə/ *n* [C] *BrE*【英】**1** someone who is employed to protect another person 保镖 **2 machine minder, child minder etc** a person whose job it is to look after a machine, a child etc 看管机器的人；照看孩子的人

mind·ful /ˈmaɪndfəl; ˈmaɪndfəl/ *adj* **mindful of** behaving in a way that shows you remember a particular rule or fact 记着…的，想着…的；留神…的；注意…的：*Mindful of the guide's warning they returned before dark.* 他们想着导游的警告，天黑前就回来了。

mind·less /ˈmaɪndlɪs; ˈmaɪndləs/ *adj* **1** completely stupid and without any purpose 愚笨的，无知的；毫无目标的：*mindless vandals* 愚昧的破坏公物者 **2** mindless work or a mindless activity can be done without intelligence or thought〔工作或活动〕无需动脑筋的：*a completely mindless task* 一项完全不需要动脑子的任务 | *mindless game shows on TV* 电视上无需动脑筋的游戏节目 **3 mindless of** not paying attention to or thinking about danger or warnings; HEEDLESS 不注意[不考虑]…的，不顾…的 —**mindlessly** *adv* —**mindlessness** *n* [U]

mind read·er /ˈ· ,··/ *n* [C] *often humorous* someone who knows what someone else is thinking without being told【常幽默】能看透别人心思的人

mind·set /ˈmaɪndset; ˈmaɪndset/ *n* [C] someone's way of thinking about things, which is often difficult to change 思维定式：*You need a logical mindset to develop computer programs.* 开发电脑程序需要逻辑思维定式。

S1 **mine[1]** /maɪn; maɪn/ *pron* [possessive form of 'I' I 的所有格形式] the one or the ones that belong to me 我的（东西）："*Whose is this coat?" "It must be mine.*" "这大衣是谁的？" "一定是我的。" | *Can I borrow your CD player? Mine's broken.* 我可以借一下你的 CD 播放机吗？我的坏了。| **a friend/cousin etc of mine** *an old teacher of mine* 我以前的一位老师

S2 W3 **mine[2]** *n* [C] **1** a deep hole or series of holes under the ground that are dug in order to find coal, gold, tin etc 矿井，矿：**coal/gold/copper mine etc** *He works in the coal mines.* 他在煤矿工作。—compare 比较 QUARRY[1] (1) **2** a type of bomb that is hidden just below the ground or under water and that explodes when it is touched 地雷；水雷 **3 a mine of information/gossip etc** someone who knows a lot about something or a book that tells you a lot about a subject 大量信息/小道消息等的来源 **4** a passage dug beneath the place where an enemy army is 在敌人阵地下挖掘的坑道

mine[3] *v* **mined, mining 1** [I,T] to make holes or passages under the ground in order to take out coal, gold etc, or to take coal, gold etc from these holes 挖掘矿井；开采：[+for] *mining for coal* 采煤 **2** [T often passive 常用被动态] to hide bombs in the sea or under the ground 在…中布水雷[地雷]：*All the roads leading to the city had been mined.* 通向该城市的所有道路都布下了地雷。**3** [T] to dig a passage under the ground beneath the place where an enemy army is 在〔敌人阵地下面〕挖坑道

mine[4] *determiner old use* a way of saying 'my', before a vowel sound or 'h', or after a noun【旧】我的〔用于元音或 /h/ 之前，或名词之后〕：*mine host* 我的房东

mine·field /ˈmaɪn,fild; ˈmaɪnfiːld/ *n* **1** [C] an area where a lot of bombs have been placed just below the ground or under water 雷区 **2** [singular] something that has hidden dangers or difficulties 隐藏着危险[困难]的事物：*The legal system is a minefield for the ordinary person.* 法律体系对普通人来说隐藏着重重危险。

min·er /ˈmaɪnə; ˈmaɪnə/ *n* [C] someone who works under the ground in a MINE[2] (1) taking out coal, gold etc 矿工：*a coal miner* 煤矿工人

min·e·ral /ˈmɪnərəl; ˈmɪnərəl/ *n* [C] **1** a substance that is formed naturally in the earth, especially a solid substance such as coal, salt, stone, or gold 矿物：*an area rich in minerals* 矿藏丰富的地区 **2** a natural substance such as CALCIUM or iron that is present in some foods and that is important for good health〔某些食物中的〕矿物质〈如钙或铁〉**3** *BrE formal* a SOFT DRINK【英，正式】汽水

min·e·ral·o·gy /,mɪnəˈælədʒɪ; ,mɪnəˈrælədʒi/ *n* [U] the scientific study of minerals 矿物学 —**mineralogist** *n* [C]

mineral wa·ter /ˈ··· ,··/ *n* [C,U] water that comes from under the ground and contains minerals 矿泉水

min·e·stro·ne /,mɪnəˈstronɪ; ,mɪnɨˈstrəʊni/ *n* [U] an Italian soup containing vegetables and small pieces of PASTA〔意大利式〕蔬菜浓汤

mine·sweep·er /ˈmaɪn,swipə; ˈmaɪn,swiːpə/ *n* [C] a ship that has equipment for removing bombs from under water 扫雷舰 —**minesweeping** *n* [U]

Ming Dyn·as·ty /ˈmɪŋ ,daɪnəstɪ; ˈmɪŋ ,dɪnəsti/ the DYNASTY (=family of rulers) which ruled China from 1368 to 1644. During this period there were many important developments in Chinese art, politics, and trade. Ming VASES (=decorated containers) are famous for being very beautiful and very valuable. 明朝〔1368-1644 年间统治中国的一个朝代。当时，中国在艺术、政治和贸易等方面取得了重大发展。明朝的花瓶以美观和珍贵闻名〕

min·gle /ˈmɪŋgl; ˈmɪŋgəl/ *v* **mingled, mingling 1** [I,T] if two feelings, sounds, smells etc mingle, they combine with each other but can still be recognized separately（使）混合：[+with] *excitement mingled with nervousness* 既兴奋又紧张 | [+together] *The smell of sweat and stale cigar smoke mingled together.* 汗臭味和污浊的雪茄烟味混杂在一起。**2** [I] to mix with different groups of people at a social occasion and talk to people that you do not already know; CIRCULATE (4)〔在社交场合与不相识的人〕相交往；来回应酬：*The cast and crew mingled as everyone started to relax.* 大家开始休息的时候，演员和摄制组工作人员凑在一起交谈起来。—**mingled** *adj*

Min·gus /ˈmɪŋgəs; ˈmɪŋgəs/, **Charlie** (1922-79) a US JAZZ musician and COMPOSER who played the DOUBLE BASS. He wrote the story of his own life called *Beneath the Underdog* (1971). 明戈斯〔(1922-1979)，美国爵士音乐家、作曲家。他演奏低音提琴，著有自传体小说《落水狗的内心戏》(1971)〕

min·gy /ˈmɪndʒɪ; ˈmɪndʒi/ *adj BrE informal* not at all generous; STINGY【英，非正式】小气的，吝啬的：*Don't be so mingy.* 别这么小气。| *mingy portions* 极少量

min·i /ˈmɪnɪ; ˈmɪni/ *n* [C] **1** a very short skirt or dress; MINISKIRT 超短裙，迷你裙 **2** a type of very small British car〔英国〕微型汽车

mini- /mɪnɪ; mɪni/ *prefix* very small compared with others of its kind〔同类中〕极小的，微型的；极短的：*a mini-break* (=a short holiday) 短暂的休假 | *a miniskirt* (=very short) 超短裙，迷你裙 —compare 比较 MICRO-

min·ia·ture[1] /ˈmɪnɪətʃə; ˈmɪnɨtʃə/ *adj* **miniature camera/railway/garden etc** a camera etc that is much smaller than a normal one 微型照相机/铁路/花园等

miniature[2] *n* **1 in miniature** exactly like something or someone but much smaller 缩影的，微小模型的：*She's her mother in miniature.* 她是她母亲的缩影。**2** [C] a very small painting, usually of a person 细密画，袖珍画；微型人像画：*a collection of Victorian miniatures* 维多利亚时代的微型画收藏品

miniature golf /,··· ˈ·/ *n* [U] *AmE* a GOLF game, played for fun, in which you hit a small ball through passages, over bridges and small hills etc【美】小型高尔夫球（运动），迷你高尔夫；CRAZY GOLF *BrE*【英】

min·ia·tur·ist /ˈmɪnɪətʃərɪst; ˈmɪnɨtʃərɨst/ *n* [C] someone who paints very small pictures 微型画画家

M

min·ia·tur·ize also 又作 **-ise** *BrE*【英】/ˈmɪnɪətʃəraɪz; ˈmɪnɪ̵tʃəraɪz/ *v* [T] to make something in a very small size 使微型化，使小型化 —**miniaturized** *adj* —**miniaturization** /ˌmɪnɪətʃərəˈzeʃən; ˌmɪnɪ̵tʃəraɪˈzeɪʃən/ *n* [U]

min·i·bus /ˈmɪnɪbʌs; ˈminibʌs/ *n* [C] *especially BrE* a small bus with seats for six to twelve people【尤英】小型公共汽车，面包车，小巴

min·i·cab /ˈmɪnɪkæb; ˈminikæb/ *n* [C] *BrE* a taxi that you can call for on the telephone but cannot stop in the street【英】〔可用电话预约但不能在街上截停的〕小型出租车

min·i·com·put·er /ˈmɪnɪkəmˌpjutɚ; ˈminikəmˌpjuːtə/ *n* [C] a computer that is larger than a PERSONAL COMPUTER and smaller than a MAINFRAME, used by businesses and other large organizations〔大于个人电脑但小于大型电脑的〕微型电脑

min·im /ˈmɪnɪm; ˈmɪnɪ̵m/ *n* [C] *BrE* a musical note that continues for half the length of a SEMIBREVE【英】〔音乐中的〕二分音符; HALF NOTE *AmE*【美】—see picture at 参见 MUSIC 图

min·i·mal /ˈmɪnɪml; ˈmɪnɪ̵məl/ *adj* very small in degree or amount, especially the smallest degree or amount possible 极小的，极少的;〔尤指〕最小的，最少的: *The storm caused only minimal damage.* 暴风雨只造成了轻微破坏。—**minimally** *adv*

min·i·mal·is·m /ˈmɪnɪmlɪzəm; ˈmɪnɪ̵məlɪzəm/ *n* [U] art, music etc that uses very simple ideas or patterns that are repeated often〔美术、音乐的〕极简主义; 极简抽象派 —**minimalist** *n* [C]

min·i·mart /ˈmɪnɪmɑrt; ˈmɪnimɑːt/ *n* [C] *especially AmE* a small shop that stays open very late and that sells food, cigarettes etc【尤美】〔营业到很晚的〕小商店

min·i·mize also 又作 **-ise** *BrE*【英】/ˈmɪnəˌmaɪz; ˈmɪnɪ̵maɪz/ *v* [T] **1** to reduce something to the smallest possible amount or degree 把…减至最小量[程度]: *We need to minimize disruptions to the schedule.* 我们需要尽可能降低对日程安排的干扰。**2** to make something seem less serious or important than it really is 对…的严重性[重要性]作最低估计; 极度轻视[贬低]: *a tendency to minimize the problem of sexual harassment in the workplace* 把工作场所中的性骚扰问题大事化小的倾向 —compare 比较 MAXIMIZE

min·i·mum¹ /ˈmɪnəməm; ˈmɪnɪ̵məm/ *adj* [only before noun 仅用于名词前] the minimum number, degree, or amount of something is the smallest or least that is possible, allowed, or needed 最小的，最少的; 最低限度的: *The minimum requirements for the job are a degree and two years' experience.* 该工作的最低要求是要有学位和两年的工作经验。| *a minimum price* 最低价格 —compare 比较 MAXIMUM¹

minimum² *n* [singular] **1** the smallest amount, number, or degree of something that is possible, allowed, or needed 最少量，最小数; 最低限度: [**+of**] *Looking after a horse costs a minimum of £2,000 a year.* 照料一匹马每年最少要花费2000英镑。| **absolute/bare minimum** (=the very least amount or number) 绝对/仅够的最少量 *Staffing levels at the hospital have been slashed to an absolute minimum.* 该医院的职员人数已经减得不能再减了。**2 keep/reduce sth to a minimum** to limit something, especially something bad, to the smallest amount or degree possible 将某事物保持在/减少到最低限度: *The school manages to keep bullying to a minimum.* 学校设法最大限度地减少恃强凌弱的行为。

minimum se·cu·ri·ty pris·on /ˌ··ˈ···ˌ··/ *n* [C] *AmE* a prison that does not restrict prisoners' freedom as much as ordinary prisons【美】〔对犯人自由比普通监狱限制少的〕不设防监狱; OPEN PRISON *BrE*【英】

minimum wage /ˌ··ˈ·/ *n* [C singular] the lowest amount of money that can legally be paid per hour to a worker〔法定每小时〕最低工资

min·ing /ˈmaɪnɪŋ; ˈmaɪnɪŋ/ *n* [U] the action or industry of getting minerals out of the earth 采矿(业) —see also 另见 STRIP MINING

min·ion /ˈmɪnjən; ˈmɪnjən/ *n* [C] a very unimportant person in an organization, who just obeys other people's orders〔某组织中〕顺从听话的小人物

mini-round·a·bout /ˌ··ˈ···/ *n* [C] *BrE* a white circle painted on the road that vehicles must drive around at a place where several roads meet【英】小环岛圈〔道路交叉处涂在路面上的白色圆圈，车辆须绕其行驶〕

min·is·cule /ˈmɪnɪskjul; ˈmɪnɪ̵skjuːl/ *adj* another spelling of MINUSCULE minuscule 的另一种拼法

min·i·se·ries /ˈmɪnɪˌsɪrɪz; ˈmɪniˌsɪəriz/ *n* [C] a television film that is divided into several parts, which are usually shown once a night for several days 电视连续短片[剧]

min·i·skirt /ˈmɪnɪskɝt; ˈminiskɜːt/ *n* [C] a very short skirt; MINI 超短裙，迷你裙

min·is·ter¹ /ˈmɪnɪstɚ; ˈmɪnɪ̵stə/ *n* [C] **1** a politician who is a member of the government and is in charge of a government department, in Britain and some other countries〔英国和其他一些国家的〕部长，大臣: [**+of/for**] *the Minister of Education* 教育部长[大臣] —see also 另见 PRIME MINISTER **2** a priest in some Christian churches〔基督教的〕牧师 —see 见 PRIEST (USAGE) **3** someone whose job is to represent their country in another country, but who is lower in rank than an AMBASSADOR 公使 **4** a MINISTER OF STATE〔英国的〕国务大臣

minister² *v*

minister to sb/sth *phr v* [T] *formal* to give help to someone who needs it【正式】给以…帮助: *ministering to the sick* 帮助生病的人

min·is·ter·i·al /ˌmɪnəsˈtɪrɪəl; ˌmɪnɪ̵ˈstɪəriəl◂/ *adj* connected with or relating to a government minister or a minister in the Christian church 部长的，大臣的;〔基督教〕牧师的: *ministerial duties* 部长的职责

minister of state /ˌ····ˈ·/ *n* [C] a member of the government in Britain who has an important job in a government department but is not the chief minister〔英国的〕国务大臣

min·i·stra·tions /ˌmɪnəˈstreʃənz; ˌmɪnɪ̵ˈstreɪʃənz/ *n* [plural] *formal* the giving of help and service, especially to people who are ill or who need the help of a priest【正式】护理病人;〔牧师的〕行宗教仪式

min·is·try /ˈmɪnɪstrɪ; ˈmɪnɪ̵stri/ *n* **1** [C] a government department that is responsible for one of the areas of government work, such as education, health, or defence〔政府的〕部: [**+of**] *the Ministry of Agriculture* 农业部 **2 the ministry** the profession of being a church leader, especially in the Protestant church〔尤指基督教新教的〕神职，牧师职位: *James wants to join the ministry.* 詹姆斯想当牧师。**3** [U] the work done by a priest or other religious person 牧师[其他宗教人物]所做的工作: *the ministry of Jesus* 耶稣的传道工作

Ministry of Ag·ri·cul·ture, Fisheries and Food /ˌ····ˌ····ˌ···ˈ·/ abbreviation 缩写为 **MAFF** the British government department that was responsible for farming, food production, and the safety of food products. In 2001, it became part of a new Department for Environment, Food and Rural Affairs. 农业、渔业和粮食部〔英国一政府部门，负责农业、粮食生产及食品安全。2001 年划归新成立的环境、食品与农村事务部〕

Ministry of De·fence, the /ˌ····ˈ·/ abbreviation 缩写为 **MOD** the British government department that is responsible for the UK's armed forces. The minister in charge of this department is the **Secretary of State for Defence**. 国防部〔英国一政府部门，主管国家军队。其首长称国防大臣〕

min·i·van /ˈmɪnɪvæn; ˈminivæn/ *n* [C] *AmE* a large car for up to eight people【美】〔可供八人乘坐的〕大轿车

mink /mɪŋk; mɪŋk/ *n plural* **mink** [C,U] a very valuable brown fur used to make coats, hats etc, or the animal from which this fur is obtained 水貂皮; 水貂

Min·ne·ap·o·lis /ˌmɪnɪˈæpəlɪs; ˌmɪniˈæpəlɪs/ a city in east Minnesota, US and an important industrial centre. It is a port on one side of the Mississippi River, with Saint Paul on the other side. Together, they are called the Twin Cities. 明尼阿波利斯〔美国明尼苏达州东部一城市，为重要的工业中心。它是密西西比河沿岸的一个港口，与圣保罗隔河相望，这两座城市被称为双子城〕

Min·ne·ha·ha /ˌmɪnɪˈhɑhɑ; ˌmɪniˈhɑːhɑː/ the wife of the Native American chief Hiawatha 明尼哈哈〔美洲土著人首领海华沙的妻子〕

Min·ne·so·ta /ˌmɪnɪˈsotə; ˌmɪnɪ̵ˈsəʊtə/ abbreviation 缩写为 **MN** a state in the north of the US, which is an industrial and farming area with many farms that produce milk 明尼苏达州〔美国北部一州，为一工农业区，建有许多牛奶场〕

Min·nie Mouse /ˌmɪnɪ ˈmaʊs; ˌmini ˈmaʊs/ *trademark* a CARTOON character invented by Walt Disney. She is a female mouse, and wife or girlfriend of Mickey Mouse.【商标】米妮鼠〔沃尔特·迪斯尼创作的一卡通形象。它是一只母鼠，为米老鼠的妻子或女友〕

Minnie the Minx /ˌ··ˈ·/ a character in the British COMIC (=a magazine for children that tells stories using sets of drawings) *The Beano*. She is a girl who enjoys behaving badly and causing problems for other people. 冒失鬼明妮〔英国连环漫画杂志《欢闹》中的一个人物。她是个女孩子，喜欢捣蛋，爱给别人惹麻烦〕

min·now /ˈmɪno; ˈmɪnəʊ/ *n* [C] **1** a very small fish that lives in rivers and lakes 米诺鱼〔一种生活在河、湖中的极小的鱼〕**2** an organization, company etc that is small and unimportant 微

不足道的组织[公司等]: *one of the minnows of the computer industry* 电脑业中微不足道的公司之一

2 2 **mi·nor¹** /ˈmaɪnə; ˈmaɪnə/ *adj* **1** small and not very important or serious, especially when compared with other things〔尤指与其他事物相比〕小的; 不很重要的; 不很严重的: *We have made some minor changes to the program.* 我们对那个计划作了一些小改动。| *an issue of minor importance* 次要的问题 | **minor illness/operation/injury** (=one that is not very serious or dangerous) 小病/小手术/轻伤 *minor head injuries* 头部轻伤 —opposite 反义词 MAJOR¹ (1) **2** based on a musical SCALE¹ (8) in which the third note of the related MAJOR¹ (4) scale has been lowered by a SEMITONE〔音乐〕小调的; 小音阶的: *a minor key* 小调 | *a symphony in D minor* D小调交响曲

minor² *n* [C] **1** *law* someone who is below the age at which they become legally responsible for their actions【法律】未成年人 **2** *especially AmE* a subject studied at university that has less importance and needs less work than your MAJOR (=main subject)【尤美】〔大学中的〕辅修科目 **3 the minors** the MINOR LEAGUES〔美国棒球的〕小联盟; 小企业, 小公司; 小的机构[组织]

minor³ *v*

minor in sth *phr v* [T] *especially AmE* to study an additional subject at university that is less important than your main subject【尤美】〔大学里〕副修〔某课程〕—opposite 反义词 MAJOR³

Mi·nor·ca /mɪˈnɔrkə; mɪ̣ˈnɔːkə/ also 又作 **Menorca** a Spanish island in the west Mediterranean Sea, one of the Balearic Islands, which is popular with tourists 梅诺卡岛〔西班牙一岛, 位于地中海西部, 属巴利阿里群岛, 深受旅游人士青睐〕

3 2 **mi·nor·i·ty¹** /məˋnɔrətɪ; maɪˈnɒrɪ̣ti/ *n* **1** [singular] a small group of people or things within a much larger group 少数派; 少数: *Gaelic is still spoken in Ireland by a tiny minority.* 在爱尔兰极少数人仍然说盖尔语。| [+of] *It's only in a minority of cases that the illness is fatal.* 只有在少数情况下这种疾病才是致命的。| [also+plural verb *BrE* 英] *Only a minority support these new laws.* 只有少数人支持这些新法律。**2** [C usually plural 一般用复数] **a)** a group of people in a country who are different from the rest in race or religion 少数民族; 宗教少数派: *People from ethnic minorities often face prejudice and discrimination.* 来自少数民族的人们常常面临偏见和歧视。**b)** *AmE* someone who belongs to a group like this【美】少数民族[宗教少数派]〔成员〕: *hiring minorities and women* 雇用少数民族和妇女 **3 be in the/a minority** to form less than half of a larger group 占少数: *Boys are very much in the minority at the dance class.* 在舞蹈班上男孩子占极少数。**4 be in a minority of one** to be the only person in a group who has a particular opinion 是孤家寡人, 得不到任何人的支持 **5** [U] *law* the period of time when someone is below the age at which they become legally responsible for their actions【法律】未成年期 —opposite 反义词 MAJORITY

minority² *adj* [only before noun 仅用于名词前] relating to people who form less than half of a larger group of people〔人〕少数的; 少数民族的: *a series of television programmes designed to appeal to minority interests* 一系列迎合少数人趣味的电视节目 | *a minority language* 少数民族语言

minority gov·ern·ment /ˌ... ˈ.../ *n* [C] a government that does not have enough politicians in parliament to control it without the support of other parties 少数党政府

minority lead·er /ˌ.'... ˌ../ *n* [C] *AmE* a leader of the political party that has fewer politicians in the lawmaking institutions than the leading party【美】〔国会中的〕少数党领袖 —compare 比较 MAJORITY LEADER

minor league /ˈ.. ./ *n* [C] **1** a group of professional BASEBALL teams in the US that are not as good as the teams in the MAJOR LEAGUES〔美国棒球的〕小联盟〔由水平低于职业棒球大联盟的球队组成〕 **2** *informal* small businesses and organizations, rather than large powerful ones【非正式】小企业, 小公司; 小的机构[组织] —**minor-league** *adj*

Min·o·taur, the /ˈmɪnəˌtɔr; ˈmɪnətɔː/ in ancient Greek stories, a creature which was half a man and half a BULL (=a male cow), which was kept in a LABYRINTH (=a complicated network of paths which it is difficult to find your way out of) and was given young men and women to eat. It was killed by Theseus. 弥诺陶洛斯〔古希腊神话中一半人半牛的怪物, 被关在迷宫, 吃的是少男少女, 后被忒修斯所杀〕

Minsk /mɪnsk; mɪnsk/ the capital city of Belarus, on the Svisloch River. It was badly damaged during the Second World War. 明斯克〔白俄罗斯首都, 位于斯维斯洛奇河上, 二战中曾遭到严重破坏〕

min·ster /ˈmɪnstə; ˈmɪnstə/ *n* [C] *BrE* a large or important church【英】大教堂: *York Minster* 约克大教堂

min·strel /ˈmɪnstrəl; ˈmɪnstrəl/ *n* [C] **1** a singer or musician in the Middle Ages〔中世纪的〕歌手; 乐师 **2** one of a group of singers and dancers who performed in popular shows in the 1920s〔20世纪20年代的〕歌舞团演员

mint¹ /mɪnt; mɪnt/ *n* **1** [C,U] a sweet that tastes of PEPPERMINT (=a strong tasting substance obtained from a plant) 薄荷糖 **2** [U] a small plant with leaves that have a fresh smell and taste and are used in cooking 薄荷属植物 **3 in mint condition** looking new and in perfect condition 崭新的; 完美的: *A copy in mint condition would fetch about £2,000.* 一份崭新的拷贝大约能卖2000英镑。**4 a mint** *informal* a large amount of money【非正式】一大笔钱: *Lynn won a mint in that competition!* 林恩在那次竞赛中赢了一大笔钱! **5** [C] a place where coins are officially made 铸币厂

mint² *v* [T] **1** to make a coin 铸〔币〕 **2** to invent new words, phrases, or ideas 创造〔新的词、短语或思想〕, 发明: *a recently minted phrase* 一个新创短语

mint ju·lep /ˌ. ˈ../ *n* [C] *AmE* a drink in which alcohol and sugar are mixed with ice and mint leaves are added【美】冰镇薄荷酒, 薄荷朱利酒

> **CULTURAL NOTE 文化注释**
>
> Americans connect this drink with summertime and the South, where it is popular. It is a custom to drink it while watching the Kentucky Derby, a famous horse race. 美国人会把冰镇薄荷酒与夏天和南方联系起来, 因为在美国南方这种酒很受欢迎。观看著名的赛马比赛肯塔基赛马会时饮用此酒是一种风俗。

mint·y /ˈmɪntɪ; ˈmɪnti/ *adj* tasting or smelling of mint 薄荷口味的; 薄荷气味的

min·u·et /ˌmɪnjuˈɛt; ˌmɪnjuˈet/ *n* [C] a slow graceful dance of the 17th and 18th century, or a piece of music for this dance〔17和18世纪的一种缓慢优美的〕小步舞, 米奴哀舞; 小步舞曲, 米奴哀舞曲

mi·nus¹ /ˈmaɪnəs; ˈmaɪnəs/ *prep* **1** used in mathematics when you SUBTRACT one number from another〔数学中〕减(去): *17 minus 5 is 12 (17−5 = 12).* 17减5等于12。**2 minus 5, 20 etc** less than zero, especially less than zero degrees in temperature 零下5度、20度等: *At night the temperature can go as low as minus 30.* 晚上气温能降至零下30度。**3** *informal* without something that would normally be there【非正式】没有, 缺少: *He came back minus a couple of front teeth.* 他回来时门牙少了两颗。—opposite 反义词 PLUS¹

minus² *n* [C] **1** also 又作 **minus sign** a sign (−) showing that a number is less than zero, or that the second of two numbers is to be subtracted (SUBTRACT) from the first 负号; 减号 **2** something that is a disadvantage because it makes a situation unpleasant 不利条件; 不足; 缺点: *There are both pluses and minuses to living in a big city.* 住在大城市里既有利也有弊。—opposite 反义词 PLUS²

minus³ *adj* **1 minus point/factor** *BrE* a quality that makes something or someone seem less good【英】弱点/不利因素: *Kirsten's very keen, but her inexperience is a definite minus factor.* 柯尔丝滕非常热心, 但她没有经验却是个明显的弱点。**2 A minus, B minus etc** a mark used in a system of marking students' work, A minus is lower than A, but higher than B plus A减(A−), B减(B−)等〔给学生打成绩时用〕—opposite 反义词 PLUS³

min·us·cule, miniscule /mɪˋnʌskjul; ˈmɪnɪ̣skjuːl/ *adj* extremely small 极小的: *a minuscule amount* 极少量 | *Her office is miniscule.* 她的办公室非常小。

min·ute¹ /ˈmɪnɪt; ˈmɪnɪ̣t/ *n* [C] 1 1

1 ►TIME 时间◄ one of the 60 parts into which an hour is divided 分, 分钟: *It takes me ten minutes to walk to work.* 我步行上班要用10分钟。| *The train arrived at four minutes past eight.* 火车于8点零4分到达。

2 at the last minute at the last possible time, just before it is too late 在最后一刻; 在紧要关头: *Clare changed her mind at the last minute and came with us.* 克莱尔在最后一刻改变了主意, 和我们一起来了。—see also 另见 LAST-MINUTE

3 by the minute also 又作 **every minute, minute by minute** *spoken* increasingly as time passes【口】每过一分钟; 越来越: *"Do you still feel sick?" "No, I'm feeling better by the minute."* "你还觉得恶心吗?" "不了, 我感觉越来越好了。"

4 love/enjoy/hate etc every minute of *informal* to love, enjoy etc all of something【非正式】特别喜欢/尽情享受/极其憎恨〔某物〕: *I went camping for a week and enjoyed every minute of it.* 我去野营了一周, 尽情享受了一下。

5 within minutes very soon after something has happened 片刻后，转瞬间：*The ambulance was there within minutes.* 片刻之后救护车就到那儿了。
6 ►MEETING 会议◄ minutes [plural] an official written record of what is said and decided at a meeting 会议记录，议事录
7 ►NOTE ON A REPORT 报告记录◄ a short official note on or about a document 简短的批示；备忘录
8 ►MATHEMATICS 数学◄ *technical* one of the 60 parts into which a degree of angle is divided【术语】分〔角的计量单位，即 1/60 度〕—see also 另见 UP-TO-THE-MINUTE

Frequencies of the noun **minute** in spoken and written English 名词 minute 在英语口语和书面语中的使用频率

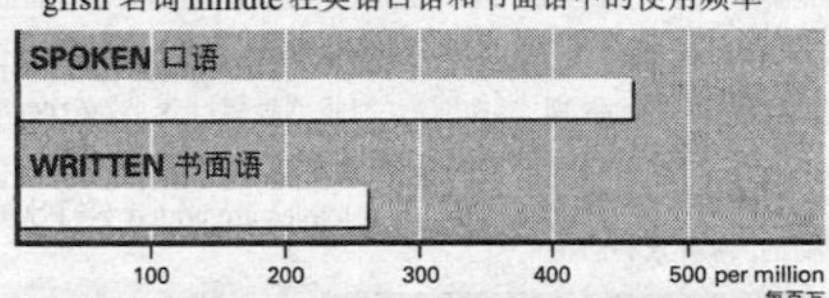

Based on the British National Corpus and the Longman Lancaster Corpus 据英国国家语料库和朗文兰开斯特语料库

This graph shows that the noun **minute** is much more common in spoken English than in written English. This is because it is used in a lot of common spoken phrases. 本图表显示，名词 minute 在英语口语中的使用频率远远高于书面语，因为口语中很多常用短语是由 minute 构成的。

minute (*n*) SPOKEN PHRASES
含 minute 的口语短语

9 a minute a very short period of time; MOMENT (2) 一会儿，片刻：*He was there a minute ago.* 他刚才还在那儿。| *Stay there a minute.* 在那里待一会儿。
10 in a minute very soon 很快，立刻，马上：*All right, I'll do it in a minute.* 好吧，我马上就做。| *Mr Gregson will be with you in a minute.* 格雷格森先生很快就到。
11 wait a minute/just a minute/hold on a minute/hang on a minute a) used to tell someone you want them to wait for a short time while you do or say something else 稍等片刻：*Wait a minute, I have to turn off the cooker.* 稍等一会儿，我得关掉炉具。| *Just a minute, I'll see if she's in.* 请等一下，我看看她在不在。**b)** used to tell someone to stop speaking or doing something for a short time because they have said or done something wrong 且慢：*Hold on a minute! That can't be right.* 且慢！那不可能是正确的。
12 any minute now used to say that something will happen extremely soon 随时，马上，在任何时刻：*We're expecting them any minute now.* 他们随时会到。
13 have you got a minute? *BrE*【英】, **do you have a minute?** *AmE*【美】used to ask someone if it is convenient for you to talk to them for a short time 能耽误你一点时间吗？：*Have you got a minute? I've got a problem.* 能耽误你一点时间吗？我有一个问题。
14 one minute a) used to say that a situation suddenly changes 一会儿〔表示情况突然变化〕：*One minute they're madly in love and the next they've split up again.* 他们一会儿爱得发狂，一会儿又分手了。**b)** used to ask someone to wait for a short time while you do something else 稍等一会儿：*One minute Stephen, let me finish this.* 斯蒂芬，请稍等片刻，让我先把这个做完。
15 the minute sb does sth as soon as someone does something 某人一做某事就…：*Tell him I need to see him the minute he arrives.* 他一到就告诉他我要见他。
16 the next minute immediately afterwards 马上，立刻，紧接着：*I put down the phone and the next minute it rang again.* 我刚放下电话，电话铃声马上又响了起来。
17 not think/believe etc for one minute used to say that you certainly do not think something, believe something etc 一点也不认为/相信等：*I don't think for one minute that he'll do it but I have to ask.* 我一点也不认为他会去做那件事，但我必须问一下。
18 this minute used to tell someone, often angrily, to do something immediately 立刻，马上〔用于叫人马上做某事，常带有怒意〕：*Johnny! Get inside, this minute!* 约翰尼！到里面来，马上！

mi·nute² /məˋnjut; maɪˈnjuːt/ *adj* **1** extremely small 极小的：*There's been a minute improvement in sales figures.* 销售额有了一点上涨。| *Her handwriting is minute.* 她的字非常小。**2** paying careful attention to the smallest details 非常仔细的，极详细的：*a minute examination of the rock* 仔细检查那块岩石 | **in minute detail** *He explained the plan in minute detail.* 他非常详细地解释了那个计划。—**minutely** *adv* —**minuteness** *n* [U]

min·ute³ /ˋmɪnɪt; ˈmɪnɪ̯t/ *v* [T] *especially BrE* to make an official note of something in the record of a meeting【尤英】将…记入议事录[会议记录]

minute hand /ˋmɪnɪt hænd; ˈmɪnɪ̯t hænd/ *n* [C] the long thin piece of metal that points to the minutes on a clock or watch〔钟、表的〕分针

min·ute·man /ˋmɪnɪtmæn; ˈmɪnɪ̯tmæn/ *n* [C] *AmE* one of a group of men in the past who were not official soldiers but who were ready to fight at any time【美】〔旧时〕随时应召的民兵

mi·nu·ti·ae /mɪˋnjuʃɪˌi; maɪˈnjuːʃiaɪ/ *n* [plural] very small and exact but unimportant details〔准确但不重要的〕微小细节，细枝末节

minx /mɪŋks; mɪŋks/ *n* [C] *old-fashioned* a girl who is not RESPECTFUL and is very good at getting what she wants【过时】无礼而工于心计的女孩

mips /mɪps; mɪps/ *n* [plural] *technical* million instructions per second; a way of measuring how fast a computer works【术语】〔电脑运行速度〕每秒百万条指令

mir·a·cle /ˋmɪrəkḷ; ˈmɪrəkəl/ *n* [C] **1** something lucky that you did not expect to happen or did not think was possible 意外的奇事，不可思议的事；奇迹：*By some miracle, we managed to catch the plane.* 令人有些不可思议的是，我们竟然赶上了飞机。| **it is a miracle (that)** *It's a miracle you weren't killed!* 你没有死真是奇迹！**2** an action or event that is impossible according to the ordinary laws of nature, believed to be done by God〔神创造的〕奇迹：*the miracles of Jesus* 耶稣创造的奇迹 **3 miracle cure/drug** a very effective medical treatment that cures even serious diseases 有奇效的疗法/药物 **4 work/perform miracles** to have a very good effect or result 创造奇迹；有奇效：*Maybe you should try yoga – it worked miracles for me.* 也许你该试一试瑜伽——它对我有惊人的效果。**5 a miracle of engineering/design etc** something that is produced or invented that is a very impressive example of a particular quality or skill 工程学/设计等上的奇迹：*This new electronic notebook is a miracle of miniaturization.* 这种新型电子笔记本是微型化技术的一项奇迹。

mi·rac·u·lous /məˋrækjələs; mɪˈrækjʊ̯ləs/ *adj* completely unexpected and usually resulting from extreme good luck 不可思议的；神奇的；非凡的：**miraculous recovery/escape/improvement** *It was thought she only had a month to live but she made a miraculous recovery.* 人们认为她只有一个月的寿命，但她却奇迹般康复了。—**miraculously** *adv*

mi·rage /məˋrɑʒ; ˈmɪrɑːʒ/ *n* [C] **1** a strange effect caused by hot air in a desert, in which you think you can see objects when they are not actually there〔沙漠里的〕海市蜃楼 **2** a dream, hope, or wish that cannot come true 梦想，幻想，妄想

Mi·ran·da /mɪˋrændə; mɪˈrændə/ the daughter of Prospero in the play *The Tempest* by William Shakespeare 米兰达〔莎士比亚剧本《暴风雨》中普洛斯彼罗的女儿〕

Miranda, Carmen (1913-55) a Brazilian actress and singer, who appeared in MUSICALS (=films that use singing and dancing to tell a story) and was famous for her hats decorated with fruit 米兰达（1913-1955），巴西女演员、歌手，主演过音乐片，以戴水果装饰的帽子闻名〕

Miranda de·ci·sion, the a 1966 decision by the US Supreme Court that said it was necessary for police, when arresting people, to tell them about their legal rights 米兰达判决〔1966 年美国最高法院作出的一项判决。根据这一判决，警方在拘捕时必须告知嫌疑人他们所拥有的合法权利〕

Miranda rights in the US, the legal rights that a person being arrested by the police must be told about. These include the 'right to remain silent' (to not say anything) and the right to get advice from a lawyer. These rights were established by the **Miranda decision** of the US Supreme Court in 1966, in the case of *Miranda v. Arizona.* 米兰达权利〔美国警察拘捕嫌疑人时必须告知他们应有的合法权利，其中包括沉默权和咨询律师权。这些权利是根据 1966 年米兰达诉亚利桑那州一案的"米兰达判决"确定的〕

mire¹ /maɪr; maɪə/ *n* [U] *literary*【文】**1 drag sb's name through the mire** to talk about someone publicly in a way that brings shame on them 玷污某人的名声，辱没某人 **2 in/into the**

mire more and more deeply involved in problems 处于/陷入困境中: *The Party sank deeper into the mire of conflict.* 该党在冲突的泥潭里陷得更深了。**3** deep mud 泥潭, 泥坑

mire² *v* **be mired (down) in** *especially literary*【尤文】**a)** to be stuck in deep mud 陷入〔泥潭〕: *The plane's wheels were deeply mired in waterlogged ground.* 飞机的轮子深深地陷进泥沼地中。**b)** to be in a very difficult situation 陷入〔困境〕

Mi·ró /mɪˋro; mɪˈrəʊ/, **Joán** /ʒʊˋan; ʒʊˈɑːn/ (1893-1983) a Spanish SURREALIST painter, famous for his use of bright colours and abstract shapes 米罗〔(1893-1983), 西班牙超现实主义画家, 以使用鲜艳色彩和抽象图案著称〕

S3 W3 **mir·ror¹** /ˋmɪrɚ; ˈmɪrə/ *n* [C] **1** a piece of special flat glass that you can look at and see yourself in 镜子: *Check your rearview and side mirrors before you drive away.* 开车之前检查一下后视镜和侧视镜。—see picture on page A2 参见 A2 页图 **2 a mirror of** something that gives a clear idea of what something else is like 清楚地反映…的东西: *We believe the polls are an accurate mirror of public opinion.* 我们认为这些民意测验结果准确地反映了公众的意见。

mirror² *v* [T] **1** if something mirrors a situation, fact, belief etc, it is very similar to it and gives a clear idea of what it is like 反映〔情况、事实、信念等〕: *The discussion mirrored the general attitudes prevalent in the local area.* 这一讨论反映了当地人的普遍态度。**2** to be very similar to something or a copy of it 与…十分相似; 与…完全一样: *Victor's expression mirrored her own, both of them staring in amazement.* 维克托的表情和她自己的一个样, 两个人都惊讶得傻了眼。

Mirror, The a British daily TABLOID newspaper owned by Mirror Group Newspapers. It usually supports the Labour Party. 《镜报》〔英国镜报报业集团每日出版的一种通俗小报, 通常支持工党〕

mirror im·age /ˈ··, ·ˈ/ *n* [C+of] **1** an image of something in which the right side appears on the left, and the left side appears on the right 镜像 **2** something that is either very similar to something else or is the complete opposite of it 与…十分相似[完全相反]的事物: *Davy's messiness is the mirror image of his sister Dora's neatness.* 戴维的邋遢与他姐姐多拉的干净整洁形成了鲜明的对照。

mirth /mɝθ; mɜːθ/ *n* [U] *literary* happiness and laughter【文】欢乐; 欢笑: *Stifled laughter and cries of suppressed mirth issued from the next room.* 隔壁房间传来了压低的欢笑声。—**mirthful** *adj* —**mirthfully** *adv*

mirth·less /ˋmɝθlɪs; ˈmɜːθləs/ *adj literary* mirthless laughter or a mirthless smile does not seem to be caused by real amusement or happiness【文】〔微笑等〕没有欢乐的, 忧郁的, 阴郁的; 悲哀的: *Now it's your turn, he said with a mirthless grin.* 现在轮到你了, 他咧嘴苦笑着说道。—**mirthlessly** *adv*

mis- /mɪs; mɪs/ *prefix* **1** bad or badly 坏的[地]: *misfortune* (=bad luck) 不幸 | *He's been misbehaving.* 他一直行为不端。**2** wrong or wrongly 错的; 错误地: *a miscalculation* 误算 | *I misunderstood what you said.* 我误解了你的话。**3** shows an opposite or the lack of something 不; 相反; 缺少: *mistrust* 不信任

mis·ad·ven·ture /ˌmɪsədˋvɛntʃɚ; ˌmɪsədˈventʃə/ *n* [C,U] **1 death by misadventure** *BrE law* the official name for an accidental death【英, 法律】意外致死[死亡] **2** *literary* bad luck or an accident【文】不幸, 灾难; 事故

mis·al·li·ance /ˌmɪsəˋlaɪəns; ˌmɪsəˈlaɪəns/ *n* [C] *informal* a situation in which two people or organizations have mistakenly agreed to work together, marry each other etc, but are not suitable for each other【非正式】不适当的结合[联合]; 不匹配的婚姻

mis·an·thro·pist /mɪsˋænθrəpɪst; mɪsˈænθrəpɪ̈st/ also 又作 **misanthrope** /ˋmɪsənˌθrop; ˈmɪsənθrəʊp/ *n* [C] *formal* someone who dislikes other people and prefers to be alone【正式】厌恶人类者; 性情孤僻的人, 遁世者 —**misanthropic** /ˌmɪsənˋθrɑpɪk; ˌmɪsənˈθrɒpɪk◂/ *adj* —**misanthropy** *n* [U]

mis·ap·ply /ˌmɪsəˋplaɪ; ˌmɪsəˈplaɪ/ *v* [T] to use a principle, rule etc incorrectly or for a wrong purpose 误用; 用错; 滥用 —**misapplication** /ˌmɪsæpləˋkeʃən; ˌmɪsæplɪ̈ˈkeɪʃən/ *n* [U+of]: *a misapplication of the law* 法律的误用

mis·ap·pre·hend /ˌmɪsæprɪˋhɛnd; ˌmɪsæprɪˈhend/ *v* [T] *formal* to understand something wrongly【正式】误解, 误会

mis·ap·pre·hen·sion /ˌmɪsæprɪˋhɛnʃən; ˌmɪsæprɪˈhenʃən/ *n* [C] *formal* a mistaken belief or a wrong understanding of something【正式】误会, 误解: **(labour) under a misapprehension** (=believe something is true when in fact it is not) 误认为 *I wonder if others are under the misapprehension that screwdrivers used to test electricity are infallible.* 我想知道其他人是否会错误地认为用螺丝刀来测试电流是绝对可靠的。

mis·ap·pro·pri·ate /ˌmɪsəˋpropriˌet; ˌmɪsəˈprəʊprieɪt/ *v* [T] *formal* to dishonestly take something that you have been trusted to keep safe, for example to take money that belongs to your employer; EMBEZZLE【正式】侵吞; 私占; 挪用; 盗用 —**misappropriation** /ˌmɪsəproprɪˋeʃən; ˌmɪsəprəʊpriˈeɪʃən/ *n* [U+of]: *the misappropriation of treasury funds* 盗用国库资金

mis·be·got·ten /ˌmɪsbɪˋgɑtn̩; ˌmɪsbɪˈgɒtn◂/ *adj* [only before noun 仅用于名词前] **1** a misbegotten plan, idea, etc is not likely to succeed because it is badly planned or not sensible〔计划、想法等〕难以成功的; 不周详的; 不合理的 **2** *formal or humorous* a misbegotten person is completely stupid or useless【正式或幽默】〔人〕非常愚蠢的; 完全无用的: *You misbegotten fool!* 你个大笨蛋!

mis·be·have /ˌmɪsbɪˋhev; ˌmɪsbɪˈheɪv/ *v* [I] also 又作 **misbehave yourself** to behave badly, and cause trouble or annoy people 行为不端; 举止不检点: *William has been misbehaving himself at school.* 威廉在学校行为不端。

mis·be·ha·viour *BrE*【英】, **misbehavior** *AmE*【美】/ˌmɪsbɪˋhevjɚ; ˌmɪsbɪˈheɪvjə/ *n* [U] behaviour that is not acceptable to other people 不良行为; 不正当的举止: *Even the most minor forms of misbehaviour were punished.* 即使最轻微的不良行为也受到了惩罚。

mis·cal·cu·late /mɪsˋkælkjəˌlet; ˌmɪsˈkælkjʊ̈leɪt/ *v* [I,T] **1** to make a mistake when deciding how long something will take to do, how much money you will need etc 误算, 算错: *The contractor miscalculated the costs of rebuilding.* 承包商算错了重建所需的费用。**2** to make a wrong judgment about a situation 对(局势)判断错误

mis·cal·cu·la·tion /ˌmɪskælkjəˋleʃən; mɪsˌkælkjʊ̈ˈleɪʃən/ *n* [C] **1** a mistake made in deciding how long something will take to do, how much money you will need etc 误算, 错算 **2** a wrong judgment about a situation 错误判断

mis·car·riage /mɪsˋkærɪdʒ; ˌmɪsˈkærɪdʒ/ *n* [C,U] the act of accidentally giving birth too early for the baby to live 流产, 小产: **have a miscarriage** *Unfortunately, she had a miscarriage at four months.* 不幸的是, 她怀孕四个月时流产了。—compare 比较 ABORTION, STILLBIRTH

miscarriage of jus·tice /ˌ·ˈ···ˈ··/ *n* [C,U] a situation in which someone is wrongly punished by a court of law for something they did not do 误判; 审判不公

mis·car·ry /mɪsˋkærɪ; mɪsˈkæri/ *v* [I] **1** to give birth to a baby too early for it to live 流产, 小产 —compare 比较 ABORT (3) **2** *formal* if a plan miscarries, it is not successful【正式】〔计划〕失败

mis·cast /mɪsˋkæst; ˌmɪsˈkɑːst/ *v past tense and past participle* **miscast** [T usually passive 一般用被动态] to choose an unsuitable actor to play a particular character in a play or film 选择不合适的演员去演〔某个角色〕

mis·ce·ge·na·tion /ˌmɪsɪdʒəˋneʃən; ˌmɪsɪ̈dʒɪ̈ˈneɪʃən/ *n* [U] *formal* the act of having children by parents of different races, especially when one of the parents is white【正式】异族通婚生育子女〔尤指父母一方为白种人〕

mis·cel·la·ne·ous /ˌmɪslˋenɪəs; ˌmɪsəˈleɪniəs◂/ *adj* [only before noun 仅用于名词前] made up of many different things or people who do not seem to be connected with each other〔人或物〕各色各样混在一起的, 混杂的; 多种多样的: *a miscellaneous assortment of books* 各种各样的书籍 | *miscellaneous expenses* 杂费, 杂项开支

mis·cel·la·ny /ˋmɪslˌenɪ; mɪˈseləni/ *n* [C] a collection of different things 大杂烩; 杂集, 杂录: *a miscellany of American short stories* 美国短篇小说杂集

mis·chance /mɪsˋtʃæns; ˌmɪsˈtʃɑːns/ *n* [C,U] bad luck, or a situation that results from bad luck 不幸, 厄运; 不幸的事: *As mischance would have it we ran into Sue – just the person we wanted to avoid.* 倒霉的是我们遇上了休 — 我们想躲着的那个人。

mis·chief /ˋmɪstʃɪf; ˈmɪstʃɪ̈f/ *n* **1** [U] bad behaviour, especially by children, that causes trouble or damage, but no serious harm 恶作剧, 捣蛋, 胡闹: **get into mischief** (=behave in a way that causes trouble) 胡闹, 捣蛋 *Now run along, and don't get into mischief.* 好了, 走吧, 不要捣乱。| **be up to mischief** (=plan or do something you know you should not do) 捣鬼, 搞恶作剧 *If you can't see Nick, you can be sure he's up to some mischief.* 如果看不到尼克, 可以肯定他又在搞什么鬼。| **keep (sb) out of mischief** *They've got enough toys to keep them out of mischief for a while.* 有足够的玩具使他们暂时不捣蛋。**2** [U] enjoyment of playing tricks on people or embarrassing them 顽皮, 调皮, 淘气: *Helena's eyes flashed with amusement and mischief.* 海伦娜的眼里闪现出快乐而顽皮的神色。**3 make mis-**

M

chief (between) *informal* to deliberately cause quarrels or unfriendly feelings between people【非正式】(在…之间)挑拨离间,搬弄是非 **4 do yourself a mischief** *BrE humorous* to injure yourself slightly【英,幽默】〔轻微地〕伤害自己: *If you try to lift that box, you'll do yourself a mischief.* 如果你试图搬起那个箱子,你会伤着自己。**5** [U] *formal* damage or harm that may or may not have been intended【正式】(有意[无心]的)损坏[伤害]

mischief-mak·er /ˈ‥ ˌ‥/ *n* [C] someone who deliberately causes trouble or quarrels 惹是生非的人; 搬弄是非者, 挑拨离间者

mis·chie·vous /ˋmɪstʃɪvəs; ˈmɪstʃɪvəs/ *adj* **1** liking to have fun, especially by playing tricks on people or doing things to annoy or embarrass them 调皮的, 淘气的; 恶作剧的: *a mischievous boy* 淘气的男孩 | **mischievous smile/expression etc** *Gabby looked at him with a mischievous grin.* 加比看着他, 调皮地咧着嘴笑。**2** causing trouble or quarrels deliberately 引起麻烦的; 造成不和的: *a mischievous remark* 挑拨离间的言论 —**mischievously** *adv* —**mischievousness** *n* [U]

mis·con·ceived /ˌmɪskənˋsivd; ˌmɪskənˈsiːvd◂/ *adj* **1** a misconceived plan will not succeed because it is stupid or has not been carefully thought about〔指计划〕愚蠢的, 考虑不周的 **2** a misconceived idea is based on a wrong understanding of something〔指想法〕建立在对…误解基础上的; 设想错误的: *a misconceived notion of what acting really involves* 对表演真正包含的内容的错误看法

mis·con·cep·tion /ˌmɪskənˋsɛpʃən; ˌmɪskənˈsepʃən/ *n* [C, U] an idea which is wrong or untrue, but which people believe because they do not understand it properly 错误想法, 误解; 错误印象: [**+that**] *the misconception that unemployment can be cured by government intervention* 认为政府干预能消除失业的错误想法 | **a popular/common misconception** (=a wrong idea that a lot of people believe) 普遍的/常见的误解 *It is a popular misconception that eye problems result in headaches.* 认为眼病会引起头痛是一个普遍的误解。

mis·con·duct /mɪsˋkɑndʌkt; ˌmɪsˈkɒndʌkt/ *n* [U] *formal* bad or dishonest behaviour by someone in a position of authority or trust【正式】不端行为; 不诚实行为; 胡作非为: *allegations of misconduct by council officials* 有关市政会官员滥用职权的指控 | **gross misconduct** (=very serious misconduct) 严重的不端行为 *One of the doctors had been dismissed for gross professional misconduct.* 其中一名医生因严重的职业行为不端已被免职。

mis·con·struc·tion /ˌmɪskənˋstrʌkʃən; ˌmɪskənˈstrʌkʃən/ *n* [C,U] *formal* an incorrect or mistaken understanding of something【正式】误解, 曲解: **open to misconstruction** (=easy to misunderstand) 易被误解 *A law must be worded so carefully that it is not open to misconstruction.* 法律措辞必须严谨以不被人曲解。

mis·con·strue /ˌmɪskənˋstru; ˌmɪskənˈstruː/ *v* [T] *formal* to misunderstand something that someone has said or done【正式】误解

mis·count /mɪsˋkaunt; ˌmɪsˈkaʊnt/ *v* [I,T] to count wrongly 算错, 数错: *Oops! Sorry, I miscounted – we need ten copies, not nine.* 哎哟! 对不起, 我数错了 —— 我们需要十份, 不是九份。

mis·cre·ant /ˋmɪskrɪənt; ˈmɪskriənt/ *n* [C] *old use* a bad person who causes trouble, hurts people etc【旧】坏蛋, 恶棍, 歹徒, 无赖

mis·deed /mɪsˋdid; ˌmɪsˈdiːd/ *n* [C] *formal* a wrong or illegal action【正式】错误行为; 违法行为; 罪行: *No one ever suspected the seriousness of his misdeeds.* 从来没有人怀疑过他违法行为的严重性。

mis·de·mea·nour *BrE*【英】, **misdemeanor** *AmE*【美】/ˌmɪsdɪˋminɚ; ˌmɪsdɪˈmiːnə/ *n* [C] **1** *formal* a bad or unacceptable action that is not very serious【正式】不很严重的恶劣行为: *Alfred beat his children for even the smallest misdemeanour.* 孩子们哪怕有最轻微的不端行为, 艾尔弗雷德也会打他们。**2** *law* a crime that is not very serious【法律】轻罪 —compare 比较 FELONY

mis·di·ag·nose /ˌmɪsdaɪəgˋnos; ˌmɪsdaɪəgˈnəʊz/ *v* [T usually passive 一般用被动态] to give an incorrect explanation of an illness, a problem in a machine etc 误诊

mis·di·rect /ˌmɪsdəˋrɛkt; ˌmɪsdʒˈrekt/ *v* [T usually passive 一般用被动态] **1** *formal* to use your efforts, energy or abilities in a wrong or unsuitable way【正式】误用, 错用〔精力或能力〕, 使用…不当: *We believe their efforts to prevent animal testing are misdirected.* 我们认为他们阻止动物实验的努力是把精力用错了地方。**2** if a judge misdirects a JURY (=the group of people who decide a legal case), he or she gives them incorrect information about the law〔法官对陪审团〕作错误引导 **3** *formal* to send someone or something to the wrong place【正式】把…送错地方 —**misdirection** /-ˋrɛkʃən; -ˈrekʃən/ *n* [U]

mise-en-scène /ˌmizɑ̃ˋsɛn; ˌmiːz ɒn ˈsen/ *n* [C] *French*【法】**1** *technical* the arrangement of furniture and other objects used on the stage in a theatre play【术语】舞台布置〔对道具等的布局安排〕; 舞台调度 **2** *formal* the environment in which an event takes place【正式】〔事件的〕环境, 背景

mi·ser /ˋmaɪzɚ; ˈmaɪzə/ *n* [C] someone who hates spending money and likes saving it 守财奴, 吝啬鬼, 小气鬼: *A typical miser, he hid his money in the house in various places.* 他是个典型的守财奴, 把钱藏在房子里多个不同的地方。

mis·e·ra·ble /ˋmɪzərəbḷ; ˈmɪzərəbəl/ *adj* **1** extremely unhappy, for example because you feel lonely, cold, or badly treated 极不愉快的, 痛苦的: *You're making my life miserable!* 你使我的生活痛苦不堪! | *There's nothing like a bad cold to make you feel miserable.* 没有什么能像重感冒那样使人感到难受。| *You look miserable. What's up?* 你看上去愁眉苦脸的, 怎么啦? **2** always unhappy, dissatisfied, or complaining 总是不高兴[不满意]的; 总是抱怨的: *He's a miserable old devil.* 他是个终日郁郁不乐的老家伙。**3** [usually before noun 一般用于名词前] making you feel very unhappy, uncomfortable etc 令人不愉快的; 令人不舒服的, 使人难受的: *They endured hours of backbreaking work in miserable conditions.* 他们忍受了数小时恶劣条件下繁重的劳动。**4** [only before noun 仅用于名词前] very bad in quality, or very small in amount 质量极差的; 数量极少的: *I can hardly afford the rent on my miserable income.* 靠我微薄的收入我几乎连房租都交不起。—**miserably** *adv*: *miserably cold and wet* 极度寒冷和潮湿

mi·ser·ly /ˋmaɪzɚlɪ; ˈmaɪzəli/ *adj* **1** a miserly amount, salary etc is one that is much too small 小[少]得可怜的: *a miserly 4% pay rise* 区区4%的工资增长 **2** a miserly person is one who hates spending money 守财奴的, 吝啬鬼的, 爱钱如命的 —**miserliness** *n* [U]

mis·e·ry /ˋmɪzərɪ; ˈmɪzəri/ *n* **1** [C,U] great suffering or discomfort, caused for example by being very poor or very sick 痛苦, 难受; 苦难: *the awful shantytowns, so full of human misery* 条件极差的棚户区, 充满了如此之多人类的苦难 | [**+of**] *The cold increased the misery of the retreating army.* 寒冷使后撤部队的状况更加悲惨。**2** [C,U] great unhappiness 极大的不幸; 愁苦, 悲苦: *Her face was a picture of misery.* 她一脸苦相。**3 make sb's life a misery** to cause so much trouble for someone that they cannot enjoy their life 使某人的日子不好过, 使某人的生活充满痛苦: *Competitive mothers can make their daughters' lives a misery.* 争强好胜的母亲会使自己女儿的日子不好过。**4 put sth/sb out of their misery a)** *informal* to make someone stop feeling worried, especially by telling them something they are waiting to hear【非正式】〔尤指通过告诉其想了解之事〕使某人不再感到忧虑[不安]: *Go on, put them out of their misery and announce the winner.* 说下去, 别再让他们忐忑不安了, 宣布谁是获胜者吧。**b)** to kill an animal in order to end its suffering 杀死动物以结束其痛苦 **5** [C] *BrE spoken* someone who is always complaining and never enjoys anything【英口】满腹牢骚的人: *Don't be such a misery.* 别埋怨个没完。| **misery guts** (=a name for someone who is like this) 牢骚包 *You don't want to be like old misery guts over there.* 你不会想成为那儿的一个老牢骚包吧?

mis·field /ˌmɪsˋfild; ˌmɪsˈfiːld/ *v* [I,T] to make a mistake in catching or throwing the ball in some ball games, such as cricket〔板球等〕接[掷]球失误 —**misfield** /ˋmɪsfild; ˈmɪsfiːld/ *n* [C]

mis·fire /mɪsˋfaɪr; ˌmɪsˈfaɪə/ *v* [I] **1** if a plan or joke misfires, it does not have the result that you intended〔计划或笑话〕未达到预期的效果; 失败 **2** if an engine misfires, the petrol mixture does not burn at the right time〔发动机〕不发火, 发动不起来 **3** if a gun misfires, the bullet does not come out〔枪〕发射不出子弹 —**misfire** /ˋmɪsfaɪr; ˈmɪsfaɪə/ *n* [C]

mis·fit /ˋmɪsˌfɪt; ˈmɪsˌfɪt/ *n* [C] someone who does not seem to belong in a place because they are very different from the other people there 不适应环境的人: *a social misfit* 与社会格格不入的人

mis·for·tune /mɪsˋfɔrtʃən; mɪsˈfɔːtʃən/ *n* [C,U] very bad luck, or something that happens to you as a result of bad luck 不幸, 厄运; 不幸事故; 灾难: *It seems the banks always profit from farmers' misfortunes.* 银行似乎总是从农民的灾祸中获益。| **have the misfortune to do sth** *The French soldiers had the misfortune to be caught in the crossfire.* 那些法国士兵不幸受到了交叉火力的袭击。

mis·giv·ing /mɪsˋgɪvɪŋ; ˌmɪsˈgɪvɪŋ/ *n* [C,U] a feeling of doubt, distrust, or fear about what might happen or about whether some-

thing is right 疑虑; 担忧; 害怕: *She eyed Bert's pistol with misgiving.* 她恐惧地盯着伯特的手枪。| **have deep/serious misgivings** *Opponents of nuclear energy have deep misgivings about its safety.* 反核人士对核能的安全性深感疑虑。

mis·guid·ed /mɪsˋgaɪdɪd; mɪsˈgaɪdɪ̣d/ *adj* **1** intended to be helpful but in fact making a situation worse 帮倒忙的: *a well-meaning but misguided attempt to bring her parents back together* 想使她父母重归于好却帮了倒忙的好心尝试 **2** a misguided idea or opinion is wrong because it is based on a wrong understanding of a situation〔基于对情况的误解而观点〕错误的: *They cling to the misguided belief that only big name managers can bring big time success.* 他们坚持只有大名鼎鼎的经理才能创造一流的业绩这一错误看法。—**misguidedly** *adv*

mis·han·dle /mɪsˋhændḷ; ˌmɪsˈhændl/ *v* [T] **1** to deal with a situation badly, because of a lack of skill or care 对…处理不当: *The Prime Minister admitted that the water privatisation had been mishandled.* 首相承认供水私营化的问题没有处理好。**2** to treat something roughly, often causing damage 粗暴对待, 胡乱使用〔某物〕

mis·hap /ˋmɪsˌhæp; ˈmɪshæp/ *n* [C,U] a small accident or mistake that does not have very serious results 小事故; 小错误: *a slight mishap with the glasses* 眼镜出的小问题 | **without mishap** *Only one horse finished the course without mishap.* 只有一匹马平安地跑完了全程。

mis·hear /mɪsˋhɪr; ˌmɪsˈhɪə/ *v past tense and past participle* **misheard** /-ˋhɝd; -ˈhɜːd/ [I,T] to not properly hear what someone says, so that you think they said something different 听错, 误听: *It seemed a strange question; I wondered if I had misheard.* 这好像是一个古怪的问题, 我怀疑自己是不是听错了。

Mish·i·ma /ˋmɪʃɪmə; ˈmɪʃɪmə/, **Yu·ki·o** /ˋjukɪo; ˈjuːkiəʊ/ (1925-70) a Japanese writer who most people consider to be the most important Japanese writer of NOVELs in the 20th century. He wrote about modern Japan and wanted to return to older, more traditional Japanese values. His best-known books include *Confessions of a Mask* and *The Sea of Fertility*. He killed himself using the traditional Japanese method of HARAKIRI after a military COUP by his small private army was unsuccessful. 三岛由纪夫〔(1925-1970), 日本作家, 被视为是20世纪最有影响力的日本小说作家。他的作品以现代日本为题材, 希望回归日本以前的传统价值观。最著名的作品有《虚假的告白》和《丰饶之海》。他率领一支小规模私家军队发动政变, 失败后按照日本传统方式剖腹自杀〕

mis·hit /ˌmɪsˋhɪt; ˌmɪsˈhɪt/ *v* [T] to hit a ball badly, especially in GOLF〔尤指在打高尔夫球中〕误击〔球〕—**mishit** /ˋmɪshɪt; ˈmɪshɪt/ *n* [C]

mish·mash /ˋmɪʃˌmæʃ; ˈmɪʃmæʃ/ *n* [singular] *informal* a mixture with no particular order in its design or in the choice of what is included【非正式】混杂物, 大杂烩; HOTCHPOTCH *BrE*【英】: [+of] *The magazine is a jumbled mishmash of jokes, stories, and serious news.* 这本杂志是把笑话、故事和严肃新闻乱凑在一起的大杂烩。

Mish·nah, the /ˋmɪʃnə; ˈmɪʃnə/ a collection of Jewish traditions that form the Jewish law, on which the Talmud is based《密西拿》〔犹太教律法汇编, 构成了《塔木德》的基础〕

mis·in·form /ˌmɪsɪnˋfɔrm; ˌmɪsɪnˈfɔːm/ *v* [T usually passive 一般用被动态] to give someone information that is incorrect or untrue 向〔某人〕提供错误信息, 向…误报

mis·in·for·ma·tion /ˌmɪsɪnfɚˋmeʃən; ˌmɪsɪnfəˈmeɪʃən/ *n* [U] incorrect information, especially when deliberately intended to deceive people〔尤指故意骗人的〕错误信息, 错误情报 —compare 比较 DISINFORMATION

mis·in·ter·pret /ˌmɪsɪnˋtɝprɪt; ˌmɪsɪnˈtɜːprɪ̣t/ *v* [T] to not understand the correct meaning of something that someone says or does, or to explain something wrongly to other people 对…误解, 错误地解释: *Liam misinterpreted her friendly offer of a lift home.* 利亚姆误解了她邀他搭车回家的友好用意。—**misinterpretation** /ˌmɪsɪnˌtɝprɪˋteʃən; ˌmɪsɪntɜːprɪ̣ˈteɪʃən/ *n* [C,U]: *a misinterpretation of the test results* 对检验结果的误解

mis·judge /mɪsˋdʒʌdʒ; ˌmɪsˈdʒʌdʒ/ *v* [T] **1** to form a wrong or unfair opinion about a person or situation 对〔人或情况〕错误判断: *The defeat showed how badly he'd misjudged the mood of the electorate.* 这次失败表明他对选民情绪的判断大错特错。**2** to guess an amount, distance etc wrongly 推测错误, 错误地估计〔数量、距离等〕: *I misjudged the turn and hit the sidewalk.* 我在拐弯处判断错误, 撞上了人行道。—**misjudgment** or **misjudgement** *n* [C,U]

mis·lay /mɪsˋle; mɪsˈleɪ/ *v past tense and past participle* **mislaid** /-ˋled; -ˈleɪd/ [T] to put something somewhere, then forget where you put it; MISPLACE 忘记把…放在何处, 一时找不到〔某物〕: *I've mislaid my glasses again.* 我又忘记把眼镜放在什么地方了。

mis·lead /mɪsˋlid; mɪsˈliːd/ *v past tense and past participle* **misled** /-ˋlɛd; -ˈled/ [T] to make someone believe something that is not true by giving them false or incomplete information 将…引入歧途, 误导: *McFarlane admitted that he had misled Congress about aid to the Contra.* 麦克法兰承认就向〔尼加拉瓜〕反政府势力提供援助一事他误导了国会。| **don't be misled by** *Don't be misled by appearances, he's a very competent worker.* 不要被表象迷惑, 他是一个非常能干的工人。

mis·lead·ing /mɪsˋlidɪŋ; mɪsˈliːdɪŋ/ *adj* likely to make someone believe something that is not true 易使人误信的; 误导人的; 骗人的: *The article was misleading, and the newspaper has apologized.* 那篇文章误导读者, 那家报纸已致歉了。—**misleadingly** *adv*: *"You imply, misleadingly, that you knew nothing about it," accused the prosecutor.* "你, 以误导人的方式, 暗示你对此一无所知。"检控官指控道。

mis·man·age /mɪsˋmænɪdʒ; ˌmɪsˈmænɪdʒ/ *v* [T] if someone mismanages something they are in charge of, they deal with it badly 对…管理不善, 对…经营不当: *The nation's finances had been badly mismanaged.* 该国的财政管理非常紊乱。—**mismanagement** *n* [U]

mis·match /ˌmɪsˋmætʃ; ˈmɪsmætʃ/ *n* [C] a combination of things or people that do not work well together or are not suitable for each other 错配; 不匹配; 不协调: *the mismatch between the demand for health care and the supply* 医疗保健供求之间的不协调 —**mismatched** /ˌmɪsˋmætʃt; ˌmɪsˈmætʃt◂/ *adj*: *a brilliant woman tragically mismatched with an incompetent, dull man* 不幸错嫁了一个无能笨汉的才女

mis·no·mer /mɪsˋnomɚ; mɪsˈnəʊmə/ *n* [C] a wrong or unsuitable name 错误[使用不当]的名字: *The word 'new' in their New Development was now something of a misnomer given that building had not even started.* 那座楼都还没有开工, 他们所说的"新建住宅区"中的"新"字用得有些不当。

mi·so·gy·nist /mɪˋsɑdʒənɪst; mɪ̣ˈsɒdʒɪ̣nɪ̣st/ *n* [C] a man who hates women 憎恨女人者, 厌恶女人者 —**misogyny** *n* [U] *formal*【正式】

mis·place /mɪsˋples; ˌmɪsˈpleɪs/ *v* [T] to lose something for a short time by putting it in the wrong place; MISLAY〔因放错地方而〕暂时丢失, 一时找不到〔某物〕; 把…放在一时记不起的地方: *Oh dear, I seem to have misplaced the letter.* 哎呀, 我好像忘了把信放在什么地方了。

mis·placed /ˌmɪsˋplest; ˌmɪsˈpleɪst◂/ *adj* misplaced feelings of trust, love etc are wrong and unsuitable, because the person that you have these feelings for does not deserve them〔把信任、爱等感情〕错给不值当人的: *her misplaced sense of loyalty* 她那用错对象的忠诚感

mis·print /ˋmɪsˌprɪnt; ˈmɪs-prɪnt/ *n* [C] a mistake, especially a spelling mistake, in a book, magazine etc 印刷错误, 手民之误

mis·pro·nounce /ˌmɪsprəˋnaʊns; ˌmɪsprəˈnaʊns/ *v* [T] to pronounce a word or name wrongly 念错, 发错〔音〕—**mispronunciation** /ˌmɪsprənʌnsɪˋeʃən; ˌmɪsprənʌnsiˈeɪʃən/ *n* [C,U]

mis·quote /mɪsˋkwot; ˌmɪsˈkwəʊt/ *v* [T] to make a mistake in reporting what someone else has said 错误地引证, 误引〔他人的话〕: *Dr Hall said he had been misquoted in the press.* 霍尔博士说新闻界错误地引用了他的话。—**misquotation** /ˌmɪskwoˋteʃən; ˌmɪskwəʊˈteɪʃən/ *n* [C,U]

mis·read /mɪsˋrid; ˌmɪsˈriːd/ *v past tense and past participle* **misread** /-ˋrɛd; -ˈred/ [T] **1** to make a wrong judgment about a person or situation 对…判断错误: *Negotiators misread the clues as to the enemy's true intentions.* 谈判者们对有关敌人真正意图的线索判断错误。**2** to read something incorrectly 读错, 念错; 看错 —**misreading** *n* [C,U]: *a misreading of the situation* 对局势的错误判断

mis·re·port /ˌmɪsrɪˋport; ˌmɪsrɪˈpɔːt/ *v* [T usually passive 一般用被动态] to give an incorrect or untrue account of an event or situation 对…报道失实: *The facts of the story have been misreported.* 事情的真相被歪曲了。

mis·rep·re·sent /ˌmɪsrɛprɪˋzɛnt; ˌmɪsreprɪˈzent/ *v* [T] to deliberately give a wrong description of someone's opinions or of a situation 故意对…作错误的描述, 歪曲: *These statistics grossly misrepresent the reality.* 这些统计资料严重歪曲了事实真相。—**misrepresentation** /ˌmɪsrɛprɪzɛnˋteʃən; ˌmɪsreprɪzenˈteɪʃən/ *n* [C,U]

mis·rule /mɪsˋrul; ˌmɪsˈruːl/ *n* [U] *formal* bad government【正式】治理不当; 苛政, 暴政: *15 years of misrule by a weak and corrupt government* 一个腐败无能的政府15年的暴政

Misrule, Lord of —see 见 the LORD OF MISRULE

M

miss¹ /mɪs; mɪs/ *v*

① NOT DO STH/FAIL TO DO STH 不做某事/未能做到某事
② BE TOO LATE 太迟
③ FEEL SAD WITHOUT 因没有…而难过
④ NOT NOTICE 不注意
⑤ AVOID STH 避免某事物
⑥ NOTICE STH ISN'T THERE 发现某物不在 那儿
⑦ OTHER MEANINGS 其他意思

① NOT DO STH/FAIL TO DO STH 不做某事/未能做到某事

1 [T] to not go somewhere or do something, especially when you want to but cannot〔尤指想去或想做而〕未去[未做]: *I'm really hungry. I missed breakfast.* 我真的饿了，我没吃上早饭。| *Donna had to miss a week of school because of chickenpox.* 唐娜因出水痘只得缺了一周的课。

2 ▶NOT HIT/GET HOLD OF 未击中/抓住◀ [I,T] to not hit something or catch something 未击中；未抓住: *She fired at the target but missed.* 她朝目标开了枪，但没有击中。| **miss sth** *He ran to catch the ball but missed it.* 他跑着去接球，但没接住。| **miss doing sth** *The car came screeching round the corner and just missed hitting a little boy who was crossing the road.* 汽车尖叫着从拐角开过来，险些撞上一个正在过马路的小男孩。—see picture on page A23 参见 A23 页图

3 miss a chance/opportunity to fail to use an opportunity to do something 错过机会: *A free trip to Jamaica was an opportunity he couldn't miss.* 免费去牙买加旅游是一个他不能错过的机会。

4 I wouldn't miss it for the world *spoken* used to say that you really want to go to an event, see something etc【口】我无论如何也不想错过

5 miss the boat/bus *informal* to fail to take an opportunity【非正式】错过机会，坐失良机: *You'll miss the boat if you don't buy these shares now.* 如果现在不买这些股票，你会坐失良机。

② BE TOO LATE 太迟

6 [T] to be too late for something 未赶上: *By the time we got there we'd missed the beginning of the movie.* 我们赶到那儿的时候电影开头已经放过去了。| **miss the train/bus etc** *I overslept and missed the train.* 我睡过了头，误了火车。—opposite 反义词 CATCH¹ (7)

③ FEEL SAD WITHOUT 因没有…而难过

7 ▶MISS SB 思念某人◀ [T] to feel sad because someone you love is not with you 思念，想念；怀念〔某人〕: *When George went away I really missed him.* 乔治走后我确实想念他。| *Will you miss me?* 你会想我吗？

8 ▶MISS STH 留恋某物◀ to feel sad because you do not have something or cannot do something you had or did before 留恋，思恋〔某物〕: *I miss the car, but the bus system is good.* 我留恋汽车，但公共交通系统也不错。| *We really missed being able to go to the beach whenever we wanted.* 我们确实留恋想去海滩就能去的日子。

④ NOT NOTICE 不注意

9 [T] to not see, hear, or notice something, especially when it is difficult to notice 未看到；未听到；未注意到〔某事物〕: *Grandpa Joe spoke very slowly so that Charlie wouldn't miss a word.* 乔爷爷说得非常慢，这样查利就不会漏听一个字。| *J.D. noticed a design fault in the engine that everyone else had missed.* J.D. 在发动机上发现了一个其他人都没有注意到的设计上的缺陷。

10 you can't miss it/him etc *spoken* used to say that it is very easy to notice or recognize someone or something【口】你不会看不到[认不出]它/他等的: *He's the one in the red hat. You can't miss him.* 他是戴红帽子的那个人，你不会认不出来的。

11 sb doesn't miss much *spoken* used to say that someone is good at noticing things, even small details【口】某人很善于察觉事物，明察秋毫: *Old Mr Staines doesn't miss much, does he?* 老斯坦斯先生对事情明察秋毫，是吧？

12 sb doesn't miss a trick *spoken* used to say that someone notices every opportunity to get an advantage【口】某人很精明，很善于把握机会: *The cunning old devil – he never misses a trick.* 这个狡猾的老家伙 —— 他总是能把握住每次机会。

⑤ AVOID STH 避免某事物

13 ▶AVOID STH 避开某事◀ [T] to avoid doing something or going somewhere, especially deliberately〔尤指故意地〕避开，躲开〔做某事或去某地〕: *If we leave now we should miss the traffic.* 如果我们现在走，就能避开交通拥堵。| *They narrowly missed being killed in the fire.* 他们差点被那场火烧死。

⑥ NOTICE STH ISN'T THERE 发现某物不在那儿

14 [T] to notice that something or someone is not in the place you expect them to be 发觉〔某人或某物〕不在应在之处: *I didn't miss my wallet till it came to paying the bill.* 直到付账时我才发现钱包没了。

⑦ OTHER MEANINGS 其他意思

15 miss the point to not understand the main point of what someone is saying 没有领会要点

16 sb's heart misses a beat used to say that someone is very excited, surprised, or frightened〔因激动、惊讶或害怕〕心跳停了一拍: *When I spotted Christophe my heart missed a beat.* 当我认出克里斯托夫时，我激动得心跳都停了一拍。

17 without missing a beat if you do something without missing a beat, you do it without showing that you are very surprised or shocked 不露声色地；镇定地: *"I hear you're a private detective," he said, without missing a beat.* "我听说你是位私家侦探。"他若无其事地说道。

18 ▶ENGINE 发动机◀ [I] if an engine misses, it stops working for a very short time and then starts again 短时熄火

miss out *phr v* **1** [I] to not have the chance to do something that you enjoy 没有做自己喜欢的事的机会: *Some children miss out because their parents can't afford to pay for school trips.* 一些孩子失去了机会，因为他们的父母没钱支付学校组织的旅行。| **[+on]** *She married young and felt she was missing out on life.* 她早早就结婚了，因而感到失去享受生活的机会。**2** [T **miss sb/sth ↔ out**] *BrE* to not include someone or something【英】不包括，漏掉: *Make sure you don't miss any details out.* 你要确保不漏掉任何细节。

miss² *n*

1 Miss Smith/Cleveland etc used in front of the family name of a woman who is not married to address her politely, to write to her, or to talk about her 史密斯/克利夫兰小姐等〔用在未婚女子姓的前面，作为礼貌的称呼〕—compare 比较 MRS, MS —see 见 MR (USAGE)

2 ▶TEACHER 教师◀ *BrE* used by children when addressing a female teacher, whether she is married or not【英】老师〔儿童对女教师的称呼〕: *I know the answer, Miss.* 老师，我知道答案。—compare 比较 SIR (5)

3 Miss Italy/Ohio/World etc used before the name of a country, city etc which a woman represents in a beauty competition 意大利/俄亥俄/世界小姐等〔用在选美比赛中某女子所代表的国家、城市等的前面〕

4 ▶YOUNG WOMAN 年轻女子◀ *old-fashioned* used as a polite way of addressing a young woman when you do not know her name【过时】小姐〔用来礼貌地称呼不知其名的年轻女子〕: *Excuse me, miss, you've dropped your umbrella.* 对不起，小姐，您的伞掉了。—compare 比较 MADAM (1), SIR (1,2)

5 ▶YOUNG GIRL 年轻姑娘◀ [C] *BrE* a young girl, especially one who has been naughty or rude【英】〔尤指顽皮或无礼的〕小姑娘，女孩，少女: *a cheeky little miss* 无礼的小姑娘

6 give sth a miss *informal especially BrE* to decide not to do something【非正式，尤英】决定不做某事: *I think I'll give aerobics a miss this week.* 我想这周不去做有氧健身运动了。

7 ▶NOT HIT/CATCH 没击中/抓住◀ [C] a failed attempt to hit, catch, or hold something 未击中；未抓住；没接住: *an exciting*

game with three shots at goal and only two misses 一场激动人心的比赛，三次射门，只两次射失

8 a miss is as good as a mile used to say that although someone failed by only a small amount to do something, they were still unsuccessful 功败垂成终是败 —see also 另见 HIT-AND-MISS

mis·sal /ˋmɪsḷ; ˈmɪsəl/ *n* [C] a book containing all the prayers said during each Mass for a whole year in the Roman Catholic church〔罗马天主教的〕弥撒经书

Miss A·mer·i·ca Pa·geant, the /,· ·ˊ··· ,·ˊ/ a beauty contest held every year in Atlantic City, New Jersey, in which women who have won beauty contests in each of the 50 states represent those states. One of them is chosen to serve as **Miss America** for one year. 美国小姐选美大赛〔一年一度在新泽西州大西洋城举行的选美比赛。参赛者均为50个州选美比赛的优胜者，选出其中一名为当年的"美国小姐"〕

mis·shap·en /mɪsˋʃepən; ˌmɪsˈʃeɪpən/ *adj* not the normal or natural shape 畸形的: *Ballerinas often have blunted, misshapen toes.* 芭蕾舞女演员的脚趾常常会磨粗、变形。

mis·sile /ˋmɪsḷ; ˈmɪsaɪl/ *n* [C] **1** a weapon that can fly over long distances and that explodes when it hits the thing it has been aimed at 导弹，飞弹: *a nuclear missile* 核导弹 **2** an object that is thrown at someone in order to hurt them〔用来伤人的〕投掷物: *Many of the hooligans were throwing missiles at the police.* 许多街头恶棍在向警察投掷东西。

S3 **miss·ing** /ˋmɪsɪŋ; ˈmɪsɪŋ/ *adj* **1** something that is missing is not in its usual place and you cannot find it 找不到的；丢失的: *We found the missing piece of the jigsaw under the chair.* 我们在椅子下面发现了那块丢失的拼图。| [+from] *Fifty dollars were missing from my wallet.* 我的钱包里少了50美元。**2** if part of something is missing, it has been removed, destroyed etc and no longer exists 缺掉的，缺少的，缺损的: *Two of her front teeth were missing.* 她的两颗门牙没有了。**3** someone who is missing has disappeared, and no one knows where they are 下落不明的，失踪的: *The soldiers were reported missing, presumed dead.* 那些士兵据报失踪，估计已经死亡。**4** not included, although it ought to have been 漏掉的，遗漏的: [+from] *Why is my name missing from the list?* 为什么名单上漏掉了我的名字? **5 go missing** *BrE* to disappear or become lost【英】失踪，走失；丢失: *My cat's gone missing again.* 我的猫又不见了。

missing link /,·· ˈ·/ *n* [C] **1** a piece of information that you need in order to solve a problem 缺少的一环: *a discovery which could provide a new direction towards finding the missing link in the search for a cure for cancer* 为探索癌症治疗方法找到所缺环节指明新方向的一项发现 **2 the missing link** an animal similar to humans that may have existed at the time when apes (APE[1] (1)) developed into humans 猿进化到人类的过程中或许存在过的一种过渡动物: *The race is on to find the missing link in our evolution.* 科学家正在进行竞赛，以找到那种被推定在人类进化过程中介于猿和人类之间的动物。

missing per·son /,·· ˈ··/ *n plural* **missing persons** [C] **1** someone who has disappeared and whose family has asked the police to try to find them 失踪者 **2 Missing Persons** the police department responsible for trying to find people who have disappeared 失踪人口调查部〔负责寻找失踪者的警察部门〕

W3 **mis·sion** /ˋmɪʃən; ˈmɪʃən/ *n* [C]

1 ►AIRFORCE/ARMY ETC 空军/陆军等◄ an important job done by a member of the airforce, army etc, especially an attack on the enemy 任务，使命: *He was sent on over 200 missions before being killed in action.* 在阵亡之前他奉命执行过二百多次军事任务。| *a space mission* 航天任务

2 ►GOVERNMENT/GROUP 政府/团体◄ a group of important people who are sent by their government to another country to discuss something or collect information 代表团，工作团；外交使团: *a British trade mission to Moscow* 派往莫斯科的英国贸易代表团

3 ►JOB 工作◄ an important job that someone has been given to do especially when they are sent to another place〔尤指给予被派遣人员的〕重要任务，使命: *His mission was to improve staff morale and output.* 他的任务是鼓舞员工的士气，提高产量。

4 ►DUTY 职责◄ something that you feel you must do because it is your duty 职责，天职；使命: **mission in life** *He always felt that his mission in life was to help old people.* 他总是认为帮助老年人是他的职责。

5 ►RELIGION 宗教◄ a) the work of a religious leader or organization, that has gone to a foreign country, in order to teach people about Christianity or help poor people〔在国外进行基督教的〕传教，布道: *After he trained as a priest he went to work for the missions in Africa.* 在受过牧师培训后，他前往非洲进行传教活动。**b)** a building where this kind of work is done 布道所用的建筑物

6 mission accomplished used when you have finished a job that someone has asked or told you to do 任务已完成

mis·sion·a·ry /ˋmɪʃən,ɛrɪ; ˈmɪʃənəri/ *n* [C] someone who has been sent to a foreign country to teach people about Christianity and persuade them to become Christians〔被派到国外传教的〕基督教传教士: *She spent 20 years in Africa as a missionary.* 她在非洲做了20年传教士。

CULTURAL NOTE 文化注释

In the past, Christian missionaries were often EXPLORERS and they were sometimes the first Europeans that people in many parts of the world had ever seen. They were greatly admired for being brave and morally good, and for helping people to learn about Christianity. But today, many people criticize what missionaries did, because they encouraged people to give up their traditional religious beliefs and social practices. Sometimes, they encouraged people to do things in a more European way, for example to dress in Western clothes and cover their bodies, even if they lived in a hot country. 过去基督教传教士常常也是探险者，他们是世界其他地方的人见到的第一批欧洲人。他们因为勇敢、道德高尚和帮助人们了解基督教而受人尊敬。但时至今日，很多人对当年传教士的所作所为提出了批评，因为他们怂恿人们放弃自己传统的宗教信仰和社会行为。有时他们倡导人们以欧洲人的方式行事，例如穿西式服装，把身体裹得严严实实，即便这些人生活在热带国度。

missionary po·si·tion /ˈ···· ·,·ˊ/ *n* [singular] the sexual position in which the woman lies on her back with the man on top of her and facing her 传教士式姿势〔指男上女下的面对面性交姿势〕

mission con·trol /,·· ·ˈ·/ *n* [singular] the people on earth who control, communicate with and guide a group of people on a space flight 航天地面指挥中心

mission state·ment /ˈ·· ,·ˊ/ *n* [C] a clear statement about the aims of a company or organization 任务说明

mis·sis /ˋmɪsɪz; ˈmɪsɨz/ *n* another spelling of MISSUS missus 的另一种拼法

Mis·sis·sip·pi /ˌmɪsəˋsɪpɪ; ˌmɪsɨˈsɪpi/ **1** abbreviation 缩写为 **MS** a state in the southeastern US, which is now an industrial area but used to produce a lot of cotton, and which was an important centre of the Civil Rights Movement in the 1950s and 1960s 密西西比州〔美国东南部一州，以前盛产棉花，现为一工业区。20世纪50、60年代曾是民权运动的一个重要中心〕**2 the Mississippi** the longest river in the US, about 2,350 miles long, which flows from Minnesota to the Gulf of Mexico 密西西比河〔美国最长的河流，长约2350英里，从明尼苏达州流至墨西哥湾〕

mis·sive /ˋmɪsɪv; ˈmɪsɪv/ *n* [C] *humorous* a letter【幽默】书信，信件: *An anonymous missive had been pushed under her door.* 一封匿名信被人从她的门下面塞了进去。

Mis·sou·ri /məˋzurɪ; mɨˈsʊəri/ **1** abbreviation 缩写为 **MO** a state in the central US, which is an industrial and farming area 密苏里州〔美国中部一州，为一工农业区〕**2 the Missouri** a long river in the US, flowing from the Rocky Mountains to join the Mississippi at St Louis 密苏里河〔美国一长河，发源自落基山脉，在圣路易斯汇入密西西比河〕

mis·spell /mɪsˋspɛl; ˌmɪsˈspel/ *v past tense and past participle* **misspelt** /-ˋspɛlt; -ˈspelt/ or **misspelled** [T] to spell a word wrongly 拼写错〔单词〕—**misspelling** *n* [C,U]

mis·spend /mɪsˋspɛnd; ˌmɪsˈspend/ *v past tense and past participle* **misspent** /-ˋspɛnt; -ˈspent◂/ [T] **1 misspent youth** *often humorous* someone who had a misspent youth wasted their time or behaved badly when they were young【常幽默】虚度的青春 **2** to use time, money, etc badly, and not carefully or effectively 滥用〔时间、金钱等〕；使用…不当

Miss Pig·gy /,·ˈ··/ *trademark* a PUPPET in the form of a pig with long BLOND hair who appears in the television programme *The Muppets*. She thinks that she is very beautiful and expects everyone to admire her, and she gets angry if the other characters do not do what she wants.【商标】猪小姐〔电视节目《木偶剧场》中留着长长金发、形态似猪的木偶。她自以为美貌盖世，期望每个人都崇拜她。别人不依她，她就大发雷霆〕

mis·step /ˋmɪs-stɛp; ˈmɪs-step/ *n* [C] *AmE* a mistake, especially one that is caused by not understanding a situation correctly【美】〔尤指判断上的〕错误；失策: *He has made a number of missteps over health care.* 在保健方面他已犯了许多错误。

M

Miss U·ni·verse /ˌ·ˈ···/ *trademark* a US competition in which women from many different countries compete to be judged the most beautiful and to win the title 'Miss Universe'. 【商标】环球小姐选美大赛〔美国举办的选美比赛。选手来自世界各国，角逐"环球小姐"称号〕

mis·sus, missis /ˈmɪsəz; ˈmɪsɨ̥z/ *n* [singular] **1** *informal* a man's wife【非正式】妻子，老婆: *How's the missus?* 老婆好吗？ **2** *spoken, especially BrE* used when addressing a woman whose name you do not know【口，尤英】太太〔用以称呼不知其名的妇女〕: *Hey, missus, are these your kids?* 喂，太太，这些孩子是你的吗？

Miss World /ˌ·ˈ·/ *trademark* a competition in which women from many different countries compete to be judged the most beautiful. The winner is given the title Miss World.【商标】世界小姐选美大赛〔一项世界性选美比赛。选手来自世界各国，角逐"世界小姐"称号〕

mist[1] /mɪst; mɪst/ *n* **1** [C,U] a light cloud low over the ground that makes it difficult for you to see very far 薄雾，雾霭: *We could just see the outline of the house through the mist.* 透过薄雾我们只能看到房子的轮廓。—compare 比较 FOG[1] (1) —see picture on page A13 参见 A13 页图 **2** [singular] air that is filled with very small drops of a particular liquid 充满雾状液体的空气: *a treatment for asthma in the form of an aerosol mist* 哮喘病的气雾剂吸入疗法 **3 lost in the mists of time** if something such as a fact or secret is lost in the mists of time, no one remembers it because it happened so long ago 淹没在时间的迷雾中〔指某事因发生的时间太久已没人能记起〕: *The real reasons for the war are now lost in the mists of time.* 那场战争爆发的真正起因现在已随着时间的推移而被人遗忘了。

mist[2] *v* [T] to cover something with very small drops of liquid in order to keep it wet 使…蒙上雾气〔以保持湿润〕: *The plant has to be misted every day.* 这棵植物必须每天喷水。

mist over *phr v* [I] **1** if someone's eyes mist over, they become filled with tears〔眼睛因充满泪水而〕变得模糊不清: *His eyes misted over at the memory of his wife.* 想起妻子，他变得泪眼模糊。**2** to mist up 蒙上水蒸气

mist up *phr v* [I,T] if a piece of glass mists up or if something mists it up, it becomes covered with very small drops of water so that you cannot see through it〔玻璃〕蒙上水蒸气; 使〔玻璃〕蒙上水蒸气: *I can't see where I'm going, the windows have misted up.* 我看不清我在往哪儿走，车窗蒙上了水汽。

S2 W2 **mis·take**[1] /məˈstek; mɨ̥ˈsteɪk/ *n* [C]

1 ►INCORRECT ACTION/OPINION ETC 不正确的行为/看法等◄ something that has been done incorrectly, or an opinion or statement that is incorrect 错误的行为，错误的看法[陈述]; 误会: *Hitting the ball too hard in golf is a typical beginner's mistake.* 击球过猛是高尔夫球初学者易犯的典型错误。| **make a mistake** *I think you've made a mistake – this isn't my coat.* 我想你弄错了 —— 这不是我的大衣。| **there must be some mistake** (=used when you think someone has made a mistake) 一定是弄错了 *There must be some mistake – I already paid my hotel bill.* 一定是弄错了 —— 旅馆的账我已经付清了。| **learn from your mistakes** (=learn how to do something correctly by doing it the wrong way first) 从错误中吸取教训 —see graph at 参见 ERROR 图表

2 by mistake if you do something by mistake, you do it without intending to 错误地〔并非故意〕: *Someone must have left the door open by mistake.* 一定是有人疏忽忘了关门。

3 ►STUPID ACTION 愚蠢的行为◄ something unwise or stupid that someone does, which they regret doing afterwards 不明智的行为; 愚蠢的失误[失策]: *Buying the house seemed a great idea at the time, but now I can see it was a mistake.* 买那座房子当时好像是一个很棒的主意，但现在我才明白是失策。| **make a mistake** *It's your decision, but I warn you – you're making a mistake.* 这是你的决定，但我要警告你 —— 你在做傻事。| **big mistake** *Marrying him was the biggest mistake she ever made.* 嫁给他是她最大的失误。| **make the mistake of doing sth** *I stupidly made the mistake of giving them my phone number.* 我真蠢，居然把我的电话号码给了他们。| **it is a mistake to do sth** *It would be a mistake to underestimate the amount of support for his victims.* 低估他的受害者所得到的支持是不明智的。

4 ►IN SPEECH OR WRITING 在言语或文字中◄ something that is said or written incorrectly, for example in a piece of school work 错误: *Ivan's work is always full of mistakes.* 伊万的作业总是错误满篇。| **make a mistake** *At this level, students tend to make a lot of basic mistakes.* 学生在这个阶段往往会犯许多基本错误。| **spelling mistake** *There are a lot of spelling mistakes in this letter.* 这封信中有许多拼写错误。

5 we all make mistakes *spoken* used when telling someone not to be worried because they have made a mistake【口】我们都有出错的时候，人谁无过

6 make no mistake (about it) *spoken* used to emphasize what you are saying, especially when you are warning someone【口】〔对这一点〕不要有半点怀疑，完全可以肯定〔用以强调，尤在警告某人时〕: *He'll get his revenge, make no mistake about it!* 他会报复，这完全可以肯定！

7 and no mistake *spoken* used to show that you are very certain about something that you have just said【口】毫无疑问，的确: *Miles was a heartbreaker, and no mistake!* 迈尔斯的确是一个令人伤心的人！—compare 比较 ERROR

mistake[2] *past tense* **mistook** /mɪsˈtuk; mɨ̥ˈstʊk/ *past participle* **mistaken** /məˈstekən; mɨ̥ˈsteɪkən/ *v* [T] **1** to understand something wrongly 弄错，误解，误会: *Ken mistook her concern, thinking she was interested in him for another reason.* 肯误解了她的关心，认为她对他感兴趣是另有原因。| *She mistook my meaning entirely.* 她完全误解了我的意思。**2 you can't mistake sb/sth** used to say that someone or something is very easy to recognize 你不会认错某人/某物: *You can't mistake her. She's the one with the long red hair.* 你不会认错人的，她就是那个留着红色长发的人。**3 there is no mistaking sb/sth** used to say that you are certain about something 决不可能搞错某人/某物: *There's no mistaking whose children they are – they all look just like Joe.* 他们是谁的孩子一清二楚 —— 他们长得都很像乔。

mistake sb/sth **for** sb/sth *phr v* [T] to think that one person or thing is someone or something else 把〔某人/某物〕误认为〔他人/他物〕: *I mistook the poor woman for my sister.* 我把那个可怜的女人误认为是我姐姐。| *The doctor mistook the symptoms for blood poisoning.* (=and it was something else) 医生把那些症状误诊为血中毒。

mis·tak·en /məˈstekən; mɨ̥ˈsteɪkən/ *adj* **1** [not before noun 不用于名词前] someone who is mistaken is wrong about something〔人〕弄错的: **be mistaken** *I thought I saw her at the movies but I guess I was mistaken.* 我以为我在电影院里看到了她，但现在想来我是弄错了。**2 mistaken idea/belief/impression etc** a mistaken belief etc is not correct or is based on bad judgment 错误[基于错误判断]的想法/信念/印象等: *Marijuana has few withdrawal effects, and this has given rise to the mistaken belief that it is not addictive.* 由于戒断作用很少，人们错误地认为大麻不会使人上瘾。**3 a case of mistaken identity** a situation in which someone believes that they have seen a particular person taking part in a crime, when in fact it was someone else 认错人的情况: *The police arrested her but it turned out to be a case of mistaken identity.* 警察逮捕了她，但结果发现抓错了人。—**mistakenly** *adv*

mis·ter /ˈmɪstɚ; ˈmɪstə/ *n* **1 Mister** the full form of MR 先生〔Mr 的全拼形式〕 **2** *spoken especially AmE* used to address a man whose name you do not know【口，尤美】先生〔用以称呼不知其名的男子〕: *Hey, mister, you dropped your paper.* 喂，先生，你的报纸掉了。

mis·time /mɪsˈtaɪm; ˌmɪsˈtaɪm/ *v* [T] to do something at the wrong time or at an unsuitable time 在错误[不适当]的时候做: *We mistimed a scene where a door slams in my face and I ended up with a broken nose.* 门在我面前砰的关上的那个场景，我们没掌握好时间，结果我的鼻子碰破了。

mis·tle·toe /ˈmɪslˌto; ˈmɪsəltəʊ/ *n* [U] a plant with small white berries, which grows over other trees, and is often used as a decoration at Christmas 槲寄生

> **CULTURAL NOTE 文化注释**
>
> Mistletoe is a traditional Christmas decoration. People hang it in their homes, and there is a custom which says that you can kiss anyone who is standing under it. 槲寄生小枝是一种传统的圣诞节装饰物。人们把它挂在家里。有这样一个习俗，说是你可以去亲吻站在槲寄生小枝下面的任何一个人。— see Feature on page F12 见 F12 页文化特写

mis·took /mɪsˈtuk; mɨ̥ˈstʊk/ the past tense of MISTAKE (2)

mis·tral /ˈmɪstrəl; ˈmiːstrɑːl/ *n* [singular] a strong cold dry wind that blows from the north into the south of France 密史脱拉风〔从北方吹到法国南部的干冷的强风〕

mis·tress /ˈmɪstrɪs; ˈmɪstrɨ̥s/ *n* [C] **1** a woman that a man has a sexual relationship with even though he is married to someone else 情妇: *The Prince had shocked society by living openly with his mistress.* 王子和他的情妇公开生活在一起，使社会大为震惊。**2** *BrE old-fashioned* a female teacher【英，过时】女教师: *the new English mistress* 新来的女英语教师 **3** the female owner of a dog, horse etc〔狗、马等的〕女主人 **4** *old-fashioned* the fe-

male employer of a servant【过时】〔仆人的〕女雇主，女主人: *You'll have to deal with the mistress of the house.* 你将不得不和家中的女主人打交道。**5 be mistress of** if a woman is a mistress of something she is in control of it, highly skilled at it etc 〔妇女〕控制着…; 是…的能手: *She appeared to be very much the mistress of the situation.* 她似乎很好地控制着局面。**6 Mistress** *old use* used with a woman's family name as a polite way of addressing her【旧】夫人; 小姐〔对女子的礼貌称呼，置于女子的姓之前〕—compare 比较 MASTER¹ (1)

mis·tri·al /mɪsˋtraɪəl; ˌmɪsˈtraɪəl/ *n* [C] a trial during which a mistake in the law is made, so that a new trial has to be held 无效审判

mis·trust¹ /mɪsˋtrʌst; mɪsˈtrʌst/ *n* [U] the feeling that you cannot trust someone, especially because you think they may treat you unfairly or dishonestly 不信任: [+of] *He had a deep mistrust of the legal profession.* 他对司法界很不信任。—compare 比较 DISTRUST¹

mistrust² *v* [T] to not trust someone, especially because you think they may treat you unfairly or dishonestly 不信任，不相信: *As a very small child she had learned to mistrust adults.* 她很小的时候就学会了不相信大人。—compare 比较 DISTRUST² —**mistrustful** *adj*: *Some people are very mistrustful of computerised banking.* 有些人非常信不过电脑化的银行业务。—**mistrustfully** *adv*

mist·y /ˋmɪstɪ; ˈmɪsti/ *adj* **mistier, mistiest 1** misty weather is weather with a lot of mist 多雾的: *The forecast says it will be wet and misty tomorrow.* 天气预报说明天潮湿多雾。**2** *literary* full of tears【文】泪汪汪的: *Her eyes became misty.* 她双眼变得泪汪汪的。**3** not clear or bright 不清楚的，朦胧的，模糊的: *Without my glasses everything is just a misty blur.* 如果我不戴眼镜，看什么都是模模糊糊的。

mis·un·der·stand /ˌmɪsʌndəˋstænd; ˌmɪsʌndəˈstænd/ *v past tense and past participle* **misunderstood** [I,T] to think that something means one thing when in fact it means something different 误解，误会: *I don't think we should be seen travelling together – people might misunderstand.* 我认为我们不应该被人看到在一起旅行 —— 别人会误解的。

mis·un·der·stand·ing /ˌmɪsʌndəˋstændɪŋ; ˌmɪsʌndəˈstændɪŋ/ *n* **1** [C,U] a problem caused by someone not understanding a question, situation, or instruction correctly 误解，误会: *I think there must have been some misunderstanding. I didn't order all these books.* 我想准是出了点误会，我并没有订购这些书。**2** [C] an argument or disagreement that is not very serious 争执; 不和: *We had a little misunderstanding with our neighbors last night.* 昨天晚上我们和邻居发生了一点小争执。

mis·use¹ /mɪsˋjuz; ˌmɪsˈjuːz/ *v* [T] **1** to use something in the wrong way or for the wrong purpose 错用，误用; 把…派作不当的用途: *The term schizophrenia is often misused.* 精神分裂症这个术语经常被误用。**2** to treat someone badly or unfairly 虐待，苛待

mis·use² /mɪsˋjus; mɪsˈjuːs/ *n* [C,U] the use of something in the wrong way or for the wrong purpose 错用，误用; 滥用: *a system designed to prevent credit card misuse* 为防止信用卡错用而设计的系统 | *the misuse of power* 滥用权力

MIT /ˌɛm aɪ ˋti; ˌem aɪ ˈtiː/ Massachusetts Institute of Technology; a respected US university in Cambridge, Massachusetts. It is an important centre for research work in scientific subjects such as mathematics and computer science. 麻省理工学院〔美国一所名牌大学，位于马萨诸塞州坎布里奇。该校为一重要理工科研究中心，以数学和计算机科学见长〕

Mitch·ell /ˋmɪtʃəl; ˈmɪtʃəl/, **Jo·ni** /ˋdʒonɪ; ˈdʒəʊni/ (1943-) a Canadian singer and songwriter, popular especially in the 1960s and 1970s. Her songs include *Big Yellow Taxi*. 米切尔〔(1943-)，加拿大歌手和歌曲作家，20 世纪 60、70 年代尤为著名。代表歌曲有《黄色出租车》〕

mite /maɪt; maɪt/ *n* [C] **1** a very small insect that lives in plants, carpets etc 螨虫 **2** a small child, especially one that you feel sorry for 〔尤指令人怜悯的〕小孩: *Poor mite! You must be starving!* 可怜的小家伙！你一定是饿坏了！**3 a mite shy/boring/nervous etc** slightly shy, boring, nervous etc 有点害羞/枯燥/紧张等 **4 a mite of** *old-fashioned* a small amount【过时】一点点，少量

Mit·ford /ˋmɪtfəd; ˈmɪtfəd/, **Nan·cy** /ˋnænsɪ; ˈnænsi/ (1904-73) a British writer who wrote NOVELs and other books about the British ARISTOCRACY. Her best-known novels are *The Pursuit of Love* and *Love in a Cold Climate*. She and her sisters were known as **the Mitford girls**, and they belonged to a well-known English upper-class family. Two of the sisters, **Diana** and **Unity**, became involved in RIGHT-WING politics. They greatly admired Adolf Hitler, and Diana married the British fascist leader Oswald Mosley. 米特福德〔(1904-1973)，英国作家。她的小说和其他作品均以英国贵族为题材，最出名的小说有《爱的追求》和《寒冷季节的爱情》。她和她的姐妹被称为"米氏姐妹"，属英国上流社会的一个名门望族。她的两个姐妹戴安娜和尤尼蒂从事右翼政治活动，狂热崇拜阿道夫·希特勒，戴安娜后来嫁给英国的法西斯领袖奥斯瓦尔德·莫斯利〕

Mith·ras /ˋmɪθræs; ˈmɪθræs/ the god of light or the sun in an ancient Persian religion known as **Mithraism**, which spread through the Roman Empire in the first and second centuries AD, and was an important religion especially among Roman soldiers 密特拉神〔古代波斯密特拉教中的光明之神或太阳神。公元 1、2 世纪密特拉教传入罗马，成为颇受罗马军人崇奉的一种重要宗教〕

mit·i·gate /ˋmɪtəˌget; ˈmɪtɪgeɪt/ *v* [T] *formal* to make a situation or the effects of something less unpleasant, harmful, or serious【正式】减轻，缓解，缓和: *Measures need to be taken to mitigate the environmental effects of burning more coal.* 需要采取措施以减轻燃烧更多的煤对环境造成的影响。

mit·i·gat·ing /ˋmɪtəˌgetɪŋ; ˈmɪtɪgeɪtɪŋ/ *adj* **mitigating circumstances/factors etc** facts about a situation that make a crime or bad mistake seem less serious 可使罪行[严重错误]减轻的情节/因素等: *a reduced prison sentence due to mitigating circumstances* 因情有可原而被缩短的刑期

mit·i·ga·tion /ˌmɪtəˋgeʃən; ˌmɪtɪˈgeɪʃən/ *n* [U] **1 in mitigation** *law* if you say something in mitigation, you try to make someone's crime or mistake seem less serious or show that they were not completely responsible【法律】为了减轻罪责: *The captain added, in mitigation, that the engines may have been faulty.* 船长为减轻罪责补充说，也许发动机出了毛病。**2** *formal* a reduction in how unpleasant, harmful, or serious a situation is【正式】减轻，缓和: *His marriage had brought slight mitigation of the monotony of his existence.* 结婚稍微缓解了一下他单调乏味的生活。

mi·tre *BrE*【英】, **miter** *AmE*【美】/ˋmaɪtə; ˈmaɪtə/ *n* [C] **1** a tall pointed hat worn by BISHOPS and ARCHBISHOPS 主教冠〔主教和大主教戴的一种尖顶高帽〕**2** also 又作 **mitre joint** a joint between two pieces of wood, in which each piece is cut at an angle 斜接口，斜面接头，斜榫

mitt /mɪt; mɪt/ *n* [C] **1** a type of GLOVE that does not have separate parts for each finger; MITTEN 连指手套，独指手套 **2** a GLOVE made of thick material, worn to protect your hand 防护手套: *an oven mitt* 烤箱防护手套 | *ski mitts* 滑雪防护手套 **3** a type of leather GLOVE used to catch a ball in BASEBALL 棒球手套 —see picture on page A22 参见 A22 页图 **4** *informal, especially BrE* someone's hand【非正式，尤英】手: *Robert's put his sticky mitts all over it.* 罗伯特用他黏糊糊的双手捂了个严实。

mit·ten /ˋmɪtn̩; ˈmɪtn/ *n* [C] a type of GLOVE that does not have separate parts for each finger 连指手套，独指手套 —see picture at 参见 GLOVE 图

Mit·ty /ˋmɪtɪ; ˈmɪti/, **Wal·ter** /ˋwɔltə; ˈwɔːltə/ the main character in a story by James Thurber called *The Secret Life of Walter Mitty* (1932). He has a very ordinary life, but spends a lot of time imagining that he is a brave and important person living a dangerous and exciting life. His name is used, especially in newspapers, to describe someone who seems very ordinary but who either imagines they have an exciting secret life or who actually does have one. 米蒂〔詹姆斯·瑟柏创作的小说《沃尔特·米蒂的秘密生活》(1932) 中的主人公。米蒂生活平淡，却整日想入非非，把自己想象成一个勇敢的大人物，生活中四处都是危险、充满刺激。报纸上尤其喜欢借用此名形容这样一类人: 要么看似平凡却想入非非，要么过着一种刺激而私密的生活〕: *Their quiet neighbour turned out to be a Walter Mitty character, running a huge drug-smuggling business from his garage.* 他们那个不声不响的邻居原来是一个沃尔特·米蒂式的人物，以车库为据点干着大宗毒品走私生意。

mix¹ /mɪks; mɪks/ *v* **1** [I,T] if you mix two or more substances or if they mix, they combine to become a single substance, and they cannot be easily separated (使)混合，拌和: *Mix the blue and yellow paint to make green.* 把蓝色和黄色颜料混成绿色。| *Oil and water don't mix.* 油水不溶。| **mix sth together/in etc** *First mix the butter and sugar together, then add the milk.* 先把黄油和糖搅拌好，然后加牛奶。| **mix sth with sth** *Shake the bottle well so that the oil mixes with the vinegar.* 使劲儿晃动瓶子，使油和醋混合。—see picture on page A11 参见 A11 页图 **2** [I,T] to combine two or more different activities, ideas, groups of things etc (使)结合: **mix sth with sth** *His books mix historical fact with fantasy.* 他的书把史实和想象结合在一起。| **mix business with pleasure** (=combine business and social activities at the same time) 使工作和娱乐相结合 **3 not mix** if two

M

different ideas, activities etc do not mix, they are not suitable for each other and cause problems when they are combined 不相协调, 不相容: *We all know that drink, drugs and knives do not mix.* 我们都知道酒、毒品和刀子不能在一块。**4** [T] to prepare something, especially food or drink, by mixing things together 调制, 配制: *Will you mix us some martinis, Bill?* 比尔, 给我们调制几杯马提尼酒好吗? **5** [I] to enjoy meeting, talking, and spending time with other people, especially people you do not know very well〔尤指与不相熟的人〕相处, 交往, 交际: **[+with]** *Charlie doesn't mix well with the other children.* 查利与其他孩子合不来。**6** [T] *technical* to control the balance of sounds in a record or film【术语】〔在制作唱片或影片时〕调谐, 混录〔声音〕**7 mix and match** to try wearing different pieces of clothing together to see whether they look good 混合着搭配〔不同的衣服〕**8 mix it (up) with** to argue or threaten to fight with someone 与…争吵; 威胁要与…打架: *You don't want to mix it with him. He's been drinking since noon.* 你别去和他争吵, 他从中午就一直在喝酒。

mix sb/sth ↔ **up** *phr v* [T] **1** [**mix** sb/sth ↔ **up**] to make the mistake of thinking that someone or something is another person or thing 混淆, 弄混〔人或物〕: **[+with]** *I always mix him up with his brother. They look so much alike.* 我总是把他和他的弟弟弄混, 他们长得太像了。**2** [**mix** sth ↔ **up**] to change the way things have been arranged, often by mistake, so that they are no longer in the same order 弄乱〔某物〕: *Don't mix up those papers, or we'll never find the ones we need.* 别把那些文件搞乱了, 否则我们永远找不到所需要的文件。**3** [**mix** sb **up**] to make someone feel confused 使糊涂: *They kept trying to mix me up.* 他们一直想要把我弄糊涂。—see also 另见 MIXED UP, MIX-UP

mix² *n* **1** [singular] the particular combination of things or people that form a group 混合; 混合体: **[+of]** *There's a real mix of ethnic groups in that area of the city.* 在该城市的那个区有许多不同民族杂居在一起。| *We have to come up with a mix of policies to please the voters.* 我们必须提出一套兼容并蓄的政策来取悦选民。**2** [C,U] a combination of substances that you mix together to make something such as a cake〔做蛋糕等用的〕混合配料: **cake/soup etc mix** *Add water to the cake mix and cook at 375°.* 往蛋糕混合料里加水, 然后以375度的温度烘烤。

2 **mixed** /mɪkst; mɪkst/ *adj* **1** [only before noun 仅用于名词前] consisting of many different types of things or people 混合的, 混杂的: *The doctor suggested a mixed diet of fruits and vegetables.* 医生建议水果蔬菜搭配着吃。| *a mixed race community* 不同种族混住的居民区 **2 mixed reaction/response/reviews etc** if something gets a mixed reaction etc, some people say they like it or agree with it, but others dislike it or disagree with it 多种不同的反应/回应/评论等: *The film has had mixed reviews from the critics.* 这部电影得到了评论家们褒贬不一的评价。**3 have mixed emotions/feelings about** to be unsure about whether you like or agree with something or someone 对…怀有复杂[矛盾]的感情: *I must admit I have rather mixed feelings about my brother's new wife.* 我必须承认, 我对新嫂子确实说不上喜欢还是不喜欢。**4** *especially BrE* for both males and females【尤英】男女混合的: *a mixed school* 男女生兼收的学校 **5 a mixed blessing** something that is good in some ways but bad in others 利弊兼有的事物: *Having your parents living nearby is a mixed blessing.* 父母住在附近有利也有弊。**6 a mixed bag** a group of things or people that are all very different from each other 混合体, 大杂烩: **[+of]** *The concert was a mixed bag of classical and modern music.* 那场音乐会是古典音乐和现代音乐的大杂烩。**7 in mixed company** when you are with people of both sexes 在男女都有的场合: *It's not the sort of joke you tell in mixed company.* 这不是那种可以在男女都有的场合讲的笑话。

mixed a·bil·i·ty /,· '···◂/ *adj* [only before noun 仅用于名词前] a mixed ability school or class teaches all children of the same age together, even if they have different levels of ability〔学校或班级〕学生年龄相同但程度参差不齐的

mixed doub·les /,· '··/ *n* [U] a game in a sport such as tennis in which a man and a woman play against another man and woman 混合双打

mixed e·con·o·my /,· ·'···/ *n* [C] *technical* an economic system in which some industries are owned by the government and some are owned by private companies【术语】〔包括公有制和私有制的〕混合经济

mixed farm·ing /,· '··/ *n* [U] a system of farming in which you grow crops and keep animals〔既种庄稼又养牲畜的〕混合农业

mixed grill /,· '·/ *n* [C] *BrE* a dish consisting of meats such as SAUSAGE, BACON, LIVER etc which have all been grilled (GRILL¹ (1))【英】烤杂排, 什锦烤肉

mixed mar·riage /,· '··/ *n* [C,U] a marriage between two people from different races or religions 异族[异教]通婚

mixed up /,· '·◂/ *adj* **1 be mixed up in** to be involved in an illegal or dishonest activity 被卷入, 被牵连到…中: *He's the last person I'd expect to be mixed up in something like this.* 我认为他最不可能牵涉到这样的事情中。**2 be mixed up with** to be involved with someone who has a bad influence on you 与〔行为不良者〕交往, 与…厮混: *When he left college he got mixed up with the wrong people.* 离开大学后, 他结交了一些不三不四的人。**3** [not before noun 不用于名词前] confused, for example because you have too many different details to remember or think about 困惑的, 糊涂的, 头脑混乱的: *I get all mixed up over the money whenever I travel abroad.* 每次去国外旅行, 钱的事我都弄不清楚。**4** *informal* confused and suffering from emotional problems【非正式】情感错乱的, 感情迷茫的: *She's just a crazy mixed up kid.* 她只是一个疯狂而迷茫的孩子。—see also 另见 **mix up** (MIX¹), MIX-UP

mix·er /ˈmɪksə; ˈmɪksə/ *n* [C] **1** a piece of kitchen equipment used to mix flour, sugar, butter etc together 食品搅拌器, 搅拌机: *an electric food mixer* 电动食品搅拌器 **2** a drink that can be mixed with alcohol, especially to make a COCKTAIL 调酒〔尤指调制鸡尾酒〕用的饮料: *We can use tonic water or orange juice as mixers.* 我们可以用奎宁水或橘子汁来调酒。**3 a good/bad mixer** someone who finds it easy or difficult to make friends with people and talk to strangers 善于/不善于交际的人 **4** someone whose job is to control the sound when making a record or tape of a piece of music, or to control the quality of the picture when making a film 调音技术员; 〔电影〕画面质量负责人 **5** *AmE old-fashioned* a party held so that people who have just met can get to know each other better【美, 过时】交谊会: *Are you going to the freshman mixer?* 你去参加新生交谊会吗?

mix·ing bowl /'·· ·/ *n* [C] a large bowl used for mixing things such as flour and sugar for making cakes 搅拌碗

mix·ture /ˈmɪkstʃə; ˈmɪkstʃə/ *n* **1** [C] a combination of two or more people, things, feelings, or ideas that are different 混合, 混合体: *People are a mixture of good and evil.* 人集善恶于一身。| *the mixture of different people living in a city* 生活在一个城市中的形形色色的人的混合体 | *He looked at her with a mixture of amusement and despair.* 他既开心又绝望地看着她。**2** [C,U] a liquid or other substance made by mixing several substances together 混合液, 混合料: *Pour the cake mixture into the pan slowly and then bake on a low heat.* 把蛋糕混合料慢慢倒进锅里, 然后用低温烘烤。**3** [C] *technical* a combination of substances that are put together but do not mix with each other【术语】混合物 —compare 比较 COMPOUND¹ **4** [U] *formal* the action of mixing things or the state of being mixed【正式】混合动作; 混合状态 

mix-up /'· ·/ *n* [C] *informal* a mistake that causes confusion about details or arrangements【非正式】〔引起混乱的〕错误: *There was a mix-up over the reservations and we had to share a room.* 旅馆预订出了差错, 我们不得不合住一个房间。

miz·zen /ˈmɪzən; ˈmɪzən/ *n* [C] **1** also 又作 **mizzen mast** the MAST behind the main mast on a sailing ship 后桅 **2** also 又作 **mizzen sail** the main sail set lengthways on a mizzen on a sailing ship 后桅纵帆

Mk the written abbreviation of 缩写= MARK² (7)

ml the written abbreviation of 缩写= MILLILITRE(*s*)

m'lady, milady /mɪˈledɪ; mɪˈleɪdi/ *n old use* a word used by a servant to address a woman who belongs to a NOBLE family【旧】夫人, 太太〔仆人对贵妇人的称呼〕: *Will that be all, m'lady?* 夫人, 还有什么吩咐?

MLitt /ˌɛm ˋlɪt; ˌem ˈlɪt/ Master of Letters; a university degree that you can get at some British universities by studying for two years after your first degree 文学硕士

M'lord /mɪˋlɔrd; məˈlɔːd/ *n* **1** a word used to address a judge 大人, 阁下〔对法官的称呼〕**2** *old use* a word used by a servant to address a man who belongs to a NOBLE family【旧】老爷, 大人〔仆人对贵族绅士的称呼〕

M'lud /məˋlʌd; məˈlʌd/ *n* used to address a judge in a British court of law (short for 'my lord') 大人, 阁下〔英国法庭上对法官的称呼〕

mm¹ /m; m/ *interjection spoken* used when someone else is speaking and you want to show that you are listening or that you agree with them【口】嗯〔表示在聆听或赞同〕

mm² the written abbreviation of 缩写= MILLIMETRE(*s*)

MN the written abbreviation of 缩写= MINNESOTA

M'Nagh·ten Rules, the /məkˋnɔtn̩ ˌrulz; məkˈnɔːtn ˌruːlz/ —see 见 the MCNAUGHTEN RULES

mne·mon·ic /niˋmɑnɪk; nɪˈmɒnɪk/ *n* something, such as a poem, or a sentence that you use to help you remember a rule, a

name etc 帮助记忆的东西〈如诗歌或句子〉—**mnemonic** *adj* —**mnemonically** /-kḷɪ; -kli/ *adv*

MO[1] /ˌɛm ˋo; ˌem ˈəʊ/ *n informal*【非正式】**1** [C] *especially BrE* medical officer; an army doctor【尤英】医官, 军医 **2** [singular] modus operandi; a way of doing something that is typical of one person or a group 典型的做事方式, 一惯的做法; 惯技

MO[2] the written abbreviation of 缩写= MISSOURI

mo /mo; məʊ/ *n* [singular] *BrE spoken* a very short period of time; MOMENT (2)【英口】极短的时间, 一会儿: *Wait a mo!* 等一会儿!

mo. *AmE*【美】the written abbreviation for 缩写= MONTH

moan[1] /mon; məʊn/ *v* **1** [I] to make a long low sound expressing pain, unhappiness, or sexual pleasure 呻吟, 呜咽, 哼哼: *The sick child moaned a little and then fell asleep.* 那个生病的小孩呻吟了一会儿后睡着了。**2** [I,T] *BrE informal* to complain in an annoying way, especially in an unhappy voice and without good reason【英, 非正式】抱怨, 发牢骚: *You've done nothing but moan all day.* 你什么也没干, 整天发牢骚。| [**+at**] *My mum never stops moaning at me.* 我妈总是没完没了地对我发牢骚。| [**+that**] *He's always moaning that we use too much electricity.* 他总是抱怨我们用电太多。**3** [I] *literary* if the wind moans it makes a long low sound【文】〔风〕发出长而低的声音, 发呜咽声: *She was awakened by the low moaning of the wind in the trees.* 树林里风声呜咽, 把她吵醒了。—**moaner** *n* [C]

moan[2] *n* [C] **1** a long low sound expressing pain, unhappiness, or sexual pleasure 呻吟声; 呜咽声: *There was a moan of pain from the injured man.* 那个受伤的男子痛苦地呻吟了一声。| **give a moan** *She gave a little moan of pleasure.* 她快活地轻轻呻吟了一声。**2 have a moan** *BrE informal* to complain about something【英, 非正式】抱怨: *We were just having a moan about work.* 我们只是在抱怨工作。**3** *literary* a low sound made by the wind【文】〔风的〕呜咽声, 萧萧声

moat /mot; məʊt/ *n* [C] **1** a deep wide hole, usually filled with water, around a castle or fort as a defence 护城河, 城壕 **2** a deep wide hole dug around an area used for animals in a zoo to stop them from escaping〔动物园为防止动物逃跑而在其场地四周挖的〕深沟 —**moated** *adj*

mob[1] /mɑb; mɒb/ *n* [C] **1** a large, noisy crowd, especially one that is angry and violent 成群的暴民[乱民]; 乌合之众: *a mob of demonstrators* 一帮示威者 | **mob rule** (=when a mob controls the situation rather than the government or the law) 暴民统治 **2** *informal* a group of people of the same type【非正式】同类的一群人: *The usual mob of teenagers were standing on the corner.* 那帮常来的少年正站在拐角处。**3 the Mob** the MAFIA (=a powerful organization of criminals) 黑手党 **4 the mob** *old use* an insulting expression meaning all the poorest and least educated people in society【旧】最穷且受教育最少的民众, 下层民众, 贱民〔侮辱性用词〕**5 a mob of sheep/cattle** *AustrE, NZE* a large group of sheep or cattle【澳, 新西兰】一大群羊/牛

mob[2] *v* **mobbed, mobbing** [T] to form a crowd around someone in order to express admiration or to attack them 围住; 围攻: *The actress was mobbed by doting fans.* 那位女演员被崇拜她的影迷围住了。

mob cap /ˈ· ·/ *n* [C] a light cotton hat with a decorative edge, worn by women in the 18th and 19th centuries〔18和19世纪〕带装饰边的女帽

Mo·bile /ˈmobḷ; ˈməʊbaɪl/ a city which is Alabama's only port and one of the busiest ports in the US 莫比尔〔亚拉巴马州唯一港口, 也是美国最繁忙的港口之一〕

mobile[1] *adj* **1** able to move or travel easily 行动方便的: *She's more mobile now that she has her own car.* 有了自己的小汽车, 她现在行动方便多了。**2** not fixed in one position, and easy to move and use in different places 移动式的; 活动的; 可动的: *mobile air-conditioners* 移动式空调器 **3 mobile library/shop/clinic etc** *BrE* a shop etc that is kept in a vehicle and driven from place to place【英】流动图书馆/商店/诊所等 **4** tending to move or able to move from one social class, job, or place to another〔在不同社会阶层、职业或地区之间〕流动的: *People these days are much more socially mobile.* 如今人们的社会地位变化得快多了。**5 mobile face/features** a face that can change its expression quickly 表情多变的脸 —see also 另见 IMMOBILE, UPWARDLY MOBILE

mo·bile[2] /ˈmobil; ˈməʊbaɪl/ *n* [C] **1** a decoration made of small objects tied to wires or string and hung up so that the objects move when air blows around them〔悬挂在绳索等上的〕风动小饰物 **2** a MOBILE PHONE 移动电话

mobile home /ˌ·· ˈ·/ *n* [C] **1** *AmE* a type of house that looks like an ordinary house but can be moved to another place【美】活动房屋 **2** *BrE* a large CARAVAN which stays permanently in one place and is used as a house【英】〔永久地安置在某一地点的〕拖车式活动住房; TRAILER (1) *AmE*【美】

mobile phone /ˌ·· ˈ·/ *n* [C] a telephone that you can carry with you and use in any place 移动电话, 手机

mobile phone
移动电话

CULTURAL NOTE 文化注释

Mobile phones are very popular and many people, especially in the UK, enjoy sending each other TEXT MESSAGES. For some people, a mobile phone is an important fashion ACCESSORY and they always want to have the newest model with the best features, such as a camera or being able to ACCESS the Internet. 手机非常流行, 而且很多人, 特别是很多英国人热衷于相互发送短信息。对有些人来说, 手机是一个重要的时尚设备, 他们总想自己的手机款式最新、最具特色, 比如拍照和能够上网等。

In the UK, it is illegal to use a mobile phone when driving, unless you have a HANDS-FREE phone. 在英国, 法律规定开车时不得使用手机, 除非手机具有免提功能。

The increase in the number of MASTS, built to provide people with a signal, has led to protests against masts being built near houses and schools because people are worried about the effects of ELECTROMAGNETIC fields on their health. 接发手机信号的天线塔数量越来越多, 这已经引起人们的不满, 由于担心电磁场对健康的危害, 他们抗议天线塔建在住宅和学校附近。

mo·bil·i·ty /moˋbɪlətɪ; məʊˈbɪlʒti/ *n* [U] **1** the ability to move easily from one job, place to live, or social class to another 流动性; 易变性: **social/job mobility** *In America, social mobility is an everyday reality.* 在美国, 所属社会阶层变动是很普通的事。**2** the ability to move easily from place to place 活动性, 机动性: *Arthritis restricted his mobility.* 关节炎限制了他的活动。| *The key to the Army's effectiveness is its increased mobility.* 增强军队战斗力的关键是提高其机动性。

mo·bil·ize also 又作 **-ise** *BrE*【英】/ˈmobḷˌaɪz; ˈməʊbʒlaɪz/ *v* **1** [T] to bring people together so that they can all work to achieve something important 调动, 鼓动起; 召集: *to mobilize the rural population in a drive for self-sufficiency* 动员农村人口开展自给自足运动 **2 mobilize support/resources etc** to bring together the supporters, resources etc that you need and prepare them for action 争取支持/动用资源等: *Owen was trying to mobilize support for a new political party.* 欧文正为一个新政党争取支持。**3** [I,T] if a country mobilizes or mobilizes its army, it prepares to fight a war〔国家军事力量〕动员起来; 动员〔军队〕—see also 另见 DEMOBILIZE —**mobilization** /ˌmoblə̩ˋzeʃən; ˌməʊbʒlaɪˈzeɪʃən/ *n* [C,U]

mob·ster /ˈmɑbstɚ; ˈmɒbstə/ *n* [C] *especially AmE* a member of an organized criminal group; GANGSTER【尤美】犯罪集团成员, 匪徒, 歹徒

Mo·by-Dick /ˌmobɪˋdɪk; ˌməʊbi ˈdɪk/ (1851) a NOVEL by Herman Melville about a man called Captain Ahab who risks his life and the lives of the other people on his ship by hunting a large, powerful white WHALE called Moby-Dick. The book is famous of containing a lot of information about hunting whales and for being very long. Many people consider it to be one of the greatest American novels.《白鲸》〔(1851), 赫尔曼·梅尔维尔创作的一部小说。书中的埃哈伯船长为了捕杀一只叫莫比·狄克的大白鲸而不惜拿自己和其他船员的生命去冒险。书中有大量关于捕鲸的知识, 篇幅极长, 被认为是最杰出的美国小说之一〕

moc·ca·sin /ˈmɑkəsn; ˈmɒkəsɪn/ *n* [C] a flat comfortable shoe made of soft leather 莫卡辛鞋, 软皮平底鞋 —see picture at 参见 SHOE[1] 图

moch·a /ˈmokə; ˈmɒkə/ *n* [U] **1** a type of coffee 摩卡咖啡, 莫加咖啡 **2** *AmE* a combination of coffee and chocolate【美】巧克力咖啡

mock- /mɑk; mɒk/ *prefix* **1** only pretendingly 假装地: *a mock-serious expression* 假装严肃的表情 **2** not real 非真实的, 假的; 仿制的: *a mock-Tudor fireplace* 仿都铎式壁炉

mock[1] /mɑk; mɒk/ *v* **1** [I,T] *formal* to laugh at someone or something and try to make them look stupid by making unkind

M

remarks about them or by copying them; make fun of【正式】嘲笑, 讥笑, 嘲弄;〔以模仿〕取笑: **mock sth/sb** *They have insulted us and mocked our religion.* 他们侮辱我们, 还嘲笑我们的宗教。| *It's easy for you to mock, but we put a lot of work into this play.* 你讲风凉话是不用费力气的, 但我们却在这场剧中费了很大力气。| *mocking laughter* 嘲弄的笑声 **2** [T] *formal* to make something seem completely useless【正式】使无效; 使失败, 挫败: *His silence mocked her efforts to start a conversation.* 他的沉默使她搭讪的努力归于失败。—**mocker** *n* [C] —**mockingly** *adv*: *His lips twisted mockingly.* 他嘲弄地噘了噘嘴。

mock sth ↔ **up** *phr v* [T] to make a full-size model of something so that it looks real〔照原尺寸〕模仿, 仿制 —see also 另见 MOCK-UP

mock² *adj* [only before noun 仅用于名词前] **1** not real, but intended to be very similar to a real situation, substance etc 非真实的; 模拟的: *war games with mock battles* 模拟战争的游戏 | *a mock interview* 模拟面试 **2 mock surprise/horror/indignation etc** surprise etc that you pretend to feel, especially as a joke 假装的吃惊/害怕/愤怒等〔尤指开玩笑〕: *He pulled at his hair in mock distress.* 他撕扯着头发, 假装很痛苦。**3 mock Tudor/Georgian** copying the style of Tudor or Georgian buildings 仿都铎/乔治王朝建筑风格的

mock³ *n* **1 mocks** [plural] *BrE* school examinations taken as practice before official examinations【英】模拟考试 **2 make mock of** *literary* to mock someone【文】嘲笑; 嘲弄: *He makes mock of my dreams.* 他嘲笑我的梦想。

mock·ers /ˈmɑkɚz; ˈmɒkəz/ *n* [plural] **put the mockers on** *BrE informal* to spoil an event or someone's plans【英, 非正式】挫败, 使告吹, 使成功无望: *Oh well, if you've got the car that puts the mockers on my plans to go out!* 算了吧, 既然你买了车, 我旅游的计划就吹了!

mock·e·ry /ˈmɑkəri; ˈmɒkəri/ *n* **1 make a mockery of** to make something such as a plan, system, or organization seem completely useless or ineffective 使…显得无用[无效]: *The continued flouting of Security Council resolutions is making a mockery of the UN.* 连续违反安理会决议的行为使联合国形同虚设。**2** [U] a feeling or attitude of laughing at someone or something or of trying to make them seem completely stupid 嘲笑, 愚弄: *There was an element of mockery in the politeness he showed the inspector.* 他对那位督察员所表现出来的客套带有一种嘲弄的成分。**3** [singular] something that is completely useless or ineffective 无用的东西; 无效的东西: *The driving test was a mockery as a test of real driving skill.* 那次驾驶测试根本不能测定实际驾驶技术。

mock·ing·bird /ˈmɑkɪŋ͵bɝd; ˈmɒkɪŋbɜːd/ *n* [C] an American bird that copies the songs of other birds 嘲鸫〔一种产于美国的鸟, 能模仿其他鸟的叫声〕

mock tur·tle /͵· ˈ··/ *n* [C] *AmE* a shirt or SWEATER with a high, close-fitting band around the neck【美】高领衫; 高领毛衣; TURTLENECK *BrE*【英】—see picture on page A17 参见 A17 页图

Mock Tur·tle, the /͵· ˈ··/ a character in the book *Alice in Wonderland* by Lewis Carroll, who is a strange and sad creature who often cries 假海龟〔刘易斯·卡罗尔小说《艾丽丝漫游奇境记》中的角色。此物性格怪异, 动不动就哭〕

mock-up /ˈ· ·/ *n* [C] a full-size model of something that is going to be made or built, which shows how it will look〔原尺寸〕实体模型: *a mock-up of the space shuttle* 航天飞机实体模型 —see also 另见 **mock up** (MOCK¹)

MOD /͵ɛm o ˈdi; ͵em əʊ ˈdiː/ the abbreviation of 缩写= MINISTRY OF DEFENCE

Mod /mɑd; mɒd/ *n* a Gaelic festival of music and poetry held in Scotland every year 盖尔文艺节〔苏格兰一年一度的音乐和诗歌节〕

mod /mɑd; mɒd/ *n* [C] *BrE* a member of a group of young people in Britain in the 1960s who wore a particular type of neat clothes, listened to SOUL MUSIC, and drove MOTOR SCOOTERS【英】摩登派成员〔指英国20世纪60年代穿着整洁时髦、听灵歌并骑小摩托车的青少年帮派成员〕—compare 比较 ROCKER (3)

mo·dal¹ /ˈmodl; ˈməʊdl/ *n* [C] a modal verb 情态动词

modal² *adj technical*【术语】**1** [only before noun 仅用于名词前] related to the MOOD (6) of a verb〔动词〕语气的 **2** related to or written in a musical MODE (5)〔音乐〕调式的 —**modally** *adv*

modal aux·il·ia·ry /͵·· ·ˈ···/ *n* [C] a modal verb 情态动词

modal verb /͵·· ˈ·/ *n* [C] *technical* one of these verb forms: can, could, may, might, shall, should, will, would, must, ought to, used to, need, had better, and DARE. They are all used with other verbs to change their meaning by expressing ideas such as possibility, permission, or intention【术语】情态动词 —see also 另见 AUXILIARY VERB

mod cons /͵mɑd ˈkɑnz; ͵mɒd ˈkɒnz/ *n* **all mod cons** *BrE informal* all the things that are fitted in modern houses to make life easy and comfortable【英, 非正式】〔家中的〕现代化生活设施: *a property with many interesting features and all mod cons* 一处风格多样而有趣、现代化生活设施一应俱全的房产

mode /mod; məʊd/ *n* [C] **1** *formal* a particular way or style of behaving, living or doing something【正式】方式, 方法, 做法: *They have a relaxed mode of life that suits them well.* 他们过着一种很适合自己的悠闲生活。| *a highly efficient mode of transport* 高效的运输方式 **2** *technical* a particular way in which a machine operates when it is doing a particular job【术语】〔机器的〕运行方式; 状态, 模式: *a spacecraft in re-entry mode* 处于重返大气层状态中的航天器 | *To get out of the 'auto' mode on the camera, turn the knob to 'M'.* 要退出相机的"自动"模式, 将旋钮转向M。**3 be in work mode/holiday mode etc** *informal* to be in a particular state of mind【非正式】思想上处于工作状态/休假状态等: *With only 10 minutes to go, we were now in panic mode.* 仅仅还剩下10分钟, 我们此刻心里很惊慌。**4 be the mode** *formal* to be fashionable at a particular time【正式】流行, 时髦: *Long skirts were then the latest mode.* 长裙当时最时兴。**5** *technical* one of various systems of arranging notes in music, such as MAJOR and MINOR in Western music【术语】〔音乐的〕调式 —see also 另见 À LA MODE, MODISH

mod·el¹ /ˈmɑdl; ˈmɒdl/ *n* [C]

1 ►SMALL COPY 小的仿制物◄ a small copy of a building, vehicle, machine etc, especially one that can be put together from separate parts 模型: *He enjoys making airplane models.* 他喜欢制作飞机模型。| **[+of]** *They brought us a little model of the Taj Mahal.* 他们带给我们一个泰姬陵小模型。| **working model** (=one in which the parts move) 工作模型 *a working model of a steam engine* 蒸汽机的工作模型

2 ►FASHION 时装◄ someone whose job is to show clothes, hair styles etc by wearing them and being photographed 时装模特儿: *a top fashion model* 高级时装模特儿 | *a male model* 男服装模特儿

3 ►ART 艺术◄ someone who is employed by an artist or photographer to be painted or photographed〔绘画或摄影〕模特儿

4 ►GOOD/SPECIAL PERSON 优秀/特殊人物◄ someone you should imitate because of their good qualities or behaviour 模范, 典范, 榜样: **[+of]** *As a politician, she was a model of integrity and decency.* 作为一名政治家, 她是诚实、正派的典范。| **role model** (=someone that you try to copy because they have qualities you would like to have)〔具有令人崇拜的品质而被仿效的〕楷模 *A woman teacher can become a role model for female students.* 女教师会成为女学生的行为榜样。

5 ►GOOD/SUCCESSFUL THING 好/成功的事物◄ a way of doing something that is successful or useful and therefore worth copying〔因成功或有用而〕值得效仿的做事方式, 典范: **[+of]** *Scarman's report is a model of fairness and clarity.* 斯卡曼的报告是公正和明确的模范。| *The science of astronomy was developed first and became a model for the other sciences.* 天文学成熟得最早并成为其他科学的典范。

6 ►DESCRIPTION 描述◄ a simple description of a system or structure that is used to help people understand similar systems or structures〔帮助理解用的〕模型: *a computer model of the main factors determining a company's market share* 对决定公司市场份额的主要因素进行分析的电脑模型

7 ►TYPE OF CAR ETC 汽车等的型号◄ a particular type or design of a vehicle or machine 样式, 型号: *the cheapest model in the Volkswagen range* 大众系列汽车中最便宜的型号 | **latest model** (=the newest design produced by a company) 最新型产品 *Our dishwasher is the latest model.* 我们的洗碗机是最新型产品。

model² *adj* **1 model airplane/train/car etc** a small copy of an airplane etc, especially one that a child can play with or put together from separate parts〔尤指儿童可玩或拼装的〕模型飞机/火车/汽车等 **2 model wife/employee/student etc** someone who behaves like a perfect wife, employee etc 模范妻子/雇员/学生等: *His lawyers tried to show him as a model husband and father.* 他的律师们竭力想证明他是一个模范丈夫、模范父亲。**3 model prison/farm/school etc** a prison etc that has been specially designed or organized to be as good as possible 模范监狱/农场/学校等

model³ *v* **modelled, modelling** *BrE*【英】, **modeled, modeling** *AmE*【美】**1** [I,T] to wear clothes in order to show them to possible buyers 当模特儿, 做模特儿向顾客展示〔服装〕: *She's modeling Donna Karan's fall collection of skirts.* 她在为唐娜·凯伦的秋季系列女裙展览当模特儿。**2 model yourself on** to try to be like someone else because you admire them 以…为榜样:

Jim had always modelled himself on his great hero, Martin Luther King. 吉姆总是以他心目中的大英雄马丁·路德·金为榜样。**3 be modelled on** to be designed in a way that copies another system or way of doing something 模仿，效仿；仿制：*Their education system is modelled on the French one.* 他们的教育体制是模仿法国的。**4** [T] to make small objects from materials such as wood or clay 用〔木头或泥巴等材料〕制作小物品，塑造：*She was modeling the plasticine into little animal figures.* 她正在用橡皮泥捏制一些小动物。

mod·el·ling *BrE*【英】，**modeling** *AmE*【美】/ˈmɑdlɪŋ; ˈmɒdlɪŋ/ *n* [U] **1** the work of a MODEL[1] (2) 模特儿的职业：*a career in modelling* 模特儿职业生涯 **2** the activity of making model ships, planes, figures etc〔船只、飞机、人物等的〕模型制作

Model T Ford /ˌmɑdl ti ˈfɔrd; ˌmɒdl tiː ˈfɔːd/ *trademark* a type of Ford car made between 1909 and 1927. It was the first car to be built on an ASSEMBLY LINE, and this made inexpensive cars available to ordinary people for the first time. The Model T Ford was sold in very large numbers, and was informally called the 'Tin Lizzie'. Henry Ford, who invented and produced this car, was speaking about the Model T when he said the famous phrase: "You can have any colour you like, so long as it's black." 【商标】福特T型汽车〔1909-1927年生产的一种福特牌汽车。这是第一批从装配线上生产出来的汽车，也是普通老百姓最早能买得起的汽车。福特T型汽车销量极好，俗称"便宜小汽车"。设计生产这款车型的亨利·福特在谈到福特T型车时曾说过一句名言："什么颜色都有，只要是黑的"〕

mo·dem /ˈmoˌdɛm; ˈməʊdəm/ *n* [C] a piece of electronic equipment that allows information from one computer to be sent along telephone wires to another computer 调制解调器 —see picture on page A14 参见A14页图

mod·e·rate[1] /ˈmɑdərɪt; ˈmɒdərɪ̮t/ *adj* **1** neither very big nor very small, very hot nor very cold, very fast nor very slow etc 中等的，适度的：*Bake the pie for 30 minutes in a moderate oven.* 把馅饼在烤炉里用中温烘烤30分钟。| *We're looking for a house with a moderate-sized garden.* 我们正在找一所带中型花园的住房。| *a moderate degree of success* 中等程度的成功 | *a student of only moderate ability* 能力一般的学生 **2** having opinions, or beliefs especially about politics, that are not extreme and that most people consider reasonable or sensible 不极端的，温和的；稳健的：*Her views represent the moderate wing of the party.* 她的观点代表该政党中温和派的观点。| *a moderate politician* 温和派政治家 **3** staying within reasonable or sensible limits 有节制的，不过分的：*a moderate smoker* 吸烟有节制的人 | *moderate wage demands* 适度的工资要求 —see also 另见 MODERATELY

mod·e·rate[2] /ˈmɑdəˌret; ˈmɒdəreɪt/ *v* [I,T] **1** *formal* to make something less extreme or violent, or to become less extreme or violent【正式】(使)和缓；(使)减轻；节制，克制：*The students moderated their demands.* 学生们降低了要求。| *We couldn't leave the harbour until the storm moderated.* 在暴风雨减弱之前我们无法离开港口。**2** *BrE* to do the work of a MODERATOR【英】做调解人；做考试监督员；做〔比赛等〕主持人

mod·e·rate[3] /ˈmɑdərɪt; ˈmɒdərɪ̮t/ *n* [C] someone whose opinions or beliefs, especially about politics, are not extreme and are considered reasonable by most people 持温和观点的人，温和派人士：*Carter appointed moderates to the Supreme Court.* 卡特任命了一些温和派法官到最高法院任职。

mod·e·rate·ly /ˈmɑdərɪtlɪ; ˈmɒdərɪ̮tli/ *adv* fairly but not very 适度地；不过分地；有限地：*a moderately successful film* 一部还算成功的电影

mod·e·ra·tion /ˌmɑdəˈreʃən; ˌmɒdəˈreɪʃən/ *n* [U] **1 in moderation** if you do something in moderation, such as drinking alcohol or smoking, you do not do it too much〔饮酒或吸烟等〕有节制地，适度地：*Some people think drinking in moderation is healthy.* 有些人认为适度饮酒对健康有益。**2** *formal* control of your behaviour, so that you keep your actions, feelings, habits etc within reasonable or sensible limits【正式】节制，克制：**[+in]** *Moderation in diet is the way to good health.* 饮食有节制是保持身体健康的方法。**3** *formal* reduction in force, degree, speed etc【正式】缓和，减轻：*Even after sunset there was little moderation in the temperature.* 甚至在日落之后气温也几乎没有降低。

mod·e·ra·to /ˌmɑdəˈrɑto; ˌmɒdəˈrɑːtəʊ/ *adj, adv* a word meaning at an average speed, used as an instruction on how fast to play a piece of music〔音乐演奏〕中速的[地]

mod·e·ra·tor /ˈmɑdəˌretə; ˈmɒdəreɪtə/ *n* [C] **1** someone whose job is to control a discussion or argument and to help people reach an agreement 仲裁人；调解人 **2** *BrE* someone who makes sure that an examination is fair, and that the marks given are fair and correct【英】〔保证考试公正、判分正确的〕考试监督员 **3** someone who asks questions and keeps the marks of competing teams in a spoken game or competition〔问答比赛中提问题并记录参赛队分数的〕主席，主持人 **4** a religious leader who is in charge of the council of the Presbyterian and United Reformed Churches〔主持长老会和联合归正会会议的〕议长

mod·ern /ˈmɑdən; ˈmɒdn/ *adj* **1** [only before noun 仅用于名词前] time belonging to the present time or most recent time 现代的，近代的：*a book about modern history* 一本关于现代史的书 | *Traditional treatments, once shunned by modern medicine, are now being examined scientifically.* 传统疗法曾一度备受现代医学的冷落，但现在又被纳入科学研究。| *The original supermarkets were small by modern standards.* 按现代的标准来看，最初的超级市场很小。**2** made or done using the most recent methods; UP-TO-DATE 现代化的；新式的：*Their offices are in a modern 25-storey skyscraper.* 他们的办公室在一幢25层高的现代化摩天大楼中。| *modern surgical techniques* 现代外科技术 **3** using or willing to use very recent ideas, fashions, or ways of thinking〔思想、时装或思维方式〕时髦的，摩登的，新潮的：*The school is very modern in its approach to sex education.* 这所学校在性教育方式上非常开放。**4** [only before noun 仅用于名词前] modern art, music, literature etc uses styles that have been recently developed and are very different from traditional styles〔艺术、音乐、文学等〕当代风格的，现代派的：*Modern dance looks more spontaneous than traditional ballet.* 现代派舞蹈看起来比传统芭蕾更自由奔放、无拘无束。**5 Modern Greek/Hebrew/English** the form of the Greek etc language that is used today 现代希腊语/希伯来语/英语 —see also 另见 SECONDARY MODERN

modern-day /ˈ·· ·/ *adj* [only before noun 仅用于名词前] existing in the present time, but considered in relation to someone or something else in the past 现代的，当代的：*She's a modern-day Joan of Arc.* 她是当代的圣女贞德。| *The modern-day diet has too little fiber in it.* 现代人的饮食含纤维太少。

mod·ern·is·m /ˈmɑdənˌɪzəm; ˈmɒdənɪzəm/ *n* [U] a style of art, building etc that was popular especially from the 1940s to the 1960s, in which artists used simple shapes and modern artificial materials〔20世纪40年代至60年代艺术、建筑等的〕现代主义，现代派 —compare 比较 POST-MODERNISM —**modernist** *adj, n* [C]: *the modernist school* 现代派

mod·ern·ist·ic /ˌmɑdəˈnɪstɪk; ˌmɒdəˈnɪstɪk◂/ *adj* designed in a way that looks very modern and very different from previous styles〔外观〕非常现代化的；现代派的：*a modernistic office building* 外观非常现代化的办公大楼

mo·der·ni·ty /məˈdɝnɪtɪ; mɒˈdɜːnɪ̮ti/ *n* [U] *formal* the quality of being modern【正式】现代性；现代状态：*a conflict between tradition and modernity* 传统与现代的冲突

mod·ern·ize also 又作 **-ise** *BrE*【英】/ˈmɑdənˌaɪz; ˈmɒdənaɪz/ *v* **1** [T] to change something so that it is more suitable for the present time by using new equipment or methods 使现代化：*NATO is determined to modernize its ground forces.* 北约决心使其地面部队现代化。| *a tastefully modernized old farmhouse* 雅致而现代化的旧农场住宅 **2** [I] to start using more modern methods and equipment 采用现代方法和设备，现代化：*The business will lose money if it doesn't modernize.* 该企业如果不现代化的话就要赔钱。—**modernization** /ˌmɑdənəˈzeʃən; ˌmɒdənaɪˈzeɪʃən/ *n* [C,U]

modern lan·gua·ges /ˌ·· ˈ···/ *n* [plural] *BrE* modern European languages, such as French or Italian, studied as a subject at school or university【英】现代语言〔指作为中小学或大学课程的现代欧洲语言，如法语或意大利语〕

mod·est /ˈmɑdɪst; ˈmɒdɪ̮st/ *adj* **1** unwilling to talk proudly about your abilities and achievements 谦虚的，谦逊的，谦恭的：**[+about]** *He was always surprisingly modest about his role in the Everest expedition.* 他总是对自己在那次珠穆朗玛峰探险中所起的作用谦虚得令人惊讶。**2** not very big, expensive etc, especially less big, expensive etc than you would expect 不太大的；不很贵的：*quite a modest salary for such an important job* 对如此重要的工作而言一点也不算高的薪水 | *his modest ambitions* 他的小小的抱负 | **a modest amount/improvement etc** *House prices rose by a modest amount in the last quarter.* 房价最近一个季度有所增长。**3** shy about showing your body or attracting sexual interest, because you are easily embarrassed 羞怯的，腼腆的；忸怩的：*Children often become very modest at around age 11.* 小孩子常常在11岁左右的时候变得非常腼腆。**4** *old-fashioned* modest clothing covers the body in a way that does not attract sexual interest【过时】〔衣服〕庄重的：*a modest knee-length dress* 长至膝部、显得庄重的连衣裙 —**modestly** *adv*

mod·es·ty /ˈmɑdəstɪ; ˈmɒdɪ̮sti/ *n* [U] **1** a modest way of behaving or talking 谦虚，谦逊，谦恭：*the great player's modesty*

那位优秀选手的谦逊 **2 in all modesty** *spoken* used to say that you do not want to seem too proud of something you have done, when in fact you are【口】〔用于不失谦逊地承认自己的功劳〕: *I think in all modesty that I can take some small credit for the team's success.* 我不是要为自己请功，但我认为球队的成功有我一份小小的功劳。**3** unwillingness to show your body or do anything that may attract sexual interest 羞怯；端庄 **4 modesty forbids** *spoken* used when saying jokingly that you do not want to talk about your achievements【口】君子不自尚其功〔开玩笑地表示不想谈论自己的成就〕—see also 另见 **false modesty** (FALSE (4))

mod·i·cum /ˋmɑdɪkəm; ˈmɒdɪkəm/ *n* **a modicum of** *formal* a small amount of something, especially a good quality【正式】〔尤指好的方面〕少量，一点点: *a modicum of common sense* 一点儿常识

mod·i·fi·ca·tion /ˌmɑdəfəˋkeʃən; ˌmɒdɪ̣fɪ̣ˈkeɪʃən/ *n* **1** [C] a small change made in something such as a design, plan, or system 修改，更改，改变: *We've made one or two minor modifications to the original design.* 我们对原先的设计作了一两处小小的修改。**2** [U] the act of modifying something, or the process of being modified 修改的行为[过程]; 改造: *The fuel can be used in diesel engines without modification.* 这种燃料柴油机无需改造就可使用。

mod·i·fi·er /ˋmɑdəˌfaɪɚ; ˈmɒdɪ̣faɪə/ *n* [C] *technical* a word or group of words that give additional information about another word. Modifiers can be adjectives (such as 'fierce' in 'the fierce dog'), adverbs (such as 'loudly' in 'the dog barked loudly'), or phrases (such as 'with a short tail' in 'the dog with a short tail').【术语】修饰语〔可以是形容词、副词或短语〕

mod·i·fy /ˋmɑdəˌfaɪ; ˈmɒdɪ̣faɪ/ *v* [T] **1** to make small changes to something in order to improve it and make it more suitable or effective〔略微地〕修改，更改；改进，改造: *The present law needs to be modified.* 目前的法律尚待改进。**2** *technical* if an adjective, adverb etc modifies another word it describes it or limits its meaning【术语】〔形容词、副词等〕修饰〔另一词〕: *In the phrase 'walk slowly', the adverb 'slowly' modifies the verb 'walk'.* 在短语 walk slowly 中，副词 slowly 修饰动词 walk。

Mod·i·glia·ni /ˌmodilˋjɑnɪ; ˌmɒdɪlˈjɑːni/, **Am·e·de·o** /ˌæməˋdeo; ˌæməˈdeɪəʊ/ (1884-1920) an Italian painter and SCULPTOR known especially for his pictures of NUDES (=women without clothes) and of people's faces, in which the bodies and faces are much longer than in real life 莫迪里阿尼〔(1884-1920)，意大利画家和雕塑家，尤以女性裸体画和肖像画闻名，作品中的人体和脸部比真人长的多〕

mod·ish /ˋmodɪʃ; ˈməʊdɪʃ/ *adj* modish ideas, designs etc are modern and fashionable 新潮的，时髦的；流行的 —**modishly** *adv*

mod·u·lar /ˋmɑdʒələ; ˈmɒdjʊ̈lə/ *adj* based on modules or made using modules 分单元的；组合式的；模块化的: *a modular course in business studies* 商业课程中一门分单元进行的课程 | *modular furniture* 组合式家具

mod·u·late /ˋmɑdʒəˌlet; ˈmɒdjʊ̈leɪt/ *v* **1** [T] *formal* to change the sound of your voice or the strength of something【正式】改变〔音质或强度〕；调整，调节 **2** [I+**from/to**] *technical* to move from one KEY to another in a piece of music using a series of related chords (CHORD (1))【术语】〔音乐〕转调；变调 **3** [T] *technical* to change the form of a radio signal so that it can be broadcast more effectively【术语】调制〔无线电信号〕—**modulation** /ˌmɑdʒəˋleʃən; ˌmɒdjʊ̈ˈleɪʃən/ *n* [C]

2 **mod·ule** /ˋmɑdʒul; ˈmɒdjuːl/ *n* [C] **1** *especially BrE* one of the units that a course of study has been divided into, each of which can be studied separately【尤英】单元〔课程学习单位〕: *a module in mathematics* 数学课的一个单元 **2** a part of a SPACECRAFT that can be separated from the main part and used for a particular purpose〔宇宙飞船的〕分离舱 **3** one of several separate parts that can be combined to form a larger object, such as a machine or building〔机器、建筑物等的〕组件，模件，模块

mo·dus op·e·ran·di /ˋmodəs ˌɑpəˋrændaɪ; ˌməʊdəs ɒpəˈrændi/ *n* [singular] *Latin formal* a way of doing something that is typical of one person or group【拉丁，正式】典型的做法；一惯的做法

modus vi·ven·di /ˋmodəs vɪˋvɛndaɪ; ˌməʊdəs vɪˈvendi/ *n* [singular] *Latin formal* an arrangement between people with very different opinions or habits that allows them to live or work together without quarrelling【拉丁，正式】〔矛盾双方的〕妥协，解决办法，权宜之计

Moët et Chandon *trademark* a type of CHAMPAGNE【商标】酩悦香槟

Mogadishu /ˌmɑgəˋdɪʃu; ˌmɒgəˈdɪʃuː/ also 又作 **Mogadiscio, Muqdisho** the capital, largest city, and main port of Somalia, on the Indian Ocean 摩加迪沙〔索马里首都和最大城市，也是该国主要港口，濒临印度洋〕

mog·gy, moggie /ˋmɑgɪ; ˈmɒgi/ *n* [C] *BrE informal* a cat【英，非正式】猫

Mogul also 又作 **Moghul, Mughal** a member of a family of Muslim rulers of northern India from 1526-1857, a period famous for beautiful art and buildings, including the Taj Mahal 莫卧儿〔指1526-1857年印度北部地方一穆斯林王朝的家族成员。这段时期以精美的艺术作品和漂亮的建筑见称，其中包括泰姬陵〕

mo·gul /ˋmogʌl; ˈməʊgəl/ *n* [C] **movie/record/tennis mogul etc** someone who has great power and influence in a particular industry or activity 电影业/唱片业/网坛等的泰斗

mo·hair /ˋmoˌhɛr; ˈməʊheə/ *n* [U] expensive wool made from the hair of the ANGORA goat〔用安哥拉羊毛制成的〕马海毛毛线: *a mohair sweater* 马海毛毛线衫 —see picture on page A16 参见 A16 页图

Mo·ham·med /moˋhæmɪd; məʊˈhæmɪ̣d/ — see 见 MUHAMMAD

Mo·ham·me·dan /moˋhæmədən; məʊˈhæmɪ̣dən/ *n* [C] an old-fashioned word for Muslim, now considered offensive by most Muslims 伊斯兰教信徒，回教徒〔穆斯林的旧称，大多数穆斯林觉得这种叫法极具冒犯性〕—**Mohammedan** *adj*

Mo·ham·me·dan·is·m an old-fashioned word for the Muslim religion, now considered offensive by most Muslims 伊斯兰教，回教〔伊斯兰教的旧称，大多数穆斯林认为这种叫法极具冒犯性〕

Mo·ha·ve Desert /moˌhɑvɪ ˋdɛzɚt; məʊˌhɑːvi ˈdezət/ — see 见 the MOJAVE DESERT

Mohican an imaginary Native American tribe of the upper Hudson River valley in New York State, invented by the writer James Fenimore Cooper for his stories, such as *The Last of the Mohicans* 莫希干族〔作家詹姆士·费尼莫尔·库珀《最后的莫希干人》等故事中虚构的北美土著，居住在纽约州哈得孙河上游河谷〕

moi /mwɑ; mwɑː/ *pron spoken humorous* me【口，幽默】我〔宾格〕: *Difficult, moi?* 不好打交道？是说我吗？

moi·e·ty /ˋmɔɪətɪ; ˈmɔɪɪ̣ti/ *n* [C+**of**] *law or literary* a half share【法律或文】一半，半份

moist /mɔɪst; mɔɪst/ *adj* slightly wet but not too wet, especially in a way that seems pleasant or suitable 潮湿的，微湿的，湿润的: *Make sure the soil is moist before planting the seeds.* 播种之前要确保土壤湿润。| *a moist chocolate cake* 松软的巧克力蛋糕 —compare 比较 DAMP[1] (1) —**moistness** *n* [U]

moist·en /ˋmɔɪsn; ˈmɔɪsən/ *v* [I,T] to become slightly wet, or to make something slightly wet（使）潮湿，（使）湿润: *Moisten the clay if it seems too dry.* 如果黏土看起来太干，就将其湿润。

mois·ture /ˋmɔɪstʃɚ; ˈmɔɪstʃə/ *n* [U] small amounts of water that are present in the air, in a substance, or on a surface 水分，水气，湿气: *Plants use their roots to absorb moisture from the soil.* 植物利用根从土壤中吸收水分。

mois·tur·ize also 又作 **-ise** *BrE*【英】/ˋmɔɪstʃəˌraɪz; ˈmɔɪstʃəraɪz/ *v* [T] **1** to make your skin less dry by using special cream 使〔皮肤〕湿润，滋润 **2 moisturizing cream/lotion/oil** cream, oil etc which you put on your skin to make it less dry 润肤霜/润肤露/润肤油

mois·tur·iz·er also 又作 **-iser** *BrE*【英】/ˋmɔɪstʃəˌraɪzɚ; ˈmɔɪstʃəraɪzə/ *n* [C,U] cream that you put on your skin to make it less dry 润肤膏，润肤霜

Mo·ja·ve Des·ert, the /moˌhɑvɪ ˋdɛzɚt; məʊˌhɑːvi ˈdezət/ also 又作 **the Mohave Desert** a large desert in southern California. Death Valley, the lowest point in the US, is found in the Mojave Desert. 莫哈韦沙漠〔加利福尼亚州南部一大沙漠。美国海拔最低点"死亡峡"即位于该沙漠〕

mo·lar /ˋmolɚ; ˈməʊlə/ *n* [C] one of the large teeth at the back of the mouth used for breaking up food 臼齿 —compare 比较 INCISOR —**molar** *adj* —see picture at 参见 TEETH 图

mo·las·ses /məˋlæsɪz; məˈlæsɪ̣z/ *n* [U] *AmE* a thick dark sweet liquid that is obtained from raw sugar plants when they are being made into sugar【美】糖浆，糖蜜；TREACLE *BrE*【英】

mold /mold; məʊld/ *n* [U] the American spelling of MOULD mould 的美式拼法 —**molding** *n* [C,U]

mol·der /ˋmoldɚ; ˈməʊldə/ *v* [I] the American spelling of MOULDER moulder 的美式拼法

Mol·do·va /mɑlˋdovə; mɒlˈdəʊvə/ a country in Eastern Europe between Romania and the Ukraine, which used to be part of the former Soviet Union. Population: 4,432,000 (2001). Capital: Kishinev. 摩尔多瓦〔东欧一国家，位于罗马尼亚和乌克兰之间，曾是前苏联一部分。人口：4,432,000 (2001)，首都：基什尼奥夫〕—**Moldavan** *n, adj*

mold·y /ˈmoldɪ; ˈməʊldi/ *adj* the American spelling of MOULDY mouldy 的美式拼法 —**moldiness** *n* [U]

mole /mol; məʊl/ *n* [C] **1** a small furry almost blind animal that usually lives under the ground 鼹鼠 **2** a small dark brown mark on the skin that is slightly higher than the skin around it 痣 **3** someone who works for an organization while secretly giving information to its enemies 内奸；长期潜伏的间谍 **4** *technical* a scientific unit for measuring the quantity of a substance【术语】摩尔，克分子（量）

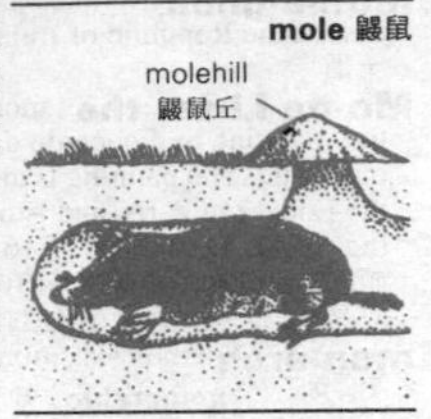

Mole, A·dri·an /ˈedrɪən; ˈeɪdriən/ the main character in a series of humorous British books written by Sue Townsend, the first of which was *The Secret Diary of Adrian Mole, Aged 13* (1982). Each book is in the form of a DIARY in which Adrian writes about his daily life and thoughts. He describes many of the emotional problems that are typical of people his age. 莫尔〔苏·汤森所著的英国幽默系列丛书中的主人公。丛书的第一本名为《13岁少年安德里安·莫尔的私人日记》。每本书都以日记形式写成。安德里安记录他的日常生活和种种想法，写到的许多情感问题在他这个年龄很典型〕

mol·e·cule /ˈmɑləˌkjul; ˈmɒlɪkjuːl/ *n* [C] the smallest unit into which any substance can be divided without losing its own chemical nature, usually consisting of two or more atoms 分子 —**molecular** /məˈlɛkjələ; məˈlekjʊ̈lə/ *adj*: *molecular structure* 分子结构

mole·hill /ˈmolˌhɪl; ˈməʊlˌhɪl/ *n* [C] a small pile of earth made by a MOLE 鼹鼠丘 —see also 另见 **make a mountain out of a molehill** (MOUNTAIN (4)) —see picture at 参见 MOLE 图

mole·skin /ˈmolˌskɪn; ˈməʊlˌskɪn/ *n* [U] **1** thick dark cloth 仿鼹鼠皮布料，厚毛头斜纹棉布 **2** the skin of a MOLE 鼹鼠皮

mo·lest /məˈlɛst; məˈlest/ *v* [T] **1** to attack or harm someone, especially a child, by touching them in a sexual way or trying to have sex with them〔尤指〕对〔儿童〕作性骚扰，猥亵；调戏：*men who molest young boys* 猥亵男童的男子 —compare 比较 ABUSE² (2) **2** *old-fashioned* to attack and physically harm someone【过时】袭击；伤害：*a dog that was molesting sheep* 一只正在袭扰绵羊的狗 —**molester** *n* [C]: *a convicted child molester* 已被判猥亵儿童罪的犯人 —**molestation** /ˌmolɛsˈteʃən; ˌməʊleˈsteɪʃən/ *n* [U]

Mol·i·ère /molˈjɛr; ˈmɒlieə/ (1622-73) a French actor and writer of plays whose real name was Jean-Baptiste Poquelin. His most famous works are comedies (COMEDY) that make fun of human behaviour, such as *Le Misanthrope*, *Tartuffe*, and *Le Bourgeois Gentilhomme*. 莫里哀〔（1622-1673），法国演员和剧作家，原名为让-巴蒂斯特·波克兰。最著名的作品皆为嘲弄人类行为的喜剧，如《愤世嫉俗者》、《伪君子》和《暴发户》〕

moll /mɑl; mɒl/ *n* [C] *old-fashioned, slang especially AmE* a criminal's girlfriend【过时，俚，尤美】罪犯的情人：*a gangster's moll* 匪徒的情人

Moll Flanders /ˈmɑl ˈflændəz; ˈmɒl ˈflɑːndəz/ the main character in the book *The Fortunes and Misfortunes of the Famous Moll Flanders*, written in 1722 by Daniel Defoe. Moll tells the story of her marriages, sexual relationships, and crimes in an amusing way that makes the reader feel sympathy for her. 摩尔〔丹尼尔·笛福1722年创作的小说《摩尔·弗兰德斯》中的主要人物。摩尔用一种逗趣的方式讲述她的婚姻、婚外情以及她犯下的罪行，使读者不由得对她产生同情〕

mol·li·fy /ˈmɑləˌfaɪ; ˈmɒlɪ̈faɪ/ *v* [T] to make someone feel less angry and upset about something 抚慰，使平静；使平息怒气：*The old man seemed mollified by the flattery.* 老头听了那些恭维话好像气消了。—**mollification** /ˌmɑləfɪˈkeʃən; ˌmɒlɪ̈fɪ̈ˈkeɪʃən/ *n* [U]

mol·lusc *BrE*【英】, **mollusk** *AmE*【美】/ˈmɑləsk; ˈmɒləsk/ *n* [C] a type of sea or land animal that has a soft body covered by a hard shell 软体动物：*snails and other molluscs* 蜗牛和其他软体动物

mol·ly·cod·dle /ˈmɑlɪˌkɑdl; ˈmɒliˌkɒdl/ *v* [T] to treat someone too kindly 溺爱；娇惯，娇养：*rather a weak young man who had always been mollycoddled as a boy* 小时候就一直娇生惯养的、懦弱的青年男子

Mol·ly Ma·guires, the /ˌmɑlɪ məˈgwaɪrz; ˌmɒli məˈgwaɪəz/ a 19th-century secret organization of Irish Americans in the coal-producing area of Pennsylvania, US, which used often violent means to try to improve working conditions 莫利社〔19世纪美国宾夕法尼亚州产煤区美籍爱尔兰人的一个秘密组织。该组织常采用暴力手段以改善工作条件〕

Mo·loch /ˈmolɑk; ˈməʊlɒk/ a god in some ancient religions, mentioned in the Old Testament of the Bible, for whom children were killed as a SACRIFICE 摩洛〔据《圣经·旧约》记载，摩洛是古代某些宗教中的神灵，信徒常杀死儿童向其献祭〕

Mol·o·tov cock·tail /ˌmɑlətɔf ˈkɑktel; ˌmɒlətɒf ˈkɒkteɪl/ *n* [C] a simple bomb consisting of a bottle filled with petrol with a piece of cloth at the end 莫洛托夫燃烧弹〔用装满汽油的瓶子和塞在瓶口的引燃布条制成的一种简易炸弹〕

molt /molt; məʊlt/ *v* [I] the American spelling of MOULT moult 的美式拼法

mol·ten /ˈmoltn̩; ˈməʊltən/ *adj* [usually before noun 一般用于名词前] molten metal or rock has been made into a liquid by being heated to a very high temperature 熔化的，熔融的：*molten lava* 熔岩

mol·to /ˈmolto; ˈmɒltəʊ/ *adv* a word used in music meaning 'very' 极，甚〔音乐用语〕：*molto allegro* (=very fast) 极快

mo·lyb·de·num /məˈlɪbdənəm; məˈlɪbdənəm/ *n* [U] a pale-coloured metal used especially to strengthen steel 钼

mom /mɑm; mɒm/ *n* [C] *AmE informal* mother【美，非正式】妈妈；MUM¹ (1) *BrE*【英】：*fourteen-year-old girls and their moms and dads arguing about a moral issue* 一群14岁女孩和她们的爸爸妈妈正在争论一个道德问题 | *"My mom got this for me." "Oh, isn't that pretty?"* "这个是我妈妈为我买的。" "哎呀，真漂亮啊！"

MOMA /ˈmomə; ˈməʊmə/ the abbreviation of 缩写= the MUSEUM OF MODERN ART

mom-and-pop /ˌ· · ˈ·◂/ *adj* [only before noun 仅用于名词前] *AmE* a mom-and-pop business is owned and operated by a family or a husband and wife【美】〔生意〕夫妻经营的，家庭经营的：*a real mom-and-pop operation* 一家真正的夫妻企业

mo·ment /ˈmomənt; ˈməʊmənt/ *n*

1 ▶POINT IN TIME 时间点◀ [C] a particular point in time 某一时刻：*They've been arguing from the moment they walked in the door.* 他们从进门那一刻就一直在争论。| *There were a few worrying moments, but on the whole the play went well.* 尽管有令人担心的时刻，但总的说来那部剧演得不错。| **at the moment** *especially spoken BrE, formal AmE* (=used to say that something is happening or true now)【尤口，英；正式，美】此刻，目前，眼下 *Julia's on holiday in Spain at the moment.* 朱莉娅目前在西班牙度假。| *At the moment, the situation in Haiti is very tense.* 眼下，海地的局势非常紧张。| **for the moment** (=used to say that something is happening or true now but will probably change in the future) 暂时，目前 *Well, for the moment we're just friends.* 好吧，目前我们仅仅是朋友。| *For the moment the troops had stopped firing and there was an eerie hush.* 部队暂时停止了射击，四周寂静得可怕。| **at this/that moment** (=used to emphasize that something is happening now or at a particular time in the past) 在此/那时 *Just at that moment there was a knock on the door.* 就在那时有人敲门了。| *John's listening to the programme at this moment, in fact.* 事实上，约翰此时正在收听这个节目。| **at this moment in time** (=used especially by politicians, newspapers etc to mean now) 此时此刻〔尤为政治家、报纸等使用〕*At this moment in time it would be inappropriate to speculate on Castro's intentions.* 此时此刻妄加猜测卡斯特罗的意图是不合适的。| **just this moment** (=used to emphasize that something has only just happened) 刚刚，方才 *I just this moment arrived, and already Dan wants to know when I'm leaving.* 我刚到，丹就想知道我什么时候要离开了。

2 ▶SHORT TIME 短时间◀ [C] a very short period of time 片刻，瞬间，刹那：*But you said a moment ago you weren't going to see him again!* 可你刚才还说你不再见他了呢！| *Can you spare a few moments to answer some questions?* 你能抽点时间回答几个问题吗？| **in a moment** (=very soon) 立刻，马上；一会儿：*I'll come back to that point in a moment.* 我马上就会再谈到那一点。| **for a moment** *It was quiet for a moment, then Rae asked what time he'd be back.* 沉默了一会儿，然后雷问他什么时候回来。| **wait/just a moment** (=used when you want someone to wait a short time while you do or say something) 请稍候，稍等一下 *Just a moment, let me put these away first.* 请等一会儿，让我先把这些放起来。

3 the moment (that) sb does/says sth as soon as someone does something or says something 某人一做/一说…就…：*He said he'd phone you the moment he got home.* 他说他一到家就给你打电话。

4 the last moment if you do something at the last moment or wait until the last moment to do it, you do it at the last possible time 最后一刻：*How could you leave buying your wed-*

ding dress to the last moment?! 你怎么能到最后一刻才去买结婚礼服呢?!

5 not believe/think/do sth for a moment *especially spoken* used to say that you did not believe etc something at all【尤口】一点儿也没相信/认识到/做某事: *He didn't fool me for a moment.* 他一点儿也骗不到我。

6 any moment extremely soon 马上, 立刻: *The plumber should be here any moment now.* 水暖工现在应该就要到这儿了。| **at any moment** *The roof could collapse at any moment.* 屋顶随时都会坍塌下来。

7 of the moment the job, person, event etc of the moment is the one that is most important or famous at the present time〔工作、人、事件等〕当前最重要[著名]的: *her boyfriend of the moment* 她那位眼下最亲密的男友

8 ►OPPORTUNITY 机会◄ [C usually singular 一般用单数] a particular period of time when you have a chance to do something 时机, 机会: **big moment** (=a time when you have a chance to show other people how skilled, intelligent etc you are) 大好机会, 绝佳时机 *It was André's big moment; he breathed deeply and began to play.* 这是安德烈大显身手的好机会, 他深深地吸了口气, 然后开始演奏起来。| **choose/pick your moment** (=an expression meaning to choose a good time to do something, often used if you choose a very bad time to do it) 选择好时机〔常为反话〕

9 have its/your moments to have periods of being good or interesting 有好[有趣]的时刻: *a movie that had its moments* 一部还有些看点的电影

10 not a moment too soon almost too late 几乎太迟, 险些迟到: *The ambulance finally arrived, and not a moment too soon.* 救护车终于到了, 但险些误事。

11 the moment of truth the time when you will find out if something will work properly, be successful etc 发现真相[实情]的关键时刻[紧要关头]

12 of great moment *old-fashioned* important【过时】重要的

mo·men·tar·i·ly /ˈmomənˌtɛrəlı; ˈməʊməntərɨli/ *adv* **1** for a very short time 片刻地; 短暂地: *She paused momentarily and glanced over her shoulder.* 她停了片刻, 转过头看了一眼。**2** *AmE* very soon【美】马上, 立刻: *Mr Johnson will be with you momentarily.* 约翰逊先生马上就来见你。

mo·men·ta·ry /ˈmomənˌtɛrı; ˈməʊməntəri/ *adj* lasting for a very short time 短暂的, 瞬间的, 片刻的: *There was a momentary pause.* 停顿了片刻。

mo·men·tous /moˈmɛntəs; məʊˈmentəs/ *adj* a momentous event, occasion, decision etc is very important or serious, especially because it will have a great influence on the future 重大的, 重要的: *a momentous decision* 重大决定 | *1789 was a momentous year in European history.* 1789 年是欧洲历史上非常重要的一年。

mo·men·tum /moˈmɛntəm; məʊˈmentəm/ *n* [U] **1** the ability to keep increasing, developing, or being more successful 动力, 势头: **lose momentum** (=stop increasing or developing) 失去〔增长或发展的〕势头 *The business did well at first but it seems to be losing momentum.* 该企业开始时很红火, 但其发展势头现在好像正在减弱。| **gain/gather momentum** (=begin to increase or develop more quickly) 势头开始日益强劲 *The trend towards political change in South Africa was gathering momentum.* 南非政治变革的势头正变得日益强劲。**2** the force that makes a moving object keep moving〔使运动物体继续运动的〕冲力, 推力, 动力: **gain/gather momentum** (=move faster) 获得动力; 加速 *The hill got steeper and the sled gained momentum.* 小山变得更陡了, 所以雪橇也滑得更快了。| **lose momentum** (=move more slowly) 失去动力; 减速 **3** *technical* the force or power contained in a moving object calculated by multiplying its weight by its speed【术语】动量

MOMI /ˈmomı; ˈməʊmi/ the abbreviation of 缩写= the MUSEUM OF THE MOVING IMAGE

mom·ma /ˈmɑmə; ˈmɒmə/ *n* [C] *AmE* another spelling of MAMA[1]【美】mama[1] 的另一种拼法

S3 **mom·my** /ˈmɑmı; ˈmɒmi/ *n* [C] *AmE* a word meaning mother, used by or to young children【美】妈咪〔儿语〕; MUMMY (1) *BrE*【英】

Mon the written abbreviation of 缩写= MONDAY

Mon·a·co /ˈmɑnəko; ˈmɒnəkəʊ/ a small PRINCIPALITY (=a country ruled by a prince) on the Mediterranean coast between France and Italy. Population: 31,842 (2001). Capital: Monaco. It is a popular place for rich people from other countries to go to live, because of its low taxes. Its main town is Monte Carlo. People from Monaco are called 'Monegasques'. 摩纳哥〔地中海沿岸一小公国, 位于法国和意大利之间。人口: 31,842 (2001), 首都: 摩纳哥。该国税率较低, 许多国家的富人都喜欢去那里定居。主要城镇: 蒙特卡洛。摩洛哥人通常被叫做 Monegasques〕

Mon·a·ghan /ˈmɑnəhən; ˈmɒnəhən/ a COUNTY in the northeast of the Republic of Ireland 莫纳亨郡〔爱尔兰共和国东北部一郡〕

Mo·na Li·sa, the /ˌmonə ˋlisə; ˌməʊnə ˈliːzə/ a 16th century painting by Leonardo da Vinci of a woman with a mysterious smile. The painting is also called *La Gioconda*. It is kept in the Louvre in Paris, and is one of the most famous paintings in the world.《蒙娜·丽莎》〔16 世纪莱奥纳多·达·芬奇创作的一幅画。画中的女性面露神秘的微笑。此画亦名《佐贡多》, 藏于巴黎卢浮宫, 是世界上最有名的画作之一〕

mon·arch /ˈmɑnək; ˈmɒnək/ *n* [C] a king or queen 君主; 国王; 女王 **—monarchic** /məˋnɑrkık; məˈnɑːkık/ also 又作 **monarchical** *adj*: *monarchic rule* 君主统治

mon·arch·ist /ˈmɑnəkıst; ˈmɒnəkɨst/ *n* [C] someone who supports the idea that their country should be ruled by a king or queen 君主主义者 **—monarchism** *n* [U]

mon·ar·chy /ˈmɑnəkı; ˈmɒnəki/ *n* **1** [U] the system in which a country is ruled by a king or queen 君主政体, 君主制: *the abolition of the monarchy* 君主制的废除 **2** [C] a country that is ruled by a king or queen 君主国: *Britain is a constitutional monarchy.* 英国是君主立宪国。—compare 比较 REPUBLIC

CULTURAL NOTE 文化注释

The UK is a CONSTITUTIONAL MONARCHY. The monarch, at present Queen Elizabeth II, is the HEAD OF STATE (=the official ruler of the country), not only of the UK, but also of some countries in the British Commonwealth, including Australia, Canada, and New Zealand. The Queen has little real power, and most of her work consists of ceremonies. Every year, the Queen performs the State Opening of Parliament, when she makes a speech that says what the government plans to do. A new law does not become official until it has had the **royal assent** (=been signed by the Queen), but she cannot refuse to agree to a law that has been decided on by Parliament. The Queen gives titles and other honours to people who have achieved important things for the country, but most honours go to people chosen by the government. 英国是一个君主立宪国家。现任的君主是女王伊丽莎白二世, 她不仅是英国的国家元首, 同时还是英联邦中一些国家的国家元首, 包括澳大利亚、加拿大和新西兰。女王没有多少实权, 她的大部分工作是礼仪方面的。女王每年要主持英国议会的开幕, 届时她会发表一个演说来阐述政府的规划。只有经过女王认可(即经过女王签署)的法律才正式生效, 但是女王对议会通过的法律并无否决权。女王授予那些为国家作出过重大贡献的人各种头衔或荣誉, 但是大多数荣誉获得者都是政府选定的。

Some British people believe that the monarchy is old-fashioned, unnecessary, and a waste of money, and that Britain should become a REPUBLIC. But many other British people like the monarchy, and feel that it is good to have someone who is not connected with a political party to represent the country on important occasions. 有些英国人认为君主制国家是过时的、不必要的, 也是浪费钱的, 因此英国应该变成一个共和国。但是有很多英国人喜欢君主制, 他们觉得在重要场合找一个与任何政党都无瓜葛的人来代表国家更好。

TABLOID newspapers often write stories about the Royal Family, especially if they think that a member of the Royal Family has been behaving badly. They do not treat them with as much respect as newspapers in many other countries treat their Royal Families. 庸俗小报经常刊发一些有关王室的消息, 特别是在他们看来某位王室成员行为不端时。与许多其他国家的报刊对待王室的态度不同, 英国小报对英国王室不是那么尊重。

mon·as·tery /ˈmɑnəsˌtɛrı; ˈmɒnəstri/ *n* [C] a building or group of buildings in which MONKs live 寺院; 修道院 —compare 比较 CONVENT, NUNNERY

mo·nas·tic /məˈnæstık; məˈnæstık/ *adj* **1** concerned with or relating to MONKs or monasteries 修道院的, 寺院的; 修士的, 僧侣的: *monastic lands* 修道院的土地 **2** someone who has a monastic way of life lives alone and very simply 简朴的; 遁世的 **—monastically** /-klı; -kli/ *adv* **—monasticism** *n* [U]

Mon·day /ˈmʌndı; ˈmʌndi/ *n* [C,U] the day between Sunday and Tuesday. In Britain, Monday is considered the first day of the week, and in the US, it is considered the second day of the week. 星期一〔在英国被认为是一周中的第一天, 而在美国则被认

为是一周中的第二天〕: *It was raining on Monday.* 星期一下雨了。| *I found it hard to get out of bed for work on Monday morning.* 我觉得星期一早上起床上班很不容易。| *Sasha will arrive Monday.* 萨莎将于星期一到达。| **on Mondays** (=each Monday) 每个星期一 *We play football on Mondays.* 我们每个星期一都踢足球。| **a Monday** (=one of the Mondays in a year) 某个星期一 *Does Christmas fall on a Monday this year?* 今年圣诞节是星期一吗?

Mon·dri·an /ˈmɑndrɪˌɑn; ˌmɒndriˈɑːn/, **Piet** /pit; piːt/ (1872-1944) a Dutch painter famous for his abstract work involving only straight lines and squares or RECTANGLES of colour 蒙德里安〔(1872-1944), 荷兰画家, 以抽象画见称。其作品只采用直线和着色的正方形或长方形〕

Mon·et /moˈne; ˈmɒneɪ/, **Claude** /klɔd; klɔːd/ (1840-1926) a French painter who helped to start the Impressionist movement. He is famous for his paintings of the countryside in which he tried to show the effects of light by painting the same picture at different times of day or in different types of weather. 莫奈〔(1840-1926), 法国画家, 印象主义绘画运动的发起人。他以描绘乡村景色见称, 曾尝试在一天的不同时间或者在不同天气状况下画同一幅画, 以显示光线的不同效果〕

mon·e·ta·ris·m /ˈmɑnətəˌrɪzəm; ˈmʌnɪtərɪzəm/ *n* [U] the belief that the best way to manage and control a country's economic system is to limit the amount of money that is available and being used 货币主义 —**monetarist** *adj, n* [C]

3 **mon·e·ta·ry** /ˈmʌnəˌtɛrɪ; ˈmʌnɪtəri/ *adj* concerned with or relating to money, especially all the money in a particular country 货币的, 金融的: *monetary growth* 货币增长 | *a monetary unit* 货币单位

1 1 **mon·ey** /ˈmʌnɪ; ˈmʌni/ *n* [U] **1** what you earn by working and what you spend in order to buy things 钱, 货币: *The repairs will cost a lot of money.* 修理要花不少钱。| **earn money** *She barely earns enough money to live on.* 她挣的钱勉强够糊口。| **save money** *We're not going on holiday this year – we're trying to save money.* 我们今年不打算去度假了 —— 我们正在设法攒钱。| **get/be given your money back** *If it doesn't fit, just take it back to the shop and they'll give you your money back.* 如果不合适, 尽管拿回商店, 他们会把钱退给你。| **spend money** *I spent so much money at the weekend I can't afford to come.* 我那个周末花钱太多, 所以没钱来了。| **borrow money** *Maybe you could borrow some money from the bank to pay for your course.* 也许你可以从银行贷些款来支付你的学费。| **make money** (=earn money or make a profit) 赚钱, 挣钱, 赢利 *John's making a lot of money from his computer games.* 约翰靠他的电脑游戏大把大把地赚钱。| *His business has finally started making money.* 他的企业终于开始赚钱了。| **charge money** *I said I didn't want it if they were going to charge me a lot of money for it.* 我说如果他们要价太高, 我就不要它了。| **good money** (=good wages for your work) 丰厚的薪水 *She's making about $40,000 a year, which is pretty good money.* 她每年挣大约4万美元, 这可是一份很丰厚的薪水。| **raise money** (=collect money for a purpose) 集资, 筹款 *We're trying to raise money for the victims of the earthquake.* 我们正在设法为地震受灾者筹集资金。| **birthday money/redundancy money etc** (=money you receive on a particular occasion or in a particular situation) 生日礼金/裁员费等 *They're using part of his redundancy money to go on a cruise.* 他们计划动用他一部分裁员补偿金去进行一次乘船游览。| **put money into** (=lend money or allow a business to use your money, especially in order to make a profit) 投资于 *George has decided to put some of his money into the business.* 乔治决定把他的一部分钱投到这家企业。| **put money on a race/horse etc** (=risk money on the result of a race etc) 在比赛/赛马等上下赌注 **2** money in the form of coins or notes; CASH[1] (1) 钱, 现款, 现金: *My bag came open, and all my money fell on the floor.* 我的包开了, 所有的钱都掉到了地上。| **have money on you** (=carry money with you) 随身带着现钱 *Do you have enough money on you to pay for the meal?* 你身上带的钱够付餐费吗? **3 French/Japanese/Turkish money** the money that is used in a particular country; CURRENCY 法国/日本/土耳其货币: *Don't forget to get some French money before you leave.* 你走之前别忘了弄点法国货币。**4** all the money that a person, organization, or country owns 资产, 财产, 财富: *The business collapsed and we lost all our money.* 企业倒闭了, 我们损失了所有的钱。| *She's only marrying him for his money.* 她只是为了他的财产才想跟他结婚。| **make your money** (=earn all your money) 发财 *I think he made his money in property speculation.* 我认为他靠房地产投机买卖发了财。**5 pay good money for** *spoken* to spend a lot of money on something【口】为…花大笔的钱: *I paid good money for that sofa, so it should last.* 我买那张沙发花了不少钱, 想来应该经久耐用。**6 there's money (to be made) in** *spoken* used to say that you can get a lot of money from a particular activity or from buying and selling something【口】在…中有钱可赚, 在…中有利可图: *Apparently there's a lot of money in ostrich farming.* 据说饲养鸵鸟能赚大钱。**7 be rolling in money/be rolling in it** *informal* to be very rich【非正式】非常富有, 财源滚滚: *They're always going on vacation – they must be rolling in money!* 他们经常去度假, 一定非常富有! **8 I'm not made of money** *spoken* used to say that you do not have a lot of money when someone asks you for some【口】我不是钱做的, 我没有很多钱 **9 he/she must have money to burn** used when you think someone is wasting their money on unnecessary things 他/她钱多得烫手, 他/她一定是钱多得可以拿去烧 **10 get your money's worth** to get something worth the price that you paid 让你的钱花得物有所值: *At that price you want to make sure you get your money's worth.* 价钱那么贵, 你该弄清楚你的钱花得是否划算。**11 be in the money** *informal* to have a lot of money, especially suddenly or when you did not expect to【非正式】〔尤指突然或出乎意料地〕发财, 拥有大笔的钱 **12 money is no object** *informal* used to say that you can spend as much money as you want to on something【非正式】钱不成问题: *Choose whatever you like, money is no object.* 喜欢什么你就选什么, 钱不成问题。**13 for my money** *spoken* used when giving your opinion about something to emphasize that you believe it strongly【口】依我之见〔用于强调对自己的观点非常有把握〕: *For my money, Torville and Dean were by far the best skaters.* 依我看, 托维尔和迪安显然滑冰滑得最好。**14 I'd put money on it** *spoken* used to emphasize that you are completely sure about something【口】我敢打赌, 我对此深信不疑: *"Do you really think that she'll get the gold medal?" "I'd put money on it."* "你真的认为她会获得金牌吗?" "我对此深信不疑。" **15 my money's on** *spoken* used to say that you think someone will probably win, or a situation will probably have a particular result【口】我认为…会…: *My money's on a draw – I don't think either team can win now.* 我想会打个平局 —— 我认为两支球队哪支现在也赢不了。**16 money for old rope/money for jam** *BrE spoken* money that you earn very easily【英口】很容易赚的钱 **17 put your money where your mouth is** *informal, often humorous* to show by your actions that you really believe what you say【非正式, 常幽默】以实际行动证明自己的观点; 说话兑现 **18 money doesn't grow on trees** *spoken* used to tell someone that they should not waste money【口】钱不是树上长的〔用以告诫某人不应乱花钱〕 **19 money talks** *spoken* used to say that money is powerful, and people who have money can get what they want【口】金钱万能 **20 be (right) on the money** *AmE spoken* used when something is perfect or exactly right for the situation【美口】(完全) 正确, 管用: *Her solution was right on the money – the clients loved it.* 她的解决办法完全对路, 客户很满意。**21 marry (into) money** to marry someone whose family is rich 和富人结婚 —see also 另见 BLOOD MONEY, HUSH MONEY, POCKET MONEY, **have a (good) run for your money** (RUN[2] (11)), **throw money at** (THROW[1] (20))

This graph shows some of the words most commonly used with the noun **money**. 本图表所示为含有名词 money 的一些最常用词组。

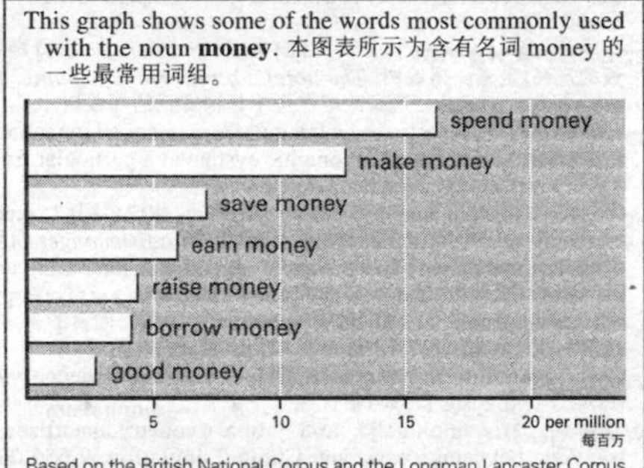

Based on the British National Corpus and the Longman Lancaster Corpus
据英国国家语料库和朗文兰开斯特语料库

USAGE NOTE 用法说明: MONEY

WORD CHOICE 词语辨析: **money, cash, change, funds**

Money is the most general word. money 是表示"钱"的最通用的词: *Where can I change money?* 我在哪儿可以兑换钱? | *How much money do you have?* 你有多少钱? | *taxpayers' money* 纳税人的钱

M

Cash usually means money in coins or notes rather than cheques or credit cards. cash通常指现金、现钞，而不是支票或信用卡: *"May I pay by Visa?" "I'm sorry, we only take cash."* "我可以用维萨信用卡付款吗?" "对不起，我们只收现金。" But it can also mean money in any form that is available to be spent. 但它也可以指能够用来消费的任何形式的钱: *We're going to Australia next year if we have the cash.* 如果有钱的话，我们明年会去澳大利亚。

Change is used for the amount of money that is given back to you when you have given more for something than the amount it costs. change用来指付款多于某物的价格时找回的钱: *three dollars fifty change* 3美元50美分的找头。 **Change** can also mean money in low-value coins or notes. change也可以指小面额的硬币或纸币，即"零钱": *Can you give me change for a ten pound note?* 你能换给我十英镑的零钱吗? | *I keep all my small change for the coffee machine.* 我留着所有的零钱以便在自动售咖啡机买咖啡用。

Money collected for a particular purpose may be called **funds**. 为某一特殊用途而筹集起来的钱可被称作funds (基金，专款; 资金): *I need more funds if I'm to study abroad.* 我如果要到国外学习则需要更多的钱。| *We're short of funds at the moment.* 我们眼下缺少资金。

mon·ey·bags /ˈmʌnɪˌbægz; ˈmʌnibægz/ *n* [singular] *informal humorous* someone who has a lot of money【非正式, 幽默】富翁, 阔佬

mon·ey·box /ˈmʌnɪˌbɑks; ˈmʌnibɒks/ *n* [C] *especially BrE* a box for saving money in【尤英】储钱盒, 储钱罐

mon·ey·chang·er /ˈmʌnɪˌtʃendʒɚ; ˈmʌniˌtʃeɪndʒə/ *n* [C] someone whose business is to exchange one country's money for money from another country, sometimes unofficially〔有时指非官方的〕钱商, 货币兑换商

mon·eyed, monied /ˈmʌnɪd; ˈmʌnid/ *adj* [only before noun 仅用于名词前] *formal* rich【正式】富有的: *the new moneyed classes* 新兴有产阶层

mon·ey·grab·bing /ˈmʌnɪgræbɪŋ; ˈmʌnigræbɪŋ/ also 又作 **moneygrubbing** /ˈmʌnɪgrʌbɪŋ; ˈmʌnigrʌbɪŋ/ *adj* [only before noun 仅用于名词前] *informal* determined to get money, even by unfair or dishonest methods【非正式】财迷的, 贪财的 —**moneygrabber, moneygrubber** *n* [C]

mon·ey·lend·er /ˈmʌnɪˌlɛndɚ; ˈmʌniˌlendə/ *n* [C] someone whose business is to lend money to people, especially at very high rates of INTEREST[1] (4)〔尤指高息〕放款人, 放债人

mon·ey·mak·er /ˈmʌnɪˌmekɚ; ˈmʌniˌmeɪkə/ *n* [C] a product or business that earns a lot of money 赚大钱的产品[生意], 摇钱树; MONEY-SPINNER *BrE*【英】: *The movie has turned into a real moneymaker.* 那部电影已变成了一棵真正的摇钱树。

money mar·ket /ˈ·· ,··/ *n* [C] the banks and other institutions who buy, sell, lend, or borrow money, especially foreign money, for profit 金融市场, 货币市场, 资金市场

money or·der /ˈ·· ,··/ *n* [C] an official document that you buy in a post office or a bank and send to someone so that they can exchange it for money in a bank 汇票 —compare 比较 POSTAL ORDER

money-spin·ner /ˈ·· ,··/ *n* [C] *BrE* MONEYMAKER【英】赚大钱的产品[生意], 摇钱树: *The hotel's a real money-spinner in the summer months.* 这家旅馆在夏季是棵真正的摇钱树。

money sup·ply /ˈ·· ·,·/ *n* [singular] *technical* all the money that exists in a country's economic system at a particular time【术语】货币供应量

-mon·ger /mʌŋgɚ; mʌŋgə/ *suffix* [in nouns 构成名词] **1** someone who sells a particular thing 商人, 贩子: *a fishmonger* 鱼贩(子) **2** someone who likes to say or encourage something unpleasant 喜欢传播[支持]坏事的人: *the rumour-mongers* (=people who say untrue things about other people) 好散布谣言的人, 好造谣的人 | *capitalist warmongers* 资本主义战争贩子

mon·gol /ˈmɑŋgəl; ˈmɒŋgəl/ *n* [C] *old-fashioned* someone with DOWN'S SYNDROME【过时】唐氏综合征患者 —**mongolism** *n* [U]

Mon·go·li·a /mɑŋˈgoljə; mɒŋˈgəʊliə/ a country in north central Asia between Russia and China. Population: 2,655,000 (2001). Capital: Ulaanbaatar (formerly Ulan Bator). Mongolia is a large country but has a small population because it includes a large area of desert and open plains. The country is sometimes informally called 'Outer Mongolia', and it is next to a part of China called 'Inner Mongolia'. 蒙古〔亚洲中北部一国家, 位于俄罗斯和中国之间。人口: 2,655,000 (2001), 首都: 乌兰巴托。蒙古幅员辽阔, 但人口稀少, 原因是国土中有大面积的沙漠和开阔平原。该国有时在非正式的场合称"外蒙古", 与中国的"内蒙古"接壤〕 —**Mongolian** *n, adj*

mon·goose /ˈmɑŋgus; ˈmɒŋguːs/ *n plural* **mongooses** [C] a small furry tropical animal that kills snakes and rats 獴

mon·grel /ˈmʌŋgrəl; ˈmʌŋgrəl/ *n* [C] a dog that is a mix of several breeds of dog 杂种狗

mon·ied /ˈmʌnɪd; ˈmʌnid/ *adj* another spelling of MONEYED moneyed的另一种拼法

mon·ies /ˈmʌnɪz; ˈmʌniz/ *n* [plural] *law* money【法律】钱, 货币

mon·i·ker /ˈmɑnɪkɚ; ˈmɒnɪkə/ *n* [C] *humorous* someone's name, signature, or NICKNAME【幽默】名字; 签名; 绰号

mon·i·tor[1] /ˈmɑnətɚ; ˈmɒnɨtə/ *v* [T] **1** to carefully watch and check a situation in order to see how it changes or progresses over a period of time 监视; 监测, 检测; 监督: *British Aerospace has built a scanner that monitors damage to the ozone layer.* 英国航空航天工业公司已建起一座扫描站, 监测对臭氧层的破坏。| *Their job is to monitor healthcare costs.* 他们的工作是监督保健费用。**2** to secretly listen to other people's phone calls, foreign radio broadcasts etc 监听: *The Security Police had monitored all of his phone calls.* 秘密警察对他所有的电话进行了监听。 S3 W3

monitor[2] *n* [C] **1** a television that shows a picture of what is happening in a particular place 监视器: *a row of monitors covering key areas of the building* 覆盖大楼关键区域的一排监视器 **2** the part of a computer that looks like a television and that shows information; VDU〔电脑的〕显示器 —see picture on page A14 参见 A14 页图 **3** a piece of equipment that receives and shows information about what is happening inside someone's body〔人体内部〕检测监视仪, 监护仪: *a monitor that shows the baby's heartbeat* 能显示婴儿心跳的监护仪 **4** a child who has been chosen to help the teacher in some way〔学校的〕班长, 级长, 值勤生: *the milk monitors*〔负责给同学分发牛奶的〕牛奶值勤生 **5** someone whose job is to listen to news, messages etc from foreign radio stations and report on them〔外国电台〕监听员

monk /mʌŋk; mʌŋk/ *n* [C] a member of an all-male religious group that lives apart from other people in a MONASTERY 修道士, 僧侣 —compare 比较 NUN —**monkish** *adj*: *a monkish silence* 一片远离俗世的寂静

mon·key[1] /ˈmʌŋkɪ; ˈmʌŋki/ *n* [C]

1 ►**ANIMAL** 动物◄ a small brown animal with a long tail, which uses its hands to climb trees and lives in hot countries 猴; 猿

2 ►**CHILD** 孩子◄ *informal* a small child who is very active and likes to play tricks【非正式】顽皮的儿童, 淘气鬼, 捣蛋鬼: *Stop that, you little monkey!* 别捣乱了, 你这个淘气鬼!

3 monkey business *informal* behaviour that may cause trouble or may be dishonest【非正式】恶作剧, 骗人把戏, 捣鬼: *The boys are awfully quiet – I think they're up to some monkey business.* 那些男孩子出奇地安静 —— 我想他们在捣什么鬼。

4 make a monkey (out) of sb to make someone seem stupid 使某人出丑, 戏弄某人, 愚弄某人: *They got into the palace in broad daylight, and made monkeys out of the security men.* 他们在光天化日之下进入了王宫, 让保安人员出了丑。

5 I don't give a monkey's *BrE spoken* used to say that you do not care at all about something【英口】我一点都不在乎: *To be honest I don't give a monkey's what they do.* 说实话, 我一点都不在乎他们做什么。

6 a monkey on your back *AmE informal* a serious problem that makes your life very difficult, especially being dependent on drugs【美, 非正式】使生活艰难的沉重负担〔尤指对毒品的依赖〕

monkey[2] *v*

monkey around also 又作 **monkey about** *phr v* [I] *BrE informal* to behave in a stupid or careless way【英, 非正式】胡闹, 捣蛋, 调皮: *They were monkeying around in the playground and one of them got hurt.* 他们在操场上打闹, 其中一人受了伤。| [**+with**] *I wish those kids would stop monkeying around with the remote control!* 我希望那些孩子别再乱动遥控器了!

monkey bars /ˈ·· ·/ *n* [plural] **1** *AmE* a structure for children to climb and play on【美】猴架〔一种供孩子攀爬玩耍的架子〕; CLIMBING FRAME *BrE*【英】**2** *BrE* bars fixed to the wall in a GYM (1)【英】〔体育馆中固定在墙上的〕攀爬架

monkey nut /ˈ·· ·/ *n* [C] *BrE informal* a PEANUT in its shell【英, 非正式】带壳花生

mon·key·shines /ˈmʌŋkɪʃaɪnz; ˈmʌŋkiʃaɪnz/ *n* [plural] *AmE informal* tricks or jokes【美, 非正式】把戏, 恶作剧; 玩笑: *Jo's monkeyshines finally cost him his job.* 乔因搞恶作剧而最终丢了工作。

monkey suit /ˈ·· ·/ *n* [C] *old-fashioned* a formal suit, especially with black trousers and jacket and a BOW TIE【过时】男子礼服

M

monkey wrench /ˈ‥ ˌ·/ *n* [C] *AmE*【美】**1** a tool that is used to hold or turn things, especially nuts (NUT[1] (2)) 活动扳手，活扳子; ADJUSTABLE SPANNER *BrE*【英】—see picture at 参见 TOOL[1] 图 **2 throw a monkey wrench in the works** *AmE informal* to do something that will cause problems or spoil what someone else is planning【美，非正式】阻挠; 破坏; 给…惹麻烦

mono- /mɑno; mɒnəʊ/ *prefix* one; single 一个，单一: *a monoplane* (=plane with only one wing on each side) 单翼（飞）机 | *a monolingual dictionary* (=dealing with only one language) 单语词典

mon·o[1] /ˈmɑno; ˈmɒnəʊ/ *n* [U] *informal*【非正式】**1** *AmE* an infectious illness that makes your LYMPH GLANDs swell and makes you feel weak and tired for a long time afterwards【美】传染性单核细胞增多症，腺热; GLANDULAR FEVER *BrE*【英】**2** a system of recording or broadcasting sound, in which the sound comes from only one direction 单声道录[放]音系统 —compare 比较 STEREO[1]

mono[2] *adj* using a system of recording or broadcasting sound in which all the sound comes from only one direction〔录音或放音〕单声道的: *a mono recording* 单声道录音 —compare 比较 STEREO[2]

mon·o·chrome /ˈmɑnəˌkrom; ˈmɒnəkrəʊm/ *adj* **1** in shades of only one colour, especially shades of grey 单色的〔尤指黑白的〕: *The landscape was dull, misty, and monochrome.* 那张风景画灰暗、朦胧、色调单一。**2** using or appearing in only black, white, and grey 黑白的，只用黑白灰三色的，仅以黑白灰三色出现的: *a monochrome television* 黑白电视 **3** a monochrome computer MONITOR uses one colour as a background and only one other colour for the letters on the SCREEN〔电脑显示器〕黑白的 —opposite 反义词 COLOUR[3]

mon·o·cle /ˈmɑnəkḷ; ˈmɒnəkəl/ *n* [C] a single LENS (=ROUND PIECE OF GLASS) that you hold in front of one eye to help you to see better 单片眼镜

mo·nog·a·my /məˈnɑgəmɪ; məˈnɒgəmi/ *n* [U] the custom or practice of being married to only one husband or wife 一夫一妻制 —compare 比较 BIGAMY, POLYGAMY—**monogamous** *adj* —**monogamously** *adv*

mon·o·gram /ˈmɑnəˌgræm; ˈmɒnəgræm/ *n* [C] two or more letters, usually the first letters of someone's names, that are put together to form a design 交织字母，花押字〔两个或两个以上字母，通常是姓和名的首字母，放在一起构成的图案〕—**monogrammed** *adj*

mon·o·graph /ˈmɑnəˌgræf; ˈmɒnəgrɑːf/ *n* [C+on] a serious article or short book about a subject 专题文章; 专题著作

mon·o·ling·ual /ˌmɑnəˈlɪŋgwəl; ˌmɒnəʊˈlɪŋgwəl◂/ *adj* speaking or using only one language 只说[使用]一种语言的，单语的: *a monolingual dictionary* 单语词典 —compare 比较 BILINGUAL, MULTILINGUAL

mon·o·lith /ˈmɑnḷˌɪθ; ˈmɒnəlɪθ/ *n* [C] **1** an organization, government etc that is very large and powerful and difficult to change 庞大而僵化的组织[政府等]: *the break-up of the Soviet monolith* 像铁板一块的苏联的解体 **2** a large tall block of stone, especially one that was put in place in ancient times, possibly for religious reasons〔尤指古代竖起、可能用于宗教目的的〕独石柱[碑]

mon·o·lith·ic /ˌmɑnḷˈɪθɪk; ˌmɒnəˈlɪθɪk◂/ *adj* **1** very large, solid, and impressive 庞大结实的; 气势宏伟的; 磐石般的: *huge monolithic office buildings* 气势雄伟、坚如磐石的办公大楼 **2** a monolithic organization, political system etc is very large and powerful and difficult to change〔组织、政治制度等〕铁板一块的

mon·o·logue also 又作 **monolog** *AmE*【美】/ˈmɑnḷˌɔg; ˈmɒnəlɒg/ *n* [C] **1** *informal* a long period of talking by one person that prevents other people from taking part in a conversation【非正式】〔使别人无法插嘴的〕滔滔不绝的讲话，长篇大论: *Charles listened patiently to a fifteen-minute monologue before finally interrupting.* 查尔斯耐心地听了持续15分钟之久的长篇大论后才插话打断对方。**2** a long speech by one character in a play or film〔戏剧或电影的〕长篇独白: *Hamlet's famous monologue* 哈姆雷特著名的独白 —compare 比较 DIALOGUE, SOLILOQUY

mon·o·ma·ni·a /ˌmɑnəˈmenɪə; ˌmɒnəʊˈmeɪniə/ *n* [U] an unusually strong interest in a particular idea or subject; OBSESSION 单狂，偏狂;〔对某一想法或问题的〕狂热: *the victims of a computing monomania* 电脑偏狂症患者 —**monomaniac** /-nɪˌæk; -niæk/ *n, adj*

mon·o·nu·cle·o·sis /ˌmɑnoˌnuklɪˈosɪs; ˌmɒnəʊnjuːkliˈəʊsɪ̇s/ *n* [U] *AmE technical* MONO[1] (1)【美，术语】传染性单核细胞增多症，腺热

mon·o·plane /ˈmɑnəˌplen; ˈmɒnəʊpleɪn/ *n* [C] a plane with only one wing on each side, like most modern planes 单翼（飞）机 —compare 比较 BIPLANE

Monopolies and Mer·gers Com·mis·sion, the /ˌ· ‥ · ˈ· · ˌ· · ˌ·/ a British government organization whose job is to examine cases where two companies plan to MERGE (=join together to form a larger company), and to decide whether this would be bad for other businesses and for ordinary customers. There is a similar organization in the US called the FTC (=the Federal Trade Commission). 垄断与合并委员会〔英国一政府组织。其职责是调查两家公司计划合并案，并裁定合并是否会对别的企业或普通客户造成不利影响。美国也有一个类似组织，简称FTC（联邦贸易委员会）〕

mo·nop·ol·is·tic /məˌnɑpəˈlɪstɪk; məˌnɒpəˈlɪstɪk◂/ *adj* controlling or trying to control something completely, especially an industry or business activity 垄断的，垄断性的: *monopolistic corporations* 垄断公司

mo·nop·o·lize also 又作 **-ise** *BrE*【英】/məˈnɑpḷˌaɪz; məˈnɒpəlaɪz/ *v* [T] **1** to have complete control over something so that other people cannot share it 垄断; 独占; 完全控制: *This small group monopolized the key positions in government for many years.* 这个小集团多年来一直占据着政府中的关键职位。| *to monopolize a conversation* 垄断谈话 **2** to demand or need a lot of someone's time and attention 占用〔时间和注意力〕: *Virtually all her time and energy is now monopolized by the children.* 现在她几乎所有的时间和精力都被孩子占去了。—**monopolization** /məˌnɑpḷəˈzeʃən; məˌnɒpəlaɪˈzeɪʃən/ *n* [U]

Mo·nop·o·ly /məˈnɑpḷɪ; məˈnɒpəli/ *trademark* a very popular type of board game that has been sold since the 1930s. Players use toy money to buy streets and buildings on squares on the board, and then make other players pay rent if they move onto those squares. The squares on the board show the names of real streets in cities in the US (=in an American Monopoly set), London (=in a British Monopoly set), or other big cities around the world. People sometimes use the expression **Monopoly money** to mean a very large amount of money.【商标】大富翁游戏〔20世纪30年代开始出售的一种非常流行的棋类游戏。游戏者用玩具钱购买棋盘方格内的街道和建筑。如果其他游戏者走进这些方格，就必须支付租金。棋盘方格内的街道采用美国城市（美国版游戏）、伦敦（英国版游戏）或世界其他大城市街道的真名。人们有时借用 Monopoly money（大富翁钞票）意指大量的钱财〕

monopoly *n* **1** [C] the control of all or most of a business activity by a single company or by a government, so that other organizations cannot easily compete with them 垄断; 独占; 专营: *Cigarette production is a state monopoly in China.* 在中国，香烟生产是国家专营的。| **[+on/of]** *For years Bell Telephone had a monopoly on phone services in the US.* 过去许多年，贝尔电话公司垄断着美国的电话业务。**2** [singular] something that belongs to only one person, group, or organization, so that other people cannot share it 垄断品，被独占的东西: *Good healthcare shouldn't be the monopoly of the rich.* 良好的保健服务不应为富人所独享。| **have/hold a monopoly on** *Universities do not hold a monopoly on intellectual life.* 知识生活不是大学所独有的。

mon·o·rail /ˈmɑnəˌrel; ˈmɒnəʊreɪl/ *n* **1** [U] a railway system that uses a single RAIL[1] (3), usually high above the ground〔通常指高架的〕单轨铁道 **2** [C] a train on this system 单轨火车

mon·o·sod·i·um glu·tam·ate /ˌmɑnəˈsodɪəm ˈgluːtəˌmet; ˌmɒnəʊˌsəʊdiəm ˈgluːtəmeɪt/ *n* [U] *technical* MSG【术语】谷氨酸钠〔味精的化学成分〕

mon·o·syl·lab·ic /ˌmɑnəsɪˈlæbɪk; ˌmɒnəsɪˈlæbɪk◂/ *adj* **1** someone who is monosyllabic or makes monosyllabic remarks seems rude because they do not say much〔说话〕简短而无礼的: *Jim became more and more monosyllabic.* 吉姆说话越来越简短无礼。**2** *technical* a monosyllabic word has only one SYLLABLE【术语】〔词〕单音节的

mon·o·syl·la·ble /ˈmɑnəˌsɪləbḷ; ˈmɒnəˌsɪləbəl/ *n* [C] *technical* a word with one SYLLABLE【术语】单音节词

mon·o·the·is·m /ˈmɑnəθiˌɪzəm; ˈmɒnəʊθiːɪzəm/ *n* [U] *technical* the belief that there is only one God【术语】一神论，一神教 —compare 比较 POLYTHEISM —**monotheist** *n* [C] —**monotheistic** /ˌmɑnəθiˈɪstɪk; ˌmɒnəʊθiːˈɪstɪk◂/ *adj*: *Christianity is a monotheistic religion.* 基督教是一神教。

mon·o·tone /ˈmɑnəˌton; ˈmɒnətəʊn/ *n* [singular] a sound or way of speaking or singing that continues on the same note without getting any louder or softer, and therefore sounds very boring 单调的声音; 单调: *Mr Major was talking in a flat, slow monotone.* 梅杰先生以一种平缓的单调声音在说话。

M

mo·not·o·nous /mə`nɑtṇəs; məˈnɒtənəs/ *adj* boring because there is no variety 单调的, 乏味的: *He was speaking in a low monotonous voice.* 他以一种低沉而单调的声音在说话。| *a monotonous factory job* 工厂里单调乏味的工作 —**monotonously** *adv*: *The rain poured monotonously out of the grey sky.* 灰蒙蒙的天空中雨令人厌烦地下个不停。

mo·not·o·ny /mə`nɑtṇɪ; məˈnɒtəni/ *n* [U] a lack of variety that makes you feel bored 单调乏味, 无变化, 千篇一律: *A small group of houses relieved the monotony of the landscape.* 一小片房子为单调乏味的景色带来生气。

mo·nox·ide /mɑn`ɑksaɪd; məˈnɒksaɪd/ *n* [C,U] *technical* a chemical compound containing one atom of oxygen to every atom of another substance【术语】一氧化物: *carbon monoxide* 一氧化碳

Mon·roe /mən`ro; mənˈrəʊ/, **James** (1758-1831) the President of the US from 1817 to 1825. He is famous especially for the speech he made to the US Congress in 1823, called the Monroe Doctrine. 门罗〔(1758-1831), 美国总统, 1817-1825年在任。他尤以1823年在国会上发表的演讲闻名, 史称"门罗主义"〕

Monroe, Mar·i·lyn /`mærəlɪn; ˈmærḷɪn/ (1926-62) a US film actress and singer, whose real name was Norma Jean Baker. People still think of her as the most typical example of a SEX SYMBOL (=someone who represents society's idea of what is sexually attractive). Her films include *Gentlemen Prefer Blondes* (1953) and *Some Like It Hot* (1959). 梦露〔(1926-1962), 美国电影女演员和歌手, 原名诺尔马·让·贝克。人们至今仍把她看成是典型的性感偶像。她主演过的影片有《绅士们更爱金发女郎》(1953) 和《热情如火》(1959)〕

Monroe Doc·trine, the /·ˈ··, ··/ the idea, stated in a speech by President James Monroe in 1823, that countries of Europe should not get involved in the affairs of the countries of North and South America, and, in exchange for this, the US would not get involved in European affairs 门罗主义〔1823年美国总统詹姆斯·门罗在一次演讲中提出的观点: 欧洲各国不应干涉北美和南美各国的事务, 这样美国才不会干涉欧洲事务〕

Mon·ro·vi·a /mən`rovɪə; mənˈrəʊviə/ a city and port which is the capital of Liberia, West Africa 蒙罗维亚〔西非国家利比里亚首都, 为一港口城市〕

Mon·sieur /mə`sjɝ; məˈsjɜː/ *n plural* **Messieurs** /me`sjɝz; meɪˈsjɜːz/ [C] *French* a way of addressing or referring to a French-speaking man【法】先生: *Monsieur Bonnet* 邦尼先生

Mon·si·gnor /mɑn`sinjə; mɒnˈsiːnjə/ *n* [C] a way of addressing or referring to a priest of high rank in the Roman Catholic Church 阁下〔对罗马天主教高级教士的称呼〕

mon·soon /mɑn`sun; mɒnˈsuːn/ *n* [C] **1** [usually singular 一般用单数] the season, from about April to October, when it rains a lot in India and other southern Asian countries〔印度等南亚国家的〕季风季节, 雨季 **2** the rain that falls during this season or the wind that brings the rain 季风雨;〔带来雨水的〕季风, 季雨风

mon·ster[1] /`mɑnstə; ˈmɒnstə/ *n* [C]

1 ▶IN STORIES 在故事中◀ a large ugly frightening creature, especially an imaginary one 怪物; 怪兽; 妖怪: *the Kraken and other legendary sea monsters*〔挪威传说中的〕北海巨妖克拉肯和其他传说中的海怪 | *a prehistoric monster* 史前怪物

2 ▶CRUEL PERSON 残忍的人◀ someone who is very cruel and evil 残忍的人; 恶人, 恶魔: *Only a monster could kill all those women and feel no remorse.* 只有恶魔才会把那些妇女杀光而毫无悔意。

3 ▶CHILD 孩子◀ *often humorous* a small child, especially one who is behaving badly【常幽默】〔尤指不守规矩的〕小孩子; 调皮精, 捣蛋鬼: *I've got to get home and feed this little monster.* 我必须回家喂这个小捣蛋。

4 ▶STH LARGE 巨大的东西◀ *informal* an object, animal etc that is unusually large【非正式】庞然大物: *That car of his is an absolute monster!* 他那辆汽车简直是个庞然大物!

5 a dangerous or threatening problem, especially one that develops gradually〔尤指渐渐恶化的〕危险[可怕]的问题: *It was years before people realized what a monster industrialization had created.* 人们经过多年后才认识到工业化带来了多么可怕的后果。

monster[2] *adj* [only before noun 仅用于名词前] *informal* unusually large【非正式】异常大的, 庞大的, 巨大的: *the monster fortunes of the Mellons and DuPonts* 梅隆和杜邦家族巨大的财富

Monster Rav·ing Loon·y Par·ty, the /,·· ·· ˈ··, ··/ a small British political party, whose ideas are not intended to be serious, but which some people vote for in order to show that they do not approve of any of the main parties. It was led by a former pop singer called **Screaming Lord Sutch** until his death in 1999. 疯狂傻瓜党〔英国一小政党。该党派的政治观念并不严肃, 但是有些人为了表示自己不支持任何一个大党, 就会投他们的票。该党的领袖人物是一个名叫"尖叫的萨奇勋爵"的流行歌手, 1999年去世以前一直领导该党〕

mon·stros·i·ty /mɑn`strɑsətɪ; mɒnˈstrɒsḷti/ *n* [C] something large and ugly, especially a building 巨大而丑陋的东西〔尤指建筑物〕: *The office complex is yet another monstrosity in the very center of the city.* 那座综合办公大楼是市中心另一个丑陋的大怪物。

mon·strous /`mɑnstrəs; ˈmɒnstrəs/ *adj* **1** very wrong, immoral, or unfair 极端错误的; 非常不道德的; 极不公正的: *It's monstrous to charge that much for a hotel room.* 一个旅馆房间就要收那么多钱真是太无理了。| *a monstrous injustice* 极端的不公正 **2** unusually large and ugly 巨大而丑陋的: *a monstrous castle* 一座丑陋的大城堡 —**monstrously** *adv*

mon·tage /mɑn`tɑʒ; ˈmɒntɑːʒ/ *n* **1** [U] an art form in which a picture, film, piece of writing etc is made from parts of different pictures etc, that are combined to form a whole 蒙太奇〔图像、电影、写作等的艺术形式, 把不同的图像等结合成整体〕, 剪辑 **2** [C] something made using this process 蒙太奇作品, 综合[组合]式作品

Montagues, the —see 见 the CAPULETS AND MONTAGUES

Mon·taigne /mɑn`ten; mɒnˈteɪn/, **Mi·chel Ey·quem de** /mi`ʃɛl i`kɛm də; miːˈʃel iːˈkem də/ (1533-92) a French writer of ESSAYs (=short pieces of writing giving someone's ideas on particular subjects) who influenced many writers with his informal but careful way of writing 蒙田〔(1533-1592), 法国散文家。他的写作风格平实而严谨, 影响了许多作家〕

Mon·ta·na /mɑn`tænə; mɒnˈtɑːnə/ abbreviation 缩写为 **MT** a state in the northwestern US that has many mountains. It is the fourth largest state in the US, but has one of the smallest populations. 蒙大拿州〔美国西北部一州, 境内多山, 为美国第四大州, 但却是人口最少的州之一〕

Mont Blanc[1] /ˌmɑŋ `blɑŋ; ˌmɒŋ ˈblɑːŋ/ a mountain in the Alps on the border between France and Italy. It is the highest mountain in western Europe, and there is a TUNNEL through it for cars to drive between France and Italy. 勃朗峰〔阿尔卑斯山一山峰, 位于法意边境, 是西欧的最高峰。勃朗峰下有一隧道, 将法意两国相连, 可通行汽车〕

Mont Blanc[2] *trademark* a very expensive type of pen【商标】万宝龙〔一种高级钢笔〕

Mon·te Car·lo /ˌmɑntɪ `karlo; ˌmɒnti ˈkɑːləʊ/ the main town of Monaco where many wealthy people live or visit. It has many casinos and is famous for a car RALLY and the Monaco Grand Prix car race, which are held there every year. 蒙特卡洛〔摩纳哥主要城镇。许多富人在此定居或到此旅游, 有许多赌场, 以每年举行的汽车拉力赛和摩纳哥汽车大奖赛闻名〕

Mon·te Cris·to /ˌmɑntɪ `krɪsto; ˌmɒnti ˈkrɪstəʊ/, **the Count of** the main character in the book *The Count of Monte Cristo* by the French writer Alexandre Dumas. He is wrongly put in prison for many years, and when he escapes he does not tell anyone who he is so that he can find and punish his enemies. 基督山伯爵〔法国作家大仲马所著的《基督山伯爵》中的主人公。他蒙冤在狱中度过多年, 逃脱后隐姓埋名, 以求报复他的仇敌〕

Montego Bay /·ˌ·· ˈ·/ a city and port in northwest Jamaica, the second largest city on the island. Its beautiful beaches make it a popular place for tourists. 蒙特哥贝〔牙买加西北部一港口城市, 该岛第二大城市。海滩景色秀美, 颇受游人青睐〕

Mon·te·ne·gro /ˌmɑntə`nigro; ˌmɒntḷˈniːgrəʊ/ a republic of the Federal Republic of Yugoslavia, which consists of Serbia and Montenegro, on the Adriatic Sea. In 2006, Montenegro became an independent country. 黑山〔南斯拉夫联盟共和国的组成共和国之一, 濒临亚得里亚海。南斯拉夫联盟共和国由塞尔维亚和黑山组成。2006年黑山独立〕

Mon·te·rey Jack /ˌmɑntəre `dʒæk; ˌmɒntəreɪ ˈdʒæk/ also 又作 **Jack, Jack cheese** a pale yellow processed cheese sold in the US 蒙特雷杰克干酪〔在美国销售的一种加工好的淡黄色干酪〕

Mon·ter·rey /ˌmɑntə`re; ˌmɒntəˈreɪ/ an industrial city in northeast Mexico, and the most important centre for producing steel in the country 蒙特雷〔墨西哥东北部一工业城市, 该国最大的炼钢中心〕

Mon·tes·so·ri /ˌmɑntə`sɔrɪ; ˌmɒntḷˈsɔːri/, **Ma·ri·a** /mə`riə; məˈriːə/ (1870-1952) an Italian teacher and writer who developed a new way of teaching young children, the **Montessori method**, which encourages each child to develop at his or her own speed, to learn through playing, and to be confident and

independent. Her method is used in **Montessori schools** in many countries. 蒙台梭利〔(1870-1952)，意大利教育家和作家，蒙台梭利教学法的创始人。这种教学法用于幼儿教育，鼓励每个儿童按自己的能力来发展，在玩耍中学习，培养自信心和独立性。这套教学法在许多国家的蒙台梭利学校广为采用〕

Mon·te·vi·de·o /ˌmɑntəvɪˋdeo; ˌmɒntʒvɪˈdeɪəʊ/ a city and port in southern Uruguay, the capital of the country 蒙得维的亚〔乌拉圭南部一港口城市及该国首都〕

Mon·te·zu·ma /ˌmɑntəˋzumə; ˌmɒntʒˈzuːmə/ (1466-1520) the last Aztec ruler of Mexico, who was taken prisoner by the Spaniards under Cortés, and later killed by his own people 蒙提祖玛〔(1466-1520)，墨西哥阿兹特克人的最后一位统治者，被科尔特斯旗下的西班牙人监禁，后为族人所杀〕

Mont·gom·e·ry /məntˋgʌmərɪ; məntˈgʌməri/ the capital city of the US state of Alabama 蒙哥马利〔美国亚拉巴马州首府〕

Montgomery, Field Marshal (1887-1976) a British military leader, known informally as **Monty**, who led the British army to victory in the Battle of El Alamein (1942) in World War II, and later became the commander of the British forces in Europe 蒙哥马利〔(1887-1976)，英国军事领袖，别名蒙迪。第二次世界大战期间，他率领英军取得阿拉曼战役 (1942) 的胜利，后成为欧洲战场的英军统帅〕

Montgomery, L.M. (1874-1942) a Canadian writer who wrote *Anne of Green Gables* 蒙哥马利〔(1874-1942)，加拿大作家，最著名的小说是《格林·盖布尔斯的安妮》〕

1 1 **month** /mʌnθ; mʌnθ/ *n* [C] **1** one of the twelve named periods of time that a year is divided into 月，月份: *It snowed heavily during the month of January.* 一月份雪下得很大。| *Phil is coming home for a visit next month.* 菲尔下个月要回家看看。| *She'll be thirteen this month.* 到这个月她就13岁了。| *a tremendous article in this month's American Indian Review* 本月《美国印第安人评论》杂志中一篇精彩的文章 **2** a period of about four weeks 一个月: *She has an eight-month old daughter.* 她有一个八个月大的女儿。| *He'll be away for two months.* 他要离开两个月。**3 once/twice etc a month** 每月一次/两次等: *We update the schedule at least once a month.* 我们每月至少更新一次时间表。**4 months** a long time, especially several months 很长一段时间〔尤指数月〕: *Redecorating the kitchen took months.* 重新装修厨房用了好长时间。| **for/in months** (=for a long time) 好长时间，很久 *I haven't seen him for months.* 我好长时间没见到他了。**5 month after month** used to emphasize that something happens regularly or continuously for several months 一月又一月，每月: *I felt I was doing the same old thing week after week, month after month.* 我感到我在周复一周、月复一月地干着相同的事。**6 month by month** used when you are talking about a situation that develops over several months 逐月: *Unemployment figures are rising month by month.* 失业数字正在逐月增加。**7 never in a month of Sundays** *spoken* used to emphasize that something will definitely never happen【口】永远也不会: *You'll never guess it in a month of Sundays.* 你永远也猜不出来。

3 **month·ly¹** /ˋmʌnθlɪ; ˈmʌnθli/ *adj* [only before noun 仅用于名词前] **1** happening once a month 每月一次的: *The mortgage is payable in monthly instalments.* 该抵押借款按月偿付。| *a monthly publication* 月刊 **2** a monthly income, figure etc is the total amount that is received, paid, measured etc in a month〔收入、数字等〕按月支付的，按月计算的；每月的: *a monthly salary of $850* 月薪850美元 | *Monthly rainfall in the area goes down from four inches in January to nothing at all in July.* 该地区的月降雨量从1月份的4英寸降到7月份的滴水全无。**3** a monthly ticket, PASS² (1) etc can be used for a period of one month〔票、通行证等〕有效期为一个月的 **—monthly** *adv*: *They meet monthly to discuss progress.* 他们每月碰一次头讨论进展情况。

monthly² *n* [C] **1** a magazine that appears once a month 月刊 **2 monthlies** *BrE old-fashioned* a woman's PERIOD (=flow of blood from the body each month)【英，过时】月经

Mont·mar·tre /monˋmartrə; mɒnˈmɑːtrə/ an area of northern Paris on a hill, which is famous for the large white church of Sacré Coeur and for its bars, restaurants, and NIGHTCLUBS, including the Moulin Rouge, where the 19th century artist Toulouse-Lautrec did paintings of the dancers and singers. Many artists used to live and work there. 蒙马特尔〔巴黎北部一区，地势较高，以白色圣心教堂、酒吧、餐厅和夜总会闻名。19世纪画家图卢斯·劳特雷克曾在此地的红磨坊夜总会画过舞女和歌手。许多艺术家曾在该地居住和工作过〕

Montpelier /mɑntˋpiljə; mɒntˈpiːljə/ the capital city of the US state of Vermont 蒙彼利埃〔美国佛蒙特州首府〕

Mon·tre·al /ˌmɑntrɪˋɔl; ˌmɒntriˈɔːl/ a city and port on **Montreal Island** in the St. Lawrence river in southern Quebec, in East Canada. Most people living in Montreal speak French as their main language. 蒙特利尔〔加拿大东部一港口城市，坐落在魁北克南部圣劳伦斯河上的蒙特利尔岛上，大多数居民主要讲法语〕

Mont·ser·rat /ˌmɑntsəˋræt; ˌmɒntsəˈræt/ an island in the Caribbean Sea, one of the Leeward Islands, which belongs to the UK. Capital: Plymouth. 蒙塞拉特〔加勒比海背风群岛一岛屿，隶属于英国。首府：普利茅斯〕**—Montserratian** /-ˋreʃən; -ˈreɪʃən◂/ *n, adj*

Mon·ty Py·thon /ˌmɑntɪ ˋpaɪθɑn; ˌmɒnti ˈpaɪθən/ also 又作 **Monty Python's Flying Circus** (1969-74) a humorous British television programme famous for its SURREAL humour and its SKETCHes (=short scenes) in which people behaved in strange or crazy ways. The programme's style of humour influenced many later COMEDIANs, and the group later made several films, including *The Life of Brian.*《蒙蒂·皮松》〔又名《飞行的马戏团》(1969-1974)，英国一喜剧系列电视节目，以超现实主义幽默短剧表演著称。剧中的人物行为疯狂古怪。节目的幽默风格对许多喜剧演员产生了影响。该剧组后来拍摄了好几部影片，其中有《布里安的生活》〕

mon·u·ment /ˋmɑnjəmənt; ˈmɒnjʒmənt/ *n* [C] **1** a building or other large structure that is built to remind people of an important event or famous person 纪念碑，纪念塔，纪念馆: **[+of/to]** *a monument to soldiers killed in battle* 阵亡将士纪念碑 | *The Victor Emmanuel monument was built to commemorate the unity of Italy.* 维克托·伊曼纽尔纪念碑是为纪念意大利的统一而建造的。**2** a very old building or place that is important historically 遗迹，遗址，名胜古迹: *The Alhambra is the last and most exquisite monument of Arab civilization in Europe.* 艾勒汉卜拉宫是阿拉伯文明在欧洲最后的也是建筑最精美的一处遗址。**3 be a monument to** to be a very clear example of what can happen as a result of a particular quality 是…的例证[见证]: *The house, built just before the stock market crash, was a monument to miscalculation.* 股票市场崩溃前不久建起的那幢房子是错误判断的见证。

mon·u·ment·al /ˌmɑnjəˋmɛntḷ; ˌmɒnjʒˈmentl◂/ *adj* **1** [usually before noun 一般用于名词前] a monumental achievement, piece of work, etc is very important and influential, and is usually based on many years of work 丰碑式的，伟大的: *a monumental contribution to the field of medicine* 对医学领域重大的贡献 | *Charles Darwin's monumental study, 'The Origin of Species'* 查尔斯·达尔文的巨著《物种起源》**2** [only before noun 仅用于名词前] extremely large, bad, good, impressive etc 极大[坏，好，令人难忘等]的: *There was a monumental traffic jam on the freeway.* 高速公路上出现了严重的交通阻塞。| *This is yet more evidence of his monumental incompetence.* 这将成为他极端无能的又一次证明。**3** [only before noun 仅用于名词前] appearing on a monument or built as a monument 出现在纪念碑[塔]上的；纪念性的: *a monumental temple* 纪念性神殿

mon·u·ment·al·ly /ˌmɑnjəˋmɛntḷɪ; ˌmɒnjʒˈmentəli/ *adv* extremely 极端，极其: [+adj/adv] *It was a monumentally stupid thing to do.* 那是一件极其愚蠢的事。

moo¹ /mu; muː/ *v* [I] to make the sound a cow makes 发牛叫声，发哞声

moo² *n* [C] **1** the sound that a cow makes 哞〔牛叫声〕**2** *BrE old-fashioned* a stupid woman【英，过时】愚蠢的女人: *You silly old moo!* 你这个傻老太婆！

mooch /mutʃ; muːtʃ/ *v* [T] *AmE informal* to get something by asking someone to give you it, instead of paying for it; CADGE【美，非正式】讨要，乞取: *He tried to mooch a drink from me.* 他想从我这儿讨杯酒喝。

mooch around also 又作 **mooch about** *BrE*【英】*phr v* [I] *informal* to walk around without any purpose【非正式】闲荡，闲逛: *"Where've you been?" "Oh, just mooching around."* "你到哪儿去了？" "噢，只是随便逛了逛。"

3 3 **mood** /mud; muːd/ *n*

1 ▶WAY YOU FEEL 心情◀ [C] the way you feel at a particular time 心情，心境，情绪: *His moods change very quickly – one moment he's cheerful and the next he's sunk in despair.* 他的情绪变化无常——一会儿兴高采烈，一会儿又心灰意冷。| *It takes a couple of days to get into the holiday mood.* 进入假日气氛需要几天的时间。| **be in a good mood/bad mood etc** (=be happy, annoyed, angry etc) 心情好/坏等 *You're in a good mood this morning!* 你今天早晨心情不错啊！| *The kids were in a really silly mood after the party.* 派对后那些年轻人感到很失落。| **be in a foul/filthy mood** (=be very angry or upset) 心情非常不好，情绪很糟 *Don't talk to Jean; she's in a filthy mood!* 别跟琼说话，她情绪糟透了！| **put sb in a good/bad mood** (=make them feel happy or annoyed) 使某人心情愉快/不愉快 *I'd been stuck*

M

in the traffic for hours, which put me in a really bad mood. 我被困在车流中好几个小时，心情都坏透了。

2 be in a mood to feel unhappy or angry 情绪不好: *She's been in a real mood all day.* 她整天在闹情绪。| **be in one of your/his moods** (=used when someone often gets in a bad mood) 情绪不好

3 be in no mood for sth/to do sth to not want to do something, or be determined not to do something 不想做某事; 决心不做某事: *The boss is in no mood for compromise on this point.* 在这一点上老板不想妥协。| *I was in no mood to argue any more.* 我不想再争论了。

4 be/feel in the mood (for sth/to do sth) to want to do something or feel that you would enjoy doing something 有意(做某事), 有(做某事)的心情: *She was in the mood for a romantic walk in the woods.* 她想在树林里浪漫地走一走。| *I don't want to talk about it now. I'm not in the mood.* 我现在不想谈论此事, 我没心情。

5 ►WAY PEOPLE FEEL 人们的情绪◄ [singular] the way a group of people feels about something or about life in general 情绪; 心态: **[+of]** *The president had misjudged the mood of the people on this issue.* 总统在这个问题上错误地判断了公众的情绪。| *The novel captures the mood of postwar France.* 这部小说如实地呈现了战后法国的社会氛围。

6 ►GRAMMAR 语法◄ [C] *technical* one of the sets of verb forms in grammar such as the INDICATIVE (=expressing a fact or action), the IMPERATIVE (=expressing a command) or the SUBJUNCTIVE (=expressing a doubt or wish)【术语】语气〈如陈述、祈使和虚拟等语气〉

mood mu·sic /ˈ· ,· ·/ *n* [U] music that is supposed to make you feel particular emotions, especially romantic feelings 气氛音乐〔引起听众某种情感、尤指浪漫情感的音乐〕, 抒情乐曲

mood·y /ˈmudɪ; ˈmuːdi/ *adj* **moodier, moodiest 1** easily becoming annoyed or unhappy when there is no good reason to feel that way 易怒的; 情绪不好的: *She had been moody and difficult all day.* 她整天一直闷闷不乐、别别扭扭的。| *They kept apart in moody silence.* 他们闷闷不乐, 一言不发, 彼此保持着距离。**2** having moods that change often and quickly 喜怒无常的, 情绪多变的: *a moody child* 喜怒无常的孩子 **—moodily** *adv*: *She was staring moodily into the fire.* 她闷闷不乐地盯着炉火。**—moodiness** *n* [U]

Moody's In·vest·ors Ser·vice /ˌ· · ˈ· · ˌ· ·/ also 又作 **Moody's** a US company that provides information about the performance of investments and companies, giving them a rating based on combinations of letters from A to C: 穆迪投资者服务公司〔美国一投资咨询公司。该公司根据投资收益和企业业绩用A至C字母组合进行等级评定〕: *The bonds have a Moody's AAA rating.* 该债券的穆迪等级为AAA级。

moo·la, moolah /ˈmulə; ˈmuːlə/ *n* [U] *AmE slang* money【美俚】钞票, 钱

3 **moon[1]** /mun; muːn/ *n* **1 the moon** the round object that you can see shining in the sky at night, and that moves around the Earth every 28 days 月亮, 月球: *the first man on the moon* 第一个登上月球的人 **2** [singular] the shape of this object as it appears at a particular time〔特定时间出现的〕月亮, 月球的形状: *a crescent moon* 新月, 娥眉月 | *There's no moon tonight.* (=it cannot be seen) 今晚没有月光。**3** [C] a round object that moves around a PLANET other than Earth 卫星: *the moons of Saturn* 土星的卫星 **4 ask for the moon** also 又作 **cry for the moon** *BrE informal* to ask for something that is difficult or impossible to obtain【英, 非正式】要求得到难以[无法]得到的东西; 妄想, 异想天开 **5 over the moon** *BrE informal* very happy【英, 非正式】非常高兴的: *She's over the moon about her new job.* 她对新工作非常满意。**6 throw a moon** *BrE*【英】, **shoot the moon** *AmE*【美】*informal* to show your bare BUTTOCKS to someone as a joke or a way of insulting someone【非正式】〔开玩笑或侮辱性地〕露出光屁股 **7 many moons ago** *poetic* a long time ago【诗】很久以前: *It all happened many moons ago.* 那一切都发生在很久以前。—see also 另见 FULL MOON, HALF MOON, NEW MOON, **once in a blue moon** (BLUE[1] (4)), **promise sb the moon** (PROMISE[1] (3))

moon[2] *v* [I,T] *informal* to bend over and show your bare BUTTOCKS as a joke or a way of insulting someone【非正式】〔开玩笑或侮辱性地〕(对着…)躬身露出光屁股

moon about/around *phr v* [I] *BrE informal* to spend your time lazily, moving around with no real purpose【英, 非正式】闲荡; 闲混: *I wish you'd stop mooning about and do something useful!* 我希望你别再闲混, 做点有用的事吧!

moon over sb/sth *phr v* [T] *informal* to spend your time thinking and dreaming about someone or something that you love【非正式】为…出神, 如梦如痴地想念〔所爱的人或物〕: *She sits mooning over his photograph for hours.* 她连坐好几个小时, 对着他的照片出神。

moon·beam /ˈmun,bim; ˈmuːnbiːm/ *n* [C] a beam of light from the moon 一道[缕]月光

moon boot /ˈ· ·/ *n* [C] a thick warm cloth or plastic boot worn in snow and cold weather 月靴〔一种在雪中及寒冷天气下所穿的厚而暖和的布靴或塑料靴〕

Moon·ie /ˈmunɪ; ˈmuːni/ *n* [C] a member of a religious group started by the Korean businessman Sun Myung Moon 统一教信徒〔韩国商人文鲜明所创始的一个宗教团体的成员〕

moon·less /ˈmunləs; ˈmuːnləs/ *adj* a moonless sky or night is dark because the moon cannot be seen 没有月光的: *a cloudy, moonless night* 一个多云、没有月色的夜晚

moon·light[1] /ˈmun,laɪt; ˈmuːnlaɪt/ *n* [U] **1** the light of the moon 月光: *The hills were bathed in pale moonlight.* 群山沐浴在淡淡的月光中。**2 do a moonlight** also 又作 **do a moonlight flit** *BrE* leave a place secretly in the middle of the night in order to avoid paying money that you owe【英】〔为躲债而〕夜间潜逃: *Two of the hotel guests had done a moonlight without paying their bills.* 旅馆房客中有两个没有付账, 夜间偷偷地逃走了。

moonlight[2] *v past tense and past participle* **moonlighted** [I] *informal*【非正式】**1** to have a second job in addition to your main job, especially without the knowledge of the government tax department 从事第二职业〔尤指不为政府税务部门所知〕, 兼职: *She's been moonlighting as a waitress in the evenings.* 她晚上一直兼职做女招待。**2** *BrE* to do paid work although you are getting money from the government because you do not officially have a job【英】〔在领取政府失业救济金的同时〕做工赚钱; DOUBLE-DIP[2] *AmE*【美】**—moonlighter** *n* [C] **—moonlighting** *n* [U]: *He's been doing some moonlighting for another company.* 他一直在另一家公司做兼职。

moon·lit /ˈmun,lɪt; ˈmuːn,lɪt/ *adj* [only before noun 仅用于名词前] made brighter by the light of the moon 月光照耀下的: *a moonlit garden* 月色下的花园

moon·scape /ˈmun,skep; ˈmuːnskeɪp/ *n* [C] a bare empty area of land that looks like the surface of the moon〔如月球表面一样的〕荒凉地带, 荒山景色

moon·shine /ˈmun,ʃaɪn; ˈmuːnʃaɪn/ *n* [U] *informal*【非正式】**1** a stupid or impractical remark, idea, or plan 愚蠢[不切实际]的言辞[想法, 计划]; 空谈; 妄想: *He regarded her plans as romantic moonshine.* 他认为她的计划不切实际。**2** *especially AmE* strong alcoholic drink that is produced illegally【尤美】非法酿造的烈性酒

moon·shot /ˈmunʃɑt; ˈmuːnʃɒt/ *n* [C] a SPACESHIP flight through space to the moon〔宇宙飞船的〕奔月飞行

moon·stone /ˈmun,ston; ˈmuːnstəʊn/ *n* [C,U] a milky-white stone used in making jewellery 月长石, 月光石: *a moonstone necklace* 月长石项链

moon·struck /ˈmun,strʌk; ˈmuːnstrʌk/ *adj informal* slightly mad【非正式】轻度神经错乱的

moor[1] /mur; mʊə/ *n* [C] **1** usually 一般作 **moors** [plural] *especially BrE* a wild open area of high land, covered with rough grass or low bushes and HEATHER, that is not farmed because the soil is not good enough【尤英】漠泽, 高沼〔因土质差无法耕种的高地荒原〕; 荒野, 旷野: *They went grouse shooting up on the moors.* 他们去荒野射猎松鸡。| *the Yorkshire moors* 约克郡漠泽 **2 Moor** one of the Muslim people of the Arab race who were in power in Spain from 711 to 1492 摩尔人〔公元711年至1492年统治西班牙的阿拉伯穆斯林〕

moor[2] *v* [I,T] to fasten a ship or boat to the land or to the bottom of the sea using ropes or an ANCHOR 停泊, 系泊〔船只〕: *We moored in the estuary, waiting for high tide.* 我们停泊在河口, 等待涨潮。

Moore /muɚ; mʊə/, **Bobby** (1941-93) a British football player, one of the greatest English players ever, who played for the English national team and led the team that won the World Cup in 1966. 穆尔〔(1941-1993), 英国足球运动员, 被认为是英国最出色的足球运动员之一。他曾效力于英格兰队, 带领该队赢得1966年世界杯冠军〕

Moore, Henry (1898-1986) a British SCULPTOR considered by many people to be the most important British sculptor of the 20th century. He made many large sculptures of people in a partly abstract style, especially of women lying down. 穆尔〔(1898-1986), 英国雕塑家。许多人认为他是20世纪英国最重要的雕塑家。他采用部分抽象风格创作了许多大型人物雕塑, 尤见于卧姿女人雕像〕

Moore, Mar·i·anne /,mærɪˈæn; ,mæriˈæn/ (1887-1972) a US poet and critic, who wrote clever and SATIRICAL poems 穆尔〔(1887-1972), 美国诗人和评论家, 以创作工巧的讽刺诗见长〕

moor·hen /ˈmʊrˌhɛn; ˈmʊəhen/ *n* [C] a black bird that lives beside streams and lakes 泽鸡, 黑水鸡

moor·ing /ˈmʊrɪŋ; ˈmʊərɪŋ/ *n* [C] **1 moorings** [plural] the ropes, chains, ANCHORs etc used to moor a ship or boat〔船的〕系泊用具〈如绳、链、锚等〉: *Several ships had broken their moorings during the storm.* 在暴风雨中好几条船挣断了缆绳。**2** the place where a ship or boat is moored〔船的〕系泊处, 停泊地, 泊位: *a temporary mooring* 临时系泊处

Moor·ish /ˈmʊrɪʃ; ˈmʊərɪʃ/ *adj* connected with the MOORs 摩尔人的: *Moorish architecture in Spain* 西班牙的摩尔式建筑

moor·land /ˈmʊrˌlænd; ˈmʊələnd/ also 又作 **moorlands** *n* [U] *especially BrE* wild open countryside covered with rough grass and low bushes【尤英】高沼地; 旷野, 荒原 —**moorland** *adj*: *a moorland cottage* 旷野中的小屋

Moors Mur·der·ers, the /ˈ· ˌ···/ Ian Brady and Myra Hindley, a British man and woman who murdered several children in the 1960s. Brady and Hindley were lovers, and they were called the Moors Murderers because they buried the murdered children in the MOORs (=wild areas of high land) in the North of England. Before they killed the children, they TORTUREd them (=treated them very cruelly), and these events caused great shock and anger in the UK. 漠泽杀人狂〔即伊恩·布雷迪和迈拉·欣德利, 英国一对恋人。20 世纪 60 年代, 他们合谋杀害了数名儿童, 并把尸体埋在英格兰北部的漠泽, 故名"漠泽杀人狂"。实施杀人前, 他们还对儿童百般折磨。这些罪行曾震惊全英国, 并激起极大公愤〕

moose /mus; muːs/ *n plural* **moose** [C] a large brown animal like a DEER that has very large flat ANTLERs (=horns that grow like branches), and lives in North America and northern Europe 麋, 驼鹿

moot¹ /mut; muːt/ *adj* **1 a moot point/question** something that has not yet been decided, and about which people have different opinions 争论未决的论点/问题: *Whether these controls will really reduce violent crime is a moot point.* 这些控制措施能否真的减少暴力犯罪是一个尚有争议的问题。**2** *AmE* a situation or possible action that is moot, is no longer likely to happen or exist【美】〔某情况或行为〕不再会发生的, 不再会存在的: *The fear that airstrikes could endanger troops is moot now that the army is withdrawing.* 由于军队正在撤退, 人们不会再害怕空袭可能危及部队的安全了。

moot² *v* [T] **be mooted** to be suggested for people to consider 被提出供考虑: *The question of changing the membership rules was mooted at the last meeting.* 修改会员章程的问题是在上一次会议上提出的。

moot court /ˈ· ·/ *n* [C] *AmE* a court in which law students practise holding trials【美】〔法学院学生实习的〕模拟法庭, 假设法庭

mop¹ /mɑp; mɒp/ *n* [C] **1** a thing for washing floors with, consisting of a long stick with threads of thick string or a piece of SPONGE¹ (1) fastened to one end 拖把 **2** a thing for cleaning dishes with, consisting of a short stick with a piece of SPONGE¹ (1) fastened to one end 洗碗刷 **3** [usually singular 一般用单数] *informal* a large amount of thick, often untidy hair【非正式】浓密(蓬乱)的头发: [+of] *a baby with a mop of golden curls* 长着一头浓密的金色鬈发的婴儿

mop² *v* **mopping, mopped 1** [I,T] to wash a floor with a wet mop 用湿拖把拖〔地板〕—see picture at 参见 CLEAN² 图 **2** [T] to dry your face by rubbing it with a cloth or something soft 擦干〔脸〕, 揩干: *It was so hot he had to keep stopping to mop his face.* 天气太热, 他只得不断地停下来擦脸。| **mop your brow** (=remove SWEAT² (1) from your forehead) 擦去额头上的汗水 **3** [I,T] to remove liquid from a surface by rubbing it with a cloth or something soft 擦掉〔液体〕, 抹掉: **mop sth from sth** *The nurse gently mopped the blood from the wound.* 护士轻轻地抹去伤口上的血。| **mop sth away** *She mopped the tears away with a lacy handkerchief.* 她用一条花边手绢擦去了泪水。**4 mop the floor with** *AmE*【美】, **wipe the floor with** *BrE*【英】 to completely defeat someone, for example in a game or argument〔在比赛或辩论中〕彻底击败: *We mopped the floor with the team from Pomona High.* 我们彻底击败了波莫纳中学参赛队。

mop sth ↔ **up** *phr v* [T] **1** to remove liquid with a mop, cloth, or something soft, especially in order to clean a surface 擦干, 抹去〔液体〕: *Can you mop up the milk you've spilled?* 把你洒了的牛奶擦干净好吗? | *Mop up the sauce with your bread.* 用你的面包把调味汁抹干净。**2** to deal with the remaining members of a defeated army by killing them or making them prisoners 肃清〔残敌〕, 扫荡〔残兵败将〕: *mopping up isolated pockets of resistance* 扫荡零星抵抗的敌人 | **mopping-up operations** *The rebellion has been crushed, but mopping-up operations may take several weeks.* 叛乱已被镇压, 但肃清残余也许还要数周时间。**3** *BrE* to complete a piece of work or finish dealing with something or someone【英】结束, 完成: *I've just got a couple of jobs to mop up before I go on holiday.* 去休假之前我还有几件工作要完成。

mope /mop; məʊp/ *v* [I] to feel sorry for yourself, without making any effort to be more cheerful 忧郁, 闷闷不乐: *Don't lie there moping on a lovely morning like this!* 这么美好的一个早晨, 你就别躺在那里闷闷不乐了!

mope around also 又作 **mope about** *phr v* [I,T] *BrE* to move around a place in a sad, slow way【英】(在…) 没精打采地闲荡, 忧郁地徘徊: *She spends her days moping around the house.* 她成天在房子里没精打采地瞎转悠。

mo·ped /ˈmopɛd; ˈməʊped/ *n* [C] a small two-wheeled vehicle with an engine 机器脚踏车, 助动车 —compare 比较 MOTORCYCLE

mo·quette /moˈkɛt; mɒˈket/ *n* [U] a thick soft material used for covering furniture〔包盖家具的〕绒布织物: *a moquette armchair* 绒面扶手椅

mo·raine /moˈren; məˈreɪn/ *n* [C] *technical* a mass of earth or pieces of rock left in a line at the bottom or edge of a GLACIER【术语】冰碛, 冰川堆石 —see picture on page A12 参见 A12 页图

mor·al¹ /ˈmɔrəl; ˈmɒrəl/ *adj* 

1 ▶ABOUT RIGHT AND WRONG 有关对与错◀ [only before noun 仅用于名词前] connected with the principles of what is right and wrong behaviour, and with the difference between good and evil 道德(上)的: *a man of high moral standards* 道德高尚的人 | *You don't know the circumstances of the divorce, so don't make moral judgments about it.* 你不了解离婚的前因后果, 所以不要对此作道德上谁是谁非的判断。| **moral dilemma/issue** (=a subject that involves morals) 道德上的困境/问题 *the abortion issue, one of the great moral dilemmas* 道德上的大难题之一——堕胎问题 | **moral sense** (=ability to understand the difference between right and wrong) 道德感, 是非感 *Babies are born without a moral sense.* 婴儿生下来并没有道德感。

2 ▶BASED ON WHAT IS RIGHT 基于是非感的◀ [only before noun 仅用于名词前] based on your ideas about what is right, rather than on what is legal or practical 基于道德的, 道义上的: **moral responsibility/duty** *You have a moral responsibility to help people in need.* 你在道义上有责任帮助有困难的人。| **moral courage** (=the courage to do what you believe is right) 道义勇气, 坚持正义的勇气 *Does he have the moral courage necessary to lead the country?* 他具有国家领导人所需的道义勇气吗? | **moral authority** (=influence that you have because people accept that your beliefs are right) 道义上的权力[权威, 影响力] *The UN feels that it has the moral authority to send troops to the area.* 联合国认为它在道义上有权向该地区派遣部队。| **moral fibre** *BrE*【英】/**fiber** *AmE*【美】(=the emotional strength to do what you believe is right) 道德力量, 正义感

3 moral support encouragement that you give by expressing approval or interest, rather than by giving practical help 道义上的支持, 精神支持: *He went along to give moral support.* 他前去给予道义上的支持。

4 moral victory a situation in which you show that your beliefs are right and fair, even if you do not win the argument 道义[精神]上的胜利: *We felt we had won a moral victory in the debate.* 我们感到在辩论中取得了道义上的胜利。

5 ▶STORY 故事◀ a moral story, play etc is one that teaches or shows good behaviour〔故事、戏剧等〕有教育意义的, 说教性的

6 ▶PERSON 人◀ always behaving in a way that is based on strong principles about what is right and wrong 有道德的, 品行端正的 —compare 比较 AMORAL, IMMORAL —see also 另见 MORALLY

moral² *n* [C] **1 morals** [plural] principles or standards of good behaviour, especially in matters of sex〔尤指男女关系上的〕道德准则[标准]; 道德, 伦理; 品行: *The novel reflects the morals and customs of the time.* 这部小说反映了当时的道德标准和社会习俗。| **public morals** (=the standards of behaviour, especially sexual behaviour, expected by society)〔尤指性行为方面的〕公众道德, 社会公德 *The sex shop was deemed a danger to public morals.* 性用品商店被认为有伤风化。| **loose morals** *old-fashioned or humorous* (=low standards of sexual behaviour resulting in someone having many sexual partners)【过时或幽默】放荡的品行, 不检点的品行 **2** a practical lesson about what to do or how to behave, which you learn from a story or from something that happens to you 寓意, 道德上的教训; 教育意义: **the moral of sth is** *The moral of the film was that crime does not pay.* 这部电影的寓意是犯罪难逃法律制裁。| **draw a moral** (=understand what a story or event is teaching you) 明白〔故事或事件的〕寓意

mo·rale /mə'ræl; mə'rɑːl/ *n* [U] the level of confidence and positive feelings, especially among a group of people who work together, belong to the same team etc 士气, 斗志; 精神面貌: *The team's morale was low after losing.* 比赛输了之后, 球队士气低落。| *A few words of praise are always good for morale.* 几句赞扬的话对提高士气总是有用的。| **keep up/maintain morale** *the benefits of regular exercise in keeping up students' morale* 定期锻炼在保持学生良好的精神状态方面所具有的好处 | **boost/raise/improve morale** *Churchill's visit did a great deal to boost morale among the troops.* 丘吉尔的慰问大大鼓舞了军队的士气。

mor·al·ist /'mɔrəlɪst; 'mɒrəlɪst/ *n* [C] **1** someone who has very strong beliefs about what is right and wrong, and who tries to control other people's morals 说教者, 卫道士 **2** a teacher of moral principles 道德家; 德育家, 德育工作者

mor·al·ist·ic /,mɔrə'lɪstɪk; ,mɒrə'lɪstɪk◂/ *adj* having very strong unchanging beliefs about what is right and wrong, especially when this makes you judge other people's behaviour 道德观念强烈的; 道德说教的: *It's difficult to talk to teenagers about drugs without sounding too moralistic.* 跟青少年谈论毒品, 很难做到听起来不过于说教。—**moralistically** /-klɪ; -kli/ *adv*

mo·ral·i·ty /mə'rælətɪ; mə'rælɪti/ *n* **1** [U] beliefs or ideas about what is right and wrong and about how people should behave 道德; 道德观: *traditional morality* 传统道德观 | *declining standards of morality* 日益低下的道德水平 **2** [U] the degree to which something is right or acceptable 道德性; 道义性; 正当性: [+of] *a discussion on the morality of abortion* 关于堕胎是否符合道德标准的讨论 **3** [C,U] a system of beliefs and values concerning how people should behave, which is accepted by a particular person or group 道德体系; 道德规范: *Christian morality* 基督教的道德体系 | *a direct clash in moralities* 不同道德体系的直接冲突 —opposite 反义词 IMMORALITY

mor·al·ize also 又作 **-ise** *BrE*【英】/'mɔrəl,aɪz; 'mɒrəlaɪz/ *v* [I] to tell other people your ideas about right and wrong behaviour, especially when they have not asked for your opinion 说教; 教化; 训导: [+about/on] *politicians moralizing about people's sexual behaviour* 就人们的性行为进行说教的政治家 —**moralizer** *n* [C]

mor·al·ly /'mɔrəlɪ; 'mɒrəli/ *adv* **1** according to moral principles about what is right and wrong 道德上, 道义上: *What you did wasn't illegal, but it was morally wrong.* 你做的事并不违法, 但从道义上讲是错误的。| *The president is morally opposed to capital punishment.* 总统从道义上反对死刑。| **morally responsible** *He held himself morally responsible for the accident.* 他认为自己应为那次事故负道义上的责任。**2** in a way which is good or right 有道德地, 品行端正地: *one of the few politicians who always behaves completely morally* 行为一贯十分端正的极少数政治家之一 **3** **morally certain** *old-fashioned* very probable【过时】很可能的: *It's morally certain that he'll be the next President.* 他很可能会成为下届总统。

Moral Ma·jor·i·ty, the /,·· ·'···/ *trademark* a US Christian organization started in 1979 by the Rev. Jerry Falwell. The group's aim is to help politicians who support its RIGHT WING ideas on subjects such as ABORTION and the rights of HOMOSEXUALs, and to actively oppose politicians who disagree with these ideas.【商标】道德多数派〔美国一基督教组织, 1979年由牧师杰里·福尔韦尔创立。就人工流产和同性恋者的权利等问题, 该组织给支援其右翼观点的政客提供帮助, 而极力反对与其观点相左的政客〕

moral ma·jor·i·ty /,·· ·'···/ *n* [singular] a group of people in the US with strong Christian principles, who have very traditional beliefs about the family, crime and punishment, people's sexual behaviour etc 道德多数派〔美国严格遵循基督教准则并对家庭、犯罪与惩罚及人们的性行为等抱有传统观念的团体〕

Moral Re·ar·ma·ment /,·· ·'···/ abbreviation 缩写为 **MRA** an international movement started in 1938 by the US EVANGELIST Frank Buchman (1878-1961), who wanted to make people behave in a more moral and spiritual way, especially in international relations 道德重建运动〔1938年由美国福音传教士弗兰克·布克曼 (1878-1961) 发起的一场国际运动, 旨在使人们的行为更符合道德和精神标准, 尤其体现在国际关系领域〕

mo·rass /mə'ræs; mə'ræs/ *n* **1** [singular] a complicated and confusing situation that is very difficult to get out of 困境; 陷阱: [+of] *We were bogged down in a morass of detail.* 我们陷进了琐碎细节的泥淖。**2** [C] *especially literary* a dangerous area of soft wet ground; MARSH【尤文】泥淖, 沼泽

mor·a·to·ri·um /,mɔrə'torɪəm; ,mɒrə'tɔːriəm/ *n* [C usually singular 一般用单数] **1** an official stopping of an activity for a period of time〔官方的〕暂停, 中止: [+on] *the proposed moratorium on nuclear testing* 拟议中的暂停核试验 **2** a law or an agreement that gives people more time to pay their debts 允许延期偿债的法律[协议]

Moray /'mʌri; 'mʌrɪ/ a COUNTY in northern Scotland, with a coast on the North Sea 马里郡〔苏格兰北部一郡, 濒临北海〕

mor·bid /'mɔrbɪd; 'mɔːbɪd/ *adj* **1** having a strong and unhealthy interest in unpleasant subjects, especially death〔兴趣、精神、思想等〕病态的, 不健康的: *He wanted to know all the morbid details about the accident.* 他想知道所有与那起事故有关的令人毛骨悚然的细节。| *a morbid fascination with instruments of torture* 对刑具的一种病态的迷恋 **2** *technical* connected with or caused by a disease【术语】疾病的; 疾病引起的; 致病的: *a morbid gene* 致病基因 —**morbidly** *adv* —**morbidity** *n* [U]

mor·dant /'mɔrdnt; 'mɔːdənt/ *adj* **mordant criticism/wit/humour** *formal* cruel and insulting criticism, wit etc【正式】尖刻的批评/妙语/幽默

Mor·dred /'mɔrdrɛd; 'mɔːdred/ also 又作 **Modred** an evil KNIGHT who is either the son or the NEPHEW of King Arthur in old stories. He tries to take Arthur's land from him, but is killed by Arthur during a battle. 莫得里德〔传说故事中的一个邪恶的骑士。此人是亚瑟王之子或侄子, 企图夺取亚瑟王的土地, 但在一场战斗中被亚瑟王杀死〕

more[1] /mɔr; mɔː/ *adv* **1** [+adj/adv] having a particular quality or characteristic to a greater degree than someone or something else 更, 更加, 较为: **more interesting/expensive etc** *We can make the test more difficult by adding a time limit.* 我们可以加上时间限制使测试更难些。| *It could have been an infection but it's more likely to have been something you ate.* 这可能是由于感染, 但更可能是由于你吃东西吃的。| **more interesting/expensive etc than** *Who knows if there are beings more advanced than ourselves out there on other planets?* 谁知道在其他行星上是否存在着比我们更高级的生物呢? | **much/a lot/far more** *Many of the children feel much more confident if they work in groups.* 许多孩子在集体协作时会感到自信得多。—opposite 反义词 LESS[1] (1) **2** used to say that something happens more often or for a longer time than before or than something else 更〔经常地或长久地〕: *He's managed to master the basics of tennis but needs to practice a bit more.* 他已经掌握了网球的基本要领, 但还需要多加练习。| **more than** *Businesses use computers more than they used to.* 企业比过去更多地使用电脑。| **far/much/a lot more** *He goes out a lot more now he has the car.* 现在有了汽车, 他出去的次数多多了。—opposite 反义词 LESS[1] (1) **3** used to say that something such as a feeling or opinion is felt or believed to a greater degree 更强烈; 更大程度地: *I couldn't agree more.* 我完全同意。| **more than** *It's her manner I dislike, more than what she actually says.* 我讨厌的倒不是她实际上说些什么, 而是她的态度。| **much/far/a lot more** *She cares far more for her dogs than she does for me.* 她关心狗远远胜过关心我。—opposite 反义词 LESS[1] (1) **4** **more and more** if something happens or is done more and more it happens or is done more than before and is becoming common 越来越: *More and more I see young boys with no prospects turning to crime or drugs.* 我看到越来越多前途无望的男孩子走上犯罪或吸毒的邪路。**5** **more and more tired/angry etc** increasingly tired, angry etc as time passes 越来越疲劳/生气等: *As the disease worsened he found walking more and more difficult.* 随着病情的恶化, 他感到走路越来越困难。**6** **once more a)** if you do something once more you do it again and usually for the last time 再次〔通常为最后一次〕: *Can we rehearse the scene once more before the show starts?* 在演出开始之前我们把这场戏再排练一次好吗? **b)** *especially literary* again【尤文】再一次, 又一次: *Once more the soldiers attacked and once more they were defeated.* 士兵们再次发动进攻, 但又一次被击败。**7** **not any more** also 又作 **no more** *literary* no longer【文】不再: *Didn't you know? Paul and Ann aren't going out together any more.* 你不知道吗? 保罗和安分手了。| *No more is it possible to stand on the football terraces and cheer on your local team.* 站在足球场看台上, 为当地球队欢呼呐喊, 这已是不再可能的事了。**8** **more often than not** used to say that something usually happens 往往, 多半, 通常: *More often than not people don't realise what their rights are.* 人们往往不知道自己有哪些权利。**9** **be more than pleased/sorry etc** used to emphasize that you are very pleased, very sorry etc 非常高兴/难过等: *The store is more than happy to deliver goods to your home.* 本商店很乐意为您送货上门。| *"I suppose you will be working late again tonight?" "More than likely, yes."* "我想今晚你又要工作到深夜, 是吧?" "是的, 极有可能。" **10** **be more than a little angry/sad etc** used to emphasize how angry or sad you are 非常生气/伤心等: *We're more than a little concerned about the state of his financial affairs.* 我们非常担心他的财务状况。**11** **more...than...** used to emphasize that one

thing is truer, more important etc than something 与其说…倒不如说…: *Don't be too hard on him. He's more misled than stupid.* 不要对他太苛刻。与其说他愚蠢,倒不如说他被误导了。| *She's known more for her wild private life than her acting ability.* 她的出名与其说靠的是演技,倒不如说是放荡不羁的私生活。**12 a)** **no more than** used to say that something is needed or suitable 正是〔需要的或合适的〕: *It's no more than you deserve.* 这完全是你该得到的。**b)** also 又作 **little more than** used to say that someone or something is less important than they seem 只不过,仅仅: *He's no more than a glorified accountant.* 他只不过是一个被美化了的会计而已。| *It was little more than a scratch.* 仅仅是一点擦伤而已。**13** **(and) what's more** used to add more information that emphasizes what you are saying 而且,更重要的是,更有甚者: *He enjoyed the meal and what's more he ate the lot!* 他喜欢那饭,而且全吃光了! **14** **no more...than...** used to emphasize that something is not true, not suitable etc 不比…更…,与…同样不…: *He's no more fit to be a priest than I am!* 他和我一样都不适合当牧师! **15** **no more can she/no more do I etc** neither can she, neither do I etc 她也不能/我也没有等: *I don't have time to do the filing and no more do you!* 我没有时间把文件归档,你也没有! **16** **(then) more fool you** *BrE* used to say that you think someone is being stupid【英】(那)你真是傻极了: *If you want to get up so early in the morning then more fool you!* 如果你想起那么早,那你真是傻透了!

USAGE NOTE 用法说明: MORE
GRAMMAR 语法
More is used with an adjective instead of the *-er* form, not as well as it. more后跟形容词的原级形式而非其-er形式,如: *This year's exam was harder for me* (NOT 不用 *more harder*). 今年的考试对我来说更难一些。
It is also used when an adjective does not have an *-er* form. 它后面也可跟没有-er形式的形容词: *This year's exam was more difficult than last year's.* 今年的考试比去年的难。

S1 W1 **more²** *quantifier comparative of many, much* many和much的比较级 **1** used to say that a particular number or amount is larger than another〔数量〕更大的,更多的;更大的数量: *"Do you want more cake?" "Uh, maybe. I'll get it."* "你还要点蛋糕吗?" "唔,也许吧。我会去拿的。" | **more people/things etc than...** *More cars are failing the emissions test than was anticipated.* 通不过尾气排放测试的汽车比预计的多。| *She makes more phone calls in one day than anyone else I know.* 我认识的人当中,她每天打的电话最多。| **more than 10/100 etc** *More than 500 people had to be helped to safety when the stadium collapsed.* 体育馆坍塌时,有五百多人需要帮忙脱险。| **more than sth** *In some places bottled water costs more than a glass of beer.* 有些地方一瓶瓶装水比一杯啤酒还贵。| *It is possible to earn $100 a day, some days more.* 一天可能挣100美元,有时还不止。| *I'd ask Veronica – she knows far more about it.* 我还是问问韦罗妮卡,她对此事知道得要多得多。| [+of] *We sell more of these maps because they're so colourful.* 这些地图我们卖得多一些,因为它们色彩非常鲜艳。| **much/far/a lot more** *Recent anti-smoking campaigns have driven a lot more smokers to give up.* 近来的反吸烟运动已经使更多的吸烟者戒了烟。—opposite 反义词 LESS² or FEWER **2** used when you mean another number or amount in addition to what you have, expect, or have mentioned〔数量〕另外的,附加的,额外的: *You'll have to pay more for a double room.* 住双人间必须多付钱。| *A free trip to Jamaica? Tell me more!* 免费到牙买加旅游?跟我具体讲讲! | **2/10 etc more** *That was Jim on the phone. He needs two more tickets for the play.* 是吉姆来的电话,他还需要两张戏票。| **some/any/a few etc more** *We have some wonderful people volunteering to help out but many more are needed.* 我们有一些很不错的人志愿帮忙,但还需要更多的人。| **more people/things etc** *I think I'd need to know some more facts before I could agree to the trip.* 我想我还需要再了解一些情况,才能同意作这次旅行。| *I'm sorry sir, your meal will be five minutes more, I'm afraid.* 对不起先生,恐怕您的饭还要再等五分钟。| [ ] *Can I have some more of that apple pie please?* 请问我可以再来一些那样的苹果馅饼吗? | *You've had a week to do it. How much more time do you need?* 已经给了你一周时间了,你还需要多少时间? —opposite 反义词 LESS² **3** **more and more** an increasing number of something 越来越多的: *More and more people are taking early retirement these days.* 现在越来越多的人提前退休。—opposite 反义词 **less and less** (LESS¹ (2)) **4** **more or less a)** almost 几乎,差不多: *By the time of the dress rehearsal she knew her lines more or less by heart.* 到最后彩排的时候,她几乎把台词都背下来了。**b)** APPROXIMATELY 大致,大约,或多或少: *We're expecting 150 delegates at the conference, more or less.* 我们预计大约会有150名代表参加会议。**5** **not/no more than** used to say that a price, distance etc is only a particular number or amount〔价格、距离等〕不超过,至多,仅仅: *It's a beautiful cottage not more than five minutes from the nearest beach.* 那是一座漂亮的小屋,离最近的海滩至多五分钟路程。**6** **the more..., the more.../the less** used to say that when you do something or something happens, a particular situation will be the result of it 越…越…: *It's simple. The more preparation you do now, the less nervous you'll be before the exam.* 这很简单,你现在准备得越充分,考试前就越不会紧张。—see also 另见 **more's the pity** (PITY¹ (5))

More, Sir Thomas (1478-1535) an English politician and writer. His most famous work is *Utopia*, which describes his idea of a perfect society. He was a powerful adviser to King Henry VIII, but he opposed the king's DIVORCE (=the official ending of a marriage) and refused to accept him as the head of the Church of England. For this the king put him in prison and ordered his head to be cut off. The Roman Catholic Church later made him a saint. 莫尔〔(1478-1535),英国政治家和作家。最著名的作品是《乌托邦》,其中描述了他构想的完美社会。他是国王亨利八世的得力顾问,但他反对国王离婚,不肯承认他是英国国教会的首领。为此国王将他投进监狱并下令将他斩首。后来,罗马天主教教会追谥他为圣徒〕

more·ish /ˈmɔrɪʃ; ˈmɔːrɪʃ/ *adj BrE spoken* food that is moreish tastes very good, and makes you want to eat more of it【英口】好吃的;令人垂涎欲滴的

more·o·ver /mɔrˋovɚ; mɔːrˈəʊvə/ *adv* [sentence adverb 句子副词] *formal* a word meaning 'in addition', used to introduce information that adds to or supports what has previously been said【正式】此外,而且,加之,再者: *The rent is reasonable and, moreover, the location is perfect.* 房租合理,而且地段极好。 W2

USAGE NOTE 用法说明: MOREOVER
FORMALITY 正式程度
Moreover is very formal and not common in spoken English. But you may see it used in a report. moreover非常正式,口语中不常见,但可见于报道中: *Local people would like a new road. Moreover, there are good economic reasons for building one.* 当地人希望修一条新公路,而且在经济方面修路也有充足的理由。
Also is a less formal way of adding a reason or idea. It can be used at the beginning of a sentence to link it to the previous one. also用以补充原因或想法,正式程度比moreover低一些,此词可用于句首把该句与前句连接起来: *You can stay at our house. Also, I can check the plane times for you.* 你可以住在我们这儿。另外,我能为你查一下班机的时间。Or it can be used within a sentence. 它也可以用于句中: *I can also check the plane times for you.* 我还能为你查一下班机的时间。
Besides (that) is more informal and used especially to add a reason. besides (that)正式程度比also又低了一个层次,尤用以补充原因: *June isn't a good month to go there. Besides, I want to finish my exams first.* 6月份不是去那儿的好时候。而且,我还想先考完试。
People also often add reasons and ideas within one sentence using **and** and made stronger with **moreover/also/besides**. 人们也经常在句中用and与moreover/also/besides连用来补充原因和想法,后者加强前者的语气: *You should switch to a healthier diet and moreover/also/besides that stop smoking.* 你应该改用更有益于健康的饮食,除此之外,还要把烟戒掉。

mo·res /ˋmɔriz; ˈmɔːreɪz/ *n* [plural] *formal* the customs, social behaviour, and moral values of a particular group【正式】习俗;惯例: *American social and sexual mores* 美国的社交和性习俗

Mor·gan le Fay /ˌmɔrgən lə ˋfe; ˌmɔːgən lə ˈfeɪ/ an evil SORCERESS (=a woman who has magic powers) who is the half-sister of King Arthur in old stories 仙女摩根〔古老传说中的一个邪恶的女巫。她是亚瑟王同母异父的妹妹〕

morgue /mɔrg; mɔːg/ *n* [C] **1** a building or room, for example in a hospital, where dead bodies are kept until they are buried or cremated (CREMATE) 停尸房;陈尸所;太平间; MORTUARY¹ (1) *BrE*【英】**2** *often humorous* a quiet place where not much happens, so that you feel sad or bored【常幽默】死气沉沉的地方

Mor·i·ar·ty, Professor /ˌmɔrɪˋartɪ; ˌmɒriˈɑːti/ an extremely intelligent criminal, who is the main enemy of Sherlock Holmes in the stories by Sir Arthur Conan Doyle 莫里亚蒂〔亚瑟·柯南·道尔爵士创作的系列小说中的一个智商极高的罪犯。他是夏洛克·福尔摩斯的主要敌手〕

mor·i·bund /ˈmɔrə,bʌnd; ˈmɒrɪ̈bʌnd/ *adj* **1** a moribund industry, institution, custom etc is no longer active or effective and therefore coming to an end〔行业、机构、风俗等〕没有活力的，死气沉沉的，行将消亡的: *The eastern region's heavy industry is inefficient and moribund.* 东部地区的重工业效率低下，已日落西山。**2** *literary* slowly dying【文】垂死的，奄奄一息的

Mor·mon /ˈmɔrmən; ˈmɔːmən/ *n* [C] a member of a religious organization formed in 1830 in the US, officially called The Church of Jesus Christ of Latter-day Saints 摩门教教徒 **—Mormon** *adj* **—Mormonism** *n* [U]

> **CULTURAL NOTE 文化注释**
> The largest groups of Mormons live in the Western US, especially in the state of Utah, where the Mormon TABERNACLE (=their most important church) is. They have strict moral rules and do not use tobacco or drink alcohol, tea, or coffee. Mormons also think that the family is very important. Young Mormons must do MISSIONARY work for a period of time, and people think of young Mormon men as wearing white shirts and ties when they go from house to house trying to persuade people to join the Mormon church. In the past, Mormon men were allowed to have more than one wife, but this is no longer common. 摩门教徒的最大群体居住在美国西部，尤以犹他州为多，那里有摩门教的大礼拜堂。摩门教有严格的戒律，禁止教徒吸烟、饮酒、喝茶和喝咖啡。摩门教徒亦有很强的家庭观念。年轻的摩门教徒必须做一段时间的传教工作。在人们的印象中，摩门教年轻男教徒衣着白衫、打着领带，挨家挨户地劝导人们皈依摩门教。过去摩门教徒允许一夫多妻，现在已不常见。

morn /mɔrn; mɔːn/ *n* [C usually singular 一般用单数] *poetic* morning【诗】早晨，黎明

morn·ing¹ /ˈmɔrnɪŋ; ˈmɔːnɪŋ/ *n* [C,U] **1** the early part of the day, from when the sun rises until the middle of the day 早晨；上午: *a sunny morning* 阳光灿烂的上午 | *six o'clock in the morning* 早上6点钟 | *I had a letter from George this morning.* 我今天上午收到了乔治的一封信。| *We're leaving on Tuesday morning.* 我们周二早上动身。**2** the part of the day from midnight until the middle of the day 半夜至中午的时间: *The phone rang at three in the morning.* 电话在凌晨3点响了起来。**3 in the morning** tomorrow morning 明天早晨[上午]: *I'll deal with that in the morning.* 我明天上午会处理那件事。**4 mornings** during the morning each day 每天早晨[上午]: *She works mornings at the local school.* 她每天上午在当地那所学校工作。**5 morning, noon, and night** used to emphasize that something happens a lot or continuously 白天黑夜地，夜以继日: *That girl is on the phone morning, noon, and night!* 那个女孩子一天到晚不停地打电话！—see also 另见 COFFEE MORNING

morning² *interjection* used to greet someone in the morning 早上好，你好〔早上见面时的问候语〕: *Morning, Dave. How are you?* 早，戴夫，你好吗？

morning-af·ter pill /,.. ˈ.. ,. / *n* [C] a drug that a woman can take after having sex to prevent her from having a baby〔女性房事后用的〕口服避孕药，应急避孕药

morning coat /ˈ.. ./ *n* [C] a formal black coat with a long back that is worn as part of morning dress 常礼服的外套

morning dress /ˈ.. ./ *n* [U] *especially BrE* men's formal clothes that include a morning coat, trousers, and a TOP HAT, worn at daytime ceremonies such as weddings【尤英】〔男式〕常礼服

Morning Edition a US news programme broadcast in the morning on National Public Radio stations 早间新闻〔美国全国公共广播电台在早晨播出的新闻节目〕

morning glo·ry /,.. ˈ.. ./ *n* [C,U] a plant that has white, blue, or pink flowers that open in the morning and close in late afternoon 牵牛花

Morning Prayer /,.. ˈ../ *n* [U] a morning church service in the Church of England and the Episcopal Church in the US; MATINS 晨祷

morning room /ˈ.. ./ *n* [C] *old-fashioned* a comfortable room that is used in the morning, usually in a large house【过时】〔通常指大宅中的〕晨室

morning sick·ness /ˈ.. ,.. / *n* [U] a feeling of sickness that some women have before they have a baby 孕妇晨吐

morning star /,.. ˈ./ *n* [singular] a bright PLANET, usually Venus, you can see in the eastern sky when the sun rises 启明星，晨星〔通常指金星〕—compare 比较 EVENING STAR

morning suit /ˈ.. ./ *n* [C] a man's suit that is worn at formal ceremonies during the day, especially weddings〔男士在日间正式场合，尤指婚礼上穿的〕晨礼服

Mo·roc·co a country in northwest Africa on the Mediterranean Sea, whose people speak Arabic, Berber, and French, and whose cities include Casablanca, Marrakesh, and Tangier. Population: 30,645,000 (2001). Capital: Rabat. 摩洛哥〔非洲西北部一国家，濒临地中海，讲阿拉伯语、柏柏尔语和法语。主要城市有卡萨布兰卡、马拉喀什和丹吉尔。人口: 30,645,000 (2001)，首都: 拉巴特〕**—Moroccan** *n, adj*

mo·roc·co /məˈrɑko; məˈrɒkəʊ/ *n* [U] fine soft leather used especially for covering books 摩洛哥皮革〔尤用来做书的封面〕

mo·ron /ˈmɔrɑn; ˈmɔːrɒn/ *n* [C] **1** *informal* someone who is very stupid【非正式】蠢人，傻子，笨蛋: *Don't leave it there, you moron!* 别把它放在那儿，你这个笨蛋！**2** *technical old use* someone whose intelligence has not developed to the normal level【术语，旧】痴愚者 **—moronic** /məˈrɑnɪk; məˈrɒnɪk/ *adj*: *a moronic grin* 傻笑，痴笑 **—moronically** /-klɪ; -kli/ *adv*

mo·rose /məˈros; məˈrəʊs/ *adj* bad-tempered, unhappy, and silent 脾气不好的；闷闷不乐的；阴郁的: *Daniel seems very morose and gloomy.* 丹尼尔好像非常乖僻，闷闷不乐。**—morosely** *adv* **—moroseness** *n* [U]

mor·pheme /ˈmɔrfim; ˈmɔːfiːm/ *n* [C] *technical* the smallest meaningful unit of language, consisting of a word or part of a word that cannot be divided without losing its meaning【术语】语素，词素: *'Gun' contains one morpheme but 'gun-fight-er' contains three.* gun 含有一个词素，但 gun-fight-er 却含有三个词素。

Mor·phe·us /ˈmɔrfiəs; ˈmɔːfiəs/ *n* **in the arms of Morpheus** *literary* asleep【文】酣睡，在梦乡中

mor·phi·a /ˈmɔrfɪə; ˈmɔːfiə/ *n* [U] *old-fashioned* morphine【过时】吗啡

mor·phine /ˈmɔrfin; ˈmɔːfiːn/ *n* [U] a powerful and ADDICTIVE drug used for stopping pain and making people calmer 吗啡

morph·ing /ˈmɔrfɪŋ; ˈmɔːfɪŋ/ *n* [U] a computer method that is used to make one image gradually change into a different one〔图像的〕渐变〔一种电脑技术〕

mor·phol·o·gy /mɔrˈfɑlədʒɪ; mɔːˈfɒlədʒi/ *n technical*【术语】**1** [U] the study of the MORPHEMES of a language and of the way in which they are joined together to make words〔语言〕词法；形态学 —compare 比较 SYNTAX **2** [U] the scientific study of how animals, plants, and their parts are formed〔生物〕形态学 **3** [C,U] the structure of an object or system or the way it was formed 结构；形态 **—morphological** /,mɔrfəˈlɑdʒɪkəl; ,mɔːfəˈlɒdʒɪkəl◂/ *adj*

Morris, William (1834-96) a British artist, CRAFTSMAN, writer, and supporter of social change. Morris was a Socialist who disliked the development of mass production in factories, and tried to support traditional methods of making things. He designed and made his own furniture and materials, and his designs are still popular. 莫利斯〔(1834-1896)，英国画家、手工艺家、作家和社会改革的支持者。他是一名社会主义者，憎恶工厂的大规模生产方式，支持传统的制作方法。他自行设计并制造过家具及各种用品，至今仍颇受欢迎〕: *William Morris wallpaper* (=wallpaper with a pattern originally designed by William Morris) 威廉·莫利斯墙纸

mor·ris danc·ing /ˈmɔrɪs ,dænsɪŋ; ˈmɒrɪ̈s ,dɑːnsɪŋ/ *n* [U] traditional English country dancing performed by men wearing white clothes 莫里斯舞〔英国传统乡村舞〕**—morris dancer** *n* [C]

Morris Mi·nor /,.. ˈ../ *trademark* a type of small British car built by the Morris company from the 1950s to the 1970s. There were several types of Morris Minor, including the **Morris Minor Traveller**, an ESTATE car, with a frame made out of wood. Morris Minors have a simple, old-fashioned design and are not very fast. They are very popular with people who care about the environment or do not like advanced modern machines. Their owners look after them well, so there are still many of these cars being driven in the UK.【商标】小莫利斯〔20世纪50至70年代由英国莫利斯公司制造的一种小型汽车。该汽车有多种款式，如车身为木制的"小莫利斯旅行车"。小莫利斯车设计简洁、老派，行驶速度不快，深受关心环保或不喜欢现代机械的人士喜爱。车主都很注意保养自己的小车，所以在英国仍有许多小莫里斯车在街上行驶〕

Mor·ri·son /ˈmɔrəsn̩; ˈmɒrɪ̈sən/, **Jim** /dʒɪm; dʒɪm/ (1943-71) the main singer with the ROCK group The Doors, known for his sexually exciting performances on stage. Many people see him as a typical example of someone whose life was destroyed by drugs, alcohol, and the problems of being famous. 莫里森〔(1943-1971)，大门摇滚乐队的主唱，以舞台上的性感表演著称。许多人认为他是毁于吸毒酗酒、被盛名所困的典型人物〕

Morrison, Toni (1931-) a US author whose NOVELs include *Song of Solomon* (1977) and *Beloved* (1987). In 1993 she won the Nobel Prize for Literature. 莫里森〔(1931-), 美国作家。代表作有《所罗门之歌》(1977) 和《心爱的人》(1987) 等小说, 1993年获诺贝尔文学奖〕

mor·row /ˈmɔro; ˈmɒrəʊ/ *n* **1 the morrow a)** the next day 次日, 翌日, 明日: *They were to arrive on the morrow.* 他们将于翌日到达。**b)** the future 将来, 未来: *We wondered what the morrow would bring.* 我们想知道将来会发生什么。**2 the morrow of** *literary* the time immediately after a particular event【文】紧接〔某事件〕之后的时间: *the morrow of victory* 得胜之初 **3 good morrow** *old use* good morning【旧】早上好

Morse /mɔrs; mɔːs/, **Inspector** a character in books written by Colin Dexter, and in British television programme based on these books. Morse is a police officer in Oxford, who rarely smiles and sometimes has a rather unfriendly manner. 莫尔斯探长〔科林·德克斯特的小说及根据小说改编的英国电视剧中的一个人物。莫尔斯是牛津的一名警官, 不苟言笑, 有时还显得很不友善〕

Morse code /ˌmɔrs ˋkod; ˌmɔːs ˈkəʊd/ *n* [U] a system of sending messages in which the alphabet is represented by signals made of DOTs (=short signals) and DASHes (=long signals) in sound or light 莫尔斯电码

mor·sel /ˈmɔrsəl; ˈmɔːsəl/ *n* [C] **1** a small piece of food〔食物的〕一小片, 一小块: [+of] *a morsel of bread* 一小片面包 | *tasty morsels* 一点可口的食物 **2 morsel of hope/wisdom/gossip etc** a small amount of hope etc 一点点希望/智慧/流言飞语等: *That's the best morsel of scandal we've had for ages.* 那是我们多年来所听到的最严重的一桩丑闻。

mor·tal¹ /ˈmɔrtl̩; ˈmɔːtl/ *adj* **1** not living for ever 凡人的, 不会长生不死的, 终有一死的: *Her father's death reminded her that she was mortal.* 父亲的去世使她认识到她总会死的。| *mortal creatures* 最终会死的生物 —opposite 反义词 IMMORTAL (1) **2 mortal blow/injuries/danger etc** causing death or likely to cause death 致命的打击/伤害/危险等: *He was dealt a mortal blow in the battle.* 他在战斗中受了致命伤。| **mortal combat** (=fighting until one person kills the other) 殊死的战斗, 你死我活的搏斗 *two gladiators locked in mortal combat* 陷入殊死搏斗的两个角斗士 —compare 比较 LETHAL (1) **3 mortal enemy/foe** an enemy that you hate very much and always will hate 不共戴天的敌人, 死敌 **4 mortal fear/terror/dread** extreme fear 极度的恐惧: *She lives in mortal fear of her husband's anger.* 她成天生活在胆战心惊之中, 生怕她丈夫发脾气。**5** [only before noun 仅用于名词前] *old-fashioned* used to emphasize the word that follows it, especially to show that you are annoyed【过时】〔用以强调后面的单词, 尤表示恼怒〕: *Now I've lost every mortal thing I owned.* 现在我已失去了我所拥有的一切。**6** *poetic* belonging to a human【诗】人的; 凡人的: *a sight as yet unseen by mortal eyes* 凡胎肉眼所未见的景象 —see also 另见 MORTALLY

mortal² *n* [C] **1 lesser/ordinary/mere mortals** *humorous* ordinary people, as compared with people who are more important or more powerful【幽默】普通人, 草民, 平民百姓: *Of course, she dines in the executive suite, while we lesser mortals use the staff cafeteria.* 当然了, 她在经理套房用膳, 而我们这些小民在职工餐厅用餐。**2** *especially literary* a word meaning a human, used especially when comparing humans with gods, spirits etc【尤文】凡人〔与神相对〕

mor·tal·i·ty /mɔrˋtælətɪ; mɔːˈtælɪ̥ti/ *n* [U] **1** also 又作 **mortality rate** /·ˈ··· ·/ the number of deaths during a certain period of time among a particular type or group of people 死亡率; 死亡数: *Mortality from heart disease varies widely across the world.* 世界不同地区心脏病死亡率差异很大。| **infant mortality** (=the rate at which babies die) 婴儿死亡率 **2** the condition of being human and having to die 必死性, 生死无常 —opposite 反义词 IMMORTALITY

mor·tal·ly /ˈmɔrtl̩ɪ; ˈmɔːtəl-i/ *adv* **1** in a way that will cause death 致命地: *Arthur, mortally wounded, was attended by Sir Bedivere.* 亚瑟受了致命伤, 由贝德维尔爵士照料着。**2** extremely or greatly 极度地; 非常: *We hid, mortally afraid, in the cellar.* 我们藏在地下室里, 害怕得要命。

mortal sin /ˌ·· ˈ·/ *n* [C] something that you do that is so bad, according to the Roman Catholic Church, that it will bring unending punishment to your soul after death unless it is forgiven〔天主教中的〕大罪〔天主教认为犯这种罪的人未得宽恕, 死后永远受苦〕

mor·tar /ˈmɔrtɚ; ˈmɔːtə/ *n* **1** [U] a mixture of LIME¹ (3), sand, and water, used in building for joining bricks or stones together 砂浆, 灰浆 **2** [C] a heavy gun that fires bombs or shells (SHELL¹ (2)) in a high curve 迫击炮 **3** [C] a hard bowl in which substances are crushed into powder with a PESTLE (=tool with a heavy round end) into very small pieces or powder 研钵; 臼: *Pound the garlic with a mortar and pestle.* 用臼和杵把蒜捣碎。—see picture at 参见 LABORATORY 图

mor·tar·board /ˈmɔrtɚˌbɔrd; ˈmɔːtəbɔːd/ *n* [C] a black cap with a flat square top worn by members of some universities on formal occasions 学士帽, 学位帽 —see picture at 参见 CAP¹ 图

Morte d'Arthur, Le /ˌmɔrt ˋdɑrθɚ; ˌmɔːt ˈdɑːθə/ the Death of Arthur; a book by Sir Thomas Malory, written in the 15th century, which describes the life of King Arthur《亚瑟王之死》〔托马斯·马洛礼爵士15世纪所著的一部小说, 描写亚瑟王的生平故事〕—see 见 ARTHURIAN LEGEND

mort·gage¹ /ˈmɔrgɪdʒ; ˈmɔːgɪdʒ/ *n* [C] **1** a legal arrangement by which you borrow money from a bank or similar organization in order to buy a house, and pay back the money over a period of years 抵押借款, 按揭: *Your building society or bank will help arrange a mortgage.* 你们的建屋互助会或银行将协助安排抵押借款。| **take out a mortgage** (=borrow money for a mortgage) 办理抵押借款 *They've taken out a 30 year mortgage.* 他们已办理了一笔30年期的抵押借款。| **pay off a mortgage** (=pay back all the money you borrowed for a mortgage) 偿清抵押借款 | **mortgage rate/payment etc** *Mortgage interest rates are set to rise again in the spring.* 抵押贷款利率春季又要上涨。**2** the amount of money you owe on a mortgage 抵押借款额: *a mortgage of $90,000* 一笔 90,000 美元的抵押借款 W3

mortgage² *v* [T] **1** to give someone, usually a bank, the right to own your house, land, or property if you do not pay back the money they lent you within a certain period of time 抵押: *He's mortgaged all his assets to try and save the business.* 他抵押了他所有的资产, 试图挽救那家企业。**2 be mortgaged to the hilt** to have everything that you own mortgaged 把全部家当抵押出去

mor·ti·cian /mɔrˋtɪʃən; mɔːˈtɪʃən/ *n* [C] *AmE* someone whose job is to arrange funerals and prepare bodies for burial【美】承办丧葬者, 殡葬业者; UNDERTAKER *BrE*【英】

mor·ti·fy /ˈmɔrtəˌfaɪ; ˈmɔːtɪ̥faɪ/ *v* [T] **1 be mortified** to feel extremely embarrassed or ashamed 深感窘迫[丢脸]: *She was mortified to think that he had read her diary.* 想到他读过她的日记, 她就感到很难堪。**2 mortify the flesh/yourself** *formal* to try to control your natural physical desires and needs by making your body suffer pain【正式】用苦行抑制〔身体的自然欲望〕, 用苦行禁欲 —**mortification** /ˌmɔrtəfəˋkeʃən; ˌmɔːtɪ̥fɪ̥ˈkeɪʃən/ *n* [U]: *To my utter mortification I could not remember his name.* 让我十分尴尬的是, 我竟想不起他的名字了。

mor·ti·fy·ing /ˈmɔrtəfaɪ·ɪŋ; ˈmɔːtɪ̥faɪ-ɪŋ/ *adj* extremely embarrassing 令人极其难堪的: *The princess now faced further mortifying revelations in the tabloid press.* 王妃现在面临着秘闻被通俗小报进一步曝光的尴尬局面。

mor·tise /ˈmɔrtɪs; ˈmɔːtɪ̥s/ *n* [C] *technical* a hole cut in a piece of wood or stone to receive the TENON (=the shaped end) of another piece and form a joint【术语】榫眼, 榫孔

mortise lock /ˈ·· ·/ *n* [C] *BrE* a lock that fits into a hole cut in the edge of a door【英】〔嵌入门里的〕榫眼锁, 插锁, 嵌锁, 暗锁; DEAD BOLT *AmE*【美】

Mor·ton /ˈmɔrtn̩; ˈmɔːtn/, **Jelly Roll** (1885-1941) a US JAZZ piano player and band leader, who helped to develop New Orleans jazz 莫顿〔(1885-1941), 美国爵士钢琴演奏家和乐队领队。他曾帮助组建了新奥尔良爵士乐〕

mor·tu·a·ry¹ /ˈmɔrtʃʊˌɛrɪ; ˈmɔːtʃuəri/ *n* [C] **1** *BrE* a building or room, for example in a hospital, where dead bodies are kept before they are buried or cremated (CREMATE); MORGUE (1)【英】停尸室, 太平间 **2** *AmE* the place where a body is kept before a funeral and where the funeral is sometimes held【美】殡仪馆

mortuary² *adj* [only before noun 仅用于名词前] *formal* connected with death or funerals【正式】死亡的; 丧葬的: *a mortuary urn* 骨灰瓮

Mo·sa·ic /moˋze·ɪk; məʊˈzeɪ-ɪk/ *adj* connected with or relating to Moses, the great leader of the Jewish people in ancient times〔古代犹太人领袖〕摩西的: *Mosaic law* 摩西律法

mosaic *n* **1** [C,U] a pattern or picture made by fitting together small pieces of coloured stone, glass etc 马赛克, 镶嵌图案: *a Roman stone mosaic* 古罗马石子镶嵌图案 | *mosaic tiles* 马赛克地砖 **2** [C usually singular 一般用单数] a group of various things that are seen or considered together as a pattern 镶嵌画般的东西; 镶嵌细工似的图案: *The forest floor was a mosaic of autumn colours.* 森林里落满各色树叶的地面是一幅秋色斑斓的镶嵌画。

Mosaic Law /ˌ·· ˈ·/ also 又作 **the Law of Moses** the rules and laws stated in the Pentateuch, which is the first five books of the Old Testament of the Bible. These rules and laws are

M

believed to have been given by God to Moses, and Jewish law is based on them. 摩西律法〔《圣经·旧约》首五卷即《五经》中的戒律与法规。该书的戒律与法规据认为是上帝向摩西授订的。犹太法律就是基于摩西律法制定的〕—see 见 TORAH

Mos·cow /ˈmɑskaʊ; ˈmɒskəʊ/ the capital of Russia, and formerly of the Soviet Union. Its many famous and beautiful buildings include the Kremlin, where the government is based, St. Basil's Cathedral, and Red Square. 莫斯科〔俄罗斯及前苏联首都。莫斯科有许多著名的漂亮建筑，其中包括政府所在地克里姆林宫、圣巴西勒大教堂和红场〕

Mo·ses /ˈmozɪz; ˈməʊzɪ̇z/ a leader of the Jewish people in ancient times. According to the story in the Bible, he brought the Israelites out of Egypt. They were able to escape from the Egyptians when God made the waters of the Red Sea move so that they could walk across. Moses received the Ten Commandments (=God's laws) from God on Mount Sinai. 摩西〔古代犹太人的领袖。据《圣经》故事所述，他曾率领以色列人离开埃及。当时，上帝将红海的海水分开，他们渡海如履平地。摩西还在西奈山上领受过上帝的十诫〕

Moses, Grandma (1860-1961) a US artist who did not begin painting until she was almost 70 years old. Her paintings of life in the American countryside are in the PRIMITIVE style (=they are very simple, and made to look like children's paintings). 摩西奶奶〔(1860-1961)，美国艺术家，70岁高龄才开始作画。她的作品以美国乡村生活为题材，画风质朴自然〕

Mo·ses bas·ket /ˈmozɪz ˌbæskɪt; ˈməʊzɪ̇z ˌbɑːskɪ̇t/ *n* [C] *BrE* a large basket with handles, in which a baby can sleep and be carried【英】手提摇篮

Moses basket 手提摇篮

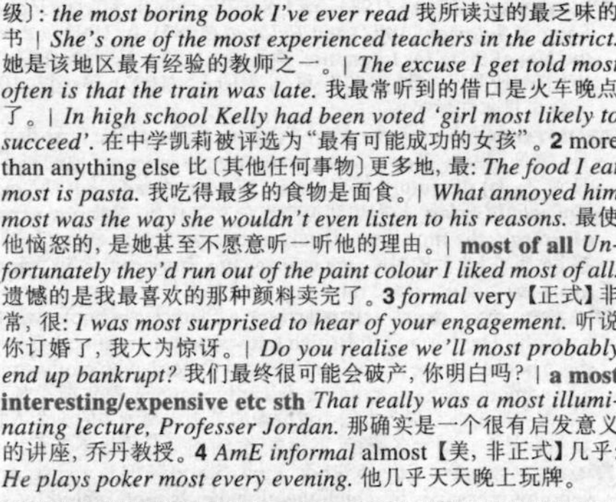

mo·sey /ˈmozɪ; ˈməʊzi/ *v* [I always+adv/prep] *AmE informal, often humorous*【美，非正式，常幽默】**1** to walk somewhere in a slow relaxed way 漫步，溜达，闲逛: **[+around/down etc]** *I guess I'll mosey on down to the store now.* 我想我可以溜达着去那家商店。**2 mosey along** to leave 离开，离去: *I'd better mosey along – it's getting late.* 我还是走吧——天晚了。—**mosey** *n* [singular]

Mos·lem /ˈmɑzləm; ˈmɒzlɪ̇m/ *n* [C] another spelling of MUSLIM, which is unacceptable to some Muslims Muslim 的另一种拼法〔这一拼法不为某些穆斯林所接受〕

Mos·ley /ˈmozlɪ; ˈməʊzli/**, Sir Oswald** (1896-1980) a British politician who started a new political group called the British Union of Fascists (BUF) in 1932. Mosley admired Mussolini and Hitler, and the BUF organized attacks on Jewish people in London. 莫斯利〔(1896-1980)，英国政客。1932年，他创建了一个新政党，名为"英国法西斯联盟"。莫利斯崇拜墨索里尼和希特勒。该联盟曾组织过对伦敦犹太人的袭击行动〕

mosque /mɑsk; mɒsk/ *n* [C] a building in which Muslims worship 清真寺: *the famous mosque in Regents Park* 摄政公园中著名的清真寺

mos·qui·to /məˈskito; məˈskiːtəʊ/ *n plural* **mosquitoes** or **mosquitos** [C] a small flying insect that sucks the blood of people and animals 蚊子

mosquito net /ˈ·ˈ·· ·/ *n* [C] a net placed over a bed as a protection against mosquitoes 蚊帐

moss /mɔs; mɒs/ *n* [C,U] a small flat green or yellow plant that grows in a thick furry mass on wet soil or rock 藓，苔藓: *rocks covered in moss* 长满苔藓的岩石 —compare 比较 LICHEN —**mossy** *adj*

Moss Side /ˈ· ·/ a poor area of central Manchester. British people think of Moss Side as a dangerous place where there are GANGS (=groups of violent criminals) who sell drugs. 莫塞区〔曼彻斯特市中心一贫民区。英国人心目中的莫塞区是一个毒品交易猖獗的危险地带〕

-most /most; məʊst/ *suffix* [in adjectives 构成形容词] nearest to something 离〔某物〕最近的: *the northernmost town in Sweden* (=the town that is furthest to the north) 瑞典最北部的城镇 | *the topmost branches of the tree* 那棵树最顶上的树枝

most¹ /most; məʊst/ *adv* [+adj/adv] **1** used for forming the SUPERLATIVE of most adjectives and adverbs with more than two SYLLABLES, and many that only have two 最〔用以构成大多数具有两个以上音节以及许多只有两个音节的形容词和副词的最高级〕: *the most boring book I've ever read* 我所读过的最乏味的书 | *She's one of the most experienced teachers in the district.* 她是该地区最有经验的教师之一。| *The excuse I get told most often is that the train was late.* 我最常听到的借口是火车晚点了。| *In high school Kelly had been voted 'girl most likely to succeed'.* 在中学凯莉被评选为"最有可能成功的女孩"。**2** more than anything else 比〔其他任何事物〕更多地，最: *The food I eat most is pasta.* 我吃得最多的食物是面食。| *What annoyed him most was the way she wouldn't even listen to his reasons.* 最使他恼怒的，是她甚至不愿意听一听他的理由。| **most of all** *Unfortunately they'd run out of the paint colour I liked most of all.* 遗憾的是我最喜欢的那种颜料卖完了。**3** *formal* very【正式】非常，很: *I was most surprised to hear of your engagement.* 听说你订婚了，我大为惊讶。| *Do you realise we'll most probably end up bankrupt?* 我们最终很可能会破产，你明白吗？| **a most interesting/expensive etc sth** *That really was a most illuminating lecture, Professer Jordan.* 那确实是一个很有启发意义的讲座，乔丹教授。**4** *AmE informal* almost【美，非正式】几乎: *He plays poker most every evening.* 他几乎天天晚上玩牌。

USAGE NOTE 用法说明: MOST

GRAMMAR 语法

Most meaning 'nearly all' is followed directly by a noun when you are speaking generally. most 意为"大多数"并在表示泛指时，后面直接跟名词: *Most cheese contains a lot of fat* (NOT 不用 *most of cheese*). 几乎所有干酪都含有大量的脂肪。| *Most Americans own cars.* 大多数美国人都有汽车。

You use **most of the** when you are talking about part of a particular thing, group, etc. 在谈论某一特定事物或群体等的一部分时用 most of the: *Greg has eaten most of the cheese that was in the fridge.* 格雷格把冰箱里的大部分干酪都吃了。| *Most of the Americans we asked owned cars.* 我们问到的美国人中大多数都有汽车。

You can also say: *Most Americans we asked own cars* without using **of the** to talk about that particular group. 也可以说 Most Americans we asked own cars, 这里不用 of the, 指的是那个特定的群体。

The most can be followed directly by a plural or uncountable noun, when it means 'more than any other(s)'. 当表示"在…中最多的"时，the most 后面可直接跟复数或不可数名词: *The most damage was done to the houses nearest the cliff*〔最靠近悬崖的房子受到的破坏最厉害〕means more damage was done to those houses than any others 意思是最靠近悬崖的那些房子比其他房子遭受了更大的破坏。

You use **most** meaning 'more than anything else' in these ways. 在下列句子中 most 可用来表示"比其他任何事物更多地": *My swimming is the thing I most want to improve.* 我最想提高的是我的游泳水平。| *I want to improve my swimming most.* 我最想提高一下我的游泳水平。| *I most want to improve my swimming* (NOT 不用 *The most thing I want to improve is my swimming*). 我最想提高一下我的游泳水平。

Remember that most short adjectives have a form ending in *-est* that you usually use when you want to say 'more than any other', and you should not use **most** with them. 记住，大多数音节少的形容词其最高级形式以 -est 结尾，不应在其前加 most: *Manhattan is the richest area in New York* (NOT 不用 *the most rich* or 或 *the most richest*). 曼哈顿区是纽约市最富有的地区。| *the dullest people I've ever met* (NOT 不用 *most dull*) 我所见到的最无聊的人

Note that you use the phrase 注意人们使用短语 **most of the time**, not 而不是 *the most time* or 或 *most of times.*

most² *quantifier* [superlative of **many, much** many, much 的最高级] **1** almost all of a particular group of people or things 大多数，大部分，几乎全部: **most things/food etc** *These days most crime is against property, not people.* 如今大多数犯罪针对的是财物，而不是人。| *Like most people, I try to take a vacation every year.* 像大多数人一样，我每年争取休一次假。| **most of** *It was afternoon and most of the shops were shut.* 当时是下午，大多数商店都关门了。| *Tim spent most of his salary on alcohol and cigarettes.* 蒂姆把大部分工资都花在喝酒和抽烟上了。| **most** *Of all the money donated, most is spent on food and clothing for the refugees.* 捐款大部分都用在为难民提供食品和衣服上了。**2** more people or things than anyone else〔人或物〕在…中最多的: **the most people/food etc** *It's the best hotel in town and it also has the most rooms.* 这是镇上最好的旅馆，客房也最

多。| *This is the most votes any candidate has ever received.* 这是有史以来候选人获得过的最高票数。| **the most** *It's unfair that you should have to pay the most when you earn so little.* 你挣得那么少却必须支付得最多，这不公平。| **most** *Whoever scores most in the penalty competition will be awarded the trophy.* 谁在罚球比赛中得分最高，谁就获得奖杯。**3** the largest number or amount possible 最大数量，最大部分: **most people/food etc** *How can we plan the campaign to reach most people?* 我们如何筹划这次宣传活动才能让最多的人知道它？| **the most people/food etc** *To get the most use out of the machine, recharge the batteries overnight.* 为了最大限度地利用机器，给电池充一晚上电。| **the most** *The most you can hope to achieve is to just get him to listen to your ideas.* 你能希望做到的充其量只是让他听听你的想法而已。**4 at (the) most** used to say that a number or amount could not be larger 至多，不超过: *You could buy a good washing machine for about £350, £400 at most.* 350英镑左右，最多400英镑，就能买一台不错的洗衣机。| **at (the) very most** *At the very most the temperature in summer goes up to about 38°C.* 夏天气温最高上升到38摄氏度左右。—compare 比较 **at (the) very least** (LEAST[1] (1)) **5 for the most part** used when a statement or fact is generally true but not completely true 就绝大部分而言；基本上，大体上: *For the most part the relationship between private investment and government interests has not been a successful one.* 总的说来，私人投资和政府利益之间的关系一直不太好。**6 make the most of sth** to get the most advantage from a good situation because it will not last a long time 最大限度地利用某物: *You should be outside making the most of the sunshine.* 你应该到户外尽量多晒晒太阳。

S2 W3 **most·ly** /ˈmostlɪ; ˈməʊstli/ *adv* in most cases or most of the time 大部分；主要地；多半；通常: *I mostly worked as a researcher, writer, or teacher.* 我主要从事研究、写作或教学工作。| *More immigrants arrived, mostly Europeans.* 更多的移民来了，大多是欧洲人。

MOT /ˌɛm o ˈti; ˌem əʊ ˈtiː/ *n* [C] a regular official examination in Britain of the condition and safety of cars that are more than three years old〔英国对三年以上车龄的车辆的〕年检: *Will the car pass its MOT?* 那辆汽车能通过车检吗？

mote /mot; məʊt/ *n* [C] *old-fashioned* a very small piece of dust【过时】微尘，尘埃

mo·tel /moˈtɛl; məʊˈtel/ *n* [C] a hotel for people travelling, where you can park your car outside your room 汽车旅馆

moth /mɔθ; mɒθ/ *n* [C] **1** an insect related to the BUTTERFLY that flies mainly at night and is attracted to lights 蛾 **2** also 又作 **clothes moth** a moth whose young eat holes in cloth 衣蛾

moth·ball[1] /ˈmɔθˌbɔl; ˈmɒθbɔːl/ *n* [C usually plural 一般用复数] **1** a small ball made of a strong-smelling chemical, used for keeping moths away from clothes 卫生球，樟脑丸 **2 in mothballs** stored and not used for a long time 封存不用；束之高阁: *With the end of the Cold War several warships were put into mothballs.* 随着冷战的结束，数艘军舰被封存起来了。

mothball[2] *v* [T] to close a factory or to decide not to use plans or machinery for a long time 长期关闭〔工厂〕；把〔计划〕束之高阁；封存〔机器设备〕: *The company announced that plans to create new offices have been mothballed.* 公司宣布成立新办事处的计划已经搁置起来了。

moth-eat·en /ˈ· ,··/ *adj* **1** cloth that is moth-eaten has holes eaten in it by moths 虫蛀的，蛀坏的: *a moth-eaten sweater* 蛀坏了的羊毛衫 **2** old and in bad condition 破旧的: *a moth-eaten old sofa* 破旧的沙发

S1 W1 **moth·er**[1] /ˈmʌðɚ; ˈmʌðə/ *n* [C]

1 ▶PARENT 母亲◀ a female parent of a child or animal 母亲，妈妈: *His mother and father are both doctors.* 他的父母都是医生。| *Can I borrow your car please, Mother?* 妈妈，我能借用一下你的车吗？| **mother hen/cat/dog etc** (=an animal that is a mother) 母鸡/母猫/母狗等 —see picture at 参见 FAMILY 图

2 be (like) a mother to to care for someone as if you were their mother 母亲般照料

3 mother's boy *BrE*【英】, **mama's boy** *AmE*【美】a man or boy who allows his mother to protect him too much and is considered weak 过分依赖母亲的男人[男孩]，娇生儿

4 mother hen someone who tries to protect her children too much and worries about them all the time 老母鸡〔过分保护子女并时时为他们操心的女人〕

5 learn/be taught sth at your mother's knee to learn something as a very young child 年幼时就学习某事: *She had learned to flirt at her mother's knee.* 她小时候就学会调情了。

6 ▶BIG 大的◀ *spoken especially AmE* something very large and usually very good【口，尤美】大家伙〔通常指很好的事物〕: *a real mother of a car* 真正的大号汽车

7 ▶SLANG 俚语◀ *AmE taboo spoken* MOTHERFUCKER【美，讳，口】不要脸的家伙，混账东西

8 every mother's son *old-fashioned* an expression meaning every man, used for emphasis【过时】人人，所有人: *I'd jail every mother's son of them.* 我要把他们全部监禁起来。

9 Mother a) used to address the woman who is head of a CONVENT 院长〔对女修道院院长的称呼〕 **b)** *old use* used by a man to address an old woman【旧】大娘，大妈〔男子用以称呼老年妇女〕

10 the mother of a) the origin or cause of something 根由，根源: *Westminster is known as 'the mother of parliaments'.* 威斯敏斯特被公认为是"议会之母"。**b)** *informal* a very bad or severe type of something【非正式】糟糕的事；艰难的事: *I woke up with the mother of all hangovers.* 我醒来后因宿醉而十分难受。

mother[2] *v* [T] to look after and protect someone as if you were their mother, especially by being too kind and doing everything for them 母亲般照管；〔尤指〕溺爱: *Tom was constantly mothered by his wife, and resented it.* 汤姆时时被妻子母亲般呵护着，他对此很反感。

moth·er·board /ˈmʌðɚbɔrd; ˈmʌðəbɔːd/ *n* [C] *technical* a board where all the circuits (CIRCUIT (4)) of a computer are placed【术语】〔电脑的〕主板，母板

mother coun·try /ˈ·· ,··/ *n* [C usually singular 一般用单数] the country where you were born 祖国

Mother Earth /,·· ˈ·/ *n* [U] the world considered as the place or thing from which everything comes〔孕育万物的〕大地，大地母亲

moth·er·fuck·er /ˈmʌðɚˌfʌkɚ; ˈmʌðəˌfʌkə/ *n* [C] *AmE taboo spoken* someone that you dislike very much or that you are very angry with【美，讳，口】不要脸的家伙，混账东西 —**motherfucking** *adj*

Mother Goose /,·· ˈ·/ *AmE* the imaginary writer of a book of NURSERY RHYMES (=old songs or poems for young children), or the nursery rhymes themselves【美】鹅妈妈〔一本童谣集虚构的作者名，或该童谣本身的名称〕: *If you're good, I'll read you some Mother Goose before you go to bed.* 你乖的话，睡觉前我就给你读鹅妈妈童谣。

moth·er·hood /ˈmʌðɚhʊd; ˈmʌðəhʊd/ *n* [U] the state of being a mother 母亲身份: *teenage motherhood* 少女妈妈 | *She's enjoying motherhood.* 她喜欢做母亲。

Mothering Sun·day /ˈ··· ,··/ *n* [C,U] *BrE old-fashioned* MOTHER'S DAY【英，过时】母亲节

mother-in-law /ˈ··· ,·/ *n plural* **mothers-in-law** *or* **mother-in-laws** [C] the mother of your wife or husband 岳母，丈母娘；婆婆 —see picture at 参见 FAMILY 图

CULTURAL NOTE 文化注释

People often make jokes about mothers-in-law, and the STEREOTYPE of a mother-in-law is that she does not like her son-in-law or daughter-in-law, and often makes trouble for them. Mothers-in-law are also thought to give a lot of unwanted advice. 人们经常开丈母娘或婆婆的玩笑。丈母娘或婆婆的典型形象是不喜欢女婿或儿媳，经常给他们添乱，还喜欢出一些不受欢迎的馊主意。

moth·er·land /ˈmʌðɚlænd; ˈmʌðəlænd/ *n* [C usually singular 一般用单数] the country where you were born or that you feel you belong to 祖国 —see also 另见 FATHERLAND, MOTHER COUNTRY

moth·er·less /ˈmʌðɚləs; ˈmʌðələs/ *adj* a motherless child is one whose mother has died 母亲已去世的，无母亲的: *Alone and motherless, David set out to find fame and fortune.* 母亲已亡且孑然一身，戴维动身寻求名利去了。

mother lode /ˈ·· ·/ *n* [C usually singular 一般用单数] *AmE*【美】**1** a mine that is full of gold, silver etc〔矿藏的〕母脉，主脉 **2** a place where you can find a lot of a particular type of object 丰富的源泉: *The Sharper Image catalog has a mother lode of men's gadgets and toys.* 《时髦形象》的目录列有许多男用小器具和小摆设。

moth·er·ly /ˈmʌðɚlɪ; ˈmʌðəli/ *adj* similar to or typical of a good mother 慈母般的，母亲一样的: *a kind, motherly woman* 慈母般善良的妇女 —see also 另见 MATERNAL (1) —**motherliness** *n* [U]

Mother Na·ture /,·· ˈ··/ *n* [U] an expression used to talk about the world and living creatures as a person 大自然〔拟人化用法〕: *We can hardly expect Mother Nature not to protest at the pollution we've been creating for the last half century.* 我们过去半个世纪一直在制造污染，大自然对此不表示抗议才怪。

M

Mother of God /ˌ· · · ˈ·/ *n* [singular] a title for Mary, the mother of Jesus Christ, used in the Roman Catholic Church 圣母〔天主教会对耶稣基督母亲马利亚的尊称〕

mother-of-pearl /ˌ· · · ˈ·/ *n* [U] a pale-coloured hard smooth shiny substance that forms the inside of some SHELLFISH, and is used for making buttons, jewellery etc 珍珠母

Mother's Day /ˈ· · ˌ·/ *n* [C,U] a day on which people give cards and presents to their mother 母亲节

mother ship /ˈ· · ˌ·/ *n* [C] a large ship or SPACECRAFT from which smaller boats or spacecraft are sent out 母舰，母船；航天运载飞船

mother's ru·in /ˌ· ˈ· ˈ·/ *n* [U] *BrE old-fashioned humorous* GIN (=a strong alcoholic drink)【英，过时，幽默】杜松子酒

Mother Su·pe·ri·or /ˌ· · ˈ· · ·/ *n* [C usually singular 一般用单数] the woman who is the leader of a CONVENT 女修道院院长

Mother Te·re·sa /ˌmʌðɚ təˈrizɚ; ˌmʌðə təˈriːzə/ (1910-97) an Albanian Roman Catholic NUN (=a member of a group of Christian religious women) who lived in India, where she worked to help the poor and the sick in the city of Calcutta. She won the Nobel Peace Prize in 1979, and people think of her as a typical example of someone who is very kind, unselfish, and morally good. 特里萨修女〔(1910-1997)，阿尔巴尼亚罗马天主教修女，居住在印度。她曾在加尔各答致力于扶助穷人和病人的慈善活动，1979 年获诺贝尔和平奖。她在人们心目中是善良无私、道德高尚的典型代表〕

mother-to-be /ˌ· · ˈ·/ *n plural* **mothers-to-be** [C] a woman who is going to have a baby 准妈妈，孕妇

mother tongue /ˌ· · ˈ·/ *n* [C] the first and main language that you learn as a child 母语：*Her mother tongue is French.* 她的母语是法语。

mo·tif /moˈtif; məʊˈtiːf/ *n* [C] **1** an idea, subject, or pattern that is regularly repeated and developed in a book, film, work of art etc〔书、电影、艺术品等的〕主题，中心思想；基本模式：*The theme of creation is a recurrent motif in Celtic mythology.* 天地万物的创造是凯尔特神话中反复出现的主题。**2** a small picture or pattern used to decorate something plain 装饰图画[图案]：*a cat motif on a child's pyjamas* 孩子睡衣裤上猫的图案 **3** an arrangement of notes that is often repeated in a musical work〔音乐作品的〕乐旨，动机

3 **mo·tion¹** /ˈmoʃən; ˈməʊʃən/ *n*

1 ►MOVEMENT 移动◄ [U] the process of moving or the way that someone or something moves 动；运动；移动：*The rocking motion of the boat made Sylvia feel sick.* 小船晃来晃去，使西维娅感到恶心。

2 ►MOVING YOUR HEAD OR HAND 动头或手◄ [C] a single movement of your hand or head, especially done in order to communicate something〔手或头的〕示意动作；手势；姿势：*He summoned the waiter with a motion of his hand.* 他做了个手势，召唤侍者。

3 ►SUGGESTION AT A MEETING 会议上的建议◄ [C] a proposal that is made formally at a meeting and then decided on by voting 提议，动议：**motion to do sth/motion that** *We will now vote on the motion that membership charges should rise by 15%.* 我们现在将对会费提高 15% 这一动议进行投票表决。| **pass/carry a motion** (=accept it by voting)〔通过投票〕通过一项动议 *The motion was carried by 15 votes to 10.* 该动议以 15 票对 10 票通过。| **propose/put forward a motion** (=make a proposal) 提出一项动议 *I'd like to propose a motion to move the weekly meetings to Thursdays.* 我提议把每周的例会改到星期四。| **reject a motion** (=not accept it) 拒绝一项提议 | **motion denied** (=used by a judge in a law court to refuse a suggestion by one of the lawyers) 动议予以否决〔法官在法庭上说的话〕

4 in motion *formal or technical* moving from one place or position to another【正式或术语】运动中的：*a photograph of a frog in motion* 运动中的青蛙的照片

5 go through the motions to do something because you have to, even though you do not want to do it 装样子，做姿态，敷衍塞责地做：*The mayor said he enjoyed the party, but you could see he was only going through the motions.* 市长说他喜欢那个聚会，但你能看出他只是在敷衍。

6 set/put sth in motion to start a process or series of events that will continue for some time 使某事开始：*The Church voted to set in motion the process allowing women to be priests.* 教会投票决定启动允许妇女当牧师的程序。

7 in slow motion if a film is shown in slow motion, it is shown more slowly than usual so that all the actions can be clearly seen 以慢动作，慢速地：*Let's look at that goal in slow motion.* 让我们看一看那个进球的慢镜头。

8 ►BOWELS 肠◄ [C] *especially BrE* a word meaning an act of emptying your BOWELS, used especially by doctors and nurses【尤英】排便〔此词尤为医护人员所用〕—see also 另见 TIME AND MOTION STUDY

motion² *v* [I,T] to give someone directions or instructions by moving your hands 用手势示意：**motion (for) sb to do sth** *The police officer motioned for me to pull over.* 警察招手示意我把车停在路边。| **motion to sb to do sth** *He motioned to her to be quiet.* 他做手势让她安静。| **motion sb in/out etc** *I saw her motioning me into the room.* 我看到她招手示意我进房间。

mo·tion·less /ˈmoʃənlɪs; ˈməʊʃənləs/ *adj* not moving at all 一动不动的，静止的：*Helen sat motionless and silent.* 海伦一动不动，默默地坐着。—**motionlessly** *adv*

motion pic·ture /ˌ· · ˈ· ·/ *n* [C] *AmE* a film made for the cinema【美】电影：*the motion picture industry* 电影业

motion sick·ness /ˈ· · ˌ· ·/ *n* [U] *AmE* travel sickness (TRAVEL-SICK)【美】晕动病〈如晕车、晕船等〉：*I always get motion sickness when I sit in the back of a car.* 坐在车后部我总是晕车。

mo·ti·vate /ˈmotəˌvet; ˈməʊtɪ̣veɪt/ *v* [T] **1** to make someone want to achieve something and make them willing to work hard in order to do it 激发，激励，促动：*A good teacher has to be able to motivate her students.* 好教师必须能激发学生积极学习。| **motivate sb to do sth** *The profit-sharing plan is designed to motivate the staff to work hard.* 制订利润分红计划是为了激励员工努力工作。**2** [often passive 常用被动态] to provide the reason why someone does something 为…的动机：*Would you say that he was motivated solely by a desire for power?* 你认为他仅仅是受权欲的驱使吗？

mo·ti·va·ted /ˈmotəˌvetɪd; ˈməʊtɪ̣veɪtɪ̣d/ *adj* **1** very keen to do something or achieve something, especially because you find it interesting or exciting 积极的；主动的：*They're a really good bunch of students – highly motivated and very intelligent.* 他们确实是一群优秀的学生 —— 学习积极性高，而且非常聪明。**2 politically/financially/commercially motivated etc** done for political, financial etc reasons 受政治/财政/商业等方面的原因所驱使的：*a politically-motivated decision* 有政治目的的决定 | *Police believe the attack was racially motivated.* 警察认为那次袭击是由于种族仇恨。

mo·ti·va·tion /ˌmotəˈveʃən; ˌməʊtɪ̣ˈveɪʃən/ *n* **1** [U] eagerness and willingness to do something without needing to be told or forced to do it 动力；积极性；兴趣：*Jack is an intelligent pupil, but he lacks motivation.* 杰克是一个很聪明的学生，但他学习不够主动。**2** [C] the reason why you want to do something 动机，原因：[**+for**] *What was your motivation for becoming a teacher?* 你为什么做教师？

mo·tive¹ /ˈmotɪv; ˈməʊtɪv/ *n* [C] **1** the reason that makes someone do something, especially when this reason is kept hidden〔尤指隐藏的〕动机，原因；目的：*The police believe the motive for this murder was jealousy.* 警察认为这次谋杀的动机是嫉妒。**2** a MOTIF 主题；装饰图画；〔音乐作品的〕乐旨 —**motiveless** *adj*: *an apparently motiveless killing* 一起没有明显动机的杀人案

motive² *adj* [only before noun 仅用于名词前] *technical* a motive power or force is one that causes movement【术语】引起运动的，起推动作用的；提供动力的

mot juste /ˌmo ˈʒust; ˌməʊ ˈʒuːst/ *plural* **mots justes** (*same pronunciation* 发音相同) *n* [C] *French* exactly the right word or phrase【法】最贴切的字眼，最恰当的词语：*How can I describe her? I'm searching for the mot juste ... Yes, that's it – slender.* 我怎么形容她呢？我在找一个最贴切的字眼…啊，有了 —— 苗条。

mot·ley¹ /ˈmɑtlɪ; ˈmɒtli/ *adj* [only before noun 仅用于名词前] **1 a motley crew/bunch/assortment etc** a group of people of very different kinds, especially people that you do not approve of 形形色色的一伙/一帮/一批人等：*I looked at the motley bunch we were sailing with and began to feel uneasy about the trip.* 看到和我们一起航行的这帮人三教九流全有，我开始对这次旅程感到不安起来。**2** a motley group of things contains objects that are all different in shape, size etc and that do not seem to belong together〔东西〕混杂的，杂七杂八的：*His pockets contained a motley collection of coins, movie ticket stubs, and old peppermint candies.* 他的口袋里乱七八糟，有硬币、电影票根和放了很久的薄荷糖。**3** *literary* having a strange mixture of many different colours【文】杂色的，五颜六色的：*a court jester in motley garb* 穿着杂色花衣的宫廷小丑

motley² *n* [U] *technical* the clothes worn by a JESTER【术语】〔小丑穿的〕杂色花衣

mo·to·cross /ˈmotoˌkrɔs; ˈməʊtəʊkrɒs/ *n* [U] the sport of racing MOTORCYCLES over rough land, up hills, through streams etc 摩托车越野赛

mo·tor¹ /ˈmotɚ; ˈməʊtə/ *n* [C] **1** the part of a machine that makes it work or move, by changing power, especially electrical power, into movement 发动机; 电动机, 马达: *The lawnmower is powered by a small motor.* 这台割草机由一个小马达提供动力。| *We had to replace the starter motor in the car's engine.* 我们不得不换掉汽车引擎上的起动电动机。**2** *BrE informal* a car【英, 非正式】汽车: *That's a nice motor you've got, Dave.* 戴夫, 你这辆汽车不错。

motor² *adj* [only before noun 仅用于名词前] **1** *especially BrE* connected with cars or other vehicles with engines【尤英】汽车的, 机动车辆的: *a motor accident* 汽车事故 | *the motor industry* 汽车工业 | *motor insurance* 汽车保险 **2** using power provided by an engine 机动的: *a motor scooter* 低座小摩托车 **3** *technical* related to a nerve that makes a muscle move【术语】运动神经的: *impaired motor function* 受到损伤的运动神经功能

motor³ *v* [I] *BrE old-fashioned* to travel by car【英, 过时】乘汽车旅行; 驾驶汽车: *Bertie is motoring down from London this weekend.* 本周末伯蒂要开车从伦敦南下。

motorbike 摩托车

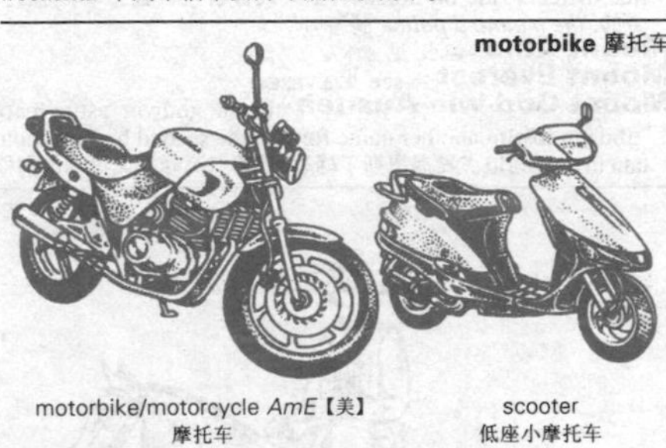

motorbike/motorcycle *AmE*【美】摩托车　　scooter 低座小摩托车

mo·tor·bike /ˈmotɚˌbaɪk; ˈməʊtəbaɪk/ *n* [C] *especially BrE* a fast two-wheeled vehicle with an engine【尤英】摩托车

mo·tor·boat /ˈmotɚˌbot; ˈməʊtəbəʊt/ *n* [C] a small fast boat with an engine 摩托艇, 汽艇; 汽船

mo·tor·cade /ˈmotɚˌked; ˈməʊtəkeɪd/ *n* [C] a group of cars and other vehicles that travel together and surround a very important person's car〔要人的〕车队: *the President's motorcade* 总统车队

motor car /ˈ· · ·/ *n* [C] *BrE formal or old-fashioned* a car【英, 正式或过时】汽车

mo·tor·cy·cle /ˈmotɚˌsaɪkḷ; ˈməʊtəˌsaɪkəl/ *n* [C] a fast, usually large, two-wheeled vehicle with an engine 摩托车 —see picture at 参见 MOTORBIKE 图

mo·tor·drome /ˈmotɚˌdrom; ˈməʊtədrəʊm/ *n* [C] *AmE* a track where people can watch car or motorcycle races【美】汽车[摩托车]赛车场

motor home /ˈ· · ·/ *n* [C] a large vehicle with beds, a kitchen, toilet etc built into it, used for travelling and holidays〔有床、厨房、卫生间等的〕旅宿汽车 —see also 另见 RV

mo·tor·ing /ˈmotərɪŋ; ˈməʊtərɪŋ/ *n* [U] *BrE old-fashioned* the activity of driving a car【英, 过时】开汽车: *a motoring enthusiast* 热衷于开汽车的人

motor inn /ˈ· · ·/ *n* [C] *AmE* a MOTEL【美】汽车旅馆

mo·tor·ist /ˈmotərɪst; ˈməʊtərɪst/ *n* [C] *especially BrE* someone who drives a car【尤英】汽车驾驶员: *12,000 motorists were stopped for speeding in the police crackdown.* 在警方惩治违章驾车的行动中, 12,000 名汽车司机因超速被拦截。

mo·tor·ized also 又作 **-ised** *BrE*【英】/ˈmotəˌraɪzd; ˈməʊtəraɪzd/ *adj* [only before noun 仅用于名词前] **1** fitted with an engine, especially when something does not usually have an engine 装发动机的, 机动的: *a motorized bicycle* 机动脚踏车, 助动车 **2** a motorized army or group of soldiers is one that uses motor vehicles〔军队或士兵〕摩托化的, 机动化的 —**motorize** *v* [T]

motor lodge /ˈ· · ·/ *n* [C] *AmE* a MOTEL【美】汽车旅馆

mo·tor·mouth /ˈmotɚˌmaʊθ; ˈməʊtəmaʊθ/ *n* [C] *informal* someone who talks too much and too loudly【非正式】"马达嘴", 喋喋不休大声喧哗的人

motor neu·rone dis·ease /ˌmotɚ ˈnuron dɪˌziz; ˌməʊtə ˈnjʊərəʊn dɪˌziːz/ *n* [U] a disease that causes a gradual loss of control over the muscles and nerves of the body, resulting in death 运动神经元病

motor pool /ˈ· · ·/ *n* [C] *AmE* CAR POOL¹ (2)【美】〔公司等组织拥有的供其工作人员使用的多辆〕合伙用车

motor rac·ing /ˈ· · ,· ·/ *n* [U] the sport of racing fast cars on a special track 赛车运动

motor scoot·er /ˈ· · ,· ·/ *n* [C] a SCOOTER (1) 低座小摩托车

motor ve·hi·cle /ˈ· · ,· · ·/ *n* [C] the official word for any vehicle which is powered by an engine, such as a car, bus, or TRUCK 机动车辆: *This road is closed to motor vehicles.* 这条路机动车禁止通行。

mo·tor·way /ˈmotɚˌwe; ˈməʊtəweɪ/ *n* [C] *BrE* a very wide road for travelling fast over long distances, especially between cities【英】高速公路 —compare 比较 EXPRESSWAY, FREEWAY, HIGHWAY (1) S2

Mo·town /ˈmotaʊn; ˈməʊtaʊn/ **1** *trademark* a US music record company, based in Detroit【商标】摩城唱片公司〔美国底特律的一家唱片公司〕**2** a style of popular music called SOUL MUSIC, performed by black musicians 摩城音乐〔即一种被称为灵乐的流行音乐, 由黑人音乐家演奏〕

mot·tled /ˈmɑtḷd; ˈmɒtld/ *adj* covered with patterns of light and dark colours of different shapes 杂色的; 斑驳的; 有花纹的; 云纹状的: *mottled like an owl's feathers* 像猫头鹰的羽毛一样斑驳的 | *His red, mottled face showed the effect of too much whiskey.* 他那张红红的、满是斑点的脸表明, 他威士忌喝得太多了。

mot·to /ˈmɑto; ˈmɒtəʊ/ *n plural* **mottos** also 又作 **mottoes** [C] **1** a short statement giving a rule on how to behave, which expresses the aims or beliefs of a person, school, or institution 箴言, 格言, 座右铭: *'Be prepared' is the motto of the boy scouts.* "时刻准备着"是童子军的格言。**2** *BrE* an amusing remark or joke printed on a piece of paper in a CHRISTMAS CRACKER【英】〔圣诞彩包爆竹中印在纸片上的〕俏皮话, 妙语

mould¹ *BrE*【英】, **mold** *AmE*【美】/mold; məʊld/ *n* **1** [U] a soft green or black substance that grows on food which has been kept too long, and on objects that are in warm, wet air 霉, 霉菌: *Throw that bread away, there's mold on it.* 把那块面包扔了吧, 上面长霉了。| *There was mould on the bathroom ceiling.* 浴室天花板发霉了。—see also 另见 LEAF MOULD **2** [C] a hollow container that you pour liquid into, so that when the liquid becomes solid, it takes the shape of the container 模子, 模具, 铸模, 铸型: *a jelly mould* 果冻模子 | *a candle mold* 蜡烛模子 **3** [singular] if someone is in, or fits into, a particular mould, they have all the attitudes, and qualities, typical of a certain type of person〔人的〕性格, 气质, 类型: *a sex symbol in the traditional Hollywood mold* 具有传统好莱坞气质的性感偶像 | *She didn't quite fit into the standard 'high-flying businesswoman' mould.* 她并不完全属于"雄心勃勃的女商人"那种类型。**4 break the mould** to change a situation completely, by doing something that has not been done before 彻底改变格局, 打破模式: *an attempt to break the mould of British politics* 打破英国政治模式的尝试

mould² *BrE*【英】, **mold** *AmE*【美】*v* **1** [T] to shape a soft substance by pressing or rolling it or by putting it into a mould 使…成形; 用模子制作; 浇铸: **mould sth into sth** *Mould the sausage meat into little balls.* 把灌香肠用的碎肉捏成丸子。| **mold sth** *moulded plastic piping* 模制塑料管材 **2** [T] to influence the way someone's character or attitudes develop 影响〔某人性格或态度〕的形成, 塑造: *I enjoy working with children, helping to mold their young minds.* 我喜欢和小孩子打交道, 帮着塑造他们稚嫩的头脑。| *an attempt to mold public opinion* 影响舆论的企图 **3** [I,T] to fit closely to the shape of something (与…的) 轮廓相符: *Her wet dress was moulded to her body.* 她的湿衣服紧贴在身上。

moul·der *BrE*【英】, **molder** *AmE*【美】/ˈmoldɚ; ˈməʊldə/ also 又作 **moulder away** *v* [I] to decay slowly and gradually 腐烂, 腐朽; 渐渐崩塌: *old papers mouldering away in the attic* 阁楼里慢慢朽坏的旧报纸 | *the discovery of a dead body, mouldering in the woods* 在树林中发现一具腐尸

mould·ing *BrE*【英】, **molding** *AmE*【美】/ˈmoldɪŋ; ˈməʊldɪŋ/ *n* **1** [C,U] a thin decorative line of stone or wood around the edge of a wall, a piece of furniture, a picture frame etc 装饰线条, 线饰, 线脚 **2** [C] an object produced from a mould 模制件; 铸造物

mould·y *BrE*【英】, **moldy** *AmE*【美】/ˈmoldɪ; ˈməʊldi/ *adj* **mouldier, mouldiest** covered with MOULD¹ (1) 发霉的: *mouldy cheese* 发霉的干酪 | **go mouldy** *BrE* (=become mouldy)【英】发霉 *The bread's gone mouldy.* 面包已发霉了。

Mou·lin Rouge, the /ˌmulæŋ ˈruʒ; ˌmuːlæŋ ˈruːʒ/ a CABARET in the Montmartre area of Paris, famous especially in the 19th century for its CANCAN dancers 红磨坊〔巴黎蒙马特区一卡巴莱夜总会, 尤以 19 世纪的康康舞女郎闻名〕

moult *BrE*【英】, **molt** *AmE*【美】/molt; məʊlt/ *v* [I] when a bird or animal moults, it loses hair or feathers so that new ones can grow〔鸟〕换羽; 〔动物〕脱毛 —**moult** *n* [C,U]

mound /maund; maʊnd/ *n* [C] **1** a pile of earth or stones that looks like a small hill 土[石]堆；土冈，土丘 **2** a large pile of something（大）堆，（大）垛：[+of] *There's a mound of papers on my desk.* 我办公桌上有一大堆文件。| *The waiter appeared with a huge mound of spaghetti.* 服务生端着一大盘小山般高的意大利面条出现了。**3** the small hill that the PITCHER stands on in the game of BASEBALL〔棒球场中的〕投球区土墩 —see picture on page A22 参见 A22 页图

mount¹ /maunt; maʊnt/ *v*
1 ▶INCREASE 增加◀ [I] to increase gradually, especially in a way that makes a situation worse 渐渐增加，增长〔尤指朝着使情况更糟的方向〕: *The tension here is mounting, as we await the final result.* 我们等待着最终结果，这里的气氛也随之越发紧张。| *For days after the accident, the death toll continued to mount.* 事故发生后的数日内死亡人数持续上升。—see also 另见 MOUNTING¹
2 mount a campaign/attack/exhibition etc to plan, organize, and begin an event or a course of action 发起战役／发动进攻／举办展览等: *Scott mounted an expedition to the South Pole.* 斯科特发起了去南极的探险。
3 ▶HORSE/BICYCLE 马/自行车◀ [I,T] to get on a horse, bicycle etc 骑上，跨上: *She mounted and rode off.* 她骑上自行车走了。—opposite 反义词 DISMOUNT (1)
4 ▶CLIMB STAIRS 爬楼梯◀ [T] *formal* to go up something such as a set of stairs【正式】走上，爬上，登上: *We mounted some stone steps to a gallery.* 我们登上几级石阶，来到一间陈列室。
5 be mounted to/on to be fixed to something and supported by it 被固定在…上: *The statue was mounted on a marble plinth.* 雕像被安放在一个大理石底座上。
6 ▶PICTURE 图画◀ [T] to fix a picture or photograph to a larger piece of stiff paper so that it looks more attractive 裱贴〔图画或照片〕
7 ▶SEX 性◀ [T] *technical* if a male animal mounts a female animal, he gets up onto her back to have sex【术语】〔雄性动物〕趴到〔雌性动物〕身上交配
8 mount guard (over) *formal* to guard a place, especially as a military duty【正式】担任警卫；站岗
mount up *phr v* [I] to gradually increase in size or amount〔规模或数量〕逐渐增加，增长: *Our debts are beginning to mount up again.* 我们的债务又开始增加了。

mount² *n* [C] **1 Mount** part of the name of a mountain …山，…峰〔山名的一部分〕: *Mount Everest* 珠穆朗玛峰 **2** a horse that you ride on 被乘骑的马，坐骑 **3** *old use* a mountain【旧】山，山岳

S3 W2 **moun·tain** /ˈmauntn; ˈmaʊntɪn/ *n* [C] **1** a very high hill 高山，山岳: *the Rocky Mountains* 落基山脉 | *a mountain rescue team* 山地救援队 —see picture on page A12 参见 A12 页图 **2** also 又作 **mountains** *plural* a very large pile or amount of something 大堆；大量: *My mother-in-law always gives me a mountain of potatoes from her garden.* 我岳母总是送给我一大堆她园子里产的马铃薯。| *I've got mountains of washing to do.* 我有一大堆衣物要洗。**3 butter/grain etc mountain** a very large amount of food that is stored in order to prevent prices from becoming lower, especially by the European Union〔尤指欧盟为防止价格下跌而〕大量积存的黄油／谷物等 —compare 比较 LAKE (2) **4 make a mountain out of a molehill** to treat a problem as if it was very serious when in fact it is not 小题大做

mountain ash /,.. ˈ../ *n* [C] a type of tree with red or orange-red berries; ROWAN 花楸树

mountain bike /ˈ.. ,./ *n* [C] a strong bicycle with a lot of GEARS and wide tyres, specially designed for riding up hills and on rough ground 山地（自行）车

moun·tain·eer /,mauntnˈɪr; ,maʊntɪˈnɪə/ *n* [C] someone who climbs mountains as a sport 登山家，登山运动员

moun·tain·eer·ing /,mauntnˈɪrɪŋ; ,maʊntɪˈnɪərɪŋ/ *n* [U] the sport of climbing mountains 登山运动

mountain goat /ˈ.. ,./ *n* [C] an animal with thick white fur which looks like a goat and lives in the western mountains of North America 石山羊〔生活在北美西部山区看似山羊的一种动物〕

mountain laur·el /,.. ˈ../ *n* [C] a bush with glossy leaves and pink or white flowers that grows in North America 山月桂

mountain li·on /ˈ.. ,../ *n* [C] a COUGAR 美洲狮

moun·tain·ous /ˈmauntnəs; ˈmaʊntɪnəs/ *adj* **1** having a lot of mountains 多山的: *the mountainous coast of Wales* 威尔士多山的海岸 | *a mountainous region* 山区 **2** very large in amount or size〔数量或规模〕巨大的；庞大的: *a mountainous woman in a floral swimsuit* 穿着花泳衣的身材高大的女人

mountain range /,.. ˈ./ *n* [C] a long row of mountains that covers a large area 山脉

moun·tain·side /ˈmauntn,saɪd; ˈmaʊntɪnsaɪd/ *n* [C] the side of a mountain 山坡；山腰: *Great rocks rolled down the mountainside.* 巨大的岩石顺着山坡滚了下去。

moun·tain·top /ˈmauntn,tap; ˈmaʊntɪntɒp/ *n* [C] the top part of a mountain 山顶

Mount Ararat —see 见 Mount ARARAT

Mount·bat·ten /mauntˈbætn; maʊntˈbætn/, **Louis** (1900-79) a British politician and military leader, also known as Earl Mountbatten of Burma. In 1947 he became the last VICEROY (=British governor) of India before its independence. He was killed by Irish terrorists. 蒙巴顿（(1900-1979)，英国政治家和军事领袖，亦称缅甸的蒙巴顿伯爵。1947 年，他被任命为印度独立前的最后一任总督，后被爱尔兰恐怖分子杀害）

moun·te·bank /ˈmauntə,bæŋk; ˈmaʊntɪbæŋk/ *n* [C] *literary* a dishonest person who tricks and deceives people【文】江湖骗子

moun·ted /ˈmauntɪd; ˈmaʊntɪd/ *adj* mounted soldiers or police officers ride on horses〔士兵或警察〕骑马的，骑马执行任务的: *the mounted police* 骑警（队）

Mount Etna —see 见 ETNA

Mount Everest —see 见 EVEREST

Mount God·win Aus·ten /maunt ,gadwɪn ˈɔstɪn; maʊnt ,gɒdwɪn ˈɒstɪn/ another name for K2, the second highest mountain in the world 戈德温奥斯丁峰〔世界第二高峰乔戈里峰的别称〕

Mountie 加拿大皇家骑警

Mount·ie /ˈmauntɪ; ˈmaʊnti/ *n* [C] *informal* a member of the Royal Canadian Mounted Police【非正式】加拿大皇家骑警

mount·ing¹ /ˈmauntɪŋ; ˈmaʊntɪŋ/ *adj* [only before noun 仅用于名词前] **1 mounting excitement/anger/violence** gradually increasing or becoming worse 越来越强烈的兴奋／愤怒／暴力: *mounting violence in urban areas* 城市地区越来越严重的暴力行为 | *With mounting excitement the children waited for Christmas morning.* 孩子们怀着越来越兴奋的心情等待着圣诞早晨的到来。**2 mounting inflation/debts/losses** gradually increasing and causing serious problems 日益严重的通货膨胀／不断增加的债务／日渐增加的损失: *the mounting costs of the project* 该工程不断增加的成本

mounting² *n* [C] an object to which other things, especially parts of a machine, are fastened to keep them in place 底座，座架: *The engine is supported by four rubberized mountings.* 发动机由四个覆有橡胶层的座架支撑着。

Mount Kilimanjaro —see 见 KILIMANJARO

Mount McKinley —see 见 DENALI

Mount of Ol·ives, the /,. . ˈ../ a mountain east of Jerusalem, mentioned in the New Testament of the Bible, especially as the place of Jesus Christ's Ascension to Heaven 橄榄山〔《圣经》中提到的位于耶路撒冷东部的一座山，尤指耶稣基督升天的地方〕

Mount Olympus —see 见 OLYMPUS

Mount Palomar —see 见 Mount PALOMAR

Mount Rainier —see 见 Mount RAINIER

Mount Saint Helens —see 见 Mount ST HELENS

Mount Sinai —see 见 Mount SINAI

Mount Ver·non /maunt ˈvɜnən; maʊnt ˈvɜːnən/ the home of George Washington between 1747 and 1799 and the place

where he is buried. It is in northeast Virginia, US and is now a museum. 芒特弗农〔乔治·华盛顿1747至1799年生活过的地方，去世后亦安葬在此地。芒特弗农位于美国弗吉尼亚州东北部，现为博物馆〕

Mount Vesuvius —see 见 VESUVIUS

mourn /mɔrn; mɔːn/ *v* [I,T] **1** to feel very sad because someone that you love has died, and show this in the way you behave 悼念，哀悼，为…哀痛: **mourn sb's death/loss** *She still mourns her son's death.* 她还在为儿子的死伤心。| **[+for]** *They mourned for their children, killed in the war.* 他们为自己死于战争的孩子哀悼。**2** to feel very sad because something no longer exists or is no longer as good as it used to be 对…感到痛心[遗憾]: *The old steam trains were much-loved, and we all mourn their passing.* 那些老蒸汽火车曾深受人们的喜爱，我们都为它们的消失而感到遗憾。

mourn·er /ˈmɔrnɚ; ˈmɔːnə/ *n* [C] someone who attends a funeral, especially a relative of the dead person 参加葬礼者，送葬者〔尤指死者的亲属〕

mourn·ful /ˈmɔrnfl; ˈmɔːnfəl/ *adj* very sad 非常伤心的，悲痛的，悲伤的: *Durant was thin, mournful and silent.* 杜兰特很消瘦，神情悲伤，默默不语。| *the slow, mournful music of the bagpipes* 风笛那缓慢、忧伤的音乐 —**mournfully** *adj* —**mournfulness** *n* [U]

mourn·ing /ˈmɔrnɪŋ; ˈmɔːnɪŋ/ *n* [U] **1** great sadness because someone has died〔因某人去世而感到的〕哀痛，悲痛，哀悼: *The drawn curtains and solemn hush told me that this was a house of mourning.* 拉上的窗帘和肃穆的寂静告诉我这户人家有丧事。**2** black clothes worn to show that you are very sad that someone has died 丧服: *She was recently widowed and wearing mourning.* 她失去丈夫不久，所以穿着丧服。**3 be in mourning a)** to be very sad because of someone's death〔因某人去世而〕悲痛，哀痛: *It was the custom to visit those in mourning and sit quietly with them.* 依照风俗，要去拜访那些因亲人去世而处于悲痛中的人，陪他们静静地坐些时候。**b)** to be dressed in black clothes to show that you are mourning 穿丧服，戴孝

mouse /maus; maʊs/ *n* [C] **1** *plural* **mice** /maɪs; maɪs/ a small furry animal with a long tail that lives in people's houses or in fields, and that looks like a small rat 小(老)鼠，家鼠，耗子: *I think we have mice in the kitchen.* 我觉得我们的厨房里有老鼠。| *a field mouse* 田鼠 **2** *technical* a small object connected to a computer by a wire, which you move with your hand to give commands to the computer【术语】鼠标，滑鼠 —see picture on page A14 参见 A14 页图 **3** [usually singular 一般用单数] *informal* a quiet, nervous person【非正式】胆小的人 —see also 另见 **play cat and mouse with** (CAT (4))

mouse 鼠

CULTURAL NOTE 文化注释

Mice are thought of as quiet, shy animals, and people sometimes tell children to be 'as quiet as a mouse', meaning that they should be very quiet. Mice are thought to like cheese, which is often used in MOUSETRAPS to catch mice. 老鼠被认为是安静、胆怯的动物，因此人们常对孩子说要"像老鼠一样安静"，意思是让他们特别安静。人们认为老鼠爱吃奶酪，捉老鼠时也常将奶酪放在鼠夹上。

There is a STEREOTYPE that women are afraid of mice, and CARTOONS often show women standing on chairs to escape from a mouse. 有一种模式化的观念，认为女人怕老鼠，因此漫画上常能看到女人站在椅子上躲避老鼠。

mous·er /ˈmausɚ; ˈmaʊsə/ *n* [C] a cat that catches mice 捕鼠的猫

mouse·trap /ˈmaus͵træp; ˈmaʊs-træp/ *n* [C] a trap for catching mice 捕鼠器，老鼠夹子

Mousetrap, The a play by Agatha Christie, which was first performed in the West End of London in 1952, and has been performed there continuously for longer than any other play in the world. It is a WHODUNIT (=a play about a murder in which you do not find out who did the murder until the end). 《捕鼠器》〔阿加莎·克里斯蒂创作的一部剧本。1952年在伦敦西区首演，成为在那里连续上演时间最长的一出戏。这是一部推理剧〕

mous·sa·ka /muˈsɑkə; muːˈsɑːkə/ *n* [U] a Greek dish made from meat, cheese, and AUBERGINES 莫萨卡〔由肉、干酪和茄子做成的一种希腊菜肴〕

mousse /mus; muːs/ *n* [C,U] **1** a sweet food made from a mixture of cream, eggs, and fruit or chocolate which is eaten when it is cold 奶油冻〔一种甜味食品〕: *chocolate mousse* 巧克力奶油冻 **2** a white slightly sticky substance that you put in your hair to make it look thicker or to hold it in place 定型发胶，摩丝

Moussorgsky /ˈmusəgskɪ; ˈmuːsəgski/, **Modest** also 又作 **Mussorgsky, Modest** (1839-81) a Russian composer known for his OPERA *Boris Gudonov* and for his other works, including *Pictures at an Exhibition* and *Songs and Dances of Death.* 穆索尔斯基〔(1839-1881)，俄国作曲家，以歌剧《鲍里斯·戈多诺夫》、钢琴组曲《图画展览会》和声乐套曲《死之歌舞》著称〕

mous·tache also 又作 **mustache** *AmE*【美】/ˈmʌstæʃ; məˈstɑːʃ/ *n* [C] hair that grows on a man's upper lip 髭，小胡子: *He's shaved off his moustache.* 他剃去了小胡子。—compare 比较 BEARD (1)

mous·tach·i·oed /məˈstæʃɪod; məˈstæʃiəʊd/ *adj* an American spelling of MUSTACHIOED mustachioed的美式拼法

mous·y, mousey /ˈmausɪ; ˈmaʊsi/ *adj* **1** mousy hair is a dull brown colour〔头发〕灰褐色的 **2** a mousy woman is quiet and unattractive〔女人〕没有生气的；不引人注目的 —**mousiness** *n* [U]

mouth¹ /mauθ; maʊθ/ *n plural* **mouths** /mauðz; maʊðz/

1 ►FACE 脸◄ [C] the part of your face which you put food into, or which you use for speaking 嘴，口；口腔: *Don't talk with your mouth full of food!* 嘴里塞满了吃的东西时别说话！—see picture at 参见 HEAD¹ 图

2 keep your mouth shut *informal*【非正式】**a)** to not tell other people about a secret 保守秘密，守口如瓶: *I don't want my parents finding out about this, so you'd better keep your mouth shut.* 我不想让我父母知道这事，所以你最好嘴严点。**b)** to not say anything because you might make a mistake, or annoy someone or upset them 保持缄默，一声不吭: *She started to cry, and I wished I'd kept my mouth shut.* 她开始哭了起来，我真希望自己什么也没说。

3 open your mouth to start to speak, especially in a situation where you feel you should not say anything 开口说话: *I didn't dare open my mouth in case I offended her.* 我不敢开口，以免得罪她。

4 ►OPENING 口状物◄ [C] **a)** the entrance to a large hole or CAVE〔洞穴等的〕入口 **b)** the open part at the top of a bottle or container〔瓶子或其他容器的〕开口处

5 ►RIVER 河流◄ [C] the part of a river where it joins the sea 入海口，河口 —see picture on page A12 参见 A12 页图

6 big mouth *informal* someone who is a big mouth or has a big mouth is annoying because they cannot keep secrets or they often say things they should not say【非正式】嘴不严的人，多嘴的人

7 me and my big mouth/you and your big mouth etc *spoken* used when you are annoyed with yourself or with someone else for telling other people a secret or saying something that should not be said【口】都怪我/你等多嘴

8 he/she is all mouth *spoken* used when you think that someone is not really brave enough, strong enough etc to do what they say they can do【口】他/她只是嘴上发发狠而已〔指某人只是嘴里嚷着要做某事但实际上不敢付诸行动〕

9 mouth to feed someone who you must provide food for, especially one of your children 需要养活的人〔尤指孩子〕: *To these parents, a new baby is just another hungry mouth to feed.* 对这些父母来说，新生一个婴儿又添了一张嗷嗷待哺的嘴。

10 make your mouth water if food makes your mouth water, it looks so good you want to eat it immediately 使某人馋得流口水 —see also 另见 MOUTH-WATERING

11 down in the mouth *informal* looking very unhappy【非正式】垂头丧气的，沮丧的: *Why's Tim so down in the mouth?* 蒂姆为什么这样闷闷不乐？

12 open-mouthed/wide-mouthed etc with an open, wide etc mouth 张着嘴的/大嘴巴的等

13 out of the mouths of babes (and sucklings) *humorous* used when a small child has just said something clever or interesting【幽默】小孩子的话也有道理 —see also 另见 **by word of mouth** (WORD¹ (29)), **foam at the mouth** (FOAM² (2)), HAND TO MOUTH, **put your foot in your mouth** (FOOT¹ (12)), **shut your mouth** (SHUT¹ (3)), **shoot your mouth off** (SHOOT¹ (7))

mouth² /mauð; maʊð/ *v* [T] **1** to move your lips as if you are saying words, but without making any sound 不出声地说，用口型默示: *Brook was waving and mouthing over the noise at the others to stand aside.* 在嘈杂声中布鲁克朝着其他人一边摆手一边用口形示意他们站到一边去。**2** to say things that you do not really believe or that you do not understand 言不由衷地说；〔自

己胡涂却）信口开河: *a third-rate politician, capable only of mouthing the current party line* 只会空谈当前政党路线的三流政客 | **mouth platitudes** (=give opinions that are not original) 信口重复一些陈词滥调 *people at cocktail parties mouthing platitudes about the starving millions* 在鸡尾酒会上信口说些数百万人正在挨饿之类的老套话的人们

mouth off *phr v* [I+at/about] *informal* to complain angrily and noisily about something, or talk as if you know more than anyone else【非正式】愤怒而大声地抱怨; 大发议论; 卖弄地说话

mouth·ful /ˈmauθˌful; ˈmaʊθfʊl/ *n* [C] **1** an amount of food or drink that you put into your mouth at one time〔食物或饮料的〕一口: *That was a great steak! I enjoyed every mouthful.* 牛排真是棒极了! 我吃得津津有味。**2 a mouthful** *informal* a long word or phrase that is difficult to say【非正式】冗长而拗口的词〔短语〕: *Her real name is a bit of a mouthful, so we just call her Dee.* 她的真名有点儿拗口, 所以我们只叫她迪伊。**3 give sb a mouthful** *informal especially BrE* to speak angrily to someone, often swearing at them【非正式, 尤英】愤怒地对某人说; 咒骂某人 **4 say a mouthful** *AmE informal* to say a lot of true and important things about something in a few words【美, 非正式】几句话说出许多真实而重要的事, 说到点子上; 话短而精

mouth or·gan /ˈ· ·ˌ··/ *n* [C] a small musical instrument which you hold close to your lips and blow or suck; HARMONICA 口琴

mouth·piece /ˈmauθˌpis; ˈmaʊθpiːs/ *n* [C] **1** [usually singular 一般用单数] a person, newspaper etc that expresses the opinions of a government or a political organization 代言人; 喉舌; 传声筒: *Pravda was the official mouthpiece of the Communist Party of Soviet Union.*《真理报》曾是苏联共产党的官方喉舌。**2** the part of a musical instrument, telephone etc that you put in your mouth or next to your mouth〔乐器的〕吹口;〔电话的〕送话口

mouth-to-mouth re·sus·ci·ta·tion /ˌ· · ·ˌ· · ·ˌ· ·ˈ· ·/ *n* [U] a method used to make someone start breathing again by blowing air into their mouth 口对口人工呼吸

mouth·wash /ˈmauθˌwɔʃ; ˈmaʊθwɒʃ/ *n* [C,U] a liquid used to make your mouth smell fresh or to get rid of infection in your mouth 漱口剂; 洗口药

mouth-wa·ter·ing /ˈ· ˌ··· / *adj* food that is mouth-watering looks or smells extremely good〔食物〕令人馋涎欲滴的, 诱人的: *a mouth-watering aroma coming from the kitchen* 从厨房里传来的诱人的香味

mov·a·ble[1], moveable /ˈmuvəbl; ˈmuːvəbəl/ *adj* able to be moved and not fixed in one place or position 活动的; 可移动的: *a teddy bear with movable arms and legs* 四肢能活动的玩具熊

movable[2] also 又作 **moveable** *n* [C usually plural 一般用复数] *law* a personal possession such as a piece of furniture【法律】动产〈如家具〉

movable feast /ˌ··· ˈ·/ *n* [C] **1** *BrE informal* something that happens at different times, so that you are not sure exactly when it will happen【英, 非正式】发生时间不固定的事 **2** a special religious day, such as Easter, the date of which changes 日期因年而异的宗教节日〈如复活节〉

move[1] /muv; muːv/ *v*

1 ►CHANGE PLACE 改变地方◄ [I,T] to change your place or position, or to make something do this (使) 改变位置, 移动, 搬动: *Don't move or I'll shoot.* 不许动, 否则我就开枪了。| *You mustn't get off the train while it's still moving.* 火车还未停稳的时候不得下车。| **move sth** *Can you move your car – it's blocking the road.* 你能不能移动一下你的汽车 —— 它挡着路。| *We'll have to move the bed closer to the wall.* 我们将不得不把床移得靠墙更近一些。| **move about** *BrE*【英】**/around** *I could hear someone moving around upstairs.* 我能听见有人在楼上来回走动。| **can't move** (=be stuck or trapped) 动弹不了, 被困住 *Get me out of here – I can't move.* 把我从这儿弄出去 —— 我动弹不了。

2 ►NEW HOUSE/OFFICE 新房子/新办公室◄ [I,T] to go to live or work in a different place 搬家; 搬迁; 迁移: [+to] *When are you moving to Memphis?* 你什么时候搬到孟菲斯去? | [+into] *They've moved into a bigger office.* 他们已搬进了一间大一些的办公室。| **move house/home** *BrE* (=go to live in a different house)【英】搬家 *My parents kept moving house because of my dad's job.* 由于父亲的工作需要, 我父母不断地搬家。

3 ►CHANGE JOB/CLASS ETC 换工作/班级等◄ [I,T] to change to a different job, class etc, or to make someone change to a different job, class etc (使) 改做〔不同工作〕; (把某人) 调到〔不同班级等〕; **move sb to/into** *His teacher wants him moved to a higher class.* 他的老师想把他调到高年级去。| **move to/from** *She's just moved from the sales department.* 她刚刚从销售部调过来。

4 ►CHANGE YOUR OPINION 改变看法◄ a) [I] to change from one opinion or way of thinking to another 改变看法: *Neither side is willing to move on the issue of territory.* 双方都不愿意在领土问题上让步。| [+towards/ away from] *The two political parties have moved closer towards each other in recent months.* 最近几个月, 这两个政党的观点已较为接近了。**b)** [T] to persuade someone to change their opinion 说服〔某人〕改变看法: *She won't be moved – it doesn't matter what you say to her.* 她是说不动的 —— 不管你对她说什么。

5 ►MAKE SB SAD 使某人难过◄ [T] to make someone feel strong feelings, especially of sadness or sympathy 激起〔某人〕的强烈情感〔尤指难过或同情〕; 使感动: **be deeply/greatly moved** *I was deeply moved by their story.* 我被他们的故事深深地感动了。| **move sb to tears** *The child's suffering moved us to tears.* 那孩子受的苦使我们难过得流泪。—see also 另见 MOVING

6 ►PROGRESS 进展◄ [I] to progress in a particular way or at a particular rate 进展, 前进; 发展: *Things moved quickly once the contract was signed.* 合同一签, 事情进展得很快。| *The negotiations seem to be moving in the right direction.* 谈判好像正朝着正确的方向进展。

7 be/feel moved to do sth to want to do something because you feel angry, sad etc〔因感到生气、难过等而〕想做某事: *Hearing so much nonsense talked, I felt moved to speak on the subject.* 听到那么多的废话, 我想就那个话题说说自己的意见。

8 get moving *informal*【非正式】**a)** used when telling someone to hurry or when saying that you must hurry 赶紧; 赶快: *We'd better get moving if we're going to catch that plane.* 如果想赶上那班飞机, 我们最好赶紧出发。**b)** *spoken* used to tell someone that you need to leave a place【口】该走了: *It's time we got moving – I have to be up early tomorrow.* 我们该走了, 我明天得早起。

9 get things moving *informal* to make a process or event start happening【非正式】开始 (做) 某事, 取得进展

10 ►CHANGE ARRANGEMENTS 改变安排◄ [T] to change the time or order of something 改变〔时间或顺序〕: **move sth to/from** *Could we move the meeting to Thursday?* 我们可以把会议改到星期四吗?

11 ►CHANGE SUBJECT/ACTIVITY 改变话题/活动◄ [I] to change from one subject or activity to another 改变话题[活动]: [+away from/off] *We seem to be moving away from the main point of the discussion.*我们好像偏离讨论的要点了。—see also 另见 **move on**

12 ►START DEALING WITH 开始处理◄ [I] to start doing something, especially in order to achieve something or deal with a problem 开始做某事, 开始采取行动: [+on/against etc] *The governor has yet to move on any of the recommendations in the report.* 州长尚未处理报告中的任何建议。| **move fast/quickly** *You'll have to move fast if you want to get a place on the course.* 如果你想报名读这门课程, 就得赶紧行动起来。

13 ►LEAVE 离开◄ [I] *BrE especially spoken* to go somewhere or leave a place【英, 尤口】去某处; 离开某地: *It's time we were moving.* 我们该离开了。

14 ►GAMES 游戏◄ [I,T] to change the position of one of the pieces used to play a game such as CHESS 移动 (棋子), 走 (棋)

15 ►AT A MEETING 在会上◄ [I,T] *formal* to officially make a proposal at a meeting【正式】提议, 提出〔动议〕: **move that** *The chairman moved that the meeting be adjourned.* 主席提议休会。| **move an amendment** *BrE* (=propose a change)【英】提出一项修正案 *They want to move an amendment to the bill.* 他们想提议修正该法案。

16 ►GO FAST 快速行进◄ [I] *informal* to travel very fast【非正式】快速行进, 飞驰: *This car can really move!* 这辆小汽车跑得真快!

17 ►SELL STH 卖掉某物◄ [I] *informal* to sell something quickly【非正式】快速销售掉, 很快脱手: *You should watch these juggling kits move. The kids love'em.* 你应该看看这些杂耍用品卖得多快, 孩子们喜欢极了。

18 not move a muscle to stay completely still 一动不动, 纹丝不动

19 move with the times to change the way you think and behave, as the world changes around you 与时俱进

20 you can't move/you can hardly move *spoken* used to say that a place is very full and there is not much space【口】〔挤得〕动不了/几乎无法动弹: *The bar was so crowded you could hardly move.* 酒吧非常拥挤, 人几乎无法动弹。

21 you can't move for *spoken* used to say that a place is full of a particular kind of people or things【口】到处都是, 挤满了〔某类人或物〕: *You couldn't move for police in town this morning.* 今天上午城里到处都是警察。

22 move in a society/world/circle to spend a lot of time with a particular kind of people and know them well 与某一团体/社会/圈子的人长期交往: *Lady Olga moved in a different social world from me.* 奥尔佳夫人出入的社交圈和我的不同。—see also 另见 **move the goalposts** (GOALPOST (2)), **move in for the kill** (KILL[2] (2)), **move heaven and earth** (HEAVEN (10)), **when the spirit moves you** (SPIRIT[1] (13))

move along *phr v* **1** [I] *BrE* to move further towards the back or front of something【英】向前[后]移动: *The bus-driver asked us all to move along.* 公共汽车司机要我们都往里边走。**2** [T **move sb along**] *especially BrE* to officially order someone to leave a public place【尤英】命令〔某人〕离开〔公共场所〕: *The police moved us along almost as soon as we started playing.* 我们刚开始玩，警察就把我们赶走了。

move away *phr v* [I] to go to live in a different area 搬走: *Her children had moved away and she was left on her own.* 她的孩子都搬走了，只剩她一个人独自生活。

move in *phr v* [I] **1** to start living in a new house 搬进新居: *We decided not to move in until we'd finished decorating.* 我们决定装修完后再搬进去。**2** to start living with someone in the same house 开始〔和某人〕同居；搬来〔和某人〕一起居住: **[+with]** *She wants her boyfriend to move in with her.* 她想让她的男朋友搬进来和她住在一起。**3** to take control of a situation, often using your power and influence unfairly 强行插手，干预: *The big multinationals moved in and started pushing up prices.* 一些大的跨国公司插手进来，开始抬高价格。**4** to go towards a place or group of people in order to attack them or take control of them〔为了进攻或控制而〕向…逼近，进逼: **[+on]** *Already a special police task force was preparing to move in on the gang.* 一支特警队已准备逼近那伙歹徒以采取行动。

move off *phr v* [I] if a vehicle or group of people moves off, they start to leave the place where they are〔车辆或人群〕离开，出发，起程: *The conductor blew his whistle and the train slowly moved off.* 列车员吹响了哨子，火车徐徐开动了。

move on *phr v*

1 ▶CONTINUE JOURNEY 继续行程◀ [I] to leave the place where you have been staying and continue your journey 继续前行: *That's enough rest – it's time to move on.* 休息够了 —— 该继续赶路了。

2 ▶CHANGE SUBJECT 改变话题◀ [I] to start talking about a new subject in a discussion, book etc〔在讨论、书籍等中〕开始谈论新话题，更换话题: *I think we've covered this topic – is it all right if we move on?* 我觉得这个话题我们谈过了，换个话题好吗？

3 ▶ CHANGE JOB/CLASS 改换工作/班级◀ [I] to leave your present job, class, or activity and start doing another one 改换工作[班级，活动]: **[+to]** *Children usually move on to secondary school at 11.* 儿童通常在11岁时升入中学。

4 ▶PROGRESS/DEVELOP 进步/发展◀ [I] **a)** to develop in your life, and become older and more experienced〔在生活中〕成长，变得更成熟: **[+from]** *I felt that I'd moved on from my college days, and didn't want to go back.* 我感到自己与大学时比变得老成了，不想再回到从前。**b)** to become more modern, advanced, or complicated than before 变得更现代[先进，复杂]，有了新发展: *In my day you could only get them in black-and-white, but things have moved on since then.* 在我那个时候，那些玩意儿只有黑白的，现在和当时已大不一样了。

5 move on to higher/better things *humorous* to get a better job or social position【幽默】高升: *I expect you'll be moving on to higher things now that you have your degree.* 你既然拿到了学位，我认为你会高升的。

6 ▶TIME 时间◀ [I] if time moves on, the year moves on etc, the time passes〔岁月〕流逝

7 time is moving on *BrE spoken* used to say that you must leave soon or do something soon, because it is getting late【英口】时间不早了: *Time's moving on – we'd better get back to the car.* 时间不早了 —— 我们最好回到车上去。

8 ▶MAKE SB LEAVE 让某人离开◀ [T **move sb on**] *BrE* to officially order someone to leave a public place【英】命令〔某人〕离开〔公共场所〕: *We got moved on by the police for making too much noise.* 我们太吵了，警察要我们走开。

move out *phr v* [I] **1** to leave the house where you are living now in order to go and live somewhere else 搬出，迁走: **[+of]** *They want to find a house somewhere and move out of their apartment.* 他们想在某个地方找栋房子，然后搬出他们的公寓套房。**2** if a group of soldiers moves out, they leave a place〔部队〕开拔，撤出 **3** *AmE informal* to leave【美，非正式】离开: *Is everything packed? Then let's move out.* 全都收拾好了吗？那咱们动身吧。

move over *phr v* [I] **1** to change position so that there is more space for someone else〔为腾出地方而〕挪动，移动: *Move over so that we can all sit down.* 挪一挪，大家都能坐下。**2** to change to a different system, opinion, group of people etc 转变，变更: **[+to]** *Most companies have moved over to computer-aided design systems.* 大多数公司已转而采用电脑辅助设计系统。

move up *phr v* [I] **1** *BrE* to change position in order to make more space for other people or things, or to be near someone else【英】〔为腾出地方而〕挪动；靠拢: *There's room for one more if everyone moves up a bit.* 如果大家都挪动一下，还会有一个人的地方。**2** to get a better job in a company, or move to a higher class in a school 升迁，晋升；升年级: *Everyone here's very ambitious – they all want to move up as quickly as possible.* 这儿所有的人都野心勃勃，都想尽快升职。**3 move up in the world** *often humorous* to get a better job or social position【常幽默】升职，高升: *John's moved up in the world since you knew him – he's a director now.* 约翰在你认识他以后高升了 —— 他现在是总裁。

move[2] *n* 

1 ▶ACTION 行动◀ [singular] something that you decide to do 步骤；行动: *She's still thinking about her next move.* 她还在考虑她的下一步行动。| **a good/wise/smart etc move** *He said he was starting his own company, which sounded like a smart move.* 他说他要自己开公司，这听起来像是不错的选择。

2 make a move a) to move in a particular direction, especially in order to attack someone or to escape〔尤指为袭击某人或逃走而〕移动；挪动: *If anyone makes a move, I'll shoot.* 谁动一下，我就开枪。| **[+towards/for]** *He suddenly made a move towards the door.* 他突然朝门口走去。**b)** to do something to achieve a particular result 采取行动: *Neither side had made a move to resolve the dispute.* 双方都没有采取行动来解决争端。**c)** *BrE informal* to leave a place【英，非正式】离开，出发: *It's getting late – we ought to make a move.* 时间不早了，我们该走了。

3 be on the move a) to be travelling from one place to the next 在迁移；在行进: *We have received reports that the rebel army is on the move.* 我们已接到报告，说叛军正在转移。**b)** to be busy and active 忙碌；活跃: *She's always on the move, isn't she?* 她总是闲不住，是不是？**c)** to be changing and developing a lot 在发展变化；在前进: *Georgian England was a society on the move.* 乔治王朝时期的英格兰是一个正处于发展变化中的社会。

4 get a move on *spoken* used to tell someone to hurry【口】快点，赶紧: *Get a move on or we'll be late!* 快点，要不我们会迟到的！

5 make the first move to do something first, especially in order to end a quarrel or start a relationship〔尤指为了结束争吵或建立关系而〕先迈出第一步，先采取行动: *Neither was willing to make the first move towards reconciliation.* 双方谁都不愿意先迈出和解的第一步。

6 watch/follow sb's every move to carefully watch everything that someone does, especially because you think they are doing something illegal 注视某人的一举一动: *I have three officers watching his every move.* 我让三名警察监视他的一举一动。

7 make no move to do sth to make no attempt to prevent someone from doing something 没有采取行动做某事: *They were staring, but made no move to stop us.* 他们瞪眼看着，但没有采取行动阻止我们。

8 ▶GOING TO A NEW PLACE 去新的地方◀ [singular] the process of leaving one house, office etc, and going to live or work in a different one 搬家；搬迁，迁移: *"How was the move?" "Exhausting!"* "搬家的滋味如何？""累死人！"

9 ▶PROGRESS 进展◀ [C] something that is done to improve a situation〔使局面改观的〕举措: *It's a move in the right direction.* 这是一个方向正确的举措。

10 ▶GAMES 游戏◀ [C] **a)** an act of changing the position of one of the objects in a game such as CHESS〔下棋的〕一步，一着 **b)** a way in which this may be done, according to the rules〔棋子的〕规定走法: *I'm learning all the different moves.* 我在学习棋的各种不同走法。**c)** the time when a player can move one of these objects〔轮到某一方的〕走棋: *It's your move.* 该你走了。

move·a·ble /ˈmuvəbḷ; ˈmuːvəbəl/ *adj* another spelling of MOVABLE movable的另一种拼法

move·ment /ˈmuvmənt; ˈmuːvmənt/ *n*

1 ▶GROUP 团体◀ [C] a group of people who share the same ideas or beliefs and work together to achieve a particular aim〔政治、社会方面的〕运动；积极开展运动的团体: *the civil rights movement* 民权运动 | *The nationalist movement did not have widespread support.* 民族主义运动没有得到广泛的支持。

2 ▶MOVING 移动◀ a) [C,U] a change in the place or position of something or someone 移动; 调动: *reports of troop movement in the area* 该地区部队动向的报道 b) [C] an act of moving your body, or the way someone moves their body 动作; 举止, 风度: *the dancer's graceful movements* 舞蹈家优美的动作
3 ▶CHANGE/DEVELOPMENT 变化/发展◀ a) [U] a change that brings progress or improvement in a situation 改进, 改善; 进步, 发展: *There's been no movement in the dispute since Thursday.* 自周四以来, 争端一直没有缓和。b) [C] a gradual change or development in people's attitudes or behaviour〔态度或行为的〕逐渐变化, 趋势, 倾向: *a growing movement among consumers away from buying processed foods* 消费者不再购买加工食品这一日益增长的趋势
4 sb's movements all of a person's activities over a certain period〔在某一期间内〕某人所有的活动: *Police are trying to trace Carter's movements over the last 48 hours.* 警方正设法追查卡特在过去48小时里的活动。
5 ▶MUSIC 音乐◀ [C] one of the main parts into which a piece of music is divided, especially in a SYMPHONY〔尤指交响曲的〕乐章
6 ▶CLOCK/WATCH 钟/表◀ the moving parts of a piece of machinery, especially a clock or watch〔活动〕机件; 〔尤指钟表的〕机芯
7 ▶BODY WASTE 人体的排泄物◀ [C] *formal* an act of getting rid of waste matter from the bowels (BOWEL (1))【正式】排便

mov·er /ˈmuvɚ; ˈmuːvə/ *n* [C] **1** someone who makes a formal proposal at a meeting〔会议上的〕提议人, 动议者: *The mover of the motion has a right of reply to the discussion.* 提出动议者有权对讨论作出答复。**2** someone or something that moves in a particular way〔以某种方式〕移动的人[物]: *Saturn is the slowest mover of all the planets.* 土星是所有行星中运行速度最慢的。**3** *especially AmE* someone whose job is to help people move from one house to another【尤美】搬家工人 **4 movers and shakers** powerful and influential people 有权势的人: *The movers and shakers in the stock market predicted a rise in share-dealing.* 证券市场中有权势的人物预测股票交易将会增加。—see also 另见 PRIME MOVER, **key mover/player** (KEY[1])

S2 W2 **mov·ie** /ˈmuvɪ; ˈmuːvi/ *n* [C] *especially AmE*【尤美】**1** a film made to be shown at the cinema 电影: *a Hollywood movie* 好莱坞影片 **2 the movies** the cinema 电影院: **go to the movies** (=go to watch a movie at the cinema) 去看电影

mov·ie·go·er /ˈmuvɪˌgoɚ; ˈmuːviˌgəʊə/ *n* [C] *especially AmE* someone who goes to see films, especially regularly【尤美】〔尤指经常〕看电影的人

movie star /ˈ / *n* [C] *especially AmE* a famous film actor or actress【尤美】电影明星

movie thea·ter /ˈ.. ,../ *n* [C] *AmE*【美】= CINEMA (1) *BrE*【英】

mov·ing /ˈmuvɪŋ; ˈmuːvɪŋ/ *adj* **1** making you feel strong emotions, especially sadness or sympathy 动人的, 感人的: *Jackson's speech was so moving, it made me cry.* 杰克逊的讲话非常感人, 我都哭了。| **moving account/experience/story etc** *a moving account of life in the refugee camps* 对难民营生活的感人叙述 **2** [only before noun 仅用于名词前] changing from one position to another 活动的, 移动的: *a moving stage* 活动舞台 | **fast/slow moving etc** *Be very careful when changing lanes in fast moving traffic.* 在快速行进的车流中换车道一定要非常小心。**3 the moving spirit** someone who makes something start to happen 发起人, 策动者: *Mr Arkwright was the moving spirit behind the founding of the union.* 阿克赖特先生是创建该协会的幕后发起人。—**movingly** *adv*: *the sufferings of the famine victims, so movingly described in Buerk's TV reports* 伯克的电视报道中描述得如此感人的饥民的苦难

moving part /,.. ˈ./ *n* [C] a part of a machine that moves when it is operating〔机器的〕活动部件: *Keep the moving parts well oiled.* 要使活动部件保持良好的润滑状态。

moving pic·ture /,.. ˈ..◂/ *n* [C] *old-fashioned, especially AmE* a film made to be shown at the cinema【过时, 尤美】电影

moving stair·case /,.. ˈ../ *n* [C] *old-fashioned* an ESCALATOR【过时】自动扶梯

moving van /ˈ.. ,./ *n* [C] *AmE*【美】搬家车, 搬运车; REMOVAL VAN *BrE*【英】

mow /mo; məʊ/ *v past participle* **mowed** *or* **mown** /mon; məʊn/ [I,T] **1** to cut grass or wheat using a machine or tool with special blades 刈, 割(草或小麦): *It's time to mow the lawn again.* 又该修剪草坪了。**2 new-mown hay/grass etc** recently cut grass etc 新割的牧草/草等

mow sb ↔ **down** *phr v* [T] to kill large numbers of people at the same time, especially by shooting them 大量杀死〔尤指射杀〕; 扫杀: *The battalion was mown down by enemy tanks.* 那个营的士兵在敌军坦克扫射下成片成片地倒下了。

mow·er /ˈmoɚ; ˈməʊə/ *n* [C] **1** a machine used for cutting grass; LAWNMOWER 割〔刈〕草机, 草坪修剪机 **2** *old use* someone who mows【旧】刈割者

Mow·gli /ˈmauglɪ; ˈmaʊgli/ a character in *The Jungle Book* (1894-95), by Rudyard Kipling, who is lost in the JUNGLE (=a tropical forest) as a small boy and is cared for and taught by the animals in the jungle 莫格利〔拉迪亚德·吉卜林《丛林故事》(1894-1895)中的一个人物。他是一个在热带丛林里迷了路的小男孩, 得到丛林中许多动物的照料和教导〕

mox·ie /ˈmɑksɪ; ˈmɒksi/ *n* [U] *AmE informal* courage and determination【美, 非正式】勇气, 胆量; 决心: *He's always had plenty of moxie.* 他向来浑身是胆。

Mo·zam·bique /ˌmozəmˈbik; ˌməʊzəmˈbiːk/ a country in southeast Africa, between Tanzania and South Africa. Population: 19,371,000 (2001). Capital: Maputo. 莫桑比克〔非洲东南部一国家, 位于坦桑尼亚和南非之间。人口: 19,371,000 (2001), 首都: 马普多〕—**Mozambiquean** *n, adj*

Mo·zart /ˈmotsɑt; ˈməʊtsɑːt/, **Wolf·gang Am·a·de·us** /ˈwulfgæŋ æməˈdeəs; ˈwʊlfgæŋ æməˈdeɪəs/ (1756-91) an Austrian COMPOSER, one of the most famous and admired CLASSICAL musicians who ever lived. His many works include 41 symphonies (SYMPHONY), 27 piano CONCERTO*s*, and some of the most famous OPERA*s* ever written, including *Don Giovanni* and *The Magic Flute*. 莫扎特〔(1756-1791), 奥地利作曲家, 最著名和最为人欣赏的古典音乐家之一。他十分多产, 创作了41部交响曲、27首钢琴协奏曲和几部有史以来最著名的歌剧, 其中有《唐·乔凡尼》和《魔笛》〕

MP /ˌɛm ˈpi; ˌem ˈpiː/ *n* [C] **1** MEMBER OF PARLIAMENT; someone who has been elected to represent the people in a parliament 国会议员; 英国下议院议员: *She's the MP for Liverpool North.* 她是利物浦市北区的下议院议员。| *Ken Newton, MP* 肯·牛顿, 下议院议员 **2** *informal* a member of the MILITARY POLICE【非正式】宪兵队队员

MPAA, the /ˌɛm pi e ˈe; ˌem piː eɪ ˈeɪ/ the Motion Picture Association of America; a US organization whose job is to watch new films and decide whether children or young people will be allowed to see them. Each film is given a rating, which shows for example that a film can be shown to anyone (G), or can be seen by children if an adult goes with them (PG). A film that has an 'X' rating probably has a lot of sex and violence in it, so can only be seen by people who are at least 18 years old. There is a similar organization in the UK called the British Board of Film Classification. 美国电影协会〔美国一组织。其职责是审查新拍摄的影片以确定是否适合儿童或年轻人观看, 该组织给每部影片定级, 如G级表示所有人可以观看, PG级表示有成年人陪伴的儿童可观看。一部影片被评定为X级, 就说明里面可能含有大量性和暴力镜头, 只允许18岁以上的人群观看。英国也有类似组织, 称 the British Board of Film Classification (英国电影分级委员会)〕

mpg /ˌɛm pi ˈdʒi; ˌem piː ˈdʒiː/ the abbreviation of 缩写 = miles per GALLON, used to describe the amount of petrol used by a car 每加仑汽油所行英里数, 英里/加仑: *a car that does 35 mpg* 每加仑汽油行驶35英里的汽车

mph /ˌɛm pi ˈetʃ; ˌem piː ˈeɪtʃ/ the abbreviation of 缩写 = miles per hour, used to describe the speed of a vehicle 英里/小时: *speeding along at 100 mph* 以每小时100英里的速度飞驰

MPhil /ˌɛm ˈfɪl; ˌem ˈfɪl/ *n* [C] *BrE* Master of PHILOSOPHY; a university degree that you get after your first degree【英】哲学硕士; 哲学硕士学位

Mr *BrE*【英】, **Mr.** *AmE*【美】/ˈmɪstɚ; ˈmɪstə/ **1** a title used before a man's family name when you are speaking to him or writing to him and want to be polite 先生〔用于男子的姓之前的尊称〕: *Mr Smith* 史密斯先生 | *Mr. John Smith* 约翰·史密斯先生 | *Mr and Mrs Smith* 史密斯先生及夫人 **2** a title used when addressing a man in an official position 先生〔对有官职的男子的称呼〕: *Mr Chairman* 主席先生 | *Mr. President* 总统先生 —compare 比较 MADAM (3) **3 Mr Right** a man who would be the perfect husband for a particular woman 理想的丈夫, 如意郎君: *She's spent years waiting for Mr Right to come along.* 多少年来她一直在等着如意郎君的出现。**4 Mr Big** *informal* the leader or most important person in a group, especially a criminal group【非正式】〔尤指犯罪集团的〕头儿, 最重要的人物 **5 Mr Clean** *informal* someone who is honest and always obeys the law【非正式】清白先生, 诚实守法的人 **6** *spoken* used before the name of a personal quality or kind of behaviour as a humorous name for a man who has that quality【口】…先生, …大王〔用于表示某种个人品质或行为的词之前, 作为对具有该品质或行为的男子的幽默称呼〕: *I don't think we need any comments from Mr Sarcasm here.* 我认为我们这里不需要利嘴先生作任何评论。—see also 另见 **no more Mr Nice Guy!** (GUY[1] (5))

USAGE NOTE 用法说明: MR
COLLOCATION 搭配

Mr, Mrs, Miss, and **Ms** are only used with full names or last names (surnames). Mr, Mrs, Miss 及 Ms 只能与全名或姓连用: *Hello, Mr Gray.* 你好，格雷先生。| *The next candidate for the job is Mrs Betty Schwarz* (NOT 不用 *Please Miss teacher* or 或 *Good morning Mr Jerry*). 该工作的下一个申请者是贝蒂·施瓦茨夫人。

When you are talking or writing to someone directly, you do not usually use their full name. 直接跟某人谈话或通信时通常不用他的全名: *Hello, Mr Smith*(NOT 不用 *Hello, Mr Alan Smith*). 你好，史密斯先生。

Usually **Mr, Ms** etc is not used with names of people you know well or who are famous. 通常情况下，在很熟的人或名人的姓名之前不用Mr, Ms等: *This is my friend Annie Walker.* 这是我的朋友安妮·沃克。| *the defeat of Adolf Hitler* 阿道夫·希特勒的失败 | *Clinton's health care policy* 克林顿的医疗保健政策 | *'The Wave' by Hokusai* 北斋画的《神奈川巨浪》

CULTURAL NOTE 文化注释

Mr, Mrs, Ms, and Miss

Mr If a man is married, his last name may be used for both the man and his wife in the expression 'Mr and Mrs': *Mr and Mrs Blair are on vacation in Italy.* In formal situations, the man's first name is sometimes also used like this: *Mr and Mrs David Clark* (=Mr David Clark and his wife). But this is now regarded as old-fashioned. 已婚男子的姓可以用于包含夫妻双方的称谓"…先生和夫人"中: 布莱尔夫妇正在意大利度假。在正式场合，男子的名有时也可以这样使用: 戴维·克拉克先生和夫人。但是现在这被看成是过时的用法。

Mrs Traditionally, a woman who gets married takes the title **Mrs** and uses her husband's last name. She can be addressed either with or without her own first name: *our neighbour, Mrs Daley* | *Mrs Nancy Reagan.* Married women sometimes used to be formally addressed by the title **Mrs** followed by their husband's first and last names: *Mrs Edward Rochester.* But this is now regarded as very old-fashioned. Many women in the UK and the US no longer take their husband's name when they marry, and if they keep their own last name, they use the title **Ms** instead of **Mrs**. Other women now use both their own and their husband's last name: for example, when the US actress Pamela Anderson married Tommy Lee, she changed her name to Pamela Anderson Lee. 传统上，女子结婚后就开始使用丈夫的姓，称"…夫人"。称呼她时带不带上她的名都可以: 我们的邻居戴利夫人 | 南希·里根夫人。过去对已婚妇女的正式称呼有时是在Mrs后加上其丈夫的名和姓: 爱德华·罗切斯特夫人。但是现在这种用法被认为极度过时。现在英美很多女性结婚后并不使用丈夫的姓名。如果她们仍使用自己原来的姓，她们就把称谓从 Mrs 换成 Ms。还有些妇女既使用自己的姓又使用丈夫的姓，例如美国女演员帕梅拉·安德森和汤米·李结婚后，她把自己的名字改成了帕梅拉·安德森·李。

Ms The title **Ms** has been used since the 1970s, and many women prefer it because it does not draw attention to whether they are married or not. Ms这一称谓从20世纪70年代开始就有使用，很多女性喜欢这个称谓的原因是它不会向人透露自己是否已婚。

Miss Traditionally, all unmarried women, whatever their age, used the title **Miss**: *Miss Elizabeth Bennet* or simply *Miss Bennet.* Some older unmarried women may still do this, but **Miss** is now regarded as rather old-fashioned, especially in the US, except when used about a very young girl. 传统上所有未婚女性，不论多大年纪，都可以使用Miss这一称谓: 伊丽莎白·贝内特小姐，或简单地称作"贝内特小姐"。Miss这一称谓现在被认为相当过时、尤其在美国，除非在称谓一个年轻姑娘时才使用; 尽管如此，还是有不少的大龄未婚女性愿意用这个称谓。— see also Cultural Note at MAIDEN NAME 另见 MAIDEN NAME 文化注释

Mrs *BrE*【英】, **Mrs.** *AmE*【美】/ˈmɪsɪz; ˈmɪsɨz/ **1** a title used before a married woman's family name when you are speaking or writing to her and want to be polite 夫人，太太〔跟已婚妇女谈话或通信时用于其姓之前的尊称〕: *Mrs. Smith* 史密斯夫人 | *Mr and Mrs David Smith* 戴维·史密斯先生及夫人 —compare 比较 MISS[2], MS —see 见 MR (USAGE) **2** *spoken* used before the name of a personal quality or type of behaviour as a humorous name for a married woman who has that quality【口】夫人〔用于表示某种个人品质或行为的词之前，作为对具有该品质或行为的已婚女子的幽默称呼〕: *Mrs Superefficiency* 超级效率夫人

Mr U·ni·verse /ˌ.. ˈ.../ a US competition in which men from many different countries who are BODYBUILDERs (=people who exercise to develop big muscles) compete to be judged the most physically attractive and to win the title 'Mr Universe' 环球先生〔美国举行的男性健美比赛。健美运动员来自世界各国，竞相展示各自的身躯魅力，以赢得"环球先生"称号〕

MS[1] /ˌɛm ˋɛs; ˌem ˈes/ *n* **1** [C] *AmE* Master of Science; a university degree in science that you get after your first degree【美】理科硕士; 理科硕士学位 **2** [U] multiple sclerosis; a serious illness that gradually destroys your nerves, making you weak and unable to move 多发性硬化 (症)

MS[2] /ˌɛm ˋɛs; ˌem ˈes/ the written abbreviation of 缩写= MISSISSIPPI

Ms *BrE*【英】, **Ms.** *AmE*【美】/mɪz; mɪz/ a title used before a woman's family name because it is not important to say whether she is married or not, or when you do not know whether she is married or not 女士〔置于女子姓前的称呼，用在没必要说明其婚姻状况或其婚姻状况不明时〕—compare 比较 MISS[2], MRS —see 见 MR (USAGE)

ms *n plural* **mss** the written abbreviation of 缩写= MANUSCRIPT

Ms. *trademark* a US magazine for women, started by the feminist writer Gloria Steinem【商标】《女士》〔美国一女性杂志，由女权主义作家格洛丽亚·斯坦内姆创刊〕

MSc /ˋɛm ɛs ˋsi; ˌem es ˈsiː/ *n* [C] Master of Science; a university degree in science that you get after your first degree 理科硕士; 理科硕士学位; MS (1) *AmE*【美】—compare 比较 MA

MS-DOS /ˌɛm ɛs ˋdɑs; ˌem es ˈdɒs/ *n* [U] *trademark* one of the most common OPERATING SYSTEMs for a computer【商标】微软磁盘操作系统

MSG /ˌɛm ɛs ˋdʒi; ˌem es ˈdʒiː/ *n* [U] MONOSODIUM GLUTAMATE; a chemical compound added to food 味精，味素〔谷胺酸钠〕

MSP Member of the Scottish Parliament; a British politician who is a member of the Scottish Parliament 苏格兰议会议员

MT the written abbreviation of 缩写= MONTANA

Mt the written abbreviation of 缩写= MOUNT[2] (1): *Mt Everest* 珠穆朗玛峰

MTV /ˌɛm ti ˋvi; ˌem tiː ˈviː/ *trademark* Music Television; a US television company whose programmes are shown around the world. It broadcasts popular music and videos of the singers or groups performing it.【商标】音乐电视公司〔美国一电视制作公司，面向全世界播出节目，有流行音乐及歌手或组合的演出录像〕

much[1] /mʌtʃ; mʌtʃ/ *adv* **1 much taller/much more difficult etc** used especially before comparatives and superlatives to mean a lot taller, a lot more difficult 高得多/难得多等: *You get a much better view if you stand on a chair.* 站在椅子上看会清楚得多。| *She looks much fatter in real life than she does on TV.* 她在现实生活中看起来比在电视上胖得多。| **much too old/much too tall etc** *You can't marry him. He's much too old.* 你不能嫁给他，他年龄实在太大了。| **much the bigger/much the more interesting** *Her second novel was much the more exciting.* 她的第二部小说要精彩得多。| **much the biggest/much the most interesting etc** *He is much the most handsome man I've ever met.* 他绝对是我所见过的最英俊的男子。| **much loved/much admired** *Maturity and wider experience are much sought after commodities in teaching these days.* 在现代教学中，人们更注重追求的是成熟的处事态度和广泛的经验。**2 too much/so much/very much/how much etc** used to show the degree which someone does something or something happens 太多/如此多/很多/多么地等: *If he didn't talk so much he'd do a lot better.* 如果他话不那么多，他会做得好很多。| *The divorce was messy and at the time upset her very much.* 那次离婚弄得乱糟糟的，令她那时很苦恼。| *I've so much looked forward to your visit.* 我十分急切地期盼着你的来访。| *However much you hate walking you still have to go to the top.* 不管你是多么不喜欢走路，你还是必须走到顶。**3 not much a)** only a little, only to a small degree etc 只一点点，不多; 不怎么: *"Did you enjoy the performance?" "Not much!"* "你喜欢那场演出吗?" "不怎么喜欢!" | *I haven't seen Tony for over 20 years. He hasn't changed much.* 我有二十多年没见托尼了，他变化不大。| *It was only a young dog – not much higher than my knee.* 那只是一条幼犬，比我的膝盖高不了多少。**b)** used to say that something does not happen often 不经常，很少: *We don't go to the theatre much these days.* 我们如今不常去看戏。| *The new compact discs mean you don't see LPs in the shops as much.* 激光唱片的普及意味着

M

如今商店里不会(像以前那样)经常看到密纹唱片了。**4 much like/much as/much the same** used to say that something is very similar to something else 很像,几乎一样: *The house was very much as I'd remembered it.* 那座房子和我记忆中的样子几乎完全一样。| *It's easy to confuse us, we're much the same build and have the same coloured hair.* 很容易把我们弄混,我们体型差不多,而且头发的颜色也一样。**5 not be much good at something** to not be able to do something such as play a sport, speak a foreign language etc very well 不太善于做某事,对某事不太在行: *Brian's never been much good at understanding other people's feelings.* 布赖恩从来就不太善于理解别人的感情。**6 much less** used to say that one thing is even less true, possible etc, than another 更不用说,更何况: *He can hardly afford beer, much less champagne.* 他几乎连啤酒都买不起,更不用说香槟了。**7 be too much/a bit much** *spoken* used to say that someone's behaviour is rude or impolite【口】太过分/有点过分: *I thought breaking your window and expecting you to pay for it was a bit much!* 打破了你的窗玻璃还指望你为此掏腰包,我认为这有点过分!**8 not so much...as...** used to show that something is bigger, more difficult etc than people may think 与其说是…不如说是…: *In many cases nursing is not so much a job as a way of life.* 在许多情况下,护理与其说是一件工作倒不如说是一种生活方式。**9 much as sb does sth** used to mean that although one thing is true, something else is also true 尽管某人做某事〔指尽管某一情况是事实,而另一情况也是事实〕: *Much as I enjoy Shakespeare, I was glad when the play was over.* 尽管我喜欢莎士比亚,但当那个戏剧演完时我还是很高兴。**10 much to sb's surprise/disgust etc** *formal* used to say that someone was very surprised, very disgusted etc【正式】令某人非常吃惊/厌恶等的是: *Much to my displeasure some of the pupils in the school have been smoking outside the gates.* 令我非常不快的是,有些小学生一直在校门外吸烟。**11 so much the better (for sb)** *especially spoken* used to say that you think a situation, idea etc is very good【尤口】那(对某人来说)更好: *If he wants to not drink and drive everyone home, so much the better for us!* 如果他打算不喝酒并开车把我们大伙都送回家,那就更好了。**12 Not much!** used to emphasize that you really do want to do something, that you really are excited about something etc 哪里的话!当然不是!未必!〔用于强调确实想做某事或确实为某事感到兴奋〕: *"You don't want any cake, do you Tom?" "Not much!"* "你不要蛋糕了,是吧汤姆?""我当然要了!"

USAGE NOTE 用法说明: MUCH

GRAMMAR POINTS 语法要点

Much, with or without *very*, is only used with nouns if they are uncountable, and then only with negative clauses or in questions. 不管带very与否,much只能和不可数名词连用,而且只能用于否定句及疑问句中: *She doesn't get out much.* 她不大出门。| *Did you get very much work done?* 你做了很多很多的工作吗? | *How much money do you have?* 你有多少钱?

For positive statements and with countable nouns, you use **a lot** or **many**. 在肯定句中或可数名词之前要用a lot或many: *She's done a lot of work.* 她已做了很多工作。| *They visited many/a lot of countries.* 他们去过许多国家。| *Were there many people there?* 那里人多吗?

You often use **(very) much** with verbs in negative or question contexts. In questions, it usually comes at the end of a clause. 在否定或疑问语境中(very) much常和动词连用,在疑问句中通常位于句末: *Do you go to London much?* 你经常去伦敦吗? In negative contexts, it may come before the verb, or, more often, at the end. 在否定语境中,可以出现在动词之前,但更常见的是在句末。So you would say 所以人们会说: *I don't much like living in London.* | *I don't like living in London much* (NOT 不用 *I don't like living much in London*). 我不太喜欢住在伦敦。

So much, as much, much more and **too much** are often used in positive contexts with verbs and uncountable nouns. so much, as much, much more和too much常用在肯定语境中,修饰动词或不可数名词: *I go to restaurants so much I'm tired of them.* 我去饭馆去得太多了,我都感到厌烦了。| *She smokes too much!* 她吸烟吸得太凶了! | *Try to relax as much as possible.* 尽量放松。| *We'll need much more money than that.* 我们将需要比那多得多的钱。

With some verbs, especially with the general meaning 'like', **very much** can be used in positive contexts as well. Using **very much** before a verb is particularly common in British English. 当和某些动词〔尤其和表示"喜欢"的动词〕连用时,very much也可用于肯定句中。动词前用very much在英国英语中特别常见: *Rhoda very much enjoys skiing* (NOT 不用 *Rhoda enjoys very much skiing*). 罗达非常喜欢滑雪。| *I love her very much.* 我很爱她。You also say 人们也说: *Thank you very much.* 非常感谢。

(Very) much is used with most adjectives only before **more** and **too**, or when they are in the **-er** form. You cannot use it simply instead of **very**. (very)much和大多数形容词连用时只能用在more和too之前,或者与形容词的-er形式连用。它不能代替very: *This is much more/too difficult.* 这事困难得多/这事实在太难了。But note that you say 但注意可以说: *I am very sorry* (NEVER 永不用 *I am much sorry*, or 或 *I am sorry very much*). 我很抱歉。

Some adjectives end in **-ed** or **-ing** and look like forms of verbs, but they take **very** rather than **much** (unless **more** or **too** is there as well). 有些形容词以-ed或-ing结尾,看起来像动词,但它们却用very而不是much作修饰语〔除非这些形容词前有more或too〕。So you would use **much** in this sentence 所以在下面这个句子中人们会用much: *She was a much-loved colleague* (她是一个很受大家喜爱的同事), because **loved** is a passive verb, but you would use **very** in this one 因为loved是一个被动动词,而在下句人们却会用very: *The kids are getting very tired* (孩子们很累了) because **tired** is an adjective. 因为tired是一个形容词。

much² *quantifier* **1** used to mean a lot of something especially in spoken English in questions and negatives or in formal written English 很多(的),大量(的)〔尤用于口语里的疑问句及否定句中,或用于正式的书面语中〕: *There isn't much time. Pack the bag quickly.* 时间不多了,赶快把包收拾好。| *He didn't say much about it but I think his wife left him.* 他没有多说,但我认为是他妻子离开了他。| *Do you get much chance to travel in your job?* 你到外地公干的机会多吗? | *After much deliberation the judges awarded the prize to Miss Venezuela.* 经过反复研究,评委们把奖颁给了委内瑞拉小姐。| **how much?** *How much is the dress with the white collar?* 那件白领连衣裙多少钱? | **much of** *Much of the city was destroyed in the attack.* 在那次进攻中城市大部分被摧毁了。**2 so much/too much** used to talk about a particularly large amount of something, especially more than necessary 那么多的/太多的: *I think it would taste nicer if you didn't use so much salt.* 我想如果你不放那么多的盐,味道会更好。| *There was too much work for one person.* 工作太多了,一个人干不了。| **far/much etc too much** *Easy on the gin! You've put in much too much!* 少搁点杜松子酒吧!你已经加得过量了!**3 not much** mean that something is not important, interesting, worthy etc 并不那么〔重要、有趣、有价值等〕: *The car may not be much to look at but it's very reliable.* 这辆汽车也许看上去不怎么样,但很靠得住。| *Spend the vacation decorating? I don't think much of that idea.* 把假期用在装修上?我认为那并不是个好主意。| *I think we should leave. There's nothing much we can do to help.* 我想我们该走了,我们帮不了多大忙。| *The sequel was slightly better than the first movie but that's not saying much.* 这部影片的续集比第一部略好,但这并不是说续集就一定好。**4 not be up to much** *spoken especially BrE* to be fairly bad【口,尤英】很糟糕: *The restaurant's very grand but the food isn't up to much.* 那饭店很气派,但饭菜却非常糟糕。**5 not be much of a dancer/swimmer etc** to not be a good dancer, swimmer etc 不怎么会跳舞/游泳等: *Greg's not much of a footballer but you can't fault his motivation.* 格雷格不太会踢足球,但他态度积极,无可挑剔。**6 it was as much as I/she etc could do** used to say that someone could only just manage to do something 我/她等尽最大努力也只能如此: *He looked so absurd, it was as much as I could do to keep a straight face.* 他看起来非常滑稽,我尽了最大努力才忍着没笑出来。**7 be too much for sb** to be too difficult for someone to do 非某人力所能及: *Climbing the stairs is too much for her now that she's in her 90s.* 她九十多岁了,爬不动楼梯了。**8 think/say etc as much** to think or say what you have just mentioned 也这样认为/说等: *She believed that the company should abandon such a risky proposal and said as much at the meeting.* 她认为公司应该放弃这样一个有风险的计划,她在会上也这么说的。**9 make much of sb/sth a)** to treat information, a situation etc as though you think it is very important or serious 重视[认真对待]某人/某物: *The press didn't make as much of the discovery as they might have done.* 新闻界没有像本该做到的那样对这个发现大大宣传一番。**b)** to think that something is very good or very impressive 高度评价: *I didn't make much of her latest novel.* 我对她最新写的小说不敢恭维。**c)** to treat someone very kindly because you like them a lot 疼爱,溺爱: *A childless couple, they*

always made much of their nephews and nieces. 那对夫妇没有子女，总是宠爱他们的侄子和侄女。**10 not/without so much as** used when you are surprised or annoyed that someone did not do something 甚至没有，连…都没有: *He left without so much as saying goodbye.* 他甚至连一声"再见"也没说就走了。| *Sonia didn't so much as thank her for her help.* 对她的帮助，索尼娅甚至连谢都没谢。**11 I'll say this/that much for** used to praise someone or something when they are being criticized a lot 我只能为…这么说，起码〔用以赞扬正遭受批评的人或事〕: *I'll say this much for Fiona – she has plenty of spirit!* 关于菲奥娜我只能这么说——起码她勇气十足！**12 so much for** used to say that it was not worth using something because it had little effect, it was useless etc …到此为止; …就谈这些; …只好作罢: *So much for worrying she'd be lonely – she's having a party tonight!* 别再担心她会寂寞了——今晚她有聚会呢！**13 as much again** the same amount or number as the one mentioned before〔和前面提到的数量〕一样多，同样多: *The car only cost me £500 but it cost as much again to get it insured.* 那辆汽车只花了我500英镑，但买保险也花了同样多的钱。

Much A·do A·bout Noth·ing /ˌ· · ˌ· · ˈ· ·/ a humorous play by William Shakespeare. People sometimes use the title as a phrase to describe a situation in which there has been a lot of excitement about something that is not really important.《无事生非》〔威廉·莎士比亚的一部喜剧。人们有时借用这一剧名来形容为无关紧要的小事而异常兴奋的情形〕

much-her·ald·ed /ˌ·ˈ···◂/ *adj* [only before noun 仅用于名词前] talked about a lot before it actually appears〔出现之前〕被广为谈论的; 被看好的: *Ford's much-heralded new family saloon* 人们十分看好的福特新款家用轿车

much·ness /ˈmʌtʃnɪs; ˈmʌtʃnəs/ *n* **be much of a muchness** *BrE informal* to be very similar【英，非正式】很相像，差不多: *It was hard to choose between the candidates – they were all much of a muchness.* 很难在候选人之间作选择——他们各方面都不相上下。

mu·ci·lage /ˈmjuslɪdʒ; ˈmjuːsəlɪdʒ/ *n* [U] a sticky liquid obtained from plants and used as a glue〔从植物中提取的〕黏液，黏胶 —**mucilaginous** /ˌmjusˈlædʒɪnəs; ˌmjuːsəˈlædʒənəs/ *adj*: *the mucilaginous fruit of the okra plant* 含黏液的秋葵果

muck[1] /mʌk; mʌk/ *n* [U] *informal*【非正式】**1** *especially BrE* something such as dirt, mud, or another sticky substance that makes something dirty【尤英】污物，污秽: *Come on, let's wipe that muck off your face.* 过来，让我们把你脸上的脏东西擦掉。**2** *BrE* waste matter from animals, especially waste matter that is put on land to make plants grow better【英】粪便; 粪肥: *dog muck* 狗粪 | *They were shovelling muck onto the fields.* 他们在把粪肥铲到田里去。**3** something that is unpleasant or of very bad quality 令人讨厌的东西; 劣质的东西: *How can you eat that muck? It looks disgusting.* 你怎么能吃那玩意儿？看着就令人恶心。| *All that paper ever prints is muck about people's sex lives.* 那张报纸刊登的尽是些关于人们性生活的令人作呕的东西。**4 as common as muck** *BrE old-fashioned* an insulting way of describing someone of a low social class【英，过时】举止粗俗; 没有教养〔对低层社会的人的侮辱性用语〕

muck[2] *v*

muck about/around *phr v BrE informal*【英，非正式】**1** [I] to behave in a silly way, especially when you should be working or paying attention to something; mess around (MESS[2]) 胡闹; 鬼混; 闲荡: *Stop mucking about and listen!* 别再胡闹了，好好听着！| *We spent the days mucking around on the beach.* 那些日子我们在海滩闲荡。**2** [T **muck** sb/sth **about/around**] to cause trouble and inconvenience for someone, especially by changing your mind a lot; mess around (MESS[2]) 耍弄〔某人〕; 瞎弄〔某物〕: *The travel agent has really been mucking me around over this holiday.* 这次休假，旅行社实在是耍弄我。

muck in *phr v* [I] *BrE informal*【英，非正式】**1** to work together with other people in order to get a job done; pitch in (PITCH[2]) 一起出力，一起干活; 参加: *Oh, stop moaning – we've all got to muck in!* 喂，别再抱怨了，我们都得干！**2** to share things with other people 分享: *We're a bit short of space. Do you mind mucking in with the other boys?* 我们地方不够，你和其他男孩子共用一处好吗？

muck sth ↔ **out** *phr v* [I,T] to clean the place where an animal lives 打扫〔牲畜棚〕: *to muck out the stables* 打扫马厩

muck sth ↔ **up** *phr v* [T] *BrE informal*【英，非正式】**1** to do something wrong or badly, so that you fail to achieve something 弄糟; 弄砸: *I really mucked up those last two exams.* 最后两门考试我确实考砸了。**2** to spoil something, especially an arrangement or plan 破坏，打乱〔尤指安排或计划〕: *The bad weather mucked up our plans for a picnic.* 坏天气打乱了我们的野餐计划。**3** to make something dirty 弄脏: *Don't muck up your shirt.* 别把你的衬衫弄脏了。

muck·heap /ˈmʌkˌhip; ˈmʌkhiːp/ *n* [C] *BrE* a pile of MANURE (=animal waste matter) in a farmyard【英】厩肥堆，粪堆

muck·rak·ing /ˈmʌkˌrekɪŋ; ˈmʌk-reɪkɪŋ/ *n* [U] the practice of telling or writing unpleasant and perhaps untrue stories about people's private lives, especially famous people 收集和披露〔尤指名人的〕隐私: *low quality magazines specializing in muckraking* 专门揭人隐私的低级杂志 —**muckraking** *adj* —**muckraker** *n* [C]

muck·spread·er /ˈmʌksprɛdə; ˈmʌkspredə/ *n* [C] *BrE* a machine used on a farm to spread MANURE (=animal waste matter) onto farm land【英】施粪肥机，粪肥撒播机 —**muck-spreading** *n* [U]

muck·y /ˈmʌkɪ; ˈmʌki/ *adj BrE informal*【英，非正式】**1** dirty, for example with mud or oil 肮脏的: *Your hands are all mucky.* 你的手肮脏不堪。**2** a mucky joke or story etc is slightly rude and about sex〔笑话等〕粗俗的，下流的 **3** mucky weather is cold and wet〔天气〕寒冷潮湿的

mu·cous mem·brane /ˌmjukəs ˈmɛmbren; ˌmjuːkəs ˈmembreɪn/ *n* [C] the thin surface that covers certain inner parts of the body, such as the inside of the nose, and produces mucus 黏膜

mu·cus /ˈmjukəs; ˈmjuːkəs/ *n* [U] a liquid produced in parts of your body such as your nose〔人体分泌的〕黏液〈如鼻涕〉—**mucous** *adj*

mud /mʌd; mʌd/ *n* [U] **1** wet earth that has become soft and sticky 泥，烂泥: *His shoes were covered with mud.* 他的鞋沾满了烂泥。**2 your name is mud** *spoken* if your name is mud, people are annoyed with you because you have caused trouble【口】某人名声扫地: *His name is mud in the office after what happened.* 那事发生之后，他在办公室里的名声就臭了。**3** earth used for building〔建筑用的〕泥土: *a mud hut* 一座小土屋 **4 here's mud in your eye** *spoken old-fashioned* used for expressing good wishes when having a drink with someone; CHEERS (1)【口，过时】祝您健康; 干杯 —see also 另见 **as clear as mud** (CLEAR[1] (19))

mud·bath /ˈmʌdbæθ; ˈmʌdbɑːθ/ *n* **1** [C] a health treatment in which heated mud is put onto your body, used especially to reduce pain 泥浴，泥疗 **2** [singular] a large area of mud 泥淖: *Heavy rain had turned the playing field into a mudbath.* 大雨把运动场变成了一片烂泥场。

mud·dle[1] /ˈmʌdl; ˈmʌdl/ *n* [C usually singular 一般用单数] **1** a state of confusion or untidiness, that results in things being done wrong 混乱，杂乱: *There was a bit of a muddle over our reservations.* 我们所作的预订有点混乱。| *We had to get an accountant in to sort out the muddle.* 我们不得不请了个会计，整理那些乱糟糟的账目。**2 be in a muddle a)** to be in an untidy and confused state 处于混乱状态，凌乱不堪: *The papers were all in a muddle.* 文件一团糟。**b)** to be confused because you have too much to do〔因事情多而〕糊涂: *I'm in such a muddle, I'd completely forgotten you were coming today.* 我真糊涂透了，我完全忘了你今天要来。

muddle[2] *v* also 又作 **muddle up** [T] *especially BrE*【尤英】**1** to put something in the wrong order or mix something up 弄乱，弄混: *Someone's muddled up all the papers on my desk.* 有人把我桌子上的文件全都弄乱了。| *Your invoice got muddled up with Mr Clark's.* 你的发票和克拉克先生的发票弄混了。**2 get muddled (up)** to get confused between one thing or person and another, and make a mistake 被弄糊涂: *Sorry, I got a bit muddled up over the dates.* 对不起，我被这些日期弄得有点糊涂了。| **get sb/sth muddled (up)** *I'm not quite sure of their ages, I get them muddled up.* 我对他们的年龄说不太准，我把他们弄混了。—**muddled** *adj*: *muddled thinking* 混乱的思维 —**muddling** *adj*

muddle along/on *phr v* [I] *BrE* to continue doing something without having any clear plan【英】混日子，得过且过; 胡乱地干下去: *We just seem to muddle along but never make any real progress.* 我们好像只是在混日子，却从来没有取得任何真正的进展。

muddle through *phr v* [I] *especially BrE* to achieve something even though you do not have a clear plan or use the best methods or equipment【尤英】胡乱应付过去: *Jack got some difficult questions but he managed to muddle through.* 杰克遇上了一些难题，但他设法稀里糊涂地应付过去了。

muddle-head·ed /ˌ··ˈ··◂/ *adj BrE* confused or not able to think clearly【英】糊涂的，头脑混乱的 —**muddle-headedness** *n* [U]

mud·dy[1] /ˈmʌdɪ; ˈmʌdi/ *adj* **muddier, muddiest 1** covered with mud or containing mud 沾满泥的; 泥泞的，多泥的: *the muddy banks of the river* 泥泞的河岸 | *Take your boots off out-*

M

side if they're muddy. 如果你的靴子沾满污泥，就在门外脱掉。**2** colours that are muddy are dull〔颜色〕不亮的，暗的 **3** confused and not clear 糊涂的，混乱的；不清晰的：*muddy thinking* 混乱的思维 —**muddiness** *n* [U]

muddy² *v* **muddied, muddying** [T] **1** to make something dirty with mud 使…沾上泥污：*She was taking care not to muddy her new shoes.* 她小心翼翼地走，不让新鞋沾上污泥。**2 muddy the waters/the issue** to make things more complicated or confusing in a situation that was simple before 把水搅浑，使事情[问题]更加复杂

mud·flap /ˋmʌdflæp; ˈmʌdflæp/ *n* [C] *BrE* a piece of rubber that hangs behind the wheel of a vehicle to prevent mud from flying up【英】〔车轮后的〕挡泥胶皮，挡泥板；SPLASH GUARD *AmE*【美】—see picture on page A2 参见 A2 页图

mud·flat /ˋmʌdflæt; ˈmʌdflæt/ *n* [C often plural 常用复数] **1** an area of muddy land, covered by the sea when it comes up at HIGH TIDE and uncovered when it goes down at LOW TIDE〔落潮时露出、涨潮时隐没的〕泥滩，潮泥滩 **2** *AmE* the muddy bottom of a dry lake【美】〔湖泊干涸后的〕泥床，泥底

mud·guard /ˋmʌdˌgɑrd; ˈmʌdgɑːd/ *n* [C] *BrE* a curved piece of metal or plastic over the wheel of a bicycle that prevents the mud from flying up【英】〔自行车的〕挡泥板；FENDER (4) *AmE*【美】—see picture at 参见 BICYCLE[1] 图

mud·pack /ˋmʌdˌpæk; ˈmʌdpæk/ *n* [C] a soft mixture containing clay that you spread over your face and leave there for a short time to improve your skin〔化妆或治疗的〕泥膏

mud pie /ˌ·ˈ·/ *n* [C] a little ball of wet mud made by children as a game〔儿童捏着玩的〕小泥饼

mud·sling·ing /ˋmʌdslɪŋɪŋ; ˈmʌdslɪŋɪŋ/ *n* [U] the practice of saying bad and often untrue things about someone in order to make other people have a low opinion of them 诽谤，中伤：*There has been a lot of political mudslinging in the battle for votes.* 在选票争夺战中出现了大量的政治诽谤。—**mudslinger** *n* [C]

Muenster /ˋmʌnstɚ; ˈmʌnstə/ a fairly soft cheese that does not have a strong taste 门斯特干酪〔一种质地非常柔软、味道清淡的法国乳酪〕

mues·li /ˋmjuzlɪ; ˈmjuːzli/ *n* [U] grains, nuts, and dried fruits, mixed together and eaten with milk as a breakfast food 穆兹利，干果全谷片〔一种把碾碎的谷物、坚果、干果混合后搀入牛奶吃的早餐食品〕；GRANOLA *AmE*【美】

mu·ez·zin /mjuˋɛzɪn; muːˈezɪn/ *n* [C] a man who calls Muslims to prayer from a MOSQUE 宣礼员〔清真寺中召唤信徒做礼拜的人〕

muff¹ /mʌf; mʌf/ *n* [C] a short tube of thick cloth or fur that you can put your hands into to keep them warm in cold weather〔御寒用的〕手笼，手筒 —see also 另见 EARMUFFS

muff² *v* [T] **1** also 又作 **muff up** *informal* to spoil a chance to do something well【非正式】错过〔机会等〕；把…弄糟：*I wanted to impress her with my efficiency but I muffed it up.* 我想让她对我的办事效率留个好印象，但是我把事情搞砸了。**2 muff a catch/muff it** to fail to catch or hold a ball in a game or sport 漏接球，接球失误

muf·fin /ˋmʌfɪn; ˈmʌfɪn/ *n* [C] **1** *BrE* a small thick round kind of bread, usually eaten hot with butter【英】〔通常涂黄油趁热吃的〕英式松饼；ENGLISH MUFFIN *AmE*【美】**2** *AmE* a small usually sweet cake that sometimes has bits of fruit in it【美】松饼：*blueberry muffins* 蓝莓松饼

muf·fle /ˋmʌfl; ˈmʌfəl/ *v* [T usually passive 一般用被动态] **1** to make a sound less loud and clear 使〔声音〕减弱[低沉]：*The falling snow muffled the noise of the traffic.* 纷纷飘落的雪花减弱了车辆的噪音。**2** also 又作 **muffle up** to cover yourself with something thick and warm〔用保暖的衣物〕裹住：*He went out into the snow muffled up in his scarf and thick overcoat.* 他用围巾和厚大衣把自己裹得严严实实，走进雪中。

muf·fled /ˋmʌfld; ˈmʌfəld/ *adj* muffled sounds or voices cannot be heard clearly, for example because they come from behind a door or wall〔声音因隔着门或墙等〕听不清楚的：*I heard the muffled thump of a car door slamming.* 我隐隐约约听到了关汽车门的声音。| *Muffled voices could be heard in the next room.* 能听到隔壁房间里隐隐约约的说话声。

muf·fler /ˋmʌflɚ; ˈmʌflə/ *n* [C] **1** a thick long piece of cloth worn to keep your neck warm 厚围巾 **2** *AmE* SILENCER (2)【美】〔汽车引擎的〕消音器，灭声器

muf·ti /ˋmʌftɪ; ˈmʌfti/ *n* **1 in mufti** *old-fashioned* wearing ordinary clothes instead of a uniform【过时】穿着便服：*soldiers in mufti* 穿着便服的士兵 **2** [C] someone who officially explains Muslim law 穆夫提〔解释伊斯兰教法典的神职人员〕

mug¹ /mʌg; mʌg/ *n* [C] **1** a large cup with straight sides used for drinking tea, coffee etc〔喝茶或咖啡等用的〕圆筒形有柄大杯 —see picture at 参见 CUP[1] 图 **2** a large glass with straight sides and a handle, used especially for drinking beer〔尤指喝啤酒用的〕圆筒形有柄大玻璃杯：*rugby players swilling mugs of beer at the bar* 在酒吧里用大杯畅饮啤酒的橄榄球运动员 **3** also 又作 **mugful** a mug and the liquid inside it 一大杯（的量）：*Two mugs of tea, please.* 请来两大杯茶。**4** *BrE spoken* someone who is stupid and easy to deceive【英口】易上当受骗的傻瓜：*I expect they'll find some poor mug to buy their car.* 我预料他们会找到某个可怜的傻瓜买他们的汽车。**5** *spoken* a face【口】脸：*What an ugly mug!* 多丑陋的一张脸！**6 a mug's game** *BrE spoken* something that is not likely to be successful or profitable【英口】不易成功的事；无利可图的事：*Gambling is a mug's game, Jonah.* 乔纳，赌博是赌不来钱的。

mug² *v* **mugged, mugging** **1** [T] to attack someone and rob them in a public place〔在公共场所〕行凶抢劫：*A lot of people won't go out alone at night for fear of being mugged.* 许多人因害怕被抢劫，晚上不愿单独出门。**2** [I] *AmE informl* to make silly expressions with your face or behave in a silly way, especially in a photograph or a play【美，非正式】〔尤指照相或演出时〕做鬼脸，扮傻相：*Scotty's always mugging for the camera.* 斯科蒂照相时总是扮鬼脸。

mug up *phr v* [I,T] *BrE informal* to study something very hard, especially when preparing for an exam【英，非正式】〔尤指为准备考试而〕用功，攻读：**mug sth ↔ up** *He's got to mug up some facts about pollution.* 他不得不拼命死记一些有关污染的情况。| [+on] *She's mugging up on Racine for her French paper.* 她正在为撰写她的法语论文而攻读拉辛的作品。

mug·ger /ˋmʌgɚ; ˈmʌgə/ *n* [C] someone who attacks people and robs them in a public place〔在公共场所的〕行凶抢劫者

mug·ging /ˋmʌgɪŋ; ˈmʌgɪŋ/ *n* [C,U] an attack on someone in which they are robbed in a public place〔在公共场所的〕行凶抢劫：*There has been an increase in muggings in the park.* 公园里的抢劫案件增多了。

mug·gins /ˋmʌgɪnz; ˈmʌgɪnz/ *n* [singular] *spoken BrE* used jokingly to mean yourself, when you know you have been stupid and let other people treat you unfairly【英口】傻瓜，笨蛋〔用于自嘲〕：*Everyone disappeared after supper, leaving muggins here to do the washing-up.* 晚饭后大家都走了，把我这个傻子留在这儿洗碗。

mug·gy /ˋmʌgɪ; ˈmʌgi/ *adj* **muggier, muggiest** *informal* muggy weather is unpleasantly warm and the air seems wet【非正式】〔天气〕闷热的：*The air was muggy and damp, threatening a storm later.* 空气闷热而潮湿，预示着暴风雨即将来临。—**mugginess** *n* [U]

mug·shot /ˋmʌgʃɑt; ˈmʌgʃɒt/ *n* [C] *informal* a photograph of a criminal's face, taken by the police【非正式】〔警方拍摄的〕犯人面部照片：*Can you look through some mugshots to identify the man who attacked you?* 你能从这些照片辨认出袭击你的那个男子吗？

Mu·ham·mad /muˋhæməd; mʊˈhæmɪd/ also 又作 **Mohammed** (?570-632) an Arab holy man, born in Mecca, who started the religion of Islam and is its most important PROPHET (=someone who has been sent by God to lead people and teach them). The things that God told him were later written down to form the holy book called the Koran. When Muslim people mention Muhammad's name, they usually add the words 'peace be upon him' in order to show their respect. 穆罕默德〔(?570-632)，阿拉伯圣人，生于麦加。他创立了伊斯兰教，是伊斯兰教中最重要的先知。他把上帝对他的启示记下来汇编成圣书，称《古兰经》。每当穆斯林提到穆罕默德的名字，通常都要随口说出“愿他安详”的字句，以示敬意〕

Muhammad, El·i·jah /ɪˋlaɪdʒə; ɪˈlaɪdʒə/ (1897-1975) a US black man who was the leader of the Black Muslims from the late 1930s until his death 穆罕默德〔(1897-1975)，“黑人穆斯林”领袖，20 世纪 30 年代末开始任职直至去世〕

Mu·ham·ma·dan /muˋhæmədən; mʊˈhæmɪdən/ *n, adj old-fashioned* a word meaning Muslim, now considered offensive by most Muslims【过时】穆斯林（的），伊斯兰教信徒（的），回教徒（的）〔现在大多数穆斯林认为此词具冒犯性〕—**Muhammadanism** *n* [U]

mu·ja·hed·din /ˌmudʒəhɛˋdin; ˌmuːdʒəheˈdiːn/ *n* [plural] Muslim soldiers with strong religious beliefs〔具有强烈宗教信仰的〕穆斯林士兵

muk·luks /ˋmʌklʌks; ˈmʌklʌks/ *n* [plural] *AmE* boots made of animal skin with a thick bottom, used for walking in snow【美】〔厚底〕雪地兽皮靴

mu·lat·to /məˋlæto; mjuːˈlætəʊ/ *n* [C] an insulting word for someone with one black parent and one white parent 穆拉托人〔侮辱性用语，指黑人与白人的混血儿〕

mul·ber·ry /ˋmʌlˏbɛrɪ; ˈmʌlbəri/ *n* **1** [C] a dark purple fruit that can be eaten, or the tree on which this fruit grows 桑椹; 桑树 **2** [U] the dark purple colour of these fruit 桑椹色, 深紫红色

mulch¹ /mʌltʃ; mʌltʃ/ *n* [singular] decaying leaves that are put on the soil to improve its quality, to protect the roots of plants, and to stop WEEDS (=unwanted plants) growing〔为改良土壤、护根及阻止杂草生长而覆在地表上的〕腐叶, 覆盖料

mulch² *v* [T] to cover the ground with a mulch 用腐叶覆盖〔地面〕

mule /mjul; mjuːl/ *n* [C] **1** an animal that has a DONKEY and a horse as parents 骡, 骡子 **2** [usually plural 一般用复数] a shoe or SLIPPER without a back, that has a piece of material across the toes to hold it on your foot 夹趾拖鞋 **3** *slang* someone who brings illegal drugs into a country by hiding them on or in their body【俚】〔体内〕携带毒品走私的人 —see also 另见 **stubborn as a mule** (STUBBORN (1))

mu·le·teer /ˏmjuləˋtɪr; ˌmjuːlɪˈtɪə/ also 又作 **mule·skin·ner** *AmE*【美】/ˋmjulskɪnɚ; ˈmjuːlskɪnə/ —*n* [C] someone who leads mules 赶骡人, 骡夫

mul·ish /ˋmjulɪʃ; ˈmjuːlɪʃ/ *adj* refusing to do something or agree to something in an unreasonable way; STUBBORN 固执的, 执拗的, 犟的: *mulish obstinacy* 骡子般的倔强, 顽固透顶 —**mulishly** *adv* —**mulishness** *n* [U]

Mull also 又作 **the Isle of Mull** a large island off the west coast of Scotland, the largest island in the Inner Hebrides. It is often visited by tourists, especially in summer. 马尔岛〔与苏格兰西海岸隔海相望的一座大岛, 内赫布里底群岛的最大岛屿。游客众多, 夏天尤其如此〕

mull¹ /mʌl; mʌl/ *v* [T] to heat wine or beer with sugar and SPICES 将〔葡萄酒或啤酒〕放糖和香料后加热

mull sth ↔**over** *phr v* [T] to think about a problem, plan etc and consider it for a long time 仔细考虑〔问题、计划等〕, 反复思考: *Victor mulled over the idea and finally decided that it made sense.* 维克托仔细考虑了那个想法, 最后认为它很合理。

mull² *n* [C] *ScotE* an area of land that sticks out into the sea; PROMONTORY【苏格兰】岬, 海角: *Mull of Kintyre* 金泰尔角

mul·lah /ˋmʌlə; ˈmʌlə/ *n* [C] a Muslim teacher of law and religion 毛拉〔伊斯兰法律及宗教教师〕

mulled wine /ˏ· ˈ·/ *n* [U] wine that has been heated with sugar and SPICES〔放糖和香料后加热而成的〕香甜热葡萄酒: *mulled wine with lots of cloves and cinnamon* 加了大量干丁香花苞和桂皮香料的香甜热葡萄酒

mul·let /ˋmʌlɪt; ˈmʌlɪ̈t/ *n* [C] a fairly small sea fish that can be eaten 鲻(鱼)〔一种可食用的小海鱼〕

mul·li·ga·taw·ny /ˏmʌlɪgəˋtɔnɪ; ˌmʌlɪgəˈtɔːni/ *n* [U] a soup that tastes hot because it contains hot SPICES 咖喱肉汤

mul·lion /ˋmʌljən; ˈmʌljən/ *n* [C] a piece of stone, metal, or wood that divides a window between the glass parts〔分隔窗扇的〕直棂, 竖框 —**mullioned** *adj*: *mullioned windows* 有直棂的窗

multi- /mʌltɪ; mʌltɪ̈/ *prefix* more than one; many 多于一的; 多的: *multicoloured* (=with many colours) 多色的 | *a multistorey office block* 多层写字楼

mul·ti·choice /ˋmʌltɪtʃɔɪs; ˈmʌltitʃɔɪs/ *adj* MULTIPLE CHOICE〔试题〕多项选择的

mul·ti·col·oured *BrE*【英】, **multicolored** *AmE*【美】/ˋmʌltɪˏkʌlɚd; ˈmʌltiˌkʌləd/ *adj* having many different colours 有多种不同颜色的, 杂色的: *a multicoloured sweatshirt* 杂色的圆领长袖运动衫

mul·ti·cul·tur·al /ˏmʌltɪˋkʌltʃərəl; ˌmʌltiˈkʌltʃərəl◂/ *adj* involving or including people or ideas from several different countries, races, or religions 多种文化的; 融合[具有]多种文化的: *a multicultural society* 融合多种文化的社会

mul·ti·cul·tu·ral·is·m /ˏmʌltɪˋkʌltʃərəlɪzəm; ˌmʌltiˈkʌltʃərəlɪzəm/ *n* [U] the belief that it is important and good to include people or ideas from many different countries, races, or religions 多元文化论 —**multiculturalist** *n* [C]

multi-faith /ˏ·· ˈ·◂/ *adj* [only before noun 仅用于名词前] including or involving people from several different religious groups 包括[涉及]不同宗教团体的: *a multi-faith service of thanksgiving* 由信仰不同宗教的人参加的感恩祈祷仪式

mul·ti·far·i·ous /ˏmʌltəˋfɛrɪəs; ˌmʌltɪ̈ˈfeəriəs◂/ *adj* of very many different kinds 多种多样的, 五花八门的: *her multifarious business activities* 她的种种商业活动 —**multifariously** *adv* —**multifariousness** *n* [U]

multi-func·tion /ˏ·· ˈ··◂/ **multi-func·tion·al** /ˏ·· ˈ···◂/ *adj* [only before noun 仅用于名词前] a multi-function machine, piece of equipment, building etc is designed to have several different uses〔机器、设备、建筑等〕多功能的, 起多种作用的

mul·ti·lat·e·ral /ˏmʌltɪˋlætərəl; ˌmʌltɪˈlætərəl◂/ *adj* **multilateral agreements/trade etc** agreements, trade etc that involve the governments of several different countries 多边协议/贸易等 —compare 比较 BILATERAL, UNILATERAL —**multilaterally** *adv*

mul·ti·lin·gual /ˏmʌltɪˋlɪŋgwəl; ˌmʌltɪˈlɪŋgwəl◂/ *adj* **1** able to speak several different languages 会说数种语言的: *a multilingual secretary* 会说好几种语言的秘书 **2** written in several different languages 用数种语言写的: *a multilingual phrasebook covering English, French, German, and Italian* 包括英语、法语、德语和意大利语的多语种常用语手册 —compare 比较 BILINGUAL, MONOLINGUAL —**multilingualism** *n* [U]

mul·ti·me·di·a /ˏmʌltɪˋmidɪə; ˌmʌltiˈmiːdiə◂/ *adj* [only before noun 仅用于名词前] using a mixture of sound, pictures, film, and writing to give information, especially with computers 多媒体的: *Encarta, the latest multimedia encyclopedia* 最新的多媒体百科全书《恩卡特》—**multimedia** *n* [U]

mul·ti·mil·lion /ˏmʌltəˋmɪljən; ˌmʌltiˈmɪljən◂/ *adj* **multimillion-pound/multimillion-dollar etc** worth or costing many millions of pounds, dollars etc〔值或花费〕数百万英镑/美元等的: *Gascoigne's multimillion-pound move to Lazio* 加斯科因以数百万英镑的身价转会到拉齐奥

mul·ti·mil·lio·naire /ˏmʌltəˏmɪljənˋɛr; ˌmʌltɪˌmɪljəˈneə/ *n* [C] an extremely rich person, who has many millions of pounds or dollars 大富豪, 巨富, 千万富翁

mul·ti·na·tion·al¹ /ˏmʌltɪˋnæʃənḷ; ˌmʌltɪˈnæʃənəl◂/ *adj* **1** a multinational company has factories, offices, and business activities in many different countries〔公司〕跨国的, 在多国经营的: *a multinational motor-manufacturing corporation* 跨国汽车制造公司 **2** involving people from several countries 由多个国家的人组成的, 多国的: *a multinational force sponsored by the UN* 由联合国提供经费的多国部队 —**multinationally** *adv*

multinational² *n* [C] a large company that has offices, factories etc in many different countries 跨国公司: *a giant food multinational* 庞大的跨国食品公司 | *the growth of the multinationals* 跨国公司的增长

mul·ti·ple¹ /ˋmʌltəpḷ; ˈmʌltɪ̈pəl/ *adj* including or involving many things, people, events etc 包括[涉及]多个人[物, 事件等]的; 多的; 多种的: **multiple injuries/burns** *Baxter was rushed to the hospital with multiple stab wounds.* 巴克斯特因多处刺伤被急速送进了医院。| **multiple collision/crash/accident** (=an accident involving many cars) 连环撞车事故 | **multiple birth** (=an occasion when several babies are born to the same mother at the same time) 多胎产

multiple² *n* [C] **1** a number that contains a smaller number an exact number of times〔数学中的〕倍数: *20 is a multiple of 5.* 20是5的倍数。—see also 另见 LOWEST COMMON MULTIPLE **2** a multiple store 连锁商店

multiple choice /ˏ··· ˈ·◂/ *adj* a multiple choice examination or question shows several possible answers and you have to choose the correct one〔试题〕多项选择的

multiple scle·ro·sis /ˏ··· ·ˈ··/ also 又作 **MS** —*n* [U] a serious illness that gradually destroys your nerves making you weak and unable to walk, often involving weakening eyesight and slow speech 多发性硬化(症)

multiple store /ˏ··· ˈ·/ *n* [C] *BrE* a word used especially in business meaning a CHAIN STORE【英】连锁商店

mul·ti·plex /ˋmʌltəˏplɛks; ˈmʌltɪ̈pleks/ *adj* **1** a multiplex cinema shows several different films at the same time〔电影院〕同时放映多部电影的, 多放映场的 **2** *technical* having several different parts【术语】复合的

mul·ti·pli·ca·tion /ˏmʌltəpləˋkeʃən; ˌmʌltɪ̈plɪ̈ˈkeɪʃən/ *n* [U] **1** a method of calculating in which you add the same number to itself a particular number of times 乘法; 乘法运算 **2** *formal* a large increase in the size or number of something【正式】〔大量〕增加; 增多: *the multiplication in the number of claim forms that have to be filled out* 需要填写的索赔表格数量激增

multiplication sign /ˏ··ˈ·· ·/ *n* [C] a sign (×) showing that one number is multiplied by another 乘号(×) —see picture at 参见 MATHEMATICS 图

multiplication ta·ble /ˏ··ˈ·· ˏ··/ *n* [C] a list showing the result of numbers between one and twelve that have been multiplied together, used by children in schools 乘法表

mul·ti·pli·ci·ty /ˏmʌltəˋplɪsətɪ; ˌmʌltɪ̈ˈplɪsɪ̈ti/ *n* [C,U] a large number or great variety of things 多, 大量; 多种多样, 多样性: [+of] *the baffling multiplicity of courses available to language students* 学语言的学生可以选修的课程多得叫人不知选哪门好

mul·ti·ply /ˋmʌltəˏplaɪ; ˈmʌltɪ̈plaɪ/ *v* **1** [I,T] to increase greatly or make something increase greatly (使)大大增加: *Our chances*

M

of success had multiplied several times over. 我们成功的机会已增加了好几倍。| *This vast stock of computerized images has multiplied the possibilities open to the artist.* 这一庞大的电脑图像库极大地增加了艺术家的创作潜力。**2** [I,T] to do a calculation in which you add a number to itself a particular number of times 乘, 乘以: **multiply sth by sth** *3 multiplied by 4 is 12.* 3乘以4等于12。—compare 比较 DIVIDE[1] (4) **3** [I] to breed 繁殖: *The bugs can easily multiply to give a nasty bout of food poisoning.* 这些病菌繁殖迅速, 容易引发严重的食物中毒。

mul·ti·pur·pose /ˌmʌltɪˋpɝpəs; ˌmʌltiˈpɜːpəs◂/ *adj* a multipurpose tool, building etc is designed to be used for many different purposes〔工具、建筑等〕多用途的, 通用的

mul·ti·ra·cial /ˌmʌltɪˋreʃəl; ˌmʌltɪˈreɪʃəl◂/ *adj* including or involving several different races of people 多种族的: *a multiracial society* 多种族的社会

multi-sto·rey[1] /ˌ‥ˋ‥◂/ *adj* [only before noun 仅用于名词前] *BrE* a multi-storey building has many levels or floors【英】〔建筑物〕多层的

multi-storey[2] *n* [C] *BrE spoken* a multi-storey CAR PARK【英口】多层停车场

mul·ti·tude /ˋmʌltəˌtud; ˈmʌltɪ̆tjuːd/ *n* [C] **1 a multitude of** *formal or literary* a very large number of people or things【正式或文】众多, 大量; 大批, 大群: *The captain sat before a multitude of dials and levers.* 船长坐在一大堆仪表盘和操纵杆前面。| *a multitude of possible interpretations* 种种可能的解释 **2 the multitude a)** ordinary people, especially when they are thought of as not being very well educated 大众, 民众, 群众: *Political power has been placed in the hands of the multitude.* 政治权力已交到群众手中。**b)** *literary or biblical* a large crowd of people【文或圣经】一大群人 **3 cover/hide a multitude of sins** *especially humorous* to make faults or problems seem less clear or noticeable【尤幽默】掩盖种种错误[问题]

mul·ti·tu·di·nous /ˌmʌltəˋtudnəs; ˌmʌltɪ̆ˈtjuːdɪ̆nəs◂/ *adj formal* very many【正式】大量的, 众多的: *language in all its multitudinous forms* 形式多种多样的语言

mum[1] /mʌm; mʌm/ *n* [C] **1** *BrE* mother【英】妈妈; MOM *AmE*【美】**2 mum's the word** used to tell someone that they must not tell other people about a secret 别声张, 不要讲出去; 要保密: *Remember, mum's the word! I don't want anyone else finding out about this!* 记住, 千万别说出去! 我不想让其他任何人知道这事!

mum[2] *adj* **keep mum** *informal* to not tell anyone about a secret【非正式】保密

mum·ble /ˋmʌmbḷ; ˈmʌmbəl/ *v* **mumbled, mumbling** [I,T] to say something too quietly and not clearly enough, so that it is difficult or impossible to hear 咕哝, 含糊地说: *The little boy mumbled something about wanting to go to the toilet.* 那个小男孩咕咕哝哝地说要去厕所。| *Stop mumbling and speak up!* 别咕咕哝哝的, 大声说! —**mumbler** *n* [C] —**mumble** *n* [C]

mum·bo-jum·bo /ˋmʌmboˋdʒʌmbo; ˌmʌmbəʊ ˈdʒʌmbəʊ/ *n* [U] **1** talk or writing on a technical subject that is difficult to understand and seems to have no sense 晦涩难懂的文字; 莫名其妙的话: *Psychology books are often full of meaningless mumbo-jumbo.* 心理学书籍常常满篇都是毫无意义、晦涩难懂的语言。**2** religious beliefs or activities that seem without sense or meaning 莫名其妙的宗教信仰[活动]

mum·mer /ˋmʌmɚ; ˈmʌmə/ *n* [C] an actor in a simple traditional play without words 哑剧演员 —**mumming** *n* [U]

mum·mi·fy /ˋmʌmɪˌfaɪ; ˈmʌmɪfaɪ/ *v* [T] to preserve a dead body by putting special oils on it and wrapping it with cloth 将〔尸体〕制成木乃伊 —**mummification** /ˌmʌmɪfəˋkeʃən; ˌmʌmɪfɪ̆ˈkeɪʃən/ *n* [U]

mum·my /ˋmʌmɪ; ˈmʌmi/ *n* [C] **1** *BrE* a word meaning mother, used by or to young children【英】妈咪〔儿语〕; MOMMY *AmE*【美】**2** a dead body that has been preserved by wrapping it in cloth, expecially in ancient Egypt〔尤指古埃及的〕木乃伊

mummy 木乃伊

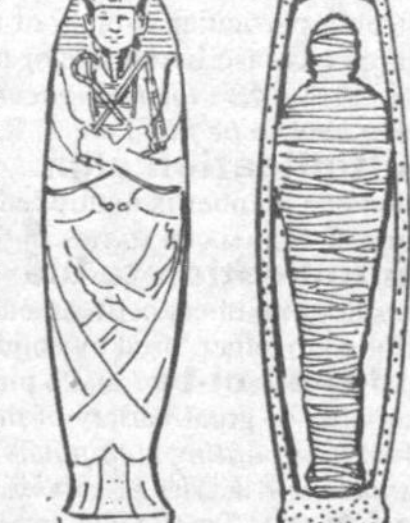

mummy's boy /ˈ‥ ˌ/ *n* [singular] *informal* a mother's boy (MOTHER[1] (3))【非正式】过分依赖母亲的男人[男孩]

mumps /mʌmps; mʌmps/ also 又作 **the mumps** *n* [U] an infectious illness which makes your neck swell and become painful, and is common among children 腮腺炎

mum-to-be /ˌ‥ˈ‥/ *n* [C] *BrE informal* a MOTHER-TO-BE【英, 非正式】准妈妈, 孕妇

munch /mʌntʃ; mʌntʃ/ *v* [I,T] to eat something noisily 出声地嚼; 用力嚼: *My father went on munching his toast.* 我爸爸继续大嚼他的烤面包片。| **[+on/at]** *She was busily munching on an apple.* 她正忙着咔哧咔哧地啃苹果。

Munch /mʊŋk; mʊŋk/, **Ed·vard** /ˋɛdvɑrd; ˈedvɑːd/ (1863-1944) a Norwegian painter whose most famous picture is *The Scream* 蒙克〔(1863-1944), 挪威画家, 以作品《呼喊》最为著名〕

munch·ies /ˋmʌntʃɪz; ˈmʌntʃiz/ *n* [plural] *informal*【非正式】**1 have the munchies** to feel hungry 感到饥饿 **2** small pieces of food, that you can eat with drinks at a party〔晚会上边喝饮料边吃的〕小片食品, 小吃

Munchkins 1 a group of very small people in the book and film *The Wizard of Oz*. 奥兹国人〔小说和电影《绿野仙踪》中的一群小矮人〕**2** unimportant people who work for a big organization 无名小卒; 无足轻重的人

mun·dane /ˋmʌnden; mʌnˈdeɪn/ *adj* **1** ordinary and uninteresting 平凡的; 平淡的; 乏味的: *Initially, the work was pretty mundane.* 刚开始, 该工作非常乏味。| *She led a mundane existence in the drab suburbs of Paris.* 她在巴黎了无生气的郊区过着一种平淡的生活。**2** *formal* concerned with ordinary daily life rather than religious matters; WORLDLY (3)【正式】世俗的; 尘世间的, 人世间的 —**mundaneness** *n* [U] —**mundanely** *adv*

mung bean /ˌmʌŋ ˋbin; ˌmʌŋ ˈbiːn/ *n* [C] a small green bean, usually eaten as a BEANSPROUT 绿豆

Mu·nich /ˋmjunɪk; ˈmjuːnɪk/ an industrial city in southern Germany, and the capital of the PROVINCE of Bavaria, whose German name is **München**. It has many attractive old buildings, and a famous beer festival takes place there every October. 慕尼黑〔德国南部一工业城市, 巴伐利亚州首府, 德语名为München。市区有许多漂亮的古建筑。每年10月在此举行的啤酒节十分有名〕

Munich A·gree·ment, the /ˌ‥ˈ‥/ the agreement signed in 1938 between Adolf Hitler from Germany, Mussolini from Italy, Daladier from France, and Neville Chamberlain from Britain. The agreement gave Germany part of Czechoslovakia, and the other countries hoped that this would prevent Hitler from trying to take control of any other areas of land. Chamberlain returned to Britain saying that the agreement would give "peace in our time". In fact, Hitler's army attacked Poland soon afterwards, and World War II began. 《慕尼黑协定》〔1938年德国的希特勒、意大利的墨索里尼、法国的达拉第和英国的张伯伦签订的一份协议。根据该协定, 捷克斯洛伐克向德国割让部分地区。其他几个国家希望这一做法可以阻止希特勒觊觎其他领土。张伯伦回到英国时曾说道, 这一协议将会带来"我们时代的和平"。但事实上希特勒的军队不久就进攻了波兰, 第二次世界大战由此爆发〕

mu·ni·ci·pal /mjuˋnɪsəpḷ; mjuːˈnɪsɪ̆pəl/ *adj* belonging to or concerned with the government of a town or city 市政府的; 市的; 市办的: *the municipal waste dump* 城市垃圾场 | *municipal elections* 市级选举 —**municipally** *adv*

mu·ni·ci·pal·i·ty /ˌmjunɪsəˋpælətɪ; mjuːˌnɪsɪ̆ˈpælɪ̆ti/ *n* [C] **1** a town, city, or other small area, which has its own government that makes decisions about local affairs 市, 自治市 **2** the government of a town, city etc, which makes decisions about local affairs 市政当局

mu·nif·i·cent /mjuˋnɪfəsnt; mjuːˈnɪfɪ̆sənt/ *adj formal* very generous【正式】慷慨的, 大方的: *a munificent gift* 丰厚的礼物 —**munificence** *n* [U]: *She thanked the committee for their munificence.* 她感谢委员会成员的慷慨。—**munificently** *adv*

mu·ni·tions /mjuˋnɪʃənz; mjuːˈnɪʃənz/ *n* [plural] military supplies such as bombs and large guns 军火〈如炸弹、大炮等〉: *a munitions factory* 兵工厂 —**munition** *adj* [only before noun 仅用于名词前]: *munition workers* 兵工厂的工人

Munro /mənˋro; mənˈrəʊ/ *n* [C] *BrE* one of the 277 mountains in Scotland that are 3000 feet high or higher. The word is used by people who climb mountains as a sport.【英】缪若〔苏格兰海拔在3000英尺以上的277座山峰之一。登山运动者常使用该词〕

Mun·ster /ˋmʌnstɚ; ˈmʌnstə/ a PROVINCE in the southwest of the Republic of Ireland, containing the counties (COUNTY) of Clare, Cork, Kerry, Limerick, Tipperary, and Waterford 芒斯特〔爱尔兰共和国西南部一省区, 包括克莱尔、科克、凯里、利默里克、蒂珀雷里和沃特福德等郡〕

Mup·pets, The /ˋmʌpɪts; ˈmʌpɪts/ also 又作 **The Muppet Show** a US television programme in which the main characters were PUPPETS such as Kermit the Frog and Miss Piggy. The

characters, who were made by Jim Henson, are called Muppets, and they perform in amusing SKETCHes (=short scenes) with well-known human entertainers. Some of the muppets also appear in the children's programme *Sesame Street*. 《木偶剧场》〔美国一电视节目，其主角皆为木偶，如青蛙克米特和猪小姐等。节目中的木偶角色由吉姆·亨森制作，以提线木偶得名。这些木偶也与著名娱乐节目演员一同表演滑稽短剧。有些木偶还出演过儿童节目《芝麻街》〕

mu·ral /ˋmjurəl; ˈmjʊərəl/ *n* [C] a painting that is painted on a wall, either inside or outside a building 壁画 —compare 比较 FRESCO —**mural** *adj* [only before noun 仅用于名词前]

S3 W2 **mur·der¹** /ˋmɝdɚ; ˈmɜːdə/ *n* **1** [C,U] the crime of deliberately killing someone 谋杀；谋杀罪: *He is charged with the horrific murder of two young boys.* 他被指控以恐怖手段谋杀了两个小男孩。| **commit (a) murder** *4600 murders were committed in the US in 1975.* 1975年美国发生了4600宗谋杀案。| *the murder weapon* 谋杀用的凶器 —compare 比较 MANSLAUGHTER **2** [U] unnecessary loss of human life caused by stupidity, especially in war〔尤指战争中因愚蠢而导致的〕无谓的死亡: *Sending untrained men into the battle was sheer murder.* 把未经训练的人送到战场上纯粹是让他们去送死。**3 get away with murder** *informal* if someone gets away with murder they are not punished for their actions and are allowed to do anything they want【非正式】犯了大错而不受惩罚；为所欲为: *She lets those kids get away with murder.* 她听任那些孩子为所欲为。**4 it's murder** *spoken* used to say that something is very difficult or unpleasant【口】某事很难办；某事令人很不快: *It's murder trying to find somewhere to park in Cambridge these days.* 如今在剑桥找个地方停车简直难死人。**5 it's murder on your feet/back etc** *spoken* used to say that something makes a part of your body feel very uncomfortable【口】脚/脊背等极难受: *It's murder on your feet wearing high-heels all day.* 整天穿着高跟鞋，两只脚难受得要命。—see also 另见 **scream/yell blue murder** (BLUE¹ (5))

murder² *v* [T] **1** to kill someone deliberately and illegally 谋杀: *She murdered him for his money.* 她为得到他的钱而谋杀了他。| *Thousands of civilians have been brutally murdered by right-wing death squads.* 数以千计的平民遭到右翼杀手小组残杀。| *the murdered man* 那个被谋杀的男子 —see 见 KILL¹ (USAGE) **2** *informal* to spoil a song, play etc completely by performing it very badly【非正式】〔因表演拙劣而〕糟蹋〔歌曲、剧本〕: *It's a beautiful song, but they murdered it.* 那是一首很美的歌曲，但他们给唱糟蹋了。**3** *informal* to defeat someone completely【非正式】彻底击败: *They murdered us in the final.* 在决赛中他们彻底击败了我们。**4 I could murder a beer/pizza etc** *BrE spoken* used to say that you very much want to eat or drink something【英口】我能消灭一杯啤酒/一张比萨饼等〔表示极想吃或喝某物〕**5 sb will murder you** *spoken* used to tell someone that another person will be very angry with them【口】某人会宰了你〔表示某人会很生气〕: *Your dad'll murder you when he hears about it.* 要是你爸听说这事，他会宰了你。

mur·der·er /ˋmɝdərɚ; ˈmɜːdərə/ *n* [C] someone who murders another person 谋杀犯，凶手: *a convicted murderer* 已定罪的谋杀犯

mur·der·ess /ˋmɝdərɪs; ˈmɜːdərɪ̣s/ *n* [C] *old-fashioned* a woman who murders another person【过时】女谋杀犯，女凶手

Murder of Roger Ackroyd, The /ˌ⋯ ˈ⋯ˈ⋯/ a famous DETECTIVE story by Agatha Christie. When the book was published in 1926, it caused a lot of CONTROVERSY (=serious disagreement) among readers because the NARRATOR is shown to be the murderer at the end of the story. Some people thought that Christie was cheating by using this type of plot. 《罗杰疑案》，又译《罗杰·艾克罗伊德谋杀案》〔阿加莎·克里斯蒂创作的一部著名侦探小说。1926年，该书一经出版就在读者当中引起不少争议，因为叙述者在故事结尾时竟成了杀人凶手。有人认为克里斯蒂正是利用这种情节在欺骗读者〕

mur·der·ous /ˋmɝdərəs; ˈmɜːdərəs/ *adj* **1** very dangerous and likely to kill people 杀气腾腾的；可能杀人的；凶残的: *Captain Bligh's murderous crew* 布莱船长的那帮杀人不眨眼的船员 | *murderous weapons of war* 杀人军火 **2 murderous look/expression** an expression or look which shows that someone is very angry 气势汹汹的表情: *She kept giving me murderous looks every time I mentioned her husband.* 每次我提到她的丈夫，她都是凶巴巴地看着我。—**murderously** *adv* —**murderousness** *n* [U]

Mur·doch /ˋmɝdɑk; ˈmɜːdɒk/, **Dame Iris** /dem ˋaɪrɪs; deɪm ˈaɪərɪ̣s/ (1919-99) a British writer born in Ireland. She wrote intelligent, humorous, and often complicated NOVELS which include *The Sea, The Sea* and *The Book and the Brotherhood*. She also wrote books about PHILOSOPHY. 默多克〔(1919-1999)，英国作家，生于爱尔兰。她的小说富于智慧，语言幽默，情节复杂。代表作为《大海啊，大海》和《书与兄弟情谊》。她还著有哲学著作〕

Murdoch, Ru·pert /ˋrupət; ˈruːpət/ (1931-) a powerful businessman, born in Australia but now a US citizen, who controls one of the world's largest MEDIA businesses, News Corporation, which owns newspapers, television companies, film companies, and book publishers. These include many British, US, and Australian newspapers, such as the *New York Post* and *The Times*, *Sky TV*, and the Fox film company. 默多克〔(1931-)，实力雄厚的企业家，生于澳大利亚，现为美国公民。他拥有世界上最大的媒体企业之一即新闻集团。该公司下属有报社、电视制作公司、电影公司和图书出版公司，其中包括《纽约邮报》和《泰晤士报》等几家英国、美国和澳大利亚报社、天空电视台和福克斯影片公司〕

murk /mɝk; mɜːk/ *n* [U] *literary* darkness caused by smoke, dirt, or cloud; GLOOM (1)【文】黑暗，昏暗，阴沉: *the misty murk of the lagoon* 环礁湖上雾蒙蒙的昏暗

murk·y /ˋmɝkɪ; ˈmɜːki/ *adj* **1** dark and difficult to see through 阴暗的，黑暗的；朦胧的: *the murky grey light of dawn* 黎明时分朦朦胧胧的灰色天光 | *He plunged into the murky waters of Honolulu harbour.* 他纵身跳进了火奴鲁鲁港浑浊的水中。**2** involving dishonest or illegal activities that are kept hidden or secret 不光彩的，不可告人的，不清白的: *It's a murky business.* 那是个见不得人的行当。| **a murky past** *a politician with a murky past* 历史不清白的政客 —**murkily** *adv* —**murkiness** *n* [U]

mur·mur¹ /ˋmɝmɚ; ˈmɜːmə/ *v* **1** [I,T] to say something in a soft low voice which is difficult to hear clearly 小声说，咕哝: *He began stroking her hair and gently murmuring her name.* 他开始抚摸她的头发，喃喃地呼唤她的名字。**2** [I] to complain to friends and people you work with, but not officially〔向朋友和同事〕私下抱怨，发牢骚: [+about/against] *Within the city there was much murmuring against the new ruler.* 该城市的市民对那位新统治者非常不满，怨声载道。**3** [I] to make a soft, low sound 发出轻柔的声音: *The wind murmured through the trees.* 风穿过树林发出沙沙声。—**murmuring** *n* [C,U]: *vague murmurings of discontent* 表示不满的叽叽咕咕声

murmur² *n* [C] **1** a soft low sound made by people speaking quietly or from a long way away 轻轻的谈话声，低语声: *the murmur of voices from down the corridor* 从走廊那端传来的絮絮低语声 | *She replied in a low murmur.* 她轻声作了回答。**2** a complaint, especially one made to friends and people you work with, but not officially〔尤指向朋友和同事的〕私下的抱怨，怨言，咕哝: *There have been some murmurs of discontent over new city taxes.* 对新的城市税已有一些不满的言论。| **without a murmur** (=without complaining or opposing) 毫无怨言，毫不反对 *Congress had accepted the treaty almost without a murmur.* 国会几乎毫无异议地认可了那个条约。**3** the soft low sound made by a stream, the wind etc〔溪流、风等发出的〕细声，轻柔的声音: *the murmur of the little brook* 小溪淙淙的流水声 **4** [usually singular 一般用单数] an unusual sound made by the heart which shows that there may be something wrong with it〔心脏的〕杂音: *a heart murmur* 心脏杂音

Mur·phy /ˋmɝfɪ; ˈmɜːfi/, **Ed·die** /ˋɛdɪ; ˈedi/ (1961-) a US film actor and COMEDIAN. His films include *Beverly Hills Cop* (1984) and *The Nutty Professor* (1997). 墨菲〔(1961-)，美国电影演员和喜剧演员。主演的影片有《妙探出差》(1984)和《肥佬教授》(1997)〕

Mur·phy's law /ˌmɝfɪz ˋlɔ; ˌmɜːfiz ˈlɔː/ *n* [singular] *especially AmE* a tendency for bad things to happen whenever it is possible for them to do so; SOD'S LAW【尤美】墨菲定律〔一种认为凡有可能出差错的事终将出差错的论断〕

Mus·ca·det /ˋmʌskəde; ˈmʌskədeɪ/ a dry white wine from France 玛斯卡特〔法国产的一种干白葡萄酒〕

Muscat /ˋmʌsˌkæt; mʌskæt/ the capital city of Oman 马斯开特〔阿曼首都〕

mus·ca·tel /ˌmʌskəˋtɛl; ˌmʌskəˈtel/ *n* [C,U] a sweet light-coloured wine, or the type of GRAPE that is used to make it 麝香葡萄酒；麝香葡萄

mus·cle¹ /ˋmʌsl; ˈmʌsəl/ *n* **1** [C,U] one of the pieces of flesh inside your body that connects your bones together and that you use when you move 肌肉: *The next day the muscles in my arm felt sore.* 第二天我胳膊上的肌肉有些酸痛。| **arm/chest/stomach muscles** *bulging chest muscles* 隆起的胸肌 | **pull a muscle** (=injure a muscle so that it becomes painful) 拉伤肌肉 *My leg hurts – I think I've pulled a muscle.* 我腿疼——我想我把肌肉拉伤了。**2** [U] physical strength and power 体力，力气: *It must have taken a lot of muscle to get that piano up those stairs.* 把那架钢琴搬上楼梯一定费了很大的力气。| **put some muscle into it** *spoken* (=used to tell someone to try harder and use more S2 W3

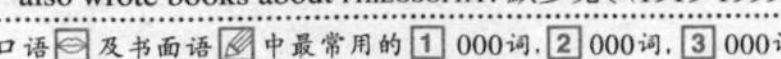

effort)【口】再加把劲，再努把力 **3** [U] military, political, or financial power or influence〔军事、政治或财政的〕实力，力量：*US military muscle* 美国的军事实力 **4 not move a muscle** to remain completely still 一动不动：*I shouted at him, but he didn't move a muscle.* 我对着他大喊，但他却一动不动。**5** [U] *slang* strong men who are paid to protect or attack someone, especially by criminals【俚】保镖；打手；暴徒 —see also 另见 **flex your muscles** (FLEX¹ (2))

muscle² *v* **muscled, muscling**

muscle in *phr v* [I] to use your strength, power, or influence to get control of someone else's business or to interfere in their affairs 强行控制[干预]：[**+on**] *Another gang was trying to muscle in on their territory.* 另一伙歹徒正企图侵占他们的地盘。

mus·cle-bound /ˈmʌsl̩baund; ˈmʌsəlbaʊnd/ *adj* having large stiff muscles because of too much physical exercise〔因运动过度而〕肌肉僵大的：*musclebound he-men with no imagination* 肌肉发达、头脑简单的强健男子

mus·cle·man /ˈmʌsl̩ˌmæn; ˈmʌsəlmæn/ *plural* **musclemen** /-ˌmɛn; -men/ *n* [C] **1** a man who has developed big strong muscles by doing exercises 肌肉发达的男子 **2** a strong man who is employed to protect someone, usually a criminal 保镖；打手；暴徒

Mus·co·vite /ˈmʌskəˌvaɪt; ˈmʌskəvaɪt/ *n* [C] someone from Moscow 莫斯科人

mus·cu·lar /ˈmʌskjələ˞; ˈmʌskjələ/ *adj* **1** having a lot of big muscles; strong-looking 肌肉发达的；强壮的：*strong muscular arms* 肌肉发达而有力的双臂 | *She liked men who were tall and muscular.* 她喜欢身材高大、体格健壮的男人。**2** concerning or affecting the muscles 肌肉的；影响肌肉的：*muscular injuries* 肌肉损伤 —**muscularly** *adv* —**muscularity** /ˌmʌskjəˈlærɪtɪ; ˌmʌskjəˈlærəti/ *n* [U]

muscular dys·tro·phy /ˌmʌskjələ˞ ˈdɪstrəfi; ˌmʌskjələ ˈdɪstrəfi/ *n* [U] a serious illness in which the muscles become weaker over a period of time 肌肉萎缩(症)

Muscular Dys·tro·phy As·so·ci·a·tion, the /ˌ‥ˈ‥ ‥ˌ‥ˈ‥/ abbreviation 缩写为 **the MDA** a US CHARITY organization that helps people who have MUSCULAR DYSTROPHY 肌肉萎缩症救助协会〔美国帮助肌肉萎缩症患者的一个慈善组织〕

muse¹ /mjuz; mjuːz/ *v* **1** [I] to think carefully about something for a long time 沉思，冥想，默想：[**+on/over**] *He lit a cigarette and sat musing over the problems of the world.* 他点上一支烟，坐着默默地思考世界上的种种问题。**2** [T] to say something in a thoughtful way, especially a question that you are trying to find the answer to 沉思着自语；沉思着自问：*"I wonder why she was killed," mused Poirot.* "她为什么被杀呢？"波洛沉思着自问。—**musingly** *adv*

muse² *n* [C] **1** someone's muse is the force or person that makes them want to write, paint, or make music, and helps them to have good ideas; INSPIRATION (3) 灵感（的源泉）；才气：*She was the artist's lover and his creative muse.* 她是那位艺术家的情人，也是他创作灵感的源泉。**2 the Muses** a group of ancient Greek goddesses, each of whom represented a particular art or a science 缪斯〔古希腊神话中掌管文艺、科学等的九位女神〕

Mu·sée d'Or·say /ˌmjuze dɔˈse; ˌmjuːzeɪ dɔːˈseɪ/ a MUSEUM in Paris, France, in a former railway station. It contains Impressionist and Post-Impressionist paintings, SCULPTUREs, and examples of Art Nouveau. 奥塞艺术馆〔法国巴黎一博物馆，坐落在一旧火车站内。该馆藏有印象派和后印象派的绘画作品、雕塑及新艺术派的代表作〕

mu·se·um /mjuˈziəm; mjuːˈziːəm/ *n* [C] a building where important cultural, historical, or scientific objects are kept and shown to the public 博物馆，博物院：*the Museum of Modern Art* 现代艺术博物馆

Museum of Lon·don, the /ˌ‥ ‥ˈ‥/ a MUSEUM in central London which tells the history of London from Roman times to the present 伦敦博物馆〔位于伦敦市中心，展示伦敦从罗马时期及至当代的历史〕

Museum of Man·kind, the /ˌ‥ ‥ˈ‥/ a MUSEUM in west central London which contains objects and information about the lives and cultures of people from many countries around the world 人类博物馆〔位于伦敦市中心西区，藏有世界各民族的生活和文化实物及信息资料〕

Museum of Mod·ern Art, the /ˌ‥ ‥ ‥ˈ/ abbreviation 缩写为 **MOMA** a MUSEUM in New York City which contains one of the world's finest collections of modern art and photography 现代艺术博物馆〔位于纽约市，藏有世界最优秀的现代艺术和摄影作品〕

Museum of the Mov·ing Im·age, the /ˌ‥ ‥ ‥ˈ‥/ abbreviation 缩写为 **MOMI** a MUSEUM on the South Bank in London, containing information about the history of the cinema and of television, and collections of equipment used in the making of films and television programmes 电影博物馆〔位于伦敦南岸，藏有电影、电视发展史料及电影、电视节目制作设备〕

museum piece /ˈ‥ ‥/ *n* [C] **1** *often humorous* a very old-fashioned piece of equipment【常幽默】陈旧过时的设备，老古董：*Some of the weapons used by the rebels are museum pieces.* 叛军使用的一些武器都是老掉牙的过时货。**2** an object that is so valuable or interesting that it should be in a museum 值得在博物馆陈列的精品

mush¹ /mʌʃ; mʌʃ/ *n* **1** [singular, U] an unpleasant soft mass of a substance, especially food, which is partly liquid and partly solid 软乎乎令人讨厌的东西，烂糊状的东西〔尤指食物〕：*The cabbage had been boiled down into a flavourless mush.* 卷心菜被熬成了一团没滋没味的烂糊糊。**2** [U] *AmE* a thick PORRIDGE made from CORN MEAL【美】稠玉米粥 **3** [U] a book or film that is mush is about love and is SENTIMENTAL 感伤的爱情书籍[电影等] —**mushy** *adj*

mush² /mʊʃ; mʊʃ/ *n* [singular] *BrE spoken* an angry and insulting way of addressing someone【英口】讨厌鬼；脏鬼〔对某人愤怒和侮辱的称呼〕：*Oi, mush! Get your hands off my car!* 喂，脏鬼！把你的手从我车上拿开！

mush·room¹ /ˈmʌʃrum; ˈmʌʃruːm/ *n* [C] one of several kinds of FUNGUS with a flat top, some of which can be eaten 蘑菇：*mushroom soup* 蘑菇汤 —see also 另见 MAGIC MUSHROOM —see picture on page A9 参见 A9 页图

mushroom² *v* [I] **1** to grow and develop very quickly 快速成长；迅速发展：*New housing developments mushroomed on the edge of town.* 在城郊雨后春笋般出现了一些新的住宅区。**2** [+adv/prep] to spread up into the air in the shape of a mushroom〔在空中〕呈蘑菇状扩散

mushroom cloud /ˈ‥ ‥/ *n* [C usually singular 一般用单数] a big cloud shaped like a mushroom, which is caused by a NUCLEAR explosion〔核爆炸后形成的〕蘑菇云

mushy peas /ˌ‥ ˈ/ *n* [plural] *BrE* soft cooked PEAs, eaten especially in the north of England【英】〔尤指英格兰北部人们食用的〕豌豆糊[泥]

mu·sic /ˈmjuzɪk; ˈmjuːzɪk/ *n* [U] **1** the arrangement of sounds made by instruments or voices in a way that is pleasant or exciting 音乐，乐曲：*loud pop music* 响亮的流行音乐 | *I like all kinds of music.* 各种音乐我都喜欢。| **a piece of music** *The Moonlight Sonata is one of my favourite pieces of music.*《月光奏鸣曲》是我最喜欢的乐曲之一。| **write/compose music** *Nyman writes the music for most of Peter Greenaway's films.* 彼得·格林纳威的大多数电影是由尼曼作曲的。**2** the art of writing or playing music 音乐艺术：*studying music at college* 在大学学习音乐 | *music lessons* 音乐课 **3** a set of written marks representing music, or paper with the written marks on it 乐谱；曲谱：**read music** (=understand the sounds that written music represents) 识谱 *Can you read music?* 你识乐谱吗？| *organ/piano/pop music* 风琴/钢琴/流行乐乐谱 **4 be music to your ears** if someone's words are music to your ears, they make you very happy or pleased〔某人的话〕听起来顺耳；动听 **5 set/put sth to music** to write music so that the words of a poem, play etc can be sung 为…谱曲 —see also 另见 **face the music** (FACE² (8))

mu·sic·al¹ /ˈmjuzɪkl̩; ˈmjuːzɪkəl/ *adj* **1** [only before noun 仅用于名词前] connected with music or consisting of music 音乐的；配乐的：*a musical entertainment* 音乐表演 | *We share the same musical tastes.* 我们有共同的音乐爱好。**2** good at or interested in playing or singing music 擅长音乐的；对音乐感兴趣的：*I wasn't very musical when I was at school.* 学生时代我不太喜欢音乐。**3** having a pleasant sound like music〔声音〕音乐般好听的，悦耳的：*She had a sweet musical voice.* 她的嗓音甜美动听。—see also 另见 MUSICALLY

musical² also 又作 **musical com·e·dy** /ˌ‥ ˈ‥/ *n* [C] a play or film that uses singing and dancing to tell a story 音乐剧，音乐影片：*'West Side Story', a musical with music by Leonard Bernstein* 由伦纳德·伯恩斯坦作曲的音乐剧《西城故事》

musical box /ˈ‥ ‥/ *n* [C] *especially BrE* a box that plays a musical tune when you open it【尤英】音乐盒，八音盒

musical chairs /ˌ‥ ˈ/ *n* [U] a children's game in which all the players must sit down when the music stops, but there are never enough chairs〔儿童玩的〕随乐声抢椅子游戏

musical in·stru·ment /ˌ‥ ˈ‥/ *n* [C] something that you use for playing music, such as a piano or GUITAR 乐器

mu·sic·ally /ˈmjuzɪkl̩ɪ; ˈmjuːzɪkli/ *adv* **1** with regard to music 在音乐方面，就音乐而言：*The band aren't much good musically, but they're very good-looking.* 这个乐队在音乐方面的水平不是很高，但他们人很漂亮。| *Musically speaking, the*

concert was only average. 就音乐而言，那次音乐会只是中等水平。**2** in a way that sounds like music 动听地，悦耳地：*Welsh people are supposed to pronounce English words musically.* 人们认为威尔士人说英语悦耳动听。

music box /ˈ‥ ˌ‧/ *n* [C] *especially AmE* a musical box【尤美】音乐盒，八音盒

music hall /ˈ‥ ‧/ *n* **1** [U] a type of entertainment in the theatre, especially in the 19th and early 20th century consisting of singers, dancers, and people telling jokes〔尤指19世纪和20世纪初在剧院进行的包括唱歌、跳舞和讲笑话的〕综艺表演；VAUDEVILLE *AmE*【美】**2** [C] *BrE* a theatre used for this kind of entertainment【英】综艺剧场，歌舞杂耍剧院

mu·si·cian /mjuˋzɪʃən; mjuːˈzɪʃən/ *n* [C] a person who plays a musical instrument, especially very well or as a job 音乐家，乐师：*a talented young musician* 有天赋的年轻音乐家

mu·si·cian·ship /mjuˋzɪʃənʃɪp; mjuːˈzɪʃənʃɪp/ *n* [U] skill in playing music 音乐演奏技巧：*His musicianship was superb, really beyond compare.* 他的音乐演奏技巧高超，简直是无与伦比。

mu·si·col·o·gy /ˌmjuzɪˋkɑlədʒɪ; ˌmjuːzɪˈkɒlədʒi/ *n* [U] the study of music, especially the history of different types of music 音乐学 **—musicologist** *n* [C] **—musicological** /ˌmjuzɪkəˋlɑdʒɪkl; ˌmjuːzɪkəˈlɒdʒɪkəl/ *adj*

music stand /ˈ‥ ‧/ *n* [C] a metal frame for holding written music, so that you can read it while playing an instrument or singing 乐谱架

musk /mʌsk; mʌsk/ *n* [U] a strong smelling substance used to make PERFUME 麝香

mus·ket /ˋmʌskɪt; ˈmʌskɪ̤t/ *n* [C] a type of gun used in former times〔旧时用的〕滑膛枪；旧式步枪，毛瑟枪

mus·ket·eer /ˌmʌskəˋtɪr; ˌmʌskɪ̤ˈtɪə/ *n* [C] a soldier who uses a musket 火枪手，滑膛枪手

musk mel·on /ˈ‧ ˌ‧‧/ *n* [C] a type of sweet MELON 甜瓜；香瓜

musk·rat /ˋmʌskræt; ˈmʌskræt/ *n* [C] an animal which lives in water in North America and is hunted for its fur〔生长于北美洲水中的〕麝鼠

musk·y /ˋmʌskɪ; ˈmʌski/ *adj* like MUSK 麝香似的：*a musky smell* 麝香味 **—muskiness** *n* [U]

Mus·lim /ˋmʌzləm; ˈmʊzlɪ̤m/ *n* [C] someone whose religion is Islam 穆斯林，伊斯兰教信徒 **—Muslim** *adj*

mus·lin /ˋmʌzlɪn; ˈmʌzlɪ̤n/ *n* [U] a very fine thin cotton cloth used for making dresses and curtains, especially in past times〔尤指以前的〕麦斯林纱；平纹细布

muss /mʌs; mʌs/ *v* [T+up] *informal especially AmE* to make something untidy, especially someone's hair【非正式，尤美】把〔某物，尤指头发〕弄乱，使凌乱；把…弄脏

mus·sel /ˋmʌsl; ˈmʌsəl/ *n* [C] a small sea animal, with a soft body that can be eaten and a black shell that is divided into two parts 贻贝，壳菜，淡菜 —see picture at 参见 SHELL[1] 图

Mus·so·li·ni /ˌmusəˋlinɪ; ˌmʊsəˈliːni/, **Be·ni·to** /bɛˋnito; beˈniːtəʊ/ (1883-1945) an Italian leader known as 'Il Duce', who established the system of FASCISM and ruled Italy as a DICTATOR from 1925-43. He fought with Germany in World War II against the Allies, but because of his armies' failures, he was forced to give up power in 1943. After the war he was shot and killed by Italian PARTISANS. 墨索里尼〔(1883-1945)，意大利领导人，又称意大利国家元首。他建立了法西斯制度，1925-1943年间在意大利实行独裁统治。二战期间，他与德国为伍，对抗盟军。由于他率领的意大利军队屡战屡败，他于1943年被迫下台。大战结束之后，他被意大利游击队击毙〕

Mussorgsky, Modest —see 见 Modest MOUSSORGSKY

must[1] /məst; məst; *strong* 强读 mʌst; mʌst/ *modal verb* [negative short form 否定缩略式为 **mustn't**] **1** [past usually 过去式一般作 **had to**] to have to do something because the situation forces you, because of a rule or law, or because you feel that you should 必须：*All passengers must wear seat belts.* 所有乘客都必须系安全带。| *You mustn't tell anyone about this – it's a secret.* 你不许跟任何人讲这件事——这是个秘密。| *I don't really want to make the appointment, but I suppose I must.* 我并不很想安排这次约见，但看来我必须这样做。| *Under no circumstances must any member of staff socialize with the patients.* 在任何情况下工作人员都不得与病人交往。| *Apologize? Must I? It was all her own fault.* 道歉？我非得道歉吗？那完全是她自己的过错。| **I must admit/say etc** *I must admit, I was surprised when he passed his driving test first time.* 我得承认，他一次就通过了驾驶考试，令我感到惊讶。—compare 比较 HAVE[3] —see graph at 参见 OBLIGE 图表 **2** [past usually 过去式一般作 **must have**] used when you are guessing that something is true or that something has happened because there seems to be no other possibility 一定，肯定：*Sam must be nearly 90 years old now.* 萨姆现在肯定快90岁了。| *Buying roses? It must be love.* 买玫瑰花？那一定是恋爱了。| *He must have been drunk to say that.* 他准是喝醉了才那样说的。| *There must have been ten of them, all hiding in my attic.* 他们肯定有10个人，都藏在我的阁楼上。**3 a)** used to suggest that someone does something, especially because you think they will enjoy it very much or you think it is a very good idea 应该：*You must go and see the new Spielberg movie, the special effects are amazing.* 你应该去看看斯皮尔伯格的那部新影片——特技效果令人惊叹。**b)** used when you want to do something and hope to do it soon 一定要：*We must come over and try out that new barbecue of yours.* 我们改天一定要来试试你那个新的烤肉架。**4 if you must** used to tell someone that they are allowed to do something but that you do not approve or agree with it 如果你硬要：*"Can I borrow your car, Mum?" "If you must."* "妈，我可以借用一下你的汽车吗？""如果你非借不可那就借吧。" | **if you must do sth** *If you must smoke, do it outside please.* 如果你非要吸烟，请到外面去吸。**5 you must be joking** used when you think someone's suggestion is silly or stupid 你准是在开玩笑〔用以表示某人的提议很愚蠢〕：*£2000 for that old car? You must be joking!* 花2000英镑买那辆旧汽车？你准是在开玩笑！

must[2] /mʌst; mʌst/ *n* **1 a must** something that you must do or must have 必须做的事；必不可少的东西：*Warm clothes are a must in the mountains.* 御寒衣服在山里是必不可少的。**2** [U] the liquid from which wine is made; GRAPE juice〔酿酒用的〕葡萄汁

mus·tache /ˋmʌstæʃ; məˈstɑːʃ/ *n* [C] the usual American spelling of MOUSTACHE moustache 的一般美式拼法

mustachioed, moustachioed /məˋstæʃɪod; məˈstæʃiəʊd/ *adj* having a large curly MOUSTACHE 留着〔大而弯的〕八字须的

Mustang *trademark* a type of fast car built by the Ford company in the US, popular especially in the 1960s and 1970s【商标】野马〔美国福特汽车公司制造的一种高速汽车，20世纪60、70年代尤为流行〕

mus·tang /ˋmʌstæŋ; ˈmʌstæŋ/ *n* [C] a small American wild horse〔产于美洲的〕小野马

mus·tard /ˋmʌstəd; ˈmʌstəd/ *n* [U] **1** a yellow sauce that tastes hot, eaten especially with meat 芥末；芥子酱 **2** a plant with yellow flowers whose seeds can be used to make the powder used

to make this 芥菜 **3 not cut the mustard** to not be good enough for a particular job 不符合要求, 不符合条件: *He'll never cut the mustard as a manager.* 他永远也不会是当经理的料。**4** a yellow-brown colour 芥末黄, 深黄色 —see also 另见 **keen as mustard** (KEEN[1] (8)) —see picture on page A5 参见 A5 页图

mustard gas /ˈ‥ ˌ/ *n* [U] a poisonous gas that burns the skin, which was used during the First World War 芥子气〔一种毒气〕

mus·ter[1] /ˈmʌstɚ; ˈmʌstə/ *v* **1 muster (up) courage/support/energy etc** to try to find as much courage, support etc as you can in order to do something difficult 鼓起勇气/争取支持/积蓄力量等: *Finally I mustered up the courage to ask her out.* 最后我鼓起了勇气约她出来。| *Senator Newbolt has been trying to muster support for his proposals.* 参议员纽博尔特一直在尽力争取人们支持他的提议。**2** [I,T] to gather a group of people, especially soldiers, together in one place, or to come together as a group 召集〔人群, 尤指士兵〕;〔人群〕集合, 集结: *In April 1185 he began to muster an army.* 他于1185年4月开始召集军队。

muster[2] *n* **1 pass muster** to be accepted as good enough 被认为合格, 通过检查: *Jackson wasn't a great player, but he just about passed muster.* 杰克逊虽然不是一个优秀的运动员, 但还算过得去。**2** [C] *especially literary* a group of people, especially soldiers, that have been gathered together【尤文】集合在一起的一群人〔尤指士兵〕

Mus·tique /muˈstik; mʊˈstiːk/ a small island in the Caribbean Sea. It is a popular place for rich and famous people to take holidays. 马斯蒂克岛〔加勒比海一小岛, 是富人和名流的度假胜地〕

must·n't /ˈmʌsn̩t; ˈmʌsənt/ the short form of 缩略式= 'must not': *You mustn't tell Jerry what I've bought.* 不准你告诉杰里我买了什么。

must·y /ˈmʌstɪ; ˈmʌsti/ *adj* a musty room, house, or object has a damp and unpleasant smell, because it is old and has not had any fresh air for a long time〔房间、屋子或东西等〕霉臭的; 发霉的; 霉烂而潮湿的: *musty old books* 发霉臭味的旧书 | *the stale musty smell of the attic* 阁楼里陈腐的霉臭味 —**mustiness** *n* [U]

mu·ta·ble /ˈmjutəbl̩; ˈmjuːtəbəl/ *adj formal* able or likely to change【正式】可变的; 易变的, 无常的 —**mutability** /ˌmjutəˈbɪlətɪ; ˌmjuːtəˈbɪlɪ̣ti/ *n* [U] —opposite 反义词 IMMUTABLE

mu·ta·gen /ˈmjutədʒən; ˈmjuːtədʒən/ *n* [C] *technical* a substance that causes a living thing to mutate【术语】诱变剂, 致突变物

mu·tant /ˈmjutənt; ˈmjuːtənt/ *n* [C] an animal or plant that is different in some way from others of the same kind, because of a change in its GENETIC structure〔动物或植物的〕突变型, 突变体 —**mutant** *adj*

mu·tate /ˈmjutet; mjuːˈteɪt/ *v* [I] if a plant or animal mutates, it develops a feature that makes it different from other plants or animals of the same kind, because of a change in its GENETIC structure〔动物或植物〕突变

mu·ta·tion /mjuˈteʃən; mjuːˈteɪʃən/ *n* [C,U] **1** a change in the GENETIC structure of an animal or plant, that makes it different from others of the same type〔动物或植物的〕突变, 变异: *random mutation* 无规则突变 **2** *technical* a change in a speech sound, especially a vowel, because of the sound of the one next to it【术语】元音变化; 语音变异

mute[1] /mjut; mjuːt/ *adj* **1** not speaking or refusing to speak 缄默的, 不说话的; 拒绝说话的: *Helena glared at me in mute anger.* 海伦娜一声不吭, 愤怒地瞪着我。**2** *old-fashioned* unable to speak; DUMB【过时】不会说话的, 哑的 **3** *technical* not pronounced【术语】〔语音中〕不发音的: *a mute 'e'* 不发音的e —**mutely** *adv* —**muteness** *n* [U]

mute[2] *v* [T] **1** to make a sound quieter 使〔声音〕减弱: *He placed a hand across her mouth to mute her screams.* 他用手捂住她的嘴, 止住了她的尖叫声。**2** to make a musical instrument sound softer 使〔乐器〕听起来柔和些, 使〔乐器声音〕弱化

mute[3] *n* [C] **1** something that is placed over or into a musical instrument to make it sound softer〔乐器上的〕弱音器 **2** someone who cannot speak 哑巴 —see also 另见 DEAF-MUTE

mut·ed /ˈmjutɪd; ˈmjuːtɪ̣d/ *adj* **1 muted criticism/support/response etc** criticism etc that is not expressed strongly 温和的批评/有分寸的支持/有克制的反应等: *At first, criticism of the war was fairly muted.* 起初人们对战争的批评相当温和。**2** quieter than usual〔声音〕减弱的, 比平常静的: *We could hear the muted cries of newspaper-sellers in the street outside.* 我们能听到外面街道上卖报人隐隐约约的叫卖声。**3** a muted colour is not bright but soft and gentle〔颜色〕柔和的, 不耀眼的: *muted pinks and blues* 各种柔和的粉红色和蓝色

mu·ti·late /ˈmjutl̩ˌet; ˈmjuːtɪ̣leɪt/ *v* [T often passive 常用被动态] **1** to severely and violently damage someone's body, especially by removing part of it 残害〔某人的身体〕, 使断肢, 使伤残: *Many people were mutilated and maimed in the blast.* 许多人在那次爆炸中被炸得肢体残缺不全。**2** to damage or change something so much that it is completely spoiled or ruined 完全损毁; 使支离破碎 —**mutilation** /ˌmjutl̩ˈeʃən; ˌmjuːtɪ̣ˈleɪʃən/ *n* [C,U]

mu·ti·neer /ˌmjutn̩ˈɪr; ˌmjuːtɪ̣ˈnɪə/ *n* [C] someone who is involved in a mutiny 叛变者, 反叛者

mu·ti·nous /ˈmjutn̩əs; ˈmjuːtɪ̣nəs/ *adj* **1** behaving in a way that shows you do not want to obey someone; REBELLIOUS 抗命的, 反抗的; 桀骜不驯的: *There was a mutinous look in Rosie's eyes.* 在罗西的目光里有一种叛逆的神情。| *mutinous teenagers* 桀骜不驯的青少年 **2** involved in a mutiny 叛变的, 反叛的: *mutinous soldiers* 叛乱的士兵 —**mutinously** *adv*

mu·ti·ny /ˈmjutn̩ɪ; ˈmjuːtɪ̣ni/ *n* [C,U] a situation in which people, especially sailors or soldiers, refuse to obey the person who is in charge of them, and try to take control for themselves〔尤指水手或士兵的〕反叛, 哗变, 叛乱: *There was already talk of mutiny among the crew.* 船员中间已经有哗变的传言。—**mutiny** *v* [I]

Mutiny on the Boun·ty, The —see 见 The BOUNTY

mutt /mʌt; mʌt/ *n* [C] *informal*【非正式】**1** a dog that does not belong to any particular breed; MONGREL 杂种狗 **2** *BrE* a stupid person; fool【英】笨蛋, 傻瓜: *You dumb mutt – look what you've done now!* 你这个笨蛋, 瞧瞧你做了些什么!

mut·ter /ˈmʌtɚ; ˈmʌtə/ *v* **1** [I,T] to speak quietly or in a low voice, usually because you are annoyed about something, or because you do not want people to hear you 咕哝, 喃喃; 悄声说: *"I didn't even want to come in the first place," he muttered.* "我原来甚至都不想来的。"他嘟哝着说。| *Mr Clarke left, muttering something about having to see a client.* 克拉克先生走了, 嘴里咕哝着必须去见一个客户什么的。**2** [I] to complain about something or express doubts about it, but without saying clearly and openly what you think 私下抱怨; 小声质疑: [+about] *Some senators muttered darkly about the threat to national security.* 一些议员私下里质疑对国家安全构成的威胁。—**mutter** *n* [singular]: *His voice subsided to a mutter.* 他的嗓音低了下来, 变成了轻轻的喃咕声。—**mutterer** *n* [C] —**muttering** *n* [C,U]

mut·ton /ˈmʌtn̩; ˈmʌtn/ *n* [U] **1** the meat from a sheep 羊肉 **2 mutton dressed as lamb** *BrE* an offensive expression meaning a woman who is trying to look younger than she really is【英】设法使自己看起来年轻些的妇女〔冒犯性说法〕

mutton chop /ˌ‥ ˈ‧/ *n* [C] **1** a piece of meat containing a bone, that has been cut from the RIBS of a sheep 羊排 **2 mutton chops** also 又作 **mutton chop whiskers** hair that grows only on the sides of a man's cheeks, not on his chin, in a style that was popular in the 19th century 羊排络腮胡子〔指仅在脸颊两旁蓄的上窄下宽的络腮胡子, 盛行于19世纪〕

mu·tu·al /ˈmjutʃʊəl; ˈmjuːtʃuəl/ *adj* **1 mutual respect/hatred/support** mutual feelings such as respect or hatred are felt equally by two people towards each other 相互尊重/仇恨/支持: *Mutual respect is necessary for the partnership to work.* 相互尊重是合作所必需的。| **the feeling is mutual** (=used to say that you have the same feeling about someone else as they have about you, especially when you dislike each other)〔感情方面〕彼此一样, 彼此彼此 *I didn't like Dev, and the feeling seemed to be mutual.* 我不喜欢迪夫, 他好像也不喜欢我。—compare 比较 RECIPROCAL **2 mutual friend/interest** a friend or interest that two people both have 共同的朋友/兴趣: *We discovered a mutual interest in gardening.* 我们在园艺方面找到了共同的爱好。**3 mutual admiration society** *humorous* a situation in which two people praise each other a lot【幽默】相互吹捧 —**mutuality** /ˌmjutʃʊˈælətɪ; ˌmjuːtʃuˈælɪ̣ti/ *n* [U]

mutual fund /ˈ‥‥ ˌ/ *n* [C] *AmE*【美】单位投资信托公司, 共同基金; a UNIT TRUST *BrE*【英】

mu·tu·al·ly /ˈmjutʃʊəlɪ; ˈmjuːtʃuəli/ *adv* **1** done or experienced equally by two people 相互, 彼此: *a mutually beneficial arrangement* 互利的安排 **2 mutually exclusive/contradictory** two ideas or beliefs that are mutually exclusive cannot both exist or be true at the same time 相互排斥/矛盾的

muu·muu /ˈmu mu; ˈmuː muː/ *n* [C] *AmE* a long loose dress【美】姆姆袍〔一种宽松的长袍〕

Muy·bridge /ˈmaɪbrɪdʒ; ˈmaɪbrɪdʒ/, **Ead·weard** /ˈɛdwɚd; ˈedwəd/ (1830-1904) an English photographer who recorded movement, especially of animals, by taking sets of photographs with several cameras arranged in a row 迈布里奇〔(1830-1904), 英国摄影家。他曾将几架照相机排成一行拍摄动物的一连串活动〕

mu·zak /ˈmjuzæk; ˈmjuːzæk/ *n* [U] *trademark* recorded music that is played continuously in airports, shops, hotels etc 【商标】背景音乐〔机场、商店、饭店等公共场所连续播放的录制好的音乐〕

muz·zle¹ /ˈmʌzl; ˈmʌzəl/ *n* [C] **1** the nose and mouth of an animal such as a dog or horse〔狗或马等动物的〕鼻口部，吻: *a grey dog with a black muzzle* 嘴和鼻子呈黑色的灰狗 —see picture at 参见 HORSE¹ 图 **2** something that you put over a dog's mouth to stop it from biting people〔狗的〕口套，口络 **3** the end of the BARREL of a gun 枪口，炮口 —see picture at 参见 GUN¹ 图

muzzle² *v* [T] **1** to prevent someone from speaking freely or expressing their opinions 使缄默，封住…的嘴；钳制…的言论: *an attempt to muzzle the press and ban opposition newspapers* 限制新闻自由并取缔反对派报纸的企图 **2** to put a muzzle over a dog's mouth so that it cannot bite people 给〔狗〕戴口套

muz·zy /ˈmʌzɪ; ˈmʌzi/ *adj BrE*【英】**1** unable to think clearly, especially because you are ill or drunk; CONFUSED〔尤指因生病或醉酒而〕头脑糊涂的，昏昏沉沉的: *I was feeling a bit muzzy by that time, and decided to go home.* 我那时已感到头脑有点昏沉，所以决定回家。**2** not clear; BLURRED 不清楚的；模糊的: *a muzzy TV picture* 不清晰的电视图像 —**muzzily** *adv* —**muzziness** *n* [U]

MW a written abbreviation for 缩写= MEDIUM WAVE

my /maɪ; maɪ/ *determiner* [possessive form of 'I' I的所有格形式] **1** of or belonging to me 我的: *Have you seen my car keys?* 你看到我的汽车钥匙了吗？| *My mother phoned last night.* 我母亲昨天晚上来电话了。| *You should take my advice.* 你应该采纳我的建议。| *I'm sure you don't want to listen to all my problems.* 我敢肯定你不想听我所有的问题。**2** used when you are surprised about something 哎呀〔表示惊奇〕: *My! What a clever boy you are.* 哎呀！你真是个聪明的孩子。**3** used when you are shocked or angry about something 天哪〔表示震惊或气愤〕: *Oh my God! The house is on fire!* 天哪！房子起火了！**4** used when addressing people who you love or like a lot 亲爱的〔用于称呼所爱或喜欢的人〕: *Good night, my dear. Sleep well.* 晚安，亲爱的。睡个好觉。

Myan·mar /ˈmjænmɑr; ˈmjænmɑː/ a country in southeast Asia, to the east of India and Bangladesh, and to the west of China and Thailand, which was called Burma until 1998. Population: 41,995,000 (2001). Capital: Nay Pyi Taw. 缅甸〔东南亚一国家，位于印度和孟加拉以东，中国和泰国以西。1998年之前的英文名为Burma。人口：41,995,000（2001），首都：内比都〕— **Myanmarese** /ˈmjænmɑriz; ˌmjænmɑːˈriːz/ *n, adj*

My·ce·nae /maɪˈsini; maɪˈsiːni/ an ancient Greek city in southern Greece, where King Agamemnon is supposed to have lived. It was a wealthy and important city in the period before about 1100 BC. In the late 19th century many beautiful and ancient objects were found there by ARCHAEOLOGISTS. 迈锡尼〔希腊南部一古城。传说阿伽门农国王曾在此居住。公元前约1100年前的一段时期，迈锡尼曾是一座富裕而重要的城市。19世纪末，许多考古学家在此发现了大量漂亮的古代文物〕—**Mycenaean** /ˌmaɪˈsɪniən; ˌmaɪˈsʒniːən/ *adj: a gold Mycenaean bracelet* 迈锡尼金手镯

my·col·o·gy /maɪˈkɑlədʒɪ; maɪˈkɒlədʒi/ *n* [U] the study of fungi (FUNGUS) 真菌学

My Coun·try 'Tis of Thee /· ˌ· ·, · · ˈ·/ a PATRIOTIC song that praises the US. It has the same tune as the British song *God Save the Queen*, and it begins: *My country 'tis of thee, /Sweet land of liberty, /Of thee I sing.*《你是我的祖国》〔一首赞美美国的爱国歌曲，曲调与英国歌曲《神佑女王》相同。歌词开首如下：你是我的祖国，/甜美自由之乡，/我要为您歌唱〕

My Fair La·dy /ˌ· · ˈ· ·/ (1964) a US MUSICAL (=a film that uses singing and dancing to tell a story) in which Audrey Hepburn plays a poor young woman from London who is taught to speak and behave like an upper-class lady by a bad-tempered professor, played by Rex Harrison. It is based on the play *Pygmalion* by George Bernard Shaw.《窈窕淑女》〔(1964)，美国一音乐剧。剧中奥黛丽·赫本扮演伦敦的一个穷女孩。她在一位脾气暴躁的教授培养下，谈吐和举止酷似上流社会的贵妇人。教授由雷克斯·哈里森饰演。该剧根据乔治·萧伯纳的剧本《皮格马利翁》改编而成〕

My Lai /ˈmi ˈlaɪ; ˈmiː ˈlaɪ/ a village in Vietnam where, in 1968, a group of US soldiers killed several hundred people, mostly old people, women, and children, during the Vietnam War. This event, known as the **My Lai Massacre**, influenced many Americans to oppose the war. 米来〔越南一小村庄。1968年越战期间，一伙美国士兵杀害了该村的几百名村民，多为老人、妇女和儿童，史称"米来大屠杀"。这一事件促使许多美国人开始反对越战〕

my·nah bird /ˈmaɪnə bɝd; ˈmaɪnə bɜːd/ also 又作 **mynah** *n* [C] a large dark Asian bird that can copy human speech 八哥，鹩哥〔产于亚洲的一种能学说话的鸟〕

my·o·pi·a /maɪˈopɪə; maɪˈəupiə/ *n* [U] **1** inability to imagine what the results of your actions will be or how they will affect other people 目光短浅，缺乏远见 **2** *formal* inability to see things clearly that are far away【正式】近视

my·o·pic /maɪˈɑpɪk; maɪˈɒpɪk/ *adj* **1** unwilling or unable to think about the future results of your actions 目光短浅的，缺乏远见的: *the government's myopic refusal to take environmental issues seriously* 政府拒绝认真对待环境问题的短视行为 **2** *technical* unable to see things clearly that are faraway; SHORTSIGHTED (1)【术语】近视的 —**myopically** /-klɪ; -kli/ *adv*

myr·i·ad¹ /ˈmɪrɪəd; ˈmɪriəd/ *adj* [only before noun 仅用于名词前] *literary* too many to count【文】无数的，不计其数的: *Myriad bright stars shone in the sky above.* 无数明亮的星星在天空中闪耀。

myriad² *n* [C] *especially literary* a very large number of something【尤文】无数，极大数量: **[+of]** *myriads of small islands* 无数的小岛屿

myrrh /mɝ; mɜː/ *n* [U] a sticky brown substance that is used for making PERFUME and INCENSE〔制香水和香用的〕没药（树脂）

myr·tle /ˈmɝtl; ˈmɜːtl/ *n* [C] a small tree with shiny green leaves and sweet-smelling white flowers 爱神木，香桃木

my·self /maɪˈsɛlf; maɪˈself/ *pron* **1** [reflexive form of 'I' I的反身形式] 我自己: *I hurt myself.* 我把自己弄伤了。| *I passed the exam so I'm feeling pretty pleased with myself.* 我通过了考试，所以对自己感到非常满意。| *Those dishwashers are great. I think I'll get one for myself.* 那些洗碗机真棒，我想给自己买一台。**2** used to emphasize the pronoun I 我本人，我亲自〔用以强调代名词I〕: *Why do I always have to do everything myself?* 为什么我总是得亲自做每一件事？| *I'm sorry, I'm a stranger here myself.* 对不起，我自己也是新来这里的。| *I myself might have done things differently.* 要是我自己也许会用不同的方式行事了。**3 not be/feel etc myself** to not feel or behave in the way you usually do because you are nervous or upset 自我感觉不正常: *I do apologise – I haven't been feeling myself lately.* 我真的表示道歉 —— 我近来一直心神恍惚。**4 (all) by myself a)** alone 独自，单独: *If you don't mind, I'd like to be by myself for a while.* 如果你不介意的话，我想独自待一会儿。**b)** without help 独力地；独自地: *It's hard to believe but I painted the house all by myself.* 真不敢相信我自己一个人刷完了房子。**5 (all) to myself** if you have something to yourself, you do not have to share it with anyone 独自占有的，独用的: *I always dreamt of having a room all to myself.* 我一直梦想着有一个完全属于自己的房间。—see also 另见 YOURSELF

mys·te·ri·ous /mɪsˈtɪrɪəs; mɪˈstɪəriəs/ *adj* **1** mysterious events, behaviour, or situations are difficult to explain or understand 神秘的，难以解释[理解]的: *His father died of a mysterious disease.* 他父亲死于一种神秘的疾病。| *a mysterious smile* 神秘的微笑 | **in mysterious circumstances** *Benson later disappeared in mysterious circumstances.* 本森后来神秘地失踪了。**2** a mysterious person is someone who you know very little about and who seems strange or interesting〔人〕神秘的: *Who was this mysterious stranger?* 这个神秘的陌生人是谁？**3** saying very little about what you are doing; SECRETIVE 故弄玄虚的；诡秘的；遮遮掩掩的: **[+about]** *Helen's being very mysterious about her plans.* 海伦在对她的计划故弄玄虚。—**mysteriously** *adv* —**mysteriousness** *n* [U]

mys·te·ry /ˈmɪstrɪ; ˈmɪstəri/ *n* **1** [C] something that is impossible to understand or explain or about which little is known 神秘的事物，无法理解[解释]的事物，谜: **remain a mystery** *Twenty years after the event, his death remains a mystery.* 事情过去20年了，他的死仍然是个谜。| **solve/unravel a mystery** (=find an explanation for it) 解开一个谜 *They never solved the mystery of Gray's disappearance.* 他们从来没有解开格雷失踪之谜。| **a mystery phone call/lover/package etc** (=one that you know very little about, which therefore seems strange and interesting) 神秘的电话/情人/包裹等 *If I tell you the mystery ingredient, my recipe won't be a secret.* 如果我告诉你那种神秘的配料，我的食谱就不会是个秘密了。| **be a mystery to** (=used to say that you do not know or understand much about something) 对…是个谜 *Jean's business affairs were always a mystery to him.* 琼生意上的事对他来说一直是个谜。**2 It's a mystery to me** *spoken* used to say that you cannot understand something at all【口】对我来说是个谜: *It's a mystery to me how she manages to work so fast.* 她怎么能干得那么快，这对我来说是个谜。**3** [U] a quality that makes someone or something seem strange, secret, or difficult to explain 神秘（性）: **an air of mystery** *There was*

M

an air of mystery about him. 他为人诡异难测。| **be shrouded/veiled in mystery** *The circumstances of his death were veiled in mystery.* 他的死笼罩着一层神秘的色彩。**4** [C] *formal* a quality that something has that cannot be explained in any practical or scientific way, especially because it is connected with God and religion【正式】〔宗教的〕奥秘，玄理: [+of] *the mystery of creation* 天地万物的奥秘 **5** [C] a story about a murder, in which you are not told who the murderer is until the end 侦探[推理，疑案]故事: *a murder mystery* 有关谋杀的侦探故事

Mystery of Edwin Drood, The/ˌ‥ ‥ ‥ ˈ‥/ the last NOVEL by Charles Dickens, which was unfinished when he died in 1870《德鲁特疑案》〔查尔斯·狄更斯的辞世之作。1870年去世时，这部小说尚未完成〕

mystery play/ˈ‥ ‥ ·/ *n* [C] a religious play from the Middle Ages based on a story from the Bible〔中世纪依据圣经故事编写的〕神秘剧，神迹剧

mystery tour/ˈ‥ ‥ ·/ *n* [C] *BrE* a trip, usually by bus, in which people do not know where they will be taken【英】〔旅客事先不知道目的地、通常乘公共汽车进行的〕神秘旅游

mys·tic[1]/ˈmɪstɪk; ˈmɪstɪk/ *n* [C] someone who practises MYSTICISM 神秘主义者，通灵论者，通灵主义信奉者

mystic[2] *adj* another word for MYSTICAL mystical 的另一说法

mys·tic·al/ˈmɪstɪkḷ; ˈmɪstɪkəl/ *adj* **1** involving religious, spiritual, or magical powers that people cannot understand 神秘的，神奇的，不可思议的: *a mystical union with nature* 与大自然的神秘结合 | *the mystical significance of names and numbers* 名字和数字的玄妙含义 **2** connected with mysticism 神秘主义的，通灵(论)的 —**mystically**/-kḷɪ, -kli/ *adv*

mys·ti·cis·m/ˈmɪstəˌsɪzəm; ˈmɪstɨsɪzəm/ *n* [U] a religious practice in which people try to get knowledge of truth and to become united with God through prayer and MEDITATION 神秘主义，通灵论，通灵主义

mys·ti·fy/ˈmɪstəˌfaɪ; ˈmɪstɨfaɪ/ *v* [T] to be impossible for someone to understand or explain; BAFFLE[1] 使困惑不解，使迷惑; 难住: *a case that mystified the police* 使警方迷惑不解的案子 —**mystifying** *adj* —**mystification**/ˌmɪstəfəˈkeʃən; ˌmɪstɨfɨˈkeɪʃən/ *n* [U]

mys·tique/mɪsˈtik; mɪˈstiːk/ *n* [U] a quality that makes someone or something seem different, mysterious, or special 神秘性，神秘色彩: *Hollywood has lost none of its mystique.* 好莱坞丝毫也没有失去其神秘色彩。

myth /mɪθ; mɪθ/ *n* **1** [C,U] an idea or story that many people believe, but which is not true〔许多人相信但不真实的〕荒诞传说，无根据的观念: *the myth of male superiority* 没有根据的男性优越论观念 | *Most people think that bats are blind, but in fact this is a myth.* 大多数人认为蝙蝠看不见东西，但事实上这是一个错误的观念。| **popular myth**(=one that a lot of people believe) 许多人的误解，普遍的误解 *Contrary to popular myth, there is no evidence that long jail sentences really deter young offenders.* 与人们的普遍看法相反，没有证据表明长期囚禁真的会吓住年轻罪犯。| **explode/dispel a myth**(=prove that it is not true) 戳穿谎言，消除误解 **2** [C] an ancient story, especially one invented in order to explain natural or historical events〔古代的〕神话: *the myth of Orpheus* 关于俄尔甫斯的神话 **3** [U] this kind of ancient story in general 神话故事: *the giants of myth and fairy-tale* 神话和童话故事中的巨人

myth·ic/ˈmɪθɪk; ˈmɪθɪk/ *adj* like something or someone in a myth 像神话中人[物]的，神话般的: *mythic powers* 神奇的力量 | *mythic beauty* 仙女般的美丽

myth·i·cal/ˈmɪθɪkḷ; ˈmɪθɪkəl/ *adj* **1** connected with or only existing in an ancient story 神话的; 只存在于神话中的: *a mythical creature like the Minotaur* 神话中像弥诺陶洛斯〔古希腊神话中半人半牛的怪物〕一样的动物 **2** imagined or invented; FICTITIOUS 想象中的; 虚构的; 非真实的: *all these mythical 'job prospects' he keeps talking about* 他一直在谈论着的种种虚幻的"就业前景"

my·thol·o·gy/mɪˈθɑlədʒɪ; mɪˈθɒlədʒi/ *n* [C,U] **1** ancient myths in general, and the beliefs they represent 神话〔统称〕; 神话学: *scenes from classical mythology* 古典神话中的场面 **2** ideas or opinions that many people believe, but that are wrong or not true〔许多人所持有的〕错误的想法，不正确的看法: *popular mythology about the lives of the royal family* 公众关于王室生活的错误想法 —**mythologist** *n* [C] —**mythological**/ˌmɪθəˈlɑdʒɪkḷ; ˌmɪθəˈlɒdʒɪkəl◂/ *adj*: *a mythological hero* 神话中的英雄

myx·o·ma·to·sis/ˌmɪksəməˈtosɪs; ˌmɪksəməˈtəʊsɨs/ *n* [U] a disease that kills rabbits 多发性黏液瘤病，兔瘟

M

N,n

N

N, n /ɛn; en/ *plural* **N's, n's***n* [C] the 14th letter of the English alphabet 英语字母表的第十四个字母

N the written abbreviation of 缩写= north or northern

n[1] the written abbreviation of 缩写= NOUN

n[2] /ən; ən/ a short form of 缩略式= 'and': *rock 'n' roll* 摇滚乐

N/A not applicable; written on a form to show that you do not need to answer a question 不适用〔写在表格中表示某项无必要填写〕

NAACP /ˌɛn e e si ˋpi; ˌen eɪ eɪ siː ˈpiː/ *n* [singular] the National Association for the Advancement of Colored People; an American organization that works for the rights of African-American people〔美国〕全国有色人种协进会

Naaf·i /ˋnæfɪ; ˈnæfi/ *n* [C] a shop or eating place in a British military establishment〔英国军营中的〕小吃部, 小卖部; 小食堂

naan /nɑn; nɑːn/ *n* [U] another spelling of NAN[2] nan[2] 的另一种拼法

nab /næb; næb/ *v* **nabbed, nabbing**[T] *informal*【非正式】**1** to catch someone doing something illegal; ARREST[1] (1) 当场抓住; 逮捕 **2** to get something quickly 快速得到; 猛然抓住; 抢: *See if you can nab a seat.* 看你能不能抢个座位。

na·bob /ˋnebɑb; ˈneɪbɒb/ *n* [C] an Englishman in the 18th or 19th century who became rich in India and returned to Europe〔18 或 19 世纪〕在印度发财后回到欧洲的英国人

Na·bo·kov /nəˋbokɑf; nəˈbəʊkɒf/ **, Vlad·i·mir** /ˋvlædɪmɪr; ˈvlædəˌmɪə/ (1899-1977) a US writer who was born in Russia, and lived most of his life in Europe. He is best known for his NOVEL *Lolita*. 纳博科夫〔(1899-1977), 美国作家, 生于俄国, 大半生在欧洲度过, 以小说《洛丽塔》最为出名〕

nach·os /ˋnætʃoz; ˈnætʃəʊz/ *n* [plural] hot-tasting Mexican food consisting of small pieces of TORTILLAs covered with cheese, beans etc 辣味乳酪玉米〔墨西哥食物〕

na·cre /ˋnekɚ; ˈneɪkə/ *n* [U] MOTHER-OF-PEARL 珍珠母: *Buzz's gift, a nacre box, lay on the table.* 桌子上放着布兹的礼物——一个珍珠母做的盒子。—**nacreous***adj*

Na·der /ˋnedɚ; ˈneɪdə/ **, Ralph** /rælf; rælf/ (1934-) a US lawyer who is famous for criticizing the government and big companies, and for fighting for the rights and protection of CONSUMERs (=people who buy goods and services). He has also tried to run for president of the United States. 纳德〔(1934-), 美国律师, 以批评美国政府和大公司而闻名, 以努力维护消费者的权益而广为人知。他也曾竞选过美国总统〕

na·dir /ˋnedɚ; ˈneɪdɪə/ *n* [singular] *literary* the time when a situation is at its worst【文】最低点, 最糟的时刻: *By 1932, the depression had reached its nadir.* 经济大萧条在 1932 年到了最糟的时刻。

naff[1] /næf; næf/ *adj BrE slang* silly, especially in a way that shows a lack of good judgement about style, fashion etc【英俚】愚蠢的; 低级的: *a really naff film* 荒唐透顶的影片

naff[2] *v* **naff off***BrE spoken* used to tell someone rudely to go away【英口】滚开

nag[1] /næg; næg/ *v* **nagged, nagging**[I,T] **1** to keep complaining to someone about their behaviour or asking them to do something, in a way that is very annoying 唠叨; 不停地抱怨; 跟…纠缠不休: *I wish you'd stop nagging!* 我希望你别再唠叨了! | **nag sb to do sth***Nadia's been nagging me to fix the lamp.* 纳迪亚一直在唠叨着要我修理那盏灯。| **nag sb for***The kids are always nagging me for new toys.* 孩子们总是缠着要我买新玩具。**2** to make someone feel continuously worried or uncomfortable 困扰, 烦扰: [**+at**] *a problem that had been nagging at him for days* 已经困扰他多日的一个问题 | **nagged by doubts/worries/fears***Karen lay awake all night, nagged by doubts.* 卡伦满心疑虑, 一整夜都没有睡着。

nag[2] *n* [C] *informal*【非正式】**1** a person who nags continuously 爱唠叨的人 **2** a horse, especially one that is old or in bad condition 马〔尤指老马或驽马〕

Nag·a·sa·ki /ˌnægəˋsɑkɪ; ˌnægəˈsɑːki/ a city and port in the west of the island of Kyushu, Japan, which was badly damaged in 1945 when a US NUCLEAR bomb was dropped on it, killing very many people 长崎〔日本九州西部一港口城市。1945 年, 美国在该市投下了一枚原子弹, 该市遭受毁灭性破坏, 死者甚众〕—compare 比较 HIROSHIMA

nag·ging /ˋnægɪŋ; ˈnægɪŋ/ *adj* [only before noun 仅用于名词前] making you worry or feel pain all the time 无法摆脱的; 烦人的; 让人头痛的: **nagging doubt/fear/feeling etc***It was a week before the wedding, and there was still the nagging doubt in the back of her mind.* 尚有一星期就举行婚礼, 但她的内心却仍然无法摆脱疑虑。| **nagging toothache/headache/pain etc***Lee had a nagging pain in her back.* 李的背一直痛个不停。

Na·gor·no-Kar·a·bakh /nəˌgɔrno kɑrəˋbɑk; nəˌgɔːnəʊ kɑrəˈbɑːk/ an AUTONOMOUS (=partly independent) area in Azerbaijan. Capital: Stepanakert. Most of its people are Armenians who want to separate from Azerbaijan and join Armenia, and in the late 1980s and early 1990s there was fighting there between Armenians and Azerbaijanis. Nagorno-Karabakh is not officially an independent country, but it has its own government and its own president. 纳戈尔诺－卡拉巴赫〔阿塞拜疆一自治区。首府: 斯捷潘纳克特。居民大多是亚美尼亚人, 他们希望脱离阿塞拜疆, 并入亚美尼亚。20 世纪 80 年代末、90 年代初, 亚美尼亚人与阿塞拜疆人之间发生过冲突。纳戈尔诺－卡拉巴赫并不是一个正式的独立国家, 但有自己的政府和总统〕

nai·ad /ˋneæd; ˈnaɪæd/ *n* [C] a female spirit who, according to ancient Greek stories, lived in a lake, stream, or river〔古希腊神话故事中的〕水精; 水泉女神

nail[1] /nel; neɪl/ *n* [C] 3 **1** a thin pointed piece of metal which you force into a piece of wood with a hammer to fasten the wood to something else 钉子 **2** the hard smooth layer on the ends of your fingers and toes 指甲; 趾甲: *Damn! I've just broken a nail.* 该死! 我的指甲断了。**3 a nail in sb's/sth's coffin**something bad which will help to destroy someone's success or hopes 促使某人/某事物失败的因素: *This latest scandal was one more nail in the coffin of Manley's ambitions.* 最近这宗丑闻是对曼利雄心壮志的又一次致命打击。**4 on the nail a)** *BrE* if you pay money on the nail, you pay it immediately【英】当即, 当场〔付款〕**b)** *AmE* completely correct in what you say or when you guess something【美】准确(地): *Ed was right on the nail when he guessed Sue's age.* 埃德猜休的年龄猜得真准。—see also 另见 **as hard as nails**(HARD[1] (27)), **hit the nail on the head**(HIT[1] (24))

nail 钉子

head

钉头

nail[2] *v* [T] **1** [always+adv/prep] to fasten something to something else with a nail or nails 钉, 将…钉牢: **nail sth to/together/down etc***A sign saying 'No Fishing' had been nailed to the tree.* 树上钉着一块牌子, 上面写着"禁止钓鱼"。| *The lid was nailed down.* 盖子被钉牢了。**2** *informal* to catch someone and prove that they are guilty of a crime or something bad【非正式】抓住, 逮住: *It took us 10 years to nail the bastard who killed our daughter.* 我们花了 10 年时间, 终于将杀害我们女儿的那个杂种抓捕归案。| **nail sb for***The state police finally nailed him for fraud.* 州警方最终以诈骗罪逮捕了他。**3 nail sb to the wall/cross***especially AmE* to punish someone severely【尤美】严惩某人 **4 nail your colours to the mast***BrE* to say clearly and publicly which ideas or which people you support【英】明确表态 **5 nail a lie/rumours***informal* to prove that what someone has said is a lie【非正式】揭穿谎言/谣言

nailsb/sth ↔ **down***phr v* [T] *informal*【非正式】**1** to force someone to say clearly what they want or what they intend to do 强迫〔某人〕表明意图: **nail sb down to sth***Before they repair the car, nail them down to a price.* 修车前, 先让他们把价钱讲明白。**2** *AmE* to reach a final and definite decision about something【美】最终确定, 对…作出定论: *Two days isn't enough time to nail down the details of an agreement.* 要把协议的所有细节都确定下来, 两天的时间是不够的。

nail-bit·er /ˈ···/ *n* [C] *informal* a very exciting story, film etc【非正式】非常刺激的故事[影片]

nail-bit·ing /ˈ···/ *adj* [only before noun 仅用于名词前] extremely exciting because you do not know what is going to hap-

N

pen next 非常刺激的; 充满悬念的: *a nail-biting finish to the tennis final* 网球决赛中令人紧张的最后时刻

nail·brush /ˈ· ·/ *n* [C] a small, stiff brush for cleaning your fingernails 指甲刷 —see picture at 参见 BRUSH 图

nail file /ˈ· ·/ *n* [C] a thin piece of metal with a rough surface used for making your fingernails a nice shape 指甲锉

nail pol·ish /ˈ· ,··/ also 又作 **nail e·nam·el** /ˈ· ·,··/, **nail var·nish** /ˈ· ,··/ *BrE*【英】*n* [U] coloured or transparent liquid which is painted on women's fingernails or toenails to make them look attractive 指[趾]甲油: *pink nail polish* 粉红色指甲油

nail scis·sors /ˈ· ,··/ *n* [plural] a small pair of scissors for cutting fingernails or toenails 指[趾]甲剪 —see picture at 参见 SCISSORS 图

Nai·ro·bi /naɪˋrobɪ; naɪˈrəʊbi/ the capital of Kenya in East Africa 内罗毕〔东非肯尼亚首都〕

na·ive /nɑˋiv; naɪˈiːv/ *adj* not having much experience of how complicated life is so that you trust people too much and believe that good things will always happen 无经验的, 幼稚的, 天真的: *a group of young, naive revolutionaries* 一群年轻幼稚的革命者 | *You really believe him? How can you be so naive?* 你竟然相信他?你怎么会这么天真呢? —**naively** *adv*: *I had naively imagined that he was in love with me.* 我一直天真地以为他爱我。—**naivety** /nɑˋivtɪ; naɪˈiːvəti/ also 又作 **naiveté** /nɑˋivte; naɪˈiːvəteɪ/ *n* [U]: *dangerous political naivety* 危险的政治幼稚性

3 **na·ked** /ˋnekɪd; ˈneɪkɪ̈d/ *adj* **1** not wearing clothes or not covered by clothes; NUDE[1] 裸体的, 赤条条的: *The children swam naked in the lake.* 孩子光着身子在湖里游泳。| **stark naked** also 又作 **buck naked/naked as a jaybird** *AmE* (=completely naked)【美】一丝不挂的 **2 with the naked eye** without the help of any instrument 凭肉眼: *Bacteria can't be seen with the naked eye.* 细菌是肉眼无法看到的。**3 naked sword/light/flame etc** a sword etc that is not enclosed by a cover 无鞘剑/无罩灯/没有遮挡的火焰: *The naked light bulb glared in her eyes.* 无罩灯泡刺得她的双眼很不舒服。**4 naked truth/self-interest/aggression etc** truth etc that is not hidden and is shocking 明摆着的事实/明显的私利/赤裸裸的侵略: *Their claim was based on naked self-interest.* 他们的要求是建立在赤裸裸的利己主义基础上的。—**nakedly** *adv* —**nakedness** *n* [U]

Naked Ape, The /,· ·ˈ·/ (1967) a book by Desmond Morris which examines similarities in the behaviour of humans and APEs. The title is based on the fact that humans are the only type of ape which is not covered in hair.《裸猿》〔(1967), 德斯蒙德·莫里斯的著作。该书研究人和猿在行为上的相似之处。人类是唯一一种没有毛发蔽体的猿类动物, 书名由此而来〕

nam·by-pam·by /ˋnæmbɪ ˋpæmbɪ; ˌnæmbi ˈpæmbi◂/ *adj informal* too weak and gentle and lacking determination【非正式】柔弱的; 无决断的: *To these soldiers writing poetry must have seemed a namby-pamby sort of occupation.* 对这些士兵来说, 写诗一定是件婆婆妈妈的事。—**namby-pamby** *n* [C]

Name /nem; neɪm/ *n* [C] a member of Lloyd's, the international group of insurance underwriters based in London. The Names are wealthy people who accept a financial risk in an insurance contract, and in return for this they usually make large profits. Sometimes, however, they lose a lot of money when events happen which affect insurance companies, such as serious accidents involving ships or planes, or severe weather conditions that cause a lot of damage. 劳埃德投资人, 劳氏公司成员〔劳埃德公司是一个国际保险商联合组织, 总部在伦敦。其成员都十分富有, 自愿承担保险合同中的金融风险, 以此换取巨额利润。不过, 一旦遇到轮船、飞机失事等重大事故或者严重天气灾害, 保险公司就会受到影响, 他们也将蒙受巨额损失〕

1 1 **name¹** *n* **1** [C] the word that someone or something is called or known by 姓名; 姓; 名字; 名称: *What's the name of that river?* 那条河的名称是什么? | *Her name is Mandy Wilson.* 她的姓名是曼迪·威尔逊。| **first name/Christian name** *Her first name is Mandy.* 她的名字叫曼迪。| **last name/surname/family name** *Her surname is Wilson.* 她姓威尔逊。| **middle name** *Lots of girls have Elizabeth as their middle name.* 很多女孩的中名都叫伊丽莎白。| **full name** (=complete name) 全名 *Please leave your full name and address with reception.* 请在接待处留下您的全名和地址。| **know sb by name** (=know what someone is called) 知道某人叫什么名字 *It's a big school but the principal knows everyone by name.* 尽管这所学校很大, 但校长叫得上每个人的名字。| **by the name of** (=whose name is...) 名叫… *Is there anyone here by the name of Sommerville?* 这里有人叫萨默维尔吗? | **go by the name of** (=call yourself a particular name which may not be your real name)自称名叫 *a wrestler who went by the name of Mazambula* 一位自称名为马赞布拉的摔跤手 | **under the name (of)** (=using a name that is different from your own) 用…为别名; 以…为笔名 *H. H. Munro wrote under the name Saki.* H. H. 芒罗以笔名萨基从事写作。**2 call sb names** to say something nasty or insulting about someone 骂某人: **call sb all the names under the sun** (=say rude and insulting things about someone) 谩骂[辱骂]某人 **3** [singular] the opinion that people have about a person or organization; REPUTATION 名声; 名誉: **have a name for** (=be known by people to have a particular quality) 以…著称 *The company has a name for reliability.* 这家公司享有可靠的名声。| **get a good/bad name** *The restaurant got a bad name for slow service.* 这家餐馆因服务效率低而名声不好。| **make a name for yourself** (=become known and admired by many people) 出名, 闻名, 扬名 *Manyac made a name for himself in the Parisian art world.* 马尼亚克在巴黎艺术界出了名。**4 big/famous/household name** *informal* someone who is famous【非正式】名人, 名家, 知名人士: *some of the biggest names in show business* 演艺界中一些最出名的人物 **5 not have a penny to your name** *informal* to be very poor【非正式】一文不名, 十分贫穷 **6 in sb's name** if an official document, a hotel room etc is in someone's name it officially belongs to them or is for them 属于某人; 以某人的名义: *The mortgage is in my husband's name.* 抵押是以我丈夫的名义申请的。**7 do sth in the name of science/religion etc** to do something that is wrong and believe that you are doing it to support the work of science etc 借科学/宗教等的名义做某事: *cruel experiments on animals carried out in the name of science* 借科学名义进行的残忍的动物试验 **8 in the name of sb** doing something as someone else's representative 代表某人: *I claim this land in the name of the King!* 我代表国王宣布拥有这块土地! **9 in name only** if something exists in name only it does not really exist although it is officially said to 只是在名义上: *a democracy in name only* 有名无实的民主国家 **10 in all but name** if a situation exists in all but name, it is the real situation but people do not admit that it is 既成事实地, 不承认但已成事实地: *She was his wife in all but name.* 她虽无妻子的名分, 但事实上已经是他的妻子了。**11 I can't put a name to it** *spoken* used when you cannot remember what something is called【口】我忘了它叫什么, 我叫不出它的名字: *I know the tune but I can't put a name to it.* 我知道这首曲子, 但说不出曲名来。**12 take sb's name in vain** *often humorous* to talk about someone without showing respect【常幽默】以不尊重的方式谈论某人, 在背后说某人的闲话 **13 the name of the game** *informal* the most important thing or quality needed for a particular activity【非正式】〔从事某种活动所需的〕最重要的东西[元素]: *In fishing, patience is the name of the game.* 就钓鱼而言, 有耐性是最重要的。**14 sb's name is mud** *informal* used to say that people are angry with someone because of something he or she has done【非正式】某人声名狼藉 —see also 另见 PEN NAME, **clear sb's name** (CLEAR² (3))

name² *v* [T] 2 2

1 ►GIVE SB A NAME 给某人取名◄ to give someone or something a particular name 给…取名, 给…命名: **name sb John/Ann etc** *We named our daughter Sarah.* 我们给女儿取名为萨拉。| *I name this ship 'Arcadia'.* 我把这艘船命名为"世外桃源"。| **name sb after** *BrE*【英】**/name sb/sth for** *AmE*【美】(=give someone the same name as) 以…的名字给某人/某物命名 *Bill is named after his father.* 比尔以其父亲的名字命名。| *The college is named for George Washington.* 这所大学以乔治·华盛顿的名字命名。

2 ►SAY SB'S OR STH'S NAME 说出某人或某物的名字[名称]◄ to say what the name of someone or something is 说出…的名字: *Can you name this tune?* 你能说出这首曲子的名字吗? | *The two murder victims have yet to be named.* 这两个被谋杀者的姓名尚未公布。| **name names** (=name the people who were involved in something, especially something bad or illegal) 点名揭发 *She has secret information and is threatening to name names.* 她掌握着秘密情报, 并恐吓要把相关人员的名字捅出来。

3 ►CHOOSE SB 选择某人◄ to officially choose someone or something 选定; 指定; 任命: **name sb as** *Gerry's been named as successor to the present manager.* 杰里已被选定接替现任经理。| **name sb to sth** *AmE*【美】*Fitzgerald was named to the committee by the chairman.* 菲茨杰拉德被主席选定进入该委员会。

4 to name but a few used after a short list of things or people to say that there are many more you could mention 略举几例: *Gina Fratini, David Neil and Benny Ong, to name but a few, became famous when the Princess wore their designs.* 略举几个例子, 吉纳·弗拉蒂尼、戴维·尼尔和本尼·翁都因王妃穿了他们所设计的时装而出了名。

5 you name it *spoken* used after a list of things to mean that there are many more you could mention【口】凡是你说得出的,

应有尽有: *Clothes, furniture, books – you name it, they sell it!* 服装、家具、书籍 —— 凡是你说得出的, 他们都卖!
6 name the day to decide on a date for your wedding 选定结婚日期
7 name your price used to mean that you can decide how much money you want to buy or sell something for (自己)出个价钱

name-cal·ling /ˈ· ,··/ *n* [U] the act of saying nasty things about someone 辱骂, 骂人〔行为〕: *children subjected to jibes and name-calling* 遭受嘲讽和辱骂的孩子们

name day /ˈ· ·/ *n* [C] the day each year when the Christian church gives honour to the particular SAINT (=holy person) whose name you have been given 命名日〔基督教教会纪念某圣徒的日子〕

name·drop /ˈnem,drɑp; ˈneɪmdrɒp/ *v* [I] *informal* to mention famous or important people's names to make it seem that you know them personally【非正式】〔在言谈中〕提及名人[要人]的名字〔表示和他们相识, 以抬高自己的身价〕—**namedropping** *n* [U]

name·less /ˈnemlɪs; ˈneɪmləs/ *adj* **1** not known by name; ANONYMOUS 不知名的; 匿名的: *the work of a nameless 13th century writer* 13世纪一位不知名作家的作品 **2 a)** [only before noun 仅用于名词前] *literary* difficult to describe【文】难以名状的, 难以形容的: *Nameless fears made her tremble.* 不可名状的恐惧使她全身颤抖。**b)** too terrible to name or describe 坏得说不出口的: *nameless crimes* 难以言喻的罪行 **3** having no name 无名的, 未取名的: *hundreds of nameless canyons* 数百个无名峡谷 **4 who shall remain nameless** *spoken* used when you want to say that someone has done something wrong but without mentioning their name【口】不便说出其名字的: *A certain person, who shall remain nameless, forgot to lock the front door.* 某位我不便说出名字的人忘了锁上前门。

name·ly /ˈnemlɪ; ˈneɪmli/ *adv* used to introduce additional information which makes it clear exactly who or what you are talking about 即, 也就是(说): *Three students were mentioned, namely John, Sarah and Sylvia.* 有三位学生被提到, 他们是约翰、萨拉和西尔维娅。

name·plate /ˈnemplet; ˈneɪmpleɪt/ *n* [C] a piece of metal or plastic fastened to something, showing the name of the owner or maker, or the person who lives or works in a place 姓名牌; 名称牌; 名牌

name·sake /ˈnem,sek; ˈneɪmseɪk/ *n* [C] **sb's namesake** another person, especially a more famous person, who has the same name as someone〔尤指较著名的〕同(姓)名的人: *Like his famous namesake, young Nelson had a brave, adventurous spirit.* 像与他同名的那位名人一样, 小纳尔逊具备勇敢、冒险的精神。

name tag /ˈ· ·/ *n* [C] a small sign with your name on it that you wear〔胸前佩戴的〕姓名牌

name-tape /ˈ· ·/ *n* [C] *BrE* a small piece of cloth with your name on it that is sewn onto clothes【英】〔缝在衣服上的〕标有姓名的布条; LABEL[1] (1) *AmE*【美】

Na·mib·i·a /nəˈmɪbɪə; nəˈmɪbiə/ a country in southwest Africa, west of Botswana and north of South Africa. Population: 1,798,000 (2001). Capital: Windhoek. Namibia was formerly called South West Africa, and until 1990 it was controlled by South Africa. 纳米比亚〔非洲西南部一国家, 位于博茨瓦纳以西和南非以北。人口: 1,798,000 (2001), 首都: 温得和克。旧称西南非洲, 1990年之前受南非控制〕—**Namibian** *n, adj*

nan[1] /næn; næn/ *n* [C] *BrE informal* a word meaning grandmother, used by children【英, 非正式】奶奶; 外婆〔儿语〕

nan[2], naan /nɑn; nɑːn/ *n* [U] a type of bread made without YEAST and eaten with Indian food〔未经发酵的〕印度式面包

Nanak /ˈnɑnək; ˈnɑːnək/, **Gu·ru** /ˈguru; ˈgʊruː/ (1469-?1539) an Indian religious leader who started the Sikh religion. He lived and taught in the Punjab region of northern India. 那纳克〔(1469-?1539), 印度一宗教领袖, 锡克教创始人。他居住在印度北部的旁遮普地区, 并在那里传教〕

nan·ny /ˈnænɪ; ˈnæni/ *n* [C] **1** a woman whose job is to take care of the children in a family, usually in the children's own home〔照看小孩的〕保姆 **2** *BrE informal* a word meaning grandmother, used by children【英, 非正式】奶奶; 外婆〔儿语〕: *It's my Nanny's birthday.* 今天是我奶奶的生日。**3 the nanny state** *especially BrE* a government which tries to control the lives of citizens too much【尤英】保姆国家; 保姆政府〔指过分干涉国民生活的政府〕

nanny goat /ˈ·· ·/ *n* [C] a female goat 雌山羊

nano- /næno; nænəʊ/ *prefix* one thousand millionth of a particular unit 纳, 毫微, 10^{-9}: *nanometre* (=one thousand millionth of a metre) 纳米, 10^{-9}米 —see table on page C4 参见C4页附录

nan·o·sec·ond /ˈnæno,sɛkənd; ˈnænəʊ,sekənd/ *n* [C] a unit for measuring time. There are one thousand million nanoseconds in a second 毫微秒, 十亿分之一秒

Nan·tuck·et /nænˈtʌkɪt; nænˈtʌkɪt/ an island off the coast of Massachusetts in the US. It used to be a port for ships hunting WHALES, but it is now a popular place for holidays, and many wealthy people have summer homes there. 楠塔基特〔美国马萨诸塞州沿海一岛屿。过去曾为捕鲸船停靠的港口, 现为度假胜地, 许多富人在岛上拥有消夏别墅〕

nap[1] /næp; næp/ *n* **1** [C] a short sleep, especially during the day〔尤指白天的〕小睡, 打盹儿: **have/take a short nap** *I usually take a nap after lunch.* 我午饭后通常要小睡一会儿。**2** [singular] the soft surface on some cloth and leather, made by brushing the short, fine threads or hairs in one direction〔布或皮革上的〕绒面, 绒毛 —compare 比较 PILE[1] (4) **3** [C] information about the horse likely to win a race〔赛马中的〕获胜预测

nap[2] *v* **napped, napping 1** [I] to sleep for a short time during the day〔在白天〕小睡, 打盹儿 **2 be caught napping** *informal* to not be ready to deal with something when it happens, although you should be ready for it【非正式】措手不及, 没有防备 **3** [T] to give advice about which horse is likely to win a race〔在赛马中〕作获胜预测

na·palm /ˈnepɑm; ˈneɪpɑːm/ *n* [U] a thick liquid made from petrol, which is used in bombs〔炸弹中使用的〕凝固汽油

nape /nep; neɪp/ *n* [singular] the back of your neck 颈背, 后颈: *He nuzzled the soft, warm nape of her neck.* 他紧贴着她那柔软温暖的后颈。

naph·tha /ˈnæfθə; ˈnæfθə/ *n* [U] a chemical compound like petrol 石脑油

nap·kin /ˈnæpkɪn; ˈnæpkɪn/ *n* [C] **1** a square piece of cloth or paper used for protecting your clothes and for cleaning your hands and lips during a meal〔布或纸质的〕餐巾 —see picture on page A10 参见A10页图 **2** SANITARY PAD *AmE*【美】卫生巾

napkin ring /ˈ·· ,·/ *n* [C] a small ring in which a napkin is put and kept for someone to use at the next meal 餐巾套环

Na·ples /ˈnepl̩z; ˈneɪpəlz/ **1** an industrial city and port in southeast Italy. Naples is the main city of southern Italy, and its beautiful position, which is on the **Bay of Naples** and near to Mount Vesuvius, makes it a popular place for tourists to visit. People from Naples are called 'Neapolitans'. 那不勒斯〔意大利东南部一港口工业城市。该市是意大利南部主要城市, 位于那不勒斯湾, 靠近维苏威火山。所在地区风景如画, 因而该市也是旅游观光的好去处 。那不勒斯人被称为Neapolitan〕**2 see Naples and die** a saying which means that once you have seen Naples, you can die, because you will never see anything more beautiful 看过那不勒斯死而无憾〔意思是目睹了那不勒斯, 即使死了, 也可瞑目, 因为再也看不到更美的景致了〕

Na·po·le·on[1] /nəˈpolɪən; nəˈpəʊliən/ **Napoleon Bonaparte** (1769-1821) the emperor of France from 1804 to 1815. He was a great and very skilful military leader and his armies took control of many European countries, which then became part of his EMPIRE. In 1815 he was defeated at the Battle of Waterloo and was forced to spend the rest of his life on the island of St Helena. Napoleon also changed the way that France was organized, and established a new system of laws, called the 'Napoleonic Code', on which modern French law is based. 拿破仑〔(1769-1821), 法国皇帝, 1804至1815年在位。他是一位伟大的、战术高超的军事领袖, 曾率军占领了欧洲许多国家, 并将这些国家并入法兰西帝国的版图。1815年, 他在滑铁卢战役中战败, 被迫在圣赫勒拿岛上度过余生。拿破仑还改革了法国的社会组织形态, 建立了一套全新的法律体系, 史称"拿破仑法典", 构成了现代法国法律的基础〕

Napoleon[2] a main character in Animal Farm, a SATIRE on the autocratic regimes by George Orwell. Napoleon is a pig who chases his RIVALS off the farm to win power. Napoleon represents a DICTATOR. 拿破仑〔《动物农场》里一主要人物。英国作家乔治·奥威尔借此小说讽刺专制制度。故事中的拿破仑是一头猪, 将对手逐出农场以赢得权力。小说中的拿破仑影射独裁者〕

Na·po·le·on·ic Wars, the /nə,polɪˈɑnɪk ˈwɔrz; nə,pəʊliɒnɪk ˈwɔːz/ a series of wars from 1799 to 1815, fought between France when it was ruled by Napoleon, and several other European countries, including Britain. They ended when Napoleon was defeated at the Battle of Waterloo. 拿破仑战争〔1799至1815年间拿破仑统治下的法国与包括英国在内的欧洲几个国家进行的一系列战争。这些战争以拿破仑在滑铁卢一役中战败而告终〕

nap·py /ˈnæpɪ; ˈnæpi/ *n* [C] *BrE* a piece of soft cloth or paper worn by a baby between its legs and fastened around its waist to hold its liquid and solid waste【英】尿布; DIAPER *AmE*【美】 S3

N

nappy rash /ˈ·· ·/ *n* [U] *BrE* sore skin between a baby's legs and on its BUTTOCKS caused by a wet or dirty nappy【英】尿布疹; DIAPER RASH *AmE*【美】

narc¹ /nɑrk; nɑːk/ *n* [C] *AmE informal* a police officer who deals with the problem of illegal drugs【美, 非正式】缉毒警察

narc² *v* [I+on] *AmE slang* to secretly tell the police about someone else's criminal activities, especially activities involving illegal drugs【美俚】告密〔尤指向警方透露有关贩毒的情报〕

nar·cis·sis·m /nɑrˋsɪsˌɪzəm; ˈnɑːsɨsɪzəm/ *n* [U] a tendency to admire your own physical appearance or abilities 自我陶醉; 自恋: *He went to the gym to train every day, driven purely by narcissism.* 他每天都去健身房健身, 纯粹出于自我欣赏。—**narcissist** *n* [C] —**narcissistic** /ˌnɑrsɪˋsɪstɪk; ˌnɑːsɨˋsɪstɪk◂/ *adj*

Nar·cis·sus /nɑrˋsɪsəs; nɑːˈsɪsəs/ in Greek MYTHOLOGY, a beautiful young man who fell in love with his own reflection when he saw his face in a pool of water. Because he became very unhappy as a result, he gradually became so weak that he died. A flower grew up in the place where he died, which was called narcissus after him. 那喀索斯〔希腊神话中一美少年。他在水中看到自己的面容, 从此便迷恋上那个倒影。他因思恋而心中不悦, 并日渐憔悴, 最后死去。他死去的地方长出了 种花, 根据他的名字取名 narcissus (水仙花)〕—see also 另见 NARCISSISM

narcissus *n* [C] a white or yellow spring flower, such as the DAFFODIL 水仙花

nar·cot·ic¹ /nɑrˋkɑtɪk; nɑːˈkɒtɪk/ *n* **1 narcotics** [plural] *especially AmE* illegal drugs that affect the mind in a harmful way【尤美】毒品: **narcotics agent** (=a police officer who deals with the problems of narcotics) 缉毒警察 **2** [C] a type of drug which makes you sleep and reduces pain 安眠药; 麻醉剂

narcotic² *adj* **1** [only before noun 仅用于名词前] *especially AmE* connected with illegal drugs【尤美】(有关) 毒品的: *narcotic addiction* 毒瘾 **2** a narcotic drug takes away pain or makes you sleep 麻醉 (性) 的; 催眠 (用) 的

nark¹ /nɑrk; nɑːk/ *n* [C] *BrE slang* someone who is friendly with criminals and who secretly tells the police about their activities【英俚】〔向警方提供情报的〕线人; STOOLPIGEON *AmE*【美】

nark² *v BrE slang*【英俚】**1 be/get narked** to be angry or get angry about something someone has done 生气, 发火: *I was really narked when she wouldn't listen to me.* 她不听我的话时, 我真的非常生气。**2** [I+on] to secretly tell the police about someone else's criminal activities〔向警方〕告密

nark·y /ˈnɑrkɪ; ˈnɑːki/ *adj BrE slang* bad-tempered【英俚】脾气坏的, 暴躁的

Nar·ni·a /ˈnɑrnɪə; ˈnɑːniə/ an imaginary land of magic people and animals visited by four children in *The Lion, the Witch and the Wardrobe* and other children's stories written by C. S. Lewis 纳尼亚〔虚构的一片大陆。那里住着一群有魔法的人和动物, 是英国小说家C.S.刘易斯创作的《狮子、女巫和衣橱》等儿童故事中的四个小孩曾去过的地方〕

nar·rate /næˋret; nəˈreɪt/ *v* [T] *formal* to tell a story by describing all the events in order【正式】讲〔故事〕; 叙述, 描述: *a wild life film narrated by David Attenborough* 一部由戴维·阿滕伯勒解说的野生动物影片

nar·ra·tion /næˋreʃən; nəˈreɪʃən/ *n* [C,U] *formal*【正式】**1** the act of telling a story 讲故事 **2** a spoken description or explanation which is given during a film, play etc〔电影、戏剧等的〕旁白; 解说

nar·ra·tive /ˈnærətɪv; ˈnærətɪv/ *n* **1** [C,U] *formal* something that is told as a story【正式】叙述, 记叙: *The last chapter of the book brings the narrative of his journey to an end.* 书的最后一章结束了对他旅途的叙述。**2** [U] the art of telling a story 叙述 (艺术) —**narrative** *adj*: *a narrative poem* 叙事诗

nar·ra·tor /næˋretɚ; nəˈreɪtə/ *n* [C] a person in some books, plays etc who tells the story〔书、戏剧等中的〕叙述者, 讲解人, 解说人

S3 W2 **nar·row¹** /ˈnæro; ˈnærəʊ/ *adj*

1 ▶NOT WIDE 不宽的◀ not wide, especially in comparison with length or with what is usual 狭窄的: *a narrow winding valley* 狭长蜿蜒的山谷 | *a long narrow room* 窄长形房间 | *There are plans to widen the narrowest sections of the road.* 有计划要拓宽该道路最狭窄的部分。—compare 比较 BROAD¹ (1) —opposite 反义词 WIDE¹ (1) —see picture at 参见 THIN¹ 图

2 narrow escape a situation in which you only just avoid danger, difficulties, or trouble 死里逃生, 险些遇险: *Peter had a narrow escape from drowning when he fell overboard.* 彼得从船上掉入水中, 险些淹死。

3 narrow majority/victory/defeat etc one that is only just achieved or happens by only a small amount 微弱多数/险胜/勉强击败

4 by a narrow margin if you win or lose by a narrow margin, you do it by only a small amount 幅度有限地, 相差不多地

5 ▶IDEAS/ATTITUDES 观点/态度◀ a narrow attitude or way of looking at a situation is too limited and does not consider enough possibilities 狭隘的; 不够全面的: *The company takes too narrow a view of possible export markets.* 公司对潜在出口市场的看法过于狭隘。| *Each group has their own narrow economic interest.* 每个群体都有自己狭隘的经济利益。—see also 另见 NARROW-MINDED

6 narrow squeak *informal* a situation in which you only just escape from danger or avoid an accident【非正式】死里逃生; 勉强避过危险

7 *formal* careful and thorough【正式】精细而严密的: *a narrow examination of events* 对所有事件进行的严密审查 —see also 另见 NARROWLY, NARROWS, **keep to/stray from the straight and narrow** (STRAIGHT³ (4)) —**narrowness** *n* [U]

narrow² *v* [I,T] **1** to become narrower or make something narrower (使) 变窄: *The river narrows at this point.* 河在这里变窄了。| *He narrowed his eyes against the sun.* 他眯起了双眼盯着太阳。**2** also 又作 **narrow down** to become less or make something less in range, difference etc 缩小…的范围: *The police have narrowed down their list of suspects.* 警方已经缩小了嫌疑犯的范围。| *New tax laws will narrow the gap between rich and poor.* 新税法将会缩小贫富差距。| *The choice of goods available is narrowing.* 可供选择的商品越来越少。

narrow boat /ˈ·· ·/ *n* [C] *BrE* a long, narrow boat for use on CANALS【英】〔运河中的〕狭长小船

narrow gauge /ˈ·· ·/ *n* [C] a size of railway track of less than standard width 窄轨 (铁路) —see also 另见 GAUGE¹ (3)

nar·row·ly /ˈnærolɪ; ˈnærəʊli/ *adv* **1** only by a small amount 勉强地, 差一点儿: *We narrowly missed hitting the other car.* 我们差一点撞上另一辆汽车。| *The amendment was narrowly defeated.* 修正案差了几票未获通过。**2** looking at or considering only a small part of something 狭隘地, 不全面地: *The law is being interpreted too narrowly.* 对该法律的诠释过于狭隘。**3** *formal* in a thorough way, looking for detail【正式】彻底地, 仔细地: *The teacher questioned the boy narrowly about why he was late.* 老师追根究底地盘问那男孩为什么迟到。

narrow-mind·ed /ˌ·· ˈ··◂/ *adj* unwilling to accept or understand new or different ideas or customs; PREJUDICED 心胸狭窄的, 气量小的; 不开放的; 有偏见的 —opposite 反义词 BROADMINDED —**narrow-mindedness** *n* [U] —**narrow-mindedly** *adv*

nar·rows /ˈnæroz; ˈnærəʊz/ *n* [plural] **1** also 又作 **Narrows** a narrow passage of water between two pieces of land which connects two larger areas of water 海峡; 江峡 **2** *AmE* a narrow part of a river, lake etc【美】〔江、湖等的〕狭窄处

na·ry /ˈnɛrɪ; ˈneəri/ *adv old use* not one【旧】一个也没有: *They said nary a word.* 他们一个字也没有说。

NASA /ˈnæsə; ˈnæsə/ *n* [singular] National Aeronautics and Space Administration; a US government organization that controls space travel and the scientific study of space 美国航空航天局, 美国太空总署

na·sal¹ /ˈnezḷ; ˈneɪzəl/ *adj* **1** related to the nose 鼻 (子) 的: *the nasal passage* 鼻腔 —see picture at 参见 RESPIRATORY 图 **2** a sound or voice that is nasal comes mainly through your nose 有鼻音的: *He spoke in a high nasal voice.* 他说话鼻音很重。**3** *technical* a nasal CONSONANT or vowel such as /n/ or /m/ is one that is produced wholly or partly through your nose【术语】〔发音〕鼻音的 —**nasally** *adv*

nasal² *n* [C] *technical* a particular speech sound, such as /m/, /n/, or /ŋ/ that is made through your nose【术语】鼻音

na·sal·ize also 又作 **-ise** *BrE*【英】/ˈnezḷˌaɪz; ˈneɪzəlaɪz/ *v* [T] to make a sound partly through your nose 使…鼻音化; 将…发成鼻音: *nasalized vowels* 鼻元音

nas·cent /ˈnæsṇt; ˈnæsənt/ *adj formal* coming into existence or starting to develop【正式】初生的, 新生的; 开始发展的: *South Africa's nascent democracy* 南非刚刚开始发展的民主

NASDAQ /ˈnæzdæk; ˈnæzdæk/ a US organization that provides information through the Internet about the price of shares of certain businesses, especially companies in the computer industry and other areas of science and technology 纳斯达克, 全国证券交易商自动报价协会〔美国一机构, 专门通过互联网提供某些企业, 尤其是计算机等科技公司的股票价格信息〕

Nash /næʃ; næʃ/, **Og·den** /ˈɑgdən; ˈɒgdən/ (1902-71) a US poet who wrote amusing poems 纳什〔(1902-1971), 美国诗人, 创作幽默诗歌〕

Nash·ville /ˈnæʃvɪl; ˈnæʃvɪl/ the capital city of the state of Tennessee, US, famous as the centre of the COUNTRY AND WEST-

ERN music industry 纳什维尔〔美国田纳西州首府，以美国乡村和西部音乐产业中心闻名〕

Nas·sau /ˈnæs,ɔ; ˈnæsɔː/ the capital city and main port of the Bahamas, on the northeast coast of New Providence Island 拿骚〔巴哈马首都和主要港口，位于新普罗维登斯岛东北沿海地区〕

Nas·ser /ˈnæsɚ; ˈnæsə/, **Ga·mal Ab·dal** /gəˈmɑl ˈæbdl; gəˈmɑːl ˈæbdəl/ (1918-70) an Egyptian army officer and politician, who was the first President of the Republic of Egypt (1956-70). He successfully took control of the Suez Canal from France and Britain in 1956, and this made him extremely popular in Egypt. 纳赛尔〔(1918-1970)，埃及军官、政治家，埃及共和国的首任总统(1956-1970)。1956年，他从法、英两国手中成功收回苏伊士运河的控制权，从而使他在埃及的声望达到极致〕

nas·tur·tium /næˈstɝʃəm; nəˈstɜːʃəm/ *n* [C] a garden plant with orange, yellow, or red flowers and circular leaves 旱金莲

2 **nas·ty** /ˈnæstɪ; ˈnɑːsti/ *adj*

1 ▶BEHAVIOUR 行为◀ nasty behaviour or remarks are extremely unkind and unpleasant; MALICIOUS 不友善的；不好的；恶毒的：*a nasty temper* 坏脾气 | *That's a nasty thing to say!* 说这话真恶毒！| *There's a nasty streak in her character.* 她性格中有坏的一面。| **be nasty to** (=treat someone in an unkind way) 对…不友善 *Don't be so nasty to your mum.* 别对你妈妈这么凶。| **get/turn nasty** *especially BrE* (=suddenly start behaving in a threatening way)【尤英】突然变凶 *Don't tease the dog. He might turn nasty.* 别逗那条狗，它会变得很凶的。

2 ▶SIGHT/SMELL ETC 景象/气味等◀ having a bad appearance, smell, taste etc 难看的；难闻的；难吃的：*The medicine tastes nasty, but it works.* 这药虽然难吃，但很管用。| **cheap and nasty** *cheap and nasty furniture* 廉价而难看的家具

3 nasty illness/cut/wound etc an illness etc that is severe or very painful 严重的疾病/割伤/伤口等：*a nasty cut on the head* 头部严重的伤口

4 ▶EXPERIENCE/SITUATION 经历/情况◀ a nasty experience, feeling or situation is unpleasant 令人不快的，糟糕的：*nasty weather* 恶劣的天气 | *It gave me a nasty shock.* 这使我非常震惊。| *I have a nasty suspicion that he's going to make us pay for everything.* 我有个不祥的感觉，他会让我们为这一切付出代价。| **leave a nasty taste in the mouth** (=make you feel upset or angry afterwards) 使人事后懊恼不已 *When you feel you've been cheated, it always leaves a nasty taste in the mouth.* 你感觉受骗时，总会有一种懊恼的感觉。

5 ▶OFFENSIVE 冒犯人的◀ morally bad or offensive; OBSCENE (1) 不道德的；下流的，猥亵的：*nasty language* 下流话 | *You've got a nasty mind.* 你的思想很肮脏。

6 a nasty piece of work *BrE* someone who is dishonest, violent, or likely to cause trouble【英】不诚实的人；凶暴的人；易惹麻烦的人 —see also 另见 VIDEO NASTY —**nastily** *adv* —**nastiness** *n* [U]

na·tal /ˈnetl; ˈneɪtl/ *adj technical* connected with birth【术语】出生的：*the salmon's natal stream* 鲑鱼出生的河流

natch /nætʃ; nætʃ/ *adv* [sentence adverb 句子副词] *slang* used to say that something is exactly as you would expect【俚】当然：*"What does he drive?" "A BMW, natch."* "他开什么车？""当然是宝马。"

3 2 **na·tion** /ˈneʃən; ˈneɪʃən/ *n* [C] **1** a country, considered especially in relation to its people and its social or economic structure 国家：*the President's radio broadcast to the nation* 总统对全国的广播讲话 | *the world's leading industrial nations* 世界上的主要工业国 **2** a large group of people of the same race and language 民族：*the Cherokee nation* 切罗基民族 —see 见 RACE[1] (USAGE)

1 1 **na·tion·al[1]** /ˈnæʃənl; ˈnæʃənəl/ *adj* **1** related to a whole nation as opposed to any of its parts 国家的，全国性的：*national and local news* 全国及地方新闻 **2** related to a nation as opposed to other nations 国内的，本国的：*We refuse to sign any treaty that is against our national interests.* 我们拒绝签署任何违反本国利益的条约。| *selling to national and international markets* 销往国内外市场 **3** [only before noun 仅用于名词前] owned or controlled by the central government of a country 国有的；国立的：*a national bank* 国有银行 | *the National Health Service* 〔英国〕国民保健制度 —see also 另见 NATIONALLY

national[2] *n* [C] someone who is a citizen of a particular country but is living in another country〔侨居国外的〕(某国)国民，侨民：*Foreign nationals were advised to leave the country.* 建议外国侨民离开该国。—compare 比较 ALIEN[2] (1), CITIZEN (2), SUBJECT[1] (6)

National, the 1 the GRAND NATIONAL (英国) 全国越野障碍大赛马 **2** the NATIONAL THEATRE (英国) 皇家国家剧院

national an·them /,···ˈ··/ *n* [C] the official song of a nation that is sung or played on certain formal occasions 国歌

National As·so·ci·a·tion for the Ad·vance·ment of Col·ored Peo·ple /,··· ··,·· · · ·,·· ˈ·· ˈ··,·/ *n* [singular] the NAACP

National Bas·ket·ball As·so·ci·a·tion /,··ˈ··· ···,·/ *n* [singular] the NBA

National Can·cer In·sti·tute, the /,··ˈ··,···/ a US organization that works to discover the causes of cancer and to find treatments and cures for it 国家肿瘤研究所〔美国一组织，致力于探究癌症致病原因、寻找诊治方法〕

National Centre for Popular Music, the /,···,·· ·,···ˈ··/ a MUSEUM of POP and ROCK music in Sheffield, UK, in a specially built building which is shaped like four very large, shiny drums, and which contains information about pop and rock music and shows films of musicians playing 国家流行音乐中心〔位于英国设菲尔德的一个流行乐和摇滚乐博物馆。该建筑造型别致，像四面闪亮的巨型鼓。馆藏有流行乐和摇滚乐资料，并放映音乐家的演出录像〕

National Child·birth Trust, the /,···ˈ··,·/ abbreviation 缩写为 NCT a British organization that provides advice and information to women who are going to have babies. It supports women who want to give birth naturally, without the use of drugs, and it encourages new mothers to BREASTFEED their babies instead of giving them milk made from powder. 全国分娩照管协会〔英国一组织，专为即将分娩的孕妇提供生育咨询和信息，提倡妇女自然分娩，不用药物，并鼓励产妇用母乳喂养新生儿，而不用奶粉〕

National Col·le·gi·ate Ath·let·ic As·so·ci·a·tion /,··· ·ˈ··· ·ˈ···,·/ *n* [singular] the NCAA

National Con·fe·rence, the /,···ˈ···/ a group of American football teams in the US that play against one another. There is another group of teams called the American Conference, and the best team from that group plays the best team from the National Conference in the Super Bowl, the most important football game of the year 全国橄榄球联盟〔由美国职业橄榄球队组成。另一个橄榄球组织称美国橄榄球联盟，其最佳球队在超级碗赛上与全国橄榄球联盟最佳球队比赛。超级碗赛是每年最重要的橄榄球比赛〕

national cos·tume /,···ˈ··/ *n* [C,U] special clothing traditionally worn by the people of a particular country; NATIONAL DRESS 民族服装：*folk dancers in national costume* 身穿民族服装的民间舞蹈演员

national debt /,···ˈ·/ *n* [C] the total amount of money owed by the government of a country 国债

national dress /,···ˈ·/ *n* [U] national costume 民族服装

National Eas·ter Seal So·ci·e·ty, the /,···,··ˈ· ·,···/ a US CHARITY organization that helps disabled children and adults. It makes sure that they are treated fairly, become independent, and have equal rights. 全国复活节誓约协会〔美国一帮助残疾人的慈善组织，旨在确保残疾人获得公平待遇，逐步独立生活，并拥有平等权利〕

National Ed·u·ca·tion As·so·ci·a·tion, the /,···,·ˈ·· ···,·/ *n* [singular] the NEA

National En·dow·ment for the Arts /,··· ·ˈ··· ·ˈ·/ abbreviation 缩写为 NEA a US government organization that provides money for artists, MUSEUMS, theatre companies etc, to help them in their work. There is a similar organization in the UK called the Arts Council. 全国艺术基金会〔美国一政府机构，专为艺术家、博物馆、剧团等提供资助以帮助其开展工作。英国也有一类似机构，名为"艺术总会"〕

National En·dow·ment for the Hu·man·i·ties, the /,···,·· · · ·ˈ··/ abbreviation 缩写为 NEH a US government organization which provides money for writers and other people working in the humanities (=subjects like history, language, and literature) to help them with their work 全国人文学科基金会〔美国一政府机构，专为作家等人文学科工作者提供资助以帮助其开展工作〕

National En·quir·er, The /,···ˈ··/ *trademark* a US weekly TABLOID newspaper that has strange, unbelievable articles about famous people and SUPERNATURAL events【商标】《国家询问者报》〔美国一小型周报，刊登有关名人和超自然现象的离奇报道〕

National Ex·hi·bi·tion Cen·tre, the /,··· ··ˈ··,··/ the full name of the NEC 国家展览中心〔NEC 的全称〕

National Farm·ers U·nion, the /,···ˈ··,·/ abbreviation 缩写为 NFU a British organization that provides advice and support for farmers. Although it is called a 'union', it is not a TRADE UNION, but it tries to influence politicians to support

口语及书面语中最常用的 1 000词，2 000词，3 000词

policies (POLICY) that help its members. 全国农场主联合会〔英国专为农场主提供建议和支援的一个组织。虽然它被称为union，但不是工会。不过，该组织力图对政治人物施加影响，让他们支持对其成员有利的政策〕

National Film Thea·tre, the /,··· '·,·/ abbreviation 缩写为 **NFT** a building containing two cinemas on the South Bank in London, which is part of the British Film Institute. It is known for showing films that are not shown at ordinary cinemas, including old films, foreign films, and films made by small companies 国家电影院〔伦敦南岸一幢建筑，内设两处电影院，属英国电影协会。该电影院以放映普通影院不上映的影片而出名，其中有老片子、外国影片以及小公司制作的影片〕

National Foun·da·tion of the Arts and the Hu·man·i·ties /,··· ·,·· ·,· · · ·'··/ an American government organization which develops and supports arts and humanities. It works with the National Endowment for the Arts and the National Endowment for the Humanities. 国家艺术与人文学科基金会〔美国一政府机构，致力于发展、扶持艺术和人文学科。该基金会与全国艺术基金会和全国人文学科基金会配合工作〕

National Front, the /,··· '·/ a small extreme RIGHTWING political party in Britain which believes that white people should have more rights than black and Asian people who live in the UK 民族阵线党〔英国一极右小政党，主张英国的白人应比黑人和亚洲人拥有更多的权利〕

National Gal·le·ry, the /,··· '···/ a large public ART GALLERY in Trafalgar Square, London, which contains the largest collection of important paintings in the UK. The National Gallery contains mostly European art, from all periods between about 1200 and the end of the 19th century. A large new part, called the **Sainsbury Wing**, was added in 1991. 国家美术馆〔位于伦敦特拉法尔加广场的一座大型公共美术馆，是英国馆藏名画最多的美术馆。馆藏以1200年前后至19世纪末各个时期的欧洲绘画作品为主，1991年新增了一个大型展厅，名为塞恩斯伯里侧翼展厅〕

National Gal·le·ry of Art, the /,··· ,··· · '·/ a large public MUSEUM of paintings, SCULPTURES etc in Washington, D.C. 国立艺术馆〔华盛顿特区一大型公共博物馆，藏有绘画、雕塑等艺术品〕

National Ge·o·graph·ic, The /,··· ··'··/ a US monthly magazine, which is produced by the National Geographic Society and has photographs, maps, and interesting articles about nature, wild animals, and people from different cultures all over the world《国家地理》〔美国国家地理学会发行的一种月刊。该杂志刊登摄影图片、地图以及有关世界各地自然、野生动物和风土人情的趣味文章〕

national grid /,··· '·/ *n* [C] the system of numbered squares printed on a map to show the exact position of a place 地图坐标网格

National Guard /,··· '·/ *n* [singular] a military force in each state of the US which can be used when it is needed by the state or the US government〔美国的〕国民警卫队

National Health Ser·vice /,··· '· ,··/ *n* [singular] the NHS〔英国〕国民保健制度

National Her·i·tage /,··· '···/ a British organization that is in charge of giving out money from the **National Heritage Memorial Fund** to MUSEUMS and other institutions to help them buy works of art, buildings of historic interest etc, or to keep these things in good condition. The money that is used in this way is provided by the UK's National Lottery. 国家遗产管理局〔英国一政府机构，负责将国家遗产纪念基金会的专款拨给博物馆等机构，资助其购买艺术品、历史建筑等，或资助其对上述物品和建筑进行维护。此项目的资金由英国国家彩票提供〕

National In·sur·ance /,··· ·'··/ *n* [U] a system of insurance organized by the British Government into which workers and employers make regular payments, and which provides money for people who are unemployed, old, or ill〔英国的〕国民保险制度〔由英国政府经管的一项保险制度，雇主和雇员必须按时缴纳钱款，以帮助失业者、老年人或病人〕

National In·sur·ance Num·ber /,··· ·'·· ,··/ a special number given to each person in the UK as soon as they are old enough to work, so that they become part of the National Insurance system. There is a similar system in the US, by which people are given a Social Security Number. 国民保险编号〔每个达到工作年龄的英国公民都会配给一个特别号码，从而纳入国民保险制度。美国也有一类似制度，加入者每人都有一个"社会保障编号"〕

na·tion·al·ise /ˈnæʃənḷ,aɪz; ˈnæʃənəlaɪz/ *v* [T] *BrE* another spelling of NATIONALIZE【英】nationalize 的另一种拼法

na·tion·al·is·m /ˈnæʃənḷ,ɪzəm; ˈnæʃənəlɪzəm/ *n* [U] **1** desire by a group of people of the same race, origin, language, etc to form an independent country 民族主义: *Scottish nationalism* 苏格兰民族主义 **2** the belief that your own country is better than any other country 本国优越感; 民族自豪感: *the rise of nationalism in Eastern Europe* 东欧民族主义的兴起

na·tion·al·ist¹ /ˈnæʃənḷɪst; ˈnæʃənələ̩st/ *adj* [only before noun 仅用于名词前] a nationalist organization, party etc wants to get or keep political independence for their country and people 国家主义的; 民族主义的

nationalist² *n* [C] someone who is involved in trying to gain or keep political independence for their country 国家主义者; 民族主义者: *Welsh nationalists* 威尔士民族主义者

na·tion·al·is·tic /,næʃənḷˈɪstɪk; ,næʃənəˈlɪstɪk◂/ *adj* someone who is nationalistic believes that their country is better than other countries, and often has no respect for people from other countries 有民族[国家]主义情绪的; 民族[国家]主义的 **—nationalistically** /-kḷɪ; -kli/ *adv*

na·tion·al·i·ty /,næʃənˈæləti; ,næʃəˈnælə̩ti/ *n* **1** [C,U] the legal right of belonging to a particular country 国籍: *people of the same nationality* 同国籍的人 | **French/Brazilian etc nationality** *He has British nationality.* 他有英国国籍。| **dual nationality** (=the legal right of being a citizen of two countries) 双重国籍 **2** [C] a large group of people with the same race, origin, language etc 民族: *the different nationalities within the former USSR* 前苏联的各个民族

na·tion·al·ize also 又作 **-ise** *BrE*【英】/ˈnæʃənḷ,aɪz; ˈnæʃənəlaɪz/ *v* [T] if a government nationalizes a very large industry or service such as water, gas or electricity, it buys or takes control of it 使国有化, 把…收归国有: *The British government nationalized the railways in 1948.* 英国政府在1948年将铁路国有化。| *a nationalised industry* 国有化工业 —compare 比较 PRIVATIZE **—nationalization** /,næʃənḷaɪˈzeʃən; ,næʃənəlaɪˈzeɪʃən/ *n* [C,U]

National La·bor Re·la·tions Board, the /,··· '·· ·'·· ,·/ abbreviation 缩写为 **the NLRB** a US government organization that tries to settle disagreements between workers and managers, especially in large companies. There is a similar organization in the UK called ACAS. 全国劳资关系局〔美国一政府机构，负责解决劳资矛盾，尤其是大公司的劳资纠纷。英国也有一类似机构，名为"咨询调解仲裁处"〕

National Lam·poon /,··· ·'·/ a humorous US magazine which is read especially by young people, and which makes fun of famous people, recent events, traditions etc. There are also *National Lampoon* films and radio and television programmes.《国民讽刺》〔美国一幽默杂志，读者大多是年轻人，以嘲讽名人、时事及传统等而闻名。此外，还有名为"国民讽刺"的影片、广播和电视节目〕

National League /ˈ··· ,·/ *n* [singular] a group of professional BASEBALL teams in the US which play against each other. Every year, the team that wins in this LEAGUE plays against the winning team of the American League in the World Series.〔美国〕全国棒球联盟〔由美国职业棒球队组成。其最佳球队在每年的世界系列赛事中都要与"美国棒球联盟"最佳球队比赛〕

National Lot·te·ry, the /,··· '···/ *trademark* the UK LOTTERY. Money collected by the lottery is partly given away in prizes, and partly given to support CHARITY organizations, sports clubs, theatres etc. Although the chances of winning the lottery are extremely small, the prizes are very large, and this makes the lottery very popular.【商标】国家彩票〔指英国国家彩票。其收入的一部分用于支付奖金，另一部分捐给慈善机构、体育俱乐部、剧院等。彩票的中奖几率极小，但奖金数额巨大，因此购者踊跃〕

na·tion·al·ly /ˈnæʃənḷɪ; ˈnæʃənəli/ *adv* by or to everyone in the nation 全国性地; 全民地: *The programme will be broadcast nationally.* 该节目将向全国播出。

National Mar·i·time Mu·se·um, the /,··· '··· ·,·/ a MUSEUM in Greenwich, South London, with models and pictures of British ships, and things relating to the sea, sailing, and famous seamen 国家海事博物馆〔位于南伦敦格林尼治的一家博物馆，藏有英国船只模型和图片以及与海洋、航海和著名航海家有关的物品〕

national mon·u·ment /,··· '···/ *n* [C] a building, special feature of the land etc that is kept and protected by a government for people to visit〔受政府保护、供参观的〕名胜古迹, 名胜区: *the Death Valley National Monument in California* 加利福尼亚州的死亡谷名胜区

National Or·gan·i·za·tion for Wom·en, the /,··· ···,·· · '··/ *n* [singular] the NOW

N

national park /ˌ··· ˈ·/ *n* [C] an area of natural, historical, or scientific interest which is kept and protected by a government for people to visit 国家公园: *Yosemite National Park*〔加州〕约塞米蒂国家公园

National Por·trait Gal·le·ry, the /ˌ···ˈ··, ···/ an ART GALLERY in Trafalgar Square in London which contains many pictures of famous men and women in British history and culture 国家肖像美术馆〔位于伦敦特拉法尔加广场的一家美术馆, 藏有大量英国历史和文化名人的肖像〕

National Pub·lic Ra·di·o /ˌ··· ,··ˈ··/ abbreviation 缩写为 **NPR** a network of independent US radio stations. National Public Radio is paid for by the people who listen to it, and has interesting high-quality programmes on news and current affairs (=important things that are happening in the world). 美国全国公共广播电台〔由美国独立广播电台组成的一个广播网, 由听众付费收听, 经常播出有趣的高质量新闻和时事节目〕

National Ri·fle As·so·ci·a·tion, the /ˌ···ˈ·· ··,··/ abbreviation 缩写为 **the NRA** a US organization that supports people's rights to buy and keep guns, and opposes attempts to change the laws and introduce more strict controls on guns. 全国步枪协会〔美国一组织, 旨在支持人们购买和拥有枪支的权利, 反对修改现行法律和采取更严格的枪支管制办法〕

National Sav·ings Bank, the /ˌ···ˈ·· ·/ a British bank that operates through local post offices. It is known for selling National Savings Certificates and PREMIUM BONDS. People consider it a very safe place for their savings, because the money is in the care of the British government. 国民储蓄银行〔英国一家通过地方邮局运作的银行。该银行销售国民储蓄存单和有奖债券。人们普遍认为在该银行存款非常安全, 因为存款是由英国政府管理的〕

National Sci·ence Foun·da·tion, the /ˌ···ˈ·· ·,··/ a US government organization that provides money and support for scientific study 国家科学基金会〔美国一政府机构, 专为科学研究提供资金和支持〕

national se·cu·ri·ty /ˌ··· ·ˈ···/ *n* [U] the idea that a country must keep its secrets safe and its army strong in order to protect its citizens 国家安全: *a matter of national security* 涉及国家安全的事

National Se·cu·ri·ty Coun·cil, the /ˌ··· ·ˈ···, ˌ·/ a powerful government committee in the US, which controls the relationship between military and foreign policy. Its members include the President, the Secretary of State, and the Defense Secretary, and its leader is the President's 'National Security Adviser'. 国家安全委员会〔美国一权力颇大的政府委员会。负责调控军事政策与外交政策的关系, 成员包括总统、国务卿和国防部长, 负责人是总统的国家安全顾问〕

national ser·vice /ˌ··· ˈ··/ *n* [U] *BrE* the system of making all men serve in the army for a limited time, whether the country is involved in a war or not【英】国民义务兵役制

National Thea·tre, the /ˌ··· ˈ··/ also 又作 **the Royal National Theatre** abbreviation 缩写为 **the NT** a modern building on the South Bank in London containing three theatres, the Olivier, the Lyttelton, and the Cottesloe. It is the home of the Royal National Theatre Company, which is famous for the high quality of its actors and which performs a wide variety of serious plays, both old and modern. 皇家国家剧院〔伦敦南岸的一幢现代化建筑, 内有三座剧院, 即奥利弗、利特尔顿和科特斯洛。这里是皇家国家剧团的所在地, 该剧团以拥有高水准的演员闻名, 经常演出古今各种严肃类剧目〕

National Trust /ˌ··· ˈ·/ *n* [singular] a British organization which owns and takes care of many beautiful places and historic buildings in England and Wales 全国名胜古迹托管协会〔英国一机构, 在英格兰和威尔士拥有许多秀丽的景点和历史建筑, 并对它们进行维护〕

National Weath·er Ser·vice, the /ˌ···ˈ··, ˌ·/ the national organization that collects information about the weather in the US, and provides weather reports and warnings of dangerous weather conditions for newspapers, radio, and TV, and also for farmers, scientists, airports etc. There is a similar organization in the UK called the Met Office. 国家气象局〔专门收集美国气象资料的国家机构, 向报刊、电台、电视台、机场以及农场主和科学家等提供天气预报和灾害性天气警报。英国也有一类似机构, 称 Met Office (气象局)〕

Nation of Is·lam, the /ˌ·· · ˈ·/ a US black rights organization, which was founded in 1930 by Farad Mohammad. For many years its leader was Elijah Muhammad until his death in 1975. Its members have included Malcolm X and Muhammad Ali. 伊斯兰联盟〔美国一黑人民权组织, 法拉德·穆罕默德于 1930 年创立。伊莱贾·穆罕默德任该组织领袖多年, 直至 1975 年去世。其成员有马尔科姆·X和穆罕默德·阿里〕

nation state /ˌ·· ˈ·/ *n* [C] a nation that is a politically independent country〔政治上独立的〕民族国家: *European union is seen as a threat to the sovereignty of the nation state.* 欧盟被视为是对民族国家主权的一种威胁。

na·tion·wide /ˌneʃənˈwaɪd; ˌneɪʃənˈwaɪd◂/ *adj* happening or existing in every part of the country 全国性的, 全国各地的: *a nationwide radio broadcast* 全国性电台广播 | *a nationwide search for the criminals* 全国性的搜捕罪犯行动 —**nationwide** *adv*: *We have 350 sales outlets nationwide.* 我们在全国各地有 350 个销售点。

na·tive[1] /ˈnetɪv; ˈneɪtɪv/ *adj* [only before noun 仅用于名词前] W3

1 ▶**COUNTRY** 国家◀ your native country, town etc is the place where you were born 出生地的: *a visit by the Pope to his native Poland* 教皇对他出生地波兰的访问 | *They never saw their native land again.* 他们从此再也没见到自己的故土。

2 native New Yorker/Londoner/Californian etc a person who has always lived in New York, London etc 土生土长的纽约人/伦敦人/加州人等

3 native language/tongue the language you spoke when you first learned to speak 本国语, 本地语; 母语: *Lara's native language is Swedish.* 劳拉的母语是瑞典语。

4 ▶**PLANT/ANIMAL** 植物/动物◀ growing, living, produced etc in one particular place; INDIGENOUS 土产的, 当地的: **[+to]** *The oregano plant is native to Italy.* 牛至是意大利的一种土生植物。| *the region's native birds* 该地区的本地鸟类

5 ▶**ART/CUSTOM** 艺术/风俗◀ related to the people of a country who were the earliest people to live there 土著的: *the native art of Peru* 秘鲁的土著艺术

6 native intelligence/wit etc a quality that you have naturally from birth 天生的才智/智慧等: *native genius* 天才

7 go native *humorous* to behave, dress, or speak like the people who live in the country where you have come to stay or work【幽默】入乡随俗, 过当地人的生活: *I once knew an anthropologist who went native and married a Masai warrior.* 我曾经认识一位人类学家, 她入乡随俗, 还与一位马萨伊族勇士结了婚。

native[2] *n* [C] **1** a person who was born in a particular place 出生于某地的人: **[+of]** *a native of Texas* 一个出生在得克萨斯州的人 **2** someone who lives in a place all the time or has lived there a long time 本地人, 当地人; 久居某地的人: **[+of]** *Are you a native of these parts?* 你是本地人吗? **3** [often plural 常用复数] a word that is now considered offensive, in former times used by Europeans to mean one of the people who lived in Africa, S. Asia etc before Europeans arrived 土著, 土人〔昔日欧洲人用来指居住在非洲、南亚等地的当地人, 现在一般认为此词具冒犯性〕 **4** a plant or animal that grows or lives naturally in a place 当地土生的植物[动物]: **[+of]** *The bear was once a native of Britain.* 熊曾是英国的土生动物。

Native A·mer·i·can /ˌ·· ·ˈ···/ *n* [C] one of the people who were living in N. America before white people arrived there 北美土著居民, 印第安人

CULTURAL NOTE 文化注释

Native Americans used to be called Indians or sometimes even Red Indians by white people, but these names, especially Red Indians, are now usually considered offensive. The word American Indian also means Native American, but can also be used about the peoples of Central and South America. 美国土著过去常被白人称为印第安人, 有时甚至被称为"红番"。这些称呼, 特别是"红番", 现在通常被认为具有冒犯性。American Indian 这个词组也可以表示"美国土著"的意思, 但是它还可以用来指称中南美洲的美洲原住民。

In the past, films and books showed Native Americans in a negative way, fighting COWBOYS, or being cruel to PIONEERS. The STEREOTYPE of a Native American was someone who did not wear many clothes, had paint on their face, feathers in their hair or in a type of hat, and who was very fierce. Films and books now try to show Native Americans in a fairer and more positive way. Many people admire the attitude that most Native Americans have toward the environment, which is that people should take care of the earth and only take what they need to live. 过去的电影和书籍常以负面形象来描写美国土著, 他们与牛仔作战, 对开拓者十分残酷。美国土著的典型形象是穿得很少, 涂面, 头发上插羽毛或佩戴羽冠, 而且非常凶狠。现在的电影和书籍尽量以更公平和正面的态度来描写美国土著。大多数美国土著善待土地、只取其生活所需, 这种对待环境的态度让人敬佩。

N

When Europeans first came to America, many Native Americans suffered greatly and had to fight in order to defend their land, their way of life, and their CULTURE. Many Native Americans died from diseases that the Europeans brought to America. Starting around the 1850s, the US government also forced whole tribes to move far away from their own lands and onto RESERVATIONS (=separate areas of land for Native Americans to live on). Often these lands were not very good for growing crops or raising animals. Many Native Americans still live on reservations today. 欧洲人刚到美洲时，很多美国土著深受其害，他们不得不为保护他们的土地、生活方式和文化而战。欧洲人将疾病带到了美洲，这夺去了很多美国土著的生命。19世纪50年代前后，美国政府强令整个整个的土著部落背井离乡迁入保留地。这些保留地条件很差，不利于种植和放牧。直至今日仍有很多美国土著生活在保留地。

Native Americans who live on reservations generally have lower wages, less education, and fewer jobs than the average US population. Many tribes are trying to improve their conditions, and some are also trying to start using old customs and religious practices again, to preserve their languages, and to get back some of their lost land. One of the ways that Native Americans can make money on their reservations is to have CASINOS on their land, so that people can come and GAMBLE. Because reservations follow FEDERAL law rather than state laws, gambling is allowed even in states that do not normally allow gambling. 在保留地生活的美国土著工资水平、教育程度、工作机会都较美国的平均水平低。很多部落在尽力改善处境，有些还重新拾起他们过去的风俗和宗教习惯，继续保留自己的语言，并且要回一些失去的土地。保留地的美国土著的一种生财之道是在他们的土地上开设赌场，吸引人前来赌博。因为保留地遵守的是联邦法律而不是州的法律，所以即便在那些不允许赌博的州的保留地上也可以进行赌博。

native speak·er /ˌ‥ ˈ‥/ *n* [C] someone who has learned a particular language as their first language, rather than as a foreign language 以某种语言为母语的人，说本族语的人: *a native speaker of English* 以英语为母语的人

Na·tiv·i·ty /nəˈtɪvətɪ; nəˈtɪvəti/ *n* **1** [singular] the birth of Jesus Christ 耶稣的诞生 **2** [C] a picture or model of the baby Jesus Christ and his parents in the place where he was born 耶稣诞生图[模型]

Nativity play /ˈ‥ ‥ ˌ/ *n* [C] a play telling the story of the birth of Jesus Christ performed by children at Christmas〔由孩子们在圣诞节时表演的〕关于耶稣降生的短剧

NATO /ˈneto; ˈneɪtəʊ/ *n* [singular] the North Atlantic Treaty Organization; a group of countries including the US and several European countries, which give military help to each other 北大西洋公约组织: *our allies in NATO* 我们在北约中的盟国 | *a NATO country* 北约成员国

nat·ter¹ /ˈnætɚ; ˈnætə/ *v* [I] *BrE informal* to talk continuously about unimportant things【英，非正式】唠叨，喋喋不休: *Lynne's been nattering on about the wedding for weeks.* 林恩几周来一直在唠叨婚礼的事。

natter² *n* [singular] *BrE informal* the act of talking about unimportant things for fun【英，非正式】闲聊，闲谈: **have a natter** *Come round after work and we'll have a natter.* 下班后到我家来，我们聊聊。

nat·ty /ˈnætɪ; ˈnæti/ *adj informal* very neat and fashionable in appearance【非正式】〔外表〕整洁而时髦的: *a natty suit* 时髦的套装 — **nattily** *adv*

S2 W1 **nat·u·ral¹** /ˈnætʃərəl; ˈnætʃərəl/ *adj*

1 ▶**NORMAL** 正常的◀ normal and what you would expect in a particular situation or at a particular time 平常的，正常的: *Don't worry – it's a perfectly natural reaction.* 别担心，这完全是正常反应。| **it's only natural** *spoken*【口】*It's only natural to be afraid sometimes.* 人有时会害怕的心理是正常的。| **it is natural for sb to do sth** *It's not natural for a child of his age to be so quiet.* 像他这个年龄的孩子这么安静不太正常。—opposite 反义词 UNNATURAL (1), ABNORMAL

2 ▶**NOT ARTIFICIAL** 非人为的◀ not caused, made, or controlled by human beings 自然的，天然的；非人为的: *an area of spectacular natural beauty* 自然风景秀丽的地区 | *natural disasters* 自然灾害 | *death from natural causes* 自然死亡 —compare 比较 ARTIFICIAL, MAN-MADE

3 ▶**TENDENCY/ABILITY** 倾向/能力◀ **a)** a natural tendency or type of behaviour is part of your character when you are born, rather than one that you learn later; INNATE 天生的，生来的；固有的: *Cats have a natural aversion to water.* 猫生来就讨厌水。**b)** [only before noun 仅用于名词前] having a particular quality or skill without needing to be taught and without needing to try hard 有天赋的；无需教导的: *a natural musician* 天生的音乐家 | *Cheryl has a natural elegance about her.* 谢里尔具有一种天生的高雅气质。

4 ▶**NOT PRETENDING** 不假装的◀ behaving in a way that is normal and shows you are relaxed and not trying to pretend 表现自然的；不做作的: *Try to look natural for your photograph.* 拍照时你要自然些。

5 **natural parent/mother etc** the parent from whom a child is born 生身父母/母亲等: *John was adopted; he never knew his natural parents.* 约翰是领养来的，他从不知道自己的生身父母是谁。

6 ▶**NOT MAGIC** 非神怪的◀ not connected with gods, fairies, or spirits 与神仙鬼怪无关的: *I'm sure there's a perfectly natural explanation.* 我相信一定有一种纯自然的解释。—opposite 反义词 SUPERNATURAL¹

7 ▶**FOOD** 食物◀ with nothing added to change the taste 天然的，没有添加其他成分的: *natural yoghurt* 原味酸乳酪

8 a musical note that is natural has been raised from a FLAT² (3) by one SEMITONE or lowered from a SHARP³ (1) by one semitone〔音符〕本位(音)的，标明本位号的

9 **natural child/son/daughter** *old use* a child whose parents are not married【旧】私生子/儿子/女儿 —**naturalness** *n* [U]

natural² *n* [C] **1** **be a natural** to be good at doing something without having to try hard or practise 是天生具有某种才能的人；是天才: *Look how he swings that bat – he's a natural.* 瞧他挥动球棒的样子，他是个天生的高手。**2 a)** a musical note that has been changed from a FLAT² (3) to be a SEMITONE higher, or from a SHARP³ (1) to be a semitone lower〔音乐中的〕本位音 **b)** the sign (♮) in written music that shows this〔音乐中的〕本位号 —see picture at 参见 MUSIC 图

natural-born /ˈ‥ ‥ˌ/ *adj* **natural-born fool/singer etc** *AmE informal* someone who has always had a particular quality or skill without having to try hard【美，非正式】天生的傻瓜/歌手等

natural child·birth /ˌ‥ ˈ‥/ *n* [U] a method of giving birth to a baby in which a woman chooses not to use drugs 自然分娩(法)

natural gas /ˌ‥ ˈ‥/ *n* [U] gas used for heating and lighting, taken from under the earth or under the sea 天然气

natural his·to·ry /ˌ‥ ˈ‥/ *n* [U] the study of plants, animals, and minerals 博物学: *the Natural History Museum* 自然博物馆

Natural His·to·ry Mu·se·um, the /ˌ‥ ˈ‥ ‥ ˌ/ **1** a MUSEUM in West London which contains objects and information about the history of plants, animals, and minerals, and is famous for its collection of DINOSAUR bones (英国) 自然历史博物馆〔位于西伦敦，藏有反映植物、动物和矿物演化的实物和史料，因保存有恐龙化石而出名〕**2** a similar museum in New York City (纽约的) 自然历史博物馆

nat·u·ral·is·m /ˈnætʃərəlˌɪzəm; ˈnætʃərəlɪzəm/ *n* [U] a style of art or literature which tries to show the world and people exactly as they are〔艺术或文学的〕自然主义

nat·u·ral·ist /ˈnætʃərəlɪst; ˈnætʃərəlɪst/ *n* [C] **1** someone who studies plants or animals, especially outdoors 博物学家〔尤指在野外研究动植物者〕**2** someone who believes in naturalism in art or literature〔艺术或文学的〕自然主义者

nat·u·ral·is·tic /ˌnætʃərəlˈɪstɪk; ˌnætʃərəˈlɪstɪk/ also 又作 **naturalist** *adj* painted, written, etc according to the ideas of naturalism 自然主义的 —**naturalistically** /-klɪ; -kli/ *adv*

nat·u·ral·ize also 又作 **-ise** *BrE*【英】/ˈnætʃərəlˌaɪz; ˈnætʃərəlaɪz/ *v* **be naturalized a)** if someone who was born outside a particular country is naturalized, they become a citizen of that country 使归化，使〔外国人〕入国籍 **b)** if a foreign word or phrase is naturalized in another language, it has become part of it 采纳，吸收〔外来词语〕—**naturalization** /ˌnætʃərələˈzeʃən; ˌnætʃərəlaɪˈzeɪʃən/ *n* [U]

nat·u·ral·ly /ˈnætʃərəlɪ; ˈnætʃərəli/ *adv* **1** [sentence adverb 句子副词] used to mean that the fact you are mentioning is just what you would have expected 当然；自然: *Naturally, you'll want to discuss this with your wife.* 自然你一定想和你妻子商量一下这件事的。| *"How do you feel about it?" "Well, naturally, we're very disappointed, but ..."* "你对此感觉如何？" "嗯，我们当然很失望，不过…" —see 见 SURELY (USAGE) **2** *spoken* used to say 'yes' when you think the person who asked the question should know that your reply will be yes【口】当然了: *"You'll write to me, won't you?" "Naturally."* "你会给我写信的，是吗？" "当然了！" —see 见 OF COURSE (USAGE) **3** as a natural

feature or quality 生来；天然地: *My hair is naturally curly.* 我的头发生来就是鬈的。| **come naturally (to)**(=be easy for you to do because you have a natural ability) 天生就会… *Speaking in public seems to come quite naturally to her.* 她似乎天生就会在公众面前讲话。**4** in a relaxed manner without trying to look or sound different from usual 表现自然地, 不做作地: *Just speak naturally and pretend the microphone isn't there.* 自然些说就行, 就当麦克风根本不存在。

natural phi·los·o·phy /,⋯ ·'⋯/ *n* [U] *old use* science 【旧】科学, 自然哲学

natural re·sourc·es /,⋯ ·'⋯/ *n* [plural] all of the land, minerals, natural energy etc that exist in a country 自然资源: *a country rich in natural resources* 自然资源丰富的国家

natural sci·ence /,⋯ '⋯/ *n* [C,U] chemistry, BIOLOGY, and PHYSICS considered together as subjects for study, or one of these subjects 自然科学〔指化学、生物和物理〕

natural se·lec·tion /,⋯ ·'⋯/ *n* [U] *technical* the process by which only plants and animals that are naturally suitable for life in their environment will continue to live, while all others will die【术语】自然淘汰, 自然选择 —see also 另见 **survival of the fittest**(SURVIVAL (2))

natural wast·age /,⋯'⋯/ *n* [U] a reduction in the number of people employed by an organization, which happens when people leave their jobs and the jobs are not given to anyone else〔由退职引起的〕自然减员

Na·ture /ˈnetʃɚ; ˈneɪtʃə/ a British weekly JOURNAL (=serious magazine) which deals with all areas of science. It is a very respected journal, and many important new discoveries are first reported in articles in *Nature*.《自然》〔英国一家周刊, 内容涉及所有的科学领域。这份杂志非常受人推崇, 科学上的许多重大新发现都最早刊登在该杂志上〕

nature *n*

1 ▶PLANTS/ANIMALS ETC 植物/动物等◀also 又作 **Nature** [U] everything in the physical world that is not controlled by humans, such as wild plants and animals, earth and rocks, and the weather 大自然, 自然界: *We grew up in the countryside, surrounded by the beauties of nature.* 我们在乡村长大, 周围是美丽的大自然。| *the fundamental forces of nature* 自然界的基本力量

2 ▶SB'S CHARACTER 某人的性格◀[C,U] someone's character 本性, 天性: *Eric's got a lovely easy-going nature.* 埃里克为人可爱随和。| **be in sb's nature** *Jana wouldn't lie, it's not in her nature.* 杰娜不会说谎, 这不是她的本性。| **by nature** *He was, by nature, a man of few words.* 他生来就是个寡言少语的人。| **sb's better nature**(=your feelings of kindness) 某人性格中善良的一面 *I've tried appealing to her better nature, but she still refuses to help.* 我竭力想唤起她善良的一面, 但她还是拒绝帮忙。| **human nature**(=the feelings and natural qualities that everyone has) 人类的天性 *Of course she's jealous – it's only human nature.* 她当然嫉妒, 这是人的天性。

3 ▶CHARACTER OF STH 某物的特性◀[C,U] a particular combination of qualities that makes something what it is and makes it different from other things 特性, 性质: *the true nature of their difficulties* 他们那些困难的真正性质 | **by its very nature** *Companies are, by their very nature, conservative.* 就本质而言, 公司都是保守的。

4 ▶TYPE 类型◀[singular] a particular kind of thing 类别, 种类: **of a personal/political/difficult nature** *books of an erotic nature* 色情书籍 | *The support being given is primarily of a practical nature.* 提供的支持主要是实用性的。| **of that nature** (=of that kind) 那类的, 那种的 *I never trouble myself with affairs of that nature.* 我从不关心那类事情。| **be in the nature of sth**(=to be like something) 属于某一类, 与某事物类似 *The cruise was to be in the nature of a 'rest cure'.* 这次乘船出游是属于"休养疗法"一类的。

5 in the nature of things according to the natural way things happen 按照事物的规律: *In the nature of things, there is bound to be the occasional accident.* 按照事物的规律, 偶尔发生事故是必然的。

6 let nature take its course to allow events to happen without doing anything to change the results 顺其自然, 任其自然发展: *Sometimes the best cure is just to let nature take its course.* 有时最好的办法就是顺其自然。

7 in a state of nature a) in a natural state, not having been affected by the modern world 处于未开化的自然状态 **b)** *humorous* not wearing any clothes【幽默】一丝不挂, 裸体

8 back to nature a style of living in which people try to live more simply 返璞归真, 回归自然(的生活方式) —see also 另见 SECOND NATURE, **the call of nature**(CALL[2] (12))

nature re·serve /'⋯ ·,·/ *n* [C] an area of land in which animals and plants, especially rare ones, are protected 自然保护区

nature stud·y /'⋯,⋯/ *n* [U] the study of plants, animals etc as a school subject〔学校里的〕自然课

na·tur·ist /ˈnetʃərɪst; ˈneɪtʃərɨst/ *n* [C] someone who enjoys not wearing any clothes because they believe it is natural and healthy; NUDIST 裸体主义者 —**naturism** *n* [U]

na·tu·ro·path /ˈnetʃərə,pæθ; ˈneɪtʃərəpæθ/ *n* [C] someone who tries to cure illness using natural things such as plants, rather than drugs〔使用植物等代替药物治病的〕自然疗法者 —**naturopathy** /,netʃəˈrɑpəθɪ; ,neɪtʃəˈrɒpəθi/ *n* [U] —**naturopathic** /,netʃərəˈpæθɪk; ,neɪtʃərəˈpæθɪk◂/ *adj*

NatWest Tro·phy, the /,⋅⋅'⋅⋅/ a one-day CRICKET competition in the UK, in which any team that loses a game leaves the competition, so that in the end there is a final game between the two remaining teams 国民威斯敏斯特银行杯板球赛〔英国一项为期一天的板球赛。任何参赛队输一场球即被淘汰出局, 最后剩下两支参赛队进行决赛〕

naught /nɔt; nɔːt/ *n* [U] *old use* nothing【旧】无; 没有什么东西; 不存在: *He cared naught for public opinion.* 他一点也不在乎公众舆论。| **come to naught**(=fail) 失败 *All their plans came to naught.* 他们所有的计划都泡了汤。

naugh·ty /ˈnɔtɪ; ˈnɔːti/ *adj* **1** a naughty child behaves badly and is rude and disobedient〔孩子〕淘气的, 顽皮的; 没有规矩的; 不听话的: *You're a very naughty boy! Look what you've done!* 你真是个淘气鬼！瞧你干了些什么！**2** *especially BrE* used jokingly about an adult when you are pretending to disapprove of their behaviour【尤英】〔开玩笑地说成年人〕不听话的; 不守规矩的: **it's naughty of sb to do sth** *spoken*【口】*It was a bit naughty of me to stay out so late last night.* 我昨天晚上很晚才回家, 真是有点不听话。**3 naughty jokes/magazines/pictures etc** *BrE* naughty jokes etc deal with sex in a rude but not very serious way【英】黄色笑话/杂志/图片等 —**naughtily** *adv* —**naughtiness** *n* [U]

Na·u·ru /nɑˈuru; nɑːˈuːruː/ an independent republic, one of the smallest nations in the world, on an island in the southwest Pacific Ocean near the Equator. Population: 12,088 (2001). Capital: Yaren. It has large amounts of PHOSPHATE salts, which are used for making plants grow better, and an important phosphate mining industry. 瑙鲁〔一独立共和国, 是世界上最小的国家之一, 位于赤道附近太平洋西南部的一座岛上。人口: 12,088 (2001), 首都: 亚伦区。该国磷酸盐储量丰富, 可用来促进植物生长。磷酸盐采矿业在该国具有重要地位〕—**Nauruan** *n, adj*

nau·se·a /ˈnɔʒə; ˈnɔːziə/ *n* [U] *formal* the feeling that you have when you think you are going to VOMIT (=bring food up from your stomach through your mouth)【正式】恶心; 呕吐感: *Early pregnancy is often accompanied by nausea.* 怀孕早期常伴有恶心。—see also 另见 AD NAUSEAM

nau·se·ate /ˈnɔʒɪ,et; ˈnɔːzieɪt/ *v* [T] to make someone feel NAUSEA 使恶心, 使作呕; 使厌恶: *Even clear fluids were making him feel nauseated.* 连清水都会使他感到恶心。| *It nauseates me the way Keith bullies you.* 基思欺侮你的样子让我觉得恶心。

nau·se·a·ting /ˈnɔʒɪ,etɪŋ; ˈnɔːzieɪtɪŋ/ *adj* **1** making you feel NAUSEA 令人恶心的, 令人作呕的: *In summer the smell of the farmyard was nauseating.* 夏天农场里的气味让人作呕。**2** making you feel angry 使人生气的: *It's nauseating how the coach always picks his favorites.* 教练总是挑他最喜欢的队员上场, 真让人生气。—compare 比较 DISGUSTING —**nauseatingly** *adv*

nau·se·ous /ˈnɔʒəs; ˈnɔːziəs/ *adj* **1** *especially AmE* feeling nausea【尤美】感到恶心的, 有呕吐感的: *I awoke from my drunken stupor feeling nauseous.* 我醉酒后醒来, 感到很恶心。**2** *formal* making you feel NAUSEA【正式】令人恶心的, 令人作呕的: *the nauseous stench of the durian fruit* 榴莲果令人恶心的气味 —**nauseously** *adv* —**nauseousness** *n* [U]

nau·ti·cal /ˈnɔtɪkl; ˈnɔːtɪkəl/ *adj* connected with ships or sailing 船舶的; 航海的 —**nautically** /-klɪ; -kli/ *adv*

nautical mile /,⋯ '·/ *n* [C] a measure of distance used at sea, equal to 1,852 metres; SEA MILE 海里〔相当于 1,852 米〕—see table on page C4 参见 C4 页附录

na·val /ˈnevl; ˈneɪvəl/ *adj* [only before noun 仅用于名词前] connected with or used by the navy 海军的: *a naval officer* 海军军官 | *naval battles* 海战

nave /nev; neɪv/ *n* [C] the long central part of a church〔教堂的〕中殿

na·vel /ˈnevl; ˈneɪvəl/ *n* [C] **1** the small hollow or raised place in the middle of your stomach 肚脐, 脐 —see picture at 参见 BODY 图 **2 gaze at/contemplate your navel** *humorous* to spend too much time thinking about your own problems【幽默】过多地考虑自己的问题

口语 书面语 中最常用的 1000词, 2000词, 3000词

N

nav·i·ga·ble /ˈnævəgəbl; ˈnævɨgəbəl/ *adj* a river, lake etc that is navigable is deep and wide enough for ships to travel on〔水域〕可通航的，可航行的: *The St Lawrence River is navigable from the Great Lakes to the Atlantic.* 圣劳伦斯河自五大湖区至大西洋的整段河道都可通航。—**navigability** /ˌnævəgəˈbɪlətɪ; ˌnævɨgəˈbɪlɨti/ *n* [U]

nav·i·gate /ˈnævəˌget; ˈnævɨgeɪt/ *v* **1** [I,T] to find the way to a place, especially by using maps〔尤指用地图〕导航；(为…) 指引方向: *I'll drive, you take the map and navigate.* 我开车，你拿着地图指方向。| **navigate by the stars/sun** *Early explorers used to navigate by the stars.* 早期的探险家往往靠星辰确定方向。**2** [T] to sail all the way across or along an area of water〔海上〕航行

nav·i·ga·tion /ˌnævəˈgeʃən; ˌnævɨˈgeɪʃən/ *n* [U] **1** the science of planning the way along which you travel from one place to another 航行学；航海术；航空术: *compasses and other instruments of navigation* 罗盘等导航仪器 **2** the act of sailing a ship or flying a plane along a particular line of travel 航行；航海；航空: *Navigation becomes more difficult further up the river.* 越往河上游，航行就越困难。**3** the movement of ships or aircraft〔船或飞机的〕航行: *open to navigation* 可通航 —**navigational** *adj*

nav·i·ga·tor /ˈnævəˌgetə; ˈnævɨgeɪtə/ *n* [C] an officer on a ship or aircraft who plans the way along which it is travelling〔船或飞机的〕领航员

nav·vy /ˈnævɪ; ˈnævi/ *n* [C] *BrE* an unskilled worker who does tiring physical work, such as building roads【英】〔从事筑路等的〕干粗活儿的工人

3 **na·vy** /ˈnevɪ; ˈneɪvi/ *n* [C] **1** the part of a country's military forces that is organized for fighting a war at sea 海军: *My father joined the Navy during the war.* 战时我父亲参加了海军。**2** the war ships belonging to a country〔某国的〕军舰，舰队: *demands for a larger navy* 扩大舰队规模的要求

navy blue /ˌ·· ˈ·◂/ also 又作 **navy** *adj* very dark blue 深蓝色的，藏青色的 —**navy blue** *n* [U] —see picture on page A5 参见 A5 页图

nay¹ /ne; neɪ/ *adv* **1** [sentence adverb 句子副词] *literary* used when you are adding something to emphasize what you have just said【文】不但如此，而且: *a bright – nay, a blinding light* 不只明亮，还令人目炫的一道光 **2** *old use or dialect* used to say no【旧或方言】不，否: *Nay, lad. It's not that bad.* 不，小伙子，没有那么糟。

nay² *n* [C] a vote against or someone who votes against an idea, plan, etc 反对票，投反对票者 —opposite 反义词 AYE¹ (1), YEA²

Naz·a·reth /ˈnæzərəθ; ˈnæzərəθ/ a town in Galilee, northern Israel. According to the New Testament of the Bible, Jesus lived there when he was a boy. 拿撒勒〔以色列北部加利利一城镇。根据《圣经·新约》记载，耶稣幼年曾在此生活过〕

Na·zi /ˈnɑtsɪ; ˈnɑːtsi/ *n plural* **Nazis** [C] **1** a member of the National Socialist Party of Adolf Hitler which controlled Germany from 1933 to 1945〔1933 年到 1945 年德国的〕纳粹党员，纳粹分子 **2** someone who likes to use their authority in an unreasonably strict way 独断专横者: *Some of the traffic wardens are real Nazis.* 有些交通管理员真霸道。—**Nazi** *adj* —**Nazism** *n* [U]

NB, nb *Latin* nota bene; used to make a reader pay attention to an important piece of information【拉丁】注意，留心〔用于提醒读者留意某个重要信息〕

NBA /ˌɛn bi ˈe; ˌen biː ˈeɪ/ *n* [singular] National Basketball Association; the American organization which arranges BASKETBALL games〔美国〕全美篮球协会

NBC /ˌɛn bi ˈsi; ˌen biː ˈsiː/ *n* [U] National Broadcasting Company; one of three main American television companies〔美国〕全国广播公司

NC the written abbreviation of 缩写= NORTH CAROLINA

NCAA /ˌɛn si dʌbl ˈe; ˌen siː dʌbəl ˈeɪ/ *n* National Collegiate Athletic Association; an organization which sets rules for sports competitions between US colleges and universities 全国大学生体育协会〔制定美国大专院校体育比赛规则的一个机构〕

NCO /ˌɛn si ˈo; ˌen siː ˈəʊ/ *n* [C] noncommissioned officer; a soldier such as a CORPORAL or SERGEANT 军士

NCT /ˌɛn si ˈti; ˌen siː ˈtiː/ the abbreviation of 缩写= the NATIONAL CHILDBIRTH TRUST

ND the written abbreviation of 缩写= NORTH DAKOTA

-nd /nd; nd/ *suffix* forms written ORDINAL numbers with 2〔构成以 2 结尾的序数词〕: *the 2nd* (=second) *of March* 3 月 2 日 | *her 22nd birthday* 她的 22 岁生日

NE the written abbreviation of 缩写= northeast or northeastern 东北；东北的: *NE Scotland* 苏格兰东北部

NEA, the /ˌɛn i ˈe; ˌen iː ˈeɪ/ **1** the National Education Association; a US organization that represents the interests of teachers and schools 全国教育协会〔美国代表教师和学校利益的一个组织〕 **2** the abbreviation of 缩写= NATIONAL ENDOWMENT FOR THE ARTS

Neagh —see 见 LOUGH NEAGH

ne·an·der·thal /nɪˈændəˌtɔl; niˈændəˌtɑːl/ *n* [C] **1** *humorous* a big, ugly, stupid man【幽默】体形巨大、相貌丑陋的蠢人，傻大粗 **2** someone who opposes all change without even thinking about it 反对变革的人；守旧的人，思想保守的人 **3** a Neanderthal man 尼安德特人 —**Neanderthal** *adj*

Neanderthal man /ˈ····· ˈ/ *n* an early type of human being who lived in Europe during the STONE AGE 尼安德特人〔石器时代住在欧洲的原始人〕

nea·pol·i·tan /ˌniəˈpɑlətn; nɪəˈpɒlɨtən/ *adj* neapolitan ICE CREAM has layers of different colours and tastes〔冰激凌〕各层味道、颜色不同的

neap tide /ˈnip taɪd; ˈniːp taɪd/ *n* [C] a very small rise and fall of the level of the sea at the times of the first and third quarters of the moon〔上弦或下弦时的〕小潮

near¹ /nɪr; nɪə/ *adv, prep* **1** only a short distance from a person or thing 接近(地)，靠近(地)；离…很近(地): *Bob was standing near enough to hear what they said.* 鲍勃站得很近，能听到他们的谈话。| *Why don't you move your chair nearer mine?* 你为什么不把你的椅子挪得离我近一些呢? | **near to** *Don't sit too near to the screen.* 别坐得离屏幕太近。| **go/come/get etc near** (=to move near someone or something) 靠近/接近 *Don't come any nearer – I have a gun.* 别再过来，我手里有枪。| *As the car drew nearer I realized the man was a stranger.* 车子驶近时，我发现那是个陌生人。**2 come/be near (to) sth** to almost do something or almost be in a particular state 差不多，几乎: *She had what came near to a perfect singing voice.* 她的歌喉几近完美。| **come/be near (to) tears/death etc** *Sarah was trembling, and near to tears.* 萨拉全身发抖，都快哭出来了。| **come/be near to doing sth** *especially BrE*【尤英】*Samuel came very near to rejecting the award before accepting graciously.* 塞缪尔差点儿拒绝接受奖项，但最后还是很有风度地接受了。**3** soon before a particular time or event 接近〔某时间或事件〕: *Near the day of the wedding she started to have second thoughts.* 临近婚礼之日，她又开始改变想法了。| *Remind me nearer the time of the meeting.* 快到开会的时候提醒我一下。| **draw near** *As my birthday drew near, I began to dread being fifty.* 临近生日的时候，我开始害怕自己 50 岁了。**4 near perfect/impossible etc** almost perfect etc 近乎完美/不可能等: *The dye left a near transparent liquid on the surface of her skin.* 染剂在她的皮肤表面留下了一层几乎透明的液体。**5 (as) near as dammit** *BrE spoken* used to say that something is very nearly true or correct【英口】几乎一点不差: *The repairs will cost us £1,000, as near as dammit.* 修理费用将高达 1000 英镑。

near² *adj* **1** only a short distance away from someone or something〔距离〕近的，接近的: *It's a beautiful house but it's 20 miles away from the nearest town.* 这是一幢漂亮的房子，但离最近的城镇也有 20 英里。| *We can meet at the pub or in the restaurant, whichever's nearer for you.* 我们可以在酒吧或餐馆见面，看哪个离你近一些。| **[+to]** *Of course I've heard of the Littleton sports centre – it's near to my college.* 我当然听说过利特尔顿体育中心，那儿离我就读的大学不远。**2** if something is near something else, it is similar to it 相似的，近似的，接近的: **[+to]** *It seems that his diaries are as near to the truth as we'll ever get.* 看来他的日记和我们掌握的事实真相很接近。| *Hyde Park is the nearest thing we have to the countryside round here.* 海德公园是附近最具乡村风情的地方了。| *It may not be an exact replica but it's pretty damn near.* 这也许说不上是完美的复制品，但的确已经十分相似了。**3 a near disaster/collapse etc** almost a disaster, a collapse etc 险些发生的灾难/几乎崩溃等: *The factory has seen a near doubling of its output this year alone.* 该厂今年的产量几乎增长了一倍。**4 be a near thing a)** if something you succeed in doing is a near thing, you manage to succeed but you nearly failed 险胜: *They won the championship, but it was a near thing.* 他们得了冠军，但只是险胜。**b)** used to say that you just managed to avoid a dangerous or unpleasant situation 好险〔表示刚好躲过危险或不愉快的情况〕: *That was a near thing – that truck was heading straight for us.* 刚才好险啊，那辆卡车朝着我们直冲过来。**5 be a near miss** if a bomb, shot etc is a near miss it seemed as if it would hit something but did not〔炸弹、子弹等〕几乎打中 **6 in the near future** soon 在不久的将来: *They promised to contact us again some time in the near future.* 他们答应不久将和我们再联系。**7 to the nearest £10/hundred etc** an amount to the nearest £10, hundred

N

etc is the number nearest to it that can be divided by £10, a hundred etc 以十英镑/一百等略算: *Give me the car mileage to the nearest thousand.* 告诉我以千位数略算，这车行驶了多少英里。**8 a) near relative/relation** a relative who is very closely related to you such as a parent 近亲: *You are only allowed time off if the funeral is for a near relative.* 你只能在参加近亲葬礼时才允许请假。**b) sb's nearest and dearest** *humorous* someone's family【幽默】某人的家人[亲人]; 某人的至爱 **9** [only before a noun, no comparative 仅用于名词前，无比较级] **a)** used to describe the side of something that is closest to where you are 离得较近的〔一侧〕: *the near bank of the river* 较近的河岸 **b)** used when talking about the wheels on a vehicle to mean the one on the left side〔车辆〕左侧的: *the near wheel of a car* 汽车的左轮 —opposite 反义词 OFF³ (3) —see also 另见 NEARLY, **nowhere near** (NOWHERE (4)) —**nearness** *n* [U]

near³ *v* **1** [T] to come closer to a particular place, time, or state; APPROACH¹ 靠近，接近: *Work is nearing completion.* 工作快完成了。| *The ship was nearing harbour.* 船正在向港口靠近。**2** [I] if a time nears, it gets closer and will come soon〔时间〕临近: *He got more and more nervous as the day of his departure neared.* 随着自己起程的日子一天天临近，他变得越来越紧张。

near·by /ˈnɪrˋbaɪ; ˈnɪəbaɪ/ *adj* [only before noun 仅用于名词前] not far away 附近的: *Lucy was staying in the nearby town of Hamilton.* 露西当时住在附近的汉密尔顿镇。—**nearby** /nɪrˋbaɪ; nɪəˈbaɪ/ *adv*: *Dan found work on one of the farms nearby.* 丹在附近的一个农场里找到了工作。

Near East, the /ˌ· ˈ·/ *n* the Middle East 近东〔即中东〕—**Near Eastern** *adj*: *Ancient Near Eastern literature* 古代近东文学

S1 W1 **near·ly** /ˈnɪrlɪ; ˈnɪəli/ *adv* **1** *especially BrE* almost, but not quite or not completely【尤英】几乎，差不多，将近: *It took nearly two hours to get here.* 花了将近两个小时才到这里。| *Michelle's nearly twenty.* 米歇尔快 20 岁了。| *Is the job nearly finished?* 这工作快干完了吗? | *He's nearly always right.* 他几乎永远都是对的。| *Louise is nearly as tall as her mother.* 路易丝几乎和她母亲一样高。| **very nearly** *He very nearly died.* 他几乎死掉。| **not nearly enough** (=much less than enough) 远远不够 *I can earn some money, but not nearly enough to live on.* 我能赚一点钱，但还远远不够养活我自己。—see 见 ALMOST (USAGE) **2** *old use* closely【旧】密切地: *a problem which concerns me nearly* 一个和我密切相关的问题

near·side /ˈnɪrˌsaɪd; ˈnɪəsaɪd/ *adj* [only before noun 仅用于名词前] *BrE* on the side of a vehicle that is nearest the edge of the road【英】〔车辆〕左侧的，左边的: *a scratch on the nearside front wing of the car* 汽车左前侧的一道划痕 —**nearside** *n* [singular] —opposite 反义词 OFFSIDE²

near·sight·ed /ˈnɪrˋsaɪtɪd; ˌnɪəˈsaɪtɪ̈d◂/ *adj* unable to see things clearly unless they are close to you 近视的; SHORTSIGHTED *BrE*【英】—**nearsightedly** *adv* —**nearsightedness** *n* [U]

S2 **neat** /nit; niːt/ *adj* **1** tidy and carefully arranged 整齐的; 整洁的: *neat handwriting* 工整的笔迹 | *She wears her hair short and neat.* 她的头发剪得又短又齐。| *He folded his clothes in a neat pile on the chair.* 他把自己的衣服在椅子上折成了整齐的一叠。| **neat and tidy** *Can't you keep your bedroom neat and tidy?* 难道你不能把卧室保持得整洁一点吗? **2** *AmE spoken* very nice or pleasant【美口】很好的，美妙的: *The party was really neat – we had a good time.* 那晚会美妙极了，我们玩得很开心。| *I liked working for him – he was a neat guy.* 我喜欢为他工作，他是个好人。**3** simple and effective 简洁的，简明的; 巧妙的: *a neat turn of phrase* 简洁的措辞 | *There are no neat solutions to this problem.* 这个问题没有简捷的解决办法。**4** neat alcoholic drinks have no ice or water or any other liquid added; STRAIGHT² (12)〔酒〕纯的〔不加冰、水或其他酒的〕: *She likes her whisky neat.* 她喜欢喝纯威士忌。**5** someone who is neat likes to keep things tidy〔人〕爱整洁的: *The new lodger was fortunately a neat person.* 幸亏新房客是个爱整洁的人。—**neatly** *adv*: *He arranged the books neatly on the shelf.* 他把书整齐地排放在架子上。—**neatness** *n* [U]

neath /niθ; niːθ/ *prep poetic* below【诗】在…之下: *neath the stars* 在星空下

Ne·bras·ka /nɪˋbræskə; nɪˈbræskə/ abbreviation 缩写为 **NE** a state in the central US which consists mainly of farmland, and which produces corn, wheat, cattle, and pigs. Its largest city is Omaha. 内布拉斯加州〔美国中部一州，以农田为主，出产玉米、小麦、牛和猪。该州最大的城市为奥马哈〕—**Nebraskan** *n, adj*

Neb·u·chad·nez·zar /ˌnɛbjəkədˋnɛzɚ; ˌnebjʊkədˈnezə/, **King** (?630-?562 BC) in the Old Testament of the Bible, a king of Babylon who destroyed Jerusalem in 586 BC 尼布甲尼撒二世〔(?公元前630-?前562)，据《圣经·旧约》记载，他是巴比伦的一位国王，公元前 586 年曾摧毁耶路撒冷〕

neb·u·la /ˋnɛbjələ; ˈnebjɪ̈lə/ *n* [C] **1** a mass of gas and dust among the stars, often appearing as a bright cloud in the sky at night 星云 **2** a GALAXY (=mass of stars) which has this appearance 星云状的星系 —**nebular** *adj*

neb·u·lous /ˋnɛbjələs; ˈnebjɪ̈ləs/ *adj formal*【正式】**1** an idea that is nebulous is not at all clear or exact; VAGUE 模糊不清的，含糊的: *The reasons he gave were rather nebulous.* 他提出的理由很含糊。**2** a shape that is nebulous is misty and has no definite edges 朦胧的，轮廓不清的: *a nebulous ghostly figure* 鬼影般朦胧的身影 —**nebulously** *adv* —**nebulousness** *n* [U]

NEC, the /ˌɛn i ˋsi; ˌen iː ˈsiː/ *n* the National Exhibition Centre; a large modern building near Birmingham in central England, which is used for conferences and exhibitions 国家展览中心〔英格兰中部伯明翰市附近一大型现代建筑，常用来举办各种会议和展览〕

ne·ces·sar·i·ly /ˈnɛsəˌsɛrəlɪ; ˈnesɪ̈sərɪ̈li/ *adv* **1 not necessarily** possibly but not certainly 不一定: *Expensive restaurants are not necessarily the best.* 昂贵的餐馆不一定是最好的。| *"We'll need to employ another engineer, then." "Not necessarily."* "那么我们需要再雇用一名工程师。" "不一定。" | *It does not necessarily follow that a larger workforce will be more productive.* 人越多不一定生产效率就越高。**2** in a way that cannot be different or be avoided; INEVITABLY 必然，必定: *Testing criteria are necessarily subjective.* 测试标准必定是主观的。 S1 W2

ne·ces·sa·ry¹ /ˋnɛsəˌsɛrɪ; ˈnesɪ̈səri/ *adj* **1** something that is necessary is what you need to have or need to do; ESSENTIAL 必要的，必需的，必不可少的: *I'll leave it to you to make all the necessary arrangements.* 我就让你来负责所有必要的准备工作了。| [+for] *Food is necessary for life.* 食物是生命所必需的。| **it is necessary (for sb) to do sth** *It's not necessary to wear a tie.* 不一定要打领带。| *The doctor says it may be necessary for me to have an operation.* 医生说也许我有必要做手术。| **make it necessary (for sb) to do sth** *The heavy rain made it necessary to close several roads.* 大雨使得有必要关闭几条道路。| **is it really necessary to do sth?** *spoken* (=used to complain about something that someone is doing)【口】真的必须做某事吗?〔表示抱怨〕*Is it really necessary to make all that noise!* 真有必要那么吵闹吗? | **if necessary** (=if it is necessary) 如果必要 *I'll stay up all night, if necessary, to get it finished.* 如果必要，我会熬个通宵把这事做完。| **hardly necessary** (=almost not necessary) 几乎没有必要 *Taking notes was hardly necessary – she had a brilliant memory.* 她记忆力很好，几乎没有必要记笔记。**2 necessary connection/consequence etc** a connection, result etc that must exist 必然的联系/结果等: *the necessary connection between wage rates and the price of food* 工资水平和食物价格之间的必然联系 **3 a necessary evil** something bad or unpleasant that you have to accept in order to achieve what you want〔为实现目的不得不接受的〕不得已的事; 难免的坏事: *Mr Hurst regarded work as a necessary evil.* 赫斯特先生把工作看成一件不得已的事情。 S1 W1

necessary² *n* **1 the necessaries** things that you need, such as food or money, especially for a journey〔尤指旅行的〕必需品 **2 do the necessary** *spoken* to do what is necessary【口】做必要的事: *Leave it to me – I'll do the necessary.* 交给我吧，我会把该办的事都办好的。

ne·ces·si·tate /nəˋsɛsəˌtet; nɪ̈ˈsesɪ̈teɪt/ *v* [T] *formal* to make it necessary for you to do something【正式】使成为必需; 需要: *Lack of money necessitated a change of plan.* 由于缺乏资金，只能改变计划。| **necessitate doing sth** *This change would necessitate starting all over again.* 这样一变动，就得从头干起。

ne·ces·si·tous /nəˋsɛsətəs; nəˈsesɪ̈təs/ *adj* a word meaning 'poor' used when people are trying to sound important or want to avoid saying 'poor' directly 贫困的，贫穷的〔夸张或委婉用语〕—**necessitously** *adv*

ne·ces·si·ty /nəˋsɛsətɪ; nɪ̈ˈsesɪ̈ti/ *n* **1** [C] something that you need to have 必需品: *A telephone is an absolute necessity for this job.* 电话是做这项工作绝对必需的。| *We went to buy the basic necessities for our stay.* 我们去购买了逗留期间用的基本必需品。| **bare necessities** (=basic things that you must have) 基本必需品 *Food and clothing are the bare necessities of life.* 食物和衣服是生活的基本必需品。—compare 比较 LUXURY (2) **2** [U] the fact of something being necessary 必要; 需要: [+for] *the necessity for decent, affordable housing* 对舒适而经济的住房的需要 | **necessity of doing sth** *Martell Bakeries was faced with the necessity of firing many of its employees.* 马特尔面包房不得不大规模裁员。| **necessity to do sth** *There's no necessity to buy tickets in advance.* 没有必要提前买票。**3** [C] something that must happen, even if it is unpleasant or undesirable 无奈的事物; 不好却必要的东西: *Taxes are a regrettable neces-*

sity. 税收是令人遗憾而又必要的东西。| *The treaty is considered a diplomatic necessity.* 该条约被认为是外交上的必要手段。
4 [U] the condition of urgently needing money or food 贫穷，窘迫: *He was forced by necessity to steal a loaf of bread.* 他迫于饥饿偷了一条面包。| **dire necessity** (=great need) 极为需要 **5 of necessity** used when something happens in a particular way because that is the only possible way it can happen 势必，必定: *The summary of his findings is, of necessity, very brief.* 他的研究成果总结必定很简短。**6 necessity is the mother of invention** used to say that if someone really needs to do something they will find a way of doing it 需要乃发明之母

S2 W2 **neck¹** /nɛk; nek/ *n*
1 ▶PART OF THE BODY 人体部位◀ [C] the part of your body that joins your head to your shoulders 颈，脖子: *She wore a string of pearls around her neck.* 她脖子上戴了一串珍珠。—see picture at 参见 HEAD¹ 图
2 ▶CLOTHING 衣服◀ [C] the part of a piece of clothing that goes around your neck 衣领，领口: *the neck of the shirt* 衬衫的领子 | *The colour's all right, but the neck's a bit low.* 颜色还不错，只是领口低了点。 see also 另见 CREW NECK, POLO NECK, SCOOP NECK, TURTLENECK, V-NECK —see picture on page A17 参见 A17 页图
3 ▶BOTTLE 瓶子◀ [C] the narrow part of a bottle 瓶颈
4 be up to your neck in to be in a difficult situation, or to be very busy doing something 深深陷入〔困境中〕; 忙于〔做某事〕: *Jim's always up to his neck in debt.* 吉姆总是债台高筑。| *I've been up to my neck in paperwork all week.* 我整个星期都在处理文件，忙得不可开交。
5 breathe down sb's neck to watch what someone is doing very carefully, in a way that makes them nervous or annoyed 密切监视某人: *How can I concentrate with you breathing down my neck all the time?* 你总是盯着我，我怎能集中精神？
6 V-necked/open-necked etc also 又作 **V-neck/open-neck etc** if a piece of clothing is V-necked etc, it has that type of neck V 字领/开领等的: *a navy V-necked sweater* 深蓝色的 V 形领套头毛衣
7 I'll break/wring your neck *spoken* used to tell someone that you are so angry with them you feel like hurting them【口】我会扭断你的脖子〔表示生气〕
8 (hanging) around your neck if a problem or difficult situation is hanging around your neck, you are responsible for it, and this makes you worry〔问题或困难〕缠着令人烦恼
9 get it in the neck *BrE spoken* to be severely punished【英口】受到严惩: *You'll really get it in the neck if you lose that watch!* 你要是把表丢了，就会受到严厉的惩罚！
10 ▶MEAT 肉◀ [U] the neck of an animal, used as food〔动物的〕颈肉: *neck of lamb* 羊颈肉
11 neck and neck *informal* if two things are neck and neck in a competition or race, they both have an equal chance of winning【非正式】〔在比赛中〕不相上下；并驾齐驱
12 in this neck of the woods *informal* in this area or part of the country【非正式】在这一带，在这地区: *What are you doing in this neck of the woods?* 你在这一带干什么？
13 by a neck *informal* if a race is won by a neck, the winner is only a very short distance in front【非正式】〔比赛中〕以些微之差〔获胜〕: *Our horse won by a neck.* 我们的马以一颈之差获胜。

neck and neck 并驾齐驱

—see also 另见 **a pain in the neck** (PAIN¹ (4)), **risk your neck** (RISK² (1)), **save sb's skin/neck/bacon etc** (SAVE¹ (10)), **stick your neck out** (STICK¹)
14 ▶LAND 土地◀ a narrow piece of land that comes out of a wider part 狭长地带

neck² *v* [I] *informal* if two people neck, they kiss for a long time in a sexual way【非正式】搂脖子深吻，拥吻 —**necking** *n* [U]

neck·band /ˈnɛkˌbænd; ˈnekbænd/ *n* [C] a narrow piece of material around the neck of a piece of clothing〔衣服上的〕领圈: *a velvet neckband* 丝绒领圈

neck·er·chief /ˈnɛkɚtʃɪf; ˈnekətʃiːf/ *n* [C] a square piece of cloth that is folded and worn tied around the neck 围巾，领巾

neck·lace /ˈnɛklɪs; ˈnekləs/ *n* [C] a string of jewels, BEADS etc or a thin gold or silver chain 项链，颈链: *a diamond necklace* 钻石项链 | *a pearl necklace* 珍珠项链 —see picture at 参见 JEWELLERY 图

neck·let /ˈnɛklɪt; ˈneklət/ *n* [C] a short necklace 短项链，短颈链

neck·line /ˈnɛkˌlaɪn; ˈneklaɪn/ *n* [C usually singular 一般用单数] the shape made by the upper edge of a piece of woman's clothing around or below the neck〔女装的〕领口: *a flattering scoop neckline* 使人显得更漂亮的汤匙领 | **low/plunging neckline** (=leaving part of the chest uncovered) 低开口领，低胸 *Her evening gown had a plunging neckline.* 她的晚礼服领口开得很低。

neck·tie /ˈnɛkˌtaɪ; ˈnektaɪ/ *n* [C] *AmE formal* a man's TIE【美，正式】领带

nec·ro·man·cy /ˈnɛkrəˌmænsɪ; ˈnekrəmænsi/ *n* [U] **1** magic, especially evil magic 魔法；〔尤指〕妖术 **2** *literary* the practice of claiming to talk with the dead【文】召亡魂问卜的巫术 —**necromancer** *n* [C]

nec·ro·phil·i·a /ˌnɛkroˈfɪlɪə; ˌnekrəʊˈfɪliə/ *n* [U] sexual interest in dead bodies 恋尸癖

nec·tar /ˈnɛktɚ; ˈnektə/ *n* [U] **1** the sweet liquid that BEES collect from flowers 花蜜: *The sunbird feeds on nectar.* 太阳鸟以花蜜为食。**2** the drink of the gods, in the stories of ancient Greece〔古希腊神话中〕众神饮的酒；琼浆玉液 **3** thick juice made from certain fruits〔未经冲淡的〕水果原汁: *mango nectar* 芒果汁

nec·ta·rine /ˈnɛktəˌrin; ˈnektəriːn/ *n* [C] a type of fruit like a PEACH that has a smooth skin, or the tree that produces this fruit 油桃（树）—see picture on page A8 参见 A8 页图

née /ne; neɪ/ *adj* a word used after a woman's married name and before the family name that she had when she was born〔已婚妇女〕婚前原名为…的；娘家姓…的: *Mrs Carol Cook née Williams* 卡萝尔·库克太太，娘家姓威廉斯

need¹ /nid; niːd/ *v* [T not in progressive 不用进行时] 
1 ▶MUST 必须◀ to feel that you must have something or must do something; REQUIRE 需要〔做某事〕: **need sth** *That was what I needed – strong, hot coffee.* 那才是我要的——一杯又浓又热的咖啡。| *I don't need your approval, thank you very much.* 我不需要你的批准，谢谢！| **need to do sth** *I need to think about this before I make a decision.* 在决定之前我需要想一想。| **need sth for** *He said he needed the information for an article he was writing.* 他说他正在写的文章需要那些资料。| **need sb to do sth** *We need volunteers to clean up after the performance.* 我们需要志愿者在演出结束后打扫卫生。| **need sth badly** *Money was tight and he needed a job badly.* 他手头很紧，急需找份工作。—see graph at 参见 REQUIRE 图表
2 to have to do something because you feel you should do it or because you think it is necessary 必须〔做某事〕: **need (to) do sth** *Do you think I need to go to the meeting?* 你认为我必须去开会吗？| *You need to work harder if you're going to pass those exams.* 如果你想通过那些考试，你就必须加倍努力。| *Nobody need feel jealous.* 谁也不必妒嫉。| **need not do sth** *BrE*【英】*You needn't worry, I've taken care of it.* 你不必担心，我已经把这事处理好了。| **do not need to do sth** *Honestly, you don't need to get changed. You look fine as you are.* 说实话，你不必换衣服，你现在穿的就不错。| **need not have done sth** *BrE* (=used when someone does something that was not necessary)【英】本来不必做某事 *Terence has done so little work, he needn't have bothered to come to school today.* 特伦斯几乎什么也没做，他今天其实就不用来学校！| **did not need to do sth** *What a beautiful day! I didn't need to bring my umbrella after all.* 天气真好！我根本不必带雨伞。| **need sb do sth?** *BrE old-fashioned*【英，过时】*Need we leave so soon? I'm having a wonderful time.* 我们一定要这么快就走吗？我正玩得开心呢！
3 need cleaning/mending/fixing etc if something needs cleaning or needs to be cleaned, someone should clean it because it is dirty 需要清洁/修补/修理等: *That fence needs fixing.* 那个栅栏需要修理。| **need washing/mending etc** *The children need collecting at 4 o'clock.* 孩子们需要在 4 点钟接回。| **need to be washed/to be mended etc** *I think these potatoes need to be cooked a little longer.* 我认为这些马铃薯需要多煮一会儿。| **need a wash/a mend etc** *He looked tired and looked like he needed a shave.* 他看起来很疲惫，好像还需要刮一刮脸。
4 if a job or activity needs a particular quality, you need to have that quality in order to do it well 要求，需要〔某种素质〕: *A job like nursing needs patience and understanding.* 做护理工作需要有耐心和通情达理。
5 I need hardly say/tell/remind etc used when you think that people should already know what you are going to say 不用我说/告诉/提醒等: *I need hardly remind you that people will judge the school by the way you behave.* 不用我说你也知道，人们会根据你的表现对学校作出判断。

6 **need you ask/need I ask** *spoken* used to say that someone already knows what they are asking about【口】这还用问: *"Who did it?" "Need you ask? It was Joe, of course."* "这是谁干的?" "那还用问? 当然是乔。"
7 **who needs it?** *spoken* used to say you are not interested in something【口】才没人想要呢!: *To hell with enlightenment, who needs it?* 去他的开导, 才没有人需要呢!

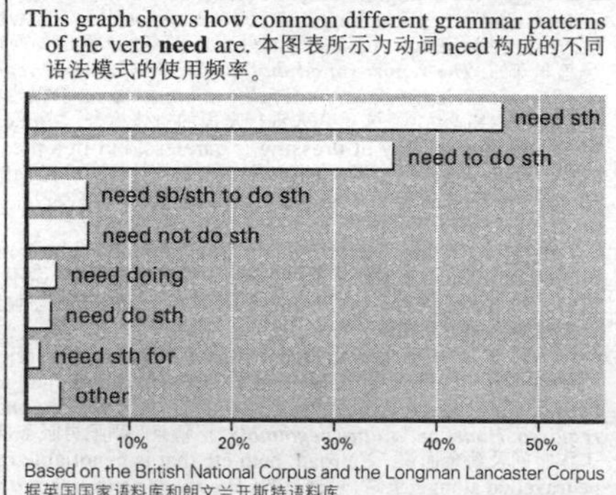

This graph shows how common different grammar patterns of the verb **need** are. 本图表所示为动词 need 构成的不同语法模式的使用频率。

Based on the British National Corpus and the Longman Lancaster Corpus
据英国国家语料库和朗文兰开斯特语料库

need² *n*
1 ▶**WHEN STH IS NECESSARY** 需要某事物时◀ [singular] a situation in which something is necessary, especially something that is not happening yet or is not yet available 需要, 需求: [+for] *the need for stricter safety regulations* 对更严格安全条例的需要 | *There's a growing need for new housing in many rural areas.* 许多农村地区对新住房的需求不断增长。| **the need to do sth** *We fully recognize the need to improve communications.* 我们充分意识到改善沟通的需要。| *Don't you ever feel the need to take a vacation?* 你难道从未想过要休假吗? | **as the need arises** (=whenever it is necessary) 有必要时 *We draw money from the account as the need arises.* 必要时我们从账户上提款。| **if need be** (=if it is necessary) 如果需要的话 *I'll work all night if need be.* 如果需要, 我将通宵工作。
2 **there's no need (for sb) to do sth a)** used to say that someone does not have to do something (某人) 不必做某事: *There's no need for you to come if you don't want to.* 如果你不想来, 就不必来了。**b)** *spoken* used to tell someone to stop doing something【口】别做某事了: *There's no need to shout; I'm not deaf!* 不用大声喊, 我不是聋子!
3 **be in need of a)** to need to be cleaned, repaired, or given attention in some way 需要〔清洁、修理或照料〕: *The whole house is in need of decorating.* 整座房子都需要装修。**b)** to need help, advice, money etc, because you are in a difficult situation 需要〔帮助、建议、金钱等〕: *I felt lonely and in need of some companionship.* 我觉得孤独, 需要有人做伴。| **be in dire need of** (=need something urgently) 急需… *Many of the refugees are in dire need of medical treatment.* 许多难民急需医治。
4 **have no need of** to not need something 不需要: *Japan has its own space technology and has no need of American help.* 日本拥有自己的太空技术, 不需要美国的帮助。
5 ▶**WHAT YOU NEED** 所需要的◀ [C usually plural 一般用复数] what someone needs to have in order to live a normal healthy comfortable life〔生活上的〕需求, 需要的东西: **sb's needs** *We must look after the needs of the elderly.* 我们必须照顾老年人的需要。| **meet/answer/fill a need** (=provide something that people want or need) 满足需求 *meeting the educational needs of every child* 满足每个儿童的教育需求 | **your every need** *a service that caters for your every need* 满足你各种需求的服务
6 ▶**LACK OF MONEY** 缺钱◀ [U] the state of not having enough food or money〔食物或金钱的〕短缺; 困窘: *cases of severe need in the inner cities* 旧城区中出现的严重食物短缺现象 | **in need** (=not having enough food or money) 缺〔食物或钱〕*Our aim is to provide adequate food for those families in need.* 我们的目标是为有困难的家庭提供足够的食物。
7 **in your hour of need** when you are in trouble 处于困境时, 患难时: *a friend you can turn to in your hour of need* 患难时会向你伸出援手的朋友

need·ful /ˈnidfəl; ˈniːdfəl/ *adj formal* necessary【正式】必要的, 需要的: *needful expenditure* 必要的开支 —**needfully** *adv*

needles 针
needle
指针
N
W
E
S
needle
注射针
knitting needles
编织针
eye
针眼
needle
缝针

nee·dle¹ /ˈnidl; ˈniːdl/ *n* [C]
1 ▶**SEWING** 缝纫◀ **a)** a small thin piece of steel, with a point at one end and a hole in the other, used for sewing 缝针: *a needle and thread* 穿了线的针 **b)** a KNITTING NEEDLE 编织针
2 ▶**DRUGS** 药◀ a very thin, pointed steel tube at the end of a SYRINGE, which is pushed into your skin to put a drug or medicine into your body or to take out blood 注射针
3 ▶**POINTING** 指示◀ a long thin piece of metal on a scientific instrument, that moves backwards and forwards and points to numbers or directions〔仪器上的〕指针
4 ▶**FROM A TREE** 树上的◀ a small needle-shaped leaf, especially from a PINE tree〔尤指松树的〕针叶: *pine needles* 松树的针叶
5 ▶**FOR PLAYING RECORDS** 播放唱片用◀ the very small, pointed part in a RECORD PLAYER that picks up sound from the records; STYLUS (1) 唱针
6 **like looking for a needle in a haystack** *informal* used to say that something is almost impossible to find【非正式】如同海底捞针
7 **a needle match** *BrE* a game in which both teams are determined to win because they do not like each other【英】充满火药味的比赛

needle² *v* [T] *informal* to deliberately annoy someone by continuously making unkind remarks or stupid jokes【非正式】〔用话〕刺激; 激怒: *She's always needling me about my accent.* 她老是嘲笑我的口音。

nee·dle·point /ˈnidlˌpɔɪnt; ˈniːdlpɔɪnt/ *n* [U] pictures made by covering a piece of material with small stitches 刺绣画; 刺绣品

need·less /ˈnidlɪs; ˈniːdləs/ *adj* **1** needless troubles, suffering, loss etc are unnecessary because they could easily have been avoided 不必要的; 不需要的: *the needless loss of life* 不必要的牺牲 | *needless expense* 不必要的开支 | *a lot of needless worry* 许多不必要的忧虑 **2 needless to say** used when you are telling someone something that they probably know or expect 不用说, 当然: *Needless to say, we'll pay your expenses.* 当然了, 我们会支付你的费用。—**needlessly** *adv*: *Thousands of women die needlessly every year because of poor medical care.* 每年成千上万的妇女因为医疗条件欠佳而白白死去。

nee·dle·wom·an /ˈnidlˌwʊmən; ˈniːdlˌwʊmən/ *n* [C] a woman who is good at sewing 精于缝纫的妇女; 缝纫女工

nee·dle·work /ˈnidlˌwɝk; ˈniːdlwɜːk/ *n* [U] the activity or art of sewing, or things made by sewing 缝纫; 刺绣; 针线活儿

need·n't /ˈnidn̩t; ˈniːdnt/ *especially BrE*【尤英】the short form of 缩略式 = 'need not': *I needn't have put on this thick coat.* 我原本不必穿这件厚外套的。

need·y /ˈnidɪ; ˈniːdi/ *adj* **1** having very little food or money 缺食物[钱]的; 贫困的; : *a needy family* 贫穷家庭 **2 the needy** needy people 穷人: *money to help the needy* 用来帮助穷人的钱 —**neediness** *n* [U]

ne'er /nɛr; neə/ *adv poetic* never【诗】永不, 决不

ne'er-do-well /ˈnɛr du ˌwɛl; ˈneə duː ˌwel/ *n* [C] *old use* a lazy useless person【旧】无用的懒人

ne·far·i·ous /nɪˈfɛrɪəs; nɪˈfeəriəs/ *adj formal* evil or criminal【正式】恶毒的, 邪恶的; 罪恶的: *nefarious activities such as drug trafficking and fraud* 贩毒和诈骗之类的犯罪活动 —**nefariously** *adv* —**nefariousness** *n* [U]

neg the written abbreviation of 缩写 = NEGATIVE

ne·gate /nɪˈget; nɪˈgeɪt/ *v* [T] *formal*【正式】**1** to prevent something from having any effect 取消, 使无效: *Efforts to expand*

the tourist industry could be negated by reports that the sea is highly polluted. 有关海洋受到严重污染的报道可能会使拓展旅游业的努力完全白费。**2** to state that something does not exist or is untrue; DENY (1) 否认; 否定 —**negation** /nɪˈgeʃən; nɪˈgeɪʃən/ *n* [U]

neg·a·tive¹ /ˈnɛgətɪv; ˈnegətɪv/ *adj*

1 ►EFFECT 效果◄ bad or harmful 不好的, 有害的: *protectionist policies that had a negative effect on the country's economy* 对该国经济产生不良影响的贸易保护主义政策 | *I think our relationship was very negative and destructive.* 我认为我们的关系很差, 并带有破坏性。—opposite 反义词 POSITIVE (7)

2 ►ATTITUDE 态度◄ considering only the bad qualities of a situation, person etc and not the good ones 消极的; 负面的: *Her negative attitude really annoys me.* 她的消极态度令我十分恼火。| *The play was criticized for its violence, and its bleak, negative message.* 该剧因带有暴力内容并宣扬悲观消极的思想而受到批评。| **be negative (about)** *Don't be so negative – of course you can win!* 别那么消极, 你当然能赢! —opposite 反义词 POSITIVE (2)

3 ►NO/NOT 不◄ a) saying or meaning no 拒绝的; 不; 否定的: *a negative response to our request* 对我们的要求说不 **b)** containing one of the words 'no', 'not', 'nothing', 'never' etc; for example 'cannot' and 'can't' are the negative forms of 'can' 否定式的 —opposite 反义词 AFFIRMATIVE (1)

4 ►SCIENTIFIC TEST 科学试验◄ not showing any sign of the chemical or medical condition that was being looked for 〔结果〕阴性的: *The pregnancy test was negative.* 妊娠试验结果为阴性。—opposite 反义词 POSITIVE (6)

5 ►ELECTRICITY 电◄ *technical* of the type that is carried by ELECTRONS【术语】阴性的, 负的 —opposite 反义词 POSITIVE (11)

6 ►NUMBER/QUANTITY 数字/数量◄ less than zero 负的: *a negative return to our investment* (=a loss) 我们投资的负收益[亏损]

7 ►BLOOD 血液◄ *technical* not having RHESUS FACTOR in your blood【术语】不含猕[Rh]因子的 —opposite 反义词 POSITIVE (13) —**negatively** *adv*

negative² *n* [C] **1** a statement or expression that means 'no' 否定; 不: **in the negative** *formal* (=saying 'no')【正式】否定; 不 *He answered in the negative.* 他作出了否定的回答。—opposite 反义词 AFFIRMATIVE(2) **2** a photographic image that shows dark areas as light and light areas as dark, from which the final picture is printed 〔照相〕底片

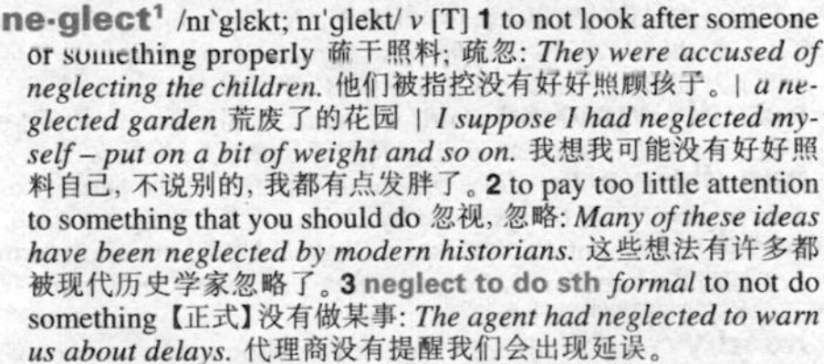
negative 底片

negative³ *v* [T] *formal*【正式】**1** to refuse to accept a proposal or request 否决; 拒绝 **2** to prove something to be untrue 否定; 否认; 证明…错误

negative pole /ˌ··· ˈ·/ *n* [C] *technical*【术语】**1** the end of a MAGNET which turns naturally to the south 〔磁铁的〕负极 **2** a CATHODE 阴极

ne·glect¹ /nɪˈglɛkt; nɪˈglekt/ *v* [T] **1** to not look after someone or something properly 疏于照料; 疏忽: *They were accused of neglecting the children.* 他们被指控没有好好照顾孩子。| *a neglected garden* 荒废了的花园 | *I suppose I had neglected myself – put on a bit of weight and so on.* 我想我可能没有好好照料自己, 不说别的, 我都有点发胖了。**2** to pay too little attention to something that you should do 忽视, 忽略: *Many of these ideas have been neglected by modern historians.* 这些想法有许多都被现代历史学家忽略了。**3 neglect to do sth** *formal* to not do something【正式】没有做某事: *The agent had neglected to warn us about delays.* 代理商没有提醒我们会出现延误。

neglect² *n* [U] **1** failure to look after something or someone properly because you do not care enough about them 忽视; 疏忽; 忽略: **[+of]** *Tenants are complaining about the landlord's neglect of the property.* 住户在抱怨房东疏忽了物业的维修。**2** the condition of not being properly looked after 被忽略的状况: *Grass grew on the sidewalk. The whole district had an air of abandonment and neglect.* 人行道上长满了草 —— 整个地区给人一种荒凉的气氛。

ne·glect·ful /nɪˈglɛktfəl; nɪˈglektfəl/ *adj formal* not looking after something properly, or not giving it enough attention【正式】疏忽的; 不注意的: **[+of]** *She became more and more neglectful of her responsibilities.* 她越来越无视自己的责任。—**neglectfully** *adv* —**neglectfulness** *n* [U]

neg·li·gee /ˌnɛglɪˈʒe; ˈneglɪ̆ʒeɪ/ *n* [C] a very thin, pretty coat, worn over a NIGHTDRESS 〔套在睡衣上的〕薄料宽松室内服

neg·li·gence /ˈnɛglədʒəns; ˈneglɪdʒəns/ *n* [U] failure to take enough care over something that you are responsible for 疏忽; 玩忽职守: *negligence in carrying out safety procedures* 在执行安全程序中的疏忽 | *The bridge's architect was sued for criminal negligence.* 该桥的建筑师被控犯玩忽职守罪。

neg·li·gent /ˈnɛglədʒənt; ˈneglɪdʒənt/ *adj* **1** not taking enough care over something that you are responsible for, with the result that serious mistakes are made 疏忽的, 粗心大意的; 玩忽职守的: *The report stated that Dr Brady had been negligent in not giving the patient a full examination.* 这份报告称布雷迪医生粗心大意, 未给病人进行全面的身体检查。**2** a negligent manner or way of dressing is careless, but in a pleasantly relaxed way 〔态度、穿着〕不拘泥的; 不计较的; 随便的: *He dresses with negligent grace.* 他穿着随便而又自然大方。—**negligently** *adv*

neg·li·gi·ble /ˈnɛglədʒəbl; ˈneglɪdʒɪ̆bəl/ *adj* too slight or unimportant to have any effect 可以忽视的, 无足轻重的, 微不足道的: *The damage done to his property was negligible.* 对他财产造成的损失十分轻微。—**negligibly** *adv*

ne·go·ti·a·ble /nɪˈgoʃɪəbl; nɪˈgəʊʃiəbəl/ *adj* **1** an offer, price, contract etc that is negotiable can be discussed and changed before being agreed on 可谈判的, 可协商的: *Part-time barman required. Hours and salary negotiable.* 招聘兼职酒吧男服务员, 工作时间及薪金面议。**2** a road, path etc that is negotiable can be travelled along 〔道路〕可通行的: *The road is only negotiable in the dry season.* 这条路只有在旱季才可通行。**3** *technical* a cheque that is negotiable can be exchanged for money【术语】〔支票〕可兑现的

ne·go·ti·ate /nɪˈgoʃɪˌet; nɪˈgəʊʃieɪt/ *v* **1** [I,T] to discuss something in order to reach an agreement, especially in business or politics 〔尤指商业或政治〕谈判, 协商: **[+with]** *The government refuses to negotiate with terrorists.* 政府拒绝和恐怖分子谈判。| **negotiate an agreement/contract etc** *Union leaders have negotiated an agreement for a shorter working week.* 工会领袖已经商定了一份缩短每周工作时间的协议。| **come to the negotiating table** (=start official discussions) 开始正式谈判 *The French have brought new proposals to the negotiating table.* 法国人在谈判桌上提出了几项新提议。**2** [T] to succeed in getting past or over a difficult place on a path, road etc 顺利通过: *Eliot negotiated the steep stairs and walked across the courtyard.* 埃利奥特顺利走下陡峭的楼梯, 然后穿过了院子。—**negotiator** *n* [C]

ne·go·ti·a·tion /nɪˌgoʃɪˈeʃən; nɪˌgəʊʃiˈeɪʃən/ *n* [C usually plural 一般用复数, U] official discussions between the representatives of opposing groups, who are trying to reach an agreement, especially in business or politics 〔尤指正式的商业或政治〕谈判, 协商: *The treaty was a result of long and complex negotiations.* 该条约是漫长而复杂的谈判的结果。| *Through negotiation we were able to reach a compromise.* 通过谈判我们达成了妥协。| **be open to negotiation** (=can be negotiated and changed) 可以协商(修改) *The terms of the contract are still open to negotiation.* 合同条款仍可协商。| **enter into negotiation** (=start negotiation) 开始[进入]谈判

Ne·gress /ˈnigrɪs; ˈniːgrɪ̆s/ *n* [C] *old-fashioned* a word meaning a black woman, which is now usually considered offensive【过时】女黑人〔现在被视为具有冒犯性〕

Ne·gro /ˈnigro; ˈniːgrəʊ/ *plural* **Negroes** *n* [C] *old-fashioned* a word meaning a black person, which is now usually considered offensive【过时】黑人〔现在被视为具有冒犯性〕—**negro** *adj*

> **USAGE NOTE 用法说明: NEGRO**
>
> POLITENESS 礼貌程度
>
> People of African origin (recent or long ago) usually prefer to be called **black**, or in the US, often **African-American**. In the UK the term **Afro-Caribbean** is often used. 非洲血统的人(最近或过去)通常都愿意被称作black, 在美国则喜欢被称作 African-American。在英国, 他们经常被称作 Afro-Caribbean。
>
> Some people think that it is polite to use the word **coloured** but this is now considered to be offensive and unacceptable. 有人觉得用 coloured 一词较为礼貌, 但现在此词被认为是不礼貌和难以接受的。

ne·groid /ˈnigrɔɪd; ˈniːgrɔɪd/ *adj technical* having the physical features of a black person from Africa【术语】带有黑人生理特征的

Negro spir·i·tu·al /ˌ‥ˈ‥‥/ *n* [C] a religious song of the type sung by the black people of the US〔美国黑人唱的带有宗教色彩的〕黑人灵歌

Neh·ru /ˈnɛru; ˈneəruː/, **Ja·wa·har·lal** /dʒəˈwɑhɚˌlɑl; dʒəˈwɑːhəˌlɑːl/ (1889-1964) an Indian politician who was one of the leaders of India's fight for independence from the UK. He became India's first Prime Minister after its independence (1947-64), and he was the father of Indira Gandhi. 尼赫鲁〔(1889-1964), 印度政治家。他是印度抗英独立战争的领袖之一, 也是印度独立后的第一任总理(1947-1964)。他是英迪拉·甘地的父亲〕

neigh /ne; neɪ/ *v* [I] if a horse neighs, it makes a long loud noise〔马〕嘶 —**neigh** *n* [C]

S2 W2 **neigh·bour** *BrE*【英】, **neighbor** *AmE*【美】/ˈnebɚ; ˈneɪbə/ *n* [C] **1** someone who lives next to you or near you 邻居, 邻人: **next-door neighbour** (=in the house next to you) 隔壁邻居 *Our next-door neighbours are so noisy we can hardly sleep some nights.* 我们隔壁的邻居爱吵闹, 有时我们晚上几乎无法睡觉。**2** someone who is sitting or standing next to you 身边的人: *The teacher saw Bobby passing a note to his neighbour.* 老师看到博比给他身旁的人递了一张条子。**3** a country's neighbour is the country next to it 邻国: *The USA is Canada's only neighbour.* 美国是加拿大唯一的邻国。

neigh·bour·hood *BrE*【英】, **neighborhood** *AmE*【美】/ˈnebɚˌhud; ˈneɪbəhʊd/ *n* [C] **1** a small area of a town, or the people who live there 社区, 住宅小区; 四邻, 街坊: *You're going to wake up the whole neighbourhood with that noise.* 你发出这么大的声音, 会把街坊邻居全都吵醒的。| *I grew up in a quiet neighborhood of Boston.* 我是在波士顿一个宁静的住宅区里长大的。| *a neighbourhood school* 社区学校 **2 in the neighbourhood** in the area around you or around a particular place 在附近地区: *Are there any hotels in the neighbourhood?* 附近有旅馆吗? | [+of] *somewhere in the neighbourhood of Chester* 在切斯特附近的某个地方 **3 in the neighbourhood of** either a little more or a little less than a particular number or amount; APPROXIMATELY 大约, 左右: *I'm hoping to buy one for something in the neighbourhood of £500.* 我希望能以500英镑左右的价钱买下。

neighbourhood watch /ˌ‥ˈ‥/ *n* [U] a system for preventing crime by which people living in an area watch each other's houses 居民区防盗制度

CULTURAL NOTE 文化注释

The people who take part in a neighbourhood watch scheme are typically honest respectable people with nice houses, living in good neighbourhoods. They report anything strange or anyone behaving badly to the police, who deal with it. 居民区防盗制度的参与者通常是那些受人尊敬而又诚实的人。他们的房子漂亮, 居住地段也很不错。他们发现了异常情况或行为诡异的人便向警察报告, 警察负责处理。

neigh·bour·ing *BrE*【英】, **neighboring** *AmE*【美】/ˈnebərɪŋ; ˈneɪbərɪŋ/ *adj* [only before noun 仅用于名词前] near the place where you are or the place you are talking about; NEARBY 邻近的, 附近的: **neighbouring country/town/house etc** *The fair attracted hundreds of people from the neighbouring towns and villages.* 集市吸引了邻近城镇及村庄的好几百人前来。

neigh·bour·ly *BrE*【英】, **neighborly** *AmE*【美】/ˈnebɚlɪ; ˈneɪbəli/ *adj* friendly and helpful towards your neighbours 睦邻的; 友好的, 友善的: *Since we've moved in people have been very neighbourly.* 自我们搬来时起, 这儿的人一直对我们十分友善。—**neighbourliness** *n* [U]

W3 **nei·ther**[1] /ˈniðɚ; ˈnaɪðə/ *determiner, pron* not one or the other of two people or things 两者都不(的); 两者中无一(的): **neither person/thing etc** *Neither parent cares what happens to the child.* 父母都不关心这孩子。| **neither of them/the people etc** *Both players have been warned, but neither of them seem to take it seriously.* 两名运动员都受到了警告, 但他们好像都不当回事。| **neither** *"Would you like tea or coffee?" "Neither, thanks."* "你喝茶还是咖啡?" "都不喝, 谢谢。" | *We went to see a couple of houses, but neither was suitable.* 我们去看了两所房子, 但都不合适。—compare 比较 EITHER, NONE[1] —see 见 EACH (USAGE)

S2 W3 **neither**[2] *adv* **1** used to add a negative statement to one that has just been mentioned 也不: **neither can I/neither does John etc** *"I have never been to Paris before." "No, neither have we."* "我从未去过巴黎。" "我们也没去过。" | *Tom didn't believe a word she said and neither did the police.* 汤姆根本不相信她说的话, 警方也不相信。| **me neither/John neither etc** *"I don't like horror movies." "Me neither."* "我不喜欢恐怖电影。" "我也不喜欢。" —see 见 ALSO (USAGE) **2** *formal* used to emphasize or add information to a negative statement【正式】更不: *The authorities were not sympathetic to the students' demands, neither would they tolerate any disruption.* 当局没有对学生提出的要求表示同情, 他们更不会容忍任何扰乱行为。—compare 比较 ANY, EITHER[4]

neither[3] *conjunction* **1 neither... nor...** used when two states, facts, actions etc are mentioned and both are not true or not possible 既不…也不…, 不…也不…, …和…都不: *The equipment is neither accurate nor safe.* 这种设备既不精确也不安全。| *She was expressionless, neither laughing nor crying.* 她毫无表情, 既不哭也不笑。**2 be neither here nor there** *especially spoken* used to say that something is not important because it does not affect or change another fact or situation【尤口】一点都不重要: *The fact that she needed the money for her children is neither here nor there, it's still stealing.* 尽管她偷钱是为了孩子, 可是毕竟还是偷窃。

nel·ly, nellie /ˈnɛlɪ; ˈneli/ *n* **not on your nelly** *BrE spoken* used to tell someone humorously or rudely that you are definitely not going to do something【英口】绝不可能, 当然不〔幽默或粗鲁口气〕

Nel·son /ˈnɛlsən; ˈnelsən/, **Ho·ra·ti·o** /həˈreʃio; həˈreɪʃiəʊ/ (1758-1805) a British ADMIRAL (=high-ranking officer in the navy) who is Britain's most famous naval leader. He lost an arm and the ability to see in one eye during the wars against Napoleon, and he became very popular after winning several important battles at sea. His most famous battle was the Battle of Trafalgar in 1805, in which he was killed. 纳尔逊〔(1758-1805), 英国海军元帅, 为英国最著名的海军将领。他在与拿破仑的连场海战中失去了一条手臂, 一只眼失明。几次重大海战取得胜利之后, 他威名大振。最著名的战役是1805年的特拉法尔加海战, 纳尔逊在此战中阵亡〕

Horatio Nelson 霍雷肖·纳尔逊

Nelson's Col·umn /ˌ‥ˈ‥/ a very tall COLUMN (=upright stone post) with a statue of Admiral Nelson on the top of it in Trafalgar Square in central London. It was built to honour Nelson, who was killed at the Battle of Trafalgar, where the British navy defeated the navy of Napoleon in 1805. It is one of the best-known sights in London. 纳尔逊圆柱〔位于伦敦市中心特拉法尔加广场上的一根非常高的圆柱, 顶部有海军元帅纳尔逊的雕像。该圆柱是为纪念纳尔逊而建的。1805年, 他曾率领英国海军在特拉法尔加海战中击败了拿破仑的海军。这根圆柱是伦敦最著名的景观之一〕

nem con /ˌnɛm ˈkɑn; ˌnem ˈkɒn/ *adv Latin law* without any opposition【拉丁, 法律】无异议地; 全体一致地: *The motion was passed nem con.* 该动议得到一致通过。

nem·e·sis /ˈnɛməsɪs; ˈneməsəs/ *n* [singular] *literary* a punishment that is deserved and cannot be avoided【文】天罚; 不可逃避的惩罚; 报应

neo- /nio; niːəʊ/ *prefix* [in nouns and adjectives 构成名词和形容词] a recent or later kind of a former system, style etc; new 新的: *neoclassical architecture* (=copying that of ancient Greece and Rome) 新古典主义建筑 | *neocolonialism* (=the control of other countries by large modern states) 新殖民主义

ne·o·clas·sic·al /ˌnioˈklæsɪkḷ; ˌniːəʊˈklæsɪkəl◂/ *adj* neoclassical art copies the style of ancient Greece or Rome 新古典主义的

ne·o·co·lo·ni·al·is·m /ˌniokəˈlonɪəˌlɪzəm; ˌniːəʊkəˈləʊniəlɪzəm/ *n* [U] the economic and political influence which a powerful country uses to control another country 新殖民主义

ne·o·lith·ic /ˌnioˈlɪθɪk; ˌniːəˈlɪθɪk◂/ *adj* connected with the latest period of the STONE AGE about 10,000 years ago, when people began to settle in villages and make stone tools and weapons 新石器时代的: *the discovery of a Neolithic burial mound* 发现一处新石器时代的坟堆

ne·ol·o·gis·m /niˈɑləˌdʒɪzəm; niːˈɒlədʒɪzəm/ *n* [C] a new word or expression, or a word used with a new meaning 新词; 旧词新义

ne·on /ˈniɑn; ˈniːɒn/ *n* [U] gas that produces a bright light when electricity is passed through it 氖

neon light /ˌ· ˈ· ·/ *n* [C] a glass tube filled with neon that produces a bright light when electricity is passed through it 氖光灯；霓虹灯：*the neon lights of Las Vegas* 拉斯韦加斯的霓虹灯

neon sign /ˌ· ˈ· ·/ *n* [C] an electric advertising sign consisting of neon lights in the form of shapes and words 霓虹灯广告牌

ne·o·phyte /ˈniəˌfaɪt; ˈniːəfaɪt/ *n* [C] *formal* 【正式】**1** someone who has just started to learn a particular skill, art, trade etc 初学者；新手 **2** a new member of a religious group 新入教者

Ne·pal /nɪˈpɔl; nɪˈpɔːl/ a country in southern Asia, in the Himalayan mountains, north of India and south of China. Population: 25,284,000 (2001). Capital: Kathmandu. Nepal is popular with tourists who want to go walking and climbing in the mountains. 尼泊尔〔南亚一国家，地处喜马拉雅山脉，位于印度以北，中国以南。人口：25,284,000（2001），首都：加德满都。尼泊尔是山间徒步旅行和爬山爱好者的好去处〕—**Nepalese** /ˌnɛpəˈliz; ˌnepəˈliːz◂/ *n, adj*

neph·ew /ˈnɛfju; ˈnefjuː/ *n* [C] the son of your brother or sister, or the son of your husband's or wife's brother or sister 侄子；外甥：*I've got one nephew. He's two.* 我有一个侄子，两岁了。—see picture at 参见 FAMILY 图 —compare 比较 NIECE

nep·o·tis·m /ˈnɛpəˌtɪzəm; ˈnepətɪzəm/ *n* [U] the practice of giving the best jobs to members of your family when you are in a position of power 任人唯亲；重用亲戚；裙带关系—**nepotistic** *adj*

Nep·tune /ˈnɛptʃun; ˈneptjuːn/ *n* [singular] the PLANET eighth in order from the sun 海王星 —see picture at 参见 SOLAR SYSTEM 图

nerd /nɝd; nɜːd/ *n* [C] *informal* 【非正式】**1** someone who is boring and unfashionable 乏味落伍的人 **2** someone who is extremely interested in computers 电脑迷—**nerdy** *adj*: *nerdy glasses* 难看落伍的眼镜

ner·e·id /ˈnɪriɪd; ˈnɪəri-ɪd/ *n* [C] a female spirit who lives in the sea according to ancient Greek stories〔古希腊神话中的〕海中仙女

Ne·ro /ˈniro; ˈnɪərəʊ/ (AD 37-68) a Roman emperor. Many people believe that he killed his mother, wives, and many others. He blamed the Christians for causing the great fire of Rome in AD 64 and many were killed. He also gave performances as an actor and musician, and is usually shown in pictures FIDDLING (=playing the violin) while Rome is on fire behind him. 尼禄〔（公元37-68），罗马皇帝。据说，他处死了自己的母亲、几位妻子和其他许多人。他把公元64年的罗马大火归咎于基督教徒，处死了许多人。他还当过演员，演奏过音乐。绘画作品中他的形象经常是以罗马大火为背景拉着小提琴〕

Neruda /nəˈrudə; nəˈruːdə/, **Pablo** /ˈpɑblo; ˈpɑːbləʊ/ (1904-73) a poet, DIPLOMAT, and Communist leader from Chile who won the Nobel Prize for Literature in 1971 聂鲁达〔(1904-73)，智利诗人、外交家、共产党领导人。1971 年获诺贝尔文学奖〕

S3 W3 **nerve¹** /nɝv, nɜːv/ *n*

1 ▶FEELINGS 情绪◀ nerves [plural] the feeling of being nervous because you are worried or a little frightened 焦虑；紧张："*What's wrong?*" "*It's just nerves. He's got his exams tomorrow.*" "怎么了？""只是紧张，他明天要考试。" | **be a bundle/bag of nerves** *informal* (=be extremely worried or frightened) 【非正式】极度焦虑[害怕] *I remember you were a bundle of nerves on your wedding day.* 我记得你在婚礼那天紧张极了。| **calm/steady your nerves** (=stop yourself feeling worried or frightened) 定神/稳住情绪 *Sean drank a large glass of brandy to calm his nerves.* 肖恩喝了一大杯白兰地，好让自己定定神。| **live on your nerves** (=be always worried) 常常感到忧虑 *He's the type of person who lives on his nerves.* 他是那种一天到晚老是担惊受怕的人。

2 get on sb's nerves *informal* to annoy someone, especially by repeatedly doing something 【非正式】烦扰某人，使人心烦不安：*She's always moaning. It really gets on my nerves.* 她老是在呻吟，真令我心烦。

3 ▶COURAGE 勇气◀ [U] the ability to stay calm and confident in a dangerous, difficult or frightening situation 镇定；勇气；意志力：**have the nerve to do sth** *Not many people have the nerve to stand up and speak in front of a large audience.* 不是很多人都有勇气站在一大群人面前讲话的。| **it takes a lot of nerve to do sth** *spoken* 【口】*It takes a lot of nerve to report a colleague for sexual harassment.* 要举报同事的性骚扰行为需要很大的勇气。| **lose your nerve** *He'd have won if he hadn't lost his nerve.* 他要不是失去勇气，就赢了。

4 have a nerve *spoken* to be surprisingly rude without seeming ashamed or embarrassed 【口】厚颜无耻；放肆：*He's got a nerve asking for more money.* 他居然有脸要更多的钱。| **have the nerve to do sth** *She lets me do all the work, and then she has the nerve to criticise my cooking.* 她让我做所有的工作，居然还有脸挑剔我的厨艺。| **what a nerve!** *What a bloody nerve! Telling me how to do something I've been doing for years!* 真是不要脸！居然指手画脚告诉我怎样做，要知道我都干了多少年了。

5 ▶BODY PART 身体部分◀ [C] one of the thin parts like threads inside your body, along which feelings and messages are sent to the brain 神经：*The dentist was drilling and he hit a nerve. The pain was incredible!* 牙医在钻我的牙齿时碰到了我的神经，真是疼死了！—see picture at 参见 TEETH 图

6 hit/touch a raw nerve to say something that someone else is very sensitive about especially accidentally〔尤指无心地〕触到敏感话题；触到痛处 —see also 另见 **touch a raw nerve** (RAW¹ (6)), **strain every nerve** (STRAIN² (7))

nerve² *v* **nerve yourself** to force yourself to be brave enough to do something difficult or dangerous 鼓起勇气：[+for] *The parachutist nerved himself for the jump.* 跳伞者鼓足勇气准备往下跳。

nerve cen·tre *BrE* 【英】, **nerve center** *AmE* 【美】/ˈ· ˌ··/ *n* [C] the place from which a system, activity, organization etc is controlled 中枢，核心；控制中心：*The bridge is the ship's nerve center.* 驾驶台是这艘船的控制中心。

nerve gas /ˈ· ·/ *n* [U] a poisonous gas that is used in war and that damages your CENTRAL NERVOUS SYSTEM 神经性毒气〔一种破坏人体中枢神经系统的毒气，于战时使用〕

nerve·less /ˈnɝvlɪs; ˈnɜːvləs/ *adj* nerveless fingers, feet, hands etc have no strength or feeling in them〔手、脚等〕无力的；神经麻木的

nerve-wrack·ing, nerve-racking /ˈ· ˌ··/ *adj* a nerve-wracking situation makes you feel very nervous because it is difficult or frightening 令人心烦的，使人紧张的：*Your first appearance on stage is always a nerve-wracking experience.* 初次上台总是让人紧张不安。

ner·vous /ˈnɝvəs; ˈnɜːvəs/ *adj* **1** worried or frightened about something that may happen so that you cannot relax 神经紧张的；焦虑不安的；害怕的，胆怯的：[+about] *I was so nervous about my exams that I couldn't sleep.* 考试让我紧张得睡不着觉。| [+of] *Jill's always been a little nervous of dogs.* 吉尔一直有点怕狗。**2** often becoming worried or frightened and easily upset 神经脆弱的，神经质的：*She's a nervous, sensitive child.* 她是一个神经脆弱而且敏感的孩子。| **nervous wreck** (=someone whose health and confidence have been destroyed by worry, fear etc)〔因焦虑或恐惧〕身心极度受损的人 *This job is turning me into a nervous wreck.* 这份工作快使我神经崩溃了。| **of a nervous disposition** *This film is unsuitable for people of a nervous disposition.* 这部影片不适合性格焦虑的人看。**3 nervous exhaustion/strain etc** a mental condition in which you feel very tired, usually caused by working too hard or by difficult emotional problems 精神极度疲劳/紧张等 **4** related to the nerves in your body 神经系统的，神经方面的：*a nervous disorder* 神经系统紊乱—**nervously** *adv*: *She smiled nervously.* 她紧张地笑了一笑。—**nervousness** *n* [U]: *Minelli's nervousness showed in his voice.* 米内里的声音里透出紧张不安。 S3 W3

USAGE NOTE 用法说明: NERVOUS

WORD CHOICE 词语辨析: **nervous, uneasy, concerned, anxious, worried**

You are **nervous** about something difficult or strange that you are doing, or when you are worried and a little frightened about something that might happen or is going to happen, so that you cannot relax. 当你做一件困难或陌生的事情，或者对某件可能发生或即将发生的事感到担心或害怕时，你会感到 nervous: *Don't drive so fast – you're making me nervous!* 别把车开那么快，这使我有些紧张。| *She gets nervous about walking home alone late at night.* 她对独自一人走夜路回家感到害怕。You are **uneasy** when you are unable to relax because you think but do not know for certain that something bad is happening or is going to happen. 当你猜想有不祥的事正在发生或即将发生而无法放松时，你会感到 uneasy: *When Jody didn't call for the next three days I started to get uneasy.* 在接下来的三天内乔迪一直没有来电话，这使我开始变得不安。

You are **concerned** when there is a problem or when someone has a problem that you wish you could do something about. 当出现某个问题，或某人遇到问题而你想帮助解决时，你会感到 concerned: *I'm rather concerned about Harvey's health.* 我对哈维的健康感到相当忧虑。**Worried** is stronger. If you are **worried** you are unhappy and cannot stop thinking about a problem or about some-

thing bad that might happen. worried 一词较为强烈。如果你感到 worried, 就说明你不开心, 总是为某个问题或可能发生的不祥之事而担心: *Martha's very worried about her son's disappearance.* 玛莎因为儿子失踪而十分担心。**Anxious** is stronger still. You are **anxious** when you are very worried and frightened about something that is happening or might happen. anxious 则更为强烈。当你为正在发生或可能发生的某事感到十分担心和害怕时, 你会感到 anxious: *the little girl's anxious face as she searched the crowds for her mother* 在人群中寻找母亲时小女孩那充满忧虑的脸。

nervous break·down /ˌ‥ˈ‥ˌ/ *n* [C] *not technical* a mental illness in which someone becomes extremely anxious and tired and cannot deal with the things they usually do【非术语】精神崩溃

nervous sys·tem /ˈ‥ ˌ‥/ *n* [C] the parts of your body, including your nerves, brain, and SPINAL CORD, by means of which you feel pain, heat etc and control your movements 神经系统

nerv·y /ˈnɜvɪ; ˈnɜːvi/ *adj* **1** *informal* nervous and easily frightened【非正式】神经质的; 紧张不安的 **2** *AmE informal* brave and confident【美, 非正式】勇敢自信的

-ness /nɪs; nə̇s/ *suffix* [in nouns 构成名词] the condition, quality, or degree of being something (…的) 状态; 性质; 程度: *loudness* 响度 | *sadness* 悲伤 | *warm-heartedness* 热心 | *the many kindnesses you've done me* 你给我的许多帮助

Nes·sie /ˈnɛsɪ; ˈnesi/ an informal name for the Loch Ness Monster 尼斯〔尼斯湖水怪的俗称〕

Nes·sun Dor·ma /ˌnɛsən ˋdɔrmə; ˌnesən ˈdɔːmə/ an ARIA (=a song sung by one person) from the OPERA *Turandot* by Puccini, which became very popular when it was sung by Luciano Pavarotti as the theme song for the 1990 football World Cup《今夜无人入眠》〔普契尼的歌剧《图兰朵》中的一段咏叹调。曾被选为 1990 年世界杯足球赛的主题歌, 由卢西亚诺·帕瓦罗蒂演唱, 从此格外有名〕

nest[1] /nɛst; nest/ *n* [C] **1** a hollow place made or chosen by a bird to lay its eggs in and to make its home in 鸟巢, 鸟窝 **2** a place where insects or small animals live〔昆虫或小动物的〕窝; 穴: *a field mouse's nest* 田鼠穴 **3 a nest of spies/criminals/vice etc** a place where there are many bad people or evil activities 间谍/罪犯/罪恶等的老巢[温床] **4 leave the nest** to leave your parents' home 搬出父母家, 离家独立 **5 nest of tables/boxes** a set of tables etc that fit inside one another〔可依大小套放的〕一套桌子/盒子 —see also 另见 **feather your nest** (FEATHER[2] (1)), **stir up a hornets' nest** (HORNET (2)), **mare's nest** (MARE (2)), **love nest** (LOVE[2] (15))

nest[2] *v* [I] to build or use a nest 筑巢; 巢居: *gulls nesting on the cliffs* 在悬崖上筑巢的海鸥

nest egg /ˈ· ·/ *n* [C] an amount of money that you have saved 个人储蓄金, 储备金

nes·tle /ˈnɛsl̩; ˈnesəl/ *v* **1** [I always+adv/prep, T always+adv/prep] to move into a comfortable position, pressing your head or body against someone or against something soft (使) 舒适地安顿下来; (使) 偎依, (使) 依靠: **nestle against/beside/by etc** *Sarah lay there peacefully, the child nestling by her side.* 萨拉安静地躺在那儿, 孩子偎依在她身边。| **nestle sth against/beside etc** *He nestled his head against her shoulder.* 他把头靠在她的肩膀上。**2** [I always+adv/prep] to be in a position that seems to be protected by the hills etc around 坐落在〔山间〕: [+among/between etc] *several small villages nestling among the mountains* 群山环抱的几个小村落

nest·ling /ˈnɛslɪŋ; ˈnestlɪŋ/ *n* [C] a very young bird 雏鸟

[3] **net**[1] /nɛt; net/ *n* **1** [C,U] a piece of material consisting of strings, threads, or wires woven across each other with regular spaces in between, used, for example, for catching fish, protecting vegetables etc 网: *a fishing net* 鱼网 **2 the net a)** a long net used in games such as tennis that the players must hit the ball over〔网球等的〕球网 —see picture at 参见 TENNIS 图 **b)** a net forming an enclosure at the back of the GOAL in football, HOCKEY etc〔足球、曲棍球等的〕球门网: *Cole slammed the ball into the back of the net.* 科尔将球狠狠地踢进网窝。**3** [U] very thin material made from fine threads woven together with very small spaces between 网眼织物; 网纱: *net curtains* 网纱窗帘 **4** [C] a bag made of net on the end of a stick used for catching butterflies (BUTTERFLY (1)) etc〔捕昆虫等的〕网〔如捕蝶网〕 **5** [C] a communications or computer network〔通讯、电脑〕网络 **6 the Net** *technical* the Internet; a system that allows millions of computer users around the world to exchange information【术语】互联网 —see also 另见 **cast your net wide** (CAST[1] (18)), HAIRNET, SAFETY NET

net[2] *v* **netted, netting** [T] **1** to catch a fish in a net 用网捕〔鱼〕: *We netted three fish in under an hour.* 不到一小时我们就网住了三条鱼。**2** *especially AmE* to earn a particular amount of money as a profit after tax has been paid【尤美】获得净收入, 净赚: *I was netting around $64,000 a year.* 我每年净赚约 64,000 美元。**3** *informal* to hit or kick the ball into the net in sport【非正式】击〔球〕入网; 踢〔球〕入网 **4** to succeed in getting something by using your skill〔靠技能〕成功获取: *a company that has netted several large contracts* 成功获取几个大合同的公司 [2]

net[3] also 又作 **nett** *BrE*【英】—*adj* [only before noun 仅用于名词前] **1** a net amount of money is the amount that remains after everything has been taken away from it〔钱〕净得的: **net profit** (=profit after tax, rent etc are paid) 纯利, 净利润 *He took 50% of the net revenue.* 他拿走了净收入的 50%。—compare 比较 GROSS[1] (1) **2 net weight** the weight of something without its container 净重: **21b/500g etc net** *jars of coffee weighing 450 grams net* 净重 450 克的瓶装咖啡 **3 net result (of)** the final result of something (…的) 最后结果: *The net result of this policy was even worse inflation.* 这项政策的最后结果是更为严重的通货膨胀。

net·ball /ˈnɛtbɔl; ˈnetbɔːl/ *n* [U] a game similar to BASKETBALL played in Britain especially by girls〔英国女子玩的〕无挡板篮球

neth·er /ˈnɛðɚ; ˈneðə/ *adj* [only before noun 仅用于名词前] *literary or humorous* lower down【文或幽默】下面的, 下部的: *the nether regions* 地狱, 阴间

Neth·er·lands, the /ˈnɛðɚləndz; ˈneðələndz/ a country in northwest Europe which is a member of the EU. Population: 15,981,000 (2001). The capital is Amsterdam, but the government is based in The Hague. Most of the country is flat and large parts of it are below sea level. British and American people often call the country Holland, but this is not officially correct because Holland is only one part of the Netherlands.People from the Netherlands are called Dutch. 荷兰〔欧洲西北部一国家, 欧盟成员国。人口: 15,981,000 (2001), 首都: 阿姆斯特丹, 政府所在地在海牙。国土大部分为平原, 大都低于海平面。英美人常把该国叫做 Holland, 但正式讲这并不准确, 因为 Holland 仅是荷兰的一部分。荷兰人称作 Dutch〕

Netherlands An·til·les, the /ˌnɛðɚləndz ænˋtɪliz; ˌneðələndz ænˈtɪliːz/ a group of islands, including Bonaire and Curaçao, in the Caribbean Sea, which belong to the Netherlands. Population: 200,000 (1995). Capital: Willemstad. 荷属安的列斯群岛〔加勒比海一群岛, 隶属荷兰, 包括博拉尔岛和库拉索岛。人口: 200,000 (1995), 首府: 威廉斯塔德〕

neth·er·most /ˈnɛðɚˌmost; ˈneðəməʊst/ *adj literary* lowest【文】最下面的, 最低的: *the nethermost fiery pit of hell* 烈火熊熊的地狱最深处

nett /nɛt; net/ *adj* a British spelling of NET[3] net[3] 的英式拼法

net·ting /ˈnɛtɪŋ; ˈnetɪŋ/ *n* [U] material consisting of string, wire etc that has been woven into a net 网; 网状物: *a fence of wire netting* 铁丝网围栏

net·tle[1] /ˈnɛtl̩; ˈnetl/ *n* [C] a wild plant with rough leaves that sting you 荨麻 —see also 另见 **grasp the nettle** (GRASP[1] (4))

nettle[2] *v* [T] **be nettled** *informal* to be annoyed by someone's behaviour【非正式】被惹怒: *She was nettled by Holman's remark.* 她被霍尔曼的话激怒了。

nettle rash /ˈ‥ ˌ/ *n* [C,U] *BrE* a condition that causes areas of red spots on your skin【英】荨麻疹, 风疹块

network 网状系统

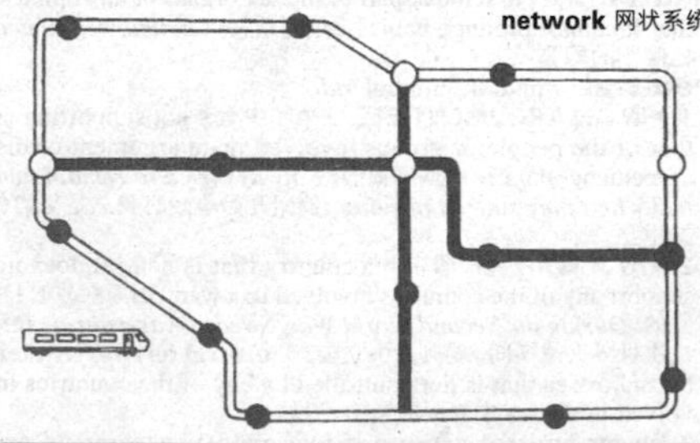

net·work[1] /ˈnɛtˌwɝk; ˈnetwɜːk/ *n* [C] **1** a group of radio or television stations, which broadcast many of the same programmes, but in different places 广播网; 电视网 **2** a system of lines, tubes, wires, roads etc that cross each other and are connected to each other 网络, 网状系统: [+of] *an elaborate net-* [3]

work of canals 四通八达的运河网 | *the network of blood vessels in the body* 人体内的血管网 **3** a group of people, organizations etc that are connected or that work together 人际关系网, 联络网: [+of] *It's important to build up a network of professional contacts.* 建立一个专业联系网是很重要的。**4** a set of computers that are connected to each other and can be used to send information or messages 电脑网络

network² *v* [I,T] **1** to broadcast a radio or television programme on several different channels (CHANNEL¹ (1,2)) at the same time 通过〔电台、电视〕网络播出 **2** to connect several computers together so that you can send information between them (使)〔电脑〕联网

net·work·ing /ˈnɛtwɝkɪŋ; ˈnetwɜːkɪŋ/ *n* [U] the practice of meeting other people involved in the same kind of work, to share information, support each other etc 联网 (技术) 〔指与同行建立联系, 旨在共享资料或相互支援〕

CULTURAL NOTE 文化注释

This word is used generally to talk about anyone improving their professional connections. In Britain, the word can be used about professional people who work from home, or in areas which do not give them the advantages enjoyed by people in other businesses or professions. 这个词一般用来指增进与同行的关系。在英国, 这个词可以用在一些职业人士的身上, 他们要么在家中工作, 要么在其工作领域不像在其他公司或职业上能享受到便利的条件。

neur- /njur; njʊə/ *prefix* another form of the prefix NEURO- 前缀 neuro- 的另一种形式

neu·ral /ˈnjurəl; ˈnjʊərəl/ *adj technical* related to a nerve or the NERVOUS SYSTEM【术语】神经的, 神经系统的: *neural networks* 神经网络

neu·ral·gia /njuˈrældʒə; njʊˈrældʒə/ *n* [U] a sharp pain along the length of a nerve 神经痛 —**neuralgic** *adj*

neuro- /ˈnjurə; ˈnjʊərəʊ/ *prefix* also 又作 **neur-** *technical* concerning the nerves【术语】(关于) 神经的: *neuropathology* 神经病理学 | *a neurosurgeon* (=who specializes in the body's nervous system) 神经外科医生

neu·rol·o·gy /njuˈrɑlədʒɪ; njʊˈrɒlədʒi/ *n* [U] the scientific study of the NERVOUS SYSTEM and its diseases 神经 (病) 学 —**neurologist** *n* [C]: *consultant neurologist David Hart* 神经病科顾问[会诊]医生戴维·哈特 —**neurological** /ˌnjurəˈlɑdʒɪkəl; ˌnjʊərəˈlɒdʒɪkəl◂/ *adj*

neu·ro·sis /njuˈrosɪs; njʊˈrəʊsɨs/ *n plural* **neuroses** /-siz; -siːz/ [C,U] a mental illness that makes someone unreasonably worried or frightened 神经机能病; 神经官能症

neu·rot·ic /njuˈrɑtɪk; njʊˈrɒtɪk/ *adj* **1** unreasonably anxious or afraid 神经质的, 神经过敏的; 极度害怕的: *He seemed a neurotic, self-obsessed character.* 他看起来像个神经质、自我陶醉的人。**2** connected with or affected by neurosis 神经官能症的: *neurotic disorders* 神经机能失调 —**neurotically** /-klɪ; -kli/ *adv* —**neurotic** *n* [C]

neu·ter¹ /ˈnjutɚ; ˈnjuːtə/ *adj* **1** plants or animals that are neuter have undeveloped sex organs or no sex organs〔动植物〕生殖器发育不完全的; 无性的; 无生殖器的 **2** *technical* a neuter noun, PRONOUN etc belongs to a class of words that have different inflections (INFLECTION (1)) from MASCULINE (4) or FEMININE (2) words【术语】〔名词、代名词等〕中性的

neuter² *v* [T] to remove part of the sex organs of an animal so that it cannot produce babies 阉割〔动物〕: *a neutered tomcat* 已阉割的雄猫

neu·tral¹ /ˈnjutrəl; ˈnjuːtrəl/ *adj*

1 ▶**IN AN ARGUMENT ETC** 在争吵中等◀ not supporting either of the people or groups involved in an argument or disagreement 中立的, 不偏不倚的: *I always tried to remain neutral when they started arguing.* 他们开始争吵时我总是努力保持中立。

2 ▶**IN A WAR** 在战争中◀ a country that is neutral does not support any of the countries involved in a war〔国家在战时〕中立的: *During the Second World War, Sweden was neutral.* 在第二次世界大战期间, 瑞典是中立国。| **neutral territory/waters** (=land or sea that is not controlled by any of the countries involved in a war) 中立国的领土/海域

3 be on neutral ground if two opposing teams or representatives are on neutral ground they are in a place that is not favourable to either of them〔对手间〕旗鼓相当, 没有一方占优势

4 ▶**LANGUAGE** 语言◀ language, words etc that are neutral are deliberately chosen to avoid expressing any strong opinion or feeling 中性的; 不带感情色彩的: *the neutral language of an official news report* 官方新闻报道采用的中性语言

5 ▶**COLOUR** 色彩◀ a neutral colour is not very strong or bright, for example grey or light brown 暗淡的; 不鲜艳的〈如灰色或浅棕色〉

6 ▶**WIRE** 电线◀ *technical* a neutral wire has no electrical CHARGE¹ (7)【术语】不带电的

7 ▶**CHEMICAL** 化学品◀ *technical* a neutral substance is neither acid nor ALKALI【术语】中性的 —**neutrally** *adv*

neutral² *n* **1** [U] the position of the gears (GEAR¹ (1)) of a car or machine in which the engine does not turn the wheels〔汽车或机器的〕空挡位置: **in/into neutral** *When you start the engine, be sure the car's in neutral.* 你在发动引擎时, 一定要让汽车处于空挡。**2** [C] a country or person that is not fighting for or helping any of the countries involved in a war〔战时的〕中立国; 中立人士

neu·tra·list /ˈnjutrəlɪst; ˈnjuːtrəlɨst/ *adj AmE* tending not to support either side in a war, quarrel etc【美】中立的 —**neutralist** *n* [C]

neu·tral·i·ty /njuˈtrælətɪ; njuːˈtrælɨti/ *n* [U] the state of not supporting either side in an argument or war 中立; 中立地位

neu·tral·ize also 又作 **-ise** *BrE*【英】/ˈnjutrəlˌaɪz; ˈnjuːtrəlaɪz/ *v* [T] **1** to prevent something from having any effect 使失效; 抵消: *Rising prices tend to neutralize increased wages.* 不断上涨的物价往往会抵消工资的增长。**2** *technical* to make a substance chemically NEUTRAL【术语】使中和: *a medicine that neutralizes the acid in the stomach* 能中和胃酸的药物 **3** to make a country or population NEUTRAL in war〔在战争期间〕使〔国家或人民〕中立 —**neutralization** /ˌnjutrələˈzeʃən; ˌnjuːtrəlaɪˈzeɪʃən/ *n* [U]

neu·tron /ˈnjutrɑn; ˈnjuːtrɒn/ *n* [C] a part of an atom that has no electrical CHARGE¹ (7) 中子

neutron bomb /ˈ··, ·/ *n* [C] a kind of NUCLEAR bomb which kills people but which does not cause much damage to property 中子弹

Ne·va·da /nɪˈvædə; nɪˈvɑːdə/ abbreviation 缩写为 **NV** a state in the western US, between California and Utah. Nevada is mostly desert, and it is the driest part of the US. Its most important industry is GAMBLING, especially in Las Vegas, and the city of Reno is famous for being an easy place to get a divorce. 内华达州〔美国西部一州, 位于加利福尼亚州与犹他州之间, 大部分土地为沙漠, 为美国最干旱的地区。该州最重要的产业是赌博, 在拉斯维加斯尤为如此。该州的里诺城也很有名气, 办理离婚手续非常容易〕—**Nevadan** *n, adj*

nev·er /ˈnɛvɚ; ˈnevə/ *adv*

1 ▶**NOT AT ANY TIME** 任何时候都不◀ not once or not at any time 从来没有; 决不, 永不: *We've never been to Paris.* 我们从未去过巴黎。| *I'll never forget what my mother said.* 我永远不会忘记母亲的话。| **never... again** *Never let me hear you use that word again!* 永远别让我再听到你用那个词! | **never in all my life** *spoken* (=used to emphasize how bad something was)【口】我这辈子从没 *Never in all my life have I felt so humiliated.* 我这辈子从未感到如此受辱。| **never ever** *spoken* (=used to emphasize 'never')【口】永不 *I'll never ever forgive him for leaving me.* 我永远不会原谅他离开我。| **never once** *spoken* (=used when you are annoyed because someone never did something although they had many opportunities)【口】一次也没有…过 *Never once did she offer to look after the children.* 她一次也没有提出过要照顾孩子们。| **never for one moment** *especially spoken* (=used to emphasize that you never thought, imagined, or doubted something)【尤口】一刻都没有 *Never for one moment did I think that we were going to encounter so many problems.* 我从未想过我们会遇到这么多问题。| **sb/sth has never been known to do something** (=used to mean that something is strange because it has never happened before) 从未听说某人/某物做某事 *Max had never been known to leave home without telling someone.* 从未听说过马克斯不跟任何人打招呼就出门。—see picture at 参见 FREQUENCY 图

2 never mind *spoken* used to tell someone that something is not important or serious, so that there is no need to worry or feel sorry【口】别担心; 没关系, 不要紧: *"We've missed the train." "Never mind, there's another one in ten minutes."* "我们没赶上火车。" "别担心, 十分钟后还有一班。"

3 never you mind *spoken* used to tell someone not to ask questions about something because you do not want to tell them about it【口】不关你的事: *"What were you talking about just now?" "Never you mind."* "你们刚才在谈论什么呢?" "不关你的事。"

4 you never know *spoken* used to say that something which seems unlikely may happen【口】说不定: *Try it! You never know, you might be lucky.* 试试看! 说不定你会有好运。

5 that would never do *spoken* used to say that you would not want something to happen【口】那就糟了: *Someone might discover our secret and that would never do.* 也许会有人发现我们的秘密，那就糟了。

6 I never knew (that) *spoken* used to mean that you did not know something until now【口】以前我一直不知道: *I never knew Texas was so big.* 我一直不知道得克萨斯州这么大。| *I've just learned something I never knew before.* 我刚听说了一件以前一直不知道的事。

7 well, I never (did)! *spoken* used to say that you are very surprised【口】啊，真没想到！: *Well, I never! I wouldn't have thought she was that old.* 啊，真出乎意料！我没想到她那么大年纪了。

8 never! *BrE spoken* used when you are surprised by something, because you think it is not possible【英口】不可能！: *He's never going to cycle all the way to Manchester!* 他不可能一路骑自行车去曼彻斯特！| *Never! I don't believe it!* 不可能！我不相信！

9 never so much as not even 甚至没有: *The thought that Laura might be having an affair had never so much as crossed his mind.* 他脑子里从未出现过劳拉可能有外遇的想法。

10 no I never! *BrE spoken* used by a child to say that they did not do something bad when someone else is saying that they did【英口】我没干过！〔儿童申辩用语〕: *"You cheated, didn't you?" "No, I never."* "你骗人了，不是吗？""不，我没有。"

11 never fear *old-fashioned* used to tell someone not to worry【过时】别怕，别担心: *She'll be back, never fear.* 别担心，她会回来的。

12 never say die used to encourage someone when they are losing hope 别放弃，别轻言放弃

nev·er-end·ing /ˌ‥ ˈ‥◂/ *adj* seeming to continue for a very long time 永远不会完结的; 不断的: *The work is never-ending.* 这工作永无休止。

nev·er·more /ˌnɛvɚˈmɔr; ˌnevəˈmɔː/ *adv poetic* never again【诗】永不再，决不再

never-never /ˌ‥ ˈ‥/ *n* **on the never-never** *BrE humorous* if you buy something on the never-never, you buy it on HIRE PURCHASE (=by making small regular payments)【英，幽默】分期付款（购买）

never-never land /ˌ‥ ˈ‥ ˌ/ *n* [U] an imaginary place where everything is perfect〔想象中的〕世外桃源，理想乐土

S3 W2 **nev·er·the·less** /ˌnɛvɚðəˈlɛs; ˌnevəðəˈles/ *adv* [sentence adverb 句子副词] *formal* in spite of a fact that you have just mentioned【正式】然而，不过；尽管如此: *What you said was true. It was, nevertheless, a little unkind.* 你说的都是实话，只不过有点刻薄。| *He insisted that everything would be alright. Nevertheless, I could not help feeling anxious.* 他坚持说一切都会好。尽管如此，我还是放心不下。

Ne·vis /ˈnivəs; ˈniːvɪs/ an island which is one of the Leeward Islands and is also part of St Kitts-Nevis, an island state in the Caribbean Sea 尼维斯岛〔背风群岛一岛屿，属于加勒比海岛国圣基茨和尼维斯联邦〕—see also 另见 BEN NEVIS

S1 W2 **new** /nju; njuː/ *adj*

1 ►RECENTLY MADE 新造的◄ recently made, built, or invented 新造的; 新建的; 新发明的: *the city's new hospital* 市里新建的医院 | *Renault's new GTI hatchback* 雷诺新推出的GTI掀背轿车 | *the new issue of 'Time' magazine* 新一期《时代周刊》| *the new fashions* 新的时装款式 | *a new way of organizing data* 数据整理的新方法

2 ►RECENTLY BOUGHT 新买的◄ recently bought 新买的: *Do you like my new dress?* 你喜欢我新买的连衣裙吗？| *That's a nice bag – is it new?* 这个手提袋不错，是新买的吗？

3 ►NOT THERE BEFORE 以前没有的◄ having just developed 新出现的: *new buds on the trees* 树上的新芽 | *a young woman with new ideas* 拥有新观念的女青年 | *the new nations of Africa* 非洲的新兴国家 | **new hope/confidence/optimism etc** (=hope etc that you have only just started to feel) 新的希望/信心/乐观态度等 *a medical breakthrough that offers new hope to cancer patients* 给癌症患者带来新希望的医学突破

4 ►NOT USED BEFORE 以前未用过的◄ [no comparative 无比较级] not used or owned by anyone before 未用过的，崭新的: *New and second hand books for sale.* 出售新书及二手书。| **buy sth new** *I got a used video camera for £300 – it would have cost £1,000 if I'd bought it new.* 我花300英镑买了一台二手摄影机，如果买新的要花1000英镑。| **brand new** (=completely new) 崭新的 *When did you buy this sofa? It looks brand new.* 这张沙发你什么时候买的？看起来像是全新的。

5 like new/as good as new in excellent condition 跟新的一样: *Your watch just needs cleaning and it'll be as good as new.* 你的手表该清洁一下了，之后会跟新的一样。| *We polished the car till it looked like new.* 我们把汽车擦亮，直到它看起来跟新的一样。

6 ►UNFAMILIAR 不熟悉的◄ not recognized or not experienced before 不认识的; 未体验过的: *learning a new language* 学习新的语言 | *Living in the city was a new experience for Philip.* 在城市里生活对菲利普来说是一种新的经历。| **be new to sb** *The fruit had a delicate taste that was completely new to me.* 这种水果带有一种我从未尝过的鲜美味道。| **that's a new one on me** *spoken* (=used to say that you have never heard a particular word, name etc before)【口】我第一次听说

7 ►RECENTLY ARRIVED 最近到达的◄ having recently arrived in a place, joined an organization, or started a new job 新来的; 新加入的; 刚开始的: *You're new here, aren't you?* 你是新来的，是吗？| **be new to sth/be new at sth** *Don't worry if you make mistakes you're still new to the job.* 别怕犯错，你才刚刚开始干这份工作呢！| **new member/employee/student etc** (=people who are not already members) 新成员/新雇员/新生等 *training for new employees* 对新员工的培训 | *The party is anxious to recruit new members.* 该党正在急切地招募新成员。| **new arrival** (=someone who has recently arrived in a place) 新来的人 *As a new arrival, Maria was obviously going to have problems with the language.* 刚到此地，玛丽亚肯定会在语言方面遇到问题。| **be the new kid on the block** *AmE informal* (=be the newest person in a job, school etc)【美，非正式】新雇员; 新生 *It's not always easy being the new kid on the block.* 做新生并非总是件轻松的事。| **be the new boy/girl** *BrE humorous* (=be the newest person in a job, organization etc)【英，幽默】新雇员; 新成员

8 new owner/address/job etc the owner etc that has recently replaced the previous one 新业主/地址/工作等: *Have you met Keith's new girlfriend?* 你见过基思的新女朋友吗？| *I'll let you have my new phone number.* 我会告诉你我的新电话号码。

9 ►RECENTLY DISCOVERED 新发现的◄ recently discovered 新发现的: *the discovery of a new planet* 一颗新行星的发现 | *new oilfields in Alaska* 阿拉斯加的新油田 | *important new evidence that may prove her innocence* 可能证明她清白的重要新证据

10 new life/day/era a period that is just beginning and seems to offer better opportunities 新的生活/一天/纪元: *They went to Australia to start a new life there.* 他们去澳大利亚开始新的生活。

11 feel (like) a new man/woman to feel much healthier and have a lot more energy than before 感到自己焕然一新

12 new blood new members of a group or organization who will bring new ideas and be full of energy〔团体或组织中的〕新血液，新成员，新生力量: *What we need in this company is some new blood.* 我们这个公司需要的是新生力量。

13 new broom someone who has just become the leader or manager of an organization and is eager to make changes〔急于变革的〕新上任官员[领导人]

14 what's new? *spoken especially AmE* used as a friendly greeting to mean 'how are you?'【口，尤美】怎么样？你好吗？〔招呼语〕

15 the new unfamiliar ideas or changes in society 新观念; 新变化: *the shock of the new* 新观念带来的震撼

16 new-made/new-formed etc recently made, formed etc 新造的/新建立的等 —see also 另见 **a new lease of life** (LEASE[1] (2)), **turn over a new leaf** (LEAF[1] (3)) —**newness** *n* [U]: *Philip was bewildered by the newness of his surroundings.* 菲利普对他四周的新环境感到迷茫。

New Age /ˌ· ˈ·◂/ *adj* concerning the belief in SPIRITUAL ideas, cures, and ways of life which became popular in Britain and the US in the late 20th century 新时代的〔形容20世纪晚期在英国和美国十分流行的一种关于精神信念、疗法和生活方式的信仰〕

New Age trav·el·lers /ˌ· ˈ· ˌ‥/ *n* [plural] people in Britain who refuse to live the way other people live in ordinary society, and go from place to place living in vehicles〔新时代中以车为家四处漫游的〕新潮一族，新时代旅行者

New·ark /ˈnjuɚk; ˈnjuːək/ **1** a large city and port in New Jersey, US, which is next to the Hudson River and across from New York City 纽瓦克〔美国新泽西州一个大的港口城市，濒临哈得孙河，与纽约市隔岸相望〕**2** a town in Nottinghamshire in central England, whose full name is Newark-on-Trent 纽瓦克〔英格兰中部诺丁汉郡一城镇，全称为特伦特河畔的纽瓦克〕

new·born /ˈnjuˌbɔrn; ˈnjuːbɔːn/ *adj* **newborn child/baby/son etc** a child that has just been born 新生儿/婴儿/儿子等: *He took his newborn baby in his arms.* 他把自己刚出生的宝宝抱在怀里。—**newborn** *n* [C]

New Bruns·wick /nju ˈbrʌnzwɪk; njuː ˈbrʌnzwɪk/ a PROVINCE of Canada on the Gulf of St Lawrence 新不伦瑞克省〔加拿大一省，濒临圣劳伦斯湾〕

N

New Cal·e·do·ni·a an island in the Pacific Ocean, east of Australia, which is a TERRITORY of France. Population: 204,863 (2001). Capital: Nouméa. 新赫里多尼亚〔澳大利亚以东，太平洋中一岛，归属法国。人口: 204,863 (2001)，首府: 努美阿〕

New·cas·tle /ˈnjuˌkæsl; ˈnjuːkɑːsəl/ **1** a large industrial city and port on the River Tyne in northeast England, whose full name is **Newcastle upon Tyne**. Newcastle used to have a large coal mining and shipbuilding industry, but much of the old industry has now closed down. People from Newcastle are informally called Geordies, and they have their own DIALECT of English and their own ACCENT (=way of pronouncing words) which is also called Geordie and is easy to recognize. 纽卡斯尔〔英格兰东北部泰恩河畔一大型工业城市和港口，其全称为泰恩河畔的纽卡斯尔。过去，该地的采煤业和造船业规模较大，如今大部分工厂都已关闭。纽卡斯尔人的绰号是泰恩赛德人，他们有自己的方言和口音，被称为泰恩赛德话，很容易辨识〕 **2** a city, port, and important industrial centre in New South Wales, southeast Australia, near where the Hunter River joins the sea 纽卡斯尔〔澳大利亚东南部新南威尔士州一城市、港口和重要的工业中心，位于亨特河入海口附近〕

Newcastle Brown /ˌ···ˈ·/ *trademark* a type of strong dark beer made in the north of England, and usually sold in tall bottles【商标】纽卡斯尔黑啤〔英格兰北部生产的一种酒精度较高的黑啤，常以高瓶装出售〕

new·com·er /njuˋkʌmɚ; ˈnjuːkʌmə/ *n* [C] someone who has only recently arrived somewhere or only recently started a particular activity 新来的人; 新手: [+to] *I'm a relative newcomer to the retail business.* 我在零售行业相对来说还是个新手。| *Promising newcomer Gillespie won outright.* 前途无量的新秀吉莱斯皮大获全胜。

New Deal, the /ˌ·ˈ·/ **1** a programme of economic and social changes that was introduced in the US by President Franklin D. Roosevelt in 1933, in order to help people who had lost their jobs or their property as a result of the Great Depression. It included money for farmers to borrow and an important programme of PUBLIC WORKS (=work on new roads, public buildings etc, paid for by the government) 新政〔1933 年美国总统富兰克林·D.罗斯福推行的一项经济和社会变革计划，旨在帮助因大萧条而失去工作或财产的民众。该计划包括向农场主提供贷款和一项重要的市政工程建设专案〕 **2** a programme introduced in the UK by the Labour government in 1998, in order to help people without jobs, especially people who have been unemployed for a long time. It offers people new jobs or the opportunity to receive training. "新政"计划〔1998 年英国工党政府推行的一项计划，目的是帮助失业者，尤其是长期失业的人。该计划为人们提供新的岗位或培训机会〕

New Del·hi /ˌ·ˈ··/ the capital city of India, built to the south of the old city of Delhi by the British in 1912 新德里〔印度首都，1912 年由英国人修建，位于德里旧城以南〕

New Dem·o·crat·ic Par·ty, the /ˌ···ˈ··ˌ··/ a political party in Canada which has fairly LEFT-WING ideas 新民主党〔加拿大一左翼政党〕

New En·gland /ˌ·ˈ··/ the states of the northeastern US: Maine, New Hampshire, Vermont, Massachusetts, Rhode Island, and Connecticut. It is called New England because it was the first part of the US where people from England, including the Pilgrim Fathers, began to settle in the 17th century. 新英格兰〔指美国东北部各州，包括缅因州、新罕布什尔州、佛蒙特州、马萨诸塞州、罗得岛州以及康涅狄格州。17 世纪，包括清教徒前辈移民在内的英格兰人到达美洲后最先在此定居，故名〕

CULTURAL NOTE 文化注释

When people in the US think of New England, they think of the brightly coloured leaves that fall from the trees in the FALL (=autumn) and neatly painted white wooden houses. New England contains most of the northern states that were part of the original colonies (COLONY), so it has a lot of small attractive old towns and some of the oldest most famous universities in the country, such as the colleges in the Ivy League. 美国人想到新英格兰时就会想起秋日的斑斓落叶、精致地漆成白色的木屋。新英格兰包括北部诸州的大多数，过去这些州是英国的殖民地，所以那里有不少古老而又迷人的小城镇。而美国那些历史悠久的、最著名的大学，像常春藤联盟里的那些大学，就分布在此地。

New England Jour·nal of Medi·cine, The /ˌ·ˌ··ˌ···ˈ·/ a US JOURNAL (=serious magazine) for doctors, SURGEONS, and other people working in medicine, which has technical reports on new methods of medical treatment, medicines, drugs etc《新英格兰医学杂志》〔美国一杂志，读者为医生、外科医生及其他医务工作者，刊载有关新疗法和新药等内容的专业报告〕— compare 比较 the LANCE, JAMA

New En·glish Bi·ble, The /ˌ·ˌ··ˈ··/ (1970) a translation of the Bible into modern English《圣经》新译本〔(1970)，《圣经》的现代英语译本〕

new·fan·gled /ˌnjuˈfæŋgḷd; ˌnjuːˈfæŋgəld◂/ *adj* newfangled ideas, machines etc have been recently invented but you think they are too complicated or unnecessary〔主意、机器等〕新而无价值的，新奇而无意义的; 新花样的: *newfangled ideas about education* 关于教育的异想天开的新想法

New For·est, the /ˌ·ˈ··/ an area in Hampshire in southern England, which has many OAK and BEECH trees, and also has large areas of HEATH (=open land with grass) 新福里斯特〔英格兰南部汉普郡一地区。该地区多橡树和山毛榉，还有大片的荒原〕

new-found /ˌ·ˈ·◂/ *adj* **newfound confidence/freedom/happiness etc** confidence, freedom etc that someone has only recently gained 新获得的信心/自由/幸福等: *At first Mozart enjoyed his new-found freedom, earning enough to rent a big apartment.* 刚开始时，莫扎特赚到足够的钱租了一套大公寓，享受着新的自由。

New·found·land /ˈnjuːfəndlənd; ˈnjuːfəndlənd/ a PROVINCE of eastern Canada consisting of the island of Newfoundland and the coast of Labrador. It is an important centre for fishing. 纽芬兰〔加拿大东部一省，包括纽芬兰岛和拉布拉多海岸地区，为重要的渔业中心〕

New·gate /ˈnjuˌget; ˈnjuːgeɪt/ also 又作 **Newgate prison** a prison in London from about 1200 to about 1900, famous for the terrible conditions in which the prisoners were forced to live and for holding some of the most famous criminals in British history 纽盖特监狱〔约 1200 年至大约 1900 年间伦敦的一座监狱。该监狱以生活条件恶劣出名，曾关押过英国历史上一些有名的犯人〕

New Guin·ea /ˌ·ˈ··/ an island in the southwest Pacific Ocean, north of Australia. It is divided into two halves, one belonging to Indonesia and the other belonging to Papua New Guinea. 新几内亚岛〔太平洋西南部一岛，位于澳大利亚以北。该岛一分为二，一半属印度尼西亚，另一半属巴布亚新几内亚〕

New Hamp·shire /ˌ·ˈ··/ abbreviation 缩写为 **NH** a state in the northeastern US, that has many lakes and mountains and old buildings. It was one of the 13 original states of the US, and was the first to publicly announce its intention to become independent from Britain on July 4th, 1776. New Hampshire is usually the first state to hold primary elections and each party's winner is generally considered to have the best chance of becoming their candidate for President in the national elections in November. 新罕布什尔州〔美国东北部一州，有湖光山色和古老建筑。该州是美国最早的 13 个州之一，也是 1776 年 7 月 4 日最早声明希望摆脱英国统治、实现独立的一个州。美国总统大选期间，新罕布什尔州通常是最早开始初选的一个州。一般认为，每个政党的获胜者最有希望成为 11 月份的全国大选的总统候选人〕

New Ha·ven /ˌ·ˈ··/ a city and port in southern Connecticut, US, where English PURITANS first lived when they came to America in 1638. It is also the home of Yale University. 纽黑文〔美国康涅狄格州南部一城市和港口。1638 年，英国清教徒抵达美洲时最早在此定居。该市亦是耶鲁大学的所在地〕

New Heb·ri·des, the /ˌ·ˈ···/ the former name of Vanuatu 新赫布里底群岛〔瓦努阿图旧称〕

New In·ter·na·tion·a·list, The /ˌ·ˌ··ˈ····/ a magazine that has articles about people in many different countries, and deals especially with the relationship between rich and poor countries and the unfair or unequal ways in which some people and countries are treated《新国际主义者》〔一份反映世界各国民情的杂志，尤其关注贫穷国家与富裕国家之间的关系以及对某些人群和国家的待遇不公或不平等问题〕

New Jer·sey /ˌ·ˈ··/ abbreviation 缩写为 **NJ** a state in the northeastern US, which has a large population and many businesses and industries. New Jersey was one of the 13 original states of the US, and the northern part of the state is across the Hudson River from New York City. It is often informally called Jersey. 新泽西州〔美国东北部一州，人口众多，工商业发达。该州是美国最早的 13 个州之一，北部与纽约市隔哈得孙河相望。俗称泽西州〕

New Je·ru·sa·lem, the /ˌ·ˌ·ˈ···/ a Christian name for Heaven 新耶路撒冷〔基督教所指的天堂、天国〕

New La·bour /ˌ·ˈ··/ an unofficial name for the British Labour Party used especially by Tony Blair and his supporters to show that the Labour Party has changed some of its ideas and become more modern. One of the main New Labour ideas is that

N

the government should not use high taxes to pay for public services. 新工党〔英国工党俗称，尤为托尼·布莱尔及其支持者所使用，以显示工党在某些观点上已有所变化，并已变得更加现代。新工党的主要观点之一是，政府不应提高税率来支付公共服务开支〕

new-laid /ˌ· ˈ◂/ *adj* a new-laid egg is fresh 〔蛋〕新下的，新鲜的

new-look /ˈ· ·/ *adj* recently made more modern or more attractive 新面孔的，新面貌的: *the new-look Labour Party* 以新面貌出现的工党

W3 **new·ly** /ˈnjulɪ; ˈnjuːli/ *adv* **newly formed/created/appointed/married etc** formed etc very recently 新成立/新创造/新任命/新婚等的: *the newly appointed director* 新任命的董事 | *newly fallen snow* 新下的雪

new·ly·weds /ˈnjulɪˌwɛdz; ˈnjuːliwedz/ *n* [plural] a man and a woman who have recently got married 新婚夫妇，〔一对〕新人 —**newlywed** *adj*

New·man /ˈnjumən; ˈnjuːmən/, **Cardinal John Henry** (1801-90) a British THEOLOGIAN (=someone who studies religion and religious beliefs) and writer. He was a priest in the Church of England and became leader of the Oxford Movement. Later he changed his religion and became a Roman Catholic, and he was made a CARDINAL (=a priest of high rank) in 1879. 纽曼〔(1801-1890)，英国神学家、作家，曾为英国国教会的牧师和牛津运动的领袖。后来，他改变了宗教信仰，成为天主教徒，1879年被任命为红衣主教〕

New Man /ˌ· ˈ·/ *n* [C] a man who is considered to be very modern because he enjoys looking after his children and helping his partner with the care of the home〔乐于照料子女及做家务的〕新男性，新派男子: *He is a New Man, freely admitting to doing cleaning in place of his career-woman wife.* 他是个新派男子，坦率地承认替自己事业型的妻子打扫房间。

New·mar·ket /ˈnjuˌmɑrkɪt; ˈnjuːmɑːkɪ̆t/ a market town in Suffolk, southeast England, which is a centre for horse racing and for breeding and training horses for racing 纽马基特〔英格兰东南部萨福克郡一集市城镇，现为赛马比赛及赛马驯养中心〕

new maths /ˌ· ˈ·/ *BrE* 【英】, **new math** *AmE* 【美】 *n* [U] a way of teaching and understanding mathematics, first used in schools in the early 1970s 新数学〔20世纪70年代初引入学校的一种数学教学和理解的新方法〕，基础数学集论教学法

New Mex·i·co /ˌ· ˈ· · ·/ abbreviation 缩写为 **NM** a state in the southwestern US, where the land is mostly desert or mountain forests. Most of New Mexico used to belong to Mexico, so there is a strong Mexican and Spanish influence on the culture, language, buildings etc. 新墨西哥州〔美国西南部一州，境内多为荒漠、山地森林。大部分地区曾为墨西哥所有，因此该州在文化、语言、建筑等方面深受墨西哥和西班牙的影响〕

New Mod·el Ar·my, the /ˌ· ˌ·· ˈ··/ an army started by Oliver Cromwell during the English Civil War in 1645, which was well-trained and skilled at fighting. It consisted of Roundheads, fighting against King Charles I and his Cavaliers. 新模范军〔1645年英格兰内战期间由奥利弗·克伦威尔创建的一支军队，训练有素，骁勇善战。新模范军由圆颅党人组成，与查理一世及其保王党人进行战斗〕

new mon·ey /ˌ· ˈ··/ *n* [U] people who have recently or suddenly become very rich, as opposed to people whose families have always been rich 暴发户

new moon /ˌ· ˈ·/ *n* **1** [C] the moon when it first appears in the sky as a thin CRESCENT〔月牙形的〕新月 **2** [C,U] the time of the month at which this is first seen 新月出现的时候 **3** [C] *technical* the time when the moon is between the Earth and the sun, and cannot be seen 【术语】新月期 —compare 比较 FULL MOON, HALF MOON

new-mown /ˌ· ˈ◂/ *adj* **new-mown hay/grass** grass that has recently been cut 新割的饲草/新剪的草坪: *the sweet smell of new-mown grass* 新剪草坪的清香

New Mu·sic·al Ex·press, The /ˌ· ˌ··· ˈ··/ abbreviation 缩写为 **NME** a British music newspaper《新音乐快讯》〔英国一份音乐报纸〕

New Or·le·ans /ˌnju ɔrˈlɪənz; ˌnjuː ɔːˈliːənz/ a city in Louisiana in the southern US, next to the Mississippi River. It was originally a French city, and its style of cooking, old buildings, and traditions were influenced by French culture. It is famous for the way it celebrates Mardi Gras every year and also for the music played there. Many people consider New Orleans as the place where JAZZ music was originally developed. 新奥尔良〔美国南部路易斯安那州一城市，濒临密西西比河。原为一法国城市，因此该市的烹饪、古建筑和许多传统都带有法国文化的烙印。该市每年四旬斋前的狂欢节甚为有名。另外，新奥尔良音乐也闻名遐迩，该市被认为是爵士乐的发源地〕

New·port /ˈnjuport; ˈnjuːpɔːt/ **1** a wealthy city in Rhode Island, US, which is also an important port for the US navy 纽波特〔美国罗得岛州一富裕城市，也是美国重要军港〕 **2** a city and port in Gwent, southeast Wales, which has many factories and used to have an important steel and coal industry 纽波特〔威尔士东南部格温特郡一城市和港口，市内现有许多工厂。钢铁和煤炭工业在该市曾具有重要地位〕 **3** a town in the Isle of Wight in southern England 纽波特〔英格兰南部怀特岛一镇〕

Newport Jazz Fes·ti·val, the /ˌ·· ˈ· ˌ···/ a US event at which many JAZZ musicians perform. It was first held in 1954 at Newport, Rhode Island, and is now held every year in New York State. 纽波特爵士音乐节〔美国一音乐盛事，吸引许多爵士音乐家前来表演。首届音乐节于1954年在罗得岛州纽波特举办，此后每年都在纽约州举行〕

new po·ta·to /ˌ· ·ˈ··/ *n* [C] a potato from one of the first crops of a year 新收获的马铃薯

new rich /ˌ· ˈ◂/ *n* **the new rich** *AmE* people who have recently or suddenly become very rich, as opposed to people whose families have always been rich 【美】新贵；暴发户 —**new rich** *adj*

news /njuz; njuːz/ *n* [U] **1** information about something that has happened recently（新）消息: *That's great news!* 那是个好消息！| *Sit down and tell me all your news.* 坐下来给我说说你最新的消息。| **[+about/of]** *There hasn't been any news of him since he left home.* 自从他离开家后，一直都没有他的消息。| **[+that]** *Our delegates returned with the news that negotiations had broken down.* 我们的代表团回来时带来了谈判破裂的消息。| **good/bad news** *You're looking upset – not bad news, I hope?* 你看起来很不高兴，我想不会有什么坏消息吧？| **hear news** (=receive news) 听到消息，得到消息 *Have you heard any news from Emily yet?* 你有埃米莉的任何音讯吗？| **piece of news** *Your brother's just told me an interesting piece of news.* 你兄弟刚告诉我一则有趣的消息。| **have news for** *I've some good news for you – they've signed the contract.* 告诉你一个好消息，他们已经签了合同。| **I've got news for you** (=some bad news) 我有坏消息要告诉你 *You may think you've fooled him, but I've got news for you – he's wise to your little trick.* 你以为你骗过了他，告诉你，他早已识破了你的小把戏。| **break the news to** (=tell someone some bad news) 告诉〔某人〕坏消息，向〔某人〕透露实情 *I don't know how to break the news to her.* 我不知道该怎样告诉她这个坏消息。 S1 W1 **2** reports of recent events in the newspapers or on the radio or television 新闻（报道）: **[+of/about]** *News is coming in of a major explosion at the World Trade Centre.* 有报道称世界贸易中心发生了大爆炸。| *We'll bring you more news about the election at 11 o'clock.* 我们将在11点报道更多有关选举的新闻。| **news that** *Several evening papers carried the news that a cabinet minister was about to resign.* 好几家晚报报道了一名内阁部长将要辞职的消息。| **latest news** *the latest news from the Olympic stadium* 来自奥林匹克运动场的最新消息 | **local/national etc news** *a programme bringing you national and international news* 国内外新闻报道 | **make the news** (=be considered important enough to be in the news) 成为新闻 *Twenty years ago environmental issues rarely made the news.* 20年前，环境问题很少被传媒报道。| **be in the news** *I see Michael Jackson's in the news again.* 我看到迈克尔·杰克逊又在新闻中出现了。| **be front page news** (=be interesting enough to be on the front page of a newspaper) 成为头版新闻 *Wallace's resignation was front page news.* 华莱士的辞职成了头版新闻。| **news story/report** *Wilks had been paid by journalists to simply invent bogus news stories.* 记者们付钱给威尔克斯为他们凭空杜撰新闻。 **3 the news** a regular television or radio programme that gives you reports of recent events〔电视或电台的〕新闻报道，新闻节目: **on the news** *It must be true – I heard it on the news last night.* 这肯定是真的，我昨晚在新闻节目中听到的。 **4 be good/bad news for** if the facts about something are good or bad news for someone, they are likely to make life better or worse for them 对〔某人〕是个好/坏消息: *House prices are very low at the moment, which is good news for first-time buyers.* 目前房价很低，这对首次置业人士来说是个好消息。 **5 he's/she's bad news** *informal* used to say that someone is likely to cause trouble 【非正式】他/她不是好东西〔指某人可能会带来麻烦〕: *Stay away from that guy, he's bad news.* 离那家伙远一点，他不是个好东西。 **6 that's news to me!** *spoken* used when you are surprised or annoyed because you have not been told something earlier 【口】我一点都不知道！: *So, the meeting's*

N

been cancelled? Well, that's news to me! 这么说，会议被取消了？啊，我一点都不知道呢！**7 no news is good news** *spoken* used when you have not received any news about someone and you hope this means that nothing bad has happened【口】没有消息就是好消息；不闻凶讯便是吉

This graph shows some of the words most commonly used with the noun **news**. 本图表所示为含有名词 news 的一些最常用的词组。

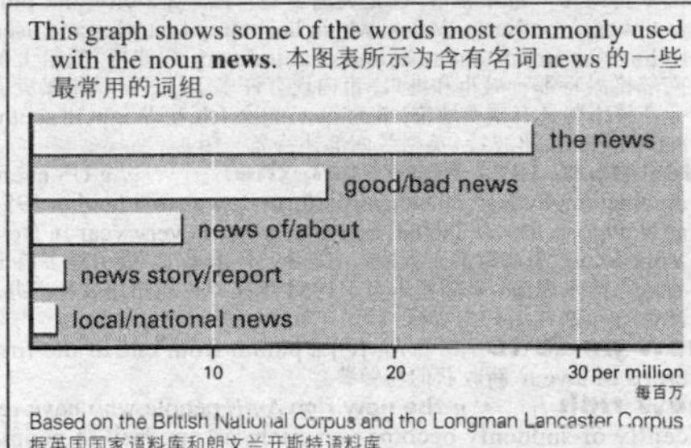

Based on the British National Corpus and the Longman Lancaster Corpus
据英国国家语料库和朗文兰开斯特语料库

news a·gen·cy /'·,···/ *n* [C] a company that supplies information to newspapers, radio and television 新闻社，通讯社

news·a·gent /ˈnjuzedʒənt; ˈnjuːzˌeɪdʒənt/ *n* [C] *BrE* someone who owns or works in a shop that sells newspapers and magazines【英】报刊经销人：**newsagent's** (=a newsagent's shop) 报刊销售店

news bul·le·tin /'·,···/ *n* [C] **1** *BrE* a short news programme on radio or television, reporting only the most important information【英】〔电台或电视的〕新闻简报 **2** *AmE* a very short news programme on radio or television, broadcast suddenly in the middle of another programme when something very important has happened【美】新闻快讯〔指插在电台或电视其他节目中播出的重要新闻〕；NEWSFLASH *BrE*【英】

news·cast /ˈnjuzˌkæst; ˈnjuːzkɑːst/ *n* [C] *AmE* a news programme on radio or television【美】〔电台或电视的〕新闻广播〔报道〕

news·cast·er /ˈnjuzˌkæstə; ˈnjuːzˌkɑːstə/ *n* [C] someone who reads the news on radio or television〔电台或电视的〕新闻播音员；NEWSREADER *BrE*【英】

New Sci·en·tist, The /,·'···/ *trademark* a British weekly magazine that provides news about recent developments and discoveries in all areas of science. There is a similar US magazine called *Scientific American*.【商标】《新科学家》〔英国一周刊，报道各学科领域的新发展和新发现。美国也有一类似杂志，名为《科学美国人》〕

news con·fer·ence /'·,···/ *n* [C] a PRESS CONFERENCE 记者招待会

New Scot·land Yard /,··'·/ the official name for Scotland Yard 新苏格兰场〔苏格兰场的正式名称〕

news·flash /ˈnjuzˌflæʃ; ˈnjuːzflæʃ/ *n* [C] *especially BrE* a very short news programme on radio or television, broadcast suddenly in the middle of another programme when something very important has happened【尤英】新闻快讯〔指插在电台或电视其他节目中播出的重要新闻〕；NEWS BULLETIN *AmE*【美】：*We interrupt this programme to bring you a newsflash from the Malabar front.* 我们暂时中断本节目，向大家报道来自马拉巴前线的新闻快讯。

news·hound /ˈnjuzˌhaund; ˈnjuːzhaʊnd/ *n* [C] *informal* someone who writes for a newspaper and is always looking for exciting new stories but sometimes upsets people by being too eager【非正式】无孔不入的新闻记者

news·let·ter /ˈnjuzˌlɛtə; ˈnjuːzˌletə/ *n* [C] one or several sheets of printed news sent regularly to a particular group of people〔给特定读者定期寄发的〕通讯；简报；业务通讯：*Have you seen the church newsletter?* 你看到教会的通讯了吗？

News of the World, The /,····'·/ a British TABLOID newspaper sold every Sunday, and which prints shocking articles about famous people, especially about their relationships and sexual experiences. It sells more copies than any other British newspaper.《世界新闻》〔每逢周日销售的一种英国小报，刊登名人猛料，尤其关涉名人的情事关系和性生活经历。销量居英国报纸之冠〕

New South Wales /,··'·/ abbreviation 缩写为 **NSW** a state in southeast Australia, next to the Pacific Ocean, which has the largest population and the most industry of any state in Australia. It produces steel, coal, grain, and wool, and its capital city, Sydney, is Australia's main business and financial centre. 新南威尔士〔澳大利亚东南部一州，濒临太平洋，是澳大利亚人口最多、工业最集中的一个州，出产钢铁、煤炭、粮食和羊毛。首府悉尼是澳大利亚主要的商业和金融中心〕

news·pa·per /ˈnjuzˌpepə; ˈnjuːsˌpeɪpə/ *n* **1** [C] a set of large folded sheets of paper containing news, articles, pictures, advertisements etc printed and sold daily or weekly 报（纸）：*a national newspaper* 一份全国性的报纸 **2** [U] sheets of paper from old newspapers〔旧〕报纸：*Wrap the plates in newspaper to stop them from breaking.* 用旧报纸把盘子包起来，以免打碎。**3** [C] a company that produces a newspaper 报社：*I think he works for a local newspaper.* 我认为他在一家本地报社工作。 S2 W2

newspaper stand /'···,·/ *n* [C] a NEWSSTAND 书报摊；报刊亭

news·print /ˈnjuzˌprɪnt; ˈnjuːzˌprɪnt/ *n* [U] *technical* cheap paper used mostly for printing newspapers on【术语】新闻纸，白报纸

news·read·er /ˈnjuzˌridə; ˈnjuːzˌriːdə/ *n* [C] *especially BrE* someone who reads the news on television or radio【尤英】〔电视或电台的〕新闻播音员，新闻广播员

news·reel /ˈnjuzˌril; ˈnjuːzriːl/ *n* [C] a cinema film of news 新闻片

news re·lease /'·,·'/ *n* [C] a PRESS RELEASE 新闻稿

news·room /ˈnjuzrum; ˈnjuːzrʊm/ *n* [C] the office in a newspaper or broadcasting company where news is received and news reports are written〔报社、广播公司的〕新闻编辑室

news·stand /ˈnjuzˌstænd; ˈnjuːzstænd/ *n* [C] a place on a street where newspapers and magazines are sold 书报摊；报刊亭

New States·man, The /,·'··/ *trademark* a British weekly magazine which contains news reports, discussions about politics, articles about art, books, etc. It expresses independent opinions and is fairly LEFT-WING.【商标】《新政治家》〔英国一周刊，刊登新闻报道、政治评论、艺术鉴赏以及新书介绍之类的文章，借此表达独立观点和左倾立场〕

news ven·dor /'·,··/ *n* [C] *especially BrE* someone who sells newspapers【尤英】报贩

News·week /ˈnjuzˌwik; ˈnjuːzwiːk/ a US weekly magazine which contains articles and photographs about news and current affairs《新闻周刊》〔美国一周刊，刊登新闻与时事文章及照片〕

news·wor·thy /ˈnjuzˌwɜðɪ; ˈnjuːzˌwɜːði/ *adj* important or interesting enough to be reported as news 有新闻价值的，值得报道的：*The reporter's task is to report what is newsworthy about an event.* 记者的职责是将事件中有新闻价值的内容报道出来。

news·y /ˈnjuzɪ; ˈnjuːzi/ *adj* a newsy letter is from a friend or relative and contains a lot of news about them〔信件〕消息丰富的

newt /njut; njuːt/ *n* [C] a small animal with a long body, four legs and a tail, that lives in water 蝾螈，水螈

New Ter·ri·to·ries, the /,·'····/ part of Hong Kong on the mainland of China, which was occupied by the UK from 1898 until 1997, when it was given back to China 新界〔中国香港位于中国大陆的一片土地，1898 年起一直被英国占领，1997 年回归中国〕

New Tes·ta·ment, the /,·'···/ *n* the part of the Bible which includes the four Gospels describing the life of Jesus Christ and what he taught〔《圣经》的〕《新约全书》〔其中包括四部福音书，讲述耶稣的生平与传教的事迹〕—compare 比较 OLD TESTAMENT

New·ton /ˈnjutn̩; ˈnjuːtn/, **Sir Isaac** (1642-1727) a British physicist and mathematician who discovered GRAVITY (=the force that causes things to fall towards the ground or to be pulled towards stars or planets in space). He made many other important scientific discoveries, and is one of the most important scientists who ever lived. Until the early 20th century, modern physics was based on Newton's work, and it is sometimes called **Newtonian physics**. 牛顿〔(1642-1727)，英国物理学家和数学家。他发现了万有引力，并取得了其他许多重要的科学发现，是有史以来最重要的科学家之一。直至 20 世纪初，近代物理学一直以牛顿的研究成果为基础，因此有时也称牛顿物理学〕

New·to·ni·an /njuˈtonɪən; njuːˈtəʊniən/ *adj* related to the laws of PHYSICS that were discovered by the scientist Isaac Newton 牛顿学说的：*Newtonian mechanics* 牛顿力学

new town /'· ·/ *n* [C] one of several towns built in Britain since 1946, each designed and built according to a plan that included houses, shops, and factories〔英国自 1946 年以来建立的〕新市镇：*A new town may not be very attractive but is certainly a very convenient place to live.* 新市镇也许不太吸引人，但肯定是一个生活十分方便的地方。

N

new wave /ˌ· ˈ·◂/ *n* [C] a group of people making a conscious effort to introduce new ideas in music, films, art, politics etc〔在音乐、电影、艺术、政治等方面引入新观念的〕新浪潮; 新潮派 —**new wave** *adj*: *new wave music* 新潮派音乐

New World /ˌ· ˈ·◂/ *n* **the New World** North, Central, and South America 新大陆, 新世界〔指美洲〕—**New World** *adj*: *New World wines* 新大陆出产的葡萄酒

New Year, new year /ˌ· ˈ·◂/ *n* [U] **1** the time at the beginning of the year when you celebrate 新年: *We're going to spend Christmas and New Year with my parents.* 我们打算和父母一起过圣诞节和新年。| **Happy New Year** (=used as a greeting) 新年快乐 | **see in the new year** (=celebrate the beginning of the year) 庆祝新年, 迎接新年 *Our neighbours invited us round to see in the new year.* 邻居邀请我们去他们家庆祝新年。**2 the new year** the first few weeks of the year 新年伊始: *Let's hope things will begin to improve in the new year.* 希望在新的一年情况会有所好转。| **new year resolution** (=a decision to improve yourself in the new year) 新年的决心 *I haven't made any new year resolutions – I never stick to them anyway.* 我没有下任何新年的决心, 反正我从未照办过。

CULTURAL NOTE 文化注释

The New Year is thought of as a time to celebrate, and people often hope that the New Year will bring good changes in their lives, and more happiness or better luck. Some people make special promises about improving their behaviour or stopping bad habits, called **New Year's resolutions**. People usually promise to do things such as lose weight or stop smoking, but most people do not manage to succeed with their resolutions for very long. 新年被认为是一个值得庆祝的时节。人们常常希望新年能给生活带来好的变化, 多福气和好运气。有些人就改进个人行为举止或戒除坏习惯而许下特别的诺言, 被称作"新年的决心"。人们通常许诺要做的事情有减肥和戒烟, 但大多数人坚持不了多久就无果而终了。

People in the US and UK celebrate **New Year's Eve** (December 31st) especially by going to parties and drinking a lot of alcohol. It is traditional to stay awake until midnight to 'see the New Year in' (=experience the start of the new year). People typically count the last few seconds until it is midnight, and then shout "Happy New Year!" Then people traditionally sing a special song called *Auld Lang Syne* and friends kiss each other. In Scotland, New Year's Eve is an especially important celebration, and is known as **Hogmanay**. The first day of the year, January 1st, is called **New Year's Day** and is a public holiday in both the US and the UK. 英美人特别会通过参加聚会或狂饮来庆祝新年前夕(12月31日)。传统上人们会一直熬到午夜来"迎接新年"。人们通常会倒计时数秒到零点, 然后高呼"新年快乐!"之后人们传统上会唱一首特别的歌曲《友谊地久天长》, 朋友们还会相互亲吻。在苏格兰, 新年前夕是个特别重要的节庆日, 叫做Hogmanay(除夕)。每年的第一天, 即1月1日, 叫做"元旦", 在英国和美国它都是一个公共假日。— see Cultural Note at HOGMANAY 见 HOGMANAY 文化注释

New Year's Day /ˌ· · ˈ·/ *n* [singular, U] 1st January, the first day of the year 元旦

New Year's Eve /ˌ· · ˈ·/ *n* [singular, U] 31st December, the last day of the year 除夕

New Year's Hon·ours, the /ˌ· · ˈ· ·/ special honours given to a number of British people each year, as a reward for their special achievements or good work, which are announced on January 1st. These include titles such as 'Sir', 'Lord', or 'OBE'. 新年荣誉称号〔一年一度给作出突出贡献或取得优秀业绩的英国人授予的特别荣誉。1月1日为授勋日。所授称号有"爵士"、"勋爵"或"英帝国军官勋章"〕

New York /ˌ· ˈ·◂/ —see 见 NEW YORK CITY, NEW YORK STATE

New York Cit·y /ˌ· · ˈ· ·/ also 又作 **New York, NYC** a large city and port in the northeastern US, on the southeast coast of New York State and east of the Hudson River. New York City is the largest city in the US and its main business centre, but it is not the capital city of the US, which is Washington, D.C. The city is divided into five BOROUGHS: Manhattan, the Bronx, Brooklyn, Queens, and Richmond. 纽约市〔美国东北部一大城市和港口, 位于纽约州东南沿岸和哈得孙河以东。纽约是美国最大城市和重要商业中心, 但不是首都。美国首都为华盛顿特区。该市划分为五个行政区, 即曼哈顿区、布朗克斯区、布鲁克林区、昆斯区和里士满区〕

CULTURAL NOTE 文化注释

New York City is one of the most popular cities in the world. It has several famous LANDMARKS, including the Statue of Liberty and the Empire State Building. The area in and around Wall Street is the financial centre of the US, and the city is also famous for its theatre productions on Broadway. It also has famous MUSEUMS. When people talk about New York City, they are usually really talking about the island of Manhattan, which contains most of the city's businesses, theatres, and hotels for tourists. Some people think that New York City is too busy and crowded, but many people love it because of all its excitement, entertainment, and culture. It is sometimes called the Big Apple or the city that never sleeps, because it is never quiet and many people go out at night. 纽约市是世界上最受人追捧的城市之一。纽约有很多地标建筑, 包括自由女神像和帝国大厦。华尔街及其附近区域是美国的金融中心, 纽约亦以百老汇的舞台演出知名。纽约还有一些著名博物馆。人们谈论纽约时实际通常指的是曼哈顿岛, 大多数面向游客的商业、剧院和宾馆都汇集于此。有人认为纽约市太过热闹和拥挤, 但还是有很多人喜欢这个刺激、有娱乐和文化的城市。纽约有时被称为"大苹果城"或"不夜城", 因为这是一个永不宁静的城市, 很多人深夜还要外出。— see Cultural Note at MANHATTAN 见 MANHATTAN 文化注释; see also 另见 CENTRAL PARK, GREENWICH VILLAGE, MADISON AVENUE, TIMES SQUARE; see map on page F5 见F5页地图

New York Dra·ma Crit·ics Cir·cle A·ward /ˌ· · ˌ· · ˌ· · ˌ· · ˈ· ·/ *n* [C] a special prize for excellent work in the theatre, given each year by a group of US THEATRE CRITICS (=writers who give their judgement on the good or bad qualities of plays, actors etc) 纽约戏剧评论家奖〔每年由美国戏剧评论家颁发的奖项, 以奖励优秀戏剧作品、演员等〕

New York·er, The /· ˈ· ·/ a serious weekly magazine, read by educated people all over the US. It contains articles on many different subjects, including art, films, etc. It also contains short stories, poetry, and clever CARTOONS, and is respected for the quality of its writing. 《纽约人》〔纽约市出版的一种严肃周刊, 读者主要是受过良好教育的美国人。该刊题材多样, 包括艺术、电影等, 另有短篇故事、诗歌及构思工巧的漫画。该杂志因高品质的文章而备受推崇〕

New York Phil·har·mon·ic, the /ˌ· · · · ˈ· ·/ an ORCHESTRA (=a large group of musicians) based in New York City, which is the oldest orchestra in the US 纽约爱乐交响乐团〔纽约一大型乐团, 为美国历史最悠久的乐团〕

New York Post, the /ˌ· · ˈ·/ a US daily newspaper produced in New York City, which includes a lot of GOSSIP (=information about famous people's private lives) and reports events in ways that make them seem as strange, exciting, or shocking as possible 《纽约邮报》〔纽约市出版的一份美国日报, 内有大量八卦消息, 以尽可能离奇、刺激或震撼的方式报道事件〕

New York Re·view of Books, The /ˌ· · · ˌ· · ˈ·/ a US magazine with long serious articles on new books, NOVELS, poetry, writers etc 《纽约书评》〔美国一杂志, 刊载风格严肃的长篇文章, 评论新书、新小说、新诗以及新作家〕

New York State /ˌ· · ˈ·/ also 又作 **New York** abbreviation 缩写为 **NY** a state in the northeastern US. Its capital is Albany and its largest city is New York City. It is famous for its beautiful countryside, especially its mountains and rivers, and it was one of the 13 original states of the US. The area in the centre and north of the state is often called upstate New York. 纽约州〔美国东北部一州, 首府奥尔巴尼, 最大城市为纽约。纽约州尤以旖旎的乡村山水风光闻名。它还是美国最早的13个州之一。纽约州中部与北部常被称为 upstate New York (上纽约州)〕

New York Stock Ex·change, the /ˌ· · ˈ· · ˌ·/ abbreviation 缩写为 **NYSE** the largest STOCK EXCHANGE in the US, where shares in companies are bought and sold. It is also called 'the Big Board', and its building is on Wall Street in New York City. 纽约证券交易所〔美国最大的证券交易所, 专门经营公司股票交易业务, 俗称 the Big Board (大盘)。交易所大楼位于纽约市华尔街〕—see also 另见 DOW JONES AVERAGE

New York Times, The /ˌ· · ˈ·/ a serious daily newspaper which is produced in New York City. It is sold everywhere in the US and in many other countries, and people in the US often just call it 'the Times'. 《纽约时报》〔纽约市出版的一种严肃类日报, 销路遍及全美及许多国家。美国人常简称之为 the Times (时报)〕

New Zealand 新西兰

Auckland 奥克兰
NORTH ISLAND 北岛
Wellington 惠灵顿
SOUTH ISLAND 南岛
Christchurch 布赖斯特彻奇
Dnedin 达尼丁

New Zea·land /nju ˋzilənd; njuː ˈziːlənd/ a country consisting of two main islands, the **North Island** and the **South Island**, and several smaller ones, in the Pacific Ocean southeast of Australia. Population: 3,864,000 (2001). Capital: Wellington. Farming, especially sheep farming, is important to the New Zealand economy. About 10% of the population are Maori people, who first came to New Zealand around the 9th century AD, and who call the country Aotearoa. Most of the rest of the population are people who came from the UK in the 19th and 20th centuries. 新西兰〔太平洋一岛国，位于澳大利亚东南，由北岛、南岛两个主岛和另外几个小岛组成。人口：3,864,000（2001），首都：惠灵顿。农业，尤其是牧羊业在该国经济中具有重要地位。大约10%的人口为毛利人，大约在公元9世纪，他们最早移居到新西兰，毛利人称新西兰为 Aotearoa（白云之乡）。其余绝大多数人口为19、20世纪移居到此的英国人后裔〕—**New Zealand** *adj: New Zealand lamb* 新西兰羔羊 —**New Zealander** *n*

next¹ /nɛkst; nekst/ *determiner* **1** the next house, room etc is the one that is closest to you〔位置〕离得最近的；隔壁的：*I asked the woman at the next table what time it was.* 我向邻桌的女人打听几点了。| *They could be heard arguing from the next room.* 能听到他们在隔壁房间争吵。**2** the next event, day, time etc is the one that happens after the present one〔时间〕紧接着来到的；下次的：**the next train/meeting/class etc** *The next episode was watched by over 10 million anxious viewers.* 接下来的一集吸引了一千多万名焦急的观众收看。| *If they win the next election they have promised to reform the health service.* 如果他们在下次大选中获胜，他们承诺要改革医疗制度。| *I've just missed the flight to Chicago, what time's the next one?* 我没赶上飞往芝加哥的航班，下一班是几点？| **the next few weeks/three years etc** *Over the next couple of months, try to relax more and take more exercise.* 在今后几个月里，要试着多放松，多运动。| **next Monday/July/year etc** *We're hoping to reopen the factory some time next year.* 我们希望能在明年某个时候重开工厂。| **(the) next day** *She called me and we arranged to meet the next day.* 她给我打了电话，我们约好第二天见面。| **(the) next time** *Next time I take a cab, I'll be more careful.* 下次坐计程车时，我会更加小心。—compare 比较 LAST¹ (1) **3** the next person or thing in a list, a series, a line of people etc is the one that you come to after the one that you are dealing with at the present time〔次序〕下一个的：*The letter continues on the next page.* 此信未完，见下页。| *The next interviewee has a degree in geography and plenty of work experience.* 下一位应试人拥有地理学学位，还有丰富的工作经验。| *The cottage is just around the next bend in the road.* 那间小屋就在公路的下一个拐弯处附近。**4 a) the next biggest/smallest etc** the one that is a bit bigger, smaller etc than the one you are talking about 第二大/小等：*The hotel was full and the next nearest was over 20 miles away.* 这家旅馆已经客满，离此地最近的下一家旅馆在20英里以外。**b) the next best thing** the thing that is almost as good as something else 仅次于…的东西：*If butter is too expensive use the next best thing – margarine.* 如果黄油太贵的话，就退而求其次用人造黄油。—see also 另见 **next of kin** (KIN (2))

next² *adv* **1** immediately afterwards 紧接下来地；下一步；然后：*Being a doctor is a great life, you never know what will happen next.* 医生的生活很奇妙，你永远无法预料下一步会发生什么事情。| *The mixture is heated to a temperature of 40°C. Next, it is poured into a mould and left to cool.* 将混合物加热至摄氏40度，然后倒进模子里冷却。| *Where do you think you'll travel next?* 你接下来要去哪儿旅行呢？**2 next to a)** situated very close to someone or something with nothing in between 紧挨着，紧靠着：*There was a little girl sitting next to him.* 有一个小女孩坐在他旁边。| *The church is on the left, next to the school.* 教堂在左边，紧靠着学校。—see picture on page A1 参见 A1 页图 **b)** used when giving a list of things you like or prefer etc in order to say what is first in the list 仅次于，在…之后：*Next to soccer, squash is the sport I'm best at.* 我最擅长的运动是足球，其次是壁球。**3 next to nothing** very little 几乎没有：*He knows next to nothing about antiques.* 他对古董几乎一窍不通。**4** the next time 下次，再次：*When I next saw her she completely ignored me.* 我再次见到她时，她压根儿就没有理我。

next³ *pron* **1** the person or thing in a list, a series, a line of people etc that you come to after the one that you are dealing with at the present time 下一个〔人或事物〕：*Un, deux, trois... what comes next?* 一、二、三…，下面是什么？| *You're next, Mrs Williams. The doctor will be ready in a moment.* 威廉斯太太，下一位轮到您了。医生很快就会准备好。**2 the day/week etc after next** the day, week etc that follows the next one 后天/下下个星期等：*Have you remembered it's Susie's birthday the week after next?* 你还记得下下星期是苏茜的生日吗？**3 the next to last** the one before the last one 倒数第二：*We'll need to buy some more ink. I'm on the next to last bottle at the moment.* 我们得买些墨水了，我正在用倒数第二瓶。**4 next (please)** used to tell someone that it is now their turn to speak or their turn to do something 下一位（请）**5 be next in line** to be the next person to become king, a leader etc〔王位、领袖等的〕下一位继任人

next door¹ /ˌ·ˈ·/ *adv* **1** in the house, room etc next to yours or someone else's 在隔壁：*the boy next door* 住在隔壁的男孩 | *the people who've just moved in next door* 隔壁刚搬来的那家人 | *Her office is just next door.* 她的办公室就在隔壁。**2 next door to a)** next to another building, room etc 在…的隔壁：*He runs that small restaurant next door to the theatre.* 他经营剧院隔壁的那家小餐馆。**b)** almost the same as 几乎等于，和…差不多：*Leaving a man to die is next door to murder.* 见死不救简直和谋杀差不多。

next door² *n* [U] *BrE informal* the people living in the house or apartment next to yours【英，非正式】隔壁邻居：*Have you seen next door's new car?* 你看到隔壁邻居的新车了吗？

next-door³ /ˌ·ˈ·◂/ *adj* **1 next-door neighbour** the person who lives in the house or apartment next to yours 隔壁邻居：*I met my new next-door neighbour for the first time last night.* 我昨晚首次见到隔壁新搬来的邻居。**2 next door apartment/office etc** the apartment etc that is next to yours 隔壁房间/办公室等

nex·us /ˋnɛksəs; ˈneksəs/ *n plural* **nexus** [C+of] *formal* a connection or network of connections between a number of people, things or ideas【正式】〔人、事物、思想等之间的〕关系，关联，联系，连结：*Beneath the apparent certainty was a nexus of contradictions.* 在表面的确定性底下是一连串矛盾。

NFC *n* National Footbal Conference; a group of teams that is part of the NFL 国家橄榄球联盟〔（美国）全国橄榄球联盟的一部分〕—see also 另见 AFC

NFL, the /ˌɛn ɛf ˋɛl; ˌen ef ˈel/ *n* National Football League; the organization in charge of professional football in the US. The NFL consists of two LEAGUES (=groups of teams who play against each other), the National Football Conference (NFC) and the American Football Conference (AFC). （美国）职业橄榄球大联盟〔负责管理美国职业橄榄球的组织，由国家橄榄球联合会和美国橄榄球联合会组成〕

NFT, the /ˌɛn ɛf ˋti; ˌen ef ˈtiː/ the abbreviation of 缩写= the NATIONAL FILM THEATRE

NFU /ˌɛn ɛf ˋju; ˌen ef ˈjuː/ the abbreviation of 缩写= the NATIONAL FARMERS UNION

NH the written abbreviation of 缩写= NEW HAMPSHIRE

NHL, the /ˌɛn etʃ ˋɛl; ˌen eɪtʃ ˈel/ *n* National Hockey League; the group of US and Canadian ICE HOCKEY teams who play games against one another 国家冰球联盟〔由美国与加拿大冰上曲棍球队组成的一个组织〕

NHS, the /ˌɛn etʃ ˋɛs; ˌen eɪtʃ ˈes/ *n* the National Health Service; the British system that provides free medical treatment for everyone, paid for by taxes 国民保健制度〔英国的一种免费医疗制度〕：*NHS hospitals* 国民保健制度所属的医院 | **on the NHS** (=paid for by the NHS) 由国民保健制度支付 *Can I get my glasses on the NHS?* 我配眼镜可以享受国民医疗保健吗？

NI /ˌɛn ˋaɪ; ˌen ˈaɪ/ the abbreviation of 缩写= NATIONAL INSURANCE

Ni·ag·a·ra Falls /naɪˋægrə ˋfɔlz; naɪˌægərə ˈfɔːlz/ two very large WATERFALLS on the border between Canada and the US, which are popular with tourists and are also used to produce electricity 尼亚加拉瀑布〔位于加拿大和美国边境的两处巨大瀑布，颇受游人喜欢，也用于发电〕

N

Nia·mey /njɑˋme; njɑːˈmeɪ/ the capital of Niger, in the southwest of the country on the Niger River, formerly called Niave 尼亚美〔尼日尔首都，位于该国西南部，濒临尼日尔河，旧称Niave〕

nib /nɪb; nɪb/ *n* [C] **1** the pointed metal part at the end of a pen 钢笔尖 **2 his/her nibs** *old-fashioned* someone of a higher social rank than you or someone who thinks they are important【过时】上司；要人；自以为了不起的人：*His nibs has wine with his meal – we get water.* 那位大人物吃饭有酒喝，我们只有水。

nib·ble¹ /ˈnɪbl; ˈnɪbəl/ *v* **1** [I,T] to eat small amounts of food by taking very small bites 啃；一点一点地咬[吃]：*He nibbled the biscuit cautiously.* 他小心地啃着饼干。| [+at] *She nibbled at her sandwich.* 她小口小口地吃着三明治。**2** [I+at] to show slight interest in an offer or suggestion〔对提议、建议〕略表兴趣

nibble away at sth *phr v* [T] to keep reducing a large amount by taking smaller amounts from it 一点一点地减少[耗掉]；蚕食：*All these expenses are nibbling away at our savings.* 所有这些开支在一点一点地耗掉我们的积蓄。

nibble² *n* [C] **1** a small bite of something 一小口：*taking tiny nibbles of a biscuit* 一小口一小口地啃饼干 **2 nibbles** [plural] *informal* small things to eat, especially at a party【非正式】〔尤指聚会上的〕小吃；少量食品 **3** an expression of slight interest in an offer or suggestion 略有兴趣的表示：*We've had the house on the market for a month and not even a nibble yet.* 我们的房子上市已有一个月了，但至今连略表兴趣的人都没有。

Nic·a·rag·u·a /ˌnɪkəˋrɑgwə; ˌnɪkəˈrægjuə/ a country in Central America between the Caribbean Sea and the Pacific Ocean, and south of Honduras and north of Costa Rica. Population: 4,918,000 (2001). Capital: Managua. Its main products are coffee, cotton, and sugar. In the 1980s there was a civil war. 尼加拉瓜〔中美洲一国家，东临加勒比海，西临太平洋，北接洪都拉斯，南临哥斯达黎加。人口：4,918,000 (2001)，首都：马那瓜。主要出产咖啡、棉花和糖。20世纪80年代发生过内战〕—**Nicaraguan** *n, adj*

Nicaragua, Lake a lake in southwest Nicaragua which is the largest lake in Central America 尼加拉瓜湖〔位于尼加拉瓜西南部，是中美洲最大的湖泊〕

Nice /nis; niːs/ a city on the Mediterranean coast of France. It is a fashionable place for tourists to stay, and also a port and industrial area. 尼斯〔法国地中海沿岸一港口工业城市，同时也是时尚的旅游目的地〕

S1 W2 **nice** /naɪs; naɪs/ *adj*

1 ►ENJOYABLE/ATTRACTIVE 令人愉快/吸引人的◄ pleasant, attractive or enjoyable 令人愉快的；吸引人的，美好的：*That's a nice dress.* 那条裙子很漂亮！| *We had a really nice day at the beach.* 我们在海滩度过了愉快的一天。| *not too hot, just a nice temperature* 不太热，温度正好 | *"We could take a picnic." "Yes, that'd be nice."* "我们可以去野餐。""对，好主意。" | **it is nice to do something** *It's nice to have a sit down.* 能坐一会儿真好。| *It's really nice to see you again.* 能再见到你真高兴。| **look/taste/smell nice** *You look nice in that suit.* 你穿那套西服看起来很不错。| *If it doesn't taste nice, don't eat it.* 如果味道不好，就别吃了。| **nice big/new/long etc** *spoken*【口】*I had a nice long letter from your mother.* 我收到你母亲的一封长信。| **nice and warm/nice and sweet etc** *Have one of these oranges – they're nice and juicy.* 吃个橙子吧，汁很多的。| **one of the nice things about...** *One of the nice things about Christmas is having all the family together.* 圣诞节的一个好处是全家团聚在一起。

2 ►FRIENDLY 友好的◄ friendly or kind 友好的；友善的，和善的：*Dave's a really nice guy.* 戴夫是个很友善的人。| *He told me, in the nicest possible way, that I was interfering too much.* 他以最友善的方式告诉我，我干涉得太多了。| *Did she really say all those nice things about me?* 她真的说了我那么多好话吗？| **be nice to** *Be nice to Grandad. He's not feeling very well today.* 对爷爷好些，他今天有点不舒服。| **it is nice of sb (to do sth)** *It was nice of you to help.* 你帮了忙，真好。

3 it's nice to know (that) *spoken* used to mean that you feel happier when you know something【口】知道…真好：*I still haven't heard any news – it would be nice to know what's happening.* 我还是没有得到任何消息，要是能知道发生了什么事就好了。

4 ►NOT NICE AT ALL 一点也不好◄ *spoken* used when you think that something or someone is not nice at all【口】压根儿不好的；令人不快的：*That's a nice way to treat a friend, I must say!* 我说，你这样对待朋友太不像话了！| *You've got us into a nice old mess, haven't you?* 你使我们陷入了这种困境，不是吗？

5 be as nice as pie *spoken* if someone is as nice as pie, they are very nice to you when you were expecting them to be angry【口】〔出乎意料地〕极好：*I told her about the broken window and she was as nice as pie about it.* 我告诉她打破窗子的事，但她却丝毫没有生气。

6 have a nice day! *spoken especially AmE* used to say goodbye to someone, especially to customers in shops and restaurants when they are leaving【口，尤美】祝你今天过得愉快！〔尤用作商店店员、餐厅侍应向顾客告别时的用语〕

7 nice to meet you *spoken* used as a friendly greeting when you meet someone for the first time【口】很高兴认识你〔初次见面时的礼貌用语〕：*Hello. It's nice to meet you at last.* 你好，终于见到你，我真高兴！

8 it's been nice meeting you *spoken* used when you say goodbye to someone you have just met【口】能认识你真高兴〔初次见面后的告别用语〕

9 nice one! *BrE spoken* used to say that you think someone has just said or done something clever, amusing, helpful etc【英口】真聪明！真好笑！好极了！：*"Dad said he'd give us some money to help pay for it." "Nice one!"* "爸爸说他会给我们一些钱，帮我们付账。""太棒了！"

10 nice work! *BrE spoken* used to praise someone when they have succeeded in doing something【英口】干得好！：*"I've traced those missing files, sir." "Nice work, Cardew!"* "先生，我找到丢失的文件了！""干得好，卡迪尤！"

11 ►DETAIL 细节◄ *formal* involving a very small difference or detail【正式】细微的；微妙的：*a nice point of law* 一项微妙的法律条款

12 ►RESPECTABLE 正派的◄ *old-fashioned* having high standards of moral and social behaviour【过时】高尚的；正派的：*the kind of nightclubs nice people don't go to* 正派人不去的那种夜总会 —**niceness** *n* [U] —see also 另见 **no more Mr Nice Guy!** (GUY¹ (5))

USAGE NOTE 用法说明：NICE

GRAMMAR 语法

Nice is often joined to another adjective by *and* when it follows **is, seems** etc without a noun. (But you do not use 'nice and' before a noun) 当 nice 用在 is, seems 等词之后，后面又没有名词时，往往要用 and 将其与另一形容词连接（但 nice and 不用于名词前）：*Your new house looks nice and big.* 你的新房子看起来真大！Compare 比较：*This is a nice big house!* 这房子真大！

SPOKEN-WRITTEN 口语－书面语

Nice is very frequent in spoken English, but many people feel you should not use it too much in writing. Often it is better to think of a word that describes what you mean more exactly. nice 在英语口语中的使用频率很高，但很多人认为书面语中不宜用得过多，而应使用一些更加具体的词来描述确切含义。For example, look at this sentence 如下句：*That area of France is really nice.* 法国的那个地区真不错！Here you could make your meaning clearer by using more specific adjectives such as **interesting** or **beautiful**. 这里可使用一些更加具体的形容词，如 interesting（有意思的）或 beautiful（美丽的），以将意思表达得更清楚。

nice-look·ing /ˌ·ˈ··/ *adj* attractive 美丽的，漂亮的；英俊的：*Do you really think he's nice-looking?* 你真的认为他长得英俊吗？

nice·ly /ˋnaɪslɪ; ˈnaɪsli/ *adv* S3

1 ►WELL 很好地◄ in a satisfactory or pleasing way 很好地；令人满意地；令人愉快地：*The car seems to be running nicely now it's been fixed.* 汽车修理过以后好像跑得很不错。| *We were managing quite nicely till you started interfering.* 你没有插手以前，我们本来进展得很顺利。| *My legs are getting nicely tanned.* 我把双腿晒成漂亮的棕褐色。

2 ►IN A FRIENDLY/PLEASANT WAY 友好/适宜地◄ in a pleasant, polite, or friendly way 友好地；礼貌地；适宜地：*I hope you thanked Mrs Deville nicely.* 我希望你已经好好谢过德维尔夫人了。

3 be doing nicely (for yourself) to be successful and be earning a lot of money（为自己）干得很出色，干得很成功：*I've heard Malcom's doing very nicely for himself out in Japan.* 我听说马尔科姆在日本干得很出色。

4 will do nicely *spoken* if something will do nicely, it is suitable for a particular purpose【口】非常好用：*"Is this knife big enough?" "Yes, it'll do nicely."* "这把刀子够大吗？""够大，它非常好用。"

5 ►EXACTLY 确切地◄ *formal* exactly or carefully【正式】精确地；仔细地：*a nicely calculated distance* 精确计算出的距离

N

ni·ce·ty /ˈnaɪsətɪ; ˈnaɪsəti/ *n* **1** [C usually plural 一般用复数] a small and exact point of difference or detail 细微区别; 细微之处; 细节: *legal niceties* 法律细节 | [+of] *the niceties of etiquette* 礼节的细微之处 **2 to a nicety** *formal* exactly【正式】精确地, 精细入微地

niche /nɪtʃ; nɪtʃ/ *n* **1** [C] a job or activity that is perfect for someone 合适的工作[活动]: *She's found a niche for herself in the book trade.* 她在图书行业找到了一份非常适合自己的工作。**2** [C] a hollow place in a wall, often made to hold a STATUE〔用来放雕像的〕壁龛 **3** [singular] *technical* all the people who buy a particular product or use a particular service【术语】〔特定产品或服务的〕用户群

niche mar·ket·ing /ˈ· ,···/ *n* [U] the practice of trying to sell a product to a particular group of people 针对特定群体的销售法, 目标群体销售法

Nich·o·las /ˈnɪkələs; ˈnɪkələs/**, St** a Christian BISHOP (=high-ranking priest) who lived in western Asia in the 4th century AD. He became connected with the custom of giving gifts to children either at Christmas (=in countries such as the UK and the US), or on the night before his saint's day (December 6th) (=in some countries, such as the Netherlands). The imaginary character Santa Claus is based on stories about him. He is also the patron saint of Russia. 圣尼古拉〔公元4世纪时生活在西亚的一位基督教主教。在圣诞节或圣尼古拉节前夜给儿童送礼物的习俗据说与他有关。虚构的圣诞老人就是根据他的故事创造的。他还是俄罗斯的主保圣人〕

Nicholas II /ˌnɪkələs ðə ˈsɛkənd; ˌnɪkələs ðə ˈsekənd/ (1868-1918) the Tsar (=ruler) of Russia from 1894 to 1917. His opposition to change led to the Revolution of 1905 and eventually to the Russian Revolution of 1917, in which he was forced to ABDICATE (=give up his position). He and his family were shot in 1918. 尼古拉二世〔(1868-1918), 俄国沙皇, 1894至1917年在位。他反对变革, 从而引发了1905年革命, 最终导致了1917年俄国革命, 他被迫退位。1918年, 沙皇一家遭到处决〕

nick[1] /nɪk; nɪk/ *n* **1 in the nick of time** just before it is too late or just before something bad happens 在紧要关头; 正是时候: *Luckily, help arrived in the nick of time.* 幸运的是援助及时来了。**2** [C] a very small cut made on the edge or surface of something 刻痕; 裂口 **3 in good nick/in bad nick etc** *BrE informal* in good condition or in bad condition【英, 非正式】状态良好/不好等: *It's an old car but it's in good nick.* 这是辆旧汽车, 但性能良好。**4 the nick** *BrE informal* prison or a POLICE STATION【英, 非正式】监狱; 警察局

nick[2] *v* [T] **1** to make a small cut in the surface or edge of something, usually by accident〔意外地〕刻痕于; 擦伤: *A bullet nicked his leg.* 一颗子弹擦伤了他的腿。**2** *BrE informal* to steal something【英, 非正式】偷: *Someone's nicked my bike.* 有人偷了我的自行车。**3** *BrE informal* if the police nick you, they catch you and charge you with a crime; ARREST[1] (1)【英, 非正式】抓获, 逮捕, 拘捕

nick·el /ˈnɪkḷ; ˈnɪkəl/ *n* **1** [U] a hard silver-white metal that is an ELEMENT (=a simple substance) and is used in the production of other metals 镍 **2** [C] a coin in the US or Canada that is worth five cents〔美国、加拿大的〕五分硬币

nickel-and-dime /ˌ· · ˈ· ◂/ *adj AmE* unimportant and not costing a lot of money【美】不重要的; 不值钱的

nick·nack /ˈnɪk ˌnæk; ˈnɪk næk/ *n* [C] another spelling of KNICK-KNACK knick-knack 的另一种拼法

nick·name /ˈnɪk ˌnem; ˈnɪkneɪm/ *n* [C] a name given to someone, especially by their friends or family, that is not their real name and is often connected with what they look like or something they have done〔尤指给朋友或家人取的〕绰号, 外号; 诨名 —**nickname** *v* [T]: *Frank Sinatra, nicknamed 'Old Blue Eyes'* 弗兰克·西纳特, 外号"老蓝眼"

Nic·o·si·a /ˌnɪkəˈsiə; ˌnɪkəˈsiːə/ the capital city of Cyprus, whose industries include leather goods, POTTERY, and TEXTILES. The city has many old buildings and walls from the time when it was ruled by Venice in the 15th and 16th centuries. 尼科西亚〔塞浦路斯首都, 其工业包括皮革业、制陶业与纺织业。该城有许多古建筑和城墙, 建于15、16世纪威尼斯统治时期〕

nic·o·tine /ˈnɪkəˌtin; ˈnɪkətiːn/ *n* [U] a substance in tobacco which makes it difficult for people to stop smoking 尼古丁, 烟碱

nicotine patch /ˈ··· ,·/ *n* [C] a small piece of material containing nicotine which you stick on your skin to help you stop smoking〔贴在某人皮肤上帮助戒烟的〕尼古丁贴片, 戒烟贴

niece /nis; niːs/ *n* [C] the daughter of your brother or sister, or the daughter of your wife's or husband's brother or sister 侄女; 外甥女 —compare 比较 NEPHEW —see picture at 参见 FAMILY 图

Niel·sen Rat·ings, the /ˈnilsn̩ ˌretɪŋz; ˈniːlsən ˌreɪtɪŋz/ also 又作 **the Nielsens** *n* [plural] *trademark* a system used to show how many people watch a particular US television programme, using information provided by **Nielsen Media Research**. The Nielsen Ratings are used to decide how much companies will have to pay to advertise their products during a particular programme, and they also help television companies to decide which shows should continue.【商标】尼尔森收视率〔一种基于"尼尔森媒体研究中心"提供的资料显示美国某一电视节目收看人数的系统。尼尔森收视率可用来决定公司在某一档节目中做产品广告应支付多少费用, 还有助于电视公司决定哪些节目应继续播出〕

Nietz·sche /ˈnitʃə; ˈniːtʃə/**, Fried·rich** /ˈfridrɪk; ˈfriːdrɪk/ (1844-1900) a German PHILOSOPHER whose most famous books are *Thus Spake Zarathustra* and *The Antichrist*. He wrote that 'God is dead', meaning that people no longer had to accept the values of the Christian religion. He believed that a new type of person would exist, the 'Übermensch' or SUPERMAN, who would be free to follow his own moral principles. 尼采〔(1844-1900), 德国哲学家。最著名的作品有《查拉图斯特拉如是说》和《敌基督》。他曾写道"上帝死了", 意指人们不必再接受基督教的价值观念。他认为世间会出现一种新人, 即"超人"。超人将有自由遵循自己的道德准则〕—**Nietzschean** /ˈnitʃiən; ˈniːtʃiən/ *adj*

niff /nɪf; nɪf/ *n* [singular] *BrE informal* a bad smell【英, 非正式】难闻的气味 —**niffy** *adj*

nif·ty /ˈnɪftɪ; ˈnɪfti/ *adj informal* very good, fast, or effective【非正式】极好的; 极快的; 极有效的: *a nifty little gadget for squeezing oranges* 榨橙汁的精巧小玩意儿 | *a nifty little car* 跑得极快的小汽车

Ni·ger /ˈnaɪdʒɚ; ˈnaɪdʒə/ **1 the Niger** the third longest river in Africa, flowing through Mali, Niger, and Nigeria 尼日尔河〔非洲第三大河, 流经马里、尼日尔和尼日利亚〕**2** a large country in West Africa, south of Algeria and north of Nigeria. Much of the land is desert. Population: 10,355,000 (2001). Capital: Niamey. 尼日尔〔西非一大国, 位于阿尔及利亚以南, 尼日利亚以北。大部分国土为沙漠。人口: 10,355,000 (2001), 首都: 尼亚美〕

Ni·ge·ri·a /naɪˈdʒɪrɪə; naɪˈdʒɪəriə/ an oil-producing country in West Africa, east of Benin and west of Cameroon. Population: 126,636,000 (2001). Its capital is Abuja, and its largest city is Lagos. Nigeria became an independent state in 1960, after being ruled by the UK for almost 100 years. About half its population are Muslims, who live mainly in the north, and the rest are Christians, living mainly in the south. 尼日利亚〔西非一石油生产国, 位于贝宁以东, 喀麦隆以西。人口: 126,636,000 (2001), 首都: 阿布贾。最大城市为拉各斯。尼日利亚被英国统治近一百年, 于1960年独立。人口中约有一半为穆斯林, 主要居住在北方, 其余为基督徒, 多住在南方〕—**Nigerian** *n, adj*

nig·gard·ly /ˈnɪgɚdlɪ; ˈnɪgədli/ *adj* **1** unwilling to spend money or be generous; STINGY 小气的, 吝啬的: *The landlord was niggardly about repairs.* 房东在维修方面很吝啬。**2** a niggardly gift, amount, salary etc is not worth very much and is given unwillingly 很少的, 勉强给的: *niggardly wages* 微薄的工资 —**niggard** *n* [C] —**niggardliness** *n* [U]

nig·ger /ˈnɪgɚ; ˈnɪgə/ *n* [C] *taboo* an extremely offensive word for a black person【讳】黑鬼〔对黑人极具冒犯性的用语〕—see 见 NEGRO (USAGE)

nig·gle /ˈnɪgḷ; ˈnɪgəl/ *v* **1** [T] if something niggles you, it worries or annoys you slightly and you cannot forget about it 惹恼, 烦扰: *Something's been niggling her all day.* 有件事一整天都在烦扰着她。**2** [I] to argue or make criticisms about small unimportant details 挑剔, 吹毛求疵: [+**about/over**] *She niggled over every detail of the bill.* 她在这账单上处处挑毛病。—**niggle** *n* [C] —**niggler** *n* [C]

nig·gling /ˈnɪglɪŋ; ˈnɪgəlɪŋ/ *adj* **niggling doubt/worry/suspicion etc** a doubt etc that keeps worrying you slightly and that you cannot stop thinking about 使人心烦的疑虑/担心/怀疑等: *A niggling doubt about Marlow's motives suddenly entered his mind.* 他心里突然怀疑起马洛的动机。

nigh /naɪ; naɪ/ *adv* **1 nigh on** *old-fashioned* almost【过时】几乎: *There were nigh on 40 people there.* 那里有近40个人。**2** *literary* near【文】接近, 临近: **draw nigh** (=come near or be about to happen soon) 接近; 即将来临 *Winter draws nigh.* 冬天快要来了。—see also 另见 WELL-NIGH

night /naɪt; naɪt/ *n*

1 ►WHEN IT IS DARK 黑夜时◄ [C,U] the dark part of each 24-hour period when the sun cannot be seen 夜晚, 夜间: *a starry night* 星夜 | **at night/by night** (=when it is dark) 在夜里 *At night the temperature drops below zero.* 温度在夜间降至零度以下。| *They travelled by night and slept during the day.* 他们

夜间旅行，白天睡觉。| **all night (long)** (=through the whole night) 整夜；通宵 *In New York, some stores stay open all night long.* 在纽约，有些商店通宵营业。| *The party went on all night.* 晚会持续了一整夜。| **night train/flight/bus** (=a train, plane, bus etc that travels at night) 夜班火车/航班/公共汽车 *We took the night train to Glasgow.* 我们坐夜班火车去格拉斯哥。| **the night sky/air** *the cold night air* 夜间寒冷的空气 | **at dead of night** (=in the middle of the night when it is quiet) 夜深人静时 *Their meetings were held in secret at dead of night.* 他们的会议是在夜深人静时秘密召开的。| **night falls** (=it becomes dark) 夜幕降临 *Night was beginning to fall as we sailed into Vera Cruz.* 当我们驶入韦拉克鲁斯港时，夜幕开始降临。

2 ▶WHEN YOU SLEEP 睡觉时◀ the time when most people are in bed 夜晚，晚上：*I didn't sleep too well last night.* 我昨晚睡得不太好。| *We had to get up in the middle of the night.* 我们不得不在半夜里起床。| *14 nights in a 5 star hotel* 在一家五星级酒店住的14夜 | **at night** (=when it is night) 在夜里 *She's so worried she can't sleep at night.* 她担心得晚上无法入睡。| **in the night** (=during the night) 在夜间 *The baby woke up twice in the night.* 婴儿夜里醒了两次。| **spend the night** *We spent the first two nights of our vacation in a cheap motel.* 我们度假的头两个晚上住在一家廉价的汽车旅馆里。| **spend the night with sb** (=and have sex with someone) 与某人过夜〔并发生性关系〕| **stay the night** (=sleep at someone's house) 借宿 *If you miss the last bus home, you can always stay the night.* 如果你没赶上末班车回家，你可以随时来借宿。| **a good night's sleep** (=when you sleep well all night) 一夜好觉 *You look exhausted! What you need is a good night's sleep.* 你看起来累坏了！你需要好好睡一夜。| **have a bad night** *BrE* (=not sleep much)【英】没睡好觉

3 ▶EVENING 傍晚◀ [C,U] the time during the evening until you go to bed 傍晚，黄昏；晚上：*Most nights we just stay at home and watch television.* 大多数晚上我们只是留在家里看电视。| **last night** *Where did you go last night?* 昨晚你去哪儿了？| **at night** *Do you mean 9:30 in the morning or 9:30 at night?* 你是说上午9点半还是晚上9点半？| **tomorrow night** *My parents are coming for dinner tomorrow night.* 我父母明晚要过来吃晚饭。| **the other night** *spoken* (=a few nights ago)【口】几天前的一个晚上 *Did I tell you I saw Nicky Ansell the other night?* 我有没有告诉你我前几天晚上看到了尼基·安塞尔？| **Friday night/Saturday night etc** *There's a party at Ben's place on Saturday night.* 星期六晚上本的家里有个聚会。| **a night out** (=a night when you go to a party, restaurant, theatre etc) 外出的一晚 *Let's go see a band – I could do with a night out.* 我们去看乐队演出吧——我想晚上出去玩会儿。| **late at night** *Anna doesn't like him walking home late at night.* 安娜不想他走夜路回家。

4 nights *especially AmE* if you do something nights, you do it regularly or often at night【尤美】每晚；晚上经常：*I lie awake nights.* 我晚上躺在床上总是睡不着。| **work nights** *I'd hate to work nights – it's so antisocial.* 我讨厌晚上工作，那太不合生活常规。

5 night! *spoken* used to say goodbye to someone when it is late in the evening or when they are going to bed【口】晚安！：*Night! See you tomorrow!* 晚安！明天见！

6 night night! *spoken* used to say goodbye to someone, especially a child, when they are going to bed【口】晚安！〔尤用于对儿童说〕

7 night after night every night for a long period〔长期以来〕每晚；一夜又一夜地：*He's out drinking night after night.* 他每天晚上都出去喝酒。

8 night and day/day and night all the time 夜以继日地，日夜不停地：*The store is guarded day and night.* 这家商店日夜都有保安人员看守。

9 late night a night when you go to bed later than usual 比通常晚睡的晚上：*You're looking sleepy this morning. Too many late nights!* 你今天上午看起来很困，熬夜太多了！—see also 另见 LATE-NIGHT

10 have an early night to go to bed earlier than usual 睡得早，〔比平常〕早睡觉：*I'm exhausted – I think I'll have an early night.* 我累极了，我想早点儿睡觉。

11 last thing at night just before you go to bed 临睡之前：*You should never eat cheese last thing at night.* 临睡之前千万不要吃乳酪。

12 at this time of night! *spoken* used when you are surprised because something happens late at night【口】夜这么深了！：*Who on earth could be calling at this time of night?* 谁会这么晚打电话来呢？

13 first night/opening night the first performance of a play or show 首场演出；首映：*We saw 'Miss Saigon' on its opening night.* 我们看了《西贡小姐》的首场演出。

14 make a night of it to stay out late drinking, dancing etc 在外痛快地玩一个晚上 —see also 另见 NIGHTLY

Night Be·fore Christ·mas, The /,· · ˈ· ·/ a poem by Clement Moore which contains many of the popular ideas and images that Americans think of about Santa Claus. It has been set to music, made into a television film, and appears printed in newspapers and magazines at Christmastime.《圣诞前夜》〔克莱门特·穆尔创作的一首诗。诗中可见美国人对圣诞老人的普遍看法以及圣诞老人在人们心目中的各种形象。这首诗已配乐，并录制成电视片，圣诞节期间还会刊登在报纸和杂志上〕

night·cap /ˈnaɪt,kæp; ˈnaɪtkæp/ *n* [C] **1** an alcoholic drink that you have just before you go to bed 临睡前喝的酒 **2** a soft cap that people in the past used to wear in bed〔旧时的〕睡帽

night·clothes /ˈnaɪtkloðz; ˈnaɪtkləʊðz/ *n* [plural] clothes that you wear in bed 睡衣

night·club /ˈnaɪt,klʌb; ˈnaɪtklʌb/ *n* [C] a place of entertainment open late at night where people can dance and drink 夜总会

night·club·bing /ˈnaɪt,klʌbɪŋ; ˈnaɪt,klʌbɪŋ/ *n* [U] **go nightclubbing** *BrE* to spend an evening at a nightclub【英】去夜总会

night de·pos·it·o·ry /ˈ· ·,· · · ·/ *n* [C] *AmE* NIGHT SAFE【美】夜用保险箱

night·dress /ˈnaɪt,drɛs; ˈnaɪtdres/ *n* [C] a piece of clothing, like a thin dress, that women wear in bed 女睡袍

night·fall /ˈnaɪt,fɔl; ˈnaɪtfɔːl/ *n* [U] the time when it begins to get dark in the evening; DUSK 黄昏，傍晚：*We rushed to reach home before nightfall.* 我们在黄昏之前赶回了家。

night·gown /ˈnaɪt,gaun; ˈnaɪtgaʊn/ *n* [C] a nightdress 女睡袍

night·hawk /ˈnaɪt,hɔk; ˈnaɪthɔːk/ *n* [C] *especially AmE informal* someone who enjoys staying awake all night【尤美，非正式】夜猫子，喜欢熬夜的人

night·ie /ˈnaɪtɪ; ˈnaɪti/ *n* [C] *informal* a NIGHTDRESS【非正式】女睡袍

nigh·tin·gale /ˈnaɪtɪŋ,gel; ˈnaɪtɪŋgeɪl/ *n* [C] a small bird that sings very beautifully, especially at night 夜莺

Nightingale, Florence (1820-1910) a British nurse who set up a hospital for soldiers in Turkey during the CRIMEAN WAR. She was called the 'Lady with the Lamp', because she walked around the hospital in the evenings with a lamp to check that everything was in order. She set up a school for nurses, making nursing (=the job of being a nurse) into a real profession. 南丁格尔〔(1820-1910)，英国一护士。克里米亚战争期间，她在土耳其建立了一所士兵医院。她有"提灯女士"之称，因为她每晚都要提着一盏灯在医院里四处查看，以确保一切正常。她还创办了一所护士学校，从而使护理工作成为一种真正的职业〕

night·life /ˈnaɪtlaɪf; ˈnaɪtlaɪf/ *n* [U] entertainment in the evening 夜生活，夜间娱乐活动：*It's a beautiful place but there's not much nightlife.* 这是个美丽的地方，但没有多少夜生活。

night·light /ˈnaɪtlaɪt; ˈnaɪtlaɪt/ *n* [C] a small electric light that you put in a child's room at night〔儿童房中的〕小夜灯

night·long /ˈnaɪt,lɔŋ; ˈnaɪtlɒŋ/ *adj* [only before noun 仅用于名词前] *literary* lasting all night【文】彻夜的，通宵的：*a nightlong vigil* 通宵守夜

night·ly /ˈnaɪtlɪ; ˈnaɪtli/ *adv* every night 每晚，每夜：*The band performed nightly.* 乐队每晚都演出。—**nightly** *adj*: *nightly news broadcasts* 晚间新闻广播

night·mare /ˈnaɪt,mɛr; ˈnaɪtmeə/ *n* [C] **1** a very frightening dream 噩梦，梦魇：*Years after the accident I still have nightmares about it.* 多年后，我仍然做噩梦梦见那次事故。**2** a very unpleasant or frightening experience 不愉快的[可怕的]经历：*He kept trying to hold my hand all the time – it was a real nightmare!* 他一直想要握住我的手，真是可怕极了！| **nightmare journey/situation etc** (=the worst journey etc you can imagine) 可怕的旅程/情景等 *a nightmare sea voyage in a raging storm* 狂风暴雨中一次可怕的海上航行 **3** something terrible that you fear may happen in the future 可能发生的恐怖事件：[+of] *the nightmare of a nuclear war* 核战争的恐怖 | **nightmare scenario** (=the worst or most frightening situation that you can imagine) 最坏[恐怖]的设想 —**nightmarish** *adj*

Nightmare on Elm Street, A /,· · ˈ· ·/ (1984) a US HORROR FILM (=a film that is intended to make you feel frightened) about a frightening character called Freddy Krueger who has knives instead of FINGERNAILs, and who appears in people's dreams and tries to kill them《猛鬼街》〔(1984)，美国一恐怖片。片中有一个名叫弗列迪·克鲁格的可怕人物，手指上长着刀子而不是指甲，常出现在人们的梦境里，企图将人杀死〕

N

night owl /ˈ· ·/ *n* [C] *informal* someone who enjoys staying awake all night【非正式】夜猫子，喜欢熬夜的人

night por·ter /ˈ· ,··/ *n* [C] someone who works at the main entrance of a hotel during the night〔旅馆门口的〕夜班服务员

night safe /ˈ· ·/ *n* [C] *BrE* a special hole in the outside wall of a bank into which a customer can put money or documents when the bank is closed【英】夜用保险箱〔银行关门后，其外墙上供顾客存放钱物的安全存放器〕；NIGHT DEPOSITORY *AmE*【美】

night school /ˈ· ·/ *n* [U] classes that take place in the evening for people who work during the day 夜校

night shift /ˈ· ·/ *n* [C] **1** a period of time at night during which people regularly work, especially in a factory 夜班：*She's on the night shift this week.* 她这星期上夜班。**2** the group of people who work at this time 上夜班的人：*The night shift was just arriving.* 上夜班的人正在陆续到来。

night·shirt /ˈnaɪt,ʃɝt; ˈnaɪt-ʃɜːt/ *n* [C] a long loose shirt that people, especially men, wear in bed〔男用〕衬衫式长睡衣

night soil /ˈ· ·/ *n* [U] *technical* human waste used in growing crops【术语】〔人的〕粪便

night spot /ˈ· ·/ *n* [C] a place people go to at night for entertainment 夜间娱乐场所；夜总会：*my favourite New York night spot* 纽约我最喜欢的一个夜间娱乐场所

night·stand /ˈnaɪt,stænd; ˈnaɪtstænd/ *n* [C] *AmE* a small table beside a bed【美】床头柜

night·stick /ˈnaɪt,stɪk; ˈnaɪt,stɪk/ *n* [C] *AmE* a short thick stick carried as a weapon by police officers【美】警棍；TRUNCHEON *BrE*【英】

night·time /ˈnaɪt,taɪm; ˈnaɪt,taɪm/ *n* [U] the time during the night 夜间：**at nighttime** *animals that hunt at nighttime* 夜间猎食的动物 —opposite 反义词 DAYTIME

night watch, the /ˈ· ·/ *n* a kind of police force in the past, who looked after a town at night〔旧时的〕巡夜警察；值夜警卫（队）

night watch·man /,· ˈ· ·/ *n* [C] someone whose job is to guard a building at night〔大楼的〕夜间守卫

night·wear /ˈnaɪt,wɛr; ˈnaɪtweə/ *n* [U] clothes that you wear in bed at night 睡衣

nig·nog /ˈnɪg ,nɑg; ˈnɪg nɒg/ *n* [C] *BrE old-fashioned taboo* an extremely offensive word for a black person【英，过时，讳】黑鬼〔对黑人极具冒犯性的用语〕

ni·hil·is·m /ˈnaɪəl,ɪzəm; ˈnaɪɪ̈lɪzəm/ *n* [U] **1** the belief that nothing has any meaning or value 虚无主义〔认为一切都没有意义或价值〕**2** the idea that all social and political institutions should be destroyed 政治虚无主义〔主张摧毁一切社会和政治机构的思想〕—**nihilist** *n* [C] —**nihilistic** /,naɪəˈlɪstɪk; ,naɪɪ̈ˈlɪstɪk◂/ *adj*

Ni·jin·sky /nɪˈdʒɪnski; nɪ̈ˈdʒɪnski/, **Vas·lav** /ˈvɑθslɑf; ˈvɑθslɑːf/ (1890-1950) a Russian BALLET dancer who worked with the ballet producer Diaghilev and was one of the greatest male dancers ever 尼任斯基（1890-1950），俄国芭蕾舞演员。他曾与芭蕾舞出品人佳吉列夫合作过，被认为是有史以来最杰出的男舞蹈演员之一

-nik /nɪk; nɪk/ *suffix* [in nouns 构成名词] *informal* someone who is connected with something or enjoys something【非正式】与…有关的人；爱好…的人：*a computernik* (=someone who works with or is very keen on computers) 用电脑工作的人；电脑迷 | *a peacenik* (=someone who supports peace) 和平爱好者

Nik·kei in·dex, the /,nɪke ˈɪndɛks; ,nɪkeɪ ˈɪndeks/ also 又作 **the Nikkei, the Nikkei Average** a number that shows how well or badly shares have performed on the Tokyo STOCK EXCHANGE on a particular day. The number is based on the share prices of about 200 important companies. 日经指数〔反映东京证券交易所某日股市行情的指数。该指数是基于大约二百家大公司的股票价格计算出来的〕—see also 另见 DOW JONES AVERAGE, the FT 100 SHARE INDEX, the HANG SENG INDEX

nil /nɪl; nɪl/ *n* [U] **1** nothing 无；零：*The new machine reduced labour costs to almost nil.* 新机器把人工成本几乎降到零。**2** *BrE* the number zero, used in sports results【英】〔体育比赛比分中的〕零：*Our team won by two goals to nil.* 我队以二比零获胜。

Nile, the /naɪl; naɪl/ a river in northeast Africa, the longest river in the world, whose water is used for most of the farming in Egypt and Sudan. It is formed from two rivers: the **Blue Nile**, which starts in Ethiopia, and the **White Nile**, which starts in Uganda. The two rivers join in Sudan, and flow north into the Mediterranean Sea. 尼罗河〔非洲东北部一河流，是世界上最长的河流，河水灌溉了埃及和苏丹的大部分农田。尼罗河有两条源流，即发源于埃塞俄比亚的青尼罗河和发源于乌干达的白尼罗河。两条河在苏丹汇合，然后流向北部注入地中海〕

nim·ble /ˈnɪmbl; ˈnɪmbəl/ *adj* **1** able to move quickly and easily with light neat movements 敏捷的，灵活的：*a nimble climber* 敏捷的爬山者 | *nimble fingers* 灵巧的手指 **2 a nimble mind/brain/wit** an ability to think quickly or understand things easily 敏捷的思维/头脑/才智：*They liked his nimble mind – his ability to come up with original ideas.* 他们喜欢他敏捷的头脑，他常常能提出一些新颖的想法。—**nimbly** *adv* —**nimbleness** *n* [U]

nim·bus /ˈnɪmbəs; ˈnɪmbəs/ *n* **1** [C,U] a dark cloud that may bring rain or snow 雨云 **2** [C] a HALO〔神像等头上的〕光轮，光环

nim·by /ˈnɪmbɪ; ˈnɪmbi/ *n* [C] not in my backyard; someone who does not want a particular activity or building near their home 反对自家附近有某种活动[建筑]的人 —**nimby** *adj*: *nimby attitudes* 反对在附近建楼或举行活动的态度

Nin /nɪn; nɪn/, **Anais** /əˈnɪəs; əˈnɪəs/ (1903-77) a French writer of NOVELS, best known work for her own personal story written in her *Journals* 阿娜伊丝·宁（1903-77），法国小说家。最有名的作品是描述她个人亲身经历的《日记》

Ni·ña, the /ˈninə; ˈniːnə/ one of the three ships that sailed to America with Christopher Columbus in 1492. The other two were the 'Pinta' and the 'Santa Maria'. "尼娜"号〔1492年克里斯托弗·哥伦布首航美洲时所用的三艘船之一，另外两艘船分别是"平塔"号和"圣马利亚"号〕

nin·com·poop /ˈnɪŋkəm,pup; ˈnɪŋkəmpuːp/ *n* [C] *old-fashioned* a stupid person【过时】笨人，傻瓜

nine /naɪn; naɪn/ *number* **1** 9 九（个）—see table on page C1 参见 C1 页附录 **2 nine times out of ten** almost always 十之八九，几乎总是，几乎每次：*Nine times out of ten it's careless driving that causes an accident.* 事故十之八九是由于驾驶不谨慎造成的。**3 nine days' wonder** a thing or event that makes people very excited for a short time 轰动一时（即被遗忘）的事物；昙花一现的新鲜事 —see also 另见 **dressed up to the nines** (DRESSED (5)), **be on cloud nine** (CLOUD[1] (4))

nine·pins /ˈnaɪn,pɪnz; ˈnaɪn,pɪnz/ *n* [U] a game in which you roll a ball at nine bottle-shaped objects to try to knock them down 九柱滚球戏

nine·teen /,naɪnˈtin; ,naɪnˈtiːn◂/ *number* **1** 19 十九（个）—see table on page C1 参见 C1 页附录 **2 nineteen to the dozen** if you talk nineteen to the dozen, you talk very quickly and without stopping 说个不停，喋喋不休 —**nineteenth** *adj*

1984, Nineteen Eighty-Four (1949) a NOVEL by George Orwell which describes an imaginary society of the future, where the government has complete control of everyone's lives, thoughts, and behaviour, and watches everything they do. The leader of this government is called Big Brother. The book has had a great influence on the way that people think about and talk about politics, and people sometimes use the phrase 1984 to describe a society that is too strictly controlled.《一九八四》〔乔治·奥威尔1949年所著的一部小说。小说描写了一个虚构的未来社会，政府完全控制每个人的生活、思想和行为，监视每个人的一举一动。其领袖人物叫"老大哥"。此书对人们思考和谈论政治问题的方式产生了重大影响，以至于大家有时会借用"1984"来形容一个控制得过于严厉的社会〕—see 见 the THOUGHT POLICE

nine·teenth /ˈnaɪnˈtinθ; ,naɪnˈtiːnθ◂/ *number* [singular] *humorous* an expression used by GOLF players meaning the bar where they drink after playing【幽默】第十九洞〔指高尔夫球员在打球后喝酒聊天的酒吧〕

nine-to-five /,· · ˈ·◂/ *adv* **work nine-to-five** to work from 9 o'clock until 5 o'clock; the normal working hours of an office worker 从早上9点工作到下午5点〔早上9点至下午5点是办公室工作人员正常的工作时间〕—**nine-to-five** *adj*: *a nine-to-five job* 一份朝九晚五的工作

nine·ty /ˈnaɪntɪ; ˈnaɪnti/ *number* **1** 90 九十（个）—see table on page C1 参见 C1 页附录 **2 the nineties** also 又作 **the '90's, the 1990's**; the years from 1990 to 1999 20世纪90年代 **3 be in your nineties** to be aged from ninety to ninety-nine 九十多岁：*My grandparents are both in their nineties.* 我的祖父母都九十多岁了。—**ninetieth** *number*

Nin·e·veh /ˈnɪnɪvə; ˈnɪnɪ̈və/ the capital of Assyria, an ancient empire, on the east bank of the River Tigris, in what is now Iraq. The ruins of many beautiful ancient buildings have been found buried there. 尼尼微〔古亚述帝国的首都，位于底格里斯河东岸，即现在的伊拉克境内。该地已发掘了许多精美古建筑的遗址〕

nin·ja /ˈnɪndʒə; ˈnɪndʒə/ *n* [C] a member of a Japanese class of professional killers in former times〔旧时的〕忍者，日本武士：*a ninja warrior* 忍者

nin·ny /ˈnɪnɪ; ˈnɪni/ *n* [C] *old-fashioned* a silly person【过时】笨人，傻瓜

N

Nin·ten·do /nɪn`tɛndo; nɪn'tendəʊ/ *trademark* a type of computer games machine made by the Japanese company Nintendo, which is used to play video games on a television screen. Nintendo also makes the GameBoy, a small games machine that you hold in your hand.【商标】任天堂游戏机〔日本任天堂公司生产的一种游戏机, 可在电视机屏幕上玩电子游戏。该公司还生产了一种叫"游戏小子"的掌上游戏机〕

ninth¹ /naɪnθ; naɪnθ/ *number* 9th 第九 —see table on page C1 参见 C1 页附录

ninth² *n* [C] one of nine equal parts of something 九分之一

nip¹ /nɪp; nɪp/ *v* **nipped, nipping 1** [T] to bite someone or something lightly 轻咬: *The dog nipped my ankles.* 那只狗轻轻地咬了一下我的脚踝。**2** [I always+adv/prep] *BrE informal* to go somewhere quickly or for a short time【英, 非正式】快走; 急忙离去; 去一会儿: [+in/down/out etc] *I'm just nipping out to the shops – I'll be back in five minutes.* 我只是去一下商店, 五分钟后就回来。| *Another car nipped in* (=nipped into a space) *in front of me.* 又一辆车突然插到我前面。**3 nip sth in the bud** to prevent something from becoming a problem by stopping it as soon as it starts 把某事物消灭在萌芽状态; 对某事物从开始即加以阻止: *If you feel a cold coming on try to nip it in the bud by keeping warm and getting a lot of sleep.* 如果你感觉要感冒了, 就穿暖些, 多睡觉, 不让它进一步恶化。**4** [T] *BrE* to suddenly and accidentally press something tightly between two edges or surfaces【英】夹; 钳; 掐; 捏: *He nipped his finger in the door.* 他的手指被门夹了一下。

nip sth ↔ **off** *phr v* [T] to remove a small part of something, especially a plant, by pressing it tightly between your finger and thumb 掐掉, 摘去〔尤指植物〕: *She nipped off a dead flower.* 她掐掉了一朵凋谢的花。

nip² *n* [C] **1** the act or result of pressing something between two edges or biting it lightly 夹; 钳; 掐; 捏; 轻咬 **2** a small amount of strong alcoholic drink 少量的烈性酒: [+of] *a nip of brandy* 一点儿白兰地酒 **3 a nip in the air** coldness in the air 寒气, 寒冷 **4 nip and tuck** *AmE informal*【美, 非正式】**a)** if two competitors are nip and tuck in a race or competition, they are doing equally well; **neck and neck** (NECK¹ (11)) 并驾齐驱, 不相上下: *They were nip and tuck in the last lap of the race.* 他们比赛到最后一圈时仍难分高低。**b)** equally likely to happen or not happen 概率相等, 均有可能: *I might just make it to the airport, but it'll be nip and tuck.* 我也许能及时赶到机场, 但这很难说。

nipp·er /`nɪpɚ; 'nɪpə/ *n* [C] *BrE informal* a child, especially a small boy【英, 非正式】小孩〔尤指男孩〕

nip·ple /`nɪpl̩; 'nɪpəl/ *n* [C] **1** the small dark circular part of a woman's breast, through which a baby sucks milk〔女人的〕乳头 —see picture at 参见 BODY 图 **2** one of the two small dark circular parts on a man's chest〔男人的〕乳头 —see picture at 参见 BODY 图 **3** *AmE* the rubber part on a baby's bottle that a baby sucks milk through【美】〔奶瓶的〕橡皮奶嘴; TEAT (1) *BrE*【英】**4** a small thing shaped like a nipple on a machine, with a hole in it which you pour oil through〔机器上的〕(乳头状) 注油口; 加油嘴

nip·py /`nɪpɪ; 'nɪpi/ *adj informal*【非正式】**1** weather that is nippy is slightly cold〔天气〕有点冷的, 冷飕飕的: *It's rather nippy out there.* 外面有点冷飕飕的。**2** *BrE* moving quickly or able to move quickly【英】敏捷的, 动作快的: *a nippy little car* 一辆快速的小汽车 —**nippiness** *n* [U] —**nippily** *adv*

Nir·va·na /nɪr`vɑnə; nɪə'vɑːnə/ a US band who developed a new style of ROCK music called grunge, which was popular in the early 1990s, and whose lead singer was Kurt Cobain. Their ALBUMS include *Nevermind* and *In Utero*. "涅槃"乐队〔美国一摇滚乐队。该乐队开创了一种新的名为 Grunge (垃圾摇滚) 的摇滚乐风格, 20 世纪 90 年代早期曾盛极一时。主唱是库尔特·科巴恩。该乐队的专辑有《别介意》和《回归母体》〕

nirvana *n* [U] **1** *technical* a state of knowledge or understanding that is beyond life and death, suffering, and change, and is the aim of believers in Buddhism【术语】〔佛教的〕涅槃; 解脱 **2** *informal* a condition of great happiness and a feeling of peace【非正式】极乐世界, 无忧无虑的境界

ni·si /`naɪsaɪ; 'naɪsaɪ/ *n* —see 见 DECREE NISI

nit /nɪt; nɪt/ *n* [C] **1** an egg of a LOUSE (=a small insect that sucks blood), that is sometimes found in people's hair 虱卵, 虮子 **2** *BrE informal* a silly person【英, 非正式】笨蛋, 傻瓜

nit·pick·ing /`nɪt,pɪkɪŋ; 'nɪt,pɪkɪŋ/ *n* [U] *informal* the annoying habit of arguing about unimportant details, especially in someone's work【非正式】〔尤指对某人的工作〕挑剔, 吹毛求疵 —**nitpicking** *adj* —**nitpicker** *n* [C]

ni·trate /`naɪtret; 'naɪtreɪt/ *n* [C,U] a chemical compound that is mainly used to improve the soil for growing crops 硝酸盐〔主要用作肥料〕

ni·tre *BrE*【英】, **niter** *AmE*【美】/`naɪtɚ; 'naɪtə/ *n* [U] one of several natural nitrates, including SALTPETRE 硝石

ni·tric ac·id /,naɪtrɪk `æsɪd; ,naɪtrɪk 'æsɪ̈d/ *n* [U] a powerful acid that is used in explosives and other chemical products 硝酸

ni·tro·gen /`naɪtrədʒən; 'naɪtrədʒən/ *n* [U] a gas that is an ELEMENT (=a simple substance) without colour or smell, that forms most of the Earth's air 氮(气)

ni·tro·gly·ce·rine, nitroglycerin /,naɪtrə`glɪsərɪn; ,naɪtrəʊ'glɪsərɪ̈n/ *n* [U] a powerful liquid explosive 硝化甘油

nit·ty-grit·ty /`nɪtɪ `grɪtɪ; ,nɪti 'grɪti/ *n informal*【非正式】**the nitty-gritty** the basic and practical facts of a subject or activity 基本内容; 实质性部分: **get down to the nitty-gritty** *Let's get down to the nitty-gritty and work out the costs, shall we?* 让我们来谈谈实质性问题, 把成本计算出来, 好吗?

nit·wit /`nɪt,wɪt; 'nɪt-wɪt/ *n* [C] *informal* a silly person【非正式】笨蛋, 傻瓜

nix¹ /nɪks; nɪks/ *adv AmE old-fashioned* no【美, 过时】不, 不行

nix² *v* [T] *AmE old-fashioned* to answer no to something or FORBID something【美, 过时】拒绝, 否决; 禁止: *They nixed the idea of filming in Ireland.* 他们否决了在爱尔兰拍摄的建议。

Nix·on /`nɪksən; 'nɪksən/, **Richard** (1913-94) a US politician in the Republican Party who was President of the US from 1969 to 1974. He helped to end the Vietnam War and improved the US's political relationship with China. He is most famous for being involved in Watergate and for officially leaving his position as President before Congress could IMPEACH him (=charge him with a serious crime). Many people thought he was dishonest, and because of this he was sometimes called 'Tricky Dicky'. 尼克松〔(1913-1994), 美国共和党政治家, 1969 年至 1974 年间任美国总统。他为结束越战付出了努力, 并改善了中美政治关系。他因卷入"水门事件"而相当出名, 未等到国会弹劾他就正式辞去总统职务。有些人认为他不诚实, 因此有时称他为"狡猾的迪克"〕

NJ the written abbreviation of 缩写= NEW JERSEY

N·kru·mah /əŋ`krumə; əŋ'kruːmə/, **Kwa·me** /`kwɑmɪ; 'kwɑːmi/ (1909-72) a Ghanaian politician who led his country's fight for independence from the UK. He was Prime Minister (1952-60) and President (1960-66), but he was eventually removed from power by the army. 恩克鲁玛〔(1909-1972), 加纳政治家。他曾领导国人进行脱离英国的独立斗争。他先后任加纳总理 (1952-1960) 和总统 (1960-1966), 最后被军方废黜〕

NLRB, the /,ɛn ɛl ɑr `bi; ,en el ɑː 'biː/ the abbreviation of 缩写= the NATIONAL LABOR RELATIONS BOARD

NM the written abbreviation of 缩写= NEW MEXICO

NME, The /,ɛn ɛm `i; ,en em 'iː/ the New Musical Express; a British weekly newspaper about ROCK and POP music《新音乐快讯》〔英国一摇滚乐和流行乐周报〕

no *plural* **nos.** the written abbreviation of 缩写= NUMBER

no¹ /no; nəʊ/ *adv* **1** *spoken* used to give a negative reply to a question, offer, or request【口】不, 不行〔对问题、提议或请求表示否定或拒绝〕: *"Are you Italian?" "No, I'm Spanish."* "你是意大利人吗?" "不, 我是西班牙人。" | *"Do you want any more?" "No thanks."* "你还要再来点儿吗?" "不要了, 谢谢。" | *"Could you help me write this?" "No, sorry, I haven't got time at the moment."* "你能帮我写吗?" "抱歉, 不行, 我现在没时间。" | **say no** *Would you be terribly offended if I said no?* 如果我拒绝的话, 你会很生气吗? | **the answer's no** *If she asks to borrow any money, the answer's no!* 她要是想借钱, 休想! —opposite 反义词 YES¹ (1) **2** *spoken* used to say that you disagree with a statement【口】不, 不是〔表示不同意〕: *"You're always complaining about things." "No, I'm not!"* "你总是爱发牢骚。" "不, 我没有。" **3** *spoken* used to say that you agree with a negative statement【口】是, 对〔对否定陈述表示赞同〕: *"They shouldn't be charging such high prices." "No, it's ridiculous!"* "他们不该要这么高的价钱。" "没错, 太离谱了!" **4 won't take no for an answer** if someone won't take no for an answer, they say firmly that you must do something 不能接受否定的回答: *You simply must come to dinner, and I won't take no for an answer.* 你必须来吃晚饭, 非来不可。**5** *spoken* used to show that you are shocked, surprised, annoyed, or disappointed by what someone has just told you, or by what has just happened【口】不会吧, 不可能〔表示惊讶、生气或失望〕: *"This skirt cost me £7." "No!"* "这条裙子花了我 7 英镑。" "不会吧!" | **Oh no** *Oh no, not another false alarm?* 哦, 不会又是一次假警报吧? **6 no good/no use etc** not at all good, not at all useful etc 没有任何好处/没有用等: *This*

map's no use – it's out of date. 这张地图毫无用处，早就过时了。| *I'm no good at physics.* 我的物理很差。**7 no better/no more/no less etc** not better, not more etc 不比…好/不多于/不少于等: *They've written no fewer than ten letters of complaint and still nothing's been done.* 他们已经写了不少于十封投诉信，但什么问题也没解决。**8 no small part/no great matter etc** *formal* a large part, a small matter etc【正式】大作用/小事等: *a question of no great importance* (=of little importance) 无关紧要的问题 | *She had no small part* (=had a large part) *in its success.* 此事成功她大有功劳。

no² *determiner* **1** not one or not any 没有，无: *Do you mind having black coffee? There's no milk.* 喝不加奶的咖啡你介意吗？没有牛奶了。| *There're no buses in this part of town.* 城里这一带没有公共汽车。| *a house with no central heating* 没有中央暖气系统的房子 | **be no reason why** *There's no reason at all why Jenny shouldn't come along too.* 珍妮不一起来完全没有理由。**2** used on a notice to say that something is forbidden 不准，不许〔用于告示中表示禁止某事〕: *No parking* 禁止停车 | *No smoking* 禁止吸烟 **3 in no time** *informal* very soon or very quickly【非正式】很快，马上: *We're almost home now – we'll be there in no time.* 我们快到家了，转眼就到。**4 there's no knowing/telling/saying etc** *spoken* used to say that it is impossible to guess what will happen or what is true【口】谁也说不准，不可能知道[说清]: *He's such a strange person – there's no knowing what he'll do next.* 他这人很怪，谁也说不准他下一步会做什么。**5 be no fool/expert/friend etc** to be not at all stupid etc 根本不是傻瓜/专家/朋友等: *Larry's no friend of mine.* 拉里根本不是我的朋友。

USAGE NOTE 用法说明: NO
GRAMMAR 语法
No is used before nouns and adjectives when it means 'not any'. no 用在名词和形容词前表示"没有"、"并不": *No problem.* 没问题。| *That's no good – it's broken.* 那没有用，已经破了。| *He's no slimmer than he was before.* 他跟以前一样胖。
Otherwise **not** is used, especially before *a, all, many, much,* and *enough.* 其他情况下则用 not, 尤其是在 a, all, many, much 和 enough 之前: *Not many tourists come here.* 来这儿的游客不多。| *not enough food for all of us* 食物不够大家吃 | *She's not stupid.* 她不笨。| *The news was not good.* 这不是一个好消息。
SPELLING 拼法
Nobody meaning 'no one' is always spelt as one word. 表示"没有人"的 nobody 是连在一起拼写的一个单词: *There was nobody there* (=no person). 那里没有人。Compare 比较: *There was no body there* (=there was not a dead body there). 那里没有尸体。

no³ *n plural* **noes 1** [singular] a negative answer or decision 不，拒绝；否定，否认: *The answer was a definite no.* 答复是明确的拒绝。**2 noes** [plural] votes against a proposal in parliament〔议会中的〕反对票

No. 10, Num·ber Ten /ˌnʌmbrə ˈten; ˌnʌmbə ˈten/ *n* [singular] also 又作 **No. 10 Downing Street** the official home of the British Prime Minister. The expression is also used, especially in newspapers and news broadcasts to mean the Prime Minister and his or her advisers 唐宁街10号〔英国首相官邸。该词多用于报纸和新闻报道，指称首相及其顾问〕: *This suggestion won't be welcomed at No. 10.* 这个建议不会得到首相的赞同。| *Sources close to Number 10 say there will be no change in the Cabinet.* 据首相圈内的消息人士透露，内阁班子将无变动。

No. 11, Number E·lev·en /ˌnʌmbər ɪˈlevən; ˌnʌmbər ɪˈlevən/ also 又作 **No. 11 Downing Street** the official home of the British Chancellor of the Exchequer (=the chief financial minister) 唐宁街11号〔英国财政大臣官邸〕

no-ac·count /ˈ· ·ˌ·/ *adj AmE*【美】another form of the word NO-COUNT no-count 的另一种形式: *a series of no-account boyfriends who drank too much* 一个接一个没出息的酗酒男友

No·ah /ˈnoə; ˈnəʊə/ in the Old Testament of the Bible, a man chosen by God to build an ARK (=a large boat) so that he could save his family and two of every kind of animal that lived on the Earth from the terrible Flood which covered the Earth 诺亚〔《圣经·旧约》中被上帝选中制造一艘方舟的人。他造舟的目的是为了拯救自己的家人，还有地球上生存的每种动物各一对，以免被席卷大地的可怕"大洪水"吞噬〕

Noah's ark *n* [singular] the large boat which Noah built, according to the Bible, to save his family and two of every type of animal from a flood sent by God 诺亚方舟〔《圣经》中诺亚建造的大船，用来拯救自己的家人，还有每种动物各一对，以免被上帝造的"大洪水"吞噬〕—see 见 the FLOOD

nob /nɑb; nɒb/ *n* [C] *BrE old-fashioned* a rich person with a high social position【英，过时】有钱有势的人，上流人物: *They watched the nobs in their satin and feathers.* 他们注视着穿着华丽的上流人物。

no ball /ˈ· ·/ *n* [C] an act of bowling (BOWL² (1, 2)) the ball, in games such as CRICKET, in a way not allowed by the rules〔板球等球类运动中的〕投球犯规

nob·ble /ˈnɑbl; ˈnɒbəl/ *v* [T] *BrE informal*【英，非正式】**1** to get someone's attention, especially in order to persuade them to do something〔尤指为说服某人做某事而〕引起〔某人〕的注意: *I'll try to nobble Jim and ask him if he'll help us.* 我会努力接近吉姆，问他能不能帮助我们。**2** to make someone do what you want by offering them money or threatening them 收买；要挟 **3** to prevent a horse from winning a race, especially by giving it drugs〔尤指给赛马服药〕使不能取胜

No·bel /noˈbɛl; nəʊˈbel/, **Al·fred** /ˈælfrɪd; ˈælfrɨd/ (1833-96) a Swedish engineer and CHEMIST who invented DYNAMITE (=a powerful explosive substance) and became very wealthy from his factories that produced explosives. When he died, he left all his money to establish the Nobel Prizes. 诺贝尔〔(1833-1896)，瑞典工程师、化学家。他发明了炸药，并创办炸药厂而成为巨富。他去世时将全部遗产捐出，设立了诺贝尔奖〕

No·bel prize /noˌbɛl ˈpraɪz; nəʊˌbel ˈpraɪz/ *n* [C] one of the prizes given each year to people who have done important work in various types of activity. There are prizes for special achievements in PHYSICS, chemistry, economics, PHYSIOLOGY or medicine, literature, and peace. The Nobel prizes were established by Alfred Nobel and are given in Sweden. It is a great honour to receive a Nobel prize, and people who have received them are sometimes called **Nobel laureates** 诺贝尔奖〔一年一度授予各领域中有重大贡献者的奖项。奖项分物理学奖、化学奖、经济学奖、生理学或医学奖、文学奖与和平奖。该奖由阿尔弗雷德·诺贝尔设立，在瑞典颁发。获得诺贝尔奖是一种极高的荣誉，获奖者有时被称作 Nobel laureate (诺贝尔奖得主)〕

no·bil·i·ty /noˈbɪlətɪ; nəʊˈbɪlɨti/ *n* **1 the nobility** the group of people in some countries who belong to the highest social class and have titles such as Duke or Countess; the ARISTOCRACY 贵族(阶层) **2** [U] the quality of being noble in character or appearance 崇高，高贵: *For him, true nobility is found in hard work.* 对他来说，真正的高尚在于勤奋。

no·ble¹ /ˈnobl; ˈnəʊbəl/ *adj* **1** someone who is noble behaves in a morally good or generous way that should be admired 高尚的，崇高的；豁达的: *It's very noble of you to spend all your weekends helping the old folk.* 你心地真好，把周末时间全部用来帮助老人。| *noble ideals* 崇高的理想 **2** something that is noble is very impressive and beautiful 宏伟的，堂皇的，壮丽的: *this noble monument to our war heroes* 宏伟的战争英雄纪念碑 **3** belonging to the nobility 贵族的，显贵的: *a man of noble birth* 贵族出身的人 **4** a noble metal, such as gold or silver, is not affected chemically by the air〔金、银等贵金属〕不〔与空气〕起化学变化的，不易锈蚀的 —compare 比较 BASE METAL

noble² *n* [C] a member of the highest social class with a title such as Duke or Countess, especially in the past〔尤指旧时的〕贵族〈如公爵或女伯爵〉: *a vast gathering of kings and nobles* 一大群王公贵族 —compare 比较 COMMONER

no·ble·man /ˈnoblmən; ˈnəʊbəlmən/ *n plural* **noblemen** /-mən; -mən/ [C] a man who is a member of the highest social class and has a title such as Duke (男)贵族〈如公爵〉

no·blesse o·blige /noˈblɛs oˈbliʒ; nəʊˌbles əˈbliːʒ/ *n French* used to mean that people who belong to a high social class should be generous and behave with honour【法】位高则任重；贵人行为理应高尚

no·ble·wom·an /ˈnoblˌwʊmən; ˈnəʊbəlˌwʊmən/ *n plural* **noblewomen** /-ˌwɪmɪn; -ˌwɪmɨn/ [C] a woman who is a member of the highest social class with a title such as Duchess 女贵族〈如女公爵或公爵夫人〉

no·bly /ˈnoblɪ; ˈnəʊbli/ *adv* **1** in a morally good or generous way that should be admired 崇高地，高尚地；豁达地: *great pain nobly borne* 从容地承受巨大的痛苦 **2 nobly born** *literary* having parents who are members of the NOBILITY (1)【文】出身于贵族的

no·bod·y¹ /ˈnoˌbɑdɪ; ˈnəʊbədi/ *pron* no one 没有人，无人，谁也不: *I knocked on the door but nobody answered.* 我敲了敲门，但没人来开。—see also 另见 **like nobody's business** (BUSINESS (24)), **be nobody's fool** (FOOL¹ (3)) —see 见 NO² (USAGE) 

nobody² *n* [C] someone who is not important and has no influence 无名小卒, 小人物, 无足轻重的人: *I'm tired of being a nobody!* 我再也不想当无名小卒了!

no-claims bo·nus /ˌ·ˈ· ,ˈ··/ *n* [C] *BrE* a reduction in the amount that you have to pay for car insurance, because you have not made any claims【英】无索偿折扣, 无索偿奖励, 无赔款回扣〔指汽车保险, 如在保险期间未有任何赔款要求, 可以给予一定回扣〕

no-count /ˈ· ·/ *adj* [only before noun 仅用于名词前] *AmE* a no-count person never achieves very much because they are very lazy【美】没出息的, 混日子的, 不长进的: *my no-count good-for-nothing nephew* 我那个一无所长没出息的侄子

noc·tur·nal /nɑkˈtɝnəl; nɒkˈtɜːnl/ *adj* **1** *technical* an animal that is nocturnal is active at night【术语】〔动物〕夜间活动的: *Hamsters are nocturnal creatures.* 仓鼠是夜间出没的动物。**2** *formal* happening at night【正式】夜间发生的: *nocturnal visits* 夜访 —**nocturnally** *adv*

noc·turne /ˈnɑktɝn; ˈnɒktɜːn/ *n* [C] a piece of music, especially a soft beautiful piece of piano music〔尤指用钢琴弹奏的〕夜曲

nod 点头

The lady nodded her head. 那位女士点了点头。

Sam shook his head. 萨姆摇了摇头。

W2 **nod¹** /nɑd; nɒd/ *v* **nodded, nodding** [I,T] **1** to move your head up and down, especially in order to show agreement or understanding〔尤指表示赞同或理解而〕点头: *I asked her if she was ready to go, and she nodded.* 我问她是否已准备好出发, 她点了点头。| **nod your head** *Jane nodded her head sympathetically.* 简同情地点了点头。| **nod your approval/agreement etc** (=show your approval etc by nodding) 点头表示赞成/同意等 **2** to move your head down and up again once in order to greet someone or give someone a sign to do something 点头〔打招呼或示意〕: [**+at/to**] *The judge nodded at the foreman to proceed.* 法官点头示意陪审团团长继续说下去。| *She nodded to us as she walked by.* 她从我们身边走过时向我们点了点头。**3 be on nodding terms (with)/have a nodding acquaintance (with)** to know someone slightly or know a little about a subject〔与某人〕只是点头之交;〔对某事〕略知一二: *Burke was already on nodding terms with a number of senators.* 伯克已经与一些参议员有了点头之交。| *a nodding acquaintance with local history* 对当地历史略知一二

nod off *phr v* [I] to begin to sleep, when you do not intend to 打盹儿, 打瞌睡: *I missed the movie because I'd nodded off.* 我打了个盹儿, 结果没有看到电影。

nod² *n* **1** [C] an act of nodding 点头: *The woman greeted us with a nod of the head.* 那个女人向我们点头打招呼。| **give a nod** *I showed the doorman my card and he gave a friendly nod.* 我向门卫出示证件, 他友善地点了一下头。**2 give sb the nod** *BrE informal* to give someone permission to do something【英, 非正式】点头同意某人〔做某事〕: *We're waiting for the boss to give us the nod on this one.* 我们都在等着老板的同意。**3 a nod's as good as a wink** *humorous* used to tell someone that you have understood something, although it was said in an indirect way【幽默】不用明说, 不用多说; 一暗示就明白 **4 on the nod** *BrE informal* by general agreement and without discussion【英, 非正式】无异议地; 无反对地: *The chairman's proposals are usually passed on the nod.* 主席的提议通常在无人反对的情况下一致通过。—see also 另见 **the land of nod** (LAND¹ (9))

no·dal /ˈnodl; ˈnəʊdl/ *adj technical* connected with nodes【术语】节的; 结的: *nodal root systems* 茎节的根系

nod·dle /ˈnɑdḷ; ˈnɒdl/ *n* [C] *BrE old-fashioned* your head or brain【英, 过时】头; 头脑; NOODLE *AmE*【美】: *It's easy enough to do if you just use your noddle.* 这事很容易, 你只要动动脑筋就行了。

Nod·dy /ˈnɑdɪ; ˈnɒdi/ *trademark* a character in children's books by the British writer Enid Blyton. He wears a little blue hat with a bell on the top, and drives a yellow and red car around Toytown, with his friend Big Ears.【商标】诺迪〔英国作家伊妮德·布莱顿创作的儿童作品中的人物。他戴着一顶蓝色小帽, 帽顶上有一只铃铛, 与朋友大耳朵一起驾着一辆红黄相间的汽车周游玩具城〕

node /nod; nəʊd/ *n* [C] **1** the place on the stem of a plant from which a leaf or branch grows 茎节〔植物茎上长叶的部分〕**2** a place where lines in a network, GRAPH etc meet or join〔线条的〕交点; 结点 **3** a LYMPH NODE 淋巴结

nod·ule /ˈnɑdʒul; ˈnɒdjuːl/ *n* [C] a small round raised part, especially a small swelling on a plant or someone's body〔植物的〕小结节;〔人体的〕小瘤 —**nodular** *adj*

No·el /noˈɛl; nəʊˈel/ *n* [U] a word used in songs, on cards etc meaning CHRISTMAS 圣诞节〔常用于歌词、贺卡中〕

noes /noz; nəʊz/ the plural of NO³

no-fly zone /ˌ·ˈ· ,·/ *n* [C] an area that no airplane is allowed to enter, and in which it would be attacked 禁飞区

nog·gin /ˈnɑgɪn; ˈnɒgɪn/ *n* [C] *old-fashioned*【过时】**1** a small amount of an alcoholic drink 一小杯酒 **2** *informal* your head or brain【非正式】头; 脑袋: *Use your noggin. Don't light a match in here.* 动动脑子, 别在这里点火柴。

no-go ar·e·a /ˌ·ˈ· ,ˈ···/ *n* [C] **1** an area in a city that is controlled by a violent group and is dangerous for anyone else to enter〔城市里由暴力分子控制的〕危险地带; 禁区: *They had taken a wrong turning and now found themselves in one of the most dangerous no-go areas in the city.* 他们拐错了弯, 结果进入了市内最危险的地区之一。**2** a subject that cannot be discussed because it may offend people 忌讳的话题

no·how /ˈnoˌhaʊ; ˈnəʊhaʊ/ *adv usually humorous* not in any way or in any situation【一般幽默】决不; 毫不, 一点也不: *I never liked her nohow.* 我从未喜欢过她。

noise¹ /nɔɪz; nɔɪz/ *n* S2 W2

1 ▶SOUND 声音◀ [C,U] sound, especially a loud or unpleasant sound 噪音, 杂音; 嘈杂声, 喧闹声: *the noise of the traffic* 交通噪音 | *a loud cracking noise* 巨大的爆裂声 | **make (a) noise** *Try not to make a noise when you go upstairs.* 上楼时尽量不要弄出声。| *Stop making so much noise.* 别吵了。

2 make polite/encouraging etc noises to talk in a way that sounds polite, encouraging etc 说客气/鼓励等的话: *My teacher made encouraging noises when I told her I wanted to go to university.* 我告诉老师我想上大学时, 她连声鼓励。| **make the right noises** (=pretend to be concerned about or interested in what someone is saying) 随声附和;〔对某人所说的话〕假装感兴趣

3 make a noise about to complain a lot about something so that other people will notice 对…不停地抱怨

4 ▶ELECTRICAL 电的◀ [U] *technical* unwanted signals produced by an electrical CIRCUIT【术语】杂音; 干扰

5 ▶COMPUTERS 电脑◀ [U] *technical* pieces of unwanted information that can prevent a computer from working effectively【术语】噪声 —see also 另见 BIG NOISE

USAGE NOTE 用法说明: NOISE

WORD CHOICE 词语辨析: **noise, sound, racket, voice**

A **sound** is anything that you hear. sound 指人所听到的任何声音: *I love the sound of the sea.* 我喜欢听大海的声音。| *the sound of voices/a guitar/breaking glass* 人声/吉他声/打碎玻璃的声音

A **noise** is usually an unpleasant sound, often not made by a person. noise 通常指难听的声音, 往往不是由人发出的: *"What's that noise?" she asked nervously.* "那是什么声音?" 她紧张地问道。| *They had to shout to make themselves heard above the noise of the machines.* 他们不得不大声叫喊, 这样才能压过机器的噪声让别人听到自己说话。

A **voice** is the sound of a person speaking or singing. voice 指人说话或唱歌的声音: *We heard voices outside.* 我们听到外面有人声。| *She has rather a high-pitched voice.* 她的嗓音很尖。

Racket is an informal word for a loud unpleasant noise. racket 是表示音量大而难听的噪音的非正式用词: *They're making a hell of a racket next door.* 他们在隔壁发出很大的噪音。

noise² *v* **be noised abroad/about/around** *old-fashioned, especially BrE* if news or information is noised abroad people are talking about it【过时, 尤英】〔消息〕传播出去: *Rumours of*

N

an election are being noised abroad. 要进行一场选举的谣言到处传开了。

noise·less·ly /ˋnɔɪzlɪslɪ; ˈnɔɪzləsli/ *adv* without making any sound 无声无息地, 静悄悄地: *We crept noiselessly down the hall.* 我们悄悄地穿过大厅。**—noiseless** *adj*: *noiseless tears* 无声的眼泪 **—noiselessness** *n* [U]

noise pol·lu·tion /ˈ· ·, ·ˈ·/ *n* [U] very loud or continuous loud noise which is considered to be harmful to people 噪声污染

noi·some /ˋnɔɪsəm; ˈnɔɪsəm/ *adj literary* extremely unpleasant【文】极糟的; 十分令人不快的: *The workers lived in noisome slums.* 工人们生活在条件十分恶劣的贫民窟里。

3 **nois·y** /ˋnɔɪzɪ; ˈnɔɪzi/ *adj* making a lot of noise, or full of noise 噪音大的, 嘈杂的, 喧闹的: *The kids have been really noisy today.* 孩子们今天实在很吵闹。| *The bar was too noisy and crowded.* 酒吧太吵太挤了。| *a noisy engine* 噪音大的发动机 **—noisily** *adv*: *The children chattered noisily.* 孩子们在哇啦哇啦地聊天。**—noisiness** *n* [U]

no·mad /ˋnomæd; ˈnəʊmæd/ *n* [C] a member of a tribe that travels from place to place, especially to find grass for their animals 游牧民, 游牧部落中的一员 **—nomadic** /noˋmædɪk; nəʊˈmædɪk/ *adj*: *a nomadic people* 游牧民族

no-man's-land /ˈ· · ,·/ *n* [singular, U] an area of land that no one owns or controls, especially an area between two borders or opposing armies〔尤指边界处或敌对阵地间的〕无人地带; 真空地带

nom de plume /ˌnɑm də ˌplum; ˌnɒm də ˈpluːm/ *n* [C] a name used by a writer instead of their real name 笔名

no·men·cla·ture /ˋnomən,kletʃɚ; nəʊˈmeŋklətʃə/ *n* [C, U] *formal* a system of naming things, especially in science【正式】〔尤指科学上的〕命名法: *medical nomenclature* 医学命名法

nom·i·nal /ˋnɑmənl; ˈnɒmɪnəl/ *adj* **1 nominal head/leader etc** someone who has the title of leader etc but is not really doing that job 名义上的负责人/领导人等: *Longo was the real power in the Communist Party while Togliatti was merely the nominal head.* 朗哥是共产党中的真正掌权人物, 而陶里亚蒂只是名义上的领袖。**2** a nominal sum of money is very small, especially when compared with the usual amount that would be paid for something〔金额〕极小的, 微不足道的, 象征性的: *Golfers may play this course for a nominal fee in the off-peak season.* 打高尔夫球者在淡季只需象征性地付一点费用就可以在这块球场上打球。**3** *technical* connected with or used as a noun【术语】名词性的, 作名词用的: *nominal endings such as 'ness' and 'ation'* 诸如 ness 和 ation 等的名词性词尾

nom·i·nal·ly /ˋnɑmənlɪ; ˈnɒmɪnəli/ *adv* officially described as something when this is not really true 名义上: *Although Banda is nominally a Christian island, few of its inhabitants actually attend church.* 虽然班达名义上是个基督教岛屿, 但居民中很少有人去教堂做礼拜。

nom·i·nate /ˋnɑmə,net; ˈnɒmɪneɪt/ *v* [T] **1** to officially suggest someone for an important position, duty, or prize 提名, 推荐: **nominate sb for sth** *He was nominated for the Nobel Prize.* 他获得诺贝尔奖提名。| **nominate sb as** *BrE*【英】*I wish to nominate Jane Morrison as president of the club.* 我想提名简·莫里森为本俱乐部的主席。| **nominate sb to do sth** *I nominate John to represent us at the meeting.* 我推荐约翰代表我们出席会议。**2** to choose someone for a particular job 任命, 委任, 指定: **nominate sb as** *The director nominated me as her official representative at the conference.* 那位董事指定我为她的正式代表出席会议。| **nominate sb to sth** *She was nominated to the legislative council.* 她被任命为立法委员会委员。

nom·i·na·tion /ˌnɑməˋneʃən; ˌnɒmɪˈneɪʃən/ *n* **1** [C,U] the act of officially suggesting someone for a position, honour or prize, or the fact of being suggested for it (被) 提名: **[+for]** *Who will get the Republican nomination for president?* 谁会被共和党提名竞逐总统呢? | *All the committee's nominations were approved.* 该委员会的所有提名均获得批准。**2** [C] the name of a book, film, actor etc that has been suggested to receive an honour or prize〔书、电影、演员等的〕(被) 提名〔获奖〕: *'Schindler's List' was an obvious nomination for an Oscar.*《辛德勒的名单》显然是角逐奥斯卡奖的提名影片。**3** [C,U] the act of choosing someone for a particular job, or the fact of being chosen (被) 任命, (被) 指定: **[+as]** *O'Neil's nomination as chief executive* 任命奥尼尔为行政总裁

nom·i·na·tive /ˋnɑmənətɪv; ˈnɒmɪnətɪv/ *n* [C] *technical* a particular form of a noun in some languages, such as Latin and German, which shows that the noun is the SUBJECT[1] (5) of a verb【术语】主格 **—nominative** *adj*

nom·i·nee /ˌnɑməˋni; ˌnɒmɪˈniː/ *n* [C] someone who has been suggested for a prize, duty, or honour 被提名者: *Oscar nominee Whoopi Goldberg* 获得奥斯卡提名的乌比·戈德堡

non- /nɑn; nɒn/ *prefix* **1** in some adjectives and nouns, shows a negative; not 非, 不 (是), 无〔用在形容词、名词前表示"否定"之意〕: *a nonalcoholic drink* 非酒精饮料 | *a nonsmoker* (=someone who does not smoke) 不吸烟的人 | *a nonstick frying pan* (=which food does not stick to) 不粘锅底的平底煎锅 **2** *informal* in some nouns, means something not deserving a particular name【非正式】名不符实的, 与名称不相符的〔用于某些名词中〕: *a non-event* (=something boring) 枯燥无味的活动

no·na·ge·nar·i·an /ˌnɑnədʒəˋnɛrɪən; ˌnəʊnədʒɪˈneəriən/ *n* [C] someone between 90 and 99 years old 90 至 99 岁的人

non-ag·gres·sion /ˌ· ·ˈ· ·/ *n* [U] the idea that countries should not attack each other〔国与国之间的〕互不侵犯: *a policy of non-aggression* 互不侵犯政策 | **non-aggression pact/treaty** *In 1939 Stalin and Hitler signed a non-aggression pact.* 斯大林和希特勒于 1939 年签订了一项互不侵犯条约。

non-al·co·hol·ic /ˌ· · ·ˈ· ·◂/ *adj* a drink that is non-alcoholic does not contain alcohol 不含酒精的

non-a·ligned /ˌ· ·ˈ·◂/ *adj* a non-aligned country does not support, or is not dependent on, any of the powerful countries in the world〔国家〕不结盟的 **—non-alignment** *n* [U]

nonce[1] /nɑns; nɒns/ *adj technical* a nonce word or phrase is only invented once for a particular occasion【术语】〔词或短语〕临时造的

nonce[2] *n* **for the nonce** *literary or humorous* for the present time or for this particular occasion【文或幽默】目前, 暂时

non·cha·lant /ˋnɑnʃələnt; ˈnɒnʃələnt/ *adj* behaving calmly and seeming not to worry or care about anything 若无其事的; 毫不在乎的: *He was leaning on the bar, trying to look nonchalant.* 他靠在酒吧台上, 装出若无其事的样子。**—nonchalance** *n* [U] **—nonchalantly** *adv*

non-com·ba·tant /ˌ· ˈ· · ·/ *n* [C] someone who is in the army, navy etc during a war but who does not actually fight, for example an army doctor〔军队中的〕非战斗人员〔如军医〕

non-com·mis·sioned of·fi·cer /ˌ· · · ˈ· · · ·/ *n* [C] an NCO 军士

non·com·mit·tal /ˌnɑnkəˋmɪtl; ˌnɒnkəˈmɪtl◂/ *adj* not expressing a definite opinion or intention 不表明意见的, 不表态的, 态度暧昧的: **[+about]** *The doctor was noncommittal about his chances of making a full recovery.* 医生对他是否可以完全康复没有明确表态。| *a noncommittal answer* 模棱两可的回答 **—noncommittally** *adv*

non com·pos men·tis /ˌnɑn ˋkɑmpəs ˋmɛntɪs; ˌnɒn ˌkɒmpəs ˈmentɪs/ *adj* [not before noun 不用于名词前] *Latin* unable to think clearly or be responsible for your actions【拉丁】神智不清的; 不能为自己的行为负责的

Non·con·form·ist[1] /ˌnɑnkənˋfɔrmɪst; ˌnɒnkənˈfɔːmɪst◂/ *adj* belonging to one of the Protestant Christian churches that have separated from the Church of England 不信奉英国国教的 **—Nonconformist** *n* [C] **—Nonconformism** *n* [U]

nonconformist[2] *n* [C] someone who does not follow ways of living, thinking, or behaving accepted by most people 不遵守规范的人; 不遵循常规的人; 不落俗套的人: *a political nonconformist* 政治主张上不随俗的人 **—nonconformist** *adj*: *nonconformist attitudes* 不顺应传统规范的态度 **—nonconformity** *n* [U]

non·con·trib·u·to·ry /ˌnɑnkənˋtrɪbjə,torɪ; ˌnɒnkənˈtrɪbjʊtəri◂/ *adj* a noncontributory PENSION or insurance plan is paid for by the employer only, and not by the worker〔退休金、保险金计划〕由雇主支付的, 非分担的

non-co·op·e·ra·tion /ˌ· · ˈ· · ·/ *n* [U] the refusal to do any more than you officially have to, as a protest 不合作〔作为抗议〕

non·cus·to·di·al /ˌnɑnkʌsˋtodɪəl; ˌnɒnkʌˈstəʊdiəl◂/ *adj* **noncustodial sentence** a form of punishment which does not involve being kept in prison 不涉及监禁的判决

non·de·script /ˋnɑndɪ,skrɪpt; ˈnɒndɪskrɪpt/ *adj* very ordinary looking and without any interesting or unusual qualities or features 没有独特之处的; 平凡无奇的: *a nondescript suburban house* 平平常常的郊区房子

none[1] /nʌn; nʌn/ *pron* **1** not any of something 全无, 没有一点儿: *I was going to offer you some cake but there's none left.* 我本来想请你吃些蛋糕, 但一点也没剩。| **none of** *Everyone was talking about it – it did not matter to them that none of it was true.* 所有人都在谈论这件事, 全然不顾这事根本不是真的。| *She had inherited none of her mother's beauty.* 她丝毫也没有遗传她母亲的美貌。| **none at all/none whatsoever** *"Any mail arrive today?" "None whatsoever."* "今天有信吗?" "一封也没有。" **2** not any of a number of people or things〔几个人或几样东西中〕没有一个: **none of** *None of my friends phone me* 1 2

anymore. 我的朋友全都不再给我打电话了。| *None of you need worry.* 你们全都不用担心。| *None of their promises were kept.* 他们所作的承诺没有一个兑现的。| **none** *Of all the movies Hepburn made none is more memorable than 'Breakfast at Tiffany's'.* 在赫本拍摄的所有影片中，没有哪部像《蒂凡尼的早餐》那样令人难忘。| *Perhaps none felt the effects more than Peter.* 也许没有哪个人受的影响有彼得那么深。**3** not one thing or person 没有任何一个〔人或物〕: *Even an old car is better than none.* 即使是一辆旧车也比没有车好。| **none at all** *It'd be better to make some sort of decision than none at all.* 作出某种决定总比什么决定都没有强。**4 have none of sth** to not allow someone to do something or to not allow someone to behave in a particular way 不允许〔做〕某事; 不接受〔做〕某事: *This time I'll have none of her tears and tantrums.* 这一次我不会再容忍她大哭大闹。| *We offered to pay our half of the cost but Charles would have none of it.* 我们提出支付一半的费用，但查尔斯不答应。**5 none but** *literary* only【文】只有: *None but she would have been capable of such strength and courage.* 只有她才有这样的力量和勇气。**6 none other (than)** used when you are surprised that a particular person, especially someone famous, has done something〔表示惊奇〕不是别的，正是…: *The mystery guest turned out to be none other than Cher herself.* 神秘嘉宾不是别人，正是雪儿她本人。—see also 另见 NONETHELESS, **be second to none** (SECOND[1] (6)), **bar none** (BAR[3] (2))

USAGE NOTE 用法说明: NONE
FORMALITY 正式程度
When **none of** is followed by a plural noun, it usually takes a plural verb in ordinary spoken English. 在日常英语口语中，当 none of 后面跟复数名词时，动词常用复数形式: *None of us are ready yet.* 我们还没有人准备好。
In formal writing a singular verb is used. 在正式的书面语中则用动词的单数形式: *None of our factories is in operation yet.* 我们的工厂还没有一个运作起来。Some people believe the singular is the only correct form. 有些人认为只有单数形式才是正确的。

none² *adv* **1 none the worse/better etc** not at all worse, better etc than before 一点也没有变得更差/更好等: *She seems none the worse for her experience.* 这次经历后她似乎一点也没有变坏。| **none the wiser** (=not knowing any more about something than you did at the beginning) 仍然不明白 *I've read the instruction book from cover to cover, but I'm still none the wiser.* 我已经将说明书从头看到尾，但仍然不明白。**2 none too** *informal* not at all【非正式】一点也不: *I was none too pleased to have to take the exam again.* 我要重考一次，一点也高兴不起来。

non·en·ti·ty /nɑnˋɛntətɪ; nɒˈnentɪ̮ti/ *n* [C] someone who has no importance, power, or ability, and who you have no respect for 无足轻重的人; 无能力的人: *Chomsky was the only speaker of any importance – the rest were nonentities.* 乔姆斯基是唯一有分量的发言人，其余的人都无足轻重。

non·es·sen·tial /ˌ· ·ˈ··◂/ *adj* not completely necessary 非必要的，非必需的: *The US has imposed a ban on non-essential aerosols.* 美国已经禁止使用非必要的喷雾器。

none·such, nonsuch /ˋnʌnˌsʌtʃ; ˈnʌnsʌtʃ/ *n* [singular] *old use* a person or thing that is better than all the others of the same kind【旧】无可匹敌的人[物]，完美无比的人[物]

none·the·less /ˌnʌnðəˋlɛs; ˌnʌnðəˈles◂/ *adv* [sentence adverb 句子副词] *formal* in spite of the fact that has just been mentioned; NEVERTHELESS【正式】然而，但是; 尽管如此，虽然如此: *These islands are not a popular holiday destination, but are worth considering nonetheless.* 虽然这些岛屿算不上什么热门的度假去处，但值得考虑。| *The region was extremely beautiful. Nonetheless Gerard could not imagine spending the rest of his life there.* 这个地方非常漂亮，然而杰勒德却无法想象自己要在那里度过余生。

non·e·vent /ˌ· ·ˈ·/ *n* [C usually singular 一般用单数] an event that is disappointing because it is much less interesting and exciting than you expected 远不如预料中那么有趣[兴奋]的事: *The conference was a bit of a non-event – hardly anyone turned up for it.* 会议令人大失所望，几乎没有人来参加。

non·ex·ec·u·tive di·rec·tor /ˌ· ····· ·ˈ··/ *n* [C] one of the directors (DIRECTOR (1)) of a company who gives advice, but does not have any responsibility for how the company is managed 非执行董事，非常务董事

non·ex·ist·ent /ˌnɑnɪgˋzɪstənt; ˌnɒnɪgˈzɪstənt/ *adj* not existing at all, or not present in a particular place 不存在的: *We were expected to sit on nonexistent chairs.* 要让我们坐在根本不存在的椅子上。| *Their sex life was practically nonexistent.* 他们实际上没有什么性生活。—**non-existence** *n* [U]

non·fic·tion /ˌ·ˈ··◂/ *n* [U] books, articles etc about real facts or events, not imagined ones 非小说类文学作品，写实作品 —**non-fiction** *adj*

non·fi·nite /ˌ·ˈ··/ *adj* **1** a non-finite verb is not marked to show a particular tense or subject, and is either the INFINITIVE or the PARTICIPLE form of the verb, for example 'go' in the sentence 'Do you want to go home?'〔动词〕非限定形式的，非限定的 **2** not having an end or limit; INFINITE 无限的，无穷无尽的 —opposite 反义词 FINITE

non·flam·ma·ble /nɑnˋflæməbḷ; ˌnɒnˈflæməbəl/ *adj* nonflammable materials or substances do not burn easily or do not burn at all 不易燃的; 不燃的 —opposite 反义词 FLAMMABLE, INFLAMMABLE

non·in·ter·ven·tion /ˌ· ··ˈ··/ *n* [U] the practice by a government of not trying to influence or become involved in the affairs of other countries or organizations 不干涉: *a policy of non-intervention in internal affairs* 不干涉内政的政策

non·i·ron /ˌ·ˈ··◂/ *adj* non-iron materials do not need to be ironed (IRON[2]) after washing 免熨的，不需熨烫的

non·ne·go·ti·a·ble /ˌ· ·ˈ····/ *adj* **1** rights and conditions that are non-negotiable are parts of a law or contract that cannot be discussed or changed 不可谈判的，无商量余地的; 不能更改的 **2** a cheque that is non-negotiable can only be exchanged for money by the person whose name is on it〔支票〕不可转让的

no-no /ˈ· ·/ *n* [C] *informal* something that you must not do because it is considered to be unacceptable behaviour【非正式】不准干的事: *Colouring your hair was a distinct no-no at that time.* 染发在那时是绝对不能做的事。

no-non·sense /ˌ·ˈ··◂/ *adj* [only before noun 仅用于名词前] very practical and direct, without wasting time on unnecessary and unimportant things 实事求是的，务实的; 直截了当的，不绕弯子的: *His clients admired his straightforward no-nonsense attitude to business.* 他的客户欣赏他那种直截了当、实事求是的经营态度。

non·pa·reil /ˌnɑnpəˋrɛl; ˈnɒnpərəl/ *n* **1 nonpareils** [plural] *AmE* very small pieces of coloured sugar used to decorate cakes【美】〔装饰蛋糕用的〕彩色珠子糖 **2** [C] *AmE* a piece of chocolate covered with nonpareils【美】沾有彩色珠子糖的巧克力 **3** [singular] *literary* someone or something that is much better than all the others【文】无可匹敌的人[物]: *reviews by film critic nonpareil Pauline Kael* 无与伦比的影评家保利娜·凯尔所写的影评 —**nonpareil** *adj*

non·par·ti·san /ˌ· ··ˈ·◂/ *adj* not supporting the ideas of any political party or group 不支持任何党派的，无党派的: *a non-partisan approach to the housing problem* 在住房问题上不支持任何一派的态度

non·pay·ment /ˌ·ˈ··/ *n* [U] failure to pay money that you owe in tax, rent etc 未能[无力]支付: **[+of]** *non-payment of rent* 付不起房租

non·plussed also 又作 **nonplused** *AmE*【美】/ˌnɑnˋplʌst; ˌnɒnˈplʌst/ *adj* so surprised by something that you do not know what to say or do 惊讶不已的; 不知所措的: *He stood, nonplussed, the letter still in his hand.* 他不知所措地站在那里，手里还捏着那封信。

non·prof·it·mak·ing /ˌnɑn ˋprɑfɪtmekɪŋ; ˌnɒn ˈprɒfɪ̮tmeɪkɪŋ/ *BrE*【英】, **non-prof·it** /ˌ·ˈ··/ *AmE*【美】*adj* a nonprofitmaking organization uses the money it earns to help people〔机构〕非营利性的，非牟利的

non·pro·lif·e·ra·tion /ˌ· ····ˈ··/ *n* [U] the aim of limiting the number of NUCLEAR OR CHEMICAL WEAPONS in the world, especially by stopping countries that do not yet have them from developing them 防止核[化学]武器扩散: *the nuclear non-proliferation treaty* 防止核扩散条约

non·re·new·a·ble /ˌ· ·ˈ···◂/ *adj* non-renewable types of energy such as coal or gas cannot be replaced after they have been used〔能源〕不可再生的: *the diminishing non-renewable resource of coal* 不断减少、不可再生的煤资源

non·res·i·dent /ˌ·ˈ···/ *n* [C] **1** someone who is not staying in a particular hotel〔旅馆的〕非住客: *The hotel restaurant is open to non-residents.* 那家旅馆的餐厅对非住客开放。**2** someone who is not living in a particular place or country 非本地居民，非本国居民 —**non-resident** *adj*

non·res·i·den·tial /ˌnɑnrɛzəˋdɛnʃəl; ˌnɒnrezɪ̮ˈdenʃəl◂/ *adj* not providing somewhere for people to live or stay at night 不提供住宿的: *The course is nonresidential.* 那个课程不提供住宿。| *nonresidential care for the elderly* 对老人的日间护理

non·re·strict·ive /ˌ· ·ˈ··◂/ *adj technical* a non-restrictive RELATIVE CLAUSE gives additional information about a particular

N

person or thing rather than saying which person or thing is being mentioned, for example in the sentence 'Perry, who is 22, was arrested yesterday.', the phrase 'who is 22' is a non-restrictive clause【术语】〔从句〕非限制性的

S3 **non·sense** /ˋnɑnsɛns; ˈnɒnsənsˌ/ *n* [U]

1 ►STUPID/UNTRUE 愚蠢/不真实的◄ ideas, opinions, statements etc that are untrue or stupid 荒谬的话[想法]; 胡说, 废话: *all this nonsense about health foods* 有关健康食品的一派胡言 | *"She says she's 39." "Nonsense!"* "她说她39岁。""胡说!" | **a load of nonsense** (=a lot of nonsense) 一派胡言 *If you ask me, these modern teaching methods are a load of nonsense.* 要我说, 这些现代化的教学方法全是一派胡言。| **talk nonsense** *He was talking utter nonsense as usual.* 他像平常一样又在胡说八道了。| **be a nonsense** *The whole idea's a complete nonsense.* 这整个想法真是太荒谬了。

2 ►WITHOUT MEANING 毫无意义的◄ speech or writing that has no meaning or cannot be understood 无意义的话[字句]: *Computer programs look like complete nonsense to me.* 在我看来, 电脑程序像是毫无意义的东西。

3 nonsense poems/verse poetry that is humorous because it does not have a normal sensible meaning 打油诗

4 ►ANNOYING BEHAVIOUR 令人不快的行为◄ behaviour that is stupid and annoying 愚蠢的行为; 胡闹: *I wish they'd stop all this nonsense and be nice to each other for a change.* 我希望他们别再胡闹, 而是相互之间变得友好一些。| **not stand any nonsense** (=be very strict) 十分严格, 不允许胡闹 *She won't stand any nonsense from the kids in her class.* 她不允许孩子们在她的课上胡闹。

5 make (a) nonsense of *BrE* to show that a previous action or idea was useless and had no meaning【英】使…失去作用[意义]: *Having the army still in power makes a nonsense of last year's democratic elections.* 让军队继续掌权使得去年的民主选举失去意义。

non·sen·si·cal /nɑnˋsɛnsɪkḷ; nɒnˈsensɪkəl/ *adj* not reasonable or sensible 无意义的; 愚蠢的; 荒谬的: *nonsensical ideas* 荒谬的想法 —**nonsensically** /-kḷɪ; -kli/ *adv*

non seq·ui·tur /nɑn ˋsɛkwɪtɚ; ˌnɒn ˈsekwɪtə/ *n* [C] a statement which does not seem to be connected in a reasonable or sensible way with what was said before 前后不连贯的陈述, 不根据前提的推论

non-shrink /ˌ·ˈ·◄/ *adj* non-shrink materials do not become smaller when they are washed 不缩水的

non-smok·er /ˌ·ˈ··/ *n* [C] someone who does not smoke 不抽烟的人

non-smok·ing /ˌ·ˈ··◄/ *adj* a non smoking area is one where you are not allowed to smoke 禁烟的, 不准吸烟的

non-stan·dard /ˌ·ˈ··◄/ *adj* **1** not the usual size or type〔尺寸等〕不标准的, 不规则的: *a non-standard disk size* 不标准的磁盘尺寸 **2** non-standard words, expressions, or pronunciations are not usually considered to be correct by educated speakers of a language, for example 'gotta' in the sentence 'I gotta go.'〔用词、发音等〕不标准的, 不规范的

non·start·er /ˌnɑnˋstɑrtɚ; ˌnɒnˈstɑːtə/ *n* [C] **1** [usually singular 一般用单数] *informal* a person, idea, or plan that has no chance of success【非正式】无成功机会的人[想法、计划]: *The whole thing sounds like a nonstarter to me.* 这件事在我听来不可能成功。**2** a horse that is supposed to take part in a race but does not run 参加了比赛, 但没有上场跑的马

non-stick /ˌ·ˈ·◄/ *adj* a non-stick cooking pan has a special inside surface which prevents food from sticking to it〔锅〕不粘食物的

non·stop /ˌnɑnˋstɑp; ˌnɒnˈstɒp◄/ *adj, adv* without stopping 不停顿的[地], 不断的[地]: *She talked nonstop for over an hour.* 她一刻不停地讲了一个多小时。| *a non-stop flight to Los Angeles* 直飞洛杉矶的航班

non·such /ˋnʌnsʌtʃ; ˈnʌnsʌtʃ/ *n* [singular] another spelling of NONESUCH nonesuch 的另一种拼法

non-u·nion /ˌ·ˈ··◄/ *adj* [usually before noun 一般用于名词前] **1** not belonging to a TRADE UNION (=official organization for workers) 不属于工会的: *non-union members* 非工会成员 **2** not officially accepting TRADE UNIONS, or not employing their members 不承认工会的; 不雇用工会会员的: *non-union factories* 不雇用工会会员的工厂 —**non-unionized** *adj*

non·ver·bal /ˌnɑnˋvɝbḷ; ˌnɒnˈvɜːbəl◄/ *adj* not using words 不用言辞表达的: *nonverbal communication* 非言语的交流 —**nonverbally** *adv*

non-vi·o·lence /ˌ·ˈ···/ *n* [U] political opposition without fighting, shown especially by not obeying laws or orders 非暴力反抗; 非暴力主义: *Gandhi's policy of non-violence and negotiation* 甘地提出的非暴力和协商的政策 —**non-violent** *adj*: *non-violent protests* 非暴力抗议 —**non-violently** *adv*

non-white /ˌ·ˈ·/ *n* [C] *especially SAfrE* someone who does not belong to a white race【尤南非】非白种人 —**non-white** /ˌ·ˈ·◄/ *adj*

noo·dle /ˋnudḷ; ˈnuːdl/ *n* **1 noodles** [plural] long thin pieces of food made from a mixture of flour, water, and eggs, usually cooked in soup or boiling water 面条: *egg noodles* 鸡蛋面 **2** [C] *old-fashioned* a silly person【过时】笨人, 傻瓜 **3** [C] *AmE old-fashioned* your head or brain【美, 过时】头; 头脑: *Use your noodle!* 动动脑子!

nook /nʊk; nʊk/ *n* [C] **1** a small quiet place which is sheltered by a rock, a big tree etc 隐蔽处: *a shady nook* 阴凉的隐蔽处 **2** a small space in a corner of a room〔房间的〕角落: *a cozy little nook next to the fireplace* 壁炉旁舒适的一隅 **3 nook and cranny** every part of a place 到处, 四处: *We searched every nook and cranny.* 我们搜遍了每个角落。

nook·ie /ˋnʊkɪ; ˈnʊki/ *n* [U] *humorous* the activity of having sex【幽默】性交

noon /nun; nuːn/ *n* [U] 12 o'clock in the daytime; MIDDAY 正午, 中午: *We left home at noon.* 我们在中午离开了家。| *He rarely gets up before noon.* 他很少在中午之前起床。—see also 另见 **morning, noon and night** (MORNING[1] (5))

noon·day /ˋnunˌde; ˈnuːndeɪ/ *adj literary* happening or appearing at noon【文】正午的: *in the heat of the noonday sun* 在正午的骄阳下

no one /ˈ· ·/ *pron* not anyone; NOBODY 没人, 无人: *No one likes being criticized.* 没有人喜欢受到批评。| *There's no one else I really want to invite apart from you.* 除你之外, 我不想再邀请别人了。| *I see no one new has joined the department in my absence.* 我发现我不在期间系里没有增加新人。| *No one can say I didn't warn you.* 谁也不能说我没有警告过你。—see 见 EACH[1] (USAGE) S1 W2

noose /nus; nuːs/ *n* **1** [C] a ring formed by the end of a piece of rope or string, which closes more tightly as it is pulled 活绳结, 绳套 **2 the noose** punishment by hanging 绞刑: *The outlaws managed to escape the hangman's noose.* 亡命之徒设法逃脱了绞刑。

nope /nop; nəʊp/ *adv spoken* used to say 'no' when you answer someone【口】不, 不是: *"Hungry?" "Nope, I just ate."* "饿吗?" "不饿, 我刚吃过了。" S3

no place /ˈ· ·/ *adv informal especially AmE* nowhere【非正式, 尤美】无处: *There's no place left to hide.* 已经无处可藏了。

nor'- /nɔr; nɔː/ *prefix* a prefix meaning 'north', used especially by sailors〔表示"北", 尤为海员所用〕: *nor'east* 东北 | *nor'west* 西北

nor[1] /nɔr; nɔː/ *conjunction* **1 neither... nor...** used when two states, facts, actions etc are mentioned and both are not true or not possible 既不…也不…: *He can neither read nor write.* 他既不会读也不会写。| *Hilary was neither shocked nor surprised by the news.* 希拉里对这个消息既没有感到震惊也没有觉得意外。**2** *formal* used after a negative statement to mean 'and not something else too'【正式】也不〔用于否定句之后〕: *I wasn't very impressed by his replies, nor his reasons.* 我对他的回答不太满意, 对他的理由也是一样。 S2 W1

nor[2] *adv* **1 nor can I/nor does John etc** *especially BrE* used to add a negative statement to one that has just been mentioned【尤英】我也不会/约翰也不等: *She couldn't work out the answer, and nor could I.* 她算不出答案, 我也算不出。**2** *formal* used to emphasize or add information to a negative statement【正式】也不〔表示强调或增加信息〕: *I don't expect children to be rude, nor do I expect to be disobeyed.* 我不希望孩子们没礼貌, 也不希望他们不听话。| *I am not, nor have I ever been a wealthy man.* 我现在不是, 从来也不是一个富人。—see also 另见 NEITHER

Nor·dic /ˋnɔrdɪk; ˈnɔːdɪk/ *adj* from or connected with the Northern European countries of Denmark, Norway, Sweden, Iceland, and Finland 来自北欧的; 北欧国家的: *Nordic beauty* 北欧美人

Nor·folk /ˋnɔrfək; ˈnɔːfək/ a COUNTY in eastern England, consisting mainly of rather flat farmland and some lakes called the Norfolk Broads, where many people spend holidays sailing in small boats or BARGES. 诺福克郡〔英格兰东部一郡。境内主要由平坦的耕地和诺福克湖区的部分湖泊组成, 众多游客来此度假泛舟〕

norm /nɔrm; nɔːm/ *n* **1** [C] the usual or normal situation, way of doing something etc 标准; 准则; 规范: *Joyce's style of writing was a striking departure from the literary norm.* 乔伊斯的写作风格与传统的文学风格大相径庭。| **be the norm** *Short term contracts are now the norm with some big companies.* 签订短期合同是目前一些大公司的惯常做法。**2 norms** [plural] generally accepted standards of social behaviour 社会准则: *terror-*

ists who violate the norms of civilized society 违反文明社会准则的恐怖分子

nor·mal /ˈnɔrml; ˈnɔːməl/ *adj* **1** not unusual in any way, but happening just as you would expect 正常的; 平常的; 意料之中的: *normal working hours* 正常工作时间 | **it is normal for sb to do sth** *In the West it's becoming quite normal for couples to live together before they are married.* 在西方, 婚前同居正在变得十分平常。| **back to normal** *Train services are back to normal again after the strike.* 罢工结束后火车服务已恢复正常。| **above/below normal** *The rainfall has been below normal for this time of year.* 这个时期的降雨量低于正常水平。**2** a normal person, especially a child, is physically and mentally healthy and does not behave strangely〔尤指儿童〕发育正常的, 身心健康的: *a normal healthy baby* 发育正常的健康婴儿 | **perfectly normal** *He seems a perfectly normal little boy.* 他看起来是个发育完全正常的小男孩。—compare 比较 ABNORMAL

nor·mal·i·ty /nɔrˋmælətɪ; nɔːˈmæləti/ also 又作 **nor·mal·cy** /ˈnɔrmlsɪ; ˈnɔːməlsi/ *AmE*【美】*n* [U] a situation in which things happen in the usual or expected way 正常状态: *a return to normality* 恢复正常 | *a comforting sense of normality* 一种一切如常的令人安心的感觉

nor·mal·ize also 又作 **-ise** *BrE*【英】/ˈnɔrml͵aɪz; ˈnɔːməlaɪz/ *v* [I,T] if you normalize a situation, or if it normalizes, it becomes normal again (使) 变得正常; (使) 正常化: **normalize relations** (=start having a normal friendly relationship with a country again after a period of war or disagreement) 使〔国家〕关系正常化, 使邦交正常化 —**normalization** /͵nɔrml̩əˋzeʃən; ͵nɔːməlaɪˈzeɪʃən/ *n* [U]

nor·mal·ly /ˈnɔrməlɪ; ˈnɔːməli/ *adv* **1** *especially BrE* usually, or under normal conditions【尤英】通常, 平常, 一般地: [sentence adverb 句子副词] *Normally, I get home about 6 o'clock.* 我通常六点左右回到家。| *The illness normally lasts about a week or ten days.* 这种病通常持续约七到十天。**2** in a normal ordinary way 正常地: *The patient started breathing normally again.* 病人又开始正常呼吸了。

Nor·man /ˈnɔrmən; ˈnɔːmən/ *adj* **1** built in the style that was popular during the 11th and 12th centuries in Europe〔建筑〕诺曼式的; 诺曼风格的〔指 11 至 12 世纪时的北欧建筑风格〕: *a Norman church* 一座诺曼式教堂 **2** connected with the Normans, the northern French people who took control of England in the 11th century 诺曼 (人) 的

Norman Con·quest, the /͵‥ ˈ‥/ the period when the Normans, led by William the Conqueror, took control of England after defeating the English king Harold II, at the Battle of Hastings in 1066. These events had a very great influence on England's history, culture, and language, and French became the main language of the ruling class. 诺曼征服〔指诺曼人在征服者威廉的率领下在1066年黑斯廷斯一役中击溃英格兰国王哈罗德二世并占领英格兰这一历史事件。诺曼征服对英格兰的历史、文化及语言产生了巨大影响, 法语遂成为统治阶级的主要语言〕

Nor·man·dy /ˈnɔrməndɪ; ˈnɔːməndi/ a part of northwest France, on the English Channel, that includes the ports of Cherbourg and Le Havre, where boats carrying passengers from England arrive 诺曼底〔法国西北部濒临英吉利海峡一地区, 包括瑟堡港和勒阿弗尔港, 英国客轮常在此停泊〕

Normandy Land·ings, the /͵‥‥ ˈ‥/ the arrival of the Allies on the coast of Normandy in 1944, when they began to force German soldiers to leave France. The day on which they landed, 6 June 1944, is called D-Day. 诺曼底登陆〔指 1944 年同盟国军队登陆诺曼底的行动。此次行动迫使德军撤离法国。1944年6月6日登陆的这一天被称作 D-day (军事进攻日)〕

nor·ma·tive /ˈnɔrmətɪv; ˈnɔːmətɪv/ *adj formal* describing or establishing a set of rules or standards of behaviour【正式】合乎规范的; 按规定准则的: *a normative social structure* 合乎规范的社会结构

Norse /nɔrs; nɔːs/ *adj* connected with the people of ancient Scandinavia or their language 古代斯堪的纳维亚人的; 古代斯堪的纳维亚语的: *Norse legends* 古代斯堪的纳维亚人的传奇故事

Norse·man /ˈnɔrsmən; ˈnɔːsmən/ *n* [C] *literary* a VIKING【文】古代斯堪的纳维亚人, 北欧海盗, 维京人

north¹, North /nɔrθ; nɔːθ/ written abbreviation 缩写为 **N** *n* [singular, U] **1** the direction that is at the top of a map of the world, above the EQUATOR, and is on the left of a person facing the rising sun 北, 北方: *Which way is north?* 哪边是北方? | **from/towards the north** *A strong wind was blowing from the north.* 一阵狂风从北方吹来。| **to the north (of)** *Cheshunt is a few miles to the north of London.* 切森特位于伦敦以北几英里处。| **in the north** *A strange light appeared in the north.* 一道奇特的光在北方出现。| *The wind is in the north.* (=is coming from the north) 风从北面吹来。**2 the North a)** the northern part of a country〔一国的〕北部, 北方: *The North will be dry and bright.* 北部地区的天气将是干燥而晴朗的。| *in the north of England* 在英格兰北部 **b)** the northeastern states of the US, which fought against the South in the American Civil War〔美国南北战争中的〕北方各州 **c)** the richer countries of the world, especially Europe and N America 北方富裕国家〔尤指欧洲和北美的一些国家〕

north² written abbreviation 缩写为 **N** *adj* **1** in the north or facing the north 北方的, 北部的; 朝北的: *The north side of the building doesn't get much sun.* 该建筑物朝北的一面很少晒到太阳。| *He lives in North Wales.* 他住在威尔士北部。**2** a north wind comes from the north〔风〕来自北面的

north³ written abbreviation 缩写为 **N** *adv* **1** towards the north 向北, 朝北: *The birds fly north in summer.* 夏季鸟儿向北飞。| *Chicago is four hours north of Indianapolis.* 芝加哥位于印第安纳波利斯以北四小时路程处。| *a north-facing window* 朝北的窗户 **2 up north** *informal* to or in the north of the country【非正式】往〔国家的〕北部; 在〔国家的〕北部: *They've moved up north.* 他们搬到北部去了。

North, the **1** the northeastern states of the US, especially during the Civil War (1861-65) when they fought against the South. Today, the six states in New England and the states of New York, New Jersey, and Pennsylvania are usually called the Northeast,and the states to the west of these are called the Midwest. People from the northern part of the US are called Northerners. (美国) 北方地区〔尤指南北战争期间 (1861-1865) 的东北方各州。如今的新英格兰六州、纽约州、新泽西州和宾夕法尼亚州通常合称为东北地区。东北地区以西各州称为中西部地区。北部地区的居民称作 Northerners (北方人)〕 **2** the northern part of England, which includes the area north of the Midlands and south of the Scottish border, and contains several large cities, including Manchester, Leeds, Liverpool, and Newcastle. (英格兰) 北部地区〔指英格兰中部地区以北、苏格兰边境以南的地区, 包括曼彻斯特、利兹、利物浦和纽卡斯尔等大城市〕

CULTURAL NOTE 文化注释

In the past, there was a lot of industry in the North of England, including coal mines, SHIPBUILDING, and factories where cloth and steel were made. Most of this industry closed down during the 1970s and 1980s, and as a result many people lost their jobs. There are more modern types of industry there now, although there are fewer jobs in the North than in the South, and the area is thought of as being less rich than the South. People from the North, who are called **Northerners**, are generally thought to be friendlier than people in the South, and more direct and honest in the way they express their opinions. 英格兰北部过去有很多工业, 包括采煤和造船, 还有纺织厂和炼钢厂。在20世纪70、80年代, 大多数工业的倒闭导致了很多人失业。尽管北部比南部的工作机会要少, 北部也被认为不如南部富裕, 现在这里还是有了更新型的工业。来自北部的人被称为北方人, 一般认为他们比南方人更加友好, 表达个人观点时也更加直接和诚恳。

North A·mer·i·ca /͵‥ ˈ‥‥/ the third largest CONTINENT in the world, consisting of Canada and the United States of America, as well as Mexico, Central America, Greenland, and other smaller islands 北美洲〔世界第三大洲, 包括加拿大、美国、墨西哥、中美洲、格陵兰及其他一些较小的岛屿〕 —**North American** *n, adj*

Nor·thamp·ton·shire /nɔrˋθæmptənʃɚ; nɔːˈθæmptənʃə/ abbreviation 缩写为 **Northants** a COUNTY in central England that consists mainly of farmland 北安普敦郡〔英格兰中部一郡, 境内大部分地区为农田〕

North At·lan·tic Treat·y Or·ga·ni·za·tion, the /͵‥ ‥ˈ‥ ˈ‥ ͵‥‥ˈ‥/ the full name of NATO 北大西洋公约组织〔NATO 的全称〕

north·bound /ˈnɔrθ͵baund; ˈnɔːθbaʊnd/ *adj* travelling or leading towards the north 向北行的; 往北的: *a northbound bus* 北行的公共汽车 | *the northbound lane of the A1* A1 号公路的北行车道

North Car·o·li·na /͵nɔrθ kærəˋlaɪnə; ͵nɔːθ kærəˈlaɪnə/ abbreviation 缩写为 **NC** a state on the east coast of the US, which produces a lot of TOBACCO. It was one of the 13 original states of the US. 北卡罗来纳州〔美国东部沿海一州, 出产烟草, 属美国最早的 13 个州之一〕

North Da·ko·ta /͵nɔrθ dəˋkotə; ͵nɔːθ dəˈkəʊtə/ abbreviation 缩写为 **ND** a state in the northern central US, on the border

N

with Canada, with a small population, good farmland, and mineral mines 北达科他州〔美国中北部一州，与加拿大接壤。该州人口少，耕地肥沃，有不少矿藏〕

north·east¹ /ˌnɔrθˋist; ˌnɔːθˈiːst◂/ written abbreviation 缩写为 NE *n* [U] **1** the direction that is exactly between north and east 东北，东北方向 **2 the northeast** the northeastern part of a country 〔一国的〕东北部 —**northeast** *adv*: *This road goes northeast.* 这条路通往东北方向。

northeast² written abbreviation 缩写为 NE *adj* **1** a northeast wind comes from the northeast 〔风〕来自东北的 **2** in the northeast of a place 东北部的: *the northeast outskirts of Las Vegas* 拉斯韦加斯东北部的郊区

Northeast, the **1** the northeastern part of the US, including the six states in New England, and the states of New York, New Jersey, and Pennsylvania (美国) 东北地区〔包括新英格兰六州、纽约州、新泽西州和宾夕法尼亚州〕 **2** the northeastern part of England, which includes the industrial areas of Tyneside (around Newcastle) and Teeside (around Middlesborough) (英格兰) 东北地区〔包括纽卡斯尔周围的泰恩赛德工业区和米德尔斯伯勒周围的蒂赛德工业区〕

Northeast Cor·ri·dor, the /ˌ‥ˈ‥‥/ an area of the northeastern US, between Boston and Washington, D.C., which has the highest population DENSITY in the country 东北走廊〔美国东北部一地区，位于波士顿和华盛顿之间。该地区的人口密度居全国之首〕

north·east·er /ˌnɔrθˋistɚ; ˌnɔːθˈiːstə/ *n* [C] a strong wind or storm coming from the northeast 东北大风[风暴]

north·east·er·ly /ˌnɔrθˋistɚlɪ; ˌnɔːθˈiːstəli/ *adj* **1** towards or in the northeast 向东北方的; 在东北方的: *They set off in a northeasterly direction.* 他们向着东北方出发。 **2** a northeasterly wind comes from the northeast 〔风〕来自东北的

north·east·ern /ˌnɔrθˋistɚn; ˌnɔːθˈiːstən/ *adj* in or from the northeast part of a country or area 东北部的; 来自东北部的: *the northeastern states of the US* 美国东北部各州

Northeast Pas·sage, the /ˌ‥ˈ‥‥/ a way by sea between the Atlantic and Pacific Oceans, going along the northern coasts of Europe and Asia. It was discovered by the Swedish EXPLORER Nils Nordenskjöld in 1878-79 东北航路〔大西洋与太平洋之间沿欧亚大陆北海岸的一条航路。该航路是瑞典探险家尼尔斯·诺登舍尔德 1878 至 1879 年间发现的〕—see 见 the NORTHWEST PASSAGE

north·east·wards /ˌnɔrθˋistwɚdz; ˌnɔːθˈiːstwədz/ also 又作 **northeastward** *adv* towards the northeast 向东北方向 — **northeastward** *adj*

nor·ther·ly /ˋnɔrðɚlɪ; ˈnɔːðəli/ *adj* **1** towards or in the north 向北的; 在北方的: *a northerly direction* 向北的方向 **2** a northerly wind comes from the north 〔风〕来自北方的

nor·thern /ˋnɔrðɚn; ˈnɔːðən/ *adj* in or from the north of a country or area 北部的; 来自北部的: *a man with a northern accent* 带有北方口音的男子 | *Northern Europe* 北欧

nor·thern·er /ˋnɔrðɚnɚ; ˈnɔːðənə/ *n* [C] someone who comes from the northern part of a country 北方人

northern hem·is·phere /ˌ‥ˈ‥‥/ *n* [singular] the half of the world that is north of the EQUATOR 北半球 —see picture at 参见 EARTH 图

Northern Ire·land /ˌ‥ˈ‥/ the northern part of the island of Ireland, which is politically part of the United Kingdom. It is sometimes called the Six Counties, because it consists of six counties, or as Ulster, or the Province. Its capital city is Belfast, and its main industries are farming and engineering, especially ship and aircraft building. The population of Northern Ireland is divided between the Protestants (over 50%) and the Roman Catholics (almost 40%). In general, the Protestants want Northern Ireland to remain part of the UK, and they are called Unionists or Loyalists. Catholics want Northern Ireland to become part of the Republic of Ireland, and are called Republicans or Nationalists. The disagreements between these groups have led to a lot of violence. 北爱尔兰〔位于爱尔兰岛北部，政治上隶属于英国。因为北爱尔兰由 6 个郡组成，有时也称为"六郡"，或称作 Ulster 或 the Province。首府: 贝尔法斯特。主要产业为农业和工程业，尤其是船舶与飞机制造。北爱尔兰 50% 以上的人口为新教徒，40% 左右为天主教徒。总的来说，新教徒主张北爱尔兰继续留在英国，这些人被称为联合派或保皇派，而天主教徒则希望北爱尔兰成为爱尔兰共和国的一部分，这些人被称为共和派或民族派。两个派别之争导致了许多暴力冲突〕

Northern Ireland Assembly, the a political ASSEMBLY set up as part of the 1998 Good Friday peace agreement. The assembly has 108 members, six from each of the 18 constituencies (CONSTITUENCY) in Northern Ireland. The assembly has an executive of up to 12 ministers, whose responsibilities include health, education, environment and finance. 北爱尔兰议会〔根据 1998 年签署的《耶稣受难日和平协定》有关条款而建立的一个政治议会，由 108 名成员组成，北爱尔兰 18 个选区每个选区 6 名。该议会由 12 名部长做行政工作，负责卫生、教育、环境以及金融等事务〕

Northern Lights, the /ˌ‥ˈ‥/ *n* [plural] bands of coloured light that are seen in the night sky in the most northern parts of the world; AURORA BOREALIS 北极光〔地球最北部夜间可见到的五彩光带〕

Northern Marianas a group of islands in the Pacific Ocean, east of the Philippines. Population: 74,612 (2001). Capital: Saipan. 北马里亚纳群岛〔太平洋一群岛，位于菲律宾群岛以东。人口: 74,612 (2001)，首府: 塞班〕

nor·thern·most /ˋnɔrðɚnˌmost; ˈnɔːðənməust/ *adj* furthest north 最北端的，极北的: *the northernmost tip of the island* 岛屿的最北端

Northern Ter·ri·to·ry, the /ˌ‥ˈ‥‥/ an area of northern central Australia whose main city is Darwin. It is an extremely large area, but most of it is very dry and its population is very small. 北部地区〔澳大利亚中北部一地区，主要城市为达尔文市。该地区地广人稀，大部分土地非常干旱〕

North Is·land /ˈ‥ˌ‥/ one of the two main islands of New Zealand, which includes Wellington, New Zealand's capital city 北岛〔新西兰两大岛屿之一，新西兰首都惠灵顿在该岛上〕—see 见 SOUTH ISLAND

North Ko·re·a /ˌ‥ˈ‥/ a country in East Asia, west of Japan and east of China, which is officially called the Democratic People's Republic of Korea. Population: 21,968,000 (2001). Capital: Pyongyang. North Korea was formed in 1945 when Korea was divided into two countries (North and South Korea) by the US and the former Soviet Union. 朝鲜〔东亚一国家，位于日本以西，中国以东。正式名称为朝鲜民主主义人民共和国。人口: 21,968,000 (2001)，首都: 平壤。1945 年，朝鲜半岛被美国和前苏联分为两个国家，朝鲜民主主义人民共和国就此成立〕— **North Korean** *n, adj*

North Pole /ˌ‥ˈ/ *n* [singular] the most northern point on the surface of the earth, or the area around it 北极; 北极地区 —see also 另见 SOUTH POLE —see picture at 参见 EARTH 图

North Sea, the /ˌ‥ˈ/ part of the Atlantic Ocean, between Great Britain and northwest Europe. It is economically important because of its fish, and also for oil and gas which were discovered there in the 1970s. 北海〔英国与欧洲西北部之间的大西洋海域。北海鱼类资源丰富，20 世纪 70 年代在此还发现了石油与天然气，因此具有重要的经济地位〕

North/South di·vide, the /ˌ‥ˈ‥ˈ/ **1** the difference between the rich and poor countries of the world, which is shown by people's standard of living and by the level of industrial and economic development. The expression the North is used to mean the richer countries which are mainly in Europe, North America, and parts of East Asia, and the South is used to mean the poorer countries of Africa, Asia, and Central and South America. 南北差距〔指富裕国家与贫困国家在人民生活水平及工业、经济发展水平方面存在的差距。北方指主要集中在欧洲、北美洲及东亚部分地区的富裕国家; 南方指非洲、亚洲、中美洲及南美洲的贫穷国家〕: *Latest statistics suggest the North/South divide is becoming even more pronounced.* 最新统计数据显示南北差距日益显著。 **2** the difference between the northern and southern parts of a country, shown for example in the amount of money people have, the quality of their health, or their general attitudes and way of life (一国的) 南北差距〔具体表现在居民收入、健康状况或总体生活态度与生活方式〕: *The 1980s property boom in and around London helped to create a North/South divide in the cost of housing.* 20 世纪 80 年代伦敦及其周边地区的房地产热致使南北方的房价差距拉大。

CULTURAL NOTE 文化注释

In the UK, the North/South divide means the difference between southern England, especially London and SE England, and northern England and Scotland. People in the South generally earn more money than people in the North. There is less unemployment in the South, and people are typically more healthy. In the North, however, the cost of living is generally lower, and houses cost less to rent or buy. 在英国，南北差距指英格兰南部，特别是伦敦和英格兰东南部与英格兰北部和苏格兰的差异。南部人一般比北部人挣的钱多。南部失业较少，人们一般也更健康。但是在北部，生活花费一般较低，无论是租房子还是买房子都比较便宜。

North·um·ber·land /nɔrˈθʌmbɚlənd; nɔːˈθʌmbələnd/ a COUNTY in northeast England, just south of Scotland and on the North Sea coast, which has many hills and forests and Hadrian's Wall 诺森伯兰〔英格兰东北部一郡。东临北海，北与苏格兰接壤。境内多丘陵、森林，还有哈德良长城〕

Nor·thum·bri·a /nɔrˈθʌmbrɪə; nɔːˈθʌmbriə/ an Anglo-Saxon KINGDOM in the north of England and south of Scotland that was politically important from the 7th to the 9th centuries. This name is often used unofficially to mean Northumberland.诺森布里亚王国〔7至9世纪具有重要政治地位的一个盎格鲁－撒克逊王国，位于英格兰北部，苏格兰以南。在非正式场合也用来指称诺森伯兰郡〕—**Northumbrian** *n, adj*

North Wales /ˌ·ˈ·/ the northern part of Wales. Its coast and mountains are popular with tourists. 北威尔士〔即威尔士北部，其海岸和山峰吸引着众多游客〕

north·wards /ˈnɔrθwɚdz; ˈnɔːθwədz/ also 又作 **northward** *adv* towards the north 向北方: *We sailed northward.* 我们向北航行。—**northward** *adj*

north·west[1] /ˌnɔrθˈwɛst; ˌnɔːθˈwest◂/ written abbreviation 缩写为 **NW** *n* [U] **1** the direction that is exactly between north and west 西北，西北方 **2 the northwest** the northwestern part of a country 〔一国的〕西北部 —**northwest** *adv*: *The house faces northwest.* 房子面向西北。

northwest[2] written abbreviation 缩写为 NW *adj* **1** a northwest wind comes from the northwest 〔风〕来自西北的 **2** in the northwest of a place 在西北部的: *the northwest suburbs of the city* 城市西北部的郊区

north·west·er /ˌnɔrθˋwɛstɚ; ˌnɔːθˈwestə/ *n* [C] a strong wind or storm coming from the northwest 西北大风[风暴]

north·west·er·ly /ˌnɔrθˋwɛstɚlɪ; ˌnɔːθˈwestəli/ *adj* **1** towards or in the northwest 向西北的; 在西北方的 **2** a northwesterly wind comes from the northwest 〔风〕来自西北的

north·west·ern /ˌnɔrθˋwɛstɚn; ˌnɔːθˈwestən/ *adj* in or from the northwest part of a country or area 西北部的; 来自西北部的: *northwestern Canada* 加拿大西北部

Northwest Pas·sage, the /ˌ··ˈ··/ a way by sea between the Atlantic and Pacific Oceans, going along the northern coast of North America. It was first sailed through by Roald Amundsen in 1903-06 西北航道〔大西洋和太平洋之间沿北美洲北部沿岸的一条海路。1903至1906年间，罗阿尔德·阿蒙森首次航行通过这条航道〕—see 见 the NORTHEAST PASSAGE

Northwest Ter·ri·to·ries, the /ˌ··ˈ···/ a very large area in northwest Canada east of the Yukon, whose capital is Yellowknife. It covers a third of the area of Canada, but it has a very small population and very cold weather. 西北地方〔指加拿大西北部育空以东的广大地区，首府为耶洛拉夫。该地区面积辽阔，占国土面积的三分之一，但人口稀少，气候严寒〕

north·west·wards /ˌnɔrθˋwɛstwɚdz; ˌnɔːθˈwestwədz/ also 又作 **northwestward** *adv* towards the northwest 向西北方向

North York Moors, the /ˌ·ˈ·ˈ·/ an area of high, open land, a National Park, in northeast England 北约克漠泽〔英格兰东北部一片空旷的高地，为国家公园〕

North York·shire /ˌ·ˈ··/ a COUNTY in northeast England. It consists mainly of farmland. The centre of local government is at Northallerton but the main city is York 北约克郡〔英格兰东北部一郡，境内主要为耕地。地方行政中心在诺萨勒顿，主要城市为约克〕

Nor·way /ˈnɔrˌwe; ˈnɔːweɪ/ a country of northern Europe, in western Scandinavia. Population: 4,503,000 (2001). Capital: Oslo. Norway's industries include fishing, oil from the North Sea, and wood products from its large forests. 挪威〔北欧一国家，位于斯堪的那维亚半岛西部。人口: 4,503,000 (2001)，首都: 奥斯陆。挪威的主要产业有渔业、北海采油业以及木材加工业〕—**Norwegian** /nɔrˋwidʒən; nɔːˈwiːdʒən/ *n, adj* —see also 另见 VIKING

Nor·wich /ˈnɔrɪdʒ; ˈnɒrɪdʒ/ a city in Norfolk, east central England, where the local government for that COUNTY is based 诺里奇〔英格兰中东部诺福克郡一城市，为郡政府所在地〕

nos. the written abbreviation of 缩写= numbers: *nos. 17–33* 17至33号

S2 W2 **nose[1]** /noz; nəʊz/ *n*

1 ▶ON YOUR FACE 在脸上◀ [C] the part of your face that you smell with and breathe through 鼻子: *a broken nose* 断了的鼻子 | *Marty punched him on the nose.* 马蒂一拳打在他鼻子上。| **blow your nose** (=clear it by blowing strongly into a piece of cloth or soft paper) 擤鼻子 *Here, take this hanky and blow your nose.* 拿着，用这条手帕擤擤鼻子。—see picture at 参见 HEAD[1] 图

2 red-nosed/long-nosed etc having a nose that is red, long etc 红鼻子/长鼻子等的

3 (right) under sb's nose so close to someone that they ought to notice, but they do not 就在某人眼前，当着某人的面；公然地: *The drugs were smuggled in right under the noses of security guards.* 毒品就在保安人员的眼皮底下被走私进来。

4 stick/poke your nose into to show too much interest in private matters that do not concern you 多管〔闲事〕，干涉〔别人的私事〕: *She always has to stick her nose into everything, doesn't she?* 她老是爱管闲事，是吗？— see also 另见 NOSY

5 keep your nose out (of) *spoken* to stop showing too much interest in private matters that do not concern you【口】别管〔闲事〕: *I'd prefer you to keep your nose right out of my business!* 我宁愿你别过问我的事！

6 turn your nose up (at) *informal* to refuse to accept something because you do not think it is good enough for you【非正式】瞧不起，(对…) 嗤之以鼻: *My children turn their noses up at home cooking.* 我的孩子们看不上家里做的饭菜。

7 look down your nose at *informal* to behave as if you think someone or something is not good enough for you【非正式】瞧不起，对…嗤之以鼻: *The Taggarts have always looked down their noses at their neighbours.* 塔格特一家人一向瞧不起他们的邻居。

8 with your nose in the air behaving as if you are more important than other people and not talking to them 目中无人地; 瞧不起人地: *Maria flounced past with her nose in the air.* 玛丽亚目中无人地大步走了过去。

9 have a nose round *BrE spoken* to look around a place or to look for something【英口】四处观看；四处寻找: *Let's have a nose round while there's no one here.* 趁这儿没人，我们四处找找吧！

10 have a (good) nose (for) a) to be naturally good at finding and recognizing something 天生擅长寻找[识别]〔某物〕: [+for] *a reporter with a nose for a story* 擅长发掘题材的新闻记者 **b)** to be good at recognizing smells 嗅觉灵敏: *a dog with a good nose* 嗅觉灵敏的狗

11 get up sb's nose *BrE spoken* to annoy someone very much【英口】使某人非常生气: *His manner really gets up my nose.* 他的态度着实惹恼了我。

12 follow your nose to keep going straight ahead 一直向前走: *Turn left at the post office and then just follow your nose.* 在邮局那儿向左转，然后一直向前走。

13 keep your nose clean *spoken* to make sure you do not get into trouble, or do anything wrong or illegal【口】遵纪守法；行为检点；不卷入是非

14 on the nose *AmE spoken* exactly【美口】确切地，精确地: *Guess how much I paid. That's right; $50 on the nose!* 猜猜我付了多少钱。没错，50美元整！

15 keep your nose to the grindstone *informal* to work very hard, without stopping to rest【非正式】努力工作，一刻不停地苦干

16 have your nose in a book to be giving all your attention to what you are reading 埋头苦读

17 by a nose if a horse wins a race by a nose, it only just wins 〔赛马〕险胜

18 put sb's nose out of joint *informal* to annoy someone, especially by attracting everyone's attention away from them【非正式】〔尤指通过抢夺众人的注意力〕使某人气歪鼻子；使某人眼红

19 nose to tail *especially BrE* cars, buses etc that are nose to tail are moving very slowly without much space between them【尤英】〔车辆〕首尾相接〔指交通堵塞〕: *Traffic was nose to tail for three miles.* 汽车首尾相接堵了三英里长。

20 ▶PLANE 飞机◀ [C] the pointed front end of a plane, ROCKET etc 〔飞机、火箭等的〕头部，机首，前端；突出部分 —see picture at 参见 AIRCRAFT 图 —see also 另见 HARD-NOSED, BROWN-NOSE, **cut off your nose to spite your face** (CUT OFF (9)), NOSE JOB, **pay through the nose (for sth)** (PAY[1] (13)), **powder your nose** (POWDER[2] (3)), **thumb your nose at** (THUMB[2] (2))

nose[2] *v* **1** [I always+adv/prep] *informal* to try to find out things about other people in a way that is annoying【非正式】窥探；探听；四处查看: **nose about** *BrE*【英】**/around/into** *The landlady was nosing around the house while we were out.* 女房东趁我们外出时在屋里四处查看。| *Stop nosing into my affairs!* 别管我的事！ **2** [I always+adv/prep, T always+adv/prep] if a vehicle, boat etc noses forward, or if you nose it forward, it moves forward slowly 〔车辆、船只等〕缓慢地前行；将〔车辆、船只等〕缓慢地向前开: **[+out/through etc]** *The boat nosed out into Nantucket Sound.* 船徐徐驶进了楠塔基特湾。| **nose sth out/through etc** *She carefully nosed the car forward through the traffic.* 她小心地在车流中将车慢慢向前开。

N

nose sth ↔ **out** *phr v* [T] *informal* to discover information by searching carefully for a long time【非正式】〔经长时间仔细查找而〕发现，察觉：*The reporters have nosed out some interesting facts about the politician's past life.* 记者们找到了这位政治家旧日的一些趣事。

nose·bag /ˋnozbæg; ˈnəʊzbæg/ *n* [C] a bag that holds food and can be hung around a horse's head〔挂在马头上的〕饲料袋；FEEDBAG *AmE*【美】

nose·bleed /ˋnoz͵blid; ˈnəʊzbliːd/ *n* [C] **have a nosebleed** to have blood coming out of your nose 鼻出血

nose·cone /ˋnozkon; ˈnəʊzkəʊn/ *n* [C] the pointed front part of a MISSILE〔导弹的〕头部，前锥体

nose·dive[1] /ˋnoz͵daɪv; ˈnəʊzdaɪv/ *n* [C] **1** a sudden drop in amount, price, rate etc〔数量、价格、比率等的〕猛跌，急降：*The pound took a nosedive on the foreign exchange market today.* 英镑今天在外汇交易市场上出现暴跌。**2** a sudden steep drop made by a plane with its front end pointing towards the ground〔飞机的〕俯冲：*Everyone screamed as the plane suddenly went into a nosedive.* 当飞机突然俯冲下来时，大家都尖叫起来。

nosedive[2] *v* [I] **1** if a price, rate, amount etc nosedives, it becomes smaller or reduces in value suddenly〔价格、比率、数量等〕猛跌，急降 **2** if a plane nosedives, it drops suddenly and steeply with its front end pointing towards the ground〔飞机〕俯冲

nose·gay /ˋnoz͵ge; ˈnəʊzgeɪ/ *n* [C] *old-fashioned* a small arrangement of flowers【过时】小花束

nose job /ˈ· ·/ *n* [C] *informal* a medical operation on someone's nose to improve its appearance【非正式】鼻子整形手术

nos·ey /ˋnozɪ; ˈnəʊzi/ *adj* another spelling of NOSY nosy 的另一种拼法

nosh[1] /nɑʃ; nɒʃ/ *n informal*【非正式】**1** [U] *BrE* food【英】食物：*They serve good nosh there.* 那里的食物不错。**2** [singular] *BrE* a meal【英】一顿饭 **3** [singular] *AmE* a small amount of food eaten between meals; SNACK【美】〔正餐之外的〕小吃，零食

nosh[2] *v* [I] *informal* to eat【非正式】吃

no-show /ˌ· ˈ·/ *n* [C] someone who is expected to arrive somewhere, for example at a restaurant or plane, but does not arrive 已预订〔餐馆坐位或飞机航班等〕但未到的人；不能如约出席者：*How many no-shows were there?* 有多少客人没来？—**no-show** *v* [I,T] *AmE*【美】

nosh-up /ˈ· ·/ *n* [singular] *BrE informal* a big satisfying meal【英，非正式】盛宴；美餐

nos·tal·gia /nɑˋstældʒɪə; nɒˈstældʒə/ *n* [U] the slightly sad feeling of remembering happy events or experiences from the past 对往昔事物的留恋，怀旧情绪：*He thought with nostalgia of his carefree childhood.* 他带着怀旧之情想起那无忧无虑的童年。| [+for] *nostalgia for the good old days* 对美好过去的留恋

nos·tal·gic /nɑˋstældʒɪk; nɒˈstældʒɪk/ *adj* feeling or expressing a slight sadness when remembering happy events or experiences from the past 留恋过去的，怀旧的：*Seeing those old school photographs has made me quite nostalgic.* 看到那些上学时拍的旧照片，我不禁产生了怀旧之情。| *a nostalgic look back at the 1950s* 对20世纪50年代的怀念 —**nostalgically** /-klɪ; -kli/ *adv*

Nos·tra·da·mus /͵nɑstrəˋdɑməs; ͵nɒstrəˈdɑːməs/ (1503-66) a French doctor and ASTROLOGER (=someone who studies the movements of the planets and their influence on events) who wrote a book describing things that he believed would happen in the future. Some people believe that Nostradamus had special powers, and that his ideas about the future are correct. 诺斯特拉达穆斯〔(1503-1566)，法国医生，占星家。他写有一本预言书，描写自己认为未来会发生的事情。有的人认为，他有特异功能，对未来的预测是准确的〕

nos·tril /ˋnɑstrəl; ˈnɒstrəl/ *n* [C] one of the two openings at the end of your nose, through which you breathe and smell things 鼻孔 —see picture at 参见 HEAD[1] 图

nos·trum /ˋnɑstrəm; ˈnɒstrəm/ *n* [C] **1** *formal* an idea that someone thinks will solve a problem easily, but probably will not help at all【正式】〔实际上也许并无用处的〕妙计，妙策：*an economic nostrum* 经济上的"灵丹妙药" **2** *old-fashioned* a medicine that is probably not effective and is not given by a doctor【过时】江湖药；骗人的假药

nos·y, nosey /ˋnozɪ; ˈnəʊzi/ *adj* always wanting to find out things that do not concern you, especially other people's private affairs 好管闲事的，爱打听别人事情的：*Don't be so nosy! It's none of your business.* 别这么爱管闲事！这不关你的事。—**nosiness** *n* [U]

nosy park·er /ˌ· ·ˈ··/ *n* [C] *BrE informal* a nosy person【英，非正式】爱管闲事的人

not /nɑt; nɒt/ *adv* **1** used to make a word or expression negative 不，没，不是〔表示否定的意思〕：*"Can we go to the park?" "No, not today, dear."* "我们可以去公园吗？""不，今天不去，亲爱的。" | *Lorna was not a tidy child and left toys everywhere.* 洛娜不是一个整洁的孩子，把玩具丢得到处都是。| *The store is open all week but not on Sundays.* 这家店每天都开，但星期天不开。| *Sally will not eat meat.* 萨莉不吃肉。| *You were wrong not to inform the police.* 你没有通知警方是不对的。| **not at all easy/difficult etc** *I was not at all surprised to see her at the meeting.* 在会上看到她，我一点也不感到惊讶。| **not at all** *I don't like his attitude at all.* 我一点也不喜欢他的态度。—compare 比较 NO[1] —see also 另见 -N'T —see 见 NO[2] (USAGE) **2** used instead of a word or expression to mean the opposite of something that has been mentioned before it〔用来代替前面提到的整个语句，表示与其相反的意思〕：*Are you ready to eat or not?* 你准备好吃饭了没有？| *I hope to see you tomorrow, but if not, leave me a message.* 我希望明天能见到你，如果不行的话，你给我留个信儿。| **hope/think/be afraid etc not** *"Is Fiona coming?" "I hope not, she's so boring."* "菲奥娜要来吗？""我希望她不要来，她实在烦人。" | *I asked if she would be able to help out but she said not.* 我问她能不能帮忙，她说不能。—compare 比较 SO[1] (3) **3** used to give a word or expression the opposite meaning 不，不是〔表示相反的意思〕：*"Will the journey take much longer?" "Oh, it's not far now."* "路途还很远吗？""哦，现在不远了。" | *Madeline is such a caring person, not without problems of her own.* 马德琳真是个热心的人，尽管她自己也不是没有困难。| *In the war years diphtheria was not an uncommon disease.* 战争年代白喉是常见病。| *They want a cheap service but they're not slow to complain if the trains break down.* 他们想要廉价服务，但火车坏了他们又急着抱怨。| **not very tall/expensive etc** (=fairly short, cheap etc) 不太高/昂贵等 *These teabags aren't very good, are they?* 这些袋泡茶不太好喝，是吗？| **not a little/a few etc** (=quite a lot) 很多，不少：*He drank not a little of the wine.* 他喝了不少酒。| **not a lot/much/many etc** (=only a few/a little etc) 不多，很少 *It's a new remedy for hay fever which not many people have heard of.* 这是治疗花粉症的一种鲜为人知的新方法。**4 not a/not one** not any person or thing 一个也没有：*Since she went abroad she hasn't even written a letter, not one word!* 她出国后一封信也没写过，一个字也没有！| **not even a** *Her face was stony, not even a smile.* 她脸上毫无表情，连一点笑容也没有。| **not a single** *He has none of his savings left, not a single penny!* 他的积蓄一点也没剩下，一分钱都没有了！**5 not at all** *especially BrE* used to be polite when someone has thanked you or asked you to do something【尤英】别客气；一点不介意：*"Would you mind helping me with my suitcase?" "Not at all."* "你能帮我提一下行李箱吗？""没问题。" **6 not only** used to say that besides someone doing one thing they have also done something else 不仅，不但：**not only...but (also)...** *Shakespeare was not only a writer but also an actor.* 莎士比亚不仅是个作家，还是个演员。| **not only do/will/can etc** *Not only do the nurses want a pay increase, they want reduced hours as well.* 护士们不仅要求提高工资，还要求缩短工作时间。**7 not that I care/not that it is important etc** used to mean that you do not care, that it is not important etc 我并不在乎/那并不重要：*Sarah's found herself a new boyfriend – not that I care about it.* 萨拉找了个新的男朋友，不过我并不在乎。**8 – not!** *spoken* used, especially by young people, to say that you really mean the opposite of what you have just said【口】才不是呢！〔年轻人常用〕：*I really like spending my Saturday afternoons tidying the house – not!* 我很喜欢在星期六下午整理房子 —— 才不是呢！—see also 另见 **not half** (HALF[3] (5)), **not to say** (SAY[1] (13))

USAGE NOTE 用法说明：NOT

FORMALITY 正式程度

In spoken English and informal writing **not** is usually shortened to **n't** with *is, are, was, were, has, have, had, do, does* etc. *Shall not* becomes *shan't*, and *will not* becomes *won't*. (Note however that **shan't** is only used in British English). 在英语口语和非正式的书面语中，not 与 is, are, was, were, has, have, had, do, does 等连用时通常缩略为 n't。shall not 变成 shan't，而 will not 则变成 won't。(注意 shan't 只在英国英语中使用)

SPELLING 拼法

The short form of **not** is **n't** not *'nt.* not 的缩略形式是 n't，而不是 'nt。

Can with the full form **not** is written as one word. can 和 not 的非缩略形式连写时为一个单词：*The two sides in the dispute still cannot reach an agreement.* 纠纷的双方仍未能达成协议。| *I simply cannot understand what he's talking about.* 我完全听不懂他在说什么。

no·tab·il·i·ty /ˌnotəˈbɪlətɪ; ˌnəʊtəˈbɪlᵻti/ *n* [C usually plural 一般用复数] *formal* an important person【正式】要人；名人

no·ta·ble /ˈnotəbḷ; ˈnəʊtəbəl/ *adj* important, interesting, excellent, or unusual and therefore deserving to be noticed or mentioned 显要的；显著的；值得注意的：*a notable achievement* 显著的成就 | *a notable lack of enthusiasm* 明显的热情不足 | [+for] *The book is notable for its striking illustrations.* 该书以引人注目的插图著称。| **a notable example/exception etc** *Most birds sing only in daylight, one notable exception being the nightingale.* 多数鸟类只在白天鸣叫，而夜莺显然是个例外。

no·ta·bles /ˈnotəbḷz; ˈnəʊtəbəlz/ *n* [plural] important or famous people 显要人物；著名人士

3 **no·ta·bly** /ˈnotəblɪ; ˈnəʊtəbli/ *adv* **1** particularly; especially 格外地；特别地：*Some early doctors, notably Hippocrates, thought that diet and hygiene were important.* 一些早期的医生，如希波克拉底，认为饮食和卫生是很重要的。**2** in a way that is noticeably different, important, or unusual 明显地，显著地：*Emigration has notably increased.* 移居国外的人明显增加。

no·ta·rize also 又作 **-ise** *BrE*【英】/ˈnotəˌraɪz; ˈnəʊtəraɪz/ *v* [T often passive 常用被动态] if a notary notarizes a document or written statement they make it official〔公证人〕对…作公证，公证

no·ta·ry /ˈnotərɪ; ˈnəʊtəri/ also 又作 **notary pub·lic** /ˌ··· ˈ··/ *n* [C] someone, especially a lawyer, who has the legal power to make a signed statement or document official 公证人，公证员

no·ta·tion /noˈteʃən; nəʊˈteɪʃən/ *n* [C,U] a system of written marks or signs used to represent something such as music, mathematics, or scientific ideas 记号，符号；记法

notch[1] /nɑtʃ; nɒtʃ/ *n* [C] **1** a V-shaped cut in a surface or edge〔V字形的〕切口，凹口；刻痕：*He made three notches in the stick.* 他在棍子上刻了三个V字形切口。**2** a degree or level on a scale of achievement, social position etc 等级，水平：*Her new book is several notches above anything else she has written.* 她的新书比她以前的作品要高出好几个等级。**3** *AmE* a passage between two mountains or hills【美】山峡，峡谷 —see also 另见 TOP-NOTCH

notch[2] *v* [T] to cut a usually V-shaped mark into something, especially as a way of showing the number of times something has been done〔尤指为记录次数而〕在…上刻下V字形切口，在…上开V形槽口

notch sth ↔ **up** *phr v* [T] to achieve something, especially a victory or a particular total or SCORE 赢得，获取：*The Houston Astros have notched up another win.* 休斯敦太空人队又赢了一场比赛。

S1 W1 **note[1]** /not; nəʊt/ *n*

1 ►TO REMIND YOU 用于提醒自己◄ [C] something that is written down to remind you of something you need to do, say, or remember 笔记，记录：*I'll write myself a note so I don't forget to ring the bank.* 我会用笔记下来，这样就不会忘了给银行打电话。| *She gave a brilliant speech – and without any notes.* 她作了个精彩的演讲，连讲稿都没有用。| **make a note of sth** (=write something down so that you can look at it later) 将某事记下来 *I made a note of her address and phone number.* 我记下了她的地址和电话号码。

2 ►SHORT LETTER 短信◄ [C] a short, usually informal letter〔通常指非正式的〕短笺，便条：*There was a note on the table – 'Gone to movies – Back about 11:30.'* 桌上有张便条："我看电影去了，大约11点半回来。" | **thank-you note** (=a note to thank someone for a present etc) 感谢信

3 ►FOR STUDYING 为了学习◄ **notes** [plural] pages written by a student containing information from a book, lesson etc〔学生的〕笔记：*There is no textbook, so you must rely on your lecture notes.* 没有教科书，因此你们必须依靠课堂笔记。| **take/make notes** (=write notes) 记笔记 *She sat quietly in the corner making careful notes.* 她静静地坐在角落里仔细地做笔记。

4 ►MUSIC 音乐◄ [C] **a)** a particular musical sound or PITCH[1] (3a) 乐音；音调：*She has a good voice but has trouble hitting the high notes.* 她的嗓音很好，但唱高音时有困难。**b)** a sign in a piece of music that represents a particular musical sound or pitch and that is of a particular length 音符 —see picture at 参见 MUSIC 图 **c) the black/white notes** the black or white KEYS of a piano〔钢琴的〕黑/白键

5 ►MONEY 钱◄ [C] *BrE* a piece of paper that is used as money【英】纸币，钞票；BILL[1] (3) *AmE*【美】：*Alice took out a ten-pound note.* 艾丽斯拿出一张10英镑的钞票。

6 ►VOICE 声音◄ [singular] if there is a particular note in someone's voice, they show what they are thinking or feeling by the way their voice sounds 口气，调子：*There was a strained note in Fischer's normally relaxed voice.* 费希尔一贯轻松的说话声中带有一点紧张的口气。| **a note of anger/jealousy/anxiety etc** *I detected a note of jealousy in his voice.* 我从他的声音里听出了嫉妒的口气。

7 ►PARTICULAR QUALITY 特征◄ [singular] something that adds a particular quality to a situation, statement, or event 特征，特点；色彩：*Her story brought a personal note to the debate on child care.* 她的故事给这场关于育儿的争论添加了一丝个人色彩。| **a note of humour/sadness/dissent etc** *We need to add a note of caution to such optimism.* 我们需要给这种乐观的态度添加一点谨慎。

8 ►ADDITIONAL INFORMATION 附加资料◄ [C] a short piece of writing at the bottom of a page or at the end of a book, that gives more information about something written in the main part〔页尾或书后的〕注释，注解；评注：*the notes at the back of the book* 书后的注释

9 ►LETTER 信◄ [C] a formal letter between governments〔外交上的〕照会；通牒：*a diplomatic note* 外交照会

10 of note important or famous 重要的；著名的：*The school has produced several architects of note.* 这所学校培养了几位著名的建筑设计师。

11 worthy/deserving of note important or interesting and deserving to be noticed 值得注意的：*History has been called 'the record of what one age finds worthy of note in another'.* 历史被称为"某一时代对自己认为值得后世注意的事件的记录"。

12 take note to pay careful attention to something 注意（到），留意（到）：[+of] *People were beginning to take note of her talents.* 人们开始注意到她的才能。

13 hit/strike the right/wrong note to succeed or not succeed in being right and suitable for a particular occasion 做对/错事 —see also 另见 **compare notes** (COMPARE[1] (6))

note[2] *v* [T] *formal*【正式】**1** to notice or pay careful attention to something 注意，留意：**note that** *Please note that the bill must be paid within ten days.* 请注意本账单必须在十天以内付清。| **note sth** *The children should be encouraged to note the colours and textures of the fabrics.* 应该鼓励孩子们注意织物的颜色和质地。| **note who/what/how etc** *I noted how her face reddened every time Ben's name was mentioned.* 我注意到每次一提到本的名字，她就会脸红。**2** to mention something because it is important or interesting 特别提到；指出：*The report noted a complete disregard for the safety regulations.* 报告特别提到人们对安全规定的漠视。| **note that** *We have already noted that soybeans are a good source of protein.* 我们已经说过，大豆含有丰富的蛋白质。**3** also 又作 **note down** to write something down so that it will be remembered 记下来：*Note any adverse reaction to the medication on the chart.* 把对药物的任何不良反应都记在这张表上。

note·book /ˈnotˌbʊk; ˈnəʊtbʊk/ *n* [C] **1** a book made of plain paper on which you can write notes 笔记本 **2** a very small PERSONAL COMPUTER that is the size of a book 笔记本电脑，手提电脑 —see picture on page A14 参见A14页图

note card /ˈ· ·/ *n* [C] *AmE* a NOTELET【美】短柬卡

not·ed /ˈnotɪd; ˈnəʊtᵻd/ *adj* well known, especially because of some special quality or ability〔尤指因有特别之处而〕著名的，知名的：*restaurants noted for the excellence of their cuisine* 以精美菜肴著称的餐馆

note·let /ˈnotlɪt; ˈnəʊtlᵻt/ *n* [C] *BrE* a small folded piece of paper with a picture on it, for writing a short letter【英】〔用来写短信的卡式〕便笺，邮简；NOTE CARD *AmE*【美】

note·pad /ˈnotpæd; ˈnəʊtpæd/ *n* [C] a number of sheets of paper fastened together at the top, used for writing notes 便条簿，记事本

note·pa·per /ˈnotˌpepɚ; ˈnəʊtˌpeɪpə/ *n* [U] paper used for writing letters etc 信纸，信笺；便条纸：**headed notepaper** (=with someone's address printed on it) 印有寄信人地址的信笺

note·wor·thy /ˈnotˌwɝðɪ; ˈnəʊtˌwɜːði/ *adj* something such as an event that is noteworthy deserves attention because it is important, interesting, or unusual 值得注意的；显著的：*a noteworthy achievement* 显著的成就 | *a noteworthy piece of architecture* 值得注意的建筑

not-for-prof·it /ˌ· · ˈ··/ *adj AmE* NON-PROFITMAKING【美】非营利性的

noth·ing[1] /ˈnʌθɪŋ; ˈnʌθɪŋ/ *pron* **1** not anything; no thing 没有任何东西；没有事：*Nothing ever happens in this town.* 这个城镇从来都不会发生什么特别的事。| *There's nothing in this box. Throw it away.* 这盒子里什么也没有，扔掉吧。| *He said nothing about it to me.* 这件事他什么都没对我说。| **nothing new/bad etc** *Why are you still in bed when there's nothing wrong with you?* 既然你没有什么不舒服，为什么还不起床呢？| **nothing to do/to eat etc** *If you have nothing to do how about helping me in the garden?* 如果你没事干，能不能来花园帮我呢？| S1 W1

N

nothing else (=nothing more) 没有别的东西 *I had nothing else to say so I signed the letter.* 我没有别的什么要说，所以就在信上签了名。| **nothing at all** (=absolutely nothing) 什么也不; 根本没有 *You must eat nothing at all before the operation.* 手术前你什么都不能吃。**2** something which is considered unimportant, not interesting or not worth worrying about 微不足道的事, 小事: *A harmless kiss. It meant nothing.* 只是一个没有恶意的亲吻, 别当回事。| *It's nothing, just a scratch.* 没什么，只是一点擦伤。| *There's nothing on television tonight.* 今晚电视上没有什么好节目。| *It was nothing for a family to have ten children in those days.* 那时一家有十个孩子不算什么。**3** *especially AmE* zero【尤美】零: *We beat them ten to nothing.* 我们以十比零击败了他们。**4 for nothing a)** without paying for something or being paid for something 不要钱; 不交钱; 免费: *Why pay a plumber when my brother will do it for nothing?* 我弟弟可以免费干，何必花钱去雇一个管子工呢? | *She knows the club manager so we always get in for nothing.* 她认识俱乐部的经理，所以我们总是不花钱就能入场。**b)** without having a good reason or purpose 平白无故地, 白白地: *We went all that way for nothing.* 我们白白地走了那么多路。| *They don't call him Babyface Dickson for nothing!* 他们并非无缘无故地叫他"娃娃脸迪克森"的。**5 have/be nothing to do with sb/sth** [not in progressive 不用进行式] **a)** if something has nothing to do with a particular fact or situation it is not connected with that fact or situation 与某事无关: *Our decision has nothing to do with the fact that her father is on the committee.* 我们的决定与她父亲是委员会成员没有关系。**b)** if a situation has nothing to do with someone, it is personal and private 不关某人的事: *It's nothing to do with you. Mind your own business.* 这事与你无关，别管闲事。**6 have/want nothing to do with** to not be involved in something, especially because you disapprove〔尤指因不赞同而〕不想牵连在内, 不想涉足〔某事〕: *He told the police that he had wanted nothing to do with the whole thing.* 他告诉警方他一直不想与那件事有任何瓜葛。**7 nothing special** not very bad and not very good; average 没什么特别之处的, 普通的: *The meal was nothing special, just a little fish with a cheese sauce.* 这顿饭很普通，只不过是一点鱼加上干酪汁罢了。**8 nothing but** *formal* only【正式】只不过: *He's nothing but a common criminal.* 他只不过是个普通的罪犯。**9 nothing much** very little 很少, 没有什么: *"What did you do last weekend?" "Oh, nothing much."* "你上个周末干了些什么?""噢, 没干什么。" **10 there's nothing like** used to say that something is very good 什么都比不上…: *There's nothing like a long hot bath after a day's climbing.* 爬了一天的山以后，什么都比不上好好泡个热水浴。**11 there's nothing in/to sth** used to say that what people are saying about someone else's personal life is not true 某事是捏造的: *It seems there's nothing in the rumours that she's pregnant.* 看来关于她怀孕的谣言是毫无根据的。**12 there's nothing for it but to do sth** used when there is only one thing you can do in a particular situation 除了做某事以外别无他法: *With the bridge destroyed there was nothing for it but to swim.* 桥被毁坏了，除了游过去别无他法。**13 nothing doing** *spoken* used to refuse to do something【口】不行, 我不干: *Lend you £500? Nothing doing!* 借给你500英镑? 不行! **14 be nothing if not** used to emphasize a particular quality that someone or something has 极其, 非常〔用于强调〕: *You've got to admit – he's nothing if not persistent.* 你必须承认，他非常执著。**15 nothing to it** *spoken* used when something is easy to do【口】〔做某事〕没有困难, 很容易: *Anyone can use a computer. There's nothing to it!* 任何人都能用电脑，很容易的! **16 it was nothing/think nothing of it** *spoken* used when someone has thanked you a lot for something you have done for them【口】别放在心上, 没什么〔用于回答他人的感谢〕: *"You really shouldn't have gone to so much trouble." "Oh, think nothing of it."* "让你这么麻烦真不好意思。""噢, 没什么。" **17 nothing of the sort** *spoken* used to strongly refuse to do something or when you feel strongly that something is not true【口】绝对不行; 绝对不可能〔用于严词拒绝或否认〕: *What do you mean you're going to borrow my car? You'll do nothing of the sort!* 你说要借我的汽车? 绝对不行! —see also 另见 **sweet nothings** (SWEET[1] (12)), **to say nothing of** (SAY[1] (47)), **nothing on earth** (EARTH[1] (11))

nothing² *adv* **1 be nothing like sb/sth** to have no qualities or features that are similar to someone or something else 一点都不像某人/某物: *She's nothing like her brother. He's dark and she's fair.* 她一点都不像她的哥哥: 她哥哥皮肤黑，她皮肤白。**2 be nothing short of sth** if someone's behaviour is nothing short of something such as laziness, corruption etc, they are extremely lazy or corrupt 完全…, 确实…: *His behaviour was nothing short of rudeness.* 他的行为非常不礼貌。

noth·ing·ness /ˈnʌθɪŋnɪs; ˈnʌθɪŋnɪs/ *n* [U] **1** empty space or the complete absence of everything 无; 空: *Natalie found him standing very still, looking into nothingness.* 纳塔莉发现他一动不动地站着，目光茫然。**2** the state of not existing 不存在: *Is there only nothingness after death?* 人死后一切便会化为乌有吗?

no·tice¹ /ˈnotɪs; ˈnəʊtɪs/ *v* [I, T not in progressive 不用进行时] S1 W2
1 to see, hear, or feel something 看到; 听到; 感觉到; 注意(到): *He spilled the tea, but Miss Whitley did not notice.* 他把茶泼出来了，但怀特利小姐没有注意到。| **notice sth/sb** *You may notice a numb feeling in your fingers.* 你可能会感觉到手指有点麻木。| **notice that** *Catherine noticed that Isabella was restless.* 凯瑟琳注意到伊莎贝拉有点坐立不安。| **notice who/what/how etc** *He was too tired even to notice how hungry and thirsty he was.* 他太累了，甚至没有意识到自己有多饿多渴。| **notice sb/sth doing sth** *Did you notice him leaving the party early?* 你注意到他提前离开了聚会吗? **2 be/get noticed** to get attention from someone 引起注意: *a young actress trying to get herself noticed* 一心想引人注目的年轻女演员

This graph shows how common different grammar patterns of the verb **notice** are. 本图表所示为动词notice构成的不同语法模式的使用频率。

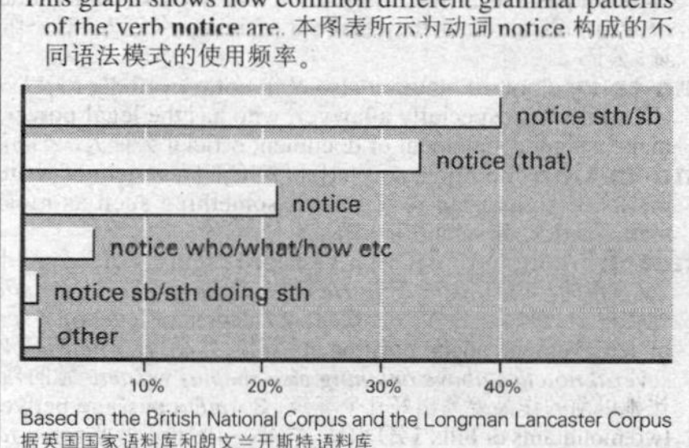

Based on the British National Corpus and the Longman Lancaster Corpus
据英国国家语料库和朗文兰开斯特语料库

notice² *n* S2 W2

1 take notice (of) to pay attention to something or someone and let them affect or influence you 注意(到): **not take any notice/take no notice** *I keep complaining but nobody takes any notice.* 我不断地抱怨，但没有人理我。| *Take no notice of Henry – he's just being silly.* 别理亨利，他在发傻。| *I hope you'll take notice of what I'm going to tell you.* 我希望你注意我下面要讲的话。

2 ►ON PAPER 在纸上◄ [C] a written or printed statement that gives information or a warning to people 布告; 通告; 启事: *That notice on the wall says 'No smoking'.* 墙上的告示写着"禁止吸烟"。| *I'll put up a notice about the meeting.* 我会贴一张开会通知的。

3 ►WARNING/TIME TO PREPARE 警告/准备时间◄ [U] information or a warning about something that is going to happen 通知, 预告: *These rules are subject to change without notice.* 这些规则可不经通知便进行更改。| **ten days' notice/three months' notice etc** (=a warning ten days etc before) 提前十天/三个月通知等 *Either party may terminate the contract upon three months' notice.* 任何一方可在提前三个月通知对方终止合同。| **at short notice/at a moment's notice** (=allowing only a short time to prepare for something) 在短时间内 *You can't expect me to produce a meal at a moment's notice.* 别指望跟我一说，我立马就能做出一顿饭。| **give sb some notice** *If they'd given me more notice, I'd have had everything ready.* 如果他们能更早些通知我，我早就把一切都准备妥当了。| **serve notice** *formal* (=officially warn someone that something is going to happen)【正式】正式通知

4 give sb notice a) to tell someone that they must leave their job in a week, a month etc 向某人发出解雇通知: *They closed the factory, giving the workers only a week's notice.* 他们只提前一周通知工人，就关闭了工厂。**b)** to tell someone officially that they must leave the place they are renting by a particular date 正式向某人发出停租通知: **give sb notice to quit/leave** *BrE*【英】*I've been given notice to leave my flat.* 我接到通知，要我搬出所住的套房。

5 hand in/give in your notice to inform your employer that you will be leaving your job soon, especially by writing a formal letter〔正式〕递交辞呈

6 come to sb's notice *formal* if a fact, problem etc comes to your notice, you notice it or find out about it【正式】引起某人的注意; 为某人察觉: *It has come to my notice that your account is overdrawn by £200.* 我注意到你的账户已透支了200英镑。|

bring sth to sb's notice (=tell someone about something) 提醒某人注意某事 *There are several important matters I'd like to bring to your notice.* 我想提醒你注意几件重要的事。| **escape sb's notice** (=not be noticed by someone) 没有被某人注意到 *It may have escaped your notice but your father is much too ill to travel.* 你可能没有注意到，你父亲病得很严重，已无法去旅行了。

7 until further notice from now until another change is announced 直至另行通知: *The office is closed until further notice.* 办事处将一直关闭，直到另行通知为止。

8 ►BOOK/PLAY ETC 书/戏等◄ [C usually plural 一般用复数] a statement of opinion, especially one written for a newspaper or magazine, about a new play, book, film etc; REVIEW[1] (2)〔尤指报刊上对新剧、新书、新电影等的〕评价; 评论; 短评: *The new play got mixed notices* (=some good, some bad) *in the newspapers.* 报纸对那出新剧的评价褒贬不一。—see also 另见 **make sb sit up (and take notice)** (SIT)

no·tice·a·ble /ˋnotɪsəbḷ; ˈnəʊtɨ̥səbəl/ *adj* easy to notice 容易注意到的; 明显的, 显著的: *However much he drank it had no noticeable effect on him.* 不管他喝了多少酒，看起来都没有什么明显的影响。| *There was a noticeable lack of interest in the idea.* 对这个想法大家显然没有兴趣。| **it is noticeable that** *It was noticeable that she invited everybody except Gail.* 显而易见，除了盖尔外，所有人都收到了她的邀请。—**noticeably** *adv*: *The atmosphere at the dinner table was noticeably less relaxed.* 饭桌上的气氛显然不像以前那么轻松。

no·tice·board /ˋnotɪsˌbord; ˈnəʊtɨ̥sˌbɔːd/ *n* [C] *BrE* a special board on a wall which notices can be fixed to【英】布告牌, 布告栏; BULLETIN BOARD *AmE*【美】—see picture at 参见 BOARD[1] 图

no·ti·fi·a·ble /ˋnotəˌfaɪəbḷ; ˈnəʊtɨ̥faɪəbəl/ *adj BrE technical* a notifiable disease is one that by law must be reported to an office of public health【英, 术语】〔疾病〕须报告卫生当局的, 应汇报的

no·ti·fi·ca·tion /ˌnotəfəˋkeʃən; ˌnəʊtɨ̥fɨ̥ˈkeɪʃən/ *n* [C,U] *formal* an act of officially informing someone about something【正式】通知, 告知: **[+of]** *Notification of any changes should be in writing.* 任何变更均应以书面形式告知。

no·ti·fy /ˋnotəˌfaɪ; ˈnəʊtɨ̥faɪ/ *v* [T] to formally or officially tell someone about something; inform〔正式地〕通知, 告知: **notify sb of** *You will be notified of any changes in the system.* 系统中如有任何变化都会通知你。

3 **no·tion** /ˋnoʃən; ˈnəʊʃən/ *n* [C] **1** an idea, belief or opinion, especially one that is false or not very clear〔尤指错误或模糊的〕概念; 观点; 看法: **[+of]** *misguided notions of male superiority* 男尊女卑的错误观念 | *We haven't the faintest notion of her whereabouts.* 我们一点也想不出她在哪儿。| **notion that** *the notion that human beings are basically good* 认为人本质上是好的这一观念 **2** a sudden desire to do something; WHIM 突然的念头, 奇想: **notion to do sth** *At midnight she had a sudden notion to go to the beach.* 半夜里她突发奇想要去海滩。**3 notions** [plural] *AmE* small things used for sewing【美】小件缝纫用品

no·tion·al /ˋnoʃənḷ; ˈnəʊʃənəl/ *adj* existing only in the mind as an idea or plan, and not existing in reality 概念上的; 理论上的: *Their calculations were based on a notional minimum wage.* 他们的计算是以理论上的最低工资为依据的。

no·to·ri·e·ty /ˌnotəˋraɪətɪ; ˌnəʊtəˈraɪəti/ *n* [U] the state of being famous or well-known because of something bad 臭名昭著, 声名狼藉: *His affairs with young actresses earned him great notoriety.* 他和几位年轻女演员的风流韵事使他声名狼藉。

no·to·ri·ous /noˋtorɪəs; nəʊˈtɔːriəs/ *adj* famous or well-known for something bad 臭名远扬的, 声名狼藉的: *a notorious bandit* 臭名昭著的歹徒 | **[+for]** *The region is notorious for its terrible snowstorms.* 该地区因可怕的暴风雪而坏名远扬。—**notoriously** *adv*: *a notoriously inefficient company* 一家人人都知道效率奇低的公司 —see 见 FAMOUS (USAGE)

Not·re Dame /ˌnotə ˋdam; ˌnɒtrə ˈdɑːm/ a famous CATHEDRAL (=a large important church) in central Paris, which is a beautiful Gothic building from the 12th century, and a popular place for tourists to visit 巴黎圣母院〔巴黎市中心一著名大教堂。该教堂是一幢漂亮的12世纪哥特式建筑, 也是热门旅游景点〕

Notre Dame, University of also 又作 **Notre Dame** a private Catholic university in Indiana, US, which is famous especially for having a very good football team 圣母大学〔美国印第安那州一私立天主教会大学, 以拥有一支非常优秀的橄榄球队而闻名〕

Not·ting·ham /ˋnɑtɪŋəm; ˈnɒtɪŋəm/ an industrial city in Nottinghamshire in central England. Its industries include chemicals, engineering, and clothing, but it is especially known as a place where LACE (=very fine cloth with patterns of very small holes) is made. The stories of Robin Hood take place in this area. 诺丁汉〔英格兰中部诺丁汉郡一工业城市。其产业包括化工、工程技术和制衣, 尤以生产蕾丝布料闻名。罗宾汉的故事就发生在该地〕

Nottingham For·est /ˌ··· ˋ··/ a well-known English football team from Nottingham 诺丁汉森林队〔英国诺丁汉市的一支知名足球队〕

Not·ting·ham·shire /ˋnɑtɪŋəmʃɚ; ˈnɒtɪŋəmʃə/ written abbreviation 缩写 = **Notts.** a COUNTY in central England consisting mainly of farmland. There also used to be many coal mines, but most of them have now closed down. 诺丁汉郡〔英格兰中部一郡, 境内主要为耕地。过去这里也曾有许多煤矿, 但大部分现已关闭〕

Not·ting Hill Car·ni·val, the /ˌnɑtɪŋ hɪl ˋkɑrnəvḷ; ˌnɒtɪŋ hɪl ˈkɑːnɨ̥vəl/ a street CARNIVAL that takes place in the Notting Hill area of West London in August every year, mostly involving black people and famous for the colourful COSTUMES worn and the steel band music played 诺丁山狂欢节〔每年8月在西伦敦诺丁山举行的街头狂欢节。参加者主要为黑人, 以色彩斑斓的服装和演奏钢盘打击乐闻名〕

Notts. /nɑts; nɒts/ the written abbreviation of 缩写 = NOTTINGHAMSHIRE

not·with·stand·ing /ˌnɑtwɪθˋstændɪŋ; ˌnɒtwɪθˈstændɪŋ/ *prep formal* in spite of something【正式】尽管: *The government is determined to proceed with the housing policies, notwithstanding public opposition.* 尽管公众反对, 政府仍决心继续执行其房屋政策。| *The EU nations embarked upon the trade agreement, a few exceptions notwithstanding.* 尽管有几个国家例外, 多数欧盟国家都开始执行这项贸易协定。—**notwithstanding** *adv*

nou·gat /ˋnugət; ˈnuːgɑː/ *n* [U] a sticky pink or white sweet made of sugar, nuts, and small pieces of fruit 鸟结糖, 牛轧糖, 果仁糖

nought /nɔt; nɔːt/ *n* **1** [C] *BrE* the number 0; zero【英】零: *A billion is 1 with 9 noughts after it.* 十亿是在1后面加9个零。**2** [U] *old use* nothing【旧】无

noughts and cross·es /ˌ· · ˋ··/ *n* [U] *BrE* a game in which two players write 0 or X in a pattern of nine squares, trying to win with a row of three 0s or three Xs【英】画圈打叉游戏, 画井游戏〔在"井"字的九个方格内, 由两人轮流填写, 谁能先把三个X或O列成一行即取胜〕; TICK-TACK-TOE *AmE*【美】

noun /naun; naʊn/ *n* [C] a word or group of words that represent a person (such as 'Michael' or 'teacher' or 'police officer'), a place (such as 'France' or 'school'), a thing or activity (such as 'coffee' or 'football'), or a quality or idea (such as 'danger' or 'happiness'). Nouns can be used as the subject or object of a verb (as in 'The teacher arrived' or 'We like the teacher') or as the object of a PREPOSITION (as in 'good at football') 名词 —see also 另见 COMMON NOUN, COUNT NOUN, PROPER NOUN, VERBAL NOUN

nour·ish /ˋnɝɪʃ; ˈnʌrɪʃ/ *v* [T] **1** to give a person or other living thing the food they need in order to live, grow, and stay healthy 滋养; 给…营养: *a well nourished baby* 营养良好的婴儿 **2** *formal* to keep a feeling, idea, or belief strong or help it to grow stronger【正式】保持, 怀有; 培养〔感情、观念等〕: *The beauty of the region has nourished the imagination of countless artists.* 该地区的美景激发了无数艺术家的想象力。

nour·ish·ing /ˋnɝɪʃɪŋ; ˈnʌrɪʃɪŋ/ *adj* food that is nourishing makes you strong and healthy〔食物〕有营养的, 滋养人的

nour·ish·ment /ˋnɝɪʃmənt; ˈnʌrɪʃmənt/ *n* [U] *formal* food that is needed to live, grow, and stay healthy【正式】食物; 滋养品; 营养: *The child has taken no nourishment all day.* 这孩子已经一整天没吃东西了。

nous /nus; naʊs/ *n* [U] *BrE informal* intelligence and the ability to make good practical decisions; COMMON SENSE【英, 非正式】良好的判断力; 常识: *She did have the nous to ring and tell us she'd be late.* 她很明事理, 打电话告诉我们她要晚到。

nou·veau riche /nuvo ˋriʃ; ˌnuːvəʊ ˈriːʃ/ *plural* **nouveaux riches** (*same pronunciation* 读音相同) *n* [C] someone who has only recently become rich and spends a lot of money 暴发户 —**nouveau riche** *adj*

nou·velle cui·sine /ˌnuvɛl kwɪˋzin; ˌnuːvel kwɪˈziːn/ *n* [U] a style of cooking from France that uses fresh fruit and vegetables cooked in a simple way and attractively served 新式烹饪〔一种源自法国的烹饪法, 它注重保持新鲜蔬果的原有风味, 并讲究食物的外观〕

> **CULTURAL NOTE 文化注释**
> People often joke that nouvelle cuisine is attractive to look at, but that there is only a very small amount of it on the plate and it is often very expensive. 人们常拿新式烹饪来开玩笑, 说它看起来很诱人, 但是盘子里的分量太少, 而且往往价格不菲。

Nov. the written abbreviation of 缩写= NOVEMBER

no·va /ˈnovə; ˈnəʊvə/ *plural* **novas** *or* **novae** /-vi; -viː/ *n* [C] a star which explodes and suddenly becomes much brighter for a short time 新星

No·va Sco·tia /ˌnovə ˋskoʃə; ˌnəʊvə ˈskəʊʃə/ a PROVINCE of southeast Canada on the Atlantic Ocean, whose capital city is Halifax. It consists mainly of farmland and forests, and it also produces minerals. 新斯科舍省〔加拿大东南部一省, 濒临大西洋, 首府: 哈利法克斯。境内主要为耕地和森林, 也有各种矿藏〕

3 **nov·el¹** /ˈnɑvḷ; ˈnɒvəl/ *n* [C] a long written story in which the characters and events are usually imaginary （长篇）小说: *an Agatha Christie novel* 阿加莎·克里斯蒂的小说

novel² *adj* not like anything known before and often thought of as new, unusual, and interesting 新的; 新颖的; 新奇的: *That's a novel idea – opening an English restaurant in France.* 在法国开一家英式餐馆, 那真是个新奇的想法。

nov·el·ist /ˈnɑvḷɪst; ˈnɒvəlɪ̈st/ *n* [C] someone who writes novels 小说家

no·vel·la /nəˋvɛlə; nəʊˈvelə/ *n* [C] a story that is shorter than a novel, but longer than a SHORT STORY 中篇小说

nov·el·ty /ˈnɑvḷtɪ; ˈnɒvəlti/ *n* **1** [C] something new and unusual which attracts people's attention and interest 新奇的事物: *Cars were still something of a novelty at the beginning of the century.* 世纪初期汽车仍是一种新奇的东西。**2** [U] the quality of being new, unusual, and interesting 新颖; 新奇性: *I was intrigued by the novelty of her ideas.* 我被她想法的新奇之处深深吸引。| **the novelty wears off** (=used to say that something gradually loses its novelty) 新奇感慢慢消失 *I enjoyed living in Paris at first but the novelty soon wore off.* 起初我很喜欢住在巴黎, 但这种新鲜感很快就消失了。**3** [C often plural 常用复数] an unusual, small, cheap object, suitable to be given as a present 新颖小巧而价廉的物品: *Christmas novelties* 圣诞小饰物 | *a novelty key ring* 一个小巧的钥匙圈

No·vem·ber /noˋvɛmbɚ; nəʊˈvembə/ written abbreviation 缩写为 **Nov.** *n* [C,U] the 11th month of the year, between October and December 十一月: **in November** *This office opened in November 1991.* 这个办事处是在1991年11月开业的。| **last/next November** *He started work here last November.* 他去年11月开始在这里工作。| **on November 6th** (also 又作 **on 6th November** *BrE*【英】) *It happened on November 6th.* (spoken as 读作 *on the sixth of November* or 或 *AmE*【美】: *on November the sixth* or 或 *on November sixth*) 这件事发生在11月6日。

> **CULTURAL NOTE 文化注释**
> In the UK and northern US, when people think of November, they think of colder weather and the days becoming shorter. In the UK, November 5th is Guy Fawkes' Night, and in the US the fourth Thursday in the month is Thanksgiving. 在英国和美国北部, 对于11月人们想到的是天气转冷和白天变短。在英国, 11月5日是盖伊·福克斯之夜, 而在美国, 11月的第四个星期四是感恩节。

nov·ice /ˈnɑvɪs; ˈnɒvɪ̈s/ *n* [C] **1** someone who has no experience in a skill, subject, or activity; beginner 新手, 生手; 初学者: *You'll have to show me what to do – I'm a complete novice.* 你得教我怎么做, 我完全是个新手。| **a novice skier/driver etc** *The novice pilot had to take the controls.* 新飞行员不得不握住操纵器。**2** someone who has recently joined a religious group to become a MONK or NUN 见习修道士; 见习修女

no·vi·ti·ate, noviciate /noˋvɪʃɪɪt; nəʊˈvɪʃi-ɪ̈t/ *n* [C] *technical* the period of being a novice【术语】见习期

No·vo·cain /ˈnovəˌken; ˈnəʊvəkeɪn/ *n* [U] *AmE trademark* a drug used for stopping pain during a small operation, especially on your teeth【美, 商标】奴佛卡因, 普鲁卡因〔一种局部麻醉药, 尤用于牙齿〕

1 1 **now¹** /naʊ; naʊ/ *adv* **1** at the present time 现在, 此刻, 目前: *If we leave now we'll be there before dark.* 如果我们现在出发, 天黑之前就能到那儿。| *They now live in the city centre.* 他们目前住在市中心。| **right now** (=exactly now) 此刻, 目前 *Right now I couldn't give a damn about your broken window.* 我此刻可顾不上你的破窗户。| **just now** *especially BrE* (=at the present time)【尤英】此刻, 目前 *There are a lot of bargains in the shops just now.* 商店里现在有许多便宜货卖。| **up to now/until now** *It's been a good game up to now but it would be nice to see a few more goals.* 这场比赛到目前为止还算不错, 但要是能再进几个球就更好了。| **by/before now** (=before the present time) 到现在 *Sonia should be home by now. Do you think she's had an accident?* 索尼娅这个时候该到家了, 你说她会不会出什么事了? | **from now on/as of now** (=starting from now) 从现在开始 *From now on Bill wishes to be addressed as Mr Wilson by all the staff.* 从现在开始, 比尔希望全体员工称他为威尔逊先生。| **for now** (=used when something is happening at the present time but may change in the future) 目前; 暂时 *That's enough talk for now. Take a break and we'll try again after lunch.* 暂时说到这里。休息一下, 我们午饭后再继续。**2** immediately 马上, 立刻: *I've already told you to clean up. I said now and I mean now.* 我告诉过你要整理干净。我说马上, 还不快去! | *The bell has rung – stop writing now.* 铃声已经响了, 立即停笔。**3** used when you know or understand something because of something you have just seen, just been told etc 这下, 一来: *Having met the rest of the family, she now saw where he got his temper from.* 见到他家里的其他成员之后, 她这才明白他的脾气是从哪儿来的。**4** **3 weeks/2 years etc now** starting 3 weeks, 2 years etc ago and continuing into the future 至今三周/两年等: *They've been going out together for a long time now.* 他们至今已经来往很长一段时间了。| *It's been over five years now since I started working here.* 自从我开始在这儿工作至今已经五年多了。| **it is now 3 weeks/2 years etc** *It's now a month since we bought the car and it's broken down three times already.* 这辆车我们买了才一个月时间, 就已坏过三次了。**5** **any day/minute etc now** very soon 很快, 不久, 随时: *The guests will arrive any minute now.* 客人马上就会到。**6** **(every) now and then/now and again** sometimes 时而, 有时, 不时: *I try to buy myself something every now and then.* 我偶尔会试着给自己买点东西。**7** used in stories when you mean at the time that the event or story is happening 这时候, 当时〔用于讲述故事时〕: *She blew out the candle. Now she could hear the sound of the wind howling in the trees outside.* 她吹灭了蜡烛, 这时她听到了外面树林里呼啸的风声。**8** **now...now...** *literary* used to say that at one moment someone does one thing and immediately after they do something else【文】时而…时而…; 忽而…忽而…: *The eagle glided through the sky, now rising, now swooping.* 鹰在天空中翱翔, 时而向上急冲, 时而向下猛扑。

Frequencies of the adverb **now** in spoken and written English 副词 now 在英语口语和书面语中的使用频率

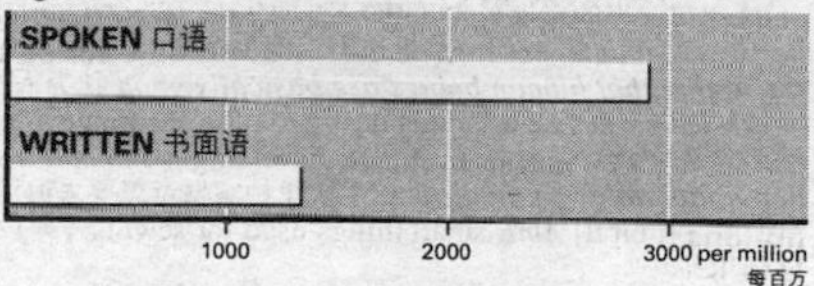

Based on the British National Corpus and the Longman Lancaster Corpus 据英国国家语料库和朗文兰开斯特语料库

This graph shows that the adverb **now** is much more common in spoken English than in written English. This is because it has some special uses in spoken English and is used in a lot of common spoken phrases. 本图表显示, 副词 now 在英语口语中的使用频率要远远高于书面语, 这是因为它在英语口语中有一些特殊的用法, 而且口语中很多常用短语是由 now 构成的。

now (*adv*) **SPOKEN PHRASES**
含 now 的口语短语

9 a) used when pausing or getting someone's attention before continuing what you are saying or changing the subject 好了〔用于停顿或引起别人的注意, 然后才继续说话或改变话题〕: *Now, what did you say your name was?* 呃, 你刚才说你叫什么名字? | *Now, let's move on to the question of payment.* 好了, 我们下面来谈付款的问题吧。**b)** used when pausing when you are thinking what to say next 好, 嗯〔在说话过程中停下来思索时用〕: *Now, let's see, oh yes – they wanted to know what time you'll be back on Friday.* 嗯, 让我想想, 噢, 对了, 他们想知道你星期五什么时候回来。**c)** used to say that if the situation was different, something different would happen 反过来, 不过〔用于假设〕: *Now, if I'd been in charge there's no way I'd have let them use the van.* 如果我负责的话, 我绝不会让他们用那辆小货车的。**d)**

used to make someone calm or comfort them when they are angry, upset etc 好了，好了〔用于安慰别人〕: *Come on now, don't cry.* 好了，别哭了。**e)** used when telling or reminding someone to do something 这下〔用于告诉或提醒某人做某事〕: *Don't forget now – put the keys in the right hand drawer.* 这下可别忘了，把钥匙放在右手边的抽屉里。| *Now hurry up! I haven't got all day.* 好了，快点儿！我没有太多的时间。**10 right now** at the moment 此刻，现在: *I'm really busy right now, can I call you back?* 我现在正忙着，过一会儿再给你打电话好吗？**11 just now** *especially BrE*【尤英】**a)** at the moment 此刻，目前: *I can't do it just now, I'm busy.* 我现在不行，我正忙着呢。**b)** a moment ago 刚才: *Where have I put that pen? I was using it just now.* 我把那支钢笔放在哪儿了？我刚才还在用呢。**12 now then** used to get someone's attention before telling them to do something or asking them a question 喂，听着〔用于引起别人的注意〕: *Now then, what's the matter?* 喂，怎么了？**13 well now** used when giving an opinion or asking someone to tell you something 听着；说吧〔用于发表意见或要求别人告知某事〕: *Well now, what's all this I hear about you getting married?* 说吧，我听别人说你要结婚了，这到底是怎么回事？**14 now for** used when saying what you are going to do next 接下来，下面: *That's that done. Now for a nice cup of coffee.* 那事就这么办了，接下来喝杯咖啡吧。**15 and now a)** used when introducing the next activity, performer etc 接下来，下面〔用于介绍下一个活动或表演者等〕: *And now, live from New York, Diana Ross.* 下面请看来自纽约的直播，黛安娜·罗丝。**b)** to ask someone what the situation is like at the moment when they have been telling you what it was like in the past 那现在呢〔在听了别人叙述某事的经过后用于询问目前情况〕: *"It was terrible, she nearly died." "And now?" "Oh, she's back to normal now."* "当时情况很糟糕，她差点儿死了。""那现在呢？""噢，她现在又恢复正常了。"**16 now now a)** used to make someone calm or comfort them when they are angry, upset etc 好了，好了〔用于安慰别人〕: *Now now, don't worry, everything will be okay.* 好了，好了，别担心，一切都会好的。**b)** *especially BrE* used when telling someone not to behave badly【尤英】行了，得了〔用于劝阻别人〕: *Now now, leave her alone, it's not fair to blame her.* 行了，行了，放过她吧，责备她是不公平的。**17 not now** used to tell someone that you do not want to talk to them or do something now, because you are busy, tired etc 现在不行: *"Tell me a story." "Not now, Daddy's working."* "给我讲个故事吧。""现在不行，爸爸在工作呢。"**18 it's now or never** used to say that if someone does not do something now, they will not get another chance to do it 机不可失，莫失良机 **19 now's the time** used to say that someone should do something now, because it is the right time to do it 现在是〔做某事〕的时候，正是时候: *Now's the time to buy a suit, while there are still sales on.* 趁现在还在减价，正是买一套西装的时候。**20 now I know** used when you have just found out something you didn't know before 我现在明白了: *Okay, now I know. I won't do it again, I'm sorry.* 好了，我现在明白了，我不会再这样做，对不起。**21 what is it now?** used when you are annoyed because someone keeps interrupting you or asking you things 又怎么了？〔表示因受到烦扰而生气〕: *What is it now? I wish you'd leave me alone!* 又怎么了？让我清静一会儿吧！**22 now you tell me!** used when you are annoyed or amused because someone has just told you something they should have told you before 为什么不早告诉我？: *Now she tells me! After I spent hours waiting for you all to arrive!* 她现在才告诉我！害我在这里等了你们半天！

1 3 **now²** *conjunction* also 又作 **now that** because of something or as a result of something 既然，由于: *Now that they've got to know each other a little better, they get along just fine.* 由于彼此之间有了进一步了解，他们相处得不错。| *Now you're here, why not have a drink.* 既然你来了，就喝一杯吧。

NOW, the /ˌɛn o ˋdʌblju; ˌen əʊ ˈdʌbəljuː/ the National Organization for Women; a large US organization started in 1966, which works for legal, economic, and social equality between women and men. Its first president was Betty Friedan, who also helped to start it 全国妇女组织〔美国一大型全国性组织，成立于1966年，旨在争取男女法律平等、经济平等和社会地位平等，第一任主席暨创始人为贝蒂·弗里登〕

2 **now·a·days** /ˋnaʊəˌdez; ˈnaʊədeɪz/ *adv* now, compared with what happened in the past〔与过去相比〕现今，现时: *Nowadays young people are much more aware of ecological issues than they used to be.* 如今，年轻人比以往更加注意生态问题。

no way /ˌ· ˋ·/ *adv spoken* certainly not【口】不行，决不: *"Are you going to offer to work over the weekend?" "No way!"* "你愿意周末加班吗？""不行！" | *No way will we be finished by five o'clock.* 我们绝不可能在五点钟前结束。| **there's no way...** *There's no way I'm going to pay £300 just for a weekend in Paris.* 我绝不会花 300 英镑就为了在巴黎度个周末。 2

no·where /ˋnoˌwɛr; ˈnəʊweə/ *adv* **1** also 又作 **no place** *AmE informal*【美，非正式】not in any place or to any place 什么地方都不，无处: *I have no job and nowhere to live.* 我没有工作，也没有地方住。| **nowhere else** (=no other place) 没有别的地方 *You've got to help me. I've nowhere else to go.* 你一定要帮我，我没有别处可去了。**2 get nowhere** to have no success or make no progress 没有结果；没有进展: *It's a good idea but it will get nowhere without more financial support.* 这个主意不错，但如果没有更多的资金支持它是不会成功的。| **get sb nowhere** *Taking that kind of attitude will get us nowhere.* 采取那种态度对我们没好处。| **get nowhere with** *Flaherty was getting nowhere with the Americans, and decided on a different approach.* 弗莱厄蒂与那些美国人在一起并没有什么进展，因此决定采用另一种方式。| **get nowhere fast** *I soon realized that being tough was getting me nowhere fast.* 不久我发现，态度强硬对我没什么帮助。**3 be nowhere to be seen/found/heard** not to be seen, found, or heard anywhere 哪儿也见/找/听不到: *Typical – another street crime and the police are nowhere to be seen.* 很典型，又是一宗街头罪案，而警察则哪儿也找不到。**4 nowhere near a)** far from a particular place 离〔某地方〕很远: *He swore he was nowhere near her house on the night she died.* 他发誓说，她死的当夜他离她家很远。**b)** not at all 远没有，远不及: **nowhere near ready/full/finished etc** *The building's nowhere near finished.* 这栋大楼还远没有建好。| **nowhere near as good as etc** *Sarah's nowhere near as fit as I am.* 萨拉远不及我健康。**5 out of/from nowhere** happening or appearing suddenly and without warning 突然发生；突然出现: *In the last few seconds Gunnell came from nowhere to win another gold medal.* 在最后几秒钟里，冈内尔不知从哪儿突然冒出来，又赢得了一枚金牌。| *From out of nowhere he asks me to marry him!* 他突如其来向我求婚！ 2

no-win sit·u·a·tion /ˌ· · ··ˋ··/ *n* [C] a situation which will end badly whatever you decide to do 无法取胜的状况；注定的败局

no·wise /ˋnoˌwaɪz; ˈnəʊwaɪz/ *adv old use* not at all【旧】一点也不，决不

nox·ious /ˋnɑkʃəs; ˈnɒkʃəs/ *adj formal* harmful or poisonous【正式】有害的；有毒的: *noxious gases* 有毒气体

noz·zle /ˋnɑzl; ˈnɒzəl/ *n* [C] a short tube fitted to the end of a HOSE, pipe etc to direct and control the stream of liquid or gas pouring out 管嘴；喷嘴

nozzle 管嘴；喷嘴

NPR /ˌɛn pi ˋɑr; ˌen piː ˈɑː/ the abbreviation of 缩写= NATIONAL PUBLIC RADIO

nr *BrE* the written abbreviation of 缩写= 'near', used in addresses【英】在…附近〔用于书写地址〕

NRA /ˌɛn ɑr ˋe; ˌen ɑːr ˈeɪ/ the abbreviation of 缩写= the NATIONAL RIFLE ASSOCIATION

NRC, the /ˌɛn ɑr ˋsi; ˌen ɑː ˈsiː/ the abbreviation of 缩写= the NUCLEAR REGULATORY COMMISSION

NSB /ˌɛn ɛs ˋbi; ˌen es ˈbiː/ the abbreviation of 缩写= NATIONAL SAVINGS BANK

NSC /ˌɛn ɛs ˋsi; ˌen es ˈsiː/ the abbreviation of 缩写= the NATIONAL SECURITY COUNCIL

NSPCC /ˌɛn ɛs ˌpi si ˋsi; ˌen es ˌpiː siː ˈsiː/ *n* the National Society for the Prevention of Cruelty to Children; a British organization that protects children who are being badly treated 全国防止虐待儿童协会〔英国机构，旨在保护受虐待的儿童〕

NSU /ˌɛn ɛs ˋju; ˌen es ˈjuː/ *n* [U] non-specific urethritis; an infection of the URETHRA 非特异性尿道炎

NT /ˌɛn ˋti; ˌen ˈtiː/ **1** the abbreviation of 缩写= NATIONAL THEATRE **2** the abbreviation of 缩写= NATIONAL TRUST

n't /nt; ənt/ the short form of 缩略式= 'not': *hadn't* | *didn't* | *wouldn't* | *isn't* —see 见 NOT (USAGE)

nth /ɛnθ; enθ/ *adj* **1** [only before noun 仅用于名词前] *informal* the most recent of a long series of similar things that have happened【非正式】无数次的，多次的: *Even after I'd reminded him for the nth time, he forgot.* 尽管我已提醒过他无数次，但他还是忘了。**2 to the nth degree** *informal* extremely, or as much as possible【非正式】极度地；无穷地: *It was boring to the nth degree.* 那事令人厌烦透顶。

N

nu·ance /nju`ɑns; 'njuːɑːns/ *n* [C,U] a very slight, hardly noticeable difference in manner, colour, meaning etc〔方式、颜色、意义等的〕细微差别: *He was aware of every nuance in her voice.* 他听得出她声音中所有细微的变化。

nub /nʌb; nʌb/ *n* **the nub of the problem/matter/argument etc** the main point of a problem etc 问题/事情/争论等的焦点[要点]: *Differing social attitudes lie at the nub of the dispute.* 不同的社会态度是这场争议的关键。

nu·bile /ˈnubḷ; 'njuːbaɪl/ *adj formal or humorous* a woman who is nubile is young and sexually attractive【正式或幽默】〔女子〕年轻性感的

W3 **nu·cle·ar** /ˈnjuklɪɚ; 'njuːkliə/ *adj* **1** using or connected with nuclear energy 核能的, 核动力的: *a nuclear power station* 核电站 | *a nuclear-powered submarine* 核动力潜艇 **2** concerning the NUCLEUS (1) of an atom〔原子〕核的: *nuclear fission* 核裂变 **3** connected with or involving the use of NUCLEAR WEAPONS 核武器的: **nuclear bomb/war** *the threat of nuclear war* 核战的威胁 | **nuclear tests** (=for testing nuclear bombs) 核试验 | **nuclear disarmament** (=getting rid of nuclear weapons) 核裁军, 裁减核军备 | **the nuclear deterrent** (=nuclear weapons used as a threat to stop an enemy attacking) 核武器威胁

nuclear en·er·gy /,··· '···/ *n* [U] the powerful force that is produced when the NUCLEUS (=central part) of an atom is either split or joined to another atom 核能

nuclear fam·i·ly /,··· '···/ *n* [C] a family unit that consists only of husband, wife and children〔仅由夫妻与子女组成的〕核心家庭, 小家庭

nuclear fis·sion /,··· '··/ *n* [U] the splitting of the NUCLEUS (=central part) of an atom which results in a lot of power being produced 核裂变

nuclear-free /,··· '·◂/ *adj* places that are nuclear-free do not allow NUCLEAR materials to be carried, stored or used in that area〔地区〕无核的: *a nuclear-free zone* 无核区

nuclear fu·sion /,··· '··/ *n* [U] a NUCLEAR (2) reaction in which the nuclei (NUCLEUS (1)) of light atoms join with the nuclei of heavier atoms, which produces power without producing any waste 核聚变

nuclear phys·ics /,··· '··/ *n* [U] the area of PHYSICS which is concerned with the structure and features of the NUCLEUS (=central part) of atoms 核物理学〔研究原子核的结构和属性的科学〕

nuclear pow·er /,··· '··/ *n* [U] power, usually in the form of electricity, from NUCLEAR ENERGY 核动力; 核电

CULTURAL NOTE 文化注释

Many people worry about the risks connected with using nuclear power, and some people oppose the building of new POWER STATIONS. People are frightened by the possibility of accidents, such as those that happened at Three Mile Island in the US in 1979 and Chernobyl in Ukraine in 1986. People also worry that people who live near nuclear power stations have a greater risk of getting some types of CANCER, and that the methods used to get rid of RADIOACTIVE waste are not safe. Some people feel that the governments and the nuclear industry do not always tell the truth about the dangerous effects that nuclear power has on people and the environment. 很多人担心核动力带来的风险, 因此有人反对建设新的核电站。人们为可能发生的事故担惊受怕, 像1979年发生在美国三英里岛和1986年发生在乌克兰切尔诺贝利的核泄漏事故。人们还担心生活在核电站附近的人患上某些癌症的风险更大, 并且处理放射性废物的方法也不安全。有人觉得, 政府和核工业部门在核能对人和环境的危害性上并没有全都讲实话。

nuclear re·ac·tion /,··· '··/ *n* [C] a process in which the parts of the NUCLEUS (=central part) of an atom are rearranged to form new substances 核反应

nuclear re·ac·tor /,··· '··/ *n* [C] a large machine that produces NUCLEAR ENERGY, especially as a means of producing electricity〔尤指用于发电的〕核反应堆

Nuclear Reg·u·la·to·ry Com·mis·sion, the /,··· '····· ,··/ abbreviation 缩写为 **the NRC** a US government organization that checks on the safety of NUCLEAR power stations 核管理委员会〔美国一政府机构, 专门检查核电站安全〕

nuclear waste /,··· '·/ *n* [U] waste material from NUCLEAR REACTORS, which is RADIOACTIVE 核废料〔核反应堆中核燃料使用后的放射性废弃物〕: *There are no easy solutions to the problems of nuclear waste disposal.* 有关核废料的处理问题并无简单的解决方法。

nuclear weap·on /,··· '··/ *n* [C] a very powerful weapon which uses atomic power to cause death and destruction over a large area 核武器: *the controversy over nuclear weapons testing* 有关核武器试验的争议

nu·cle·ic ac·id /nju,kliɪk 'æsɪd; njuː,kliːɪk 'æsɪ̣d/ *n* [C,U] one of the two acids, DNA and RNA, that exist in the cells of all living things 核酸

nucleus 核心

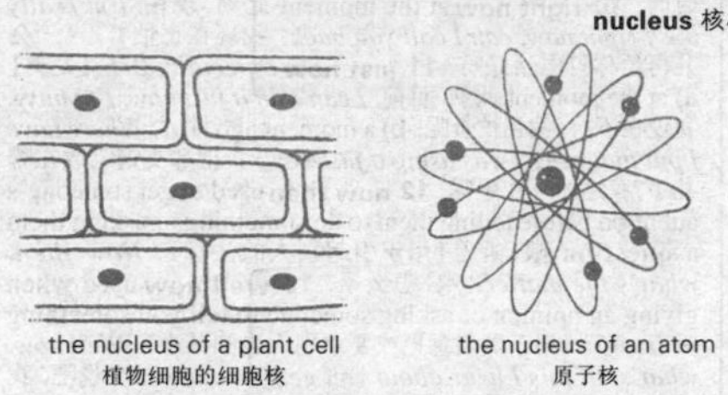

the nucleus of a plant cell 植物细胞的细胞核 | the nucleus of an atom 原子核

nu·cle·us /ˈnjuklɪəs; 'njuːkliəs/ *n plural* **nuclei** /-klɪaɪ; -kliaɪ/ [C] **1** the central part of an atom, made up of NEUTRONS, PROTONS, and other ELEMENTARY PARTICLES〔原子〕核 **2** the central part of almost all the cells of living things 细胞核 **3** a small, important group at the centre of a larger group or organization 核心, 中心: *the nucleus of an effective team* 高效团队的核心

nude[1] /njud; njuːd/ *adj* **1** not wearing any clothes; NAKED 赤裸的, 裸体的 **2** done by or involving people who are not wearing any clothes 裸体者的: *There are several nude scenes in the film.* 影片中有几个裸体镜头。

nude[2] *n* **1** [C] a painting, STATUE etc of someone not wearing clothes 裸体艺术品〈如人体画、人体雕塑等〉**2 in the nude** not wearing any clothes 裸体的[地], 赤裸的[地]: *He was standing there in the nude.* 他光着身子站在那里。

nudge /nʌdʒ; nʌdʒ/ *v* **1** [T] to push someone gently, usually with your elbow, in order to get their attention〔通常用肘〕轻推〔以引起某人的注意〕: *"Look!" Benjamin nudged his mother. "There's my teacher, Miss Watts."* "看!"本杰明轻轻碰了一下母亲, "那是我的老师, 沃茨小姐。" —see picture on page A21 参见A21页图 **2** [T always+adv/prep] to move something or someone a short distance by gently pushing 轻推移动, 推开: **nudge sth/sb towards/away etc** *She nudged the glass towards me.* 她将杯子轻轻推向我。| *David nudged me out of the way.* 戴维把我挤到一边。**3** also 又作 **nudge your way** [I always+adv/prep] to move forward slowly by pushing gently 往前挤: **[+to/through/forward etc]** *I started to nudge my way to the front of the crowd.* 我慢慢地挤到人群前面。**4** [T always+adv/prep] to gently persuade or encourage someone to take a particular decision or action 劝说; 鼓励: **[+into/towards]** *We're trying to nudge them towards a practical solution.* 我们正在努力促使他们找到一种切实可行的解决方法。**5** [T usually in progressive 一般用进行时] to almost reach a particular level or amount 接近, 靠近〔某程度或数量〕: *For the first time in my life I was nudging 80kg.* 我这辈子第一次体重接近80公斤。—**nudge** *n* [C]: *Hannah gave me a sharp nudge.* 汉纳突然推了我一下。

nud·ist /ˈnjudɪst; 'njuːdɪ̣st/ *n* [C] someone who enjoys not wearing any clothes because they believe it is natural and healthy; NATURIST 裸体主义者 —**nudist** *adj*: *a nudist camp* 裸体营 —**nudism** *n* [U]

nu·di·ty /ˈnjudətɪ; 'njuːdɪ̣ti/ *n* [U] the state of not wearing any clothes 裸体, 赤裸, 裸露

nug·get /ˈnʌgɪt; 'nʌgɪ̣t/ *n* [C] **1** a small rough piece of a valuable metal found in the earth〔天然〕块金; 矿块: *gold nuggets* 天然金块 **2** a small, round piece of food〔食物〕小圆块儿: *chicken nuggets* 鸡块 **3 nugget of information/wisdom etc** a piece of valuable information, advice etc 有价值的资料/几句至理名言等: *It took ages to extract that nugget of information from him.* 费了好长时间才从他那儿套出一点资料来。

nui·sance /ˈnjusns; 'njuːsəns/ *n* **1** [C usually singular 一般用单数] a person, thing, or situation that annoys you or causes problems 讨厌或麻烦的人[事物, 情况]: *Those dogs next door are a thorough nuisance.* 隔壁的那几只狗真是讨厌极了。| **What a nuisance!** *spoken*【口】*What a nuisance! I've forgotten my ticket.* 真讨厌!我忘了带票。| **make a nuisance of yourself** (=behave in a way that annoys other people) 惹人讨厌 *Stop making a nuisance of yourself.* 别那样惹人讨厌。**2** [C,U] *law* the use of a place or property in a way that causes public annoyance【法律】妨害公共利益的行为: *She was charged with caus-* S3

ing a nuisance in a public place. 她被控在公共场所滋扰他人。
3 nuisance value *BrE* something that has nuisance value is useful because it causes problems for your opponents【英】给对手造成麻烦的价值, 阻扰[骚扰]作用

NUJ, the /ˌɛn ju ˋdʒe; ˌen juː ˈdʒeɪ/ the National Union of Journalists; the professional TRADE UNION in the UK for people working in newspapers, magazines, and book production 全国记者联合会〔英国报刊、杂志以及图书出版行业从业人员工会〕

nuke¹ /njuk; njuːk/ *v* [T] *informal* to attack a place using NUCLEAR WEAPONS【非正式】用核武器攻击

nuke² *n* [C] *informal* a NUCLEAR WEAPON【非正式】核武器

null /nʌl; nʌl/ *adj* **null result/effect etc** *technical* a result etc that is zero or nothing【术语】零结果/无效等

null and void /ˌ· · ˈ·/ *adj law* having no legal effect; INVALID¹ (1)【法律】无效的: *The contract was declared null and void.* 该合同被宣布无效。

nul·li·fy /ˈnʌləˌfaɪ; ˈnʌlɪ̣faɪ/ *v* [T] **1** *law* to officially state that something has no legal force【法律】宣布…在法律上无效: *The claim was nullified by the court.* 法庭宣布该要求无效。**2** *formal* to make something lose its effect or value【正式】使无效; 使无价值: *Inflation has nullified the recent wage increases.* 通货膨胀抵消了最近的工资增长。—**nullification** /ˌnʌləfəˋkeʃən; ˌnʌlɪ̣fɪ̣ˈkeɪʃən/ *n* [U]

nul·li·ty /ˈnʌlətɪ; ˈnʌlɪ̣ti/ *n* [U] *law* the fact that a marriage or contract no longer has any legal force【法律】〔婚姻或合约等〕法律上无效: *a decree of nullity* 宣布在法律上无效的判决

null set /ˌ· ˈ·/ *n* [C] *technical* a mathematical set with no members, usually written { }【术语】〔数学中通常用 { } 表示的〕零集; 空集

numb¹ /nʌm; nʌm/ *adj* **1** a part of your body that is numb is unable to feel anything, for example because you are very cold〔身体部位〕麻木的; 失去感觉的: *My fingers were so numb I could hardly write.* 我的手指都麻木了, 几乎不能写字。| *The anaesthetic had made his whole face go numb.* 麻醉剂使他整个脸部都失去了知觉。**2** unable to think, feel, or react in a normal way〔思维、感觉、反应〕迟钝的; 麻木的: **numb with shock/fear/terror etc** *I just sat there, numb with terror.* 我只是坐在那儿, 吓呆了。—**numbly** *adv* —**numbness** *n* [U]

numb² *v* [T] **1** to make someone unable to feel pain or other sensations 使麻木; 使失去感觉: *fingers numbed with cold* 冻僵了的手指 | *the numbing effect of the drug* 药物的麻醉作用 **2** to make someone unable to think, feel, or react in a normal way 使迟钝; 使麻木: *He was numbed by the shock of his wife's death.* 他受到妻子去世的打击而变得麻木。

num·ber¹ /ˈnʌmbɚ; ˈnʌmbə/ *n*
1 ▶NUMBER 数字◀ [C] a word or sign which represents an amount or a quantity 数; 数字: *Add together the following numbers: 1027, 643, and 378.* 将下列数字相加: 1027, 643 和 378。| **…/low number** *Choose a fairly low number – under 100, so…* 选择一个较小的数字, 比如低于100的。| **even number** (=2, 4, 6…) 偶数 | **odd number** (=1, 3, 5, 7, 9 etc) 奇数 | … **number** (=a number ending in 0) 整数 *I'll give her £17 … £20. That's a good round number.* 我要给她 17 英镑…吧, 那是个吉利的整数。| **be good/no good etc** … *formal* (=to be good, bad etc at calculating …)【非正式】擅长/不擅长计算 —see also 另见 CARD… …INAL NUMBER, PRIME NUMBER, WHOLE NUMBER
2 ▶IN A S… …中◀ [C] a number used to show the position … …ered set or list 号码; …号, 第…号: *We … Street.* 我们住在城堡街 107号。| *An…* …第4题。| *a number 17 bus* 17路… —see also … …BER, NO. 10, NUMBER ONE
3 model/accou… …
4 ▶TELEPHONE 电… …o communicate with some… …one or something etc 型… …
…number, please? …
NUMBER, PIN, SERIAL …
new number is 502655…
office/work number …
wrong …

6 ▶AMOUNT 数量◀ [singular] also 又作 **numbers** *plural* an amount of something that can be counted; a QUANTITY 数目; 数量: *The number of cars on our roads rose dramatically last year.* 去年道路上的汽车数量剧增。| *Estimates put the number of deaths at between three and five thousand.* 估计死亡人数在三千到五千之间。| **a large/great/small etc number of** also 又作 **large/great/small etc numbers of** *Doctors believe only a tiny number of people are at risk.* 医生认为只有极少数人有危险。| **in large/great/small etc numbers** *They were printed in limited numbers.* 印数有限。| **bring the number of sth to five/ten etc** *This latest bomb brings the number of terrorist attacks this year to seven.* 最近一次爆炸事件使今年的恐怖袭击次数达到七次。| **ten/twelve etc in number** *formal*【正式】*A small number of protesters, about 20 in number, gathered outside.* 一小群大约 20 人的抗议者聚集在外面。—see also 见 AMOUNT¹ (USAGE)
7 numbers [plural] how many people there are, especially people attending an event or doing an activity together〔尤指参加某一活动的〕人数: *Can you give me some idea of numbers?* 你能告诉我一个大致的人数吗? | **student/client etc numbers** *Visitor numbers increase in the summer.* 游客人数在夏季有所增加。
8 by (sheer) force/weight of numbers if a group of people is defeated by force of numbers, it is defeated because many more people are attacking or opposing it (纯粹) 靠数量上的优势〔取胜〕
9 a number of *formal* several【正式】几个, 若干 (个): *She has written a number of articles for the local paper.* 她为当地报纸写过几篇文章。| **a good number of/quite a number of** (=a lot of) 许多 *Darke knew a good number of people with government connections.* 达克认识不少和政府有联系的人。| **a number of ways/reasons/factors etc** (=various different ways etc) 几个不同的方式/原因/因素等 *These paintings differ from his earlier ones in a number of ways.* 这些画与他以前的作品相比有好几个不同之处。| **any number of** *There could be any number of reasons why she's late.* 她迟到的原因有很多。
10 some/none/20 etc of sb's number *formal* some etc of a group of people【正式】一群人中的一些/一个也没有/20个等: *Only three of our number could speak Italian.* 我们当中只有三人会讲意大利语。
11 ▶MUSIC 音乐◀ [C] a piece of popular music that forms part of a longer performance 一首流行乐曲: *Madonna sang several numbers from her latest album.* 麦当娜唱了她最新唱片中的几首歌曲。—see also 另见 PRODUCTION NUMBER
12 a recent/an old/last month's number *BrE* a copy of a magazine printed recently, a long time ago etc【英】最新一期/过期/上月的杂志; ISSUE¹ (2) *AmE*【美】: **back number** (=an old copy of a magazine) 过期的杂志
13 have sb's number *informal* to understand something about someone that helps you deal with them【非正式】对某人心中有数, 摸透某人的底: *You'll never fool her, Mike – she's got your number!* 你是骗不了她的, 迈克, 她对你了如指掌。
14 sb's number is up/has come up *informal* someone will suffer or be punished【非正式】轮到某人遭殃[受罚]: *Your number's up, Hanks!* 你会受到惩罚的, 汉克斯!
15 black/elegant etc (little) number *informal* a black etc dress【非正式】黑色/高贵等的礼服: *Sue turned up in a very elegant number.* 休穿着一件十分高贵的礼服出现。
16 sb's number comes up someone has the winning number in a competition 某人的号码中了
17 the number of times I've... *spoken* used to say that you have done something many times, without any result【口】我已经说过无数次…: *Honestly, the number of times I've told that girl not to walk home alone.* 说实话, 我已多次告诉过那个女孩不要独自一人步行回家。
18 the numbers an illegal game in the US in which people risk money on the appearance of a combination of numbers in a newspaper〔美国的〕数字 (彩票) 赌博〔通常是非法的, 就报纸上出现的某种数字组合下赌注〕: *playing the numbers* 赌数字
19 beyond/without number *literary* if things are beyond …umber, there are so many of them that no one could count them …文】数不胜数
…**RAMMAR** 语法◀ [U] *technical* the form of a word, de… …whether one thing or more than one thing is being … …术语】数: *'Horses' is plural in number, 'horse' is …* …是复数, horse 是单数。
… …give a number to something that is part … 给…编号: *They haven't numbered the …* …未给报告编页码。| *All the seats in …* …里的所有座位都编了号。| **num-**

N

ber sth (from) 1 to 10/100 etc *Number the questions 1 to 25.* 把这些问题从1到25编号。| *a numbering system* 编号系统 **2 his/their/its days are numbered** someone or something cannot live or continue much longer 生命垂危; 活着[存在]的日子屈指可数 **3 number several thousands/almost a million etc** to be several thousands etc 数量有几千/近一百万等: *The crowd numbered at least 7,000.* 聚集的人群至少有7000人。| *The men on strike now number 5% of the workforce.* 罢工人数目前约占工人总数的5%。**4 number among/be numbered among** *formal* to be included as one of a particular group【正式】被认为; 被算作: *Amis numbers among the best of our younger writers.* 埃米斯被视为当代最优秀的年轻作家之一。**5** [T] *literary* to count【文】计算, 数: *Who can number the stars?* 谁能数清星星有多少?

number off *phr v* [I] *BrE technical* if soldiers number off, they call out their number when their turn comes【英, 术语】〔士兵〕报数; COUNT off *AmE*【美】

Number 10 /ˌnʌmbə`tɛn; ˌnʌmbə ˈten/ —see 见 NO. 10

Number 11 /ˌnʌmbə ɪˈlɛvən; ˌnʌmbər ɪˈlevən/ —see 见 NO. 11

number crunch·er /ˈ‥ ˌ‥/ *n* [C] *informal humorous*【非正式, 幽默】**1** someone who works with numbers, such as an ACCOUNTANT 捣弄数字者〈如会计师〉**2** a computer designed to work with numbers and calculate results〔运算用的〕计算机, 电脑

number crunch·ing /ˈ‥ ˌ‥/ *n* [U] *informal humorous* the process of working with numbers and calculating results【非正式, 幽默】数字捣弄 —**number-crunching** *adj*

num·ber·less /ˈnʌmbəlɪs; ˈnʌmbələs/ *adj* too many to be counted; INNUMERABLE 数不胜数的, 多到数不清的, 无数的: *numberless possibilities* 无数种可能

number one[1] /ˌ‥ ˈ◂/ *n* [singular] **1** the most important or successful person or thing 最重要的人物[事物], 头号人物[事物]: *George is number one in this organization.* 乔治是这个组织的头号人物。| *Kline had so many great plans – number one being to star in a movie.* 克兰有许多重大的计划, 最重要的就是要在某部影片中担任主角。**2** the musical record that is the most popular at a particular time 最热门的唱片: *number one in the charts* 排行榜榜首的唱片 **3 look out for number one/look after number one** *spoken* to look after yourself and not worry about other people【口】只顾自己: *Suzanne's only bothered about looking after number one.* 苏珊娜只知道顾自己。

number one[2] /ˌ‥ ˈ◂/ *adj* **1** most important or successful in a particular situation 头号的; 最重要的; 最成功的: *Obedience was the organization's number one priority.* 服从是该组织最为看重的事情。| *Sweden's number one model* 瑞典的头号模特儿 **2** first on a list of several things to be considered, done etc 首要的; 第一的: *item number one on the agenda* 议程上的第一项

num·ber·plate /ˈnʌmbəˌplet; ˈnʌmbəpleɪt/ *n* [C] *BrE* one of the signs at the front and back of a car showing its REGISTRATION NUMBER【英】〔汽车的〕牌照, 号码牌; LICENSE PLATE *AmE*【美】—see picture on page A2 参见A2页图

Number Ten /ˌ‥ ˈ/ *n* [singular] —see 见 NO. 10

numb·skull /ˈnʌmˌskʌl; ˈnʌmskʌl/ *n* [C] another spelling of NUMSKULL numskull 的另一种拼法

nu·me·ral /ˈnjumərəl; ˈnjuːmərəl/ *n* [C] a written sign that represents a number 数字 —**numeral** *adj*

nu·me·rate /ˈnjuməˌret; ˈnjuːmərə̇t/ *adj* able to do calculations and understand simple mathematics 会计算的; 能做算术的: *We need someone who's numerate.* 我们需要一个懂计算的人。—opposite 反义词 INNUMERATE —compare 比较 LITER…
—**numeracy** *n* [U]

nu·me·ra·tion /ˌnjuməˈreʃən; ˌnjuːməˈr…
nical a system of counting or the proc…
数法, 读数法; 计算法; 计算

nu·me·ra·tor /ˈnjuməˌr…
number above the line in …
numerator in 5/6【术语】(…
NATOR

nu·mer·i·cal /njuˈmɛr…
sidered in numbers 用数…
code 数字代码 | *the nu…*
forces (=the fact that th…
量上的优势 —**numeri…**
数字上相等的

3 **nu·me·rous** /ˈnju…
式】许多的, 很多的: …
the truth. 为掩盖事…
很多次

nu·mi·nous /ˈnjumənəs; ˈnjuːmɪ̇nəs/ *adj literary* having a mysterious and holy quality, which makes you feel that God is present【文】神秘的; 神圣的

nu·mis·mat·ics /ˌnjumɪzˈmætɪks; ˌnjuːmɪ̇zˈmætɪks/ *n* [U] *technical* the activity of collecting and studying coins and MEDALS【术语】钱币[徽章]收集; 古钱学, 钱币学; 徽章学 —**numismatic** *adj* —**numismatist** /njuˈmɪzmətɪst; njuːˈmɪzmətɪ̇st/ *n* [C]

num·skull, numbskull /ˈnʌmˌskʌl; ˈnʌmskʌl/ *n* [C] *informal* a very stupid person; IDIOT【非正式】笨蛋, 傻瓜, 白痴: *Look what you've done now, you numskull!* 看看你干了些什么, 你这个笨蛋!

nun /nʌn; nʌn/ *n* [C] a member of an all female religious group who live together in a CONVENT 修女; 尼姑 —compare 比较 MONK

nun·ci·o /ˈnʌnʃɪˌo; ˈnʌnsiəʊ/ *n* [C] *plural* **nuncios** a representative of the Pope in a foreign country 罗马教皇的使节; 教廷大使

nun·ne·ry /ˈnʌnərɪ; ˈnʌnəri/ *n* [C] *literary* a CONVENT【文】女修道院; 尼姑庵

nup·tial /ˈnʌpʃəl; ˈnʌpʃəl/ *adj formal or humorous* connected with marriage or the marriage ceremony【正式或幽默】婚姻的, 结婚的; 婚礼的: *the nuptial day* 结婚日 | *nuptial bliss* 美满婚姻

nup·tials /ˈnʌpʃəlz; ˈnʌpʃəlz/ *n* [plural] *formal or humorous* a wedding【正式或幽默】婚礼

Nu·rem·berg /ˈnjurəmbɝg; ˈnjʊərəmbɜːg/ an industrial city in Bavaria, southern Germany, whose German name is Nürnberg. People think of Nuremberg because of the Nuremberg Rallies of the 1930s, when the Nazi Party held very large well-organized public meetings. In 1945-46 the Nuremberg Trials took place there, when many Nazi leaders were judged in a court of law for their war crimes, and some of them were punished by death. 纽伦堡〔德国南部巴伐利亚州一工业城市, 德文名为Nürnberg。人们想起纽伦堡是因为20世纪30年代的纽伦堡集会。当时, 纳粹党在此地举行组织周密的大型公共集会。1945至1946年的"纽伦堡审判"也在该地进行, 许多纳粹头目因战争罪受审, 其中一些人被判处死刑〕

Nu·re·yev /njuˈreɛf; ˈnjʊərief/, **Ru·dolf** /ˈrudɑlf; ˈruːdɒlf/ (1938-93) a Russian BALLET dancer who escaped from the former Soviet Union in 1961 to live in the West. He often danced with Dame Margot Fonteyn and was one of the greatest male dancers ever. 努里耶夫〔(1938-1993), 俄罗斯芭蕾舞演员, 1961年从前苏联逃往西方定居。他常与玛格特·芳廷女士搭档, 是有史以来最出色的男舞蹈演员之一〕

nurse[1] /nɝs; nɜːs/ *n* [C] **1** someone who is trained to look after people who are ill or injured, usually in a hospital〔通常指医院里的〕护士: *The nurse is coming to give you an injection.* 护士很快会来给你打针。| *a student nurse* (=someone learning to be a nurse) 实习护士 | *Nurse Jones* 琼斯护士 | *a male nurse* 男护士 **2** *old-fashioned* a woman employed to look after a young child; NANNY (1)【过时】保姆 —see also 另见 WET NURSE 3 3

nurse[2] *v*

1 ►SICK PEOPLE 病人◄ a) [T] to look after someone who is ill or injured 护理; 照顾, 照料: *nursing an elderly* … usually in … 一位年老的亲戚 | **nurse sb back to health** (… *She spent* … until they are well again) 照料某人直至… progressive 一般用进行时] to …: 不用被动态] to … *for a long time,* … *several years nursing in* … 里当了几年护士 … **nurse a grudge/grievance** … *had nursed a grievance* … 一直对自己的前任雇主 …

2 ►YOUR FEE… … an illness or injury so that it … [T not in passive 不 … secret … *area was at home, nursing a cold.* … **nurse sth through/along etc** … during a difficult situation … [T] to take special care … *the company through a financially difficult* … 使公司成功地渡过了财政困难时期。… [T] to hold something carefully in your hands … your body 小心地捧[抱]着; 爱惜地搂抱: *a child* … | *Frank sat there nursing his* … 手里捧着一杯啤酒。… 弗兰克坐在那里 …

… **A BABY** 喂婴儿◄ **a)** [I,T] if a woman nurses a baby, … breast … 喂奶 **b)** [I] if a baby nurses, it sucks milk from her breasts; BREAST-FEED 哺乳, … 吃〔母亲的〕奶

N

nurse·ling /ˈnɜ·slɪŋ; ˈnɜːslɪŋ/ *n* [C] another spelling of NURSLING nursling 的另一种拼法

nurse·maid /ˈnɜ·sˌmed; ˈnɜːsmeɪd/ *n* [C] *old-fashioned* a woman employed to look after young children【过时】保姆

nur·se·ry /ˈnɜ·sərɪ; ˈnɜːsəri/ *n* [C] **1** a place where young children are taken care of during the day while their parents are at work, shopping etc 托儿所 —see also 另见 DAY CARE CENTRE (1) **2 nursery education/school/unit/teacher etc** education etc for young children from three to five years old 幼儿园教育/幼儿园/幼儿园机构/幼儿园教师等 —see also 另见 KINDERGARTEN **3** *old-fashioned* a baby's bedroom or a room where young children play, in a private house【过时】〔私人住宅中的〕婴儿房; 儿童活动室 **4** a place where plants and trees are grown and sold 苗圃; GARDEN CENTRE *BrE*【英】

nur·se·ry·man /ˈnɜ·sərɪmən; ˈnɜːsərimən/ *n* [C] *plural* **nurserymen** /-mən; -mən/ someone who grows plants and trees in a nursery 苗圃工人; 苗木培养工

nursery nurse /ˈ· · · , ·/ *n* [C] *BrE* someone who has been trained to work with and look after young children【英】〔受过训练的〕保育员

nursery rhyme /ˈ· · · ·/ *n* [C] a short traditional song or poem for children 童谣, 儿歌

nursery slope /ˈ· · · , ·/ *n* [C] *BrE* a slope that is not very steep, where people are taught to SKI【英】〔供初学滑雪者使用的〕练习坡地; BUNNY SLOPE *AmE*【美】

nurs·ing /ˈnɜ·sɪŋ; ˈnɜːsɪŋ/ *n* [U] the job or skill of looking after people who are ill, injured, or old 护士[护理]工作; 护士[护理]技巧: *I'd love to go into nursing.* 我很乐意加入护理行业。

nursing home /ˈ· · ·/ *n* [C] a type of small private hospital for old people who cannot look after themselves 私立养老院, 私立疗养院

> **CULTURAL NOTE 文化注释**
>
> In the US and UK, some people put their parents in a nursing home when their parents are too old to take care of themselves. 在美国和英国, 有些人在父母年老生活不能自理的时候就将他们送到私人疗养院去。

nursing moth·er /ˌ· · ˈ· ·/ *n* [C] a mother who is feeding her baby from her breast 哺乳期妇女

nurs·ling, nurseling /ˈnɜ·slɪŋ; ˈnɜːslɪŋ/ *n* [C] *old use* a baby who is being fed from the breast, or who is being looked after by a nurse【旧】乳婴; 〔由保姆照料的〕婴儿

nur·tur·ance /ˈnɜ·tʃərəns; ˈnɜːtʃərəns/ *n* [U] *AmE* loving care and attention that you give to someone【美】关爱, 关怀; 养育: *the feminine virtue of nurturance* 女性关爱的美德 —**nurturant** *adj*

nur·ture¹ /ˈnɜ·tʃə; ˈnɜːtʃə/ *v* [T often passive 常用被动态] *formal*【正式】**1** to feed and take care of a child or a plant while it is growing 养育; 培育: *children nurtured in an overprotective environment* 在过分保护的环境下养育出来的孩子 | *plants nurtured in the greenhouse* 在温室里培育的植物 **2** to help a plan, idea, feeling etc to develop 发展〔计划、想法等〕; 培养〔感情等〕: *European union is an ideal that has been nurtured since the post-war years.* 建立欧盟是战后多年来一直发展的一个理想。

nurture² *n* [U] *formal* the education and care that you are given as a child, and the way it affects your later development and attitudes【正式】〔儿时所受的〕教育; 教养; 培育

NUS, the /ˌɛn ju ˋɛs; ˌen juː ˈes/ National Union of Students; an organization that represents students at colleges and universities in the UK. As well as supporting the rights of students, it also arranges entertainment, travel, advice centres etc for students. 全国学生联合会〔代表英国各大专院校学生的一个组织。其职能是维护学生的权益, 为学生安排娱乐与旅行, 建立咨询中心等〕

S3 **nut¹** /nʌt; nʌt/ *n* [C]
1 ▶FOOD 食物◀ a dry brown fruit inside a hard shell, that grows on a tree 坚果; 坚果仁: *crack a nut* 砸开坚果 | *a cashew nut* 腰果
2 ▶TOOL 工具◀ a small piece of metal with a hole through the middle which is screwed onto a BOLT¹ (2) to fasten things together 螺母, 螺帽
3 ▶CRAZY PERSON 疯子◀ *informal especially AmE* someone who is crazy or behaves strangely【非正式, 尤美】疯子; 怪人: *He's kind of a nut, but I like him.* 他是个怪人, 但我喜欢他。
4 a golf/opera etc nut *informal* someone who is very interested in golf etc【非正式】高尔夫球迷/歌剧迷等: *She's a Clark Gable nut.* 她是克拉克·盖博的忠实影迷。
5 ▶SEXUAL ORGAN 性器官◀ *slang* a man's testicles【俚】睾丸: *He got kicked in the nuts.* 他被人踢中了睾丸。
6 the nuts and bolts of *informal* the practical details of a subject or job【非正式】基本要点, 实质性要点: *the nuts and bolts of the project* 该计划的基本要点
7 a tough/hard nut *informal* someone who is difficult to deal with【非正式】难对付的人: *Johnny Stone was a tough nut.* 约翰尼·斯通是个难对付的家伙。
8 a hard/tough nut to crack a difficult problem or situation 棘手的问题; 难办的事: *Saturday's match will be a tough nut to crack.* 周六的比赛将是场硬仗。
9 ▶HEAD 头◀ *BrE spoken* your head or brain【英口】头; 头脑: *Oh come on, use your nut!* 加油, 动动脑筋吧!
10 be off your nut *BrE spoken* to be crazy【英口】发疯: *You must be off your nut!* 你一定是疯了!
11 do your nut *BrE spoken* to become very angry or worried【英口】大发雷霆; 极度忧虑: *I didn't get home till three – my Mum did her nut!* 我3点才到家, 妈妈都担心坏了!
12 sb can't... for nuts *spoken* used to say that someone is completely unable to do something【口】某人对…一窍不通: *She can't sing for nuts.* 她一点也不会唱歌。—see also 另见 NUTS¹

nut² *v* [T] *BrE informal* to hit someone with your head; HEADBUTT【英, 非正式】用头撞: *He just turned round and nutted me!* 他干脆转过身来用头撞我!

NUT, the /ˌɛn ju ˋti; ˌen juː ˈtiː/ National Union of Teachers; one of the main professional TRADE UNIONs which represents teachers in England and Wales, in both government and private schools 全国教师联合会〔代表英格兰和威尔士公立和私立学校教师的一个重要的行业工会组织〕

nut·case /ˈnʌtˌkes; ˈnʌtkeɪs/ *n* [C] *informal humorous* someone who is crazy or mentally ill【非正式, 幽默】疯子: *That man's a complete nutcase.* 那个男人完全是个疯子。

nut·crack·er /ˈnʌtˌkrækə; ˈnʌtˌkrækə/ *n* [C] also 又作 **nutcrackers** [plural] *BrE* a tool for cracking the shells of nuts【英】夹碎坚果的钳子, 胡桃钳

Nutcracker, The (1892) a BALLET with music by Tchaikovsky about a girl who dreams that her NUTCRACKER becomes a prince. It is one of the most popular ballets, and is often performed at Christmas. 《胡桃夹子》〔(1892), 柴可夫斯基谱曲的一部芭蕾舞剧。该剧讲述一个女孩梦见自己的胡桃夹子变成一个王子的故事。这部作品是最受欢迎的芭蕾舞剧之一, 常在圣诞节期间上演〕

nut·house /ˈnʌtˌhaus; ˈnʌthaʊs/ *n* [C] *slang* an offensive word for a PSYCHIATRIC HOSPITAL【俚】疯人院〔对精神病医院的冒犯性用语〕

nut·meg /ˈnʌtmɛg; ˈnʌtmeg/ *n* **1** [U] a brown powder used as a SPICE¹ (1) to give a particular taste to food 肉豆蔻粉〔用作调味品〕 **2** [C] the seed of a tropical tree from which this powder is made 肉豆蔻

nu·tri·ent /ˈnjutrɪənt; ˈnjuːtriənt/ *n* [C] a chemical or food that provides what is needed for plants or animals to live and grow 养分, 营养物: *The plant absorbs nutrients from the soil.* 植物从土壤中吸取养分。—**nutrient** *adj*

nu·tri·ment /ˈnjutrəmənt; ˈnjuːtrɪ̣mənt/ *n* [U] *formal* substances that plants and animals need in order to live and grow; NOURISHMENT【正式】养分; 营养

nu·tri·tion /njuˋtrɪʃən; njuːˈtrɪʃən/ *n* [U] the process of giving or getting the right kind of food for good health and growth 营养(作用); 滋养: *Nutrition and exercise are essential to fitness and health.* 营养和运动是保持健康所必不可少的。—**nutritional** *adj*: *the nutritional value of fresh vegetables* 新鲜蔬菜的营养价值 —**nutritionally** *adv*

nu·tri·tious /njuˋtrɪʃəs; njuːˈtrɪʃəs/ *adj* food that is nutritious is full of the natural substances that your body needs to stay healthy or to grow properly; NOURISHING〔食物〕有营养的, 滋养的, 营养价值高的: *Wholemeal bread is more nutritious than white bread.* 全麦面包比白面包更有营养。

nu·tri·tive /ˈnjutrətɪv; ˈnjuːtrɪ̣tɪv/ *adj* **1** [no comparative 无比较级] *technical* relating to nutrition【术语】有关营养的 **2** *formal* nutritious【正式】有营养的, 营养价值高的

nuts¹ /nʌts; nʌts/ *adj* [not before noun 不用于名词前] *informal*【非正式】**1** crazy 发疯的, 发狂的: **go nuts** (=become crazy) 发疯 *I'll go nuts if I have to wait any longer.* 再等下去我会发疯的。| **drive sb nuts** (=annoy someone very much) 使某人发疯 *Turn that radio off. It's driving me nuts.* 把那个收音机关掉, 吵得我快发疯了。**2 be nuts about/on/over** to like someone or something very much 对…着迷; 热衷于…: *She's nuts about the boy next door.* 她迷恋上了隔壁的男孩。

nuts² *interjection AmE old-fashioned* used when you are angrily refusing to listen to someone【美, 过时】去你的; 混蛋〔表示生气、拒绝〕: *"Nuts to you, wise guy," he sneered.* "去你的, 自作聪明的人。"他讥笑道。

N

nut·shell /ˈnʌt,ʃɛl; ˈnʌt-ʃel/ *n* [C] **1 (to put it) in a nutshell** *spoken* used when you are stating the main facts about something in a short, clear way【口】一言以蔽之，简括地说，用一句话概括：*To put it in a nutshell, the show was a total disaster.* 概括说来，这场演出糟糕透了。**2** the hard outer part of a nut 坚果的外壳

nut·ter /ˈnʌtə; ˈnʌtə/ *n* [C] *BrE informal* a crazy person【英，非正式】疯子：*an absolute nutter* 十足的疯子

nut·ty /ˈnʌtɪ; ˈnʌti/ *adj* **1** tasting like nuts 有坚果味的：*This coffee has a rich nutty flavour.* 这种咖啡带有浓郁的坚果味道。**2** containing or filled with nuts 含坚果的，放了很多坚果的：*a nutty cake* 果仁蛋糕 **3** *informal* crazy【非正式】发疯的：*another of his nutty ideas* 他又一个古怪的主意 | **nutty as a fruitcake** (=completely crazy) 彻底疯掉的 —**nuttiness** *n* [U]

nuz·zle /ˈnʌzḷ; ˈnʌzəl/ also 又作 **nuzzle up** *v* [I always+adv/prep, T] to gently rub or press your nose or head against someone to show you like them〔为表示喜爱〕用鼻子触碰；用头挨擦；把头紧挨在：*The horses were nuzzling up against each other.* 马用鼻子相互蹭来蹭去。| *Tim nuzzled Clare's neck.* 蒂姆把头紧挨在克莱尔的脖子上。

NV the written abbreviation of 缩写= NEVADA

NW the written abbreviation of 缩写= NORTHWEST OR NORTHWESTERN

NY the written abbreviation of 缩写= NEW YORK

NYC the written abbreviation of 缩写= NEW YORK CITY

Nye·re·re /njəˈrɛrɪ; njəˈreəri/, **Jul·i·us** /ˈdʒuljəs; ˈdʒuːliəs/ (1922-99) a Tanzanian politician who was one of the leaders of the country's fight for independence from the UK. He was the first President of Tanzania (1964-85) and he strongly believed that African countries should develop their own farming and industry without copying Western economic ideas. 尼雷尔〔(1922-1999)，坦桑尼亚政治家，反英独立斗争的领袖之一。他是坦桑尼亚第一任总统(1964-1985)，坚信非洲国家应发展自己的工农业，不应照搬西方的经济理念〕

ny·lon /ˈnaɪlɑn; ˈnaɪlɒn/ *n* [U] **1** a strong artificial material that is used to make plastics, clothes, rope etc 尼龙；耐纶：*shirts made of nylon* 尼龙衬衫 | *nylon thread* 尼龙线 **2 nylons** *old-fashioned* women's STOCKINGs or TIGHTs made of nylon【过时】〔妇女的〕尼龙长袜；尼龙连裤袜

nymph /nɪmf; nɪmf/ *n* [C] **1** one of the spirits of nature, who, according to ancient Greek and Roman stories, appeared as young girls living in trees, mountains, streams etc〔希腊和罗马神话中居于山林水泽中的〕仙女 **2** *poetic* a girl or young woman【诗】少女；少妇

nym·phet /nɪmˈfɛt; nɪmˈfet/ *n* [C] *humorous* a young girl who is very sexually attractive【幽默】性感少女

CULTURAL NOTE 文化注释

This word became popular after it was used in Vladimir Nabokov's book *Lolita*. 这个词自从在弗拉基米尔·纳博科夫的小说《洛丽塔》中用过之后就流行起来。

nym·pho·ma·ni·ac /ˌnɪmfəˈmenɪæk; ˌnɪmfəˈmeɪniæk/ also 又作 **nympho** *informal*【非正式】*n* [C] a woman who always wants to have sex, with a lot of different men 女色情狂；慕男狂 —**nymphomaniac** *adj*: *nymphomaniac tendencies* 慕男狂倾向 —**nymphomania** /-nɪə; -niə/ *n* [U]

NYPD the abbreviation of 缩写= the New York Police Department 纽约警察局

NYSE /ˌɛn waɪ ɛs ˈi; ˌen waɪ es ˈiː/ the abbreviation of 缩写= the NEW YORK STOCK EXCHANGE

NZ the written abbreviation of 缩写= New Zealand

O,o

O

O, o /o; əʊ/ *plural* **O's, o's 1** the 15th letter of the English alphabet 英语字母表的第十五个字母 **2** *spoken* a zero【口】零

O /o; əʊ/ *interjection* **1** *poetic* used when addressing someone or something【诗】啊〔用于称呼前〕: *O Death, where is thy sting?* 啊！死亡，你的毒钩在哪里？**2** another form of OH oh 的另一种形式

o' /ə; ə/ *prep* **1** a way of writing 'of' as it is usually said in speech〔口语中通常所说的 of 的书写形式〕: *a pint o' beer* 一品脱啤酒 **2** *literary*【文】= on

oaf /of; əʊf/ *n* [C] a stupid awkward man or boy 蠢人，呆子〔指男性〕: *You clumsy oaf!* 你这个笨手笨脚的蠢货！—**oafish** *adj* —**oafishly** *adv* —**oafishness** *n* [U]

S3 **oak** /ok; əʊk/ *n* [C,U] a large tree that is common in northern countries, or the hard wood of this tree 栎树，橡树；栎木，橡木: *ancient oaks* 古老的橡树 | *an oak door* 橡木做的门 | *polished oak* 抛光的栎木

oak ap·ple /ˈ· ·ˌ·/ *n* [C] a raised part on the leaf or stem of an oak tree, caused by an insect 栎瘿，栎五倍子〔栎树叶或树干上由昆虫引致的瘤状物〕

oak·en /ˈokən; ˈəʊkən/ *adj especially literary* made of oak【尤文】栎[橡]木制的

Oak·ley /ˈoklı; ˈəʊkli/, **An·nie** /ˈænı; ˈæni/ (1860-1926) a US woman who was very skilled at shooting, and who performed in Buffalo Bill's *Wild West Show*. The musical show and film *Annie Get Your Gun* is based on her life. 奥克利〔(1860-1926)，美国女子，精通射击，曾参加过野牛比尔的"西大荒演艺会"。《飞燕金枪》这一音乐剧和影片就是基于她的生平故事而创作的〕

Oaks, the /oks; əʊks/ a horse race for fillies (FILLY = young female horses) held every year at Epsom in the UK, one of the most important events in British FLAT RACING (=racing on level ground, not jumping over fences) 欧克斯赛〔每年在英国埃普瑟姆举行的小母驹赛，是英国平地赛马最重要的赛事之一〕

oa·kum /ˈokəm; ˈəʊkəm/ *n* [U] small pieces of old rope used for filling up small holes in the sides of wooden ships 麻絮，填絮〔用于填塞木船帮上的小洞〕

OAP /ˌo e ˈpi; ˌəʊ eɪ ˈpiː/ *n* [C] *BrE* Old Age Pensioner; a person who is old enough to receive a PENSION from the state【英】领取养老金者

oar /ɔr; ɔː/ *n* [C] **1** a long pole with a wide flat blade at one end, used for rowing a boat 橹，桨 —compare 比较 PADDLE[1] (1) **2 put/shove/stick your oar in** *BrE informal* to join in a discussion without being asked to【英，非正式】多嘴，插嘴

oar·lock /ˈɔrˌlɑk; ˈɔːlɒk/ *n* [C] *AmE* a ROWLOCK【美】桨叉，桨架

oars·man /ˈɔrzmən; ˈɔːzmən/ *n plural* **oarsmen** /-mən; -mən/ [C] someone who rows a boat, especially in races〔尤指划船比赛中的〕划手，桨手

oars·wom·an /ˈɔrzˌwʊmən; ˈɔːzˌwʊmən/ *n plural* **oarswomen** /-ˌwımın; -ˌwımın/ [C] a woman who rows a boat, especially in races〔尤指划船比赛中的〕女划手，女桨手

OAS, the /ˌo e ˈɛs; ˌəʊ eɪ ˈes/ the Organization of American States; an organization whose members include the US and Canada and most of the countries of Central and South America. Its aims are to preserve peace and to help the economic development of the area. 美洲国家组织〔由美国、加拿大以及中美洲和南美洲大部分国家组成的一个组织。其宗旨是维护本地区的和平，促进本地区的经济发展〕

OASDHI /ˌo e ˌɛs ˌdi etʃ ˈaı; ˌəʊ eɪ ˌes ˌdiː eɪtʃ ˈaɪ/ Old Age, Survivors, Disability, and Hospital Insurance; the Social Security insurance programme provided by the US government for people who have worked in the US for a certain number of years. The programme provides PENSIONS (=money for older people who have stopped working), money for people who have been permanently injured, and MEDICARE (=medical care for older people). 养老、遗孤、伤残和医疗保险〔美国政府为在美国工作过一定年限的人士安排的一项社会保障计划。该计划包括养老金、永久性伤残补助以及老年医疗保障等项目〕

o·a·sis /oˈesıs; əʊˈeɪsɪs/ *n plural* **oases** /-siz; -siːz/ [C] **1** a place with water and trees in a desert〔沙漠中的〕绿洲 **2** a peaceful or pleasant place that is very different from everything around it 宁静宜人的地方: *the one oasis of calm in the war-torn city* 饱经战祸的城市中一片宁静之地

oast house /ˈost ˌhaus; ˈəʊst haʊs/ *n* [C] *BrE* a round building with a pointed top, built for drying HOPS[2] (4)【英】〔烘烤啤酒花的〕尖顶圆形烘房

oat cake /ˈot ˌkek; ˈəʊt keɪk/ *n* [C] a flat cake made of oatmeal 燕麦饼

Oates /ots; əʊts/, **Captain Law·rence** /ˈlɔrəns; ˈlɒrəns/ (1880-1912) a British EXPLORER who went with Captain Scott on his journey to the South Pole. On the way back, Oates was suffering from FROSTBITE and could no longer walk fast enough, so he deliberately killed himself by going out into the snow, because he did not want to delay the other members of the team. His last words, "I am just going outside, and may be some time", are now often said humorously by someone when they are about to do something difficult or slightly dangerous, and they are not sure when they will return. 欧茨〔(1880-1912)，英国探险家，曾随同斯科特上尉奔赴南极探险，回程途中饱受冻伤之苦，行走步履艰难。为了不耽误队友的行程，他走入雪堆结束了自己的生命。他说的最后一句话是："我出去一下，可能一时回不来。"现在，有人常诙谐地借用这句话来表示自己要去做一件困难或有点危险的事情，并且说不准何时才能回来〕

oath /oθ; əʊθ/ *n* [C] *plural* **oaths** /oðz; əʊðz/ **1** a formal and very serious promise 誓言，誓约，誓词: **swear/take an oath** *The knights swore an oath of loyalty to their king.* 骑士们宣誓效忠于国王。**2 be on/under oath** *law* to have made a formal promise to tell the truth in a court of law【法律】【在法庭上】已发誓要讲真话，在宣誓的约束下: *evidence given under oath* 宣誓后提供的证词[证据] **3 take the oath** to make an official promise to tell the truth in a court of law〔在法庭上〕宣誓，立誓，发誓 **4** an expression of strong feeling that uses religious or sexual words in an offensive way 诅咒，咒骂: *He shouted oaths and curses as they took him away.* 他们带走他时，他大声诅咒谩骂。

oat·meal /ˈotˌmil; ˈəʊtmiːl/ *n* [U] **1** crushed OATS used for making cakes and PORRIDGE (1) 燕麦片 **2** *AmE* a soft breakfast food made by boiling crushed oats【美】燕麦片粥; PORRIDGE (1) *BrE*【英】

oats /ots; əʊts/ *n* [plural] **1** a grain that is eaten by people and animals 燕麦 **2** oatmeal 燕麦片 **3 feel your oats** *informal* to feel full of energy【非正式】精力充沛，精神饱满 **4 get your oats** *BrE informal* to have sex regularly【英，非正式】定期行房 **5 be off your oats** *BrE informal* to have lost the desire to eat【英，非正式】食欲不振，胃口不好

OAU, the /ˌo e ˈju; ˌəʊ eɪ ˈjuː/ the former name of the African Union 非洲统一组织〔非洲联盟旧称〕

ob·du·ra·cy /ˈɑbdjərəsı; ˈɒbdjərəsi/ *n* [U] *formal* an unreasonable refusal to change your beliefs or feelings【正式】执拗，倔强，顽固

ob·du·rate /ˈɑbdjərıt; ˈɒbdjərɪt/ *adj formal* unreasonably determined not to change your beliefs or feelings; STUBBORN【正式】执拗的，倔强的，顽固的: *She remained obdurate despite their pleas.* 不管他们怎样恳求，她依然倔强如初。—**obdurately** *adv*

OBE /ˌo bi ˈi; ˌəʊ biː ˈiː/ *n* Officer of the Order of the British Empire; a special honour given to some British people for things they have done for their country. OBE is written after someone's name to show that they have been given this honour 英帝国官佐勋章(获得者)〔英国给为国家做出杰出贡献的人士授予的一种特殊荣誉。获此殊荣的人，其姓名后附有 OBE 的字样〕: *John Smith, OBE* 英帝国官佐勋章获得者约翰·史密斯 | *She's been given an OBE.* 她被授予英帝国官佐勋章。

o·be·di·ence /əˈbidıəns; əˈbiːdiəns/ *n* [U] obedient behaviour; doing what you are told to do by your parents etc 服从，顺从；遵从: [+to] *obedience to her father's wishes* 遵从她父亲的意愿 | **demand obedience** *a master who demanded absolute obedience from his servants* 要求仆人绝对服从的主人

o·be·di·ent /əˈbidıənt; əˈbiːdiənt/ *adj* **1** always doing what you are told to do by your parents, by someone in authority etc 服从的，顺从的，听话的: *an obedient and dutiful child* 听话而孝顺的孩子 **2 your obedient servant** *old use* used to end a very formal letter【旧】您恭顺的仆人〔正式信尾用语〕—opposite 反义词 DISOBEDIENT —**obediently** *adv*: *She obediently did as she was told.* 她顺从地按吩咐做了。

o·bei·sance /o`besn̩s; əʊ'beɪsəns/ *n* [C,U] *formal* an act of showing respect and obedience, by bending your head or the upper part of your body【正式】敬礼〈如鞠躬等〉

ob·e·lisk /`ɑbl̩,ɪsk; 'ɒbəlɪsk/ *n* [C] **1** a tall pointed stone PILLAR (1) 方尖碑; 方尖塔 **2** a DAGGER (1) sign used in printing〔印刷品中的〕剑号

O·ber·am·mer·gau /,obɚ`æmɚgau; ,əʊbər'æməgaʊ/ a town in Bavaria, southern Germany, where a PASSION PLAY (=a play telling the story of Jesus' suffering and death) has been performed by the people of the town every ten years since 1634, as a way of thanking God for saving them from the PLAGUE (=a very infectious disease that killed large numbers of people) 上阿默高〔德国南部巴伐利亚一城镇。1634年至今, 镇上的居民每10年就会表演一次耶稣受难复活剧, 以感谢上帝使他们逃过瘟疫〕

O·be·ron /`obərɑn; 'əʊbərɒn/ the king of the fairies and the husband of Titania in the play *A Midsummer Night's Dream* by William Shakespeare 奥伯伦〔威廉·莎士比亚的剧本《仲夏夜之梦》中的仙王, 为泰坦尼娅之夫〕

o·bese /o`bis; əʊ'biːs/ *adj technical* very fat in a way that is unhealthy【术语】肥胖的; 臃肿的 —see 见 FAT[1] (USAGE)

CULTURAL NOTE 文化注释

More and more people seem to be becoming obese, and it is considered an important health problem in the US. The UK also now has more obese people than it did in the past, though not as many as in the US. Doctors are especially worried because more children are becoming obese, and they will probably have many health problems, such as heart disease or DIABETES when they are older. Doctors and other people think that the main cause is that people do not get enough exercise and eat too much JUNK FOOD. Some people who are obese have even tried to SUE restaurants that serve FAST FOOD, saying that there should be more warnings about the fat levels in fast food and how it can affect your health. Most people who are obese have tried many different DIETS, and some even have medical operations to try to lose weight. 胖人越来越多, 在美国这被认为是严重的健康问题。尽管没有美国那么多, 现在英国的胖人也比过去增加了很多。医生对此事尤为担忧, 因为少年儿童中的小胖墩越来越多, 等他们长大了就很可能会遇到健康问题, 如患上心脏病、糖尿病等。医生还有其他人都认为, 肥胖的主要原因是人们缺乏锻炼和摄入太多的垃圾食品。一些肥胖患者甚至把快餐店告上了法庭, 理由是应该对快餐有更多的警示提醒, 标明脂肪含量以及对健康的影响。很多肥胖者也尝试了不同的节食疗法, 有些甚至通过做手术来减肥。

o·be·si·ty /o`bisətɪ; əʊ'biːsɪ̮ti/ *n* [U] *technical* the condition of being too fat in a way that is dangerous to your health【术语】肥胖症

o·bey /ə`be; əʊ'beɪ/ *v* [I,T] to do what someone in a position of authority tells you to do, or to do what a law or rule says you must do 服从〔权威等〕; 遵守〔法规等〕: *The men always obey him.* 他手下的人总是听命于他。| *"Stand still!" he bellowed. Only a few obeyed.* "站着别动!"他大声喝道, 但只有几个人服从。| **obey an order/command** *Soldiers are expected to obey orders.* 军人必须服从命令。| **obey the law/laws/rules** *You'll have to obey the rules if you want to live here.* 要想在这里住, 你就得守规矩。—opposite 反义词 DISOBEY

ob·fus·cate /`ɑbfəs,ket; 'ɒbfəskeɪt/ *v* [T] *formal* to deliberately make something unclear or difficult to understand【正式】〔有意地〕使模糊, 使费解 —**obfuscation** /,ɑbfəs`keʃən; ,ɒbfəs'keɪʃən/

ob/gyn /,o bi ,dʒi waɪ `ɛn; ,əʊ biː ,dʒiː waɪ 'en/ *n* [U] *informal, especially AmE* OBSTETRICS and GYNAECOLOGY【非正式, 尤美】妇产科(学)

O·bie A·ward /`obɪ ə,wɔrd; 'əʊbi ə,wɔːd/ *n* [C] also 又作 **The Village Voice Off-Broadway Award** a prize given to plays in the theatres of the off-Broadway area of New York City 奥比奖〔颁发给纽约的外百老汇剧场内演出的戏剧奖〕

o·bit·u·a·ry /ə`bɪtʃʊ,ɛrɪ; ə'bɪtʃuəri/ *n* [C] a report in a newspaper about the life of someone who has just died〔报纸上的〕讣告, 讣闻, 讣文

3 2 **ob·ject**[1] /`ɑbdʒɪkt; 'ɒbdʒɪkt/ *n*

1 ▶THING 东西◀ [C] a solid thing, especially something that you can hold or touch 实物, 物体: *some kind of heavy blunt object* 某种笨重的东西

2 an object of pity/desire/contempt etc someone or something that is pitied, desired etc 让人怜悯/渴望/鄙视等的对象: *Once famous, he was now a mere object of pity.* 他曾经名噪一时, 但现在不过是一个让人怜悯的对象。—see also 另见 SEX OBJECT

3 ▶AIM 目的◀ [singular] the intended result of a plan, action, or activity 目的, 目标; 宗旨: **[+of]** *The object of the game is to score 100 points.* 这个游戏的目标是得到100分。| *His primary object was to gain publicity.* 他的主要目的是想出名。| **the object of the exercise** (=the object of whatever you are doing) 做事的目的 *The customer will benefit most, and that after all is the object of the exercise.* 客户将是最大的得益者, 说到底, 这正是此举的目的。

4 money/expense is no object used to say that you are willing to spend a lot of money 钱/费用不成问题

5 object lesson an event or story that shows you the right or wrong way of doing something 有教诲的事件[故事]; 可引以为训的事例: *The whole weekend was an object lesson in how not to attract a woman.* 这整个周末可引以为训, 像那样做吸引不了女人。

6 ▶IN GRAMMAR 语法◀ [C] a noun, noun phrase, or PRONOUN representing **a)** the person or thing that something is done to, for example 'the house' in 'We built the house.'; DIRECT OBJECT 直接宾语[受词]〈如We built the house中的the house〉 **b)** the person who is concerned in the result of an action, for example 'her' in 'I gave her the book.'; INDIRECT OBJECT 间接宾语[受词]〈如I gave her the book中的her〉 **c)** the person or thing that is joined by a PREPOSITION to another word or phrase, for example 'table' in 'He sat on the table.' 介词宾语[受词]〈如He sat on the table中的table〉

ob·ject[2] /əb`dʒɛkt; əb'dʒekt/ *v* **1** [I] to complain or protest about something, or to feel or say that you oppose it or disapprove of it 反对, 不赞成: *Do you think anyone would object if I park my car here?* 如果我把车停在这里, 你认为会有人反对吗? | **[+to]** *My mother objected to every boy I brought home.* 我带回家的男孩, 我母亲一个都不喜欢。| **object to being called/being told etc** *I object to being spoken to like that.* 我不喜欢别人那样对我说话。| **I object** (=used in formal arguments) 我反对〔用于正式辩论中〕 *Mr. Chairman, I object. That is an unfair allegation.* 主席先生, 我反对, 这是不公正的指控。**2** [T+that] to state a fact or opinion as a way of opposing something or complaining 提出…作为反对的理由; 反对说: *Mom objected that we were too young to go on vacation alone.* 妈妈表示反对, 说我们年纪太小, 不能单独去度假。| *"My name's not Sonny," the child objected.* "我的名字不叫小家伙。"那孩子反驳道。—see also 另见 OBJECTOR 2

object code /'‥ ,‥/ *n* [U] MACHINE CODE〔电脑中的〕目标代码

ob·jec·tion /əb`dʒɛkʃən, əb'dʒekʃən/ *n* [C] **1** something that you say to show that you oppose or disapprove of an action, idea etc 反对, 不赞成; 异议: **[+to]** *objections to the Governor's plan* 对州长计划的反对意见 | **have an objection** *If no one has any objection, I'll declare the meeting closed.* 如果没有人反对的话, 我将宣布会议结束。| **raise/voice an objection** (=state an objection) 提出反对(意见) **2** a reason against doing something 反对的原因: **[+to/against]** *The only objection to hiring him is that he can't drive.* 反对雇用他的唯一理由是他不会开车。 3

ob·jec·tion·a·ble /əb`dʒɛkʃənəbl̩; əb'dʒekʃənəbəl/ *adj* unpleasant and likely to offend people; offensive 令人不快的; 可能得罪人的; 讨厌的: *a most objectionable remark* 很令人讨厌的言辞 | *What an objectionable man he is!* 他真讨厌! —**objectionably** *adv*

ob·jec·tive[1] /əb`dʒɛktɪv; əb'dʒektɪv/ *n* [C] **1** an aim that you are trying to achieve, especially in business or politics〔尤指生意或政治方面的〕目的, 目标: *The main objective of this policy is to reduce unemployment.* 这项政策的主要目的是减少失业。**2** a place that you are trying to reach, especially in a military attack 出击目标〔尤指军事攻击目标〕: *The valley was our primary objective.* 这山谷是我们主要的出击目标。 3

objective[2] *adj* **1** not influenced by your own feelings or opinions, when you have to make a judgment or decision 客观的, 公正的: *I need an objective opinion from someone who's not involved.* 我需要一个与此事无涉的人的客观看法。—opposite 反义词 SUBJECTIVE (1) **2** *formal* existing outside the mind; real【正式】客观存在的; 真实的: *objective facts* 客观事实 **3** *technical* connected with the object【术语】宾格的, 受格的 —**objectivity** /,ɑbdʒɛk`tɪvətɪ; ,ɒbdʒek'tɪvɪ̮ti/ *n* [U] 3

ob·jec·tive·ly /əb`dʒɛktɪvlɪ; əb'dʒektɪvli/ *adv* if you consider something objectively, you try to think about it without being influenced by your own feelings or opinions 客观地

ob·jec·tor /əb`dʒɛktɚ; əb`dʒektə/ *n* [C] someone who states or shows that they oppose something 反对者: *objectors to the new motorway* 反对修建这条新公路的人

ob·jet d'art /ˌɑbʒe `dɑr; ˌɒbʒeɪ `dɑː/ *plural* **objets d'art** (*same pronunciation* 发音相同) *n* [C] a small object, used for decoration, that has some value as art 小艺术[工艺、装饰]品

ob·la·tion /əb`leʃən; ə`bleɪʃən/ *n* [C,U] *formal* a gift that is offered to God or a god, or the act of offering the gift【正式】〔给上帝或神的〕祭品, 供物; 供奉

ob·li·gat·ed /`ɑbləˌgetɪd; `ɒblɪ̧geɪtɪ̧d/ *adj especially AmE*【尤美】**1 be obligated (to do something)** to have to do something or have a duty to do it 不得不(做某事); 有义务(做某事): *IBM's European customers will be obligated to make more drastic cutbacks in mainframe expenditure.* 国际商业机器公司的欧洲客户将不得不更大幅度地缩减在大型电脑主机方面的开支。**2 be/feel obligated to someone** to owe someone loyalty, thanks, or money, because they have done something for you 欠某人人情, 对某人感恩图报

W3 **ob·li·ga·tion** /ˌɑblə`geʃən; ˌɒblɪ̧`geɪʃən/ *n* [C,U] **1** a moral or legal duty to do something〔道义或法律上的〕义务, 职责, 责任: **obligation to do sth** *You can look at the books without any obligation to buy.* 你可以看看这些书, 不一定非要买。| **[+to]** *I have certain obligations to my family.* 我对自己的家庭负有一定的义务。| **meet/fulfil an obligation** (=do something that is your duty) 履行义务[职责] *Have the employers met their contractual obligations?* 雇主履行合同规定的义务了吗? | **a sense of obligation** (=feeling that you ought to do something) 责任感 *I helped you because I wanted to, not out of any sense of obligation.* 我帮你是因为我想这样做, 而不是出于什么责任感。**2 be under an obligation a)** to have to do something because it is a legal or moral duty 有义务〔做某事〕: **be under no obligation to do sth** *We are invited but we are under no obligation to go.* 我们接到了邀请, 但我们没有义务一定要去。| **place sb under an obligation** *Signing a contract places you under a long-term obligation.* 签署一项合同就使人在很长一段时期内负有责任。**b)** to owe someone loyalty, thanks, or money because they have done something for you 欠〔某人〕人情: **[+to]** *I don't want to be under an obligation to anyone.* 我不想欠任何人的人情。

ob·lig·a·to·ry /ə`blɪgəˌtorɪ; ə`blɪgətəri/ *adj* **1** *formal* something that is obligatory must be done because of a law, a rule etc; COMPULSORY, MANDATORY【正式】〔因法律、规定等〕必须履行的, 有义务的; 强制性的: *Attendance is obligatory.* 必须出席。**2** *often humorous* used to describe something that is usually done, worn, or included because many people also do it, or you have always done it in the past【常幽默】惯常的, 习惯上的: *Paula was smartly dressed in a new tweed suit with the obligatory matching bag and shoes.* 葆拉穿的很时髦, 一身新花呢套服以及必不可少与之相配的手提袋和鞋子。

Frequencies of **be obliged to, must,** and **have to/have got to** in spoken and written English 英语口语和书面语中 be obliged to, must 和 have to/have got to 的使用频率

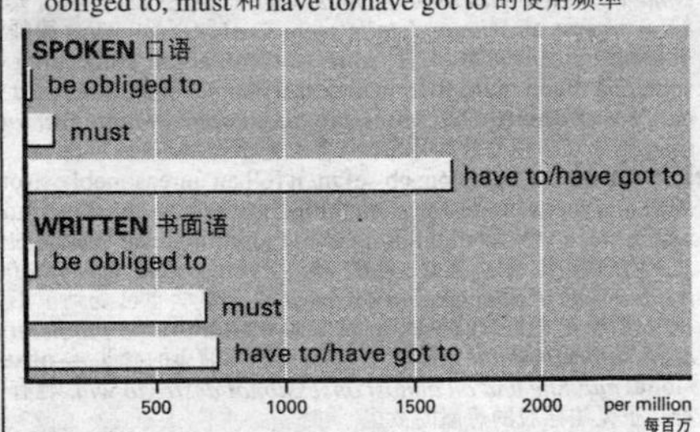

Based on the British National Corpus and the Longman Lancaster Corpus
据英国国家语料库和朗文兰开斯特语料库

This graph shows that the expressions **have to** and **have got to** are much more common in spoken English than **must** or **be obliged to**. **Have got to** is only used in British English. **Must** is more common in written English. **Be obliged to** is much less common than the others and is only used to say that someone must do something because of a rule or law, or because the situation forces them to do it. 本图表显示, 在英语口语中 have to 和 have got to 的使用频率远远高于 must 或 be obliged to。have got to 仅用于英国英语。must 更多用于书面语。be obliged to 的使用频率要低得多, 且仅用于表示某人因受某规定或法律所约束, 或因为情况所迫而必须做某事。

o·blige /ə`blaɪdʒ; ə`blaɪdʒ/ *v formal*【正式】**1** [T usually passive 一般用被动态] to make it necessary for someone to do something 使[某人]非做…不可, 迫使; 责成: **be obliged to do sth** *As a result of falling profits we were obliged to close the factory.* 由于利润下降, 我们被迫关闭这家工厂。| **feel obliged to do sth** (=feel that you have a duty to do something) 觉得有义务做某事 *Don't feel obliged to play if you don't want to.* 你不想玩就不要勉强。**2** [I,T] to do something that someone has asked you to do 帮忙; 答应[某人的]请求: *Would you oblige me by taking this letter to the Director?* 劳驾你帮我把这封信捎给主任好吗? | **happy/glad/ready to oblige** *If you need a ride home, I'd be happy to oblige.* 如果你需要搭车回家, 我很乐意效劳。**3 I'd be obliged if** *spoken* used to make a polite request【口】多谢〔请别人帮忙时的客气话〕: *I'd be obliged if you'd treat this matter as strictly confidential.* 此事如你能严格保密, 我将非常感激。**4 (I'm) much obliged (to you)** *spoken* used to thank someone very politely【口】(我) 非常感谢 (你)〔用于有礼貌地向某人致谢〕 S3

o·blig·ing /ə`blaɪdʒɪŋ; ə`blaɪdʒɪŋ/ *adj* willing and eager to help 乐于助人的, 热心相助的: *What an obliging child!* 一个多么热心助人的孩子呀! —**obligingly** *adv*: *"Of course I'll do it," she said obligingly.* "这事我当然要做。"她热情地说。

o·blique[1] /ə`blik; ə`bliːk/ *adj* **1** not expressed in a direct way 间接的, 不直截了当的: *oblique references to his drinking problems* 拐弯抹角地提及他的酗酒问题 **2** not looking or pointing directly at something 斜的, 倾斜的: *an oblique glance* 睨视 **3 oblique line/stroke etc** a sloping line etc 斜线 **4 oblique angle** *technical* an angle that is not 90°, 180°, or 270°【术语】斜角 —**obliquely** *adv* —**obliqueness** *n* [U]

oblique[2] *n* [C] a mark (/) used for writing FRACTIONS (2) or for separating numbers, letters, words etc; SLASH[2] (2) 斜线符号

o·blit·er·ate /ə`blɪtəˌret; ə`blɪtəreɪt/ *v* [T] **1** to destroy something so completely that no sign of it remains 完全毁灭〔不留痕迹〕: *The entire village was obliterated by incendiary bombs.* 整个村子被燃烧弹夷为平地。**2** to cover something completely so that it cannot be seen 涂抹; 遮蔽 **3** to remove a thought, feeling, or memory from someone's mind 忘却, 抹去〔想法、感情或记忆〕: *Nothing could obliterate the memory of those tragic events.* 什么也不能让人忘却对那些悲惨事件的记忆。—**obliteration** /əˌblɪtə`reʃən; əˌblɪtə`reɪʃən/ *n* [U]

o·bliv·i·on /ə`blɪvɪən; ə`blɪviən/ *n* [U] **1** the state of being completely forgotten 被完全忘却 (的状态); 遗忘: *The loser's name is consigned to oblivion.* 那败者的姓名湮没无闻了。**2** the state of being unconscious or of not noticing what is happening 无感觉[知觉]的状态; 漠视: *the oblivion of sleep* 睡眠中的无知觉状态

o·bliv·i·ous /ə`blɪvɪəs; ə`blɪviəs/ *adj* [not before noun 不用于名词前] not knowing about, or not noticing, something that is happening around you; UNAWARE 不在意的, 未觉察到的: **[+of/to]** *Mallory set off, utterly oblivious of the danger.* 马洛里出发了, 全然没有觉察到有危险。—**obliviousness** *n* [U]

ob·long /`ɑblɔŋ; `ɒblɒŋ/ *adj* **1** *AmE* an oblong shape is much longer than it is wide【美】长椭圆形的: *an oblong leaf* 长椭圆形的叶子 **2** *BrE* an oblong shape has four straight sides at 90° to each other, two of which are much longer than the other two【英】长方形的: *an oblong frame* 长方形的框架 —compare 比较 RECTANGLE —**oblong** *n* [C]

ob·lo·quy /`ɑbləkwɪ; `ɒbləkwi/ *n* [U] *formal*【正式】**1** very strong, offensive criticism 辱骂, 痛责 **2** loss of respect and honour 丧失尊严, 耻辱

ob·nox·ious /əb`nɑkʃəs; əb`nɒkʃəs/ *adj* extremely unpleasant or rude 可憎的, 讨厌的; 粗暴无礼的: *You obnoxious little creep!* 你这个烦人的小讨厌鬼! | *an obnoxious smell* 难闻的气味 —**obnoxiously** *adv* —**obnoxiousness** *n* [U]

o·boe /`obo; `əʊbəʊ/ *n* [C] a wooden musical instrument, shaped like a narrow tube, which you play by blowing air through a REED (2) 双簧管

o·bo·ist /`oboɪst; `əʊbəʊɪ̧st/ *n* [C] someone who plays the oboe 双簧管吹奏者

O'Brien an important character in the book *1984* by George Orwell. O'Brien pretends to be a friend of the main character Winston Smith, but tricks and tortures him. 奥布莱恩〔乔治·奥威尔的作品《一九八四》中的重要人物。奥布莱恩表面上对主人公温斯顿·史密斯以友相待, 实际却在欺骗他, 折磨他〕

ob·scene /əb`sin; əb`siːn/ *adj* **1** dealing with sex in a socially unacceptable and offensive way; INDECENT (1) 猥亵的, 淫猥的, 下流的: *The condemned man made an obscene gesture at the jury.* 受判者向陪审团做了个下流的手势。| *obscene publications* 淫秽出版物 | **obscene phone calls** (=from an unknown person saying obscene things) 〔来自陌生人的〕下流电话 **2** extremely

immoral and unfair in a way that makes you angry 令人震怒的，使人震惊的：*an obscene indifference to the needs of the poor* 对贫民的需求无动于衷，令人震怒 **—obscenely** *adv*

ob·scen·i·ty /əbˋsɛnətɪ; əbˈsenʲti/ *n* **1** [U] sexually offensive language or behaviour, especially in a book, play, film etc〔尤指书籍、戏剧、电影等中的〕猥亵语言；下流举动 **2** [C usually plural 一般用复数] a sexually offensive word or action 淫话；淫行：*He ran off, shouting obscenities at them.* 他跑开了，对他们大声说着淫话。

O

ob·scu·ran·tis·m /əbˋskjurəntˌɪzəm; ˌɒbskjʊˈræntɪzəm/ *n* [U] *formal* the practice of deliberately stopping ideas and facts from being known【正式】蒙昧主义，愚民政策 **—obscurantist** *adj*

ob·scure[1] /əbˋskjur; əbˈskjʊə/ *adj* **1** not at all well-known and usually not very important 无名的；微贱的：*an obscure poet* 没有名气的诗人 | *The exact origin of the paisley design is obscure.* 佩斯利花纹图案的确切起源不明。**2** difficult to understand 难理解的，晦涩的：*obscure legal phrases* 费解的法律词语 **—obscurely** *adv*

obscure[2] *v* [T] **1** to make something difficult to know or understand 搞混，使难理解：**obscure the fact/issue etc** *Recent successes obscure the fact that the company is still in trouble.* 近来的一些成功使人看不清公司依然处于困境。**2** to prevent something from being seen or heard clearly 遮蔽，使朦胧；使听不清：*Thick cloud obscured the stars from view.* 厚厚的云层遮住了星星。

ob·scu·ri·ty /əbˋskjurətɪ; əbˈskjʊərʲti/ *n* **1** [U] the state of not being known or remembered 无名，默默无闻：**[+in]** *O'Brien retired from politics and died in obscurity.* 奥布赖恩退出政坛后默默无闻地死去。**2** [C,U] something that is difficult to understand, or the quality of being difficult to understand 费解的事物；费解，晦涩：*After years of analysis, a great many obscurities remain in the text.* 虽经多年分析探讨，文中仍存有大量难解之处。**3** [U] *literary* darkness【文】黑暗

ob·se·quies /ˋɑbsɪkwɪz; ˈɒbsʲkwiz/ *n* [plural] *formal* a funeral ceremony【正式】葬礼，丧礼

ob·se·qui·ous /əbˋsikwɪəs; əbˈsiːkwiəs/ *adj* too eager to serve people and agree with them; SERVILE (1) 谄媚的，奉承的；奴颜婢膝的：*The salesman's obsequious manner was beginning to irritate me.* 那推销员逢迎的样子让我恼怒起来。**—obsequiously** *adv* **—obsequiousness** *n* [U]

ob·ser·va·ble /əbˋzɝvəbl; əbˈzɜːvəbəl/ *adj* something that is observable can be seen or noticed 看得见的，能观察到的：*unemployment and other observable effects of the recession* 失业及其他可看得到的经济衰退带来的影响 **—observably** *adv*

ob·ser·vance /əbˋzɝvəns; əbˈzɜːvəns/ *n* **1** [U] the practice of obeying a law or doing what is expected according to a custom or ceremony〔对法律、风俗或仪式的〕遵守，奉行：**[+of]** *strict observance of the rules* 对规则的严格遵守 | *the observance of Chinese New Year* 奉行过中国农历新年的习俗 **2** [C] a part of a religious ceremony 宗教的典礼，仪式：*ritual observances* 例行的宗教仪式

ob·ser·vant /əbˋzɝvənt; əbˈzɜːvənt/ *adj* **1** good or quick at noticing things 观察力敏锐的，机警的：*Luckily, an observant passerby spotted the broken cable.* 幸亏一位机警的过路人发现了那根断裂的电缆。| **[+of]** *Artists tend to be more observant of their surroundings.* 艺术家往往对他们周围的环境更为留意。**2** **[+of]** obeying laws, religious rules etc 遵守法律[宗教教规等]的

3 **ob·ser·va·tion** /ˌɑbzɚˋveʃən; ˌɒbzəˈveɪʃən/ *n* **1** [C,U] the process of watching something or someone carefully for a period of time 观察，注意；监视：*a study based on detailed observation of a group of 20 patients* 基于对一组20位患者详细观察的研究 | *a result of scientific observation* 科学观察的结果 | **under observation** (=being watched continuously by police, doctors etc) 受〔警方或医生等的〕监视[观察] *She's in hospital under observation.* 她在医院接受观察。| *Detectives are keeping the place under observation.* 侦探们监视着这个地方。**2** [C] a spoken or written remark about something you have noticed〔对所注意到的事物的〕评述，评论：**[+on]** *Darwin's observations on the habits of certain birds* 达尔文对某些鸟类习性的评述 | **make an observation** *I'd like to make a few observations about the current style of management.* 我想对当前的管理方式提出一些看法。**3 powers of observation** a natural ability to notice what is happening around you 观察力 **4 escape observation** to avoid being noticed 避免被人看见 **5** [U] the act of obeying a law etc; OBSERVANCE (1)〔对法律等的〕遵守，奉行 **—observational** *adj*

observation post /ˌ‥ˋ‥ ˌ/ *n* [C] a position from which an enemy can be watched 监视哨，瞭望哨

ob·ser·va·to·ry /əbˋzɝvəˌtorɪ; əbˈzɜːvətəri/ *n* [C] a special building from which scientists watch the moon, stars, weather etc 天文台；观象台；气象台：*the Greenwich Observatory* 格林尼治天文台

ob·serve /əbˋzɝv; əbˈzɜːv/ *v* [T] **1** [not in progressive 不用进行式] *formal* to see and notice something【正式】看到，注意到：**observe sb doing sth** *Ben knew that someone had observed him meeting Ryan.* 本知道有人看到他和瑞安见面了。| **[+that]** *She observed that the pond was drying up.* 她注意到池塘日渐干涸。| **observe sth** *The car I had observed earlier was no longer there.* 我早些时候看到的那辆汽车不在那里了。**2** to watch something or someone carefully 观察，监视，观测：*The police have been observing his movements.* 警方一直监视着他的一举一动。| **observe what/how/where** *I sat in a corner and observed what was going on.* 我坐在一个角落里观察当时发生的事情。**3** to do what you are supposed to do according to a law, agreement, or custom 遵守，奉行〔法律、协议或习俗〕：*So far the ceasefire has been observed by both sides.* 到目前为止，双方都遵守着停火协定。| **observe Christmas/May Day etc** (=celebrate a traditional holiday) 庆祝[纪念]圣诞节/五一劳动节等 **4** *formal* to say what you have noticed about a situation【正式】评述，评论，说：*"Michael's looking very anxious," I observed.* "迈克尔看上去很着急。"我说道。| **observe that** *Keynes observed that humans fall into two classes.* 凯恩斯说人类分为两个阶级。**5 closely observed** a play, character etc that is closely observed is very like a situation, character etc in real life〔戏剧、人物等〕与现实生活非常相似的，逼真的 2

ob·serv·er /əbˋzɝvɚ; əbˈzɜːvə/ *n* [C] **1** someone who sees or notices something 目击者：*Shocked observers told police about the robbery.* 震惊的目击者将抢劫案的情况告知了警方。| **casual observer** (=one who is not specially interested) 漫不经心的目击者 *To a casual observer she may have seemed fine, but I knew better.* 对于不是很留意她的人来说，她也许看上去不错，但我知道得更清楚。**2** someone who regularly watches or pays attention to particular things 观察者，观测员：**[+of]** *an impartial observer of the current political scene* 对当今政治局面不带偏见的观察者 | *an observer of nature* 自然界的观察者 **3** someone who attends meetings, classes etc to check what is happening〔会议等的〕观察员；〔课程的〕旁听者：*The UN sent a team of observers to the peace talks.* 联合国派出一个观察员小组出席和平会谈。

Observer, The a serious British Sunday newspaper which generally supports fairly LEFT-WING political ideas. *The Observer* is owned by the same company that owns *The Guardian*.《观察家报》〔英国一严肃类星期日报纸，通常支持相当左翼的政治观点，与《卫报》同属一家公司〕

ob·sess /əbˋsɛs; əbˈses/ *v* **1** [T usually passive 一般用被动态] if something or someone obsesses you, you think about them all the time and you cannot think of anything else 使着迷；使缠绕；使心神不宁：**be obsessed with** *You've always been obsessed with making money.* 你总是鬼迷心窍想着挣钱。| *He had become obsessed with another man's wife.* 他迷恋上一名有夫之妇。| **obsess sb** *Minute details seem to obsess lawyers.* 律师似乎总纠缠于细节问题。**2** [I] *AmE* to think about something or someone much more than is necessary or sensible【美】过分担心：**[+over/about]** *Stop obsessing about your weight. You look fine.* 不要过于担心你的体重，你看上去很好。

ob·ses·sion /əbˋsɛʃən; əbˈseʃən/ *n* [C] an unreasonably strong and continuous interest in something, or worry about something, which stops you from thinking about anything else 困扰人的想法；无法摆脱的意念；着迷，着魔：*He's convinced he was unfairly treated and it's become an obsession.* 他认为自己受到了不公正的对待，这想法一直困扰着他。| **[+with/about]** *an unhealthy obsession with death* 一种总是想到死的不健康的念头 **—obsessional** *adj*: *She had an almost obsessional desire to win.* 她有一种几乎无法摆脱的想赢的欲望。

ob·ses·sive[1] /əbˋsɛsɪv; əbˈsesɪv/ *adj* an obsessive feeling, interest or attitude makes you think all the time about a particular thing or person 着迷的；缠住不放的；〔在某方面〕过分的：*an obsessive need for excitement* 对刺激感着魔般的需求 | *She's becoming obsessive about hygiene.* 她变得有洁癖了。**—obsessively** *adv*

obsessive[2] *n* [C] *technical* someone whose behaviour is obsessive【术语】着迷的人；强迫症患者

ob·sid·i·an /əbˋsɪdɪən; əbˈsɪdiən/ *n* [U] a type of dark rock which looks like glass 黑曜岩

ob·so·les·cence /ˌɑbsəˋlɛsəns; ˌɒbsəˈlesəns/ *n* [U] **1** the state of becoming old-fashioned and no longer useful, because something else that is newer and better has been invented 过时；

淘汰，废弃 **2 planned/built-in obsolescence** the practice of making a product in such a way that it will soon become unfashionable or impossible to use〔商品等〕计划报废，有计划的淘汰〔指让产品具有不久就会过时或淘汰的特征〕

ob·so·les·cent /ˌɑbsəˈlɛsənt; ˌɒbsəˈlesənt◂/ *adj* becoming obsolete 逐渐被废弃的；即将过时的

ob·so·lete /ˈɑbsəˌlit; ˈɒbsəliːt◂/ *adj* no longer useful because something newer and better has been invented 废弃的，淘汰的；过时的：*obsolete weapons* 老式的武器 | **render sth obsolete** (=make it obsolete) 使某物变过时 *Current production methods will soon be rendered obsolete.* 现在的生产方法将很快被淘汰。

ob·sta·cle /ˈɑbstəkl; ˈɒbstəkəl/ *n* [C] **1** something that makes it difficult for you to achieve your aim 障碍，阻碍，妨碍：**[+to]** *Fear of change is the greatest single obstacle to progress.* 害怕变革是进步的一个最大障碍。| **put obstacles in the way (of)** (=try to prevent something by causing difficulties) 设法阻挠，设置障碍 *They tried to put obstacles in the way of our marriage.* 他们想阻挠我们的婚姻。**2** an object which blocks your way, so that you must try to go around it 障碍物

obstacle course /ˈ···ˌ·/ *n* [C] **1** a line of objects which runners in an OBSTACLE RACE have to jump over, climb through etc 障碍赛跑道 **2** a series of difficulties which must be dealt with to achieve a particular aim 重重困难 **3** *AmE* an ASSAULT COURSE【美】突击训练场，军事训练场地

obstacle race /ˈ···ˌ·/ *n* [C] a type of race in which runners have to jump over or climb through various objects 障碍赛跑

ob·ste·tri·cian /ˌɑbstɛˈtrɪʃən; ˌɒbstəˈtrɪʃən/ *n* [C] a doctor who has special training in obstetrics 产科医生

ob·stet·rics /əbˈstɛtrɪks; əbˈstetrɪks/ *n* [U] the part of medical science concerned with the birth of children 产科学 —**obstetric** *adj*

ob·sti·na·cy /ˈɑbstənəsɪ; ˈɒbstənəsi/ *n* [U] an unreasonable determination not to change your mind 固执，顽固；倔强

ob·sti·nate /ˈɑbstənɪt; ˈɒbstənət/ *adj* **1** unreasonably refusing to change your ideas of behaviour, even though people try to persuade you 固执的，顽固的；倔强的：*Harry was obstinate and wouldn't admit he was wrong.* 哈里很固执，不肯承认他错了。| *a sulky, obstinate child* 爱生闷气的倔强孩子 | *an obstinate refusal to face facts* 顽固地拒绝面对事实 **2** [only before noun 仅用于名词前] difficult to deal with or get rid of 难以对付的；难以去除的；难治的：*strong enough to remove the most obstinate stains* 效力很强，足以去除最难对付的污渍 | *an obstinate cough* 难治的咳嗽 —**obstinately** *adv*

ob·strep·e·rous /əbˈstrɛpərəs; əbˈstrepərəs/ *adj* obstreperous behaviour is noisy and cheerful or angry 喧哗的，喧闹的；吵嚷的 —**obstreperously** *adv* —**obstreperousness** *n* [U]

ob·struct /əbˈstrʌkt; əbˈstrʌkt/ *v* [T] **1** to block a road, passage etc 阻塞，堵塞〔道路、通道等〕：*A small aircraft now obstructed the runway.* 一架小型飞机现在堵塞了跑道。| *an accident obstructing northbound traffic* 一宗堵塞了南北方向交通的事故 | *Our view was obstructed by a high wall.* 我们的视线被一堵高墙挡住了。**2** to try to prevent someone from doing something by making it difficult for them 阻挠，妨碍，阻止：*A small minority obstructed policies that would help the majority of people.* 一小撮人阻挠了将对大多数人有益的若干政策。| *obstructing a police officer in the course of his duty* 妨碍警官执行公务

ob·struc·tion /əbˈstrʌkʃən; əbˈstrʌkʃən/ *n* **1** [U] the act of trying to prevent or delay a legal or political process〔对立法或议事等的〕阻挠；拖延：**[+of]** *obstruction of vital legislation* 对重要立法的阻挠 **2** [U] the act of blocking a road, passage, tube etc〔道路、通道、管道等的〕阻塞，堵塞：**[+of]** *obstruction of the public highway* 阻塞公共交通干线 **3** [C] something that blocks a road, passage, tube etc〔堵塞道路、通道、管道等的〕障碍物：*There's an obstruction in the fuel pipe.* 燃料管道中有阻塞物。**4** [C] an offence in football, HOCKEY etc in which a player gets between an opponent and the ball〔足球、曲棍球等中的〕阻挡(犯规) —see picture on page A23 参见 A23 页图

ob·struc·tion·is·m /əbˈstrʌkʃənɪzm; əbˈstrʌkʃənɪzəm/ *n* [U] the practice of trying to prevent or delay a legal or political process〔对立法或议事等的〕蓄意阻挠；故意拖延 —**obstructionist** *n* [C]

ob·struc·tive /əbˈstrʌktɪv; əbˈstrʌktɪv/ *adj* trying to prevent someone from doing something by deliberately making it difficult for them 蓄意阻挠的；故意妨碍的：*an obstructive official* 蓄意阻挠的官员 | *obstructive tactics* 故意妨碍的策略 —**obstructively** *adv* —**obstructiveness** *n* [U]

S2 W2 **ob·tain** /əbˈten; əbˈteɪn/ *v formal*【正式】**1** [T] to get something that you want, especially through your own effort, skill, or work〔尤指通过自身的努力、技能或工作等〕获得，得到：*Further information can be obtained from head office.* 详细资料可从总公司得到。| *They've extended the growing season to obtain a larger crop.* 他们延长了作物的生长期以获得更好的收成。| *the difficulty of obtaining credit* 得到信任的困难 **2** [I not in progressive 不用进行式] if a situation, system, or rule obtains, it continues to exist〔情况、系统、规则等〕继续存在，通用：*These conditions no longer obtain.* 这些条件已不复存在。

USAGE NOTE 用法说明: OBTAIN

WORD CHOICE 词语辨析: **obtain, get, get hold of, find out, achieve, receive**

Obtain is formal and often sounds unnatural in spoken English or in a personal letter. obtain 属正式用语，用于口语或私人信函时常会令人感觉不自然：*Where can I obtain a list of restaurants?* 我从哪里能得到一份各餐馆的名录？| *Fresh fruit and vegetables were especially difficult to obtain.* 新鲜的水果和蔬菜尤其难以买到。

Get is the most common word in spoken English and informal writing meaning to come to have something. However, some people feel that **get** should not be used too often in writing. get是口语及非正式书面语中最常用的词，意为“得到某物”。但有人认为get不应过多地用于书面语中：*Where did you get that painting?* 你从哪里得到那幅画的？| *He gets about $200 a week at the textile mill.* 他在纺织厂工作，周薪为200美元左右。

You can also **get hold of** things, or information, especially after some difficulty (informal). get hold of〔非正式〕也可用来表示得到东西或资料，尤指在经历了困难之后：*I need to get hold of a powerful computer.* 我需要弄到一台功能强大的电脑。| *At last I managed to get hold of her address.* 最终我设法得到了她的地址。

You **find out** information. find out 指查获资料：*I need to find out where my classes are.* 我需要搞清楚我的课都在哪里上。

If you get yourself into a better situation through your own efforts, you **achieve** something. achieve 指通过个人努力改善自身的状况：*We are working to achieve better results/equality/independence.* 我们正在努力以争取更好的成绩/平等/独立。| *Regular exercise helps people achieve better health.* 经常锻炼使人身体更健康。

If what you get comes naturally or is given to you, you can use the word **receive** (slightly formal). receive〔稍正式〕指所得之物是自然而来的或是馈赠的：*The charity receives most of its money through private donations.* 那个慈善机构收到的善款大多来自私人捐赠。

ob·tain·a·ble /əbˈtenəbl; əbˈteɪnəbəl/ *adj* something that is obtainable can be obtained 能得到的，可获得的：*Most of the ingredients for Chinese cooking are obtainable at the supermarket.* 中式菜肴的配料大部分都能在超级市场里买到。

ob·trude /əbˈtrud; əbˈtruːd/ *v* [I,T] *formal*【正式】**1** if something obtrudes, or you obtrude something, it becomes noticed where it is not wanted (使)强行进入[闯入]；强加：**[+into/upon]** *Personal taste is bound to obtrude into a book about wine.* 评酒的书中肯定掺有个人的喜好。—compare 比较 INTRUDE (1), PROTRUDE **2** to stick out or make something stick out (使)凸出，(使)伸出

ob·tru·sive /əbˈtrusɪv; əbˈtruːsɪv/ *adj* noticeable in a way that is unpleasant 过分突出而难看[讨人嫌]的，突兀的：*large obtrusive TV antennas* 高耸扎眼的电视天线 | *He was here just now, being kind of obtrusive and polite at the same time.* 他刚才还在这里，表现得既有点惹眼又彬彬有礼。—opposite 反义词 UNOBTRUSIVE —**obtrusively** *adv* —**obtrusiveness** *n* [U]

ob·tuse /əbˈtus; əbˈtjuːs/ *adj* **1** slow to understand things, in a way that is annoying 迟钝的，愚笨的：*an obtuse lout of a man* 迟钝的笨人 | **be obtuse** (=pretend to not understand something) 装傻 *Is he being deliberately obtuse?* 他在故意装傻吗？**2 obtuse angle** *technical* an angle between 90 and 180 degrees【术语】钝角 —**obtusely** *adv* —**obtuseness** *n* [U] —see picture at 参见 ANGLE[1]图

ob·verse /ˈɑbvɝs; ˈɒbvɜːs/ *n* **1** *formal* the opposite of a particular situation or feeling【正式】对立面；对应物：**[+of]** *Defeat is the obverse of victory.* 与失败相对的是胜利。**2 the obverse** *technical* the front side of a coin or MEDAL【术语】〔硬币或奖章的〕正面 —opposite 反义词 REVERSE[2] (6)

ob·vi·ate /ˈɑbvɪˌet; ˈɒbvieɪt/ *v* [T] **1 obviate the need** *formal* to make something unnecessary【正式】使成为不必要，避免：*The use of a credit card obviates the need to carry a lot of money.*

使用信用卡就不必随身携带大量现金。**2** to remove a difficulty 排除，消除〔困难〕

ob·vi·ous /ˈɑbvɪəs; ˈɒbviəs/ *adj* **1** easy to notice or understand 显然的，显而易见的，明白的：*the obvious advantages of cooperation* 合作的明显好处 | *For obvious reasons we have had to cancel tonight's performance.* 基于显而易见的原因，我们不得不取消了今晚的演出。| *"Why is she leaving?" "Well, it's pretty obvious isn't it?"* "她为什么要走？""哦，这很明白，不是吗？" | **it is obvious (to sb) that** *It was obvious to everyone that Gina was lying.* 大家都很清楚吉娜在撒谎。**2 obvious statement/remark etc** a statement that is unnecessary because it states what is obvious to everyone 明显多余的说明/话语等 **3 the obvious choice** the person or thing that you would expect everyone to choose 明摆着的选择：*Nicholson was the obvious choice for team leader.* 尼科尔森是明摆着的队长人选。**4 the obvious thing (to do)** what clearly seems the best thing to do 最好的做法：*The obvious thing would have been to travel with her husband, but she couldn't.* 明显地最好的做法是她和丈夫一起去旅游，但她不能去。**5 state the obvious** to say something that is already obvious and is therefore unnecessary 说出明摆着的大实话 —**obviousness** *n* [U]

ob·vi·ous·ly /ˈɑbvɪəslɪ; ˈɒbviəsli/ *adv* used to mean that a fact can easily be noticed or understood 明显地，显而易见地，明白地：[sentence adverb 句子副词] *We're obviously going to need more help.* 显然我们将需要更多的帮助。| *"Is she sorry?" "Obviously not! Look at her."* "她难过吗？""显然不！你看她那个样子。" | [+adj/adv] *The woman was lying across the chairs, obviously unwell.* 那女子横躺在椅子上，显然是身体不舒服。—see 见 OF COURSE (USAGE) —compare 比较 APPARENTLY, EVIDENTLY

oc·ca·sion[1] /əˈkeʒən; əˈkeɪʒən/ *n*

1 ►TIME 时间◄ **a)** [C] a time when something happens〔某事发生的〕时刻，时候，时节：**on an occasion** *She had met Zahid on an earlier occasion.* 她早些时候曾见过扎希德。| *I've seen Jana with them on several occasions.* 我几次看见贾娜和他们在一起。**b)** [singular] a suitable or favourable time〔合适的〕机会，〔有利的〕时机：[+for] *We used the meeting as an occasion for announcing the restructuring.* 我们把握这次会议的机会宣布重组。

2 ►SPECIAL EVENT 特殊活动◄ [C] an important social event or ceremony 重要的社交活动，盛会：*I'm saving this bottle of champagne for a special occasion.* 我要把这瓶香槟酒留到特殊场合用。| **quite an occasion** (=a very exciting or impressive occasion) 重大场合，盛大的场面 *The opening of the new library turned out to be quite an occasion.* 新图书馆的开幕典礼成了一次盛事。

3 ►CAUSE/REASON 起因/缘由◄ [singular] *formal* a direct cause or reason【正式】直接的原因[诱因]：**be the occasion of** *His remark was the occasion of a bitter quarrel.* 他的话引起了一场激烈的争吵。| **have occasion to do sth** (=need to do something) 有必要做某事 *More than once Dr Standish had occasion to warn his son about his irresponsible behaviour.* 对儿子不负责任的行为，斯坦迪什博士不得不多次向他提出告诫。

4 if (the) occasion arises *formal* if a particular action ever becomes necessary【正式】如有必要，必要时：*I am ready to defend our policies if the occasion arises.* 必要时，我准备为我们的政策进行辩护。

5 on occasion sometimes but not often 有时，间或，偶尔：*I have on occasion visited her at home.* 有时我去登门拜访她。

6 on the occasion of *formal* at the time of an important event【正式】在〔重要事件〕之际：*on the occasion of her 50th birthday* 在她50岁生日之际

7 rise to the occasion to deal well with an unexpected and difficult situation 随机应变，善于应付突如其来的困难局面 —see also 另见 **sense of occasion** (SENSE[1] (20))

occasion[2] *v* [T] *formal* to cause something【正式】引起，惹起：*disputes occasioned by greed and intolerance* 因贪婪和偏狭引起的纠纷 | **occasion sb sth** *Your behaviour has occasioned us a great deal of anxiety.* 你的行为让我们极为不安。

oc·ca·sion·al /əˈkeʒənḷ; əˈkeɪʒənəl/ *adj* **1** happening sometimes but not often 偶尔的，偶然的，不经常的：*Expect occasional showers today.* 今天偶尔有阵雨。| *He smokes an occasional cigar.* 他偶尔抽一支雪茄烟。**2** *formal* written or intended for a special occasion【正式】为特殊场合写作[使用]的，应景的：*occasional poems* 应景诗

oc·ca·sion·al·ly /əˈkeʒənḷɪ; əˈkeɪʒənəli/ *adv* sometimes, but not regularly and not often 偶尔，偶然，间或：*Occasionally Alice would look up from her books.* 艾丽斯偶尔从书本中抬起头来。| **very occasionally** (=rarely) 难得，不常 *We only see each other very occasionally.* 我们极少见面。—see picture at 参见 FREQUENCY 图

occasional ta·ble /.ˈ.. ,../ *n* [C] *BrE* a small light table that can be easily moved【英】〔易于挪动的〕轻便小桌，备用小桌

Oc·ci·dent, the /ˈɑksədənt; ˈɒksɪ̈dənt/ *n literary* the western part of the world, especially Europe and the Americas【文】西方，西方国家，西半球〔尤指欧洲和美洲〕—compare 比较 ORIENT[2]

oc·ci·den·tal /ˌɑksəˈdɛntḷ; ˌɒksɪ̈ˈdentəl◄/ *n* [C] *formal* someone from the western part of the world【正式】西方人，西洋人，欧美人 —compare 比较 ORIENTAL[2] —**occidental** *adj*

oc·cult[1] /əˈkʌlt; ˈɒkʌlt/ *n* **the occult** mysterious practices and powers involving magic and spirits 神秘学；神秘仪式；魔法：*He was a strange man who dabbled in the occult.* 他是个怪人，懂一点魔法。

occult[2] *adj* magical and mysterious 玄妙的；奥秘的；神秘的；超自然的：*the occult powers* 魔力[超自然力量]

oc·cu·pan·cy /ˈɑkjəpənsɪ; ˈɒkjʊ̈pənsi/ *n* [U] *formal* someone's use of a building, piece of land, or other space, for living or working in【正式】〔对房产、土地等的〕占有，占用；居住：*their occupancy of the apartment* 他们对那套公寓的占用

oc·cu·pant /ˈɑkjəpənt; ˈɒkjʊ̈pənt/ *n* [C] *formal*【正式】**1** someone who lives in a house, room etc, though without necessarily owning it 居住者，住户：*furniture left by the previous occupants* 先前的住户留下的家具 **2** someone who is in a room, vehicle etc at a particular time〔房间、汽车等某一时期的〕使用者，占有人：*Neither of the car's two occupants was injured.* 车里的两个人都没有受伤。

oc·cu·pa·tion /ˌɑkjəˈpeʃən; ˌɒkjʊ̈ˈpeɪʃən/ *n* **1** [C] a job or profession 工作，职业：*Please state your name, address and occupation.* 请说明你的姓名、地址和职业。—see 见 JOB (USAGE) **2** [C] a way of spending your time; PASTIME 消遣，业余活动：*Marcus regarded stamp-collecting as a childish occupation.* 马库斯把集邮视为一种幼稚的消遣。**3** [U] the act of living or staying in a building or place 居住；占用：*In many of the caves there is evidence of human occupation.* 其中许多洞穴有人类居住过的痕迹。**4** [U] the act of entering a place in a large group and keeping control of it, especially by military force〔尤指用军事力量的〕占领，占据，控制：[+of] *the German occupation of France* 德军对法国的占领 | *Demonstrators are continuing their occupation of the building.* 示威者继续占据着那栋大楼。

Occupation, the the period from 1940-44 during World War II, when France was occupied by the German army 德军占领期〔指1940至1944年二战期间德军对法国的占领〕

oc·cu·pa·tion·al /ˌɑkjəˈpeʃənḷ; ˌɒkjʊ̈ˈpeɪʃənəl◄/ *adj* [only before noun 仅用于名词前] related to, or caused by your job 职业的，工作的；由职业引起的：*an occupational disease* 职业病 | **occupational hazard** (=a risk that always exists in a particular job) 职业上的风险 —**occupationally** *adv*

occupational ther·a·py /,..... ˈ.../ *n* [U] a form of treatment for helping people to get back their health after illness by giving them special work 职业[作业]疗法 —**occupational therapist** *n* [C]

oc·cu·pi·er /ˈɑkjəˌpaɪɚ; ˈɒkjʊ̈paɪə/ *n* [C] *especially BrE* someone who lives in or uses a particular house, piece of land etc, especially temporarily【尤英】〔房屋、土地等的暂时〕占用者，居住者 —see also 另见 OWNER-OCCUPIER

oc·cu·py /ˈɑkjəˌpaɪ; ˈɒkjʊ̈paɪ/ *v* [T]

1 ►STAY IN A PLACE 住在某处◄ *formal* to live or stay in a place【正式】占居，居住：*The Jackson family have occupied this apartment for the past six months.* 过去半年中，杰克逊一家住在这套公寓里。

2 be occupied if a room, seat, or bed is occupied, someone is in it or using it〔房间、座位、床位等〕有人使用，被占用

3 ►SEIZE AND CONTROL 占据并控制◄ to enter a place in a large group and keep control of it, for example by military force〔被军队等〕占领，占据：*Rebel forces have occupied the city for 8 months.* 叛军占领该城市已有八个月。| *an occupying army* 占领军

4 ►FILL TIME/SPACE 占时间/空间◄ to fill a space or period of time 占用〔空间或一段时间〕：*Soccer occupies most of my leisure time.* 足球占去了我大部分闲暇时间。| *Traditional paintings occupy most of the wall-space in the gallery.* 传统绘画占去了美术馆的大部分墙面。

5 occupy sb's mind/thoughts/attention if something occupies your mind etc, you think about that thing more than anything else 占据某人的头脑/思想/注意力

6▶BUSY 忙碌◀ a)occupy sb/keep sb occupied to keep someone busy 使某人忙碌: *I've invented a game that will keep the kids occupied for hours.* 我发明了一种游戏，够孩子们玩上几个小时的。| *Hannah gets so bored – she needs something to occupy her.* 汉娜很是腻烦，她需要点东西使自己忙碌起来。**b)be occupied with** to be busy doing something 忙于〔做某事〕: *Helen was fully occupied with business matters, so we didn't want to bother her.* 海伦公务缠身，所以我们不想打扰她。**7▶OFFICIAL POSITION 正式职位◀** to have an official position or job 担任〔正式职位或工作〕: *Before becoming prime minister, Mrs Thatcher had already occupied several cabinet posts.* 在成为首相之前，撒切尔夫人曾出任过好几个内阁职位。

oc·cur /əˋkɝ; əˈkɜː/ *v* **occurred, occurring** [I] *formal*【正式】**1** to happen 发生: *Many accidents occur in the home.* 许多事故都在家中发生。| *Climatic changes have occurred at intervals throughout the millenium.* 整个千年中，气候变化时有发生。**2** [always + adv/prep] to happen or exist in a particular place or situation〔在特定地点或情况下〕发生；存在: [**+in/among etc**] *Whooping cough occurs mainly in young children.* 百日咳多发于幼儿。

occur to sb *phr v* [T not in passive 不用被动态] if an idea or thought occurs to you, it suddenly comes into your mind〔主意或想法突然〕浮现于脑中；被想起，被想到: **it occurs to sb that** *Didn't it occur to you that your husband might be late?* 你当时没有想到你丈夫也许会晚到吗？| *The possibility that she might be wrong never occurred to her.* 她压根儿没想到自己可能会错。| **it occurs to sb to do sth** *I suppose it never occurred to you to phone the police?* 我想你根本就没想到打电话报警吧？

USAGE NOTE 用法说明: OCCUR

WORD CHOICE 词语辨析: **occur to, strike, occur, there is, happen, take place, arise, crop up**

If a thought comes into your mind it **occurs to** you or **strikes** you. 倘有一个想法出现在某人脑海中，可用 occur to 或 strike (某人): *It suddenly occurred to/struck me I hadn't seen Peter all day.* 我突然想到，我一整天都没看见彼得。

Occur meaning 'happen' is rather formal and not common in spoken English. occur 作"发生"解时，是相当正式的用语，且很少用于口语: *The court will decide what really occurred.* 法庭会判定到底发生了什么事。**Occur to** is not used in this sense: *A problem occurred to me* means 'I thought of a problem' NOT 'I had a problem'. occur to 则不用于此意: A problem occurred to me 意为"我想到了一个问题"，而不是"我有一个麻烦"。

Usually people use **there is...** 人们通常使用 there is ...: *There was a loud bang from outside.* 外面传来砰的一声巨响。| *There's been an accident.* 发生了一起事故。| *There's going to be a meeting next Tuesday.* 下周二有个会议。When the person who something happens to is mentioned, you use **have**. 当提及某人遭遇某事时，则用 have: *He had an interview last week.* 上周他去面试了。| *She's bound to have trouble with the customs officials.* 她肯定要和海关官员纠缠。

Events and processes **happen** or **happen to** you, especially if they are not planned. happen 或 happen to 用以指某事情和过程发生，或某事件和过程发生在某人身上，尤其是未经计划的事情: *All sorts of unexpected things might happen.* 什么样的意外都有可能发生。| *The Industrial Revolution happened in the eighteenth century.* 工业革命发生在18世纪。| *What's happening to us?* 我们这是怎么啦？

If you are talking about something that is planned or arranged, you often use **take place**. 在谈论有计划或预先安排的事情时，常使用 take place: *The wedding will take place in St Peter's Church.* 婚礼将在圣彼得教堂举行。

Problems or difficulties **arise** (formal) and something that happens suddenly and unexpectedly **crops up** (informal). 问题或困难的"出现"用 arise〔正式〕，某事"突然发生"则用 crop up〔非正式〕: *Let's consider what kind of difficulties might arise from the situation.* 让我们考虑一下，这种情况下可能会出现哪些困难。| *I have to go home early – something's cropped up.* 我得早点回家——出了点事。

SPELLING 拼法

Remember that there are two 'r's in *occurred* and *occurring*. 切记 occurred 和 occurring 中都有两个 r。

oc·cur·rence /əˋkɝəns; əˈkʌrəns/ *n* **1** [C] something that happens 发生的事，事件: **a common/rare/regular occurrence** *Flooding under this bridge is a common occurrence.* 这桥下经常洪水泛滥。| *Laughter was a rare occurrence in his classroom.* 他的课堂上难得有笑声。**2** [U] the fact of something happening〔事件的〕发生，出现: *the frequent occurrence of violent storms in the area* 该地区强风暴的频繁发生

o·cean /ˋoʃən; ˈəʊʃən/ *n* **1 the ocean** *especially AmE* the great mass of salt water that covers most of the Earth's surface【尤美】海洋，大海: *She stood on the beach, gazing at the ocean.* 她站在海滩上，凝视着大海。**2** [C] one of the very large areas of sea on the Earth's surface …洋: *the Pacific Ocean* 太平洋 **3 oceans of** *informal* a great mass or amount of something【非正式】大量，许多 —see also 另见 **a drop in the ocean** (DROP[2] (8)) —**oceanic** /ˌoʃɪˋænɪk; ˌəʊʃiˈænɪk◂/ *adj*

o·cean·go·ing /ˋoʃənˌgoɪŋ; ˈəʊʃənˌgəʊɪŋ/ *adj* an oceangoing ship is designed to sail across the sea〔船只〕用于越洋的，远洋航行的；行驶外洋的: *an oceangoing tanker* 远洋油轮

o·cean·og·ra·phy /ˌoʃɪənˋɑgrəfɪ; ˌəʊʃənˈɒgrəfi/ *n* [U] the scientific study of the ocean 海洋(地理)学 —**oceanographer** *n* [C]

oc·e·lot /ˋosəˌlɑt; ˈɒsḷɒt/ *n* [C] a large American wild cat that has a pattern of spots on its back〔美洲的一种背部有斑点的大型〕豹猫

och /ɑk; ɒk/ *interjection ScotE* used to express surprise or to emphasize a remark; OH (3)【苏格兰】啊，呀，哎哟〔用于表示惊讶或加强语气〕

o·chre usually 一般作 **ocher** *AmE*【美】/ˋokɚ; ˈəʊkə/ *n* [U] **1** a reddish-yellow earth used in paints 赭石〔用作颜料〕**2** the colour of ochre 赭色，黄褐色 —**ochre** *adj*

ock·er /ˋɑkɚ; ˈɒkə/ *n* [C] *AustrE, NZE* a word for an Australian man, also used in Australia by men speaking to or about each other【澳，新西兰】澳大利亚人；老兄〔澳大利亚男人互相称呼对方的用语〕: *G'day Ocker – how's it going?* 你好，老兄！过得怎么样？

o'clock /əˋklɑk; əˈklɒk/ *adv* **one o'clock/two o'clock etc** one of the times when the clock shows the exact hour as a number from 1 to 12 一点钟/两点钟等: *"What time is it?" "It's 9 o'clock."* "现在几点钟？" "9点钟。"

USAGE NOTE 用法说明: O'CLOCK

UK-US DIFFERENCE 英国英语和美国英语的差异

O'clock is used only when you are talking about the exact hour. o'clock 只用于表示正点时间: *nine o'clock* 9点钟。Compare 比较: *ten to nine* 8点50分

Minutes after the hour are expressed with **past** (usually **after** in American English). 说几点过几分可用 past〔美国英语中通常用 after〕: *five/a quarter/ten past nine* 9点5分/15分/10分。Compare 比较: *five/ten/a quarter after nine* (American English only 只用于美国英语) 9点5分/10分/15分。In British English you can say 'half past' the hour, but it is not possible in American English to say 'half after' the hour. 在英国英语中，可说 half past (the hour)〔几点半〕，但在美国英语中则不能说 half after (the hour)。

You talk about minutes before the hour using **to** (and also **of** in American English). e.g. 说几点差几分可用 to〔美国英语中也用 of〕，如: *twenty/a quarter to eight.* 8点差20分/15分。Compare 比较: *It's five minutes of two/a quarter of eight* (American English only 只用于美国英语). 现在是2点差5分/8点差15分。

Time can also be expressed by using the numbers alone. 时间也可以单用数字表示: *The meeting is at 10.15.* 会议定于10点15分召开。| *I'll pick you up about 3.20.* (=said 口语中说 three-twenty). 我将在3点20分来接你。

O Come All Ye Faith·ful /ˌ·ˌ·ˌ··ˈ··/ the title and first words of a popular Christmas CAROL (=a traditional religious song)《齐来崇拜》〔一首家喻户晓的圣诞颂歌歌名及首句〕

O'Con·nell /oˋkɑnl; əʊˈkɒnl/, **Daniel** (1775-1847) an Irish politician who forced the government to give rights to Catholics, and worked for an end to the union with Britain 奥康奈尔〔(1775-1847)，爱尔兰政治家。他迫使政府赋予天主教徒应有的权利，并致力于结束爱尔兰与英国的合并〕

O'Connor, San·dra Day /ˋsændrə de; ˈsændrə deɪ/ (1930-) a US judge who became the first woman member of the Supreme Court in 1981 奥康纳〔(1930-)，美国法官，1981年成为美国最高法院的首位女性大法官〕

-oc·ra·cy /ɑkrəsɪ; ɒkrəsi/ also 又作 **-cracy** *suffix* [in nouns 构成名词] **1** government by a particular sort of people or according to a particular principle〔由某一类人或根据某一原则管理

的〕政府, 政体; 统治; 政治: *democracy* (=government by the people) 民主政府; 民主政体 | *mobocracy* 暴民统治; 暴民政治 **2** a society or country governed in this way 有…政体的社会[国家]: *the Western democracies* (=countries governed by their people) 西方的民主国家 | *a meritocracy* 精英管理的社会; 精英领导[统治]集团 **3** the powerful social class made up of a particular sort of people 〔由特定的某类人组成的强大的〕社会阶层: *the aristocracy* (=people with noble titles) 贵族

O

-o·crat /əkræt; əkræt/ also 又作 **-crat** *suffix* [in nouns 构成名词] **1** a believer in a particular principle of government 某种政体的信奉者: *a democrat* (=someone who believes in government by the people) 民主主义者 **2** a member of a powerful or governing social class or group 有权势的社会阶层或统治阶级的一分子: *a technocrat* (=scientist who controls organizations etc) 技术专家官员 —**-ocratic** /əkrætɪk; əkrætɪk/ *suffix* —**-ocratically** /əkrætɪklɪ; əkrætɪkli/ *suffix*

Oct the written abbreviation of 缩写= October

oc·ta·gon /ˋɑktəˌgɑn; ˈɒktəgən/ *n* [C] a flat shape with eight sides and eight angles 八边形, 八角形 —**octagonal** /ɑkˋtægənl; ɒkˈtægənəl/ *adj*: *an octagonal room* 八角形的房间

oc·tane /ˋɑkten; ˈɒkteɪn/ *n* [U] **high octane petrol/fuel etc** petrol etc of the highest quality 辛烷值高的汽油/燃料等

oc·tave /ˋɑktɪv; ˈɒktɪ̣v/ *n* [C] **a)** the range of musical notes between the first note of a SCALE[1] (8) and the last one 八度, 八度音程 **b)** the first and last notes of a musical SCALE[1] (8) played together 八度和音

oc·tet /ɑkˋtɛt; ɒkˈtet/ *n* [C] **1** eight singers or musicians performing together 八重唱[八重奏]演出小组 **2** a piece of music for an octet 八重唱(曲), 八重奏(曲)

Oc·to·ber /ɑkˋtobə; ɒkˈtəʊbə/ written abbreviation 缩写为 **Oct** *n* [C,U] the tenth month of the year, between September and November 十月: *It happened on October the third.* 事情在10月3日发生。| *on the third of October* 在10月3日 | *on October third* 在10月3日 | *in October 1991* 在1991年10月

CULTURAL NOTE 文化注释

In the UK and northern US, when people think of October, they think of the leaves on the trees turning brown. Halloween is on October 31st. 在英国和美国北部, 对于10月人们想到的是树叶渐渐变黄。万圣节前夕即在10月31日这天。

oc·to·ge·nar·i·an /ˌɑktədʒəˋnɛrɪən; ˌɒktəʊdʒɪ̣ˈneəriən/ *n* [C] a person who is between 80 and 89 years old 80至89岁之间的人, 八旬老人

oc·to·pus /ˋɑktəpəs; ˈɒktəpəs/ *n plural* **octopuses** [C] a sea creature with eight TENTACLES (=arms) 章鱼, 八爪鱼

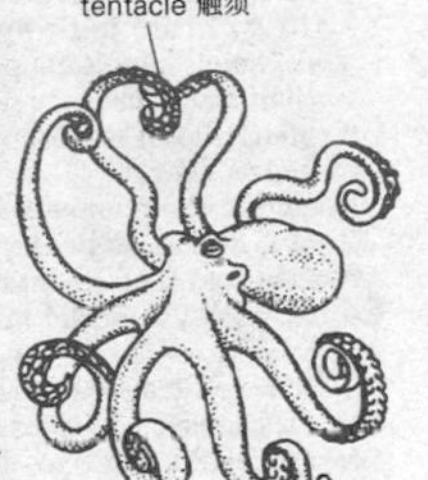

octopus 章鱼, 八爪鱼

oc·u·lar /ˋɑkjələ; ˈɒkjɪ̣lə/ *adj technical* related to the eyes【术语】眼睛的; 视觉的: *ocular muscles* 眼部肌肉

oc·u·list /ˋɑkjəlɪst; ˈɒkjɪ̣lɪst/ *n* [C] *old-fashioned* a doctor who examines and treats people's eyes【过时】眼科医生[医师]

OD /ˌo ˋdi; ˌəʊ ˈdiː/ *v* [I+on] *slang*【俚】**1** to take too much of a dangerous drug; OVERDOSE 服用过量的毒品 **2** to see, hear too much of something 沉溺〔于看、听某物〕—**OD** *n* [C]

ODA, the /ˌo di ˋe; ˌəʊ diː ˈeɪ/ the Overseas Development Administration; the former name of the DFID (the British government's Department for International Development) 海外开发部〔英国政府国际开发部旧称〕

o·da·lisque /ˋodlˌɪsk; ˈəʊdəlɪsk/ *n* [C] *literary* a beautiful female slave in former times【文】〔古时貌美的〕女奴

1 3 **odd** /ɑd; ɒd/ *adj*

1 ▶STRANGE 奇怪的◀ different from what is normal or expected 奇特的, 异常的, 古怪的: *an odd character* 古怪的人 | *Isn't that odd? She's never done that before.* 难道这不奇怪吗? 她以前可从来没这样做过。| *An odd thing happened last night!* 昨晚发生了一件怪事! | **it is odd (that)** *It's odd that Diana never answered your letter.* 很奇怪, 戴安娜从不回你的信。| **the odd thing is...** *The odd thing is no one seems to know who actually bought the picture.* 奇怪的是好像没有人知道到底是谁买走了那幅画。

2 odd-looking/sounding looking or sounding strange or unusual 看上去/听上去奇特[异常]的: *He was an odd-looking bloke.* 他是个模样古怪的家伙。

3 the odd drink/word/moment etc *especially BrE* a few drinks etc at various times but not often and not regularly; OCCASIONAL (1)【尤英】偶尔喝酒/得到消息/有时间等: *We get the odd complaint from customers.* 我们偶尔会收到客户的投诉。| *We have the odd drink together now and again.* 我们偶尔一起去喝上几杯。

4 ▶VARIOUS 各种各样的◀ [only before noun 仅用于名词前] not specially chosen or collected 非特意挑选[收集]的; 零碎的: *He'd written the addresses on odd scraps of paper.* 他把地址写在零零碎碎的纸片上。| **odd jobs** (=many different small pieces of work) 零工, 杂活 *He sometimes does odd jobs around the estate.* 他有时在这一区干点零活。

5 ▶NOT IN A PAIR/SET 不成对/套◀ [only before noun 仅用于名词前] separated from its pair or set 〔一双、一套中〕单只的, 不成对的: *an odd shoe* 单只鞋 | **odd socks/gloves etc** (=not a matching pair of socks etc) 不配对的袜子/手套等

6 odd number a number that cannot be divided exactly by two, for example 1, 3, 5, 7 etc 奇数, 单数〔不能被2整除的数, 如1、3、5、7等〕—opposite 反义词 EVEN[2] (4)

7 20-odd/30-odd etc *spoken* a little more than 20 etc【口】二十多一点/三十多一点等: *I have 20-odd years to work before I retire.* 我还要工作二十多年才退休。

8 odd man out/odd one out a) *especially BrE* someone or something that is different from the rest of the group【尤英】与众不同的人/物: *Which of these three shapes is the odd one out?* 这三种形状中哪一个是不一样的? **b)** *BrE informal* someone who is not usually included in groups of people or friends【英, 非正式】不合群的人: *I was always the odd one out in my class at school.* 在学校我总是跟班上的同学合不来。—see also 另见 ODDLY —**oddness** *n* [U]

odd·ball /ˋɑdˌbɔl; ˈɒdbɔːl/ *n* [C] *especially AmE informal* someone who behaves in a strange or unusual way【尤美, 非正式】举止古怪的人 —**oddball** *adj*: *Ernest, the oddball comedian in 'Ernest Goes to Jail'* 欧内斯特, 在《欧内斯特入狱》中那个举止古怪的喜剧演员

odd·i·ty /ˋɑdətɪ; ˈɒdɪ̣ti/ *n* **1** [C] a strange or unusual person or thing 怪人; 怪事; 奇特的东西: *He was something of an oddity in the neighborhood with his neat suits.* 他穿着笔挺的西装, 在街坊四邻中有点像个怪人。**2** [C,U] a strange quality in someone or something 奇怪, 古怪, 奇特: *fashions that are remembered for their oddity* 因款式怪异而让人记住的时装

odd-job man /ˌ· ˈ· ˌ·/ *n* [C] a man who does various jobs in or around people's houses〔在他人家里或周围〕打零工的人

odd·ly /ˋɑdlɪ; ˈɒdli/ *adv* **1** in a strange or unusual way 奇怪地, 古怪地; 异常地: *Brenda's been acting oddly this week.* 布伦达这一周表现得相当古怪。**2** also 又作 **oddly enough** [sentence adverb 句子副词] used to say that something seems strange or surprising 奇怪的是; 令人惊讶的是: *Oddly enough, her anger made her seem more attractive.* 说也奇怪, 她一生气倒使她显得更迷人了。**3 oddly matched/assorted** very different and looking strange together 不相配的/搭配怪异的

odd·ments /ˋɑdmənts; ˈɒdmənts/ *n* [plural] small things of no value, or pieces of stuff that were not used when something was made 零头, 碎屑, 零碎物件; 残剩物

odds /ɑdz; ɒdz/ *n* [plural] 3

1 ▶PROBABILITY 可能性◀ how likely it is that something will or will not happen, especially when this can be stated in numbers〔事物发生的〕可能性, 机会〔尤用于可用数字表示时〕: *If you are male, the odds are about 1 in 12 of being colour-blind.* 如果你是男性, 患色盲的可能性在十二分之一左右。| **the odds are (that)** (=it is likely) 可能会… *Invest now – the odds are that the share prices will rise after the budget.* 现在就投资吧 —— 预算完成后股价可能会上涨。| **odds in favour of** *The odds are in favour of a Russian victory.* 俄罗斯获胜的机会居多。| **odds against** *The odds against you getting killed in a plane crash are around a million to one.* 死于空难的可能性极小, 大约为百万分之一。

2 ▶DIFFICULTIES 困难◀ **a) enormous/heavy odds** difficulties which make a good result seem very unlikely 巨大的困难/非常不利的条件: *Theresa has overcome enormous odds to get where she is today.* 特雷莎克服了巨大的困难才取得今天这样的成就。**b) against all (the) odds** in spite of great difficulties 尽管困难重重: *Against all the odds, racing driver Lauda recovered from his terrible injuries.* 尽管非常困难, 赛车手劳达从严重的受伤中康复过来。

3 be at odds (with) a) to disagree (与…) 不合, 争吵: *Briggs*

found himself at odds with his colleagues at NASA. 布里格斯发现自己与国家航空航天局的同事们意见不合。**b)** if two statements, descriptions, actions etc are at odds with each other, they are different although they should be the same〔说法、描述、行为等〕不一致: *Burt's latest evidence is at odds with his earlier statements.* 伯特的最新证据与他早前的说法有矛盾。

4 ▶HORSE RACING ETC 赛马等◀ numbers based on the probability of a horse winning a race, or a particular result in any competition, which show by how much you can increase your money if you BET[1] (1) on the one that wins〔打赌时用数字表示的〕可能性; 赔率: *I bet £10 on Broadway Flyer with the odds at 6-1.* 我在"百老汇飞人"上押注 10 英镑, 赔率为 6 比 1。| **lay/offer (sb) odds** *I laid him odds of 7-2.* 我向他提出以 7 比 2 的赔率打赌。| **long/short odds** (=odds based on a high or low risk of losing) 赢面不大的/较大的押注

5 it makes no odds/what's the odds? *BrE spoken* it makes no difference【英口】没有多大差别[无关紧要]/那有什么关系?: *You can pay me now or later – it makes no odds.* 你现在或以后付我钱都行 — 没关系的。

6 pay/charge over the odds *BrE informal* to pay or charge a higher price than is usual or reasonable【英, 非正式】花高价/索要高价: *There's always somebody ready to pay over the odds for a designer jacket.* 总有人乐意花高价买一件由著名设计师设计的夹克。—see also 另见 **have the odds stacked against you** (STACK[2] (3))

odds and ends /ˌ· · ˈ·/ *n* [plural] small things of various kinds without much value 琐碎物品, 零星杂物: *He didn't keep much in his desk – just odds and ends.* 他书桌里没放多少东西, 只是些零碎物品。

odds and sods /ˌ· · ˈ·/ *n* [plural] *BrE informal* odds and ends【英, 非正式】琐碎物品, 零星杂物

odds-on /ˌ· ˈ·◂/ *adj* **1 the odds-on favourite** a competitor that is very likely to win, especially a horse in a race 大有希望赢的竞赛者〔尤指参赛的赛马〕**2** *informal* **it's odds-on (that)** used to say that something is very likely to happen【非正式】〔某事〕很有可能发生: *It's odds-on that she won't come.* 她很可能不来。

ode /od; əʊd/ *n* [C] a long poem addressed to a person or thing 颂诗, 颂歌: *Keats' 'Ode to a Grecian Urn'* 济慈的《希腊古瓮颂》

O·de·on /ˈodiən; ˈəʊdiən/ a British cinema run by a company which operates cinemas in most British towns and cities 奥登影院〔英国一公司经营的一家老电影院, 该公司经营的影院遍布英国大部分城镇〕

O·din /ˈodɪn; ˈəʊdɪn/ in Norse MYTHOLOGY, the king of the gods. He made the universe, and is also the god of war and WISDOM. In German mythology his name is Wotan, and in Anglo-Saxon mythology his name is Woden. 奥丁〔北欧神话中的众神之王。他创造了宇宙, 同时还是战神和智慧之神。德国神话中称沃坦, 盎格鲁-撒克逊神话中称沃登〕

o·di·ous /ˈodiəs; ˈəʊdiəs/ *adj formal* extremely unpleasant【正式】十分讨厌的; 可憎的; 丑恶的: *an odious and conceited little man* 丑恶而又自负的小个子男人 —**odiously** *adv*

o·di·um /ˈodiəm; ˈəʊdiəm/ *n* [U] *formal* hatred that a lot of people feel for someone【正式】反感; 憎恨; 公愤

o·dom·e·ter /oˈdɑmətə; əʊˈdɒmɪtə/ *n* [C] *AmE*【美】〔汽车等的〕里程计; MILEOMETER *BrE*【英】

o·do·rif·er·ous /ˌodəˈrɪfərəs; ˌəʊdəˈrɪfərəs◂/ *adj old use* odorous【旧】有气味的; 有香味的, 芳香的

o·do·rous /ˈodərəs; ˈəʊdərəs/ *adj literary* having a smell, especially a pleasant one【文】有气味的; 〔尤指〕有香味的, 芳香的

o·dour *BrE*【英】, **odor** *AmE*【美】/ˈodə; ˈəʊdə/ *n* [C] **1** a smell, especially an unpleasant one 气味; 〔尤指〕臭气: *Get rid of unpleasant household odours with new Fleur!* 请使用全新的 Fleur, 消除室内的异味! **2 be in bad odour (with)** if you are in bad odour with someone, they are not pleased with something you have done 不得宠; 不受青睐[欢迎] —see also 另见 BODY ODOUR

o·dour·less *BrE*【英】, **odorless** *AmE*【美】/ˈodələs; ˈəʊdələs/ *adj* not having a smell 没有气味的: *Water is a colorless, odorless liquid.* 水是一种无色、无味的液体。

O·dys·se·us /oˈdɪsiəs; əˈdɪsiəs/ in ancient Greek stories, the King of Ithaca and husband of Penelope, who is the main character in the poem *The Odyssey* by Homer. He spent ten years fighting in the Trojan War, and another ten years travelling home after the war. He is brave, clever, and good at tricking people in order to get what he wants. In ancient Roman stories his name is Ulysses. 奥德修斯〔古希腊神话中伊萨卡国王、佩内洛普之夫, 荷马史诗《奥德赛》中的主人公。他在特洛伊战争中作战 10 年, 战后又花了 10 年才回到故里。他勇敢、聪明, 工于心计以求达到目的。罗马神话中称尤利西斯〕—see also 另见 The ILIAD, the TROJAN WAR

od·ys·sey /ˈɑdəsɪ; ˈɒdʒsi/ *n* [C] *literary* a long journey with lots of adventures【文】漫长的历险旅程

OECD, the /ˌo i si ˈdi; ˌəʊ iː siː ˈdiː/ *n* the Organization for Economic Cooperation and Development; a group of rich countries who work together to develop trade and economic growth 经济合作与发展组织〔一些发达国家致力于发展贸易和经济增长的组织〕

OED, the /ˌo i ˈdi; ˌəʊ iː ˈdiː/ the abbreviation of 缩写= the OXFORD ENGLISH DICTIONARY

oe·di·pal /ˈɛdəpəl; ˈiːdɪpəl/ *adj* related to an Oedipus complex 俄狄浦斯的, 恋母情结的: *oedipal fantasies* 恋母幻想

Oe·di·pus /ˈɛdɪpəs; ˈiːdɪpəs/ in ancient Greek stories, the son of King Laius and Queen Jocasta of Thebes. When he was a baby Oedipus was left to die on a mountain by his father, but he was found and taken to live with the King of Corinth, so he did not know who his real parents were. When he became an adult, Oedipus returned to Thebes and, without knowing who they were, killed his father and married his mother. His story is told in the play *Oedipus Rex* by Sophocles. 俄狄浦斯〔古希腊神话中底比斯国王拉伊俄斯和王后伊俄卡斯特之子。俄狄浦斯幼时被父亲弃于山上等死, 但却被人发现, 后带回科林斯王国与国王一起生活, 因此他不知道自己的生身父母。长大成人后, 他回到底比斯。由于不明真相, 他杀死了父亲, 娶了自己的母亲。他的故事见于索福克勒斯创作的剧本《俄狄浦斯王》〕

Oe·di·pus com·plex /ˈɛdəpəs ˌkɑmplɛks; ˈiːdɪpəs ˌkɒmpleks/ *n* an unconscious sexual desire that a son feels for his mother, combined with a hatred for his father, according to Freudian PSYCHOLOGY〔弗洛伊德心理学中所说的〕俄狄浦斯情结, 恋母情结

o'er /or; əʊə/ *adv, prep poetic* over【诗】在…之上: *o'er vales and hills* 在溪谷和群山之上

oe·soph·a·gus *especially BrE*【尤英】, usually 一般作 **esophagus** *AmE*【美】/ɪˈsɑfəgəs; ɪˈsɒfəgəs/ *n* [C] the tube from your mouth to your stomach, down which food passes 食道, 食管 —see picture at 参见 DIGESTIVE SYSTEM 图

oes·tro·gen *BrE*【英】, **estrogen** *AmE*【美】/ˈɛstrədʒən; ˈiːstrədʒən/ *n* [U] a substance that is produced in a woman's ovaries (OVARY), and causes changes in her body that prepare it for having babies 雌激素

oeu·vre /ˈɜvrə; ˈɜːvrə/ *n* [C] *French* all the works of an artist, such as a painter or writer【法】〔画家、作家等的〕全部作品

of /əv; əv; *strong* 强读 ɑv; ɒv/ *prep* **1 a)** used to show a feature or quality that something has …的〔表示某物的特征或品质〕: *the colour of her dress* 她裙子的颜色 | *the width of the road* 马路的宽度 | *the size of John's overdraft* 约翰透支的数额 **b)** used to say that something is part of something else …的一部分: *the leg of the table* 桌子的腿 | *the roots of her hair* 她的头发根 | *the last scene of the movie* 电影的最后一幕 **2** used to show that something belongs to someone〔属于某人〕的: *a friend of my parents* 我父母的一个朋友 | *a computer of her own* 她自己的电脑 | *a habit of his* 他的习惯 **3** used to talk about a group or collection of particular people or things〔说明一组或一类特定的人或物〕: *a herd of elephants* 一群大象 **4** used to talk about a particular amount or measurement of something〔说明某物的特定数量〕: *two kilos of sugar* 两公斤糖 | *lots of money* 许多钱 | *a drop of water* 一滴水 | *a cup of coffee* 一杯咖啡 **5** used to talk about a particular person or thing from a larger group of the same people or things〔用于指同类的群体中的某一人或物〕: *a member of the soccer team* 足球队的一个队员 | *both of us* 我们俩 | *The Mona Lisa is one of his finest works.*《蒙娜·丽莎》是他最优秀的作品之一。| *the leading brand of shampoo* 洗发剂的头号品牌 **6 a)** used in dates〔用于日期〕: *the 27th of July* 7 月 27 日 **b)** *AmE* used in giving the time to mean before【美】在…之前〔用于报时〕: *a quarter of seven* (=6.45) 7 点差一刻 **7** used when giving the name of something or being more specific about something that is very general〔用于某物的名称, 或表明泛指事物的具体范畴〕: *the city of New York* 纽约市 | *the art of painting* 绘画艺术 | *the age of eight* 八岁 | *the problem of unemployment* 失业问题 **8 a)** used after nouns describing actions, to show who the action is done to〔用于说明动作的名词之后, 表示动作的对象〕: *the killing of innocent children* (=the children are killed) 对无辜儿童的杀害 **b)** used after nouns describing actions, to show who does the action〔用于说明动作的名词之后, 表示动作的发出者〕: *the barking of the dogs* (=the dogs bark) 狗的吠叫 **9** used to say what subject, person, thing etc another subject, person or thing is connected with or deals

with 关于…的, 与…有关的〔用于说明论题之间、人物之间、事物之间等的相互关系〕: *the Queen of England* 英格兰女王 | *disease of the liver* 肝病 | *the results of the meeting* 会议的结果 | *the advantages of using a computer* 使用电脑的好处 **10** used to say what something is made from 用…制的〔用于说明某物是由何种材料制作的〕: *a dress of pure silk* 真丝连衫裙 | *These bowls are made of plastic.* 这些碗是塑料做的。**11 a)** **the day/year etc of** the day, year etc that something happened〔某事发生的〕那天/那年等: *the day of the accident* 出事那天 | *the week of the festival* 节日的那周 **b)** **of the day/year etc** the best or most important person or thing on a particular day or year 某日/某年等最佳的[最重要的]: *She has been voted 'Woman of the Year'.* 她被选为"年度最杰出女性"。**c)** **of an evening/of a weekend** used to say that you often do something in the evenings, at weekends etc 晚上/周末经常…: *We always like to walk by the river of an evening.* 我们总喜欢傍晚到河边去散步。**12** used to show that something is the result of something else 因, 由〔用于表示事物之间的因果关系〕: *She left of her own free will.* 她是自愿离开的。| *He died of cancer.* 他死于癌症。| *the effects of radiation* 辐射的影响 **13 a)** used to say who writes a play, who paints a painting etc 由…著作的; 由…画的〔用于说明谁写的剧本、谁画的画等〕: *the plays of Shakespeare* 莎士比亚的戏剧 | *The building is the work of a great artist.* 这幢建筑是一位艺术大师的作品。**b)** used to show what a picture, story etc is about or who is in it 关于…的, 以…为主题的〔用于说明图片、故事等是何内容, 或是有关何人的〕: *a photo of Elizabeth* 伊丽莎白的照片 | *a map of Indonesia* 印度尼西亚地图 | *a story of love and loss* 有关爱情与迷惘的故事 **14** about 关于: *He's never heard of John Lennon.* 他从未听说过约翰·列侬。| *Rumours of his infidelity filled the newspapers.* 报上满是关于他不忠行为的传闻。**15** used to show where something is or how far something is from something else〔用于表示某物的方位或与另一物之间的距离〕: *east of Suez* 苏伊士以东 | *I live within a mile of here.* 我住的地方距离这里不到一英里。**16** used to describe a particular person or thing〔用于描述某人或物〕: *a woman of tremendous spirit* 一名具有无比勇气的女子 | *a matter of no importance* 无关紧要的事 **17** *especially literary* used to say where someone comes from 【尤文】来自…的〔用于说明某人来自何方〕: *Jesus of Nazareth* 拿撒勒的耶稣 | *the people of China* 中国人民 **18** **it is kind of/it was wrong of etc** used to say that something that someone has done shows that they are kind, wrong etc〔某人做某事〕是仁慈的/错误的: *It was silly of him to think he could cheat.* 他以为他可以作弊, 这是很愚蠢的。

USAGE NOTE 用法说明: OF

GRAMMAR 语法

You use **'s** or plural **s'** rather than **of** to mean 'belonging to someone'. 常用's或复数的s', 而不用of, 来表示"属于某人"之意: *the students' grades* 学生的成绩 | *my friend's car* 我朋友的汽车 | *Clive's new hairstyle* 克莱夫的新发型

When you talk about something that belongs to or is part of something, you can use **of**. 表示某物属于另一物或是其部分时, 可用of: *the corner of the street* 街角 | *the top of the mountain* 山顶 | *the street corner* 街角 | *the mountain top* 山顶

You also use **'s and s'** to talk about periods of time, for example 表示一段时间也可用's和s', 如: *a day's work* 一天的工作 | *three weeks' vacation* 三周的假期

's is increasingly used with the names of places, especially in newspapers and American English. 's越来越多地用于地名, 尤其是在报纸上和美国英语中: *Chicago's favorite son* 芝加哥的宠儿 | *China's recent history* 中国近代史

When you use words like **a, some, the, this** etc with the word for something that belongs to someone, or the person you are talking about in connection with them, you can use both **of** and **'s** together. 当a, some, the, this等与表示属于某人之物的词, 或与某人有关之人的词连用时, 可同时使用of和's: *that old bike of Cathy's* 凯茜的那辆旧自行车 | *a friend of Terry's* 特里的一位朋友

S1 W1 **of course** /ˌ·ˈ·/ *adv* **1** certainly 当然: *Of course I'll give you your money back.* 我当然要还你钱。| *"Were you glad to leave?" "Of course not!"* "你愿意离开吗?""当然不愿意!" | *Of course you must make a profit, but not if it involves exploiting people.* 当然你得赚取利润, 但是这要以不剥削人为前提。**2** used when you think that someone should know something, or should not be surprised by something 理当, 自然: *You should of course keep copies of all correspondence.* 所有信件你自然都该留底存档。| *Well, she won, of course.* 嗯, 她赢了, 当然喽。

USAGE NOTE 用法说明: OF COURSE

POLITENESS 礼貌程度

You use **of course** as a polite and friendly way of agreeing to something or agreeing to do something someone has asked you. 可用of course作为一种礼貌而友好的方式来表示同意某事或同意做某人要求你做的事: *"May I borrow this book?" "Of course you can."* "我可以借这本书吗?""当然可以。" | *"Do you think I was wrong?" "Of course not."* "你认为我错了吗?""当然没有。"

It is not usually polite to use **of course** or **of course not** as a reply to a request for information. If for example someone asked you 用of course或of course not来回答询问的请求, 通常是不礼貌的: *"Is this the way to the station?"* and you replied *"Of course (it is)"*, this would sound as if you think the answer to the question is very clear and you think the person is stupid to need to ask you. 如某人问你: "这是去车站的路吗?" 而你回答说: "当然(是啦)", 这听上去好像你认为答案十分明显, 那人这样问很愚蠢和多余。

STYLE 文体

Except when you are answering questions, **of course** is not usually used at the beginning of a sentence. 除了在回答问题时, of course通常不用在句首。Instead of saying 我们不说: *We play a lot of tennis and polo. Of course we have our own swimming pool,* you would say 而说: *We also have our own swimming pool, of course* or 或 *...and of course we have our own swimming pool.* 我们经常打网球和马球。当然喽, 我们还有自己的游泳池。

off[1] /ɔf; ɒf/ *adv, adj* [not before noun 不用于名词前] **1** away or from where something is 离开, 离去: *Travis got into his car and drove off.* 特拉维斯上汽车后就开走了。| *Suddenly they turned off and parked in a side road.* 突然他们转向停在一条岔路上。| **be off** (=to leave) 离开 *We're off now. Thanks for the meal!* 我们要走了。谢谢你的饭菜款待! | **be off to** (=to go to a particular place) 去, 前往〔某处〕*They're off to Jamaica for a hard-earned vacation.* 他们要去牙买加度一个来之不易的假期。**2** out of a bus, train, car etc 下〔公共汽车、火车、汽车等〕: *I'll get off at the next stop.* 我将在下一站下车。**3** removed; no longer connected or fastened to something 脱落, 脱离, 脱掉: *Can anyone get the lid off?* 谁能掀开这个盖子? | *Take off your shoes.* 把你的鞋子脱掉。| *Waxing the table is a really good way of keeping the dust off.* 给桌子上蜡的确是一种保持洁净的好办法。**4** a machine, piece of equipment etc that is off is not working or operating〔机器、设备等〕不在工作; 不在运转; 停止: *Will someone switch the radio off?* 谁把收音机关掉好吗? —opposite 反义词 ON[2] (6) **5** not at work, school etc because you are ill or on holiday〔因病或假日〕不工作; 不上学; 休息: *You look tired. Why don't you take tomorrow off?* 你看上去很疲惫, 为什么明天不休息一天呢? | **day/afternoon etc off** *I'm entitled to 25 days off a year.* 我每年可享受25天的年假。| **be off** (=to be absent) 缺席 *Mary is off with the flu today.* 玛丽因患流感今天没来。**6 a)** **be/go off** *especially BrE* food that is off is beginning to decay【尤英】〔食品〕腐坏, 变质: *Ugh! This milk is off.* 呀, 这牛奶酸掉了! **b)** **be off** not be available to be eaten in a restaurant〔餐馆里〕不供应的: *The fish is off today, sir.* 今天没有鱼了, 先生。**7 a)** **4 kilometres/3 days' walk etc off** a particular distance away 离开有四公里/三天的步行距离: *The hostel is at least two more miles off.* 旅舍至少还有两英里路。**b)** **4 hours/10 years etc off** a particular amount of time away in the future 相隔四小时/十年等: *The game is only two days off and our top player has been injured.* 距离比赛只有两天, 而我们最好的队员受伤了。**8** a particular amount of money off is how much the price has been reduced by 扣除, 减掉: *If you buy more than ten, they knock 10% off.* 如果你买十个以上, 他们会打九折。**9** *BrE* behaviour that is off is rude or not what is expected【英】〔行为〕粗鲁; 失常: *I thought it was a little off when he said he wished he'd never been invited.* 我认为, 他说但愿自己永远没受到邀请时是有点失常了。| *Look, I know when someone's being off with me. OK?* 听着, 别人对我不客气时我是知道的, 明白吗? **10** an arranged event that is off will no longer happen 不再举行的, 取消了的: *The wedding's off!* 婚礼取消了! —compare 比较 ON[2] (8) **11 a)** **be badly/well off** to be poor or rich 贫穷的/富有的: *They have to be fairly well off to have that big a house.* 拥有那么大的一栋房子, 他们得相当有钱才行。**b)** **be badly/well off for sth** *informal* to have a small amount or large amount of something【非正式】少量/大量拥有某物: *The school's fairly well off for books these days.* 学校如今拥有很多书。| **how are you off for**

sth? *How are you off for jeans?* (=do you have enough pairs of jeans?) 你有足够的牛仔裤吗？**12 be better off** *especially spoken* to be in a situation where you would gain more advantage【尤口】处于较有利的境况：**be better off with** *I always said she was better off with a boyfriend of her own age.* 我总是说，她找个同龄的男朋友会好一些。| **be better off doing sth** *You'd be better off resigning and working part time.* 你辞去工作干兼职会好些。**13 off and on** also 又作 **on and off** for short periods but not regularly, over a long period of time 断断续续地：*We've been going out together for five years, off and on.* 我们两人交往断断续续有五年了。**14 right off/straight off** *especially BrE informal* immediately【尤英，非正式】立即，立刻，马上 **15** not on the stage but still able to be heard in the theatre; OFFSTAGE (1) 幕后的，舞台后面的：*noises off* 幕后的噪音

1 1 **off²** *prep* **1** not on something or not touching something 离开；不触及：*Keep off the grass.* 勿踩草地。| *Get off your backside and start digging.* 别坐着了，开始挖吧。| *I hope your dirty feet are off my clean floor.* 我希望你的脏脚不要踩我干净的地板。—opposite 反义词 ON¹(1) **2** away from a particular person or thing 离开〔某人或某物〕：*Once we were off the main freeway the trip felt more like a vacation.* 我们一旦驶离了干道高速公路，这趟旅行感觉更像是一次度假。| *The referee ordered three players off the field.* 裁判命令三名球员离场。**3** taken from someone or something 从〔某人处〕拿走；从〔某物中〕去掉：*Tom borrowed £500 off his sister.* 汤姆从他姐姐那里借了500英镑。| *I got this necklace off a woman outside the market.* 我从市场外的一位女子那里买了这条项链。| *What do you plan to live off while you're studying?* 在学习期间你打算靠什么生活呢？**4** out of a bus, train, car etc 离开〔公共汽车、火车、汽车等〕：*Both robbers jumped off the train while it was still moving.* 抢劫者双双跳离了还在行驶的火车。**5** no longer held or supported by a particular thing 从…上脱落[脱离]：*Take your coat off the hook.* 把你的外套从钩上取下来。| *Suddenly the trophy fell off the platform.* 奖杯突然从台上掉了下来。**6** no longer connected or fastened to something; REMOVED 从…分开，从…去掉：*A button has come off my shirt.* 我衬衫上的一颗纽扣掉了。| *Cut about an inch off my bangs please.* 请把我的刘海剪短一英寸左右。**7 a)** at a particular distance from something; REMOVED 与〔某物〕相隔；离…：*My house is about 50 yards off Main Street.* 我的房子离主街约有50码。**b)** in the sea but near the land 在〔陆地附近〕的海面：*an island off the coast of France* 法国海岸附近的一个岛屿 | *The ship began to sink 30 miles off Portsmouth.* 那艘船在距离朴次茅斯30英里的海面上开始沉没。**8** if one room is off another, you get to the second room by passing through the first 穿过〔某屋〕到〔另一屋〕；经由〔某处〕到〔另一处〕：*Off the main bedroom was a beautiful en suite bathroom.* 穿过主卧室是一个漂亮的配套的浴室。**9** *informal* not in a particular building, area etc【非正式】不在〔某建筑物或地区内〕：*Smoking is only allowed off the hospital premises.* 只准在医院外面吸烟。**10 a)** no longer interested in something 不再对…感兴趣：*Toby's been off his food for a few days.* 托比有几天不想吃东西了。| **go right off** *BrE*【英】*I've gone right off her books.* 我已不再喜欢看她的书了。**b)** no longer taking something such as medicine 不再吃〔药等〕：*The operation was a success, and she's off the morphine.* 手术很成功，她已不再服用吗啡了。**11 off the top of your head** if you say something off the top of your head, you are guessing 猜测，猜想

off³ *adj* [only before noun, no comparative 仅用于名词前，无比较级] **1 off day/ week etc** a day, week etc when you are not doing something as well as you usually do 发挥不正常的[失水准的]一天/一个星期等：*Brian never forgets the words – he must be having one of his off days.* 布赖恩从来都不会忘记台词——今天他肯定是状态不好。**2 off period/season etc** a period or season which is not as busy as other times of the year 清淡的时期/淡季等：*In the off season there's hardly anyone in the hotel at all.* 在淡季，这家旅馆几乎没什么人。**3** used when talking about a pair of things such as wheels on a car, to mean the one on the right 〔一对东西之中〕右边的，右侧的 —opposite 反义词 NEAR² (9)

off⁴ *n* **the off** the start, especially of a race or a journey 〔尤指比赛或旅程的〕开始，出发：*The horses were in line, ready for the off.* 赛马已站成一排，准备出闸。

off⁵ *v* [T] *AmE slang* to kill someone【美俚】杀死〔某人〕

of·fal /ˈɔfl; ˈɒfəl/ *n* [U] the inside organs of an animal, for example the heart, LIVER, and KIDNEYs used as food 〔用作食物的〕动物内脏，下水，杂碎

Of·fa's Dyke /ˌɔfəz ˋdaɪk; ˌɒfəz ˈdaɪk/ a long wall of earth, originally over 100 miles long, put up to mark the border between Wales and the Anglo-Saxon kingdom of Mercia, by King Offa of Mercia in the 8th century. Parts of it can still be seen. 奥发大堤〔麦西亚国王奥发于公元8世纪修建的一道土质屏障，绵延100余英里，为威尔士和盎格鲁－撒克逊王国麦西亚的界标。部分残段留存至今〕

off-bal·ance /ˌ·ˈ··/ *adj* [not before noun 不用于名词前] **1** in an unsteady position so that you are likely to fall 不平衡的，不稳定的：**throw/knock/push sb off-balance** *Lee caught hold of my wrist and pulled me off-balance.* 李抓住我的手腕，拽得我失去了平衡。**2** unprepared for something, so that it surprises or shocks you 突然的，冷不防的：**catch sb off-balance** *This time poor old Simpson had been caught off-balance by events.* 这一次可怜的老辛普森猝不及防。

off·beat /ˈɔfˌbit; ˌɒfˈbiːt◂/ *adj informal* unusual and not what people normally expect【非正式】不寻常的；异常的；不落俗套的：*a slightly offbeat lifestyle* 有点别具一格的生活方式

off-cen·tre *BrE*【英】, **off-center** *AmE*【美】/ˌ·ˈ··◂/ *adj* not exactly in the centre of something 偏离中心的，中心错位的：*Here, the photo is slightly off-centre.* 这儿，照片稍微有点偏离了中心。

off-chance /ˈ··/ *n* **on the off-chance** hoping that something will happen, although it is unlikely 怀有万分之一的希望；希望极小的可能性：*I just stopped by on the off-chance that Pippa might be here.* 我怀着万分之一的希望来这里看看，心想或许皮帕会在这儿。

off-col·our *BrE*【英】, **off-color** *AmE*【美】/ˌ·ˈ··◂/ *adj* **1** sexually offensive 下流的，有伤风化的，猥亵的：*Lou followed that up with some fairly off-color jokes.* 卢随后又讲了一些相当下流的笑话。**2** [not before noun 不用于名词前] *especially BrE* slightly ill【尤英】稍有不适的，脸色不好的：*She's been feeling a bit off-colour lately.* 近来她一直感到身体有点不舒服。

off-cut /ˈ··/ *n* [C] a piece of wood, paper etc that is left after the main piece has been cut and removed 〔木头、纸张等的〕边料

off day /ˈ··/ *n* [C] **have an off day** to not do things as well as you usually do on a particular day 发挥失常，状态不好

off-du·ty /ˌ·ˈ··◂/ *adj* someone such as a policeman, nurse, or soldier is off-duty during the hours when they are not working 不在值班的，下了班的：*an off-duty guard* 不当班的警卫 | *Sorry, I'm off-duty now.* 对不起，我现在已下班了。

of·fence *BrE*【英】, usually 一般作 **offense** *AmE*【美】/əˋfɛns; əˈfens/ *n* **1** [C] an illegal action or a crime 违法行为，违章；犯罪：*Driving while drunk is a serious offence.* 醉酒驾车属严重违章。| *a parking offense* 停车违章 | [**+against**] *sexual offences against children* 对儿童的性犯罪 | **commit an offence** (=do something that is an offence) 犯罪 | **first offence** (=the first illegal thing that someone has done) 初犯 | **criminal offence** *Possession of stolen property is a criminal offence.* 私藏赃物属刑事犯罪。| **serious offence** *serious offences under the Prevention of Terrorism Act* 严重触犯《反恐怖主义法案》| **capital offence** (=a crime for which death is the punishment) 死罪 | **minor offence** (=one that is not very serious) 轻微犯罪[违章] **2** [U] behaviour which offends someone 得罪；冒犯行为：**cause/give offence** (=offend someone) 得罪；使伤感情 *The problem was how to get rid of her without causing offence.* 问题是怎样摆脱她而又不得罪她。| **mean no offence** (=have no intention of offending someone) 并无冒犯某人之意 *Don't be upset by what he said; he meant no offence.* 不要为他的话感到生气，他没有冒犯你的意思。**3 no offence** *spoken* used to tell someone that you do not want to offend them by what you are saying【口】请别见怪，没有冒犯你的意思：*No offense, but this cheese tastes like rubber.* 请别见怪，这乳酪吃起来像是嚼橡胶。**4 take offence** to feel offended because of something someone has said or done 对…生气；因…见怪：*She's always quick to take offence.* 她老是动不动就生气。**5** [U] *formal* the act of attacking【正式】进攻，攻击行为：*It depends on whether it was used as a weapon of offence or defence.* 那要看这武器是用来攻击的还是用来防卫的。**6** [U] *BrE* the part of a game such as football concerned with getting points and winning【英】〔足球等比赛中的〕进攻 —see also 另见 OFFENSE² 3

of·fend /əˋfɛnd; əˈfend/ *v* **1** [T usually passive 一般用被动态] to make someone angry or upset 使生气，使恼火：**be offended** *Richard was deeply offended that people thought he'd faked the story.* 人们认为理查德说的事情是编造的，这使他大为恼火。| *I hope you won't be offended if I leave early.* 我如果早走，希望你不要生气。| **offend sb** *I'm sorry; have I done something to offend you?* 对不起，我做什么事让你生气了？**2** [T] to seem bad or unpleasant to someone 使反感，使不快；冒犯：*Cruelty to animals offends many people.* 许多人对虐待动物很反感。| **offend the eye/ear** (=look very ugly or sound very bad) 刺眼/刺耳 **3** [I] to do something that is a crime 犯罪：*Many criminals offend again within a year of their release from prison.* 许多罪犯出狱不到一年又再犯罪。**4** [I,T] *formal* to go against people's feelings of what is morally right【正式】违背，有失〔道德准则〕：

[+against] *behaviour that offends against common decency* 有悖日常礼节的行为

of·fend·er /əˋfɛndə; əˈfendə/ *n* [C] **1** someone who is guilty of a crime 罪犯, 有罪者: *an institute for young offenders* 青少年罪犯教养院 | **first offender** (=one who has done a criminal action for the first time) 初犯 **2** someone or something that is the cause of something that is bad 引发坏事的人[事物]: *Among causes of air pollution, car exhaust fumes may be the worst offender.* 在造成空气污染的多种原因中, 汽车排放的废气可能是罪魁祸首。

of·fend·ing /əˋfɛndɪŋ; əˈfendɪŋ/ *adj* **the offending ...** *often humorous* the thing that is causing a problem【常幽默】引起问题的…, 造成不便的…: *I decided to have the offending tooth removed.* 我决定把这颗讨厌的牙拔掉。

of·fense¹ /əˋfɛns; əˈfens/ *n* [C,U] the usual American spelling of OFFENCE offence的一般美式拼法

of·fense² /ˋɔfɛns; əˈfens/ *n* [U] *AmE* the part of a game such as football concerned with getting points and winning【美】〔足球等比赛中的〕进攻: *The Bears are going to have to work on their offense this season.* 本赛季熊队将不得不加强进攻。—opposite 反义词 DEFENSE²

of·fen·sive¹ /əˋfɛnsɪv; əˈfensɪv/ *adj* **1** very rude or insulting and likely to upset people 无礼的; 冒犯的; 令人恼火的: *I found her remarks deeply offensive.* 我发现她的话令人非常恼火。| [+to] *crude jokes that are offensive to women* 冒犯女士的粗鄙笑话 —opposite 反义词 INOFFENSIVE¹ (1) **2** *formal* unpleasant【正式】令人不快的: *an offensive smell* 令人讨厌的气味 **3** [only before noun 仅用于名词前] for attacking 攻击的, 进攻性的: *offensive weapons* 攻击性武器 | *The troops took up offensive positions.* 部队已准备发动攻击。—opposite 反义词 DEFENSIVE **4** *AmE* concerned with getting points and getting a game, as opposed to stopping the other team from getting points【美】〔体育比赛中〕进攻的, 攻势的: *offensive play* 进攻型打法 | *an offensive coach* 进攻型教练 —opposite 反义词 DEFENSIVE —**offensively** *adv*: *His clothes smelled slightly, but not offensively.* 他的衣服有点发臭, 但不是臭得令人作呕。| *The planes were too few to be used offensively.* 飞机太少, 难以展开攻势。—**offensiveness** *n* [U]

offensive² *n* [C] **1** a planned military attack involving large forces over a long period〔军事〕进攻, 攻势: *On March 6th they launched a full-scale offensive.* 3月6日他们发起了全面进攻。**2 be on the offensive** to be ready to attack or criticize people 采取攻势, 出击; 批评 **3 take the offensive/go on the offensive** to be the first to make an attack or strong criticism 率先攻击; 先发制人 **4 sales/charm/PR offensive** a planned set of actions intended to influence a lot of people 销售/魅力/公关攻势

of·fer¹ /ˋɔfə; ˈɒfə/ *v* **1** [T] to say that you are willing to give someone something, or to hold something out to them so that they can take it 提出, 提供: **offer sb sth** *You haven't offered Grandma any ice cream.* 你没给奶奶吃冰激凌。| *They offered him a very good job but he turned it down.* 他们给他提供了一份很好的工作, 但他拒绝了。| **offer sth to sb** *Offer some coffee to the guests.* 端些咖啡给客人。**2** [T] to say that you are willing to pay a particular amount of money 出价, 开价: **offer (sb) sth for** *They've offered us £75,000 for the house.* 他们已向我们出价7.5万英镑买这幢房子。| *The police are offering a reward for any information.* 警方在悬赏奖金获取任何情报。**3** [I,T] to say that you are willing to do something 愿意〔做某事〕: *I don't need any help, but it was nice of you to offer.* 我不需要任何帮助, 但是我很感激你的好意。| **offer to do sth** *My dad has offered to pick us up.* 我爸爸表示愿意开车来接我们。| *Shelly didn't even offer to help.* 雪莉甚至都不愿意帮忙。**4** [T] to provide something that people need or want 提供, 给予: *He offered no explanation for his actions.* 他对自己的行为未作任何解释。| **offer sth to sb** *Senator Joseph's speech will have offered little comfort to bankrupt businessmen.* 参议员约瑟夫的讲话不会对破产的商人有多大安慰。| **have sth to offer (to sb)** *Edinburgh has a great deal to offer to visitors in the way of entertainment.* 爱丁堡能给游客提供大量的娱乐活动。**5 offer (up) a prayer/sacrifice etc** to pray to God or give something to God 作祷告/献祭等 **6 offer itself** *formal* if an opportunity offers itself, it happens for you【正式】〔机会〕出现: *I shall be ready to raise the matter with him when a suitable occasion offers itself.* 等有合适的机会, 我会乐意向他提出这个问题的。**7 offer your hand to sb** to hold out your hand in order to shake hands with someone 向某人伸出手来〔握手〕

offer² *n* [C] **1** a statement that you are willing to give someone something or do something for them〔愿给某人某物或愿为某人做某事的〕提议; 提供: [+of] *an offer of assistance* 愿提供帮助的建议 | **offer to do sth** *an offer to help* 愿意帮忙的提议 | **turn down/refuse/decline an offer** (=say no to an offer) 拒绝提议[建议] *He turned down the offer of a free trip to Milan.* 他拒绝了免费去米兰的提议。**2** an amount of money that you are willing to pay for something 出价, 开价, 报价: **make (sb) an offer (for)** *I'm prepared to make you a generous offer for the house.* 这幢房子我愿意给你出一个高价。| **accept an offer** *They've accepted our offer of £50,000.* 他们已接受了我们5万英镑的报价。| **be open to offers** (=be ready to consider people's offers) 愿意考虑还价 *We're asking £2,500, but we're open to offers.* 我们要价2500英镑, 但允许还价。**3** a reduction of the price of something in a shop for a short time 特价〔售货〕: **special offer** *They have a special offer on this week – buy two, get one free.* 本周他们特价售货, 买二赠一。**4 on offer a)** available to be bought or used 供购买的; 供使用的: *a whole range of services on offer* 提供的一整套服务 **b)** *BrE* for sale at a very cheap price for a short time【英】〔短期〕削价[特价]出售的: *Olive oil is on offer this week.* 橄榄油本周削价出售。**5 be under offer** *BrE* if a house that is for sale is under offer, someone has offered money for it【英】〔待售房屋〕已有人出价要买

of·fer·ing /ˋɔfərɪŋ; ˈɒfərɪŋ/ *n* **1** [C] a book, play, piece of music etc that someone has written recently〔新近完成的〕作品: *the latest offering from Nancy Griffith* 南希·格里菲思的最新作品 **2** something that is given to God or given as a present to please someone 供品, 祭品; 赠品 —see also 另见 **burnt offering** (BURNT² (2)), PEACE OFFERING

of·fer·to·ry /ˋɔfə˞ˌtorɪ; ˈɒfətəri/ *n plural* **offertories** [C] **1** the money people give during a religious ceremony in church 宗教仪式上的献金 —see also 另见 COLLECTION (2a) **2** the offering of the bread and wine to God at COMMUNION (2)〔圣餐礼中向上帝奉上面包和酒的〕奉献仪式

off-guard /ˌ· ˈ·◂/ *adj* [not before noun 不用于名词前] not expecting something surprising or dangerous to happen, and not prepared to deal with it 未加提防的, 措手不及的: **catch/take sb off-guard** *Caught off-guard, Paul blushed and looked away in embarrassment.* 措手不及之下, 保罗脸红了, 尴尬地移开了目光。

off·hand¹ /ˌɔfˈhænd; ˌɒfˈhænd◂/ *adj* not giving people much time or attention, when you are talking to them 说话漫不经心的, 简慢的: *She said you were a bit offhand with her this afternoon.* 她说你今天下午对她有点简慢无礼。—**offhandedly** *adv* —**offhandedness** *n* [U]

offhand² *adv* immediately, without time to think about it or find out about something 立刻; 不假思索地: *I can't remember offhand what shifts I'm working next week.* 我一时记不起来下周我上什么班。

of·fice /ˋɔfɪs; ˈɒfɪs/ *n* 

1 ►BUILDING 建筑物◄ [C] the building that belongs to a company or organization, with a lot of rooms where people work〔公司或组织的〕办公楼, 办事处: *The company is moving to new offices in central London.* 公司准备迁往伦敦市中心的新办事处。| **head office** (=main office) 总部 | **the office** *Did you go to the office today?* 你今天去办公了吗? | **at the office** *I must have left my keys at the office.* 我准是把钥匙忘在办公室了。| **work in an office** *I'd hate to work in an office, but I could use a regular income.* 我讨厌在办公室里工作, 但倒是能有一份固定的收入。

2 ►ROOM 房间◄ [C] a room where you do work that involves writing, calculating, or talking to people 办公室: *the manager's office* 经理办公室 | *My office gets really hot and sticky in the summer.* 夏天时我的办公室真的又热又闷。—see picture on page A14 参见A14页图

3 office hours the time between about nine in the morning and five in the afternoon, when the people in offices are working 办公时间〔大约为上午九点至下午五点〕: *You can contact us during office hours.* 你可以在办公时间跟我们联系。

4 information/ticket etc office a room or building where people go to ask for information 询问处/售票处等 —see also 另见 BOX OFFICE, POST OFFICE

5 ►IMPORTANT JOB 要职◄ [C,U] an important job or position with power, especially in government〔尤指政府中拥有权力的〕重要职位: *the office of President* 总统的职位 | **in office** (=in an important position) 执政 *His decision to resign after 30 years in office came as a great shock.* 他在执政30年后作出退职的决定, 令人大为震惊。| **hold office** *She had previously held office as Minister of Education.* 她曾担任过教育部长一职。| **take office** (=start an important job) 就职, 上任

6 Office used in the names of British government departments〔英国政府的〕部, 局, 处: *the Foreign Office* 外交部

7 sb's good offices *formal* help given by someone who has authority or can influence people【正式】某人的得力相助: *I managed to get a visa through the good offices of a friend in*

the Service. 我通过政府部门里一个朋友的大力帮助而设法获得了签证。

office block /ˈ‥ ˌ/ *n* [C] *BrE* a large building with many offices in it【英】办公大楼; OFFICE BUILDING *AmE*【美】

office build·ing /ˈ‥ ˌ‥/ *n* [C] *AmE* a large building with many offices in it【美】办公大楼; OFFICE BLOCK *BrE*【英】

office girl /ˈ‥ ˌ/ *n* [C] a young woman who does unimportant work in an office〔担任的工作相对不重要的〕办公室小姐

office hold·er /ˈ‥ ˌ‥/ *n* [C] someone who has an official position, especially in the government 任公职者，公务员，政府官员

Office of Fair Trad·ing, the /ˌ‥ ‥ ˈ‥/ abbreviation 缩写为 **OFT** a British government organization whose job is to protect people from being cheated by shops and other businesses, and to help customers who have been cheated or treated unfairly 公平贸易局〔英国一政府机构。其职责是保护消费者免受商店和其他经营实体的欺诈，并对蒙受欺骗或不公待遇的顾客提供帮助〕

Office of Man·age·ment and Bud·get, the /ˌ‥ ‥ ‥ ‥ ˈ‥/ abbreviation 缩写为 **the OMB** a US government organization that provides help for the President in organizing the work of government departments and especially in preparing the BUDGET (=the official plan for how government money will be used) 行政管理和预算局〔美国一政府机构。其职责是协助总统组织政府各部门的工作，尤其是编制预算方案〕

office par·ty /ˈ‥ ˌ‥/ *n* [C] a party just before Christmas in the office of a company, government department etc for the people who work there〔圣诞节前夕在办公室为员工举办的〕办公室派对，联欢会

> **CULTURAL NOTE 文化注释**
>
> Office parties are usually relaxed occasions, at which managers and workers behave less formally than usual towards each other and most people drink a lot of alcohol. People often make jokes about office parties, suggesting that some people have brief sexual relationships at these events. The jokes usually refer to people kissing or having sex 'behind the filing cabinets'. 办公室派对的气氛通常轻松愉快，经理和下属相互之间也不同于平时那样一本正经，而多数人都会痛饮一番。人们常拿办公室派对开玩笑，说有人趁此场合与人偷欢片刻。笑话经常说有人"躲在档案柜后面"亲吻和交欢。

1 1 **of·fi·cer** /ˈɔfəsɚ; ˈɒfɪsə/ *n* [C] **1** someone who is in a position of authority in the army, navy etc 军官: *a naval officer* 海军军官 | *Report to your commanding officer.* 去向你的指挥官报告。**2** someone who has an important position in an organization, such as a government, company etc〔政府的〕高级官员;〔公司等的〕高级职员: *a local government officer* 地方政府官员 | *a personnel officer* 人事部主管 **3** a policeman or policewoman 警察，警官: *What's the problem, officer?* 什么问题，警官？| *the officer in charge of the murder inquiry* 负责调查谋杀案的警察 **4 Officer** *AmE* a title for a policeman or policewoman【美】警官〔用于对男女警察的称呼〕: *Officer Maloney will help you.* 马洛尼警官会帮助你。

3 **of·fi·cial**[1] /əˈfɪʃəl; əˈfɪʃəl/ *n* [C] someone who has a responsible position in an organization 官员；高级职员: *trade union members and officials* 工会会员和干事 | *a government official* 政府官员

3 2 **official**[2] *adj* **1** approved of or done by someone in authority, especially the government 官方的，正式的: *You have to get official permission to build a new house.* 你要盖一幢新房必须得到官方的许可。| *an official inquiry* 官方调查 | *The official languages of Canada are English and French.* 加拿大的官方语言是英语和法语。**2** done as part of your job and not for your own private purposes 公务上的，公职的: *Are you here in your official capacity?* 你是以官方身份来这里的吗？| *the Queen's official visit to the Bahamas* 女王对巴哈马的正式访问 **3** official information, reasons etc are given formally and publicly, but may not always be true 正式公布的，公开宣称的〔但并非总是事实〕: *The official motive for his resignation was that he wanted to spend more time with his children.* 官方公布他辞职的原因是他想多花些时间和孩子在一起。| *The news is not yet official.* (=has not been publicly announced) 这消息尚未正式公布。**4** chosen to represent someone or an organization, or do something for them 被正式选用的: *official photographer to the Royal Family* 王室专职摄影师 | *their official logo* 他们选用的标志 **5** an official event is a formal, public event〔事件〕正式的，公开的: *the official opening of the new store* 新商店的正式开张

Official Birth·day, the /ˌ‥ ˈ‥/ the day when the British Queen or King's birthday is officially celebrated, especially with the ceremony of Trooping the Colour in London. It is not the same as the Queen or King's own personal birthday, and it is always on the second Saturday of June. 官方诞辰日〔指英国官方庆祝女王或国王诞辰的日子。官方诞辰日定于每年6月的第二个星期六，届时在伦敦要专门举行军旗敬礼分列式。这天并非女王或国王的实际生日〕

of·fi·cial·dom /əˈfɪʃəldəm; əˈfɪʃəldəm/ *n* [U] a word meaning government departments or the people who work in them, used when you think they are unhelpful 官场；官僚

of·fi·cial·ese /əˌfɪʃəˈliz; əˌfɪʃəlˈiːz/ *n* [U] *informal* a way of talking or writing used by government officials, that is unnecessarily difficult to understand【非正式】官话；官场公文体

of·fi·cial·ly /əˈfɪʃəlɪ; əˈfɪʃəli/ *adv* **1** publicly and formally 官方地；正式地: *They have officially announced their engagement.* 他们已正式宣布订婚。| *The new clinic was officially opened this morning.* 新诊所今天上午正式开业。| *The two countries are still not officially at war.* 两国尚未正式交战。**2** [sentence adverb 句子副词] according to what you say publicly, even though this may not be true 根据公布所说〔不一定是事实〕: *Officially, he's on vacation, but there's a rumor that he's very ill.* 据公布所说，他正在休假，但传言说他病得很重。

official re·ceiv·er /ˌ‥ ‥ ˈ‥/ *n* [C] someone whose job is to take care of the financial affairs of a company or a person that is BANKRUPT〔负责处理公司或私人破产事务的〕官方接管人，破产管理人

Official Se·crets Act, the /ˌ‥ ˈ‥ ˌ/ a UK law by which people who work for the government are not allowed to discuss their work with people who do not work for the government or to make known information which should be kept secret. Government workers must 'sign the Official Secrets Act' (=agree to obey this law), and they can be put in prison if they break this agreement. 《官方保密法》〔英国一法律。该法规定政府工作人员不得与非政府工作人员讨论自己的工作，也不得泄露相关机密。政府工作人员必须签名保证遵守该法，如有违反，则会被判入狱〕

of·fi·ci·ate /əˈfɪʃɪˌet; əˈfɪʃieɪt/ *v* [I+at] to do official duties, especially at a religious ceremony 行使职责；主持宗教仪式

of·fi·cious /əˈfɪʃəs; əˈfɪʃəs/ *adj* too eager to tell people what to do 爱发号施令的，好管闲事的: *An officious little guard came and told me not to whistle in the museum.* 一位耍权威的小警卫走过来，叫我不要在博物馆里吹口哨。—**officiously** *adv* —**officiousness** *n* [U]

off·ing /ˈɔfɪŋ; ˈɒfɪŋ/ *n* **be in the offing** to be about to happen or to be possible 即将发生，即将来到: *Everything's topsy-turvy at the moment with this big trip in the offing.* 这次大规模的旅行活动即将开始，此刻一切都很混乱。

off·ish /ˈɔfɪʃ; ˈɒfɪʃ/ *adj informal* behaving in a slightly unfriendly or impolite way【非正式】(有点)冷淡的，疏远的: *I don't know why but she seemed a bit offish to me.* 我不知道为什么，她好像对我有点冷淡。

off-key /ˌ ˈ◂/ *adj* music that is off-key sounds unpleasant because it is played slightly above or below the correct PITCH[1] (3)〔音乐〕走调的，不和谐的: *The band sounds slightly off-key.* 乐队的演奏稍有点走调。—**off-key** *adv*: *Someone upstairs was singing off-key.* 楼上有人唱歌走调了。

off-li·cence /ˈ ‥/ *n* [C] *BrE* a shop that sells wine, beer, and other alcoholic drinks, in bottles or cans【英】出售瓶装或罐装含酒精饮料的商店; LIQUOR STORE *AmE*【美】

off lim·its /ˌ ˈ‥/ *adj* **be off limits** if a place is off limits, you are not allowed to go there 禁止入内: [**+to**] *Under the proposal, the Antarctic would be declared off-limits to whalers.* 根据这项提议，南极洲将被宣布为捕鲸船禁入区。

off·line /ˈɔflaɪn; ˈɒflaɪn/ *adj* not directly connected to a computer or directly controlled by it〔电脑〕脱机的；离线的: *an offline terminal* 离线终端 | *offline storage of data* 脱机数据储存 —opposite 反义词 ONLINE —**offline** *adv*

off-load /ˌ ˈ/ *v* **1** [T] to get rid of something that you do not need by giving it to someone else〔通过送给别人来〕清除〔不需要之物〕: **off-load sth onto sb** *We managed to off-load all those old typewriters onto a friend of mine.* 我们设法将那些旧打字机全都清理给了我的一个朋友。**2 off-load your problems/guilt/troubles etc** to tell someone about your problems etc in order to make yourself feel better〔为了减轻心理负担而〕倾诉困难/愧疚/麻烦等

off-peak /ˌ ˈ◂/ *adj* **1** off-peak hours or periods are times when fewer people want to do or use something 非高峰时间的；非繁忙的: *Telephone charges are lower during off-peak periods.* 非繁忙时间电话收费要低一些。**2** off-peak travel, electricity etc is cheaper because it is done or used at these times 非繁忙时间所做[用]的

off·print /ˈɔfprɪnt; ˈɒfprɪnt/ *n* [C] an article from a magazine that is printed and sold separately〔杂志中选出的文章的〕单印本, 选印本

off·put·ting /ˈ·,··/ *adj* if someone's behaviour or the appearance of something is off-putting, it is strange or unpleasant and stops you from liking or being interested in them〔某人的举止或某物的外观〕令人气恼的, 令人讨厌的: *Jack's aggressiveness is really off-putting.* 杰克的挑衅行为的确很令人讨厌。—see also 另见 **put sb/sth off** (PUT)—**off-puttingly** *adv*

off-ramp /ˈ· ·/ *n* [C] *AmE* a road for driving off a HIGHWAY (1)【美】〔主要公路或高速公路上的〕驶出坡道, 驶出匝道

off-road ve·hi·cle /,· ˈ· ··/ *n* [C] a vehicle that is built very strongly so that it can be used on rough ground 越野车, 非道路车辆

> **CULTURAL NOTE 文化注释**
>
> In Britain and the US, many people who spend most of their time in towns and cities still buy off-road vehicles because they are fashionable and look impressive. 在英国和美国, 很多大部分时间都生活在城市和小镇上的人也会买越野车, 因为开越野车既时髦又抢眼。

off-screen /,· ˈ·◂/ *adv* when a film actor is not acting〔电影演员〕在银幕外, 在私人生活中: *What's he like off-screen?* 他在银幕外是什么模样的?—**off-screen** *adj*: *The fan magazines are full of her off-screen romances.* 各种影迷杂志中满是她银幕外的风流韵事。

off-sea·son, the /,·ˈ··◂/ *n* the time of the year when there is not much work or activity, especially in farming or the tourist industry〔尤指农业或旅游业的〕淡季: *Most hotels are closed in the off-season.* 在淡季时, 大多数旅馆都关门停业。—**off-season** *adj, adv*: *Take advantage of our special off-season fares.* 我们提供淡季特惠票价, 请莫失良机。

off-set[1] /ɔfˋsɛt; ˈɒfset/ *v past tense and past participle* **offset** *present participle* **offsetting** [T] **1** if something such as a cost or sum of money offsets another cost, sum etc or is offset against it, it has an opposite effect so that the situation remains the same 补偿, 抵消: **be offset by** *In 1992 the cost of the layoffs was offset by the savings on the payroll.* 在1992年, 裁员的成本费用因工资总额的减少而得以弥补。| **offset sth against sth** *He was able to offset his travel expenses against tax.* 他用旅费抵消了他的税。**2** to make something look better by being close to it and different 衬托出: *Streaks of blond in his hair offset his deep tan.* 他头发中一缕缕的金色衬托出他黝黑的肤色。

off-set[2] /ˈɔfsɛt; ˈɒfset/ *n* [C,U] a method of printing in which ink is put onto rollers (ROLLER (1)) and the paper then passes between the rollers 胶印(法)—**offset** *adj*

off-shoot /ˈɔf,ʃut; ˈɒfʃuːt/ *n* [C] **1** an organization, system of beliefs etc which has developed from a larger or earlier one〔组织、信仰等的〕分支, 衍生事物: *Marxism-Leninism and its various offshoots* 马列主义及其诸多不同的分支 | [+of] *The company was originally an offshoot of Bell Telephones.* 该公司原本是贝尔电话公司的一家分支机构。**2** a new stem or branch on a plant〔植物的〕新茎, 分枝, 分株

off-shore /,ɔfˋʃɔr; ,ɒfˈʃɔː/ *adj* **1** connected with work that is done on or under the sea 海上[海下]作业的: **offshore fishing/oil rig/exploration etc** *more than 10,000 offshore workers based in Orkney* 以奥克尼为基地的一万多海上作业的工人 **2 offshore bank/company/investment etc** a bank etc that is based abroad in a country where you pay less tax than in your home country 境外[海外]银行/公司/投资等 **3 offshore wind/current etc** a wind etc that is blowing or moving away from the land 从陆地吹向海面的风/离岸的水流 —compare 比较 INSHORE, ONSHORE—**offshore** *adv*: *a boat anchored offshore* 在近海岸锚泊的船

off-side[1] /,ɔfˋsaɪd; ,ɒfˈsaɪd◂/ *adj, adv* in a position where you are not allowed to play the ball in sports such as football〔足球等运动中〕越位(的) —opposite 反义词 ONSIDE

offside[2], **the** /ˈɔfsaɪd; ˈɒfsaɪd/ *n BrE* the side of a car that is nearest to the middle of the road when you are driving it【英】〔汽车的〕右侧, 右边 —opposite 反义词 NEARSIDE—**offside** *adj*: *the offside headlight* 右边的前灯

off-spring /ˈɔf,sprɪŋ; ˈɒf,sprɪŋ/ *n plural* **offspring** [C] **1** someone's child or children〔某人的〕子女, 子孙, 后代: *one of her numerous offspring* 她众多儿女中的一个 **2** an animal's baby or babies〔动物的〕崽

off-stage /,ɔfˋstedʒ; ,ɒfˈsteɪdʒ◂/ *adv* **1** just behind or to the side of a stage in a theatre, where the people watching a play cannot see 幕后, 舞台后, 舞台旁: *There was a loud crash offstage.* 后台发出很大的碰撞声。**2** when an actor is not acting〔演员〕在台下, 在私生活中: *Offstage Peter always seemed a quiet, shy sort of person.* 舞台下, 彼得总是显得那么文静腼腆。—**offstage** *adj*

off-street /ˈ· ·/ *adj* **off-street parking** places for parking that are not on main streets 离开主要街道的停车处

off-the-cuff /,· · ˈ·◂/ *adj* [usually before noun 一般用于名词前] an off-the-cuff remark, reply etc is one that you make without thinking about it first 未经准备的, 随口作出的, 当场的, 即席的—**off-the-cuff** *adv*

off-the-peg /,· · ˈ·/ *adj BrE* off-the-peg clothes are not made to fit one particular person but are made in standard sizes【英】〔衣服〕现成的, 非定做的; OFF-THE-RACK *AmE*【美】—compare 比较 MADE-TO-MEASURE—**off-the-peg** *adv*: *It was only a cheap suit, bought off-the-peg.* 这不过是一套便宜的西服, 是现成买来的。

off-the-rack /,· · ˈ·◂/ *adj AmE* OFF-THE-PEG【美】〔衣服〕现成的, 非定做的

off-the-rec·ord /,· · ˈ··◂/ *adj* an off-the-record remark is unofficial and is not supposed to be made public 非正式的; 不准公开的: *The Prime Minister's remarks were strictly off-the-record.* 首相的讲话是非正式的, 严禁发表。—**off-the-record** *adv*

off-the-shelf /,· · ˈ·◂/ *adj, adv* already made and available in shops 现成的[地]: *off-the-shelf database software* 现成的数据库软件

off-the-wall /,· · ˈ·◂/ *adj informal* a little strange or unusual【非正式】有点古怪的, 异乎寻常的: *an off-the-wall idea* 古怪的想法

off-track /ˈɔftræk; ˈɒftræk/ *adj AmE* away from a place where horses race【美】〔赛马赌博等〕场外进行的: *Few states allow offtrack betting.* 只有几个州允许场外赛马赌博。

off-white /,· ˈ·◂/ *n* [U] a white that has some yellow or grey in it 黄白色, 灰白色, 米色—**off-white** *adj*: *an off-white blouse* 一件黄白色的女衬衫

off-year /ˈ· ·/ *n* [C usually singular 一般用单数] **1** a year when something is not as successful as usual 情况较差的年头, 小年: [+for] *an off-year for car sales* 汽车滞销的一年 **2** *AmE* a year in which no elections happen【美】非选举年

Of·gas /ˈɔfgæs; ˈɒfgæs/ the British government organization whose job is to make sure that the UK gas industry operates safely and does not charge unfair prices 燃气管理处〔英国一政府机构。其职责是确保燃气行业操作安全, 收费合理〕

Of·sted /ˈɔfstɛd; ˈɒfsted/ the Office for Standards in Education; the government organization that is responsible for checking the quality of education in British schools 教育标准局〔英国一政府机构。其职责是检查英国学校的教育质量〕

oft /ɔft; ɒft/ *adv poetical or formal* often【诗或正式】经常, 时常: **oft-repeated/quoted etc** *oft-repeated advice* 多次重复的忠告

Of·tel /ˈɔftɛl; ˈɒftel/ the British government organization whose job is to make sure that the UK telephone industry treats its customers fairly and does not charge unfair prices 电信管理局〔英国一政府机构。其职责是确保电信行业公平对待客户, 收费合理〕

of·ten /ˈɔfən; ˈɒfən/ *adv* **1** if something happens often, or you do something often, it happens regularly or many times 经常, 时常, 多次: *Rosi often works till 7 or 8 o'clock in the evening.* 罗西经常工作到晚上七八点钟。| *If you wash your hair too often, it tends to make it greasy.* 如果洗头过勤, 会使头发变得油光光的。| **how often?** *How often do you go to the movies?* 你多久去看一次电影? | **very/quite often** *Tom quite often goes to his Mum's on Saturday for tea.* 汤姆星期六常去他妈妈家喝茶。| **not often** *It's not often that you meet people who are so willing to help.* 这样乐于助人的人不是经常能遇到的。—see picture at 参见 FREQUENCY 图 **2** [sentence adverb 句子副词] if something happens often, it happens in many situations or cases 在许多情况下: *It's often difficult to translate poetry.* 诗歌通常不容易翻译。| **very/quite often** *Very often you find that children with behavioral problems come from broken homes.* 你会发现行为有问题的孩子大都来自破裂的家庭。**3 all too often** also 又作 **only too often** used to say that something sad, disappointing, or annoying happens too much 过于频繁, 屡次三番: *All too often victims of bullying are too frightened to ask for help.* 往往都是这样, 受欺侮的人因太害怕而不敢求助。| *These loopholes in the tax laws are exploited only too often.* 这些税法中的漏洞屡屡被人利用。**4 every so often** sometimes 有时, 偶尔: *An inspector would come round every so often to check the premises.* 偶尔有检查员来查看这地方的情况。**5 as often as not** also 又作 **more often than not** *spoken* usually【口】通常: *More often than not he'll come and apologize within minutes of shouting at us.* 他跟我们吵嚷过后通常没几分钟就会来道歉。

of·ten·times /ˈɔfən,taɪmz; ˈɒfəntaɪmz/ *adv old use* often【旧】经常, 时常

Of·wat /ˋɔfwɔt; ˈɒfwɒt/ the British government organization whose job is to make sure that the UK water industry provides safe water, protects the environment, and does not charge unfair prices 供水管理局〔英国一政府机构。其职责是确保自来水行业供水安全,保护环境,收费合理〕

o·gle /ˋogl; ˈəʊgəl/ *v* [I,T] to look at someone in an offensive way that shows you think they are sexually attractive 色迷迷地看着,盯视: *A small fat man sat there most days, ogling girls' legs.* 一个矮胖的男子多数日子都会坐在那里,色迷迷地盯着姑娘们的腿看。

O grade /ˋo gred; ˈəʊ greɪd/ *n* [C] an examination in a particular subject, taken in Scotland, usually at the age of 16 O级考试〔苏格兰地区对某一特定科目的考试,考生年龄通常在16岁〕—see also 另见 O LEVEL

o·gre /ˋogɚ; ˈəʊgə/ *n* [C] **1** a large character in children's stories who eats people〔童话中的〕吃人大妖魔 **2** someone who seems fierce, cruel, and frightening 凶残可怕的人: *My boss is a real ogre.* 我们老板真是可怕。

OH the written abbreviation of 缩写= OHIO

oh /o; əʊ/ *interjection* **1** used to make a slight pause, especially before replying to a question or giving your opinion on something 噢〔用于稍作停顿,尤其是在回答问题或对某事发表看法时〕: *"What time are you going into town?" "Oh, I haven't decided yet."* "你什么时候去城里?""噢,我还没决定呢。" | *"I don't like the new boss." "Oh, I think she's quite nice."* "我不喜欢新来的老板。""噢,我认为她很不错呀。" **2** used to get or keep someone's attention so that you can ask them a question or continue what you are saying 喂,哦〔用于让人注意〕: *Oh, Janet, could you get me a paper while you're out?* 喂,珍妮特,外出时给我买份报纸好吗? | *Milk, cereal, juice – oh, and put lettuce on the list too.* 牛奶、麦片、果汁——哦,把生菜也加到购物单上去。**3** used to express a strong emotion or to emphasize what you think about something 啊,呀〔用于表示强烈的情感或强调对某事的看法〕: *Oh, aren't those flowers gorgeous!* 呀,那些花可真漂亮! | *Oh, how awful!* 啊,真糟糕! | *She got the job? Oh great!* 她得到那份工作啦? 啊,太好了! **4 oh, did he?/oh, are you?/oh, was she? etc** used to show that you did not previously know what someone has just told you 哦,真的吗?〔用于表示以前不知道刚听说的事〕: *"Frances has left her husband, you know." "Oh, has she?"* "你知道,弗朗西丝跟她丈夫分手了。""哦,真的吗?"

O'Ha·ra /oˋhærə; əʊˈhɑːrə/, **Scar·lett** /ˋskarlɪt; ˈskɑːlɪ̣t/ the main female character in the book and film *Gone With the Wind*. She is a beautiful, determined, and clever woman. 郝思嘉,又译斯佳丽〔小说和电影《乱世佳人》中的女主人公。她是一个漂亮、坚定而又聪明的女人〕

O'Hare /oˋhɛr; əʊˈheə/ the main airport in Chicago, Illinois, US 奥黑尔国际机场〔美国伊利诺伊州芝加哥市的主要机场〕

O·hi·o /oˋhaɪo; əʊˈhaɪəʊ/ written abbreviation 缩写为 **OH 1** a state in the Midwest of the US, an important centre of engineering, coal mining, and farming. Its largest city is Cleveland. 俄亥俄州〔美国中西部一州,为重要的工程、采煤及农业中心。最大城市为克利夫兰〕**2 the Ohio** a long river in the central US, which used to carry a lot of industrial goods 俄亥俄河〔美国中部一河流,以前曾大量运输工业品〕

ohm /om; əʊm/ *n* [C] *technical* the standard unit of electrical RESISTANCE (5) which allows one AMP (1) to flow under a pressure of one VOLT【术语】欧姆〔电阻单位〕

o·ho /oˋho; əʊˈhəʊ/ *interjection old-fashioned* used to show surprise or satisfaction【过时】哦嗬,嗳哟,嘿嘿〔用于表示惊讶或满意〕

Oh Su·san·na /ˌo suˋzænə; ˌəʊ suːˈzænə/ a 19th century US FOLK SONG written by Stephen Foster. Some of the words are: Oh, Susanna! Now don't you cry for me, / For I've come from Alabama / With my banjo on my knee. 《噢,苏珊娜》〔美国19世纪民歌,由斯蒂芬·福斯特创作。歌中唱道: 噢,苏珊娜! / 别为我哭泣, / 我已从亚拉巴马赶来, / 膝上放着我那班卓琴〕

-oid /ɔɪd; ɔɪd/ *suffix technical* [in adjectives 构成形容词] like or in the form of something【术语】像…的,似…的: *humanoid creatures* (=similar to humans) 类人动物 | *ovoid* (=egg shaped) 卵型的

oik /ɔɪk; ɔɪk/ *n* [C] *BrE slang* a rude unintelligent man who is likely to cause trouble【英俚】蠢人,笨人;乡巴佬;举止粗鲁的人 —**oikish** *adj*

oil[1] /ɔɪl; ɔɪl/ *n* **1** [U] a smooth thick mineral liquid that is burned to produce heat, or used to make machines run easily 油;燃料油;润滑油: *Check the oil level in your car every week.* 每周检查一下你汽车的油量。| **oil-burning/oil-fired** *oil-fired central heating* 燃油集中供暖系统 **2** [U] the thick, dark liquid from under the ground from which oil and petrol are produced; PETROLEUM 石油: *the oil industry* 石油工业 **3** [C,U] a smooth, thick liquid made from plants or animals, used in cooking or for making beauty products〔用于烹调或生产美容用品的〕植物油,动物油: *olive oil* 橄榄油 | *coconut oil shampoo* 椰子油洗发剂 **4 oils** [plural] paints that contain oil; OIL PAINTS 油漆;油性涂料;油画颜料: **in oils** *Mostly I paint in oils.* 大多数情况下,我都用油画颜料作画。—see also 另见 **burn the midnight oil** (BURN[1] (24)), **pour oil on troubled waters** (POUR (8))

oil[2] *v* [T] **1** to put oil into or onto something, such as a machine, in order to make it work more smoothly 加油于…;给…加润滑油: *Isabel went upstairs to oil the attic lock and door hinges.* 伊莎贝尔上楼去给阁楼的锁和门的合叶上油。**2 oil the wheels** to help something to be done in business, politics etc successfully and easily 使某事顺利进行

oil-bear·ing /ˋ·,··/ *adj* oil-bearing rock contains oil〔岩石〕含油的

oil·cake /ˋɔɪlkek; ˈɔɪlkeɪk/ *n* [C] a type of food for cattle〔作牛饲料用的〕油渣饼

oil·can /ˋ··/ *n* [U] a metal container for oil with a long thin tube for pouring 油壶,加油罐

oil·cloth /ˋɔɪlˌklɔθ; ˈɔɪlklɒθ/ *n* [U] cloth treated with oil to give it a smooth surface 油布

oiled /ɔɪld; ɔɪld/ *adj* **well oiled** *BrE informal* very drunk【英,非正式】烂醉的

oil·field /ˋɔɪlˌfild; ˈɔɪlfiːld/ *n* [C] an area of land or sea under which there is oil 油田

oil-fired /ˋ··/ *adj* an oil-fired heating system burns oil to produce heat〔供暖系统〕燃油的,烧油的

oil·man /ˋɔɪlmæn; ˈɔɪlmæn/ *n plural* **oilmen** /-mən; -mən/ [C] someone who owns an oil company or works in the oil industry 石油商;石油工人

oil paint /ˋ··/ *n* [C,U] paint that contains oil 油漆;油性涂料;油画颜料

oil paint·ing /ˋ·,··/ *n* **1** [C] a picture painted with oil paint 油画 **2** [U] the art of painting with oil paint 油画艺术 **3 he's/she's no oil painting** *BrE humorous* used to say that someone is unattractive or ugly【英,幽默】某人一点都不漂亮

oil pan /ˋ··/ *n* [C] *AmE* a part of an engine that holds the supply of oil【美】〔发动机底部的〕油盘,润滑油箱; SUMP (2) *BrE*【英】

oil plat·form /ˋ·,··/ *n* [C] an oil rig 石油钻台[塔]

oil rig /ˋ··/ *n* [C] a large structure with equipment for getting oil from under the ground, especially from under the sea bottom〔尤指从海底取油的〕石油钻台[塔];油井设备

oil·seed rape /ˌɔɪlsid ˋrep; ˌɔɪlsiːd ˈreɪp/ *n* [U] RAPE[2] (3) 欧洲油菜

oil·skin /ˋɔɪlˌskɪn; ˈɔɪl-skɪn/ *n* **1** [U] cloth treated with oil so that water will not pass through it 防水油布 **2 oilskins** [plural] a coat and trousers made of oilskin 油布[防水布]衣裤

oil slick /ˋ··/ *n* [C] a layer of oil floating on water〔水面上的一层〕浮油

oil tank·er /ˋ·,··/ *n* [C] a ship that has large containers for carrying oil 油轮,运油船

oil well /ˋ··/ *n* [C] a hole that is dug in the ground to obtain oil 油井

oil·y /ˋɔɪlɪ; ˈɔɪli/ *adj* **1** covered with oil or containing a lot of oil 涂油的;含油的;油腻的: *oily skin* 油性皮肤 | *oily rags* 油腻的抹布 **2** looking or feeling like oil 似油的,油质的: *an oily liquid* 油质液体 **3** unpleasantly polite 圆滑的,会奉承人的,讨好的 —**oiliness** *n* [U]

oink /ɔɪŋk; ɔɪŋk/ *interjection* used to represent the sound that a pig makes 哼哼〔猪的叫声〕—**oink** *n* [C]

oint·ment /ˋɔɪntmənt; ˈɔɪntmənt/ *n* [C,U] a soft substance made of solid oil that you rub into your skin, especially as a medical treatment 油膏,软膏,药膏 —see also 另见 **fly in the ointment** (FLY[3] (5))

OJ /ˋo dʒe; ˈəʊ dʒeɪ/ *n* [U] *AmE informal* orange juice【美,非正式】橙汁,橘子汁

OK the written abbreviation of 缩写= OKLAHOMA

OK! *trademark* a British magazine which publishes pictures and articles about famous people【商标】《OK!》〔英国一杂志,主要刊登名人照片和相关文章〕

o·ka·pi /oˋkapɪ; əʊˈkɑːpi/ *n* [C] an African animal like a GIRAFFE, but with a shorter neck 獾㹢狓〔产于非洲,类似长颈鹿,但颈短〕

o·kay[1], **OK** /oˋke; əʊˈkeɪ/ *adj spoken*【口】**1** [not before noun 不用于名词前] not ill, injured, unhappy etc 身体好的;未受伤的;愉快的: *Do you feel OK now?* 现在你感觉好吗? **2** used to say that something is acceptable 行的,可以的: *"Sorry I'm late."*

"That's okay." "对不起, 我来晚了。" "没关系。" | *Does my hair look OK?* 我的头发看上去行吗? **3** [not before noun 不用于名词前] satisfactory but not extremely good 不错的, 还算满意的: *Well, it was OK, but I liked the other one better.* 嗯, 这个不错, 但我更喜欢那一个。**4 is it OK...?/...OK?** used to ask if you can do something or to tell someone they can do it …好吗?/…行吗?〔用于征求同意或表示允许〕: *Is it OK if I take Monday off?* 我星期一休假, 行吗? | *I'll go first, OK?* 我先走, 行吗? | **it is okay for sb to do sth** *It's okay for you to go home now.* 你现在可以回家了。| **it is okay with/by sb** *If it's OK with your mom, it's OK by me.* 如果你妈同意, 我也就没意见。**5** *especially AmE* nice, helpful, honest etc【尤美】很好的; 有用的; 诚实的: *Dwight's OK – you can trust him.* 德怀特是好人, 你可以信任他。| *an OK kind of guy* 一个挺好的小伙子 —**okay, OK** *adv*: *Mum's doing OK now.* 妈现在过得不错。| *Yeah, the TV's working okay.* 对, 这电视机性能不错。

1 **okay², OK** *interjection* **1** used when you start talking about something else, or when you pause before continuing 好(了)〔用于转换话题或停顿〕: *OK, let's go on to item B.* 好, 我们接着来看 B 项吧。| *OK, any questions so far?* 好, 到现在为止有什么问题吗? **2** used to express agreement or give permission 行, 可以〔用于表示同意或给予许可〕: *"Can I take the car today?" "Okay."* "今天我能用这车吗?" "可以。" **3** used to stop people arguing with you 行了, 好了〔用于停止他人与你争吵〕: *OK, OK, so I made a mistake, I've told you I'm sorry.* 好了, 好了, 是我出了错, 我已经跟你说对不起了。**4** used when you think people are being unreasonable 难道不是, 还要怎样〔用于认为他人不近情理时〕: *Look, I'm doing my best, OK?* 瞧, 我正拼命干着呢, 不是吗?

okay³, OK *v* **okayed, okaying** [T] *informal* to say officially that you will agree to something or allow it to happen【非正式】〔正式表明〕对…同意; 批准, 允许: *Has the bank okayed your request for a loan?* 银行批准你的贷款申请了吗?

okay⁴, OK *n informal* **give (sb) the okay/get the okay** to give or get permission to do something【非正式】给(某人)以批准/获得批准: *I got the OK to leave early today.* 我获准今天早走。

Frequencies of the word **okay** in spoken and written English 单词 okay 在英语口语和书面语中的使用频率

SPOKEN 口语

WRITTEN 书面语

200 300 400 500 1000 per million 每百万

Based on the British National Corpus and the Longman Lancaster Corpus 据英国国家语料库和朗文兰卡斯特语料库

This graph shows that the word **okay** is much more common in spoken English than in written English. 本图表显示, 单词 okay 在英语口语中的使用频率远远高于书面语。

OK Cor·ral, the /ˌo ke kəˈræl; ˌəʊ keɪ kəˈrɑːl/ a CORRAL (=an area surrounded by fences where animals can be kept) in the town of Tombstone, Arizona. In 1881 it was the scene of a famous GUNFIGHT in which Wyatt Earp fought with his brothers Morgan and Virgil, who was the Marshal of Tombstone, and with Doc Holliday, against a group of criminals called the Clanton GANG. Three of the Clantons were killed, and Virgil Earp lost his job as SHERIFF because the people believed that the Earps had murdered the Clantons.The phrase 'gunfight at the OK Corral' is sometimes used humorously when talking about a fight involving several people. 奥凯镇畜栏〔指亚利桑那州汤姆斯通镇一畜栏。1881 年, 此处发生过一场著名枪战。一方是汤姆斯通治安官怀雅特·厄普, 他的两个兄弟摩根和维吉尔以及霍利迪医生, 另一方是克兰顿匪帮。枪战中, 克兰顿匪帮有三人丧生。维吉尔·厄普丢了治安官一职, 因为镇上的人认为厄普三兄弟杀了人。有时, 人们诙谐地借用"奥凯镇畜栏大决斗" 这一短语表示几个人参加的打斗〕: *It was more like the gunfight at the OK Corral than a football game.* 这场比赛与其说是足球赛, 还不如说是奥凯镇畜栏大决斗。

O·kee·cho·bee /ˌokɪˈtʃobɪ; ˌəʊkɨˈtʃəʊbi/, **Lake** a large lake of fresh (=not containing salt) water in southern Florida, US. Water flows from it into the Atlantic Ocean through the Everglades. 奥基乔比湖〔美国佛罗里达州南部一大型淡水湖。湖水流经佛罗里达的大沼泽地注入大西洋〕

O'Keeffe /oˈkif; əʊˈkiːf/, **Georgia** (1887-1986) a US artist who painted large beautiful paintings of flowers and animal bones. Her later paintings were often influenced by the desert scenery of New Mexico, where she went to live. 奥基夫〔(1887-1986), 美国艺术家。其作品幅面较大, 画得漂亮好看, 入画之物有花卉和兽骨。她曾在新墨西哥州居住过, 晚期作品深受当地沙漠风光的影响〕

O·ke·fe·no·kee Swamp, the /ˌokɪfɪnokɪ ˈswɑmp; ˌəʊkɨfɨnəʊki ˈswɒmp/ a large area of SWAMP land in the US, in southeast Georgia and northeast Florida. It is the home of many ALLIGATORS and many kinds of snakes and birds. Most of the area is now included in the Okefenokee National Wildlife Refuge. 奥克弗诺基沼泽〔美国一大沼泽地, 位于佐治亚州东南部和佛罗里达州东北部。当地有许多短吻鳄及多种蛇类和鸟类。沼泽地的大部分现已划入奥克弗诺基国家野生生物保护区〕

o·key-doke /ˌokɪ ˈdok; ˌəʊki ˈdəʊk/ also 又作 **okey-do·key** /-ˈdokɪ; -ˈdəʊki/ *adj, adv spoken* used like 'okay' to express agreement【口】行, 好〔用法同 okay, 表示同意〕

Ok·i·na·wa /ˌokɪˈnawə; ˌɒkɨˈnɑːwə/ a Japanese island in the west Pacific Ocean, southwest of Kyushu, where an important battle took place between the US and Japan in 1945 near the end of World War II 冲绳岛〔太平洋西部日本一岛屿, 位于九州西南面。1945 年二战结束前夕, 美日双方在此进行过一场至关重要的决战〕

O·kla·ho·ma /ˌokləˈhomə; ˌəʊkləˈhəʊmə/ abbreviation 缩写为 **OK** a state in the Great Plains in the western central US, whose products include oil and grain. Oklahoma has a large Native American population. Its farmlands became part of the Dust Bowl in the 1930s, when very dry conditions forced many people to leave their farms and look for work in other places, especially California. 俄克拉何马州〔美国中西部大平原上一州, 出产石油和谷物。境内有大批印第安人。20世纪30年代, 该州的农场成为沙尘暴区的一部分。当时, 极度干旱的自然条件迫使许多人背井离乡去别处寻找工作, 尤其是去加利福尼亚州〕

Oklahoma! (1943) a MUSICAL (=a play that uses singing and dancing to tell a story) by Richard Rodgers and Oscar Hammerstein about people who moved to Oklahoma in the late 1800s. It was made into a successful film in 1955, and it includes many well-known songs, such as 'Oh What a Beautiful Morning!'《俄克拉何马之恋》〔(1943), 理查德·罗杰斯和奥斯卡·哈默斯坦合作的一部音乐剧, 讲述 19 世纪末一批人移居到俄克拉何马州的故事。1955年, 该剧被改编成一部优秀影片, 其中有许多著名歌曲, 如《啊, 清晨多美丽!》〕

Oklahoma Cit·y /ˌ····ˈ··/ the capital and largest city of the US state of Oklahoma. The city was established in one day in 1889, when 10,000 people went to the area and quickly put up tents, so that they could become the owners of land that had just been made available for settlers. 俄克拉何马城〔美国俄克拉何马州首府和最大城市。该城建于 1889 年。当年, 10,000 人在一日之内蜂拥而至, 搭起帐篷安顿下来, 以便成为刚刚可以认领的土地的主人〕

o·kra /ˈokrə; ˈɒkrə/ *n* [U] a green vegetable used in cooking in Asia and the southern US 秋葵〔亚洲和美国部用于烹调的一种绿色蔬菜〕—see picture on page A9 参见 A9 页图

old /old; əʊld/ *adj* 1 1

1 ▶USED OR NOT NEW 用过的或旧的◀ having existed for a long time, or having been used a lot before 古老的, 年代久远的; 用旧了的: *an old winter coat* 冬天穿的旧大衣 | *a big old house* 很大的老房子 | *an old saying* 古老的格言 | *My car's older than yours.* 我的汽车比你的旧。| **be (as) old as the hills** (=be extremely old) 极老的, 陈年老旧的

2 ▶NOT YOUNG 不年轻的◀ having lived for a long time 年老的, 年迈的: *an old man* 老人 | **get/grow old** (=become old) 变老, 上年纪 *The next time Robbie saw Mrs Dawes he thought she had grown very old.* 再次见到道斯夫人时, 罗比认为她已变得很老了。

3 the old old people 老(年)人: *taking care of the old and the sick* 照料老人和病人

4 ▶AGE 年龄◀ **be ... old** to be a particular age 有…岁: *How old are you?* 你多大年纪? | **be 5/10/50 etc years old** *Our house is 60 years old.* 我们的房子有 60 年了。| **5-year-old/10-year-old etc** *our 12-year-old son* 我们 12 岁大的儿子 | *a six-week-old baby* 六星期大的宝宝 | **old enough/too old** *I think you're old enough to make your own decisions.* 我认为你已经到了自己拿主意的年龄了。

5 old house/job/teacher etc a house, job etc that you had before but do not have now 从前的房子/工作/老师等: *I saw Phil with one of my old girlfriends.* 我看见菲尔和我以前的一个女朋友在一起。| *My old car didn't have air conditioning.* 我从前的那辆汽车没有空调。

6 he's old enough to be your father/she's old enough to be your mother *informal* used to say that someone is too old for someone to have a sexual relationship with【非正式】他都

能当你爸了/她都能当你妈了〔用于表示某人年龄过大，不适合成为性伴侣〕

7 be old beyond your years to be wiser or more sensible than most people your age 比你的实际年龄来得聪明[明智]

8 be old before your time to behave like someone much older than you, because bad things have happened to you〔因有过不好的经历而〕比你的实际年龄来得老成，未老先衰的，老气横秋的

9 sb is old enough to know better used to say that you think someone should have behaved more sensibly 某人已经长大该知好歹了

10 an old friend/enemy etc someone you have known for a long time 老朋友/夙敌等: *Bob's an old friend of mine.* 鲍勃是我的一个老朋友。

11 an old head on young shoulders a young person who seems to think and behave like an older person 少年老成

12 ►FAMILIAR 熟悉的◄ [only before noun 仅用于名词前] experienced, heard, or seen many times before; familiar 已经历[见闻]过多次的; 熟悉的: *It's good to get back into the old routine.* 还是恢复老一套的例行做法为好。| *the old familiar faces* 熟悉的老面孔 | **the same old** (=often used to say that you are bored with something) 老生常谈的〔常用于指对某事厌烦〕*We get tired of hearing the same old stuff.* 我们对这老一套都听烦了。—see also 另见 **it's the same old story** (STORY (10))

13 old flame someone with whom you used to have a romantic relationship 老相好，旧情人

14 the old country *especially AmE* the country that you were born in, but that you no longer live in, used especially to mean Europe【尤美】〔移民等的〕祖国，故国〔尤指欧洲国家〕

15 the old days times in the past 旧日的时光，以前: *In the old days people used to fetch water from the pump.* 过去，人们都用抽水泵来打水。

16 the good old days/the bad old days an earlier time in your life, or in history, when things seemed better or worse than now 过去的好/坏日子: *We like to chat about the good old days.* 我们喜欢聊聊过去的好时光。

17 of old a) *literary* long ago in the past【文】往日的，从前的: *in days of old* 在从前的日子 **b)** if you know someone of old you know them from a long time ago 从前，很久以前〔便认识某人〕

18 for old times' sake if you do something for old times' sake, you do it to remind yourself of a happy time in the past 看在旧日的情分上; 为了老交情; 为怀念往日之故

19 be/feel/look like your old self to feel or look better again after you have been ill or very unhappy 感觉/看上去恢复了正常状态: *Glad to see you looking more like your old self again.* 很高兴看到你又恢复过去的老样子。

20 Old English/Old Icelandic etc an early form of English, Icelandic etc 古英语/古冰岛语等

21 good old/poor old/silly old etc *spoken* used to talk to or about someone you are fond of【口】〔与喜欢之人说话或谈论喜欢之人的用语〕: *Good old Keith!* 老友基思! | *You poor old thing!* 你这个可怜的老东西!

22 the old... used to talk about something that you often use or are very familiar with 用惯了的; 很熟悉的: *So I got the old paint brushes out and set to work.* 于是，我拿出那些用惯了的漆刷，开始干活。

23 you old .../the old ... used to show that you are surprised or amused by what someone has said or done〔表示对某人所说或所做的事情感到吃惊或好笑的用语〕: *You told her that? You old liar!* 你把那事告诉她了?你这个老骗子! | *Don't ask him, the old miser.* 别求他，那个吝啬鬼!

24 old fool/old cow etc *spoken* used to talk about someone you do not like【口】老糊涂/讨厌鬼等〔用于谈论不喜欢之人〕: *the old bastard* 老杂种 | *silly old fool* 老糊涂

25 a good old also 又作 **a right old** *BrE spoken* used to talk about something you enjoy【英口】〔用于谈论欣赏之事〕: *We had a good old talk.* 我们畅快地聊了一阵子。

26 any old thing/hat/place etc *informal* used to say that it does not matter which thing, place etc you choose【非正式】随便哪个东西/帽子/地方等都行: *Oh, just wear any old thing.* 噢，就随便穿一件吧。| *You can't just turn up at any old time, you know.* 你知道，你不能随便找个时间就来。

27 any old how/way *informal* untidily or carelessly【非正式】不整洁地; 粗心地: *Put these away properly, don't shove them in any old how.* 把这些收拾利索，不要乱塞乱放。

28 pay/settle an old score to punish someone for something wrong that they did to you in the past 清算旧仇，了结宿怨

29 of the old school old-fashioned and believing in old ideas and customs 老派的，守旧的: *a real English lady of the old school* 地道的老派英国女士

30 old wives' tale a belief based on old ideas that are now considered to be untrue 愚蠢的信仰; 陈腐的思想; 无稽之谈

31 be an old hand at to have a lot of experience of something 是…的老手，在…方面经验老到: *I'm an old hand at this game.* 我是玩这种把戏的老手。

32 the old guard a group of people within an organization or club who do not like changes or new ideas〔机构、俱乐部等内的〕守旧派，保守派，保守分子: *The old guard will vote against letting women into the club.* 那些保守派将投票反对妇女加入俱乐部。

33 the Old Bill *BrE informal* the police【英，非正式】警察，警察当局 —see also 另见 **the old school tie** (SCHOOL TIE (2))

USAGE NOTE 用法说明: OLD

WORD CHOICE 词语辨析: **older, elder, elderly, senior citizen, OAP**

You can use **older** to describe either people or things. **Elder** means the same thing but you only use it to talk about people and usually only your close family. 可用 older 来描述人或事物。elder 意思相同，但只可用于人，而且通常只用于关系密切的家庭成员: *My elder/older daughter is at university.* 我的大女儿在上大学。| *Shane is the elder brother of the two.* 沙恩是两人中的哥哥。But you can also say 但也可以说: *elder members of the community* 社区中的年长成员

Older but not **elder** can be used with **than**. older 可与 than 连用，而 elder 则不能: *Shane is older than Mark* (NOT 不用 *elder than*). 沙恩比马克年龄大。

When you are talking about people, **elderly** (NOT 不用 *elder*) is a polite way of saying **old**. 当讲到人时，elderly（上了年纪的）比 old（老的）更有礼貌。Compare 比较 *an old church*（一座古老的教堂）and 和 *an old/elderly lady*（一位年老/上了年纪的女士）。Most people however now prefer to be called **senior citizens**, and this is the most common, polite, and acceptable expression to use. 但现在，大多数人更乐意被叫作 senior citizen（年长公民），这是最普遍、最礼貌和最能被接受的叫法。

In British English, especially in official notices, you might see OAP, which is short for 'old age pensioner'. 在英国英语中，尤其是在官方通告中，还可能会见到 OAP 一词，这是 old age pensioner（领取养老金者）的缩写。

old age /ˌ· ˈ·◄/ *n* [U] the part of your life when you are old 老年，晚年: *the effects of old age* 因年老而出现的问题 | **in your old age** *My aunt needed to be cared for in her old age.* 我姨母在晚年时需要照顾。

old age pen·sion /ˌ· · ˈ··/ *n* [U] *BrE* money paid regularly by the state to old people【英】〔政府付给的〕养老金; SOCIAL SECURITY (1) *AmE*【美】

old age pen·sion·er /ˌ· · ˈ···/ *n* [C] *BrE* someone who does not work any more and who receives an old age pension【英】领取养老金者 —see also 另见 OAP

Old Bai·ley, the /ˌold ˋbelɪ; ˌəʊld ˈbeɪli/ the most famous law court in the UK, officially called the Central Criminal Court. It is a CROWN COURT (=a court that deals with very serious crimes) in London, named after the street it is on. 老贝利刑事法院〔英国最著名的法院，正式名称为"中央刑事法庭"，位于伦敦，名称取自所在街道〕

old boy /ˈ· ·/ (for 适用于义项 1, 2), ˌ· ˈ· (for 适用于义项 3, 4)/ *n* [C] **1** *BrE* a man who used to be a student at a particular school【英】男校友，老同学: *an old boys' reunion* 男校友聚会 **2 the old-boy network** the system by which men from rich families, men who went to the same school, belong to the same club etc, use their influence to help each other 男校友关系网，男校友会 **3** *BrE spoken* an old man【英口】老汉，老头儿: *the old boy from down the road* 沿路走来的那位老头儿 **4** *BrE old-fashioned* a way of addressing a male friend【英，过时】老朋友，老兄〔对男性朋友的一种称呼〕: *How are you, old boy?* 你好吗，老朋友。—compare 比较 OLD GIRL

Old Curiosity Shop, The /ˌ· ˈ···· ˌ·/ (1841) a NOVEL by Charles Dickens about a girl called Little Nell and her grandfather, who are forced to leave their shop and give it to a cruel man called Quilp, because the grandfather owes him money. The scene at the end of the book in which Little Nell dies is famous for being very sad.《老古玩店》〔(1841)，查尔斯·狄更斯所著的一部小说。一个名叫小内尔的姑娘，她和爷爷不得不离开自家的老古玩店，把店转让给一个名叫奎尔普的凶残男人，因为老爷爷还不起欠他的钱。小说结尾部分小内尔死去的场景令人十分伤感，是一个有名的悲剧结局〕

old·e /ˈoldɪ; ˈəʊldi/ *adj* another spelling of old, used in the names of shops, products etc to make them seem traditional 老的〔old 的另一种拼写形式，用于商号、产品等名称，以示传统悠久〕: *ye olde tea shoppe* 老（字号）茶庄

old·en /ˈoldn̩; ˈəʊldən/ *adj* **in olden days/times** a long time ago 往昔，从前: *In olden times life was simpler.* 从前的生活比较简朴。

Ol·den·burg /ˈoldənbɝg; ˈəʊldənbɜːg/**, Claes** /klɔs; klɔːs/ (1929-) a US SCULPTOR, born in Sweden, important in the POP ART movement and famous for his large SCULPTURES of small ordinary objects, often made of soft materials 奥尔登伯格〔(1929-)，美国雕塑家，生于瑞典，在波普艺术运动中占有重要地位。他的雕塑以刻画小物件的大雕塑著称，小物件均以普通生活物品为原型，且常采用软性材料〕

Old En·glish Sheep·dog /ˌ· ·· ˈ·· / *n* [C] a large dog with long thick grey and white hair 老英格兰牧羊犬〔体型大，有长而密的灰白相间的毛发〕

CULTURAL NOTE 文化注释
In the UK, an Old English Sheepdog has appeared in advertisements for Dulux paint, and these dogs are sometimes called 'Dulux dogs' because of this. 在英国，因为有只老英格兰牧羊犬出现在多乐士油漆广告中，所以这种狗有时也被称为"多乐士狗"。

Old Faith·ful /ˌ· ˈ·· / a large GEYSER in Yellowstone National Park in the northwestern US, which sends a stream of hot water high up into the air about once every hour 老忠实喷泉〔美国西北部黄石国家公园一大型间歇喷泉，大约每隔一小时就喷发一次烫热的泉水〕

olde-world·e /ˌoldɪ ˈwɝldɪ; ˌəʊldi ˈwɜːldi◂/ *adj BrE informal* a place that is olde-worlde has been decorated so that it looks old-fashioned【英，非正式】古色古香的，古老奇趣的: *an olde-worlde country pub* 一家古色古香的乡村小酒馆

old-fash·ioned[1] /ˌ· ˈ··◂/ *adj* **1** not modern and considered not to be fashionable any more 旧式的，老式的；过时的: *Gwen's clothes are so old-fashioned!* 格温的衣服太过时了！| *'Wireless' is an old-fashioned word for 'radio'.* wireless（无线电）是 radio（收音机）的旧称。**2** someone who is old-fashioned believes in ways of doing things that are not usual any more〔人〕老派的，守旧的: *Dad's kind of old-fashioned in his views on sex before marriage.* 老爸对婚前性行为的看法有点守旧。 **3 an old-fashioned look/expression** *BrE old use* a disapproving look or expression【英旧】不以为然的目光/表情

old-fashioned[2] *n* [C] *AmE* an alcoholic drink made with WHISKEY【美】古典鸡尾酒〔用威士忌等调制的含酒精饮料〕

old fo·gey /ˌold ˈfogɪ; ˌəʊld ˈfəʊgi/ *n* [C] *informal* someone who is old, or has old-fashioned ideas about things【非正式】老家伙；极守旧的人，老顽固: *Oh come on, it's only 10 o'clock, don't be such an old fogey!* 喂，得啦！才10点钟，别那么死板嘛！

old folk /ˈ· ˌ·/ *BrE*【英】also 又作 **old folks** *especially AmE*【尤美】*n* [plural] an expression meaning old people, used especially when speaking of them in a kind way 老人，长辈: *We always try to do something for the old folk at Christmas.* 圣诞节时，我们总想着为老人家们做点事。

old folks' home /ˌ· ˈ· ˌ·/ *n* [C] *informal* an OLD PEOPLE'S HOME【非正式】养老院

old girl /ˈ· ·(for 适用于义项 1), ˌ· ˈ·(for 适用于义项 2)/ *n* [C] *BrE*【英】**1** a woman who is a former student of a particular school 女校友 **2** *spoken* an old woman【口】老妇人: *Don't tell me the old girl still drives!* 那老太太不至于还开车吧！—compare 比较 OLD BOY

Old Glo·ry /ˌ· ˈ··/ *n* [U] *AmE* the flag of the US【美】古老的荣耀〔指美国国旗〕

Old Har·ry /ˌ· ˈ··/ *n BrE old-fashioned* the devil【英，过时】"老哈里"〔指魔鬼〕

old hat /ˌ· ˈ·/ *adj* [not before noun 不用于名词前] familiar or old-fashioned, and therefore boring 旧式的；过时的；老套的: *Most of this is probably old hat to you, isn't it?* 对你来说，这其中大部分很可能是陈年老套了，是吗？

old·ie /ˈoldɪ; ˈəʊldi/ *n* [C] *informal* someone or something that is old【非正式】老人；古老的东西，陈旧之物: **oldie but goodie** *It's all nostalgia – they play the oldie-but-goodie records.* 这全是怀旧情愫——他们爱放那些经典的老唱片。—see also 另见 **golden oldie** (GOLDEN (6))

old·ish /ˈoldɪʃ; ˈəʊldɪʃ/ *adj* not very old, but not young or new either 有点老的；稍旧的

Old King Cole /ˌ· · ˈ·/ a character in a NURSERY RHYME (=an old song or poem for young children). 老国王科尔〔一首童谣中的人物〕The rhyme goes 该童谣唱道: *Old King Cole /Was a merry old soul, /And a merry old soul was he; /He called for his pipe, /And he called for his bowl, /And he called for his fiddlers three.* 老国王科尔 / 一位快乐的老顽童，/开心快乐当数他；/一会儿要烟斗，/一会儿要碗碟，/还叫人找来三位琴师。

Old Labour /ˌ· ˈ··/ an unofficial name used to talk about the British Labour Party before it was changed by Tony Blair in the 1990s. Old Labour was more LEFT WING, and supported the idea of increasing taxes to pay for public services such as education and health. 老工党〔非正式名称，指20世纪90年代托尼·布莱尔进行改革之前的英国工党。老工党较为左倾，主张提高税收以支付教育、医疗等公共事业项目的费用〕

old la·dy /ˌ· ˈ··/ *n slang*【俚】**1** an expression meaning someone's wife 老婆，妻子: *Gotta go home to my old lady, I guess.* 我想我要回家去会老婆了。**2** an expression meaning your mother 老娘，母亲

Old La·dy of Thread·nee·dle Street /ˌ· ˌ·· · ˈ··· ˌ·/ a NICKNAME for the Bank of England, which is in Threadneedle Street, London 针线街上的老妇人〔英格兰银行的诨名，因该银行位于伦敦针线街，故名〕

old lag /ˌ· ˈ·/ *n BrE old-fashioned* someone who has been in prison many times【英，过时】惯犯，多次坐牢的人

old maid /ˌ· ˈ·/ *n* [C] **1** an offensive expression meaning a woman who has never married and is not young any more 老姑娘，老处女〔具冒犯性的称呼〕**2** *informal* someone who pays too much attention to unimportant matters and has old-fashioned ideas【非正式】斤斤计较的人；思想保守的人；谨小慎微的人 —**old-maidish** *adj*

CULTURAL NOTE 文化注释
The STEREOTYPE of an old maid is of an unpleasant unattractive woman who is too concerned with unimportant details. She is typically thought of as being shocked by anything to do with sex, but there are also many jokes about old maids having sex with men who are not particularly interested or excited. 老处女的典型形象是相貌平平，不讨人喜欢，她们老是纠缠于鸡毛蒜皮的小事。人们认为，只要一提起性，老处女一般就会张皇失措。但也有不少笑话说老处女与男人发生性关系，尽管这些男人对她们并没有特别的感觉和激情。

old man /ˌ· ˈ·/ *n* [C] **1** *slang* an expression meaning someone's husband【俚】老公，丈夫: *I heard her old man beats her.* 我听说她老公经常打她。**2** *slang* an expression meaning your father【俚】老爹，父亲 **3** *BrE old-fashioned* used to address a male friend【英，过时】老兄，伙计，老朋友〔用于称呼男性朋友〕: *Could I have a word with you, old man?* 我可以和你谈一下吗，老兄？

Old Man of the Sea, The /ˌ· · · · ˈ·/ a character in the story of *'Sinbad the Sailor'* in *The Arabian Nights*, who persuades Sinbad to carry him on his back, and then twists his legs around Sinbad so that Sinbad cannot get him off. Sinbad makes the old man drunk, gets him off his back, and kills him. 海中老人〔《天方夜谭》中"水手辛巴德"故事里的一个人物。海中老人劝说辛巴德把他背在背上，接着用双腿缠住他的身体，以免辛巴德甩掉他。后来，辛巴德把老家伙给灌醉了，把他从背上弄下来杀死〕

old mas·ter /ˌ· ˈ··/ *n* [C] a famous painter, especially from the 15th to 18th century, or a painting by one of these painters〔尤指15至18世纪的〕古典名画家（作品）: *a priceless collection of old masters* 一批古典名画家的珍贵收藏品

Old Moore's Almanack /ˌ· · ˈ· ···/ a small British ALMANAC (=a book giving information about the movement of the sun and moon, the times of the tides etc) which is produced each year and sold in large numbers. It also makes PREDICTIONS (=saying what will probably happen in the future) based on such things as the position of the planets in the sky. Its predictions are often about political events or famous people. 老穆尔历书〔英国一小型历书，每年出版，销路很好。该书根据天体中行星的位置主要对政治事件或知名人士作出预测〕

Old Moth·er Hub·bard /ˌ· ·· ˈ··/ a character in a NURSERY RHYME (=an old song or poem for young children). 哈伯德老妈〔童谣中的一个人物〕The rhyme goes 该童谣唱道: *Old Mother Hubbard / Went to the cupboard / To get her poor dog a bone; / But when she came there / The cupboard was bare, / And so the poor dog had none.* 哈伯德老妈，/走到橱柜边，/想找根骨头喂狗儿;/但往橱门里一看，里面什么也没有，/可怜狗儿空喜欢。The expression 'the cupboard is bare' is sometimes used about a situation in which a person, organization, or government has no money left.〔"橱柜里什么也没有"这一说法有时用来指个人、组织或政府面临囊空如洗的状况〕

Old Nick /ˌ·ˈ·/ *n BrE old-fashioned* the devil【英, 过时】"老尼克"〔指魔王或魔鬼〕

old peo·ple's home /ˌ·ˈ··ˌ·/ *n* [C] a place where old people live together and are cared for 养老院, 老人院

Old Pre·tend·er, the /ˌ·ˈ··/ —see 见 James Edward STUART

old salt /ˌ·ˈ·/ *n* [C] *old-fashioned* a SAILOR who has had a lot of experience of sailing【过时】有经验的老水手

old·ster /ˈoldstɚ; ˈəʊldstə/ *n* [C] *informal* an old person【非正式】老家伙, 老年人

Old Tes·ta·ment, the /ˌ·ˈ···◂/ *n* the first part of the Christian Bible containing ancient Hebrew writings about the time before the birth of Christ〔《圣经》的〕《旧约全书》—compare 比较 NEW TESTAMENT

old tim·er /ˌ·ˈ··/ *n* [C] **1** someone who has been in a particular job, place etc for a long time and knows a lot about it 老资格的人, 老前辈, 老手 **2** *especially AmE* an old man【尤美】老人, 上了年纪的人

Old Vic, the /ˌold ˈvɪk; ˌəʊld ˈvɪk/ a theatre in South London, famous especially for its productions of plays by William Shakespeare 老维克剧院〔南伦敦一剧场, 尤以上演威廉·莎士比亚的戏剧而闻名〕

old wom·an /ˌ·ˈ··/ *n BrE slang*【英俚】**1 the old woman** an offensive expression meaning someone's wife or mother 老婆; 老娘〔具冒犯性的说法〕**2** [C] a man who pays too much attention to unimportant details 斤斤计较[婆婆妈妈]的男人—**old womanish** *adj*

Old Wom·an Who Lived in a Shoe, The /ˌ·ˌ···ˌ···ˈ·/ a character in a NURSERY RHYME (=old song or poem for children) 住在鞋里的老妇人〔童谣中的一个人物〕, which starts 该童谣唱道: *There was an old woman who lived in a shoe,/Who had so many children she didn't know what to do /...* 有位老妇人, 住在鞋子里, /孩子养得多, 她不知所措 /...

Old World, the /ˌ·ˈ·◂/ *n old use* the Eastern Hemisphere, especially Europe, Asia and Africa【旧】旧世界, 东半球〔尤指欧洲、亚洲和非洲〕—compare 比较 NEW WORLD

old-world /ˈ··/ *adj* [only before noun 仅用于名词前] an old-world place or quality is attractive because it is old or reminds you of the past〔地方、品质等〕老式的, 古色古香的: *the old-world charm of the village* 那村庄古朴的魅力

ole /ol; əʊl/ *adj* used in written English to represent the way some people say 'old' 老的〔英语书面语中用以表示一些人说old的方式〕: *The poor ole guy!* 可怜的老家伙!

o·le·ag·i·nous /ˌolɪˈædʒənəs; ˌəʊliˈædʒɪnəs/ *adj technical* containing, producing, or like oil【术语】含油的; 产油的; 油质的

o·le·an·der /ˌolɪˈændɚ; ˌəʊliˈændə/ *n* [C,U] a green bush with white, red, or pink flowers 夹竹桃

O lev·el /ˈo ˌlɛvl; ˈəʊ ˌlevəl/ *n* **1** [U] Ordinary level; an examination taken in schools in England and Wales before 1988, usually at the age of 16 O级, 普通级 (考试)〔指英格兰和威尔士在1988年前对中学生进行的考试, 考生年龄通常在16岁〕**2** [C] one of these examinations in a particular subject〔某一学科的〕O级证书考试, 普通级证书考试: *He left school with five O levels.* 他毕业时通过了五门学科的普通级证书考试。| *O level German* 普通级证书的德语考试 —compare 比较 A LEVEL, GCSE

ol·fac·to·ry /ɑlˈfæktərɪ; ɒlˈfæktəri/ *adj technical* connected with the sense of smell【术语】嗅觉的: *the olfactory ducts* 嗅觉管

ol·i·gar·chy /ˈɑlɪˌgɑrkɪ; ˈɒlɪgɑːki/ *n* **1** [U] government or control by a small group of people 寡头政治; 寡头统治 **2** [C usually singular 一般用单数] a state governed by a small group of people, or the group who govern such a state 寡头统治的国家; 寡头政治集团—**oligarch** *n* [C]

O Lit·tle Town of Beth·le·hem /ˌ·ˌ··ˌ·ˈ···/ the title and first words of a Christmas CAROL (=a traditional religious song).《美哉, 小城伯利恒》〔一首圣诞颂歌的曲名和首句〕It begins 开首是: *O little town of Bethlehem,/How still we see thee lie,/Above thy deep and dreamless sleep,/The silent stars go by.* 美哉, 小城伯利恒, /瞧你何等宁静! /沉然安眠, 无梦无惊, /群星悄然前行。

ol·ive /ˈɑlɪv; ˈɒlɪv/ *n* **1** [C] a tree grown in Mediterranean countries that has small bitter egg-shaped fruits, usually black or green 橄榄树: *an olive grove* 一片橄榄树林 **2** [C] the fruit of this tree, used for food and also for its oil〔作食品或榨油用的〕橄榄 **3** a deep yellowish green colour 橄榄色, 黄绿色, 茶青色 —see picture on page A5 参见A5页图 **4 olive skin/complexion** skin colour that is yellowish brown 橄榄色的皮肤/肤色 **5 offer/hold out/extend the olive branch** to do something to show that you want to end an argument 伸出橄榄枝〔做某事以表示愿意和解〕—**olive** *adj*: *an olive sweatshirt* 橄榄色的圆领长袖运动衫

olive drab /ˌ··ˈ·/ *n* [U] *especially AmE* a greyish green colour, used especially in military uniforms【尤美】草绿色〔尤指军服颜色〕—**olive drab** *adj*

olive oil /ˌ··ˈ·/ *n* [U] a pale yellow or green oil obtained from olives and used in cooking 橄榄油

Ol·i·ver Twist /ˌɑlɪvɚ ˈtwɪst; ˌɒlɪvə ˈtwɪst/ (1837-38) a NOVEL by Charles Dickens about a poor boy called Oliver Twist. The most famous scene in the book takes place in the WORKHOUSE when Oliver holds out his bowl and asks for more food, but is punished instead. He runs away to London and then lives with Fagin, the leader of a group of young thieves who include the Artful Dodger.《奥利弗·特威斯特》, 又译《雾都孤儿》〔(1837-1838), 查尔斯·狄更斯创作的一部小说, 讲述一个名叫奥利弗·特威斯特的穷孩子的故事。书中最著名的一幕发生在济贫院, 当奥利弗伸出碗想再要点吃的时候, 他得到的却是惩罚。于是, 他逃到了伦敦, 与费金一起生活。费金是一帮少年小偷的头目, 其中一个小偷叫"逮不着的机灵鬼"〕

Olives, the Mount of —see 见 the MOUNT OF OLIVES

O·liv·i·er, Laur·ence /əˈlɪvɪe; əˈlɪvieɪ, ˈlɔrəns; ˈlɒrəns/ (1907-89) a British actor officially called Lord Olivier, who worked in the theatre and cinema for over 50 years and is one of the greatest actors of the 20th century. He is famous for directing and acting in three films of plays by Shakespeare: *Henry V* (1944), *Hamlet* (1948), and *Richard III* (1956). Other films include *Wuthering Heights* (1939), *Rebecca* (1940), and *Marathon Man* (1976). He was also the first DIRECTOR of the National Theatre in London. 奥利弗〔(1907-1989), 英国演员, 正式称奥利弗勋爵。他从事戏剧与电影表演长达50多年, 被认为是20世纪最伟大的演员之一。他自导、自演了三部由莎士比亚剧本改编的影片, 并以此知名, 即《亨利五世》(1944)、《哈姆雷特》(1948) 和《理查三世》(1956)。他导演的其他影片有《呼啸山庄》(1939)、《蝴蝶梦》(1940) 和《霹雳钻》(1976)。他还是伦敦国家剧院的首任院长〕

-ol·o·gist /ɑlədʒɪst; ɒlədʒɪst/ also 又作 **-logist** *suffix* [in nouns 构成名词] a person who studies or specializes in a particular kind of science …学家: *a biologist* 生物学家

-ology /ɑlədʒɪ; ɒlədʒi/ also 又作 **-logy** *suffix* [in nouns 构成名词] **1** the scientific study of something …学, 学科: *geology* (=the study of rocks and the Earth) 地质学 | *climatology* (=the study of CLIMATE) 气候学 | *Egyptology* (=the study of ancient Egypt) 古埃及学 **2** *informal* something that is done or talked about as though it was a scientific study【非正式】…学科, 学说〔把某物说成是一门学说似的〕: *futurology* (=the practice of trying to say how the future will develop) 未来学 **3** the things studied by a particular science〔某种科学研究的〕对象: *The geology of north Devon is particularly interesting* (=it has interesting rocks, etc). 德文郡北部的地质格外有意思。—**-ological** /əlɑdʒɪkl; əlɒdʒɪkəl/ *suffix* [in adjectives 构成形容词]—**-ologically** /əlɑdʒɪklɪ; əlɒdʒɪkli/ *suffix* [in adverbs 构成副词]: *geologically interesting* 地质上有趣的

O·lym·pi·a /əˈlɪmpɪə; əˈlɪmpiə/ **1** an area of flat land and an ancient religious centre in the west of the Peloponnese in Greece, where the Olympic Games were held in ancient times 奥林匹亚〔希腊伯罗奔尼撒半岛西部一平原和古代宗教中心。古时的奥林匹克运动会即在此举行〕**2** a set of large buildings in West London, used for exhibitions 奥林匹亚〔位于西伦敦的一组大型建筑, 常用来举办各种展览会〕**3** the capital city of the US state of Washington 奥林匹亚市〔美国华盛顿州首府〕

O·lym·pi·ad /əˈlɪmpɪˌæd; əˈlɪmpi-æd/ *n* [C] *formal* a particular occasion of the modern Olympic Games【正式】〔现代〕奥林匹克运动会: *Welcome to the games of the 23rd Olympiad.* 欢迎光临第23届奥运会。

O·lym·pi·an[1] /əˈlɪmpɪən; əˈlɪmpiən/ *n* one of the ancient Greek Gods 奥林匹斯山诸神之一

Olympian[2] *adj* **1** like a god, especially by being calm and not concerned about ordinary things 神仙般逍遥自在的, 超脱世俗的: *to view the world with an Olympian detachment* 以一种超然的态度看待世界 **2** connected with the ancient Greek gods 奥林匹斯山诸神的

O·lym·pic /əˈlɪmpɪk; əˈlɪmpɪk/ *adj* [only before noun 仅用于名词前] connected with the Olympic Games 奥运会的: *an Olympic runner* 奥运会赛跑选手

Olympic Games /ˌ·ˌ··ˈ·/ *n* [plural] **1** an international sports event held every four years in different countries 奥林匹克运动会〔每四年一次在不同国家举行〕**2** a sports event held at Olympia in Greece every four years in ancient times〔古希腊〕奥林匹克竞技会〔每四年在奥林匹亚城举行一次〕

O·lym·pics /əˈlɪmpɪks; əˈlɪmpɪks/ *n* [plural] the Olympic Games 奥林匹克运动会

O·lym·pus /ə`lɪmpəs; ə'lɪmpəs/ also 又作 **Mount Olympus** a mountain in northern Greece, the highest mountain in Greece. In Greek MYTHOLOGY, it was the place where the gods lived. 奥林匹斯山〔位于希腊北部, 希腊境内最高的山, 希腊神话中众神的住所〕

OM /,o`ɛm; ,əʊ'em/ *n* [C] the abbreviation of 缩写= the ORDER OF MERIT

O·magh /o`mɑr; əʊ'mɑː/ a town in Northern Ireland which became well known in 1998 when a terrorist group called 'the Real IRA' planted a bomb there, killing 29 people 奥马〔北爱尔兰一城镇。1998年, 一帮自称"真爱尔兰共和军"的恐怖主义分子在此埋设了一枚炸弹, 结果炸死29人。该镇因此广为人知〕

O·man /o`mæn; əʊ'mɑːn/ a country in the Middle East, east of Saudi Arabia and northeast of Yemen. Population: 2,622,000 (2001). Capital: Muscat. Oman is a SULTANATE. Its people are Muslims, and its main product is oil. 阿曼〔中东一国家, 位于沙特阿拉伯以东、也门东北。人口: 2,622,000 (2001), 首都: 马斯喀特。阿曼是一个苏丹统治的国家, 国民为穆斯林, 主要物产是石油〕 —**Omani** *n, adj*

O·mar Khay·yám /,omɑr kaɪ`jɑm; ,əʊmɑː kaɪ'æm/ (?1048-?1123) a Persian MATHEMATICIAN and poet. He is famous in the west for his romantic poem, the *Rubaiyat*, produced in a popular English translation by Edward Fitzgerald in 1859, which is mainly about love, nature and pleasure. 欧玛尔·海亚姆〔(?1048-?1123), 波斯数学家、诗人。他以浪漫诗歌《鲁拜集》享誉西方。1859年, 爱德华·菲茨杰拉德将其译成英文, 广受欢迎。主要涉及爱情、自然与享乐三个主题〕

OMB, the /,o ɛm `bi; ,əʊ em 'biː/ the abbreviation of 缩写= the OFFICE OF MANAGEMENT AND BUDGET

om·buds·man /`ɑmbudzmən; 'ɒmbʊdzmən/ *n* [C] someone who deals with complaints made by ordinary people against the government, banks, insurance companies etc 民情调查员, 巡视官, 申诉专员〔专门处理民众对政府、银行、保险公司等投诉的人〕

o·me·ga /o`mɛgə; 'əʊmɪ̈gə/ *n* [C] the last letter of the Greek alphabet 奥米伽〔希腊字母表的最后一个字母〕

ome·lette also 又作 **omelet** *AmE*【美】/`ɑmlɪt; 'ɒmlɪ̈t/ *n* [C] **1** eggs mixed together and cooked in hot fat, sometimes with other foods added 煎蛋卷, 摊鸡蛋: *a cheese omelette* 乳酪煎蛋卷 **2 you can't make an omelette without breaking eggs** used to say that it is impossible to do something important without causing problems 要煎蛋卷就得打破鸡蛋, 有失才有得〔指要做大事必会引起一些问题〕

o·men /`omən; 'əʊmən/ *n* [C] a sign of what will happen in the future 前兆, 预兆, 兆头: **a good/bad/ill omen** *The sudden change in weather seemed to Frank to be a good omen.* 对弗兰克来说, 天气突变似乎是个好兆头。—see also 另见 ILL-OMENED

om·i·nous /`ɑmənəs; 'ɒmɪ̈nəs/ *adj* making you feel that something bad is going to happen〔使人感到〕不吉利的, 不祥的: *The car is making an ominous rattling sound.* 汽车在发出一种不祥的卡嗒卡嗒声。—**ominously** *adv*: *The sky looked ominously dark.* 天空黑沉沉的, 像要变天。

o·mis·sion /o`mɪʃən; əʊ'mɪʃən/ *n* **1** [U] the act of not including or not doing something 省略; 删节; 遗漏: *The omission of her name was not a deliberate act.* 她的名字不是故意遗漏的。**2** [C] something that has been omitted 省略的东西; 遗漏的东西: *It was one of many errors and omissions pushing up the cost of the road works.* 有许多失误和疏漏造成了道路施工费用的增加, 而这只是其中之一。| **a glaring omission** (=one that is very bad and easily noticed) 显而易见的严重疏忽

o·mit /o`mɪt; əʊ'mɪt/ **omitted, omitting** *v* [T] **1** to not include someone or something, either deliberately or because you forget to do it; **leave out** (LEAVE[1]) 省去, 略去, 删去; 遗漏: *Please don't omit any details, however trivial they may seem.* 请勿省略任何细节, 不管这些细节看似多么琐碎。**2 omit to do sth** *formal* to not do something, either because you forgot or deliberately【正式】忘记做某事; 故意不做某事: *Oliver omitted to mention that he was married.* 奥利弗没有提及他已结婚。

om·ni- /ɑmnɪ; ɒmnɪ/ *prefix* everything or everywhere; all 一切; 到处; 全部: *an omnivore* (=animal that eats all sorts of food) 杂食动物

om·ni·bus /`ɑmnɪbəs; 'ɒmnɪbəs/ *n* [C] *especially BrE*【尤英】**1** a book containing several stories, especially by one writer, that have already been printed separately〔尤指某作家的〕选集, 文集; 汇编 **2** a radio or television programme made of several programmes that have previously been broadcast separately 节目荟萃, 多集节目的一次播出〔由曾分别播出过的几个节目组成的广播或电视节目〕: *the Brookside omnibus* 布鲁克塞德节目荟萃 **3** *old use* a bus【旧】公共汽车

om·nip·o·tent /ɑm`nɪpətənt; ɒm'nɪpətənt/ *adj formal* able to do everything【正式】全能的 —**omnipotence** *n* [U]: *God's omnipotence* 上帝的全能

om·ni·pres·ent /,ɑmnɪ`prɛznt; ,ɒmnɪ'prezənt◂/ *adj formal* present everywhere at all times【正式】〔任何时候都〕无所不在的; 普遍存在的 —**omnipresence** *n* [U]

om·nis·ci·ent /ɑm`nɪʃənt; ɒm'nɪʃənt/ *adj formal* knowing everything【正式】无所不知的, 全知的: *Only God is omniscient.* 唯有上帝是无所不知的。—**omniscience** *n* [U]

om·ni·vore /`ɑmnɪvɔr; 'ɒmnɪ̈vɔː/ *n* [C] *technical* an animal that eats both meat and plants【术语】杂食动物, 肉草兼食的动物

om·niv·o·rous /ɑm`nɪvərəs; ɒm'nɪvərəs/ *adj technical*【术语】**1** an animal that is omnivorous eats both meat and plants〔动物〕杂食性的, 肉草兼食的 **2** interested in everything, especially in all books 对什么都感兴趣的; 〔尤指〕什么书都看的: *an omnivorous reader* 什么书都读的人

on[1] /ɑn; ɒn/ *prep* **1** touching or being supported by a particular surface 在…上〔表示接触或由某一表面支撑着〕: *The plate's on the table.* 盘子在桌上。| *You have mud on your shoes.* 你的鞋子上有泥。| *The answer is written on page 25.* 答案在第25页上。—see picture on page A1 参见A1页图 **2** hanging from, supported by or connected to a particular thing 自…悬下; 由…支持; 与…连接[有联系]: *Stand on one foot.* 用单脚站立。| *pictures stuck on the wall* 贴在墙上的图画 | *a ball on a string* 吊在绳上的球 **3 a)** in a particular place, building or area of land 在〔某个场所、建筑物或地区〕内: *Several bombs landed on the runway.* 几颗炸弹落在飞机跑道上。| *He grew up on a ranch in California.* 他在加利福尼亚的一个大牧场上长大。**b)** *AmE* in a particular road【美】在〔某条道路、街道〕上: *We live on Mulberry Drive.* 我们住在马尔伯里大道。| *I met Amy on the street the other day.* 前几天我在街上遇到了埃米。**4** in a particular direction 向…, 朝…方向: *On my right sat the Chancellor.* 我的右边坐着校长。| *As the troops marched on the city, the leaders planned their escape.* 大军向该城市进发时, 那些头脑人物已筹划好逃跑了。**5** used to show the person or thing affected by an action or someone's behaviour 受〔某种行动或某人行为〕的影响: *a tax on cigarettes* 烟草税 | *The divorce has had a particularly bad effect on the children.* 离婚已对孩子们造成了极坏的影响。**6** on one of the sides of something such as a river or road 在〔河流或道路等的〕一边: *a cafe on the river* 河边的咖啡馆 | *a beautiful village on the Austrian border* 位于奥地利边界的美丽村庄 | *trees on both sides of the street* 街道两旁的树 **7 on Friday/August 2nd/my birthday** at some time during a particular day 在星期五/8月2日/我的生日: *They arrive on Tuesday.* 他们于星期二到达。| *I was born on July 1st.* 我出生于7月1日。**8** about a particular subject 关于〔某一主题〕: *a book on India* 一本关于印度的书 | *advice on what to wear* 关于衣着方面的建议 **9** in a bus, train, aircraft etc 乘坐〔公共汽车、火车、飞机等〕: *Everyone on the plane was frightened.* 飞机上所有的人都被吓坏了。| *He managed to be on the first train back to London.* 他设法坐上了返回伦敦的头班火车。—see also 另见 **on foot** (FOOT[1](2)), **on horseback** (HORSEBACK) **10** used to say what food someone needs to survive, what FUEL[1](1) something needs to operate etc 以〔某种食物〕为生; 靠〔某种燃料〕运转: *We can't live on rice and water forever.* 我们不能总以大米和水来过日子。| *Many cars nowadays run on lead free petrol.* 如今许多汽车都用无铅汽油(为燃料)来行驶。**11** used to say what money people use to live, the amounts of money someone earns etc 靠〔某种钱财〕为生; 赚〔钱的数额〕: *Some families in the ghettos have been on welfare all their lives.* 贫民区的一些家庭终生靠福利救济金过活。| *People on high salaries should pay more tax.* 高薪人士应该多纳税。**12** *informal* used to say that someone takes a particular drug or medicine【非正式】吸食〔毒品〕; 服用〔药物〕: *Since she's been on Prozac she's been a different person.* 自从服用"百忧解"抗抑郁药以来, 她完全变了一个人。**13 on the radio/telephone** using a radio or telephone 使用收音机/电话: *Shut up! I'm on the phone.* 别说话! 我在打电话呢。**14 on a trip/journey etc** during a trip, journey etc 在旅途中: *I met several people on the voyage.* 在这次航行中, 我结识了好几个人。| *On my way to work the car broke down.* 在去上班的路上, 我的汽车坏了。**15** used to say what has been used to do something 使用…〔做某事〕: *Phil had torn his shirt on a nail.* 菲尔的衬衫被钉子划破了。| *It's amazing what you can do on these new word processors.* 这些新的文字处理器的功能真让人不可思议。**16** *formal* immediately after something has happened or after someone has done something【正式】一…就, 在…后立即: **on doing sth** *On hearing the news of the air attack most foreigners headed for the border.* 一听到空袭的消息, 大多数外国人便涌向边境。| **on arrival/sb's return etc** *On arrival at*

reception, guests should sign the visitors' book. 客人一到接待处就要在来宾签名簿上签名。| **on sth** *On the general's command, all soldiers must salute.* 一听到将军的命令，全体士兵必须立即敬礼。**17** used to say that someone is a member of a team, organization etc 是…的成员: *What team did you say your boyfriend was on?* 你说你的男朋友是什么球队的? **18** compared with another person or thing 与〔其他人或东西〕相比较: *This essay is a definite improvement on your last one.* 与上一篇相比，你这篇文章有了明显的改进。| *Sales are 10% up on last year.* 销量比去年增加了10%。**19 have/carry etc sth on you** *informal* to have a particular thing in your pocket, your bag etc【非正式】有/携带某物在身上: *How much cash do you have on you?* 你身上带了多少现金? **20** *spoken* used to say that someone will pay for something such as a drink, a meal etc【口】由某人支付〔饮料、饭菜等的费用〕: *Drinks are on Harold!* 喝酒由哈罗德请客! **21** *informal* if a machine stops, breaks etc on you, it stops or breaks while you are using it【非正式】在〔某人〕使用时出现故障: *Suddenly the telephone went dead on me.* 我的电话突然断了。

S1 W1 **on²** *adj, adv* [not before noun 不用于名词前] **1** used to say that someone continues to do something or something continues to happen, without stopping 继续的[地]; 不停的[地]: **play/read/talk etc on** (=to continue playing, reading etc) 继续玩耍/阅读/谈话等 *Both teams managed to play on into overtime, despite the blistering heat.* 尽管天气炎热，两队都坚持不懈，进入了加时赛。| **carry/ keep/go on etc doing sth** *If you keep on eating like that you'll need to diet.* 如果照那样吃下去，你就得节食了。| **carry/keep/go on etc** *Carry on. You're doing very well.* 坚持下去，你干得很好。**2** if you move, walk etc on, you move forward to a particular place (再) 往前，向前: *If you walk on a little, you can see the coast.* 再往前走一点，你就会看见海岸了。| *You can have your letters sent on to you at your new address.* 你可以把信件转到你的新地址。| **straight on** *Keep straight on and turn left at the bank.* 一直往前走，到了银行向左拐弯。**3** used to say that something happens at a time that is before or after another time〔指某事发生的时间〕早于或晚于另一时间: **earlier/later on** *Later on we learned that he got back to France safely.* 后来我们得知，他平安回到了法国。| **from then on/from that day on etc** *From that moment on I never believed a word she told me.* 自那一刻起，我不再相信她跟我说的任何一句话。**4** if you have something on, you are wearing it 穿[戴]上: *Put your coat on. It's freezing outside.* 穿上大衣吧，外面冷极了。| *The poor child had absolutely nothing on.* 那可怜的孩子身上一丝不挂。**5** in a bus, train, aircraft etc 上〔汽车、火车、飞机等〕: *The bus stopped and everyone rushed to get on.* 公共汽车停下来后，人们一拥而上。**6** if a machine, light etc is on, it is operating〔机器、灯等〕工作[运转]着的: *Who left the hot water faucet on?* 谁让热水龙头开着? | *The TV's on but nobody seems to be watching it.* 电视开着，但好像没人在看。—opposite 反义词 OFF¹ (4) **7** if a film, TV programme etc is on, it is being broadcast or shown at a theatre〔电影、电视节目等〕正在播放[放映]的: *That new sitcom is on tonight.* 那部新拍的情景喜剧将于今晚播映。**8** if an event is on, it is happening or will still happen 正在[将要]发生: *There's a jazz festival on in Vancouver this week.* 本周在温哥华要举行爵士音乐节。| *Are you sure the party's on for tonight?* 你肯定聚会是今晚举行吗? **9 have a lot on** *informal* to be very busy【非正式】十分忙碌: *We don't have much on at the moment. I could see you tomorrow.* 我们眼下不怎么忙，明天我可以见你。**10 be on at sb** *informal* to keep asking someone to do something, so that they become annoyed【非正式】向某人唠叨，不停地催促某人〔做某事〕: *Mildred's been on at him to fix that cupboard for weeks now.* 米尔德丽德要他修理那个碗柜，都唠叨了好几个星期了。**11 be/go on about sth** *informal BrE* to keep talking about something, in a way that is boring【非正式，英】〔令人生厌地〕不断谈论某事: *Will you stop going on about that goal! It was definitely a penalty.* 你别再唠叨那个进球啦! 那肯定是个点球。**12 on and off** also 又作 **off and on** if you do something during a period of time on and off, you do it for several short periods in that time but not continually 断断续续地，间歇地: *He's been smoking for 10 years now, on and off.* 到现在，他吸烟断断续续已有10年了。**13 it's not on** *spoken BrE* used to say that you do not think something is socially acceptable or reasonable【口，英】这不可以，这不能接受，这不合理: *It's not on, is it? Leaving your children alone like that.* 这是说不过去的，不是吗? 就那样把你的孩子撇下不管。**14 head on/full on** if two things hit each other head on, they hit the front part of each other, usually very hard 迎面地，迎头地: *Both cars skidded, crashing head on at 80 miles an hour.* 两辆车都打滑了，以每小时80英里的速度迎头相撞。**15** if an actor is on, they are performing〔演员〕正在演出，在表演中: *You're on in two minutes.* 你两分钟后上场。

on-air /ˈ· ·/ *adj* [only before noun 仅用于名词前] broadcast while actually happening 现场直播的: *an on-air interview* 现场采访

O·nas·sis /oˈnæsɪs; əʊˈnæsɪs/, **Aristotle** /ˈærɪstɑtl; ˈærɪstɒtl/ (1906-75) a Greek ship owner, famous for being extremely rich, who married Jackie Kennedy, the WIDOW of US President John F. Kennedy, in 1968. Before that he had a long relationship with Maria Callas. 奥纳西斯〔(1906-1975)，希腊船王，以极为富有而著称。1968年，他与美国总统约翰·F.肯尼迪的遗孀杰奎琳·肯尼迪结婚。此前，他与玛丽亚·卡拉斯有过很长一段时间的情人关系〕

O

Onassis, Jackie —see 见 Jackie KENNEDY

once¹ /wʌns; wʌns/ *adv* S1 W1

1 ▶ONE TIME 一次◀ on one occasion 一次，一回: *I've only met her once.* 我只见过她一面。| **once before** *Paul's been to Wexford once before.* 保罗曾去过韦克斯福德一次。

2 once a week/year etc one time every week etc as a regular activity 每周/每年等一次: *We do aerobics once a week.* 我们每周做一次有氧健身操。

3 at once a) immediately or without delay 立刻，马上: *Young lady, get upstairs and clean your room at once!* 小姐，赶快上楼去打扫你的房间! **b)** at the same time, together 同时; 一起: *Don't all talk at once.* 不要同时都发言。

4 all at once if something happens all at once, it happens suddenly when you do not expect it 一下子; 突然: *All at once there was a loud banging on the door.* 突然传来一记重重的敲门声。

5 once more one more time or again 再一次: *Can we go please Daddy, just once more!* 请让我们去吧，爸爸，就再去一次嘛!

6 once again/once more again, after happening several times before〔像从前那样〕再次，又一次: *Once again she's refusing to help.* 她再一次拒绝帮忙。

7 once or twice a few times 一两次，几次: *I've driven down here once or twice before.* 我以前开车来过这里几次。

8 once in a while sometimes, although not often 偶尔，有时，间或: *It'd be nice if you'd write to me once in a while.* 你要是能偶尔给我来封信就好了。

9 ▶IN THE PAST 从前◀ at some time in the past, but not now 过去，以前: *Franklyn had obviously been handsome once.* 显然富兰克林以前挺英俊的。| **once-great/beautiful etc** *It was sad to see the once-great man looking so frail.* 看见那个曾经叱咤一时的人如此虚弱，真令人难过。

10 once in a blue moon *informal* very rarely【非正式】极为罕见，难得一次

11 (just) for once *spoken* used to say that something hardly ever happens, although it should happen often【口】难得一次，就这一回: *Just for once I'd like to see him cook dinner.* 我就想看看他做一次饭。| *Well, for once he's being nice to me.* 嗯，他就这一回对我好。

12 (just) this/the once *spoken* used to emphasize that this is the only time that you will let someone do something, or ask someone to do something【口】仅这一回，就这一次: *Go on, lend me the car, just this once.* 来吧，把车借给我吧，就这一次。

13 once and for all a) if you deal with something once and for all, you deal with it definitely and finally 一劳永逸地: *Let's settle this matter once and for all.* 让我们一劳永逸地解决这个问题吧。**b)** *spoken* used to say that you are asking someone to do something for the last time, and they must do it【口】最后一次〔要求某人必须做某事〕: *Once and for all, will you switch off that television!* 最后说一次，把那电视关掉!

14 once upon a time a) used at the beginning of children's stories 从前，很久以前〔用于儿童故事的开头〕**b)** *spoken* at a time in the past that you think was much better than now【口】那时候〔指比现在好得多的过去某一时期〕: *Once upon a time you used to be able to leave your front door unlocked.* 曾经，你的前门总是可以不上锁。

15 do sth once too often to be hurt because of something dangerous or stupid that you have done 某事做得太多〔而遭殃〕

16 the once *spoken* on one particular occasion【口】一次，一回: *I've only met her the once.* 我就见过她那么一次。

17 once bitten, twice shy used to say that people will not do something again if it has been a bad experience 一次被咬，下次胆小; 一朝被蛇咬，十年怕草绳

once² *conjunction* from the moment that something happens 一…便，一旦，一经: *Once she arrives, we can start.* 她一到，我们就可以开始。| *Once in bed, the children usually stay there.* 小孩子一上床一般就不再下来。 S1 W1

Once in Roy·al Da·vid's Cit·y /ˌ· · ˌ·· ˌ·· ˈ··/ the title and first words of a well-known Christmas CAROL (=a traditional religious song)《昔日皇家大卫城中》〔一首有名的圣诞颂歌的歌名和首句〕

once-o·ver /'·, ··/ *n* **give sb/sth the once-over** to look at someone or something quickly to check who they are or what they are like 粗略地看某人/某物一眼，草草过目：*A guard gave us the once-over before letting us in the door.* 警卫扫了一眼就让我们进门了。

on·com·ing /ˈɑnˌkʌmɪŋ; ˈɒnˌkʌmɪŋ/ *adj* **oncoming car/traffic etc** a car etc that is coming towards you 迎面而来的汽车/车流等

one[1] /wʌn; wʌn/ *number* **1** the number one〔数字〕1，一：*one hundred and twenty one pounds (£121)* 121英镑 | *The answer is on page forty-one.* 答案在第41页上。| *Can I have one coffee and two milkshakes please?* 请给我一杯咖啡、两杯奶昔好吗？**2 one or two** a small number of people or things 一两个，很少的：*There are one or two things to sort out before I leave.* 我在走之前还要处理一两件事。**3 in ones and twos** if people do something in ones and twos they do it on their own or in small groups 三三两两地，零零落落地：*Guests arrived in ones and twos.* 客人三三两两地到来了。**4 a)** *AmE* a one dollar bill【美】一张一美元的纸币 **b)** *BrE* a one pound coin【英】一个一英镑的硬币 **5 for one thing** *spoken* used to introduce the first of several reasons【口】其中一个理由是，一则：*You can't see in that fridge, for one thing the light's gone and for another the button's broken.* 你看不清那个冰箱里的东西，一是灯不亮，二是开关坏了。**6 one-armed/one-eyed/one-legged etc** having only one arm, eye, leg etc 独臂的/独眼的/一条腿的

one[2] *determiner* **1** a person or thing, especially when there are other people or things of the same type or kind〔尤指同类中的〕一个人；一样东西，一件事：*Sam's just heard that one of his houses has caught fire.* 萨姆刚得知他的其中一栋房子着火了。| *If there's one thing I can't stand it's people who bite their nails.* 如果说有一件事让我无法忍受，那就是有些人咬自己的指甲。| *There's one person I really must thank.* 有一个人我真的要感谢。**2 one day/afternoon/year etc a)** a particular day, afternoon etc in the past 过去的某一天/某个下午/某一年等：*We first met one cloudy day last July.* 我们初次见面是在去年7月的一个阴天。| *One morning I was sitting at my desk when a policeman knocked at my door.* 一天上午我正坐在书桌旁，突然有个警察敲门。**b)** any day, afternoon etc at any time in the future 未来的任何一天/一个下午/一年等：*One evening you and I should go out for a drink.* 改天晚上我和你去外面喝一杯。**3 sb's one fear/worry/concern etc** someone's main fear, worry etc 某人主要的担心/忧虑/挂虑等：*My one fear is that her nerves will get the better of her.* 我最担心的是她会神经紧张。**4 the one man/place etc** the only man, place etc 唯一的人/地方等：*Claire is the one person I can trust.* 克莱尔是我唯一能信任的人。| *I'm sorry madam, we've only the one ticket left.* 对不起，夫人，我们只剩下这一张票。**5** used to talk about one person or thing in comparison with other similar or connected people or things〔一群类似的或有关的人或物中的〕某一个：*It's impossible to tell one child from another in that family.* 那家的孩子让人难以分清谁是谁。| *One of the gang broke into the safe while the other was keeping watch.* 歹徒中的一人撬开保险箱，另一人在把风。| **It's one thing... but...** *It's one thing passing your driving test but being a good driver is another.* 通过驾驶考试是一回事，但成为一个好司机则是另一回事。**6** *formal* used before the name of someone who you do not know well【正式】某位〔用于不太熟悉之人的姓名之前〕：*It seems the inheritance went to an old family friend, one Joseph Nelson.* 继承权似乎归于家族的一位老朋友，一个叫约瑟夫·纳尔逊的人。**7 one wonderful woman/one interesting job etc** *spoken especially AmE* a very wonderful woman, a very interesting job etc【口，尤美】一位非常出色的女性/一份很有趣的工作等：*Hey, your brother is one amazing guy!* 嗨，你兄弟真是个不寻常的家伙！**8 one by one/one after another** if people do something one by one, first one person does it, then the next, then the next etc 一个接一个地/依次地：*One by one each soldier approached the coffin and gave a final salute.* 士兵一个个地依次走到灵柩跟前，致以最后的敬礼。**9 I/John etc for one** used to emphasize that you are doing something, believe something etc and hope others will do the same 拿我/约翰等来说〔用于强调某人会怎么做、怎么认为等，并希望别人也会如此〕：*If they continue to abuse civil rights, I for one will be boycotting any food they produce.* 如果他们继续滥用公民权，我首先就会罢买他们生产的任何食品。**10 (all) in one** if someone or something is many different things all in one, they are all of those things 合为一体，一起，兼：*She's president, secretary and treasurer all in one.* 总裁、秘书和会计都由她一个人兼任。**11 be one up (on sb)** to have an advantage over someone 比（某人）占优势，占（某人的）上风，略胜一筹 —see also 另见 ONE-UPMANSHIP **12 put one over on sb** *informal* to trick someone【非正式】哄骗某人：*No one's going to put one over on me!* 谁也别想哄骗我！**13 get one over on sb** *informal* to get an advantage over someone【非正式】胜[强]过某人：*The easiest way to get one over on bullies is to answer them back.* 打败恃强凌弱者最简单的办法就是以牙还牙。**14 the one and only** *informal* used to emphasize that someone is very famous【非正式】真正的〔用于强调某人非常有名〕：*"That wasn't George Best I saw you talking to, was it?" "The one and only!"* "我看到和你在说话的不会是乔治·贝斯特吧？""正是他！" **15 be at one with sb/sth a)** to feel very calm or relaxed because of the calm situation or environment you are in〔在安详的环境中〕感到很镇定[放松]：*a weekend in the country, when you can feel at one with nature* 在乡村度过的一个周末，有一种与大自然融为一体的感觉 **b)** *formal* to agree with someone about something【正式】与某人意见一致：**16 a) be as one** *formal* to agree about something【正式】赞同〔某事〕：*The whole committee is as one on this – no women are allowed on the golf course.* 委员会全体赞同这一点——女子不得进入高尔夫球场。**b) as one** if many people do something as one they all do it at the same time〔许多人〕同时，一起〔做某事〕：*The whole team stood up as one and marched out of the room.* 全队同时站立起来，迈着大步走出房间。**17 got it in one!** *spoken* used to say that someone has guessed correctly【口】猜对了！：*"You're not painting the house again are you?" "Got it in one!"* "你不会又要刷房子吧？""猜对了！" **18 have one for the road** *informal* to have an alcoholic drink, especially the last one before you leave a place【非正式】喝一杯饯行[壮行]酒；〔告辞前〕喝最后一杯酒 **19 you are/he is a one** *old-fashioned especially BrE* used to tell someone that they are being rude, foolish etc【过时，尤英】你/他真是粗鲁[愚蠢]：*The patient in the end bed is a real one, I can tell you.* 最里头那张床上的病人真是粗鲁，我能肯定。—see also 另见 ONE-TO-ONE

one[3] *pron plural* **ones 1** used instead of a noun that has already been mentioned or which the person you are talking to already knows about〔用于代替已提及的某个名词或对方已知道的某个名词〕：*I've always wanted a CD player and I've just saved enough money to buy one.* 我一直想要一个CD唱机，现在我刚攒够了买一个的钱。| *The train was crowded so we decided to catch a later one.* 这班火车太挤了，我们决定乘坐下一班。| **the one that/who/which etc** *Soufflés are so hard to cook. Why is it that the ones I make always sink?* 蛋奶酥真是难做，为什么我做的那些总是塌下去？| **this one/that one/these ones/those ones** *I'll take that one, the one with all the chocolate on top.* 我要那个，就是上头全是巧克力的那个。**2** *formal* used when you mean YOU (2), especially when you do not mean any one person in particular【正式】任何人〔尤用于泛指时〕：*One asks oneself where children learn to behave so badly.* 谁都该问问自己，孩子是从哪里学坏的。**3 the one about ...** *especially spoken* a joke or humorous story【尤口】关于…的笑话[幽默故事]：*Have you heard the one about the dog that thought it was a cat?* 你听过那个关于狗把自己当作猫的笑话吗？**4 a...one** a particular kind of problem, question, story etc 一个…的难题[问题、故事等]：*"Excuse me, can you tell me the way to the bank?" "Oh, that's a hard one, it's either the second or the third road on the left."* "对不起，你能告诉我去银行的路吗？""噢，这有点难说，该是左边第二条或是第三条马路。" **5 not be one to do sth/not be one who does sth** *informal* to never do a particular thing, especially something that annoys people【非正式】决不做某事〔尤指让人生气的事〕：*I'm never one to complain, as you know, but I do think you could come and visit me more often.* 你知道，我这人从来不爱抱怨，但我真的认为你可以多来看看我。**6 be one for** *informal* to enjoy doing a particular sport, subject etc【非正式】喜爱〔某种体育运动、学科等〕：*I've never been (a great) one for watersports.* 我一向都不（很）喜欢水上运动。**7 one and the same** the same person or thing 同一个人[物]：*Muhammad Ali and Cassius Clay are one and the same.* 穆罕默德·阿里和凯萨斯·克莱是同一个人。**8 one and all** *old-fashioned* everyone【过时】每个人，全体：*The bride was welcomed by the family, one and all.* 新娘受到全家所有人的欢迎。**9 be one of the family/the boys** to be accepted as a member of a particular group of people 接纳为家庭/男孩中的一员：*It took me a while to settle in but I just feel like one of the family now.* 我过了一段时间才适应，但现在感觉就像是家庭中的一员了。**10 one of us** *especially spoken* used to say that someone is a member of the same group that you are in and has the same ideas, beliefs etc【尤口】我们自己人：*You can talk in front of Terry – he's one of us.* 你可以在特里面前说话，他是我们自己人。**11 the little/young ones** *humorous or old-fashioned* children, especially young children【幽默或过时】孩子，小家伙〔尤指小孩子〕

USAGE NOTE 用法说明: ONE
FORMALITY 正式程度
One meaning 'people in general' is very formal. Most people usually use **you** with the same meaning. one 作"任何人"解时是非常正式的词。大多数人通常用you来表示同样的意思。Compare 比较: *One can do what one likes here.* | *You can do what you like here.* 在这里，人们爱干什么就干什么。
You use **one** instead of repeating a noun phrase in both spoken and written English. 在英语口语和书面语中，都可以用one来避免重复一个名词短语: *The reason is basically an economic one.* 原因主要是经济方面的。
You can use **ones** when two adjectives are used to compare things, but it is best to avoid this in formal written English. 当两个形容词用于比较复数之物时，可以用ones，但在正式书面语中最好避免这种用法: *He buys German rather than British cars* (formal 正式). 他买德国汽车而非英国汽车。| *He buys German cars rather than British ones* (informal 非正式). 他买德国汽车而不买英国的。

S3 W3 **one an·oth·er** /ˌ· ·ˈ··/ *pron* each other 互相，彼此: *Liz and I have known one another for years.* 我和利兹相识好多年了。| *They often stay at one another's houses.* 他们经常住在彼此的家里。—compare 比较 EACH OTHER

one-armed ban·dit /ˌ· · ˈ··/ *n* [C] a machine with a long handle, into which you put money in order to try to win more money 吃角子老虎，独臂强盗〔指用一臂状杆操纵放入硬币赌博的机器〕; FRUIT MACHINE *BrE*【英】; SLOT MACHINE *AmE*【美】

one-horse /ˈ· ·/ *adj* **1 one-horse town** *informal* a small and boring town【非正式】沉闷的小镇: *I can't wait to get out of this one-horse town!* 我恨不得马上就能离开这个死气沉沉的乡下小镇! **2** pulled by one horse 由一匹马拉的: *a one-horse plough* 单匹马拉的犁

One Hundred and One Dalmatians /ˌ· ˌ··· · ˌ· ·ˈ··/ (1961) a CARTOON film made by Walt Disney, about 99 young DALMATIANS which an evil woman called Cruella de Vil wants to kill so that she can use their skins to make a coat. Two more adult Dalmatians save them. Another film was made of the story in 1996 with human actors.The films are based on the book by Dodie Smith.《101斑点狗》〔(1961)，沃尔特·迪斯尼公司出品的一部卡通电影。一位名叫库伊拉的邪恶女人为了用狗皮给自己做一件外套而想杀掉99条小斑点狗，而这些小狗最终被两条成年斑点狗所救。1996年，该故事被改编成另一部真人版影片。两部影片均根据多迪·史密斯的同名小说改编〕

O'Neill /oˈnil; əʊˈniːl/, **Eu·gene** /ˈjudʒin; ˈjuːdʒiːn/ (1888-1953) a US writer of plays, who won the Nobel Prize for Literature in 1936. His plays include *The Iceman Cometh* and *Long Day's Journey into Night*. 奥尼尔〔(1888-1953)，美国剧作家，1936年获诺贝尔文学奖，其剧本有《卖冰的人来了》和《长夜漫漫路迢迢》〕

one-lin·er /ˌ· ˈ··/ *n* [C] a very short joke or humorous remark 很短的笑话; 俏皮话，打趣话

one-man /ˈ· ·/ *adj* [only before noun 仅用于名词前] performed, operated, controlled etc by one person 由一人表演[经营、控制]的: *He does a one-man show in Las Vegas.* 他在拉斯韦加斯表演独角戏。| *a one-man business* 一人经营的生意

one-man band /ˌ· · ˈ·/ *n* [C] **1** *informal* an organization or activity in which one person does everything【非正式】唱独角戏式的组织[活动]: *The company is really a one-man band.* 这家公司其实只有一个人在唱独角戏。**2** a street musician who plays several instruments at the same time 单人乐队〔一个同时演奏多种乐器的街头艺人〕

one-night stand /ˌ· · ˈ·/ *n* [C] **1** *informal*【非正式】**a)** an occasion when two people have sex, but do not intend to meet each other again 一夜情，一宿风流: *I'm not into one-night stands.* 我对一夜情不感兴趣。**b)** a person that you have sex with once and do not see again 一夜情人〔有过一夜性关系后再未见过的人〕**2** a performance of music or a play that is given only once in a particular place 在某地仅表演一次的(巡回)演出: *The band had a series of one-night stands around the country.* 这支乐队在全国各地巡回演出，每个地方只表演一场。

one-off[1] /ˌ· ˈ·◂/ *adj* [only before a noun 仅用于名词前] *BrE* happening or done only once, not as part of a regular series【英】只发生一次的; 一次完成的; ONE-SHOT *AmE*【美】: *Yours for a one-off payment of only £200.* 只要一次付完200英镑，这东西就是你的了。

one-off[2] *n* [C] *BrE*【英】**1** something that is done or made only once 只做过一次的事; 一次性事物: *I missed my chance. The deal was a one-off.* 我错过了机会，这种事情只有一次。**2** *informal* someone who is completely different from anyone else【非正式】与他人完全不同者

one-pa·rent fam·i·ly /ˌ· ·· ˈ···/ *n* [C] a family in which there is only one parent who looks after the children 单亲家庭

one-piece /ˈ· ·/ *adj* [only before noun 仅用于名词前] consisting of only one piece, not separate parts 单件的，上下连身的: *a one-piece bathing suit* 连衣裤泳装

o·ner·ous /ˈɑnərəs; ˈɒnərəs/ *adj formal* work or RESPONSIBILITY that is onerous is difficult and worrying or makes you tired【正式】繁重的，艰巨的，困难的: *an onerous task* 艰巨的任务 | *onerous duties* 繁重的职责 —**onerously** *adv* —**onerousness** *n* [U]

one-self /wʌnˋsɛlf; wʌnˈself/ *pron formal* the reflexive form of ONE[3] (2)【正式】自己，自身〔one 的反身代词〕: *It is only through study that one really begins to know oneself.* 人只有通过学习才能逐渐认识自己。—see 见 ONE (USAGE)

one-shot /ˈ· ·/ *adj AmE* happening or done only once【美】只发生一次的; 一次完成的; ONE-OFF *BrE*【英】: *It's a one-shot deal. You don't get any second chances.* 这是一锤子买卖，不会有第二次机会的。

one-sid·ed /ˌ· ˈ··◂/ *adj* **1** considering or showing only one side of a question, subject etc in a way that is unfair 片面的，偏颇的，偏于一方的，不公正的: *The newspapers give a very one-sided account of the war.* 报纸对这场战争作了非常片面的报道。**2** an activity or competition that is one-sided is one in which one person or side does what they want and the other can do nothing〔活动、比赛等〕一边倒的; 不均衡的: *a very boring, one-sided game* 一场很乏味的、一边倒的比赛 | *I'd say the conversation was pretty one-sided.* 要我说呀，这次对话很不对等。—**one-sidedly** *adv* —**one-sidedness** *n* [U]

one-star /ˈ· ·/ *adj* **one-star hotel/restaurant etc** a hotel etc that is not of a very high standard 一星级酒店/餐馆等〔指质量不高〕

one-stop /ˈ· ·/ *adj AmE* **one-stop shop/store etc** a shop where you can buy many different things【美】一站式[综合性]商店

one-time /ˈ· ·/ *adj* [only before noun 仅用于名词前] former 从前的，一度的: *Neil McMurtry, a one-time busdriver, is the lead singer.* 尼尔·麦克默特里以前是公共汽车司机，现在成了领唱歌手。

one-to-one /ˌ· · ˈ·◂/ *adj* **1** between only two people 只在两人之间的，一对一的: *tuition on a one-to-one basis* 一对一的辅导 **2** matching each other exactly 完全对应的: *a one-to-one correlation* 完全对应的相互依存关系 —**one-to-one** *adv*: *I need to discuss it with him one-to-one.* 我需要和他面对面地商讨此事。

one-track mind /ˌ· · ˈ·/ *n* **have a one-track mind** to be continuously thinking about one particular thing 脑子里只想着一件事: *All you ever talk about is sex! You've got a one-track mind.* 你讲的都是关于性的问题！你满脑子只有这一样东西。

one-two /ˌ· ˈ·/ *n* [C] a movement in which a BOXER hits his opponent with one hand and then quickly with the other〔拳击中〕连续左右猛击: *Ali gives his opponent the old one-two, and it's all over.* 阿里左右开弓，向对手施展出他那一贯的二连击，比赛就此结束了。

one-up-man-ship /ˌwʌnˋʌpmənˌʃɪp; wʌnˈʌpmənʃɪp/ *n* [U] the skill of making yourself seem better than other people 胜人一筹的本领

one-way /ˌ· ˈ·◂/ *adj* [usually before noun 一般用于名词前] **1** moving or allowing movement in only one direction 单向的，单行的: *one-way traffic* 单向交通 | *a one-way street* 单行街道 **2** *especially AmE* a one-way ticket is for travelling from one place to another but not back again【尤美】单程的; SINGLE[1] (6) *BrE*【英】—opposite 反义词 RETURN[3], ROUND-TRIP **3** a one-way process, relationship etc is one in which only one person makes any effort 单方面的

one-way mir·ror /ˌ· · ˈ··/ *n* [C] a mirror which can be used as a window by people secretly watching from the other side of it 单向玻璃镜

one-wom·an /ˈ· ˌ··/ *adj* [only before noun 仅用于名词前] performed, operated, controlled etc by only one woman 只有一个女子表演[经营、控制等]的: *a one-woman show* 女子独角戏

on·go·ing /ˈɑnˌgoɪŋ; ˈɒnˌgəʊɪŋ/ *adj* [usually before noun 一般用于名词前] continuing, or continuing to develop 继续进行的; 不断发展中的: *an ongoing search for a new director* 继续寻找一位新主管 | *ongoing negotiations* 正在进行的谈判

S3 **on·ion** /ˈʌnjən; ˈʌnjən/ *n* [C,U] **1** a round white vegetable with a brown skin and many layers, that has a strong taste and smell 洋葱(头) —see picture on page A9 参见 A9 页图 **2 know your onions** *BrE informal* to know a lot about something【英，非正式】精通某事

on·ion·skin /ˈʌnjənskɪn; ˈʌnjənskɪn/ *n* [U] *AmE* very thin light paper, used especially for writing letters on【美】〔尤用于写信的〕薄光泽纸

on·line /ˈɑnˌlaɪn; ˈɒnlaɪn/ *adj* directly connected to or controlled by a computer 〔电脑〕联机的; 在线的, 〔与电脑〕联线的: *an online printer* 联机打印机 —**online** *adv*

on·look·er /ˈɑnˌlʊkɚ; ˈɒnˌlʊkə/ *n* [C] someone who watches something happening without being involved in it 旁观者, 观看者: *A crowd of onlookers had gathered at the scene of the accident.* 一群旁观者围聚在事故现场。—see also 另见 **look on** (LOOK[1])

on·ly[1] /ˈonlɪ; ˈəʊnli/ *adv* **1** not more than a particular amount, number, age etc 仅仅, 才: *Naomi was only 17 when she got married.* 娜奥米结婚时才17岁。| *Only five minutes more, and then we can go home.* 只要再过五分钟, 我们就可以回家了。**2** nothing or no one except 只限, 只有: *Only the president can authorize a nuclear attack.* 只有总统才能授权发动核攻击。| *Get me some peaches, but only pick the ones that are ripe.* 给我弄些桃子来, 但只能摘那些熟了的。| **staff/women/men etc only** *The car park is for staff only.* 那个停车场只限员工使用。**3** not better, worse, or more important than 只不过, 只是: *I didn't mean what I said. It was only a joke.* 我说的并不算数, 那不过是一个玩笑。| *It's no good asking me. I'm only the cleaner.* 问我没有用, 我只是一个清洁工。**4** in one place, situation, or way and no other, or for one reason and no other 只在; 只因为: *a plant that is only found in Madagascar* 一种只产于马达加斯加的植物 | *I only did it for the money.* 我做这事只是为了那笔钱。| *I'll tell you, but only if you promise not to tell anyone else.* 如果你保证不告诉任何人, 我就告诉你。—see 见 UNIQUE (USAGE) **5** no earlier than a particular time 不早于: *I only got here last night.* 我昨晚才到这里。| **only yesterday/last week/recently** *They got married five weeks ago but I only heard about it yesterday.* 他们五周前已经结了婚, 但我只是昨天才听说。| **only then** (=at that moment and not before) 只在那时 *Trevor sat in the dark, and it was only then that he realised how unhappy he was.* 特雷弗坐在一片漆黑中, 直到那时他才意识到自己是多么的不快乐。**6** **only just** especially *BrE* 【尤英】**a)** a moment ago 刚刚, 刚才: *No wonder she looks sleepy – she's only just got up.* 难怪她看上去睡眼惺忪的 — 她刚刚才起床。**b)** almost not; hardly 几乎不: *There's only just room for the two of us on the back seat.* 后排座位的空间只够我们俩勉强坐下。| *The dress fits her, but only just.* 这连衣裙她能穿上, 不过很勉强。**7** **I only wish/hope** *spoken* used to express a strong wish or hope 【口】但愿/希望: *"What's going to happen after the divorce?" "I only wish I knew."* "离婚后会发生什么事?" "但愿我能知道。" **8** **if only** used to express a strong wish 但愿, 真希望, 要是…就好了〔表示强烈的愿望〕: *If only I had a car, I could get out of this place.* 要是我有辆车, 我就能离开这个地方了。**9** **you'll only ...** used to tell someone that what they want to do will have a bad effect 你只会…: *Don't interfere, you'll only make things worse.* 别插手, 你只会把事情弄得更糟。**10** **you only have to read/look at/listen to etc** *spoken* used to mean that it is easy to realise that something is true because you can see or hear things that prove it 【口】你只要读一读/看一看/听一听等〔就会明白〕: *The situation's getting worse – you only have to look at the crime statistics.* 情况在恶化 — 你只要看看这犯罪的统计数字就会明白。**11** **I can only assume/suppose etc** used to say that you can only think of one explanation for something surprising or disappointing 我只能认为: *I can only assume that there has been some kind of mistake.* 我只能认为出现了某种差错。**12** **only to...** used to say that someone did something, with a disappointing or surprising result 结果只是…: *Scott arrived at the South Pole on January 18th, only to find that Amundsen had got there before him.* 斯科特于1月18日到达南极, 结果却发现阿蒙森已先于他到了那里。**13** **only too** very or completely 很, 非常; 完全: *Mark was only too ready to agree with her.* 马克非常同意她。| **only too true/likely etc** (=used when something unpleasant is true etc) 〔某件令人不快的事〕完全是事实/完全有可能等 *"Is it true that there's going to be a war?" "Only too true, I'm afraid."* "真的会发生一场战争吗?" "恐怕很有可能。" — see also 另见 **not only...but (also)** (NOT (6)), **only have eyes for sb** (EYE[1] (25))

only[2] *adj* [only before noun 仅用于名词前] **1** **the only thing/person/way etc** **a)** the one single thing, person etc that there is when there are no others 唯一的东西/人/方法等: *Dan's the only guy in this office who smokes.* 丹是这个办公室里唯一抽烟的人。| *The only reason I came here was to see you.* 我来这里的唯一原因是看望你。**b)** the best 最好的东西/人/方法等: *She's the only person for this job.* 她是担任这一工作的最佳人选。| *I'd recommend Kensington. Honestly – it's the only place to live.* 我会推荐肯辛顿区。说实话, 这是最好的居住地点。**2** **the only thing is...** *spoken* used when you are going to mention a problem or disadvantage about something 【口】唯一的问题是…: *I'd be happy to take you to the airport. The only thing is I think my mother needs the car.* 我很乐意送你去机场, 唯一的问题是我想我母亲要用这辆车。**3** **an only child** a child who has no brothers or sisters 独生子[女] — see also 另见 **the one and only** (ONE[2] (14)), **(only) time will tell** (TIME[1] (66))

only[3] *conjunction informal* used like 'but' to introduce the reason why something is not possible 【非正式】只是, 但是, 可是: *I'd offer to help you, only I'm really busy just now.* 我是想帮你的, 但眼下我实在很忙。

o.n.o. *BrE* the written abbreviation of 缩写 = 'or nearest offer', used in advertisements to show that you may be willing to sell something for slightly less money than you have asked for 【英】或最接近的出价〔广告用语〕: *Bicycle for sale; £60 o.n.o.* 有自行车出售; 价格60英镑, 可适当还价

O·no /ˈono; ˈəʊnəʊ/**, Yo·ko** /ˈjoko; ˈjəʊkəʊ/ (1933-) a Japanese artist and musician who was married to John Lennon. She made several records with Lennon as part of their group the Plastic Ono Band. 大野洋子〔(1933-), 日本艺术家、音乐家, 约翰·列侬的妻子。她作为"人造大野乐队"的一员, 与列侬合作推出了几张唱片〕

on·o·mat·o·poe·ia /ˌɑnəˌmætəˈpiə; ˌɒnəmætəˈpiːə/ *n* [U] *technical* the use of words that sound like the thing that they are describing, like 'hiss' or 'boom' 【术语】拟声法构词, 拟声词〈如"嘶嘶声"; "隆隆声"〉 —**onomatopoeic** *adj*

on-ramp /ˈ· ·/ *n* [C] *AmE* a road for driving onto a HIGHWAY(1) 【美】〔高速公路的〕驶入坡道[匝道], 高速公路的支路 —see picture on page A3 参见A3页图

on·rush /ˈɑnˌrʌʃ; ˈɒnrʌʃ/ *n* [singular] a strong fast movement forward 向前猛冲, 急冲: [+of] *the second onrush of demonstrators* 示威者的第二次向前猛冲 —**onrushing** *adj*: *the onrushing tide* 汹涌的潮水

on-screen /ˌ· ˈ·◂/ *adv* if information appears or is written onscreen, it appears on the SCREEN of a computer 在电脑屏幕上: *I prefer to edit on-screen rather than on paper.* 我喜欢在屏幕上修改, 不喜欢在纸上。—**on-screen** *adj*

on·set /ˈɑnsɛt; ˈɒnset/ *n* **the onset of** the beginning of something, especially something unpleasant 〔尤指某种不好事情的〕开始, 发作: *The enemy had to withdraw before the onset of winter.* 敌人不得不在冬季到来前撤退。

on·shore /ˈɑnˌʃɔr; ˌɒnˈʃɔː◂/ *adj* **1** on or near the land rather than in the sea 在陆地上的, 在岸上的, 在近岸处的: *onshore oil production* 近海石油生产 **2** moving towards the land 向陆地的, 朝向岸的: *strong onshore winds* 吹向陆地的强风 —**onshore** *adv*

on·side /ˌɑnˈsaɪd; ɒnˈsaɪd◂/ *adj, adv* in a position where you are allowed to play the ball in sports such as football 〔足球等运动中〕没有越位(的) —opposite 反义词 OFFSIDE[1]

on·slaught /ˈɑnˌslɔt; ˈɒnslɔːt/ *n* [C] a very strong attack against someone or something 猛攻, 猛击, 攻击: *He was confident his armies could withstand the Allied onslaught.* 他有信心他的军队能够抵挡盟军的猛攻。| [+on] *an onslaught on their whole culture and way of life* 对他们整个文化和生活方式的猛烈抨击

on-stream /ˌ· ˈ·◂/ *adv* in operation or ready to begin operation 投入生产; 处于开工状态: *More hotel developments are due to come on-stream for the 1998-99 season.* 更多新开发的酒店要在1998年至1999年赛季投入使用。—**on-stream** *adj*

On·ta·ri·o /ɑnˈtɛrɪo; ɒnˈteəriəʊ/ a PROVINCE in the east of central Canada, containing the country's largest city, Toronto, and over a third of its population. 安大略省〔加拿大中东部一省份。其境内的多伦多为加拿大最大城市。该省人口占全国总人口的三分之一以上〕

Ontario, Lake the smallest of the five Great Lakes, between the US and Canada. Its main port is the Canadian city of Toronto. 安大略湖〔北美五大湖中最小的一个湖, 位于美国和加拿大边境, 其主要港口为加拿大的多伦多〕

On the Or·i·gin of Spe·cies /· ·, ···· ˈ··/ (1859) a book written by Charles Darwin in which he explains his ideas about EVOLUTION《物种起源》〔(1859), 查尔斯·达尔文所著的一部著作, 阐述他的进化论观点〕

on·to /ˈɑntu; ˈɒntu; *before consonants* 辅音前 ˈɑntə; ˈɒntə/ *prep* **1** used with verbs expressing movement meaning in or on a particular place 在…中; 到…之上: *The men managed to jump onto the train while it was moving.* 那些人设法跳上了正在行驶的火车。| *Some paint was dripping off the ceiling onto the floor.* 一些油漆正由天花板滴落到地板上。**2 a)** **be onto sb** *informal* to know who did something wrong, committed a crime etc 【非正式】知道某人的错事[罪行等]: *The police are onto him.* 警察盯上他了。**b)** **be/get onto sb** *especially BrE* to get in contact with someone 【尤英】与某人联络: *Get onto the hospital and see if they can spare extra nurses.* 与这家医院联络, 看他们能不能抽调一些额外的护士。**3** **be onto a good thing/a winner** *in-*

formal to be in a very good situation that gives you many advantages【非正式】处境不错, 处于很有利的形势: *She's onto a real winner with that job.* 有了那份工作, 她就是一个真正的赢家。**4** if something such as a room looks or gives onto another room, a view etc, that is what you can see from that room or where that room leads〔房间等〕面向, 面对; 通向: *The main sitting area looked out onto a beautiful view of the hills.* 主要的起居生活区面对着一片峰峦叠嶂的美景。

on·tol·o·gy /ɑn`tɑlədʒɪ; ɒn'tɒlədʒi/ *n* [U] a subject of study in PHILOSOPHY that is concerned with the nature of existence〔哲学中的〕本体论, 实体论 **—ontological** /ˌɑntə`lɑdʒɪkḷ; ˌɒntə'lɒdʒɪkəl◂/ *adj*

o·nus, the /`onəs; 'əʊnəs/ *n* the responsibility for something〔对某事的〕责任, 义务: **the onus is on sb (to do sth)** *The onus is on the prosecution to provide proof of guilt.* 控方有责任提供(疑犯)有罪的证据。

on·ward /`ɑnwəd; 'ɒnwəd/ *adj* [only before noun 仅用于名词前] **1** moving forward or continuing 向前的; 继续的: *the onward journey* 继续向前的旅程 **2** developing over a period of time〔在某一时期内〕发展的, 进步的: *the onward march of scientific progress* 科学发展的前进步伐

on·wards /`ɑnwədz; 'ɒnwədz/ usually 一般作 **onward** *AmE*【美】*adv* **1** forwards 向前: *The ship sailed majestically onwards.* 那艘船威风凛凛地向前驶去。**2 from...onwards** beginning at a particular time and continuing after that time 从…起: *I'm on call at the hospital from midnight onwards.* 我从半夜起在医院值班。

on·yx /`ɑnɪks; 'ɒnɪks/ *n* [U] a stone with lines of different colours in it, often used in jewellery 缟玛瑙〔常用于珠宝首饰〕

oo·dles /`udḷz; 'uːdlz/ *n* [plural] *informal* a large amount of something【非正式】大量, 许多: [+of] *Give me oodles of cream. I love it.* 给我多来些奶油, 我爱吃。

oof /uf; uːf/ *interjection* the sound that you make when you have been hit, especially in the stomach 哎哟, 哎唷〔挨打时发出的声音, 尤被打中肚子时〕

ooh /u; uː/ *interjection* used when you think something is very beautiful, unpleasant, surprising etc 嗬〔用于觉得某事物很美丽、很讨厌、很令人惊讶等时〕: *"Look what I've bought." "Ooh!"* "看我买了什么。""嗬!"

ooh la la /ˌu lɑ `lɑ; ˌuː lɑː 'lɑː/ *interjection French humorous* used when you think that something or someone is surprising, unusual, or sexually attractive【法, 幽默】嗬啦啦〔觉得某事或某人令人惊讶、异乎寻常或漂亮性感时的用语〕

oomph /umf; ʊmf/ *n* [U] *informal*【非正式】**1** energy 精力, 活力: *It's not a bad song, but it needs more oomph.* 这是一首不错的歌曲, 但还要更强劲些。**2** sexual attractiveness 性感, 魅力

oops /ups; ʊps/ *interjection* used when someone has fallen, dropped something, or made a small mistake 哎哟, 啊呀〔某人摔倒、掉了某物或出了点小差错时的用语〕: *Oops! Sorry, Calvin, I didn't mean to bump into you like that.* 啊呀, 对不起, 卡尔文, 我不是故意这么撞你的。

oops-a-dai·sy /`· · ,· · ·/ *interjection* used when someone has fallen, especially a child 一, 二, 三, 起来了〔用于某人摔倒时, 尤指小孩〕

ooze[1] /uz; uːz/ *v* **1** [I always+adv/prep, T] if a liquid oozes from something or if something oozes a liquid, liquid flows from it very slowly 渗出; 慢慢地冒出; 分泌出: [+from/out] *Great tears oozed out from between her tight-shut eyelids.* 止不住的泪水从她那紧闭的双眼中渗出。| **ooze sth** *The stone walls of the cottage oozed moisture.* 小屋的石墙上渗出水分。**2** [I,T] to show a lot of a particular quality or feeling 显示出〔特质或情感〕: *oozing charm from every pore* 每一个毛孔都散发着魅力 | [+with] *oozing with sexuality* 显示性征

ooze[2] *n* **1** [U] very soft mud, especially at the bottom of a lake or the sea〔尤指湖底或海底的〕淤泥, 软泥 **2** [singular] a very slow flow of liquid〔液体的〕缓缓流动, 流淌

ooz·y /`uzɪ; 'uːzi/ *adj* soft and wet like mud 泥泞的, 淤泥的

Op the written abbreviation of 缩写= OPUS

op /ɑp; ɒp/ *n* [C] *BrE informal* a medical operation【英, 非正式】医疗手术

o·pac·i·ty /o`pæsɪtɪ; əʊ'pæsɪ̣ti/ *n* [U] **1** the quality of being difficult to understand 难解, 晦涩 **2** the quality of being difficult to see through 不透明性[度]: *different degrees of opacity and translucence* 不同程度的不透明性和半透明性

o·pal /`opḷ; 'əʊpəl/ *n* [C,U] a type of white stone with changing colours in it, or a piece of this stone used in jewellery 蛋白石

o·pa·les·cent /ˌopḷ`ɛsṇt; ˌəʊpə'lesənt◂/ *adj* having colours that shine and seem to change 乳白的, 乳色的; 发乳光的: *The sky shone a pale, opalescent blue.* 天空发出一种朦胧的乳光蓝。**—opalescence** *n* [U]

o·paque /o`pek; əʊ'peɪk/ *adj* **1** glass, liquid etc that is opaque is too thick or too dark to see through〔玻璃、液体等〕不透明的: *There was a shower with an opaque glass door.* 有一个淋浴间装着不透明的玻璃门。**2** speech or writing that is opaque is difficult to understand〔演讲或文章〕难理解的, 晦涩的: *very opaque style of writing* 晦涩的写作风格 **—opaquely** *adv* **—opaqueness** *n* [U] —compare 比较 TRANSPARENT —see also 另见 OPACITY

op art /`· ·/ *n* [U] a form of art using patterns that seem to move or to produce other shapes as you look at them 欧普艺术, 视幻艺术, 光效应艺术

op cit an abbreviation used in formal writing to refer to a book that has been mentioned before 在前面所引用的书中〔用于正式的文章中〕

ope /op; əʊp/ *v* [I,T] *poetic* to open【诗】打开; 把…张开

OPEC /`opɛk; 'əʊpek/ *n* [U] Organization of Petroleum Exporting Countries; an organization of nations that produce and sell oil and which fixes the price of the oil 石油输出国组织, 欧佩克

op-ed /ˌ· `·/ *adj AmE informal* **op-ed page** the page in a newspaper that has articles containing opinions on various interesting subjects【美, 非正式】〔报纸的〕专栏版, 特写稿版

S1 W1

o·pen[1] /`opən; 'əʊpən/ *adj*

① NOT CLOSED 未关闭的
② NOT ENCLOSED 敞开的, 开旷的
③ NOT UNDER A ROOF/COVER 无遮盖的/未覆盖的
④ READY FOR SERVICE 准备好提供服务的
⑤ AVAILABLE 现成可使用的
⑥ NOT RESTRICTED 不受限制的
⑦ NOT DECIDED 未决定的
⑧ NOT HIDING ANYTHING 不加隐瞒的
⑨ OTHER MEANINGS 其他意思

open 开着的

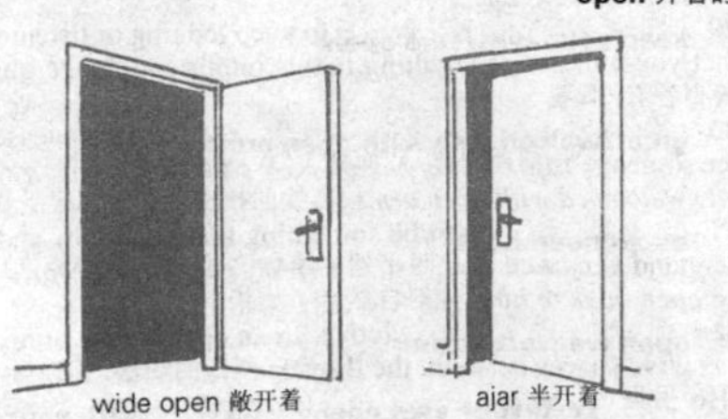

① NOT CLOSED 未关闭的

1 ►DOOR/CONTAINER 门/容器◄ not closed, so that you can go through, take things out, or put things in 开着的: *an open window* 开着的窗子 | *I guess I did leave the door open.* 我想我的确没关门。| *I can't get this milk open.* 我打不开这瓶牛奶。| **wide open** (=completely open) 敞开着 *The door was wide open and we could hear everything she said.* 门大开着, 她说什么我们都能听见。| **fly/blow/burst open** *A suitcase fell off the cart and burst open.* 箱子掉下马车, 一下子撞开了。| **push/slide/throw sth open** *Fran flung the window open and screamed.* 弗兰猛地推开窗子, 尖叫起来。| **tear/rip sth open** *He snatched the envelope from me and ripped it open.* 他从我手中抢过信去撕开了。

2 ►EYES/MOUTH 眼睛/嘴巴◄ not closed 未合上的, 张开的:

I was so sleepy, I couldn't keep my eyes open. 我困得眼睛都睁不开了。| **wide open**(=completely open) 大张着 *Ben gaped at me, his mouth wide open.* 本愣愣地看着我，张大着嘴巴。

3 ▶**BOOK** 书◀ a book that is open has its pages moved apart so that you can read it 打开的: *A book lay open on the table.* 桌上放着一本打开的书。

4 ▶**NOT BLOCKED** 无障碍的◀ if a road or line of communication is open, it is not blocked and can be used 可通行的: *We try to keep the mountain roads open all through the winter.* 我们要尽力保证那些山路在整个冬季都畅通无阻。

5 ▶**CLOTHES** 衣服◀ not fastened 未系好的; 未扣上的: *His shirt was open at the neck.* 他衬衫的领口敞开着。

② NOT ENCLOSED 敞开的，开旷的

6 [only before noun 仅用于名词前] not behind a cover or surrounded by a structure 敞开的; 未被围起的: *goods displayed on the open shelves* 开架陈列的商品 | *An open fire is cosier than central heating.* 明火比集中供暖系统更舒适。

7 **open country/fields/space** countryside where there are no buildings, walls etc 空旷[开阔]的郊野/田野/地方: *To the east, through miles of suburban streets, lay the open country.* 往东穿过数英里的市郊大街就是空旷的郊外。

8 **the open sea** sea that is far from any land 外海，外洋; 公海: *The battered boat slowly drifted out towards the open sea.* 那艘撞坏的船只缓慢地漂向外海。

9 **the open road** roads that you can travel on freely or quickly 畅通无阻的道路: *The thought of the open road is already making my feet itch.* 想起那条快捷的公路我就脚板发痒，跃跃欲试。

③ NOT UNDER A ROOF/COVER 无遮盖的/未覆盖的

10 **in the open air/(out) in the open** outdoors 在户外，在露天: *In the summer we have our meals in the open air.* 夏天我们在户外吃饭。| *It was too cold to spend the night out in the open.* 在露天过夜太冷了。—see also 另见 OPEN-AIR

11 ▶**NOT COVERED** 未覆盖的◀ without a roof or cover 无顶的，无遮盖的: *an open limousine* 敞篷豪华大轿车 | *an open sewer* 排污明沟 | **open to the sky/elements**(=without a roof) 无顶的，露天的

④ READY FOR SERVICE 准备好提供服务的

12 ▶**SHOP/BANK ETC** 商店/银行等◀ [not before noun 不用于名词前] allowing customers to enter and ready to serve them 准备好营业的: *The bank is open until 12:00 on Saturdays.* 这家银行星期六一直营业到12点。

13 **declare sth open** to officially state that a building is ready to be used, or that an organized event is ready to start 宣布〔大楼〕落成; 宣布〔活动〕开始: *I now declare the exhibition open.* 我现在宣布展览会正式开幕。

⑤ AVAILABLE 现成可使用的

14 ▶**OPPORTUNITY** 机会◀ **be open to sb** if an opportunity or possible action is open to you, you have the chance to do it 对某人开放: *training opportunities open to science graduates* 面向理科毕业生的培训机会 | *There is only one course of action open to me.* 我可采取的行动只有一个。

15 ▶**JOB** 工作◀ [not before noun 不用于名词前] a job that is open is available 〔职位〕空额的，空缺的: *Is the vacancy still open?* 这职位还空缺着吗?

⑥ NOT RESTRICTED 不受限制的

16 an open competition, discussion etc is one that anyone can join in 〔竞赛、讨论等〕公开的: *the British Open Squash Championships* 英国壁球公开锦标赛 | [+to] *The competition is open to men and women of all ages.* 这项比赛男女都可以参加，年龄不限。| **throw sth open to sb** *The discussion was thrown open to the studio audience.* 演播室现场观众可自由参加讨论。

17 **be open to the public/be open to visitors etc** if a place is open to the public etc, anyone can enter or visit it 向公众/参观者等开放: *The bar is open to non-residents.* 那家酒吧对非住客开放。

18 **on the open market** if something is sold on the open market, it is made available for anyone to buy 在公开市场上〔任何人都可购买〕: *This house would sell for £300,000 on the open market.* 这所房子在公开市场上会卖到30万英镑。

19 **an open invitation a)** an invitation to visit someone whenever you like 随时欢迎的邀请 **b)** something that makes it easier for criminals to steal, cheat etc 给罪犯以方便之门的东西: *An unlocked car is an open invitation to thieves.* 汽车没上锁等于是请盗贼来偷。

⑦ NOT DECIDED 未决定的

20 a choice or question that is open has been considered but not finally decided 〔选择或问题〕未决定的，悬而未决的: *Who will lead the new party is still an open question.* 谁将领导这个新党派还是个悬而未决的问题。| **leave it open**(=not decide yet) 暂不作决定

21 **keep/leave your options open** to delay any decision so that you can choose later 留有选择余地: *a flexible fare package for executives who need to keep their options open* 给需要自行选择的主管们准备的一整套灵活票价

22 **be open to discussion/negotiation** if something is open to discussion etc, you can discuss it and suggest changes 尚可讨论/谈判: *The terms are open to negotiation.* 这些条款还可以谈判。

23 **keep/have an open mind** to deliberately not make a decision or form a definite opinion about something 有意不作决定; 不对某事存先入之见: *Try to keep an open mind on the subject until you've heard all the evidence.* 对这个问题先不要作定论，听完所有的证词再说吧。

24 **be open to suggestions/offers** to be ready to consider people's suggestions, or prices that people offer to pay 愿意考虑建议/接受报价: *We're always open to suggestions about how we can improve our service.* 我们随时欢迎您对于如何改进我们的服务提出建议。

⑧ NOT HIDING ANYTHING 不加隐瞒的

25 [only before noun 仅用于名词前] actions, feelings, or intentions that are open are not hidden or secret 〔行为、感情或目的〕公开的: *open threats against the president* 对总统公开的威胁 | *Ralph was looking at her in open admiration.* 拉尔夫不加掩饰地以欣赏的目光看着她。| **open hostility/rivalry/rebellion** *open rivalry between two of the big TV channels* 其中两个主要电视频道之间的公开竞争 | **open government**(=a system of government where information is freely available) 公开的政府 | **in open court**(= in a court of law where everything is public) 在公开法庭上 *allegations made in open court* 在公开法庭上所作的指控 | **(out) in/into the open**(=no longer secret) 公开〔出来〕*The public has a right to know what has been happening. Let's get it out in the open.* 公众有权知道发生了什么事。我们把情况公开出来吧。| **an open secret**(=something that is supposed to be secret but that most people know about) 公开的秘密 *It was an open secret that he had links with far-right extremists.* 他与极右翼极端分子有瓜葛是公开的秘密。

26 ▶**HONEST** 诚实的◀ honest and not wanting to hide any facts from other people 坦率的，坦诚的: [+with] *Let's be completely open with each other.* 让我们彼此完全坦诚相对吧。| *frank and open discussions* 真诚坦率的讨论 | *a friendly open smile* 友好坦诚的微笑 | **open and above board**(=done in a completely honest and legal way) 光明正大的 *We don't have to bribe anyone. It's all open and above board.* 我们没必要贿赂任何人，这完全是光明正大的。

⑨ OTHER MEANINGS 其他意思

27 **be open to criticism/blame/suspicion** to be likely to be criticized, blamed etc 易受批评/指责/怀疑的: *Such a remark is open to misinterpretation.* 这种话易受曲解。| **lay yourself (wide) open to criticism etc**(=do or say something that will make it much easier for people to criticize you etc) 使自己易遭受批评等

28 **be open to question** if someone's honesty, judgment etc is open to question there are doubts about it 〔某人的诚信、判断等〕有疑问的，令人怀疑的: *Their motives are open to question.* 他们的动机令人生疑。

29 **keep your eyes/ears open** to keep looking or listening so that you will notice anything that is important, dangerous etc 留心看着/听着

30 **greet/welcome sb with open arms** to be very pleased to see someone 热情地迎接/欢迎某人: *Wealthy investors are usually welcomed with open arms.* 有钱的投资者通常都很受欢迎。

31 **be an open book** to be something that you know and understand very well 是一目了然的事物: *The natural world was an open book to him.* 他对自然界了如指掌。

32 **open weave/texture** cloth with an open weave or texture has wide spaces between the threads 粗疏的织法/质地 — see also 另见 **keep your eyes open**(EYE[1] (15)), **with your eyes open**(EYE[1] (38)), OPEN-EYED

open² *v*

① OPEN（打）开
② START 开始
③ SPREAD/UNFOLD 展开/打开
④ OTHER MEANINGS 其他意思

① OPEN（打）开

1▶DOOR/WINDOW ETC 门/窗等◀ **a)** [T] to move a door, window etc so that people, things, air etc can pass through 打开，开启：*Open all the windows and let some fresh air in.* 打开所有的窗子，让新鲜空气进来。**b)** [I] to be moved in this way 开：*The bus doors open and close automatically.* 公共汽车的门是自动开关的。

2▶CONTAINER/PACKAGE 容器/包装盒◀ [T] to unfasten or remove the lid, top, or cover of a container, package etc 开；撕开；揭开：*I've asked the waiter to open a bottle of champagne.* 我叫了服务员开一瓶香槟。| *She opened the letters one by one and read them in silence.* 她把信一封一封地拆开，默默地看。

3▶EYES 眼睛◀ **a)open your eyes** to raise your EYELIDS so that you can see 睁开眼睛 **b)open sb's eyes (to)** to make someone realize something that they had not realized before 使某人认清[了解]…：*Dan's remarks opened my eyes to the fact that he was only interested in my money.* 丹的话使我看清了这一事实：他只是对我的钱财感兴趣。

4▶MOUTH 嘴巴◀ **open your mouth** to move your lips apart 张开嘴巴

5▶BOOK 书◀ [T] to turn the covers and pages of a book so that you can read it 翻开，打开：*Open your books to page 29.* 把书翻到第29页。

6▶OPEN A WAY THROUGH 开出一条通道◀ [T] to make it possible for cars, goods etc to pass through a place 开通，打通：*They were clearing away snow to open the tunnel.* 他们在清扫积雪以开通隧道。|**open a border/frontier (to)** *The new republic has opened its borders to foreign trade.* 新的共和国已开放其边境地区进行外贸。

② START 开始

7▶SHOP/RESTAURANT ETC 商店/餐馆等◀ **a)** [I] if a shop or office opens at a particular time, it starts business at that time 开始营业：*What time do the banks open?* 银行什么时候开门（营业）？**b)** [I,T] if a new business such as a shop or restaurant opens or is opened, someone starts it〔商店、餐馆等〕开业，开张：*A new supermarket has opened.* 一家新的超市开张了。| *plans to open a chain of restaurants* 开办连锁式餐馆的计划

8▶START AN ACTIVITY 开始一项活动◀ **open an inquiry/investigation** to start gathering information or opinions from a lot of people 展开调查：*Police have opened an investigation into the girl's disappearance.* 警方对那女孩的失踪展开了调查。

9▶MEETING/EVENT 会议/事情◀ [I,T] if a meeting etc opens or is opened in a particular way, it starts in that way〔会议等〕开幕，（使）开始：*Our chairman opened the conference by welcoming new delegates.* 我们的主席以欢迎新代表来宣布大会揭幕。| [+with] *The concert opens with Beethoven's Egmont Overture.* 音乐会以贝多芬的《埃格蒙特序曲》开场。

10▶FILM/PLAY ETC 电影/戏剧等◀ [I] to start being shown to the public 开始公演[公映]：*Bertolucci's new film opens in London on March 15th.* 贝托鲁奇的新电影于3月15日在伦敦首映。

11▶OFFICIAL CEREMONY 正式仪式◀ [T] to perform a ceremony in which you officially state that a building is ready to be used 为〔大楼等〕举行揭幕典礼；宣布…落成

12 open an account to start an account at a bank or other financial organization by putting money into it 开立账户

③ SPREAD/UNFOLD 展开/打开

13 [I,T] if something that is folded opens or you open it, you make it spread out into a wide shape（使）展开，打开：*His parachute failed to open.* 他的降落伞无法打开。| *I opened my umbrella.* 我打开了雨伞。

14▶FLOWER/LEAF 花/叶◀ [I] if a flower or BUD opens, it spreads out wide 绽开，绽放：*The buds are starting to open.* 花蕾开始绽放。

15 open your arms to stretch your arms wide apart 张开双臂：*Marcus opened his arms in a welcoming gesture.* 马库斯张开双臂以示欢迎。

④ OTHER MEANINGS 其他意思

16 open sth to the public to let people come and visit a house, garden etc 向公众开放〔房屋、花园等〕：*For the first time, Buckingham Palace has been made open to the public.* 白金汉宫破天荒第一次向公众开放。

17 open the door/way to to make an opportunity for something to happen 给…以机会，给…敞开方便之门：*a joint venture that opens the way to wider international co-operation* 开拓更广阔的国际合作之路的合资企业 |**open doors** *A degree no longer opens doors in the way it used to.* 学位不再像以前那样敞开门提供了。

18 open fire (on) to start shooting at someone or something（向…）开火：*Troops opened fire on the rioters.* 部队向暴徒开火了。

19 open your mind to to be ready to consider or accept new ideas 乐于考虑[接受]〔新观念〕

20 the heavens opened it started to rain heavily 天开始下大雨

21 open your heart (to) to tell someone your real thoughts and feelings because you trust them（对…）敞开心扉，（向…）倾吐心事 —see also 另见**open the floodgates** (FLOODGATE (1))

open onto/into sth *phr v* [T] if a room, door etc opens onto or into another place, you can enter that other place directly through it〔房间、门等〕通往，通向：*The living room opens into the dining room.* 起居室通往饭厅。| *patio doors opening onto the garden* 通向花园的露台门

open out *phr v* [I] **1** if a road, path, or passage opens out, it becomes wider〔道路或通道〕变宽，变开阔：[+into] *Beyond the forest the path opened out into a track.* 过了森林，这条小径就拓宽成了小路。**2** *BrE* if someone opens out, they become less shy【英】变得不羞怯：*As she got to know us better, Lizzie gradually started to open out.* 莉齐跟我们熟了之后，渐渐地就放开了。

open up *phr v*

1▶LAND 土地◀ [I,T] if someone opens up an area of land, they make it easier to reach and ready for development 开发，开拓，开辟：**open sth ↔up** *They saw the new railroad as a means of opening up the far west of the country.* 他们把这条新铁路视为开发国家大西部的一种途径。

2▶SHOP/RESTAURANT ETC 商店/餐馆等◀ **a)** [I,T] if a shop, restaurant etc opens up or is opened up, someone starts it（使）开张，开办，开设 **b)** [I] if a shop, office etc opens up at a particular time, it starts business at that time〔商店、办公室等〕开始营业[办公]

3▶DOOR/BOX 门/箱子◀ [I,T] an expression meaning to open a door or something such as a box or case, often used to order someone to do this 开门，打开，开启〔常用于命令某人〕：*Open up, this is the police.* 开门，我们是警察。|**open sth ↔up** *Is this your suitcase? Right, open it up.* 这是你的旅行箱吗？好，把它打开。

4▶OPPORTUNITY 机会◀ [I,T] if an opportunity opens up or is opened up, it develops 展现；（使）显现；开拓：*A new life was opening up before her.* 新生活展现在她面前。|**open sth ↔up** *A move to New York would open up all kinds of exciting new possibilities.* 迁到纽约会带来各种令人振奋的新机遇。

5▶WITH A GUN 用枪炮◀ [I] to start shooting 开火，射击：*The enemy opened up with machine guns.* 敌人的机关枪开火了。

6▶DISAGREEMENT 分歧，不一致◀ [I,T] if a disagreement opens up or is opened up between people, it starts to divide them（使）产生分歧，（使）分裂：*A rift has opened up, splitting the committee down the middle.* 分歧出现了，使委员会分裂成两派。|**open sth ↔up** *The abortion issue may open up a split in the Democratic party.* 人工流产的问题可能会在民主党中引起分歧。

7▶TALK 讲话◀ [I] to stop being shy and say what you really think〔不拘束地〕畅谈，倾吐心事：*Once she knew she could trust me, Melissa started to open up.* 梅莉莎知道可以信任我之后，便开始没有顾忌地谈了起来。

8▶HOLE/CRACK ETC 洞/隙缝等◀ [I,T] if a hole, crack etc opens up or is opened up, it appears and becomes wider（使）变宽；（使）扩大

USAGE NOTE 用法说明: OPEN

WORD CHOICE 词语辨析: **open, shut, close, undo, do up, turn on/off, switch on/off, open up**

You **open**, **shut** or **close** your mouth, eyes, doors, windows, boxes, bottles, and shops. 张开或闭上嘴巴、眼睛, 打开或关上门、窗、箱子、瓶子, 使商店开门或关门用open, shut或close。

You **open** meetings and debates, but you can only **close** (NOT **shut**) them. 开始会议和辩论用open, 但结束只能用close (不用shut): *Madam Chair, I think we should close the meeting at eight.* 主席女士, 我想我们应该在八点结束会议。

You **undo** or **do up** clothes. 解开或扣上衣服用undo或do up: *She did up her boots/shirt.* 她系上靴子/扣上衬衫。

You **turn** water or gas **on** or **off**. 开关水或煤气用turn on和turn off。

You **turn** or **switch** electrical things **on** or **off**. 开关电器用turn/switch on和turn/switch off: *Turn that radio off.* 把那收音机关掉。| *She opened her laptop and switched it on.* 她打开手提电脑, 按下了启动的开关。

You **open up** new opportunities or possibilities. 开辟新的机会和可能性用open up: *plans to open up the world of higher education to people from poor backgrounds* 将高等教育的天地向来自贫穷家庭的人开放的计划

open³ *n* **1 the open** outdoors 户外, 野外: **in the open** *It must be wonderful to be able to take your meals in the open every day.* 每天都能在户外吃饭一定很快活。**2 in the open** not hidden or secret 公开的[地]: *It was a great relief to know that it was all in the open at last.* 得知最后一切都公布于众, 真让人大松了一口气。| **bring sth (out) into the open** *an opportunity to bring all your gripes out into the open* 倾诉所有苦恼的机会 **3 the Open** a national GOLF competition 全国高尔夫球公开赛: *the US Open* 美国高尔夫球公开赛

Open, the an important national GOLF competition, especially the British Open Championship or the US Open Championship 高尔夫球公开锦标赛〔尤指全英高尔夫球公开锦标赛或美国高尔夫球公开锦标赛〕

open-air /ˌ‥ ˈ‥◂/ *adj* [usually before noun 一般用于名词前] happening or existing outdoors, not in a building 户外的, 露天的: *open-air concerts* 露天音乐会 | *an open-air swimming pool* 室外游泳池

open-and-shut case /ˌ‥ · · ˈ·/ *n* [C] a law case that is easy to prove and will not take a long time in court 昭然若揭[容易证明]的案子

open bar /ˌ‥ ˈ·/ *n* [C] *AmE* a bar at an occasion such as a wedding, where drinks are served free【美】〔在婚礼等场合提供饮料的〕免费酒柜[吧台]

o·pen·cast /ˈopənˌkæst; ˈəʊpənkɑːst/ *adj BrE* **opencast mine/mining** mines where minerals, especially coal, are dug from large open holes in the ground【英】露天矿山/采矿〔尤指煤矿〕

Open Col·lege, the /ˌ‥ ˈ‥/ a British organization which teaches adults in their own homes by means of radio and television programmes and CORRESPONDENCE COURSEs (=courses of study in which work is sent between teachers and students by post). It teaches courses on business and the skills needed to work in many jobs and industries 开放学院〔英国一机构, 通过广播、电视、函授等方式对成人进行教学, 开设商务课程及适应许多岗位和行业需要的技能课程〕—compare 比较 OPEN UNIVERSITY

open-cut /ˈ‥ ·/ *adj AmE* opencast【美】露天开采的

open day /ˈ‥ ·/ *n* [C] *BrE* a day or time when a school, organization etc allows anyone to come in and see the work that is done there【英】〔学校、机构等允许公众参观的〕开放日; 开放时间; OPEN HOUSE (2) *AmE*【美】

open door pol·i·cy /ˌ‥ ˈ·, ˈ‥ ·/ *n* [C] **1** the principle of allowing people and goods to move into your country〔国家的〕对外开放政策 **2** the principle of allowing anyone to come and talk to you while you are working 对外〔指公众〕接待政策

open-end·ed /ˌ‥ ˈ‥◂/ *adj* **1** without a fixed ending time 无最终限期的, 无时间限制的: *hiring workers on open-ended contracts* 按无固定期限的合同雇用工人 **2** not having rules that limit or restrict anything 无限制的, 无拘束的: *These interviews are fairly open-ended in format.* 这些采访在形式上是相当轻松随意的。

o·pen·er /ˈopənɚ; ˈəʊpənə/ *n* [C] **1** a tool or machine used to open letters, bottles, or cans〔拆信或开启瓶罐等用的〕开具: *an electric can opener* 电动开罐器 **2** the first of a series of things such as sports competitions〔体育比赛的〕首场比赛: *the opener against the 49ers* 与"49人"队的首场赛事 **3 for openers** as a beginning or first stage 首先, 作为开始: *Well, for openers, it would be nice to know your name.* 嗯, 首先, 请告知您的尊姓大名。

open-eyed /ˌ‥ ˈ·◂/ *adj, adv* **1** awake, or with your eyes open 醒着的[地], 睁着眼睛的[地] **2** accepting or taking notice of all the facts of a situation 警觉的[地], 留神的[地], 警惕的[地]: *clear, open-eyed reasoning* 清晰而严谨的推论

open-faced sand·wich /ˌ‥ · ˈ‥/ *n* [C] *AmE*【美】〔馅露在外面的〕单片三明治, 开口三明治; an OPEN SANDWICH *BrE*【英】

open-hand·ed /ˌ‥ ˈ‥◂/ *adj* generous and friendly 慷慨的, 出手大方的; 友好的: *an open-handed offer of help* 慷慨地提供帮助 —**open-handedness** *n* [U]

open-heart·ed /ˌ‥ ˈ‥◂/ *adj* kind and sympathetic 心地善良的; 富同情心的

open-heart sur·ge·ry /ˌ‥ ˌ· ˈ‥ ·/ *n* [U] a medical operation in which doctors operate on someone's heart 心脏直视手术, 开心 (外科) 手术

open house /ˌ‥ ˈ·/ *n* **1** [U] a situation in which visitors are welcome at any time 热情好客: *It's always open house at Beryl's.* 贝丽尔一家一向都热情好客。**2** [C] *AmE* an occasion when a college, factory, or organization allows the public to come in and see the work that is done there【美】〔大学、工厂或机构的〕对外开放参观日, 开放日; OPEN DAY *BrE*【英】**3** [C] *AmE* an occasion on which someone who is selling their house lets everyone who is interested in buying it come to see it【美】售房参观日

o·pen·ing¹ /ˈopənɪŋ; ˈəʊpənɪŋ/ *n* **1** [C] a hole or space in something through which air, light, objects etc can pass〔空气、光、物体等进出的〕通路, 孔洞, 开口: *There was another opening to the cave.* 这个洞穴另有一个出口。**2** [C] an occasion when a new business, building, road etc starts working or being used〔新的公司、大楼、公路等的〕开张, 开业, 启用: **[+of]** *the opening of the new theatre* 新剧院的开幕 **3** [C usually singular 一般用单数] the beginning or first part of something 开始, 开端: **[+of]** *The opening of the novel is dull.* 这部小说的开头部分很乏味。| *at the opening of each school day* 每天上学开始时 **4** [C] a good chance for someone to do or say something〔某人做或说某事的〕良机, 机遇: **[+for]** *His question left an opening for me to say exactly what I thought.* 他的提问给了我一个确切地表述自己想法的好机会。**5** [C] a job or position that is available〔工作或职位的〕空缺, 空额: *Are there any openings for computer programmers?* 电脑程序员有空缺吗? **6** [U] the act of opening something 开, 启: **[+of]** *the opening of markets in Eastern Europe* 打开东欧的市场

opening² *adj* [only before noun 仅用于名词前] first or beginning 首先的; 开始的: *the opening speech of the debate* 辩论会的开场白

opening hours /ˈ‥ ·, ·/ *n* [plural] the hours during which a shop, building etc is open to the public〔商店、建筑物等的〕营业时间, 对外开放时间

opening night /ˌ‥ ˈ·/ *n* [C] the first night that a new play, film etc is shown to the public〔新戏剧或新电影等的〕首演之夜, 首映之夜

opening time /ˈ‥ ·, ·/ *n* [C] the time that a business opens to the public, especially the time a PUB begins serving drinks〔尤指酒馆的〕开始营业时间: *It was nearly an hour till opening time.* 离开门营业时间差不多还有一小时。

opening up /ˌ‥ ˈ·/ *n* [singular] **1** the process of making something, especially land, available for use or development〔尤指土地的〕开发, 开拓, 开辟: *The opening up of new land brought a rush of immigrants.* 开发新土地引起了一阵移民潮。**2** the process of becoming less restricted or limited 开放〔限制〕: *the opening up of jobs for women* 为妇女开放就业机会

open let·ter /ˌ‥ ˈ‥/ *n* [C] a letter to an important person, which is printed in a newspaper or magazine in order to protest or complain about something〔刊于报章上的〕公开信

o·pen·ly /ˈopənlɪ; ˈəʊpənli/ *adv* in a way that does not hide your feelings or opinions 公开地, 公然地: *Sarah talked openly about her abusive parents.* 萨拉公开谈起父母滥用暴力。| *He was openly contemptuous of his colleagues.* 他公然蔑视自己的同事。

open mike /ˌ‥ ˈ·/ *n* [U] *AmE* a time when anyone is allowed to tell jokes, sing etc in a bar or NIGHTCLUB【美】〔酒吧或夜总会里〕自愿者的即兴表演〈如讲笑话或唱歌等〉

open-mind·ed /ˌ‥ ˈ‥◂/ *adj* willing to consider and accept other people's ideas, opinions etc 愿意考虑他人观点的, 思想开放的: *I'm quite open-minded about this subject.* 对于这个问题我是相当开通的。—**open-mindedly** *adv* —**open-mindedness** *n* [U]

open-mouthed /ˌ· ˈ· ◂/ *adj, adv* with your mouth wide open, because you are very surprised or shocked〔因惊讶或震惊而〕张大嘴的[地], 吃惊的[地]: *They stared open-mouthed at the extraordinary spectacle.* 他们张着大嘴凝视着那奇妙的壮观景象。

open-necked /ˌ· ˈ· ◂/ *adj* an open-necked shirt is one on which the top button has not been fastened〔衬衫〕开领的 —see picture on page A17 参见 A17 页图

o·pen·ness /ˈopənnɪs; ˈəʊpən-nə̥s◂/ *n* [U] **1** the quality of being honest and not keeping things secret 公开, 坦率: *dealing based on honesty and openness* 以坦诚为本的买卖 **2** the quality of being willing to accept new ideas or people 开明, 思想开通: *his openness to new experience* 他乐于体验新事物的开明态度 **3** the quality of being open and not enclosed 开阔, 敞开, 空旷: *the openness of the landscape* 景色的壮阔

open-plan 敞开式的

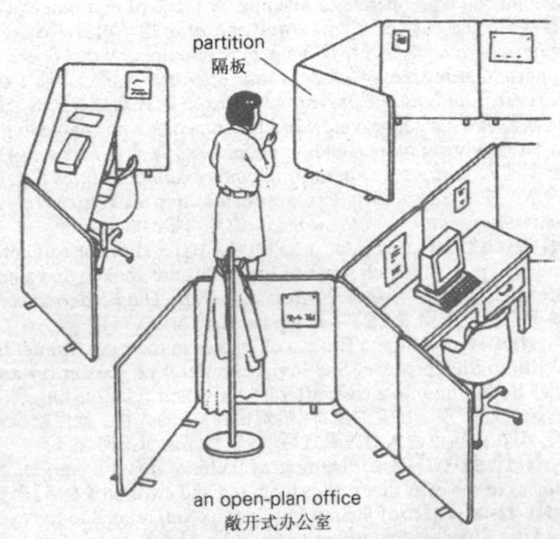

an open-plan office
敞开式办公室

open-plan /ˌ· ˈ· ◂/ *adj* an open-plan office, school etc does not have walls dividing it into separate rooms〔办公室、学校等〕敞开式的, 无隔墙的

open pri·ma·ry /ˌ· ˈ· · · ◂/ *n* [C] a PRIMARY ELECTION in the US in which any voter may vote for someone from any party〔美国的〕开放预选

open pris·on /ˌ· ˈ· ◂/ *n* [C] *BrE* a prison that does not restrict the actions or freedom of prisoners as much as ordinary prisons【英】〔对囚犯行动限制较少的〕开放式监狱; MINIMUM SECURITY PRISON *AmE*【美】

open sand·wich /ˌ· ˈ· ·/ *n* [C] *BrE* a single piece of bread with meat, cheese, etc on top【英】〔馅露在外面的〕单片三明治, 开口三明治; OPEN-FACED SANDWICH *AmE*【美】

open sea·son /ˈ· ·, · ˈ· ·/ *n* [singular] **1** the period of time each year when it is legal to kill certain animals or fish as a sport〔渔猎的〕开禁期, 狩猎期: **[+for/on]** *open season for deer* 允许猎鹿的季节 —opposite 反义词 CLOSE SEASON (1) **2 open season (on sb)** a time when a lot of people take the opportunity to criticize someone〔对某人的〕自由批评期〔指许多人同时批评某人的一段时期〕: *The CNN broadcast, in effect, declared open season on Lester Coleman.* 实际上, 美国有线新闻电视网的广播节目已宣布对莱斯特·科尔曼开始自由批评。

open ses·a·me /ˌ· ˈ· · ·/ *n* [singular] a way to achieve something that is nearly impossible "芝麻开门", 开门咒; 诀窍, 法宝: *A degree isn't an open sesame to a good job.* 大学学位并非是获得一份好工作的敲门砖。

Open Soft·ware Foun·da·tion, the /ˌ· ˈ· · · ·, · ˈ· ·/ abbreviation of 缩写为 **OSF** an international organization, whose members include large computer companies, TELECOMMUNICATIONS companies, and important computer scientists, which is trying to set international standards for the systems that make computers operate. Its aim is for computers made by different companies to be able to work together. 开放软件基金会〔一国际性组织。成员包括大型电脑公司、电信公司和重要的电脑科学家。该组织试图制定电脑作业系统的国际标准, 从而使不同公司生产的电脑相互兼容〕

open sys·tem /ˈ· ·, · ˈ· ·/ *n* [C] *technical* a computer system that is made so that it can be connected with similar computer systems made by other companies【术语】〔电脑〕开放系统〔根据已设定的标准而开发的电脑系统, 可与其他公司开发的类似系统相连接〕

Open U·ni·ver·si·ty /ˌ· · · ˈ· · ·/ *n* [singular] a British university that teaches adult students mainly in their own homes by means of radio and television programmes and courses of study sent by mail〔英国采用广播、电视和函授对成人学生进行教学的〕开放大学, 公开进修大学

O

open ver·dict /ˌ· · ˈ· ·/ *n* [C] a decision of a JURY (1) in a British court that the cause of someone's death is not known〔陪审团作出的〕死因未定裁决: *Johnson returned an open verdict.* 约翰逊裁决死因不详。

open vow·el /ˌ· · ˈ· ·/ *n* [C] *technical* a vowel that is pronounced with your tongue flat on the bottom of your mouth【术语】开元音〔发音时舌位较低〕

o·pen·work /ˈopənˌwɝk; ˈəʊpənˌwɜːk/ *adj* [only before noun 仅用于名词前] using or containing a pattern that has spaces in between metal bars, pieces of thread etc〔金属条、细纱等上的〕透雕细工; 网状细工; 透孔样式: *a beautiful openwork screen* 漂亮的镂雕屏风 —**openwork** *n* [U]

op·e·ra /ˈɑpərə; ˈɒpərə/ *n* **1** [C] a musical play in which all of the words are sung 歌剧: **go to the opera** (=go to a performance of an opera) 去看歌剧 *Helena had never been to the opera until that night.* 海伦娜直到那天晚上才看过歌剧。**2** [U] these plays considered as a form of art 歌剧艺术: *Do you enjoy opera?* 你喜欢歌剧吗? | *an opera lover* 歌剧爱好者 —see also 另见 COMIC OPERA, GRAND OPERA, SOAP OPERA —compare 比较 OPERETTA —**operatic** *adj* —**operatically** *adv*

op·e·ra·ble /ˈɑpərəbl̩; ˈɒpərəbəl/ *adj* a medical condition that is operable can be treated by an operation〔疾病〕可施手术的, 可开刀的

opera glass·es /ˈ· · · ·, · ˈ· ·/ *n* [plural] a small pair of special glasses used at the theatre for making things seem closer〔看戏用的〕小型双筒望远镜

opera house /ˈ· · · ·/ *n* [C] a theatre where operas are performed 歌剧院: *the Sydney Opera House* 悉尼歌剧院

op·e·rate /ˈɑpəˌret; ˈɒpəreɪt/ *v* S3 W2

1 ►MACHINE 机器◄ **a)** [T] to use and control a machine or equipment 使用, 操作, 操纵〔机器或设备〕: *If affected by drowsiness, do not drive or operate heavy machinery.* 如果感到犯困, 不要开车或操作重型机器。| *instructions for operating the central heating* 集中供暖设备的操作说明 **b)** [I always+adv/prep] if a machine operates in a particular way, it works in that way; FUNCTION[2] 运转, 运行: **[+in/at]** *a motor operating at high speeds* 高速运转的电动机

2 ►SYSTEM/PROCESS/SERVICE 制度/程序/服务◄ **a)** [I] if a system, process etc operates, it works in a particular way or for a particular purpose 运作; 有效, 起作用: *How well does your company's decision-making system operate in practice?* 你们公司的决策系统实际效果如何? | *The new law doesn't operate in our favour.* 这项新法规对我们不利。**b)** [T] if you operate a system, service etc, you make it work 实行, 实施: *St. Mark's School operates a system of rewards and punishments.* 圣马可学校实行一套奖惩制度。

3 ►MEDICAL 医学的◄ [I] to cut open someone's body in order to remove or repair a part that is damaged 开刀, 动手术: *It's serious. We'll have to operate immediately.* 情况严重, 我们得马上动手术。| **[+on/for]** *Doctors had to operate on his spine.* 医生不得不给他做脊椎手术。

4 ►BUSINESS/ORGANIZATION 公司/机构◄ [I always+adv/prep] to work in a particular place or way 经营, 做生意; 活动: **[+in/within/from]** *rival gangs that operate in the south side of the city* 在城南一带活动的几个敌对匪帮 | *a small company operating out of a converted barn* 在一家改头换面的仓库里经营业务的小公司

5 ►WORK 工作◄ [I] to do your job or try to achieve things in a particular way 行事; 行使职责: *Soldiers cannot operate effectively without good food.* 士兵吃不好就不能好好作战。| *That's just the way she operates.* 那就是她做事的方法。

6 operate as to have a particular purpose 起…作用, 作…之用: *The word 'onward' can operate as an adjective and an adverb.* onward 一词可用作形容词和副词。| *Our consciences operate as a check on our behaviour.* 我们的行为受控于自己的良知。

7 ►LAWS/PRINCIPLES 定律/原理◄ [I] to have an effect on something 起作用; 发生影响: *evolutionary principles operating in the physical world* 在物质世界起作用的进化原理

op·e·rat·ing room /ˈ· · · ·, · ˈ·/ *n* [C] *AmE* an OPERATING THEATRE【美】手术室

operating sys·tem /ˈ· · · ·, · ˈ· ·/ *n* [C] a system in a computer that helps all the programs (PROGRAM[1] (1)) in it to work together〔电脑的〕操作系统

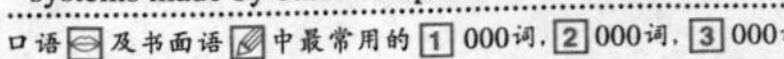

operating ta·ble /ˈ····,·/ *n* [C] a special table that you lie on to have a medical operation 手术台

operating thea·tre /ˈ····,·/ *n* [C] *BrE* a room in a hospital where operations are done【英】手术室; OPERATING ROOM *AmE*【美】

op·e·ra·tion /ˌɑpəˈreʃən; ˌɒpəˈreɪʃən/ *n*
1 ▶**MEDICAL** 医学的◀[C] the process of cutting into someone's body to repair or remove a part that is damaged 手术: *a heart bypass operation* 心脏搭桥手术 | *She had a bad operation, she had a hysterectomy.* 她动了个大手术, 被切除了子宫。| [**+on/for**] *She's going to have an operation on her knee.* 她准备去医院接受膝部手术。| **perform an operation** *an operation only the most skilled surgeon could perform* 只有最老练的外科医生才能做的手术
2 ▶**SET OF ACTIONS** 整个行动◀[C] a set of planned actions or activities for a particular purpose〔为达到某一目的而计划好的〕整个行动[活动]: *The whole operation should only take about ten minutes to perform.* 整个行动应该只要十分钟左右就完成。| *a search and rescue operation, expertly performed* 一次搜救行动, 干得很专业
3 ▶**MACHINE/SYSTEM** 机器/系统◀[U] **a)** the way the parts of a machine or system work together 运转, 运作: *to maintain proper engine operation* (=working) 维持引擎正常运转 | **in operation** (=working) 运转着, 操作中 *Protective clothing must be worn when the machine is in operation.* 操作这机器时必须穿着防护服。**b)** the process of making a machine or system work 操作: *Operation of the system is automatic.* 该系统的操作是自动的。
4 ▶**BUSINESS** 经营◀**a)** [C] a business, company, or organization, especially one with many parts〔尤指有许多分支的〕商号, 公司, 机构: *Their huge interstate operation reportedly brings in $20 million a year.* 据报道, 他们庞大的州际公司每年挣得2000万美元的收益。**b)** [C,U] the work or activities done by a business, organization etc, or the process of doing this work 经营; 业务: *Many small businesses fail in the first year of operation.* 许多小商行在经营的第一年常常亏本。| **be in operation** *Chris's courier service has only been in operation for two months.* 克里斯的快递服务才经营了两个月。
5 ▶**PRINCIPLE/LAW/PLAN ETC** 原理/定律/计划等◀[U] the way something such as a principle, law etc works or has an effect 作用, 效力: *the operation of the laws of gravity* 万有引力定律的作用 | **in operation** *a clear example of Murphy's law in operation* 墨菲定律起了作用的一个明显例子 | **come/go into operation** (=begin to have an effect) 开始生效 *The Act will come into operation later this year.* 该法案将于今年晚些时候实施。| **put/bring sth into operation** (=make something start to work) 使…开始工作[生效]
6 ▶**MILITARY/POLICE ACTION** 军事的/警方的行动◀[C] a planned military or police action, especially one that involves a lot of people〔尤指涉及众多人员的〕军事行动; 警方行动: *an espionage operation* 谍报行动
7 ▶**COMPUTERS** 电脑◀[C] *technical* an action done by a computer【术语】运算: *a multitasking machine performing millions of operations per second* 每秒运算数百万次的多任务处理机

op·e·ra·tion·al /ˌɑpəˈreʃənl; ˌɒpəˈreɪʃənəl◀/ *adj* **1** working and ready to be used 工作着的; 即可使用的: *The new vehicle could be operational as early as 1994.* 这种新车早在1994年就可使用。| **fully operational** *The new laboratory is fully operational and open for business.* 新实验室已经全面投入使用, 并对外开放。—compare 比较 OPERATIVE¹ (1) **2** [only before noun 仅用于名词前] related to the operation of a business, government etc〔公司、政府等〕运作的, 操作上的, 经营上的: *operational and budgetary planning officer* 运作及预算规划官员 —**operationally** *adv*

operational re·search /,····ˈ·/ *n* [U] *technical* the study of how best to build and use machines or plan organizations【术语】运筹学

Operation Des·ert Storm /,····,··ˈ·/ the name given to the military operation that forced the army of Iraq to leave Kuwait in 1991 during the Gulf War 沙漠风暴行动〔指1991年海湾战争期间迫使伊拉克军队撤离科威特的军事行动〕

Operation O·ver·lord /,····ˈ··/ the secret name given to the Allied invasion of northwest Europe, on D-Day 1944 霸王计划〔1944年6月6日盟军进攻欧洲西北部计划的代号〕

op·e·ra·tive¹ /ˈɑpə,retɪv; ˈɒpərətɪv/ *adj* **1** working and able to be used 运作中的, 工作着的; 可使用的: *We had only one radar station operative.* 我们只有一个雷达站在工作。| *operative missiles* 可发射的导弹 —compare 比较 OPERATIONAL (1) **2 the operative word** used when you repeat a word from a previous sentence to draw attention to its importance 最重要[关键]的词〔用于重复前一句中的某个词, 使人注意其重要性〕: *He is supposed to supervise their work. 'Supposed', unfortunately, is the operative word.* 他应该监督他们的工作。不幸的是, "应该"这个词才是关键。

operative² *n* [C] **1** a word meaning a worker, especially a factory worker, used in business 工人, 技工: *increased productivity from the operatives* 由工人提高的生产力 **2** *AmE* someone who does work that is secret in some way, especially for a government organization【美】〔尤指为政府部门服务的〕特工, 特务; 间谍; 密探: *Hunt was no ordinary consultant, but a political operative.* 亨特不是个普通的顾问, 而是个政治间谍。

op·e·ra·tor /ˈɑpə,retɚ; ˈɒpəreɪtə/ *n* [C] **1** someone who works on a telephone SWITCHBOARD, who you can call for help when you have problems 电话接线员: *Ask the operator to put you through.* 让接线员接通你的电话。—see 见 TELEPHONE (USAGE) **2** someone who operates a machine or piece of equipment〔机器或设备的〕操作员: *a tow truck operator* 拖车司机 | *a computer operator* 电脑操作员 **3** a person or company that operates a particular business 经营者: *a tour operator* 旅游经营商 | *the largest road haulage operator in Alaska* 阿拉斯加最大的公路运输公司 **4** a disapproving word for someone who is able to get what they want by persuading people 善于摆布他人的人; 精明圆滑的人: *a supreme operator in congressional politics* 国会政治事务中的头号大骗子 | **a smooth/sharp operator** *He's a smooth operator with the women.* 他是欺骗妇女的老手。

op·e·ret·ta /ˌɑpəˈrɛtə; ˌɒpəˈretə/ *n* [C] a short or romantic musical play in which some of the words are spoken and some are sung 小歌剧, 轻歌剧: *Strauss's operetta Die Fledermaus* 斯特劳斯的轻歌剧《蝙蝠》—compare 比较 OPERA (1)

O·phe·li·a /oˈfiljə; əˈfiːliə/ a character in the play *Hamlet* by William Shakespeare. She loves Hamlet, but goes crazy and dies by falling into a river after he ends their relationship. 奥菲莉娅〔威廉·莎士比亚的剧本《哈姆雷特》中的人物。她爱哈姆雷特, 但在他结束两人的关系之后, 她精神错乱而投河自尽〕

oph·thal·mi·a /ɑfˈθælmɪə; ɒfˈθælmiə/ *n* [U] *technical* an illness of the eyes that makes them red and swollen【术语】眼炎

oph·thal·mic /ɑfˈθælmɪk; ɒfˈθælmɪk/ *adj* related to the eyes and the illnesses that affect them 眼的; 眼炎的: *an ophthalmic surgeon* 眼外科医生

oph·thal·mol·o·gist /ˌɑfθælˈmɑlədʒɪst; ˌɒfθælˈmɒlədʒɪst/ *n* [C] a doctor who treats people's eyes and does operations on them 眼科医生[师] —compare 比较 OPTICIAN (1), OPTOMETRIST

oph·thal·mol·o·gy /ˌɑfθælˈmɑlədʒɪ; ˌɒfθælˈmɒlədʒi/ *n* [U] *technical* the study of the eyes and diseases that affect them【术语】眼科学

o·pi·ate /ˈopɪ,et; ˈəʊpiɪt/ *n* [C] a type of drug that contains OPIUM and makes you want to sleep〔用以安眠的〕鸦片制剂

o·pine /oˈpaɪn; əʊˈpaɪn/ *v* [T **+that**] *formal* to say that you think something is true【正式】认为, 以为; 发表意见: *"She did right, if you ask me," opined Moreau.* "要问我的话, 她做对了。"莫罗发表意见说。

o·pin·ion /əˈpɪnjən; əˈpɪnjən/ *n* **1** [C] your ideas or beliefs about a particular subject 意见, 看法, 主张: [**+about**] *Sarah's parents have strong opinions about divorce.* 萨拉的父母强烈反对离婚。| [**+on**] *I went to my boss to ask him for his opinion on the matter.* 我去找过老板问他对此事的看法。| [**+of**] *What's your opinion of her as a teacher?* 你认为她这个老师怎么样? | **the general opinion** (=what most people believe) 普遍的看法 *The general opinion is that the new working hours are a good thing.* 人们普遍认为实行新的工作时间是件好事。—compare 比较 VIEW¹ (1) **2** [C] judgement or advice from a professional person about something 专家意见, 专业意见: *When choosing an insurance policy it's usually best to get an independent opinion.* 选择保险时, 通常最好去听听(专家)独立的意见。| **a second opinion** (=advice from a second person to make sure that the first advice is right) 他人的忠告[意见] *My doctor says I need an operation, but I've asked for a second opinion.* 我的医生说我需要开刀, 不过我又征询了其他医生的意见。**3 have a high/low/good/bad etc opinion of** to think that someone or something is very good or very bad 对…评价很高/很低/很好/很差等: *They seem to have a very high opinion of Paula's work.* 他们似乎对葆拉的工作评价很高。**4 in my opinion/if you want my opinion** used to tell someone what you think about a particular subject 依我看/如果要听我的意见: *If you want my opinion, Phil's gone crazy.* 我的意见是, 菲尔发疯了。**5 be of the opinion (that)** to think that something is true 认为, 主张: *Aristotle was of the opinion that there would always be rich and poor in society.* 亚里士

多德认为，社会上总有贫富存在。—see also 另见 **a difference of opinion** (DIFFERENCE (4)), **it's/that's a matter of opinion** (MATTER[1](21)), PUBLIC OPINION

o·pin·ion·at·ed /ə`pɪnjən͵etɪd; əˈpɪnjəneɪtɪ̈d/ *adj* expressing very strong opinions about things 固执己见的，武断的：*an opinionated old fool* 固执的老糊涂

opinion-mak·ers /·ˈ·· ͵··/ *n* [plural] people who have great influence over the way other people think 观念制造者〔指对他人的思维方式有巨大影响的人〕

opinion poll /·ˈ·· ·/ *n* [C] an attempt to find out what the public thinks about something, especially politics, by asking many people the same questions 民意测验[调查]: *The latest opinion polls show the Social Democrats leading by 10%.* 最新的民意测验显示，社会民主党领先 10%。

o·pi·um /ˈopɪəm; ˈəʊpiəm/ *n* [U] a powerful illegal drug made from POPPY seeds, that used to be used legally as a PAINKILLER 鸦片 —see also 另见 HEROIN

o·pos·sum /əˈpɑsəm; əˈpɒsəm/ also 又作 **possum** *n* [C] one of various small animals from America and Australia that has fur and climbs trees 负鼠〔产于美洲和澳大利亚〕

opp. the written abbreviation of 缩写= OPPOSITE

Op·pen·hei·mer /ˈɑpənhaɪmɚ; ˈɒpənhaɪmə/ **J. Robert** (1904-67) a US physicist who led the team of scientists on the Manhattan Project (1942-45), the secret plan to develop the first ATOM BOMB 奥本海默〔(1904-1967)，美国物理学家。他曾带领一个科学家团队致力于研发首枚原子弹的绝密计划，即"曼哈顿计划"(1942-1945)〕

3 **op·po·nent** /əˈponənt; əˈpəʊnənt/ *n* [C] **1** someone who tries to defeat another person in a competition, game, fight, or argument〔竞争、比赛等的〕对手，敌手：*Tyson knocked his opponent out in the first round.* 泰森在第一回合中把对手击倒了。| *Rumpole was a formidable opponent in court.* 在法庭上，朗波尔是个令人生畏的对手。**2** someone who disagrees with a plan, idea etc, and wants to try and stop it 反对者：[+ **of**] *opponents of the Administration's plans to cut the Federal budget* 反对政府削减联邦预算的人

op·por·tune /͵ɑpɚˈtjun; ˈɒpətjuːn/ *adj formal*【正式】**1 an opportune moment/time** a time that is suitable for doing something 合适的时机/时间：*Deborah was waiting for an opportune moment to ask for a raise.* 德博拉在等待合适的时机要求加薪。**2** done at a very suitable time 适时的，及时的：*an opportune remark* 合时宜的话 —opposite 反义词 INOPPORTUNE —**opportunely** *adv*

op·por·tun·is·m /͵ɑpɚˈtjunɪzəm; ͵ɒpəˈtjuːnɪzəm/ *n* [U] trying whenever possible to gain power or unfair advantages over other people 机会主义；投机取巧：*a blatant piece of political opportunism* 一宗无耻的政治投机事件

op·por·tun·ist /͵ɑpɚˈtjunɪst; ɒpəˈtjuːnɪ̈st/ *n* [C] someone who uses every chance to gain power or unfair advantage over others 机会主义分子 —**opportunist** *adj*: *the opportunist policies of war-time leaders* 战时领导人的机会主义政策 —**opportunistic** /͵ɑpɚtjuˈnɪstɪk; ͵ɒpətjuːˈnɪstɪk/ *adj*: *A recent police video reflects the increasing number of opportunistic thefts from drivers in heavy urban traffic.* 警方最近的一份录像显示，在城市交通繁忙之时，伺机向驾车者下手的盗窃案数目在增加。

1 1 **op·por·tu·ni·ty** /͵ɑpɚˈtjunətɪ; ͵ɒpəˈtjuːnɪ̈ti/ *n* **1** [C,U] a chance to do something or an occasion when it is easy for you to do something 机会，时机：*I just thought it was too good an opportunity to miss.* 我当时只是想这是个不可错过的好机会。| **opportunity to do sth** *You have had plenty of opportunity to observe our way of doing things.* 你已有很多机会观察我们如何办事。| [+ **for**] *When you're in school there are lots of opportunities for meeting people of the opposite sex.* 上学时，你会有很多机会接触异性。| **take the opportunity to do sth** (=use a chance to say something you want to) 借机做某事 *I'd like to take this opportunity to wish you a good trip.* 我想借此机会祝你旅途顺利。| **at the earliest/first opportunity** (=as soon as possible) 一有机会〔就…〕*He must have got rid of the body at the first opportunity.* 他准是一有机会便把那尸体弃掉了。| **at every opportunity** (=whenever possible) 利用一切机会 *I try to speak French at every available opportunity.* 我努力抓住各种机会讲法语。—CHANCE[1] (USAGE) **2** [C] a chance to get a job 就业机会：*There are fewer opportunities for new graduates this year.* 对今年新毕业的大学生来说，就业机会要少一些。—see also 另见 **equal opportunities** (EQUAL[1] (2))

opposable thumb /·͵··· ˈ·/ *n* [C] a thumb that human beings, MONKEYs etc have that can be used for holding things〔人类、猴等的〕拇指

op·pose /əˈpoz; əˈpəʊz/ *v* [T] **1** to disagree with something such as a plan or idea and try to prevent it from happening or succeeding 反对；阻碍：*Congress is continuing to oppose the President's healthcare budget.* 国会继续反对总统的卫生保健预算。| **be opposed to sth** *Most of us are opposed to the death penalty.* 我们大多数人反对死刑。**2** to fight or compete against another person or group in a battle, competition, or election 与…对抗，与…较量：*He is opposed by two other candidates.* 还有两名候选人和他较量。 3

op·posed /əˈpozd; əˈpəʊzd/ *adj* [not before noun 不用于名词前] **1** two ideas that are opposed to each other are completely different from each other 相反的，对立的：[+ **to**] *The principles of capitalism and socialism are diametrically opposed to each other.* 资本主义与社会主义所遵循的原则彼此截然相反。**2 as opposed to** used to compare two things and show that they are different from each other 与…对照之下；而非：*Students discuss ideas, as opposed to just copying from books.* 学生们一起交流思想，而不是单纯抄袭书本。| *his private as opposed to his public life* 他的私生活而非他的社会生活

Frequencies of **oppose, be opposed to** and **be against** in spoken and written English 英语口语和书面语中 oppose, be opposed to 和 be against 的使用频率

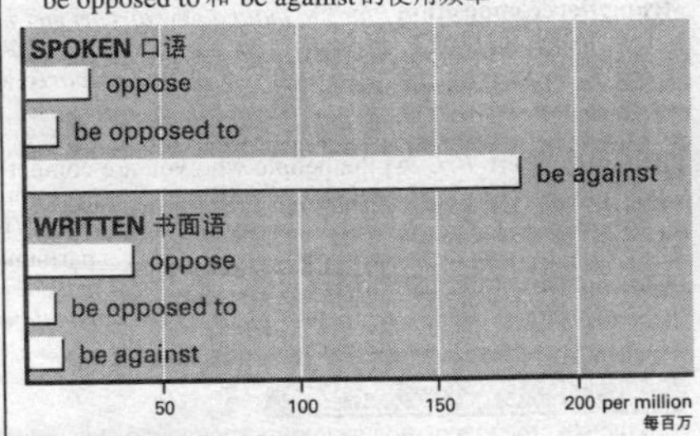

Based on the British National Corpus and the Longman Lancaster Corpus
据英国国家语料库和朗文兰开斯特语料库

This graph shows that it is much more usual in spoken English to say that you **are against** something, rather than to say that you **oppose** it or **are opposed to** it. This is because **be against** is more informal and more general than **oppose** and **be opposed to**, which often suggest not only disagreeing with and disapproving of something, but also taking action to prevent it.
本图表显示，英语口语中说"反对某事"时，大多使用 are against，而少用 oppose 或 are opposed to。这是因为相比而言，be against 比较非正式且较为通用，而 oppose 和 be opposed to 常不仅表示不同意和不赞成某事，而且还含有采取行动加以阻止的意思。

op·pos·ing /əˈpozɪŋ; əˈpəʊzɪŋ/ *adj* **1** opposing teams, groups, forces etc are competing, arguing, or fighting against each other 对抗的，对立的，反对的，敌对的：*The opposing armies were already preparing for war.* 敌对双方的军队已经在备战了。| *The Socialist Party has split into two opposing camps.* 社会党分裂成两个对立的阵营。**2** opposing ideas, opinions etc are completely different from each other〔观点、意见等〕相反的，相对立的，截然不同的：*Bobbie and Jo have opposing views on abortion.* 鲍比和乔对人工流产持截然相反的观点。

op·po·site¹ /ˈɑpəzɪt; ˈɒpəzɪ̈t/ *prep* if one thing or person is opposite another, they are facing each other 在…的对面：*The people sitting opposite us looked very familiar.* 坐在我们对面的人看上去很面熟。| *It's easy to find – there's a church just opposite my house.* 我家很容易找，正对面有座教堂。 2 2

opposite² *adj* **1** as different as possible from something else 对立的，截然相反的，完全不同的：*I thought the medicine would make him sleep, but it had the opposite effect.* 我以为这药会使他入睡，但效果却完全相反。| *two parties at opposite ends of the political spectrum* 政治派别中截然对立的两个党派 **2** the opposite direction, way etc is directly away from someone or something〔方向〕相反的：*The woman turned and walked off in the opposite direction.* 那妇女转身朝着相反的方向走了。**3** one thing that is opposite another is on the other side of the same area, often directly across from it（在…）对面的，相对的：*The grocery store was on the opposite side of the street.* 杂货店在街对面。| *the houses opposite* 对面的房子 —see 见 FRONT[1] (USAGE) **4 at opposite ends of the city/country etc** on different sides of a city etc, and a long way apart 在城市/国家等的两端：*We live at opposite ends of the city, so it's not always easy to meet.*

我们住在城市的两头，所以见面并不总是很容易。**5 the opposite sex** the other sex 异性: *He doesn't feel comfortable with the opposite sex.* 与异性相处时，他觉得不自在。**6 opposite number** someone who has the same job in another similar organization〔在别的机构中〕居相同职位的人，职务对等的人: *his opposite number in the KGB* 在克格勃中与他的职务对等的人

opposite³ *n* [C] **1** a person or thing that is as different as possible from someone or something else 相反的人[事物]，对立物: *The colors 'black' and 'white' are opposites.* 黑色与白色相反。| **be the opposite (of)** *She's tall and slim, and he's the complete opposite.* 她高挑而苗条，他则全然相反。**2 not ... just/quite the opposite** used to say that something is completely different from what has just been said 不…，正好/完全相反: *Martha's not shy at all – just the opposite in fact.* 玛莎一点都不腼腆，事实上正好相反。

opposite⁴ *adv* in a position on the other side of the same area 在对面，对过: *The Browns live just opposite.* 布朗一家就住在对面。

S2 W1 **op·po·si·tion** /ˌɑpəˋzɪʃən; ˌɒpəˈzɪʃən/ *n* [U] **1** strong disagreement with, or protest against, something such as a plan, law, or system etc 反对；反抗: **opposition to sth** *There was a great deal of opposition to the war.* 对这场战争有很多反对意见。| **strong/fierce opposition** *Plans to build a new airport met with fierce opposition from local farmers.* 兴建新机场的计划遭到当地农民的强烈反对。| **in opposition to (sth)** *The party was founded in opposition to the more moderate policies of the government.* 该党的成立是为了反对政府较为温和的政策。**2** [also+plural verb *BrE* 英] the people who you are competing against 对手，对抗者: *He passed the ball to the opposition by mistake.* 他把球误传给了对方。—see also 另见 RIVAL¹ (1) **3 the opposition** the main political party in a country's parliament that is not part of the government 反对党，在野党: *the leader of the Opposition* 反对党的领袖 | *protests from the opposition* 反对党的抗议

CULTURAL NOTE 文化注释

In the UK, the Opposition is an important part of the political system. The members of the Opposition sit in Parliament. Their main job is to criticize the government, but they also work with the government on special committees set up to examine particular problems. The official title of the Opposition is 'Her Majesty's Loyal Opposition', which shows that the Opposition is considered to be loyal to the Queen and to the country, although it does not agree with the government's ideas. 反对党是英国政治制度的一个重要组成部分。英国议会中设有反对党党员的议席。反对党的主要工作是给政府提批评意见，但在为调查某个特别问题而成立特别委员会时，他们也与政府合作。反对党的正式称号是"女王陛下的忠实反对党"，这表明尽管反对党与政府的观点有分歧，它还是忠于女王和国家的。

4 in opposition a political party that is in opposition is in parliament, but is not part of the government〔政党〕在野的: *The Socialists were elected to power after 10 years in opposition.* 在野十年后，社会党人当选执政。

op·press /əˋprɛs; əˈpres/ *v* [T often passive 常用被动态] **1** to treat a group of people unfairly or cruelly, and prevent them from having the same rights that other people in society have 压迫，压制: *Native tribes had been oppressed by the government and police for years.* 多年来，土著部落一直受到政府和警方的压迫。**2** to make someone feel unhappy by restricting their freedom in some way 使压抑；使烦恼: *The solitude of her little apartment oppressed her.* 独居于那套小公寓房使她感到压抑。

op·pressed /əˋprɛst; əˈprest/ *adj* **1** a group of people who are oppressed are treated unfairly or cruelly and prevented from having the same rights as other people have 受压迫的，受压制的: *oppressed minorities* 受压迫的少数民族 | **the oppressed** (=people who are oppressed) 受压迫者，被压迫的人民 **2** someone who is oppressed feels unhappy because their freedom has been restricted in some way〔因受压制而〕烦恼的，忧郁的

op·pres·sion /əˋprɛʃən; əˈpreʃən/ *n* [U] the act of oppressing a group of people, or the state of being oppressed 压迫，压制: *immigrants taking refuge from the oppression of a dictatorship* 为了躲避专制压迫而寻求避难的移民

op·pres·sive /əˋprɛsɪv; əˈpresɪv/ *adj* **1** powerful, cruel, and unfair 暴虐的，残酷的；不公平的: *an oppressive military regime* 暴虐的军事政权 **2** weather that is oppressive is unpleasantly hot with no movement of air〔天气〕闷热的，令人烦闷的: *The evening gradually grew more and more oppressive.* 夜晚渐渐变得越来越闷热。**3** a situation that is oppressive makes you feel too uncomfortable to do or say anything 难以忍受的，郁闷的: *The silence in the meeting was becoming oppressive.* 会场上一片寂静，让人开始难以忍受。—**oppressively** *adv* —**oppressiveness** *n* [U]

op·pres·sor /əˋprɛsɚ; əˈpresə/ *n* [C] a person or group that oppresses people 压迫者；暴君: *They rose up against their colonial oppressors.* 他们奋起反抗殖民地的压迫者。

op·pro·bri·ous /əˋprobrɪəs; əˈprəʊbriəs/ *adj formal* showing great disrespect【正式】极无礼的，鄙俗的；表示轻蔑的 —**opprobriously** *adv*

op·pro·bri·um /əˋprobrɪəm; əˈprəʊbriəm/ *n* [U] *formal* strong public criticism, hatred, or shame【正式】〔公众强烈的〕批评，羞辱: *in the face of public opprobrium* 面对公众猛烈的批评

opt /ɑpt; ɒpt/ *v* [I] to choose one thing or one course of action instead of another 选择，挑选: **[+for]** *GM workers opted for job security over pay increases.* 通用汽车公司的工人宁愿选择就业保障，而不是加薪。| **opt to do sth** *Many young people are opting to go on to further education.* 许多年轻人都在选择继续学习深造。

opt out *phr v* [I] **1** to avoid doing a duty 躲避职责: **[+of]** *You can't just opt out of all responsibility for the child!* 你不能对孩子全然撒手不管！**2** to decide not to join in a group or system 决定不参与: *Britain wants to opt out of the European Social Chapter.* 英国不想加入《欧洲社会宪章》。**3** if a school or hospital in Britain opts out, it decides to control its own money, that it is given by the government, instead of being controlled by local government〔英国学校或医院〕自主管理〔政府拨给的经费，而非由地方政府来管理〕

op·tic¹ /ˋɑptɪk; ˈɒptɪk/ *adj* [only before noun 仅用于名词前] concerning the eyes 眼睛的；视觉的: *the optic nerve* 视觉神经 —see picture at 参见 EYE¹ 图

optic² *n* **1 optics** [U] the scientific study of light 光学 **2** [C] *BrE* a small plastic object on a bottle of alcohol that measures the amount to be poured into a glass【英】奥普蒂克量杯〔一种烈酒量杯，罩在酒瓶上〕

op·ti·cal /ˋɑptɪkl; ˈɒptɪkəl/ *adj* **1** used for seeing images and light 视觉的，有助于视力的；光学的: *microscopes and other optical instruments* 显微镜和其他光学仪器 **2** concerned with the way light is seen 光像的: *an optical diagram* 光学图像 **3** using light, especially for the purpose of sending or storing information for use in a computer system 光学的，利用光的〔尤指为电脑系统所使用发送或储存信息〕: *optical character recognition* 光学符识别（技术），感光字元辨识 —**optically** /-klɪ; kli/ *adv*

optical fi·bre /ˌ··ˈ··/ *n* [U] a thread-like piece of glass or plastic which is used for sending information, for example in a telephone or computer system 光学纤维，光纤

optical il·lu·sion /ˌ···ˈ··/ *n* [C] a picture or image that tricks your eyes and makes you see something that is not actually there 视错觉，光幻觉

op·ti·cian /ɑpˋtɪʃən; ɒpˈtɪʃən/ *n* [C] **1** *BrE* someone who tests people's eyes and sells SPECTACLES in a shop【英】〔眼镜店的〕验光配镜技师 **2** *AmE* someone who makes lenses (LENS (1)) for SPECTACLES【美】镜片制造商

op·ti·mal /ˋɑptəməl; ˈɒptɪməl/ *adj* the best or most suitable; OPTIMUM (1) 最佳的；最适宜的

op·ti·mis·m /ˋɑptəˌmɪzəm; ˈɒptɪmɪzəm/ *n* [U] a tendency to believe that good things will always happen 乐观；乐观主义: *the optimism of the postwar years* 战后几年的乐观（情绪）—opposite 反义词 PESSIMISM

op·ti·mist /ˋɑptəmɪst; ˈɒptɪmɪst/ *n* [C] someone who always believes that good things will happen 乐观者，乐观主义者: *I'm a born optimist.* 我是个天生的乐天派。—opposite 反义词 PESSIMIST

op·ti·mis·tic /ˌɑptəˋmɪstɪk; ˌɒptɪˈmɪstɪk◂/ *adj* **1** believing that good things will happen in the future 乐观的；乐观主义的: **[+about]** *Foreign bankers are cautiously optimistic about the country's economic future.* 外国银行家对该国的经济前景持谨慎乐观的态度。**2** thinking that things will be better, easier or more successful than is actually possible〔对未来〕（过于）有信心的，（过分）乐观的: **over-optimistic** *They're being over-optimistic if they think that car can make an 800 mile trip.* 如果他们以为那辆车能胜任一趟800英里的旅行，那他们想得过于乐观了。—**optimistically** /-klɪ; -kli/ *adv* —opposite 反义词 PESSIMISTIC

op·ti·mize also 又作 **-ise** *BrE*【英】/ˋɑptəˌmaɪz; ˈɒptɪmaɪz/ *v* [T] to make the way that something is done or used as effective as possible 使最优化，使尽可能完善；使尽量有效: *The company is seeking to optimize its use of financial resources by introduc-*

ing performance-related pay. 公司正寻求采取将薪酬与业绩挂钩的方式来尽力优化资金的使用。

op·ti·mum /ˈɑptəməm; ˈɒptɪməm/ *adj* [only before noun 仅用于名词前] **1** the best or most suitable for a particular purpose 最优的; 最有利的; 最适宜的: *the optimum temperature for keeping wine* 储存酒的最适宜温度 **2 the optimum** the best possible situation, conditions, amount of time etc for something to happen 最佳条件, 最佳状况

S1 W2 **op·tion** /ˈɑpʃən; ˈɒpʃən/ *n*

1 ▶A CHOICE 选择◀ [C] a choice you can make in a particular situation 选择: *As I see it, we have two options – either we sell the house or we rent it out.* 依我看, 我们有两种选择 —— 或是卖掉房子, 或是出租。| *I usually choose the vegetarian option in restaurants.* 我在餐馆里通常都点素菜。| **the option of doing sth** *I always had the option of going back to Canada.* 我当时随时都可以选择回加拿大。| **have no option but to do sth** (=be forced to do something because there are no other choices) 不得不做某事, 除做某事外别无选择 *Teenage mothers often have no option but to live with their parents.* 少女妈妈经常只能与父母同住, 别无选择余地。

2 keep/leave your options open to wait before making a decision 暂不作决定, 留有选择余地: *We should keep our options open until Jim can study the results of the survey.* 我们暂且不作决定, 等吉姆对调查结果研究过以后再说。

3 ▶RIGHT TO BUY/SELL 买/卖的选择权◀ [C] the right to buy or sell something in the future〔将来〕买卖某物的选择权利: [+on] *The Saudi government has agreed to buy 20 planes, with an option on a further 10.* 沙特政府已同意购买20架飞机, 并拥有再买10架的选购权。

4 ▶COMPUTERS 电脑◀ [C] one of the possible choices you can make when using a computer PROGRAM[1] (1)〔电脑程序的〕选项: *Press 'P' to select the print option.* 按P键选择打印。

5 ▶STH THAT IS ADDITIONAL 附件, 配件◀ [C] something that is offered in addition to the standard equipment when you buy something new, especially a car〔购买新商品, 尤指汽车时标准设备之外可供选择的〕附件, 配件

6 ▶AT COLLEGE/UNIVERSITY 在大学◀ [C] *BrE* a subject that you can choose to study as part of a course【英】选修课: *I did an option in Korean Studies.* 我选修了一门朝鲜语研究课程。

7 first option the chance to buy or get something before anyone else 第一选择; 优先权: *They've agreed to give us the first option on their apartment.* 他们同意给予我们那套房子的优先购买权。

8 the soft/easy option the course of action that needs the least effort, chosen because you are being lazy 最轻松/最容易的选择: *Some people consider studying Expressive Arts to be a soft option.* 一些人认为选修表现艺术最容易及格。

op·tion·al /ˈɑpʃənl; ˈɒpʃənəl/ *adj* if something is optional, you do not have to do it or use it, but you can choose to if you want to 可选择的, 非强制的: *Woodwork was an optional subject at our school.* 木工手艺在我们学校是一门选修课。| **an optional extra** (=something that you can choose to have in addition to what you would normally get) 可选的额外之物 *Leather seats are an optional extra in the hatchback.* 这款掀背式汽车另有皮革座椅可供选择。

op·tom·e·trist /ɑpˈtɑmətrɪst; ɒpˈtɒmɪtrɪst/ *n* [C] someone who tests people's eyes and orders SPECTACLES for them 验光师, 配镜师

op·u·lence /ˈɑpjələns; ˈɒpjʊləns/ *n* [U] great wealth 富裕; 财富: *the opulence of ancient Rome* 古罗马的富足

op·u·lent /ˈɑpjələnt; ˈɒpjʊlənt/ *adj* **1 a)** very beautiful, highly decorated, and made from expensive materials; LUXURIOUS 华丽的, 豪华的, 奢侈的: *the opulent splendour of the Sultan's palace* 苏丹王宫的金碧辉煌 **b)** very rich 阔绰的, 非常富有的: *opulent officials in large limousines* 坐着大型豪华轿车的富有官员 **2** growing healthily and in large amounts; LUXURIANT 繁茂的; 大量的; 浓密的

o·pus /ˈopəs; ˈəʊpəs/ *n* [usually singular 一般用单数] **1** a piece of music by a great musician, numbered according to when it was written〔根据创作时间先后〕编号的音乐作品: *Beethoven's Opus 95 quartets* 贝多芬的四重奏, 作品第95号 **2** an important work of art by a famous writer, painter etc〔著名作家、画家等的〕大作, 杰作, 主要作品: *Verdi's Requiem, his greatest opus* 威尔第的《安魂曲》, 他最伟大的作品 —see also 另见 MAGNUM OPUS

OR the written abbreviation of 缩写= OREGON

-or /ɚ; ə/ *suffix* [in nouns 构成名词] the form used for -ER in certain words〔在某些词中用以代替 -ER 的(后缀)形式〕: *an actor* (=someone who acts) 演员 | *an inventor* 发明家; 创造者

or /ɚ; ə; *strong* 强读 ɔr; ɔː/ *conjunction* S1 W1 **1** used between two things or before the last in a list of possibilities, things that people can choose from etc 或, 或者; 还是: *Do you want to leave now or would you rather set off later?* 你想现在动身还是愿意晚点出发? | *Was it London, Paris or Rome where you first met Maxim?* 你初次见到马克西姆是在伦敦、巴黎还是罗马? | **or anything/something** *spoken* (=or something of the same kind)【口】或其他什么的, 诸如此类的什么 *Would you like a coffee or something?* 你想来杯咖啡或别的什么饮料? | *I wasn't trying to push in or anything.* 我并不想挤进去或怎么的。| **either... or...** *If either Lennie or Miranda calls, I'm not at home.* 如果伦尼或米兰达来电话就说我不在家。—compare 比较 EITHER[1] **2** used after a negative verb when you mean not one thing and also not another thing 也不〔用于含否定意思的动词后〕: *He doesn't have a television or a video.* 他没有电视机, 也没有录像机。| *Sonia never cleans or even offers to wash the dishes.* 索尼娅从不收拾整理, 连主动提出洗碗碟也没有。**3** used to warn or advise someone that if they do not do something, something they do not want will happen 否则, 要不然: *Wear your coat or you'll catch cold.* 穿上外套, 要不你会着凉的。| **or else** *You have to roll the clothes very tightly or else they won't all fit in the rucksack.* 你得把衣服裹紧, 要不没法全都塞进帆布包里。| *You'd better be there, or else.* (=used to threaten someone) 你最好去那里, 要不够你受的。**4** used to correct something that you have said or to give more specific information 即, 那就是, 或者说〔用于更正说法或给予更确切的信息〕: *It's going to snow tomorrow, or that's what the forecast says.* 明天将要下雪, 确切地说, 气象预报是这样说的。| *She was born in Saigon, or Ho Chi Minh City as it is now called.* 她出生于西贡, 即现在所称的胡志明市。| **or rather** *The computer software is old, or rather very out of date.* 这个电脑软件很老了, 更确切地说是早就过时了。**5** used to explain why something happens or to show that something must be true 要不然〔用以解释某事发生的原因或说明某事必定是真的〕: *He must be very drunk or he wouldn't keep falling down.* 他准是喝得烂醉了, 要不然他不会老是摔倒。| **or else** *It's either a coincidence they're so alike, or else they are related in some way.* 要不就是他们碰巧这么相像, 要不就是他们有某种血缘关系。**6 a minute/a mile/twenty etc or so** a particular amount or a little more 一分钟/一英里/二十等左右: *They had to wait an hour or so for the police to arrive.* 他们得等上一小时左右警察才到来。**7 a minute/a dollar etc or two** a small amount or number of something 大约一两分钟/一两块钱等: *I saw Nigel leaving a second or two ago.* 我看见奈杰尔一两秒钟前刚离开。

or·a·cle /ˈɔrəkl; ˈɒrəkəl/ *n* [C] **1** someone the ancient Greeks believed could communicate with the gods, who gave advice to people or told them what would happen〔古希腊时〕宣示神谕的人, 传神谕者: *Spartans would consult the oracle before going into battle.* 斯巴达人总要先请示神谕后再去打仗。**2** a message given by an oracle 神谕 **3** *humorous* a person or book that gives advice and information【幽默】提供意见[信息]的人[书籍]

o·rac·u·lar /ɔˈrækjəlɚ; ɒˈrækjʊlə/ *adj* **1** said by an oracle 神谕的 **2** difficult to understand 难解的; 玄妙深奥的

o·ral[1] /ˈɔrəl; ˈɔːrəl/ *n* [C] **1** *BrE* a spoken test, especially in a foreign language【英】〔尤指外语的〕口试: *I've got my French oral tomorrow.* 我明天有法语口试。**2** *AmE* a spoken test for a MASTER'S DEGREE【美】〔硕士学位中的〕口试

oral[2] *adj* **1** spoken, not written 口头的, 口述的: *oral history* 口述的历史 | *a brief oral report* 简短的口头报告 **2** concerned with or involving the mouth 口的, 口腔的: *oral hygiene* 口腔卫生 —**orally** *adv*

oral con·tra·cep·tive /ˌ.. ..ˈ../ *n* [C] a drug that a woman takes by mouth, so that she can have sex without having a baby; the PILL (2) 口服避孕药

oral ex·am /ˈ.. .ˌ./ *n* [C] an ORAL 口试

oral sex /ˌ.. ˈ./ *n* [U] touching someone's sex organs with the lips and tongue, to give sexual pleasure 口交, 舐淫

oral sur·geon /ˈ.. ˌ../ *n* [C] **1** a DENTIST who performs operations in the mouth 口腔外科医生 **2** *AmE* a DENTIST【美】牙医

or·ange /ˈɔrɪndʒ; ˈɒrɪndʒ/ *n* [C] **1** a round fruit that has a thick orange skin and is divided into parts inside 柑橘, 橙 —see picture on page A8 参见A8页图 **2** a colour that is between red and yellow 橘黄色, 橙色: *The sky turned a brilliant orange.* 天空转而呈现出鲜艳的橙色。—**orange** *adj*: *Carrots are orange.* 胡萝卜是橘黄色的。—see picture on page A5 参见A5页图 S3

or·ange·ade /ˌɔrɪndʒˈed; ˌɒrɪndʒˈeɪd/ *n* [U] a drink that tastes like oranges 橘子水, 橙汁饮料

Orange Bowl, the /ˈ.. ˌ./ an important college football game, held every year in Miami, Florida 柑橘杯赛〔大学生美式橄榄球比赛的重要赛事, 每年在佛罗里达州迈阿密举行〕

Orange Free State /ˌ· · ˈ·/ —see 见 FREE STATE

Or·ange·man /ˈɔrɪndʒmən; ˈɒrɪ̣ndʒmən/ *n plural* **Orangemen** /-mən; -mən/ a member of a Protestant society in Northern Ireland, known as the **Orange Order**. Orangemen strongly support the idea that Northern Ireland should remain as part of the UK, and they oppose Catholic groups who want Northern Ireland to become part of Ireland 奥兰治党员，橙带党党员〔北爱尔兰一新教社团(取名"橙带党")成员。他们极力支持北爱尔兰与联合王国合一的主张，反对天主教群体企图将北爱尔兰纳入爱尔兰共和国的做法〕

Orangemen's Day /ˈ· · ·, ·/ July 12, celebrated by Protestants in Northern Ireland with the Orangemen's Day Parade, which remembers the Protestant success over James II and his Catholic supporters at the Battle of the Boyne 奥兰治日〔即7月12日。这天，北爱尔兰的新教教徒举行"奥兰治日大游行"纪念博恩河战役。新教教徒曾在此次战役中打败了詹姆斯二世及其信仰天主教的支持者〕

or·an·gery /ˈɔrɪndʒri; ˈɒrɪ̣ndʒəri/ *n* [C] a place where orange trees are grown 柑橘园

orange squash /ˌ· · ˈ·/ *n* [U] *BrE* a drink that tastes like oranges, made by adding water to a strong tasting liquid【英】橙子水，鲜橘水，橘子汽水

o·rang·u·tang /əˈræŋəˌtæŋ; ɔːˌræŋuːˈtæŋ/ also 又作 **o·rang·u·tan** /-tæn; -tæn/ *n* [C] a large APE[1] (1) with long arms and long orange hair 猩猩

o·ra·tion /ɔˈreʃən; əˈreɪʃən/ *n* [C] a formal public speech〔正式的〕演说，演讲

or·a·tor /ˈɔrətə; ˈɒrətə/ *n* [C] someone who makes speeches and is good at persuading people 演讲者，演说家

or·a·to·ri·o /ˌɔrəˈtɔrio; ˌɒrəˈtɔːriəʊ/ *n* [C] a long piece of music in which a large group of people sing 清唱剧，神剧

or·a·tory /ˈɔrəˌtɔri; ˈɒrətri/ *n* **1** [U] the skill of making powerful and persuasive speeches 演讲术，雄辩术: *a dazzling display of oratory* 令人赞叹的口才展示 **2** [U] language that includes long and formal words〔含长而正式词语的〕华丽言辞 **3** [C] a small building or part of a church where people can go to pray 小礼拜堂，祈祷室 —**oratorical** /ˌɔrəˈtɔrɪkḷ; ˌɒrəˈtɒrɪkəl◂/ *adj*: *Churchill's formidable oratorical skills* 丘吉尔令人钦佩的雄辩技巧 —**oratorically** /-kḷɪ; -kli/ *adv*

orb /ɔrb; ɔːb/ *n* [C] **1** *literary* a bright ball-shaped object, especially the sun or the moon【文】明亮的球体〔尤指太阳或月亮〕: *the red orb of the sun* 红彤彤的太阳球体 **2** a ball decorated with gold, carried by a king or queen on formal occasions as a sign of power〔国王或女王在正式场合作为王权标志携带的〕宝球

or·bit[1] /ˈɔrbɪt; ˈɔːbɪ̣t/ *v* [I,T] to travel in a circle around a much larger object such as the Earth, the sun etc 环绕…轨道运行: *The satellite orbits the Earth every 48 hours.* 那颗人造卫星每48小时绕地球轨道运行一周。

orbit[2] *n* [C] **1** the path travelled by an object which is moving around another much larger object such as the Earth, the sun etc〔环绕地球或太阳等运行的〕轨道: *the Moon's orbit around the Earth* 月球环绕地球运行的轨道 | **in orbit** (=travelling in this kind of path) 在轨道上运行 *The Space Shuttle is now in orbit.* 航天飞机已进入轨道飞行。**2** an area of power and influence 势力范围: *brought within orbit of the Central Office* 纳入总局的势力范围

or·bit·al /ˈɔrbɪtḷ; ˈɔːbɪtl/ *adj* **1** concerned with the orbit of one object around another 轨道的: *the Earth's orbital path* 地球的运行轨道 **2** *BrE* an orbital road goes around a large city【英】〔公路〕环城的: *the London orbital motorway* 伦敦外环高速公路 —**orbital** *n* [C]

or·chard /ˈɔrtʃəd; ˈɔːtʃəd/ *n* [C] a place where fruit trees are grown 果园: *a cherry orchard* 樱桃园

or·ches·tra /ˈɔrkɪstrə; ˈɔːkɪ̣strə/ *n* [C also+plural verb *BrE* 英] a large group of musicians playing many different kinds of instruments and led by a CONDUCTOR (1)〔大型的〕管弦乐队

or·ches·tral /ɔrˈkɛstrəl; ɔːˈkestrəl/ *adj* concerned with or written for an orchestra 管弦乐队(演奏)的；为管弦乐队创作的: *orchestral music* 管弦乐

orchestra pit /ˈ· · · ·/ *n* [C] the space below the stage in a theatre where the musicians sit〔剧场舞台前凹陷的〕乐池 —see picture at 参见 THEATRE 图

or·ches·trate /ˈɔrkɪsˌtret; ˈɔːkɪ̣streɪt/ *v* [T] **1** to organize an important event or a complicated plan, especially secretly〔尤指秘密地〕精心策划: *The coup was orchestrated by the CIA.* 这次政变是中央情报局一手策划的。**2** to arrange a piece of music so that it can be played by an orchestra 将〔乐曲〕编成管弦乐曲 —**orchestrated** *adj* —**orchestration** /ˌɔrkɪˈstreʃən; ˌɔːkɪ̣ˈstreɪʃən/ *n* [C,U]

or·chid /ˈɔrkɪd; ˈɔːkɪ̣d/ *n* [C] a plant that has flowers with three parts, the middle one being shaped like a lip 兰花

or·dain /ɔrˈden; ɔːˈdeɪn/ *v* [T] **1** to officially make someone a priest or religious leader 正式任命〔某人〕为牧师，授予〔某人〕圣职: *Desmond Tutu was ordained in 1960.* 德斯蒙德·图图于1960年被授予圣职。| **ordain sb (as) sth** *Paulson was ordained deacon.* 保尔森被任命为执事牧师。—see also 另见 ORDINATION **2** *formal* to order that something should happen【正式】命令，规定；判定: *a duty ordained by God* 上帝规定的职责 | [+that] *The King ordained that a feast should be prepared.* 国王命令准备一场盛宴。

or·deal /ɔrˈdil; ɔːˈdiːl/ *n* [C] a terrible or painful experience 可怕的经历，痛苦的折磨: [+of] *the ordeal of having your child kidnapped* 孩子遭绑架的痛苦经历 | **it is an ordeal to do sth** *Some people find it an ordeal to appear before the TV camera.* 有些人觉得面对电视摄像机是一种煎熬。

or·der[1] /ˈɔrdə; ˈɔːdə/ *n*

1 ▸FOR A PURPOSE 为某一目的◂ a) in order to do sth for the purpose of doing something 为了做某事: *politicians who make promises simply in order to win more votes* 纯粹为了赢得更多选票而作出种种承诺的政客 | *In order to understand how the human body works, you need to have some knowledge of chemistry.* 为了了解人体是如何运转的，你需要懂一些化学知识。**b) in order for/that** *formal* so that something can happen or so that someone can do something【正式】为了，以便: **in order for sb/sth to do sth** *Sunlight is needed in order for photosynthesis to take place.* 需要阳光来进行光合作用。| **in order that** *I locked the door in order that we might continue our discussions undisturbed.* 我锁上门以便我们能不受干扰地继续商谈。

order 顺序 1 1

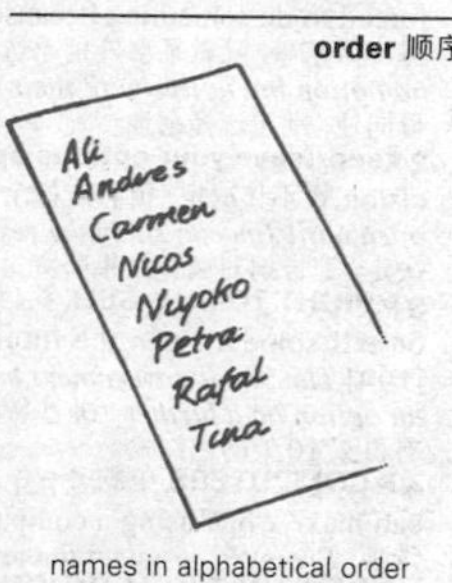

names in alphabetical order
按字母顺序排列的姓名

2 ▸ARRANGEMENT 安排◂ [C,U] the way that several things, events etc are arranged or put on a list, showing whether something is first, second, third etc; SEQUENCE 顺序，次序: *The programme shows the order of events for the day.* 节目单列出了当天节目的顺序。| **in order** (=arranged in a particular way) 整齐，有条理 *You should keep the files in order.* 你应当把文件都归放整齐。| *What order are these videos supposed to be in?* 这些录像节目应该怎样排序？| **do sth in order** (=do things one after another, according to a plan) 做事有条不紊 *Then they call out our names in order and we answer yes or no.* 随后，他们依次点我们的名字，我们则回答是与否。| **out of order** (=in the wrong order) 次序颠倒，不按顺序 | **in chronological/alphabetical/numerical order** *Let us examine these events in chronological order.* 我们按年代顺序来考察一下这些事件吧。| **in the right/wrong order** *Wait a minute, we've got these photos in the wrong order.* 等一下，我们把这些照片的顺序弄错了。| **in order of importance/preference/appearance etc** *Characters are listed in order of appearance.* 人物是按出场顺序排列的。| **in reverse order** (=in the opposite order to what is usual) 次序颠倒 | **in ascending/descending order** (=starting with the lowest or highest number) 按递增/递减的顺序

3 ▸REQUEST FOR GOODS 订货◂ [C] a request by a customer for a company to supply goods or for a meal in a restaurant 订货；订购；点菜: **place an order** (=make an order) 订货，下订单 *The Canadian Air Force has placed a large order for electronic equipment.* 加拿大空军订购了一大批电子设备。| **order form** (=special piece of paper for writing orders on) 订单，订购表格 *Have you filled out the order form?* 你填好订单了吗？| **on order** (=ordered but not yet received) 订购中的，已订购但尚未交货的 *It's on order – it should be in next week.* 货已订购，下周该到了。| **have sth on order** (=be waiting for something you have ordered) 等待着已订购之物的交货 | **take sb's order** (=write down what a customer in a restaurant wants) 记下顾客点的饭菜 *The waiter came over to take my order.* 服务员过来请我点菜。| **make/supply sth to order** (=produce something especially for a particular customer) 按订单要求生产/供应货物 *We supply hand-made shoes to order.* 我们供应手工订做的鞋。

4 ▸GOODS/MEAL 货物/饭菜◂ [C] goods or a meal that a customer has asked for〔客户订的〕货物；点的饭菜: *Your order has arrived – you can collect it from the store any time.* 你订的货已

经到了，你可以随时来店铺提取。| **side order**(=a small plate of food in addition to your main meal) 主菜以外另点的小菜

5 ►NO TROUBLE OR CRIME 无动乱或犯罪◄[U] a situation in which rules are obeyed and authority is respected 治安，秩序；规矩：**law and order** *the work of the police in maintaining law and order* 警方在维持法律和秩序方面的工作 | **public order** *Their speeches were clearly a threat to public order.* 他们的言论无疑是对社会治安的一种威胁。| **keep order/keep sb in order**(=stop people from behaving badly) 维持秩序/使某人守规矩 *Some of the new teachers can't keep order.* 年轻老师中有一些人无法维持课堂秩序。| *Don't worry, I'll keep them in order.* 别担心，我会让他们规规矩矩的。| **restore order** *The army was called in to restore order.* 军队被召来恢复秩序。| **call sb to order**(=order someone in a formal meeting or court of law to obey the rules)〔在正式会议或法庭上〕要某人遵守秩序 | **Order! Order!**(=used in parliament or in court to tell people to be quiet and obey the rules) 秩序！秩序！〔在议会里或法庭上说的话〕

6 ►COMMAND 命令◄also 又作 **orders**[C] a command given by someone in authority 命令；指示：*I expect my orders to be obeyed.* 我希望大家能服从我的命令。| *You will report to me at eight o'clock tomorrow – and that's an order.* 你要在明天8点向我报告，这是命令。| **give orders** *I'm the one who gives the orders around here – just remember that.* 在这里我才是发号施令的人，你们要记着。| **take orders from**(=obey someone) 接受…的命令 *I'm not taking orders from you!* 我不接受你的命令！| **order to do sth** *General Bradley gave the order to advance.* 布拉德利将军下令前进。| **have orders to do sth**(=have been commanded to do something) 奉命做某事 *I have orders to search your house.* 我奉命搜查你的房子。| **by order of/on the orders of**(=because of someone's order) 奉…之命 *On Stalin's orders the target for the five year plan was raised once again.* 奉斯大林之命，五年计划的目标又一次提高了。| **under orders to do sth**(=having been commanded to do something) 奉命做某事 *A warship was dispatched, under orders to sail directly to Georgetown.* 军舰奉命出发，直驶乔治敦。

7 ►LEGAL DOCUMENT 法律文件◄[C] an official statement from a court of law that something must be done; COURT ORDER 法院决议；法院指令

8 be out of order **a)** if a machine or piece of equipment is out of order, it is not working〔机器或设备等〕发生故障，失灵：*The phone at the street corner is out of order again.* 街角的电话又坏了。**b)** if things on a list or in a series are out of order, they are not correctly arranged 次序颠倒[紊乱]；排列错误：*Some of the pages in this book are out of order.* 这本书的一些书页次序颠倒了。**c)** *BrE informal* if someone's behaviour is out of order it is unacceptable【英，非正式】举止不当；OUT OF LINE (LINE¹ (32)) *AmE*【美】**d)** to be breaking the rules in a committee, court, parliament etc 违反〔委员会、法庭、议会等的〕规程：*The MP's remarks were ruled out of order.* 该议员的意见被裁定为违反章程。

9 be in order **a)** if things on a list or in a series are in order they are correctly arranged〔排列〕顺序正确 **b)** if an official document is in order it is legal and correct〔正式文件等〕合法，无误，妥当：*Is your passport in order?* 你的护照有效吗？**c)** if something that you do is in order, it is allowed by the rules in a committee, court, parliament etc 符合〔委员会、法庭、议会等的〕规程 **d)** to be a suitable thing to do or say on a particular occasion 适宜，合适，恰当：*I hear congratulations are in order.* 听说该向你道喜了。

10 be in (good) working/running order if a vehicle or machine is in good working or running order, it is working well〔车辆或机器等〕状况良好：*a 1927 Model A Ford, still in good running order* 一辆1927年的A型福特汽车，车况依然良好

11 ►WELL-ORGANIZED STATE 井然有序的状态◄[U] a situation in which everything is controlled, well organized, and correctly arranged 有条理，整齐：*Let's have some order in here. Someone put those desks straight.* 我们把这里整理一下，谁去把那些书桌摆整齐吧。| **put sth in order**(=organize or arrange something properly) 把某事安排妥当 *Uncle Bob put his business affairs in order before he died.* 鲍勃大叔在去世前把生意方面的事情都安排妥当了。| **in apple-pie order** *AmE informal* (=very tidy and correctly arranged)【美，非正式】井然有序，有条不紊 *Tim's room was in apple-pie order.* 蒂姆的房间井然有序。

12 leave/retreat/retire in good order to leave in a controlled way, when people are angry or attacking you〔在他人生气或攻击时〕以克制的方式离开/退出/离去

13 ►POLITICAL/SOCIAL SITUATION 政治/社会的状况◄[singular] the political, social, or economic situation at a particular time〔某一时期政治、社会或经济的〕状况，秩序，制度：*the present economic order* 当前的经济模式 | **the established order**(=the traditional rules and customs of society) 现存制度；传统社会习俗 *The gay rights movement emerged to challenge the established order.* 同性恋者争取权益的运动对现存制度发起了挑战。| **the new order**(=the new situation after an important change in politics or society)〔重大政治或社会变革之后的〕新秩序 *the new world order since the end of the Cold War* 自冷战结束以来的世界新秩序

14 the (natural) order of things the way that life and the world are organized and intended to be 事物的正常秩序：*People accepted the class system as part of the natural order of things.* 人们曾把等级制度看作是自然而然的事。

15 of a high/the highest/the first order of a very good or of the best kind 优秀的/最高级的/一流的：*an achievement of the highest order* 最出色的成就

16 be the order of the day **a)** to be suitable for a particular occasion or situation〔在某场合或情况中〕适宜的，恰当的：*Casual clothes are the order of the day.* 休闲服装很合时宜。**b)** to be very common at a particular time 在某一时期变得很寻常，非常普遍：*Sexual explicitness seems to be the order of the day.* 公开讨论性的话题当今似乎已成为寻常之事。

17 in the order of/of the order of also 又作 **on the order of** *AmE*【美】a little more or a little less than a particular amount; APPROXIMATELY 大约：*a figure in the order of $7 million* 大约700万美元的一笔数字

18 in short order *especially AmE* immediately【尤美】立即，毫不耽搁地：*The crisis was resolved in relatively short order.* 这场危机很快就化解了。

19 ►RELIGIOUS GROUP 宗教团体◄[C] a society of MONKS or NUNS (=people who live a holy life according to religious rules) 修道会，修士[修女]会：*the Benedictine Order* 本笃会 | [+of] *the order of Jesuits* 耶稣会

20 take (holy) orders to become a priest 担任圣职

21 ►SECRET SOCIETY 秘密会社◄[C] an organization or society whose members meet for secret ceremonies 秘密组织[会社]：*a Masonic order* 共济会 | *the Royal Ancient Order of Boars* 皇家古野猪会

22 ►OFFICIAL HONOUR 正式荣誉◄[C] **a)** a group of people who have received a special official reward from a king, president etc for their services or achievements 获得勋位的一批人，勋爵士团：*the Order of the Garter* 获得嘉德勋位的勋爵士团 **b)** a special piece of metal, silk etc that members of the order wear at ceremonies〔获勋位者佩戴的〕勋章

23 ►MONEY 钱财◄[C] an official piece of paper that can be exchanged for money 汇票，汇单 —see also 另见 POSTAL ORDER, BANKER'S ORDER, MONEY ORDER

24 the lower orders *BrE old-fashioned* people who belong to the lowest social class【英，过时】低下阶层

25 ►OF ANIMALS/PLANTS 动物的/植物的◄[C] *technical* a group of animals or plants that are considered together because they are descended from the same plant or animal in EVOLUTION (1)【术语】〔动、植物分类用的〕目 —compare 比较 CLASS¹ (6), KINGDOM (3), SPECIES

26 ►COMPUTER 电脑◄[C] *AmE technical* a list of jobs that a computer has to do in a particular order【美，术语】任务排序；等待队列；QUEUE *BrE*【英】—see also 另见 POINT OF ORDER, **tall order**(TALL (3)), STANDING ORDER, PECKING ORDER, **be given/get your marching orders**(MARCH¹ (5)), **under starter's orders** (STARTER (3)), **set/put your own house in order**(HOUSE¹ (7))

This graph shows some of the words most commonly used with the noun **order**. 本图表所示为含有名词 order 的一些最常用词组。

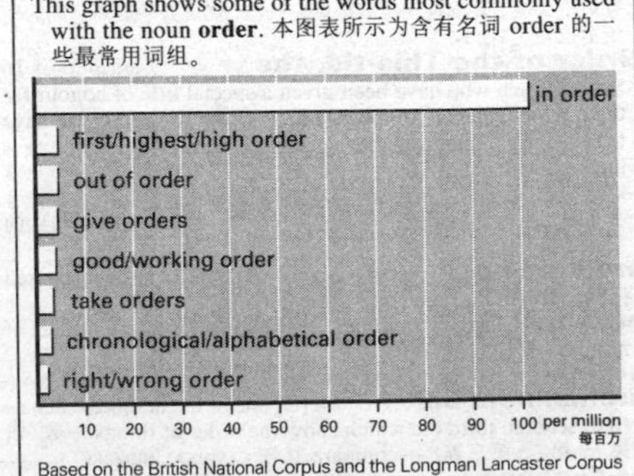

Based on the British National Corpus and the Longman Lancaster Corpus
据英国国家语料库和朗文兰开斯特语料库

order² *v* **1** [I,T] to ask for goods or services 点菜; 订购: *Have you ordered yet, madam?* 夫人, 您点过菜了吗? | **order sth** *She ordered a double brandy.* 她要了一杯双份白兰地。| **order sb sth** *We'll order you a taxi from the station.* 我们会为你在车站预订一辆出租车。| **order sth for sb/sth** *I've ordered new curtains for the living room.* 我已经为起居室订购了新窗帘。**2** [T] to tell someone to do something, using your authority or power 命令, 指令; 嘱咐: *"Stay right there," she ordered.* "就待在这里。" 她命令道。| **order sb in/out etc** *If you make any more noise I'll order you out of the room.* 要是你再吵, 我就要你离开这个房间。| **order sb to do sth** *The commandant ordered them to line up against the wall.* 指挥官命令他们靠墙排成一行。| **order sth** *Only the king has the power to order the release of the prisoners.* 只有国王有权下令释放囚犯。| **[+that]** *A grand jury has ordered that Schultz be sent for trial.* 大陪审团已下令将舒尔茨送审。**3** [T] to arrange something in an order 安排, 整理: *The diamonds are ordered according to size.* 这些钻石是按规格大小整理排列的。**4** [T] *old use* to arrange things neatly or effectively【旧】将…收拾整齐; 有效地安排

order sb **about/around** *phr v* [T] *BrE* to continuously give someone orders in an annoying or threatening way【英】不断地支使〔某人〕, 〔专横地〕将〔某人〕差来遣去: *Keith's older brother is always ordering him around.* 基思的大哥总是支使他干这干那。

order sb ↔ **out** *phr v* [T] to order soldiers or police to go somewhere to stop violent behaviour by a crowd 下令出动〔军警等〕: *The Governor decided to order out the National Guard.* 州长决定出动国民警卫队。

or·dered /ˈɔrdəd; ˈɔːdəd/ also 又作 **well-ordered** *adj* well arranged or controlled 有条理的, 有秩序的: *a well-ordered household* 井然有序的家庭 | *an ordered existence* 有条不紊的生活 —compare 比较 DISORDERED (1)

or·der·ly¹ /ˈɔrdəlɪ; ˈɔːdəli/ *adj* **1** arranged or organized in a sensible or neat way 有条理的, 整齐的: *an orderly household* 整洁的家庭 | *an orderly mind* 有条理的头脑 **2** peaceful or well-behaved 守秩序的: *An orderly crowd assembled at the gate.* 一群守秩序的人聚集在大门口。—**orderliness** *n* [U]

orderly² *n* [C] **1** someone who does unskilled jobs in a hospital〔医院里从事简单工作的〕护理员, 勤杂人员 **2** a soldier who does unskilled jobs 勤务兵

Order of Mer·it, the /,··ˈ··/ abbreviation 缩写为 **OM** a special honour given to British people who have done something unusually good in military or civilian life. Only 24 people have the Order of Merit at any one time. 功绩勋位〔英国授予有突出贡献的军职或文职人员的一种特殊勋衔。一次只有24人可获此殊荣〕

Order of the Bath, the /,····ˈ·/ a group of British people who have been given a special title of honour for their achievements. Members of the Order of the Bath have the title 'Sir' (for a man) or 'Dame' (for a woman), and it is regarded as a very special honour. 巴思勋位[勋爵士团]〔授予业绩杰出的一批英国人士的一种特殊荣誉称号。巴思勋位获得者, 男士冠以"爵士"头衔, 女士冠以"女爵士"头衔。该勋衔被认为是一种极为特殊的荣誉〕

Order of the Gar·ter, the /,····ˈ··/ a group of 24 British men who have been given a special title of honour for their achievements. Members of the Order of the Garter have the title 'Sir', and, together with the Order of the Thistle, it is the highest level of knighthood. 嘉德勋位[勋爵士团]〔授予业绩杰出的24名英国男士的一种特殊荣誉称号。嘉德勋位获得者享有爵士头衔。嘉德勋位与蓟花勋位一样, 被认为是最高级别的骑士勋位〕

Order of the This·tle, the /,····ˈ··/ a group of 16 Scottish men who have been given a special title of honour for their achievements. Members of the Order of the Thistle have the title 'Sir', and, together with the Order of the Garter, it is the highest level of knighthood. 蓟花勋位[勋爵士团]〔授予业绩杰出的16名苏格兰男士的一种特殊荣誉称号。蓟花勋位获得者享有爵士头衔。蓟花勋位与嘉德勋位一样, 被认为是最高级别的骑士勋位〕

order pa·per /ˈ··,··/ *n* [C] a list of subjects to be discussed in the British Parliament〔英国议会的〕议事日程表

or·di·nal¹ /ˈɔrdnəl; ˈɔːdɪnəl/ *adj* showing a position in a set of numbers 顺序的, 依次的

ordinal² *n* [C] an ordinal number 序数

ordinal num·ber /,···ˈ··/ *n* [C] one of the numbers such as first, second, third etc which show the order of things 序数〈如第一、第二、第三等〉—compare 比较 CARDINAL NUMBER

or·di·nance /ˈɔrdṇəns; ˈɔːdɪnəns/ *n* [C] **1** an order given by a ruler or governing organization 条例, 法令, 法规: *a Royal ordinance* 圣旨 **2** *AmE* a law, usually of a city or town, that forbids or restricts an activity【美】〔城镇颁布的〕法规, 条例: *contravening city ordinances* 违反城市法规

or·di·na·ri·ly /,ɔrdṇˈɛrɪlɪ; ˈɔːdənərəli/ *adv* **1** [sentence adverb 句子副词] usually 通常: *Ordinarily, the process of buying clothes irritates me.* 买衣服的过程通常都使我感到烦躁。| *It is ordinarily possible to predict the results with some accuracy.* 准确预测结果通常是可能的。**2** in an ordinary or normal way 平常地, 普普通通地: *He was walking along quite ordinarily.* 他很平常地走着。

or·di·na·ry /ˈɔrdṇ,ɛrɪ; ˈɔːdənəri/ *adj* **1** average, common, or usual, not different or special 普通的, 平常的, 通常的: *part of a politician's ordinary routine* 政治家例行公事的一部分 | *The new taxes came as a shock to ordinary Americans.* 新税费使普通美国人大为震惊。| **out of the ordinary** (=unusual or unexpected) 不寻常的; 例外的 *Nothing out of the ordinary had happened.* 没发生什么意外之事。| **in the ordinary way** *BrE* (=normally)【英】一般, 通常 *Jim was not in the ordinary way a romantic, but he decided to bring Joanna some roses.* 吉姆通常并不是一个浪漫的人, 但他决定送一些玫瑰花给乔安娜。**2** not particularly good or impressive 平淡无奇的: *I thought the paintings were pretty ordinary.* 我认为这些画是泛泛之作。—see also 另见 EXTRAORDINARY (1,2) —**ordinariness** *n* [U]

ordinary sea·man /,···ˈ··/ *n* [C] a low rank in the British Navy〔英国海军的〕二等水兵, 见习水兵 —see table on page C6 参见 C6 页附录

ordinary shares /,···ˈ·/ *n* [plural] *technical* the largest part of a company's CAPITAL¹ (2), which is owned by people who have the right to vote at meetings and to receive part of the company's profits【术语】普通股〔公司资本的最大一部分。拥有普通股的股东可在股东会上投票及在公司赢利时分享红利〕

or·di·na·tion /,ɔrdṇˈeʃən; ,ɔːdɪˈneɪʃən/ *n* [C,U] the act or ceremony making someone a priest 授圣职(礼): *the ordination of women* 授予妇女圣职

> **CULTURAL NOTE 文化注释**
>
> For many years, most Protestant churches in the US have allowed women to be ordained, and there are also some women BISHOPS (=high-ranking priests) in the US. In the UK, however, many people opposed the idea of women becoming priests, and the Church of England did not allow the ordination of women until 1992. There are no women priests in the Roman Catholic Church, and some Protestants who oppose women's ordination have become Catholics because of this. 在美国新教教会中授予女性圣职已有多年的历史, 美国亦因此有不少女性主教。可是在英国, 很多人反对让女人当牧师, 英国圣公会直到1992年才授予女性圣职。因为罗马天主教会中没有女性牧师, 一些反对授予女性圣职的新教教徒因此皈依了天主教。

ord·nance /ˈɔrdnəns; ˈɔːdnəns/ *n* [U] **1** large guns with wheels; ARTILLERY (1) 大炮 **2** weapons, explosives, and vehicles used in fighting 军械〈如武器、弹药、军车等〉

Ordnance Sur·vey, the /,··ˈ··/ abbreviation 缩写为 **the OS** an official organization which makes very detailed and correct maps of Britain and Ireland. The maps are used by people walking in the country, and each map has its own OS number. 地形测量局〔英国一官方机构, 专门绘制精细且准确的不列颠和爱尔兰地图, 可供人们在该国徒步旅行时使用。每幅地图上都有地形测量局的编码〕—see 见 US GEOLOGICAL SURVEY

ordnance sur·vey map /,··ˈ···/ *n* [C] *BrE* a map which shows all the roads, paths, hills etc of an area in detail【英】〔精细准确的〕地形测量图

or·dure /ˈɔrdʒə; ˈɔːdjʊə/ *n* [U] *formal* dirt, especially waste matter from the body【正式】污物; 排泄物, 粪便

ore /ɔr; ɔː/ *n* [C,U] rock or earth from which metal can be obtained 矿石, 矿砂: *iron ore* 铁矿石 | *veins of rich ore* 富矿脉

o·reg·a·no /əˈrɛgəno; ,ɒrɪˈgɑːnəʊ/ *n* [U] a plant used in cooking, especially in Italian cooking 牛至〔可用作调味品的植物, 尤用于意大利烹调〕

Or·e·gon /ˈɑrɪgən; ˈɒrɪgən/ abbreviation 缩写为 **OR** a state in the northwestern US which has beautiful mountains, rivers, and forests, and produces fish and fruit. Its largest city is Portland. 俄勒冈州〔美国西北部一州, 山水秀丽, 森林葱绿, 盛产鱼类和水果。最大城市是波特兰〕

Oregon Trail, the /ˈ···,·/ one of the main paths across the US to the western part of the country, used by PIONEERS (=people who are the first to go and live in an unknown land) in the mid-19th century. The Trail crossed the Great Plains and the Rocky Mountains before turning towards Idaho, Washington, and

…journey took around six months, and was extremely … The pioneers did not have good equipment, and they …ffered from illness or were attacked by Native …ans. 俄勒冈小道〔19 世纪中期的拓荒者前往美国西部的…道之一。俄勒冈小道穿越大平原和落基山脉，然后通向爱…、华盛顿州和俄勒冈州。整个旅程大约需要6个月，沿途异…险。早期的拓荒者没有良好的装备，经常会患上疾病或遭遇…第安人袭击〕

…res·tes /əˈrestiz; ɒˈrestiːz/ in ancient Greek stories, the son of Agamemnon, King of Mycenae, and Clytemnestra. Clytemnestra and her lover Aegisthus kill Agamemnon when Orestes is a child. When he becomes an adult, Orestes kills his mother and Aegisthus. 俄瑞斯忒斯〔古希腊传说中迈锡尼国王阿伽门农和克吕泰墨斯特拉之子。当俄瑞斯忒斯还是小孩时，克吕泰墨斯特拉和情人埃癸斯托斯合伙害死了阿伽门农。俄瑞斯忒斯长大成人后，杀死了母亲和埃癸斯托斯〕

3 **or·gan** /ˈɔrgən; ˈɔːgən/ *n* [C]

1 ▶BODY PART 人体部位◀ a) a part of the body, such as the heart or lungs, that has a particular purpose 器官: *inflammation affecting the internal organs* 影响内脏的炎症 | *an organ transplant* 器官移植 **b)** a word meaning PENIS, used because you want to avoid saying this directly〔委婉语〕阴茎

2 ▶MUSICAL INSTRUMENT 乐器◀ a large musical instrument used especially in churches, with one or more keyboards (KEYBOARD¹ (1)) and large pipes out of which the sound comes 管风琴: *an organ recital in Westminster Cathedral* 威斯敏斯特大教堂的管风琴独奏会

3 ▶ORGANIZATION 机构◀ an organization that is part of, or works for, a larger organization or group 部门, 机关, 机构: **[+of]** *Giving too much power to any organ of government should be avoided.* 应避免给予任何一个政府部门过多的权力。

4 ▶NEWSPAPER/MAGAZINE 报纸/杂志◀ *formal* a newspaper or magazine which gives information, news etc for an organization【正式】机关报刊, 宣传工具, 喉舌: **[+of]** *This publication is the organ of the Conservative Party.* 这份刊物是保守党的机关报。

5 ▶PLANT 植物◀ a part of a plant, such as a leaf or stem, that has a special purpose 植物器官〈如叶子、茎等〉

or·gan·die also 又作 **organdy** *AmE*【美】/ˈɔrgəndi; ˈɔːgəndi/ *n* [U] very thin, stiff cotton, used as dress material〔做女装用的〕蝉翼纱, 玻璃纱

organ grind·er /ˈ· ·, ·ˈ/ *n* [C] a musician who plays a BARREL ORGAN in the street〔街头的〕手摇风琴师

or·gan·ic /ɔrˈgænɪk; ɔːˈgænɪk/ *adj*

1 ▶LIVING THINGS 生物◀ living, or produced by or from living things 生物的, 有机物的: *Peat is decomposed organic matter.* 泥炭是已分解的有机物。—opposite 反义词 INORGANIC (1)

2 ▶BODY ORGANS 人体器官◀ concerning the organs of the body 器官的: *organic diseases* 器官疾病

3 ▶PART OF STH 某物的部分◀ a) made up of many parts that …depend on each other 有组织[系统]的: *an organic system* 有…组…的系统 | *an organic link between the music and the mean…* …乐与含义之间的有机联系 **b)** connected with the relation… between these parts 有机的; 关联的

…ARMING 农业◀ using farming or gardening methods with…ificial chemicals, or produced or grown by these meth…用化肥的, 有机的: *organic vegetables* 有机蔬菜 | *an …armer* 用有机肥料耕作的农民

…RAL NOTE 文化注释

…d is more expensive than non-organic food, but … it because they are concerned about the PESTI…nicals used to prevent insects and diseases … the crops) and FERTILIZERS (=chemicals used …grow better) used for growing most food. … to protect the environment, and believe … buy food that has been grown naturally, … so many harmful chemicals. 虽然比…人们…还是购买有机食物, 原因在于他们很…人购买…, 这是种植大多数作物都要使用的。…多的有…境的目的, 他们认为如果有更多的…来的食物, 农民就会不再用那么… HEALTH …ultural Note at HEALTH FOOD 见

5 ▶DEVELO… organic happ… or forcing it t… …ge or development which is … without anyone planning it …自然发展的 —**organically** /-klɪ; -kli/ *adv*

organic chem·is·try /·,·· ˈ···/ *n* [U] the study of CARBON (1) compounds 有机化学 —compare 比较 INORGANIC CHEMISTRY

or·gan·is·m /ˈɔrgən,ɪzəm; ˈɔːgənɪzəm/ *n* [C] **1** an animal, plant, human, or any other living thing 生物, 有机体: *the human organism* 人体组织 | *a microscopic organism living in the cow's stomach* 寄生在牛胃里的微生物 **2** a system made up of parts that are dependent on each other 有机组织[体系]: *A society is essentially an organism.* 就本质而言, 社会是一个有机整体。 3

or·gan·ist /ˈɔrgənɪst; ˈɔːgənɪst/ *n* [C] someone who plays the ORGAN (2) 管风琴手, 管风琴演奏家: *a church organist* 教堂的管风琴手

or·gan·i·za·tion also 又作 **organisation** *BrE*【英】/,ɔrgənəˈzeʃən; ,ɔːgənaɪˈzeɪʃən/ *n* **1** [C] a group such as a club or business that has formed for a particular purpose 组织, 团体, 机构: *a charitable organization* 慈善机构 **2** [U] the act of planning and arranging things effectively 统筹安排, 组织, 协调: *Organisation's never been my strong point.* 做组织工作向来不是我的长处。| **[+of]** *The organization of the fund raisers has been left to Ellen.* 募捐活动的筹备工作交给了埃伦。**3** [U] the way in which the different parts of a system are arranged and work together 结构, 体制: **[+of]** *the social organization of primitive cultures* 各种原始文化的社会结构 —**organizational** *adj*: *organizational ability* 组织能力 —**organizationally** *adv* 2 1

Organization of African Unity /·······/ the former name of the African Union 非洲统一组织〔非洲联盟旧称〕

Organization of A·mer·i·can States, the /······/ the full name of the OAS 美洲国家组织〔OAS 的全称〕

or·gan·ize also 又作 **-ise** *BrE*【英】/ˈɔrgən,aɪz; ˈɔːgənaɪz/ *v* **1** [T] to make the necessary arrangements so that an activity can happen 筹划, 筹办: *They organized a protest march.* 他们筹划了一次抗议游行。| *Who's going to organise the party this year?* 谁来筹办今年的聚会? **2** [T] to arrange information, work, a group etc so that it works correctly 组织; 安排; 将…编组: *Organize your thoughts before you begin to speak.* 把思绪理清楚再说话。| *A team of professionals will organize the volunteers.* 一个专家小组将给志愿人员编队。| **be organized in/along/around** *The political system is organized along party lines.* 这一政治体制是按照党的路线建立的。| *industrial towns organized around places of work* 环绕工作场所建立的工业城镇 **3** [I,T] *especially AmE* to form a TRADE UNION (=an organization that protects workers' rights) or persuade people to join one; UNIONIZE【尤美】组织工会; 使加入工会 1 2

or·gan·ized also 又作 **organised** *BrE*【英】/ˈɔrgən,aɪzd; ˈɔːgənaɪzd/ *adj* **1** achieving aims in an effective, ordered, and sensible way 有序的, 有组织[条理]的: *I'm sorry I forgot – I'm not very organized these days.* 对不起我忘了——我这些天脑子有点乱。| *You can be sure the conference will be well organised if Barb is in charge.* 如果由巴布来负责, 你可以肯定大会将组织得有条不紊。| **get organized** *spoken*【口】*I have to get organized and get some things done.* 我得理顺一下头脑, 处理完一些事情。| **highly organized** (=very well organized) 高度组织化的, 很有条理的 *a highly organized social system* 高度组织化的社会体系 —opposite 反义词 DISORGANIZED **2** an organized activity is arranged for and done by many people〔活动〕有组织的, 安排有序的: *organized religion* 有组织的宗教 | *organized sports* 安排有序的体育活动 3

organized crime /,··· ˈ·/ *n* [U] a large and powerful organization of criminals 有组织犯罪, 集团犯罪: *moves to combat terrorism, drug trafficking and organized crime* 打击恐怖主义、毒品贩卖及有组织犯罪的行动

or·gas·m /ˈɔrgæzəm; ˈɔːgæzəm/ *n* [C,U] the greatest point of sexual pleasure 性高潮

or·gas·mic /ˈɔrgæzmɪk; ˈɔːgæzmɪk/ *adj* **1** *technical* related to orgasm【术语】性高潮的 **2** *slang* extremely exciting or enjoyable【俚】极度兴奋的; 令人非常愉快的

or·gy /ˈɔrdʒɪ; ˈɔːdʒi/ *n* [C] **1** a wild party with a lot of eating, drinking, and sexual activity〔纵欲的〕狂欢宴会, 纵酒宴乐 **2** sexual activity in a group 集体纵欲, 群交 **3 an orgy of** a short time spent doing too much of an activity in a way that is not sensible or controlled 无节制的〔行为、活动〕: *an orgy of shopping* 无节制的购物 —**orgiastic** *adj*

o·ri·el win·dow /ˈɔrɪəl ,wɪndo; ˈɔːriəl ,wɪndəʊ/ *n* [C] *technical* an upper window that is built out from a wall【术语】凸肚窗

o·ri·ent¹ /ˈɔrɪənt; ˈɔːriənt/ also 又作 **orientate** *BrE*【英】*v* **1 be oriented to/towards** to be developed, trained, made etc for a particular purpose 针对, 面向; 以…为方向; 为…设计: *an English language course oriented towards the needs of businessmen* 针对商务人士需求而开设的英语课程 **2 be oriented**

around if something is oriented around a particular idea, that idea is very important to it 围绕，以…为重点: *Wanda's whole life has been oriented around the children.* 万达的一生全是在为孩子们操心。**3 orient yourself a)** to find your position with a map or a COMPASS (1)〔依据地图或指南针〕确定自己的方位: *The climbers stopped to orientate themselves.* 登山者停下来确定自己所在的位置。**b)** to become familiar with a new situation 使自己熟悉新环境[新情况]: *I'll need a few days to orient myself.* 我需要几天时间来熟悉新环境。

o·ri·ent² *n* **the Orient** *old-fashioned* the eastern part of the world, especially China and Japan and the countries near them【过时】东方(世界)〔尤指中国和日本及邻近国家〕—compare 比较 **the East** (EAST (1a)), OCCIDENT

orient³ *adj poetic*【诗】**1** eastern 东方的 **2 orient star/sun** a rising star or sun 正在升起的星星/太阳

o·ri·en·tal¹ /ˌɔrɪˋɛntḷ; ˌɔːriˈentl◂/ *adj* concerning or from the East or South-East Asia 东方的; 东亚[东南亚]的: *oriental countries* 东方国家 | *oriental culture* 东方文化

oriental² *n* [C] *old-fashioned* a word meaning someone from an oriental country, which is now usually considered offensive【过时】东方人〔现通常视为具冒犯性〕—compare 比较 OCCIDENTAL

o·ri·en·tal·ist /ˌɔrɪˋɛntḷɪst; ˌɔːriˈentəlɨst/ *n* [C] someone who studies the languages and culture of oriental countries〔研究东方国家语言、文化等的〕东方学专家，东方通

o·ri·en·tate /ˋɔrɪɛnˌtet; ˈɔːriənteɪt/ *v BrE* another form of the word ORIENT¹【英】orient¹ 的另一种形式

o·ri·en·ta·tion /ˌɔrɪɛnˋteʃən; ˌɔːriənˈteɪʃən/ *n* [C,U] **1** the aims or interests of a particular activity or organization 目标，目的; 兴趣: **[+towards/to]** *an orientation to world affairs* 对世界事务的兴趣 | **[+of]** *the orientation of post-war policy* 战后政策的目标 **2 political/religious orientation** the political views or religious beliefs that you have 政治/宗教倾向 **3 sexual orientation** the fact that someone is HETEROSEXUAL or HOMOSEXUAL 性取向〔指某人是异性恋还是同性恋〕: *questions about race and sexual orientation* 有关种族和性取向的问题 **4** [U] *especially AmE* training and preparation for a new job or activity【尤美】〔为熟悉新工作或活动的〕培训，准备: *This is orientation week for all the new students.* 这是让全体新生熟悉情况的迎新周。**5** [C] the angle or position of an object in relation to another object or a direction 定向; 定位

o·ri·ent·ed /ˋɔrɪɛntɪd; ˈɔːrientɨd/ also 又作 **o·ri·en·ta·ted** /ˋɔrɪɛnˌtetɪd; ˈɔːriənteɪtɨd/ *BrE*【英】*adj* **politically oriented/family oriented etc** giving a lot of time, effort, or attention to politics, family etc 重视政治的/家庭的等: *The new generation doesn't seem to be politically oriented at all.* 新一代人好像对政治全无兴趣。

o·ri·en·teer·ing /ˌɔrɪɛnˋtɪrɪŋ; ˌɔːriənˈtɪərɪŋ/ *n* [U] a sport in which people have to find their way quickly across unknown country using a map and a COMPASS (1) 定向运动，定向越野比赛〔一种靠地图和指南针快速寻找目的地的运动〕

Orient Ex·press, the /ˌ·· ·ˈ·/ a famous LUXURY railway train, used especially by rich people. It used to run (1883-1977) between Paris and Istanbul in Turkey, but there is now a luxury Orient Express train that goes from London to Venice. The train appears in many stories, including Agatha Christie's NOVEL *Murder on the Orient Express* (1934). 东方快车〔一著名豪华列车，多为富人乘坐，1883至1977年间往返于巴黎和土耳其的伊斯坦布尔之间。现在，伦敦和威尼斯之间开通了东方快车。这列火车在许多故事中都有记述，如阿加莎·克里斯蒂的《东方快车谋杀案》(1934)〕

or·i·fice /ˋɔrəfɪs; ˈɒrɨfɨs/ *n* [C] **1** *technical or humorous* one of the holes in your body, such as your mouth, nose etc【术语或幽默】〔身体上的〕孔，洞: *the dental orifice* 牙洞 **2** *formal* a hole or entrance【正式】孔，洞; 入口

o·ri·ga·mi /ˌɔrəˋgɑmɪ; ˌɒrɪˈgɑːmi/ *n* [U] the Japanese art of folding paper to make attractive objects〔日本的〕折纸艺术，折纸手工

or·i·gin /ˋɔrədʒɪn; ˈɒrɨdʒɨn/ *n* **1** also 又作 **origins** [plural] the situation, place, or physical matter from which something begins 起源，开端: **[+of]** *the origins of language* 语言的起源 | **have your/its origin in sth** (=begin in a particular place, situation etc) 起源于… *Many of the problems had their origin in post-war Europe.* 其中的许多问题起源于战后的欧洲。**2** also 又作 **origins** [plural] the country, race or class from which someone or their family comes 出身，血统; 来历: *They are proud of their aristocratic origins.* 他们为自己的贵族血统感到自豪。**3** [C] *technical* the point where two axes (AXIS (3)) cross on a GRAPH【术语】〔曲线图上两根轴线相交处的〕原点

o·rig·i·nal¹ /əˋrɪdʒənḷ; əˈrɪdʒɨnəl/ *adj* **1** [only b... 用于名词前] existing or happening first, before be... or replaced by something or someone else 原先的，... 初的: *The land was returned to its original owner.* 这... 归还给原主。| *We still have the original stone floor.* 我... 留着原先的石头地面。**2** completely new and different fro... thing that anyone has thought of before 新颖的，独特的; ... 同的，独创的: *a highly original style* 极为独特的风格 | *an o... nal thinker* 富有创见的思想家 | *What an original idea!* 多么... 出心裁的主意啊! **3** [only before noun 仅用于名词前] not cop... ied 原版的，非抄袭的，非模仿的: *an original Holbein drawing* 霍尔拜因的原画

original² *n* [C] **1** a painting, document, etc that is not a copy, but is the one produced by the writer or artist〔绘画、文件等的〕原件，原物，原稿，原作品: *The colour was paler in the original.* 原作的色彩要淡一些。| *I'll keep a copy, and give you the original.* 我将留一份副本，把原件给你。**2 in the original** in the language that a book, play etc was first written in, before it was translated 原著的语言，原文: *I read it in the original.* 我读过它的原文。**3** *informal* someone whose behaviour, clothing etc is unusual and amusing【非正式】〔举止、服饰等〕怪异滑稽的人

o·rig·i·nal·i·ty /əˌrɪdʒəˋnælətɪ; əˌrɪdʒɨˈnælɨti/ *n* [U] the quality of being completely new and different from anything that anyone has thought of before 独创性; 创见; 创造力; 新颖: *poems of great originality* 非常新颖独特的诗

o·rig·i·nal·ly /əˋrɪdʒənḷɪ; əˈrɪdʒɨnəli/ *adv* in the beginning 最初，原先: *The family originally came from France.* 那个家族最初来自法国。| *The book was originally conceived as an autobiography, but it became a novel.* 该书最初的构思是一部自传，但后来却写成了一本小说。| [sentence adverb 句子副词] *Originally, we had planned a tour of Scotland but we never got further than Edinburgh.* 我们原先计划周游苏格兰，但结果最远只到了爱丁堡。

original sin /·ˌ··· ˈ·/ *n* [U] the state of disobedience to God which everyone is in from birth, according to some Christian teaching 原罪〔基督教教义中的指人类与生俱来的罪孽〕

o·rig·i·nate /əˋrɪdʒəˌnet; əˈrɪdʒɨneɪt/ *v* **1** [I always+adv/prep, not in progressive 不用进行时] *formal* to start to develop in a particular place or from a particular situation【正式】发源; 开始; 起因: **[+in/from/with]** *a custom originating in Chinese culture* 源自中国文化的一种习俗 | *How did the idea originate?* 这主意是怎么来的? **2** [T] to have the idea for something and start it 创始; 创造; 发起: *Who originated the present complaints procedures?* 谁最先创建了现在这套投诉程序?

o·rig·i·nat·or /əˋrɪdʒəˌnetə; əˈrɪdʒɨneɪtə/ *n* [C] the person who first has the idea for something and starts it 创始人; 发明者: **[+of]** *the originator of a whole genre of detective fiction, Edgar Allan Poe* 埃德加·艾伦·坡，侦探小说体裁的创始者

Origin of Species, the —see 见 ON THE ORIGIN OF SPECIES

or·i·ole /ˋɔrɪˌol; ˈɔːriəʊl/ *n* [C] **1** a N. American bird that is bl... with a red and yellow stripe on its wing 拟黄鹂〔产于北美洲... 色羽毛，翅膀带红黄色条纹〕**2** a European bird with black... and a yellow body 金黄鹂〔产于欧洲，黄色羽毛，翅膀为...

or·i·son /ˋɔrɪzn; ˈɒrɨzən/ *n* [C] *old use* a prayer【旧...

Ork·ney /ˋɔrknɪ; ˈɔːkni/ also 又作 **the Orkney I...** **Orkneys** a group of islands off the north coast of S... of the Shetland Islands. Farming and fishin... industries, but the islands are also a base for... industry. 奥克尼群岛〔与苏格兰北部沿岸隔... 位于设得兰群岛以南。该群岛以农业和渔... 石油工业基地〕

Or·lan·do /ɔrˋlændo; ɔːˈlændəʊ/ a c... attracts large numbers of tourists, ... World and the Epcot Center. 奥兰... 该市的迪斯尼世界、未来世界等...

Orly /ˋɔrlɪ; ˈɔːli/ one of France... 主要机场之一〕

or·mo·lu /ˋɔrməˌlu; ˈɔːm... of metals, not containing... *an ormolu clock* 镀金的...

or·na·ment¹ /ˋɔrn... you keep in your ho... 装饰品，点缀物，... decoration that ... *tecture with* ... **ornament t...** beauty to s... *She is an* ...

ornament² *v* **be ornamented with** to be decorated with something 用…装饰, 装饰有…: *a silver goblet ornamented with pearls* 缀有珍珠的银制高脚酒杯

or·na·men·tal /ˌɔrnəˋmɛntḷ; ˌɔːnəˈmentl◂/ *adj* designed to decorate something 装饰(用)的, 观赏(用)的: *ornamental gardens* 观赏用的花园 | *These buttons are only ornamental.* 这些扣子只是用作装饰。—**ornamentally** *adv*

or·na·men·ta·tion /ˌɔrnəmɛnˋteʃən; ˌɔːnəmenˈteɪʃən/ *n* [U] decoration 装饰, 修饰; 装饰性: *the Victorian love of ornamentation* 维多利亚时代对装饰的喜爱

or·nate /ɔrˋnet; ɔːˈneɪt/ *adj* a lot of decoration, or too much decoration, especially with many complicated details 装饰华美的, 华丽的, 过分修饰的: *a heavy ornate gold cigarette case* 一个很重的华丽的金质烟盒 —**ornately** *adv* —**ornateness** *n* [U]

or·ne·ry /ˋɔrnərɪ; ˈɔːnəri/ *adj humorous AmE* behaving in an unreasonable and angry way【幽默, 美】脾气坏的, 执拗的

or·ni·thol·o·gist /ˌɔrnɪˋθɑlədʒɪst; ˌɔːnɪ̣ˈθɒlədʒɪ̣st/ *n* [C] someone who studies birds 鸟类学家

or·ni·thol·o·gy /ˌɔrnəˋθɑlədʒɪ; ˌɔːnɪ̣ˈθɒlədʒi/ *n* [U] the scientific study of birds 鸟类学 —**ornithological** /ˌɔrnɪθəˋlɑdʒɪkḷ; ˌɔːnɪ̣θəˈlɒdʒɪkəl◂/ *adj*

o·ro·tund /ˋɔrəˌtʌnd; ˈɒrəʊtʌnd/ *adj formal*【正式】**1** an orotund sound or voice is strong and clear〔声音〕洪亮的, 嘹亮的, 高昂的 **2** orotund speech or writing is trying to sound important and impressive〔演说、文笔等〕做作的, 浮夸的, 夸张的

Orozco /oˋrosko; əʊˈrɒːskəʊ/, **José** (1883-1949) a Mexican painter of MURALS whose most famous work is *Man of Fire* (1936-39). 奥罗兹科〔(1883-1949), 墨西哥壁画家, 其最著名作品是《火人》(1936-1939)〕

or·phan¹ /ˋɔrfən; ˈɔːfən/ *n* [C] a child whose parents are both dead 孤儿: *the plight of thousands of war orphans* 数以千计的战争孤儿的困境

orphan² *v* **be orphaned** to become an orphan 成为孤儿: *She was orphaned when her parents died in a plane crash.* 父母死于空难后, 她便成了孤儿。

or·phan·age /ˋɔrfənɪdʒ; ˈɔːfənɪdʒ/ *n* [C] a place where orphan children live 孤儿院: *He was raised in a Catholic orphanage.* 他是在一家天主教会办的孤儿院里长大的。

Or·phe·us and Eu·ry·di·ce /ˌɔrfɪəs ənd juˋrɪdɪsɪ; ˌɔːfiəs ənd juːˈrɪdɪ̣si/ in ancient Greek stories, a husband and wife who love each other very much. When Eurydice died, Orpheus was so upset that he followed her down into Hades (=the place under the ground where the spirits of dead people live) and sang to the king and queen there. They allowed Eurydice to leave so long as Orpheus did not look back to see if she was following him. He did look back, however, and so she had to return to Hades. Many stories, plays, and pieces of music have been based on this story. 奥菲士和欧律狄刻〔古希腊神话中一对非常恩爱的夫妻。欧律狄刻死后, 奥菲士难过不已, 就跟着去了冥界。奥菲士在冥界为国王和王后唱歌, 于是他们就允许欧律狄刻离开冥界, 条件是奥菲士不能回头看她是否跟在身后。可是, 奥菲士最终还是忍不住回了头, 欧律狄刻也只好重回冥界。许多故事、戏剧和音乐作品都根据这一传说创作而成〕

or·tho·don·tics /ˌɔrθəˋdɑntɪks; ˌɔːθəˈdɒntɪks/ *n* [U] the practice or skill of making teeth grow straight when they have not been growing correctly 正牙术; 畸齿矫正术 —**orthodontic** *adj*: *orthodontic treatment* 畸齿矫正治疗

or·tho·don·tist /ˌɔrθəˋdɑntɪst; ˌɔːθəˈdɒntɪ̣st/ *n* [C] a DENTIST who is a specialist in making teeth grow straight when they have not been growing correctly 正牙医生

or·tho·dox /ˋɔrθəˌdɑks; ˈɔːθədɒks/ *adj* **1** ideas or behaviour that are orthodox are considered by most people to be normal, correct and acceptable 传统的, 正统的: *orthodox theories of medicine* 传统医学理论 —see also 另见 UNORTHODOX **2** believing in and following all the traditional beliefs, laws, and practices of a religion〔宗教观念〕正统的; 信奉宗教观念的; 循规蹈矩的: *an orthodox Jew* 正统派犹太教徒 **3** believing in or following the usual form of a particular set of ideas 正统观念的: *orthodox monetarism* 正统货币主义

Orthodox Church /ˌ···ˈ·/ *n* [U] one of the Christian churches in eastern Europe and parts of Asia〔东欧及亚洲部分地区的〕正教(会), 东正教(会)

Orthodox Jew /ˌ···ˈ·/ *n* [C] a believer in the religion known as Orthodox Judaism, a form of the Jewish religion that strictly follows the laws given in the holy books called the *Torah*, including rules about food and clothes. Men who are Orthodox Jews wear black clothes and large black hats and usually have long beards. 正统派犹太教教徒〔他们所信仰的正统派犹太教严格遵从《律法书》的教规, 其中包括衣食方面的规定。男性教徒身穿黑衣, 头戴宽大檐帽, 通常留有长须〕

or·tho·dox·y /ˋɔrθəˌdɑksɪ; ˈɔːθədɒksi/ *n* **1** [C,U] an idea or set of ideas considered by most people to be normal, correct and acceptable 正统观念: *The early feminists challenged the social and political orthodoxy of their time.* 早期的女权主义者对她们那个时代的社会及政治方面的正统观念提出了挑战。**2** the traditional ideas and beliefs of a group or religion, or the practice of following these strictly〔团体或宗教的〕传统观念[信仰]; 传统习俗

or·thog·ra·phy /ɔrˋθɑgrəfɪ; ɔːˈθɒgrəfi/ *n* [U] *technical*【术语】**1** the spelling of words 拼字法 **2** correct spelling 正确拼字法 —**orthographic** /ˌɔrθəˋgræfɪk; ˌɔːθəˈgræfɪk◂/ *adj* —**orthographically** /-klɪ; -kli/ *adv*

or·tho·pe·dic, orthopaedic /ˌɔrθəˋpidɪk; ˌɔːθəˈpiːdɪk◂/ *adj* **1** connected with or providing medical treatment for problems affecting bones, muscles etc 矫形学的; 整形外科的: *an orthopaedic surgeon* 整形外科医生 **2 orthopedic bed/chair/shoe etc** one that is designed to cure or prevent medical problems affecting your bones, muscles etc 矫形床/矫形椅/矫形鞋等 —**orthopedically** /-klɪ; -kli/ *adv*: *orthopedically designed seats* 为矫形设计的座椅

or·tho·pe·dics, orthopaedics /ˌɔrθəˋpidɪks; ˌɔːθəˈpiːdɪks/ *n* [U] the area of medical science or treatment that deals with problems, diseases, or injuries of bones, muscles etc 矫形学; 整形外科

or·tho·pe·dist, orthopaedist /ˌɔrθəˋpidɪst; ˌɔːθəˈpiːdɪ̣st/ *n* [C] a doctor with special training in orthopedics 整形外科医生

Orton /ˋɔrtn; ˈɔːtən/, **Joe** (1933-67) an English writer of BLACK COMEDY, whose most famous plays are *Entertaining Mr Sloan* (1964) and *Loot* (1966). He was murdered by his lover Keith Halliwall. 奥顿〔(1933-1967), 英国黑色喜剧作家。代表作有《款待斯隆先生》(1964)和《掠夺》(1966)。他被同性爱侣基思·哈利韦尔杀害〕

Or·well /ˋɔrwɛl; ˈɔːwel/, **George** (1903-50) a British writer and journalist who wrote books about politics and who also wrote NOVELS. His real name was Eric Blair. His books *Animal Farm* and *Nineteen Eighty-Four* are both about political systems in which ordinary people have no power, and are completely controlled by the government. Both novels have had a great influence on the way people think about and write about politics, and political systems like those described in the books are sometimes called Orwellian. Orwell fought on the Republican (=left wing) side in the Spanish Civil War. 奥威尔〔(1903-1950), 英国作家、记者。作品有政治论著和小说。真名为埃里克·布莱尔。他创作的《动物农庄》和《一九八四》两部小说均关乎政治制度, 其中的普通人没有权力, 完全受制于政府。这两部作品对人们思考和论述政治问题的方式产生了重大影响。书中描写的政治制度有时被称为奥威尔式制度。西班牙内战期间, 奥威尔站在共和派一边〕

-ory¹ /ɔrɪ; əri/ *suffix* [in nouns 构成名词] a place or thing used for doing something 作…之用的场所[东西]: *an observatory* (=where people look at things, especially the stars) 天文台, 观测台 | *a directory* 号码簿

-ory² *suffix* [in adjectives 构成形容词] describes something that does a particular thing 作…之用的: *an explanatory note* (=that gives an explanation) 注释 | *a congratulatory telegram* (=that CONGRATULATES) 贺电

OS /ˌo ˋɛs; ˌəʊ ˈes/ **1** the abbreviation of 缩写= the ORDNANCE SURVEY **2** the abbreviation of 缩写= OUTSIZE

O·sa·ka /oˋsɑkə; əʊˈsɑːkə/ the second largest city in Japan, on the island of Honshu. Osaka is an important port and industrial centre. 大阪〔日本第二大城市, 位于本州岛, 是日本重要港口和工业中心〕

Os·borne /ˋɑzbɔrn; ˈɒzbɔːn/, **John** (1929-94) a British writer of plays who became known as an Angry Young Man when he criticized British society in the 1950s. His most famous work is *Look Back in Anger*. 奥斯本〔(1929-1994), 英国剧作家。20世纪50年代, 他因抨击英国社会而以"愤怒青年"的形象著称。最著名的作品是《愤怒的回顾》〕

Os·car /ˋɑskɚ; ˈɒskə/ *n* [C] an American prize given each year for the best film, actor etc in the film industry; it is the usual name for an 'Academy Award' 奥斯卡奖〔美国每年颁发给电影界人士的奖项, 设有最佳影片奖、最佳演员奖等奖项; 是"学院奖"的俗称〕: *the Oscar for best actress* 奥斯卡最佳女主角奖

os·cil·late /ˋɑsḷˌet; ˈɒsɪ̣leɪt/ *v* [I] **1** *technical* to keep moving regularly from side to side, between two limits【术语】〔两点间有规律地〕来回摆动, 振动 **2** *formal* to keep changing between one feeling or attitude and another; VACILLATE【正式】摇摆不

定, 踌躇: [+**between**] *Her attitude towards her husband oscillated between tender affection and deep mistrust.* 她对丈夫时而温柔体贴, 时而疑虑重重, 态度飘忽。**3** if an electric current oscillates, it changes direction very regularly and very frequently〔电流很有规律并很频繁地来回〕振荡, 波动 —**oscillatory** /ˈɑsələˌtɔrɪ; ˈɒsɨlətəri/ *adj*

os·cil·la·tion /ˌɑslˈeʃən; ˌɒsɨˈleɪʃən/ *n technical*【术语】**1** [U] the regular movement of something from side to side between two limits〔两点间有规律的〕来回摆动 **2** [C] a single movement from side to side of something that is oscillating〔来回摇摆的〕一次摆动, 振幅

os·cil·la·tor /ˈɑslˌetɚ; ˈɒsɨleɪtə/ *n* [C] a machine that produces electrical oscillations 振荡器

-oses /osiz; əʊsiːz/ *suffix* the plural form of the suffix -osis 后缀 -osis 的复数形式

OSF /ˌo ɛs ˈɛf; ˌəʊ es ˈef/ the abbreviation of 缩写= the OPEN SOFTWARE FOUNDATION

OSHA /ˈoʃə; ˈəʊʃə/ the Occupational Safety and Health Administration; a US government organization that looks after the safety and health of people at work 职业安全健康局〔美国一政府机构。其职责是关注在职人员的安全和健康状况〕—see 见 the HEALTH AND SAFETY EXECUTIVE

o·si·er /ˈoʒɚ; ˈəʊziə/ *n* [C] a type of WILLOW tree whose branches are used for making baskets 杞柳, 青刚柳〔枝条可编筐篮〕

O·si·ris /oˈsaɪrɪs; əʊˈsaɪərɨs/ in ancient Egyptian MYTHOLOGY, the god of the dead, who was the husband and brother of Isis 俄赛里斯〔古埃及神话中的冥王, 伊西斯的丈夫和兄弟〕

-osis /osɪs; əʊsɨs/ *suffix plural* **-oses** /osiz; əʊsiːz/ [in nouns 构成名词] **1** *technical* a diseased condition【术语】病, 病变状态: *silicosis* (=a lung disease) 硅肺病 | *neuroses* (=disorders of the mind) 神经机能病 **2** a condition or process 状态; 过程: *a metamorphosis* (=change from one state to another) 变形; 变态 —**-otic** /ɑtɪk; ɒtɪk/ [in adjectives 构成形容词]: *neurotic* 神经机能病的 | *hypnotic* 催眠(术)的 —**-otically** /ɑtɪklɪ; ɒtɪkli/ [in adverbs 构成副词]

Os·lo /ˈɑzlo; ˈɒzləʊ/ a city in southeast Norway, the country's capital and main port 奥斯陆〔挪威东南部一城市, 为该国首都和主要港口〕

Oslo Agreement, the /ˈ‥ ·,‥/ an official peace agreement made between Israel and the PLO (=Palestine Liberation Organization) in Oslo in 1993, by which Israel agreed to remove its military forces from the Gaza Strip and Jericho《奥斯陆协议》〔以色列和巴勒斯坦解放组织于1993年在奥斯陆签署的一项正式和平协议。根据该协议, 以色列同意从加沙地带和杰里科撤出军队〕

os·mo·sis /ɑzˈmosɪs; ɒzˈməʊsɨs/ *n* [U] **1 by osmosis** if you learn facts or receive ideas by osmosis, you gradually learn them by hearing them often 通过耳濡目染, 靠潜移默化: *I must have learnt it by osmosis.* 这事我准是靠耳濡目染慢慢学会的。**2** *technical* the gradual process of liquid passing through a MEMBRANE (2)【术语】渗透(作用) —**osmotic** /ɑzˈmɑtɪk; ɒzˈmɒtɪk/ *adj* —**osmotically** /-klɪ; -kli/ *adv*

os·prey /ˈɑsprɪ; ˈɒspri/ *n* [C] a type of large bird that eats fish 鹗, 鱼鹰

os·si·fy /ˈɑsəˌfaɪ; ˈɒsɨfaɪ/ *v* **1** [I] to become unwilling to consider new ideas or change your behaviour 墨守陈规; 僵化 **2** [I, T] *technical* to change into bone or to make something change into bone【术语】(使)骨化 —**ossification** /ˌɑsəfəˈkeʃən; ˌɒsɨfɨˈkeɪʃən/ *n* [U]: *the rapid ossification of the Soviet hardline position* (前)苏联强硬立场的急速僵化

Os·tend /ɑstˈɛnd; ɒstˈend/ a town and port in northwest Belgium, which is on the North Sea coast and is a popular place for tourists. It used to be well known in the UK because of the many ferries (FERRY) that went there from the south of England, but fewer ferries now make this journey. 奥斯坦德〔比利时西北部一城镇和港口, 濒临北海, 为旅游胜地。过去, 曾有许多渡船从英格兰南部驶往该镇, 因此该镇在英国十分有名。如今, 往返两地之间的渡船已减少〕

os·ten·si·ble /ɑsˈtɛnsəbl; ɒˈstensɨbəl/ *adj* seeming to be the reason for or the purpose of something but usually hiding the real reason or purpose〔指理由或动机〕表面上的, 貌似真实的, 诡称的: *The ostensible purpose of the war was to liberate a small nation from tyranny.* 这场战争的目的表面上是要把一个小国从专制政权下解放出来。

os·ten·si·bly /ɑsˈtɛnsəblɪ; ɒˈstensɨbli/ *adv* if something is done ostensibly for a particular reason, it is not really done for this reason but people pretend that it is 表面上; 假装地: *The big bosses went to Hawaii, ostensibly to launch the new project.* 大老板都去了夏威夷, 表面上是要启动那个新项目。

os·ten·ta·tion /ˌɑstənˈteʃən; ˌɒstənˈteɪʃən/ *n* [U] an unnecessary show of wealth or knowledge intended to make people admire you〔财富或学识的〕炫耀, 卖弄: *Their simple style of dress and complete lack of ostentation made me like them even more.* 他们简朴的衣着和全无炫耀卖弄的作风令我更加喜欢他们。

os·ten·ta·tious /ˌɑstənˈteʃəs; ˌɒstənˈteɪʃəs◂/ *adj* **1** something that is ostentatious is large, looks expensive and is designed to make people think that its owner must be very rich 摆阔气的, 讲排场的, 铺张的: *The hotel loomed huge and ostentatious above the street.* 那家饭店赫然耸现在街道前方, 显得巨大而阔气。**2** someone who is ostentatious likes to show everyone how rich they are 夸示的, 炫耀的, 卖弄的: *I was vaguely annoyed by his generosity which seemed almost ostentatious.* 他大方得几乎就像在炫耀, 让我隐隐地感到一丝不快。—**ostentatiously** *adv*

osteo- /ɑstɪə; ɒstiəʊ/ *prefix technical* concerning bones【术语】骨的

os·te·o·ar·thri·tis /ˌɑstɪoɑrˈθraɪtɪs; ˌɒstiəʊɑːˈθraɪtɨs/ *n* [U] *technical* a condition which makes your knees and other joints stiff and painful【术语】骨关节炎

os·te·o·path /ˈɑstɪəˌpæθ; ˈɒstiəpæθ/ *n* [C] someone trained in osteopathy 整骨医师, 按骨医师

os·te·op·a·thy /ˌɑstɪˈɑpəθɪ; ˌɒstiˈɒpəθi/ *n* [U] the practice or skill of treating physical problems such as back pain by moving and pressing muscles and bones 整骨术, 按骨术

os·tler /ˈɑslɚ; ˈɒslə/ also 又作 **hostler** *AmE*【美】*n* [C] a man who, in former times, took care of guests' horses at a hotel〔旧时旅店照料客人马匹的〕马夫

os·tra·cize also 又作 **-cise** *BrE*【英】/ˈɑstrəˌsaɪz; ˈɒstrəsaɪz/ *v* [T] if a group of people ostracize someone, they stop accepting them as a member of the group〔一伙人〕把…排除在外, 排斥: *Reg was ostracized by the whole squadron, who cursed his actions.* 雷格遭到整个中队的排斥, 他们咒骂他的行动。—**ostracism** /-sɪzəm; -sɪzəm/ *n* [U]

os·trich /ˈɔstrɪtʃ; ˈɒstrɪtʃ/ *n* [C] **1** a large African bird with long legs, that runs very quickly but cannot fly 鸵鸟 **2** *informal* someone who refuses to accept that unpleasant problems exist instead of dealing with them【非正式】不愿正视现实的人, 逃避现实的人

Os·wald /ˈɑzwəld; ˈɒzwəld/, **Lee Harvey** (1939-63) the man who was believed by the police to have shot and killed the US President John F. Kennedy in 1963. Two days after the President's death, Oswald was shot and killed by Jack Ruby. Some people believe that Oswald was not the real killer. 奥斯瓦尔德〔(1939-1963), 被警方认为是1963年谋杀美国总统肯尼迪的男子。总统遇难两天后, 他被杰克·鲁比开枪打死。有些人认为奥斯瓦尔德并不是真正的凶手〕

OT the written abbreviation of 缩写= OLD TESTAMENT

OTC /ˌo ti ˈsi; ˌəʊ tiː ˈsiː◂/ the abbreviation of 缩写= OVER-THE-COUNTER (2)

O·thel·lo /əˈθɛlo; əˈθeləʊ/ the main character in the play *Othello* by William Shakespeare. Othello, a black man, is a very jealous husband, and kills his wife, Desdemona, because his friend Iago makes him believe, wrongly, that she is having a sexual relationship with another man. 奥赛罗〔威廉·莎士比亚的剧作《奥赛罗》中的主人公。黑人奥赛罗是一个妒忌心很强的丈夫。在他的朋友伊阿古的诱骗下, 他误以为自己的妻子苔丝狄蒙娜与别的男人有染而把她杀死〕

oth·er /ˈʌðɚ; ˈʌðə/ *determiner, adj, pron* **1** used when there are two people, things etc to mean the one that is not being used, the one that you do not already have etc〔两者中的〕另一个, 其他的人[东西]: **the other** *She was driving the car with one hand and wiping the window with the other.* 她一只手开车, 另一只手擦车窗。| *I've got mud all over my trousers – are my others clean?* 我裤子上全是泥, 我的另一条干净吗? | **the other person, thing etc** *On weekends I do all my housework on one day so the other day I'm free to relax.* 周末我把所有的家务一天干完, 另一天就有空放松一下。| **the other one** *I recognize one of the guitarists but who's the other one?* 我认得其中一个吉他手, 但另一个是谁? **2** used to mean all the people, things etc that are not the particular one you are talking about 所有其他的, 其余的: **the other people/things etc** *Olivia is cleverer than all the other children in the class.* 奥利维娅比班上别的孩子都聪明。| *The museum may be closed but the other tourist places are open.* 博物馆可能已经关门, 但其他旅游景点还开着。| **the others** *The wine glasses got broken but some of the others are alright.* 葡萄酒杯都破了, 但其他的一些还是完好的。| **other ones** *I bought this dress on sale. There were other ones that*

were nicer but I could only afford this one. 这裙子我是在减价时买的，还有几条更好看的，但我只买得起这一条。**3** used to mean more people or things in addition to the ones you already have or are talking about 更多的，另外的：**other people/things etc** *I know you've met Peter but I have two other brothers as well.* 我知道你见过彼得，但我还有两个兄弟呢。| *I'm sure if you asked other people they would say the same.* 我敢肯定，如果你问别的人，他们也都会这么说。**4** used to mean the people or things which are different from the ones you already have or are talking about 不同的：*Making omelettes is one way to cook eggs but there are others you know.* 蛋的一种做法是煎蛋卷，但你知道，还有别的做法呢。| **some/any/no etc other thing** *I'm busy – we'll have to meet some other time.* 我很忙，我们只能改天见面了。| *Do you know of any other job where you get as many benefits as this one?* 你知道还有什么工作有这么多的福利待遇吗？**5 others** [plural] other people or things 其他的人[物]：*Some of these lapel microphones are better than others.* 这些微型麦克风中一部分的质量比其他的更好。**6 other than** apart from a particular person or thing; except 除了：*You should get a little stiffness but other than that there should be no side effects.* 你会有一点僵硬的感觉，但除此之外应该不会有别的副作用。| *How can you say that religion is anything other than a way of controlling people?* 你怎么能说宗教不是一种摆布人的手段呢？**7 none other than** used when saying who someone is when you are surprised or shocked to find out exactly who they are 不是别人而正是：*The winner of 'journalist of the year' was none other than the editor's daughter.* 赢得"年度最佳记者"称号的不是别人，正是主编的女儿。**8 a) on the other side/bank etc** on the opposite side of the road, river etc, facing you 在对面/对岸等：*There is a book store on the other side of the road.* 马路对面有一家书店。**b) the other way/direction etc** in the opposite direction to the one you are moving in already 相反的方向等：*She thought it unusual that all the traffic was going the other way.* 所有车辆都跟她反向而行，她觉得很奇怪。**9 the other end/side etc** the end, side etc of something that is furthest away from where you are now 另一端/另一边等：*My car broke down on the other side of town.* 我的汽车在城的另一边出故障了。| *The woman on the other end of the phone didn't really understand what I'd asked for.* 电话另一端的女士不太明白我要些什么。**10 the other way around/round** *BrE* if the situation is the other way around, it is actually the opposite of how you thought it was【英】相反地，倒过来，以相反方式：*If you look at it the other way around, the soldiers were only trying to protect themselves.* 如果你反过来看，士兵们其实只是为了自卫而已。**11 the other day/morning etc** *especially spoken* on a recent day, morning etc【尤口】那天/那天早上等〔指前不久的日子〕：*I saw Rufus the other day.* 前些天我看见了鲁弗斯。**12 something/someone etc or other** used to mean a particular thing, person etc or anything or person that is similar 诸如此类的事/人等：*Don't worry, we'll get the money somehow or other.* 别担心，我们会想个什么办法弄到钱的。**13 in other words** used to express an idea or opinion in a way that is easier to understand 换句话说，换言之：*The company claims it's got to rationalize its workforce, in other words many of the staff will lose their jobs.* 公司宣称必须合理配置劳动力，换言之，许多员工将失去工作。—compare 比较 ANOTHER —see also 另见 EACH OTHER, **every other** (EVERY (7)), **on the one hand ... on the other hand** (HAND[1] (36))

oth·er·ness /ˋʌðɚnɪs; ˈʌðənɪs/ *n* [U] the quality of being strange or different 另一性；不同性；特异性

1 2 **oth·er·wise** /ˋʌðɚˌwaɪz; ˈʌðəwaɪz/ *adv* **1** [sentence adverb 句子副词] a word meaning 'if not', often used when there will be a bad result if something does not happen 否则，要不然：*You'll have to go now, otherwise you'll miss your bus.* 你现在得走了，要不然就赶不上公共汽车了。| *They got two free tickets to Canada, otherwise they'd never have been able to afford to go.* 他们得到了两张去加拿大的免费机票，否则他们绝对出不起旅费的。| *A surveyor's inspection of the building revealed faults that might otherwise have been overlooked.* (=if there had not been an inspection) 检视员检查大楼时找出了一些毛病，要不然的话，这些毛病可能就被忽视了。**2 say/think/decide etc otherwise** to say, think etc something different from what has been mentioned 说/认为/决定等并非如此：*The government claims that the economy is improving, but this survey suggests otherwise.* 政府宣称经济状况在好转，但这份调查显示情况并非如此。**3** [sentence adverb 句子副词] except for what has just been mentioned 除此之外；在其他方面：*I could hear the distant rumbling of traffic. Otherwise all was still.* 我能听见远处车辆的隆隆声，除此之外，万籁俱寂。| *He was tired but otherwise in good health.* 他很疲倦，但除此之外身体很健康。| [+adj/adv] *a few mistakes in an otherwise excellent piece of work* 瑕不掩瑜的一件作品 **4 or otherwise** *especially BrE* or not【尤英】或相反，或其反面：*We welcome any comments from viewers, favourable or otherwise.* 观众的任何意见，无论是褒是贬，我们都欢迎。**5 otherwise engaged** *formal* busy doing something else【正式】忙于别的事情：*I was unable to attend the conference because I was otherwise engaged.* 我无法出席会议，因为我在忙别的事情。**6 otherwise known as** also called 又称，也叫：*Albert DeSalvo, otherwise known as the Boston strangler* 阿尔伯特·德萨尔沃，又称波士顿扼杀者 **7 it cannot be otherwise/how can it be otherwise?** used to mean that it is impossible for something to be different from the way it is 不可能是别的/怎么可能会是别的?：*Life in the military is hard – how can it be otherwise?* 军队生活是艰苦的，怎么可能不艰苦呢？

oth·er·world·ly /ˌʌðɚˋwɝldlɪ; ˌʌðəˈwɜːldli◂/ *adj* more concerned with religious or SPIRITUAL[1] (1) thoughts than with normal daily life 超俗的，超脱尘世的

o·ti·ose /ˋoʃɪˌos; ˈəʊʃiəʊs/ *adj formal* ideas or words that are otiose are unnecessary; REDUNDANT (2)【正式】〔想法或言辞等〕不必要的，多余的

OTT /ˌo ti ˋti; ˌəʊ tiː ˈtiː/ *adj BrE informal* OVER-THE-TOP【英，非正式】〔言行等〕过于夸张的，荒唐的

Ot·ta·wa /ˋɑtəwə; ˈɒtəwə/ the capital city of Canada, in the southeast of the country. One third of its people are French-speaking. 渥太华〔加拿大首都，位于该国东南部，其三分之一的人口讲法语〕

ot·ter /ˋɑtɚ; ˈɒtə/ *n* [C] a swimming animal that has smooth brown fur and eats fish 水獭

ot·to·man /ˋɑtəmən; ˈɒtəmən/ *n* [C] **1** a piece of furniture like a big box with a soft top, used as a seat and for storing things 褥榻；〔可存放东西的〕软垫椅 **2** *AmE* a soft piece of furniture shaped like a box, used to rest your feet on when you are sitting down【美】软垫搁脚凳

Ottoman Em·pire, the /ˌ··· ˈ··/ a large EMPIRE, based in Turkey and with its capital in Istanbul, which also included large parts of Eastern Europe, Asia, and North Africa. It continued from the 13th century until after World War I, but it was most powerful in the 16th century, at the time of its most famous ruler, Suleiman. 奥斯曼帝国〔以土耳其为中心的一个庞大帝国，首都为伊斯坦布尔，包括欧洲东部、亚洲和北非的大片土地。其历史自13世纪一直延续到第一次世界大战后，但全盛时期是在16世纪，即奥斯曼帝国最有名的统治者苏莱曼一世统治时期〕

OU /ˌo ˋju; ˌəʊ ˈjuː/ the abbreviation of 缩写= OPEN UNIVERSITY

ou·bli·ette /ˌublɪˋɛt; ˌuːbliˈet/ *n* [C] a small room or prison in an old castle where prisoners were kept〔古堡中关押囚犯的〕土牢，地牢

ouch /autʃ; aʊtʃ/ *interjection* a sound that you make when you feel sudden pain 哎唷！〔突然感到疼痛时的叫声〕：*Ouch! That hurt!* 哎唷！那好疼！

ought /ɔt; ɔːt/ *modal verb* **1** used to say that someone should do something because it is the best or most sensible thing to do 应该〔指做最好或最明智的事〕：**ought to do sth** *I think you ought to make more time for yourself to relax.* 我认为你应该多给自己一些放松的时间。| *What you ought to have done is call the police.* 你当时应该做的是报警。| *If Veronica's trying to get to college she ought to study more.* 要是韦罗妮卡想上大学，她就应该多学习。**2** used to say that someone should do something because it is right 应该〔指做正确的事〕：**ought to do sth** *You ought to be ashamed of yourself.* 你应该感到羞耻。| *I don't care what you say – I still think he ought to have apologised.* 我不在乎你说什么——我还是认为他本该道歉的。| **ought (to)** *"I can't decide whether to tell him the truth." "Well you ought to."* "我无法决定是否要告诉他真相。""哦，你应该告诉他。" **3** used to say that you think something will probably happen, probably be true etc 可能会，预料会：**ought to do sth** *He left 2 hours ago so he ought to be there by now.* 他两小时前动身的，现在该到那里了。| *They ought to win, they've trained hard enough.* 他们应该能赢，他们训练够刻苦的。| *This ought to be good.* 这应该不错。—see also 另见 SHOULD 1 2

oughtn't /ˋɔtnt; ˈɔːtnt/ the short form of 缩略式= 'ought not' 不应该：*You oughtn't to drive if you are feeling so drowsy.* 你要是感到这么困倦的话就不该开车。

Oui·ja board /ˋwidʒə ˌbɔrd; ˈwiːdʒə bɔːd/ *n* [C] *trademark* a board with letters and signs on it, used to try to receive messages from the spirits of dead people【商标】灵应牌，灵乩板〔一种上有字母和符号，用于接收亡灵信息的乩板〕

ounce /auns; aʊns/ *n* **1** [C] written abbreviation 缩写为 oz a unit for measuring weight equal to 28.35 grams 盎司，安士，英 3

两〔等于 28.35 克〕—see table on page C3 参见 C3 页附录 —see also 另见 FLUID OUNCE **2 not an ounce of sense/truth/decency** no sense etc at all 毫无头脑/真实性/礼节: *If you had an ounce of sense you wouldn't believe these stupid rumors!* 你要是有一点头脑就不会相信这些愚蠢的谣言! **3 every (last) ounce of courage/energy/strength** all the courage etc that you have (最后) 全部的勇气/精力/力量: *He clung to the rock with every last ounce of strength in his body.* 他用体内最后一点儿力气紧抓着岩石。

our /aur; aʊə/ *determiner* [possessive form of **we** we 的所有格] **1** of or belonging to us (属于) 我们的: *Our daughter is in France at the moment.* 我们的女儿目前在法国。| *Winning the Grand Prix was one of our finest sporting achievements.* 赢得大奖赛是我们最杰出的体育成就之一。| *It is important that we preserve our natural resources.* 保护我们的自然资源很重要。**2** *N Eng spoken* used to show that the person mentioned is your child, brother, or sister【英格兰北部, 口】我们的, 我家的: *Our Sharon did really well in her exams.* 我家莎伦各科考试都考得非常好。

Our Fa·ther /,· ˈ··/ *n* [singular] the LORD'S PRAYER〔基督教的〕主祷文

Our La·dy /,· ˈ··/ *n* [singular] Mary, the mother of Christ 圣母马利亚

Our Lord /,· ˈ·/ *n* [singular] Jesus Christ〔基督教的〕耶稣

ours /aurz; aʊəz/ *pron* [possessive form of **we** we 的所有格] the one or the ones that belong to us or that are of us (属于) 我们的 (人、物): *I'll show you to your room. Ours is the one next door.* 我带你去你的房间, 我们的房间在你的隔壁。| *We wouldn't dream of wasting your time, so don't waste ours.* 我们不会想着去浪费你的时间, 所以你也别浪费我们的。

our·selves /aurˋsɛlvz; aʊəˈselvz/ *pron* **1** the reflexive form of 'we'〔we 的反身代词〕我们自己: *It was strange seeing ourselves on television.* 在电视上看到我们自己很奇怪。| *We all introduced ourselves before the meeting started.* 会议开始前我们都作了自我介绍。**2** used to emphasize the pronoun we, a plural noun etc 我们亲自, 我们自己〔用于强调〕: *Not many people realise we built the house ourselves.* 没多少人知道这座房子是我们自己盖的。| *As we are parents ourselves we can understand what you've gone through.* 我们自己也是父母, 所以我们能理解你所经受的一切。**3 (all) by ourselves a)** alone 我们独自地: *Our teacher left us by ourselves for over an hour.* 老师让我们独自待了一个多小时。**b)** without help 我们独力地, 无他人帮助地: *My sister and I learnt to use the computer all by ourselves.* 我和妹妹完全是自己学会使用电脑的。**4 to ourselves** if we have something to ourselves, we do not have to share it with any other people 归我们单独使用, 非合用: *Once Sam left town we had the house to ourselves.* 萨姆一离开城里, 房子就归我们单独使用了。—see also 另见 YOURSELF

-ous /əs; əs/ *suffix* [in adjectives 构成形容词] describes something that causes or has a particular quality 具有…的; 有…特性的: *dangerous* (=full of danger) 危险的 | *spacious* (=with much space) 宽敞的

Ouse, the /uz; uːz/ **1** also 又作 **the Great Ouse** a river in eastern England which begins in Northamptonshire and flows northeast to the Wash 乌斯河〔英格兰东部一河流, 发源于北安普敦郡, 流向东北注入沃什湾〕**2** a river in northeast England which flows southeast to the Humber 乌斯河〔英格兰东北部一河流, 流向东南注入亨伯河〕

oust /aust; aʊst/ *v* [T] to force someone out of a position of power, especially so that you can take their place 强迫〔某人〕放弃职权; 把…撵走〔以取代之〕: **oust sb from** *an attempt to oust the Conservatives from power* 把保守党人撵下台的企图

ous·ter /ˈaustə; ˈaʊstə/ *n* [C] *AmE* an act of moving someone from a position of power in order to take their place【美】撤职, 罢黜; 撵走

out¹ /aut; aʊt/ *adv, adj* [adv only after verb 作副词仅用于动词后, adj not before noun 作形容词不用于名词前]

1 ▶NOT INSIDE STH 不在某物里面◀ from the inside of something 由〔某物〕里面出来, 到外面: *She opened the envelope and took the letter out.* 她打开信封取出信来。| **[+of]** *The diary must have fallen out of her pocket.* 日记本准是从她的口袋里掉出来的。| *Someone has torn the last page out of the book I'm reading.* 有人把我在看的这本书的最后一页撕掉了。

2 ▶LEAVE A PLACE 离开某处◀ from the inside part of something such as a building to the outside part 由〔建筑物等的〕内部到外部: *Lock the door on your way out.* 外出时锁好门。| **[+of]** *I don't think I'd have the courage to jump out of a plane.* 我想我没有胆量跳出飞机。| **out jumped/walked etc** *The plane door slid open, and out walked the princess.* 飞机舱门拉开后, 公主迈步而出。—see picture on page A1 参见 A1 页图

3 ▶NOT HOME 不在家◀ away from your home, especially because you are in a restaurant, party etc 在外面 (的)〔尤指因在餐馆或参加聚会等而不在家〕: *Let's go out to eat tonight.* 我们今晚去外面吃吧。| *That guy she likes has finally asked her out.* 她喜欢的那个男人终于约她出去了。

4 ▶ABSENT 不在的◀ not in the place where you usually are, especially for a short time〔尤指短暂〕外出 (的), 不在通常的地方 (的): *I'm sorry, my mother is out at the moment.* 对不起, 我母亲这会儿出去了。| *He went out at 11 o'clock.* 他 11 点外出的。

5 ▶OUTSIDE 外面◀ outside 在[到]外面, 在[到]室外: *Many of the homeless have been sleeping out for years.* 许多无家可归者常年露宿街头。| *Billy was out playing in the street.* 比利在外面街上玩耍。—see 见 OUTSIDE (USAGE)

6 ▶GIVEN TO MANY PEOPLE 给许多人◀ used to say that something is given to many people, a situation affects many people etc〔分发〕出去; 向四面八方: *The examination will start when all the question papers have been handed out.* 试卷全部分发完后考试就开始。

7 ▶GET RID OF STH 去除某物◀ used to say that something no longer exists or that someone has got rid of something 去除; 不再存在: *These eggs are old, throw them out.* 这些鸡蛋不新鲜, 把它们扔了吧。| **[+of]** *There's this stuff you can buy to get the stains out of delicate fabrics.* 你可以买这种东西来去除精细织物上的污渍。

8 ▶NOT INCLUDED 排除在外◀ used to say that someone or something has not been included, not allowed to enter somewhere etc 不包括在内的; 不允许进入的: *The house had a 'Keep Out' sign in front.* 房子前面有一块"禁止入内"的标牌。| **[+of]** *Daniels has been left out of the team due to injury.* 丹尼尔斯因受伤而被排除在队外。

9 ▶FIND STH 发现某物◀ used to say that someone finds or discovers something 发现, 弄明白: **[+of]** *If she knows what the plan is I'll soon get it out of her.* 如果她知道计划的内容, 我会很快让她说出来的。

10 ▶PRODUCE STH 制造某物◀ used to say that someone or something produces something 制造出来: *factories throwing out pollution into the atmosphere* 向大气中排放污染物的工厂 | **[+of]** *A lot of good music came out of the hippy culture in the 1960s.* 许多好的音乐来源于 20 世纪 60 年代的嬉皮士文化。

11 ▶STICK OUT 突出◀ used to say that something is very easy to see, feel etc because it is not part of the main part of something 伸出 (的), 显眼 (的): **[+of]** *the nail sticking out of the chair* 椅子上凸出的钉子 | *a small peninsula jutting out into the sea* 伸进海中的小半岛

12 ▶CHOOSE STH 选择某物◀ used to say that one person or thing is chosen or taken from a larger group〔从一组人或东西中〕挑选, 选出: *Pick out something to wear.* 找件衣服穿上吧。| *singled out for punishment* 挑出来加以惩罚

13 ▶DO STH COMPLETELY 彻底地做某事◀ used to say that something is done carefully and completely 彻底地, 完全地: *When the cupboard was cleared out I found some of my old books.* 我在清理柜子时发现了自己的一些旧书。| *The work rota is a little confused but we'll sort it out.* 工作轮值表有点混乱, 但我们会排好的。

14 ▶PRODUCT 产品◀ used to say that a product is available to be bought〔产品〕问世, 推出: *When's Archer's new book out?* 阿切尔的新书什么时候出版? | *Sony have brought out a new portable music system.* 索尼公司推出了一种新的便携式音响系统。

15 ▶FREE 自由的◀ used to say that someone is no longer in prison or locked in a place against their will 不再囚禁的, 不再关起来的: *Once he was out it was only a matter of time till he reoffended.* 他出狱以后必定会再次犯罪, 这是迟早的事。| **[+of]** *I like to let my parrots out of their cage once in a while.* 我喜欢偶尔把鹦鹉放出笼子来。

16 ▶NOT FASHIONABLE 不时髦◀ used to say that something is no longer fashionable 不再时兴 (的), 过时 (的): *You can't wear that, maxi skirts have been out for years.* 你不能穿那条超长裙, 它已经多年不时兴了。

17 ▶SECRET 秘密◀ used to say that some information is no longer a secret 暴露 (的), 泄露 (的): *Her secret was out.* 她的秘密泄露了。| *The word's out that Mel Gibson is in town.* 有消息传出, 梅尔·吉布森在城里。

18 ▶APPEAR 出现◀ used to say that someone or something has suddenly appeared (突然) 显露出来 (的): *You don't often see daffodils out at this time of year.* 在一年的这个时候, 你很少见到水仙花开放的。| *The house looks so much better when the sun comes out.* 太阳出来一照, 这房子看上去要漂亮很多。

19 read/shout etc sth out (loud) to say something in a voice that is loud enough for others to hear 大声念出/叫出某物: *The teacher made Ben read the note out to the whole class.* 老师让本把笔记大声地念给全班听。| *As I call out the winners' names, will you please approach the stage?* 我念到获胜者的姓名时，请你们走到台前来好吗？

20 watch/listen/mind etc out *especially spoken* used to tell someone to be careful【尤口】当心，小心: *Look out! There's a van coming.* 当心！有辆小货车开过来了。

21 a fire or light that is out is no longer burning or shining〔火或灯等〕熄灭(的)；燃尽(的): *Blow the candles out.* 把蜡烛吹灭。| *Suddenly the lights went out.* 灯突然灭了。

22 ►NOT AWAKE 未醒的◄ a) used to say that someone is asleep 沉睡(的)，酣睡(的): **be/go out like a light** *The poor kid's exhausted. He went out like a light.* 那可怜的孩子累坏了，一下子就睡着了。| **flat out** *Ray spent the whole afternoon flat out on the sofa.* 雷整个下午都在沙发上沉睡。**b)** used to say that someone is no longer conscious 昏迷(的)，失去知觉(的): *He was out for about 10 minutes.* 他昏迷了大约10分钟。| **be out cold** *How hard did you hit him? He's out cold.* 你使了多大劲打他？他都昏过去了。

23 ►DISTANT PLACE 遥远之处◄ used to say that someone goes to a place that is a long way away, very difficult to get to etc 去很远的地方，去很难到达之处: *They've just moved out to a farm in Massachusetts.* 他们刚搬走，去了马萨诸塞州的一个农场。| *He went out to Africa.* 他出远门去非洲了。

24 wear/tire etc out to make someone feel extremely tired 使精疲力竭: *By the time she'd tidied up she was worn out.* 她拾掇完后已经疲惫不堪。

25 be/run/sell etc out to not have something because you have used it all, sold it all etc 没有了/用完/售完等: *The album was sold out within minutes.* 专辑几分钟就销售一空。| **[+of]** *We've run out of coffee.* 我们没有咖啡了。

26 think/plan etc it out to think, plan etc something very carefully before you do it 周详地考虑/计划等: *It would be wiser to work it out with your financial advisors.* 较明智的做法是和你的财务顾问一起来细商此事。

27 ►NOT WORKING 出了毛病的◄ *especially AmE* if a machine, piece of equipment etc is out it is not working【尤美】〔机器、设备等〕出了毛病(的)，发生故障(的): *I don't believe it – the elevator's out again!* 我真不敢相信——电梯又坏了！— see also 另见 **out of order** (ORDER[1] (8))

28 before the day/year etc is out before the day, year etc has ended 在一天/一年等过去之前: *Don't cry, I'll be back before the week's out.* 别哭，我不出一周就会回来。

29 ►MEASUREMENT 计量◄ if a measurement, result etc is out, it is wrong because the numbers have not been calculated correctly 错误的，不正确的: *He was out in his calculations, so there was a lot of carpet left over.* 他计算错了，所以地毯还剩下很多。| **be out by £4/$5 etc** *The bill was out by over £10.* 账单算错了十多英镑。| **be way out** *These accounts are way out – the tax people will never accept them.* 这些账目差错严重，税务人员绝不会认可的。

30 be out for sth/be out to do sth *informal* to have a particular intention【非正式】试图得到某物/力图做某事: *Mark my words – he's only out for one thing and that's her money.* 听我说——他只想得到一样东西，那就是她的钱。| *These salesmen are out to trick you into buying something you just don't need.* 这些推销员是想哄骗你买下你根本就不需要的东西。

31 ►NOT IN POWER 下台◄ used to say that someone, especially a political party, no longer has power or authority 在野(的)，下台的: *It's time we voted the Republicans out.* 该是我们把共和党人选下台的时候了。

32 be the stupidest/silliest etc person out *BrE* to be extremely stupid, silly etc【英】最愚蠢/最呆笨等的人: *You've got to be the luckiest man out!* 你算是所有人中最走运的了！

33 ►OFFICIAL PROTEST 正式抗议◄ *BrE* used to say that someone has stopped working as a way of protesting about something【英】罢工: *The doctors have come out in sympathy with the miners.* 医生罢诊以声援矿工。

34 ►HOMOSEXUAL 同性恋者◄ if a homosexual is or comes out, they tell people that they are homosexual 公开承认〔自己是同性恋者〕

35 sth's out used to say that a suggestion is not possible (做)某事不行[不可能]: *"What are we going to do?" "Well bowling's out because my wrist is killing me."* "我们去做什么？""噢，打保龄球不行，我的手腕正痛得厉害呢。"

36 ►SEA 大海◄ if the sea, the TIDE[1] (1) etc is out, it is at its lowest level〔海水、潮汐等〕最低水位的，落[退]潮(的)

37 ►SPORT 体育◄ a) a player or team that is out in a game such as cricket or baseball is no longer allowed to play in the game〔板球或棒球等比赛中选手或球队〕出局(的): *Sussex were all out for 365.* 萨塞克斯队得了365分后便全部出局了。**b)** a ball that is out in a game such as tennis or basketball is outside the line〔网球或篮球等比赛中的球〕出界(的)

38 out with it! used to tell someone to say something that they are having difficulty saying 说出来！〔要某人说出难以启齿的事〕: *OK, out with it! What really happened?* 好啦，说出来吧！到底出了什么事？

39 out you go! used to order someone to leave a room 滚出去！

40 be out of luck/condition etc used to say that someone or something is no longer in a particular state or situation 不走运/健康状况不好等: *She's not completely cured but at least she's out of danger.* 她还未痊愈，但至少已经脱离了危险。| *This whole situation is getting out of control.* 整个局面越来越失控了。

41 be out of earshot/sight to be so far away from someone that they cannot hear you, see you etc 在听觉/视线所及的范围之外: *I thought she was out of earshot or I wouldn't have said that.* 我以为她听不见的，否则我就不说了。

42 out of curiosity/interest etc because you are curious, interested etc 出于好奇/兴趣等: *Just out of curiosity, why did you take that job?* 我只是有点好奇，你为什么接受那份工作？

43 out of wood/metal etc used to say what substance a particular thing is made of 由木头/金属等制成: *a little box made out of wood and decorated with flowers* 用花装饰的木制小盒子

44 9 out of 10/4 out of a hundred etc used to say that there are ten people or things and you are talking about nine of them 十个中有九个/一百个中有四个等: *Apparently they've lost three games out of seven already.* 很明显，他们七盘比赛已输了三盘。

45 be out of work/a job etc to not have a job 失业: *those who have been out of work for over 6 months* 那些失业已超过半年的人

46 ►MONEY 金钱◄ used to say where the money has come from to pay for something or buy something 从…取钱〔来付账或购物〕: *Can you believe he used money out of our bank account to pay for his trips with another woman?* 你能相信他动用我们的银行存款去和别的女人游山玩水吗？

47 out of the way a) a place that is out of the way is fairly far from any town 偏僻的，偏远的: *The camp site is a little out of the way but the views are magnificent.* 营地有点偏僻，但景色壮丽。**b)** if you get a problem out of the way you solve it so that you can do something else 解决〔难题〕: *So, that's got the salary thing out of the way, let's move on to productivity.* 那么，薪水的问题就这么定了。我们接下来谈生产力的问题吧。

48 be out of your head/mind *informal*【非正式】**a)** to be very worried 非常焦虑: *His parents were out of their minds with worry when he didn't come home.* 他没有回家，使父母急得团团乱转。**b)** to be very drunk 烂醉，醉得不省人事: *By the time I got to the party most people were out of their heads.* 等我赶到聚会上时，大多数人已喝得醉醺醺的。

49 be/feel out of it (all) a) *informal* to feel different from the rest of a group of people【非正式】感到格格不入: *It was nice but I felt really out of it because I was the only one who couldn't speak French.* 活动搞得很不错，但我感到很像个局外人，因为我是唯一不会说法语的人。**b)** *informal* to be drunk【非正式】喝醉: *You were really out of it last night. What were you drinking?* 昨晚你真的醉了，你喝的什么？

50 ►HORSE 马◄ *technical* having a particular horse as a mother【术语】生自〔特定的母马〕: **[+of]** *Golden Trumpet, by Golden Rain out of Silver Trumpet* 由"金雨"和"银喇叭"交配所生的"金喇叭" —compare 比较 BY[1] —see also 另见 **out of the blue** (BLUE[2] (4)), **out of the question** (QUESTION[1] (8)), **out of sorts** (SORT[1] (5)), **out of this world** (WORLD[1] (13))

out² *prep informal*【非正式】**a)** *AmE* used to say that someone or something is removed from inside something, leaves somewhere etc【美】从…里面出去；离开〔某处〕: **[+of]** *When I first came out of the army I worked in a drug store.* 我刚离开军队时，去了一家药店工作。**b)** *BrE* used in a way which some people think is incorrect, to say that someone or something is removed from inside something, leaves somewhere etc【英】从…里面出去；离开〔某处〕〔有人认为这一用法不正确〕: *Get out the car and push with the rest of us!* 下车，跟我们一起推车！ S1 W1

out³ *v* **1** [T usually passive 一般用被动态] to publicly say that someone is homosexual when that person would prefer to keep it private 揭发〔某人〕为同性恋者；使〔同性恋者〕曝光: *Several gay politicians have been outed in recent months.* 近几个月来，数名政客的同性恋身份被曝光了。**2 truth/murder etc will out!**

used to say that it is difficult to hide the truth, a murder etc 真相/谋杀案等终将水落石出!

out⁴ *n* **1** [singular] an excuse for not doing an activity or to avoid being blamed for something 推托的借口, 逃脱的托辞: *I have tons of work to do. At least that gives me an out.* 我有大量的工作要做, 起码这可以给我一个推托的借口。**2** [C] the state of no longer being allowed to take part in a particular game in a sport such as baseball〔棒球等的〕出局 —see also 另见 INS AND OUTS

out- /aʊt; aʊt/ *prefix* **1** used to form nouns and adjectives from verbs followed by 'out'〔与后接 out 的动词构成名词和形容词〕: *an outbreak of flu* (=from 'break out') 流感的爆发 | *outspoken comments* (=from 'speak out') 直言不讳的评论 **2** in some nouns and adjectives, means outside; beyond 在外; 超过〔与某些名词及形容词合用〕: *an outhouse* (=small additional building) (附属于正屋的) 外屋 | *outlying areas* (=far from the centre) 边缘地区 **3 a)** beyond; further 超过; 更进一步: *She outlived her brother.* (=he died before her) 她比她哥哥活得长。| *He's outgrown his clothes.* (=become too big for them) 他个子长得衣服穿不下了。**b)** better than someone, so that you defeat them 强于…, 胜过…: *I can out-argue you any day.* 我任何时候都能辩过你。

out·age /ˈaʊtɪdʒ; ˈaʊtɪdʒ/ *n* [C] *AmE* a period when a service such as the electricity supply is not provided【美】〔电力等的〕断供期: *a power outage* 停电期

out-and-out /ˌ· · ˈ·◂/ *adj* [only before noun 仅用于名词前] having all the qualities of a particular kind of person or thing; complete 十足的, 彻头彻尾的: *an out-and-out villain* 十足的恶棍

out·back, the /ˈaʊtbæk; ˈaʊtbæk/ *n* the Australian countryside far away from cities, where few people live〔澳大利亚远离城市、人烟稀少的〕内地

out·bid /aʊtˋbɪd; aʊtˈbɪd/ *v past tense* **outbid** *present participle* **outbidding** [T] to offer a higher price than someone else, especially at an AUCTION[1]〔尤指在拍卖中〕出价高过〔别人〕

out·board mo·tor /ˈaʊtˌbɔrd ˋmotɚ; ˌaʊtbɔːd ˈməʊtə/ *n* [C] a motor fixed to the back end of a small boat〔小船的〕舷外[尾挂]发动机

out·bound /ˌaʊtˋbaʊnd; ˈaʊtbaʊnd/ *adj* moving away from you or away from a town, country etc 向外去的; 向城外的; 向国外的: *outbound traffic* 驶向城外的车流

out·break /ˈaʊtˌbrek; ˈaʊtbreɪk/ *n* [C] a sudden appearance or start of war, fighting, or serious disease〔战争、战斗、恶疾的〕突然发生, 爆发: *a cholera outbreak* 霍乱的爆发 | **[+of]** *renewed outbreaks of fighting* 战斗的持续爆发 | *the outbreak of World War II* 第二次世界大战的爆发 —see also 另见 **break out** (BREAK[1])

out·build·ing /ˈaʊtˌbɪldɪŋ; ˈaʊtˌbɪldɪŋ/ *n* [C] a building such as a BARN (1) or SHED[1] (1) near a main building〔主要建筑物旁如谷仓或棚屋的〕附属建筑, 外屋: *the farm and its outbuildings* 农场及其附属建筑物

out·burst /ˈaʊtˌbɝst; ˈaʊtbɜːst/ *n* [C] **1** a sudden powerful expression of strong emotion〔感情的〕突然爆发: *He later came to apologize to me for his outburst.* 他后来为自己乱发脾气而向我道歉。| **[+of]** *I was surprised by this outburst of resentment.* 我对这突然爆发的怨恨感到吃惊。**2** a sudden temporary increase in activity〔活动的〕突发, 激增: *an outburst of creative energy* 创作力的勃发

out·cast /ˈaʊtˌkæst; ˈaʊtkɑːst/ *n* [C] someone who is not accepted by the people they live among, or has been forced out of their home 被〔家庭、社会等〕遗弃[排斥]的人; 被逐出者: *In these health-conscious times smokers are often treated as social outcasts.* 在如今注重健康的时代, 吸烟者在社会上常常成了被排斥的一群。—**outcast** *adj*

out·caste /ˈaʊtˌkæst; ˈaʊtkɑːst/ *n* [C] someone who does not belong to or who has been forced out of a CASTE (=a traditional social class) in India〔印度〕被逐出种姓者; 贱民

out·class /aʊtˋklæs; aʊtˈklɑːs/ *v* [T often passive 常用被动态] to be much better than someone at doing something, or to be much better than something else 远远胜过; 比…等级高: *The Pittsburgh Steelers were completely outclassed by their rivals.* 匹兹堡钢人队完全敌不过对手。| *There's never been a jet engine to outclass the Rolls Royce Avon.* 从未有哪种喷气式引擎能超过劳斯莱斯埃文牌的。

3 **out·come** /ˈaʊtˌkʌm; ˈaʊtkʌm/ *n* [singular] the final result of a meeting, discussion, war etc, especially when no-one knows what it will be until it actually happens〔尤指未发生前无人知晓的〕结果, 后果: **[+of]** *We are anxiously awaiting the outcome of the negotiations.* 我们急切地等待着谈判的结果。

out·crop /ˈaʊtˌkrɑp; ˈaʊtkrɒp/ *n* [C] a rock or group of rocks above the surface of the ground 露头, 露出地面的岩石[岩层]

out·cry /ˈaʊtˌkraɪ; ˈaʊtkraɪ/ *n* [singular] an angry protest by a lot of ordinary people 公众的强烈抗议[反对], 呐喊: *The closure of our local hospital has caused a huge public outcry.* 我们当地医院的关闭激起了大规模的公开抗议。| **[+against]** *an outcry against this waste of public money* 反对如此浪费公共资金

out·dat·ed /aʊtˋdetɪd; ˌaʊtˈdeɪtɨd◂/ *adj* **1** unsuitable for the modern world and no longer used much; old-fashioned 不适合现代社会的; 过时的, 陈旧的: *outdated teaching methods* 不合时宜的教学方法 | *We reject outdated notions of national sovereignty.* 我们拒绝过时的国家主权概念。**2** a document that is outdated cannot be used because it is no longer effective〔文件等〕过期的, 失效的: *an outdated passport* 过期的护照

out·did /aʊtˋdɪd; aʊtˈdɪd/ the past tense of OUTDO

out·dis·tance /aʊtˋdɪstəns; aʊtˈdɪstəns/ *v* [T] to run, ride etc faster than other people, especially in a race, so that you are far ahead〔尤指在赛跑、赛车等中〕遥遥领先于, 超过: *Laura quickly outdistanced her pursuers.* 劳拉很快就把追赶者远远地抛在后面。

out·do /aʊtˋdu; aʊtˈduː/ *v past tense* **outdid** /-ˋdɪd; -ˈdɪd/, *past participle* **outdone** /-ˋdʌn; -ˈdʌn/, *3rd person singular present tense* **outdoes** [T] **1** to be better or more successful than someone else at doing something 胜过, 超过; 比…更成功: *The economies of South East Asia are already outdoing Western competitors.* 东南亚各经济体已经超越了西方的竞争对手。| **outdo sb in** *skaters trying to outdo the others in grace and speed* 想在动作的优美程度及速度上胜过他人的滑冰者 **2 not to be outdone** in order not to let someone else do better than you (为了) 不让别人超过自己: *Not to be outdone by the rival country-clubs, the Glen Hills golf club put in a new swimming pool.* 格伦·希尔高尔夫球俱乐部建了一个新的游泳池, 为的是不让对手的乡村俱乐部超过自己。

out·door /ˈaʊtˌdɔr; ˈaʊtdɔː/ *adj* **1** [only before noun 仅用于名词前] existing, happening, or used outside, not inside a building (在) 户外的; 用于户外的: *outdoor activities* 户外活动 | *outdoor clothing* 户外活动服装 | *a healthy outdoor life* 有益健康的户外生活 —opposite 反义词 INDOOR **2 outdoor type** a person who enjoys camping, walking in the countryside etc 野外活动爱好者

out·doors¹ /ˌaʊtˋdɔrz; ˌaʊtˈdɔːz/ *adv* outside, not inside a building; OUT OF DOORS 在户外, 在野外: *I reckon it's warm enough to eat outdoors this evening.* 我想今晚够暖和, 可以在室外吃饭。—opposite 反义词 INDOORS

outdoors² *n* **the (great) outdoors** the countryside far away from buildings and cities〔远离建筑物和城市的〕野外: *a love of the great outdoors* 对野外大自然的喜爱

out·door·sy /aʊtˋdɔrzɪ; aʊtˈdɔːzi/ *adj informal* enjoying outdoor activities【非正式】爱好野外活动的: *She's a real outdoorsy type.* 她是真正爱好野外活动的一类人。

out·draw /aʊtˋdrɔ; aʊtˈdrɔː/ *v* [T] to pull a gun out faster than someone else 比〔他人〕更快地拔出手枪: *The kid could outdraw any man in Texas.* 那小子拔枪的速度快过得克萨斯州的任何男子。

out·er /ˈaʊtɚ; ˈaʊtə/ *adj* [only before noun 仅用于名词前] **1** on the outside of something 在外的, 外面的: *Remove the tough outer leaves before cooking.* 煮之前先把外面的老叶子去掉。**2** further from the centre of something 远离中心的: *the outer suburbs* 远郊 —opposite 反义词 INNER (1)

Outer He·br·i·des, the /ˌ· · ˈ· · ·/ also 又作 **the Western Isles** a group of islands northwest of the Inner Hebrides to the west of Scotland. The main islands are Lewis and Harris, North Uist, South Uist, Benbecula, and Barra. The main town, Stornoway, is on Lewis. Many people there still speak Scottish Gaelic, and the main industries are sheep farming and producing goods made of wool, especially Harris TWEED. The area attracts many tourists in summer. English people sometimes use this name to represent any place that is very far away from the places where most people live. 外赫布里底群岛〔苏格兰以西内赫布里底群岛西北方一群岛屿。主要岛屿有路易斯—哈里斯岛、北尤伊斯特岛、南尤伊斯特岛、本贝丘拉岛和巴拉岛。主要城镇是位于路易斯岛的斯托诺韦。那里的许多岛民仍讲苏格兰盖尔语。该地以养羊业和羊毛产品制造业为主, 主要产品为哈里斯毛呢。该岛是游人消夏的好去处。有时, 英格兰人借用"外赫布里底岛"指任何远离众人居住的地方〕: *You would have to be living in the Outer Hebrides not to have heard about Harry Potter.* 你准是住在那个偏远的外赫布里底群岛, 你连哈利·波特都没听说过!

Outer Mon·go·li·a /ˌ· · ˈ· · ·/ another name for Mongolia 外蒙古〔蒙古人民共和国的别称〕

out·er·most /ˈautə͵most; ˈaʊtəməʊst/ *adj* [only before noun 仅用于名词前] furthest outside or furthest from the middle 最外面的, 离中心最远的: *the outermost stars* 最远的恒星 —opposite 反义词 INMOST (2), INNERMOST (2)

outer space /͵‥ ˈ‥/ *n* [U] the space outside the Earth's air, where the PLANETs and stars are 外层空间, 太空

out·er·wear /ˈautə͵wɛr; ˈaʊtəweə/ *n* [U] clothes, such as coats, that are worn over ordinary clothes 外衣, 外套

out·face /autˋfes; aʊtˈfeɪs/ *v* [T] to deal bravely with a difficult situation or opponent 勇敢地面对〔困境或对手〕

out·fall /ˈaut͵fɔl; ˈaʊtfɔːl/ *n* [C] a place where water flows out, especially from a DRAIN² (1) or river 排水口; 河口: *a sewage outfall* 污水排出口

out·field, the /ˈaut͵fild; ˈaʊtfiːld/ *n* **1** the part of a cricket or BASEBALL field furthest from the player who is batting (BAT² (1)) 〔板球或棒球场的〕外野, 外场 **2** the players in this part of the field 外场手 —compare 比较 INFIELD —**outfielder** *n* [C]

3 **out·fit¹** /ˈaut͵fit; ˈaʊtfɪt/ *n* [C] **1** a set of clothes worn together, especially for a special occasion〔尤指在特殊场合穿着的〕全套服装: *She bought a new, elegant two-piece outfit in shades of apricot for the wedding.* 她为婚礼买了一身两件套的新礼服, 款式雅致, 颜色是有深有浅的杏黄色。**2** *informal* a group of people who work together as a team or organization【非正式】〔一起工作的〕一群人, 全班人马: *a small advertising outfit* 广告业务小组 **3** a set of equipment that you need for a particular purpose or job〔为特定目的或工作所需的〕全套设备: *a tyre repair outfit* 修理轮胎用的整套工具

outfit² *v* **outfitted, outfitting** [T] to provide someone with a set of clothes or equipment for a special purpose 为…提供全套服装[设备], 配备, 装备

out·fit·ter /ˈaut͵fitə; ˈaʊtfɪtə/ *n* [C] **1** *BrE old-fashioned* a shop that sells men's clothes【英, 过时】男式服装商店: *a firm of gentlemen's outfitters* 销售男子全套服装的商行 **2** *AmE* a shop that sells equipment for outdoor activities such as camping【美】〔出售户外活动所需装备的〕旅行用品商店

out·flank /autˋflæŋk; aʊtˈflæŋk/ *v* [T] **1** to go around the side of an enemy during a battle and attack them from behind 包抄〔敌人〕, 迂回攻击 **2** to gain an advantage over an opponent, especially in politics〔尤指在政治上〕出奇制胜, 智胜: *The Tories found themselves outflanked by Labour on the issue of law and order.* 保守党人发现他们在法律和秩序的问题上被工党占了上风。

out·flow /ˈaut͵flo; ˈaʊtfləʊ/ *n* [C,U] **1** the process in which money, goods etc leave a bank, country etc〔钱、货物等从银行、国家等的〕外流: *the outflow of gold from the US Federal Reserve* 黄金由美国联邦储备银行外流出去 **2** the flow of water or air from something〔水或空气由某物中的〕流出: *an outflow of gas escaping from the main duct* 从主管道泄漏的煤气 | *the outflow valve* 外流阀

out·fox /autˋfɑks; aʊtˈfɒks/ *v* [T] to gain an advantage over someone by being cleverer than they are; OUTWIT 智胜, 以计谋胜过; 比…更狡猾

out front /͵· ˈ·/ *adv AmE informal*【美, 非正式】**1** honest, in a way that other people can clearly see 坦诚地, 直率地: *I just want you to know, out front, that I can't stand the guy, and I don't like spending time with him.* 我就是要坦率地让你知道, 我实在不能忍受那家伙, 而且我也不愿意浪费时间和他待在一起。**2** taking a leading position 带头, 担起领导职责: *The President has to be out front, not ducking responsibility for important issues.* 总统必须作出表率, 对重大问题不逃避责任。—**out front** *adj*

out·go·ing /ˈaut͵goɪŋ; ͵aʊtˈgəʊɪŋ◂/ *adj* **1** liking to meet and talk to new people 好交际的, 外向的: *She's got a warm, outgoing personality.* 她具有一种热心、外向的个性。**2 the outgoing president/chancellor etc** someone who is finishing their time as a president etc 即将离任的总统/总理等 **3** [only before noun 仅用于名词前] going out or leaving a place 外出的, 离开的: *the tray for outgoing mail* 放置外发邮件的公文格 | *outgoing phone calls* 外拨电话

out·go·ings /ˈaut͵goɪŋz; ˈaʊt͵gəʊɪŋz/ *n* [plural] *especially BrE* amounts of money that you spend, especially money that you have to spend regularly【尤英】支出, 开销〔尤指定期的必要花费〕: *My monthly outgoings come to about £500.* 我每月的开支在500英镑左右。

out·grow /autˋgro; aʊtˈgrəʊ/ *v past tense* **outgrew** /-ˋgru; -ˈgruː/, *past participle* **outgrown** /-ˋgron; -ˈgrəʊn/ [T] **1** to grow too big for something; GROW OUT OF 长得太大而不适用…: *You've outgrown that coat; I'll have to buy you another one.* 你已长大, 穿不下这件外套了; 我得给你再买一件。**2** to change as you become older, and no longer enjoy the things that you used to do 因年长而放弃…; 随年长而改变…: *Callahan had outgrown the radical idealism of his younger days.* 卡拉汉长大了, 也改变了自己少年时的激进理想主义。**3** to grow faster than someone or something else 长得比…快: *a population outgrowing its resources* 增长速度超过资源开发的人口 **4 outgrow your strength** *BrE* to grow too quickly when you are a child, so that you become weak or unhealthy【英】个子长得太快而营养跟不上

out·growth /ˈaut͵groθ; ˈaʊtgrəʊθ/ *n* [C] **1** a natural result of something, especially an unpleasant one〔尤指令人不悦的〕自然结果; 后果; 副产品: *Crime is often an outgrowth of poverty.* 犯罪往往是贫困的产物。**2** *technical* something that grows out of something else【术语】〔某物上的〕生长物, 长出物

out·house /ˈaut͵haus; ˈaʊthaʊs/ *n* [C] **1** *BrE* a small building which is near to and belongs to a larger main building【英】〔主建筑物外面的〕附属建筑物, 外屋 **2** *AmE* an outside toilet【美】户外厕所

out·ing /ˈautɪŋ; ˈaʊtɪŋ/ *n* **1** [C] a short pleasure trip for a group of people〔一群人的〕短途旅游, 远足: **a school/church/class etc outing** *a class outing to the ballet* 班级组织外出观看芭蕾舞 **2** [C,U] the practice of publicly naming people as HOMOSEXUALs, when they do not want anyone to know this 公开指出某些人为同性恋者的行为

out·land·ish /autˋlændɪʃ; aʊtˈlændɪʃ/ *adj* strange and unusual 古怪的, 奇异的: *He used to play guitar and wear outlandish costumes in a punk band.* 他以前常在一支朋克摇滚乐队中身着奇装异服弹吉他。—**outlandishly** *adv* —**outlandishness** *n* [U]

out·last /autˋlæst; aʊtˈlɑːst/ *v* [T] to continue to exist for a longer time than something else 比…经久[持久] —compare 比较 OUTLIVE

out·law¹ /ˈaut͵lɔ; ˈaʊtlɔː/ *n* [C] someone who has done something illegal, and who is not protected by the law 不法之徒, 无法无天的人; 不受法律保护的罪犯

outlaw² *v* [T] **1** to completely stop something by making it illegal or socially unacceptable 将〔某事〕定为非法; 全面禁止: *Certain counties have outlawed the sale of alcohol.* 一些郡已禁止售酒。**2** to officially state that someone is an outlaw 宣布〔某人〕为不法之徒

out·lay /ˈaut͵le; ˈaʊtleɪ/ *n* [C,U] the amount of money that you have to spend in order to start a new business, activity etc〔用于开设新商号、进行某活动等的〕花费, 开支: *For a relatively small outlay you can start manufacturing T-shirts.* 如果可用的资金相对较少, 你可以先开始生产T恤。| **[+on/for]** *House buyers usually have a large initial outlay on carpets and furniture.* 购房者通常先要为买地毯和家具花去一大笔钱。

out·let /ˈaut͵lɛt; ˈaʊtlet/ *n* [C] **1** a way of expressing or getting rid of strong feelings〔强烈情感的〕发泄途径, 释放方式, 出路: **[+for]** *I play racquet ball as an outlet for stress.* 我用打壁球来排解压力。**2** a shop, company, or organization through which products are sold 批发商店, 商行; 销售公司: **retail outlet** *Benetton has retail outlets in every major European city.* 贝纳通公司在欧洲各主要城市都有零售店。**3** a way through which something such as a liquid or gas can flow out〔液体或气体的〕出口; 排水口; 通风口 **4** *AmE*【美】电源插座; a POWER POINT *BrE*【英】

out·line¹ /ˈaut͵laɪn; ˈaʊtlaɪn/ *n* [singular] **1** the main ideas or facts about something, without the details 纲要, 梗概, 要点: *I'd like to see the proposal outline.* 我想看看这份建议书的概要。| *an outline of world history* 世界史纲 | **broad/rough outline** (=a very general outline) 大致的/粗略的纲要 | **in outline** (=giving an outline) 扼要地 *Chapter I describes in outline the way money circulates through the economy.* 第一章扼要地讲述了货币在经济中的流通方式。**2** a line around the edge of something which shows its shape 外形; 轮廓: *the outline of a footprint in the snow* 雪中脚印的轮廓 | **outline map/sketch etc** *an outline map of Europe* 欧洲略图 **3** *especially AmE* a plan for a report, story etc in which each new idea is separately recorded【尤美】〔报告、故事等的〕设想, 草案

outline 外形, 轮廓

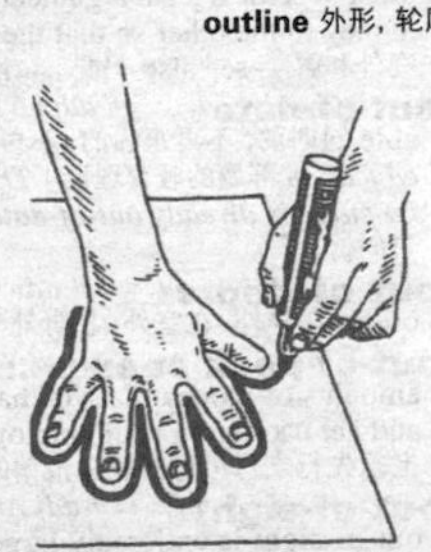

She is drawing an outline of her hand. 她在勾画自己手的轮廓。

outline² *v* [T] **1** to describe something in a general way, giving the main points but not the details 概述; 提出…的纲要: *The President outlined his peace plan for the Middle East.* 总统概述了他的中东和平计划。**2** [often passive 常用被动态] to make the outline of a shape very clear 画…的轮廓, 描…的外形: *a map of the area with our property outlined in red* 一张用红色勾画出来的我们物业的区位图

O

out·live /aʊtˋlɪv; aʊtˈlɪv/ *v* [T] **1** to live longer than someone else 比…活得长: *She outlived her husband by twenty years.* 她比她丈夫多活了 20 年。**2** to continue to exist after something else has ended or disappeared 比…经久: *The military regime has outlived its statutory term by three years.* 这一军事政权的存在已超过法定期限三年。| **outlive its usefulness** (=become no longer useful) *As a commuter service the Seacombe Ferry had outlived its usefulness.* 作为通勤服务设施, 西库姆渡轮已不再有用了。

out·look /ˋaʊtˌlʊk; ˈaʊtlʊk/ *n* [C] **1** your general attitude to life and the world〔对生活、世界的〕看法, 观点, 态度: [**+on**] *He's got a very positive outlook on life.* 他持有一种非常积极的人生观。| *The farmers were narrowly provincial in their outlook.* 这些农民观念偏狭, 见识不广。**2** what is expected to happen in the future 前景, 远景: [**+for**] *The weather outlook for the weekend is bad.* 本周末的天气情况不佳。| *The outlook for sufferers from this disease is not good.* 这种疾病的患者希望渺茫。**3** a view from a particular place〔从某处望见的〕景色, 风光: *a very pleasing outlook from the bedroom window* 从卧室窗户看到的非常宜人的景色

out·ly·ing /ˋaʊtˌlaɪɪŋ; ˈaʊtˌlaɪ-ɪŋ/ *adj* [only before noun 仅用于名词前] far from the centre of a city, town etc or from a main building 边远的; 远离市中心的; 远离主要建筑物的: *one of the outlying suburbs* 边远郊区之一 | *the outlying barns* 外围的谷仓

out·ma·noeu·vre *BrE*【英】, **outmaneuver** *AmE*【美】 /ˌaʊtməˋnuvɚ; ˌaʊtməˈnuːvə/ *v* [T] to gain an advantage over someone by using cleverer plans or methods than they do 智胜〔对手〕, 比〔对手〕计高一筹, 使〔对手〕处于下风: *a woman who could outmanoeuvre even the Prime Minister* 一个甚至能比首相计高一筹的女人

out·mod·ed /aʊtˋmodɪd; aʊtˈməʊdɪ̤d/ *adj* no longer fashionable or useful 过时的, 不再流行的; 废弃的: *an outmoded set of values* 一套过时的价值观

out·most /ˋaʊtˌmost; ˈaʊtməʊst/ *adj* furthest outside or furthest from the middle; OUTERMOST 最外面的, 离中心最远的

out·num·ber /aʊtˋnʌmbɚ; aʊtˈnʌmbə/ *v* [T usually passive 一般用被动态] to be more in number than another group 比…多, 在数量上胜过: *We were completely outnumbered by the enemy.* 在数量上我们完全被敌人压倒。| *In the nursing profession women still outnumber men by four to one.* 在护理行业, 女性依然多于男性, 人数比例为四比一。

out-of-bod·y /ˌ. . ˈ. .◂/ *adj* **out-of-body experience** the feeling that sometimes happens when someone is close to death that they are outside of their body and can look down on it from above 游离体外的感觉, 灵魂出窍的感觉〔人临死前有时产生的一种游离于体外俯视自己身体的感觉〕

out-of-court /ˌ. . ˈ.◂/ *adj* **out-of-court settlement** an agreement to settle a legal argument, in which one side agrees to pay money to the other so that the problem is not brought to court 庭外和解 —see also 另见 **settle sth out of court** (COURT¹ (1))

out-of-date /ˌ. . ˈ.◂/ *adj* no longer useful, correct or fashionable 过时的, 不再正确的, 不再流行的: *out-of-date theories on education* 陈腐的教育理论 | *The information in last year's tourist guide is already out-of-date.* 去年的旅游指南上的资料已经过时。

out of doors /ˌ. . ˈ./ *adv* outside, not in a building; OUTDOORS 在户外, 在室外; 在野外 —see 见 OUTSIDE (USAGE)

out-of-pock·et ex·pens·es /ˌ. . ˌ. . . ˈ. . ./ *n* [plural] small amounts of money that you have to spend as part of your job, and get back from your employer 先自行垫付的开销〔指在工作上须先行支付但可向雇主报销的小额开支〕

out-of-sight /ˌ. . ˈ./ *adj AmE* an amount of money that is out-of-sight is extremely large【美】金额极大的, 非常昂贵的: *The hotel bill was out-of-sight.* 旅馆的账单数额极大。—see also 另见 **out of sight, out of mind** (SIGHT¹ (18))

out-of-the-way /ˌ. . . ˈ.◂/ *adj* **1** far from other towns and villages and often difficult to find 边远的, 偏僻的, 人迹罕至的: *Don't you find it inconvenient living in such an out-of-the-way place?* 你住在这样荒僻的地方难道不觉得不方便吗? **2** *BrE* unusual or strange【英】不寻常的; 怪异的: *Her taste in music is a bit out-of-the-way.* 她对音乐的品味有点怪异。

out-of-work /ˌ. . ˈ.◂/ *adj* unemployed 失业的, 未受雇用的: *out-of-work actors* 未受聘用的演员

out-pa·tient /ˋaʊtˌpeʃənt; ˈaʊtˌpeɪʃənt/ *n* [C] someone who goes to a hospital for treatment but does not stay there 门诊病人 —compare 比较 INPATIENT

out-per·form /ˌaʊtpɚˋfɔrm; ˌaʊtpəˈfɔːm/ *v* [T] to perform better than someone or something else 做得比…好; 胜过: *The new Pentium computers outperform our 486s.* 新的奔腾电脑比我们的 486 好。

out-place·ment /ˋaʊtˌplesmənt; ˈaʊtˌpleɪsmənt/ *n* [C,U] the process of a company helping people to find new jobs after asking them to leave their employment〔公司解雇员工后的〕新岗位安排, 再就业服务

out-play /aʊtˋple; aʊtˈpleɪ/ *v* [T] to beat an opponent in a game by playing with more skill than they do〔比赛中〕胜过〔对手〕, 击败

out-point /aʊtˋpɔɪnt; aʊtˈpɔɪnt/ *v* [T] to defeat an opponent in BOXING by gaining more points〔拳击赛中〕以得分多而击败〔对手〕

out-post /ˋaʊtˌpost; ˈaʊtpəʊst/ *n* [C] a small town or group of buildings in a distant lonely place, usually established as a military camp or a place for trade〔通常作为军营或贸易点而建的〕前哨(基地), 偏远居民区

out-pour-ing /ˋaʊtˌporɪŋ; ˈaʊtpɔːrɪŋ/ *n* **1** **outpourings** [plural] continuous expressions of strong feeling〔强烈感情的〕不断流露: [**+of**] *outpourings of grief* 悲伤的倾吐 **2** [C,U] a lot of something that is produced suddenly 进发; 涌出(物); 泻出(物): *an outpouring of creative energy* 创造力的迸发

out-put¹ /ˋaʊtˌpʊt; ˈaʊtpʊt/ *n* [C,U] **1** the amount of goods or work produced by a person, machine, factory etc 产量; 输出量: *Output is up 30% on last year.* 产量比去年增加了 30%。**2** *technical* the information produced by a computer【术语】〔电脑的〕输出信息 **3** *technical* the amount of electricity produced by a GENERATOR【术语】〔发电机的〕发电量, 输出功率 —compare 比较 INPUT¹ 2

output² *v past tense and past participle* **output** [T] if a computer outputs information, it produces it〔电脑〕输出〔信息〕

out-rage¹ /ˋaʊtˌredʒ; ˈaʊtreɪdʒ/ *n* **1** [U] a feeling of great anger and shock 愤慨, 义愤; 震怒: *The injustice of the situation filled him with a sense of outrage.* 这种不公正的情况使他满腔愤慨。**2** [C] a very cruel, violent, and shocking action or event 残忍的行径, 暴行; 令人震惊的事情: [**+against**] *These terrorist attacks are an outrage against society.* 这些恐怖袭击是一种反社会的暴行。

outrage² *v* [T usually passive 一般用被动态] to make someone feel very angry and shocked 激起〔某人〕的义愤; 使〔某人〕震怒: *People were outraged at the idea of the murderer Hindley being released.* 人们对释放凶手欣德利的主意义愤填膺。

out-ra-geous /aʊtˋredʒəs; aʊtˈreɪdʒəs/ *adj* **1** very shocking and extremely unfair or offensive 骇人的; 极不公正的; 蛮横的: *outrageous prices* 骇人的价格 | *I can't believe he's been allowed to spread such outrageous lies!* 我无法相信竟然会允许他散布这种耸人听闻的谎言! | **it is outrageous that** *It's outrageous that the poor should have to pay such high taxes.* 穷人得缴纳这么高的税额, 真是令人骇然。**2** extremely unusual and slightly amusing or shocking 极不寻常的; 有点可笑[吓人]的: *an outrageous hairstyle* 怪里怪气的发型 | *Mark will say the most outrageous things, especially when he's supposed to be polite.* 马克常会出言不逊, 尤其是在要他讲究礼貌时。

out-ran /aʊtˋræn; aʊtˈræn/ the past tense of OUTRUN

out-rank /aʊtˋræŋk; aʊtˈræŋk/ *v* [T] **1** to have a higher rank than someone else in the same group 级别高于〔同一团体中的某人〕; 地位高于 **2** to be more important than something else 重要性超过〔某物〕

ou-tré /uˋtre; ˈuːtreɪ/ *adj French* strange, unusual, and slightly shocking【法】怪诞的, 异常的; 有点吓人的: *the genius of artists as outré as Beardsley or Toulouse-Lautrec* 像比尔兹利或土鲁斯－劳特累克一样怪诞的艺术家之天赋

out-reach /ˋaʊtritʃ; ˈaʊtriːtʃ/ *n* [U] *especially AmE*【尤美】**1** services based close to people's homes to help those who cannot easily come to an office, hospital etc〔靠近人们家庭, 以帮助不便上班或去医院看病等的人为主要业务的〕扩大范围的服务, 外展服务: **outreach service/center etc** *outreach centers for drug addicts* 戒毒外展服务中心 **2** the work a church does to teach or serve people who are not its members〔教堂为非教民所做的〕布道; 善事

out-ride /aʊtˋraɪd; aʊtˈraɪd/ *v past tense* **outrode** /-ˋrod; -ˈrəʊd/ *past participle* **outridden** /-ˋrɪdn̩; -ˈrɪdn/ [T] to ride faster or further than someone or something else 骑得比…快[远]

out·rid·er /ˈaut͵raɪdɚ; ˈaʊt͵raɪdə/ *n* [C] a guard or police officer who rides on a MOTORCYCLE or horse beside or in front of a vehicle in which an important person is travelling〔为重要人物的车辆开路的〕驾摩托车的警卫, 骑马的警官

out·rig·ger /ˈaut͵rɪgɚ; ˈaʊt͵rɪgə/ *n* [C] **1** a piece of wood shaped like a small narrow boat which is fixed to the side of a boat, especially a CANOE[1], to prevent it from turning over in the water〔尤指独木舟的〕舷外浮木〔形如一小船的木头, 固定在船侧以防船在水中翻转〕 **2** a boat fitted with one of these 装有舷外浮木的小艇

out·right[1] /͵autˈraɪt; aʊtˈraɪt/ *adv* **1** without trying to hide your feelings or intentions 直率地; 无掩饰地; 痛快地: *They laughed outright at my suggestion.* 他们听了我的建议后爽快地笑了。| *Tell him outright exactly what you think.* 把你的想法坦白告诉他。**2** completely 完全地, 彻底地: *The town was destroyed outright.* 城镇被彻底毁掉了。| *She won outright.* 她大获全胜。**3 buy/own sth outright** to own something such as a house completely because you have paid the full price with your own money 一次性付款买下某物/完全拥有某物 **4 be killed outright** to be killed immediately 被当场杀死

out·right[2] /ˈaut͵raɪt; ˈaʊtraɪt/ *adj* [only before noun 仅用于名词前] **1** clear and direct 明白无误的; 直截了当的: *an outright refusal* 断然拒绝 **2** complete 彻底的, 完全的: *outright ban on the sale of pornographic films* 彻底禁止色情影片的销售 **3 outright winner/victor** someone who has definitely and easily won 毫无疑问的轻松获胜者

out·ri·val /autˈraɪvl; aʊtˈraɪvəl/ *v* [T] to defeat someone in a competition〔在竞争中〕击败, 胜过

out·rode /autˋrod; aʊtˈrəʊd/ the past tense of OUTRIDE

out·run /autˋrʌn; aʊtˈrʌn/ *v past tense* **outran** /-ˋræn; -ˈræn/ *past participle* **outrun** *present participle* **outrunning** [T] **1** to run faster or further than someone 比…跑得快[远], 跑得比…更快[更远] **2** to develop more quickly than something else 发展快于…, 比…发展得更快: *The Reverend believes that technological progress has outrun our moral development.* 那位牧师认为科技发展已经超过了人类道德的进化。

out·sell /autˋsɛl; aʊtˈsel/ *v past tense and past participle* **outsold** /-ˋsold; -ˈsəʊld/ [T] **1** to be sold in larger quantities than something else 卖得比…多, 销量胜过: *a detergent that outsells every other brand* 销量超过其他任何牌子的洗涤剂 **2** to sell more goods or products than a competitor 比〔竞争对手〕销售得多

out·set /ˈaut͵sɛt; ˈaʊtset/ *n* **at/from the outset** at or from the beginning of an event or process 在开头时/从一开始: *It was clear right from the outset that there were going to be problems.* 从一开始就很清楚, 会有问题出现的。

out·shine /autˋʃaɪn; aʊtˈʃaɪn/ *v past tense and past participle* **outshone** /autˋʃon; aʊtˈʃɒn/ *present participle* **outshining** [T] **1** to be better at something than someone else 优于; 使…黯然失色: *Vera's flowers outshone all the others in the competition.* 在比赛中, 维拉的花让别的花都黯然失色。**2** to shine more brightly than something else 照耀得比…更亮

S1 W1 **out·side**[1] /autˋsaɪd; aʊtˈsaɪd/ *prep* **1** out of a particular building or room 到〔建筑物或房间〕的外面, 由…向外: *As soon as we were outside the door we burst out laughing.* 我们一出门便放声大笑起来。—opposite 反义词 INSIDE[1] (2) **2** out of a building but still close to it 在〔离建筑物不远〕的外边: *I'll meet you outside the hardware store at 2 o'clock.* 我两点钟会在五金商店外边见你。**3** beyond the limits of a city, country etc 超出〔城市、乡村等的〕界限: *Add the area code 212 if you are calling from outside the New York area.* 如果在纽约市范围以外打电话, 要加上区号 212。| **just outside** *Bolton is a beautiful mill town just outside Manchester.* 博尔顿是一座美丽的磨坊之城, 就在曼彻斯特边上。**4** beyond the limits or range of a situation, activity etc 超出〔情况、活动等的〕界限, 在…范围之外: *It's outside my experience I'm afraid.* 恐怕我没有这方面的经验。| *I don't care who you see outside working hours.* 我并不在意你在上班时间以外见什么人。—opposite 反义词 WITHIN —compare 比较 BEYOND[1] **5** if someone is outside a group of people, an organization etc they do not have the same ideas and beliefs 与〔团体、组织等的想法、看法〕不一致: *Outside the party the official story was that he needed to spend more time with his family.* 该党对外的官方口径是, 他需要多花些时间和家人在一起。

S1 W3 **out·side**[2] /autˋsaɪd; aʊtˈsaɪd/ *adv* **1** not inside a building 在外面, 在户外: *Can't you kids go and play outside?* 你们这些小孩子不能去外头玩吗? | *What do you want to go out for? It's still dark outside.* 你想出去干什么? 外面天还黑着呢。**2** not in a room or building but close to it 在〔房屋、建筑物附近的〕外面, 在室外: *I don't have time to chat, my husband's waiting outside.* 我没时间聊天, 我丈夫在外面等着呢。| *What's happening at the stadium? There are lots of people standing outside.* 体育场出什么事了? 好多人在外头站着。**3 outside of** *informal especially AmE*【非正式, 尤美】**a)** apart from a particular person or thing; except 除…以外, …除外: *What else can we do, outside of tearing the work up and starting from the beginning?* 除了推翻一切重来之外, 我们还能做什么? **b)** outside a particular place, building etc 在〔某处、某建筑物等〕的外面: *It was decided to run a campaign outside of Washington.* 已决定在华盛顿附近举行一场〔竞选〕活动。

USAGE NOTE 用法说明: OUT

WORD CHOICE 词语辨析: **out, outside, outdoors/out of doors**

If you are **outside** a room or building, you are not in it but are close to it. outside 指在房间或建筑物外面, 但相距很近: *You have to go outside if you want to smoke.* 你如果想吸烟, 就得到外面去。| *It's cold outside.* 外面很冷。

If you are **out**, you are away from a building, especially somewhere you live or spend a lot of time. out 指离开某建筑物, 尤指居住或待很长时间的地方: *Let's go out for a meal/drive.* 我们出去吃饭吧/我们开车出去兜兜风吧。| *I'm sorry, Mr. Davies is out at the moment.* 对不起, 戴维斯先生这会儿外出了。

You use **outdoors** (or **out of doors**) more informally to mean being out of any building. outdoors〔或 out of doors〕为较非正式的用语, 意指在任何建筑物之外: *I'd like a job where I can work outdoors.* 我想找一份能在室外干活的工作。

GRAMMAR 语法

People or things go or come **out of** somewhere. 人或物由某处出来用 out of: *He comes out of prison next week.* (NOT 不用 *out from prison*) 他下周出狱。| *Water poured out of the pipe.* 水从管道中流出。(Also *out the pipe* in American English and informal spoken British English. 美国英语及非正式的英国口语中也用 out the pipe。)

You go/are **out of** *the house*, but **away from** *home*. 出屋用 out of the house, 离家用 away from home。

Outside may be used alone or with **of** (especially in spoken and American English). outside 可以单用, 也可与 of 连用〔尤在口语和美国英语中〕: *He lives outside (of) Miami.* (NOT 不用 *outside from...*) 他住在迈阿密附近。

out·side[3] /ˈautˋsaɪd; ˈaʊtsaɪd/ *adj* [only before noun 仅用于名词前] S2 W2 **1 outside wall/toilet etc** a wall, toilet etc that is not inside a building 外墙/室外的厕所等: *Most apartments have outside staircases in case of emergency.* 大多数公寓都有供紧急情况用的室外楼梯。| *The house will need a lot of outside repairs before we can sell it.* 房子外部要好好修缮才能出售。—opposite 反义词 INSIDE[4] (1) —see also 另见 OUTDOORS[1], OUTER **2 outside help/interest etc** help etc from people who do not belong to the same group or organization as you 外援/外界的关注等: *My family solved its problems without any outside interference.* 我家没靠外人干预, 自己解决了问题。**3 outside expert/consultant etc** an expert, consultant etc who does not work for your company or organization but who you pay to do some work for you 外聘专家/顾问等: *A firm of outside caterers were brought in especially for the function.* 这次宴会请了一家对外承办酒席的公司来专门供应酒食。**4 outside interests/experiences etc** interests, experiences etc that are different from those that you have in your job 业余爱好/工作以外的经历等: *Ex-scientists can bring their outside knowledge into the teaching profession.* 曾经当过科学家的人可以把他们独到的知识用于教学。**5 the outside world** the rest of the world which is unknown to you because you have no communication with it, you are not involved in it etc 外界: *Since the attack the city has been cut off from the outside world.* 那个城市自遭受袭击以来, 与外界的联系已被隔绝。**6 an outside chance** a very small possibility that something will happen 极小的可能性, 不大可能的机会: *There's an outside chance that Regis might be sent to Uganda on business.* 派里吉斯去乌干达出差的可能性不大。**7 an outside figure/estimate etc** a number or amount that is the largest something could possibly be 最大限度的数字/估计等 **8 outside line/call etc** a telephone line or telephone call which is to or from someone not inside a building 外线/外线电话等 **9 the outside lane** the LANE (2) that is nearest the middle of the road 外车道 —see picture on page A3 参见 A3 页图

out·side[4] /autˋsaɪd; aʊtˈsaɪd/ *n* **the outside** **1** the outer walls, windows etc of something such as a building or vehicle〔某物的〕外墙; 外层窗; 外面: [+of] *We've decided to paint the outside of the house brown.* 我们决定把房子的外墙刷成棕色。**2** the

area of land around something such as a building, vehicle etc〔建筑物、车辆等的〕周围, 周边地带, 外围: *From the outside the hotel looked fairly rundown.* 从外面看, 这家旅馆已经相当破旧。**3** the outer part or surface of something〔某物的〕外部; 表面: [+of] *The outside of the cheese is red but this is just a protective wax.* 乳酪的外表呈红色, 但这只是一层保护蜡而已。—opposite 反义词 INSIDE[3] (1a) **4** someone who is on or from the outside is not involved in an activity or does not belong to a particular group, organization etc 局外〔人士〕; 外界〔人士〕: *To anyone on the outside our discipline methods may seem a little severe.* 对任何局外人而言, 我们的训练方法看来也许有些严厉。**5 on the outside a)** used to describe the way someone appears to be or to behave 表面上, 由表面来看: *On the outside she appeared gentle and kind but really she was the meanest person I ever met.* 从表面上看, 她温柔可亲, 但实际上她是我所遇到的最卑鄙的人。**b)** not in prison 在监狱外(的): *Life on the outside was not as easy as he'd first thought.* 出狱后的生活并非像他原来想的那样轻松。**6 at the (very) outside** used to say that a particular number or amount could be the largest something, and it might be less 最多, 充其量: *It's only a 20 minute walk, half an hour at the outside.* 那只是20分钟的路程, 最多半个小时。**7** the LANE (2) on a road that is nearest to the middle of the road 外车道: *In some countries it is only permissible to overtake on the outside.* 有些国家只允许在外车道超车。—opposite 反义词 INSIDE[3] (1b)

out·sid·er /aʊtˋsaɪdɚ; aʊtˈsaɪdə/ *n* [C] **1** someone who is not accepted as a member of a particular social group〔不被某一社会团体接受的〕局外人, 外人; 非成员: *We felt like complete outsiders when we first moved here.* 刚搬来这里时, 我们感到自己完全像外人。**2** someone who does not seem to have much chance of winning a race or competition〔比赛中〕赢面不大的人: *The champion was knocked out by an outsider.* 冠军被一位不被看好的拳击手击倒了。**3** someone who does not belong to a particular company or organization 公司[组织]外的人: *The firm was obliged to seek the help of outsiders.* 该商行被迫寻求外援。

out·size /ˋaʊtˌsaɪz; ˈaʊtsaɪz/ *adj* also 又作 **out·sized** /-ˌsaɪzd; -saɪzd/ **1** larger than normal 超过正常尺寸的, 特大号的: *peering through outsize spectacles* 透过特大号眼镜凝视 **2** made for people who are very large 为非常高大的人裁制的, 超人号的: *outsize clothes* 超大号服装

out·skirts /ˋaʊtˌskɝts; ˈaʊtskɜːts/ *n* [plural] the parts of a town or city that are furthest from the centre 远离城市中心的地区, 远郊区: **on the outskirts** *They live on the outskirts of Paris.* 他们住在巴黎的远郊区。

out·smart /aʊtˋsmɑrt; aʊtˈsmɑːt/ *v* [T] to gain an advantage over someone using tricks or clever plans; OUTWIT 比…更精明; 智胜…: *The lizard can outsmart any predators by leaving its tail behind to confuse them.* 蜥蜴比任何食肉动物都机灵, 它会甩掉自己的尾巴来迷惑其他动物。

out·sour·cing /ˋaʊtˌsɔrsɪŋ; ˈaʊtˌsɔːsɪŋ/ *n* [U] the practice of using workers from outside a company 外包, 外判〔使用公司外聘员工的做法〕

out·spo·ken /aʊtˋspokən; aʊtˈspəʊkən/ *adj* expressing your opinions honestly, even when it is not popular to do so 坦率的, 直言不讳的: *an outspoken critic of the country's human rights policies* 对该国人权政策直言不讳的批评家 —**outspokenly** *adv* —**outspokenness** *n* [U]

out·spread /ˋaʊtˌsprɛd; ˌaʊtˈspred◂/ *adj* spread out flat or completely 张开的, 伸开的: *He was lying on the beach with arms outspread.* 他两臂摊开躺在沙滩上。

out·stand·ing /aʊtˋstændɪŋ; aʊtˈstændɪŋ/ *adj* **1** extremely good 杰出的, 优秀的, 出色的: *an area of outstanding natural beauty* 极佳的自然风景区 | *an outstanding performance* 出色的表演 **2** not yet done, solved, or paid 未完成的; 未解决的; 未付款的: *We've got quite a few debts still outstanding.* 我们尚有好多欠债未曾偿还。| *an outstanding problem* 悬而未决的问题

out·stand·ing·ly /aʊtˋstændɪŋlɪ; aʊtˈstændɪŋli/ *adv* extremely well 出色地, 极好地: *Varese played outstandingly.* 瓦雷塞打得很出色。| [+adj/adv] *an outstandingly talented musician* 一位才华出众的音乐家

out·stare /aʊtˋstɛr; aʊtˈsteə/ *v* [T] to look at someone for so long that they feel too uncomfortable to look at you 以目光逼视; 盯得…局促不安

out·stay /aʊtˋste; aʊtˈsteɪ/ *v* [T] to stay somewhere longer than someone else 停留较〔他人〕长久, 比〔他人〕待得久: *As usual she outstayed all the other guests at the party.* 晚会上, 她照例比其他客人都待得久。—see also 另见 **outstay your welcome** WELCOME[3] (3)

out·stretched /aʊtˋstrɛtʃt; ˌaʊtˈstretʃt◂/ *adj* stretched out to full length 张开的, 伸开的: *She ran to meet them with outstretched arms.* 她张开双臂跑过去迎接他们。

out·strip /aʊtˋstrɪp; aʊtˈstrɪp/ *v* **outstripped, outstripping** [T] **1** to do something better than someone else 比…做得好, 胜过: *We outstripped all our competitors in sales last year.* 去年我们在销售方面超过了所有的竞争对手。**2** to be greater in quantity than something else 数量上大于…: *Demand for energy is outstripping the supply.* 能源目前求大于供。**3** to run or move faster than someone or something else 跑步[移动]快于…; 把…抛在后面: *Dawson outstripped the other runners on the last lap.* 道森在最后一圈超越了其他赛跑者。

out·take /ˈ· ·/ *n* [C] a piece of a film or television show that is removed before it is broadcast, especially because it contains a mistake〔尤指因内容有错而在播放前〕被临时撤掉的电影[电视节目]片段

out tray /ˈ· ·/ *n* [C] a box on an office desk to hold work and letters which are ready to be sent out or put away〔办公桌上存放已处理或待发文件的〕发文匣[格] —compare 比较 IN TRAY

out·vote /aʊtˋvot; aʊtˈvəʊt/ *v* [T] to defeat a person or an idea by voting against them 以票数多击败…, 比…得到更多选票

out·ward /ˋaʊtwɚd; ˈaʊtwəd/ *adj* **1** [only before noun 仅用于名词前] concerning how someone seems to other people, rather than what they are actually like 外表的, 表面上的: *She managed to maintain her outward composure.* 她保持着外表的镇静。| *His house shows few outward signs of worldly success.* 他的房子看不出他有取得世俗成就的迹象。| **to all outward appearances** (=as much as you can judge by the way things seem) 从外表上看 *To all outward appearances, Jayne seems to be dealing with the tragedy well.* 从外表看, 杰恩似乎对那件惨剧应付得很好。**2 outward journey/voyage etc** a journey in which you are travelling away from home 外出旅行/出航等 **3** [only before noun 仅用于名词前] directed towards the outside or away from something 往外的, 向外的: *an outward movement of the arm* 手臂的向外运动 **4 outward bound** a train, ship, etc that is outward bound is leaving a place that it will return to later〔列车、船只等〕开往外地的; 出海的

Outward Bound /ˌ·· ˈ·/ *trademark* an educational organization that provides adventure programmes and team activities for schoolchildren and adults, who are taught skills such as how to live outside in wild areas of land. These programmes and activities aim to develop qualities such as leadership, courage, and respect for the environment.【商标】拓展训练中心〔为学龄儿童及成年人组织冒险性训练专案和团队活动的一个教育机构。参加者须学习野外生存技能等诸多内容, 旨在培养其领导才能、勇敢精神和尊重自然环境等素质〕

out·ward·ly /ˋaʊtwɚdlɪ; ˈaʊtwədli/ *adv* according to the way things seem 外表上, 从表面上看: *Calvin remained outwardly calm but inside he was seething.* 卡尔文表面上不露声色, 但内心却澎湃不已。| [sentence adverb 句子副词] *Outwardly, nothing seemed to have changed.* 从表面上看, 似乎一无变化。

out·wards /ˋaʊtwɚdz; ˈaʊtwədz/ also 又作 **outward** *AmE*【美】*adv* towards the outside or away from the centre of something 往外, 向外: *The door opens outwards.* 这门是朝外开的。

out·weigh /aʊtˋwe; aʊtˈweɪ/ *v* [T] to be more important or valuable than something else 比…更重要; 比…更有价值: *The advantages of this plan far outweigh the disadvantages.* 该计划的利远大于弊。

out·wit /aʊtˋwɪt; aʊtˈwɪt/ *v* **outwitted, outwitting** [T] to gain an advantage over someone using tricks or clever plans 智胜, 以计谋击败: *My father spent years trying to build a bird feeder that would outwit the squirrels.* 我父亲花了数年的时间, 想造一个让松鼠无计可施的喂鸟器。

out·work /ˋaʊtˌwɝk; ˈaʊtwɜːk/ *n* [U] work for a business that is done by people at home〔由人们在家中完成的〕外包活 —**outworker** *n* [C]

out·worn /ˌaʊtˋwɔrn; ˌaʊtˈwɔːn◂/ *adj* [only before noun 仅用于名词前] old-fashioned, and no longer useful or important 过时的, 废弃了的; 不再重要的: *A lot of schools have abolished these outworn traditions.* 许多学校已废除了这些过时的传统习俗。

ou·zo /ˋuzo; ˈuːzəʊ/ *n* [U] a Greek alcoholic drink that is drunk with water〔希腊的〕茴香烈酒

o·va /ˋovə; ˈəʊvə/ *n* the plural form of OVUM

o·val /ˋovl; ˈəʊvəl/ *n* [C] a shape like a circle, but longer than it is wide 卵形, 椭圆形 —**oval** *adj*: *an oval mirror* 椭圆形的镜子 —see picture at 参见 SHAPE[1] 图

Oval Of·fice /ˌ·· ˈ··/ *n* the office of the US president, in the White House, Washington DC〔美国华盛顿白宫内的〕椭圆形

办公室，总统办公室：*We're waiting for a reaction from the Oval Office.* 我们在等候总统办公室的反应。

o·var·i·an /o`vɛrɪən; əʊ'veəriən/ *adj* related to the ovary 卵巢的；子房的：*ovarian cancer* 卵巢癌

o·va·ry /`ovərɪ; 'əʊvəri/ *n plural* **ovaries** [C] **1** the part of a female that produces eggs〔雌性动物的〕卵巢 **2** the part of a female plant that produces seeds〔植物的〕子房

o·va·tion /o`veʃən; əʊ'veɪʃən/ *n* [C] *formal* if a group of people give someone an ovation they CLAP¹ (1) to show approval【正式】〔以鼓掌表示的〕赞同；欢呼，喝彩：*60,000 fans gave the rock group a thunderous ovation.* 6万名歌迷向摇滚乐队报以雷鸣般的掌声。| **standing ovation** (=one in which people stand) 起立鼓掌

S3 **ov·en** /`ʌvən; 'ʌvən/ *n* [C] **1** a thing inside which food is cooked, shaped like a box with a door on the front 烘箱；烤箱，烤炉：**a medium/moderate oven** (=an oven that has not been made very hot) 温度调在中挡的烘箱 *Bake in a medium oven for 40 minutes.* 用中挡温度在烘箱内烤 40 分钟。**2 like an oven** *informal* uncomfortably hot【非正式】很热的：*It's like an oven in here! Open the window.* 这里热得像火炉！快把窗户打开吧。—see also 另见 **have a bun in the oven** (BUN (4))

ov·en·proof /`ʌvən,pruf; 'ʌvənpru:f/ *adj* a dish, plate etc that is ovenproof will not be harmed by the high temperatures in an oven〔碟子、盘子等〕耐热的，经得起烘箱温度而不致碎裂的

oven-read·y /,‥ '‥◂/ *adj* oven-ready food is already prepared when you buy it, so you only have to cook it〔购买时已加工好的食物〕即可入炉烤制的

ov·en·ware /`ʌvən,wɛr; 'ʌvənweə/ *n* [U] cooking pots that can be put in a hot oven without cracking〔经得起烘箱高温烘烤的〕耐热器皿

S1 W1 **over¹** /`ovɚ; 'əʊvə/ *prep* **1** above or higher than something, without touching it 在…上面[上方]〔但未触及〕，在…上空：*A lamp hung over the table.* 桌子上方悬吊着一盏灯。| *She leaned over the desk to answer the phone.* 她俯身靠在书桌上接电话。| *The sign over the door said 'Mind your head'.* 门上方的警示牌写着"小心碰头"。—opposite 反义词 UNDER¹ (1) —see also 另见 ABOVE¹, ACROSS¹—see picture at 参见 ABOVE¹ 图 **2** on something, so that it is covered 蒙在…上，覆盖在…的上面：*Over the body lay a thin white sheet.* 尸体上盖着一层薄薄的白布单。| *She wore a large jacket over her sweater.* 她在毛衣外面穿了件宽大的夹克。—opposite 反义词 UNDER¹ (1) **3** from one side of something to the other side of it 从〔某物〕的一边到另一边：*Somehow the sheep had jumped over the fence.* 不知怎么地，那只羊跳过了围栏。| *The road over the mountains is steep and dangerous.* 这条翻越山区的路陡峭而危险。**4 over on** also 又作 **over** *BrE*【英】on the opposite side of something from where you already are 在〔所在之处〕的另一边：*We live over on the other side of town.* 我们住在城镇的那一边。**5** down from the edge of something 从…边缘上掉下：*Apparently the car fell over a cliff.* 汽车显然是从悬崖边上掉下去的。| *The shirt was hanging over the back of the chair.* 衬衫搭在椅子的靠背上。**6** in many parts of a particular place, organization etc 遍及〔某一地方、组织等〕，到处：*I've travelled over most of Europe but my favourite place was Austria.* 我游历了欧洲的大多数地方，最喜欢之处是奥地利。| **all over** (=in every part) 到处，各处 *They said they had cleaned up but there were bottles all over the place.* 他们说已经清扫过了，但那里到处都是瓶子。**7 be over sth** to feel better after an illness or bad situation 从〔疾病或困境之后〕恢复过来：*I think I'm over the worst of it now.* 我想我现在已经熬过了最困难的时候。**8** in control of someone or having authority to give orders to someone 控制；统治；支配：*He rules over a large kingdom.* 他统治着一个疆域辽阔的王国。| *In this office there is one manager over a staff of 15 workers.* 在这个办公室里有一位经理及下属 15 名员工。—opposite 反义词 UNDER¹ (9) **9** more than a particular number, amount or level 超出〔某一数目、数额或程度〕，比…多：*I've lost over 3 kilos in weight.* 我的体重已减了三公斤多。| *Children over 12 are not allowed in the swimming area.* 12岁以上的儿童不得进入本游泳区。| *The driver was found to have over the legal alcohol limit in his blood.* 司机被查出血液里的酒精含量超出了法律许可之限度。| **the over-30s/the over-50s etc** (=people who are more than a particular age) 30岁/50岁等以上者 *a social club for the over-60s* 为 60 岁以上者而设的联谊俱乐部 **10** during 在…期间：*Will you be home over the Christmas vacation?* 圣诞节期间你在家吗？| *Over a period of ten years he stole a million pounds from the company.* 他在十年间从公司偷走了 100 万英镑。| *Can we talk about this over dinner?* 我们能否边吃饭边谈这问题？**11** using something such as a telephone or radio 使用〔电话或收音机等〕：*I don't want to talk about this over the telephone.* 我不想在电话里谈这件事。**12** about a particular subject, person or thing 与…有关，关于：*He's having problems over his income tax.* 他在所得税方面出了问题。| *a row over public expenditure* 有关公共开支的争论 **13 over and above** an amount that is over and above another is an extra amount 除…外（还）：*He gets a travel allowance over and above his existing salary.* 他除目前的薪水以外，还有一份出差津贴。—see also 另见 **all over** (ALL² (6))

over² *adv* **1 fall over/knock sth over etc** to fall etc so that you are lying down or knock something etc so that it is flat on a surface after being upright 摔倒/弄倒某物等：*He was so drunk he fell over in the road.* 他喝得烂醉，跌倒在马路上。| *A lot of work is being done to prevent the tower from toppling over.* 正在进行大量工作以避免塔楼倒塌。**2 bend over/fold sth over etc** to bend etc so that you are no longer upright or fold something etc so that it is no longer straight or flat and is folded in the middle 弯腰/折叠某物等：*As Sheila bent over, a sudden pain shot up her back.* 希拉弯腰时，背部突然一阵疼痛。| *He silently folded the paper over and put it in his pocket.* 他默默地把纸折叠起来放入口袋。**3** [only after verb 仅用于动词后] from one side of something to the other side 从…的一边到另一边；穿越：*There are only 3 canoes so some people will have to swim over.* 仅有三艘独木舟，所以一部分人得游过去。| *I went over to say hello but Vincent didn't recognize me.* 我走过去打招呼，但文森特没有认出是我。| **over to/from** *We flew over to the US to visit my Aunt Polly.* 我们飞往美国去探望我的姨母波莉。| *I took her over to Saginaw because she had a doctor's appointment.* 我带她去萨吉诺，因为她约好了医生。**4** [only after verb 仅用于动词后] to or in a particular house, city etc 到，在〔某处〕：*You really should come over and see our new house.* 你真的该过来看看我们的新房子。**5 hand over/sign over etc** to give something to another person 移交/签字转让等：*The attacker was ordered to hand over his weapon and lie on the ground.* 袭击者被命令交出武器并就地趴下。| *Most of the money has been signed over to his children.* 大部分钱已签字过户给了他的孩子。**6 change over/swap over** if you change two things over you put one of the things in the place of the other 交换/对调：*The vases had been swapped over and nobody had spotted the fake.* 花瓶被人调包了，谁也没认出那个赝品。| *The guards change over at midnight.* 卫兵午夜时换岗。**7 turn over/roll over** if you turn something over you move it so that the side of it which could not be seen can now be seen 翻转/翻滚：*Turn the page over.* 把这一页翻过去。| *The children spent hours rolling over and over in the sand.* 孩子们在沙地里打滚玩耍了几个小时。**8 twelve years/90% etc and over** more than 12 years, 90% etc 12岁/90%等以上：*The film is suitable for people of 18 and over.* 这部影片适合 18 岁及 18 岁以上人士观看。| *Sorry, this agency only deals with properties worth $200,000 and over.* 对不起，本事务所只接手财产价值在 20 万美元以上的生意。—opposite 反义词 UNDER **9** a particular amount of something that is over is what remains after some of it has been used 剩下，余下：*We were over by about $300!* 我们还剩下大约 300 美元！| **left over** *We had so much food left over we donated it to charity.* 我们剩了很多食品，都赠给了慈善机构。**10 covered over/painted over etc** covered with a particular substance or material 覆盖/涂抹等：*Most of the windows have been boarded over.* 大部分窗户都用木板封死了。| **[+with]** *The door had been painted over with a bright red varnish.* 门用鲜红的漆刷过了。**11 read/think/talk etc sth over** to read something, think about something etc very carefully before deciding what to do 认真地阅读/思考/商量某事：*After talking it over with my wife, I've decided to retire.* 和妻子认真商量之后，我决定退休。**12 over and over (again)** repeatedly 再三地，重复地：*The only way to learn the script is to say it to yourself over and over again.* 要背熟剧本，唯一的办法是自己反复地念。**13 over to sb** used to say that it is now someone else's turn to do something, to speak etc 轮到某人：*I've done my best. Now it's over to the professionals.* 我已经尽了全力，现在该到专家们出手了。| *We're going over live to our correspondent at the scene of the explosion.* 我们现在转给在爆炸现场的记者作进一步的报道。**14 over!** *spoken* used when using a radio to show that you have finished speaking【口】〔无线电通话用语〕完毕！**15 over against** compared to someone or something else 与…相比，与…成对照 —see also 另见 **all over** (ALL² (6))

over³ *adj* [not before noun 不用于名词前] **1** if an event or period of time is over, it has finished〔指一件事或一段时间〕完结的，结束的：*When the game was over all the players shook hands.* 比赛结束时，所有球员都互相握手。**2 be over (and done) with** if an unpleasant situation or experience is over with, it has finished〔不愉快之事或经历〕已了结，已过去：*We don't have to*

mention the court case again! It's all over and done with now. 我们不要再提这桩官司！现在一切已经了结了。| **get sth over (and done) with** (=to do something so that the situation no longer exists) 把某事了结掉 *The sooner you get it over with the better, so phone up and make the appointment.* 这事你早了早好，所以打电话预约一下吧。

over⁴ *n* [C] the period of time in the game of CRICKET (2) during which six or eight balls are thrown by the same BOWLER (1) in one direction〔板球比赛中投球手连续投出六次或八次的〕一轮投球数

over- /ovɚ; əʊvə/ *prefix* **1** too much 过多，过头，过分: *over-population* 人口过剩 | *overcooked cabbage* 煮过头的洋白菜 **2** above; beyond; across 在上面；超过；横越: *overhanging branches* 悬垂的树枝 | *the overland route* (=not by sea or air) 陆路 **3** outer; covering 外面的；覆盖的: *an overcoat* 外套 **4** additional 额外的: *working overtime* (=beyond the usual time) 加班[超时]工作

over·a·chiev·er /,‥ ·ˈ‥/ *n* [C] someone who works very hard to be successful and is very unhappy if they do not achieve everything they want to 成就欲望过强者〔指非常努力地工作以获取成功的人，他们如未能获得想要的一切便会非常恼怒〕— **over-achieve** *v* [I]

o·ver·act /,ovɚˋækt; ,əʊvərˈækt/ *v* [I,T] to act a part in a play with too much emotion or movement 把〔角色〕演得过火[过于夸张]

o·ver·ac·tive /ˊovɚˋæktɪv; ,əʊvərˈæktɪv◂/ *adj* too active, in a way that produces a bad result 过度活跃的: *Paul's illness was due to an overactive thyroid.* 保罗的病是因甲状腺过于活跃而引起的。| **have an overactive imagination** (=tend to imagine things that are untrue) 有过于丰富的想象力 *The rumor is probably just the result of someone's overactive imagination.* 这谣言或许只是某些人想象力过于丰富的结果。

over-age /,‥ ˈ‥◂/ *adj* too old for a particular purpose or activity 过老的；超龄的: *He looked like an over-age drummer from some sixties band.* 他看上去像一个老去的来自60年代某个乐队的鼓手。—compare 比较 UNDERAGE

3 2 **o·ver·all¹** /,ovɚˋɔl; ,əʊvərˈɔːl◂/ *adj* including everything 包括一切的，全部的: *My overall impression of his work is good.* 我对他的作品总的印象是良好的。| *What's the overall cost of repairs?* 修理费用总共是多少?

overall² *adv* **1** including everything 全部地；总共: *The fish measures 1.7 metres overall.* 那条鱼全长为1.7米。| *What will it cost, overall?* 这总共要花多少钱? **2** [sentence adverb 句子副词] generally 一般地，总体上: *Overall, prices are still rising.* 总的来说，价格仍在上涨。

o·ver·all³ /ˊovɚɔl; ˈəʊvərɔːl/ *n* **1** [C] *BrE* a loose-fitting piece of clothing like a coat, that is worn over clothes to protect them【英】〔穿在其他衣服外面的〕宽大罩衫 **2 overalls** [plural] *especially AmE* heavy cotton trousers with a piece covering your chest and held up by pieces of cloth that go over your shoulders【尤美】粗布工装裤；DUNGAREES (1) *BrE*【英】**3 overalls** [plural] *BrE*【英】also 又作 **overall** [C] *AmE*【美】a piece of clothing like a shirt and trousers in one piece worn over other clothes to protect them〔上下连身的〕工作服

overall ma·jor·i·ty /,‥‥ ·ˈ‥‥/ *n* [C] **1** more votes than all the other political parties together 压倒多数票，绝对多数票〔指得票数多于所有其他政党的总和〕**2** *BrE* the difference between this number of votes and the total votes gained by all the other parties【英】多得票数〔指得票数与所有其他政党得票数总和之间的差额〕

o·ver·arch·ing /,ovɚˋartʃɪŋ; ,əʊvərˈɑːtʃɪŋ◂/ *adj* **1** including or influencing every part of something 包罗万象的；支配一切的: *The project's overarching aim is the improvement of education.* 这项计划的宗旨在于提高教育水平。**2** forming a curved shape over something 在…上成圆拱形的: *the overarching sky* 苍穹

o·ver·arm /ˊovɚ,arm; ˈəʊvərɑːm/ *adj, adv especially BrE* an overarm throw in a sport is when you throw the ball with your arm high above your shoulder【尤英】〔运动中掷球或投球时〕挥臂[举手]过肩的[地]; OVERHAND *AmE*【美】—see picture on page A23 参见A23页图

o·ver·awe /,ovɚˋɔ; ,əʊvərˈɔː/ *v* [T] to make someone feel respect or fear so that they become very quiet 使敬畏，使慑服: *overawed by the great man's booming voice* 被那伟人深沉的嗓音所镇服

o·ver·bal·ance /,ovɚˋbæləns; ,əʊvəˈbæləns/ *v* [I,T] **1** *especially BrE* to shake and start to fall because you lose balance, or to make someone or something do this【尤英】(使)失去平衡而歪倒: *The horse reared, overbalanced, and fell.* 马用后腿直立起来，失去平衡而倒下了。**2** *AmE* OUTWEIGH【美】比…更重要，重要性超过…: *The lack of social life is overbalanced by the amount of money I'll save living here.* 比起住在这里我将省下的钱数，缺少社交生活就不那么重要了。

o·ver·bear /,ovɚˋbɛr; ,əʊvəˈbeə/ *v* [T usually passive 一般用被动态] *past tense* **overbore**, *past participle* **overborne** to defeat someone or something 击败；战胜

o·ver·bear·ing /,ovɚˋbɛrɪŋ; ,əʊvəˈbeərɪŋ◂/ *adj* always trying to control other people without considering their wishes or feelings; DOMINEERING 专横的，好指使人的；飞扬跋扈的: *self-important overbearing attitudes of these high-up doctors* 这些高级医生那自视甚高且盛气凌人的态度—**overbearingly** *adv*

o·ver·bid /,ovɚˋbɪd; ,əʊvəˈbɪd/ *v* **1** [I+for] to offer too high a price for something, especially at an AUCTION¹〔尤指在拍卖中〕出价太高 **2** [I,T] to offer more than the value of your cards in a card game such as BRIDGE¹ (4)〔在桥牌赛中〕叫牌超过〔自己的实力〕

o·ver·bite /ˊovɚbaɪt; ˈəʊvəbaɪt/ *n* [C] a condition in which someone's upper jaw is too far forwards beyond their lower jaw〔牙齿的〕覆咬合；上包齿

o·ver·blown /,ovɚˋblon; ,əʊvəˈbləʊn◂/ *adj* **1** *formal* made to seem greater or more impressive; EXAGGERATED (1)【正式】夸张的；过分渲染的: *overblown news stories* 夸大的新闻报道 **2** overblown flowers have opened too wide and become less beautiful〔指花〕已过盛期的，开得太大的

o·ver·board /ˊovɚ,bord; ˈəʊvəbɔːd/ *adv* **1** over the side of a ship or boat into the water 从船舷掉入水中: *One of the crew fell overboard and drowned.* 船员中有一人从船边跌入水中淹死了。| *Man overboard!* 有人落水了! **2 go overboard** *informal* to do or say too much because you are too eager or excited【非正式】〔因太急切或激动而〕做事[说话]过分，走极端: *Dean knew he had gone overboard by sending six dozen roses.* 迪安知道自己送六打玫瑰是做过头了。**3 throw sth overboard** to get rid of an idea etc that is useless or unnecessary 抛弃某物，去除某物

o·ver·book /,ovɚˋbʊk; ,əʊvəˈbʊk/ *v* [I,T] to sell more tickets for a theatre, plane etc than there are seats available 超量售出〔戏票、机票等〕，超额订出[预订]

o·ver·bur·den /ˊovɚˋbɝdn̩; ,əʊvəˈbɜːdn/ *v* [T usually passive 一般用被动态] to give someone or a system too much work or too many problems to deal with 使负担过多；使负荷过重: *an overburdened donkey* 负载过重的驴 | [+with] *a student overburdened with essays* 因作文繁多而不堪重负的学生

o·ver·came /,ovɚˋkem; ,əʊvəˈkeɪm/ *v* the past tense of OVERCOME

o·ver·cap·i·tal·ize also 又作 **-ise** *BrE*【英】/ˊovɚ,kæpətl̩,aɪz; ,əʊvəˈkæpɪtl-aɪz/ *v* [I,T] **1** to supply too much money for a business 对〔企业〕投资过多 **2** to put too high a value on a business 对〔企业的〕资本估价过高—**overcapitalization** /ˊovɚ,kæpətl̩əˈzeʃən; ,əʊvəkæpɪtl-aɪˈzeɪʃən/ *n* [U]

o·ver·cast /,ovɚˋkæst; ,əʊvəˈkɑːst◂/ *adj* dark with clouds 阴天的，多云的: *an overcast day* 多云的日子 | *an overcast sky* 阴沉沉的天空 —see picture on page A13 参见A13页图

o·ver·charge /ˊovɚˋtʃardʒ; ,əʊvəˈtʃɑːdʒ/ *v* **1** [I,T] to charge someone too much money for something 对〔某人〕索价过高: **overcharge sb** *The cashier overcharged me by at least $2.00.* 收银员至少多收了我两美元。**2** too full of emotion or excitement 充满〔过度的〕感情[激情]: *The atmosphere in the stadium was overcharged with excitement.* 体育场里的气氛充满了激情。**3** [T] to put too much power into a BATTERY (1) or electrical system 使〔电池〕充电过度；使〔电路系统〕超负荷

o·ver·cloud /,ovɚˋklaud; ,əʊvəˈklaʊd/ *v* [T usually passive 一般用被动态] **1** to cover the sky, sun etc with clouds〔天空、太阳等〕布满云层，给云遮盖 **2** to fill someone or a situation with unhappy or worried feelings 使悲伤，使忧郁: *a look of fear suddenly overclouding his face* 突然笼罩在他脸上的恐惧神色

o·ver·coat /ˊovɚ,kot; ˈəʊvəkəʊt/ *n* [C] a long, thick, warm coat worn over other clothes in cold weather 大衣

o·ver·come /,ovɚˋkʌm; ,əʊvəˈkʌm/ *v past tense* **overcame** /-ˋkem; -ˈkeɪm/ *past participle* **overcome** **1** to control a feeling or problem that prevents you from achieving something 控制〔感情〕；克服〔困难〕: *He struggled to overcome his shyness.* 他努力克服自己的羞怯。**2** [I,T] to fight and win against someone or something 征服，战胜: *They overcame the enemy after a long battle.* 经过一场漫长的战斗，他们击败了敌人。| *We shall overcome!* 我们一定会胜利! **3** [T usually passive 一般用被动态] to have such a strong effect on someone that they become weak, unconscious, or unable to control their feelings 被〔感情〕制服；使无能为力: *She was overcome by emotion.* 她激动得难以自持。| *Those who died in the fire were overcome by the gas fumes.* 那些死于大火的人是被煤气熏倒的。 3 3

o·ver·com·pen·sate /ˌovɚˋkɑmpənset; ˌəʊvə'kɒmpənseɪt/ *v* [I] to try to correct a weakness or mistake by doing too much of the opposite thing〔为弥补缺陷或过失而〕矫枉过正，过度补偿: *Zoe overcompensates for her shyness by talking a lot.* 佐伊为克服自己的羞怯而说话过多，真是矫枉过正。—**overcompensation** /ˌovɚkɑmpənˋseʃən; ˌəʊvəkɒmpən'seɪʃən/ *n* [U]

o·ver·crowd /ˌovɚˋkraud; ˌəʊvə'kraʊd/ *v* [T] to fill a space or period of time with too many things or people 使〔某处〕过分拥挤；使〔某段时间〕安排过满: [**+with**] *The courts overcrowd their calendars with too many trials.* 法庭安排了过多的庭审，日程表排得太满了。

o·ver·crowd·ed /ˌovɚˋkraudɪd; ˌəʊvə'kraʊdɪ̵d◂/ *adj* filled with too many people or things 过分拥挤的: *an overcrowded room* 拥挤不堪的房间

o·ver·crowd·ing /ˌovɚˋkraudɪŋ; ˌəʊvə'kraʊdɪŋ/ *n* [U] the condition of living or working too close together, with too many people in a small space 过度拥挤

o·ver·de·vel·oped /ˋovɚdɪˋvɛləpt; ˌəʊvədɪ'veləpt◂/ *adj* too great or large 过度的；过大的: *Ryan has an overdeveloped sense of his own importance.* 瑞安自视过高。

o·ver·do /ˋovɚˋdu; ˌəʊvə'duː/ *v past tense* **overdid** /-ˋdɪd; -'dɪd/ *past participle* **overdone** /-ˋdʌn; -'dʌn/ [T] **1** to do something more than is suitable or natural 把〔某事〕做得过火[过于夸张]: *Don't overdo the praise. She wasn't that good.* 不要过分赞扬，她没那么好。| **overdo it** *I think Trudy's overdone it with all the lace and frills in the bedroom.* 特鲁迪在卧室里弄了那么多饰带和花边，我认为有点过火。**2** to use too much of something 使用…过多: *I think I overdid the salt.* 我想是盐放多了。**3** **overdo it** to work too hard or be too active so that you become tired 工作过度；过于劳碌: *She's been overdoing it lately.* 近来她劳碌过度。

o·ver·done /ˋovɚˋdʌn; ˌəʊvə'dʌn◂/ *adj* cooked too much 煮得过度的，烧得太久的: *The beef was overdone.* 牛肉煮过头了。—compare 比较 UNDERDONE

o·ver·dose /ˋovɚˌdos; 'əʊvədəʊs/ *n* [C] too much of a drug taken at one time〔药物的〕使用过量: *a massive overdose of heroin* 过量服用海洛因 —**overdose** /ˌovɚˋdos; ˌəʊvə'dəʊs/ *v* [I **+on**] *He overdosed on heroin.* 他服用了过量的海洛因。

o·ver·draft /ˋovɚˌdræft; 'əʊvədrɑːft/ *n* [C] the amount of money you owe to a bank when you have taken out more money than you had in your bank account 透支额: *I have to find the money to pay off this overdraft.* 我得弄点钱来偿还这笔透支款。

overdraft fa·cil·i·ty /ˈ‧‧‧ ‧ˌ‧‧/ *n* [C] *BrE* an agreement with the bank that a customer may take more money from the bank than they have in their account, up to a certain amount【英】透支服务〔银行按协议允许客户提取超出其账户存款一定数目的钱款〕

o·ver·drawn /ˋovɚˋdrɔn; ˌəʊvə'drɔːn/ *adj* **be overdrawn** if your bank account is overdrawn you have spent more than is in it and you owe the bank money〔存款账户〕透支的: *I'm overdrawn at the moment.* 我现已透支了。| **be overdrawn by £50/$600 etc** *My account is overdrawn by £300.* 我的存款账户透支了300英镑。—**overdraw** *v* [I]

o·ver·dressed /ˋovɚˋdrɛst; ˌəʊvə'drest◂/ *adj* dressed in clothes that are too formal for the occasion〔对某种场合来说〕穿着过于正式的: *I felt distinctly overdressed beside all those young people in jeans.* 与那些全是穿着牛仔裤的年轻人相比，我感觉自己显然穿得过于隆重。—**overdress** *v* [I]

o·ver·drive /ˋovɚˋdraɪv; 'əʊvədraɪv/ *n* [U] **1** an additional GEAR[1] (2) which allows a car to go fast while its engine produces the least power necessary〔汽车的〕超速挡: *Put the car in overdrive when you hit 50 mph.* 你开到每小时50英里的速度时，把车挂到超速挡。**2** **go into overdrive** to become very excited or active 变得非常激动[活跃]: *You could see his imagination go into overdrive at the thought.* 你能看出来，他一想到这个，想象力就会变得十分活跃。

o·ver·due /ˋovɚˋdju; ˌəʊvə'djuː◂/ *adj* **1** a payment that is overdue should have been paid earlier 过期未付的: *an overdue gas bill* 逾期未付的煤气账单 **2** **be overdue for** to have needed something done for a long time 早就需要，早该: *The car is overdue for a tune-up.* 这辆汽车早该检修了。**3** something that is overdue should have happened or been done a long time ago 早该发生的；早该完成的；期待已久的: **long overdue** *This is a major, but long overdue reform which will benefit around 4 million low-paid people.* 这是一项早该实行的重大改革，它将会使约400万低收入人士获益。**4** [not before noun 不用于名词前] a baby that is overdue was not born at the time that it was expected〔婴儿〕超过预产期的: *Collette's baby is a week overdue.* 科利特的胎儿已超过预产期一周了。**5** a library book that is overdue was not returned to the library when it should have been〔图书馆的书〕逾期未还的

o·ver·eat /ˋovɚˋit; ˌəʊvər'iːt/ *v past tense* **overate** /-ˋet; -'et/ *past participle* **overeaten** /-ˋitn̩; -'iːtn/ [I] to eat too much, or eat more than is healthy 吃得过饱，暴食: *Pete's gained so much weight because he can't stop overeating.* 皮特体重增加了那么多，是因为他不停地暴食。

o·ver·egg /ˌovɚˋɛg; ˌəʊvər'eg/ *v* **overegg the pudding** *BrE informal* to do more than is necessary, or add something that is not needed【英，非正式】做不必要的事；画蛇添足

o·ver·es·ti·mate[1] /ˋovɚˋɛstəˌmet; ˌəʊvər'estɪ̵meɪt/ *v* **1** [T] to judge something to be better than it really is 对〔某事〕估计过好，估计过高: *I'm afraid we overestimated his abilities.* 恐怕我们对他的能力评价过高。**2** [I,T] to guess an amount or value that is too high 对〔数额或价值〕估计过高: *We overestimated the number of people who would come.* 我们高估了到场的人数。| [**+by**] *I think Jo's overestimated by about 300.* 我认为乔多估了300左右。—compare 比较 UNDERESTIMATE[1]

o·ver·es·ti·mate[2] /ˋovɚˋɛstəmɪt; ˌəʊvər'estɪ̵mɪ̵t/ *n* [C] a calculation, judgment, or guess that is too large 过高的估计[评价]

o·ver·ex·cit·ed /ovərɪkˋsaɪtɪd; əʊvərɪk'saɪtɪ̵d/ *adj* children who are overexcited are too excited to behave sensibly〔指儿童〕过于激动的，过度兴奋的

o·ver·ex·pose /ˋovərɪkˋspoz; ˌəʊvərɪk'spəʊz/ *v* [T] **1** to allow too much light to reach the film when taking or developing a photograph 使〔底片或照片〕过度感光[曝光] **2** **be overexposed** become less popular because of appearing too many times on television, in the newspapers etc 曝光率过高〔指在电视、报纸等上面出现次数过多而使受欢迎程度下降〕—opposite 反义词 UNDEREXPOSE

over·ex·po·sure /ˌ‧ ‧ˈ‧ ‧/ *n* [U] the state of having received too much light, sunlight, RADIATION etc, that is harmful to someone's skin, a photographic film etc〔皮肤、胶片等受光线、阳光、辐射等的〕过度照射，过度曝光

o·ver·ex·tend /ˋovərɪkˋstɛnd; ˌəʊvərɪk'stend/ *v* [T] to try to do or use too much of something, causing problems, illness, or damage 把…做得过分；把…使用过头: *The accountants have advised us not to overextend our resources.* 会计师告诫我们不要过度动用我们的财力。| **overextend yourself** *Be careful not to overextend yourself. You've been very ill!* 注意不要让自己操劳过度，你已经重病在身了！

o·ver·flow[1] /ˌovɚˋflo; ˌəʊvə'fləʊ/ *v* **1** [I,T] if a river, lake, or container overflows, it is so full that the water, material etc inside flows over its edges〔从…中〕溢出；泛滥: *The toilet's just overflowed again.* 马桶的水刚才又溢出来了。| [**+with**] *a trash can overflowing with papers* 被报纸塞得满出来的垃圾箱 | **overflow sth** *The river had overflowed its banks.* 河水溢出河堤了。**2** **overflow with love/gratitude etc** to have a very strong feeling of love etc 充满爱意/感激等: *My heart was overflowing with gratitude for the old man.* 我心里充满了对那位老人的感激之情。**3** [I,T] if people overflow a place, there are too many of them to fit into it〔人〕多得使…无法容纳；挤出: [**+into/onto**] *The crowd overflowed into the street.* 人群涌到了大街上。

overflow 溢出

o·ver·flow[2] /ˋovɚˌflo; 'əʊvəfləʊ/ *n* [C] **1** [singular] the amount of something or the number of people that cannot be contained in a place because it is already full 容纳不下的东西[人]；溢出物；超出的数额: *The overflow will be accommodated in another hotel.* 接纳不下的人将安排下榻另一家旅馆。| [**+of**] *the overflow of water from the lake* 由湖里外溢的水 **2** [U] an act of overflowing something 溢流，泛滥 **3** [C] a pipe through which water flows out of a container when it becomes too full 排水管；溢流道

o·ver·fly /ˌovɚˋflaɪ; ˌəʊvə'flaɪ/ *v* [T] to fly over an area or country in an aircraft 在〔某地区或国家的〕上空飞行

o·ver·grown /ˋovɚˋgron; ˌəʊvə'grəʊn◂/ *adj* **1** covered with plants that have grown in an uncontrolled way 长满〔野生植物等〕的: [**+with**] *The garden will be overgrown with weeds by the time we get back.* 我们回来的时候，花园里将长满杂草。**2** **overgrown child/schoolboy/baby** used to describe an adult

who behaves like a child 长得太大[太快]的小孩/男生/婴儿〔用于形容孩子气的成人〕: *Stop acting like an overgrown schoolboy.* 不要表现得像个大孩子似的。

o·ver·growth /ˈovɚˌgroθ; ˈəʊvəgrəʊθ/ *n* [U] plants and branches of trees growing above your head, usually in a forest 蔓生的植物〔通常指森林里长得比人高的植物或树枝〕

o·ver·hand /ˈovɚˌhænd; ˈəʊvəhænd/ *adj, adv AmE* an overhand throw in a sport is when you throw the ball with your arm above the level of your shoulder【美】〔体育运动中投掷球时〕举手过肩的[地]; OVERARM *especially BrE*【尤英】—opposite 反义词 UNDERHAND[2]

o·ver·hang[1] /ˌovɚˈhæŋ; ˌəʊvəˈhæŋ/ *v past tense and past participle* **overhung** /-ˈhʌŋ; -ˈhʌŋ/ [I,T] to hang over something 悬在…的上方: *Our apple trees overhang the neighbors' yard.* 我们的苹果树俯临着邻居的院子。

o·ver·hang[2] /ˈovɚˌhæŋ; ˈəʊvəhæŋ/ *n* [usually singular 一般用单数] **1** a rock, roof etc that hangs over something else 悬垂物〈如岩石、屋顶等〉: *We stood under the overhang while it rained.* 下雨时我们站在悬伸的遮蔽物之下。**2** the amount by which something hangs over something else 悬伸量, 伸出量

o·ver·haul[1] /ˌovɚˈhɔl; ˌəʊvəˈhɔːl/ *v* [T] **1** to repair or change all the parts that need it, in a machine, system etc that is not working correctly 彻底检修; 全面改革[革新]: *overhaul an engine* 检修引擎 **2** to move up to a vehicle, ship, or person from behind and pass them; OVERTAKE (1) 赶上并超过〔车辆、船或人〕

o·ver·haul[2] /ˈovɚˌhɔl; ˈəʊvəhɔːl/ *n* [C] necessary changes or repairs made to a machine or system〔对机器的〕大检修;〔对体制的〕彻底改革: *The Chevy needs a complete overhaul.* 这辆雪佛兰汽车需要彻底检修一下。| *an overhaul of civil court procedures to speed up and simplify cases* 彻底改革民事法庭的办案程序以加快并简化案件的审理

o·ver·head[1] /ˈovɚˌhɛd; ˌəʊvəˈhed◂/ *adv* above your head 在头顶上, 在空中: *A plane flew overhead.* 一架飞机从空中飞过。| *Bullets whizzed overhead.* 子弹飕飕地掠过头顶。—**overhead** *adj*: *overhead wires* 架空电线 —see picture on page A1 参见 A1 页图

o·ver·head[2] /ˈovɚˌhɛd; ˈəʊvəhed/ *n* **1** [singular] *especially AmE*【尤美】also 又作 **overheads** [plural] *especially BrE*【尤英】money spent regularly on rent, insurance, electricity, and other things that are needed to keep a business operating〔企业的〕经常性支出, 管理费用〈如租金、保险费、电费等〉: *Their offices are in London so the overheads are very high.* 他们的办事处在伦敦, 所以经常性开支非常大。**2** [C] a piece of transparent material used with an overhead projector to show words, pictures etc〔用于投影仪显示文字、图片等的〕透明胶片

overhead pro·jec·tor /ˌ··· ·ˈ··/ *n* [C] a piece of electrical equipment used for making words, pictures etc look larger by showing them on a wall or large SCREEN[1] (1) so that many people can see 投影仪, 高射投影器 —see picture on page A14 参见 A14 页图

o·ver·hear /ˌovɚˈhɪr; ˌəʊvəˈhɪə/ *v past tense and past participle* **overheard** /-ˈhɝd; -ˈhɜːd/ [T] to accidentally hear what other people are saying, when they do not know that you have heard 无意中听到, 偶然听到: *I overheard part of their conversation.* 我无意中听到了他们的一些谈话。| **overhear sb saying sth** *Christie overheard the men saying they were going to rob the bank!* 克里斯蒂不经意间听到那几个人说要去抢劫银行! | **overhear sb say (that)** *We overheard the teacher say there would be a pop quiz today.* 我们无意中听到老师说今天有突击测验。—compare 比较 EAVESDROP

o·ver·heat /ˌovɚˈhit; ˌəʊvəˈhiːt/ *v* [I,T] to become too hot, or to make something too hot 变得过热; 使…太热: *I think the engine's overheating again.* 我想引擎又过热了。| **overheat sth** *Try not to overheat the sauce.* 注意别把调味汁热过头了。

o·ver·heat·ed /ˌovɚˈhitɪd; ˌəʊvəˈhiːtɪd◂/ *adj* **1** too hot 过热的: *the overheated waiting room* 过热的等候室 **2** full of angry feelings 充满愤怒的: *an overheated quarrel that turned into a fight* 最终演变成打架的激烈口角 **3** an ECONOMY[1] (1) that is overheated is too active to work properly〔指经济〕过热的, 发展过快的

o·ver·hung /ˌovɚˈhʌŋ; ˌəʊvəˈhʌŋ/ *v* the past tense and past participle of OVERHANG[1]

o·ver·in·dulge /ˈovərɪnˈdʌldʒ; ˌəʊvərɪnˈdʌldʒ/ *v* **1** [I] to eat or drink too much 吃喝过度: *I'm getting too fat, so I mustn't overindulge.* 我变得太胖了, 所以决不能大吃大喝。**2** [T] to let someone have everything they want, or always let them do what they want 过分放任〔某人〕: *Penny was overindulged by her parents.* 彭妮被她的父母宠坏了。—**overindulgence** *n* [U]

o·ver·joyed /ˈovɚˈdʒɔɪd; ˌəʊvəˈdʒɔɪd/ *adj* [not before noun 不用于名词前] extremely pleased or happy 极为高兴的, 十分开心的: **overjoyed to hear/find/see sth** *We were overjoyed to hear that they were safe.* 听到他们都安全, 我们感到非常高兴。| [+at] *Richard was overjoyed at the prospect of becoming a father.* 理查德为将要成为父亲而欣喜若狂。

o·ver·kill /ˈovɚˌkɪl; ˈəʊvəkɪl/ *n* [U] **1** more of something than is necessary or desirable 过分, 过火: *I thought 24 hours of television coverage of the election verged on overkill.* 我认为对大选作 24 小时电视实况报道有点过分。**2** more than enough weapons, especially NUCLEAR (3) weapons, to kill everyone in a country〔尤指核武器〕过大的杀伤力

o·ver·la·den /ˌovɚˈledn̩; ˌəʊvəˈleɪdn/ *v* a past tense and past participle of OVERLOAD

o·ver·laid /ˌovɚˈled; ˌəʊvəˈleɪd/ *v* the past tense and past participle of OVERLAY[1]

o·ver·land /ˈovɚˌlænd; ˌəʊvəˈlænd◂/ *adv* across land, not by sea or air 经陆路的, 陆上的: *travelling overland to China* 从陆路去中国 —**overland** *adj*

o·ver·lap[1] /ˌovɚˈlæp; ˌəʊvəˈlæp/ *v* **overlapped, overlapping** [I,T] **1** if two or more things overlap, part of one thing covers part of another thing 与〔某物〕部分重叠, 交搭, 叠盖: *One of Jilly's front teeth overlaps the other.* 吉里的一颗门牙与另一颗有些交叠。| *The tiles on the roof overlap.* 屋顶的瓦片相互交搭在一起。**2** if two sets, subjects, ideas etc overlap, they include some but not all of the same things〔两种倾向、学科、观念等〕部分交叉: [+with] *This is where sociology overlaps with economics.* 这就是社会学与经济学在内容上的交叉之处。| **overlap sth** *Maxwell's responsibilities overlap yours, so you will be sharing some of the work.* 马克斯韦尔的职责中有一部分与你重叠, 所以你得分担一些工作。**3** if two events or activities overlap, the first one finishes a short time after the second one starts〔时间上〕重叠, 与…部分同时发生: [+with] *My vacation overlaps with yours, so we won't see each other for a month or so.* 我的假期和你的假期前后挨着, 所以我俩将有一个月左右见不着面。| **overlap sth** *The first shift overlaps the second.* 第一轮换班与第二轮换班之间有一段交接的时间。

overlap 交搭, 重叠

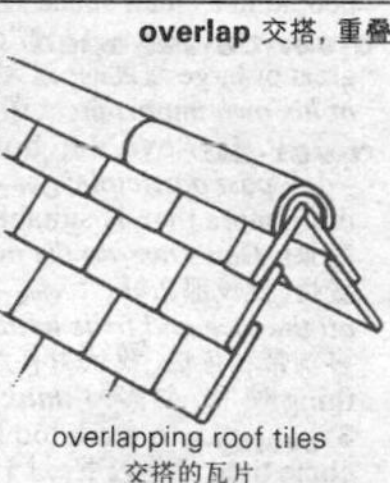

overlapping roof tiles
交搭的瓦片

o·ver·lap[2] /ˈovɚˌlæp; ˈəʊvəlæp/ *n* [C,U] the amount by which two things, activities etc overlap〔两种事物、活动等〕交搭的数量, 重叠: [+between] *The overlap between the two subjects is considerable.* 这两门学科间重叠的内容极多。

o·ver·lay[1] /ˌovɚˈle; ˌəʊvəˈleɪ/ *v past tense and past participle* **overlaid** /-ˈled; -ˈleɪd/ [T] *technical*【术语】**1 be overlaid with** to be thinly covered with something 在…上涂[盖、包、贴]薄薄的一层: *wood overlaid with silver* 包着一层薄银的木料 **2** [usually passive 一般用被动态] to add an outer appearance to something that hides its real character 遮盖〔某物的本质〕: [+with] *His ordinarily cheerful face was overlaid with gloom.* 他脸上没有了平日的开朗, 却添了一层忧郁。

o·ver·lay[2] /ˈovɚˌle; ˈəʊvəleɪ/ *n* [C] **1** something laid over something else 覆盖物 **2** a transparent sheet with a picture or drawing on it which is put on top of another picture to change it〔上有图片或画样, 用于覆盖在另一图片上对其进行修改的〕套图塑料膜 **3** an additional quality or feeling 附加的特性[情感]: *sad stories with an overlay of humour* 幽默掩盖下的悲惨故事

o·ver·leaf /ˈovɚˈlif; ˌəʊvəˈliːf/ *adv* on the other side of the page 在一页的另一面, 在一页的背面: *See the diagram overleaf.* 参见背页的示意图。

o·ver·lie /ˌovɚˈlaɪ; ˌəʊvəˈlaɪ/ *v* [T] *technical*【术语】**1** to lie over something 躺在〔某物〕上面: *A thick layer of soil overlies the rocks.* 一层厚厚的泥土压在岩石上。**2** if a parent animal overlies its young it kills them by lying on them 压在〔幼小动物〕上面使闷死, 使窒息

o·ver·load /ˌovɚˈlod; ˌəʊvəˈləʊd/ *v past participle* **overloaded** *or* **overladen** /-ˈledn̩; -ˈleɪdn/ [T] **1** to load something with too many things 使过量载重, 使超载: [+with] *The bus was overloaded with tourists and their luggage.* 公共汽车因游客和行李过多而超载。**2** to put too much electricity through an electrical system or piece of equipment 使〔电路系统或设备〕超过负荷: *Don't overload the outlet by plugging in too many appliances.* 不要同时使用太多的电器而使电源插座超过负荷。**3** to give someone too much work 给〔某人〕过多的工作: [+with] *All the staff are overloaded with work.* 所有的员工都已是超负荷工作了。—**overload** /ˈovɚˌlod; ˈəʊvələʊd/ *n* [C,U]

o·ver·long /ˌovɚˋlɔŋ; ˌəʊvəˈlɒŋ/ *adj* continuing for too long 持续过久的，时间太长的: *an overlong performance* 表演时间过长的节目

o·ver·look /ˌovɚˋlʊk; ˌəʊvəˈlʊk/ *v* [T] **1** to not notice something 没有注意到，忽视: *It is easy to overlook a small detail like that.* 那样的细枝末节很容易被忽略。**2** to ignore and forgive someone's mistake, bad behaviour etc 不计较，宽恕〔某人的过错、不良举止等〕: *I'll overlook your mistake this time.* 这次我会原谅你的过失。**3** if a building, room, or window overlooks a place, you can look down on that place from it 俯视，俯瞰: *Our room overlooks the ocean.* 从我们的房间能眺望大海。| *My garden is overlooked by the neighbours.* 我的花园被居高临下的邻居看得一清二楚。

o·ver·lord /ˋovɚˌlɔrd; ˈəʊvəlɔːd/ *n* [C] a lord who ruled over other lords in the past〔昔日的〕封建君主；大领主

o·ver·ly /ˋovɚlɪ; ˈəʊvəli/ *adv* [often in negatives 常用于否定句] too or very 太，非常，极为: *I wasn't overly impressed with her performance.* 她的表演并没有给我留下太深的印象。| *You're being overly critical.* 你过于吹毛求疵了。

o·ver·manned /ˌovɚˋmænd; ˌəʊvəˈmænd◂/ *adj* having more workers than are needed for a job; OVERSTAFFED 人手过多的，人员配备太多的 —**overmanning** *n* [U]

o·ver·mas·ter /ˌovɚˋmæstɚ; ˌəʊvəˈmɑːstə/ *v* [T] *literary* to gain control or power over someone【文】控制，压倒〔某人〕

o·ver·much /ˋovɚˋmʌtʃ; ˌəʊvəˈmʌtʃ◂/ *adv literary or humorous* too much【文或幽默】太多，过多: *It is unwise to indulge overmuch in strong drink.* 过度饮用烈酒是不明智的。| **not overmuch** *We didn't like each other overmuch.* 我们彼此不大喜欢对方。

o·ver·night¹ /ˋovɚˋnaɪt; ˌəʊvəˈnaɪt/ *adv* **1** for or during the night 夜里，在夜间: **stay overnight** *Pam's staying overnight at my house.* 帕姆将在我家过夜。**2** *informal* suddenly【非正式】突然，一下子: *Logan became famous overnight.* 洛根一夜之间成名了。

o·ver·night² /ˋovɚˋnaɪt; ˈəʊvənaɪt/ *adj* **1** continuing all night 持续整夜的: *an overnight flight from Boston to London* 从波士顿到伦敦的一整夜飞行 **2** done in one night 一夜间完成的: *an overnight delivery service* 隔夜就能送达的快递服务 **3 an overnight success** something that suddenly becomes very popular or successful 突如其来的成功: *The show was an overnight success on Broadway.* 这场表演在百老汇一举成功。

o·ver·night·er /ˌ‥ˋ‥/ *n* [C] a bag or small case which holds a few clothes and other things you need for a short trip〔短途旅行用的〕小旅行包，小提箱

over·op·ti·mis·tic /ˌ‥‥ˋ‥◂/ *adj* expecting that things will be better than is possible or likely 过分乐观的，盲目乐观的: *over-optimistic forecasts of economic growth* 对经济增长过于乐观的预测

o·ver·pass /ˋovɚˌpæs; ˈəʊvəpɑːs/ *n* [C] *AmE* FLYOVER (1)【美】立交桥，高架公路 —see picture on page A3 参见 A3 页图

o·ver·pay /ˋovɚˋpe; ˌəʊvəˈpeɪ/ *v past tense and past participle* **overpaid** /-ˋped; -ˈpeɪd/ [T] to pay someone too much 多付给〔某人〕钱；给〔某人〕过高的报酬: *I think lawyers are overpaid for what they do.* 我认为律师的工作报酬过高。

o·ver·play /ˌovɚˋple; ˌəʊvəˈpleɪ/ *v* [T] **1** to make something seem more important than it is 夸大…的重要性；把…做得过头: *The poet's importance is overplayed by his biographer.* 该诗人的重要性被其传记作者夸大了。—opposite 反义词 UNDERPLAY (1) **2 overplay your hand** to try to gain more advantage than you know you can reasonably expect 不自量力，试图获取应得之外的更多好处: *If you're asking for more vacation time, don't overplay your hand by bringing salary into it too.* 你要是想得到更多的假期，就别太贪心还要提薪水的问题。

o·ver·pop·u·lat·ed /ˌovɚˋpɑpjəˌletɪd; ˌəʊvəˈpɒpjʊleɪtɪd◂/ *adj* a city or country that is overpopulated has too many people〔城市或国家等〕人口过密〔过多〕的: *a programme of resettlement from the most overpopulated areas* 从人口最过于稠密的地区重新安置居民的计划 —**overpopulation** /ˌovɚpɑpjəˋleʃən; ˌəʊvəpɒpjʊˈleɪʃən/ *n* [U]

o·ver·pow·er /ˌovɚˋpaʊɚ; ˌəʊvəˈpaʊə/ *v* [T] **1** to defeat someone because you are stronger〔以更强的力量〕打败，制服〔某人〕: *The policeman and a dog handler struggled to overpower the man.* 警察和警犬训练员努力想制服那名男子。**2** if a smell, task, emotion etc overpowers someone or something it is too strong; OVERCOME (3)〔气味、任务、情感等〕使…无法忍受；压倒，压服: *a full flavour slightly overpowered by saltiness* 咸味略重的醇厚风味

o·ver·pow·er·ing /ˌovɚˋpaʊərɪŋ; ˌəʊvəˈpaʊərɪŋ◂/ *adj* **1** very strong; INTENSE (1) 很强的，强烈的；不可抗拒的: *an overpowering smell* 浓烈的气味 | *an overpowering desire to slap her* 想掴她一个耳光的强烈欲望 **2** someone who is overpowering has such a strong character that they make other people feel uncomfortable or afraid; OVERBEARING〔人〕个性强的；专横的 —**overpoweringly** *adv*

o·ver·priced /ˌovɚˋpraɪst; ˌəʊvəˈpraɪst◂/ *adj* too expensive 过于昂贵的，定价过高的: *The patisserie has good food, but it's overpriced.* 这家法式糕点店的糕点很好，但价钱太贵。

o·ver·print /ˌovɚˋprɪnt; ˌəʊvəˈprɪnt/ *v* [T+with/on] to print additional words over a document, stamp etc that already has printing on it 在〔已印的文件、邮票等〕上加印〔文字〕

o·ver·proof /ˋovɚˋpruf; ˌəʊvəˈpruːf/ *adj* **10%/15% overproof** containing 10% etc more alcohol than PROOF SPIRIT does 酒精含量超标 10%/15% 以上的

o·ver·pro·tec·tive /ˌovɚprəˋtɛktɪv; ˌəʊvəprəˈtektɪv◂/ *adj* so anxious to protect someone from harm, danger etc that you restrict their freedom〔对某人〕过分保护的，溺爱的: *I suppose I've been overprotective, but Mike's my only son.* 我相信我是过分保护孩子，但迈克毕竟是我的独生子。

o·ver·qual·i·fied /ˌovɚˋkwɑləfaɪd; ˌəʊvəˈkwɒlɪfaɪd◂/ *adj* having so much experience or training that people do not want to employ you for particular jobs〔对某职位而言〕资历过高的: *The firm told me not to bother applying because I was overqualified.* 那家公司叫我不必费心去应招，因为我的资历过高。

o·ver·ran /ˌovɚˋræn; ˌəʊvəˈræn/ *v* the past tense of OVERRUN

o·ver·rate /ˋovɚˋret; ˌəʊvəˈreɪt/ *v* [T] to think that something is better or more important than it is 对…评价过高: *'Titus Andronicus' is an overrated play in my opinion.* 我认为人们对《泰特斯·安德洛尼克斯》这部戏剧评价过高了。—opposite 反义词 UNDERRATE

o·ver·reach /ˌovɚˋritʃ; ˌəʊvəˈriːtʃ/ *v* [T] **overreach yourself** to try to do more than you have the ability or money to do 试图做能力[财力]不及之事: *The company overreached itself financially.* 该公司的做法超过了自己的经济实力。

o·ver·re·act /ˌovɚrɪˋækt; ˌəʊvəriˈækt/ *v* [I] to react to something with too much emotion, especially anger 对〔某事〕反应过火〔尤指愤怒〕: **[+to]** *You always overreact to criticism.* 你对待批评总是反应过激。—**overreaction** /-rɪˋækʃən; -riˈækʃən/ *n* [C,U]

o·ver·ride /ˌovɚˋraɪd; ˌəʊvəˈraɪd/ *v past tense* **overrode** /-ˋrod; -ˈrəʊd/ *past participle* **overridden** /-ˋrɪdn̩; -ˈrɪdn/ [T] **1** to ignore a decision or order made by someone with less authority than you 无视，不顾〔下属的决定或命令〕: *The principal overrode the teacher's rule and let the children stay outside.* 校长不顾那位老师的规定，让孩子们待在外面。**2** to be regarded as more important than something else 视为比…更重要: *The needs of the mother should not override the needs of the child.* 母亲的需要不应优先于孩子的需要。

o·ver·rid·ing /ˌovɚˋraɪdɪŋ; ˌəʊvəˈraɪdɪŋ/ *adj* [only before noun 仅用于名词前] more important than anything else 最重要的；压倒一切的: *a question of overriding importance* 压倒一切的重要问题 | *Our overriding obligation is to prepare our graduates for their future.* 我们最重要的职责是要为毕业生的前途着想。

o·ver·rule /ˌovɚˋrul; ˌəʊvəˈruːl/ *v* [T] to change someone's order, or decision that you think is wrong, using your official power〔用职权〕推翻，否决，驳回〔认为是错误的命令或决定〕: *Parliament overruled the local authorities.* 议会否决了地方政府的意见。

o·ver·run /ˌovɚˋrʌn; ˌəʊvəˈrʌn/ *v past tense* **overran** /-ˋræn; -ˈræn/ *past participle* **overrun** **1** [T] if something unwanted overruns a place or area, it spreads over it in great numbers〔讨厌的事情在某地〕大量蔓延；侵扰: *Rats had overrun the barn in the few years since we'd been there.* 我们初到那儿的几年间，谷仓里老鼠成灾。| **overrun by/with** *a tiny island overrun with tourists* 布满游客的小岛 **2** [I,T] to continue longer than intended 超越，超出〔预期的时间〕: *The final speaker overran by at least half an hour.* 最后那位演讲者至少多用了半个小时。

o·ver·seas¹ /ˋovɚˋsiz; ˌəʊvəˈsiːz◂/ *adv* to or in a foreign country somewhere across the sea 向国外，在海外，在外国: *Carmen is going to work overseas.* 卡门打算去国外工作。| *Most applications came from overseas.* 申请大部分来自海外。 W3

o·ver·seas² /ˋovɚˋsiz; ˈəʊvəsiːz/ *adj* [only before noun 仅用于名词前] coming from or happening abroad 来自海外的，外国来的；发生在国外的: *overseas students* 外国留学生 | *overseas trade* 海外贸易

o·ver·see /ˌovɚˋsi; ˌəʊvəˈsiː/ *v past tense* **oversaw** /-ˋsɔ; -ˈsɔː/ *past participle* **overseen** /-ˋsin; -ˈsiːn/ [T] to be in charge of a group of workers and check that a piece of work is done satisfactorily 监管，监察，监督: *A team leader was appointed to over-*

see the project. 任命了一位组长来监管该工程。| *overseeing the workers* 监督工人

o·ver·seer /ˈovɚˌsiɚ; ˈəʊvəsɪə/ *n* [C] someone in charge of a group of workers, who checks that their work is done properly 监工; 工头; 监督人

o·ver·sell /ˌovɚˈsɛl; ˌəʊvəˈsel/ *v past tense and past participle* **oversold** /-ˈsold; -ˈsəʊld/ [T] to praise someone or something too much 对〔某人或某事〕赞扬过多; 过分吹嘘

o·ver·sen·si·tive /ˈovɚˈsɛnsɪtɪv; ˌəʊvəˈsensɪtɪv◂/ *adj* easily upset or offended 易于烦恼[生气]的, 过分敏感的: *I didn't mean that. Rod's just being oversensitive.* 我不是那个意思, 罗德过于敏感了。

o·ver·sexed /ˌovɚˈsɛkst; ˌəʊvəˈsekst◂/ *adj* having too much interest in or desire for sex 性欲过强的

o·ver·shad·ow /ˌovɚˈʃædo; ˌəʊvəˈʃædəʊ/ *v* [T] **1** to make someone or something else seem less important 使〔别的人或事〕显得较不重要, 使相形见绌[黯然失色]: *Her success has been overshadowed by her fears for her daughter, Maggie.* 她对女儿玛吉的担忧使她的成功显得无足轻重。**2** if a tall building, mountain etc overshadows a place, it is very close to it〔高楼、高山等〕使〔周围某处〕阴暗: *a dark valley overshadowed by towering peaks* 被高耸的山峰遮蔽的阴暗山谷 **3** to make an occasion or period of time less enjoyable by making people feel sad or worried 给〔某一场合或某段时间〕蒙上阴影, 使感到难过[忧虑]: *The threat of war overshadowed the summer of 1939.* 战争的威胁给 1939 年的夏天蒙上了一层阴影。

o·ver·shoe /ˈovɚˌʃu; ˈəʊvəʃuː/ *n* [C] a rubber shoe that you wear over an ordinary shoe to keep your feet dry〔穿在普通鞋子外面的〕橡胶套鞋; 罩靴

o·ver·shoot /ˌovɚˈʃut; ˌəʊvəˈʃuːt/ *v past tense and past participle* **overshot** /-ˈʃɑt; -ˈʃɒt/ [I,T] **1** to drive past the place where you intended to stop or turn 驶过〔原想停下或拐弯之处〕: *I didn't see the sign and overshot the turning.* 我没看见标志, 驶过了拐弯处。**2** **overshoot the mark** to make the mistake of going higher or further than the amount or distance you had aimed for 超过原定高度[距离]: *We realized after a half hour that we'd overshot the mark, and had to turn back.* 半小时后我们意识到我们走过头了, 只得掉头而行。

o·ver·sight /ˈovɚˌsaɪt; ˈəʊvəsaɪt/ *n* [C,U] **1** a mistake that you make by not noticing something or by forgetting to do something 失察; 疏忽: *I assure you that this was purely an oversight on my part.* 我向你保证, 这纯粹是我的一个疏忽。**2** **have oversight of** to be in charge of a piece of work and check that it is satisfactory 监管, 监督: *The works manager will have general oversight of the project.* 厂长将全面监督这项工程。

o·ver·sim·pli·fy /ˌovɚˈsɪmpləˌfaɪ; ˌəʊvəˈsɪmplɪfaɪ/ *v* [I,T] to make a situation or problem seem less complicated than it really is, by ignoring important facts〔以忽略重要事实〕使〔情况或问题〕看似比实际简单, 使…过于简单化: *My research has been grossly oversimplified in your account.* 在你的报道中, 我的研究只是被一带而过。—**oversimplification** /ˈovɚˌsɪmpləfəˈkeʃən; ˌəʊvəsɪmplɪfɪˈkeɪʃən/ *n* [C,U]

over-six·ties /ˌ· ˈ··/ *n* [plural] people who are over sixty years old 六十岁以上的人: *holidays for the over-sixties* 针对六十岁以上人士的度假安排

o·ver·size /ˈovɚˈsaɪz; ˌəʊvəˈsaɪz◂/ also 又作 **o·ver·sized** /-ˈsaɪzd; ˈsaɪzd◂/ *adj* bigger than usual or too big 大于一般的; 太大的: *His features were dwarfed by a pair of oversize spectacles.* 他戴了一副大号的眼镜, 相形之下五官便显得很小了。

o·ver·sleep /ˈovɚˈslip; ˌəʊvəˈsliːp/ *v past tense and past participle* **overslept** /-ˈslɛpt; -ˈslept/ [I] to sleep for longer than you intended 睡过头, 睡得过久: *I had overslept that morning, and was late for work.* 那天早上我睡过了头, 所以上班迟到了。—compare 比较 **sleep in** (SLEEP[1])

o·ver·spend /ˈovɚˈspɛnd; ˌəʊvəˈspend/ *v past tense and past participle* **overspent** /-ˈspɛnt; -ˈspent/ [I] to spend more money than you can afford 支出超过〔自己的财力〕, 超支: *Credit cards have encouraged people to overspend.* 信用卡鼓励人们透支消费。—**overspend** /ˈovɚspɛnd; ˈəʊvəspend/ *n* [C]: *an overspend of £200,000* 20 万英镑的超支额

o·ver·spill /ˈovɚˌspɪl; ˈəʊvəˌspɪl/ *n* [U] *BrE* people who move out of a big city because there are too many people living there, and go to live in new houses outside the city【英】〔因城市人口过多而迁移到市外新居的〕过剩人口: *a new town built to accommodate London's overspill* 为容纳伦敦的过剩人口而建的一座新城镇

o·ver·staffed /ˌovɚˈstæft; ˌəʊvəˈstɑːft◂/ *adj* a company, organization etc that is overstaffed has more workers than it needs〔公司、机构等〕人员过多的 —opposite 反义词 UNDERSTAFFED

o·ver·state /ˈovɚˈstet; ˌəʊvəˈsteɪt/ *v* [T] to talk about something in a way that makes it seem more important, serious etc than it really is; EXAGGERATE 把…讲得过分; 夸大, 夸张: *We must not frighten people by overstating the dangers.* 我们绝不能夸大这些危险来吓唬人。—opposite 反义词 UNDERSTATE

o·ver·state·ment /ˈovɚˈstetmənt; ˌəʊvəˈsteɪtmənt/ *n* [C,U] the act of talking about something in a way that makes it seem more important, serious etc than it really is, or an example of this; EXAGGERATION 言过其实; 夸张, 大话: *It's a bit of an overstatement to say that the man's a fool, but he's not brilliant.* 说这个人蠢是有点过分, 不过他不聪明。

o·ver·stay /ˈovɚˈste; ˌəʊvəˈsteɪ/ *v* [T] to stay somewhere longer than you intended or longer than you should〔在某处〕逗留超过时限, 待得时间过久 —see also 另见 **overstay your welcome** (WELCOME[3] (3))

o·ver·step /ˌovɚˈstɛp; ˌəʊvəˈstep/ *v* **overstepped, overstepping** [T] **1** **overstep the rules/limits etc** to behave in a way that is not polite or not allowed by the rules〔行为〕超越规定/限度等 **2** **overstep the mark** to do or say more than you should, and offend people or make them angry 言行过分〔得罪人或让人生气〕: *I've been very patient with him so far, but he's really overstepped the mark this time!* 迄今为止我已经够能忍耐的了, 但他这次也确实太过分了!

o·ver·stock /ˌovɚˈstɑk; ˌəʊvəˈstɒk/ *v* [I,T] to obtain more of something than is needed for a shop, hotel etc〔商店、旅馆等〕进货过多; 使存货过多

o·ver·sub·scribe /ˌovɚsəbˈskraɪb; ˌəʊvəsəbˈskraɪb/ *v* [T] **be oversubscribed** if an activity, sale, service etc is oversubscribed, people are asking for more places, tickets etc than there are available〔活动、销售、服务等〕被超额预订, 被过量订购: *Hostels for single people are normally oversubscribed.* 单身客人住的旅舍通常供不应求。

o·vert /ˈovɝt; ˈəʊvɜːt/ *adj formal* actions that are overt are done publicly, without trying to hide anything【正式】〔行动〕公开的, 不加隐瞒的: *an overt attempt to silence their political opponents* 想让他们的政敌闭嘴的明显企图 | *overt discrimination* 公然的歧视 —opposite 反义词 COVERT —**overtly** *adv*

o·ver·take /ˌovɚˈtek; ˌəʊvəˈteɪk/ *v past tense* **overtook** /-ˈtʊk; -ˈtʊk/ *past participle* **overtaken** /-ˈtekən; -ˈteɪkən/ **1** [I,T] to go past a moving vehicle or person because you are going faster than them and want to get in front of them 追上; 赶上并超过〔汽车或人〕: *He pulled out to overtake the red van.* 他开出车道去超越那辆红色的货车。—see picture on page A3 参见 A3 页图 **2** [T] if something bad overtakes you, it happens to you suddenly and prevents you from doing what you had planned to do〔不愉快的事〕突然降临〔使人不能按计划行事〕, 意外侵袭: [+by] *We'd both been overtaken by sheer fatigue.* 我们俩都累坏了。**3** [T] to develop or increase more quickly than someone or something else and become bigger, better, or more advanced than them〔发展或增长〕赶超: *By 1970 the Americans had overtaken the Russians in space technology.* 到 1970 年, 美国人在太空技术方面已领先于苏联人。**4** **be overtaken by events** if you are overtaken by events, the situation changes, so that your plans or ideas are not useful any more 因情况有变而不再有用: *His last years were spent working from a theory that was rapidly being overtaken by events.* 他在生命最后的几年应用了一套很快就被淘汰的理论。

o·ver·tax /ˈovɚˈtæks; ˌəʊvəˈtæks/ *v* [T] **1** to make someone do more than they are really able to do, so that they become very tired 使〔某人〕负担过重[过度疲劳]: **overtax yourself** *Don't overtax yourself!* 别让自己过于劳累! **2** to make people pay too much tax 对〔人民〕征税过重

over-the-coun·ter /ˌ· · ˈ··◂/ *adj* [only before noun 仅用于名词前] **1** over-the-counter drugs can be obtained without a PRESCRIPTION (=a written order) from a doctor〔药品〕无医生处方也可买到的, 非处方的 **2** *AmE* abbreviation 缩写为 **OTC** over-the-counter business shares are ones that do not appear on an official STOCK EXCHANGE (2) list【美】〔股票买卖〕场外的, 买卖双方直接交易的, 非挂牌的

over-the-top /ˌ· · ·ˈ·◂/ *adj* abbreviation 缩写为 **OTT** *BrE informal* remarks, behaviour etc that are over-the-top are so exaggerated (EXAGGERATE) or unreasonable that they seem stupid or offensive【英, 非正式】〔言行等〕过于夸张的, 荒唐的: *It's a bit over-the-top to call him a fascist.* 把他叫做法西斯分子有点夸张了。

o·ver·throw[1] /ˌovɚˈθro; ˌəʊvəˈθrəʊ/ *v past tense* **overthrew** /-ˈθru; -ˈθruː/ *past participle* **overthrown** /-ˈθron; -ˈθrəʊn/ [T] **1** to remove a leader or government from a position of power 颠覆, 推翻〔某领导或政府〕: *Rebels were already plotting to over-*

throw the government. 反叛者已在密谋颠覆政府。**2** to get rid of the rules of a society 背弃，摒弃〔社会制度〕: *a social revolution that has overthrown basic standards of morality* 摒弃了基本道德标准的社会变革

o·ver·throw² /ˈovə-ˌθro; ˈəʊvəθrəʊ/ *n* [U] the defeat and removal from power of a leader or government, especially by force 〔尤指用武力〕打倒，推翻〔某领导或政府〕: [+of] *The organization was dedicated to the overthrow of capitalism.* 该组织致力于推翻资本主义。| *the overthrow of Mussolini* 推翻墨索里尼政府

o·ver·time /ˈovə-ˌtaɪm; ˈəʊvətaɪm/ *n* [U] **1** time that you spend working in your job in addition to your normal working hours 超时工作，加班时间，额外工作时间: *six hours' overtime* 六小时的加班 | *overtime pay* 加班费 | **work overtime** *They're working overtime to get the job finished.* 他们正在加班以完成那项工作。**2** the money that you are paid for working more hours than usual 加班费: *A miner could earn £250 a week, including overtime.* 连加班费在内，矿工一周能挣250英镑。**3 be working overtime** *informal* to be very active【非正式】变得非常活跃: *After nine months of pregnancy your hormones are working overtime.* 怀孕九个月后，你体内的荷尔蒙会变得异常活跃。**4** *AmE*【美】〔足球比赛等的〕加时，延长时间; EXTRA TIME *BrE*【英】

o·ver·tone /ˈovə-ˌton; ˈəʊvətəʊn/ *n* **1 overtones** [plural] signs of an emotion or attitude that is not expressed directly 〔情感或态度〕含蓄的表示，暗示；弦外之音: *His words were polite, but there were overtones of anger in his voice.* 他的话很客气，但声音里却暗含怒气。| *heavy moral overtones* 浓重的说教意味 **2** [C] *technical* a higher musical note that sounds together with the main note: HARMONIC【术语】〔高于主音并与之合为一个单音的〕泛音 —see also 另见 UNDERTONE

o·ver·took /ˌovə-ˈtʊk; ˌəʊvəˈtʊk/ the past tense of OVERTAKE

o·ver·top /ˌovə-ˈtɑp; ˌəʊvəˈtɒp/ *v* **overtopped, overtopping** [T] *formal* to be higher or more important than something【术语】高于〔某物〕；比…更重要；胜过，超过

o·ver·ture /ˈovə-tʃə-; ˈəʊvətjʊə/ *n* **1** [C] a short piece of music written as an introduction to a long piece of music, especially an OPERA〔尤指歌剧的〕前奏曲，序曲 **2 overtures** an attempt to begin a friendly relationship with a person, country etc 〔试图与某人、某国等开始友好关系的〕主动表示；姿态: [+of] *overtures of friendship* 希望友好的表示 | **make overtures to** *They began making overtures to the Irish government in the hope of gaining their support.* 他们主动向爱尔兰政府表示友好，希望获得他们的支持。**3 be an overture** if an event is an overture to a more important event, it happens just before it and makes you expect it 是一个序幕〔表示某事是另一更为重要之事的开端〕: *This encounter was a sort of overture to their first real meeting.* 这次见面是他们首次正式会谈的一个序幕。

o·ver·turn /ˌovə-ˈtɝn; ˌəʊvəˈtɜːn/ *v* **1** [I,T] if you overturn something or if it overturns, it turns upside down or falls over on its side (使)翻倒，(使)倾覆；打翻: *Leslie leapt to her feet, overturning her chair.* 莱斯莉一跃而起，弄倒了椅子。| *One of the boats had overturned.* 有一艘船翻了。**2** [T] **overturn a decision/verdict etc** to change a decision or result so that it becomes the opposite of what it was before 推翻决定/裁决等: *The decision was finally overturned by the Supreme Court last year.* 这项判决去年最终被最高法院推翻了。**3** [T] to suddenly remove a government from power, especially by using violence; OVERTHROW¹ (1)〔尤指用暴力突然〕推翻，颠覆〔政府〕

o·ver·val·ue /ˌovə-ˈvælju; ˌəʊvəˈvæljuː/ *v* [T] to believe or say that something is more valuable or more important than it really is 对…估价过高；高估…的重要性 —**overvaluation** *n* [U]

o·ver·view /ˈovə-ˌvju; ˈəʊvəvjuː/ *n* [C] a short description of a subject or situation that gives the main ideas without explaining all the details 概述；概要: [+of] *an overview of the issues involved* 对所涉及问题的概述 | **give an overview** *Professors often give an overview of the subject at the start of the lecture.* 教授经常在讲课开始时先扼要介绍一下主要内容。

o·ver·ween·ing /ˈovə-ˈwinɪŋ; ˌəʊvəˈwiːnɪŋ◂/ *adj formal* too proud and confident; ARROGANT【正式】过于傲慢的，过分自信的；傲慢无礼的: *overweening vanity* 妄自尊大的虚荣心 —**overweeningly** *adv*

o·ver·weight /ˈovə-ˈwet; ˌəʊvəˈweɪt◂/ *adj* **1** someone who is overweight is too heavy and fat 〔人〕体重超常的，过重的，肥胖的: **10 kilos/20 lbs etc overweight** *Sally was three stone overweight.* 萨莉体重超了3英石。**2** something such as a package that is overweight weighs more than it is supposed to weigh 〔包裹等〕超重的: *My luggage was overweight by five kilos.* 我的行李超重五公斤。—compare 比较 UNDERWEIGHT —see 见 FAT¹ (USAGE)

o·ver·whelm /ˌovə-ˈhwɛlm; ˌəʊvəˈwelm/ *v* [T]

1 ▶EMOTION 感情◀ if someone is overwhelmed by an emotion, they feel it so strongly that they cannot think clearly 〔感情上〕使〔某人〕感到不能自持，使不知所措: *He was suddenly overwhelmed by a strong feeling of his insignificance.* 一股强烈的卑微感突然袭上他的心头。| *Grief overwhelmed me.* 我不胜悲伤。

2 ▶SURPRISE SB 使某人吃惊◀ to surprise someone very much, so that they do not know how to react 使〔某人〕非常惊讶: *I was completely overwhelmed by his generosity.* 他的慷慨让我惊讶万分。

3 ▶DEFEAT SB 击败某人◀ to defeat an army completely 彻底击败，击溃〔军队〕: *In 1532 the Spaniards finally overwhelmed the armies of Peru.* 1532年，西班牙人最终打垮了秘鲁军队。

4 ▶PROBLEM 问题◀ if a problem overwhelms someone or something, it has such a great effect that nothing can be done to deal with it 使不可解决，毁坏，摧毁: *Decades of war and natural catastrophes had overwhelmed the city's finances.* 几十年的战争和自然灾害摧毁了这座城市的经济。

5 ▶WATER 水◀ *literary* if water overwhelms an area of land, it covers it completely and suddenly【文】突然淹没〔某地〕

o·ver·whelm·ing /ˌovə-ˈhwɛlmɪŋ; ˌəʊvəˈwelmɪŋ/ *adj* **1** having such a great effect on you that you feel confused and do not know how to react 令人迷惘而不知所措的: *The sheer size of the place will seem overwhelming and confusing at first.* 一开始的时候，单是这地方的幅员之广已令人感到势不可挡，不知所措。| *overwhelming generosity* 极其宽宏大量[慷慨] **2 overwhelming numbers/majority/odds etc** very large numbers etc 压倒性的数字/多数/几率等: *An overwhelming majority of the members were against the idea.* 反对这项主张的成员占压倒多数。—**overwhelmingly** *adv*: *Congress voted overwhelmingly in favor of the bill.* 国会表决时，这项提案得到压倒性的支持。

o·ver·win·ter /ˌovə-ˈwɪntə-; ˌəʊvəˈwɪntə/ *v* [I,T] to live through the winter, or to make it possible for something to live through the winter 过冬；(使)越冬: *These birds generally overwinter in tropical regions.* 这些鸟通常在热带地区过冬。

o·ver·work¹ /ˌovə-ˈwɝk; ˌəʊvəˈwɜːk/ *v* [I,T] to work too much, or to make someone work too much (使)过度工作，(使)过分劳累: *Batson overworked his staff mercilessly.* 巴特森冷酷无情地让员工承担过于繁重的工作。| *You've been overworking – why don't you take a week off?* 你已经劳累过度了——为什么不休息一周呢?

overwork² *n* [U] too much hard work 过于繁重的工作；过分劳累: *a heart attack brought on by overwork* 因过度劳累导致的心脏病发作

o·ver·worked /ˌovə-ˈwɝkt; ˌəʊvəˈwɜːkt◂/ *adj* **1** made to work too hard 操劳过度的: *an overworked doctor* 劳累过度的医生 **2** a word or phrase that is overworked is used too much and has become less effective 〔词语〕使用过度的，陈词滥调的: *overworked metaphors* 用得过滥的比喻

o·ver·wrought /ˈovə-ˈrɔt; ˌəʊvəˈrɔːt◂/ *adj* very upset, nervous, and worried 非常烦恼的；神经很紧张的；十分忧虑的: *Clara was tired and overwrought after the upheavals of the last few days.* 经历了过去几天的剧变之后，克拉拉既疲惫又紧张。

Ov·id /ˈɑvɪd; ˈɒvɪd/ (43 BC-17 AD) a Latin poet whose Roman name was Publius Ovidius Naso, who is famous for the *Metamorphoses*, a set of poems telling ancient stories (MYTHS) 奥维德〔(公元前43年-公元17年)，拉丁文诗人，其罗马名字为普布利乌斯·奥维迪乌斯·纳索，以讲述古代神话的诗集《变形记》闻名〕

o·vi·duct /ˈovɪˌdʌkt; ˈəʊvidʌkt/ *n* [C] *technical* one of the two tubes in a female through which eggs pass to the WOMB【术语】输卵管

o·vip·a·rous /oˈvɪpərəs; əʊˈvɪpərəs/ *adj technical* an animal, fish, bird etc that is oviparous produces eggs that develop outside its body【术语】〔动物、鸟、鱼等〕卵生的；产卵的

o·void /ˈovɔɪd; ˈəʊvɔɪd/ *adj* shaped like an egg 卵形的 —**ovoid** *n* [C]

ov·u·late /ˈɑvjulet; ˈɒvjʊleɪt/ *v* [I] when a woman or female animal ovulates, she produces eggs inside her body 排卵；产卵 —**ovulation** /ˌɑvjuˈleʃən; ˌɒvjʊˈleɪʃən/ *n* [U]

o·vum /ˈovəm; ˈəʊvəm/ *n plural* **ova** /ˈovə; ˈəʊvə/ [C] *technical* an egg, especially one that develops inside the mother's body【术语】卵(子)，卵细胞

ow /aʊ; aʊ/ *interjection* used to express sudden pain 哎唷〔用于表示突然的疼痛〕: *"Ow, that hurts!"* "哎唷，好痛!"

owe /o; əʊ/ *v* [T] S2 W3

1 ▶MONEY 钱◀ to have to pay someone for something that they have done for you or sold to you, or to have to give someone back money that they have lent you 欠〔钱〕；负债: **owe sb sth** *I owe my brother $50.* 我欠我弟弟50美元。| **owe sb for**

sth *We still owe the garage for those repairs.* 我们还欠着汽车修理厂那笔修理费呢。| **owe sth** *How much do you owe?* 你欠了多少钱?

2 ▶**STH DONE/GIVEN** 做过的事情/已给的东西◀ to feel that you should do something for someone, give someone something etc because they have done something for you or given something to you 应该做; 应给予; 对…负有…的义务: **owe sb a drink/letter etc** *I'll write and tell Marie, I owe her a letter anyway.* 我将写信告诉玛丽; 不管怎样, 我该给她写封信了。| **owe sb a favour** *One of the neighbours owes me a favor, I'm sure they'll take care of the cat.* 邻居中有一家欠我一个人情, 我肯定他们会帮我照料这只猫的。| **I owe you one** (=used when saying thank you, when they have helped you and you are willing to help them) 我得报答你〔用于别人帮助你后, 你愿意回报并表示感谢之时〕 *Thanks a lot for being so understanding about all this – I owe you one!* 非常感谢你对这一切这么通情达理 —— 我得报答你! | **owe sb** *informal* (=be in a position in which someone has helped you, so that you should help them)【非正式】报答某人 *Let's go and see Joe – he owes me!* 我们去看看乔 —— 他该报答我!

3 **owe sb an explanation/apology** to feel that you should give someone an explanation of why you did something, or say you are sorry 该向某人解释/致歉: *"I owe you an apology, Margaret," he said sheepishly.* "我得向你道歉, 玛格丽特。"他腼腆地说道。

4 ▶**STH YOU HAVE/ACHIEVE** 你所拥有/获得的东西◀ **a)** to have something or achieve something because of what someone else has done 把…归功于, 有…是由于: **owe sth to sb** *Helena probably owed her rapid recovery to her husband's devoted care.* 海伦娜的迅速痊愈也许应归功于她丈夫的悉心照料。| **owe sb sth** *I knew that I owed Shanklin my life.* 我知道我能活下来全亏了尚克林。**b)** to know that someone's help has been important to you in achieving something 感激: **owe sb a lot/owe sb a great deal** *"I owe my parents a lot," he admitted.* "我非常感激我的父母。"他承认道。| *He owes a great deal to his publishers.* 他对他的出版商感激涕零。| **owe it all to/owe everything to** *I owe it all to you.* 我把这一切都归功于你。| **owe sb a debt (of gratitude)** *the debt that we owe to our teachers* 我们对老师们的感激之情

5 **owe it to sb to do sth** to feel you should do something for someone because they have helped you or given you support 认为应该为某人做某事: *You owe it to your supporters not to give up now.* 为了你的支持者, 你现在不应该放弃。

6 **owe it to yourself to do sth** to feel you should try to achieve something because it is what you deserve 认为自己应该做某事: *You owe it to yourself to take some time off.* 你该让自己休息一下了。

7 ▶**GOOD EFFECT** 良好的作用◀ to be successful because of the good effect of something 归功〔于某事〕: *Their success owes more to good luck than to careful management.* 他们的成功靠的是好运气, 而不是苦心经营。

8 **owe loyalty/allegiance etc** to have a duty to obey someone 负有尽忠的义务: *From then on English and Scottish citizens owed allegiance to the same king.* 自那时起, 英格兰和苏格兰的公民便效忠于同一个国王。

9 **think that the world owes you a living** to be unwilling to work in order to get things, and expect them to be provided for you 认为生来就该过舒服的日子

Owen /ˈoɪn; ˈəʊɪ̬n/, **Wil·fred** /ˈwɪlfrɪd; ˈwɪlfrɪ̬d/ (1893-1918) a British poet who was a soldier in World War I and whose poems are mainly about the terrible events and experiences of the war. Some of his best-known poems, such as *Anthem for Doomed Youth*, are a protest against the idea that it is honourable to die for your country. He was killed just before the end of the war, and his poems were published after his death. 欧文〔(1893-1918), 英国诗人, 一战时期军人。其诗作大多取材于一战中的可怕事件和经历。他的一些著名诗歌, 如《厄运青春的颂歌》, 是对为国捐躯无上光荣这一观念的抗议之声。他在战争结束前夕阵亡, 死后其诗作得以出版〕

Ow·ens /ˈoɪnz; ˈəʊɪ̬nz/, **Jes·se** /ˈdʒɛsɪ; ˈdʒesi/ (1913-80) a very successful black US ATHLETE, who won four gold medals at the 1936 Olympic Games in Berlin. This disproved the Nazi idea that the 'Aryans' (=white people from Northern Europe) were better than people of other races. Hitler refused to attend the ceremonies at which Owens was given his gold medals. 欧文斯〔(1913-1980), 一位十分出色的美国黑人运动员, 在1936年柏林奥运会上获四枚金牌。欧文斯的成绩是纳粹的雅利安人种族优秀论的反证, 希特勒因此拒绝出席他的颁奖典礼〕

ow·ing /ˈo·ɪŋ; ˈəʊɪŋ/ *adj* **1** [not before noun 不用于名词前] *especially BrE* if money is owing, it has not yet been paid to the person who should receive it【尤英】未付的, 欠着的: *There's still over £100 owing to the bank.* 还欠着银行一百多英镑。**2** **owing to** because of 因为, 由于: *Owing to a lack of funds, the project will not continue next year.* 由于缺乏资金, 该项目明年将停止进行。

USAGE NOTE 用法说明: OWING

WORD CHOICE 词语辨析: **owing to, due to, because of, thanks to**

Owing to is less common in spoken English than **due to**, but both are slightly formal and are often used in official notices or public statements. owing to 在英语口语中不如 due to 那么常用, 但二者都略为正式, 并经常用于正式的通告或公开声明中: *All flights into London Heathrow have been delayed due to/owing to thick fog.* 所有进入伦敦希思罗机场的航班均因大雾而延误。

You would usually use **because of** in spoken English. 英语口语中通常用 because of: *All the flights have been delayed because of fog.* 由于大雾, 所有的航班都延误了。

Thanks to is not formal and is used especially to explain why or how something good has happened. thanks to 是非正式用语, 尤用于解释某件好事发生的原因或过程: *Thanks to the public's generosity, we've been able to build two new schools in the area.* 多亏公众慷慨解囊, 我们才得以在该地区建造了两所新学校。

GRAMMAR 语法

You do not use **owing to** directly after the verb **to be**, but with other verbs. owing to 不能直接用于动词 be 之后, 而要和别的动词连用。

Some people think **due to** should only be used after the verb **to be**, but many people use it with other verbs as well. 有些人认为 due to 只能用于 be 动词之后, 但许多人也将其与别的动词连用: *The accident was largely due to human error.* 这次事故主要是由人为错误造成的。| *Prices have risen due to an increase in demand.* 价格因需求增加而上涨。

owl /aʊl; aʊl/ *n* [C] a bird with large eyes that hunts at night 鸮, 猫头鹰

Owl and the Pus·sy·cat, The /ˌaʊl ənd ðə ˈpʊsɪkæt; ˌaʊl ənd ðə ˈpʊsikæt/ (1871) a NONSENSE POEM (=a humorous poem that uses strange words and describes impossible events) by Edward Lear《猫头鹰和猫咪》〔(1871), 爱德华·李尔的一首打油诗〕, which begins 开首如下: *The owl and the pussycat went to sea/In a beautiful pea-green boat./They took some honey and plenty of money,/Wrapped up in a five-pound note...* 猫头鹰小猫咪出海一起玩儿, /坐的是豆绿色漂亮小船儿。/带了点儿蜜, 也没少带钱儿, /五镑的钞票一张裹成个团儿…

owl·et /ˈaʊlɪt; ˈaʊlɪ̬t/ *n* [C] a young owl 小鸮, 小猫头鹰

owl·ish /ˈaʊlɪʃ; ˈaʊlɪʃ/ *adj* looking like an owl and seeming serious and clever 像猫头鹰的; 看似严肃而聪明的: *Professor Jay looked owlish in his hornrimmed spectacles.* 杰伊教授戴着角质镜架的眼镜, 看上去严肃而富有智慧。—**owlishly** *adv*

own[1] /on; əʊn/ *determiner, pron* **1** belonging to you and no one else 自己的, 属于自己的: **your own house/car etc** *He was so drunk he even forgot his own name.* 他醉得竟然忘了自己的名字。| *He tells people how to bring up their children but is so lenient with his own.* 他常教导人们该怎样教育孩子, 但对自己的孩子却如此宽容。| **a house/car etc of your own** *He left the company to start a business of his own.* 他离开公司去开办自己的企业。| **your very own** (=used to add emphasis) 完全属于自己的〔用于加强语气〕 *When you grow up you can have your very own room.* 等你长大以后你便会有一间完全属于自己的房间。**2** done or caused without the help or influence of someone else 自己做[造成]的: *Why buy clothes when you can make your own more cheaply?* 既然你自己会做衣服, 还更便宜, 为什么还要买衣服呢? | *You've got to learn to make your own decisions.* 你得学会自己作决定。| *It's your own fault for leaving the window open.* 让窗户开着是你自己的过错。**3** **get your own back (on sb)** *informal* to get REVENGE[1] (1) for something someone has done to you【非正式】(向某人) 复仇, 报复 (某人): *All I wanted was to get my own back on my stepfather for punishing me.* 我想做的一切就是要报复继父对我的惩罚。**4** **(all) on your own** **a)** alone 单独地, 独自地: *I've been living on my own for four years now.* 我独自生活迄今已四年了。**b)** without anyone's help 无援地, 独立地: *I made this wardrobe all on my own.* 这个衣柜是我自己打的。—see graph at 参见 ALONE[1] 图表 **5** **be your own man/woman** to have your opinions and not be influenced by others〔不受他人影响〕自己拿主意, 自己做主 —see also 另见 **come into your own** (COME INTO (5)), **hold your own** (HOLD[1] (39))

USAGE NOTE 用法说明: OWN
GRAMMAR 语法
You use **own** only after possessive words like *my, John's, the company's,* etc. own 只能用在如 *my, John's, the company's* 等表示所属关系的词之后: *He has his own room/a room of his own.* 他有自己的房间。
Own can be made stronger by adding **very**. 加上 very 可使 own 的语气更强: *He has his very own room/a room of his very own.* 他有一间完全属于自己的房间。

2 2 **own²** *v* [T not in progressive 不用进行时] **1** to have something when it is legally yours, especially because you have bought it, been given it etc〔尤指因购买或赠与等而合法地〕拥有〔某物〕: *Who owns that beautiful house?* 谁拥有那幢漂亮的房子? | *Mr Silver owned a large printing firm.* 西尔弗先生拥有一家大型印刷公司。**2 behave as if you own the place** also 又作 **act like you own the place** *informal* to behave in a way that is too confident and upsets other people【非正式】弄得好像是这里的主人似的〔指表现过于自信而令他人不快〕: *She's only been here five minutes and she's already acting like she owns the place!* 她到这里不过五分钟, 但却表现得像这里的主人! **3** *old-fashioned* to admit that something is true【过时】承认: **own (that)** *I own that I judged her harshly at first.* 我承认原先我对她的评价很苛刻。| **[+to]** *I must own to a feeling of anxiety.* 我得承认有焦虑感。

own up *phr v* [I] to admit that you have done something wrong, especially something that is not serious 承认〔犯错误, 尤指小错〕: *Unless the guilty person owns up, the whole class will be punished.* 除非犯错者自己认错, 否则全班都要受罚。| **own up to sth/to doing sth** *No one owned up to breaking the window.* 没人承认打碎了窗子。

own brand /ˌ·ˈ·◂/ *adj BrE* own brand goods are specially produced and sold by particular shops and have the name of the shop on them【英】本店商标的, 自有商标的〔指产品由店家自产自销并标有店家名称的〕; STORE BRAND *AmE*【美】: *Sainsbury's own brand tomato sauce* 赛恩斯伯里商店以自己商标出品的番茄酱

2 2 **own·er** /ˈonɚ; ˈəʊnə/ *n* [C] someone who owns something 所有人, 物主, 业主: **[+of]** *I met the owner of the local hotel.* 我碰见了那家当地旅馆的业主。| **the proud owner of** *the proud owner of a bright red sports car* 那位得意的大红跑车车主 | **car-owner/dog-owner etc** *Dog-owners have been warned to keep their animals under control.* 狗主已被告诫要看管好自己的狗。| **home-owner** (=someone who owns their house) 住宅拥有者, 房主

owner-oc·cu·pied /ˌ··ˈ···◂/ *adj* houses, apartments etc that are owner-occupied are lived in by the people who own them〔房子等〕业主居住的, 业主自用的: *Most of these properties are owner-occupied.* 这些房产大部分都是业主自用的。

owner-oc·cu·pi·er /ˌ··ˈ····/ *n* [C] someone who owns the house or apartment etc that they live in 业主居住者

3 3 **own·er·ship** /ˈonɚˌʃɪp; ˈəʊnəʃɪp/ *n* [U] the fact of owning something 所有权: *a dispute over the ownership of the land* 关于土地所有权的纠纷

own goal /ˌ·ˈ·/ *n* [C] *BrE*【英】**1** a GOAL that you accidentally SCORE² (1) against your own team without intending to in a game of football, HOCKEY etc 乌龙球〔足球、曲棍球等比赛中误入自己球门的一球〕**2** *informal* an action or remark that has the opposite effect from what you intended【非正式】〔不利于自己的〕错事, 蠢话, 自打嘴巴: *the minister's spectacular own goal when he admitted that his own department had leaked the document* 那位部长承认是他的部门泄露文件内容, 这显然是在自打嘴巴

own la·bel /ˌ·ˈ··◂/ *adj BrE* OWN BRAND【英】自有商标的, 本店商标的

ox /ɑks; ɒks/ *n plural* **oxen** /ˈɑksn̩; ˈɒksən/ [C] **1** a BULL whose sex organs have been removed, often used for working on farms etc〔常用于干农活的〕阉牛 **2** a large cow or BULL 牛〔指大的母牛或公牛〕

Ox·bridge /ˈɑksˌbrɪdʒ; ˈɒksˌbrɪdʒ/ *n* [U] the universities of Oxford and Cambridge 牛津大学和剑桥大学 —compare 比较 REDBRICK

CULTURAL NOTE 文化注释
Oxford and Cambridge are the two oldest and most respected universities in the UK. They are considered to give a very high standard of education, and students need very good examination results if they want to study at these universities. Oxbridge GRADUATE*s* often become powerful and successful members of British society, and many of the leading people in professions such as the law, politics, and the Civil Service have traditionally been 'Oxbridge-educated', though this is beginning to change. 牛津和剑桥是英国两所历史最悠久、最受尊敬的大学。人们认为它们能提供高水平的教育, 而且只有成绩优异的学生才有资格进入这两所大学学习。牛津和剑桥的毕业生很多都成了英国社会中的权势人物和成功人士, 例如法律界、政界中的佼佼者和公职人员的头面人物都有"在牛津或剑桥受过教育"的经历, 尽管这一传统正在发生变化。
Oxbridge is sometimes criticized for the fact that about half its students come from PUBLIC SCHOOL*s* (=expensive private schools), even though most British children do not attend these schools. Some people also think of Oxbridge colleges as too old-fashioned, traditional, and ELITIST (=considering themselves as very special and as more important than ordinary universities). They believe that these institutions do not really understand how ordinary people think and live. 也有不少针对牛津和剑桥的批评声音, 因为它们一半左右的学生来自公学, 而大多数英国孩子上的并不是公学。也有些人认为牛津和剑桥过于守旧、传统和自大。他们认为这样的机构并不真正理解普通人的想法和生活。— see also Cultural Note at IVY LEAGUE 另见 IVY LEAGUE 文化注释

ox·cart /ˈɑksˌkɑrt; ˈɒkskɑːt/ *n* [C] a vehicle pulled by oxen 牛车

ox-eye /ˈ· ·/ *n* [C] a yellow flower like a DAISY 牛眼菊, 春白菊

Ox·fam /ˈɑksfæm; ˈɒksfæm/ *n* [singular] the Oxford Committee for Famine Relief; a British CHARITY organization that aims to help people in poor countries 乐施会, 牛津饥荒救济委员会〔英国专门帮助贫困国家人民的慈善机构〕

Ox·ford /ˈɑksfɚd; ˈɒksfəd/ **1** a city on the Rivers Thames and Cherwell in Oxfordshire, southern England. It has many beautiful old buildings and is famous for its university 牛津市〔英格兰南部牛津郡一城市, 位于泰晤士河与查韦尔河交汇处。该市有许多漂亮的古建筑, 以牛津大学闻名〕**2** also 又作 **Oxford University** one of the two oldest and most respected universities in the UK, established in the 13th century. The university is made up of about 35 separate colleges, where the students live and also receive some of their teaching 牛津大学〔英国最古老、最受尊敬的两所大学之一, 建于 13 世纪。该大学共有 35 个独立学院, 是学生生活和听讲一些课程的地方〕: *A lot of well-known politicians went to Oxford.* (=were students there)许多著名政治家曾就读于牛津大学。| *an Oxford graduate* 一名牛津大学毕业生 —see 见 CAMBRIDGE, OXBRIDGE, OXON

oxford *n AmE*【美】**1** [C] a type of shirt made of thick cotton 牛津衬衫〔一种用厚棉布做的衬衫〕**2 oxfords** [plural] a type of leather shoes that fasten with SHOELACE*s* 牛津鞋〔一种缚带的男式皮鞋〕

Oxford Cir·cus /ˌ··ˈ··/ the place in central London where Regent Street and Oxford Street cross, and also the name of the underground station there. It is one of the busiest places in London, and is always full of people going shopping. 牛津广场〔位于伦敦市中心摄政街与牛津街的交汇处, 也是广场地铁站的站名。牛津广场是伦敦市区最繁华的地段之一, 购物的人群总是熙熙攘攘〕

Oxford En·glish Dic·tion·a·ry, the /ˌ··, ˌ··ˈ····/ abbreviation 缩写为 **OED** a very large dictionary of English, started in the 1880s, which is famous for its completeness and for its explanations of the origins of words and their history. It is available either as a book in several large volumes, or as a CD-ROM.《牛津英语大词典》〔一大型英语词典, 编纂于 19 世纪 80 年代, 以收词全及对词源和词义演变的诠释而闻名。该词典既有分卷套装版, 也有光碟版〕

Oxford Group, the /ˈ··ˌ·/ a group that was formed in Oxford in the mid-19th century, which tried to bring some of the ceremonies and beliefs of the Catholic religion into the Church of England 牛津集团, 牛津派〔19 世纪中叶形成于牛津的一个团体。该团体试图将天主教的一些仪式和信仰引入英国国教会〕

Ox·ford·shire /ˈɑksfɚdʃɚ; ˈɒksfədʃəʳ/ abbreviation 缩写为 **Oxon** a COUNTY in south central England, in and around the Thames Valley. It is mainly farmland, with some old towns and villages. 牛津郡〔英格兰中南部一郡, 遍及泰晤士河谷及其周边地区, 大部分为耕地, 可见一些古老村镇〕

Oxford Street /ˈ··ˌ·/ one of the main streets of central London, famous for its shops and for being very busy 牛津街〔伦敦市中心的主要街道之一, 以店铺林立、热闹繁华出名〕

ox·ide /ˈɑksaɪd; ˈɒksaɪd/ *n* [C,U] *technical* a chemical compound in which another substance is combined with oxygen【术语】氧化物: *iron oxide* 氧化铁

ox·i·dize also 又作 **-ise** *BrE*【英】/ˈɑksəˌdaɪz; ˈɒksɨdaɪz/ *v* [I, T] *technical* to combine with oxygen, or make something combine with oxygen, especially in a way that causes RUST【术语】(使) 氧化; (使) 生锈 —**oxidation** /ˌɑksəˋdeʃən; ˌɒksɨˈdeɪʃən/ also 又作 **oxidization** /ˌɑksədəˋzeʃən; ˌɒksɨdaɪˈzeɪʃən/ *n* [U]

Ox·on /ˈɑksɑn; ˈɒksɒn/ **1** Oxfordshire 牛津郡 **2** used after the title of a degree to show that it is from Oxford University 牛津大学的〔用于学位名称之后〕: *David Jones, BA (Oxon)* 戴维·琼斯, 牛津大学文学学士 — compare 比较 CANTAB

ox·tail /ˈɑksˌtel; ˈɒksteɪl/ *n* [U] the meat from the tails of cattle, used especially in soup〔尤指做汤用的〕牛尾: *oxtail soup* 牛尾汤

ox·y·a·cet·y·lene /ˌɑksɪəˋsɛtḷˌin; ˌɒksiəˈsetəliːn◂/ *n* [U] *technical* a mixture of oxygen and ACETYLENE that produces a hot white flame that can cut steel【术语】氧 (乙) 炔

ox·y·gen /ˈɑksədʒən; ˈɒksɪdʒən/ *n* [U] a gas with no colour, smell, or taste, that is present in air and is necessary for most animals and plants to live 氧, 氧气

ox·y·gen·ate /ˈɑksədʒənˌet; ˈɒksɪdʒəneɪt/ *v* [T] *technical* to add oxygen to something【术语】充氧于 —**oxygenation** /ˌɑksədʒənˋeʃən; ˌɒksɪdʒəˈneɪʃən/ *n* [U]

oxygen mask /ˈ··· ·/ *n* [C] a piece of equipment that fits over someone's mouth and nose to provide them with oxygen 氧气面罩

oxygen tent /ˈ··· ·/ *n* [C] a piece of equipment shaped like a tent that is put around people who are very ill in hospital, to provide them with oxygen〔给医院病人用的〕氧气帐

ox·y·mo·ron /ˌɑksɪˋmɔrɑn; ˌɒksiˈmɔːrɒn/ *n* [C] *technical* a deliberate combination of two words that seem to mean the opposite of each other, such as 'cruel kindness'【术语】矛盾修辞法, 逆喻〈如残酷的善良〉

o·yez /ˈojɛz; əʊˈjez/ *interjection* a word used by law officials or by TOWN CRIERS in the past to get people's attention 肃静! 静听!〔法官或过去的城镇公告员在街上宣布要事时要人注意听的喊声〕

Oyl /ɔɪl; ɔɪl/, **Olive** a character in the US CARTOON STRIP, television cartoons, and film about Popeye. Olive Oyl is a tall very thin woman who is Popeye's girlfriend. 奥利弗〔反映大力水手的美国连环漫画、电视卡通片和影片中的一个人物。她身材高挑, 极为瘦削, 是大力水手的女朋友〕

oy·ster /ˈɔɪstɚ; ˈɔɪstə/ *n* [C] **1** a type of SHELLFISH that can be eaten cooked or uncooked, and that produces a jewel called a PEARL (1) 牡蛎, 蚝 —see picture at 参见 SHELL[1] 图 **2 the world is your oyster** used to tell someone that they can achieve whatever they want 你可以随心所欲; 想要什么就能得到什么

oyster bed /ˈ·· ·/ *n* [C] an area at the bottom of the sea where oysters live〔海底〕牡蛎养殖场

oyster-catch·er /ˈ·· ,··/ *n* [C] a black and white bird that eats SHELLFISH 蛎鹬〔一种捕食水生有壳动物的海鸟〕

Oz /ɑz; ɒz/ *n BrE, AustrE informal* Australia【英, 澳, 非正式】澳大利亚

oz the written abbreviation of 缩写= OUNCE or ounces

O·zarks, the /ˈozɑrks; ˈəʊzɑːks/ an area of high land covered by forests in the US states of Missouri and Arkansas 欧扎克高原〔美国密苏里州和阿肯色州境内一片森林茂密的高原地区〕

o·zone /ˈozon; ˈəʊzəʊn/ *n* [U] **1** *technical* a poisonous blue gas that is a type of oxygen【术语】臭氧〔有毒的蓝色气体, 氧的同素异形体〕 **2** *informal* air near the sea, thought to be fresher and healthier【非正式】〔近海处的〕清新空气

ozone-friend·ly /ˌ·· ˈ··◂/ *adj* not containing chemicals that damage the ozone layer 对臭氧层无害的: *an ozone-friendly aerosol* 对臭氧层无害的喷雾剂

ozone lay·er /ˈ·· ,··/ *n* [singular] a layer of gases that prevents harmful RADIATION (2) from the sun from reaching the Earth 臭氧层: *CFCs, the chemicals responsible for the hole in the ozone layer* 氯氟烃, 造成臭氧层空洞的化学物

P,p

P, p /pi; piː/ *plural* **P's, p's** *n* [C] the 16th letter of the English alphabet 英语字母表的第十六个字母 —see also 另见 **mind your p's and q's** (MIND[2] (7))

p **1** the written abbreviation of 缩写= page **2** *BrE* pence or PENNY【英】便士: *'The Times' now costs only 30p.*《泰晤士报》现在只售30便士。**3** the written abbreviation of 缩写= PARTICIPLE **4** the written abbreviation of 缩写= POPULATION **5** used in written music to show that a part should be played or sung quietly 柔声地, 轻轻地〔用于乐谱中表示该部分演奏或演唱时应用轻声〕

p & p the written abbreviation of 缩写= **postage and packing**: *Please send 20p to cover p & p.* 请寄20便士支付邮资和包装费。

P45 in the UK, an official document that is given to you by your employer when you leave a job. It gives details of the money you have earned and the taxes you have paid during this period of employment, and if you start a new job you have to give it to your new employer. P45表〔在英国雇员离职时雇主给其出具的一份正式文件。该文件记录有雇员受聘期间的收入与缴税信息。雇员找到新的工作时须将该文件提交给新雇主〕

P60 in the UK, an official document which is given to you by your employer each year and which gives details of the money you have earned and the taxes you have paid during that year P60表〔在英国雇主每年给雇员出具的一份正式文件, 上面记录有雇员当年的收入和缴税信息〕—see 见 w-2

PA[1] /ˌpi ˋe; ˌpiː ˈeɪ/ *n* **1** [C, usually singular 一般用单数] public address system; a set of electronically controlled pieces of equipment that makes someone's voice loud enough to be heard by large groups of people 有线广播系统; 扩音系统 **2** [C] *BrE* personal assistant; a special secretary who looks after the affairs of just one person【英】私人助理

PA[2] the written abbreviation of 缩写= PENNSYLVANIA

p.a. the written abbreviation of 缩写= PER ANNUM

pa /pɑ; pɑː/ *n* [C] *old-fashioned* a word meaning 'father' used by or to children【过时】爸爸〔儿语〕

Pac 10, Pac Ten /ˌpæk ˋtɛn; ˌpæk ˈten/ also 又作 **Pacific Ten** a group of ten university football teams from the area of the US along the Pacific coast who play against each other 太平洋十强〔美国太平洋沿岸十支相互角逐的大学橄榄球队〕

W3 **pace[1]** /pes; peɪs/ *n*

1 ▶WALK/RUN 走/跑◀ [singular] the speed at which you walk or run 步速, 走[跑]的速度: *They've run the first mile in under six minutes – can they keep up this pace?* 他们不到六分钟就跑完了头一英里——他们能保持这个速度吗? | **at a steady/gentle/brisk pace** *The troops marched at a steady pace.* 部队稳步行进。

2 ▶SPEED STH HAPPENS 某事发生的速度◀ [singular] the rate or speed at which something happens or at which someone does something 速度, 进度: [**+of**] *The pace of change in Eastern Europe has been breathtaking.* 东欧的变化速度是惊人的。| **at your own pace** (=at the pace that suits you) 以适合自己的速度 *He liked to work at his own pace.* 他喜欢以自己的进度工作。

3 ▶A STEP 一步◀ [C] a single step when you are running or walking, or the distance moved in one step〔跑或走的〕一步; 一步之距: *I moved forward a couple of paces.* 我向前移动了几步。

4 force the pace to make something happen or develop more quickly than it would do normally 使加快速度, 使加速发展: *Gorbachev favoured gradual reform and felt it was dangerous to force the pace.* 戈尔巴乔夫支持循序渐进的改革, 并认为加速改革是很危险的。

5 keep pace (with) to move or change as fast as someone or something else (与…) 并驾齐驱, 齐头并进; 跟上…: *She followed Bobby, barely keeping pace with him.* 她走在博比的后面, 只能勉强跟上他。| *Pensions and benefits have failed to keep pace with the rate of inflation.* 养老金和救济金的增加跟不上通货膨胀的速度。

6 put sb/sth through their paces to make a person or a machine show how well they can do something 测试某人/某物的本领[性能]; 使某人/某物展示本领[性能]: *a series of tests to put candidates through their paces* 考察候选人能力的一连串测试

7 set the pace a) to establish a speed at which others try to do something, or a quality they try to achieve 起带头作用, 树立榜样: *Japanese firms have been setting the pace in electronic engineering.* 日本公司一直在电子工程方面处于领先地位。**b)** to run at a speed that other runners try to keep to, at the beginning of a race〔在比赛开始时〕定步速〔使其他赛跑者跟从〕

8 stand the pace to be able to deal with situations where you are very busy and have to think and act very quickly 能够适应紧张的节奏: *If you can stand the pace, working in advertising pays well.* 要是你能适应紧张的工作节奏, 在广告行业工作报酬很高。

9 show your paces to show your skill or speed in an activity 显示自己的本领[才能], 显身手; 展示自己的速度

10 the pace of life the amount of activity in people's lives and how busy they are 生活节奏: *The pace of life in the village was slow and restful.* 这个乡村的生活节奏缓慢而悠闲。

11 ▶HORSE 马◀ [C] one of the ways that a horse walks or runs〔马的〕步法, 步态

pace[2] *v* **1** [I always+adv/prep,T] to walk with slow, regular, steady steps, usually backwards and forwards 慢步走(于), 踱步; 以规律的步伐行走: **pace up and down** *He paced nervously up and down the hospital room, waiting for news.* 他紧张不安地在医院的房间里踱来踱去, 等待消息。| **pace the floor/room etc** *Ben stood up and paced the floor, deep in thought.* 本站起来踱来踱去, 陷入了沉思。—see picture on page A24 参见A24页图 **2 pace yourself a)** to set a controlled regular speed for yourself, especially in a race〔尤指在比赛中〕控制自己的步速: *I paced myself so that I was not too far ahead of the others.* 我控制好自己的速度, 以使自己不领先别人太多。**b)** to do something at a steady speed without rushing 以平稳的速度做某事; 掌握速度 **3 pace someone** to set a speed for someone running or riding, especially in a race〔尤指在比赛中〕为某人定步速 **4** also 又作 **pace off, pace out** [T] to measure a distance by taking steps of an equal length 用脚步测量, 步测: *The director paced out the length of the stage.* 那位导演用步子测量了舞台的长度。

pace·mak·er /ˋpesˌmekɚ; ˈpeɪsˌmeɪkə/ *n* [C] a small machine that is fixed inside someone's chest in order to make weak or irregular beats of the heart regular〔心脏〕起搏器

pace·set·ter /ˋpesˌsɛtɚ; ˈpeɪs-setə/ *n* [C] **1** a team that is ahead of others in a competition〔比赛中〕领先队伍 **2** someone or something that sets an example for others 带头人, 榜样: *Industry is the pacesetter of modern life.* 工业是现代生活的先导。**3** someone who runs at the front at the beginning of a race and sets the speed at which others must run〔赛跑中其他参赛者跟随其速度的〕领跑者, 定步速者

Pachelbel /ˋpæxəlbɛl; ˈpæxəlbel/, **Johann** /ˋjohɑn; ˈjəʊhæn/ (1653-1706) a German COMPOSER of Baroque music, famous especially for his *Canon and Gigue in D major.* 帕黑尔贝尔〔(1653-1706), 德国巴洛克音乐作曲家, 尤以《D大调卡农和吉格变奏曲》闻名〕

pach·y·derm /ˋpækəˌdɝm; ˈpækɪdɜːm/ *n* [C] *technical* a thick-skinned animal such as an elephant or a RHINOCEROS【术语】厚皮动物〈如象或犀牛〉

pa·cif·ic /pəˋsɪfɪk; pəˈsɪfɪk/ *adj literary*【文】**1** peaceful or loving peace 平静的, 安宁的; 爱好和平的: *a normally pacific community* 通常很平静的社区 **2** helping to cause peace 求和的, 和解的; 息事宁人的 —**pacifically** /-klɪ; -kli/ *adv*

Pacific North·west, the /ˌ·ˌ·· ˌ·ˋ·/ the area of the US which includes Washington State, Oregon, and northern California, especially along the Pacific coast. The area is famous for its wild beauty, cliffs, and forests.〔美国〕太平洋西北部地区〔包括华盛顿州、俄勒冈州、加利福尼亚州北部在内的太平洋沿岸地区, 以优美的野外风光、峭壁和森林闻名〕

CULTURAL NOTE 文化注释

When people in the US talk about the Pacific Northwest, they usually think of Seattle and Portland, which are the main cities in the states of Washington and Oregon. These cities are considered to be quieter and less busy than cities on the East Coast, and they have forests, the coast, and the mountains nearby. Seattle is also known as a place where coffee shops and microbreweries (MICROBREWERY) started to become popular in the late 1980s and early

1990s. 美国人谈起太平洋西北岸地区时通常会想到西雅图和波特兰，二者分别是华盛顿州和俄勒冈州的主要城市。这两个城市被认为比东海岸的那些城市更安静、更悠闲，城市周边还有森林、海岸和群山。西雅图还以 20 世纪 80 年代后期和 90 年代早期兴起的咖啡店和小啤酒厂而广为人知。

Pacific Ocean, the /ˌ·ˌ·· ˈ··/ also又作 **the Pacific** the world's largest ocean, covering one third of the Earth's surface between the continents of North and South America to the east and Asia and Australia to the west 太平洋〔世界上最大的洋，即南、北美洲大陆以西与亚洲和澳大利亚以东的水域，占地球面积的三分之一〕

Pacific Rim /ˌ·ˌ·· ˈ·/ *n* **the Pacific Rim (countries)** the countries or parts of countries that border the Pacific Ocean, such as Japan, Australia, and the west coast of the US, considered as an economic group 太平洋沿岸国家[地区]〔如日本、澳大利亚和美国西海岸，被视为一个经济群体〕

Pacific Ten /ˌ·ˌ·· ˈ·/ —see 见 PAC 10

pac·i·fi·er /ˈpæsəˌfaɪɚ; ˈpæsɪ̵faɪə/ *n* [C] **1** *AmE* a specially shaped rubber object that you give a baby to suck so that it does not cry【美】〔哄婴孩用的〕橡皮奶头[奶嘴]; DUMMY[1] (3) *BrE*【英】 **2** something that makes people calm 镇静剂; 使人安定的东西

pac·i·fis·m /ˈpæsəˌfɪzəm; ˈpæsɪ̵fɪzəm/ *n* [U] the belief that all wars and all forms of violence are wrong 和平主义; 反战主义

pac·i·fist /ˈpæsəfɪst; ˈpæsɪ̵fɪ̵st/ *n* [C] someone who believes that all wars are wrong and who refuses to use violence 和平主义者; 反战主义者

pac·i·fy /ˈpæsəˌfaɪ; ˈpæsɪ̵faɪ/ *v* [T] **1** to make someone calm, quiet, and satisfied after they have been angry or upset 使平静，使安静，安抚: *Gregory knew his wife would be furious and he was trying to think how to pacify her.* 格雷戈里知道妻子会大发雷霆的，所以他在想如何安抚她。**2** to bring peace to an area or to end war in a place 给〔某个地区〕带来和平; 使〔某地〕结束战争，平定; 绥靖: *It was hoped the new ruler could pacify the region.* 人们希望这位新的统治者能给这一地区带来和平。—**pacification** /ˌpæsəfəˈkeʃən; ˌpæsɪ̵fɪ̵ˈkeɪʃən/ *n* [U]

pack (把…)装箱

pack[1] /pæk; pæk/ *v*

1 ▶**IN BOXES, CASES ETC** 在箱子、盒子等中◀ also 又作 **pack up** [I,T] to put things into cases, boxes etc for taking somewhere or storing (把…) 打包; (把…) 装箱: *I forgot to pack my razor.* 我忘记把剃须刀放入行李包。| *They packed up the contents of their house.* 他们把屋子里的东西打好捆。| *We're off to Greece tomorrow and I haven't even started packing yet.* 我们明天就动身去希腊，但我还没有开始收拾行李呢。| **pack sb sth** *Have you packed the kids a lunch?* 你为孩子们备好盒装午餐了吗?

2 **pack a bag/case etc** to put things into a bag, case etc 把东西装入袋[包]/箱[盒]等: *She packed her suitcase and headed for the airport.* 她把东西装入手提箱，然后动身去机场。—opposite 反义词 UNPACK (1)

3 ▶**CROWD OF PEOPLE** 人群◀ [I always+adv/prep, T always+adv/prep] to go in large numbers into a space that is not big enough, or to make a lot of people or things do this 挤进, 涌进; 塞满, 使挤满: [**+into/in/onto**] *When the door was opened people began to pack into the hall.* 门一打开，人们就开始涌入大厅。| *They packed as many people as possible onto the bus.* 他们尽量让多些人挤上那辆公共汽车。

4 ▶**PROTECT STH** 保护某物◀ [T] to cover, fill, or surround an object closely with a protective material〔用保护材料〕把…裹[包]起来: *Pack the newspaper around the china so that it doesn't break.* 用报纸把瓷器包起来以免打破。| [**+in/with**] *china cups packed with paper* 用纸包起来的瓷杯

5 **pack your bags** *informal* to leave a place and not return, especially because of a disagreement【非正式】〔尤指由于意见不合而〕离开: *Why don't you pack your bags and find another job?* 你为什么不离开再找一份工作呢?

6 ▶**SNOW/SOIL ETC** 雪/土壤等◀ [T] to press soil, sand etc into a firm mass 把〔土壤、沙等〕结实地堆积起来; 压紧; 捣固: *pack soil firmly around the stem* 把树干周围的培土拍实

7 ▶**MEAT ETC** 肉等◀ [T] to prepare food and put it into containers for preserving or selling 把〔食品〕装罐[制成罐头]

8 **pack a committee/jury/meeting etc** [T] to secretly and dishonestly arrange for a committee etc to be filled with people who support you〔秘密及不正当地〕在委员会/陪审团/会议等中安插[安排]支持自己的人

9 **pack a gun** *AmE* to regularly carry a gun【美】携带枪支

10 **pack a (hard) punch** *informal*【非正式】**a)** to be able to hit another person hard in a fight〔在打斗中〕能有力地击拳，用力出拳 **b)** to be able to speak very effectively in an argument or discussion〔在辩论或讨论中〕措辞有力 —see also 另见 **send sb packing** (SEND (9))

pack sth ↔ **away** *phr v* [T] to put something back in a box, case etc where it is usually kept 将〔某物〕收拾起来: *We packed away the picnic things.* 我们把野餐用的东西收拾起来。

pack sb/sth ↔ **in** *phr v* [T] **1** *informal* to attract people in large numbers【非正式】吸引〔大批的人〕: *'Pulp Fiction' is really packing them in.*《低俗小说》确实把他们吸引住了。**2** also 又作 **pack** sth **into** sth to fit a lot of something into a space, place, or period of time 把〔太多事物〕塞入，挤入: *They packed so much into their holiday, they returned exhausted.* 他们把假期安排得太紧密，结果回来时筋疲力尽。**3** *informal especially BrE* to stop doing something, especially a job that you find unpleasant or annoying【非正式，尤英】停止〔尤指不愉快或令人讨厌的工作〕: *At times like this I feel like packing it all in and going off travelling.* 像这种时候我就想丢下所有的事情去旅行。**4** **pack it in** *spoken* used to tell someone to stop doing something that is annoying you【口】〔用于告诉别人〕停止〔做令人讨厌的事〕: *Pack it in you two. I'm tired of hearing you arguing.* 你们两个别争了，我都听厌了。**5** *BrE informal* to end a romantic relationship with someone【英，非正式】结束与…的恋情，与…分手

pack sb/sth **off** *phr v* [T] *informal* to send someone away quickly, to avoid trouble or because you want to get rid of them【非正式】〔为避免麻烦或摆脱某人而〕把…打发走，撵走: *My parents packed us off to camp every summer.* 我的父母每到夏天就打发我们去夏令营。

pack up *phr v* **1** [I] *informal* to finish work【非正式】完成工作，停工，收工: *Business was slack and she packed up early.* 由于生意清淡，她早早就收工了。**2** [I] *informal especially BrE* if a machine packs up it stops working【非正式，尤英】〔机器〕停止运转，出故障，失灵: *The engine's packed up!* 引擎坏了! **3** [T] *informal BrE* to stop doing something such as a job【非正式，英】停止〔做某事〕; 停止工作: *He's packed up his job after only three months.* 仅三个月后他就放弃了自己的工作。

pack[2] *n* [C]

1 ▶**THINGS WRAPPED TOGETHER** 包在一起的东西◀ several things wrapped or tied together or put in a case, to make them easy to carry, sell, or give to someone 包，捆，包裹: *Send away for your free information pack today.* 今天就写信索取免费资料包。—see also 另见 SIX-PACK

2 ▶**SMALL CONTAINER** 小容器◀ *especially AmE* a small container, usually made of paper, with a set of things in it; PACKET (1,2)【尤美】〔一般用纸造的〕小盒，小包: [**+of**] *a pack of cigarettes* 一包香烟 | *a pack of gum BrE*【英】一包口香糖 —see picture at 参见 CONTAINER 图

3 ▶**BAG** 包◀ [C] *BrE* a bag carried by a climber, walker, or soldier, that is fastened to their shoulders and is used to carry equipment, clothes etc【英】背包

4 ▶**ANIMALS** 动物◀ a group of wild animals that hunt together, or a group of dogs trained together for hunting〔野兽或猎犬的〕一群: *a wolf pack* 狼群 | *a pack of hounds* 一群猎狗

5 ▶**GROUP OF PEOPLE** 一群人◀ a group of people who do something together, especially a group who you do not approve of 一帮，一伙: *a pack of thieves* 一伙贼 | *the Hollywood brat pack* 一帮好莱坞的青年名演员

6 ▶**MILITARY** 军事◀ a group of aircraft, SUBMARINEs, etc that fight the enemy together〔作战飞机或潜艇的〕一队，一群

7 **be a pack of lies** *informal* to be completely untrue【非正式】一派谎言: *Don't you believe what it says in the paper – it's a pack of lies.* 别相信报纸上说的—那全是一派谎言。

8 ►**CARDS** 纸牌◄ a complete set of PLAYING CARDS〔纸牌的〕一副: *Please shuffle the pack and deal.* 请洗牌并发牌。

9 **Cub/Brownie pack** a group of children belonging to a children's organization 一队幼年男/女童子军 —see 见 CUB SCOUT, BROWNIE

10 ►**ON A WOUND** 在伤口上◄ a thick mass of soft cloth that you press on a wound to stop the flow of blood; COMPRESS[2]〔压在伤口上止血用的〕敷布, 裹布, 绷带 —see also 另见 ICE PACK

11 ►**BEAUTY TREATMENT** 美容◄ a substance, often a special mud or clay, that you put on your skin to make you feel better 美容敷剂 —see also 另见 FACE PACK, MUDPACK

pack·age[1] /ˈpækɪdʒ; ˈpækɪdʒ/ *n* [C] **1** an amount of something, or several things, packed together firmly and wrapped in paper etc; PARCEL[1] (1) 包, 包裹: **[+of]** *Can you deliver a large package of books?* 你能递送一大包书吗? **2** *AmE* the box, bag etc that foods are put in for selling【美】〔包装食物的〕盒, 包 **3** a set of related things or services sold or offered together〔出售或提供的相关东西或服务的〕一套, 一揽子: *a new software package* 一套新的软件包 | *The bank is offering a special financial package for students.* 这家银行正给学生提供一整套特殊的金融服务。

package[2] also 又作 **package up** *v* [T] **1** to make something into a package or tie it up as a package 把…包成一包[扎成一捆]: *She packaged up the clothes to send to her daughter.* 她把衣服包成一包寄给她的女儿。**2** to put something in a special package ready to be sold 将…包装〔以备出售〕

pack·aged /ˈpækɪdʒd; ˈpækɪdʒd/ *adj* specially wrapped and put in a container for selling〔作销售用途〕包装的, 装盒的: *The soap was beautifully packaged in a special gift box.* 那块肥皂被放在一个特制的礼品盒里, 包装非常精美。

package deal /ˈ· · ˌ·/ *n* [C] an offer or agreement that includes several things that must all be accepted together 一揽子交易, 整批交易

package hol·i·day /ˈ· · ˌ· · ·/ *n* [C] *BrE* a package tour【英】包办旅游, 包价旅游

package store /ˈ· · ˌ·/ *n* [C] *AmE old-fashioned* a store where alcohol is sold【美, 过时】销售酒的商店; OFF LICENCE *BrE*【英】

package tour /ˈ· · ˌ·/ *n* [C] a completely planned holiday arranged by a company at a fixed price, which includes travel, hotels, meals etc〔一切由旅行社安排且费用固定的〕包办旅游, 包价旅游

CULTURAL NOTE 文化注释

In the UK, package tours are very popular. The STEREOTYPE of someone who goes on a package tour is a tourist who wants to go to a beach in a foreign country where the weather is hot, but still expects to speak English and eat British food. Sometimes package tours do not happen as they were planned, and people make jokes about having to wait for a long time at the airport, or about the fact that their hotel was only half built. 在英国, 包价旅游很受欢迎。一般选择包价旅游的是那些想去国外海滩旅游的人, 他们去的地方天气炎热, 可他们又希望能在那里说英语和吃英国饭菜。有时包价旅游并不像原先定好的那样, 因此人们拿这个开玩笑, 说要在机场等待很长时间或者要住的旅馆还没有完全建好。

In the US, people do not go on package tours as often as people in the UK. They are usually bought by older couples or by large organized groups, such as the students of a particular class or the employees of a particular office. US package tours often visit several different places as part of the trip, for example a ten-day tour stopping in six European cities. US tourists also tend to buy package tours for special trips or events, such as a CRUISE to Alaska or a family vacation to Disneyland or the Olympics. 美国人不像英国人那样经常选择包价旅游。选择包价旅游的人是老年夫妇或组织起来的大团体, 如一个班级的学生或一个办公室的雇员。美国的包价旅游常常会分别游览几个不同的地方, 例如会在欧洲六个城市停留的、为期十天的旅游。美国的旅游者还会购买特殊旅程和特别活动的包价旅游, 例如乘游轮去阿拉斯加或者去迪斯尼乐园或观看奥运会的举家度假。

pack·ag·ing /ˈpækɪdʒɪŋ; ˈpækɪdʒɪŋ/ *n* [U] **1** material used to cover a product that is sold in a shop 包装材料: *Packaging adds to the cost of food.* 包装材料增加了食品的成本。**2** [U] the process of wrapping food for sale 包装; 打包: *Prepacked bacon carries the date of packaging.* 预先包装好的熏肉均有包装日期。**3** a way of making a plan or a politician seem better than they are〔对某项计划或某个政客进行的〕包装, 美化: *the imaginative packaging of an unacceptable tax* 对于一项难以接受的税收进行的富于想象力的包装

pack an·i·mal /ˈ· ˌ· · ·/ *n* [C] an animal, such as a horse, used for carrying heavy loads 驮畜〈如马〉

packed /pækt; pækt/ *adj* **1** extremely full of people 挤满人的, 非常拥挤的: *a packed dance floor* 挤满人的舞池 **2 packed with/packed full of** containing a lot of a particular kind of thing 充满…的; 含有很多…的: *a new magazine packed with exciting recipes* 内有很多诱人食谱的新杂志 **3** [not before noun 不用于名词前] if you are packed, you have put everything you need into boxes or cases before going somewhere 收拾好行李的 **4 loosely packed** packed without being pressed closely together 包装松散的: *loosely packed cigarettes* 包装松散的香烟 **5 tightly packed** pressed into a small space 包装密实的; 压得紧密的: *tightly packed fibres* 压得紧实的纤维

packed lunch /ˌ· ˈ·/ *n* [C] *BrE* a cold meal of SANDWICHes, fruit etc packed into a box【英】〔三明治、水果等〕盒装午餐

packed out /ˌ· ˈ·/ *adj* [not before noun 不用于名词前] *informal* a cinema, restaurant etc that is packed out is completely full【非正式】〔电影院、餐馆等〕挤得满满的, 满座的

pack·er /ˈpækə; ˈpækə/ *n* [C] someone who works in a factory, preparing food and putting it into containers 包装工, 打包工; 装罐头食品的工人

pack·et /ˈpækɪt; ˈpækɪt/ *n* [C] **1** *BrE* a small container, usually made of paper, with several things of the same kind in it【英】〔通常用纸制作的〕小包, 小盒, 小袋; PACK *AmE*【美】: **[+of]** *a packet of envelopes* 一扎信封 | *a packet of cigarettes* 一包香烟 **2** a very small packet like an envelope〔像信封一样的〕小包: *a packet of seeds* 一包种子 —see picture at 参见 CONTAINER 图 **3 cost a packet** *BrE informal* to cost a lot of money【英, 非正式】花费一大笔钱: *That car cost me a packet.* 那辆汽车花了我一大笔钱。**4** a packet boat 定期邮船, 班轮 **5 catch/cop/get/stop a packet** *BrE old-fashioned* to get into serious trouble or receive a severe punishment【英, 过时】陷入严重困境; 受到严厉惩罚

packet boat /ˈ· · ˌ·/ *n* [C] *old-fashioned* a boat that carries mail and usually passengers at regular times【过时】定期邮船, 班轮

packet-switch·ing /ˈ· · ˌ· ·/ *n* [C] a method of sending DATA (=information stored on a computer) on telephone lines, that breaks long messages into pieces and puts them together again when they are received 小包交换法; 封包交换, 分封交换〔一种通过电话线传送电脑数据的方法, 即把长信息分割成片断传送, 在信息收到之后再组合在一起〕

pack horse /ˈ· ˌ·/ *n* [C] a horse used for carrying heavy loads〔用来驮重物的〕驮马

pack ice /ˈ· ˌ·/ *n* [U] sea ice in a large floating mass〔海上的〕大片浮冰, 浮冰群

pack·ing /ˈpækɪŋ; ˈpækɪŋ/ *n* [U] **1** the act of putting things into cases or boxes so that you can send or take them somewhere 包装, 打包, 装箱; 收拾行李: **do the packing** *I'll do my packing the night before we leave.* 我会在我们动身前一晚收拾行李。**2** paper, plastic, cloth etc used for packing things 包装材料〈如纸、塑料、布等〉

packing case /ˈ· · ˌ·/ *n* [C] a large strong wooden box in which things are packed to be sent somewhere or stored 粗板箱, 装货大木箱

pack rat /ˈ· ˌ·/ *n* [C] *AmE* someone who collects and stores things that they do not really need【美】收藏无用东西的人

pack sad·dle /ˈ· ˌ· ·/ *n* [C] a SADDLE[1] (1) that you fasten bags to so that a horse or other animal can carry them 驮鞍

pack trip /ˈ· ˌ·/ *n* [C] *AmE* a trip through the countryside on horses, for fun or as a sport【美】〔为消遣或运动的〕乡间骑马旅行; PONY-TREKKING *BrE*【英】

pact /pækt; pækt/ *n* [C] a formal agreement between two groups, nations, or people, especially to help each other or fight together against an enemy〔尤指团体、国家之间为互相援助或共同抗击敌人而订的正式〕条约, 协定, 协议: **make/sign a pact** *The two countries signed a non-aggression pact.* 这两个国家签署了互不侵犯条约。| **a pact to do sth** *an electoral pact to keep out the Fascists* 为排挤法西斯主义者而订立的选举协议 —see also 另见 SUICIDE PACT

pad[1] /pæd; pæd/ *n* [C]

1 ►**SOFT MATERIAL** 柔软材料◄ something made of or filled with soft material, that is used to protect something or make it more comfortable 垫, 衬垫; 护垫: *She put a sterile pad of cotton over the wound.* 她把一团消过毒的棉花敷在伤口上。| *a*

foam rubber pad 泡沫橡胶衬垫 | **knee/elbow/shoulder pad** (=a pad sewn into someone's clothes to protect their knee etc or make them look bigger) 护膝/护肘/护[垫]肩

2 ▶PAPER 纸◀ several sheets of paper fastened together, used for writing letters, drawing pictures etc 便笺本, 拍纸簿: *a writing pad* 拍纸簿

3 ▶ANIMAL'S FOOT 动物的足◀ the flesh on the bottom of the foot of a cat, dog, etc〔猫、狗等动物的〕肉趾, 爪垫

4 ▶APARTMENT 公寓◀ *informal* a room or apartment where someone lives【非正式】住所, 房间, 公寓: *a bachelor pad in Mayfair* 在〔伦敦〕梅费尔区的单身人士公寓

5 ▶QUIET SOUND 轻声◀ [singular] a soft sound made by someone walking quietly 轻轻走路的声音: *I heard the pad and squeak of footsteps in the snow.* 我听到走在雪地里低沉而吱吱作响的脚步声。

6 ▶WATER PLANT 水生植物◀ *technical* the large floating leaf of some water plants such as the WATER LILY【术语】〔睡莲等水生植物的〕浮叶

7 ▶FOR WOMEN 供妇女用的◀ a soft material like paper, worn by a woman during her PERIOD[1] (4) to take up the blood〔妇女经期使用的〕卫生巾

8 ▶FOR INK 盛墨水用的◀ a piece of material that has been made wet with ink and is used for covering a STAMP[1] (1) with ink; INK PAD 印色盒, 印(泥)台 —see also 另见 LAUNCH PAD, HELICOPTER PAD

pad² *v* **padded, padding 1** [I always+adv/prep] to walk softly and quietly 轻轻地走, 放轻脚步走: *The boy's dog padded after him.* 那个男孩的狗轻轻地跟在他后面。**2** [T] to protect something, shape it, or make it more comfortable by covering or filling it with soft material 给…装衬垫; 用软物覆盖[填塞] **3** [T] *AmE* to dishonestly make bills more expensive than they really are【美】虚报, 夸大〔账目〕: *padding the bills of medicare patients* 虚报医疗保健病人的账目

pad sth ↔ **out** *phr v* [T] to make a sentence, speech etc longer by adding unnecessary words〔用增加不必要的空话来〕拉长, 充斥〔句子、演讲等〕: *The last two chapters are padded out with boring stories.* 最后两章被加进乏味的故事而拉长了。

pad·ded /ˈpædɪd; ˈpædɪd/ *adj* something that is padded is filled or covered with a soft material to make it thicker or more comfortable 装有衬垫的, 有护垫的: *a jacket with padded shoulders* 装垫肩的短上衣

padded cell /ˌ‥ ˈ·/ *n* [C] a special room with thick, soft walls in a MENTAL HOSPITAL, used to stop people who are being violent from hurting themselves〔精神病院里墙上装有护垫以防病人自伤的〕软墙病房, 软壁小室

pad·ding /ˈpædɪŋ; ˈpædɪŋ/ *n* [U] **1** soft material used to fill or cover something to make it softer or more comfortable 衬料, 衬垫, 填料 **2** unnecessary words that are added to make a sentence, speech etc longer 凑篇幅的词句, 冗词赘句

Pad·ding·ton /ˈpædɪŋtən; ˈpædɪŋtən/ a railway station in the western part of central London, from which trains go to the west and southwest of England and to South Wales 帕丁顿站〔伦敦市中心西部一小火车站。该站有开往英格兰西部、西南部和南威尔士的列车〕

Paddington Bear /ˌ‥ ˈ·/ also 又作 **Paddington** the main character in children's stories by the British writer Michael Bond. Paddington is a TEDDY BEAR from Peru who gets lost at Paddington Station in London, and goes to live with an English family. 帕丁顿熊〔英国作家迈克尔·邦德创作的儿童作品中的主角。帕丁顿是一只来自秘鲁的玩具熊, 在伦敦的帕丁顿车站迷了路, 后来跟一个英国家庭在一起生活〕

pad·dle¹ /ˈpædl; ˈpædl/ *n* [C] **1** a short pole that is wide and flat at one end or both ends, used for moving a small boat along〔小船的〕短桨, 桨 —compare 比较 OAR —see picture at 参见 CANOE 图 **2** [singular] *BrE* the action of walking about in water which is not very deep【英】涉水, 蹚水: **have a paddle/go for a paddle** *I'm just going for a quick paddle to cool my feet down.* 我正要去蹚一蹚水使我的脚凉快下来。**3** *AmE* a small round BAT[1] (2b) with a short handle, used for hitting the ball in TABLE TENNIS【美】〔乒乓球的〕球拍 **4** one of the wide blades on the wheel of a PADDLE STEAMER〔明轮船的〕轮叶, 明轮翼 **5** a tool like a flat spoon, used for mixing food〔平匙状〕搅拌器: *a paddle for making the butter* 制作黄油的搅拌棒 **6** *AmE* a piece of wood with a handle, used for hitting a child to punish them【美】〔用于惩罚孩子的〕带柄木板 —see also 另见 DOG PADDLE

paddle² *v* **paddled, paddling 1** [I,T] to move a small light boat through water, using one or more paddles 用桨划〔小船〕: [+**along/upstream/towards**] *We got out the canoe and paddled upstream.* 我们取出独木舟向上游划去。| **paddle sth** *They paddled the canoe across the lake.* 他们划着独木舟过了那个湖。—compare 比较 ROW[3] **2** [I] *BrE* to walk about in water that is not very deep【英】涉水, 蹚水: *The children paddled in the sea.* 孩子们在海边蹚水。—see picture on page A24 参见 A24 页图 **3** [I] to swim by moving your hands and feet up and down〔游泳时用手脚〕拨水 **4** [T] *AmE informal* to hit a child with a piece of wood as a punishment【美, 非正式】用木板打孩子〔作为惩罚〕 **5 paddle your own canoe** *informal* to depend on yourself and no one else【非正式】独立自主; 自力更生

paddle boat /ˈ‥ ·/ *n* [C] a paddle steamer 明轮船

paddle steam·er /ˈ‥ ˌ‥/ *n* [C] *BrE* a STEAMBOAT (=a large boat driven by steam) which is pushed forward by two large wheels at the sides【英】明轮船; SIDE-WHEEL *AmE*【美】

paddling pool /ˈ‥ ·/ *n* [C] *BrE*【英】**1** a small pool, which is not very deep, for children to play in〔供孩子玩水用的〕嬉水池 **2** a plastic container that is filled with water, for small children to play in〔灌水供孩子在里面玩的〕塑料嬉水池; WADING POOL *AmE*【美】

pad·dock /ˈpædək; ˈpædək/ *n* [C] **1** a small field near a house or STABLE in which horses are kept or exercised〔住宅或马厩附近的〕小牧场; 练马场 **2** a place where horses are brought together before a race so that people can look at them〔赛马前的〕马匹检阅场 **3** *AustrE, NZE* a field, especially one with grass【澳, 新西兰】牧场, 草场

Pad·dy /ˈpædɪ; ˈpædi/ *n* [C] *informal* a joking word for an Irishman, that is often considered offensive【非正式】爱尔兰人〔常被认为具冒犯性的戏称〕

pad·dy /ˈpædɪ; ˈpædi/ *n* [C] **1 be in a paddy** *BrE* to be in a bad temper【英】发脾气, 大怒 **2** a paddy field 水稻田

paddy field /ˈ‥ ·/ *n* [C] a field in which rice is grown in water; RICE PADDY 水稻田

paddy wag·on /ˈ‥ ˌ‥/ *n* [C] *AmE informal* a police vehicle【美, 非正式】警车

Pad·e·rew·ski /ˌpædəˈrɛfskɪ; ˌpædəˈrefski/, **Jan** /jæn; jæn/ (1860-1941) a Polish politician who became the first Prime Minister of Poland after World War I. He was also a CLASSICAL musician who played the piano. 帕岱莱夫斯基〔(1860-1941), 波兰政治家, 一战后波兰第一任总理。他还是一位古典钢琴演奏家〕

pad·lock /ˈpædˌlɑk; ˈpædlɒk/ *n* [C] a small lock that you can put on a door, cupboard, bicycle etc〔用于锁门、柜橱、自行车等的〕挂锁, 扣锁 —**padlock** *v* [T]

pa·dre /ˈpɑdrɪ; ˈpɑːdri/ *n* [C] *informal* a priest, especially one in the army【非正式】牧师, 〔尤指〕随军牧师 —see 见 PRIEST (USAGE)

pae·an /ˈpiən; ˈpiːən/ *n* [C] *literary* a happy song of praise, thanks, or victory【文】赞歌; 感恩歌; 凯歌

paed·e·rast *BrE*【英】, **pederast** *AmE*【美】/ˈpɛdəˌræst, ˈpedəræst/ *n* [C] *technical* a man who has sex with a boy【术语】鸡奸者〈指对男童发生性行为的男子〉—**paederasty** *n* [U]

pae·di·a·tri·cian *BrE*【英】, **pediatrician** *AmE*【美】/ˌpidɪəˈtrɪʃən; ˌpiːdiəˈtrɪʃən/ *n* [C] a doctor who looks after children and treats their illnesses 儿科医生

pae·di·at·rics *BrE*【英】, **pediatrics** *AmE*【美】/ˌpidɪˈætrɪks; ˌpiːdiˈætrɪks/ *n* [U] the branch of medicine connected with children and their illnesses 儿科学 —**paediatric** *adj*: *a paediatric hospital* 儿科医院

pae·do·phile *BrE*【英】, **pedophile** *AmE*【美】/ˈpidəfaɪl; ˈpiːdəfaɪl/ *n* [C] someone who is sexually attracted to young children 恋童癖患者

pa·el·la /pɑˈɛlə; paɪˈelə/ *n* [U] a Spanish dish of rice cooked with pieces of meat, fish, and vegetables〔用肉、鱼和蔬菜烹制的〕西班牙肉菜饭, 西班牙什锦饭

pa·gan¹ /ˈpegən; ˈpeɪgən/ *adj* pagan religious beliefs and customs do not belong to any of the main religions of the world, and may come from a time before these religions 异教的: *Christmas is held around the time of an old pagan festival.* 圣诞节是在一个旧的异教节日前后。

pagan² *n* [C] **1** someone who believes in a pagan religion 异教徒 **2** *humorous* someone who has few or no religious beliefs【幽默】无宗教信仰的人 —**paganism** *n* [U]

Pag·a·ni·ni /ˌpægəˈninɪ; ˌpægəˈniːni/, **Nic·co·lò** /ˈnɪkəlo; ˈnɪkələʊ/ (1782-1840) an Italian VIOLIN player and COMPOSER who was one of the greatest violin players ever 帕格尼尼〔(1782-1840), 意大利小提琴演奏家、作曲家, 有史以来最伟大的小提琴演奏家之一〕

page¹ /pedʒ; peɪdʒ/ *n* [C]

1 ▶PAPER 纸◀ one side of a sheet of paper in a book, newspaper etc, or the sheet of paper itself〔书、报纸等的〕页; 〔纸的〕一

张: *There's a picture on the next page.* 下一页有一幅图画。| *I've made several pages of notes.* 我已经做了好几页笔记。| *an eight-page booklet* 一本八页的小册子 | **front/back page** (=of a newspaper)〔报纸的〕头版/末版 *The story was all over the front page.* 这篇报道占据了整个头版。| **see/turn to page 5/20 etc** *See page 5 for further details.* 详情见第五页。| **turn a page** *idly turning the pages* 懒洋洋地翻阅 | **the opposite/facing page** *the diagram on the facing page* 在对页上的示意图 | **over the page** (=on the next page) 在下页 | **the sports pages/the fashion page etc** (=part of a newspaper)〔报纸的〕体育版/时尚版等 | **a blank page** (=a page that is empty) 空白页

2 ►COMPUTER 电脑◄ **a)** a piece of TEXT (=writing) or a picture on a computer screen that will fill one side of a piece of paper when it is printed 页〔指电脑屏幕上可打满一页纸的文本或图片〕 **b)** all the text that can be seen at one time on a computer screen 页面〔指电脑屏幕上一次所见的所有文本内容〕

3 ►BOY 男孩◄ a PAGEBOY (1,2) 男侍童

4 ►MIDDLE AGES 中世纪◄ a boy who served a KNIGHT during the Middle Ages as part of his training to become a knight himself〔中世纪为接受骑士训练并服侍某个骑士的〕学习骑士

5 ►STUDENT 学生◄ *AmE* a student who works as a helper to a member of the US Congress【美】〔美国国会成员的〕青年听差

6 page in history an important event or period of time 历史上的一页〔指某重要事件或某段重要时期〕: *a significant page in our country's history* 我们国家历史上重要的一页

7 ►SERVANT 侍从, 仆人◄ *old use* a boy who is a servant to a person of high rank【旧】〔高层人员的〕男侍从

page² *v* [T] **1** to call someone's name out in a public place, especially using a LOUDSPEAKER, in order to find them〔尤指用扩音器在公共场合〕呼喊找〔人〕: *I couldn't find Jenny at the airport, so I had her paged.* 我在机场找不到珍妮, 只好通过扩音器呼叫她。**2** to call someone by sending a message to their PAGER (=a small machine they carry that receives signals)〔通过传呼机〕传呼〔某人〕: *If you need me for anything, just page me.* 如果你需要我做什么, 就传呼我。

page through sth *phr v* [T] *AmE* to look at a book, magazine etc【美】翻阅〔书本、杂志等〕: *paging through old newspapers* 翻看旧报纸

pag·eant /ˈpædʒənt; ˈpædʒənt/ *n* **1** [C] a public show or ceremony, often performed outdoors, with people dressed in beautifully decorated clothes or actors acting historical scenes〔历史性场面的〕(露天) 演出; 盛大庆典; 盛装的游行 **2** [singular] *literary* history or a continuous series of events that are interesting and impressive【文】历史场景; 一系列有趣而难忘的事件: *the dramatic pageant of life in the upland valleys* 高地山谷中富有戏剧性的生活场景 **3** [C] *AmE* a public competition for young women in which their appearance, and sometimes other qualities, are compared and judged; BEAUTY CONTEST【美】选美(竞赛) **4** [U] behaviour or ceremonies which look impressive or grand, but have no real meaning〔无实际意义的〕炫耀; 虚饰

pag·eant·ry /ˈpædʒəntrɪ; ˈpædʒəntri/ *n* [U] impressive ceremonies or events, involving many people wearing special clothes〔许多人穿着特殊服装的〕盛大庆典; 盛况: *the pageantry of a military ceremony* 军事典礼的盛况

page·boy /ˈpedʒbɔɪ; ˈpeɪdʒbɔɪ/ *n* [C] **1** *BrE* a boy chosen to help a BRIDE as part of a wedding ceremony【英】〔婚礼中陪伴新娘的〕男侍童, 男小傧相 **2** *old-fashioned* a boy or young man employed in a hotel, club, theatre etc to deliver messages, carry bags etc【过时】〔酒店、俱乐部、剧院等雇用的〕侍童, 门童; 青年男侍 **3** a style of cutting women's hair in which the hair is cut fairly short and has its ends turned under 娃娃头, 侍童式发型〔一种发梢向内卷曲的女式短发型〕

pag·er /ˈpedʒɚ; ˈpeɪdʒə/ *n* [C] a small machine that you carry in a pocket, that makes short high noises to tell the person who is wearing it that they must telephone someone 传呼机〔可放入口袋, 会发出短且高的声响提醒机主给某人回电话的一种小装置〕

pa·gi·na·tion /ˌpædʒəˈneʃən; ˌpædʒɪˈneɪʃən/ *n* [U] *technical* the process of giving a number to each page of a book, magazine etc【术语】〔书、杂志等的〕页码标注 **—paginate** /ˈpædʒəˌnet; ˈpædʒɪneɪt/ *v* [T]

pa·go·da /pəˈgodə; pəˈgəʊdə/ *n* [C] a Buddhist TEMPLE that has several levels with a decorated roof at each level (佛)塔

pah /pɑ; pɑː/ *interjection* used to show that you disapprove strongly of something 呸, 哼〔表示强烈的不赞同〕

S2 **paid** /ped; peɪd/ the past tense and past participle of PAY —see also 另见 **put paid to** (PUT (19))

paid-up /ˌ· ˈ·◄/ *adj* **1 paid-up member** someone who has paid the money necessary to be a member of a club, political party etc 已缴纳会[党]费的会[党]员 **2 a fully paid-up** used when saying that someone who is definitely a particular kind of person or a member of a particular group 十足的, 绝对的; 忠实的〔用于表示某人确属某种人或某个团体的成员〕: *a fully paid-up heavy metal fan* 十足的重金属音乐迷

Paige /pedʒ; peɪdʒ/, **Satch·ell** /ˈsætʃəl; ˈsætʃəl/ (1906-82) a US BASEBALL player, famous as a PITCHER, who played in the National Negro Leagues from 1926 to 1947, and became one of the first black players in the Major Leagues when he joined the Cleveland Indians team in 1948. 佩奇〔(1906-1982), 美国棒球运动员, 著名投手。1926至1947年间效力于全国黑人棒球联盟, 1948年加盟克利夫兰印第安人队, 成为棒球大联盟的首批黑人球手之一〕

pail /pel; peɪl/ *n* [C] *especially AmE*【尤美】**1** a container with a handle for carrying liquids or used by children when playing on the beach〔用来运送液体或供孩子在海滩上玩耍的〕桶: *a milk pail* 牛奶桶 | *The kids brought shovels and pails to the beach.* 孩子们把铲子和桶带到沙滩上。**2** also 又作 **pail·ful** /-ˌful; -fʊl/ the amount a pail will hold 一桶的量: *It takes about ten pails of water to fill the trough.* 要装满这条槽需要十桶水。

pail·lasse /ˌpælˈjæs; ˈpæliæs/ *n* [C] another spelling of PALLIASSE palliasse 的另一种拼法

S2 W2 **pain¹** /pen; peɪn/ *n*

1 ►PHYSICAL 肉体的◄ [C,U] the feeling you have when part of your body hurts〔肉体上的〕疼, 痛, 疼痛: **be in pain** (=having a pain in part of your body) 疼痛 *Take these tablets if you're in pain.* 要是疼痛就服下这些药片。| **feel pain** *We've given him an anaesthetic so he shouldn't feel any pain.* 我们已给他用了麻醉剂, 所以他不会感到任何疼痛。| **be in great pain** *Her face was contorted and she was clearly in great pain.* 她脸部都扭曲了, 显然在经受着剧烈疼痛。| **severe pain** *She started getting severe back pains and had to stay off work.* 她背部开始剧烈疼痛, 只得停止工作。| **relieve pain** (=stop pain) 缓解疼痛; 止痛 *drugs to relieve the pain* 缓解疼痛的药物, 止痛药 | **ease the pain** (=reduce the pain) 减轻疼痛 | **a sharp pain** (=one that you feel very severely, usually for a short time) 剧烈的疼痛 | **a dull pain** (=one that is not very strong but which continues for a long time) 钝痛 | **have a pain in your chest/leg/back etc** *I've got a terrible pain in my left side.* 我的左肋非常疼。| **labour pains** (=pain felt by women beginning to have a baby)〔分娩时的〕阵痛 —see also 另见 GROWING PAINS (1)

2 ►MENTAL 精神的◄ [C,U] emotional or mental suffering, or a particular experience of this suffering〔感情或精神上的〕痛苦; 痛苦经历: *life with its pleasures and pains* 充满欢乐和痛苦的人生 | **cause (sb) pain/inflict pain on sb** *She hated to say the words, for fear of causing pain.* 她不愿说那些话, 怕引起悲痛之情。

3 a pain in the ass/butt *AmE*【美】also 又作 **pain in the arse/backside** *BrE*【英】*spoken* an impolite expression meaning someone or something extremely annoying【口】令人极其讨厌的人[事物]〔不礼貌的说法〕: *What's wrong with Dave? He's becoming a total pain in the ass.* 戴夫怎么了? 他变得十分令人讨厌。

4 a pain also 又作 **a pain in the neck** *spoken* someone or something that you have to do that is very annoying【口】令人非常讨厌的人[事物]: *My commute to work is a real pain.* 我每天乘车上下班真烦人。| *He's such a pain in the neck.* 他是个非常讨厌的家伙。

5 aches and pains many small pains in various parts of your body 各种各样的疼痛, 周身疼痛: *everyday aches and pains increase* 每天全身疼痛加剧

6 take pains to do sth also 又作 **take pains with/over sth** to make a special effort to do something, or to be very careful in doing something 煞费苦心[尽心竭力]做某事; 小心谨慎地做某事: *Take pains to present a smart, efficient appearance.* 费尽心思表现出聪明能干的样子。

7 be at pains to do sth to be especially careful to do something, or try very hard to do something 小心翼翼地做某事; 费尽苦心[尽心竭力]做某事: *Major and Clinton were clearly at pains to avoid a row.* 很明显, 梅杰和克林顿在尽力避免争吵。

8 for your pains used when saying that you got something, especially an unfairly small payment, as a reward for your efforts 作为辛劳的报酬〔尤指少量报酬〕: *I drive them sixty miles, and I only get a fifty-cent tip for my pains!* 我开车载他们行驶了六十英里, 到头来却只得到五十美分的小费作为酬劳!

9 on/under pain of death at the risk of being killed as punishment 违则处死: *You are sworn to keep the secret, on pain of death.* 你要发誓保守秘密, 违则处死。

This graph shows some of the words most commonly used with the noun **pain**. 本图表所示为含有名词 pain 的一些最常用词组。

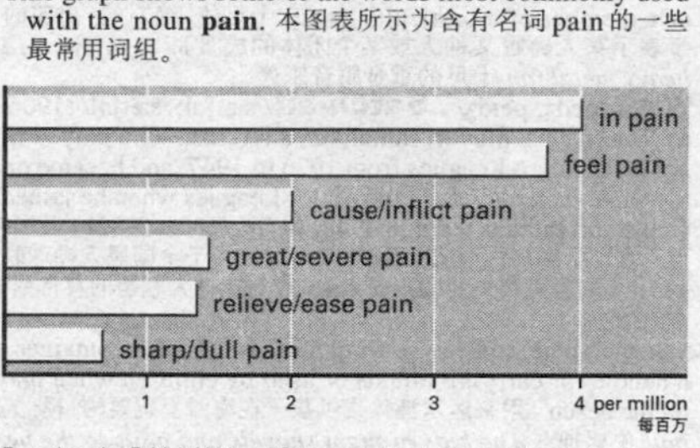

Based on the British National Corpus and the Longman Lancaster Corpus
据英国国家语料库和朗文兰开斯特语料库

pain² *v* [T] **1 it pains sb to do sth** *formal* it is very difficult and upsetting for someone to have to do something【正式】必须做某事使某人难受: *It pains me to leave you.* 离开你使我感到痛苦。**2** *old use* if a part of your body pains you, it hurts【旧】〔身体某一部分〕疼痛

Paine /pen; peɪn/, **Thomas** (1737-1809) a US political PHILOSOPHER and writer, born in England. He supported the American states in their fight to become independent of Britain, and he also supported the French Revolution and had to escape from England to France because of this. His most famous books, which have had a great influence on political thinking, are *The Rights of Man* and *The Age of Reason*. 潘恩〔(1737-1809), 美国政治思想家、作家, 生于英格兰。他支持美国各州为摆脱英国统治争取独立而斗争, 而且还支持法国大革命, 并因此被迫从英格兰逃亡到法国。最有名的著作是《人权论》和《理性时代》, 对政治思想具有重大影响〕

pained /pend; peɪnd/ *adj* worried and upset 痛苦的, 难过的: *Every time she saw us smoking, my mother got a pained look on her face.* 妈妈每次看到我们在抽烟, 脸上就露出难过的样子。

pain·ful /ˈpenfəl; ˈpeɪnfəl/ *adj* **1** making you feel very upset, or very difficult and unpleasant for you 令人痛苦[难受]的; 困难的, 令人不快的: **be painful for sb (to do sth)** *It's still painful for her to talk about the divorce.* 她谈到离婚仍然觉得心里不好受。| **painful memories/experience** *Hearing about the war again brings back painful memories for many people.* 再次听到有关那场战争的事勾起许多人痛苦的回忆。| **painful decision/choice/task etc** *Wendy took the painful decision to switch off their son's life support system.* 温迪痛苦地决定切断儿子的生命维持系统。| **painful to watch/hear etc** *It was painful to hear those words.* 听到那样的话真令人痛心。**2** if part of your body is painful, you feel pain in it〔身体某个部位〕疼痛的: *My leg's still really painful.* 我的腿还很痛。**3** causing physical pain 引起疼痛的, 痛苦的: *painful cosmetic surgery* 痛苦的整容手术 | *Brynner's excruciatingly painful death from cancer* 布林纳极痛苦地死于癌症 **4** very bad and embarrassing for other people to watch, hear etc 难看的; 不好听的; 〔看着或听着〕令人难堪的: *The poor script and bad acting make the film painful to watch.* 拙劣的剧本和糟糕的表演让那部电影十分难看。| *the boy's painful shyness* 那个男孩让人看着难受的羞怯 —**painfulness** *n* [U]

pain·ful·ly /ˈpenfəlɪ; ˈpeɪnfəli/ *adv* **1** with pain or causing pain 疼痛地; (令人)痛苦地: *The prince walked slowly and painfully.* 王子缓慢而痛苦地走着。| *The ball hit him painfully on the shin.* 那个球打在他的胫部使他很痛。**2 painfully obvious/clear/evident** easy to see and disappointing or embarrassing 明显地令人失望; 显而易见地令人尴尬: *It was becoming painfully obvious that I would never be a singer.* 越来越清楚我永远成不了一名歌手, 这真叫人痛心。**3** with a lot of effort and trouble 费力地, 困难地: *all the knowledge that he had so painfully acquired* 他尽心竭力地获得的所有知识 | **painfully slow** *Progress in the negotiations has been painfully slow.* 谈判的进程吃力而缓慢。**4** in a way that makes you sad or upset 令人伤心地, 令人痛苦地: *the painfully early death of someone who was very close to her* 她某个至亲令人痛心的早逝

pain·kill·er /ˈpenˌkɪlɚ; ˈpeɪnˌkɪlə/ *n* [C] a medicine which reduces or removes pain 止痛药, 祛痛药

pain·less /ˈpenlɪs; ˈpeɪnləs/ *adj* **1** causing no pain 无痛的: *A visit to the dentist should be quite painless.* 看牙医应该没什么痛苦。**2** *informal* needing no effort or hard work【非正式】不费力的: *a painless way to learn a foreign language* 一种不费力的学习外语的方法 —**painlessly** *adv*

pains·tak·ing /ˈpenzˌtekɪŋ; ˈpeɪnzˌteɪkɪŋ/ *adj* very careful and thorough 小心的; 费尽心思的; 精心的: *fourteen months of painstaking investigation* 十四个月的艰苦调查 —**painstakingly** *adv*

paint¹ /pent; peɪnt/ *n* **1** [U] a liquid that you put on a surface to make it a particular colour 油漆; 涂料; 颜料: *a can of blue paint* 一罐蓝色油漆 | **a coat of paint** (=a layer of paint) 一层油漆[涂料] *The whole house could do with a fresh coat of paint.* 整个房子需要涂一层新的油漆。| **wet paint** (=used as a warning on a sign) 油漆未干 **2 paints** [plural] a set of small tubes or dry blocks of coloured substance, used for painting pictures〔绘画用的呈管状或块状的〕(一套) 颜料: *oil paints* 油画颜料 **3** [U] *old-fashioned* MAKE-UP【过时】化妆品 S2 W3

paint² *v* **1** [I,T] to put paint on a surface 给…上油漆; 给…涂颜料: *I wear old clothes when I'm painting.* 我油漆东西时穿上旧衣服。| *The ceiling needs painting.* 天花板需要上油漆了。| **paint sth blue/red/green etc** *We painted the door blue.* 我们把那扇门漆成蓝色。**2 a)** [T] to make a picture, design etc using paint〔用颜料〕画; 给…上色: **paint a picture/portrait etc** *Turner is famous for painting landscapes.* 透纳以画风景画而闻名。**b)** [I] to use paint to make pictures or designs〔用颜料〕绘画: **paint in oils/watercolours etc** (=using a particular kind of paint) 画油画/水彩画等 *Jana likes to paint in watercolours.* 贾娜喜欢画水彩画。**c)** [T] to make a picture of someone or something using paint〔用颜料〕画像, 描绘: *I'll paint the view from the window.* 我要画窗外的风景。**3** [T] to put a coloured substance on part of your face or body to make it more attractive〔用化妆品〕涂, 搽, 擦: **paint your lips/fingernails etc** *Her lips and fingernails were painted bright red.* 她把嘴唇和指甲涂成了鲜红色。**4 paint a picture of sth** to describe something in a particular way〔以某种方式〕描绘[描写]某物: **paint a grim/rosy/gloomy picture of sth** *Dickens painted a grim picture of Victorian factory conditions.* 狄更斯描绘了一幅维多利亚时代工厂环境的阴暗画面。**5 paint sth with a broad brush** to describe something without giving many details 对某事物作概括[大致]的描述 —see also 另见 BROADBRUSH **6 paint the town red** *informal* to go out to bars, clubs etc to enjoy yourself【非正式】〔到酒吧、夜总会等处〕痛饮[狂欢]作乐, 寻欢作乐 **7** [T] to put medicine on a part of your body with a brush〔用小刷子〕搽药于 —see also 另见 **not be as black as you are painted** (BLACK¹ (7)) S2 W3

paint sth ↔ **in** *phr v* [T] to fill a space in a picture or add more to it using paint〔用颜料〕在画上加绘, 补画: *The additional figures were painted in at a later date.* 另外的一些人物是后来补画上去的。

paint sth ↔ **out** *phr v* [T] to remove a design, figure etc from a picture or surface by covering it with more paint 用漆[颜料]涂掉, 覆盖: *On the side of the van the company name had been painted out.* 货车侧面的公司名称已用颜料涂掉了。

paint sth ↔ **over** *phr v* [T] to cover a picture or surface with new paint 用新的颜料[涂料]覆盖…的画面[表面]

paint·box /ˈpentˌbɑks; ˈpeɪntbɒks/ *n* [C] a small box containing dry blocks of paint that can be mixed with water 颜料盒

paint·brush /ˈpentˌbrʌʃ; ˈpeɪntbrʌʃ/ *n* [C] a brush for spreading paint on a surface 漆刷; 画笔 —see picture at 参见 BRUSH¹ 图

Painted Des·ert, the /ˌ· ˈ··/ a desert area in Arizona in the southwestern US, east of the Little Colorado River. It is famous for the red, brown, and purple rock surfaces on the PLATEAUS (=large areas of flat land higher than the land around them). 彩绘沙漠, 又译佩恩蒂德沙漠〔美国西南部亚利桑那州一沙漠区, 位于小科罗拉多河以东。该沙漠以遍布高原的红、棕、紫色岩面闻名〕

paint·er /ˈpentɚ; ˈpeɪntə/ *n* [C] **1** someone who paints pictures; ARTIST 画家: *a landscape painter* 风景画家 | *a portrait painter* 肖像画家 **2** someone whose job is painting houses, rooms etc 油漆工 **3** a rope for tying a small boat to a ship or to a post on land 缆索; 系船索

paint·er·ly /ˈpentɚlɪ; ˈpeɪntəli/ *adj* typical of painters or painting 画家的; 美术的; 绘画艺术的: *painterly images* 美术形象

paint·ing /ˈpentɪŋ; ˈpeɪntɪŋ/ *n* **1** [C] a painted picture 图画; 水彩画; 油画: *A large painting hung in the hallway.* 一幅巨大的油画挂在门厅里。**2** [U] the act of making a picture using paint 绘画: *I've always admired O'Keefe's style of painting.* 我一向敬慕奥基夫的绘画风格。**3** [U] the act of covering a wall, house etc with paint〔给墙壁、房屋等〕(上) 油漆: *painting and decorating* 油漆和装修 S3 W2

paint strip·per /ˈ· ˌ··/ *n* [U] a substance used to remove paint from walls, doors etc〔用以清除墙壁、门等上涂料的〕脱漆剂

paint·work /ˋpent͵wɝk; ˈpeɪntwɜːk/ *n* [U] paint on a car, house etc〔汽车、房子等上的〕油漆层，漆面：*the drab office with its faded paintwork and nicotine-stained ceiling* 油漆褪色、天花板染有尼古丁污迹的色调灰暗的办公室

S2 W2 **pair**[1] /pɛr; peə/ *n plural* **pairs** *or* **pair** [C]

1 ▶TROUSERS ETC 裤子等◀ a single thing made of two similar parts that are joined together〔由连在一起的相同两部分构成的〕一副，一把，一条：**a pair of jeans/ trousers/scissors/ glasses etc** *Go put on a clean pair of jeans.* 去穿上一条干净的牛仔裤。| *a new pair of sunglasses* 一副新的太阳镜

2 ▶SHOES ETC 鞋子等◀ two things of the same kind that are used together〔由两个一起使用的同类东西组成的〕一双，一对：**a pair of shoes/socks/gloves etc** *three pairs of socks* 三双袜子 | *a pair of candlesticks* 一对烛台 | **a matching pair** (=two things that are exactly alike) 匹配的一双[对]

3 in pairs in groups of two 两个一组地，成对地，成双地：*OK class, get in pairs for the next activity.* 好，同学们，分成两人一组进行下一个活动。| *earrings sold in pairs* 成对出售的耳环

4 ▶TWO PEOPLE 两个人◀ [singular] two people who are standing or doing something together, or are connected with each other in some way〔站在一起或合做某事或相互关联的〕两个，一对〔人〕：**[+of]** *a pair of dancers* 一对舞伴 | *a pair of scruffy kids* 两个邋遢的孩子

5 the pair of you/them *BrE spoken* used when you are angry or annoyed【英口】你们/他们两个〔用于生气或厌烦时〕：*Oh get out, the pair of you.* 喂，走开，你们两个。| *They're crooks, the pair of them.* 他们是一对骗子。

6 ▶TWO ANIMALS 两个动物◀ [singular] **a)** two animals, one male and one female, that come together to have sex 雌雄成对的动物：**[+of]** *a pair of doves* 一对鸽子 | *the mating pair* 交配的一对 **b)** *old use* two horses that work together【旧】〔一起干活的〕两匹马，双套马：*a carriage and pair* 双驾马车

7 I've only got one pair of hands *spoken* used to say that you are busy and cannot do any more than you are doing【口】我只有一双手〔意指干不了更多的工作〕

8 ▶CARDS 纸牌◀ two PLAYING CARDS which have the same value 两张同点的牌，〔牌的〕一对：**[+of]** *a pair of jacks*〔牌中的〕一对杰克

9 the happy pair two people who have just become married 新婚夫妇

USAGE NOTE 用法说明：PAIR

WORD CHOICE 词语辨析：**pair, couple**

A **pair** is a set of two things which are joined or normally used together, or two people who work or do something together. pair 指两件连在一起或通常一起使用的物品，或指两个一起工作或合做某事的人：*a pair of jeans/slippers* 一条牛仔裤/一双拖鞋 | *Drug dealers often work in pairs.* 毒品贩子常常两个人一组。

A **couple** is two or a few things of the same kind. couple 指同类的两个或几个物品：*I've found two/a couple of socks but they aren't a pair.* 我找到了两只袜子，但它们不是一对。| *Can you lend me a couple of dollars (=a few dollars)?* 你能借给我几块钱吗？

Note that two married people or two people in a lasting relationship are a **couple** not a **pair**. 注意，结了婚的两个人或持续保持关系的两个人是 a couple，而不是 a pair：*a childless couple* 没有孩子的一对夫妇

GRAMMAR 语法

Things that come in pairs and are joined can only be counted using the word **pair**, even though they are plural. 成对出现并连在一起的物品即使是复数也只能用 pair 来表示：*two pairs of jeans* 两条牛仔裤 | *a pair of glasses* (NOT 不用 *a glasses*) 一副眼镜 | *both pairs of scissors* 两把剪刀

Things that come in pairs but are not joined can be counted either in pairs or separately. 成对出现但不连在一起的物品可以成对地数，也可以单个地数：*one shoe* 一只鞋 | *two/ both shoes* 两只鞋 | *a pair of shoes* 一双鞋

pair[2] also 又作 **pair up** *v* [I,T usually passive 一般用被动态] to form groups of two or be put into groups of two（使）结成一对；（使）配成一对：**be paired with sb** *We were each paired with a newcomer to help with training.* 我们被安排每人和一名新手组成一对，以帮助他们训练。

pair off *phr v* [I,T] to come together or bring two people together to have a romantic relationship（使）结成一对，（使）结合，（使）结婚：*All the others were pairing off and I was left on my own.* 其他人都在出双入对，就剩我独身一人。| **pair sb off with sb** *They want to pair their daughters off with rich men.* 他们想让自己的女儿都嫁给有钱的男人。

pair up *phr v* [I] **1** to become friends and start to have a relationship 成对，成搭档 **2** to agree to start to work together with someone 同意〔与某人〕一起开始工作，同意〔与某人〕结成搭档

pais·ley /ˋpezlɪ; ˈpeɪzli/ *adj* made from cloth that is covered with a pattern of shapes that look like curved drops of rain 佩斯利涡旋纹花呢的：*a paisley shawl* 佩斯利纹呢披肩 —see picture on page A16 参见 A16 页图

Paisley, the Reverend I·an /ˋiən; ˈiːən/ (1926-) a Northern Irish protestant political leader who speaks very strongly in favour of Northern Ireland remaining part of the United Kingdom 伯斯利〔(1926-)，北爱尔兰新教政治领袖。他极力主张北爱尔兰留在联合王国〕

pa·ja·mas /pəˋdʒæməz; pəˈdʒɑːməz/ *n* [plural] the usual American spelling of PYJAMAS pyjamas 的一般美式拼法 —**pajama** *adj*

Pa·ki /ˋpækɪ; ˈpæki/ *n* [C] *BrE taboo* a very offensive word for a person from Pakistan, or a person born in Britain whose parents were from Pakistan【英讳】〔严重冒犯用语〕巴基斯坦佬，老巴〔指来自巴基斯坦或生在英国但父母来自巴基斯坦的人〕

Pa·kis·tan /͵pækɪˋstæn; ͵pɑːkɪˈstɑːn/ a Muslim country in Asia, west of India and east of Afghanistan and Iran. Population: 144,617,000 (2001). Capital: Islamabad. Pakistan was formed as a new, independent country in 1947, when the British left India and India was divided into separate parts in a process known as 'Partition'. The mainly Hindu part of India became the country now called India, and the mainly Muslim part became Pakistan. Pakistan was also divided into East Pakistan and West Pakistan, but they separated in 1971. East Pakistan became the new country of Bangladesh, and West Pakistan became Pakistan. 巴基斯坦〔亚洲一伊斯兰教国家，位于印度以西，阿富汗和伊朗以东。人口：144,617,000 (2001)，首都：伊斯兰堡。1947年英军撤离印度后，印度实行"印巴分治"。印度按印度教和伊斯兰教分为两个部分，即印度和巴基斯坦。巴基斯坦成了一个新的独立国家，包括东巴基斯坦和西巴基斯坦。1971年，东西巴基斯坦分离，东巴基斯坦成了一个新的国家，即孟加拉国。西巴基斯坦则成为今天的巴基斯坦〕

Pak·i·sta·ni /͵pækɪˋstænɪ; ͵pækɪˈstɑːni◂/ **1** *n* [C] someone from Pakistan 巴基斯坦人 **2** *adj* from or connected with Pakistan 巴基斯坦的；来自巴基斯坦的

pal[1] /pæl; pæl/ *n* [C] **1** *informal* a close friend【非正式】密友，好友：*an old pal of mine* 我的一位老朋友 | *We just weren't pals any more.* 我们只是不再是好朋友了。**2** *spoken* used to address a man in an unfriendly way【口】老兄，小子〔对男性不友好的称呼〕：*Listen, pal, I don't want you hanging around my sister any more.* 听着，小子，我不许你再纠缠我妹妹。

pal[2] *v*

pal around *phr v* [I+with] *AmE* to go to places and do things with someone as a friend【美】〔与某人〕结伴〔去某地或做某事〕：*It was nice having someone to pal around with.* 有人作伴真好。

pal up *phr v* [I+with] *BrE* to become someone's friend【英】〔与某人〕结成朋友：*They palled up while travelling round Europe.* 他们在欧洲旅行时结成朋友。

pal·ace /ˋpælɪs; ˈpælɪ̣s/ *n* [C] **1** often 常作 **Palace** a large grand house where a ruling king or queen, or a British BISHOP or ARCHBISHOP, officially lives 皇宫，宫殿；〔主教或大主教的〕宅邸：*Buckingham Palace* 白金汉宫 **2** a large, grand, beautifully decorated house 富丽堂皇的大房子，豪宅：*The nobles of Florence built splendid palaces.* 佛罗伦萨的贵族建造了许多富丽堂皇的住宅。 W3

Palace, the *BrE* an informal name for Buckingham Palace, used especially to mean the British queen or king and his/her advisers【英】白金汉宫〔非正式叫法，尤用来指英国女王或国王及其顾问〕：*A spokesman for the Palace confirmed that Her Majesty would be visiting South Africa next year.* 白金汉宫发言人证实，女王陛下明年将出访南非。

Palace of West·min·ster, the /͵‥ ˈ‥/ the official name of the Houses of Parliament in London 威斯敏斯特宫〔英国议会大厦正式名称，位于伦敦〕

palace rev·o·lu·tion /͵‥ ‥ˈ‥/ *n* [C] a situation in which a ruler or an important person in a large organization, has their power taken away by the less important people who work with them 宫廷政变

pal·a·din /ˋpælədɪn; ˈpælədɪn/ *n* [C] **1** *literary* a respected person who strongly supports a particular action or opinion; CHAMPION[1] (2)【文】〔强烈支持某项行动或某种看法的〕卫士；捍卫者，拥护者 **2** a KNIGHT (=a soldier of high rank) in the Middle Ages who fought loyally for his prince〔中世纪王公的〕武士，骑士

palaeo- /pelɪə; pæliəʊ/ *prefix* another spelling of PALEO- paleo-的另一种拼法

pal·ae·o·lith·ic /ˌpelɪə`lɪθɪk; ˌpæliəʊ`lɪθɪk◂/ *adj* the British spelling of PALEOLITHIC paleolithic 的英式拼法

pal·ae·on·tol·o·gy /ˌpelɪɑn`tɑlədʒɪ; ˌpæliɒn`tɒlədʒi/ *n* [U] the British spelling of PALEONTOLOGY paleontology 的英式拼法

pal·ais /`pæle; `pæleɪ/ also 又作 **palais de danse**/ˌpæle də `dɑns; ˌpæleɪ də `dɑ:ns/ *n* [C] *BrE* a large public building used for dancing in the past【英】〔旧时的〕大舞厅

pal·an·quin, palankeen/ˌpælən`kin; ˌpælən`ki:n/ *n* [C] a box-shaped container with a seat or bed inside it for one person, carried on poles by other people 轿子

pal·a·ta·ble /`pælətəbḷ; `pælətəbəl/ *adj* **1** having a pleasant or acceptable taste 美味的, 可口的: *a palatable wine* 美味的葡萄酒 **2** something such as an idea, suggestion etc that is palatable is acceptable or pleasant〔主意、建议等〕合意的, 受欢迎的: [+to] *We need to find a compromise that's more palatable to the voters.* 我们需要寻求一种更合选民心意的折中方案。—opposite 反义词 UNPALATABLE —**palatably** *adv*

pal·a·tal /`pælətḷ; `pælətl/ *n* [C] *technical* a CONSONANT[1] (1) sound made by putting your tongue against or near your HARD PALATE【术语】〔辅音中的〕腭音 —**palatal** *adj*

pal·ate /`pælɪt; `pæl¦t/ *n* **1** [C] the ROOF (=top inside part) of the mouth 腭〔口腔的顶盖〕—see also 另见 CLEFT PALATE, HARD PALATE, SOFT PALATE **2** [C,U] the sense of taste 味觉: *a crisp salad to refresh the palate* 鲜嫩爽口的沙拉[色拉] | *too spicy for my palate* 就我的口味来说太辣

pa·la·tial /pə`leʃəl; pə`leɪʃəl/ *adj* very large and beautifully decorated, like a palace 豪华的, 富丽堂皇的, 宫殿似的: *a palatial home* 富丽堂皇的住宅 —**palatially** *adv*

pa·lat·i·nate /pə`lætṇɪt; pə`læt¦n¦t/ *n* [C] an area which in past times was ruled over by a man of high rank who was the representative of a higher ruler 巴拉丁领地〔旧时指享有特权的贵族或伯爵的领地〕

Palau /pə`laʊ; pə`laʊ/ a country consisting of a group of many islands in the western Pacific Ocean, southeast of the Philippines. Population: 190,092 (2001). Capital: Melekeok. 帕劳〔西太平洋一国, 由多个岛屿组成, 位于菲律宾东南。人口: 190,092 (2001), 首都: 梅莱凯奥克〕

pa·la·ver /pə`lævɚ; pə`lɑ:və/ *n* **1** [U, singular] *informal* unnecessary trouble and anxiety over small matters; BOTHER[2] (1); FUSS[1] (1)【非正式】〔不必要的〕麻烦, 不便, 〔琐事引起的〕烦恼: *all the palaver of booking a flight and getting a passport* 订机票和领取护照的麻烦(手续) | *What a palaver!* 真麻烦! **2** [U] *informal* a lot of silly and meaningless talk【非正式】废话, 空谈: *What's all the palaver about?* 这些废话都在说些什么? **3** [C] *old use* a long talk about something important【旧】〔重要事件的长时间〕谈判, 交涉, 商谈

W3 **pale[1]** /pel; peɪl/ *adj* **1** having a much whiter skin colour than usual, especially because you are ill, worried etc〔尤指由于生病、忧虑等而造成肤色〕苍白的: *She suddenly noticed how pale and drawn he looked.* 她突然注意到他看起来那么苍白憔悴。| *a pale complexion* 苍白的脸色 —see picture on page A6 参见 A6 页图 **2** a pale colour is much lighter than the standard colour〔颜色〕浅的, 淡的: **pale blue/pink/green etc** *pale blue curtains* 淡蓝色的窗帘 —compare 比较 DEEP[1] (7), LIGHT[2] (1) **3** pale light is not bright〔光线〕微弱的, 暗淡的: *the pale light of early morning* 晨曦的微光 —**palely** *adv* —**paleness** *n* [U]

pale[2] *v* [I] **1** if your face pales, it becomes much whiter than usual because you have had a shock〔脸色〕变苍白: *Kent's face paled when he saw Rob had a knife.* 肯特看到罗布有把刀子, 顿时面无血色。**2 pale into insignificance** to seem much less important when compared to something else, especially something much worse that has happened〔尤指与更糟的事情相比〕显得微不足道[无足轻重]: *All her anger, her jealousy, paled into insignificance beside this momentous news.* 与这一重大新闻比起来, 她所有的愤怒、嫉妒都显得微不足道了。**3 pale in/by comparison** to seem small or unimportant compared to something else 与…相比显得微不足道, 相形见绌: *This year's profits pale in comparison to last year's.* 今年的利润与去年的相比显得大为逊色。

pale[3] *n* **1 beyond the pale** behaviour that is beyond the pale is offensive or unacceptable〔行为〕不可容忍的, 越轨的 **2** [C] a PALING〔做栅栏用的〕尖板条, 桩

pale ale /ˌ· `·/ *n* [C,U] a type of beer that does not contain much ALCOHOL and is sold in bottles〔酒精含量低的〕淡啤酒

pale·face /`pelˌfes; `peɪlfeɪs/ *n* [C] an insulting word for a white person used by Native Americans in films 白人〔电影中美洲土著印第安人对白人的侮辱性用语〕

paleo-, palaeo- /pelɪo; pæliəʊ/ *prefix technical* extremely ancient, before historical times【术语】非常古老的, 史前的: *paleobotany* 古植物学

pal·e·o·lith·ic, palaeolithic, often 常作 **Paleolithic** /ˌpelɪo`lɪθɪk; ˌpæliəʊ`lɪθɪk◂/ *adj* connected with the earliest period of the STONE AGE (=the period thousands of years ago when people made stone tools and weapons) 旧石器时代的: *a paleolithic axe* 旧石器时代的石斧 —compare 比较 NEOLITHIC

pal·e·on·tol·o·gy, palaeontology /ˌpelɪɑn`tɑlədʒɪ; ˌpæliɒn`tɒlədʒi/ *n* [U] the study of FOSSILS (=ancient animals and plants that have been preserved in rock) 古生物学, 化石学 —**paleontologist** *n* [C]

Pal·es·tine /`pæləsˌtaɪn; `pæl¦staɪn/ a country in the Middle East, which includes the West Bank of the River Jordan, the city of Jericho, and the Gaza Strip. 巴勒斯坦〔中东一国, 区域包括约旦河西岸、杰里科城及加沙地带〕

Palestine Lib·e·ra·tion Or·ga·ni·za·tion, the /ˌ·······, ··/ the full name of the PLO 巴勒斯坦解放组织〔PLO 的全称〕

Palestine Na·tion·al Au·thor·i·ty /ˌ···, ·····/ also 又作 **Palestinian National Authority** the government of the Palestinian people, which controls Gaza and part of the West Bank area 巴勒斯坦民族权力机构〔巴勒斯坦人的政府, 控制着加沙地带和约旦河西岸的部分地区〕

pal·ette /`pælɪt; `pæl¦t/ *n* [C] **1** a board with a curved edge and a hole for your thumb, on which a painter mixes colours〔画家用的〕调色板 **2** [usually singular 一般用单数] *technical* the particular colours used by a painter or for a picture【术语】〔画家或一幅画所用的〕一组颜色; 一套颜料

palette knife /`·· ·/ *n* [C] a thin knife that bends easily and has a rounded end, used in cooking and by painters〔烹调用的〕铲刀; 〔画家用的〕调色刀

pal·frey /`pɔlfrɪ; `pɔ:lfri/ *n* [C] *old use* a horse trained to be ridden, especially by a woman【旧】〔尤指供妇女骑的〕驯马

pa·li·mo·ny /`pæləmonɪ; `pæl¦məni/ *n* [U] *AmE* money that someone is ordered to pay regularly to a former partner, when they have lived together without being married【美】〔非婚同居者分居后一方被判令付给另一方的〕同居生活费

pal·imp·sest /`pælɪmpˌsɛst; `pæl¦mpsest/ *n* [C] an ancient written document which had its original writing rubbed out, not always completely, so that it could be used again〔古时可擦去原有文字供再次使用的〕羊皮纸

pal·in·drome /`pælɪnˌdrom; `pæl¦ndrəʊm/ *n* [C] a word or phrase such as 'deed' or 'level', which is the same when you read it backwards 回文〔指顺读和倒读都一样的词或短语, 如deed或level〕

pal·ing /`pelɪŋ; `peɪlɪŋ/ *n* **1** [C usually plural 一般用复数] a pointed piece of wood used with other pointed pieces in making a fence〔做栅栏用的〕尖板条, 桩 **2 palings** [plural] a fence made out of palings 栅栏, 围篱

pal·i·sade /ˌpælə`sed; ˌpæl¦`seɪd/ *n* [C] **1** a fence made of strong pointed poles, used for defence in past times〔古时用于防御的坚固的〕尖木栅; 栅栏 **2** [plural] also 又作 **palisades** *especially AmE* a line of high straight cliffs, especially along a river or beside the sea【尤美】〔尤指河边或海边的〕一排陡崖

pal·ish /`pelɪʃ; `peɪlɪʃ/ *adj* slightly pale 略带苍白的

pall[1] /pɔl; pɔ:l/ *v* [T +on/upon] if something palls on you, it becomes uninteresting or unpleasant, because you have done, used, heard, or seen it too often or for too long〔因过多、过久而〕失去吸引力, 令人发腻: *Gradually the novelty of city life began to pall.* 渐渐地, 城市生活的新奇之处开始失去它的吸引力。

pall[2] *n* **1 a pall of smoke/dust etc** something heavy or dark, which covers something else, like a cloud 一层烟/灰尘等: *A pall of grey smoke hung over the buildings.* 那些建筑物的上空笼罩着一层灰色的烟幕。**2 cast a pall on/over** to spoil an event or occasion that should have been happy and enjoyable 给〔原本应该高兴和愉快的事情〕蒙上一层阴影: *The drugs scandal cast a pall over the athletics championships.* 违禁药丑闻给那次田径锦标赛蒙上了一层阴影。**3** [C] a large piece of cloth spread over a COFFIN (=box in which a dead body is carried) 棺罩; 柩衣 **4** [C] a COFFIN with a body inside〔内有尸体的〕棺材

pall·bear·er /`pɔlˌbɛrɚ; `pɔ:lˌbeərə/ *n* [C] someone who walks beside a COFFIN (=a box with a dead body inside) or helps to carry it at a funeral〔葬礼中的〕护柩者, 扶灵人, 抬棺者

pal·let /`pælɪt; `pæl¦t/ *n* [C] **1** a large metal plate or flat wooden frame on which heavy goods can be lifted, stored, or moved〔供提起、储存或移动重物用的金属或木制〕托盘, 托板, 货板, 集装架 **2** *old-fashioned* a temporary bed, or a cloth bag filled with STRAW (1a) for sleeping on【过时】临时床铺; 草垫

pal·li·asse, paillasse /ˌpæl`jæs; 'pæliæs/ *n* [C] *old use* a cloth bag filled with STRAW (1a) for sleeping on【旧】草褥, 草垫

pal·li·ate /ˈpælɪˌet; 'pælieɪt/ *v* [T] *formal*【正式】**1** to reduce the unpleasant effects of illness, pain etc without curing them 减轻, 缓和〔病痛等〕**2** to make a bad situation seem better than it really is by giving excuses 掩饰; 为…找借口 —**palliation** /ˌpælɪ`eʃən; ˌpæli'eɪʃən/ *n* [U]

pal·li·a·tive /ˈpælɪˌetɪv; 'pæliətɪv/ *n* [C] *formal*【正式】**1** an action taken to make a bad situation seem better, but which does not solve the problem 缓和(之举): *Promises of reform are mere palliatives.* 改革的承诺只不过是缓兵之计。**2** a medical treatment that will not cure a problem but will reduce the pain 治标之药, 舒缓剂 —**palliative** *adj*: *palliative surgery* 治标手术

pal·lid /ˈpælɪd; 'pælɨd/ *adj* **1** unusually or unhealthily pale 苍白的, 无血色的: *Paul was still pallid and sick.* 保罗仍然脸色苍白, 一副病容。**2** boring, without any excitement 乏味的, 无趣的; 无生气的 —**pallidly** *adv* —**pallidness** *n* [U]

Pall Mall /ˌpæl `mæl; ˌpæl 'mæl/ a wide street in west central London, between Trafalgar Square and St James's Palace, where there are a lot of gentleman's clubs 蓓尔美尔街〔伦敦市中心西面的一条宽阔大街, 位于特拉法尔加广场和圣詹姆斯宫之间, 许多男士俱乐部集中于此〕

pal·lor /ˈpælɚ; 'pælə/ *n* [singular] unhealthy paleness of the skin or face〔肤色或脸色〕苍白: *Her skin had a deathly pallor.* 她的肤色如死一般地苍白。

pal·ly /ˈpælɪ; 'pæli/ *adj* [not before noun 不用于名词前] *informal* very friendly with someone【非正式】与…非常友好的, 亲密的: *She's getting very pally with the boss these days.* 这些日子她与老板相处得很好。| **be pally with sb** *I didn't know you were pally with her.* 我不知道你和她要好。

palm[1] /pɑm; pɑːm/ *n* [C] **1** the inside surface of your hand between the base of your fingers and your wrist 手掌, 手心, 掌部: *He held the pebble in the palm of his hand.* 他把那颗卵石握在手中。**2** a palm tree 棕榈树 **3 hold/have sb in the palm of your hand** to have a strong influence on someone, so that they do what you want them to do 把某人攥在手心里, 完全掌握[控制]某人: *She's got the whole committee in the palm of her hand.* 她已完全控制了整个委员会。**4 read sb's palm** to tell someone what is going to happen to them by looking at their hand 看某人的手相 —see also 另见 **itchy palm** (ITCHY (6)), **cross sb's palm (with silver)** (CROSS[1] (17)), **grease sb's palm** (GREASE[2] (2))

palm[2] *v* [T] to hide something in the palm of your hand, especially when performing a magic trick or stealing something〔尤指变戏法或偷东西时〕把…藏在手心里[藏于手中]

palm off *phr v* [T **palm** sth/sb ↔ **off**] to persuade someone to accept or buy something, especially by deceiving them 哄骗某人接受…, 把…骗卖给: **palm sth off on/onto sb** *The fruit seller palmed some damaged apples off onto an old lady.* 那个水果贩子把一些坏苹果骗卖给了那位老太太。| **palm sth off as** *He tried to palm it off as a real Renoir.* 他企图把那幅画冒充雷诺阿的真迹骗卖出去。| **palm sb off with sth** *They palmed her off with an obsolete computer.* 他们骗她买下了一台已过时的电脑。

Palm Beach /ˌ· `·/ a city in the southeast of Florida in the US, which is a popular tourist centre, especially as a place for rich people to go in the winter 棕榈滩市〔美国佛罗里达州东南部一城市, 为旅游胜地, 冬季富人尤其爱去〕

pal·met·to /pæl`mɛto; pæl'metəʊ/ *n* [C] a small PALM TREE that grows in the south-eastern US〔生长于美国东南部的〕扇形叶矮棕榈, 蒲葵

palm·ist /ˈpɑmɪst; 'pɑːmɨst/ *n* [C] *BrE* someone who claims they can tell what a person is like or what will happen to them, by looking at the palm of their hand【英】看手[掌]相者 —compare 比较 FORTUNE-TELLER

palm·ist·ry /ˈpɑmɪstrɪ; 'pɑːmɨstri/ *n* [U] the art of looking at the palm of a person's hand to tell what they are like or what will happen to them 手[掌]相术

palm oil /ˈ· ·/ *n* [U] the oil obtained from the nut of an African PALM TREE〔非洲油棕榈的〕棕榈油

palm read·ing /ˈ· ˌ··/ *n* [U] palmistry 手[掌]相术 —**palm reader** *n* [C]

Palm Springs /ˌ· `·/ a city to the east of Los Angeles in California, which is popular with rich and famous people 棕榈泉市〔加利福尼亚州洛杉矶以东一城市, 颇受名流富豪喜爱〕

Palm Sun·day /ˌ· `··/ *n* the Sunday before Easter in the Christian Church〔基督教的〕棕榈主日〔指复活节前的星期日〕

palm·top /ˈpɑmtɑp; 'pɑːmtɒp/ *n* [C] a very small computer that you can hold in your hand 掌上型电脑

palm tree /ˈ· ·/ *n* [C] a tropical tree which typically grows near beaches or in deserts, with a long straight trunk and large pointed leaves at the top 棕榈树

palm·y /ˈpɑmɪ; 'pɑːmi/ *adj* used to describe a period of time when people have money and life is good 繁荣的, 兴旺的: *in the palmy days of Elizabeth I* 在伊莉莎白一世时的兴盛时期

Pal·o·mar /ˈpæləmɑr; 'pæləʊmɑː/, **Mount** a mountain near San Diego, California, where the **Mount Palomar Observatory** (=a special building from which scientists study the stars) is based. Its equipment includes a very large telescope. 帕洛马山〔位于加利福尼亚州圣迭戈附近。山上有帕洛马山天文台, 其中有一架巨型望远镜〕

pal·o·mi·no /ˌpælə`mino; ˌpælə'miːnəʊ◂/ *n* [C] a horse of a golden or cream colour, with a white MANE and tail 帕洛米诺马〔毛呈金黄或淡黄色, 有白色鬃毛和尾毛〕

pal·pa·ble /ˈpælpəbḷ; 'pælpəbəl/ *adj formal*【正式】**1** easily and clearly noticed; OBVIOUS (1) 明显的, 显而易见的: *a palpable lie* 明显的谎言 **2** able to be touched or physically felt; TANGIBLE (2) 可触知的, 摸得到的: *an almost palpable atmosphere of mistrust* 几乎一下就能察觉出的不信任气氛 —opposite 反义词 IMPALPABLE —**palpably** *adv*: *What he said was palpably false.* 他的话显然是假的。

pal·pate /ˈpælpet; pæl'peɪt/ *v* [T] *technical* to give someone a medical examination by touching their body【术语】〔检查身体时〕摸, 触: *The doctor palpated his abdomen.* 医生摸了摸他的腹部。—**palpation** /pæl`peʃən; pæl'peɪʃən/ *n* [C,U]

pal·pi·tate /ˈpælpəˌtet; 'pælpɨteɪt/ *v* [I] **1** if your heart palpitates, it beats quickly and irregularly〔心脏〕急速而不规则地跳动, 悸动 **2** to tremble 颤抖, 发抖: [+**with**] *He was positively palpitating with excitement.* 他兴奋得全身发颤。

pal·pi·ta·tions /ˌpælpə`teʃənz; ˌpælpɨ'teɪʃənz/ *n* [plural] irregular or extremely fast beating of your heart, caused by illness or too much effort〔因疾病或劳累引起的〕心悸, 心跳不规则[过速]

pal·sied /ˈpɔlzɪd; 'pɔːlzid/ *adj not technical* suffering from an illness that makes your arms and legs shake because you cannot control your muscles【非术语】〔因患病而〕四肢颤抖的; 麻痹的, 瘫痪的

pal·sy /ˈpɔlzɪ; 'pɔːlzi/ *n* [U] **1** *old use* PARALYSIS (1)【旧】麻痹, 瘫痪 **2** an illness that makes your arms and legs shake because you cannot control your muscles 麻痹性震颤(症) —see also 另见 CEREBRAL PALSY

pal·sy-wal·sy /ˈpɔlzɪ `wɔlzɪ; ˌpælzi 'wælzi/ *adj BrE spoken* very friendly, especially in a way that seems insincere【英口】亲密的, 友好的〔尤指显得不真诚〕; 伪善的

pal·try /ˈpɔltrɪ; 'pɔːltri/ *adj* **1** a paltry amount of something such as money is too small to be useful or important〔钱等〕太少的, 微不足道的: *The management offered us a paltry 3% pay increase.* 资方提出给我们的加薪幅度是微不足道的3%。**2** worthless and silly 无价值的; 愚蠢的: *paltry excuses* 拙劣的借口 | *her paltry little observations on Russia* 她对俄罗斯的毫无价值的评论

pam·pas /ˈpæmpəz; 'pæmpəz/ *n* **the pampas** the large wide flat areas of land covered with grass in some parts of South America 阿根廷草原, 南美大草原

pampas grass /ˈ·· ·/ *n* [U] a kind of tall grass with silver-white feathery flowers 蒲苇

pam·per /ˈpæmpɚ; 'pæmpə/ *v* [T] to look after someone too kindly or very kindly 宠, 娇惯, 过分呵护: *a pampered cat* 被娇养的猫 | *Pamper yourself with a long, luxurious bath.* 好好地泡个澡, 善待一下自己。

Pam·pers /ˈpæmpɚz; 'pæmpəz/ *trademark* a type of NAPPY for babies, which is thrown away after being used, sold in the US and the UK【商标】帮宝适〔一种一次性婴儿纸尿布, 美国、英国均有销售〕

pam·phlet /ˈpæmflɪt; 'pæmflɨt/ *n* [C] a very thin book with paper covers, giving information about something 小册子

pam·phle·teer /ˌpæmflɪ`tɪr; ˌpæmflɨ'tɪə/ *n* [C] someone who writes pamphlets giving political opinions〔涉及政治见解的〕小册子作者

pan-, Pan- /pæn; pæn/ *prefix* including all 全, 总, 泛: *pan-African unity* 泛非团结 | *Pan-Arabism* (=political union of all Arabs) 泛阿拉伯主义

Pan in Greek MYTHOLOGY, the god of fields, forests, and SHEPHERDS. Pan is usually shown in pictures as a man with a goat's horns, ears, and legs, playing the PANPIPES. He is also famous for his strong sexual desire. 潘神〔希腊神话中主土地、森林和牧羊人之神。画中的潘神是一个长着羊角、羊耳朵及羊腿, 吹奏排箫的男子。他还以性欲旺盛出名〕

pans 锅

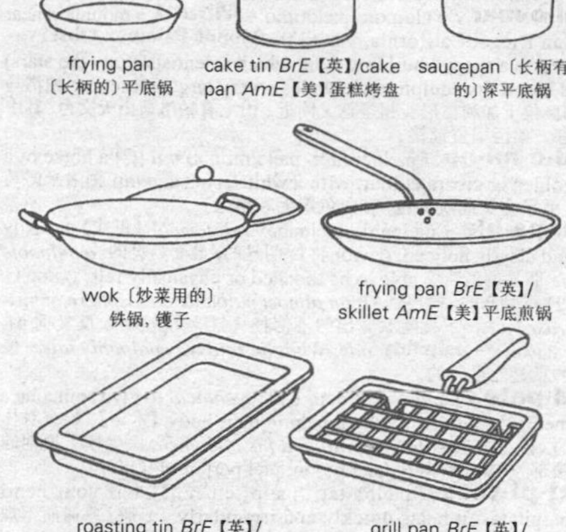

pan¹ /pæn; pæn/ *n* [C]
1 ►FOR COOKING 用于烹饪◄ a round metal container used for cooking usually, with one long handle and a lid; SAUCEPAN〔长柄有盖的〕锅，平底锅：*Cook the pasta in a large pan of boiling salted water.* 在大锅盐开水里煮意大利面。
2 ►FOR BAKING CAKES ETC 用于烘烤糕饼等◄ *AmE* a metal container for baking things in【美】蛋糕烤盘；TIN *BrE*【英】：*a 9" cake pan* 9英寸的蛋糕烤盘
3 ►FOR WEIGHING 用于量重◄ one of the two dishes on a pair of SCALES (=a small weighing machine)〔天平的〕秤盘
4 ►TOILET 厕所◄ *especially BrE* the bowl of a toilet【尤英】抽水马桶，便池
5 ►DRUM 鼓◄ a metal drum that is played in a STEEL BAND〔钢鼓乐队中的〕钢鼓
6 ►FOR FINDING GOLD 用于淘金◄ *AmE* a container used to separate gold from other substances, by washing them in water【美】淘（金）盘
7 go down the pan *BrE slang* to be wasted or become useless or ruined【英俚】被破坏[糟蹋]，变得无用 —see also 另见 FRYING PAN, SKIDPAN, WARMING PAN, **a flash in the pan** (FLASH² (8))

pan² *v* **panned, panning**
1 ►CRITICIZE 批评◄ [T] *informal* to strongly criticize a film, play etc in a newspaper or on television or radio【非正式】〔在报纸、电视或广播上〕严厉批评〔电影、戏剧等〕：*a production that was panned by the critics* 受到评论家严厉批评的一部作品
2 ►CAMERA 摄影[像]机◄ **a)** [I always+adv/prep] if a film or television camera pans in a particular direction, it moves and follows the thing that is being filmed〔制作电影或电视时摄影机随着被拍摄对象移动而〕摇动拍摄，移动拍摄：*The camera panned slowly across the crowd.* 摄影机镜头慢慢移动摇向那群人。**b)** [I, T] to move a camera in this way 使〔摄影机〕摇摄，移动拍摄
3 ►GOLD 金子◄ **a)** [I,T] to wash soil in a pan to separate gold from it 用淘金盘淘洗〔含金砂砾〕：[+for] *panning for gold* 淘金 **b)** also 又作 **pan out, pan off** to get or separate gold in this way〔用淘金盘淘洗的方法〕淘出金子

pan out *phr v* [I] to happen or develop in a particular way〔以某种方式〕发生，进展：*I wonder how it will all pan out.* 我想知道其结果会怎么样。

Pan, Peter —see 见 PETER PAN

pan·a·cea /ˌpænəˋsiə; ˌpænəˈsɪə/ *n* [C] **1** something that people think will make everything better and solve all their problems〔解决所有问题的〕万全之策，解决一切弊病的方法：*Battery-powered cars are not a panacea for the pollution problem.* 以电池为动力的汽车不是解决污染问题的万全之策。**2** a medicine or form of treatment that is supposed to cure any illness 包治百病的药，万灵药

pa·nache /pəˋnæʃ; pəˈnæʃ/ *n* [U] a way of doing things that is exciting and makes them seem easy, and makes other people admire you 神气活现，潇洒：*a designer with flair and panache* 风格独特而潇洒的设计师 | *They sang their songs with great panache.* 他们神气十足地唱着歌。

Pan·a·ma /ˌpænəˋmɑ; ˌpænəˈmɑː◄/ a country on the Isthmus of Panama, a narrow piece of land connecting Central and South America, between Costa Rica and Colombia. Population: 2,846,000 (2001). Capital: Panama City. The Panama Canal, a long narrow stretch of water, was built across the country in 1914 in order to allow ships to sail between the Atlantic and Pacific Oceans. 巴拿马〔位于连接中、南美洲的巴拿马地峡的一个国家，地处哥斯达黎加和哥伦比亚之间。人口：2,846,000（2001），首都：巴拿马城。巴拿马运河是一条横穿全国的狭长水道，建于1914年，船舶借此可在大西洋和太平洋之间通行〕— **Panamanian** /ˌpænəˋmenɪən; ˌpænəˈmeɪniən/ *n, adj*

panama also 又作 **panama hat** /ˌ··ˈ·/ *n* [C] a light hat for men, made from STRAW 巴拿马（式）草帽 —see picture at 参见 HAT 图

Panama Canal /ˌ···ˈ·/ a CANAL (=artificial river) that connects the Pacific and Atlantic Oceans across the Isthmus of Panama, allowing ships to avoid having to sail around the southern part of South America. It opened in 1914, after ten years of building, and is 64 km/40 miles long. 巴拿马运河〔一条连接太平洋和大西洋的运河。它切过巴拿马地峡，船舶不必再绕行南美洲南部。运河工程历时10年，1914年通航，全长64公里或40英里〕

Pan A·mer·i·can Games, the /ˌ··,···ˈ·/ a number of sports competitions which take place every four years in which the countries of South, Central, and North America take part 泛美运动会〔每四年举行一次，包括多项比赛项目。参赛国为南美洲、中美洲及北美洲国家〕

Pan-American High·way, the /ˌ··,···ˈ··/ a road that goes all the way from Canada to Argentina, connecting North, Central, and South America. It is about 25,000 kilometres/16,000 miles long. 泛美公路〔一条从加拿大到阿根廷的公路，贯通北美洲、中美洲和南美洲，全长约25,000公里，即16,000英里〕

pan·a·tel·la /ˌpænəˋtɛlə; ˌpænəˈtelə/ *n* [C] a long thin CIGAR 细长雪茄烟

pan·cake /ˋpænˌkek; ˈpænkeɪk/ *n* **1** [C] *BrE* a very thin, flat round cake made from flour, milk, and eggs, that has been cooked in a flat pan, and is eaten hot【英】薄烤[煎，烙]饼；CREPE *AmE*【美】**2** [C] *AmE* a thick round cake made from flour, milk, and eggs that has been cooked in a flat pan and is eaten for breakfast, often with MAPLE SYRUP; FLAPJACK (2); HOT CAKE【美】〔当早点吃的〕厚煎饼〔通常和枫糖浆一起食用〕**3** [U] very thick MAKE-UP for the face〔化妆用的〕粉饼

Pancake Day /ˈ·· ·/ *n* [C,U] *BrE informal* SHROVE TUESDAY, when people in Britain traditionally eat pancakes【英，非正式】〔按传统吃薄煎饼的〕薄煎饼日〔即忏悔星期二〕

pancake land·ing /ˌ··ˈ··/ *n* [C] an act of bringing an aircraft down to the ground in such a way that it drops flat from a low height〔飞机的〕平坠着陆，平降

pancake roll /ˌ··ˈ·/ *n* [C] *BrE* a SPRING ROLL【英】春卷

Pancake Tues·day /ˌ··ˈ··/ *n* [C,U] Pancake Day 薄煎饼日〔即忏悔星期二〕

pan·cre·as /ˋpæŋkrɪəs; ˈpæŋkriəs/ *n* [C] a GLAND inside your body, near your stomach, that produces INSULIN and a liquid that helps your body to use the food that you eat 胰，胰腺 — **pancreatic** /ˌpæŋkrɪˋætɪk; ˌpæŋkriˈætɪk◄/ *adj* —see picture at 参见 DIGESTIVE SYSTEM 图

pan·da /ˋpændə; ˈpændə/ *n* [C] **1** a large black and white animal that looks like a bear and lives in the mountains of China; GIANT PANDA 大熊猫，大猫熊 **2** a small animal with red-brown fur and a long tail, living in the south-eastern Himalayas〔产于喜马拉雅山东南部的〕小熊猫，小猫熊

Panda car /ˈ·· ·/ *n* [C] *BrE* a small police car used by local police; PATROL CAR【英】巡逻警车

pan·dem·ic /pænˋdɛmɪk; pænˈdemɪk/ *n* [C] *technical* an illness or disease that affects the population of a large area【术语】广泛地区流行的病 —**pandemic** *adj* —compare 比较 ENDEMIC

pan·de·mo·ni·um /ˌpændɪˋmonɪəm; ˌpændɪ̥ˈməʊniəm/ *n* [U] a situation in which there is a lot of noise because people are angry, confused or frightened〔人们因感到愤怒、迷惑或恐惧而引起的〕大混乱，嘈杂，骚乱：*Pandemonium broke out when the results were announced.* 结果公布之后一片混乱。

pan·der /ˋpændɚ; ˈpændə/ *v*

pander to sth/sb *phr v* [T] to give someone what they want, when you know it is not good for them 迎合〔不良需求〕：*newspapers that pander to people's interest in sex* 迎合人们性趣味的报纸

pan·dit /ˋpʌndɪt; ˈpʌndɪt/ *n* [C] a title of respect for a wise man, used in India 博学之士, 学者〔在印度对智者、贤人的尊称〕: *Pandit Nehru* 博学之士尼赫鲁

Pan·do·ra's box /pænˌdorəz ˋbɑks; pænˌdɔːrəz ˈbɒks/ *n* **open Pandora's box** to cause a lot of problems that did not exist before 打开潘多拉的盒子, 引发种种祸患

pane /pen; peɪn/ *n* [C] a sheet of glass used in a window or door〔窗或门上的〕一块玻璃 —see also 另见 WINDOWPANE —see picture on page A7 参见 A7 页图

pan·e·gyr·ic /ˌpænəˋdʒɪrɪk; ˌpænɪˈdʒɪrɪk/ *n* [C+**on/upon**] *formal* a speech or piece of writing that praises someone or something very highly【正式】颂词; 颂文

S1 W2 **pan·el¹** /ˋpænl̩; ˈpænl/ *n* [C]
1 ▶PART 部分◀ a) a flat piece of wood, glass etc with straight sides, which forms part of a door, wall, fence etc〔门、墙、栅栏等的〕镶板, 嵌板; 窗玻璃片: *a stained glass panel* 一块彩色玻璃 **b)** a piece of metal that forms part of the outer structure of a vehicle〔车身的〕金属板 **c)** a piece of material that forms part of a piece of clothing〔衣服上的〕镶条, 饰片
2 ▶GROUP OF PEOPLE 一组人◀ a) a group of people with skills or specialist knowledge who have been chosen to give advice or opinions on a particular subject〔由选定人员组成的〕专门小组; 专题讨论小组: *A panel of experts was consulted.* 专家小组提供了咨询。| *a crime prevention panel* 防止犯罪专门小组 **b)** a group of well-known people who answer questions on a radio or television programme〔由知名人士组成在广播或电视节目中回答问题的〕答问小组: *Let me introduce tonight's panel.* 让我介绍一下今晚的答问小组。—see also 另见 PANELLIST **c)** a group of people who are chosen to listen to a case in a court of law and to decide the result; JURY 陪审团
3 instrument/control panel a board in a car, plane, boat etc on which the controls are fixed〔汽车、飞机、船等的〕仪表板/控制面板
4 ▶PICTURE 图画◀ a thin board with a picture painted on it 画板 —see also 另见 SOLAR PANEL

panel² *v* **panelled, panelling** *BrE*【英】, **paneled, paneling** *AmE*【美】[T usually passive 一般用被动态] to cover or decorate something with flat pieces of wood, glass etc〔用木头、玻璃镶板等〕覆盖; 装饰〔某物〕: **be panelled with** *The walls were panelled with oak.* 这些墙壁都镶着橡木板。| **oak-panelled/glass-panelled etc** *an oak-panelled library* 镶有橡木板的图书馆

panel-beat·er /ˈ· ·, ·ˌ/ *n* [C] *BrE* someone whose job is to repair the outer structure of cars, for example after an accident, by beating the metal with a hammer【英】汽车板金工

pan·el·ling *BrE*【英】, **paneling** *AmE*【美】/ˋpænl̩ɪŋ; ˈpænəl-ɪŋ/ *n* [U] wood, especially in long or square pieces, used to decorate walls etc〔用于装饰墙壁的〕嵌板, 镶板: *oak panelling* 橡木镶板

pan·el·list *BrE*【英】, **panelist** *AmE*【美】/ˋpænl̩ɪst; ˈpænəl-ɪst/ *n* [C] one of a group of well-known people who answer questions on a radio or television programme 答问小组成员〔在广播或电视节目中回答问题的一组知名人士之一〕

panel pin /ˈ·· ·/ *n* [C] a short, thin nail used for fastening thin pieces of wood together〔用来把薄木板钉在一起的短而细的〕镶板钉

panel truck /ˈ·· ·/ *n* [C] *AmE* a small motor vehicle used for delivering goods【美】小型货车

pang /pæŋ; pæŋ/ *n* [C] a sudden feeling of pain, sadness etc 一阵剧痛; 一阵伤心: [+**of**] *pangs of jealousy* 一阵阵忌妒 | *hunger pangs* 饥饿引起的阵阵剧痛

Pan·gae·a /pænˋdʒiə; pænˈdʒiːə/ the very large area of land that existed as the only land on Earth about 300-225 million years ago, before it broke apart to form two large land masses, called Laurasia and Gondwanaland. These later broke apart to form the modern continents. 盘古大陆, 原始大陆, 泛古陆〔约3亿至2.25亿年前地球上唯一一块巨大陆地。这块大陆后来断裂为两大块, 分别称作劳亚古陆和冈瓦纳古陆。这两块大陆继续分裂, 形成现在的几个大洲〕

pan·han·dle¹ /ˋpænˌhændl̩; ˈpænˌhændl/ *n* [C] *AmE* a thin piece of land that is joined to a larger area like the handle of a pan【美】〔锅柄状的〕狭长地带: *the Alaskan panhandle* 阿拉斯加狭长地带

panhandle² *v* [I] *especially AmE* to ask for money in the streets【尤美】在街上行乞, 乞讨: *a ban on panhandling in New York's subway* 纽约地铁里的行乞禁令 —**panhandler** *n* [C]

S3 **pan·ic¹** /ˋpænɪk; ˈpænɪk/ *n* **1** [C usually singular 一般用单数, U] a sudden strong feeling of fear or nervousness that makes you unable to think clearly or behave sensibly 惶恐, 惊恐, 惊慌: **get into a panic/be thrown into (a) panic** *She got into a real panic when she thought she'd lost the tickets.* 她十分惊慌, 以为自己把入场券丢了。| **in (a) panic** *Shoppers fled the street in panic after two bombs exploded in central London.* 两枚炸弹在伦敦市中心爆炸之后, 购物者惊慌失措地逃离了那条街。| **panic attack** *Philip sometimes gets panic attacks and can't breathe properly.* 菲利普有时会突然恐慌起来, 不能正常呼吸。**2** [C usually singular 一般用单数, U] a situation in which people are suddenly made very anxious, and make quick decisions without thinking carefully 大恐慌: *the recent panic over the contamination of food by listeria and salmonella* 最近对于食物受到李氏杆菌和沙门氏菌污染的恐慌 | **panic buying/selling** *A wave of panic selling in Hong Kong shook the city yesterday.* 昨天香港的恐慌性抛售浪潮震动了整个城市。**3** [singular] *especially BrE* a situation in which there is a lot to do and not much time to do it in【尤英】忙乱, 慌乱: *There was the usual last minute panic just before the deadline.* 在截止时间到来之前的最后一刻, 通常总是一阵忙乱。**4 press/push the panic button** *BrE* to do something quickly without thinking enough about it, because something unexpected or dangerous has suddenly happened【英】惊慌失措, 在紧急情况下慌乱行事 **5 panic stations** *BrE* a state of confused anxiety because something needs to be done urgently【英】紧急慌乱的状态, 惊慌: *It was panic stations here on Friday.* 星期五这里是一片慌乱。

panic² *v* **panicked, panicking** [I, T] to suddenly become so frightened that you cannot think clearly or behave sensibly, or to make someone do this (使)恐慌, (使)惊慌失措: *The crowd panicked at the sound of the gunfire.* 炮火声一响, 群众便惊慌失措。| *He panicked thinking it was a shark.* 他以为那是一条鲨鱼, 因而惊慌起来。| **Don't panic!** (=used to tell people to stay calm) 别慌! | **panic sb into doing sth** *The protests became more violent and many landowners were panicked into leaving the country.* 抗议愈演愈烈, 许多地主慌忙地离开了那个国家。

pan·ic·ky /ˋpænɪkɪ; ˈpænɪki/ *adj informal* very nervous or anxious【非正式】惊惶的, 紧张不安的: *Emily always gets panicky about exams.* 埃米莉总是害怕考试。

panic-strick·en /ˈ·· ˌ··/ *adj* so frightened that you cannot think clearly or behave sensibly 惊惶失措的, 恐慌不已的: *the panic-stricken faces of the hostages* 那些人质惶恐不安的表情

Pank·hurst /ˋpæŋkhɝst; ˈpæŋkhɜːst/, **Mrs Em·me·line** /ˋɛməlin; ˈeməliːn/ (1858-1928) a famous member of the British SUFFRAGETTES, who fought for women's rights, especially the vote, in Britian. She was put in prison many times for her actions. Her daughters, **Christobel** and **Sylvia**, were also suffragettes and worked for the rights of poor women. 潘克赫斯特夫人〔(1858-1928), 英国著名的女权运动代表人物, 曾为妇女的权利尤其是投票权而斗争, 并因此多次入狱。她的女儿克里斯托贝尔和西尔维亚也为妇女投票权与贫穷妇女的权利而奋斗〕

pan·ni·er /ˋpænɪɚ; ˈpæniə/ *n* [C] **1** one of a pair of baskets or bags carried one on each side of an animal or a bicycle〔挂在动物或脚踏车两边的〕驮篮, 挂篮; 挂包 **2** a basket used to carry a load on someone's back 背篓

pan·ni·kin /ˋpænəkɪn; ˈpænɪkɪn/ *n* [C] *BrE old use* a small metal drinking cup【英旧】金属小杯

pan·o·ply /ˋpænəplɪ; ˈpænəpli/ *n* [U+**of**] **1** an impressive show of special clothes, decorations etc, especially at an important ceremony 盛装; 盛大的场面: *the whole panoply of a royal wedding* 王室婚礼的整个盛大场面 **2** a large amount of equipment, weapons etc 大量装备[武器等] —**panoplied** *adj*

pan·o·ra·ma /ˌpænəˋræmə; ˌpænəˈrɑːmə/ *n* [C usually singular 一般用单数] **1** an impressive view of a wide area of land 风景的全貌, 全景: *A breathtaking panorama of mountains and lakes spread out in front of them.* 一大片令人惊叹的湖光山色展现在他们面前。| [+**of**] *a vast panorama of roof tops* 一大片屋顶的全景 **2** a description or series of pictures that shows all the features of a subject, historical period etc 概述, 概论; 概观; 概貌: [+**of**] *a panorama of life in England 400 years ago* 400 年前英格兰生活的概貌 —**panoramic** /ˌpænəˋræmɪk; ˌpænəˈræmɪk◂/ *adj*: *a panoramic view of the valley* 山谷的全景 —**panoramically** /-kl̩ɪ; -kli/ *adv*

pan·pipes /ˋpænˌpaɪps; ˈpænpaɪps/ *n* [plural] a simple musical instrument made of several short wooden pipes of different lengths, that are played by blowing across their open ends 排箫; 潘神箫

pan·sy /ˋpænzɪ; ˈpænzi/ *n* [C] **1** a small garden plant with flat brightly coloured flowers 三色堇, 三色紫罗兰 **2** *informal* an insulting word for a man who seems weak and too much like a woman【非正式】脂粉[女人]气的男子〔称呼男子的侮辱性词语〕

pant /pænt; pænt/ *v* **1** [I] to breathe quickly with short noisy breaths because you have been running, climbing etc or because it is very hot〔累得或热得〕气喘, 喘息: *He was panting after his exertions.* 他在用力之后累得气喘吁吁。| *The dog lay panting on the doorstep.* 那只狗躺在门阶上喘着气。**2** [T] to say something while panting 喘着气说: *"I can't run any farther," she panted.* 她气喘吁吁地说:"我实在跑不动了。"

pant for sth *phr v* [T] to want something very much 渴望…, 迫切想要…: *He was panting for a chance to speak.* 他渴望得到说话的机会。—**pant** *n* [C]

pan·ta·loons /ˌpæntl̩ˋunz; ˌpæntəˈluːnz/ *n* [plural] long trousers with wide legs, which are gathered in again at the ankles〔裤腿宽大、脚踝处收紧的〕灯笼裤

pan·tech·ni·con /pænˋtɛknɪˌkɑn; pænˈteknɪkən/ *n* [C] *BrE old-fashioned* a REMOVAL VAN【英, 过时】搬运车

pan·the·is·m /ˋpænθiˌɪzəm; ˈpænθi-ɪzəm/ *n* [U] the religious idea that God and the universe are the same thing and that God is present in all natural things 泛神论 —**pantheist** *n* [C] —**pantheistic** /ˌpænθiˋɪstɪk; ˌpænθi-ˈɪstɪk◂/ *adj*

pan·the·on /ˋpænθɪən; ˈpænθiən/ *n* [C] **1** all the gods of a particular people or nation〔某一民族所信奉的〕诸神, 众神: *the Roman pantheon* 罗马众神 **2** *literary* a group of famous and important people【文】〔一批〕名人; 要人: *a leading figure in the pantheon of 20th century designers* 20世纪著名设计师中的领导人物 **3** a TEMPLE built in honour of all gods 万神殿, 万神庙

Pantheon, the a well-preserved building of ancient Rome which was a temple to the gods. It has a DOME which is 43 metres across, and it was built by the Roman emperor Hadrian between AD 118 and 128. 万神殿[庙]〔一座保存完好的古罗马建筑, 用以供奉诸神。该殿有一直径为43米的穹顶, 是罗马大帝哈德良于公元118至128年间建造的〕

pan·ther /ˋpænθɚ; ˈpænθə/ *n plural* **panthers** or **panther** [C] **1** a black LEOPARD 黑豹 **2** *AmE* a COUGAR or JAGUAR【美】美洲狮; 美洲豹

pan·ties /ˋpæntɪz; ˈpæntiz/ *n* [plural] a piece of women's underwear that covers the area between their waist and the top of their legs〔妇女的〕短衬裤, 内裤; KNICKERS *BrE*【英】: *a pair of lacy panties* 一条带花边的短衬裤 —see picture at 参见 UNDERWEAR 图

pan·ti·hose /ˋpæntɪˌhoz; ˈpæntihəʊz/ *n* [plural] *AmE*【美】another spelling of PANTYHOSE pantyhose 的另一种拼法

pan·tile /ˋpænˌtaɪl; ˈpæntaɪl/ *n* [C usually plural 一般用复数] a curved roof TILE〔屋顶的〕波形瓦

pan·to /ˋpænto; ˈpæntəʊ/ *n* [C] *BrE informal* pantomime【英, 非正式】童话剧

pan·to·graph /ˋpæntəˌgræf; ˈpæntəgrɑːf/ *n* [C] **1** an instrument used to make a smaller or larger exact copy of a drawing, plan etc〔绘画、制图等使用的〕缩放仪 **2** the metal structure on top of an electric train that takes power from the wires above the track〔电气列车顶上的〕导电弓架, 受电弓

pan·to·mime /ˋpæntəˌmaɪm; ˈpæntəmaɪm/ *n* **1** [C,U] a type of play for children that is performed in Britain around Christmas, in which traditional stories are performed with jokes, music, and songs〔英国在圣诞节前后演出, 用笑话、音乐和歌曲演绎传统故事的〕童话剧 **2** [C,U] a method of performing using only actions and not words, or a play performed using this method; MIME[1] (1) 哑剧[默剧]表演艺术; 哑剧, 默剧

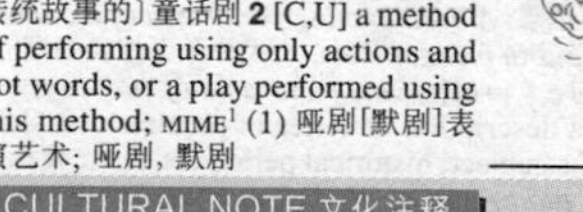

pantomime horse 童话剧中的马

CULTURAL NOTE 文化注释

Pantomimes are based on traditional children's stories, such as *Cinderella*, *Jack and the Beanstalk*, and *Aladdin*, and are performed around Christmas time. They traditionally have three types of characters. The main male character is called the **Principal Boy** and is played by an attractive young woman. The funniest character is the **Dame** who is a fat old woman, played by a man. There is also usually a funny animal character such as a PANTOMIME HORSE. The children who are watching the pantomime are encouraged to sing along with the actors and are also expected to warn them and shout "He's behind you!" when the bad character appears. The actor pretends not to believe them and says "Oh no he isn't!" The children then shout "Oh yes he is!" Most cities have their own pantomimes, and famous singers and television actors often play the main characters. 英国童话剧取材于传统童话, 如《灰姑娘》、《杰克和仙豆茎》和《阿拉丁》等, 在圣诞节前后演出。剧中传统上有三种角色。主要的男性角色叫 Principal Boy (男一号), 由漂亮的女子扮演。最滑稽的、又老又肥的Dame (老太婆) 角色是由一个男人来演。通常还有一个好玩的动物角色, 如童话剧的马。人们鼓励孩子们观看儿童剧时参与互动, 他们和演员一起唱, 坏角色出现的时候他们要大喊: "他在你后面!" 而演员却装作不信, 说: "噢, 不, 他没在这儿!" 孩子们接着喊: "不, 没错, 他就在那儿呢!" 大多数城市都有自己的童话剧, 知名歌手和电视演员常会出演主要角色。

pan·try /ˋpæntrɪ; ˈpæntri/ *n plural* **pantries** [C] **1** a very small room in a house where food is kept; LARDER〔家庭中的〕食品储藏室 **2** a room in a big house, hotel etc where glasses, dishes etc are kept〔大宅第、酒店等的〕餐具室

pants /pænts; pænts/ *n* [plural] **1** *AmE* a piece of clothing that covers you from your waist to your feet and has a separate part for each leg【美】(长) 裤子; TROUSERS *especially BrE*【尤英】—see graph at 参见 TROUSERS 图表 —see picture on page A17 参见 A17 页图 **2** *BrE* a piece of underwear that covers the area between your waist and the top of your legs【英】短衬裤, 内裤 **3 bore/charm/beat etc the pants off** *spoken* to make you feel very bored, very frightened etc【口】使…厌烦透顶/把…迷倒/把…彻底打败等: *She always bores the pants off me.* 她总是让我厌烦透顶。**4 he/she puts his/her pants on one leg at a time** *AmE spoken* used to say that someone is just like everyone else【美口】他/她也是个普通人: *Go on, ask him for his autograph – he puts his pants on one leg at a time just like you do.* 去吧, 问他要一个亲笔签名——他和你一个样子, 没什么特别的。**5 be in short pants** *informal* to still be a very young boy【非正式】还是小孩, 未成年: *I've known Eric since he was in short pants.* 埃里克还是小孩子时我就认识他了。—see also 另见 **by the seat of your pants** (SEAT[1] (9)), **catch sb with their pants down** (CATCH[1] (3)), **wear the pants/trousers** (WEAR[1] (8))

pant·suit /ˋpæntsut; ˈpæntsuːt/ *n* [C] *AmE*【美】女式裤套装; a TROUSER SUIT *BrE*【英】

pan·ty·hose, pantihose /ˋpæntɪˌhoz; ˈpæntihəʊz/ *n* [plural] *AmE* a very thin piece of women's clothing that covers their legs from the toes to the waist and is usually worn with dresses or skirts【美】(女用) 连裤袜; TIGHTS *BrE*【英】

pan·ty·lin·er /ˋpæntɪˌlaɪnɚ; ˈpæntilaɪnə/ *n* [C] a very thin SANITARY PAD〔薄型的〕卫生护垫

pap /pæp; pæp/ *n* [U] **1** books, television programmes etc that people read or watch for entertainment but which have no serious value〔无甚价值的〕消遣性读物; 娱乐节目: *Telly snobs dismiss the show as lightweight pap.* 自以为对电视在行的人轻率地把这个节目视为思想浅薄的娱乐节目。**2** very soft food eaten by babies or sick people〔婴儿或病人吃的〕软食, 半流质食物 —see also 另见 PAP SMEAR

pap·a /ˋpɑpə; pəˈpɑː/ *n* [C] *AmE or old-fashioned BrE* a way of talking about your father【美或过时, 英】爸爸: *Good morning, Papa!* 早上好, 爸爸!

pa·pa·cy /ˋpepəsɪ; ˈpeɪpəsi/ *n* **1 the papacy** the position and authority of the POPE 教皇的职位; 教皇的职权 **2** [U] the time during which a particular POPE is in power 教皇的任期

Papa Doc /ˌpɑpə ˋdɑk; ˌpɑːpə ˈdɒk/ an informal name for François Duvalier, the President of Haiti from 1957 to 1971 爸爸医生〔弗朗索瓦·杜瓦利埃的绰号。他1957至1971年间任海地总统〕

pap·a·dum /ˋpæpədəm; ˈpæpədəm/ *n* [C] another spelling of POPADUM popadum 的另一种拼法

pa·pal /ˋpepl̩; ˈpeɪpəl/ *adj* [only before noun 仅用于名词前] connected with or belonging to the POPE 教皇的: *papal authority* 教皇的权威

pap·a·raz·zi /ˌpɑpəˋrɑtsɪ; ˌpæpəˈrætsi/ *n* [plural] newspaper writers or photographers who follow famous people 追逐名人的 (摄影) 记者, 狗仔队

CULTURAL NOTE 文化注释

The paparazzi became very unpopular after the death of Diana, Princess of Wales in 1997, because it was thought that they had followed her continuously and made it impossible for her to have a private life. Some people even believed they were partly responsible for causing her death by chasing her car in Paris. 威尔士王妃戴安娜1997年去

世后，人们对跟踪拍摄名人的狗仔队变得极为反感。人们认为正是这些狗仔队不断地追踪戴妃，才让她很难有私人空间。有人甚至认为这些狗仔队对戴妃的死负有部分责任，因为他们在巴黎追逐她所乘坐的汽车，导致了车祸的发生。

pa·pa·ya /pə`paɪə; pə'paɪə/ *n* [C] the large yellow-green fruit of a tropical tree 番木瓜，木瓜 —see picture on page A8 参见A8页图

S1 W1 **pa·per¹** /`pepɚ; 'peɪpə/ *n*

1 ▶FOR WRITING ON 用于在上面书写◀ [U] material in the form of thin sheets that is used for writing on, wrapping things etc 纸: *a piece of paper* 一张纸 | *wrapped in brown paper* 用棕色纸包起来 | **writing/wrapping/drawing paper** *sheets of writing paper* 几张信纸

2 ▶NEWSPAPER 报纸◀ [C] a newspaper 报纸: *Have you seen today's paper?* 你看到今天的报纸了吗？| *Why don't you put an ad in the local paper?* 你为什么不在当地报纸上刊登一则广告呢？| **daily/evening/Sunday paper** *The story was all over the Sunday papers.* 这则报道刊登在周日的所有报纸上。

3 ▶DOCUMENTS/LETTERS 文件/信件◀ **a) papers** [plural] pieces of paper with writing on them that you use in your work, at meetings etc〔工作、会议等上用的〕文件，文献: *I left some important papers in my briefcase.* 我把一些重要的文件遗落在公文包里了。**b)** documents and letters concerning someone's private or public life〔私人的〕文件；书信: *I found this photograph among his private papers.* 我在他的私人书信里找到了这张照片。**c)** official documents such as your PASSPORT, IDENTITY CARD etc 公文文件；证件〈如护照、身份证等〉: *After checking our papers, the border guards let us through.* 边境卫兵检查了我们的证件之后便让我们通过了。—see also 另见 WHITE PAPER, GREEN PAPER, ORDER PAPER

4 on paper a) if you put ideas or information on paper, you write them down 在纸上: *As soon as you have an idea, get it down on paper so you don't forget it.* 一有想法就把它写下来，这样就不会忘记了。**b)** if something seems true on paper, it seems to be true as an idea, but may not be true in a real situation 理论上: *It's a nice idea on paper, but you'll never get it to work.* 这在理论上是个好主意，但你永远无法把它付诸实践。

5 ▶EXAMINATION 考试◀ **a)** [C] *BrE* a set of printed questions used as an examination in a particular subject【英】试卷〔指未做的考卷〕: *an exam paper* 考卷 | **history/French etc paper** *The history paper was really easy.* 那份历史试卷真容易。**b)** the answers that have been written to these questions 试卷〔指已完成的答卷〕: *I have a stack of papers to mark.* 我有一叠试卷要批改。

6 ▶ABOUT A SUBJECT 关于某个主题◀ [C] **a)** a piece of writing or a talk by someone who has made a study of a particular subject〔研究〕论文；讲话: *a scientific paper* 科学论文 | **give a paper on** (=give a talk about) 就…发表讲话，谈一谈… *Professor Usborne gave a paper on recent developments in the field of cognitive psychology.* 厄斯本教授就认知心理学领域的新动态发表了讲话。| **working paper** (=an official document that makes suggestions about a subject or problem) 建议书〔关于一个题目或问题提出建议的正式文件〕 **b)** *especially AmE* a piece of writing that is done as part of a course at school or university【尤美】文章，论文〔学生的作业〕: **[+on]** *I have a paper to write on the Civil War.* 我有一篇关于南北战争的文章要写。

7 ▶FOR WALLS 用于墙壁◀ [C,U] paper for covering and decorating the walls of a room; WALLPAPER 墙纸，壁纸: *We've chosen a floral paper for Pauline's bedroom.* 我们为保利娜的卧室选了一种有花卉图案的墙纸。

8 not worth the paper it is written on/printed on if something such as a contract is not worth the paper it is written on, it has no value because whatever is promised in it will not happen〔合同等〕毫无价值的，不会兑现的 —see also 另见 **put/set pen to paper** (PEN¹ (3)), TOILET PAPER, WASTE PAPER

paper² *adj* [only before noun 仅用于名词前] **1** made of paper 用纸做的，纸制的: *a paper cup* 纸杯 **2 paper qualifications** an expression meaning documents showing that you have passed certain examinations, used specially when you think that someone's experience and knowledge of a subject are more important 纸上资历〔尤用在你认为某人的经验及对某一学科的了解更重要时〕 **3** existing only as an idea but not having any real value 纸上的，有名无实的: *paper profits* 纸上盈利，账面利润 | *paper promises* 一纸空文的保证 **4 paper tiger** an enemy or opponent who seems powerful but actually is not 纸老虎〔指外强中干的敌人或对手〕

paper³ *v* [T] **1** to decorate the walls of a room by covering them with special paper 用墙纸裱糊〔墙壁〕 **2 paper over the cracks/a problem etc** to try to hide disagreements or difficulties 隐瞒[掩盖]分歧/困难等

pa·per·back /`pepɚ͵bæk; 'peɪpəbæk/ *n* [C] a book with a stiff paper cover 平装书，简装书: *a shelf full of paperbacks* 放满了平装书的书架 | **in paperback** *His first novel sold over 20,000 copies in paperback.* 他的第一部小说卖了20,000册平装本。—compare 比较 HARDBACK

pa·per·boy /`pepɚ͵bɔɪ; 'peɪpəbɔɪ/ *n* [C] a boy who delivers newspapers to people's houses 送报的男孩，报童

paper chase /`‥ ˌ/ *n* [C] **1** *especially BrE* a game in which someone runs ahead of a group of people dropping pieces of paper which they have to follow【尤英】逐纸游戏〔跑在前面的人沿途撒下纸屑供后面的一群人循踪追逐〕 **2** *AmE* an attempt to gain a university degree【美】追逐文凭

pa·per·clip /`pepɚ͵klɪp; 'peɪpəklɪp/ *n* [C] a small piece of curved wire used for holding sheets of paper together 曲别针，回形针

paper doll /͵‥ `ˌ/ *n* [C] a piece of stiff paper cut in the shape of a person〔用硬纸剪出的〕纸人，纸娃娃

paper fas·ten·er /`‥ ͵‥ˌ/ *n* [C] *BrE* a small metal object like a button used to hold several pieces of paper together【英】圆形纸夹，曲头钉，平头钉; BRAD *AmE*【美】

paper girl /`‥ ˌ/ *n* [C] a girl who delivers newspapers to people's houses 送报的女孩，女报童

pa·per·hang·er /`pepɚ͵hæŋɚ; 'peɪpə͵hæŋə/ *n* [C] someone whose job is to decorate rooms with WALLPAPER 裱糊工人，糊墙纸工人

paper knife /`‥ ˌ/ *n* [C] *BrE* a knife for opening envelopes【英】拆信刀

paper mon·ey /`‥ ͵‥/ *n* [U] money consisting of small sheets of paper, not coins 纸币

paper-push·er /`‥ ͵‥/ *n* [C] someone whose job is doing unimportant office work〔办公室中处理琐事的〕文书，办事员

paper round /`‥ ˌ/ *n* [C] *BrE* the job of delivering newspapers to a group of houses【英】挨户送报: *Harry used to do a paper round before breakfast.* 哈里过去常常在早餐之前挨家挨户送报。

paper route /`‥ ˌ/ *n* [C] *AmE* a paper round【美】送报路线

paper shop /`‥ ˌ/ *n* [C] *BrE* a shop that sells newspapers and magazines【英】报刊店; NEWSAGENT *AmE*【美】

paper-thin /͵‥ `◂/ *adj* very thin 薄如纸的，极薄的

paper tow·el /͵‥ `‥/ *n* [C] a sheet of soft thick paper that you use to dry your hands (擦手) 纸巾

pa·per·weight /`pepɚ͵wet; 'peɪpəweɪt/ *n* [C] a small heavy object used to hold pieces of paper in place 镇纸，压纸器

pa·per·work /`pepɚ͵wɝk; 'peɪpəwɜːk/ *n* [U] **1** work such as writing letters or reports, which must be done but is not very interesting 日常文书工作〈如写信或写报告等〉: *The job involves a lot of paperwork.* 这项工作涉及大量的文书工作。**2** the documents that you need for a business deal, a journey etc〔商贸、旅行等所需的〕资料，文件: *I'm leaving the solicitors to sort out the paperwork.* 我把整理资料的工作留给律师们去做。

pa·per·y /`pepərɪ; 'peɪpəri/ *adj* something such as skin or leaves that is papery is very dry and thin and a little stiff〔皮肤、树叶等〕像纸的，纸一样的，质地似纸的: *the papery skin of her hands* 她双手像纸一般又干又硬的皮肤

pap·ier-mâ·ché /`pepɚ mə`ʃe; ͵pæpieɪ 'mæʃeɪ/ also 又作 **paper-mâché** *AmE*【美】*n* [U] a soft substance made from a mixture of paper, water, and glue, which becomes hard when it dries and is used for making boxes, pots etc〔制纸箱等用的〕混凝纸浆

pa·pist /`pepɪst; 'peɪpɪ̣st/ *n* [C] an insulting word for a member of the Roman Catholic Church 教皇党〔对天主教徒的侮辱性称呼〕

pa·poose /pæ`pus; pə'puːs/ *n* [C] **1** a type of bag fixed to a frame, used to carry a baby on your back〔背负幼儿用的〕有框架的背袋 **2** *old use* a Native American baby or young child【旧】北美土著婴[幼]儿

pap·py /`pæpɪ; 'pæpi/ *n* [C] *AmE old-fashioned* a father【美，过时】爸爸

pap·ri·ka /pə`prikə; 'pæprɪkə/ *n* [U] a red powder made from a type of SWEET PEPPER, used to give a strong taste to food 辣椒粉

Pap smear /`‥ ˌ/ *n* [C] *AmE* a medical test that takes cells from a woman's CERVIX and examines them for signs of CANCER【美】帕氏涂片试验〔一种探查早期癌变的子宫颈涂片检查〕; SMEAR TEST *BrE*【英】

Pap·u·a New Guin·ea /͵pæpjuə nju `gɪnɪ; ͵pæpuə njuː 'gɪni/ a country in the southwest Pacific Ocean, north of Australia, which includes the eastern half of the island of New Guinea and various small islands. Population: 5,049,000 (2001).

Capital: Port Moresby. 巴布亚新几内亚〔太平洋西南部一国，位于澳大利亚以北。领土包括新几内亚岛的东部一半和其他一些小岛。人口: 5,049,000 (2001)，首都: 莫尔兹比港〕—**Papuan** *n, adj*

pa·py·rus /pəˈpaɪrəs; pəˈpaɪərəs/ *n plural* **papyruses** or **papyri** /-raɪ; -raɪ/ **1** [U] a plant like grass that grows in water 纸莎草 **2** [C,U] a type of paper made from this plant and used in ancient Egypt, or a piece of this paper〔古埃及人用的〕纸莎草纸

par /pɑr; pɑː/ *n* [U] **1** **be on a par (with)** to be at the same level or standard (与…) 水平[标准]相同: *The wages of clerks were on a par with those of manual workers.* 文员的工资和体力劳动者的工资是一样的。**2** **be below/under par a)** to feel a little ill or lacking in energy 感觉有些不舒服，健康状况欠佳；没精神: *I've been feeling a little under par the last couple of weeks.* 几个星期以来我一直感觉有些不舒服。**b)** also 又作 **not be up to par** to be less good than usual or below the proper standard 在一般水平以下；达不到标准: *None of the people who'd auditioned were really up to par.* 试镜的人中没有一个真的达到标准。**3** **be par for the course** to be what you would normally expect to happen 不出所料，意料之中: *The train's late again – I guess that's about par for the course.* 火车又晚点了——我想这几乎是意料中的事。**4** the number of STROKEs a player should take to hit the ball into a hole in the game of GOLF〔高尔夫球击球入洞的〕标准杆数 **5** also 又作 **par value** the value of a STOCK or BOND that is printed on it when it is first sold〔证券或债券的〕票面价值，面值: *a par value of $40 million* 4000 万美元的票面价值 —see also 另见 PAR EXCELLENCE

para- /pærə; pærə/ *prefix* **1** beyond 超: *the paranormal* (=strange unnatural events) 超自然现象 **2** very similar to something 和…相似[接近]: *terrorists wearing paramilitary uniforms* 穿着准军事部队制服的恐怖分子 | *paratyphoid* 副伤寒 **3** connected with a profession and helping more highly trained people 辅助: *paramedical workers such as ambulance drivers* 如救护车司机等医务辅助人员

par·a[1] /ˈpærə; ˈpærə/ *n BrE informal* a PARATROOPER【英，非正式】伞兵

para[2] also 又作 **par** the written abbreviation of 缩写= PARAGRAPH

par·a·ble /ˈpærəbḷ; ˈpærəbəl/ *n* [C] a short simple story that teaches a moral or religious lesson, especially one of the stories told by Jesus in the Bible〔道德或宗教〕说教寓言 (故事)〔尤指《圣经》中耶稣所讲的故事〕

pa·rab·o·la /pəˈræbələ; pəˈræbələ/ *n* [C] *technical* a curve in the shape of the imaginary line a ball makes when it is thrown high in the air and comes down a little distance away【术语】抛物线 —**parabolic** /ˌpærəˈbɑlɪk; ˌpærəˈbɒlɪk◂/ *adj*

par·a·ce·ta·mol /ˌpærəˈsitəmɑl; ˌpærəˈsiːtəmɒl/ *n* [C, U] *BrE* a common drug used to reduce pain, which does not contain ASPIRIN【英】扑热息痛，止痛退热药，对乙酰氨基酚，醋氨酚〔一种不含阿斯匹林的常用镇痛药〕

par·a·chute[1] /ˈpærəˌʃut; ˈpærəʃuːt/ *n* [C] the thing that you wear fastened to your back to make you fall through the air slowly when you jump out of a plane 降落伞: *a parachute jump* 跳伞

parachute 跳伞

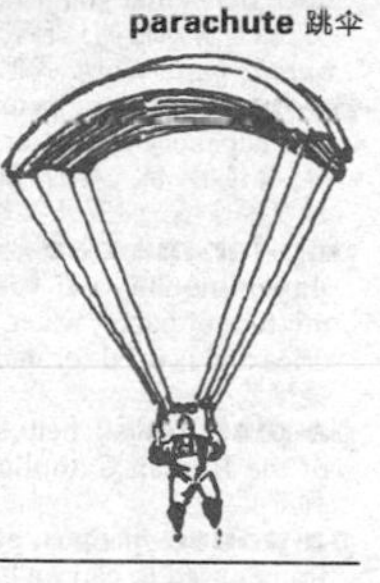

parachute[2] *v* **1** [I always+adv/prep] to jump from a plane using a parachute 跳伞: [+**into/on**] *We parachuted into Vietnam in September 1968.* 我们于1968年9月跳伞降落在越南境内。**2** [T always+adv/prep] to drop something from a plane with a parachute〔用降落伞〕空投: **parachute sth to/into** *It may be possible to parachute supplies to the garrison.* 或许可以给卫戍部队空投补给品。

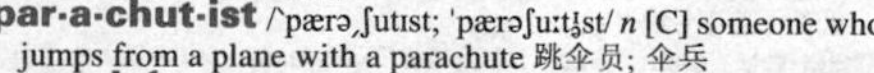

par·a·chut·ist /ˈpærəˌʃutɪst; ˈpærəʃuːtɪst/ *n* [C] someone who jumps from a plane with a parachute 跳伞员；伞兵

pa·rade[1] /pəˈred; pəˈreɪd/ *n* [C] **1** a public celebration when musical bands, brightly decorated vehicles etc move down the street〔庆祝〕游行；列队行进: *a victory parade* 庆祝胜利的游行 **2** a military ceremony in which soldiers stand or march together so that important people can examine them 阅兵式: *a passing-out parade* 军校学生毕业阅兵式 | **be on parade** (=be standing or marching in a parade) 在接受检阅；在列队行进 **3** a line of people moving along so that other people can watch them 列队表演，展示: **fashion parade** (=a show of different styles of clothes) 时装表演 **4** *especially BrE* a street with a row of small shops【尤英】商业街 —see also 另见 IDENTIFICATION PARADE, HIT PARADE

> **CULTURAL NOTE 文化注释**
>
> Many big celebrations in the US include a parade, and some parades are traditional events. Some of the most famous parades that take place every year are Macy's Thanksgiving Day Parade in New York City, and the Rose Parade on New Year's Day in Pasadena, California. Both these parades are shown on television. Parades are also common at special town events, holidays such as the Fourth of July, or for a university's HOMECOMING celebrations. In a parade there are usually MARCHING BANDs, MAJORETTEs, FLOATs, and famous or important people who ride in big cars. 美国的很多大庆典都有一场游行，而有些游行是传统节目。每年都举行的最著名的游行有纽约的梅西公司感恩节大游行和加利福尼亚州帕萨迪纳在元旦这天举行的蔷薇游行，这两场游行都有电视转播。在城市的特别活动或赶在假日时举行游行也很普遍，例如7月4日独立纪念日的游行；此外还有大学校友返校聚会的游行。游行队伍中经常有游行乐队、乐队女指挥、彩车和乘坐大轿车的要人和名流。

parade[2] *v*

1 ▶CELEBRATE/PROTEST 庆祝/抗议◀ [I always+adv/prep] to walk or march together to celebrate or protest about something 游行；列队行进: [+**around/past etc**] *The marchers paraded peacefully through the center of the capital.* 游行者有秩序地列队穿过首都中心。

2 ▶SHOW STH 展示某物◀ [T] to show your possessions, knowledge etc in order to make people admire you 夸示，炫耀〔财产、知识等〕: *He loves to parade his knowledge in front of his students.* 他喜欢在学生面前卖弄自己的知识。

3 ▶WALK AROUND 四处走动◀ [I always+adv/prep] to walk around, especially in a way that shows that you want people to notice and admire you 炫耀地走来走去，招摇而过: [+**around/past etc**] *A trio of girls in extremely brief bikinis paraded up and down.* 三个女孩穿着极暴露的比基尼泳装招摇地走来走去。

4 ▶SHOW SB 展示某人◀ [T always+adv/prep] to proudly show someone to other people, often to prove that you have control over them 使示众: *The prisoners were paraded in front of the TV cameras.* 囚犯在电视摄影机前曝光。

5 ▶SOLDIERS 士兵◀ [I,T] if soldiers parade or if an officer parades them, they march together so that an important person can watch them (使) 列队行进接受检阅: *Two thousand of his warriors paraded before him.* 他的两千名武士在他面前列队行进接受检阅。

6 **parade as/be paraded as** if something parades as something else that is better, someone is pretending that it is the other better thing 冒充为/被冒充为: *It's just self-interest parading as concern for your welfare.* 这只是假装关心你幸福的利己表现。

parade ground /.ˈ. ,./ *n* [C] a large flat area where soldiers practise marching or standing together in rows 阅兵场，练兵场

par·a·digm /ˈpærəˌdaɪm; ˈpærədaɪm/ *n* [C] **1** *formal* a very clear or typical example of something【正式】示例，范例，样式: [+**of**] *The Holocaust, to me, is a paradigm of evil.* 纳粹对犹太人的大屠杀在我看来是邪恶的典型。**2** *technical* a model or example that shows how something works or is produced【术语】〔展示工作或制作方法的〕模型，例子 **3** *technical* an example or pattern of a word, showing all its forms in grammar, like child's, children, children's【术语】词形变化 (表) —**paradigmatic** /ˌpærədɪgˈmætɪk; ˌpærədɪgˈmætɪk◂/ *adj* —**paradigmatically** /-klɪ; -kli/ *adv*

par·a·dise /ˈpærəˌdaɪs; ˈpærədaɪs/ *n* **1** [U] a place or situation that is extremely pleasant, beautiful, or enjoyable 极乐 (世界)；至美，至福: *the beautiful Thai holiday paradise of Phuket* 美丽的泰国度假乐园普吉岛 | *The hotel felt like paradise after two weeks of camping.* 两个星期的野营之后，那酒店让人感觉像是天堂。**2** [singular] a place that has everything you need for doing a particular activity〔所需物一应俱全的〕乐园，乐土: *The market is a shopper's paradise.* 这个市场是购物者的天堂。| [+**for**] *Hawaii is a paradise for surfers.* 夏威夷是冲浪者的理想去处。**3** **Paradise** [singular] **a)** Heaven, thought of as the place where God lives and where there is no illness, death, or evil 天堂，天国 **b)** the garden where Adam and Eve lived (=the first humans, according to the Bible)〔《圣经》中人类始祖亚当和夏娃居住的〕伊甸园 —see also 另见 BIRD OF PARADISE, **be living in a fool's paradise** (FOOL[1] (8))

Paradise Lost /,. ... ˈ./ (1667) a long EPIC poem by John Milton which tells the story of Adam and Eve, and why God punished them. The story is continued in a later poem called *Paradise Regained.*《失乐园》〔(1667)，约翰·弥尔顿创作的一

部长篇史诗，讲述亚当与夏娃的故事以及他们被上帝惩罚的原因。这则故事在后来创作的史诗《复乐园》中继续讲述〕

par·a·dox /ˈpærə͵dɑks; ˈpærədɒks/ *n* **1** [C] a situation that seems strange because it involves two ideas or qualities that are very different 自相矛盾(的情况): *It's a paradox that in such a rich country there can be so much poverty.* 在如此富有的国家却有这么多的贫穷现象，真是自相矛盾。**2** [C] a statement that seems impossible because it contains two opposing ideas that are both true 反论，悖论；似非而是的说法[隽语] **3** [U] the use of such statements in writing or speech 反论[悖论]运用，似非而是的隽语运用 —**paradoxical** /͵pærəˋdɑksɪkḷ; ͵pærəˈdɒksɪkəl◂/ *adj*

par·a·dox·i·cally /͵pærəˋdɑksɪklɪ; ͵pærəˈdɒksɪkli/ *adv* in a way that is surprising because it is the opposite of what you would expect 自相矛盾地；反常地: [sentence adverb 句子副词] *Paradoxically, the prohibition of liquor caused an increase in alcoholism.* 十分矛盾的是，禁酒反而导致了酗酒的增加。

par·af·fin /ˈpærəfɪn; ˈpærəfə̇n/ *n* [U] **1** *BrE* an oil used for heating and in lamps, made from PETROLEUM or coal【英】〔取暖、点灯用的〕煤油；KEROSENE *AmE*【美】**2** paraffin wax 石蜡

paraffin wax /ˈ···, ·ˈ/ *n* [U] a soft white substance used for making CANDLES, made from PETROLEUM or coal 石蜡

par·a·glid·ing /ˈpærəˋglaɪdɪŋ; ˈpærə͵glaɪdɪŋ/ *n* [U] a sport in which you jump off a hill and use a PARACHUTE to float back down to the ground 滑翔伞飞行运动，翼伞滑翔运动

par·a·gon /ˈpærə͵gɑn; ˈpærəgən/ *n* [C] someone who is perfect or is extremely brave, good etc 完(美的)人；典范，模范: [+of] *a paragon of virtue* 美德的典范

3 3 **par·a·graph** /ˈpærə͵græf; ˈpærəgrɑːf/ *n* [C] a group of several sentences in a piece of writing, the first sentence of which starts on a new line〔文章的〕段，段落 —**paragraph** *v* [T]

Par·a·guay /ˈpærə͵gwe; ˈpærəgwaɪ/ a country in South America between Brazil and Argentina. Population: 5,734,000 (2001). Capital: Asunción. It has no sea coast and its main industry is farming 巴拉圭〔南美洲一国，位于巴西和阿根廷之间。人口：5,734,000(2001)，首都：亚松森。巴拉圭为内陆国家，以农业为主〕—**Paraguayan** /͵pærəˋgwaɪən; ͵pærəˈgwaɪən/ *n, adj*

par·a·keet /ˈpærə͵kit; ˈpærəkiːt/ *n* [C] a small brightly coloured bird with a long tail 长尾(小)鹦鹉

par·a·le·gal /͵pærəˋligḷ; ͵pærəˈliːgəl/ *n* [C] *AmE* LEGAL EXECUTIVE【美】法律事务助理；律师助手

par·al·lel¹ /ˈpærə͵lɛl; ˈpærəlel/ *n* [C] **1** a connection between two things, especially things that exist or happen in different places or at different times〔尤指不同地点或不同时间的两事物之间的〕联系，相似(之处): [+between] *There are certain parallels between Europe today and 100 years ago.* 今天的欧洲和100年前的欧洲存在某些相似之处。| [+with] *The study of philosophy has close parallels with the study of linguistics.* 哲学研究和语言学研究非常相似。| **draw a parallel between** (=show that two things are similar) 在…之间作比较〔以显示其相似处〕*The book draws a parallel between ancient and modern theories of education.* 这本书把古代和现代的教育理论作了比较。**2** something that is very similar to something else 和…相似的事物: *Modern styles of painting have their parallels in music and literature.* 现代绘画风格与现代音乐和现代文学的风格有相似之处。| **have no parallel/be without parallel** (=be greater, better, worse etc than anything else) 没有可相比拟的事物；无可匹敌 *a social revolution without parallel in history* 历史上独一无二的社会革命 **3 in parallel with** together with and at the same time as something else 和…一起，和…同时；并行: *private organizations working in parallel with the state education system* 与国家教育体制平行运作的私人机构 **4** an imaginary line drawn on a map of the Earth, that is parallel to the EQUATOR 纬线，纬度圈: *the 38th parallel* 38 度纬线 **5 be in parallel** *technical* if two electrical CIRCUITS (=complete circular paths) are in parallel, they are connected so that any electric current is divided equally between them【术语】〔电路的〕并联

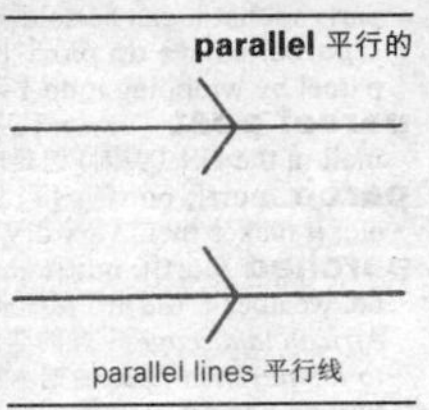

parallel² *adj* **1** two lines that are parallel to each other are the same distance apart along their whole length 平行的，并行的: *Lines AB and CD are parallel.* AB 线和 CD 线平行。| [+to/with] *Parallel with the old fence was a new one of barbed wire.* 和旧栅栏平行的是一排新的带刺铁丝栅栏。| *The road runs parallel to the railway.* 这条公路与铁路(线)相平行。**2** *formal* similar and happening at the same time【正式】相似的；同时发生的: *Social changes in Britain are matched by parallel trends in other countries.* 在英国发生社会变革的同时，其他国家也出现了相似的趋势。

parallel³ *v* [T] *formal*【正式】**1** to be as good as something else 与…相当，与…相匹敌: *a level of economic prosperity paralleled by few other countries* 只有少数几个国家能比得上的经济繁荣水平 **2** to be similar to something else 与…相似: *Does the geology of Mars parallel in any way that of Earth?* 火星和地球的地质状况有什么相似之处吗？

parallel bars /͵···ˈ·/ *n* [plural] two wooden bars that are held parallel to each other on four posts, used in GYMNASTICS (1)〔体操的〕双杠

par·al·lel·is·m /ˈpærəlɛl͵ɪzəm; ˈpærəlelɪzəm/ *n* **1** [U] the state of being PARALLEL with something 平行；类似；对应 **2** [C] a similarity 相似；相似点

par·al·lel·o·gram /͵pærəˋlɛlə͵græm; ͵pærəˈleləgræm/ *n* [C] a flat shape with four sides in which each side is the same length as the side opposite it and parallel to it 平行四边形 —see picture at 参见 SHAPE¹ 图

parallel pro·cess·ing /͵···ˈ··/ *n* [U] *technical* the method of using several computers to work on a single problem at one time【术语】〔电脑〕并行处理(技术)〔用多台电脑一次处理一个问题的方法〕

par·a·lyse *BrE*【英】, **paralyze** *AmE*【美】/ˈpærə͵laɪz; ˈpærəlaɪz/ *v* [T] **1** to make someone lose the ability to move part or all of their body, or to feel anything in it 使瘫痪；使麻痹: *Mrs Burrows had been paralysed by a stroke.* 伯罗斯夫人因中风瘫痪了。**2 be paralysed** to be unable to move, or to deal with a situation, because you are frightened or surprised〔因害怕或惊吓而〕无法动弹；不知所措: *She was paralysed by shock and disbelief.* 她由于震惊和怀疑而不知所措。**3** to make something unable to operate normally 使不能正常运作，使陷入瘫痪: *The electricity failure paralysed the city.* 停电使这个城市陷于瘫痪。

par·a·lysed *BrE*【英】, **paralyzed** *AmE*【美】/ˈpærə͵laɪzd; ˈpærəlaɪzd/ *adj* **1** unable to move part or all of your body or feel things in it 瘫痪的；麻痹的: *The accident left him permanently paralysed.* 那次意外事故使他永久瘫痪了。**2** unable to think clearly or deal with a situation 不知所措的: *paralysed in the face of danger* 面对危险不知所措

pa·ral·y·sis /pəˋræləsɪs; pəˈræləsəs/ *n* [U] **1** the loss of the ability to move all or part of your body or feel things in it 瘫痪；麻痹: *He suffered a stroke and partial paralysis.* 他患了中风，身体局部瘫痪。**2** a state of being unable to take action, make decisions, or operate normally 不知所措；〔行动、决策、运行等〕瘫痪，停顿 —see also 另见 INFANTILE PARALYSIS

par·a·lyt·ic¹ /͵pærəˋlɪtɪk; ͵pærəˈlɪtɪk◂/ *adj* **1** [not before noun 不用于名词前] *BrE informal* very drunk【英，非正式】酩酊大醉的 **2** [only before noun 仅用于名词前] suffering from PARALYSIS 瘫痪的；患麻痹的 —**paralytically** /-klɪ; -kli/ *adv*

paralytic² *n* [C] someone who is PARALYSED 麻痹症患者；瘫痪病人

par·a·lyze /ˈpærə͵laɪz; ˈpærəlaɪz/ the American spelling of PARALYSE paralyse 的美式拼法

par·a·med·ic /͵pærəˋmɛdɪk; ͵pærəˈmedɪk/ *n* [C] someone who has been trained to help people who are hurt or to do medical work, but who is not a doctor or nurse〔非医生或护士的〕护理人员，医务辅助人员

par·a·med·i·cal /͵pærəˋmɛdɪkḷ; ͵pærəˈmedɪkəl◂/ *adj* helping or supporting doctors, nurses, or hospitals 辅助医务的: *paramedical staff* 医务辅助人员

pa·ram·e·ter /pəˋræmətɚ; pəˈræmə̇tə/ *n* [C usually plural 一般用复数] a set of fixed limits that control the way that something should be done 起限定作用的因素；界限，范围: **establish/set/lay down parameters** *The inquiry has to stay within the parameters laid down by Congress.* 调查要局限在国会设定的范围之内。

par·a·mil·i·ta·ry /͵pærəˋmɪlɪ͵tɛrɪ; ͵pærəˈmɪlə̇təri◂/ *adj* [usually before noun 一般用于名词前] **1** a paramilitary organization fights and kills people illegally in order to achieve political aims 准军事的: *extremist paramilitary groups* 极端分子的非法准军事组织 **2** connected with or helping a military organization 与正规军有联系的；辅助正规军的: *Their police have paramilitary duties.* 他们的警察有辅助正规军的职责。—**paramilitary** *n* [C]

Par·a·mount /ˈpærə͵maunt; ˈpærəmaʊnt/ *trademark* a large US film and television company based in Hollywood, which has made many famous films【商标】派拉蒙电影公司〔美国一大型电影电视制作公司，总部设在好莱坞，拍过许多著名影片〕

paramount *adj* more important than anything else 至高无上的, 最重要的: *The interests of the consumer should be paramount.* 消费者的利益应是至高无上的。| **of paramount importance** *A balanced budget is of paramount importance.* 保持预算平衡是最重要的。—**paramountcy** *n* [U]

par·a·mour /ˈpærəˌmʊr; ˈpærəmʊə/ *n* [C] *literary* someone who you have a romantic or sexual relationship with, but who you are not married to; LOVER (2)【文】情人, 情妇[夫]

par·a·noi·a /ˌpærəˈnɔɪə; ˌpærəˈnɔɪə/ *n* [U] **1** an unreasonable belief that you cannot trust other people, or that they are trying to harm you or saying bad things about you 多疑, 瞎猜疑: *No one's blaming her – it's pure paranoia!* 没有人会责怪她——那纯粹是瞎猜疑! **2** *technical* a serious mental illness that makes someone believe that people hate them and treat them badly【术语】偏执狂; 妄想狂

P

par·a·noi·ac /ˌpærəˈnɔɪæk; ˌpærəˈnɔɪæk◂/ *adj* paranoid 多疑的; 患偏执狂的; 患妄想狂的 —**paranoiac** *n* [C]

par·a·noid /ˈpærənɔɪd; ˈpærənɔɪd/ *adj* **1** believing unreasonably that you cannot trust other people, or that they are trying to harm you or are saying bad things about you 多疑的, 疑神疑鬼的: *You think I'm just being paranoid, but something's going on!* 你认为我只是多疑, 但是确实发生了一些事! | *She's getting paranoid about being burgled.* 她总是疑神疑鬼, 怕有人入室盗窃。**2** *technical* suffering from a mental illness that makes you believe that other people are trying to harm you【术语】患偏执狂的; 患妄想狂的

par·a·nor·mal /ˌpærəˈnɔrməl; ˌpærəˈnɔːməl◂/ *adj* **1** paranormal events cannot be explained by science and seem strange and mysterious 不能用科学解释的; 超自然的, 神秘的: *ESP and other paranormal phenomena* 超感知觉及其他超自然现象 **2 the paranormal** these events in general 超自然现象, 超自然事件 —compare 比较 SUPERNATURAL[1]

par·a·pet /ˈpærəpɪt; ˈpærəpɪt/ *n* [C] **1** a low wall at the edge of a high roof, bridge etc (屋顶、桥梁等边上的)矮墙, 护墙 **2** a protective wall of earth or stone built in front of a TRENCH (2) in a war (堑壕前作掩护用的)胸墙

par·a·pher·na·li·a /ˌpærəfəˈnelɪə; ˌpærəfəˈneɪlɪə/ *n* [U] **1** a lot of small things that belong to someone, or are needed for a particular activity 个人随身物品; (某项活动所需的)用具, 装备: *camping paraphernalia* 野营用品 **2** the things and events that are connected with a particular activity (与某项活动有关的)烦琐手续, 复杂程序: *all the usual paraphernalia of bureaucracy* 官僚作风一贯的繁文缛节

par·a·phrase[1] /ˈpærəˌfrez; ˈpærəfreɪz/ *v* [T] to express in a shorter or clearer way what someone has written or said (把书面或口头的文字以简短、清晰的方式)意译, 释义; 改述: *To paraphrase Finkelstein: mathematics is a language, like English.* 芬克尔斯坦所说的意思是: 数学就像英语一样是一门语言。

paraphrase[2] *n* [C] a statement that expresses in a shorter or clearer way what someone has said or written (对一段口头或书面文字的)意译, 释义; 改述

par·a·ple·gi·a /ˌpærəˈplidʒɪə; ˌpærəˈpliːdʒɪə/ *n* [U] inability to move your legs and the lower part of your body 截瘫, 下身瘫痪[麻痹]

par·a·ple·gic /ˌpærəˈplidʒɪk; ˌpærəˈpliːdʒɪk◂/ *n* [C] someone who is unable to move the lower part of their body including their legs 截瘫患者, 下身瘫痪[麻痹]者 —**paraplegic** *adj*

par·a·psy·chol·o·gy /ˌpærəsaɪˈkɑlədʒɪ; ˌpærəsaɪˈkɒlədʒi/ *n* [U] the scientific study of mysterious abilities that some people claim to have, such as knowing what will happen 通灵学, 心理玄学(对于某些人所声称具有的神奇能力的科学研究)

par·a·quat /ˈpærəˌkwɑt; ˈpærəkwɒt/ *n* [U] a strong poison used to kill WEEDs 百草枯(一种强力除草剂)

> **CULTURAL NOTE 文化注释**
>
> In the US, paraquat is remembered for having been used on CANNABIS plants by the government, which led to cannabis users being poisoned. 在美国, 百草枯为人所知是因为政府曾把它喷洒在大麻植株上, 导致大麻吸食者中毒。

par·a·sail·ing /ˈpærəˌselɪŋ; ˈpærəˌseɪlɪŋ/ *n* [U] a sport in which you wear a PARACHUTE and are pulled behind a motor boat so that you sail through the air (由汽船拖引在空中滑翔的)帆伞运动, 水上拖伞运动

par·as·cend·ing /ˈpærəˌsɛndɪŋ; ˈpærəˌsendɪŋ/ *n* [U] a sport in which you wear a PARACHUTE, go up into the sky by being pulled along behind a car, and float back down to the ground (由汽车拖引升到空中然后飘降地面的)拖引式降落伞运动

par·a·site /ˈpærəˌsaɪt; ˈpærəsaɪt/ *n* [C] **1** a plant or animal that lives on or in another plant or animal and gets food from it 寄生植物; 寄生动物, 寄生虫 **2** a lazy person who does not work but depends on other people 靠他人为生的人, 寄生者: *He thinks students are just parasites.* 他认为学生只是靠他人为生的人。

par·a·sit·ic /ˌpærəˈsɪtɪk; ˌpærəˈsɪtɪk◂/ also 又作 **parasitical** /-ˈsɪtɪkl; -ˈsɪtɪkəl/ *adj* **1** living in or on another plant or animal and getting food from them 寄生的: *parasitic fungi* 寄生真菌 **2** a parasitic person is lazy, does no work, and depends on other people (人)寄生虫似的, 靠他人为生的 **3** a parasitic disease is caused by parasites (疾病)由寄生虫引起的 —**parasitically** /-klɪ; -kli/ *adv*

par·a·sol /ˈpærəˌsɔl; ˈpærəsɒl/ *n* [U] a type of UMBRELLA used to provide shade from the sun (遮)阳伞

par·a·troop·er /ˈpærəˌtrupə; ˈpærəˌtruːpə/ *n* [C] a soldier who is trained to jump out of a plane using a PARACHUTE 伞兵

par·a·troops /ˈpærəˌtrups; ˈpærətruːps/ *n* [plural] a group of paratroopers that fights together as a military unit 伞兵部队

par·a·ty·phoid /ˌpærəˈtaɪfɔɪd; ˌpærəˈtaɪfɔɪd/ *n* [U] a disease that causes fever and severe pain in your INTESTINE 副伤寒(可引起高热和剧烈的肠痛)

par·boil /ˈpɑrˌbɔɪl; ˈpɑːbɔɪl/ *v* [T] to boil something until it is partly cooked 把…煮到半熟

par·cel[1] /ˈpɑrsl; ˈpɑːsəl/ *n* [C] **1** *especially BrE* an object that 3
has been wrapped in paper or put in a special envelope, especially so that it can be sent by mail【尤英】(小)包裹; 邮包; PACKAGE[1] (1) *AmE*【美】: *She tied up the parcel with string.* 她用绳子把包裹绑紧。**2** an area of land that is part of a larger area which has been divided up (土地的)一块, 一片(指已被分割的较大块土地的一部分): *a parcel of farmland* 一块农田 **3** *BrE* a small quantity of food that has been wrapped up, usually in PASTRY (1)【英】(通常指油酥点心的)馅: *parcels of cod* 鳕鱼馅 —see also 另见 **be part and parcel of** (PART[1] (25))

parcel[2] *v* **parcelled, parcelling** *BrE*【英】, **parceled, parceling** *AmE*【美】

parcel sth ↔ **out** *phr v* [T] to divide or share something among several people 把…分成; 分配: *Government posts have already been parcelled out among the President's friends.* 政府职位已经在总统的朋友们中间瓜分了。

parcel sth ↔ **off** *phr v* [T] to divide something into small parts so that it can be sold 把…分成小份(待售)

parcel sth ↔ **up** *phr v* [T] *BrE* to make something into a parcel by wrapping it up【英】把…包起来, 把…打包

parcel post /ˈ·· ˌ·/ *n* [U] the system of sending parcels by mail in the US (美国)包裹邮递系统

parch /pɑrtʃ; pɑːtʃ/ *v* [T] if sun or wind parches land, plants etc, it makes them very dry 晒[吹]干; 使焦干[干枯]

parched /pɑrtʃt; pɑːtʃt/ *adj* **1** very dry, especially because of hot weather (尤指由于天气炎热而)焦干的, 干枯的: *the parched African landscape* 干燥的非洲地貌 | *He raised the water bottle to his parched lips.* 他把水瓶举到自己干裂的唇边。—see picture on page A13 参见 A13 页图 **2 be parched** *informal* to be very thirsty【非正式】渴得要命

Par·chee·si /pɑrˈtʃizɪ; pɑːˈtʃiːzi/ *n* [U] *AmE trademark* a children's game in which you move a small piece of plastic around a board after throwing DICE【美, 商标】巴棋戏(一种儿童游戏, 掷色子后在板上移动一小块塑料的棋戏), LUDO *BrE*【英】

parch·ment /ˈpɑrtʃmənt; ˈpɑːtʃmənt/ *n* **1** [U] a material used in the past for writing on, made from the skin of a sheep or a goat (古时写字用的)羊皮纸 **2** [U] thick yellow-white writing paper, sometimes used for official documents (用于书写正式文件的)仿羊皮纸 **3** [C] a document written on this paper or material 羊皮纸文件; 仿羊皮纸文件

pard·ner /ˈpɑrdnə; ˈpɑːdnə/ *n AmE humorous spoken* a way of addressing someone you know well【美, 幽默, 口】伙伴, 老兄: *Howdy, pardner!* 你好, 朋友!

par·don[1] /ˈpɑrdn̩; ˈpɑːdn/ *interjection especially BrE*【尤英】**1** 2
used when you want someone to repeat something because you did not hear it 请重复一遍, 请再说一遍(没听清对方的话希望重复一遍时的用语): *Pardon, you'll have to talk louder, I can't hear you.* 请再说一遍, 你得大声点说, 我听不见。| *"Is it hanging up in your bedroom?" "Pardon?" "I said is it in your bedroom?"* "那东西是不是挂在你的卧室里?" "请原谅, 你说什么?" "我说那东西是不是在你的卧室里?" **2** used to say 'sorry' after you have made an impolite sound such as a BURP or YAWN 对不起, 请原谅(在发出不礼貌的声音如打嗝或打哈欠后的道歉语)

pardon[2] *v* [T] **1** to officially allow someone to be free without being punished, although a court has proved that they are guilty

of a crime 赦免: *The governor pardoned the two offenders.* 州长赦免了那两名罪犯。**2** [not in progressive 不用进行时] *old-fashioned* to forgive someone for behaving badly【过时】宽恕, 原谅: *I hope you will pardon my son's little outburst at dinner.* 我希望你能原谅我儿子在晚餐时耍的小脾气。**3 sb may be pardoned for doing sth** used to say that it is easy to understand why someone has done something or why they think something 某人做某事情有可原: *Anyone reading the advertisement might be pardoned for thinking that the offer was genuine.* 无论谁看了那则广告认为那个开价名符其实, 也许都是情有可原的。

Frequencies of the verb **pardon** in spoken and written English 动词 pardon 在英语口语和书面语中的使用频率

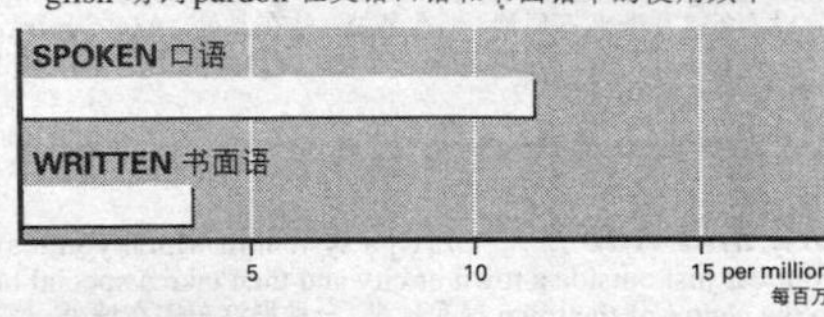

Based on the British National Corpus and the Longman Lancaster Corpus
据英国国家语料库和朗文兰开斯特语料库

This graph shows that the verb **pardon** is much more common in spoken English than in written English. This is because it is used in a lot of common spoken phrases. 本图表显示, 动词 pardon 在英语口语中的使用频率远远高于书面语, 因为口语中很多常用短语是由 pardon 构成的。

pardon (*v*) SPOKEN PHRASES
含 pardon 的口语短语

4 a) pardon me used to say 'sorry' politely when you have accidentally pushed someone, interrupted them etc 对不起, 请原谅〔无意中碰到某人、打断某人等时的礼貌用语〕: *Oh, pardon me, I didn't mean to disturb you.* 噢, 对不起, 我不是有意要打扰你。**b)** used to say 'sorry' politely after you have made an impolite sound such as a BURP (1) or a YAWN[2] (1) 对不起, 很抱歉〔在发出不礼貌的声音如打嗝、打哈欠后的道歉用语〕 **c)** used before you politely correct someone or disagree with them 对不起, 不好意思〔在纠正或不同意某人时的礼貌用语〕: *Pardon me, but I think you've got your facts wrong.* 对不起, 我想你把事情搞错了。**d)** *old-fashioned, especially AmE* used to politely get someone's attention in order to ask them a question【过时, 尤美】对不起, 劳驾〔为问问题而吸引别人注意力时的礼貌用语〕: *Pardon me, can you direct me to City Hall?* 劳驾, 你能告诉我去市政厅怎么走吗? **5 pardon me for interrupting/asking/saying** *especially BrE* used to politely ask if you can interrupt someone, ask something etc【尤英】请原谅我打断/问/说: *Pardon me for saying so, but you're doing that all wrong.* 请原谅我这么说, 但是你全做错了。**6 pardon my ignorance/rudeness etc** used when you think that you may seem not to know enough, not to be polite enough etc 请原谅我的无知/无礼等: *Pardon my ignorance, but what does OPEC stand for?* 请原谅我的无知, OPEC 代表什么? **7 if you'll pardon the expression** used when you are saying sorry for using a slightly impolite phrase 请原谅我用这个词语: *It was a bit of a cock-up, if you'll pardon the expression.* 这事搞得有点儿一团糟, 请原谅我用这个词。**8 pardon my French** *humorous* used to say sorry after you have said an impolite word【幽默】请原谅我讲了这样的话〔说了无礼的话之后使用〕 **9 pardon me for breathing/living** used when you are annoyed because you think someone has answered you angrily for no good reason 请原谅我活着让你受气了〔对别人无缘无故气冲冲地回答你表示恼火〕

pardon[3] *n* **1 (I) beg your pardon a)** *spoken* used when politely saying sorry because you have just made a mistake【口】对不起, 请原谅〔用于对自己的过错表示歉意〕: *I beg your pardon, I meant the green one.* 对不起, 我说的是绿色的那个。| *I do beg your pardon, I thought you were someone else.* 请原谅, 我认错人了。**b)** used to politely ask someone to repeat something because you did not hear it 对不起, 你说什么? 〔用于礼貌地请求别人重复说过的话〕: *"I think the radiator's leaking." "Beg your pardon?" "The radiator, I think it's leaking."* "我想散热器在漏水。" "对不起, 你说什么?" "那散热器, 我想它在漏水。" **c)** used to politely say sorry because you have accidentally touched someone, stepped on their foot, burped (BURP (1)) etc 对不起, 很抱歉〔无意中碰到别人、踩了别人的脚、打嗝等时的道歉用语〕 **d)** used when you are strongly or angrily disagreeing with what someone has just said 对不起〔用于对某人所说的话感到强烈反对〕: *I beg your pardon, I never said that at all.* 对不起, 我从来没有那样说过。**e)** used when you are surprised or shocked by what someone has just said 对不起, 不好意思〔对别人刚说过的话表示惊奇或震惊时的用语〕: *"I'm ready to pay £20,000." "I beg your pardon, are you serious?"* "我准备付 20,000 英镑。" "对不起, 你是认真的吗?" —see 见 EXCUSE[1] (USAGE) **2** [C] an official order allowing someone to be free and stopping their punishment, although a court has proved them guilty of a crime 赦免令, 赦免状: **grant/give sb a pardon** *Tyler was convicted but was granted a royal pardon.* 泰勒被判有罪, 但得到了国王的赦免。**3** [U] *old-fashioned* the act of forgiving someone【过时】宽恕, 原谅: **ask/beg sb's pardon (for)** (=ask someone to forgive you) 请求某人的原谅 *Walter begged her pardon for all the pain he had caused her.* 沃尔特请求她原谅自己给她造成的所有痛苦。

P

par·don·a·ble /ˈpɑrdn̩əbl̩; ˈpɑːdənəbəl/ *adj formal* pardonable behaviour or mistakes are not very bad and can be forgiven; EXCUSABLE【正式】〔行为或过失〕可宽恕的, 可原谅的 —**pardonably** *adv*

pare /pɛr; peə/ *v* [T] **1** to cut off the thin outer part of something using a sharp knife〔用刀子〕削去…的皮: *Pare the onions then cut them.* 先削去洋葱的外皮, 然后再将其切开。**2** to cut your nails so that they look neat 修剪〔指甲〕

pare sth **down** *phr v* [T] to gradually reduce an amount or number〔逐步〕削减, 减少: *The workforce has been pared down from 1,400 to 700.* 职工总数已从 1400 人裁减至 700 人。| **pare sth down to the bone** (=reduce an amount or number as much as possible) 尽可能地削减某物, 将某物减到极限[最低] —**pared-down** *adj*

par·ent /ˈpɛrənt; ˈpeərənt/ *n* [C] **1** the father or mother of a person or animal〔人的〕父; 母; 〔动物的〕亲体, 母体: *I don't really get on with my boyfriend's parents.* 我和我男朋友的父母相处得不怎么好。| *a parent substitute, such as an aunt* 代替母亲的人如姨妈 —see picture at 参见 FAMILY 图 **2** something that produces other things of the same type 母体, 母公司: *Shares in Mercury parent Cable and Wireless went up by 3p.* 墨丘利电讯公司的母公司英国大东电报局的股价上涨了三便士。—see also 另见 ONE-PARENT FAMILY, SINGLE PARENT 1 1

par·ent·age /ˈpɛrəntɪdʒ; ˈpeərəntɪdʒ/ *n* [U] someone's parents and the country and social class they are from 出身, 身世: *a child of unknown parentage* (=we do not know who its parents are) 身世不明的孩子

pa·rent·al /pəˈrɛntl̩; pəˈrentl/ *adj* connected with one parent or both parents 父亲的; 母亲的; 父母的: *parental responsibilities* 父母的责任

parent com·pa·ny /ˈ· ··, ···/ *n* [C] a company that controls a smaller company or organization 母公司, 总公司

pa·ren·the·sis /pəˈrɛnθəsɪs; pəˈrenθɪ̣sɪ̣s/ *n plural* **parentheses** /-ˌsiz; -siːz/ [usually plural 一般用复数] *especially AmE* a round BRACKET【尤美】圆括号: **in parentheses** *The figures in parentheses refer to page numbers.* 圆括号内的数字指的是页码。—see picture at 参见 PUNCTUATION MARK 图

par·en·thet·i·cal /ˌpærənˈθɛtɪkl̩; ˌpærənˈθetɪkəl◂/ also 又作 **parenthetic** *adj* said or written as an extra remark about something you are talking about 补充性质的, 附带[加]说明的 —**parenthetically** /-kl̩ɪ; -kli/ *adv*

par·ent·hood /ˈpɛrəntˌhʊd; ˈperənthʊd/ *n* [U] the state of being a parent 父母的身份

par·ent·ing /ˈpɛrəntɪŋ; ˈpeərəntɪŋ/ *n* [U] the skill or activity of looking after children as a parent 父母对孩子的养育[照顾]

par ex·cel·lence /pɑr ˋɛksəˌlɑns; ˌpɑːr ˈeksəlɑːns/ *adj* [only after noun 仅用于名词后] *French* the very best【法】最卓越的, 出类拔萃的: *Auguste Escoffier, master-chef par excellence* 奥古斯特·埃斯科菲耶, 技艺超群的厨师长

par·fait /pɑrˋfe; pɑːˈfeɪ/ *n* [U] *AmE* a sweet food made of layers of ICE CREAM and fruit【美】冰激凌水果冻〔由多层冰激凌和水果制成的甜点〕

pa·ri·ah /pəˈraɪə; pəˈraɪə/ *n* [C] **1** someone who is hated and avoided by other people 被痛恨和排斥的人, 被遗弃的人: *a social pariah* 被社会遗弃者 **2** *old use* a member of a very low social class in India【旧】〔印度社会下层的〕贱民

par·i·mu·tu·el /ˈpærɪˋmjutʃʊəl; ˌpæriˈmjuːtʃuəl/ *n French*【法】**1** [U] a system in which the money that people have risked on a horse race is shared between the people who have won〔赛马赌博中由赢家分享全部赌金的〕同注分彩赌博法 **2** [C] *AmE* a machine used to calculate the amount of money people can win

by risking it on horse races【美】〔计算赛马赌金的〕赌金计算器, 同注分彩计算器; TOTE² *BrE*【英】

par·ings /ˈpɛrɪŋz; ˈpeərɪŋz/ *n* [plural] thin pieces of something that have been cut off 削下的薄片: *nail parings* 剪下的指甲 | *cheese parings* 削下的乳酪片

Pa·ris¹ /ˈpærɪs; ˈpærɪ̇s/ the capital city of France, on the River Seine, which is also the country's business and financial centre. Many people think of Paris as a very romantic city where many famous artists lived, especially in the 19th and early 20th centuries. People from Paris are called Parisians. 巴黎〔法国首都, 位于塞纳河畔, 亦为法国的商业和金融中心。巴黎一直被认为是一个浪漫的城市, 曾居住过许多著名艺术家, 19世纪和20世纪初尤为如此。巴黎人被称作 Parisian〕

Paris² in ancient Greek stories, a prince of Troy who caused the Trojan War by taking Helen away from Greece, and who killed Achilles in this war 帕里斯〔古希腊传说中的特洛伊王子。他因把海伦从希腊带走而引发了特洛伊战争, 期间他杀死了阿喀琉斯〕—see 见 the ILIAD

Paris-Dak·ar Ral·ly, the /ˌpærɪs dəˈkɑr ˌrælɪ; ˌpærɪs ˈdækɑːˌræli/ a race over public roads from Paris, France to Dakar, Senegal, including the crossing of the Sahara Desert. All kinds of motor vehicles can take part in the Paris-Dakar Rally. 巴黎-达喀尔汽车拉力赛〔赛程从法国的巴黎到塞内加尔的达喀尔, 沿途要穿越撒哈拉沙漠。各种类型的机动车辆均可参赛〕

par·ish /ˈpærɪʃ; ˈpærɪʃ/ *n* [C] **1** the area that a priest is responsible for〔由一名牧师管理的〕教区: *a parish priest* 教区牧师 **2** *BrE* a small area, especially a village, that has its own local government【英】〔有其地方政府的〕郡以下的小行政区〔尤指村庄〕: *a parish boundary* 小行政区边界 **3 the parish** the people who live in a particular area, especially those who go to church〔尤指参加教区教堂活动的〕教区居民 **4 sb's parish** *BrE old-fashioned* something which someone knows a lot about or which they are responsible for【英, 过时】某人的知识领域[职责范围]

Parish, Max·field /ˈmæksfild; ˈmæksfiːld/ (1870-1966) a US artist famous for his ILLUSTRATIONS (=pictures in books), which are romantic and colourful, and show light in a slightly SURREAL way 帕里什〔(1870-1966), 美国艺术家, 以插图闻名。其插图具有浪漫气息, 色彩明快, 以略带超现实的手法表现画中的亮度〕

parish church /ˌ‥ ˈ‥/ *n* [C] the main church in a particular area 教区教堂

parish clerk /ˌ‥ ˈ‥/ *n* [C] an official who works for a church in a particular town or area 教区执事

parish coun·cil /ˌ‥ ˈ‥/ *n* [C] a group of people who are responsible for taking decisions about a small area, especially a village 行政区议会

pa·rish·io·ner /pəˈrɪʃənɚ; pəˈrɪʃənə/ *n* [C] someone who lives in a parish, especially someone who regularly goes to the church there〔尤指定期参加教区教堂活动的〕教区居民

parish pump /ˌ‥ ˈ‥/ *adj* [only before noun 仅用于名词前] *BrE old-fashioned* concerned only with a small local area【英, 过时】区域性的, 地方性的: *parish pump politics* 区域性政治

parish re·gis·ter /ˌ‥ ˈ‥‥/ *n* [C] an official record of the births, deaths, and marriages in a parish〔有关教区居民出生、死亡、婚姻的〕教区记事录

Pa·ris·i·an /pəˈrɪʒən; pəˈrɪziən/ *adj* coming from or connected with Paris 来自巴黎的; 巴黎的 —**Parisian** *n* [C]

par·i·ty /ˈpærətɪ; ˈpærɪ̇ti/ *n* [U] **1** the state of being equal, especially having equal pay, rights, or power〔尤指薪金、权利、权力的〕相同, 相等, 同等: [+with] *Women workers are demanding parity with their male colleagues.* 女职工在要求与男同事享有同等的待遇。**2** *technical* equality between the units of money from two different countries【术语】〔两个不同国家的货币单位的〕平价, 等价: *until the time the pound has parity with the dollar* 直到英镑和美元等价的时候 **3** *technical* a system for finding mistakes in the sending of information from one computer to another【术语】〔在两台电脑之间发送信息时发现错误的〕奇偶校验, 同位核对: *parity checking* 奇偶校验

park¹ /pɑrk; pɑːk/ *n* [C] **1** a large open area with grass and trees, especially in a town, where people can walk, play games etc 公园: *Let's go for a walk in the park.* 我们去公园散步吧。| *a park bench* 公园长凳 **2** a large enclosed area of land, with grass and trees, around a big house in the countryside〔乡村别墅周围的〕庭园, 园林 **3 the park** *BrE informal* the field where a game of football or RUGBY is played【英, 非正式】足球场; 橄榄球场 **4** *AmE informal* the field where a game of BASEBALL is played【美, 非正式】棒球场 —see also 另见 AMUSEMENT PARK, BALL PARK, CAR PARK, NATIONAL PARK, SAFARI PARK, SCIENCE PARK, THEME PARK, TRAILER PARK

park² *v* **1** [I,T] to put a car or other vehicle in a particular place for a period of time 停放〔汽车或其他车辆〕: *You can't park here – it's private property.* 这里不能停车 —— 这是私人地产。| **park sth** *We couldn't find anywhere to park the van.* 我们找不到地方停放那辆小型货车。| *There's a police car parked outside our house.* 一辆警车停在我们的房子外面。| *parked cars* 停放的汽车 | *I'm parked over there.* (=I've parked my car over there) 我的汽车停在那边。**2** [T] *spoken* to put something in a particular place for a period of time, in a way that is inconvenient or annoying【口】〔引起不便或令人讨厌地〕把〔某物〕放在〔某处〕: **park sth in/on/here etc** *He parked a load of papers on my desk.* 他把一大摞文件放在我桌上。**3 park yourself** *spoken* to sit or stand in a particular place, that is inconvenient for other people【口】〔给别人带来不便地〕坐在某处; 站在某处: *Alma parked herself in the hotel lobby and refused to budge.* 阿尔玛站在酒店大厅里不肯动。

par·ka /ˈpɑrkə; ˈpɑːkə/ *n* [C] a thick warm JACKET with a HOOD 风雪大衣, 派克大衣〔带兜帽的御寒夹克〕—see picture at 参见 COAT¹ 图

park and ride /ˌ· · ˈ·/ *n* [U] a system in which you leave your car just outside a town or city and then take a special bus to the centre of the town 换车通勤〔一种把汽车停在城外, 换乘公共汽车进城的交通体制〕

Par·ker /ˈpɑrkɚ; ˈpɑːkə/, **Bonnie** —see 见 BONNIE AND CLYDE

Parker, Charlie (1920-55) a US JAZZ musician and SAXOPHONE player, who was also called 'Bird', and who invented the Bebop style of jazz with Dizzy Gillespie 帕克〔(1920-1955), 美国爵士音乐家、萨克斯管演奏家, 绰号"菜鸟"。他与迪齐·吉莱斯皮一起首创了"比博普"爵士乐风格〕

Parker, Dor·o·thy /ˈdɔrəθɪ; ˈdɒrəθi/ (1893-1967) a US writer of poetry and short stories, who also wrote reviews of books, plays etc for magazines such as *The New Yorker*. She was one of the main members of the Algonquin Round Table, a group of writers who met regularly at a hotel in New York City. She is famous especially for her many clever and funny sayings in which she criticized US society and well-known people. 帕克〔(1893-1967), 美国诗人、短篇小说家, 也为《纽约人》等杂志撰写书评和剧评。她是阿尔冈昆圆桌会的中坚人物之一。该会成员定期在纽约市一家酒店聚会。她尤以抨击美国社会及名人的连珠妙语闻名〕

Park·hurst pris·on /ˌpɑrkhɝst ˈprɪzn; ˌpɑːkhɜːst ˈprɪzən/ also 又作 **Parkhurst** a British prison on the Isle of Wight for men who have received long prison sentences for serious crimes 帕克赫斯特监狱〔英国一男子监狱, 位于怀特岛。在押犯人均因重罪而被判长期监禁〕

par·kin /ˈpɑrkɪn; ˈpɑːkɪn/ *n* [U] *BrE* a type of cake made with OATMEAL and GINGER【英】〔用燕麦片和姜制成的〕燕麦姜饼

park·ing /ˈpɑrkɪŋ; ˈpɑːkɪŋ/ *n* [U] **1** the act of parking a car or other vehicle〔车辆等的〕停放: *No Parking.* 禁止停车。| *a parking fine* 违章停车罚款 | *a parking space* 停车位 **2** spaces in which you can leave a car or other vehicle 停车处, 停车位: *There's plenty of parking at the shopping mall.* 那个购物中心有许多停车位。

parking ga·rage /ˈ‥ ˌ‥/ *n* [C] *AmE* MULTISTOREY CAR PARK【美】公共停车库, 多层停车场

parking light /ˈ‥ ˌ·/ *n* [C] *AmE* SIDELIGHT【美】侧灯; 旁灯, 停车信号灯 —see picture on page A2 参见 A2 页图

parking lot /ˈ‥ ·/ *n* [C] *AmE* an open area for cars to park in【美】露天停车场[区]; CAR PARK *BrE*【英】

parking me·ter /ˈ‥ ˌ‥/ *n* [C] a machine which you put money into when you park your car next to it 停车计时收费器 —see picture on page A3 参见 A3 页图

parking tick·et /ˈ‥ ˌ‥/ *n* [C] an official notice fixed to a vehicle, saying that you have to pay money because you have parked your car in the wrong place or for too long 违章停车罚款通知单

Par·kin·son's dis·ease /ˈpɑrkɪnsənz dɪˌziz; ˈpɑːkɪ̇nsənz dɪˌziːz/ also 又作 **Parkinson's** *n* [U] a serious illness in which your muscles become very weak and your arms and legs shake 帕金森(氏)病, 震颤性麻痹

Parkinson's law /ˈ‥ ˌ·/ *n* [singular] the idea that the amount of work you have to do increases to fill the amount of time you have to do it in 帕金森定律〔指工作总是到时限最后一刻才会完成的一种观点〕

park keep·er /ˈ· ˌ‥/ *n* [C] *BrE* someone whose job is to look after a park【英】公园管理员

park·land /ˈpɑrkˌlænd; ˈpɑːklænd/ *n* [U] **1** *BrE* an area of land with grass and trees, surrounding a big house in the countryside【英】〔环绕乡村宅邸的〕邸园, 草木区 **2** land with grass

and trees which is used as a park〔用作公园的〕公园用地，公共绿地

Park Lane /ˌ· ˈ·/ a wide street in central London between Marble Arch and Hyde Park Corner. It has buildings on one side and Hyde Park on the other, and it is famous for its expensive hotels and houses. 柏丽大道〔伦敦市中心一宽阔大街，位于大理石拱门和海德公园角之间。大街一边建筑林立，一边是海德公园，以高档酒店和住宅闻名〕

park ran·ger /ˈ· ˌ··/ *n* [C] *AmE* a RANGER (1)【美】公园管理员

Parks /pɑrks; pɑːks/, **Ro·sa** /ˈrozə; ˈrəʊzə/ (1913-2005) a black woman in the US who became famous in 1955 because she refused to give her seat on a bus to a white man. This action was illegal in the US state of Alabama and she was arrested by the police. As a result, Martin Luther King persuaded people not to use these buses, and in 1956 the US Supreme Court said that SEGREGATION (=keeping black people separate from white people) on buses was not legal. 帕克斯〔(1913-2005)，美国一黑人女子，1955年因拒绝在公共汽车上给一名白人男子让座而声名远扬。这一做法在美国当时的亚拉巴马州属违法行为，警察因此逮捕她。事发后马丁·路德·金动员大家罢乘公共汽车来抗议。1956年，美国联邦最高法院宣称公共汽车上的种族隔离是不合法的〕

park·way /ˈpɑrkˌwe; ˈpɑːkweɪ/ *n* [C] *AmE* a wide road with an area of grass and trees in the middle or along the sides【美】〔中间或两旁有草地和树木的〕林园式大路，林荫大路

par·ky /ˈpɑrkɪ; ˈpɑːki/ *adj BrE informal* cold【英，非正式】寒冷的: *It's a bit parky outside today.* 今天外面有点儿冷。

par·lance /ˈpɑrləns; ˈpɑːləns/ *n* **in common/medical/advertising etc parlance** expressed in words that most people, or a particular group of people, would use 用一般的/医学上的/广告上等的说法[用语]等: *This is called a unique selling proposition in advertising parlance.* 在广告用语中，这叫做独特的销售主张。

par·lay /ˈpɑrlɪ; ˈpɑːli/ *v* [T] *AmE* to increase the value of something that you have, especially your abilities, previous success, or money, by using all your opportunities well【美】使增值，使更有价值；成功地利用〔尤指才能、以往的成功或金钱等〕: **parlay sth into** *He parlayed his athletic achievements into a successful sports broadcasting career.* 他利用自己的体育成就成为了一名成功的体育播音员。

par·ley /ˈpɑrlɪ; ˈpɑːli/ *n* [C] *old-fashioned* a discussion in which enemies try to achieve peace【过时】〔与敌人谋求和平的〕和谈，会谈 —**parley** *v* [I]

W2 **par·lia·ment** /ˈpɑrləmənt; ˈpɑːləmənt/ *n* [C] **1** the group of people who are elected to make a country's laws and discuss important national affairs 议会，国会 **2 Parliament** the main law-making institution in the United Kingdom, which consists of the HOUSE OF COMMONS and the HOUSE OF LORDS 英国议会〔由上议院和下议院组成〕: **enter Parliament/get into Parliament** (=be elected as a member of Parliament) 被选为议员 **3** the period during which this institution meets 一届议会[国会]: *We expect to get these laws passed during the present parliament.* 我们期望这些法律能在本届议会中通过。

par·lia·men·tar·i·an /ˌpɑrləmɛnˈtɛrɪən; ˌpɑːləmənˈteəriən/ *n* [C] a skilled and experienced member of a parliament 有经验的议员

W3 **par·lia·men·ta·ry** /ˌpɑrləˈmɛntərɪ; ˌpɑːləˈmentəri◂/ *adj* connected with or governed by a parliament 议会的，国会的；由议会[国会]支配的: *the world's oldest parliamentary democracy* 世界上最古老的议会民主制

par·lor /ˈpɑrlɚ; ˈpɑːlə/ *n* [C] the American spelling of PARLOUR parlour 的美式拼法

parlor car /ˈ·· ˌ·/ *n* [C] *AmE* a special railway carriage which has comfortable seats【美】豪华型列车车厢 —compare 比较 PULLMAN

par·lour *BrE*【英】, **parlor** *AmE*【美】/ˈpɑrlɚ; ˈpɑːlə/ *n* [C] **1 ice cream/massage/funeral etc parlour** a shop or type of business that provides a particular service 冰激凌店/按摩院/殡仪馆等〔专门提供某种服务的店〕 **2** *old-fashioned* a room in a house which has comfortable chairs and is used for meeting guests【过时】〔家庭的〕起居室，会客室，客厅 —see also 另见 MILKING PARLOUR

parlour game *BrE*【英】, **parlor game** *AmE*【美】/ˈ·· ˌ·/ *n* [C] *old-fashioned* a game that can be played indoors, such as a guessing game or a word game【过时】室内游戏〈如猜谜或文字游戏〉

parlour maid *BrE*【英】, **parlor maid** *AmE*【美】/ˈ·· ˌ·/ *n* [C] a female servant who was employed in former times in a large house to clean the rooms, serve guests etc〔旧时受雇清理房间、服侍客人等的〕客厅女仆

par·lous /ˈpɑrləs; ˈpɑːləs/ *adj formal* in a very bad or dangerous condition【正式】糟糕的；危险的: *the parlous state of the country* 该国的危险状况

Par·me·san /ˌpɑrməˈzæn; ˌpɑːmɪ̵ˈzæn◂/ also 又作 **Parmesan cheese** /ˌ··· ˈ·/ *n* [U] a hard strong-tasting Italian cheese 帕尔梅森干酪〔一种味道很重的意大利硬牛奶干酪〕

Par·nas·sus /pɑrˈnæsəs; pɑːˈnæsəs/ a high mountain in central Greece. In ancient times people thought it was a holy place of the gods Apollo and Dionysus, and of the Muses (=goddesses of art and science) 帕尔纳索斯山〔希腊中部一高山。古时被认为是阿波罗、狄俄尼索斯、缪斯等神的圣地〕

Par·nell /pɑrˈnɛl; pɑːˈnel/, **Charles Stewart** (1846-91) an Irish politician who was a member of the British Parliament. He was a leading supporter of the idea of Home Rule (=self-government) for Ireland. 巴涅尔〔(1846-1891)，爱尔兰政治家，曾任英国议会议员。他是爱尔兰自治主张的主要支持者〕

pa·ro·chi·al /pəˈrokɪəl; pəˈrəʊkiəl/ *adj* **1** only interested in the things that affect you and your local area, and not interested in more important matters〔兴趣、视野等〕褊狭的，狭隘的: *Local newspapers tend to be very parochial.* 地方报纸一般视野很狭隘。**2** [only before noun 仅用于名词前] concerned with a PARISH 教区的 —**parochialism** *n* [U] —**parochially** *adv*

parochial school /ˈ···· ˌ·/ *n* [C] *especially AmE* a private school which is run by or connected with a church【尤美】〔由教会兴办或与教会有关的〕教区学校，教会学校

par·o·dy¹ /ˈpærədɪ; ˈpærədi/ *n* **1** [C,U] a piece of writing or music that copies a particular well-known style in an amusing way〔文章或音乐的〕诙谐性模仿作品，滑稽的模仿作品: [+on/of] *The play is a parody of James Joyce's book 'Ulysses'.* 该剧是对詹姆斯·乔伊斯作品《尤利西斯》的滑稽模仿。**2** [C] something that is so bad that it seems like a very bad copy of another thing 拙劣的模仿: *a grotesque parody of her former self* 对她自己以前样子的怪诞模仿 **3 a parody of justice** something that is extremely unfair 极不公平的事，对正义的嘲弄

parody² *v* [T] to copy someone's style or attitude 模仿〔某人的风格或态度〕: *East end working class attitudes have been parodied by the TV character Alf Garnett.* 电视人物阿尔夫·加尼特滑稽地模仿了伦敦东区工人阶层的态度。—**parodist** *n* [C]

pa·role¹ /pəˈrol; pəˈrəʊl/ *n* [U] permission for someone to leave prison, on the condition that they promise to behave well 假释(出狱)，有条件释放: **on parole** *He was released on parole after serving 2 years.* 服刑两年后他获假释出狱。| **break parole** (=not behave as you are supposed to when you are on parole)(假释期间)违誓

parole² *v* [T] to allow someone to leave prison on the condition that they promise to behave well 准许假释；使获假释

par·ox·ys·m /ˈpærəksˌɪzəm; ˈpærəksɪzəm/ *n* [C] **1 a paroxysm of rage/jealousy/laughter etc** a sudden uncontrollable expression of strong feeling 勃然大怒/顿生妒忌/一阵狂笑等: *Joshua suddenly broke out into a paroxysm of sobbing.* 乔舒亚突然一阵啜泣。**2** a sudden, short attack of pain, coughing, shaking etc〔疼痛、咳嗽、颤抖等的〕发作，阵发: [+of] *paroxysms of coughing* 一阵咳嗽 —**paroxysmal** /ˌpærəkˈsɪzml; ˌpærəkˈsɪzməl◂/ *adj*

par·quet /pɑrˈke; ˈpɑːkeɪ/ *n* [U] small flat blocks of wood fitted together in a pattern that cover the floor of a room 镶木地板: *a parquet floor* 镶木地板

par·ri·cide /ˈpærəˌsaɪd; ˈpærɪ̵saɪd/ *n* **1** [U] *formal* the crime of killing your father, mother, or any other close relative【正式】弑父[母]罪；弑近亲罪 **2** [C] *technical* someone who is guilty of this crime【术语】弑父[母]者；弑近亲者 —compare 比较 MATRICIDE, PATRICIDE

par·rot¹ /ˈpærət; ˈpærət/ *n* [C] **1** a tropical bird with a curved beak and brightly coloured feathers that can be taught to copy human speech 鹦鹉 **2 parrot fashion** *BrE* repeating what someone has just said without understanding it【英】鹦鹉学舌般地，重复而不解其义地: *reciting poems parrot-fashion* 鹦鹉学舌般地背诵诗歌 —see also 另见 **sick as a parrot** (SICK¹ (8))

CULTURAL NOTE 文化注释

Polly is a TRADITIONAL name for a parrot, and parrots are often taught to say 'pretty Polly'. In stories PIRATES often have a parrot which sits on their shoulder and says "pieces of eight" (old, valuable coins). 鹦鹉传统上常被取名为波莉，因此人们通常教鹦鹉说"靓波莉"。在故事中，海盗的肩膀上常常蹲坐着一只鹦鹉，鹦鹉嘴里说着"几个古银币"。— see also 另见 LONG JOHN SILVER, PIRATE

parrot² *v* [T] to repeat someone else's words or ideas without really understanding what you are saying 不假思索[不解其义]地重复, 鹦鹉学舌般地重复, 机械地模仿

par·ry /ˈpæri; ˈpæri/ *v* [T] **1** to avoid answering a difficult question 回避〔难以回答的问题〕: *White House spokesmen tired of parrying journalists' questions.* 白宫发言人对回避记者的问题感到厌倦。**2** to defend yourself against someone who is attacking you by pushing their weapon or hand to one side; DEFLECT 挡开, 避开〔武器、手〕 —**parry** *n* [C]

parse /pɑrs; pɑːz/ *v* [T] *technical* to describe the grammar of a word when it is in a particular sentence, or the grammar of the whole sentence【术语】对〔句中的词或句子〕作语法分析 —**parser** *n* [C]: *a powerful parser that analysed errors in word processed letters* 对计算机打出来的信件中的错误进行分析的强大语法分析程序

P

Par·see, Parsi /ˈpɑrsi; pɑːˈsiː/ *n* [C] a member of an ancient Persian religious group in India 帕西人〔印度的古波斯祆教教徒〕 —**Parsee** *adj*

par·si·mo·ni·ous /ˌpɑrsəˈmoniəs; ˌpɑːsɪ̍ˈməʊniəs◂/ *adj formal* extremely unwilling to spend money; MEAN² (2)【正式】过分节俭的, 吝啬的, 小气的 —**parsimoniously** *adv* —**parsimony** /ˈpɑrsəˌmoni; ˈpɑːsɪ̍məni/ *n* [U]

pars·ley /ˈpɑrslɪ; ˈpɑːsli/ *n* [U] a small plant with curly leaves that have a strong taste, used in cooking or as decoration on food 欧芹〔可供食用或作食品上的装饰〕

pars·nip /ˈpɑrsnɪp; ˈpɑːsnɪp/ *n* [C,U] a plant with a thick white or yellowish root that is eaten as a vegetable 欧洲防风〔其根部可食用, 呈白色或淡黄色〕—see picture on page A9 参见 A9 页图

par·son /ˈpɑrsn; ˈpɑːsən/ *n* [C] *old-fashioned* a Christian priest or minister responsible for a small area, especially in the Church of England【过时】〔尤指英国国教的〕教区牧师

par·son·age /ˈpɑrsnɪdʒ; ˈpɑːsənɪdʒ/ *n* [C] the house where a parson lives 教区牧师住宅

parson's nose /ˌ.. ˈ. / *n* [C] *BrE informal* the piece of flesh at the tail end of a bird, usually a chicken, that has been cooked【英, 非正式】〔烹调过的禽类的, 通常指鸡的〕尾部[屁股]肉; POPE'S NOSE *AmE*【美】

part¹ /pɑrt; pɑːt/ *n*

1 ▶**PIECE OF** 部分◀ [C,U] a piece of something such as an object, area, event, or period of time …的(一)部分: **[+of]** *The front part of the car was badly damaged.* 这辆汽车的前部损坏严重。| *In parts of Canada, French is the first language.* 在加拿大的部分地区, 法语是第一语言。| *What part of America do you come from?* 你来自美国的哪个地区? | *I only saw the first part of the programme.* 我只看了那个节目的第一部分。| **be (a) part of** *Falling over is part of learning how to ski.* 学滑雪少不了要摔倒。| **late/early part** *She spent the early part of her life in Belfast.* 她的早年是在贝尔法斯特度过的。| **best/worst part** *The best part of the holiday was the trip to the Islands.* 假期中最开心的一段是去那座岛上旅行。| **hard/easy part** *Getting dad to agree will be the hard part.* 让爸爸同意会是很难的。

2 ▶**MACHINE/OBJECT** 机器/物体◀ [C] one of the separate pieces that something such as a machine, object etc is made of 〔机器、物体等的〕零件, 部件: *I've glued it back together, but this part won't fit properly.* 我已重新用胶把它粘好了, 但这一块不怎么合适。| *They send you the parts and you build it yourself.* 他们寄给你部件, 你要自己组装。| **spare part** (=kept for when a part breaks, needs replacing etc) 备品, 备件

3 ▶**NOT ALL** 不是全部◀ [C,U] some but not all of a particular thing or group of things 〔东西的〕部分, 局部: **[+of]** *Part of the castle was destroyed in the fire.* 这个城堡的一部分毁于火灾。| **in parts** *The film is very violent in parts.* 这部电影有些片段是非常暴力的。| **(only) part of the story/problem/explanation etc** *Poor working conditions are only part of the problem.* 恶劣的工作条件仅仅是问题的一方面。

4 play a part a) if something plays a part in something, it is one of the several causes that make it happen or be successful 起作用, 有影响: **[+in]** *This innovation has played a part in the company's success.* 这项革新对于公司的成功起了作用。| **play a big/important part in** *Besides dieting, exercising plays an important part in losing weight.* 除节食之外, 锻炼对减肥也起着重要的作用。**b)** to perform the actions, words etc of a particular character in a play, film etc 扮演…角色: **play the part of** *Kenneth Brannagh played the part of Henry V.* 肯尼思·布兰纳扮演亨利五世。**c)** to be involved in something 参与, 参加: *Britain should play its full part in these negotiations.* 英国应在这些谈判中充分发挥作用。

5 take part to be involved in an activity, sport, event etc together with other people 参加, 参与: **[+in]** *About 400 students took part in the protest.* 大约 400 名学生参加了抗议活动。| *She wanted to take part but she was too ill.* 她想参加, 但她病得太厉害了。| **take an active/leading part** *At college I took an active part in student politics.* 在大学里我积极参与学生政治活动。

6 the best/better part of nearly all of something 绝大部分/大部分, 大半: *We waited for the best part of an hour.* 我们等了近一个小时。

7 a good/large part of a lot or more than half of something 多半, 大半: *A large part of the budget will be spent on advertising.* 大部分预算将花费在广告上。

8 in large part/for the most part mostly, to a great extent, or in most places 多半, 在很大程度上; 在大多数地方: *The team, for the most part, was confident of success.* 这个队的队员大多有获胜的信心。| *The money was in large part raised by sponsorship.* 这些钱多半是筹集得来的赞助费。

9 form part of/form a part of to be one of the things that together make up something larger or more important 组成…的(一)部分: *Practical work forms an integral part of the course.* 实习是这门课必不可少的部分。

10 ▶**HAIR** 头发◀ *AmE* a PARTING【美】〔头发的〕分缝

11 ▶**ACTING** 表演◀ [C] the words and actions of a particular character in a play, film etc, performed by an actor 〔角色的〕台词和动作: *I have to learn the part of Romeo by Tuesday.* 我必须在星期二之前背熟罗密欧这一角色的台词。

12 part of the body a particular piece or area of a body 身体部位: *More heat is lost through the head than through any other part of the body.* 身体热量通过头部散发比通过其他部位散发来得多。—see also 另见 PRIVATE PARTS

13 ▶**BOOK** 书◀ [C] the different parts of something written such as a book, sometimes used as a title 〔书等的〕部分, 篇, 章: **first/last part** *Please turn to the first part of the report.* 请翻到报告的第一部分。| **Part One/Three/Six etc** *The first chapter of Part Two begins at the funeral.* 第二部分的第一章是从葬礼开始的。

14 ▶**MUSIC** 音乐◀ [C] a tune that a particular type of instrument or voice within a group plays or sings 〔乐器或声音的〕部, 声部, 音部: *The tenor part carried the melody.* 男高音部唱主旋律。

15 take/have/play/want no part in not be involved in something, because you do not agree with or approve of it 〔因不同意或不赞成而〕不(想)参与; 和…没有关系: *I played no part in leaking the information to the press.* 我没有把消息泄露给新闻界。

16 ▶**YOUR PART IN** 某人在…中的作用◀ what you yourself did, in an activity that was shared by several people, especially something bad 〔尤指坏事中的〕份儿; 责任; 作用: *They were sentenced for their part in a £14 million fraud.* 他们因参与1400万英镑的诈骗活动而被判刑。

17 in/round these parts in the particular area, part of a country etc that you are in 在这一带: *We don't get many tourists in these parts.* 我们这一带没有多少游客。

18 part of me/him etc used when you have many different feelings or thoughts about something, so it is difficult to decide what you feel or what you should do 我/他等有点…〔用于表示你无法断定自己的想法或感觉〕: *Part of me just wants to leave, but I know I will be unhappy if I do.* 我有点想一走了之, 但我知道如果我走了, 我会不开心的。

19 take sb's part to support someone when they are being criticized or attacked 站在某人一边, 支持[袒护]某人: *The school took the teacher's part and told Jamie to leave.* 校方支持那位老师, 要杰米退学。

20 ▶**QUANTITY** 数量◀ [C] a particular quantity of a substance used when measuring different substances together into a mixture …中的一份, …分之一: *Prepare the glue with one part powder to three parts water.* 用一份粉末和三份水来配制胶水。

21 for the part of/for his part etc used to say what someone's opinions are, when compared to someone else's opinions 就…而言[对…来说]/就他而言[对他来说]等: *For my part I prefer living in the country.* 对我来说, 我更愿住在乡下。

22 on sb's part/on the part of sb used to say that someone has done something or feels something 由某人所作出的; 就某人而言: *It was probably just a mistake on her part.* 这可能只是她的一个失误。| *There has never been any jealousy on my part.* 我从没有感到嫉妒。

23 in part to some degree, but not completely 在某种程度上; 部分地: *The accident was due in part to my own carelessness.* 这次事故在某种程度上是由于我的粗心大意造成的。

24 take sth in good part *old-fashioned* to be able to laugh at a joke, which is about you or affects you【过时】对某事一笑置之, 对某事物并不见怪

25 be part and parcel of included in something else or connected with it 是…的一部分, 是…不可或缺的部分: *Working irregular hours is all part and parcel of being a journalist.* 工作时间无规律是从事记者工作的基本特征。

part² *v* **1** [T] to pull the two sides of something apart, making a space in the middle 使分开, 使分离: *The sunlight flooded the room when he parted the curtains.* 他拉开窗帘, 阳光洒满了整个房间。| **parted lips** (=your mouth open) 张开的嘴 *Ralph's lips parted into a delighted smile.* 拉尔夫咧开嘴, 露出了开心的笑容。**2** [I] to separate from someone, or end a relationship with them 分手, 分别; 断绝关系: *They parted on amicable terms.* 他们友好地分手了。| *I hope we will never part.* 我希望我们永不分离。| **be parted** *They were hardly ever parted in thirty years of marriage.* 在三十年的婚姻生活中, 他们几乎从没有分开过。**3 part company a)** to separate from someone, or end a relationship with them 分手, 分别; 断绝关系: *The two women parted company outside their rooms.* 那两个女人在她们的屋外分了手。**b)** to no longer agree with or think the same as someone else (和…)意见不合, 有分歧: *He parted company with Lloyd George over post-war diplomacy.* 他和劳合·乔治在战后外交问题上意见不合。**4** [T] if you part your hair you separate it into two parts with a comb so that it looks tidy 用梳子给〔头发〕分缝

part with sth *phr v* [T] to unwillingly give something to someone else or stop having it yourself〔不情愿地〕放弃, 舍弃: *I'm reluctant to part with any of the kittens, but we need the money.* 我不愿卖掉任何一只小猫, 但是我们需要钱。

part³ *adv* **part sth, part sth** if something is part one thing, part another, it consists of both of those things 部分是某物, 部分是某物; 既有某物, 又有某物: *The medical exams are part written, part practical.* 医学考试部分是笔试, 部分是考实践。| *The room is really part sitting room, part bedroom.* 这个房间实际上既是起居室, 又是卧室。

part⁴ *adj* **part owner/payment etc** only owning, paying etc a bit of something, not all of it 共同所有者/部分付款等: *I gave them £10 in part payment.* 我给了他们10英镑作为部分付款。

par·take /pɑr`tek; pɑː'teɪk/ *v past tense* **partook** /-`tuk; -'tʊk/ *past participle* **partaken** /-`tekən; -'teɪkən/ [I] *formal*【正式】**1** to eat or drink something that is offered to you 吃; 喝: **[+of]** *Will you partake of a glass of wine?* 你要喝杯酒吗? **2** to take part in an activity or event; PARTICIPATE 参加, 参与: **[+in]** *I like to partake in the festivities.* 我想参加这次庆祝活动。

partake of sth *phr v* [T] *formal* to have a certain amount of a particular quality【正式】有点…, 带有几分〔某种性质或特征〕: *a self-confident manner that partakes of arrogance* 自信中带有几分傲慢的态度

par·terre /pɑr`tɛr; pɑː'teə/ *n* [C] a part of a garden with flat areas of grass and flowers that make a formal pattern〔庭园的〕花坛, 花圃

part-ex·change /ˌ· ·ˈ·/ *n* [C,U] *BrE* a way of buying a new car, television etc in which you give your old car, television etc as part of the payment【英】以旧换新, 部分抵价交易(法); TRADE-IN *AmE*【美】

par·the·no·gen·e·sis /ˌpɑrθəno`dʒɛnəsɪs; ˌpɑːθɪ̣nəʊ-'dʒenɪ̣sɪ̣s/ *n* [U] *technical* the production of a new plant or animal from a female without the sexual involvement of the male【术语】孤雌生殖, 单性生殖

Par·the·non, the /`pɑrθənɑn; 'pɑːθɪ̣nən/ an ancient building on the Acropolis in Athens, built in the 5th century BC and the most famous example of a Greek temple 帕台农神庙〔雅典卫城上的一座古建筑, 建于公元前5世纪, 为希腊神殿最著名的典范〕

par·tial /`pɑrʃəl; 'pɑːʃəl/ *adj* **1** not complete 部分的, 不完全的: *a partial success* 部分成功 | *The patient may only make a partial recovery.* 那病人或许只能部分康复。**2 be partial to sth** *formal* to like something very much【正式】特别喜欢某物, 偏爱某物: *I'm very partial to cream cakes.* 我特别喜欢吃奶油蛋糕。**3** unfairly supporting one person or one side against another 偏向一方的, 偏袒的, 不公平的 —opposite 反义词 IMPARTIAL

par·ti·al·i·ty /ˌpɑrʃɪ`ælətɪ; ˌpɑːʃi'ælɪ̣ti/ *n* [U] **1** unfair support of one person or one side against another; BIAS¹ (1) 偏袒, 偏向; 不公平: *Councillors were accused of partiality on land issues.* 市政委员们被指控在土地问题上有失公正。**2 partiality for** *formal* a special liking for something【正式】对…的特别喜爱, 偏爱, 癖好: *a partiality for Moorish architecture* 对摩尔式建筑的偏爱

par·tial·ly /`pɑrʃəlɪ; 'pɑːʃəli/ *adv formal*【正式】**1** not completely; partly 不完全地; 部分地: *He was only partially to blame for the accident.* 他对这次事故只应负部分责任。**2** in a way that shows you unfairly support one person, side etc against another 偏向一方地, 偏袒地

par·tic·i·pant /pɑr`tɪsəpənt; pɑː'tɪsɪ̣pənt/ *n* [C] someone who is taking part in an activity or event 参加者, 参与者: **[+in]** *Would participants in the next race come forward?* 下个项目参赛者请到前面来好吗? W3

par·tic·i·pate /pɑr`tɪsəˌpet; pɑː'tɪsɪ̣peɪt/ *v* [I] *formal* to take part in an activity or event【正式】参加, 参与: **[+in]** *Everyone in the class is expected to participate in these discussions.* 希望全班同学都参加这些讨论。—see 见 JOIN¹ (USAGE) W3

par·ti·ci·pa·tion /pɑrˌtɪsə`peʃən; pɑːˌtɪsɪ̣'peɪʃən/ *n* [U] the act of taking part in an activity or event 参加, 参与: **[+in]** *We want more participation in the decision-making.* 我们想更多地参与决策。| *entertainment with plenty of audience participation* 有许多观众参与的娱乐活动 W3

par·ti·ci·pa·tory /pɑr`tɪsəˌpətorɪ; pɑːˌtɪsɪ̣'peɪtəri◂/ *adj formal* a way of making decisions that is participatory involves everyone who is affected by the decisions【正式】〔决策〕众人参与的: *a participatory democracy* 公众参与决策的民主

par·ti·cip·i·al /ˌpɑrtə`sɪpɪəl; ˌpɑːtɪ̣'sɪpiəl/ *adj technical* using a participle, or having the form of a participle【术语】分词的; 有分词形式的 **—participially** *adv*

par·ti·ci·ple /`pɑrtəˌsɪpl̩; 'pɑːtɪ̣sɪpəl◂/ *n* [C] *technical* the form of a verb, usually ending in -ing or -ed, which is used to make compound forms of the verb or as an adjective【术语】分词 —see also 另见 PAST PARTICIPLE, PRESENT PARTICIPLE

par·ti·cle /`pɑrtɪkl̩; 'pɑːtɪkəl/ *n* [C] **1** a very small piece of something 微粒, 粒子: *dust particles* 尘埃 —see also 另见 ELEMENTARY PARTICLE **2 not a particle of truth/evidence etc** no truth etc at all 没有一点真实性/证据等: *There's not a particle of truth in what he says.* 他所说的没有半点是真的。**3** *technical* a type of word in grammar, such as a CONJUNCTION (3) or PREPOSITION, that is usually short and is not as important in a sentence as the subject or verb【术语】〔语法中的〕质词, 小品词, 虚词〈如连词、介词〉

particle ac·cel·e·ra·tor /ˈ· ··ˌ···/ *n* [C] *technical* an ACCELERATOR (2)【术语】粒子加速器

particle phys·ics /ˈ··· ˌ··/ *n* [U] the study of the way ELEMENTARY PARTICLES (=very small bits of substance inside atoms) develop and behave 粒子物理学

par·ti-col·oured /`pɑrtɪˌkʌlɚd; ˌpɑːti'kʌləd◂/ *adj* having different colours in different parts 杂色的, 斑驳的

par·tic·u·lar¹ /pɚ`tɪkjələ; pə'tɪkjɪ̣lə/ *adj* **1** [only before noun 仅用于名词前] a particular thing or person is the one that you are talking about, and not any other 特定的, 特指的: *Fred hasn't seen that particular film.* 弗雷德还没有看过那部电影。| *We expect budget pressures in this particular area.* 我们预计这一地区会出现经费紧张。**2** special or important enough to mention separately 特殊的, 特别的; 值得特别一提的: *You should pay particular attention to spelling.* 你应特别注意拼写。| *There was nothing of particular interest in the letter.* 这封信中没有什么特别要注意的事。| *Is there any particular thing that's worrying you?* 有什么特别的事让你烦恼吗? **3** very careful about choosing exactly what you like and not easily satisfied 讲究的; 挑剔的, 吹毛求疵的: **[+about]** *Marty's very particular about his food.* 马蒂吃东西非常挑剔。**4 I'm not particular** *spoken* used to say that you do not care what is decided【口】我不在意, 我不管: **[+what/how/where etc]** *I'm not particular how you do it, as long as it gets done.* 你怎么做我不管, 只要把它做完就行。**5** *formal* giving exact details【正式】详细的, 详尽的; 细致的: *She gave us a full and particular account of what had happened.* 她全面而详尽地向我们叙述了所发生的事情。 S1 W1

particular² *n* **1 in particular** especially 尤其, 特别: *It was a good concert – I enjoyed the last song in particular.* 那是一场不错的音乐会——我尤其喜欢最后一首歌。| **anything/anyone in particular** *Was there anything in particular that you wanted to talk about?* 你有什么特别想谈的吗? | **nothing/no one in particular** *"What did you want?" "Oh, nothing in particular."* "你想要什么?" "噢, 没什么特别的。" **2 particulars** [plural] the facts and details 细节, 详情: **[+of]** *I am not familiar with the particulars of the case.* 我对这个案子的详细情况并不熟悉。| **sb's particulars** (=details such as their name, address, profession etc) 某人的详细资料〈如名字、地址、职业等〉 **3 in every particular/in all particulars** *formal* in every detail【正式】在每个/所有细节上: *The documents were identical in almost every particular.* 这些文件几乎在每个细节上都是完全一样的。

par·tic·u·lar·i·ty /pəˌtɪkjəˋlærətɪ; pəˌtɪkjʊˈlærɪ̩ti/ *n formal*【正式】**1** [U] the quality of being exact and paying attention to details 详细, 详尽, 仔细, 细致 **2** [C] a detail 细节

par·tic·u·lar·ize also 又作 **-ise** *BrE*【英】/pəˋtɪkjələˌraɪz; pəˈtɪkjʊləraɪz/ *v* [I,T] *formal* to give the details of something; ITEMIZE【正式】详述; 具体列出, 列举 **—particularization** /pəˌtɪkjələrəˋzeʃən; pəˌtɪkjʊləraɪˈzeɪʃən/ *n* [U]

par·tic·u·lar·ly /pəˋtɪkjələlɪ; pəˈtɪkjʊləli/ *adv* **1** more than usual or more than others; ESPECIALLY 特别, 尤其: *Steve was in a particularly bad mood when he got back.* 史蒂夫回来时情绪特别差。| *The restaurant is particularly popular with young people.* 那家餐馆尤其受到年轻人的欢迎。| *We are hoping to expand our business, particularly in Europe.* 我们希望扩大我们的业务, 尤其是在欧洲。**2 not particularly a)** not very 不太, 不是非常: *I'm not particularly impressed with their performance.* 我对他们的表演印象不太深。**b)** *spoken* not very much【口】不(是)特别…: *"Do you want to come to the party?" "Not particularly."* "你想去参加聚会吗?" "不是特别想。"

par·tic·u·lates /pəˋtɪkjəlets; pəˈtɪkjʊlɪ̩ts/ *n* [plural] substances that consist of very small separate parts, especially substances in the air that come from car engines and seriously damage your health〔尤指空气中由汽车引擎排出的对人体十分有害的〕微粒, 颗粒

part·ing¹ /ˋpɑrtɪŋ; ˈpɑːtɪŋ/ *n* **1** [C,U] an occasion when two people leave each other 分离, 分开, 离别: *It had been a melancholy parting in the rain.* 那曾是一场令人伤感的雨中别离。**2** [C] *BrE* the line on your head made by dividing your hair with a comb【英】〔头发的〕分缝; PART *AmE*【美】: *a centre parting*〔头发的〕中分 —see picture on page A6 参见 A6 页图 **3 the parting of the ways** the point at which two people or organizations decide to separate〔两个人或组织〕决定分手的时刻, 决定分道扬镳的时刻; (十字) 路口

parting² *adj* **1 a parting kiss/gift/glance etc** a kiss etc that you give someone as you leave 临别的一吻/礼物/一瞥等 **2 parting shot** an unpleasant remark that you make just as you are leaving, especially at the end of an argument 临别时说的令人不快的话; 〔尤指〕争论结束时的尖刻话: *As her parting shot, she told me never to phone her again.* 临别时, 她居然告诉我再也不要打电话给她。

par·ti·san¹ /ˋpɑrtəzn; ˌpɑːtɪ̩ˈzæn/ *adj* **1** supporting a particular party, plan or leader and disliking all others 党派的, 帮派性的; 〔对某个政党、计划或领导〕热忱(而盲目)支持的: *a partisan report* 党派性的报告 **2 partisan struggle/conflict** the continuing fight of an armed group against an enemy that has defeated its country 游击斗争/冲突

partisan² *n* [C] **1** someone who supports a party, plan, or leader〔某个政党、计划或领导人的〕盲目支持者; 党徒, 党羽 **2** a member of an armed group that continues to fight against an enemy that has defeated its country〔抗击占领者的〕游击队员

par·ti·tion¹ /pɑrˋtɪʃən; pɑːˈtɪʃən/ *n* **1** [C] a thin wall that separates one part of a room from another 隔墙, 隔板 —see picture at 参见 OPEN-PLAN 图 **2** [U] the division of a country into two or more independent countries〔国家的〕分裂, 分割: *the partition of India* 印度的分治

partition² *v* [T **+into**] to divide a country, building, or room into two or more parts 分割; 把…分成部分; 分隔

partition sth ↔ **off** *phr v* [T] to divide part of a room from the rest by using a partition〔用隔墙、隔板〕将…隔开, 分隔: *They partitioned off part of the living room to make a study.* 他们把客厅隔出一部分做书房。

par·ti·tive /ˋpɑrtətɪv; ˈpɑːtɪ̩tɪv/ *n technical* a word which comes before a noun and shows that part of something is being described, not the whole of it, for example the word 'some' in the phrase 'some of the cake'【术语】表示部分的词〈如短语 some of the cake 中的 some〉 **—partitive** *adj*

part·ly /ˋpɑrtlɪ; ˈpɑːtli/ *adv* to some degree, but not completely 在某种程度上; 部分地: *It was partly my fault.* 那件事部分是我的错。| *The company's problems are partly due to bad management.* 那家公司的问题部分是由于管理不善造成的。| *The track was partly covered by long grass.* 那条小路有一部分被深草覆盖住了。

part·ner¹ /ˋpɑrtnə; ˈpɑːtnə/ *n* [C]

1 ►MARRIAGE ETC 婚姻等◄ one of two people who are married, or who live together and have a sexual relationship 配偶; (性) 伴侣; 情人

2 ►BUSINESS 生意◄ one of the owners of a business, who share the profits and losses 合伙人, 股东: *She's a partner in a law firm.* 她是一家法律事务所的合伙人。—see also 另见 SLEEPING PARTNER

3 ►DANCING/GAMES ETC 跳舞/游戏等◄ someone you do a particular activity with, for example dancing or playing a game against two other people〔跳舞、玩游戏等的〕搭档, 同伴: *Clare's my tennis partner.* 克莱尔是我的网球搭档。

4 ►COUNTRY 国家◄ a country that your country has an agreement with 伙伴: *Britain's new trading partners in Eastern Europe* 英国在东欧的新贸易伙伴

5 partners in crime *humorous* two people who have planned and done something together, especially something that slightly annoys other people【幽默】〔尤指恶作剧的〕同伙, 共犯

partner² *v* [T] to be someone's partner in a dance, game etc〔在跳舞、游戏等中〕做…的同伴[搭档]: *I used to partner him in tennis matches.* 我过去常在网球比赛中做他的搭档。

partner up also 又作 **partner off** *phr v* [I,T] to become or make people become partners (使) 成为伙伴[搭档]: **partner sb ↔ up with sb** *The host tried to partner me up with Janice.* 主人设法让我和贾尼斯成为舞伴。

part·ner·ship /ˋpɑrtnəˌʃɪp; ˈpɑːtnəʃɪp/ *n* **1** [U] the state of being a partner in business〔生意中的〕合伙(关系): **be in partnership** *We've been in partnership for five years.* 我们合伙经营已经五年了。| **go into partnership** *She's gone into partnership with two local doctors.* 她已和当地的两名医生合伙开业。**2** [C] a business owned by two or more partners who share the profits and losses 合伙企业, 合股公司: *It's one of the most profitable partnerships in the country.* 那是该国最赚钱的合伙企业之一。**3** [C] a relationship between two people, organizations, or countries that work together regularly〔两个人、组织或国家之间的〕合作关系; 伙伴关系: *Laurel and Hardy – a comedy partnership that lasted all through the 1930s* 劳莱和哈代 —— 整个20世纪30年代一直合作的一对喜剧搭档

part of speech /ˌ· · ˈ·/ *n* [C] *technical* one of the types into which words are divided in grammar according to their use, such as noun, verb, or adjective【术语】词类, 词性

par·took /pɑrˋtuk; pɑːˈtʊk/ the past tense of PARTAKE

par·tridge /ˋpɑrtrɪdʒ; ˈpɑːtrɪdʒ/ *n* [C] a fat bird with a short tail which is shot for sport and food 山鹑, 鹧鸪

part-sing·ing /ˈ· ˌ··/ *n* [U] the singing of part-songs 多声部合唱

part-song /ˋpɑrtsɔŋ; ˈpɑːtsɒŋ/ *n* [C] a song that consists of three or more musical lines that are sung together〔三个或三个以上声部的〕多声部合唱歌曲

part-time /ˌ· ˈ·◄/ *adj* [only before noun 仅用于名词前] a part-time worker works regularly for a part of the usual working time 部分时间的, 兼职的: *Mattie had a part-time job in the evenings.* 马蒂有一份在晚上兼职的工作。—compare 比较 FULL-TIME **—part-time** *adv*: *She'll work part-time after she's had the baby.* 她生完孩子以后将做兼职工作。**—part-timer** *n* [C] *informal*【非正式】: *A part-timer helps us out in the mornings.* 一名兼职人员每天早上过来帮我们的忙。

part·way /ˋpɑrtˋwe; ˈpɑːtweɪ/ *adv informal* some of the way into a space, or after some of a period of time has passed【非正式】(到) 中途; 一段时间过后: *She slid partway into the room.* 她中途悄悄地溜进了房间。| *He came in partway through the presentation.* 他在演出[演讲]进行到一半时进来了。

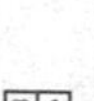

par·ty¹ /ˋpɑrtɪ; ˈpɑːti/ *n plural* **parties** [C]

1 ►FOR FUN 为娱乐◄ an occasion when people meet together, to enjoy themselves by eating, drinking, dancing etc〔社交或娱乐性的〕聚会, 宴会: *a birthday party* 生日聚会 | *a garden party* 游园会 | *Want to come to a party on Saturday?* 星期六想来参加聚会吗? | *Let's have a party here before we move out.* 我们搬出去之前在这里举行一次聚会吧。| **give/throw a party** *Robin threw a party while his parents were away.* 罗宾趁他父母不在时举行了一次聚会。| **party dress/clothes/hat** (=worn at a party) 宴会装/礼服/宴会[礼]帽 | **party game/trick** (=played or done at a party) 晚会游戏/把戏 | **party animal** *informal* (=someone who enjoys parties)【非正式】热衷于社交聚会的人 | **party house/school** *AmE informal* (=a place that often has noisy parties)【美, 非正式】经常举行聚会的场所/学校 —see also 另见 HEN PARTY, HOUSE PARTY, STAG PARTY

2 ►IN POLITICS 政治上◄ an organization of people with the same political beliefs and aims, that you can vote for in elections 政党: *The Democratic Party increased its majority.* 民主党扩大了自己的多数优势。| [also+plural verb] *BrE*【英】*The Labour party have launched their manifesto.* 工党已发表了他们的宣言。| *an all-party committee* 由所有政党组成的委员会 | **party leader/member** *Party leaders met to discuss their housing policy.* 党的领导人开会讨论他们的住房政策。| **the party faithful** (=its most loyal members) 忠诚的党员 —see also 另见 PARTY LINE (1)

3 ▶GROUP OF PEOPLE 一组人◀ a group of people that someone has formed in order to go somewhere or do something in an organized way〔共同去某地或做某事的〕一组，一队，一群：*a search party* 搜索队 | *a rescue party* 援救小组 | *The bus was rented by a party of tourists.* 一群游客租用了那辆公共汽车。—see also 另见 WORKING PARTY

4 ▶IN AN ARGUMENT/LAW 在争论中/法律上◀ one of the people or groups involved in an argument, agreement etc, especially a legal one〔法律上争论、协议等的〕一方；当事人：*The two parties are having difficulty agreeing.* 双方争执不下。—see also 另见 THIRD PARTY

5 **the guilty party** the person who has done something illegal or wrong 有罪的一方；有错的一方

6 **be (a) party to sth** *formal* to be involved in or have your name connected with an activity【正式】参与某事，参加；与某事有牵连：*I insist on being a party to this discussion.* 我坚持要求参与这次讨论。

party² also 又作 **party down** *v* [I] *informal especially AmE* to enjoy yourself, especially by drinking alcohol, eating, dancing etc【非正式，尤美】〔尤指饮酒、吃饭、跳舞等〕尽情欢乐：*All right! Let's party!* 好吧！大家尽兴吧！

party fa·vors /ˌ‥ ˈ‥/ *n* [plural] *especially AmE* small gifts such as paper hats or toys given to children at a party【尤美】〔社交聚会上送给孩子的〕聚会小礼物〈如纸帽或玩具〉

party line /ˈ‥ ˌ/ *n* [C] 1 the official opinion of a political party, which its members are expected to agree with and support 政党的路线：*He follows the party line fairly closely.* 他相当严格地遵循党的路线。—see also 另见 **toe the line** (TOE²) 2 a telephone line connected to two or more telephones belonging to different people 电话合用线

party piece /ˈ‥ ˌ/ *n* [C] something that you usually do to entertain people at a party, for example a song that you sing〔某人〕经常在社交聚会上表演的节目〈如唱歌〉

party po·lit·i·cal /ˌ‥ ‥ˈ‥‥/ *adj* [only before noun 仅用于名词前] *especially BrE* related to party politics【尤英】党派政治的：*party-political conflict* 党派政治冲突 | *a party political broadcast* 党派政治的广播[电视]节目

party pol·i·tics /ˌ‥ ˈ‥‥/ *n* [U] activities that are concerned with getting support for a political party rather than with doing things to improve the situation in a country 党派政治

party poop·er /ˈpɑrti ˌpupɚ; ˈpɑːti ˌpuːpə/ *n* [C] *informal* someone who spoils other people's fun【非正式】社交聚会上令人扫兴[煞风景]的人

party wall /ˌ‥ ˈ/ *n* [C] a dividing wall between two houses, apartments etc which belong to both owners〔两座房屋或公寓等之间的〕界墙，共有墙

par·ve·nu /ˈpɑrvəˌnu; ˈpɑːvənjuː/ *n* [C] *formal* someone from a low social position who suddenly becomes rich or powerful【正式】暴发户；新贵：*Aristocratic families found themselves associating with parvenus.* 贵族家庭发现他们自己在与新贵们来往。—**parvenu** *adj*

PASCAL /pæˈskæl; ˈpæskæl/ *n* [U] a computer language that works well on small computer systems and is used in teaching PASCAL 语言〔一种用于教学的电脑语言〕

Pas·cal /pæˈskæl; pæˈskæl/, **Blaise** /blez; bleɪz/ (1623-62) a French PHILOSOPHER, MATHEMATICIAN, and PHYSICIST, who wrote about religion, and made many important scientific discoveries. His inventions include an early type of calculating machine and the BAROMETER. 帕斯卡〔(1623-1662)，法国哲学家、数学家和物理学家。他写有宗教作品，曾做出大量有价值的科学发现。其发明包括早期的一种计算器和气压计〕

pas·chal /ˈpæskl; ˈpæskəl/ *adj* 1 related to the Jewish holiday of Passover〔犹太人〕逾越节的 2 related to the Christian holiday of Easter〔基督教〕复活节的

pas de deux /ˌpɑ də ˈdu; ˌpɑː də ˈdɜː/ *n* [C] a dance in BALLET performed by a man and a woman〔芭蕾〕双人舞

Pas·o·li·ni /pæsəˈlini; pæsəˈliːni/, **Pier Pao·lo** /pjɛr ˈpaulo; pjeə ˈpaʊləʊ/ (1922-75) an Italian film DIRECTOR, poet, and writer, who was murdered on a beach near Rome. He used his films, which include *Oedipus Rex* (1967) and *Medea* (1970), to criticize society. 帕索里尼〔(1922-1975)，意大利电影导演、诗人和作家，在罗马附近的海滩上被人杀害。他以自己导演的《俄狄浦斯王》(1967)和《美狄亚》(1970)等影片对社会现象进行批判〕

pass¹ /pæs; pɑːs/ *v* S1 W1

1 ▶GO PAST 通过◀ [I,T] to come up to a particular point or object and go past it 经过，越过：*The crowd parted to let the truck pass.* 人群散开让卡车通过。| *They kept quiet until the soldiers had passed.* 他们在士兵走过之前一直保持安静。| **pass sb/sth** *We passed each other on the staircase.* 我们在楼梯上擦肩而过。| *I pass the sports centre on the way to work.* 我去上班的路上经过体育中心。

2 ▶MOVE/GO 移动/行进◀ a) [I always+adv/prep] to move, go, or travel from one place to another, following a particular direction 前行，穿过：[+through/into/from etc] *We saw her arrive, passing through the little gate into the garden.* 我们看见她到了，看到她穿过那道小门进了花园。| *A few seconds later, I heard his footsteps pass along the deck above my head.* 几秒钟后，我听到他沿着我头顶上的甲板走过的脚步声。| *Light bends as it passes from air to water.* 光从空气进入水中时会折射。| **be (just) passing through** *spoken* (=be travelling through a place)【口】(恰好)经过 *We were just passing through and thought we'd call in and see you.* 我们正好经过，于是就想到你家看看你。b) [T always+adv/ prep] to move something or place something across, through, around etc something else 使通过，使穿过；使环绕：**pass sth around/along/across etc** *Pass the rope around the tree.* 把绳子绕在树上。

3 ▶ROAD/RIVER ETC 道路/河流等◀ [I always+adv/prep] if a road, river, railway line etc passes through a place, it goes through that place〔道路、河流、铁路线等〕经过，通过，穿过：*The new road passes immediately behind the theatre.* 那条新公路紧挨着剧院后面经过。

4 ▶TIME 时间◀ a) [I] if time passes, it goes by〔时间〕过去，流逝：*The days passed slowly.* 日子慢慢地过去。| *Several years passed before she realized the truth.* 好几年过去了，她才知道事情的真相。| **with each day that passes/with every passing day** *The situation seems to get worse with each day that passes.* 情况好像一天比一天糟。| **not a day/hardly a day passes without** *Hardly a day passes without me thinking about Ian.* 我几乎没有一天不想念伊恩。b) [T] if you pass time or pass your life in a particular way, you spend it in that way 度过〔时间〕：*We passed the winter pleasantly enough.* 我们非常愉快地度过了那个冬天。| **pass the time** (=when you are bored or waiting for something) 消磨时间 *We played cards to pass the time until morning.* 我们打牌消磨时光，直到次日凌晨。

5 ▶EXAM/TEST 考试/测试◀ [I,T] a) to succeed in an examination or test 考试及格；通过〔考试〕：*Do you think you'll pass?* 你觉得你考试会及格吗？| *I passed my driving test first time.* 我第一次驾驶考试就通过了。| **pass (sth) with flying colours** (=get very high marks) 以优异成绩通过(某事) b) [T] to officially decide that someone has passed an examination or test 让〔某人〕通过考试[测试]：*The examiners finally passed her.* 考官们最终还是让她通过了。

6 ▶LAW/PROPOSAL 法律/提案◀ a) [T] to officially accept a law or proposal, especially by voting〔尤指以投票方式〕通过〔法律或提案〕：**pass a law/motion/resolution etc** *Parliament passed a series of important measures in 1994.* 议会在1994年通过了一系列重要举措。| *The motion was passed unanimously.* 那项动议获一致通过。b) [I,T] if a law or proposal passes an official group, it is officially accepted by that group〔法律、提案等〕被…接受，被…通过：*The bill failed by 17 votes to pass the House of Representatives.* 那项法案以17票之差没有被众议院通过。

7 ▶GIVE 给◀ [T] to take something and put it in someone's hand, especially because they cannot reach it 传递，递给：*Pass the salt, please.* 请把盐递过来。| **pass sb sth** *Can you pass me that bag that's on the floor by your feet?* 你能把地板上你脚边的那个包递给我吗？| **pass sth to sb** *I passed the note back to her.* 我把便条递还给她。—see also 另见 **pass around**

8 ▶SAY/COMMUNICATE 说/交流◀ a) [I always+adv/ prep] if words, looks, or signs pass between two or more people, they exchange them with one another 交流；交换〔眼色、信号等〕：[+between/through etc] *A glance of understanding passed between them.* 他们会意地互相看了一眼。| *The news passed quickly through the crowd outside the palace.* 那消息在王宫外的人群中传得很快。b) **pass a remark/comment/opinion etc** to say something or give your opinion 发表评论/意见等：*She sat and watched the game, passing the occasional witty comment.* 她坐在那里观看比赛，时而发表一些言辞风趣的评论。

9 **let sth pass** to deliberately not say anything or not react when someone says or does something that you do not like 对某事物不予理会[不加追究]：*Carla made some comment about my work but I decided to let it pass.* 卡拉对我的工作作了一些评论，但我决定不予理会。

10 ▶END 结束◀ [I] to gradually come to an end 渐渐终止[消失]：*The storm soon passed.* 暴风雨很快就过去了。| *You may feel a little stiff, but it'll pass.* 你会感到有点儿僵硬，但这种感觉会渐渐消失。

11 ▶SPORT 体育运动◀ [I,T] to kick, throw, or hit a ball etc to a member of your own team〔给己方队员〕传〔球〕: *Maradona quickly passed to Jaires.* 马拉多纳迅速把球传给雅尔伊。| **pass sth** *Pass the baton, you idiot!* 把接力棒传过来，你这个蠢货！—see picture on page A22 参见 A22 页图

12 **pass 600/pass the $5,000 mark etc** to go past a particular number or amount, as a total gradually increases or is added to 超过 600/超过 5000 美元大关等: *Contributions to the disaster fund have already passed the $2 million mark.* 救灾捐款已超过 200 万美元大关。

13 **pass unnoticed** to happen without anyone noticing or saying anything 不被注意地发生

14 **pass the time of day (with sb)** to talk to someone for a short time in order to be friendly（与某人）寒暄

15 ▶CHANGE CONTROL 改变控制◀ [I] *formal* to go from one person's control or ownership to someone else's【正式】〔控制权或所有权〕转移; 转让: [+to/into] *On his death his lands passed to his son.* 他死后，土地传给了儿子。

16 ▶CHANGE 变化◀ [I] *formal* if a substance passes from one condition into another, it changes into another condition【正式】转变, 转化: [+from/to] *Ice passes from a solid to a liquid state.* 冰从固态变成液态。

17 ▶FALSE MONEY 假币◀ [T] to use false money to pay for something 使用〔假币〕付款: *She tried to pass a counterfeit $100 bill.* 她企图使用一张 100 美元的假钞付款。

18 ▶PROBLEM 问题◀ [T always+adv/prep] to send a problem or question to another person or group so that they can deal with it 把〔难题或问题〕转给: **pass sth (across/back/on) to sb** *They passed your enquiry over to us.* 他们把你询问的事转给了我们。

19 **pass (a) sentence (on sb)** to officially decide how a criminal will be punished, and to announce what the punishment will be（对某人）宣判, 宣布判决

20 **pass judgment (on sb)** to give your opinion about someone's behaviour（对某人）作出评论

21 ▶GIVE NO ANSWER 不予回答◀ [I] to give no answer to a question because you do not know the answer〔因不知问题答案而〕不予回答; 略过: *"Who won the Cup in 1966?" "Pass."* "1966 年谁赢了那奖杯?" "过。"

22 **pass urine/stools/blood etc** *formal or technical* to send out something as waste material or in waste material from your BLADDER OR BOWELS【正式或术语】排尿/排便/便血等

23 **pass water** *technical* to send out URINE (=liquid waste) from your body【术语】排尿, 小便

24 **pass understanding/comprehension/belief** *formal* to be impossible to understand or believe【正式】难以理解/相信

25 **come to pass** *literary or biblical* to happen【文或圣经】发生 —see also 另见 PASSING, **pass the buck** (BUCK[1] (2)), **pass muster** (MUSTER[2] (1))

pass as sb/sth *phr v* [T] **pass for** (PASS[1])〔错误地〕被看[当]作, 被认为是

pass sth ↔ **around** *phr v* [T] **1** to offer something to each person in a group 分发〔某物〕. *Pass the cookies around, would you?* 请把小甜饼分发给大家, 好吗? **2** to give something to one person in a group for them to give to the person next to them 传递〔某物〕: *He took a cigar and passed the box around.* 他拿了一支雪茄, 然后把盒子传下去。—see also 另见 **pass the hat round** (HAT (5))

pass away *phr v* [I] an expression meaning to die, used because you want to avoid upsetting someone by saying this directly 去世〔委婉说法〕

pass by *phr v* **1** [I, T] to move past or go past a person, place, vehicle etc 经过: *I'd lie on my back and look at the clouds passing by.* 我常常仰面躺着, 看片片的云彩掠过。| **pass by sb/sth** *Call in and see us if you're ever passing by the house.* 如果你什么时候经过我家, 就来看看我们。—see also 另见 PASSERBY **2** [T **pass** sb ↔ **by**] if something passes you by, it is there but you do not get any profit or advantage from it〔某人〕没有从中受益[获益]; 忽视, 忽略: *She felt that life was passing her by.* 她觉得自己从未受到生活的眷顾。

pass sth ↔ **down** *phr v* [T often passive 常用被动态] to give or teach something, such as knowledge or traditions, to people who are younger than you or live after you 把〔知识、传统等〕传给后人; 把…往下传: **pass sth down (from sb) to sb** *They pass their knowledge down from one generation to the next in stories and rhymes.* 他们把自己的知识以故事和韵诗的形式一代一代地传下去。

pass for sb/sth *phr v* [T] if someone or something passes for something, people think that they are that thing, although they are not really〔错误地〕被看[当]作, 被认为是: *With my hair cut short I could have passed for a boy.* 我要是把头发剪短, 或许会被当作是一个男孩。| **what passes for** *Davis then encountered the police, or what passed for the police in those peculiar conditions.* 就在那时, 戴维斯遇到了警察, 或者说在那种特定条件下被当作是警察的人。

pass off *phr v* **1** [T **pass** sb/sth **off as** sth] to try to make people think that something or someone is something that it is not, especially something valuable 把…冒充为, 假称…是: *There is rarely any attempt to pass these copies off as originals.* 很少有人试图把这些复制品冒充为原作。**2 pass off well/badly etc** if an event passes off well, badly etc, it happens and is completed in that way 进行顺利/不顺利等: *The presidential tour passed off without a hitch.* 总统的巡访非常成功。

pass on *phr v* **1** [T **pass** sth ↔ **on**] to tell someone a piece of information that someone else has told you 把〔信息〕传给〔其他人〕: **pass sth on to sb** *She said she'd pass the message on to the other students.* 她说她会把口信传给其他学生。**2** [T **pass** sth ↔ **on**] **a)** to give something, especially a disease, to your children through your GENES〔尤指把疾病〕遗传给 **b)** to give a slight illness to someone else 传染〔疾病〕: *I stayed off work, as I didn't want to pass my cold on to anyone.* 我没有去上班, 因为我不想把感冒传给别人。**3** [T **pass** sth ↔ **on**] to make someone else pay the cost of something 把〔费用〕转嫁给…: *Any increase in wage costs is bound to be passed on to the consumer.* 增加工资的成本必然会转嫁到消费者的头上。**4** [I] **pass away** (PASS[1]) 去世

pass out *phr v* **1** [I] to faint 昏过去, 晕倒, 失去知觉: *He always passes out at the sight of blood.* 他总是一见到血就晕过去。**2** [T **pass** sth ↔ **out**] to give something to each one of a group of people 分[散]发〔某物〕: *Their teacher passed out the dictionaries.* 老师把词典分发给他们。**3** [I] *especially BrE* to finish a course of study at a military school or police college【尤英】〔从军校或警校〕毕业

pass over *phr v* [T] **1** [**pass** sb ↔ **over** usually passive 一般用被动态] if you pass someone over for a job, you choose someone else who is younger or lower in the organization than them〔就某项工作〕对〔某人〕不加考虑: **be passed over for promotion** (=someone else got the promotion) 不被考虑提升 **2** [**pass over** sth] if you pass over a remark or a subject in a conversation, you do not spend any time discussing it〔谈话中〕忽略…, 对…不加理会: *I think we'd better pass over that last remark.* 我想我们最好不理会最后那句话。

pass sth ↔ **round** *phr v* [T] *BrE* to pass something around【英】分发〔某物〕; 传递〔某物〕

pass up *phr v* **pass up a chance/opportunity/offer** to not make use of a chance to do something 放过[放弃, 错过]机会: *Why did you pass up the opportunity to go to university?* 你为什么放弃了上大学的机会?

pass² *n* [C] **1** an official piece of paper which shows that you are allowed to enter a building, travel on something without paying, etc 出入证, 通行证; (免费) 乘车证: *The guard checked our passes.* 警卫检查了我们的通行证。| **bus pass/train pass etc** *She issued us with a one-day bus pass.* 她给我们发了一天有效的公共汽车免费乘车证。**2** a successful result in an examination（考试）及格: **a pass in** *delighted with her pass in geography* 为她地理考试及格感到高兴 | **pass mark** (=the mark you need to succeed in an examination) 及格分数 **3** a single act of kicking, throwing, or hitting a ball etc to another member of your team 传球: *Holden intercepted a short pass by Maradona.* 霍尔登拦截了马拉多纳的一个短距离传球。**4 make a pass at** *informal* to try to kiss or touch another person with the intention of starting a sexual relationship with them【非正式】向…调情, 勾引… **5** a road or path which goes through a place that is difficult to cross 山道, 山口, 要隘: *The road wound over a narrow mountain pass.* 那条路蜿蜒越过狭窄的山道。| *at the top of the pass into Italy* 在进入意大利的要隘的顶端 —see picture on page A12 参见 A12 页图 **6 this pass/the first etc pass** this, the first etc stage in a process, especially one which involves separating unwanted things out from a group 这一轮/第一轮筛选等, 这一个/第一个回合等: *On the second pass we eliminated all the candidates with less than a year's experience.* 在第二轮筛选中, 我们淘汰了所有经验不足一年的候选人。**7 a pretty/sorry/fine etc pass** *old-fashioned informal* an unpleasant situation【过时, 非正式】令人不快的处境, 困境: **come to a pretty pass** *Things have come to a pretty pass if we can't even afford to get a newspaper!* 如果我们连一张报纸都买不起, 那情况就糟透了! **8 a)** a single movement of your hands or of a WAND over something〔用手或魔杖做的〕遮掩动作, 障眼法动作 **b)** a single

movement of an aircraft over a place which it is attacking〔飞机等对攻击目标的〕一次俯冲

pass·a·ble /ˈpæsəbl; ˈpɑːsəbəl/ *adj* **1** just good enough to be acceptable, but not very good 过得去的, 尚可的, 还好的: *a passable piece of work* 还可以接受的一项工作 **2** a road or river that is passable is not blocked, so you can travel along or across it〔道路、河流〕可通行的, 能通过的: *The mountain path is not passable in winter.* 这条山路冬天无法通行。**—passably** *adv*: *passably well* 还不错

pas·sage /ˈpæsɪdʒ; ˈpæsɪdʒ/ *n*
1 ▶IN A BUILDING 建筑物内◀ [C] a long narrow way with walls on either side which connects one room or place to another; CORRIDOR (1) 过道, 走廊: *Vaughan's room is just along the passage.* 沃恩的房间就在过道前边。| *an underground passage* 地下通道
2 ▶A WAY THROUGH 穿行的路◀ [singular] a way through something 通道, 通路: **[+through]** *We forced a passage through the crowd.* 我们从人群中挤出一条通道。
3 ▶FROM A BOOK ETC 来自一本书等◀ [C] a short part of a book, poem, speech, piece of music etc〔书、诗、演讲、乐曲等的〕一段, 一节
4 ▶OF A LAW 关于一项法律◀ [U] the process of getting a BILL through a parliament or Congress so that it can become law〔法案的〕通过: **[+through]** *The bill was amended several times during its passage through Congress.* 那项法案在国会通过期间作过几次修正。
5 ▶MOVEMENT 移动◀ [U] *formal* the action of going across, over, along etc something【正式】穿过; 越过; 经过: *The bridge isn't strong enough to allow the passage of heavy vehicles.* 那座桥不够坚固, 无法让重型车辆通过。
6 the passage of time the passing of time 时间的流逝: *With the passage of time, things began to look more hopeful.* 随着时间的流逝, 事情开始显得更有希望。
7 ▶INSIDE A BODY 体内◀ a tube in your body that air or liquid can pass through〔人体的〕管道: *nasal passages* 鼻道
8 ▶JOURNEY 旅行◀ [singular] the cost of a journey on a ship 乘船旅行的费用, 船费: **[+to]** *My parents couldn't afford the passage to America.* 我父母付不起去美国的船费。| **work your passage** (=pay for a journey by working on the ship) 在船上做工以支付船费 —see also 另见 **rite of passage** (RITE (2))

Passage to In·di·a, A /ˌ· · · ˈ· · · / (1924) a book by E. M. Forster about the relationships in India between British people and Indians during the early 1900s, when Britain controlled India's government《印度之行》〔(1924), E. M.福斯特创作的一部小说, 讲述20世纪初英国人控制印度政府期间英国人与印度人的关系〕

pas·sage·way /ˈpæsɪdʒˌwe; ˈpæsɪdʒweɪ/ *n* [C] a PASSAGE (1) 过道, 走廊

pas·sant /pɑˋsɑn; ˈpæsɒŋ/ *adv* —see 见 EN PASSANT

pass·book /ˈpæsˌbuk; ˈpɑːsbʊk/ *n* [C] **1** a book in which a record is kept of the money you put into and take out of a BUILDING SOCIETY OR SAVINGS AND LOAN ASSOCIATION〔房屋互助协会或储蓄贷款协会的〕存款提款记录簿, 存折 **2** *AmE* a BANK BOOK【美】(银行) 存折

Pas·schen·daele /ˈpæʃəndel; ˈpæʃəndeɪl/ an important battle during World War I in 1917, in northwest Belgium, in which over 200,000 British soldiers were killed. The MUD (=soft wet earth) made the terrible conditions in which the soldiers lived and fought even worse. 帕森达勒战役〔1917年一战期间在比利时西北部进行的一场重要战役, 其间20万英军战死。泥泞的战地使英军的日常起居及作战尤为艰难〕

pas·sé /pæˋse; ˈpæseɪ/ *adj* no longer modern or fashionable 过时的, 老式的, 陈旧的: *passé colours typical of the 80s* 过时的80年代典型色彩

pas·sel /ˈpæsəl; ˈpæsəl/ *n* [C **+of**] *AmE old-fashioned* a group of people or things【美, 过时】一群; 一批: *a whole passel of kids* 一大群孩子

pas·sen·ger /ˈpæsn̩dʒɚ; ˈpæsɪndʒə/ *n* [C] **1** someone who is travelling in a vehicle, plane, boat etc, but is not driving it or working on it〔车辆、飞机、船舶等的〕乘客, 旅客: *Neither the driver nor the passengers were hurt.* 司机和乘客均未受伤。| **passenger train/carriage/car** (=for people, not for goods)〔火车〕客车 **2** *BrE* someone in a team who does not do their share of the group's work【英】〔团体中〕不做分内事的成员, 不干活的人

passenger seat /ˈ· · · ˌ· / *n* [C] the seat in the front of a vehicle next to the driver〔汽车驾驶员旁边的〕乘客座位

Passe·par·tout /ˌpæspɑrˋtu; ˌpæspɑːˈtuː/ a character in the book *Around the World in 80 Days* (1873) by Jules Verne. He is the servant and friend of Phileas Fogg, and goes with him when he makes his journey around the world. 百事通〔儒勒·凡尔纳的小说《八十天环游地球》(1873) 中的人物。他是菲莱亚斯·弗格的仆人和朋友, 陪伴弗格完成环游世界的旅程〕

pass·er·by /ˌpæsɚˋbaɪ; ˌpɑːsəˈbaɪ/ *n plural* **passersby** [C] someone who is walking past a place by chance (过) 路人: *A few passersby witnessed the accident.* 有几个过路人目击了那次事故。

pas·sim /ˈpæsɪm; ˈpæsɪm/ *adv technical* used in the notes to a book or article to show that a particular word or name appears many times【术语】多处, 到处, 各处〔用于书籍或文章后面的注释, 表示某个词或名称在书中或文章中出现多次〕

pass·ing¹ /ˈpæsɪŋ; ˈpɑːsɪŋ/ *n* [U] **1 the passing of time/the years** the process of time going by 时间/岁月的流逝: *With the passing of years, he grew more bad-tempered.* 随着岁月的流逝, 他的脾气更坏了。**2 mention/note in passing** if you say something in passing, you mention it while you are mainly talking about something else〔在谈论别的事情时〕顺便 (说起), 附带 (提及): *He did mention his brother's wife, but only in passing.* 他确实提到了他的弟媳, 但只是顺带而已。**3** the fact of something ending or disappearing 终止; 消失: *The old regime was defeated, and few people mourned its passing.* 旧政权被打垮, 但很少有人对其消失感到痛惜。**4** a word meaning death, used when you want to avoid saying this directly 去世, 逝世〔委婉说法〕

passing² *adj* [only before noun 仅用于名词前] **1** going past 经过的, 通过的: *Michael watched the passing cars.* 迈克尔望着来往的汽车。**2 with each passing day/week/year** *literary* continuously as time passes【文】随着一天天/一周周/一年年的过去: *With each passing day she grew stronger.* 她一天天变得更加强健[坚强]。**3** short, or disappearing after only a short time; BRIEF¹ (1) 短暂的; 一时的: *He didn't even give the matter a passing thought.* 他对那件事甚至连想都没想一下。| *a passing reference* 顺带提及

passing³ *adv old use* very【旧】很, 非常: *passing strange* 很奇怪

pas·sion /ˈpæʃən; ˈpæʃən/ *n* **1** [C,U] a very strong, deeply felt emotion, especially of sexual love, of anger, or of belief in an idea or principle 强烈的情感, 激情〔尤指性爱、愤怒或对某种思想、原则的信念〕: *a sermon full of passion and inspiration* 充满激情和灵感的布道 | **[+for]** *Paolo's burning passion for an older woman* 保罗对一位比他年长的女子燃烧的激情 | **fly into a passion** (=suddenly become very angry) 勃然大怒 **2** [C] a strong liking for something 对…的强烈爱好, 热爱: **[+for]** *the Cubans' passion for baseball* 古巴人对棒球的热爱 **3 the Passion** *technical* the suffering and death of Christ【术语】耶稣的受难 —see also 另见 **crime of passion** (CRIME (5)) **—passionless** *adj*

pas·sion·ate /ˈpæʃənɪt; ˈpæʃənət/ *adj* **1** having or involving very strong feelings of sexual love 情欲强烈的; 多情的: *a passionate kiss* 充满激情的亲吻 **2** having or expressing a very strong feeling, especially belief in an idea or principle〔尤指对某种思想、原则〕具有[表现出]强烈感情的; 激昂的: *Lewis is a passionate supporter of women's rights.* 刘易斯是女权运动的狂热支持者。**3** very eager; INTENSE 热切的; 强烈的: *Brian is passionate about football.* 布赖恩酷爱足球。**—passionately** *adv*: *Peter is passionately involved in environmental issues.* 彼得热烈地参与有关环境的议题。

pas·sion·flow·er /ˈpæʃənˌflauɚ; ˈpæʃənˌflaʊə/ *n* [C] a climbing plant with large flowers 西番莲〔一种攀缘植物〕

passion fruit /ˈ· · ˌ· / *n* [C,U] a small fruit that grows on some types of passionflower 西番莲果实 —see picture on page A8 参见A8页图

passion play /ˈ· · ˌ· / *n* [C] a play telling the story of the suffering and death of Christ 耶稣受难 (复活) 剧

Passion Sun·day /ˌ· · ˈ· · / in the Christian church, the Sunday two weeks before Easter 受难主日, 棕枝主日〔基督教复活节前第二个星期日〕

pas·sive¹ /ˈpæsɪv; ˈpæsɪv/ *adj* **1** tending to accept situations or things that other people do, without attempting to change or fight against them; SUBMISSIVE 被动的; 消极的; 顺从的: *They accepted their defeat with passive resignation.* 他们以无可奈何的消极心态接受了失败。| *Kathy seems to take the passive role in the relationship.* 凯西在这一关系中似乎扮演着被动的角色。**2** *technical* a verb or a sentence that is passive has as its subject the person or thing to which an action is done, as in 'The boy was thrown from his horse.'【术语】〔动词或句子〕被动的 —compare 比较 ACTIVE¹ (7) **—passively** *adv* **—passiveness, passivity** *n* [U]

passive² *n* **the passive** *technical* the passive form of a verb, for example 'was kicked' in the sentence 'The ball was kicked

by the boy.' 【术语】〔动词的〕被动式; 被动语态〈如句子 'The ball was kicked by the boy.' 中的 'was kicked'〉 —compare 比较 ACTIVE[2]

passive re·sis·tance /ˌ··ˈ···/ *n* [U] a way of opposing or protesting against something without using violence 消极抵抗, 非暴力抵抗: *Gandhi's campaign of passive resistance* 甘地的非暴力抵抗运动

passive smok·ing /ˌ··ˈ··/ *n* [U] the act of breathing in smoke from someone else's cigarette, PIPE etc 被动吸烟, 吸二手烟

passive voice /ˈ··, ·ˈ/ *n* [singular] the PASSIVE[2]〔动词的〕被动式; 被动语态

pas·siv·ize also 又作 **-ise** *BrE*【英】/ˈpæsɪˌvaɪz; ˈpæsɪvaɪz/ *v* [I,T] *technical* to make a verb PASSIVE, or to become passive 【术语】(使) 变成被动式 —**passivization** /ˌpæsɪvəˈzeʃən; ˌpæsɪvaɪˈzeɪʃən/ *n* [U]

pass·key /ˈpæsˌki; ˈpɑːskiː/ *n* [C] **1** a key given to a few people for a door that only they are allowed to use〔只有少数人拥有的〕专用钥匙 **2** a key that will open a number of different locks〔能开启若干不同锁的〕万能钥匙

Pass·o·ver /ˈpæsˌovə; ˈpɑːsəʊvə/ *n* [singular] an important Jewish religious holiday when the escape of the Jews from Egypt is remembered〔犹太教纪念犹太人逃离埃及的〕逾越节

pass·port /ˈpæsˌport; ˈpɑːspɔːt/ *n* [C] **1** a small official book given by a government to a citizen that proves who that person is and allows them to leave the country and enter other countries 护照 **2 a passport to success/romance/a good job etc** something that makes success, romance etc possible and likely 获取成功/爱情/好工作等的手段: *Erin saw marriage as a passport to happiness.* 埃琳把婚姻看作是获取幸福的一个手段。

passport con·trol /ˈ··, ·ˈ/ *n* [U] the place where your passport is checked when you leave or enter a country 护照检查处

pass·word /ˈpæsˌwɝd; ˈpɑːswɜːd/ *n* [C] **1** a secret word or phrase that someone has to speak before they are allowed to enter a place such as a military camp〔进入某地如军营的〕口令 **2** a secret group of letters or numbers that must be put into a computer before you can use a system or PROGRAM〔使用电脑系统或程序所用的〕通行密码

past[1] /pæst; pɑːst/ *adj*

1 ▶PREVIOUS 以前的◀ [only before noun 仅用于名词前] done, used, or experienced before now 以前的, 过去的, 曾经的: *Judging by her past performance, I'd say Rowena should do very well.* 从罗伊娜以往的表现来看, 我要说她会干得很好的。| *From past experience she knew not to ask him where he'd been.* 根据过去的经验, 她知道不能问他去了哪里。| *Study some past exam papers to get an idea of the questions.* 研究一些以前的考卷, 大致了解一下所考的问题。

2 ▶RECENTLY 最近◀ a little earlier than the present or up until now 刚过去的: **in the past 24 hours/year/few weeks etc** *In the past year Shane's changed jobs 3 times.* 在过去一年里, 沙恩更换了三次工作。| **for the past 24 hours/year/few weeks etc** *Ben hasn't been feeling too good for the past week.* 这一星期来本一直感到不太舒服。

3 ▶FINISHED 完成的◀ finished or having come to an end 完成的, 结束的: *Winter is past and spring has come at last.* 冬天过去了, 春天终于来临。| *Sarah's eyes shone with memories of past happiness.* 萨拉的眼睛闪耀着对以往幸福的回忆。| **past life** (=part of your life that you have no connection with any more) 昔日的生活 *a sleep filled with dreams of my past life in the East* 梦境中尽是昔日我在东方的生活

4 ▶FORMER 以往的◀ [only before noun 仅用于名词前] achieving something in the past, or holding a particular important position in the past 以往的; 前任的: **past president/champion/heroes etc** *celebrating in honour of all our nation's past heroes* 纪念我们以往所有的民族英雄

5 be past it *spoken* to be too old to do something【口】年纪太大干不了什么; 太旧而不能用: *Talbot's past it – they should have dropped him.* 塔尔博特年纪太大——他们本该把他除名的。

6 ▶GRAMMAR 语法◀ [only before noun 仅用于名词前] *technical* being the form of a verb that is used to show a past action or state【术语】〔动词形式〕过去的: *the past tense* 过去时[式]

past[2] *prep* **1** further than 在…的更远处: *The hospital's just up this road about a mile past the school on your left.* 医院就在这条路上离你左手边的学校大约一英里外的地方。| **just past** (=a little further than) 比…远一点 *There are parking spaces over there, just past the garage.* 那边有停车的地方, 就在那个车库过去一点儿。—see picture on page A1 参见 A1 页图 **2** up to and beyond 越过: *Will you be going past my house on your way home?* 你回家的路上会经过我家吗? | **straight past** (=directly past without stopping) 径直经过 *Eva had changed so much I walked straight past her and didn't recognize her.* 伊娃变化太大了, 我从她旁边径直走过竟没有认出她来。**3 I wouldn't put it past sb (to do sth)** *spoken* used to say that you would not be surprised if someone did something bad or unusual because it is typical of them to do that type of thing【口】我认为某人很有可能〔做坏事或不寻常的事〕: *I'm not sure if he actually did cheat in the exams, but I wouldn't put it past him!* 我不能肯定他考试是否真的作弊了, 但我认为他会做出这种事来的! **4 be past caring/being interested/hope etc** to not care any more, be interested in something any more etc 不再在乎/感兴趣/抱希望等: *I used to get really upset when he wouldn't see me, but I'm past caring now.* 当他不愿见我, 我曾一度非常伤心, 但我现在已不再在乎了。

past[3] *n* **1 the past a)** the time that existed before the present 过去, 以前, 昔日: *James has done many things in the past, but he's happiest now in his job as a teacher.* 詹姆斯以前做过很多工作, 但他对现在当教师感到最开心。| **a thing of the past** (=something that does not exist any more) 往事 *Good manners seem to have become a thing of the past.* 以礼待人似乎已成了往事。**b)** the form of a verb that shows that the action or state described by the verb happened or existed some time before the present time〔动词的〕过去式: *Change the following verbs into the past.* 把以下动词改变成过去式。**2 it's all in the past** *spoken* used to say that an unpleasant experience has ended and can be forgotten【口】一切都已过去了: *You mustn't think about it. It's all in the past now.* 你千万不要再想那件事, 现在一切都已过去了。**3 sb's/sth's past** all the things that have happened to someone or something in the past 某人/某物的过去: *There were certain things in his past which were very painful for Neil to remember.* 尼尔的一些往事对他来说是非常痛苦的记忆。**4** [singular] part of someone's life that they try to keep secret because they did things that are considered to be wrong〔某人做过错事而试图保密的〕经历: **a shady past** *There was something odd about him which suggested he had a shady past.* 他有点怪, 这表明他有见不得人的过去。

past[4] *adv* **1** up to and beyond a particular place 经过: *Hal and his friends came running past at top speed.* 哈尔和他的朋友以最快的速度跑过去了。**2 go past** if a period of time goes past, it passes〔一段时间〕过去: *Weeks went past without any news of them.* 几个星期过去了, 一点关于他们的消息也没有。

pasta 意大利面食

spaghetti 意大利面条

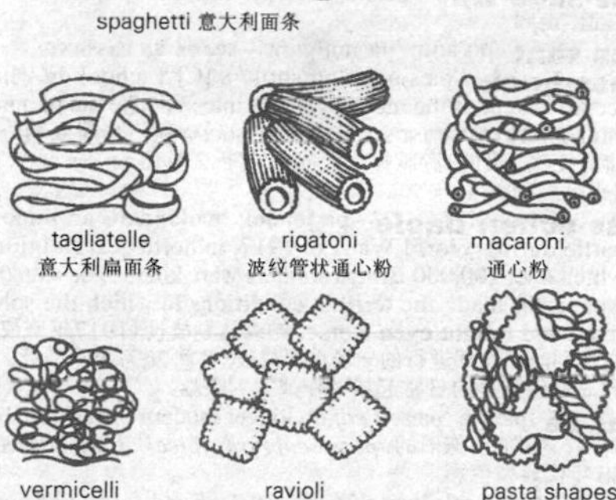

pas·ta /ˈpɑstə; ˈpæstə/ *n* [U] an Italian food made from flour, eggs, and water and cut into various shapes, usually eaten with a sauce〔常拌以调味汁的〕意大利面食

paste[1] /pest; peɪst/ *n* **1 meat/fish/tomato etc paste** a soft mixture made from crushed solid food that is used in cooking or is spread on bread〔用于烹调或涂面包的〕肉酱/鱼酱/番茄酱等 **2** [C,U] a soft thick mixture that can easily be shaped or spread 糊状物; 膏: *Mix the powder with enough water to make a smooth paste.* 把粉末和足够的水混合调成均匀的糊状。**3** [C, U] a kind of glue that is used for sticking paper onto things 糨糊: *wallpaper paste* 贴墙纸用的糨糊 **4** [U] artificial diamonds 人造钻石

paste² *v* **1** [T always+adv/prep] to stick paper to a surface using paste〔用糨糊〕粘贴〔纸〕: **[+on/over/down etc]** *A notice had been pasted to the door.* 一张告示贴在门上。| *Paste down the edges of the label.* 用糨糊把标签的边粘牢。**2** [I,T] to make words appear in a new place on a computer SCREEN〔在电脑屏幕上〕粘贴〔词语〕—see also 另见 PASTE-UP, PASTING

paste·board /ˈpestˌbɔrd; ˈpeɪstbɔːd/ *n* [U] flat stiff CARDBOARD made by sticking sheets of paper together (硬) 纸板

pas·tel¹ /pæsˈtɛl; ˈpæstl/ *n* **1 a)** [C,U] a small coloured stick for drawing pictures with, made of a substance like CHALK 彩色粉笔[蜡笔] **b)** [C] a picture drawn with pastels 彩色粉笔画; 蜡笔画 **2** [C usually plural 一般用复数] a soft pale colour, such as pale blue or pink 淡而柔和的色彩〈如淡蓝色或粉红色〉

pastel² *adj* [only before noun 仅用于名词前] **1** a pastel colour is pale and light〔色彩〕浅的, 淡的, 柔和的: *pastel blue* 淡蓝色 **2** drawn using pastels 用彩色粉笔画的; 用蜡笔画的

pas·tern /ˈpæstɚn; ˈpæstɜːn/ *n* [C] *technical* the narrow upper part of a horse's foot, just above the HOOF【术语】〔马脚的〕骹 —see picture at 参见 HORSE¹ 图

Pas·ter·nak /ˈpæstɚnæk; ˈpæstənæk/, **Bor·is** /ˈbɔrɪs; ˈbɒrɪ̧s/ (1890-1960) a Russian poet and writer. His most famous work is his NOVEL about the Russian revolution Doctor Zhivago. In 1958 he won the Nobel Prize for Literature. 帕斯捷尔那克〔(1890-1960), 苏联诗人和作家。其最有名的作品是反映俄国革命的小说《日瓦戈医生》。1958年获得诺贝尔文学奖〕

paste-up /ˈ· ·/ *n* [C] a piece of paper with writing and pictures stuck on it that show what a page will look like when a book or magazine is produced 拼贴版样〔用于看书页或杂志页的效果〕

Pas·teur /pæˈstɚ; pæˈstɜː/, **Louis** (1822-95) a French scientist who established the study of MICROBIOLOGY (=the study of very small living things such as bacteria), and proved that disease can be caused by GERMS. He also studied FERMENTATION (=the process by which substances change chemically and become filled with gas by the action of bacteria), and invented the process of PASTEURIZATION. He also developed some VACCINES (=substances that are put into people's bodies to protect them from diseases). 巴斯德〔(1822-1895), 法国科学家。他曾创立了微生物学, 证明细菌可引发疾病。他还研究过发酵, 并研发出消毒法和几种疫苗〕

pas·teur·ize also 又作 **-ise** *BrE*【英】/ˈpæstəˌraɪz; ˈpɑːstʃəraɪz/ *v* [T] to heat a liquid in a special way that kills any BACTERIA in it 用巴斯德[巴氏]杀菌法给〔液体〕消毒: *pasteurized milk* 消毒牛奶 —**pasteurization** /ˌpæstərəˈzeʃən; ˌpɑːstʃəraɪˈzeɪʃən/ *n* [U]

pas·tiche /pæsˈtiʃ; pæˈstiːʃ/ *n* **1** [C] a piece of writing, music etc that is deliberately made in the style of another artist〔文章、音乐等的〕模仿作品: *The concert was a weird mixture of traditional classics and slightly embarrassing Beatles pastiches.* 这场音乐会是传统的经典作品和有点令人难堪的模仿甲壳虫乐队作品的奇怪混合。**2** [C] a work of art that consists of a variety of different styles put together 拼凑的艺术作品, 混成作品, 集锦 **3** [U] the style or practice of making works of art in either of these ways 模仿[混成]的艺术风格[手法, 实践]

pas·tille /pæsˈtil; pæˈstiːl/ *n* [C] *especially BrE* a small round sweet, sometimes containing medicine for a sore throat; LOZENGE (1)【尤英】〔含治喉疾药物的〕锭剂; 润喉糖: *fruit pastilles* 水果润喉糖

pas·time /ˈpæsˌtaɪm; ˈpɑːstaɪm/ *n* [C] something that you do because you find it enjoyable or interesting 消遣; 娱乐: *Reading was her favourite pastime.* 阅读是她最喜爱的消遣。

past·ing /ˈpestɪŋ; ˈpeɪstɪŋ/ *n* **1 give sb a pasting** *informal especially BrE*【非正式, 尤英】**a)** to punish someone by hitting them hard 痛打[毒打]某人: *You'll get a pasting if your dad finds out.* 如果被你爸爸发现, 你会挨一顿痛打的。**b)** to defeat someone easily in a game or other competition〔在比赛或其他竞赛中〕轻易击败某人 **2** [U] the activity of moving words from one place to another on a computer screen〔词语在电脑屏幕上的〕粘贴: *cutting and pasting* 剪切和粘贴

pas·tor /ˈpæstɚ; ˈpɑːstə/ *n* [C] a Christian priest in some protestant churches〔某些新教教会的〕牧师

pas·tor·al /ˈpæstərəl; ˈpɑːstərəl/ *adj* **1** connected with the duties of a priest, minister etc towards the members of their religious group 牧师的; 牧师职责的: *The Rabbi makes pastoral visits on Tuesdays.* 拉比每星期二作履行神职的访问。**2** *literary* typical of the simple peaceful life in the country【文】田园生活的; 田园式的: *a charming pastoral scene* 迷人的田园景象 **3** connected with the duties of a teacher in advising students about their personal needs outside of lessons 精神上指导的〔指教师在课外对学生个人需求提供咨询的〕

past par·ti·ci·ple /ˌ· ˈ····/ *n* [C] *technical* a participle that can be used in compound forms of a verb to show the PASSIVE or the PERFECT tenses (for example 'broken' in 'I have broken my leg'), or sometimes as an adjective (for example 'broken' in 'a broken leg')【术语】过去分词

past per·fect /ˌ· ˈ··/ *n* [singular] *technical* the form of a verb that shows that the action described by the verb was completed before a particular time in the past, formed in English with 'had' and a past participle【术语】过去完成时[式] —**past perfect** *adj*

pas·tra·mi /pəˈstrɑmɪ; pəˈstrɑːmi/ *n* [U] smoked BEEF that contains a lot of SPICES 五香烟熏牛肉

pas·try /ˈpestrɪ; ˈpeɪstri/ *n* **1** [U] a mixture of flour, fat, and milk or water, used to make the outer part of baked foods such as PIES〔用来做烘烤食物外层的〕油酥面团 **2** [C] a small sweet cake, made using this substance 油酥点心[糕饼]: *a Danish pastry* 丹麦油酥糕饼 S3

pas·tur·age /ˈpæstʃərɪdʒ; ˈpɑːstʃərɪdʒ/ *n* [U] **1** *technical* the right to use an area of land for feeding your sheep, cattle, horses etc【术语】放牧权 **2** pasture 牧场

pas·ture¹ /ˈpæstʃɚ; ˈpɑːstʃə/ *n* [C,U] **1** land or a field that is covered with grass and is used for cattle, sheep etc to feed on 牧场: *Stone walls divided pasture from arable land.* 道道石墙把牧场和可耕地分隔开了。| *the rolling pastures of southern England* 英格兰南部绵延起伏的牧场 **2 put sth/sb out to pasture a)** to move cattle, horses etc into a field to feed on the grass 放〔牛、马等〕到牧场吃草 **b)** *informal* to make someone leave their job because you think they are too old to do it properly【非正式】〔认为某人年纪太大而〕使离职, 使退休 **3 pastures new/greener** *humorous* a new and exciting or better job, place or activity【幽默】更刺激[更好]的新职位[活动, 地方]: *"I'd like to say goodbye to Paul who leaves us for pastures new."* "我想向保罗道别, 他要离开我们奔更好的前程去了。"

pasture² *v* **1** [T] to put animals outside in a field to feed on the grass 放牧 **2** [I+on] if animals pasture on a particular area of land, they eat the grass that is growing there〔牛、羊等〕在草地上吃草

pas·ture·land /ˈpæstʃɚˌlænd; ˈpɑːstʃəlænd/ *n* [U] pasture 牧场

past·y¹ /ˈpestɪ; ˈpeɪsti/ *adj* a pasty face looks very pale and unhealthy〔脸色〕苍白的; 不健康的

past·y² /ˈpæstɪ; ˈpæsti/ *n* [C] *BrE* a small case of PASTRY (1) filled with meat, vegetables etc and baked【英】〔用肉、蔬菜等做馅的〕肉馅饼: *a Cornish pasty* 康沃尔肉馅饼

pasty-faced /ˈpestɪ ˈfest; ˈpeɪsti feɪst/ *adj* having a very pale face that looks unhealthy 脸色苍白的

pat¹ /pæt; pæt/ *v* **patted, patting** [T] **1** to repeatedly touch someone or something lightly with your hand flat, especially to give comfort 轻拍〔尤指给予安慰〕: *He patted the dog affectionately as he spoke.* 他边说边疼爱地轻轻拍了拍那只狗。**2 pat sb/yourself on the back** to praise someone or yourself for doing something well〔因干得好而〕赞扬某人/自己: *You can pat yourselves on the back for a job well done.* 你们可以因为工作干得出色而赞扬一下自己。—see picture on page A21 参见 A21 页图

pat² *n* [C] **1** a friendly act of touching someone with your hand flat〔表示友善的〕轻拍: *Mrs Dodd gave the child a pat on the head.* 多德夫人轻轻地拍了拍那个孩子的头。**2** the sound made by hitting something lightly with a flat object〔用扁平物轻轻击打某物时发出的〕轻拍声 **3 a pat of butter** a small flat lump of butter 一小块黄油 **4 a pat on the back** *informal* praise for something that you have done well【非正式】称赞, 赞扬: *Alex deserves a pat on the back for all his hard work.* 亚列克斯干活十分卖力, 应该受到表扬。—see also 另见 COWPAT

pat³ *adj* [usually before noun 一般用于名词前] a pat answer or explanation is made quickly and sounds as if it has been used before〔回答或解释〕脱口而出的, 预先准备好似的: *Don't give me any of your pat answers.* 我不想听你那早有准备的回答。

pat⁴ *adv* **1 have sth off pat** *BrE*【英】, **have sth down pat** *AmE*【美】to know something thoroughly so that you can say it, perform it etc immediately without thinking about it 对…了如指掌, 对…熟悉得可随口说出[随即表演等] **2 stand pat** *especially AmE* to refuse to change your opinion or decision【尤美】坚持自己的意见[决定]

Pat·a·go·ni·a /ˌpætəˈgonɪə; ˌpætəˈgəʊniə/ a large area in southern Argentina, which has a small population and many sheep farms 巴塔哥尼亚〔阿根廷南部一广大地区。那里人口稀少, 有许多牧羊场〕—**Patagonian** *adj*: *the Patagonian plains* 巴塔哥尼亚平原

patch¹ /pætʃ; pætʃ/ *n* [C]
1 ►PART OF AN AREA 小块，小片◄ a part of an area that is different or looks different from the parts that surround it〔与周围部分不同的〕斑；小块：*Lost: a small dog, white with brown patches.* 寻动物启事：一只小狗，白色带有棕色斑点。| **patch of dirt/grease/damp etc** *Watch out for icy patches on the roads.* 小心路上结冰的地方。| **patch of light/sky etc** *Patches of blue sky peeked through the clouds.* 片片蓝天从云层中显露出来。
2 ►OVER A HOLE 在破洞上◄ a small piece of material used to cover a hole in something 补片，补丁：*a jacket with leather patches at the elbows* 肘部有皮革补丁的短上衣
3 ►FOR GROWING STH 用于种植某物◄ a small area of ground for growing fruit or vegetables〔用于种水果或蔬菜的〕小块土地：*a strawberry patch* 一小块草莓地
4 ►ON YOUR EYE 在眼睛上◄ a piece of material that you wear over your eye to protect it when it has been hurt〔保护受伤眼睛的〕眼罩
5 ►DECORATION 装饰◄ a small piece of cloth with words or pictures on it that you can stitch onto clothes〔用于缝在衣服上的带有文字或图画的〕小布片
6 a bad/difficult/sticky patch *informal especially BrE* a period of time when you are having a lot of difficulty【非正式，尤英】〔碰到许多困难的〕倒霉时期：*Gemma's going through a bad patch right now.* 杰玛目前正处于困难时期。
7 sb's patch *BrE informal* an area that someone knows very well because they work or live there【英，非正式】某人的地盘[管辖区]〔指某人因在某工作或生活而对之非常了解〕；TURF¹ (4) *AmE*【美】：*The boss knows everything that's going on in our patch.* 那位老板对发生在我们这里的任何事情都了如指掌。
8 not be a patch on *BrE informal* to be much less attractive, good etc than something or someone else【英，非正式】远不如，比…差得远：*She's no great beauty – not a patch on Maria.* 她根本算不上大美人 —— 比玛丽亚差远了。
9 good/interesting/boring etc in patches *especially BrE* good etc in some parts, but not all the time【尤英】有些部分不错/有趣/乏味

patch² *v* [T] to put a piece of cloth over a hole, especially in a piece of clothing〔尤指用布块〕缝补〔衣服〕

patch 缝补

patch sth ↔ **together** *phr v* [T] to make something quickly or carelessly from a number of different pieces or ideas〔用碎料〕仓促拼制；〔把不同的观点〕草草拼凑：*A new plan was quickly patched together.* 一项新计划被匆匆拼凑起来了。

patch sth/sb ↔ **up** *phr v* [T] **1** to end an argument because you want to stay friendly with someone 平息〔争吵〕；解决〔分歧〕：*Try to patch up your differences before he leaves.* 在他离开之前努力解决你们之间的分歧。| **patch it up (with)** *I've patched it up with the landlord.* 我已和房东和解了。**2** to repair something by adding a new piece of material to it 修补：*We'd better patch up the roof – we can't afford a new one.* 我们最好把屋顶修一下 —— 我们没有钱盖新的。**3** to give quick and basic medical treatment to someone who is hurt〔给伤者〕草草包扎：*We just patch up the wounded as best we can.* 我们只是尽可能地给伤者草草包扎一下。

patch pock·et /ˌ· ˈ··/ *n* [C] a pocket made by SEWING a square piece of cloth onto a piece of clothing〔缝在衣服外面的〕贴袋

patch·work /ˈpætʃˌwɝk; ˈpætʃwɜːk/ *n* [U] **1** a type of needlework in which many coloured squares of cloth are stitched together to make one large piece〔由各色方形布片拼缝而成的〕拼布工艺(品)；拼缝物：*a patchwork quilt* 用各色布片拼缝的被子，百衲被 —see picture on page A16 参见A16页图 **2 a patchwork of fields/villages etc** a pattern that fields and villages seem to make when you see them from far above 片片田野/村庄等〔自空中俯看时似由田野和村庄等拼缀而成的图案〕**3 a patchwork of ideas/techniques etc** a combination of many different ideas etc 不同观念/技术等的拼凑物：*a patchwork of architectural styles* 各种建筑风格的拼凑物

patch·y /ˈpætʃɪ; ˈpætʃi/ *adj* **1** happening or existing irregularly in a number of small separate areas 局部地区的；零散的，斑驳的：*patchy fog* 零散薄雾 **2** not complete enough to be useful 不完整的，零零碎碎的：*His knowledge of French remained pretty patchy.* 他对法语仍然是一知半解。| *patchy evidence* 零零碎碎的证据 **3** *especially BrE* good in some parts but bad in others【尤英】只有部分好的：*I thought the performance was patchy.* 我认为那场演出只有部分是不错的。—**patchiness** *n* [U]

pate /pet; peɪt/ *n* [C] *old use* the top of your head【旧】头顶：*his bald pate* 他的秃头顶

pâ·té /pɑˈte; ˈpæteɪ/ *n* [C,U] a smooth, soft substance made from meat or fish that can be spread on bread〔可涂抹在面包上的〕肉酱；鱼酱

pa·tel·la /pəˈtɛlə; pəˈtelə/ *n* [C] *technical* your KNEE CAP【术语】髌骨，膝盖骨 —see picture at 参见 SKELETON 图

pa·tent¹ /ˈpætn̩t; ˈpeɪtnt/ *n* **1** [C] a special document that says that you have the right to make or sell a new INVENTION or product and that no one else is allowed to do so 专利证书；许可证：*When does the patent expire?* 这项专利什么时候到期？| **take out a patent on sth** (=get one officially) 获得某物的专利 **2** [U] the right given by this document to make or sell something that no one else is allowed to copy 专利，专利权：*The machine is protected by patent.* 这种机器受专利保护。

patent² *adj* [only before noun 仅用于名词前] **1** a patented INVENTION or product is protected by a patent, so that nobody else can copy it〔发明或产品〕受专利保护的；专利的：*a patent lock* 专利锁 **2 patent lie/nonsense/impossibility etc** *formal* something that is clearly a lie etc; OBVIOUS (1)【正式】明显的谎言/胡说/不可能等 —see also 另见 PATENTLY

Patent and Trade·mark Of·fice, The /ˌ· · ˈ· ·, ˌ·/ the US government department that decides which new inventions can be given a PATENT (=the right to make and sell a new invention). There is a similar department in the UK called the Patent Office. 专利商标局〔美国一政府部门，负责决定哪些新发明可授予专利权。英国也有一个类似机构，名为the Patent Office(专利局)〕

patent leath·er /ˌpætn̩t ˈlɛðɚ; ˌpeɪtnt ˈleðə◄/ *n* [U] thin shiny leather, usually black 漆皮〔通常为黑色〕：*patent leather shoes* 漆皮鞋

pa·tent·ly /ˈpetn̩tlɪ; ˈpeɪtntli/ *adv formal* a word meaning clearly, used about something that is so clearly bad that no reasonable person could disagree with that fact【正式】〔指坏事〕显然地，明显地：*The treatment is patently not working.* 这种疗法显然没有什么效果。| **patently false/impossible/absurd/obvious etc** *Her denial was swift and patently false.* 她的否认来得那么快，显然是虚假的。

patent medi·cine /ˌ·· ˈ···/ *n* [C] a medicine which can be bought without a PRESCRIPTION (=a written order from your doctor) 专卖药；成药〔指不要处方就能买到的药〕

Patent Of·fice, the /ˈ·· ˌ··/ the British government department that decides which new inventions can be given a patent (=the right to make and sell a new invention). There is a similar department in the US called the Patent and Trademark Office. 专利局〔英国一政府机构，负责决定哪些新发明可授予专利权。美国有一个类似机构，名为the Patent and Trademark Office(专利商标局)〕

pa·ter /ˈpetɚ; ˈpeɪtə/ *n* [C] *BrE old-fashioned* father【英，过时】父亲，爸爸

pa·ter·fa·mil·ias /ˈpetɚfəˈmɪlɪˌæs; ˌpeɪtəfəˈmiːliæs/ *n* [C] *formal* a father or a man who is the head of a family【正式】父亲；〔男性〕家长，户主

pa·ter·nal /pəˈtɝnl; pəˈtɜːnl/ *adj* **1** paternal feelings or behaviour are like those of a father for his children〔感情或行为〕父亲(般)的：*Dan took a paternal interest in my work.* 丹像父亲般关注我的工作。**2 paternal grandmother/uncle etc** your father's mother, brother etc 祖母/叔叔等〔父方的亲戚〕—compare 比较 MATERNAL —**paternally** *adv*

pa·ter·nal·is·m /pəˈtɝnl̩ˌɪzəm; pəˈtɜːnəlɪzəm/ *n* [U] a system of controlling people or organizations in which people are protected, and their needs are satisfied, but they do not have any freedom or responsibility 家长式统治[管理] —**paternalist, paternalistic** /pəˌtɝnl̩ˈɪstɪk; pəˌtɜːnəlˈɪstɪk◄/ *adj*

pa·ter·ni·ty /pəˈtɝnətɪ; pəˈtɜːn̩ti/ *n* [U] *law* the fact of being the father of a particular child, or the question of who the child's father is【法律】父亲的身份，生父：*The paternity of the child is in dispute.* 这个孩子的生父是谁尚在争论之中。

paternity leave /ˈ· ˈ··· ˌ·/ *n* [U] a period of time away from work that a father of a new baby is allowed〔父亲享有的〕陪产假

paternity suit /ˈ· ˈ··· ˌ·/ *n* [C] a legal action in which a mother asks a court of law to say that a particular man is the father of her child 生父确认诉讼程序

pa·ter·nos·ter /ˌpætɚˋnɑstɚ; ˌpætəˈnɒstə/ *n* [C] the LORD'S PRAYER 主祷文

path /pæθ; pɑːθ/ *n plural* **paths** /pæðz; pɑːðz/ [C]

1 ▶TRACK 小径◀ a track that people walk along over an area of ground〔人走出来的〕小径;〔人走的〕小道: *I walked nervously up the path towards the front door.* 我提心吊胆地沿着小道向前门走去。| *A path had been worn across the grass.* 草地上被踩出了一条小径。

2 ▶WAY THROUGH STH 通道◀ a way through something, that is made by opening a space to allow you to move forward〔开出的〕通道: *The crowd moved aside to make a path for them.* 人们挪往一旁给他们让路。| **[+through]** *They used axes to clear a path through the jungle.* 他们用斧头开辟出一条穿过密林的小道。

3 ▶DIRECTION 方向◀ the direction or line along which someone or something moves〔人或事物移动的〕方向; 路线; 轨道: *Sherman's army burned and looted everything that lay in its path.* 谢尔曼的军队烧毁并劫掠了所经之地的一切东西。| *the orbital path of the moon around the earth* 月亮绕地球的轨道

4 ▶PLAN 计划◀ what you intend to do over a long period of time 道路; 途径: *a career path* 职业发展途径 | **[+to]** *Shamira saw a college degree as her path to independence.* 沙米拉把大学学位看作是她走向独立的一条途径。

5 sb's paths cross if two people's paths cross, they meet by chance〔两个人〕不期而遇: *Our paths did not cross again until 1941.* 我们直到1941年才再次相遇。—see also 另见 **beat a path (to sb's door)** (BEAT[1] (23)), **lead sb up the garden path** (LEAD[1] (18)), **stand in sb's way/path** (STAND[1] (42))

pa·thet·ic /pəˋθɛtɪk; pəˈθetɪk/ *adj* **1** something or someone that is pathetic is so useless, unsuccessful, or badly done that they annoy you 无用的; 差劲的; 令人生厌的: *You're pathetic! Here, let me do it.* 你真没用! 让我来做吧。| *It's a pretty pathetic computer, basically.* 这实际上是一台很差劲的电脑。| *Vic made a pathetic attempt to apologise.* 维克很不像样地试图道歉。**2** making you feel pity or sympathy 招人怜悯的, 可怜的: *a pathetic sight* 悲惨的景象 **—pathetically** /-klɪ; -kli/ *adv*

pathetic fal·la·cy /ˌ·,·ˋ···/ *n* [U] *technical* the idea of describing the sea, rocks, weather etc in literature as if they were human【术语】感情的误置〔文学中对大海、石头、气候等的拟人化描述〕

Path·find·er /ˋpæθˌfaɪndɚ; ˈpɑːθˌfaɪndə/ a US government space programme in which NASA sent a space vehicle to Mars in 1997 in order to find out more information about the PLANET 探路者计划〔美国政府推出的一项太空计划。国家航空和航天局据此于1997年向火星发送了一个航天探测器, 以获取有关该星球的更多资料〕

pathfinder *n especially AmE*【尤美】**1** [C] a person who goes ahead of a group and finds the best way through unknown land 探路者, 开路先锋 **2** a person who discovers new ways of doing things; TRAILBLAZER 先驱, 开拓者, 探索者

path·o·gen /ˋpæθədʒən; ˈpæθədʒən/ *n* [C] *technical* something that causes disease in your body【术语】病原体, 致病菌 **—pathogenic** /ˌpæθəˋdʒɛnɪk; ˌpæθəˈdʒenɪk◂/ *adj*

path·o·log·i·cal /ˌpæθəˋlɑdʒɪkḷ; ˌpæθəˈlɒdʒɪkəl◂/ *adj* **1** pathological behaviour or feelings happen regularly, are unreasonable, and impossible to control〔行为或感情〕非理智的, 无法控制的, 病态的: *a pathological liar* 病态说谎者 | *a pathological hatred of women* 对女人的病态的憎恨 **2** a mental or physical condition that is pathological is caused by disease 由疾病引起的, 病理的 **3** *technical* connected with pathology【术语】病理学的 **—pathologically** /-klɪ; -kli/ *adv*: *pathologically jealous* 病态妒忌的

pa·thol·o·gy /pəˋθɑlədʒɪ; pəˈθɒlədʒi/ *n* [U] the study of the causes and effects of illnesses 病理学 **—pathologist** *n* [C]

pa·thos /ˋpeθɑs; ˈpeɪθɒs/ *n* [U] the quality that a person or a situation has that makes you feel pity and sadness〔人或境况具有的〕激起怜悯[伤感]的性质, 伤感力: *a scene full of pathos* 充满伤感的场面

path·way /ˋpæθˌwe; ˈpɑːθweɪ/ *n* [C] a path 小道, 小径

pa·tience /ˋpeʃəns; ˈpeɪʃəns/ *n* [U] **1** the ability to wait calmly for a long time and accept delays without becoming angry or anxious〔忍受长时间等待的〕耐心, 忍耐(性): *You'll need patience if you want to be served in this shop.* 如果你想在这家商店得到服务, 你需要有耐心。| *Marianna listened to his story with patience.* 玛丽安娜耐心地倾听他的叙述。**2** the ability to accept trouble and other people's annoying behaviour without complaining or becoming angry〔忍受麻烦事或他人讨厌行为的〕耐心, 耐性, 忍受力, 克制力: **have no patience with** *She has no patience with time-wasters.* 她对浪费时间的人没有耐性。| **lose patience (with)** (=stop being patient and get angry)(对…)失去耐心 *I'm beginning to lose patience with you people.* 我开始对你们这些人失去耐心了。| **the patience of Job/the patience of a saint** (=very great patience when someone is annoying you) 约伯/圣人的耐心〔指极大的耐心〕| **try sb's patience** (=make someone lose their patience) 使…失去耐心, 使…无法忍受 *Henry began to try Isabel's patience with his negative attitude.* 亨利消极的态度开始让伊莎贝尔无法忍受了。**3** the ability to continue to give your attention to work that is difficult or tiring 坚忍; 韧性; 毅力: **have the patience to do sth** *I wouldn't have the patience to sit sewing all day.* 我可没有整天坐着做针线活的毅力。**4** *BrE* a card game for one player【英】单人纸牌戏; SOLITAIRE (3) *AmE*【美】

pa·tient[1] /ˋpeʃənt; ˈpeɪʃənt/ *n* [C] someone receiving medical treatment from a doctor〔接受治疗的〕病人, 患者

patient[2] *adj* able to wait calmly for a long time or to accept difficulties, people's annoying behaviour etc without becoming angry 有耐心的; 忍耐的: **[+with]** *Louise was very patient with me when I was ill and crabby.* 在我生病而且脾气乖戾的日子里, 路易丝对我很有耐心。**—patiently** *adv*

pat·i·na /ˋpætɪnə; ˈpætɪ̣nə/ *n* [singular, U] **1** a greenish layer that forms naturally on the surface of copper or BRONZE〔铜或青铜表面的〕铜绿, 铜锈 **2** a smooth, shiny surface that gradually develops on wood, leather etc〔木头、皮革等表面因年久而产生的〕光泽 **3 the patina of wealth/success etc** the attractive or impressive appearance of wealth etc 有钱人/成功者等的神采[气派]

pat·i·o /ˋpɑtɪˌo; ˈpætiəʊ/ *n plural* **patios** [C] a flat area with a stone floor next to a house, used for sitting outside〔与房屋相连并铺有石头地面的、作户外歇息用的〕露台, 平台

patio doors /ˋ···ˌ·/ *n* [plural] *especially BrE* glass doors that open from a living room onto a patio【尤英】〔起居室通往露台的〕玻璃门

pa·tis·se·rie /pəˋtisərɪ; pəˈtiːsəri/ *n* [C] *French* a shop that sells French cakes and pies, or the cakes it sells【法】法式糕点店; 法式糕点

pa·tois /ˋpætwɑ; ˈpætwɑː/ *n plural* **patois** /-twɑz; -twɑːz/ [C, U] a spoken form of a language used by the people of a small area and different from the national or standard language 方言; 土语

Pa·ton /ˋpetṇ; ˈpeɪtn/, **Al·an** (1903-88) a South African writer and schoolteacher. He wrote about political and social subjects, but is best known for his NOVEL *Cry, the Beloved Country.* 佩顿〔(1903-1988), 南非作家、教师。他的作品多涉及政治和社会题材, 但以小说《哭吧, 亲爱的祖国》最为著称〕

patri- /petrɪ; peɪtrɪ̣/ *prefix* **1** concerning fathers 父亲的: *patricide* (=killing one's father) 弑父(罪) **2** concerning men 男人的: *a patriarchal society* (=controlled by men) 男人统治的社会, 父权制社会 —compare 比较 MATRI-

pa·tri·al /ˋpetrɪəl; ˈpeɪtriəl/ *n* [C] *BrE technical* someone who has a legal right to come to live in the United Kingdom because their parents, grandfather, or grandmother were born there【英, 术语】〔因父母或祖父母在英国出生而〕有英国居留权的人

pa·tri·arch /ˋpetrɪˌɑrk; ˈpeɪtriɑːk/ *n* [C] **1** an old man who is respected as the head of a family or tribe〔年长而受人尊敬的〕家长; 族长; 年高德劭的人 —compare 比较 MATRIARCH **2** a BISHOP (1) in the early Christian church〔早期基督教的〕主教 **3** a chief BISHOP (1) of the Orthodox Christian churches〔东正教的〕大主教

pa·tri·arch·al /ˌpetrɪˋɑrkḷ; ˌpeɪtriˈɑːkəl◂/ *adj* **1** ruled or controlled only by men 由男性控制[统治]的: *a patriarchal system* 父权制 **2** connected with being a patriarch, or typical of a patriarch 家长的; 族长的; 家长[族长]特有的: *patriarchal attitudes* 家长式的态度

pa·tri·arch·y /ˋpetrɪˌɑrkɪ; ˈpeɪtriɑːki/ *n* [C,U] **1** a social system in which the oldest man rules his family and passes power and possessions on to his sons 父权制(社会) **2** a social system in which men have all the power 男权至上的社会制度; 男性政体 —compare 比较 MATRIARCHY

pa·tri·cian /pəˋtrɪʃən; pəˈtrɪʃən/ *adj* **1** typical of a member of the highest class in society; ARISTOCRATIC 贵族的; 贵族似的: *a patrician face* 高贵的面容 **2** belonging to the governing classes in ancient Rome〔属于古罗马〕统治阶层的 —compare 比较 PLEBEIAN **—patrician** *n* [C]

pat·ri·cide /ˋpætrɪˌsaɪd; ˈpætrɪ̣saɪd/ *n* [U] the crime of murdering your father 弑父(罪) —compare 比较 MATRICIDE, PARRICIDE (1)

Pat·rick /ˋpætrɪk; ˈpætrɪk/, **Saint** (?389-461) the PATRON SAINT of Ireland, who helped to spread the Christian religion

there and who people think got rid of snakes in Ireland. **St Patrick's Day**, 17th March, is celebrated in Ireland and in the US, where people drink Irish beer and often wear green clothes. 圣帕特里克〔(公元?389-461), 爱尔兰主保圣人。他在当地传播基督教, 人们认为是他除掉了爱尔兰的蛇。每年3月17日, 爱尔兰和美国都要庆祝圣帕特里克节, 届时人们喝爱尔兰啤酒, 且常穿着绿色衣服〕

pat·ri·mo·ny /ˈpætrəˌmonɪ; ˈpætrɪməni/ *n* [U, singular] *formal* property given to you after the death of your father, which was given to him by your grandfather etc; INHERITANCE (1)【正式】祖传的财产; 遗产 —**patrimonial** /ˌpætrəˈmonɪəl; ˌpætrɪˈməʊniəl◂/ *adj*

pat·ri·ot /ˈpetrɪət; ˈpætriət/ *n* [C] someone who loves their country and is willing to defend it 爱国者: *Mr Bush praised Weinburger as 'a true American patriot'.* 布什先生称赞温伯格为"美国真正的爱国者"。

pat·ri·ot·ic /ˌpetrɪˈɑtɪk; ˌpætriˈɒtɪk◂/ *adj* having or expressing a great love of your country 爱国的, 有爱国心的: *good patriotic Americans* 正直爱国的美国人 | *patriotic songs* 爱国歌曲 —**patriotism** /ˈpetrɪətɪzəm; ˈpætriətɪzəm/ *n* [U]

pa·trol¹ /pəˈtrol; pəˈtrəʊl/ *v* **patrolled, patrolling** [I always+adv/prep, T] **1** to go around the different parts of an area or building at regular times to check that there is no trouble or danger 巡逻, 巡查: *waters patrolled by enemy submarines* 敌方潜水艇巡逻的水域 | *Armed guards with dogs patrolled the exhibition.* 武装卫兵带着狗在展览会上巡逻。**2** to drive or walk repeatedly around an area in a threatening way 以威胁性的架势在〔某地带〕走来走去[驾着车转来转去]: *Gangs of youths patrolled the streets at night.* 晚上一帮一帮的年轻人在街上摆出威胁性的架势走来走去。

patrol² *n* **1** [C,U] the act of going around different parts of an area at regular times to check that there is no trouble or danger 巡逻, 巡查: *Security guards carry out regular patrols of the factory premises.* 保安人员对厂房进行定时巡查。| *patrol duty* 巡逻任务 | **on patrol** *submarines on patrol in the North Atlantic* 在北大西洋巡逻的潜水艇 | **patrol boat/car** (=used by the army or police)〔军队或警察用的〕巡逻船/巡逻车 **2** [C] a group of police, soldiers, vehicles, planes etc sent out to search a particular area 巡警队; 巡逻兵; 巡逻车; 巡逻机队: *the US border patrol* 美国边境巡逻队 **3** [C] a small group of BOY SCOUTS or GIRL GUIDES 童子军小队 —see also 另见 HIGHWAY PATROL

patrol car /ˈ· · ˌ·/ *n* [C] a police car that drives around the streets of a city 巡逻警车

pa·trol·man /pəˈtrolmən; pəˈtrəʊlmən/ *n* [C] **1** *AmE* a police officer who regularly walks or drives around a particular area to prevent crime from happening【美】巡警 **2** someone employed by a car owners' association in Britain who drives along roads to give help to drivers〔由英国车主协会雇用, 在道路上驾车巡逻给司机提供帮助的〕流动汽车修理工

patrol wag·on /ˈ· ˌ· ·, ·ˈ· ·/ *n* [C] *AmE* a police vehicle used to move prisoners【美】囚车; BLACK MARIA *BrE*【英】

pa·tron /ˈpetrən; ˈpeɪtrən/ *n* [C] **1** someone who supports the activities of an organization, for example by giving money; BENEFACTOR 赞助者, 资助人: *a patron of the arts* 艺术的赞助者 | *patron companies* 赞助公司 **2** *formal* someone who uses a particular shop, restaurant or hotel【正式】〔商店、餐馆、酒店的〕(老)顾客, (老)主顾 —compare 比较 CUSTOMER (1)

pat·ron·age /ˈpetrənɪdʒ; ˈpætrənɪdʒ/ *n* [U] **1** the support, especially financial support, that is given to an organization or activity by a patron 赞助, 资助 **2** *AmE* the support that you give a particular shop, restaurant etc by buying their goods or using their services【美】〔对商店、餐馆等的〕惠顾, 光顾; CUSTOM (3) *BrE*【英】: *Thank you for your patronage.* 感谢您的惠顾。**3** a system by which someone in a powerful position gives people generous help or important jobs in return for their support〔有权势者为回报人们的支持而给予慷慨帮助或重要职位的〕恩惠制; 任命权

pat·ron·ize /ˈpetrənˌaɪz; ˈpætrənaɪz/ *v* [T] **1** to talk to someone as if they are stupid when in fact they are not 以高人一等的态度对待: *Don't patronize me – I'm not a fool.* 别对我摆出高人一等的臭架子 —— 我不是傻瓜。**2** *formal* to use or visit a shop, restaurant etc【正式】光顾, 惠顾〔商店、餐馆等〕: *tourists who patronize the shopping and recreational facilities* 光顾购物和娱乐场所的游客 **3** to support or give money to an organization or activity 赞助, 资助〔机构或活动〕

pat·ro·niz·ing /ˈpetrənˌaɪzɪŋ; ˈpætrənaɪzɪŋ/ *adj* someone who is patronizing talks to you as if they think you are less intelligent or important than them〔说话时〕高人一等的, 屈尊俯就的: *Try not to sound so patronizing when you talk to the students.* 和学生谈话时, 尽量不要用这种高人一等的口吻。| *a patronizing attitude* 屈尊俯就的态度 —**patronizingly** *adv*

patron saint /ˌ·· ˈ·/ *n* [C **+of**] a Christian SAINT (=very holy person) who is believed to give special protection to a particular place, activity, or person〔某个地方、某种活动、某个人的〕守护神, 主保圣人: *St. Christopher, patron saint of travellers* 圣克里斯托弗, 旅行者的守护神

pat·ro·nym·ic /ˌpætrəˈnɪmɪk; ˌpætrəˈnɪmɪk/ *n* [C] *technical* a name formed from the name of your father, grandfather etc【术语】源自父名[祖父名等]的名字 —**patronymic** *adj*

pat·sy /ˈpætsɪ; ˈpætsi/ *n* [C] *AmE informal* someone who is easily tricked or deceived, especially into taking the blame for someone else's crime【美, 非正式】易上当受骗的人,〔尤指〕替罪羊, 替死鬼

pat·ten /ˈpætn̩; ˈpætn/ *n* [C] a wooden shoe with pieces of iron on the bottom〔底部钉有铁片的〕木套鞋

pat·ter¹ /ˈpætɚ; ˈpætə/ *v* [I] **1** to make the quiet sound of something hitting a surface lightly, quickly, and repeatedly 发出急速的轻拍声: *rain pattering on the window panes* 雨啪嗒啪嗒地打在窗玻璃上 **2** [always+adv/prep] to walk or run with light steps making this sound 以轻快的脚步走[跑], 笃笃地跑: [**+around/along etc**] *I can hear the dog pattering around downstairs.* 我能听到狗儿在楼下嗒啦嗒啦地到处走动。

patter² *n* **1** [singular] the repeated sound of something hitting a surface lightly and quickly 急促的轻拍声: [**+of**] *the patter of hooves on the street* 大街上嘚嘚的马蹄声 **2** [U, singular] very fast, continuous, and usually amusing talk, used by someone telling jokes or trying to sell something〔讲笑话等时的〕急口词, 顺口溜;〔推销物品时〕喋喋不休的叫卖语: *It's difficult to look at the cars without getting the sales patter.* 看汽车时总免不了要听推销员喋喋不休的花言巧语。**3 the patter of tiny feet** *humorous* used to mean that someone is going to have a baby【幽默】将要有小宝宝了: *Are we going to hear the patter of tiny feet?* 我们要有小宝宝了吗?

pat·tern¹ /ˈpætɚn; ˈpætən/ *n* [C]

1 ▶**OF EVENTS** 关于事件◀ the regular way in which something happens, develops, or is done〔事情发生、发展、完成的〕模式; 方式, 形式: *Watch for changes in her breathing pattern.* 注意她呼吸方式的变化。| *a strange pattern of events* 事件发生的奇特方式 | **follow a set pattern** (=always happen or develop in the same fixed way) 遵循固定的模式 *Romantic novels tend to follow a set pattern.* 浪漫爱情小说趋向于遵循一定的模式。

2 ▶**DESIGN** 设计◀ **a)** a regularly repeated arrangement of shapes, colours, or lines on a surface usually intended as decoration 图案, 花样, 式样: *a cotton dress with a flowery pattern* 带有花卉图案的棉布连衣裙 | *tracing an intricate pattern in the sand* 在沙地上画出一个错综复杂的图形 **b)** a regularly repeated arrangement of sounds or words〔声音或词汇有规则排列的〕模式: *A sonnet has a fixed rhyming pattern.* 十四行诗有固定的押韵模式。

3 ▶**EXAMPLE** 范例◀ [usually singular 一般用单数] a thing, form, or person that is an example to copy 模范, 典范, 榜样: **set a pattern (for)** (=become a pattern) 为…树立典范[榜样] *a successful course that set a pattern for the training of all new employees* 为所有新雇员的培训树立典范的成功课程

4 ▶**MAKING THINGS** 制造东西◀ a shape used as a guide for making something, especially a thin piece of paper used when cutting material to make clothing〔用以制作某物的〕模型;〔服装的〕纸样: *a dress pattern* 连衣裙的纸样

5 ▶**CHOOSING** 选择◀ a small piece of cloth, paper etc that shows what a larger piece will look like; SAMPLE¹〔布、纸等的〕样品

pattern² *v* **be patterned on** to be designed or made in a way that is copied from something else 仿制; 模仿: *a planned economy patterned on the Stalinist model* 仿效斯大林模式的计划经济

pat·terned /ˈpætɚnd; ˈpætənd/ *adj* decorated with a pattern 有图案装饰的: *a patterned carpet* 有图案的地毯 | *wallpaper patterned with roses* 有玫瑰图案的壁纸

pat·tern·ing /ˈpætɚnɪŋ; ˈpætənɪŋ/ *n* [U] **1** *technical* the development of fixed ways of behaving, thinking, doing things etc as a result of copying and repeating actions, language etc【术语】〔行为、思维等的〕模式(化): *cultural patterning* 文化的模式化 **2** patterns of a particular kind, especially on an animal's skin〔尤指动物毛皮上的〕图案结构

Pat·ton /ˈpætn̩; ˈpætn/, **George Smith** (1885-1945) a US army general who was one of the most important US military leaders in World War II, and was known as 'Old Blood and Guts' 巴顿〔(1885-1945), 美国陆军将领, 二战期间美军最重要的将领之一, 人称"血胆老将"〕

pat·ty /ˈpæti; ˈpæti/ *n plural* **patties** [C] **1** *especially AmE* small, flat pieces of cooked meat or other food【尤美】小肉饼; 饼状食品: *a hamburger patty* 一块牛肉饼 **2** *BrE dialect* a PASTY【英, 方言】肉馅饼

patty melt /ˈ· · ˌ·/ *n* [C] a flat round piece of BEEF that is cooked with cheese on top and served on bread in the US〔美国的〕扁圆形牛肉饼

pau·ci·ty /ˈpɔsəti; ˈpɔːsɪ̇ti/ *n* **a paucity of** *formal* less than is needed of something【正式】(…的) 不足; 缺乏: *a paucity of information* 缺乏资料[信息]

Paul /pɔl; pɔːl/**, Saint** (?3AD-?68AD) a Christian APOSTLE (=someone chosen by Jesus to teach and spread the Christian religion) whose original name was **Saul of Tarsus**. As a young man he refused to accept Christian beliefs and treated Christians very cruelly. He was sent to Damascus to punish the Christians who lived there, but on his way there a very bright light suddenly appeared and he heard Jesus ask "Saul, Saul, why do you persecute me?" He then became a Christian, changed his name to Paul, and spent the rest of his life teaching people about Jesus. He wrote many of the Epistles in the New Testament of the Bible. 圣保罗〔(公元?3-?68), 基督教使徒, 原名塔尔苏斯的扫罗。保罗年轻时拒绝接受基督教信仰, 对待基督徒非常残忍。他被派往大马士革去惩罚那里的基督徒, 途中突然出现一道耀眼的亮光, 同时, 他听到耶稣问道: "扫罗, 扫罗, 你为什么迫害我?" 从此之后, 他成了基督徒, 改名保罗, 将余生奉献给传教事业。《圣经·新约》中的许多使徒书信都是他写的〕

Pau·ling /ˈpɔlɪŋ; ˈpɔːlɪŋ/**, Li·nus** /ˈlaɪnəs; ˈlaɪnəs/ (1901-94) a US scientist who studied how atoms join together and form larger structures. He strongly opposed the use of NUCLEAR weapons, and won two Nobel Prizes, one for Chemistry and one for Peace. 泡令, 又译鲍林〔(1901-1994), 美国科学家, 专门研究原子组合并形成更大结构的原理。他极力反对使用核武器。他两次荣获诺贝尔奖, 分别是化学奖及和平奖〕

paunch /pɔntʃ; pɔːntʃ/ *n* [C] *often humorous* a man's fat stomach【常幽默】〔男人的〕大肚子 —**paunchy** *adj*

pau·per /ˈpɔpə; ˈpɔːpə/ *n* [C] *old-fashioned* someone who is very poor【过时】穷人, 贫民

pau·per·ize also 又作 **-ise** *BrE*【英】/ˈpɔpəˌraɪz; ˈpɔːpəraɪz/ *v* [T] *technical* to make people poor【术语】使贫穷, 使贫困 —**pauperization** /ˌpɔpərəˈzeʃən; ˌpɔːpəraɪˈzeɪʃən/ *n* [U]

3 **pause¹** /pɔz; pɔːz/ *v* [I] to stop speaking or doing something for a short time before starting again 暂停, 停顿: *I paused for breath, almost choking with rage.* 我停下来喘口气, 愤怒得几乎说不出话来。| *Please pause to consider the matter.* 请停下来考虑一下这个问题。

pause² *n* [C] **1** a short time during which someone stops speaking or doing something before starting again 暂停, 停顿: *"Yes," said Philip after a moment's pause.* "是的。" 菲利普停顿了一下说。| [+in] *an awkward pause in the conversation* 谈话中令人尴尬的停顿 **2** a mark (𝄐) over a musical note, showing that the note is to be played or sung longer than usual〔音乐中的〕延长记号〔标在音符上, 表示该音符应比通常演奏或唱得长一些〕 **3 give sb pause (for thought)** to make someone stop and consider carefully what they are doing 使某人停下来〔仔细考虑〕: *an avoidable accident that should give us all pause for thought* 值得我们都停下来仔细考虑的一次可以避免的事故

pa·vane /pəˈvɑn; pəˈvæn/ *n* [C,U] a formal dance of the 16th and 17th centuries, or the music for this dance 帕凡舞; 帕凡舞曲〔16 和 17 世纪很正式的舞蹈或舞曲〕

Pav·a·rot·ti /ˌpævəˈrɑtɪ; ˌpævəˈrɒti/**, Lu·cia·no** /luˈtʃɑno; luːˈtʃɑːnəʊ/ (1935-2007) an Italian OPERA singer, one of the greatest TENORS (=men with fairly high singing voices) of the 20th century. He has helped to make opera more popular by performing concerts of songs from operas in large parks and sports stadiums. Many people know him as one of the Three Tenors. 帕瓦罗蒂〔(1935-2007), 意大利歌剧演唱家, 20 世纪最伟大的男高音之一。他曾在大型公园和露天体育场举行演唱会, 以此促进歌剧艺术的不断普及。许多人都知道他是世界三大男高音之一〕

pave /pev; peɪv/ *v* [T usually passive 一般用被动态] **1** to cover a path, road, area etc with a hard level surface such as blocks of stone or CONCRETE〔用石板或混凝土板〕铺〔路、地面等〕, 铺砌, 铺筑: *The road was only paved last year.* 这条路是去年刚铺成的。| *a paved courtyard* 地面铺砌过的院子 **2 pave the way for** to make a later event or development possible by producing the right conditions 为…铺平道路; 为…创造条件: *The Supreme Court decision paved the way for further legislation on civil rights.* 最高法院的这个决定为人权的进一步立法铺平了道路。 **3 the streets are paved with gold** used to say that it is easy to become rich quickly in a particular place〔某地〕遍地是黄金〔表示在某地很容易快速变富〕

pave·ment /ˈpevmənt; ˈpeɪvmənt/ *n* **1** [C] *BrE* a hard level surface or path at the side of a road for people to walk on【英】人行道; SIDEWALK *AmE*【美】—see picture on page A4 参见 A4 页图 **2** [U] *AmE* the hard surface of a road【美】〔道路的〕硬路面 **3** [C,U] paved surface or area of any kind; PAVING (2) 铺过的地面[路面]

This graph shows how common the nouns **pavement** and **sidewalk** are in British and American English. 本图表所示为名词 pavement 和 sidewalk 在英国英语和美国英语中的使用频率。

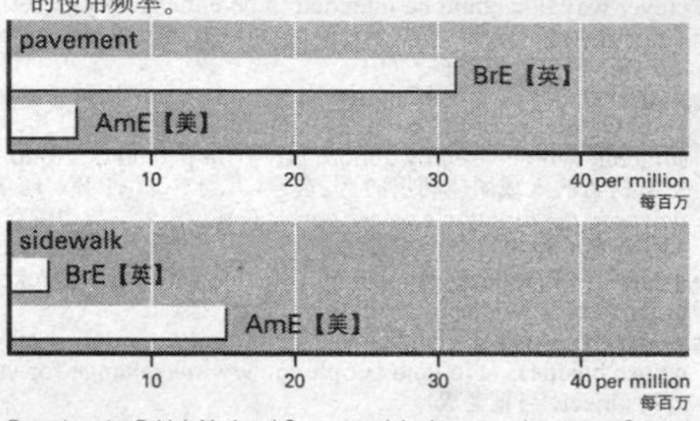

Based on the British National Corpus and the Longman Lancaster Corpus
据英国国家语料库和朗文兰开斯特语料库

In British English the word **pavement** means the path for people to walk on at the side of a road. Americans use the word **sidewalk** for this meaning. In American English, **pavement** is used to mean the hard surface of a road, or a paved surface. 在英国英语中, pavement 一词意为 "〔路边的〕人行道", 美国人则用 sidewalk 表示这种意思。在美国英语中, pavement 用于表示 "硬路面" 或 "铺过的地面"。

pavement art·ist /ˈ· · ˌ· ·/ *n* [C] *BrE* someone who draws coloured pictures on a pavement, hoping that people passing will give them money【英】马路画家〔在人行道上画彩色图画, 以此向路人讨钱的人〕; SIDEWALK ARTIST *AmE*【美】

pa·vil·ion /pəˈvɪljən; pəˈvɪljən/ *n* [C] **1** a large, light structure that is built to be used for only a short time especially for public entertainments or EXHIBITIONS〔尤用于公共娱乐或展览的〕临时建筑物; 亭子; 大帐篷: *the German pavilion at the World Trade Fair* 世界贸易博览会的德国国家馆 **2** *especially BrE* a building beside a sports field, especially a CRICKET field, used by the players and people watching the game【尤英】〔尤指板球场旁供运动员和观众使用的〕选手席; 看台

pav·ing /ˈpevɪŋ; ˈpeɪvɪŋ/ *n* **1** [U] material used to form a hard, level surface on a path, road, area etc 铺筑材料, 铺面材料 **2** [U] any kind of paved (PAVE) surface 铺过的路面[地面] **3** [C] a paving stone 铺路石 (板)

paving stone /ˈ· · ˌ·/ *n* [C] one of the flat square pieces of stone that are used to make a hard surface to walk on 铺路石板

Pav·lov /ˈpævlɑv; ˈpævlɒv/**, I·van Pet·ro·vich** /ˈaɪvən ˈpɛtrəvɪtʃ; ˈaɪvən ˈpetrəvɪtʃ/ (1849-1936) a Russian scientist who won the Nobel Prize for Medicine for his work on the DIGESTIVE system. He is famous especially for his work with dogs, which proved the existence of the CONDITIONED REFLEX (=a physical reaction that you cannot control, caused by repeated training or experiences). Each time he fed his dogs he rang a bell before giving them their food. The dogs learned to connect the ringing of the bell with the arrival of the food, and they got excited and began to SALIVATE when they heard the bell, even if there was no food. 巴甫洛夫〔(1849-1936), 俄国科学家, 以有关消化系统的研究成果获诺贝尔医学奖。他尤以通过对狗做实验证明条件反射的存在而闻名。他每次给狗喂食时都摇铃, 于是狗就习惯将铃声与食物联系起来。每次听到铃声时, 即使没有食物, 它们也会兴奋起来, 开始流口水〕 —**Pavlovian** /pævˈlovɪən; pævˈləʊviən/ *adj*

pav·lo·va /pævˈlovə; pævˈləʊvə/ *n* [C,U] a light cake made of MERINGUE, cream, and fruit〔用蛋白酥、奶油和水果做成的〕奶油蛋白饼

Pavlova, An·na /ˈænə; ˈænə/ (1885-1931) a Russian BALLET dancer especially famous for her dancing of *The Dying Swan*. Many people consider her to have been the world's greatest ballet dancer. 巴甫洛娃〔(1885-1931), 俄国芭蕾舞演员, 尤以表演的《天鹅之死》而著名。许多人都认为她是世界上最出色的芭蕾舞演员〕

paw¹ /pɔ; pɔː/ *n* [C] **1** an animal's foot that has nails or CLAWS〔动物的〕爪子: *a lion's paw* 狮爪 **2** *informal* someone's hand【非正式】〔人的〕手: *Keep your filthy paws off me!* 别用你的脏爪子碰我!

paw² *v* [I,T] **1** if an animal paws a surface, it touches or rubs one spot repeatedly with its paw 用爪子[前足、蹄等]抓[触, 扒, 刨]: **[+at]** *The dog's pawing at the door again – let him out.* 那只狗又在扒门了 — 让它出去吧。**2** *informal* to feel or touch someone in a rough or sexual way that is offensive【非正式】〔粗鲁或放肆地〕摸弄: *First he drank too much, then he started pawing me.* 他先是喝多了酒, 然后开始对我动手动脚。

paw·ky /ˈpɔkɪ; ˈpɔːki/ *adj especially ScotE* humorous in a quiet clever way that could be intended to be either funny or serious【尤苏格兰】俏皮的; 狡诈的; 冷面滑稽的: *a pawky sense of humour* 俏皮的幽默感

pawn¹ /pɔn; pɔːn/ *n* [C] **1** one of the eight smallest and least valuable pieces in the game of CHESS〔国际象棋中的〕兵, 卒 **2** someone who is used by a more powerful person or group〔被更有权势的人或团体利用的〕马前卒, 爪牙: **[+in]** *We're just pawns in the director's power game.* 在那位主管的权力游戏中, 我们只是一批小卒子。

pawn² *v* [T] to leave something valuable with a pawnbroker in order to borrow money from them 典当; 抵押

pawn·bro·ker /ˈpɔnˌbrokə; ˈpɔːnˌbrəʊkə/ *n* [C] someone whose business is to lend people money in exchange for valuable objects 当铺老板

pawn·shop /ˈpɔnˌʃɑp; ˈpɔːnʃɒp/ *n* [C] a pawnbroker's shop 当铺

paw·paw /ˈpɔˌpɔ; ˈpɔːpɔː/ *n* [C] *especially BrE and CarE* the large yellow-green fruit of a tall tropical tree; PAPAYA【尤英和加勒比】番木瓜, 木瓜

pax /pæks; pæks/ *interjection* a word used by children when they want to end an argument or fight 别吵了! 别打了! 算了吧!〔小孩在劝别人停止争吵或打架时的用语〕

Pax A·mer·i·ca·na /ˌpæks əmɛrɪˈkɑnə; ˌpæks əmerɪˈkɑːnə/ the peace that is supposed to be established in the world by the power of the US 美国强权下的和平

Pax Bri·tan·ni·ca /ˌpæks brɪˈtænɪkə; ˌpæks brɪˈtænɪkə/ the peace that is supposed to have been established by British rule in the countries of the British Empire, especially during the 19th century 英国强权下的和平〔大英帝国时期, 尤其是19世纪, 英国以强权在英联邦成员国建立的和平〕

pay¹ /pe; peɪ/ *v past tense and past participle* **paid** /ped; peɪd/

1 ▶GIVE MONEY 付钱◀ [I,T] to give someone money for something you have bought, or for something they have done for you 给〔某人〕付款; 付钱给〔某人〕: *They ran off without paying.* 他们没有付钱就逃走了。| *Didn't pay 'em a penny, just asked 'em to do it.* 没付给他们一个子儿, 只是让他们去干活。| **[+for]** *Mum and Dad paid for my driving lessons.* 妈妈和爸爸支付了我学驾驶所需的费用。| **pay sb for sth** *When can you pay me for the work?* 你什么时候付给我工钱? | **pay sb sth** *I paid her $200 for this painting.* 我付给她200美元买这幅画。| **pay sb to do sth** *Ray paid some kids to wash the car.* 雷花钱雇一些孩子洗车。| **pay (in) cash** *You'd get a discount for paying cash.* 用现金付款你可以享有折扣。| **pay by cheque/credit card** *May I pay by credit card?* 我可以用信用卡付款吗?

2 ▶DEBT/BILL/TAX 债务/账单/税◀ [T] to pay money that you owe to a person, company etc 偿还; 交付; 缴纳: *I forgot to pay the gas bill!* 我忘记交煤气费了! | *How much tax did you pay last year?* 去年你缴了多少税?

3 ▶WAGE/SALARY 工资/薪水◀ [I,T] to give someone money for the job they do 付给〔某人〕报酬: *How much do they pay you?* 他们付给你多少报酬? | *Home workers are very poorly paid.* 在家工作的人工资很低。| **pay sb $100 a day/£200 a week etc** *Programmers are paid about £200 a day.* (电脑)程序员每天的报酬约为200英镑。

4 pay attention (to) to give your attention to something (对…)注意: *I'm sorry, I wasn't paying attention to what you were saying.* 对不起, 我没有仔细听你说的话。

5 pay a call/visit on sb or **pay sb a call/visit** to visit someone 拜访某人

6 pay the penalty/price to experience something unpleasant because you have done something wrong, made a mistake etc〔因做坏事、犯错误等而〕吃苦头, 付出代价: **pay the price for (doing) sth** *You'll pay the price for drinking so much tomorrow.* 你喝酒太多, 明天你将会为此吃苦头。

7 ▶GOOD RESULT 好的结果◀ [I] if a particular action pays, it brings a good result or advantage for you 合算, 值得, 有利, 有好处: *Crime doesn't pay.* 犯罪不会有好结果。| **it pays to do sth** *It usually pays to tell the truth.* 讲真话通常有好处。| **it would/it might pay (you) to do sth** *It would pay you to ask if there are any jobs going at the London office.* 问一下伦敦分公司是否有工作做或许对你有好处。| **pay dividends** *Getting some qualifications now will pay dividends in the long term.* 现在取得一些资格证明将会给你带来长期的好处。

8 ▶PROFIT 利润◀ [I] if a shop or business pays, it makes a profit〔商店或公司〕有利可图, 有收益: *If the pub doesn't start to pay, we'll have to sell it.* 如果这家酒馆还没有开始赢利, 我们将不得不把它卖掉。

9 pay sb a compliment to say nice things about someone's appearance, behaviour etc 恭维[赞扬]某人: **pay sb the compliment of doing sth** *Gretta paid me the compliment of saying I was a good judge of character.* 格利塔恭维说我很擅长识别人品。

10 pay your respects (to sb) *formal* to send polite greetings to someone or to visit them【正式】(向某人)表示敬意; 问候[拜访](某人): **pay your last respects** (=go to someone's funeral)〔向某人〕致以最后的敬意, 参加某人的葬礼

11 pay for itself if something you buy pays for itself, it makes you save as much money as you bought it for 省下相当于购买某物的钱: *A new boiler would pay for itself within two years.* 一台新锅炉两年内就可以为你省下买它的钱。

12 pay your way to pay for everything that you want without having to depend on anyone else for money 支付自己应付的费用, 不负债

13 pay through the nose (for sth) *spoken* to pay far too much for something【口】(为某物)付费过高; (为某事)花代价过大: *I had to pay through the nose for these tickets.* 我得花高价去买这些票。

14 pay tribute to to say how much you admire or respect someone or something 对…表示赞赏[敬佩]; 称赞: *Doctors paid tribute to her courage at the end.* 最后, 医生们对她的勇气表示赞赏。

15 pay court to sb *old-fashioned* to treat someone, especially a woman, with great respect and admiration【过时】向某人〔尤指女人〕大献殷勤, 讨好某人 —see also 另见 **pay lip service to** (LIP SERVICE), **pay your dues** (DUE² (2))

pay sb/sth ↔ **back** *phr v* [T] **1** to give someone the money that you owe them; REPAY 偿还〔欠款〕: **pay sb back** *Can you lend me £10 and I'll pay you back on Friday?* 你能借给我10英镑吗? 我星期五就还你。| **pay sth ↔ back** *We're paying back the loan over 15 years.* 我们要在15年内偿还贷款。| **pay sb back sth** *Did I pay you back that £5?* 那5英镑我还给你了吗? **2** to make someone suffer for doing something wrong or unpleasant 向…报复: **pay sb back for sth** *I'll pay Jenny back for what she did to me!* 珍妮这样对待我, 我一定要向她报复!

pay for sth *phr v* [T] to suffer or be punished for something you have done 为…而受苦; 因…而受惩罚: *These people should pay for their crimes.* 这些人应为他们的罪行受到惩罚。| *You'll pay for that!* 你一定会为那事而受到惩罚的! | **pay for doing sth** *I'll make her pay for ruining my chances.* 她毁了我的机会, 我要她为此吃苦头。| **pay dearly** *Nick's paid dearly for his unfaithfulness to his wife.* 尼克因对妻子不忠而付出了巨大的代价。

pay sth ↔ **in/into** *phr v* [T] to put money in your bank account etc 把〔钱〕存入〔银行账户〕: *Did you remember to pay that cheque in?* 你记得把那张支票存入银行账户了吗? | **pay sth into sth** *I've paid $250 into my account.* 我已把250美元存入了我的账户。

pay off *phr v* **1** [T **pay** sth ↔ **off**] to give someone all the money you owe them 付清, 还清〔债务〕: *I've paid off the balance on the dishwasher.* 我已付清了那台洗碗机的余款。**2** [T **pay** sb ↔ **off**] to pay someone their wages and dismiss them from their job 付清工资解雇〔某人〕: *Two hundred workers have been paid off.* 两百个工人已被结清工资后解雇了。**3** [T **pay** sb ↔ **off**] to pay someone to keep quiet about something illegal or dishonest 用钱封住〔某人〕的嘴〔使其对非法或不诚实的事情保持沉默〕, 付封口费 **4** [I] if a plan or something that you try to do pays off, it is successful〔计划等〕取得成功: *They took a hell of a risk but it paid off.* 他们冒了很大的风险, 但事情成功了。—see also 另见 PAYOFF

pay out *phr v* **1** [I,T **pay** sth ↔ **out**] to pay a lot of money for something 为〔某事〕付出大笔款项: *Why is it always me who has to pay out?* 为什么总是得我付款? | **pay out sth for sth** *I paid out a lot of money for that car.* 我为那辆汽车花了很多钱。**2** [T **pay** sth ↔ **out**] to let a piece of rope be unwound 放出, 松开〔绳索〕—see also 另见 PAYOUT

pay sth ↔ **over** *phr v* to make an official payment of money 正式付款: **pay sth over to** *The solicitor arranged for Clancy's share of the inheritance to be paid over to him.* 律师安排正式支付克兰西应得的那份遗产。

pay up *phr v* [I] to pay money that you owe, especially when you do not want to or you are late〔尤指不情愿地或迟迟地〕付清, 偿还〔欠款〕—see also 另见 PAID-UP

USAGE NOTE 用法说明: PAY
GRAMMAR 语法
You **pay** the cost of something. pay 表示支付某物的费用: *pay $100/the bill/postage/the cost of removal* 支付100美元/账款/邮资/搬迁费 | *Will they pay my traveling expenses/accommodation costs?* 他们会支付我的旅行费/住宿费吗?
You **pay for** something you buy. pay for 表示为所买的东西付款: *I'll pay for the tickets.* 我会付买这些票的钱。| *You'll have to pay for any stationery you use.* 你必须为你所使用的任何文具付钱。You also say **pay for** when both the cost and what is bought are mentioned. 当同时提到所买的东西及其费用时, 也用 pay for: *She paid $200 for the use of the room.* 她为使用那个房间花了 200 美元。
You **pay** a person etc. pay 后可接人等: *Could you pay the taxi driver?* 你来付钱给出租车司机可以吗? You also pay someone something, or pay something to someone. 也可以用 pay someone something 或 pay something to someone: *He paid the assistant £30.* 他付给助手 30 英镑。| *He has to pay half his salary to his ex-wife every month.* 他每月得把一半的薪水付给他的前妻。
You **pay by** cheque/credit card etc. pay by 表示用支票/信用卡等支付: *Can I pay by Visa?* 我可以用威世信用卡付款吗?
SPELLING 拼法
The past tense of **pay** is **paid** (NOT 不用 *payed*). pay 的过去式为 paid。

This graph shows how common the different grammar patterns of the verb **pay** are. 本图表所示为动词 pay 构成的不同语法模式的使用频率。

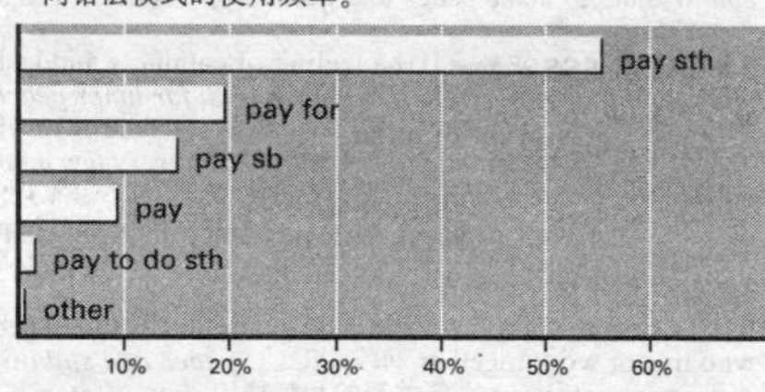

Based on the British National Corpus and the Longman Lancaster Corpus
据英国国家语料库和朗文兰开斯特语料库

pay² *n* [U] **1** money that you are given for doing your job; SALARY 工资, 薪金: *Wayne gets his pay every Friday.* 韦恩每星期五领工资。| *I like the work but the pay's terrible.* 我喜欢这份工作, 但报酬太低了。| **holiday/sick pay** (=money your employer gives you when you are on holiday or are ill) 节假日/病假工资 | **a pay rise/increase** *I've been promised a pay rise in January.* 我已得到许诺一月份给我加薪。**2 in the pay of** someone who is in someone else's pay is working for them, often secretly〔多指秘密地〕受雇于〔某人〕: *an informer in the pay of the police* 一名受警察雇用的线人[告密者]

USAGE NOTE 用法说明: PAY
WORD CHOICE 词语辨析: **pay, salary, wages, fee, income**
Money given to someone in return for work is called **pay**. pay 表示支付给某人的工资、薪金: *Truck drivers are demanding higher pay.* 卡车司机正在要求增加工资。| *a compaign against low pay* 反对低薪酬的运动
A **salary** is paid to someone once a month, especially to professional people, managers etc and usually goes directly into their bank account. salary 指每月发给某人〔尤指专业人员、经理等〕的薪金, 通常直接存入其银行账户: *a salary of $100,000 a year* 每年 10 万美元的薪金
Wages are paid weekly, usually in the form of coins and notes, especially to people whose job is not professional, in management etc. wages 指每周付给某人〔尤指非专业人员、非管理人员等〕的报酬, 通常以现金形式支付: *Wages at the cannery are very low.* 那家罐头食品厂的工资很低。
A **fee** is money that some professions charge for a particular service they have done. fee 指从事某些职业的人收取的服务费: *doctor's/lawyer's fees* 医生的诊金/律师费
Income means any money you receive regularly, from work or anywhere else. income 意为从工作或其他地方得到的经常性收入: *Unearned income* (=money you get but not from work) *is taxed at a higher rate.* 对于非工作所得的收入, 所征的税更高。

pay·a·ble /ˈpeəbl; ˈpeɪəbəl/ *adj* [not before noun 不用于名词前] **1** a bill, debt etc that is payable must be paid〔账单、债务等〕应支付的: *payable in advance* 可预付的 **2 payable to** a cheque etc that is payable to someone has that person's name written on it and should be paid to them〔支票等〕写明给〔某人〕的, 应付给…的

pay·bed /ˈpebɛd; ˈpeɪbed/ *n* [C] a hospital bed in a publicly owned hospital in Britain, used by someone who is paying to have better conditions, such as a private room〔英国公立医院中的〕自费病床

pay·cheque *BrE*【英】, **paycheck** *AmE*【美】/ˈpètʃɛk; ˈpeɪtʃek/ *n* [C] **1** a cheque that pays someone's wages 支付工资的支票: *a weekly paycheque* 支付周薪的支票 **2** *especially AmE* the amount of wages someone earns【尤美】薪金, 工资; PAY PACKET *BrE*【英】: *a nice fat paycheck* 丰厚的工资

pay·day /ˈpeˌde; ˈpeɪdeɪ/ *n* [U] the day on which you get your wages 发放工资日, 发薪日: *When's payday?* 哪一天是发薪日?

pay·dirt /ˈpedɝt; ˈpeɪdɜːt/ *n* [U] *AmE*【美】**1 hit paydirt** *informal* to make a valuable or useful discovery【非正式】作出有价值[有用]的发现 **2** earth found to contain valuable minerals such as gold 贵金属砂土〔含有金等的矿砂〕

PAYE /ˌpi e waɪ ˋi; ˌpiː eɪ waɪ ˈiː/ *n* [U] pay as you earn; a system in Britain by which tax is taken away from your wages before you are paid〔英国的〕所得税预扣法〔未发工资前预先从工资中扣除所得税〕

pay·ee /peˋi; peɪˈiː/ *n* [C] *technical* the person to whom money, especially a cheque, should be paid【术语】〔钱, 尤指支票的〕受款人, 收款人

pay en·ve·lope /ˈ· ˌ···/ *n* [C] *AmE* an envelope containing your wages【美】工资袋; PAY PACKET *BrE*【英】

paying guest /ˌ·· ˈ·/ *n* [C] someone who lives in someone else's house with them and pays them rent; LODGER〔私人家中的〕房客

paying-in book /ˌ·· ˈ· ·/ *n* [C] *BrE* a book of forms that you use when you pay money into your bank account【英】〔银行〕存款单簿

paying-in slip /ˌ·· ˈ· ·/ *n* [C] *BrE* a form that you use to pay money into your bank account【英】〔银行〕存款单; DEPOSIT SLIP *AmE*【美】

pay·load /ˈpelod; ˈpeɪləʊd/ *n* **1** [C,U] the amount of goods or passengers carried by a vehicle or aircraft, for which payment is received〔车辆或飞机的〕收费载重, 酬载 **2** [C] the instruments and equipment carried in a SPACECRAFT 有效载重〔宇宙飞船携带的仪器设备〕: *The shuttle had a maximum payload of 65,000 pounds.* 这架航天飞机的最大载重量为 65,000 磅。**3** [C] the amount of explosive that a MISSILE can carry〔导弹的〕有效载荷, 炸药量

pay·mas·ter /ˈpeˌmæstɚ; ˈpeɪˌmɑːstə/ *n* [C] **1** an official in a factory, the army etc, who gives people their wages〔工厂、军队等发放工资、军饷的〕出纳员; 军需官 **2** someone who pays someone else to do something, especially something illegal〔雇用别人做非法勾当的〕操纵者: *The assassin's paymasters were never identified.* 那位刺客的幕后操纵者始终没有查出来。

pay·ment /ˈpemənt; ˈpeɪmənt/ *n* **1** [C] an amount of money that has been or must be paid 已[应]支付的金额: *discounts offered for cash payments* 给予现金付款的折扣 | *Tom's gotten into arrears with his mortgage payments.* 汤姆已开始拖欠抵押贷款了。| **make a payment** *Interest payments are made quarterly.* 利息是按季度支付的。**2** [U] the act of paying 支付, 付款: *We expect prompt payment.* 我们期望即时付款。| *payment by instalments* 分期支付 | **in payment of** (=to pay) 支付 *I enclose a cheque in full payment of my account.* 我(随信)附上一张支付我全部欠账的支票。| **on payment of** (=when an amount has been paid) 支付…之后 *Any item can be reserved on payment of a small deposit.* 付一小笔订金后就可以预订任何物品。**3** [U] someone's reward for doing something 报偿: [+for] *All the payment I got for my troubles was insults.* 我辛苦了一番, 结果还要受辱。**4 payment in kind** a way of paying for something with goods or services instead of money 以货物[服务]代替钱款的支付方式 —see also 另见 BALANCE OF PAYMENTS, DOWN PAYMENT

pay·off /ˈpeˌɔf; ˈpeɪɒf/ *n* [C] *informal*【非正式】**1** a payment that you make to someone in order to stop them from causing

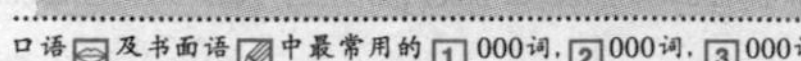

you any trouble, or when you make them leave their job〔为使某人不来找麻烦而付的〕贿赂款;〔辞退某人时的〕付款: *A network of police payoffs was discovered.* 贿赂警察的网络被发现了。| *The redundancies were bought by offering massive payoffs.* 以巨额的遣散费解雇冗员。**2** the good result of a particular series of actions〔一系列行动的〕良好结果 —see also 另见 **pay off**

pay·o·la /peˈolə; peɪˈəʊlə/ *n informal, especially AmE*【非正式,尤美】**1** [singular] a secret or indirect payment made to someone who uses their influence to make people buy what your company is selling〔暗中付给某人以利用其影响推销公司产品的〕贿赂 —compare 比较 BRIBE² **2** [U] the practice of giving or taking these payments 行贿; 受贿

pay·out /ˈpeˌaut; ˈpeɪ-aʊt/ *n* [C] *informal* a large payment of money in an insurance claim, competition etc or the act of making this payment【非正式】〔保险索赔、竞赛等中的〕大笔付款: *a big payout on this month's lottery* 本月彩票的大额奖金 —see also 另见 **pay out**

pay pack·et /ˈ· ,··/ *n* [C] *BrE*【英】**1** the amount of money someone earns; PAYCHEQUE (2) 工资 **2** an envelope containing your wages 工资袋; PAY ENVELOPE *AmE*【美】

pay phone /ˈ· ·/ *n* [C] a public telephone that you can use when you put in a coin or a CREDIT CARD〔投币式或插卡式〕公用电话

pay rise /ˈ· ·/ *BrE*【英】, **pay raise** *AmE*【美】*n* [C] an increase in the amount of money you are paid for doing your job 增加工资, 加薪: *Some company directors have awarded themselves huge pay rises.* 一些公司董事已给他们自己大幅加薪了。

pay·roll /ˈpeˌrol; ˈpeɪrəʊl/ *n* **1** [C] a list of people who are employed by a company and the amount of wages each of them is paid〔公司员工的〕在职人员名册, 发薪员工表: **be on the payroll** (=be employed by a company) 被雇用 *Nathan's still on the company payroll.* 内森仍受雇于这家公司。**2** [singular] the total amount of wages paid to all the people working for a particular company〔某家公司的〕发放工资总额

payroll tax /ˈ··,·/ *n* [C,U] a tax that an employer must pay to the government in the US, and that is a PERCENTAGE of the total wages they pay〔在美国雇主必须向政府缴纳的〕薪金税, 工资税〔占雇主所付工资总额的一定比例〕

pay set·tle·ment /ˈ· ,···/ *n* [C] an agreement, after a long argument, between managers and a union, on how much workers should be paid〔管理者和工会经过长时间争论之后达成的〕工人工资协议

pay·slip /ˈpeslɪp; ˈpeɪslɪp/ *n* [C] a piece of paper that shows how much money an employed person has been paid and how much has been taken away for tax etc〔显示工资额、扣税额等的〕工资单

Paz /pæz; pæz/, **Octavio** /ɑkˈtavɪo; ɒkˈtɑːviəʊ/ (1914-98), a Mexican poet and DIPLOMAT who won the Nobel Prize for Literature in 1990 帕斯〔(1914-1998), 墨西哥诗人、外交官。1990 年获诺贝尔文学奖〕

PBS /ˌpi bi ˈɛs; ˌpiː biː ˈes/ Public Broadcasting Service; a US television company whose aim is to show good-quality programmes and not to make profits. It broadcasts no advertisements, but its programmes are paid for partly by the people who watch them and partly by money from the government and from large companies. Two programmes for which PBS is famous are *Sesame Street* and *Masterpiece Theater*. 公共广播公司〔美国一电视公司, 其经营目的是播出高质量的节目, 而不是营利。该公司不插播广告, 节目制作费用部分来自观众, 部分来自政府拨款和大企业的赞助。该公司的两个著名节目是《芝麻街》和《经典剧场》〕

P.C. /ˌpi ˈsi; ˌpiː ˈsiː◂/ *n* [C] *BrE* police constable; a policeman of the lowest rank【英】警员〔警衔最低的警察〕: *P.C. Williams* 警员威廉斯 | *Two P.C.s were attacked.* 两名警员遭到了袭击。—see also 另见 WPC

PC¹ /ˌpi ˈsi; ˌpiː ˈsiː◂/ *n* [C] a personal computer; a small computer that is used by one person at a time, in business or at home 个人电脑

PC² *adj* POLITICALLY CORRECT 政治上正确的

pcm per calendar month; used when stating the amount of rent to be paid each month 每月〔用于说明每月应付的房租〕: *£500 pcm* 每月 500 英镑

PCP /ˌpi si ˈpi; ˌpiː siː ˈpiː/ *n* [U] phencyclidine hydrochloride; an ANAESTHETIC that is also taken as an illegal drug 苯环己哌啶〔别称"天使粉", 一种被当作毒品使用的麻醉剂〕

pd the written abbreviation of 缩写= paid

pdq /ˌpi di ˈkju; ˌpiː diː ˈkjuː/ *adv slang* pretty damn quick; used to say that something should be done immediately【俚】马上, 立刻: *If Jeff doesn't get back here pdq there's going to be trouble.* 杰夫如果不马上回到这里, 就要有麻烦了。

PDT /ˌpi di ˈti; ˌpiː diː ˈtiː/ the abbreviation of 缩写= PACIFIC DAYLIGHT TIME

PE /ˌpi ˈi; ˌpiː ˈiː/ *n* [U] physical education; sport and physical activity taught as a school subject 体育(课); PT *BrE*【英】

pea /pi; piː/ *n* [C] **1** a large round green seed that is cooked and eaten as a vegetable〔作为蔬菜食用的〕豌豆: *frozen peas* 冰冻豌豆 | *garden peas* 庭园豌豆 | *pea soup* 豌豆汤 | **shell peas** (=take them out of their seed container) 剥豌豆 —see picture on page A9 参见 A9 页图 **2** a plant that produces long green PODs that contain these seeds 豌豆〔一种植物〕**3 like two peas in a pod** *informal* exactly the same in appearance, behaviour etc【非正式】〔容貌、行为等〕一模一样 —see also 另见 SPLIT PEA, SWEET PEA

peace /pis; piːs/ *n* 2 2

1 ▶NO WAR 没有战争◀ a) [U] a situation in which there is no war between countries or in a country 和平: **world peace** *a dangerous situation that threatens world peace* 威胁世界和平的危险局势 | **peace agreement/treaty etc** *the Geneva peace talks* 日内瓦和谈 | **be at peace with** *Germany has been at peace with France for fifty years.* 德国已与法国和平相处了五十年。**b)** [singular] a period of time in which there is no war 和平时期: *a lasting peace* 持久和平 **c) peace movement/campaign etc** organized efforts to prevent war 和平运动

2 ▶AGREEMENT 协议◀ [singular] an agreement that ends a war 和约: *the Peace of Nijmegen* 奈梅亨和约 | *a negotiated peace* 谈判后达成的和约

3 ▶NO NOISE 无噪声◀ [U] a peaceful situation with no unpleasant noise 安静, 平静: *A single gunshot shattered the peace of the May afternoon.* 一声枪响划破了五月那个下午的宁静。| **in peace** (=without being interrupted) 安静地; 不被打断地 *I wish you'd leave me in peace – I've got work to do.* 我希望你不要打扰我 — 我有工作要做。| **peace and quiet** *We're going to the countryside for some peace and quiet.* 我们打算去乡下过清静一些的日子。

4 ▶CALMNESS 平静◀ [U] a feeling of calmness and lack of worry and problems 平静, 安宁: *the search for inner peace* 寻求内心的平静 | **peace of mind** (=to stop you from worrying) 心境的平静, 安心 *Ann had to check the baby every few minutes for her own peace of mind.* 为使自己安心, 安不得不每隔几分钟就查看一下婴儿。| **at peace with yourself** (=calm and happy) 平静而快乐 *Lynn never seems to be at peace with herself.* 琳恩好像永不会平静下来似的。

5 [U] a situation in which there is no quarrelling between people who live or work together 和睦〔相处〕: *peace and stability in industrial relations* 劳资关系的和睦稳定 | **keep the peace** (=stop people from quarrelling, fighting, or causing trouble) 维持治安

6 disturb the peace *law* to behave in a noisy and unpleasant way in public【法律】扰乱治安: *Macklin was charged with disturbing the peace.* 麦克林被指控扰乱治安。—see also 另见 **breach of the peace** (BREACH¹ (4)), JUSTICE OF THE PEACE

7 hold/keep your peace to keep quiet even though there is something you would like to say 保持缄默: *In spite of John's provocative remarks, I held my peace.* 不管约翰说什么挑衅的话, 我都保持缄默。

8 make (your) peace with to end your quarrel with someone, especially by telling them you are sorry 与〔某人〕和解〔尤指主动表示道歉〕: *Ann wanted to make her peace with her father before he died.* 安想在她父亲死之前与他和解。

9 at peace an expression meaning dead, used when you want to say this in a gentle way 长眠〔"死"的委婉说法〕

10 rest in peace a prayer for someone who has died, said during a funeral service or written on a GRAVESTONE 安息吧〔在葬礼上说的或刻在墓碑上的祷辞〕

peace·a·ble /ˈpisəbl̩; ˈpiːsəbəl/ *adj* **1** a situation or way of doing something that is peaceable is calm, without any violence or fighting 平和的; 太平的, 和平的 **2** someone who is peaceable dislikes arguing 不爱争吵的, 温和的, 和睦的 —**peaceably** *adv*: *The two tribes live peaceably together.* 这两个部落和睦相处。

Peace Corps, the /ˈ· ·/ a US government organization that aims to help poorer countries, by sending them VOLUNTEERS (=people who work without payment), especially young people, who teach skills in education, health, farming etc 和平队〔美国一政府组织。该组织向贫困国家派遣主要由年轻人组成的志愿者, 以传授教育、保健和农业技能等方式扶助贫困国家〕

peace div·i·dend /ˈ· ,···/ *n* [singular] the money saved on weapons and available for other purposes, when a government

reduces its military strength〔政府通过削减军费而节省下来用于其他用途的〕和平红利，和平效益

peace·ful /ˈpisfəl; ˈpiːsfəl/ *adj* **1** quiet and calm without any worry or excitement 平静的，安宁的，宁静的: *We had a peaceful afternoon without the children.* 孩子们不在，我们度过了一个宁静的下午。| *into a deep and peaceful sleep* 进入安详的熟睡 **2** without war 没有战争的，和平的: *a state of peaceful coexistence between nations* 国家之间和平共处的状态 **3** deliberately avoiding any violence 有意避免暴力的: *a peaceful demonstration* 和平示威 —**peacefully** *adv* —**peacefulness** *n* [U]

peace·keep·ing /ˈpisˌkipɪŋ; ˈpiːsˌkiːpɪŋ/ *adj* **peacekeeping force/troops etc** soldiers that are sent to a place where the people are fighting, to try to stop more violence 维持和平部队

peace·lov·ing /ˈ· ˌ··/ *adj* believing strongly in peace rather than war 爱好和平的

peace·mak·er /ˈpisˌmekɚ; ˈpiːsmeɪkə/ *n* [C] someone who tries to persuade other people or nations to stop fighting 调解人，调停者: *Eisenhower was anxious to play the role of peacemaker in his last year in office.* 艾森豪威尔在他执政的最后一年渴望扮演调解人的角色。

peace march /ˈ· ·/ *n* [C] a march by people who are protesting against violence or military activities 反战[反暴力]游行

peace of·fer·ing /ˈ· ˌ···/ *n* [C] *informal* something you give to someone to show them that you are sorry and want to be friendly, after you have annoyed or upset them【非正式】〔为表示歉意和友好而赠送的〕和平礼物，谢罪礼: *I took along a box of chocolates as a peace offering.* 我带了一盒巧克力作为谢罪礼。

peace pipe /ˈ· ·/ *n* [C] a pipe which Native Americans use to smoke tobacco, which is shared in a ceremony as a sign of peace; PIPE OF PEACE〔美洲土著用作和平象征的〕长杆烟斗，和平烟斗

peace·time /ˈpisˌtaɪm; ˈpiːstaɪm/ *n* [U] a period of time when a nation is not fighting a war 和平时期 —opposite 反义词 WARTIME

peach /pitʃ; piːtʃ/ *n* **1** [C] a round fruit with soft yellow or red skin, that has sweet juicy flesh, and a large seed in its centre, or a tree that produces this fruit 桃(子); 桃树 —see picture on page A8 参见 A8 页图 **2** [U] a pale pinkish-orange colour 桃红色 —see picture on page A5 参见 A5 页图 **3** [singular] *old-fashioned* someone or something that you think is attractive or like very much【过时】有吸引力的人[物]，特别惹人喜爱的人[物]: *a peach of a hat* 漂亮的帽子 | *Jan's a real peach.* 简真是个美人儿。**4 a peaches and cream complexion** skin with an attractive pink colour 白皙红润的肤色

Peach Mel·ba /ˌpitʃ ˈmɛlbə; ˌpiːtʃ ˈmelbə/ *n* [C,U] half a peach served with ice cream and RASPBERRY juice〔浇以悬钩子汁的〕蜜桃加冰激凌

pea·cock /ˈpiˌkɑk; ˈpiːkɒk/ *n* [C] a large male bird which has long tail feathers that it can spread out, showing their beautiful blue and green colours and patterns (雄)孔雀

Peacock, Thomas Love (1785-1866) a British writer and poet who used SATIRE (=a way of writing in which you make someone seem funny in order to show their faults) to criticize the politicians and writers of his time. His most famous works are NOVELs such as *Headlong Hall* and *Nightmare Abbey*. 皮科克〔(1785-1866)，英国作家、诗人。他曾以讽刺手法批评同时代的政客和作家，以小说《险宫》和《噩梦隐修院》最为著名〕

peacock blue /ˌ·· ˈ·◂/ *n* [U] a deep greenish-blue colour 孔雀蓝(色) —**peacock blue** *adj*

pea·fowl /ˈpiˌfaʊl; ˈpiːfaʊl/ *n* [C] a peacock or peahen〔雄或雌的〕孔雀

pea green /ˌ· ˈ·◂/ *n* [U] a light green colour, like that of PEAS 青豆色，嫩绿色 —**pea green** *adj*

pea·hen /ˈpiˌhɛn; ˈpiːhen/ *n* [C] a large, brownish bird, the female peafowl 雌孔雀

peak¹ /pik; piːk/ *n* [C]

1 ►TIME 时间◄ [usually singular 一般用单数] the time when something or someone is strongest, most successful, or best 顶峰，顶点: *Her career was at its peak.* 她的事业正处于鼎盛时期。| *Sales have reached a new peak.* 销售额达到了新的最高点。| **be at your peak/reach your peak** *Most athletes have reached their peak by the time they're 20.* 大多数运动员在 20 岁时已达到巅峰时期。—compare 比较 OFF-PEAK

2 ►MOUNTAIN 山◄ **a)** the sharply pointed top of a mountain 山顶，山峰: *peaks covered with snow all the year round* 终年被白雪覆盖的山峰 —compare 比较 SUMMIT (1) —see picture on page A12 参见 A12 页图 **b)** a whole mountain with a pointed top 有尖峰的山: *K2 is one of the world's highest peaks.* 乔戈里峰是世界上最高的山峰之一。

3 ►POINT 尖◄ a part that curves to a point above a surface 尖端，尖顶: *Whisk the egg whites until they form stiff peaks.* 把蛋白打到发稠且顶端耸起为止。

4 ►CAP 帽子◄ the flat curved part of a cap that sticks out in front above your eyes 帽檐，帽舌 —see picture at 参见 CAP 图

peak² *v* [I] to reach the highest point or level 达到顶峰，达到最高水平: *Sales peaked in August, then fell sharply.* 销售额于八月份达到最高点，然后急剧下降。| **[+at]** *Around 1950 Chicago's population peaked at about 3.6 million.* 在 1950 年左右，芝加哥的人口达到高峰，约有 360 万之多。

peak³ *adj* **1 peak level/rate/value** the highest level etc of something 最高水平/(速)率/值: *The factory is running at peak productivity.* 这家工厂的生产能力正处于最高峰。**2** *BrE* the peak time or period is when the greatest number of people are doing the same thing, using the same service etc【英】〔时间、阶段〕高峰的: *the peak time for electricity consumption* 用电的高峰时间 | *Extra buses run at peak times.* 交通高峰期有加开的公共汽车。

Peak Dis·trict, the /ˈ· ˌ··/ a hilly area and national park, mostly in Derbyshire, northern England, which is popular for climbing, walking, and POTHOLING. 皮克区〔英国一丘陵地带和国家公园。大部分在英格兰北部德比郡境内，是爬山、步行及岩洞探险的好去处〕

Peake /pik; piːk/, **Mer·vyn** /ˈmɝvɪn; ˈmɜːvɪn/ (1911-68) a British writer and ILLUSTRATOR (=someone who draws pictures for books), whose NOVELs *Titus Groan*, *Gormenghast*, and *Titus Alone* describe the strange imaginary world of Gormenghast castle 皮克〔(1911-1968)，英国作家、插画家。他的三部曲《泰特斯·格罗恩》、《歌门鬼城》和《泰特斯独行》描写了歌门鬼城城堡这一奇特的虚幻世界〕

peak·ed¹ /ˈpikɪd; ˈpiːkɪd/ *adj especially AmE* pale and ill【尤美】苍白的，有病容的; peaky *BrE*【英】: *You're looking a bit peaked this morning.* 今早你看起来有点憔悴。

peaked² /pikt; piːkt/ *adj* a peaked cap has a flat curved part at the front above the eyes 有帽檐的 —see picture at 参见 CAP 图

pea·ky /ˈpikɪ; ˈpiːki/ *adj informal especially BrE* pale or ill【非正式，尤英】苍白的，有病容的，不适的: *Jane's feeling a bit peaky today.* 简今天感到有点不舒服。

peal¹ /pil; piːl/ *n* [C] **1** a sudden loud sound of laughter or thunder 洪亮的笑声; 隆隆的雷声: **[+of]** *Peal of laughter came from the other room.* 阵阵笑声从另一个房间传来。**2** the sound of the loud ringing of bells 响亮的钟声[铃声]: **[+of]** *a joyous peal of bells* 欢快的铃声 **3** *technical*【术语】**a)** a musical pattern made by ringing a number of bells one after the other 钟乐 **b)** a set of bells 编钟

peal² *v* also 又作 **peal out** [I] if bells peal, they ring loudly〔钟或铃〕发出响亮的声音，鸣响: *The bells pealed out across the churchyard.* 教堂墓地对面的钟声当当地响起。

pea·nut /ˈpiˌnʌt; ˈpiːnʌt/ *n* **1** [C] a nut which grows in a soft shell under the ground and which can be eaten (落)花生: *salted peanuts* 咸花生 **2 peanuts** [U] *informal* a sum of money that is so small that it is hardly worth mentioning【非正式】微不足道的一小笔钱: *The hotel workers get paid peanuts.* 酒店工人的报酬十分微薄。

peanut but·ter /ˌ·· ˈ··/ *n* [U] a soft substance made from crushed peanuts, eaten on bread or used in cooking 花生酱

peanut gal·ler·y /ˈ·· ˌ···/ *n* [C] *AmE humorous* the cheap rows of seats at the back of a theatre or cinema【美，幽默】〔剧院或影院里票价较低的〕后排座位

Peanuts /ˈpiːˌnʌt; ˈpiːnʌt/ a humorous US CARTOON STRIP (=a set of drawings that tell a story in a newspaper or magazine) by Charles Schultz, about a boy called Charlie Brown, who is nice

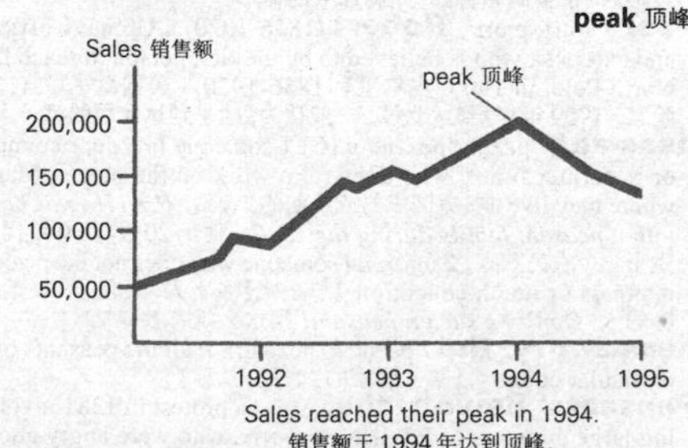

Sales reached their peak in 1994.
销售额于 1994 年达到顶峰。

but not very confident and often unlucky. Other characters include his dog Snoopy, his sister Sally, and his friends Lucy, Linus, Pigpen, Peppermint Patty, and Schroeder.《花生》〔查尔斯·舒尔茨创作的美国幽默卡通连环画。故事中有一个男孩，名叫查利·布朗。他是个好孩子，但不十分自信，常常运气不佳。其他角色包括他的小狗史努比和妹妹萨莉，还有他的朋友露西、莱纳斯、皮格彭、薄荷·帕蒂和施罗德〕

S3 **pear** /pɛr; peə/ *n* [C] a sweet juicy fruit that has a round base and becomes thinner nearer the top, or the tree that produces this fruit 梨; 梨树 —see also 另见 PRICKLY PEAR—see picture on page A8 参见 A8 页图

pearl /pɝl; pɜːl/ *n*
1 ►JEWEL 首饰◄ [C] **a)** a small round hard white object with a silvery shine, that is formed inside the shell of an OYSTER, and is very valuable as a jewel 珍珠: *a string of pearls* 一串珍珠 | *a pearl necklace* 珍珠项链 **b)** an artificial copy of this jewel 人造珍珠
2 ►LIQUID 液体◄ [C] *literary* a small round drop of some liquid【文】〔液体的〕珠状物: *Pearls of dew sparkled on the grass.* 草地上露珠闪烁。
3 ►HARD SUBSTANCE 坚硬物质◄ [U] a hard shiny, variously coloured substance formed inside some SHELLFISH, which is used for decorating objects; MOTHER-OF-PEARL 珍珠母: *a knife with a pearl handle* 一把带珍珠母柄的小刀
4 ►EXCELLENT THING/PERSON 出色的东西/人◄ [C usually singular 一般用单数] someone or something that is especially good or valuable 极其优秀的人; 特别珍贵的东西: *a pearl among women* 女中俊杰 | **a pearl beyond price** *Good health is a pearl beyond price.* 健康的身体是无价之宝。
5 cast pearls before swine to give something valuable to someone who does not understand its value 把贵重的东西给不懂其价值的人; 明珠暗投
6 pearls of wisdom an expression meaning wise remarks, often used jokingly to mean slightly stupid remarks 有见识的评说, 智慧的结晶〔常用于开玩笑, 表示其中略有点愚蠢〕: *Have you any more pearls of wisdom you'd like to share with us?* 你还有什么"至理名言"要让我们分享吗?

pearl bar·ley /,· '··/ *n* [U] small grains of BARLEY that have been polished smooth 珍珠大麦

pearl div·er /'· ,··/ *n* [C] someone who swims underwater in the sea, looking for shells that contain pearls (潜水)采珠人

Pearl Har·bor /,· '··/ an important US naval base in Hawaii, which was suddenly attacked by Japanese planes in December 1941. Many warships were destroyed or damaged, and this caused great shock and anger in the US, and made the US start fighting in World War II. 珍珠港〔美国一重要海军基地, 位于夏威夷。1941年12月遭到日军飞机突袭, 许多战舰被击毁或破坏。此次偷袭事件在美国引起震惊和愤怒, 促使其加入二战〕

pearl·y /'pɝlɪ; 'pɜːli/ *adj* like pearls or having the colour of pearls 珍珠似的; 珍珠色的: *pearly white teeth* 珍珠般洁白的牙齿

pearly gates /,·· '·/ *n* [plural] *often humorous* the entrance to heaven【常幽默】天国之门

Pears /pɪrz; pɪəz/, **Sir Peter** (1910-86) a British TENOR (=a male singer with a fairly high voice). In 1948 he started the Aldeburgh Festival with his partner, the musician Benjamin Britten, who wrote a lot of vocal music and OPERAS for him. 皮尔斯〔(1910-1986), 英国男高音。1948年, 他与自己的搭档音乐家本杰明·布里顿共同创办了奥尔德堡音乐节。布里顿曾为皮尔斯创作过大量声乐作品和歌剧〕

pear-shaped /'· ·/ *adj* someone who is pear-shaped is larger around their waist and HIPS than around their chest〔人的体形〕梨形的〔指腰部和臀部宽, 胸部窄的体形〕

Peary /pɪrɪ; pɪəri/, **Robert** (1856-1920) a US navy officer and EXPLORER who is believed to be the first person to reach the North Pole, in 1909. 皮尔里〔(1856-1920), 美国海军军官、探险家。1909 年, 他到达北极。一般认为, 他是到达北极的第一人〕

peas·ant /'pɛzn̩t; 'pezənt/ *n* [C] **1** someone in a poor country or in former times, who does farm work on the piece of land where they live〔贫穷国家的或从前的〕农民, 农夫: *He was born into a peasant family during the 1930s.* 他于 20 世纪 30 年代出生于一个农民家庭。**2** *informal* someone who does not have good manners or much education【非正式】乡下人, 土包子; 缺乏教养的人: *Don't be such a peasant!* 别这么没有教养!

peas·ant·ry, the /'pɛzn̩trɪ; 'pezəntri/ *n* all the peasants of a particular country〔某一国家的〕农民〔总称〕

Peasants' Re·volt, the /,·· '·/ a protest in 1381 involving large numbers of English PEASANTS, who were angry about unfair social and economic conditions and about high taxes. They formed an unoffical army, led by Wat Tyler, and marched to London, where they demanded better conditions and took control of the Tower of London. The English king, Richard II, pretended to agree to some of their demands, but after their leaders were killed he changed his mind, so the revolt failed. 农民起义〔众多英格兰农民因对不公的社会经济条件和沉重的税负不满于1381年掀起的一场反抗运动。他们组成了一支非正规军队, 由瓦特·泰勒率领向伦敦进发。到了伦敦, 他们强烈要求改善生活条件, 并控制了伦敦塔。英王理查二世表面上答应了他们的某些要求, 但起义领袖遇害后, 国王却改变了主意, 起义因此遭到失败〕

pease pud·ding /,piz 'pudɪŋ; ,piːz 'pʊdɪŋ/ *n* [U] *BrE* a dish made of dried PEAS, boiled with ham to make a thick yellow substance that is eaten with bread【英】豌豆布丁

pea·shoot·er /'pi,ʃutɚ; 'piː,ʃuːtə/ *n* [C] a small tube used by children to blow small objects, especially dried PEAS, at someone or something 射豆枪〔一种儿童用来吹射豆子等的玩具枪〕

pea soup·er /,pi 'supɚ; ,piː 'suːpə/ *n* [C] a very thick FOG 浓雾

peat /pit; piːt/ *n* **1** [U] a substance formed from decaying plants under the surface of the ground in some areas, which can be burned instead of coal, or mixed with soil to help plants grow well 泥炭, 泥煤: *a peat bog* 泥炭沼泽 **2** [C] a piece of this used for burning on a fire〔用作燃料的〕泥炭[泥煤]块 —**peaty** *adj*: *brown peaty water* 泥炭似的黑水

peb·ble /'pɛbl̩; 'pebəl/ *n* [C] **1** a small smooth stone found on the beach or on the bottom of a river〔见于海滩或河底等的〕卵石, 小圆石, 砾石 **2 you're not the only pebble on the beach** used to say that someone is not the only person who has to be considered or who deserves attention 你并非绝无仅有的人; 除了你还大有人在 —**pebbly** *adj*: *a pebbly beach* 多卵石的海滩

peb·ble·dash /'pɛbl̩,dæʃ; 'pebəldæʃ/ *n* [U] *BrE* a surface for the outside walls of houses, made of CEMENT with a lot of very small pebbles set into it【英】〔房屋外墙面上的〕灰泥卵石涂层 —**pebbledash** *v* [T]

pe·can /prɪ'kɑn; prɪ'kæn/ *n* [C] a long thin nut with a dark red shell, or the tree that it grows on 山核桃; 山核桃树: *pecan pie* 山核桃馅饼

pec·ca·dil·lo /,pɛkə'dɪlo; ,pekə'dɪləʊ/ *n* [C] a small unimportant thing that someone does wrong 小错误, 小过失: *Bernard's wife had learnt to put up with his little peccadillos.* 伯纳德的妻子已学会了忍受他的小过失。

pec·ca·ry /'pɛkərɪ; 'pekəri/ *n* [C] a wild animal like a pig that lives in Central and South America〔生活在中、南美洲的〕西貒

peck[1] /pɛk; pek/ *v* **1** [I,T] if a bird pecks something, it makes quick repeated movements with its beak to try to bite it〔鸟〕啄; 啄食: [+at] *sparrows pecking at breadcrumbs* 啄食面包屑的麻雀 | **peck sth** *A bird flew down and pecked my hand.* 一只鸟飞下来啄了我的手。| *It had pecked a hole in the bottom of its cage.* 它在笼底啄了一个洞。**2 peck sb on the cheek** to kiss someone quickly and lightly 匆匆地轻吻某人的面颊 —see also 另见 HENPECKED

peck at sth ↔ *phr v* [T] to eat only a little bit of a meal because you are not hungry; **pick at** (PICK[1])〔因不饿而〕吃一点点

peck[2] *n* [C] **1 give sb a peck** to kiss someone quickly and lightly 匆匆地轻吻某人 **2** an act of pecking 啄 **3** a measure of amount for dry substances such as fruit or grain 配克〔水果、谷物等的计量单位〕

peck·er /'pɛkɚ; 'pekə/ *n* [C] **1 keep your pecker up** *BrE spoken* used to tell someone to stay cheerful even when it is difficult to do so【英口】打起精神, 振作起来 **2** *AmE slang* PENIS【美俚】阴茎

pecking or·der /'·· ,··/ *n* [C] *often humorous* the social system of a particular group of people or animals, in which each one knows who is more important and less important than themselves【常幽默】〔人或动物特定群体中的〕社群等级, 权势等级: *Patients seem to be very low down in the pecking order as far as making changes to hospital policy is concerned.* 就改变医院的政策而言, 病人好像处于最无足轻重的地位。

peck·ish /'pɛkɪʃ; 'pekɪʃ/ *adj BrE informal* slightly hungry【英, 非正式】有点饿的

Peck·sniff /'pɛksnɪf; 'peksnɪf/, **Mr** a character in the book *Martin Chuzzlewit* (1843-44) by Charles Dickens. He is a HYPOCRITE (=someone who pretends to be morally good but is not), and pretends to like people who have power or money in order to get an advantage. 佩克斯涅夫〔查尔斯·狄更斯的小说《马丁·朱述尔维特》(1843-1844) 中的人物。他是一个伪君子, 经常讨好有钱或有势的人, 以求落到好处〕

pecs /pɛks; peks/ *n* [plural] *informal* PECTORALS【非正式】胸肌

pec·tic /ˈpɛktɪk; ˈpektɪk/ *adj technical* containing pectin【术语】果胶的；含果胶的

pec·tin /ˈpɛktɪn; ˈpektɪn/ *n* [U] *technical* a chemical substance like sugar that is found in some fruits and is important in making JAM¹ (1) and JELLY (1,2)【术语】果胶

pec·to·ral /ˈpɛktərəl; ˈpektərəl/ *adj technical* of or connected with the chest【术语】胸的；胸部的：*pectoral muscles* 胸肌

pectoral fin /ˌ····ˈ·/ *n* [C] the FIN that is on the side of a fish's head and helps it to control the direction it swims in〔鱼的〕胸鳍

pec·to·rals /ˈpɛktərəlz; ˈpektərəlz/ *n* [plural] your chest muscles 胸肌：*strong men with bulging pectorals* 胸肌发达的强壮男人

pe·cu·li·ar /pɪˈkjuljə; pɪˈkjuːliə/ *adj* **1** strange, unfamiliar, and a little surprising, especially in a way that is unpleasant or worrying 奇怪的；异常的；乖僻的：*This meat tastes peculiar.* 这肉味道很古怪。| *It seems very peculiar that no one noticed Kay had gone.* 没有人注意到凯已经走了，这好像很奇怪。**2 be peculiar to** if something is peculiar to a particular person, place, or situation, it is a feature that only belongs to that person etc〔某人、某地方或某情况所〕特有的：*The problem of racism is not peculiar to this country.* 种族歧视问题并不是这个国家特有的。**3** behaving in a strange and slightly crazy way〔行为〕怪癖的；有点疯狂的：*Auntie May's gone a bit peculiar lately.* 梅姑妈最近有点古怪。**4 feel peculiar** *informal* to feel slightly ill【非正式】感到有点不舒服

pe·cu·li·ar·i·ty /pɪˌkjulɪˈærətɪ; pɪˌkjuːliˈærəti/ *n* **1** [C] something that is a feature of only one particular place, person, or situation〔仅为某人、某地方或某情况所独有的〕特点，独特性：[+of] *The lack of a written constitution is a peculiarity of the British political system.* 没有一部成文宪法是英国政治制度的一大特点。**2** [C] a strange or unusual habit, quality etc 奇异的性质；怪癖：*It took some time for Theresa to get used to her husband's peculiarities.* 特雷莎花了好一段时间才习惯了她丈夫的怪癖。**3** [U] the quality of being strange or unfamiliar 奇特；怪异；古怪

pe·cu·li·ar·ly /pɪˈkjuljəlɪ; pɪˈkjuːliəli/ *adv* **1** especially 特别；尤其(是)：*a peculiarly difficult question* 特别难的问题 **2** in a strange or unusual way 奇怪地，古怪地：*Theo had been behaving most peculiarly.* 西奥的举止一直很古怪。**3 peculiarly British/middle-class/Christian etc** something that is peculiarly British etc is a feature only of British people etc 英国人/中产阶级/基督教徒等特有的：*a peculiarly American phenomenon* 美国特有的一种现象

pe·cu·ni·a·ry /pɪˈkjunɪˌɛrɪ; pɪˈkjuːniəri/ *adj formal* connected with or consisting of money【正式】钱的；金钱上的：*a pecuniary advantage* 金钱上的优势

ped·a·gog·i·cal /ˌpɛdəˈgɑdʒɪkl; ˌpedəˈgɒdʒɪkəl/ *adj technical* concerning teaching methods or the practice of teaching【术语】教学(法)的：*training in pedagogical skills* 教学技巧的培训 —**pedagogically** /-klɪ; -kli/ *adv*

ped·a·gogue /ˈpɛdəˌgɑg; ˈpedəgɒg/ *n* [C] **1** a teacher who cares too much about rules 过分拘泥条条框框的老师，学究 **2** *old use* a teacher【旧】老师

ped·a·go·gy /ˈpɛdəˌgɑdʒɪ; ˈpedəgɒdʒi/ *n* [U] *technical* the practice of teaching or the study of teaching【术语】教学(法)；教育学

ped·al¹ /ˈpɛdl; ˈpedl/ *n* [C] **1** one of the two parts of a bicycle that you push round with your feet to make the bicycle go forward〔脚踏车的〕踏板，脚蹬 —see picture at 参见 BICYCLE¹ 图 **2** a part in a car or on a machine that you press with your foot to control it〔汽车或机器的〕踏板：*the accelerator pedal* 油门踏板 **3** a part on a piano or organ that you press with your foot to change the quality of the sound〔钢琴或风琴的〕踏板

pedal² *v* **pedalled, pedalling** *BrE*【英】, **pedaled, pedaling** *AmE*【美】[I, T] **1** [always+adv/prep] to ride a bicycle 骑〔脚踏车〕：[+up/along/down etc] *Andrew pedalled up the road towards the town centre.* 安德鲁骑着自行车在通往市中心的路上行驶。—see also 另见 SOFT PEDAL **2** to turn or push the pedals on a bicycle or other machine 踩动〔自行车或机器的〕踏板：*pedalling furiously on her exercise bike* 飞快地踏着她的健身车

pedal bin /ˈ··ˌ·/ *n* [C] a container for waste that has a lid which is opened by pressing a pedal with your foot〔用脚一踩盖子即开启的〕脚踏式垃圾桶

ped·ant /ˈpɛdn̩t; ˈpednt/ *n* [C] someone who pays too much attention to rules and details 过分注重规则和细节的人，学究，迂夫子：*She is something of a pedant when it comes to intellectual argument.* 说到知性的讨论时，她多少有点像一个迂夫子。—**pedantry** *n* [U]

pe·dan·tic /pɪˈdæntɪk; pɪˈdæntɪk/ *adj* paying too much attention to rules and details 过分注重规则和细节的；学究式的；书呆子气的：*He was meticulous, but never pedantic.* 他非常谨慎，但决不迂腐。—**pedantically** /-klɪ; -kli/ *adv*

ped·dle /ˈpɛdl; ˈpedl/ *v* [T] **1** to go from place to place, trying to sell something 沿街叫卖，挨户兜售：*An old woman was peddling goods on a street corner.* 一位老妇人正在街角处兜售物品。| **peddle drugs** (=sell illegal drugs) 贩卖毒品 **2** to try to get people to accept opinions, false information etc 散播，兜售〔观点、假信息等〕：*a magazine that peddles scandal and gossip* 散播丑闻和流言的杂志 **3** *informal, especially AmE* to sell goods that are of low quality【非正式，尤美】兜售〔劣质货物〕

ped·dler /ˈpɛdlə; ˈpedlə/ *n* [C] **1** the American form of the word PEDLAR pedlar的美式拼法 **2** *old-fashioned* someone who sells illegal drugs【过时】贩卖毒品的人：*a dope peddler* 毒品贩子 —compare 比较 PUSHER

ped·e·rast /ˈpɛdəræst; ˈpedəræst/ *n* [C] a man who has sex with a boy 鸡奸者〈指与男孩发生性行为的男子〉

ped·es·tal /ˈpɛdɪstl; ˈpedɪstəl/ *n* [C] **1** the base on which a PILLAR OR STATUE stands〔柱子或雕像的〕基座，台座，柱脚：*a Grecian bust on a pedestal* 放在基座上的古希腊半身人像 **2 pedestal basin/table** *especially BrE* a BASIN or table that is supported by a single COLUMN【尤英】〔只有一根支柱支撑的〕支柱式洗脸盆/独脚桌 **3 put/place sb on a pedestal** to admire someone so much that you treat them or talk about them as though they are perfect 非常敬慕某人，把某人当作偶像崇拜：*You shouldn't put him on a pedestal – he doesn't deserve it.* 你不应把他当作偶像崇拜 —— 他不值得你那样做。

pe·des·tri·an¹ /pəˈdɛstrɪən; pɪˈdestriən/ *n* [C] someone who is walking, especially in a street or other place used by cars 行人，步行者 —see picture on page A3 参见 A3 页图

pedestrian² *adj* **1** ordinary and uninteresting and without any imagination 平淡无奇的；乏味的；缺乏想象力的：*a pedestrian description* 单调乏味的描述 | *a rather pedestrian student* 相当平凡的学生 **2 pedestrian walkway/footbridge etc** a path, bridge etc used by pedestrians 人行道/步行桥等

pedestrian cross·ing /·ˌ····ˈ··/ *n* [C] *BrE* a special place for people to cross the road【英】人行横道；CROSSWALK *AmE*【美】

pe·des·tri·a·nize also 又作 **-ise** *BrE*【英】/pɪˈdɛstrɪənˌaɪz; pɪˈdestriənaɪz/ *v* [T] to change a street or shopping area into a place where vehicles are not allowed 使成为行人专用区，使成为步行购物区 —**pedestrianization** /pɪˌdɛstrənəˈzeʃən; pɪˌdestrənaɪˈzeɪʃən/ *n* [U]

pedestrian pre·cinct /·ˌ····ˈ··/ *BrE*【英】, **pedestrian mall** /·ˌ····ˈ·/ *AmE*【美】*n* [C] a shopping area in the centre of a town where traffic cannot go〔市中心禁止车辆通行的〕步行购物区，行人区

pe·di·a·tri·cian /ˌpidɪəˈtrɪʃən; ˌpiːdiəˈtrɪʃən/ *n* [C] the American spelling of PAEDIATRICIAN paediatrician 的美式拼法

pe·di·at·rics /ˌpidɪˈætrɪks; ˌpiːdiˈætrɪks/ *n* [U] the American spelling of PAEDIATRICS paediatrics 的美式拼法

ped·i·cel /ˈpɛdəsl; ˈpedɪsel/ *n* [C] *technical* a long thin part of a plant below each flower【术语】花梗

ped·i·cure /ˈpɛdɪˌkjur; ˈpedɪkjʊə/ *n* [C, U] treatment for feet and toenails, to make them more comfortable or beautiful 足部治疗；修脚趾甲 —**pedicurist** *n* [C]

ped·i·gree¹ /ˈpɛdəˌgri; ˈpedɪgriː/ *n* [C, U] the past family, especially the parents, grandparents etc, of a person or animal, or an official written record of this 血统；家系，家谱；〔动物的〕纯种系谱

pedigree² *adj* [only before noun 仅用于名词前] a pedigree animal comes from a family that has been recorded for a long time and is considered to be of a very good breed〔动物〕纯种系谱的：*a pedigree greyhound* 纯种灵猩 —compare 比较 PUREBRED, THOROUGHBRED (1)

ped·i·ment /ˈpɛdəmənt; ˈpedɪmənt/ *n* [C] a three-sided piece of stone or other material placed above the entrance to a building, especially in the buildings of ancient Greece〔尤指古希腊建筑门顶上的〕三角顶饰[楣饰]

ped·lar /ˈpɛdlə; ˈpedlə/ *n* [C] *BrE* someone who used to walk from place to place selling small things【英】流动小贩，货郎；PEDDLER *AmE*【美】

pe·dom·e·ter /pɪˈdɑmətə; pɪˈdɒmɪtə/ *n* [C] an instrument used for measuring how far you walk 计步器，步程计

pe·do·phile /ˈpidəfaɪl; ˈpiːdəfaɪl/ *n* [C] the American spelling of PAEDOPHILE paedophile 的美式拼法

pee¹ /pi; piː/ *v* [I] *informal* to pass liquid waste from your body; URINATE【非正式】撒尿

pee² *n informal*【非正式】**1** [singular] an act of passing liquid waste from your body 撒尿: **go for a pee/have a pee** *Have I got time to go for a pee before we leave?* 在我们离开前我有时间去小便吗？**2** [U] liquid waste passed from your body; URINE 尿

peek /pik; piːk/ *v* [I] to look quickly at something, especially something that you are not supposed to see 偷看, 窥视: *The children were peeking from behind the wall.* 孩子们在从墙后面偷看。—compare 比较 PEEP¹ —**peek** *n* [C]: *I noticed Diane taking a quick peek at herself in the mirror.* 我注意到黛安娜快速地照了一下镜子。

peek·a·boo /ˈpikəˌbu; ˌpiːkəˈbuː/ *interjection, n* [U] a game played to amuse babies, in which you repeatedly hide your face and then show it again, or the word you say when you play this game 躲猫猫〔把脸一隐一现地逗小孩的一种游戏〕; 做躲猫猫时所说的话

P

peel¹ /pil; piːl/ *v* **1** [T] to remove the skin from fruit or vegetables 剥去, 削去〔水果、蔬菜〕的皮: *peeling potatoes* 削马铃薯皮 —see picture on page A11 参见 A11 页图 **2 peel sth from/away/off etc** [T always+adv/prep] to remove the outer layer from something 除去[剥去]…的外皮: *Jessie peeled the wrapper from the sweet.* 杰西把糖纸剥掉了。**3** [I] **a)** to lose an outer layer or surface〔外层或表面〕脱落, 剥落: *The walls were peeling with the damp.* 墙面因受潮而正在剥落。**b)** if skin, paper, or paint peels, it comes off, usually in small pieces〔皮肤、纸或油漆〕脱皮, 剥落: *My skin always peels when I've been in the sun.* 我的皮肤在晒了太阳后总要脱皮。—see picture on page A18 参见 A18 页图 —see also 另见 **keep your eyes open/peeled** (EYE¹ (15))

peel off *phr v* **1** [I,T **peel** sth ↔ **off**] to take your clothes off 脱去〔衣服〕: *The children peeled off their clothes and leapt into the pool.* 孩子们脱去衣服, 跳进了水池。**2** [I] to leave a moving group of vehicles, aircraft etc and go in a different direction〔车辆、飞机等〕离队, 离群: *The last two motorcycles peeled off from the convoy.* 最后的两辆摩托车离开了车队。

peel² *n* [U] the outer layer of some fruits, especially the ones that you usually peel before you eat them〔尤指某些水果在吃前要剥掉的〕外皮: *orange peel* 橙皮

Peel, Rob·ert (1788-1850) a British Conservative politician who established the first official British police force and introduced freedoms for Roman Catholics. He was prime minister from 1834 to 1835 and 1841 to 1846. 皮尔〔(1788-1850), 英国保守党政治家。他组建了英国第一支正规警察部队, 允许罗马天主教徒自由信教, 1834-1835 年、1841-1846 年两度出任首相〕

peel·er /ˈpilɚ; ˈpiːlə/ *n* [C] **1** a special type of knife for removing the skin from fruit or vegetables〔水果或蔬菜的〕削皮刀, 剥皮器 —see picture on page A11 参见 A11 页图 **2** *BrE old-fashioned* a police officer【英, 过时】警官

peel·ings /ˈpilɪŋz; ˈpiːlɪŋz/ *n* [plural] pieces of skin that have been removed from fruit or vegetables〔水果或蔬菜〕剥下[削下]的皮

peep¹ /pip; piːp/ *v* [I] **1** to look at something quickly and secretly, especially through a hole〔尤指从小孔〕窥视, 偷看: [**+into/through etc**] *I caught him peeping through the keyhole.* 他从钥匙孔偷看时, 我当场抓住了他。**2** [always+adv/prep] if something peeps from somewhere, it is just possible to see it 隐约出现, 微现: [**+through/from etc**] *The sun peeped briefly through the clouds.* 太阳从云中短暂地露出了一会儿。—compare 比较 PEEK, PEER²

peep² *n* [C] **1** a quick or secret look at something 一瞥; 偷看; 窥视: **take a peep** *Mike had taken a peep at the answers.* 迈克偷偷看了一下答案。**2 not hear a peep out of** *spoken* to not hear a sound from someone【口】听不到…的说话声: *I don't want to hear a peep out of you until you've done your homework.* 在你完成作业之前, 我不想听到你在说话。**3** *BrE* a word meaning the sound of a car's horn, used especially by or to children【英】汽车的喇叭声〔尤用于儿语〕**4** a short weak high sound like the sound a mouse or a young bird makes〔老鼠或幼鸟发出的〕吱吱声, 啾啾声

peep-bo /ˈpipbo; ˈpiːpbəʊ/ *interjection, n* [U] PEEKABOO 躲猫猫; 做躲猫猫时所说的话

peep·ers /ˈpipɚz; ˈpiːpəz/ *n* [plural] *old-fashioned* your eyes【过时】眼睛

peep·hole /ˈpipˌhol; ˈpiːphəʊl/ *n* [C] a small hole in a door or wall that you can see through〔门或墙上的〕窥视孔

peeping Tom /ˌpipɪŋ ˈtam; ˌpiːpɪŋ ˈtɒm/ *n* [C] someone who secretly watches people, especially when they are undressing, having sex etc 窥视者〔尤指偷看别人脱衣服、性交等〕

peep·show /ˈpipˌʃo; ˈpiːpʃəʊ/ *n* [C] **1** a type of show in which a man pays for a woman to take her clothes off while he watches〔男人付钱让女人脱去衣衫以观看的〕脱衣表演 **2** a box containing moving pictures that you look at through a small hole or LENS 西洋景; 西洋镜

peer¹ /pɪr; pɪə/ *n* [C] **1** someone of the same age, social class etc as you 同龄人; 社会地位相同的人: *Children compete to win the approval of their peers.* 孩子互相竞争以赢得同龄人的认同。| *The jury system gives you the right to be judged by your peers.* 陪审团制度使你有权利接受与自己地位相同的人的审判。—see also 另见 PEER GROUP, PEER PRESSURE **2** a member of the British NOBILITY, who has the right to sit in the House of Lords〔英国可出席上议院的〕贵族 —see also 另见 LIFE PEER

peer² *v* [I always+adv/prep] to look very carefully or hard, especially because you are having difficulty in seeing〔尤指因看起来费劲而〕盯着看, 凝视: [**+at/across/through etc**] *Every few paces they stopped to peer ahead into the gloom.* 每走几步, 他们就停下来张望着黑暗的前方。

peer·age /ˈpɪrɪdʒ; ˈpɪərɪdʒ/ *n* **1 the peerage** all the British peers (PEER¹ (2)) considered as a group 贵族〔总称〕**2** [C] the rank of a British PEER¹ (2) 贵族爵位: *After ten years in the government she was given a peerage.* 她在政府工作 10 年后被授予贵族爵位。

peer·ess /ˈpɪrɪs; ˈpɪərɪ̱s/ *n* [C] **1** a woman who is a member of the British NOBILITY and has the right to sit in the House of Lords; a female peer (PEER¹(2))〔英国可出席上议院的〕女贵族; 上议院女议员 **2** the wife of a British PEER¹ (2) 上议院议员夫人

peer group /ˈ· ·/ *n* [C] a group of people, especially young people of the same age, social class etc as yourself 同辈群体, 年龄、社会地位等相同的一群人〔尤指年轻人〕: *Establishing good peer group relationships is very important.* 同龄人之间建立良好的关系是非常重要的。

peer·less /ˈpɪrlɪs; ˈpɪələs/ *adj* better than any other 无与匹敌的; 无双的: *Torvill and Dean's peerless performances in ice dancing* 托维尔和迪安无与伦比的冰上舞蹈表演

peer pres·sure /ˈ· ˌ··/ *n* [C] a strong feeling that you must do the same things as other people of your age if you want them to like you 同辈间的压力, 同龄人间的压力: *Teenagers often start smoking because of peer pressure.* 青少年通常出于同龄人的压力而开始吸烟。

peeve /piv; piːv/ *n* [C] *informal* something that annoys you【非正式】令人气恼的事情: **pet peeve** *Car alarms going off at night is one of my pet peeves.* 夜间响起的汽车警报声是最令我头痛的事情之一。

peeved /pivd; piːvd/ *adj informal* annoyed【非正式】生气的, 恼怒的: *Ranulf felt peeved that she had not thanked him properly for his help.* 雷纳夫感到生气的是她没有好好感谢自己对她的帮助。

peev·ish /ˈpivɪʃ; ˈpiːvɪʃ/ *adj* easily annoyed by small and unimportant things; bad-tempered 易动怒的, 脾气坏的: *The kids were peevish after so long in the car.* 孩子们坐了这么长时间的汽车, 心情很烦躁。—**peevishly** *adv* —**peevishness** *n* [U]

pee·wit /ˈpiwɪt; ˈpiːwɪt/ *n* [C] a LAPWING 田凫, (凤头) 麦鸡

pegs 短钉, 桩, 琴栓

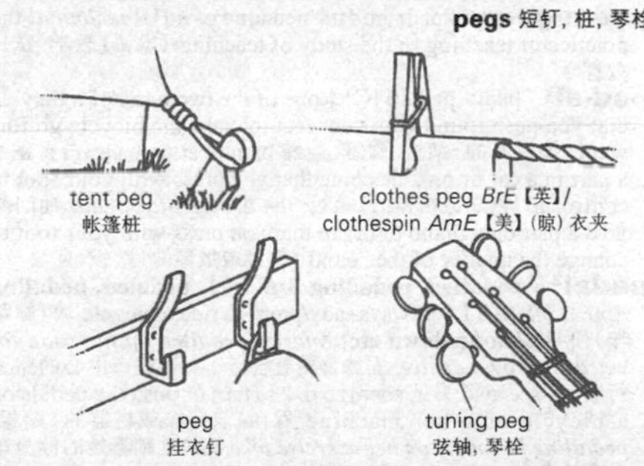

peg¹ /pɛg; peg/ *n* [C]
1 ►CLOTHES 衣服◄ a) a short piece of wood, metal etc fixed to a wall or door, used for hanging things on, especially clothes〔木头或金属制的〕短钉; 挂衣钉: *Hang your coat up on the peg.* 把你的外套挂在挂衣钉上。**b)** *BrE* a small piece of plastic or wood used for fastening wet clothes to a line to dry; CLOTHES PEG【英】〔晾衣服用的塑料或木制〕衣夹 **c) off the peg** *BrE*

clothes that are off the peg are made to a standard size and have not been specially made to fit you【英】〔衣服〕现成的，非订做的；OFF-THE-RACK *AmE*【美】—see also 另见 OFF-THE-PEG

2 take/bring sb down a peg (or two) to make someone realize that they are not as important or as good at something as they think they are 煞某人的威风，挫某人的傲气：*It's time that young man was brought down a peg or two.* 是煞煞那个年轻人傲气的时候了。

3 ▶FOR A TENT 用于帐篷◀ a pointed piece of wood or metal that you push into the ground in order to keep a tent in the correct position〔用于固定帐篷的木制或金属〕桩

4 ▶MUSICAL INSTRUMENT 乐器◀ a wooden screw used to tighten or loosen the strings of a VIOLIN, GUITAR etc; TUNING PEG〔用于调节小提琴、吉他等弦线松紧的〕弦轴，琴栓

5 a peg to hang sth on something that is used as a reason or excuse when you are trying to prove or explain something〔做〕某事的理由[借口]

6 ▶DRINK 饮料◀ *BrE old-fashioned* a small amount of strong alcoholic drink, especially WHISKY or BRANDY【英，过时】少量威士忌[白兰地]—see also 另见 **square peg in a round hole** (SQUARE[1] (11))

peg[2] **pegged, pegging** *v* [T] **1** to fasten something somewhere with a peg 用钉或桩等固定〔某物〕，把…钉牢 **2** to fix prices, wages etc at a particular level, or fix them in relation to something else 把〔价格、工资等〕固定在一定水平，限定：**peg sth to** *Most industrial countries stopped pegging their currencies to the US dollar in the early 1970s.* 在20世纪70年代早期，大部分工业化国家不再把他们的货币与美元挂钩。**3 have sb pegged as** *especially AmE* to regard someone's character in a particular way【尤美】认定某人为〔某种性格的人〕：*I never had you pegged as an idler.* 我从来没有认定你是游手好闲的人。**4 peg it** *AmE slang* to die【美俚】死

peg away at sth *phr v* [T not in passive 不用被动态] *BrE informal* to work hard and with determination【英，非正式】坚持不懈地努力工作：*Vicky's been pegging away at her books all week.* 整个星期维基都在苦读她的那些书。

peg out *phr v* **1** [I] *BrE informal* to die, or fall down because you are tired【英，非正式】死；〔因筋疲力尽而〕倒下 **2** [T **peg** sth ↔ **out**] *BrE* to fasten wet clothes to a washing line to dry【英】把〔湿衣服〕夹在晾衣绳上晾晒 **3** [T **peg** sth ↔ **out**] to mark a piece of ground with wooden sticks 用木桩标明〔某块土地〕

Peg·a·sus /ˈpɛgəsəs; ˈpegəsəs/ in ancient Greek and Roman stories, a horse with wings 珀加索斯〔古希腊和古罗马神话故事中长有双翼的飞马〕

peg·board /ˈpɛgbɔrd; ˈpegbɔːd/ *n* **1** [C] a small piece of board with holes in it, used to record the players' points in some games, especially card games〔在某些游戏中，尤指纸牌戏中记录选手得分的〕插孔记分板 **2** [U] thin board with holes in it, into which you can put PEGs or hooks to hang things on〔有孔眼可装挂物钉的〕配挂板

peg leg /ˈ· ·/ *n* [C] *informal* an artificial leg, especially a wooden one【非正式】〔尤指木制的〕假腿

Pei /pe; peɪ/, **I.M.** (1917-) a US ARCHITECT (=someone who designs buildings), born in China, who has built many important public buildings, most of which are known because of their simple style and the way they look good with the environment 贝聿铭〔(1917-)，美籍华裔建筑师。他设计建造了许多重要的公共建筑，多以风格简约、与环境和谐著称〕

Peirce /pɪrs; pɪəs/, **Charles San·ders** /tʃɑrlz ˈsændəz; tʃɑːlz ˈsɑːndəz/ (1838-1914) a US PHILOSOPHER, who said that an idea on its own does not have any value, and that there is only value in the results produced by the idea. His most important writings were put together after his death in a book called *Chance, Love and Logic*. 皮尔斯〔(1838-1914)，美国哲学家。他认为一个观点就其本身而言并没有任何价值，唯有观点产生的结果才有价值。在他去世之后，他的多数名篇结集出版，书名为《机遇、爱情与逻辑》〕

pe·jo·ra·tive /pɪˈdʒɔrətɪv; pɪˈdʒɒrətɪv/ *adj formal* a word or expression that is pejorative expresses disapproval or criticism【正式】〔单词或片语〕贬义的：*'Spinster' is a pejorative word for an unmarried woman.* spinster（老处女）是对未婚妇女的贬抑言词。—**pejoratively** *adv*

peke /pik; piːk/ *n* [C] *informal* a pekinese【非正式】北京狗，狮子狗

pe·kin·ese /ˌpikɪnˈiz; ˌpiːkɪˈniːz◂/ *n* [C] a very small dog with a short flat nose and long silky hair 京巴，狮子狗 —see picture at 参见 DOG[1] 图

Pe·king /ˌpiˈkɪŋ; ˌpiːˈkɪŋ/ a former name for Beijing 北京〔Beijing 的旧拼法〕

pe·lag·ic /pəˈlædʒɪk; pɪˈlædʒɪk/ *adj technical* connected with or living in the deep sea, far from shore【术语】深海的，远洋的：*pelagic fish* 深海鱼类

Pel·é /pɛˈle; ˈpeleɪ/ (1940-) a Brazilian football (soccer) player, considered by many people to be the best player ever. He played for Brazil's national team in four World Cups, and then went to the US, where he helped to make football more popular. In 1994, he became Brazil's minister of sports. 贝利〔(1940-)，巴西足球运动员。许多人认为他是有史以来的最佳球员。他曾代表巴西国家队参加过四次世界杯，之后前往美国促进足球运动的普及。1994年，他开始担任巴西体育部长〕

pel·i·can /ˈpɛlɪkən; ˈpelɪkən/ *n* [C] a large water bird that catches fish for food and stores them in a deep bag under its beak 鹈鹕，塘鹅〔一种食鱼鸟〕

pelican cross·ing /ˌ··· ˈ··/ *n* [C] a place on some roads in Britain, where someone who wants to cross the road can stop the traffic by pushing a button that makes TRAFFIC LIGHTS change to red〔行人想横过马路时可按下按钮使交通灯转为红色的〕自控人行横道 —compare 比较 ZEBRA CROSSING

pel·lag·ra /pəˈlægrə; pɪˈlægrə/ *n* [U] a disease caused by a lack of a type of B VITAMIN, that makes you feel tired and causes problems with your skin and CENTRAL NERVOUS SYSTEM 陪拉格病，糙皮病〔因缺乏维生素B而引起的一种病。患者会感到疲倦，皮肤和中枢神经系统均会出毛病〕

pel·let /ˈpɛlɪt; ˈpelɪt/ *n* [C] **1** a small ball of any soft substance, sometimes made by rolling it between your fingers〔软的〕小丸；〔用手指搓成的〕小球，小丸 **2** a small ball of metal made to be fired from a gun〔枪中射出的〕小弹丸，子弹

pell-mell /ˈpɛl ˈmɛl; ˌpel ˈmel◂/ *adv old-fashioned* rushing very quickly, and in a way that seems uncontrolled【过时】匆忙地，忙乱地：*The children ran pell-mell out of school.* 孩子一窝蜂地跑出学校。

pel·lu·cid /pəˈlusɪd; pɪˈluːsɪd/ *adj literary* very clear; TRANSPARENT (1)【文】清澈的；透明的：*a pellucid stream* 清澈的小溪 —**pellucidly** *adv*

pel·met /ˈpɛlmɪt; ˈpelmɪt/ *n* [C] *BrE* a narrow piece of wood or cloth above a window that hides the rod that the curtains hang on【英】〔窗帘上方用以遮蔽帘子拉杆的〕窗帘盒；布帷幔；VALANCE *AmE*【美】

Pel·o·pon·nese, the /ˌpɛləpəˈnis; ˌpeləpəˈniːs◂/ the southern part of Greece, which is connected to the rest of Greece by the Isthmus of Corinth. The ancient state of Sparta was in the Peloponnese. 伯罗奔尼撒〔希腊南部地区，经由柯林斯地峡与希腊其余地区相连。古希腊城邦斯巴达即位于该区〕

Pel·o·pon·ne·sian War, the /ˌpɛləpənɪʃən ˈwɔr; ˌpeləpəniːʃən ˈwɔː/ (431-404BC) a long war between the ancient Greek states of Athens and Sparta. It ended with the defeat of Athens, and this led to the end of Athens' political power in ancient Greece. The history of the war by the ancient Greek writer Thucydides is one of the most famous European works of history. 伯罗奔尼撒战争〔(公元前431-前404)，古希腊城邦雅典与斯巴达之间一场旷日持久的战争。战争以雅典的失败而告终，从而推翻了古希腊的雅典政权。古希腊作家修昔底德的《伯罗奔尼撒战争史》是最著名的欧洲史书之一〕

pelt[1] /pɛlt; pelt/ *v* **1** [T] to attack someone by throwing a lot of things at them 向…连续投掷：**pelt sb with sth** *The Senator was pelted with rotten eggs.* 那位参议员遭人投掷臭鸡蛋。**2 it is pelting down/it is pelting with rain** used to mean that it is raining very heavily〔雨〕倾盆而下 **3** [I always+adv/prep] *informal* to run somewhere very fast【非正式】向…飞快地跑去：[**+along/into/past etc**] *Three huge dogs came pelting out into the street.* 三条大狗飞快地跑到街上。

pelt[2] *n* [C] **1 a)** the skin of a dead animal with the fur or hair still on it〔死动物的〕生皮，带毛的兽皮 **b)** the skin of a dead animal with the fur or hair removed and ready to be prepared as leather〔清理掉毛准备做皮革用的〕兽皮 **2** the fur or hair of a living animal〔活动物身上的〕毛皮 **3 (at) full pelt** moving as fast as possible 全速地，开足马力地；尽快地：*Nancy drove her car at full pelt down the road.* 南希驾着汽车全速地沿大路驶去。

pel·vic /ˈpɛlvɪk; ˈpelvɪk/ *adj* in or connected with the pelvis 骨盆内的；盆腔的

pel·vis /ˈpɛlvɪs; ˈpelvɪs/ *n* [C] the large frame of bones at the base of your SPINE, to which your legs are joined 骨盆 —see picture at 参见 SKELETON 图

Pembrokeshire a COUNTY in western Wales 彭布罗克郡〔威尔士西部一郡〕

pem·mi·can /ˈpɛmɪkən; ˈpemɪkən/ *n* [U] dried meat, beaten into small pieces and pressed into flat round shapes 干肉饼

P

pens〔墨水〕笔

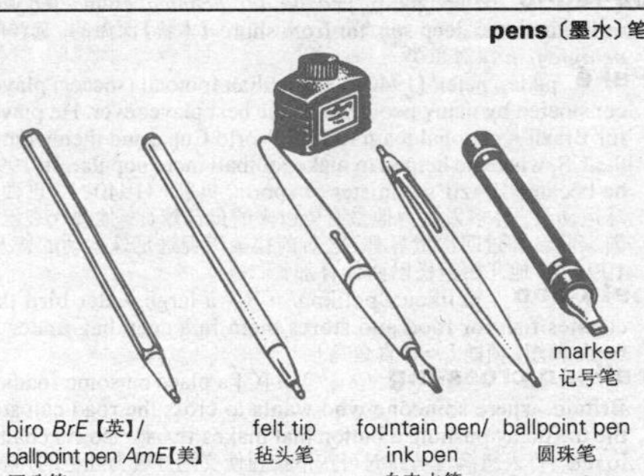

pen¹ /pɛn; pen/ *n* [C] **1** an instrument for writing or drawing with ink〔墨水〕笔: *a ballpoint pen* 圆珠笔 | *a fountain pen* 自来水笔 | *a felt-tip pen* 毡头笔 **2** a small piece of land enclosed by a fence, used for keeping farm animals in〔围养家畜的〕栏, 圈, 棚: *a sheep pen* 羊圈 —see also 另见 PLAYPEN **3 put/set pen to paper** to begin to write 开始书写 **4** *AmE slang* PENITENTIARY; a prison【美俚】监狱

pen² *v* **penned, penning** [T] *formal* to write a letter or note with a pen【正式】用笔写〔信或便条〕

pen sb/sth ↔ **up/in** *phr v* [T] **1** to shut an animal in a small enclosed area 把〔动物〕关入围栏中 **2 be penned in** to be restricted, as if you are being kept in a small place 被约束的, 被束缚的: *They were penned in watching TV with their parents all night.* 他们被管束着, 与父母看了一整夜电视。

pe·nal /ˈpinḷ; ˈpiːnl/ *adj* **1** [only before noun 仅用于名词前] connected with the legal punishment of criminals, especially in prisons〔尤指在狱中〕刑罚的, 惩戒(性)的: *penal reform* 刑罚改革 | *the penal system* 刑罚制度 | **penal colony/settlement** (=a special area of land where prisoners are kept) 罪犯流放地 | **penal servitude** *law* (=a period of being kept in prison with hard physical work)【法律】劳役监禁 **2** [only before noun 仅用于名词前] a penal offence can be punished by the law 当受处罚的, 当受刑罚的 **3** very severe 非常严厉的: *penal rates of taxation* 极苛刻的税率

penal code /ˈ· ·, ·ˈ/ *n* [C] a system of laws and statements of the punishments for breaking those laws 刑法典

pe·nal·ize also 又作 **-ise** *BrE*【英】/ˈpinḷˌaɪz; ˈpiːnəlaɪz/ *v* [T] **1** to treat someone unfairly or make them have a disadvantage 对待…不公平; 使…处于不利地位: *The whole class is being penalized just because one student behaved badly.* 只因一位学生行为恶劣, 全班同学都要受到不公平的对待。| *Sales taxes penalize the consumer.* 销售税对消费者不利。**2** to punish a team or player in sports by giving an advantage to the other team〔在体育运动中〕对…处罚: *In one game the All Blacks were penalized for wasting time.* 在一场比赛中, 全黑队因拖延时间而受罚。—**penalization** /ˌpinḷɪˈzeʃən; ˌpiːnəlaɪˈzeɪʃən/ *n* [U]

pen·al·ty /ˈpɛnḷtɪ; ˈpenlti/ *n plural* **penalties** [C] **1** a punishment for breaking a law, rule, or legal agreement〔因违反法律、规则或合约而受到的〕惩罚, 处罚: *No littering. Penalty $500.* 不要乱扔东西, 违者罚款500元。| [+for] *The penalty for murder was death.* 对谋杀罪的刑罚是死刑。| **impose a penalty** (=force someone to accept a penalty) 对…施加惩罚 *the highest penalty the court can impose* 法庭能够施加的最重处罚 | **stiff/heavy penalty** (=a severe penalty) 严厉的惩罚[处罚] | **the death penalty** *Some MPs are calling for the death penalty to be brought back.* 一些下议院议员正在要求恢复死刑。**2** something unpleasant that happens to you because of something unwise that you have done or because of the situation you are in〔行为或处境所造成的〕不利结果; 苦恼: [+of] *One of the penalties of being famous is the loss of privacy.* 成名的麻烦之一是失去个人隐私。| **pay the penalty (for)** (=suffer the penalty for something) (为…)受到惩罚 *They never insured their property and now they're paying the penalty for their foolishness.* 他们从不为自己的财产投保, 现在他们正为自己的愚蠢而自食苦果。**3** a disadvantage in sports given to a player or team for breaking a rule〔体育运动中对犯规者的〕处罚 **4** a chance to kick the ball into the GOAL (3) in a game of football, given because the other team has broken a rule〔足球中因一方犯规而给予对方的〕点球

penalty ar·e·a /ˈ···, ··ˈ/ also 又作 **penalty box** /ˈ···, ·ˈ/ *n* [C] the area in front of the GOAL (3) in football, in which the breaking of a rule means that the opposing team gets a PENALTY (4)〔足球的〕禁区 —see picture on page A23 参见 A23 页图

penalty clause /ˈ···, ·ˈ/ *n* [C] the part of a contract which says what someone will have to pay or do if they break the agreement, for example if they fail to complete work on time〔合同中对违约方的〕惩罚条款

penalty kick /ˈ···, ·ˈ/ *n* [C] a penalty (PENALTY (4)) 罚点球

penalty point /ˈ···, ·ˈ/ *n* [C] *BrE* a note made on a driver's LICENCE to show that they have done something wrong while they were driving【英】〔对违章司机的〕处罚记分

penalty shoot-out /ˌ···ˈ·ˈ·/ *n* [C] a series of penalty kicks used as a way of deciding which team has won a football game (罚)点球大战〔足球中决定胜负的一种方式〕

pen·ance /ˈpɛnəns; ˈpenəns/ *n* **1** [C,U] the action of willingly making yourself suffer, especially for religious reasons, to show you are sorry for having done something wrong〔表示忏悔的〕自我惩罚: **do penance (for)** *Bianca has confessed and done penance for her sins.* 比安卡已悔过, 并为赎罪而自我惩罚。**2** [singular] something that you have to do but do not enjoy doing 不喜欢做而又不得不做的事情, 苦差事: *Visiting old Uncle Edgar had become more of a penance than a pleasure.* 去探望老埃德加叔叔已成为一件苦差事而不是乐事。

pence /pɛns; pens/ abbreviation 缩写为 **p** *BrE*【英】the plural of PENNY (4): *a few pence* 几便士 | *a 13 pence stamp* 一枚面值13便士的邮票

pen·chant /ˈpɛntʃənt; ˈpɒnʃɒn/ *n* [C] *French* a liking for something, especially something that is slightly disapproved of by other people【法】嗜好, 爱好〔尤指别人有点不赞成的事物〕: [+for] *a penchant for fast cars* 对高速汽车的强烈爱好

pen·cil¹ /ˈpɛnsḷ; ˈpensəl/ *n* [C, U] **1** a narrow pointed wooden instrument, used for writing or drawing, containing a thin stick of a black or coloured substance 铅笔; 颜色铅笔: *written in pencil* 用铅笔书写的 | *drawn with a pencil* 用铅笔画的 | *a pencil sketch* 铅笔速写画 **2 a pencil of light** a narrow beam of light beginning from or ending in a small point 一束光 —see also 另见 EYEBROW PENCIL

pencil² *v* **pencilled, pencilling** *BrE*【英】, **penciled, penciling** *AmE*【美】[T] to write something or make a mark with a pencil 用铅笔写[标记]〔某物〕: *Mark pencilled a note to his wife.* 马克用铅笔写了一张便条给他妻子。

pencil sb/sth ↔ **in** *phr v* [T] to include someone or something in a list or an arrangement, knowing that this might have to be changed later〔在清单或安排中〕暂时添入, 暂时填入; 暂定: *Let's pencil in Friday at 10 for the meeting.* 让我们暂定星期五早上10点开会。

pencil push·er /ˈ· ˌ··/ *n* [C] *AmE* PEN PUSHER【美】文员, 文书

pencil sharp·en·er /ˈ·· ˌ···/ *n* [C] a small thing with a blade inside, used for sharpening pencils 削铅笔器, 转笔刀

pencil skirt /ˈ··, ·ˈ/ *n* [C] a long narrow straight skirt 直筒长裙, 笔杆裙(一种窄而直的长裙)

pen·dant, pendent /ˈpɛndənt; ˈpendənt/ *n* [C] a piece of jewellery hanging from a thin chain that you wear around your neck〔项链上的〕垂饰, 挂件, 坠子: *a ruby pendant* 红宝石坠子

pen·dent /ˈpɛndənt; ˈpendənt/ *adj literary or technical*【文或术语】**1** hanging from something 悬挂着的, 下垂的, 吊着的: *a pendent lamp* 吊灯 **2** sticking out beyond a surface 向外伸出的, 突出的: *pendent ledges of rocks* 突出的岩礁

pend·ing¹ /ˈpɛndɪŋ; ˈpendɪŋ/ *prep formal* while waiting for something, or until something happens【正式】在等待…之际; 直到…时: *A decision has been delayed pending further inquiries.* 在进一步调查之前暂不作出决定。

pending² *adj* **1** [not before noun 不用于名词前] *formal* not yet decided or settled【正式】未定的, 未决的; 待定的, 待决的: *As my divorce was pending, I had to stay where I was.* 因为我的离婚诉讼还未判决, 我不得不待在原来的地方。**2 pending file/tray** a container for keeping papers, letters etc that have not yet been dealt with 待处理文件夹/格 **3** *formal* something that is pending is going to happen soon【正式】将要发生的, 迫近的: *a pending criminal trial* 待审的刑事案件

pen·du·lous /ˈpɛndʒələs; ˈpendjʊləs/ *adj literary* hanging down loosely and swinging freely【文】松垂的, 悬垂而自由摆动的: *pendulous breasts* 松垂的乳房 —**pendulously** *adv*

pen·du·lum /ˈpɛndʒələm; ˈpendjʊləm/ *n* [C] **1** a rod with a weight at the bottom that swings regularly from side to side to control the working of a clock 钟摆 **2 the pendulum of opinion/fashion etc** something that tends to change regularly from

one position to an opposite one 摇摆不定的观点/时尚等: *The pendulum of public opinion has swung back.* 摇摆不定的舆论已转过来了。

Pe·nel·o·pe /pəˈnɛləpɪ; pəˈneləpi/ in ancient Greek stories, the wife of Odysseus, who remained faithful to him for more than 20 years while he was away from home, fighting in the Trojan War 佩内洛普〔古希腊传说中奥德修斯之妻。丈夫离家20余年, 出征特洛伊战争, 她依然忠贞不渝〕

pen·e·trate /ˈpɛnəˌtret; ˈpenɪ̈treɪt/ *v*

1 ▶GO THROUGH 穿过◀ [I,T] to enter something or pass through it, especially when this is difficult 进入; 渗入; 刺入; 穿过, 穿透: *shells that penetrate thick armour plating* 穿过厚厚装甲层的炮弹 | **[+into]** *Explorers penetrated into unknown regions.* 探险者深入到未知的区域。

2 ▶BUSINESS 生意◀ [T] to start to sell things to an area or country, or to have an influence there 打进〔某地区或国家的市场〕: *Their goal is to penetrate undeveloped markets in the Third World.* 他们的目标是打入第三世界国家的未开发市场。

3 ▶ORGANIZATION 组织◀ [T] to get yourself accepted into a group or an organization in order to find out their secrets〔为发现秘密而〕渗入〔某团体或组织〕: *KGB agents had penetrated most of their intelligence services.* 克格勃特工人员已渗透到他们的大部分情报部门。

4 ▶SEE THROUGH 看穿◀ [T] to see into or through something even though it is difficult 透过…看见, 看穿: *My eyes couldn't penetrate the gloom.* 我的眼睛在黑暗里看不见。

5 ▶UNDERSTAND 理解◀ a) [T] to succeed in understanding something 洞察, 了解: *Science has penetrated the mysteries of nature.* 科学已揭开了大自然的奥秘。 **b)** [I] *informal* to be fully understood by someone【非正式】被完全理解: *I heard what you said but it didn't fully penetrate.* 你的话我听见了, 但没有完全明白。

6 ▶SEX 性◀ [T] *technical* if a man penetrates a woman, he puts his PENIS into her VAGINA when having sex【术语】〔性交时〕把阴茎插入…的阴道 —see also 另见 IMPENETRABLE —**penetration** /ˌpɛnəˈtreʃən; ˌpenɪ̈ˈtreɪʃən/ *n* [U]: *the CIA's penetration of left wing organizations* 〔美国〕中央情报局对左翼组织的渗透 —**penetrable** /ˈpɛnətrəbl̩; ˈpenɪ̈trəbəl/ *adj* —**penetrability** /ˌpɛnətrəˈbɪlətɪ; ˌpenɪ̈trəˈbɪlɪ̈ti/ *n* [U]

pen·e·trat·ing /ˈpɛnəˌtretɪŋ; ˈpenɪ̈treɪtɪŋ/ *adj* **1 penetrating look/eyes/gaze** a look etc which makes you feel uncomfortable and seems to see inside your mind 锐利的目光/眼睛/凝视: *an attempt to avoid her husband's penetrating gaze* 试图避开她丈夫犀利的目光 **2** a penetrating sound is loud, clear, and often unpleasant〔声音〕响亮的, 刺耳的, 尖锐的: *a penetrating whistle* 尖得刺耳的汽笛声 **3** showing an ability to understand things quickly and completely 有洞察力的, 思维敏锐的: *Parker had prepared some penetrating questions.* 帕克准备了一些尖锐的问题。**4** spreading and reaching everywhere 弥漫的; 渗透的: *penetrating dampness* 无孔不入的潮气 —**penetratingly** *adv*

pen·e·tra·tive /ˈpɛnəˌtretɪv; ˈpenɪ̈trətɪv/ *adj* **1** able to get into or through something easily 容易穿透〔某物〕的 **2** showing an ability to understand things quickly and completely 思想敏锐的, 有洞察力的: *penetrative observations* 敏锐的观察

pen friend /ˈ· ·/ *n* [C] *BrE* someone you make friends with by writing letters, especially someone in another country whom you have never met; PEN PAL【英】笔友

pen·guin /ˈpɛŋgwɪn; ˈpeŋgwɪ̈n/ *n* [C] a large black and white Antarctic sea bird, which cannot fly but uses its wings for swimming 企鹅

pen·i·cil·lin /ˌpɛnɪˈsɪlɪn; ˌpenɪ̈ˈsɪlɪ̈n/ *n* [U] a substance used as a medicine to destroy bacteria; an ANTIBIOTIC 青霉素, 盘尼西林

pe·nile /ˈpinaɪl; ˈpiːnaɪl/ *adj technical* relating to the penis【术语】阴茎的

pe·nin·su·la /pəˈnɪnsələ; pɪ̈ˈnɪnsjʊ̈lə/ *n* [C] a piece of land almost completely surrounded by water but joined to a large mass of land 半岛 —**peninsular** *adj*

Peninsular War, the /·,··· ˈ·/ a war that was fought in Spain and Portugal between the armies of France, led by Napoleon, and of Britain, led by the Duke of Wellington. It began when Napoleon attacked Spain in 1808 and ended when he was defeated and forced to leave Spain in 1813. 半岛战争〔拿破仑率领的法军和威灵顿公爵率领的英军在西班牙和葡萄牙进行的一场战争。1808年, 拿破仑进攻西班牙, 战争由此开始, 直到1813年拿破仑战败并撤离西班牙〕

pe·nis /ˈpinɪs; ˈpiːnɪ̈s/ *n* [C] the outer sex organ of men and male animals that is used for urinating (URINATE) and in sexual activity 阴茎

pen·i·tent[1] /ˈpɛnətənt; ˈpenɪ̈tənt/ *adj formal* feeling sorry because you have done something wrong, and intending not to do anything wrong again; REPENTANT【正式】后悔的; 悔过的; 忏悔的: *He knelt and put his head on her knee like a penitent dog.* 他像一只做了错事的狗那样跪了下来, 把头放在她的膝上。—**penitently** *adv* —**penitence** *n* [U]

penitent[2] *n* [C] someone who is doing religious PENANCE 悔过者; 忏悔者; 告解者; 苦行赎罪者

pen·i·ten·tial /ˌpɛnəˈtɛnʃəl; ˌpenɪ̈ˈtenʃəl◂/ *adj formal* connected with being sorry for having done something wrong【正式】后悔的, 忏悔的: *penitential journeys to famous shrines* 去著名圣地的赎罪之旅 —**penitentially** *adv*

pen·i·ten·tia·ry /ˌpɛnəˈtɛnʃərɪ; ˌpenɪ̈ˈtenʃəri/ *n* [C] a prison, especially in the US〔尤指美国的〕监狱: *the North Carolina state penitentiary* 北卡罗来纳州监狱

pen·knife /ˈpɛnˌnaɪf; ˈpen-naɪf/ *n plural* **penknives** /-ˌnaɪvz; -naɪvz/ [C] a small knife with blades that fold into the handle, usually carried in your pocket 折叠式小刀 —see picture at 参见 KNIFE[1] 图

pen·man·ship /ˈpɛnmənˌʃɪp; ˈpenmənʃɪp/ *n* [U] *formal* the art of writing by hand, or skill in this art【正式】书法; 书写技巧

Penn /pɛn; pen/, **William** (1644-1718) an English leader of the Quakers (=a Christian religious group), who was put in prison for having unacceptable religious beliefs. After he was let out of prison, he was given some land in North America, and he established a COLONY there as a place of religious freedom for Quakers and others to go and live in. He called the colony Pennsylvania, and planned and built the city of Philadelphia in 1682. 佩恩〔(1644-1718), 英国贵格派领袖。他曾因持有异端邪说而遭到监禁, 释放出狱后得到北美的一些土地。于是, 他建立了一个殖民地, 取名宾夕法尼亚, 贵格会教徒等人可前去定居, 自由信教。1682年, 他还规划并开始建设费城〕

pen name /ˈ· ·/ *n* [C] a name used by a writer instead of their real name; PSEUDONYM 笔名

pen·nant /ˈpɛnənt; ˈpenənt/ *n* [C] **1** a long narrow pointed flag used on ships or by schools, sports teams, etc〔船只, 学校, 运动队等用的〕三角旗 **2 the pennant** the prize given to the best team in the American and National BASEBALL competitions〔发给美国国家棒球比赛中最好球队的〕锦旗, 奖旗

pen·nies /ˈpɛnɪz; ˈpeniz/ *n* the plural of PENNY

pen·ni·less /ˈpɛnɪlɪs; ˈpenɪləs/ *adj* having no money 一文不名的, 一贫如洗的: *The old lady died penniless.* 那位老妇人死的时候一贫如洗。

Pen·nines, the /ˈpɛnaɪnz; ˈpenaɪnz/ a range of hills in a line down the middle of England from the Scottish border to central England, which are sometimes called the 'backbone of England' 奔宁山脉〔从苏格兰边境沿英格兰中路一线而下直至英格兰中部的一条山脉, 有时称作"英格兰的脊梁"〕

Pennine Way, the /ˌ·· ˈ·/ a very long path (250 miles) along the Pennines, which people walk along for pleasure or exercise 奔宁小径〔一条穿越奔宁山脉、长达250英里的小径。人们在此或漫步散心或锻炼身体〕

pen·non /ˈpɛnən; ˈpenən/ *n* [C] a long narrow pointed flag, especially one carried on the end of a long pole by soldiers on horses in the Middle Ages〔尤指中世纪骑士长矛上的〕三角矛旗; 小三角旗

pen·n'orth /ˈpɛnəθ; ˈpenəθ/ *n* [singular+**of**] *BrE old-fashioned* a PENNYWORTH【英, 过时】一便士的价值; 值一便士的东西

Penn·syl·va·ni·a /ˌpɛnslˈvenɪə; ˌpensəlˈveɪniə◂/ abbreviation 缩写为 **PA** a state in the northeastern US, which produces large amounts of steel and coal. It was one of the 13 original US states, and was an important centre in the fight to become independent from Britain during the American Revolutionary War. 宾夕法尼亚州〔美国东北部一州, 出产大量钢铁和煤炭。它是美国最早的13州之一, 也是美国独立战争期间美国人民摆脱英国统治、争取独立的一个举足轻重的中心〕

Pennsylvania Dutch, the /ˌ···· ˈ·/ *n* [plural] a group of people living in the US state of Pennsylvania, who came from Germany in the 1600s and 1700s to find religious freedom, and still live in the style of that time. They wear very old-fashioned clothes, and do not have cars or other modern machines. They are Protestants, and include the Amish and the Mennonites 德裔宾州人〔17至18世纪期间为寻求宗教自由从德国来到美国宾夕法尼亚州定居的一批人。他们至今仍保留着当初的生活方式, 穿着非常老式的服装, 也没有汽车或现代机械。他们都是新教徒, 其中包括阿曼派教徒和门诺派教徒〕—**Pennsylvania Dutch** *adj*

pen·ny /ˈpɛnɪ; ˈpeni/ *n plural* **pennies** or **pence** /pɛns; pens/ *BrE*【英】[C] **1** a small BRONZE coin, used in Britain since 1971, worth one hundredth (1/100th) of a pound〔英国1971年起使用 S1

的〕一便士铜币〔值 1/100 英镑〕: *a bag of pennies* 一袋一便士的硬币 **2** *plural* **pence** abbreviation 缩写为 **p** a unit of money used in Britain since 1971 便士〔英国 1971 年起使用的货币单位〕: *There are 100 pence in one pound.* 一英镑等于 100 便士。| *It only costs a few pence.* 这东西只要几便士。| *a 20 pence piece* 一枚 20 便士的硬币 **3** *AmE* a coin worth a CENT in the US or Canada【美】〔美国或加拿大的〕一分钱硬币: *I only have pennies and nickels in my pocket.* 我口袋里只有一分和五分的硬币。**4** written abbreviation 缩写为 **d** *plural* **pence** a unit of money in Britain before 1971, equal to one 12th (l/12th) of a SHILLING〔英国 1971 年前使用的〕便士〔等于 1/12 先令〕: *pounds, shillings and pence* 镑、先令和便士 | **twopence/threepence etc** *a book costing only sixpence* 只卖六便士的书 **5 fourpenny/sixpenny etc** worth or costing fourpence, sixpence etc of the money used in Britain before 1971〔英国 1971 年前的〕值四便士/六便士等的: *a sixpenny piece* 一枚六便士的硬币 **6 not a penny** no money at all 一个便士也没有, 一文不名: *Not a penny of the money came to me.* 我一个便士也没有拿到。| *She'll never get a penny from me.* 她一个便士也别想从我这儿拿走。**7 every penny** all of an amount of money 一笔钱的全部, 全部的钱: *You'd better pay it back – every penny!* 你最好还钱——一便士都不能少! **8 the/your last penny** the only money that is left 仅剩的钱: *She had given away her last penny.* 她把最后一个便士都送掉了。**9 a penny for your thoughts/a penny for them** *spoken* used to ask someone what they are thinking about when they are silent【口】告诉我你在想什么〔用于对沉默不语的人说〕**10 the penny (has) dropped** *BrE informal* used to mean that someone has finally understood something that had been said【英, 非正式】最后终于明白了 **11 be two/ten a penny** *BrE* to be very cheap and easy to obtain, and therefore of little value【英】廉价而易得的; 多得不值钱的: *Computer experts are two a penny nowadays.* 如今电脑专家多的是。**12 not have two pennies/half-pennies to rub together** *BrE informal* to be very poor【英, 非正式】非常穷的 **13 in for a penny, in for a pound** *BrE* used to mean that if something has been started, it should be finished, whatever the cost may be【英】一不做, 二不休; 一旦开始就干到底 **14 turn up like a bad penny** *BrE* if someone you dislike turns up like a bad penny, they keep appearing in situations where they are not wanted【英】〔不喜欢的人〕又来了 —see also 另见 HALFPENNY, **spend a penny** (SPEND (5)), **cost a pretty penny** (PRETTY[2] (7))

penny an·te /ˈ‥, ‥ˈ/ *adj AmE informal* involving very small sums of money【美, 非正式】涉及金额很小的, 没什么价值的: *his penny ante schemes to make money* 他赚取蝇头小利的计划

Penny Black /‚‥ ˈ‥/ *n* [C] the first British stamp for sticking on envelopes. It was introduced in 1840, and its value was one penny, which was the cost of sending a letter by post in Britain. The stamp shows the head of Queen Victoria on a dark background, and stamp collectors consider it to be very important, although it is not the rarest British stamp. 黑便士邮票〔英国最早贴在信封上的邮票, 1840 年投入使用, 面值为1便士, 是当时英国境内邮寄一封信的费用。邮票上印有维多利亚女王的头像, 背景为深色。集邮者认为这枚邮票虽然算不上最为稀缺, 但却非常具有收藏价值〕

penny can·dy /ˈ‥ ‚‥/ *n* [C,U] *AmE old-fashioned* a sweet that costs one cent for a piece【美, 过时】一便士一块的糖果

penny dread·ful /‚‥ ˈ‥/ *n* [C] *BrE* a cheap and badly written book about violent crime【英】〔描写暴力犯罪的〕廉价低劣的小说

penny-far·thing /‚‥ ˈ‥/ *n* [C] a bicycle with a very large front wheel and a very small back wheel, used in the late 19th century〔19 世纪晚期使用的〕前轮大后轮小的自行车

penny-half-penny /‚‥ ˈ‥‥/ *n BrE* one and a half old pence【英】〔旧便士的〕一个半便士

penny-pinch·ing /ˈ‥ ‚‥/ *adj* unwilling to spend or give money 吝啬的, 小气的 —**penny pinching** *n* [U] —**penny pincher** *n* [C]

penny whis·tle /‚‥ ˈ‥/ *n* [C] a simple musical instrument shaped like a tube that you blow down 六孔小笛〔一种简单的管状吹奏乐器〕

pen·ny·worth /ˈpɛnɪ͵wɝθ; ˈpenɪwəθ/ *n* [singular+**of**] *old-fashioned* as much as you can buy with a penny【过时】一便士的价值; 值一便士的东西

pe·nol·o·gy /piˋnɑlədʒɪ; piːˈnɒlədʒi/ *n* [U] the scientific study of the punishment of criminals and the operation of prisons 刑罚学; 监狱(管理)学 —**penologist** *n* [C]

pen pal /ˈ‥ ‚/ *n* [C] *especially AmE* someone you make friends with by writing letters, especially someone in another country whom you have never met【尤美】笔友; PEN FRIEND *BrE*【英】

pen push·er /ˈ‚ ‚‥/ *n* [C] *BrE* someone who has a boring unimportant job in an office【英】〔在办公室做枯燥而不重要工作的〕文员, 文书; PENCIL PUSHER *AmE*【美】

pen·sion¹ /ˋpɛnʃən; ˈpenʃən/ *n* [C] an amount of money paid regularly by a government or company to someone who is officially considered to be too old or too ill to earn money by working 养老金; 退休金; 抚恤金: *They both have their pensions to live on now that they've retired.* 由于已经退休, 他们俩都靠退休金生活。| *a disability pension* 残疾抚恤金 | **draw a pension** *BrE* (=receive or collect a pension)【英】领取退休金 | **pension rights/plan/scheme** *a company pension plan* 公司退休金计划 | **occupational/company pension** (=one that you get from your former employer)〔从前雇主那里获得的〕职业退休金/公司退休金 | **old age pension** *BrE* (=paid regularly by the government to old people; SOCIAL SECURITY *AmE*【美】)【英】养老金; 社会保障金

pension² *v* [T] *BrE*【英】

pension sb/sth ↔ **off** [T] **1** *informal* to make someone leave their job, especially because of old age or illness, and pay them a pension【非正式】〔尤指由于年老或疾病而〕发给〔某人〕养老金使其(提早)退休: *Jean was pensioned off at 55.* 琼在 55 岁时被迫领养老金退休。**2** *informal* to get rid of something because it is too old or not useful any more【非正式】〔因太旧或不再有用而〕丢弃某物

pension³ *n* [C] a house like a small hotel, where you can get a room and meals, in France or some other European countries〔在法国或其他欧洲国家的〕膳宿公寓 —compare 比较 BOARDING HOUSE

pen·sion·a·ble /ˋpɛnʃənəbl; ˈpenʃənəbəl/ *adj* **1** giving someone the right to receive a pension 有享受养老金[退休金, 抚恤金]资格的: *a pensionable age* 领取养老金的年龄 | *appointments that were not pensionable* 不能领取养老金的职位 **2 pensionable pay/salary** pay from which money is regularly taken for a pension 扣除养老金的报酬/薪水

pen·sion·er /ˋpɛnʃənɚ; ˈpenʃənə/ *n* [C] *BrE* someone who is receiving a pension, especially an OLD AGE PENSION【英】领取退休金〔尤指养老金〕的人

pension fund /ˈ‥ ‚/ *n* [C] a sum of money which is invested (INVEST (1)) and used to pay PENSIONs to those people who have regularly paid money into it 退休[养老, 抚恤]基金

pension plan /ˈ‥ ‚/ *n* [C] a system by which your employer, insurance company etc provides you with a pension after you have made regular payments to them over many years 退休金[养老金]计划 —compare 比较 RETIREMENT PLAN

pension scheme /ˈ‥ ‚/ *n* [C] *BrE* a pension plan【英】退休金[养老金]计划

pen·sive /ˋpɛnsɪv; ˈpensɪv/ *adj* thinking deeply about something and seeming a little sad 沉思的; 郁郁不乐的: *Jan was pensive.* 简心事重重。| *a pensive expression* 忧伤的表情 —**pensively** *adv* —**pensiveness** *n* [U]

penta- /pɛntə; pentə/ *prefix* five 五(个): *a pentagon* (=shape with five sides) 五边形, 五角形

Pent·a·gon, the /ˋpɛntə͵gɑn; ˈpentəgən/ *n* the building in Washington DC from which the army, navy etc of the US are controlled, or the military officers who work in this building 美国五角大楼, 美国国防部; 美国国防部军事官员

pen·ta·gon *n* [C] a flat shape with five, usually equal, sides and five angles 五边形, 五角形 —**pentagonal** *adj*

Pentagon Pa·pers, the /ˈ‥‥ ‚‥/ secret government documents that discussed the US's military involvement in Vietnam during the 1960s. These papers were taken from the Pentagon and printed in the *New York Times* in 1971. President Nixon tried to prevent the papers being printed, but the US Supreme Court said that the newspaper had a right to print them, because of the First Amendment. The court case examined the government's right to keep important information secret, and showed that the public has the right to know what its government is doing. 五角大楼文件〔有关 20 世纪 60 年代美军介入越战的政府机密文件。1971 年, 这些文件被人从五角大楼窃取, 最后刊登在《纽约时报》上。尼克松总统曾试图阻止这一行为, 但联邦最高法院裁定, 鉴于《第一修正法案》的规定, 该报有权刊登这些文件。这宗庭审案就美国政府对重要信息保密的权利问题进行了审查, 结果表明公众有了解政府行为的权利〕

pen·ta·gram /ˋpɛntə͵græm; ˈpentəgræm/ *n* [C] a five-pointed star, used as a magic sign 五角星形(符号)〔巫术的标记〕

pen·tam·e·ter /pɛnˋtæmətɚ; penˈtæmɪtə/ *n* [C] a line of poetry with five main beats 五音步诗行 —see also 另见 IAMBIC PENTAMETER

Pen·ta·teuch, the /ˋpɛntətuk; ˈpentətjuːk/ the Christian name for the first five books of the Old Testament of the Bible, which people believe were written by Moses, and which Jewish people call the 'Torah'《摩西五经》〔《圣经·旧约》中的首五卷。据说为摩西所作，犹太人称其为 Torah（《托拉》）〕

pen·tath·lon /pɛnˋtæθlən; penˈtæθlən/ *n* [singular] a sports event involving five different sports〔体育中的〕五项全能运动

Pen·te·cost /ˋpɛntɪˌkɔst; ˈpentɪkɒst/ *n* [singular] **1** a Jewish religious holiday 50 days after Passover〔犹太教的〕五旬节〔为逾越节后第50日〕 **2** the seventh Sunday after Easter when Christians celebrate the coming of the Holy Spirit〔基督教的〕圣灵降临节〔复活节后第七个星期日〕; WHITSUN *BrE*【英】

Pen·te·cos·tal /ˌpɛntɪˋkɔstl̩; ˌpentɪˈkɒstəl◂/ *adj* **1** belonging to or connected with a group of Christian churches with particular interest in the gifts of the HOLY SPIRIT 五旬节派教会的〔注重圣灵的恩赐〕 **2** connected with the holiday of Pentecost〔犹太人的〕五旬节的；〔基督教的〕圣灵降临节的

Pen·te·cos·tal·ist /ˌpɛntɪˋkɔstl̩ɪst; ˌpentɪˈkɒstəl̩ɪst/ *n* [C] someone who belongs to a Pentecostal church 五旬节派教会的教徒 —**Pentecostalist** *adj* —**Pentecostalism** *n* [U]

Pent·house /ˋpɛntˌhaus; ˈpenthaʊs/ *trademark* a magazine for men which has pictures of young women wearing very few clothes and articles about sex【商标】《阁楼》〔美国一男士杂志，主要刊登半裸年轻女子的照片和有关性事的文章〕

penthouse *n* [C] a very expensive and comfortable apartment or set of rooms built on top of a tall building〔建在大厦屋顶的昂贵舒适的〕楼顶公寓[套房]: *a magnificent penthouse apartment* 一套豪华的楼顶公寓

Pen·ton·ville /ˋpɛntənvɪl; ˈpentənvɪl/ also 又作 **Pentonville prison** a large prison for men, in north London 佩顿维勒监狱〔伦敦北部一大型男子监狱〕

pent up /ˌpɛnt ˋʌp; ˌpent ˈʌp◂/ *adj* pent up emotions are not freely expressed〔感情〕被压抑的: *She began to cry, letting her pent up grief come out.* 她哭了起来，让自己郁结的悲痛发泄出来。

pe·nul·ti·mate /pɪˋnʌltəmɪt; peˈnʌltɪ̈mɪ̈t/ *adj* [only before noun 仅用于名词前] *literary* next to the last【文】倒数第二的: *the penultimate chapter* 倒数第二章

pe·num·bra /pɪˋnʌmbrə; pɪ̈ˈnʌmbrə/ *n* [C] *technical* a slightly dark area between full darkness and full light【术语】半阴影；半影

pe·nu·ri·ous /pəˋnurɪəs; pɪ̈ˈnjʊəriəs/ *adj formal* very poor【正式】非常贫穷的

pen·u·ry /ˋpɛnjərɪ; ˈpenjʊ̈ri/ *n* [U] *formal* the state of being very poor; POVERTY【正式】贫穷，贫困: *families living in penury* 生活非常贫困的家庭

pe·on /ˋpiən; ˈpiːən/ *n* [C] **1** *AmE usually humorous* someone who works at a boring or physically hard job for low pay【美，通常幽默】〔从事枯燥或重体力工作、报酬很低的〕劳工，苦工 **2** *AmE* someone in Mexico or South America who works as a kind of slave to pay his debts【美】〔墨西哥或南美的〕抵债苦工，抵债奴 **3** an office messenger in India〔印度的〕办公室信差

pe·o·ny /ˋpiənɪ; ˈpiːəni/ *n* [C] a garden plant with large round flowers that are dark red, white, or pink 牡丹，芍药

Peo·ple /ˋpipl̩; ˈpiːpəl/ also 又作 **People Magazine** *trademark* a US magazine that contains short articles and pictures of famous people, especially people who appear on television and in films or sports people【商标】《人物》〔美国一杂志，刊登有关名人的短讯和照片，尤其是影视界或体育界名人〕

S1 W1 **people¹** *n*

1 [plural] persons 人: *Were there many people at the meeting?* 开会的人多吗？| *Most people in our neighborhood drive to work.* 我们家附近的人大多开车去上班。| *a retirement home for elderly people* 老年之家 —see 见 PERSON (USAGE)

2 ▶PEOPLE IN GENERAL 人的总称◀ [plural] people in general, or people other than yourself 人们: *Sometimes people think we're sisters.* 有时候人们认为我们是姐妹。| *People enjoy reading about the rich and famous.* 人们喜欢阅读有关富人和名人的书。| **theatre/business etc people** *Computer people are notoriously bad at arithmetic.* 搞电脑的人算术差是出了名的。

3 the people [plural] all the ordinary people in a country or a state who do not have special rank or position 平民，民众，老百姓: *Abraham Lincoln spoke of 'government of the people, by the people, for the people'.* 亚伯拉罕·林肯曾讲到"民有，民治，民享的政府"。| *the common people* 老百姓 | **man of the people** *a politician who was regarded as a man of the people because his father had been a miner* 因为父亲曾是矿工而被视为平民政治家

4 [C] a race or nation 种族；民族: *the national heritage of the American people* 美国的民族遗产 | *the peoples of Africa* 非洲各民族 | *The Chinese people share a common written language.* 中国人使用的是同一种书面语言。—see 见 RACE¹ (USAGE)

5 sb's people [plural] **a)** the people that God, a king, or a leader rules or leads〔上帝、国王的〕臣民；〔领袖的〕拥护者: *the exaltation of God's people* 上帝子民的狂喜 **b)** your parents, grandparents etc 家族: *His people have lived in this valley for centuries.* 他的家族已在这山谷中生活了几个世纪。**c)** *old-fashioned* your close relatives, especially parents【过时】家属，亲属〔尤指父母〕: *Come home with me to meet my people.* 跟我回家见见我的父母。

6 of all people *spoken* used to say that someone is the one person who you would not have expected to do something【口】在所有人中(偏偏): *Why should he, of all people, get a promotion?* 在所有人中为什么偏偏是他获得晋升呢？| *You of all people should have known better.* 在所有人中尤其是你本应该更明智一些。

7 *AmE spoken* used to get the attention of a group of people【美口】诸位〔用于引起众人的注意〕: *Listen up, people!* 注意听，各位！—compare 比较 FOLK¹ (3) —see also 另见 LITTLE PEOPLE, PERSON

people² *v* **1 be peopled with/by** *literary* to be filled with people or things of a particular type【文】充满〔某种类型的人或物〕；充斥: *Her little world was peopled with imaginary friends.* 她的小世界里满是假想的朋友。**2** [T] *technical* to live in a place; INHABIT【术语】居住于: *the tribes who first peopled the peninsula* 最早居住在该半岛上的部落

People, The *trademark* a British TABLOID newspaper sold every Sunday, which is known for printing shocking articles about famous people, especially about their relationships and their sexual experiences【商标】《人民报》〔英国一份周日发行的小报，以刊载名人猛料著称，尤其热衷于报道名人的绯闻〕

People's Dai·ly, The /ˌ‥ˈ‥/ the official daily newspaper of China, which is controlled by the Chinese government《人民日报》〔中国一官方日报，由中国政府主办〕

Pe·o·ri·a /pɪˋɔrɪə; piˈɔːriə/ a city in Illinois, US, which is an important port on the Illinois River 皮奥里亚〔美国伊利诺伊州一城市，为伊利诺伊河沿岸重要港口〕

pep¹ /pɛp; pep/ *v* **pepped, pepping**

pep sb/sth ↔ **up** *phr v* [T] *informal* to make something or someone more active, interesting or full of energy【非正式】使〔某人[物]〕更活跃[更有意思，充满活力]: *You need something to pep you up – how about a drink?* 你需要点东西让自己振作起来——来杯酒怎么样？| *Pep up the dish with some curry powder.* 给这份菜加点咖喱粉提提味儿。

pep² *n* [U] *informal* physical energy; VIGOUR【非正式】精力，活力: *His exercise routine keeps him full of pep.* 他的日常锻炼使他充满活力。—see also 另见 PEP TALK

pep·per¹ /ˋpɛpɚ; ˈpepə/ *n* **1** [U] a grey or pale yellow powder used to add a slightly hot taste to food 胡椒粉: *Pass the salt and pepper, please.* 请把盐和胡椒粉递过来。—see also 另见 BLACK PEPPER, WHITE PEPPER **2** a red powder like this, especially CAYENNE PEPPER or PAPRIKA 辣椒粉 **3** [C] a hollow red, green or yellow vegetable that is used in hot or cold dishes 辣椒 —see also 另见 BELL PEPPER, SWEET PEPPER —see picture on page A9 参见A9页图 S3

pepper² *v* [T] **1** to scatter things all over or all through something 在…上撒；使…布满: **be peppered with** *a report peppered with statistics* 满篇都是统计数字的报告 **2** to hit something repeatedly with many bullets 连续射击，频繁射击: **pepper sth with** *He peppered the side of the barn with buckshot.* 他用大号铅弹连续击打谷仓的侧面。**3** to add pepper to food 给〔食物〕加胡椒粉

pepper-and-salt /ˌ‥ˈ‥◂/ *adj* coloured with small areas of black and white mixed together 花白的，黑白相间的: *a pepper-and-salt beard* 花白胡子

pep·per·corn /ˋpɛpɚˌkɔrn; ˈpepəkɔːn/ *n* [C] the small dried fruit from a tropical plant which is crushed to make pepper 胡椒粒[子]

peppercorn rent /ˌ‥ˈ‥/ *n* [C] *BrE* a very small amount of rent, much less than you would expect to pay【英】象征性租金，极少的租金

pep·per mill /ˈ‥ ˌ/ *n* [C] a small piece of kitchen equipment which is used to crush peppercorns into pepper 胡椒研磨器

pep·per·mint /ˋpɛpɚˌmɪnt; ˈpepəˌmɪnt/ *n* **1** [U] a MINT plant with a strong taste which is often used in sweets and medicine〔常用来做成糖果和药的〕胡椒薄荷 **2** the taste of this plant 薄荷味: *peppermint candy* 薄荷糖 **3** [C] a sweet with the taste of peppermint 薄荷糖

P

pep·pe·ro·ni /ˌpɛpəˋronɪ; ˌpepəˈrəʊni/ *n* [C,U] an Italian spicy dry SAUSAGE 意大利辣香肠

pepper pot /ˈ··ˌ/ *BrE*【英】, **pepper shak·er** /ˈ··ˌ··/ *AmE*【美】*n* [C] a small container with little holes in the top used for shaking pepper onto food〔盖子上有小孔的〕胡椒(粉)瓶

pep·per·y /ˋpɛpərɪ; ˈpepəri/ *adj* **1** tasting of pepper 胡椒味的，辛辣的 **2** easily made angry; IRRITABLE 易怒的，暴躁的

pep pill /ˈ··/ *n* [C] *informal* a PILL containing a drug that gives you more energy or makes you happier for a short time; STIMULANT (1)【非正式】兴奋药丸[片]

pep ral·ly /ˈ·ˌ··/ *n* [C] *AmE* a meeting of all the students at a school before a sports event when CHEERLEADERS lead students in encouraging their team to win【美】〔全体学生参加的〕学校运动会赛前动员大会

Pep·si /ˋpɛpsɪ; ˈpepsi/ also 又作 **Pepsi Cola** *trademark* a type of COLA drink (=a dark, sweet, non-alcoholic drink with bubbles) that is sold all over the world by an American company【商标】百事可乐〔美国一公司生产的一种可乐饮料，畅销全球〕

pep·sin /ˋpɛpsɪn; ˈpepsɪ̇n/ *n* [U] a liquid in your stomach that changes food into a form that can be used by your body 胃蛋白酶

pep talk /ˈ··/ *n* [C] *informal* a speech that is intended to encourage you to work harder, win a game etc【非正式】鼓舞士气的讲话，激励性讲话: *The manager gave his team a pep talk at half time.* 主教练在半场休息时给队员作了鼓舞士气的讲话。

pep·tic ul·cer /ˌpɛptɪk ˋʌlsɚ; ˌpeptɪk ˈʌlsə/ *n* [C] a sore painful place inside the stomach caused by the action of pepsin 消化性溃疡

Pep·to-bis·mol /ˌpɛptoˋbɪzmɔl; ˌpeptəʊˈbɪzmɒl/ *trademark* a type of medicine for the stomach which you take when you have INDIGESTION. It is a thick, pink, sweet-tasting liquid.【商标】佩托比斯摩，碱式水杨酸铋〔美国一种胃药。专治消化不良，为粉红色稠状甜味制剂〕

Pepys /pips; piːps/, **Sam·u·el** /ˋsæmjuəl; ˈsæmjuəl/ (1633-1703) an English writer famous for his diary, which describes his personal life and the important events of the time, such as the Great Fire of London, and gives a lot of information about what life was like at the time 佩皮斯〔(1633-1703)，英格兰作家。以其日记闻名，描述了他的个人生活和当时的重大事件，如伦敦大火，比较详尽地反映了当时的生活状况〕

per /pɚ; pə; strong 强读 pɝ; pɜː/ *prep* **1** for each 每: **per kilo/gallon/metre etc** (=for each kilo etc) 每公斤/每加仑/每米等 *Apples are 60 cents per pound.* 苹果每磅60美分。| *My car does about 12 miles per litre* (=for each litre of petrol). 我的汽车每升汽油大约跑12英里。| **per head** (=for or by each person) 每人 *How much food should we allow per head?* 我们应允许每人吃多少食物? **2 per hour/day/week etc** during each hour etc 每小时/每天/每星期等: *How many calls do you make per day?* 你每天打多少个电话? | **miles/kilometres per hour** (=used for measuring speed) 每小时…英里/公里〔用以测量速度〕 *a train travelling at 150 miles per hour* 每小时行驶150英里的火车 **3** according to 按照: **as per sth** *work carried out as per your instructions* 按照你的指示完成的工作 **4 as per usual** *spoken* used when something annoying happens which has often happened before【口】〔令人讨厌的事情〕照常，照旧: *Hardy was late, as per usual.* 哈迪同往常一样迟到了。—see also 另见 PER ANNUM, PER CAPITA

per·ad·ven·ture /ˌpɚədˋvɛntʃɚ; ˌperədˈventʃə/ *adv old use*【旧】**1** perhaps 也许；或许 **2** by chance 偶然；碰巧: *if peradventure we should meet* 如果我们碰巧相遇的话

per·am·bu·late /pəˋræmbjəˌlet; pəˈræmbjɡleɪt/ *v* [I,T] *old-fashioned* to walk around or along a place without hurrying【过时】徘徊于；漫步于 —**perambulation** /pəˌræmbjəˋleʃən; pəˌræmbjɡˈleɪʃən/ *n* [C,U]

per·am·bu·la·tor /pəˋræmbjəˌletɚ; pəˈræmbjɡleɪtə/ *n* [C] *old-fashioned especially BrE* a PRAM【过时，尤英】婴儿车

per an·num /pɚ ˋænəm; pər ˈænəm/ written abbreviation 缩写为 **p.a.** *adv formal* for or in each year【正式】每年: *a salary of $20,000 per annum* 两万美金的年薪

per·cale /pɚˋkel; pəˈkeɪl/ *n* [C,U] *AmE* cotton cloth, used especially for making sheets【美】〔尤指用来做床单的〕棉布

per cap·i·ta /pɚ ˋkæpɪtə; pə ˈkæpɪ̇tə/ *adj, adv formal* for or by each person in a particular place【正式】〔某个特定地方〕每人(的)，人均(的): *What is the average per capita income in this country?* 这个国家的人均收入是多少?

per·ceive /pɚˋsiv; pəˈsiːv/ *v* [T not in progressive 不用进行时] **1** to understand or think of something in a particular way〔以某种方式〕理解，领悟: **perceive that** *People now perceive that green issues are important to our future.* 人们现在认识到环境问题对我们的未来很重要。| **perceive sth as sth** *Holly began to perceive her father as a loser.* 霍莉开始认为她父亲是一个失败者。| **perceive sth to be sth** *The past is often perceived to be better than the present.* 过去常常被认为比现在好。| **perceive what/where/who etc** *We were able to perceive where the problem lay.* 我们能够看出问题出在何处。**2** to notice something that is difficult to notice 察觉，注意到，发觉: *That morning, he perceived a change in Franca's mood.* 那天早上，他发觉弗兰卡的情绪有些变化。| **perceive that** *Jill could just perceive that someone was inside the house.* 吉尔完全能察觉到有人在房子里。

percent¹ also 又作 **per cent** *BrE*【英】/pɚˋsɛnt; pəˈsent/ *adj, adv* **1 5 percent (5%)/10 percent (10%) etc** equal to 5, 10 etc parts out of a total that consists of 100 parts 5%/10%等: *Leave the waitress a 15 percent (=15%) tip.* 留给服务员15%的小费。**2 a/one hundred percent** completely, totally 百分之百地，完全地: *I agree with you a hundred percent.* 我百分之百地同意你的看法。

percent² also 又作 **per cent** *BrE*【英】*n* **5 percent (5%)/10 percent (10%) etc** an amount equal to 5, 10 etc parts out of a total that consists of 100 parts 5%/10%等: *30 percent (=30%) of our profits* 我们利润的30% | *The bank charges interest at fourteen per cent (=14%).* 银行收取14%的利息。

per·cen·tage /pɚˋsɛntɪdʒ; pəˈsentɪdʒ/ *n* **1** [C,U] *technical* an amount stated as if it is part of a whole which is 100【术语】百分比，百分率: *"What percentage of school leavers go to university?" "About five per cent."* "毕业生上大学的百分比是多少?""大约5%。" | **high/low percentage** *A high percentage of married women have part-time jobs.* 已婚妇女拥有兼职工作的比例很高。| **in percentage terms** *The numbers are small in percentage terms, but significant.* 按百分比来说，这些数目并不大，但意义重大。**2** [C usually singular 一般用单数] a share of profits 利润分成: *She gets a percentage for every record sold.* 每卖一张唱片她都可得到一份利润。**3 there is no percentage in** *informal* used to say that there is no advantage or profit in doing something【非正式】〔做某事〕没有好处[利益]

per·cep·ti·ble /pɚˋsɛptəbl; pəˈseptɪ̇bəl/ *adj formal* something that is perceptible can just be noticed, although it is small【正式】可察觉的: *a barely perceptible sound* 几乎察觉不出的声响 | *a small but perceptible change* 微小但可以察觉的变化 —opposite 反义词 IMPERCEPTIBLE—**perceptibly** *adv*

per·cep·tion /pɚˋsɛpʃən; pəˈsepʃən/ *n* **1** [C] the way you regard something and your beliefs about what it is like 认识，观念；看法: *Parents' views influence their children's perceptions of the world.* 父母的观点影响其孩子对世界的看法。**2** [U] the way that you notice things with your senses 感觉，感知方式: *This drug alters perception.* 这种药物会改变感知。**3** [U] the natural ability to understand or notice something quickly 感知能力；认识能力；洞察力: *Ross shows unusual perception for a boy of his age.* 罗斯所表现出的洞察力对于他这个年龄的男孩来说是非凡的。

per·cep·tive /pɚˋsɛptɪv; pəˈseptɪv/ *adj approving* good at noticing and understanding what is happening or what someone is thinking or feeling【褒】观察敏锐的，洞察力强的: *a perceptive woman* 一位洞察力强的女士 | *perceptive comments* 颇有见地的评论—**perceptively** *adv*—**perceptiveness** *n* [U]: *trust in their own powers of perceptiveness and intuition* 相信他们自己的理解力和直觉

perch¹ /pɝtʃ; pɜːtʃ/ *n* [C] **1** a branch, stick, rod etc where a bird sits, especially in a bird cage〔尤指鸟笼中的〕栖木，栖枝 **2** *informal* a high place where a person sits or where a building is placed【非正式】〔人或建筑物所处的〕高位，高处: *From our perch on the hill, we can see the whole city.* 从这山岗的高处，我们能鸟瞰全市。**3** a fish that lives in lakes and rivers〔生活在湖和河中的〕鲈鱼

perch² *v* **1 be perched on/upon/over etc** to be in a position on top of, or on the edge of something 处在…的顶上[边上]: *a house perched on a cliff above the town* 一幢位于悬崖之上俯瞰城镇的房屋 **2 perch (yourself) on** to sit on top of, or on the edge of, something〔使自己〕坐在…的上面[边上]: *Linda perched herself on a bar stool.* 琳达坐在酒吧的凳子上。**3** [I+on] if a bird perches on something, it flies down and sits on it〔鸟〕落，歇

per·chance /pɚˋtʃæns; pəˈtʃɑːns/ *adv old use or literary*【旧或文】**1** perhaps 或许，也许 **2** by chance 偶然，碰巧: *Leave now, lest perchance he should find you.* 现在就离开，以免他碰巧找到你。

per·cip·i·ent /pɚˋsɪpɪənt; pəˈsɪpiənt/ *adj formal* quick to notice and understand things; PERCEPTIVE【正式】目光敏锐的，洞察[理解]力强的—**percipience** *n* [U]

per·co·late /ˈpɝkəˌlet; ˈpɜːkəleɪt/ *v* **1** [I always+adv/prep] if liquid, light etc percolates somewhere, it passes slowly through a material that has very small holes in it〔液体、光等〕渗透，滤出：[**+through/down**] *Water percolated down through the rock.* 水从岩石中渗漏下来。**2** [I always+adv/prep] if information percolates among people, it is passed gradually from one person to another〔信息〕逐渐传播开来：[**+through/down**] *News of the war percolated through to us after a few days.* 几天后，战争的消息逐渐传到我们这里。**3 a)** [I] if coffee percolates, it is made in a special pot in which hot water is passed through crushed coffee beans〔咖啡在渗滤式咖啡壶中〕滤煮 **b)** [T] to make coffee by this method〔用渗滤式咖啡壶〕滤煮〔咖啡〕—**percolation** /ˌpɝkəˈleʃən; ˌpɜːkəˈleɪʃən/ *n* [C,U]

per·co·la·tor /ˈpɝkəˌletɚ; ˈpɜːkəleɪtə/ *n* [C] a pot in which coffee is percolated 咖啡渗滤壶，煮咖啡壶

per·cus·sion /pɚˈkʌʃən; pəˈkʌʃən/ *n* **1** [U, singular] musical instruments, especially drums, that are played by being hit with an object such as a stick or hammer, or the group of people who play these instruments in an ORCHESTRA 打击乐器〔尤指鼓〕；〔管弦乐队中的〕打击乐器演奏组：*The percussion is too loud.* 打击乐器声音太响。**2** [U] the sound or effect of two things hitting each other with great force〔两物猛烈相撞产生的〕撞击声；振动，震动

per·cus·sion·ist /pɚˈkʌʃənɪst; pəˈkʌʃənɪst/ *n* [C] someone who plays percussion instruments 打击乐器演奏者

per di·em[1] /pɚ ˈdiəm; pə ˈdiːəm/ *n* [C] *especially AmE* money paid by an employer to workers who are paid by the day【尤美】〔雇主付给工人的〕日工资：*What's the per diem for the job?* 这份工作每日的报酬是多少？

per diem[2] *adv* happening every day or from one day to another 每日地，按日：*We are paid per diem.* 我们按日计酬。

per·di·tion /pɚˈdɪʃən; pəˈdɪʃən/ *n* [U] *formal*【正式】**1** punishment after death 死后的惩罚，永劫；恶报 **2** *old use* complete destruction【旧】彻底毁灭：*He had gambled his way to perdition.* 他因赌博走上了灭亡之路。

per·e·gri·na·tion /ˌpɛrəgrɪˈneʃən; ˌperɪgrɪˈneɪʃən/ *n* [C] *literary or humorous* a long journey, especially in foreign countries【文或幽默】〔尤指在外国的〕旅行；游历：*His peregrinations took him to India and China.* 他游历到了印度和中国。

per·e·grine fal·con /ˈpɛrəgrɪn ˈfælkən; ˌperɪgrɪn ˈfɔːlkən/ also 又作 **peregrine** *n* [C] a hunting bird with a black and white spotted front 游隼

pe·remp·to·ry /pəˈrɛmptərɪ; pəˈremptəri/ *adj formal*【正式】**1** peremptory behaviour, speech etc is not polite or friendly and shows that the person speaking expects to be obeyed at once〔行为、说话等〕专横的，霸道的；盛气凌人的：*a peremptory tone of voice* 专横的语调 **2** a peremptory command must be obeyed〔命令〕强制性的，必须服从的，不容抗拒的 —**peremptorily** *adv*

pe·ren·ni·al[1] /pəˈrɛnɪəl; pəˈreniəl/ *adj* **1 perennial problem/concern/struggle etc** a problem etc that people are concerned with all the time 长期存在的问题/担忧/斗争等：*The film addresses the perennial theme of marital discord.* 这部电影关注的是夫妻不和这个永恒的主题。**2** a plant that is perennial lives for more than two years〔植物〕多年生的 —**perennially** *adv*

perennial[2] *n* [C] a plant that lives for more than two years〔两年以上的〕多年生植物 —see also 另见 HARDY PERENNIAL

Per·es /ˈpɛrɛs; ˈperes/, **Shi·mon** /ʃɪˈmon; ʃɪˈmɒn/ (1923-) an Israeli Socialist politician, Prime Minister from 1984 to 1986. He won the Nobel Peace Prize with Yitzhak Rabin and Yasser Arafat in 1994. 佩雷斯〔(1923-)，以色列工党政治家，1984至1986年任总理。1994年，他与伊扎克·拉宾和亚西尔·阿拉法特一起获得诺贝尔和平奖〕

pe·re·stroi·ka /ˌpɛrəˈstrɔɪkə; ˌperɪˈstrɔɪkə/ *n* [U] a Russian word meaning rebuilding, used to describe the policies of social, political, and economic change started by Mikhail Gorbachev in the former USSR 重建，改革〔俄语词，用于指前苏联米哈伊尔·戈尔巴乔夫开始的社会、政治和经济变革的政策〕

S2 W2 **per·fect**[1] /ˈpɝfɪkt; ˈpɜːfɪkt/ *adj* **1** of the very best possible kind or standard 完美的，理想的：*It's a perfect day for a picnic.* 这是个适合野餐的理想日子。| *a perfect example of Gothic architecture* 哥德式建筑的完美典范 | *a perfect marriage* 美满的婚姻 | **the perfect crime** (=one in which the criminal is never discovered) 掩盖得天衣无缝的罪行 *There is no such thing as the perfect crime.* 没有什么永不败露的罪行。**2** complete, without any faults or weaknesses 完整的，完好的，完美的：*a perfect performance* 完美的演出 | *a perfect set of teeth* 一口完好无缺的牙齿 | *in perfect condition* 状况完好的 | **nobody's perfect** *spoken* (=used when you are answering someone who has criticized you)【口】人无完人〔用来回答批评自己的人时用〕*So I did the wrong thing! Well nobody's perfect.* 我确是做错事了！嗯，人无完人嘛。**3** exactly right and just what is needed for a particular purpose; IDEAL[1] (1) 完美的，最适当的；理想的：*That's perfect! – just the way I wanted it to look.* 那太完美了——正是我想要的样子。| *"D'you want some more soup?" "No, this is perfect."* (=enough; plenty) "你再要点汤吗？""不要啦，这些足够了。" | *We've found the perfect actor to play the part.* 我们找到了最适合扮演这个角色的演员。| [**+for**] *The house is perfect for our family.* 这房子对我们家来说是最合适不过的。**4** completely correct and accurate 完全正确的，精确的：*Your English is perfect.* 你的英语说得很地道。| *a perfect copy of the original* 与原件一字不差的副本 | **perfect timing** (=when something happens at exactly the right time) 精确的时间掌握 *"Have you been waiting?" "No, it was perfect timing. I've just arrived."* "你一直在等吗？""没有，是时间算得正好。我刚到。" **5 the perfect gentleman/wife/host** someone who behaves exactly as a typical gentleman etc ought to behave 十足的绅士/理想的妻子/完美（待客）的主人 **6 a perfect stranger/fool/angel etc** complete stranger etc 完全陌生的人/十足的傻瓜/十足的好人等：*I felt a perfect idiot.* 我感到自己是个十足的傻瓜。—see also 另见 PERFECTLY, **practice makes perfect** (PRACTICE (11)), PRESENT PERFECT, PAST PERFECT

per·fect[2] /pɚˈfɛkt; pəˈfekt/ *v* [T] to make something perfect or as good as you are able to 使…完美[完善]：*It's just a working model; we haven't perfected it yet.* 这只是个工作模型，我们还没有使它完善。

per·fect[3] /ˈpɝfɪkt; ˈpɜːfɪkt/ *n technical*【术语】**the perfect** the form of a verb which shows a period of time up to and including the present, and in English is usually formed with 'have' and the past participle; PRESENT PERFECT〔动词的〕完成式 —see also 另见 PAST PERFECT

per·fec·ti·ble /pɚˈfɛktəbl; pəˈfektɪbəl/ *adj* something that is perfectible can be improved or made perfect 可臻完美的，可完善的，可改进[改善]的 —**perfectibility** /pɚˌfɛktəˈbɪlətɪ; pəˌfektɪˈbɪlɪti/ *n* [U]

per·fec·tion /pɚˈfɛkʃən; pəˈfekʃən/ *n* [U] **1** the state of being perfect 完美，完善：**to perfection** (=perfectly) 完美地，恰到好处 *The meat was cooked to perfection.* 这肉煮得恰到好处。**2** the process of making something perfect 达到完美的过程：*the perfection of his technique* 他的技术的完善过程 **3** a perfect example of something〔某物的〕完美典型：*Her performance was pure perfection.* 她的表演达到了尽善尽美的地步。

per·fec·tion·ist /pɚˈfɛkʃənɪst; pəˈfekʃənɪst/ *n* [C] someone who is not satisfied with anything unless it is completely perfect 力求完美者，完美主义者，凡事求全者：*You did fine! Don't be such a perfectionist.* 你做得不错了！不要苛求尽善尽美。—**perfectionist** *adj* —**perfectionism** *n* [U]

per·fect·ly /ˈpɝfɪktlɪ; ˈpɜːfɪktli/ *adv* **1** in a perfect way 完美地；极佳地：*She speaks English perfectly.* 她英语说得很地道。| *The colors match perfectly.* 这些颜色搭配得非常好。**2** a word meaning very or completely, used especially when you are annoyed about something 十分地，完全地〔尤用于表示对某事讨厌时〕：*We want to make our position perfectly clear!* 我们想把我们的立场完全说清楚！| *You know perfectly well what I mean.* 你完全知道我是什么意思。 S2 W3

perfect par·ti·ci·ple /ˌ.. ˈ..../ *n* [C] the PAST PARTICIPLE 过去分词

perfect pitch /ˌ.. ˈ./ *n* [U] the ability to correctly name any musical note that you hear, or to sing any note at the correct PITCH without the help of an instrument 绝对音高，绝对音感〔不借助乐器而正确地说出或唱出任何一个乐音的能力〕

per·fid·i·ous /pɚˈfɪdɪəs; pəˈfɪdiəs/ *adj literary* someone who is perfidious is disloyal and cannot be trusted; TREACHEROUS (1)【文】不忠实的，背信弃义的 —**perfidiousness** *n* [U]

per·fi·dy /ˈpɝfədɪ; ˈpɜːfɪdi/ *n* [U] *literary* disloyalty to someone who trusts you; TREACHERY【文】不忠，背信弃义

per·fo·rate /ˈpɝfəˌret; ˈpɜːfəreɪt/ *v* [T] **1** to make a hole or holes in something 在…上打洞[穿孔]：*A broken rib had perforated her lung.* 一根折断的肋骨把她的肺刺穿了。**2** [usually passive 一般用被动态] to make a line of small holes in a piece of paper so that a part of it can be torn off easily 在〔纸〕上打孔眼线〔以便撕开〕—**perforated** *adj*: *a perforated sheet of paper* 一张打有齿孔的纸

per·fo·ra·tion /ˌpɝfəˈreʃən; ˌpɜːfəˈreɪʃən/ *n* **1** [C usually plural 一般用复数] a small hole in something, or a line of holes made in a piece of paper so that it can be torn easily 孔；〔纸上的〕孔眼线：*the perforations in a sheet of stamps* 整版邮票上的齿孔 **2** [U] the making of a hole or holes in something 穿孔；打齿孔

per·force /pɚˋfɔrs; pəˈfɔːs/ *adv literary* because it is necessary【文】由于需要，不得已：*He fell sick and had perforce to stay at home.* 他感到不舒服，所以不得不待在家里。

per·form /pɚˋfɔrm; pəˈfɔːm/ *v* **1** [I,T] to do something to entertain people, for example by acting a play, or playing a piece of music 表演，演出〈如演戏、演奏〉：*I've never seen 'Othello' performed so brilliantly.* 我从未看过《奥赛罗》这出戏表演得如此精彩。| *Chris will be performing in public next week.* 克里斯下星期将进行公开演出。**2** [T] to do something such as a piece of work, a duty, or a ceremony, especially according to a usual or established method 做；执行；履行；实行：*an operation performed by surgeons at Guy's Hospital* 盖伊医院的外科医生进行的一个手术 | *The advice service performs a useful function.* 咨询服务发挥了有益的作用。| **perform miracles** (=do things that seem impossible) 创造奇迹 **3 perform well/badly** to work or do something well, badly etc 表现得好/差：*Our team performed very well on Saturday.* 我们队星期六表现得很好。| *The car performs badly in the wet.* 这辆汽车在下雨天不好开。

per·form·ance /pɚˋfɔrməns; pəˈfɔːməns/ *n* **1 a)** [C] an act of performing a play or a piece of music 表演；演出；演奏：[+of] *Stern's performance of the Bruch concerto* 斯特恩演奏的布鲁赫协奏曲 | **give a performance** *The orchestra will give two more performances this week.* 这个管弦乐队本周将加演两场。**b)** an occasion on which a play, piece of music etc is performed〔戏剧、音乐等的〕表演，演出：*This evening's performance will begin at 8:00 pm.* 今晚的演出八点开始。**2** [U] **a)** the act of doing a piece of work, duty etc 履行，执行：*the performance of his official duties* 履行他的公务 **b)** how well or badly you do a particular job or activity〔工作或活动中的〕表现：*Jodie's performance in the exams was disappointing.* 乔迪考试的成绩令人失望。**3** [U] how well a car or other machine works〔汽车或机器的〕性能：*The car's performance on mountain roads was impressive.* 这辆汽车在山路上表现出的性能给人留下深刻的印象。| *high-performance cars* (=very powerful cars) 性能很好的汽车 **4 a) a performance** *spoken* a process that takes too much time and effort【口】费时费力的事：*What a performance!* 真是麻烦事！**b)** an example of bad behaviour that involves angry shouting〔带有愤怒叫喊的〕糟糕的行为[举止]

performance-re·lat·ed pay /ˌ···ˌ···ˈ·/ *n* [U] money that you earn which increases if you work well and decreases if you work badly 与工作表现挂钩的报酬

per·form·er /pɚˋfɔrmɚ; pəˈfɔːmə/ *n* [C] **1** an actor, musician etc, who performs to entertain people 表演者；演奏者；演员：*circus performers* 马戏演员 **2 skilful/brilliant/poor etc performer** someone who does a particular job or activity well or badly 技术娴熟的/才华横溢的/表演欠佳的演奏者[演员]：**star performer** (=the best performer) 明星演员

performing arts, the /·ˌ··ˈ·/ *n* arts such as dance, music, or DRAMA, which are performed to entertain people 表演艺术〈如舞蹈、音乐或戏剧〉

per·fume¹ /ˋpɝfjum; ˈpɜːfjuːm/ *n* [C,U] **1** a liquid that has a strong pleasant smell, that you put on your skin or clothing to make yourself smell nice 香水：*She never wears perfume.* 她从来不用香水。**2** a sweet or pleasant smell 香味：*the rose's heady perfume* 令人陶醉的玫瑰香味

per·fume² /pɚˋfjum; ˈpɜːfjuːm/ *v* **1** *literary* to fill something with a sweet, pleasant smell【文】使充满香气：*The flowers in her garden perfumed the evening air.* 她花园里的鲜花使夜间的空气充满了香味。**2** to put perfume on something 喷[擦]香水于：*Use lavender oil to perfume your handkerchiefs.* 把薰衣草油洒在你的手绢上。—**perfumed** *adj*: *perfumed soap* 香皂

per·fum·er·y /pɚˋfjumərɪ; pəˈfjuːməri/ *n* **1** [C] a place where perfumes are made or sold 香水制造厂；香水商店：*the store's perfumery counter* 商店中的香水（经销）柜台 **2** [U] the process of making perfumes 香水调制法

per·func·to·ry /pɚˋfʌŋktərɪ; pəˈfʌŋktəri/ *adj formal*【正式】 **1** a perfunctory action is done quickly, and is only done because people expect it〔行动〕草率的，马虎的；敷衍的：*Olivia dismissed him with a perfunctory nod.* 奥利维娅敷衍地点了点头，把他打发走了。| *a perfunctory kiss on the cheek* 在脸颊上漫不经心的一吻 **2** someone who is perfunctory does things in this way〔指人〕做事敷衍塞责的 —**perfunctorily** *adv*: *The two men shook hands perfunctorily.* 那两个人敷衍地握了握手。

per·go·la /ˋpɝgələ; ˈpɜːgələ/ *n* [C] a structure made of posts built for plants to grow over in a garden〔花园中的〕藤架，蔓棚

per·haps /pɚˋhæps; pəˈhæps/ *adv* **1** possibly; MAYBE 也许，可能：*This is perhaps her finest novel yet.* 这或许是她迄今为止写得最好的一部小说。| *Perhaps she's next door.* 也许她住在隔壁。| *"Do you think Mark's upset?" "Perhaps."* "你觉得马克很难过吗？""也许是吧。" | **perhaps not** *"Do you think I dare ask him?" "Perhaps not."* "你认为我敢问他吗？""也许不敢。" **2** used to say that a number is only a guess 也许，可能〔用于表示某个数字仅仅是猜测〕：*The room was large, perhaps twenty feet square.* 这个房间很大，可能有20平方英尺。**3** *spoken* used to politely ask or suggest something【口】也许，或许〔用于表示礼貌的请求或建议〕：*I thought perhaps we'd have lunch in the garden.* 我想或许我们可以在花园里吃午餐。| *Perhaps you'd like to join us?* 也许你愿意加入我们吧？**4** *spoken formal* used to say what you are going to do, or what someone else should do【口，正式】也许〔用于表示你自己要做或别人应该做的事情〕：*Perhaps in closing I could repeat a statement from our Chairman's opening address.* 在结束时，我也许可以重复我们的主席在开幕词中说的一句话。—see 见 MAYBE (USAGE)

per·il /ˋpɛrəl; ˈperɪ̵l/ *n* **1** [U] *literary* great danger, especially of being harmed or killed【文】〔尤指遭伤害或杀害的〕巨大的危险：**in peril** *a prayer for those in peril on the sea* 为遇上海难的人祈祷 **2 the perils of a)** *literary* things that can cause great danger【文】可招致极大危险的事物：*Cook faced the perils of the Atlantic seas.* 库克面临着充满危险的大西洋。**b)** things that might cause you problems in life 可能招致麻烦的事物：*Her mother had warned her about the perils of living alone.* 她母亲告诫过她独居的难处。**3 you do sth at your peril** used to warn someone that what they intend to do is very dangerous 你做某事要自担风险〔用于告诫某人他们打算做的事情很危险〕：*Those who ignore the gale warning do so at their peril.* 那些无视大风警告的人这样做要自担风险。

per·il·ous /ˋpɛrələs; ˈperɪ̵ləs/ *adj especially literary* very dangerous【尤文】非常危险的：*a perilous journey across the mountains* 穿越群山的危险旅程 —**perilously** *adv*: *perilously close to the precipice* 离悬崖太近，十分危险 —**perilousness** *n* [U]

pe·rim·e·ter /pəˋrɪmətɚ; pəˈrɪmɪ̵tə/ *n* [C] **1** the border around an enclosed area such as a military camp〔军营等的〕四周，周围；周边，边缘：*the perimeter of the airfield* 机场的四周 | *a perimeter fence* 环形的篱笆围墙 **2** the whole length of the border around an area or shape 周长：*Calculate the perimeter of this rectangle.* 计算这个长方形的周长。—compare 比较 CIRCUMFERENCE

pe·ri·na·tal /ˌpɛrəˋnetl; ˌperɪ̵ˈneɪtl◂/ *adj technical* at or around the time of birth【术语】围产期的，接近出生时期的：*a high rate of perinatal mortality* 很高的围产期死亡率

pe·ri·od¹ /ˋpɪrɪəd; ˈpɪəriəd/ *n* [C] 

1 ▶LENGTH OF TIME 时间长度◀ a particular length of time with a beginning and an end 一段时间；时期：*Tomorrow's weather will be dry with sunny periods.* 明天天气干燥，间或有太阳。| *the period 1910–1917* 1910–1917年间 | *a period of six weeks* 六周的时间 | *a six-week period* 六周的时间 | **trial period** (=a period of testing) 试用期 *Helen has been taken on for a three month trial period.* 海伦已被录用，试用期为三个月。

2 ▶IN DEVELOPMENT 发展中的◀ a particular period in the development of a country or a person〔国家或个人发展的〕时期；阶段：*Van Gogh's early period* 梵高的早期阶段

3 ▶IN HISTORY 历史上的◀ a particular period in history〔历史上的〕时期；阶段；时代：*Which period are you studying?* 你在学哪一段历史？

4 ▶WOMAN 妇女的◀ the MONTHLY flow of blood from a woman's body 月经

5 ▶DOT 点◀ *AmE* a DOT (.) in a piece of writing that shows the end of a sentence or an ABBREVIATION【美】句点；FULL STOP *BrE*【英】—see picture at 参见 PUNCTUATION MARK 图

6 ▶FOR EMPHASIS 用于强调◀ period! *AmE spoken* used to say that you have made a decision and that you do not want to discuss the subject any more【美口】到此为止，就这样定了〔用于表示已作出决定，不想再讨论某话题〕：*I'm not going, period!* 我不去，就这样决定了！

7 ▶SCHOOL 学校◀ one of the equal parts that the school day is divided into; lesson 课时，学时，一节（课）：*What class do you have first period?* 你第一节课上什么？| *a double period of Science* 自然科学这门课程的双节课时

period² *adj* **period costume/furniture** clothes or furniture in the style of a particular time in history 具有特定历史时期特点的服装/家具：*actors dressed in period costume* 穿着当时式样的服装的演员

pe·ri·od·ic /ˌpɪrɪˋɑdɪk; ˌpɪəriˈɒdɪk◂/ also 又作 **periodical** *adj* [only before noun 仅用于名词前] happening repeatedly, usually at regular times 周期（性）的；定期的：*periodic bouts of depression* 抑郁症的定期发作 —compare 比较 SPASMODIC (1) —**periodically** /-klɪ; -kli/ *adv*: *Teachers meet periodically to discuss progress.* 教师定期开会讨论进展情况。

pe·ri·od·i·cal /ˌpɪrɪˋɑdɪkḷ; ˌpɪəriˈɒdɪkəl/ *n* [C] a magazine, especially one about a serious or technical subject, that comes out at regular times such as once a month 期刊, 杂志

periodic ta·ble /ˌ‧‧‧‧ˈ‧ ‧/ *n* [singular] a list of ELEMENTS (=simple chemical substances) arranged according to their ATOMIC STRUCTURE（元素）周期表

period pain /ˈ‧‧‧ ˌ‧/ *n* [U] pain that a woman gets when she has her PERIOD[1] (4) 月经痛, 痛经; CRAMPS[1] (2) *AmE*【美】

period piece /ˈ‧‧‧ ˌ‧/ *n* [C] **1** something that was very modern when it was first made, written etc, but now seems old-fashioned 一度时兴但现已过时的物品[作品] **2** a typical example of something, such as a piece of furniture or work of art, from a particular period in history 具有某一历史时期特点的东西〈如家具或艺术品〉

per·i·pa·tet·ic /ˌpɛrəpəˋtɛtɪk; ˌperǝpəˈtetɪk◂/ *adj formal* travelling from place to place, especially in order to do your job【正式】〔尤指为工作而〕到处旅行的, 到处走的: *a peripatetic music teacher* 巡回音乐教师 —**peripatetically** /-kḷɪ; -kli/ *adv*

pe·riph·e·ral¹ /pəˋrɪfərəl; pəˈrɪfərəl/ *adj* **1** connected to the main idea, question or activity, but much less important, and given much less attention 次要的, 非主要的: *Can we leave the peripheral issues till later?* 我们能不能把这些次要问题留待以后再说? | **[+to]** *The love interest is peripheral to the main plot of the movie.* 对爱情的关注相对整部电影的主要情节来说是次要的。**2** in the outer area of something or related to this area 外围的, 周边的, 边缘的: *the city's peripheral suburbs* 这个城市的市郊住宅区 **3** peripheral equipment can be connected to a computer and used with it〔电脑设备〕外围的, 周边的, 外部的: *peripheral software*（电脑）外围软件 —**peripherally** *adv*

peripheral² *n* [C] a piece of equipment that is connected to a computer and used with it, for example a PRINTER[1]〔电脑的〕外围[周边]设备〈如打印机〉

pe·riph·e·ry /pəˋrɪfərɪ; pəˈrɪfəri/ *n* **1** [C usually singular 一般用单数] the outer area or edge that surrounds a place 外围, 边缘: **[+of]** *a residential area on the periphery of the city* 位于城市边缘的住宅区 —compare 比较 OUTSKIRTS **2 be on the periphery** to be only slightly involved in a group or activity〔与某团体或活动〕稍有牵连的, 处于…外围的: *extremists on the periphery of the animal rights movement* 与动物权利运动稍有牵连的极端分子

pe·riph·ra·sis /pəˋrɪfrəsɪs; pəˈrɪfrəsǝs/ *n plural* **periphrases** [C,U] *formal*【正式】**1** the unnecessary use of long words or phrases or unclear expressions 迂说(法)〔指不必要地使用较长的单词、短语或不清晰的表达法〕**2** *technical* the use of AUXILIARY words instead of inflected (INFLECT (1)) forms【术语】迂说法〔用助动词而不用屈折变化的表达法〕—**periphrastic** /ˌpɛrəˋfræstɪk; ˌperǝˈfræstɪk◂/ *adj*

per·i·scope /ˋpɛrəˌskop; ˈperǝskəʊp/ *n* [C] a long tube with mirrors fitted in it used to look over the top of something, especially to see out of a SUBMARINE〔尤指潜水艇上用的〕潜望镜

per·ish /ˋpɛrɪʃ; ˈperɪʃ/ *v* **1** [I] *especially literary* to die, especially in a terrible or sudden way【尤文】死亡〔尤指惨死或猝死〕: *Hundreds perished when the ship went down.* 轮船沉没, 数百人遇难。**2** [I,T] *BrE, technical in AmE* if a material such as rubber or leather perishes, it decays and loses its natural strength【英, 美术语】〔橡胶或皮革的〕损坏, 腐烂, 老化 **3 Perish the thought!** *spoken* used as a reply to an unacceptable idea or suggestion, to say that you hope this never happens【口】但愿这事永远不会发生! 死了心吧!〔用来答复不能接受的观点或建议〕

per·ish·a·ble /ˋpɛrɪʃəbḷ; ˈperɪʃəbəl/ *adj* food that is perishable is likely to decay if it is not kept in the proper conditions〔食品〕易腐烂的, 易变质的: *perishable goods such as butter, milk, fruit and fish* 黄油、牛奶、水果和鱼等易变质的商品 —**perishables** *n* [plural]

per·ished /ˋpɛrɪʃt; ˈperɪʃt/ *adj* **1** *BrE spoken* feeling very cold【英口】感到很冷的: *I wish I'd brought a jacket – I'm perished!* 我真希望带了件夹克来——我现在冷得要命! **2** *BrE,technical in AmE* material such as rubber that is perished has lost its strength and become useless【英, 美术语】〔橡胶等〕老化的; 无用的: *The rubber hoses were found to be perished and had to be replaced.* 这些橡胶软管已经老化, 需要更换。

per·ish·er /ˋpɛrɪʃɚ; ˈperɪʃə/ *n* [C] *BrE old-fashioned* a child that behaves badly【英, 过时】淘气的小孩: *Come here, you little perisher!* 到这儿来, 你这个小淘气鬼!

per·ish·ing /ˋpɛrɪʃɪŋ; ˈperɪʃɪŋ/ *adj spoken especially BrE*【口, 尤英】**1** weather that is perishing is very cold〔天气〕非常冷的: *It's really perishing this morning!* 今天早上简直冷死了! **2** feeling very cold 感到非常冷的: *Let's go indoors. I'm perishing!* 我们进屋去吧——我冷死了! **3** *old-fashioned* used to describe someone or something that is annoying you【过时】讨厌的; 该死的〔用于描述令人讨厌的人或事〕: *Tell those perishing kids to shut up!* 叫那些该死的孩子别吵了! —**perishingly** *adv*: *perishingly cold* 冷得要命

per·i·style /ˋpɛrəˌstaɪl; ˈperǝstaɪl/ *n* [C] *technical* a row of PILLARS around an open space in a building or the open space itself【术语】列柱廊; 列柱中庭

per·i·to·ni·tis /ˌpɛrətəˋnaɪtɪs; ˌperǝtəˈnaɪtǝs/ *n* [U] *technical* a poisoned and sore condition of the inside wall of your ABDOMEN (=part around and below your stomach)【术语】腹膜炎

per·i·wig /ˋpɛrəˌwɪg; ˈperɪwɪg/ *n* [C] a white WIG with rolls or curls at the sides, worn in the 18th century〔18 世纪戴的白色〕假发

per·i·win·kle /ˋpɛrəˌwɪŋkḷ; ˈperɪwɪŋkəl/ *n* **1** [C] a small plant with light blue or white flowers that grows close to the ground 长春花 **2** [C] a small sea animal that lives in a shell and can be eaten; WINKLE[2] 滨螺, 玉黍螺 **3** [U] a light blue colour 淡蓝色

per·jure /ˋpɝdʒɚ; ˈpɜːdʒə/ *v* [I] **perjure yourself** to tell a lie after promising to tell the truth in a court of law〔在法庭上〕作伪证; 起[发]假誓

per·jur·er /ˋpɝdʒərɚ; ˈpɜːdʒərə/ *n* [C] someone who tells a lie after promising to tell the truth in a court of law〔在法庭上〕作伪证者; 发假誓者

per·ju·ry /ˋpɝdʒərɪ; ˈpɜːdʒəri/ *n* [C,U] the crime of telling a lie after promising to tell the truth in a court of law, or a lie told in this way 伪证罪; 伪誓: *Hall was found guilty of perjury.* 霍尔被判犯有伪证罪。

perk¹ /pɝk; pɜːk/ *n* [C usually plural 一般用复数] something that you get legally from your work in addition to your wages such as goods, meals, or a car〔工资以外的〕额外收入〈如实物、膳食或汽车〉, 津贴: *With all the perks, she's really earning over £20,000 a year.* 加上她的全部津贴, 她每年实际上的工资超过两万英镑。| **one of the perks of the job** *I get a company car – it's one of the perks of the job.* 我得到公司的一辆汽车——这是该项工作的额外津贴之一。

perk² *v* [I,T] *informal* to percolate (PERCOLATE (3))【非正式】滤煮〔咖啡〕

perk up *phr v informal*【非正式】**1** [I,T] to become more cheerful and interested in what is happening around you, or to make someone feel this way（使）快活[振作]起来: *Zara perked up when her boyfriend's letter arrived.* 扎拉收到男朋友的来信后, 精神为之一振。| **perk sb ↔ up** *Have a cup of tea – that'll perk you up.* 喝杯茶——那会帮你提提神。**2** [T **perk** sb/sth ↔ **up**] to make someone or something look brighter, neater etc 使看起来较为鲜亮[整洁]: *You can soon perk the room up with a coat of paint.* 刷一层漆, 一下子就能使这个房间焕然一新。

perk·y /ˋpɝkɪ; ˈpɜːki/ *adj informal* confidently cheerful and interested in what is happening around you【非正式】自信而愉快的; 活泼的, 生气勃勃的: *You're very perky today!* 你今天看起来很精神! —**perkily** *adv* —**perkiness** *n* [U]

perm¹ /pɝm; pɜːm/ *n* [C] a process of putting curls into straight hair, by chemical treatment〔用化学剂的〕烫发: *I'm going to have a perm to give my hair more body.* 我要把头发烫一下, 让它显得浓密一些。

perm² *v* [T] **1** to put curls into straight hair by means of a chemical treatment 烫〔发〕: *I'm having my hair permed today.* 我今天要去烫发。**2** *BrE* to choose and combine a number of football games from the list given in the FOOTBALL POOLS【英】〔足球赛赌博中〕选定并组合〔数字〕

per·ma·frost /ˋpɝməˌfrɔst; ˈpɜːməfrɒst/ *n* [U] a layer of soil, in very cold countries, that is always frozen〔寒冷国家的〕永久冻土

per·ma·nence /ˋpɝmənəns; ˈpɜːmənəns/ also 又作 **per·ma·nen·cy** /-nənsɪ; -nənsi/ *n* [U] the state of being permanent 持久（性）; 永久（性）, 永恒（性）: *There's no feeling of permanence about our relationship.* 我们的关系不会长久。

per·ma·nent¹ /ˋpɝmənənt; ˈpɜːmənənt/ *adj* continuing to exist for a long time or for all future time 长久的; 永久的, 永恒的: *a paint that gives woodwork permanent protection against the weather* 长久保护木制品不受风雨侵蚀的涂料 | *I need a permanent job.* 我需要一份固定的工作。| *Natalie seems to have a permanent grin on her face.* 纳塔莉脸上好像永远挂着笑容。| **permanent fixture** (=someone or something that is always there) 总是在某处的人[物] *Dan seems to have become a permanent fixture in her life now.* 丹现在好像已成为她生活中的一部分了。—compare 比较 TEMPORARY —**permanently** *adv*: *The accident left him permanently disabled.* 那次意外事故使他永远残疾了。 S2 W2

permanent² *n* [C] *AmE* a PERM[1]【美】〔用化学剂的〕烫发

permanent wave /ˌ‧‧‧ ˈ‧/ *n* [C] *formal* a PERM[1]【正式】〔用化学剂的〕烫发

permanent way /ˌ‧‧‧ ˈ‧/ *n* [C] *BrE* a railway track and the stones and beams on which it is laid【英】铁路路基, 轨道

per·man·ga·nate /pɚˋmæŋgəˏnet; pəˈmæŋgənɪ̀t/ also 又作 **permanganate of potash** *n* [U] a dark purple chemical compound used for killing BACTERIA 高锰酸钾

per·me·a·ble /ˋpɝmɪəbl; ˈpɜːmiəbəl/ *adj formal or technical* material that is permeable allows water, gas etc to pass through it【正式或术语】可渗透的, 具渗透性的: *a fine-grained permeable rock* 纹理细密的渗水岩 —opposite 反义词 IMPERMEABLE —**permeability** /ˏpɝmɪəˋbɪlətɪ; ˌpɜːmiəˈbɪlɪ̀ti/ *n* [U]

per·me·ate /ˋpɝmɪˏet; ˈpɜːmieɪt/ *v* **1** [I always+adv/prep, T] if liquid, gas etc permeates something, it enters it and spreads through every part of it〔液体、气体等〕渗透, 渗入; 弥漫(于): *Toxic chemicals may permeate the soil, threatening the environment.* 有毒化学品会渗入土壤, 威胁环境。| [**+through/into**] *Water had permeated through cracks in the wall.* 水从墙缝里渗了进来。**2** [T] if ideas, beliefs, emotions etc permeate something, they are present in every part and have an effect on all of it〔观点、信念、感情等〕充满于: *A feeling of sadness permeates all his music.* 他的音乐全都充满着悲哀的情绪。—**permeation** /ˏpɝmɪˋeʃən; ˌpɜːmiˈeɪʃən/ *n* [U]

per·mis·si·ble /pɚˋmɪsəbl; pəˈmɪsɪ̀bəl/ *adj formal* allowed by law or by the rules【正式】〔根据法律或规定〕允许的, 许可的, 准许的: *maximum permissible levels of radiation* 允许的最大辐射强度 —**permissibly** *adv*

2 3 **per·mis·sion** /pɚˋmɪʃən; pəˈmɪʃən/ *n* [U] an act of officially allowing someone to do something 允许, 许可, 准许: **permission to do sth** *I applied to the authorities for permission to cross the frontier.* 我向当局申请批准我越过边境。| **give sb permission (to do sth)** *Who gave you permission to leave class early?* 谁准许你提早离开课堂的? | **ask permission (from sb)** *If you want to take photographs, you must ask permission from the warden.* 要想拍照必须征得管理员的许可。| **with your permission** *spoken* (=used to politely ask someone for permission to do something)【口】如果你准许的话〔用于礼貌地征求某人的许可〕*With your permission, I'll send a copy of this letter to the doctor.* 如果你准许的话, 我就把这封信的副本寄给那位医生。—see also 另见 PLANNING PERMISSION

per·mis·sive /pɚˋmɪsɪv; pəˈmɪsɪv/ *adj* allowing behaviour, especially sexual behaviour, that many other people disapprove of〔尤指对许多人反对的性行为〕纵容的, 宽容的: *parents who are too permissive* 过分纵容的父母 | *the permissive society of the 1960s* 20世纪60年代性开放的社会 —**permissiveness** *n* [U]: *permissiveness in education* 教育上的放任 —**permissively** *adv*

3 **per·mit¹** /pɚˋmɪt; pəˈmɪt/ *v* **permitted, permitting** [T] **1** *formal* to allow something to happen, especially by an official order or decision【正式】〔尤指根据正式命令或决定〕允许, 准许, 许可: *Smoking is only permitted in the public lounge.* 只允许在公共休息室里抽烟。| **permit sb sth** *You are not permitted access to confidential files.* 你不准翻看机密档案。| **permit sb to do sth** *I am afraid I cannot permit my daughter to marry you.* 恐怕我不会允许我的女儿嫁给你。| **permit sth in/near etc** *Dogs are not permitted inside the shop.* 狗不准进入店内。**2** [I] to make it possible for something to happen 容许, 许可: *I'll see you after the meeting, if time permits.* (=if it finishes early enough) 如果时间许可的话, 我开完会去见你。| **weather permitting** (=if the weather is good enough) 如果天气允许的话, 假如天气好的话 *We'll have a picnic in the woods, weather permitting.* 如果天气好, 我们将在树林里野餐。**3** also 又作 **permit of** [T] *formal* to make something possible【正式】容许有; 允许有: *The facts permit of no other explanation.* 这些事实不容有其他解释。

Frequencies of the verbs **let**, **allow** and **permit** in spoken and written English 动词let, allow 和 permit 在英语口语和书面语中的使用频率

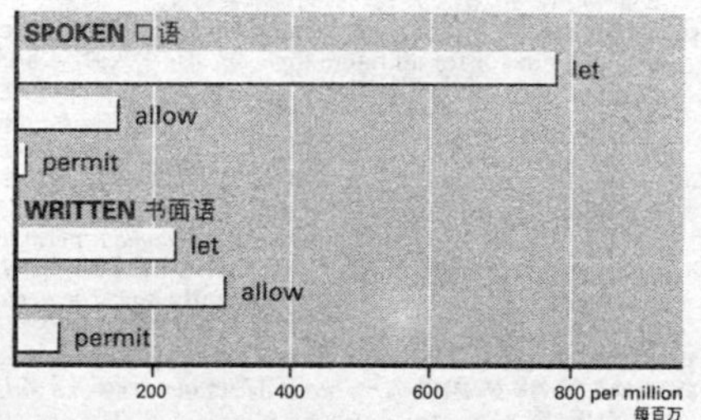

Based on the British National Corpus and the Longman Lancaster Corpus 据英国国家语料库和朗文兰开斯特语料库

This graph shows that **let** is much more common in spoken English than **allow** and **permit**. **Allow** is more common in written English. **Permit** is a formal word meaning to officially let someone do something. 本图表显示, let 在英语口语中的使用频率远远高于 allow 和 permit。allow 在书面语中较常用。permit 较正式, 意思为正式地准许某人做某事。

per·mit² /ˋpɝmɪt; ˈpɜːmɪt/ *n* [C] an official written statement giving you the right to do something 许可证: *You're not allowed to park here unless you have a permit.* 除非你有许可证, 否则不许在这儿停车。| **a travel/work/export etc permit** *The authorities may refuse to issue an export permit.* 当局可以拒绝签发出口许可证。—see also 另见 WORK PERMIT

per·mu·ta·tion /ˏpɝmjəˋteʃən; pɜːmjʊˈteɪʃən/ *n* [C] one of the different ways in which a number of things can be arranged in order〔数学的〕排列, 置换: *The six possible permutations of two letters chosen from ABC are AB, BA, CB, BC, AC, and CA.* 从ABC中取两个字母有六组可能的排列, 即AB, BA, CB, BC, AC及CA。—compare 比较 COMBINATION —**permute** *v* [T]

per·ni·cious /pɚˋnɪʃəs; pəˈnɪʃəs/ *adj formal* very harmful or evil, often in a way that you do not notice easily【正式】很有害的; 恶性的: *the pernicious effect of horror videos on children* 恐怖录像对少年儿童的极坏影响 | *a pernicious lie* 恶毒的谎言 —**perniciously** *adv* —**perniciousness** *n* [U]

pernicious a·nae·mi·a /·ˏ·· ··ˋ··/ *n* [U] *technical* a form of severe ANAEMIA (=too few red blood cells in the blood) that will kill the sick person if it is not treated【术语】恶性贫血

per·nick·e·ty /pɚˋnɪkɪtɪ; pəˈnɪkɪ̀ti/ *adj BrE informal*【英, 非正式】**1** worrying too much about small and unimportant things; FUSSY (1)【英】吹毛求疵的; 爱挑剔的; PERSNICKETY *AmE*【美】**2** difficult to do because you have to deal with a lot of small objects; FIDDLY (1) 精细的, 需要仔细的: *Changing this fridge lightbulb is a pernickety job.* 更换这个冰箱的灯泡是一项精细的工作。

Per·nod /pɛrˋno; ˈpɜːnəʊ/ *trademark* a type of strong alcoholic drink from France, tasting of ANISEED. Pernod is a clear liquid, but it becomes cloudy when it is mixed with water.【商标】佩诺〔一款法国出产的烈酒, 有茴香味, 清澈透明, 掺水即变浑浊〕

Pe·rón /pɛˋron; peˈrɒn/, **E·va** /ˋevə; ˈeɪvə/ (1919-52) an Argentinian actress who married Juan Perón in 1945. When he became president of Argentina in 1946, she became active in social and educational work in the country, and this made her extremely popular. 庇隆夫人〔(1919-1952), 阿根廷女演员, 1945年与胡安·庇隆结婚。1946年, 庇隆就任阿根廷总统, 她开始积极参与阿根廷的政治和教育事业, 深受民众喜爱〕

Perón, Juan Do·min·go /hwɑn dəˋmɪŋgo; wɑːn dəˈmɪŋgəʊ/ (1895-1974) an army officer who became president of Argentina in 1946. He and his wife Eva Perón were very popular but after she died he lost a lot of his popularity and had to leave the country in 1955. He returned and became president again in 1973. 庇隆〔(1895-1974), 阿根廷军官, 1946年就任总统。他与妻子伊娃·庇隆深受民众喜爱, 但妻子去世后, 他名声大跌, 1955年只好离开阿根廷。1973年回国后再次担任总统〕

per·o·ra·tion /ˏpɛroˋreʃən; ˌperəˈreɪʃən/ *n* [C] *technical*【术语】**1** the last part of a speech, especially a part in which the main points are repeated〔演说的〕结束语, 总结 **2** *formal* a long speech that sounds impressive but does not have much meaning【正式】夸夸其谈的长篇演说

per·ox·ide /pəˋrɑksaɪd; pəˈrɒksaɪd/ *n* [U] a chemical liquid used to make dark hair lighter or to kill BACTERIA 过氧化氢〔用作漂染头发剂或防腐剂〕

peroxide blonde /·ˏ·· ˈ·/ *n* [C] *old-fashioned* a woman who has changed the colour of her hair to very light yellow by using peroxide【过时】用过氧化氢把头发漂染成浅黄色的女人

per·pen·dic·u·lar¹ /ˏpɝpənˋdɪkjəlɚ; ˌpɜːpənˈdɪkjɪ̀lə◂/ *adj* **1** not leaning to one side or the other but exactly upright; VERTICAL¹ (1) 直立的, 垂直的: *a perpendicular line* 垂直线 | *a perpendicular wall of rock* 笔直的石墙 **2 be perpendicular to** if one line is perpendicular to another line, they form an angle of 90 degrees〔线〕与…成直角 **3 Perpendicular** in the style of 14th and 15th century English churches which are decorated with straight, upright lines〔14、15世纪英格兰教堂〕垂直式装饰风格的 —**perpendicularly** *adv* —**perpendicularity** /ˏpɝpəndɪkjəˋlærətɪ; ˌpɜːpəndɪkjɪ̀ˈlærɪ̀ti/ *n* [U]

perpendicular² *n* **the perpendicular** an exactly upright position or line 直立姿势; 垂直线: *at an angle to the perpendicular* 与垂直线成一定角度

per·pe·trate /ˋpɝpəˏtret; ˈpɜːpɨtreɪt/ *v* [T] *formal* to do something that is morally wrong or criminal【正式】做〔错事〕; 犯〔罪〕: *crimes that have been perpetrated in the name of religion* 以宗教名义犯下的罪行 —**perpetrator** *n* [C]: *We'll bring the perpetrators to justice.* 我们将把罪犯缉拿归案。—**perpetration** /ˏpɝpəˋtreʃən; ˌpɜːpɨˈtreɪʃən/ *n* [U]: *the perpetration of crime* 犯罪

per·pet·u·al /pɚˋpɛtʃuəl; pəˈpetʃuəl/ *adj* **1** continuing all the time without stopping, especially in a way that is worrying 连续不断的, 无休止的: *the perpetual noise of the machines* 不绝于耳的机器噪音 | *His wife lived in perpetual fear of his fiery temper.* 他的妻子一直生活在对他暴躁脾气的恐惧之中。**2** repeated many times in a way that annoys you〔令人讨厌地〕一再重复的: *Ella's perpetual moaning nearly drove me mad.* 埃拉没完没了的呻吟几乎把我逼疯了。**3** *literary* permanent【文】永久的, 永恒的: *the perpetual snows of the mountaintops* 山顶上的终年积雪 —**perpetually** *adv*

per·pet·u·ate /pɚˋpɛtʃuˏet; pəˈpetʃueɪt/ *v* [T] to make something continue to exist for a long time 使长存; 使永恒: *an education system that perpetuates the divisions in our society* 使我们的社会长期分化的一种教育制度 —**perpetuation** /pɚˏpɛtʃuˋeʃən; pəˌpetʃuˈeɪʃən/ *n* [U]

per·pe·tu·i·ty /ˏpɝpəˋtuətɪ; ˌpɜːpɨˈtjuːɨti/ *n* **in perpetuity** *law* for all future time【法律】永久; 永恒; 永远: *The community does not own land in perpetuity.* 公众对土地并没有永久的拥有权。

per·plex /pɚˋplɛks; pəˈpleks/ *v* [T usually passive 一般用被动态] if something perplexes you, it makes you feel worried and confused because it is difficult to understand 使困惑, 使茫然, 使费解: *I was somewhat perplexed by his response.* 我有点儿被他的回答弄糊涂了。| *a perplexing problem* 一个令人困惑的问题

per·plexed /pɚˋplɛkst; pəˈplekst/ *adj* confused and worried by something that you do not understand 困惑的, 茫然的; 糊涂的: *She looked up at me with a perplexed stare.* 她抬起头迷惑地盯着我。—**perplexedly** /pɚˋplɛkstlɪ; pəˈpleksɨdli/ *adv*: *Florian was examining her perplexedly.* 弗洛里安正迷惑地打量着她。

per·plex·i·ty /pɚˋplɛksətɪ; pəˈpleksɨti/ *n* **1** [U] the feeling of being confused or worried by something you cannot understand 困惑, 茫然 **2** [C usually plural 一般用复数] something that is complicated or difficult to understand 复杂的事物; 使人困惑的事物; 令人费解的事物: *moral perplexities* 道德上的复杂性

per·qui·site /ˋpɝkwəzɪt; ˈpɜːkwɨzɪt/ *n* [C] *formal* a PERK[1]【正式】〔工资以外的〕额外收入, 津贴

Per·ri·er /ˋpɛrɪe; ˈperieɪ/ *trademark* a type of MINERAL WATER from Vergèze in the south of France, which naturally has a lot of BUBBLES in it【商标】巴黎水, 沛绿雅〔法国南部维里耶出产的一种矿泉水, 这种矿泉水中有许多天然的气泡〕: *Could I have two beers and a Perrier, please?* 请来两杯啤酒和一杯巴黎水。

per·ry /ˋpɛrɪ; ˈperi/ *n* [U] *especially BrE* an alcoholic drink made from PEARS【尤英】梨子酒

Perry, Fred /frɛd; fred/ (1909-95) a British TENNIS player who won the men's singles competition at Wimbledon three times (1934-36). He later started a successful company making sports clothes. 佩里〔(1909-1995),英国网球运动员, 1934-1936 年三次获温布尔登网球赛男单冠军。后来, 他成功创建了一个体育服装公司〕

per se /pɝ ˋsi; ˌpɜː ˈseɪ/ *adv Latin* a word meaning 'in itself' or 'by itself', used to say that something is being considered alone, not in connection with other things【拉丁】本身; 就本身而言: *The music per se was not very good, but it did help to create the right atmosphere.* 这音乐本身并不太好, 但它的确帮助营造了合适的气氛。

per·se·cute /ˋpɝsɪˏkjut; ˈpɜːsɪkjuːt/ *v* [T] **1** to treat someone cruelly over a period of time, especially because of their religious or political beliefs〔尤指因宗教、政治信仰不同而在一段时期中〕迫害: *Puritans left England to escape being persecuted.* 清教徒离开了英格兰以躲避迫害。**2** to deliberately cause trouble for someone by continually annoying them; HARASS 骚扰, 烦扰; 纠缠: *Actors complained of being persecuted by the press.* 演员抱怨说受到新闻界的纠缠。—**persecutor** *n* [C] —**persecution** /ˏpɝsɪˋkjuʃən; ˌpɜːsɪˈkjuːʃən/ *n* [C,U]: *the persecution of writers who criticize the government* 对批评政府的作家的迫害

persecution com·plex /ˏ··ˋ·· ˏ··/ *n* [C] a mental illness in which someone believes that other people are continually trying to harm them 受迫害妄想症, 被迫害情结

Per·se·pho·ne /pɚˋsɛfənɪ; pəːˈsefəni/ in Greek MYTHOLOGY, the daughter of Zeus who was taken to the Underworld (=the place under the ground where the spirits of dead people live) by Pluto, the god of the Underworld, and made queen there. Zeus allowed her to return, but only for six months each year, from the beginning of spring to the end of summer. As a result, she represents death and rebirth, and the change from winter into spring. In Roman mythology her name is **Proserpina**, and in English she is sometimes called **Proserpine**. 珀耳塞福涅〔希腊神话中宙斯之女。她被冥王普路托带到阴间做了冥后。宙斯允许她回家, 但每年只能从早春到夏末在家住六个月。于是, 她成了死亡与再生、冬春季节变换的化身。罗马神话中称她为 Proserpina (普罗塞耳皮娜), 英语中有时称她为 Proserpine (普罗塞耳皮恩)〕

Per·se·us /ˋpɝsɪəs; ˈpɜːsiəs/ in ancient Greek stories, a HERO who killed Medusa 珀尔修斯〔古希腊神话中杀死美杜萨的英雄〕

per·se·ver·ance /ˏpɝsəˋvɪrəns; ˌpɜːsɨˈvɪərəns/ *n* [U] *approving* determination to keep trying to achieve something in spite of difficulties【褒】不屈不挠, 坚持不懈: *Beth has shown great perseverance in trying to overcome her handicap.* 贝丝在努力克服残疾的过程中表现出坚忍的毅力。

per·se·vere /ˏpɝsəˋvɪr; ˌpɜːsɨˈvɪə/ *v* [I] *approving* to continue trying to do something in a very determined way in spite of difficulties【褒】坚韧不拔, 坚持不懈: [+at/in/with] *Rob keeps persevering in his efforts to learn French.* 罗布坚持不懈地学习法语。—**persevering** *adj*

Per·sia /ˋpɝʒə; ˈpɜːʃə/ the name used for Iran from ancient times until the early 20th century 波斯〔伊朗旧称, 从古代一直沿用至20世纪初〕

Per·sian[1] /ˋpɝʒən; ˈpɜːʃən/ *n* **1** [U] the language of Iran; FARSI 波斯语, 伊朗语 **2** [C] someone from Iran 波斯人, 伊朗人

Persian[2] *adj* from or connected with Iran, which used to be known as Persia 波斯的, 伊朗的: *a Persian carpet* 波斯地毯

Persian cat /ˏ·· ˋ·/ *n* [C] a cat with long silky hair 波斯猫

Persian Gulf, the also 又作 **the Arabian Gulf, the Gulf** a part of the Indian Ocean between Iran and the Arabian Peninsula 波斯湾〔印度洋的一部分, 位于伊朗和阿拉伯半岛之间〕

per·si·flage /ˋpɝsɪˏflɑʒ; ˈpɜːsɪflɑːʒ/ *n* [U] *formal* amusing talk, which usually includes laughing at other people【正式】〔通常含有嘲弄别人意味的〕打趣; 玩笑; 挖苦

per·sim·mon /pɚˋsɪmən; pəˈsɪmən/ *n* [C] a soft orange-coloured fruit that grows in hot countries 柿, 柿子 —see picture on page A8 参见 A8 页图

per·sist /pɚˋsɪst; pəˈsɪst/ *v* **1** to continue to do something, although this is difficult, or other people warn you not to do it 坚持; 执意: **persist in (doing) sth** *If you persist in causing trouble, the company may be forced to dismiss you.* 如果你坚持制造麻烦, 公司可能不得不解雇你。| *"I'm sorry, I just don't think it's right," John persisted.* "我很抱歉, 我只是认为那不对。"约翰坚持说道。**2** [I] to continue to exist or happen 继续存在[发生]: *Despite official denials, the rumours persisted.* 尽管官方否认, 谣言仍在继续流传。

per·sis·tent /pɚˋsɪstənt; pəˈsɪstənt/ *adj* **1** continuing to do something, although this is difficult, or other people warn you not to do it 坚持的; 执意的: *Paul is amazingly persistent in trying to get Gina to go out with him.* 保罗以惊人的执著在追求吉娜。| *Persistent attempts to interview Garbo were fruitless.* 试图采访嘉宝的不懈努力毫无结果。| **persistent offender** (=someone who continually breaks the law) 惯犯 **2** continuing to exist or happen, especially for longer than is usual or desirable 持续存在[发生]的: *the persistent bad weather* 持续的坏天气 | *persistent headaches* 持续的头疼 —**persistently** *adv*: *He persistently called her at home.* 他不断地往她家里打电话。—**persistence** *n* [U]

per·snick·e·ty /pɚˋsnɪkɪtɪ; pəˈsnɪkɨti/ *adj AmE* PERNICKETY【美】吹毛求疵的; 爱挑剔的

per·son /ˋpɝsn; ˈpɜːsən/ *n* **1** [C] *plural* **people** a human being, especially considered as someone with their own particular character 人: *Tessa's a very intense person.* 特莎是个非常热情的人。| *Hank's not the sort of person I find easy to talk to.* 汉克不是那种我觉得容易交谈的人。| *I like her as a person, but not as a boss.* 我喜欢的是她本人, 而不是因为她是老板。| *What nice young people!* 多好的年轻人啊! | *The person I need to speak to isn't here.* 我要找他[她]谈的那个人不在这儿。—see 见 MAN[1] (USAGE) | **a city/cat etc person** (=someone who likes a particular thing or activity) 喜欢城市/猫等的人 *Are you one of those drama people?* 你属于那种喜欢戏剧的人吗? **2 in person** if you do something in person, you do it by going somewhere yourself, not by letter or asking someone else to do it 亲自: *You have to go sign for it in person, they can't just mail it.* 你必须亲自去签收, 他们不能直接邮寄过来。**3 business-person/salesperson etc** someone who works in business,

selling etc 生意人/推销员等 —see also 另见 CHAIRPERSON, SPOKESPERSON **4** [C] *plural* **persons** *formal or law* someone who is not known or not named【正式或法律】〔不认识或不知其名的〕人: *Any person found trespassing will be prosecuted.* 禁止非法侵入,违者必起诉。| *murder committed by a person or persons unknown* 凶手不明的谋杀案 **5 about/on your person** *formal* on your body or hidden in your clothes【正式】在你身上; 藏在你衣服里: *Customs Officers found a gun concealed about his person.* 海关人员发现他身上藏有一支枪。**6 first/second/third person** one of the three special forms of verbs or PRONOUNs that show the speaker (first person), the one who is being spoken to (second person), or the one who is being spoken about (third person) 第一/第二/第三人称: *The third person singular of the verb 'go' is 'goes'.* 动词 go 的第三人称单数是 goes。| *'I', 'me', and 'we' are all first person pronouns.* I, me 和 we 都是第一人称代词。—see also 另见 FIRST PERSON **7 in the person of** *formal* used before someone's name to emphasize that this is the person who represents a particular group【正式】名叫…的; 即; 那就是〔用在某人的名字前强调此人代表某个团体〕: *I was met by the police in the person of Sergeant Black.* 代表警方接待我的是布莱克警官。—see also 另见 MISSING PERSON, PERSON-TO-PERSON

USAGE NOTE 用法说明: PERSON
GRAMMAR 语法
The usual plural of **person** is **people**. person 通常的复数形式是 people: *Only one person turned up.* 仅有一个人露面。| *A lot of people replied to our advert.* 很多人对我们的广告作出了回应。| *young people* 年轻人
People meaning 'more than one person' is already plural and cannot form a plural with 's'. It always takes a plural verb. people 表示"人们",是复数形式,故不能再加 s 构成复数。它总是与复数动词连用: *Most people are basically honest.* 大多数人基本上是诚实的。| *People are dying of starvation every day* (NOT 不用 *...is dying*). 每天都有人死于饥饿。
People meaning 'race' or 'nation' is countable and you can add 's' in the normal way. people 表示"种族"或"民族"时是可数的,可以用通常的方式加 s 构成复数: *the peoples of South East Asia* 东南亚各民族
Persons is very formal and used, for example, in official language. persons 非常正式,可用于譬如官方语言中: *He was murdered by a person or persons unknown.* 他被不知姓名的人杀害了。You may also see it on offical notices. 也可见于正式公告: *This elevator may only carry eight persons.* 本电梯限乘八人。

per·so·na /pɚˋsonə; pəˈsəʊnə/ *n plural* **personae** /-ni; -niː/ [C] the way you behave when you are with other people, that makes them think that you are a particular type of person〔在公开场合装出的〕伪装外表,表面形象: *Joel has a very cheerful public persona but in private he's very different.* 乔尔在公开场合显得很开朗,但私下里就很不一样了。

per·son·a·ble /ˈpɝsṇəbḷ; ˈpɜːsənəbəl/ *adj* having an attractive appearance and a pleasant, polite way of talking and behaving 英俊的; 有风度的,有魅力的: *a very personable young man* 一位英俊潇洒的年轻人

per·son·age /ˈpɝsṇɪdʒ; ˈpɜːsənɪdʒ/ *n* [C] *formal*【正式】**1** a famous or important person 名人,要人: *a royal personage* 皇室要人 **2** a character in a play or book, or in history〔戏剧、书籍或历史中的〕人物,角色

per·son·al¹ /ˈpɝsṇl; ˈpɜːsənəl/ *adj*
1 ►DONE YOURSELF 本人做的◄ [only before noun 仅用于名词前] done, learned, or experienced by you yourself 亲自的,亲身的: *I know from personal experience that you can't trust Ralph.* 从我的亲身经历来说,我认为你不能相信拉尔夫。| *The Mayor promised to give the matter his personal attention.* 市长答应亲自处理此事。| *I'll take personal responsibility if this doesn't work.* 如果这行不通,由我本人负责。| **personal contact** (=meeting and dealing with people yourself directly) 直接与人接触,亲自与人打交道 *As you get promoted in a firm you lose that personal contact.* 当你在公司里得到提升,你就失去了与人直接接触的机会。
2 ►PRIVATE 私人的◄ concerning only you, especially the private areas of your life 个人的: *May I ask you a personal question?* 我可以问你一个私人问题吗? | *personal problems* 个人隐私问题 | *personal letters* 私人信件 | *I'd tell you what's wrong, but it's a bit personal.* 我会告诉你问题出在哪里,但那有点涉及隐私。| **personal details** (=where you live, how old you are etc)〔住址、年龄等〕个人资料 *You will have to fill out a form giving your personal details.* 你必须要填一张表格提供你的个人资料。
3 ►YOUR OWN 你自己的◄ yours and no one else's 个人的: *Well, that's my personal view, anyway.* 好吧,不管怎样,那是我的个人观点。| *Modern art isn't to my personal taste.* 我个人不喜欢现代艺术。| **my/their etc own personal** *They paid for everything and then he was given his own personal chauffeur to drive him home.* 他们包下了他的一切开支,而且还给他派了一名私人司机送他回家。| **personal possessions/property/belongings** (=things belonging only to you) 私人财物 | **personal effects** *formal* (=small possessions)【正式】随身物品,私人物品 *personal effects scattered all around the wreckage of an aircraft* 散落在飞机残骸周围的私人物品
4 ►CRITICIZING 批评◄ involving rude or upsetting criticism of someone 人身攻击的: *It's unprofessional to make such personal remarks.* 进行这样的人身攻击是违反职业准则的。| **get personal** *You don't have to get so personal!* 你不必进行人身攻击! | **(it's) nothing personal** *spoken* (=used to tell someone that you do not intend to be rude to them)【口】无意冒犯〔用于告诉某人你无意对他们无礼〕*It's nothing personal, I just have to go home now.* 我无意冒犯,我只是现在必须回家了。
5 personal friend someone that you know well, especially a famous or important person 私人朋友〔尤指名人或要人〕: *Apparently the director is a personal friend of hers.* 显然,那位主任是她的私人朋友。
6 ►NOT OFFICIAL 非公务的◄ not concerned with your work, business, or official duties 与公务无关的,私人的: *Please try not to make personal phone calls at work.* 上班时请尽量不要打私人电话。| **sb's personal life** *I don't answer questions about my personal life.* 我不回答有关我私生活的问题。
7 ►YOUR BODY 你的身体◄ [only before noun 仅用于名词前] concerning your body or the way you look 身体的; 容貌的: *Grant was always fussy about his personal appearance.* 格兰特总是过于讲究自己的外表。| *personal hygiene* 个人卫生
8 personal touch something you do to make something special, or that makes someone feel special 个人风格[特色]: *It's those extra personal touches that make our service better.* 正是那些额外的个性化特点使得我们的服务更出色。
9 personal development the improvements in your character that come from your experiences in life 个性发展: *the role of physical activities in the child's personal development* 体育活动在孩子个性发展中所起的作用

personal² *n* [C] *AmE* a short advertisement put in a newspaper or magazine by someone who wants a friend or LOVER【美】〔报纸或杂志上的〕征友[婚]广告

personal al·low·ance /,… ˈ··/ *n* [C] *BrE* the amount of money that you are allowed to earn each year before you start to pay INCOME TAX【英】〔计算所得税时的〕个人免税额; EXEMPTION *AmE*【美】

personal as·sis·tant /,… ·ˈ··/ *n* [C] a PA; a special secretary who works for one person 私人助理,私人秘书

personal col·umn /ˈ… ,··/ *n* [C] a part of a newspaper in which people can have private or personal messages printed〔报纸上的〕人事栏,私人广告栏

personal com·pu·ter /,… ·ˈ··/ *n* [C] a PC; a small computer that is used by one person for business or at home 个人电脑

personal i·den·ti·fi·ca·tion num·ber /,… ….ˈ.. ,.·/ *n* [C] a PIN 个人身份识别码,私人密码

per·son·al·i·ty /,pɝsṇˋælətɪ; ,pɜːsəˈnælɪti/ *n* **1** [C,U] someone's character, especially the way they behave towards other people 个性; 性格: *Iain has a very dynamic personality.* 伊恩是个精力很充沛的人。| *Childhood experiences have a strong influence on forming personality.* 童年经历对个性的形成有很大的影响。| **personality clash** (=when two people find it impossible to work together in a friendly way) 性格冲突 **2** [U] the qualities that make someone interesting, friendly and enjoyable to be with〔使某人有趣、友好、受人喜爱的〕品质; 个性: *The boss likes people with personality.* 那位老板喜欢有个性的人。**3** [C] someone who is well-known to the public, because they are often in the newspapers, on television etc〔因常出现在报纸、电视等上而知名的〕名人: *a TV personality* 电视名人 | *a sports personality* 体育名人 **4 personalities** [plural] *BrE old-fashioned* unkind or rude remarks about someone's appearance, character etc【英,过时】人身攻击,诽谤: *Let's keep personalities out of the conversation, shall we!* 我们谈话时不要带有人身攻击好吗? **5** [C usually singular 一般用单数] the qualities which make a place or thing special〔地方或事物的〕特色: *It's partly the architecture which gives the town its personality.* 这个城镇具有特色一部分原因在于它的建筑。

personality cult /ˌ‥ˈ‥‥ˌ/ *n* [C] the officially encouraged practice of giving too much admiration, praise, love etc to a political leader〔对政治领袖的〕个人崇拜

per·son·al·ize also 又作 **-ise** *BrE*【英】/ˈpɝsn̩ˌaɪz; ˈpɜːsənəlaɪz/ *v* [T usually passive 一般用被动态] **1** to put your name or INITIALS on something, or decorate it in your own way to show that it belongs to you 在…上标出个人的姓名[姓名的首字母], 使个性化: *Why not do something to personalize your office?* 为什么不布置一下使你的办公室具有个性呢? **2** to make something suitable for someone's particular needs or desires 使〔某物〕符合某人的特定需求: *The bank is trying to personalize its service to customers.* 这家银行在努力使自己的服务满足客户的个性化需求。**3** to change the subject of your remarks, arguments etc so that they are more concerned with personal matters or relationships than with facts 使〔评论、争论等〕针对个人, 使个人化: *In the later stages the campaign became highly personalized.* 这项运动在后期变成了过分针对个人的运动。—**personalized** *adj*: *personalized license plates* 个性化车牌—**personalization** /ˌpɝsn̩ləˈzeʃən; ˌpɜːsənəlaɪˈzeɪʃən/ *n* [U]

per·son·al·ly /ˈpɝsn̩lɪ; ˈpɜːsənəli/ *adv*

1 ▶IN YOUR OPINION 以你的观点◀ [sentence adverb 句子副词] *especially spoken* used to emphasize that you are only giving your own opinion about something【尤口】就个人而言; 就自己的看法而言: *Personally, I don't think much of the idea.* 就我本人而言, 我认为这个主意不怎么样。

2 ▶DIRECTLY 直接地◀ doing or having done something yourself rather than through someone else 本人直接地, 亲自地: *I'm holding you personally responsible for this mess!* 出了这样的乱子, 我要唯你是问! | *The managing director wrote personally to thank me.* 那位总经理亲自写信向我表示感谢。

3 take sth personally to let yourself get upset or hurt by the things other people say or do 为某人的言行感到不快: *Don't take it personally; she's rude to everyone.* 不要为此感到不高兴, 她对每个人都没有礼貌。

4 ▶CRITICISM 批评◀ directed against someone's character or appearance in an unpleasant way 攻击人地: *Sue didn't mean those criticisms personally you know.* 你知道, 休所作的那些批评并不是针对某个人的。

5 ▶FRIEND 朋友◀ as a friend, or as someone you have met 作为一个朋友, 作为熟人: *I don't know her personally, but I like her work.* 我并不认识她本人, 但我喜欢她的作品。

personal or·ga·niz·er /ˌ‥ˈ‥‥ˌ/ *n* [C] a small book with loose sheets of paper, or a very small computer, for recording information, addresses, meetings etc〔记录资料、地址、会议等的活页〕记事本;〔记事用的〕掌上电脑

personal pro·noun /ˌ‥ˈ‥ˌ/ *n* [C] *technical* a PRONOUN used for the person who is speaking, being spoken to, or being spoken about, such as 'I', 'you', and 'they'【术语】人称代词〈如 I, you 和 they〉

personal ster·e·o /ˌ‥ˈ‥ˌ/ *n* [C] a small CASSETTE PLAYER which you carry around with you and listen to through small HEAD-PHONES; WALKMAN〔可随身携带, 使用耳机的〕小型放音机, 随身听

personal stereo 小型放音机, 随身听

earphones 耳机

persona non gra·ta /pɚˈsonə ˌnɑn ˈgretə; pəˌsəʊnə nɒn ˈgrɑːtə/ *n* [U] *Latin* someone who is not acceptable to a government or not welcome in someone's house【拉丁】不受欢迎的人: *He was declared persona non grata.* 他被宣布为不受欢迎的人。

per·son·i·fi·ca·tion /pɚˌsɑnəfəˈkeʃən; pəˌsɒnɪ̣fɪ̣ˈkeɪʃən/ *n* **1 the personification of** someone who is a perfect example of a quality because they have a lot of it …的化身: *the personification of evil* 罪恶的化身 **2** [C,U] the representation of a thing or a quality as a person, in literature or art〔文学或艺术中的〕拟人化, 人格化: *the personification of Justice as a woman* 正义之神用一位女性的形象来表现

per·son·i·fy /pɚˈsɑnəˌfaɪ; pəˈsɒnɪ̣faɪ/ *v* [T] **1** to think of or represent a quality or thing as a person 把…拟人化[人格化]: *Time is often personified as an old man with a scythe.* 时间经常被拟人化地表现为一位拿着一把长柄镰刀的老人。**2** to represent a particular quality or thing by having a lot of that quality or by being a typical example of that thing 是…的化身[典型]: *Our son is laziness personified.* 我们的儿子是懒惰的典型。| *The President seemed to personify American people in general.* 总统好像代表了全体美国人民。

per·son·nel /ˌpɝsn̩ˈɛl; ˌpɜːsəˈnel/ *n* **1** [plural] the people who work in a company or organization, or in the army, navy etc〔公司、组织或军队等中的〕全体人员; 员工, 全体职员: *medical personnel* 医疗人员 | *All personnel are to receive security badges.* 所有人员都将收到安全徽章。**2** [U] the department in an organization that appoints people to jobs and deals with their complaints, problems etc; HUMAN RESOURCES 人事部门: *Fay finally decided to take her grievance to Personnel.* 费伊最后决定把她的不满向人事部门申诉。

person-to-person /ˌ‥ˈ‥◂/ *adj* **person-to-person call** *AmE* a telephone call that is made to one particular person and does not have to be paid for if they are not there【美】指定受话人的电话, 叫人电话〔如果指定受话人不在则不必付电话费〕

perspective 透视图

a chessboard drawn in perspective
用透视法绘制的国际象棋棋盘

per·spec·tive /pɚˈspɛktɪv; pəˈspektɪv/ *n* **1** [C] a way of thinking about something which is influenced by the kind of person you are or by your experiences〔思考问题的〕角度; 观点; 想法: [+on] *His father's death gave him a whole new perspective on life.* 他父亲的死使他对生活有了全新的看法。| **from the perspective of** *The novel is written from the perspective of a child.* 这部小说是从一个孩子的视角写的。| **from a…perspective** *From a white male perspective, it's hard to understand oppression.* 从一个白人男性的角度来看, 很难理解什么是压迫。**2** [C,U] a sensible way of judging and comparing situations so that you do not imagine that something is more serious than it really is〔对事物的〕合理判断, 正确认识: *I think Viv's lost all sense of perspective.* 我认为维夫已不能明察事理。| **get/keep sth in perspective** (=judge the importance of something correctly) 正确判断某事物的重要性 **3** [U] a method of drawing a picture that makes objects look solid and shows distance and depth, or the effect this method produces in a picture 透视(画)法; 透视效果, 透视感: *Children's drawings often have no perspective.* 儿童画的画通常没有透视感。| **in perspective/out of perspective** (=drawn with or without the effect of perspective) 有透视感/没有透视感 *The background is all out of perspective.* 这背景整个没有透视感。**4** [C] a view, especially one that stretches into the distance〔尤指由近而远的〕景, 远景

per·spex /ˈpɝspɛks; ˈpɜːspeks/ *n* [U] *BrE* a strong plastic material that can be seen through and is used instead of glass【英】珀斯佩有机玻璃〔一种高强度透明塑胶〕; PLEXIGLASS *AmE*【美】

per·spi·ca·cious /ˌpɝspɪˈkeʃəs; ˌpɜːspɪˈkeɪʃəs◂/ *adj formal* good at judging and understanding people and situations【正式】判断力强的; 敏锐的; 有洞察力的: *a perspicacious literary critic* 睿智的文学评论家 | *a perspicacious remark* 有见地的评论—**perspicaciously** *adv*—**perspicacity** /-ˈkæsətɪ; -ˈkæsɪ̣ti/ *n* [U]

per·spi·ra·tion /ˌpɝspəˈreʃən; ˌpɜːspəˈreɪʃən/ *n* [U] **1** liquid that appears on your skin when you are hot; SWEAT[2] (1) 汗, 汗水 **2** the process of perspiring 出汗, 流汗

per·spire /pɚˈspaɪr; pəˈspaɪə/ *v* [I] to become wet on parts of your body, especially because you are hot or have been doing hard work; SWEAT[1] (1) 出汗, 流汗

per·suade /pɚˈswed; pəˈsweɪd/ *v* [T] **1** to make someone decide to do something, especially by repeatedly asking them or telling them reasons why they should do it 说服; 劝服: **persuade sb to do sth** *I finally managed to persuade her to go out for a drink with me.* 我最后终于想法子说服她跟我一起出去喝一杯。| **persuade sb** *Leo wouldn't agree, despite our efforts to persuade him.* 尽管我们努力说服利奥, 他还是不同意。| **persuade sb into doing sth** *Don't let yourself be persuaded into buying things you don't really want.* 不要被别人说服去买那些根本不想要的东西。**2** to make someone believe something or

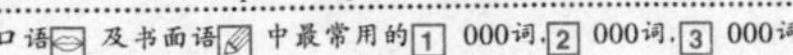

feel sure about something; CONVINCE 使相信，使信服: *I was persuaded by the sheer strength of this argument.* 我被这个极具说服力的论点劝服了。| **persuade sb of sth** *We finally persuaded Ben of the wisdom of this decision.* 我们最终使本相信这项决定是明智的。| **persuade sb (that)** *Carla failed to persuade us that she was innocent.* 卡拉没能使我们相信她是无辜的。

per·sua·sion /pə`sweʒən; pəˈsweɪʒən/ *n* **1** the act or skill of persuading someone to do something 说服; 劝服: *After a little gentle persuasion, Debbie agreed to let us in.* 经过一小会儿温和的劝说，黛比同意让我们进去。| **powers of persuasion** (=skills used for persuading) 说服的技巧 **2** [C] *formal* a particular kind of belief, especially a political or religious one【正式】〔尤指政治或宗教的〕信仰; 信念: *people of all political persuasions* 各种政治信仰的人 **3** [singular] *formal* a strongly held belief or opinion【正式】坚定的信念[看法]: *It has always been my persuasion that capital punishment is wrong.* 我一直坚定地认为死刑是错误的。**4 of the... persuasion** *formal or humorous* of a particular kind【正式或幽默】…种类的，…派别的: *an artist of the modern persuasion* 一位现代派的艺术家

per·sua·sive /pə`swesɪv; pəˈsweɪsɪv/ *adj* good at influencing other people to believe or do what you want 有说服力的: *They used some very persuasive arguments.* 他们用了一些很有说服力的论据。—**persuasively** *adv* —**persuasiveness** *n* [U]

pert /pɝt; pɜːt/ *adj* **1** a girl or woman who is pert is amusing, but slightly disrespectful〔女孩或妇女〕俏皮的; 有点不规矩但有趣的: *Angie gave him one of her pert little glances.* 安吉调皮地瞥了他一眼。**2** clothing that is pert is neat and attractive in a cheerful way〔衣服〕别致的; 俏丽的: *a pert little red hat set well back on her head* 戴在她头顶后的一顶俏丽的小红帽 —**pertly** *adv* —**pertness** *n* [U]

per·tain /pə`ten; pəˈteɪn/ *v*

pertain to sth *phr v* [T] *formal* to be directly connected with something【正式】与…直接相关; 有关，关于: *legislation pertaining to employment rights* 与就业权利有关的立法

Perth /pɝθ; pɜːθ/ **1** a city in southwest Australia, capital of the state of Western Australia and the largest city in the western part of the country 珀斯〔澳大利亚西南部一城市，西澳大利亚州首府。该市是澳大利亚西部最大城市〕**2** a city in central Scotland on the River Tay 珀斯〔苏格兰中部一城市，位于泰河河畔〕

Perth and Kinross a COUNTY in central Scotland 珀斯-金罗斯郡〔苏格兰中部一郡〕

per·ti·na·cious /ˌpɝtn̩`eʃəs; ˌpɜːtɪ̵ˈneɪʃəs◂/ *adj formal* continuing to believe something or to do something in a very determined way; TENACIOUS【正式】固执的; 坚持的; 顽固的 —**pertinaciously** *adv* —**pertinacity** /-n̩`æsətɪ; -ˈnæsɪ̵ti/ *n* [U]

per·ti·nent /`pɝtn̩ənt; ˈpɜːtɪ̵nənt/ *adj formal* directly concerned with something that is being considered: RELEVANT【正式】直接相关的，有关的: *The investigator asked several highly pertinent questions.* 那位调查员问了几个高度相关的问题。| [+to] *Your remarks are not pertinent to today's discussion.* 你的话与今天的讨论不相干。—**pertinently** *adv* —**pertinence** *n* [U] —see also 另见 IMPERTINENT

per·turbed /pə`tɝbd; pəˈtɜːbd/ *adj* worried or annoyed because of something that has happened〔由于发生某事而〕忧虑的，不安的，烦恼的: *Fritz did not seem unduly perturbed when asked to change rooms.* 当弗里茨被要求更换房间时，他好像并没有过分不安。—**perturbation** /ˌpɝtə`beʃən; ˌpɜːtəˈbeɪʃən/ *n* [U] —**perturb** /pə`tɝb; pəˈtɜːb/ *v* [T]

Pe·ru /pə`ru; pəˈruː/ a country on the west coast of South America, north of Bolivia and south of Ecuador. Population: 27,484,000 (2001). Capital: Lima. The high Andes Mountains cover a large part of the country. 秘鲁〔南美洲西海岸一国家，位于玻利维亚以北，厄瓜多尔以南。人口: 27,484,000 (2001)，首都: 利马。耸立的安第斯山脉占据了秘鲁的大部分国土〕

pe·ruse /pə`ruz; pəˈruːz/ *v* [T] *formal or humorous* to read something, especially in a careful way【正式或幽默】〔尤指仔细〕阅读，精读: *I'll give you the leaflet so you can peruse it at your leisure.* 我会把小册子给你，以便你可以在闲暇时仔细阅读。—**perusal** *n* [C,U]

perv /pɝv; pɜːv/ *n* [C] *BrE spoken* a PERVERT² 【英口】性行为反常者，性变态者 —**pervy** *adj*

per·vade /pə`ved; pəˈveɪd/ *v* [T] if a feeling, idea, or smell pervades a place, it spreads through every part of it〔感觉、想法或气味〕弥漫于，遍及，充满: *After the war a spirit of hopelessness pervaded the country.* 战争过后，全国普遍存在着一种绝望的情绪。

per·va·sive /pə`vesɪv; pəˈveɪsɪv/ *adj* existing or spreading everywhere 到处存在的; 到处弥漫着的，遍布的: *the pervasive influence of television* 电视无所不在的影响 | **all-pervasive** (=extremely pervasive) 无所不在的，极其普遍的 *the all-pervasive mood of apathy* 无处不在的冷漠情绪 —**pervasiveness** *n* [U] —**pervasively** *adv*

per·verse /pə`vɝs; pəˈvɜːs/ *adj* continuing to behave in an unreasonable way, especially by deliberately doing the opposite of what people want you to do 任性的; 不合情理的，一意孤行的: *He gets some kind of perverse satisfaction from embarrassing people.* 他有一种不正常的心态，以使别人难堪而获得某种满足。—**perversely** *adv* —**perverseness** *n* [U]

per·ver·sion /pə`vɝʒən; pəˈvɜːʃən/ *n* **1** [C,U] a type of sexual behaviour that is considered unnatural and unacceptable 性反常行为，性变态 **2** [C,U] the process of changing something that is natural and good into something that is unnatural and wrong, or the result of such a change 歪曲，曲解; 堕落，变坏: *a perversion of the true meaning of democracy* 对民主的真正含义的歪曲

per·ver·si·ty /pə`vɝsətɪ; pəˈvɜːsɪ̵ti/ *n* [U] the quality of being perverse 任性，执拗; 反常; 执迷不悟: *Max refused the money out of sheer perversity.* 马克斯拒收那些钱完全是出于任性。

per·vert¹ /pə`vɝt; pəˈvɜːt/ *v* [T] **1** to change something in an unnatural and often harmful way〔以不合自然规律且通常有害的方式〕改变: *Genetic scientists are often accused of perverting nature.* 遗传学家经常被指责破坏了自然状态。**2** to influence someone so that they begin to think or behave in an immoral way; CORRUPT² (1) 使走上邪路，使堕落，使变坏; 腐蚀: *TV sex and violence perverts the minds of young children.* 电视上的性和暴力镜头腐蚀了青少年的心灵。**3 pervert the course of justice** *law* to deliberately prevent a fair examination of the facts about a crime【法律】妨碍司法公正

per·vert² /`pɝvɝt; ˈpɜːvɜːt/ *n* [C] someone whose sexual behaviour is considered unnatural and unacceptable 性行为反常者，性变态者: *What are you, some kind of pervert?* 你是什么? 性变态者吗?

per·vert·ed /pə`vɝtɪd; pəˈvɜːtɪ̵d/ *adj* **1** perverted ways of thinking and behaving, especially sexual behaviour, are unacceptable and unnatural〔思维和行为方式〕反常的;〔尤指性行为〕反常的，变态的 **2** morally wrong or unnatural 道德上错误的; 有悖常理的: *the perverted logic of Nazi propaganda* 纳粹宣传的荒谬逻辑

pe·se·ta /pə`setə; pəˈseɪtə/ *n* [C] the standard unit of money in Spain before the euro 比塞塔〔原西班牙货币单位，现在已为欧元取代〕

pes·ky /`pɛskɪ; ˈpeski/ *adj informal especially AmE* annoying and causing trouble【非正式，尤美】令人讨厌的，惹麻烦的: *Those pesky kids!* 那些令人讨厌的孩子!

pe·so /`peso; ˈpeɪsəʊ/ *n* [C] the standard unit of money in Mexico, Colombia and Cuba 比索〔墨西哥、哥伦比亚和古巴的货币单位〕

pes·sa·ry /`pɛsərɪ; ˈpesəri/ *n* [C] **1** a solid medicine or CONTRACEPTIVE chemical which is put into a woman's VAGINA〔治疗或避孕的〕阴道栓〔剂〕**2** an instrument put into a woman's VAGINA to support her WOMB or as a CONTRACEPTIVE 子宫帽，子宫托

pes·si·mist /`pɛsəmɪst; ˈpesɪ̵mɪst/ *n* [C] someone who always expects that the worst thing will happen 悲观主义者: *Don't be such a pessimist – you're not going to fail.* 别这么悲观——你不会失败的。—opposite 反义词 OPTIMIST —**pessimism** *n* [U]

pes·si·mis·tic /ˌpɛsə`mɪstɪk; ˌpesɪ̵ˈmɪstɪk◂/ *adj* expecting that bad things will happen in the future or that a situation will have a bad result 悲观的; 悲观主义的: [+about] *He remains deeply pessimistic about the peace process.* 他对和平进程仍持极度悲观的态度。—opposite 反义词 OPTIMISTIC —**pessimistically** /-klɪ; -kli/ *adv*

pest /pɛst; pest/ *n* [C] **1** a small animal or insect that destroys crops or food supplies〔毁坏庄稼或食物的〕有害小动物[昆虫]; 害虫: *a chemical used in pest control* 用于防治虫害的化学品 **2** *informal* an annoying person, especially a child【非正式】令人讨厌的人〔尤指孩子〕; 害人精: *Giles was being a thorough pest.* 贾尔斯是个十足的害人虫。

pes·ter /`pɛstə; ˈpestə/ *v* [T] to annoy someone repeatedly, especially by asking them to do something 不断烦扰，纠缠〔尤指不断要求某人做某事〕: **pester sb for sth** *Beggars kept pestering us for money.* 乞丐纠缠着我们要钱。| **pester sb to do sth** *The kids have been pestering me to buy them new trainers.* 孩子一直缠着我，要我给他们买新运动鞋。

pes·ti·cide /`pɛstɪsaɪd; ˈpestɪ̵saɪd/ *n* [C] a chemical substance used to kill insects and small animals that destroy crops 杀虫剂，农药

pes·ti·lence /`pɛstləns; ˈpestɪ̵ləns/ *n* [C,U] *literary* a disease that spreads quickly and kills large numbers of people【文】瘟疫

pes·ti·lent /ˈpɛstḷənt; ˈpestɪ̣lənt/ also 又作 **pes·ti·len·tial** /ˌpɛstḷˈɛnʃəl; ˌpestɪ̣ˈlenʃəl◂/ *adj* **1** *literary or humorous* extremely unpleasant and annoying【文或幽默】特别令人讨厌的; 极其令人不快的 **2** *old use* causing a pestilence【旧】引起瘟疫的

pes·tle /ˈpɛsl; ˈpesəl/ *n* [C] a short stick with a heavy round end, used for crushing things in a MORTAR (=a special bowl)〔捣研用的〕杵, 捣锤 —see picture at 参见 LABORATORY 图

pet¹ /pɛt; pet/ *n* [C] **1** an animal such as a cat or a dog which you keep and look after at home 供玩赏的动物, 宠物〈如猫、狗〉: *Rabbits can make very good pets.* 兔子可以成为很好的宠物。| *a pet tortoise* 宠物乌龟 —see also 另见 TEACHER'S PET **2** *BrE spoken* a way of addressing someone who you like or love【英口】宝贝儿〔用于称呼你喜欢[爱]的人〕**3** **be in a pet** *BrE old-fashioned* to be annoyed【英, 过时】烦恼的, 不痛快的

pet² *v* [T] **1** to touch and stroke someone, especially a child or an animal, in a kind loving way 抚弄; 爱抚: *Our cat loves being petted.* 我们的猫喜欢被人爱抚。**2** to kiss and touch someone as part of a sexual activity〔两性间〕亲吻, 爱抚 —see also 另见 HEAVY PETTING

pet³ *adj* **1** **pet theory/project/subject** a plan, idea, or subject that you particularly like or are interested in 特别喜爱的理论/计划/主题 **2** **pet hate** *BrE*【英】, **pet peeve** *AmE*【美】something that you strongly dislike because it always annoys you 特别讨厌的事物; 极可恶的事物: *TV game shows are one of my pet hates.* 电视游戏节目是我最讨厌的节目之一。

PETA /ˈpɛtə; ˈpetə/ People for the Ethical Treatment of Animals; a US organization that works to prevent cruelty to animals. Its members protest against VIVISECTION and against people wearing clothes made of fur 人道对待动物协会〔美国一组织, 旨在保护动物, 使其免遭虐待。该组织成员既反对动物活体解剖, 也反对人们穿毛皮衣物〕

Pé·tain /peˈtæŋ; peˈtæŋ/, **Marshal Hen·ri** /ɑnˈri; ɒnri/ (1856-1951) a French soldier and politician who was one of the main military commanders of World War I. During World War II, he became Prime Minister of France and was head of the RIGHT WING government in Vichy, which helped the Nazi army that controlled France. After the war he was put in prison for being a COLLABORATOR (=someone who helps an enemy during war). 贝当〔(1856-1951), 法国军人、政治家, 一战主要军事指挥之一。二战期间, 他担任法国总理, 也是维希右翼政府的首脑。维希政府曾给统治法国的纳粹军队提供援助, 二战结束之后, 他以通敌罪被判入狱〕

pet·al /ˈpɛtḷ; ˈpetl/ *n* [C] **1** the coloured part of a flower that is shaped like a leaf 花瓣: *rose petals* 玫瑰花瓣 | *Each of these flowers has seven petals.* 这些花每朵有七个花瓣。**2** **eight-petalled, blue-petalled etc** *BrE*【英】, **-petaled** *AmE*【美】having eight petals, blue petals etc 有八瓣的/有蓝色花瓣的等

pe·tard /pɪˈtɑrd; pɪ̣ˈtɑːd/ *n* —see 见 **be hoist with your own petard** (HOIST¹ (2))

Peter —see 见 **rob Peter to pay Paul** (ROB (3))

pet·er /ˈpitə; ˈpiːtə/ *v*

peter out *phr v* [I] to gradually become smaller or happen less often and then come to an end 逐渐变小; 逐渐减少; 逐渐消失: *The road became narrower and eventually petered out.* 那条路变得越来越窄, 最后消失了。| *Public interest in the environment is in danger of petering out.* 公众对环境的兴趣面临逐渐消失的危险。

Peter, Saint the leader of Jesus Christ's twelve DISCIPLES (=his close friends and followers), who became the leader of the first Christians. He is considered by Catholics to be the first Pope, and Christians think of him as being in charge of the keys of the gates to Heaven. He is sometimes called **Simon Peter**. 圣彼得〔基督耶稣12门徒的第一门徒, 也是早期基督教徒的首领。天主教视其为首任教皇, 基督教徒认为他掌管着天堂之门的钥匙。他有时也叫做西门·彼得〕

Peter Pan /ˌ.. ˈ../ **1** the main character in the play *Peter Pan* (1904) by J. M. Barrie, which has also been made into films. He is a young boy who never grows up but lives in a magic place called Never-Never Land and can fly. Three children, Michael, John, and Wendy, are taken by Peter Pan and a FAIRY called Tinkerbell to stay in Never-Never Land, where they have many adventures. 彼得·潘〔J. M.巴里的剧作《彼得·潘》(1904) 中的主人公。该剧也已改编成了电影。他是个小男孩, 可永远长不大, 住在一个叫梦幻岛的魔界, 具有飞翔的本领。彼得·潘和仙女小叮当还把迈克尔、约翰和温蒂三个孩子一同带到了梦幻岛, 经历了不少奇遇〕**2** a man who never seems to get older or grow up 孩子气的男人: *the Peter Pan of the music business* 音乐界那个看似长不大的男子

Peter Rab·bit /ˌ.. ˈ../ a character from children's stories by Beatrix Potter. He is a young RABBIT who often does things that he is not supposed to do, but his mother still forgives him and loves him. 兔子彼得〔比阿特丽克斯·波特创作的童话故事中的一角色。它是只小兔子, 经常惹祸, 可它的妈妈仍然会原谅它, 也会爱它〕

Peter's pence /ˌ.. ˈ./ **1** money given by Roman Catholics in many countries to help to pay for the running of the Vatican (=the offices of the Pope) 一便士奉金, 圣座献金〔许多国家的罗马天主教徒给梵蒂冈交纳的奉金〕**2** a tax of one penny which each person in England had to pay to the Pope until Henry VIII stopped it in 1534 一便士税金〔英格兰每人必须向教皇缴纳的赋税, 1534年被亨利八世废止〕

Peter the Great /ˌ.. . ˈ./ also 又作 **Peter I** /ˌpitə ðə ˈfɜst; ˌpiːtə ðə ˈfɜːst/ (1672-1725) the TSAR (=ruler) of Russia from 1682 to 1725 彼得大帝〔(1672-1725), 俄国沙皇, 1682至1725年在位〕

Petipa /ˈpɛtɪpɑ; ˈpetipɑː/, **Marius** /ˈmɛrɪəs; ˈmeəriəs/ (1819-1910) a French BALLET dancer and CHOREOGRAPHER (=someone who arranges the way dancers move) who began the modern classical ballet. He was the choreographer for more than sixty ballets, including the famous ballets *The Nutcracker*, *Swan Lake*, and *The Sleeping Beauty*. 佩季帕 (1819-1910), 法国芭蕾舞演员、舞蹈编导, 现代古典芭蕾舞的先驱。他曾担任60多部芭蕾舞剧的编导, 其中有著名芭蕾舞剧《胡桃夹子》、《天鹅湖》和《睡美人》〕

pet·it bour·geois /ˌpɛtɪ ˈburʒwɑ; ˌpeti ˈbʊəʒwɑː/ *adj* another spelling of PETTY BOURGEOIS petty bourgeois 的另一种拼法

pe·tite /pəˈtit; pəˈtiːt/ *adj* a woman who is petite is short and attractively thin〔女子〕娇小的

petit four /ˈpɛtɪ ˈfɔr; ˌpeti ˈfɔə/ *n* [C] *French* a small sweet cake or BISCUIT served with coffee【法】〔配咖啡吃的〕小蛋糕; 小饼干

pe·ti·tion¹ /pəˈtɪʃən; pɪ̣ˈtɪʃən/ *n* [C] **1** a written request signed by a lot of people, asking someone in authority to do something or change something 请愿(书): [+against] *They wanted me to sign a petition against experiments on animals.* 他们要我在反对用动物做实验的请愿书上签名。| **draw up a petition** *Local residents have drawn up a petition to protest the hospital closure.* 当地居民已草拟了抗议医院关闭的请愿书。**2** an official letter to a law court, asking for a legal case to be considered〔向法院递交的〕陈情书, 诉状: *She is threatening to file a petition for divorce.* 她在威胁说要提起离婚诉讼。**3** *formal* a formal prayer or request to someone in authority or to God or to a ruler【正式】〔向当局、上帝或统治者的〕正式请求; 祈求; 祈祷

petition² *v* [I,T] **1** to ask the government or an organization to do something by sending it a petition 向〔政府或组织〕请愿, 请求: **petition sb to do sth** *Villagers petitioned the local authority to provide better bus services.* 村民请求地方当局提供更好的公共汽车服务。| [+against/for] *Residents are petitioning against the new road.* 居民正在请愿反对修建这条新路。**2** to make a formal request to someone in authority, to a court of law, or to God〔向当权者、法庭或上帝〕正式请求, 祈求

pe·ti·tion·er /pəˈtɪʃənə; pɪ̣ˈtɪʃənə/ *n* [C] **1** someone who writes or signs a petition 请愿人; 请愿书签名人 **2** *law* someone who asks for their marriage to be legally ended【法律】离婚申请人, 离婚诉讼原告

petit mal /ˌpɛtɪ ˈmɑl; ˌpeti ˈmæl/ *n* [U] *technical* a form of EPILEPSY which is not very serious【术语】〔癫痫〕小发作 —compare 比较 GRAND MAL

Peter Pan 彼得·潘

pet name /ˌ· ˈ·/ *n* [C] a name you call someone you like very much 爱称, 昵称

Pet·o In·sti·tute, the /ˈpɛto ˌɪnstətjut; ˈpetəʊ ˌɪnstɪ̈tjuːt/ an institution in Budapest, Hungary, started by Dr Andras Peto in 1945, which teaches children who have CEREBRAL PALSY and cannot control their bodies properly to lead more independent lives by means of conductive education 皮托学院〔1945年安德拉斯·皮托博士在匈牙利布达佩斯建立的一个机构, 通过引导式教育教会因脑瘫而无法支配肢体的患儿独立生活〕

Pet·ra /ˈpɛtrə; ˈpetrə/ an ancient city in Jordan, where buildings are cut into pink-coloured rock. It is sometimes called 'the rose-red city, half as old as time', and is visited by many tourists. 佩特拉〔约旦一古城。城内的建筑是在红岩上开凿出来的。该城有时也叫做"玫瑰红古城", 常有不少游人前去观赏〕

Pet·rarch /ˈpetrɑrk; ˈpɛtrɑːk/ (1304-74) an Italian poet whose best known works include the *Canzoniere*, a collection of poems, mostly SONNETS, about his love for a woman named Laura 彼特拉克〔(1304-1374), 意大利诗人。最有名的作品是《抒情诗集》, 其中多为十四行诗, 抒发了他对一位名叫劳拉的女子的爱情〕

pet·rel /ˈpɛtrəl; ˈpetrəl/ *n* [C] a black and white sea bird; STORMY PETREL 海燕

pet·ri·fied /ˈpɛtrəˌfaɪd; ˈpetrɪ̈faɪd/ *adj* **1** extremely frightened, especially so frightened that you cannot move or think 吓呆的, 惊呆的: *She stood there, petrified at the thought of the crowds waiting outside.* 一想到在外面等待的人群, 她吓得一动不动地站在那里。**2 petrified wood/trees/insects etc** wood, trees etc that have changed into stone over a long period of time 石化木/树/昆虫等 **—petrify** *v* [T]: *My new boss absolutely petrifies me.* 我的新老板简直把我吓呆了。**—petrifaction** /ˌpɛtrəˈfækʃən; ˌpetrɪ̈ˈfækʃən/ *n* [U]

Petrified For·est, the /ˌ··· ˈ··/ a large national park in eastern Arizona, US, where the rock surfaces show FOSSILS (=ancient plants and trees that have been preserved in rock) 石化森林〔美国亚利桑那州东部一大型国家公园。园内岩石的表面可见古植物化石的痕迹〕

pet·ro·chem·i·cal /ˌpɛtroˈkɛmɪkl; ˌpetrəʊˈkemɪkəl/ *n* [C] a chemical substance obtained from PETROLEUM or natural gas 石(油)化(学)产品: *the petrochemical industry* 石(油)化(学)工业

pet·ro·dol·lar /ˈpɛtroˌdɑlə; ˈpetrəʊˌdɒlə/ *n* [C] a dollar earned by the sale of oil 石油美元〔出售石油所得的美元〕: *in search of petrodollars from Iran* 从伊朗寻求石油美元

Pet·ro·grad /ˈpɛtrəgræd; ˈpetrəgræd/ the name used from 1914 to 1924 for the Russian city of St Petersburg 彼得格勒〔俄国圣彼得堡旧称, 用于1914至1924年间〕

3 **pet·rol** /ˈpɛtrəl; ˈpetrəl/ *n* [U] *BrE* a liquid that is used to supply power to the engine of cars and other vehicles, which is obtained from PETROLEUM【英】汽油; GASOLINE *AmE*【美】

pet·ro·la·tum /ˌpɛtrəˈletəm; ˌpetrəˈleɪtəm/ *n* [U] *AmE* VASELINE【美】凡士林, 矿脂

petrol bomb /ˈ·· ˌ·/ *n* [C] *BrE* a simple bomb consisting of a bottle filled with petrol with a lighted cloth in the end【英】汽油弹, 燃烧弹

pe·tro·le·um /pəˈtrolɪəm; pɪ̈ˈtrəʊliəm/ *n* [U] oil that is obtained from below the surface of the Earth and is used to make petrol, PARAFFIN and various chemical substances 石油: *petroleum-based products* 石油产品

petroleum jel·ly /ˌ····ˈ··/ *n* [U] *especially BrE* VASELINE【尤英】凡士林, 矿脂, 石油冻

petrol sta·tion /ˈ·· ˌ··/ *n* [C] *BrE* a place where you can take your car and fill it with petrol【英】汽车加油站; GAS STATION *AmE*【美】

pet·ti·coat /ˈpɛtɪˌkot; ˈpetikəʊt/ *n* [C] **1** *especially BrE* a piece of women's underwear that hangs from your shoulders or waist; SLIP[2] (6)【尤英】〔从双肩或腰部垂下的〕衬裙 **2** a long skirt that was worn under a skirt or dress by women in the past〔过去妇女穿在外衣内的〕长衬裙

Petticoat Lane /ˌ··· ˈ·/ a street in the East End of London, where a market is held every week on Sunday morning 衬裙巷, 佩蒂科特街〔伦敦东区一小巷, 每周星期天上午有集市〕

pet·ti·fog·ging /ˈpɛtɪˌfɑgɪŋ; ˈpetiˌfɒgɪŋ/ *adj BrE old-fashioned*【英, 过时】**1** too concerned with small details 过分关注细节的; 吹毛求疵的 **2** too unimportant to be worth considering 无足轻重的, 微不足道的; 琐碎的

pet·ti·ness /ˈpɛtɪnɪs; ˈpetinɪ̈s/ *n* [U] behaviour and attitudes that are ungenerous and are too much concerned with unimportant matters 小心眼; 心胸狭窄: *the jealousy and pettiness of Hollywood* 好莱坞的妒嫉和狭隘

petting zoo /ˈ·· ˌ·/ *n* [C] *AmE* part of a zoo which has baby animals in it for children to touch【美】〔有供儿童抚摸的小动物的〕爱畜动物园

pet·tish /ˈpɛtɪʃ; ˈpetɪʃ/ *adj* PETULANT 任性的; 耍孩子脾气的; 脾气暴躁的 **—pettishly** *adv* **—pettishness** *n* [U]

pet·ty /ˈpɛtɪ; ˈpeti/ *adj* **1** a problem, detail, worry etc that is petty is small and unimportant〔问题、细节、担心等〕小的, 琐碎的, 不重要的: *He said he wasn't interested in petty details.* 他说他对细枝末节不感兴趣。| *petty squabbles* 小事引起的口角 **2** not generous and caring only about small unimportant things 小气的, 小心眼的, 心胸狭窄的; 只关注琐事的: *petty jealousy and spitefulness* 心胸狭窄的嫉妒和怨恨 —see also 另见 PETTINESS **3 petty tyrant/dictator etc** someone who is not really important but uses their power as if they were important 小暴君/小独裁者等: *Some petty bureaucrat wanted all the documents in triplicate.* 一些小官僚想要所有的文件一式三份。**4 petty crime** a crime that is not serious, for example stealing things that have little value 轻罪〈如小偷小摸〉: **petty criminal/thief etc** *Big-time gangsters despise petty thieves.* 大匪徒看不起那些小偷小摸的贼子。

petty bour·geois /ˌ·· ˈ··/ also 又作 **petit bourgeois** *adj* **1** paying too much attention to unimportant matters concerning social position, private possessions etc 小资产阶级的〔过分注重社会地位和个人财物, 过分注重名利〕: *a petty bourgeois mentality* 小资产阶级心理 **2** belonging to the group of MIDDLE CLASS people who own small businesses, shops etc 小资产阶级的 **—petty bourgeois** *n* [C]

petty cash /ˌ·· ˈ·/ *n* [U] an amount of money in coins or notes that is kept in an office for making small payments 零用现金; 小额现金[备用金]

petty lar·ce·ny /ˌ·· ˈ···/ *n* [U] *law* the crime of stealing things that are only worth a small amount of money【法律】轻微盗窃罪, 小偷小摸

petty of·fi·cer /ˌ·· ˈ···/ *n* [C] an officer of low rank in the Navy 海军军士 —see table on page C6 参见C6页附录

pet·u·lant /ˈpɛtʃələnt; ˈpetʃʊ̈lənt/ *adj* behaving in an impatient and angry way for no reason at all, like a child 任性的; 耍孩子脾气的; 脾气暴躁的 **—petulantly** *adv*: *Kara stamped her foot and frowned petulantly.* 卡拉暴躁地跺着脚, 皱着眉。**—petulance** *n* [U]

pe·tu·ni·a /pəˈtunɪə; pɪ̈ˈtjuːniə/ *n* [C] a garden plant which has pink, purple, or white TRUMPET-shaped flowers 矮牵牛

pew[1] /pju; pjuː/ *n* [C] **1** a long wooden seat in a church〔教堂里的〕长条木座椅 **2 take a pew** *BrE spoken* used to invite someone to sit down【英口】请坐下

pew[2] *interjection AmE spoken* used when there is a very unpleasant smell【美口】呸!〔用来表示气味非常难闻〕; POOH *BrE*【英】

pew·ter /ˈpjutə; ˈpjuːtə/ *n* [U] **1** a grey metal made by mixing LEAD and TIN 白镴〔铅和锡的合金〕: *a pewter tankard* 一个用白镴制作的有柄大酒杯 **2** objects made from this metal 白镴制品

pey·o·te /peˈotɪ; peɪˈəʊti/ *n* **1** [U] a drug made from a Mexican CACTUS, which makes people imagine that strange things are happening to them; MESCALIN 佩奥特碱〔取自一种墨西哥仙人掌的致幻药〕**2** [C] the plant that produces this drug〔提取这种致幻药的〕佩奥特掌

Pey·ton Place /ˌpetn̩ ˈples; ˌpeɪtn ˈpleɪs/ a NOVEL by Grace Metalious that was made into a very popular television SOAP OPERA (1964-68), about the lives of a group of people in a small town in New England. People sometimes say that a situation is like Peyton Place when they mean that a group of people have many secrets and complicated emotional relationships.《佩顿镇》, 又译《冷暖人间》〔格雷丝·麦泰莉创作的一部颇受欢迎的电视肥皂剧(1964-1968)。该剧反映生活在新英格兰一小镇的一群人的生活。人们有时会把一群人有着许多秘密和复杂情感关系的情形说成是"像在佩顿镇一样"〕

pfen·nig /ˈfɛnɪg; ˈfenɪg/ *n* [C] a unit of money worth 1/100th of a German MARK[2] (8) 芬尼〔德国货币单位, 相当于 1/100 马克〕

PG /ˌpi ˈdʒi; ˌpiː ˈdʒiː/ *adj* parental guidance; a film that is PG may include parts that are unsuitable for children under 15 需在家长指导下观看的, 家长指引级影片〔指电影部分镜头不适宜15岁以下的儿童观看〕: *Jurassic Park (PG)*《侏罗纪公园》(家长指引级) —compare 比较 G, U, R, X-CERTIFICATE

PGA, the /ˌpi dʒi ˈe; ˌpiː dʒiː ˈeɪ/ Professional Golfers' Association; a US organization for those who make money from GOLF, either by playing it, running golf courses, or teaching. The organization runs the **PGA Championship**, a golfing competition. 职业高尔夫球协会〔美国一组织。会员皆为高尔夫球运动员、球场经营者或教练等职业人士。该组织定期举办PGA锦标赛〕

pH /ˈpi ˋetʃ; piː ˈeɪtʃ/ also 又作 **pH val·ue** /ˈ· ˈ·, ·ˈ/ *n* [singular] a number on a scale of 0 to 14 which shows how acid or ALKALINE a substance is pH值, 酸碱度

phae·ton /ˋfeətn̩; ˈfeɪtn/ *n* [C] a light open carriage used in the past, usually pulled by two horses〔旧时用的通常由两匹马拉的〕轻便敞篷马车

phag·o·cyte /ˋfægə,saɪt; ˈfægəsaɪt/ *n* [C] a blood cell that protects your body by destroying harmful BACTERIA etc 吞噬细胞〔杀死有害细菌保护身体的血液细胞〕

pha·lanx /ˋfelæŋks; ˈfælæŋks/ *plural* **phalanxes** *n* [C] **1** a large group of people who stand close together so that it is difficult to go through them 密集的人群; 密集队形: *A solid phalanx of policemen blocked the road.* 警察排成密集的队形封锁了那条道路。**2** a group of soldiers who stand or move closely together in battle〔作战时的〕士兵方阵

phal·lic /ˋfælɪk; ˈfælɪk/ *adj* like or related to the phallus 阴茎状的; 阴茎的: *phallic symbols* 阴茎的象征

phal·lus /ˋfæləs; ˈfæləs/ *n* [C] **1** a model of the male sex organ, used to represent sexual power〔用来象征生殖力的〕男性生殖器形象 **2** *technical* the male sex organ; PENIS【术语】阴茎

phan·tas·m /ˋfæntæzəm; ˈfæntæzəm/ *n* [C,U] *literary* something that exists only in your imagination; an ILLUSION【文】幻象; 幻影; 幻觉 —**phantasmal** /fænˋtæzməl; fænˈtæzməl/ *adj*

phan·tas·ma·go·ri·a /ˌfæntæzməˋgɔriə; ˌfæntæzməˈgɔːriə/ *n* [C] *literary* a confused, changing strange scene like something from a dream【文】如梦般变幻无常的情景, 梦幻景象 —**phantasmagorical** /-ˋgɑrɪkl̩; -ˈgɒrɪkəl/ *adj*

phan·ta·sy /ˋfæntəsɪ; ˈfæntəsi/ *n* [C,U] an old spelling of FANTASY fantasy 的旧式拼法

phan·tom /ˋfæntəm; ˈfæntəm/ *n* [C] *literary*【文】**1** a frightening and unclear image, especially of a dead person; GHOST[1] (1) 可怕而模糊的影像〔尤指鬼魂〕; 幽灵: **phantom horseman/hound/ship etc** *The phantom hound loomed suddenly out of the mist.* 那只幽灵猎犬突然从雾中隐现。**2** something that exists only in your imagination 幻象; 幻觉; 幻影: *the phantoms that troubled his dreams* 困扰他梦境的幻影 **3** *humorous* used to describe an unknown person that you blame for something annoying【幽默】幽灵〔用来描述做了令人讨厌的事又不为人知的人〕: *The phantom pen stealer strikes again!* 那个偷笔的幽灵又出击了!

Phantom of the Op·e·ra, The /ˌ· · · ˈ· ·/ (1910) a book by the French writer Gaston Leroux about a frightening man whose face has been DISFIGURED (=injured in an ugly way) and who wears a MASK to hide it. He KIDNAPS a beautiful OPERA singer because he loves her. Several films and plays have been based on the story.《歌剧魅影》〔(1910), 法国作家卡斯顿·勒鲁创作的一部小说。书中有一令人生畏的男子, 毁过容, 常戴面具。他爱上了一位美丽的女歌剧演员, 结果绑架了她。这部小说已改编成好几部电影和戏剧〕

phantom preg·nan·cy /ˌ· ·ˈ· · ·/ *n* [C] a medical condition in which a woman seems to be PREGNANT, but in fact is not 精神性假妊娠

pha·raoh /ˋfero; ˈfeərəʊ/ *n* [C] a ruler of ancient Egypt 法老〔古埃及统治者的称号〕

phar·i·see /ˋfærə,si; ˈfærɨsiː/ *n* [C] **1** someone who pretends to be religious or to be concerned about morals〔假装虔诚或关注道德的〕伪善者 **2** **Pharisee** a member of a group of Jews who lived at the time of Christ and who believed in strictly obeying religious laws 法利赛人〔生活在耶稣基督时代, 相信应严守宗教法规的犹太人〕—**pharisaic** /ˌfærəˋse·ɪk; ˌfærɨˈseɪ-ɪk/ *adj*

phar·ma·ceu·ti·cal /ˌfɑrməˋsutɪkl̩; ˌfɑːməˈsjuːtɪkəl◂/ *adj* concerned with the production of drugs and medicine 制药的: *the large pharmaceutical companies* 大型制药公司

phar·ma·ceu·ti·cals /ˌfɑrməˋsutɪkl̩z; ˌfɑːməˈsjuːtɪkəlz/ *n* [plural] drugs and medicines 药物, 药品

phar·ma·cist /ˋfɑrməsɪst; ˈfɑːməsɨst/ *n* [C] someone who is trained to prepare drugs and medicines and who works in a shop or in a hospital〔药店或医院的〕药剂师 —compare 比较 CHEMIST

phar·ma·col·o·gy /ˌfɑrməˋkɑlədʒɪ; ˌfɑːməˈkɒlədʒi/ *n* [U] the scientific study of drugs and medicines 药理学, 药物学 —**pharmacologist** *n* [C] —**pharmacological** /ˌfɑrməkəˋlɑdʒɪkl̩; ˌfɑːməkəˈlɒdʒɪkəl◂/ *adj*

phar·ma·co·poe·ia /ˌfɑrməkəˋpiə; ˌfɑːməkəˈpiːə/ *n* [C] *technical* an official book giving information about medicines【术语】药典

phar·ma·cy /ˋfɑrməsɪ; ˈfɑːməsi/ *n* **1** [C] *especially AmE* a shop or a part of a shop where medicines are prepared and sold【尤美】药店; 药房; 〔商店的〕药品部: *an all-night pharmacy* 通宵营业的药房 **2** [U] the study or practice of preparing drugs and medicines 药剂学; 制[配]药(学)

phar·yn·gi·tis /ˌfærɪnˋdʒaɪtɪs; ˌfærɪnˈdʒaɪtɨs/ *n* [U] a medical condition in which you have a sore swollen pharynx 咽喉炎

phar·ynx /ˋfærɪŋks; ˈfærɪŋks/ *n plural* **pharynxes** [C] the tube that goes from the back of your mouth to where the separate passages for food and air divide 咽 —see picture at 参见 RESPIRATORY 图

phase[1] /fez; feɪz/ *n* [C] **1** a part of a process of development or growth〔发育或生长的〕阶段; 时期: *a transitional phase before democratic elections are held* 举行民主选举前的过渡阶段 —compare 比较 STAGE[1] (1) **2** **in phase/out of phase (with)** *BrE* working together in a way that produces the right effect, or not working together in this way【英】同相/异相的; 协调/不协调的; 同步/不同步的: *The traffic lights were out of phase with each other.* 交通信号灯相互不同步变化了。**3** one of a fixed number of changes in the appearance of the moon or a planet when it is seen from the Earth〔月球、行星的〕位相 2

phase[2] *v* [T] to make something happen gradually in a planned way 使…逐步进行, 使…分阶段进行: *a phased withdrawal of military forces* 军队的分阶段撤出

phase sth ↔ **in** *phr v* [T] to introduce something such as a new law, rule etc gradually 逐步采用[实施]〔新的法律、规定等〕: *The government is going to phase in the new pension system over the next five years.* 在今后的五年中, 政府将逐步实施新的退休金计划。

phase sth ↔ **out** *phr v* [T] to gradually stop using or providing something 逐步停止使用[提供]; 逐步淘汰: *Leaded gas was phased out in the 1970s.* 含铅汽油在20世纪70年代就被逐渐淘汰了。

PhD /ˌpi etʃ ˋdi; ˌpiː eɪtʃ ˈdiː/ *n* [C] Doctor of Philosophy; a university degree of very high rank, above an MA or an MSc, which involves doing RESEARCH, or someone who has this degree 哲学博士学位; 哲学博士: *Jacqueline Hope, PhD* 哲学博士杰奎琳·霍普 —see also 另见 DOCTORATE

pheas·ant /ˋfɛznt; ˈfezənt/ *n* [C,U] a large bird with a long tail, often shot for food, or the meat of this bird 雉, 野鸡; 野鸡肉

> **CULTURAL NOTE 文化注释**
>
> Pheasants can legally be shot in certain seasons in Britain and the US. In Britain, this is a mainly UPPER-CLASS sport. 在英国和美国的某些季节射猎野鸡是合法的。在英国这主要是上层阶级的运动。

phe·no·bar·bi·tone /ˌfinoˋbɑrbɪ,ton; ˌfiːnəʊˈbɑːbɨtəʊn/ *BrE*【英】, **phe·no·bar·bi·tal** /-bɪ,tɔl; -bɨtl/ *AmE*【美】*n* [U] a powerful drug that helps you to sleep 苯巴比妥〔一种强效安眠药〕

phe·nom·e·nal /fəˋnɑmənl̩; fɪˈnɒmɨnəl/ *adj* very unusual and impressive 非凡的; 惊人的: *phenomenal strength* 惊人的力气 | *phenomenal economic growth* 不寻常的经济增长 —**phenomenally** *adv*: *phenomenally successful* 极成功的

phe·nom·e·non /fəˋnɑmə,nɑn; fɪˈnɒmɨnən/ *n plural* **phenomena** [C] **1** something that happens or exists, especially something that is studied because it is not understood〔尤指因不理解而加以研究的〕现象: **[+of]** *the phenomenon of international terrorism* 国际恐怖主义现象 | *violent natural phenomena such as hurricanes* 诸如飓风之类猛烈的自然现象 **2** something or someone that is very unusual because of a rare quality or ability that they have 非凡的人[事物]; 奇才; 奇迹 3

phew /fju; fjuː/ *interjection* used when you feel tired, hot, or RELIEVED 啊! 唷! 唉!〔表示疲倦、感到炎热或放心〕

phi·al /ˋfaɪəl; ˈfaɪəl/ *n* [C] a small bottle, especially for liquid medicines〔尤指盛药水的〕小药瓶: *a phial of morphine* 一小瓶吗啡

Phi Be·ta Kap·pa /ˌfaɪ ˌbitə ˋkæpə; ˌfaɪ ˌbiːtə ˈkæpə/ *n* [singular] an American society for university and college students who have reached a high level in their studies〔美国的〕大学优秀生联谊会

-phil /fɪl; fɪl/ *suffix* another form of the suffix -PHILE 后缀 -phile 的另一种形式

Phil·a·del·phi·a /ˌfɪləˋdɛlfɪə; ˌfɪləˈdelfiə◂/ a city in the US state of Pennsylvania, which is an important port and an industrial and financial centre. Philadelphia, which is informally called **Philly**, is the fifth largest city in the US. The Declaration of Independence from Britain was signed in Philadelphia in 1776, and the city was the first capital of the new United States. 费城〔美国宾夕法尼亚州一城市, 重要港口, 工业与金融中心, 俗称Philly (费利), 美国第五大城市。1776年在此签署了

宣布脱离英国的《独立宣言》。该市是美利坚合众国新成立时的第一个首都〕

Philadelphia Or·ches·tra, the /,……'……/ a US ORCHESTRA (=a large group of musicians) based in Philadelphia, Pennsylvania 费城交响乐团〔美国一管弦乐队，总部在宾夕法尼亚州的费城〕

phi·lan·der·er /fə'lændərə; fɪ'lændərə/ *n* [C] *old-fashioned* a man who has sex with many women, without intending to have any serious relationships【过时】玩弄女性的男人 —**philandering** *adj* —**philandering** *n* [U]

phil·an·throp·ic /,fɪlən'θrɑpɪk; ,fɪlən'θrɒpɪk◂/ *adj* a philanthropic person or institution gives money and help to people who are poor or in trouble 〔人或机构〕慈善的；仁慈的 —**philanthropically** /-klɪ; -kli/ *adv*

phi·lan·thro·pist /fə'lænθrəpɪst; fɪ'lænθrəpɪst/ *n* [C] a rich person who gives a lot of money to help poor people 慈善家，乐善好施者

phi·lan·thro·py /fə'lænθrəpɪ; fɪ'lænθrəpi/ *n* [U] the practice of giving money and help to people who are poor or in trouble 慈善行为

phi·lat·e·ly /fə'lætḷɪ; fɪ'lætəli/ *n* [U] the activity of collecting stamps for pleasure 集邮 —**philatelic** /,fɪlə'tɛlɪk; ,fɪlə'telɪk◂/ *adj* —**philatelist** /fə'lætḷɪst; fɪ'lætəlɪst/ *n* [C]

Phil·by /'fɪlbɪ; 'fɪlbi/, **Kim** /kɪm; kɪm/ (1911-88) a British SPY (=someone who gives secret information to a country's enemies). He was a member of the British Secret Intelligence Service during and after World War II, but all the time he was secretly working for the Soviet Union. He escaped to Russia in 1963. 菲尔比〔(1911-1988)，英国间谍。二战以来，他一直为英国情报部门工作，同时也秘密为苏联服务。1963年，他叛逃到苏联〕

-phile /faɪl; faɪl/ *suffix* also 又作 **-phil** [in nouns 构成名词] someone who likes something 喜爱…的人；爱好…的人：*a bibliophile* (=who likes books) 书籍爱好者 | *an Anglophile* (=who likes England or Britain) 亲英者，崇英者

Phil·har·mo·ni·a Or·ches·tra, the /,fɪlə·monɪə 'ɔrkɪstrə; ,fɪləməʊniə 'ɔːkɪstrə/ an important British ORCHESTRA (=large group of musicians playing together), based in London and started in 1945〔英国〕爱乐乐团〔英国一重要管弦乐队，总部在伦敦，成立于1945年〕

Phil·har·mon·ic /,fɪlə'mɑnɪk; ,fɪlə'mɒnɪk◂/ *adj* used in the names of ORCHESTRAs 爱乐的〔用于管弦乐队的名称中〕

-philia /fɪlɪə; fɪliə/ *suffix* [in nouns 构成名词] **1** *technical* a tendency to feel sexually attracted in a way that is not approved of, that may be part of a mental illness【术语】〔病态地〕爱恋…的倾向，〔不正常的〕癖好：*necrophilia* (=a sexual attraction to dead bodies) 恋尸癖 **2** *technical* a diseased or unhealthy tendency to do something【术语】〔不健康地〕做…的倾向，瘾癖：*haemophilia* (=a tendency to bleed) 血友病 **3** a tendency to like something 喜爱…的倾向，爱好…的倾向，亲…：*Francophilia* (=liking France) 亲法

-philiac /fɪlɪæk; fɪliæk/ *suffix technical*【术语】[in nouns 构成名词] **1** someone who feels sexually attracted in a way that is not approved of〔不正常地〕爱恋…的人：*a necrophiliac* 恋尸癖者 **2** someone who has a particular illness 患某种病的人：*a haemophiliac* 血友病患者

Phil·ip /'fɪlɪp; 'fɪlɪp/, **Prince** —see 见 the DUKE OF EDINBURGH

phi·lip·pic /fə'lɪpɪk; fɪ'lɪpɪk/ *n* [C] *literary* a strong angry speech publicly attacking someone【文】猛烈的抨击性演说；痛斥

Phil·ip·pines, the /'fɪlə,pinz; 'fɪlɪpiːnz/ a country made up of over 7000 islands off the southeast coast of Asia. Population: 82,842,000 (2001). Capital: Manila. The Philippines were a COLONY of the US from 1898 until they became fully independent in 1948. People from the Philippines are called Filipinos. 菲律宾〔与亚洲东南沿海地区隔海相望一国家，由7000多个岛屿组成。人口：82,842,000 (2001)，首都：马尼拉。1898年起，菲律宾一直是美国的殖民地，直到1948年独立。菲律宾人被称作Filipino〕

Phil·is·tine /'fɪləs,tin; 'fɪlɪstaɪn/ *n* [C] in the Bible, a member of a race of people who lived in Palestine, and who were the enemies of the Israelites 非利士人〔《圣经》中居住在巴勒斯坦的一个民族。他们是以色列人的敌人〕

philistine *n* [C] someone who does not like or understand art, literature, music etc 不喜欢[懂]艺术、文学或音乐等的人；没有教养的人 —**philistine** *adj* —**philistinism** *n* [U]

Phil·ly /'fɪlɪ; 'fɪli/ an informal name for Philadelphia费利〔费城的俗称〕

phi·lol·o·gy /fɪ'lɑlədʒɪ; fɪ'lɒlədʒi/ *n* [U] *old-fashioned* the study of words and of the way words and languages develop【过时】语文学 —compare 比较 LINGUISTICS —**philologist** *n* [C] —**philological** /,fɪlə'lɑdʒɪkḷ; ,fɪlə'lɒdʒɪkəl◂/ *adj* —**philologically** /-klɪ; -kli/ *adv*

phi·los·o·pher /fə'lɑsəfə; fɪ'lɒsəfə/ *n* [C] **1** someone who studies and develops ideas about the nature and meaning of existence and reality, good and evil etc 哲学家：*Plato, Aristotle, and other Greek philosophers* 柏拉图、亚里士多德和其他希腊哲学家 **2** someone who thinks deeply about the world, life etc 思想深刻的人，思想家

philosopher's stone /,·,···'·/ *n* [singular] an imaginary substance that was thought in the past to have the power to change any other metal into gold 点金石〔旧时被认为能使任何金属变成黄金的物质〕

phil·o·soph·i·cal /,fɪlə'sɑfɪkḷ; ,fɪlə'sɒfɪkəl◂/ also 又作 **phil·o·soph·ic** /,fɪlə'sɑfɪk; ,fɪlə'sɒfɪk◂/ *adj* **1** related to philosophy 哲学的：*the philosophical writings of Sartre* 萨特的哲学著作 **2** someone who is philosophical calmly accepts a difficult or unpleasant situation because they know it cannot be changed 豁达的，达观的：[+about] *Robert was surprisingly philosophical about losing his job.* 罗伯特对于失去工作表现得惊人地达观。—**philosophically** /-klɪ; -kli/ *adv*: *Marne took her defeat philosophically.* 玛内以豁达的态度对待失败。

phi·los·o·phize also 又作 **-ise** *BrE*【英】/fə'lɑsə,faɪz; fɪ'lɒsəfaɪz/ *v* [I+about] to make remarks about the nature and meaning of things as if you were a philosopher 像哲学家似地谈论〔事物的本质和意义〕

phi·los·o·phy /fə'lɑsəfɪ; fɪ'lɒsəfi/ *n* **1** [U] the study of the nature and meaning of existence and reality, good and evil, etc 哲学 **2** [C] one of the many systems of thought that has this study as its base〔以哲学为基础的〕思想体系；哲学体系：*the philosophy of Kant* 康德的哲学体系 **3** [C] a rule you follow in living your life, doing your job etc 人生哲学；生活[工作]准则：*current management philosophy* 目前的管理准则 —see also 另见 NATURAL PHILOSOPHY

phil·tre also 又作 **philter** *AmE*【美】/'fɪltə; 'fɪltə/ *n* [C] *literary* a magic drink or object that makes someone fall in love【文】催情药，春药

phiz·og /'fɪzɑg; 'fɪzɒg/ *n* [C] *BrE old-fashioned* your face【英，过时】脸，面孔；容貌

phle·bi·tis /flɪ'baɪtɪs; flɪ'baɪtɪs/ *n* [U] a swollen condition of the VEINS (=tubes that carry blood through your body) 静脉炎

phlegm /flɛm; flem/ *n* [U] **1** the thick yellowish substance produced in your nose and throat, especially when you have a cold; MUCUS 痰 **2** unusual calmness in worrying, frightening, or exciting situations 冷静，沉着；不冲动

phleg·mat·ic /flɛg'mætɪk; fleg'mætɪk/ *adj* calm and not easily excited or worried 冷静的；沉着的；镇定的：*Even the most phlegmatic individual would get stressed out under such pressure.* 即使最镇静的人在这样的压力下也会变得很紧张。—**phlegmatically** /-klɪ; -kli/ *adv*

phlox /flɑks; flɒks/ *n* [C] **1** a tall garden plant with red, purple, or white flowers 福禄考〔一种园艺植物，开红色、紫色或白色的花〕 **2** *AmE* a low, spreading plant with pink or white flowers【美】丛生福禄考〔一种低矮蔓生植物，开粉色或白色的花〕

Phnom Penh /,nɑm 'pɛn; ,nɒm 'pen/ the capital of Cambodia. The Khmer Rouge took control of it in 1975, and sent most of the population to work in the country, but people started to come back to the city in 1979 when the Vietnamese took control of it. 金边〔柬埔寨首都。1975年，该市被红色高棉占领，多数居民被迫到乡下做工。1979年，越南人控制该市之后，他们又开始返回城里〕

-phobe /fob; fəʊb/ *suffix* [in nouns 构成名词] a person who dislikes or hates something 憎恶…的人，仇视…的人：*an Anglophobe* (=someone who hates England or Britain) 仇英者 | *a xenophobe* (=someone who hates foreigners) 憎恶外国人的人

pho·bi·a /'fobɪə; 'fəʊbiə/ *n* [C] a strong unreasonable fear of something〔对某物无端的〕强烈恐惧：[+about] *Owen has a phobia about heights.* 欧文有恐高症。—**phobic** *adj*

-phobia /fobɪə; fəʊbiə/ *suffix* [in nouns 构成名词] **1** a dislike or hatred of something 憎恶，仇视：*Anglophobia* (=dislike of England or Britain) 仇英 **2** *technical* a strong dislike or fear of something, that is unusual and may be part of a mental illness; a phobia【术语】〔不正常的〕憎恶，恐惧：*claustrophobia* (=fear of being in a small enclosed space) 幽闭恐惧(症) | *aquaphobia* (=fear of water) 恐水(症)

-phobic /fobɪk; fəʊbɪk/ *suffix technical*【术语】**1** [in nouns 构成名词] someone suffering from a particular phobia 患…恐惧症的人：*He's a claustrophobic.* 他是一个患有幽闭恐惧症的人。**2** [in adjectives 构成形容词] suffering from or connected with a

particular phobia 患恐惧症的，惧怕…的：*I'm a bit agoraphobic.* 我有点恐旷症。—**-phobically**/fobɪklɪ; fəʊbɪkli/ [in adverbs 构成副词]

Phoe·nix /ˋfinɪks; ˈfiːnɪks/ the capital and largest city of Arizona, US. It is an extremely hot city. It is growing very quickly, because many old people go there to live. 菲尼克斯，又译凤凰城〔美国亚利桑那州首府及最大城市。该市非常炎热。许多老人前往该地居住，城市发展十分迅速〕

phoenix *n* [C] **1** a magic bird that is born from a fire according to ancient stories 凤凰〔古代传说中一种生于火中的神奇的鸟〕 **2 rise like a phoenix from the ashes** to become successful again after seeming to have failed completely 在看似彻底失败后取得成功；起死回生

phon- /fən; fən; *strong* 强读 fon; fəʊn/ *prefix* another form of the prefix PHONO- 前缀 phono- 的另一种形式

-phone /fon; fəʊn/ *suffix* **1** [in nouns 构成名词] an instrument or machine connected with sound or hearing, especially a musical instrument 与声音[听力]有关的乐器[机器]：*earphones* (=for listening to a radio, etc) 耳机 | *a saxophone* 萨克斯管 **2** *technical* [in nouns 构成名词] someone who speaks a particular language【术语】讲某种语言的人：*a Francophone* (=who speaks French) 讲法语的人 **3** [in adjectives 构成形容词] speaking a particular language 讲某种语言的：*Francophone nations* (=where French is spoken) 讲法语的国家

S1 W2 **phone¹** /fon; fəʊn/ *n* [C] **1** a telephone 电话：*Could you answer the phone, please?* 请你接一下电话，好吗？| *a long-distance phone call* 长途电话 | *What's your phone number?* 你的电话号码是多少？| **by phone/over the phone** (=using a telephone) 用电话，通过电话 *I made a booking by phone.* 我打电话进行了预订。**2** the part of a telephone into which you speak; RECEIVER (1)〔电话的〕听筒：*Greg slammed down the phone angrily.* 格雷格生气地把电话听筒砰地放下。**3 be on the phone a)** to be making a telephone call 在通电话：*Turn down the TV! I'm on the phone!* 把电视音量关小！我正在打电话！**b)** *BrE* to have a telephone in your home or office【英】〔在家或办公室〕装有电话：*Are you on the phone?* 你安装了电话没有？

S1 **phone²** also 又作 **phone up** *v* [I,T] to speak to someone by telephone; TELEPHONE² 给…打电话：*Has Anna phoned yet?* 安娜打电话了吗？| *I bet they'll phone up with some excuse.* 我敢肯定他们会打电话来为自己找借口。| **phone sb (up)** *I phoned Jim up last night.* 昨晚我给吉姆打了电话。—see graph at 参见 TELEPHONE 图表

phone in *phr v* [I,T] **1** to telephone the place where you work, especially to report something〔尤指为报告某事而〕打电话到自己的工作处：*Why don't you phone in and say you are ill?* 为什么你不给单位打电话说你病了？| **phone** sth ↔ **in** *How many salespeople have phoned in their figures so far?* 到目前为止，有多少推销员已打电话回来汇报了他们的销售额？**2** to telephone a radio or television show to give your opinion or ask a question〔给无线电台或电视节目〕打电话〔发表意见或提问〕：*We encourage viewers to phone in during the program.* 我们鼓励观众在节目进行期间打电话进来。—see also 另见 PHONE-IN

phone book /ˈ· ·/ *n* [C] a book that contains an alphabetical list of the names, addresses, and telephone numbers of all the people who have a telephone in a particular area; TELEPHONE DIRECTORY 电话（号码）簿

phone booth /ˈ· ·/ *n* [C] *AmE* a small structure that is partly or completely enclosed, containing a public telephone【美】〔公用〕电话亭

phone box /ˈ· ·/ *n* [C] *BrE* a small structure that is partly or completely enclosed, containing a public telephone【英】〔公用〕电话亭

phone·card /ˋfonkard; ˈfəʊnkɑːd/ *n* [C] a plastic card that can be used in some public telephones instead of money〔在公用电话上使用的〕电话卡

phone-in /ˈ· ·/ *n* [C] a radio or television programme in which you hear ordinary people expressing opinions or asking questions over the telephone 公众打电话参与的电台[电视]节目，听众[观众]来电话参加的直播节目

pho·neme /ˋfonim; ˈfəʊniːm/ *n* [C] *technical* the smallest unit of speech that can be used to make one word different from another word, such as the 'b' and the 'p' in 'big' and 'pig'【术语】音素；音位 —**phonemic** /foˋnimɪk; fəˈniːmɪk/ *adj* —**phonemically**/-klɪ; -kli/ *adv*

pho·ne·mics /fəˋnimɪks; fəˈniːmɪks/ *n* [U] *technical* the study and description of the phonemes of languages【术语】音位学

phone-tap·ping /ˈ· ˌ· ·/ *n* [U] the activity of listening secretly to other people's telephone conversations using special ELECTRONIC equipment〔利用特殊电子设备进行的〕电话窃听

pho·net·ic /fəˋnɛtɪk; fəˈnetɪk/ *adj technical*【术语】**1** related to the sounds of human speech 语音的 **2** using special signs, often different from ordinary letters, to represent the sounds of speech 使用音标代表语音的，表示发音的：*a phonetic alphabet* 音标 | *phonetic symbols* 音标符号

pho·net·ics /fəˋnɛtɪks; fəˈnetɪks/ *n* [U] the science and study of speech sounds 语音学 —**phonetician** /ˌfonəˋtɪʃən; ˌfəʊnɪ̥ˈtɪʃən/ *n* [C]

pho·ney also 又作 **phony** *AmE*【美】/ˋfonɪ; ˈfəʊni/ *adj informal*【非正式】**1** false or not real, and intended to deceive someone; FAKE 假冒的，伪造的：*a phoney British accent* 假冒的英国口音 | *I gave the police a phoney address.* 我给了警察一个假地址。**2** someone who is phoney pretends to be good, clever, kind etc when they are not 伪善的；假装聪明的；骗人的 —**phoney** *n* [C]: *Grant's such a phoney!* 格兰特是个大骗子！—**phoniness** *n* [U]

phoney war /ˌ·· ˈ·/ *n* [singular] a period during which a state of war officially exists but there is no actual fighting 假战；静坐战

phon·ic /ˋfanɪk; ˈfɒnɪk/ *adj technical*【术语】**1** related to sound 声音的 **2** related to speech sounds 语音的

phon·ics /ˋfanɪks; ˈfɒnɪks/ *n* [U] a method of teaching people to read in which they are taught to recognize the sounds that letters represent 读音法〔一种教人阅读的方法〕

phono- /fono; fəʊnəʊ/ *prefix* also 又作 **phon-** *technical*【术语】**1** concerning the voice or speech 音，语音：*phonetics* (=science of speech sounds) 语音学 **2** concerning sound 声：*a phonoreceptor* (=hearing organ) 感声器

pho·no·graph /ˋfonəˌgræf; ˈfəʊnəgrɑːf/ *n* [C] *AmE old-fashioned* a RECORD PLAYER【美，过时】留声机，唱机

pho·nol·o·gy /foˋnalədʒɪ; fəˈnɒlədʒi/ *n* [U] *technical* the study of the system of speech sounds in a language, or the system of sounds itself【术语】音系学；音韵学；语音体系 —**phonologist** *n* [C] —**phonological**/ˌfonəˋladʒɪkḷ; ˌfəʊnəˈlɒdʒɪkəl◂/ *adj* —**phonologically**/-klɪ; -kli/ *adv*

pho·ny /ˋfonɪ; ˈfəʊni/ *adj* the usual American spelling of PHONEY phoney 的一般美式拼法

phoo·ey /ˋfuɪ; ˈfuːi/ *interjection* used to express strong disbelief or disappointment 呸，啐〔用于表示强烈的不信任或失望〕

phos·gene /ˋfazdʒin; ˈfɒzdʒiːn/ *n* [U] a poisonous gas used in war and in industry〔战争或工业中使用的〕光气，碳酰氯

phos·phate /ˋfasfet; ˈfɒsfeɪt/ *n* [C,U] **1** one of the various forms of a SALT¹ (3) of PHOSPHORUS, widely used in industry 磷酸盐 **2** [usually plural 一般用复数] a substance containing a phosphate used for making plants grow better 磷肥

phos·pho·res·cence /ˌfasfəˋrɛsṇs; ˌfɒsfəˈresəns/ *n* [U] a slight steady light that can only be noticed in the dark 磷光，磷火

phos·pho·res·cent /ˌfasfəˋrɛsṇt; ˌfɒsfəˈresənt◂/ *adj* shining slightly in the dark but producing little or no heat 发磷光的：*a strange phosphorescent light at night* 夜晚奇异的磷光 —**phosphorescently** *adv*

phos·pho·rus /ˋfasfərəs; ˈfɒsfərəs/ *n* [U] a poisonous yellowish ELEMENT (=simple substance) that starts to burn when brought out into the air 磷 —**phosphoric**/fasˋfɔrɪk; fɒsˈfɒrɪk/ *adj*

pho·to /ˋfoto; ˈfəʊtəʊ/ *n plural* **photos** [C] *informal* a photograph【非正式】照片，相片：*the family photo album* 家庭相册 | **take a photo** *Let's take a photo of the hotel.* 让我们拍一张酒店的照片。

photo- /foto; fəʊtəʊ/ *prefix technical*【术语】**1** concerning light 光的：*photosensitive paper* (=that changes when light acts on it) 感光纸 **2** concerning photography 照相的，摄影的：*photojournalism* (=use of photographs in reporting news) 摄影新闻（工作）

photo booth /ˈ·· ·/ *n* [C] a small structure in which you can sit to have photographs taken by a machine〔立等可取的〕自助照相亭

pho·to·cop·i·er /ˋfotoˌkapɪə; ˈfəʊtəʊˌkɒpiə/ *n* [C] a machine that quickly makes photographic copies of documents 复印机，影印机；摄影复制机 —see picture on page A14 参见 A14 页图

pho·to·cop·y¹ /ˋfotoˌkapɪ; ˈfəʊtəʊˌkɒpi/ *n* [C] a photographic copy, especially of something printed, written, or drawn 复印件，影印本：*Make three photocopies of the report, please.* 请把这份报告影印三份。

photocopy² *v* [T] to make a photographic copy of something 复印，影印：*Could you get this photocopied in the office?* 你把这个在办公室复印一下好吗？

pho·to·e·lec·tric /ˌfoto·ɪˋlɛktrɪk; ˌfəʊtəʊ-ɪˈlektrɪk◂/ *adj* using an electrical effect that is controlled by light 光电的

photoelectric cell /,·····'·/ *n* [C] **1** an electronic instrument that changes light into electricity 光电池 **2** an electronic instrument that uses light to start an electrical effect, often used in BURGLAR ALARMS〔常用于防盗警报器的〕光电管, 电眼

photo fin·ish /,··'··/ *n* [C] the end of a race in which the leading runners finish so close together that a photograph has to be taken to decide which is the winner 摄影定胜负〔参赛者到达终点时非常接近, 需借照片决定胜负〕

Pho·to·fit /ˈfotofɪt; ˈfəʊtəʊfɪt/ *n* [U] *BrE trademark* a way of making a picture of a face using a collection of photographs of parts of different faces, used to help the police catch a criminal【英, 商标】〔由多张照片拼成, 用于帮助警方捉拿罪犯的〕拼图像法

pho·to·gen·ic /,fotəˈdʒɛnɪk; ,fəʊtəʊˈdʒenɪk◂/ *adj* always looking attractive in photographs 上镜的, 上相的: *Helen is very photogenic.* 海伦非常上相。

pho·to·graph[1] /ˈfotə,græf; ˈfəʊtəgrɑːf/ also 又作 **photo** *informal*【非正式】*n* [C] a picture obtained by using a camera and film that is sensitive to light 照片, 相片: *a passport photograph* 护照照片 | *wedding photographs* 结婚照 | *an old black-and-white photograph of the city* 一张这个城市的黑白旧照片 | **take a photograph** *Visitors are not allowed to take photographs inside the museum.* 游客不许在博物馆内拍照。| **sb's photograph** (=a photograph of someone) 某人的照片 *Did you see Leo's photograph in the newspaper?* 你在报纸上看到利奥的照片了吗?

photograph[2] *v* **1** [T] to make a picture of someone or something by using a camera and film sensitive to light 给…拍照, 拍摄: *Michelle doesn't like being photographed.* 米歇儿不喜欢被拍照。**2 photograph well/badly** to always look attractive or unattractive in photographs 上相/不上相

pho·tog·ra·pher /fəˈtɑgrəfɚ; fəˈtɒgrəfə/ *n* [C] someone who takes photographs, especially as a professional or as an artist 摄影者〔尤指专业摄影师或艺术摄影师〕: *a fashion photographer* 时装摄影师

pho·to·graph·ic /,fotəˈgræfɪk; ,fəʊtəˈgræfɪk◂/ *adj* **1** connected with photographs, using photographs, or used in producing photographs 摄影的; 使用照片的; 摄影用的: *a photographic history of the West* 西方历史画册 | *photographic equipment* 摄影器材 **2 photographic memory** the ability to remember exactly every detail of something you have seen 准确得惊人的记忆力 —**photographically** /-klɪ; -kli/ *adv*

pho·tog·ra·phy /fəˈtɑgrəfɪ; fəˈtɒgrəfi/ *n* [U] the art, profession, or method of producing photographs or the scenes in films 摄影业; 摄影(艺)术: *a documentary with marvellous wildlife photography* 有精彩的野生动物镜头的纪录片

pho·ton /ˈfotɑn; ˈfəʊtɒn/ *n* [C] *technical* a unit of energy (ENERGY (2)) that carries light and has zero MASS【术语】光子, 光量子

photo-op·por·tu·ni·ty /'·· ··,··/ *n* [C] a chance for someone such as a politician to be photographed for a newspaper in a way that will make them look good〔政治家等〕接受媒体拍照的时间

pho·to·sen·si·tive /,fotəˈsɛnsətɪv; ,fəʊtəʊˈsensətɪv◂/ *adj* sensitive to the action of light, for example by changing colour or form 感光的: *photosensitive paper* 感光纸

pho·to·sen·si·tize also 又作 **-ise** *BrE*【英】/,fotəˈsɛnsə,taɪz; ,fəʊtəʊˈsensətaɪz/ *v* [T] to make something photosensitive 使具感光性

photo shoot /'·· ·/ *n* [C] an occasion during which a professional PHOTOGRAPHER takes pictures of a fashion model or an actor for advertisements〔由职业摄影师进行拍摄的〕时装拍照会; 明星广告拍照

pho·to·stat /ˈfotə,stæt; ˈfəʊtəstæt/ *n* [C] *trademark* a type of machine used for making photographic copies, or the copy itself【商标】复[影]印机; 复[影]印件 —**photostat** *v* [T] —**photostatic** /,fotəˈstætɪk; ,fəʊtəˈstætɪk◂/ *adj*

pho·to·syn·the·sis /,fotəˈsɪnθəsɪs; ,fəʊtəʊˈsɪnθəsəs/ *n* [U] the production by a green plant of special substances like sugar that it uses as food, caused by the action of sunlight on CHLOROPHYLL (=the green substance in leaves) 光合作用

phras·al /ˈfrezl; ˈfreɪzəl/ *adj* consisting of or connected with a phrase or phrases 词组的; 短语的; 片语的

phrasal verb /,··'·/ *n* [C] a group of words that is used like a verb and consists of a verb with an adverb or PREPOSITION, such as 'set off', 'look after', 'put up with'. In this dictionary phrasal verbs are marked *phr v.* 短语动词, 片语动词〔在本辞典中短语动词以 *phr v* 表示〕

phrase[1] /frez; freɪz/ *n* [C] **1** a group of words that together have a particular meaning, especially when they express the meaning well in a few words〔尤指简洁的〕说法, 用语, 警句: *He said the President was – what was the phrase he used? – 'trigger-happy'.* 他说总统 —— 他用什么词来着? ——"好战"。| *Mrs Thatcher was, in Gorbachev's phrase, 'the iron lady'.* 用戈尔巴乔夫的说法, 撒切尔夫人是个"铁娘子"。**2** *technical* a group of words without a FINITE verb, especially when they are used to form part of a sentence, such as 'walking along the road' and 'a bar of soap'【术语】短语, 片语 —compare 比较 CLAUSE (2), SENTENCE[1] (1) **3** a short group of musical notes that is part of a longer piece 乐句 —see also 另见 **to coin a phrase** (COIN[2] (2)), **a turn of phrase** (TURN[2] (10))

phrase[2] *v* [T] **1** to express something in a particular way 以某种方式表达, 以…措辞表达: *Criticisms were phrased in careful terms.* 对批评的用词十分谨慎。| *a politely-phrased refusal* 婉言拒绝 **2** to perform music so as to produce the full effect of separate musical phrases 把〔乐曲〕分成短句演奏〔以充分表现每个乐句的效果〕

phrase·book /ˈfrezbʊk; ˈfreɪzbʊk/ *n* [C] a book that explains phrases of a foreign language, for people to use when they travel to other countries〔供游客到国外旅行时用的〕(外语) 常用语手册

phra·se·ol·o·gy /,frezɪˈɑlədʒɪ; ,freɪziˈɒlədʒi/ *n* [U] the way that words and phrases are chosen and used in a particular language or subject 专门用语; 术语

phras·ing /ˈfrezɪŋ; ˈfreɪzɪŋ/ *n* [U] **1** the way that something is said 措辞, 说法; 用语: *I don't remember her exact phrasing.* 我不记得她原话是怎么说的了。**2** a way of playing music, reading poetry etc that separates the notes, words, or lines into phrases〔演奏音乐时的〕乐句划分;〔朗诵诗歌时的〕分句法

phre·nol·o·gy /frəˈnɑlədʒɪ; frəˈnɒlədʒi/ *n* [U] the study of the shape of the human head as a way of showing someone's character and abilities, which was popular especially in the 19th century 颅相学〔通过研究头颅的形状来判断一个人的性格和能力, 尤在19世纪流行〕—**phrenologist** *n* [C]

phut /fʌt; fʌt/ *n* [singular] *BrE informal*【英, 非正式】**1 go phut** to stop working completely 停止运作, 出故障, 坏了: *The microwave's gone phut.* 微波炉坏了。**2** a sound like air suddenly escaping from something 啪〔气体突然排出的声音〕: *The engine gave a phut, and stopped.* 引擎发出啪的一声响, 然后就停止运转了。

phy·lum /ˈfaɪləm; ˈfaɪləm/ *n plural* **phyla** /-lə; -lə/ [C] *technical* one of the main groups into which scientists divide plants, animals, and languages, above a CLASS【术语】〔动植物分类的〕门;〔语言的〕语系, 语群

physi- /fɪzɪ; fɪzi/ *prefix* another form of the prefix PHYSIO- 前缀 physio- 的另一种形式

phys·ic /ˈfɪzɪk; ˈfɪzɪk/ *n* [C,U] *old use* medicine【旧】药品

phys·i·cal[1] /ˈfɪzɪkl; ˈfɪzɪkəl/ *adj*

1 ▶BODY NOT MIND 身体而非精神的◀ related to someone's body rather than their mind or soul 身体的, 肉体的: *physical exercise* 体育活动, 体操 | *physical abuse* 肉体上的虐待 | *people with mental or physical disabilities* 精神或身体有残疾的人

2 ▶REAL/SOLID 真实的/固体的◀ related to real objects or structures that can be touched, seen, felt, etc 物质的, 有形的: *man's domination of his physical environment* 人类对物质环境的主宰 | *They were kept in appalling physical conditions.* 他们被困在物质条件极差的地方。

3 ▶NATURAL 自然的◀ related to or following natural laws 自然的; 按照自然规律的: *There must be a physical explanation for the strange lights in the sky.* 天空中这些奇怪的光一定可以根据自然规律作出解释。

4 ▶PERSON 人◀ *informal* someone who is physical likes touching people a lot【非正式】(人) 喜欢动手动脚的

5 ▶VIOLENT 粗暴的◀ a word meaning violent, used to avoid saying this directly 粗暴的, 粗野的: *That was a very physical tackle!* 那是个非常粗野的擒抱动作!

6 ▶SCIENCE 科学◀ [only before noun 仅用于名词前] a physical science is the part of an area of scientific study that is connected with PHYSICS 物理学的: *physical chemistry* 物理化学 —see also 另见 PHYSICALLY

physical[2] also 又作 **physical ex·am·i·na·tion** /,···· ····'··/ *n* [C] a thorough examination of someone's body and general health by a doctor, especially to decide whether they are fit to do a particular job〔尤指为决定是否适合做某种工作而做的〕身体[体格]检查

physical ed·u·ca·tion /,··· ··'··/ *n* [U] sport and physical exercise taught as a school subject 体育教育; 体育课

physical ge·og·ra·phy /,··· ·'···/ *n* [U] the study of the Earth's surface and of its rivers, mountains etc rather than of

the countries it is divided into 自然地理学 —compare 比较 POLITICAL GEOGRAPHY

physical jerks /ˌ··· ˈ·/ *n* [plural] *BrE old-fashioned* physical exercises such as bending and stretching etc【英, 过时】体操

phys·i·cally /ˈfɪzɪkl̩ɪ; ˈfɪzɪkli/ *adv* **1** in relation to the body rather than the mind or soul 身体上, 体格上: *She is young and physically fit.* 她年轻而且身体健康。| *He's all right physically, but he's still very confused.* 他身体并没有问题, 但仍然十分糊涂。**2** **physically impossible** not possible according to the laws of nature or what is known to be true〔根据自然法则或已知事实〕不可能的; 完全不可能的: *Surely it's physically impossible to go a week without water?* 在没有水的情况下坚持一个星期想必也是完全不可能的吧?

physically chal·lenged /ˌ··· ˈ··/ *adj especially AmE* a word meaning physically HANDICAPPED, used when you want to avoid offending people【尤美】身体残疾的〔避免冒犯人的委婉说法〕

physical sci·ence /ˌ··· ˈ··/ *n* [U] also **the physical sciences** [plural] the sciences, such as CHEMISTRY, PHYSICS etc, that are concerned with things that are not living 自然科学〈如化学、物理等非生命科学〉

phy·si·cian /fəˈzɪʃən; fɪ̈ˈzɪʃən/ *n* [C] *AmE formal* a doctor【美, 正式】(内科) 医生

phys·i·cist /ˈfɪzəsɪst; ˈfɪzɪ̈sɪ̈st/ *n* [C] someone who studies or works in PHYSICS 物理学家

phys·ics /ˈfɪzɪks; ˈfɪzɪks/ *n* [U] the science concerned with the study of physical objects and substances, and of natural forces such as light, heat and movement 物理学

phys·i·o /ˈfɪzɪo; ˈfɪziəʊ/ *n plural* **physios** [C] *informal* a PHYSIOTHERAPIST【非正式】理疗师, 物理治疗师

physio- /fɪzɪo; fɪziəʊ/ *prefix* also 又作 **physi-** *technical*【术语】**1** concerning nature and living things 关于自然和生物的: *physiology* (=study of how the body works) 生理学 **2** physical 物理的: *physiotherapy* (=treatment using exercises etc) 物理疗法

phys·i·og·no·my /ˌfɪzɪˈɑgnəmɪ; ˌfɪziˈɒnəmi/ *n* [C] *technical or humorous* the general appearance of a person's face【术语或幽默】相貌, 容貌

phys·i·ol·o·gy /ˌfɪzɪˈɑlədʒɪ; ˌfɪziˈɒlədʒi/ *n* [U] **1** the science concerned with the study of how the bodies of living things work 生理学 **2** the way the body of a person or an animal works and looks〔人或动物的〕生理机能; 生理: *A newborn's physiology is not the same as an older baby's.* 新生儿的生理机能和大一些的婴儿是不一样的。—compare 比较 ANATOMY —**physiologist** *n* [C] —**physiological** /ˌfɪzɪəˈlɑdʒɪkl; ˌfɪziəˈlɒdʒɪkəl◂/ *adj*: *The doctors could find no physiological cause for his illness.* 医生们找不出他患病的生理方面的原因。

phys·i·o·ther·a·pist /ˌfɪzɪoˈθɛrəpɪst; ˌfɪziəʊˈθerəpɪ̈st/ *n* [C] someone whose job is to give PHYSIOTHERAPY as a treatment for medical conditions 理疗师; 物理治疗师

phys·i·o·ther·a·py /ˌfɪzɪoˈθɛrəpɪ; ˌfɪziəʊˈθerəpi/ *n* [U] a treatment for illnesses and problems with muscles which uses special exercises, rubbing, heat etc 物理疗法, 理疗

phy·sique /fɪˈzik; fɪ̈ˈziːk/ *n* [C] the shape and appearance of a human body, especially a man's body〔尤指男人的〕体格, 体形: *exercises designed to improve your physique* 为改善你的体形而设计的运动

pi /paɪ; paɪ/ *n* [U] *technical* a number that is represented by the Greek letter (π) and is equal to the distance around a circle, divided by its width【术语】圆周率 (π)

PIA Personal Investment Authority; a British organization which checks that financial companies do not give people bad advice or sell them the wrong type of insurance or PENSION. The PIA can fine companies and order them to pay money to people who have been given the wrong advice. 个人投资局〔英国一组织。其职责是监管金融公司, 以免向个人投资者提供恶意投资建议或出售不良险种或养老保险。个人投资局有权处罚违规公司并责令其对个人投资者赔偿〕

Pi·af /piˈɑf; ˈpiːæf/, **E·dith** /ˈidɪθ; ˈiːdɪθ/ (1915-63) a French CABARET singer and songwriter, sometimes called 'The Little Sparrow'. She is famous for her powerful and emotional performances, for songs such as *Non, je ne regrette rien.* 皮亚芙〔(1915-1963), 法国夜总会歌手、词作家, 有时称"小麻雀"。她以富有感染力的动情表演闻名, 最出名的歌曲是《不, 我从不后悔》〕

pi·a·nist /pɪˈænɪst; ˈpiːənɪ̈st/ *n* [C] someone who plays the piano, especially very well 钢琴演奏者, 钢琴家

pi·an·o¹ /pɪˈæno; piˈænəʊ/ *n* [C] a large musical instrument that you play by sitting in front of it and pressing the KEYS (=narrow black and white bars) 钢琴

piano² *adj, adv* played or sung quietly〔弹或唱时〕轻柔的[地]

pi·a·no·la /ˌpiəˈnolə; ˌpiːəˈnəʊlə/ *n* [C] a PLAYER PIANO 自动钢琴

piano stool /ˈ··· ˌ·/ *n* [C] a small seat for sitting on while you play the piano〔弹奏钢琴时坐的〕琴凳

pi·az·za /pɪˈæzə; piˈætsə/ *n* [C] a public square (=large open area in a city) or market place, especially in Italy〔尤指意大利的〕广场; 市场

pic·a·dor /ˈpɪkəˌdɔr; ˈpɪkədɔː/ *n* [C] a man in a BULLFIGHT who rides a horse, and annoys and weakens the BULL by sticking a long spear into it〔斗牛中用长矛刺牛使之发怒并变虚弱的〕骑马斗牛士

Pi·card /pɪˈkɑr; pɪˈkɑː/, **Cap·tain Jean Luc** /ˈkæptɪn ˈʒɑŋ ˈljuk; ˈkæptɪ̈n ˈʒɔːŋ ˈljuːk/ the main character in the television programme *Star Trek: The Next Generation.* Picard is a Frenchman played by the British actor Patrick Stewart. Picard is clever and brave and in charge of the Starship Enterprise. *Star Trek: The Next Generation* was the SEQUEL to *Star Trek.* 皮卡尔上校〔电视剧《星舰迷航记: 下一代》的主人公。皮卡尔是法国人, 由英国演员帕特里克·斯图尔特饰演。他聪明、勇敢, 掌管着"进取号"星舰。《星舰迷航记: 下一代》是《星舰迷航记》的续篇〕

pic·a·resque /ˌpɪkəˈrɛsk; ˌpɪkəˈresk◂/ *adj* a picaresque story or NOVEL tells the adventures and travels of a character whose behaviour is not always moral but who is still likeable〔指故事或小说〕以流浪汉冒险事迹为题材的

Pi·cas·so /pɪˈkɑso; pɪˈkæsəʊ/, **Pab·lo** /ˈpɑblo; ˈpæbləʊ/ (1881-1973) a Spanish artist who was one of the greatest and most original artists of the 20th century. After training as an artist in Barcelona and Madrid he moved to Paris in 1900 and stayed there for many years. He helped to develop CUBISM and other styles of abstract art, and his work is divided into periods, such as the 'Blue Period' and the 'Rose Period'. His many famous paintings include *Les Demoiselles d'Avignon* and *Guernica*, a criticism of war and FASCISM. 毕加索〔(1881-1973), 西班牙艺术家, 20世纪最伟大、最富创造力的艺术家之一。他曾在巴塞罗那和马德里接受过艺术的熏陶, 于1900年去了巴黎并在那里生活了许多年。他促进立体主义等抽象艺术风格的发展。其艺术创作可分为若干时期, 如"蓝色时期"与"粉色时期"等。他创作了大量名画, 包括《亚威农的少女》和《格尔尼卡》, 其中《格尔尼卡》是抨击战争和法西斯主义的一幅作品〕

pic·a·yune /ˌpɪkəˈjun; ˌpɪkəˈjuːn/ *adj AmE* small and unimportant【美】微不足道的, 无关紧要的, 琐细的: *the picayune squabbling of party politicians* 政党的政客为琐事进行的争论

Pic·ca·dil·ly /ˌpɪkəˈdɪlɪ; ˌpɪkəˈdɪli◂/ a street in central London along the northern edge of Green Park, between Hyde Park Corner and Piccadilly Circus, where there are many expensive hotels and shops 皮卡迪利大街〔伦敦市中心沿格林公园北缘的一条大街, 地处海德公园角和皮卡迪利广场之间。此处有多家高档酒店和商店〕

Piccadilly Cir·cus /ˌ··· ˈ··/ a round, open area in central London, where several streets join together, famous for being very busy, for its advertising signs made of NEON lights, and for the statue of Eros in its centre. People sometimes say that a place is like Piccadilly Circus to mean that it is very busy. 皮卡迪利广场〔伦敦市中心一圆形露天广场。此地是几条大街的交汇点, 以繁华热闹、霓虹灯看板以及广场中央的爱神厄洛斯雕像著称。人们有时说某一地方像皮卡迪利广场, 意指该地方繁华热闹〕

pic·ca·lil·li /ˌpɪkəˈlɪlɪ; ˌpɪkəˈlɪli/ *n* [U] a hot-tasting sauce made with small pieces of vegetables and eaten with cold meat 辣泡菜

pic·co·lo /ˈpɪkəˌlo; ˈpɪkələʊ/ *n plural* **piccolos** [C] a musical instrument that looks like a small FLUTE 短笛

pick¹ /pɪk; pɪk/ *v* [T]

1 ▶CHOOSE STH 选择某物◀ to choose someone or something good or suitable from a group or range of people or things 挑选; 选择: *Students have to pick three courses from a list of 15.* 学生必须从15门学科中选修3门。| *Let me pick a few examples at random.* 让我随便选取几个例子。| **pick your words** (=be careful about what you say) 斟酌词句 *Trevor was picking his words with great care.* 特雷弗正在小心地斟字酌句。| **pick sb as** *The group picked me as their spokesperson.* 这个组选我作为他们的发言人。| **pick sb/sth for** *Harris was picked for the England team.* 哈里斯被选进了英格兰队。| **pick sb to do sth** *She has been picked to represent us in Rome.* 她已被挑选为我们在罗马的代表。—see also 另见 PICKED, **pick out** (PICK¹)

2 ▶FLOWERS/FRUIT ETC 花/水果等◀ to pull off or break off a flower, fruit, nut etc from a plant or tree 采, 摘〔花果等〕: *The cotton was picked by teams of men.* 棉花是由男队采摘的。| *We*

picked some blackberries to eat on the way. 我们采了一些黑莓以备路上吃。| **pick sb sth** *He picked her a single red rose.* 他采了一朵红玫瑰给她。| **pick a bunch/a basketful etc** *Amy picked a small bunch of wild flowers.* 埃米采了一小束野花。| **newly/freshly picked** *Runner beans should be eaten young and freshly picked.* 红花菜豆应趁幼嫩新鲜的时候吃。| **go grape/strawberry etc picking** (=pick something either for your own use or as a part-time job) 去摘葡萄/采草莓等

3 ▶SMALL THINGS/PIECES 小东西/小碎片◀ to remove small things from something, or pull off small pieces of something 挖, 剔: **pick sth from/off/out of** *Ahmed picked the melon pips from his teeth.* 阿米德剔去牙缝里的瓜子。| *She was nervously picking bits of fluff off her sweater.* 她正在紧张地揪去毛衣上的小绒毛。| **pick a hole in sth** (=make a hole in something by repeatedly pulling off small pieces of it) 在某物上挖[凿, 掘]出一个洞

4 pick your teeth to remove bits of food from between your teeth, with your fingers or something pointed 剔牙

5 pick your nose to take MUCUS from your nose with your finger 〔用手〕挖鼻孔

6 pick sth clean to take all the meat from a bone 把〔骨头〕剔[啃]干净

7 pick your way through/across/among etc to move slowly and carefully, choosing exactly where to put your feet down 小心翼翼地穿过: *She picked her way between the piles of books.* 她小心翼翼地走在书堆中间。

8 pick and choose to choose only the people or things you really like 仔细挑选〔真正喜欢的人或物〕, 挑挑拣拣: *We can't pick and choose, we'll have to take what they give us.* 我们不能挑挑拣拣, 只能是他们给什么, 我们就要什么。

9 pick a quarrel/fight (with sb) to deliberately start a quarrel or fight with someone 〔故意〕(向某人) 挑衅, 找碴儿: *He got drunk one night and picked a quarrel with his girlfriend.* 有一天晚上他喝醉了, 就向女朋友找碴儿吵架。

10 pick sb's brains to ask someone who knows a lot about something for information and advice about it 请教某人: *Have you got a minute? I need to pick your brains.* 你有时间吗? 我需要向你请教请教。

11 pick a lock (with) to use something that is not a key to unlock a door, drawer etc 〔用钥匙之外的东西〕打开[撬开]锁: *She picked the lock with a hairpin.* 她用发夹把锁打开了。

12 pick holes (in) to criticize a plan, an idea etc 批评〔计划、观点等〕; 挑…的毛病; 找…的漏洞: *I had no trouble picking holes in her theory.* 我毫不费事地找出了她理论中的漏洞。| *Stop picking holes! I bet you couldn't do any better.* 别再挑毛病了! 我敢肯定要你做也好不到哪里去。

13 pick sb's pocket to quietly steal something from someone's pocket 〔从口袋里〕偷, 扒窃: *When all the fuss died down I found my pocket had been picked.* 当所有的忙乱平息下来时, 我发现口袋里的东西被扒窃了。—see also 另见 PICKPOCKET

14 pick a winner *informal* an expression meaning to make a very good choice, sometimes used jokingly when you think someone has made a very bad choice 【非正式】挑选得极好〔有时戏谑地用作反话〕

15 pick sb/sth to pieces *informal* to criticize someone or something very severely and in a very detailed way 【非正式】把某人/某物驳得体无完肤; 对某人/某物吹毛求疵

16 ▶MUSICAL INSTRUMENT 乐器◀ *AmE* to play a musical instrument by pulling at its strings with your fingers; PLUCK¹ (5) 【美】弹拨〔琴弦〕; 弹奏〔弦乐器〕 —see also 另见 **have a bone to pick with sb** (BONE¹ (2))

pick at sth *phr v* [T] **1** to eat something taking small bites and without much interest, for example because you feel unhappy 〔因不高兴而〕一点一点地吃, 挑挑拣拣地吃: *He picked gloomily at his lamb chop.* 他沮丧地一点一点吃着羊排。**2** to touch something repeatedly with your fingers, often pulling it slightly 拉扯: *The little boy was picking at his mother's sleeve, trying to get her attention.* 这个小男孩正在拉扯他妈妈的袖子, 试图引起她的注意。

pick sb/sth ↔ **off** *phr v* [T] to shoot people or animals that are some distance away one at a time, by taking careful aim 逐个地仔细瞄准射杀〔人或动物〕: *The sniper was picking off our men one by one.* 那个狙击手正在把我们的人逐个瞄准打死。

pick on sb/sth *phr v* [T] *spoken* 【口】**1** to choose someone to do an unpleasant job or blame someone for something, especially unfairly 选中〔某人做不愉快的工作〕; 〔尤指不公平地〕责备〔某人〕: *Why does the boss always pick on me?* 为什么老板总是跟我过不去? | *You big bully – pick on someone your own size!* 你这个恃强凌弱的大坏蛋 —— 挑一个跟你个头一样大的人欺负呀! **2** to decide to choose someone or something 选中〔某人或某物〕: *First, pick on some daily task that you all share.* 首先, 挑选出某项你们都要分担的日常工作。

pick sb/sth ↔ **out** *phr v* [T] **1** to choose someone or something carefully 认真挑选〔人或物〕: *Pick out all the words in the poem that suggest despair.* 挑出这首诗中所有表示绝望的词。**2** to recognize someone or something in a group of people or things 分辨出, 辨认出: *It was easy to pick out Bob's father.* 鲍勃的父亲很容易被认出来。| *I could just pick out a few landmarks in the gloom.* 在黑暗中我只能分辨出几处地标。**3 a)** if you pick out a shape, letter etc in a particular colour, you make it that colour so that it can be clearly seen 〔用某种颜色〕把…衬托出来: *Every name on the memorial was picked out in scarlet edged with gold.* 纪念碑上的每个名字都是深红色的, 并镶上了金边, 十分显眼。**b)** if a light picks someone or something out, it shines directly on it 〔光〕直接照射在…上: *The searchlight picked out a figure on the roof.* 探照灯照在屋顶的一个人身上。**4** to play a tune on a stringed musical instrument slowly or with difficulty 凭记忆〔缓慢或困难地在弦乐器上〕弹奏〔曲调〕: *He picked out a moody chord on his guitar.* 他缓慢地拨动吉他, 凭记忆弹奏起忧伤的和弦。

pick over ↔ sth *phr v* [T] to examine a group of small things very carefully in order to choose the ones you want 仔细检查…以选出想要的东西, 甄选, 精选: *He turned the drawer upside-down and picked over the spilled contents.* 他把抽屉翻个底朝天, 仔细从倒出来的东西中挑选。

pick through sth *phr v* [T] to search through a pile or group of things, and take the one that you want 在…里搜寻〔以发现想要的东西〕

pick up 捡起, 拿起, 拾起

Steve is picking up the can.
史蒂夫正在捡起罐子。

Mom picked up her jacket from the dry cleaner's.
妈妈从干洗店取回她的短上衣。

The truck driver picked up a hitchhiker.
卡车司机接载了一个搭便车的人。

pick up *phr v*

1 ▶LIFT STH UP 捡起, 拿起, 拾起◀ [T **pick** sth ↔ **up**] to lift something up from a surface 捡起, 拿起, 拾起: *She kept picking up magazines and putting them down again.* 她不断地把那些杂志拿起来又放下。| *My wife picks the baby up whenever it cries.* 每次婴儿一哭, 我妻子就把他抱起来。| *The phone rang and I picked it up.* 电话响起, 我拿起了话筒。| *The vacuum cleaner won't pick this stuff up.* 吸尘器不能把这东西吸起来。| **pick sth up by sth** *The lioness picked up her cub by its neck.* 母狮叼住幼

狮的脖子把它衔起来。| **bend/stoop (down) and pick sth up** *Seth bent to pick up the papers.* 塞思弯腰捡起文件。| **pick your feet up** (=used to tell someone to walk properly) 把你的脚提起来〔用于告诉某人好好走路〕

2 pick yourself up to get up from the ground after a fall〔跌倒后〕再站起来: *Carol picked herself up and dusted herself off.* 卡萝尔跌倒后爬了起来，拍去自己身上的灰尘。

3 ►TIDY STH 整理某物◄ [T **pick** sth ↔ **up**] **a)** to put toys, magazines etc away neatly 把〔玩具、杂志等〕收拾起来; 整理〔某物〕: *Please pick up your slippers.* 请把你的拖鞋收拾好。**b)** *AmE* to make a place tidy【美】整理，收拾某个地方: *Connie had made some effort to pick up the apartment.* 康妮费了一些功夫才把公寓收拾干净。

4 pick up after sb *informal especially AmE* to tidy things that someone else has left untidy【非正式，尤美】跟在某人后面收拾[整理]东西: *Who wants to get married and spend their life picking up after some man?* 谁愿意结了婚就一辈子跟在某个男人后面收拾东西?

5 ►GET STH 获得某物，得到某物◄ [T **pick** sth ↔ **up**] *informal*【非正式】**a)** to find or get something, especially unexpectedly〔尤指无意中〕发现，得到: *I picked up a bug on holiday.* (=became ill) 我度假时染上了病。| *Hill only picked up four points from the two races.* 希尔两次赛跑只得了四分。| *We picked up some nice souvenirs.* 我们买到一些很不错的纪念品。| *Where can I pick up a cheap video camera?* 我到哪里可以买到一台廉价的摄像机? **b)** to get or buy something, while you are going somewhere or doing something〔去某地或做某事时〕得到，买到〔某物〕: *I picked up an evening paper on the way home.* 我在回家的路上买了一份晚报。| *For more details, pick up a leaflet in your local post office.* 要了解更多细节，你可以在当地的邮局领取一份小册子。

6 ►COLLECT SB/STH 接某人/取某物◄ [T **pick** sth ↔ **up**] to collect someone who is waiting for you or something that you have left somewhere or need 接〔某人〕，取〔某物〕: *I'll pick my things up later.* 我过一会儿来取我的东西。| *She just dropped by to pick up her mail.* 她只是顺便过来取她的邮件。| *My husband will pick you up in the car.* 我丈夫会开车来接你。| *Pick me up at 8:00.* 8点来接我。

7 ►SKILL/INFORMATION ETC 技术/信息等◄ [T **pick** sth ↔ **up**] to get a skill, language, habit, idea or piece of information by chance rather than by deliberately trying to get it〔偶然、无意间〕学会〔技术、语言〕; 染上〔习惯〕; 想到〔主意〕; 得到〔信息〕: *"Where did you study Greek?" "I didn't, I just sort of picked it up when I lived there."* "你在哪里学的希腊语?" "我没学，只是在希腊生活时偶然会了一点。" | *If you sing it several times, your children will begin to pick up the words.* 如果你把它唱上几遍，你的孩子就会不知不觉地学会歌词。| *There's a tip I picked up from a professional model.* 我偶然从一位职业模特儿那里学到了一个小窍门。

8 ►RADIO/RECORDING 无线电/录音◄ if a machine picks up a sound, a movement or the presence of something, it is able to receive it, record it, or TRANSMIT (1) it 收看[收听]到; 记录; 传送: *The sensors pick up faint vibrations in the Earth.* 这些传感器可记录地球内部微弱的振动。| *I managed to pick up an American news broadcast.* 我设法收听到一档美国的新闻广播节目。

9 ►LET SB INTO A VEHICLE 让某人进入车辆◄ [T **pick** sb ↔ **up**] to stop and let someone get into your car, boat etc 搭载，接载: *They were picked up by a fishing boat.* 他们被一艘渔船接走了。| *It is an offence to pick up or set down a hitchhiker on a motorway.* 在高速公路上让搭便车的人上下车是违章的。

10 ►BECOME FRIENDLY WITH SB 与某人关系变得友好起来◄ [T **pick** sb ↔ **up**] to become friendly with someone you have just met because you find them sexually attractive 结识，勾搭上〔某人〕; 结识: *I wish I could just go out and pick up a nice man.* 我希望我能够走出去就结识一位好男人。| *Are you trying to pick me up?* 你在设法勾搭我吗?

11 ►NOTICE STH 注意到某事物◄ [T **pick** sth ↔ **up**] **a)** [U] to smell a slight smell or hear a quiet sound 闻到〔轻微的味道〕; 听到〔轻微的声音〕: *Then he picked up the even fainter aroma of apple pie.* 然后他闻到一点更弱的苹果派的香味。| *The dogs picked up the scent and raced off.* 那些狗嗅出了气味，飞快地跑了。**b)** to see something that you are looking for 发现[找到]〔某事物〕: *She picked up a flicker of movement just beyond the fence.* 她发现篱笆那边晃动了一下。| *We picked up the car again within a block.* 我们在一个街区内又发现了那辆轿车。| **pick up the track/trail/traces** *Cody picked up the track of their horses but lost it again.* 科迪发现了他们的马的足迹，但过后又找不到了。

12 ►START AGAIN 重新开始◄ [I,T **pick** sth ↔ **up**] **a)** if a conversation, meeting etc picks up or if you pick it up, it starts again from the point where it was interrupted〔谈话、会议等〕重新开始，继续: **pick up where you left off** *informal*【非正式】*He left her for two years and then came back expecting to pick up where they had left off!* 他离开她两年后又回来了，希望重新开始两人的关系! **b)** if you pick up a point or an idea that has been mentioned, you return to it and develop it further 回过头来进一步阐述〔某观点〕: *Tocqueville picks up this theme in his later works.* 托克维尔在他后来的著作中进一步阐述了这个主题。

13 ►IMPROVE 改进，提高◄ [I] **a)** if business, your social life etc picks up, it improves〔生意、社交生活等〕改进，提高，好转: *Trade is picking up nicely.* 生意很有起色。| *The economy is finally beginning to pick up again.* 经济最终又开始有所好转。**b)** [T **pick** sb ↔ **up**] if a medicine, drink etc picks you up, it makes you feel better〔药物、饮料等〕使感觉好些，使好转 —see also 另见 PICK-ME-UP

14 sb's speed/the wind/the beat etc picks up if someone's speed etc picks up, it increases or grows stronger 某人的速度/风力/节拍等增加[增强]: *The breeze had now picked up considerably.* 微风现在已刮得大起来了。

15 pick up speed/steam to go faster 加快速度: *The train was gradually picking up speed.* 火车逐渐加快了速度。

16 pick up the bill/tab (for sth) *informal* to pay for something【非正式】(为某物)付款: *Why should the taxpayer pick up the tab for a private company's mistakes?* 为什么纳税人要为一家私人公司的过错所造成的损失付账呢?

17 ►A COLOUR 颜色◄ [T **pick** sth ↔ **up**] if a colour or a piece of furniture picks up the colour of something else, it has small amounts of that colour in it〔颜色或家具〕有少量的…颜色: *I like the way the curtains pick up the red and yellow in the rug.* 我喜欢那些窗帘带一点地毯中的红色和黄色。

18 ►A CRIMINAL 罪犯◄ [T **pick** sb ↔ **up**] if the police or another organized group of people pick someone up, they find them and take them somewhere, to answer questions or to be locked up 逮捕; 拘捕: *The coastguard picked him up at Dover.* 海岸警卫队员在多佛尔逮捕了他。| *She was picked up on prostitution charges.* 她因被控卖淫而遭拘捕。

19 pick up the pieces (of sth) if you pick up the pieces of a business, relationship etc that has gone seriously wrong, you try to get it back to the point where it was before 重整旗鼓; 恢复正常; 重修旧好: *Small agricultural communities are picking up the pieces after the long depression.* 长时间的萧条之后，小型的农业社区正在重整旗鼓。

20 pick up the threads (of sth) if you pick up the threads of a relationship, a way of life, or an idea that has been interrupted, you try to return to it again 恢复〔被中断的关系、生活方式、观念〕: *When I got home after the war it wasn't so easy to pick up the threads of my ordinary life again.* 战后我回到家中，要重新过起普通人的生活可不那么容易。

pick up on *phr v* [T] **1** [**pick up on** sth] **a)** to notice something that other people do not notice 注意到〔别人没有注意到的事物〕: *It was very smart of you to pick up on the undercurrents between those two.* 你注意到了那两人之间潜在的情绪，真是很聪明。**b)** to notice something and react to it 理解并作出反应: *I was trying to indicate that I didn't want to go, but they didn't pick up on it.* 我试图暗示我不想去，但他们没有会意到这点。**c)** to return to a point or an idea that has been mentioned and discuss it further 重新回到〔已被提到的论点或观点〕并作进一步讨论: *Can I just pick up on your objections to the project?* 我能否回过头来进一步谈谈你反对这项计划的问题呢? **2** [**pick** sb **up on** sth] to criticize someone slightly for something they have said〔因某人说了某种话而〕指责，责备: *The Senator picked him up on his use of the word 'deception'.* 那位参议员因他使用了"欺骗"一词而批评了他。

pick² *n* **1** [U] choice 挑选，选择: **take your pick** (=choose) 选择，挑选 *You can have any one you like – take your pick!* 你想要哪一个都行 —— 自己挑吧! | **have your pick of** (=to be able to choose any one of a group of things) 任意挑选 *Sarah could have had her pick of any university in the country, but she chose her local college.* 萨拉原本可以挑选全国任何一所大学，但她选择了当地的一所学院。**2 the pick of sth** *informal* the best thing or things of a group【非正式】某物中的精华[最好的东西]: *It's the pick of this month's new movies.* 这是本月上映的新影片中最好的。| **the pick of the bunch** (=the best in the group) 一批中最好的，出类拔萃者 *It's not much good, but it's the pick of the bunch.* 它虽不特别好，但它是这一批中的佼佼者。**3** [C] *AmE informal* someone or something that is chosen from among other people or things【美，非正式】挑选出来的人[物]: *Reno was able to name his own pick for the Criminal Division.* 雷诺可以自行挑选任命刑事组人员。**4** [C] a pickaxe 镐，鹤嘴锄: *He put his*

pick and shovel over his shoulder. 他把镐和铲扛在肩膀上。**5** [C] *AmE informal* a small, flat object for pulling at the strings of an instrument such as a GUITAR; PLECTRUM【美, 非正式】〔拨吉他等弦乐器用的〕拨子 —see also 另见 ICE PICK

pick·a·nin·ny /ˌpɪkəˋnɪnɪ; ˌpɪkəˈnɪni/ *n* [C] word for a small African child, used in the past but now considered very offensive 黑人小孩〔过去使用、现被认为是冒犯用语〕

pick·axe *BrE*【英】, **pickax** *AmE*【美】/ˋpɪkˌæks; ˈpɪkæks/ *n* [C] a large tool used for breaking up roads, which consists of a curved iron bar with a sharp point on each end and a long handle 镐, 鹤嘴锄

picked /pɪkt; pɪkt/ *adj* [only before noun 仅用于名词前] chosen as being very suitable for a particular job or purpose 仔细挑选的, 精选的: *The assault group consisted of six picked men.* 突击队由六名精选出来的男子组成。—see also 另见 HANDPICKED

pick·er /ˋpɪkɚ; ˈpɪkə/ *n* [C] **cotton picker/fruit picker etc** a person or machine that picks things, especially crops 摘棉工[机]/摘水果工[机]: *Orange pickers are on strike in California.* 加利福尼亚的柑橘采摘工在罢工。

pick·et¹ /ˋpɪkɪt; ˈpɪkɨt/ *n* [C] **1** also 又作 **picket line** a group or line of people who stand or march in front of a shop, factory, government building etc to protest about something or to stop people from going in during a STRIKE〔罢工时设置的〕纠察队; 纠察线: *a picket on the steps of the Federal court building* 联邦法院大楼台阶上的纠察队 | *None of the workers crossed the picket lines.* 没有一个工人越过纠察线。**2** one person in a picket 纠察队员: *The pickets persuaded some drivers not to enter the factory.* 罢工纠察队员劝阻一些司机不要进入工厂。—see also 另见 FLYING PICKET **3** a soldier or a group of soldiers with the special duty of guarding a military camp 警戒哨; 警戒队: **picket duty** *Hanks, you're on picket duty tonight.* 汉克斯, 今晚该你放哨。

picket² *v* **1** [I,T] to stand or march in front of a shop, factory, government building etc to protest about something or to stop people from going in during a STRIKE 在…处抗议, 在…设置纠察队, (派…) 担任纠察队员: *protesters picketing outside the White House gates* 在白宫门外示威的抗议者 | **picket sth** *Miners picketed every pit for months.* 矿工已有好几个月在每个矿井进行纠察了。**2** [T] to place soldiers around or near a place as guards 派士兵担任警戒哨

picket fence /ˋ‥ˌ·/ *n* [C] *AmE* a fence made up of a line of strong pointed sticks fixed in the ground【美】〔用尖板条连成的〕尖桩篱栅, 栅栏, 篱笆 —see picture on page A4 参见 A4 页图

Pick·ford /ˋpɪkfɚd; ˈpɪkfəd/, **Mary** (1893-1979) a Canadian-born actress who became Hollywood's most famous silent film actress and was called 'America's Sweetheart'. She was married to the famous actor Douglas Fairbanks from 1920 to 1936, and formed United Artists with Fairbanks and Charlie Chaplin in 1919. 璧克馥〔(1893-1979), 生于加拿大的电影女演员, 好莱坞最有名的无声电影演员, 有"美国甜心"之称。1920至1936年, 她与著名演员道格拉斯·范朋克结婚, 1919年与范朋克和查理·卓别林共同创建了联美公司〕

pick·ings /ˋpɪkɪŋz; ˈpɪkɪŋz/ *n* [plural] *informal*【非正式】**rich/easy pickings** money or profits that you can get easily 容易得来的钱[利润]: *There were rich pickings to be had if you played the stock market.* 如果你玩股票, 就可轻而易举地赚到许多钱。

pick·le¹ /ˋpɪkl̩; ˈpɪkəl/ *n* **1** [U] a strong-tasting liquid made with VINEGAR, used to preserve vegetables〔腌菜用的〕醋渍液 **2** [U] *BrE* a thick cold sauce eaten with food, made from pieces of vegetables preserved in VINEGAR【英】腌菜酱, 泡菜酱: *sweet pickle* 甜味泡菜酱 | *cheese and pickle sandwiches* 干酪和腌菜酱三明治 **3** [C,U] *AmE* a CUCUMBER preserved in VINEGAR or salt water, or a slice of this【美】腌黄瓜(片), 醋渍黄瓜(片): *Would you like pickle on your cheeseburger?* 你的干酪汉堡包上要配些腌黄瓜吗? **4 be in a (pretty) pickle** *old-fashioned* to be in a difficult or confusing situation【过时】处于困境; 处于混乱境地

pickle² *v* [T] to preserve food in VINEGAR or salt water〔用醋或盐水〕腌制〔食物〕; 腌渍: *pickled onions* 腌洋葱

pick·led /ˋpɪkl̩d; ˈpɪkəld/ *adj old-fashioned informal* drunk【过时, 非正式】醉的

pick-me-up /ˋ· · ˌ·/ *n* [C] *informal* something that makes you feel more cheerful and gives you more energy, especially a drink or medicine【非正式】兴奋饮料, 提神的饮料[食品]; 兴奋剂

pick·pock·et /ˋpɪkˌpɑkɪt; ˈpɪkˌpɒkɨt/ *n* [C] someone who steals things from people's pockets, especially in a crowd 扒手

pick-up /ˋ· ·/ *n* **1** [C] *especially AmE* a small open motor vehicle with low sides, used for carrying goods【尤美】敞篷小货车: *We used the pick-up to carry the lumber to the building site.* 我们用敞篷小货车把木材运到了建筑工地。**2** [C] *informal* a stranger that you meet in a bar, at a party etc and spend a short time with, often in order to have sex【非正式】〔在酒吧、派对等中为调情而〕偶然结识的人; 勾搭的人 **3** [U] *AmE* the rate at which a vehicle can increase its speed; ACCELERATION【美】〔汽车的〕加速能力: *It was a tiny car, but it had good pick-up.* 这是一部很小的汽车, 但它有很好的加速能力。**4** [C] the part of a record player that receives and plays the sound from a record〔唱机的〕拾音器, 电唱头

pick-up truck /ˋ· · ˌ·/ *n* [C] *AmE* a PICK-UP (1)【美】敞篷小货车

Pick·wick /ˋpɪkwɪk; ˈpɪkwɪk/, **Mr** the main character in the book *The Pickwick Papers* by Charles Dickens. Pickwick is kind, happy, and not easily made angry, and always has a good opinion of other people. Many people think of him as a typical Victorian English gentleman. 匹克威克〔查尔斯·狄更斯的小说《匹克威克外传》中的主人公。他心地善良, 性格开朗, 脾气温和, 而且总是觉得别人好。在许多人看来, 他是典型的维多利亚时期的英国绅士〕

Pickwick Pa·pers, The /ˌ‥ ˈ‥/ (1836-37) a book by Charles Dickens about the adventures of the members of the Pickwick Club, who include Mr Pickwick《匹克威克外传》〔(1836-1837), 查尔斯·狄更斯创作的一部小说, 讲述匹克威克俱乐部会员的冒险故事, 其中包括匹克威克先生〕

pick·y /ˋpɪkɪ; ˈpɪki/ *adj AmE informal* someone who is picky only likes very particular things【美, 非正式】挑剔的: *a picky eater* 挑食的人 | *She's so picky about her clothes.* 她对穿什么衣服很挑剔。

picnic 野餐

pic·nic¹ /ˋpɪknɪk; ˈpɪknɪk/ *n* [C] **1** an occasion when people take food and eat it outdoors, especially in the country 野餐: *We're having a picnic in the park this afternoon.* 今天下午我们要在公园野餐。| *a picnic basket* (=for carrying food for a picnic) 野餐食品篮 **2 be no picnic** *informal* to be difficult or unpleasant and need a lot of work【非正式】不是件轻松愉快的事: *Taking 60 kids to the museum will be no picnic!* 带60个孩子去博物馆不会是件轻松愉快的事! **3 picnic lunch/supper** *especially AmE* the food you take for a picnic【尤美】野外午餐/晚餐: *Vera packed a picnic lunch and headed for the river.* 薇拉把野外午餐装好, 朝河边走去。**4** *BrE* the food you take for a picnic【英】野餐用的食物: *We'll take a picnic with us.* 我们会带野餐食物。

picnic² *v* **picnicked, picnicking** [I] to have a picnic 举行野餐; 去郊游野餐: *holidaymakers picnicking on the grass* 在草地上野餐的度假者 —**picnicker** *n* [C]

picnic ar·e·a /ˋ‥ ˌ‥·/ *n* [C] an area near a road where people in cars can stop and have a picnic〔公路附近供开车的人停下野餐的〕野餐区

pic·to·ri·al /pɪkˋtorɪəl; pɪkˈtɔːriəl/ *adj* related to paintings, drawings, or photographs 画的; 图画的; 图片的

pic·ture¹ /ˋpɪktʃɚ; ˈpɪktʃə/ *n* 

1 ►IMAGE 影像◄ [C] a painting, drawing, or photograph 画, 图画; 照片: *A picture of a waterfall hung on the wall.* 一幅瀑布画挂在墙上。| *Get the children to draw a picture of their dream house.* 让孩子画出梦想中房子的图画。| *Gary got his picture in the papers.* 加里的照片上了报纸。

2 ►SITUATION 情况◄ [singular] the general situation in a place, organization etc〔某地方、组织等的〕情况, 局面: *The general picture appears to be of low levels of union membership.* 总体情况好像是工会会员的人数处于较低水平。| *the wider political picture* 更广泛的政治局面

3 ▶DESCRIPTION 描述◀ [C usually singular 一般用单数] a description that gives you an idea of what something is like 描述, 描绘; 描写: [+of] *Archaeologists are trying to build up a picture of life in Mayan cities.* 考古学家正试图复现玛雅人的城市生活。| **paint a picture** (=describe something in a particular way) 〔以某种方式〕描述[绘] *Lee's film paints a bleak picture of life in the inner city.* 李的电影描绘了内城区的黯淡生活。

4 ▶TELEVISION 电视◀ [C usually singular 一般用单数] the image that appears on a television or cinema SCREEN 〔电视或电影的〕图像, 画面: *Something's wrong with the TV – the picture is blurry.* 这台电视机出毛病了 —— 画面模糊不清。

5 ▶MENTAL IMAGE 头脑中的形象◀ [C usually singular 一般用单数] an image or memory that you have in your mind 〔脑中的〕形象; 印象: *I still have a vivid picture of the first time I saw Paris.* 我还清晰地记得我第一次见到巴黎时的情形。

6 **take a picture** to use a camera to take a photograph 拍一张照片: *Dad took a picture of us standing by a huge redwood tree.* 父亲拍了一张我们站在一棵巨大红杉树旁的照片。

7 **put sb in the picture** to give someone information about something, so that they can understand it 使某人明白[了解]实情: *I've been away for a month so you'll have to put me in the picture.* 我离开了一个月, 所以你必须告知我详情。

8 **get the picture** *especially spoken* to understand a situation 【尤口】了解情况: *"Her parents are separated and she's being raised by her sister." "I get the picture."* "她的父母分居了, 她目前由她姐姐抚养。" "我明白了。"

9 **out of the picture** if someone is out of the picture, they are not involved in a situation 不相干; 不知情: *"Is Pam still with Eric?" "No, he's out of the picture."* "帕姆还和埃里克在一起吗?" "不, 他已经和她不相干了。"

10 ▶FILM 电影, 影片◀ **a)** [C] a word meaning a film, used especially by people in the film industry 电影〔尤被电影界人士使用〕: *It was voted the year's best picture.* 它被选为本年度最佳影片。**b) the pictures** *old-fashioned* the cinema 【过时】电影院: *Do you want to go to the pictures on Saturday?* 星期六你想去电影院看电影吗? | **be in pictures** (=act in films or work in making films) 从事电影 (表演、制作) 工作

11 **be the picture of health/innocence/despair etc** to look very healthy, innocent etc 看上去很健康/天真/绝望等: *Head bowed and sobbing, she was the picture of misery.* 她低头啜泣, 看上去非常痛苦。

12 **the big picture** *AmE informal* a situation considered as a whole, rather than its details 【美, 非正式】整体情况, 大局: *Try and get an idea of the big picture before you suggest any changes.* 在你建议进行任何改变前, 尽量了解一下整体情况。

13 **be/look a picture** *especially BrE* to be beautiful or unusual to look at 【尤英】美丽如画, 漂亮; 看起来不寻常: *Madge's garden is a picture in the summer.* 玛奇的花园在夏季美不胜收。— see also 另见 **pretty as a picture** (PRETTY² (8))

picture² *v* [T] **1** to imagine something, especially by creating an image in your mind 想象, 设想: **picture sb/sth as sth** *Rob had pictured her as kind of serious, but she wasn't like that at all.* 罗布想象她有些严肃, 但她根本不是那样。| **picture sb doing sth** *I really can't picture him skiing. He's so clumsy!* 我真的无法想象他滑雪的样子, 他那么笨拙! | **picture my surprise/horror/annoyance etc** (=used when saying how surprised, annoyed etc you were) 想象我有多么惊奇/恐惧/烦恼等〔用于表示你有多么惊奇、烦恼等〕 *Picture my surprise on finding everyone had left!* 想象一下, 当我发现每个人都离开了, 我有多么惊讶! **2** to show something or someone in a photograph, painting, or drawing 画, 绘; 拍摄: *The billboard pictured a handsome, thirtyish man smoking a cigarette.* 在这个广告牌上是一位30岁左右的英俊男子在抽烟的照片。**3** [often passive 常用被动态] to describe something clearly 〔清楚地〕描绘, 描述: *This situation is realistically pictured in the first chapter.* 第一章真实地描绘了这一状况。

picture book /ˈ‥ ·/ *n* [C] a children's book that has a lot of pictures and usually a simple story 〔儿童看的〕图画书

picture card /ˈ‥ ·/ *n* [C] a FACE CARD 花牌, 人头牌

Picture of Do·ri·an Gray, The /ˌpɪktʃə əv ˌdɔriən ˈgre; ˌpɪktʃər əv ˌdɔːriən ˈgreɪ/ (1891) a NOVEL by Oscar Wilde about a beautiful young man, Dorian Gray, who has a painting of himself that he keeps in the ATTIC (=a room under the roof) of his house. Dorian Gray's own face remains young and beautiful, but the face in the painting looks older and more ugly as Gray becomes more and more evil and immoral 《道林·格雷的肖像》〔(1891), 奥斯卡·王尔德创作的一部小说。小说中有一名叫道林·格雷的英俊青年, 他在自家屋顶的阁楼上存有一幅自己的肖像画。道林·格雷本人看上去年轻而英俊, 可随着他作恶多端、道德沦丧, 画中的他看上去却越来越老态, 越来越丑陋〕

picture pal·ace /ˈ‥ ,‥/ *n* [C] *old-fashioned, especially BrE* a large building used for showing films to the public; CINEMA 【过时, 尤英】电影院

picture-per·fect /ˌ‥ ˈ‥◂/ *adj AmE* exactly right in appearance or quality 【美】外表[品质]完美的: *Doesn't the bride look picture-perfect?* 新娘子真是太漂亮了, 对吗?

picture post·card /ˌ‥ ˈ‥/ *n* [C] *BrE* a POSTCARD with a photograph or picture on the front of it 【英】〔印有照片或图画的〕明信片

picture-postcard /ˌ‥ ˈ‥◂/ *adj* [only before noun 仅用于名词前] *BrE* very pretty 【英】非常漂亮的: *picture-postcard villages* 风景如画的村庄

picture rail /ˈ‥ ·/ *n* [C] a long narrow piece of wood fixed high on a wall, from which pictures can be hung 〔固定在墙的高处用来悬挂图画的〕挂镜线, 画镜线

pic·tur·esque /ˌpɪktʃəˈrɛsk; ˌpɪktʃəˈresk◂/ *adj* **1** a place that is picturesque is pretty and interesting, especially in an old-fashioned way 〔某个地方〕美丽的, 风景如画的: *a picturesque New England village in the fall* 秋天风景如画的新英格兰村庄 **2** language that is picturesque uses unusual, interesting, or sometimes rude words to describe things 〔语言〕生动的, 形象化的, 绘声绘色的: *He gave a picturesque account of his trip to New York.* 他绘声绘色地叙述了他的纽约之行。**3** someone who is picturesque looks or behaves in an interesting, unusual, or slightly strange way 〔人的外表或行为〕奇特的, 独特的, 不同寻常的: *a picturesque character with a long beard and a large pipe* 一个蓄着长胡须、叼着大烟斗的奇人 —**picturesquely** *adv* —**picturesqueness** *n* [U]

picture win·dow /ˈ‥ ,‥/ *n* [C] a large window made of a single piece of glass 〔一整块大玻璃做的〕观景窗

pid·dle /ˈpɪdl; ˈpɪdl/ *v* [I] *informal* to URINATE 【非正式】撒尿

piddle around also 又作 **piddle about** *BrE* 【英】 *phr v* [I] *informal* to waste time doing unimportant things 【非正式】做无关紧要的事情浪费时间; 混日子 —**piddle** *n* [U]

pid·dling /ˈpɪdlɪŋ; ˈpɪdlɪŋ/ *adj* small and unimportant 无关紧要的, 微不足道的; 琐碎的: *I can't be bothered with all these piddling details.* 我不想为那些琐碎的细节操心。

pid·gin /ˈpɪdʒɪn; ˈpɪdʒɨn/ *n* [C,U] **1** a language that is a mixture of two other languages and is used especially between people who do not speak each other's languages well 〔两种语言混合在一起的〕混杂语言, 洋泾浜语 **2 pidgin English/French etc** English, French etc that is either not very good or is mixed with the words or grammar of another language 洋泾浜英语/法语等

pie /paɪ; paɪ/ *n* [C,U] **1** a sweet food usually made with fruit baked inside a PASTRY covering 水果馅饼: *apple pie* 苹果馅饼[派] | *a slice of pie* 一块馅饼 —compare 比较 TART¹ (1) **2** *especially BrE* a food made of meat or vegetables baked in a PASTRY covering 【尤英】肉饼; 蔬菜馅饼: *He bought a pie for lunch.* 他买了个肉饼当午餐。| *steak and kidney pie* 牛排和腰子馅饼 **3 slice/share/piece of the pie** a share of something such as money, profits etc 〔钱、利润等的〕一份: *The smaller companies want a bigger share of the pie.* 那些较小的公司想分到更大的一杯羹。**4 pie in the sky** something good that someone is promising or suggesting, but which you do not think will happen 天上掉的馅饼, 不大可能实现的允诺[建议]: *The idea of full employment is just pie in the sky.* 充分就业的想法只不过是空中楼阁。—see also 另见 MUD PIE, PIE CHART, **easy as pie** (EASY¹ (1)), **eat humble pie** (HUMBLE¹ (6)), **have a finger in every pie** (FINGER¹ (11)), **be as nice as pie** (NICE (5)) S2

pie·bald /ˈpaɪˌbɔld; ˈpaɪbɔːld/ *adj* a piebald animal has large areas of skin of two different colours, usually black and white 〔动物〕有花斑的〔通常指有黑白斑的〕 —**piebald** *n* [C]

piece¹ /pis; piːs/ *n* [C] S1 W1

1 ▶SEPARATE PART 分离的部分◀ a part of something that has been separated, broken, or cut from the rest of it 碎块, 碎片; 断片, 切片: *She cut the cake into 8 pieces.* 她把蛋糕切成八块。| [+of] *How many pieces of toast would you like?* 你想要几片烤面包? | *pieces of broken glass* 碎玻璃片 | **in pieces** (=broken into many pieces) 摔成碎片 *The vase had slipped and lay in pieces on the floor.* 那只花瓶滑动了一下, 摔到地板上碎了。

2 ▶OBJECT 物体◀ a single thing of a particular type, often one that is part of a set of things 一块, 一片, 一件, 一张, 一首: *Each piece of clothing had her name written in it.* 每件衣服都写上了她的名字。| *Can I have another piece of paper?* 再给我一张纸, 好吗? | *a beautifully made piece of furniture* 做得很漂亮的一件家具 | **24-piece/60-piece etc** (=with 24, 60 etc pieces in the set) 24件/60件等的 *an 80-piece orchestra* 80人[80件乐器]组成的管弦乐队

3 ▶CONNECTED PART 相关联的部分◀ one of several different parts that must be joined together to make something 部件, 部分: *Some of the jigsaw pieces are missing.* 这套拼图的一些部分找不到了。| **in pieces** (=separated into pieces) 拆成部分 *The shelves are sold in pieces that you have to assemble.* 这些架子是以散件卖的, 你必须自己安装。| **take sth to pieces** (=separate it into pieces) 把某物拆开 *We'll have to take the whole engine to pieces to fix it.* 我们必须把整个引擎拆开才能修理。| **come to pieces** (=be designed to be separated into pieces)〔被设计成〕可以拆开的 *The table comes to pieces so it's easy to deliver.* 那张桌子可以拆卸, 所以它很容易运送。

4 piece of advice/information/gossip etc some advice, information etc 一条建议/消息/流言飞语等: *Let me give you a piece of advice – sell the car.* 让我给你一点忠告 — 把那辆汽车卖掉吧。| *a juicy piece of gossip* 有趣的小道消息

5 piece of luck/stupidity/willfulness etc something lucky, stupid etc 幸运/愚蠢/任性等的事情: *Finding that store sure was a piece of luck.* 找到那家商店确实是件幸运的事。

6 ▶LAND 土地◀ an area of land 一片土地: *The factory had been built on a piece of waste ground.* 该工厂建在一片废弃的土地上。

7 fall to pieces to become very old and damaged 变旧并损坏: *All my clothes are falling to pieces.* 我所有的衣服都破损了。

8 go to pieces to be so upset or nervous that you cannot think or behave normally〔因伤心、紧张不安而〕崩溃, 垮掉: *We're looking for someone who won't go to pieces in a crisis.* 我们在寻找一个在危机时刻不会垮下来的人。

9 smash/rip/tear sth to pieces to damage something very severely 把某物摔成/撕成碎片; 彻底毁坏某物: *The city had been shot to pieces in the air strike.* 这个城市在空袭中遭到彻底的摧毁。| *In a rage, I tore the letter to pieces.* 我一怒之下把信撕得粉碎。

10 pull/rip/tear sb to pieces to criticize someone or their ideas very severely 把某人驳得体无完肤, 严厉批评某人[某人的观点]: *After she had finished speaking, Hayes tore her to pieces.* 她说完之后, 海斯把她驳得一无是处。

11 (all) in one piece not damaged or injured 完好无损的: *Luckily the parcel arrived all in one piece.* 所幸的是, 那个包裹完好无损地送到了。| *The car was a wreck, but we got out in one piece.* 虽然那辆汽车受到严重损坏, 我们却安然无恙地出来了。

12 give sb a piece of your mind *informal* to tell someone that you are very angry with them【非正式】告诉某人你很生他们的气, 责备[申斥]某人

13 be a piece of cake *informal* to be very easy to do【非正式】很容易做的, 轻松的: *Learning to drive was a piece of cake for me.* 学开车对我来说是件很容易的事。

14 a piece of the action *informal* a share of the profits from a business activity, especially an illegal one【非正式】〔尤指从非法的商业活动中获得的〕一份收益

15 be (all) of a piece a) to be the same as something else〔与…〕相似的, 〔与…〕一样的: *The testimony was all of a piece with Mandeville's version of events.* 那份证词和曼德维尔对事件的叙述一致。**b)** to be the same in all parts 完全一样: *The style of the book is all of a piece, both in illustrations and text.* 这本书无论是插图还是文字, 都是统一的风格。

16 ▶MONEY 钱◀ a) a coin of a particular value〔某种币值的〕硬币: **ten pence/fifty-cent etc piece** *Does anyone have change for a 50 pence piece?* 有谁能给我换 50 便士的零钱吗? **b)** *old use* a coin【旧】硬币: *30 pieces of silver* 30 块银元

17 ▶ART/MUSIC ETC 艺术/音乐等◀ something that has been produced by an artist, musician, or writer〔艺术家、音乐家或作家创作的〕作品: *The 1812 Overture is one of Tchaikovsky's finest pieces.*《1812 序曲》是柴可夫斯基最好的作品之一。

18 ▶IN A NEWSPAPER 报纸上◀ a short written ARTICLE (2) in a newspaper or magazine〔报纸或杂志上的〕文章, 短文: *Did you see that piece in the Observer about censorship?* 你看到《观察家报》上那篇有关审查制度的文章了吗?

19 ▶IN GAMES 游戏中◀ a small object or figure used in playing games such as CHESS〔棋类游戏等中的〕棋子

20 ▶GUN 枪◀ *AmE slang* a small gun【美俚】小型的枪

21 be a piece of shit/crap *spoken* a rude way of saying that something is of very low quality【口】是一件废物〔表示某物质量非常低劣的粗鲁说法〕: *Why did you buy that car? It's a piece of crap!* 你为什么买那辆汽车? 那是一件废物!

22 piece of ass *AmE* an offensive expression meaning a woman, used by men when they are talking about sex【美】女人, 雌儿〔男人谈论性时的冒犯用语〕

23 a piece *AmE old-fashioned* a short distance away【美, 过时】〔路程的〕一小段: *The store is down the road a piece.* 沿着这条路往前走一小段就到那个商店了。—see also 另见 MUSEUM PIECE, PARTY PIECE, SET PIECE, **a nasty piece of work** (NASTY (6)), **pick up the pieces** (PICK UP (19)), **say your piece** (SAY¹ (2)), **the villain of the piece** (VILLAIN (3))

piece² *v*

piece sth ↔ **together** *phr v* [T] **1** to use all the facts or information you have about a situation in order to understand it〔把所有事实或信息〕拼凑起来: *Police are still trying to piece together his movements before the murder.* 警方还在设法拼凑他在谋杀案前的行动。**2** to put all the separate parts of an object into the correct order or position〔把物体的部件〕拼合起来: *He was slowly piecing together torn fragments of a letter.* 他正在慢慢地把撕碎的信拼起来。

pi·èce de ré·sis·tance /ˌpjɛs də ˌrezisˋtɑ̃s; piˌes də reziːˈstɑːns/ *n* [C] *French* the best or most important thing or event in a series, especially when it comes after all the others【法】最佳项目; 最重要的事件: *The pièce de résistance was an enormous birthday cake with 21 candles.* 最重要的东西是一个巨大的插着 21 支蜡烛的生日蛋糕。

piece·meal /ˈpisˌmil; ˈpiːsmiːl/ *adj* a process that is piecemeal happens slowly in separate unconnected stages and is not planned 一步一步的, 逐渐的, 逐个的: *The airport had been developed in a piecemeal fashion.* 这个机场是逐步发展起来的。— **piecemeal** *adv*: *The house was filled with odd furniture they'd bought piecemeal.* 那屋子里满是他们一件一件零买来的不配套的家具。

piece rate /ˈ· ·/ *n* [C] an amount of money that is paid for each thing a worker produces 计件工资; 按件计酬: *The piece rate was $2.00 per skirt.* 每条裙子的计件工资为两美元。

pieces of eight /ˌ· · ˈ·/ *n* [plural] silver coins used in the past in Spain 西班牙古银币

piece·work /ˈpisˌwɝk; ˈpiːswɜːk/ *n* [U] work that is paid according to the number of things you complete or produce rather than the number of hours you work 按件计酬的工作, 计件工作

pie chart /ˈ· ˌ·/ *n* [C] a circle divided into several parts that shows how something such as an amount of money or the population is divided 圆形统计图, 饼分图〔以大小扇形表示比例〕—see picture at 参见 CHART¹ 图

pie crust /ˈ· ·/ *n* [C,U] the PASTRY (1) that is underneath and sometimes covering the meat or fruit in a PIE 馅饼皮

pied /paɪd; paɪd/ *adj* [only before noun 仅用于名词前] a pied animal, especially a bird, has two colours on its feathers or fur, usually black and white〔尤指某些鸟〕杂色的; 〔通常为〕黑白的

pied-à-terre /ˌpjed ɑ ˋtɛr; ˌpjeɪd æ ˈteə/ *n* [C] *French* a small apartment or house that is not your main home but which you own and stay in sometimes【法】备用小公寓, 临时寓所: *The Maines keep a pied-à-terre in London for theatre evenings.* 梅因一家在伦敦有一所备用房屋供看戏时过夜。

Pied Piper 花衣魔笛手

Pied Pip·er /ˌ· ˈ·· ·/ *n* **1 the Pied Piper (of Hamelin)** the main character in an old story about a man who got rid of all the rats from the town of Hamelin in Germany, by playing his FLUTE and making the rats follow him into the river and drown in it. When he was not paid for this job, the Pied Piper played his flute again and led away all the town's children too. 花衣魔笛手〔一古代神话故事中的主人公。他吹奏魔笛把德国哈默尔恩镇的老鼠引入河里全部给淹死, 从而解除了该镇的鼠患, 但因没有得到相应的报酬而再次吹响魔笛, 结果把全城的孩子都给引跑了〕**2** someone that other people like or admire, who attracts many followers 有魅力的人; 受尊崇的人

pie-eyed /ˈpaɪ ˌaɪd; ˌpaɪ ˈaɪd◂/ *adj old-fashioned* very drunk【过时】烂醉的

pier /pɪr; pɪə/ *n* [C] **1** a structure that is built out into the water so that boats can stop next to it〔伸向海中的〕突堤码头; 凸式码头: *The troop transport ship docked at Pier Five.* 运兵船停靠在5号码头。—compare 比较 JETTY **2** *especially BrE* a structure that is built out into the sea and has small buildings on it where people can eat, play games, and enjoy themselves【尤英】〔伸入海中, 上面有小型建筑物供人们游乐的〕突堤, 长堤: *Brighton pier* 布赖顿长堤 | *a concert on the pier* 在长堤上举行的音乐会 —compare 比较 BOARDWALK **3** a thick post of stone, wood, or metal used to support something such as a bridge〔石头、木头或金属的〕桥墩, 支柱

pierce /pɪrs; pɪəs/ *v* [T] **1** to make a small hole in or through something using an object with a sharp point 刺入, 刺穿, 刺破: *Maybe you can pierce another hole in your belt.* 也许你可以在皮带上再穿一个洞。| *Steam the corn until it can easily be pierced by a fork.* 把玉米蒸到可以用叉子一扎就破的程度。**2 have your ears/nose etc pierced** to have a small hole made in your ears, nose etc so that you can wear jewellery 给耳朵/鼻子等穿孔 **3** if sound, light, pain etc pierces something you can suddenly hear it, see it, or feel it〔声音、光、痛苦等〕被突然听到〔看到、感觉到〕: *The sun finally pierced the haze and the day was beautiful.* 太阳终于划破了阴霾, 天很好。| *A sudden scream pierced the air.* 突然一声尖叫划破了长空。**4 pierced ear/nose etc** a part of your body that has had small holes made in it so that you can wear jewellery 穿了孔的耳朵/鼻子等

Pierce, Franklin (1804-69) the fourteenth president of the US, from 1853 to 1857 皮尔斯〔(1804-1869), 1853至1857年担任美国第十四任总统〕

pierc·ing /ˈpɪrsɪŋ; ˈpɪəsɪŋ/ *adj*

1 ▶**SOUND** 声音◀ high, sharp, and usually unpleasant 尖锐的, 刺耳的: *Raimundo grinned and let out a piercing whistle.* 雷蒙多咧嘴一笑, 接着发出一声刺耳的口哨声。

2 ▶**COLD/WIND** 寒冷/风◀ very cold and seeming to cut through your clothes 凛冽的, 刺骨的: *The wind whipped off the water with a piercing bite.* 凛冽刺骨的寒风掠过水面。

3 ▶**EYES/LOOK** 眼睛/目光◀ seeming to examine things and notice and understand more than other people would 敏锐的, 锐利的, 有洞察力的: *Her piercing brown eyes scanned their faces.* 她犀利的棕色眼睛扫视了他们的脸。

4 ▶**REMARK/QUESTION** 评论/问题◀ piercing questions, criticisms etc seem to notice and express the main point of something very clearly 深刻的, 尖锐的, 直指要害的

5 ▶**EMOTION** 感情◀ affecting your emotions very much, especially in a sad way 强烈的〔尤指伤心的〕: *She had a piercing vision of what life would be like without David.* 她很担心没有戴维生活将会怎么过。—**piercingly** *adv*

Pierre /pɪr; pɪə/ the capital city of the US state of South Dakota 皮尔〔美国南达科他州首府〕

Pier·rot /ˈpɪəro; ˈpɪərəʊ/ a character from old French PANTOMIME who has a sad, white face, and wears loose, white clothes with a stiff circular collar 定型男丑角〔法国古代哑剧中一角色。通常涂白脸, 面容悲伤, 身着硬圆领的宽松白衣〕

pierrot *n* [C] a CLOWN with white clothes and a white painted face〔穿白衣、涂白脸的〕丑角, 小丑

Piers Plow·man /pɪrz ˋplaumən; ˌpɪəz ˈplaʊmən/ a religious poem written in Middle English by William Langland (?1332-?1400)《农夫皮尔斯》〔威廉·朗格兰 (?1332-?1400) 用中世纪英语创作的一首宗教诗歌〕

pi·e·ty /ˈpaɪətɪ; ˈpaɪəti/ *n* [U] respect for God and religion, often shown in the way you behave 虔诚, 虔敬 —opposite 反义词 IMPIETY —see also 另见 PIOUS

pie·zo·e·lec·tric /paɪˌizo·ɪˋlɛktrɪk; ˌpiːzəʊ-ɪˈlektrɪk◂/ *adj* operated by electricity which is produced by pressure on a CRYSTAL 压电的

pif·fle /ˈpɪfl; ˈpɪfəl/ *n* [U] *BrE old-fashioned* nonsense【英, 过时】废话, 无聊话; 胡说

pif·fling /ˈpɪflɪŋ; ˈpɪflɪŋ/ *adj BrE old-fashioned* unimportant or useless【英, 过时】不重要的; 无用的: *Even these sums seem piffling in comparison.* 相比之下, 甚至这些钱也显得微不足道。

2 **pig**[1] /pɪg; pɪg/ *n* [C]

1 ▶**ANIMAL** 动物◀ a farm animal that is usually pink or black and has short legs, a fat body, and a curved tail 猪 —see also 另见 GUINEA PIG (1)

2 ▶**PERSON** 人◀ *spoken*【口】**a)** someone who eats too much or eats more than their share 贪吃的人: *Greedy pig, you ate all the candy!* 贪吃的家伙, 你把所有的糖果都吃了! **b)** someone who is very dirty or untidy 不整洁的人, 肮脏的人: *How can you live in this mess? You're such a pig!* 你怎么能住在这么乱的地方? 你可真脏! **c)** someone who is unpleasant or offensive 令人讨厌的人; 无礼的人: *You're a selfish pig.* 你是个自私鬼。| **male chauvinist pig** (=unpleasant man who thinks women are not equal to men) 大男子主义者

3 ▶**POLICE** 警察◀ *slang* an insulting word meaning a police officer【俚】警察猪猡〔对警察的侮辱性称呼〕

4 a pig (of a...) *BrE spoken* something that is very difficult or unpleasant to do【英口】困难的事情; 讨厌的事: *Stripping wallpaper is a pig of a job.* 撕去墙纸是件令人讨厌的工作。

5 make a pig's ear of *BrE spoken* to do something very badly【英口】把…弄糟: *Jon's made a complete pig's ear of the decorating.* 乔恩把装修完全搞砸了。—see also 另见 **in a pig's eye** (EYE[1] (21))

pig[2] *v* [I,T] *BrE spoken* to eat a lot of food, even when you are not very hungry【英口】狼吞虎咽, 贪婪地吃: *There's no ice cream left, Tony pigged the lot.* 冰激凌没有了, 托尼把它全吃了。

pig out *phr v* [I] *informal* to eat a lot of food【非正式】大吃大喝, 狼吞虎咽: *We pigged out on pizza and beer.* 我们大吃比萨饼, 大喝啤酒。

pi·geon /ˈpɪdʒən; ˈpɪdʒɪn/ *n* **1** [C] a grey bird with short legs that is common in cities 鸽子 **2 sb's pigeon** *BrE old-fashioned* something that a particular person is responsible for【英, 过时】某人的职责[事务]: *It's not my pigeon – someone else can deal with it.* 那不是我的事, 别人会处理的。—see also 另见 CARRIER PIGEON, CLAY PIGEON SHOOTING, HOMING PIGEON 3

CULTURAL NOTE 文化注释

In the UK, people used to think of Trafalgar Square in London as a place where you could go to feed the pigeons, and tourists used to have photographs taken with pigeons sitting on their shoulders. But people are not allowed to feed them any more, and most of the pigeons have been removed. There is also a STEREOTYPE about people from the North of England who keep pigeons and race them, to see which pigeon returns home first. Pigeons are generally disliked in both the US and the UK, however, because large numbers of them live in towns, leaving their DROPPINGS (=waste matter) everywhere. Some people call them 'flying RATS'. 在英国, 人们过去通常会想到伦敦的特拉法尔加广场是可以去喂鸽子的地方, 而游客也会和停落在他们肩头的鸽子合影留念。但是现在已经不允许去喂这些鸽子了, 那里的很多鸽子也被清理走了。人们对生活在英格兰北部的人有个先入为主的印象, 即他们饲养鸽子, 并观察哪只鸽子最早归巢。可是无论在英国还是美国, 鸽子都不怎么招人喜欢, 因为城市里的鸽子数量太多, 到处拉屎。有人把鸽子叫做"飞老鼠"。

pigeon-chest·ed /ˌ‥ˈ‥◂/ *adj* someone who is pigeon-chested has a narrow chest that sticks out〔人〕鸡胸的

pi·geon·hole[1] /ˈpɪdʒənˌhol; ˈpɪdʒɪnhəʊl/ *n* [C] **1** one of a set of small boxes built into a desk or into a frame on a wall, in which letters or papers can be put〔办公桌上或墙上的〕鸽笼式分类架, 信件格, 文件格 **2 put sb/sth into a pigeonhole** to have a very fixed idea about a person, activity etc, which is too simple and therefore unfair 把某人/某物简单分类

pigeonhole[2] *v* [T] to consider a person, activity etc as belonging to a particular type or group, in a way that is too simple and therefore unfair; CATEGORIZE 把〔某人或某活动等〕简单分类, 把…归档: *People tend to pigeonhole her just because she's a feminist.* 只因为她是个女权主义者, 人们往往将她简单地对号入座。

pigeon-toed /ˈ‥ˌ/ *adj* someone who is pigeon-toed has feet that point inwards rather than straight forwards〔人〕脚向内弯的, 内八字的

pig·ge·ry /ˈpɪgərɪ; ˈpɪgəri/ *n* [C] *BrE*【英】**1** a pig farm 养猪场 **2** a place where pigs are kept, usually with a building and an outdoor area; PIGSTY (1) 猪圈, 猪栏

pig·gish /ˈpɪgɪʃ; ˈpɪgɪʃ/ *adj* someone who is piggish eats too much or is dirty, or is unpleasant 贪吃的; 肮脏的, 邋遢的; 令人讨厌的: *piggish behaviour* 令人生厌的行为 —**piggishly** *adv* —**piggishness** *n* [U]

Pig·gy /ˈpɪgɪ; ˈpɪgi/ a character in the book *Lord of the Flies* by William Golding, about a group of boys who are on a small island and cannot escape. Piggy is fat and wears glasses, and the other boys treat him cruelly, and finally kill him. 皮吉〔威廉·戈尔丁的小说《蝇王》中的人物。小说讲述一群孩子被困在一座小岛上的故事。皮吉长得胖胖的, 戴副眼镜。别的孩子虐待他, 最后将他杀害〕

piggy[1] *n* [C] **1** a word meaning a pig, used especially by or to children 猪仔, 小猪〔尤用作儿语〕**2 piggy in the middle** *BrE*

【英】**a)** *informal* someone who is between two opposing groups or people and is unable to influence either side【非正式】〔夹在对立双方之间而又无法影响任何一方的〕夹在中间的人 **b)** a game in which a ball is thrown between two people who try to prevent a third person in the middle from catching it 掷球游戏〔两个人互相掷球尽量不让中间的第三人接到球的游戏〕; KEEP-AWAY *AmE*【美】

piggy² *adj* **1** like a pig 猪似的: *little piggy eyes* 猪似的小眼睛 **2** *informal* wanting or taking more food than you really need; GREEDY【非正式】贪婪的, 贪吃的: *Don't be so piggy, Ed.* 别这么贪吃, 埃德。

pig·gy·back¹ /ˋpɪgɪˌbæk; ˈpɪgibæk/ *n* [C] a ride on someone's back or shoulders 骑在…的背[肩]上, 驮, 扛: *Please, Uncle Jack, give me a piggyback!* 求求你了, 杰克叔叔, 背我一下嘛! —**piggyback** *adv*

piggyback 骑在…的背[肩]上

piggyback² *v* [I] *AmE informal* to join or be joined with something that is larger, more important or more effective【美, 非正式】〔与更大、更重要、更有效的东西〕连接起来, 附带出现[发生]: [+on/onto] *videos that simply piggyback onto the success of proven TV programs* 仅仅是靠攀上公认成功的电视节目而沾光的录像带

piggy-bank /ˊ·· ˏ/ *n* [C] a small container, usually in the shape of a pig, in which children can save coins〔猪形〕储钱罐, 扑满

pig·head·ed /ˋpɪgˋhɛdɪd; ˌpɪgˈhedɪ̣d◂/ *adj* determined to do things the way you want and refusing to change your mind, even when there are good reasons to do so; STUBBORN 顽固的, 固执的: *Stop being so pigheaded and admit that you were wrong!* 别再这么固执了, 承认你错了吧! —**pigheadedly** *adv* —**pigheadedness** *n* [U]

pig i·ron /ˊ· ˌ·· / *n* [U] a form of iron that is not pure, obtained directly from a BLAST FURNACE 生铁

Pig·let /ˋpɪglɪt; ˈpɪglɪ̣t/ a character in the stories about Winnie the Pooh by A.A. Milne. He is a small pig who walks on two legs and has no tail, and he is a friend of Winnie the Pooh. 小猪皮杰〔A.A.米尔恩创作的故事《小熊维尼》中的一个角色。它是一头小猪, 两条腿走路, 没尾巴, 是小熊维尼的朋友〕

piglet *n* [C] a young pig 小猪, 猪仔

pig·ment /ˋpɪgmənt; ˈpɪgmənt/ *n* [C,U] **1** a dry coloured powder that is mixed with oil, water etc to make paint 颜料(粉) **2** one of the natural substances in humans, plants, and animals that gives colour to skin, blood, hair etc〔人和动植物的〕天然色素

pig·men·ta·tion /ˌpɪgmənˋteʃən; ˌpɪgmənˈteɪʃən/ *n* [U] **1** the colouring of plant or animal cells caused by too much pigment 色素沉着 **2** the colouring of living things〔生物的〕天然颜色: *Pigmentation is biologically inherited.* 生物体的天然颜色是遗传的。

pig·my /ˋpɪgmɪ; ˈpɪgmi/ *n* [C] another spelling of PYGMY pygmy 的另一种拼法

Pig·pen /ˋpɪgpɛn; ˈpɪgpen/ a character in the US CARTOON STRIP called *Peanuts*, who always has a cloud of dirt all around him 皮格彭〔美国连环漫画《花生》中的一个人物。他非常脏, 满身总是蒙着一层灰〕

pigpen *n* [C] *AmE*【美】**1** a place where pigs are kept, usually with a building and an outdoor area; PIGSTY 猪圈, 猪栏 **2** *informal* a very dirty or untidy place; PIGSTY (2)【非正式】非常肮脏的地方

Pigs, Bay of —see 见 BAY OF PIGS

pig·skin /ˋpɪgˌskɪn; ˈpɪgˌskɪn/ *n* **1** [U] leather made from the skin of a pig 猪皮(革) **2** [singular] *AmE informal* the ball used in American football【美, 非正式】橄榄球: *tossing the pigskin around* 把橄榄球掷来掷去

pig·sty /ˋpɪgˌstaɪ; ˈpɪgstaɪ/ *n* [C] **1** a place where pigs are kept, usually with a building and an outdoor area 猪圈, 猪栏 **2** a very dirty or untidy place 非常肮脏的地方: *Clean up your room. It's a pigsty!* 清扫一下你的房间, 简直太脏了!

pig·swill /ˋpɪgˌswɪl; ˈpɪgˌswɪl/ *n* [U] *BrE* **1** food that is given to pigs 猪食, 泔水, 潲水 **2** tasteless or unpleasant food 无味的食物; 难吃的食物

pig·tail /ˋpɪgˌtel; ˈpɪgteɪl/ *n* [C] **1** one of two lengths of hair that have been pulled together on either side of the head and usually plaited (PLAIT¹), worn especially by very young girls 女孩垂在头两侧的长发〔通常编着〕, 发辫: **in pigtails** *Jenny wore her hair in pigtails.* 珍妮梳着辫子。**2** all of the hair pulled to the back of the head and plaited so that it hangs down 辫子〔指独辫〕; BRAID¹ (2) *AmE*【美】—compare 比较 BUNCH¹ (5), PLAIT², PONYTAIL —see picture at 参见 HAIRSTYLE 图

pike /paɪk; paɪk/ *n* [C] **1** a large fish that eats other fish and lives in rivers and lakes 狗鱼 **2** a TURNPIKE (收费)高速公路 **3** a long-handled weapon used in the past by soldiers〔古时士兵使用的〕长矛, 长枪 **4** *NEngE* a mountain or hill with a pointed top【英格兰北】尖峰: *Scafell Pike* 斯科费尔峰

Pike, Zeb·u·lon /ˋzɛbjulən; ˈzebjʊlən/ (1779-1813) a US army general and explorer who travelled through Louisiana and along the Mississippi River. Pike's Peak is named after him. 派克〔(1779-1813), 美国陆军将军、探险家。他的足迹遍布路易斯安那州及密西西比河沿岸。派克峰以他的姓氏命名〕

pike·man /ˋpaɪkmən; ˈpaɪkmən/ *n* [C] a soldier who fought in the past with a pike〔旧时的〕长矛兵

Pike's Peak /ˌ·ˈ·/ one of the Rocky Mountains in the US state of Colorado 派克峰〔美国科罗拉多州境内落基山脉的一座山峰〕

pike·staff /ˋpaɪkˌstæf; ˈpaɪkstɑːf/ *n* [C] the long wooden handle of a pike (PIKE (3)) 长矛柄, 长枪柄

pi·laff, pilaf /pəˋlɑf; ˈpiːlæf/ *n* [C,U] a pilau (菜)肉饭

pi·las·ter /pəˋlæstɚ; pɪ̣ˈlæstə/ *n* [C] a square COLUMN that sticks out partly beyond the wall of a building and is usually only a decoration〔装饰性的〕壁柱, 半露柱

Pi·late /ˋpaɪlət; ˈpaɪlət/, **Pon·tius** /ˋpɑntʃɪəs; ˈpɒnʃəs/ (1st century AD) the Roman GOVERNOR of Judaea, a former country in the area that is now Palestine, at the time when Jesus Christ was judged and killed. According to the New Testament of the Bible, Pilate offered to let Jesus go free, but the Jewish leaders would not accept this. Pilate then washed his hands and said he was not to blame for Jesus's death. People mention Pilate, or talk about someone 'washing their hands of' a problem, when they are talking about someone who is not morally strong enough to do what they think is right. 彼拉多〔(公元1世纪), 旧时犹太国(今巴勒斯坦境内)罗马总督。时值耶稣基督被审判并处死。据《圣经·新约》记载, 彼拉多提出放走耶稣, 但犹太人领袖不同意。彼拉多于是洗了洗手, 言明耶稣的死与自己无关。某人在道义上立场不够坚定, 不能坚持做自己认为正确的事, 人们就说他是彼拉多, 或者说他对某个问题"不再负责"〕

pi·lau /pɪˋlo; ˈpiːlaʊ/ *n* [C,U] a dish made from rice mixed with vegetables and often meat (菜)肉饭〔由大米加蔬菜和肉煮成〕: *mushroom pilau* 磨菇肉饭

pil·chard /ˋpɪltʃɚd; ˈpɪltʃəd/ *n* [C] a small fish that lives in the sea and can be eaten 沙丁鱼: *pilchards in tomato sauce* 番茄酱沙丁鱼

pile¹ /paɪl; paɪl/ *n* 2

1 ▶LARGE AMOUNT/MASS 大量◀ [C] **a)** a tidy collection of several things of the same kind placed on top of each other; STACK¹ (1)〔由同类东西堆成的整齐的〕堆, 叠, 摞: *We put the newspapers in piles on the floor.* 我们把报纸在地板上堆叠起来。| *The record I want is at the bottom of the pile.* 我要的那张唱片在这一摞的最底层。| [+of] *a pile of blankets* 一叠毯子 —compare 比较 HEAP¹ (1) **b)** a large mass of things collected together 一大堆: *big pile of brushwood* 一大堆柴枝

2 a pile of also 又作 **piles of** *informal* a lot of something【非正式】一大堆, 大量: *I've got piles of work to do this evening.* 我今晚有一大堆事情要做。

3 at the bottom of the pile in a very weak position in society or in an organization 处于〔社会或组织的〕底层: *At the bottom of the pile are young people in their first jobs.* 处于底层的是那些刚开始工作的年轻人。

4 ▶CLOTH/CARPETS 布料/地毯◀ [C,U] the soft surface of short threads on a CARPET or some types of cloth, especially VELVET〔地毯、某些布料, 尤指天鹅绒上的〕绒面: *a deep pile carpet* 厚绒地毯 —compare 比较 NAP¹ (2)

5 ▶POST 柱; 桩◀ [C] a heavy post made of wood, stone, or metal, pushed into the ground as a support for a building, bridge etc〔建筑物、桥梁等的〕柱, 桩

6 make a/your pile *informal* to make a lot of money【非正式】赚很多钱, 发财: *He made his pile in the antiques business.* 他做古董生意赚了大钱。

7 ▶BUILDING 建筑物◀ [C] *especially BrE* a large tall old building or group of buildings【尤英】高大的古建筑物; 建筑群: *They live in a rambling Victorian pile.* 他们居住在布局零乱的维多利亚式建筑群中。

8 ▶MEDICAL 医药的◀ piles *BrE not technical* HAEMORRHOIDS【英, 非术语】痔(疮)

pile² *v* **1** also 又作 **pile up** [T] to make a pile by collecting things together; STACK² (1) 把…堆积[堆叠]起来: *Ma stacked the cups and piled the plates.* 妈妈把杯子和盘子摞好。| *We piled the books up on the table.* 我们把书堆放在桌子上。| **pile sth high** (=make a tall pile) 高高地堆起 *Clothes were piled high on the chair.* 衣服高高地堆放在椅子上。**2** [T] to fill something or cover a surface with a lot of something 把…堆放在; 塞满, 堆满: *Anna piled spaghetti onto her plate.* 安娜把意大利面条堆在她的碟子里。| **be piled (high) with** *The cart was piled high with fruit and vegetables.* 马车上堆满了水果和蔬菜。

pile in/into sth *phr v* [T] to go quickly into a place or vehicle in a disorganized way 拥进, 挤进, 蜂拥进入: *We all piled into the back of his car.* 我们一窝蜂地挤进他车子的后座。

pile on *phr v* [T] *informal*【非正式】**1 pile on the praise/criticism etc** also 又作 **pile it on** to talk about something in a way that makes it seem much better or much worse than it really is; EXAGGERATE 过分地称赞/批评等: *Mitch was really piling on the compliments!* 米奇确实恭维得过分了! | *It can't be that bad – Nellie tends to pile it on.* 情况不可能那么糟 —— 内莉往往夸大其词。**2 pile on the agony** *BrE* to enjoy making something seem worse than it really is【英】大肆渲染坏的情况, 过分夸大坏的情况

pile out *phr v* [I] to quickly leave a place or get out of a vehicle in a rather disorderly way 挤出, 蜂拥而出: [+of] *As soon as the bell went the kids piled out of the building.* 铃声一响, 孩子们就一窝蜂地从大楼里出来了。

pile up *phr v* [I,T] to become much larger in quantity or amount, or to make something do this; ACCUMULATE (使)堆积, (使)积累: *Work is really piling up.* 工作确实越积越多。| **pile sth ↔ up** *Greg has managed to pile up enormous debts.* 格雷格已负债累累。—see also 另见 PILE-UP

pile driv·er /ˈ· ˌ··/ *n* [C] **1** a machine for pushing heavy posts into the ground 打桩机 **2** *informal* a very hard PUNCH² (1), especially in BOXING【非正式】(尤指拳击中的)重(重一)击

pile-up /ˈ· ·/ *n* [C] *informal* a road traffic accident in which several vehicles crash into each other【非正式】多车相撞, 连环撞车: *There had been several motorway pile-ups in the fog.* 雾中高速公路上发生了几起连环撞车事故。

pil·fer /ˈpɪlfɚ; ˈpɪlfə/ *v* [I,T] to steal small amounts of things, or things that are not worth much, especially from the place where you work (尤指从工作的地方)偷窃(少量或不值钱的东西), 小偷小摸: *They'd been caught pilfering building materials from the construction site.* 他们在从建筑工地偷窃建筑材料时被当场抓住。—**pilferer** *n* [C] —**pilfering** *n* [U]

pil·grim /ˈpɪlgrɪm; ˈpɪlgrɨm/ *n* [C] someone who travels a long way to a holy place for a religious reason 朝圣者, 香客: *pilgrims at Lourdes* 卢尔德的朝圣者

pil·grim·age /ˈpɪlgrəmɪdʒ; ˈpɪlgrɨmɪdʒ/ *n* [C,U] **1** a journey to a holy place for religious reasons 朝圣者的旅程: *a pilgrimage to Mecca* 去麦加朝圣 **2** a journey to a place connected with someone or something famous (去因某人或某物而有名的地方)旅行: *Elvis Presley's home has become a place of pilgrimage.* 埃尔维斯·普雷斯利的家已成了人们参观的地方。

Pilgrim Fa·thers, the /ˌ·· ˈ··/ *n* the group of English people who arrived to settle at Plymouth, Massachusetts in the US in 1620 清教徒前辈移民(1620年到达美洲创立普利茅斯殖民地的英国移民)

Pilgrim's Pro·gress, The /ˌ·· ˈ··/ a book by John Bunyan (1628-88). It is an ALLEGORY of the difficult journey of the human soul through life to Heaven. The main character, Christian, leaves his family and travels through places such as the Slough of Despond and Vanity Fair, facing many dangers on his way. 《天路历程》(约翰·班扬(1628-1688)一部寓言式作品, 讲述人的灵魂从人世到天国的艰难历程。作品中的主人公基督徒离家踏上天路历程, 途经绝望深渊和名利场等地, 一路上经历了重重危险)

Pilgrim's Way, the /ˌ·· ˈ·/ the name of an old path from Winchester to Canterbury in southern England, which pilgrims travelled along in the past 朝圣之路(从英格兰南部的温切斯特到坎特伯雷的一条古道。过去的朝圣者常取此道)

S3 **pill** /pɪl; pɪl/ *n* **1** [C] a small solid piece of medicine, that you swallow whole 药丸; 药片: *He has to take pills to control his blood pressure.* 他必须服药控制他的血压。| *sleeping pills* 安眠药 **2 the Pill** a pill taken regularly by some women in order to prevent them having babies (女用)口服避孕药: **on the Pill** *My doctor advised me to go on the Pill.* 我的医生建议我服避孕药。**3 sugar the pill** *BrE*【英】, **sweeten the pill** *AmE*【美】to do something to make an unpleasant job or situation less unpleasant for the person who has to accept it 给药丸加糖衣, 使不愉快的工作[局面]变得较易接受 **4** *AmE informal* someone who annoys you, often a child【美, 非正式】令人讨厌的人(通常指小孩): *Luke can be a real pill sometimes.* 卢克有时候确实很讨厌。—see also 另见 **a bitter pill (to swallow)** (BITTER¹ (7)), MORNING-AFTER PILL

> **CULTURAL NOTE 文化注释**
>
> **The Pill** The Pill is one of the most popular and EFFECTIVE forms of CONTRACEPTIVE used in the US and the UK. There are certain religions that do not allow women to **go on the pill** (take the pill) because they believe it is morally wrong. Many people in the US and UK, however, believe that it is acceptable to have sex for pleasure, and use the pill so that they can have sex without the risk of PREGNANCY. The Pill first became available in the 1960s, and some people connect it with the increased sexual freedom of that period of time. 口服避孕药是英美最流行、最有效的避孕手段。某些宗教不允许女性服用避孕药, 认为此举不合道德。可是在英美, 很多人都接受性爱是为了快乐的观点, 使用避孕药就不用担心不慎怀孕的问题。20世纪60年代开始有避孕药出现, 因此有人认为避孕药与那个时期逐渐开放的性自由有关。

pil·lage /ˈpɪlɪdʒ; ˈpɪlɪdʒ/ *v* [I,T] if an army pillages a place, it uses violence to steal from and damage a place that it has taken control of in a war; PLUNDER¹ (军队)抢劫, 劫掠, 掠夺 —compare 比较 LOOT² —**pillage** *n* [U] —**pillager** *n* [C]

pil·lar /ˈpɪlɚ; ˈpɪlə/ *n* [C] **1 a)** a tall upright round post used as a support for a roof 房柱, 柱子: *Huge pillars support the cathedral roof.* 巨大的柱子支撑着大教堂的屋顶。—see picture on page A4 参见 A4 页图 **b)** a tall upright round post, usually made of stone, put up to remind people of an important person or event (通常为石制的)纪念柱 **2 pillar of the community/church etc** an active and important member of a group, organization etc 社区/教会等的活跃而重要的成员[栋梁、中坚分子] **3** a very important part of a system of beliefs, especially religious beliefs (尤指宗教信仰的)非常重要的部分: *These tenets are the pillars on which our faith is founded.* 这些信条是我们信仰得以建立的基础。**4 be driven/passed from pillar to post** to go from one difficult situation to another without achieving much 到处碰壁, 走投无路 **5 pillar of dust/smoke/flame etc** a tall upright mass of dust, smoke, flame etc 一缕灰尘/烟柱/火柱等

pillar box /ˈ·· ·/ *n* [C] *old-fashioned* a large red tube-shaped box for posting letters that stands on streets in Britain【过时】(英国的)邮筒, 信筒 —compare 比较 LETTERBOX (2)

Pillars of Her·cu·les, the /ˌ·· ·ˈ···/ two very tall rocks on either side of the Strait of Gibraltar, a narrow area of sea at the western end of the Mediterranean Sea. According to ancient Greek stories, the rocks had been moved apart by Hercules, and they showed the limits of the known world. 赫拉克勒斯之柱(位于地中海西端直布罗陀海峡两岸的两块高耸的岩石。据古希腊神话记载, 赫拉克勒斯把岩石一分为二, 标明已知世界的尽头)

pill·box /ˈpɪlˌbɑks; ˈpɪlbɒks/ *n* [C] **1** a small round box for holding pills (PILL (1)) (圆形)药丸盒, 药片盒 **2** a small, strong, usually circular shelter with a gun inside it, built as a defence 碉堡, 坚固的机枪掩体 **3** also 又作 **pillbox hat** /ˌ·· ˈ·/ a small round hat for a woman (女性戴的)圆形小帽

pil·lion /ˈpɪljən; ˈpɪljən/ *n* [C] **1** a seat for a second person behind the driver of a motorcycle or a rider on a horse 摩托车后座; (马鞍后的)附座, 加鞍 **2 ride pillion** to sit behind someone who is driving a motorcycle or riding a horse 骑在摩托车后座上; 骑在马的后鞍上

pil·lock /ˈpɪlək; ˈpɪlək/ *n* [C] *BrE slang* a very stupid person【英俚】非常愚蠢的人

pil·lo·ry¹ /ˈpɪlərɪ; ˈpɪləri/ *v* [T usually passive 一般用被动态] if someone is pilloried, they are publicly criticized by a lot of people 使(某人)受公众责备: *The education secretary was pilloried by the press for his latest proposals.* 教育部长因他最近的提议而受到新闻界公开的批评。

pillory 颈手枷

pillory² *n* [C] a wooden frame with holes for the head and hands to be locked into, used in the past as a way of publicly punishing someone 颈手枷(将罪犯的颈和手夹住示众的古代刑具) —compare 比较 **the stocks** (STOCK¹ (14))

3 **pil·low¹** /ˈpɪlo; ˈpɪləʊ/ *n* [C] **1** a cloth bag filled with soft material, that you put your head on when you are sleeping 枕头 —compare 比较 CUSHION¹ (1) **2** any object used to support your head while you are sleeping 用作枕头的东西: *Paula used her rucksack as a pillow.* 葆拉把背包当作枕头。**3 pillow fight** a game in which children hit each other with pillows 枕头战〔小孩玩的游戏, 即用枕头互相打闹〕**4 pillow talk** *informal* conversation between lovers in bed【非正式】〔情人间的〕枕边话

pillow² *v* [T] to rest your head somewhere, especially so that you can go to sleep〔尤指为睡觉而〕把〔头〕枕在…: **pillow your head on sth** *Don fell asleep with his head pillowed on a sack.* 唐把头枕在一个麻袋上睡着了。

pil·low·case, pillow case /ˈpɪloˌkes; ˈpɪləʊkeɪs/ *n* [C] a cloth cover for a pillow 枕头套

3 **pi·lot¹** /ˈpaɪlət; ˈpaɪlət/ *n* [C] **1** someone who operates the controls of an aircraft or spacecraft〔飞机、宇宙飞船上的〕驾驶员, 飞行员: *an airline pilot* 航空公司飞行员 **2** someone with a special knowledge of a particular area of water, who is employed to guide ships across it〔船舶的〕领航员: *a harbour pilot* 海港领航员 **3** a television programme that is made in order to test whether people like it and would watch it〔为测试观众是否喜欢和观看的〕电视试播节目 **4 pilot test/project/scheme etc** a test that is done to see if an idea, product etc will be successful 小规模试验/试点项目/试验性计划等: *If the pilot survey goes well, we'll go into full production.* 如果这次试销调查顺利的话, 我们将投入全面生产。—see also 另见 AUTOMATIC PILOT

pilot² *v* [T] **1** to guide an aircraft, spacecraft, or ship as its pilot 驾驶〔飞机或宇宙飞船〕; 给〔船舶〕领航 **2** to help someone to go to a place 引领, 带领, 指引: **pilot sb toward/out etc** *He took my hand and piloted me through the corridors.* 他拉着我的手领着我穿过走廊。**3** to be responsible for making sure that a new law or plan is officially approved 使〔新的法律、计划〕顺利通过: **pilot sth through** *I'm relying on your skill in piloting this through Parliament.* 我要靠你的技巧使它得以在议会顺利通过。**4** to test a new idea, product etc on people to find out whether it will be successful 试用〔新想法、新产品等〕, 试行: *They are piloting parts of the book in language schools.* 他们正在语言学校试用这本书的部分内容。

pilot light /ˈ· · ·/ also 又作 **pilot burner** *n* [C] **1** a small gas flame that burns all the time and is used for lighting larger gas burners〔用于点燃大煤气用具的〕常燃引火小火苗 **2** a small electric light on a piece of electrical equipment that shows when it is turned on〔电器上显示通电的〕指示灯, 信号灯

pilot of·fi·cer /ˈ· · , · · ·/ *n* [C] a middle rank in the Royal Air Force, or someone who has this rank 英国皇家空军少尉〔军阶〕—see table on page C7 参见 C7 页附录

pi·men·to also 又作 **pimiento** /pɪˈmɛnto; pȷ̊ˈmentəʊ/ *n* [C,U] a small red PEPPER often used for putting inside OLIVES 甜辣椒, 番椒

Pimms /pɪmz; pɪmz/ *trademark* a type of alcoholic drink containing GIN, whose full name is **Pimms Number One Cup**. Pimms is drunk with ice, LEMONADE, and small pieces of fruit, and in the UK it is connected in people's minds with fashionable summer events such as the Henley Regatta or Wimbledon.【商标】飘仙甜酒〔含有杜松子酒的一款酒精饮料, 全称"飘仙第一杯"。这款酒喝时可加冰块、柠檬和水果丁。英国人常把飘仙甜酒与亨利赛船大会、温布尔登网球公开赛等时尚夏季活动联系在一起〕

pimp /pɪmp; pɪmp/ *n* [C] a man who makes money by controlling PROSTITUTES (=women who have sex with men for money) 拉皮条的男子, 妓院男老板 —**pimp** *v* [I]

pim·per·nel /ˈpɪmpɚˌnɛl; ˈpɪmpənel/ *n* [C] a small wild plant with flowers that are blue, white, or especially red 海绿〔矮小野生植物, 开蓝色白色、尤其是红色的花〕

pim·ple /ˈpɪmpḷ; ˈpɪmpəl/ *n* [C] a small raised red spot on your skin, especially on your face〔尤指长在脸上的〕丘疹, 小脓疱, 粉刺 —see also 另见 GOOSE PIMPLES —**pimpled** *adj* —**pimply** *adj*

PIN /pɪn; pɪn/ also 又作 **PIN num·ber** /ˈ· , · · ·/ *n* [C] Personal Identification Number; a number that you use when you get money from a CASHPOINT using a plastic card 个人身份识别号码, 私人密码〔用银行卡在自动提款机上取款时的密码〕

3 **pin¹** /pɪn; pɪn/ *n* [C]

1 ▶FOR CLOTH 用于布料◀ a short thin piece of metal with a sharp point at one end, used especially for fastening together pieces of cloth while making clothes〔尤在做衣服时固定布料用的〕别针, 大头针

2 ▶JEWELLERY 首饰◀ a) *AmE* an attractively shaped piece of metal, sometimes containing jewels, that you fasten to your clothes and wear as a decoration【美】胸针; BROOCH *BrE*【英】 **b)** *BrE* a short thin piece of metal with a decoration at one end, used as jewellery【英】〔一端有装饰的〕饰针

3 ▶ELECTRICAL 电的◀ one of the pieces of metal that sticks out of an electric PLUG〔电器插头的〕插脚: *a three-pin plug* 三脚插头

4 ▶FOR SUPPORT 用于支撑◀ a thin piece of metal or wood used as a support for something, or to fasten things together〔用于支撑或固定物品的〕钉, 楔, 销, 栓: *When I broke my leg, I had to have a pin inserted.* 我腿骨折后, 需植入一根钢钉。

5 ▶GAMES 游戏◀ one of the bottle-shaped objects that you try to knock down in a game of BOWLING〔保龄球运动中的〕球柱

6 you could hear a pin drop *spoken* used to say that it is very quiet and no one is speaking【口】静得可以听到针掉下来的声音〔用于表示非常安静〕

7 for two pins I'd ... *BrE old-fashioned* used to say that you would like to do something to someone because they have annoyed you【英, 过时】恨不得, 巴不得〔用于表示你想要对惹恼你的人做某事〕: *For two pins, I'd tell him to get lost.* 我真想叫他滚开。

8 pins [plural] *BrE informal* legs【英, 非正式】腿 —see also 另见 DRAWING PIN, PIN MONEY, PINS AND NEEDLES, ROLLING PIN, SAFETY PIN

pin² *v* **pinned, pinning 1** [T always+adv/prep] to fasten something somewhere, or to join two things together, using a pin〔用别针〕把…别住,〔用钉〕把…钉住; 固定住: **pin sth together** *Pin the pieces together before sewing them.* 把布片用别针别在一起, 然后再缝起来。| **pin sth to/on/onto** *Can you pin this to the notice board?* 你能把这钉在布告板上吗? **2 pin your hopes on** to hope that something will happen or someone will help you, because all your plans depend on this 把你的希望寄托在…上, 指望: *Chris is pinning his hopes on getting into Yale.* 克里斯正寄望于进入耶鲁大学。**3 pin the blame on** to blame someone for something, often unfairly〔通常不公平地〕把某事归罪于〔某人〕, 把责任加在〔某人〕身上: *It's your fault – don't try to pin the blame on me!* 这是你的错——别想把过错推在我身上! **4** [T always+adv/prep] to make someone unable to move by putting a lot of pressure or weight on them 按住, 压住; 使不能动: **pin sb to/under** *In the accident she was pinned under the car.* 在那次事故中, 她被压在汽车底下, 动弹不得。**5 pin your ears back!** *BrE spoken* used to tell someone to listen carefully【英口】注意听! 竖起耳朵听!〔用于告诉别人仔细听〕

pin sb/sth **↔ down** *phr v* [T] **1** to make someone give clear details or make a definite decision about something 使〔某人〕详细说明, 使〔某人〕明确表态: *I've been trying to pin him down all week, but he won't say what's going on.* 我一整个星期都在努力让他把事情说个明白, 但他就是不肯说发生了什么事。**2** to understand something clearly or be able to describe it exactly 清楚地知道, 确切地描述, 确定: *We know someone's been stealing, but it's difficult to pin down who it is.* 我们知道有人一直在偷窃, 但难以确定那人是谁。

pins 针

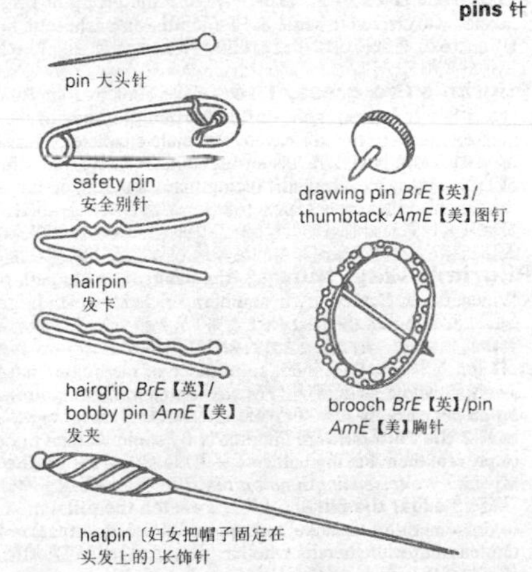

pi·ña co·la·da /ˌpinjə koˋlɑdə; ˌpiːnə kəˈlɑːdə/ *n* [C,U] an alcoholic drink made from COCONUT juice, PINEAPPLE juice, and RUM[1] 椰子菠萝鸡尾酒〔用椰子汁、菠萝汁和朗姆酒掺杂而成〕

pin·a·fore /ˋpɪnəˌfɔr; ˈpɪnəfɔː/ *n* [C] **1** also 又作 **pinafore dress** /ˈ· · · ˌ·/ *BrE* a dress that does not cover your arms and under which you wear a shirt or BLOUSE【英】无袖连衣裙〔一般穿在衬衫外面〕; JUMPER (2) *AmE*【美】**2** a loose piece of clothing that does not cover your arms, worn over your clothes to keep them clean 连胸围裙

Pina·tubo /ˌpɪnəˋtubo; ˌpɪnəˈtuːbəʊ/**, Mount** a mountain that is an active VOLCANO in the Philippines. It was inactive for 600 years before ERUPTing in 1991 and killing 343 people. 皮纳图博山〔菲律宾一活火山，于1991年爆发，造成343人死亡，而在此之前的600年间一直处于休眠状态〕

pin·ball /ˋpɪnˌbɔl; ˈpɪnbɔːl/ *n* [U] a game played on a machine with a sloping board down which a ball rolls, which the player has to prevent reaching the bottom 弹球戏，玩弹子机

pince-nez /ˋpæns ˌne; ˌpæns ˈneɪ/ *n* GLASSES worn in the past that were held in position on the nose by a spring, instead of by pieces fitting round the ears〔从前使用的〕夹鼻眼镜

pin·cer /ˋpɪnsɚ; ˈpɪnsə/ *n* **1** [C usually plural 一般用复数] one of the pair of claws (CLAW[1] (3)) that some SHELLFISH and insects have, used for holding and cutting food, and for fighting〔一些甲壳类动物和昆虫的〕螯(针) —see picture at 参见 LOBSTER 图 **2 pincers** [plural] a tool made of two crossed pieces of metal used for holding things tightly 钳子 —see picture at 参见 TOOL[1] 图

pincer move·ment /ˈ· · ˌ · ·/ *n* [C] a military attack in which two groups of soldiers come from opposite directions in order to trap the enemy between them〔军事进攻中的〕钳形攻势[运动]

pinch[1] /pɪntʃ; pɪntʃ/ *v* **1** [T] to press a part of someone's flesh very tightly between your finger and thumb, especially so that it hurts 捏，掐，拧；夹: *Mum, he pinched me!* 妈妈，他拧我! —see picture on page A20 参见 A20 页图 **2** [T] *informal* to steal something, especially something small or not very valuable【非正式】偷窃〔尤指小的物品或不很值钱的东西〕: *Someone's pinched my coat!* 有人偷了我的大衣! **3** [I,T] if something you are wearing pinches you, it presses painfully on your flesh, because it is too tight〔穿的东西〕夹痛，挤痛: *Her head was aching and her new shoes pinched dreadfully.* 她感到头痛，新买的鞋子又夹脚夹得很厉害。**4 I had to pinch myself** *especially spoken* used to say that you needed to make sure a situation was real and that you were not imagining it【尤口】我不得不拧自己一下〔以证实某情况是真的〕**5 pinch and scrape** to be very careful about how much money you spend, because you do not have very much 尽量节省，省吃俭用 —see also 另见 PENNY-PINCHING **6** [T usually passive 一般用被动态] *old-fashioned BrE* to ARREST[1] (1) someone【过时，英】逮捕，拘留

pinch[2] *n* **1 pinch of salt/pepper etc** a small amount of salt, pepper etc that you can hold between your finger and thumb 一撮盐/胡椒粉等: *Add a pinch of cayenne pepper.* 加一撮辣椒粉。**2** [C] an act of pressing someone's flesh between your finger and thumb 捏，拧，掐；夹: *She gave him a playful pinch.* 她闹着玩地拧了他一把。**3 at a pinch** *BrE*【英】, **in a pinch** *AmE*【美】if necessary in a particularly difficult or urgent situation 必要时；在紧要关头: *We can squeeze one more person in the car, at a pinch.* 如果有必要，我们的轿车里可以再挤一个人。| *In a pinch, I could manage $60.* 必要时我能够拿得出60美元。**4 take sth with a pinch of salt** to not completely believe what someone says to you 对所说的事半信半疑，对某事不完全相信 **5 feel the pinch** to have financial difficulties, especially because you are not making as much money as you used to make〔尤指因赚钱不如以前多而〕感到拮据: *Local stores and businesses are beginning to feel the pinch.* 本地的商店和公司开始感到资金短缺。

pinched /pɪntʃt; pɪntʃt/ *adj* a pinched face looks thin and unhealthy, for example because the person is ill, cold, or tired〔脸〕消瘦的，不健康的: *Years of working in the mine had left their faces pinched and haggard.* 多年的井下工作使他们形容枯槁。

pinch-hit /ˈ· ·/ *v* [I+for] *AmE*【美】**1** to do something for someone else because they are unexpectedly not able to do it〔紧急时〕代替某人做某事 **2** to HIT[1] (4a) for someone else in BASEBALL (1)〔在棒球运动中〕替补击球 —**pinch-hitter** *n* [C]: *Mark is sick – we're sending Jim as a pinch-hitter.* 马克病了——我们要安排吉姆为替补击球员。

pin·cush·ion /ˋpɪnˌkuʃən; ˈpɪnˌkʊʃən/ *n* [C] a soft filled bag for sticking pins in until you need to use them〔供插缝纫针用的〕针垫

pine[1] /paɪn; paɪn/ *n* **1** [C,U] a tall tree with long hard sharp leaves that do not fall off in winter 松树: *a pine forest* 松树林 **2** the soft pale-coloured wood of this tree, used to make furniture, floors etc 松木: *a pine table* 松木桌子

pine[2] also 又作 **pine away** *v* [I] to gradually become weaker, less active, and less healthy, especially because you feel very unhappy〔尤指因不开心而逐渐〕衰弱，憔悴: *After my grandfather died, my grandmother just pined away.* 祖父死后，祖母就一天比一天憔悴了。

pine for sth/sb *phr v* [T] to become unhappy or ill because you cannot be with someone you love or in a place you love 想念〔某人或某地〕，苦苦思念〔某人或某地〕: *She won't touch her food. I think she's pining for home.* 她不愿吃一点东西，我想她在想家。

pin·e·al gland /ˋpaɪnɪəl glænd; ˈpɪniəl ˌglænd/ *n* [C] a part of the brain that is thought to be sensitive to light in some way〔脑部的〕松果腺，松果体

pine·ap·ple /ˋpaɪnˌæpl; ˈpaɪnæpəl/ *n* [C,U] a large yellow-brown tropical fruit or its sweet juicy yellow flesh 菠萝，凤梨: *pineapple chunks* 菠萝块 | *pineapple juice* 菠萝汁 —see picture on page A8 参见 A8 页图

pine·cone /ˋpaɪnkon; ˈpaɪnkəʊn/ *n* [C] a fruit of the PINETREE 松果，松球

pine mar·ten /ˈ· ˌ· ·/ *n* [C] a small European animal that lives in forests 松貂〔欧洲一种生活在森林中的小动物〕

pine nee·dle /ˈ· ˌ· ·/ *n* [C] a leaf of the pinetree, that is thin and sharp like a needle 松针；松叶

pine·tree /ˋpaɪntri; ˈpaɪnˌtriː/ *n* [C] a tall tree with long hard sharp leaves that do not fall off in winter; a PINE[1] (1) 松树

Pine·wood /ˋpaɪnwud; ˈpaɪnwʊd/ also 又作 **Pinewood Studios** a large film STUDIO (=place where films are made), to the west of London, near Slough 派伍德电影制片厂〔一大型电影制片厂，位于伦敦以西，斯劳附近〕

pinewood *n* **1** [C] a forest of pinetrees 松林 **2** [U] the wood from a pinetree 松木

ping[1] /pɪŋ; pɪŋ/ *n* [C] a short high ringing sound 砰，乒；铛: *The bell on the counter let out a sharp ping.* 柜台上的铃发出铛的一声响。

ping[2] *v* **1** [I] to make a short high ringing sound 发出砰[铛铛]的声响 **2** [I] *AmE* PINK[3]【美】〔汽车引擎有毛病时〕咯噔咯噔地响

ping-pong /ˈ· ·/ *n* [U] an indoor game played on a table top by two people with a small plastic ball and two BATS; TABLE TENNIS 乒乓球运动

pin·head /ˋpɪnˌhɛd; ˈpɪnhed/ *n* [C] the head of a pin〔大头针的〕针头，钉头

pin·ion[1] /ˋpɪnjən; ˈpɪnjən/ *v* **1** [T always+adv/prep] to hold or tie up someone's arms or legs very tightly, so that they cannot move freely 捆住〔手臂或腿〕: *Her arms were pinioned tightly behind her.* 她的双臂被紧紧地反绑在背后。**2** [T usually passive 一般用被动态] *technical* to cut off the big strong feathers from a bird's wings so that it cannot fly【术语】剪去〔鸟的〕飞羽

pinion[2] *n* **1** [C] a small wheel, with teeth on its outer edge, that fits into a larger wheel and turns it or is turned by it 小齿轮 —compare 比较 COGWHEEL **2** [C] *literary* a bird's wing【文】〔鸟的〕翅膀，翼 **3** [C] *technical* the outer part of a bird's wing, where the strongest flying feathers grow【术语】〔鸟的〕翼梢，翼尖，前翼

pink[1] /pɪŋk; pɪŋk/ *adj* **1** pale red 粉红色的: *a wedding cake with pink and white icing* 有粉红色和白色糖霜的结婚蛋糕 | *The western sky was glowing pink.* 西边的天空闪着粉红色的光。**2** [only before noun 仅用于名词前] a word used to talk about HOMOSEXUAL people 同性恋的: *a campaign aimed at the pink consumer* 面向同性恋消费者的宣传活动 —see also 另见 **be tickled pink** (TICKLE[1] (3)) S2 W3

pink[2] *n* **1** [C,U] a pale red colour 粉红色 —see picture on page A5 参见 A5 页图 **2** [C] a garden plant with pink, white, or red flowers 石竹〔一种园艺植物，开粉红色、白色或红色的花〕**3 in the pink** *old-fashioned* in very good health【过时】非常健康(的)，身体很好(的)

pink[3] *v* [I] *BrE* if a car engine pinks, it makes knocking sounds because it is not working properly【英】〔汽车引擎有毛病时〕咯噔咯噔地响; PING[2] *AmE*【美】

pink-col·lar /ˌ· ˈ· ·◂/ *adj* **pink-collar jobs/workers/industries etc** *especially AmE* low-paid jobs done mainly by women, for example in offices and restaurants, or the women who do these jobs【尤美】粉领工作/工人/行业等〔指主要由妇女做的报酬很低的工作，如办公室和餐馆工作〕—compare 比较 WHITE-COLLAR, BLUE-COLLAR

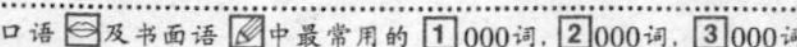

Pink·er·ton's /ˋpɪŋkə·tnz; ˈpɪŋkətənz/ also **Pinkerton's National Detective Agency** a private DETECTIVE business in the US, started by Allan Pinkerton (1819-84) 平克顿全国侦探事务所〔美国一家私人侦探事务所，由艾伦·平克顿（1819-1884）创办〕

pink gin /ˌ· ˈ·/ *n* [C,U] an alcoholic drink made of GIN and ANGOSTURA which gives it a pink colour 红杜松子酒

pink·ie, pinky /ˋpɪŋkɪ; ˈpɪŋki/ *n* [C] *especially AmE or ScotE* the smallest finger of the human hand【尤美或苏格兰】小（手）指

pink·ing shears /ˈ· · ·/ also 又作 **pinking scissors** /ˈ· ·, · ·/ *n* [plural] a special type of scissors with blades that have V-shaped teeth, used for cutting cloth〔用于剪布的〕锯齿剪刀，齿边布样剪刀 —see picture at 参见 SCISSORS 图

pink·ish /ˋpɪŋkɪʃ; ˈpɪŋkɪʃ/ *adj* slightly pink 浅粉红色的: *a pinkish tinge* 淡淡的粉红色

pink·o /ˋpɪŋko; ˈpɪŋkəʊ/ *n* [C] **1** *AmE* an insulting word for a SOCIALIST or COMMUNIST[2] (1)【美】赤色分子〔称呼社会主义者或共产主义者的冒犯用语〕**2** *BrE* someone who supports LEFT WING ideas, but is not a strong believer in SOCIALISM【英】准左倾分子，略带左倾色彩的人 —compare 比较 RED[1] (4) —**pinko** *adj*

Pink Pan·ther, the /ˌ· ˈ··/ **1** a character in humorous CARTOON films who is a pink PANTHER (=a large wild animal of the cat family). The music from the cartoon, the 'Pink Panther theme', is very well known.粉红豹，顽皮豹〔一卡通喜剧片中的角色，是一只粉红色的美洲豹。该片的《粉红豹主题曲》广为人知〕**2** a valuable jewel which is stolen in a series of humorous films about a French police officer called Inspector Clouseau. The first of these films is called *The Pink Panther*. 粉红豹〔法国警察克劳索系列喜剧影片中被盗的一颗珍贵珠宝。该系列片的第一部取名为《粉红豹》〕

pink·y /ˋpɪŋkɪ; ˈpɪŋki/ *n* [C] a PINKIE 小（手）指

pin mon·ey /ˈ· ,· ·/ *n* [U] a small amount of money that you can spend on yourself rather than on necessary things 零用钱

pin·na·cle /ˋpɪnəkḷ; ˈpɪnəkəl/ *n* **1** [singular] the most successful, powerful, exciting etc part of something〔某事物最成功、最强大、最激动人心的〕部分；顶点，顶峰: **[+of]** *By the age of 40, she had reached the pinnacle of her political career.* 到了40岁，她已达到了政治生涯的顶峰。**2** [C] a pointed stone decoration, like a small tower, on a building such as a church or castle〔教堂或城堡等上作装饰用的〕尖顶，小尖塔 **3** [C] *especially literary* a high mountain top【尤文】山峰；山顶

pin·nate /ˋpɪnet; ˈpɪneɪt/ *adj technical* a pinnate leaf is made of two rows of little leaves arranged opposite each other along a stem【术语】〔叶〕羽状的

pin·ny /ˋpɪnɪ; ˈpɪni/ *n* [C] *BrE informal* a PINAFORE (2)【英，非正式】连胸围裙

Pi·no·cchi·o /pɪˋnokɪo; pɪˈnəʊkiəʊ/ a character in an Italian children's story that was later made into a CARTOON film. Pinocchio is a wooden PUPPET who at the end of the story comes alive as a real boy. At one point in the story, Pinocchio's nose grows longer when he tells lies. People sometimes mention the idea of someone's nose growing longer to mean that someone is lying. 匹诺曹〔意大利一儿童故事中的人物。该故事后来被改编成一部卡通电影。匹诺曹是个木偶，后来变成了一个真的男孩。故事中，他一说谎话鼻子就会变长。人们有时会提及某人的鼻子在变长，意指他在说谎〕

pin·point[1] /ˋpɪn,pɔɪnt; ˈpɪnpɔɪnt/ *v* **1** [T] to say exactly what the facts about something really are 准确地说出，描述〔事实真相〕: *This new report pinpoints the failings of the welfare system.* 这份新的报告准确地指出了福利制度的缺点。| **pinpoint what/how/why etc** *When children have learning difficulties, it's often difficult to pinpoint what the problem really is.* 当儿童有学习困难时，往往很难确定问题到底是什么。**2** [T] to find or show the exact position of something 准确地找出〔某物的位置〕；为…准确定位: *The team went behind enemy lines to pinpoint the exact locations of missile launchers.* 那一队人到了敌人的后方，以确定导弹发射器的精确位置。

pinpoint[2] *n* [C] **1** a very small point or dot of something 极小的点: **[+of]** *tiny pinpoints of light* 点点亮光 **2 with pinpoint accuracy/precision** very exactly 非常精确地: *Radar can locate an underwater target with pinpoint accuracy.* 雷达可以非常精确地确定水下目标的位置。

pin·prick /ˋpɪn,prɪk; ˈpɪn,prɪk/ *n* [C] **1** a very small area or DOT of something〔某物的〕极小区域[点]: **[+of]** *a pinprick of light* 一丝亮光 **2** a very small hole in something, similar to one made by a pin〔似针刺的〕小孔 **3** something that slightly annoys you 小烦恼

pins and nee·dles /ˌ· · ˈ··/ *n* **1** [U] the uncomfortable prickly feeling you get in a part of your body when a full supply of blood comes back to it after having been partly blocked 酸痛，发麻，针刺感: **get pins and needles** *If you sit like that for too long you'll get pins and needles.* 如果你那样坐太久了就会感到酸麻。**2 be on pins and needles** *AmE* to be very nervous and unable to relax, especially because you are waiting for something important【美】〔尤指等待重要事情时〕如坐针毡，坐立不安: *I wish Billy would give her a call. She's been on pins and needles all day.* 我希望比利会给她打个电话。她一整天都坐立不安。

pin·stripe /ˋpɪn,straɪp; ˈpɪnstraɪp/ *n* [C] **1** one of the thin light-coloured lines that forms a pattern on cloth against a darker background〔织物上的〕细条花纹 —see picture on page A16 参见 A16 页图 **2 pinstripe suit** a man's suit made from cloth with a pinstripe pattern, worn especially by business people〔尤指商界人士穿的〕细条纹布西装: *a navy-blue pinstripe suit* 一套海军蓝色细条纹布西装 —**pin-striped** *adj*

pint /paɪnt; paɪnt/ *n* **1** [C] a unit for measuring an amount of liquid, especially beer or milk, in the US and Britain. In the US a pint contains 16 ounces of liquid, and in Britain it contains 20 ounces 品脱〔美国和英国的液量单位，尤指啤酒或牛奶。在美国，一品脱等于16盎司，而在英国，一品脱等于20盎司〕: *Add two pints of water to the mixture.* 在混合物中加入两品脱的水。| *half a pint of milk* 半品脱牛奶—see table on page C3 参见 C3 页附录 **2** [C] *BrE* a pint of beer, especially one that you drink in a bar【英】〔尤指在酒吧喝的〕一品脱啤酒: *He's gone down the pub for a quick pint.* 他去小酒馆喝一品脱啤酒。| *My dad remembers when a pint cost sixpence.* 我爸爸还记得买一品脱啤酒才花六便士的时候。—compare 比较 HALF[2] (1) 2

Pin·ta, the /ˋpaɪntə; ˈpaɪntə/ one of the three ships that sailed to America with Christopher Columbus in 1492. The other two were the Nina and the Santa Maria. "平塔"号〔1492年克里斯托弗·哥伦布首航美洲时的三艘船之一。另外两艘为"尼娜"号和"圣玛丽亚"号〕

pin·ta·ble /ˋpɪn,tebḷ; ˈpɪn,teɪbəl/ *n* [C] *BrE* a machine for playing PINBALL on【英】弹球机，弹子机

Pin·ter /ˋpɪntə; ˈpɪntə/**, Harold** (1930-2008) a British writer of plays, whose works include *The Birthday Party* and *The Caretaker*. His plays include very realistic conversations, with long silences, and show the misunderstandings and problems of communication in ordinary social situations. 品特〔(1930-2008)，英国剧作家。代表作有《生日晚会》和《看房者》。剧中设计的对白十分贴近现实生活，有时会穿插一段沉默。作品反映的是日常交际情景下的诸多误解和问题〕

pin·to /ˋpɪnto; ˈpɪntəʊ/ *n* [C] *AmE* a horse with irregular markings of two or more colours【美】杂色马；花斑马; PIEBALD *BrE*【英】

pinto bean /ˈ· · ·/ *n* [C] a small light brown bean 斑豆

pint-size /ˈ· ·/ also 又作 **pint-sized** *adj* [only before noun 仅用于名词前] small, and unimportant or unsatisfactory 微小的；无足轻重的；不能令人满意的

pin-up /ˈ· ·/ *n* **1** [C] a picture of an attractive person, often a woman with not many clothes on, that is put up on a wall to be looked at and admired〔被钉[挂]在墙上供欣赏的〕半裸美女图片 **2** [C] someone who appears in one of these pictures 这类图片中的人物

pin·wheel /ˋpɪn,hwil; ˈpɪnwiːl/ *n* [C] *AmE* WINDMILL (2)【美】玩具风车

pi·o·neer[1] /,paɪəˋnɪr; ,paɪəˈnɪə/ *n* **1** [C] one of the first people to do something that other people will later develop or continue to do 先驱，先锋，创始人: **[+of]** *the pioneers of the Women's Liberation movement* 妇女解放运动的先驱 | **[+in]** *Hans Richter, a pioneer in experimental cinema* 汉斯·李克特，实验电影的创始人 | **pioneer photographer/geologist etc** (=one of the first people to develop photography etc) 摄影术/地质学等的创始人 **2** [C] one of the first people to travel to a new country or area and begin living there, farming etc 拓荒者，开拓者，开发者: *the early pioneers of the Dakota territory* 达科他地区的早期拓荒者

pioneer[2] *v* [T] to be the first person to do, invent or use something 开创，开发；倡导: *The new cancer treatment was pioneered in the early eighties by Dr Sylvia Bannerjee.* 这种新的癌症治疗方法是由西尔维娅·班纳基医生在80年代初期开创的。

pi·o·neer·ing /,paɪəˋnɪrɪŋ; ,paɪəˈnɪərɪŋ◂/ *adj* [only before noun 仅用于名词前] introducing new and better methods or ideas for the first time 开创性的，先驱的: *the pioneering work of NASA scientists* 美国国家航空和航天局科学家们的开创性工作 | *his pioneering discoveries in the field of dynamics* 他在动力学领域的开创性发现

pi·ous /ˈpaɪəs; ˈpaɪəs/ *adj* **1** having strong religious beliefs, and showing this in the way you behave〔对宗教〕虔诚的 **2** pretending to have sincere religious feelings in order to make people think you are better than you really are 假虔诚的, 虚伪的, 伪善的: *Don't believe any of his pious talk.* 不要相信他那些虚伪的话。**3 pious hope/wish** something that you want to be true or to happen, but that probably will not 不大可能实现的希望/愿望 —see also 另见 PIETY —**piously** *adv* —**piousness** *n* [U]

pip¹ /pɪp; pɪp/ *n* [C] *BrE*【英】**1** a small seed from a fruit such as an apple or orange〔苹果、柑橘等水果的〕果核, 种子, 籽 **2** a high note that is part of a series of short sounds, used for example on the radio to show the time, or in the operation of public telephones 短而尖的声音;〔电台的〕报时信号;〔电话中的〕哔哔声; BEEP² (1) *AmE*【美】**3** *old-fashioned* one of the stars on the shoulders of the coats of army officers that shows their rank【过时】〔军官肩章上表示等级的〕星 **4 give sb the pip** *old-fashioned* to annoy someone【过时】使某人恼怒[烦恼]

pip² **pipped, pipping** *v* [T] *BrE informal*【英, 非正式】**1 pip sb at the post** to beat someone at the last moment in a race, competition etc, when they were expecting to win 在最后关头击败某人: *I nearly got the job, but was pipped at the post by the other candidate.* 我几乎得到了这份工作, 但在最后关头败在了另一位应聘者手里。**2** to beat someone in a race, competition etc, by only a small amount〔在比赛、竞争等中〕险胜, 以微弱优势击败〔对手〕

pi·pal /ˈpipəl; ˈpiːpəl/ *n* [C] a large Indian tree〔印度的〕菩提树

pipe¹ /paɪp; paɪp/ *n* [C]

1 ▶TUBE 管子◀ a tube through which a liquid or gas flows, often under the ground〔通常埋在地下的〕管, 管子, 管道: *A pipe had burst in the kitchen and flooded the floor.* 厨房的一根管道爆裂了, 弄得满地都是水。| *Workmen were laying pipes under the road.* 工人正在道路下面铺设管道。| *The pipe's blocked again!* 管道又堵塞了! | *a gas pipe* 煤气管

2 ▶FOR SMOKING 用于抽烟◀ a thing used for smoking tobacco, consisting of a small tube with a container shaped like a bowl at one end 烟斗: *Peters filled and lit his pipe.* 彼得斯装上烟斗, 然后把它点着。| *pipe tobacco* 烟斗用的烟丝

3 ▶MUSIC 音乐◀ a) a simple musical instrument shaped like a tube and played by blowing 笛(子); 管乐器 **b)** one of the metal tubes through which air passes when an ORGAN (2) is played〔管风琴的〕音管, 风管 **c) the pipes** *BrE informal* BAGPIPES【英, 非正式】〔苏格兰的〕风笛

4 pipe dream a hope, idea, plan etc that is impossible or will probably never happen 白日梦, 幻想, 空想: *Arsenal lost 4-0, making winning the league something of a pipe dream.* 阿森纳队以0比4输了, 这使他们获得联赛冠军的好梦成空。

5 Put that in your pipe and smoke it! *spoken* used to say that someone must accept what you have just said, even though they do not like it【口】不管喜欢不喜欢你都得接受我所说的!

6 the pipes BAGPIPES 苏格兰风笛

pipe² *v*

1 ▶SEND LIQUID/GAS 输送液体/气体◀ [T usually passive 一般用被动态] to send a liquid or gas through a pipe to another place 用管道输送〔液体或气体〕: *a piped water supply* 管道供水 | **pipe sth into/to** *Eighty per cent of sewage is piped directly into the sea.* 80%的污水通过管道被直接排入海中。

2 ▶SPEAK/SING 说话/唱歌◀ [I,T] to speak or sing in a high voice 用尖嗓子说话; 尖声唱; 高声鸣叫: *A moorhen piped suddenly from the lake.* 一只黑水鸡突然从湖中发出鸣叫声。

3 ▶MAKE MUSIC 演奏音乐◀ [I,T] to make a musical sound using a pipe 吹奏〔管乐〕: *He piped a jaunty tune for us to dance to.* 他吹奏了一支轻快的曲子让我们随之跳舞。

4 ▶FOOD 食物◀ to decorate food, especially a cake, with thin lines of ICING or cream 用糖霜[奶油]细线条装饰食物〔尤指蛋糕〕

5 pipe sb aboard *technical* to welcome someone important onto a ship by blowing a special whistle【术语】〔通过吹特殊的哨子〕欢迎…上船

pipe down *phr v* [I] *spoken* to stop talking or making a noise, and become calmer and less excited【口】停止讲话[吵闹]; 安静下来: *Pipe down! I'm trying to listen to the news.* 别吵! 我在听新闻呢。

pipe up *phr v* [I] *informal* to begin to say something or start speaking, especially when you have been quiet until then【非正式】突然开始说话〔尤指之前一直很安静〕: *The smallest child suddenly piped up with the answer.* 最小的那个孩子突然说出了答案。

pipe clean·er /ˈ· ˌ··/ *n* [C] a length of wire covered with soft material, used to clean the inside of a tobacco pipe〔清理烟斗用的〕烟斗通条

piped mu·sic /ˌ· ˈ··/ *n* [U] quiet recorded music played continuously in shops, hotels, restaurants etc〔商店、旅店、餐馆等地〕不断播放的轻音乐

pipe fit·ter /ˈ· ˌ··/ *n* [C] someone who puts in and repairs pipes for water, gas etc 管道安装修理工

pipe·line /ˈpaɪpˌlaɪn; ˈpaɪp-laɪn/ *n* [C] **1** a line of connecting pipes, often under the ground, used for taking gas, oil etc over long distances〔用来长距离输送气、油等的地下〕管道, 管线 **2 be in the pipeline** if a plan, idea or event is in the pipeline, it is still being prepared, but it will happen or be completed soon〔计划、观点或事件〕在准备中; 在进行中: *We've made several changes lately, and there are more in the pipeline.* 我们最近做了一些改动, 但还有一些改动正在进行之中。

pipe of peace /ˌ· · ˈ·/ *n* [C] a PEACE PIPE 长杆烟斗, 和平烟斗

pip·er /ˈpaɪpɚ; ˈpaɪpə/ *n* [C] a musician who plays a PIPE¹ (3) or the BAGPIPES 吹笛人, 风笛吹奏者

pipe rack /ˈ· ·/ *n* [C] a small frame for holding several tobacco pipes 烟斗架

pi·pette /pɪˈpɛt; pɪˈpet/ *n* [C] a thin glass tube for sucking up exact amounts of liquid, used especially in chemistry〔尤指化学实验用的〕吸量管, 移液管 —see picture at 参见 LABORATORY 图

pip·it /ˈpɪpɪt; ˈpɪpɪt/ *n* [C] a small brown or grey singing bird 鹨〔一种棕色或灰色的鸣禽〕

pip·pin /ˈpɪpɪn; ˈpɪpɪn/ *n* [C] a small sweet apple〔一种小而甜的〕苹果

pip·squeak /ˈpɪpˌskwik; ˈpɪpskwiːk/ *n* [C] someone that you think is not worth attention or respect, especially because they are small or young 无足轻重的人, 小人物: *Shut up, you little pipsqueak!* 闭嘴, 你这个小东西!

pi·quant /ˈpikənt; ˈpiːkənt/ *adj* **1** having a pleasantly sharp taste or flavour 辛辣的; 开胃的: *a piquant tomato sauce* 辣味番茄酱 **2** interesting and exciting; INTRIGUING 有趣的; 激动人心的: *The disappearance of the letter made the situation all the more piquant.* 那封信的消失使情况更加令人感兴趣。—**piquantly** *adv* —**piquancy** *n* [U]

pique¹ /pik; piːk/ *n* [U] **1** a feeling of being annoyed or upset, especially because someone has ignored you or made you look stupid〔尤指因被人忽视或被人愚弄而〕不悦, 生气: **a fit of pique** (=sudden anger) 一怒之下 *Greta stormed off in a fit of pique.* 格蕾塔一赌气, 气冲冲地离开了。**2** also 又作 **piqué** a type of material made of cotton, silk, or RAYON 一种用棉花、丝或人造丝制成的织物

pique² *v* **1** [T usually passive 一般用被动态] to make someone feel annoyed or upset, especially by ignoring them or making them look stupid〔尤指因忽视或愚弄而〕使〔某人〕生气, 激怒: **be/feel piqued** *We did feel a little piqued when nobody even bothered to ask us.* 甚至都没有人询问我们一下, 我们的确感到有点生气。**2 pique your interest/curiosity** *especially AmE* to make you feel interested in something or someone【尤美】激起你的兴趣/好奇心

pi·ra·cy /ˈpaɪrəsɪ; ˈpaɪərəsi/ *n* [U] **1** the illegal copying and sale of books, TAPES, VIDEOS etc 非法翻印〔书籍等〕; 非法翻录〔磁带、录像带等〕, 盗版: *software piracy* 软件的盗版 **2** the crime of attacking and stealing from ships at sea 海上抢劫, 海盗行为

Pir·an·del·lo /ˌpɪrənˈdɛlo; ˌpɪrənˈdeləʊ/, **Lu·i·gi** /luˈidʒɪ; luˈiːdʒi/ (1837-1936) an Italian writer of plays and NOVELs, whose most famous play is *Six Characters in Search of an Author.* His work examines the relationship between what is real and what is imaginary, and had an important influence on modern theatre. 皮蓝德娄〔(1837-1936), 意大利剧作家、小说家。代表剧作为《六个寻找作者的剧中人》, 探究真实与虚幻的关系, 对现代戏剧产生了重要影响〕

pi·ra·nha /pɪˈrɑnjə; pɪ̵ˈrɑːnjə/ *n* [C] a South American fish with sharp teeth that lives in rivers and eats flesh 锯脂鲤〔南美一种有尖利牙齿的食肉河鱼〕

pi·rate¹ /ˈpaɪrət; ˈpaɪərət/ *n* [C] **1** someone who dishonestly copies and sells another person's work 剽窃者; 侵犯版权者, 非法翻印者; 侵犯专利权者 **2 pirate radio/TV (station)** illegal radio or television broadcasts, or the station sending them out 非法无

pirate 海盗

线电广播[台]/非法电视[台]: *a pirate channel* 非法电视频道 **3** someone who sails on the seas, attacking other boats and stealing things from them 海盗 —**piratical** /paɪˈrætɪk; paɪˈrætɪkəl/ *adj* —**piratically** /-kḷɪ; -kli/ *adv*

CULTURAL NOTE 文化注释

Pirates in stories and films often speak roughly, drink a lot, especially RUM, and have a PARROT on their shoulder. The STEREOTYPE of a pirate is someone who wears a black PATCH over one eye, has a wooden leg, and uses expressions such as 'Shiver me timbers!' (=a phrase used to show great surprise). 故事和电影中的海盗通常说话粗声粗气, 很能喝酒, 尤其是喝朗姆酒。他们的肩膀上蹲着一只鹦鹉。海盗的典型形象是一只眼睛上戴着黑眼罩, 拖着一条木腿, 喜欢说"真见鬼!"之类的话。

pirate² *v* [T] to illegally copy and sell another person's work such as a book, design, or invention 剽窃, 盗用; 非法翻印; 非法仿制 —**pirated** *adj*: *pirated video tapes* 非法翻录的录像带

Pirates of Pen·zance, The /ˌpaɪrəts əv penˋzæns; ˌpaɪrəts əv penˈzæns/ (1879) a COMIC OPERA by Gilbert and Sullivan about a group of PIRATES who never succeed in robbing anyone. It contains the well-known songs *The Very Model of a Modern Major General* and *A Policeman's Lot Is Not a Happy One*.《彭赞斯的海盗》〔(1879), 吉伯特和沙利文合作的一部滑稽歌剧。剧中有一帮海盗, 他们抢劫多次都没有成功。剧中的两首歌曲十分著名, 即《现代少将的典范》和《警察的命也真叫苦》〕

pir·ou·ette /ˌpɪruˋɛt; ˌpɪruˈet/ *n* [C] a very fast turn made on one toe or the front part of one foot, especially by a BALLET dancer〔尤指芭蕾舞演员的〕足尖旋转, 单足旋转 —**pirouette** *v* [I]

Pi·sa /ˋpizə; ˈpiːzə/ a city in north central Italy, famous for the Leaning Tower of Pisa and for its CATHEDRAL 比萨〔意大利中北部一城市, 以比萨斜塔和大教堂闻名〕

pis·ca·to·ri·al /ˌpɪskəˋtɔrɪəl; ˌpɪskəˈtɔːriəl◂/ *adj formal* connected with fishing or fishermen【正式】捕鱼业的; 渔民的

Pis·ces /ˋpaɪsiz; ˈpaɪsiːz/ *n* **1** [singular] the twelfth sign of the ZODIAC, represented by two fish, and believed to affect the character and life of people born between February 21 and March 20 双鱼座, 双鱼宫〔黄道第十二宫〕: *Nick's a Pisces.* 尼克是双鱼座的。**2** [C] someone who was born between February 21 and March 20 出生于双鱼座时段〔2月21日至3月20日〕的人

pish /pɪʃ; pɪʃ/ *interjection old use* used to express annoyance or impatience【旧】呸!〔表示不愉快或不耐烦〕

piss¹ /pɪs; pɪs/ *v* **1** [I] *informal* an impolite word meaning to URINATE【非正式】撒尿〔不礼貌的说法〕**2 piss all over sb** *spoken* an impolite expression meaning to thoroughly defeat a person or a team【口】把某人[某队]打得屁滚尿流〔不礼貌的说法〕**3 piss in the wind** *spoken* an impolite expression meaning to waste time or effort trying to do something that is impossible【口】浪费时间[精力]做不可能的事〔不礼貌的说法〕**4 be pissing (it) down (with rain)** *BrE informal* to rain very heavily【英, 非正式】下大雨: *By the time we got there, it was absolutely pissing down!* 我们到那里时, 天下起了倾盆大雨! **5 piss yourself (laughing)** *BrE spoken* an impolite expression meaning to laugh uncontrollably【英口】笑得尿都出来了〔不礼貌的说法〕: *When Michelle fell in that puddle we absolutely pissed ourselves.* 当米歇尔跌倒在那个水坑里时, 我们都笑得不得了。**6 go piss up a rope!** *AmE spoken* a very impolite expression used to tell someone to go away【美口】滚开! 滚蛋!〔非常不礼貌的说法〕**7 not have a pot to piss in** *AmE spoken* a very impolite expression meaning to be extremely poor【美口】穷得连个尿壶都没有〔非常不礼貌的说法〕

piss about/around *phr v BrE spoken*【英口】**1** [I] an impolite expression meaning to waste time doing stupid things with no purpose or plan 胡闹, 浪费时间, 游手好闲〔不礼貌的说法〕: *Stop pissing about and get some work done!* 别再瞎混了, 找些事干干吧! **2** [T **piss** sb **about/around**] an impolite expression meaning to treat someone badly by not doing what you have promised to do, or by not being honest with them〔不礼貌的说法, 以不履行承诺或不坦诚的方式〕愚弄, 欺骗: *I wish he'd say yes or no – he's been pissing me around for weeks.* 我希望他能给予明确的答复 —— 他已经愚弄我好几个星期了。

piss sth ↔ **away** *phr v* [T] *spoken* a very impolite expression meaning to waste something very stupidly【口】〔不礼貌的说法〕非常愚蠢地浪费〔某物〕, 糟蹋: *Jean inherited a load of money, but she pissed it all away.* 琼继承了一大笔钱, 但她全挥霍掉了。

piss off *phr v* [I] *spoken*【口】**1** [usually imperative 一般用于祈使句] an offensive expression meaning to go away 滚开, 滚蛋〔冒犯用语〕: *Why don't you just piss off and leave me alone!* 你为什么不滚开, 让我一个人待着! **2** an offensive expression used to say no or to refuse to do something 没门儿, 不行〔不礼貌的说法; 用以说不或拒绝做某事〕: *"Johnny, will you do the dishes?" "Piss off!"* "约翰尼, 你去洗碗好吗?" "不行!"

piss sb ↔ **off** *phr v* [T] *spoken* an impolite expression meaning to annoy someone very much【口】激怒〔某人〕, 使〔某人〕非常恼火〔不礼貌的说法〕: *It really pisses me off when my car won't start in the morning.* 早上要是汽车发动不了, 那真会把我气死。

piss² *n* **1** [singular] *spoken* an impolite word for an act of urinating (URINATE)【口】撒尿〔不礼貌的说法〕: **have/take a piss** *I need to have a piss.* 我需要去撒尿。**2** [U] *spoken* an impolite word meaning URINE【口】尿〔不礼貌的说法〕**3 take the piss (out of sb/sth)** *BrE spoken* to make fun of someone, especially by copying them or trying to make them believe something untrue【英口】〔尤指通过模仿某人或使某人相信不真实的事情而〕取笑〔某人〕: *Stop taking the piss out of Dave!* 别捉弄戴夫了! | *£900 for that stereo? You're taking the piss!* 900英镑买那台立体声音响? 你在开玩笑吧! **4 be on the piss** *BrE spoken* to be drinking a lot of alcohol【英口】在大量喝酒: *"Where's Jo?" "Out on the piss somewhere."* "乔在哪里?" "在外面某个地方喝酒呢。" **5 a piece of piss** *BrE spoken* something very easy【英口】非常容易的事: *That test was a piece of piss!* 那考试非常容易! **6 full of piss and vinegar** *AmE spoken* full of energy【美口】充满活力, 精力充沛

piss³ *adv spoken*【口】**piss poor/piss easy etc** an impolite expression meaning very poor, very easy etc 非常蹩脚/非常容易等〔不礼貌的说法〕: *"You'd make a piss-poor lawyer," he replied.* "你只能当一个非常蹩脚的律师。" 他回答道。

piss-ant¹, pissant /ˋpɪsænt; ˈpɪsænt/ *adj* [only before noun 仅用于名词前] *AmE informal* an impolite word meaning of very low value, quality, or importance【美, 非正式】没什么价值的; 质量低劣的; 无足轻重的〔不礼貌的说法〕: *I get really fed up doing these piss-ant little jobs.* 我对于干这些无足轻重的琐碎工作真的感到烦透了。

piss-ant², pissant *n AmE informal* an impolite word meaning an annoying person with a weak character【美, 非正式】令人讨厌的胆小鬼〔不礼貌的说法〕: *The stupid little piss-ant!* 那个愚蠢的胆小鬼!

Pis·sar·ro /pɪˋsɑro; pɪˈsɑːrəʊ/**, Ca·mille** /kæˋmil; kæˈmiːl/ (1830-1903) a French artist who was a leading member of the Impressionists 毕沙罗〔(1830-1903), 法国艺术家, 印象派画家的先驱〕

piss ar·tist /ˋ· ·ˌ·/ *n* [C] *BrE informal* an impolite word for someone who drinks a lot of alcohol【英, 非正式】酒鬼〔不礼貌的说法〕

piss-ass /ˋ· ·/ *adj AmE spoken* [only before noun 仅用于名词前] a very impolite word meaning not at all important, or very silly【美口】一点也不重要的; 非常愚蠢的〔非常不礼貌的说法〕: *Seth thinks his piss-ass little job makes him somebody!* 赛思居然以为就凭他那个不值一提的工作会让他成为什么大人物呢!

pissed /pɪst; pɪst/ *adj* **1** *BrE spoken* drunk【英口】喝醉的: *They rolled in pissed at three in the morning.* 他们早上3点醉醺醺地拥进来。| **pissed as a newt/pissed out of your head** (=extremely drunk) 酩酊大醉的 **2** *AmE spoken* an impolite word meaning annoyed, disappointed, or unhappy【美口】生气的, 恼火的, 失望的〔不礼貌的说法〕: *Oh God, I'm really pissed, I screwed up on my exam.* 噢上帝, 我真的很烦, 我考试考糟了。| **[+with/at]** *Are you still pissed at me?* 你还在生我的气吗? **3 pissed off** *especially BrE* annoyed, disappointed, or unhappy【尤英】生气的, 恼火的, 失望的, 不快的: **[+with]** *I'm a bit pissed off with my job at the moment.* 我现在对我的工作感到有点厌烦。

pis·ser /ˋpɪsɚ; ˈpɪsə/ *n* [C] *spoken*【口】**1** an impolite word meaning a difficult job or activity, or a bad or annoying situation 难事, 苦差事; 糟糕的情况, 令人讨厌的局面〔非常不礼貌的说法〕: *"I'm grounded." "What a pisser."* "我被罚不准出去。" "真糟糕。" **2** an impolite word meaning a toilet 茅[屎]坑〔不礼貌的说法〕**3** *AmE* a very impolite word meaning a good situation【美】好的情况; 好事〔非常不礼貌的说法〕: *I got the job! What a pisser!* 我得到了那份工作! 真太好了!

piss·head /ˋpɪsˌhɛd; ˈpɪshed/ *n* [C] *BrE spoken* an impolite word for someone who drinks a lot of alcohol【英口】酒鬼〔不礼貌的说法〕

pis·soir /piˋswar; ˈpɪswɑː/ *n* [C] *French* a public toilet【法】公共厕所

piss-take /ˋ· ·/ *n* [C usually singular 一般用单数] *BrE spoken* a joke in which you try to make fun of someone, for example by copying them or laughing at them【英口】嘲弄[取笑]某人的玩笑 —see also 另见 **take the piss out of** (PISS² (3))

piss-up /'· ·/ *n* [C] *BrE spoken* an occasion when several people drink a lot of alcohol together【英口】痛饮, 狂饮: *I'm not going to the party – it sounds like just a piss-up to me.* 我不会去参加聚会——它听起来像是一场狂欢痛饮。

pis·sy /ˈpɪsɪ; ˈpɪsi/ *adj spoken* an impolite word meaning small or unimportant and annoying【口】微小的, 琐碎的; 令人讨厌的〔不礼貌的说法〕

pis·ta·chi·o /pɪsˈtæʃɪˌo; pɪ̥ˈstɑːʃiəʊ/ *plural* **pistachios** *n* [C] a small green nut 阿月浑子(核果), 开心果: *pistachio ice cream* 阿月浑子[开心果]冰激凌

piste /pist; piːst/ *n* [C] a snow-covered slope which has been prepared for people to SKI² down 滑雪道

pis·til /ˈpɪstḷ; ˈpɪstl/ *n* [C] *technical* the female seed-producing part of a flower【术语】雌蕊

pis·tol /ˈpɪstḷ; ˈpɪstl/ *n* [C] a small gun you can use with one hand 手枪

pistol-whip /'· · ·/ *v* [I,T] to hit someone many times with a pistol 用手枪多次击打〔某人〕

pis·ton /ˈpɪstn̩; ˈpɪstən/ *n* [C] a part of an engine consisting of a short solid piece of metal inside a tube, that moves up and down to make the other parts of the engine move 活塞

piston ring /'· · ·/ *n* [C] a circular metal spring used to stop gas or liquid escaping from between a piston and the tube that it moves in 活塞环

pit¹ /pɪt; pɪt/ *n*

1 ▶HOLE 洞◀ [C] **a)** a hole in the ground, especially one made by digging〔尤指在地上挖出的〕坑: *Dig a pit and bury the rubbish in it.* 挖一个坑, 然后把垃圾埋进去。| *a sand pit* 沙坑 | *a barbecue pit* 烧烤坑 **b)** a large hole in the ground from which stones or minerals have been dug〔地上采掘石头或矿物的〕大坑; 矿坑: *a gravel pit* 砂砾采掘场, 砂砾坑

2 ▶MARK 痕迹◀ [C] **a)** a small hollow mark in the surface of something〔某物表面的〕微小凹痕: *There are tiny scratches and pits on the windshield.* 挡风玻璃上有微小的刮痕和凹痕。**b)** a small hollow mark that is left on your face by some diseases, especially SMALLPOX〔某些疾病, 尤指天花留下的〕疤痕, 麻子

3 ▶MINE 矿井◀ [C] a mine, especially a coal mine 矿井〔尤指煤矿〕: *We have no choice but to close unprofitable pits.* 我们别无选择, 只得关闭无利可图的矿井。

4 ▶UNTIDY PLACE 不整洁的地方◀ [C] *spoken* a house or room that is dirty, untidy, or in bad condition【口】很脏的房屋[房间]; 状况很差的房屋[房间]: *No, we decided not to rent it – the place is an absolute pit!* 不, 我们决定不租了——那屋子状况太差了!

5 be the pits *usually spoken* used to say that something is extremely bad【通常口】极差, 极糟糕: *Rap music? That stuff is the pits!* 说唱乐? 那东西是最糟糕的。

6 in/at the pit of your stomach if you feel nervous, frightened etc at the pit of your stomach, you experience these emotions strongly, often as an unpleasant feeling in your stomach 在你的胸口[心窝]: *a knot of fear in the pit of my stomach* 我心中的一阵恐慌

7 ▶CAR RACING 赛车◀ **the pit** *AmE*【美】, **the pits** *BrE*【英】the place beside the track in car RACES¹ (1) where cars can come in during a race to be quickly repaired〔赛车时设在车道边的〕汽车快修站

8 ▶IN A GARAGE 在汽车修理厂◀ [C] a hole in the floor of a garage that lets you get underneath a car to repair it〔修车处可钻入汽车下的〕检修坑

9 ▶IN FRUIT 在水果中◀ [C] *AmE* the single, large hard seed in some fruits; STONE¹ (4)【美】〔某些水果的〕核: *a peach pit* 桃核

10 ▶IN A THEATRE 在剧院里◀ [C] **a)** an ORCHESTRA PIT〔剧场舞台前面的〕乐池 **b)** *BrE old use* the seats at the back of the ground floor of a theatre【英旧】〔剧院里的〕(楼下)正厅后座

11 the pit of despair/dismay/depression etc *literary* a situation in which you feel extremely sad and without hope【文】极其绝望/惊愕/沮丧等

12 ▶BUSINESS 交易◀ [C] *AmE* the area of a STOCK EXCHANGE where people buy and sell shares (SHARE² (5))【美】证券交易所的交易区; FLOOR¹ (8) *BrE*【英】

13 ▶BODY PART 身体部位◀ [C] *AmE informal* an ARMPIT【美, 非正式】腋窝

14 the pit *biblical* HELL¹ (3)【圣经】地狱: *cast into the pit of eternal damnation* 投入永受诅咒的地狱

pit² *v past tense and past participle* **pitted** **1 pit your wits against** to compete with someone or something in a situation in which you need all your intelligence 绞尽脑汁与〔某人〕较量, 用尽智慧对付〔某事物〕: *Pit your wits against the Double or Dare computer!* 与挑战者电脑游戏斗智去吧! **2** [T] *AmE* to take out the single, hard seed inside some fruits; STONE² (2)【美】除去…的核 **3** [T usually passive 一般用被动态] to put small marks or holes in the surface of something 使留下疤痕; 使有凹陷: *Heavy rain had pitted and blurred the trail.* 大雨使小径变得坑坑洼洼, 都有些看不清了。—see also 另见 PITTED

pit sb/sth **against** sb/sth *phr v* [T] to test your strength, ability, power etc against someone else 使与…竞争, 使相斗: *a chance to pit our strength against pro ball players* 一次让我们与职业球员比实力的机会

pit sth ↔**out** *phr v* [T] *AmE informal* to SWEAT so much that your clothes become wet under your arms【美, 非正式】汗湿〔腋下的衣服〕

pit·a bread /ˈpɪtə brɛd; ˈpɪtə bred/ *n* [U] the American spelling of PITTA BREAD pitta bread 的美式拼法

pit-a-pat /'· · ,·/ *adv informal* PITTER-PATTER【非正式】噼噼啪啪地 —**pit-a-pat** *n* [singular]

pit bull ter·ri·er /,· ' · · ·/ also 又作 **pit bull** /,· '·◀/ *n* [C] a small but extremely strong and sometimes violent fighting dog 斗牛㹴狗〔一种体小但极其强壮、有时凶猛的斗犬〕—see picture at 参见 DOG¹ 图

> **CULTURAL NOTE 文化注释**
>
> Pit bull terriers are considered to be very dangerous, especially when their owners are unable to control them properly, and they have caused terrible injuries to children and adults. In Britain, the law prevents pit bull terriers being sold, bred, or brought into the country, and they must wear a MUZZLE (=a covering round the mouth to prevent the dog from biting) when they are in a public place. 斗牛㹴狗被认为是一种危险的动物, 尤其当主人对其失控时更是凶猛。它们曾严重咬伤很多儿童和成人。英国法律禁止此种犬的买卖、饲养和入境。此种犬在公共场所出现时必须戴上口套。

pitch¹ /pɪtʃ; pɪtʃ/ *n* 3

1 ▶SPORTS FIELD 运动场地◀ [C] *BrE* a specially marked out area of ground on which a sport is played【英】比赛场地; FIELD¹ (4) *AmE*【美】: *The crowd invaded the pitch at the end of the match.* 比赛一结束, 人群涌入了球场。| *a cricket pitch* 板球场

2 ▶STRONG FEELINGS 强烈的感情◀ [singular, U] the strength of your feelings or opinions about something〔感情、意见的〕程度, 强度: *Disagreement reached such a pitch that we thought a fight would break out.* 分歧达到如此程度, 以至于我们认为会爆发一场打斗。| **at fever pitch** (=with a lot of excited feeling) 高度兴奋, 到狂热程度 *Speculation about the election was at fever pitch.* 有关选举的各种预测已达到了高潮。

3 ▶MUSIC 音乐◀ **a)** the highness or lowness of a musical note 音调; 音高 —see also 另见 PERFECT PITCH **b)** the ability of a musician to play or sing a note at exactly the correct pitch 乐感; 音乐家以精确的音高演奏[演唱]的能力: *She's got good pitch.* 她乐感很好。

4 ▶SELLING 销售◀ [C] *informal* what a sales person says about a product to persuade people to buy it; SALES PITCH【非正式】〔推销员的〕叫卖语, 广告语

5 ▶BASEBALL 棒球◀ [C] a throw of the ball, or a way in which it can be thrown 投球; 投球姿式: *His first pitch went wide.* 他的第一球投偏了。

6 ▶BLACK SUBSTANCE 黑色物质◀ [U] a black, sticky substance that is used on roofs, the bottoms of ships etc to stop water coming through 沥青: **as black as pitch** (=very dark) 漆黑的 —see also 另见 PITCH-BLACK, PITCH-DARK

7 ▶SHIP/AIRCRAFT 船/飞行器◀ [C] a backward and forward movement of a ship or an aircraft〔船或飞机的〕颠簸 —compare 比较 ROLL² (4)

8 ▶SLOPE 斜坡◀ [singular, U] the degree to which a roof slopes〔屋顶的〕斜度, 坡度

9 ▶STREET/MARKET 街道/市场◀ [C] *BrE* a place in a public area where a street trader or entertainer goes to sell things or perform【英】〔街道小商贩的〕摆摊处;〔街头艺人的〕表演场地 —see also 另见 **queer sb's pitch** (QUEER³)

pitch² *v*

1 ▶THROW 扔, 投, 掷◀ [T] to throw something with a lot of force, often aiming carefully〔通常仔细瞄准后〕用力投, 扔, 抛, 掷: *Men slouched on the corner, pitching pennies.* 男人们懒洋洋地坐在街角, 掷钱币赌博。| **pitch sth over/into/through etc**

Fran screwed up the letter and pitched it into the fire. 弗兰把信揉成一团，扔进火中。

2 ►BALL GAMES 球类运动◄ **a)** [I,T] to aim and throw a ball in BASEBALL〔棒球中〕投（球）—see picture on page A22 参见A22页图 **b)** [I] if a ball pitches in CRICKET or GOLF, it hits the ground〔板球或高尔夫球中〕（球）落地，击地 **c)** [T] to hit the ball in a high curve in golf〔高尔夫球中〕把〔球〕击成下旋高球 **d)** [T] to make the ball hit the ground when you are bowling (BOWL[2] (2)) in cricket〔板球中〕使球击地[触地]

3 ►FALL 跌倒◄ [I always+adv/prep, T always+adv/prep] to fall suddenly and heavily in a particular direction, or to make someone or something fall in this way（使）突然重重地跌倒：**pitch forward/backward/over etc** *Jim pitched forward as the train jerked to a halt.* 火车突然停下，吉姆向前栽倒了。

4 ►SHIP/AIRCRAFT 船/飞行器◄ [I] if a ship or an aircraft pitches, it moves along with the back and front going up and down 颠簸：*The old frigate pitched violently on the massive waves.* 那艘旧护航舰在巨浪中剧烈地颠簸着。—compare 比较 ROLL[2] (4), YAW

5 ►SET A LEVEL 确定水平◄ [T always+adv/prep] **a)** if you pitch an examination, explanation, speech etc at a particular level of difficulty, you make sure that it can be understood by people at that level 把〔考试、解释、演说等〕定于某一特定难度：*Pitch the test at your average students' level of ability.* 按照普通学生的能力水平确定考试的难度。| *They're a young audience, so don't pitch it too high.* 他们是年轻的听众，所以别讲得太深了。**b)** to set prices at a particular level 把价格定在某个水平：*Prices for the new hatchbacks are pitched very competitively.* 这种新型掀背式汽车售价定得很有竞争力。

6 ►MUSIC 音乐◄ [T always+adv/prep] if you pitch your voice or another sound at a particular level, the sound is produced at that level 为…定音高，为…定调：**pitch sth high/low etc** *This song is pitched too high for my voice.* 对我的嗓子来说，这首歌的音定得太高了。—see also 另见 HIGH-PITCHED, LOW-PITCHED

7 pitch camp/pitch a tent to set up a tent or a camp for a short time 扎营/搭帐篷：*We pitched our tents beside a stream.* 我们在一条小溪边搭起帐篷。

8 ►BUSINESS DEALS 交易◄ [I,T] *informal, especially AmE* to try to make a business agreement, or to sell something by saying how good it is【非正式，尤美】竭力推销：*sales reps pitching the latest gadgets* 竭力推销最新小玩意的销售代表 | [+for] *Jack's trying to pitch for a deal.* 为达成交易，杰克正在竭力推销。

9 ►SLOPE 斜坡◄ [I always+adv/prep] to slope downwards 向下倾斜：**pitch gently/steeply etc** *The roof pitches sharply to the rear of the house.* 屋顶向后大幅度倾斜。—see also 另见 PITCHED

10 pitch sb a line/yarn *AmE informal* to tell someone a story or give them an excuse that is difficult to believe【美，非正式】给某人编造荒诞无稽的故事，给某人编造令人难以相信的借口：*She pitched me some yarn about a bomb scare on the metro.* 她向我大谈有关地铁上炸弹恐慌的骗人故事。

pitch in *phr v* [I] *informal*【非正式】**1** to start to work eagerly as a member of a group〔作为小组中的一员〕开始大干特干，拼命地干起来：*If we all pitch in, we'll have it finished in no time.* 我们如果都全力投入地干起来，那么立刻就可以把它完成。**2** to add your help or support 提供帮助[支持]：**pitch in with sth** *The local council pitched in with the offer of a free van.* 当地市议会免费提供轻型货车予以协助。**3** to start to eat hungrily 开始狼吞虎咽，开始大吃特吃：*Pitch in – there's plenty for everyone.* 放开肚子吃吧——足够每个人吃的。

pitch into sb *phr v* [T] *spoken* to attack someone by hitting them or insulting them【口】〔武力或口头〕攻击〔某人〕

pitch up *phr v* [I] *BrE spoken* to arrive somewhere; TURN UP【英口】出现；到达：*Guess who just pitched up on Saturday night?* 猜猜星期六晚上谁来了？

pitch-and-putt /ˌ· · ˈ·/ *n* [U] *BrE* a game of GOLF played on a very small course【英】在小型高尔夫球场进行的比赛

pitch-black /ˌ·ˈ·◄/ *adj* completely black or dark 乌黑的；漆黑的：*Night in the city is never pitch-black.* 这个城市的夜晚从来不会漆黑一片。

pitch·blende /ˈpɪtʃˌblɛnd; ˈpɪtʃblend/ *n* [U] a dark shiny substance dug from the earth, from which URANIUM and RADIUM are obtained 沥青铀矿

pitch-dark /ˌ·ˈ·◄/ *adj* completely dark 漆黑的

pitched /pɪtʃt; pɪtʃt/ *adj* a roof that is pitched is sloping rather than flat〔屋顶〕倾斜的，有坡度的

pitched bat·tle /ˌ· ˈ··/ *n* [C] **1** an angry and usually long quarrel or argument 激烈的长期争执[辩论]：*We had a pitched battle with the council before they'd agree to repair the road.* 在市议会同意修路之前，我们曾有过长期激烈的争论。**2** a battle between armies who have already chosen and prepared their positions〔布好阵式的〕阵地战，对阵战 —compare 比较 SKIRMISH[1] (1)

pitch·er /ˈpɪtʃɚ; ˈpɪtʃə/ *n* [C] **1** *AmE or BrE old-fashioned* a container for holding and pouring liquids with a handle and a SPOUT (=shaped part for pouring); JUG[1] (1)【美或英，过时】〔带柄和嘴的〕壶，罐：*a pitcher of water* 一壶水 —see picture at 参见 JUG[1] 图 **2** *BrE* a large container for holding and pouring liquids, usually made of clay, with two handles【英】有两个柄的陶制大水壶 **3** the player in BASEBALL who throws the ball〔棒球运动中的〕投手 —see picture on page A22 参见A22页图

pitch·fork¹ /ˈpɪtʃˌfɔrk; ˈpɪtʃfɔːk/ *n* [C] an old-fashioned farm tool with a long handle and two long curved metal points, used especially for lifting HAY (=dried cut grass) 干草叉，长柄草耙〔一种老式农具〕—see picture at 参见 FORK[1] 图

pitchfork² *v* [T +into/in/onto] to put someone suddenly into a situation for which they are not properly prepared 使…突然处于某种境地：*She was pitchforked into this predicament by her husband's early death.* 她丈夫的早逝使她突然陷入这种困境。

pitch·out /ˈpɪtʃaut; ˈpɪtʃaʊt/ *n* [C] a ball in BASEBALL that the PITCHER deliberately throws too far to the side for it to be hit〔棒球〕投手故意投的坏球，战术性坏球

pitch pine /ˈ· ·/ *n* [C,U] a type of PINETREE that grows in North America, or the wood from this tree 北美油松；北美油松木

pit·e·ous /ˈpɪtɪəs; ˈpɪtiəs/ *adj especially literary* expressing suffering and sadness in a way that makes you feel pity【尤文】可怜的，让人怜悯的：*piteous sobs* 可怜的抽泣声 —**piteously** *adv*

pit·fall /ˈpɪtˌfɔl; ˈpɪtfɔːl/ *n* [C] a problem or difficulty that is likely to happen in a particular job, course of action, or activity 可能出现的问题[困难]，隐患，陷阱：*English spelling presents many pitfalls for foreign learners.* 英语拼写有很多意想不到的难点，外国学生很容易出错。| **avoid a pitfall** *This little booklet will help you avoid the more obvious pitfalls of travelling alone.* 这本小册子将帮助你在单独旅行时避开那些较明显的陷阱。

pith /pɪθ; pɪθ/ *n* [U] **1** a white substance just under the outside skin of oranges and similar fruit 柑橘等外皮之下的海绵层，中果皮 **2** a soft white substance that fills the stems of some plants〔某些植物茎中的〕木髓 **3 the pith of an argument/issue etc** the most important and necessary part of an argument etc 论证/问题等的核心[精髓，最重要部分]

pit·head /ˈpɪtˌhɛd; ˈpɪt-hed/ *n* [C] the entrance to a coal mine and the buildings around it 坑口，矿井口〔煤矿和周围建筑物的入口〕

pith hel·met /ˌ· ˈ··/ *n* [C] a large light hat worn especially in the past in hot countries, to protect your head from the sun; TOPEE〔尤指从前在热带地区戴的〕遮阳帽 —see picture at 参见 HELMET 图

pith·y /ˈpɪθɪ; ˈpɪθi/ *adj* **pithy comments/saying/advice etc** strongly and cleverly stated, without wasting any words 简练的评论/谚语/忠告等 —**pithily** *adv* —**pithiness** *n* [U]

pit·i·a·ble /ˈpɪtɪəbl̩; ˈpɪtiəbəl/ *adj formal* making you feel pity【正式】令人怜悯的，可怜的：*refugees living in pitiable conditions* 生活条件差得可怜的难民 —**pitiably** *adv*

pit·i·ful /ˈpɪtɪfəl; ˈpɪtɪfəl/ *adj* **1** someone or something that is pitiful looks so sad and unfortunate that you feel very sorry for them〔人或物〕令人同情的，可怜的：*The animals were a pitiful sight, in their small cages.* 那些动物在小小的笼子里，看着令人可怜。**2** not good enough to deserve respect or serious consideration 可鄙的，可耻的，不值得认真考虑的：*You don't expect me to believe that pitiful excuse.* 你别指望我会相信那个拙劣的借口。—**pitifully** *adv*: *pitifully thin* 瘦得可怜的

pit·i·less /ˈpɪtɪlɪs; ˈpɪtɪləs/ *adj* **1** showing no pity; cruel 没有怜悯心的，冷酷的，无情的：*a pitiless tyrant* 冷酷无情的暴君 **2** pitiless wind, rain, sun etc is very severe and shows no sign of changing〔风、雨、太阳等〕严酷的，无情的：*the pitiless desert sun* 无情的沙漠烈日 —**pitilessly** *adv* —**pitilessness** *n* [U]

pi·ton /ˈpitɑn; ˈpiːtɒn/ *n* [C] a piece of metal used in climbing, that you fix into the rock to hold the rope〔攀登用的〕钢锥

pit po·ny /ˈ· ˌ··/ *n* [C] a small horse that was used in the past for moving coal in a mine〔过去在煤矿中运煤的〕小马

pit prop /ˈ· ·/ *n* [C] a support for the roof of an underground passage in a coal mine〔支撑矿井巷道顶用的〕坑柱，支柱

pit stop /ˈ· ·/ *n* [C] **1** a time when you stop in the pits (PIT[1] (7)) during a car race to get more petrol or have repairs done〔汽车赛中的〕进站时间，加油时间，停车维修时间 **2 make a pit stop** *AmE informal* to stop when driving on a long journey, for food, petrol etc【美，非正式】〔驾车长途旅程中旨在用餐或加油等的〕中途停车

pit·ta bread *BrE*【英】, **pita bread** *AmE*【美】/ˈpɪtə brɛd; ˈpɪtə bred/ *n* [C,U] a type of bread which is flat and hollow〔扁平且中空的〕椭圆面包

pit·tance /ˈpɪtn̩s; ˈpɪtəns/ *n* [singular] a very small or unfairly small amount of money 少量的钱，少得可怜的钱：*She gets paid a pittance.* 她的收入少得可怜。

pit·ted /ˈpɪtɪd; ˈpɪtɪ̣d/ *adj* **1** having small marks or holes in the surface 有麻点的，有凹陷的，有坑洼的：*His skin was pitted like orange peel.* 他的皮肤像橙皮一样满是麻点。| **[+with]** *The cylinders were pitted with corrosion.* 这些钢瓶锈迹斑斑。**2** a pitted fruit has had the single, hard seed removed from it〔水果〕去核的：*pitted cherries* 去核樱桃 | *pitted olives* 去核橄榄

pit·ter-pat·ter /ˈpɪtɚ ˌpætɚ; ˈpɪtə ˌpætə/ *adv* **go pitter-patter** to make a sound consisting of many quick light beats or sounds 发出噼噼啪啪的声音，发出噗噗的声音：*Anna's heart went pitter-patter as she opened the letter.* 安娜打开信时，心噗噗直跳。—**pitter-patter** *n* [singular]: *the pitter-patter of rain on the roof* 雨落在屋顶上噼噼啪啪的声音

Pitts·burgh /ˈpɪtsbɝg; ˈpɪtsbɜːg/ an industrial city in the US state of Pennsylvania. It used to be an important centre of the steel industry. 匹兹堡〔美国宾夕法尼亚州一工业城市，曾是美国重要的钢铁工业中心〕

pi·tu·i·ta·ry /pɪˈtuəˌtɛrɪ; pɪ̣ˈtjuːɪ̣təri/ also 又作 **pituitary gland** /·ˈ····, ·/ *n* [C] the small organ at the base of your brain which produces HORMONES that control the growth and development of your body（脑）垂体 —**pituitary** *adj*

3 **pit·y[1]** /ˈpɪtɪ; ˈpɪti/ *n* **1 (it's a) pity** *spoken* used to show that you are disappointed about something and you wish things could happen differently【口】真可惜，真遗憾：**[+(that)]** *Ralph's a really nice guy – pity he's not better looking.* 拉尔夫真是个好人——遗憾的是他长得不怎么好看。| *It's a pity that Jan and George can't make it to the party.* 真可惜，简和乔治不能来参加这次聚会。| *Pity they didn't think of that earlier.* 可惜的是他们没有早想到那点。| **a pity to do sth** *It seems a pity to waste it.* 把它浪费掉似乎可惜。| **what a pity** *"Did you know the concert was cancelled?" "No, what a pity."* "你知道音乐会取消了吗？""不知道，真遗憾。" | **a great pity** *There were very few locals at the meeting, which is a great pity.* 会上没有几个当地人，真是一大遗憾。**2** [U] sympathy for someone who is suffering or unhappy 怜悯，同情：*London's homeless need more than pity – they need practical help.* 伦敦的无家可归者需要的不仅仅是怜悯，他们需要的是实实在在的帮助。| *Poor man, she thought with pity, he's given up.* 真可怜，她满怀同情地想，他已经放弃了。**3 for pity's sake** *spoken* used to show that you are very annoyed and impatient【口】请发发慈悲吧，请可怜可怜吧〔用于表示非常烦恼和不耐烦〕：*For pity's sake just shut up and let me drive!* 请发发慈悲，闭上嘴让我开车！**4 take pity on** to feel sorry for someone and do something to help them 同情，可怜：*We walked on through the pouring rain until a kind driver took pity on us.* 我们走在倾盆大雨中，直到一位好心的司机对我们发了善心。**5 more's the pity** *spoken* used after describing a situation, to show that you wish it was not true【口】太不幸了，太可惜了〔用于描述某个情况并希望那不是真的〕：*The new staff are all women, more's the pity.* 新的工作人员都是女性，太可惜了。**6 have pity on** *formal* to forgive someone or treat them sympathetically【正式】原谅；同情，怜悯

pity[2] *v* [T not usually in progressive 一般不用进行时] to feel sorry for someone because they are in a very bad situation 同情，怜悯；可怜：*I pity anyone who has to feed a family on such a low income.* 我同情所有那些须以如此微薄的收入养活全家的人。| *I pity Sophie having to live with that awful woman.* 我很同情索菲，她不得不和那个可恶的女人住在一起。

Pius XII /ˈpaɪəs ˌðə twɛlfθ; ˈpaɪəs ˌðə twelfθ/ (1876-1958) an Italian priest who became Pope (=the leader of the Roman Catholic religion) in 1939. He was Pope during World War II. 庇护十二世〔(1876-1958)，意大利牧师。1939年任教皇，也是二战时期的教皇〕

piv·ot[1] /ˈpɪvət; ˈpɪvət/ *n* [C] **1** a fixed central point or pin on which something balances or turns 枢，枢轴，支点，支轴 **2** the one central thing that a whole plan depends on, and that everything is arranged around 核心，中心：**[+of]** *The village chapel was the pivot of community life.* 这个村子的小礼拜堂是社区生活的中心。

pivot[2] *v* **1** [I,T] to turn or balance on a central point, or to make something do this（使）在枢轴上转动[平衡]：**[+on]** *The tabletop pivots on two metal pins.* 那个桌面以两个金属钉为支轴旋转。**2** [I] to turn quickly on your feet so that you face in the opposite direction〔以脚为支点〕转身

pivot on sth *phr v* [T] to depend on or be planned around a particular event, or to have a particular idea as the central one 依靠，依赖；以…为中心：*This meeting with the board is crucial – our entire project pivots on it.* 与董事会的这次见面至关重要——我们整个项目都取决于此了。

piv·ot·al /ˈpɪvət̩l; ˈpɪvətəl/ *adj* **1 a pivotal event/role/moment etc** an event etc that has a very important effect on the way something develops 关键事件/作用/时刻等：*Mandela's release was a pivotal event in South Africa's history.* 曼德拉的获释是南非历史上的一个关键事件。| *The Small Business Act had a pivotal role in job creation.*《小型企业法案》在创造就业机会方面起了关键作用。**2** like or being a pivot 似枢轴的；以枢轴为支点的：*a pivotal movement* 旋转动作

pix /pɪks; pɪks/ *n* [plural] *slang* pictures or photographs【俚】图片；照片

pix·el /ˈpɪksl̩; ˈpɪksəl/ *n* [C] *technical* the smallest unit of an image on a computer SCREEN[1] (1)【术语】像素，像点〔电脑屏幕上图像最小的单元〕

pix·ie, pixy /ˈpɪksɪ; ˈpɪksi/ *n* [C] an imaginary creature that looks like a very small human being, has magical powers, and likes to play tricks on people 小妖精，小精灵〔一种想象中的生物，身材矮小、有法术且喜爱捉弄人〕

Piz·ar·ro /pɪˈzɑro; pɪˈzɑːrəʊ/, **Fran·cis·co** /frænˈsɪsko; frænˈsɪskəʊ/ (?1475-1541) a Spanish EXPLORER and CONQUISTADOR, who went to South America in 1524. He defeated the Incas, killed their king, and took control of Peru for Spain. He was famous for his cruelty and his love of gold. 皮萨罗〔(?1475-1541)，西班牙探险家、征服者。1524年，他奔赴南美，打败了当地的印加人，杀死了印加国王，为西班牙夺取了秘鲁的控制权。此人以残忍、贪恋黄金出名〕

piz·za /ˈpitsə; ˈpiːtsə/ *n* [C,U] a thin flat round bread, baked with tomato, cheese, and sometimes vegetables or meat on top 比萨饼，意大利薄饼〔饼上放番茄、乳酪，有时加蔬菜或肉等烘烤而成〕 2

CULTURAL NOTE 文化注释

Pizza is originally an Italian food but is now very popular in Britain and the US. Some restaurants specialize in pizzas and will deliver them hot to your door when you make your order by telephone. 比萨饼原本是意大利食品，但现在在英美却广受欢迎。有不少专卖比萨饼的饭店，顾客只需电话订餐，饭店就能将热腾腾的比萨饼送到家门口。

pizza par·lor /ˈ· ·, ·ˈ/ *n* [C] *AmE* a restaurant that serves pizza; PIZZERIA【美】比萨饼餐厅，意大利薄饼店

piz·zazz /pəˈzæz; pəˈzæz/ *n* [U] *informal* an exciting strong quality or style【非正式】活力，激情，生气：*This song and dance show needs more pizzazz.* 这场歌舞表演需要更多活力。

piz·ze·ri·a /ˌpitsəˈriə; ˌpiːtsəˈriːə/ *n* [C] a restaurant that serves pizza 比萨饼餐厅，意大利薄饼店

piz·zi·ca·to /ˌpɪtsɪˈkato; ˌpɪtsɪˈkɑːtəʊ/ *n* [U] musical notes played by pulling on the strings (STRING[1] (4a)) of an instrument 拨奏；拨奏曲

pj's /ˌpi ˈdʒez; ˌpiː ˈdʒeɪz/ *n* [plural] *AmE informal* PYJAMAS【美，非正式】（一套）睡衣裤

Pk the written abbreviation of 缩写= PARK

pkt the written abbreviation of 缩写= PACKET

Pl the written abbreviation of 缩写= PLACE

pl the written abbreviation of 缩写= PLURAL

plac·ard /ˈplækɑrd; ˈplækɑːd/ *n* [C] a large notice or advertisement put up or carried in a public place 广告；广告牌；布告；标语牌；招贴：*The demonstrators carried placards attacking the government.* 示威者拿着攻击政府的标语牌。

pla·cate /ˈpleket; pləˈkeɪt/ *v* [T] *formal* to make someone stop feeling angry; APPEASE【正式】使息怒，使平静；安抚，抚慰：*I tried to placate her by offering to pay for the repairs.* 我提出支付修理费，试图让她平静下来。—**placatory** /ˈplekəˌtorɪ; pləˈkeɪtəri/ *adv*: *placatory words* 安抚的话 —**placation** /pləˈkeʃən; pləˈkeɪʃən/ *n* [U]

place¹ /ples; pleɪs/ *n* [C]

① PLACE, POSITION, OR AREA 地方, 位置, 地区
② TAKE PLACE 发生, 举行
③ IN PLACE 在适当的位置
④ FIRST/SECOND PLACE 第一/第二名
⑤ OTHER MEANINGS 其他意思

place 位置

There are two places at the back.
There's still some room at the back.
后面有两个位置。后面还有一些空位。

① PLACE, POSITION, OR AREA 地方, 位置, 地区

1 ►POINT/POSITION 地点/位置◄ **a)** any area, point, or position in space 地方, 地点, 〔空间的〕位置: *This is the place where the accident happened.* 这就是事故发生的地点。| *Make sure you keep it in a safe place.* 一定要把它存放在安全的地点。| *We kept moving from place to place.* 我们不停地搬家。| *The whole place was covered in dust.* 整个地方满是灰尘。**b)** a particular point in a larger area 〔较大区域的〕部位; 地方; 处: *a sore place on my shoulder* 肩膀的伤痛处 | *There's a place on the wall where the paint's coming off.* 墙上有块地方的漆脱落了。—see 见 POSITION (USAGE) —see graph at 参见 LOCATION 图表

2 ►PLACE FOR DOING STH 做某事的地方◄ a place that is used for, or is suitable for, a particular purpose or activity 〔适合特定用途或活动的〕地方, 场所: **place to live/eat/park etc** *What they need is a decent place to live.* 他们所需要的是一个像样的住处。| *I couldn't find a place to park.* 我找不到一个停车的地方。| **place for** *It's a great place for a vacation.* 这是度假的很好去处。| **sth's place** (=where something is usually kept) 某物常处的[原来的]位置 *Put it back in its place when you've finished with it.* 你用完以后把它放回原处。

3 ►BUILDING/TOWN/COUNTRY ETC 建筑物/城镇/国家等◄ a particular place such as a shop, factory, town, or country 场所; 地区; 地方〈如商店、工厂、城镇、国家〉: *They've just bought a little place in Wales.* 他们刚在威尔士买了一所小房子。| *We were living then in a place called Alberigu.* 那时候我们正住在一个叫阿尔伯里格的地方。| *I got it at that big furniture place on the ring road.* 我是在环城路上的那个大家具店买到的。| *a nice Korean place* (=restaurant) *on the corner* 拐角处一家很好的朝鲜餐馆

4 ►SB'S HOUSE 某人的家◄ **your place/my place etc** *informal* the house, apartment, or room where you live, I live etc【非正式】你的住所/我的住所等: *Do you want to come back to our place for coffee?* 你想回到我们家喝咖啡吗?

5 be no place for to be a completely unsuitable place 完全不适合…的地方[场所]: *A damp bedsit was no place for a baby.* 潮湿的卧室兼起居室完全不适合婴儿。

6 place of work *formal* a factory, office etc where you work【正式】工作的地方〈如工厂、办公室等〉

7 place of worship *formal* a building such as a church, where people have religious ceremonies【正式】做礼拜的场所〈如教堂〉

② TAKE PLACE 发生, 举行

8 take place to happen, especially after being planned or arranged 〔尤指经过计划或安排后〕发生, 举行: *The next meeting will take place on Thursday.* 下次会议将在星期四举行。| *the changes taking place in Indian society* 印度社会发生的变化

9 take the place of to exist or be used instead of someone or something else; REPLACE 代替, 取代: *Electric trains have now taken the place of steam ones.* 电气化火车现在已取代了蒸汽机火车。| *No-one could take the place of her mother.* 没有人能够代替她的母亲。

10 take second place to to be less important than someone or something else 处于次要地位: *Our personal wishes must take second place to the needs of the children.* 和孩子的需要相比较, 我们的个人愿望必须置于次要地位。

11 take your place a) to go to a particular position that you need to be in for an activity 站好位置, 就位: *Take your places for the next dance.* 各就各位, 准备跳下一个舞。**b)** to join, and form an important part of, a group of people or things 占据一席之地, 跻身于: *This new work will take its place among the most important paintings of the century.* 这一新作将跻身于本世纪最重要的绘画作品之列。

③ IN PLACE 在适当的位置

12 in place in the correct or usual position 在适当[通常]的位置: *Have you got all the lights in place yet?* 你把所有的灯都布置好了吗?

13 in place of instead of 代替: *In place of our advertised programme, we will be showing a film.* 我们将放映一部电影来代替广告节目。

14 in sb's place a) if you do something in someone's place, you do it because they were supposed to but could not 代替某人: *Jane was ill, so I went to the conference in her place.* 简生病了, 所以我代替她出席了这次会议。**b)** *spoken* used when talking about what you would do if you were in someone else's situation【口】处于某人的处境[情况]: *What would you do in my place?* 你要是处于我的地位, 你会怎么做?

15 in places in some parts or areas, but not everywhere 在一些地方, 有几处: *In places, there was even mould on the walls.* 墙上有些地方甚至长了霉。

④ FIRST/SECOND PLACE 第一/第二名

16 first/second/third etc place first, second etc position in a race or competition 第一/第二/第三名等: *I finished in fifth place.* 我得了第五名。

17 in the first place a) used to introduce a series of points in an argument, discussion etc 首先, 第一: *Well, in the first place, I can't afford it, and in the second place I'm not really interested.* 首先我没钱, 其次我也不怎么感兴趣。**b)** *spoken* used when talking about what was done, or should have been done, at the start of a situation【口】一开始, 起初: *I should never have gone in the first place!* 当初我压根儿就不该去!

⑤ OTHER MEANINGS 其他意思

18 ►AT COLLEGE ETC 在大学等◄ an opportunity to take part in a course, activity, event etc 〔修读课程、参加活动、项目等的〕机会, 名额: *He's been offered a place at York University.* 他已被约克大学录取。| *There are only two places left on the word-processing course.* 文字处理课程只剩两个名额了。

19 ►AVAILABLE SPACE 可利用的空间◄ a seat on a bus, room in a hotel etc that is available for someone to use 〔公共汽车上的〕座位, 位子; 〔酒店里的〕房间: *There are still a few places left on the coach.* 长途汽车上还有几个空位。

20 all over the place *informal*【非正式】**a)** everywhere 到处: *There were policemen all over the place.* 这个地方到处都有警察。**b)** in a very untidy state 凌乱, 杂乱: *Her hair was all over the place.* 她的头发乱蓬蓬的。

21 ►AT A TABLE 在桌子上◄ a knife, fork, spoon, plate etc arranged on a table for one person to use 〔餐桌上供一人使用的〕餐具; 餐位: *Shall I lay places for five or for six?* 我要摆五个人的餐具还是六个人的?

22 put sb in their place to show someone that they are not as clever or important as they think they are 使某人明白自己的地位; 杀某人的气焰: *A few curt remarks from the chairperson soon put Bates in his place.* 主席几句冷淡无礼的话很快就使贝茨明白了他自己是谁。
23 out of place a) not suitable for a particular situation or occasion 不适当的; 不相称的: *I felt completely out of place among all those smart rich people.* 在那些精明的富人中间, 我觉得完全格格不入。**b)** not in the correct or usual position 不在适当[通常]的位置上: *Nothing was ever out of place in Kitty's house.* 在姬蒂的家里, 每样东西都摆放得整整齐齐。
24 not your place if it is not your place to do something, it is not your responsibility to do it, especially because you do not have enough power 你无权…, 你没有责任…: *It's not my place to tell the directors what to do!* 我无权吩咐董事们做什么!
25 lose your place to not know what point you had reached in a book, speech etc 找不到刚才读到[讲到]的地方: *The lecturer seemed to have lost his place.* 那位讲师好像想不起刚才讲到哪儿了。
26 save/keep sb a place to make sure that people do not sit in a particular chair that you want to save for someone else 给某人留位置/占位置: *I might arrive a bit late, so could you save me a place?* 我可能会晚来一会儿, 你能给我留个位置吗?
27 have no place *formal* to be completely unacceptable【正式】完全不能被接受的: *People with racist views have no place in this union.* 带有种族主义观点的人该工会是不吸纳的。
28 fall into place a) if things fall into place in your mind, you suddenly realize and understand what is really happening〔情况〕变得清楚: *When I found out who he was, everything suddenly fell into place.* 当我查明他是谁时, 一切都突然变得豁然开朗。**b)** if plans or events fall into place, they start to happen in the way that you hoped they would〔计划或事件〕按所希望的方式发生, 变得有条不紊: *Eventually I got a job, moved house, and my life began to fall into place.* 最后我得到了一份工作, 搬了家, 我的生活开始步入正轨。
29 be going places *informal* to start becoming successful in your life【非正式】开始取得成功: *He's really going places as an actor.* 作为演员, 他真的开始走红了。
30 know your place *often humorous* to behave in a way that shows that you know which people are more important than you【常幽默】知道你自己的位置〔指你知道哪些人比你更重要〕, 有自知之明: *I'll get back to the kitchen then – I know my place!* 我会回厨房去 —— 我知道自己的位置! —see also 另见 DECIMAL PLACE, **have/take pride of place** (PRIDE[1] (6))

USAGE NOTE 用法说明: PLACE
WORD CHOICE 词语辨析: **room, space, place, somewhere, anywhere**
The uncountable nouns **room** and **space** can both mean an empty area that can be used for any purpose. 不可数名词 room 和 space 两者都能用来指可作任何用途的空间: *Is there (any) room/space for me/us to sit down in here?* 这里有我/我们坐的地方吗? | *Is there room/space for more books on this shelf?* 书架上有可以放更多书的地方吗? | *There's not enough room/space to move in here!* 这里没有足够的活动空间!
A place or **a space** [C] is a single piece of space that can be used for something. However, **a place** in this sense often has a planned or official purpose, while **a space** may be unplanned and smaller. a place 或 a space 指用于做某事的单个空间, 但 a place 用于此义时常指计划好的或有正式的用途, 而 a space 可能没有计划, 而且很小: *I need a place to work* (=an office, a study, or desk). 我需要一个工作的地方〔指办公室、书房或书桌〕。| *I need a space to work* (=a part of a room or table). 我需要一个工作的空间〔屋子或桌子的一部分〕。You say *a public place* but usually *a parking space* (=for one car) and, *an open/green space.* 人们可以说 a public place (公共场所), 但通常说 a parking space (停车位) 和 an open/green space (一块空地/绿地)。
In spoken English people often use **somewhere** or **anywhere** 在英语口语中人们常用 somewhere 或 anywhere: *I can't find anywhere to park.* 我找不到停车的地方。| *He's looking for somewhere to park his car.* 他正在找停车的地方。
GRAMMAR 语法
Place is singular, with the plural **places**. place 是单数形式, 复数形式是 places: *I visited a lot of different places* (NOT 不用 *place*). 我参观过很多不同的地方。

S3 W1 **place[2]** *v*
1 ►POSITION 位置◄ [T always+adv/prep] to put something somewhere, especially with care〔尤指小心地〕放置: **place sth in/on/under etc** *He placed the book back on the shelf.* 他把那本书放回到了书架上。| *She had placed a tape recorder in front of her on the table.* 她把一台录音机放在自己面前的桌子上。
2 ►SITUATION 处境◄ [T always+adv/prep] to put someone or something in a particular situation 使…处于某种境地: *Her request places me in a very difficult position.* 她的请求使我非常为难。
3 ►HOW IMPORTANT 多重要◄ [T] to decide how good or important something is, as compared to something else〔按好坏或重要性〕排列, 安排: *Place the wines in order of preference.* 把这些葡萄酒按口味偏好排列好。| **place value/importance etc on sth** *The company places emphasis on training its staff.* 这家公司很重视对员工的培训。
4 ►IN A JOB 在工作中◄ [T] *formal* to find a suitable job for someone【正式】为…找到合适的工作; 安插; 安排; 任命: *The agency had placed her with a local firm.* 该介绍所为她在当地一家公司找到了一份工作。
5 can't place sb to be unable to remember why you recognize someone, what their name is etc 不能想起[不记得]某人的详情〈如为什么自己会认出某人或知道其名字等〉: *I'm sure I've met that girl before somewhere, but I can't quite place her.* 我肯定以前在什么地方见过那个女孩, 但她的具体情况我就想不起来了。
6 place a bet to risk money by guessing the result of a future event 下赌注
7 place an order to ask a shop or business to provide a product that you need 下订单, 订购: *We placed an order with Whiteley's for 200 shirts.* 我们向怀特利商店订购了 200 件衬衫。
8 be placed to do sth/be placed for sth to be in a situation where you have the ability or opportunity to do or have something 处于有能力[机会]做某事[拥有某物]的境地: *You're better placed to arrange the meeting than I am.* 你比我更有能力筹备这次会议。| *How are you placed for money?* (=do you have enough money?) 你的资金情况怎么样?
9 ►RACES 比赛◄ **a) be placed first/second etc** to be first, second etc in a race or competition〔在赛跑或竞赛中〕得第一/第二名等 **b)** [T] *BrE* if a horse is placed in a race, it comes second or third【英】〔赛马中〕得第二/第三名 **c)** [I] *AmE* if a horse places in a race, it comes second【美】〔赛马中〕得第二名

pla·ce·bo /plə`sibo; plə`si:bəʊ/ *n* [C] a substance given to a patient instead of medicine, without telling them it is not real, so that they get better because they think they are taking medicine〔用来代替真的药物使病人误以为自己是在服药而病情好转的〕安慰剂: **placebo effect** (=the positive effect achieved by this) 安慰剂效应〔服用安慰剂后病情好转〕

place card /ˈ· ·/ *n* [C] a small card with someone's name on it, put on a table to show where they are going to sit〔放在桌子上、写明名字的〕座位卡[牌]

place kick /ˈ· ·/ *n* [C] a kick at a ball, especially in RUGBY or American football, when the ball is placed or held on the ground〔尤在橄榄球或美式橄榄球中的〕定位踢

place mat /ˈ· ·/ *n* [C] a mat that you put on a table for each person who is eating there〔餐桌上用餐人面前的〕餐具垫(子)

place·ment /`plesmənt; ˈpleɪsmənt/ *n* **1** [U] the act of finding a place for someone to live or work 安置; 就业安排 **2** [C] *especially BrE* a job, usually as part of a course of study, which gives you experience of a particular type of work【尤英】〔通常作为学习的一部分的〕工作; 实习职位 **3** [C,U] the act of placing something in position 放置, 布置, 摆放

pla·cen·ta /plə`sɛntə; plə`sentə/ *n* [C] a thick mass of flesh that joins an unborn child to its mother in the WOMB 胎盘

place set·ting /ˈ·, ·ˈ/ *n* [C] an arrangement of knives, forks, spoons, glasses etc to be used by one person〔进餐前〕餐位餐具的摆放

plac·id /`plæsɪd; ˈplæsɪ̣d/ *adj* **1** a placid person or animal does not easily get angry or excited〔人或动物〕平和的, 温和的: *He had a placid nature, well-suited to teaching.* 他天性温和, 非常适合教书。**2** calm and peaceful 平静的, 宁静的: *The lake was placid and still under the moonlight.* 月光下, 湖面水平如镜。—**placidly** *adv*: *Dobbs stood at the entrance, placidly smoking his pipe.* 多布斯站在入口处, 平静地抽着烟斗。—**placidity** /plə`sɪdətɪ; pləˈsɪdɪ̣ti/ *n* [U]

pla·gia·ris·m /`pledʒəˌrɪzəm; ˈpleɪdʒərɪzəm/ *n* **1** [U] the act of using someone else's words, ideas, or work and pretending they are your own 剽窃, 抄袭: *He was accused of plagiarism in*

his doctoral thesis. 他被指责在博士论文中有剽窃行为。**2** [C] an idea, phrase, story etc that has been copied from someone else's work, without stating that this is where it came from 剽窃物〈如观点、短语、故事等〉: *an article full of plagiarisms* 一篇东抄西拼的文章 —**plagiarist** *n* [C]

pla·gia·rize also 又作 **-ise** *BrE*【英】/ˈpledʒəˌraɪz; ˈpleɪdʒəraɪz/ *v* [I,T] to take words, ideas etc from someone else's work and use them in your work, as if they were your own ideas 剽窃, 抄袭〔别人的作品〕: *Half the ideas in his talk were plagiarized from an article I wrote last year.* 他讲话中有一半的观点是从去年我写的一篇文章中剽窃来的。

plague[1] /pleg; pleɪg/ *n* **1** [C,U] an attack of a disease that causes death and spreads quickly to a large number of people 瘟疫, 传染病, 疫病: *Europe suffered many plagues in the Middle Ages.* 欧洲在中世纪遭受过多次瘟疫。**2** [U] also 又作 **the plague** a very infectious disease that produces high fever and swellings on the body, and often leads to death, especially BUBONIC PLAGUE 瘟疫, 鼠疫〔尤指淋巴腺鼠疫〕: *an outbreak of plague* 鼠疫的爆发 —see also 另见 BLACK DEATH **3 a plague of rats/locusts etc** an uncontrollable and harmful increase in the numbers of a particular animal or insect 鼠灾/蝗灾等 **4 a plague on** *literary* used to show that you are extremely annoyed with someone or something【文】愿上天降祸于〔表示非常气恼〕—see also 另见 **avoid sb/sth like the plague** (AVOID (2))

plague[2] *v* [T usually passive 一般用被动态] **1** to cause continual discomfort, suffering, or trouble to someone 不断困扰, 折磨, 使苦恼: *Nick was plagued by ill health throughout his short life.* 尼克短暂的一生中一直遭受着疾病的折磨。| *street crime, riots, and other social problems plaguing our community* 困扰我们社区的街头犯罪、骚乱以及其他社会问题 **2** [T] to annoy someone, especially by continually asking them for something 使烦恼[生气], 打搅: **plague sb with sth** *The kids have been plaguing me with questions.* 孩子们一直缠着问我问题。

plaice /ples; pleɪs/ *n plural* **plaice** [C,U] a flat sea fish that is a popular food 鲽〔颇受欢迎的一种食用海鱼〕

plaid /plæd; plæd/ *n* **1** [U] thick cloth with a pattern of squares, especially of a type (TARTAN) originally from Scotland〔尤指起源于苏格兰的〕彩格呢, 格子花呢 —see picture on page A16 参见 A16 页图 **2** [C] a piece of plaid worn over the shoulder and across the chest by people from Scotland as part of their NATIONAL COSTUME〔作为苏格兰民族服装一部分的〕彩格呢披肩

Plaid Cym·ru /ˌplaɪd ˈkʌmrɪ; ˌplaɪd ˈkʌmri/ a political party in Wales, with several MPs in the British parliament, which wants Wales to become an independent country, and also wants the Welsh language to be used more 威尔士民族党〔威尔士一政党。该政党在英国议会中有数个席位, 主张威尔士独立和推广使用威尔士语〕

S2 W3 **plain**[1] /plen; pleɪn/ *adj*

1 ▶CLEAR 清楚的◀ very clear, and easy to understand or recognize; OBVIOUS (1) 清楚的, 明白的, 显而易见的, 明显的: *He spoke in Russian, but his message was plain enough.* 他虽是用俄语说的, 但意思表达得十分清楚。| **it is plain (that)** *It was plain that management policies would have to change.* 显然, 管理方针将不得不加以改变。| **as plain as day/as plain as the nose on your face** (=very clear) 极为明显(的), 非常清楚(的) *Phil loves her – that's as plain as day.* 菲尔爱她 — 这是显而易见的。

2 ▶SIMPLE 简单的◀ without anything added or without decoration; simple 无花纹的, 简单的, 朴素的, 单纯的: *a plain white blouse* 一件朴素的白衬衫 | *It's just a plain wooden table but it looks just right in this room.* 这只是一张普通的木头桌子, 但它放在这个房间正合适。| *plain food* 清淡的食物 | *a plain gold wedding ring* 一枚纯金的结婚戒指 —see picture on page A16 参见 A16 页图

3 ▶HONEST 诚实的◀ showing clearly and honestly what you think about something, without trying to hide anything; FRANK[1] (1) 坦白的, 直率的, 爽快的: *Let's have some plain, truthful answers.* 让我们听听坦率而真实的回答吧。

4 make sth plain/make yourself plain to state something very clearly, in a way that cannot be misunderstood 把某事/自己的意思说明白: *They made their position plain from the start.* 他们一开始就表明了自己的立场。| *Let me make myself plain – we are not prepared to accept the deal as it stands.* 让我把自己的立场说清楚 — 我们不准备接受目前的这个协议。—see also 另见 PLAINLY

5 the plain truth/fact is *especially spoken* used to say what you think is the simple and honest truth about a situation【尤口】简单的事实是, 明显的事实是: *The plain truth is he's just not good enough.* 简单的事实是, 他就是不够好。

6 plain stupidity/greed etc stupidity etc, and nothing else 十足的愚蠢/贪婪等: *His motive was plain greed.* 他的动机纯粹是贪婪。

7 ▶NOT BEAUTIFUL 不漂亮的◀ a word meaning ugly or unattractive, often used because you want to avoid saying this directly 不好看的, 不漂亮的, 相貌平平的〔丑陋、难看的委婉说法〕: *Mrs Cookson was a rather plain woman.* 库克森夫人是个相貌平庸的女人。

8 ▶PAPER 纸◀ plain paper does not have lines on it 不画线的, 空白的

9 (just) plain Mr/Mrs etc used to say that someone does not have a title, rank, or special name (仅仅是)不带头衔[称号]的先生/夫人等〔用来表示某人没有头衔、特殊名称等〕: *No, it's not Doctor, just plain Mister.* 不, 不是博士, 直接称呼先生就行了。

10 in plain English simply or clearly expressed, especially without using technical language 用简单的英语: *The computer system is explained in plain English.* 电脑系统是用简单的英语解释的。

11 in plain clothes police officers in plain clothes are not wearing uniform〔警察〕穿便衣的

12 be plain sailing to be very easy to do or achieve 一帆风顺, 非常顺利 —**plainness** *n* [U]

plain[2] *n* **1** also 又作 **plains** [C] a large area of flat dry land (大)平原: *The grassy plain gave way to an extensive swamp.* 青草覆盖的草原被广阔的沼泽地所取代。| *the vast plains of central China* 华中地区的广阔平原 **2** [U] the ordinary stitch in knitting; KNIT (2)〔编织的〕平针

plain[3] *adv* **plain stupid/wrong/rude etc** *informal* simply or completely stupid etc【非正式】简直愚蠢/完全错误/十分粗鲁: *It's just plain crazy to spend all your pay as soon as you get it.* 报酬一拿到手就花光, 简直是疯了。

plain·chant /ˈplentʃænt; ˈpleɪntʃɑːnt/ *n* [U] PLAINSONG〔昔日教堂中齐唱而无伴奏的〕素歌, 单旋律圣歌

plain choc·olate /ˌ· ˈ···/ *n* [U] *BrE* chocolate made without milk and with very little sugar【英】〔不加牛奶只加少量糖的〕黑[素, 纯]巧克力; DARK CHOCOLATE *AmE*【美】

plain-clothes /ˌ· ˈ·◂/ *adj* plain-clothes police are police who wear ordinary clothes so that they can work without being recognised〔警察〕穿便衣的: *plain-clothes detectives* 便衣侦探

plain flour /ˌ· ˈ·/ *n* [U] *BrE* flour that contains no BAKING POWDER【英】无发酵粉的面粉: *sift 6 oz plain flour* 筛六盎司不含发酵粉的面粉 —compare 比较 SELF-RAISING FLOUR

plain·ly /ˈplenlɪ; ˈpleɪnli/ *adv* **1** in a way that is easy to hear, see etc 清楚地〔听见、看见等〕: *We could hear Tom's voice plainly over the noise of the crowd.* 在人群的喧闹声中, 我们可以清楚地听到汤姆的声音。| *The mountains were plainly visible from our window.* 从我们的窗户望去, 群山清晰可见。**2** speaking honestly, and without trying to hide the truth 坦白地, 直率地: *She told him plainly that she had no intention of marrying him.* 她坦率地告诉他自己不打算嫁给他。**3** if something is plainly true, necessary, correct etc it is easy to see that it is true etc; OBVIOUSLY [sentence adverb 句子副词] 很清楚, 显然: *Plainly an investigation into the tragedy would be necessary.* 显然有必要对这场悲剧进行调查。**4** simply or without decoration 简单地, 简朴地, 朴素地: *a plainly dressed young girl* 穿着简朴的年轻女孩

plain sail·ing /ˌ· ˈ··/ *n* [U] **be plain sailing** to be easy and not cause any trouble 一帆风顺, 非常顺利

plain·song /ˈplenˌsɔŋ; ˈpleɪnsɒŋ/ *n* [U] a type of old Christian church music in which a group of people sing a simple tune together, without musical instruments〔昔日教堂中齐唱而无伴奏的〕素歌, 单旋律圣歌

plain·spo·ken /ˈplenˈspokən; ˌpleɪnˈspəʊkən◂/ *adj* saying exactly what you think, especially in a way that people think is honest rather than rude 直言不讳的, 坦率的, 不拐弯抹角的

plain·tiff /ˈplentɪf; ˈpleɪntɪf/ *n* [C] someone who brings a legal action against someone in a court of law; COMPLAINANT 起诉人, 原告 W3

plain·tive /ˈplentɪv; ˈpleɪntɪv/ *adj* a plaintive sound is high, like someone crying, and sounds sad〔声音〕凄厉的, 哀伤的: *the plaintive cry of the seagull* 海鸥凄厉的叫声 —**plaintively** *adv*

plait[1] /plet; plæt/ *v* [T] *BrE* to twist 3 long pieces of hair, rope etc over and under each other to make one long piece【英】把…编成辫[绳]; BRAID[2] *AmE*【美】: *a plaited leather belt* 编成辫状的皮带 | *She plaited her hair hurriedly.* 她匆匆地把头发编成辫子。—see picture at 参见 HAIRSTYLE 图

plait[2] *n* [C] *BrE* a length of something, especially hair, made by plaiting【英】发辫, 辫子; 辫绳; BRAID[1] (2) *AmE*【美】: *Jenni wore her hair in plaits.* 珍妮梳着辫子。

plan¹ /plæn; plæn/ *n* [C]

1 ▶INTENTION 意图◀ something you have decided to do or achieve 计划, 打算, 目标: *His plan is to get a degree in economics and then work abroad for a year.* 他的计划是取得一个经济学学位, 然后去国外工作一年。| **sb's best plan** *BrE* (=the best course of action) 【英】某人最好的办法 *Your best plan would be to catch a taxi – it's much too far to walk.* 你最好的办法是乘出租车 —— 走路太远了。| **change your plans/a change of plan** *There's been a change of plan – we're going on Monday instead.* 计划有变 —— 我们打算改为星期一去。| **have plans (for)** (=intend to do something) 有安排[打算] *We don't have any plans for the weekend – why don't you come over?* 我们周末没有什么安排 —— 你为何不过来呢? | **make plans (for)** (=prepare for something that you intend to do) 为…制订计划 *Julia's been busy making plans for her wedding.* 朱莉娅一直在忙于筹划她的婚礼。

2 ▶METHOD/ARRANGEMENT 方法/安排◀ a set of actions for achieving something in the future, especially one that has been considered carefully and in detail〔尤指经过仔细考虑的〕规划, 计划, 方案: *the government's five-year economic plan* 政府的五年经济计划 | **plan for** *NASA announced plans for a new space station to be launched in 1998.* 美国国家航空和航天局公布了1998年发射新空间站的计划。| **plan to do sth** *Have you heard about the plan to build a new science park?* 你听说过要建造一个新的科技园的计划吗? | **keep to/stick to a plan** *If we keep to the plan the work should be completed in two weeks.* 如果我们按照计划去做, 这项工作应该在两周内完成。| **work out/draw up/devise a plan** *They devised a plan to reduce costs.* 他们制订了一个降低成本的计划。| **a plan falls through** (=it becomes impossible because something unexpected happens) 计划落空 | **go according to plan** (=happen in the way that was expected or arranged) 按计划进行 *If everything goes according to plan the first stage will be completed by December.* 如果一切按计划进行, 第一期将在12月之前完成。

3 ▶MAP 地图◀ a drawing similar to a map, showing roads, towns, and buildings〔显示道路、城镇和建筑物的〕详图: *a street-plan of London* 伦敦街道图

4 ▶DRAWING 图画◀ a) *technical* a drawing of a building, room, or machine as it would be seen from above, showing the shape, measurements, position of the walls etc【术语】〔建筑物、房间等的〕平面图; 〔机器的〕图样, 图纸 —compare 比较 ELEVATION (4), SECTION¹ (6) —see also 另见 GROUND PLAN (1) **b)** a drawing that shows exactly how something will be arranged〔显示如何安排某物的〕示意图: *I have to organise a seating plan for the dinner.* 我得为这次宴会设计一个座位示意图。

5 plan of action/campaign a series of actions that you plan to carry out in order to achieve a particular thing 行动/活动计划[方案]: *Get your team around a table and agree a plan of action to reach this season's targets.* 让你的小组集中起来商定一套能实现本季度目标的行动计划。

6 Plan A your first plan, which you will use if things happen as you expect 第一方案〔指事情按预料的情况发展时用的计划〕

7 Plan B your second plan, which you can use if things do not happen as you expect 第二方案, 备用方案〔指事情超出预期时用的计划〕

plan² *v* **planned, planning 1** [I,T] to think carefully about something you want to do in the future, and decide exactly how you will do it 计划; 筹划, 策划: *We've been planning this visit for months – you can't cancel now.* 这次参观我们已经计划了好几个月 —— 你不能现在就把它取消。| *The whole operation went exactly as planned.* 整个行动严格按计划进行。| **[+on]** *We hadn't planned on having so many guests – we'll never have enough food for them all!* 我们没料到会来这么多客人 —— 我们根本没有足够的食物给他们吃! | **plan ahead** (=make plans for a long time in the future) 事先计划 *Now that you're pregnant, you'll have to plan ahead.* 你既然怀孕了, 就必须预先把事情都安排妥当。**2** [T] to intend to do something, especially when you have definite plans for how you will do it 打算: **plan to do sth** *Josie planned to work until she had saved enough money to go to nursing school.* 乔西打算先工作, 等储足钱了再去上护士学校。**3** [T] to think about something you are going to make, and decide what it will be like; DESIGN² 设计: *Planning a small garden is often difficult.* 设计一个小花园常常都很困难。

plan sth ↔ **out** *phr v* [T] to plan something carefully, considering all the possible problems〔周密地〕计划: *I'll get the maps so we can plan out our route.* 我去拿地图, 让我们来设计一下路线。

Planck /plɑŋk; plæŋk/, **Max** (1858-1947) a German scientist who developed the ideas on which QUANTUM theory is based 普朗克〔(1858-1947), 德国科学家。他提出的观点为量子论奠定了基础〕

plane¹ /plen; pleɪn/ *n* [C]

1 ▶AIRCRAFT 飞行器◀ a vehicle that flies in the air and has wings and at least one engine 飞机; AEROPLANE *BrE*【英】, AIRPLANE *AmE*【美】: *The next plane to New York departs in 20 minutes.* 下一班飞往纽约的航班将于20分钟后起飞。| *It's quicker to go by plane.* 乘飞机去会快一些。

2 ▶LEVEL 水平◀ a level or standard of thought, conversation etc〔思想、谈话等的〕水平, 程度; 标准: *You can't really compare the two newspapers – they're on completely different intellectual planes.* 你实在无法比较这两份报纸, 它们提供的知识层次完全不一样。

3 ▶TOOL 工具◀ a tool that has a flat bottom with a sharp blade in it, used for making wooden surfaces smooth 刨子, 平刨 —see picture at 参见 TOOL¹ 图

4 ▶TREE 树◀ a PLANE TREE 悬铃木

5 ▶SURFACE 表面◀ *technical* a completely flat surface in GEOMETRY【术语】〔几何学中的〕平面

plane² *adj* [only before noun 仅用于名词前] *technical* completely flat and smooth【术语】平的, 平面的: *a plane surface* 平面

plane³ *v* [T] to use a PLANE¹ (3) on a piece of wood to make it smooth 用刨子把…刨平: *He planed the edge of the door.* 他把门的边缘刨平。

plane ge·om·e·try /ˌ· ·ˈ···/ *n* [U] the study of lines, shapes etc that are TWO-DIMENSIONAL (=with measurements in only two directions, not three) 平面几何(学)

plan·er /ˈplenɚ; ˈpleɪnə/ *n* [C] an electric tool for making wooden surfaces smooth 刨机, 刨床 —see picture at 参见 TOOL¹ 图

plan·et /ˈplænɪt; ˈplænɨt/ *n* [C] **1** a very large round object in space that moves around the sun or another star; Earth is a planet 行星〈如地球〉: *Is there life on other planets?* 在其他行星上有生命吗? | *Planet Earth* 地球 **2 be (living) on another planet/what planet is sb on?** *spoken* humorous expressions used to say that someone's ideas are not at all practical or sensible【口】异想天开〔一种幽默的说法, 表示某人的想法毫不实际或不明智〕 **3 the planet** an expression meaning the world, used when talking about the environment 世界, 地球〔用于谈论环境〕: *the future of the planet* 地球的未来 —**planetary** *adj*

plan·e·tar·i·um /ˌplænəˈtɛrɪəm; ˌplænɨˈteəriəm/ *n* [C] a building where lights on a curved ceiling show the movements of planets and stars 天文馆, 天象馆, 太空馆

Planet of the Apes /ˌ· · · · ˈ·/ (1968) a US film about a society in the future in which intelligent monkeys, who can speak, rule the world and control humans.《决战猩球》〔(1968), 美国一影片, 讲述一个有关未来社会的故事。故事中有一群会说话的智猿, 他们统治世界, 控制人类〕

plane tree /ˈ· ·/ *n* [C] a large tree with broad leaves that is often planted along streets; PLANE¹ (4) 悬铃木

Plan·ets, The /ˈplænɪts; ˈplænɨts/ (1916) a very popular piece of CLASSICAL music by Gustav Holst, in which each of the different parts represents one of the planets (such as Mars or Jupiter) and the Roman god after whom it is named《行星》〔(1916), 古斯塔夫·霍尔斯特创作的一曲广为流传的古典音乐, 其中一段乐曲代表一颗行星及其指称的罗马人的神〕

plan·gent /ˈplændʒənt; ˈplændʒənt/ *adj literary* a plangent sound is loud and deep and sounds sad【文】〔声音〕凄切的, 悲戚的, 如泣如诉的 —**plangently** *adv* —**plangency** *n* [U]

plank /plæŋk; plæŋk/ *n* [C] **1** a long narrow, usually heavy piece of wooden board, used especially for making structures to walk on (厚)木板: *a small bridge made of planks* 用厚木板搭成的小桥 **2 plank of an argument/agenda/programme etc** one of the main features or principles of an argument etc 论证/议程/计划等的要点: *The main plank of their election strategy is to reduce taxes on business.* 他们竞选策略的主要一条是降低企业的税收。—see also 另见 **walk the plank** (WALK¹ (12))

plank·ing /ˈplæŋkɪŋ; ˈplæŋkɪŋ/ *n* [U] planks when they are put together to make a floor 板材; 地板

plank·ton /ˈplæŋktən; ˈplæŋktən/ *n* [U] the very small forms of plant and animal life that live in water, especially the sea, and are eaten by fish〔尤指海中被鱼类吞食的〕浮游生物

planned ob·so·les·cence /ˌ· ··ˈ··/ *n* [U] the practice of making products that will soon become unfashionable or less advanced than the newest ones, so that people will have to buy new ones more often 计划报废〔指生产很快就会过时或落后的产品, 以使人们不得不经常购买新的产品〕

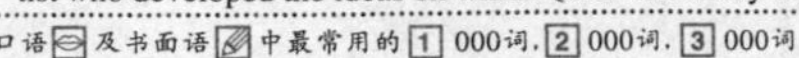

Planned Pa·rent·hood /ˌ· ˈ···/ a US organization, with offices all over the country, that provides free advice on family planning (=ways of controlling the number of children a woman has) 计划生育联合会〔美国一组织。该组织在全美各地设有办事机构，免费提供计划生育咨询服务〕

plan·ner /ˈplænɚ; ˈplænə/ *n* [C] someone who plans something, especially someone whose job is to plan the way towns grow and develop 策划者，设计者；〔尤指城市发展的〕规划者

planning per·mis·sion /ˈ·· ·ˌ··/ *n* [U] official permission to build a new building or change an existing one〔兴建或改建建筑物的〕建筑许可

2 1 **plant¹** /plænt; plɑːnt/ *n*

1 ►LIVING THING 生物◄ [C] a living thing that has leaves and roots and grows in earth, especially one that is smaller than a tree〔尤指比树小的〕植物；树秧：*Don't forget to water the plants.* 别忘记给植物浇水。| *a potato plant* 一棵马铃薯苗 | *plant pots* 花盆 —see also 另见 HOUSEPLANT

2 ►FACTORY 工厂◄ [C] a factory or building where an industrial process happens 工厂；车间：*a huge chemical plant* 一座庞大的化工厂 —see also 另见 POWER PLANT

3 ►MACHINERY 机械◄ [U] *BrE* heavy machinery that is used in industrial processes【英】重型机械，机械设备：*We are investing in new plant for the factory.* 我们正为工厂投资购置新的机械设备。| *a plant hire business* 出租重型机械的公司

4 ►STH ILLEGAL 非法的东西◄ [C usually singular 一般用单数] something illegal or stolen that is hidden in someone's clothes or possessions to make them seem guilty〔陷人入罪的〕赃物，被栽的赃物

5 ►PERSON 人◄ [C] someone who is put somewhere or sent somewhere secretly to find out information 线人；间谍

plant² *v* [T]

1 ►PLANTS/SEEDS 植物/种子◄ to put plants or seeds in the ground to grow 种植，栽种；播种：*to plant a tree* 种一棵树 | *We've planted tomatoes and carrots in the garden.* 我们在花园里种了番茄和胡萝卜。

2 plant a field/garden/area etc (with sth) to plant seeds, plants, or trees in a field etc 在田地里/花园里/某地方种植[栽种]（某物）：*a hillside planted with fir trees* 种满杉树的山坡

3 ►PUT STH SOMEWHERE 把某物放在某处◄ [always +adv/prep] *informal* to put something firmly in or on something else【非正式】牢牢插进；安置：**plant sth in/on etc** *My grandmother planted a big wet kiss on my cheek.* 祖母在我的脸颊上使劲地印上一个大大的湿吻。| *She planted her feet firmly to the spot and refused to move.* 她双脚稳稳地站在那里，拒绝移动。

4 ►ILLEGAL GOODS 非法物品◄ *informal* to hide stolen or illegal goods in someone's clothes, bags, room etc in order to make them seem guilty【非正式】栽〔赃〕：**plant sth on sb** *Someone must have planted the drugs on her.* 一定是有人把这些毒品栽赃于她。

5 plant a bomb *informal* to put a bomb somewhere【非正式】放置炸弹：*Two men are accused of planting a bomb on the plane.* 两名男子被控在飞机上放置炸弹。

6 ►PERSON 人◄ [T] to put or send someone somewhere, especially secretly, so that they can find out information〔尤指秘密地〕安插〔眼线、密探等以获取信息〕：**plant sb in/at etc** *The police had planted undercover detectives at every entrance.* 警方在每个入口处都安插了密探。

7 plant an idea/doubt/suspicion (in sb's mind) to make someone begin to believe an idea, especially so that they do not realize it was you who gave them the idea 把思想/怀疑/猜疑注入（某人的头脑），（给某人）灌输思想/怀疑/猜疑

plant sth ↔ **out** *phr v* [T] to put a young plant into the soil outdoors, so that it has enough room to grow 把〔幼苗〕移植到户外

Plan·ta·ge·nets, the /plænˋtædʒənəts; plænˈtædʒənəts/ the royal family of England from 1154 to 1399, including the kings Henry II, Richard II, and Richard III 金雀花王朝〔指1154至1399年的英格兰王室，包括亨利二世、理查二世和理查三世〕

plan·tain /ˈplæntɪn; ˈplæntɪn/ *n* **1** [C,U] a kind of BANANA that is cooked before it is eaten, or the plant on which it grows 大蕉（果实）—see picture on page A8 参见A8页图 **2** [C] a common wild plant with small green flowers and wide leaves 车前草

plan·ta·tion /plænˋteʃən; plænˈteɪʃən/ *n* [C] **1** a large area of land in a hot country, where crops such as tea, cotton, and sugar etc are grown〔热带国家的〕种植园[场]：*a rubber plantation* 橡胶园 **2** a large group of trees grown to produce wood 造林地，林场

plant·er /ˈplæntɚ; ˈplɑːntə/ *n* [C] **1** a decorative container for growing plants in 花盆 **2** someone who owns or is in charge of a plantation 种植园主；种植园管理者：*a tea planter* 茶场主，茶叶种植园园主 **3** a machine used for planting 种植机，播种机

plaque /plæk; plɑːk/ *n* **1** [C] a piece of flat metal or stone with writing on it that is fixed to a building and reminds people of an event or person connected with the place〔用金属或石板制的、刻有纪念文字的〕饰板，匾：*The mayor unveiled a special commemorative plaque.* 市长为一块有特别意义的纪念牌匾揭幕。**2** [U] a substance which forms on your teeth, which BACTERIA can live and breed in〔牙齿上的〕牙斑

plas·ma /ˈplæzmə; ˈplæzmə/ *n* [U] **1** the yellowish liquid part of the blood that contains blood cells 血浆 **2** the living substance inside a cell; PROTOPLASM 原浆，原生质 **3** a gas at a very high temperature inside stars, in flashes of electricity etc 等离子体

plas·ter¹ /ˈplæstɚ; ˈplɑːstə/ *n* **1** [U] a substance used to cover walls and ceilings and give a smooth surface, consisting of LIME, water, and sand〔涂抹墙壁、天花板等用的〕灰泥 **2** [U] PLASTER OF PARIS 熟石膏 **3** [C,U] *BrE* a piece of thin material that is stuck on to the skin to cover cuts and other small wounds【英】膏药；（窄条）橡皮膏；BANDAID *AmE*【美】**4 in plaster** *BrE* if you have a leg, arm etc in plaster you have a PLASTER CAST around a bone that is broken to keep it in place while it mends【英】打了石膏（的）

plaster² *v* [T usually passive 一般用被动态] **1** to spread or stick something all over a surface so that it is thickly covered 在…上厚厚地涂抹；覆盖：**plaster sth with sth** *Her face was plastered with makeup.* 她的脸上涂着厚厚的化妆品。**2** to cover the pages of a newspaper with a particular story or report〔新闻报道等〕覆盖，占满〔报纸的版面〕：*The news of the wedding was plastered all over the morning papers.* 有关这场婚礼的新闻覆盖了所有早报。**3** to put wet plaster on a wall or ceiling 在〔墙或天花板〕上涂灰泥 **4** to make your hair lie flat or stick to your head 使〔头发〕紧贴，粘贴：**[+down/to etc]** *His hair was plastered to his forehead with sweat.* 他的头发沾了汗水，紧贴在前额上。

plaster sth **over** *phr v* [T] to cover a hole or an old surface by spreading plaster over it〔通过涂灰泥〕覆盖〔洞或旧的表面〕

plas·ter·board /ˈplæstɚˌbɔrd; ˈplɑːstəbɔːd/ *n* [U] board made of large sheets of cardboard held together with plaster, which is used to cover walls and ceilings 灰泥板，石膏板

plaster cast /ˌ·· ˈ·/ *n* [C] **1** a cover made from plaster of Paris used to keep a broken bone in place while it mends; CAST² (2)〔用熟石膏制成的〕石膏绷带，石膏夹 **2** a copy of a STATUE made of plaster of Paris 石膏模型

plas·tered /ˈplæstɚd; ˈplɑːstəd/ *adj* [not before noun 不用于名词前] *informal* very drunk【非正式】烂醉的：*Chris was plastered after five beers.* 克里斯喝了五瓶啤酒后就烂醉如泥了。

plas·ter·er /ˈplæstərɚ; ˈplɑːstərə/ *n* [C] someone whose job is to cover walls and ceilings with PLASTER¹ (1) 泥水匠，涂灰泥工人

plaster of Par·is /ˈplæstɚ əv ˋpærɪs; ˌplɑːstər əv ˈpærɪs/ *n* [U] a quick-drying mixture of a white powder and water used for making plaster casts and to decorate buildings 熟石膏，烧石膏

plas·tic¹ /ˈplæstɪk; ˈplæstɪk/ *n* **1** [C,U] a light strong material that is chemically produced, which can be made into different shapes when soft and is used to make many things 塑料，塑胶：*children's toys made of plastic* 塑料制的儿童玩具 | *the plastics industry* 塑料工业 **2** [singular,U] *informal* small plastic cards that are used to pay for things instead of money; CREDIT CARDS【非正式】信用卡：*"I haven't got any cash." "Don't worry, I'll stick it on the plastic."* "我没带现金。" "别担心，给你记在信用卡上。" 2 2

plastic² *adj* **1** made of plastic 塑料制的：*a plastic spoon* 塑料汤匙 | *plastic bags* 塑料袋 **2** *technical* a plastic substance can be formed into many different shapes and keeps the shape【术语】（物质）可塑的，塑性的 **3** something that is plastic looks or tastes artificial or unnatural 人造的；非自然的：*plastic food* 人造食品 | *I hate that plastic smile of hers.* 我讨厌她那做作的笑容。

plastic art /ˌ·· ˈ·/ *n* [C,U] *technical* art which shows things in ways in which they can be clearly seen, especially painting or SCULPTURE【术语】造型艺术（尤指绘画或雕塑）

plastic bul·let /ˌ·· ˈ··/ *n* [C] a large bullet made of hard plastic that is intended to injure but not kill, and is used for controlling violent crowds 塑料[塑胶]子弹〔用于控制暴乱人群〕

plastic ex·plo·sive /ˌ·· ·ˈ··/ *n* [C,U] an explosive substance that can be shaped by hand, or a small bomb made from this 可塑炸药；〔由可塑炸药制成的〕可塑炸弹

plas·ti·cine /ˈplæstəˌsin; ˈplæstɪ̣siːn/ *n* [U] *BrE trademark* a soft substance like clay made in many different colours, used by young children for making models or shapes【英, 商标】〔儿童用以制作模型的〕橡皮泥, 塑胶黏土

plas·tic·i·ty /plæsˈtɪsətɪ; plæˈstɪsɪ̣ti/ *n* [U] *technical* the quality of being easily made into any shape【术语】可塑性

plastic mac /ˌ‥ ˈ·/ *n* [C] a cheap coat made of plastic, used to keep you dry in the rain〔廉价的〕塑料雨衣

plastic sur·ge·ry /ˌ‥ ˈ‥·/ *n* [U] the medical practice of changing the appearance of people's faces or bodies, either to improve their appearance or to repair injuries 整形外科, 整容手术 —**plastic surgeon** /ˌ‥ ˈ‥·/ *n* [C]

plastic wrap /ˌ‥ ˈ·/ *n* [U] *AmE* CLINGFILM【美】〔食物的〕保鲜塑料薄膜

plat du jour /ˌplɑ də ˈʒur; ˌplɑː dʊ ˈʒʊə/ *n* [C] *French* a dish that a restaurant prepares specially on a particular day in addition to its usual food【法】〔餐厅的〕当日特制菜, 当日推荐菜

S2 W2 **plate**[1] /plet; pleɪt/ *n*

1 ▶**FOOD** 食物◀ **a)** [C] a flat and usually round dish that you eat from or serve food from 盘, 碟: *The plates were piled high with rice.* 盘子里盛满了米饭。| *a dinner plate* 茶盘, 餐碟 | **clear/empty your plate** (=eat everything on your plate) 把盘子里的东西吃干净 **b)** also 又作 **plateful** [C] the amount of food that is on a plate〔食物〕一满盘[碟]: [**+of**] *He's eaten a whole plate of french fries.* 他吃了一整盘炸薯条。

2 ▶**SIGN** 标牌◀ **a)** [C] a flat piece of metal with words or numbers on it, for example on a door or a car〔印有文字或数字的〕金属牌, 牌子, 名牌〈如门牌、车牌等〉: *The plate on the door said 'Dr Rackman'.* 门牌上写着"雷克曼博士"。| *A plate below the statue indicated that it had been donated by the artist.* 塑像下面的牌子写着它是由这位艺术家捐赠的。| **number/licence/registration plate** (=on a car) 汽车的牌照[号码牌] *Did anyone see the car's license plate?* 有人看见那辆汽车的牌照吗? —see also 另见 L-PLATE, NAMEPLATE **b) plates** [plural] the flat pieces of metal on a car which give information about who the car belongs to or which country it is from〔显示汽车归谁所有或来自哪个国家等资料的〕车牌

3 **have a lot on your plate** *informal* to have a lot of problems to deal with or a lot of things to worry about【非正式】要应付的问题很多, 要操心的事情很多

4 **hand sth to sb on a plate** *informal* to let someone have what they want without making them work to achieve it【非正式】把某事物奉送给某人; 让某人轻易获得某事物: *Liverpool virtually handed the game to United on a plate.* 利物浦队几乎是拱手将这场比赛让给了曼联队。

5 ▶**PROTECTIVE COVERING** 保护性覆盖物◀ [C] **a)** *technical* one of the thin sheets of bone, horn etc that covers and protects the outside of an animal【术语】〔骨质、角质等的〕盾片, 鳞甲: *The reptile's body is covered with horny protective plates.* 爬虫的身体表面覆盖着保护性的角质鳞甲。**b)** a thin sheet of metal used to protect something〔用于保护某物的〕金属板[片]: *steel plates used in the construction of ships* 造船用的钢板

6 ▶**EARTH'S SURFACE** 地球表面◀ [C] *technical* one of the very large sheets of rock that form the surface of the Earth【术语】板块 —see also 另见 PLATE TECTONICS

7 ▶**GOLD/SILVER ETC** 金/银等◀ **a) gold/silver etc plate** ordinary metal with a thin covering of gold, silver etc 镀金/镀银等的金属 **b)** [U] articles such as plates, cups, forks or knives made of gold or silver 金银器具[餐具]

8 ▶**FOR COOKING** 用于烹饪◀ [C] *especially BrE* a metal ring on an electric COOKER that you put pans on when cooking【尤英】〔电炉上用于放锅的〕金属灶眼[炉板]

9 ▶**PICTURES/PHOTOS** 图片/照片◀ [C] **a)** a sheet of metal that has been cut or treated in some way so that words or pictures can be printed from its surface〔印刷用的〕金属版, 印版, 图版 **b)** a picture in a book, printed on good-quality paper and usually coloured〔书中的〕整页(彩色)插图 **c)** *technical* a thin sheet of glass used especially in the past in photography, with chemicals on it that are sensitive to light【术语】〔尤指过去摄影用的〕感光板[片]

10 ▶**IN CHURCH** 在教堂里◀ **the plate** a small plate or container, used to collect money in a Christian church〔教堂中的〕捐献盘[箱]

11 ▶**BASEBALL** 棒球◀ HOMEPLATE 本垒板

12 ▶**TEETH** 牙齿◀ [C] **a)** a thin piece of plastic shaped to fit inside a person's mouth, into which false teeth are fixed 假牙床, 假牙托 **b)** a thin piece of plastic with wires fixed to it, that people wear to straighten their teeth; BRACE[2] (1) 牙箍, 牙齿矫正器

plate[2] *v* [T] **be plated with a)** to be covered with a thin covering of gold, silver etc 用〔金、银等〕覆镀, 镀上〔金、银等〕: *a beautiful necklace, plated with 22 carat gold* 一条漂亮的22开镀金项链 | **gold-plated/silver-plated** *a gold-plated bracelet* 镀金手镯 **b)** to be covered in sheets of a hard material such as metal or bone 用〔金属板或骨头等坚硬材料〕覆盖: *The ship had been heavily plated with protective sheets.* 那艘船有厚厚的保护性金属板覆盖着。

plat·eau /plæˈto; ˈplætəʊ/ *n plural* **plateaus** or **plateaux** /-ˈtoz; -təʊz/ [C] **1** a large area of flat land that is higher than the land around it 高原 —see picture on page A12 参见A12页图 **2** a period during which the level of cost, achievement etc does not change, especially after a period when it was increasing 平稳时期, 稳定状态; 停滞时期: *Inflation rates have reached a plateau.* 通货膨胀率已趋平稳。| *learning plateaus among 14-year-olds* 14岁孩子的学习停滞期

plate·ful /ˈpletfʊl; ˈpleɪtfʊl/ *n* [C] all the food that is on a plate 一整盘[碟]〔食物〕

plate glass /ˌ· ˈ·◂/ *n* [U] big pieces of glass made in large thick sheets for use especially in shop windows〔尤用于商店橱窗的〕厚玻璃板, 平板玻璃

plate-lay·er /ˈ· ˌ‥/ *n* [C] *BrE* someone whose job is to make or repair railway tracks【英】〔铁路的〕铺路工; 〔维修轨道的〕养路工; TRACKLAYER *AmE*【美】

plate·let /ˈpletlɪt; ˈpleɪtlɪ̣t/ *n* [C] one of the very small plate-shaped cells in your blood that help it become solid when you bleed 血小板

plate tec·ton·ics /ˌ· ·ˈ‥/ *n* [U] the study of the forming and movement of the large sheets of rock that lie under the surface of the Earth 板块构造学

plat·form /ˈplætˌfɔrm; ˈplætfɔːm/ *n* [C] W3

1 ▶**TRAIN** 火车◀ the raised place beside a railway track where you get on and off a train in a station 站台, 月台: *The Edinburgh train will depart from platform six.* 开往爱丁堡的火车将从六号站台开出。

2 ▶**FOR SPEECHES** 用于演讲◀ a raised floor or stage for people to stand on when they are making a speech, performing etc 讲台; 戏台, 舞台: *He climbed on to the platform and began to address the crowd.* 他登上讲台开始向群众讲话。| *Please address your comments to the platform.* (=the people on the platform) 请把你的意见向台上的讲话者提出来。| *a popular platform speaker* 一位受欢迎的公开演讲者

3 ▶**STRUCTURE** 结构◀ a tall or high structure built so that people can stand or work above the surrounding area 高台, 平台: *an oil exploration platform* 石油勘探平台

4 ▶**POLITICS** 政治◀ **a)** [usually singular 一般用单数] the main ideas and aims of a political party, especially the ones that they state just before an election〔尤指政党竞选之前发表的〕政纲, 纲领: *He's running for mayor on a platform of low taxation.* 他正以低税收的政纲竞选市长。—see also 另见 PLANK (2) **b)** a chance for someone to express their opinions, especially their political opinions 发表观点的机会〔尤指政治观点〕: *The conference provides a platform for people on the left wing of the party.* 这次会议给该党的左翼人士提供了发表意见的机会。

5 ▶**BUS** 公共汽车◀ *BrE* the open part at the back of a DOUBLE-DECKER bus, where passengers get on and off the bus【英】〔双层公共汽车后部的〕出入口平台

6 ▶**SHOES** 鞋子◀ also 又作 **platform shoe** a shoe that has a thick layer of wood, leather etc underneath the front part and the heel 厚底鞋

7 ▶**COMPUTERS** 电脑◀ used to describe the type of computer system or SOFTWARE that you are using 平台〔指使用中的电脑系统或软件〕: *We're changing from an IBM to a Macintosh platform.* 我们正在把IBM操作平台换成苹果操作平台。

plat·form game /ˈ‥ ˌ·/ *n* [C] a computer game in which the action happens against a background that does not move 平台游戏〔背景不动的电脑游戏〕

Plath /plæθ; plæθ/, **Syl·vi·a** /ˈsɪlvɪə; ˈsɪlviə/ (1932-63) a US poet who was famous for her poems about women and death, and for her NOVEL *The Bell Jar*, and who was married to the British poet Ted Hughes. She killed herself after many years of unhappiness. 普拉斯〔(1932-1963), 美国女诗人, 以描写女性和死亡的诗作及小说《钟罩》闻名。她与英国诗人特德·休斯结婚, 多年生活不幸福, 最后自杀了结一生〕

plat·ing /ˈpletɪŋ; ˈpleɪtɪŋ/ *n* [U] a thin layer of metal that covers another metal surface 金属镀层: *gold plating* 镀金层

plat·i·num /ˈplætṇəm; ˈplætɪ̣nəm/ *n* [U] a silver-grey metal that does not change colour or lose its brightness, used in making expensive jewellery and in industry. Platinum is an ELE-

MENT (1) 铂, 白金〔一种化学元素〕: *a platinum ring* 白金戒指 | *jewellery made of platinum* 白金首饰

platinum blonde /, ··· ˈ ·/ *n* [C] *informal* a young woman whose hair is a silver-white colour, especially one whose hair has been coloured with chemicals【非正式】(染) 银白色头发的年轻女子

plat·i·tude /ˈplætəˌtud; ˈplætɪ̣tjuːd/ *n* [C] a statement that has been made many times before and is not interesting or clever 老生常谈, 陈词滥调: *a typical politician's speech, full of platitudes* 充满陈词滥调的典型的政客演讲 —**platitudinous**/ˌplætəˈtudn̩əs; ˌplætɪ̣ˈtjuːdɪ̣nəs◀/ *adj*

Pla·to /ˈpleto; ˈpleɪtəʊ/ (?427-347BC) an ancient Greek PHILOSOPHER, who had a very great influence on European PHILOSOPHY. He explained his ideas in the form of written conversations. His teacher was Socrates, and after Socrates' death he established a school called the Academy, where Aristotle was one of his students. His most famous work is *The Republic*, about the perfect state and form of government. 柏拉图〔(公元前?427-前347), 古希腊哲学家, 对欧洲哲学产生过重大影响。他采用书面会话形式阐述自己的观点。他的老师是苏格拉底。老师去世后, 他创办了一所学校, 名为"学苑"(Academy), 亚里士多德是学苑的一名学生。柏拉图的代表作为《理想国》, 论述完美的政体与组织形式这一主题〕

pla·ton·ic /pləˈtɑnɪk; pləˈtɒnɪk/ *adj* a relationship that is platonic is just friendly or affectionate, not a sexual relationship〔关系〕亲密而无性爱的, 柏拉图式的, 纯精神恋爱的, 纯友谊的 —**platonically** /-klɪ; -kli/ *adv*

pla·toon /pləˈtun; pləˈtuːn/ *n* [C] a small group of soldiers which is part of a COMPANY and is commanded by a LIEUTENANT〔士兵的〕排

plat·ter /ˈplætɚ; ˈplætə/ *n* [C] **1** *especially AmE* a large plate from which food is served【尤美】大浅盘 **2 chicken/seafood etc platter** chicken etc and other foods arranged on a plate and served in a restaurant〔餐馆里的〕鸡肉/海鲜等拼盘 **3** *BrE old use* a large plate, usually made of wood【英旧】〔一般为木制的〕浅盘 **4** *AmE old-fashioned* a RECORD[1] (3)【美, 过时】唱片

plat·y·pus /ˈplætəpəs; ˈplætɪ̣pəs/ *n* [C] a small, furry Australian animal that has a beak and feet like a duck, lays eggs, and gives milk to its young; DUCKBILLED PLATYPUS 鸭嘴兽

plau·dits /ˈplɔdɪts; ˈplɔːdɪ̣ts/ *n* [plural] *formal* praise and admiration【正式】喝彩, 赞扬, 赞美: *Her performance won the plaudits of the critics.* 她的表演赢得了评论家的赞扬。

plau·si·ble /ˈplɔzəbl̩; ˈplɔːzɪ̣bəl/ *adj* **1** a statement that is plausible is reasonable and seems likely to be true 似乎是真的, 貌似有理的: *His explanation sounds fairly plausible to me.* 他的解释我听起来似乎颇有道理。**2** someone who is plausible is good at talking in a way that sounds reasonable and truthful, although they may in fact be lying〔人〕花言巧语的, 能言善辩的, 能说会道的: *a plausible rogue* 花言巧语的无赖 —opposite 反义词 IMPLAUSIBLE —**plausibly** *adv*: *It could plausibly be argued that these improvements are due to government policy.* 有人可能会争辩说这些进步都归功于政府的政策, 这似乎有点儿道理。—**plausibility** /ˌplɔzəˈbɪlətɪ; ˌplɔːzɪ̣ˈbɪlɪ̣ti/ *n* [U]

S1 W1 **play[1]** /ple; pleɪ/ *v*

1 ►CHILDREN 儿童◄ [I,T] when children play, they do things that they enjoy, often together or with toys 玩, 玩耍: *The children ran off to play on the beach.* 孩子们跑到海滩上玩耍。| **play sth** *The boys were playing soldiers.* 孩子们在扮士兵玩。| *I don't want to play that game!* 我不想玩那个游戏! | **[+with]** *play with your new toys* 玩你的新玩具 | *He loves playing with his grandchildren.* 他喜欢和孙儿们一起玩。

2 ►SPORTS/GAMES 运动/比赛◄ [I,T] to take part in a game or sport 参加〔比赛或运动〕: **play sth** *Do you play a lot of golf?* 你常打高尔夫球吗? | *I enjoy playing chess.* 我喜欢下棋。| **[+against]** *They're a terrible team to play against.* 他们是一支很难对付的球队。| **[+for]** *He has played for England fifteen times now.* 他现在已为英格兰队打了15场比赛。| **play sb** *She's playing Helen Evans in the semi-final.* (=playing against her) 她将在半决赛中与海伦·埃文斯相遇。

3 play a ball to hit a ball in a game or sport〔在比赛或运动中〕击球, 打球: *She played the ball low, just over the net.* 她把球打得很低, 刚刚过网。

4 play games to hide your real feelings or wishes in order to achieve something in a clever or secret way 与…耍花招, 耍手段〔指为获得某物而隐藏真实的感情或愿望〕

5 play the game to behave in a fair and honest way 办事公道, 行为光明正大

6 ►MUSIC 音乐◄ [I,T] **a)** to perform a piece of music on a musical instrument 演奏, (用…) 演[弹]奏〔乐曲〕: *I've always wanted to learn to play the piano.* 我一直想学弹钢琴。| *She tried to play a Bach Prelude.* 她试着演奏了巴赫的一首前奏曲。| *Please play a tune on your concertina for me.* 请用你的六角手风琴为我弹奏一曲吧。**b)** to produce music 播放[演奏]〔音乐〕: *The bedside radio played softly.* 床边的收音机轻柔地播放着音乐。| *I could hear a violin playing a waltz in the background.* 我可以听到背景中有小提琴在演奏华尔兹舞曲。| **play a record/tape/CD** (=produce music from it) 播放唱片/录音带/激光唱片 *He just sits in his bedroom all day playing records.* 他只是整天坐在卧室里放唱片。

7 ►THEATRE/ACTING 剧院/表演◄ **a)** [T] to perform the actions and say the words of a particular character in a theatre performance 扮演〔角色〕: *He had always wanted to play Hamlet.* 他一直想扮演哈姆雷特。| **play a role/part** *The role of Mrs Goodfire was played by Jane Easton.* 古德费尔太太这个角色是由简·伊斯顿扮演的。**b)** [I] if a play is playing at a particular theatre, it is being performed there〔戏剧〕上演: *'Macbeth' is now playing at the Theatre Royal in York.* 《麦克白》目前正在约克皇家剧院上演。**c)** [T] if actors play a theatre, they perform there in a play〔演员〕在…演出

8 play a part/role in sth to have an effect or an influence on something 在某事中起作用, 在某事中有影响: *The press plays an important role in the life of a democracy.* 新闻界在民主国家的生活中起着很重要的作用。

9 ►PRETEND 假装◄ [linking verb 系动词] to behave as if you are a particular kind of person or have a particular feeling or quality, even though it is not true 假装, 装扮: **play dumb/dead etc** *The snake fools predators by playing dead.* 蛇以装死来欺骗捕猎者。| **play the idiot/the teacher etc** *If he is captured, he must play the idiot and reveal nothing.* 如果他被抓获, 就必须装傻, 不透露任何事情。| **play policeman/soldier etc** *These are ordinary people who think they'll play policeman for a while.* 这些是自认为可以扮一会儿警察的普通人。| **play the fool** (=behave in a silly way) 做蠢事

10 play hard to get to pretend that you are not sexually interested in someone so that they will become more interested in you 对〔异性〕欲擒故纵〔故意装出对某人不感兴趣的样子以吸引对方〕

11 ►BEHAVE 表现◄ [T always+adv/prep] to behave in a particular way in a situation in order to achieve the result or effect that you want〔以某种方式〕表现, 行事: *We always discuss how the event will be played.* 我们总是讨论如何让这件事发展下去。| **play it carefully/cool etc** *I think he might offer me the job, but I must play it carefully.* 我想他可能会给我这份工作, 但我必须谨慎对待。| **play (it) safe** (=avoid taking any risks) 稳重[谨慎]行事, 不冒险 | **play it by ear** (=decide what to do according to the way a situation develops) 见机行事, 随机应变 *Let's just play it by ear.* 我们见机行事吧。

12 play a joke/trick on sb to do something to someone as a joke or trick 跟某人开玩笑/捉弄某人: *I was trying to play a joke on you.* 我本想跟你开个玩笑。

13 ►CARDS 纸牌◄ [T] to show a card in a game of cards by putting it down on the table 出〔牌〕: *She couldn't decide which card to play.* 她无法决定出哪一张牌。| *He played his ace and won the game.* 他出了张A牌赢了那一局。

14 play your cards right to behave in a clever or skilful way in a situation so that you gain as much as possible from it 做事精明, 处理得当: *If I play my cards right, I should do very well out of the deal.* 如果我处理得当的话, 应该可以从这项交易中大赚一笔。

15 play second fiddle (to sb) to be in a lower position or rank than someone else (给某人) 当第二把手[副手], 居次要地位

16 play for time to try to delay something so that you have more time to prepare for it or prevent it from happening 为争取时间而拖延: *He was playing for time until the others arrived.* 在其他人到齐之前, 他一直在拖延时间。

17 ►SMILE 笑容◄ [I always+adv/prep] if a smile plays over someone's lips, they smile quickly and only a little〔嘴唇〕露出〔一丝微笑〕

18 ►LIGHT 光线◄ [I always+adv/prep] if light plays on something, it shines on it and moves about on it〔在…上〕闪烁, 移动: *She watched the sunlight playing on the water.* 她注视着水面上闪烁的阳光。

19 play the system to use the rules of a system in a clever way, to gain advantage for yourself 钻制度的空子〔使自己得益〕: *These accountants know how to play the tax system.* 这些会计知道如何钻税收制度的空子。

20 play the market to risk money on the STOCK MARKET as a way of trying to earn more money〔在证券市场〕买卖证券谋利

21 play hooky *AmE*【美】/**play truant** *BrE*【英】to stay away from school without permission 逃学；旷课

22 play with fire to do something that could have a very dangerous or harmful result 做危险的事，玩火

23 play a hose/light on sth to direct a HOSE or light towards something so that water or light goes onto it 把水龙头[光线]对着某物喷射[照射]

24 not play ball to refuse to do something that someone else wants you to do 拒绝做〔别人要你做的事〕，拒绝合作：*She wanted Dean to lend her the money, but he wouldn't play ball.* 她想让迪安借钱给她，但他拒绝了。

25 play the field to have sexual relationships with a lot of different people 与很多异性发生性关系，滥交

26 play sb for a sucker *AmE* to show by the way that you behave towards someone that you think they are stupid【美】把某人当成傻瓜：*It seems to me they are playing me for a sucker in this hotel.* 在我看来，他们好像把我当作这酒店里的傻瓜。

27 play fast and loose with sb *old-fashioned* to treat someone in a selfishly careless way【过时】玩弄某人，轻率地对待某人

play about/around with sb/sth *phr v* [T] **1** to have a sexual relationship with someone that is not serious or not intended to last very long 玩弄〔某人〕；与〔某人〕有不正当性关系，跟…乱搞[厮混]：*Her husband accused her of playing around with other men.* 她的丈夫指控她与别的男人鬼混。**2** to keep moving something around in your hands〔在手中〕摆弄，把玩：*Stop playing around with that knife!* 别再摆弄那把刀子了！

play along *phr v* **1** [I+with] to pretend that you agree with someone's ideas because you want to gain an advantage for yourself or to avoid a quarrel 假装同意〔某人的观点以获得好处或避免争吵〕，暂且附和 **2** [T] **play sb along** to tell someone something that is not true because you need their help in some way〔为取得某人的帮助而〕对某人撒谎，欺骗某人

play at sth *phr v* [T] **1** if you play at doing something, you do not do it properly or seriously 不认真地干，对…敷衍了事：*He just plays at being an artist.* 他当艺术家只是玩玩而已。**2** if children play at doctors, soldiers etc, they pretend to be doctors or soldiers〔小孩〕假扮…玩 **3 What is he/she etc playing at?** used when you do not understand what someone is doing or what they are trying to achieve 他/她等在干什么?：*What do you think you're playing at?* 你到底在搞什么鬼？| *I don't know what on earth he's playing at.* 我不知道他究竟在干什么。

play sth ↔ **back** *phr v* [T] to play something that has been recorded on a machine so that you can listen to it or watch it 重新播放〔已录制的录音带、录像带等〕：*I recorded my brother singing a song then played it back to him.* 我把弟弟唱的歌录下来然后放给他听。

play sth ↔ **down** *phr v* [T] to try to make something seem less important than it really is 使…看起来不那么重要，贬低…，对…轻描淡写：*The government has tried to play down its defeat in the local elections.* 政府极力淡化它在地方选举中的失败。

play sb **off against** sb *phr v* [T] if you play one person off against another, you encourage them to argue or quarrel with each other so that you can gain something〔为从中渔利而〕挑拨离间，使…相斗[对立，争吵]

play on sth *phr v* [T] to use a feeling or an idea in order to gain an advantage for yourself 利用〔别人的感情、观点等〕：*They are playing on the fact that we don't like to appear ignorant.* 他们在利用我们不喜欢显得无知这一事实。

play sth ↔ **out** *phr v* [T] if you play out an event, you take part in it in a way that seems to have been planned or thought about before 实际参加，亲身体验：*The weekend gives you a chance to play out your fantasies.* 周末使你有机会亲身实践你所幻想的事情。| *She watched the farce that was being played out before her.* 她看着正在自己面前上演的闹剧。

play up *phr v* **1** [T **play** sth ↔ **up**] if you play something up, you make it seem more important than it really is 夸大…的重要性；抬高；大肆渲染：*She knew the newspapers would try to play it up.* 她知道各家报纸将极力渲染这件事。**2** [I,T **play** sb ↔ **up**] if children play up, they behave badly〔孩子〕捣蛋；使〔某人〕恼火，给〔某人〕制造麻烦：*The children have really been playing up this afternoon.* 今天下午孩子们一直在调皮捣蛋。| *I hope the kids don't play you up.* 我希望孩子们不会给你捣乱。**3** [I,T **play** sb ↔ **up**] to hurt you or cause problems for you 使〔某人〕感到痛苦；给〔某人〕造成麻烦：*My leg's been playing me up recently.* 我的腿最近老是疼。| *The car's playing up again.* 这辆汽车又出毛病了。

play up to sb *phr v* [T] to behave in a very polite or kind way to someone because you want something from them 投〔某人〕所好，逢迎，讨好，巴结：*politicians playing up to popular opinion* 迎合公众舆论的政客

play with sb/sth *phr v* **1** [T] to keep touching something or moving it about 摆弄，玩弄：*Stop playing with the light switch!* 别再摆弄电灯开关了！**2 play with the idea of doing sth** to consider the possibility of doing something〔不大认真地〕考虑做某事：*I'm playing with the idea of writing a novel.* 我正在考虑写部小说。**3 play with yourself** to touch your own sex organs for pleasure 手淫 **4 play with words** to use words in a clever or amusing way 玩文字游戏，玩弄词藻 **5 have time/money to play with** to have extra time or money that is available to be used 有多余的时间[金钱]可用：*The budget is very tight; there isn't much money to play with.* 经费很紧，没有很多钱可用。

play² *n* S1 W2

1 ▶THEATRE 剧院◀ [C] a piece of writing performed in a theatre or on television or radio, consisting of speeches and conversations between several characters 剧本；戏剧；电视[广播]剧：*one of Shakespeare's best-known plays* 莎士比亚最著名的戏剧之一 | *When he retired, he wrote plays.* 他退休后开始写剧本。| **put on a play** (=perform a play) 上演戏剧 *The school will be putting on a play in the summer term.* 这所学校将在夏季学期中上演一出戏剧。

2 ▶AMUSEMENT 娱乐◀ [U] things that people, especially children, do for amusement rather than as work〔尤指儿童的〕游戏，玩耍；娱乐：*Soon Henry tired of his play, and wandered off along the beach.* 亨利很快就玩厌了，他于是沿着海滩漫无目的地走去。| **at play** (=playing) 在玩耍，玩耍时 *the happy laughter of children at play* 孩子玩耍时快乐的笑声 | **in play** (=done only for amusement, not seriously) 开玩笑地，闹着玩地 *She had hidden his books, in play.* 她闹着玩地把他的书藏了起来。

3 ▶ACTION IN A GAME OR SPORT 比赛或体育活动中的动作◀ [U] the actions that form part of a game or a sport〔比赛或体育活动中的〕动作；比赛：*The changes in rules were agreed upon before the next day's play began.* 在第二天的比赛开始之前，人们一致同意对比赛规则进行修改。| *The match began on time, but rain stopped play after only an hour.* 比赛准时开始，但仅仅进行了一小时便因下雨而中止。| *We have seen some very good play this afternoon.* 今天下午我们看了一些很精彩的比赛。

4 in play/out of play if a ball is in play or out of play, it is inside or outside the area allowed by the rules of the game 界内/界外：*He kicked the ball out of play.* 他把球踢出界外。

5 bring sth into play to use something or make it have an effect 利用某物；使某物发挥作用：*A whole complex system of muscles is brought into play for each movement of the body.* 身体做出的每个动作都牵涉到全身复杂的肌肉系统运动。

6 come into play to be used or have an effect 被利用[运用]；起作用，产生影响：*Several factors came into play to make this possible.* 几个因素同时发挥作用使此事变得可能。

7 the play of light the pattern made by light as it moves gently over a surface 光的闪烁[掩映]：*the play of light on the water* 水面上光的闪动

8 play on words a use of a word that is interesting or amusing because it can be understood as having two very different meanings 说[用]双关语

9 ▶LOOSENESS 松动◀ [U] if there is some play in something, it is loose and can be moved 松动：*There's too much play in that rope.* 那根绳子太松了。

10 make a play for sth to make an attempt to gain something 设法得到某物：*He made a play for the leadership last year.* 他去年费尽心机想当领导。

play·a·ble /ˈpleəbḷ; ˈpleɪəbəl/ *adj* **1** a piece of ground used for sports that is playable is in good condition and suitable for playing on〔场地〕可用于运动比赛的 **2** a piece of music that is playable is not too difficult to be played〔乐曲〕可演奏的，不难演奏的

play-act·ing /ˈ· ·,··/ *n* [U] behaviour that is not serious or sincere but is made to look as if it is 装腔作势，假装，装扮 — **play-act** *v* [I]

play·back /ˈple,bæk; ˈpleɪbæk/ *n* [C] *especially BrE* a recording of something that you play as soon as it is made, so that you can study it carefully; REPLAY² (2)【尤英】〔录音、录像等供仔细再听再看的〕重放，回放

play·bill /ˈplebɪl; ˈpleɪbɪl/ *n* [C] a printed notice advertising a play 戏剧海报

Play·boy /ˈple,bɔɪ; ˈpleɪbɔɪ/ *trademark* a magazine for men which has pictures of young women wearing very few clothes and articles about sex【商标】《花花公子》〔一男性杂志，登载年轻女子裸照与性爱文章〕

playboy *n* [C] a rich man who does no work and spends his time enjoying himself with beautiful women, fast cars etc 花花公子，寻欢作乐的有钱男子: *a middle-aged playboy* 一个中年的花花公子

play-by-play /ˌ· · ˈ·◂/ *n* [C usually singular 一般用单数] *AmE* a report on what is happening in a game of sport, given at the same time as the game is being played【美】〔体育比赛的〕实况报道

Play-Doh /ˈple do; ˈpleɪ dəʊ/ *n* [C] *trademark* a soft substance like clay made in many different colours, used by children for making models or shapes【商标】"培乐多"橡皮泥〔一种像黏土一样松软的多色物质。儿童用其制作各种模型或造型〕

played-out /ˌ· ˈ·◂/ *adj* **1** someone who is played-out is not as strong, powerful etc as they used to be〔人〕衰竭的；筋疲力尽的；已丧失权力的 **2** old-fashioned and no longer useful 过时的，陈旧的: *played-out ideas* 过时的观念 —see also 另见 **play out** (PLAY[1])

play·er /ˈpleɚ; ˈpleɪə/ *n* [C] **1** someone who takes part in a game or sport 运动员，选手，球员: *a basketball player* 篮球运动员 **2** one of the important people or companies involved in a new or competitive type of business〔新型或竞争性商业的〕重要参与者: *Murdoch is one of the major players in the multimedia industry.* 默多克是多媒体产业的巨头之一。**3** someone who plays a musical instrument〔乐器的〕演奏者 **4** *old-fashioned* an actor【过时】演员—see also 另见 **key mover/player** (KEY[1])

player pi·an·o /ˌ· · ˈ· ·/ *n* [C] a piano that is played by machinery, with the music controlled by a continuous roll of paper with holes cut into it for the notes 自动钢琴 —see also 另见 PIANOLA

play·fel·low /ˈpleˌfɛlo; ˈpleɪˌfeləʊ/ *n* [C] *old-fashioned* someone that you play with when you are a child【过时】〔儿时〕一起玩耍的朋友，玩伴

play·ful /ˈplefəl; ˈpleɪfəl/ *adj* **1** happily active and full of fun 活泼可爱的；爱玩的: *a playful little dog* 活泼可爱的小狗 **2** not intended in a serious way 闹着玩的，开玩笑的，不认真的: *a playful kiss on the cheek* 在面颊上闹着玩地吻一下 | *She tried to sound playful.* 她极力用开玩笑的语气说。—**playfully** *adv* —**playfulness** *n* [U]

play·go·er /ˈpleˌgoɚ; ˈpleɪˌgəʊə/ *n* [C] someone who often goes to see plays 经常看戏的人，戏迷

play·ground /ˈpleˌgraʊnd; ˈpleɪgraʊnd/ *n* [C] **1** a piece of ground for children to play on, especially at a school or in a park〔学校的〕操场，运动场；〔公园的〕游乐场 **2** a place where a particular group of people go to enjoy themselves 娱乐的地方，享乐的地方: *the playground of the rich* 有钱人享乐的地方

play·group /ˈplegrup; ˈpleɪgruːp/ *n* [C,U] *BrE* a kind of school where children aged 2-5 meet to learn and play【英】〔二至五岁孩子的〕幼儿游戏班；幼儿园；PRESCHOOL *AmE*【美】: *Robert's at playgroup today.* 罗伯特今天上幼儿园了。

play·house /ˈpleˌhaʊs; ˈpleɪhaʊs/ *n* [C] **1** a word meaning a theatre used in its name 剧场，戏院: *the Oxford Playhouse* 牛津戏院 **2** a small structure like a little house for children to play in〔像房子一样的〕儿童游戏屋

playing card /ˈ· · ·/ *n* [C] *formal* a CARD[1] (7)【正式】纸牌，扑克牌

playing field /ˈ· · ·/ *n* [C] a large piece of ground with particular areas marked out for playing football, cricket etc〔足球、板球等的〕运动场 —see also 另见 LEVEL PLAYING-FIELD

play·mate /ˈpleˌmet; ˈpleɪmeɪt/ *n* [C] *old-fashioned* someone who you play with when you are a child【过时】〔儿时〕一起玩耍的朋友，玩伴

play-off /ˈ· ·/ *n* [C] an additional game played to decide who will win after a game has ended with no winner〔因不分胜负而进行的〕加时赛，延长赛

play·pen /ˈpleˌpɛn; ˈpleɪpen/ *n* [C] a frame made of bars or a net that provides an area for a small child to play safely in〔让幼儿安全地在其中玩耍的〕游戏围栏

play·room /ˈpleˌrum; ˈpleɪrʊm/ *n* [C] a room for children to play in 儿童游戏室

play·school /ˈpleskul; ˈpleɪskuːl/ *n* [C] *BrE* another word for PLAYGROUP【英】playgroup 的另一种说法

Play·sta·tion /ˈpleˌsteʃən; ˈpleɪˌsteɪʃən/ *trademark* a type of special computer made by Sony for playing games on【商标】游戏站，PS 游戏机〔索尼公司出品的一款游戏机〕

play·thing /ˈpleˌθɪŋ; ˈpleɪˌθɪŋ/ *n* [C] **1** a person that you treat like a toy, using them only for your own amusement and not caring about them 玩物，被玩弄的人: *I'm not just your plaything, you know.* 你要知道我可不是你的玩物。| *Humanity has become the plaything of scientists, engineers and planners.* 人类已成了科学家、工程师和规划者的玩物。**2** *formal* a toy【正式】玩具

play·time /ˈpleˌtaɪm; ˈpleɪtaɪm/ *n* [U] a period of time at a school, when children can go outside and play〔学校里的〕游戏〔娱乐〕时间

play·wright /ˈpleˌraɪt; ˈpleɪraɪt/ *n* [C] someone who writes plays 剧作家

pla·za /ˈplæzə; ˈplɑːzə/ *n* [C] **1** a public square or market place, especially in towns in Spanish-speaking countries〔尤指讲西班牙语国家的城市中的〕广场；集市场所 **2** a group of shops and other business buildings in a town〔城市的〕购物区；商业区: *Central Plaza* 中心商业区 —compare 比较 MALL

plc /ˌpi ɛl ˈsi; ˌpiː el ˈsiː/ *n* PUBLIC LIMITED COMPANY; a large company in Britain which has shares that the public can buy〔英国的〕公开股份有限公司: *Marks & Spencer plc* 马莎公开股份有限公司

plea /pli; pliː/ *n* **1** [C] an urgent, serious or emotional request 恳求，请求: **make a plea (for)** *The missing girl's parents made a desperate plea for her to contact them.* 那个失踪女孩的父母绝望地祈求女儿与他们联络。**2** [C usually singular 一般用单数] a statement by someone in a court of law saying whether they are guilty or not〔法庭上所作的〕答辩，辩护，抗辩: **make/enter a plea** *Your Honor, we enter a plea of 'not guilty'.* 法官大人，我们作"无罪"辩护。**3** [singular] an excuse for something 借口，托词，口实

plea bar·gain·ing /ˈ· ˌ· · ·/ *n* [U] the practice of agreeing to admit in a court that one is guilty of a small crime, in exchange for not being charged with a more serious crime〔为避免受到较重处罚而在法庭上承认轻罪的〕认罪求情协议；辩诉交易

plead /plid; pliːd/ *v past tense* **pleaded** *or* **pled** /plɛd; pled/ *especially AmE*【尤美】**1** [I] to ask for something that you want very much, in a sincere and emotional way 恳求，祈求，央求: *"Don't go!" Robert pleaded.* "别走！"罗伯特央求道。| [**+for**] *The hostages' families pleaded for their safe return.* 人质的家属祈求他们能平安回来。| **plead with sb to do sth** *Moira pleaded with her mother to let her go out.* 莫伊拉恳求母亲让她出去。| *a pleading voice* 恳求的声音 **2** [I,T not in passive 不用被动态] *law* to state in a court of law whether or not you are guilty of a crime【法律】〔在法庭上〕认罪；不认罪；申辩，答辩: *You are charged with grand theft. How do you plead?* 你被控犯有严重的盗窃罪，你认罪吗？| **plead guilty/not guilty/innocent** *Henderson pled not guilty to the charge of murder.* 亨德森不承认谋杀的指控。| *The accused is mentally unstable, and unfit to plead.* 被告精神不稳定，不适合出庭申辩。—see graph at 参见 GUILTY 图表 **3** **plead ignorance/illness/insanity etc** to give a particular excuse for your actions 以不知情/生病/精神错乱等为理由[借口]: *Well, if a cop stops you for speeding, you can always plead ignorance.* 如果你因超速而被警察拦下，你总是可以以不知道作为借口。| *She left early, pleading a headache.* 她以头痛为由提早离开了。**4** [T] to speak or argue in support of something 为…争辩[辩护，说话]，发表见解支持: **plead that** *Politicians pleaded that raising teachers' salaries would make the job more attractive.* 政客们为提高教师工资争辩，说这将使这项工作更有吸引力。

plead·ing·ly /ˈplidɪŋlɪ; ˈpliːdɪŋli/ *adv* if you say something pleadingly, or look at someone pleadingly, you speak to them or look at them as though you are asking them to do something in a sincere and emotional way 恳求地，乞求地

pleas·ant /ˈplɛzn̩t; ˈplezənt/ *adj* **1** enjoyable and making you feel happy; nice 令人愉快的，惬意的，舒适的: *Well, do have a pleasant weekend.* 好啦，周末愉快。| *Nora! What a pleasant surprise to see you!* 诺拉！见到你真让人惊喜！| *Yes, the cider's sweet, but it's pleasant.* 是的，这苹果酒很甜，但它喝起来味道不错。**2** friendly, polite, and easy to talk to 礼貌而友善的，和蔼可亲的: *I know you don't like her, but at least try to be pleasant.* 我知道你不喜欢她，但至少尽量对她友善一点。| *Nick seemed very pleasant on the phone.* 尼克在电话里好像非常友善。**3** weather that is pleasant is dry and not too hot or cold〔天气〕好的，宜人的: *It's overcast, but quite pleasant.* 天虽然阴沉，但相当宜人。—opposite 反义词 UNPLEASANT —**pleasantly** *adv*: *pleasantly surprised* 又惊又喜 

pleas·ant·ry /ˈplɛzn̩trɪ; ˈplezəntri/ *plural* **pleasantries** *n* [C usually plural 一般用复数] a funny or not very serious remark, made in order to be polite〔为表示礼貌而说的〕打趣的话，客气话: *A couple of old men stopped to exchange pleasantries in the street.* 几位老人在街上停下来互相寒暄一番。

please[1] /pliz; pliːz/ *interjection* **1** used when you want to ask for something politely 请，好吗〔用于礼貌地请求〕: *I'd like a cup of coffee, please.* 请给我来杯咖啡。| *Please can we go now?* 

我们现在就走，好吗？| *"Would you like some more?" "Yes please."* "你想再来一点吗？""好的，谢谢。" **2** used to emphasize a request or wish 好吗，请〔用于加强请求或愿望的语气〕：*"May I have some water?" "Please do."* "我可以喝点水吗？""请吧。" | *Please don't be too long, because I have to go out soon.* 请别待得太久，因为我很快就得出去。| *Will you children please be quiet!* 你们这些孩子安静些好吗！ **3** used when you want to accept something that someone has offered you and show that you are grateful 好，行，谢谢〔用于接受别人的好意并表示感谢〕：*"Would you like a cup of tea?" "Please, I'd love one."* "你想来杯茶吗？""好的，请给我来一杯。" **4 Please!** *informal, often humorous* used to ask someone to stop behaving badly【非正式，常幽默】够了〔用于要求别人停止做某事〕：*Alison! Please!* 艾莉森！够了！| *Please, John, this isn't the time to discuss it!* 好了，约翰，现在不是谈论这件事的时候！ **5 please Sir/Mrs Towers etc** *spoken* used by children to get an adult's attention【口】请听我说，先生/托尔斯太太等〔小孩用来引起成人的注意〕

W3 **please²** *v* [not in progressive 不用进行时] **1** [I,T] to make someone happy or satisfied（使）高兴，（使）欢喜，（使）满意，讨好：**please sb** *I only got married to please my parents.* 我是为了让父母高兴才结婚的。| *The child is very eager to please.* 那个孩子非常热衷于讨好人。| **be hard/ easy etc to please** *Mark's a hard one to please.* 马克是个难以取悦的人。—opposite 反义词 DISPLEASE **2 please yourself a)** *spoken* used to tell someone that they can do whatever they like because you are annoyed and do not care what they do【口】〔表示不耐烦〕随你的便，我不在乎：*Well I'm going to the party – you can please yourself!* 那么我要去参加聚会了——随你的便吧！ **b)** to do whatever you like because you do not have to obey anyone or follow any rules 愿意怎样就怎样，随自己的便去做：*We don't have to be back in the hotel by any particular time, we can just please ourselves.* 我们不必一定要在某个时间以前回到旅馆去，我们想什么时候回去就什么时候回去。 **3 as sb pleases a)** doing whatever you want to do 想做什么就做什么；随意：*He just does as he pleases and never thinks of anyone else.* 他只是想做什么就做什么，从不考虑别人。 **b)** *formal* used to tell someone that they will have to decide something and you do not mind what they do【正式】愿意怎么做都行〔用于表示不介意别人做什么〕 **4 whatever/however etc sb pleases** whatever, however etc someone wants 某人喜欢的任何…：*They can appoint whoever they please.* 他们喜欢任命谁就可以任命谁。 **5 bold/cool as you please** *spoken* used to express surprise about someone's behaviour, when they have done something strange as if it is completely normal【口】竟然若无其事地〔表示惊讶〕：*He was walking down the road carrying a rifle, as bold as you please.* 他竟若无其事地拿着一支步枪在大路上走。 **6 if you please a)** *formal* used to make a polite request【正式】请，劳驾〔用于礼貌地提出请求〕：*Close the door, if you please.* 请关上门。 **b)** *old-fashioned* used to say that you find something difficult to believe, or are very surprised or angry about it【过时】真奇怪；真是岂有此理；真令人难以置信〔用于表示难以置信、惊讶或气愤〕：*And now she says she needs yet another new dress, if you please!* 她现在竟然说还需要一件新衣服，真是岂有此理！ **7 please God** used to express a very strong hope or wish 但愿，希望〔用于表示非常强烈的愿望〕：*They should have got back by now – please God they're OK.* 他们现在应该已经回去了，但愿他们平安无事。

S2 W3 **pleased** /plizd; pliːzd/ *adj* **1** *especially BrE* happy or satisfied【尤英】快乐的，高兴的；满意的：*I was so pleased when they said they'd be able to stay another week.* 当他们说能多留一星期时，我非常高兴。| **[+about]** *Are you pleased about the results?* 你对结果感到满意吗？| **pleased (with)** *Di seems pleased with her new car.* 迪好像对她的新车很满意。| **pleased (that)** *I'm pleased you decided to come.* 我很高兴你决定来。| **very/really pleased** *We asked our lawyer to check the contract, and we're really pleased we did.* 我们要求律师检查一下合同，我们非常高兴自己那样做了。| **be pleased to hear/see/report etc** *I'm pleased to hear about your new job.* 听说你找到新工作，我感到很高兴。 **2 be pleased to help/assist** to be very willing or happy to help 非常乐意帮助：*If there's anything we can do, we'd be pleased to help.* 如果我们可以做些什么，我们将非常乐意帮忙。 **3 (I'm) pleased to meet you** *spoken* used as a polite greeting when you meet someone for the first time【口】幸会，很高兴见到[认识]你〔初次会面时的礼貌说法〕 **4 pleased with yourself** feeling unreasonably proud or satisfied because you think you have done something clever 自鸣得意：*She was looking very pleased with herself so I guessed she'd passed her driving test.* 她显得非常得意，我猜她是通过了驾驶考试。 **5 not very pleased** *informal, often humorous* rather annoyed【非正式，常幽默】相当生气的：*She wasn't very pleased when she found out about the dent in her car.* 她发现自己的汽车上有凹痕后很不高兴。

pleas·ing /ˈplizɪŋ; ˈpliːzɪŋ/ *adj formal*【正式】**1** giving pleasure or enjoyment; pleasant 使人愉快的；惬意的：**[+to]** *The painting is very pleasing to the eye.* 那幅画非常悦目。 **2** making you feel pleased and satisfied 使人高兴的，令人满意的：*He has made pleasing progress in French this year.* 今年他在法语方面取得了令人满意的进步。—**pleasingly** *adv*

plea·sur·a·ble /ˈplɛʒərəbl; ˈpleʒərəbəl/ *adj formal* enjoyable【正式】令人愉快的，令人快乐的，舒适的：*a pleasurable feeling of anticipation* 愉快的期待心情 —**pleasurably** *adv*

S2 W2 **plea·sure** /ˈplɛʒɚ; ˈpleʒə/ *n*

1 ►ENJOYMENT 愉快，乐趣◄ [U] the feeling of happiness or satisfaction that you get from an experience you enjoy 愉快，快乐；满足：*The children used to get a lot of pleasure out of that game when they were young.* 这些孩子小时候从那个游戏中得到过很多乐趣。| **give/bring pleasure** *Small gifts give pleasure and don't cost much.* 小礼物使人得到很多乐趣而且花费不多。| **great pleasure** *a film that has given great pleasure to millions* 一部给数百万人带来无穷欢乐的电影

2 ►ENJOYABLE EXPERIENCE 令人愉快的经历◄ [C,U] an activity or experience that you enjoy very much 愉快的活动[经历]，乐事：*the simple pleasures of life* 简单的生活乐趣 | **it is a pleasure to do sth** *It's been a great pleasure to meet you.* 见到你真是一大乐事。

3 take pleasure in to be pleased about and proud of something 以…为乐；为…感到骄傲：*He took great pleasure in his grandchildren's achievements.* 他为孙辈的成就感到骄傲。

4 take pleasure in doing sth to enjoy doing something bad to other people 喜欢做某事〔指对别人不好的事〕：*Charlie seems to take pleasure in bullying the younger kids.* 查利似乎很喜欢欺负比自己小的孩子。

5 (it's) my pleasure *spoken* used when someone has thanked you for doing something and you want to say that you were glad to do it【口】别客气，不用谢〔表示乐意做某事〕

6 with pleasure *spoken* used to say politely that you are happy to do something that someone has just asked you to do【口】非常愿意，非常乐意：*"Will you come?" "With pleasure madam."* "你愿意来吗？""非常愿意，夫人。"

7 have the pleasure of (doing) sth a) *formal* to enjoy the experience of something【正式】有幸（做），荣幸：*I don't think I've had the pleasure of meeting your wife.* 我想我还未有幸见到你的妻子。 **b)** *humorous* used when you do not think something is enjoyable【幽默】有幸[福气]（做）…〔用于表示某事令人不愉快〕：*We had the pleasure of Rob's company last week.* 我们上星期真荣幸有罗布做伴〔反话〕。

8 at his/her Majesty's pleasure *BrE law* if someone is put in prison at his or her Majesty's pleasure, there is no fixed limit to the time they have to spend there【英，法律】（犯人）被无期限地随意监禁，随意在押

9 at your pleasure if you can do something at your pleasure, you can do it when and as you want to 随你的便，随你的意愿

10 sb's pleasure *formal* what someone wants【正式】某人的意愿[愿望]：*You can go there if that's your pleasure.* 你如果想去那里就可以去。

pleasure seek·er /ˈ· · ,· ·/ *n* [C] someone who does things just for enjoyment without considering other people〔不考虑他人的〕寻欢作乐者，玩乐的人

pleat¹ /plit; pliːt/ *n* [C] a flat narrow fold in cloth〔布料上的〕褶 —see picture on page A17 参见 A17 页图

pleat² *v* [T] to make a lot of flat narrow folds in a piece of cloth 使起褶 —**pleated** *adj*: *a pleated skirt* 百褶裙

pleb /plɛb; pleb/ *n* [C usually plural 一般用复数] *informal or humorous* an insulting word meaning someone who is from a low social class【非正式或幽默】下层平民〔侮辱性说法〕：*Plebs like me can never aspire to such perfect manners.* 像我这样的草根阶层永远不会追求如此完美的礼仪。—**plebby** *adj*

plebe /plib; pliːb/ *n* [C] *AmE informal* a first year student at a military or naval college or university【美，非正式】〔美国陆军或海军学院的〕一年级新生

ple·be·ian /plɪˈbiən; plɪˈbiːən/ *n* [C] **1** an insulting word for someone who is from a low social class 下层平民〔侮辱性说法〕 **2** an ordinary person who had no special rank in ancient Rome〔古罗马的〕平民，庶民 —compare 比较 PATRICIAN —**plebeian** *adj*

pleb·is·cite /ˈplɛbə,saɪt; ˈplebɪ̣sɪ̣t/ *n* [C,U] a system by which everyone in a country votes to decide a matter of national importance 公民投票（制）：*The choice of whether to join the federation was decided by plebiscite.* 是否加入联邦是由公民投票决定的。—compare 比较 REFERENDUM

plec·trum /ˈplɛktrəm; ˈplektrəm/ *n* [C] a small thin piece of plastic, metal, or wood, that you hold and use for playing some stringed musical instruments such as a GUITAR; PICK² (5)〔弹奏吉他等弦乐器用的〕拨子, 琴拨

pled /plɛd; pled/ *ScotE and AmE*【苏格兰和美】the past tense and past participle of PLEAD

pledge¹ /plɛdʒ; pledʒ/ *n* [C]

1 ►PROMISE 保证, 诺言◄ *formal* a firm promise or agreement, especially one made publicly or officially【正式】〔尤指公开或正式作出的〕誓言, 誓约; 保证: *Industrial conflicts continued in spite of a no-strike pledge by the unions.* 尽管各工会都作出了不罢工的承诺, 但是劳资冲突仍在继续。| **a pledge to do sth** *the government's pledge to make no deals with terrorists* 政府不向恐怖分子妥协的保证 | **fulfil a pledge** (=do what you promised) 履行诺言 *Eisenhower fulfilled his election pledge to end the war in Korea.* 艾森豪威尔履行了他竞选时所作的结束朝鲜战争的承诺。

2 sign/take the pledge *old-fashioned* to promise never to drink alcohol, for religious or moral reasons【过时】〔出于宗教或道德原因而〕发誓戒酒

3 a pledge of love/friendship etc a serious promise of love etc made by two people 发誓相爱/友好等

4 ►SOMETHING VALUABLE 有价值的东西◄ something valuable that you leave with someone else as proof that you do what you have agreed to do, pay back what you owe etc 抵押物: *She borrowed £50 and left her gold bracelet as a pledge.* 她借了 50 英镑, 并留下她的金手镯作抵押品。

5 ►AT US COLLEGES 在美国的大学里◄ someone who has promised to become a member of a university FRATERNITY or SORORITY in the US but must pass a test before they can join〔美国大学的〕宣誓加入男生[女生]联谊会的人〔他们在成为正式会员前须先通过一些测试〕

pledge² *v* [T] **1** to make a formal, usually public, promise that you will do something 发誓, 作保证: **pledge to do sth** *They have pledged to fight any changes to the abortion laws.* 他们已发誓竭力阻止对堕胎法所作的任何改动。| **pledge that** *The UK government has pledged that the wishes of the minority community in Northern Ireland will be respected.* 英国政府已作出允诺, 北爱尔兰少数民族的意愿都将受到尊重。| **pledge support/loyalty/solidarity etc** (=promise to give your support etc) 发誓支持/效忠/团结等 **2** to make someone give a firm promise 使〔某人〕发誓[保证, 许诺]: *75% of members were pledged in advance to vote for the labor program.* 75% 的成员事先被要求发誓投票支持工会的计划。| **pledge yourself to sth** *The Republicans pledged themselves to a tough stand against crime.* 共和党已保证会采取强硬态度抵制犯罪。**3** to leave something with someone as a PLEDGE¹ (4) 抵押, 典当 **4** to promise to become a member of a university FRATERNITY or SORORITY in the US〔在美国的大学〕宣誓加入男生[女生]联谊会

Pledge of Al·le·giance, the /,· · ˈ· ·/ a speech that US citizens learn, which is a promise to respect the US and be loyal to it. In schools children usually say the Pledge of Allegiance every morning, while looking at the national flag and putting their right hand over their heart: *I pledge allegiance to the flag of the United States of America, and to the republic for which it stands, one nation under God, indivisible, with liberty and justice for all.* 效忠宣誓词〔美国公民熟知的一段话, 即为尊重和效忠国家的誓言。学校的孩子们通常每天早晨都一边仰望国旗, 一边把右手放在胸前诵读这段誓词: 我宣誓忠于美国国旗, 忠于它所象征的共和国, 一个在上帝的指引下不可分割的、给全体人民以自由和正义的国家〕

Plei·a·des, the /ˈpliə,diz; ˈplaɪədiːz/ **1** a group of stars in the CONSTELLATION called Taurus 昴星团〔金牛星座中的一个星团〕**2** in ancient Greek MYTHOLOGY, the seven daughters of Atlas, who were changed into stars by Zeus 普勒阿得斯〔古希腊神话中, 阿特拉斯的七个女儿, 被宙斯变成了天上的群星〕

pleis·to·cene /ˈplaɪstə,sin; ˈplaɪstəsiːn/ *adj* belonging to the period in the Earth's history that started about a million years ago and lasted about 800,000 years, when much of the Earth was covered with ice 更新世的〔地球上大约 100 万年前开始并持续了约 80 万年的一段时期, 那时地球表面大部分被冰覆盖〕

ple·na·ry /ˈplinərɪ; ˈpliːnəri/ *adj* [only before noun 仅用于名词前] *formal*【正式】**1** a plenary meeting is one that is attended by everyone who has a right to attend〔会议〕全体出席的: *The conference ended with a plenary debate.* 这次会议以一场全体出席的辩论结束。**2** plenary power or authority is complete and has no limit〔权力或权威〕全权的, 充分的, 无限制的: *The envoy was given plenary powers to negotiate with the rebels.* 该特使被授予全权同反叛者谈判。—**plenary** *n* [C]

plen·i·po·ten·tia·ry /,plɛnəpəˈtɛnʃərɪ; ,plenɪ̥pəˈtenʃəri/ *n* [C] *formal or technical* someone who has full power to take action or make decisions, especially as a representative of their government in a foreign country【正式或术语】〔尤指在外国代表本国政府的〕全权大使, 全权代表 —**plenipotentiary** *adj*: *plenipotentiary powers* 全权

plen·i·tude /ˈplɛnə,tjud; ˈplenɪ̥tjuːd/ *n literary*【文】**1** [U] completeness or fullness 完全, 充分 **2 a plenitude of** a large amount of something 大量的, 丰富的, 充足的: *a plenitude of sunshine* 充足的阳光

plen·te·ous /ˈplɛntɪəs; ˈplentiəs/ *adj poetic* plentiful【诗】丰富的, 充足的, 富裕的 —**plenteously** *adv* —**plenteousness** *n* [U]

plen·ti·ful /ˈplɛntɪfəl; ˈplentɪfəl/ *adj* more than enough in quantity 丰富的, 充足的: *a plentiful supply of food and wine* 食物和(葡萄)酒的大量供应 | *Opportunities to practice the language are plentiful.* 练习该语言的机会很多。—**plentifully** *adv*

plen·ty¹ /ˈplɛntɪ; ˈplenti/ *pron* a large quantity that is enough or more than enough 丰富, 充足, 众多, 大量: *If you want some more chairs, there are plenty more in here.* 如果你还想要椅子, 这里多的是。| **[+of]** *Make sure she eats well and gets plenty of fresh air.* 要确保她吃得好并多呼吸新鲜空气。| *You've got plenty of time.* 你有充足的时间。| *I don't want any more work, I already have plenty to do.* 我不想再做什么工作了, 我要做的已经够多了。—compare 比较 FEW, LOT 

plenty² *adv informal*【非正式】**1 plenty big enough, plenty bright enough etc** more than big enough, bright enough etc 非常[足够]大/明亮等: *This apartment's plenty big enough for two.* 这套公寓非常大, 足够两个人住。**2** *AmE* to a large degree; a lot【美】十分, 非常; 很多: *I sleep plenty, but I always wake up feeling tired.* 虽然我睡得很多, 但醒来后总是感到疲倦。

plenty³ *n* [U] *formal*【正式】**1** a situation in which there is a large supply of something, especially something that is needed for life〔尤指生活所需东西的〕充裕, 富足: *In years of plenty everyone has enough to eat.* 丰年时人人都吃得饱。**2 in plenty** in large supply; more than enough 供应充足, 多得很: *There was food and wine in plenty.* 食物和(葡萄)酒都很充足。—see also 另见 HORN OF PLENTY

ple·o·nas·m /ˈpliə,næzəm; ˈpliːənæzəm/ *n* [C,U] *technical* the use of more words than are needed to express an idea【术语】冗笔, 赘述, 冗词[句]: *The phrase 'an apple divided into two halves' is a pleonasm.* 短语 an apple divided into two halves (分成两个一半的苹果)是赘述。—**pleonastic** /,pliəˈnæstɪk; ,pliːəˈnæstɪk◄/ *adj*

Ples·sy v. Fer·gu·son /ˈplɛsɪ vɝsəs ˈfɝgəsn̩; ˈplesi vɜːsəs ˈfɜːgəsən/ a decision by the US Supreme Court in 1896 that the SEGREGATION (=separation) of black people from white people was legal, as long as black people were given services, such as schools or restaurants, that were described as "separate but equal" services. The decision specifically concerned segregation on trains, but led in some states to separate schools, hotels, restaurants, and seats in theatres, buses etc. The decision made in this court case was changed in 1954 by the Supreme Court's decision in the case of Brown v. Board of Education of Topeka. 普莱西诉弗格森案〔1896 年美国联邦最高法院做出如下裁决: 虽然黑人在学校就读或餐馆用餐时被隔离, 但只要能得到均等的服务, 那么这样的隔离就不算违法。这一裁决原本仅限于火车上实行的种族隔离, 但最终却引发某些州在学校、旅馆、饭店、剧院和公共汽车等场合全面实行种族隔离。此判决结果在 1954 年的布朗诉托皮卡教育局一案中得以修正〕

pleth·o·ra /ˈplɛθərə; ˈpleθərə/ *n* **a plethora of** *formal* an amount of something that is larger than is needed or more than you can deal with【正式】过多, 过剩, 过量: *a plethora of suggestions* 一大堆建议 | *a plethora of paperwork* 过多的文书工作

pleu·ri·sy /ˈplurəsɪ; ˈplʊərɪ̥si/ *n* [U] a serious illness which affects your lungs, causing severe pain in your chest and sides 胸膜炎, 肋膜炎

plex·i·glass /ˈplɛksɪ,glæs; ˈpleksi,glɑːs/ *n* [U] *AmE trademark* the name of a particular type of plastic, that is often just used to mean any plastic【美, 商标】珀斯佩有机玻璃; 透明塑胶; PERSPEX *BrE*【英】

plex·us /ˈplɛksəs; ˈpleksəs/ *n* —see 见 SOLAR PLEXUS

pli·a·ble /ˈplaɪəbl̩; ˈplaɪəbəl/ *adj* **1** easy to bend without breaking or cracking 柔韧的, 易弯的; 柔软的: *The clay should be moistened regularly to keep it soft and pliable.* 这黏土应定期湿润使之保持柔软易塑。**2** able and willing to change and accept new ideas and ways of doing things; ADAPTABLE 能够变通的, 乐意接受新思想[方法]的; 适应力强的: *The committee would benefit from having members who are more pliable.* 委员会拥有适

应力强的成员将大有好处。**3** too easily influenced by other people 易受影响的; 顺从的 —**pliability** /ˌplaɪəˋbɪlətɪ; ˌplaɪəˈbɪləti/ *n* [U]

pli·ant /ˋplaɪənt; ˈplaɪənt/ *adj* pliable 易弯的; 柔韧的; 能够变通的; 适应力强的; 易受影响的; 顺从的 —**pliantly** *adv* —**pliancy** *n* [U]

pli·ers /ˋplaɪɚz; ˈplaɪəz/ *n* [plural] a small tool made of two crossed pieces of metal, used to hold small things or to bend and cut wire 钳子, 手钳, 老虎钳 —see picture at 参见 TOOL[1] 图

plight[1] /plaɪt; plaɪt/ *n* [usually singular 一般用单数] a bad, serious, or sad condition or situation〔坏的、严重的或悲伤的〕境况, 困境, 苦境: *the plight of homeless children* 无家可归的儿童的苦况

plight[2] *v* **plight your troth** *old use* to make a promise to someone that you will marry them【旧】答应结婚, 订婚

plim·soll /ˋplɪmsḷ; ˈplɪmsəl/ *n* [C] a light shoe with a top made of thick cotton cloth and a flat rubber SOLE[2] (2) 橡胶底帆布鞋, 胶底运动鞋; SNEAKER *AmE*【美】—see picture at 参见 SHOE 图

Plimsoll line /ˈ·· ·/ also 又作 **Plimsoll mark** *n* [C] a line painted on the outside of a ship, showing the depth to which it can safely be allowed to float in the water when it is loaded〔船的〕载重线标志, 载重吃水线

plinth /plɪnθ; plɪnθ/ *n* [C] a square block, usually made of stone, that is used as the base for a PILLAR or STATUE〔石柱或雕像的〕柱基; 底座

Plin·y the El·der /ˌplɪnɪ ðɪ ˋɛldɚ; ˌplɪni ði ˈeldə/ (23-79 AD) an ancient Roman writer who wrote *Natural History*, a very long book about plants, animals, minerals etc. He was killed when Mount Vesuvius ERUPT*ed*, and he was the uncle of Pliny the Younger. 老普林尼〔(公元23-79), 古罗马作家。著有《博物志》, 是一部有关植物、动物、矿物等知识的洋洋巨著。他死于维苏威火山爆发期间, 是小普林尼的叔叔〕

Pliny the Young·er /ˌ·· ·ˈ··/ (?61-113 AD) an ancient Roman politician and writer whose letters provide a detailed picture of Roman life at that time. He was the nephew of Pliny the Elder. 小普林尼〔公元?61-113〕, 罗马政治家、作家。其信札详细描述了当时罗马人的生活。他是老普林尼的侄子〕

Pli·o·cene /ˋplaɪəˌsin; ˈplaɪəsiːn/ *adj* belonging to the period in the Earth's history that started about thirteen million years ago and lasted about twelve million years 上新世的〔地球上始于约1300万年前并持续了约1200万年的一段历史时期〕

PLO, the /ˌpi ɛl ˋo; ˌpiː el ˈəʊ/ the Palestine Liberation Organization; a political group of Palestinians, whose aim is to establish a separate state of Palestine existing together with Israel 巴勒斯坦解放组织, 巴解组织〔巴勒斯坦人的一个政治组织。其宗旨是建立一个与以色列并存且独立的巴勒斯坦国〕

plod /plɑd; plɒd/ *v* **plodded, plodding 1** [I always+adv/prep] to walk along slowly, especially with difficulty and great effort; TRUDGE[1] 沉重缓慢地走, 步履艰难地走: **[+through/along etc]** *The children were plodding through the snow.* 孩子们正步履艰难地走过雪地。| *The mule plodded up the hill.* 那头骡子艰难缓慢地往山上走。**2 plod on/along** to keep working steadily, especially at something that is uninteresting or difficult 孜孜不倦地干, 埋头苦干: *I'll just plod on for another hour or so.* 我再埋头苦干一小时左右。

plod·der /ˋplɑdɚ; ˈplɒdə/ *n* [C] someone who works slowly and is not very clever 工作很慢且不太聪明的人: *I've always been a bit of a plodder.* 我一向是个有点干活迟钝的人。

plonk[1] /plɑŋk; plɒŋk/ *v* [T] *informal*【非正式】**1** to put something down somewhere, especially noisily and carelessly 重重地放下: **plonk sth in/on etc** *Just plonk those bags anywhere in my room.* 把那些袋子随便放在我房间里就行了。**2 plonk yourself (down)** to sit down heavily and then relax 重重地坐下放松: *We plonked ourselves in front of the telly.* 我们咚的一声坐在电视机前。

plonk[2] *n* [U] *BrE informal* cheap wine【英, 非正式】廉价酒

plonk·er /ˋplɑŋkɚ; ˈplɒŋkə/ *n* [C] *BrE slang*【英俚】**1** a stupid person 愚蠢的人 **2** a PENIS 阴茎

plop[1] /plɑp; plɒp/ *n* [C] a sound like something solid dropping into liquid〔物体掉入液体中的〕扑通声, 啪哒声: *The soap fell into the bath with a loud plop.* 肥皂扑通一声掉进了浴缸。

plop[2] *v* **plopped, plopping 1** [I always+adv/prep] to fall somewhere making a sound like a plop 扑通[啪哒]地落下: **[+on/down etc]** *A few drops of rain began to plop on to the roof.* 几滴雨开始啪哒啪哒地落到屋顶上。**2** [T] to put something into a liquid so that it makes a sound like a plop 把…扑通[啪哒]一声放入〔液体里〕: **[+into]** *I plopped a couple of ice cubes into the drink.* 我把几块冰啪哒一声放入饮料之中。**3 plop (yourself) down** to sit down or lie down heavily 重重地坐下[躺下]: *She plopped down on a chair.* 她扑通一声坐在椅子上。

plo·sive /ˋplosɪv; ˈpləʊsɪv/ *n* [C] *technical* a CONSONANT sound that is made by completely stopping the flow of air out of your mouth and then suddenly letting it out, done, for example, when saying /b/ or /t/【术语】〔辅音〕爆破音〈如/b/和/t/音〉—**plosive** *adj*

plot[1] /plɑt; plɒt/ *n* [C]

1 ▶STORY/FILM 故事/电影◀ the set of connected events that a story, film etc is based on〔故事、电影等的〕情节: *The plot of 'Twin Peaks' was so complicated that I couldn't follow it.*《双峰》的情节太复杂了, 我跟不上。

2 ▶PLAN 计划◀ a secret plan, involving several people, to do something harmful or illegal 密谋, 阴谋, 秘密计划: **[+to]** *There have been rumors of a plot to overthrow the President.* 谣传说有人密谋推翻总统。| **hatch a plot** (=start making a plan) 策划阴谋

3 the plot thickens *spoken humorous* used to say that events seem to be becoming more complicated and difficult to understand【口, 幽默】情况开始复杂起来; 事情越来越纠缠不清了

4 ▶PIECE OF LAND 一块土地◀ a) a small piece of land for building or growing things on〔建筑或种植用的〕小块土地[地皮] **b)** a piece of land that a particular family owns in a CEMETERY, in which members of the family are buried when they die〔属于某家族的〕一块墓地

5 ▶DRAWING 图画◀ *AmE* a drawn plan of a building at ground level; GROUND PLAN【美】楼层平面图

plot[2] *v* **plotted, plotting 1** [I,T] to make a secret plan to harm a person or organization, especially a political leader or government 密谋, 策划, 图谋: *We spent all week plotting our revenge.* 我们花了整整一星期策划报复行动。| **[+against]** *They were plotting against the government.* 他们正在密谋反对政府。| **plot to do sth** *It was alleged that they had plotted to blow up the White House.* 据说他们密谋要炸毁白宫。**2** [T] to draw a line or curve that shows facts, figures etc 绘制…的图表[平面图, 曲线图]: *We plotted a graph to show the increase in sales figures this year.* 我们绘制了一个图表来显示今年销售额的增长。**3** [T] to mark, calculate, or follow the position of a moving aircraft or ship 标绘[计算, 追踪]〔移动中的飞行器或船只的〕位置: *He was already bent over the table, plotting a new course.* 他已经趴在桌子上绘制新航线了。—**plotter** *n* [C]

plough[1] *usually* 一般作 **plow** *AmE*【美】/plaʊ; plaʊ/ *n* [C] **1** a large piece of farm equipment used to turn over the earth so that seeds can be planted 犁 **2 under the plough** used for growing crops 用于种植庄稼; 在耕种中 **3 the Plough** *especially BrE* the group of seven bright stars seen only from the northern part of the world【尤英】北斗七星; BIG DIPPER (2) *AmE*【美】—see also 另见 SNOW PLOUGH

plough[2] *usually* 一般作 **plow** *AmE*【美】*v* **1** [I,T] to turn over the earth using a plough so that seeds can be planted 犁(地), 耕(地): *a ploughed field* 犁过的地 **2** [I always+adv/prep] to move with a lot of effort or force 奋力前进: **[+along/across etc]** *The ship ploughed slowly across the bay.* 那艘船缓慢地艰难前行, 驶过海湾。

plough sth ↔ **back** *phr v* [T] to put money that you have earned back into a business in order to make the business bigger and more successful 把〔赚来的钱〕再投资: *Profits from ticket sales are ploughed back into further conservation projects.* 售票所得的利润被再投放到更多的(自然)保护项目之中。

plough into sb/sth *phr v* [T] to hit something hard, especially while driving, because you are going too fast or not paying attention〔尤指驾车过快或不留神而〕猛撞上〔某物〕: *I ploughed into the car in front.* 我猛地撞上了前面的一辆车。

plough on *phr v* [I] to continue doing something that is difficult or boring 继续做〔困难或枯燥的事情〕: *Julia ploughed on through the endless exam papers.* 朱莉娅继续批改那些没完没了的考卷。

plough through *phr v* [T] to read all of something, even though it is boring and takes a long time 费力地坚持读[看]完: *After ploughing through all those textbooks, it was a relief to read a novel.* 费力地看完那些课本之后, 读本小说是一种放松。

plough sth ↔ **up** *phr v* [T] to break up the surface of the ground by repeatedly travelling over it 碾坏; 踩坏(地面); 使有沟脊: *Horses plough up the paths and make them muddy for walkers.* 马匹把条条小路踏出许多沟脊, 使行人走起来泥泞不堪。

Plough, the *BrE* a group of seven bright stars that can only be seen from the northern part of the world. They form part of the CONSTELLATION (=group of stars) called Ursa Major【英】北

斗七星〔在地球北部才能看到的一组闪亮的恒星，由七颗组成，是大熊星座的组成部分〕

plough·boy /ˈplaʊˌbɔɪ; ˈplaʊbɔɪ/ *n* [C] *old use* a boy who led a horse that pulled a PLOUGH【旧】耕童，牵耕畜的男孩

plough·man /ˈplaʊmən; ˈplaʊmən/ *n* [C] *old use* a man whose job was to guide a PLOUGH that was being pulled by a horse【旧】把[扶]犁人，驾着马拉犁的人

plough·man's lunch /ˌ·· ˈ·/ *n* [C] *BrE* a simple meal that people eat especially in PUBS, consisting of bread, cheese, onion, and PICKLE【英】〔尤指在小酒馆吃的〕简单午餐〔通常是面包、乳酪、洋葱和泡菜〕

plough·share *BrE*【英】*usually* 一般作 **plowshare** *AmE*【美】/ˈplaʊˌʃɛr; ˈplaʊʃeə/ *n* [C] the broad curved metal blade of a PLOUGH, which turns over the soil 犁头，犁铧

P

plov·er /ˈplʌvɚ; ˈplʌvə/ *n* [C] a small bird that lives near the sea〔栖于海边的〕鸻

plow /plaʊ; plaʊ/ *n, v* the usual American spelling of PLOUGH plough 的一般美式拼法

ploy /plɔɪ; plɔɪ/ *n* [C] a clever method of getting an advantage, especially by deceiving someone〔尤指欺骗性的〕计策，手段，花招：*His usual ploy is to pretend he's ill.* 他惯用的花招是装病。| *a cynical ploy to win votes* 为博取选票而耍的让人不齿的手段

pluck¹ /plʌk; plʌk/ *v*

1 ▶TAKE STH 拿，取某物◀ [T] to take hold of something and remove it from somewhere by pulling it 拔；扯，拉：**pluck sth from/off etc** *She bent forward to pluck a thread off the lapel of his jacket.* 她俯下身从他上衣的翻领上扯去一根线。

2 pluck up (the) courage to force yourself to be brave and do something you are afraid of doing 鼓起勇气，振作精神：*He finally plucked up enough courage to ask her out on a date.* 他终于鼓足勇气约她出去。

3 ▶CHICKEN ETC 鸡等◀ [T] to pull the feathers off a dead chicken or other bird before cooking it 拔去〔死鸡或其他禽类〕的毛〔准备烹调〕

4 ▶FLOWER 花◀ *literary* to pick a flower or fruit【文】采，摘，掐〔花或果实〕：*Eve plucked an apple and offered it to Adam.* 夏娃摘了一个苹果给亚当。

5 ▶MUSIC 音乐◀ [I,T] to pull sharply at the strings of a musical instrument 拨〔弦〕，弹奏：**[+at]** *Someone was plucking at the strings of an old guitar.* 有人在拨弄一把旧吉他的弦。

6 ▶TAKE SB AWAY 带某人离开◀ [T always+adv/prep] to take someone away from a place or situation 带〔某人〕离开〔某地或某处境〕：**pluck sb from/off/away etc** *She was plucked from obscurity by a film producer.* 一位电影制片人使她从无名之辈中脱颖而出。

7 pluck sth out of the air to say or suggest a number, name etc that you have just thought of without thinking about it carefully〔未经仔细考虑〕随口说出〔一个数字或名字等〕：*I'm just plucking a figure out of the air here, but let's say it'll cost about $15,000.* 我只是随口说一个数字，比如说这东西要花大约15,000美元。

8 pluck your eyebrows to pull out hairs from the edges of your EYEBROWS 拔眉毛

pluck at sth *phr v* [T] to pull something quickly and repeatedly with your fingers〔用手指〕猛揪[拉，扯]：*The little boy plucked at her sleeve.* 那个小男孩不停地拉她的袖子。| *Sally was staring into space, plucking nervously at her pearl choker.* 萨莉凝视着天空，紧张不安地扯着她那条贴颈的珍珠项链。

pluck² *n* [U] *old-fashioned* courage and determination【过时】勇气，胆量；决心：*I really admire him for cycling to Paris on his own – it must have taken a lot of pluck.* 他独自一人骑车去巴黎，我真的很佩服他——那一定需要极大的勇气。

pluck·y /ˈplʌkɪ; ˈplʌki/ *adj* **pluckier, pluckiest** *informal* brave and determined【非正式】勇敢的，有勇气的，有胆量的：*It took guts to stand up to those bullies – she's a plucky kid.* 站起来反抗那些恃强凌弱者需要勇气——她是个很勇敢的孩子。—**pluckily** *adv* —**pluckiness** *n* [U]

S3 **plug¹** /plʌg; plʌg/ *n* [C]

1 ▶ELECTRICITY 电◀ a) a thing used for connecting a piece of electrical equipment to the main supply of electricity〔电〕插头：*a two-pin plug* 两相插头 **b)** *BrE informal* a piece of plastic, usually on a wall, where electrical equipment is connected to the main electricity supply; SOCKET (1)【英，非正式】〔电〕插座：*Make sure you turn the television off at the plug.* 记住拔掉插头来关掉电视机。**c)** an object used for connecting a wire from one piece of electrical equipment such as a computer to another〔连接两台电器的〕接头

2 ▶BATH 浴缸◀ a round flat piece of rubber or plastic used for stopping the water flowing out of a bath or SINK²〔浴缸、洗涤槽的〕塞子，栓

3 ▶ADVERTISEMENT 广告◀ *informal* an attempt to persuade people to buy a book, see a film etc, by talking about it publicly, especially on television or radio【非正式】〔尤指电视或电台上的〕推销广告；推荐：**give sth a plug** *She appeared on all the talk shows to give her new book a plug.* 她在所有的访谈节目中出现，极力推销她的新书。

4 ▶IN AN ENGINE 在引擎中◀ *informal* the part of a petrol engine that makes a SPARK and explodes the petrol mixture; SPARK PLUG【非正式】火花塞：*Change the plugs every 10,000 miles.* 每〔行驶〕1万英里换一次火花塞。

5 pull the plug (on sth) to prevent a plan or business from being able to continue, especially by deciding not to give it any more money〔尤指通过不再提供资金〕使〔某事物〕不能继续，突然中断[停止]：*We were doing fine until the bank pulled the plug on us.* 在银行终止给我们提供资金以前，我们一直干得还是不错的。

6 ▶PIECE 块◀ a piece of something pressed tightly together〔紧紧压在一起的〕块：*a cotton wool plug* 药棉块 | *a plug of tobacco* 烟草块

7 ▶FOR HOLDING SCREWS 用于固定螺钉◀ [C] a small plastic tube put in a hole to hold a screw tightly〔置于孔内使螺钉固定的〕塑料螺钉衬套

plug² *v* [T]

1 also 又作 **plug up** to fill or block a small hole 把…塞住，堵塞；填塞：*I used cement to plug the holes in the plaster.* 我用水泥填补灰泥上的洞。**2** to try to persuade people to buy a book, see a film etc by talking about it on television or radio〔在电视或电台上〕为…做广告，宣传，推销：*Arnold was only on the show to plug his new movie.* 阿诺德上节目只是为了宣传他的新影片。**3 plug the gap/gaps** to provide more of something that is needed 填补空缺：*With so few trained doctors, paramedics were brought in to plug the gap.* 由于受过培训的医生寥寥无几，所以引进了医务辅助人员以填补空缺。**4** *AmE old-fashioned* to shoot someone【美，过时】射击，枪击〔某人〕

plug away *phr v* [I] to keep working hard at something 坚持努力做〔某事〕，拼命地干：**[+at]** *I'm sure if you keep plugging away at it, your English will improve.* 我相信只要你坚持下去，你的英语水平就会提高。

plug in 插上

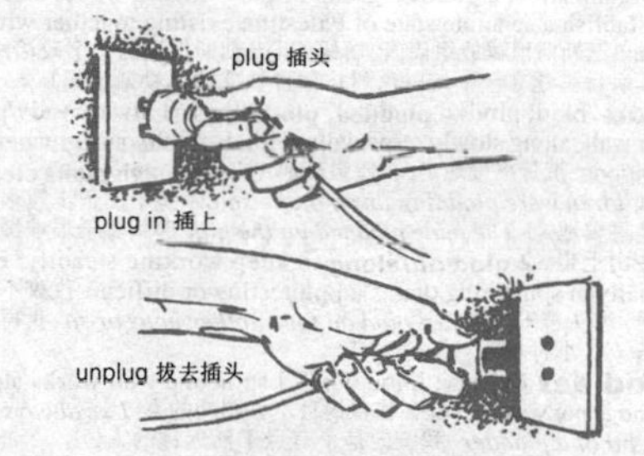

plug sth **↔ in** *phr v* [T] to connect a piece of electrical equipment to the main supply of electricity, or to another piece of electrical equipment 给〔电器〕接通电源；把〔一电器与另一电器〕接上，插上：*I don't think the antenna's plugged in right.* 我觉得天线没接好。

plug into sth *phr v* [T] **1** to connect one piece of electrical equipment to another〔把一台电器与另一电器〕连接起来，接通：**plug sth into sth** *The TV was plugged into the stereo system.* 电视与立体声系统接通了。**2** to connect your computer to a big computer system〔把电脑与大的电脑系统〕接通

plug·hole /ˈplʌgˌhol; ˈplʌghəʊl/ *n* [C] *BrE*【英】**1** a hole in a bath or SINK² where water can flow out, which you can put a PLUG¹ (2) into〔浴缸或洗涤槽中可用塞子堵住的〕排水孔；DRAIN² (2) *AmE*【美】**2 go down the plughole a)** if work or effort goes down the plughole it is completely wasted〔工作或努力〕完全白费，付诸东流：*Two years of hard work went right down the plughole.* 两年来的努力工作全都白费了。**b)** if a business goes down the plughole, it fails〔企业〕失败；破产

plum¹ /plʌm; plʌm/ *n* **1** [C] a small round juicy fruit which is dark red or yellow and has a hard part in the middle, or the tree that produces this fruit 李(子), 梅子; 李树: *stewed plums and custard* 焖李子牛奶蛋糊 | *plum blossoms* 李(子)花 —see picture on page A8 参见 A8 页图 **2** [U] a dark red colour, like a plum 李子色, 深红色 —see also 另见 PLUM PUDDING

plum² *adj* **1 a plum job** *BrE informal* a good, well-paid, and often easy job that other people wish they had【英, 非正式】轻松而报酬丰厚的工作, 优差 **2** having a dark red colour, like a plum 李子色的, 深红色的

plum·age /ˈplumɪdʒ; ˈpluːmɪdʒ/ *n* [U] the feathers covering a bird's body (鸟的)全身羽毛, 羽衣: *the parrot's brilliant blue plumage* 那只鹦鹉亮丽的蓝色羽毛

plumb¹ /plʌm; plʌm/ *v* [T] **1 plumb the depths of despair/misery/bad taste etc** to express a bad quality or feel an unpleasant emotion in a very extreme way 陷入绝望[痛苦]的深渊; 趣味低级到了极点: *When his wife left him Matt plumbed the very depths of despair.* 妻子离他而去, 马特绝望极了。**2** to succeed in understanding something completely; FATHOM² 查明, 探明, 完全理解: *Psychologists are trying to plumb the deepest mysteries of the human psyche.* 心理学家正努力探究人类心理最深层的奥秘。

plumb sth ↔ **in** *phr v* [T] to connect a piece of equipment such as a washing machine to the water supply 将(洗衣机等电器)与水源接通

plumb² *adv* **1** [always+adv/prep] *informal* exactly【非正式】精确地, 正, 恰恰: *The bullet hit him plumb between the eyes.* 子弹不偏不倚地击中他的两眼之间。**2** *AmE informal, often humorous* completely【美, 非正式, 常幽默】完全地: *I'm plumb tuckered out.* (=very tired) 我累极了。| *The whole idea sounds plumb crazy to me.* 整个想法在我听起来简直是疯了。

plumb³ *adj technical*【术语】**1** exactly upright or level 垂直的; 水平的 **2 out of plumb** not exactly upright or level 不垂直[水平]的, 倾斜的

plumb·er /ˈplʌmɚ; ˈplʌmə/ *n* [C] someone whose job is to repair water pipes, baths, SINKS etc 管子工, 水暖工, 铅管工

plumb·ing /ˈplʌmɪŋ; ˈplʌmɪŋ/ *n* [U] **1** the pipes that water flows through in a building (建筑物内的)管道设备, 水管: *We keep having problems with the plumbing.* 我们的水管老是出问题。**2** the work of fitting and repairing water pipes, baths etc 水管[浴缸等]安装及修理工作

plumb line /ˈ· ·/ *n* [C] a piece of string with a piece of LEAD tied to one end, used for measuring the depth of water or for finding out if a wall is built exactly upright 铅锤线, 铅垂线

plume¹ /plum; pluːm/ *n* [C] **1** a small cloud of smoke, dust etc which rises up into the air 升上空中的羽状物〈如烟、尘等〉: [+of] *After the explosion, a plume of black smoke hung over the horizon.* 爆炸过后, 一团黑烟悬在地平线上方。**2** a large feather or bunch of feathers, especially one that is used as a decoration on a hat (尤指用于装饰帽子的)羽毛, 大羽; 羽饰 —see also 另见 NOM DE PLUME

plume² *v* **1** [T] if a bird plumes its feathers, it cleans them and makes them smooth (鸟)整理(羽毛) **2 plume yourself on** *literary* to feel proud about a quality you have【文】为(自己的某种品性)感到骄傲[自豪]: *Meg plumed herself on her superior virtue.* 梅格为自己高尚的品德感到骄傲。

plumed /plumd; pluːmd/ *adj* [only before noun 仅用于名词前] having or decorated with feathers 有[饰有]羽毛的: *the knights' plumed helmets* 饰有羽毛的骑士头盔

plum·met /ˈplʌmɪt; ˈplʌmɪ̥t/ *v* [I] **1** to suddenly and quickly go down in value or amount (价值或数量)骤然跌落, 暴跌: *House prices have plummeted.* 房价已经暴跌。**2** to fall very suddenly and quickly from a great height (从高处突然而迅速地)坠落, 堕下: *The plane plummeted towards the earth.* 那架飞机直向地面坠落。—compare 比较 PLUNGE¹

plum·my /ˈplʌmɪ; ˈplʌmi/ *adj* **1** a plummy British voice sounds very upper-class and old-fashioned (英国发音)拿腔拿调的, 上层阶级腔调的: *the plummy Oxford tones of the newsreader* 新闻广播员拿腔拿调的牛津音 **2** tasting of or containing a lot of PLUMS 李子味的; 含有很多李子的

plump¹ /plʌmp; plʌmp/ *adj* **1** a word meaning pleasantly fat, often used when you want to avoid saying the word fat 丰满的, 胖乎乎的: *The nurse was a cheerful plump woman.* 那位护士是一位性格开朗、体形丰满的女人。| *Dad's getting a bit plump – he needs to go on a diet.* 爸爸有点儿发胖了, 他需要节食。**2** having a full, round shape 圆鼓鼓的: *plump, soft pillows* 圆鼓鼓的柔软枕头 | *plump juicy tomatoes* 圆鼓鼓的多汁的番茄 —compare 比较 CHUBBY, PORTLY —**plumpness** *n* [U] —see 见 FAT¹ (USAGE)

plump² *v* **1 plump sth in/on etc** to put something down suddenly and carelessly 把某物突然重重地放进…里面/扔在…上面等: *Otto plumped a sheaf of papers on my desk and told me to get on with it.* 奥托把一叠文件重重地扔在我的桌子上, 告诉我快点儿处理。| *You can plump the bags down anywhere you like.* 你可以把袋子随便放下。**2 plump (yourself) down** to sit down suddenly and heavily 突然重重地坐下

plump for sth *phr v* [T] *informal* to choose something after thinking carefully about it【非正式】(经过仔细考虑后)选择; 选定: *We finally plumped for a bottle of pink champagne.* 我们最后选定了一瓶粉红色的香槟酒。

plump sth ↔ **up** *phr v* [T] to make CUSHIONS, PILLOWS etc bigger and softer by shaking them (用手轻拍)使(软垫、枕头等)松软鼓起, 把…拍松

plum pud·ding /ˌ· ˈ· ·/ *n* [C,U] *BrE* CHRISTMAS PUDDING.【英】圣诞布丁

plum to·ma·to /ˈ· ·ˌ· ·/ *n* [C] a type of tomato which is shaped like a PLUM¹ (1) and is used in cooking (烹调用)李形番茄

plun·der¹ /ˈplʌndɚ; ˈplʌndə/ *v* [I,T] to steal large amounts of money or property from somewhere, especially in a violent way that causes damage (尤指以暴力)窃取; 侵占; 掠夺, 抢劫: *The rich provinces of Asia Minor were plundered by the invaders.* 小亚细亚的富饶地区遭到侵略者的劫掠。| *greedy tycoons who plunder their companies' pension funds* 侵吞了公司的退休基金的贪婪大亨 | *plundered treasures* 抢劫得来的财宝 —**plunderer** *n* [C]

plunder² *n* [U] **1** things that have been stolen during a violent attack, especially during a war 赃物; (尤指战时的)战利品; 掠夺物: *Henry's army returned loaded down with plunder.* 亨利的部队满载战利品而归。**2** the act of plundering 掠夺, 抢劫: *the plunder of Africa by the European nations* 欧洲国家对非洲的掠夺

plunge¹ /plʌndʒ; plʌndʒ/ *v* **1** [I, T always+adv/prep] to move, fall, or be thrown suddenly forwards or downwards (使)突然向前倒下[跌落]: [+off/into etc] *Her car swerved and plunged off the cliff.* 她的车突然转向冲下了悬崖。| **plunge to your death** *The rope broke and both the climbers plunged 500 feet to their death.* 绳子断了, 两名登山者从500英尺的高处跌下来摔死了。| **plunge sb/sth forward/through etc** *The car stopped suddenly and he was plunged forward through the windshield.* 汽车突然停下, 他被猛地抛出了挡风玻璃。**2** [I] if a price, value, or rate plunges it suddenly goes down by a large amount (价格、价值等)暴跌, 骤降: *The price of oil has plunged to a new low.* 石油价格已跌至新低。**3** [I] if a ship plunges, it moves violently up and down, usually because of high waves (船)猛烈地颠簸

plunge in *phr v* [I] to start talking, doing sth etc quickly and confidently, without worrying (迅速而自信地)开始谈论[做](某事): *Zoe plunged in and started chatting happily.* 佐伊开始愉快地聊了起来。

plunge into *phr v* [T] **1 plunge sth into sth** to push something firmly and deeply into something else 把某物投[插, 刺]入某物中: *Plunge the asparagus into boiling water.* 把芦笋投入沸水中。| *Jill plunged her hands deep into her pockets.* 吉尔把双手深深地插入口袋中。**2 plunge sb/sth into sth** to make someone or something experience a particular type of situation, especially one that is difficult or unpleasant 使某人/某物陷入[遭受]某种情况: *This latest scandal has plunged the Administration into controversy.* 最近的丑闻已使政府陷入争议之中。| *The hall was suddenly plunged into darkness.* 大厅突然陷入一片黑暗之中。| **be plunged into gloom/despair etc** (=suddenly experience great unhappiness) 突然陷入忧伤/绝望等之中 *The whole regiment was plunged into despair by this news.* 这个消息使全团陷入绝望之中。**3 plunge into sth** to begin to do something suddenly, without thinking about the possible results 突然[仓促]地开始做某事: *Stuart was always plunging into risky ventures.* 斯图尔特总是贸然地参与一些冒险的投资项目。

plunge² *n*

1 take the plunge to decide finally to do something, especially after delaying it or worrying about it for a long time (尤指经过拖延或踌躇之后)最终决定做某事, 决定冒险一试: *In 1990 Pam took the plunge and set up her own business.* 1990年帕姆毅然决定设立她自己的公司。

2 ►DOWNWARD MOVEMENT 向下移动◄ [C usually singular 一般用单数] a sudden quick downward movement 突降; 俯冲: *Without warning, the plane began a plunge towards the Earth.* 那架飞机没有发出警告就开始向地面俯冲下来。

3 ►INTO WATER 进入水中◄ [C usually singular 一般用单数] a DIVE[2] (1) or jump into water, or a quick swim 跳水;〔短时间的〕游泳: *Sue felt refreshed after a quick plunge in the lake.* 休在湖中游了一会儿泳后感到精神焕发。

4 ►DECREASE 降低◄ [C] a sudden large fall in the value of property, SHARES[2] (5) etc〔财产、股票等价值的〕暴跌, 骤降: *a dramatic plunge in house prices* 房价的突然暴跌

plung·er /ˈplʌndʒɚ; ˈplʌndʒə/ *n* [C] **1** a rubber cup on the end of a rod used for unblocking kitchen or bathroom pipes〔用于疏通厨房或浴室水管的〕搋子, 手压皮碗泵 **2** *technical* a part of a machine that moves up and down【术语】〔机器的〕活塞, 柱塞 **3** *AmE informal* someone who GAMBLES a lot【美, 非正式】赌徒

plung·ing neck·line /ˌ.. ˈ../ *n* [C] a very low curve or V shape on the top edge of the front of a woman's dress〔女服的〕低领口, V 形领

plu·per·fect, the /pluˈpɝfɪkt; pluːˈpɜːfɪkt/ *n technical* the PAST PERFECT tense of a verb【术语】〔动词的〕过去完成式[时]

plu·ral[1] /ˈplurəl; ˈplʊərəl/ *n* [C] a word or form that shows you are talking about more than one object, person etc. For example, 'dogs' is the plural of 'dog' 复数(形式)

plural[2] *adj* **1** a plural word or form shows you are talking about more than one object, person etc. For example 'we' is a plural pronoun 复数的〈如 we 是复数代词〉 **2** *formal* involving more than one person or thing or different kinds of people or things【正式】〔人或事物〕多种的; 多元的: *plural cultures* 多元文化 | *plural marriage* 一夫多妻制[一妻多夫制]

plu·ral·is·m /ˈplurəlɪzm; ˈplʊərəlɪzəm/ *n* [U] *formal*【正式】 **1** the principle that people of different races, religions, and political beliefs can live together peacefully in the same society 多元主义, 多元文化〔在同一社会中不同民族、宗教和政治信仰的人和平共处的原则〕 **2** the holding of more than one job at a time, especially in the Church〔尤指在教会中的〕兼职, 兼任 **—pluralist** *n* [C] **—pluralistic, pluralist** /ˌplurəˈlɪstɪk; ˌplʊərəˈlɪstɪk◂/ *adj*: *living in a pluralist society* 生活在多元主义的社会中

plu·ral·i·ty /pluˈrælətɪ; plʊˈræləti/ *n* **1** [C] *formal* a large number of different things【正式】大量不同事物: **[+of]** *a plurality of cultures* 多元文化 **2** [C,U] *especially AmE technical* the largest number of votes in an election, especially when this is less than the total number of votes that all the other people or parties have received【尤美, 术语】〔尤指选举中未超过半数的〕相对多数(票) **3** [U] *technical* the state of being plural【术语】复数(形式)

plus[1] /plʌs; plʌs/ *prep* **1** used when one number or amount is added to another 加: *Three plus six equals nine. (3+6=9)* 3 加 6 等于 9。| *The book has 250 pages, plus 28 pages of appendices.* 这本书有 250 页, 另有 28 页附录。| *All employees are paid $3 an hour plus $1.50 for time worked on the weekend.* 所有雇员的报酬都是每小时 3 美元, 周末工作每小时另加 1.5 美元。**2** and also 和, 加上: *The unit deals with all lung and heart conditions, plus many other lesser ailments.* 该科治疗所有的肺部和心脏疾病, 还有各种较轻微的疾病。**3 plus four/six etc** *technical* four, six etc more than zero【术语】正(数) 4/6 等 —opposite 反义词 MINUS[1]

plus[2] *n* [C] **1** *informal* something that gives you an advantage in a situation【非正式】有利因素[条件]: *Knowledge of French and Spanish could be a plus in this job.* 懂法语和西班牙语可能是做这份工作的有利条件。**2** a sign (+) showing that you should add two or more numbers together, or that a number is more than zero 加号; 正号

plus[3] *adj* **1 plus factor/point** an advantage or favourable feature that something has 有利因素[条件]/优点: *Another plus point for the VHS system is that you can record three or four hours of material onto one tape.* 家用录像系统的另一优点是你可以把三、四小时的材料录制到一盘带子上。**2 10/50 etc plus** more than a particular amount, number or level 多于 10/50 等: *She earns $50,000 a year plus.* 她一年多一点挣了 5 万美元。| *All the children in the class are six plus.* (=more than six years old) 这班里所有的孩子都在六岁以上。**3** [only before noun 仅用于名词前] greater than zero 大于零的, 在零以上的, 正的: *Daytime temperatures vary between minus 5° and plus 12°.* 日间的气温介乎零下 5 度至零上 12 度。

plus[4] *conjunction* and also 并且, 而且: *He's been studying for the exams all week, plus he's been working in a bar at night.* 他整个星期都在为应考温习, 而且晚上还在一家酒吧里工作。| *It's an old, draughty house. Plus the plumbing's not fixed yet.* 这是一座透风的破旧房子, 而且里面的水管还没有安装。

plus fours /ˌ. ˈ./ *n* [plural] trousers with loose wide legs that are fastened just below the knee, worn by men especially in the 1920s when playing GOLF〔尤指 20 世纪 20 年代打高尔夫球时穿的〕灯笼裤

plush[1] /plʌʃ; plʌʃ/ also 又作 **plush·y** /ˈplʌʃɪ; ˈplʌʃi/ *adj informal* expensive, comfortable, and of good quality【非正式】昂贵而舒适的; 高级的; 豪华的: *a plush hotel* 豪华酒店

plush[2] *n* [U] silk or cotton cloth with a surface like short fur 长毛绒: *plush curtains* 长毛绒窗帘

plus sign /ˈ. ./ *n* [C] the sign (+) 加号; 正号

Plu·tarch /ˈplutɑrk; ˈpluːtɑːk/ (?46-?120 AD) an ancient Greek historian who wrote about famous Greek and Roman politicians and military leaders in a book known as *Plutarch's Lives*. Plays by William Shakespeare that are set in ancient times, such as *Julius Caesar*, are based on Plutarch's writings. 普卢塔克〔(公元?46-?120), 古希腊历史学家。著有《希腊罗马名人传》, 记述希腊、罗马著名政治家与军事领袖的生平故事。威廉·莎士比亚的《尤利乌斯·凯撒》等其他以古代为背景的剧作皆取材于普卢塔克的作品〕

Plu·to /ˈpluto; ˈpluːtəʊ/ *n* [singular] an object that goes around the sun, usually beyond Neptune, which was called a PLANET until 2006 冥王星〔绕太阳运行的一个星体, 比海王星距离太阳更远, 2006 年之前被认为是一颗行星〕—see picture at 参见 SOLAR SYSTEM 图

plu·toc·ra·cy /pluˈtɑkrəsɪ; pluːˈtɒkrəsi/ *n* [C] a ruling class of rich people, or a country ruled by such people, or a government that consists of them 富豪[财阀]统治阶层; 由财阀统治的国家; 由财阀组成的政府

plu·to·crat /ˈplutəˌkræt; ˈpluːtəkræt/ *n* [C] someone who has power because they are rich 有钱有势的人, 财阀, 富豪: *bloated plutocrats who exploit the workers* 剥削工人的趾高气扬的财阀 **—plutocratic** /ˌplutəˈkrætɪk; ˌpluːtəˈkrætɪk◂/ *adj*

plu·to·ni·um /pluˈtonɪəm; pluːˈtəʊniəm/ *n* [U] an element (=simple substance) that is used in the production of NUCLEAR power〔用于生产核能的〕钚

ply[1] /plaɪ; plaɪ/ *v past tense and past participle* **plied** **1** [I always+adv/prep, T] *literary* if a vehicle or boat plies between two places or across a place it makes that journey regularly【文】〔车、船〕定期地来回[往返]: **[+between/across etc]** *Small fishing boats plied to and fro across the harbor.* 小渔船定期往返于港口之中。| **ply sth** *a regular boat service that plies the lake* 定期在湖上往返的船运服务 **2 ply your trade** *literary* to work at your job or business【文】从事工作, 经营生意: *Flower sellers were plying their trade in the marketplace.* 卖花者在市场上做生意。**3** [T] *old use or literary* to use or work skilfully with a tool【旧或文】使用〔工具〕; 熟练地用〔工具〕工作 **4 ply for hire** *BrE* if a taxi driver plies for hire, they drive around or wait somewhere looking for passengers【英】〔出租车司机〕候客, 等生意, 揽客

ply sb **with** sth *phr v* [T] **1** to keep giving someone large quantities of food and drink 不断地给〔某人大量食物和饮料〕: *They plied us with sandwiches and mugs of strong coffee.* 他们不停地给我们三明治和一大杯又一大杯的浓咖啡。**2 ply sb with questions** to keep asking someone questions 不断地向某人提问题

ply[2] *n* [U] **two/three etc ply a)** used as a measurement of the thickness of thread, rope etc, according to the number of single threads it is made from〔线、绳等的〕股 **b)** used as a measurement of the thickness of plywood according to the number of thin sheets of wood it is made from〔夹板的〕层片

Plym·outh[1] /ˈplɪməθ; ˈplɪməθ/ a port and base for the British navy, in Devon, southwest England. In the UK people think of it in connection with Francis Drake, the 16th century EXPLORER and navy commander. People in the US think of it as the place from which the Pilgrim Fathers sailed to America. 普利茅斯〔英格兰西南部德文郡一港口, 也是英国一海军基地。英国人通常把普利茅斯与 16 世纪探险家、海军司令弗朗西斯·德雷克相联系。美国人心中的普利茅斯则是清教徒前辈移民美洲之行的起航港口〕

Plymouth[2] *trademark* a type of US car made by the Chrysler company【商标】普利茅斯〔一款美国汽车, 由克莱斯勒公司制造〕

Plym·outh Breth·ren /ˌplɪməθ ˈbrɛðrən; ˌplɪməθ ˈbreðrən/ *n* [plural] a Christian organization that has very strict moral rules and is opposed to religious ceremony 普利茅斯兄弟会〔一个基督教组织, 有非常严格的道德准则, 并反对宗教仪式〕

Plymouth Col·o·ny /ˈ.. ˌ.../ the second English town to be built in North America, in 1620, in what is now Plymouth, Massachusetts. The first town was in Jamestown in Virginia. The settlers, known as the Pilgrim Fathers, were Puritans who sailed on the ship Mayflower from Plymouth, England. Only half of them were still alive after the first winter in America, but the town grew. According to old stories, the settlers' first steps when they landed in America were on a large rock, today called

Plymouth Rock. 普利茅斯殖民地〔英国人在北美的第二个城镇，建于1620年，位于今马萨诸塞州普利茅斯。第一个殖民镇是弗吉尼亚的詹姆斯敦。历史上的清教徒前辈移民是从英格兰的普利茅斯乘坐"五月花"号到达北美的。他们在美国捱过第一个严冬后，仅有一半人活了下来。尽管如此，小镇还是发展了起来。根据传说故事，早期移民到达美洲时首先踏上的是一块巨石，今称"普利茅斯巨石"〕

Plymouth Rock /,‥ ˈ‥/ a large rock on the coast at Plymouth, Massachusetts. According to old stories, the Pilgrim Fathers took their first steps in America when they landed there in 1620. 普利茅斯巨石〔马萨诸塞州普利茅斯沿岸一巨石。据传，1620年清教徒前辈移民到达美洲时首先踏上的便是这块岩石〕

ply·wood /ˋplaɪˌwʊd; ˈplaɪwʊd/ *n* [U] a material made of several thin sheets of wood stuck together to form a strong board 胶合板，夹板

PM /ˌpi ˋɛm; ˌpiː ˈem/ *n* [C] *informal, especially BrE* the PRIME MINISTER【非正式，尤英】首相: *an urgent meeting with the PM* 与首相的紧急会议

pm /ˌpi ˋɛm; ˌpiː ˈem/ *Latin* post meridiem; used after numbers expressing the time to show that it is after midday【拉丁】下午〔用于表示钟点的数字之后〕: *The meeting starts at 2.30 pm.* 会议下午两点半开始。

PMS /ˌpi ɛm ˋɛs; ˌpiː em ˈes/ *n* [U] *AmE* premenstrual syndrome; unpleasant physical and emotional feelings felt by many women just before their PERIOD【美】经前综合征; PMT *BrE*【英】

PMT /ˌpi ɛm ˋti; ˌpiː em ˈtiː/ *n* [U] *BrE* premenstrual tension【英】经前紧张症; PMS *AmE*【美】

pneu·mat·ic /nuˋmætɪk; njuːˈmætɪk/ *adj* **1** *technical* filled with air【术语】充气的: *pneumatic tyres* 充气轮胎 **2** worked by air pressure 由压缩空气推动的: *a pneumatic pump* 气压泵 — **pneumatically** /-kḷɪ; -kli/ *adv*

pneumatic drill /‥ˌ‥ ˈ‥/ *n* [C] *especially BrE* a large powerful tool worked by air pressure which is used for breaking up hard materials, especially road surfaces【尤英】〔尤指用于开凿路面的〕风钻; JACKHAMMER *AmE*【美】—see picture at 参见 DRILL¹ 图

pneu·mo·ni·a /nuˋmonjə; njuːˈməʊniə/ *n* [U] a serious disease of the lungs that makes it difficult for you to breathe 肺炎

PO /ˌpi ˋo; ˌpiː ˈəʊ/ **1** the written abbreviation of 缩写= POST OFFICE **2** the written abbreviation of 缩写= PETTY OFFICER **3** the written abbreviation of 缩写= POSTAL ORDER

Po, the /po; pəʊ/ the largest river in northern Italy 波河〔意大利北部最大河流〕

poach /potʃ; pəʊtʃ/ *v*

1 ▶COOK 烹调◀ [T] **a)** to cook eggs in a special pan over boiling water 用沸水煮〔荷包蛋〕: *poached eggs on toast* 烤面包片上的水煮荷包蛋 **b)** to cook fish or meat in boiling water or other liquid 在沸水或其他液体中煮〔鱼或肉〕: *Salmon is usually poached in a fish kettle.* 鲑鱼通常在煮鱼锅中炖煮。

2 ▶ANIMALS 动物◀ [I,T] to catch or shoot animals, birds, or fish illegally, especially on private land without permission〔尤指未经允许在私人土地上〕偷猎，偷捕: *the poaching of elephants and the illegal trading of ivory* 偷猎大象和非法买卖象牙

3 ▶PEOPLE/IDEAS 人/想法◀ [I,T] **a)** to persuade someone to leave a team or company and join yours 挖走〔球队或公司的成员〕: *Foreign football clubs seem to be poaching all our best players.* 国外的足球俱乐部似乎要挖走我们所有优秀的球员。**b)** to unfairly or illegally use someone else's ideas 剽窃; 窃取〔他人的想法〕: *screenwriters poaching from literature* 剽窃文学作品的电影剧本作家

4 poach on sb's territory/preserve to do something that is someone else's responsibility, especially when they do not want you to do it 越权行事

poach·er /ˋpotʃɚ; ˈpəʊtʃə/ *n* [C] **1** someone who catches or shoots animals, birds, or fish on private land without permission 偷猎者，偷捕者 **2** a pan with small containers shaped like cups for poaching eggs 荷包蛋锅，煮锅〔内有数个杯形煮蛋容器的平底锅〕**3 poacher turned gamekeeper** *BrE* someone who was previously a criminal and now has responsibility for stopping crime【英】由罪犯摇身一变成为执法者的人

PO Box /ˌpi o ˋbɑks; ˌpiː əʊ ˈbɒks◂/ *n* [C] a numbered box in a post office to which someone's mail can be sent and from which they can collect it 邮政信箱: *For further information, write to PO Box 714, Key Largo, Florida.* 欲知详情，请函寄佛罗里达州基拉戈岛714号邮政信箱。

Poc·a·hon·tas /ˌpokəˋhɑntəs; ˌpɒkəˈhɒntəs/ (1595-1617) a Native American woman, who was the daughter of **Chief Powhatan** of the Powhatan tribe. Pocahontas saved the life of **Captain John Smith**, leader of the English people who had gone to live in Jamestown, Virginia, when he was about to be killed by her father. She then helped to develop friendly relations between the English and the Native Americans. Later Pocahontas married an Englishman and went to England, where she died of SMALLPOX. 波卡洪塔斯〔(1595-1617)，一印第安女子，波瓦坦部落的首领之女。约翰·史密斯上尉是弗吉尼亚州詹姆斯敦英国移民的首领，波卡洪塔斯在父亲准备处死上尉的时候救了他一命。于是，她便致力于建立英国人与印第安人的友好关系。后来，她与一位英国人结婚，并一起去了英国，最后死于天花〕

pocked /pɑkt; pɒkt/ *adj* covered with small holes or marks; POCKMARKED 布满小洞的; 满是麻点的: *His face was pocked with scars.* 他的脸上布满了疤痕。

pock·et¹ /ˋpɑkɪt; ˈpɒkɪ̣t/ *n* [C] S2 W2

1 ▶IN CLOTHES 衣服上的◀ a small bag sewn onto or into a coat, trousers etc so that you can put things such as money or keys into it 衣袋，口袋: *Joseph always stands with his hands in his pockets.* 约瑟夫总是把双手插在衣袋里站着。| **coat/trouser/jacket etc pocket** *The keys are in my coat pocket.* 钥匙在我的外衣口袋里。| **turn out your pockets** (=empty your pockets) 把口袋翻出来 —see picture on page A17 参见 A17 页图

2 ▶MONEY 金钱◀ the amount of money available for you to spend 钱; 收入; 财力: *When will the new taxes start hitting people's pockets?* 新税收会在什么时候开始影响人们的收入? | **suit every pocket** *We offer a range of repayment plans to suit every pocket.* 我们提供一系列还款计划以适应各种收入人士的需求。| **from/out of your own pocket** (=using your own money instead of money from your company, the government etc) 自掏腰包，用自己的钱〔而不是公司、政府等的钱〕*The prince offered to pay for the restoration out of his own pocket.* 王子提出自掏腰包支付修复所需的费用。| **have deep pockets** (=have a lot of money) 财力充足，有很多钱

3 ▶IN A BAG/DOOR ETC 袋子里/门上等◀ a small bag or piece of material fastened to an object so that you can put small things into it〔固定于某物上用于容纳小东西的〕小袋: *All passengers should read the air safety card in the pocket of the seat in front.* 所有的乘客都应该读一下放在前面座位袋里的飞行安全卡。

4 ▶SMALL AREA/AMOUNT 小的区域/数量◀ a) a small area where the situation is very different from the area surrounding it〔与周围区域情况不同的〕一小片[小块]区域: *Apart from a few pockets of resistance, the new government is firmly established.* 除了一些零星的抵抗之外，新政府已稳固地建立起来。| *a poor country dotted with pockets of wealth* 有着零星富裕地区的贫穷国家 **b)** a small amount of something that is different from what surrounds it〔与周围事物不同的〕少量: *The mine has a few remaining pockets of iron ore.* 那个矿井有少量残留的铁矿石。

5 be/live in each other's pockets *informal, especially BrE* if two people are in each other's pockets, they are together too much【非正式，尤英】〔两人〕经常在一起，形影不离

6 have sb/sth in your pocket a) to be able to control someone such as a police officer or politician, by threatening them, paying them money etc〔通过威胁、收买等手段〕控制[支配]某人: *a powerful organization with many local politicians in its pockets* 操纵着许多本地政客的强大组织 **b)** to be very sure that you are going to win something such as a competition or election〔在比赛或选举中〕稳操胜券: *It looks like the Democrats have this election in their pockets already.* 看来民主党在这次选举中已稳操胜券。

7 be out of pocket *BrE informal* to have less money than you should have, after some form of exchange or business deal【英，非正式】赔钱的: *Unless you handle the deal carefully, you could be badly out of pocket.* 如果你不小心处理这笔交易，会赔大钱的。| **£10/£50 etc out of pocket** *Selling the car so cheaply left her £100 out of pocket.* 这么便宜卖掉那部车使她赔了100英镑。

8 pick sb's pocket to steal from someone by taking money from their pocket without them realizing〔从某人的口袋里〕扒窃，偷窃

9 put your hand in your pocket to give money to someone who needs it or in order to help someone 出钱〔帮助某人〕: *I hope everyone will put their hands in their pockets and give generously to the fund.* 我希望每个人都慷慨解囊，捐款给这个基金。

10 ▶FOR BALLS 用于装球◀ a small net bag fastened to a BILLIARD OR SNOOKER table which you have to hit the ball into〔桌球或斯诺克桌上的〕球囊，球袋 —see also 另见 AIRPOCKET, **line your own pockets** (LINE² (4))

pocket² *v* [T] **1** to put something into your pocket 把…装入口袋[衣袋]中: *Roy pocketed his wallet and car keys and left the house.* 罗伊把他的钱包和汽车钥匙放进衣袋里，然后离开了房子。**2 a)** to steal money, especially money that you are respon-

sible for 窃取, 盗用, 侵吞〔公款〕: *The society's treasurer was accused of pocketing some of the profits.* 该协会的财务主管被控侵吞了部分利润。**b)** to get money in a slightly dishonest way 捞取〔钱财〕: *It's simple – we buy them for $5, sell them for $8, and pocket the difference.* 这很简单 —— 我们以五美元买进, 以八美元卖出, 捞取其中的差价。**3** to hit a ball into a pocket in games such as BILLIARDS〔桌球等〕击〔球〕落袋

pocket³ *adj* [only before noun 仅用于名词前] small enough to be carried in your pocket 可放在衣袋内的, 袖珍的: *a pocket dictionary* 袖珍词典

pocket bat·tle·ship /ˌ·· ˈ··· / *n* [C] a fairly small fighting ship 小型战舰

pock·et·book /ˈpɑkɪtˌbʊk; ˈpɒkɪ̣tbʊk/ *n* [C] **1** *AmE* a small flat case for holding papers and paper money; WALLET【美】皮夹, 钱包 **2** a small NOTEBOOK 小笔记本 **3** *AmE old-fashioned* a woman's HANDBAG, especially one without a STRAP[1]【美, 过时】〔尤指无肩带的〕女用手袋

pocket cal·cu·lat·or /ˌ·· ˈ····/ *n* [C] a small piece of electronic equipment which you use to do calculations 袖珍计算器

pock·et·ful /ˈpɑkɪtˌfʊl; ˈpɒkɪ̣tfʊl/ *n* [C] the amount that a pocket will hold 一口袋, 一袋之量: [+of] *a pocketful of pebbles* 一口袋卵石

pocket hand·ker·chief /ˌ·· ˈ···/ *n* [C] *old-fashioned* a handkerchief made of cloth not of paper【过时】手帕

pocket-handkerchief *adj informal, especially BrE* small and square in shape【非正式, 尤英】又小又方的: *a pocket-handkerchief garden* 一小片花园

pocket knife /ˈ·· ·/ *n plural* **pocket knives** /-ˌnaɪvz; -naɪvz/ [C] a small knife with one or more blades that fold into the handle〔有一个或几个刀片、可折叠的〕小刀 —see picture at 参见 KNIFE[1] 图

pocket mon·ey /ˈ·· ˌ··/ *n* [U] **1** *especially BrE* money given regularly to a child by its parents to spend on small things【尤英】〔父母定期给小孩的〕零花钱; ALLOWANCE (4) *AmE*【美】: *Sophie spends her pocket money on sweets and magazines.* 索菲把零花钱用在买糖果和杂志上。**2** *informal* a small amount of money that you can use to buy small things【非正式】零用钱: *Gavin gives private lessons to earn himself a bit of pocket money.* 加文给私人授课为自己赚点零用钱。

pocket ve·to /ˌ·· ˈ··/ *n* [C] a method used by the US President to stop a BILL (=proposal for a new law), by keeping it without signing it until Congress is no longer working 袋中否决, 搁置否决〔美国总统把议案搁置起来不予签署直到国会休会从而阻止议案通过的一种方法〕

pock·mark /ˈpɑkˌmɑrk; ˈpɒkmɑːk/ *n* [C] a hollow mark on someone's skin left by a disease such as SMALLPOX〔由于天花之类的疾病而留在皮肤上的〕痘痕, 麻子, 麻点

pock·marked /ˈpɑkˌmɑrkt; ˈpɒkmɑːkt/ *adj* covered with pockmarks; POCKED 有麻子[麻点]的: *a pockmarked face* 有麻子的脸

Po·co·nos, the /ˈpokənoz; ˈpəʊkənəʊz/ also 又作 **the Pocono Mountains** /ˌ··· ˈ··/ a group of mountains in Pennsylvania, US, which are part of the Appalachians. The mountains are a popular place for short holidays, especially HONEYMOONS and many people from New York City and New Jersey go there to get away from their busy cities. 波科诺山〔美国宾夕法尼亚州一山脉, 属阿巴拉契亚山系, 是短期度假、尤其是度蜜月的好去处。不少纽约市人和新泽西人常去那里, 远离城市的喧嚣〕

pod¹ /pɑd; pɒd/ *n* [C] **1** a long narrow seed container that grows on various plants, especially PEAS and beans 豆荚: *a pea pod* 豌豆荚 **2** a part of a space vehicle that can be separated from the main part〔航天器的〕可分离舱 **3** a long narrow container for petrol or other substances, especially one carried under an aircraft wing〔尤指飞机翼下的〕容器, 箱; 吊舱 **4** a container which holds the eggs of some types of insects〔某些昆虫的〕卵囊

pod² *v* [T] to take beans, PEAS etc from their POD[1] (1) before cooking them 把〔豆等〕剥出荚

podg·y /ˈpɑdʒɪ; ˈpɒdʒi/ *adj* another form of PUDGY pudgy 的另一种形式

po·di·a·trist /pəˈdaɪətrɪst; pəˈdaɪətrɪ̣st/ *n* [C] *especially AmE* someone who looks after people's feet and treats foot diseases【尤美】足病医生; CHIROPODIST *especially BrE*【尤英】—**podiatry** *n* [U]

po·di·um /ˈpodɪəm; ˈpəʊdiəm/ *n* [C] **1** a small raised area for a performer, speaker, or musical CONDUCTOR to stand on 表演台; 讲台; 乐队指挥台 **2** *AmE* a tall sloping desk for putting an open book, notes for a speech etc on; LECTERN【美】〔用于放置打开的书或演讲笔记等的〕斜面高桌

po·dunk /ˈpodʌŋk; ˈpəʊdʌŋk/ *adj AmE informal* a podunk place is small and unimportant【美, 非正式】〔地方〕小的; 不重要的; 无名的: *Brad comes from some podunk town east of the mountains.* 布拉德来自该山区以东某个无名小镇。

Poe /po; pəʊ/, **Ed·gar Al·lan** /ˈɛdgə ˈælən; ˈedgə ˈælən/ (1809-49) a US poet and writer of short stories. He is most famous for his strange, frightening stories about death and evil powers such as *The Fall of the House of Usher*. Another story, *The Murders in the Rue Morgue*, was one of the first DETECTIVE stories. His most famous poem is *The Raven*. 爱伦·坡〔(1809-1849), 美国诗人、短篇小说家, 以描写死亡与邪恶力量的诡异恐怖小说闻名, 代表作为《厄舍古厦的倒塌》。他的另一部作品《莫格街凶杀案》是最早的侦探小说之一。最著名的诗作为《乌鸦》〕

p.o.ed /piˈod; piːˈəʊd/ *adj AmE informal* very annoyed【美, 非正式】非常烦恼的, 很生气的: *She was really p.o.ed when she didn't get the job.* 她因没有得到那份工作而感到非常恼怒。

po·em /ˈpo·ɪm; ˈpəʊɪ̣m/ *n* [C] a piece of writing arranged in patterns of lines and of sounds which often RHYME, expressing thoughts, emotions, and experiences in words that excite your imagination 诗, 韵文 3

po·e·sy /ˈpo·ɪsɪ; ˈpəʊɪ̣zi/ *n* [U] *old use* poetry【旧】诗歌

po·et /ˈpo·ɪt; ˈpəʊɪ̣t/ *n* [C] someone who writes poems 诗人 3

po·et·as·ter /ˈpo·ɪtˌæstɚ; ˌpəʊɪ̣ˈtæstə/ *n* [C] *literary* someone who writes bad poems【文】蹩脚诗人

po·et·ess /ˈpoətɪs; ˌpəʊɪ̣ˈtes◂/ *n* [C] *old-fashioned* a female poet【过时】女诗人

po·et·ic /poˈɛtɪk; pəʊˈetɪk/ also 又作 **poetical** /poˈɛtɪkl̩; pəʊˈetɪkəl/ *adj* **1** concerning poetry or typical of poetry 诗(一般)的, 诗歌特有的: *poetic drama* 诗体戏剧 | *poetic imagery* 诗的意象 **2** having qualities of deep feeling or graceful expression 富有诗意的; 表达优雅的; 诗一般的: *Their dancing has a kind of poetic intensity.* 他们的舞蹈有一种如诗一般的激情。—**poetically** /-klɪ; -kli/ *adv*

poetic jus·tice /ˌ·ˌ·· ˈ··/ *n* [U] a situation in which someone is made to suffer for something bad they have done, in a way that seems perfectly suitable or right 恶有恶报, 应得的惩罚: *After being bullied by her for so long, it struck me as poetic justice that she was now being victimized.* 我被她欺负了这么久之后, 现在她成了受害者, 我觉得真是恶有恶报。

poetic li·cence /ˌ·ˌ·· ˈ··/ *n* [U] the freedom to change facts, not to obey the usual rules etc, that is allowed to poets and other artists 诗或其他艺术形式的破格

Poet Lau·re·ate /ˌ·· ˈ···/ *n* [C] a poet who is appointed by the king or queen in Britain to write poems on important occasions〔英国的〕桂冠诗人

po·et·ry /ˈpo·ɪtrɪ; ˈpəʊɪ̣tri/ *n* [U] **1** poems 诗, 诗歌: *Wordsworth's poetry* 华兹华斯的诗 **2** the art of writing poems 写诗的艺术, 作诗法: *the art of poetry* 诗歌艺术 **3** *approving* a quality of beauty, grace, and deep feeling【褒】诗意, 诗情; 诗一般的美: *The way Martina moves around the court is sheer poetry.* 马丁娜在球场上移动的姿态如诗一般的优美。 3

Poets' Cor·ner /ˌ·· ˈ··/ a part of Westminster Abbey in London where many famous English poets are buried, including Chaucer and Shakespeare 诗人角〔伦敦威斯敏斯特教堂一隅, 是乔叟、莎士比亚等许多著名英国诗人的安息之地〕

po-faced /ˌpoˈfest; ˌpəʊ ˈfeɪst◂/ *adj BrE informal* having an unfriendly disapproving expression on your face【英, 非正式】板起面孔的, 面无表情的, 一本正经的: *That po-faced woman behind the bar refused to serve us.* 吧台后面那个板着脸的女人拒绝招待我们。

po·go stick /ˈpogo ˌstɪk; ˈpəʊgəʊ stɪk/ *n* [C] a pole with a spring near the bottom and a bar which you can stand on while holding the top in order to jump about for fun〔底部装有脚踏弹簧跳跃用的〕弹簧单高跷

pog·rom /poˈgrɑm; ˈpɒgrəm/ *n* [C] a planned killing of large numbers of people, especially Jews, usually done for reasons of race or religion (有组织的) 大屠杀, 集体迫害〔尤指屠杀犹太人〕

poi·gnant /ˈpɔɪnjənt; ˈpɔɪnjənt/ *adj* making you feel sad or full of pity 令人伤心的, 令人充满同情[惋惜]的: *I was struck by the poignant contrast between his lively mind and his old frail body.* 他活跃的思想和老弱的身体之间的对比给我留下深刻印象。—**poignancy** *n* [U] —**poignantly** *adv*: *The road between Hue and Danang was poignantly named 'Street without Joy'.* 越南顺化和岘港之间的路被命名为"无欢乐街", 真令人伤感。

Poin·ca·ré /ˌpwæŋkɑˈre; ˈpwæŋkæreɪ/, **Hen·ri** /ɑnˈri; ˈɒnri/ (1854-1912) a French MATHEMATICIAN, one of the greatest of his time 庞加莱〔(1854-1912), 法国数学家, 是当时最伟大的数学家之一〕

poin·set·ti·a /pɔɪn`sɛtɪə; pɔɪn'setiə/ *n* [C] a tropical plant with groups of large bright red leaves that look like flowers 一品红〔热带植物，其鲜红色叶子似花瓣〕

point¹ /pɔɪnt; pɔɪnt/ *n*

1 ▶IDEA 想法◀ [C] a single fact, idea, or opinion that is part of an argument or discussion 某一事实；某一想法；某一观点：*There was one point on which everyone agreed.* 有一点大家都同意。| *She had brought a list of points for discussion.* 她列出了一些讨论要点。| *One important point must be borne in mind.* 有很重要的一点必须记住。| *That's a very interesting point.* 那一点很有趣。| **make a point** (=give a fact, idea, or opinion) 提出一个想法[论点、意见] *John made an interesting point about the role of the artist in society.* 约翰就艺术家在社会中的作用提出了有趣的看法。| **sb's point** *I agree with Jane's point that we need to look more closely at the costs.* 我同意简关于我们需要更仔细地审查成本的看法。| **make/prove your point** (=show that your idea or opinion is right) 证明你的观点[主张]正确 *He brought along a handful of documents to help prove his point.* 他带来了一些文件以帮助证实他的观点。| **the finer points** (=details that are difficult to understand) 难以理解的细节 *the finer points of political theory* 政治理论的微妙难解之处

2 ▶MAIN MEANING/IDEA 主要的意思/观点◀ the point the main idea in something that is said or done which gives meaning to all of it 要点，重点；中心意思，主要含义；核心问题：**the point is...** (=the most important thing is) 最重要的是…，问题是… *The point is that you should have told me where you were going.* 问题是你应该告诉我你要去哪儿。| **beside the point** (=not important) 不重要的，不相干的，离题的 *She is young, but that's beside the point.* 她很年轻，但这并不要紧。| **come/get to the point** (=used to tell someone to reach the most important part of what they want to say) 谈正题，谈关键问题 *I wish you would get to the point!* 我希望你能进入正题！| **miss the point** (=not understand the main meaning of something) 不理解[明白]要点 *Was I hearing him right, or had I completely missed the point?* 我是听明白了他说的话呢，还是完全没有领会他的意思？| **to the point** (=saying something important about the matter being dealt with) 切题的；中肯的 *The message was short and to the point.* 这消息简短扼要。

3 ▶PLACE 地方◀ [C] an exact place or position〔确切的〕地方，地点；位置：*Line A crosses line B at point C.* A线和B线于C点相交。| *a border crossing point* 跨越边境处

4 ▶IN TIME/DEVELOPMENT 在时间上/在发展中◀ [C] an exact moment, time, or stage in something's development 时候，时刻；〔发展的〕阶段；程度；地步：**at this point** *It was at this point the surgeon realized things were going wrong.* 那位外科医生就在这时意识到情况不妙。| **at this point in time** (=now) 现在，此时 *It is impossible to give a definite answer at this point in time.* 现在不可能给予一个明确的答复。| **starting point** (=a time or stage from which something can start) 起点，开头 *We can use this document as a starting point for our discussions.* 我们可以以这份文件为出发点来进行讨论。| **to the point of** (=to a particular stage) 到…的阶段[程度，地步] *The beams had weakened to the point of being dangerous.* 那些横梁已经老化到危险的地步。| **if it comes to the point** (=if a particular situation is reached when a decision has to be made) 到了关键时刻，到必须作出决定的时候 *If it comes to the point, I am prepared to resign over this.* 必要时我愿为此辞职。

5 boiling point/freezing point/melting point etc the temperature at which something boils, freezes, melts etc 沸点/冰点/熔点等

6 the high/low point of the best or worst stage, or best or worst moment of something 最佳/最糟[差]阶段[时期，时刻]：*The firework display was the high point of the evening.* 烟火表演是当晚的高潮。| *This was the low point of his teaching career.* 这是他教学生涯的低谷。

7 the point of no return a stage in a process or activity when it becomes impossible to stop it or do something different 有进无退[欲罢不能]的地步

8 be on the point of (doing) something to be going to do something very soon 正要做某事：*I was on the point of leaving when the phone rang.* 我正要走时，电话铃响了。

9 ▶QUALITY/FEATURE 特质/特点◀ [C] a particular quality or feature that something or someone has 特点，特质，特征：*She tried to remind herself of his good points.* 她极力使自己想起他的种种优点。| *What are the points to look out for when buying a new computer?* 在买一台新电脑时需要特别注意哪些性能？| **the finer points of** (=the small details of quality) 细节 *He went on to educate us all on the finer points in choosing champagne.* 他继续教我们在选择香槟酒时应注意的细节。| **it has its points** (=used to say that something has some good features or qualities) 它自有它的优点[好处] *It's not a car that I would buy, but it does have its points.* 我不会买那辆车，但它确实有自己的优点。| **selling point** (=a feature that will help to sell sth) 卖点 *The main selling point of the product is its price.* 该产品的主要卖点是它的价格。| **strong/weak point** (=a part of someone or something that is good or bad) 长处，优点；短处，缺[弱]点 *Neatness is not his strong point.* 他这个人不大注重整洁。

10 ▶PURPOSE 目的◀ [U] the purpose or aim of something 目的；目标；意义：*The whole point of this experiment is to show how the chemicals react in water.* 这项实验的目的是要显示这些化学品在水中是如何起反应的。| **there is no point** *I could see that there was no point in arguing with him.* 我觉得与他争论没有什么意义。| **not see the point** *I couldn't see the point of trying to explain.* 我看不出极力解释有什么用处。| **what is the point?** *What was the point in working to pass exams if there were no jobs available?* 如果没有空缺的职位，努力通过考试还有什么意思呢？

11 up to a point to some extent, but not completely 在某程度上：*I agree with you up to a point.* 我不完全同意你的看法。

12 ▶SHARP END 尖端◀ [C] a sharp end of something〔某物的〕尖(端)：*a knife with a very sharp point* 很尖的刀子

13 at the point of a gun/at gun point if you do something at gun point, you do it while someone is pointing a gun towards you 在枪口(威逼)之下

14 ▶GAMES/SPORT 比赛/运动◀ [C] a unit used to show the score in a game or sport〔比赛或运动中的〕分数，得分：*Steve Jones is 15 points ahead.* 史蒂夫·琼斯领先15分。| **win/lose a point** *She lost three points for that fall.* 她因为那次摔倒而丢了3分。| **beat sb on points/win on points** (=win a boxing match by gaining more points than your opponent rather than by defeating them completely)〔拳击比赛中〕以点数击败某人/以点数获胜

15 ▶NUMBERS 数字◀ [C] a sign (.) used to separate a whole number from any decimals that follow it 小数点

16 ▶MEASURE ON A SCALE 刻度表上的测量单位◀ [C] a mark or measure on a scale 点；度：*The cost of living has risen by three percentage points.* 生活指数已增长了三个百分点。

17 ▶SMALL SPOT 小点◀ [C] a very small spot 一小点：*The stars shone like tiny points of light in the sky.* 星星像一个个小光点一样在天空中闪烁。

18 ▶DIRECTION 方向◀ [C] one of the marks on a COMPASS that shows direction 罗盘(方位)点：*the points of the compass* 罗盘上的方位点

19 ▶PIECE OF LAND 一块土地◀ [C] a long thin piece of land that stretches out into the sea 尖岬，岬角

20 ▶ELECTRICITY 电◀ [C] a piece of plastic with holes in it which is fixed to a wall and to which electrical equipment can be connected 插座

21 make a point (of doing sth) to do something deliberately so that people notice 特意做某事〔以使人注意〕：*I always make a point of introducing new members to the chairman.* 我总是特意把新成员介绍给主席。

22 ▶RAILWAYS 铁路◀ points [plural] a piece of railway track that can be moved to allow a train to cross over from one track to another〔铁路上的〕道岔，转辙器

23 ▶DANCING 跳舞◀ points [plural] *technical* the ends of a dancer's feet, on which they balance when they are dancing in BALLET【术语】〔芭蕾舞中的〕足尖

Frequencies of the noun **point** in spoken and written English
名词point在英语口语和书面语中的使用频率

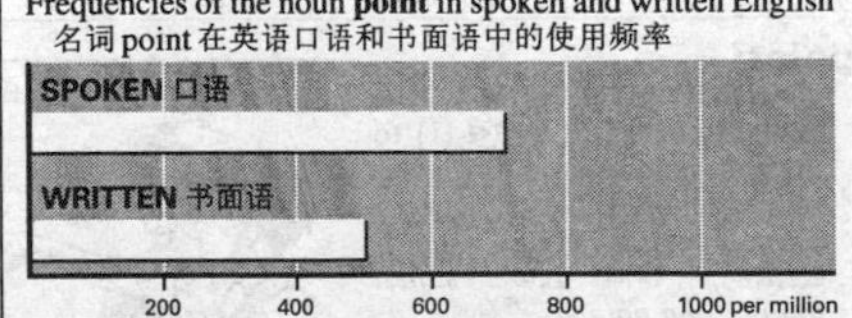

Based on the British National Corpus and the Longman Lancaster Corpus
据英国国家语料库和朗文兰开斯特语料库

This graph shows that the noun **point** is more common in spoken English than in written English. This is because it is used in a lot of common spoken phrases. 本图表显示，名词point在英语口语中的使用频率远远高于书面语，因为口语中很多常用短语是由point构成的。

point (*n*) **SPOKEN PHRASES**
含 point 的口语短语

24 what's the point?/there's no point used to say that you do not think something is worth doing 有什么意义[用处]呢?/没有意义[用处]: *I could try to help but what's the point? He never listens to anyone.* 我可以尽力帮忙, 但有什么用呢? 他根本不听任何人说的话。| **what's the point in doing sth?/there's no point in doing sth** *There's no point in lying, I'll find out anyway.* 撒谎没有什么用, 无论如何我都会发现的。

25 I can't see any point in used to say that you do not think something has any real purpose 我看不出…有什么意义[用处]: *I've got no time for politics – I can't see any point in it.* 我没有时间勾心斗角 —— 我看不出那有什么意义。| **I can't see any point in doing sth** *I can't see any point in going there when we can just call instead.* 既然我们打个电话就行了, 我看不出去那里还有什么意义。

26 that's the point used when emphasizing what the main fact, idea or purpose of something is 那才是重要的, 那才是问题所在: *It costs me more but it lasts much longer, you see. That's the point.* 你瞧这东西虽然贵点, 但它也更耐用。这才是最重要的。| **that's the whole point** *But that's the whole point – the richer you are, the more you should pay.* 但问题是 —— 你越富有, 你应付的钱就越多。

27 that's a good point used when someone mentions an important fact or detail that you had not thought of 说得对(我没有想到这一点), 所言极是: *"But how will you get there?" "That's a good point, I won't have the car, will I?"* "但你如何到那里去呢?" "说的也是, 我拿不到那辆车, 不是吗?"

28 that's not the point used to tell someone that the fact or reason they are mentioning is not at all important 那并不重要, 那并不是问题所在: *Maybe you were trying to be helpful, but that's not the point, is it?* 或许你极力想帮忙, 但那并不重要, 是吗?

29 (that's) more to the point used to say that a particular fact or reason is more important than the one that was just mentioned 那才更重要: *Yes, she has stolen the money, but why? That's more to the point.* 对, 她是偷了钱, 但是为了什么? 这才是更重要的问题。

30 I see your/his point used to say that you can understand why someone has a particular idea or opinion 我明白你/他的意思: *He thought the meeting was a waste of time, and I could see his point.* 他认为那次会议是浪费时间, 我能明白他的意思。

31 I take your point used to tell someone you accept that their idea or opinion is correct 我接受你的看法, 你说的是: *I take your point about that picture. It does look better here.* 我认为你对那幅画的看法很正确, 它在这里看起来确实更好一些。

32 point taken used to tell someone that you accept that you were wrong and they were right about something 我承认我是错了, 你说的是: *OK, point taken. I won't interfere any more.* 好吧, 你说得对。我不会再干预了。

33 you/they have a point used to say that someone has an idea or opinion that is right 你(们)/他们说得有道理: *Sue thinks it would be better to go by train, and I think she has a point.* 休认为乘火车去更好, 我认为她说得有道理。

34 not to put too fine a point on it used when you are saying something in a very direct way that might upset someone 直言不讳地说, 直话直说, 说句老实话: *She was being a real pain in the ass, not to put too fine a point on it.* 直话直说, 她真是个令人讨厌的家伙。

point² *v*

1 ►SHOW STH WITH YOUR FINGER 用手指向某物◄ [I] to show someone something by holding up one of your fingers or a thin object towards it (用手指或细物)指, 指向: *"Look!" said a soldier, and pointed.* "看!"一个士兵指着说。| *John leaned over her and pointed ahead.* 约翰向她俯过身来, 指着前方。| **[+at]** *I could see him pointing at me and telling the other guests what I had said.* 我看见他一边指着我, 一边告诉其他客人我说过的话。| **[+to]** *He shook his head, and pointed to a gate at the bottom of the field.* 他摇摇头, 指向田地尽头的一个大门。| **[+with]** *The driver pointed with his whip.* 马车夫用他的鞭子指着。

point 指, 指向

2 ►BE AIMED 对着◄ [I always+adv/prep] to be aimed in a particular direction 面向, 对着: *The arrow always points north.* 箭头总是指向北方。| **[+at]** *There were TV cameras pointing at us.* 有电视摄像机对着我们。| **[+to]** *The hands of the clock pointed to a quarter past one.* 时钟的指针指向1点1刻。

3 ►AIM STH 瞄准某物◄ [T] to hold something so that it is aimed towards a person or thing 用(某物)对准(某人或某物), 使指向: **point sth at** *I wish you'd stop pointing that gun at men.* 我希望你别再用那支枪对着别人。| *Lionel had stood up and was pointing an accusing finger at his brother.* 莱昂内尔站了起来, 用手指着弟弟以示谴责。

4 ►SHOW SB WHERE TO GO 为某人指明方向◄ [T always+adv/prep] to show someone which direction they should go in 为(某人)指明方向, 指路: **point sb down/along/to etc** *The receptionist pointed her down the corridor to the manager's office.* 接待员指引她沿着走廊去经理办公室。| *He pointed Mrs Morel to a large armchair.* 他指引莫雷尔太太坐上一把大扶手椅。

5 ►WALLS/BUILDINGS 墙/建筑物◄ [T] to put new CEMENT between the bricks of a wall (用水泥)勾嵌(墙的砌缝)

6 point your toes to stretch the ends of your feet downwards when you are dancing (跳舞时)向下绷直脚尖

7 point the finger at to blame someone or say that they have done something wrong 指责(某人), 责怪: *I don't want to point the finger at anyone in particular – I think we are all to blame for this.* 我不想指责某个人 —— 我认为我们所有人对此都有责任。

8 point the way a) to show the direction that something is in 指明方向: *A line of buildings pointed the way to the village.* 一排建筑物指明了村子的所在。**b)** to show how something could change or develop successfully 指明如何改变[成功地发展], 指明方向: *We feel that this report points the way forward for the water industry.* 我们觉得这份报告为水工业的发展指明了方向。

point sth ↔ **out** *phr v* **1** [T] to show something to someone by pointing at it 把(某物)指出来(给某人看), 指出: *They walked into the car park and Cook pointed out his new car.* 他们走进停车场, 库克指出了他的新车。| *My mother pointed him out to me.* 妈妈把他指给我看。**2** [T] to tell someone something that they did not already know or had not thought about 指出, 指明: *He pointed out the dangers of setting out without proper equipment.* 他指出了没有适当的装备就出发的种种危险。| **point out that** *The officer pointed out that the story was somewhat hard to believe.* 那位官员指出, 那种说法有点令人难以置信。| **point sth out to sb** *Mr Rogers had pointed out to us that we should keep well away from the lake.* 罗杰斯先生向我们指出我们应远离那个湖。

point to sth *phr v* [T] to mention something because you think it is important (因认为重要而)提到(某事物): *Many politicians have pointed to the need for a written constitution.* 很多政客都提出需要一部成文宪法。

point to/towards sb/sth *phr v* [T] if something points to a fact, it makes it seem very likely that it is true 表明…大有可能: *All the evidence pointed to Blake as the murderer.* 所有的证据都表明布莱克很可能是凶手。

point sth ↔ **up** *phr v* [T] *formal* to make something seem more important or more noticeable【正式】使(某事)显得更重要[明显], 清楚地表明, 强调: *The latest economic figures point up the failure of the government's policies.* 最近的经济数字表明了政府政策的失败。

point-blank /ˌ·ˈ·◂/ *adv* **1** if you say or refuse something point-blank, you do it directly and without trying to explain your reasons 直截了当地, 干脆地, 断然地: *I told him point-blank that I did not want to be involved in the deal.* 我直截了当地告诉他我不想卷入这宗交易。**2** a gun fired point-blank is fired very close to the person or thing it is aimed at 近距离平射地, 直射地: *Dodds fired both barrels point-blank at his former lover.* 多兹双管齐发, 近距离向他的旧情人射击。—**point-blank** *adj*: *shot at point-blank range* 近距离中弹

point du·ty /ˈ· ˌ··/ *n* [U] *BrE* a police officer who is on point duty stands at a place where two roads cross and controls the traffic passing through【英】(交通警察在十字路口的)岗位值勤

point·ed /ˈpɔɪntɪd; ˈpɔɪntɨd/ *adj* [usually before noun 一般用于名词前] **1** having a point at the end 尖的: *Poirot was a dapper little man with a pointed beard.* 波洛是一个矮小精悍、留着尖胡子的男人。—see picture on page A6 参见 A6 页图 **2 a pointed comment/look/remark** something you say or do in a deliberately direct and noticeable way, in order to show your annoyance or disapproval 尖锐的评论/犀利的目光/一针见血的

话: *Mark's father made a pointed remark about his hair just as we were leaving.* 我们正要离开时，马克的父亲就他的头发说了句尖刻的话。**—pointedly** *adv*: *He looked at his watch pointedly. "Are you ready to go or not?"* 他故意看了看自己的手表。"你准备走还是不走?"

point·er /ˈpɔɪntə; ˈpɔɪntə/ *n* [C]
1 ▶SHOWS NUMBER/DIRECTION ETC 显示数字/方向等◀ a thin piece of metal that points to a number or direction on a piece of equipment, for example on a measuring instrument〔仪器等的〕指针: *The pointer is halfway between 105 and 110 pounds.* 指针指在105和110磅中间。
2 ▶STICK 棍棒◀ a long stick used to point at things on a map, board etc 指示棒, 教鞭
3 ▶ADVICE 忠告◀ a useful piece of advice or information that helps you do or understand something 提示; 忠告; 点子: **[+on]** *Ralph gave me some pointers on my golf swing.* 拉尔夫就我打高尔夫球的挥杆姿势提出了一些建议。
4 ▶SIGN 标志◀ something that shows how a situation is developing, or is a sign of what might happen in the future 标志; 线索; 暗示: **[+to]** *A pointer to the growing interest in healthy eating has been the rise in sales of fresh fish.* 鲜鱼销售量的增长表明人们对健康饮食日益关注。
5 ▶DOG 狗◀ a hunting dog that stands very still and points with its nose to where birds or animals are hiding〔能站着不动用鼻子指示猎物所在处的〕指示猎犬

poin·til·lis·m /ˈpwæntəlɪzm; ˈpwæntɪlɪzəm/ *n* [U] a style of painting popular in the late 19th century that uses small spots of colour all over the painting, rather than brush strokes 点彩派, 点彩画法〔19世纪晚期流行的一种绘画风格〕**—pointillist** *adj* **—pointillist** *n* [C]

point·less /ˈpɔɪntlɪs; ˈpɔɪntləs/ *adj* **1** without any purpose or meaning 无目的的; 无意义的: *a pointless waste of money* 无意义地浪费金钱 | *Life just seemed so pointless.* 人生好像没有什么意义。**2** not likely to have any useful result 无益的, 无用的: *a pointless quarrel* 无用的争吵 | **it is pointless to do sth** *I think it would be pointless to discuss this issue again.* 我认为再讨论这个问题没有什么用处。| **it is pointless doing sth** *It's pointless telling her to clean her room – she'll never do it.* 叫她打扫自己的房间是没有用的, 她决不会干的。**—pointlessly** *adv* **—pointlessness** *n* [U]

point man /ˈ· ·/ *n* [C] *AmE* a soldier who goes ahead of a group to see if there is any danger【美】先头侦察兵

point of or·der /ˌ· · ˈ··/ *n* [C] *formal* a rule connected with the organization of an official meeting【正式】〔正式会议的〕议事程序问题: *One MP raised an objection on a point of order.* 一名下议院议员就议事程序问题提出反对意见。

point of ref·e·rence /ˌ· · ˈ···/ *n* [C] something you already know about that helps you understand a situation 参照依据, 参照标准

point of sale /ˌ· · ˈ·◂/ *n* [C] the place or shop where a product is sold 销售处[点]: *an advertising campaign in which posters and leaflets would be displayed at the point of sale* 于销售点张贴海报和派发小册子的宣传攻势

point of view /ˌ· · ˈ·/ *n* [C] **1** a particular way of thinking about or judging a situation 视角, 角度: *From a purely environmental point of view, this is not a good decision.* 从纯粹环保的角度来看, 这不是一个好决定。**2** someone's own personal opinion or attitude about something 观点, 看法, 意见: *I respect your point of view, but I really don't agree with you.* 我尊重你的观点, 但是我真的不敢苟同。| *My parents never seem to be able to see my point of view.* 我的父母好像从来都不能理解我的观点。

points·man /ˈpɔɪntsmən; ˈpɔɪntsmən/ *n* [C] *BrE* someone who operates the short RAILs that move so that a train can change from one set of tracks to another【英】铁路扳道工

point-to-point /ˌ· · ˈ·◂/ *n* [C] *BrE* a race for horses that goes across country areas【英】定点越野赛马

Poi·rot /pwɑˋro; ˈpwɑːrəʊ/, **Her·cule** /ˈɛrkjul; ˈeəkjuːl/ a character in books by Agatha Christie. He is a clever Belgian DETECTIVE (=someone whose job is to solve crimes and catch criminals), who always discovers who the criminal is by using the 'little grey cells' (=his brain). 波洛〔阿加莎·克里斯蒂小说中一人物。他是一名聪明的比利时侦探, 脑筋一动总能找出罪犯〕

Hercule Poirot
赫尔克里·波洛

poise¹ /pɔɪz; pɔɪz/ *n* [U] **1** a calm, confident way of behaving, combined with an ability to control your feelings or reactions in difficult situations 镇定, 自信, 泰然自若, 沉着: *Travelling around Europe by herself seems to have given Louisa more poise and confidence.* 路易莎只身一人遍游欧洲, 这好像使她变得更加沉着自信了。**2** a graceful way of moving or standing, so that your body seems balanced and not awkward〔优雅的〕体态, 姿态: *the poise of a dancer* 舞蹈者优美的体态

poise² *v* [T always+adv/prep] to put or hold something in a carefully balanced position, especially above something else 使平衡, 使平稳: **poise sth over/above etc** *Benjamin poised the bottle over the second glass and glanced at Consuela to see if she wanted a drink.* 本杰明稳稳地拿着瓶子, 停在第二个玻璃杯上方, 然后瞥了孔苏埃拉一眼, 看她是否想喝。

poised /pɔɪzd; pɔɪzd/ *adj* **1** [not before noun 不用于名词前] not moving but ready to move or do something at any moment (摆好姿势) 准备行动的: **[+for/on etc]** *She saw Matthew poised on the board for a swift, controlled racing dive.* 她看见马修在跳板上摆好姿势准备来一个敏捷而且控制得很好的入水动作。| **poised to do sth** *He was waiting with the door open, poised to jump, as the train pulled into the station.* 火车进站时, 他开着门等着, 准备随时跳下车去。**2** [not before noun 不用于名词前] completely ready to do or achieve something, and about to do it 准备就绪的, 完全作好准备的: **poised to do sth** *At this point, Spain was poised to become the dominant power in Europe.* 这时, 西班牙作好了成为欧洲大国的一切准备。**3** [not before noun 不用于名词前] not moving and seeming to hang in the air 似悬着不动的: **[+over/above etc]** *Noriko was holding her chopsticks poised in the air, as though waiting for me to say something.* 诺里科拿着筷子没动, 似乎在等我说些什么。| *Stanley's hand remained poised over the open box as the footsteps came closer.* 随着脚步的临近, 史坦利的手悬在打开了的箱子上面。**4** [not before noun 不用于名词前] in a position in which two things have an equally strong influence 平衡的; 介乎两者的: **[+between]** *The tone of the book is poised between comedy and moral seriousness.* 这本书的格调介乎喜剧和道德教训之间。**5** behaving in a calm, confident way, and able to control your feelings and reactions 镇定的, 自信的, 泰然自若的, 沉着的: *Abbey walked to the microphone, poised and smiling.* 阿比泰然自若、笑容满面地走向麦克风。

poi·son¹ /ˈpɔɪzn̩; ˈpɔɪzən/ *n* **1** [C,U] a substance that can cause death or serious illness if you eat it, drink it etc 毒, 毒物, 毒药: *These fruits contain a deadly poison.* 这些水果含有剧毒。| *Joanna committed suicide by swallowing poison.* 乔安娜服毒自杀了。**2** [C,U] something such as an emotion or idea that makes you behave badly or become very unhappy 使人不愉快的事物, 有危害的东西: *Anger and hatred are poisons that destroy a person's emotional life.* 愤怒和仇恨是毁掉一个人的感情生活的毒素。**3 what's your poison?** *spoken* a humorous way of asking someone which alcoholic drink they would like【口】〔幽默说法〕你想喝什么酒? —see also 另见 **one man's meat is another man's poison** (MEAT (8))

poison² *v* [T] **1** to harm or kill someone by giving them poison 毒害; 毒杀: *The whole family had been poisoned with strychnine.* 这家人全被马钱子碱毒死了。**2** to add poison to something 放毒于, 下毒于: *Germanicus feared that someone had poisoned his food.* 杰马尼库斯害怕有人在他的食物中下了毒。| *poisoned arrows* 毒箭 **3** to make land, rivers, air etc impure, especially by the use of harmful chemicals〔尤指通过使用有害化学品而〕污染〔土地、河流、空气等〕: *We are poisoning our rivers with pesticides and toxic waste.* 我们以杀虫剂和有毒废弃物污染着我们的河流。**4** to have very harmful and unpleasant effects on someone's mind and emotions 毒害, 对…有不良的影响, 危害: *Her father's tyranny had poisoned her childhood.* 她父亲的专制对她的童年产生了不良影响。| *these violent videos that poison the minds of the young* 这些毒害年轻人思想的暴力录影带 **5 poison sb's mind against sb** to make someone dislike another person by saying bad and untrue things〔通过说坏话、撒谎〕使某人对另一人产生厌恶感 **6** *especially BrE* to infect a part of the body【尤英】使〔身体的某部分〕受感染 **7 poisoned chalice** an important job that someone is given, which is likely to cause them a lot of trouble 可能带来很多麻烦的重要工作 **—poisoner** *n* [C]

poison gas /ˌ·· ˈ·/ *n* [U] gas that causes death or serious injury, used especially against an enemy in a war〔尤指战争中使用的〕毒气

poi·son·ing /ˋpɔɪzn̩ɪŋ; ˈpɔɪzənɪŋ/ *n* [C,U] illness caused by swallowing, touching, or breathing in a poisonous substance 中毒: *Several cases of poisoning have been reported.* 已接获数宗中毒事件的报告。| **alcohol/mercury/radiation poisoning** (=caused by a particular substance) 酒精/水银/辐射中毒 —see also 另见 FOOD POISONING

poison i·vy /ˌ··ˈ··/ *n* [U] a bush or VINE that causes pain on your skin when you touch it 毒漆, 气根毒藤〔触碰会引起皮肤疼痛〕

poison oak /ˌ··ˈ·/ *n* [U] a North American plant that causes painful spots on your skin when you touch it 栎叶漆树〔北美植物〕

poi·son·ous /ˋpɔɪzn̩əs; ˈpɔɪzənəs/ *adj* **1** containing poison or producing poison 有毒的; 引起中毒的: *poisonous mushrooms* 有毒蘑菇 | *poisonous snakes* 毒蛇 **2** full of unpleasant and unfriendly feelings 充满敌意的, 令人很不愉快的: *There was a poisonous atmosphere in the household that made Bonita feel very uneasy.* 家里充满了敌意, 这使博尼塔感到很不自在。**3** someone who is poisonous seems to get pleasure from causing arguments, unhappiness etc〔人〕以引起争论[不快]而取乐的; 讨厌的; 恶毒的: *That poisonous bastard Lucett told Morris I was seeing his wife.* 那个搬弄是非的坏蛋卢塞特告诉莫里斯我在和他的妻子约会。—**poisonously** *adv*

poison-pen let·ter /ˌ··ˈ·ˌ··/ *n* [C] a letter that is not signed and that says nasty and unpleasant things about the person it has been sent to 匿名〔诽谤〕信

Poi·ti·er /ˋpwɑtje; ˈpwɒtieɪ/, **Sid·ney** /ˋsɪdnɪ; ˈsɪdni/ (1924-) a US film actor and DIRECTOR, who was one of the first black actors to appear in films playing serious characters. His films include *The Blackboard Jungle* (1955), *In the Heat of the Night* (1967), and *Guess Who's Coming to Dinner* (1967). 普瓦蒂耶〔(1924-), 美国电影演员、导演。他是最早在影片中饰演严肃角色的黑人演员之一。演过的影片有《黑板丛林》(1955)、《炎热的夜晚》(1967) 和《猜猜谁来吃晚餐》(1967)〕

poke¹ /pok; pəʊk/ *v*

1 ►WITH A FINGER/STICK ETC 用手指/棒等◄ [T] to quickly push into something or someone with your finger, a stick, or something pointed 戳, 捅, 刺: *Andy poked the fish to see if it was still alive.* 安迪戳了戳那条鱼, 看它是否还活着。| *Be careful with that umbrella, or you'll poke someone in the eye.* 小心那把伞, 否则你会戳到别人的眼睛。—see picture on page A21 参见 A21 页图

2 ►THROUGH A SPACE/HOLE 通过空隙/洞◄ **a)** [T always+adv/prep] to move or push something through a space or opening 插; 伸出; 探出: *He poked his hands deep into his pockets.* 他把双手深深地插进口袋里。| **poke your head around the door/through the window etc** *One of the nurses poked her head around the door.* 一名护士从门后探出头来。**b) ►BE SEEN** 被看见◄ [I always+adv/prep] if something is poking through or out of something else, you can see part of it but not all of it 从…中露出[伸出, 探出]: *Ella looked at the tiny face poking out of the wool blanket.* 埃拉看着那张从毛毯里露出的小脸。| *Weeds had started poking through the cracks in the path.* 杂草已开始从小径的缝隙中钻了出来。

3 poke a hole to make a hole or hollow area in something by pushing something pointed into or through it〔在某物上〕戳出[捅出]一个洞: *Poke a hole in the dough and form it into a doughnut shape.* 在面团上戳一个洞, 把它做成面包圈的形状。

4 poke fun at make fun of someone in an unkind way 嘲弄, 取笑: *Some of the kids were poking fun at Judy because of the way she dressed.* 一些孩子因朱迪的衣着而取笑她。

5 poke your nose into *informal* to take an interest or get involved in someone else's private affairs【非正式】干预[插手]〔别人的私事〕; 管闲事: *I don't want him poking his nose into our marriage.* 我不想让他插手我们的婚姻。

6 poke the fire to move coal or wood in a fire with a stick to make it burn better〔用棍棒〕拨[捅]火〔使之烧得更旺〕

7 ►SEX 性◄ [T] *slang taboo* to have sex with a woman【俚, 讳】与〔女人〕性交

poke around/about *phr v* [I] *BrE informal*【英, 非正式】**1** to look for something by moving a lot of things around 到处寻找, 乱翻: *James began poking about in the cupboard, looking for the sugar.* 詹姆斯开始在橱柜中乱翻, 希望能找到些糖。**2** to try to find out information about other people's private lives, business etc, in a way that annoys them 打听, 刺探〔别人的私事〕: *I don't want you poking around in my business.* 我不想你管我的闲事。

poke at sth *phr v* [T] to keep pushing something by making repeated movements with something pointed 反复地戳[轻推]〔某物〕; 拨弄: *He was poking at the dust with his stick, making little patterns.* 他用拐杖拨弄灰尘, 画出一些小图案来。

poke² *n* **1 give sb/sth a poke** to quickly push your fingers, a stick etc into something or someone 戳, 刺: *Vanessa gave me a poke in the ribs.* 瓦妮莎碰了一下我的肋骨。**2** [C] *AmE old-fashioned slang* a WALLET containing money【美, 过时, 俚】装有钱的钱包

pok·er /ˋpokɚ; ˈpəʊkə/ *n* **1** [U] a card game that people usually play for money〔通常指赌钱的〕扑克牌戏, 纸牌戏 **2** [C] a metal stick used to move coal or wood in a fire to make it burn better 拨火棒

poker-faced /ˌ··ˈ·◄/ *adj* showing no expression on your face 面无表情的, 不动声色的, 一本正经的: *Melanie waited poker-faced for their next offer.* 梅拉妮面无表情地等着他们下一次出价。—**poker face** *n* [singular]

po·ker·work /ˋpokɚˌwɝk; ˈpəʊkəwɜːk/ *n* [U] pictures or patterns burned onto the surface of wood or leather with hot tools, or the art of making these pictures〔在木头或皮革上的〕烙画(艺术)

pok·ey /ˋpokɪ; ˈpəʊki/ *n* [C] *AmE old-fashioned* a jail【美, 过时】监狱

pok·y, pokey /ˋpokɪ; ˈpəʊki/ *adj* **1** too small and not very pleasant or comfortable 简陋的, 不舒适的, 狭小的: *The whole family was crammed into two poky little rooms.* 全家人挤在两间狭小的房间里。**2** *AmE* doing things very slowly, especially in a way that you find annoying【美】慢吞吞的, 缓慢的, 磨磨蹭蹭的: *I got behind some poky driver on the freeway.* 在高速公路上, 我落在了一些慢吞吞的司机后面。

pol /pɑl; pɒl/ *n* [C] *AmE informal* a politician【美, 非正式】政客

Po·lack /ˋpolæk; ˈpəʊlæk/ *n* [C] *AmE* an insulting word for someone from Poland【美】波兰佬〔侮辱性词语〕

Po·land /ˋpolənd; ˈpəʊlənd/ a country in central Europe, east of Germany and west of Belarus. Population: 38,634,000 (2001). Capital: Warsaw. Poland was an important European power between the 14th and 17th centuries. After World War II, Poland became a Communist country, and its government was strongly influenced by the former Soviet Union. It is now a member of the European Union. Poland's main industries traditionally include coal, shipbuilding, and farming. People from Poland are called **Poles**. 波兰〔中欧一国家, 位于德国以东, 白俄罗斯以西。人口: 38,634,000 (2001), 首都: 华沙。14 至 17 世纪的波兰是欧洲强国。二战之后, 波兰成为社会主义国家, 其政府颇受前苏联的影响。如今, 波兰成为欧盟成员国, 其主要行业传统上包括采煤、造船及农业。波兰人的英文为Pole〕—**Polish** *n, adj*

po·lar /ˋpolɚ; ˈpəʊlə/ *adj* **1** close to, or connected with the North Pole and the South Pole 近南极[北极]的, 极地的: *As our climate warms up, the polar ice caps will begin to melt.* 随着我们的气候逐渐变暖, 极地的冰冠也将融化。**2** *technical* related to one of the POLES of a MAGNET【术语】磁极的 **3 polar opposite/extreme** something exactly or completely opposite in character or nature〔性格或性质〕完全相反, 正好相反

polar bear /ˌ··ˈ·/ *n* [C] a large white bear that lives near the North Pole 北极熊

Polaris /pəˋlærɪs; pəˈlɑːrɨs/ another name for the Pole Star 北极星〔Pole Star 的别称〕

po·lar·ise /ˋpoləˌraɪz; ˈpəʊləraɪz/ *v* a British spelling of POLARIZE polarize 的英式拼法

po·lar·i·ty /poˋlærətɪ; pəˈlærɨti/ *n* [C,U] **1** *formal* the fact of people, opinions, or ideas being completely different or opposite to each other【正式】〔人、意见或观点的〕截然相反, 截然对立, 分歧: **[+between]** *the supposed polarity between the intellect and the emotions* 理智和感情之间假定的对立 **2** *technical* the state of having either a positive or negative electric charge【术语】〔电的〕极性; 正负极

po·lar·ize also 又作 **-ise** *BrE*【英】/ˋpoləˌraɪz; ˈpəʊləraɪz/ *v* [I,T] *formal* to divide into clearly separate groups with opposite beliefs, ideas, or opinions, or to make people do this【正式】(使)两极分化: *a highly controversial issue that has polarized the country* 使该国两极分化的极具争议的问题 | *Patterns of political support had become polarized between the north and south.* 南北之间政治支持模式已变得两极化了。—**polarization** /ˌpoləraˋzeʃən; ˌpəʊləraɪˈzeɪʃən/ *n* [U]

Po·lar·oid /ˋpoləˌrɔɪd; ˈpəʊlərɔɪd/ *n trademark*【商标】**1** [C] a camera that uses a special film to produce a photograph very quickly 宝丽来一次成像照相机, 拍立得照相机 **2** [C] a photograph taken with a Polaroid camera 宝丽来一次成像照片 **3** [U] a special material which is put on the glass in SUNGLASSES, car windows etc to make the sun seem less bright〔用于太阳镜、汽车玻璃等的〕偏振片, 宝丽来偏光薄膜 **4 Polaroids** [plural] dark glasses with Polaroid material on them〔含有偏振材料的〕太阳眼镜, 柔光眼镜

pole¹ /pol; pəʊl/ *n* [C]
1 ▶STICK/POST 棒/杆◀ a long stick or post usually made of wood or metal, often set upright in the ground to support something 杆, 柱, 竿: *a telephone pole* 电话线杆 | *a flagpole* 旗杆 | *The dusty curtains hung from unpolished brass poles.* 满是灰尘的窗帘挂在未磨光的黄铜杆上。
2 ▶NORTH/SOUTH POLE 北极/南极◀ the most northern or most southern point on a PLANET, especially the Earth〔尤指地球的〕南[北]极; 地极: *Amundsen's expedition was the first to reach the pole.* 阿蒙森的探险队是第一支到达极地的队伍。
3 **be poles apart** two people or things that are poles apart are as different from each other as it is possible to be〔两人或两事物〕截然相反, 大相径庭: *Both brilliant pianists, Powell and Monk are poles apart in style.* 两位卓越的钢琴家 —— 鲍威尔和蒙克 —— 在风格上截然不同。
4 ▶OPPOSITE IDEAS/BELIEFS 相反的观点/信仰◀ one of two situations, ideas, or opinions that are the complete opposite of each other〔两种情况、观点或意见〕截然相反的两极之一; 极端: *We have the accumulation of wealth at one pole and poverty and misery at the other.* 在一端, 我们有财富堆积如山的人, 而在另一端却又有贫苦不堪的人。
5 ▶ELECTRICAL 电的◀ **a)** one of two points at the ends of a MAGNET where its power is the strongest 磁极 **b)** one of the two points at which wires can be fixed onto a BATTERY (1) in order to use its electricity 电极
6 ▶IN THE SKY 天空中◀ one of the two points in the sky, one to the north of the Earth and one to the south, around which the stars appear to turn 天空中的南[北]极

Pole² *n* [C] someone who comes from Poland 波兰人

pole³ *v* [I,T] to push a boat along in the water using a pole 用篙撑〔船〕

pole·axed /ˈpol,ækst; ˈpəʊlækst/ *adj* [not before noun 不用于名词前] **1** *informal* very surprised and shocked【非正式】非常惊讶的, 目瞪口呆的, 震惊的: *I was poleaxed when I heard I'd passed the exam.* 我听到自己通过考试的消息时简直惊呆了。**2** unable to stand because something has hit you very hard〔因受重击而〕不能站立的; 被击倒的: *The big Texan staggered and collapsed as if poleaxed.* 那个大块头得克萨斯人摇摇晃晃, 最后像猛挨了一下似的瘫倒在地。

pole·cat /ˈpol,kæt; ˈpəʊlkæt/ *n* [C] **1** a small dark brown wild animal that lives in northern Europe and can defend itself by producing an unpleasant smell〔北欧产的〕艾鼬, 臭貂 **2** *AmE informal* a SKUNK【美, 非正式】臭鼬

po·lem·ic /poˈlɛmɪk; pəˈlemɪk/ *n formal or technical*【正式或术语】**1** [C] a written or spoken statement that strongly criticizes or defends a particular idea, opinion, or person〔口头或书面的〕争辩, 辩论, 论战 **2** [U] also 又作 **polemics** the practice or skill of making such statements 争辩, 辩论; 辩论术, 辩论法: *Before long, the dispute had degenerated into heated polemics.* 不久, 分歧就演变成激烈的争辩。

po·lem·i·cal /poˈlɛmɪkḷ; pəˈlemɪkəl/ also 又作 **polemic** *adj formal or technical* using strong arguments to criticize or defend a particular idea, opinion, or person【正式或术语】争辩的, 辩论的, 论战的: *The health reforms were attacked in a highly polemical piece in the 'New Yorker'.* 医疗改革在《纽约客》的一篇措辞强烈的文章中遭到了抨击。—**polemically** /-kḷɪ; -kli/ *adv*

pole po·si·tion /ˈ· ·,··/ *n* [C,U] the front position at the beginning of a car or bicycle race〔汽车或自行车赛开始时的〕杆位, 前排位置, 有利位置

Pole Star, the /ˈ· ·/ *n* a star that is almost directly over the North Pole and that can be seen from the northern part of the world 北极星〔几乎正对北极的一颗恒星, 在地球的北部可以观测到〕

pole vault, the /ˈ· ·/ *n* the sport of jumping over a high bar using a long pole 撑竿跳高 —**pole vaulter** *n* [C]

po·lice¹ /pəˈlis; pəˈliːs/ *n* [plural] **1 the police** an official organization whose job is to make sure that people obey the law, to catch criminals, and to protect people and property 警察机关, 警方: *I heard the sound of a window breaking and called the police.* 我听到一扇窗户被打破的声音就叫了警察。| *Accidents involving injuries must be reported to the police.* 伤亡事故必须报警。| *a police car* 警车 **2** the people who work for this organization 警察: *Armed police surrounded the courthouse.* 武警包围了法院。| *Several police were injured when violence broke out.* 暴力事件发生后, 有几名警察受了伤。—see also 另见 MILITARY POLICE, SECRET POLICE

police² *v* [T] **1** to keep control over a particular area in order to make sure that laws are obeyed and people and property are protected, using a police or military force〔动用警察或军队对某地区〕实施管制, 维持治安, 管治: *The army was brought in to police the riot-torn city.* 军队受命对这个遭受骚乱蹂躏的城市实施管制。| *new methods of policing the neighborhood* 维持社区治安的新方法 **2** to control a particular activity or industry by making sure that people follow the correct rules concerning what they do 控制, 监督〔某活动或行业〕: *The agency was set up to police the nuclear power industry.* 设立这个机构是为了监督核电工业。—**policing** *n* [U]: *policing in rural areas* 农村地区的治安维持

police con·sta·ble /·ˈ· ˈ···/ *n* [C] *BrE formal* a police officer of the lowest rank【英, 正式】〔普通〕警员〔最低一级的警察〕

police court /·ˈ· ·/ *n* [C,U] *AmE* a court of law for small crimes【美】警察法庭〔审理轻微违法行为的法庭〕

police de·part·ment /·ˈ· ·,··/ *n* [C] *AmE* the official police organization in a particular area or city【美】〔某地区或城市的〕警察局, 警察部门

police dog /·ˈ· ·/ *n* [C] a dog trained by the police to find hidden drugs or catch criminals 警犬

police force /·ˈ· ·/ *n* [C] the official police organization in a country or area 警队, 警察部门: *Marshall joined the police force in 1983.* 马歇尔于1983年加入了警队。

po·lice·man /pəˈlismən; pəˈliːsmən/ *n plural* **policemen** /-mən; -mən/ [C] a male police officer 男警察

police of·fi·cer /·ˈ· ,···/ *n* [C] a member of the police 警察, 警员

CULTURAL NOTE 文化注释

In the US, there is a STEREOTYPE of police officers sitting in places that sell DOUGHNUTs all night, and eating too much while they are waiting to be given police work to do. In the UK, the old-fashioned stereotype of a policeman is of a friendly man who walks along the street and helps people, for example by telling them how to get to a place, or by telling them the time. 在美国, 警察的一种典型形象是夜间坐在卖炸面圈的地方, 等接到任务时已吃得太多了。在英国, 人们对警察有点过时的印象是, 他们很友好, 走街串巷地帮助别人, 例如为人指路或者告诉别人是什么时间了。

police state /·ˈ· ·/ *n* [C] a country where the government strictly controls people's freedom to meet, write or speak about politics, travel where they like etc 警察国家; 极权国家

police sta·tion /·ˈ· ,··/ *n* [C] the local office of the police in a town, part of a city etc〔城镇等的〕警察(分)局, 派出所

po·lice·wom·an /pəˈlis,wʊmən; pəˈliːs,wʊmən/ *n plural* **policewomen** /-,wɪmɪn; -,wɪmɪn/ [C] a female police officer 女警察

pol·i·cy /ˈpɑləsɪ; ˈpɒlḷsi/ *n* **1** [C,U] a course of action that has been officially agreed and chosen by a political party, business, or other organization 政策, 方针: *the government's disastrous economic policies* 政府灾难性的经济政策 | [**+on**] *The company operates a very strict policy on smoking.* 这家公司在抽烟方面有非常严格的规定。| **defence/housing/foreign etc policy** *the President's new health policy* 总统的新保健政策 | **policy maker** (=someone who helps to decide what an organization's policies will be) 政策制定者, 决策人 **2** [C] a contract with an insurance company, or an official written statement giving all the details of such a contract 保险单: *You should obtain a separate policy covering valuable household items.* 你应该给家里的贵重物品另外投保。**3** [C,U] a particular principle that you believe in and that influences the way you behave〔处事〕原则, 策略: *Well, it's always been my policy not to talk behind people's backs.* 不在背后谈论别人是我一贯的做人原则。| *You know what they say – honesty is the best policy.* 常言道 —— 人贵乎诚。

po·li·o /ˈpolɪo; ˈpəʊliəʊ/ also 又作 **po·li·o·my·e·li·tis** /,polɪo,maɪəˈlaɪtɪs; ,pəʊliəʊmaɪəˈlaɪtḷs/ *technical*【术语】*n* [U] a serious infectious disease of the nerves in the SPINE, often resulting in permanent PARALYSIS (=complete inability to move particular muscles) 脊髓灰质炎, 小儿麻痹症

pol·i sci /,pɑlɪ ˈsaɪ; ,pɒli ˈsaɪ/ *n* [U] *AmE informal* political science【美, 非正式】政治学

pol·ish¹ /ˈpɑlɪʃ; ˈpɒlɪʃ/ *v* [T] to make something smooth, bright, and shiny by rubbing it 擦亮, 擦光: *The floor had been polished to a satiny sheen.* 地板已被擦得光亮如缎。| *It was my duty to polish the silver on Saturdays.* 我的职责是每星期六把银器擦亮。—**polisher** *n* [C]: *an electric floor polisher* 电动地板磨光机[打蜡机] —**polishing** *n* [U] —see picture at 参见 CLEAN 图

polish sth ↔ **off** *phr v* [T] *informal* to finish food, work etc, quickly or easily【非正式】快速[轻易]做完〔工作等〕; 很快吃完

〔食物〕: *At lunch, Rowan polished off six sandwiches!* 吃午饭时，罗恩一转眼就吃掉了六份三明治！

polish sb ↔ **off** *phr v* [T] *AmE informal* to kill or defeat someone【美，非正式】杀死〔某人〕；击败〔某人〕: *Mather was polished off with a shotgun in another gangland killing.* 马瑟在另一次黑社会仇杀中被人用猎枪打死了。

polish sth ↔ **up** *phr v* [T] **1** to improve a skill or an ability by practising it〔通过练习〕提高，改善〔技术、能力〕: *I need to polish up my Spanish before we go on vacation.* 我们去度假前，我需要练习一下我的西班牙语。**2** to polish something 擦亮，擦光

polish² *n* **1** [C,U] a liquid, powder, or other substance used for rubbing into a surface to make it smooth and shiny 上光剂；擦光剂；上光蜡；鞋油；亮漆: *pine panelling gleaming with wax polish* 用上光蜡擦得闪闪发亮的松木镶板 | *furniture polish* 家具上光剂 | *shoe polish* 鞋油 —see also 另见 FRENCH POLISH **2** [U] a special quality of great skill and style in the way someone performs, writes, or behaves 优美，高雅，精致，完善: *Carla's writing has potential, but it lacks polish.* 卡拉的文章很有潜力，但不够优美。**3** [singular] a smooth shiny surface produced by polishing〔因摩擦而产生的〕光亮的表面 **4** [singular] an act of polishing a surface to make it smooth and shiny 擦亮，磨光: *An occasional wipe and polish with a soft cloth will keep wall tiles looking good.* 偶尔用软布擦拭能使墙砖保持美观。—see also 另见 **spit and polish** (SPIT² (5))

Pol·ish³ /ˈpolɪʃ; ˈpəʊlɪʃ/ *adj* from or connected with Poland, its people, or their language 来自波兰的；波兰的；波兰人的；波兰语的

Pol·ish⁴ *n* [U] the language of Poland 波兰语

pol·ished /ˈpɑlɪʃt; ˈpɒlɪʃt/ *adj* **1** shiny because of being rubbed, usually with polish〔通常使用上光剂来〕擦亮的，磨光的: *highly polished boots* 擦得很亮的靴子 **2** a polished performance, piece of writing etc is done with great skill and style〔表演、作品等〕完美的，优雅的，精致的 **3** polished social behaviour, speech etc is polite, confident, and graceful〔行为、言谈等〕彬彬有礼的，文雅的

po·lit·bu·ro /ˈpɑlɪtbjʊro; ˈpɒlɪtbjʊərəʊ/ *n* [C] the chief decision-making committee of a Communist party or Communist government〔共产党或其政府的〕政治局

S3 **po·lite** /pəˈlaɪt; pəˈlaɪt/ *adj* **1** behaving or speaking in a way that is correct for the social situation you are in, and showing that you are careful to consider other people's needs and feelings 有礼貌的，客气的: *a polite refusal* 婉言谢绝 | *What polite well-behaved children!* 多么懂礼貌的乖孩子！| **it is polite to do sth** *We left as soon as it was polite to do so.* 我们在不失礼节的情况下提早离开了。| *It's not polite to talk with your mouth full.* 嘴里塞满了食物讲话是不礼貌的。—opposite 反义词 RUDE (1), IMPOLITE **2** polite conversation, remarks etc are made because it is considered socially correct to do this 客套的，出于礼貌的: *a few polite remarks about the weather* 几句谈论天气的客套话 | *Nathaniel's sexual exploits are hardly the subject of polite conversation.* 纳撒尼尔的艳遇不能作为优雅谈话的话题。**3 in polite society/circles/company** *often humorous* among people who are considered to have a good education and correct social behaviour【常幽默】上流社会，上流阶层: *You can't use words like that in polite company.* 在上流阶层你不能使用那样的词语。**4 just/only being polite** *spoken* saying something you may not really believe or think, in order to avoid offending someone【口】只是出于礼貌: *I know Ian said he liked her singing, but he was just being polite.* 我知道伊恩说他喜欢她唱的歌，但这只是出于礼貌。—**politely** *adv* —**politeness** *n* [U]

pol·i·tic /ˈpɑləˌtɪk; ˈpɒlətɪk/ *adj formal* sensible and likely to bring advantage; PRUDENT【正式】明智的，精明的；考虑周到的，深谋远虑的；慎重的: *It would not be politic to ignore the reporters.* 忽视记者是不明智的。—see also 另见 POLITICS, BODY POLITIC

S3 W1 **po·lit·i·cal** /pəˈlɪtɪkl; pəˈlɪtɪkəl/ *adj* **1** [no comparative 无比较级] connected with the government or public affairs of a country and its relations with other countries 政治（上）的；政府的；政权的；有关行政的: *a loss of political freedom* 丧失政治上的自由 | *a long period of political stability* 长期的政治稳定 | *The UN is seeking a political solution rather than a military one.* 联合国正在寻求政治上的而不是军事上的解决方法。| *Cuba's political structure* 古巴的政治结构 | *one of the main political parties* 主要政党之一 **2** [no comparative 无比较级] connected with the ideas, activities, or advantage of a particular party or group in politics 与（政党）政治有关的，党派的: *a decision that was taken for purely political reasons* 纯粹出于政治原因而作出的决定 | *There were obvious political advantages in cutting taxes.* 减税在政治上有明显的好处。| *political propaganda* 政治宣传 **3** [no comparative 无比较级] a political offence or crime is harmful to a government〔罪行等〕危害政府的: *the summary execution of a political offender* 对一名政治犯的即时处决 **4** interested in or active in politics 对政治感兴趣的，政治上活跃的: *Most students these days aren't very political.* 如今大多数学生对政治都不怎么感兴趣。**5 political football** *especially BrE* a difficult problem which opposing politicians argue about or which each side deals with in a way that will bring them advantage【尤英】政治皮球〔对立的政客互相争议的难题。他们各以对自己有利的方式处理这问题〕: *It is unfortunate that education has become something of a political football.* 不幸的是教育在某种程度上已成了被踢来踢去的政治皮球。—see also 另见 POLITICALLY

political ac·tion com·mit·tee /ˌ·,···ˈ··,·ˈ/ *n* [C] *AmE* an organization formed by a business, union, or INTEREST GROUP to help raise money so that people who support their ideas can try to be elected for Congress; PAC【美】政治行动委员会〔由某个企业、工会或利益集团等组织的机构，旨在筹集资金帮助支持其想法的人竞选国会议员〕

political a·sy·lum /ˌ·,···ˈ··/ *n* [U] the right to remain safely in another country if you cannot live safely in your own because of the political situation there 政治避难（权），政治庇护: *refugees seeking political asylum* 寻求政治庇护的难民

political e·con·o·my /ˌ·,···ˈ···/ *n* [U] the study of the way nations organize the production and use of wealth 政治经济学

political ge·og·ra·phy /ˌ·,···ˈ···/ *n* [U] the study of the way the Earth's surface is divided up into different countries, rather than the way it is marked by rivers, mountains etc 政治地理学

po·lit·ic·ally /pəˈlɪtɪklɪ; pəˈlɪtɪkli/ *adv* in a political way 政治上: *Women were becoming more politically active.* 妇女在政治上变得愈来愈活跃。| *a politically motivated strike* 出于政治动机的罢工 | [sentence adverb 句子副词] *Politically, the organization was still very divided.* 从政治上来说，该组织仍然四分五裂。

politically cor·rect /ˌ·,···ˈ·/ *adj* language, behaviour, and attitudes that are politically correct are regarded as right and acceptable because they are careful to avoid offending women, black people, DISABLED people etc〔语言、行为、态度〕政治上正确的〔即避免冒犯妇女、黑人、残疾人士等〕: *It's not politically correct to say 'handicapped' anymore.* "残废"这种说法在政治上已不再适当。—see also 另见 PC² —**political correctness** /ˌ·,···ˈ··/ *n* [U]

CULTURAL NOTE 文化注释

When people talk about political correctness, they mean the language used to describe some groups of people, that other people may find offensive. For example, people no longer use words such as CRIPPLED to describe someone who is unable to walk because of an illness. Instead, you might use DISABLED or PHYSICALLY CHALLENGED. You can also say that someone 'has a DISABILITY'. Although it is still acceptable to say that someone is DEAF, some people now use HEARING IMPAIRED instead. Some people think that this practice has become too extreme, and they often make jokes about it, for example by saying that someone who is short is VERTICALLY CHALLENGED. 人们谈起"政治上正确"的时候，他们的意思是一些用来描述某个群体的语言在另一些人看来可能具有冒犯性。例如，人们不再用"瘸腿的"形容那些因患病不能行走的人；相反，可以用"腿脚不灵便"或"腿脚欠佳"来表述，也可以说某人"…不好使"。说某人聋虽然现在仍能过得去，但人们更愿意用"有听力障碍"来表达这个意思。也有人认为这样做太过火，还常常拿这个逗乐子，例如说个子矮的人"垂直高度困难"。

Political correctness has had an effect on everyday language too, particularly language used for describing jobs that were typically done in the past by men. These days, it is more common, for example, to refer to the person who is in charge of a committee as the CHAIRPERSON or simply 'the Chair' rather than call them a CHAIRMAN. Similarly, a FIREMAN is now often referred to as a FIREFIGHTER and a woman who acts is often called an actor rather than an actress. 政治上正确对日常语言也有所影响，特别是在谈及那些过去常由男人从事的职业的措辞上。例如，现在指某个委员会的负责人（主席）时，常用 chairperson 或者简单地叫 the Chair，而不用过去的指称 chairman。同样，fireman（消防员）现在常被叫做 firefighter，叫女演员 actor，而不是 actress。

political ma·chine /ˌ· ˌ·· ˈ·/ *n* [singular] *AmE* the system used by people with the same political interests to make sure that political decisions bring advantage to themselves or to their group【美】政治机器〔政治利益相同的人为确保政治决策给自己或自己的团体带来好处而采用的体制〕

political pris·on·er /ˌ· ˌ·· ˈ···/ *n* [C] someone who is put in prison because they oppose and criticize the government of their own country 政治犯〔因反对或批评本国政府而被投入监狱的人〕

political sci·ence /ˌ· ˌ·· ˈ··/ *n* [U] the study of politics and government 政治学 —**political scientist** *n* [C]

W2 **pol·i·ti·cian** /ˌpɑləˈtɪʃən; ˌpɒlɪ̆ˈtɪʃən/ *n* [C] **1** someone who works in politics, especially an elected member of a parliament or similar institution 政治家〔尤指议员等〕 **2** someone who is skilled at dealing with people or using the situation in an organization to bring advantage to themselves 政客，善于玩弄权术者: *You really have to be a politician to succeed in this place.* 你要在这个地方获得成功，就一定得有政客的手腕。

po·li·ti·cize also 又作 **-ise** *BrE*【英】/pəˈlɪtəˌsaɪz; pəˈlɪtɪ̆saɪz/ *v* [T] to make something more political or more involved in politics 使政治化，使具有政治性: *an attempt to politicise the police* 使警察部门政治化的尝试

po·lit·i·cized also 又作 **-ised** *BrE*【英】/pəˈlɪtəˌsaɪzd; pəˈlɪtɪ̆saɪzd/ *adj* having become involved in or interested in politics 卷入政治的，政治化的；关心政治的: *The public-sector unions are the most politicized.* 公营部门的工会政治化程度最高。—**politicization** /pəˌlɪtəsəˈzeʃən; pəˌlɪtɪ̆saɪˈzeɪʃən/ *n* [U]

pol·i·tick·ing /ˈpɑlətɪkɪŋ; ˈpɒlɪ̆tɪkɪŋ/ *n* [U] political activity, usually done only for your own advantage〔通常为了个人利益而进行的〕政治活动: *the politicking behind the scenes at the party conference* 政党大会上的幕后政治活动

po·lit·i·co /pəˈlɪtɪˌko; pəˈlɪtɪkəʊ/ *n* [C] a disapproving word meaning a politician or someone who is active in politics 政客，政治上活跃的人〔带有贬义〕: *east-coast politicos seeking Irish-American votes* 寻求爱尔兰裔美国人选票的东岸政客

politico- /pəlɪtɪko; pəlɪtɪkəʊ/ *prefix* political and 政治和…的: *politico-scientific* 政治和科学的

S2 W2 **pol·i·tics** /ˈpɑləˌtɪks; ˈpɒlɪ̆tɪks/ *n* **1** [U] ideas and activities that are concerned with the gaining and using of power in a country, city etc 政治；政治活动[事务]: *Most people are fairly cynical about politics.* 大多数人对政治都抱讥讽的态度。| *She became quite active in student politics.* 她变得很热衷于学生的政治活动。| [also+plural verb *BrE* 英] *Politics have always interested Anita.* 安尼塔对政治一直感兴趣。**2** [U] the profession of being a politician 政治事业: *Flynn retired from politics in 1986.* 弗林于1986年退出政坛。| **go into politics** (=become a politician) 从政 *Smith went into politics in his early twenties.* 史密斯20岁出头就进入了政界。**3** [U] the activities of people in a group, organization etc that are concerned with gaining personal advantage〔某组织内的〕争权活动；权术；派别之争: *Try not to get involved in office politics.* 尽量不要卷入办公室内的派别之争。| *sexual politics* 性政治 **4** [plural] someone's political beliefs and opinions 政治信仰；政治观点；政见: *I've always been open about my politics.* 我从不隐瞒自己的政见。**5** [U] the study of political power and systems of government 政治学: *Tom is studying for a degree in politics.* 汤姆正在攻读政治学的学位。

pol·i·ty /ˈpɑlətɪ; ˈpɒlɪ̆ti/ *n* [C,U] *formal* a particular form of political or government organization, or a condition of society in which political organization exists【正式】政治[政府]组织；政体；国体

Polk /pok; pəʊk/, **James Knox** /dʒemz nɑks; dʒeɪmz nɒnks/ (1795-1849) the eleventh president of the US, from 1845 to 1849 波尔克〔(1795-1849)，1845至1849年担任美国第十一任总统〕

pol·ka /ˈpolkə; ˈpɒlkə/ *n* [C] a very quick, simple dance for people dancing in pairs, or a piece of music for this dance 波尔卡舞(曲) —**polka** *v* [I]

polka dot /ˈ·· ·/ *n* [C] one of a number of DOTS (spots) that form a pattern, especially on material for clothing〔尤指衣料上的〕圆点图案: *a white scarf with red polka dots* 有红色圆点图案的白色围巾 —**polka-dot** *adj*: *a polka-dot dress* 有圆点图案的连衣裙 —see picture on page A16 参见A16页图

W3 **poll**[1] /pol; pəʊl/ *n* **1** [C] **a)** an attempt to find out what the public think about something, especially about a political subject, done by questioning a large number of people; OPINION POLL 民意调查，民意测验: *Another poll asked respondents if they favoured nuclear power.* 另一项民意调查询问被访者是否赞成利用核能。| **carry out/conduct a poll** *MORI carried out a poll among senior managers to get their views on taxation.* 英国国际市场研究公司在高级经理中间进行了一项民意调查，以收集他们对税收的看法。**b)** a record of the result of this; OPINION POLL 民意测验[调查]的结果: *Recent polls show Labour well in the lead.* 最近的民意调查结果显示工党遥遥领先。—see also 另见 DEED POLL, EXIT POLL, STRAW POLL **2 the poll** also 又作 **the polls** an election to choose a government or political representative 选举: *a fourth successive defeat at the polls* 连续第四次在选举中失利 | *The result of the poll won't be known until around midnight.* 选举投票结果要到午夜前后方能揭晓。| **go to the polls** (=vote in an election) 参加投票 *It's only one more week until the country goes to the polls.* 距离全国进行选举投票仅有一星期。**3** [singular] the number of votes recorded at an election 选票数: *In most constituencies the largest party can pull 40% of the poll.* 在大多数选区中，最大的政党可以拉到40%的选票。**4 the polls** *especially AmE* the place where you can go to vote in an election【尤美】投票处，投票地点: *The polls won't close for another hour.* 投票处再过一小时才会关闭。

poll[2] *v* [T] to try to find out what the public thinks about a subject by questioning a large number of people 对…进行民意测验[调查]: *18% of the women we polled said their husbands had a drinking problem.* 我们调查的妇女当中有18%的人说她们的丈夫有嗜酒的毛病。

pol·lard[1] /ˈpɑlɚd; ˈpɒləd/ *n* [C] a tree that has had the top cut off to make the lower branches grow more thickly 截去树梢的树，截头树

pollard[2] *v* [T] to cut the top off a tree in order to make the lower branches grow more thickly〔为使枝叶更繁茂而〕截去〔树的〕树梢 —**pollarded** *adj*

pol·len /ˈpɑlən; ˈpɒlən/ *n* [U] a fine powder produced by flowers, which is carried by the wind or by insects to other flowers of the same type making them produce seeds 花粉

pollen count /ˈ·· ·/ *n* [C] a measure of the amount of pollen in the air, usually given as a guide for people who are made ill by it 散布在空中的花粉量，花粉计数〔通常用作花粉过敏症者的指引〕: *an unusually warm day with a very high pollen count* 花粉计数很高的不寻常的热天

pol·li·nate /ˈpɑləˌnet; ˈpɒlɪ̆neɪt/ *v* [T] to make a flower or plant produce seeds by giving it pollen 给〔花、植物〕传授花粉: *flowers pollinated by bees* 由蜜蜂传授花粉的花 —**pollination** /ˌpɑləˈneʃən; ˌpɒlɪ̆ˈneɪʃən/ *n* [U]

poll·ing /ˈpolɪŋ; ˈpəʊlɪŋ/ *n* [U] the activity of voting in a political election〔在政治选举中的〕投票: *Polling started at 8.00 this morning.* 投票于今早8点钟开始。| **heavy/light polling** (=with many/few people voting) 投票人数很多/很少

polling booth /ˈ·· ·/ *n* [C] *especially BrE* a small partly enclosed space in a polling station where you can vote secretly in an election【尤英】〔投票站里供秘密写选票用的〕投票亭，写票处; VOTING BOOTH *AmE*【美】

polling day /ˈ·· ·/ *n* [C] *BrE* the day on which people vote in an election【英】投票日，选举日

polling sta·tion /ˈ·· ˌ··/ *especially BrE*【尤英】**polling place** *AmE*【美】*n* [C] the place where people go to vote in an election 投票站

pol·li·wog, pollywog /ˈpɑlɪˌwɑg; ˈpɒliwɒg/ *n* [C] *AmE* a TADPOLE【美】蝌蚪

Pol·lock /ˈpɑlək; ˈpɒlək/, **Jackson** (1912-56) a US artist famous for his very large abstract paintings which are full of colour. He often made them by putting the painting on the floor and then walking around it, letting the paint drip from sticks. 波洛克〔(1912-1956)，美国艺术家，以色彩丰富的巨幅抽象画闻名。他常将画布放在地板上，然后绕着画布一边走一边从画棒上滴溅颜料作画〕

poll·ster /ˈpolstɚ; ˈpəʊlstə/ *n* [C] someone who prepares and asks questions to find out what people think about a particular subject 民意调查者，民意测验者

poll tax /ˈ· ·/ *n* **1** [C] a tax of a fixed amount collected from every citizen of a country 人头税 **2 the poll tax** a British tax of a fixed amount which was paid by each person during the late 1980s and early 1990s〔英国20世纪80年代晚期至90年代初期的〕人头税，国民税，丁税

pol·lut·ant /pəˈlutn̩t; pəˈluːtənt/ *n* [C,U] a substance that makes air, water, soil etc dangerously dirty, and is caused by cars, factories etc 污染物，污染物质: *emissions of chemical pollutants* 化学污染物的排放

pol·lute /pəˈlut; pəˈluːt/ *v* [T] **1** to make air, water, soil etc dangerously dirty and not suitable for people to use 污染〔空气、水、土壤等〕: *beaches polluted by raw sewage* 被未经处理的污水污染的海滩 | *industrial emissions that pollute the air* 污

染空气的工业排放物 **2 pollute sb's mind** to give someone immoral thoughts and spoil their character 毒害[荼毒]某人的思想: *fears that Lawrence's novels would pollute young minds* 害怕劳伦斯的小说会毒害年轻人的思想 —**polluted** *adj*: *polluted rivers* 受污染的河流 —**polluter** *n* [C]

2 **pol·lu·tion** /pə`luʃən; pə'luːʃən/ *n* [U] **1** the process of making air, water, soil etc dangerously dirty and not suitable for people to use 污染: *California's tough anti-pollution laws* 加利福尼亚州严厉的反污染法 | *chronic pollution of the atmosphere* 长期的大气污染 **2** substances that make air, water, soil etc dangerously dirty 污染物: *industries and other sources of pollution* 工业及其他污染源| *a national programme to cut sulphur dioxide pollution* 减少二氧化硫污染物的全国性计划

P

Pollux —see 见 CASTOR AND POLLUX

Pol·ly·an·na /,pɑlɪ`ænə; ,pɒli'ænə/ *n* [C usually singular 一般用单数] someone who is always cheerful and always thinks something good is going to happen 一贯乐观的人, 盲目乐观者

po·lo /`polo; 'pəʊləʊ/ *n* [U] a game played between two teams of players riding horses, who hit a small ball with long-handled wooden hammers 马球(运动) —see also 另见 WATER POLO

Polo, Mar·co /`mɑrko; 'mɑːkəʊ/ (?1254-1324) an Italian traveller whose writings gave Europeans their first knowledge of life in the Far East. He went to India, southeast Asia, and China, and spent several years working for the Chinese emperor Kublai Khan. 马可·波罗〔(?1254-1324), 意大利旅行家。其著作让欧洲人最早了解到远东的社会生活。他去过印度、东南亚和中国, 在中国皇帝忽必烈手下当过几年差〕

pol·o·naise /,pɑlə`nez; ,pɒlə'neɪz/ *n* [C,U] a slow Polish dance popular in the 19th century, or the music for this dance 波洛奈兹舞〔19世纪盛行的一种波兰慢步舞〕; 波洛奈兹舞曲

polo neck /'· · ,·/ *n* [C] *BrE* a shirt or SWEATER with a high, close-fitting band around the neck that is rolled down【英】高圆领衬衫[羊毛衫]; TURTLENECK *AmE*【美】—**polo-neck** *adj*: *a polo-neck sweater* 高圆领羊毛衫 —see picture on page A17 参见 A17 页图

Po·lo·ni·us /pə`lonɪəs; pə'ləʊniəs/ an old man who is the father of Ophelia and Laertes in the play *Hamlet* by William Shakespeare. Hamlet accidentally kills Polonius when Polonius is hiding behind the ARRAS (=a sort of thick curtain). 波洛涅斯〔威廉·莎士比亚的剧本《哈姆雷特》中的一位老人。他是奥菲利娅和雷欧提斯的父亲, 躲藏在帐幕背后时被哈姆雷特误杀〕

polo shirt /'· · ,·/ *n* [C] a shirt with short SLEEVES and a collar, made out of soft cotton material 马球衬衫〔棉制开领短袖衬衫〕

Pol Pot /,pol `pɑt; ,pɒl 'pɒt/ (1926-98) the leader of the Khmer Rouge group, and Prime Minister of Cambodia from 1975 to 1979, during which time about 3 million people were killed. Pol Pot died in an internal conflict in 1998. 波尔布特〔(1926-1998), 柬埔寨红色高棉领导人。1975至1979年任总理, 期间约有300万柬埔寨人遭到杀害。1998年, 波尔布特死于一次内部冲突中〕

pol·ter·geist /`poltɚ,gaɪst; 'pɒltəgaɪst/ *n* [C] a spirit that makes objects move around and causes strange noises 捉弄人的鬼怪〔使物体到处移动并制造奇怪噪声的鬼怪〕

pol·troon /pɑl`trun; pɒl'truːn/ *n* [C] *old use* a COWARD【旧】懦夫, 胆小鬼

pol·y /`pɑlɪ; 'pɒli/ *n* [C] *BrE informal* a POLYTECHNIC【英, 非正式】综合性理工学院, 工艺专科学校

poly- /pɑlɪ; pɒlɪ/ *prefix* many 多: *polysyllabic* (=with three or more SYLLABLES) 多音节的 | *polyandry* 一妻多夫(制)

pol·y·an·dry /`pɑlɪ,ændrɪ; ,pɒli'ændri/ *n* [U] *technical* the custom or practice of having more than one husband at the same time【术语】一妻多夫(制) —compare 比较 BIGAMY, POLYGAMY —**polyandrous** /,pɑlɪ`ændrəs; ,pɒli'ændrəs◂/ *adj*

pol·y·an·thus /,pɑlɪ`ænθəs; ,pɒli'ænθəs/ *n* [C,U] a small garden plant with a group of round brightly-coloured flowers at the top of each stem 西洋樱草

pol·y·es·ter /,pɑlɪ`ɛstɚ; 'pɒliestə/ *n* [U] a man-made material used to make cloth 聚酯纤维

pol·y·eth·y·lene /,pɑlɪ`ɛθɪlin; ,pɒli'eθəliːn/ *n* [U] *AmE* a strong light plastic used to make bags, sheets for covering food, small containers etc【美】聚乙烯; POLYTHENE *BrE*【英】

po·lyg·a·my /pə`lɪgəmɪ; pə'lɪgəmi/ *n* [U] *technical* the custom or practice of having more than one husband or wife at the same time in a society where this is allowed【术语】多配偶(制); 一夫多妻(制); 一妻多夫(制) —compare 比较 BIGAMY, MONOGAMY —**polygamous** *adj*

pol·y·glot /`pɑlɪ,glɑt; 'pɒlɪglɒt/ *adj formal* speaking or using many languages; MULTILINGUAL【正式】使用[通晓]多种语言的 —**polyglot** *n* [C]

pol·y·gon /`pɑlɪ,gɑn; 'pɒlɪgən/ *n* [C] *technical* a flat shape with three or more sides【术语】多边形, 多角形 —**polygonal** /pə`lɪgənl; pə'lɪgənəl/ *adj*

pol·y·graph /`pɑlɪ,græf; 'pɒlɪgrɑːf/ *n* [C] *technical* a piece of equipment that is used by the police to find out whether someone is telling the truth; LIE DETECTOR【术语】测谎器[仪]

pol·y·he·dron /,pɑlɪ`hidrən; ,pɒlɪ'hiːdrən/ *n* [C] a solid shape with many sides 多面体

pol·y·math /`pɑlɪ,mæθ; 'pɒlɪmæθ/ *n* [C] *formal* someone who has a lot of knowledge about many different subjects【正式】博学之士, 博学的人

pol·y·mer /`pɑlɪmɚ; 'pɒlɪmə/ *n* [C] a chemical compound that has a simple structure of large MOLECULES 聚合物[体]

pol·y·mor·phous /,pɑlɪ`mɔrfəs; ,pɒlɪ'mɔːfəs◂/ also 又作 **pol·y·mor·phic** /-fɪk; -fɪk◂/ *adj technical* having many forms, styles etc during different stages of growth or development【术语】〔生长或发展等过程中〕多种形式的, 多形(态)的

Pol·y·ne·si·a /,pɑlə`niʒə; ,pɒlǀ'niːziə/ the islands in the central and southern Pacific Ocean, including the Hawaiian islands, Tonga, Samoa, and the islands of French Polynesia 波利尼西亚〔太平洋中南部群岛, 包括夏威夷群岛、汤加、萨摩亚群岛和法属波利尼西亚群岛〕

pol·yp /`pɑlɪp; 'pɒlǀp/ *n* [C] **1** a very simple sea animal that has a body like a tube 水螅(体) **2** a small lump that grows inside someone's body and is caused by an illness 息肉

po·lyph·o·ny /pə`lɪfənɪ; pə'lɪfəni/ *n* [U] a kind of music in which several different tunes or notes are sung or played together at the same time 复调音乐(作品) —**polyphonic** /,pɑlɪ`fɑnɪk; ,pɒlɪ'fɒnɪk◂/ *adj*

pol·y·pro·py·lene /,pɑlɪ`propəlin, ,pɒlɪ'prəʊpǀliːn/ *n* [U] a hard light plastic material 聚丙烯

po·lys·e·mous /pə`lɪsɪməs; pə'lɪsǀməs/ *adj technical* a polysemous word has two or more different meanings【术语】(一词)多义的 —**polysemy** *n* [U]

pol·y·sty·rene /,pɑlɪ`staɪrin; ,pɒlɪ'staɪriːn◂/ *n* [U] *especially BrE* a soft light plastic material that prevents heat or cold from passing through it, used especially for making containers【尤英】聚苯乙烯; STYROFOAM *AmE trademark*【美, 商标】

pol·y·syl·la·ble /`pɑlə,sɪləbl; 'pɒlɪ,sɪləbəl/ *n* [C] *technical* a word that contains more than three SYLLABLES【术语】多音节词〔含有三个以上音节〕—**polysyllabic** /,pɑləsɪ`læbɪk; ,pɒlɪsɪ'læbɪk◂/ *adj*

pol·y·tech·nic /,pɑlə`tɛknɪk; ,pɒlɪ'teknɪk/ *n* [C] a kind of British college similar to a university, which provided training and degrees in many subjects, and existed until 1993〔1993年以前英国的〕综合性理工学院, 工艺专科学校

pol·y·the·is·m /`pɑləθi,ɪzəm; 'pɒlɪθiːɪzəm/ *n* [U] the belief that there is more than one god 多神论[主义]; 多神教 —compare 比较 MONOTHEISM —**polytheistic** /,pɑləθi`ɪstɪk; ,pɒlɪθiː'ɪstɪk◂/ *adj*

pol·y·thene /`pɑlɪθin; 'pɒlǀθiːn/ *n* [U] *BrE* a strong light plastic used to make bags, sheets for covering food, small containers etc【英】聚乙烯; POLYETHYLENE *AmE*【美】

pol·y·un·sat·u·rate /,pɑlɪʌn`sætʃərɪt; ,pɒliʌn'sætʃərǀt/ *n* [C] a FATTY ACID (=chemical that helps your body produce energy) that is POLYUNSATURATED 多不饱和物, 多不饱和脂肪酸

pol·y·un·sat·u·ra·ted /,pɑlɪʌn`sætʃəretɪd; ,pɒliʌn'sætʃəreɪtǀd/ *adj* polyunsaturated fats or oils come from vegetables and plants, and are considered to be better for your health than animal fats〔脂肪或油脂〕多不饱和的 —compare 比较 SATURATED FAT

pol·y·u·re·thane /,pɑlɪ`jurəθen; ,pɒlɪ'jʊərǀθeɪn/ *n* [U] a plastic used to make paints and VARNISH 聚氨酯

pom /pɑm; pɒm/ *n* [C] *AustrE, NZE slang* an insulting word for an English person, especially one who has gone to live in Australia or New Zealand【澳, 新西兰, 俚】英国佬〔侮辱性说法, 尤指迁居澳大利亚或新西兰的英国人〕

CULTURAL NOTE 文化注释

In Australia and New Zealand, the popular image of an English person is of someone who is lazy and who complains all the time, and someone like this is called 'a whinging (WHINGE) Pom'. 在澳大利亚和新西兰, 英国人的通俗形象是懒惰而且抱怨个没完, 因此有这种陋习的人被称为"满腹唠叨的英国佬"。

po·made /po`med; pə'meɪd/ *n* [U] a sweet-smelling oily substance rubbed on men's hair to make it smooth, which was used especially in former times〔尤指旧时的〕男用润发油, 男用头油

po·man·der /ˋpomændə; pəʊˈmændə/ *n* [C] a box or ball that contains dried flowers and HERBS and is used to make clothes or a room smell pleasant〔用于放出香味的〕香盒, 香球, 香丸

pom·e·gran·ate /ˋpɑm,grænɪt; ˈpɒmɪ̯grænɪ̯t/ *n* [C] a round fruit that has a lot of small seeds, red juicy flesh, and a thick reddish skin 石榴

pom·mel¹ /ˋpʌml̩; ˈpʌməl/ *n* [C] **1** the high, rounded part at the front of a SADDLE¹ (1) on a horse〔马鞍的〕前桥, 鞍头 —see picture at 参见 HORSE¹ 图 **2** the round end of a sword handle〔刀剑柄上的〕圆头

pommel² *v* [T] *especially AmE*【尤美】another spelling of PUMMEL pummel 的另一种拼法

pommel horse /ˈ· · ·/ *n* [C] a piece of equipment used in GYMNASTICS with two handles on top, which you hold onto and jump over 鞍马〔体操运动器械〕

pom·my /ˋpɑmɪ; ˈpɒmi/ *n* [C] *AustrE, NZE slang* a POM【澳, 新西兰, 俚】英国佬

pomp /pɑmp; pɒmp/ *n* [U] *formal* all the impressive clothes, decorations, music etc that are traditional for an important official or public ceremony【正式】〔典礼等的〕盛况, 壮观场面: *all the usual pomp that surrounds occasions such as the royal wedding* 诸如皇家婚礼之类场合常见的壮观场面

Pom·pa·dour /ˋpɑmpədɔr; ˈpɒmpədʊə/, **Madame de** (1721-64) the lover of King Louis XV of France from 1745 until her death. She often influenced the king, especially when he had to choose government officials and make political decisions. 蓬巴杜夫人〔(1721-1764), 从1745年至去世一直为法国国王路易十五的情人。她经常对国王施加影响, 在国王选任官员和政治决策时尤其如此〕

Pom·pei·i /pɑmˋpe-ɪ; pɒmˈpeɪ-i/ an ancient city in southern Italy, southeast of Naples, which was buried under the ash and LAVA (=hot liquid rock) from the VOLCANO Mount Vesuvius when it suddenly ERUPTed in 79AD. Everything was preserved exactly as it was then, because the ash and lava covered it completely. When scientists started to dig the city up in the 18th century, they learned a lot about how ordinary people lived in Roman times. 庞贝, 又译庞培〔意大利南部一古城, 位于那不勒斯东南。公元79年, 维苏威火山突然爆发, 火山灰与熔岩将该城完全覆盖。因为此原因, 庞贝城当初的原样保存得十分完好。18世纪, 科学家开始挖掘庞贝城, 了解了不少有关古罗马平民生活的情况〕

Pom·pey /ˋpɑmpɪ; ˈpɒmpi/ (106-48 BC) a Roman GENERAL (=military leader) and politician who opposed Julius Caesar but was defeated by him in 48 BC 庞培〔(公元前106-前48), 古罗马将军、政治家。他反对尤利乌斯·凯撒, 公元前48年被凯撒打败〕

Pompidou Cen·tre, the /ˈ· · ·, · ·/ a MUSEUM in central Paris which has paintings by important 20th century artists. The building, which is very modern, is made of glass and has metal tubes in bright colours on the outside. 蓬皮杜中心〔巴黎市中心一博物馆。馆藏有20世纪重要艺术家的作品。该馆的建筑风格十分现代, 以玻璃和金属管为材料建成, 整个外观色彩亮丽〕

pom·pom /ˋpɑm,pɑm; ˈpɒmpɒm/ also 又作 **pom·pon** /-pɑn; -pɒn/ *n* [C] **1** a small woollen ball used as a decoration on clothing, especially hats〔尤指装饰帽子用的〕小绒球 **2** a large round ball of loose plastic strings connected to a handle, used by CHEERLEADERs〔拉拉队用的〕塑料线球, 丝球 —see picture at 参见 CHEERLEADER 图

pom·pous /ˋpɑmpəs; ˈpɒmpəs/ *adj* trying to make people think you are important, especially by using very formal and important-sounding words 自命不凡的, 自高自大的; 浮华的, 虚夸的: *The principal gave a very pompous speech about 'the portals of learning'.* 那位校长夸夸其谈地发表了关于"知识门户"的演讲。—**pompously** *adv* —**pompousness, pomposity** /pɑmˋpɑsətɪ; pɒmˈpɒsɪ̯ti/ *n* [U]

ponce¹ /pɑns; pɒns/ *n* [C] *BrE informal*【英, 非正式】**1** a PIMP 拉皮条的男子, 淫媒 **2** an offensive word meaning a man who is too concerned about his appearance 过分注重外表的男人, 女人气的男人, 脂粉气十足的男人〔不礼貌的说法〕

ponce² *v*

ponce about/around *phr v* [I] *BrE informal*【英, 非正式】**1** to waste time doing silly things 瞎混, 闲逛, 游手好闲: *At least I haven't been poncing about all day with theatre people.* 至少我没有整天和那些搞戏剧的人瞎混。**2** if a man ponces about, he behaves in a way that is thought to be how a woman behaves〔男人〕矫揉造作, 举止似女人

ponce off sb *phr v* [T] *BrE* to ask someone to give you something such as a cigarette or drink without offering to pay【英】向〔某人〕要〔烟、饮料等〕: *I'd no money, you know, so I ponced off him.* 你知道的, 我没有钱嘛, 所以我就向他要。

Ponce de Le·ón /,pɑns də ˋliən; ,pɒns də ˈliːən/, **Juan** /hwɑn; wɑːn/ (1460-1521) a Spanish EXPLORER who took control of Puerto Rico for Spain in 1508. He discovered Florida in 1513, when he was searching for the Fountain of Youth, a flow of water coming from the ground which was supposed to make anyone who drank it stay young for ever. 庞赛·德·莱昂〔(1460-1521), 西班牙探险家。1508年为西班牙夺得波多黎各的控制权, 1513年发现了佛罗里达, 当时他在寻找一种据说可以永葆青春的地下泉水, 名叫"青春泉"〕

pon·cho /ˋpɑntʃo; ˈpɒntʃəʊ/ *n plural* **ponchos** [C] **1** a coat consisting of one large piece of thick wool cloth like a BLANKET, with a hole in the middle for your head 披风, 斗篷〔形似毡子, 中间有领口〕**2** *AmE* a coat that keeps out rain and is made of one large piece of material with a cover for your head【美】雨披

ponc·y, poncey /ˋpɑnsɪ; ˈpɒnsi/ *adj BrE informal* poncy clothes or behaviour are typical of a man who is too concerned about his appearance【英, 非正式】〔衣服、行为〕女人气的, 脂粉气的, 娘娘腔的

pond /pɑnd; pɒnd/ *n* [C] **1** a small area of still water, especially one that has been artificially made〔尤指人工的〕池塘: *a duck pond* 养鸭池 **2 across the pond/on the other side of the pond** *informal* on the other side of the Atlantic Ocean in the US or in Britain【非正式】在大西洋的另一边〔指美国或英国〕 S3

pon·der /ˋpɑndə; ˈpɒndə/ *v* [I,T] *formal* to spend time thinking carefully and seriously about a problem, a difficult question, or something that has happened【正式】仔细考虑, 深思, 默想: *Lisa pondered for a while before answering.* 莉萨仔细考虑了一会儿才回答。| **[+on/over/about]** *As I pondered over the whole business, an idea struck me.* 我在思考整件事情的时候, 突然想出了一个主意。| **ponder how/what/whether etc** *His critics might well ponder what would happen if he quit.* 批评他的人很可能会充分考虑他一旦辞职将会发生什么事。| **ponder sth** *Esteban sat pondering the state of his marriage.* 埃斯特班坐了下来, 细细地思考着他的婚姻状况。

pon·der·ous /ˋpɑndərəs; ˈpɒndərəs/ *adj* **1** moving slowly or awkwardly because of being very big and heavy 行动迟缓的, 笨拙的: *an elephant's ponderous walk* 大象笨拙的行走方式 **2** boring and too serious 严肃而乏味的, 呆板的; 生硬的: *a ponderous and difficult book, intended for experts* 一本为专家写的沉闷而又难懂的书 **3** very big and heavy 大而重的, 笨重的: *Calvin's way was blocked by the ponderous body of his host.* 卡尔文被主人庞大的身躯挡住了去路。—**ponderously** *adv* —**ponderousness** *n* [U]

pone /pon; pəʊn/ *n* [U] *AmE informal* CORN PONE【美, 非正式】玉米饼

pong¹ /pɑŋ; pɒŋ/ *n* [C usually singular 一般用单数] *BrE informal* an unpleasant smell【英, 非正式】难闻的气味: *There's an awful pong in the fridge!* 冰箱里有股可怕的气味!

pong² *v* [I] *BrE informal* to have a strong and unpleasant smell【英, 非正式】有强烈的异味, 发出难闻的气味: *Ugh! Your socks really pong!* 哎呀! 你的袜子真难闻! —**pongy** *adj*

pon·iard /ˋpɑnjəd; ˈpɒnjəd/ *n* [C] a small pointed knife used as a weapon in former times〔旧时用作武器的〕匕首, 短剑

Pon·ti·ac /ˋpɑntɪæk; ˈpɒntiæk/ *trademark* a type of US car made by General Motors.【商标】庞蒂亚克〔一款美国汽车, 由通用汽车公司制造〕

pon·tiff /ˋpɑntɪf; ˈpɒntɪ̯f/ *n* [C] *technical* the POPE【术语】教皇, 教宗

pon·tif·i·cal /pɑnˋtɪfɪkl̩; pɒnˈtɪfɪkəl/ *adj formal*【正式】**1** speaking as if you think your judgment or opinion is always right〔说话〕武断的, 专横的, 自负的 **2** connected with the POPE 教皇的, 教宗的 —**pontifically** /-klɪ; -kli/ *adv*

pon·tif·i·cate¹ /pɑnˋtɪfɪket; pɒnˈtɪfɪ̯keɪt/ *v* [I] to give your opinion about something in a way that shows you think you are always right 武断地谈论, 自以为是地发表意见: **[+about/on]** *He's always pontificating about the evils of modern society.* 他总是自以为是地对现代社会的种种弊病大发议论。

pon·tif·i·cate² /pɑnˋtɪfɪkɪt; pɒnˈtɪfɪkɪ̯t/ *n* [C] *technical* the position or period of being POPE【术语】教皇的职位[任期]

Pontius Pilate —see 见 Pontius PILATE

pon·toon /pɑnˋtun; pɒnˈtuːn/ *n* [C] **1** *BrE* a card game, usually played for money【英】〔通常用来赌钱的〕纸牌游戏, 二十一点牌戏; BLACKJACK *AmE*【美】**2** one of several metal containers or boats that are fastened together to support a floating bridge〔架设浮桥用的〕浮舟, 平底船 **3** one of two hollow metal containers fastened to the bottom of a plane so that it can come down onto water and float〔固定在飞机底部的〕浮筒

pontoon bridge /ˈ· · ·/ *n* [C] a floating bridge which is supported by several pontoons 浮桥

po·ny /ˈponɪ; ˈpəʊni/ *n* [C] a small horse 小马，驹；矮种马 —see also 另见 PIT PONY, SHETLAND PONY

Pony Club, the /ˈ· · ·/ a British organization that arranges horse riding activities for children 少年马术会〔英国一机构，专为青少年组织骑马活动〕

po·ny·tail /ˈponɪˌtel; ˈpəʊniteɪl/ *n* [C] hair tied in a bunch at the back of your head and falling like a horse's tail 马尾辫，马尾发 —see picture at 参见 HAIRSTYLE 图

pony-trek·king /ˈ· ·, ˌ· ·/ *n* [U] *BrE* the activity of riding through the countryside on ponies【英】乡间骑马旅行；PACK TRIP *AmE*【美】

poo /pu; puː/ *n informal*【非正式】**1** [U] a word meaning solid waste from your BOWELS, used especially by children 屎，大便〔尤儿语〕；POOP[1] (3) *AmE*【美】**2** [C usually singular 一般用单数] a word meaning the act of passing waste from your BOWELS, used especially by children 拉屎，大便〔尤儿语〕；POOP[1] (4) *AmE*【美】—**poo** *v* [I,T] *informal*【非正式】

pooch /putʃ; puːtʃ/ *n* [C] *informal often humorous* a dog【非正式，常幽默】狗

poo·dle /ˈpudḷ; ˈpuːdl/ *n* [C] **1** a dog with thick curly hair 卷毛狗，贵妇犬 —see picture at 参见 DOG[1] 图 **2 be sb's poodle** *BrE humorous* if someone is another person's poodle, they always do what the other person tells them to do【英，幽默】当某人的走狗[走卒]

poof[1] /puf; pʊf/ also 又作 **poof·ter** /ˈpuftə; ˈpʊftə/ *n* [C] *BrE* an offensive word for a HOMOSEXUAL man【英】搞同性恋的男人，男同性恋者〔具冒犯性的说法〕—**poofy** *adj* —compare 比较 POUF

poof[2] *interjection* **1** used when talking about something that happened suddenly 噗！〔表示某事突然发生〕：*Then poof! She was gone.* 于是，噗！她消失了。**2** used to show that you do not agree with or believe what someone has said 呸！啐！〔用于表示不同意或不相信〕：*Poof! He doesn't know what he's talking about.* 呸！他不知道自己在说些什么。

Pooh /pu; puː/ also 又作 **Pooh Bear** —see 见 WINNIE THE POOH

pooh *interjection BrE spoken* used when there is a very unpleasant smell【英口】哼！呸！〔表示对难闻气味的厌恶〕；PEW[2] *AmE*【美】

pooh-pooh /ˌ· ˈ·/ *v* [T] *informal* to say that you think that an idea, suggestion, effort etc is silly or not very good【非正式】对〔主意、建议、努力等〕嗤之以鼻[不以为然]：*Critics pooh-poohed the idea at first.* 评论家起初对这观点嗤之以鼻。

Pooh·sticks /ˈpustɪks; ˈpuːstɪks/ a game played especially by children, in which each child throws a stick into a stream whose current is flowing towards a bridge. The winner of the game is the one whose stick appears first at the other side of the bridge. The name comes from the stories about Winnie the Pooh by A. A. Milne, in which the game is described. 漂流木游戏〔一种儿童游戏。每个孩子将一根木棒扔进河水，木棒随着水流从一座桥下漂过，谁的木棒最先在桥的另一边出现，谁就是赢家。游戏的名称源自 A.A.米尔恩的小说《小熊维尼》，其中对此有所描述〕

pool[1] /pul; puːl/ *n*

1 ►WATER 水◄ [C] **a)** a SWIMMING POOL or PADDLING POOL 游泳池；嬉水池：*Does the hotel have a pool?* 这家酒店有游泳池吗？| *an inflatable rubber wading pool* 可充气的橡皮嬉水池 **b)** a small area of still water in a hollow place 水洼，水坑，水池：*The children hunted for crabs in the pools between the rocks.* 孩子们在岩石间的水坑里寻找螃蟹。| *where the stream formed a shallow pool* 溪流形成一个浅水池的地方

2 a pool of water/blood/light etc a small area of liquid or light on a surface 一摊水/一摊血/一小片光等：*Trautman lay unconscious in a pool of blood.* 特劳特曼躺在血泊之中，不省人事。| *His desk lamp cast a pool of light on the documents.* 他的台灯在文件上投下一小片光。

3 ►GAME 游戏◄ [U] a game in which you use a stick to knock numbered balls into holes around a table, which is often played in bars 落袋撞球戏 —compare 比较 SNOOKER

4 ►FOOTBALL 足球◄ the pools a system in Britain in which people try to win money each week by guessing the results of football games 足球赌博〔英国的一种赌博方式，通过竞猜足球比赛的结果以赢钱〕

5 ►GROUP OF THINGS/PEOPLE 一组事物/人◄ [C] **a)** a number of things or an amount of money that is shared by a group of people 合伙使用的钱[物品] **b)** a group who are available to work when they are needed 可招之即来的人员，备用人员：*a pool of volunteers for community projects* 一批为社区项目提供服务的志愿者 —see also 另见 CAR POOL, GENE POOL, TYPING POOL

pool[2] *v* [T] to combine your money, ideas, skills etc with those of other people so that you can all use them 合伙[集中]使用，共用：**pool your resources** *Investors agreed to pool their resources to develop the property.* 投资者同意集资开发房地产。

pool hall /ˈ· ·/ *n* [C] *AmE* a building where people go to practise playing pool【美】撞球室，弹子房

pool·room /ˈpulˌrum; ˈpuːlruːm/ *n* [C] a room used for playing pool, especially in a bar〔尤指酒吧里的〕撞球室，弹子房，桌球房

poop[1] /pup; puːp/ *n* **1** [C] *technical* the raised part at the back end of an old sailing ship【术语】〔旧帆船的〕船尾楼甲板 **2 the poop** *AmE informal* the latest news about something that has happened, which is told to you unofficially by someone; LOWDOWN【美，非正式】小道消息，最新消息，内幕：*Come on, Dan, what's the poop? Are they hiring Collins?* 来吧，丹，有什么内幕消息吗？他们要雇用柯林斯吗？**3** [U] *AmE informal* a word meaning solid waste from your BOWELS, used especially by children【美，非正式】大便，屎〔尤儿语〕；POO (1) *BrE*【英】**4** [singular] *AmE informal* a word meaning the act of passing waste from your BOWELS, used especially by children【美，非正式】大便，拉屎〔尤儿语〕；POO (2) *BrE*【英】

poop[2] *v* [I,T] *AmE informal* a word meaning to pass solid waste from your BOWELS, used especially by children【美，非正式】拉屎，大便〔尤儿语〕；POO *BrE*【英】—see also 另见 PARTY POOPER

poop out *phr v* [I] *AmE informal*【美，非正式】**1** to stop trying to do something because you are tired, bored etc〔由于劳累、厌烦等而〕停止做〔某事〕：*Ouida pooped out about halfway through the race.* 韦达在赛跑中跑到中途就筋疲力尽停了下来。**2** to decide not to do something you have already said you would do, because you are tired or not interested〔由于劳累或没有兴趣而〕决定不做〔已经说好要做的事〕：**poop out on sb** *"Is Bill coming along?" "Nah, he's pooping out on us."* "比尔要来吗？" "不，他又决定不跟我们去了。"

poop deck /ˈ· ·/ *n* [C] the floor on the raised part at the back of an old sailing ship〔旧帆船的〕船尾楼甲板

pooped /pupt; puːpt/ also 又作 **pooped out** /ˌ· ˈ·/ *adj* [not before noun 不用于名词前] *AmE informal* very tired; EXHAUSTED (1)【美，非正式】很累的，筋疲力尽的

poop·er scoop·er /ˈpupə ˌskupə; ˈpuːpə ˌskuːpə/ *n* [C] *informal* a small SPADE and a container, used by dog owners for removing their dogs' solid waste from the streets【非正式】〔供狗主人捡狗粪用的〕长柄粪铲及盛粪容器

poo-poo /ˈ· ·/ *n* [U] POO 屎，大便

poop sheet /ˈ· ·/ *n* [C] *AmE informal* written official instructions or information【美，非正式】〔书面的〕详细指示；〔官方的〕书面材料

poor /pur; pɔː/ *adj*

1 ►NO MONEY 无钱◄ having very little money and not many possessions 贫穷的，贫困的：*Her family were so poor they couldn't afford to buy her new clothes.* 她家很穷，买不起新衣服给她。| *Ethiopia is one of the poorest countries in the world.* 埃塞俄比亚是世界上最贫困的国家之一。| *a poor neighborhood* 贫困居民区

2 the poor people who are poor 穷人：*state subsidies to help the poor buy basic foods* 帮助穷人购买基本食品的国家补助

3 ►NOT GOOD 不好的◄ not as good as it could be or should be; INFERIOR[1] (1) 不佳的，差的，次等的，低劣的：*Poor sanitation can lead to the spread of diseases.* 卫生状况不佳会导致疾病的传播。| *The soil in this area is very poor.* 这地区的土壤很贫瘠。| *poor rates of pay* 很低的报酬 | **poor hearing/eyesight/memory** *You'd better read it to me – my eyesight's pretty poor.* 你最好读给我听，我的视力很不好。

4 poor boy/girl/Joe etc *especially spoken* used to show pity for someone because they are so unlucky, unhappy etc【尤口】可怜的[不幸的]男孩/女孩/乔等：*Poor kid, he's had a rough day.* 可怜的孩子，他度过了倒霉的一天。| *I feel sorry for the poor horse with me riding it.* 这匹可怜的马要由我来骑，我为它感到难过。| **poor thing** *You poor thing, you've had a hard time of it, haven't you?* 可怜的东西，你吃了不少苦头，是吗？| **poor old** *Poor old Lou, having to work at weekends.* 可怜的老卢，周末还得工作。

5 ►NOT GOOD AT STH 不善于某事的◄ not good at doing something 不善于…的，对…不熟练的，差的：*a poor public speaker* 不善于演讲的人 | **[+at]** *poor at spelling* 拼写很差

6 make a poor job of to do something badly 把〔某事〕做得很糟：*The builders have made a really poor job of fixing our roof.* 那些建筑工人把我们的屋顶修得很糟糕。

7 ►HEALTH 健康◄ someone whose health is poor is ill or weak for a long period of time〔身体〕虚弱的，衰弱的：**be in poor health** *My parents are both in rather poor health.* 我父母的身体都不好。

8 poor in sth lacking things that people need 缺乏某物: *fatty snacks that are poor in nutrients* 缺乏营养的高脂肪小吃
9 poor loser someone who behaves badly if they lose a game 输不起的人
10 be a poor second/third etc to finish a race, competition etc a long way behind the person ahead of you〔在比赛中〕被远远抛在后面的第二名/第三名等
11 poor man's *spoken often humorous*【口，常幽默】**a)** used to say that someone is like a very famous performer, writer etc but is not as good as they are 稍逊一筹的，较差的，无实的: *He's a kind of poor man's Richard Gere.* 他的样子跟理查·基尔很相像，但其他的都不及他。**b)** used to say that something can be used for the same purpose as something else, and is much cheaper〔可作同样用途但〕价格较低廉的，次等的: *The abacus is the poor man's pocket calculator.* 算盘算是廉价的袖珍计算器。
12 poor relation someone or something that is not treated as well as other members of a group or is much less successful than they are 同类中较次者: *Theatre musicians tend to be the poor relations of the musical profession.* 剧院乐师往往被看作是音乐界中地位稍低的人。—see also 另见 **be in bad/poor taste** (TASTE[1] (6)), POORLY, POORNESS

poor boy /ˈ· ·/ *n* [C] *AmE* a long bread roll that is cut open and filled with meat, cheese etc; SUBMARINE SANDWICH【美】〔切开后中间夹肉、干酪等的〕长面包卷，大型三明治

poor·house /ˈpurˌhaus; ˈpɔːhaʊs/ *n* [C] a building in former times where people could live and be fed, which was paid for with public money〔旧时的〕济贫院

poor law /ˈ· ·/ *n* **the Poor Law** a group of British laws which controlled the help given to poor people in former times〔英国旧时的〕济贫法，恤贫法令

poor·ly[1] /ˈpurlɪ; ˈpɔːli/ *adv* badly 糟糕地，不好地，拙劣地，蹩脚地: *poorly paid* 报酬很低 | *Jana's doing poorly in school.* 简娜在学校里的成绩很差。| *a poorly written article* 一篇写得很差的文章

poorly[2] *adj* [not before noun 不用于名词前] *informal especially BrE* ill【非正式，尤英】身体不舒服的，健康不佳的: *Matt's wife's been feeling poorly.* 马特的妻子一直感觉不舒服。

poorly off /ˌ·· ˈ·/ *adj* [not before noun 不用于名词前] **1** someone who is poorly off does not have very much money 贫困的，贫穷的 **2 be poorly off for** to not have enough of something 不够…的，缺…的: *We have enough textbooks but we're poorly off for lab equipment.* 我们有足够的教科书，但是缺少实验室设备。

poor·ness /ˈpurnɪs; ˈpɔːnǝs/ *n* [U] *formal* lack of skill or good qualities【正式】差，拙劣，低劣: [+of] *the poorness of my German accent* 我那蹩脚的德语口音 —compare 比较 POVERTY

poor-spir·it·ed /ˌ· ˈ···◂/ *adj literary* having no confidence or courage【文】缺乏信心的，胆怯的，懦弱的 —**poor-spiritedly** *adv*

Poo·ter /ˈputɚ; ˈpuːtǝ/, **Mr** the main character in the humorous book *The Diary of a Nobody* (1892). Mr Pooter is a very ordinary man, and he describes his daily life in the book. He is sometimes not sure about the socially correct way to behave, and he often makes mistakes that make him feel very embarrassed. 波特〔幽默读物《无名小卒日记》(1892) 中的主人公。波特先生是个极为普通的人，他在日记中讲述自己的日常生活。他有时候拿不准何为得体的社会行为规范，常常言行失当，弄得自己十分难堪〕

poo·tle /ˈputl; ˈpuːtl/ *v* [I+about/around] *BrE spoken* to spend time pleasantly, doing things that are not very important【英口】玩，愉快地度过

pop[1] /pɑp; pɒp/ **popped, popping** *v* (S3)
1 ▸GO SOMEWHERE QUICKLY 迅速去某处◂ [I always+adv/prep] *spoken* to go somewhere quickly, suddenly, or unexpectedly【口】迅速[突然，出人意料]地去〔某处〕: [+in/out/round/to etc] *Could you pop round to the store for some bread?* 你能不能快去商店买些面包回来？| *Pat's just popped next door for ten minutes.* 帕特刚去了隔壁 10 分钟。
2 ▸COME OUT OF STH 从某物中出来◂ [I always+adv/prep] to come suddenly or unexpectedly out of or away from something 突然[出人意料]地从〔某物〕中出来，蹦出，离开，脱落: [+out/off/up etc] *A button popped off my shirt when I sneezed.* 我打喷嚏时，一颗纽扣突然从我的衬衫上掉了下来。| **out/up popped** *The egg cracked open and out popped a tiny head.* 那只蛋裂开了，里面冒出一个小脑袋来。
3 ▸PUT STH SOMEWHERE 把某物放在某处◂ [T always+adv/prep] *informal* to put something somewhere quickly for a short time【非正式】迅速地把〔某物〕放在〔某处〕一会儿: **pop sth in/round/over etc** *I'll just pop these cakes into the oven.* 我来把这些蛋糕放到烤箱里烤一会儿。| *Barry popped his head round the door to say hello.* 巴里从门口探进头来问好。
4 ▸SHORT SOUND 短促的声音◂ [I,T] to make a short sound like a small explosion, or to make something make this sound (使) 噼啪作响: *Champagne corks were popping.* 香槟酒的瓶塞噗噗作响。| **pop sth** *Please don't pop all the balloons before the party starts.* 请不要在聚会开始前就把所有的汽球都噼啪弄破。
5 ▸EARS 耳朵◂ [I] if your ears pop, you feel the pressure in them suddenly become less when you go quickly up or down in a plane, lift etc〔在飞机、电梯等中迅速升降时〕耳膜鼓起〔因耳内压力降低〕
6 sb's eyes popped (out of their head) used to say that someone looked extremely surprised or excited〔极度惊讶或兴奋〕某人的眼睛都瞪出来了
7 pop the question *informal* to ask someone to marry you【非正式】求婚: *Hasn't Bill popped the question yet?* 比尔还没有求婚吗？
8 pop pills *informal* to take PILLS too often【非正式】过度地服药
9 pop your clogs *BrE humorous* to die【英，幽默】死，死亡
10 ▸CORN 玉米◂ [I,T] to cook corn until it swells and bursts open, or to be cooked in this way 爆玉米花；〔玉米〕爆成玉米花
11 ▸BORROWING MONEY 借钱◂ [T] *BrE old-fashioned* to PAWN[2] something【英，过时】典当，抵押
pop off *phr v* [I] *informal* to die suddenly【非正式】突然死掉，猝死
pop sth ↔ **on** *phr v* [T] *spoken*【口】**1** to quickly put on a piece of clothing 迅速穿上〔衣服〕: *Just pop this jacket on and we'll see if it fits.* 快把这件短上衣穿上，我们看合不合身。**2** to quickly turn on a piece of electrical equipment 迅速打开〔电器〕: *Pop the kettle on, would you.* 把水壶开关打开，好吗？
pop up *phr v* [I] **1** to appear suddenly and unexpectedly 突然[意外]地出现，冒出来: *Mushrooms tend to pop up overnight.* 蘑菇往往会在一夜之间长出来。| *She popped up in Munich after all that time.* 经过那么长的时间以后，她突然在慕尼黑出现。—see also 另见 POP-UP **2** to hit a ball into the air in a game of BASEBALL so that it only travels a short distance〔棒球比赛中〕击出小腾空球: *O'Malley popped up to first base.* 奥马利朝一垒击出个小腾空球。

pop[2] *n* (S3) (W3) **1** [U] modern music that is popular with young people, and usually consists of simple tunes with a strong beat 流行音乐，流行歌曲: **pop singer/concert/festival etc** *a pop record* 流行音乐唱片 | *pop culture* 通俗文化 **2** [singular] *AmE informal* a word meaning your father, used especially to address him【美，非正式】爸爸: *Can I borrow the car, Pop?* 爸爸，我可以借用一下汽车吗？**3** [U] *informal* a sweet FIZZY drink such as LEMONADE【非正式】苏打水，汽水; SODA (2) *AmE*【美】: *a bottle of pop* 一瓶汽水 **4** [C] a sudden short sound like a small explosion 砰[啪、噗]的一声: *the pop of a champagne cork* 香槟酒瓶塞发出的砰的一声 | **go pop** (=make this sound) 发出砰[啪]的一声 *The balloon went pop.* 汽球砰的一声破了。—see picture on page A19 参见 A19 页图

pop[3] the written abbreviation of 缩写=POPULATION

pop·a·dum, poppadum /ˈpɑpǝdǝm; ˈpɒpǝdǝm/ *n* [C] a large circular piece of very thin flat Indian bread cooked in oil〔印度的〕油煎薄饼

pop art /ˌ· ˈ·◂/ *n* [U] a kind of art that was popular in the 1960s, which shows ordinary objects, such as advertisements, or things you see in people's homes〔反映日常生活事物的〕波普艺术，通俗艺术，大众艺术〔20 世纪 60 年代流行的一种艺术〕

pop·corn /ˈpɑpˌkorn; ˈpɒpkɔːn/ *n* [U] a kind of corn that swells and bursts open when heated, and is usually eaten warm with salt or sugar 爆玉米花，爆谷

Pope /pop; pǝʊp/ *n* [C] **1** the leader of the Roman Catholic church〔罗马天主教的〕教皇，教宗: *The Pope will visit El Salvador this year.* 教皇今年将访问萨尔瓦多。| *Pope John XXIII* 教皇约翰二十三世 —see also 另见 PAPAL **2 Is the Pope (a) Catholic?** *informal humorous* used to say that something is clearly true or certain【非正式，幽默】教皇是天主教徒吗？这还用问？〔用于表示某事毫无疑问是真实的或确定的〕: *"Do you think they'll win?" "Is the Pope Catholic?"* "你认为他们会赢吗？""这还用问？"

Pope, Al·ex·an·der /ˌælɪgˈzændɚ; ˌælɪgˈzɑːndǝ/ (1688-1744) a British poet and SATIRIST. Many people consider him the most important poet of his time, and admire his use of the HEROIC COUPLET. His best known works are *The Rape of the Lock* and *The Dunciad*. He also produced very popular translations of the poems of Homer. 蒲柏〔(1688-1744)，英国诗人、讽刺作

家。许多人认为他是当时最重要的诗人，欣赏他的英雄双韵体作诗风格。代表作为《夺发记》和《群愚史诗》。他翻译的《荷马史诗》广为流传〕

pope's nose, the /,· ˈ·/ *n AmE, IrishE, ScotE* the piece of flesh at the tail end of a cooked bird, such as a chicken【美，爱尔兰，苏格兰】〔煮熟的〕鸡〔禽类〕的尾部〔屁股〕肉; PARSON'S NOSE *BrE*【英】

Pop·eye /ˈpɑpaɪ; ˈpɒpaɪ/ a character also called **Popeye the Sailorman**, in a US CARTOON STRIP and cartoon films. Popeye is a sailor who smokes a pipe, and when he eats cans of SPINACH (=a vegetable with large dark green leaves) his muscles immediately grow much bigger and he becomes very strong. 大力水手〔美国卡通连环画和卡通电影中的一角色。他是个抽烟斗的水手，吃了菠菜，身上的肌肉就会发达起来，也会非常有力气〕

pop-eyed /,· ˈ·◂/ *adj informal* having your eyes wide open, because you are surprised or excited【非正式】〔由于惊讶或兴奋而〕目瞪口呆的，瞪大眼睛的

pop fly /ˈ· ·/ *n* [C] a type of hit in BASEBALL in which the ball is hit straight up into the air and only travels a short distance〔棒球的〕小腾空球 —see picture on page A22 参见 A22 页图

Pop Goes the Wea·sel /,· · ˈ· ·/ an old British song for children《鼬鼠溜了》〔英国一首古老的儿歌〕: *Half a pound of tuppenny rice, /Half a pound of treacle; /That's the way the money goes, /Pop goes the weasel!* 两便士的米买半磅，/外加蜜糖又半磅；/就像鼬鼠哧溜一声，/钱儿溜得没影踪！In the US, children also know this song, but the words are〔美国也有一类似儿歌，但歌词有所不同〕: *Round and round the mulberry bush,/ the monkey chased the weasel; / The monkey said 'twas all in fun, / Pop goes the weasel!* 环绕一片桑树林，/鼬鼠跑来猴子追;/猴子自称真好玩，/鼬鼠溜得无踪影！

pop group /ˈ· ·/ *n* [C] a group of people who sing and play POP MUSIC 流行乐队，流行音乐组合

pop-gun /ˈ· ·/ *n* [C] a toy gun that fires small objects, such as corks (CORK[1] (2)), with a loud noise〔发射软木塞等的〕玩具汽枪

pop·in·jay /ˈpɑpɪn,dʒe; ˈpɒpɪ̣ndʒeɪ/ *n* [C] *old use* a young man who is too proud of his appearance【旧】讲究衣着的年轻男人，花花公子〔过分以外貌为荣的年轻人〕

pop·lar /ˈpɑplɚ; ˈpɒplə/ *n* [C] a very tall straight thin tree 杨树

pop·lin /ˈpɑplɪn; ˈpɒplɪ̣n/ *n* [U] a strong shiny cotton cloth 毛葛，府绸

pop mu·sic /ˈ· ,· ·/ *n* [U] modern music that is popular with young people and usually consists of simple tunes with a strong beat 流行音乐

Pop·o·cat·é·pet·l /,popəkætəˈpɛtl; ,pɒpəkætəˈpetl/ a mountain in Mexico which is a VOLCANO 波波卡特佩特〔墨西哥一火山〕

pop·o·ver /ˈpɑp,ovɚ; ˈpɒpəʊvə/ *n* [C] *AmE* a light, hollow cake made with eggs, milk, and flour【美】空心酥脆饼，膨松饼〔用鸡蛋、牛奶和面粉制成〕

pop·pa /ˈpɑpə; ˈpɒpə/ *n* [singular] *AmE informal* father【美，非正式】爸爸

pop·pa·dum /ˈpɑpədəm; ˈpɒpədəm/ *n* [C] another spelling of POPADUM popadum 的另一种拼法

pop·per /ˈpɑpɚ; ˈpɒpə/ *n* [C] *informal especially BrE* a small metal thing used for fastening a piece of clothing which consists of two parts, one of which is pressed into the hollow part of the other; SNAP[2] (6)【非正式，尤英】按扣，揿扣，子母扣 —see picture at 参见 FASTENER 图

Popper, Sir Karl /kɑrl; kɑːl/ (1902-94) a British PHILOSOPHER, born in Austria, who believed that ideas about the world must be proved scientifically. His best known book, *The Open Society and its Enemies*, is an attack on political systems in which the state has too much control. 波普尔〔(1902-1994)，英国哲学家，生于奥地利。他认为所有世界观都须经过科学验证。代表作为《开放社会及其敌人》，抨击过于专制的政治制度〕

pop·pet /ˈpɑpɪt; ˈpɒpɪ̣t/ *n* [C] *BrE spoken* a way of talking to or about a child or animal you are fond of【英口】宝宝，宝贝儿，乖乖〔指宠爱的小孩或动物〕: *Isn't he a poppet?* 他真是个小宝贝，不是吗？| *Come here, poppet.* 到这儿来，宝宝。

pop·py /ˈpɑpɪ; ˈpɒpi/ *n* [C] **1** a plant that has brightly coloured, usually red, flowers and small black seeds 罂粟 **2** a red colour 深橘红色 —see picture on page A5 参见 A5 页图

CULTURAL NOTE 文化注释

For British people, the poppy represents the soldiers who died in the two World Wars, especially World War I, because these flowers grew in the fields of France where many soldiers were killed in battle. People buy red poppies made of paper and wear them on their coats on **Remembrance Day** (informally known as **Poppy Day**) in order to show respect for all the people who died. 英国人认为罂粟代表着在两次世界大战，特别是一战中阵亡的将士，因为这些花长在有很多将士牺牲的法国战场上。人们在荣军纪念日（非正式的情况下亦称"罂粟花日"）买来纸做的红色罂粟花别在上衣上，以表达对那些阵亡者的崇敬之情。

pop·py·cock /ˈpɑpɪ,kɑk; ˈpɒpikɒk/ *n* [U] *old-fashioned* nonsense【过时】废话，胡扯: *He's talking absolute poppycock!* 他完全是在胡说八道！

pop·py·seed /ˈpɑpɪsid; ˈpɒpisiːd/ *n* [U] the small black seeds of the poppy plant used in cakes, bread etc 罂粟籽〔用于做糕点、面包等〕

pop quiz /ˈ· ·/ *n* [C] *AmE* a short test which is given without any warning in order to check that students have been studying【美】突击测验，突击考试

pops /pɑps; pɒps/ *adj* **pops concert/orchestra** *AmE* a concert or ORCHESTRA which performs CLASSICAL and popular music【美】〔演奏古典和流行音乐的〕通俗音乐会/管弦乐团: *the Boston Pops Orchestra* 波士顿通俗管弦乐团

Pop·si·cle /ˈpɑpsɪkl; ˈpɒpsɪ̣kəl/ *n* [C] *AmE trademark* a piece of ice, usually tasting of fruit, that you suck on a stick【美，商标】冰棍，冰棒，雪条; ICE LOLLY *BrE*【英】

pop star /ˈ· ·/ *n* [C] a famous and successful entertainer who plays or sings POP MUSIC 流行乐歌星

Pop Tarts /ˈ· ·/ *trademark* a type of square, flat PASTRY filled with fruit or chocolate, which you heat in a TOASTER and eat for breakfast【商标】果酱馅饼〔一种四方形扁平面饼。内有水果馅或巧克力馅，在烤箱中加热可作早餐〕

pop·u·lace /ˈpɑpjələs; ˈpɒpjɪ̣ləs/ *n* [singular] *formal* the ordinary people who live in a country【正式】平民，百姓，大众: *breaking the news to a joyful populace* 把这消息透露给欢乐的老百姓

pop·u·lar /ˈpɑpjəlɚ; ˈpɒpjɪ̣lə/ *adj* **1** liked by a lot of people 受大众喜爱的，受欢迎的: *Hilary was popular at school.* 希拉里在学校里很受欢迎。| **[+with]** *Video games are very popular with children.* 电子游戏很受孩子的喜爱。| *a popular holiday resort* 人们喜欢的度假胜地 —opposite 反义词 UNPOPULAR **2 popular belief/view/misconception** a belief etc that a lot of people have 普遍的信念/观点/误解: **contrary to popular belief** *Contrary to popular belief, gorillas are basically shy, gentle creatures.* 与人们普遍的看法相反，大猩猩其实是一种羞怯、温和的动物。**3** [only before noun 仅用于名词前] popular entertainment, newspapers, programmes etc are intended to be suitable for ordinary people〔娱乐、报纸、节目等〕通俗的，大众（化）的: *pilloried by the popular press* 受到通俗报刊的嘲笑 **4** [only before noun 仅用于名词前] done by a lot of people in a society, group etc 由〔社会、团体等中〕多数人做的，公众的: *popular protest* 公众的抗议 | *It was decided by popular vote.* 这是由公众投票决定的。**5 you'll be popular** *spoken* used when telling someone that other people will be annoyed with them【口】你会"走红"的〔用于告诉某人别人将会生他们的气〕: *You'll be popular when they find out you've lost their tickets.* 他们一旦知道你把他们的票丢了，你可就要"走红"了。

pop·u·lar·i·ty /,pɑpjəˈlærətɪ; ,pɒpjɪ̣ˈlærɪ̣ti/ *n* [U] the quality of being liked or supported by a large number of people 流行，普及，受欢迎; 声望: **gain in popularity** (=start to be liked by many people) 开始流行 *Western music is steadily gaining in popularity.* 西方音乐逐渐流行起来。| *The president's popularity has declined considerably.* 总统的受欢迎程度已大大降低。

pop·u·lar·ize /ˈpɑpjələ,raɪz; ˈpɒpjɪ̣ləraɪz/ also 又作 **-ise** *BrE*【英】*v* [T] **1** to make something well-known and liked 使〔某物〕受欢迎; 宣传，推广: *Reggae music was popularized by Bob Marley in the 1970s.* 雷盖音乐由鲍勃·马利在20世纪70年代推广开来。**2** to make a difficult subject or idea easily understandable for ordinary people who have no special knowledge about it 使〔困难的学科或观点〕通俗化，使大众化，使易懂，普及: *books aimed at popularizing modern science* 致力于普及现代科学的书籍 —**popularization** /,pɑpjələrəˈzeʃən; ,pɒpjɪ̣ləraɪˈzeɪʃən/ *n* [U]

pop·u·lar·ly /ˈpɑpjələlɪ; ˈpɒpjɪ̣ləli/ *adv* **popularly believed/thought/known etc** believed, thought, known etc by many people（人们）普遍相信/认为/知道等: *Vitamin C is popularly believed to prevent colds.* 人们普遍认为维生素C有预防感冒的作用。

pop·u·late /ˈpɑpjə,let; ˈpɒpjɪ̣leɪt/ *v* **be populated** if an area is populated by a particular group of people, they live there〔某地区〕居住着: **[+by]** *The Central Highlands are populated mainly by peasant farmers.* 在中部苏格兰高地居住的主要是农民。| **densely/heavily/highly/thickly populated** (=a lot of

people live in that place in relation to its size) 人口密集的 *densely populated urban areas* 人口稠密的市区 | **thinly/sparsely populated** (=few people live in that place in relation to its size) 人口稀少的 *The northern islands are very sparsely populated.* 北部各岛人烟稀少。

S2 W1 **pop·u·la·tion** /ˌpɑpjəˋleʃən; ˌpɒpjʊˈleɪʃən/ *n* [U] **1** the number of people living in a particular area, country etc 人口: *a city with a population of over two million* 一个有两百多万人口的城市 | *What is the population of Mexico?* 墨西哥有多少人口? **2** [C usually singular 一般用单数] all of the people who live in a particular area〔某一地区的〕全体居民: *The whole population had turned out to welcome us home.* 所有居民都出来欢迎我们回家。| *Most of the world's population don't get enough to eat.* 世界上大多数人都吃不饱。| **the white/French/urban etc population** (=part of the group of people who live in a particular area who are white, French etc) 白人/法国人/城市等的人口 *By the middle of the 19th century, the urban population of England exceeded the rural population.* 到19世纪中期, 英格兰的城市人口已经超过了农村人口。**3 population explosion** a rapid increase in the population of an area or the whole planet 人口爆炸 **4 centre of population/population centre** a city, town etc 城市, 城镇: *far from most centres of population* 远离大多数城市

pop·u·list /ˋpɑpjəlɪst; ˈpɒpjʊlɪst/ *adj* claiming to represent ordinary people 声称代表人民的, 平民主义的: *a populist leadership* 声称代表民众利益的领导人 —**populist** *n* [C] —**populism** *n* [U]: *the switch from Marxism to populism* 从马克思主义到平民主义的转变

pop·u·lous /ˋpɑpjələs; ˈpɒpjʊləs/ *adj formal* a populous area has a large population in relation to its size【正式】人口稠密的: *Hong Kong is one of the most populous areas in the world.* 香港是世界上人口最稠密的地区之一。—**populousness** *n* [U]

pop-up /ˈ· ·/ *adj* **pop-up book/card/toaster etc** a book, card, TOASTER etc that is designed to make something suddenly spring out of it〔可以将内部的东西突然弹出的〕弹出式书籍/贺卡/烤面包机等

Pop War·ner /ˌ· ˈ· ·/ a US organization that teaches children to play American football in teams. It was named after Pop Warner, a famous football COACH. 波普·沃纳〔美国一青少年美式橄榄球培训组织, 以著名教练波普·沃纳的名字命名〕

porce·lain /ˋpɔrslɪn; ˈpɔːslɪn/ *n* [U] **1** a hard shiny white substance that is used for making expensive plates, cups etc 瓷 **2** plates, cups etc made of this 瓷器

porch /pɔrtʃ; pɔːtʃ/ *n* [C] **1** an entrance covered by a roof outside the front door of a house or church〔房子或教堂前门外有顶的〕入口处, 门廊 **2** *AmE* an open area with a floor and a roof, often made of wood, fixed to the side of a house on the ground floor; VERANDA【美】〔房屋侧面有屋顶和地板的〕游廊, 走廊; 阳台: *sitting out on the porch* 坐在外面的游廊上 —see picture on page A4 参见 A4 页图

por·cu·pine /ˋpɔrkjəˌpaɪn; ˈpɔːkjʊpaɪn/ *n* [C] an animal with long, sharp, needle-like parts growing all over its back and sides which it can make point upwards 豪猪, 箭猪

pore[1] /pɔr; pɔː/ *n* [C] one of the small holes in your skin that liquid, especially SWEAT can pass through, or a similar hole in the surface of a plant〔皮肤的〕毛孔;〔植物表面的〕气孔, 细孔: *Witch-hazel can help to unblock greasy pores.* 金缕梅酊剂有助于疏通含油脂的毛孔。

pore[2] *v*

pore over sth *phr v* [T] to read or look at something very carefully for a long time 仔细阅读; 凝视, 注视: *They expected to find him poring over his notes the night before the exam.* 他们原以为会看到他在考试的前一天晚上仔细地研读笔记。

pork /pork; pɔːk/ *n* [U] **1** the meat from pigs 猪肉: *pork chops* 猪排 **2** *AmE slang* government money spent in a particular area in order to get political advantages【美俚】政治恩惠〔为获得政治上的好处而拨给某一地区的政府资金〕

pork bar·rel /ˈ· ˌ· ·/ *n* [singular, U] *AmE slang* a government plan to increase the amount of money spent in a particular area in order to gain political advantage【美俚】〔政府为争取选票而给予地方的〕国库拨款, 政治分肥: *the pork barrel politics of military production contracts* 军用生产合同方面的政治分肥

pork·er /ˋpɔrkɚ; ˈpɔːkə/ *n* [C] **1** a young pig that is made fat before being killed for food〔宰杀前经过催肥的〕食用小猪 **2** *informal* an insulting word for a fat person【非正式】肥猪, 胖猪〔对肥胖者的侮辱性称呼〕**3** *slang* a lie【俚】谎言, 谎话

pork pie /ˌ· ˈ·◂/ *n* [C,U] *BrE* a small round PIE which contains pieces of cooked pork【英】猪肉馅饼

pork rinds /ˌ· ˈ·/ *n* [plural] *AmE* SCRATCHINGS【美】猪肉皮

pork·y[1] /ˋpɔrkɪ; ˈpɔːki/ *adj informal* an insulting word meaning fat【非正式】肥的, 肥胖的〔侮辱性词语〕

porky[2] /ˋpɔrkɪ; ˈpɔːki/ *n* [C] also 又作 **porky pie** /ˌ· · ˈ·/ *BrE slang* a lie【英俚】谎言, 谎话

porn /pɔrn; pɔːn/ *n* [U] *informal* pornography【非正式】色情作品; 色情描写: *the porn industry* 色情业 | *Computer porn is the latest threat.* 电脑色情是最新的威胁。—see also 另见 HARD PORN, SOFT PORN

porn·o /ˋpɔrno; ˈpɔːnəʊ/ *adj* [usually before noun 一般用于名词前] *informal* PORNOGRAPHIC【非正式】色情的: *a porno movie* 色情电影

por·nog·ra·phy /pɔrˋnɑgrəfɪ; pɔːˈnɒgrəfi/ *n* [U] **1** magazines, films etc that show sexual acts and images in a way that is intended to make people feel sexually excited 色情作品[杂志, 电影等]: *a major campaign against pornography* 一场反对色情作品的重大运动 **2** the treatment of sexual acts in pictures, film or writing in a way that is intended to make people feel sexually excited〔图片, 电影或文字作品中的〕色情描绘 —**pornographer** *n* [C] —**pornographic** /ˌpɔrnəˋgræfɪk; ˌpɔːnəˈgræfɪk◂/ *adj*: *The script was condemned as pornographic.* 这个剧本被指责为淫秽作品。—**pornographically** /-klɪ; -kli/ *adv*

po·rous /ˋporəs; ˈpɔːrəs/ *adj* porous rock or soil allows liquid, air etc to pass through slowly〔岩石或土壤〕能渗透的, 透水[气]的 —**porousness** *n* [U]

por·phy·ry /ˋpɔrfərɪ; ˈpɔːfəri/ *n* [U] a type of hard dark red or purple rock containing CRYSTAL*s* 斑岩

por·poise /ˋpɔrpəs; ˈpɔːpəs/ *n* [C] a sea animal rather like a DOLPHIN, that swims in groups 鼠海豚

por·ridge /ˋpɔrɪdʒ; ˈpɒrɪdʒ/ *n* [U] **1** a soft breakfast food made by boiling OATMEAL (=crushed grain) in milk or water 燕麦片[麦片]粥; OATMEAL *AmE*【美】**2** *BrE slang* a period of time spent in prison【英俚】关押, 监禁(期): **do porridge** (=spend time in prison) 坐牢, 服刑

Porsche /pɔrʃ; pɔːʃ/ *trademark* a type of fast German sports car【商标】保时捷〔一款高速德国跑车〕

port /port; pɔːt/ *n* W2

1 ►WHERE SHIPS STOP 轮船停泊的地方◄ [C,U] a place where ships can load and unload people or things; HARBOUR[1] 港, 港口, 海港: **come into port/leave port** *The ferry was just about to leave port.* 那艘渡船正要离港。| **in port** *We're going to have two days ashore while the ship is in port.* 轮船在港口停靠时, 我们将有两天的上岸时间。

2 ►TOWN 城镇◄ [C] a town or city with a HARBOUR[1] or DOCK*s* 港口城市, 港市; 口岸: *Britain's largest port* 英国最大的港口城市 | *the Israeli port of Haifa* 以色列港市海法

3 ►WINE 葡萄酒◄ [C,U] strong sweet Portuguese wine, usually drunk after a meal 波尔图葡萄酒〔葡萄牙产的一种葡萄酒, 通常在饭后饮用〕: *port and Stilton* 波尔图葡萄酒和斯第尔顿乳酪

4 ►LEFT OF SHIP 轮船的左侧◄ [U] the left side of a ship or aircraft when you are looking towards the front〔轮船或飞机航行方向的〕左舷: *on the port side* 在左舷一边 | **to port** *After the collision, the ship began leaning over to port.* 碰撞之后, 那艘轮船开始向左舷倾斜。—opposite 反义词 STARBOARD

5 ►COMPUTER 电脑◄ [C] *technical* a part of a computer where you can connect another piece of equipment such as a PRINTER【术语】端口, 接口〔电脑与其他设备的接口〕

6 any port in a storm *usually spoken* an expression meaning that you should take whatever help you can when you are in trouble, even if it has some disadvantages【一般口】〔即使有不利之处也应接受的〕摆脱困境的任何帮助, 穷途之策 —see also 另见 FREE PORT, PORT OF ENTRY

por·ta·ble /ˋportəbl; ˈpɔːtəbəl/ *adj* light and able to be carried or moved easily 手提式的, 便携式的, 轻便的: *a portable typewriter* 便携式打字机 —**portable** *n* [C]: *We swapped the colour television for a black and white portable.* 我们用彩色电视机换了一台手提式黑白电视机。—**portability** /ˌportəˋbɪlətɪ; ˌpɔːtəˈbɪlɪti/ *n* [U]

por·ta·crib /ˋportəkrɪb; ˈpɔːtəkrɪb/ *n* [C] *AmE trademark* a small bed with handles in which a baby lies and can be carried【美, 商标】手提式婴儿床; CARRYCOT *especially BrE*【尤英】—see picture at 参见 BED[1] 图

port·age /ˋportɪdʒ; ˈpɔːtɪdʒ/ *n* [U] the act of carrying boats over land from one river to another〔两条河之间的〕路运, 陆运〔将船从一条河经陆地运至另一条河〕

Por·ta·kab·in /ˋportəkæbɪn; ˈpɔːtəkæbɪn/ *n* [C] *trademark* a small hut that can be used as a temporary office, classroom etc, and can be moved by TRUCK【商标】活动房屋〔一种可用大卡车搬运的临时房屋, 可用作临时办公室、教室等〕

por·tal /ˋpɔrtḷ; ˈpɔːtl/ *n* [C usually plural 一般用复数] *literary* a tall and impressive gate or entrance to a building【文】〔建筑物高大壮观的〕大门, 正门: *the carved Gothic portals of the college* 这所学院带有雕饰的哥特式大门

Port-au-Prince /ˌpɔtoˋprɪns; ˌpɔːtəʊˈprɪns/ the capital city of Haiti 太子港〔海地首都〕

port·cul·lis /pɔrtˋkʌlɪs; pɔːtˈkʌlɨs/ *n* [C] a strong iron gate that can be lowered over the entrance of a castle〔城堡的〕吊门, 吊闸

por·tend /pɔrˋtɛnd; pɔːˈtend/ *v* [T] *literary* to be a sign that something is going to happen, especially something unpleasant【文】预示〔不祥之事〕, 为…的凶兆: *strange events that portend some great disaster* 预示着巨大灾难的奇怪事件

por·tent /ˋpɔrtɛnt; ˈpɔːtent/ *n* [C] *literary* a sign or warning that something is going to happen【文】迹象, 征兆, 预兆: [+of] *This was a striking portent of things to come.* 这明显地预示着即将发生的事情。—compare 比较 OMEN

por·ten·tous /pɔrˋtɛntəs; pɔːˈtentəs/ *adj* **1** *literary* events that are portentous are very important, especially because they show that something unpleasant is going to happen【文】预示未来的; 凶兆的, 征兆不祥的: *portentous events that boded ill* 预示凶兆的不祥事件 **2** trying to appear important and serious 自命不凡的, 摆架子的, 自大的: *The book is portentous and badly edited.* 这本书煞有介事, 编得很差劲。—**portentously** *adv* —**portentousness** *n* [U]

por·ter /ˋpɔrtɚ; ˈpɔːtə/ *n* **1** [C] someone whose job is to carry travellers' bags at railway stations, airports etc〔火车站、机场等的〕行李搬运工人, 脚夫: *I hailed a porter and then a cab.* 我叫了一名搬运工人, 然后又叫了一辆出租车。**2** [C] *especially BrE* someone in charge of the entrance to a hotel, hospital etc【尤英】〔酒店、医院等的〕守门人 **3** [C] someone whose job is to carry heavy goods at markets〔在市场搬运重物的〕货物搬运工 **4** [C] *AmE* someone whose job is to look after a sleeping carriage in a train【美】〔火车卧铺车厢的〕服务员 **5** [U] *old-fashioned* a dark brown bitter beer【过时】黑啤酒, 深褐色苦啤酒

Porter, Cole /kol; kəʊl/ (1891-1964) a US musician who wrote many popular songs and MUSICALS (=plays or films that use singing and dancing to tell a story). His songs are still popular, and are admired for their clever and amusing words. They include *Night and Day*, *Let's Do It*, and *I've Got You Under My Skin*. 波特〔(1891-1964), 美国音乐家, 写过不少流行歌曲和音乐剧。创作的歌曲流行至今, 歌词工巧风趣, 颇受赞赏。代表作有《夜以继日》、《干起来吧》和《肌肤之亲》〕

por·ter·house steak /ˌpɔrtɚhaus ˋstek; ˌpɔːtəhaʊs ˈsteɪk/ *n* [C,U] a thick, flat piece of high quality BEEF[1] (1) 上等牛排

port·fo·li·o /pɔrtˋfolɪˌo; pɔːtˈfəʊliəʊ/ *n* [C] **1** a large flat case used especially for carrying drawings, documents etc 公事包, 文件夹 **2** a collection of drawings, paintings or other pieces of work by an artist, photographer etc〔艺术家、摄影师等的〕画作[相片]选辑, 作品选辑 **3** a collection of shares (SHARE[2] (5)) owned by a particular person or company〔某人或某公司持有的〕有价证券组合; 资产组合; 投资搭配: *an investment portfolio* 投资组合 **4** *formal, especially BrE* the area of responsibility of a particular government minister【正式, 尤英】部长[大臣]的职责[职务]: *the foreign affairs portfolio* 外交部长职务

port·hole /ˋpɔrtˌhol; ˈpɔːthəʊl/ *n* [C] a small round window on the side of a ship or plane〔轮船或飞机的〕舷窗: *a row of illuminated portholes* 一排张灯结彩的舷窗

por·ti·co /ˋpɔrtɪˌko; ˈpɔːtɪkəʊ/ *n* [C] a covered entrance to a building, consisting of a roof supported by PILLARS (有圆柱的) 门廊, 柱廊: *Above the portico is an commemorative plaque.* 门廊上面是一块纪念匾。

por·tion[1] /ˋpɔrʃən; ˈpɔːʃən/ *n* [C] **1** a part of something larger, especially a part that is different from the other parts〔东西的〕一部分〔尤指与其他部分不同〕: [+of] *The front portion of the rocket breaks off.* 火箭的前部脱落了。| *The factory represents only a small portion of the company's interests.* 这家工厂只占公司股份的一小部分。**2** an amount of food for one person, especially served in a restaurant〔尤指餐馆中食物的〕一份, 一客: *They're good-sized portions.* 它们是大份的。| [+of] *Another portion of chips?* 再来一份薯条好吗? **3** [usually singular 一般用单数] a share of something, such as responsibility, blame, or profits that is divided between a small number of people〔责任、利润等的〕一份, 一部分: [+of] *The other driver must bear a portion of the blame for the accident.* 另一位司机必须对这次事故承担部分责任。**4 sb's portion** *formal or literary* something that happens in your life that you cannot avoid; FATE (1)【正式或文】某人的命运: *Sorrow has always been her portion.* 她命中注定悲伤不断。

portion[2] *v*

portion sth ↔ **out** *phr v* [T] to divide something into parts and give them to several people 分配: **portion sth out among** *The money was portioned out among them.* 那笔钱被他们分了。

Port·land /ˋpɔrtlənd; ˈpɔːtlənd/ a port on the Columbia and Willamette Rivers, in northern Oregon in the northwestern US, which is the largest city in the Oregon 波特兰〔哥伦比亚河与威拉米特河沿岸一港口。位于美国西北的俄勒冈州北部, 为该州最大城市〕

port·ly /ˋpɔrtlɪ; ˈpɔːtli/ *adj* someone who is portly, especially a rather old man, is fat and round〔尤指年长男子〕肥胖的, 发福的: *a portly old gentleman* 一位发福的老先生 —**portliness** *n* [U]

port·man·teau[1] /pɔrtˋmænto; pɔːtˈmæntəʊ/ *n* [C] *old-fashioned* a very large SUITCASE that opens into two parts【过时】〔对开的〕手提箱, 皮箱

portmanteau[2] *adj* [only before noun 仅用于名词前] *formal* a portmanteau word is made by combining the sound and meaning of two other words【正式】〔由两个词的词义和读音合并〕组成的, 混合的, 紧缩的: *'Edutainment' is a portmanteau word meaning education by entertainment.* edutainment 是一个紧缩词, 意思为寓教于乐。

Port·mei·ri·on /pɔrtˋmɛrɪən; pɔːtˈmeriən/ a small village on the coast of North Wales, designed and built by Clough Williams-Ellis. It is based on an Italian fishing village and is popular with tourists. It is also the place where the popular 1960s British television programme *The Prisoner* was filmed. 波特梅里恩〔威尔士北部沿海一小村庄, 由克拉夫·威廉斯-埃利斯设计建造。该村以意大利的一个渔村为原型建成, 游人颇为喜欢。20 世纪 60 年代, 英国著名电视剧《囚徒》曾在该村拍摄〕

Port Moresby /ˌpɔrt ˋmɔrzbɪ; ˌpɔːt ˈmɔːzbi/ the capital city of Papua New Guinea 莫尔斯比港〔巴布亚新几内亚首都〕

Port·o·bel·lo Road /ˌpɔrtəbɛlo ˋrod; ˌpɔːtəbeləʊ ˈrəʊd/ a street in West London, where a market is held every Friday and Saturday and ANTIQUES (=valuable old furniture, jewellery etc) are sold 波托贝洛路〔伦敦西部一街道。此处周五、周六有一古董集市〕

port of call /ˌ· · ˈ·/ *n* [C usually singular 一般用单数] **1** *informal* one of a series of places that you visit【非正式】旅途中的落脚点[停留地]; 沿途要拜访的地方: *My next port of call was the City Records Department.* 我下一个要去的地方是市档案局。**2** a port where a ship stops on a journey from one place to another〔船的〕沿途停靠港: *Our next port of call was Istanbul.* 我们下一个要停泊的港口是伊斯坦布尔。

port of en·try /ˌ· · ˈ· ·/ *n* [C] a place, such as a port or airport, where people or goods can enter a country〔人或货物的〕入口港, 进口港, 入境地点

Por·ton Down /ˌpɔrtn̩ ˋdaun; ˌpɔːtn ˈdaʊn/ a place in the south of England where there is a government laboratory used for studying chemical weapons and biological weapons (=weapons that use bacteria to kill people by giving them diseases) 朴顿中心〔位于英格兰南部, 英国政府生化武器研究实验室所在地〕

Porto-Novo /ˌpɔrto ˋnovo; ˌpɔːtəʊ ˈnəʊvəʊ/ the capital city of Benin 波多诺伏〔贝宁首都〕

por·trait /ˋpɔrtrɪt; ˈpɔːtrɨt/ *n* **1** [C] a painting, drawing, or photograph of a person〔人的〕画像; 照片; 肖像: [+of] *a portrait of Lenin* 列宁的画像 | *She's been commissioned to paint Andrew's portrait.* 她已受托画安德鲁的肖像。**2** [C] a description or representation of something〔对某物的〕描绘, 描述, 表现: [+of] *The article's portrait of Owen's career was very interesting.* 这篇文章对欧文职业生涯的描述非常有趣。**3** [U] *informal* portrait mode【非正式】纵向格式 —see also 另见 SELF-PORTRAIT

portrait mode /ˈ· · ·/ *adj* a photograph, picture, book, or page that is portrait has the longer edges at the sides〔照片、图片、书或页〕竖排的, 纵向的 —opposite 反义词 LANDSCAPE

Portrait of the Ar·tist as a Young Man, A /ˌ· · · ,· · · ·, · ˈ·/ (1916) a NOVEL by James Joyce which is based on his own life《青年艺术家的肖像》〔(1916), 詹姆斯·乔伊斯的自传体小说〕

por·trai·ture /ˋpɔrtrɪtʃɚ; ˈpɔːtrɨtʃə/ *n* [U] the art of painting or drawing pictures of people 肖像画技法

por·tray /pɔrˋtre; pɔːˈtreɪ/ *v* [T] **1** to describe or represent something or someone 描绘, 描写, 描述: *His most famous painting portrayed the death of Nelson.* 他最出名的一幅画描绘了纳尔逊死时的情景。| *Levi portrays the sheer horror of the concentration camps very powerfully.* 利瓦伊将集中营的恐怖描绘得极有感染力。**2 portray sb/sth as sth** to describe or show

someone or something in a particular way, according to your opinion of them 把某人/某物描写为[刻画为]某物: *women portrayed as sex objects in Hollywood movies* 在好莱坞电影中被刻画成性对象的女人 | *Joan Crawford's daughter portrayed her as a maniac.* 琼·克劳福德的女儿把她说成是个疯子。**3** to act the part of a character in a play 扮演〔角色〕: *She portrayed a doomed woman in the TV film 'Right to Die'.* 她在电视电影《死的权利》中扮演一位遭遇厄运的女性。

por·tray·al /pɔrˋtreəl; pɔːˈtreɪəl/ *n* [C,U] the action of portraying someone or something 描绘, 描写, 描述; 扮演; 表现: *Does the film give an accurate portrayal of life under Stalin?* 这部电影如实地表现斯大林统治下的生活了吗?

Ports·mouth /ˋpɔrtsməθ; ˈpɔːtsməθ/ a town and port on the south coast of England. It is an important navy base and a place from which ferries (FERRY) take cars and passengers to France. 朴茨茅斯〔英格兰南部沿海一港市。该镇为英国一重要海军基地, 也是英法车运和客运船只的停泊港口〕

Port Stan·ley /, ·ˈ··/ the capital of the Falkland Islands, and the place where the Falklands War of 1982 began and ended 斯坦利港〔福克兰群岛首府, 也是 1982 年福克兰群岛战争所在地〕

Por·tu·gal /ˋpɔrtʃəgl; ˈpɔːtʃʊgəl/ a country in southwest Europe, west of Spain. It is a member of the EU. Population: 10,066,000 (2001). Capital: Lisbon. Portugal's traditional industries include fishing and wine, and its more modern industries include clothing and car parts. Portugal's southern coast, the Algarve, is a popular place for holidays. 葡萄牙〔欧洲西南部一国家, 位于西班牙以西, 欧盟成员国。人口: 10,066,000 (2001), 首都: 里斯本。葡萄牙的传统行业有捕鱼业和酿酒业, 较为新兴的行业为制衣和汽车零部件生产。葡萄牙的南部海岸阿尔加维是著名的度假胜地〕

Por·tu·guese /ˋpɔrtʃə,giz; ˌpɔːtʃʊˈgiːz◂/ *n* [U] **1** the language of Portugal, Brazil, and some other countries 葡萄牙语: *Do you speak Portuguese?* 你说葡萄牙语吗? **2 the Portuguese** the people of Portugal 葡萄牙人 —**Portuguese** *adj*: *Portuguese wine* 葡萄牙的葡萄酒

Portuguese man-of-war /ˌ·····ˈ·/ *n* [C] a very large JELLYFISH, which has long poisonous parts hanging down from its body 僧帽水母

W3 **pose¹** /poz; pəʊz/ *v* **1 pose a problem/threat/challenge etc** to cause a problem, danger, difficulty etc 引起问题/造成威胁/提出挑战等: *Newton's challenge poses no threat to the leadership.* 牛顿的挑战对领导层造不成任何威胁。| *Rising unemployment is posing serious problems for the administration.* 不断上升的失业率正给政府造成严重的困难。**2** [I,T] to sit or stand in a particular position in order to be photographed or painted, or to make someone do this 〔为照相或画像而〕(使)摆好〔某种〕姿势: **[+for]** *We posed for photographs after the graduation ceremony.* 毕业典礼之后, 我们摆好姿势拍照。**3 pose a question** to ask a question, especially one that needs to be carefully thought about 提出问题〔尤指需要仔细考虑的问题〕: *The first chapter poses the question: What constitutes a democracy?* 第一章提出的问题是: 民主国家是由什么构成的? **4 pose as sb** to pretend to be someone else, in order to deceive people 假装成某人, 假扮成某人: *Bryce was caught posing as a lawyer.* 布赖斯因冒充律师而被捕。**5** [I] *especially BrE* to dress or behave like a fashionable, rich etc person in order to make other people notice you or admire you 【尤英】装腔作势

pose² *n* [C] **1** the position in which someone stands or sits, especially in a painting, photograph etc 〔为画像、拍照而摆的〕姿势, 姿态: **in a pose** *a painting of the Duchess in a dramatic pose* 摆着演戏般姿势的公爵夫人画像 | **strike a pose** (=stand or sit in a particular position) 摆个姿势 **2** *especially BrE* behaviour in which someone pretends to behave like a fashionable, rich, intelligent etc person in order to make other people notice them or admire them 【尤英】做作; 装腔作势的举止: **it's just a pose** *He's always talking about his deep interest in philosophy – it's just a pose.* 他总在谈论他对哲学有浓厚的兴趣 —— 那只是装腔作势罢了。

Po·sei·don /pəˋsaɪdn̩; pəˈsaɪdn/ in Greek MYTHOLOGY, the god of the sea. In Roman mythology his name is Neptune. 波塞冬〔希腊神话中的海神, 罗马神话中称尼普顿〕

pos·er /ˋpozɚ; ˈpəʊzə/ *n* [C] **1** *informal* someone who tries to behave like a fashionable, rich, intelligent etc person to make people notice or admire them 【非正式】装腔作势的人: *Kate's such a poser.* 凯特真会装腔作势。**2** *old-fashioned* a difficult question or problem 【过时】难题, 棘手的问题

po·seur /poˋzɝ; pəʊˈzɜː/ *n* [C] *French* a POSER (1) 【法】装腔作势的人

posh /pɑʃ; pɒʃ/ *adj* **1** a posh restaurant, hotel, car etc is expensive and looks as if it is used or owned by rich people 〔餐馆、酒店、汽车等〕高档的, 豪华的, 时髦的: *a posh nightclub in Mayfair* (伦敦) 梅费尔区的高级夜总会 **2** *BrE* behaving or speaking in a way which is typical of upper class people 【英】〔行为或说话方式〕上流社会的: *My mum has a really posh voice when she's on the phone.* 我妈妈打电话时有一口上流社会的口音。—**posh** *adv*: *Doesn't he talk posh?* 他说话时难道没有上流社会的腔调吗?

pos·it /ˋpɑzɪt; ˈpɒzɪt/ *v* [T] *formal* to suggest that a particular idea should be accepted as a fact; POSTULATE¹ 【正式】假定, 假设: *positing the existence of even smaller particles* 假定存在更小的粒子

po·si·tion¹ /pəˋzɪʃən; pəˈzɪʃən/ *n* S3 W1

1 ►STANDING/SITTING/POINTING ETC 站/坐/指等◄ [C] the way someone stands or sits, or the direction in which an object, SWITCH etc is pointing 〔人的〕姿态, 姿势; 〔物体等的〕所指方向, 位置: *I had to work in an uncomfortable position, lying under the car.* 我只得不舒服地躺在汽车底下工作。| **a sitting/kneeling/standing position** *The prisoners were kept in a kneeling position.* 那些囚犯被迫跪着。| **a vertical/upright/horizontal position** *Make sure the container remains in an upright position.* 要确保那个容器保持直立。| *She turned the switch to the 'on' position.* 她把开关扭到"开"的位置。

2 ►SITUATION 情况, 状况◄ [C usually singular 一般用单数] the situation that someone is in, or the situation concerning a particular subject 处境, 状况, 状态; 形势: *What's the present position with regard to import restrictions?* 有关进口限制的现状如何? | **in a good/strong/enviable etc position** *Reuters are now in an enviable position in the news and current affairs industry.* 路透社目前在新闻和时事行业中处于令人羡慕的地位。| **in your/her etc position** *I'm not sure what I'd do if I were in your position.* 我不能肯定如果我身在你的处境会怎么办。| **put sb in a difficult/awkward position** *You're putting me in rather a difficult position.* 你让我陷入一个相当困难的处境。

3 ►LEVEL/RANK 水平/级别◄ [C] someone's or something's level or rank in a society or organization 地位, 级别, 身份: **[+in]** *the position of women in society* 妇女在社会中的地位 | **position of authority/influence** *You need to ask someone in a position of authority.* 你需要问一位权威人士。| **position of trust/responsibility** (=a position in which people depend on you to be honest or careful) 责任重大的职务 | **abuse your position** (=use your authority wrongly) 滥用职权

4 ►OPINION 观点, 看法◄ [C] an opinion or judgment on a particular subject, especially the official opinion of a government, party, or someone in authority; ATTITUDE 〔尤指政府、政党、当权者的〕立场, 态度: **[+on]** *What's the party's position on tax reform?* 该党对于税制改革持什么态度? | **take the position that** *The principal took the position that the students didn't need music classes.* 那位校长认为学生不需要上音乐课。| **reconsider your position** *The administration should reconsider its position.* 政府应重新考虑自己的立场。

5 ►PLACE WHERE SB/STH IS 某人/某物的位置◄ [C] the place where someone or something is, especially in relation to other objects and places 位置, 方位: *I checked our position by the compass.* 我用指南针查看我们的方位。| *the position of the sun in the sky* 太阳在天空中的位置 | **a strategic position** (=one that is suitable for a particular purpose) 战略位置, 〔适合某一目的的〕有利位置 *He placed himself in a strategic position next to the doorway.* 他使自己处于靠近门口的有利位置。

6 ►CORRECT PLACE 适当的位置◄ [U] the place where someone or something is supposed to be 适当的位置: **in position/out of position** *After the shelves were in position we realized we'd forgotten to paint them.* 我们把那些架子放好之后才意识到忘了给它们上漆。| *One of the legs was out of position.* 其中的一条支架错位了。

7 take up (your) position to move to a particular place so that you are ready to take part in a planned activity 站好位置〔准备参加活动〕, 就位: *Police marksmen took up their positions around the bank.* 警方的神射手在银行周围站好了位置。

8 ►JOB 工作◄ [C] your job 职位, 职务, 工作: *Richard had to give up his position with the company.* 理查德不得不放弃在这家公司的工作。| **hold a position** (=have a particular job) 担任某个职务 *She held the position of sales manager.* 她担任销售经理的职务。| **the position has been filled** (=the company has found someone to do the job) 这职位已经有人担任了 —see 见 JOB (USAGE)

9 be in a position to do sth to be able to do something because you have the ability, money, or power to do it 〔因为有能力、金钱或权力而〕能够做某事: *When I know all the facts, I'll*

be in a position to advise you. 在我了解所有的事实之后,我就能给你提出建议了。

10 be in no position to do sth to be unable to do something because you do not have the ability, money or power to do it〔因为没有能力、金钱或权力而〕不能够做某事: *While I'm unemployed, I'm in no position to support a family.* 在我没有工作时,我没有能力养家。

11 sb is in no position to talk *spoken* used to say that someone should not criticize another person, because they have made the same mistakes【口】某人没有资格说话[批评别人]〔因为他们犯有同样的错误〕

12 ▶RACE/COMPETITION 赛跑/比赛◀ [C,U] the place of someone or something in a race, competition, list etc 名次: **2nd/3rd/4th position** *Alesi has moved up into 3rd position.* 阿莱西已经升至第三名。

13 ▶SPORT 体育运动◀ [C] the place where someone plays in a game of football, HOCKEY etc〔足球、曲棍球等运动中的〕球员位置: *"What position do you play?"* "你打什么位置?"

14 be in a position of strength to be in a situation in which you should be able to succeed or win 处于能够成功[获胜]的境况,处于优势地位: *workers bargaining from a position of strength* 谈判中处于优势的工人

15 jockey/manoeuvre/jostle for position to try to get an advantage over other people who are all trying to succeed in doing the same thing 想尽办法使自己处于有利的位置[地位]: *On the eve of the election the candidates were all jockeying for position.* 在大选前夕,各候选人都在尽力争取有利的地位。

16 ▶ARMY 军队◀ [C] a place where an army has put soldiers, guns etc 阵地: *UN forces attacked Serb military positions around Sarajevo.* 联合国部队袭击了塞尔维亚人在萨拉热窝的军事阵地。

17 ▶SEX 性◀ [C] one of the ways in which two people can have sex〔性交〕姿势: *Most people prefer face-to-face positions.* 大多数人都喜欢脸对脸的正面性交姿势。

USAGE NOTE 用法说明: POSITION

WORD CHOICE 词语辨析: **place, position, location, spot, where**

Place is the usual word you use to talk about where something is or happens. place 是谈论某物所在或某事所发生的地点常用的词: *the place where I was born* 我出生的地方 | *one of the coldest places in the world* 世界上最寒冷的地方之一

Position is used to talk about the place where something is in relation to other things or places. position 用来表示相对于其他事物或地点而言的某个位置: *Plant the flowers in a sunny position.* 把花种在有阳光的地方。| *a plan that shows the position of everything in the room* 显示房间内所有东西的位置的平面图

Location is a more formal word for a place where someone works or lives, or where something is built. It may be used, for example, in business English or in advertising. location 表示某人工作或生活的地方,或某建筑物所在的位置,较为正式。例如,它可用在商业英语或广告中: *The company has found a new location for its offices.* 这家公司已找到了新的办公地点。| *a hotel in an extremely attractive location* 一家位置优越的酒店

Spot is a more informal word used especially for a pleasant place. spot 比较非正式,尤用于表示令人愉快的地方: *This part of the beach is my favourite spot.* 沙滩的这部分是我最喜欢的地方。

In spoken English you usually use **where, anywhere, somewhere, someplace** etc instead of these words. 在英语口语中,通常用 where, anywhere, somewhere, someplace 等来代替上述的词语: *I'll show you where I was born.* 我带你去看我出生的地方。| *She looked everywhere, but still couldn't find the letter.* 她到处都找遍了,但还是没有找到那封信。| *Can we put the TV someplace else?* 我们能把电视放在其他地方吗? | *It depends on where they are from.* 这视乎他们是从哪里来的。

position² *v* [T] to put something in a particular position 把〔某物〕放在〔某个位置上〕,安置: *Position the cursor before the letter you want to delete.* 把光标放在你想删去的字母前。

position pa·per /'· ··, ·'/ *n* [C] a written statement that shows how a department, organization etc intends to deal with something〔部门、组织等关于处理某事的〕立场声明

pos·i·tive /ˈpɑzətɪv; ˈpɒzɪtɪv/ *adj* S2 W2

1 ▶SURE 确信的,肯定的◀ [not before noun 不用于名词前] very sure, with no doubt at all that something is right or true 确信的,肯定的,有把握的: *"Are you sure?" "Positive."* "你能肯定吗?" "我能肯定。" | **positive (that)** *Are you absolutely positive you locked the door?* 你能绝对肯定你已把门锁好了吗? | **[+of/about]** *It was definitely his fault – James was positive of that.* 那一定是他的错——詹姆斯对那点很有把握。

2 ▶CONFIDENT 有信心的◀ believing that you will be successful or that a situation will have a good result 有信心的,积极的,乐观的: *You've got to be more positive about your work.* 你必须更积极地对待自己的工作。| **positive attitude/approach/outlook etc** *She started to have a more positive outlook on life.* 她开始拥有更积极的人生观。| **think positive** *Think positive and all your problems will be solved.* 往积极的方面去想,你所有的问题都会迎刃而解。—compare 比较 NEGATIVE[1] (2)

3 ▶LIKELY TO BE SUCCESSFUL 可能成功的◀ showing that something is likely to succeed or improve 很可能成功[改善]的: *All the signs are extremely positive – he'll be well again soon.* 所有迹象都表示非常良好——他将很快恢复健康。

4 ▶AGREEMENT/SUPPORT 同意/支持◀ showing that someone agrees with you, supports what you are doing, and wants you to succeed 予以肯定的,表示赞同的,支持的;有建设性的: *The response we've had so far from the public has been very positive.* 到目前为止,公众对我们一直十分支持。| **positive criticism/feedback** (=criticism which includes praise for things done well, and encourages you to do better) 建设性的批评/积极的反馈意见

5 positive proof/evidence/identification etc proof, EVIDENCE etc that shows that there is no doubt that something is definitely true 确凿的证据/确切的证明等: *The fingerprints are positive proof that Elliott is the murderer.* 那些指纹是证明埃利奥特就是凶手的确实证据。

6 ▶SCIENTIFIC TEST 科学试验◀ showing signs of the chemical or medical condition that was being looked for 阳性的: *The test results came back positive.* 测试结果呈阳性。—opposite 反义词 NEGATIVE[1] (4)

7 ▶GOOD/USEFUL 好的/有用的◀ having a good or useful effect 有用的,有助益的: *At least something positive has come out of the situation.* 至少这个情况也产生了一些积极的东西。| *a very positive experience* 非常有益的经历

8 ▶MORALLY GOOD 道德上好的◀ [usually before noun 一般用于名词前] showing or encouraging someone, especially a child, to behave in a way that is morally good 引人向善的,正面的: *a positive social environment* 良好的社会环境 | *positive role models* 正面的榜样

9 a positive miracle/delight/thrill etc *spoken* used to emphasize how good, surprising, exciting etc something is【口】绝对是奇迹/享受/令人兴奋的事等: *It was a positive miracle that she survived.* 她能生存下来简直是奇迹。

10 ▶MATHEMATICS 数学◀ *technical* a positive number is more than zero【术语】正的,正数的: *+ is the positive sign* +是正号

11 ▶ELECTRICITY 电◀ [no comparative 无比较级] *technical* having the type of electrical charge that is carried by PROTONS【术语】正的,阳性的: *a positive charge* 正电荷 —opposite 反义词 NEGATIVE[1] (5)

12 positive pole the end of a MAGNET which turns naturally towards the Earth〔磁铁的〕北极

13 ▶BLOOD 血液◀ *technical* having RHESUS FACTOR in your blood【术语】〔血液〕含Rh因子的 —opposite 反义词 NEGATIVE[1] (7) —**positiveness** *n* [U]

positive di·scrim·i·na·tion /,······'··/ *n* [U] the practice of giving a certain number of jobs, places in universities etc to a group of people who are often treated unfairly because of their race or sex; AFFIRMATIVE ACTION 逆向歧视〔提供一定数量的工作、大学学位等给那些由于种族或性别原因而常常受到不公平对待的人〕

pos·i·tive·ly /ˈpɑzətɪvlɪ; ˈpɒzɪtɪvli/ *adv* **1** *spoken* used to emphasize that something is true about someone or something, or when saying something surprising about them【口】确实,事实上: *Gabi isn't pretty, she's positively beautiful!* 盖拜不是漂亮,而是美貌绝伦! | *Some patients positively enjoy being in hospital.* 一些病人确实喜欢待在医院里。**2** *spoken* used to emphasize that you really mean what you are saying, especially when it may seem surprising【口】(用以加强语气)真的,确实: *This is positively the last time you'll hear me say this.* 这确确实实将是你最后一次听到我说这些话。**3** in a way that shows you agree with something or want it to succeed 表示赞同地,肯定地: *The mayor spoke positively about the work that had been done so far.* 市长对于到目前为止已做的工作给予了积极的评价。

4 think positively to believe that you are going to be success-

ful or that a situation is going to have a good result 持积极[乐观]的态度 **5** in a way that leaves no possibility of doubt 确信地, 肯定地, 有把握地: *Otto said quite positively that he would come.* 奥托十分肯定地说他会来。**6 positively charged** *technical* having the type of electrical charge that is carried by PROTONS【术语】带正电的

pos·i·tiv·is·m /ˈpɑzətɪv,ɪzəm; ˈpɒzɮtɪvɪzəm/ *n* [U] a kind of PHILOSOPHY that is based only on real facts which can be scientifically proved, rather than on ideas〔哲学中的〕实证主义, 实证论 —**positivist** *n* [C]

poss /pɑs; pɒs/ **1** *BrE*【英】the written abbreviation of 缩写= possible: *Please send a photo if poss.* 如果可能的话寄张照片来。**2** the written abbreviation of 缩写= POSSESSIVE[1] (3)

pos·se /ˈpɑsɪ; ˈpɒsi/ *n* [C] **1 a posse of** a large group of the same kind of people〔同类人的〕一群, 一队, 一批: *I was surrounded by a posse of photographers.* 我被一群摄影师围住了。**2** a group of men gathered together by a SHERIFF (=local law officer) in the US in past times to help catch a criminal〔美国旧时由县治安官召集的帮助抓捕罪犯的〕民防团 **3** *slang* someone's group of friends【俚】〔某人的〕一群朋友

W3 **pos·sess** /pəˈzɛs; pəˈzes/ *v* [T not in progressive 不用进行时] **1** *formal* to own or have something, especially something valuable or important, something illegal, or an ability or quality【正式】拥有, 具有, 持有〔尤指贵重或重要的东西、非法物品、某种能力或品质〕: *Campbell was found guilty of possessing heroin.* 坎贝尔被判犯有持有海洛因罪。| *The prison inmates possess a considerable degree of autonomy.* 狱中犯人有相当大的自主权。**2** *formal* a word meaning to own or have something, used especially when you are surprised that someone does not have something, or when saying that this is all they have【正式】拥有, 具有〔尤用来表示某人居然没有某物或某物竟是他们的全部所有〕: *I don't think Joe possesses a suit.* 我想乔没有一套正经的西服。| *They used all the money they possessed.* 他们用尽了所有的钱。**3 what (on earth) possessed you to...?** used to say that you cannot understand why someone did something stupid (究竟) 什么驱使你…〔表示不明白某人为何做傻事〕: *What on earth possessed her to do such a thing?* 究竟是什么使她鬼迷心窍做了这样的事呢? **4** *literary* if a feeling possesses you, you suddenly feel it very strongly and it affects your behaviour【文】〔感觉〕缠住, 控制, 支配, 影响: *A sense of fear possessed him as he walked into the old house.* 他走进那所老房子时感到非常恐惧。

pos·sessed /pəˈzɛst; pəˈzest/ *adj* [not before noun 不用于名词前] **1** if someone is possessed, their mind is controlled by an evil spirit 着了魔的, 鬼迷心窍的: *Her family believed that she was possessed, and called in a priest.* 她的家人认为她着了魔, 就把牧师请来了。| **like a man possessed/like one possessed** (=violently or with a lot of energy) 猛烈地, 拼命地, 着了魔似地 *He threw himself around like a man possessed.* 他发了疯似地四处乱撞。**2 be possessed of** *literary* to have a particular quality, ability etc【文】具有〔某种品质、能力等〕: *Charles was possessed of a sound intellect and a happy manner.* 查尔斯具有健全的智力和得体的举止。—see also 另见 SELF-POSSESSED

W3 **pos·ses·sion** /pəˈzɛʃən; pəˈzeʃən/ *n*

1 ►STH YOU OWN 个人拥有的东西◄ [C usually plural 一般用复数] something that someone owns and keeps or uses themselves 所有物; 财产, 财物: *The police went through all the dead girl's possessions.* 警方检查了那个死去的女孩的所有财物。| *I packed my remaining possessions into the trunk.* 我把剩下的财物装进箱子里。

2 ►STATE OF HAVING STH 拥有某物的状态◄ [U] *formal* the state of having or owning something, especially a valuable object, piece of information etc【正式】拥有, 持有, 占有〔尤指贵重物品、资料等〕: **be in sb's possession** *The house has been in the family's possession since the 1500s.* 这所房子自16世纪以来一直归这个家族所有。| **be in possession of sth/have sth in your possession** (=have something) 拥有[占有, 持有]某物 *She was found in possession of stolen goods.* 她被发现藏有赃物。| *I have in my possession a number of secret documents.* 我掌握着一些秘密文件。| **come into sb's possession** (=if something comes into your possession, you get it) 为某人所得到[占有], 落入某人手中 *How did the painting come into your possession?* 你是怎么得到那幅画的? | **have possession of** (=to own or have something, after you have bought it or taken it from someone else) 拥有〔指买来或从别人那里拿来〕*The finance company now has possession of the house.* 该金融公司现在拥有这所房子的所有权。

3 take possession of sth if you take possession of a house, car, or valuable object, you get it after it has become yours 拥有[占有]某物, 拿到某物: *We didn't take possession of the car until a few days after the auction.* 拍卖会过后几天, 我们才真正拿到了那辆汽车。

4 ►DRUGS/GUN 毒品/枪支◄ [U] *law* the crime of having illegal drugs or a gun with you or in your home【法律】〔毒品或枪支的〕私藏, 持有, 管有: *He faces trial on charges of possession of a loaded firearm.* 他因被控持有装上子弹的枪支而面临审判。

5 ►COUNTRY 国家◄ [C] a country controlled or governed by another country 领地, 属地, 殖民地: *Britain's former overseas possessions* 英国过去的海外领地

6 ►BALL 球◄ [U] the state of having control of the ball in some sports〔一些体育运动中对球的〕控制: **get/lose possession** *Waddell gets possession, and he scores!* 沃德尔控制着球, 他得分了!

7 ►AMERICAN FOOTBALL 美式橄榄球◄ [C] a period of time in American football when one team is playing OFFENSE[2] and has control of the ball〔进攻一方球队的〕控球时间

8 ►EVIL SPIRITS 魔鬼◄ [U] a situation in which someone's mind is being controlled by an evil spirit 鬼魂附体, 着魔: *tales of possession and poltergeists and exorcisms* 有关魔鬼附体、恶作剧鬼和驱魔的传说

9 in (full) possession of your faculties/senses able to think in a clear and intelligent way and not crazy, or affected by old age 神智[头脑] (非常) 清醒: *She's over 80 now, but she's still in full possession of all her faculties.* 她八十多岁了, 但头脑仍然非常清醒。

10 possession is nine-tenths of the law used to mean that someone who has something is likely to keep it 现实占有, 败一胜九〔实际占有者在财产诉讼中十有九胜〕

pos·ses·sive[1] /pəˈzɛsɪv; pəˈzesɪv/ *adj* **1** wanting someone to have feelings of love or friendship only for you〔爱情或友情上〕占有欲强的, 自私的: *Men are very protective and sometimes possessive towards their daughters.* 男人对女儿很有保护之心, 有时还有很强的占有欲。**2** unwilling to let other people use something you own 不愿与别人分享的, 占有欲强的: [+about] *He's so possessive about his new car.* 他不愿让别人用他的新汽车。**3 possessive adjective/pronoun/form** used in grammar for words such as 'my', 'its', 'their' etc, which mean belonging to someone or something〔语法中的〕所有格形容词/代词/形式 —**possessively** *adv* —**possessiveness** *n* [U]

possessive[2] *n* [C] *technical* a possessive adjective, pronoun, or form of a word【术语】所有格形容词[代(名)词, 形式]

pos·ses·sor /pəˈzɛsə; pəˈzesə/ *n* **be the proud possessor of** *often humorous* to have or own something【常幽默】拥有, 持有: *He's now the proud possessor of two satellite dishes.* 他现在拥有两个卫星电视碟形天线, 这使他引以为荣。

pos·si·bil·i·ty /,pɑsəˈbɪlətɪ; ,pɒsɮˈbɪlɮti/ *n* **1** [C,U] something that may happen or may be true 可能的事; 可能性: [+of] *the possibility of an enemy attack* 敌人进攻的可能性 | **a distinct/real possibility** (=something that is quite likely to happen) 很可能发生的事 *A peace settlement now looks like a real possibility.* 和平解决现在看来很有可能。| **there's a possibility (that)** (=used to say that you think something might happen or be TRUE) 有可能…: *There's always a possibility that he might go back to Seattle.* 他随时可能会回到西雅图去。**2** [usually plural 一般用复数] something that gives you an opportunity to do what you want 余地; 潜力: [+for] *The possibilities for improvement are endless.* 改善的余地是无限的。| **a world of possibilities** (=many opportunities) 许多机遇 *China's economic expansion has opened up a new world of possibilities for Western companies.* 中国的经济发展为西方公司打开了一个充满机遇的新天地。**3 exhaust all the possibilities** to try every possible way of doing something 试尽了所有可能的办法 **4 have possibilities** if something has possibilities it could be made into something much better 有改善的余地, 有潜力, 有发展的可能性: *The house has great possibilities!* 那所房子有极大的潜在价值! —see also 另见 **within the realms of possibility** (REALM (2)) S2 W2

pos·si·ble[1] /ˈpɑsəbl; ˈpɒsɮbəl/ *adj* **1** able to be done or likely to happen or exist 可能的; 可能做到的; 可能发生的; 可能存在的: *Accidents are always possible in this kind of situation.* 在这种情况下, 事故随时可能发生。| *Sony and Showscan are discussing possible joint projects.* 索尼和肖斯康公司正在讨论可能的合资项目。| **it is possible to do sth** *Is it possible to predict what will happen in Russia?* 有可能预测俄罗斯将会发生什么事吗? | **it is possible (that)** (=used to say that you think something might happen or be true) 可能…, 也许… *It's possible that she might have got lost on the way home.* 她有可能在回家的路上迷路了。| **it is possible for** (=used to say that someone is S1 W1

able to do something)〔某人〕能做… *It should soon be possible for most people to work from home.* 让大多数人在家里办公应该是很快就能实现的事。| **if (at all) possible** (=if it is possible to do it) 如果可能的话 *I want to avoid the rush hour traffic if possible.* 如果可能的话，我想避开高峰时间的交通。**2 would it be possible** *spoken* used when asking politely if you can do or have something【口】可以吗？〔用于礼貌地询问某人是否能做某事或拥有某物〕: **would it be possible (for sb) to do sth** *Would it be possible to have brown bread instead of white?* 可不可以要黑面包而不要白面包呢？**3** acceptable or suitable 可接受的，合适的: *This is only one of many possible answers to the problem of air pollution.* 这仅仅是解决空气污染问题的众多可行办法之一。**4 as long/much/soon as possible** as long, soon, quickly etc as you can 尽可能长/多/快: *I need the money as soon as possible.* 我需要尽快拿到这笔钱。| *Sharon always does as little work as possible.* 沙伦总是尽可能少做事。**5 the best/biggest/fastest possible** the best that can exist or be achieved 尽可能好/大/快的: *Try to get the best possible price.* 尽可能获得最好的价格。**6 where/wherever/whenever possible** every time you have an opportunity to do something 一有机会: *I send a donation whenever possible.* 我一有机会就捐款。

possible² *n* [C] someone or something that might be suitable or acceptable for a particular purpose 可能适合的人[事物]: *Frank's a possible for the job.* 弗兰克是那份工作的一个可能人选。

pos·si·bly /ˈpɑsəblɪ; ˈpɒsɨbli/ *adv* **1** used when saying that something may be true or likely, although you do not know exactly; perhaps 可能，也许，或许: *"Are you coming with us tomorrow?" "Possibly. I'm not sure yet."* "你明天要和我们一起去吗？""可能吧，我还不能肯定。" | *This novel is his most accessible, and possibly his most beautiful, book.* 这本小说是他的作品中最易懂、而且可能是最美的一本。| **quite possibly** (=used to say that something is very likely) 很有可能 *"Do you think it was murder?" "Quite possibly."* "你认为这是谋杀吗？""很可能是。" **2 could you possibly/can you possibly** *spoken* used when making a polite request【口】请你…可以吗？〔用于礼貌地请求〕: *Could you possibly lend me another $20 till Monday?* 你能再借给我20美元到星期一吗？**3** *spoken* used to say that you are very surprised or shocked by something, or you cannot understand it【口】究竟; 怎么〔用于表示惊讶、震惊或不理解〕: **can/could sb possibly** *What on earth can she possibly mean?* 她究竟是什么意思呢？| *How could anyone possibly do such a thing?* 怎么会有人做出这样的事呢？**4** used to emphasize that someone tried as hard as they could to achieve something〔用于强调某人为获得某物尽了最大努力〕: **do everything you possibly can/could** *Doctors did everything they possibly could to save the little boy's life.* 医生尽了一切可能来挽救这个小男孩的生命。**5 sb can't/couldn't possibly** used to say strongly that you refuse to do something or that someone cannot do something 某人不可能〔用于强烈地表示拒绝做某事或某人不能做某事〕: *I can't possibly allow you to go home in this weather.* 我不可能让你在这种天气下回家。

pos·sum /ˈpɑsəm; ˈpɒsəm/ also 又作 **opossum** *especially BrE*【尤英】*n* [C] **1** one of various types of small furry animals that climb trees and live in America or Australia〔产于美洲或澳洲的〕负鼠; 袋貂 **2 play possum** *informal* to pretend to be asleep or dead so that someone will not annoy or hurt you【非正式】〔为避免某人打扰或伤害而〕假装睡着; 装死

post- /post; pəʊst/ *prefix* later than; after 在…之后: *postwar* (=after a war) 战后 | *We'll have to postpone the meeting.* (=make it later) 我们不得不把会议延期。—compare 比较 ANTE-

post¹ /post; pəʊst/ *n*

1 ▶POSTAL SYSTEM 邮政系统◀ the post *especially BrE* the official system for carrying letters, parcels etc from one place to another【尤英】邮政，邮递; MAIL¹ (1) *especially AmE*【尤美】: *The letter must have got lost in the post.* 那封信一定是在邮递过程中丢了。| **be in the post** *Your cheque is in the post.* 你的支票已寄出。| **by post** *If you send the book by post it should get there by Friday.* 如果邮寄这本书，它应该在星期五之前寄到。

2 put sth in the post to send something to someone 把某物寄给〔某人〕: *I'll put a copy in the post to you today.* 我今天将给你寄上一本。

3 ▶COLLECTING/DELIVERING LETTERS 收集/投递信件◀ [C, U] *especially BrE* the time when letters are collected or delivered, or the act of collecting or delivering them【尤英】信件收集[投递]时间; 收信; 投递信件; MAIL¹ *especially AmE*【尤美】: **first/second post** (=the first collection or delivery of letters each day)〔每天的〕第一次/第二次收信[投递] *The parcel arrived in the second post.* 那包裹是随第二批邮件送到的。| **catch/miss the post** *If you hurry, you should catch the last post.* 你如果快一点儿的话，应该能赶上最后一次收信。—see also 另见 **by return (of post)** (RETURN² (8))

4 ▶LETTERS 信件◀ [U] *especially BrE* letters, parcels etc delivered to someone's house, office etc【尤英】邮件〈如信件、包裹等〉; MAIL¹ (2) *especially AmE*【尤美】: *Was there any post for me today?* 今天有寄给我的邮件吗？

5 ▶PIECE OF WOOD/METAL 一块木头/金属◀ [C] a strong upright piece of wood, metal etc that is fixed into the ground, especially to support something 柱，杆，桩: *a fence post* 栅栏桩

6 ▶JOB 工作◀ [C] *formal especially BrE* a job, especially an important one; POSITION¹ (8)【正式，尤英】〔尤指重要的〕工作; 职位: *She has been offered the post of ambassador to India.* 她获委任为驻印度大使。| **take up a post** (=start doing an important job) 开始担任一个职务 *When he took up his present post at the BBC he was only 33.* 他到英国广播公司出任目前的职位时才33岁。| **resign (from) your post** *As a result of the scandal, Profumo was forced to resign his post.* 由于这宗丑闻，普罗富莫被迫辞职。—see 见 JOB (USAGE)

7 ▶SOLDIER/GUARD ETC 士兵/卫兵等◀ sb's post the place where someone is expected to be in order to do their duty 岗位，哨位: *The guard was punished for falling asleep at his post.* 那个卫兵由于站岗时睡觉而受到了处罚。

8 ▶FOOTBALL/HOCKEY ETC 足球/曲棍球等◀ [C] one of the two upright pieces of wood which players try to kick or hit the ball between in football, HOCKEY etc; GOALPOST 球门柱

9 ▶RACE 竞赛◀ the post also 又作 **the finishing post** the place where a race finishes, especially a horse race〔竞赛，尤指赛马的〕终点标志: *Dandyboy fell ten yards from the post.* "花花公子"在离终点10码的地方摔倒了。—see also 另见 **deaf as a post** (DEAF (1)), **pip sb at the post** (PIP² (1)), **second-class post** (SECOND-CLASS (3)), LAST POST, STAGING POST, TRADING POST

post² *v* [T]

1 ▶LETTER 信件◀ *especially BrE* to send a letter, parcel etc by post【尤英】邮寄，寄出〔信件、包裹等〕; MAIL² *AmE*【美】: *She's just gone to post a letter.* 她刚出去寄信了。| **post sb sth/post sth to sb** *I posted John the cheque last Friday.* 我上星期五把支票寄给约翰了。| *I must post a card to Clara today.* 我今天必须寄张贺卡给克拉拉。

2 keep sb posted to keep telling someone the latest news about something 不断向某人提供有关某事的最新消息: *Please, keep us posted about your financial situation, and let us know if we can help.* 请随时告诉我们你的经济状况，看看我们能否帮上忙。

3 ▶GUARD 卫兵◀ to send someone somewhere, to guard a building, check who enters or leaves a place, watch something etc; STATION² 设置〔岗哨等〕: *Two National Guardsmen had been posted at the gate.* 两名国民警卫队队员被安排在大门口站岗。

4 ▶JOB 工作◀ [usually passive 一般用被动态] *especially BrE* to send someone to a different country or place to work for a company or to do a period of duty for the army, navy, or government【尤英】派驻，调派; STATION² *AmE*【美】: **post sb abroad/overseas etc** *Roger's been posted overseas for a few years.* 罗杰被派往国外工作了几年。| **post sb to** *Two years later he was posted to Buenos Aires.* 两年后他被派往布宜诺斯艾利斯。—see 见 JOB (USAGE)

5 ▶PUBLIC NOTICE 公告◀ also 又作 **post up** to put up a public notice about something on a wall or notice board 张贴，贴出〔公告〕: *The exam results were posted on the bulletin board yesterday.* 昨天布告板上张贴了考试成绩。

6 be posted missing if someone is posted missing, it is announced officially that they have disappeared〔某人〕被正式宣布失踪

Post, Em·i·ly /ˈɛmɪlɪ; ˈemɨli/ (1872-1960) a US writer of books and newspaper articles which gave advice on ETIQUETTE (=correct and polite social behaviour) 波斯特〔(1872-1960)，美国作家、报纸撰稿人。文章内容多为社交礼仪方面的建言〕

Post, the 1 the Washington Post《华盛顿邮报》**2** the New York Post《纽约邮报》**3** the Sunday Post《星期日邮报》

post·age /ˈpostɪdʒ; ˈpəʊstɪdʒ/ *n* [U] the money charged for carrying a letter, parcel etc by post 邮资，邮费: *Please enclose $9.99, including $1.00 for postage.* 请在信中附上9.99美元，其中包括1美元的邮资。| **postage and packing** (=charge for packing and sending something you have bought) 包装加邮寄费 *Yours for only £16.95 plus postage and packing!* 你的只需16.95英镑，另加包装和邮费。

postage me·ter /ˈ‥ ˌ‥/ *n* [C] *AmE* a machine used by businesses which puts a mark on letters and packages to show that postage has been paid【美】邮资机〔在信封或包裹上盖印以示邮资已付〕

postage stamp /ˈ·· ·/ *n* [C] *formal* a stamp【正式】邮票

post·al /ˈpostl; ˈpəʊstl/ *adj* [only before noun 仅用于名词前] connected with the official system which takes letters from one place to another 邮政的: *postal workers* 邮政工人 | *an increase in postal charges* 邮资的上涨

postal or·der /ˈ·· ˌ··/ *n* [C] *BrE* an official paper that you buy at a post office as a safe way of sending money through the post【英】邮政汇票: *a £2.00 postal order* 一张两英镑的邮政汇票 —compare 比较 MONEY ORDER

postal ser·vice /ˈ·· ˌ··/ *n* [C] *especially AmE* the public service for carrying letters, parcels etc from one part of a country or the world to another【尤美】邮政服务

Postal Ser·vice, the /ˈ·· ˌ··/ also **the US Postal Service** the official name for the US government department responsible for collecting and delivering mail (美国) 邮政管理局

postal vote /ˈ·· ˌ·/ *n* [C] *BrE* a vote sent through the post, especially by someone who cannot be present to vote on the day of an election【英】邮寄投票; ABSENTEE VOTE *AmE*【美】

post·bag /ˈpostˌbæg; ˈpəʊstbæg/ *n BrE*【英】**1** [singular] *informal* all the letters received by an important person, television programme etc on a particular occasion【非正式】〔要人、电视节目等的〕一次收到的邮件: *We've had an enormous postbag on the recent programme changes.* 我们就最近的节目变更收到了大批来信。**2** [C] a bag for carrying letters, used by the person who delivers them〔邮递员的〕邮袋; MAILBAG *AmE*【美】

post·box /ˈpostˌbɑks; ˈpəʊstbɒks/ *n* [C] *BrE* a box in a public place, into which you put letters you want to send【英】〔投寄信件用的〕邮箱，邮筒; MAILBOX (2) *AmE*【美】—see also 另见 LETTERBOX, PILLAR BOX

postbox 邮箱，邮筒

post·card /ˈpostˌkɑrd; ˈpəʊstkɑːd/ *n* [C] a card that can be sent in the post without an envelope, especially one with a picture on it 明信片: *Don't forget to send us a postcard!* 别忘了给我们寄张明信片！

post·code /ˈpostˌkod; ˈpəʊstkəʊd/ *n* [C] *BrE* a group of letters or numbers which shows the exact area where a house is, so that letters, parcels etc can be delivered more quickly【英】邮政编码; ZIP CODE *AmE*【美】

post·date /ˌpostˈdet; ˌpəʊstˈdeɪt/ *v* [T] **1** to write a cheque with a date that is later than the actual date, so that it cannot be used or become effective until that time〔在支票上〕填写比实际晚的日期，把…的日期填迟 **2** to happen, live, or be made later in history than something else 发生于…之后; 生活在…之后; 在历史上发生的时间后于…: *The mosaic postdates this period, although the style is quite similar.* 尽管风格很相似，但这种镶嵌图案是晚于这个时期的作品。—compare 比较 ANTEDATE, BACKDATE

post doc /ˌ· ˈ·/ *n* [C] *informal especially AmE* someone who is studying after they have finished their PHD【非正式，尤美】博士后研究人员

post doc·tor·al /ˌ· ˈ···◂/ *adj* connected with study done after a PHD 博士后的

S3 **post·er** /ˈpostɚ; ˈpəʊstə/ *n* [C] a large printed notice, picture, or photograph, used to advertise something or as a decoration 招贴(画); 海报; 广告(画): *The bedroom wall was covered in posters.* 卧室的墙壁上贴满了海报。

poste res·tante /ˌpost rɛsˈtɑnt; ˌpəʊst ˈrestɒnt/ *n* [U] *BrE* a post office department which keeps letters for people who are travelling, until they arrive to collect them【英】〔邮局的〕邮件存局候领处; GENERAL DELIVERY *AmE*【美】

pos·te·ri·or[1] /pɑsˈtɪrɪɚ; pɒˈstɪəriə/ *n* [C] *humorous* the part of the body you sit on; BOTTOM[1] (7)【幽默】臀部，屁股: *plonking his substantial posterior down on the bench* 他肥大的臀部重重地坐在长凳上

posterior[2] *adj* [only before noun 仅用于名词前] *technical* near or at the back of something【术语】(靠近) 后部的，后端的; 后面的，背部的: *the posterior end of the abdomen* 下腹部 —opposite 反义词 ANTERIOR (1)

pos·ter·i·ty /pɑsˈtɛrətɪ; pɒˈsterɪ̥ti/ *n* [U] people who will live after you are dead 后裔，后代，子孙: **preserve sth for posterity** *We must preserve these songs for posterity.* 我们必须把这些歌曲保存下来传给子孙后代。

poster paint /ˈ·· ·/ *n* [C, U] *BrE* brightly coloured paint that contains no oil, used especially by children to paint pictures【英】〔尤指供儿童画画用的不含油的〕广告颜料

post-free /ˌ· ˈ·◂/ *adv BrE* a letter sent post-free has no charge for the person who sends it【英】邮资免付地; 邮资已付地; POST-PAID *AmE*【美】—**post-free** *adj*

post-grad /ˌ· ˈ·◂/ *n* [C] *informal* a postgraduate【非正式】研究生 —**post-grad** *adj*

post·grad·u·ate[1] /postˈgrædʒuɪt; ˌpəʊstˈgrædjuɪ̥t/ *n* [C] **1** *especially BrE* someone who is studying at a university to get a MASTER'S DEGREE or a PHD【尤英】〔硕士或博士〕研究生 **2** *AmE* someone who is studying after finishing a PHD【美】博士后研究人员

postgraduate[2] *adj* **1** *BrE* connected with studies done at a university after completing a first degree【英】研究生的; GRADUATE[2] *AmE*【美】: *postgraduate qualifications* 研究生资格 **2** *AmE* connected with studies done after completing a PHD【美】博士后的

post-haste /ˌ· ˈ·/ *adv literary* very quickly【文】很快地，尽快地，急忙地: *departing post-haste* 匆匆离开

post hoc /ˌ· ˈ·/ *adj formal* a post hoc explanation, argument etc make a connection between two events that have happened simply because one happened after the other【正式】〔解释、论证等〕仅仅因为一件事发生在另一件事之后，即把二者联系起来的: *spurious post hoc analyses of the causes of the war* 错误地根据发生在其后必然是其结果来分析战争的原因

post horn /ˈ· ·/ *n* [C] a horn used in the 18th and 19th centuries as a warning by people riding on a carriage〔18和19世纪马车上用的〕驿车号

post·hu·mous /ˈpɑstʃʊməs; ˈpɒstjʊ̈məs/ *adj* happening after someone's death, or given to someone or printed after their death 死后发生的; 死后获得的; 死后出版的 —**posthumously** *adv*: *The medal was awarded posthumously.* 这枚勋章是死后颁发的。

post·ie /ˈpostɪ; ˈpəʊsti/ *n* [C] *informal* a POSTMAN【非正式】邮递员，邮差

post-in·dus·tri·al /ˌ· ·ˈ···◂/ *adj* connected with the period in the late 20th century when the older types of industry became less important, and computers became more important 后工业化的，工业化之后的〔指20世纪晚期旧的工业类型的重要性日渐下降，而电脑工业的重要性则与日俱增〕: *work patterns in post-industrial soceity* 后工业化社会的工作模式

post·ing /ˈpostɪŋ; ˈpəʊstɪŋ/ *n* [C] *especially BrE* the act of sending someone to a place to do their job, especially a soldier【尤英】〔尤指士兵的〕任命，派任: [+to] *still waiting for a posting to France* 还在等待去法国的任命

Post-it /ˈ· ·/ *n* [C] *trademark* a small piece of sticky coloured paper, used for leaving notes to people【商标】〔用于留便条的〕告示贴

postman 邮递员，邮差

post·man /ˈpostmən; ˈpəʊstmən/ *n plural* **postmen** /-mən; -mən/ [C] *especially BrE* someone whose job is to collect and deliver letters【尤英】邮递员，邮差; MAILMAN *AmE*【美】

Postman Pat /ˌ·· ˈ·/ a character in British books and television programmes for children. Postman Pat is a happy POSTMAN who drives around in his van delivering letters and packages with his black and white cat, Jess. 邮差帕特〔英国儿童读物和电视剧中的人物。帕特是位快活的邮差，常开着邮车，带着他那只黑白相间的猫咪杰斯送信件和包裹〕

post·mark /ˈpostˌmɑrk; ˈpəʊstmɑːk/ *n* [C] an official mark made on a letter, parcel etc that shows the place and time it was sent〔信件、邮包等上的〕邮戳 —**postmark** *v* [T]: *The letter was postmarked Iowa.* 这封信上盖着衣阿华州的邮戳。

post·mas·ter /ˈpost,mæstɚ; ˈpəʊst,mɑːstə/ *n* [C] the person who is in charge of a post office 邮局局长

post·mis·tress /ˈpost,mɪstrəs; ˈpəʊstmɪstrɪ̈s/ *n* [C] a woman who is in charge of a post office 邮局女局长

post·mod·ern·is·m /,· ˈ····/ *n* [U] a style of building, painting etc which uses an unusual mixture of old and new styles and was popular in the 1980s 后现代主义〔建筑、绘画等的一种风格，盛行于20世纪80年代，特征为新旧形式的奇妙混合〕—**post-modernist** *adj*: *a post-modernist painting* 后现代主义绘画 —**post-modernist** *n* [C]

post-mor·tem /,postˋmɔrtəm; ,pəʊstˈmɔːtəm/ *n* [C] **1** also 又作 **postmortem examination** *formal* an examination of a dead body to discover why the person died; AUTOPSY【正式】尸体检验，验尸，尸体解剖: *The post-mortem revealed that Mills had been strangled.* 尸体检验显示米尔斯是被勒死的。**2** an examination of a plan or event that failed, in order to discover why it failed〔对失败的计划或事件进行的〕事后剖析，事后检讨: *a post-mortem on the company's poor results* 对公司业绩不佳所作的事后剖析

post·na·tal /,postˋnetl; ,pəʊstˈneɪtl◂/ *adj technical* connected with the time after a baby is born【术语】产后的，分娩后的: *postnatal care* 产后护理 —compare 比较 ANTENATAL, PRENATAL

postnatal de·pres·sion /,··· ·ˈ··/ *n* [U] an illness in which a woman feels DEPRESSED (1) after her baby has been born 产后抑郁症

post of·fice /ˈ· ,··/ *n* **1** [C] a place where you can buy stamps, send letters and parcels etc 邮（政）局 **2 the Post Office** *BrE* the national organization which is responsible for collecting and delivering letters【英】〔英国〕邮政部: *a Post Office van* 邮政货车

Post Of·fice, the the government organization responsible for the mail in the UK. The Post Office also manages the payment of state PENSIONs and social security payments. 邮电部〔英国一政府机构。负责英国的邮政业务，管理国家养老金和社会保障金的支付〕

post office box /ˈ· ·· ,·/ *n* [C] *formal* a PO BOX【正式】邮政信箱

Post Office Coun·ters /,· ·· ˈ··/ the part of the British Post Office that deals with sales of stamps to the public, and provides other services such as the payment of state PENSIONs and social security payments, and the selling of road tax DISCs for people's cars 邮电部柜台服务，邮电部营业部〔隶属英国邮电部，负责出售邮票，提供支付国家养老金和社会保障金等服务，向车主销售路税牌〕

Post Office Tow·er, the /,· ·· ˈ··/ a former name for the Telecom Tower 邮政大楼〔英国电信塔的旧称〕

post·paid /ˈpostˋped; ,pəʊstˈpeɪd◂/ *adv AmE* a letter sent postpaid has no charge for the person sending it【美】邮资已付; POST-FREE *BrE*【英】—**postpaid** *adj*

post·pone /posˋpon; pəʊsˈpəʊn/ *v* [T] to change an event, action etc to a later time or date 使〔事件、行动等〕延期，延迟，推迟: *The match had to be postponed.* 比赛不得不延期举行。| **postpone sth until** *We're postponing our holiday until we have some more money.* 我们把度假日期推迟到我们有较多钱的时候。| **postpone doing sth** *Gail and Jim have decided to postpone having a family for a while.* 盖尔和吉姆决定暂缓要孩子。—**postponement** *n* [C,U]

post·pran·di·al /postˋprændɪəl; ,pəʊstˈprændiəl◂/ *adj formal* happening just after dinner【正式】饭后的: *a postprandial nap* 饭后小睡

post·script /ˈpos·skrɪpt; ˈpəʊs,skrɪpt/ written abbreviation 缩写为 **PS** *n* [C] **1** a message written at the end of a letter below the place where you sign your name〔信末签名后的〕附笔，附言，又及: *The postscript at the end said, 'See you soon'.* 信末的附言写道，"希望很快见到你。" **2** something that you add at the end of a story or account that you have been telling someone〔加在故事、叙述等末尾的〕附言，补充说明: *an interesting postscript to this tale* 对这个故事有趣的补述

post-trau·mat·ic stress dis·or·der /,· ··ˈ·· ˈ· ·ˈ··/ *n* [U] *technical* a mental illness which can develop after a very bad experience such as a plane crash【术语】创伤后应激障碍〔遭遇创伤性事件如飞机失事后患上的精神疾病〕

pos·tu·late¹ /ˈpɑstʃə,let; ˈpɒstjʊ̈leɪt/ *v* [T] *formal* to suggest that something might have happened or be true【正式】假定…是真的，假设…发生过: **[+that]** *One theory postulates that the ancient Filipinos came from India and Persia.* 一种理论假设古代菲律宾人来自印度和波斯。—**postulation** /,pɑstʃəˈleʃən; ,pɒstjʊ̈ˈleɪʃən/ *n* [C,U]

pos·tu·late² /ˈpɑstʃələt; ˈpɒstjələ̈t/ *n* [C] *formal* something believed to be true, but not proven, on which an argument or scientific discussion is based【正式】假定，假设: *the basic postulates of Marxism* 马克思主义的基本假设

pos·ture¹ /ˈpɑstʃɚ; ˈpɒstʃə/ *n* **1** [C,U] the position you hold your body in when you sit or stand 姿势；姿态: *Poor posture can lead to muscular problems in later life.* 不良的姿势可能导致以后生活中肌肉的障碍。**2** [singular] the way you behave or think in a particular situation 态度，立场: *the administration's posture towards China* 该政府对中国的态度

posture² *v* [I] **1** to stand or behave in a way that you hope will make other people notice and admire you 摆姿势〔以引起注意和赞赏〕: *Alexi stood posturing in front of the mirror.* 亚历克西在镜子面前站着摆姿势。**2** to pretend to have a particular opinion or attitude 假装持某种观点[态度]，故作姿态: *pseudo-intellectual posturing* 伪知识分子的装腔作势 —**posturing** *n* [C,U]

post-vi·ral syn·drome /,· ,·· ˈ··/ *n* [U] an illness that lasts for a long time and causes weakness, tiredness, and pain in your muscles; ME 肌痛性脑脊髓炎

post-war /,· ˈ·◂/ *adj* [only before noun 仅用于名词前] happening or existing after a war, especially the Second World War 战后的；〔尤指〕第二次世界大战之后的: *economic conditions in post-war Britain* 战后英国的经济状况 —**post-war** *adv* —compare 比较 PRE-WAR

po·sy /ˈpozi; ˈpəʊzi/ *n* [C] *especially literary* a small BUNCH of flowers【尤文】小花束: *a posy of African violets* 一小束非洲紫罗兰

pot¹ /pɑt; pɒt/ *n* 2 3

1 ▶TEA/COFFEE 茶/咖啡◀ [C] a container with a handle and a small tube for pouring, used to make tea or coffee 壶

2 ▶COOKING 烹饪◀ [C] a container used for cooking which is round, deep, and usually made of metal〔圆而深的〕锅: *The sink was full of dirty pots and pans.* 洗涤池里满是肮脏的锅碗瓢盆。

3 ▶STORING FOOD 储存食物◀ [C] a glass or clay container used for storing food 用于储存食物的容器，罐: *a jam pot* 果酱罐 | *a pot of honey* 一罐蜂蜜

4 ▶FOR A PLANT 用于植物◀ [C] a container for a plant, usually made of plastic or baked clay 花盆

5 ▶BOWL 碗◀ [C] a dish, bowl, plate or other container that is made by shaping clay and then baking it 陶罐，陶壶，陶盆

6 have pots of *BrE informal* to have a lot of something, especially money【英，非正式】有很多〔尤指钱〕: *Julie's Dad's got pots of money!* 朱莉的爸爸有很多钱！

7 go to pot *informal* if something such as a place or an organization goes to pot, it becomes much worse because no one is interested in looking after it or making it work【非正式】衰落；荒芜；垮掉: *This government has let the whole country go to pot.* 该政府已使整个国家垮了。

8 ▶DRUG 毒品◀ [U] *old-fashioned* MARIJUANA【过时】大麻

9 ▶STOMACH 肚子◀ [singular] *informal* a large rounded stomach that sticks out; POTBELLY【非正式】大肚子

10 ▶CARD GAMES 扑克牌戏◀ the pot all the money that people have risked in a game of cards, especially POKER (1)〔尤指扑克牌戏中一局的〕赌注总额

11 the pot calling the kettle black *informal* used to say that you should not criticize someone for a fault that you also have【非正式】锅嫌壶黑；五十步笑百步

12 take a pot at *informal* to shoot at something without aiming carefully【非正式】胡乱朝…开枪 —see also 另见 CHAMBER POT, MELTING POT

pot² *v* **potted, potting** [T] **1** to shoot at animals in order to kill them 射杀〔动物〕: *Giles was out with his gun, potting rabbits.* 贾尔斯带着枪出去打野兔。—see also 另见 POT SHOT **2** to put a plant in a pot filled with soil 把〔植物〕栽种在花盆中 —see also 另见 POTTED (1) **3** [T] to hit a ball into one of the bags at the edge of the table in games such as BILLIARDS, POOL¹ (3), and SNOOKER 击〔台球〕入袋

pot sth ↔ on *phr v* [T] *BrE* to move a plant into a large pot because it has grown too big for the pot it is in【英】把〔植物〕移栽到大盆中

po·ta·ble /ˈpotəbl; ˈpəʊtəbəl/ *adj formal* water that is potable is suitable for drinking【正式】〔水〕可饮用的

pot·ash /ˈpɑt,æʃ; ˈpɒtæʃ/ *n* [U] a sort of potassium used especially in farming to make the soil better 钾碱，碳酸钾

po·tas·si·um /pəˋtæsɪəm; pəˈtæsiəm/ *n* [U] a silver-white soft metal that is an ELEMENT (1) and usually exists in compounds formed with other substances 钾

po·ta·to /pəˋteto; pəˈteɪtəʊ/ *n plural* **potatoes 1** [C,U] a round white vegetable with a brown skin, that grows as a root 马铃 2

薯, 土豆: *mashed potato* 马铃薯[土豆]泥 | *roast potatoes* 烤马铃薯[土豆] —see picture on page A9 参见 A9 页图 **2** [C] a plant that has potatoes growing at its roots 马铃薯植株 —see also 另见 SWEET POTATO

potato chip /ˈ· ·· ˌ·/ *n* [C] *AmE* a thin piece of fried potato which is sold in packets【美】炸马铃薯片; CRISP[1] *BrE*【英】

Potato Fam·ine, the /ˈ·ˈ··, ˌ·/ a FAMINE in Ireland in 1845-46, caused when the failure of the potato crop led to a serious lack of food all over the country. As a result, many people died of hunger and many others left Ireland to go to live in the US. The British government, which at that time ruled Ireland, did very little to help people who were suffering, and some Irish people still feel upset and angry about this. 大饥荒, 马铃薯饥荒〔1845-1846 年的一场大饥荒。爱尔兰马铃薯歉收, 境内严重缺粮, 许多人饿死, 不少人移居美国。当时统治爱尔兰的英国政府对饥民的疾苦置之不理。对此, 一些爱尔兰人至今仍感沮丧和愤怒〕

potato peel·er /ˈ·ˈ··, ˌ·/ *n* [C] a small tool like a knife, used for removing the skin of a potato 马铃薯削皮器

pot·bel·lied /ˈpɑtˌbɛlɪd; pɒtˈbelid/ *adj* having a large stomach that sticks out 肚子大的, 大腹便便的: *naked potbellied children begging for food* 赤身裸体讨饭的大肚皮孩子

pot·bel·ly /ˈpɑtˌbɛlɪ; ˈpɒtˌbeli/ *n* [C] a large round stomach that sticks out 大肚子

pot·boil·er /ˈpɑtˌbɔɪlɚ; ˈpɒtˌbɔɪlə/ *n* [C] a book that is written quickly to make money〔为赚钱而〕粗制滥造的书

pot·bound /ˈpɑtˌbaʊnd; ˈpɒtbaʊnd/ *adj BrE* a plant that is potbound cannot grow any more because its roots have grown to fill the pot it is in【英】〔盆栽植物〕根满盆的, 盆缚的; ROOTBOUND *AmE*【美】

po·teen /poˈtin; pəˈtʃiːn/ *n* [U] Irish WHISKY made secretly and illegally to avoid paying tax〔为逃税而〕私酿的爱尔兰威士忌酒

po·ten·cy /ˈpotn̩sɪ; ˈpəʊtənsi/ *n* [U] **1** the power that an idea, argument, action etc has to influence people 力量, 威力; 影响力: *The spectre of mass unemployment had lost none of its political potency.* 大规模失业的恐惧丝毫没有失去它的政治影响力。 **2** the strength of the effect of a drug, medicine, alcohol etc on your mind or body〔毒品、药物、酒等的〕效力, 效能: *a high potency drug* 强效毒品 **3** the ability of a man to have sex〔男子的〕性交能力

po·tent /ˈpotn̩t; ˈpəʊtənt/ *adj* **1** having a powerful effect or influence on your body or mind 有效力的, 效力大的; 有影响力的: *a particularly potent cider* 特别浓烈的苹果酒 | *The film is full of potent images of war.* 这部电影充满了震撼人心的战争场面。 **2** powerful and effective 强有力的, 有威力的; 有说服力的: *a potent new weapons system* 有强大威力的新武器系统 —**potently** *adv* —see also 另见 IMPOTENT

po·ten·tate /ˈpotn̩ˌtet; ˈpəʊtənteɪt/ *n* [C] *literary* a ruler with direct power over his people【文】〔直接统治民众的〕君主, 统治者: *Eastern potentates* 东方君主

S3 W2 **po·ten·tial[1]** /pəˈtɛnʃəl; pəˈtenʃəl/ *adj* [only before noun 仅用于名词前] a potential customer, problem, effect etc is not a customer, problem etc yet, but may become one in the future 潜在的, 可能的: *The agents were eager to impress potential buyers.* 这些代理商急于给潜在的买主留下深刻的印象。 | *a potential threat to national security* 对国家安全的潜在威胁

W3 **potential[2]** *n* [U] **1** the possibility that something will develop in a certain way, or have a particular effect 可能性, 潜在性: [+for] *The potential for abuse in such a system is enormous.* 在这样的体制下, 滥用职权的可能性极大。 | *sales potential* (=the amount of something that is likely be sold) 销售潜力 **2** natural ability that could develop to make you very good at something 潜力, 潜能: *a young player with great potential* 有很大潜力的年轻选手 | **have/show potential** (=to be likely to be successful) 有潜力/表现出潜力 | **achieve/fulfil/realize your potential** (=succeed in doing as well as you possibly can) 发挥你的潜力 *We want each student to realize their full potential.* 我们想让每一位学生发挥他们最大限度的潜力。 **3** *technical* the difference in VOLTAGE between two points on an electrical CIRCUIT (4)【术语】电势, 电位, 电压

po·ten·ti·al·i·ty /pəˌtɛnʃɪˈælətɪ; pəˌtenʃiˈælʃti/ *n* [C,U] *formal* the possibility that something may develop in a particular way【正式】潜力, 可能性

po·ten·tial·ly /pəˈtɛnʃəlɪ; pəˈtenʃəli/ *adv* [+adj/adv] something that is potentially dangerous, useful etc is not actually dangerous etc at the present time but is likely to become so 潜在地, 可能地: *I knew that I was in a potentially dangerous situation.* 我知道我处于潜在的危险之中。 | *The benefits of computerised ordering are potentially very great.* 电脑订货有很大的潜在好处。

pot·ful /ˈpɑtfʊl; ˈpɒtfʊl/ *n* [C] the amount that a pot can contain 一(满)罐, 一(满)壶; 一(满)锅

pot·head /ˈpɑthɛd; ˈpɒthed/ *n* [C] *informal* someone who smokes a lot of MARIJUANA【非正式】吸大麻者

pot·hold·er /ˈpɑtˌholdɚ; ˈpɒthəʊldə/ *n* [C] a piece of thick material used for holding hot cooking pans〔用于端热锅等的〕防烫厚布垫

pot·hole /ˈpɑtˌhol; ˈpɒthəʊl/ *n* [C] **1** a hole in the surface of a road that makes driving difficult or dangerous〔路面上的〕凹坑, 坑洞: *swerving to avoid the potholes* 突然转向避开地面的凹坑 **2** a long hole that goes deep under the ground, formed by natural processes 锅穴, 壶穴, 瓯穴 —**potholed** *adj*

pot·hol·ing /ˈpɑtˌholɪŋ; ˈpɒtˌhəʊlɪŋ/ *n* [U] the sport of climbing down inside holes under the ground 地下洞穴探险〔一种体育运动〕—**pothole** *v* [I] —**potholer** *n* [C]

po·tion /ˈpoʃən; ˈpəʊʃən/ *n* [C] **1** *literary* a drink intended to have a special or magic effect on the person who drinks it【文】〔有特效或魔力的〕饮剂: *a love potion* 春药饮剂 **2** *humorous* a medicine, especially one that seems strange, old-fashioned, or unnecessary【幽默】药物〔尤指看上去奇怪、过时或不必要的药物〕: *treating herself with pills and potions* 用各种药剂给她自己治疗

pot luck /ˌ·ˈ·/ *n* **take pot luck a)** to choose something without knowing very much about it and hope that it will be what you want 碰运气: *We hadn't booked a hotel so we had to take pot luck.* 我们没有预订酒店, 所以只能碰碰运气。 **b)** to have a meal at someone's home in which you eat whatever they have available 吃家常便饭: *I'm not sure what there is in the fridge – you'll have to take pot luck.* 我不清楚冰箱里有什么, 你只能有什么吃什么。

pot·luck /ˈpɑtˌlʌk; ˌpɒtˈlʌk◂/ *n AmE* a meal made up of dishes of food brought by many different people【美】〔多人带食物拼成的〕百乐餐

Pot Noo·dle /ˈ·ˌ··, ˌ·/ *trademark* a dish sold in the UK, consisting of dried PASTA, meat, and vegetables. You mix it with boiling water and it is ready to eat almost immediately.【商标】波特方便面〔英国出售的一种快餐食品, 成分为干面、肉和蔬菜, 加入沸水浸泡后即可食用〕

Po·to·mac, the /pəˈtomæk; pəˈtəʊmæk/ a river in the east of the US which separates Maryland and Washington, D.C. from Virginia and West Virginia 波托马克河〔美国东部一河流, 是马里兰州和华盛顿特区与弗吉尼亚州和西弗吉尼亚州的分界线〕

pot plant /ˈ· ·/ *n* [C] **1** *BrE* a plant that is grown indoors in a pot as a decoration【英】盆栽植物; POTTED PLANT *AmE*【美】 **2** *informal* a MARIJUANA plant【非正式】大麻植株

pot·pour·ri /pɑtˈpʊrɪ; pəʊˈpʊri/ *n* **1** [U] a mixture of pieces of dried flowers and leaves kept in a bowl to make a room smell pleasant 百花香〔放在钵内的干花和叶子, 能使室内空气芳香〕 **2** [C] a mixture of things that are not usually put together, for example different pieces of music or writing〔音乐或文学作品等的〕集锦; 集锦曲; 杂集: *a potpourri of literary styles* 多种文学风格的杂集

pot roast /ˈ· ·/ *n* [C] a dish that consists of a piece of meat cooked in a pan with potatoes or other vegetables 罐炖肉菜〔用一块肉和马铃薯或其他蔬菜一起炖成〕

Pots·dam A·gree·ment, the /ˌpɑtsdæm əˈgrimənt; ˌpɒtsdæm əˈgriːmənt/ an agreement by the countries that won World War II (the US, Britain, the USSR, and France) to divide control of Germany between them《波茨坦协定》〔美国、英国、苏联和法国几个二战战胜国达成的一项协定。该协议涉及战后对德国控制权的分配问题〕

pot·sherd /ˈpɑtˌʃɝd; ˈpɒt-ʃɜːd/ *n* [C] *technical* a piece of a broken clay pot from long ago【术语】〔时代久远的〕陶器碎片: *Roman coins and potsherds* 古罗马时代的钱币和陶器碎片

pot shot /ˈ· ·/ *n* **take a pot shot at** to shoot at someone or something without aiming very carefully 对…任意射击[盲目射击, 乱射]

pot·ted /ˈpɑtɪd; ˈpɒtʃd/ *adj* [only before noun 仅用于名词前] **1** a potted plant grows indoors in a pot 盆栽的: *a potted palm* 盆栽棕榈 **2 a potted history/version** *especially BrE* a short explanation or description of something that gives only the main facts【尤英】简史/节本: *short potted histories of all the teams in the league* 俱乐部联合会所有球队的简史 **3** *BrE* potted meat or fish has been made into a PASTE for spreading on bread【英】〔肉、鱼〕制成酱的

potted plant /ˌ·ˈ· ·/ *n* [C] a plant that is grown indoors in a pot as a decoration 盆栽植物; POT PLANT *BrE*【英】

pot·ter[1] /ˈpɑtɚ; ˈpɒtə/ *n* [C] **1** someone who makes pots, dishes etc out of clay 陶工, 制陶工人 —see also 另见 POTTERY **2 have**

a potter/go for a potter *spoken* to move around a place in a slow unhurried way【口】随便走走, 闲逛

potter² also 又作 **potter about/around** *v* [I] *BrE* to spend time doing pleasant things that are not important without hurrying【英】悠然地做些轻松的工作[琐碎的事情]; PUTTER² *AmE*【美】: *I spent the morning pottering about in the garden.* 我花了一个上午在花园里随便干了些琐碎的事。—**potterer** *n* [C]

Potter, Bea·trix /ˈbɪətrɪks; ˈbɪətrɪks/ (1866-1943) a British writer who wrote stories for young children and also drew the pictures for her books. The characters in her stories are animals who dress and behave like humans, and they include Peter Rabbit, Tom Kitten, and Mrs Tiggy-Winkle (a HEDGEHOG). Her stories are still very popular today. 波特〔(1866-1943), 英国作家。她不仅创作儿童作品, 而且还为自己的作品绘制插图。书中的角色全是穿着、举止像人一样的动物, 其中包括兔子彼得、小猫汤姆以及刺猬蒂吉-温克勒太太。她的作品至今仍很受欢迎〕

Potter, Den·nis /ˈdɛnɪs; ˈdenɪs/ (1935-94) a British writer of plays for television, whose many plays include *Pennies from Heaven* and *The Singing Detective*. He is one of the most important and original writers of plays for television, which often use popular songs as part of serious stories. 波特〔(1935-1994), 英国电视剧作家。他创作了不少剧本, 其中包括《天降财神》和《奇探心魔》。他是英国最重要、也是最富原创性的电视剧作家之一, 经常在严肃的故事中穿插流行歌曲〕

Potter, Harry a boy MAGICIAN (=person who uses magic) who is the main character in a very successful series of books by the British writer J.K. Rowling. Harry goes to the Hogwarts School of Witchcraft and Wizardry, and he has an evil enemy, Lord Voldemort. 哈利·波特〔英国作家J.K.罗琳创作的优秀系列长篇小说中的主人公。他去霍格沃斯魔法学校学习魔法。他有一个邪恶的敌人, 名叫伏地魔〕

Pot·ter·ies, the /ˈpɑtərɪz; ˈpɒtəriz/ a part of Staffordshire in the Midlands of England which is a centre for the CHINA and POTTERY industry 波特里斯〔英格兰中部斯塔福德郡一区, 为陶瓷工业中心〕

potter's wheel /ˌ‥ˈ ˌ/ *n* [C] a special round flat object that spins around very fast, onto which wet clay is placed so that it can be shaped into a pot 陶轮, 拉坯轮

pot·ter·y /ˈpɑtərɪ; ˈpɒtəri/ *n* **1** [U] objects made out of baked clay 陶器: *a fine collection of medieval pottery* 精美的中世纪陶器收藏品 **2** [U] clay that has been shaped and baked in order to make pots,dishes etc 陶: *a pottery dish* 陶碟 **3** [U] the activity of making pots, dishes etc out of clay 制陶: *Pottery and basket-making were usually done by the women.* 制陶和编篮子通常由妇女来做。| *a pottery class* 制陶手工学习班 **4** [C] a factory where pottery objects are made 陶瓷厂

pot·ting shed /ˈ‥ ˌ/ *n* [C] *BrE* a small building, usually made of wood, where garden tools, seeds etc are kept【英】〔存放园艺工具、种子等的〕小木屋, 园圃棚

pot·ty¹ /ˈpɑtɪ; ˈpɒti/ *adj BrE informal*【英, 非正式】**1** crazy or silly 疯狂的; 愚蠢的: *What a potty idea!* 多么愚蠢的主意! | **drive sb potty** (=make someone crazy) 使某人发疯 *Your radio is driving me potty.* 你的收音机吵得我快发疯了。**2 potty about** extremely interested in something, or liking someone very much 迷恋…的, 对…着迷的: *Gemma's potty about riding.* 杰玛迷上了骑马。| *He's completely potty about her.* 他完全迷上了她。—**pottiness** *n* [U]

potty² *n* [C] *informal* a container shaped like a bowl, used by very young children as a toilet【非正式】小孩用的便盆

potty-train /ˈ‥ ˌ/ *v* [T] to teach a child to use a potty or toilet 训练〔小孩〕使用便盆[厕所] —**potty-training** *n* [U] —**potty-trained** *adj*

pouch /paʊtʃ; paʊtʃ/ *n* [C] **1** a small leather bag used for keeping things such as tobacco or money in〔储物的皮制〕小袋; 小烟袋; 小钱袋: *a rucksack with pouches on the sides* 两侧有小袋的帆布背包 **2** a pocket of skin which KANGAROOS use for carrying their babies〔袋鼠的〕育儿袋 **3** a fold of skin like a bag which animals such as SQUIRRELS have inside each cheek to carry and store food〔松鼠等的〕颊囊, 颊袋〔用于携带和储存食物〕**4** *AmE* an area of loose skin under someone's eyes【美】眼袋

pouf /puf; puːf/ *n* [C] *BrE*【英】**1** a round soft piece of furniture used to sit on or rest your feet on 坐垫, 脚垫; HASSOCK *AmE*【美】**2** *BrE informal* an insulting word for a male HOMOSEXUAL【英, 非正式】男同性恋者〔侮辱性词语〕—compare 比较 POOF¹

pouffe /puf; puːf/ *n* [C] *BrE* a POUF (1)【英】坐垫, 脚垫

Poulenc /puˋlæŋk puːˈlæŋk/**, Francis** /ˈfrænsɪs; ˈfrɑːnsɪs/ (1899-1963) a French COMPOSER of modern music who wrote OPERAS, piano music, songs, and BALLET music. His works include *Mouvements Perpetuels, Les Biches*, and *Dialogue des Carmélites*. 普朗克〔(1899-1963), 法国现代音乐作曲家。他写过歌剧、钢琴曲、歌曲和芭蕾舞曲, 代表作有《无穷动》、《母鹿》和《加尔默罗会修女们的对话》〕

poul·ter·er /ˈpoltərə; ˈpəʊltərə/ *n* [C] *BrE old-fashioned* someone who sells poultry【英, 过时】家禽商贩

poul·tice /ˈpoltɪs; ˈpəʊltɪs/ *n* [C] something that is put on someone's skin to make it less swollen or painful, often made of bread and milk〔常由面包和牛奶制成的〕泥敷剂, 泥罨剂

poul·try /ˈpoltrɪ; ˈpəʊltri/ *n* **1** [plural] birds that are kept on farms for supplying eggs and meat 家禽: *large-scale poultry farms* 大型家禽饲养场 **2** [U] meat from birds such as chickens, ducks etc 家禽肉

pounce /pauns; paʊns/ *v* [I] to suddenly jump on an animal or person after waiting to attack them 猛扑, 突然袭击: *crouching, ready to pounce* 弓着身子准备猛扑过去 | **[+on]** *The cat pounced on an unsuspecting mouse.* 那只猫猛然扑向一只丝毫没有戒备的老鼠。—**pounce** *n* [C]

pounce on sb/sth *phr v* [T] **1** to notice a mistake and immediately criticize or disagree with it 发现错误并立即批评[反对]: *The boss was quick to pounce on any error in her work.* 老板能够一眼看出她工作中的错误。**2** to accept an offer or invitation eagerly 欣然接受〔提议、邀请〕

pound¹ /paund; paʊnd/ *n*

1 ▶WEIGHT 重量◀ written abbreviation 缩写为 **1b** [C] a unit for measuring weight, equal to 16 OUNCES or about 0.454 kilograms 磅〔重量单位, 相当于16盎司或0.454千克〕: *a pound of apples* 1磅苹果 | *Moira weighs about 130 pounds.* 莫伊拉重约130磅。| *The grapes cost $2 a pound.* 葡萄的价格是2美元1磅。—see table on page C3 参见 C3 页附录

2 ▶MONEY 钱◀ [C] **a)** written abbreviation 缩写为 **£** the standard unit of money in Britain, which is divided into 100 pence 英镑〔英国标准货币单位, 等于100便士〕: *a five pound note* 5英镑的钞票 | *They spent over a thousand pounds on their holiday.* 他们度假花了一千多英镑。| *a multi-million pound business* 价值数百万英镑的企业 **b)** the standard unit of money in various other countries, such as Egypt and the Sudan 镑〔埃及、苏丹等国的标准货币单位〕**c)** a coin or note worth this amount 一英镑的硬币[纸币]: *Can you change a pound?* 你能把一英镑换成零钱吗?

3 the pound the value of British money in relation to the money of other countries 英镑兑换其他国家货币的比值: *There was pressure on the pound in the foreign exchange markets.* 外汇市场上英镑的压力很大。

4 ▶PLACE 地方◀ [C] a place where lost dogs and cats, or cars that have been illegally parked, are kept until the owner claims them〔走失的狗、猫的〕待领所; 〔违规停放车辆的〕临时扣押场

5 a quarter/half pounder a HAMBURGER with a quarter or half pound of meat in it 1/4 磅肉的/1/2 磅肉的汉堡(包): *a quarter-pounder with cheese* 1/4磅肉的加乳酪汉堡

6 get your pound of flesh to get something that is legally yours from someone, even though it makes them suffer and you do not really need it 要回合法但不合情理的东西: *merciless creditors, demanding their pound of flesh* 要求如数偿还欠款的无情债主

7 a 3-pounder/24-pounder etc a) animal, or fish that weighs 3 pounds, 24 pounds etc 3磅/24磅重的兽[鱼] **b)** a gun that fires a SHELL¹ (2) that weighs 3 pounds, 24 pounds etc 发射3磅/24磅等重炮弹的大炮

pound² *v*

1 ▶HIT 击打◀ [I,T] to hit something several times, making a lot of noise 连续重击, 猛打: **[+against/on]** *A heavy sea pounded against the pier.* 巨浪猛烈地拍击着码头。| **pound sth** *Thomas pounded the door with his fist.* 托马斯用拳头猛烈地敲打着门。

2 ▶MOVE 移动◀ [I always+adv/prep] to walk or run quickly with heavy, loud steps 脚步重重地快走[快跑]: **[+along/through/down]** *He pounded up the stairs in front of her.* 他在她前面嗵嗵嗵地跑上楼。

3 ▶HEART 心脏◀ [I] if your heart pounds, it beats very quickly〔心脏〕剧烈地跳动: *Patrick rushed to the door, his heart pounding with excitement.* 帕特里克冲到门口, 他的心激动得怦怦直跳。

4 ▶BREAK 弄碎◀ [T] to hit something many times with a tool in order to break it into pieces or make it flat 捣碎, 舂烂: *Pound the almonds and mix with breadcrumbs.* 把杏仁捣碎与面包屑混在一起。

5 ▶MUSIC 音乐◀ also 又作 **pound out, pound away** [T] to play music loudly by hitting your piano, drum etc very hard 猛烈地敲打〔钢琴、鼓等〕, 弹奏出: *Mrs Jones pounded out the hymns on the old piano.* 琼斯太太在那架旧钢琴上重重地弹奏出圣歌。

6 ▶ARMY 军队◀ [T] to attack a place continuously for a long time with bombs or shells (SHELL[1] (2)) 猛烈袭击，向…猛烈开火: *Enemy forces have been pounding the city for over two months.* 敌军两个多月来一直在猛烈袭击那个城市。

7 pound the beat *BrE* if a policeman pounds the beat, he walks regularly around the area he is responsible for【英】〔警察〕在辖区做例行徒步巡逻

Pound, Ez·ra /ˈɛzrə; ˈezrə/ (1885-1972) a US poet who lived mostly in Europe, and whose poems include the *Cantos*. He broadcast on the radio in support of FASCISM and Mussolini during World War II. As a result, after the war the US government charged him with TREASON, but he was judged to be mentally ill and sent to a mental hospital until 1958. 庞德〔(1885-1972)，长期旅居欧洲的美国诗人。诗作包括《诗章》等。二战期间，他发表过支持法西斯主义和墨索里尼的广播演说。战后，美国政府指控他犯有叛国罪，但法庭裁定他患有精神病，于是就把他送进精神病院，直至1958年才出院〕

pound·age /ˈpaʊndɪdʒ; ˈpaʊndɪdʒ/ *n* [U] **1** *technical* an amount charged for every pound in weight, or for every British £1 in value【术语】每磅重量的收费额；每英镑收费额 **2** *informal* weight【非正式】重量: *trying to shed that extra poundage* 极力想减掉多余的重量

pound cake /ˈ· ·/ *n* [C] *AmE* a heavy cake made from flour, sugar, and butter【美】磅蛋糕，重奶油蛋糕

pound·ing /ˈpaʊndɪŋ; ˈpaʊndɪŋ/ *n* **1** [singular, U] the action or the sound of something repeatedly hitting a surface very hard, or of your heart beating 猛击（声）；猛跳（声）；沉重的脚步（声）: *The pounding of hooves was getting nearer.* 隆隆的马蹄声越来越近了。**2 take a pounding a)** to be completely defeated 被彻底击败: *Our football team took a real pounding.* 我们的足球队遭到惨败。**b)** to be hit many times by a lot of bombs or shells (SHELL[1] (2)) 遭到猛烈袭击

pound ster·ling /ˌ· ˈ··/ *n* [singular] *technical* the standard unit of money in Britain, which is divided into 100 pence【术语】英镑〔英国标准货币单位，等于100便士〕

S2 W3 **pour** /pɔr; pɔː/ *v*

pour 灌，注，倒

1 ▶LIQUID 液体◀ [T] to make a liquid or a substance such as salt or sand flow out of or into a container 灌，注，倒: **pour sth into/out/down etc** *Kim poured some water into a glass.* 金往一只玻璃杯里倒了些水。| *You might as well pour the oil down the drain.* 你还是把油倒进排水管吧。| **pour sb sth** *Why don't you pour yourself another drink?* 你为什么不给自己再倒一杯酒呢?

2 ▶TEA 茶◀ also 又作 **pour out** [I] *BrE* to fill cups with tea【英】倒茶，斟茶: *Shall I pour or will you?* 我来给你倒茶还是你自己来?

3 ▶LIQUID/SMOKE 液体/烟◀ [I always+adv/prep] to flow quickly and in large amounts 倾泻，大量涌出: **[+from/down/out]** *Smoke was pouring out of the chimney.* 那烟囱正冒出浓烟。

4 ▶ARRIVE/LEAVE 到达/离开◀ [I always+adv/prep] if people or things pour into or out of a place, a lot of them arrive or leave at the same time 涌进[出]: **[+into/from/through]** *The men poured into the hall for the meeting.* 男人们涌进大厅开会。| *Offers of help poured in from all over the country.* 全国上下纷纷伸出援助之手。

5 ▶RAIN 雨◀ also 又作 **pour down** [I] to rain heavily without stopping〔雨〕倾盆而下: *The rain poured down endlessly.* 倾盆大雨下个不停。| **it's pouring/it poured** *It poured all night.* 倾盆大雨下了一整夜。| **It's pouring rain/hail etc** *AmE*【美】: *It's pouring rain out there!* 外面正下着倾盆大雨!

6 pour money/aid/dollars into to provide a lot of money over a period of time to pay for something 提供大笔的钱/大量援助/大量美元给…: *pouring millions of dollars into education* 把上百万美元投入到教育中

7 pour cold water over/on to spoil someone's plan, idea or keenness to do something by criticizing them 对…泼冷水: *pouring cold water on suggestions that he might resign* 对认为他可能会辞职的提法泼冷水

8 pour oil on troubled waters to try to stop a quarrel by talking to people and making them calmer 平息风波，调解争端，息事宁人

9 pour scorn on to say that something or someone is stupid and not worth considering 鄙夷地谈论〔某物或某人〕，对…嗤之以鼻: *The press is pouring scorn on the 'do nothing' Congress.* 报界正以鄙夷的口气谈论"毫无作为"的国会。

10 pour well if a container pours well, you can pour liquid easily from it〔容器〕倒起来容易

11 pour it on *informal* to tell someone about a situation in a way that makes it seem much worse than it really is, in order to make them feel sorry for you【非正式】〔为获得同情而〕夸大其词，极力渲染: *She was really pouring it on.* 她实际上在夸大其词。

pour sth ↔ **out** *phr v* [T] if you pour out your thoughts, feelings etc, you tell someone everything about them, especially because you feel very unhappy 倾吐，倾诉，尽情地诉说: **pour sth out to sb** *Liam poured out his feelings of loneliness to Laura.* 利亚姆向劳拉倾诉了自己的孤独感。| **pour out your heart/soul** (=tell someone all your feelings including your most secret ones) 诉说心里话

Pous·sin /puˈsæn; ˈpuːsæn/, **Nic·o·las** /ˈnɪkləs; ˈnɪkələs/ (1594-1665) a French painter whose most important works are his LANDSCAPES (=paintings showing an area of countryside or land) 普桑〔(1594-1665)，法国画家，尤以风景画闻名〕

pout /paʊt; paʊt/ *v* [I,T] to push out your lips because you are annoyed or to look sexually attractive 撅起〔嘴唇〕，撅嘴〔表示不高兴或显得性感〕: *The child pouted, cried, and went into a tantrum.* 那孩子撅起嘴哭着喊着，然后是大发脾气。—**pout** *n* [C] —**pouty** *adj*

pov·er·ty /ˈpɑvətɪ; ˈpɒvəti/ *n* **1** [U] the situation or experience of being poor 贫穷，贫困: **dire/abject/grinding poverty** (=very bad poverty) 极其贫困，赤贫 *Thousands of children live in dire poverty.* 成千上万的儿童生活极为贫困。**2 the poverty line/level** the income below which a person or a family is officially considered to be very poor and in need of help 贫困线: *More than 20% of American families now live below the poverty line.* 现在有超过20%的美国家庭生活在贫困线以下。**3** [singular,U] *formal* a lack of a particular quality【正式】缺少，贫乏: **[+of]** *a surprising poverty of imagination* 惊人地缺乏想象力 —compare 比较 POORNESS

poverty-strick·en /ˈ··· ,··/ *adj* extremely poor and having problems because of this 极度贫穷[贫困]的: *a poverty-stricken area* 贫困不堪的地区

poverty trap /ˈ··· ,·/ *n* [C] a situation in which a poor person will not get any advantage from taking a job because they would then lose their payments from the government 贫困陷阱〔因穷人找到了工作就会失去政府救济款，以致从工作中并没得到好处的情况〕

POW /ˌpi o ˈdʌblju; ˌpiː əʊ ˈdʌbəljuː/ *n* [C] a PRISONER OF WAR 战俘: *Thousands of POWs died in the camps.* 成千上万的战俘死在战俘营里。

pow /paʊ; paʊ/ *interjection* used to represent the sound of a gun firing, an explosion, or someone hitting another person hard, especially in children's COMICS〔尤指在儿童连环漫画中〕啪！砰！〔表示射击声、爆炸声或某人猛打另一人的声音〕

pow·der[1] /ˈpaʊdɚ; ˈpaʊdə/ *n* **1** [C,U] a dry substance in the form of very small grains 粉，粉末: *Grind the sugar into a powder.* 把糖碾成粉末。| *Zara put down some insect powder to kill the ants.* 扎拉放了一些杀虫粉以杀死蚂蚁。| **milk/custard etc powder** (=food that is stored as a powder and which you add water to in order to make it back into a liquid) 奶粉/蛋奶浆汁粉等 **2 take a powder** *AmE informal* to leave a place quickly, especially to avoid a difficult situation【美，非正式】〔尤指为避免困难局面而〕匆忙离去: *When she shows up I'll take a powder.* 她一到，我就会赶快离开。**3 a powder keg** a dangerous situation or place where violence or trouble could suddenly start 火药桶〔比喻暴力或麻烦随时可能发生的危险局面或地方〕: *Since the riot the city has been a powder keg waiting to blow.* 这个城市自骚乱以来已变成一个随时会爆发的火药桶。**4 powder snow** snow consisting of extremely small pieces 粉状雪

powder[2] *v* **1** [T] to put powder on something, especially your skin 给〔某物，尤指皮肤〕搽粉: *Dana took out her compact and began powdering her cheeks.* 达娜拿出她的小粉盒开始往脸颊上抹粉。**2 be powdered with** to be covered with small pieces of something 撒满；铺满〔某种粉状东西〕: *Their shoulders were powdered with snow.* 他们的肩膀上落满了雪。**3 powder your nose** an expression meaning to go to the TOILET, used by women to avoid saying this directly 上厕所〔女士使用的委婉说法〕

powder blue /ˌ·· ˈ·◂/ *n* [U] pale blue 淡蓝色: *a powder blue dress* 淡蓝色的服装

pow·dered /ˈpaʊdəd; ˈpaʊdəd/ *adj* **1** produced or sold in the form of a powder (制成)粉状的, 以粉状出售的: *powdered milk* 奶粉 **2** covered with powder 布满粉的: *powdered hair* 满是粉的头发

powder puff /ˈ·· ·/ *n* [C] a small piece of soft material used by women to spread POWDER on their face or body 粉扑

powder room /ˈ·· ·/ *n* [C] **1** an expression meaning a toilet for women in a theatre, hotel, restaurant etc, used to avoid saying this directly〔剧院、酒店、餐馆等内的〕女厕所〔委婉说法〕**2** *AmE* a small room with a toilet and WASHBASIN next to the main living room in a house or apartment【美】〔主起居室旁的〕盥洗室

pow·der·y /ˈpaʊdərɪ; ˈpaʊdəri/ *adj* **1** like powder or easily broken into powder 粉末状的; 易碎成粉末的: *The snow was dry and powdery.* 雪干干的而且像粉末一样。**2** covered with powder 布满粉的; 搽了粉的

Pow·ell /ˈpaʊəl; ˈpaʊəl/, **An·tho·ny** /ˈæntənɪ; ˈæntəni/ (1905-2000) a British writer who wrote a series of 12 NOVELs *A Dance to the Music of Time*, which describes the lives of a group of UPPER-CLASS friends over a long period. 鲍威尔〔(1905-2000), 英国作家。他创作了一套12本的系列小说, 名为《与时代合拍的舞蹈》, 以跨时代手法描述一群上流社会朋友的生活〕

Powell, Co·lin /ˈkolɪn; ˈkəʊlɪn/ (1937-) a US military leader who became famous during the Gulf War and who was the first black person to become Chairman of the Joint Chiefs of Staff (=leader of all the US military forces). In 2001 President George W Bush made him US Secretary of State. 鲍威尔〔(1937-), 美国军事领导人, 海湾战争期间声名鹊起, 是任参谋长联席会议主席的首位黑人。2001年, 布什总统任命他为美国国务卿〕

Powell, E·noch /ˈinɑk; ˈiːnɒk/ (1912-98) a British politician in the Conservative Party, who was a government minister in the early 1960s, and later left the Conservative Party and became an MP in Northern Ireland. He made a speech in 1968 in which he said that if the UK allowed too many black people to come and live there, there would be fighting and "rivers of blood" in the streets. Many people criticized him for this speech, because they believed that it encouraged RACIST attitudes. 鲍威尔〔(1912-1998), 英国保守党政治家, 20世纪60年代初任政府大臣, 脱离保守党后任北爱尔兰议员。1968年, 他发表了一次演讲, 声称假如允许大量黑人进入英国定居的话, 那么街头上就会出现打架斗殴、"血流成河"的现象。他因此遭到许多人的批评, 因为大家认为他的演讲助长了英国的种族主义情绪〕

Powell, Michael (1905-90) a British film DIRECTOR, who made most of his important films with the Hungarian-born director Emeric Pressburger (1902-88). They included *The Life and Death of Colonel Blimp* (1943), *A Matter of Life and Death* (1946), *The Red Shoes* (1948), and *The Battle of the River Plate* (1956). Powell also directed *Peeping Tom* (1960), the controversial film of a murderer who filmed his VICTIMS as he killed them. 鲍威尔〔(1905-1990), 英国电影导演。他的多数重要影片都是与出生于匈牙利的导演埃默里克·普雷斯伯格 (1902-1988) 合作拍摄的, 其中包括《百战将军》(1943)、《生死攸关》(1946)、《红菱艳》(1948)、《柏拉特河海战》(1956)。他还导演过一部有争议的影片, 名为《偷窥狂》(1960), 讲述一位杀了人还给死者拍照的变态杀手的故事〕

S1 W1 **pow·er**[1] /ˈpaʊə; ˈpaʊə/ *n*

1 ▶CONTROL 控制◀ [U] the ability or right to control people or events 权力, 权势; 支配力: *We all felt that the chairman had too much power.* 我们都觉得主席的权力太大了。| *He was motivated by greed, envy, and the lust for power.* 他受贪婪、嫉妒、权力欲的驱使。| [+over] *She has a lot of power over the people in her team.* 她对她队里的人有很大的影响力。| **power struggle** (=a situation in which groups or leaders try to defeat each other and get complete control) 权力斗争 *engaged in a bitter power struggle against Chairman Sir George Scott* 卷入反对议长乔治·斯科特爵士的残酷的权力斗争中

2 ▶CONTROL OF A COUNTRY 对一个国家的控制◀ [U] the position of having political control of a country or government 政权: **be in power** *The dictator had been in power for seven years.* 那个独裁者已执政七年了。| **come/rise to power** (=start having political control) 开始掌权, 上台 *De Gaulle came to power in 1958.* 戴高乐是1958年上任的。| **return to power** *The Labour Party returned to power after 13 years.* 工党于13年之后重新执政。| **get into power** *If the Social Democrats got into power, they would change the whole system of local government.* 如果社会民主党上台, 他们就会改变地方政府的整个体制。| **take/seize power** *The Communists seized power in 1962.* 共产党于1962年夺取了政权。| **lose power** *Left-wing parties lost power in several European countries last year.* 去年左翼政党在几个欧洲国家都垮台了。

3 ▶INFLUENCE 影响◀ [U] the ability to influence people or give them strong feelings 影响力, 感染力: [+of] *We were stunned by the power of his speech.* 我们惊叹于他演讲的感染力。| *the immense power of television* 电视的巨大影响力

4 ▶RIGHT/AUTHORITY 权利/权威◀ [C,U] the right or authority to do something 职权, 权限: *The police have been given special powers to help them in the fight against terrorism.* 警方被赋予特殊的权力以帮助他们打击恐怖主义。| **the power to do sth** *She was the one who had the power to hire or fire people.* 有权雇用或解雇人的是她。| **the power of** *The chairman has the power of veto on all decisions.* 议长对所有的决定都有否决权。

5 ▶ABILITY 能力◀ [C,U] a natural or special ability to do something 能力, 本领: [+of] *After the accident she lost the power of speech.* 那次事故之后, 她失去了语言的能力。| **the power to do sth** *Local people believe that the plant has the power to cure all kinds of ailments.* 当地人相信这种植物具有治愈各种疾病的效能。

6 earning/purchasing/bargaining power the ability to earn money, buy things etc 赚钱能力/购买力/议价能力: *Average earning power has shot up by more than 50%.* 平均赚钱能力已迅速增长了超过50%。

7 student/black/parent etc power the political or social influence that an organized group has 学生/黑人/家长的势力等: *another victory for student power* 学生势力的又一次胜利

8 ▶STRENGTH 力量◀ the strength of something such as an explosion, animal or natural force and its ability to move or destroy things 力量, 威力: *the sheer power and majesty of the elephant* 大象的力量和威严 | *the power of the explosion* 爆炸的威力

9 ▶ENERGY 能量◀ [U] energy that can be used to make a machine work or to make electricity 能, 动力: **nuclear/wind/solar etc power** *Many people are opposed to the use of nuclear power.* 很多人反对使用核动力。| **under its own power** (=without help from another machine, ship etc) 靠它自己的动力 *The cruiser was able to leave port under its own power.* 这艘巡洋舰能靠自己的动力离港。| **lose/run out of power** *It keeps losing power when I take a sharp bend.* 我急转弯时它老是熄火。

10 ▶ELECTRICITY 电◀ [U] electricity that is used in houses, factories etc 电, 电力: *She plugged the machine in and switched the power on.* 她把机器的插头插上, 并打开电源开关。| *Power is provided by a small 9 volt battery.* 电是由一节小小的9伏特电池提供的。| **power cut/failure/outage** (=a short time when the electricity supply is not working) 断电, 停电 *Parts of the country have had power cuts because of the storms.* 这个国家的部分地区由于暴风雨而停电了。

11 ▶STRONG COUNTRY 强国◀ [C] a country that is strong and important, or has a lot of military strength 强国; 军事强国: *Egypt is still an important power in the Middle East.* 埃及仍然是中东地区一个重要的强国。| **world power** (=a very important country that can influence events in different parts of the world) 世界强国

12 air/sea power ships or aircraft that help an army in the air or on the sea 空军/海军力量: *The outcome will be decided by air power.* 结果将取决于空军实力。

13 be in sb's power to be in a situation in which someone has complete control over you 在某人的控制下

14 be in sb's power to do sth if it is in someone's power to do something, they have the authority or ability to do it 某人有权[有能力]做某事: *It is not in my power to tell you the results of the exam.* 我无权告诉你考试的结果。

15 be beyond/outside sb's power to do sth if it is beyond someone's power to do something, they do not have the authority or ability to do it 某人无权[无能力]做某事: *I am afraid it is beyond my power to do what you are asking.* 我恐怕无力做你要求做的事。

16 do everything in your power to do everything that you are able or allowed to do 尽你的所能: *The ambassador promised to do everything in his power to get the hostages released.* 那位大使答应尽他所能使人质获释。

17 do sb a power of good *BrE informal* to make someone feel more healthy, happy, and hopeful about the future【英, 非正式】对某人大有好处: *It looks as if your holiday has done you a power of good.* 看起来你的假期对你大有好处。

18 the powers of good/evil spirits or magical forces that are believed to influence events in a good or evil way 正义/邪恶的力量

19 ▶MATHEMATICS 数学◀ [C] if a number is increased to the power of three, four, five etc, it is multiplied by itself three, four, five etc times 幂, 乘方

20 high-powered/low-powered etc having a motor that is very powerful, not very powerful etc 高功率的/低功率的等: *irresponsible young men in high-powered sports cars* 开着大马力赛车的不负责任的年轻人

21 a power in the land *old-fashioned* someone who has a lot of power and influence in a country【过时】有权势的人物

22 the power behind the throne someone who is able to secretly control and influence decisions made by the leader or government of a country, but does not have an official government position themselves 太上皇, 幕后掌权者

23 the powers that be *informal* the unknown people who have important positions of authority and power, and whose decisions affect your life【非正式】掌权者; 当权派: *The powers that be have decided that smoking is a Bad Idea.* 权威人士已断定抽烟不好。

24 be on a power trip *informal* to be enjoying the new power or authority that you have been given, in a way that other people find unpleasant【非正式】过权力瘾 —see also 另见 STAYING POWER, BALANCE OF POWER, HIGH-POWERED

power[2] *v* **1** [T usually passive 一般用被动态] to supply power to a vehicle or machine 给〔车辆或机器〕提供动力, 以动力驱动: *The motor is powered by a solar battery.* 这台发动机是由太阳能电池驱动的。**2** [I+adv/prep] to move powerfully and quickly 飞速行驶, 快速行进: **[+through/up/down]** *His strong body powered through the water.* 他强壮的身体在水中快速地游动。**3 battery-powered/nuclear-powered etc** working or moving by means of power from a BATTERY, NUCLEAR energy etc 电池驱动的/核能驱动的等: *an atomic-powered ship* 原子能动力轮船 —see also 另见 HIGH-POWERED

power[3] *adj* **1** driven by a motor 电动机驱动的: *power tools* 电动工具 **2** *informal* showing that you are important in a business organization【非正式】〔显示某人在企业组织中是〕重要的: *a power lunch* 由重要商业人士参加的商务午餐

power base /ˈ‥ ˌ/ *n* [C] an area or group of people whose support gives a politician or leader their power 权力基础, 支持某人的势力[地区]: *Texas remained Johnson's political power base.* 得克萨斯州一直是约翰逊的政治权力基础所在。

pow·er·boat /ˈpaʊəˌbot; ˈpaʊəbəʊt/ *n* [C] a powerful MOTORBOAT that is used for racing 摩托赛艇; 汽艇, 快艇

power bro·ker /ˈ‥ ˌ‥/ *n* [C] someone who controls who should have political power in an area〔操纵某地区政治势力的〕权力掮客

power cut /ˈ‥ ˌ/ *n* [C] a period of time when there is no electricity supply 停电, 断电

power dres·sing /ˈ‥ ˌ‥/ *n* [U] a way of dressing in which the colour and style of your clothes is intended to emphasize how important your job is 突显工作重要性的穿着方式; 职业强人装束: *Eighties power dressing at its brashest* 20世纪80年代极其花哨的职业装

power drill /ˈ‥ ˌ/ *n* [C] a tool for making holes that works by electricity 电钻

W2 **pow·er·ful** /ˈpaʊəfəl; ˈpaʊəfəl/ *adj*

1 ▶IMPORTANT 重要的◀ a powerful person, organization, group etc is able to control and influence events and other people's actions 权力强大的, 有势力的: *The president is the most powerful man in America and probably the world.* 总统是美国而且很可能是世界上权力最大的人。| *a powerful consortium of European companies* 强大的欧洲企业集团

2 ▶AFFECTING SB'S FEELINGS/IDEAS 影响某人的感情/观念◀ having a strong effect on someone's feelings or on the way they think 强有力的, 有影响[感染]力的: *Jealousy is such a powerful emotion.* 嫉妒是一种如此强烈的感情。| *a powerful speech* 有感染力的演讲 | *The film uses a powerful blend of images and words.* 这部电影将图像和语言很有感染力地融合在一起。| **powerful reasons/arguments** (=reasons that make you think that something must be true) 有说服力的推理/论证

3 ▶MACHINE/WEAPON ETC 机器/武器等◀ a powerful machine, engine, weapon etc works very effectively and quickly or with great force〔机器、引擎、武器等〕功率大的, 效能大的: *a new generation of more powerful PCs* 更高效的新一代个人电脑 | *The Jaguar XJ12 features a powerful 24 valve engine.* "捷豹XJ12"型汽车的特点是有一个大功率的24气门发动机。

4 ▶MEDICINE 药◀ a powerful medicine or drug has a very strong effect on your body〔药物〕强效的: *The drug is a thousand times more powerful than LSD.* 这种违禁药是LSD（迷幻药）的效力的1000倍。

5 ▶PHYSICALLY STRONG 身体强壮的◀ physically strong 强壮的, 强健的: *Jed was a powerful, well-built man.* 杰德是个强壮结实的男人。| *powerful jaws that can kill in seconds* 可在数秒钟之内咬死猎物的强有力的嘴

6 ▶TEAM/ARMY ETC 球队/部队等◀ a powerful team, army etc is very strong and can easily defeat other teams or armies 强大的: *The Allies had assembled a powerful fighting force.* 同盟国集结了一支强大的战斗队伍。

7 ▶LIGHT/SOUND/TASTE/SMELL 光/声/味道/气味◀ very strong, bright, loud etc 非常强的, 浓烈的, 强烈的: *The alarm emits a powerful high-pitched sound.* 警报器发出很响的声音。

8 ▶EXPLOSION/KICK/PUNCH ETC 爆炸/踢/猛击等◀ a powerful blow, explosion etc hits someone with a lot of force or has a lot of force 猛烈的, 用力的: *an explosion ten times more powerful than Hiroshima* 是广岛原子弹爆炸威力10倍的爆炸 | *a powerful header just over the bar* 越过球门横梁的有力的头球 —**powerfully** *adv*: *Christie is very powerfully built.* 克里斯蒂身材魁梧。—see also 另见 ALL-POWERFUL

pow·er·house /ˈpaʊəˌhaus; ˈpaʊəhaʊs/ *n* [C] *informal*【非正式】**1** an organization or place that produces a lot of ideas and has a lot of influence 很有影响力的机构[地方]: *In the 60s, MIT was an intellectual powerhouse.* 在20世纪60年代, 麻省理工学院是一个具有很大影响力的学术机构。**2** someone who is very strong and has a lot of energy 身强力壮的人, 精力充沛的人: *a powerhouse of a man* 精力充沛的男人

pow·er·less /ˈpaʊəlɪs; ˈpaʊələs/ *adj* [not before noun 不用于名词前] unable to stop or control something because you do not have the power, strength, or legal right to do so 无权力的; 无力量的; 无能为力的: **powerless to do sth** *The fire was so big that firefighters were powerless to prevent it from spreading.* 火势太大, 消防人员没有能力阻止它蔓延。| **[+against]** *The Hungarians were powerless against the might of the Red Army.* 匈牙利人无力对抗苏联红军的力量。—**powerlessly** *adv* —**powerlessness** *n* [U]

power line /ˈ‥ ˌ/ *n* [C] a large wire carrying electricity above or under the ground 电力线, 输电线: *overhead power lines* 架空输电线

power of at·tor·ney /ˌ‥ ‥ ˈ‥ˌ/ *n* [C,U] *law* the legal right to do things for another person in their personal or business life, or a document giving this right【法律】〔法律上的〕委任权, 代理权; 委任书[状], 授权书

power plant /ˈ‥ ˌ/ *n* [C] **1** *technical* the machine or engine that supplies power to a factory, plane, car etc【术语】动力设备, 发电装置 **2** *AmE* a building where electricity is produced to supply a large area; POWER STATION【美】发电厂, 发电站

power point /ˈ‥ ˌ/ *n* [C] *especially BrE* a place on a wall where electrical equipment can be connected to the electricity supply; SOCKET【尤英】〔墙上的〕电源插座

power pol·i·tics /ˈ‥ ˌ‥/ *n* [U] the use or threat of armed force in international politics〔国际上的〕强权政治: *mere pawns in a game of international power politics* 世界强权政治游戏中的区区走卒

power sta·tion /ˈ‥ ˌ‥/ *n* [C] a building where electricity is produced to supply a large area 发电站, 发电厂

power steer·ing /ˈ‥ ˌ‥/ *n* [U] a system for steering (STEER[1] (1)) a vehicle which uses power from the vehicle's engine and so needs less effort from the driver〔汽车的〕动力转向装置〔利用引擎动力减轻司机操纵方向盘时的力的装置〕

power tool /ˈ‥ ˌ/ *n* [C] a tool that works by electricity 电动工具

pow-wow /ˈ‥ ˌ/ *n* [C] **1** *humorous* a meeting or discussion【幽默】会议, 讨论会 **2** a meeting or council of Native Americans 北美印第安人的议事会

Pow·ys /ˈpauɪs; ˈpaʊɪs/ a COUNTY in central Wales 波伊斯郡〔威尔士中部一郡〕

pox /pɑks; pɒks/ *n old use*【旧】**1 the pox** the disease SYPHILIS 梅毒（病）**2** [U] the disease SMALLPOX 天花（病）**3 a pox on** *old use* used to show that you are angry or annoyed with someone【旧】让…倒大霉, 叫…见鬼去, 降灾祸于…〔表示生气或厌烦〕—see also 另见 CHICKENPOX

pox·y /ˈpɑksɪ; ˈpɒksi/ *adj BrE slang* used to show that you do not like someone or something【英俚】令人讨厌的: *Keep your poxy money.* 收好你的臭钱!

pp **1** the written abbreviation of 缩写= pages: *See pp 15–17.* 见第15–17页。**2** written before the name of another person when you are signing a letter for them 代表…〔代别人签署信件时写在别人名字前〕

PPS /ˌpi pi ˈɛs; ˌpiː piː ˈes/ *n* [C] **1** a note added after a PS in a letter or message〔信末附言后的〕再附言 **2** Parliamentary Private Secretary; a member of the British parliament who is appointed to help a minister〔英国的〕议会私人秘书〔指定协助一位大臣工作的议员〕

PR /ˌpi ˈɑr; ˌpiː ˈɑː/ *n* [U] **1** PUBLIC RELATIONS; the work of persuading people to think that a company or organization is a good one 公共关系: *a leading PR agency in the city* 该市一家主要的公关公司 | *It's not very good for your PR, is it?* 这不利于你的公共关系，是吗？ **2** PROPORTIONAL REPRESENTATION〔议会选举中的〕比例代表制

prac·ti·ca·ble /ˈpræktɪkəbḷ; ˈpræktɪkəbəl/ *adj* an idea or way of doing something that is practicable is able to be used successfully in a particular situation〔观点、方法〕可行的，行得通的: *The only practicable course of action is to sell the company.* 唯一可行的做法是卖掉这家公司。—**practicably** *adv* —**practicability** /ˌpræktɪkəˈbɪlətɪ; ˌpræktɪkəˈbɪlɪ̣ti/ *n* [U]

3 2 **prac·ti·cal¹** /ˈpræktɪkḷ; ˈpræktɪkəl/ *adj*

1 ▶CONCERNED WITH REAL SITUATIONS 与实际情况相关的◀ concerned with real situations and events rather than ideas 实践（中）的，实际的: *How much practical experience do you have of working with computers?* 你有多少操作电脑的实践经验？| *a practical knowledge of simple medicine* 关于简单药物的实用知识 | *Most of the things you learn at school have no practical value in the real world.* 在学校里学的大多数东西在现实生活中并没有实际的价值。—compare 比较 THEORETICAL

2 ▶SENSIBLE 明智的◀ sensible and basing your decisions on what is possible and what will really work 注重实际的，务实的: *Be practical! We can't afford the car and the vacation!* 实际点吧！我们没有足够的钱既去买车又去度假。—opposite 反义词 IMPRACTICAL (1)

3 ▶LIKELY TO WORK 可行的◀ practical plans, methods, advice etc are likely to succeed or be effective in a situation〔计划、方法、建议等〕可行的，行得通的: *The only practical solution is to sell the company.* 唯一可行的解决办法是把公司卖掉。| *The agency provides practical advice and support to pregnant teenagers.* 这家机构为怀孕的少女提供切实可行的建议和支持。| **practical alternative** (=another way of doing something that is likely to work) 可行的其他方案 —opposite 反义词 IMPRACTICAL (1)

4 ▶USEFUL 有用的◀ designed to be useful rather than attractive 讲求实用的: *Majorie always gets us practical Christmas presents – last year we got a kettle.* 梅杰里总是给我们买实用的圣诞礼物 —— 去年我们得到一个水壶。

5 ▶SUITABLE 合适的◀ suitable for a particular purpose or for normal life 切合实际的，实用的: *I always wanted a Ferrari, but it's not a very practical car.* 我一直想要一辆法拉利，但那不是一种很实用的车。| *Jeans would be the most practical thing to wear.* 牛仔裤将是最适于穿着的衣服。—opposite 反义词 IMPRACTICAL (1)

6 ▶GOOD AT REPAIRING/MAKING THINGS 擅长修理/制作东西◀ good at repairing or making things 心灵手巧的: *I'm not very practical – I don't know the first thing about cars.* 我动手能力不强，我对汽车一窍不通。

7 a practical certainty/disaster/sell-out etc something that is almost certain, almost a DISASTER etc 几乎确定无疑/是灾难/满座: *Sampras looks a practical certainty to win Wimbledon this year.* 桑普拉斯看起来几乎确定无疑会赢得今年温布尔登网球赛的冠军。

8 for/to all practical purposes used when saying what the real effect of a situation is 实际上，事实上: *For all practical purposes the federation no longer exists.* 实际上该联盟已不存在了。

practical² *n* [C] *BrE* a lesson or examination in science, cooking etc in which you have to do or make something yourself rather than write or read about it【英】〔科学、烹饪等的〕实验课，实习课；实用知识考试: *We have chemistry practicals after Christmas.* 圣诞节过后我们要上化学实验课。

prac·ti·cal·i·ty /ˌpræktɪˈkælətɪ; ˌpræktɪˈkælɪ̣ti/ *n* **1 practicalities** [plural] the real facts of a situation rather than ideas about how it might be 实际的事情，实际问题: *concerned with the practicalities of planning lessons and courses* 关注课程设计的实际问题 **2** [U] how suitable an idea, method, or plan is for a situation, and whether or not it will work 可行性，实用（性）: *doubts about the practicality of your suggestion* 对于你所提建议的可行性表示的怀疑 **3** [U] the quality of being sensible and basing your plans on what you know will work 实际，务实

practical joke /ˌ··· ˈ·/ *n* [C] a trick that is intended to give someone a surprise or shock and make other people laugh 恶作剧 —**practical joker** *n* [C]

prac·ti·cally /ˈpræktɪklɪ; ˈpræktɪkli/ *adv* **1** *especially spoken* almost【尤口】几乎，差不多: *The hall was practically empty.* 这个大厅几乎空无一人。| *Practically all my friends are gay.* 我的朋友几乎全是同性恋者。**2** in a sensible way which takes account of problems 讲究实际地；从实际出发: *"But how can we pay for it?" said John practically.* "但我们如何付款呢？"约翰很实际地问道。

prac·tice /ˈpræktɪs; ˈpræktɪ̣s/ *n* 2 1

1 a) ▶A SKILL 技能◀ [U] regular activity that you do in order to improve a skill 练习: *It takes hours of practice to learn to play the guitar.* 学会弹吉他需要练习好长时间。| *With a little more practice you should be able to pass your test.* 再练练，你应该能通过考试。**b)** [C] a period of time you spend training to improve your skill in doing something 进行练习的一段时间，练习期间: *choir practice* 唱诗班合唱练习 | *We have two rugby practices a week.* 我们一星期进行两次橄榄球训练。

2 in practice used when saying what really happens rather than what should happen or what people think happens 实际上；在实践中: *In practice women receive much lower wages than their male colleagues.* 实际上妇女所得的工资比她们的男同事低得多。

3 ▶CUSTOM 习俗◀ [C] something that you do often because of your religion or your society's tradition 惯常做法，惯例；习俗: *religious beliefs and practices* 宗教信仰和习俗 | **the practice of doing sth** *The Navy has abandoned the practice of serving rum to the men.* 海军终止了给士兵供应朗姆酒的惯例。—see 见 HABIT (USAGE)

4 ▶STH DONE OFTEN 经常做的事◀ [C,U] something that people do often, especially a particular way of doing something 习惯做法: *the widespread practice of under-declaring taxable income* 低报应纳税收入的普遍做法 | *unsafe sexual practices* 不安全的性习惯 | *dangerous working practices* 危险的工作方法

5 ▶DOCTOR/LAWYER 医生/律师◀ [C] the work of a doctor or lawyer or the place where they work〔医生或律师的〕业务；诊所；律师事务所: **medical/legal practice** *Mary Beth had a busy legal practice in Los Angeles.* 玛丽·贝丝在洛杉矶有一家业务繁忙的律师事务所。—see also 另见 GENERAL PRACTICE, PRIVATE PRACTICE

6 common/standard/general/normal practice the usual and accepted way of doing something 普遍/通常/一般的做法: *In Scandinavian countries it is common practice for the husband to stay at home to look after the baby.* 在斯堪的纳维亚国家，丈夫待在家里照料婴儿是很普遍的做法。

7 good/bad practice an example of a good or very bad way of doing something, especially in a particular job〔尤指工作中〕良好的/不好的习惯做法: *It's not considered good practice to reveal clients' names.* 泄露客户的姓名被认为是不好的做法。

8 be out of practice to have not done something for a long time so that you are unable to do it well〔因久不练习而〕荒废，生疏

9 be in practice if you are in practice you have practised something regularly and are able to do it well 经常练习，熟练

10 put sth into practice if you put an idea, plan etc into practice, you start to use it and see if it is effective 把某物付诸实施: *The hard part is putting it all into practice.* 困难的是将它全部付诸实施。

11 practice makes perfect used to say that if you do an activity regularly, you will become very good at it 熟能生巧

prac·tise *BrE*【英】, **practice** *AmE*【美】/ˈpræktɪs; ˈpræktɪ̣s/ 3 3
v **1** [I,T] to do an activity regularly in order to improve your skill or to prepare for a test 练习，实践，实习: **practise (doing) sth** *John's practising the violin.* 约翰在练习拉小提琴。| *Today we're going to practise parking.* 今天我们要练习停车。| **practise for sth** *She's practising for her driving test.* 她正在为驾驶考试进行练习。| **practise sth on sb** *Everybody wants to practise their English on me.* 每个人都想与我练习英语。| **practise hard** (=practise a lot) 刻苦练习 *If you practise hard you might be the next Carl Lewis.* 你如果刻苦练习，或许会成为下一个卡尔·刘易斯。**2** [T] to use a particular method or custom 实行，奉行: *Polyandry is still practised in some parts of the world.* 世界上一些地区仍然实行着一妻多夫制。**3** [I,T] to work as a doctor or lawyer〔医生、律师〕执业，从业: [+as] *Gemma is now practising as a dentist.* 杰玛现在执业当一名牙医。| **practise sth** *He went on to practise law.* 他继续当律师。**4** [T] if you practise a religion, system of ideas etc, you live your life according to its rules 遵照〔教义、观念等〕行事 **5 practise what you preach** to do the things that you advise other people to do 躬行己说，以身作则: *The Green candidate should practise what she preaches and sell her car.* 那位绿党候选人应该身体力行，卖掉她的汽车。

prac·tised *BrE*【英】, **practiced** *AmE*【美】/ˈpræktɪst; ˈpræktɪ̣st/ *adj* **1** someone who is practised in a particular job or skill is good at it because they have done it many times before

老练的，有经验的；熟练的：*a practised hunter* 有经验的猎人 | **practised in (doing) sth** *Kate became practised in the art of disguising her emotions.* 凯特变得很善于掩饰自己的感情。| **to the practised eye** (=to someone who has seen something many times and knows a lot about it) 对于目光老练的人，对于见多识广的人 **2** [only before noun 仅用于名词前] a practised action has been done so often that it now seems very easy〔动作〕娴熟的：*With practised ease he slit open the sack.* 他熟练轻松地拆开了袋子。

prac·tis·ing *BrE*【英】, **practicing** *AmE*【美】/ˈpræktɪsɪŋ; ˈpræktɪsɪŋ/ *adj* **1 a practising Catholic/Muslim/Jew etc** someone who follows the rules and customs of a particular religion 虔诚的天主教徒/穆斯林/犹太教徒等 **2 a practising doctor/lawyer/teacher etc** someone who is working as a doctor, lawyer etc 执业医生/律师/教师等：*Few practising teachers have time for such research.* 很少正在从事教学工作的教师有时间做这样的研究。

3 **prac·ti·tion·er** /prækˋtɪʃənə; prækˈtɪʃənə/ *n* [C] **1 medical/legal practitioner** someone who works as a doctor or a lawyer 执业医生/律师 **2** someone who regularly does a particular activity 从事者，实践者：*skilful public relations practitioners* 老练的公关人员 | [+of] *a practitioner of Taoist philosophy* 道家哲学的实践者 —see also 另见 GENERAL PRACTITIONER

Pra·do, the /ˈprɑdo; ˈprɑːdəʊ/ the national Spanish MUSEUM of painting and sculpture, in Madrid, which has many very important works of art by painters such as El Greco, Goya, Velasquez, and Rubens 普拉多博物馆〔西班牙国家绘画与雕刻艺术博物馆，位于马德里。收藏有如埃尔·格列柯、戈雅、委拉斯开兹、鲁本斯等画家的许多重要艺术珍品〕

prae·sid·i·um /prɪˈsɪdɪəm; prɪˈsɪdiəm/ *n* [C] another spelling of PRESIDIUM presidium 的另一种拼法

prag·mat·ic /prægˋmætɪk; prægˈmætɪk/ *adj* dealing with problems in a sensible, practical way instead of strictly following a set of ideas 讲求实际的，务实的，重实效的：*a pragmatic approach to politics* 对政治的务实态度 **—pragmatically** /-klɪ; -kli/ *adv*

prag·mat·ics /prægˋmætɪks; prægˈmætɪks/ *n* [U] *technical* the study of how words and phrases are used with special meanings in particular situations【术语】语用学

prag·ma·tis·m /ˈprægməˌtɪzəm; ˈprægmətɪzəm/ *n* [U] a way of dealing with problems in a sensible, practical way instead of following a set of ideas 实用主义；务实的方法：*conditioned more by political pragmatism than religious zeal* 较多取决于政治实用性而不是宗教狂热 **—pragmatist** *n* [C]

Prague /prɑg; prɑːg/ the capital city of the Czech Republic, which is an important industrial centre. It has many beautiful buildings and is visited by many tourists. 布拉格〔捷克共和国首都，为一重要工业中心。布拉格有许多漂亮建筑，前去观赏的游人众多〕

Prague spring, the /ˌ· ˈ·/ a short time in 1968 when the Communist government of Czechoslovakia, under Alexander Dubcek, allowed people to have more freedom than before. The Soviet Union did not agree with these changes and invaded Czechoslovakia and forced the government to return to the way things were before. 布拉格之春〔指1968年亚历山大·杜布切克领导的捷克斯洛伐克共产党政府赋予公民更多自由的一段短暂时期。然而，苏联却反对这样的变革，进而入侵捷克斯洛伐克，迫使该国政府恢复以往的政策〕

prai·rie /ˈprɛrɪ; ˈpreəri/ *n* [C] a wide open area of land in North America which is covered in grass or wheat〔北美洲的〕大草原

prairie dog /ˈ·· ˌ·/ *n* [C] a small animal with a short tail, which lives in holes on the prairies 草原犬鼠

praise¹ /prez; preɪz/ *v* [T] **1** to say that you admire and approve of someone or something, especially publicly〔尤指公开地〕称赞，赞扬，表扬：*The play was praised by the critics when it was first shown on Broadway.* 该剧首次在百老汇上演时就受到了评论家的赞扬。| **praise sb/sth for sth** *The Mayor praised the rescue team for their courage.* 市长赞扬救援队的勇气。| **praise sb/sth highly** *a highly praised novel* 备受称道的小说 | **praise sb/sth to the skies** (=to praise someone or something very much) 对某人/某事赞叹不已，把某人/某事捧上天 **2** to give thanks to God and show your respect to him, especially by singing in a church〔尤指在教堂以唱赞美诗〕赞美〔上帝〕 **3 God/Heaven be praised** also 又作 **Praise the Lord** used to say that you are pleased something has happened and thank God for it 谢天谢地，感谢上帝

praise² *n* [U] **1** words that you say or write in order to praise someone or something 赞扬；赞美：**be full of praise for** (=praise something a lot) 对…大加赞扬 *Mrs George was full of praise for her nurses' caring attitude.* 乔治太太对照顾她的护士们充满爱心的态度大加赞扬。| **high praise** (=a lot of praise) 高度的赞扬 *Bork received high praise for his efforts to cut spending.* 博克由于为削减开支所作的努力而受到了高度的赞扬。| **win praise** (=receive praise) 受到赞扬 *The film has won praise from audiences and critics alike.* 这部电影赢得了观众和评论家的一致赞扬。**2** the expression of respect and thanks to God〔对上帝的〕崇拜，赞颂：*Let us give praise unto the Lord.* 让我们赞美上帝吧。**3 praise be!** *old-fashioned* used when you are very pleased about something that has happened【过时】谢天谢地！感谢上帝！—see also 另见 **sing sb's praises** (SING (5))

praise·wor·thy /ˈprezˌwɝðɪ; ˈpreɪzwɜːði/ *adj* deserving praise, especially when not completely successful 值得赞扬的，精神可嘉的〔尤用于未取得彻底成功时〕：*the Italian team's praiseworthy attempts to reach a draw* 意大利队为打成平局所作出值得赞扬的努力 **—praiseworthiness** *n* [U]

pra·line /ˈprɑlin; ˈprɑːliːn/ *n* [C,U] a sweet food made of nuts cooked in boiling sugar 果仁糖

prams（四轮手推）婴儿车

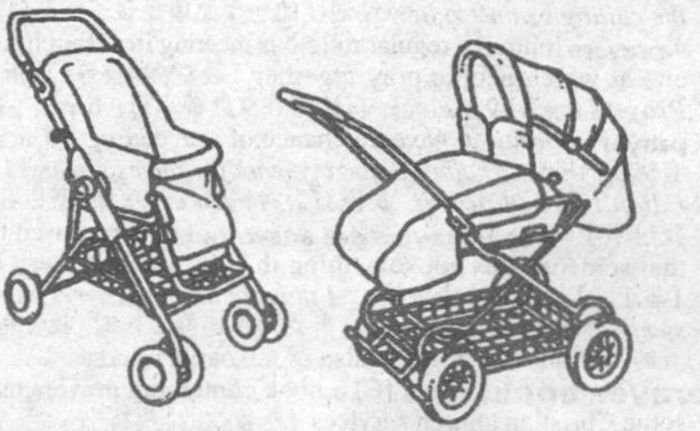

pushchair *BrE*【英】/ stroller *AmE*【美】（折叠式）轻便婴儿手推车

pram *BrE*【英】/ baby buggy *AmE*【美】婴儿车

pram /præm; præm/ *n* [C] *BrE* a small vehicle with four wheels in which a baby can lie down while being pushed【英】〔婴儿可躺在里面的〕（四轮手推）婴儿车；BABY CARRIAGE *AmE*【美】—compare 比较 BUGGY (3) 3

prance /præns; prɑːns/ *v* [I] **1** [always+adv/prep] to walk moving your body in a confident way in order to make people notice and admire you 趾高气扬地走，昂首阔步：[+around/in/up] *Leo's always prancing around as if he owns the place.* 利奥总是神气十足地走来走去，好像那地方是他的。**2** if a horse prances, it moves with high steps〔马〕腾跳，腾跃

prang /præŋ; præŋ/ *v* [T] *BrE informal* to damage a vehicle in an accident【英，非正式】〔在事故中〕撞毁〔车辆〕，损坏 **—prang** *n* [C]

prank /præŋk; præŋk/ *n* [C] a trick, especially one which is played on someone to make them look silly〔尤指使人难堪的〕玩笑，恶作剧：*a childish prank* 孩子的胡闹

prank·ster /ˈpræŋkstɚ; ˈpræŋkstə/ *n* [C] someone who plays tricks on people to make them look silly 恶作剧者

prat /præt; præt/ *n* [C] *BrE informal* a stupid person【英，非正式】傻瓜，愚蠢的人：*Don't be such a prat.* 别这么愚蠢。**—prattish** *adj*

prate /pret; preɪt/ *v* [I +on/about] *old-fashioned* to talk in a meaningless, boring way about something【过时】唠叨；瞎扯

prat·fall /ˈprætfɔl; ˈprætfɔːl/ *n* [C] an embarrassing accident or mistake 令人尴尬的事故[失误]：*another one of the Vice-President's pratfalls* 副总统的另一次令人尴尬的失误

prat·tle /ˈprætl; ˈprætl/ *v* [I] to talk continuously about silly and unimportant things 喋喋不休，闲扯，唠叨：**prattle on (about)** *What's Sarah prattling on about?* 萨拉在喋喋不休地讲什么？**—prattle** *n* [U] **—prattler** *n* [C]

Prav·da /ˈprɑvdə; ˈprɑːvdə/ a Russian newspaper, which was formerly the official newspaper of the Communist Party of the Soviet Union《真理报》〔俄罗斯一报纸，为前苏联共产党的官方报纸〕

prawn /prɔn; prɔːn/ *n* [C] a small pink SHELLFISH that is used for food 对虾，明虾，大虾：*a prawn salad sandwich* 明虾沙拉三明治

pray¹ /pre; preɪ/ *v* **1** [I,T] to speak to God in order to ask for help or give thanks 祈祷；祷告：*They went to the mosque to pray.* 他们去清真寺做祷告。| [+for] *Let us pray for peace.* 让我们为和平祈祷吧。| [+to] *Martha prayed to God every night.* 玛莎每 3

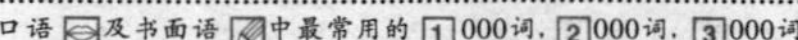

晚都向上帝祈祷。| **pray sth** *"Dear Lord, show me my duty," she prayed.* "亲爱的主，请向我指明我的义务。"她祈祷道。**2** [I, T] to wish or hope very strongly that something will happen 强烈地希望，祈望，祈求：**pray that** *Paul was praying that no one had noticed his absence.* 保罗正在祈求没有人注意到他的缺席。| **[+for]** *We're praying for a fine day tomorrow.* 我们正在祈望明天是个好天气。

pray² *adv* [sentence adverb 句子副词] *old-fashioned* used when politely asking a question or telling someone to do something 【过时】请，恳请〔用于礼貌地问问题或叫某人做某事〕：*Pray be seated.* 请坐下。| *And who, pray, is this?* 请问是谁？

3 3 **prayer** /prɛr; preə/ *n* **1** [C] words that you say when praying to God, especially a fixed form of words 祈祷文，祷辞：*We all had to say our prayers before going to bed.* 上床睡觉前我们都得做祷告。| **[+for]** *a prayer for the deceased* 为死者所做的祷告 **2** [U] the act of praying or the regular habit of praying 祈祷(的习惯)：*the power of prayer* 祈祷的力量 | *a prayer meeting* 祈祷会 | **in prayer** (=praying) 在祈祷 *The congregation knelt in prayer.* 教堂的会众跪下祈祷。**3** [C] a wish or hope that something will happen 愿望，希望，祈望：*Nadia's one prayer is that the children won't suffer.* 纳迪娅的一个愿望是孩子们不要受罪。**4 prayers** [plural] a regular religious meeting in a church, school etc. at which people pray together〔教堂、学校等的〕祈祷式：*Prayers are at 9 o'clock.* 祈祷式在9点钟举行。**5 not have a prayer** *informal* to have no chance of succeeding【非正式】没有成功的机会：*I hadn't done any work for the exam, and I knew I didn't have a prayer.* 我没有为考试做任何功课，所以我知道我过不了。**6 sb's prayers are answered** *informal* used to say that someone has got something that they wanted very much【非正式】某人的祷告应验了：*I thought all my prayers were answered when I got that job.* 当我得到那份工作时，我觉得我所有的祈求都应验了。—see also 另见 LORD'S PRAYER

prayer book /'· ·/ *n* [C] a book containing prayers used in some Christian church services〔基督教的〕祈祷书

Prayer Book, the /'· ·/ another name for the BOOK OF COMMON PRAYER 英国国教祈祷书〔The Book of Common Prayer 的别称〕

prayer mat /'· ·/ also 又作 **prayer rug** *n* [C] a small mat which Muslims kneel on when praying〔穆斯林祈祷时用的〕跪垫，跪毯

prayer wheel /'· · ·/ *n* [C] a piece of wood or metal that is shaped like a drum and turns around on a pole, on which prayers are written, used in Tibet〔西藏用的上面刻有祈祷文的〕转经筒，祈祷轮

pray·ing man·tis /,· · '· ·/ *n* [C] a large insect that eats other insects 螳螂

pre- /pri; pri:/ *prefix* **1** before someone or something 在…之前：*prewar* (=before a war) 战前的 **2** in preparation 预先：*a prearranged signal* 预定的信号 | *Preset the video.* 预先设置好录影机。—compare 比较 ANTE-

preach /pritʃ; pri:tʃ/ *v* **1** [I,T] to give a talk in public about a religious subject, especially about the correct moral way for people to behave 布道，讲道：**[+to/on/about]** *Christ began preaching to large crowds.* 基督开始向大批群众布道。| **preach sth** *The pastor preached a sermon on brotherly love.* 牧师在布道会上宣讲兄弟之爱。**2** [T] to talk about how good or important something is and try to persuade other people about this 宣扬，鼓吹：**preach the virtues of** *Imran's always preaching the virtues of a healthy outdoor life.* 伊姆兰一直在宣扬健康户外生活的好处。**3** [I] to give someone advice in a way that they think is boring or annoying 唠叨地劝诫：*I'm sorry, I didn't mean to preach.* 对不起，我无意说教。**4 preach to the converted** to talk about what you think is right or important to people who already have the same opinions as you 对已持有相同观念的人作宣传 —see also 另见 **practise what you preach** (PRACTISE (5))

preach·er /'pritʃɚ; 'pri:tʃə/ *n* [C] someone who gives talks at religious meetings but who is not actually a priest〔实际上本身并不是牧师的〕说教者，讲道者

preach·y /'pritʃɪ; 'pri:tʃi/ *adj informal* trying too much to persuade people to accept a particular opinion【非正式】爱说教的

Preak·ness, the /'priknəs; 'pri:knəs/ an important US horse race for three-year-old horses, held each year in Maryland 普利克内斯有奖赛〔美国马里兰州一年一度举行的一项重要的三龄马赛事〕

pre·am·ble /'priæmbl; pri'æmbəl/ *n* [C] *formal* a statement at the beginning of a book, document, or talk, explaining what it is about【正式】〔书、文件、讲话的〕前言；序言；开场白：**without preamble** (=immediately and without any explanation) 开门见山地 *"Murder," he said, without preamble. "No doubt about it."* "谋杀，"他开门见山地说，"毫无疑问是谋杀。"

pre·arranged /,priə'rendʒd; ,pri:ə'reɪndʒd◂/ *adj* planned in advance 预先安排的，预定的：*At a prearranged signal, everyone stood up.* 一见到预定的信号，大家都站了起来。—**prearrangement** *n* [U]

pre·car·i·ous /prɪ'kɛrɪəs; prɪ'keəriəs/ *adj* **1** a precarious situation or state is likely to become very dangerous〔局势、情况〕不稳定的，不安全的；危险的：*The refugees live a precarious existence in shanty towns.* 难民在城市贫民窟过着不安定的生活。| *a precarious peace* 不稳固的和平 **2** someone or something precarious is likely to fall 可能倒的，不稳的，不牢靠的 —**precariously** *adv*: *a cup of tea balanced precariously on her knee* 她膝盖上放置不稳的一杯茶 —**precariousness** *n* [U]

pre·cast /pri'kæst; ,pri:'kɑ:st◂/ *adj* precast CONCRETE is already formed into blocks ready for use to make buildings〔混凝土〕预浇的，预制的

pre·cau·tion /prɪ'kɔʃən; prɪ'kɔ:ʃən/ *n* [C usually plural 一般用复数] something you do in order to prevent something dangerous or unpleasant from happening 预防措施：*Fire precautions were neglected.* 防火措施被忽视了。| *elaborate precautions to avoid detection* 为避免被发现而采取的精心预防措施 | **[+against]** *You should save your work often as a precaution against computer failure.* 你要经常保存所做的工作以防电脑发生故障。| **take the precaution of doing sth** *I took the precaution of insuring my camera.* 我把我的照相机投了保以防万一。

pre·cau·tion·a·ry /prɪ'kɔʃən,ɛrɪ; prɪ'kɔ:ʃənəri/ *adj* **precautionary measures/steps etc** things that you do in order to prevent something dangerous or unpleasant from happening 预防措施：*The ward will be closed for a week as a precautionary measure.* 作为预防措施，该病房将关闭一星期。

pre·cede /prɪ'sid; prɪ'si:d/ *v* [T] *formal*【正式】**1** to happen or exist before something or someone or to come before something else in a series 先于…(发生、存在)；位于…之前：*The numbers on the license plate are preceded by a letter.* 汽车车牌的号码数字前面有一个字母。| *He was a much stronger leader than the man who preceded him.* (=was leader before him) 比起他的前任，他是个强得多的领导人。**2** to go somewhere before someone else 在…之前去[到]：*John preceded his guests into the lounge.* 约翰带客人进入大厅。**3** to say or write something as an introduction to a speech, book etc 在…前先说；给…加上引言：*The author preceded his speech with a few words of welcome.* 这位作者在演讲之前先说了几句表示欢迎的话作为开场白。 3

pre·ce·dence /'prɛsədəns; 'presɪdəns/ *n* [U] **1 take/have precedence over** to be considered more important than someone or something else and therefore come or be done before them 优先于，〔重要性〕高于：*Saving the child's life took precedence over everything else.* 救这个孩子的命比其他任何事情都重要。**2** the relative importance of different things or people and the need to deal with the most important first, then the second most important, and so on 优先权；地位先后，级别高低：**in order of precedence** *Arrange the tasks in order of precedence.* 按轻重缓急安排这些任务。

pre·ce·dent /'prɛsədənt; 'presɪdənt/ *n* **1** [C] an action or official decision which can be used to give legal support to later actions or decisions〔可援引的〕先例；判例：**set/create a precedent** *The invasion of Panama set a dangerous precedent.* 对巴拿马的入侵开了一个危险的先例。**2** [C,U] something of the same type that has happened or existed before 先例，前例：**[+for]** *Is there any precedent for this?* 这事有先例吗？| **without precedent** (=never happening before) 无先例的 *An epidemic on this scale is without precedent.* 如此规模的流行病以前从未发生过。**3** [U] the way that things have always been done 惯例：**break with precedent** (=to do something in a new way) 打破惯例

pre·ced·ing /prɪ'sidɪŋ; prɪ'si:dɪŋ/ *adj* [only before noun 仅用于名词前] *formal* happening or coming before the time, place, or part mentioned【正式】在前的，在先的；前面的：*We made more money this month than in the whole of the preceding quarter.* 我们本月赚的钱比前一整个季度还多。—opposite 反义词 FOLLOWING

pre·cept /'prisɛpt; 'pri:sept/ *n* [C] *formal* a rule on which a way of thinking or behaving is based【正式】戒律，格言，准则：*basic moral precepts* 基本的道德准则

pre·cinct /'prisɪŋkt; 'pri:sɪŋkt/ *n* **1** [C] *AmE* an area within a town or city that has its own police force, local government representatives etc【美】〔城镇中拥有自己的警队、地方政府代表等的〕分区：*the 44th Precinct* 第44分区 **2** [C] *AmE* the main police station in a particular area of a town or city【美】〔城镇分区的〕警察分局：*Book him and take him down to the precinct.*

将他记录在案并把他带到警察分局。**3** [C] **shopping/pedestrian precinct** *BrE* an area of a town where people can walk and cars are not allowed【英】商业/行人专用区 **4 precincts** [plural] the area that surrounds an important building〔某主要建筑物的〕周围地区: *the precincts of the cathedral* 大教堂周围地区

pre·ci·os·i·ty /ˌprɛʃiˋɑsətɪ; ˌpreʃiˈɒsɨti/ *n* [U] *literary* the attitude of being too concerned about style or detail in your writing or speech, so that it sounds unnatural【文】〔写作或讲话的〕矫揉造作; 故作风雅

pre·cious¹ /ˋprɛʃəs; ˈpreʃəs/ *adj* **1** precious memories or possessions are important to you because they are connected with people you like or events in your life〔记忆或财物〕珍贵的; 宝贵的: *The doll is very precious to me because it was my mother's.* 这个玩具娃娃对我来说很珍贵, 因为它是我妈妈的。**2** something that is precious is valuable and important and should not be wasted or used without care 宝贵的: *Don't waste precious time talking to him, he's not worth it.* 别浪费宝贵的时间跟他交谈, 他不值得。**3** rare and worth a lot of money 贵重的; 珍贵的: *a precious jewel* 贵重的首饰 **4** [only before noun 仅用于名词前] *spoken* used to show that you are annoyed that someone seems to care too much about something【口】"宝贵"的, 宝贝似的〔用于对某人似乎太过注重某事表示讨厌〕: *Your precious career is becoming more important than your family.* 你"宝贵"的事业正变得比家庭还重要。**5** someone who is precious is formal and unnatural because they are trying too hard to be perfect〔某人〕矫揉造作的, 过分讲究的 —**preciously** *adv* —**preciousness** *n* [U]

precious² *adv informal*【非正式】**precious little/few** very little or very few 非常少: *He has precious little experience of computing.* 他没有多少电脑方面的经验。

precious met·al /ˌ‥ˈ‥/ *n* [C,U] a rare and valuable metal such as gold or silver 贵金属〔如指金、银等〕

precious stone /ˌ‥ˈ‥/ *n* [C] a rare and valuable jewel such as a DIAMOND or an EMERALD¹ 宝石 —compare 比较 SEMIPRECIOUS

prec·i·pice /ˋprɛsəpɪs; ˈpresɨpɨs/ *n* [C] a very steep side of a high rock, mountain or cliff 悬崖, 峭壁: *towards the edge of the precipice* 向悬崖边缘

pre·cip·i·tate¹ /prɪˋsɪpəˌtet; prɨˈsɪpɨteɪt/ *v* **1** [T] *formal* to make something serious happen more quickly than was expected; HASTEN【正式】促成, 加速: *The economic crisis was precipitated by the US's inability to deal with the budget deficit.* 美国无力应付预算赤字, 这加速了经济危机。**2** [T] to force someone or something into a particular state or condition 使陷入〔某种状态〕: *The rise in the value of oil precipitated a world economic crisis.* 油价的上涨引发了世界经济危机。**3 precipitate sb somewhere** *formal* to make someone fall forwards or downwards with great force【正式】把某人猛摔[猛抛]到某处 **4** [I, T+out] *technical* to separate a solid substance from a liquid by chemical action, or to be separated in this way【术语】(使) 沉淀, (使) 淀析

precipitate² /prɪˋsɪpətɪt; prɨˈsɪpɨtɨt/ *n* [C,U] *technical* a solid substance that has been chemically separated from a liquid【术语】沉淀物

precipitate³ *adj formal* done too quickly, especially without thinking carefully enough【正式】仓促的; 贸然的, 轻率的 —**precipitately** *adv*

pre·cip·i·ta·tion /prɪˌsɪpəˋteʃən; prɨˌsɪpɨˈteɪʃən/ *n* **1** [C,U] *technical* rain, snow etc that falls on the ground, or the amount of rain, snow etc that falls【术语】〔雨、雪等的〕降落; 降水量 **2** [C,U] *technical* a chemical process in which a solid substance is separated from a liquid【术语】沉淀 **3** [U] *formal* the act of doing something too quickly in a way that is not sensible【正式】仓促, 鲁莽, 轻率

pre·cip·i·tous /prɪˋsɪpətəs; prɨˈsɪpɨtəs/ *adj* **1** dangerously high or steep 险峻的, 陡峭的: *A precipitous path led down the cliff.* 一条陡峭的小路沿悬崖而下。**2** PRECIPITATE³ —**precipitously** *adv* —**precipitousness** *n* [U]

pré·cis /preˋsi; ˈpreɪsiː/ *n plural* **précis** /ˋpresiz; ˈpreɪsiːz/ [C] a statement which gives the main ideas of a piece of writing, speech etc〔文章或演说等的〕摘要; 梗概; 概要: *a concise and accurate précis* 简明而精确的概要 —**précis** *v* [T]

W3 **pre·cise** /prɪˋsaɪs; prɪˈsaɪs/ *adj* **1** precise details, costs, measurements etc are exact 精确的, 准确的: *The precise details of the sale have not yet been released.* 这次销售的精确细节还没有发布。**2** [only before noun 仅用于名词前] used to emphasize that something happens exactly in a particular way or that you are describing something correctly and exactly 恰好的, 正是的: *Just at that precise moment her husband walked in.* 恰恰就在那个时候, 她的丈夫走了进来。| *The precise nature of the job will be made clear when you start.* 这项工作的确切性质将在你开始进行时明确地告知你。**3 to be precise** used to show that you are giving more exact details relating to something you have just said 精确地说, 确切地说: *My parents live abroad – in North Borneo to be precise.* 我父母生活在国外, 确切地说, 生活在北婆罗洲。**4** someone who is precise is very careful about small details or about the way they behave〔人〕周密的, 细心的, 一丝不苟的 —**preciseness** *n* [U]

pre·cise·ly /prɪˋsaɪslɪ; prɪˈsaɪsli/ *adv* **1** exactly 精确地, 确切地, 准确地: **precisely what/how/where etc** *I won't know precisely what the job involves until I actually start.* 直到我真正开始做时, 我才会确切地知道这项工作所涉及的内容。| *Be there at precisely 4 o'clock.* 4点整到那里。**2** used to emphasize that a particular thing is completely true or correct 恰好, 正是〔表示强调〕: *I didn't go precisely because I thought he might be there.* 我没有去正是因为我认为他可能在那儿。| *She's precisely the kind of person we're looking for.* 她正是我们要找的那种人。**3** *spoken* used to say that you agree completely with someone【口】对, 确实如此〔表示同意〕: *"Roberts should resign." "Precisely."* "罗伯茨应该辞职。" "的确如此。" S2 W3

pre·ci·sion¹ /prɪˋsɪʒən; prɪˈsɪʒən/ *n* [U] the quality of being very exact 精确 (性), 准确 (性)

precision² *adj* [only before noun 仅用于名词前] **1** made or done in a very exact way 精确的, 精密的: *precision grinding* 精磨 **2 precision tool/ instrument** a precision tool or instrument is used for making or measuring something in a very exact way 精密工具/仪器

pre·clude /prɪˋklud; prɪˈkluːd/ *v* [T] *formal* to prevent something or make something impossible【正式】阻止, 防止, 使不可能; 排除, 消除: **preclude sb from doing something** *Age alone will not preclude him from standing as a candidate.* 单是年龄不会妨碍他作为候选人参加竞选。—**preclusion** /-ˋkluʒən; -ˈkluːʒən/ *n* [U]

pre·co·cious /prɪˋkoʃəs; prɪˈkəʊʃəs/ *adj often spoken* a precocious child behaves more like an adult than a child, for example by asking difficult and intelligent questions【常口】早熟的, 智慧超前的: *At school he revealed precocious talents as a painter and writer.* 在学校他表现出作为画家和作家的超前才能。—**precociously** *adv* —**precociousness** also 又作 **precocity** /prɪˋkɑsətɪ; prɪˈkɒsɨti/ *n* [U]

pre·cog·ni·tion /ˌprikɑgˋnɪʃən; ˌpriːkɒgˈnɪʃən/ *n* [U] *formal* the knowledge that something will happen before it does【正式】预知, 预感

pre·con·ceived /ˌprikənˋsivd; ˌpriːkənˈsiːvd◂/ *adj* [only before noun 仅用于名词前] preconceived ideas, opinions etc are formed before you really have enough knowledge or experience〔思想、观点等〕预先形成的, 先入为主的: *preconceived notions about art* 对于艺术的先入之见

pre·con·cep·tion /ˌprikənˋsɛpʃən; ˌpriːkənˈsepʃən/ *n* [C] a belief or opinion you have already formed before you know the actual facts 事先形成的看法[想法]; 先入之见, 成见: *widely held but largely unexamined preconceptions about girls' attitudes towards science* 人们普遍持有但大多未经验证的关于女孩对科学的态度的成见

pre·con·di·tion /ˌprikənˋdɪʃən; ˌpriːkənˈdɪʃən/ *n* [C] something that must happen or exist before something else can happen 前提, 先决条件: [+of/for] *A ceasefire is a precondition for talks.* 停火是对话的先决条件。

pre·cooked /ˌpriˋkukt; ˌpriːˈkʊkt◂/ *adj* precooked food has been partly or completely cooked in advance so that it can be quickly heated up later〔食物〕预先煮过[熟]的 —**precook** *v* [T]

pre·cur·sor /prɪˋkɝsɚ; prɪˈkɜːsə/ *n* [C] *formal* something that happened or existed before something else and influenced its development【正式】〔事物的〕前身, 初期形式: [+of/to] *a precursor of modern jazz* 现代爵士乐的早期形式

pre·date /priˋdet; priːˈdeɪt/ *v* [T] to happen or exist earlier in history than something else 在历史上早于: *The kingdom predates previously known African cultures by over 3,000 years.* 该王国比先前所知道的非洲文化早三千多年。

pred·a·tor /ˋprɛdətɚ; ˈpredətə/ *n* [C] **1** an animal that kills and eats other animals 食肉动物, 捕食其他动物的动物 **2** someone who tries to use another person's weakness to get advantages 利用别人的弱点谋取利益的人, 损人利己的人

pred·a·to·ry /ˋprɛdəˌtorɪ; ˈpredətəri/ *adj* **1** a predatory animal kills and eats other animals for food 以捕食其他动物为生的, 食肉的 **2** trying to use someone's weakness to get advantages for yourself 利用别人的弱点谋取利益的, 损人利己的: *predatory share-buying by large foreign companies* 大型外国公司损人利己的股票收购

pre·de·ces·sor /ˌprɛdɪˋsɛsɚ; ˈpriːdɪsesə/ *n* [C] **1** someone who had your job before you started doing it 前任, 前辈: *The President inherited his economic problems from his predecessor.* 该总统的前任遗留给他很多经济问题。**2** a machine, system etc that existed before another one in a process of development〔被取代的〕原有事物, 前身: *The Julian calendar was more accurate than its predecessor.* 儒略历〔公历〕比其前身较为精确。—opposite 反义词 SUCCESSOR

pre·des·ti·na·tion /prɪˌdɛstəˋneʃən; prɪˌdestɪˈneɪʃən/ *n* [U] the belief that God has decided everything that will happen and that people cannot change this 宿命论〔认为上帝决定万事万物, 人无力改变〕

pre·des·tined /prɪˋdɛstɪnd; prɪˈdestɪnd/ *adj* something that is predestined is certain to happen because it has been decided by God or FATE（命中）注定的: **predestined to do sth** *All our plans seemed predestined to fail.* 我们所有的计划好像都注定要失败。

pre·de·ter·mined /ˌpridɪˋtɝmɪnd; ˌpriːdɪˈtɜːmɪnd/ *adj formal* if something is predetermined, it has been formed or arranged before it happens, and does not happen by chance【正式】预先决定[确定]的: *The colour of your eyes is predetermined by those of your parents.* 你眼睛的颜色是由父母眼睛的颜色决定的。| *a predetermined location* 预先确定的地点 —**predetermination** /ˌpridɪˌtɝməˋneʃən; ˌpriːdɪtɜːmɪˈneɪʃən/ *n* [U]

pre·de·ter·min·er /ˌpridɪˋtɝmɪnɚ; ˌpriːdɪˈtɜːmɪnə/ *n* [C] *technical* a word that is used before a DETERMINER (=a word such as 'the', 'that', 'his' etc). In the phrases 'all the boys' and 'both his parents', the words 'all' and 'both' are determiners【术语】前置限定词〈如 the, that, his 等〉

pre·dic·a·ment /prɪˋdɪkəmənt; prɪˈdɪkəmənt/ *n* [C] a difficult or unpleasant situation in which you do not know what to do, or you have to make a difficult choice 困境, 窘况, 尴尬的处境: *There is no painless way out of America's current economic predicament.* 美国要摆脱当前的经济困境可没有轻而易举的方法。

pred·i·cate[1] /ˋprɛdɪkɪt; ˈpredɪkɪt/ *n* [C] the part of a sentence that makes a statement about the subject, such as 'swim' in 'Fishes swim' and 'is an artist' in 'She is an artist'〔语法中的〕谓语 —compare 比较 SUBJECT[1] (5)

pred·i·cate[2] /ˋprɛdɪˌket; ˈpredɪkeɪt/ *v* [T] *formal*【正式】**be predicated on** to be based on something as the reason for doing something else 基于, 取决于: *The company's decision to take on more staff was predicated on the belief that the recession was over.* 该公司雇用更多员工的决定是基于经济衰退已经结束的看法。

pre·dic·a·tive /ˋprɛdɪˌketɪv; prɪˈdɪkətɪv/ *adj* a predicative adjective or phrase comes after a verb, for example 'happy' in the sentence 'She is happy.' 谓语性的, 表语的 —**predicatively** *adv*

pre·dict /prɪˋdɪkt; prɪˈdɪkt/ *v* [T] to say that something will happen or that something will happen in a particular way 预言, 预料; 预测: *Economists are predicting a fall in interest rates.* 经济学家预言利率将会下降。| **predict (that)** *The report predicted that more jobs would be lost in the coal industry.* 这项报告预言煤炭业将失去更多的工作职位。| **predict whether/what/how etc** *It is difficult to predict what the long-term effects of the accident will be.* 很难预料这次事故会有什么长期的后果。

pre·dic·ta·ble /prɪˋdɪktəbl; prɪˈdɪktəbəl/ *adj* **1** if the result of something is predictable, you know what it will be before it happens 可预言[预料]的: *The outcome of these experiments is not always entirely predictable.* 这些实验的结果并不总是完全可以预料的。**2** behaving or happening in the way that you expect, especially when this seems boring or annoying 不出所料的; 墨守成规的; 按老一套办事的: *I used to be interested in politics, but now it's all getting very predictable.* 我过去对政治感兴趣, 但现在它整个变得完全是老一套了。| *You're just so predictable!* 你太墨守成规了! —**predictably** *adv* [sentence adverb 句子副词]: *Predictably it was the demonstrators who were blamed for the violence.* 不出所料, 暴力行为的责任推到了示威者身上。—**predictability** /prɪˌdɪktəˋbɪlɪtɪ; prɪˌdɪktəˈbɪlɪti/ *n* [U]

pre·dic·tion /prɪˋdɪkʃən; prɪˈdɪkʃən/ *n* [C,U] something that you say is going to happen, or the act of saying what you think is going to happen 预言的事物; 预言, 预告: [+of] *Earlier predictions of a Republican victory began to look increasingly unlikely.* 对于共和党获胜的早期预测开始显得越来越不可能了。| **make a prediction** *I'd find it very hard to make a prediction.* 我发现这非常难以预料。—**predictive** /-tɪv; -tɪv/ *adj*

pre·di·gested /ˌpridəˋdʒɛstɪd; ˌpriːdaɪˈdʒestɪd/ *adj* predigested new information etc has been put in a simple form and explained so that it is easy to understand 简化的

pre·di·lec·tion /ˌprɛdlˋɛkʃən; ˌpriːdɪˈlekʃən/ *n* [C] *formal* if you have a predilection for something, especially something rather unusual, you like it very much【正式】偏爱, 偏好

pre·dis·pose /ˌpridɪsˋpoz; ˌpriːdɪsˈpəʊz/ *v* [T] to make someone more likely to behave or think in a particular way or suffer from a health problem 使预先倾向于; 使易于感染

pre·dis·posed /ˌpridɪsˋpozd; ˌpriːdɪsˈpəʊzd/ *adj* **predisposed to/towards** tending to behave in a particular way, or to have a particular health problem 对…预先有倾向的; 易感染…的: *Men are more likely to be predisposed towards violence than women.* 男人比女人较有实施暴力的倾向。

pre·dis·po·si·tion /ˌpridɪspəˋzɪʃən; ˌpriːdɪspəˈzɪʃən/ *n* [C] a tendency to behave in a particular way or suffer from a particular illness〔以某种方式行事的〕倾向; 易患某疾病的倾向: **[+to/towards]** *a predisposition towards seasickness* 容易晕船

pre·dom·i·nance /prɪˋdɑmənəns; prɪˈdɒmɪnəns/ *n* **1** [singular] if there is a predominance of one type of person or thing in a group, there are more of that type than of any other type〔数量的〕优势: **[+of]** *the predominance of white people in the audience* 观众中占绝大多数的是白人 **2** [U] someone or something that has predominance has the most power or importance in a particular group or area 主导地位, 支配地位: *The company has finally achieved predominance in Asia.* 该公司最终获得了在亚洲的主导地位。

pre·dom·i·nant /prɪˋdɑmənənt; prɪˈdɒmɪnənt/ *adj* more powerful, more common, or more easily noticed than others 占优势的; 占主导地位的; 最普遍[显著]的, 突出的: *the predominant group in society* 社会中的主导群体

pre·dom·i·nant·ly /prɪˋdɑmənəntlɪ; prɪˈdɒmɪnəntli/ *adv* mostly or mainly 绝大多数, 主要地: *The city's population is predominantly Irish.* 该城市的人口绝大多数是爱尔兰人。

pre·dom·i·nate /prɪˋdɑməˌnet; prɪˈdɒmɪneɪt/ *v* [I] **1** to have the most importance or influence, or to be most easily noticed 占主导地位, 占支配地位: *The views of the leftwing have tended to predominate within the party.* 左翼的观点趋向于在该党内部占支配地位。**2** if one type of person or thing predominates in a group or area, there are more of this type than any other〔数量上〕占优势, 占绝大多数: *Pine trees predominate on the west coast.* 西海岸以松树居多。

pree·mie /ˋprimɪ; ˈpriːmi/ *n* [C] *AmE informal* a PREMATURE (2) baby【美, 非正式】早产儿

pre·em·i·nent /prɪˋɛmənənt; priˈemɪnənt/ *adj* much more important, more powerful, or much better than any others of its kind 卓越的, 杰出的, 超群的: *Hollywood's pre-eminent role in the film industry* 好莱坞在电影业中超群的角色 —**pre-eminently** *adv* —**pre-eminence** *n* [U]

pre·empt /prɪˋɛmpt; priˈempt/ *v* [T] to make what someone has planned to do or say unnecessary or ineffective by saying or doing something first 抢在…之前行动; 先发制人: *I didn't want to pre-empt what you were about to say.* 我不想抢先说出你要说的话。—**pre-emption** /-ˋɛmpʃən; -ˈempʃən/ *n* [U]

pre·emp·tive /prɪˋɛmptɪv; priˈemptɪv/ *adj* a pre-emptive action is done to harm someone else before they can harm you, or to prevent something bad from happening〔行动〕抢先的, 先发制人的: **pre-emptive strike/attack** *a series of pre-emptive strikes on guerilla bases* 对游击队根据地一系列先发制人的打击 —**pre-emptively** *adv*

preen /prin; priːn/ *v* **1** [I,T] if a bird preens or preens itself, it cleans itself and makes its feathers smooth using its beak〔鸟〕用喙整理〔羽毛〕**2** [I] to look proud because of something you have done 为…感到骄傲 **3 preen yourself a)** to spend a lot of time in front of a mirror making yourself look tidier and more attractive 精心打扮 **b)** to be very pleased with yourself 得意扬扬, 沾沾自喜

pre·ex·ist /ˌpriɪgˋzɪst; ˌpriːɪgˈzɪst/ *v* [I,T] *formal* to exist before something else【正式】先存在; 先于…存在: *Inform your doctor of any pre-existing medical condition, eg, diabetes.* 要告知医生原先就有的任何内科疾病, 如糖尿病。—**pre-existing** *adj*

pre·fab /ˋpriˋfæb; ˈpriːfæb/ *n* [C] *informal* a small prefabricated building【非正式】预制装配式小房屋

pre·fab·ri·cate /priˋfæbrəˌket; priːˈfæbrɪkeɪt/ *v* [T] to make the parts of a building, ship etc in a factory in standard sizes, so that they can be fitted together somewhere else 预制〔房屋、船等的构件〕—**prefabricated** *adj*: *a prefabricated building* 预制装配式房屋 —**prefabrication** /priˌfæbrəˋkeʃən; priːˌfæbrɪˈkeɪʃən/ *n* [U]

pref·ace[1] /ˋprɛfɪs; ˈprefɪs/ *n* [C] an introduction at the beginning of a book or speech〔书籍的〕序言, 前言, 绪言;〔演讲的〕开场白

preface² *v* [T] *formal* to say or do something before the main part of what you are going to say【正式】作为…的开端, 作为…的开场白: *I'd like to preface my remarks by saying a little about myself.* 我先简单介绍一下我自己, 作为我讲话的开场白。

pref·a·to·ry /ˈprɛfəˌtɔrɪ; ˈprefətəri/ *adj formal* forming a preface or introduction【正式】序言的, 引言的; 作为开场白的: *a few prefatory remarks* 几句开场白

pre·fect /ˈprifɛkt; ˈpriːfekt/ *n* [C] **1** an older student in some British schools, who has special duties and helps to control younger students〔英国某些学校中帮助管理年幼学生的〕级长 **2** a public official in France, Italy etc who is responsible for a particular area〔法国、意大利等负责某个地区的〕地方行政长官, 省长

pre·fec·ture /ˈprifɛktʃə; ˈpriːfektʃʊə/ *n* [C] a large area which has its own local government in France, Italy, Japan etc〔法国、意大利等的〕省;〔日本的〕县: *Saitama prefecture*〔日本〕崎玉县

S2 W2 **pre·fer** /prɪˋfɝ; prɪˈfɜː/ *v* **preferred, preferring** [T not in progressive 不用进行时] **1** to like someone or something more than someone or something else 更喜欢: *"What kind of music do you like?" "These days I prefer classical music."* "你喜欢什么样的音乐?" "这些日子我更喜欢古典音乐。" | **prefer sb/sth to sb/sth** *I much prefer dogs to cats.* 猫和狗两者之中我更喜欢狗。| **prefer to do sth** *Many people living in cities would actually prefer to live in the country.* 很多生活在城市的人实际上宁愿生活在乡下。| **prefer doing sth** *Chantal prefers travelling by train.* 钱特尔较喜欢乘火车旅行。**2 would prefer** if you would prefer to do something, you want to do it more than another thing you could do instead, or that you are doing now 更愿意, 更希望, 宁愿: **would prefer to do sth** *We would prefer to live in the US, but I can't get a visa.* 我们更愿意生活在美国, 但我得不到签证。**3 I would prefer it if** *spoken*【口】**a)** used to say that you wish a situation was different 我更愿意[希望]: *Of course, I'd prefer it if I didn't have to do so much work.* 当然我更希望我不必做那么多工作。**b)** used when telling someone politely not to do something〔用于礼貌地告诉别人不要做某事〕我希望: *I'd prefer it if you didn't smoke in front of the children.* 我希望你不要在孩子面前抽烟。**4 prefer charges** *law* to make an official statement that someone has done something illegal【法律】起诉, 提出控告

pref·e·ra·ble /ˈprɛfrəbl; ˈprefərəbəl/ *adj* better or more suitable 更好的, 更合适的, 更可取的: **preferable to (doing) sth** *I think France would be preferable to Majorca in August.* 我认为8月份的法国比马略卡岛更好。| **infinitely preferable** (=much better or much more suitable) 好得多, 可取得多, 适合得多 *Leah finds novels infinitely preferable to poetry.* 利娅觉得小说比诗歌好得多。—**preferably** *adv*: *Can you tidy your room please – preferably today?* 你能整理一下你的房间吗? 最好是今天。

W3 **pref·e·rence** /ˈprɛfərəns; ˈprefərəns/ *n* **1** [C,U] if you have a preference for something, you like it more than another thing〔两者之中〕较喜欢的东西; 偏爱, 偏好: **have a preference** *We could eat Chinese, Italian, or Indian – do you have any preference?* 我们可以吃中餐、意大利餐或印度餐——你有什么偏爱的吗? | **have a preference for** *I must admit I have a preference for younger men.* 我必须承认我更喜欢年轻一些的男人。| **have no strong/particular preference** (=not prefer one thing more than anything else) 没有特别的偏好 | **express a preference** (=say that you like one person or thing more than others) 表示对…的偏爱 *I asked her where she wanted to go on vacation, but she didn't express any preference.* 我问她假期想去哪里, 但她没有表示较喜欢去哪里。**2** [C] the thing that you like best in a group of things〔一组东西中〕最喜欢的东西, 偏爱的事物: *Taste both drinks and make a note of your preference.* 尝一下两种酒并记下你最喜欢哪种。**3 give/show preference to** to treat someone more favourably than you treat other people 偏爱…; 给予…优先权; 流露出对…的偏爱: *In allocating housing, preference is given to those who have young children.* 在分配房屋时, 有小孩的人有优先权。**4 in preference to** if you choose one thing in preference to another, you choose it instead because you think it is better 优先于…: *Many people choose the train in preference to driving.* 很多人宁愿乘火车而不愿自己驾车。

pref·e·ren·tial /ˌprɛfəˋrɛnʃəl; ˌprefəˈrenʃəl◂/ *adj* [only before noun 仅用于名词前] preferential treatment, rates etc are deliberately different in order to give an advantage to particular people 优先的; 优待的; 优惠的: *preferential credit terms* 优惠的贷款条件 —**preferentially** *adv*

pre·fer·ment /prɪˋfɝmənt; prɪˈfɜːmənt/ *n* [U] *formal* appointment to a more important job【正式】提升, 晋升

pre·fig·ure /priˋfɪgjə; ˌpriːˈfɪgə/ *v* [T] *formal* to be a sign that shows that something will happen later【正式】预示; 成为…的预兆 —**prefiguration** /ˌprifɪgjəˋreʃən; ˌpriːfɪgəˈreɪʃən/ *n* [C,U]

pre·fix¹ /ˈpriˌfɪks; ˈpriːfɪks/ *n* [C] **1** a group of letters that is added to the beginning of a word to change its meaning and make a new word, such as 'un' in 'untie' or 'mis' in 'misunderstand' 前缀 —compare 比较 AFFIX, SUFFIX **2** a title such as 'Ms' or 'Dr' used before someone's name〔人名前的〕称谓〈如 Ms, Dr〉

prefix² *v* [T] **1** to add a prefix to a word, name or set of numbers 在…前加前缀 **2** *formal* to say something before the main part of what you have to say【正式】加…作为前言[开场白]

preg·nan·cy /ˈprɛgnənsɪ; ˈpregnənsi/ *n* [C,U] the condition of being pregnant or the period of time when a woman is pregnant 怀孕(期), 妊娠(期): *This drug should not be taken during pregnancy.* 这种药不应在妊娠期间服用。| *her third pregnancy* 她的第三次怀孕 | *teenage pregnancies* 少女怀孕

preg·nant /ˈprɛgnənt; ˈpregnənt/ *adj* **1** having an unborn baby growing inside your body 怀孕的, 妊娠的: *On the same day I started the job I found out I was pregnant.* 我开始工作的那一天, 发现自己已经怀孕了。| **twenty weeks/three months etc pregnant** *She went skiing when she was 7 months pregnant!* 她怀孕七个月时还去滑雪! | **get pregnant** *It came as a shock – I thought I was too old to get pregnant.* 这是个令人震惊的消息——我以为自己老得不能怀孕了。| **get sb pregnant** (=make a woman pregnant by having sex with her) 使某人怀孕 *I didn't mean to get her pregnant.* 我没打算使她怀孕。| **fall pregnant** *old-fashioned* (=become pregnant)【过时】怀孕 | **heavily pregnant** (=having a baby inside your body that is almost ready to be born) 怀孕后期的, 快临产的 **2 a pregnant pause/silence** a pause or silence which is full of meaning or emotion, even though no one says anything 耐人寻味[意味深长]的停顿/沉默: *Dave's outburst was followed by a pregnant pause.* 戴夫的冲动之后是一段耐人寻味的停顿。**3 pregnant with** *formal* containing a lot of a quality or feeling【正式】包含, 孕育着: *Every phrase in this poem is pregnant with meaning.* 这首诗的每一组词语都富含意义。 S3

pre·heat /priˋhit; ˌpriːˈhiːt/ *v* [T] to heat an OVEN to a particular temperature before it is used to cook something 预热〔炉灶等到一定的温度以便进行烹调〕: *Preheat the oven to 375°.* 把烤箱预热到375度。

pre·hen·sile /prɪˋhɛnsl; prɪˈhensaɪl/ *adj technical* a prehensile tail, foot etc can curl round things and hold on to them【术语】〔尾巴、脚等〕能卷缠和抓牢〔某物〕的

pre·his·tor·ic /ˌprihɪsˋtɔrɪk; ˌpriːhɪˈstɒrɪk◂/ *adj* **1** connected with the time in history before anything was written down 史前的, 有历史记载以前的: *prehistoric burial grounds* 史前墓地 | *prehistoric animals* 史前动物 **2** *often humorous* very old-fashioned【常幽默】非常陈旧的, 老掉牙的: *Keith's ideas about educating girls are positively prehistoric.* 基思关于教育女孩的观念实在太陈旧了。—**prehistorically** /-klɪ; -kli/ *adv*

pre·his·to·ry /priˋhɪstərɪ; priːˈhɪstəri/ *n* [U] the time in human history before anything was written down〔有历史记载以前的〕史前时期

pre·judge /priˋdʒʌdʒ; ˌpriːˈdʒʌdʒ/ *v* [T] to form an opinion about someone or something before you know or have considered all the facts 对〔人或事〕预先判断, 过早判断: *Try not to prejudge the issue.* 不要过早对这个问题下判断。—**prejudgment** *n* [C,U]

prej·u·dice¹ /ˈprɛdʒədɪs; ˈpredʒədəs/ *n* **1** [C,U] an unreasonable dislike and distrust of people who are different from you in some way, especially because of their race, sex, religion etc 偏见, 成见; 歧视: *Women still have to face a great deal of prejudice in the workplace.* 女性在工作场所仍然必须面对很多的偏见。| [+against] *Prejudice against black people is common in many parts of America.* 在美国很多地方仍普遍存在着对黑人的偏见。| **racial/sexual prejudice** (=prejudice against people who belong to a different race or sex) 种族/性别歧视 *victims of racial prejudice* 种族歧视的受害者 **2** [U] **to the prejudice of** *formal* having a harmful effect or influence on something else【正式】对…不利; 有损于: *Harry continued to smoke, to the prejudice of his health.* 哈里继续抽烟, 这不利于他的健康。**3 without prejudice** *law* without harming or affecting something else【法律】〔对…〕没有不利; 无损〔于〕

prejudice² *v* [T] **1** to influence someone so that they have an unfair or unreasonable opinion about someone or something 使有偏见, 使有成见; 使不公正地偏向: **prejudice sb against sth** *My own schooldays prejudiced me against all formal education.* 我自己的学生时代使我对所有的正规教育产生了偏见。| **preju-**

dice sth/sb in sb's favour *Johnson's pleasant manner prejudiced the jury in his favour.* 约翰逊令人愉快的举止使陪审团对他产生了偏心。**2** to have a bad effect on your opportunities, chances etc of succeeding in doing something 损害, 不利于: *I don't want to do anything that would prejudice my chances of getting the job.* 我不想做任何不利于我得到这份工作的事情。

prej·u·diced /ˋprɛdʒədɪst; ˈpredʒᵊdᵻst/ *adj* **1** having an unreasonable dislike of a particular group of people who are different from you in some way, especially because they belong to a different race, sex, or religion 有偏见的, 有成见, 歧视的: **[+against]** *He denied being prejudiced against black people.* 他否认对黑人存有偏见。**2** having an unreasonable dislike of something 反感的: **[+against]** *I don't know why they're all so prejudiced against the idea.* 我不知道他们为何全都对这个想法如此反感。

prej·u·di·cial /ˌprɛdʒəˋdɪʃəl; ˌpredʒᵊˈdɪʃəl◂/ *adj formal* having a bad effect on something【正式】不利的, 有损害的

prel·ate /ˋprɛlɪt; ˈprelᵻt/ *n* [C] *technical* a BISHOP, CARDINAL, or other important priest in the Christian church【术语】高级教士〈如主教、红衣主教〉

pre·lim·i·na·ry[1] /prɪˋlɪməˌnɛrɪ; prɪˈlɪmᵻnəri/ *adj* [only before noun 仅用于名词前] happening before something that is more important, often in order to prepare for it 初步的; 预备的: *the preliminary rounds of the competition* 比赛的预赛 | *a preliminary draft* 初稿 | **[+to]** *Speeches are preliminary to the real debate.* 演讲是为真正的辩论作准备。

preliminary[2] *n* [C usually plural 一般用复数] **1** something that is done first, to introduce or prepare for something else 初步行动, 准备工作: *After the usual preliminaries, we made a start on the food.* 在通常的客套之后, 我们开始吃饭。**2 the preliminaries** the first part of a competition, when it is decided who will go on to the main competition 预赛, 预试

pre·lit·e·rate /priˋlɪtərɪt; priːˈlɪtərᵻt/ *adj technical* a society that is preliterate has not developed a written language【术语】无文字的, 尚未使用文字的 —compare 比较 ILLITERATE

prel·ude /ˋprɛljud; ˈpreljuːd/ *n* [C] **1 be a prelude to** if an event is a prelude to a more important event, it happens just before it and makes people expect it 是…的序幕[前奏, 开端]: *The fighting in the streets may be a prelude to more serious trouble.* 街头打斗可能是更严重事端的序幕。**2** *technical* a short piece of music for piano or ORGAN【术语】〔钢琴或风琴的〕短篇作品 **3** a short piece of music at the beginning of a large musical piece〔音乐作品的〕序曲: *Chopin's preludes* 肖邦的序曲

pre·mar·i·tal /priˋmærətl; priːˈmærᵻtəl/ *adj* happening or existing before marriage 婚前的: *premarital sex* 婚前性行为 —**premaritally** *adv*

pre·ma·ture /ˌpriməˋtjur; ˈpremətʃə/ *adj* **1** happening before the natural or proper time 过早的, 提早的: *His premature death at the age of 32 is a great loss.* 他32岁就早逝是一大损失。| *premature ageing of the skin* 皮肤的早衰 **2** PREGNANCY a premature baby is born before the usual time of birth〔婴儿〕早产的: *a premature birth* 早产 | *The baby was six weeks premature.* 那婴儿早产了六个星期。**3** done too early or too soon〔做事〕过早的, 过快的; 仓促的, 草率的; 不成熟的: *I think your criticism of the new law is a bit premature, as we don't yet know all the details.* 我认为你对这项新法律的批评未免太早了一点, 因为我们还不了解其全部细节。—**prematurely** *adv*: *The baby was born prematurely.* 这婴儿早产了。

pre·med·i·tat·ed /priˋmɛdəˌtetɪd; priːˈmedᵻteɪtᵻd/ *adj* a premeditated crime or attack is planned in advance and done deliberately〔犯罪、袭击〕预谋的, 预先策划的: *The defense claim that the killing was not premeditated.* 被告方声称杀人不是预先策划好的。

pre·med·i·ta·tion /ˌprimɛdəˋteʃən; priːˌmedᵻˈteɪʃən/ *n* [U] the act of thinking about something and planning it before you actually do it 预先考虑; 预先策划, 预谋: *cold-blooded premeditation* 冷酷的预谋

pre·men·stru·al /priˋmɛnstruəl; priːˈmenstruəl/ *adj technical* happening just before a woman's PERIOD (=the time each month when blood flows from her body)【术语】月经前的

premenstrual syndrome /ˌ· ˌ·· ˈ· ˌ·/, **premenstrual tension** *BrE*【英】*n* [U] the tiredness, headache, bad temper etc experienced by many women in the days before their PERIOD[1] (4) 经前 (期) 综合征[紧张症]

prem·i·er[1] /ˋprimɪə; ˈpremiə/ *n* [C] a PRIME MINISTER 总理, 首相: *the Irish Premier* 爱尔兰总理

premier[2] *adj formal* [only before noun 仅用于名词前] best or most important【正式】最好的; 最重要的: *the Shelbourne, one of Dublin's premier hotels* 谢尔本, 都柏林最好的酒店之一

Premier Di·vi·sion, the /ˌ··· ·ˈ··/ the top group of professional football clubs in Scotland, consisting of 10 teams who play against each other 超级足球联赛〔苏格兰最高级别的职业足球联赛, 有10支球队参赛〕

prem·i·ere, première /prɪˋmɪr; ˈpremieə/ *n* [C] the first public performance of a film or play〔电影的〕首映,〔戏剧的〕首演: **world premiere** (=the first performance in the world) 世界首演 *Spielberg's new movie gets its world premiere tonight.* 斯皮尔伯格的新电影今晚进行世界首映。—**premiere** *v* [I,T]: *Her film was premiered in New York.* 她的电影在纽约首次上映。

prem·i·ere·ship /prɪˋmɪəʃɪp; ˈpremiəʃɪp/ *n* [C,U] the period when someone is PRIME MINISTER 首相[总理]的任期

Prem·i·er·ship, the /prɪˋmɪrʃɪp; ˈpremiəʃɪp/ also 又作 **the Premier League** the top group of professional football clubs in England and Wales, consisting of 20 teams who play against each other 超级足球联赛〔英格兰和威尔士最高级别的职业足球俱乐部联赛, 有20支球队参赛〕

prem·ise /ˋprɛmɪs; ˈpremᵻs/ *n* [C] **1 premises** the buildings and land that a shop, restaurant, company etc uses〔商店、餐馆、公司等使用的〕房屋及土地: *We hope to be moving to new premises shortly.* 我们希望很快搬到新址。| *business premises* 企业经营场所 | **off the premises** *The manager escorted him off the premises.* 那位经理把他送出门外。| **on the premises** *No food or drink is to be consumed on the premises.* 场内禁止饮食。**2** also 又作 **premiss** *BrE* a statement or idea that you accept as true and use as a base for developing other ideas【英】前提: *American justice works on the premise that an accused person is innocent until they are proved guilty.* 美国司法运作的前提是被告在被证明有罪之前是清白的。 3

pre·mi·um /ˋprimɪəm; ˈpriːmiəm/ *n* **1** [C] the cost of insurance, especially the amount to pay each year〔尤指每年支付的〕保险费: *Insurance premiums are set to rise again.* 保险费很有可能再次上涨。| *the annual premium* 每年的保险费 **2** [U] *especially AmE* HIGH-OCTANE (=good quality petrol)【尤美】优质汽油 **3 premium quality** very high quality 优质: *premium quality British potatoes* 优质英国马铃薯 **4** [C] an additional amount of money, above a standard rate or amount 加付款; 额外费用; 津贴; 花红; 奖金: *Farmers are being offered a premium for organically grown vegetables.* 人们出高价购买农民种植的有机蔬菜。| *premium payments for weekend work* 周末工作津贴 **5 at a premium a)** if something is at a premium, there is little of it available or it is difficult to get 奇缺, 难以取得: *Foldaway furniture is the answer where space is at a premium.* 对于空间很小的地方, 可折叠家具是个好的解决办法。**b)** if something is sold at a premium, it is sold at a higher price than usual 以高价, 以超出一般的价格 **6 put/place a premium on** to consider one quality as being much more important than others 高度重视: *The new management puts a premium on efficiency.* 新的管理人员十分注重效率。**7 premium prices** prices that are higher than usual, especially because there is not much of something available〔尤指因某物稀罕而超过一般价格的〕高价

premium bond /ˈ··· ˌ·/ *n* [C] a document that you buy from the government in Britain, giving you the chance to win a large prize each month〔英国〕政府发行的有奖债券

pre·mo·ni·tion /ˌpriməˋnɪʃən; ˌpreməˈnɪʃən/ *n* [C] a strange and unexplainable feeling that something, especially something unpleasant, is going to happen〔尤指不祥的〕预感, 预兆: **have a premonition** *When Anne didn't arrive, Paul had a premonition that she was in danger.* 当安妮没有到达时, 保罗预感到她有危险。| **[+of]** *a premonition of death* 死亡的预感

pre·mon·i·to·ry /prɪˋmɑnəˌtorɪ; prɪˈmɒnᵻtəri/ *adj formal* giving a warning that something unpleasant is going to happen【正式】给予警告的; 预兆的: *a disease with few premonitory symptoms* 几乎没有什么先兆的疾病

pre·na·tal /priˋnetl; ˌpriːˈneɪtl◂/ *adj* [only before noun 仅用于名词前] concerning unborn babies and the care of PREGNANT women 产前的; 孕期的; ANTENATAL *BrE*【英】: *prenatal care* 产前保健[护理] —compare 比较 POSTNATAL —**prenatally** *adv*

pre·oc·cu·pa·tion /priˌɑkjəˋpeʃən; priːˌɒkjᵊˈpeɪʃən/ *n* **1** [singular, U] a strong interest in something, usually because you are worried about it, with the result that you do not pay attention to other things 全神贯注; 入神: **[+with]** *the Bundesbank's preoccupation with keeping down inflation* 德意志联邦银行对于控制通货膨胀的关注 **2** [C] something that you give all your attention to 使人全神贯注的事物, 使人入神的事物: *Brad's main preoccupations were eating and sleeping.* 布拉德主要关心的事情就是吃和睡。

pre·oc·cu·pied /priˋɑkjəˌpaɪd; priːˈɒkjᵊpaɪd/ *adj* thinking about something a lot, with the result that you do not pay atten-

tion to other things 全神贯注的，入神的: *I tried to speak to Bella, but she seemed a little preoccupied.* 我试图和贝拉说话，但她好像有点若有所思。| **[+with]** *Rod's completely preoccupied with all the wedding preparations at the moment.* 罗德此时整个心思想的就是婚礼的所有准备工作。

pre·oc·cu·py /pri`ɑkjə,paɪ; priː'ɒkjʊpaɪ/ *v* [T] *formal* if something preoccupies someone, they think or worry about it a lot【正式】使对…全神贯注，使专心于；占据〔某人的思想〕: *Something's been preoccupying you – what is it?* 你心里老是在想着什么事情——是什么事呢?

pre·or·dain /,priɔr`den; ,priːɔː'deɪn/ *adj* [not before noun 不用于名词前] *formal* if something is preordained, it is certain to happen in the future because God or FATE has decided it【正式】命中注定的，预先注定的

prep¹ /prɛp; prep/ *n* [U] *BrE informal* school HOMEWORK【英，非正式】〔学校安排的〕家庭作业

prep² **prepped, prepping** *v* [T] *AmE informal*【美，非正式】**1** to prepare someone for an operation or an examination 使〔某人〕作好进行手术[考试]的准备 **2** to prepare food for cooking in a restaurant〔在餐馆中〕为〔烹调〕作好准备

prep³ *n* [C] the written abbreviation of 缩写= PREPOSITION

pre·packed /,pri`pækt; ,priː'pækt◂/ also 又作 **pre·pack·aged** /-`pækɪdʒd; -'pækɪdʒd◂/ *adj* prepacked or prepackaged food or other goods are already wrapped or are sold ready to use〔食物等〕预先包装好的: *prepacked fresh fruit and vegetables* 预先包装好的新鲜果蔬

pre·paid /,pri`ped; ,priː'peɪd◂/ *adj* a prepaid envelope does not need a stamp because the cost of posting it has already been paid by the person who will receive it〔信封〕邮资预付的

S2 W3 **prep·a·ra·tion** /,prɛpə`reʃən; ,prepə'reɪʃən/ *n* **1** [U] the act or process of preparing something 预备，准备: **[+for]** *Business training is a good preparation for any career.* 商业培训对任何职业都是良好的基础。| **[+of]** *Richard's currently involved in the preparation of the budget.* 理查德当前在忙于编制预算。| **in preparation for** (=in order to prepare for something) 为…作准备 *Justin had opened several bottles of wine in preparation for the party.* 贾斯廷已开了好几瓶葡萄酒为聚会作准备。| **be in preparation** (=being prepared) 在准备中 *Plans for the new school are now in preparation.* 建造新校舍的图正在绘制之中。**2 preparations** [plural] arrangements for something that is going to happen 准备工作，筹备工作: **[+for]** *preparations for the Queen's visit* 女王访问的准备工作 | **make preparations** *The army is making preparations for a full-scale invasion.* 军队正在为全面侵略作准备。**3** [C] a medicine, COSMETIC etc 配制剂；药剂: *a new preparation for cleansing the skin* 清洁皮肤的新护肤剂

pre·par·a·to·ry /prɪ`pærə,torɪ; prɪ'pærətəri/ *adj* **1** [only before noun 仅用于名词前] done in order to get ready for something 预备的，准备的: *preparatory talks to clear the way for a peace settlement* 为和平解决问题扫清道路的预备性会谈 **2 preparatory to** *formal* before something else and in order to prepare for it【正式】作为…的准备；在…之前: *The partners held several meetings preparatory to signing the agreement.* 合伙人在签订协议之前举行了几次预备性会议。

preparatory school /·'····· ,·/ *n* [C] **1** a private school in Britain for children between the ages of 8 and 13〔英国供8至13岁孩子读书的〕私立小学 **2** a private school in the US that prepares students for college〔美国为学生上大学作准备的〕私立预备学校

S1 W1 **pre·pare** /prɪ`pɛr; prɪ'peə/ *v*

1 ▶MAKE STH READY 使某事物作好准备◀ to make something such as a machine, a place, or a piece of writing ready to be used 把…准备好，使…作好准备: *Mansell's team were up all night preparing the car for the race.* 曼塞尔车队整夜未眠准备比赛用车。| *I'd better go upstairs and prepare her room.* 我最好上楼去把她的房间整理好备用。| *Have you prepared your speech yet?* 你准备好演讲稿了吗?

2 ▶MAKE PLANS/ARRANGEMENTS 制订计划/作出安排◀[I, T] to make plans or arrangements for something that will happen in the future 筹备，进行各项准备工作: *Olympus is preparing to launch a new range of cameras.* 奥林巴斯正在筹备将一批新照相机投放市场。| **[+for]** *We only heard about the meeting yesterday, so we haven't started preparing for it yet.* 我们昨天才刚听说这次会议，所以我们还没有开始筹备呢。| **prepare sth** *They've prepared a special surprise party for him.* 他们已为他筹备了一次让他感到惊喜的特别聚会。| *The airlines have prepared contingency plans in case the strike goes ahead.* 各航空公司已准备了应急计划以防罢工继续下去。| **prepare to do sth** *Her parents were busy preparing to go on holiday.* 她的父母正忙于为度假进行各项准备工作。

3 ▶MAKE YOURSELF READY 使自己准备好◀ [T] to make yourself mentally or physically ready for something that you expect to happen soon 使〔某人〕在思想上[身体上]作好准备: **prepare yourself (for)** *Prepare yourself for a shock.* 有件事会让你大吃一惊，你得作好心理准备。| *They prepared themselves for a long wait.* 他们作好了长时间等待的思想准备。| *Can you just give me a couple more moments to prepare myself?* 你能否再给我一点时间让我作好心理准备? | **prepare for action** *The captain told the men to prepare for action.* 上尉命令士兵准备战斗。

4 ▶TRAINING/EXPERIENCE 培训/经历◀[T] to provide someone with the training, skills, experience etc that they will need to do something or to deal with an unpleasant situation〔通过提供培训、技能、经验等〕使〔某人〕作好准备: **prepare sb for sth** *a course that prepares students for English examinations* 为学生参加英语考试而开设的课程 | *Schools should do more to prepare children for the world of work.* 学校应该为培养孩子适应职业场合做更多的事情。| **prepare sb to do sth** *Nothing in his life had prepared him for this ordeal.* 他一生中没有经历过这样的严酷考验。

5 ▶FOOD 食物◀ [T] to make food or a meal ready to eat 准备〔食物、饭菜〕: *Prepare the sauce while the pasta is cooking.* 在煮意大利面食的同时准备好调味汁。| **prepare sth for sb** *John's preparing supper for us.* 约翰正在为我们准备晚餐。| **prepare sb sth** *Helen had prepared us a wonderful meal.* 海伦为我们准备了一顿丰盛的饭菜。

6 prepare the way for/prepare the ground for to provide the conditions that make it possible for something to be achieved, or for someone to succeed in doing something 为…准备条件，为…打好基础: *Curie's research prepared the way for the work of modern nuclear scientists.* 居里的研究为现代核科学家的工作打下了基础。

7 ▶MEDICINE/CHEMICAL 药物/化学品◀[T] to make a medicine or chemical ready to be used, usually by mixing several substances 制作；调制；配制: *Preparing herbal medicines requires a lot of skill and knowledge about different kinds of herbs.* 配制草药需要很多技能和有关各种药草的知识。

Frequencies of **prepare, get ready** and **make preparaions** in spoken and written English 英语口语和书面语中 prepare, get ready 和 make preparations 的使用频率

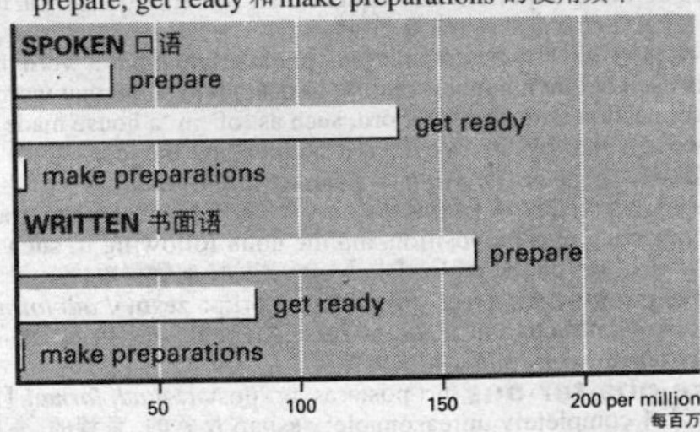

Based on the British National Corpus and the Longman Lancaster Corpus
据英国国家语料库和朗文兰开斯特语料库

This graph shows that **get ready** is more common in spoken English than **prepare** or **make preparations**. However, in written English, **prepare** is the most common of the three. **Make preparations** is the least common in both spoken and written English. It is less general, and suggests making a lot of arrangements for something that is going to happen. 本图表显示，get ready 在英语口语中的使用频率远远高于 prepare 和 make preparations。但是在书面语中，prepare 是三者中最常用的。make preparations 在口语和书面语中都是最不常用的。它较少使用，表示为将要发生的某事做很多安排。

pre·pared /prɪ`pɛrd; prɪ'peəd/ *adj* S2

1 be prepared to do sth to be willing to do something, especially something difficult or something that you do not usually do 愿意做某事〔尤指难做或通常不做的事〕: *You have to be prepared to take risks in this kind of work.* 你必须自愿承担做这种工作的风险。| *How much is she prepared to pay?* 她愿意付多少钱?

2 I'm not prepared to do sth *spoken* used when saying strongly that you refuse to do something【口】我不愿意做某事: *I'm not prepared to sit here and listen to this rubbish!* 我不愿意坐在这里听这些废话!

3 ►READY TO DEAL WITH STH 准备应付某事◄[not before noun 不用于名词前] ready to do something or deal with a situation because you were expecting it to happen or because you have made careful and thorough preparations 有准备的, 准备好的: [+for] *I wasn't prepared for all their questions.* 对于他们所有的问题我都没有准备。| **well/badly prepared** *Luckily we were well prepared for the storm.* 幸运的是我们为这次暴风雨作好了准备。| **ill-prepared** (=not prepared to deal with a difficult situation) 没有准备好的 *The country was ill-prepared to fight another war.* 该国并没有作好再打一场战争的准备。| **be prepared for the worst** (=expect that something very bad may happen and be ready for it) 作最坏的打算 *There was no news and we were prepared for the worst.* 由于没有任何消息, 我们作好了最坏的打算。

P

4 ►READY TO BE USED 准备被使用◄[not before noun 不用于名词前] arranged and ready to be used 安排好的, 配备好的: *The boss is due any minute – is everything prepared?* 老板随时会到, 一切都准备好了吗? | **get sth prepared** *By the time we'd got all our stuff prepared it was time to go on stage.* 我们把所有东西准备好时, 也该上台了。

5 ►MADE EARLIER 事先做好的◄planned, made, or written at an earlier time 事先准备好的: *The president read out a prepared statement.* 总统宣读了一份事先准备好的声明。| **hastily prepared** (=prepared very quickly because you were not expecting something) 仓促[匆忙]准备的 *Hastily prepared arrangements were made to welcome the new visitor.* 为欢迎新的访客, 进行了一些仓促的准备。

pre·pared·ness /prɪˋpɛrɪdnɪs; prɪˈpeədnɪ̈s/ *n* [U] the state of being ready for something 有准备 (的状态), 作好准备: *the country's lack of military preparedness* 该国在军事上的准备不足

pre·pon·der·ance /prɪˋpɑndərəns; prɪˈpɒndərəns/ *n formal* **a preponderance of** if there is a preponderance of people or things of a particular type in a group, there are more of that type than of any others【正式】…数量上的优势: *There is a preponderance of female students in the music department.* 在音乐系中女学生占大多数。

pre·pon·der·ant /prɪˋpɑndərənt; prɪˈpɒndərənt/ *adj formal* main or most important【正式】主要的; 最重要的 —**preponderantly** *adv*

pre·pon·der·ate /prɪˋpɑndəˌret; prɪˈpɒndəreɪt/ *v* [I] *formal* to be more important or frequent than something else【正式】〔重要性或频率上〕占优势, 胜过

prep·o·si·tion /ˌprɛpəˋzɪʃən; ˌprepəˈzɪʃən/ *n* [C] a word that is used before a noun, PRONOUN, or GERUND to show that word's connection with another word, such as 'of' in 'a house made of wood', and 'by' in 'We open it by breaking the lock' 介词, 前置词 —**prepositional** *adj* —**prepositionally** *adv*

prepositional phrase /ˌ····ˈ·/ *n* [C] *technical* a phrase consisting of a preposition and the noun following it, such as 'in bed' or 'on the table'【术语】介词短语, 前置词短语

pre·pos·sess·ing /ˌpripəˋzɛsɪŋ; ˌpriːpəˈzesɪŋ◄/ *adj formal* looking attractive or pleasant【正式】有吸引力的, 给人好感的: *a prepossessing smile* 动人的微笑

pre·pos·ter·ous /prɪˋpɑstərəs; prɪˈpɒstərəs/ *adj formal*【正式】**1** completely unreasonable; ABSURD 反常的, 荒谬的, 荒唐的: *The whole idea sounds absolutely preposterous!* 整个想法听起来荒谬透顶! **2** extremely unusual and silly 极异常且可笑的: *Look at that preposterous car!* 看那辆荒谬可笑的汽车! —**preposterously** *adv* —**preposterousness** *n* [U]

prep·py /ˋprɛpɪ; ˈprepi/ *adj AmE informal* typical of students who go to expensive private schools in the US, especially by dressing very neatly【美, 非正式】私立学校学生的, 衣着讲究[整洁]的: *preppy clothes* 讲究而又整洁的学生装

prep school /ˈ· ·/ *n* [C] *informal* a PREPARATORY SCHOOL【非正式】私立小学; 私立预备学校

pre·pu·bes·cent /ˌpripjuˋbɛsənt; ˌpriːpjuːˈbesənt◄/ *adj formal* concerned with the time just before a child reaches PUBERTY【正式】青春期前的

pre·quel /ˋprikwəl; ˈpriːkwəl/ *n* [C] a book, television programme, etc that tells you what happened before the story that is told in a popular book or film〔故事的〕前篇, 先行篇

Pre-Raph·ae·lite /priˋræfəˌlaɪt; priːˈræfəlaɪt/ *n* [C] a member of a group of late 19th century English painters and artists〔英国 19 世纪晚期的〕拉斐尔前派画家[艺术家] —**Pre-Raphaelite** *adj*

pre·re·cord /ˌpririˋkɔrd; ˌpriːrɪˈkɔːd/ *v* [T] to record music, a radio programme etc on a machine so that it can be used later 将〔音乐、电台节目等〕预先录下, 预先录制 —**prerecorded** *adj*: *prerecorded videos* 预先录制的录影[像]带 —**prerecording** *n* [C,U]

pre·req·ui·site /priˋrɛkwəzɪt; priːˈrekwɪ̈zɪ̈t/ *n* [C] *formal* something someone must have before they can be allowed to do something, or which must exist before something else can happen【正式】先决条件, 前提; 必备条件: [+for/to/of] *A reasonable proficiency in English is a prerequisite for the course.* 掌握适当程度的英语是学习这门课程的先决条件。

pre·rog·a·tive /prɪˋrɑgətɪv; prɪˈrɒgətɪv/ *n* [C, usually singular 一般用单数] a right that someone has because of their importance or position 独有的权利[权力], 特权: *the royal prerogative* 皇家的特权

pres 1 the written abbreviation of 缩写= present **2** the written abbreviation of 缩写= president

pre·sage /prɪˋsɛdʒ; ˈpresɪdʒ/ *v* [T] *literary* to be a warning or a sign that something is going to happen especially something bad【文】预示, 预兆: *A chill breeze blows, presaging winter.* 冷风吹起, 预示着冬天的来临。—**presage** *n* [C]

Pres·by·te·ri·an /ˌprɛzbəˋtɪrɪən; ˌprezbɪ̈ˈtɪəriən/ *n* [C] a member of the Presbyterian church, one of the largest churches in the US and the national church of Scotland 长老会教友〔长老会为美国最大的教会之一, 并为苏格兰国教〕—**Presbyterian** *adj* —**Presbyterianism** *n* [U]

pres·by·ter·y /ˋprɛzbəˌtɛrɪ; ˈprezbɪ̈təri/ *n* [C] **1** a local court or council of the Presbyterian church or the area controlled by that church〔长老会的〕教务评议会(管区) **2** a house in which a Roman Catholic priest lives〔天主教的〕神父住宅 **3** the eastern part of a church, behind the area where the CHOIR (=trained singers) sit〔教堂内的〕司祭席〔位于教堂东侧, 唱诗班席之后的神职人员座席〕

preschool /ˋpriskul; ˈpriːskuːl/ *n* [C] *AmE* a school for young children between two and five years of age, where they learn such things as numbers, colours, and letters【美】学龄前学校,〔二到五岁孩子的〕幼儿园; **nursery school** (NURSERY (2)) *BrE*【英】

pre-school /priˋskul; ˌpriːˈskuːl◄/ *adj* connected with the time in a child's life before they are old enough to go to school 学龄前的: *a pre-school playgroup* 学龄前的幼儿游戏班

pre-school·er /ˌpri ˋskulɚ; ˌpriː ˈskuːlə/ *n* [C] *AmE* a child who does not yet go to school【美】学龄前儿童

pre·sci·ent /ˋprɛʃɪənt; ˈpreʃiənt/ *adj formal* able to imagine or know what will happen in the future【正式】有预知能力的, 能预知未来的 —**prescience** *n* [U]

pre·scribe /prɪˋskraɪb; prɪˈskraɪb/ *v* [T] **1** to say what medicine or treatment a sick person should have (给…) 开药, 开处方; 指示〔疗法〕: **prescribe sb sth** *If these don't work I may have to prescribe you something stronger.* 如果这些药无效, 我也许得给你开一些药效更强的。| **prescribe sth for sth** *one of the most commonly prescribed drugs for treating depression* 治疗抑郁症最常见的处方药之一 **2** to state officially what someone can and cannot do, or what should be done in a particular situation 规定, 指定: *What punishment does the law prescribe for this crime?* 按照法律规定, 这种罪该怎么处罚? | **prescribe who/how/what etc** *You have no right to prescribe how others should behave.* 你无权规定别人的行为举止。

pre·scribed /prɪˋskraɪbd; prɪˈskraɪbd/ *adj* decided by a rule 规定的: *a prescribed number of hours* 规定的小时数

pre·script /ˋpriskrɪpt; ˈpriːˌskrɪpt/ *n* [C] *formal* an official order or rule【正式】规定, 命令, 条例

pre·scrip·tion /prɪˋskrɪpʃən; prɪˈskrɪpʃən/ *n* **1** [C] a piece of paper on which a doctor writes what medicine a sick person should have, so that they can get it from a PHARMACIST 处方, 药方 **2** [C] a particular medicine or treatment ordered by a doctor for a sick person〔医生开的〕处方药; 治疗方法: *Prescriptions used to be free when the National Health Service started.* 在国民保健制度刚启动时, 处方药一度是免费的。| **prescription charges** (=the fixed amount of money you have to pay in Britain for drugs which your doctor has ordered) 处方费 **3 on prescription** a drug that you get on prescription can only be obtained with a written order from the doctor 凭处方的, 根据药方的 —compare 比较 **over the counter** (COUNTER[1] (2)) **4** [C usually singular 一般用单数] an idea or suggestion about how to make a situation, activity etc successful 解救方法, 诀窍: [+for] *Her prescription for the advancement of women was education.* 她为妇女进步提出的诀窍是教育。**5** [U] the act of prescribing a medicine or drug 开处方, 开药; 指示疗法

pre·scrip·tive /prɪˋskrɪptɪv; prɪˈskrɪptɪv/ *adj* **1** stating or ordering how something should be done or what someone should do 规定的, 指定的: *prescriptive teaching methods* 规定的教学方法 **2** *technical* stating how a language should be used, rather than describing how it is used【术语】〔语言〕规定性的, 指定的; 规范的: *prescriptive grammar* 规定性语法 —**prescriptively** *adv*

prescriptive right /ˌ· ˌ· ˈ·/ *n* [C] *law* a right that has existed for so long that it is as effective as a law【法律】因时效[长期存在]而取得的权利

3 2 **pres·ence** /ˈprɛzn̩s; ˈprezəns/ *n* **1** [U] the state of being present in a particular place 出席; 到场; 存在: *Your presence is requested at the club meeting on Friday.* 俱乐部会议定于星期五举行, 敬请出席。| [+of] *The police scientists detected the presence of poison in the dead woman's blood.* 警方的化验师检测到该女性死者的血液中有毒药。—opposite 反义词 ABSENCE (1) **2 in sb's presence** with someone or in the same place as them 在某人面前, 当着某人的面: *John never seemed at ease in my presence.* 约翰在我面前总是显得不自在。| *The police will only interview a child in the presence of an adult.* 警方只有在成人在场时才能向孩子提出询问。**3** [U] the ability to impress people and make them believe you 仪态, 风度; 风采: *a man of great presence* 很有风度的男子 **4** [singular] a group of people from another country, an army, or the police, who are in a place to watch and influence what is happening〔某国在外国的〕势力;〔部队或警察的〕驻扎; 存在: *the American presence in the war zone* 战区的美国人 | *a strong police presence at the march* 在游行现场的大批警察 **5** [C usually singular 一般用单数] a spirit or influence that cannot be seen but is felt to be near〔看不见的〕灵气, 鬼怪: *They felt a strange presence in the deserted house.* 他们感到在那所废弃的房屋里有奇特的幽灵。**6 make your presence felt** to have a strong and obvious effect on the people around you or the situation you are in 使周围的人感到你的重要: *Since Webb joined the team he has really made his presence felt.* 韦布加入这个队以来, 他就使人感到他是个举足轻重的队员。

presence of mind /ˌ· · ˈ·/ *n* [U] the ability to deal with a dangerous situation calmly and quickly 镇定自若, 沉着冷静: **have the presence of mind to do sth** *Luckily Isabel had the presence of mind to take down the car's registration number.* 所幸的是, 伊莎贝尔沉着镇定地记下了那辆汽车的车牌号码。

2 2 **pres·ent¹** /ˈprɛznt; ˈprezənt/ *adj* **1 be present a)** to be in a particular place 出席的, 到场的; 存在的: *How many people were present at the meeting yesterday?* 昨天出席会议的有多少人? | *small amounts of gas present in the atmosphere* 大气中存在的少量气体 **b)** to be felt strongly or remembered for a long time 强烈感觉到的; 历历在目的: *The memory of her brother's death a year ago is still present in her mind.* 她哥哥一年前去世时的情景仍留在她脑海中。**2** [only before noun 仅用于名词前] happening or existing now 现存的; 目前的, 现在的: *What is your present address?* 你现在的住址在哪里? | *Usually I'd advise you to wait, but in the present situation I think it's best to act without delay.* 通常情况下我会建议你等着, 但在目前的情况下, 我认为最好是立即采取行动。**3** [only before noun 仅用于名词前] *technical* related to a verb that shows an existing state or action【术语】〔动词〕现在时的: *'He wants' and 'They are coming' are examples of verbs in the present tense.* He wants 和 They are coming 是动词现在时的例子。**4 all present and correct** *BrE*【英】also 又作 **all present and accounted for** *AmE*【美】used to say that everyone who is supposed to be in a place, at a meeting etc is now here 所有该到的都到了, 如数到齐 **5 present company excepted** used when you are saying something rude about someone to tell the people you are with that you do not mean to include them in the statement 在座者除外: *Women are never satisfied with anything! Present company excepted, of course.* 女人总是对什么事都不满足! 当然在座者除外。—see also 另见 PRESENTLY

Frequencies of **present** *(adj)*, **now** and **at the moment** in spoken and written English 英语口语和书面语中 present *(adj)*, now 和 at the moment 的使用频率

SPOKEN 口语
present
now
at the moment
WRITTEN 书面语
present
now
at the moment
500 1000 1500 per million 每百万

Based on the British National Corpus and the Longman Lancaster Corpus 据英国国家语料库和朗文兰开斯特语料库

This graph shows that **now** is much more common than **present** and **at the moment** in both spoken and written English. **At the moment** is more common in spoken English than in written English. **Present** is the least common of the three. It is formal, and is only used before a noun, for example in expressions such as 'the present situation', 'the present leader' etc. 本图表显示, now 在英语口语和书面语中的使用频率远远高于 present 和 at the moment。at the moment 在英语口语中的使用频率远远高于书面语。present 是三个中最不常用的, 它较为正式, 而且只用于名词前, 譬如在 the present situation(目前情况), the present leader(现任领导人)之类的表达法中。

pres·ent² /prɪˋzɛnt; prɪˈzent/ *v* [T] 2 1

1 ▶GIVE 给予◀ to give something to someone, especially at a formal or official occasion〔尤指在正式场合〕颁发, 授予, 赠送; 呈献; 呈递: **present sb with sth** *David's manager presented him with the award for best sales in the region.* 由于戴维在这一地区的销售业绩最出色, 他的经理向他颁了奖。

2 ▶CAUSE STH TO HAPPEN 使某事发生◀ to cause something to happen or exist 使发生[存在], 引起, 造成: *Slippery floors in the work area present a hazard to employees.* 工作区很滑的地板对雇员是一种危险。| **present sb with sth** *His resignation presents us with a tricky situation.* 他的辞职给我们造成一个尴尬的局面。| **present a problem/difficulty** *This equation should present no problems if you know some basic trigonometry.* 如果你懂一些三角学的基本知识的话, 这个方程式应该不会造成什么困难。

3 ▶SHOW 呈现◀ to offer or show information about something in a particular way 呈现; 展现; 表现: *The movie presents its characters in a way that I find difficult to believe in.* 我觉得这部电影表现人物的方式很难让人相信。| *Tobacco companies are trying to present a more favorable image.* 烟草公司正试图展现出较取悦人的形象。

4 ▶A SPEECH 讲话◀ to give a speech in which you offer an idea, plan etc to be considered or accepted 提出〔观点、计划等〕; 陈述: **present sth to sb** *The team is presenting its report to the board on Tuesday.* 该工作组将在星期二向董事会提出报告。

5 ▶DOCUMENT/TICKET 文件/入场券◀ to show something such as an official document or ticket to someone in an official position 呈递, 出示: *You must present your passport to the customs officer.* 你必须向海关人员出示护照。

6 ▶THEATRE/CINEMA 剧院/电影院◀ to give a performance in a theatre, cinema, etc, or broadcast a programme on television or radio 上演; 演出; 上映; 播出〔广播或电视节目〕: *This evening PBS presents the first of a six-part historical drama about the Civil War.* 今晚公共广播公司播出有关内战的六集历史剧的第一集。

7 ▶TELEVISION/RADIO 电视/广播◀ *BrE* if you present a television or radio programme, you introduce its different parts【英】主持〔广播或电视节目〕: *Tonight's edition of Newsnight, presented by Jeremy Paxman.* 今晚的晚间新闻由杰里米·帕克斯曼主持。

8 sth presents itself if a situation, opportunity etc presents itself, it suddenly happens or exists〔情况、机会等〕出现, 发生: *As soon as the opportunity presents itself, I'm going to talk to Mr Boyer about that job.* 一旦机会来了, 我就会找博耶先生谈那份工作。

9 ▶FORMALLY INTRODUCE SB 正式介绍某人◀ to introduce someone formally, especially to someone of a very high rank〔正式地〕介绍; 引见〔尤指向地位极高者〕: *I was presented to the Queen in 1964.* 我有幸于1964年被引见给女王。

10 present arms a command to soldiers to hold their weapons upright in front of their bodies as a greeting to a person of high rank 举枪〔于胸前〕敬礼〔用于军令〕

11 present your apologies/compliments etc *formal* used to greet someone, apologize to them etc very politely【正式】致歉/致意等: *Mrs Gottlieb presents her apologies and regrets she will not be able to attend.* 戈特利布夫人表达歉意, 并为她不能出席感到遗憾。

pres·ent³ /ˈprɛznt; ˈprezənt/ *n* [C] something you give someone on a special occasion or to thank them for something; gift 礼物, 赠品: *One of my Japanese students gave me a beautiful fan as a present.* 我的一位日本学生送给我一把漂亮的扇子作为礼物。| **birthday/Christmas present** *Christmas presents under the tree* 树下的圣诞礼物

present⁴ *n* [singular] **1** the time that we are experiencing now 现在, 目前: *You have to stop worrying about the past and start thinking about the present!* 你必须停止为过去担忧, 2 2

而开始为现在考虑! | **no time like the present** (=used to say that if you are going to do something at all, you should do it now) 没有比现在更合适的时机 *"I was thinking of asking Maura to marry me." "Do it! There's no time like the present!"* "我正想向毛拉求婚。" "去啊! 没有比现在更合适的时机了。" **2** *technical* the form of a verb that shows what exists or is happening now 【术语】〔动词的〕现在时形式 —see also 另见 HISTORIC PRESENT **3 at present** at this time; now 现在, 目前: *Ms Hellman is busy at present, can she ring you later?* 赫尔曼女士现在正忙着, 过一会儿她给你回电话好吗? —see 见 PRESENTLY (USAGE)

pre·sen·ta·ble /prɪˋzɛntəbl; prɪˈzentəbəl/ *adj* tidy and attractive enough to be introduced or shown to someone 拿得出手的; 像样的; 体面的: *a presentable piece of work* 摆得出去的作品 | **make yourself presentable** *I must go and make myself presentable before the guests arrive.* 客人来以前, 我得去把自己打扮得体面一点。—**presentably** *adv*

pre·sen·ta·tion /ˌprɛzn̩ˋteʃən; ˌprezənˈteɪʃən/ *n*
1 ▶**PROOF** 证据◀ [C,U] the act of showing someone something so that it can be checked or considered 提出; 出示: [+of] *On presentation of the relevant identity documents you may collect your property.* 在出示相关身份证件之后, 你就可以领走你的财物。
2 ▶**APPEARANCE** 外貌◀ [U] the way in which something is said, offered, shown, explained etc to others 讲述, 描绘; 外观, 外貌: *This word processor is excellent for presentation and layout of complex documents.* 这种文字处理机非常适于处理复杂文件的外观和版式。| *The presentation of food can be as important as the taste.* 食物的外观和味道同样重要。
3 ▶**PRESENT PRIZE** 颁奖◀ [C] the act of giving someone a prize or present at a formal ceremony 授予, 颁发: [+of] *The presentation of prizes will begin at three o'clock.* 颁奖仪式将在3点钟开始。
4 ▶**TALK** 讲话◀ [C] an event at which a new product or idea is described and explained 报告; 〔新产品的〕介绍; 〔观点的〕陈述, 说明: **give a presentation** *I've been asked to give a short presentation on the aims of the project.* 我被要求简短地介绍一下该项目的目标。
5 ▶**PERFORMANCE** 表演◀ [C] the act of performing something in front of an audience 表演, 演出: [+of] *There are two presentations of the cabaret every night.* 每晚有两场卡巴莱歌舞表演。
6 ▶**BABY** 婴儿◀ [C,U] *technical* the position in which a baby is lying in its mother's body just before it is born 【术语】〔胎儿的〕先露位置, 产位: *a breech presentation* 臀产位 —**presentational** *adj*

presentation cop·y /ˈ·····, ···/ *n* [C] a book that is given to someone, especially by the writer or PUBLISHER 〔尤指作者或出版者提供的〕赠(阅)书

pres·ent-day /ˋprɛzn̩t ˋde; ˌprezənt ˈdeɪ◂/ *adj* modern or existing now 现代的; 当今的, 当前的: *present-day Sicily* 当今的西西里岛

pre·sent·er /prɪˋzɛntɚ; prɪˈzentə/ *n* [C] *BrE* someone who introduces the different parts of a television or radio show 【英】〔电视或广播节目的〕主持人, 主播; ANNOUNCER *AmE* 【美】: *radio presenter, Libby Purves* 广播节目主持人: 利比·珀维斯

pre·sen·ti·ment /prɪˋzɛntəmənt; prɪˈzentɪ̣mənt/ *n* [C] *formal* a strange and uncomfortable feeling that something is going to happen; PREMONITION 【正式】〔尤指不祥的〕预感: [+of] *a presentiment of danger* 有危险的预感

pres·ent·ly /ˋprɛzn̩tlɪ; ˈprezəntli/ *adv formal* 【正式】 **1** in a short time; soon 马上, 一会儿, 不久, 很快: *The doctor will be here presently.* 医生一会儿就到。| *Presently a bell rang and they all trooped into school.* 很快铃响了, 他们全都成群地涌入学校。**2** *especially AmE and ScotE* now; at this time 【尤美和苏格兰】现在, 目前, 此刻: *Scientists are presently working on identifying the cause of the disease.* 科学家正致力于确认该病的病因。

USAGE NOTE 用法说明: PRESENTLY
UK-US DIFFERENCE 英美差别
In both British and American English **presently** can mean the same as **soon**, but is a little old-fashioned. 在英语和美语中, presently 都可表示 soon (马上、很快), 但有点过时: *If you take a seat, the doctor will see you presently.* 请坐, 医生一会儿就来看你。
In American English, and formal British English, it can also be used to mean 'at the present time' or to talk about something that is happening now. 在美语和正式英语中, 该词也可用来表示"目前, 现在"或谈论目前正在发生的事情: *He is presently living in Seoul.* 他现在住在首尔。| *District councils are presently making good progress on the development plans.* 区委员会目前在发展规划方面进展顺利。

present par·ti·ci·ple /ˌ·· ˈ····/ *technical* a PARTICIPLE that is formed in English by adding 'ing' to the verb, as in 'sleeping'. It can be used in COMPOUND[1] (4) forms of the verb to show PROGRESSIVE tenses, as in 'she's sleeping', or as an adjective, as in 'the sleeping child' 【术语】现在分词

present per·fect /ˌ·· ˈ··/ *n technical* the form of a verb that shows a period of time up to and including the present, formed in English with the present tense of the verb 'have', as in 'he has gone' and a PAST PARTICIPLE 【术语】现在完成时[式]

pres·er·va·tion /ˌprɛzɚˋveʃən; ˌprezəˈveɪʃən/ *n* [U] **1** the act of keeping something unharmed or unchanged 维护; 保护; 保持, 维持: [+of] *The police are responsible for the preservation of law and order.* 警察负责维护治安。**2** the degree to which something has remained unchanged or unharmed by weather, age etc 保养(程度): *The old building is in a good state of preservation.* 这所老房子保养得很好。—see also 另见 SELF-PRESERVATION

pres·er·va·tion·ist /ˌprɛzɚˋveʃənɪst; ˌprezəˈveɪʃənɪ̣st/ *n* [C] *especially AmE* someone who works to prevent historical places, buildings etc from being destroyed 【尤美】〔对古迹、古建筑物等的〕保护主义者

preservation or·der /ˌ··ˈ·· ˌ··/ *n* [C] *especially BrE* an official order that something, especially a tree or building, must be preserved and not damaged 【尤英】文物保护法令

pre·ser·va·tive /prɪˋzɝvətɪv; prɪˈzɜːvətɪv/ *n* [C,U] a chemical substance that is used to stop food or wood from decaying 防腐剂

pre·serve[1] /prɪˋzɝv; prɪˈzɜːv/ *v* [T] **1** to save something or someone from being harmed or destroyed 维护, 保护; 保存〔使免受破坏〕: *I think these traditional customs should be preserved.* 我认为这些传统习俗应该保存下去。| *The wreck was preserved by the muddy sea bed.* 失事船只的残骸被泥泞的海床保护了起来。| **preserve sb/sth from sth** *They were determined to preserve their leader from humiliation.* 他们决心保护他们的领导人免受侮辱。**2** to store food for a long time after treating it so that it will not decay 腌制; 保存〔食物〕: *figs preserved in brandy* 用白兰地浸渍的无花果 **3** to make something continue without changing 保持, 维持: *The Baroness had managed to preserve her good looks.* 那位男爵夫人设法留驻了自己姣好的面容。—see also 另见 WELL-PRESERVED —**preservable** *adj*

preserve[2] *n* **1** [C, U] a substance made from boiling fruit or vegetables with sugar, salt, or VINEGAR 果酱 **2** [singular] an activity that is only suitable or allowed for a particular group of people 〔某群体〕独有[专有]的活动: *Banking used to be a male preserve.* 银行业过去是男人独占的领域。| [+of] *Gardening is sometimes considered the preserve of the elderly.* 园艺有时被认为是老年人独有的活动。**3** [C] an area of land or water that is kept for private hunting or fishing 私人渔猎区

pre·set /priˋsɛt; priːˈset/ *present participle* **pre-setting** *past tense and past participle* **pre-set** *v* [T] to set a piece of electrical equipment, so that it will start to work 预先设置, 预先调好

pre-shrunk /ˌpriˋʃrʌŋk; ˌpriːˈʃrʌŋk◂/ *adj* clothes that are pre-shrunk are made to SHRINK (=became smaller when washed) before they are sold 〔衣服在出售之前〕已预缩的, 缩过水的: *pre-shrunk Levis* 预先缩过水的李维斯牌牛仔裤

pre·side /prɪˋzaɪd; prɪˈzaɪd/ *v* [I] to be in charge of a formal ceremony, meeting etc 〔在正式仪式、会议等〕担任主持, 负责: *They could find no clergyman who would agree to preside at the funeral.* 他们找不到愿意主持葬礼的牧师。

preside over *phr v* [T] **1** to be in charge of a situation over which you do not have much control 负责〔无力控制的局面〕: *The president found himself presiding over the worst economic depression in the history of the US.* 该总统发现自己无可奈何地面临美国历史上最严重的经济萧条。**2** to be the head of a company or organization 掌管, 管辖, 领导 **3** to be in charge of a meeting or a formal meal 主持

pres·i·den·cy /ˋprɛzədənsɪ; ˈprezɪ̣dənsi/ *n* [C] **1** the job of president 总统[主席、校长等]的职位: *Roosevelt was elected four times to the presidency of the US.* 罗斯福四次当选美国总统。**2** the period of time for which a person is president 总统[主席、校长等]的任期: *During his presidency he undertook a great initiative towards world peace.* 在他担任总统期间, 他积极地倡导世界和平。

pres·i·dent /ˈprɛzədənt; ˈprezɪ̥dənt/ *n* [C] **1** the official leader of a country that does not have a king or queen 总统: *the President of France* 法国总统 | *President Kennedy* 肯尼迪总统 **2** the person in charge of a club, college, government department etc 〔俱乐部〕会长; 〔大学〕校长; 〔政府部门〕首长 **3** *AmE* the head of a business, bank etc【美】〔公司〕董事长; 〔银行〕行长; 总裁: *the president of General Motors* 通用汽车公司总裁

president-e·lect /ˌ‥ ·ˈ·/ *n* [singular] someone who has been elected as a new president, but who has not yet started the job〔尚未就职的〕当选总统

pres·i·den·tial /ˌprɛzəˈdɛnʃəl; ˌprezɪ̥ˈdenʃəl◂/ *adj* connected with a president 总统的: *a presidential election* 总统大选 | *the party's presidential candidate* 该党的总统候选人

Presidents' Day /ˈ‥ ˌ·/ a US public holiday on the third Monday in February, which celebrates the birthdays of Presidents George Washington and Abraham Lincoln 总统日〔美国公众假日, 每年2月份的第三个星期一, 纪念美国总统乔治·华盛顿和亚伯拉罕·林肯的诞辰〕

Presiding Officer /ˌ‥ ˈ‥/ the person who officially controls the meetings and discussions in the Scottish Parliament or the Welsh Assembly. The Presiding Officer's position is the same as that of the Speaker of the House of Commons. 议会主席〔苏格兰议会或威尔士国民议会中负责主持会议和讨论的议员, 地位相当于下议院议长〕

pre·sid·i·um, praesidium /prɪˈsɪdɪəm; prɪˈsɪdiəm/ *n plural* **presidia** [C] a committee chosen to represent a large political organization, especially in a COMMUNIST country〔尤指共产党执政国家的〕常务委员会, 主席团

Pres·ley /ˈprɛzlɪ; ˈprezli/, **El·vis** /ˈɛlvɪs; ˈelvɪ̥s/ (1935-77) a US singer and GUITAR player, who first became popular as a ROCK 'N' ROLL singer in the mid-1950s, and became one of the most successful and popular singers ever. His many records had a great influence on popular music, and they include *Heartbreak Hotel*, *Blue Suede Shoes*, and *Are you Lonesome Tonight?* He also appeared in many films, such as *Jailhouse Rock* (1957) and *G.I. Blues* (1960). He is often called 'The King', and some people say that they do not believe that he is dead. Millions of people go to visit his home in Memphis, Tennessee, which is called Graceland. 普雷斯利〔(1935-1977), 美国歌手、吉他手。20世纪50年代中期以演唱摇滚歌曲开始走红, 成为有史以来最成功、最受欢迎的歌手之一。他的许多唱片对流行音乐产生了重要影响, 其中有《心碎旅馆》、《蓝色绒面鞋》和《今夜你寂寞吗?》。他还出演过不少电影, 如《监狱摇滚》(1957) 和《军士布鲁斯》(1960)。人们常称他为"猫王"。一些人说他们不相信普雷斯利已经不在了。他的故居名为格雷斯兰华丽大厦, 位于田纳西州的孟菲斯, 前去观赏的游人有数百万之众〕

press¹ /prɛs; pres/ *n*

1 ▸NEWS 新闻◂ a) [U] also 又作 **the press** people who write reports for newspapers, radio, or television〔报纸、电台、电视台的〕记者们; 新闻界: *the freedom of the press* 新闻自由 | [also+plural verb *BrE* 英] *In August the press are desperate for news.* 8月份记者们不顾一切地捕捉新闻。| *press photographers* 新闻摄影记者 **b)** [singular,U] reports in newspapers and on radio and television〔报纸、电台、电视台的〕新闻报道: *To judge from the press, the concert was a great success.* 据新闻报道来看, 这次音乐会取得了巨大成功。| *press clippings* 剪报 | **press coverage** (=the reports written about something in newspapers)〔报纸上有关某事的〕新闻报道

2 get/be given a bad press to be criticized in the newspapers or on radio or television 受到舆论界的批评: *The police have been getting a bad press in the last few months.* 在过去的几个月里, 警方一直受到舆论界的批评。

3 get/be given a good press to be praised in the newspapers or on radio or television 受到舆论界的好评: *Our recycling policy is getting a good press.* 我们的回收利用政策正获得新闻舆论的好评。

4 ▸PRINTING 印刷◂ [C] **a)** a business that prints and sometimes also sells books 出版社: *the Clarendon Press* 克拉伦登出版社 **b)** also 又作 **printing press** a machine that prints books, newspapers, or magazines 印刷机

5 trouser/flower/wine press a piece of equipment used to put weight on something to make it flat or to force liquid out of it 裤子熨烫机/压花器/葡萄榨汁机: *You can still buy old cheese presses in some areas.* 在一些地区, 你仍可以买到旧的压酪机。

6 ▸PUSH 推◂ a light steady push against something small 按, 揿: *Give the button another press.* 再按一下这个按钮。

7 go to press if a newspaper, magazine, or book goes to press, it is printed 付印, 开印

8 ▸CROWD 人群◂ a crowd of people pushing against each other 拥挤的人群

press² *v*

1 ▸AGAINST STH 靠着某物◂ [T always+adv/prep] to push something firmly against a surface 按; 压: *The little boys pressed their noses against the glass.* 那些小男孩把他们的鼻子贴在玻璃上。| *Viv tried to press himself back against the wall.* 维夫尽量往后紧贴墙壁。| *The old man pressed a coin into her hand.* 老人把一枚硬币塞进她的手里。

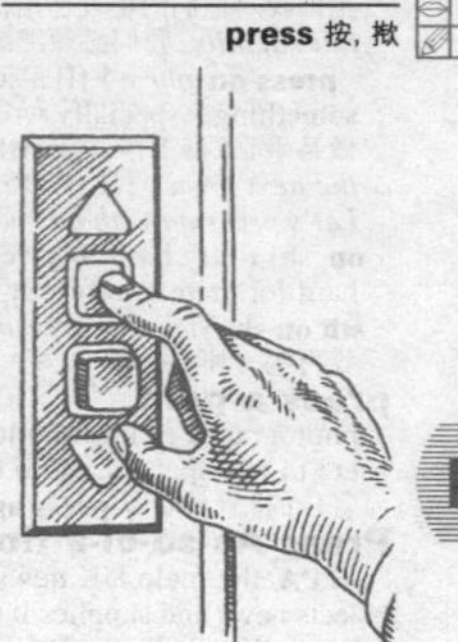
press 按, 揿

2 ▸BUTTON 按钮◂ [T] to push something with your finger to make a machine start, a bell ring etc 按, 揿: *What happens if I press the reset button?* 要是我按reset (重新设置) 按钮, 会发生什么事呢?

3 ▸CLOTHES 衣服◂ [T] to make clothes smooth using heat; IRON 熨平〔衣物〕: *I'll need to press my suit.* 我需要烫一下我的西装。

4 ▸CROWD 人群◂ [I always+adv/prep] to move in a particular direction by pushing 拥挤着移动, 挤着走: *The crowds pressed around her, hoping for her autograph.* 人群围挤在她身旁, 希望得到她的签名。

5 ▸PERSUADE 劝说◂ [T] to try hard to persuade someone to do something 极力劝说, 敦促, 催促: *Please don't press me on this point, I have no more to say.* 在这一点上请不要逼我, 我无话可说了。| **press sb to do sth** *Katie pressed me to stay a little longer.* 凯蒂极力劝我再多待一会儿。| **press sb for sth** *The bank is pressing us for a quick decision.* 银行催促我们迅速作出决定。

6 ▸FOR JUICE 为取得果汁◂ [T] to put a heavy weight on something to get liquid from it 挤取, 榨取: *The grapes must be pressed to extract the juice.* 葡萄必须经压榨才能提取葡萄汁。

7 ▸MAKE STH FLAT 使某物平整◂ [T] to put pressure or a weight on something to make it flat 把…压平[压扁]: *pressing flowers* 把花压平

8 ▸HOLD SB/STH CLOSE 抱紧某人/某物◂ [T] to hold someone or something close to you because you feel upset, are protecting them etc 使紧贴; 紧抱, 紧握: **press sb/sth to you** *Prue pressed the photograph to her chest and wept.* 普吕把照片紧贴在她胸前哭了。

9 press sb's hand/arm to hold someone's hand or arm tightly for a short time, to show friendship, sympathy etc 紧握某人的手/手臂〔表示友好、同情等〕: *Frank pressed my hand warmly when we met.* 我们见面时弗兰克热情地紧握我的手。

10 press charges to say officially that someone has done something illegal and must go to court 提出诉讼: *Police are often reluctant to press charges in such cases.* 在这些情况下, 警方常常不愿提起诉讼。

11 ▸CLAIM/STATEMENT 声称/声明◂ [T] to continue to try to make someone accept a claim or statement that you are making 坚持, 竭力要求: *We shall not press our claim for compensation.* 我们将不再坚持赔偿要求。| *I don't want to press the point, but we are late.* 我不想老提这一点, 但我们迟到了。

12 press sb/sth into service to use someone or something not completely suitable, because of an unexpected problem〔因意外问题而〕将就使用[暂用]某人/某物: *My scarf was pressed into service as a bandage.* 我的围巾被临时用作了绷带。

13 press sth home a) to push something into its place 把某物推入[压入, 按入, 塞入]适当的位置: *Jane slammed the door and pressed the bolt home.* 简砰地把门关上并插好插销。**b)** to repeat or emphasize something, so that people remember it 重复[强调]某事物〔以使人们记住它〕: *We must press home the case for action.* 我们必须令人信服地阐明这件案子以便采取行动。

14 press home your advantage to try to succeed completely, using an advantage that you have gained 尽量利用优势大获成功

15 press the flesh *humorous* to shake hands with a lot of people【幽默】与许多人握手: *politicians pressing the flesh* 与众人握手的政客

16 ▸RECORD 唱片◂ [T] to make a copy of a GRAMOPHONE record etc 压制〔唱片〕

press (sb) **for** sth *phr v* [I,T] to keep asking for something or to try hard to achieve something 敦促, 催促; 迫切要求; 努力取得: *The firm is pressing me for a decision on their offer.* 该公司

正催我对他们的提议作出决定。| *We must continue to press for full equality.* 我们必须继续争取完全平等。

press on *phr v* **1** [I] also 又作 **press ahead** to continue doing something, especially working, in a determined way 继续坚定做某事〔尤指工作〕: [**+with**] *Shall we stop here, or press on to the next town?* 我们是在这里停下还是继续赶往下一个城镇? | *Let's press on with our work.* 我们继续工作吧。**2** [T **press** sth **on** sb] to try hard to give something to someone, so that it is hard for them to refuse it 硬给, 强迫〔某人〕接受〔某物〕: **press sth on sb** *Nick was pressing yet another drink on me.* 尼克硬要我再喝一杯酒。

press a·gent /ˈ·, ·ˌ/ *n* [C] someone whose job is to supply photographs or information about a particular actor, musician etc to newspapers, radio or television〔为演员、音乐家等进行宣传的〕宣传员 —**press agency** *n* [C]

Press As·so·ci·a·tion, the /ˈ· ···,·ˌ/ abbreviation 缩写为 **PA** the main UK news agency (=an organization that collects news and supplies it to newspapers, radio, and television). As well as news, the Press Association also supplies sports and business reports and information about the weather. 英国国家通讯社〔英国一主要新闻机构。该机构除报道新闻外还提供体育、商业报道与气象信息〕

press bar·on /ˈ·, ·ˌ/ *n* [C] *informal, especially BrE* someone who owns and controls one or more important national newspapers【非正式, 尤英】报业巨头, 报业大王

press box /ˈ· ·/ *n* [C] an enclosed area at a sports ground used by people from newspapers, radio, or television〔运动场上的〕记者席

Press·bur·ger /ˈprɛsˌbɝgɚ; ˈpresˌbɜːgə/, **E·me·ric** /ˈɛmərɪk; ˈemərɪk/ (1902-88) a Hungarian-born film DIRECTOR who made films together with Michael Powell, including *A Matter of Life and Death* (1946) 普雷斯伯格〔(1902-1988), 匈牙利出生的电影导演。他常与迈克尔·鲍威尔合作拍片, 如《生死攸关》(1946) 等〕

Press Com·plaints Com·mis·sion, the /ˌ· ·ˈ· ·,·ˌ/ a British organization which tries to make sure that the British PRESS (=newspapers and magazines) give professional, high quality news reports, and which deals with complaints about the press 新闻投诉委员会〔英国一机构, 旨在确保英国新闻报道的品质和职业化水准, 同时受理读者对报刊杂志的投诉〕

press con·fer·ence /ˈ·, ···ˌ/ *n* [C] a meeting at which someone makes an official statement to people who write news reports and answers questions 记者招待会: *The Green Party held a press conference the next day.* 绿党第二天召开了一个记者招待会。

press corps /ˈ· ·/ *n* [C] a group of people who write news reports, at a place where something important is happening 记者团, 联合报道组

press cut·ting /ˈ·, ·ˌ/ also 又作 **press clipping** *n* [C] a short piece of writing or a picture, cut out from a newspaper or magazine 剪报

pressed /prɛst; prest/ *adj* **be pressed for time/money etc** to not have enough time, money etc 时间紧迫/缺钱等: *I'm a bit pressed for time – could you call back tomorrow?* 我现在没有时间, 你能明天打电话过来吗?

press gal·le·ry /ˈ·, ···ˌ/ *n* [C] an area above or at the back of a hall, used by news reporters 新闻记者席

press-gang[1] /ˈ· ·/ *n* [C] a group of sailors employed in the past to take men away by force to join the navy〔过去为海军强抓壮丁的〕征兵队, 招募水手队

press-gang[2] *v* [T] **press-gang sb into doing sth** *informal* to force someone to do something【非正式】强迫某人做某事: *I was press-ganged into doing the dishes.* 我是被强行拉去洗碗的。

pre·ssie, **prezzie** /ˈprɛzɪ; ˈprezi/ *n* [C] *BrE spoken* a present【英口】礼物, 赠品: *Did you get some nice pressies?* 你收到一些精美的礼品没有?

press·ing[1] /ˈprɛsɪŋ; ˈpresɪŋ/ *adj* **1** needing to be discussed or dealt with very soon; URGENT 紧迫的; 迫切的: *There is a pressing need for reform in this area.* 这一地区迫切需要改革。**2** demanding something in a way that is hard to refuse 恳切要求的, 坚持的: *a pressing invitation* 恳切的邀请 —**pressingly** *adv*

pressing[2] *n* [C] **1** a number of GRAMOPHONE records made at one time 同一批压制的唱片 **2** an act of pressing 按, 压, 挤, 推; 压平; 压榨

press·man /ˈprɛsmæn; ˈpresmæn/ *plural* **pressmen** /-mɛn; -men/ *n* [C] *BrE informal* someone who writes news reports【英, 非正式】记者

press of·fice /ˈ·, ·ˌ/ *n* [C] the office of an organization or government department which gives information to the newspapers, radio, or television〔组织或政府部门的〕新闻处 —**press officer** *n* [C]

press re·lease /ˈ· ·, ·ˌ/ *n* [C] an official statement giving information to the newspapers, radio, or television 新闻稿

press sec·re·ta·ry /ˈ·, ···ˌ/ *n* [C] a secretary to an important organization or person, who gives information about them to the newspapers, radio, or television 新闻秘书

press-stud /ˈ· ·/ *n* [C] *BrE* a small metal FASTENER for a piece of clothing, in which one part is pressed into a hollow part in the other【英】摁扣, 子母扣; SNAP[2] (6) *AmE*【美】

press-up /ˈ· ·/ *n* [C] *especially BrE* a type of exercise in which you lie facing the ground, and push your body up with your arms【尤英】俯卧撑; PUSH-UP *especially AmE*【尤美】

pres·sure[1] /ˈprɛʃɚ; ˈpreʃə/ *n*

1 ▶**FORCE 力**◀ [U] the act of force or weight being put on to something 压, 按, 挤, 榨: *The pressure of the water turns the wheel.* 水压使轮子转动。| *factors such as temperature and pressure* 诸如温度和压力之类的因素

2 ▶**STRENGTH 力量**◀ [C,U] the strength of the force or weight put on something 压力: **high/low pressure** *The gas containers burst at high pressures.* 在高压下这些瓦斯容器会爆炸。| *Low atmospheric pressure often brings rain.* 低气压常常带来降雨。—see also 另见 BLOOD PRESSURE

3 ▶**STRONG 有力的**◀ [U] an attempt to persuade someone by using influence, arguments, or threats〔利用影响、辩论、威胁施加的〕压力: [**+for**] *pressure for change inside the party* 党内要求变革的压力 | **pressure to do sth** *There was great pressure to conform to existing standards.* 要求遵循现行标准的压力很大。| **under pressure from** *John only agreed to go under pressure from his parents.* 约翰是在父母的压力下才同意去的。| **be/come under pressure (to do sth)** *The company is under pressure to improve pay and conditions.* 该公司面临提高工资并改善工作条件的压力。| **give in to pressure** (=agree to do something that someone has persuaded you to do) 屈服于压力 | **put pressure on** (=to try to persuade someone to do something because it is their duty) 向…施加压力 *Their parents were putting pressure on them to get married.* 他们的父母在对他们施加压力, 要求他们结婚。| **exert pressure on/bring pressure to bear on** *formal*【正式】*Special interest groups can bring great pressure to bear on legislation.* 一些特殊利益集团会给立法施加很大的压力。

4 ▶**PROBLEMS/DEMANDS 问题/要求**◀ [C,U] conditions of work or a way of living that cause anxiety or difficulties〔工作或生活的〕压力: *Paul changed jobs because he couldn't stand the pressure.* 保罗因受不了这种压力而换了工作。| [**+on**] *There are a lot of pressures on young people today.* 如今的年轻人有很多的压力。| **under pressure** *You need to be able to work accurately under pressure.* 你必需能够在压力下准确无误地进行工作。| **pressure of work** *Lou couldn't stay long because of pressure of work.* 卢因为工作压力而不会待得很久。

5 pile on the pressure to increase the amount of pressure on someone 增加〔某人的〕压力: *Just when she was at her weakest, Martin started piling on the emotional pressure.* 就在她最脆弱的时候, 马丁开始增加她感情上的压力。

pressure[2] *v* [T] to try to make someone do something by making them feel it is their duty to do it 对…施加压力; PRESSURIZE *BrE*【英】: **pressure sb into doing sth** *I've been pressured into helping with the decorating.* 我被迫帮助装修。| **pressure sb to do sth** 对某人施加压力使其做某事

pressure cook·er /ˈ··, ·ˌ/ *n* [C] a tightly covered cooking pot in which food is cooked very quickly by the pressure of hot steam 压力锅, 高压锅

pres·sured /ˈprɛʃɚd; ˈpreʃəd/ *adj* feeling worried, or making you feel worried because of the number of things you have to do (感到) 有压力的; PRESSURIZED (2) *BrE*【英】: *This is the most pressured job I've ever had.* 这是我做过的压力最大的一份工作。

pressure group /ˈ·· ·/ *n* [C] a group or organization that tries to influence the opinions of ordinary people and persuade the government to do something 压力集团〔为影响舆论或政府行为而开展活动的团体〕: *environmental pressure groups* 环境保护压力集团 —see also 另见 INTEREST GROUP

pressure point /ˈ·· ·/ *n* [C] **1** a point on the body where an ARTERY (=a tube that carries blood) that runs near a bone can be pressed and closed off, to stop blood loss〔身体上按之即可止血的〕压迫点, 加压止血点 **2** a place on the body that is massaged (MASSAGE[2] (1)) or used in treatments such as REFLEXOLOGY or

ACUPUNCTURE〔指压按摩中的〕压(觉)点, 穴位 **3** a place or situation that may involve trouble or problems 可能有麻烦[问题]的地方[局面]: *a pressure point for racial tension* 会出现种族间紧张局势的地方[局面]

pres·sur·i·za·tion /ˌprɛʃərə`zeʃən; ˌpreʃəraɪˈzeɪʃən/ *n* [U] the quality of being (PRESSURIZED (1)) or the degree to which something is pressurized 增压, 加压; 加压[增压]的程度

pres·sur·ize also 又作 **-ise** /`prɛʃəˌraɪz; ˈpreʃəraɪz/ *v* [T] *BrE* to try to make someone do something by making them feel it is their duty to do it; PRESSURE[2]【英】对…施加压力: **pressurize sb into doing sth** *They would have enjoyed the party more if they hadn't been pressurised into going.* 如果他们不是被逼迫去的, 他们在聚会上可能会玩得更好。| **pressurize sb to do sth** *Normally apathetic members were pressurized to vote.* 通常漠不关心的成员都会被迫进行投票。

pres·sur·ized also 又作 **-ised** *BrE*【英】/`prɛʃərˌaɪzd; ˈpreʃəraɪzd/ *adj* **1** containing air that has controlled pressure 耐压的, 密封的: *a pressurized container* 密封容器 | *pressurised high altitude aircraft* 耐高压的高空飞行器 **2** *BrE* feeling worried or making you feel worried, because of the amount of things you have to do; PRESSURED【英】〔感到〕有压力的: *today's pressurized society* 如今压力重重的社会

pres·tige /prɛs`tidʒ; preˈstiːʒ/ *n* [U] **1** the respect and importance a person, organization, or profession has, because of their high position in society, or the quality of their work 威望, 声望, 威信: *striving for prestige, status and power* 为声望、地位和权力而努力奋斗 | *The teaching profession has lost the prestige it used to have.* 教学职业已失去以往具有的那种威望。**2 prestige car/position/neighbourhood etc** a car etc that is expensive and important-looking in a way that other people admire 有气派的汽车/令人羡慕的职位/有气派的住宅区等 —compare 比较 STATUS (2)

pres·ti·gious /prɛ`stɪdʒəs; preˈstɪdʒəs/ *adj* admired as one of the best and most important 有威望[声望, 威信]的: *a prestigious job* 受人尊敬的工作 | *a prestigious award* 享有盛名的奖项

pres·to[1] /`prɛsto; ˈprestəʊ/ *adj, adv technical* played or sung very quickly【术语】〔演奏或演唱〕急板的[地]

presto[2] *n* [C] *technical* a piece or section of music played or sung very quickly【术语】急板; 急板乐段[乐章, 乐曲]

presto[3] *interjection spoken* used when you show someone something unbelievable or magical【口】嘿〔用于给人看令人难以置信或不可思议的东西时〕; HEY PRESTO *BrE*【英】: *And presto! The rabbit disappears.* 嘿! 那只兔子不见了。

pre·stressed /ˌpri `strɛst; ˌpriː ˈstrest◂/ *adj* pre-stressed CONCRETE has been made stronger by having wires put inside it〔混凝土〕预加应力的, 加了钢筋的

1 3 **pre·su·ma·bly** /prɪ`zuməblɪ; prɪˈzjuːməbli/ *adv* [sentence adverb 句子副词] used to say that you think something is likely to be true 可能, 大概, 据推测: *If you're eating beforehand, presumably you won't want to go to a restaurant.* 如果你要提前吃, 看来你就不想去餐馆了。| *Presumably you've all seen this notice now.* 现在你们大概都已看到这则告示了。

3 **pre·sume** /prɪ`zum; prɪˈzjuːm/ *v* **1** [T] to think you can be sure of something because it is likely, although there is no proof〔没有证据地〕相信, 认为; 推测: *Each of you will make a speech, I presume?* 我想你们每个人都要演讲, 是吗? | **presume (that)** *I presume we'll be there by six o'clock.* 我想我们将在6点之前到达那里。| **presume sb/sth to be sb/sth** *From the way they talked I presumed them to be married.* 从他们谈话的样子看, 我想他们已经结婚了。| **be presumed to do sth** *The temple is presumed to date from the first century BC.* 这座寺庙被认为建于公元前1世纪。**2** [T] to accept something as true until it is proved untrue, especially in law 认定, 视为, 推定〔尤用于法律〕: *We must presume innocence until we have evidence of guilt.* 除非我们有罪证, 否则我们应作无罪推定。| **be presumed dead/innocent etc** *Their nephew was missing, presumed dead.* 他们的侄子失踪了, 据推定已经死亡。**3** [I] *formal* to behave without respect or politeness by doing something that you have no right to do【正式】冒昧做某事, 放肆, 擅作主张: **presume to do sth** *Are you presuming to tell me how to treat my family?* 如何对待我的家人难道我还要你来教吗? **4** [T usually in present tense 一般用现在时] *formal* to accept something as being true and base something else on it; PRESUPPOSE【正式】意味着, 以…为先决条件: *The statement that everyone is free presumes equality of opportunity.* 人皆自由这一说法意味着机会是平等的。| **presume that** *Our recommendations presume that a capable person is in charge.* 我们推荐的先决条件是要有一个有能力的人来负责。

presume on/upon sth *phr v* [T] *formal* to use someone's kindness, or a relationship, to ask them for more than you should【正式】滥用, 不正当地利用〔某种关系、某人的好心〕: *I felt it would be presuming on our friendship to ask him to lend me that much money.* 我觉得向他借那么多钱是在利用我们的友情。

pre·sump·tion /prɪ`zʌmpʃən; prɪˈzʌmpʃən/ *n* **1** [C] an act of thinking that something is true because it is very likely 假定; 推测; 设想: *the presumption that she would leave* 关于她要离开的推测 **2** [U] disrespectful or impolite behaviour that shows you are too confident 放肆, 冒昧; 自以为是: *Ryan's presumption in telling her when they would meet* 瑞安自作主张地告诉她他们将在什么时候见面 **3** [C,U] *law* the act of thinking something is true because it is very likely, although there is no certain proof【法律】〔无证据的〕推定, 认定: *the presumption of innocence* 无罪认定

P

pre·sump·tive /prɪ`zʌmptɪv; prɪˈzʌmptɪv/ *adj formal or technical* based on a reasonable belief about what is likely to be true【正式或术语】推定的, 假定的: *a presumptive diagnosis* 推定的诊断 —**presumptively** *adv* —see also 另见 HEIR PRESUMPTIVE

pre·sump·tu·ous /prɪ`zʌmptʃuəs; prɪˈzʌmptʃuəs/ *adj* showing disrespect as a result of being too confident 专横的, 自以为是的; 冒失的; 放肆的: *She found Conrad charming but rather presumptuous.* 她发现康拉德长得迷人, 只是颇为专横。—**presumptuously** *adv* —**presumptuousness** *n* [U]

pre·sup·pose /ˌprisə`poz; ˌpriːsəˈpəʊz/ *v* [T] *formal*【正式】**1** to depend on something that is thought to be true; ASSUME 预先假定, 假设, 预料: **presuppose that** *The plans presuppose that people usually respond to calls for help.* 这些计划是预先假定人们通常会对呼救作出反应。**2** to depend on something in order to exist or be true 以…为先决条件, 意味着: *Every form of human society presupposes some kind of division of labour.* 每一种人类社会形式都以某种分工为先决条件。

pre·sup·po·si·tion /ˌprisʌpə`zɪʃən; ˌpriːsʌpəˈzɪʃən/ *n formal*【正式】**1** [C] something that someone thinks is true without proof; ASSUMPTION 预先假定(的事), 预想(的事), 假设(的事): **[+that]** *the presupposition that crime is just another form of sickness* 对于犯罪只是另一种形式的病态的假设 **2** [U] the act of thinking something is true without proof 预先假定, 假设

pre·teen /ˌpri`tin; ˌpriːˈtiːn◂/ *adj* connected with, or made for children who are 11 or 12 years old 青春期前儿童的; 为青春期前儿童制造的: *preteen clothing* 青春期前的童装 —**preteen** *n* [C] *AmE*【美】

pre·tence also 又作 **pretense** *AmE*【美】/prɪ`tɛns; prɪˈtens/ *n* [singular, U] **1** an attempt to pretend that something is true 假装, 作假, 做作: **[+that]** *Susie abandoned the pretence that she didn't want to go to the party.* 苏茜不再假装不想去参加聚会了。| **keep up the pretence of being/doing sth** *How long are you going to keep up the pretence of being ill?* 你装病还要装多久呢? | **under (the) pretence of sth** *John waited for her under pretence of tying his shoelaces.* 约翰假装在系鞋带等着她。| **make a pretence of doing sth** *Tollitt made no pretence of hiding his surprise.* 托利特没有假装掩饰他的惊讶。**2 under/on false pretences** if you do something under false pretences, you do it by pretending that something is true 以欺诈手段, 以虚假的借口: *Mellors obtained credit under false pretences.* 梅勒斯以欺诈手段骗得了贷款。**3 no pretence to superiority/faith/education etc** no claim that you are SUPERIOR[1] (4) etc 不自称高人一等/信仰上帝/受过教育等: *a simple man, with little pretence to education* 不自吹受过教育的纯朴的人

pre·tend[1] /prɪ`tɛnd; prɪˈtend/ *v* **1** [I,T] to behave as if something is true when in fact you know it is not 假装, 佯称: *We're not really sisters; we were just pretending.* 我们不是真姐妹, 只是装着是姐妹。| **pretend (that)** *The candidate pretended she had worked for a newspaper before.* 这位候选人佯称她以前在一家报社工作过。| **pretend to do sth** *Sarah pretended to be cheerful and said nothing about the argument.* 萨拉假装很开心, 没有说起争吵的事。| **pretend sth** *Dennis often pretends deafness when you ask him an awkward question.* 当被问及难以回答的问题时, 丹尼斯经常装聋作哑。**2** [T, usually in questions and negatives 一般用于疑问句及否定句] to claim that something is true, especially something that cannot be shown to be true 声称, 自称, 自命: **pretend (that)** *I can't pretend I understand these technical terms.* (=I admit I do not understand them) 我不能假装懂这些专业用语。| **pretend to sth** *I can't pretend to much expertise in computing.* 我不敢自命有很多电脑方面的专门知识。 2 3

3 [I,T] to imagine something is true as a game〔作为游戏〕装扮, 假装: **pretend (that)** *Let's pretend we're on the moon.* 让我们假装成是在月亮上吧。

This graph shows how common the different grammar patterns of the verb **pretend** are. 本图表所示为动词 pretend 构成的不同语法模式的使用频率。

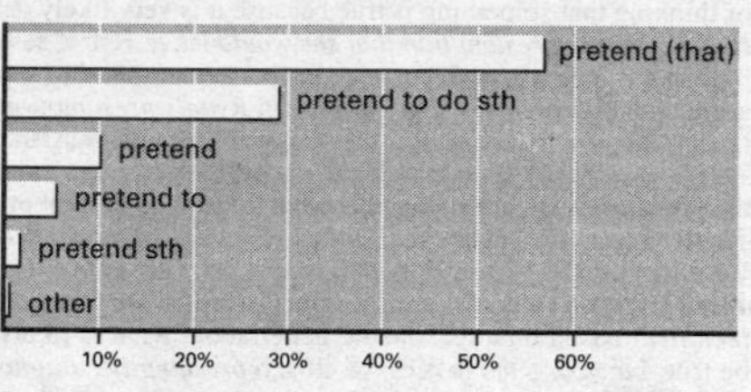

Based on the British National Corpus and the Longman Lancaster Corpus 据英国国家语料库和朗文兰开斯特语料库

pretend² *adj* a word meaning imaginary, used especially by or with children〔尤儿语〕假装的, 想象的, 假想的: *We sang songs around a pretend campfire.* 我们围在假想的营火旁唱歌。

pre·tend·ed /prɪˋtɛndɪd; prɪˈtendɪ̵d/ *adj* false or unreal, in spite of seeming to be true or real 假装的; 虚假的: *pretended sorrow* 假装的悲伤

pre·tend·er /prɪˋtɛndɚ; prɪˈtendə/ *n* [C] someone who claims a right to be king, leader etc, that many people do not accept 觊觎高位[王位]者: *the pretender to the English throne* 觊觎英国王位者

pre·tense /prɪˋtɛns; prɪˈtens/ *n* [singular, U] an American spelling of PRETENCE pretence 的美式拼法

pre·ten·sion /prɪˋtɛnʃən; prɪˈtenʃən/ *n* [C usually plural 一般用复数] an attempt to seem richer, more important etc than you really are 自命不凡; 虚荣; 炫耀: [+to] *a man with pretensions to grandeur* 妄自尊大的男人 | *an area with upper-class pretensions* 具有上流社会虚荣的地区

pre·ten·tious /prɪˋtɛnʃəs; prɪˈtenʃəs/ *adj* trying to seem more important, clever etc than you really are 自以为是的, 自我炫耀的, 矫饰的: *It's pretentious of him to keep the complete works of Proust on full display.* 为了炫耀他把普鲁斯特全集都摆了出来。| *a pretentious movie* 狂妄的影片 —opposite 反义词 UNPRETENTIOUS —**pretentiously** *adv* —**pretentiousness** *n* [U]

pret·er·ite, the also 又作 **preterit** *AmE*【美】/ˋprɛtərɪt; ˈpretərɪ̵t/ *n technical* the tense or verb form that expresses a past action or condition【术语】过去时[式] —**preterite** *adj*

pre·ter·nat·u·ral /ˌpritəˋnætʃərəl; ˌpriːtəˈnætʃərəl◂/ *adj formal*【正式】**1** beyond what is usual or normal 超乎寻常的, 异常的: *He felt possessed of a preternatural strength and fearlessness.* 他感到拥有异乎寻常的力量和勇气。**2** strange, mysterious, and unnatural 奇特的; 神秘的; 超自然的: *twisted images emerging through the preternatural green light* 从神秘的绿光中现出的扭曲的影像 —**preternaturally** *adv*: *preternaturally strong* 异常强壮的

pre·text /ˋpritɛkst; ˈpriːtekst/ *n* [C] a reason given for an action, in order to hide the real intention; EXCUSE² (1,2) 借口: [+for] *The riots were used as a pretext for banning all political activity.* 骚乱被利用来作为禁止一切政治活动的托辞。| **on/under the pretext of doing sth** *Tom called at her apartment on the pretext of asking for a book.* 汤姆借口要一本书到她的公寓去。—see 见 EXCUSE² (USAGE)

Pre·to·ri·a /prɪˋtorɪə; prɪˈtɔːriə/ a city in the northern part of South Africa. It is the administrative capital of South Africa. 比勒陀利亚〔南非北部一城市, 为南非的行政首都〕

pret·ti·fy /ˋprɪtɪˌfaɪ; ˈprɪtɪfaɪ/ *v* [T] to change something with the intention of making it pretty, but often with the effect of spoiling it 装饰, 美化; 粉饰: *The new owners have prettified the house.* 新的主人给那所房子进行了装饰。

S2 W3 **pret·ty¹** /ˋprɪtɪ; ˈprɪti/ *adv* [+adj/adv] *spoken*【口】**1** fairly, though not completely 颇, 相当: *I'm pretty sure he'll say yes.* 我相当肯定他会说行。| *Life on the farm was pretty tough.* 农场的生活相当艰苦。—see 见 RATHER (USAGE) **2** very 很, 非常: *It's pretty hard to see how we'll manage.* 很难想象我们将如何应付。**3 pretty well** also 又作 **pretty much** very nearly; almost 差不多, 几乎: *I'd say that's pretty well impossible.* 我要说那几乎是不可能的。| *"How is he feeling today?" "Pretty much the same."* "他今天觉得怎么样?" "差不多还是老样子。" **4 pretty near** *especially AmE* almost【尤美】几乎, 差不多: *That bout of pneumonia pretty near killed Roy.* 那次肺炎发作几乎致罗伊于死地。—see also 另见 **be sitting pretty** (SIT⁶)

pretty² *adj* **prettier, prettiest** **1** a woman or child who is pretty is good-looking in an ordinary way 漂亮的, 好看的, 标致的: *Susan's certainly a pretty girl, but I wouldn't call her beautiful.* 苏姗确实是一个标致的女孩, 但我认为她称不上美丽。| *Maria looks much prettier with her hair cut short.* 玛丽亚把头发剪短看起来好看得多。**2** something that is pretty is pleasant to look at or listen to without being very beautiful or impressive 悦目的; 悦耳的, 优美的: *a pretty dress* 漂亮的裙子 | *a pretty tune* 优美的曲调 | *What a pretty little garden!* 多么好看的小花园! **3** a boy who is pretty looks attractive in a way that is typical of a girl〔男孩〕俊俏的, 女孩子气的: *She said, "Oh Nick's the pretty one really."* 她说, "噢, 尼克确实是长得俊俏的那个。" **4 not a pretty sight** *often humorous* very unpleasant to look at【常幽默】让人看起来非常不舒服: *After a night's drinking, Al was not a pretty sight.* 喝了一整夜酒之后, 阿尔看上去糟透了。**5 not just a pretty face** *humorous spoken* to have qualities or abilities as well as an attractive appearance【幽默, 口】不仅相貌好〔还有其他优点〕: *I'm not just a pretty face, you know!* 你知道的, 我不仅仅徒有其表。**6 come to a pretty pass** *old-fashioned* used to say that a very bad situation has developed【过时】情况变得很糟糕: *Things have come to a pretty pass, if you can't say what you think without causing a fight.* 如果你说出自己的想法就会引起争吵的话, 情况就糟糕了。**7 cost a pretty penny** *old-fashioned* to cost a lot of money【过时】花费很多钱 **8 pretty as a picture** very pretty 非常漂亮的 **9 pretty pretty** *BrE* spoilt by too much pretty decoration【英】装饰得过分的, 过分华丽的 —**prettily** *adv*: *Charlotte sang very prettily.* 夏洛特唱得很优美。—**prettiness** *n* [U]

pret·zel /ˋprɛtsl; ˈpretsəl/ *n* [C] a hard salty BISCUIT or CRACKER (1) baked in the shape of a stick or a loose knot 棒状饼干, 纽结状咸饼干

pre·vail /prɪˋvel; prɪˈveɪl/ *v* [I] *formal*【正式】[not in progressive 不用进行时] **1** if a belief, custom etc prevails, it exists among a group of people〔信念、风俗等〕盛行, 流行: [+in/among etc] *Belief in magic still prevails in some rural parts of the country.* 这个国家的一些农村地区至今仍然相信魔法。**2** if someone or their ideas prevail, they win an argument or fight after a long time〔某人或其观点〕获胜; 占优势, 占上风: [+over] *The military finally prevailed over the civilian resistance movement.* 军队最终战胜了平民的反抗运动。| *Justice prevailed in the end.* 正义最终获得了胜利。

prevail on/upon sb *phr v* [T] *formal* to persuade someone【正式】劝说, 说服〔某人〕: **prevail on sb to do sth** *David was prevailed upon to propose a vote of thanks.* 人们劝戴维致答谢辞。

pre·vail·ing /prɪˋvelɪŋ; prɪˈveɪlɪŋ/ *adj* [only before noun 仅用于名词前] **1** existing or accepted in a particular place or at a particular time; CURRENT¹ 流行的, 盛行的: *the prevailing state of education* 普遍的教育状况 | *prevailing trends* 流行趋势 **2 prevailing wind** a wind that blows over a particular area most of the time 盛行风

prev·a·lent /ˋprɛvələnt; ˈprevələnt/ *adj* common at a particular time or in a particular place〔在某时或某地〕普遍的, 盛行的, 流行的: [+in/among etc] *Solvent abuse is especially prevalent among younger teenagers.* 吸胶毒在青少年中特别普遍。| *prevalent attitudes* 普遍的态度 —**prevalence** *n* [U]

pre·var·i·cate /prɪˋværəˌket; prɪˈværɪ̵keɪt/ *v* [I] to try to hide the truth by not answering questions directly 支吾, 搪塞, 推诿, 含糊其辞 —**prevarication** /prɪˌværəˋkeʃən; prɪˌværɪ̵ˈkeɪʃən/ *n* [C,U]

S2 W1 **pre·vent** /prɪˋvɛnt; prɪˈvent/ *v* [T] to stop something from happening, or stop someone from doing something 阻止, 阻挡; 预防, 防止: *The rules are intended to prevent accidents.* 这些规定旨在防止事故发生。| **prevent sb/sth (from) doing sth** *Lacey has a back injury that may prevent him from playing in tomorrow's game.* 莱西背上受了伤, 这可能使他不能打明天的比赛。—**preventable** *adj*

pre·ven·ta·tive /prɪˋvɛntətɪv; prɪˈventətɪv/ *adj* another form of the word PREVENTIVE 预防(性)的, 防备的: *preventative measures* 预防措施

pre·ven·tion /prɪˋvɛnʃən; prɪˈvenʃən/ *n* [U] the act of preventing something, or the actions that you take in order to prevent something happening 预防; 防止; 阻止; 预防行动: [+of] *the prevention of war* 防止战争 | **crime/accident prevention** *Accident prevention is one of the main aims of the campaign.* 预防事故发生是这次活动的主要目标之一。

Prevention of Ter·ror·is·m Act, the /,· · · ˈ· · · · , ·/ a British law made in 1989 which gives the army, police, and government more powers to deal with TERRORISTs, such as being able to keep someone in prison for 7 days without charging them with a crime《防止恐怖主义法》〔英国于1989年制定的法律。该法赋予军队、警察及政府更大的权力，以应对恐怖分子，如无需对某人提出控罪即可扣留七天〕

pre·ven·tive /prɪˋvɛntɪv; prɪˈventɪv/ also 又作 **preventative** *adj* [only before noun 仅用于名词前] intended to prevent something you do not want to happen, such as illness, or crime 预防（性）的，防备的：*preventive health programs* 预防性保健计划 | **preventive actions/measures** (=actions intended to stop something happening or a situation getting worse) 预防行动/措施 *Simple preventive measures will reduce the risk of infection.* 简单的预防措施将会减少感染的危险。—**preventively** *adv* —**preventatively** *adv*

preventive de·ten·tion /·,·· ˈ··/ *n* [U] *BrE law* a system in which people who are guilty of many crimes are kept in prison for a long time【英，法律】〔对于惯犯的〕预防性拘留

preventive medi·cine /·,·· ˈ··/ *n* [U] medical treatment, advice, and health education that is designed to prevent disease happening rather than cure it 预防医学

pre·verb·al /,· ˈ··◂/ *adj* [only before noun 仅用于名词前] happening before a child has learned to speak〔幼儿〕获得语言能力前的：*the pre-verbal stages* 尚未获得语言能力阶段

pre·view /ˋpri,vju; ˈpriːvjuː/ *n* [C] **1** an occasion when you can see a film, play etc before it is shown to the public〔戏剧、电影的〕预演，预映：**sneak preview** *a sneak preview of his new play* 他的新剧的内部预演 **2** an advertisement for a film or television programme that often consists of short parts from it〔电影或电视节目的〕预告（片）；TRAILER (3) *BrE*【英】

S1 W1 **pre·vi·ous** /ˋpriviəs; ˈpriːviəs/ *adj* **1** [only before noun 仅用于名词前] happening or existing before the event, time, or thing that is being mentioned 以前的，先前的，前的：*a better result than we've had in previous years* 比我们前些年好的结果 | *She has two children from a previous marriage.* 她前一次婚姻有两个孩子。| **previous experience** *Do you have any previous experience of this kind of work?* 你以前有过做这种工作的经验吗？| **previous offences/convictions** (=things that a criminal has done, or been judged guilty of, before) 前科 **2** **a bit previous** *BrE informal* done before the right or sensible time【英，非正式】有点操之过急的；有点过早的：*It's a bit previous to ask for the money before they've done the job.* 他们还没做工作就要钱未免有点操之过急。**3** **previous to sth** before a particular time or event 在某事物以前：*There were almost no women MPs previous to 1945.* 1945年前几乎没有女性议员。

S3 W2 **pre·vi·ous·ly** /ˋpriviəslɪ; ˈpriːviəsli/ *adv* before the present time 以前，先前：*The world record was previously held by a Spanish athlete.* 这个世界纪录以前是由一位西班牙运动员保持的。| **two days/three years etc previously** *The car was now worth twice what we'd paid for it six months previously.* 这部车现在的价钱比我们六个月前花的钱多一倍。

pre·vi·sion /prɪˋvɪʒən; ,priːˈvɪʒən/ *n* [C,U] *formal* something you see in your mind or knowledge you have of an event before it happens【正式】预知；预感；预见 —compare 比较 PREMONITION

pre-war /,· ˈ·◂/ *adj, adv* happening or existing before a war, especially the First or Second World Wars 战前（的）〔尤指第一次或第二次世界大战之前〕：*conditions in pre-war Europe* 战前欧洲的情况 —compare 比较 POST-WAR

prey[1] /pre; preɪ/ *n* **1** [U] an animal that is hunted and eaten by another animal or by a person 被〔其他动物或人〕捕食的动物，猎物：*a tiger stalking its prey* 潜步跟踪猎物的老虎 **2** **bird/beast of prey** a bird or animal which lives by killing and eating other animals 食肉猛禽/猛兽：*falcons and other birds of prey* 猎鹰和其他食肉猛禽 **3** **be/fall prey to sth** to be unable to avoid being affected by something unpleasant 为某事物所折磨：*During the long wait she was prey to all sorts of doubts and anxieties.* 在长时间的等待中，她为各式各样的疑惑和焦虑所折磨。**4** [U] someone who can easily be deceived or influenced 容易受骗[受影响]的人：*Some salesmen consider young housewives easy prey.* 一些推销员认为年轻的家庭主妇很容易被他们蒙骗。

prey[2] *v*

prey on sb/sth *phr v* [T] **1** if an animal or bird preys on another animal or bird it hunts and eats it 捕食：*Cats prey on birds and mice.* 猫捕食鸟和老鼠。**2** to try to influence or deceive weaker people 试图影响；欺骗〔弱者〕：*religious cults that specialize in preying on young people* 专门欺骗年轻人的宗教派别 **3** **prey on your mind** to make you worry continuously 使你持续苦恼，折磨你：*The accident has been preying on my mind all week.* 那次事故使我整个星期惴惴不安。

prez·zie /ˋprɛzɪ; ˈprezi/ *n* [C] *BrE spoken* another spelling of PRESSIE【英口】pressie的另一种拼法

Pri·am /ˋpraɪəm; ˈpraɪəm/ in ancient Greek stories, the king of Troy and the father of Hector and Paris 普里阿摩斯〔古希腊传说中的特洛伊国王，赫克托耳和帕里斯之父〕—see also 另见 the ILIAD, the TROJAN WAR

price[1] /praɪs; praɪs/ *n* S1 W1

1 ►MONEY 钱◄ [C,U] the amount of money for which something is sold, bought, or offered 价格，价钱：*Fuel prices are rising steadily.* 燃料价格正稳步上涨。| [+of] *Can you tell me what the price of a new window would be?* 你能告诉我一个新窗户要多少钱吗？| *They agreed on a price of £2,000 for the car.* 他们商定的这辆车的价钱为2000英镑。| **high/low price** *You can get cars in Europe at very low prices.* 在欧洲可以以很低的价钱买到汽车。| **price increase/rise** *Experts say that price rises will be gradual.* 专家说价格将逐渐上涨。| **right price** *We don't have to sell to the first buyer, we can wait for the right price.* 我们不必卖给第一个买主，我们可以等待合适的价格。| **at a good/fair etc price** *You can get a three-course meal at a fairly reasonable price.* 你可以以相当公道的价格吃到一顿三道菜的饭菜。| **half/full price** *I bought these jeans half price in the sale.* 我在一次大减价中以半价买了这条牛仔裤。| **in price** *Videos vary in price depending on the make.* 录像带根据牌子不同而价格不同。—see also 另见 ASKING PRICE, COST[1] (USAGE), COST PRICE, LIST PRICE, MARKET PRICE

2 **at a price** **a)** used to say that you can buy something, but only if you pay a lot of money 以很高的价钱：*You can get goat's cheese at the local delicatessen – at a price!* 你可以在当地的熟食店买到山羊乳酪 —— 不过价格很高！**b)** used to say that something can be achieved, but that it involves something unpleasant 以很高的代价：*She was finally made senior executive, but at what price!* 她最终当上了高级经理，但那是以什么样的代价呀！

3 **at any price** if you want to do something at any price you are determined to do it, even if it is very difficult 不惜任何代价，无论如何：*She was determined to have a child at any price.* 她决心不惜任何代价要一个孩子。

4 **not at any price** used to say that you would never sell something, or do something, even for a lot of money 无论多高的价钱也不卖；无论如何不：*Sorry, that painting's not for sale at any price.* 对不起，那幅画无论出多高的价钱也不卖。

5 **put a price on sth** **a)** to say how much something costs 给某物定价：*Could you put a price on the damage the storm caused?* 你能说出这次暴风雨造成的损失有多少钱吗？**b)** to give something a financial value 定出某物的金钱价值：*You just can't put a price on their fighting spirit.* 他们的战斗精神是无法用金钱衡量的。

6 **the price of success/freedom etc** the unpleasant or unwelcome things that you must suffer in order to be successful, free etc 成功/自由等的代价：*Monroe paid the ultimate price of success, dying alone in her room.* 梦露为成功付出了最高的代价 —— 孤身死在她的房间里。

7 **What price fame/glory etc?** *usually spoken* used to say that it is possible that it was not worth achieving something good, because too many bad things have happened as a result【一般口】名声/荣耀等又有什么用?：*Homeless widows and orphans viewing tonight's carnage may well ask, what price political independence?* 无家可归的寡妇和孤儿看了今晚的大屠杀很可能会问，政治独立有什么用？

8 ►AT HORSE RACE 在赛马时◄ [C] the chance that a horse will win a race expressed in numbers; ODDS (4)〔赛马中的〕投注赔率："*What price are you offering on 'Lucky Shot'?*" "*Seven to four.*" "你给'幸运射手'的赔率是多少?" "七赔四。"

9 **be above/beyond/without etc price** to be extremely valuable or important 极其珍贵的，极其重要的；无价的

10 **a price on sb's head** a reward for catching or killing someone 悬赏缉拿[杀死]某人的赏额：*running scared with a price on his head* 被悬赏缉拿而仓皇逃窜

11 **everyone has their price** used to say that you can persuade people to do anything if you give them what they want 人各有其价〔指人都是可以收买的〕—see also 另见 **cheap at the price** (CHEAP[1] (8)), **name your price** (NAME[2] (7)), **pay the price** (PAY[1] (6))

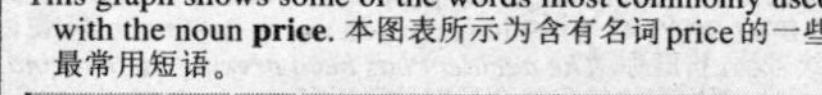

This graph shows some of the words most commonly used with the noun **price**. 本图表所示为含有名词price的一些最常用短语。

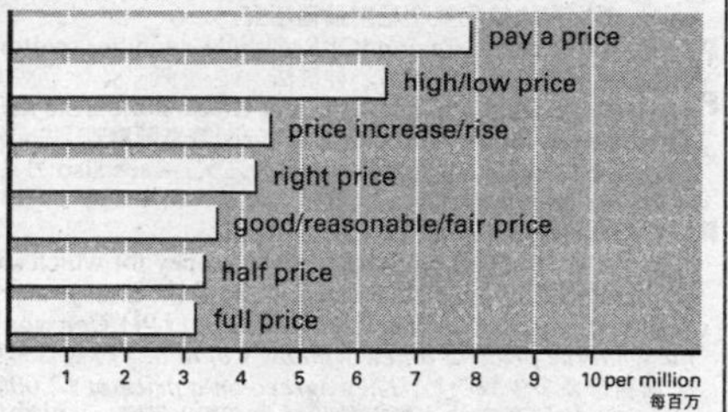

Based on the British National Corpus and the Longman Lancaster Corpus
据英国国家语料库和朗文兰开斯特语料库

price² *v* [T] **1** [usually in passive 一般用被动态] to fix the price of something that is for sale 给…定价钱: *a moderately priced apartment* 定价适中的公寓 | **be priced at** *The tennis rackets are priced at £75 each.* 这种网球拍的定价为每只75英镑。**2** to put the price on goods to show how much they cost 给…标价 **3** to compare the prices of things 比较…的价钱: *We spent Saturday morning pricing microwaves.* 我们花了星期六一上午的时间比较微波炉的价钱。**4 price yourself out of the market** to demand too much money for the services or goods that you are selling 漫天要价致使〔自己的服务或商品〕失去市场

Price, Vincent /ˈvɪnsn̩t; ˈvɪnsənt/ (1911-93) a US film actor famous for appearing in horror films, including *House of Wax* (1953),*The Mad Magician* (1954),*The Fly* (1958),*The Pit and the Pendulum* (1961),*Witchfinder General* (1968), and *Edward Scissorhands* (1990) 普莱斯〔(1911-1993), 美国电影演员。以出演恐怖影片闻名, 其中包括《恐怖蜡像馆》(1953)、《疯狂魔术师》(1954)、《苍蝇》(1958)、《地窖与钟摆》(1961)、《驱魔人》(1968)和《剪刀手爱德华》(1990)〕

price con·trol /ˈ· ·,·/ *n* [U] a system in which the government sets the prices of things〔政府实行的〕价格管制, 物价控制

price fix·ing /ˈ· ,··/ *n* [U] **1** a system in which the government sets the prices of things; PRICE CONTROL 价格管制, 物价控制 **2** an agreement between producers and sellers of a product to fix its price at a high level 价格垄断, 操纵物价

price in·dex /ˈ· ,··/ *n* [C] a system of numbers by which the prices of goods can be compared with what they were in the past 价格指数, 物价指数 —see also 另见 RETAIL PRICE INDEX

price·less /ˈpraɪslɪs; ˈpraɪsləs/ *adj* **1** so valuable that it is difficult to give a financial value 极其贵重的; 无价的: *priceless antiques* 极其贵重的古董 **2** a quality or skill that is priceless is extremely important or useful〔品质或技能〕极其重要的, 极其有用的: *The ability to motivate people is a priceless asset.* 能够激发人们的积极性是难能可贵的优点。**3** *informal* extremely funny or silly【非正式】极其荒唐的, 极其可笑的: *The look on his face when I walked in was priceless.* 我走进来时他脸上的表情极为可笑。

price list /ˈ· ·/ *n* [C] a list of prices for things being sold 价目表, 价格单

pric·es and in·comes pol·i·cy /,··· ˈ·· ,···/ *n* [C] government actions to prevent prices and incomes increasing, in order to stop or limit INFLATION 价格和收入政策〔政府为避免或限制通货膨胀而阻止价格和收入增加的措施〕

price sup·port /ˈ· ·,·/ *n* [U] a system in which the government keeps the price of a product at a fixed level by giving the producer money or buying the product itself〔政府以给制造商补贴或收购等形式给予的〕价格支持, 物价补贴

price tag /ˈ· ·/ *n* [C] **1** a small ticket showing the price of something 价格标签 **2** the amount that something costs 价格, 价值, 费用: *It's difficult to put a price tag on such a project.* 很难确定这样的项目将耗资多少。

price war /ˈ· ·/ *n* [C] a period when two or three companies reduce the prices of what they sell, all trying to get the most customers 价格战

pric·ey, pricy /ˈpraɪsɪ; ˈpraɪsi/ *adj* **pricier, priciest** *informal* expensive【非正式】昂贵的, 价钱高的: *New books are pretty pricey nowadays.* 如今的新书相当贵。

prick 刺(破), 戳(穿), 扎(穿)

prick¹ /prɪk; prɪk/ *v* **1** [T] to make a small hole in something, using a sharp point 刺(破), 戳(穿), 扎(穿): *Prick the pastry lightly with a fork.* 用叉子轻轻地在油酥面团上扎孔。| **prick yourself/prick your finger** *Ouch! I've pricked my finger with the needle.* 哎哟! 我的手指被针扎了一下。**2** [I,T] to feel an unpleasant stinging feeling on your skin, or to make someone feel this (使)感到刺痛: **prick sth** *The coarse material was beginning to prick my whole body.* 这种粗糙的布料开始使我全身感到刺痛。—see also 另见 PRICKLE² (1) **3 prick sb's conscience** to make someone feel guilty or ashamed 使某人的良心受到谴责, 使某人的良心不安: *a documentary that should prick the consciences of the comfortable middle classes* 会使舒适的中产阶级良心不安的记录片 **4 prick (up) its ears** if an animal pricks up its ears it raises them and points them towards a sound〔动物〕竖起耳朵听: *The rabbit stopped suddenly, pricking up its ears.* 那只兔子突然停下来, 竖起耳朵听。**5 prick (up) your ears** to listen carefully because you have heard something interesting〔人〕仔细倾听: *Jay pricked up his ears when I mentioned vacation.* 我提到假期时, 杰伊竖起耳朵仔细地听。**6 prick the bubble (of sth)** to make someone see the uncomfortable truth of a situation 使〔对某事物的〕幻想破灭

prick sth **out** *phr v* [T] to place a young plant in a specially prepared hole 把〔幼苗〕移植到专门挖好的坑中

prick² *n* [C]

1 ▶PAIN 疼痛◀ a slight pain you get when something sharp goes into your skin 刺痛: *Don't worry, it's just a little needle prick.* 别担心, 只是有点刺痛感。

2 ▶SMALL HOLE 小洞◀ **a)** a small hole made by a sharp point in your skin or the surface of something 刺孔; 刺痕; 刺点: *A sample of blood was drawn from a prick in the skin.* 从皮肤的刺孔采集了血样。**b)** an act of pricking something 刺, 戳; 扎: *Give the sausages a prick.* 在那些香肠上扎孔。—see also 另见 PINPRICK

3 ▶SEX ORGAN 性器官◀ *slang taboo* a PENIS【俚, 讳】阴茎

4 ▶PERSON 人◀ *slang taboo* a stupid unpleasant man【俚, 讳】蠢材, 笨蛋; 讨厌的家伙

5 prick of conscience an uncomfortable feeling that you have done something wrong 良心的不安

6 a prick of light a small point or circle of light 小光点, 小光圈

prick·le¹ /ˈprɪkḷ; ˈprɪkəl/ *n* [C] **1** a long thin sharp point on the skin of some plants and animals〔动植物的〕皮刺; 刺, 棘 **2** a stinging feeling on your skin〔皮肤上的〕刺痛感: *prickles of perspiration* 汗水的刺痛感

prickle² *v* **1** [T] to give someone a stinging feeling on their skin 引起刺痛: *The bush prickled the back of his legs.* 这种灌木刺痛了他双腿后部。**2** [I] if your skin prickles it begins to sting or feel cold because you are very frightened, angry etc〔由于非常害怕、生气等皮肤〕感到刺痛, 感到发冷: *The skin on the back of her neck prickled as she heard the door creak open.* 她听到门吱的一声打开时, 后颈直起鸡皮疙瘩。| **prickle with anger/excitement etc** (=to feel strong anger, excitement etc) 感到非常生气/兴奋等 *She spoke brusquely, prickling with an increasing dislike of Damien Flint.* 她说话粗鲁, 对达米恩·弗林特感到越来越讨厌。

prick·ly /ˈprɪklɪ; ˈprɪkli/ *adj* **1** covered with prickles 布满刺的, 多刺的: *Prickly brambles grew on either side of the path.* 那条小路两边长着多刺的灌木。**2** *informal* someone who is prickly gets annoyed or offended easily【非正式】〔人〕易生气的, 易动怒的: *Fiona's in a very prickly mood this morning.* 菲奥纳今天

早上动不动就发火。**3** something prickly makes you feel a small stinging sensation on your skin 引起刺痛的: *a prickly woollen sweater* 使皮肤感到刺痛的毛线衣 | **a prickly feeling** *I've got a prickly feeling in my leg.* 我的一条腿感到发麻。**4** causing problems, disagreements, and difficulties 棘手的, 难处理的: *Nuclear power is still a prickly issue.* 核能仍然是一个棘手的问题。—**prickliness** *n* [U]

prickly heat /,·· '·/ *n* [U] a skin condition caused by strong sunlight that consists of uncomfortable red spots on the skin 〔皮肤上的〕痱子

prickly pear /,·· '·/ *n* [C,U] a kind of CACTUS with yellow flowers, or the fruit of this plant 仙人果 (的果实)

pric·y /ˈpraɪsi; ˈpraɪsi/ *adj* another spelling of PRICEY pricey 的另一种拼法

3 3 **pride¹** /praɪd; praɪd/ *n* [U]

1 ▶FEELING OF PLEASURE 愉快的感觉◀ a feeling of satisfaction and pleasure in what you have done, or in what someone connected with you has done 自豪 (感); 得意: **show/feel/take pride in (doing) sth** *The employees all show great pride in their company.* 所有的雇员都对公司感到非常自豪。| *She takes pride in doing a job well.* 她为能很好地完成一项工作而感到自豪。| **show/feel/take (a) pride in sth** *Scott takes a great pride in his appearance.* 斯科特为自己的相貌深感自豪。| **a glow of pride** (=pride that is very clearly shown) 明显的自豪 | **with pride** *They talked about their son with obvious pride.* 他们带着明显的自豪感谈论他们的儿子。

2 ▶RESPECT 尊敬◀ a feeling that you like and respect yourself and that you deserve to be respected by other people 自尊(心): **hurt sb's pride** *Don't offer her money, you'll hurt her pride.* 别提出要给她钱, 你会伤害她的自尊心的。| **give sb their pride back** *Getting a job gave Sam his pride back.* 找到一份工作使萨姆重新获得了自尊。

3 ▶TOO MUCH PRIDE 过分的自尊◀ a feeling that you are better than other people because you are cleverer, more important etc 骄傲, 傲慢: *His pride would not allow him to ask for help.* 他自尊心作祟, 不会向别人求助。

4 sb's pride and joy someone or something that someone is very proud of, and that is important to them 某人的快乐和骄傲: *The garden is my father's pride and joy.* 这个花园是我爸爸的快乐和骄傲。

5 the pride of a) the thing or person that the people in a particular place are most proud of …引为自豪的人[事物]: *Wigan's rugby team was the pride of the town.* 威根的橄榄球队是镇里的骄傲。**b)** the best thing in a group 〔一组中〕最好的事物: *This Japanese sword is the pride of my collection.* 这把日本刀是我收藏品中的精品。

6 have/take pride of place to have the most important position in a group 占据最重要的位置: *A huge birthday cake took pride of place on the table.* 桌子上最显眼的位置放着一个巨大的生日蛋糕。

7 swallow your pride/put your pride in your pocket to forget your feelings of pride and do something that seems necessary, although you do not want to do it 放下你的架子: *Jerry swallowed his pride and apologised.* 杰里放下架子道了歉。

8 a group of lions 狮群: *A young lion had strayed some distance from the pride.* 在与狮群有一段距离的地方有一只幼狮离了群。

pride² *v* **pride yourself on sth** to be especially proud of something that you do well, or of a quality that you have 以某事物而自豪, 对某事物感到得意: *The school prides itself on its academic record.* 这所学校为它的学术成就感到自豪。

Pride and Prej·u·dice /,· · '· · ·/ (1813) a NOVEL by Jane Austen about Mr and Mrs Bennet and their daughters. The most important characters are Elizabeth Bennet, a clever and amusing young woman, and the rich, attractive Mr Darcy, who finally realize that they love each other, although previously Elizabeth thought that Darcy was too proud, and he thought that she disliked him without any good reason. The first sentence of *Pride and Prejudice* is one of the most famous sentences in English literature: "It is a truth universally acknowledged, that a single man in possession of a good fortune must be in want of a wife". 《傲慢与偏见》〔(1813), 简·奥斯汀创作的一部小说, 讲述贝内特夫妇及其女儿的故事。小说中最重要的人物是智趣的姑娘伊丽莎白·贝内特和富有迷人的达西先生, 两人最终意识到彼此是相爱的, 虽然之前伊丽莎白认为达西过于傲慢, 达西以为伊丽莎白莫名其妙地讨厌自己。小说开首是英国文学中的名句: "有钱的单身男子必定想娶位太太, 这是条举世公认的真理。"〕

3 **priest** /prist; priːst/ *n* [C] **1** someone who is specially trained to perform religious duties and ceremonies in the Christian church 〔基督教的〕牧师 **2** a man with religious duties and responsibilities in some non-Christian religions 〔基督教之外一些宗教的〕神职人员

USAGE NOTE 用法说明: PRIEST

WORD CHOICE 词语辨析: **priest, clergyman, clergy, minister, pastor, chaplain, padre**

A **priest** is someone in charge of the prayers, services etc for the people who attend a particular church, especially in the Roman Catholic Church. priest 指为参加某个教会的人们主持祈祷、宗教仪式的人, 尤在罗马天主教教会中使用。

A priest in a Protestant church is often called a **minister**, and this is the most usual word in American English. A **vicar** is a priest who is in charge of a church in the Church of England. In the US **pastor** is also used for someone in charge of a particular church in the Protestant religion. 在新教教会中, priest 常称作 minister, minister 在美国英语中是最常用的词。vicar 指在英国国教中负责某个教会的牧师。在美国, pastor 也用来指负责某个新教教会的人。

More general words for priests include **the clergy, clergymen**, or a **clergyman**. 表示神职人员的较笼统的词语包括 the clergy, clergymen, 或 a clergyman: *talks between education chiefs and the clergy* 教育长官和牧师之间的对话 | *She married an impoverished clergyman.* 她嫁给了一个贫穷的牧师。

A priest who looks after the religious needs of an organization such as a university, hospital, or prison is a **chaplain**. A priest who looks after the religious needs of soldiers in the army, navy etc, is also called a **chaplain**, but can also be called a **padre**. 负责大学、医院或监狱等机构宗教需求的神职人员称为 chaplain。负责陆军、海军等士兵的宗教需求的神职人员也称作 chaplain, 但也可称作 padre。

priest·ess /ˈpristɪs; ˈpriːstes/ *n* [C] a woman with religious duties and responsibilities in some non-Christian religions 〔基督教之外一些宗教的〕女神职人员

priest·hood /ˈpristhʊd; ˈpriːsthʊd/ *n* **1 the priesthood** the job or position of a priest 神职人员的工作, 神职人员的职位: *He decided to enter the priesthood.* 他决定成为神父。**2** [C,U] all the priests of a particular religion or country 〔某一宗教或国家的〕全体神职人员

Priest·ley /ˈpristlɪ; ˈpriːstli/, **J. B.** (1894-1984) a British writer of NOVELS, such as *The Good Companions*, and plays, such as *An Inspector Calls* and *Dangerous Corner* 普里斯特利〔(1894-1984), 英国作家。代表作有小说《好伙伴》和剧本《巡官登门》、《危险角落》等〕

priest·ly /ˈpristlɪ; ˈpriːstli/ *adj* connected with a priest 神职人员的, 牧师的: *priestly garments* 牧师袍

prig /prɪg; prɪg/ *n* [C] someone who obeys moral rules very carefully, and shows in an annoying way that they think they are better than other people 一本正经的人; 道学先生 —**priggish** *adj* —**priggishness** *n* [U]

prim /prɪm; prɪm/ *adj* **1** very formal and careful in the way you behave, and easily shocked by anything rude 一本正经的, 拘谨的, 古板的: *a prim and studious manner* 古板认真的样子 | **prim and proper** *Andy's much too prim and proper to enjoy your jokes.* 安迪太古板了, 不会喜欢你开的那些玩笑。**2** small and neat 小而整洁的: *a prim apron* 整洁的围裙 —**primly** *adv* —**primness** *n* [U]

pri·ma bal·le·ri·na /ˈprimə ˌbæləˋrinə; ˌpriːmə bæləˈriːnə/ *n* [C] the main woman dancer in a BALLET company 芭蕾舞团的主要[首席]女演员

pri·ma·cy /ˈpraɪməsɪ; ˈpraɪməsi/ *n* [U] *formal* the state of being the most important thing or person【正式】第一位, 首位, 首要: [+over] *the primacy of practical skill over theoretical knowledge* 实际技能重于理论知识

prima don·na /ˌprimə ˋdɑnə; ˌpriːmə ˈdɒnə/ *n* [C] **1** the most important woman singer in an OPERA company 歌剧团的主要[首席]女歌手 **2** someone who thinks that they are very good at what they do, and demands a lot of attention, admiration etc from other people 自以为了不起的人, 妄自尊大的人: *In my view, football players are a bunch of overpaid pampered prima donnas.* 依我看, 足球运动员是一帮收入过高、被宠坏了的自大的家伙。

pri·mae·val /praɪˋmivl; praɪˈmiːvəl/ *adj* a British spelling of PRIMEVAL primeval 的英式拼法

pri·ma fa·cie /ˌpraɪmə ˋfeʃɪ; ˌpraɪmə ˈfeɪʃi/ *adj Latin law* [only before noun 仅用于名词前] based on what seems to be true, even though it may be disproved later【拉丁, 法律】表面上的; 貌似真实的, 建立在表象基础上的: *a prima facie case against him* 表面证据对他不利的案件 —**prima facie** *adv*

3 **pri·mal** /ˈpraɪml; ˈpraɪməl/ *adj* [only before noun 仅用于名词前] *formal*【正式】**1** primal feelings seem to belong to a part of people's character that is ancient and animal-like 最初的, 原始的: *man's primal urge to explore the unknown* 人类探索未知世界的原始冲动 **2** basic 基本的, 根本的: *the primal truths of human existence* 人类生活的基本真理

3 **pri·ma·ri·ly** /ˈpraɪˌmɛrəlɪ; ˈpraɪmərəli/ *adv* mainly 主要地: *This research is concerned primarily with prevention of the disease.* 这项研究主要关注的是疾病的预防。

3 2 **pri·ma·ry**[1] /ˈpraɪˌmɛrɪ; ˈpraɪməri/ *adj* **1** most important; main 首要的, 主要的: *Our primary concern is to provide the refugees with food and health care.* 我们关注的首要问题是给难民提供食物和保健护理。| *a matter of primary importance* 至关重要的问题 **2 primary school/teacher/level etc** concerning the education of children between five and eleven years old 小学/小学教师/初级水平等; ELEMENTARY (3) *AmE*【美】: *a primary teacher* 小学教师 | *at primary level* 处于初级水平 **3** happening or developing before other things 原始的; 最初的

primary[2] *n* [C] **1** *technical* one of the longest feathers on a bird's wing【术语】〔鸟的〕初级飞羽〔指鸟翼上最长的羽毛〕**2** a primary election 初选

primary col·our /ˌ···ˈ··/ *n* [C] one of the three colours red, yellow, and blue, which you can mix together to make any of the other colours 原色, 基色〔指红、黄、蓝三色〕

primary e·lec·tion /ˌ··· ·ˈ··/ *n* [C] an election in the US at which members of a political party in one area vote to decide who will be their party's CANDIDATE for a political position〔美国推举党内候选人的〕初选

primary health care /ˌ···ˈ··/ also 又作 **primary med·i·cal care** /ˌ···ˈ···ˈ·/ *n* [U] the medical care that someone receives first when they become ill or have an accident 最初保健护理

primary school /ˈ··· ˌ·/ *n* [C] *BrE* a school for children between five and eleven years old in England and Wales【英】〔英格兰和威尔士5至11岁儿童上的〕小学; ELEMENTARY SCHOOL *AmE*【美】

primary stress /ˌ···ˈ·/ *n* [C,U] *technical* the strongest force given in speech to a part of a long word, like the force given to 'pri' in 'primary'. It is shown in this dictionary by the mark (ˈ).【术语】主重音, 第一重音

Pri·mate /ˈpraɪmɪt; ˈpraɪmɪ̈t/ *n* [C] the most important and powerful priest in a country or an area, especially in the Church of England; ARCHBISHOP〔尤指英国国教的〕大主教

pri·mate /ˈpraɪmet; ˈpraɪmeɪt/ *n* [C] a member of the group of MAMMALS that includes humans and monkeys 灵长目动物〔包括人、猴子等〕

prime[1] /praɪm; praɪm/ *adj* [only before noun 仅用于名词前] **1** most important 最重要的, 首要的: *Smoking is the prime cause of heart disease.* 抽烟是引发心脏病的首要原因。| *Our prime concern is getting the economy back on its feet.* 我们关注的首要问题是恢复经济。**2** of the very best quality or kind 质量最好的, 第一流的: *The hotel is in a prime location overlooking the valley.* 这个酒店俯瞰山谷, 位置极佳。| *prime cuts of beef* 上等牛肉切块 **3 be a prime candidate/target etc** to be the person or thing that is most suitable or most likely to be chosen for a particular purpose 最适合的[最有可能被选中的]人[物]: *The railways are a prime candidate for privatization.* 铁路最有可能私有化。**4 prime example** a very typical example of something 最好的例证, 非常典型的例子: *Sherlock Holmes is the prime example of the great detective.* 夏洛克·福尔摩斯是伟大侦探的杰出典型。

prime[2] *n* **1 be in your prime/be in the prime of life** to be at the time in your life when you are strongest and most active 正值盛年, 在壮年时期, 风华正茂: **past your prime** *Sadly I think the team are past their prime.* 很遗憾, 我认为这个队的最佳时期已经过去。| **be cut off in your prime** (=die when you are in your prime) 英年早逝 **2** [C] a PRIME NUMBER 质数, 素数

prime[3] *v* [T] **1** [usually passive 一般用被动态] to prepare someone for a situation so that they know what to do 使〔某人〕准备好〔应付某个情况〕: *I felt fully primed by the day of the meeting.* 到了会面的那天, 我感到完全作好了准备。| **prime sb to do sth** *The witness had been primed to say nothing about the car.* 那名证人受人指使过, 要对有关汽车的事只字不提。| **prime sb for sth** *primed for action* 准备行动 **2** to prepare a gun or mine so that it can fire or explode 为〔枪〕装填火药; 为〔地雷〕装雷管 **3** to put a special layer of paint on a surface, to prepare it for the next layer 在…上涂底漆[底色] **4 prime the pump** to encourage a business, industry, or activity to develop by putting money or effort into it 投入资金[精力]促使〔某企业、产业或活动〕得到发展

prime cost /ˌ·ˈ·/ *n* [C,U] the actual cost of producing something as opposed to money spent on selling it, renting factories etc 主要成本, 直接成本〔指生产商品的实际成本〕—compare 比较 OVERHEAD[2] (1)

prime fac·tor /ˌ·ˈ··/ *n* [C] a number that can be divided only by itself and the number one, and is a FACTOR of another number 质因数, 质因子: *7 is a prime factor of 21.* 7是21的质因数。

Prime Me·rid·i·an /ˌ·ˈ····/ *n* the imaginary line drawn from north to south on the earth, from which east and west are measured in degrees on a map 本初子午线〔从地球北部到南部设定的一条假想线。地图上是从本初子午线起分别向东和向西计量经度的〕

Prime Min·is·ter /ˌ·ˈ···/ abbreviation 缩写为 **PM** *n* [C] the chief minister and leader of the government in some countries with a parliamentary system of government 首相; 总理

Prime Minister's Ques·tion Time /ˌ·ˈ···ˈ···ˌ·/ a period of time each week when any member of the British House of Commons may ask the Prime Minister questions. There are often loud and angry disagreements during Question Time, which are broadcast on radio and television. 质询首相时间〔英国下议院议员每周向首相提问的时间。议员提问、首相应答期间常会有怒不可遏的大声争吵, 这些都会在广播和电视中播出〕

prime mov·er /ˌ·ˈ··/ *n* [C] **1** someone who has great influence in the development of something important 对某重要事业的发展有很大影响的人; 倡导者, 推动者: *She's one of the prime movers in the Republican movement.* 她是共和运动的发起者之一。**2** *technical* a natural force, such as wind or water, that can be used to produce power【术语】原动力〈如风力或水力〉

prime num·ber /ˌ·ˈ··/ *n* [C] a number that can be divided only by itself and the number one 质数, 素数

prim·er[1] /ˈpraɪmɚ; ˈpraɪmə/ *n* **1** [C,U] paint that is spread over the bare surface of wood, metal etc before the main covering of paint is put on 涂底料, 底层涂料; 底漆 **2** [C] a tube containing explosive, used to fire a gun, explode a bomb etc 雷管; 火帽 **3** [C] *BrE old-fashioned* a beginner's book in a school subject【英, 过时】入门书, 初级读本

pri·mer[2] /ˈprɪmɚ; ˈpraɪmə/ *n* [C] *AmE* a set of basic instructions【美】入门指南: *a primer of good management* 成功管理入门指南

prime rate /ˈ· ˌ·/ *n* [C] the lowest rate of interest at which money can be borrowed, which banks offer to their largest customers〔银行给最大客户提供的〕优惠贷款利率, 最低贷款利率 —compare 比较 BASE RATE

prime rib /ˌ·ˈ·/ *n* [singular, U] a piece of good quality BEEF that is cut from the chest of the animal 上等肋条牛肉

prime time /ˈ· ˌ·/ *n* [U] *especially AmE* the time in the evening when the greatest number of people are watching television【尤美】〔电视的〕黄金时间, 收视高峰时间

pri·me·val also 又作 **primaeval** *especially BrE*【尤英】/praɪˈmivl; praɪˈmiːvəl/ *adj* **1** belonging to the earliest period in the existence of the universe or the Earth 太古的, 太初的: *Primeval clouds of gas formed themselves into stars.* 太初的气团发展成为星球。**2** very ancient 原始的, 远古的: *primeval forests* 原始森林 **3** primeval emotions or attitudes are very strong, and seem to come from a part of people's character that is ancient and animal-like〔感情或态度〕出于人之原始天性的, 基于人类固有之本能的

prim·i·tive[1] /ˈprɪmətɪv; ˈprɪmɪ̈tɪv/ *adj* **1** belonging to a society that has a very simple way of life, without modern industries and machines 原始的, 远古的: *primitive tools made from stones and animal bones* 用石头和兽骨制成的原始工具 | *primitive art* 原始艺术 **2** belonging to an early stage of the development of humans, or of plants or animals〔人类或动植物〕原始的; 早期的: *primitive man* 原始人 | *a primitive fish* 原始鱼 **3** very simple when compared to modern things 简陋的, 粗糙的, 简单的: *primitive machinery* 简陋的机械 | *The house was primitive, with an earthen floor and mud walls.* 那所房子是泥土地面、泥墙, 很简陋。**4** old-fashioned and uncomfortable 过时的; 老式的; 简陋的; 不舒适的: *Conditions at a lot of our football stadiums are primitive.* 我们许多足球场的条件非常简陋。—**primitively** *adv* —**primitiveness** *n* [U]

primitive[2] *n* **1** someone who comes from a simple society and is not used to modern machines and modern ways of life 原始人 **2** a painter who paints simple pictures like those of a child 原始派画家 **3** a painter or SCULPTOR of the time before the Renaissance 文艺复兴时期以前的画家[雕塑家]

pri·mo·gen·i·ture /ˌpraɪməˈdʒɛnətʃɚ; ˌpraɪməʊˈdʒenɪ̈tʃə/ *n* [U] *technical* the system by which property owned by a man goes to his eldest son after his death【术语】长子继承制[权]

pri·mor·di·al /praɪˋmɔrdɪəl; praɪˈmɔːdiəl/ *adj formal*【正式】**1** existing at the beginning of time or the beginning of the Earth 原始的, 原始时代存在的; 太古的, 太初的: *the primordial seas* 原始海洋 **2** in the simplest form 形式最简单的, 基本的: *primordial passions* 最基本的情感 **3 primordial soup** the mixture of substances, gases etc thought to have existed before the beginning of life on Earth 原生浆液〔据认为地球上生命开始之前存在的物质、气体等混合物〕—**primordially** *adv*

primp /prɪmp; prɪmp/ *v* [I,T] to make yourself look attractive by arranging your hair, putting on MAKE-UP etc 梳妆打扮: *primping in front of the mirror* 在镜子前梳妆打扮

prim·rose /ˋprɪm,roz; ˈprɪmrəʊz/ *n* **1** [C] a small wild plant with light yellow flowers, or the flower from this plant 报春花 **2** [U] primrose yellow 报春花色, 淡黄色 **3 the primrose path** *literary* a way of life full of pleasure that harms the soul【文】贪图享乐使人堕落的道路

primrose yel·low /,‥ˋ‥◂/ *n* [U] a light yellow colour 淡黄色 —**primrose yellow, primrose** *adj*

prim·u·la /ˋprɪmjulə; ˈprɪmjʊlə/ *n* [C] a plant of the primrose family with brightly coloured flowers 报春花属植物

Pri·mus /ˋpraɪməs; ˈpraɪməs/ also 又作 **primus stove** /ˋ‥ ˌ/ *n* [C] *trademark BrE* a small STOVE (=a piece of equipment for cooking) that burns oil and can be easily carried around【商标, 英】普赖默斯便携式煤油炉

3 **prince** /prɪns; prɪns/ *n* [C] **1** the son of a king or queen, or one of their close male relatives 王子; 亲王; 王孙; 王室男成员: *Prince Albert* 艾伯特亲王 **2** a male ruler of a small country or state〔小国的〕国君, 君主: *Prince Rainier of Monaco* 摩纳哥国王雷尼尔 **3** the best man in a group〔一组中〕最好的男人: **the prince of/a prince among** *a prince among waiters* 男侍应生中的佼佼者 **4 merchant prince** someone who has become very rich in business 商业巨头; 商业巨子

Prince, The (1532) a book by Machiavelli which discusses what a ruler should do in order to gain and keep power and be an effective ruler, even if this means being cruel, dishonest, or immoral《君主论》〔(1532), 马基雅弗利的一部著作。该书探讨统治者获得政权、维护统治并成为卓有成效的君主应采取的手段, 即使是残酷的、欺诈的或不道德的手段〕

Prince Albert —see 见 Prince ALBERT

Prince Andrew —see 见 Prince ANDREW

Prince Charles —see 见 Prince CHARLES

Prince Charm·ing /,‥ˋ‥/ *n* [C] *informal or humorous* a perfect man who a young girl might dream about meeting【非正式或幽默】〔少女理想中的〕完美男子, 白马王子

prince con·sort /,‥ˋ‥/ *n* [C] a title sometimes given to the husband of a ruling queen 女王[女皇]的丈夫, 王夫

prince·dom /ˋprɪnsdəm; ˈprɪnsdəm/ *n* [C usually singular 一般用单数] *formal* a country ruled by a prince; PRINCIPALITY【正式】公国, 侯国; 封邑

Prince Edward —see 见 Prince EDWARD

Prince Ed·ward Is·land /,‥ˋ‥,‥/ a PROVINCE in southeast Canada that is an island in the Gulf of St Lawrence 爱德华王子岛〔加拿大东南部一省, 圣劳伦斯湾一岛屿〕

Prince Harry —see 见 Prince HARRY

prince·ly /ˋprɪnslɪ; ˈprɪnsli/ *adj* **1 princely sum** an expression meaning a large amount of money, often used jokingly to mean a very small amount of money 一大笔钱〔通常开玩笑地用来表示很少的钱〕: *My Dad offered me the princely sum of ten pence to wash his car!* 我爸爸给了我10便士的巨款让我帮他洗车! **2** *formal* fine, splendid, or generous【正式】精美的; 壮观的; 堂皇的; 慷慨的: *a princely gift* 精美的礼物 | *a princely man* 慷慨的男人 **3** belonging to or connected with a prince 王子的, 亲王的; 属于王子[亲王]的: *the princely states* 由王公贵族统治的小国[公国, 侯国]

Prince of Dark·ness, the /,‥ˋ‥/ a poetic name for the Devil 撒旦; 魔鬼〔诗歌用语〕

Prince of Peace, the /,‥ˋ/ a poetic name for Jesus Christ 救世主; 耶稣基督〔诗歌用语〕

Prince of Wales, the /,‥ˋ/ *n* a title given to the first son of a British king or queen 威尔士亲王〔英王或英女王长子的封号〕

Prince Philip —see 见 the DUKE OF EDINBURGH

Prince Re·gent, the /,‥ˋ‥/ the son of the British king George III, who was also called George and acted as king from 1811 to 1820 because his father was mentally ill. This period of British history is called 'the Regency'. When George III died in 1820, the Prince Regent became King George IV. 摄政王〔英王乔治三世之子, 1811-1820年期间因父王患有精神病而代理国王一职。英国历史上的这一时期被称做"摄政时期"。1820年乔治三世去世后, 摄政王即为乔治四世〕

Princes in the Tow·er, the /,‥‥ˋ‥/ the English boy king Edward V and his brother Richard, who in 1483 were put in prison in the Tower of London by their uncle, who later became King Richard III. Many people believe that Richard ordered the two boys to be murdered. 塔中王子〔指英国的少年国王爱德华五世及其弟弟理查德。他俩于1483年被叔叔——即后来的英王理查三世关进伦敦塔。许多人认为这两个男孩是理查三世下令杀死的〕

prin·cess /ˋprɪnsɪs; ,prɪnˈses◂/ *n* [C] **1** a close female relation of a king and queen, especially a daughter 公主; 王室女成员: *Princess Anne* 安妮公主 **2** the wife of a prince 王妃; 亲王夫人: *Princess Diana* 戴安娜王妃

Princess and the Pea, The /,‥‥ˋ/ a FAIRY TALE by Hans Christian Andersen in which a young woman proves that she is a princess by noticing that there is a PEA (=a small round green vegetable) under the pile of MATTRESSes she has been sleeping on. A queen has put the pea under her bed as a test to see if the young woman will feel it, because only a real princess would be so delicate that she would notice a small pea. As a result, the queen allows the young woman to marry her son, a prince.《公主与豌豆》〔安徒生创作的一则童话故事。故事中有一个姑娘, 她察觉到自己睡的床垫下有一粒豌豆, 并以此证明了她的公主身份。原来, 王后预先在她的床下放了一粒豌豆, 以检验姑娘能否感觉得出来, 因为唯有真正的公主才细致入微, 才可觉察到小豌豆的存在。最后, 王后终于同意姑娘跟王子结婚〕

Princess Anne —see 见 Princess ANNE

Princess Diana —see 见 Princess of Wales DIANA

Princess Margaret —see 见 Princess MARGARET

Princess of Wales /,‥ˋ/ —see 见 Princess of Wales DIANA

Princess Roy·al, the /,‥ˋ‥/ a title that is given to the eldest daughter of a British king or queen. Princess Anne was given the title by her mother, Queen Elizabeth II, in 1987. 大公主〔授予英王或英女王长女的封号。安妮公主于1987年由母亲伊丽莎白二世女王授予此封号〕

Princes Street /ˋ‥ ˌ/ the main street in Edinburgh, Scotland, with many shops and banks 王子街〔苏格兰爱丁堡市内一主要街道。街上有许多商店和银行〕

Prince·ton U·ni·ver·si·ty /,prɪnstn junəˋvɝsətɪ; ,prɪnstən juːnɪˈvɜːsɪti/ a private university in Princeton, New Jersey which is one of the oldest and most respected universities in the US and is part of the Ivy League 普林斯顿大学〔位于新泽西州普林斯顿的一所私立大学。它是美国历史最悠久、最负盛名的大学之一, 也是常春藤联合会成员之一〕

Prince William —see 见Prince WILLIAM

prin·ci·pal¹ /ˋprɪnsəpl; ˈprɪnsɪpəl/ *adj* [only before noun 仅用于名词前] most important; main 最重要的, 首要的; 主要的: *My principal source of income is teaching.* 我主要的收入来源是教学。| *The principal character in the book is called Scarlett.* 这本书的主人公叫斯卡利特。—see also 另见 PRINCIPALLY 2

principal² *n* **1** [singular] *technical* an amount of money lent to someone, put into a business etc, on which INTEREST is paid【术语】本金; 资本 **2** [C] *AmE* someone who is in charge of a school【美】〔中小学的〕校长; HEAD TEACHER *BrE*【英】**3** [C] *especially BrE* someone who is in charge of a university, college, or school【尤英】〔大学、学院或中小学的〕校长 **4** [C] the main performer in a play, group of musicians etc〔戏剧、音乐等演出的〕主角, 主要演员 **5** [C often plural 常用复数] a person for whom you are acting as a representative, especially in business〔代理关系中的〕委托人, 本人, 被代理人: *I will have to consult my principals before I can give you an answer on that.* 我得同我的委托人商量后才能就这个问题给你答复。

principal boy /,‥ˋ/ *n* [C] *BrE* the main male character in a PANTOMIME, usually played by a young woman【英】〔童话剧中的〕男主角〔通常由年轻女子扮演〕

prin·ci·pal·i·ty /,prɪnsəˋpælətɪ; ,prɪnsɪˈpælɪti/ *n* [C] a country ruled by a PRINCE 公国, 侯国; 封邑

Principality, the *BrE* another name for Wales, used especially by politicians and in news reports【英】威尔士〔Wales的别称, 尤为政治家及新闻报道所使用〕

prin·ci·pally /ˋprɪnsəplɪ; ˈprɪnsɪpli/ *adv* mainly 主要地: *The money is principally invested in government stock.* 这笔钱主要投资于政府债券上。

principal parts /,‥ˋ/ *n* [plural] *technical* the parts of a verb from which other parts are formed in English; the INFINITIVE, past tense, present participle, past participle【术语】〔动词的〕主要变形〔指英语动词的不定式、过去式、现在分词、过去分词〕

prin·ci·ple /ˈprɪnsəpl; ˈprɪnsḷpəl/ *n*
1 ►MORAL RULE 道德准则◄ **a)** [C,U] a moral rule or set of ideas which makes you behave in a particular way 道德, 操守, 准则, 为人之道: *She resigned on a matter of principle.* 她因原则性问题而辞职了。| **the principle of the thing** *spoken*【口】*You shouldn't just take the car without asking, it's the principle of the thing.* 你不应该不说一声就把车开走, 这是为人之道。| **on principle** (=because of a moral rule you follow) 由于道德准则 *I don't eat meat on principle.* 我出于道德准则而不吃肉。| **on the principle that** *We charge no fees on the principle that education should be available for all.* 我们不收取费用是出于每个人都应该受到教育的准则。**b)** strong ideas about what is morally right or wrong, that you try to follow in everything you do〔行为的〕准则, 规范: *He has no principles; he'll do anything, as long as it's profitable.* 他没有丝毫的道德准则, 只要有利可图, 他什么都会干。| **against sb's principles** (=morally wrong to that person) 违背某人的行为准则
2 ►RULES OF A PROCESS 某个过程的规则◄ **a)** [C] a rule which explains the way something such as a machine works, or which explains a natural force in the universe 原理; 定律: *the principle of the internal combustion engine* 内燃机的原理 | *Archimedes' principle* 阿基米德定律 **b) principles** *plural* the general rules on which a skill, science etc is based 基本原理: *Einstein's theories form the basic principles of modern physics.* 爱因斯坦的理论构成了现代物理学的基本原理。| **first principles** (=the most important and basic rules) 基本原则[原理]
3 ►BELIEF 信念◄ [C] a belief that is accepted as a reason for an action, way of thinking etc 原则; 信念: *the principle of free markets* 自由市场原则
4 man/woman of principle someone who has strong ideas about what is morally right or wrong 正直的男人/女人, 是非分明的人
5 in principle a) if something is possible in principle, there is no good reason why it should not happen, but it has not actually happened yet 按道理, 在理论上: *In principle you are entitled to a financial grant, but they're difficult to claim.* 按道理你有资格获得经济补助, 但是很难索取到。**b)** if you agree in principle, you agree about a general plan or idea without the details 原则上, 基本上, 大体上: *The scheme seems O.K. in principle, but I'd like to know more details.* 这项计划大体上还可以, 但我想知道更多细节。

prin·ci·pled /ˈprɪnsəpld; ˈprɪnsḷpəld/ *adj* **1** having a strong belief about what is morally right and wrong 原则性强的: *a principled woman* 原则性强的女人 **2** based on truths, beliefs or morals 原则性的; 依据行为准则的: *a principled distinction between physical and emotional injury* 身体伤害和感情伤害的原则性区别

print¹ /prɪnt; prɪnt/ *v*
1 a) ►WORDS BY MACHINE 机器印刷的文字◄ [I,T] to produce words, numbers, or pictures on paper, using a machine which puts ink onto the surface 印; 印刷: *That's what your letter's going to look like when it's printed.* 那就是你的信打印出来的样子。| *Press this key to print a copy of the text.* 按这个键打印一份文本。| **print sth on/across** *the address printed on the form* 印在表格上的地址 | **print sth in** *The menu was printed in Japanese and English.* 这份菜单是用日语和英语印制的。| *The word 'scandal' was printed in bold type.* scandal 一词是用粗体印刷的。| **be printed with** *cards printed with his name and address* 印着他的名字和地址的卡片 | **a printed card/acknowledgement/text etc** *You will receive a printed acknowledgement of your payment.* 你将收到一份打印的付款回执。| **the printed page/word** (=language in printed form) 打印页/打印文字 **b)** [I] to be printed by a computer〔电脑〕打印: *The document will print as it appears on the screen.* 该文件将如屏幕上显示的那样打印出来。
2 ►BOOKS/NEWSPAPERS 书/报纸◄ [T] to produce many copies of a book, newspaper etc in printed form 印刷, 印发〔书、报纸等〕: *the first cookery book to be printed in America* 将在美国印发的第一本烹饪书
3 ►IN A NEWSPAPER 在报纸上◄ [T] to print a letter, speech etc in a newspaper, magazine etc; PUBLISH〔在报章、杂志等上〕刊登, 刊载: *The Telegraph has printed numerous articles criticising these sales techniques.*《电讯报》已刊登了许多批评这些销售技巧的文章。| *If you print that, I'll sue you.* 要是你把它刊登出来, 我就控告你。
4 ►ON A SCREEN 在屏幕上◄ also 又作 **print sth out** [I,T] if a computer prints words and numbers on a screen it puts them there〔电脑屏幕上〕弹出〔文字、数字〕: *An error message is printed and the program ends.* 一条错误信息出现在屏幕上, 程序随即关闭。
5 ►PHOTOGRAPH 照片◄ [T] to produce a photograph from a photographic film 印制, 冲印〔相片〕: *The pictures have to be developed and printed.* 这些照片必须冲印。
6 ►CLOTH 布料◄ [T] to decorate cloth with a pattern put all over its surface by a machine 印图案于: **printed with** *a new sari printed with brown and violet flowers* 印有棕色和紫色花的新莎丽
7 print money if a government prints money, it produces too many bank notes in order to pay for something〔政府为支付某物而〕大量印发钞票
8 a licence to print money a way of making a lot of money easily 轻易赚大钱的门路: *This policy is a scandal – it's a licence to print money!* 这项政策是件丑闻 —— 它是为某些人捞大钱而制定的。
9 ►WRITE 写◄ [I,T] to write words by hand without joining the letters 用印刷体书写: *Please print your name.* 请用印刷体书写你的姓名。| **print sth in** *a thin brown envelope with the address printed in capitals* 印有大写字母地址的薄牛皮纸信封
10 ►MARK 印记◄ [T] to make a mark on a surface or in a soft substance by pressing something on to it 印上〔印痕〕: *The mark of the man's shoe was clearly printed in the mud.* 那名男子的鞋印清楚地印在泥地上。

print sth ↔ **off/out** *phr v* [T] to produce a printed copy of a computer document〔电脑〕打印出: *Once you've designed your poster, you can print off as many copies as you like.* 一旦设计好宣传海报, 你就可以喜欢打印多少份就打印多少份。

print² *n*
1 ►BOOKS/NEWSPAPERS 书/报纸◄ [U] writing that has been printed in books, newspapers etc 印刷品: *The information is available in many forms including print, microfilm, and CD-ROM.* 这些资料可以以多种形式获得, 包括印刷品、缩微胶卷和光盘。| **in print** (=printed in a book, newspaper etc) 已印出来, 已发表出来 *He believed everything he saw in print.* 凡是印出来的东西他都信以为真。| **see your name in print** *a politician who likes to see his name in print* 喜欢看见自己的名字出现在出版物中的政客 | **get into print** (=be printed) 付印; 发表 *It was the first of his stories to get into print.* 这是他发表的第一篇故事。| **get sth into print** (=have your work printed) 使某物发表 | **print unions/workers** (=those involved in printing newspapers, books etc) 印刷工人工会/印刷工人
2 be out of print if a book is out of print, it is no longer being printed and you cannot buy new copies〔书〕已绝版, 已停印: *This volume is now out of print.* 该卷现已绝版了。
3 be in print if a book is in print new copies of it are still being printed〔书〕仍可买到, 仍在印行: *Her book is still in print, a hundred years after its original publication.* 她的书在初版一百年之后仍在印刷。
4 ►LETTERS 字母◄ [U] the letters in which something is printed 印出的字;〔印刷用的〕字体: *books with large print for elderly people* 用大号字体为老年人印的书 | *This printer can produce high quality print.* 这台打印机打印质量很高。
5 the small/fine print the details of a legal document, often in very small writing〔法律文件的〕细节〔常常字体很小〕: *You should always read the small print before signing anything.* 在签署任何东西之前, 务必读一下用小号字印的细节。
6 ►MARK 印记◄ [C] a mark made on a surface or in a soft substance by something that has been pressed onto it 印记, 印痕: *His feet left prints in the soft soil.* 他在松软的泥土上留下了脚印。| *The children had decorated the walls with hand prints.* 孩子们用手印装饰了墙壁。
7 prints [plural] the marks made by the pattern of lines on the ends of your fingers; FINGERPRINTS 指纹
8 ►CLOTH 布料◄ [C,U] cloth, especially cotton, on which a coloured pattern has been printed 印花布〔尤指棉布〕: **a print dress/blouse** *She stood there in her print dress and white apron.* 她穿着印花布连衣裙、戴着白围裙站在那里。
9 ►PATTERN 图案◄ [C] the pattern printed on a piece of cloth〔织品上的〕印花, 图案: *The curtains were green with a print of sunflowers.* 窗帘是绿色的, 上面有向日葵印花。
10 ►PHOTOGRAPH 照片◄ [C] a photograph in the form of a picture that has been produced from a film〔印出的〕照片: *You get three sets of prints, plus a free film.* 你得到三套照片, 外加一个免费胶卷。
11 ►PICTURE 图片◄ [C] a picture that has been printed from a small sheet of metal or block of wood, or a copy of a painting produced by photography 印出的版画, 印出的木刻书;〔用摄影术制作的〕油画复制品

prin·ta·ble /ˈprɪntəbl; ˈprɪntəbəl/ *adj* suitable to be printed and read by everyone 可以印刷出版的; 适合大众阅读的: *Her*

remarks were scarcely printable (=were very rude). 她的话粗野得不适合刊出。—compare 比较 UNPRINTABLE

printed cir·cuit /ˌ· · ˈ· ·/ *n* [C] a set of connections between points in a piece of electrical equipment which uses a thin line of metal, not wire, to CONDUCT (=carry) the electricity 印制电路

printed mat·ter /ˈ· · ˌ· ·/ *n* [U] printed articles, such as advertisements, that can be sent by post at a cheap rate〔邮寄的〕印刷品

W3 **print·er** /ˈprɪntə; ˈprɪntə/ *n* [C] **1** a machine which is connected to a computer and makes a printed record of computer information〔与电脑连接的〕打印机 —compare 比较 PRINTING PRESS **2** someone employed in the trade of printing 印刷业从业人员, 印刷工人

printer's ink /ˈ· · ˌ·/ *n* [U] printing ink 打印机油墨

print·ing /ˈprɪntɪŋ; ˈprɪntɪŋ/ *n* **1** [U] the act or process of making a book, magazine, etc by pressing or copying letters or photographs onto paper 印刷(术): *the invention of printing* 印刷术的发明 | *a printing error* 印刷错误 **2** [C] an act of printing a number of copies of a book〔书的〕一次印刷: *the third printing* 第三次印刷

printing ink /ˈ· · ˌ·/ *n* [U] a type of ink that dries very quickly and is used in printing books and newspapers etc 打印机油墨

printing press /ˈ· · ˌ·/ also 又作 **printing machine** /ˈ· · · ˌ·/ *n* [C] a machine that prints newspapers, books etc; press 印刷机

print·out /ˈprɪntˌaut; ˈprɪntˌaʊt/ *n* [C,U] a sheet or length of paper with printed information on it, produced by a computer〔电脑〕打印出来的资料, 打印件

W3 **pri·or¹** /ˈpraɪə; ˈpraɪə/ *adj* **1 prior to** *formal* before【正式】在…之前; 先于: *All the arrangements should be completed prior to your departure.* 所有安排都应在你离开之前完成。| *Guests can relax in the lounge prior to entering the theatre.* 客人在进入剧院前可在大堂休息一会儿。**2 prior warning/notice/discussion etc** a warning etc happening before something else happens 预先警告/通知/讨论等: *The bomb exploded without any prior warning.* 炸弹没有任何预先警报就爆炸了。**3 prior agreement/arrangement etc** an arrangement made before the present situation 事先协议/安排等: *Under a prior agreement the company will sell the land in ten years time.* 根据事先协议, 该公司将在10年后卖掉这块土地。| **a prior engagement** *formal* (=something you have planned to do)【正式】预先的约会 *I won't be at the meeting as I have a prior engagement.* 由于我预先已有约会, 所以不能参加会议。

prior² *n* [C] **1** the man in charge of a PRIORY 小修道院男院长 **2** the priest next in rank to the person in charge of an ABBEY 大修道院副院长

pri·or·ess /ˈpraɪərɪs; ˈpraɪərɪ̵s/ *n* [C] the woman in charge of a PRIORY 小修道院女院长

pri·o·ri·tize also 又作 **-ise** *BrE*【英】/praɪˈɔrətaɪz; praɪˈɒrɪ̵taɪz/ *v* [T] **1** to put several things, problems etc in order of importance, so that you can deal with the most important ones first 按优先顺序列出; 确定〔事项、问题等的〕优先顺序: *Prioritize your tasks to ensure maximum efficiency.* 把你的工作按优先顺序列出, 以确保最高的效率。**2** to deal with one thing first, because it is the most important 优先考虑; 给…优先权: *The public wants to see the fight against crime prioritized.* 公众希望打击犯罪能得到优先考虑。—**prioritization** /praɪˌɑrətəˈzeʃən; praɪˌɒrɪ̵taɪˈzeɪʃən/ *n* [U]

S2 W2 **pri·or·i·ty** /praɪˈɔrətɪ; praɪˈɒrɪ̵ti/ *n* **1** [C] the thing that you think is most important and that needs attention before anything else 优先考虑的事: *First let's decide what our priorities are.* 首先让我们决定优先考虑的事项。| *Manufacturers are making safety a design priority.* 制造商以安全为产品设计中需要优先考虑的事项。| **top/high/low priority** (=important or unimportant thing) 应予以最优先考虑的事/非常重要的事/不重要的事 *Women's issues are often seen as a low priority.* 妇女问题常被看作不重要的事情。**2 have/take/get priority** also 又作 **be given priority** to be considered most important and dealt with before anything or anyone else 享有优先权: *If medical supplies are short, children will be given priorty.* 如果医疗供应品短缺的话, 儿童将得到优先考虑。| [**+over**] *Roosevelt decided that the war in Europe would take priority over the war in the Pacific.* 罗斯福认为当务之急是欧洲战争, 而不是太平洋战争。**3 get your priorities right** used to tell someone they should consider the most important things first 按照事情的轻重缓急行事: *Peter should get his priorities right and spend more time with his family.* 彼得应该按照轻重缓急, 花更多的时间与家人在一起。

pri·o·ry /ˈpraɪərɪ; ˈpraɪəri/ *n* a Christian religious house or group of MONKS or NUNS, (=men or women living a religious life) which is smaller and less important than an ABBEY〔基督教的〕小修道院; 女小修道院

prise /praɪz; praɪz/ *v* [T] a British spelling of PRIZE³ (2) prize³ (2) 的英式拼法

pris·m /ˈprɪzəm; ˈprɪzəm/ *n* [C] **1** a transparent block of glass that breaks up white light into different colours 棱镜 **2** *technical* a solid object with matching ends and several sides which are the same width all the way up【术语】棱柱(体)

pris·mat·ic /prɪzˈmætɪk; prɪzˈmætɪk/ *adj* **1** using or containing a PRISM 使用棱镜的; 含棱柱体的: *a prismatic compass*〔测量用〕棱镜罗盘 **2** a prismatic colour is very clear and bright〔颜色〕明亮的, 灿烂的

pris·on /ˈprɪzn̩; ˈprɪzən/ *n* **1** [C,U] a large building where people are kept as a punishment for a crime, or while waiting to go to court for their TRIAL¹ (1) 监狱; 看守所, 拘留所: *a maximum security prison* 防备措施最为严密的监狱 | *Forbes will be released from prison next week.* 福布斯将在下星期从狱中获释。| **in prison** (=being kept in prison) 在狱中 *Bates was sentenced to three years in prison.* 贝茨被判三年监禁。| **prison cell** (=a room where prisoners are locked up) 牢房 | **prison sentence** (=the length of time someone has to stay in prison) 监禁期, 服刑期 | **send sb to prison** (=to officially order someone to be in prison) 将某人投入监狱 *Dow was sent to prison for six years for rape.* 道由于强奸罪被判入狱六年。| **put sb in prison** *He will be put in prison for a very long time.* 他将被判处长期监禁。**2** [U] the system of sending people to be kept in a prison 监禁, 关押: *I don't believe that prison deters criminals from offending.* 我认为监禁并不能阻止罪犯犯罪。 S2 W2

prison camp /ˈ· · ˌ·/ *n* [C] a special prison in which PRISONERS OF WAR are kept 战俘营

pris·on·er /ˈprɪzn̩ə; ˈprɪzənə/ *n* [C] **1** someone who is kept in a prison as a punishment for a crime 犯人, 囚犯: *The prisoners are allowed an hour's exercise every day.* 囚犯获准每天活动一小时。**2** someone who is taken by force and kept somewhere, for example during a war 被拘押的人; 俘虏; 战俘: *enemy prisoners* 敌军俘虏 | *political prisoners* 政治犯 | **hold/keep sb prisoner** *The guerillas kept her prisoner for three months.* 游击队员将她囚禁了三个月。| **take sb prisoner** *The captain was taken prisoner by enemy soldiers.* 那位上尉被敌军士兵俘虏了。 S3 W2

prisoner of con·science /ˌ· · · ˈ· ·/ *n* [C] someone who is put in prison because of their political ideas 政治犯

prisoner of war /ˌ· · · ˈ·/ *n* [C] a soldier, member of the navy etc who is caught by the enemy during a war and kept as a prisoner 战俘

Prisoner of Zen·da, The /ˌprɪznə əv ˈzɛndə; ˌprɪzənər əv ˈzendə/ (1894) a NOVEL by Anthony Hope, which has been made into several films, about the adventures of an Englishman in the imaginary country of Ruritania《曾达的囚徒》〔(1894), 安东尼·霍普的一部小说, 讲述一个英国人在虚构的卢里坦尼亚国的历险故事, 曾几度被改编成电影〕

prison vis·i·tor /ˌ· · ˈ· · ·/ *n* [C] someone who visits prisoners in Britain to help them〔英国探望囚犯以帮助他们的〕探监工作者

pris·sy /ˈprɪsɪ; ˈprɪsi/ *adj informal* behaving very correctly and easily shocked by anything rude【非正式】谨小慎微的; 一本正经的; 拘谨的, 刻板的: *"She's not a very nice girl," Jinny said in her prissy little voice.* "她不是很好的女孩。" 吉妮用她一本正经的细嗓门说。—**prissily** *adv* —**prissiness** *n* [U]

Pristina the regional capital of Kosovo 普里什蒂纳〔科索沃首府〕

pris·tine /ˈprɪstin; ˈprɪstiːn/ *adj* extremely fresh or clean 极其新鲜的; 洁净的: *the pristine whiteness of newly fallen snow* 新降雪的洁白无瑕 | **in pristine condition** (=in the same condition as when it was made) 崭新的; 完好无损的 *a '68 Volvo in pristine condition* 完好无损的1968年产的沃尔沃汽车

Pritch·ett /ˈprɪtʃɪt; ˈprɪtʃɪt/, **V. S.** (1900-97) a British writer whose best-known works are his short stories 普里切特〔(1900-1997), 英国作家, 以短篇小说最为著称〕

prith·ee /ˈprɪðɪ; ˈprɪði/ *interjection old use* please【旧】请

priv·a·cy /ˈpraɪvəsɪ; ˈprɪvəsi/ *n* [U] **1** the state of being able to be alone, and not seen or heard by other people 隐居; 独处; 清静: *With seven people squashed in one house, you don't get much privacy.* 七个人挤在一间屋子里, 想要独处不大可能。**2** the state of being free from public attention 隐私: *each individual's right to privacy* 每个人的隐私权

pri·vate¹ /ˈpraɪvɪt; ˈpraɪvɪ̵t/ *adj* S1 W1

1 ►NOT FOR EVERYONE 不是供每个人的◄ only for use by one particular person or group, not for everyone 私人(用)的; 私有的, 个人的: *a private road* 私人道路 | *private property* 私人财产

2 ►SECRET 秘密的◄ a) private feelings, information, or opinions are personal or secret and not for other people to know about〔感情、消息、意见等〕个人的; 秘密的, 非公开的: *What I told you was private – I thought you would respect that.* 我告诉你的事不宜公开 —— 我想你会遵守这一点。**b)** a private meeting, conversation etc involves only a small number of people, and is not for other people to know about〔会议、谈话等〕秘密的, 私下的: *a peace deal hammered out in a series of private talks* 在一系列秘密会谈中达成的和平协议

3 ►NOT GOVERNMENT 非政府的◄ [only before noun 仅用于名词前] not connected with, owned by, or paid for by the government 私立的, 私营的, 民间的: *a private hospital* 私立医院 | *private pension plans* 个人退休金计划 | **go private** *BrE* (=pay for medical treatment instead of getting it free at a public hospital)【英】自付医疗费

P

4 ►NOT PART OF YOUR WORK 非工作的一部分◄ separate from and not connected with your work or your official position 与公事无关的, 与官职无关的, 私人的: *The president is paying a private visit to Europe.* 总统将对欧洲作私人访问。| **private life** (=the parts of your life not connected with your job or your public life, especially your relationships) 私生活 *I never discuss my private life in interviews.* 我从不在采访时谈及我的私生活。

5 ►QUIET PLACE 安静的地方◄ quiet and without lots of people 安静的; 人不多的: *Is there a private corner where we can have a talk?* 有没有一个僻静的角落让我们可以谈一谈?

6 ►PERSON 人◄ [only before noun 仅用于名词前] a private person is one who likes being alone, and does not talk much about their thoughts or feelings〔人〕喜欢独处的; 不喜欢谈论自己的想法[感情]的: *Although he spends a lot of time in the public eye, he is really a very private man.* 尽管他经常在公开场合露面, 但他其实性格很孤僻。

7 private joke a joke made between friends, family members etc that other people do not understand〔朋友、家庭成员等之间的〕私人玩笑 —see also 另见 PRIVATELY

private² *n* **1 in private** without other people being present 秘密地, 私下地: *I have something to tell you, but I'll speak to you about it in private.* 我有事情要告诉你, 但我要单独跟你说。**2** [C] a soldier of the lowest rank 士兵, 列兵; 二等兵 —see table on page C6 参见 C6 页附录 **3 privates** [plural] *informal* PRIVATE PARTS【非正式】阴部, 私处

private de·tec·tive /,‥ ·'‥/ *n* [C] someone who can be employed to look for information or missing people, or to follow people and report on what they do 私人侦探, 私家侦探

private ed·u·ca·tion /,‥ ‥'‥/ *n* [U] education provided for money, rather than free education provided by the government 私立教育

CULTURAL NOTE 文化注释

Quite a large number of people in Britain are against private education because they think it strengthens class differences and makes people less equal, but some people in Britain and the US are willing to pay for private education because they feel it gives their children a better standard of education. 相当多的英国人反对私立教育, 因为他们认为私立教育加深阶级分化并让人与人之间不平等。但是在英美还是有人愿意付钱接受私立教育, 因为他们认为私立教育能给他们的子女带来更好的教育。

private en·ter·prise /,‥ '‥·/ *n* **1** [U] the economic system in which private businesses are allowed to compete freely with each other, and the government does not control industry 私营企业制, 自由企业制 —see also 另见 PRIVATE SECTOR **2** [C] a business established by an individual person or group 私营企业

pri·va·teer /,praɪvəˈtɪr; ,praɪvəˈtɪə/ *n* [C] **1** an armed ship in former times that was not in the navy but attacked and robbed enemy ships carrying goods〔旧时攻击并抢夺敌人货船的〕武装民船; 私掠船 **2** someone who commanded or sailed on a ship of this kind 私掠船船长[船员]

Private Eye /,‥ '‥/ a British SATIRICAL magazine which criticizes and makes jokes about famous people, and prints stories about dishonest or embarrassing behaviour by people in public life. Many people have taken *Private Eye* to court because they say its articles about them are untrue or unfair.《私家侦探》〔英国一讽刺类杂志, 专门批评和嘲弄社会名流, 披露公众人物的欺诈或尴尬行为。不少人将《私家侦探》告上法庭, 理由是该杂志的报道失实或有所偏颇〕

private eye /,‥ '‥/ *n* [C] *informal* a PRIVATE DETECTIVE【非正式】私人侦探, 私家侦探

private in·come /,‥ '‥/ *n* [C] money that someone gets regularly, not from working but because they own part of a business or have money which earns INTEREST¹ (4) 私人收入〔指来自投资、利息等的非工资性〕

private in·ves·ti·gat·or /,‥ ·'‥·‥/ *n* [C] a PRIVATE DETECTIVE 私人侦探, 私家侦探

private law /'‥ ,·/ *n* [U] *law* the part of the law concerned with ordinary people, private property, and relationships【法律】〔处理私人关系、私人财产的〕私法

pri·vate·ly /ˈpraɪvɪtlɪ; ˈpraɪvɪ̯tli/ *adv* **1** with no one else present 单独, 私下: *Could I speak to you privately?* 我可以单独跟你谈谈吗? **2** if you feel or think something privately, you do not tell anyone about it [sentence adverb 句子副词] 私下地; 没有公开地: *Privately, Prue felt that the whole exercise was a waste of time.* 普吕私下认为整个练习就是浪费时间。**3** *especially BrE* using or involving private rather than government institutions【尤英】私立地, 私营地: *Both children are privately educated.* 两个孩子接受的都是私立教育。| *a privately-owned company* 私有公司

private medi·cine /,‥ '‥/ *n* [U] *BrE* the system in which medical treatment and advice is not provided by the government but is paid for by the person who needs it, or by their insurance company【英】自费医疗〔医疗和医疗咨询由个人或其保险公司支付而非政府提供的体制〕—compare 比较 NHS

CULTURAL NOTE 文化注释

Most people in Britain are proud of the National Health Service, mainly paid for by the government, which provides free health care for everyone in the country. Some people feel that the growth of private medicine will reduce standards in the public service. People who 'go private' (=have private medicine) often do so because they are treated more quickly. 大多数英国人都对国民保健制度感到自豪, 它主要是靠政府支付费用来为每个国民提供免费的保健服务。有人担心自费医疗的增长会削弱公共服务的质量。那些花钱支付自费医疗的人通常是为了能得到更快速的治疗。

private mem·ber /,‥ '‥/ *n BrE* [C] a member of parliament who is not a minister in the government【英】〔非内阁成员的〕下议院议员, 无公职议员

private member's bill /,‥ '‥ ,·/ *n* [C] a law introduced to the British parliament by a member of parliament who is not a minister in the government 非内阁成员的下议院议员提出的法案

private parts /,‥ '·/ *n* [plural] an expression meaning 'sex organs', used when you want to avoid naming them directly 私处, 阴部, (外)生殖器

private pa·tient /,‥ '‥/ *n* [C] *BrE* someone who pays for medical treatment or advice, rather than receiving it free through the government's system【英】自费病人

private prac·tice /,‥ '‥/ *n* [U] **1** the business of a professional person that is independent of a bigger or government controlled organization〔职业人士的〕私人企业[公司]: *Richard set up in private practice.* 理查德设立了私人事务所。**2** *AmE* the business of a professional person, especially a doctor, who works alone rather than with others【美】私人开业〔尤指医生〕

private school /,‥ '·/ *n* [C] a school not supported by government money, where education must be paid for by the parents of the children 私立学校

private sec·re·ta·ry /,‥ '‥·‥/ *n* [C] a secretary who is employed to help one person, especially with CONFIDENTIAL business 私人秘书

private sec·tor, the /,‥ '‥ ◂/ *n* the industries and services in a country that are owned and run by private companies, and not by the state or government 私营企业: *pay increases in the private sector* 私营企业的工资增长 | *private sector employers* 私营企业的雇主 —compare 比较 PUBLIC SECTOR

private sol·dier /,‥ '‥/ *n* [C] *formal* a soldier of the lowest rank; PRIVATE² (2)【正式】士兵, 列兵; 二等兵

private view /,‥ '·/ also 又作 **private view·ing** /,‥ '‥/ *n* [C] an occasion when a few people are invited to see a show of paintings before the rest of the public〔画展在公开展出前只邀请少数人参观的〕预展

pri·va·tion /praɪˋveʃən; praɪˈveɪʃən/ *n* [C,U] *formal* a lack or loss of the things that everyone needs, such as food, warmth, and shelter【正式】〔生活必需品的〕匮乏, 丧失: *Despite the privations of wartime she managed to keep the children healthy.* 尽管战时生活必需品匮乏, 她仍设法使孩子们保持健康。

pri·vat·ise /ˈpraɪvɪtaɪz; ˈpraɪvḁtaɪz/ *v* a British spelling of PRIVATIZE privatize 的英式拼法

pri·vat·i·za·tion also 又作 **-isation** *BrE*【英】/ˌpraɪvətə-ˋzeʃən; ˌpraɪvətaɪˈzeɪʃən/ *n* [C, U] the act of privatizing something 私有化, 私营化

pri·vat·ize also 又作 **-ise** *BrE*【英】/ˈpraɪvətaɪz; ˈpraɪvətaɪz/ *v* [T] to sell an organization, industry, or service that was previously controlled and owned by a government 使私营化, 使归私有 —compare 比较 NATIONALIZE

priv·et /ˈprɪvɪt; ˈprɪvḁt/ *n* [U] a bush with leaves that stay green all year, often grown to form a HEDGE 女贞〔常用作树篱的常青灌木〕

priv·i·lege /ˈprɪvlɪdʒ; ˈprɪvḁlɪdʒ/ *n* **1** [C] a special advantage that is given only to one person or group of people〔特定个人或群体的〕特权: *Don't forget that using the car is a privilege, not a right!* 别忘了使用这辆汽车是特权, 而不是权利! | **the privilege of (doing) sth** *the privilege of having an office of my own* 拥有我自己办公室的特权 **2** [U] a situation in which people who are rich or of a high social class have many more advantages than other people〔某些有权有势者的〕特权, 特别待遇: *an outdated system based on aristocratic privilege* 基于贵族特权的陈旧制度 **3** [singular] something that you are lucky to have the chance to do, and that you enjoy very much 荣幸: **the privilege of doing sth** *Ladies and gentlemen, I have the great privilege of introducing our speaker for tonight.* 女士们、先生们, 我非常荣幸地介绍我们今晚的演讲者。| *It was a privilege to hear her play.* 能听她演奏真是荣幸。**4** [C,U] the right to do or say something which might not normally be acceptable without being punished, especially in parliament 言行自由权;〔尤指〕议员〔言行不受惩罚〕权: **a breach of privilege** (=a breaking of the rules about what a member of parliament can do or say) 侵犯议会言行自由权

priv·i·leged /ˈprɪvlɪdʒd; ˈprɪvḁlɪdʒd/ *adj* **1** having a special advantage or a chance to do something that most people cannot do 有特权的; 荣幸的, 幸运的: **privileged to do sth** *Francis felt privileged to work for such a man.* 弗朗西斯觉得为这样的人工作很荣幸。| *Recently I was privileged to view his private collection.* 最近我很荣幸地看到了他的个人收藏。**2** having advantages because of your wealth, social position etc〔因为有钱有势而〕有特权的: **the privileged few** *Only the privileged few were able to afford university then.* 那时, 只有享有特权的少数人才能上得起大学。**3** *law* privileged information does not have to be given even if a court of law asks for it【法律】无须公开的; 有权保守秘密的

priv·y[1] /ˈprɪvɪ; ˈprɪvi/ *adj* **1 privy to** sharing in the knowledge of facts that are secret 了解内情的, 私下知情的: *Colby was privy to the committee's decisions.* 科尔比知道委员会的秘密决定。**2** *old use* secret and private【旧】秘密的, 私下的 —**privily** *adv*

privy[2] *n* [C] *old use* a toilet, especially one outside a house【旧】〔尤指室外的〕厕所

Privy Coun·cil, the /ˌ‥ˈ‥/ *n* a group of important people in Britain who advise the king or queen on political affairs〔英国的〕枢密院 —**Privy Councillor** *n* [C]

Privy Purse /ˌ‥ˈ·/ *n* **the privy purse** money given by the British government to the king or queen for their personal use〔英国政府拨给国王或女王的〕私用经费

Privy Seal, the /ˌ‥ˈ·/ —see 见 the LORD PRIVY SEAL

prize[1] /praɪz; praɪz/ *n* [C] **1** something that is given to someone who is successful in a competition, race, game of chance etc〔给予获胜者的〕奖品, 奖赏: *First prize was a weekend for two in Paris.* 头奖是巴黎周末二人游。| **[+for]** *Festival judges awarded 'Victims' the prize for the best feature film.* 电影节评委授予《受害者》最佳故事片奖。| **win a prize** *Hundreds of cash prizes to be won!* 可以赢得数以百计的现金奖! | **prize winner** *a list of prize winners* 获奖者名单 | **award (sb) a prize** (=decide who will have a prize) 授予〔某人〕奖赏 **2** something that is very valuable to you or that it is very important to have 有价值的事物, 值得争取的事物: *Toulouse was a rich prize, and the Count's army fought hard to keep it.* 图卢兹是块富饶的宝地, 伯爵的军队奋勇战斗守卫它。**3 (there are) no prizes for guessing sth** *spoken* used to say that it is very easy to guess something【口】某事一猜就知: *No prizes for guessing who told you that!* 是谁告诉你的, 一猜就能猜出来! **4** an enemy ship caught at sea in the past, or the goods it contained 捕获的敌船[船上的货物]

prize[2] *adj* [only before noun 仅用于名词前] **1** good enough to win a prize or to have won a prize 可获奖的; 优等的; 已获奖的: *a herd of prize cattle* 一群优选的牛 —see also 另见 PRIZE-WINNING **2 prize money** money that is given to the person who wins a competition, race etc〔赢得比赛者所获的〕奖金 **3 a prize idiot/fool** *informal* a complete IDIOT, fool etc【非正式】十足的白痴/傻瓜 **4** best, most important, or most useful 最好的; 最重要的; 最有用的: *The resource centre is one of our prize assets.* 那个资源中心是我们一个非常重要的资产。

prize[3] *v* [T] **1** [often passive 常用被动态] to think that someone or something is very important or valuable 珍视; 高度重视: *a necklace which his mother had prized* 他母亲珍爱的一条项链 **2** [T always+adv/prep] also 又作 **prise** *BrE* to move or lift something, by pushing it away from something else【英】撬; 撬开; PRY (2) *AmE*【美】: **prize sth off/up/apart etc** *Eventually we prized the lid off with a knife.* 最后我们用刀把盖子撬开了。

prize sth **out** *phr v* [T] to get information from someone with difficulty or by using force〔从某人那里〕挖出〔情报等〕, 强迫〔某人〕供出〔消息、情报〕: **prize sth out of sb** *It took an hour to prize the address out of him.* 花了一个小时才让他供出那个地址。

prized /praɪzd; praɪzd/ *adj* extremely important or valuable to someone〔对某人〕非常重要的, 非常有价值的, 极其珍贵的: **prized possession** *Nathaniel's bicycle is his most prized possession.* 纳撒尼尔的自行车是他最宝贵的财产。

prize day /ˈ· ·/ *n* [C] *BrE* an occasion when prizes are given to pupils who have done well in particular subjects【英】〔学校的〕颁奖日

prize-fight /ˈpraɪzˌfaɪt; ˈpraɪzfaɪt/ *n* [C] **1** a public BOXING match, in which two men fight each other with bare hands, in order to win money〔以赢钱为目的的〕公开徒手拳击赛 **2** *AmE* a professional BOXING match【美】职业拳击赛 —**prizefighter** *n* [C] —**prizefighting** *n* [U]

prize-win·ning /ˈ· ‥/ *adj* [only before noun 仅用于名词前] a prize-winning film, book etc has won a prize〔电影、书籍等〕获奖的: *a prize-winning science reporter* 获奖的科学记者

PRO /ˌpi ɑr ˋo; ˌpiː ɑːr ˈəʊ/ *n* [C] a public relations officer; someone whose job is to supply information about an organization, so that people have a good opinion of it 公(共)关(系)人员 —see also 另见 PR (1)

pro- /pro; prəʊ/ *prefix* **1** in favour of or supporting something 赞成; 支持; 亲: *pro-American* 亲美的 | *the pro-abortion lobby* 赞成人工流产合法化的议院外活动集团 —compare 比较 ANTI- **2** *technical* doing a job instead of someone【术语】代, 代理: *the pro-vice-chancellor* 代理副大臣

pro[1] /pro; prəʊ/ *n* [C] **1** a PROFESSIONAL (=someone who earns money because they are good at a particular sport or skill) 专门职业者, 职业人员 **2** *informal* also 又作 **old pro** someone who has had a lot of experience with a particular type of situation【非正式】〔有经验的〕老手: *Ben's an old pro at this type of thing – leave it to him.* 班恩是处理这种事情的老手, 交给他吧。**3 the pros and cons** the advantages and disadvantages of something〔某事物的〕利与弊: *the pros and cons of owning your own home* 拥有自己住所的利与弊 **4** *BrE informal* a PROSTITUTE【英, 非正式】妓女 —see also 另见 PRO FORMA, PRO RATA

pro[2] *prep* if you are pro an idea, plan, suggestion etc, you support it and hope that it will succeed 赞成的, 支持的: *As a party, they had always been pro nuclear power.* 作为一个政党, 他们一直支持核能。

pro[3] *adj informal* PROFESSIONAL【非正式】职业性的; 专业的: **turn/go pro** (=become pro) 成为职业人员 *Both skaters turned pro last year.* 两名滑冰运动员去年都成为了职业选手。

pro-ac·tive /ˈ·ˈ‥/ *adj* able to change events rather than react to them, and make things happen 积极的; 主动的, 预先采取行动的, 先发制人的: *a pro-active approach to staffing requirements* 人员需求问题的积极处理方法

pro-am /ˌpro ˋæm; ˌprəʊ ˈæm◂/ *n* [C] a competition, especially in GOLF, for PROFESSIONALs (=people who play for money) and AMATEURs (=people who play just for pleasure) 职业选手和业余选手混合赛〔尤指高尔夫球赛〕 —**pro-am** *adj*

prob·a·bil·i·ty /ˌprɑbəˋbɪlətɪ; ˌprɒbəˈbɪlḁti/ *n* **1** [singular,U] how likely it is that something will happen, exist, or be true 可能性: **[+of]** *very little probability of finding it again* 再次找到它的微乎其微的可能性 | **there is a strong probability that** *There is a very strong probability that she will make a full recovery.* 她非常有可能完全康复。| **the probability is that** (=it is likely that) 可能… *If you can answer these questions, the probability is that you'd be good at the job.* 如果你能回答这些问题, 你就有可能胜任这份工作。**2 in all probability** an expression meaning very probably, used especially when you are making a judgment about something 很可能, 十有八九〔尤用于对某事物作出判断时〕: *There will, in all probability, be parts that you do not understand.* 很有可能会有你不懂的部分。**3** [C] something that is likely to happen or exist 可能发生的事; 可能存在

的事: *A peace agreement now seems a real probability.* 达成和平协议现在似乎成了完全可能的事。**4** the mathematically calculated chance that something will happen〔数学的〕概率, 或然率: *a probability of one in four* 四分之一的概率

prob·a·ble¹ /ˋprɑbəbḷ; ˈprɒbəbəl/ *adj* likely to exist, happen, or be true 可能存在的; 可能发生的; 很可能的; 大概的: *A victory doesn't seem very probable at this stage.* 在这个阶段获胜好像不大可能。| **it is probable that** *It seems highly probable that they'll have to move house.* 他们很有可能得搬家。| **probable result/outcome/effect etc** *The new building will go ahead at a probable cost of £2.5 million.* 新的大楼将要开工, 大概需花费250万英镑。—opposite 反义词 IMPROBABLE

probable² *n* [C] someone who is likely to be chosen for a team, to win a race etc 很有可能入选的人; 很有可能获胜的人

prob·a·bly /ˋprɑbəblɪ; ˈprɒbəbli/ *adv* [sentence adverb 句子副词] used to say that something is likely to happen, likely to be true etc 很可能; 大概: *I probably still have my old army pictures.* 我大概还保留着我在部队时的老照片。| *Probably the best way to learn Spanish is by actually going to live in Spain.* 学习西班牙语最好的方法大概是亲身到西班牙生活。| *"Do you think you'll return to work after the baby?" "Yeah, probably."* "你认为生完孩子后你会再回来工作吗?" "是的, 很可能会。" | **very/most probably** *She most probably thinks she's right when she says things like that.* 她极有可能认为自己是对的才会说出那种话。

pro·bate¹ /ˋprobet; ˈprəʊbeɪt/ *n* [U] *law* the legal process of deciding that someone's WILL² (2) has been properly made and can be carried out【法律】遗嘱检验; 遗嘱认证

probate² *v* [T] *AmE law* to prove that a WILL² (2) is legal【美, 法律】验证〔遗嘱〕的合法性

pro·ba·tion /proˋbeʃən; prəˈbeɪʃən/ *n* [U] **1** a system that allows some criminals not to go to prison, if they behave well and see a PROBATION OFFICER (=special adviser) regularly, for a fixed period of time 缓刑 (制): *The court fined Kevin and gave him two years' probation.* 法庭对凯文处以罚款并判他缓刑两年。| **(put sb) on probation** *Mike was put on probation for stealing a car.* 迈克因偷一辆汽车而被判缓刑。**2** a period of time, during which someone who has just started a job is tested to see whether they are suitable for what they are doing 试用 (期), 见习 (期): *After six months' probation, Helen became a permanent member of staff.* 经过六个月的试用, 海伦成了一名正式职员。| **on probation** *I'm on probation for another month yet.* 我还有一个月的试用期。**3** *AmE* a fixed period of time in which you must improve your work or behave well so that you will not have to leave your job【美】〔留任〕察看期: **(put sb) on probation** *I'm afraid I have no choice but to put you on probation.* 恐怕我没有别的选择, 只能把你留下察看。—**probationary** *adj*: *a probationary period* 缓刑期; 试用期 | *probationary teachers* 试用中的老师

pro·ba·tion·er /proˋbeʃənɚ; prəˈbeɪʃənə/ *n* [C] **1** someone who has recently started a job, especially nursing or teaching, and who is being tested to see whether they are suitable for it 见习人员〔尤指见习护士或见习教师〕**2** someone who has broken the law, and has been put on probation 缓刑犯 **3** someone who is being tested to see if they are suitable to be a member of a church or religious group〔教会中的〕准会员

probation of·fi·cer /ˈ·ˈ·· ˌ···/ *n* [C] someone whose job is to watch, advise, and help people who have broken the law and are on probation 监视缓刑犯的官员, 缓刑监督官

probe¹ /prob; prəʊb/ *v* [I, T] **1** to ask questions in order to find things out, especially things that other people do not want you to know 调查; 打探, 探究: **[+into]** *I don't want to probe too deeply into your personal affairs.* 我不想太深入地打探你的私事。| **probe sth** *a report probing the official's involvement with drug dealing* 关于官员与贩毒活动有牵连的调查报告 **2** to look for something or examine something, using a long thin instrument〔用细长的工具〕寻找, 探测, 探查: *Jules probed the mud gingerly with a stick.* 朱尔斯小心翼翼地用棍子探着泥地。—**probing** *adj*: *probing questions* 刨根究底的问题 —**probingly** *adv*

probe² *n* [C] **1** a long thin metal instrument that doctors and scientists use to examine parts of the body〔医生和科学家用的〕探针 **2** a SPACE PROBE 宇宙探测器, 太空探测器 **3** an expression meaning a very thorough INQUIRY into something, used by newspapers 深入调查, 彻底调查〔报纸用语〕: *a police corruption probe* 对警察贪污行为的彻底调查

pro·bi·ty /ˋprobətɪ; ˈprəʊbḷti/ *n* [U] *formal* complete honesty【正式】诚实, 正直: *I have always found Bentner to be a model of probity in our dealings.* 在我们的交往中, 我一直觉得班特纳是诚实的典范。

prob·lem /ˋprɑbləm; ˈprɒbləm/ *n* [C] 

1 ▶DIFFICULTY 困难◀ a situation that causes difficulties 问题; 难题, 困难: *There was rarely any problem in motivating the students to study.* 在激励学生学习方面很少有什么问题。| **have a problem with** *I've been having a few problems with the car.* 我这车子一直都有些毛病。| **a drug/crime problem** *tough new measures to combat the drug problem* 打击毒品问题的严厉的新措施 | **pose a problem** *The shortage of trained staff poses a serious problem.* 缺乏训练有素的员工是个严重的问题。| **solve a problem** *a policy that will solve the unemployment problem* 将可解决失业问题的政策 —see 见 TROUBLE (USAGE)

2 no problem *spoken*【口】**a)** used to say that you are very willing to do something 没问题〔用于表示很愿意做某事〕: *"Could you make the booking in her name?" "Yes, no problem."* "你用她的名字预订好吗?" "好的! 没问题。" | *No problem! I'd love to show you around.* 没问题! 我很愿意带你到处看看。**b)** used after someone has said thank you or said that they are sorry 没什么〔用于回答对方的感谢或道歉〕: *"Thanks so much for all your help." "Oh, no problem!"* "非常感谢你所有的帮助。" "噢, 没什么!"

3 that's your problem *spoken* used to tell someone to deal with their own problem or situation by themselves【口】那是你的问题〔用于告诉别人自己处理自己的问题〕: *If you can't get yourself there on time, that's your problem.* 如果你不能准时到达那里, 那是你的问题。

4 it's/that's not my problem *spoken* used to say you do not care about a problem someone else has【口】那不是我的问题, 那不关我的事〔用来表示你不关心别人的问题〕: *"Your brother's under a lot of pressure." "That's not my problem."* "你的哥哥正在承受很大的压力。" "那不是我的问题。"

5 What's your problem? *spoken* used to ask someone what is wrong, in a way that is not sympathetic, and shows that you think they are being unreasonable【口】你出什么问题了?〔这句问话并无同情意味, 而且表现出你认为对方不理智〕: *Look, what's your problem? I've never seen you act like this!* 喂, 你犯什么毛病了? 我从未见过你这样!

6 a problem child/family/drinker etc a child etc who behaves in a way that is difficult for other people to deal with 问题儿童/问题家庭/难对付的饮酒者等

7 Do you have a problem with that? *spoken* used to ask someone why they oppose you or disagree with you, in a way that shows you think they are wrong【口】对此你有问题吗?〔用于询问别人为什么反对你, 表现出你认为别人是错的〕

8 ▶QUESTION 问题◀ a question, especially one connected with numbers or facts, that must be answered〔尤指与数字、事实相关的〕问题, 题: *The teacher gave them 20 mathematical problems.* 老师给他们出了20道数学题。

prob·lem·at·ic /ˌprɑbləˋmætɪk; ˌprɒbləˈmætɪk◂/ *adj* full of problems and difficult to deal with 有很多问题的, 难对付的, 成问题的: *The situation might become slightly problematic as more people are involved.* 随着更多的人牵涉进来, 形势可能变得有点难以对付。—**problematically** /-klɪ; -kli/ *adv*

problem page /ˈ·· ·/ *n* [C] a page in a magazine where letters about personal problems are printed, and answers are suggested 个人问题专页〔指杂志中刊登反映个人问题的来信和建议的解决办法的专页〕

problem-solv·ing /ˈ·· ˌ··/ *n* [U] finding ways of doing things, or finding answers to problems 解决问题: *Involve the class in a problem-solving activity.* 使全班同学参与到解决问题的活动中来。

pro bo·no pub·li·co /pro ˌbono ˋpublɪko; prəʊ ˌbəʊnəʊ ˈpʊblɪkəʊ/ also 又作 **pro bono** *adj Latin* used to descibe work that someone, especially a lawyer, does without getting paid for it【拉丁】〔尤指律师〕免费工作的: *Some law firms will take on pro bono cases when possible.* 一些律师事务所在可能的情况下会承接免费服务的案子。

pro·bos·cis /proˋbɑsɪs; prəˈbɒsḷs/ *n* [C] *plural* **proboscises** /-sɪsɪz; -sḷsiːz/ **1** a long thin tube that forms part of the mouth of some insects and worms〔某些昆虫的〕针状吻, 长嘴 **2** the long thin nose of certain animals, such as the elephant〔某些动物的〕长鼻; 〔尤指〕象鼻

pro·ce·du·ral /prəˋsidʒərəl; prəˈsiːdʒərəl/ *adj formal* connected with a procedure, especially in a law court【正式】〔尤指法庭〕程序性的, 手续上的

pro·ce·dure /prəˋsidʒɚ; prəˈsiːdʒə/ *n* **1** [C] the correct or normal way of doing something〔正确或通常做事的〕步骤, 手续: **[+for]** *What's the procedure for renewing your car tax?* 续交汽车税的正确步骤是什么? | **correct/proper/standard procedure** *A lie-detector test is standard procedure.* 用测谎仪进行测试是

标准的做法。**2** [U] the accepted method and order of doing things, especially in an official meeting, a law case etc〔尤指正式会议、法律诉讼等的〕程序: *Too much time was spent arguing about procedure.* 太多的时间花在了争论程序问题上。

[3] [3] **pro·ceed** /prəˋsid; prəˈsiːd/ *v* [I] **1** to continue to do something that has already been started 继续进行, 继续做: *The work is proceeding according to plan.* 那项工作正按计划进行。| **[+with]** *Travis paused to consult his notes, then proceeded with his questions.* 特拉维斯停下来看了看笔记, 然后继续提问。| **[+to]** *We can now proceed to the main business of the meeting.* 我们现在可以进入会议的主要议程。**2 proceed to do sth** an expression meaning to do something next, used especially about something annoying or surprising 接着做某事〔尤指令人讨厌或惊奇的事〕: **proceed to do sth** *Patrick said he liked my work, and then proceeded to tell me everything was wrong with it!* 帕特里克说他很欣赏我的作品, 接着又告诉我一切都不对! **3** [always+adv/prep] *formal* to move in a particular direction【正式】〔向某一方向〕前进, 移动: **[+in/to etc]** *Passengers for the Miami flight should proceed to gate 25.* 搭乘迈阿密航班的旅客请前往25号门登机。—see also 另见 PROCEEDS

proceed against sb *phr v* [T] *law* to begin a legal case against someone【法律】起诉〔某人〕, 对〔某人〕提起诉讼

proceed from sth *phr v* [T not in passive 不用被动态] *formal* to happen or exist as a result of something【正式】源于某物, 出自: *diseases that proceed from poverty* 由贫困引起的疾病

[2] **pro·ceed·ings** /prəˋsidɪŋz; prəˈsiːdɪŋz/ *n* [plural] **1** also 又作 **proceeding** [C] an event or series of actions, especially an unusual or annoying one〔尤指不寻常或令人讨厌的〕事件;〔一连串的〕行为: *We watched the proceedings in the street from the window.* 我们通过窗户注视着大街上的活动。**2** actions taken in a law court or in a legal case 诉讼: *Legal proceedings can be enormously expensive.* 法律诉讼可能会耗费非常大。**3** the official records of meetings 会议记录: *the proceedings of the London Historical Society* 伦敦历史学会会议记录

pro·ceeds /ˋprosidz; ˈprəʊsiːdz/ *n* [plural] the money that has been gained from doing something or selling something〔做某事或出售某物所获的〕收入, 收益: *We sold the business and bought a retirement condo with the proceeds.* 我们卖了公司, 并用所得的钱买了一套退休养老的公寓。

[2] [1] **pro·cess¹** /ˋprɑsɛs; ˈprəʊses/ *n* [C] **1** a series of natural developments or events that produce gradual change 过程, 进程; 变化过程: *Coal was formed out of dead forests by a slow process of chemical change.* 煤是由枯死的森林经过长期而缓慢的化学变化形成的。| *the digestive process* 消化过程 **2** a series of actions that someone takes in order to achieve a particular result〔为取得某个结果而采取的〕步骤, 程序, 方法: *Teaching him to read was a slow process.* 教他认字是一个缓慢的过程。| *the electoral process* 选举程序 | **by a process of elimination** (=by proving that no other possibility is true) 通过排除法 *The identity of the dead man was established by a process of elimination.* 死者的身份是通过排除法来确认的。**3 be in the process of doing sth/be in process** to have started doing something and not yet be finished 在做某事的过程中, 在进行中: *The company is in the process of moving to new offices.* 该公司正在搬往新的办公室。| *New guidelines are in process.* 新的指导方针正在制订中。**4** a system or a treatment of materials that is used to produce goods 制作法; 工序, 工艺流程: *an advanced industrial process* 先进的工业生产流程 **5 in the process** while you are doing something or something is happening 同时; 在…过程中: *Katie jumped out of the tree, spraining her ankle in the process.* 凯蒂从树上跳下来时扭伤了脚踝。**6** *technical* a legal case, considered as a series of actions【术语】诉讼程序 —see also 另见 DUE PROCESS

process² *v* [T] **1** to treat food or some other substance by adding substances to give it colour, keep it fresh etc 加工〔食品或其他物质〕: *processed cheese* 经过加工的乳酪 **2** to print a picture from a photographic film 冲印〔照片〕 **3** to deal with a document 处理〔文件〕: *Your application for a mortgage is being processed.* 你申请抵押贷款的事正在审理中。**4** to put information into a computer to be examined〔电脑〕处理〔数据〕—see also 另见 DATA PROCESSING, WORD PROCESSOR

pro·cess³ /proˋsɛs; prəˈses/ *v* [I always+adv/prep] to move in a procession, or to move very slowly and seriously 列队行进; 缓慢而严肃地行进

processed food /ˌ‥ ˈ·/ *n* [U] food that has been specially treated before it is sold, in order to make it look more attractive or last longer 加工食品

pro·ces·sion /prəˋsɛʃən; prəˈseʃən/ *n* [C] **1** a line of people or vehicles moving slowly as part of a ceremony〔人或车辆的〕行列, 队列, 游行队伍: *the funeral procession* 送葬行列 | *a carnival procession* 狂欢节的巡游队伍 | **in procession** *They marched in procession to the Capitol Building.* 他们排着队向国会大厦行进。**2** several people or things of the same kind, appearing or happening one after the other 一(长)排; 一(长)串; 一连串: **[+of]** *a never-ending procession of unwelcome visitors* 源源不断的不受欢迎的来访者

pro·ces·sion·al /prəˋsɛʃənḷ; prəˈseʃənəl/ *adj* [only before noun 仅用于名词前] connected with or used during a procession 列队行进的; 列队行进时用的: *Flags lined the processional route.* 队伍行进路线的两边插满了旗帜。

pro·ces·sor /ˋprɑsɛsɚ; ˈprəʊsesə/ *n* [C] the central part of a computer that does the calculations needed to deal with the information it is given; CENTRAL PROCESSING UNIT〔电脑的信息〕处理器[机] —see also 另见 FOOD PROCESSOR

pro-choice /ˌ·ˈ·/ *adj* someone who is pro-choice believes that women have a right to ABORTION, and uses this word to describe their views 主张女人有权人工流产的: *pro-choice activists* 主张人工流产为合法的积极分子

pro·claim /proˋklem; prəˈkleɪm/ *v* [T] *formal*【正式】**1** to say publicly that something important is true or exists 宣布, 声明: *Their religion encouraged them to proclaim their faith.* 他们的宗教鼓励他们公开表明信仰。| *A national holiday was proclaimed.* 宣布全国放假一天。| **proclaim sb sth** *His son was immediately proclaimed king.* 他的儿子立即被宣布为国王。**2** to show something clearly or be a sign of something 显示, 表明: *The two gold stripes on Tanya's uniform proclaimed her seniority.* 塔尼娅制服上的两条金条纹表明了她的高级别。

proc·la·ma·tion /ˌprɑkləˋmeʃən; ˌprɒkləˈmeɪʃən/ *n* **1** [C] an official public statement about something that is important 公告; 声明(书), 宣言: *the country's proclamation of independence* 该国的独立宣言 | *a royal proclamation* 王室公告 **2** [U] the act of stating something officially and publicly 宣布, 公布, 声明

pro·cliv·i·ty /proˋklɪvətɪ; prəˈklɪvɪ̣ti/ *n* [C+to/towards/for] *formal* a strong liking for something or natural tendency to do something, especially something bad【正式】〔尤指坏的〕嗜好, 癖性; 倾向: *The child shows no proclivity towards aggression as far as I can see.* 就我的观察, 这孩子没有表现出攻击他人的倾向。

pro·con·sul /proˋkɑnsḷ; prəʊˈkɒnsəl/ *n* [C] someone who governed a part of the ancient Roman Empire〔古罗马帝国的〕地方总督 —**proconsular** /-ˋkɑnslɚ; -ˈkɒnsjʊ̣lə/ *adj*

pro·con·su·late /proˋkɑnsḷɪt; prəʊˈkɒnsjʊ̣lɪ̣t/ also 又作 **pro·con·sul·ship** /-ˋkɑnsḷˌʃɪp; -ˈkɒnsəlʃɪp/ *n* [C] the rank of a proconsul, or the time during which someone was a proconsul 古罗马帝国地方总督的职位[任期]

pro·cras·ti·nate /proˋkræstəˌnet; prəˈkræstɪ̣neɪt/ *v* [I] *formal* to delay doing something that you ought to do, usually because you do not want to do it【正式】耽搁, 拖延: *Stop procrastinating – just go and tell her.* 别耽搁了——去告诉她吧。—**procrastination** /proˌkræstəˋneʃən; prəˌkræstɪ̣ˈneɪʃən/ *n* [U]

pro·cre·ate /ˋprokrɪˌet; ˈprəʊkrieɪt/ *v* [I, T] *formal or technical* to produce children or baby animals【正式或术语】生育, 生殖 —**procreation** /ˌprokrɪˋeʃən; ˌprəʊkriˈeɪʃən/ *n* [U]

proc·tor¹ /ˋprɑktɚ; ˈprɒktə/ *n* [C] **1** a university officer, especially at Oxford or Cambridge, whose duties include making sure that students keep the rules〔尤指牛津或剑桥大学的〕校监, 学监〔负责监督学生的纪律〕 **2** *AmE* someone who watches students in an exam to make sure that they do not cheat【美】监考人

proctor² *v* [T] *AmE* to watch students in an exam to make sure that they do not cheat【美】监〔考〕; INVIGILATE *BrE*【英】

pro·cu·ra·tor fis·cal /ˌ‥‥ ˈ‥/ *n* [C] an official in Scotland who decides whether someone should be sent to court for a TRIAL¹ (1)〔苏格兰的〕〔地方〕检察官

pro·cure /proˋkjur; prəˈkjʊə/ *v formal*【正式】**1** [T] to obtain something, especially something that is difficult to get 获得, 取得〔尤指难以得到的事物〕: **procure sb sth/procure sth for sb** *Somehow he had procured us an invitation.* 他设法给我们弄到了一张请帖。**2** [I,T] *old-fashioned* to provide a PROSTITUTE for someone【过时】为〔某人〕介绍妓女, 给…拉皮条 —**procurable** *adj* —**procurement** *n* [U] —**procurer** *n* [C]

prod¹ /prɑd; prɒd/ *v* **prodded, prodding** [I,T] **1** to push or press something with your finger or a pointed object; POKE¹ (1)〔用手指或尖物〕刺, 戳, 捅: *She prodded me sharply in the ribs.* 她用力捅了捅我的肋骨。| **[+at]** *Theo prodded at the dead snake.* 西奥戳了戳那条死蛇。—see picture on page A21 参见A21页图 **2** to strongly encourage someone to do something 激励; 促

使，督促：*She's not lazy, but she needs prodding.* 她并不懒，但她需要人加以督促。| **prod sb into (doing) sth** *We just need something to prod them into action.* 我们只是需要点什么促使他们采取行动。

prod² *n* [C usually singular 一般用单数] **1** a sudden pressing or pushing movement, using your finger or a pointed object; POKE² (1) 刺，戳，捅：*Jerry gave me a sharp prod in the back.* 杰里在我背上猛戳了一下。**2 give sb a prod** to encourage or remind someone to do something 激励[提醒]某人〔做某事〕：*You'll need to give him a prod to get him to clean his room.* 你得提醒他让他打扫自己的房间。**3** an instrument used for prodding something 刺戳的工具；刺针；刺棒：*a cattle prod* 赶牛刺棒

prod·i·gal¹ /ˈprɑdɪgl; ˈprɒdɪgəl/ *adj* **1** tending to waste what you have, especially money 浪费的，挥霍的；奢侈的：*a prodigal lifestyle* 奢侈的生活方式 | **[+of/with]** *Don't be so prodigal of your time.* 别这样浪费你的时间。**2** *formal* giving or producing large amounts of something; LAVISH¹ (1)【正式】慷慨的；丰富的，大量的：*a prodigal feast* 丰盛的宴会 | **[+of]** *The garden was filled with blossom and prodigal of scent.* 花园开满了花，香气四溢。—**prodigally** *adv* —**prodigality** /ˌprɑdɪˈgæləti; ˌprɒdɪˈgæləti/ *n* [U]

prodigal² *n humorous* someone who spends money carelessly and wastes their time【幽默】浪费〔时间与金钱〕者，挥霍者；浪子

pro·di·gious /prəˈdɪdʒəs; prəˈdɪdʒəs/ *adj* extremely or surprisingly large or powerful 巨大的，庞大的，大得惊人的：*a prodigious feat* 惊人的业绩 —**prodigiously** *adv*

prod·i·gy /ˈprɑdədʒɪ; ˈprɒdɪdʒi/ *n* [C] **1** a young person who is extremely clever or good at doing something 奇才，天才〔尤指神童〕：*a mathematical prodigy* 数学天才 | **a child/infant prodigy** *Mozart was a child prodigy.* 莫扎特是个神童。**2** something strange and wonderful 奇迹；奇物；奇观：**[+of]** *prodigies of endurance* 忍耐力的奇迹

pro·duce¹ /prəˈdus; prəˈdjuːs/ *v*

1 ▶NATURALLY 自然地◀ [T] to grow something or make it naturally〔自然地〕生产，产生，出产：*Canada produces high-quality wheat.* 加拿大出产优质小麦。| *The pancreas produces insulin in the body.* 胰腺在体内产生胰岛素。| *More sun produces riper grapes.* 日照越充沛，葡萄越成熟。

2 ▶RESULT 结果◀ [T] to make something happen or develop, or have a particular result or effect 引起；造成；产生：*New medicines are producing remarkable results in the treatment of cancer.* 新的药物在治疗癌症方面正产生显著的效果。| *a remark which produced howls of protest* 引起阵阵抗议吼声的话 | *courses designed to produce better teachers* 为培养出更好的教师而设计的课程

3 ▶SHOW 出示◀ [T] to show, bring out, or offer something so it can be seen or considered 出示；拿出；提出：*When challenged, he suddenly produced a gun.* 当受到别人挑战时，他突然掏出一支枪。| *She produced no evidence in support of her argument.* 她拿不出证据支持她的论点。

4 ▶WITH SKILL 用技巧◀ [T] to make something using skill and imagination 制作，创作：*In this play Eliot produces some of his most expressive poetry.* 在这部剧本中艾略特创作了他最具表现力的一些诗歌。| *Diane produced a fantastic meal.* 黛安娜做出了一顿美味的饭菜。

5 ▶GOODS 货物◀ [I,T] to make things to be sold 生产，制造：*The factory produces an incredible 100 cars per hour.* 该厂每小时生产100辆汽车，真不可思议。| *Gas can be produced from coal.* 煤气可从煤中提制。—see also 另见 MASS-PRODUCED

6 ▶PLAY/FILM 戏剧/电影◀ [T] to control the preparation of a play, film etc and then show it to the public 制作〔电影、戏剧等〕；上演，演出，上映：*Jane's play was produced at a London theatre.* 简的戏剧安排在伦敦的一家剧院演出。—see also 另见 PRODUCER (2)

7 ▶BABY 婴儿◀ [T] to have a baby 生，生育：*Anthea felt pressure from the family to produce a son.* 安西娅感受到家里人想让她生儿子的压力。

8 ▶MATHS 数学◀ [T] *technical* to lengthen or continue a line to a point, in GEOMETRY【术语】〔几何中〕使〔线〕延长〔至某一点〕—see also 另见 PRODUCTION

prod·uce² /ˈprɑdjus; ˈprɒdjuːs/ *n* [U] something that has been produced, especially by growing or farming 产品；〔尤指〕农产品：*agricultural produce* 农产品 | *mangoes labelled 'produce of India'* 标有"印度产品"的芒果 —see 见 PRODUCTION (USAGE)

pro·duc·er /prəˈdusə; prəˈdjuːsə/ *n* [C] **1** a person, company, or country that makes or grows goods, foods, or materials 生产者，制造者，生产公司[国]：**[+of]** *England is a producer of high quality wool.* 英国是出产优质羊毛的国家。| **a coffee/wine/car etc producer** *one of the world's largest beef producers* 世界上最大的牛肉生产国之一 —compare 比较 CONSUMER **2** someone who has general control of the preparation of a play, film, or broadcast, but who does not direct the actors〔戏剧、电影、广播的〕制作人，制片人：*Ned's been the news producer at Channel 7 for some time now.* 内德现在在第七频道做新闻节目制作人已经有一段时间了。—see 见 PRODUCTION (USAGE)

prod·uct /ˈprɑdʌkt; ˈprɒdʌkt/ *n* **1** [C,U] something useful that is made in a factory, grown, or taken from nature 产品；制品；物产：*A product with a strong brand name is very important for good sales.* 一种具有强大品牌的产品对于获得好的销量很重要。| *investing in product development* 投资于产品开发 | *Demand for products like coal and steel is declining.* 对于像煤和钢这些产品的需求正在下降。| *I'm allergic to dairy products.* 我对奶制品过敏。—see 见 PRODUCTION (USAGE) **2 the product of a)** someone whose behavior, opinions etc can be explained by their experiences 产物，结果：*Although he reacted violently against the society of his day, Nietsche's philosophy is a direct product of the Germany of that time.* 尽管尼采强烈反对他当时的社会，但他的哲学是那时候德国的直接产物。**b)** something that is a result of someone's actions or of good or bad conditions 结果：*Today's housing problems are the product of years of neglect.* 今天的住房问题是多年来忽视的结果。**3** [C] *technical* the number you get by multiplying two or more numbers in MATHEMATICS【术语】〔数学〕（乘）积：**[+of]** *The product of 3 times 5 is 15.* 3乘5的积是15。**4** [C] *technical* a new chemical compound produced by chemical action【术语】〔化学反应的〕生成物

pro·duc·tion /prəˈdʌkʃən; prəˈdʌkʃən/ *n* **1** [U] the process of making or growing things to be sold as products, or the amount that is produced 生产；产量：*The production of consumer goods has increased throughout the world.* 全世界消费品的产量都增加了。| *Smoking is banned in the factory's production areas.* 工厂的生产区禁止吸烟。| **production costs/manager/process etc** *Production costs for the plane were too high.* 飞机的生产成本太高了。| **go into (full) production** (=begin to be produced in large numbers) 开始（大量）生产，投产 *The prototype engines never went into production.* 这种引擎机型从未投产。**2** [U] the act or process of making something new, or of bringing something into existence 产生，生成：*The skin's natural production of oil slows down as we get older.* 随着我们年龄的增长，皮肤自然分泌油脂的速度逐渐减缓。**3** [C] something produced by skill or imagination, especially a play, film, or broadcast 艺术作品〔尤指戏剧、电影或广播〕：*the new Shakespeare production at the Arts Theatre* 艺术剧院新排演的莎士比亚戏剧 **4** [U] the act of showing something 拿出，出示：*Entrance is permitted only on production of a ticket.* 出示门票方可进入。**5 make a production (out) of sth** *informal* to do something in a way that takes more effort than is necessary【非正式】就…小题大做：*They only want a sandwich, Bella, don't make a production out of it!* 他们只想要一个三明治，贝拉，不要太麻烦！

USAGE NOTE 用法说明: PRODUCTION

WORD CHOICE 词语辨析: **production, product, produce, producer.**

Production [U] is the process in which things are made, usually with the help of people, or in a factory. production 作不可数名词时指生产过程，通常是在人的帮助下或在工厂中进行：*We need to increase production* (NOT 不用 *the production*). 我们需要扩大生产。| *mass production of computers* 电脑的大量生产

A **production** [C] is a play, film etc made for the theatre, television, or radio etc. production 作可数名词时指供剧院、电视台或广播电台上演、播放或播送的戏剧、电影等：*a new production of 'King Lear'* 新上演的《李尔王》

A **product** [C] is something that is made to be sold, often in a factory, or a natural substance like wood, coal etc that is taken from the ground or land to sell. product 作可数名词时常指工厂制造的用来出售的产品，或用来出售的自然产物如木材、煤等：*Glaxo produces a lot of pharmaceutical products.* 葛兰素公司生产大量的药品。| *food products such as cakes and ketchup* 诸如蛋糕和番茄酱之类的食品 | *The country's main products are timber, coal and sugar.* 该国的主要物产是木材、煤和蔗糖。**Product** can also be used to show where something is made, for example on a whiskey bottle you might see: *Product of Scotland.* product 也可用于表明某产品的产地，如在威士忌酒瓶上可能会看到：苏格兰出品。

In business, selling and advertising language, a wider range of things are beginning to be called products. For example

a life insurance company might call the services it sells its products. 在商业、销售和广告用语中，更广泛的东西开始被称为产品。如人寿保险公司可能会称它们所售的服务为产品。

Produce [U] (which is pronounced differently from the verb) is a general word for food grown, especially on farms, and sold without being changed much. produce 作不可数名词时〔其发音与动词不同〕是农产品的一般用词: *He works in the produce section at the local supermarket.* 他在当地超市的农产品部工作。

If a person, company or country produces something, they are a **producer** [C]. 生产产品的人、公司或国家称为 producer〔可数名词〕: *Brazil, the world's most important producer of coffee.* 巴西，世界上最重要的咖啡生产国。

production line /ˈ· · ˌ·/ *n* [C] an arrangement of machines and workers in a factory where each worker or machine does one job in the making of a product and it is then passed on to the next worker or machine; ASSEMBLY LINE 生产线; 装配线

production num·ber /ˈ· ·, ˌ·/ *n* [C] a scene in a MUSICAL involving many people singing and dancing〔音乐剧中〕很多演员一起唱歌跳舞的场景

production plat·form /ˈ· ·, ˌ·/ *n* [C] a large piece of equipment standing on very long legs, used for getting oil out of the ground under the sea; OIL RIG〔从海底开采石油的〕钻井平台，石油钻塔

pro·duc·tive /prəˋdʌktɪv; prəˈdʌktɪv/ *adj* **1** producing or achieving a lot 多产的; 丰饶的; 富有成效的: *Most of us are more productive in the morning.* 我们大多数人在早上较有效率。| *productive land* 肥沃的土地 | *a productive meeting* (=having useful results) 富有成果的会议 —opposite 反义词 UNPRODUCTIVE **2** producing goods, crops, or wealth 生产〔成品、庄稼或财富〕的; 生产性的: *Increased demand means developing more productive capacity in the factory.* 需求的增加意味着要加强工厂的生产能力。**3 productive of sth** *formal* causing or producing something【正式】造成…; 产生…: *Few ideas have been more productive of controversy than the redistribution of wealth.* 几乎没有什么观点比财富的再分配更能引发争议。—**productively** *adv* —**productiveness** *n* [U]

pro·duc·tiv·i·ty /ˌprɑdʌkˋtɪvətɪ; ˌprɒdʌkˈtɪvəti/ *n* [U] the rate at which goods are produced, and the amount produced, compared with the work, time, and money needed to produce them 生产力; 生产率，生产效率: *Management is always seeking ways to increase worker productivity.* 管理层总是在寻求提高工人生产效率的方法。| *a productivity bonus* 生产效率奖金

prof /prɑf; prɒf/ *n* [C] **1** *informal* a PROFESSOR【非正式】教授 **2 Prof** the written abbreviation of 缩写= PROFESSOR

pro·fane[1] /prəˋfen; prəˈfeɪn/ *adj* **1** showing disrespect for God or for holy things, using rude words, or religious words wrongly 渎神的，亵渎上帝的; 不敬圣物的;〔语言〕亵渎的，下流的: *a profane action* 亵渎行为 | *uttering profane curses* 说些下流的骂人话 **2** *formal* not religious or holy but dealing with human life【正式】世俗的，非宗教的: *sacred and profane art* 宗教艺术和世俗艺术 —opposite 反义词 SACRED —**profanely** *adv*

profane[2] *v* [T] *formal* to treat something holy in a disrespectful way【正式】亵渎〔圣物〕—**profanation** /ˌprɑfəˋneʃən; ˌprɒfəˈneɪʃən/ *n* [C,U]

pro·fan·i·ty /prəˋfænətɪ; prəˈfænəti/ *n plural* **profanities** [C, U] **1** rude words, or religious words used wrongly 亵渎的语言; 下流话 **2** an act of showing disrespect for God or for holy things 渎神，亵渎圣物

pro·fess /prəˋfɛs; prəˈfes/ *v* [T] *formal*【正式】**1** [T] to make a claim about something, especially a false one 自称; 伪称，妄称: **profess to do sth** *Leon professes to love his son, but he shows precious little evidence of it.* 利昂声称爱他的儿子，但他很少表现出这一点。| **profess to be sth** *Tusker professed to be an expert on Islamic art.* 塔斯克自称是伊斯兰艺术的专家。**2** to declare a personal feeling or belief openly and freely 声称，公开表明〔个人感情或信仰〕: *Rodin always professed his admiration for Greek and Gothic sculpture.* 罗丹总是公开表示他对希腊和哥特式雕塑的赞赏。| **profess yourself (to be) sth** *The composer professed himself to be delighted with the way we played his work.* 这位作曲家表示喜欢我们演奏他的作品的方式。**3** [T] to have a religion or belief 信仰〔某宗教〕; 具有…信仰: *Matt professed no religion.* 马特不信教。

pro·fessed /prəˋfɛst; prəˈfest/ *adj* [only before noun 仅用于名词前] *formal*【正式】**1** clearly stating what you believe 公开表示的，公开声称的: *a professed atheist* 公开声称为无神论者的人 **2** pretended, rather than real or sincere 假装的: *Holly's professed uncertainty* 霍莉装出来的犹豫 —**professedly** /prəˋfɛsɪdlɪ; prəˈfesɪdli/ *adv*

pro·fes·sion /prəˋfɛʃən; prəˈfeʃən/ *n* [C] **1** a job that needs special education and training〔需要专业教育和训练的〕职业: *What made you choose law as a profession?* 是什么使你选择法律作为职业的? —see 见 JOB (USAGE) **2 by profession** as your job 作为职业: *Castillo is a social worker by profession.* 卡斯蒂罗的职业是社会工作者。**3** all the people in a particular profession 某职业的全体人员; 同业，同行: [also+plural verb *BrE* 英] *The medical profession are divided on the main causes of heart attacks.* 医学界对于心脏病的主要病因意见不一。**4** a declaration of your belief, opinion, or feeling〔信念、观点或感情的〕公开表示，表白: *His speech was simply a profession of old-fashioned socialism.* 他的讲话只是表白自己对老式社会主义的信仰。**5 the oldest profession** *humorous* the job of being a PROSTITUTE【幽默】卖淫

pro·fes·sion·al[1] /prəˋfɛʃənl; prəˈfeʃənəl/ *adj*

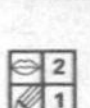

1 ►JOB 工作◄ [only before noun 仅用于名词前, no comparative 无比较级] connected with a job that needs special education and training 职业的，专业的: *What professional qualifications does he have?* 他有哪些专业资格? | *on the basis of professional advice* 根据专业人士的指导

2 ►WELL TRAINED 受过良好训练的◄ showing that someone has been well trained and is good at their work 专业的，内行的: *This business plan looks very professional.* 这个商业计划看上去很有专业水平。| *a more professional approach to work* 更内行的工作方法

3 ►PAID 有报酬的◄ [no comparative 无比较级] doing a job, sport or activity for money 职业性的; 专业的; 非业余的: *a professional tennis player* 职业网球运动员 | *a professional army* 职业军队 | **turn professional** (=start to do something as a job) 开始以做某事为职业 —compare 比较 AMATEUR[1] (1)

4 ►TEAM/EVENT 球队/比赛项目◄ [no comparative 无比较级] done by or connected with people who are paid 由职业人员参加的; 职业性的: *Jim's the manager of a professional hockey team.* 吉姆是一支职业曲棍球队的经理。| *The golf tournament is a professional event.* 这场高尔夫球锦标赛是职业球员参加的比赛。—compare 比较 AMATEUR[1] (1)

5 professional person/man/woman etc someone who works in a profession, or who has an important position in a company or business 专业人员; 专家: *We'd prefer to rent the house to a professional couple.* 我们更愿意把房子租给一对专业人士夫妇。

6 a professional liar/complainer etc *humorous* someone who lies or complains too much【幽默】撒谎过多的人/抱怨过多的人等

7 professional foul *BrE* a FOUL (=a rule broken in a sport) done deliberately to gain some advantage【英】〔体育运动中的〕故意犯规

professional[2] *n* [C] **1** someone who earns money by doing a job, sport, or activity that many other people do just for enjoyment 把…作为职业的人，专门职业者; 职业选手: *Hurd signed as a professional in 1978.* 赫德于 1978 年签约成为职业选手。—compare 比较 AMATEUR[2] **2** someone who works in a job that requires special education and training 专业人士，专家: *the relationship between health professionals and patients* 健康专家和病人之间的关系 **3** someone who has a lot of experience and does something very skilfully 内行，行家: *You read that like a real professional.* 你读起来像个行家。**4 tennis/golf/swimming etc professional** someone who is very good at a sport and is employed by a private club to teach its members〔私人俱乐部的〕网球/高尔夫球/游泳等教练

Professional Golf·ers' As·so·ci·a·tion of A·me·ri·ca /·,··· ···,····'··/ —see 见 the PGA

pro·fes·sion·al·is·m /prəˋfɛʃənl̩ɪzəm; prəˈfeʃənəlɪzəm/ *n* [U] **1** the skill and high standards of behaviour expected of a professional person 专业技巧，高超的水准; 专业道德: *The success of the orchestra is due to the professionalism of its members.* 该管弦乐队的成功是由于乐队成员高超的专业水平。**2** the practice of using professional players in sports〔体育竞赛的〕职业化

pro·fes·sion·al·ly /prəˋfɛʃənl̩ɪ; prəˈfeʃənəli/ *adv* **1** as part of your work 在工作中，在职业中: *Many foreign students will go on to use their English professionally.* 很多外国学生将继续在工作中使用英语。**2** in a way that shows high standards and good training 专业地，职业地: *Where did you learn to ski so professionally?* 你的滑雪水平这么高，是在哪里学的? **3** as a paid job rather than just for enjoyment 作为职业，职业性地: *a chance to play football professionally* 当职业足球员的机会

pro·fes·sor /prəˋfɛsɚ; prəˈfesə/ *n* [C] **1** *especially BrE* a teacher of the highest rank in a university department【尤英】〔大学〕教授; FULL PROFESSOR *AmE*【美】: *Thank you, Professor Barclay, for your comments.* 谢谢您的评论, 巴克利教授。| *my science professor* 我的理科教授 | *a professor of history* 历史学教授 **2** *AmE* a teacher at a university or college【美】大学教师: *Ted's a college professor.* 特德是一名大学教师。| *Professor, can I ask you a question?* 老师, 我能问你个问题吗? —see also 另见 ASSISTANT PROFESSOR, ASSOCIATE PROFESSOR **3** a title taken by some people who teach various skills 师傅; 专家〔对传授技艺者的称呼〕: *Madame Clara, professor of dancing* 克拉拉女士, 舞蹈专家

P

USAGE NOTE 用法说明: PROFESSOR
BRITISH AND AMERICAN ENGLISH 英国英语和美国英语

In many countries all university teachers are called **professor**. In Britain **professor** is used only for members of the highest rank of university teachers. 在很多国家, 所有的大学教师都称为professor。在英国, professor只用来称呼等级最高的大学教师: *a research professor* 研究教授 | *Professor Leech is in charge of the department here.* 利奇教授是本系的负责人。Lower ranks in a university are **lecturer, senior lecturer,** and **reader**. 大学里较低的等级有lecturer〔讲师〕, senior lecturer〔高级讲师〕和reader〔仅低于professor的教授〕。

In the US many more university teachers are called **professor**, which is used of any full member of the teaching staff of a university or college. There are three specific ranks: **associate professor, assistant professor,** and **full professor**. 在美国, 称为professor(教授)的大学教师比较多, professor可用来称大学中所有的正式教师。它有三个特定的级别: associate professor (副教授), assistant professor (助理教授), 和full professor (正教授)。

School teachers are never called professors in English. 在英语中, 中小学教师从不称为professor。

pro·fes·so·ri·al /ˌprɑfəˋsorɪəl; ˌprɒfəˈsɔːriəl◂/ *adj* connected with the job of a professor, or considered typical of a professor 教授的; 教授特有的: *His speech was clipped and precise – almost professorial.* 他的讲话急促而精确 —— 几乎像教授讲话一样。—**professorially** *adv*

pro·fes·sor·ship /prəˋfɛsɚˌʃɪp; prəˈfesəʃɪp/ *n* [C] the job or position of a university or college professor〔大学〕教授职位: *a professorship in Japanese* 日语教授职位

prof·fer /ˋprɑfɚ; ˈprɒfə/ *v* [T] *formal*【正式】**1** to offer something to someone, especially by holding it out in your hands〔给某人〕拿出, 递给: *Sarah sipped from the glass proffered by the attendant.* 萨拉从服务员端过来的玻璃杯中小口啜饮。| **proffer sb sth** *Poirot proffered him a cigarette.* 普瓦罗递给他一根烟。**2** to give someone advice, an explanation, etc 提出〔建议、解释等〕: *the proffered invitation* 提出的邀请 —**proffer** *n* [C]

pro·fi·cien·cy /prəˋfɪʃənsɪ; prəˈfɪʃənsi/ *n* [U] a high standard of ability and skill 熟练; 精通: **[+in]** *a high level of proficiency in grammar* 精通语法

pro·fi·cient /prəˋfɪʃənt; prəˈfɪʃənt/ *adj* able to do something well or skilfully 熟练的, 精通的: **[+in/at]** *Martha's proficient in Swedish.* 玛莎精通瑞典语。| *a proficient typist* 熟练的打字员 —**proficiently** *adv*

W3 **pro·file¹** /ˋprofaɪl; ˈprəʊfaɪl/ *n* [C] **1** a side view of someone's head〔人头部的〕侧面(像), 侧影: *Dani has a lovely profile.* 丹尼的侧面轮廓很可爱。| **in profile** *I only saw her face in profile.* 我只是从侧面看到她的脸。**2** a short description that gives important details about a person, a group of people, or a place 人物简介, 传略; 〔某地方的〕概况: **[+of]** *The company has an employee profile of everyone working for them.* 该公司有每个雇员的简介。| *We need a profile of the area: population, main roads, water supplies, etc.* 我们需要这一地区的概况: 人口、主要道路、供水系统等。**3 have a high profile/give sth a high profile** to be noticed by many people, or to make something get a lot of attention (使)引人注目: *Jack runs a department with a high public profile.* 杰克管理一个受到公众高度关注的部门。**4 keep a low profile** to behave quietly and avoid doing things that will make people notice you 保持低姿态[低调] **5** an edge or shape of something seen against a background 外形, 轮廓: *the sharp profile of the western foothills against the sky* 在天空衬托下西边山麓小丘的清晰轮廓

profile² *v* [T] to write or give a short description of someone or something 写…的传略[概况]: *The new editor was profiled in the Sunday paper.* 星期天的报纸登载了这位新编辑的简历。

pro·fil·ing /ˋprofaɪlɪŋ; ˈprəʊfaɪlɪŋ/ *n* **offender profiling** the process of studying a crime, especially a murder, and making judgments about the character of the person who did it 罪犯〔尤指谋杀犯〕特征分析

prof·it¹ /ˋprɑfɪt; ˈprɒfɪt/ *n* **1** [C,U] money that you gain by selling things or doing business 利润, 收益, 赢利: *They sold the business and bought a yacht with the profits.* 他们卖了公司并用所得的利润买了一艘游艇。| *The profit each day from the snack bar is usually around $500.* 这家小吃店每天所得利润通常是500美元左右。| **make (a) profit** *The telephone companies are making handsome profits every day.* (=very large ones) 电话公司每天获利丰厚。| **at a profit** *They sold their house at a huge profit.* 他们以高额利润卖掉了房子。| **clear profit** *Suzanne made a clear profit of £200 on the car sale.* 苏珊妮出售汽车净得利润200英镑。| **net profit** (=after tax etc is paid) 净利润, 纯利润 | **gross profit** (=before tax etc is paid) 毛利 | **bring sth into profit** (=gain money from it) 从…中获利 **2** [U] an advantage that you gain from doing something 益处, 好处: *reading for profit and pleasure* 为受益和乐趣而阅读 —see also 另见 NON-PROFITMAKING S1 W1

profit² *v* [T] *formal* to be useful or helpful to someone【正式】有益于, 对〔某人〕有好处: *It will profit you nothing to follow his example.* 以他为榜样对你没什么好处。

profit by/from sth *phr v* [T] to learn from something that happens, or get something good from a situation 从…中获益, 从…中得到教训: *My wardrobe definitely profited from having a stylish older sister.* 我穿的衣服无疑得益于有一位时髦的姐姐。

prof·it·a·bil·i·ty /ˌprɑfɪtəˋbɪlətɪ; ˌprɒfɪtəˈbɪləti/ *n* [U] the state of producing a profit, or the degree to which a business or activity is profitable 获利(能力), 赢利(能力): *a decline in company profitability* 公司赢利能力的下降

prof·i·ta·ble /ˋprɑfɪtəbl; ˈprɒfɪtəbəl/ *adj* producing a profit or a useful result 有利可图的; 有益的, 有用的: *The advertising campaign proved very profitable.* 事实证明, 这次广告宣传活动很有用。| *a highly profitable business* 非常有利可图的企业 | *a profitable afternoon* 有收获的下午 —opposite 反义词 UNPROFITABLE —**profitably** *adv*

profit and loss ac·count /ˌ···ˈ··ˌ·/ *n* [C] a financial statement showing a company's income, spending, and profit over a particular period 损益账〔反映公司某时期收支和利润情况的报表〕

prof·i·teer /ˌprɑfəˋtɪr; ˌprɒfɪˈtɪə/ *n* [C] someone who makes unfairly large profits, especially by selling things at very high prices when they are difficult to get 投机商, 奸商, 牟取暴利者: *black market profiteers* 黑市上牟取暴利的商人 —**profiteer** *v* [I] —**profiteering** *n* [U]

pro·fit·e·role /prəˋfɪtərol; prəˈfɪtərəʊl/ *n* [C] *BrE* a small round PASTRY with a sweet filling and chocolate on the top【英】〔内有甜馅顶部有巧克力的〕小圆饼

prof·it·less /ˋprɑfɪtləs; ˈprɒfɪtləs/ *adj* not making a profit, or not worth doing 无利的, 无利可图的; 无益的, 不值得做的 —**profitlessly** *adv*

profit mar·gin /ˈ··ˌ··/ *n* [C] the difference between the cost of producing something and the price you sell it at 利润空间, 赢利空间

profit shar·ing /ˈ··ˌ··/ *n* [U] a system by which all the people who work for a company share in its profits 分红制〔公司人员分享利润的制度〕

prof·li·gate¹ /ˋprɑflәgɪt; ˈprɒflɪgɪt/ *adj formal*【正式】**1** wasting money in a silly and careless way 恣意挥霍的; 极其浪费的: *profligate spending of the taxpayer's money* 恣意挥霍纳税人的钱 **2** behaving in an immoral way and not caring about it at all 放荡的, 行为不检点的 —**profligacy** *n* [U]

profligate² *n* [C] *formal* someone who is profligate【正式】恣意挥霍的人; 放荡的人

pro for·ma /pro ˈformə; prəʊ ˈfɔːmə/ *adj adv Latin* if something is approved, accepted etc pro forma, this is part of the usual way of doing things, but does not involve any actual choice or decision【拉丁】形式上的[地]: *pro forma approval* 形式上的同意

pro forma in·voice /ˌ··ˈ···/ *n* [C] a bill sent to a customer to show what a price would be if he made an order; QUOTATION 形式发票, 估价单

pro·found /prəˋfaʊnd; prəˈfaʊnd/ *adj* **1** showing strong, serious feelings〔感情〕强烈的; 深切的; 严肃的: *I owe you a profound apology.* 我应向你深深地道歉。**2** having a strong influ-

ence or effect〔影响〕深刻的, 极大的: *The mother's behavior has a profound impact on the developing child.* 母亲的行为对于正在成长的孩子有极大的影响。**3** showing great knowledge and understanding 知识渊博的; 见解深刻的: *a profound remark* 精辟的话 | *Jenner is a profound thinker.* 詹纳是学识渊博的思想家。**4** *literary* deep or far below the surface of something【文】深的; 深处的: *Her work engages something profound in the human psyche.* 她的作品涉及了人类心灵深处的某种东西。**5** *technical* complete【术语】完全的: *profound deafness* 全聋 —**profoundly** *adv*: *profoundly disturbing news* 令人极其不安的消息

pro·fun·di·ty /prəˋfʌndətɪ; prəˈfʌndəti/ *n formal*【正式】**1** [U] the quality of knowing and understanding a lot, or having strong, serious feelings〔知识〕渊博;〔情感〕深刻: *a young woman of extraordinary profundity* 一个思想非常深刻的年轻女人 | *Fairy tales have a profundity absent in most children's literature.* 童话思想深刻、意味深长, 为大多数儿童文学所缺乏。**2** [C usually plural 一般用复数] something that someone says that shows this quality 渊博[深刻]的话: *The profundities of his speech were lost on the young audience.* 他深奥的讲话对那些年轻的听众没有影响力。

pro·fuse /prəˋfjus; prəˈfjuːs/ *adj* **1** given, flowing, or growing freely and in large quantities 大量〔给予、流出、生长〕的; 丰富的; 充沛的: *profuse tears* 泪如泉涌 **2** too eager or generous with your praise, thanks etc〔称赞或感谢〕毫不吝惜的, 十分慷慨的; 过多的, 过滥的: **[+in]** *Stella was profuse in her thanks.* 斯特拉一再道谢。—**profusely** *adv*: *sweating profusely in the heat* 在高温下大汗淋漓 —**profuseness** *n* [U]

pro·fu·sion /prəˋfjuʒən; prəˈfjuːʒən/ *n* [singular,U] a supply or amount that is almost too large 大量; 丰富; 充沛: **[+of]** *The house was overflowing with a profusion of strange ornaments.* 这个房子里摆满了奇特的装饰品。| **in profusion** *Corn marigolds grow in profusion in the fields.* 田野里长着茂盛的珍珠菊。

pro·gen·i·tor /proˋdʒɛnətɚ; prəʊˈdʒenɪ̥tə/ *n* [C] *technical*【术语】**1** a person or animal that lived a long time ago, to whom someone or something living now is related; ANCESTOR〔人或动物的〕祖先 **2** *formal* someone who first thought of an idea a long time ago; PRECURSOR【正式】创始人, 前辈, 先驱: **[+of]** *a progenitor of modern music* 现代音乐的创始人

prog·e·ny /ˋprɑdʒənɪ; ˈprɒdʒɪ̥ni/ *n* [U] **1** *technical or formal* the DESCENDANTS of a person, animal, or plant form, or the things that can develop from something else【术语或正式】〔人、动植物或事物的〕后代; 后裔: *The drug-resistant cells' progeny are also drug-resistant.* 抗药细胞的后代同样抗药。**2** *old-fashioned or humorous* someone's children【过时或幽默】〔某人的〕儿女, 孩子: *Sarah with her numerous progeny* 萨拉和她的一大群孩子

pro·ges·ter·one /proˋdʒɛstəˌron; prəʊˈdʒestərəʊn/ *n* [U] a female sex HORMONE that is produced by a woman when she is going to have a baby and is also used in CONTRACEPTIVE drugs 孕酮, 黄体酮〔一种女性性激素〕

prog·na·thous /ˋprɑgnəθəs; prɒgˈneɪθəs/ *adj technical* with a jaw that sticks out more than the rest of your face【术语】凸颚的, 下巴突出的

prog·no·sis /prɑgˋnosɪs; prɒgˈnəʊsɪ̥s/ *n plural* **prognoses** [C] **1** *technical* a doctor's opinion of how an illness or disease will develop【术语】预后, 预断〔医生对于病情如何发展的预测〕: *The doctor's prognosis for Mum wasn't hopeful.* 医生对妈妈病情的发展不乐观。—compare 比较 DIAGNOSIS **2** *formal* a judgement about the future based on information or experience【正式】〔基于资料和经验而作出的〕预测, 展望: **[+of]** *a hopeful prognosis of the country's future development* 对于该国未来发展的乐观展望

prog·nos·ti·cate /prɑgˋnɑstɪˌket; prɒgˈnɒstɪ̥keɪt/ *v* [T] to say what will happen, or to be a sign of what will happen 预言; 预示; 是…的预兆 —**prognostication** /prɑgˌnɑstɪˋkeʃən; prɒgˌnɒstɪ̥ˈkeɪʃən/ *n* [C,U]

pro·gram[1] /ˋprogræm; ˈprəʊgræm/ *n* [C] **1** a set of instructions given to a computer to make it perform an operation〔电脑的〕程序, 程式: *a new program for forecasting sales figures* 用于预测销售数字的新程序 **2** the American spelling of PROGRAMME programme 的美式拼法

program[2] *v* **programmed, programming** [T] **1** to give a computer a set of instructions that it can use to perform a particular operation〔为电脑〕编制程序, 编程: **program sth to do sth** *Scientists are trying to program computers to think in the same way as humans.* 科学家正试图为电脑设计一套能像人类那样进行思维的程序。**2** the American spelling of PROGRAMME programme 的美式拼法 —see also 另见 PROGRAMMER

pro·gram·ma·ble /ˋprogræməbl̩; ˈprəʊgræməbəl/ *adj* able to be controlled by a computer or electronic program 可电脑控制的, 可程序控制的: *a programmable heating system* 程控供暖系统

pro·gramme[1] *BrE*【英】, **program** *AmE*【美】/ˋprogræm; ˈprəʊgræm/ *n* [C] **1** an important plan, especially one organized by a government or large organization〔尤指政府或大型机构的〕重大计划, 方案: *a United Nations programme to control the spread of AIDS* 联合国控制艾滋病传播的计划 | *the US space program* 美国太空计划 **2** a show or performance on television or radio, especially one that is played regularly〔电视或广播的〕节目: *Northern Exposure is my favorite TV program.*《北国风云》是我最喜欢的电视节目。| **[+about]** *There's a programme on about organic gardening.* 有一个关于使用有机肥栽培植物的节目正在播映。**3** a set of planned activities in education or training, with a specific purpose〔教育或训练安排好的〕课程, 活动, 方案: *Stanford University's MBA program* 斯坦福大学的工商管理硕士课程 | *Lucy's new fitness programme includes a 5 mile jog every morning.* 露西的新健身计划包括每天早上五英里的慢跑。**4** a printed description of what will happen at a play, concert etc and of the people who will be performing〔戏剧、音乐会等的〕节目单 **5** the planned order of activities or events at a performance or meeting; SCHEDULE[1] (1)〔表演或会议的〕程序单, 计划表, 活动安排, 进度表: *The next race on today's programme is the King George V Handicap.* 在今天的比赛程序单上, 下一场比赛是乔治五世让步赛。**6** a series of actions done in a particular order by a machine such as a washing machine〔洗衣机等机器按固定步骤工作的〕工作程序: *The light goes off when it finishes its program.* 完成工作程序之后, 灯就会熄灭。—see also 另见 PROGRAM[1]

programme[2] *BrE*【英】, **program** *AmE*【美】*v* [T] **1 be programmed** to be made to behave or think in a particular way because of the influence of a society, group, or situation〔由于社会、群体或情况的影响〕使〔某人〕按某种方式行事[思考]: **[+to]** *Are girls programmed at an early age not to be interested in science subjects?* 女孩年幼时就受外界影响而对科学科目不感兴趣吗? **2** to set a machine to operate in a particular way 调好, 设置〔机器, 使之按某种方式运作〕: *I've programmed the video to come on at ten.* 我已经把这台录像机设置好在10点钟开机。—see also 另见 PROGRAM[1] **3** to arrange for something to happen as part of a series of planned events or activities 安排, 计划: *What's programmed for this afternoon?* 今天下午有什么安排?

programmed course /ˌ‥ˈ‥/ *n* [C] a course of study that is part of programmed learning 程序课程

programmed learn·ing /ˌ‥ˈ‥/ *n* [U] a method of learning in which the subject to be learned is divided into small parts, and you have to get one part right before you can go on to the next 程序学习〔一种学习方法, 要学习的科目被分成小部分, 学习者必须把一部分掌握之后才能进入下一部分〕

programme mu·sic *BrE*【英】, **program music** *AmE*【美】/ˈ‥ ˌ‥/ *n* [U] descriptive music which uses sound to suggest a story, picture etc 标题音乐〔利用声音描绘故事、画面等的音乐〕

pro·gram·mer /ˋprogræmɚ; ˈprəʊgræmə/ *n* [C] someone whose job is to write computer PROGRAMS〔电脑的〕程序编制员, 程序设计员

pro·gram·ming /ˋprogræmɪŋ; ˈprəʊgræmɪŋ/ *n* [U] **1** the activity of writing PROGRAMS for computers〔电脑的〕程序编制, 编程: *programming languages* 编程语言 **2** television or radio programmes, or the activity of producing them〔电视或广播〕节目; 电视[广播]节目制作: *nearly 200 hours of sports programming* 将近200小时的体育节目

pro·gress[1] /ˋprɑgrɛs; ˈprəʊgres/ *n* **1** [U] the process of getting better at doing something, or getting closer to finishing or achieving something 进步; 进展: **[+of/on/towards]** *Nico had been candid with Stern about the progress of the investigation.* 尼科已把调查的进展情况向斯特恩坦言相告。| *tests designed to monitor the student's progress* 旨在检查学生进步情况的测试 **2 make progress a)** to get better at doing something or come closer to finishing or achieving something 取得进步, 取得进展: *Nick has made good progress with his studies this year.* 今年尼克的学习有了很大进步。| *I'm afraid we're not making much progress.* 恐怕我们进步不大。**b)** to move towards a place〔向某地〕前进, 行进: *By nighttime we had still made very little progress.* 到了夜间我们仍然没怎么前行。**3** [U] change towards a better society because of developments in science or fairer methods of social organization〔社会的〕进步: *the great march of progress* 社会进步的巨大步伐 **4 in progress** *formal* happening now, and not yet finished【正式】在进行中: *No Talking. Examination in Progress.* 不要讲话, 考试正在进行。**5** [U] slow

or difficult movement towards a place〔向某地的〕缓慢[艰难]行进: *We watched with apprehension their progress across the face of the cliff.* 我们提心吊胆地看着他们在崖面上缓慢前行。**6** [C] *old use* a journey, especially by a king or queen【旧】〔尤指国王或女王的〕巡行, 巡游

progress² /prəˋgrɛs; prəˈgres/ *v* [I] **1** to develop over a period of time and become something better or more complete 进步; 进展: *Work on the ship progressed quickly.* 轮船的建造进展迅速。| *I asked the nurse how my son was progressing.* 我向护士询问我儿子身体恢复得如何。| **[+to]** *Cindy has progressed to reading on her own.* 辛迪进步了, 开始自己阅读了。**2** if an activity or situation progresses, it continues to happen or develop gradually〔活动等〕继续进行; 逐步发展: *As the meeting progressed, Nina grew more and more bored.* 随着会议的进行, 尼娜越来越感到无聊。**3** to move forward slowly 缓慢行进: *Our taxi seemed to be progressing with agonizing slowness.* 我们的出租车仿佛以令人难以忍受的缓慢速度向前行驶。**4** to move on from doing one thing to doing another〔从做一件事〕转向〔做另一件事〕: **[+to]** *We started with a bottle of wine, and then progressed to whisky.* 我们先喝了一瓶葡萄酒, 之后便喝起了威士忌。—compare 比较 REGRESS

pro·gres·sion /prəˋgrɛʃən; prəˈgreʃən/ *n* **1** [U] a gradual process of change or development 进步; 进展: *They offer rapid career progression.* 他们提供迅速的职业晋升。| **progression from sth to sth** *The progression from infection to disease can take up to 7 years.* 从感染到发病可能长达七年。**2** [U] movement towards a goal or particular place〔向某一目标或地点的〕移动, 前行: *the river's stately progression towards the Gulf of Mexico* 这条河向墨西哥湾气势磅礴的奔流 **3** a number of things coming one after the other 接连, 连续, 一系列 —see also 另见 ARITHMETIC PROGRESSION, GEOMETRIC PROGRESSION

pro·gres·sive¹ /prəˋgrɛsɪv; prəˈgresɪv/ *adj* **1** supporting new or modern ideas and methods, especially in politics and education〔尤指在政治和教育方面〕进步的, 先进的: *a progressive administration* 进步的政府 | *progressive and forward-looking policies* 进步并有前瞻性的政策 **2** happening or developing gradually over a period of time 逐步发生的, 逐步发展的: *the progressive elimination of rural poverty* 农村贫困的逐步消除 | *Britain's progressive decline as a world power* 英国作为世界强国的逐步衰落 **3** the progressive form of a verb is used to show that an action or activity is continuing to happen, and is shown in English by the verb 'be', followed by a PRESENT PARTICIPLE, as in 'I was waiting for the bus'〔动词形式〕进行式的 —**progressively** *adv*: *The situation became progressively worse.* 情况变得越来越糟。—**progressiveness** *n* [U]

progressive² *n* [C] someone with modern ideas who wants to change things 进步人士; 革新派人士

Progressive Con·ser·va·tive Par·ty, the /.,.. '...., '.·/ one of the main political parties in Canada 进步保守党, 激进保守党〔加拿大主要政党之一〕

Progressive Par·ty, the /.'.. ,./ one of the three US political parties which existed in the first half of the 20th century and supported progressive ideas, such as better working conditions and government help for poor people, people without jobs etc. The Progressive Party was active in the US presidential elections of 1912, 1924, and 1948, but these were in fact three separate organizations. 进步党〔20 世纪上半叶美国三大政党之一。该党支持进步思想, 如改善工作条件、政府应扶助穷人及失业者等主张。进步党在1912、1924和1948年三次美国总统大选中表现活跃, 但实际上却是彼此独立的三个政党〕

progressive tax /.,.. '.·/ *n* [singular] a tax that takes a larger PERCENTAGE of money from people with higher incomes than from people with lower incomes 累进税 —compare 比较 REGRESSIVE TAX

progress re·port /'.. .,./ *n* [C] a statement about how something, especially work, is advancing or developing〔尤指工作的〕进展报告

pro·hib·it /proˋhɪbɪt; prəˈhɪbɪt/ *v* [T] **1** to officially stop an activity by making it illegal or against the rules〔以法令、规则等〕禁止: *Smoking is strictly prohibited inside the factory.* 工厂内严禁吸烟。| **prohibit sb from doing sth** *Nuclear powers are prohibited from selling this technology.* 禁止核大国出售该项技术。**2** to make something impossible or prevent it from happening 使不可能; 阻止: *High costs had prohibited the building work from being completed.* 高额费用使这项建筑工程无法完工。

Pro·hi·bi·tion /ˌproəˋbɪʃən; ˌprəʊhɪˈbɪʃən/ the period from 1920 to 1933 in the US, when it was illegal to make or sell alcoholic drinks. It was impossible to make people obey the law, and criminals made a lot of money from selling illegal alcohol. Prohibition is the subject of many US GANGSTER films. 禁酒时期〔美国1920-1933年禁止生产或销售含酒精饮品的时期。尽管如此, 当时尚无法使每个人都遵守法令, 犯罪分子反而靠非法出售私酒大获其利。"禁酒时期"是许多美国匪盗影片的主题〕

prohibition *n* **1** [U] the act of officially stopping something by law〔以法律〕禁止: **[+of]** *prohibition of the sale of firearms* 禁止出售枪支 **2** [C] an order stopping something 禁令, 禁律: **[+on/against]** *a prohibition on Sunday trading* 禁止星期天交易的法令

pro·hi·bi·tion·ist /ˌproəˋbɪʃənɪst; ˌprəʊhɪˈbɪʃənɪst/ *n* [C] someone who supported Prohibition 赞成禁酒者; 禁酒主义者 —**prohibitionism** *n* [U]

pro·hib·i·tive /proˋhɪbɪtɪv; prəˈhɪbɪtɪv/ *adj* **1** prohibitive prices are so high that they prevent people from buying something〔价格〕高得负担不起的, 贵得使人望而却步的: *The cost of land in Tokyo is prohibitive.* 东京的地价高得让人不敢问津。**2** a prohibitive tax or rule prevents people from doing things〔税收、规定〕禁止性的; 起阻止作用的: *a prohibitive tax on imports* 对进口物品征收的高额税 —**prohibitively** *adv*: *prohibitively expensive* 贵得使人负担不起

pro·hib·i·to·ry /proˋhɪbəˌtorɪ; prəˈhɪbɪtəri/ *adj* intended to stop something 禁止的, 禁止性的

proj·ect¹ /ˋprɑdʒɛkt; ˈprɒdʒekt/ *n* [C] **1** an important and carefully planned piece of work, that is intended to build or produce something new, or to deal with a problem 项目; 工程; 计划; 规划: *the Channel Tunnel project* 海峡隧道工程 | *a long-term project to help the homeless* 一项帮助无家可归者的长期计划 **2** a part of a school course that involves careful study of a particular subject over a period of time〔学校的〕课题, 研究项目: **[+on]** *We're doing a project on pollution.* 我们正在做一个有关污染的课题。**3** also 又作 **the projects** *AmE informal* a HOUSING PROJECT【美, 非正式】〔低收入人群的〕住宅区, 公屋区

pro·ject² /prəˋdʒɛkt; prəˈdʒekt/ *v*

1 ►CALCULATE 计算◄ [T] to calculate the size, amount, or rate of something as it will be in the future, using the information you have now 预计; 推断: *The company projected an annual growth rate of 3%.* 该公司预计每年的增长率为3%。| *projected sales forecasts* 预计的销售数字

2 ►STICK OUT 突出◄ [I,T] to stick out beyond an edge or surface 凸出, 突出: **[+out/from/through etc]** *The huge guns projected outwards from the deck of the ship.* 巨炮从船甲板向外伸出。

3 ►FILM 电影◄ [T] to make the picture of a film, photograph etc appear in a larger form on a SCREEN¹ (2) or flat surface 放映; 投射

4 ►YOURSELF 你自己◄ [T] to make other people have a particular idea about you 使别人对自己有某种看法; 使〔自己的特点〕呈现; 表现〔自己〕: **project an image** *Regina always projects an image of quiet self-confidence.* 雷吉娜总是表现出安静自信的样子。| **project yourself** *You'll need to project yourself well in the interview.* 你必须在面试时好好表现自己。

5 ►FEELING 感情◄ [T] *technical* to avoid dealing with your own feelings by imagining that someone else is feeling them【术语】想象〔他人〕具有〔本人的思想感情〕; 把〔自己的感情〕投射给别人: **project sth on/onto sb** *You're projecting your insecurity onto me.* 你在把你的不安全感往我身上转移。

6 ►PLAN 计划◄ be projected to be planned to happen in the future 计划; 预定: *A visit by President Clinton is projected for March.* 克林顿总统拟定于3月份出访。

7 ►THROW 扔, 投◄ [T] *technical* to throw something up or forward with great force【术语】投掷; 发射

8 ►PICTURE 图画◄ *technical*【术语】**a)** to make a picture of a solid object on a flat surface 作〔立体物的〕投影图 **b)** to make a map using this method 用投影法制作地图

9 project yourself into the future/past etc to imagine that you are in the future, past etc 设想自己身处将来/过去等: *I kept trying to project myself back into a time when I thought those kind of parties were fun.* 我总是竭力想象自己回到从前, 当时我认为那种聚会很有趣。

10 project your voice to speak clearly and loudly so that you can be heard by everyone in a big hall or room 放开声音〔使大厅或大房间的每个人都能听见〕

pro·jec·tile /prəˋdʒɛktl; prəˈdʒektaɪl/ *n* [C] an object that is thrown or is fired from a weapon, such as a bullet, stone, or SHELL¹ (2, 3) 投掷物; 抛射体; 发射物〈如子弹, 石头或炮弹〉—**projectile** *adj*

pro·jec·tion /prəˋdʒɛkʃən; prəˈdʒekʃən/ *n* **1** [C] a calculation of the amount or rate of something as it will be in the future, which is used for making official plans〔对于未来情况的〕预 

测，估算: [+of] *projections of declining natural gas production* 对于下降的天然气产量的预测 **2** [C] a statement about what will happen, based on information available now〔根据已知资料进行的〕推断，预测: *Early projections show a three point lead for the Socialists.* 早期预测显示社会党人领先三个百分点。**3** [C] *formal* something that sticks out from a surface【正式】凸出物: *small projections of weathered rock on the hillside* 山坡上许多凸出的小块风化岩石 **4** [U] the act of projecting a film or picture 投射〔电影等〕; 投影; 放映: *projection equipment* 投影器材 **5** [U] *technical* the act of imagining that someone else is feeling what you are in fact feeling【术语】投射〔想象别人与自己有同样的感受〕 **6** [C] *technical* an image of something that has been projected, especially an image of the world's surface on a map【术语】投影图;〔尤指〕投影的地图 —see also 另见 MERCATOR PROJECTION

pro·jec·tion·ist /prəˋdʒɛkʃənɪst; prəˈdʒekʃənɪst/ *n* [C] someone whose job is to operate the projector in a cinema 电影放映员

pro·jec·tor /prəˋdʒɛktɚ; prəˈdʒektə/ *n* [C] a piece of equipment that makes a film appear on a SCREEN[1] (2a) or a flat surface 电影放映机; 投影仪

Pro·kof·i·ev /prəˋkɔfɪɛf; prəˈkɒfief/**, Ser·gei** /sɛrˋge; ˈseəgeɪ/ (1891-1953) a Russian COMPOSER, whose works include the *Classical Symphony*, the BALLET *Romeo and Juliet*, and the MUSICAL story *Peter and the Wolf* 普罗科菲耶夫〔(1891-1953)，俄罗斯作曲家。其作品包括《古典交响乐》、芭蕾舞剧《罗密欧与朱丽叶》及音乐剧《彼得与狼》等〕

pro·lapse /proˋlæps; ˈprəʊlæps/ *n* [C] *technical* the falling down or slipping of an inner part of your body, such as the WOMB, from its usual position【术语】〔身体内部器官的〕脱垂; 脱出; 下垂

prole /prol; prəʊl/ *n* [C] *BrE informal* an insulting word for a working class person【英，非正式】无产者〔对工人的侮辱性说法〕

pro·le·tar·i·an /ˌproləˋtɛrɪən; ˌprəʊlɪ̵ˈteəriən◂/ *adj* concerning or involving the proletariat 无产阶级的

pro·le·tar·i·at /ˌproləˋtɛrɪət; ˌprəʊlɪ̵ˈteəriət/ *n* **the proletariat** the class of workers who own no property and work for wages, especially in factories, building things etc 无产阶级

pro-life /ˌ· ˈ·/ *adj* someone who is pro-life is opposed to ABORTION and uses this word to describe their views 反对堕胎的，反对人工流产的

pro-lif·er /ˌ· ˈ· ·/ *n* [C] a member of a pro-life group 反对堕胎者，反对人工流产者

pro·lif·e·rate /proˋlɪfəˌret; prəˈlɪfəreɪt/ *v* [I] if something proliferates it increases rapidly and spreads to many different places 激增; 扩散: *Self-help groups have proliferated all over London.* 自助小组迅速增加，遍及整个伦敦。

pro·lif·e·ra·tion /proˌlɪfəˋreʃən; prəˌlɪfəˈreɪʃən/ *n* **1** [singular, U] a rapid increase in the amount or number of something〔数量的〕激增; 扩散: [+of] *the proliferation of nuclear weapons* 核武器的扩散 | *a proliferation of cafes and restaurants* 咖啡馆和餐馆的大量涌现 **2** [U] *technical* the very fast growth of new parts of a living thing, such as cells or BUDS【术语】增殖，增生

pro·lif·ic /prəˋlɪfɪk; prəˈlɪfɪk/ *adj* **1** a prolific artist, writer etc produces many works of art, books etc〔艺术家、作家等〕多产的，作品丰富的 **2** an animal or plant that is prolific produces many babies or many other plants〔动物或植物〕多产的，多育的 **3** *literary* existing in large numbers【文】大量存在的: *the prolific bird life* 大量的鸟类 —**prolifically** /-klɪ; -kli/ *adv*

pro·lix /proˋlɪks; ˈprəʊlɪks/ *adj formal* a prolix piece of writing has too many words and is boring【正式】〔文章〕冗长乏味的，啰唆的

PROLOG /ˋprolɔg; ˈprəʊlɒg/ *n* [U] *trademark* a computer language that is similar to human language【商标】PROLOG 语言，逻辑程序设计语言，逻辑编程语言〔一种类似人类语言的电脑语言〕

pro·logue /ˋprolɔg; ˈprəʊlɒg/ *n* [C usually singular 一般用单数] **1** the introduction to a play, a long poem etc〔戏剧、长诗等的〕序幕; 开场白; 序诗; 序 **2** *literary* an act or event that leads to a much more important event【文】〔重大事件的〕开端，序幕 —compare 比较 EPILOGUE

pro·long /prəˋlɔŋ; prəˈlɒŋ/ *v* [T] **1** to deliberately make something such as a feeling or activity last longer 延长，拖长〔感觉、活动等〕: *I was trying to think of some way to prolong the conversation.* 我正在努力想出某种拖长交谈时间的办法。**2 prolong the agony** *informal* to delay telling someone something that they very much want to know【非正式】延长痛苦〔拖延告诉某人他很想知道的事情〕: *There's no point in prolonging the agony. The situation won't get any better.* 让痛苦延续下去没有什么意义——情况不会有什么好转。

pro·lon·ga·tion /ˌprolɔŋˋgeʃən; ˌprəʊlɒŋˈgeɪʃən/ *n* **1** [U] the act of making something last longer 延长，拉长; 拖延 **2** [C+of] something added to another thing which makes it longer 增加[延长]的部分

pro·longed /prəˋlɔŋd; prəˈlɒŋd/ *adj* continuing for a long time 持续很久的; 长期的: *a prolonged absence* 长时间的缺席

prom /prɑm; prɒm/ *n* [C] **1** *AmE* a formal dance party for HIGH SCHOOL students, often held at the end of a school year【美】〔常在学年末为高中生举行的〕正式舞会 **2** *BrE informal* a PROMENADE (1)【英，非正式】滨海散步道 **3** *BrE informal* a PROMENADE CONCERT【英，非正式】漫步音乐会

prom·e·nade /ˌprɑməˋned; ˌprɒməˈnɑːd/ *n* [C] **1** *BrE* a wide road next to the beach where people can walk for pleasure【英】〔供人们散步的〕滨海散步道 **2** *old-fashioned* a walk for pleasure in a public place【过时】〔在公共场所的〕散步

promenade con·cert /ˈ· · ˌ· ·/ *n* [C] *BrE* a concert at which many of the listeners stand rather than sit【英】逍遥音乐会，漫步音乐会〔很多听众站着听的音乐会〕

promenade deck /ˈ· · ˌ·/ *n* [C] the upper level of a ship where people can walk for pleasure〔轮船的〕上层甲板，散步甲板

Pro·me·the·us /prəˋmiθɪəs; prəˈmiːθiəs/ in Greek MYTHOLOGY, one of the Titans (=the first gods who ruled the universe). He stole fire from heaven to give to human beings, and as a result he was punished by Zeus by being kept in chains, and was finally set free by Herakles. 普罗米修斯〔古希腊神话中的巨人之一。他从天界偷来火种给人类使用，结果受到宙斯的惩罚，戴上了锁链，后被赫拉克勒斯解救〕

prom·i·nence /ˋprɑmənəns; ˈprɒmɪ̵nəns/ *n* **1** [U] the fact of being important and well-known 重要; 杰出; 著名: **come to/gain prominence** (=become important and well-known) 成名，崭露头角 *Gandhi first came to prominence in South Africa in the 1920s.* 甘地最初于20世纪20年代在南非崭露头角。**2 give sth prominence/give prominence to sth** to put something in a position where it is easily noticed because you think it is important 把某事物置于显著位置: *The topic didn't deserve the prominence it was given.* 这个主题本不应放在如此显著位置。**3** *formal* a part or place that is higher or larger than what is around it【正式】突出部分; 突起; 凸地

prom·i·nent /ˋprɑmənənt; ˈprɒmɪ̵nənt/ *adj* **1** [C] well-known and important 著名的; 卓越的，杰出的; 重要的: *a prominent Russian scientist* 杰出的俄罗斯科学家 | **play a prominent role** *Mandela played a prominent role in the early years of the ANC.* 曼德拉在非洲人国民大会的最初几年起着重要的作用。**2** something that is prominent is large and sticks out 突出的，凸出的: *a prominent nose* 高鼻子 **3 a prominent place/position** somewhere that is easily seen and is usually used for things that are important 突出的[显著的，显眼的]位置: *The Kaiser's photo displayed in a prominent position on the piano.* 德国皇帝的照片摆在钢琴上一个显眼的位置。

pro·mis·cu·ous /prəˋmɪskjuəs; prəˈmɪskjuəs/ *adj* **1** having sex with a lot of people 与多人发生性关系的，淫乱的，滥交的: *Single men were the most promiscuous group.* 单身男人是最不约束自己性行为的一伙人。**2** *old use* made of many different parts【旧】由很多不同部分组成的，混杂的 **3** *old use* not choosing carefully; INDISCRIMINATE【旧】不加区别的; 随便的 —**promiscuously** *adv* —**promiscuity** /ˌprɑmɪsˋkjuətɪ; ˌprɒmɪ̵ˈskjuːɪ̵ti/ *n* [U]

prom·ise[1] /ˋprɑmɪs; ˈprɒmɪ̵s/ *v* **1** [I,T] to tell someone that you will definitely do something or that something will happen 保证，答应，许诺: **promise (that)** *Hurry up, we promised that we wouldn't be late.* 快点，我们保证过不会迟到。| **promise sb (that)** *You promised me the car would be ready on Monday.* 你答应过我这辆车星期一可以用。| **I/we promise** *"Promise me you won't do anything stupid." "I promise."* "答应我你不会做蠢事。""我答应。" | **promise to do sth** *The children have promised to give us a hand with the packing.* 孩子们已答应帮我们打包。| **promise sb sth** (=promise to give someone something) 答应给某人某物 *The company promised us a bonus this year.* 公司答应今年给我们发奖金。| **Promise?** *spoken* (=used to ask if someone promises)【口】(你) 保证? *"I'll be back by 1.00." "Promise?" "Yes! Don't worry."* "我1点钟前会回来。""你能保证?""是的! 别担心。" | **promise sth to sb** *I can't give you the book – I've promised it to Ian.* 我不能把这本书给你——我已经答应给伊恩了。| **as promised** (=at the time or place that is promised) 正如许诺的 *Here you are – one new watch as promised.* 给你——一只向你许诺过的新手表。| **I promise you** *spoken* (=I warn you)【口】我警告你 *I promise you, the work won't be easy.* 我警告你，这项工作可不容易。**2** [T] to make you

expect that something will happen 有…的希望，使…很有可能；给人以…的指望：**promise to be** *Tonight's meeting promises to be a difficult one.* 今晚的会面有可能不容易对付。| *dark clouds promising showers later* 预示着稍后有阵雨的黑云 **3 promise sb the moon/the earth** to promise to give someone something that is impossible for you to give 向某人作无法兑现的承诺 **4 I can't promise anything** *spoken* used to tell someone that you will try to do what they want, but may not be able to【口】我不能保证什么：*I'll try my best, but I can't promise anything.* 我会尽我所能，但我不能保证什么。

promise² *n* **1** [C] a statement that you will definitely do something or that something will definitely happen 保证，承诺，诺言：*I'll never lie to you again. That's a promise.* 我再也不对你撒谎了，我向你保证。| **[+of]** *a promise of help* 答应给予帮助的承诺 | **a promise to do sth** *They've given a promise to introduce equal pay for women.* 他们已许诺给妇女同等报酬。| **[+that]** *I kept thinking of my mother's promise that she'd read me the story if I was good.* 我老是想起我母亲的承诺，说如果我表现好，她就给我读故事。| **keep/break a promise** (=to do or fail to do something you promised) 信守/违背诺言 *Don't make promises you can't keep.* 不要作出你不能信守的诺言。| *You broke your promise to give up smoking.* 你违背了戒烟的诺言。**2** [U] signs that something or someone will be good or successful〔某事或某人有好结果或成功的〕迹象，征兆：*a young man full of promise* 一个大有前途的年轻人 | **[+of]** *the promise of future profits* 未来赢利的预兆 | **show promise** (=to be likely to become very good) 很有前途，大有希望 *My son shows great promise as a chess player.* 我的儿子表现出成为棋手的巨大潜力。

Promised Land /ˌ‥ ˈ‥/ *n* [singular] **1** a situation or condition that you have wanted for a long time because it will bring you happiness and security 期盼中的乐土，福地：*the promised land of full employment* 充分就业的希望之乡 **2** the land of Canaan, which was promised by God to Abraham and his people in the Bible 迦南，应许之地〔《圣经》中上帝赐给亚伯拉罕和他的族人的土地〕

Promise Keep·ers, the /ˈ‥ ˌ‥/ a US Christian religious organization for men that started in 1990 and has over 2 million members. It holds very large, public meetings, often in sports grounds. The Promise Keepers have very strong Christian beliefs, and members are expected to behave in a very moral and honest way. Some people say that they have old-fashioned traditional beliefs, including the belief that men should control their wives' lives and be the leaders of their families. 基督教守信派〔美国一男性基督教派，创立于1990年，现有教友200余万。该教派经常在体育场等公共场所举行大型集会。基督教守信派笃信基督教教义，要求教徒做事做人符合道德，诚实可信。然而，有些人却认为该教派恪守的传统观念早已过时，如男人应掌控妻子的日常生活，男人应成为一家之主等等〕

prom·is·ing /ˈprɑmɪsɪŋ; ˈprɒmɪ̇sɪŋ/ *adj* showing signs of being successful in the future 大有希望的，很有前途的：*a promising career in law* 很有前途的司法界职业 | *a promising young actor* 大有前途的年轻演员 —**promisingly** *adv*

prom·is·so·ry note /ˈprɑmɪsɔrɪ ˌnot; ˈprɒmɪ̇səri ˌnəʊt/ *n* [C] a document promising to pay money before a particular date 期票；本票

pro·mo /ˈpromo; ˈprəʊməʊ/ *plural* **promos** *n* [C] *informal* a short film that advertises an event or product【非正式】广告短片

prom·on·to·ry /ˈprɑmənˌtɔrɪ; ˈprɒməntəri/ *n* [C] a high long narrow piece of land which goes out into the sea 岬（角），海角 —see picture on page A12 参见A12页图

pro·mote /prəˈmot; prəˈməʊt/ *v* [T] **1** to help something to develop and be successful 促进，增进：*a meeting to promote trade between France and the U.K.* 促进法国和英国之间贸易的会议 | *Fertilizer promotes leaf growth.* 肥料促进叶子的生长。**2** [usually passive 一般用被动态] to give someone a better, more responsible job in a company 擢升，提升，晋升〔某人〕：**promote sb to sth** *Helen was promoted to senior manager.* 海伦被提升为高级经理。—opposite 反义词 DEMOTE **3** to make sure people know about a new product, film etc by offering it at a reduced price or advertising it on television 促销，推销〔货物〕；推广〔产品〕 **4** to be responsible for arranging a large public event such as a concert or a sports game 筹办，主办〔大型活动〕〈如音乐会或体育比赛〉 **5** to try to persuade people to believe or support an idea or way of doing things 倡议；提倡：*a passionate speech promoting equality* 一篇充满激情的宣扬平等的演讲 **6 be promoted** if a sports team is promoted, they play in a different group of better teams the next year〔运动队〕被升级 —opposite 反义词 RELEGATE (2)

pro·mot·er /prəˈmotɚ; prəˈməʊtə/ *n* [C] **1** someone who arranges and advertises concerts or sports events〔音乐会或体育比赛的〕主办者，承办者 **2** someone who tries to make people believe or support an idea or way of doing things 倡导者，提倡者：*promoters of solar energy* 提倡使用太阳能的人

pro·mo·tion /prəˈmoʃən; prəˈməʊʃən/ *n* **1** [C,U] a move to a more important job or rank in a company or organization 擢升，提升，晋升：*I want a job with good promotion prospects.* 我想要一份有良好晋升机会的工作。| **[+to]** *Your promotion to Senior Editor is now official.* 现在你被正式提升为高级编辑。**2** [C, U] an activity intended to help sell a product, or the product that is being promoted〔产品的〕促销，推销；促销[推销]的产品：*a winter sales promotion* 冬季促销活动 **3** [U] the activity of persuading people to support an idea or way of doing things 提倡，倡导：*the promotion of equal opportunities* 提倡机会平等 **4** [U] the activity of helping something develop and succeed 促进，增进：*the promotion of technology development centers* 促进技术开发中心的发展 **5** [U] a move by a sports team from playing in one group of teams to playing in a better group〔运动队的〕升级 —opposite 反义词 **relegation** (RELEGATE (2))

pro·mo·tion·al /prəˈmoʃənəl; prəˈməʊʃənəl/ *adj* promotional films, events etc are made or organized to advertise something〔电影、活动等〕旨在推销[宣传]〔某物〕的：*a series of interviews and promotional appearances* 一系列访谈和旨在宣传的露面

prompt¹ /prɑmpt; prɒmpt/ *v* **1** [T] to make someone decide to do something, especially something that they had been thinking of doing 促使；激励：**prompt sb to do sth** *Her situation prompted me to do something about getting a new job.* 她的境况促使我设法找一份新工作。**2** to make people say or do something as a reaction 引起，激起〔某人说或做某事〕：*What prompted that remark?* 那句话是由什么事引起的？**3** [T] to help a speaker who pauses, by suggesting how to continue 为〔说话者〕提示：*"I can't decide...." said Beatrice. "Decide what?" prompted Marlon.* "我不能决定…"比阿特丽斯说。"决定什么？"马龙提示道。**4** [I,T] to remind an actor or actress of the next words in a speech 为〔演员〕提示台词

prompt² *adj* **1** done quickly, immediately, or at the right time 迅速的；立刻的；及时的：*prompt delivery of your purchases* 你所购买物品的迅速送货 **2** [not before noun 不用于名词前] someone who is prompt arrives at the right time or does something on time 准时的：*Lunch is at two. Try to be prompt.* 两点钟吃午饭，要尽量准时。| *Grandma is always prompt in answering letters.* 祖母总是及时回信。—**promptly** *adv*: *The performance begins promptly at nine o'clock.* 演出于9点钟准时开始。—**promptness** *n* [U]

prompt³ *adv informal* happening at the exact time【非正式】准时：*We're meeting at 6.30 prompt, so don't be late.* 我们要6点半准时会面，所以不要迟到。

prompt⁴ *n* [C] **1** a word or words said to an actor in a play, to help them remember what to say〔给演员的〕提词，提白 **2** a sign on a computer screen which shows that the computer has finished one operation and is ready to begin the next〔电脑屏幕上的〕提示〔显示电脑已完成某项操作，准备进入下一项〕：*When you see the 'C' prompt type 'WP'.* 当看到提示符C时，就键入WP。

prompt·er /ˈprɑmptɚ; ˈprɒmptə/ *n* [C] someone who tells actors in a play what words to say when they forget 提词员，提白员

Proms, the /prɑmz; prɒmz/ a series of concerts of CLASSICAL music which take place every summer at the Albert Hall in London, over a period of several weeks. Part of the hall has no seats, so that more people can attend the concerts and pay less, and many people, especially young people, stand there to listen to the concerts. The Proms were started by Sir Henry Wood in 1895, and they are a well-known part of British life. The final concert each year, called the Last Night of the Proms is always shown on television. 逍遥音乐会，漫步音乐会〔每年夏天在伦敦艾伯特音乐厅举行的系列音乐会，为期数周。大厅的部分区域不设座位，以便更多的人以低价欣赏音乐会。许多观众，尤其是年轻人往往站着欣赏音乐会。逍遥音乐会由亨利·伍德爵士于1895年初创，现已成为英国人生活中家喻户晓的一项艺术活动。每年的最后一场音乐会，即逍遥音乐会终场之夜，电视台总是要安排现场直播〕

prom·ul·gate /prəˈmʌlˌget; ˈprɒməlgeɪt/ *v* [T] **1** to spread an idea or belief to as many people as possible 传播〔思想、信仰〕；散布 **2** to make a new law come into effect by announcing it officially 颁布，公布〔法律〕 —**promulgator** *n* [C] —**promulgation** /ˌprɑmәlˈgeʃən; ˌprɒməlˈgeɪʃən/ *n* [U]

pron the written abbreviation of 缩写= PRONOUN

prone /pron; prəʊn/ *adj* **1** likely to do something or suffer from something, especially something bad or harmful 易发生某事〔尤指不好或有害的事〕的; 很可能…的; 有…倾向的: **[+to]** *Some plants are prone to a particular disease.* 有些植物容易生某种特定的疾病。| **prone to do sth** *Kids are all prone to eat junk food.* 孩子往往都喜欢吃垃圾食品。| **strike-prone/accident-prone etc** *I never saw a girl more accident-prone.* 我从未见过比她更容易出事故的女孩。**2** *formal* lying down with the front of your body facing down【正式】脸朝下卧倒的, 俯卧的: *Colley lay prone in his bunk.* 科利俯卧在铺位上。—compare 比较 PROSTRATE[1] (1) —**proneness** *n* [U]

prong /prɔŋ; prɒŋ/ *n* [C] **1** a thin sharp point of something such as a fork that has several points〔叉子等的〕尖头, 尖齿: *a pitchfork with three huge prongs* 有三个大叉头的干草叉 **2** **two-pronged, three-pronged etc a)** having two, three etc prongs 两齿的, 三齿的 **b)** a two-pronged or three-pronged attack is made on two or three parts of something at the same time〔进攻〕分两路[三路]的, 从两面[三面]的 **3** *AmE slang* a PENIS (=male sexual organ)【美俚】阴茎

pro·nom·i·nal /prə`nɑmənl; prəʊ'nɒmɪ̣nəl/ *adj technical* related to or used like a PRONOUN【术语】代词的; 代词性的 —**pronominally** *adv*

pro·noun /'pronaun; 'prəʊnaʊn/ *n* [C] a word that is used instead of a noun or noun phrase, such as 'he' instead of Peter or instead of 'the man' 代词, 代名词 —see also 另见 DEMONSTRATIVE PRONOUN, PERSONAL PRONOUN

pro·nounce /prə`nauns; prə'naʊns/ *v* **1** [T] to make the sound of a letter, word etc, especially in the correct way〔尤指正确地〕发音, 读音: *How do you pronounce your name?* 你的名字怎么念? **2** to officially state that something is true〔正式〕宣布, 宣告; 宣称: **pronounce sb/sth (to be) sth** *The victim was pronounced dead on arrival.* 受害者送抵时被宣布已死亡。| *I now pronounce you man and wife.* 我现在宣布你们结为夫妻。**3** [I, T+**on/against**] *law* to give a legal judgment【法律】宣判 **4** **pronounce on/upon sth** to state your opinion about a subject, especially when you do not really know much about it 对某事物〔尤指不甚了解的事物〕发表意见: *I don't want to listen to him pronounce on wine all night.* 我不想听他整晚滔滔不绝地大谈葡萄酒。**5** **pronounce sentence** *law* if a judge pronounces sentence, he or she tells the court what kind of punishment a criminal will have【法律】宣布判决

pro·nounce·a·ble /prə`naunsəbl; prə'naʊnsəbəl/ *adj* a word, name etc that is pronounceable is easy to say〔词、名字等〕容易念的, 容易发音的 —opposite 反义词 UNPRONOUNCEABLE

pro·nounced /prə`naunst; prə'naʊnst/ *adj* very strong or noticeable 明显的; 明确的: *a pronounced Polish accent* 明显的波兰口音 | *a pronounced effect in reducing crime* 减少犯罪的明显效果 —**pronouncedly** /prə`naunstlɪ; prə'naʊnsɪ̣dli/ *adv*

pro·nounce·ment /prə`naunsmənt; prə'naʊnsmənt/ *n* [C] *formal* an official public statement【正式】公告, 声明: *the Pope's latest pronouncement on birth control* 罗马教皇关于控制生育的最新声明

pron·to /`prɑnto; 'prɒntəʊ/ *adv spoken* quickly or immediately【口】很快地; 马上, 立刻: *Bring that hose over here, pronto!* 把那条软管拿过来, 快点!

pro·nun·ci·a·tion /prə,nʌnsɪ`eʃən; prə,nʌnsi'eɪʃən/ *n* **1** [C, U] the way in which a language or a particular word is pronounced 发音, 读音: *Make sure you give each word its correct pronunciation.* 要确保把每个词念正确。**2** [singular,U] a particular person's way of pronouncing a word or words〔某人的〕发音, 读音

-proof /pruf; pruːf/ *suffix* **1** [in adjectives 构成形容词] treated or made so as not to be harmed by something, or to protect people against something 耐…的; 防…的; 抗…的: *a bulletproof car* 防弹汽车 | *an ovenproof dish* (=that cannot be harmed by heat) 耐热盘 **2** [in verbs 构成动词] to treat or make something so that it cannot be harmed by something, or gives protection against it 防; 抗; 使不受…影响: *to soundproof a room* (=so that sound cannot get into or out of it) 给房间隔音

2 3 **proof¹** /pruf; pruːf/ *n* **1** [C,U] facts, information, documents etc that prove something is true 证明; 证据: **[+of]** *Bring a passport as proof of identity.* 带上护照作为身份证明。| **[+(that)]** *Do you have any proof that this man stole your bag?* 你有什么证据证明这个人偷了你的包吗? | **conclusive proof** (=that cannot be doubted) 确凿的证据 | **proof positive** (=definite proof) 确切的证据 **2** [C] *technical* a printed copy of a piece of writing used to find and remove mistakes before the final printing is done【术语】校样: *Can you check these proofs?* 你能核对一下这些校样吗? **3** [C] a photograph that is used as a test copy before an official copy is made 照片样片 **4** [C] **a)** a test in MATHEMATICS of the correctness of a calculation〔数学的〕验算; 验证 **b)** a list of reasons that shows a THEOREM (=statement) in GEOMETRY to be true〔几何定理等的〕证(明), 证法 **5** **the proof of the pudding (is in the eating)** used to say that you can only know whether something is good or bad after you have tried it 布丁好不好, 吃了才知道〔评价事物的好坏只能凭实践检验〕**6** [U] *technical* the standard strength of some kinds of alcoholic drink compared with that of PROOF SPIRIT【术语】〔酒类的〕标准酒精度: *This gin is 15% under proof.* 这种杜松子酒比标准酒精度低15%。**7** **put sth to the proof** to test the quality or strength of something 检验某事物〔的品质或强度〕

proof² *adj* **1** **waterproof/bulletproof etc** something that is waterproof etc will not let water etc through it or into it 防水/防弹等: *a soundproof room* 隔音的房间 **2** **child-proof/vandal-proof** not easily affected or damaged by someone or something 不易受到孩子/破坏者破坏的: *a child-proof latch on the cupboard* 橱柜上不易被孩子弄坏的门闩 **3** **be proof against** to be too strong or good to be affected by something bad 能抵挡…的; 能耐…的; 可防…的: *a faith that is proof against temptation* 能抵挡诱惑的信念 **4** **30° proof/40° proof etc** *BrE*【英】, also 又作 **30 proof/40 proof etc** *AmE*【美】whisky, bourbon etc that has a particular proof contains a specific amount of alcohol〔威士忌、波旁酒等〕30度/40度等

proof³ *v* [T usually passive 一般用被动态] to treat a material with a substance in order to protect it against water, oil etc 把〔某材料〕作防水[油]处理: **[+against]** *climbing gear proofed against water* 作过防水处理的攀缘用具

proof·read /`pruf,rid; 'pruːf,riːd/ *past tense and past participle* **proofread** /-rɛd; -red/ *v* [I,T] to read through something written or printed in order to correct any errors in it 校对 —**proofreader** *n* [C]

proof spir·it /,· '··/ *n* [U] a standard mixture of alcohol and water with which the strength of some acoholic drinks is compared for the purposes of taxation 标准强度的酒〔用以测定一些酒的强度以定其税率〕

prop¹ /prɑp; prɒp/ *v* **propped, propping** [T always+adv/prep] to support something by leaning it against something, or by putting something else under, next to, or behind it 把…靠在…上; 支撑, 撑住: **prop sth against/on** *He propped his bike against a tree.* 他把自行车靠在一棵树上。| **prop sth open** *Give me something to prop the door open.* 给我个东西顶住门, 不让它关上。

prop sth ↔ **up** *phr v* [T] **1** to prevent something from falling by putting something against it or under it 支撑, 撑住〔某物〕: *The builders are trying to prop up the crumbling walls of the church.* 建筑工人正试图撑住快要坍塌的教堂墙壁。**2** if a government props up another government it helps it with financial or military support so that it can continue to exist〔在财政上或军事上〕支持〔某政府〕**3** **prop yourself up** to stand or sit straight by leaning against something 靠着某物站直[坐直]; 撑着站起[坐起]

prop² *n* [C] **1** an object placed under or against something to hold it in a position 支柱, 支撑物 —see also 另见 PIT PROP **2** a small object such as a book, weapon etc used by actors in a play or film〔戏剧或电影中的〕道具 **3** *informal* a short form of the word PROPELLER【非正式】螺旋桨; 推进器 **4** something or someone that helps you to feel strong, or that an idea or system needs in order to exist 支持者; 后盾; 靠山: *The big house and the car were all props to his ego.* 那座大房子和那辆汽车都是他自负的资本。

prop·a·gan·da /,prɑpə`gændə; ,prɒpə'gændə/ *n* [U] false or partly false information used by a government or political party to make people agree with them〔政府或政党为了影响民意而带有虚假性质的〕宣传: *pure Fascist propaganda* 纯粹的法西斯宣传 | *a propaganda film* 宣传影片 | **propaganda campaign** (=an organised plan to spread propaganda) 宣传活动 —**propagandize** also 又作 **-ise** *BrE*【英】*v* [I,T] —**propagandist** *n* [C]

prop·a·gate /`prɑpə,get; 'prɒpəgeɪt/ *v formal*【正式】**1** [I, T] to grow and produce new plants or to make a plant do this〔植物〕繁殖; 使〔植物〕繁殖: *a species that propagates by spores* 靠孢子繁殖的物种 | *You can propagate these plants by root cuttings.* 你可以用根插的方法使这些植物繁殖。**2** [T] to spread an idea, belief etc to many people 传播, 散播〔观点、信仰等〕; 宣传: *The group started a magazine to propagate its ideas.* 这群人办了一本杂志来宣传他们的主张。**3** [T] if an animal, insect, or CELL etc propagates itself or is propagated, it increases in number by reproducing; REPRODUCE (1)〔动物、昆虫或细胞等〕繁衍, 繁殖 —**propagation** /,prɑpə`geʃən; ,prɒpə'geɪʃən/ *n* [U]

prop·a·gat·or /ˋprɑpə͵getɚ; ˈprɒpəgeɪtə/ *n* [C] **1** someone who spreads ideas, beliefs etc 传播〔思想、信仰等〕的人，宣传者 **2** a covered box of soil in which seeds are planted to grow quickly〔供种子迅速生长的〕培育箱

pro·pane /ˋpropen; ˈprəʊpeɪn/ *n* [U] a colourless gas used for both cooking and heating 丙烷（气）

pro·pel /prəˋpɛl; prəˈpel/ *v* **propelled, propelling** [T] to move, drive, or push something forward 推动；推进；驱动：*old ships propelled by steam* 由蒸汽推进的旧轮船｜*a rocket-propelled grenade* 用火箭炮发射的榴弹 —see also 另见 PROPULSION

pro·pel·lant, propellent /prəˋpɛlənt; prəˈpelənt/ *n* [C,U] **1** an explosive for firing a bullet or ROCKET[1]〔发射子弹或火箭的〕推进剂 **2** gas pressed into a small space in a container of liquid, which pushes out the liquid when the pressure is taken away〔置于喷雾容器中提供压力的〕喷射剂 —**propellant** *adj*

pro·pel·ler /prəˋpɛlɚ; prəˈpelə/ *n* [C] a piece of equipment consisting of two or more blades that spin around, that makes an aircraft or ship move〔飞机或轮船的〕螺旋桨；推进器

pro·pel·ling pen·cil /͵· ͵·· ˈ··/ *n* [C] *BrE* a pencil made of plastic or metal, in which the stick of the LEAD can be pushed out as it is used up【英】活动铅笔，自动铅笔；MECHANICAL PENCIL *AmE*【美】

pro·pen·si·ty /prəˋpɛnsətɪ; prəˈpensɪ̣ti/ *n* [C] *formal* a natural tendency to behave in a particular way【正式】倾向；习性：**a propensity to do sth** *the male propensity to fight* 男性好斗的倾向｜**a propensity for (doing) sth** *The child shows a propensity for disrupting class.* 这个孩子表现出喜欢扰乱课堂的倾向。

prop·er[1] /ˋprɑpɚ; ˈprɒpə/ *adj* **1** [only before noun 仅用于名词前，no comparative 无比较级] *especially BrE* right, suitable, or correct【尤英】正确的；合适的，适当的；恰当的：*She needs proper medical attention.* 她需要妥善的治疗。｜*Put that back in its proper place.* 把那东西放回原处。｜*I went through the proper process, I wrote to my MP.* 我遵循应有的步骤，给我的下议院议员写了信。**2** socially or legally correct and acceptable 合适的；合理的；合乎体统的；正规的；〔法律上〕正确的，可接受的：*I don't feel that it would be proper for me to give you that information.* 我觉得我把那资料给你不合适。｜**be only (right and) proper** *It's only right and proper that Shari apologize for what she said!* 莎丽为她所说的话道歉是再合理不过了！**3** [only before noun 仅用于名词前] *BrE spoken* real【英口】真正的：*Can't you get a proper job?* 你就不能找一份真正的工作吗？｜*Try to eat proper meals instead of chips and baked beans.* 尽量好好吃饭而不要吃炸马铃薯条和烘豆。**4** [only after noun 仅用于名词后] according to the real, most exact meaning of the word 严格意义上的：*Monkeys proper only began to evolve thirty five million years ago.* 真正意义上的猴子在3500万年前才开始进化。**5** **proper to sth** **a)** *formal* belonging to one particular type of thing【正式】…特有的，为…专有的：*the reasoning abilities proper to our species* 我们这个物种所特有的推理能力 **b)** natural or normal in a particular place or situation 适宜的，适合的：*dressed in a way that was proper to the occasion* 穿得适合这种场合 **6** [only before noun 仅用于名词后] *BrE spoken* complete【英口】完全的，彻底的：*He's made a proper fool of himself this time!* 这次他真是出够了丑！｜*You're in a proper old mess.* 你真是狼狈不堪。**7** very polite, and careful to do what is socially correct 非常有礼貌的；循规蹈矩的：*Andrew's behaviour was so proper that she couldn't help laughing.* 安德鲁的行为如此循规蹈矩以至她忍不住笑起来。—see also 另见 PROPERLY

proper[2] *adv BrE spoken*【英口】**1** used by some people to mean PROPERLY, although most people think that this is incorrect 好好地，适当地〔有些人把此词当作 properly 用，尽管大多数人认为这样用不正确〕：*Why don't you talk proper?* 你为什么不好好说话？**2** **good and proper** completely 完全地，彻底地：*Tom drove the car into a wall and wrecked it good and proper.* 汤姆开车撞到了墙上，把车完全撞毁了。

proper frac·tion /͵·· ˈ··/ *n* [C] a FRACTION such as ¾ in which the number above the line is smaller than the one below it〔数学的〕真分数 —compare 比较 IMPROPER FRACTION

prop·er·ly /ˋprɑpɚlɪ; ˈprɒpəli/ *adv* **1** correctly, or in a way that is considered right 正确地；适当地：*Make sure the job is done properly.* 要确保把这项工作做好。｜*He never explains anything properly.* 他从来不好好解释任何事情。｜*Granny will be there, so behave properly.* 祖母会在那里，所以要规矩点。**2** *especially BrE informal* completely; thoroughly【尤英，非正式】完全地，彻底地：*Is that cake properly defrosted?* 那蛋糕完全解冻了吗？**3** really; in fact 真正地；实际上：*Documents which properly belong to the family were taken away by the authorities.* 实际上属于这个家庭的文件被当局拿走了。｜**properly speaking** *especially BrE* (=really)【尤英】实际上 *He's not a policeman at all, properly speaking.* 其实他根本不是个警察。**4** used to say that someone was right to do something〔用于表示某人做某事是正确的〕：**quite/very/perfectly properly** *She told me, perfectly properly, that it was no business of mine.* 她告诉我这事与我无关，她说得很对。

proper noun /͵·· ˈ·/ also 又作 **proper name** *n* [C] a noun such as 'James', 'New York', or 'China' that is the name of one particular thing and is spelt with a CAPITAL[2] (1) letter 专有名词〈如 James, New York, China〉—see also 另见 NOUN

prop·er·tied /ˋprɑpɚtɪd; ˈprɒpətid/ *adj* [only before noun 仅用于名词前] owning a lot of property or land 有很多财产的；有大量地产的：*the propertied classes* 有产阶级

prop·er·ty /ˋprɑpɚtɪ; ˈprɒpəti/ *plural* **properties** *n* **1** [U] the thing or things that someone owns 所有物；资产，财产：*That's my personal property! Leave it alone!* 那是我的私人财产！别动它！｜*Some of the stolen property was found in Mason's house.* 在梅森的房子里找到了一些偷来的财物。**2** [U] land, buildings, or both together 房产；地产；房地产：*Property prices have shot up recently.* 最近房地产的价格暴涨。**3** [C] a word meaning a building, a piece of land, or both together, used especially by lawyers or ESTATE AGENTS〔尤指律师或房地产经纪人所指的〕房产，建筑；地产，房地产：*Several properties on this street are for sale.* 这条街上有几处房地产要出售。**4** [C] a quality or power that belongs naturally to something 特性，性质；属性：*a herb with healing properties* 具有治疗功效的药草｜*One of the most important properties of gold is its malleability.* 金的一个最重要特性是它的延展性。**5** [U] ownership of land, goods etc 所有权；财产权：*a belief in the idea of communal property* 对公有财产思想的信仰 —see also 另见 LOST PROPERTY, REAL PROPERTY

property de·vel·op·er /ˈ·· ·͵···/ *n* [C] someone who makes money by buying land and building on it 房地产开发商

property tax /ˈ··· ͵·/ *n* [C,U] a tax based on the value of someone's house 财产税；不动产税

proph·e·cy also 又作 **prophesy** *AmE*【美】/ˋprɑfəsɪ; ˈprɒfɪ̣si/ *n plural* **prophecies** **1** [C] a statement that something will happen in the future, especially one made by someone with religious or magic powers 预言：**[+that]** *The prophecy that David would become king was fulfilled.* 大卫将成为国王的预言果然应验了。**2** [U] the making of statements about what will happen in the future〔尤指拥有宗教权力或魔力的人作出的〕预言 —see also 另见 **self-fulfilling prophecy** (SELF-FULFILLING)

proph·e·sy[1] /ˋprɑfə͵saɪ; ˈprɒfɪ̣saɪ/ *v* **prophesies, prophesying, prophesied** [I,T] to use religious or magical knowledge to say what will happen in the future; FORETELL 预言：**[+that]** *The soothsayer prophesied that the war would be won.* 那个占卜者预言这场战争将会打赢。｜**prophesy who/what/how etc** *He even prophesied how the crops would fail.* 他甚至预言农作物将如何歉收。

proph·e·sy[2] /ˋprɑfəsɪ; ˈprɒfəsi/ *n* [C] an American spelling of PROPHECY prophecy 的美式拼法

proph·et /ˋprɑfɪt; ˈprɒfɪ̣t/ *n* [C] **1** a man whom people in the Christian, Jewish, or Muslim religion believe has been sent by God to lead them and teach them their religion〔基督教、犹太教、伊斯兰教的〕先知 **2** **the Prophet** Muhammad, who formed the Muslim religion 先知穆罕默德〔伊斯兰教的创始人〕：*followers of the Prophet* 先知穆罕默德的追随者 **3** **the Prophets** the Jewish holy men whose writings form part of the OLD TESTAMENT, or the writings themselves 犹太教诸先知〔其著作构成《圣经·旧约》的一部分〕，《先知书》的作者们；《先知书》**4** **prophet of doom/disaster** someone who believes that bad or unpleasant things will happen in the future 预言厄运/灾难的人 **5** someone who introduces and teaches a new idea〔新观念、新思想的〕提倡者，首倡者，倡导者：**[+of]** *Rontgen was regarded as the prophet of the new materialism.* 伦琴被认为是新唯物论的倡导者。

proph·et·ess /ˋprɑfɪtɪs; ͵prɒfɪ̣ˈtes/ *n* [C] a woman whom people believe has been sent by God to lead them 女先知

pro·phet·ic /prəˋfɛtɪk; prəˈfetɪk/ *adj* correctly saying what will happen in the future 预见正确的；预言性的：*Nick's remark proved prophetic two months later.* 尼克的话在两个月后被证明是正确的预言。—**prophetically** /-klɪ; -kli/ *adv*

pro·phet·i·cal /prəˋfɛtɪkl; prəˈfetɪkəl/ *adj* like a prophet, or related to the things a prophet says or does 似先知的；预言的

Proph·ets, the /ˋprɑfɪts; ˈprɒfɪ̣ts/ **1** one of the main parts of the Old Testament of the Bible, consisting of the writings of Jewish holy men such as Isaiah, Joshua, and Jeremiah 先知书〔基督教《圣经·旧约》的主要篇章之一，再现以赛亚、约书亚、耶利米等犹太先知的事迹〕**2** the Jewish holy men who did these writings 先知书的作者

pro·phy·lac·tic¹ /ˌprɑfəˋlæktɪk; ˌprɒfɪˈlæktɪk◂/ *adj technical* intended to prevent disease【术语】预防〔疾病〕(性)的

prophylactic² *n* [C] *technical*【术语】**1** something used to prevent disease 预防疾病的东西 **2** *AmE often humorous* a CONDOM【美, 常幽默】避孕套

pro·phy·lax·is /ˌprɑfəˋlæksɪs; ˌprɒfɪˈlæksɪs/ *n* [C,U] *technical* a treatment for preventing disease【术语】〔疾病的〕预防(法)

pro·pin·qui·ty /proˋpɪŋkwətɪ; prəˈpɪŋkwɪti/ *n* [U+**of**/**to**] *formal* the fact of being near someone or something, or of being related to someone【正式】〔空间上的〕接近, 邻近;〔血统上的〕近亲关系

pro·pi·ti·ate /prəˋpɪʃɪet; prəˈpɪʃieɪt/ *v* [T] *formal* to make someone who has been unfriendly or angry with you feel more friendly by doing something to please them【正式】抚慰; 劝解; 哄…息怒; 取悦 —**propitiation** /prəˌpɪʃɪˋeʃən; prəˌpɪʃiˈeɪʃən/ *n* [U]

pro·pi·ti·a·to·ry /prəˋpɪʃɪəˌtɔrɪ; prəˈpɪʃiətəri/ *adj formal* intended to please someone and make them feel less angry and more friendly【正式】抚慰的, 劝解的; 讨好的; 哄人息怒的: *a propitiatory gift of flowers* 为讨好某人而赠送的鲜花

pro·pi·tious /prəˋpɪʃəs; prəˈpɪʃəs/ *adj formal* good and likely to bring good results【正式】吉利的, 有利的, 吉祥的: *a propitious moment* 有利时机 | [**+for**] *Conditions after the 1905 revolution were propitious for stable development.* 1905年革命之后的形势有利于稳定发展。—**propitiously** *adv*

pro·po·nent /prəˋponənt; prəˈpəʊnənt/ *n* [C] someone who supports something or persuades people to do something; ADVOCATE² (1) 支持者; 拥护者; 鼓吹者: [**+of**] *Steinem has always been a strong proponent of women's rights.* 斯泰纳姆一向是妇女权利的强烈支持者。—compare 比较 OPPONENT (2)

proportion 比例

The car is out of proportion to the man.
这辆汽车与这个人不成比例。

S2 W2 **pro·por·tion¹** /prəˋpɔrʃən; prəˈpɔːʃən/ *n*

1 ▶**AMOUNT** 数量◀ [C] a part or share of a larger amount〔更大数量中的〕部分, 份额: [**+of**] *Quite high proportions of their incomes are spent on fuel.* 他们收入的很大部分花在了燃料上。

2 ▶**NUMBER** 数目◀ [C] a number of people or things, considered as a part or share of a larger number〔更大数目的人或东西的〕部分: [**+of**] *Far higher proportions of part-time workers have no health insurance at all.* 较大部分的兼职工人根本没有健康保险。| [also+plural verb *BrE* 英] *A large proportion of the people are illiterate.* 这些人中很大部分是文盲。

3 ▶**RELATIONSHIP** 关系◀ [C,U] the relationship between the amounts, numbers, or sizes of different things that go together to form a whole 比例: *eating the right foods in the right proportions* 按适当比例吃适当的食物 | **proportion of sth to sth** *The proportion of men to women in the population has changed in recent years.* 人口中男性与女性的比例最近几年有了改变。| **the proportion of** *Make salad dressing in the proportion of three parts oil to one part vinegar.* 按三份油、一份醋的比例制作凉拌菜的调味料。

4 ▶**ATTRACTIVENESS** 吸引力◀ [U] **a)** the correct relationship between the size, shape and position of the different parts of something, which gives it an attractive appearance〔某物各组成部分的〕相称; 协调; 均衡; 匀称: *Builders must learn about scale and proportion.* 建筑工必须学习比例和均衡。| **in proportion** *Reduce the drawing so that all the elements stay in proportion.* 缩小这幅画以便所有组成部分保持比例协调。**b)** the correct relationship between the size or shape of something and the place where it is〔某物与所处地方的〕协调, 相称: **out of proportion (to/with)** *They've built a house that's completely out of proportion with the size of the lot.* 他们建了一所与地皮面积完全不成比例的房子。

5 in proportion (to/with sth) according to a particular relationship in size, amount etc 与…成比例; 按某比例: *If you use a whole pineapple, increase the other ingredients in proportion.* 如果你用一整个菠萝, 就要按比例增加其他配料。| *Tax is then calculated in proportion to what you earn.* 所得税则是根据你的收入额按比例计算的。

6 in proportion (to sth) when you compare sizes, amounts etc 与…相比: *Her feet are small in proportion to her height.* 她的脚相对于她的身高来说很小。

7 ▶**SIZE/IMPORTANCE** 大小/重要性◀ **proportions** [plural] the size and shape of something, or the degree to which something is important 大小; 形状; 重要性: *a building of classic proportions* 古典式的建筑物 | *It may reduce the task to more manageable proportions.* 那可把工作缩小到大致可行的范围。| **immense/huge/massive etc proportions** *an ecological tragedy of enormous proportions* 极其严重的生态悲剧 | **epic/heroic/mythic proportions** *For most of us, Scott was a hero of mythic proportions.* 对我们大多数人来说, 斯科特是一个神话般的英雄。| **crisis/epidemic etc proportions** *a fall in silk prices of catastrophic proportions* 丝绸价格灾难性的下跌

8 keep things in proportion to react to a situation sensibly, and not think that it is worse or more serious than it really is 办事情[看问题]恰如其分; 不把事情看得太糟[太严重]: *Try to keep things in proportion; you won't die if you don't get the job.* 要尽量恰如其分地看问题, 得不到那份工作也不至于会死掉。—see also 另见 PERSPECTIVE (2)

9 get/blow things (all) out of proportion to react to a situation as if it is worse or more serious than it really is 把某事物想得过糟[过于严重]

10 out of (all) proportion (to sth) a reaction, result, emotion etc that is out of proportion is too strong or great, compared to the situation in which it happens〔反应、结果、感情等〕(相对…来说)过分; 与…不相称: *The fear of violent crime has now risen out of all proportion to the actual risk.* 对于暴力犯罪的恐惧现在已大大超出了其实际危险。

11 sense of proportion the ability to judge what is most important in a situation 区别轻重缓急的能力; 主次观念: **keep/lose a sense of proportion** *You can protest by all means, but keep a sense of proportion.* 无论你怎样抗议都可以, 但是要分清轻重。

12 ▶**MATHEMATICS** 数学◀ [U] *technical* equality in the mathematical relationship between two sets of numbers, as in the statement '8 is to 6 as 32 is to 24'【术语】比例〈如8∶6 = 32∶24〉

proportion² *v* [T usually passive 一般用被动态] *formal*【正式】**1 well/badly/beautifully etc proportioned** having a size and shape that is either pleasant or unpleasant to look at, or is either right or wrong for its use 匀称的/比例不协调的/比例恰到好处的等: *a well proportioned room* 比例很协调的房间 | *long, beautifully proportioned legs* 修长而匀称的双腿 **2** to make something stay in a particular relationship with something else according to size, amount, position etc 使均衡; 使相称; 使成比例: **proportion sth to sth** *Allowances for expenditure have been proportioned to your income.* 消费津贴与你的收入一直是成比例的。

pro·por·tion·al /prəˋpɔrʃənl̩; prəˈpɔːʃənəl/ *adj* something that is proportional to something else stays in a correct or suitable relationship to the other thing in size, amount, importance etc 成比例的; 相称的: [**+to**] *Carlow will have to pay an amount of compensation proportional to the damage he did.* 卡罗必须根据他所造成的损失按比例支付赔偿金。—**proportionally** *adv*

proportional rep·re·sen·ta·tion /ˌ· ··· ···ˋ·/ *n* [U] PR; a system of voting in elections by which all political parties are represented in the government according to the number of votes they receive in the whole country 比例代表制〔各政党按其在全国所得票数而获得议席的一种选举制度〕

pro·por·tion·ate /prəˋpɔrʃənɪt; prəˈpɔːʃənɪt/ *adj* something that is proportionate to something else stays in a correct or suitable relationship to the other thing in size, amount, importance etc 成比例的; 相称的: *The decline in production was offset by a proportionate increase in federal aid.* 产量的下降由相应增加的联邦政府补助来弥补。—opposite 反义词 DISPROPORTIONATE —**proportionately** *adv*

pro·pos·al /prəˋpozl̩; prəˈpəʊzəl/ *n* **1** [C,U] a plan or suggestion which is made formally to an official person or group, or the act of making it 计划; 建议, 提议; 建议等的提出: *Clinton is facing a battle to get Congress to accept his budget proposals.* 克林顿为使国会接受他的预算方案正面临着一场论战。| **proposal to do sth** *The proposal to build a new bypass is meeting with stiff opposition.* 修建一条支路的提议遭到强烈反对。| **proposal that** *The company had to put forward a proposal that* S3 W1

layoffs be considered. 该公司不得不提出考虑解雇工人的建议。 —see 见 PROPOSE (USAGE) **2** [C] the act of asking someone to marry you 求婚

propose 求婚

pro·pose /prəˋpoz; prəˈpəʊz/ *v*

1 ▶PLAN 计划◀ [T] *formal* to suggest something as a plan or course of action【正式】提议，建议: *Lyle proposed large cuts in the training budget.* 莱尔提出大量削减培训经费。| **propose that** *Hansen has proposed that I become his business partner.* 汉森建议我成为他的生意伙伴。| *the proposed budget cuts* 所提议的预算削减

2 ▶AT A MEETING 在会议上◀ [T] to formally suggest a course of action at a meeting and ask people to vote on it〔在会议上〕正式提议，提付表决: *I propose the admission of Peter King as a new member.* 我提议接受彼得·金为新成员。| **propose a motion** (=formally suggest a plan at a meeting) 提出动议 | **propose sb** (=formally suggest someone for an official position) 提名[推举]某人〔担任某职位〕*Mrs Banks has been proposed for the position of Treasurer.* 班克斯夫人已被提名担任财务主管。

3 ▶THEORY 理论◀ [T] to suggest an idea, method etc as an answer to a scientific question or as a better way of doing something 提出〔某观点、方法等〕: *His theory proposes the existence of black holes in the universe.* 他的理论提出宇宙中存在黑洞。

4 ▶MARRIAGE 结婚◀ **a)** [I] to ask someone to marry you, especially in a formal way〔尤指正式地向某人〕求婚: **[+to]** *Shaun proposed to me only six months after we met.* 肖恩在我们相识仅六个月后就向我求婚。**b) propose marriage** *formal* to ask someone to marry you【正式】求婚

5 propose a toast to sb also 又作 **propose sb's health** to formally ask a group of people at a social event to join you in wishing someone success, happiness, etc, while raising a glass of wine and then drinking from it 为某人[某人的健康]祝酒

6 ▶INTEND 打算◀ [T] *formal* to intend to do something【正式】打算，计划: **propose to do sth** *How do you propose to explain your long absence?* 你打算如何解释你的长时间缺席？| **propose doing sth** *Just how do you propose paying for all this?* 你究竟打算如何付清这一切？ —**proposer** *n* [C]

USAGE NOTE 用法说明: PROPOSE

WORD CHOICE 词语辨析: **propose, intend, suggest, proposal, suggestion, let's, why don't we**

Propose followed by the *to* form of a verb is a more formal way of saying you intend to do something. propose后接不定式是表示打算做某事的较正式说法: *What are you proposing to do with that old car of yours?* 你打算如何处理你那辆旧车？

Propose followed by a noun means that you are formally suggesting something should be considered. propose后接名词表示正式地提议某事物应得到考虑: *propose a motion/solution/course of action etc* 提出动议/解决方案/做法等

Propose followed by a *that* clause has a similar meaning to **suggest**. propose后接that-从句，意思与suggest相同: *I propose/suggest that we buy a new car* (=I think that this is what we should do). 我建议我们买辆新车。

Propose followed by the *ing* form of a verb may have either of the above senses. propose后接动词的-ing形式，可能有以上两个意思中的任意一个。

The difference between **suggest** and **propose** is that **propose** is more formal and often means that you have already thought about what you are proposing. But you may **suggest** an idea without a lot of careful thought. suggest和propose的区别在于propose较正式，而且常意味着你已经考虑过所建议的事情。但suggest可以表示未经太多仔细考虑: *At the meeting conservationists proposed a different route for the highway.* 在会上，自然环境保护论者提出了一条不同的公路路线。| *As we came out of the theater, Jean suggested a Chinese meal.* 我们走出剧院时，琼建议去吃中餐。

With similar differences you can also make a **proposal** or a **suggestion**. proposal和suggestion的区别与其动词形式相似: *the committee's proposal to raise local taxes* 委员会提出的提高地方税收的建议 | *George's suggestion that we go skating tonight* 乔治要我们今晚去滑冰的建议

In spoken English people do not usually say **I suggest that** but rather **Let's** or **Why don't we?** 在英语口语中，人们一般不说I suggest that，而用Let's或Why don't we?: *Let's go for a Chinese meal.* 我们去吃中餐吧。| *Why don't we get a new car?* 我们何不买一辆新车呢？

GRAMMAR 语法

You **propose** or **suggest** something always **to** someone. 对某人建议某事可以用propose/suggest something to someone的结构: *He proposed a business deal to her* (NOT 不用 *He proposed her a business deal* or 或 *He proposed her to a business deal*). 他提出与她做一笔交易。Also you would say 你也可以说: *I suggested to her that we go to the disco* (NOT 不用 *I suggested her that we go to the disco*). 我向她提议我们去跳迪斯科。

Suggest is not used with the *to* form of the verb. suggest后不接不定式: *He suggested leaving/that we leave* (NOT 不用 *He suggested to leave*). 他提议我们离开。

proposed /prəˋpozd; prəˈpəʊzd/ *adj* a proposed charge, arrangement etc is one that has been formally suggested to an official person or group〔正式〕提议的，建议的: *How will the proposed study be carried out?* 拟议中的研究将如何实施？| *The proposed site has several drawbacks.* 计划的地点有几个不利之处。

prop·o·si·tion¹ /ˌprɑpəˋzɪʃən; ˌprɒpəˈzɪʃən/ *n* [C]

1 ▶JUDGMENT 判断◀ a statement that consists of a carefully considered opinion or judgment 主张；观点，见解: *Marx accepted several of the key propositions developed by Adam Smith.* 马克思接受了亚当·斯密阐发的几个主要观点。| **proposition that** *We were asked to discuss the proposition that women are satisfied with less money.* 我们被要求就妇女满足于较少的金钱这一说法进行讨论。

2 ▶SUGGESTION 建议◀ an offer or suggestion, especially in business or politics〔尤指商业、政治上的〕提议，建议: *I'll consider your proposition and let you know.* 我会考虑你的建议然后告诉你结果。| *We have a proposition to make.* 我们要提个建议。

3 an attractive/interesting/practical etc proposition something that is an attractive etc idea, especially in business or politics〔尤指商业、政治上〕有吸引力的/有趣的/切实可行的提议: *The newest software makes computerized recruitment an attractive proposition.* 最新的软件使电脑招聘成为一个很有吸引力的提议。

4 ▶MATHEMATICS 数学◀ *technical* a word used in GEOMETRY meaning something that must be proved, or a question to which the answer must be found【术语】〔几何〕命题

5 ▶SEX 性◀ a statement that you would like to have sex with someone which avoids saying this to them directly〔男女间的〕求欢〔委婉向某人提出发生性关系的要求〕

6 ▶LAW 法律◀ also 又作 **Proposition** a suggested change or addition to the law of a state of the US, which citizens vote on〔由公民表决的美国某个州提出的〕法律修正案 —**propositional** *adj*

proposition² *v* [T] to suggest to someone that they have sex with you 提出〔与某人〕发生性关系，向〔某人〕求欢: *prostitutes propositioning the passers-by* 提出要与过路人上床的妓女

Proposition 13 /ˌprɑpəzɪʃən θɝˋtin; ˌprɒpəzɪʃən θɜːˈtiːn/ also 又作 **Prop 13** *informal* a law made in California in 1978 that reduced taxes on property. It was voted on directly by the people of California instead of being passed by California's state government. It encouraged voters in other US states to vote for similar laws, and was the first of many tax cuts introduced by the state and national governments in the 1980s.【非正式】《第13项提案》〔1978年加利福尼亚州制定的一项削减财产税的法律。这项法律不是由加州政府通过的，而是由该州公民直接投票决定的。此举促使其他各州也采取投票方式对类似法律进行全民公决。《第13项提案》是20世纪80年代美国国家政府和各州政府实施的许多减税方案的首例〕

pro·pound /prə`paʊnd; prə'paʊnd/ *v* [T] *formal* to suggest an idea, explanation etc for other people to consider【正式】提出〔观点，解释等〕供考虑

pro·pri·e·ta·ry /prə`praɪə,tɛrɪ; prə'praɪətəri/ *adj formal*【正式】**1** a proprietary medicine, cleaning liquid etc is one that is sold under a TRADE NAME〔药物、清洁液等〕有商标的 **2** proprietary behaviour makes it seem that you think you own something or someone〔行为〕像所有者那样的; 所有者(似)的: *Arnold wrapped his arm around his fiancée with a proprietary air.* 阿诺德用胳膊搂住他的未婚妻，仿佛搂住自己的财产。**3 proprietary information** information about a company's products, methods etc which is known only to people who work for the company〔公司的〕专有信息〔只有内部人员才了解的有关公司产品、方法等的信息〕

pro·pri·e·tor /prə`praɪətə; prə'praɪətə/ *n* [C] *formal* an owner of a business【正式】所有者; 业主; 老板: *Echenard was proprietor of the famous Hotel du Louvre.* 埃希纳尔是有名的卢浮宫酒店的老板。**—proprietorial** /prə,praɪə`torɪəl; prə,praɪə'tɔːriəl/ *adj* **—proprietorially** *adv*

pro·pri·e·tress /prə`praɪətrɪs; prə'praɪətrɪs/ *n* [C] *old-fashioned* a woman who owns a business【过时】女所有人; 女业主; 女老板

pro·pri·e·ty /prə`praɪətɪ; prə'praɪəti/ *n formal*【正式】**1** [singular, U] correctness of social or moral behaviour, especially between men and women or between people of different social ranks, age etc〔尤指男女之间或不同社会等级或年龄的人之间的〕礼貌, 规矩: *Jonathan behaved with the utmost propriety on our first date.* 乔纳森在我们第一次约会时举止极其得体。**2 the proprieties** the accepted rules of correct social behaviour 礼仪, 礼节: *strict in observing the proprieties* 严格遵守礼节 —see also 另见 IMPROPRIETY

pro·pul·sion /prə`pʌlʃən; prə'pʌlʃən/ *n* [U] *technical*【术语】**1** the force that drives a vehicle forward〔尤指车辆的〕推进力 **2 jet propulsion** the use of engines which push out hot gases to make an aircraft fly 喷气推进 **—propulsive** /-sɪv; -sɪv/ *adj*: *propulsive force* 推(进)力

pro ra·ta /pro `retə; ,prəʊ 'rɑːtə/ *adj technical* a payment or share that is pro rata is calculated according to exactly how much of something is used, how much work is done, etc【术语】〔报酬或份额〕按比例计算的 **—pro rata** *adv*

pro·rate /pro`ret; prəʊ'reɪt/ *v* [T] *AmE* to calculate a charge, price, etc according to the actual amount of service received rather than by a standard sum【美】按实际接受的服务计算〔价钱等〕

pro·rogue /pro`rog; prəʊ'rəʊg/ *v* [T] *technical* to leave any unfinished business of a PARLIAMENT to be dealt with at the next meeting【术语】使〔议会〕休会 **—prorogation** *n* [U]

pros /proz; prəʊz/ *n* [plural] —see 见 **the pros and cons** (PRO[1] (3))

pro·sa·ic /pro`ze·ɪk; prəʊ'zeɪ-ɪk/ *adj* boring, ordinary, or lacking in imagination 乏味的, 平淡无奇的; 缺乏想象力的: *a prosaic writing style* 乏味的写作风格 | *People said he'd been a pirate, but the truth was more prosaic.* 人们说他曾是一名海盗，但事实却没那么复杂。**—prosaically** /-klɪ; -kli/ *adv*

pro·sce·ni·um /pro`sinɪəm; prə'siːniəm/ *n* [C] **1** the part of a theatre stage which comes forward beyond the curtain〔剧院的〕幕布前的舞台部分, 前舞台 **2 proscenium arch** the arch at the front of a theatre stage where a curtain can be lowered 舞台前台的拱架; 台口

pro·sciut·to /pro`ʃuto; prəʊ'ʃuːtəʊ/ *n* [U] uncooked, dried, Italian HAM (=salted meat) which is eaten in very thin pieces 意大利熏火腿片

pro·scribe /pro`skraɪb; prəʊ'skraɪb/ *v* [T] **1** *formal* to try to stop the existence of something such as a political organization【正式】禁止〔政治组织等〕**2** *old use* to state publicly that a citizen is no longer protected by the law【旧】宣布剥夺〔公民的〕法律保护权, 使失去法律保护 **—proscription** /-`skrɪpʃən; -'skrɪpʃən/ *n* [C,U]

prose /proz; prəʊz/ *n* **1** [U] written language in its usual form, as opposed to poetry 散文〔与韵文相对的文体〕: *Gilbert's clear, simple prose* 吉尔伯特简洁而明快的散文 **2** [C] *BrE* a student's exercise in which you translate a piece of writing into a foreign language【英】〔学生的〕把原文译成外文的练习

pros·e·cute /`prɑsɪ,kjut; 'prɒsɪkjuːt/ *v* **1** [I,T] to officially say that someone is guilty of a crime and must be judged by a court of law 起诉, 检控: *Shoplifters will be prosecuted.* 在商店偷东西者将被起诉。| **prosecute sb for sth** *Buxton's being prosecuted for assault.* 巴克斯顿由于袭击罪而被起诉。| *If payment is not received by 1 March we'll be forced to prosecute.* 如果3月1日之前还没有收到付款, 我们将不得不提出诉讼。**2** [I,T] to represent someone in court as their lawyer, when they are bringing a criminal charge against someone else〔律师〕代表原告 —compare 比较 DEFEND (6) **3** [T] *formal* to continue doing something【正式】继续: *We cannot prosecute the investigation further.* 我们不能继续调查。

prosecuting at·tor·ney /'·····,··/ *n* [C usually singular 一般用单数] *AmE* a DISTRICT ATTORNEY【美】地方检察官

pros·e·cu·tion /,prɑsɪ`kjuʃən; ,prɒsɪ'kjuːʃən/ *n* **1** [C,U] the process or act of bringing a charge against someone for a crime, or of being judged for a crime in a court of law (被)起诉, (被)检控: *The evidence is now sufficient to bring a prosecution against him.* 现有的证据足以对他提出诉讼。| *I want immunity from prosecution before I give you any names.* 在我向你提供任何名字前, 我想要求免于起诉。**2 the prosecution** the lawyers who represent the person bringing a criminal charge against someone in a court of law 检控方, 控方: *the chief witness for the prosecution* 控方的主要证人 —compare 比较 DEFENCE (5) **3** [U] *formal* the doing of something that is your job【正式】执行, 履行〔职责〕: *the prosecution of her duties* 履行她的职责 W3

pros·e·cu·tor /`prɑsɪ,kjutə; 'prɒsɪkjuːtə/ *n* [C] a lawyer who represents the person who is bringing a criminal charge against someone 代表起诉人的律师; 控方律师

pros·e·lyte /`prɑsḷ,aɪt; 'prɒsḷaɪt/ *n* [C] *formal* someone who has recently been persuaded to join a religious group, political party etc; CONVERT[2]【正式】〔被说服的〕新皈依某宗教者; 新加入政党者

pros·e·lyt·ize also 又作 **-ise** *BrE*【英】/`prɑsəlɪt,aɪz; 'prɒsələtaɪz/ *v* [I,T] *formal* to try to persuade someone to join a religious group, political party etc, especially in a way that people find offensive【正式】极力劝诱〔某人〕入教[加入政党等]〔常含贬义〕**—proselytizer** *n* [C]

Pro·ser·pi·na /prə`sɝpɪnə; prə'sɜːpɪnə/ in Roman MYTHOLOGY, the name for Persephone 普罗塞耳皮娜〔罗马神话中称Persephone (珀尔塞福涅)〕

Pros·er·pine /`prɑsɚ,paɪn; 'prɒsəpaɪn/ an English name for Persephone 普罗塞耳皮恩〔珀尔塞福涅的英文名〕

pros·o·dy /`prɑsədɪ; 'prɒsədi/ *n* [U] the rules for arranging the patterns of sounds and beats in poetry, or the study of these rules〔诗歌的〕韵律(学), 诗体(学) **—prosodic** /prə`sɑdɪk; prə'sɒdɪk/ *adj*

pros·pect[1] /`prɑspɛkt; 'prɒspekt/ *n* **1** [C,U] a possibility that something which you hope for will happen soon〔成功的〕可能性, 机会: **[+of]** *There's little prospect of employment, I'm afraid.* 恐怕就业的可能性很小。| **[+for]** *There are good prospects for growth in the retail sector.* 零售行业有很好的发展前景。| **every prospect** (=a strong possibility) 很大的可能性 | *Peace talks start today with every prospect of success.* 和谈今天开始, 成功的可能性很大。**2** [singular] something that is possible or is likely to happen in the future 可能的事情, 很可能发生的事情; 前景: **[+of]** *The prospect of marriage terrified Alice.* 想到要结婚艾丽斯就感到害怕。| *a depressing prospect* 令人沮丧的前景 **3 prospects** [plural] chances of future success 将来成功的机会; 前途, 前程: *You can't marry a man with no job and no prospects!* 你不能嫁给一个没有工作也没有前途的男人! **4** [C] a person, job, plan etc that has a good chance of success in the future 有前途的人[工作, 计划等]: *Reg was the brightest schoolboy rugby prospect in years.* 雷格是多年来最有希望的学生橄榄球队员。**5** [C usually singular 一般用单数] *formal* a view of a wide area of land, especially from a high place【正式】〔尤指从高处看到的〕景象, 开阔的景观, 景色: *a fine prospect across the valley* 山谷那边的美好景色 **6 in prospect** *formal* likely to happen in the near future【正式】即将可能发生的 S2 W2

pro·spect[2] /`prɑspɛkt; prə'spekt/ *v* [I+for, T] to examine an area of land or water, in order to find gold, silver, oil etc 勘探, 勘察〔以寻找金、银、石油等矿藏〕

pro·spec·tive /prə`spɛktɪv; prə'spektɪv/ *adj* [only before noun 仅用于名词前] **1** likely to do a particular thing or achieve a particular position 预期的; 未来的; 可能的: **prospective employee/candidate/buyer etc** *I'm meeting a prospective buyer for the house today.* 今天我要见一位可能购买这所房子的人。**2** likely to happen 很可能发生的: **prospective costs/career/changes etc** *What are the prospective returns from an investment of $10,000 over five years?* 投资一万美元五年有可能收益多少?

pro·spec·tor /`prɑspɛktə; prə'spektə/ *n* [C] someone who looks for gold, minerals, oil etc 勘探者, 探矿者

pro·spec·tus /prə`spɛktəs; prə'spektəs/ *n* [C] **1** a small book that advertises a college, university, new business etc〔学院、

大学、新企业等的〕简介，广告宣传册子 **2** a formal statement giving details of a future event in business, such as the sale of shares (SHARE² (5))〔商业企业等拓股之类的〕计划书；说明书

pros·per /ˋprɑspɚ; ˈprɒspə/ *v* **1** [I] to be successful and become rich 成功；兴旺，发达，繁荣：*My father was no longer prospering in business.* 我父亲生意不再兴旺发达。**2** [I] to grow and develop in a healthy way; THRIVE 健康成长；顺利发展，蓬勃发展：*The children seemed to prosper under their care.* 在他们的照管下，孩子们看来在健康成长。**3** [T] *old use* to make something succeed【旧】使成功；使繁荣

pro·sper·i·ty /prɑsˋpɛrətɪ; prɒˈsperɪ̵ti/ *n* [U] a condition of having money and everything that is needed for a good life 兴隆，发达，昌盛，繁荣：*an era of unparalleled peace and prosperity* 空前和平与繁荣的时代

Pros·pe·ro /ˋprɑspəro; ˈprɒspərəʊ/ the main character in the play *The Tempest* by William Shakespeare 普洛斯彼罗〔威廉·莎士比亚的剧本《暴风雨》中的主角〕

pros·per·ous /ˋprɑspərəs; ˈprɒspərəs/ *adj* successful and rich 成功的；繁荣的，兴旺的，发达的：*working for a strong, prosperous and united Europe* 为实现强大、繁荣、统一的欧洲而努力 —**prosperously** *adv*

pros·tate /ˋprɑstet; ˈprɒsteɪt/ also 又作 **prostate gland** *n* [C] the organ in the male body that produces a liquid in which SPERM (=seeds) are carried 前列腺

pros·the·sis /prɑsˋθisɪs; prɒsˈθiːsɪ̵s/ *plural* **prostheses** /-siz; -siːz/ *n* [C] *technical* an artificial leg, tooth, or other part of the body which takes the place of a missing part【术语】义肢，假体〈如假肢、假牙等〉

pros·ti·tute¹ /ˋprɑstə,tut; ˈprɒstɪ̵tjuːt/ *n* [C] **1** someone, especially a woman, who earns money by having sex with people who pay for it 娼妓，妓女 **2 male prostitute** a man who earns money in this way 男妓

> **CULTURAL NOTE 文化注释**
>
> The STEREOTYPE of a prostitute is of a woman wearing a short skirt, HIGH HEELS, and a lot of MAKE-UP. 妓女的典型形象是穿短裙和高跟鞋，浓妆艳抹。

prostitute² *v* [T] **1** *formal* to use your skills, abilities etc in a way that does not show their true value, in order to earn money【正式】出卖〔才能〕，为钱而滥用〔才能〕：*Olivier never prostituted his acting talent by appearing in TV commercials.* 奥利维尔从不做电视广告来出卖自己的表演才华。**2 prostitute yourself a)** to have sex in return for money 卖淫 **b)** to do unpleasant work just to get money 为挣钱而做难堪的工作

pros·ti·tu·tion /ˌprɑstəˋtuʃən; ˌprɒstɪ̵ˈtjuːʃən/ *n* [U] **1** the work of prostitutes 卖淫〔业〕：*an alarming rise in teenage prostitution* 少年卖淫的惊人增长 **2** *formal* the use of your skill, ability etc, in a way that does not show its true value【正式】滥用〔才能〕

> **CULTURAL NOTE 文化注释**
>
> In Britain, since 1959, the law allows the practice of prostitution but it does not allow a person to openly offer himself or herself as a prostitute, or to provide a prostitute for someone else. KERB CRAWLING (=the activity of driving a car slowly along a road looking for a prostitute) is also illegal, and the police often arrest KERB CRAWLERS when they want to reduce the level of prostitution in an area. In the US, prostitution is legal only in the state of Nevada, but it is practised everywhere. Prostitution is sometimes described as 'the oldest profession in the world'. 英国法律从1959年开始就允许卖淫，但是不允许公开揽客或者介绍卖淫。沿路开车慢行以寻觅妓女是非法的，当警方想整治一个地区的卖淫时，这些人也常遭到逮捕。美国只有在内华达州卖淫是合法的，但卖淫行为各地都有。有时卖淫被称为"世界上最古老的职业"。

pros·trate¹ /ˋprɑstret; ˈprɒstreɪt/ *adj* **1** lying on your front with your face towards the ground, for example because you are injured, or are praising God 俯卧的；拜倒的，匍伏的 —compare 比较 PRONE (2) **2** so shocked, upset etc that you can no longer do anything 非常震惊[伤心]而不能做任何事的：**[+with]** *Judy was prostrate with grief after her father's death.* 朱迪在她父亲死后悲痛不已。

pro·strate² /ˋprɑstret; prəˈstreɪt/ *v* [T] **1 prostrate yourself** to lie on your front with your face towards the ground as an act of praise or a sign of obedience 拜倒，匍伏〔表示顺从或崇拜〕**2 be prostrated** *formal* to have lost all your strength, courage, or energy【正式】衰竭，一蹶不振，筋疲力尽：*prostrated by illness* 病倒 —**prostration** /prɑˋstreʃən; prɒˈstreɪʃən/ *n* [C,U]

pros·y /ˋprozɪ; ˈprəʊzi/ *adj* a prosy style of writing or speech is boring and shows no imagination〔文章或讲话〕乏味的，无想象力的 —**prosily** *adv* —**prosiness** *n* [U]

prot- /prot; prəʊt/ *prefix* another form of the prefix PROTO- 前缀 proto- 的另一种形式

pro·tag·o·nist /proˋtægənɪst; prəʊˈtægənɪ̵st/ *n* [C] **1** one of the main supporters of a new aim or policy, especially a social one〔新目标或政策的〕主要支持者，主要拥护者：**[+of]** *Ogden was one of the earliest protagonists of educational reform.* 奥格登是教育改革的最早支持者之一。**2** *formal* the most important character in a play, film, or story【正式】〔戏剧、电影或故事的〕主要人物，主角 **3** *formal* someone who is in a competition, battle, or struggle【正式】〔竞赛、战役、斗争的〕参加者，参与者：*the protagonists in America's 'software wars'* 美国"软件战"的参与者 —compare 比较 ANTAGONIST

pro·te·an /ˋprotɪən; ˈprəʊtiən/ *adj literary* having the ability to change continually in appearance or behaviour【文】〔外表或行为〕多变的，变化多端的

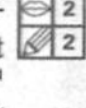

pro·tect /prəˋtɛkt; prəˈtekt/ *v* [T] **1** to keep someone or something safe from harm, damage, or illness 保护；防护：**protect sb/sth from sth** *Try to protect your skin from the sun.* 尽量保护皮肤不受太阳晒。| *Kids should be protected from all that violence.* 应保护孩子免受那些暴力的侵害。| **protect sth** *laws protecting the rights of disabled people* 保护残疾人权利的法律 | *I have to protect my reputation.* 我必须保护自己的声誉。| **protect sb/sth against** *a natural camouflage that protects them against predators* 保护它们免受食肉动物捕食的天然伪装 | **[+against]** *locks to protect against burglars* 防盗锁 **2** [usually passive 一般用被动态] to keep something such as an old building or a rare animal safe from harm or destruction, by means of special laws〔以特殊法律〕保护〔古老建筑物或稀有动物〕**3** to help the industry and trade of your own country by taxing foreign goods〔通过征收进口税〕保护〔国内工商业〕—see also 另见 PROTECTIONISM, PROTECTIVE —**protected** *adj*: *Spotted owls are a protected species.* 斑点猫头鹰是受保护的物种。

pro·tec·tion /prəˋtɛkʃən; prəˈtekʃən/ *n* **1** [U] the act of protecting or state of being protected 保护；受保护：*You're guaranteed police protection if you testify in court.* 如果你在法庭上作证，你一定会受到警方的保护。| **[+against]** *Take these vitamins daily for protection against minor infections.* 每天服用这些维生素片以预防轻微感染。| **give/offer/provide protection** (=protect) 提供保护 *Helen's thin coat gave little protection against the cold.* 海伦单薄的外衣几乎不能御寒。**2** [U] the promise of payment from an insurance company if something bad happens〔保险公司的〕保障：*Our Five-Star Policy offers complete protection in case of fire.* 我们的五星保险单在发生火灾时提供完全的保障。**3** [singular] something that protects 防护物：**[+against]** *Wear a bullet-proof vest as a protection against snipers.* 穿一件防弹背心以防狙击手。**4** [U] protection money 保护费

pro·tec·tion·is·m /prəˋtɛkʃənɪzm̩; prəˈtekʃənɪzəm/ *n* [U] the system of helping your country's trade, especially by taxing foreign goods 贸易保护主义 —**protectionist** *adj* —**protectionist** *n* [C]

protection mon·ey /-ˈ.. ˌ../ *n* [U] money paid to criminals to stop them from damaging your property〔付给不法分子的〕保护费

protection rack·et /-ˈ.. ˌ../ *n* [C] *informal* a system in which criminals demand money from you to stop them from damaging your property【非正式】〔不法分子的〕勒索保护费的勾当

pro·tec·tive /prəˋtɛktɪv; prəˈtektɪv/ *adj* **1** [only before noun 仅用于名词前] used or intended for protection 保护的，防护的：*protective clothing* 防护服 | *protective legislation* 保护性法规 | *a protective layer of varnish* 一层保护性清漆 **2** wanting to protect someone from harm or danger, often in a way that unintentionally restricts their freedom〔对人〕关切保护的；〔过于〕爱护的：**[+towards/of]** *I can't help feeling protective towards my kids.* 我忍不住想保护我的孩子。**3** intended to give an advantage to your own country's industry〔对本国工业〕保护性的：*a protective tariff on imports of foreign cars* 对进口外国汽车的保护性关税 —**protectively** *adv* —**protectiveness** *n* [U]

protective cus·to·dy /-ˌ.. ˈ.../ *n* [U] a situation in which the police make you stay somewhere to protect you from other people 保护性拘留

Protector —see 见 LORD PROTECTOR

pro·tec·tor /prə`tɛktɚ; prəˈtektə/ *n* [C] something or someone that protects 保护者, 保护物: *He sees himself as her protector.* 他把自己看成是她的保护者。

pro·tec·tor·ate /prə`tɛktərɪt; prəˈtektərɪ̈t/ *n* [C] a country that is protected and controlled by a more powerful country, especially in the areas of defence and foreign affairs 保护国〔由一个更强的国家保护并控制其国防和外交〕

prot·é·gé /ˈprotə,ʒe; ˈprɒtəʒeɪ/ *n* [C] a young person who is guided and helped by someone who has influence, power, or more experience 受保护人〔有影响、有权势、有经验的人对年轻人给予指导和帮助〕; 门生, 门徒

prot·é·gée /ˈprotə,ʒe; ˈprɒtəʒeɪ/ *n* [C] a young woman who is guided and helped by someone who has influence, power, or more experience 女性受保护人; 女门生, 女门徒

W2 **pro·tein** /ˈprotin; ˈprəʊtiːn/ *n* [C,U] one of the many substances that exist in food such as meat, eggs, and beans, which help your body to grow and keep it strong and healthy 蛋白质

pro tem /,pro `tɛm; ,prəʊ ˈtem/ also 又作 **pro tem·po·re** /-`tɛmpəre; -ˈtempəreɪ/ *Latin* 【拉丁】 *adj, adv* happening now but only for a short time 暂时的[地], 临时的[地]: *a pro tem committee of nine men* 临时九人委员会

W3 **pro·test¹** /ˈprotɛst; ˈprəʊtest/ *n* **1** [C,U] a strong complaint that shows you disagree with, or are angry about something that you think is wrong or unfair 抗议, 反对: *a written protest alleging police brutality* 指控警察行为粗暴的书面抗议 | *I turned off the TV, despite loud protests from the kids.* 尽管孩子们大声反对, 我还是关掉了电视机。| **[+against]** *American flags were burned as a protest against US intervention.* 作为对美国干涉的抗议, 美国国旗被烧了。| *a protest song* 抗议歌曲 | **in protest** (=as a way of making a protest) 作为抗议 *Seven prisoners are on hunger strike in protest against their treatment.* 七名囚犯在绝食以抗议他们所受的待遇。| *the protest movements of the 1960s* 20世纪60年代的抗议运动 | **a storm of protest/wave of protest** (=a lot of angry protest) 抗议风暴/抗议浪潮 *The price rises caused a storm of protest.* 价格上涨引起了抗议风暴。**2** [C] an occasion when people come together in public to express disapproval or opposition to something 抗议; 抗议活动: *Student protests swept across the nation's campuses.* 学生抗议活动席卷了全国的校园。**3 without protest** calmly and without complaining 平静地; 毫无怨言地: *Ben accepted his punishment without protest.* 本毫无怨言地接受了惩罚。**4 under protest** unwillingly, and with the feeling that you have been unfairly treated 不情愿地; 认为是不公正地: *I only signed the document under protest.* 我不情愿地签了这份文件。

pro·test² /prə`tɛst; prəˈtest/ *v* **1** [I,T] to say or do something publicly to show that you disagree with, or are angry about something that you think is wrong or unfair 抗议, 反对: **[+against/at/about]** *Someone has to keep protesting against human rights violations.* 必须有人不断抗议侵害人权的行为。| *I heard him protesting loudly as the medics took him away.* 医务人员把他带走时, 我听到他在大声抗议。| *"Let me go!" Sarah protested angrily.* "放开我!"萨拉生气地提出抗议。| **protest sth** *AmE* 【美】 *a large crowd protesting the war* 反对这场战争的一大群人 **2** [T] to state very firmly that something is true, especially when other people do not believe you〔尤指当别人不相信你时〕坚持说, 坚称; 声言, 申明: **protest that** *Even if Mandy protests that she's not drunk, don't let her drive.* 即使曼迪坚称她自己没有醉, 也不要让她开车。| **protest your innocence** (=keep saying that you are innocent) 坚称自己无罪

Prot·es·tant /ˈprɑtɪstənt; ˈprɒtɪ̈stənt/ *n* [C] a member of a part of the Christian church that separated from the Roman Catholic church in the 16th century 新教徒〔16世纪脱离罗马天主教的基督教教派成员〕 **—Protestant** *adj* **—Protestantism** *n* [U]

prot·es·ta·tion /,prɑtəs`teʃən; ,prɒtɪ̈ˈsteɪʃən/ *n formal* 【正式】 [C+of] a strong statement that saying that something is true, especially when other people say it is not 宣言; 声明; 断言

pro·test·er /prə`tɛstɚ; prəˈtestə/ *n* [C] someone who takes part in a public activity to show their opposition to something 抗议者

proto- /ˈproto; ˈprəʊtəʊ/ *prefix* also 又作 **prot-** *technical* first in time or order, before other things of the same kind are developed; original 【术语】第一的, 最初的, 原始的: *the huge protogalaxy from which all the galaxies developed* 所有星系赖以形成的巨大原星系

pro·to·col /ˈprotə,kɔl; ˈprəʊtəkɒl/ *n* **1** [U] the system of rules on the correct and acceptable way to behave on official occasions 礼节, 礼仪: *a breach of diplomatic protocol* 违反外交礼节 **2** [C] *technical* a method for connecting computers so that they can exchange information 【术语】〔电脑间为交换信息的〕协议

pro·ton /ˈprotɑn; ˈprəʊtɒn/ *n* [C] a very small piece of matter that carries POSITIVE electricity and that together with a NEUTRON forms the NUCLEUS (=central part) of an atom 质子 —see also 另见 ELECTRON

pro·to·plas·m /ˈprotə,plæzəm; ˈprəʊtəplæzəm/ *n* [U] *technical* the colourless substance that forms the cells of plants and animals 【术语】原生质, 原浆

pro·to·type /ˈprotə,taɪp; ˈprəʊtətaɪp/ *n* [C] the first form that a new design of a car, machine etc has〔新型汽车、机器等的〕原型; 雏形: **[+of/for]** *a complete working prototype of the new model* 新款的完整工作样机原型

pro·to·zo·a /,protə`zoə; ,prəʊtəˈzəʊə/ *n* [plural] very small living things that only have one cell 原生动物

pro·to·zo·an /,protə`zoən; ,prəʊtəˈzəʊən/ also 又作 **pro·to·zo·on** /-`zoɑn; -ˈzəʊɒn/ *n* [C] a single member of the protozoa〔单个的〕原生动物 **—protozoan** *adj*

pro·trac·ted /pro`træktɪd; prəˈtræktɪ̈d/ *adj* lasting a long time, especially longer than usual, or necessary 长时间的; 延长的, 拖延的: *the likelihood of an ugly and protracted guerilla war* 发生一场可怕而持久的游击战的可能性 **—protract** *v* [T] **—protraction** /-`trækʃən; -ˈtrækʃən/ *n* [U]

pro·trac·tor /pro`træktɚ; prəˈtræktə/ *n* [C] an instrument usually in the shape of a half-circle, used for measuring and drawing angles 量角器; 分度规

pro·trude /pro`trud; prəˈtruːd/ *v* [I] to stick out from somewhere 伸出, 突出: *protruding eyes* 突出的眼睛 | **[+from]** *A pair of shoes protruded from under the bed.* 一双鞋子从床底下露出来。

pro·tru·sion /pro`truʒən; prəˈtruːʒən/ *n* **1** [C] something that protrudes 伸出物, 突出物 **2** [U] the act of protruding 伸出, 突出

pro·tu·be·rance /pro`tubərəns; prəˈtjuːbərəns/ *n* [C] *formal* something that sticks out from the surface of something else 【正式】隆起, 突出物

pro·tu·be·rant /pro`tubərənt; prəˈtjuːbərənt/ *adj* curving outwards from a surface 隆起的, 突出的 **—protuberantly** *adv*

S2 W3 **proud** /praʊd; praʊd/ *adj*

1 ▶PLEASED 高兴的◀ feeling pleased with your achievements, family, country etc because you think they are very good 自豪的, 得意的, 引以为荣的: *You should see them with the baby – they're so proud!* 你该看看他们与婴儿在一起的样子——他们多么自豪! | **[+of]** *Jane's very proud of her new car.* 简为她的新车颇感得意。| **proud (that)** *We are proud that a pupil from our school has won a prize.* 我们学校的一个学生得了奖, 我们感到很自豪。| **proud to do/be sth** *She was proud to be part of such a prestigious project.* 她很自豪能够成为如此声誉卓著的项目的一员。—see also 另见 HOUSEPROUD

2 ▶TOO PROUD 过分得意的◀ thinking that you are more important, skilful etc than you really are 骄傲的, 傲慢的, 自负的: *Proud and boastful, Jaggers was typical of the young brokers.* 贾格尔斯是典型的年轻经纪人, 傲慢且喜欢自吹自擂。

3 ▶REFUSE HELP 拒绝帮助◀ having so much respect for yourself that you will not let other people help you when you are in a difficult situation 高傲的; 自尊心强的: *My grandfather's penniless, but he's too proud to ask for help.* 我祖父身无分文, 但他自尊心太强, 不愿求助于人。

4 do sb proud a) *informal* to provide a lot of good food, drink etc when people are visiting you or celebrating something 【非正式】盛情款待某人, 待某人以上宾之礼: *Clare did us proud last Christmas.* 去年圣诞节克莱尔盛情款待了我们。**b)** to make people feel proud of you by doing something well 使某人为你感到自豪: *Congratulations Bobby, you've done us proud!* 祝贺你, 博比, 你给我们争了光!

5 as proud as a peacock feeling very pleased with yourself because you have done something well 骄傲如孔雀, 非常骄傲

6 ▶IMPRESSIVE 给人以深刻印象的◀ *literary* tall and impressive 【文】宏伟的, 壮观的: *the proud cathedral spire* 壮观的教堂尖顶 —see also 另见 PRIDE¹ **—proudly** *adv*

Proust /prust; pruːst/, **Mar·cel** /mar`sɛl; ˈmɑːsel/ (1871-1922) a French writer of NOVEL*s*, who many people consider one of the greatest writers of modern times. His best known work is a series of novels called in English *Remembrance of Things Past*, which is a detailed description of French society in the late 19th century, and is sometimes mentioned as a typical example of a very long book. Many people also know how the book begins, when one of the characters eats a MADELEINE (=a type of small cake) and the taste reminds him of an earlier time. 普鲁斯特〔(1871-1922), 法国小说家, 被认为是最杰出的

现代作家之一。最著名的作品是系列长篇小说《追忆逝水年华》，书中详尽描述19世纪晚期法国的社会状况。该书有时被看作是鸿篇巨制的典型之作。不少人还记得小说开头的一幕：有一个人物吃着玛德琳蛋糕，蛋糕的味道令他想起早年的时光〕

prove /pruv; pruːv/ *v past tense* **proved** *past participle* **proved** also 又作 **proven** /ˈpruvən; ˈpruːvən/ *especially AmE*【尤美】
1 ►SHOW THE TRUTH 展示真实情况◄ [T] to show that something is true by providing facts, information etc 证明，证实：*Evidence has been found that proves his innocence.* 证明他无罪的证据已经找到。| **prove (that)** *It is impossible to prove that God exists.* 无法证明上帝存在。| **prove sb wrong/innocent etc** *It would give me great pleasure to prove Sam wrong.* 能证明萨姆有错我将感到非常高兴。—see also 另见 DISPROVE
2 ►BE SOMETHING 是某事物◄ [linking verb 连系动词, T] if someone or something proves difficult, helpful etc, you find out that this is what they are like 证明是；被发现是；显示出是：*Working from home proved a real advantage after my son was born.* 我儿子出生后，我发现在家工作是非常便利的。| **prove to be sth** *Your computing experience should prove to be useful.* 你使用电脑的经验应该证明是有用的。
3 prove yourself to show how good you are at something by trying hard to do it well 证明自己的实力：*When I started the job, I felt I had to prove myself.* 当我开始干这份工作时，我觉得必须证明一下我自己。
4 ►BREAD 面包◄ [I] if DOUGH (=unbaked bread mixture) proves, it rises and becomes light because of the YEAST in it〔面团〕发酵
5 ►LAW 法律◄ [T] *law* to show that a WILL has been made properly【法律】检验，认证〔遗嘱〕 —**provable** *adj* —**provably** *adv*

prov·en¹ /ˈpruvən; ˈpruːvən/ *adj*
1 [usually before noun 一般用于名词前] tested and shown to be true 被证实的，经过验证的：*a woman of proven ability* 被证实确有才能的女人 **2 not proven** an expression used in Scottish law when a court cannot decide definitely that someone is guilty of a crime〔苏格兰法律用语〕证据不足的

proven² *especially AmE*【尤美】a past participle of PROVE

prov·e·nance /ˈprɑvənəns; ˈprɒvənəns/ *n* [U] *formal* the place where something originally came from【正式】起源（地）；出处：*a rug of Iranian provenance* 原产自伊朗的小地毯

Pro·vence /proˈvɑns; prɒˈvɒns/ an area in southeast France which includes the coast of the Mediterranean Sea and the hills and mountains away from the coast. It produces wine, fruit, OLIVE oil and LAVENDER (=a strong-smelling purple flower). Its beaches, beautiful countryside, and warm weather make it a popular place for tourists to visit. Its main towns are Nice and Marseilles. 普罗旺斯〔法国东南部一地区。该地区包括地中海沿岸地区和远离海岸的丘陵和山脉，盛产葡萄酒、水果、橄榄油和薰衣草。这里有海滩，有美丽的田野，还有和暖的气候，是一个旅游胜地。主要城市有尼斯和马赛〕

prov·en·der /ˈprɑvəndɚ; ˈprɒvɨndə/ *n* [U] *old-fashioned* dry food for horses and cattle【过时】〔牲畜的〕干饲料，粮秣

prov·erb /ˈprɑvɝb; ˈprɒvɜːb/ *n* [C] a short well-known statement that contains advice about life in general 谚语，格言

pro·ver·bi·al /prəˈvɝbɪəl; prəˈvɜːbiəl/ *adj* **1 the proverbial** used when describing something using a well-known expression 俗话所说的：*This was not the proverbial free lunch!* 这不是俗话所说的免费午餐！**2** well-known by a lot of people 众所周知的：*It was a level of corruption which became proverbial.* 那是众所周知的腐败。**3** connected with a proverb 谚语（性）的：*a proverbial saying* 谚语式的格言 —**proverbially** *adv*

Prov·erbs /ˈprɑvɝbz; ˈprɒvɜːbz/ a book of the Old Testament of the Bible consisting of a collection of PROVERBS which people believe were written by King Solomon《箴言》〔《圣经·旧约》中的一卷，收有相传为所罗门王所写的格言〕

pro·vide /prəˈvaɪd; prəˈvaɪd/ *v* [T] **1** to make sure that someone gets what they need, especially by giving it to them 提供，供应，供给：**provide sth for sb** *The hotel provides a shoe-cleaning service for guests.* 该酒店为客人提供擦鞋服务。| **provide sb with sth** *a project designed to provide young people with work* 一项旨在为年轻人提供工作的计划 | **provide sth** *I'll provide the food if you bring the wine.* 你带酒我就提供吃的。**2** to produce a useful result, opportunity etc 产生有益的结果；制造[提供]机会：*We are hoping the enquiry will provide an explanation for the accident.* 我们希望这次调查将为该事故提供一种解释。| **provide sb with sth** *This has provided police with a vital clue.* 这为警方提供了一条关键的线索。**3 provide that** *formal* if a law or rule provides that something must happen, it states that it must happen【正式】〔法律、规章〕规定

provide against sth *phr v* [T] *formal* to make plans in order to deal with a bad situation that might happen【正式】预防，防备，防止

provide for sb/sth *phr v* [T] **1** to give someone the things they need, such as money, food etc 供养，抚养：*Without work, how can I provide for my children?* 没有工作，我如何供养我的孩子？**2** *formal* to make plans in order to deal with something that might happen in the future【正式】为…作准备；防备：*The policy provides for a 60% increase in traffic.* 这项政策旨在应付车辆增加60%的局面。**3** *formal* if a law or rule provides for something, it makes doing that thing possible【正式】〔法律、规章〕使〔某事〕可能；准许

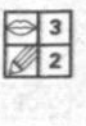
pro·vid·ed /prəˈvaɪdɪd; prəˈvaɪdɨd/ also 又作 **provided that** *conjunction* used to say that something will only be possible if something else happens or is done 只要；如果…的话：*I don't mind Guy coming with us, provided he pays for his own meals.* 只要盖伊自付餐费，我不介意他和我们一起去。

Prov·i·dence¹, providence /ˈprɑvədəns; ˈprɒvɨdəns/ *n* [singular,U] a force that some people believe controls our lives, especially because it is what God wants 天意，天命

Providence² the capital city of the US state of Rhode Island 普罗维登斯〔美国罗得岛州首府〕

prov·i·dent /ˈprɑvədənt; ˈprɒvɨdənt/ *adj formal* careful and sensible, especially by saving money for the future【正式】顾及未来的，未雨绸缪的，深谋远虑的 —opposite 反义词 IMPROVIDENT —**providently** *adv*

prov·i·den·tial /ˌprɑvəˈdɛnʃəl; ˌprɒvɨˈdenʃəl◄/ *adj formal* happening just when you need it; LUCKY【正式】幸运的，凑巧的；及时的：*To Robyn, it seemed a providential opportunity to make the break with Charles.* 对罗宾来说，那好像是与查尔斯分手的大好机会。—**providentially** *adv*

pro·vid·er /prəˈvaɪdɚ; prəˈvaɪdə/ *n* [C] someone who provides something, especially someone who supports a family 供应者；〔尤指〕供养家庭的人

pro·vid·ing /prəˈvaɪdɪŋ; prəˈvaɪdɪŋ/ also 又作 **providing that** *conjunction* used to say that something will only be possible if something else happens or is done 只要；如果…的话：*Sure you can borrow the car, providing you get it back to me before 10 o'clock.* 只要你在10点钟之前还我，你当然可以借车。

prov·ince /ˈprɑvɪns; ˈprɒvɨns/ *n* **1** also 又作 **Province** [C] one of the large areas into which some countries are divided 省：*It is China's most populous province.* 这是中国人口最多的省份。**2 the provinces** *especially BrE* the parts of a country that are not near to the capital city【尤英】外省，外地〔指首都以外的地区〕**3 sb's province** a subject that someone knows a lot about or something that they are responsible for〔知识、研究的〕范围，领域；职责范围：*Sales forecasts are outside my province – talk to the Sales Manager.* 销售预测不属我的职责范围——去找销售经理谈吧。**4** an area that an ARCHBISHOP (=a priest of the highest rank) is responsible for 大主教辖区 —compare 比较 DIOCESE

pro·vin·cial¹ /prəˈvɪnʃəl; prəˈvɪnʃəl/ *adj* **1** connected with the parts of a country that are not near the capital city 外省的，地方的〔指首都以外的地区〕：*a small provincial town* 一座地方小城镇 **2** a provincial attitude shows that you are unwilling to accept new ideas or to think about things in new ways〔态度〕褊狭的，守旧的 —**provincially** *adv*

provincial² *n* [C] someone who comes from the parts of a country that are not near the capital city（来自）首都以外的人；地方居民

pro·vin·cial·is·m /prəˈvɪnʃəlɪzəm; prəˈvɪnʃəlɪzəm/ *n* [U] the attitude of not wanting to accept new ideas and not being interested in new things 褊狭守旧的态度

prov·ing ground /ˈ.. ./ *n* [C] **1** a place or situation in which something new is tried out or tested〔新事物的〕试验场所[环境]：*High-crime areas make ideal proving grounds for new officers.* 犯罪高发地区是考验新任警察的理想场所。**2** an area for scientific testing, especially of vehicles〔尤指车辆的〕检验场，试验场

pro·vi·sion¹ /prəˈvɪʒən; prəˈvɪʒən/ *n* **1** [C,U] the act of providing something that someone needs 供应，供给，提供：**[+of]** *Many women would welcome the provision of childcare facilities at work.* 很多妇女都会欢迎在工作地点提供托儿设施。| **[+for]** *provision for people with disabilities* 满足残疾人士的需要 **2 make provision for** to make plans for future needs 为…作好准备，为…预先采取措施：*Ralph wanted to make proper provision for his children.* 拉尔夫想为他孩子的将来作好准备。**3 provisions** food supplies, especially for a journey〔尤指为旅行储备的〕粮食，食物 **4** [C] a condition in an agreement or law

〔协议或法律中的〕规定, 条款, 条件: *Let me set out the main provisions of the contract.* 让我阐明这份合同的主要条款。

provision² *v* [T] to provide someone or something with a lot of food and supplies, especially for a journey〔尤指为旅行〕提供大量的食品和其他供应品

pro·vi·sion·al /prəˋvɪʒənḷ; prəˈvɪʒənəl/ *adj* **1** intended to exist for only a short time and likely to be changed in the future 临时的〔指短期存在〕, 暂时的, 暂定的: *a provisional government* 临时政府 —compare 比较 TEMPORARY **2** provisional offers, arrangements etc are not yet definite but should become definite in the future 临时的〔指尚待确定〕: *We accept provisional bookings by phone.* 我们接受电话临时预约。—**provisionally** *adv*

Provisional IRA, the /ˌ·˙····ˈ·/ military organization that wants Northern Ireland to leave the UK. In 1969, a group that favoured the use of violence, bombing etc separated from the main IRA, and officially this group is called the 'Provisional IRA'. But in fact when people talk about the 'IRA', they usually mean this group. 爱尔兰共和军临时派〔一非法军事组织, 旨在使北爱尔兰脱离英国。1969年, 有一支主张使用暴力、爆炸等手段的力量脱离爱尔兰共和军的主体, 官方称其为"爱尔兰共和军临时派"。实际上, 人们讲到"爱尔兰共和军"时, 一般都指该组织〕

provisional li·cence /·˙···ˈ··/ *n* [C] *BrE* an official document that you need when you are learning to drive【英】〔学习驾驶时需用的〕临时驾驶执照; LEARNER'S PERMIT *AmE*【美】

pro·vi·so /prəˋvaɪzo; prəˈvaɪzəʊ/ *plural* **provisos** *n* [C] a condition that you ask for before you will agree to something〔同意某事的〕(前提) 条件, (附带) 条件: *The only proviso is that your vacation has to be for a minimum of five nights.* 唯一的条件是你的假期必须至少有五个晚上。

prov·o·ca·tion /ˌprɑvəˋkeʃən; ˌprɒvəˈkeɪʃən/ *n* [C,U] an action or event that makes someone angry or that is intended to do this 激怒; 挑衅; 挑衅性事件: *It was a vicious attack, with absolutely no provocation.* 那是在事先未发生任何挑衅情况下的恶意攻击。

pro·voc·a·tive /prəˋvɑkətɪv; prəˈvɒkətɪv/ *adj* **1** provocative behaviour, remarks etc are intended to make people angry or to cause a lot of discussion〔行为、话语等〕使人生气的; 挑衅的; 煽动的; 引起争论的: *Some would say he wrote a deliberately provocative book.* 有人会说他写了一本故意引起争论的书。**2** provocative clothes, movements etc are intended to make someone sexually excited〔衣服、动作〕挑逗性的 —**provocatively** *adv*

pro·voke /prəˋvok; prəˈvəʊk/ *v* [T] **1** to cause a sudden reaction that is often very extreme or unpleasant 激起, 引起: *The decision to invade provoked storms of protest in the UN.* 这一侵略的决定激起联合国的强烈抗议。| **provoke sb to do sth** *It's the first time an article has provoked me to write in to the newspaper.* 一篇文章激发我给这家报纸写信发表意见, 这是第一次。**2** to try to make someone angry by doing or saying things that you know annoy them 激怒; 使恼火: **provoke sb into doing sth** *Don't let him provoke you into losing your temper!* 别让他故意惹你发脾气!

Pro·vos, the /ˋprovoz; ˈprəʊvəʊz/ *n* [plural] *informal* the PROVISIONAL IRA【非正式】爱尔兰共和军临时派

Prov·ost also 又作 **provost** /ˋprɑvəst; ˈprɒvəst/ *n* [C] **1** a person in charge of a college in a British university〔英国大学中学院的〕院长 **2** *AmE* an important university official【美】大学教务长 **3** the leader of a Scottish town council〔苏格兰的〕市长 —compare 比较 MAYOR **4** the main priest in a group of priests connected with a CATHEDRAL in Britain〔英国大教堂的〕教长

pro·vost court /ˋprovo kɔrt; prəˈvəʊ kɔːt/ *n* [C] a type of military court 军事法庭

provost mar·shal /ˌprovo ˋmɑrʃəl; prəˌvəʊ ˈmɑːʃəl/ *n* [C] an officer who is in charge of military police 宪兵司令

prow /praʊ; praʊ/ *n* [C] *especially literary* the front part of a ship or boat【尤文】船头, 船首

prow·ess /ˋpraʊɪs; ˈpraʊɪ̣s/ *n* [U] *formal* great skill at doing something【正式】〔做某事的〕高超技艺[技能, 技巧]: *Peregrines are known for their hunting prowess.* 游隼以它们高超的捕猎技巧而闻名。

prowl¹ /praʊl; praʊl/ *v* **1** [I,T] if an animal prowls, it moves around an area quietly, especially because it is hunting another animal〔尤指捕猎的动物在某处〕悄悄来回游走 **2** [I,T] if someone prowls, they move around an area quietly, especially because they are involved in some criminal activity〔尤指参与某些犯罪活动的人在某处〕秘密[悄悄]来回游走: *gangs prowling the streets* 在大街上鬼鬼祟祟四处游荡的匪帮 **3** [I always+adv/prep] to walk around a place because you do not have anything to do 徘徊, 闲荡: [**+around/ about**] *Kim prowled restlessly around the room.* 金在房间里不安地踱来踱去。

prowl² *n* [singular] **1 be on the prowl** to be moving around quietly looking for something or someone 悄悄地四处搜寻: *police cars on the prowl* 在巡逻的警车 **2** an act of prowling 四处觅食; 悄悄走动

prowl·er /ˋpraʊlə; ˈpraʊlə/ *n* [C] someone who follows people or waits near their home, especially at night, and frightens or harms them〔尤指晚上心怀不轨的〕盯梢的人, 潜伏的人: *If you think there is a prowler outside, don't go out to check – call the police.* 如果你觉得外面有潜伏的人, 不要出去查看——要叫警察。

prox·i·mate /ˋprɑksəˌmɪt; ˈprɒksɪ̣mɪ̣t/ *adj formal*【正式】**1** nearest in time, order, or family relationship〔时间、顺序、亲属关系〕最近的, 最接近的 **2** a proximate cause is a direct one〔原因〕直接的 —**proximately** *adv*

prox·im·i·ty /prɑkˋsɪmətɪ; prɒkˈsɪmɪ̣ti/ *n* [U] *formal* nearness in distance or time【正式】【距离或时间的】接近, 临近; 邻近: [**+to**] *Proximity to a good school is important.* 靠近一所好的学校很重要。| **in close proximity** (=very near) 非常靠近, 紧挨

prox·y /ˋprɑksɪ; ˈprɒksi/ *n* [C] **1** someone that you choose to represent you, especially to vote for you〔由个人委托的〕代理人; 代表〔尤指代人投票〕**2 by proxy** if you do something by proxy, you arrange for someone else to do it for you 由委托人代理

proxy vote /ˈ·· ˌ·/ *n* [C] a vote you make by officially sending someone else to vote for you 委托他人代投的选票

Prozac /ˋprozæk; ˈprəʊzæk/ *trademark* a type of drug used for treating DEPRESSION (=when you feel very unhappy) and ANXIETY (=when you feel very worried)【商标】百忧解〔一种治疗抑郁、焦虑的药物〕

prude /prud; pruːd/ *n* [C] someone who is too easily shocked by anything connected with sex〔在性方面〕过分拘谨的人

pru·dence /ˋprudəns; ˈpruːdəns/ *n* [U] a sensible and careful attitude that makes you avoid unnecessary risks 小心谨慎, 慎重, 审慎

pru·dent /ˋprudn̩t; ˈpruːdənt/ *adj* sensible and careful, especially by trying to avoid unnecessary risks 明智而谨慎的; 慎重的, 审慎的: *It might be prudent to get a virus detector for the network.* 为网络装上病毒检测软件可能是一种明智的做法。—opposite 反义词 IMPRUDENT —**prudently** *adv*

pru·den·tial /pruˋdɛnʃəl; pruːˈdenʃəl/ *adj old-fashioned* PRUDENT【过时】谨慎的, 审慎的 —**prudentially** *adv*

prud·er·y /ˋprudərɪ; ˈpruːdəri/ *n* [U] prudish behaviour〔在性方面的〕拘谨

prud·ish /ˋprudɪʃ; ˈpruːdɪʃ/ *adj* too easily shocked by things connected with sex〔在性方面〕过分拘谨的 —**prudishly** *adv* —**prudishness** *n* [U]

prune¹ /prun; pruːn/ *v* [T] **1** also 又作 **prune back** to cut some of the branches of a tree or bush to make it grow better 修剪〔树枝〕: *I need to prune the roses this weekend.* 本周末我需要修剪这些玫瑰。**2** also 又作 **prune down** to get rid of the unnecessary parts of something 删除, 删节: *The essay's too long, you need to prune it down.* 这篇文章太长了, 你需要把它删节一下。

prune² *n* [C] a dried PLUM, usually cooked before eating 西梅干, (洋) 李脯

pruning hook /ˈ·· ˌ·/ *n* [C] a knife that is shaped like a hook and is usually on a long pole, used for cutting branches off trees〔用于剪树枝的〕修枝钩刀

pru·ri·ent /ˋprurɪənt; ˈprʊəriənt/ *adj formal* too strongly interested in sex【正式】好色的, 荒淫的 —**pruriently** *adv* —**prurience** *n* [U]

Prus·sia /ˋprʌʃə; ˈprʌʃə/ a former German state in northern Europe, which was a powerful military state between the 17th and 19th centuries. After World War II, its land was divided between Germany, the Soviet Union, and Poland. 普鲁士〔旧时北欧一日耳曼国家, 17至19世纪一军事强国。二战之后, 其领土被德国、苏联和波兰瓜分〕

Prus·sian blue /ˌprʌʃən ˋblu; ˌprʌʃən ˈbluː/ *n* [U] a deep blue colour 普鲁士蓝; 深蓝色 —**Prussian blue** *adj*

prus·sic ac·id /ˌprʌsɪk ˋæsɪd; ˌprʌsɪk ˈæsɪ̣d/ *n* [U] a very poisonous acid 氢氰酸〔一种剧毒性酸〕

pry /praɪ; praɪ/ *v present participle* **prying** *past tense* **pried** **1** [I] to try to find out details about someone else's private life in an impolite way 打听, 探听〔别人的私生活〕: *I don't wish to pry, but is it true that you're having problems at home?* 我并不想多管闲事, 但是你家出了问题是真的吗? **2** [T always+adv/prep] *especially AmE* to force something open, or force it away from something else; PRIZE³ (2)【尤美】撬开, 撬起: **pry sth open/away**

etc *We finally managed to pry open the door with a screwdriver.* 我们最后设法用螺丝刀撬开了门。**3 away from prying eyes** in private, where people cannot see 避开窥视的目光, 私下地: *I'd like to show you something, away from prying eyes.* 我想私下给你看样东西。

PS /ˌpi ˋɛs; ˌpiː ˈes/ *n* [C] postscript; a note added at the end of a letter, giving more information〔信末的〕附言, 又及: *She added a PS asking me to send her some money.* 她在信末附言要我寄些钱去。| *Best wishes, Julie. PS If Thursday is not convenient, let me know.* 祝好, 朱莉。又及, 若星期四不便, 请告知。

psalm /sɑm; sɑːm/ *n* [C] a song or poem praising God 赞美诗; 圣歌

psalm·ist /ˋsɑmɪst; ˈsɑːmɨst/ *n* [C] someone who has written a psalm 赞美诗作者, 圣歌作者

psal·ter /ˋsɔltɚ; ˈsɔːltə/ *n* [C] a book containing the psalms from the Bible, often with music, for use in a church〔《圣经》中的〕《诗篇》集〔礼拜时用的赞美诗集, 常配有音乐〕

psal·ter·y /ˋsɔltərɪ; ˈsɔːltəri/ *n* [C] an ancient musical instrument with strings stretched over a board 萨泰利琴〔古代的一种弦乐器〕

pse·phol·o·gy /siˋfɑlədʒɪ; seˈfɒlədʒi/ *n* [U] the study of how people vote in elections 选举学 —**psephologist** *n* [C]

pseud /sud; sjuːd/ *n* [C] *BrE informal* someone who pretends to know a lot about art, literature etc【英, 非正式】〔在艺术、文学等方面的〕假专家, 假内行, 假充有知识的人 —**pseudy** *adj*

pseudo- /sudo; sjuːdəʊ/ *prefix* not real; false 假, 伪: *pseudo-intellectuals* (=who pretend to be clever) 假知识分子 | *He says astrology's just a pseudoscience.* 他说占星术只是一种伪科学而已。

pseu·do·nym /ˋsudn̩ˌɪm; ˈsjuːdənɪm/ *n* [C] an invented name used by someone, especially a writer, instead of their real name〔尤指作家的〕笔名, 假名: *Charlotte Bronte wrote under the pseudonym of Currer Bell.* 夏洛蒂·勃朗特用柯勒·贝尔的笔名写作。—**pseudonymy** /suˋdɑnəmɪ; sjuːˈdɒnəmi/ *n* [U]

pseu·don·y·mous /suˋdɑnəməs; sjuːˈdɒnɨməs/ *adj* written or writing under a pseudonym 用笔名写的, 署假名的: *the pseudonymous writer of the 'Insider' column* "局内人"专栏使用笔名的作者 —**pseudonymously** *adv*

pshaw /ʃɔ; pʃɔː/ *interjection old-fashioned* used to express annoyance, disapproval, or disagreement【过时】哼! 哼!〔表示厌恶、反对〕

pso·ri·a·sis /səˋraɪəsɪs; səˈraɪəsɨs/ *n* [U] an illness which makes your skin dry, red, and FLAKY (=coming off in small bits) 牛皮癣

psst /ps; ps/ *interjection* used to attract someone's attention without other people noticing 嘘〔一种暗中引起某人注意的声音〕: *Psst! There's someone coming!* 嘘! 有人来了!

PST /ˌpi ɛs ˋti; ˌpiː es ˈtiː/ the abbreviation of 缩写= PACIFIC STANDARD TIME

psych /saɪk; saɪk/ *v*

psych sb/sth ↔ **out** *phr v* [T] *informal* to do or say things that will make your opponent in a game or competition feel nervous or confused, so that it is easier for you to win【非正式】〔在比赛、竞赛中〕吓住, 镇住〔对手〕; 使〔对手〕心烦意乱: *Leonard stared hard at Duran before the fight, trying to psych him out.* 伦纳德在开打前使劲瞪着杜兰, 试图镇住他。

psych sb **up** *phr v* [T] *informal*【非正式】**1 psych yourself up** to prepare yourself mentally before doing something so that you feel confident 使自己心理上作好准备: [+for] *So George, tell us how the players psych themselves up for the big game.* 那么乔治, 告诉我们选手是如何为这场大战作好心理准备的。**2 be psyched up** also 又作 **be psyched** *especially AmE* to be mentally prepared for an event and excited about it【尤美】〔为…〕作好心理准备; 斗志昂扬

psych- /saɪk; saɪk/ *prefix* another form of the prefix PSYCHO- 前缀psycho-的另一种形式

psy·che /ˋsaɪkɪ; ˈsaɪki/ *n* [C usually singular 一般用单数] *technical or formal* someone's mind, or their basic nature, which controls their attitudes and behaviour【术语或正式】心灵; 灵魂, 精神: *The image of the independent pioneer lies at the heart of the American psyche.* 独立的拓荒者形象深深植根于美国精神之中。

psy·che·del·ic /ˌsaɪkɪˋdɛlɪk; ˌsaɪkɨˈdelɪk◂/ *adj* **1** psychedelic drugs such as LSD make you HALLUCINATE (=see things that do not really exist)〔药物、毒品〕引起幻觉的, 致幻的 **2** psychedelic art, clothing etc has complicated patterns of strong bright colours, shapes etc〔艺术、服装等〕产生迷幻效果的 —**psychedelically** *adv*

psy·chi·at·ric /ˌsaɪkɪˋætrɪk; ˌsaɪkiˈætrɪk◂/ *adj* connected with the study and treatment of mental illness 精神病学的, 精神病治疗的: *He'll have to undergo psychiatric treatment at the hospital.* 他必须在医院接受精神病治疗。| *psychiatric unit* 精神病科 —**psychiatrically** /-klɪ; -kli/ *adv*

psychiatric hospital /ˌ··ˋ·· ˌ··; ˌ··ˈ·· ˌ··/ *n* [C] a hospital where people with mental illnesses are treated 精神病医院

psy·chi·a·trist /saɪˋkaɪətrɪst; saɪˈkaɪətrɨst/ *n* [C] a doctor trained in the treatment of mental illness 精神科医生 —compare 比较 PSYCHOLOGIST

psy·chi·a·try /saɪˋkaɪətrɪ; saɪˈkaɪətri/ *n* [U] the study and treatment of mental illnesses 精神病学, 精神病治疗学

psy·chic¹ /ˋsaɪkɪk; ˈsaɪkɪk/ *adj* [no comparative 无比较级] **1** also 又作 **psychical** /ˋsaɪkɪkl̩; ˈsaɪkɪkəl/ connected with mysterious events involving the power of the human mind 通灵的, 对超自然力敏感的: *psychic phenomena* 通灵现象 | *psychic research* 通灵研究 **2** having the ability to know what other people are thinking or what will happen in the future 能洞察人心的; 能知未来的: *How did you know I was here? You must be psychic!* 你怎么会知道我在这儿? 你一定能未卜先知! —compare 比较 CLAIRVOYANT **3** also 又作 **psychical** affecting the mind rather than the body 精神(上)的: *psychic disorders* 精神错乱 —**psychically** /-klɪ; -kli/ *adv*

psychic² *n* [C] someone who has mysterious powers, especially the ability to receive messages from dead people 对超自然力敏感的人, 有神秘能力的人;〔尤指〕通灵的人

Psy·cho /ˋsaɪko; ˈsaɪkəʊ/ (1960) a US HORROR FILM (= a film that is intended to make you feel frightened) made by Alfred Hitchcock. Its most famous scene is the one in which the character acted by Janet Leigh is killed with a knife by Norman Bates, played by Anthony Perkins, while she is in the SHOWER. 《精神病患者》〔(1960), 美国恐怖片, 由阿尔弗雷德·希区柯克执导。影片的女角色(珍妮特·李饰)在淋浴时被诺曼·贝茨用匕首所杀一幕最为著名〕

psycho *n* [C] *informal* someone who is likely to suddenly behave in a violent or crazy way【非正式】精神失常的人, 精神病患者

psycho- /saɪko; saɪkəʊ/ *prefix* also 又作 **psych-** *technical* concerning the mind, as opposed to the body【术语】心理: *psychotherapy* (=treatment of the mind) 心理疗法

psy·cho·a·nal·y·sis /ˌsaɪkoəˋnæləsɪs; ˌsaɪkəʊəˈnælɨsɨs/ *n* [U] a way of treating someone who is mentally ill by talking to them about their past life, feelings etc, in order to find out the hidden causes of their problems 精神分析(治疗法); 心理分析(治疗法) —**psychoanalytic** /ˌsaɪkoˌænl̩ˋɪtɪk; ˌsaɪkəʊænəˈlɪtɪk◂/ —**psychoanalytical** /-tɪkl̩; -tɪkəl/ *adj*: *psychoanalytic dream interpretation* 用精神分析法释梦 —**psychoanalytically** /-klɪ; -kli/ *adv*

> **CULTURAL NOTE 文化注释**
> Psychoanalysis is fairly common in the US, but British people often have a negative view of it and are not certain that it is effective. 精神分析治疗法在美国相当普遍, 但是英国人常对此持有消极观点, 他们怀疑其治疗效果。

psy·cho·an·a·lyst /ˌsaɪkoˋænlɪst; ˌsaɪkəʊˈænəl-ɨst/ *n* [C] someone who is trained in psychoanalysis 精神分析专家

psy·cho·an·a·lyze *BrE*【英】also 又作 **-ise** /ˌsaɪkoˋænlˌaɪz; ˌsaɪkəʊˈænəlaɪz/ *v* [T] to treat someone by psychoanalysis 用精神分析法治疗

psy·cho·bab·ble /ˋsaɪkoˌbæbl̩; ˈsaɪkəʊˌbæbəl/ *n* [U] *informal* the language that sounds scientific but is often annoying, that some people use when talking about their emotional problems【非正式】心理呓语〔某些人用来谈论感情问题时使用的听起来具有科学性但常令人讨厌的语言〕

psy·cho·bi·ol·o·gy /ˌsaɪkobaɪˋɑlədʒɪ; ˌsaɪkəʊbaɪˈɒlədʒi/ *n* [U] the study of the body in relation to the mind 生物心理学, 精神生物学

psy·cho·drama /ˋsaɪkoˌdrɑmə; ˈsaɪkəʊˌdrɑːmə/ *n* [C] a way of treating mental illness in which people are asked to act in a situation together to help them understand their emotions 心理戏剧疗法, 精神表演疗法〔一种治疗精神疾病的方法, 人们被要求在某场景中一起表演从而帮助他们了解自己的情感〕

psy·cho·ki·ne·sis /ˌsaɪkokɪˋnisɪs; ˌsaɪkəʊkaɪˈniːsɨs/ *n* [U] the moving of solid objects using only the power of the mind, which some people believe is possible 心灵致动, 意念移物 —**psychokinetic** /-kɪˋnɛtɪk; -kaɪˈnetɪk◂/ *adj* —**psychokinetically** /-klɪ; -kli/ *adv*

psy·cho·log·i·cal /ˌsaɪkəˋlɑdʒɪkl̩; ˌsaɪkəˈlɒdʒɪkəl◂/ *adj* **1** connected with the way that people's minds work and the way that this affects their behaviour 心理(上)的 **2** illness, fears etc

that are psychological are in someone's mind and are not real〔疾病、恐惧等只存在于〕心理上的: *Max says he's got some sort of virus, but I'm sure it's psychological.* 马克斯说他感染了某种病毒, 但我相信那是心理作用。**3 psychological warfare** [U] behaviour intended to make your opponents less confident 心理战 **4 the psychological moment** *informal* the exact time in a situation when you have the best chance to achieve what you want【非正式】〔做某事的〕最恰当的时机 —**psychologically** /-kḷɪ; -kli/ *adv*: *psychologically disturbed* 精神上受到困扰的 | *Psychologically* (=from a psychological point of view) *it's a good idea to praise a child for their efforts.* 从心理的角度讲, 赞扬一个孩子所作的努力是个好主意。

psy·chol·o·gist /saɪˋkɑlədʒɪst; saɪˈkɒlədʒ̩ɪst/ *n* [C] someone who is trained in psychology 心理学家: *child psychologists* 儿童心理学家 —compare 比较 PSYCHIATRIST

3 **psy·chol·o·gy** /saɪˋkɑlədʒɪ; saɪˈkɒlədʒi/ *n* **1** [U] the study of the mind and how it works 心理学: *educational psychology* 教育心理学 **2** [C,U] the usual way in which a particular person or group thinks and reacts〔某个人或某群体的〕心理: *the psychology of the mob* 暴民的心理 **3** [U] *informal* knowledge of the way that people think, that makes you able to control what they do【非正式】心机, 心计: *Use a bit of psychology. Tell them you think they'd do it better!* 用点心思, 告诉他们你认为他们会做得更好!

psy·cho·met·ric /ˌsaɪkoˋmɛtrɪk; ˌsaɪkəʊˈmetrɪk◂/ *adj* for measuring mental abilities and qualities 心理测量的: *psychometric tests* 心理测量测试

psy·cho·path /ˋsaɪkəˌpæθ; ˈsaɪkəpæθ/ *n* [C] someone who has a serious and permanent mental illness that makes them behave in a violent or criminal way 精神严重失常的人; 精神变态者 —compare 比较 SOCIOPATH —**psychopathic** /ˌsaɪkəˋpæθɪk; ˌsaɪkəˈpæθɪk◂/ *adj*: *a psychopathic personality* 精神变态人格 —**psychopathically** /-kḷɪ; -kli/ *adv*

psy·cho·sis /saɪˋkosɪs; saɪˈkəʊs̩ɪs/ *n plural* **psychoses** /-siz; -siːz/ [C,U] a serious mental illness that can change your character and make you unable to behave in a normal way 精神病, 精神失常 —see also 另见 PSYCHOTIC

psy·cho·so·mat·ic /ˌsaɪkəsəˋmætɪk; ˌsaɪkəʊsəˈmætɪk◂/ *adj* **1** a psychosomatic illness is caused by fear or anxiety rather than by any physical problem〔疾病〕心因性的, 由惧怕[焦虑]引起的 **2** concerned with the relationship between the mind and physical illness 身心的 —**psychosomatically** /-kḷɪ; -kli/ *adv*

psy·cho·ther·a·py /ˌsaɪkoˋθɛrəpɪ; ˌsaɪkəʊˈθerəpi/ *n* [U] the treatment of mental illness, for example DEPRESSION, by talking to someone and discussing their problems rather than using drugs or medicine 心理疗法, 精神疗法 —**psychotherapist** *n* [C]

psy·chot·ic /saɪˋkɑtɪk; saɪˈkɒtɪk/ *adj* suffering from psychosis 精神病的, 精神失常的: *psychotic behaviour* 精神病患者行为 —**psychotic** *n* [C] —**psychotically** /-kḷɪ; -kli/ *adv*

pt **1** the written abbreviation of 缩写= PART: *Pt. II, Chapter 7, p. 157* 第二部分第七章第157页 **2** the written abbreviation of 缩写= PAYMENT **3** the written abbreviation of 缩写= PINT: *Add 1 pt stock.* 加一品脱的原汤。**4** the written abbreviation of 缩写= POINT **5** often 常作 **Pt** the written abbreviation of 缩写= PORT (1): *Pt Moresby* 莫尔斯比港

PT /ˌpi ˋti; ˌpiː ˈtiː/ *n* [U] *especially BrE* physical training; organized games, physical exercises etc at school【尤英】体育锻炼: *a PT instructor* 体育教师 | *PT lessons at school* 学校的体育课 —compare 比较 GYM (2)

PTA /ˌpi ti ˋe; ˌpiː tiː ˈeɪ/ *n* [C] Parent-Teacher Association; an organization of parents and teachers that tries to help and improve a particular school〔帮助改进学校工作的〕家长教师协会: *an active member of the PTA* 一名家长教师协会的活跃分子 —compare 比较 PTO²

PT boat /ˌpi ˋti bot; ˌpiː ˈtiː bəʊt/ a small, fast boat used by the US military forces, especially during World War II. It was used especially for firing TORPEDO*es* (=explosive weapons that travel under the sea) at enemy ships. Many Americans remember that President John F. Kennedy fought during World War II in a PT boat, called PT 109, and that when it was sunk, Kennedy led the men to safety. 鱼雷快艇〔尤指二战期间美军使用的一种体积小、速度快的舰艇, 主要用于向敌舰发射鱼雷。许多美国人还记得约翰·F.肯尼迪总统二战时指挥鱼雷快艇109号作战的情景。快艇沉没之时, 肯尼迪率众到了安全地带〕

Pte *BrE*【英】the written abbreviation of 缩写= PRIVATE² (2): *Pte Larry Grossman* 二等兵拉里·格罗斯曼

pter·o·dac·tyl /ˌtɛrəˋdæktḷ; ˌterəˈdæktɪl/ *n* [C] a type of large flying animal that lived many millions of years ago 翼指龙〔一种远古动物〕

PTO¹ /ˌpi ti ˋo; ˌpiː tiː ˈəʊ/ *BrE* please turn over; written at the bottom of a page to tell the reader to look at the next page【英】见下页, 请翻至下页〔注于页末的字样〕

PTO² *n* [C] *especially AmE* Parent-Teacher Organization; an organization of parents and teachers that tries to help and improve a particular school【尤美】〔帮助改进学校工作的〕家长教师组织

Ptol·e·ma·ic sys·tem /ˌtɑləˋme·ɪk ˌsɪstəm; ˌtɒl̩ɪˈmeɪ-ɪk ˌsɪst̩ɪm/ *n* [singular] the old system of belief that the Earth was at the centre of the universe, with the sun, stars and PLANETS moving around it 托勒密体系〔旧时认为地球是宇宙的中心, 太阳、星辰绕地球旋转的一种学说〕

Ptol·e·my¹ /ˋtɑləmɪ; ˈtɒləmi/ (?AD100-AD170) a Greek ASTRONOMER and MATHEMATICIAN who lived and worked in Egypt. He studied the stars, and believed that the Earth was at the centre of the universe, and that the stars, the sun, and the PLANETS all travelled in circles around the Earth. This idea is known as the **Ptolemaic System**, and most people believed it to be true until Nicholas Copernicus proved that it was wrong at the beginning of the 16th century. 托勒密〔(公元?100-170), 希腊天文学家、数学家, 曾在埃及生活和工作。他研究过星象之后认为地球处于宇宙的中心, 恒星、太阳及行星均围绕地球运行。这一观点被称为托勒密体系, 多数人一直信以为真, 直到尼古拉斯·哥白尼16世纪初证明它是错误的〕

Ptolemy² the name used by the family of kings who ruled Egypt from the 4th century BC to the 1st century BC 托勒密〔公元前4世纪至公元前1世纪期间统治埃及的王族〕

pto·maine /ˋtomen; ˈtəʊmeɪn/ *n* [C,U] a poisonous substance formed by BACTERIA in decaying food〔由腐烂食物中的细菌产生的〕尸碱, 尸毒

pty the written abbreviation of 缩写= PROPRIETARY, used in Australia, New Zealand, and South Africa after the name of a business company 专营…的公司〔用于澳大利亚、新西兰和南非公司的名字后面〕: *Australian Wine Growers Pty* 澳大利亚酒业专营公司

pub /pʌb; pʌb/ *n* [C] a building in Britain where alcohol can be bought and drunk〔英国的〕酒馆, 酒吧: *Do you fancy going to the pub?* 你想去酒吧吗? | *a pub lunch* 小酒馆供应的午餐 —compare 比较 BAR¹ (1) S3 W3

pub-crawl /ˋ· ,·/ *n* [C] *informal, especially BrE* a visit to several pubs, one after the other, during which you have a drink in each pub【非正式, 尤英】串游小酒馆〔从这家酒馆喝到另一家酒馆〕: *a Saturday night pub-crawl* 星期六晚上接连到好几家酒馆喝酒

pu·ber·ty /ˋpjubəːtɪ; ˈpjuːbəti/ *n* [U] the stage of physical development during which you change from a child to an adult able to have children 青春期

pu·bes·cent /pjuˋbɛsənt; pjuːˈbesənt/ *adj* a pubescent boy or girl is going through puberty〔男孩或女孩〕处于青春期的

pu·bic /ˋpjubɪk; ˈpjuːbɪk/ *adj* [only before noun 仅用于名词前] related to or near to the sexual organs〔靠近〕阴部的: *pubic hair* 阴毛

pub·lic¹ /ˋpʌblɪk; ˈpʌblɪk/ *adj* S1 W1

1 ▶ORDINARY PEOPLE 普通人◀ [no comparative 无比较级] connected with all the ordinary people in a country, who are not members of the government or do not have important jobs 公众的, 大众的: *The law was changed as a result of public pressure.* 这项法律由于公众的压力而作了修改。| **in the public interest** (=helpful or useful to ordinary people) 对公众有益的 *Publishing this story was definitely in the public interest.* 发表这个故事肯定会对公众有益。| **public outcry** (=strong objections from many people) 公众的强烈抗议 *New taxes provoked a public outcry.* 新的税收激起了公众的强烈抗议。

2 ▶FOR ANYONE 为每个人◀ [no comparative 无比较级] available for anyone to use 公共的, 公用的: *a public telephone* 公用电话 | *a public beach* 公共沙滩 | *proposals to ban smoking in public places* 在公共场所禁止吸烟的建议

3 ▶GOVERNMENT 政府◀ [no comparative 无比较级] connected with the government and with the services it provides for people 公务的, 公众事务的: **public money** *Simply pumping public money into the railways is not the answer.* 仅仅把公共资金投入铁路不是解决方法。| **public office** (=the job of being part of a government) 公职 *We do not believe he is fit for public office.* 我们认为他不适合担任公职。—see also 另见 PUBLIC SERVICE

4 ▶KNOWN ABOUT 大家知道的◀ [no comparative 无比较级] known about by most people 公开的: **make sth public** (=tell everyone) 使某事公开 *The name of the victim has not been made public.* 受害人的姓名还未公开。| **be public knowledge** (=not

secret) 众所周知 *It's public knowledge that Ann has an alcohol problem.* 众所周知,安有酗酒的毛病。| **in the public eye/view** (=on television, radio etc a lot because you are famous)〔电视、广播等上〕公众熟悉的,公众常见的 | **public figure** (=famous person) 公众人物,名人

5 ►NOT HIDDEN 非隐秘的◄ intended for anyone to know, see or hear 公开的: *Demands for a public investigation have been ignored.* 进行公开调查的要求没有被理会。| **public display of grief/affection etc** (=showing your emotions so that everyone can see) 公开表现悲伤/爱慕等

6 ►PLACE WITH A LOT OF PEOPLE 有很多人的地方◄ a public place usually has a lot of people in it〔地方〕公开的,公共的: *Don't talk about it here; this place is too public.* 别在这里谈这件事,这地方人太多。

7 public life work that you do, especially for the government, that makes you well-known to many people 公共事务: *Judge Carson retired from public life in 1944.* 卡森法官于1944年退出公共事务。

8 public image the character or attitudes that a famous person, organization etc is thought by most people to have 公众形象: *Marilyn tried hard to protect her public image.* 玛丽莲极力保护她的公众形象。| *Violence doesn't help the game's public image.* 暴力对这项运动在公众心目中的形象不利。

9 go public a) to tell everyone about something that was secret 公开,公布于众: *We have all the evidence, so now we can go public!* 我们有所有的证据,所以现在我们可以公之于众了! **b)** to become a PUBLIC COMPANY〔公司〕公开发售股票,上市

10 public appearance a visit by a famous person in order to make a speech, advertise something etc〔名人的〕公开露面

11 public property a) something that is provided for anyone to use, and is usually owned by the government 公共财物: *Two demonstrators were charged with damaging public property.* 两名示威者被控破坏公共财产。**b)** *informal* something that everyone has a right to know about【非正式】人人有权知道的事物: *When you're a TV star you're public property it seems!* 一旦你成为电视明星,人人都好像有权知道你的一切!

12 public enemy number one the criminal, problem etc that is considered the most serious threat to people's safety 头号公敌〔指被认为是对人民安全构成最严重威胁的罪犯、问题等〕: *Drugs have become public enemy number one.* 毒品已成为头号人民公敌。—compare 比较 PRIVATE[1] —**publicly** *adv*: *publicly humiliated* 当众受辱

S2 W2 **public²** *n* **1 the public** ordinary people who do not belong to the government or have any special position in society 公众,民众,大众: *The castle is open to the public daily.* 这座城堡每天都向公众开放。| [also+plural verb in *BrE* 英] *The public are not interested in this issue.* 公众对这个问题不感兴趣。| **the general public** *Our special offer is not available to the general public.* 一般公众不能享受我们的特价。**2 in public** if you do something in public you do it where anyone can see 公开地,当众: *Her husband was always nice to her in public.* 她丈夫在公开场合总是对她很好。—opposite 反义词 **in private** (PRIVATE² (1)), —see also 另见 **wash your dirty linen in public** (WASH¹ (6)) **3** [singular, U] the people who like listening to a particular singer, reading a particular writer etc〔喜欢听某歌手的歌、读某作家作品等的〕大众: *A star has to try to please her public.* 一个明星必须尽力取悦她的支持者。| [also+plural verb in *BrE* 英] *Today's theatre-going public are very demanding.* 当今喜欢看戏的人们要求很苛刻。

public ac·cess /ˌ·· ˈ··/ *n* [U] the right of ordinary people to go onto particular areas of land or read particular documents 公众进入某区域[读某些文献]的权利: [+to] *public access to information* 公众获取信息的权利

public access chan·nel /ˌ·· ˈ·· ˌ··/ *n* [C] a television CHANNEL provided by CABLE¹ (3) television companies in the US on which anyone can broadcast 公共频道〔美国有限电视公司提供的每个人都能使用的电视频道〕

public-ad·dress sys·tem /ˌ·· ˈ· ˌ··/ *n* [C] a PA (1) 有线广播系统;扩音系统

public af·fairs /ˌ·· ˈ·/ *n* [plural] events and questions, especially political ones, which have an effect on most people 公众事务〔尤指影响大多数人的政治事件和问题〕: *a public affairs programme on TV* 电视上的公众事务节目

pub·li·can /ˈpʌblɪkən; ˈpʌblɪkən/ *n* [C] *formal, especially BrE* someone who is in charge of a PUB【正式,尤英】小酒馆老板

W2 **pub·li·ca·tion** /ˌpʌblɪˈkeʃən; ˌpʌblɪˈkeɪʃən/ *n* **1** [U] the action of making a book available for sale, or the time at which you do this 出版;出版日期[时间]: *The book is ready for publication.* 这本书已经准备好出版了。**2** [C] a book, magazine etc 出版物,书刊: *a monthly publication* 月刊 **3** [U] the act of making something known to the public 发表,公布: *the publication of the election results* 选举结果的公布

public bar /ˌ·· ˈ·/ *n* [C] *BrE* a room with plain furniture in a PUB, hotel etc where you can buy drinks【英】〔有简单家具,可从中买饮料的〕公众酒吧

public com·pa·ny /ˌ·· ˈ···/ *n* [C] *BrE* a company that offers its SHARES for sale on the STOCK EXCHANGE【英】公开出售股份的公司,股票上市公司; PUBLIC CORPORATION *AmE*【美】

public con·ve·ni·ence /ˌ·· ·ˈ···/ *n* [C] *BrE* a small building with toilets in it, provided for anyone to use【英】公厕

public cor·po·ra·tion /ˌ·· ··ˈ··/ *n* [C] **1** *AmE* a company that offers its SHARES for sale on the STOCK EXCHANGE【美】公开出售股份的公司,股票上市公司; PUBLIC COMPANY *BrE*【英】**2** *BrE* a business that is run by a government【英】由政府经营的企业

public de·fend·er /ˌ·· ·ˈ··/ *n* [C] *AmE* a lawyer who is paid by the government to defend people in court, because they cannot pay for themselves【美】公设辩护律师〔由政府出钱为付不起律师费的人们辩护的律师〕—compare 比较 DISTRICT ATTORNEY

public do·main /ˌ·· ·ˈ·/ *n law* **in the public domain** a play, idea etc that is in the public domain is available for anyone to perform or use【法律】〔戏剧、观点等〕不受版权[专利权]限制的

public ex·pen·di·ture /ˌ·· ·ˈ···/ *n* [U] the money that the government spends on public services 公共开支〔政府花在公共事业上的钱〕

public foot·path /ˌ·· ˈ··/ *n* [C] *BrE* a path that everyone has the right to use【英】公用人行小径

public fund·ing /ˌ·· ˈ··/ also 又作 **public funds** /ˌ·· ˈ·/ *n* [U] money that the government gives to support organizations or events〔政府用来支持公共组织或活动的〕公共资金

public health /ˌ·· ˈ·/ *n* [U] **1** health care provided by the government, including medical care and public cleaning services〔由政府提供的〕公共卫生保健〔包括医疗保健和公共卫生服务〕**2** the health of all the people in an area 公众健康: *a danger to public health* 对公众健康的一个威胁

public hol·i·day /ˌ·· ˈ···/ *n* [C] a special day when people do not go to work and shops do not open 公共假日;公休日

public house /ˌ·· ˈ·/ *n* [C] *BrE formal* a PUB【英,正式】小酒馆,酒吧

public hous·ing /ˌ·· ˈ··/ *n* [U] *AmE* houses or apartments built by the US government for poor people【美】公共住房〔政府为贫民建的房子〕—compare 比较 COUNCIL HOUSE

public in·quiry /ˌ·· ·ˈ··/ *n* [C] an official attempt to find out the cause of something, especially an accident 公开调查

pub·li·cist /ˈpʌblɪsɪst; ˈpʌbləsəst/ *n* [C] someone whose job is to make sure that people find out about a new product, film, book etc or about what a famous person is doing 广告员,宣传员

pub·lic·i·ty /pʌbˈlɪsətɪ; pʌˈblɪsəti/ *n* [U] **1** the attention that someone or something gets from newspapers, television etc〔报纸、电视等对某人或某物的〕关注: *The case has received massive publicity.* 这个案子受到媒体的极大关注。| **bad/adverse publicity** (=publicity that makes you look bad) 不利的宣传 | **publicity stunt** (=something that is only done to get publicity) 吸引公众注意的花招[噱头] **2** the business of making sure that people know about a new product, film etc or what a particular famous person is doing 宣传,推广: *Who's going to do the show's publicity?* 谁来做这个节目的宣传工作? | **publicity campaign** (=a series of activities intended to give something publicity) 宣传运动 S2 W3

pub·li·cize also 又作 **-ise** *BrE*【英】/ˈpʌblɪˌsaɪz; ˈpʌbləsaɪz/ *v* [T] to give information about something to the public, so that they know about it 公布;宣传,宣扬: *Schools need to publicize their exam results.* 学校需要公布考试结果。| **well-/widely/highly publicized** (=receiving a lot of attention) 广受关注 *the well-publicized financial difficulties that Rochford has faced* 罗奇福德所面临的被传得沸沸扬扬的财政困难

public lend·ing right /ˌ·· ˈ·· ˌ·/ *n* [C] a system in Britain by which writers are paid if their books are borrowed from public libraries〔英国的作者对公共图书馆出借其著作所享有的〕公共出借报酬权

public li·bra·ry /ˌ·· ˈ···/ *n* [C] a building where people can go to read or borrow books without having to pay 公共图书馆

public lim·it·ed com·pa·ny /ˌ·· ˌ··· ˈ···/ also 又作 **plc** *n* [C] a British company owned by at least two people and whose shares (SHARE² (5)) are available to everyone〔英国的〕公共有限公司〔至少为两人所有、任何人可购其股份的公司〕

public nui·sance /ˌ‥ˈ‥/ *n* [C] **1** *law* an action that is harmful to everyone【法律】妨害公众利益的行为: *He committed a public nuisance by blocking the road.* 他堵塞道路，妨害了公众。**2** a person who does things that annoy a lot of people 妨害公众者，做事令大家讨厌的人

public o·pin·ion /ˌ‥ ‥ˈ‥/ *n* [U] the opinions or beliefs that ordinary people have about a particular subject（公共）舆论，民意: *The government is bowing to public opinion on this issue.* 在这个问题上，政府正向民意屈从。

public own·er·ship /ˌ‥ˈ‥‥/ *n* [U] businesses, property etc in public ownership are owned by the state〔企业、财产等〕国家所有（制），公有（制）: *The steel and coal industries were taken into public ownership.* 钢铁和煤炭工业被收归国有。

public pros·e·cu·tor /ˌ‥ˈ‥‥/ *n* [C] a British lawyer who works for the government, and tries to prove in a court of law that someone has done something illegal 检察官，检控官，公诉人 —compare 比较 DISTRICT ATTORNEY

Public Rec·ord Of·fice, the /ˌ‥ˈ‥ˌ‥/ abbreviation 缩写为 **the PRO** a building in West London that holds all British government records and documents, from the 11th century onwards. Most of the records, including secret government papers, can be examined by the general public after 30 years. 公共档案馆〔英国伦敦西部一幢建筑，保管有11世纪以来英国历届政府的全部档案和文献。大部分档案，包括政府机密文件在内，只要超过30年，公众均可查阅〕

public re·la·tions /ˌ‥ ‥ˈ‥/ *n* **1** [U] PR; the work of explaining to the public what an organization does, so that they will understand it and approve of it 公共关系；公关（工作）: *a public relations officer in a big oil company* 一家大石油公司的公关人员 **2** [plural] the relationship between an organization and the public〔组织机构〕与公众的关系: *Helping the theatre would be good for public relations.* 帮助剧院会有利于公共关系。

public relations ex·er·cise /ˌ‥ ‥ˈ‥ˌ‥/ *n* [C] something that an organization does just to make itself popular, rather than because it is the right thing to do 公关活动，宣传推广活动: *The conference was largely a public relations exercise.* 这次大会很大程度上是一种公关活动。

public school /ˌ‥ˈ/ *n* [C] **1** a private British school, paid for by parents, where children usually live as well as study〔英国私立的〕公学，私立寄宿学校 **2** a free local school, especially in the US and Scotland, controlled and paid for by the government〔尤指美国和苏格兰免费的〕公立学校 —compare 比较 PRIVATE SCHOOL

public sec·tor /ˌ‥ˈ‥/ *n* [singular] the industries and services in a country that are owned and run by the government 公营部门，国营部门: *a job in the public sector* 公营部门的工作 | *public sector employees* 国营部门雇员 —compare 比较 PRIVATE SECTOR

public serv·ant /ˌ‥ˈ‥/ *n* [C] someone who works for the government, especially someone who is elected 公务员

public serv·ice /ˌ‥ˈ‥/ *n* **1** [C usually plural 一般用复数] a service or product that a government provides, such as electricity, TRANSPORT, etc 公用事业〈如供电、交通等〉: *What the people want is decent, local public services.* 人们需要的是良好的本地公共服务。**2** [C] a service provided to people because it will help them, and not for profit 公益服务: *This directory is provided as a public service to the community.* 这本名录簿是作为公益服务提供给公众的。**3** [singular,U] the government or its departments 政府；政府部门: *a career in public service* 政府部门的职业

Public Service Agreement a promise by a department of the British government that it will make particular improvements or reach particular standards, for example in health services or education《公共服务协议》〔英国政府部门作出的承诺，声称他们将在卫生服务或教育等领域改善具体工作或达到特定标准〕

public service an·nounce·ment /ˌ‥ˈ‥ˌ‥/ *n* [C] *especially AmE* a special message on television or radio, giving information about an important subject【尤美】〔电视或收音机里的〕重大事情通告

public speak·ing /ˌ‥ˈ‥/ *n* [U] the activity of making speeches in public 公开演说: *a clear voice, used to public speaking* 惯于公开演说的清晰嗓音

public spend·ing /ˌ‥ˈ‥/ *n* [U] the money that the government spends on public services〔政府花在公用事业上的〕公共开支: *We must cut public spending or impose higher taxes.* 我们必须削减公共开支或征收更高的税。

public-spir·it·ed /ˌ‥ˈ‥‥◂/ *adj* willing to do what is helpful for everyone in society 热心公益的: *decent, public-spirited people* 正派而热心公益的人们

public tel·e·vi·sion /ˌ‥ˈ‥‥/ *n* [U] a television service in the US which is paid for by the government, by large companies, and by the public〔美国由政府、大型公司和公众出资的〕公共电视

public trans·port /ˌ‥ˈ‥/ *BrE*【英】, **public trans·por·ta·tion** /ˌ‥ ‥ˈ‥/ *AmE*【美】*n* [U] bus services, train services etc, provided for everyone to use 公共交通

public works /ˌ‥ˈ/ *n* [plural] buildings, roads, PORTS etc provided and built by the government 公共工程，公共建设〈如公共建筑物、公路、港口等〉

pub·lish /ˈpʌblɪʃ; ˈpʌblɪʃ/ *v* **1** [I,T] to arrange the writing, production and sale of a book, magazine etc 出版，发行〔书刊等〕: *Her second novel was published in July.* 她的第二部小说于7月份出版了。| *We publish education books.* 我们出版教育书籍。**2** [T] if a book, magazine etc publishes a letter, article etc, it prints it for people to read〔书、杂志等〕刊登，登载，发表: *We can't publish all the letters we receive.* 我们无法刊登收到的全部信件。**3** [T usually passive 一般用被动态] to make official information such as a report available for everyone to read 公布；公开；宣布: *The latest unemployment figures will be published tomorrow.* 最新的失业数字将于明天公布。**4** [I,T] if a writer or musician publishes their work, they arrange for it to be printed and sold〔作家或音乐家等〕发表〔自己的作品〕 S3 W1

pub·lish·er /ˈpʌblɪʃə; ˈpʌblɪʃə/ *n* [C] a person or company whose business is to arrange the writing, production and sale of books, newspapers etc〔书、报纸等的〕出版者，出版商，出版社 W3

pub·lish·ing /ˈpʌblɪʃɪŋ; ˈpʌblɪʃɪŋ/ *n* [U] the business of producing books and magazines 出版业: *Tony wants to get a job in publishing.* 托尼想在出版业找一份工作。| *a new publishing house* 一家新出版社 —see also 另见 **desktop publishing** (DESKTOP (2))

Puc·ci·ni /puˈtʃini; puˈtʃiːni/, **Gia·co·mo** /ˈdʒɑkəmo; ˈdʒækəməʊ/ (1858-1924) an Italian COMPOSER famous for his OPERAS, especially *La Bohème*, *Tosca*, and *Madame Butterfly* 普契尼〔(1858-1924)，意大利作曲家，尤以歌剧《绣花女》、《托斯卡》和《蝴蝶夫人》闻名〕

puce /pjus; pjuːs/ *adj* dark brownish purple 紫褐色的 —**puce** *n*

Puck /pʌk; pʌk/ a character who enjoys playing tricks on people in the play *A Midsummer Night's Dream* by William Shakespeare 帕克〔威廉·莎士比亚的戏剧《仲夏夜之梦》中的人物，以捉弄人为乐〕—see 见 PUCKISH

puck *n* [C] a hard flat circular piece of rubber that you hit with the stick in the game of ICE HOCKEY 冰球〔冰球运动中当球用的橡皮圆盘〕

puck·er /ˈpʌkə; ˈpʌkə/ also 又作 **pucker up** *v* [I,T] **1** if your mouth puckers or if you pucker it, the lips are pulled tightly together 撅起（嘴）: *Her mouth puckered up and she started to cry.* 她撅起嘴哭了起来。**2** [I] if cloth puckers, it gets lines or folds in it and is no longer flat〔布料〕起皱 —**pucker** *n* [C] —**puckered** *adj*

puck·ish /ˈpʌkɪʃ; ˈpʌkɪʃ/ *adj literary* showing that you are amused by other people, and like to make jokes about them【文】淘气的，顽皮的: *a puckish grin* 调皮的一笑 —**puckishly** *adv*

pud /pʊd; pʊd/ *n* [C,U] *BrE informal* a PUDDING【英，非正式】布丁

pud·ding /ˈpʊdɪŋ; ˈpʊdɪŋ/ *n* **1** [C,U] a hot sweet dish, made from cake, rice, bread etc with fruit, milk or other sweet things added 布丁〔由蛋糕、大米、面包等加水果、牛奶或其他甜味东西制成的热甜食〕: *another helping of rice pudding* 再来一份大米布丁 | *bread and butter pudding* 面包黄油布丁 **2** [C,U] a thick sweet creamy dish, usually made with milk, eggs, sugar, and a little flour, and served cold 布丁〔通常用牛奶、蛋、糖和少许面粉制成的黏稠冷甜食〕: *chocolate pudding* 巧克力布丁 **3** [C,U] *BrE* any sweet dish served at the end of a meal【英】〔餐末食用的〕甜食，甜点心: *There's ice-cream for pudding.* 有冰激凌作为甜点。—see also 另见 DESSERT **4** [C,U] *BrE* a boiled dish that is not sweet, made of a mixture of flour, fat etc, with meat or vegetables inside【英】〔用油和面粉混和、内包有肉馅或蔬菜馅的〕不加糖布丁: *steak and kidney pudding* 牛排加腰子布丁 **5** [C] *BrE informal* someone who is fat and stupid【英，非正式】肥胖而蠢笨的人 —see also 另见 BLACK PUDDING, CHRISTMAS PUDDING, MILK PUDDING, PLUM PUDDING, YORKSHIRE PUDDING, **the proof of the pudding is in the eating** (PROOF[1] (5)) S3

pudding ba·sin /ˈ‥ ˌ‥/ *n* [C] *BrE*【英】**1** a deep round dish in which puddings are cooked〔烹制布丁的圆而深的〕布丁盘 **2** a way of cutting someone's hair so that it is in the shape of an upside down bowl 碗状发型〔一种像倒置的碗状的发型〕

pud·dle /ˈpʌdl; ˈpʌdl/ *n* [C] a small pool of water, especially rainwater, on a path, road etc〔小径、道路等上的〕水坑〔尤指雨

水坑〕: *Children splashed through the puddles.* 孩子们溅泼着水走过一个个小水坑。

pu·den·dum /pju`dɛndəm; pjuːˈdendəm/ *n plural* **pudenda** /-də; -də/ [C] *old-fashioned* the sexual organs, especially of a woman【过时】〔尤指女性的〕阴部

pudg·y /ˈpʌdʒɪ; ˈpʌdʒi/ *adj* rather fat 肥胖的: *pudgy fingers* 胖嘟嘟的手指 —**pudginess** *n* [U]

pueb·lo /ˈpwɛblo; ˈpwebləʊ/ *n* [C] *Spanish* a small town, especially in the south west US【西班牙】〔尤指美国西南部的〕小城镇

pu·er·ile /ˈpjuəˌrɪl; ˈpjʊəraɪl/ *adj formal* puerile jokes, remarks etc are silly and stupid; CHILDISH【正式】〔笑话、话等〕愚蠢的; 幼稚的: *He's got such a puerile sense of humour.* 他有如此幼稚的幽默感。—**puerility** /ˌpjuəˈrɪlətɪ; pjʊəˈrɪlɨti/ *n* [U]

P

pu·er·per·al /pju`ɝpərəl; pjuːˈɜːpərəl/ *adj technical* happening while giving birth to a child or in the period after this【术语】分娩的; 产后的: *puerperal depression* 产后抑郁症

Puer·to Ri·co /ˌpwɛrtə `riko; ˌpwɜːtəʊ ˈriːkəʊ/ an island in the Caribbean Sea, southeast of the US state of Florida. Population: 3,937,000 (2001). Capital: San Juan. People who live in Puerto Rico are US citizens, but Puerto Rico is not a US state and it governs itself. Many people from Puerto Rico go to live and work in the US. It was a COLONY of Spain from 1509 to 1898, and most people speak Spanish as their first language. 波多黎各〔加勒比海一岛屿, 位于美国佛罗里达州东南。人口: 3,937,000 (2001), 首府: 圣胡安。波多黎各居民属美国国籍, 但波多黎各实行自治, 并非是美国的一个州。许多波多黎各人到美国去生活和工作。1509至1898年, 波多黎各为西班牙殖民地, 因此大多数居民的第一语言是西班牙语〕—**Puerto Rican** *n, adj*

Puerto Val·lar·ta /ˌpɔrtə vaɪ`ɑrtə; ˌpwɜːtəʊ vaɪˈɑːtə/ a town in western Mexico on the Pacific Ocean, popular with US tourists 巴亚尔塔港〔墨西哥西部一镇, 濒临太平洋, 为美国游人所喜爱〕

puff[1] /pʌf; pʌf/ *v* **1** [I] to breathe quickly and with difficulty after running, carrying something heavy etc 喘粗气: *Catherine was puffing loudly as she carried the box into the room.* 凯瑟琳喘着粗气把那个箱子搬进房间。| **[+up/along etc]** *Duncan passed me, puffing up the hill.* 邓肯从我旁边经过, 气喘吁吁地往那座小山上爬。—see also 另见 **huff and puff** (HUFF[1] (1)) **2** [I,T] to breathe in and out while smoking a cigarette, pipe etc〔抽烟等时〕吸[喷]〔烟〕: **puff at/on sth** *Dr Foulger paused to puff on his pipe before answering.* 福尔杰博士回答之前停下来抽了口烟斗。**3 a)** [T always+adv/prep] to blow smoke or steam out of something 使〔烟、气〕喷出: *Don't puff smoke into my face.* 别把烟朝我脸上喷。**b)** [I] if smoke or steam puffs from somewhere, it comes out in little clouds〔烟或气〕一阵阵喷出, 冒出: *Steam puffed out of the chimney.* 蒸汽从烟囱里一股一股地喷出来。**4** [I always+adv/prep] if a steam train puffs along, it moves while sending out little clouds of steam〔蒸汽火车〕喷着气前进: *By now we were puffing along at a good speed.* 至此, 我们的火车喷着一股股的烟, 正快速前进。

puff sth ↔ out *phr v* [T] **puff out your cheeks/chest** to make your cheeks etc bigger by filling them with air 鼓起双颊/挺起胸膛: *George puffed out his chest proudly.* 乔治骄傲地挺起胸膛。

puff up *phr v* **1** [I,T **puff** sth ↔ **up**] to become bigger by increasing the amount of air inside, or to make something bigger in this way (使)膨胀, (使)鼓起: *Bake for 25-30 minutes until the souffle puffs up about 5cm.* 烘烤25至30分钟直到蛋奶酥胀起5厘米。| *Birds puff up their feathers to keep warm.* 鸟膨起羽毛以保暖。**2** [I] if your eye, face etc puffs up, it swells painfully because of injury or infection〔眼睛、脸等〕肿胀: *My eye had puffed up because of a mosquito bite.* 我的一只眼睛由于蚊子叮咬而肿了起来。**3** [T **puff** sb **up**] to make someone feel very pleased or proud 使〔某人〕感到高兴[自豪]

puff[2] *n* [C] **1** the action of taking the smoke from a cigarette etc into your lungs 吸, 抽〔烟〕: **[+at]** *a puff at a cigarette* 吸一口香烟 | **have/take a puff** *"May I have just one puff?" "Sure, I thought you didn't smoke."* "我就抽一口可以吗?" "当然可以, 我以为你不抽烟呢。" **2** a sudden small movement of wind, air, or smoke〔风、空气、烟雾的〕一阵, 一团, 一股: **[+of]** *puffs of smoke coming from the chimney* 从烟囱里冒出的一股股的烟 | *The water was calm and there wasn't even a puff of wind.* 水面平静, 连一丝风也没有。—see picture on page A7 参见A7页图 **3 cheese/cream/lemon puff** a piece of light PASTRY (2) with a soft mixture inside 干酪/奶油/柠檬松饼 **4 get your puff back** *BrE informal* to be able to breathe normally again after doing something that made you breathe very hard【英, 非正式】喘过气来 **5 out of puff** *BrE informal* breathing hard and very tired【英, 非正式】喘不过气来: *He only has to climb the stairs and he's out of puff!* 他只要爬爬楼梯就累得喘不过气来了!

puff·ball /ˈpʌfbɔl; ˈpʌfbɔːl/ *n* [C] a type of round FUNGUS that bursts to release its seeds 马勃〔一种菌类〕

puffed /pʌft; pʌft/ *adj* [not before noun 不用于名词前] *BrE informal* breathing quickly because you have been using lots of energy【英, 非正式】气喘吁吁的

puffed sleeve /ˌ· ˈ·/ *n* [C] a short sleeve that is wider in the middle than at each end 泡泡袖〔中间比两端宽大的袖子〕

puffed up /ˌ· ˈ·◂/ *adj* behaving in a way that shows you are too proud 得意扬扬的: *All these pompous, puffed up television pundits make me sick.* 所有这些傲慢自负的电视评论家使我感到厌恶。

puffed wheat /ˌ· ˈ·/ *n* [U] grains of wheat that have been cooked to make them very light and are eaten with milk〔与牛奶一起食用的〕膨化小麦

puf·fin /ˈpʌfɪn; ˈpʌfɨn/ *n* [C] a North Atlantic seabird with a black and white body and a large brightly coloured beak 海鹦〔一种北大西洋海鸟, 有黑白相间的身体和大而色彩鲜艳的喙〕

puff pas·try /ˌ· ˈ··/ *n* [U] a kind of very light PASTRY with a lot of air in it 千层酥面团, 油酥面团

puff·y /ˈpʌfɪ; ˈpʌfi/ *adj* **puffier, puffiest** puffy eyes, faces, or cheeks are swollen〔眼睛、脸或脸颊〕肿的, 鼓起的 —**puffiness** *n* [U]

pug /pʌg; pʌg/ *n* [C] a small fat short-haired dog with a wide flat face and a short flat nose 哈巴狗

Pu·get Sound /ˌpjudʒət `saund; ˌpjuːdʒɨt ˈsaʊnd/ an area of water leading from the Pacific Ocean into the US state of Washington. The cities of Seattle and Tacoma are on its shores. 皮吉特湾, 又译普杰湾〔太平洋通向美国华盛顿州的海域, 西雅图、塔科马等城市位于该海湾〕

pu·gi·lis·m /ˈpjudʒəˌlɪzəm; ˈpjuːdʒɨlɪzəm/ *n* [U] *formal* the sport of BOXING (=fighting with your hands)【正式】拳击(运动)

pu·gi·list /ˈpjudʒəlɪst; ˈpjuːdʒɨlɨst/ *n* [C] *formal* a BOXER (=a sportsman who fights with his hands)【正式】拳击手, 拳师

pug·na·cious /pʌgˈneʃəs; pʌgˈneɪʃəs/ *adj formal* very eager to quarrel or fight with people【正式】爱争吵的, 爱争斗的, 好斗的 —**pugnaciously** *adv* —**pugnacity** /pʌg`næsətɪ; pʌgˈnæsɨti/ *n* [U]

puke[1] /pjuk; pjuːk/ also 又作 **puke up** *v* [I,T] *informal*【非正式】**1** to bring food back up from your stomach through your mouth; VOMIT 呕吐 **2 it makes me puke!** *informal* used to say that something makes you very angry or annoyed【非正式】真让我恶心!: *It makes me puke when I hear rich people complaining about taxes!* 我听到富人抱怨纳税时, 就感到恶心!

puke[2] *n* [U] *informal* food brought back up from your stomach through your mouth; VOMIT[2]【非正式】呕吐物

puk·ey, puky /ˈpjukɪ; ˈpjuːki/ *adj slang* very unpleasant or unattractive【俚】令人不舒服的; 令人不愉快的; 令人讨厌的

puk·ka also 又作 **pukha** /ˈpʌkə; ˈpʌkə/ *adj especially IndE, PakE*【尤印, 巴】**1** very good 很好的, 上等的 **2** real, or properly made 真正的; 品质优良的: *It can't compete with pukka racing cars.* 它比不过真正的赛车。**3** *humorous* too formal【幽默】太正式的

pul·chri·tude /ˈpʌlkrɪˌtjud; ˈpʌlkrɨtjuːd/ *n* [U] *formal* beauty, especially of a woman【正式】美丽〔尤指女性〕

Pul·it·zer Prize /ˈpulɪtsɚ ˌpraɪz; ˈpʊlɪtsə ˌpraɪz/ *n* [C] one of the eight prizes given every year in the US to people who have produced especially good work in JOURNALISM (=writing for newspapers), literature, or music. The prizes were started by the US newspaper owner Joseph **Pulitzer** (1847-1911), and winning a Pulitzer Prize is a great honour. 普利策奖〔美国每年向优秀新闻作品、文学作品或音乐作品的作者颁发的八大奖项之一。该奖由美国报业巨头约瑟夫·普利策(1847-1911)设立, 获得普利策奖是一种极高的荣誉〕

pull[1] /pul; pʊl/ *v*

1 ►MOVE STH TOWARDS YOU 把某物拉过来◄ [I,T] to use your hands to make something move towards you or in the direction that you are moving〔用手〕把〔某物〕拉过来; 拉: *Help me move the piano; you push and I'll pull.* 帮我搬一下钢琴, 你来推, 我来拉。| **pull sth** *I pulled the handle and it just snapped off!* 我拉了一下那把手, 它就啪一声断掉了。| **pull sth into/away from/over etc** *Pull the chair nearer to the fire.* 把那张椅子拉到火旁。| **pull sth open/shut** *Ally tried to pull the drawer open.* 艾丽试图拉开抽屉。| **pull hard** *They pulled hard on the rope.* 他们用力拉那绳子。—see picture on page A3 参见A3页图

2 ►PUT ON/TAKE OFF 穿上/脱下◄ [T always+adv/prep] to put on or take off clothing, usually quickly〔常指迅速地〕穿上

[脱下]〔衣服〕: *Ted pulled his socks on.* 特德穿上袜子。| *pulling off her hat and coat* 脱下她的帽子和外套

3 ▶MOVE YOUR BODY 移动身体◀ [T always+adv/prep] **a)** to move your arm or your whole body away from someone or something that is holding it or touching it 挣脱; 移开; 抽出: **pull sth away/off/out of etc** *She pulled her arm out of his grasp.* 她抽出被他抓着的胳膊。**b)** to hold onto something and use force to move your body〔抓住某物〕用力移动〔身体〕: **pull yourself up/through etc** *Harry pulled himself up onto the wall.* 哈里抓住墙爬了上去。

4 ▶CARRIAGE/TRAIN 马车/火车◀ [T usually passive 一般用被动态] if horses or a railway ENGINE pull a carriage etc, they make it move along behind them〔马〕拉〔马车〕;〔火车机车〕牵引

5 ▶USE A CONTROL 用控制装置◀ [T] to move a control such as a SWITCH[2] (1) or TRIGGER towards you to make a piece of equipment work 拉〔开关〕; 扣〔扳机〕: *She raised the gun, and pulled the trigger.* 她举起枪, 扣动了扳机。

6 ▶REMOVE 去掉◀ [T always+adv/prep] to use force to take something out of the place where it is fixed or held 拔: **pull sth out/up/away** *Gemma pulled the cork from the bottle.* 杰玛拔出瓶塞。

7 ▶SMOKE 烟◀ [T always+adv/prep] to take smoke from a cigarette, pipe etc into your lungs 吸〔烟、烟斗等〕: **pull on/at sth** *Todd sat thinking, pulling on his pipe.* 托德一边抽着烟斗, 一边坐着思考。

8 ▶MUSCLE 肌肉◀ [T] to injure one of your muscles by stretching it too much during physical activity; STRAIN[2] (4) 拉伤, 扭伤〔肌肉〕: *Paul pulled a muscle trying to lift the freezer.* 保罗想把冰箱抬起来, 结果拉伤了肌肉。

9 ▶CROWD/VOTES ETC 人群/选票等◀ [T] if an event, performer etc pulls crowds or a politician pulls a lot of votes, a lot of people come to see them or vote for them 吸引〔观众〕; 获得〔选票〕: *The big match pulled an enormous crowd.* 这场大赛吸引了大量观众。| *She's unlikely to pull many votes.* 她不大可能获得很多选票。| **pull the punters** *informal* (=attract customers)【非正式】吸引顾客

10 ▶SEXUALLY ATTRACT 勾引◀ [I,T] *BrE spoken* to attract someone in order to have sex with them【英口】勾引: *Ken's hoping to pull the girls with his flashy new car.* 肯希望用他俗艳的新车勾引那些女孩子。

11 ▶GUN/KNIFE 枪/刀◀ [T] to take out a gun or knife ready to use it 掏出, 拔出〔枪、刀等〕: **pull sth on sb** *He suddenly pulled a gun on me.* 他突然拔出枪对准我。

12 ▶BEER 啤酒◀ [T] *especially BrE* to get beer out of a BARREL by pulling a handle【尤英】拉酒桶把手放出〔啤酒〕: *to pull a pint* 从酒桶里放出一品脱啤酒

13 ▶CAR 汽车◀ [I] if a car pulls to the left or right as you are driving, it moves in that direction because of a mechanical problem〔汽车由于机械故障而〕侧斜: *The car seems to be pulling to the left.* 那辆车好像在向左打斜。

14 pull sb's leg to tell someone something that is not true, as a joke 开某人的玩笑; 耍弄某人; 诓骗某人

15 pull the other one (it's got bells on) *spoken* used to tell someone that you think they are joking or not telling the truth【口】别逗了: *A racing driver? Pull the other one!* 赛车手? 别逗了!

16 pull a fast one *spoken* to deceive someone【口】欺骗, 蒙骗〔某人〕: *He was trying to pull a fast one when he told you he'd paid.* 他告诉你他已付过款时, 其实他在试图欺骗你。

17 ▶SUCCEED 成功◀ [T] *slang, especially AmE* to do something illegal or dishonest such as a crime or trick【俚, 尤美】做〔坏事〕; 犯罪: *The gang have pulled another bank robbery.* 那伙匪徒又抢劫了一家银行。| *What are you trying to pull?* 你们想干什么勾当?

18 pull the curtains/the blind to open or close curtains or a BLIND 拉开[拉上]窗帘/百叶窗: *Could you just pull the blind, please?* 请你把百叶窗拉开, 好吗?

19 ▶HORSE 马◀ [I] if a horse pulls it struggles and presses hard against the piece of metal in its mouth〔马〕咬嚼子〔不听指挥〕

20 pull sb's licence *informal* to take away someone's DRIVING LICENCE because they have done something wrong【非正式】吊销某人的驾驶执照

21 pull a punch to deliberately hit someone with less force than you could do, so that it hurts less 故意不使出全力打某人〔以避免伤害〕—see also 另见 **not pull any punches** (PUNCH[2] (7))

22 ▶CRICKET/GOLF 板球/高尔夫球◀ [I,T] *technical* to hit the ball in CRICKET or GOLF so that it does not go straight but moves to one side【术语】拉击〔板球、高尔夫球〕

23 ▶ROW A BOAT 划船◀ [I,T] to make a boat move by using OARS 划〔船〕—see also 另见 PUSH[1] —see also 另见 **make/pull a face** (FACE[1] (2)), **pull your finger out** (FINGER[1] (7)), **pull rank (on)** (RANK[1] (5)), **pull the rug (out) from under sb's feet** (RUG (3)), **pull your socks up** (SOCK[1] (3)), **pull strings** (STRING[1] (7)), **pull your weight** (WEIGHT[1] (13)), **pull the wool over sb's eyes** (WOOL (4))

pull ahead *phr v* [I] if one vehicle pulls ahead of another it gets in front of it by moving faster〔车辆〕加快速度赶到〔…的〕前面; 加速超〔车〕

pull sb/sth **apart** *phr v* [T] **1** to separate people or animals when they are fighting 拉开, 分开〔打架的人或争斗的动物〕**2** to make someone feel very unhappy 使〔某人〕感到很不开心: *The constant rows were pulling her apart.* 没完没了的争吵使她很不开心。

pull at sth *phr v* [T] **1** to take a hold of something and pull it several times 抓住并不断拉扯: *The child pulled at his mother's coat.* 那孩子不断拉扯他母亲的外套。**2** to take smoke from a pipe or cigarette into your lungs 吸〔烟或烟斗〕: *He pulled at his pipe a couple of times.* 他抽了几口烟斗。**3** *old-fashioned* to take a long drink from a bottle or glass【过时】从〔瓶子或玻璃杯〕中大口地喝

pull away *phr v* [I] **1 a)** to start to drive away from a place where you had stopped 开始驶离, 开走: *Matt jumped onto the bus just as it was pulling away.* 公共汽车正要开走时, 马特跳了上去。**b)** to drive or run more quickly than another vehicle or person and leave them behind you 超越〔另一车辆或人〕, 把…抛在后面: **pull away from sth/sb** *Nikoku is pulling away from the other runners.* 尼可库把其他跑步选手抛在后面。**2** to move backwards quickly when someone is trying to touch you or hold you 迅速后退避开〔触摸等〕: *I tried to kiss her but she pulled away.* 我想吻她, 但她避开了。

pull down *phr v* [T] **1** [**pull** sth ↔ **down**] to destroy a building that is no longer used 拆毁, 拆掉〔建筑物〕: *The old chapel is dangerous and will have to be pulled down.* 那座旧的小教堂很危险, 所以将不得不被拆除。**2 pull down a menu** to make a computer PROGRAM show you a list of the things it can do 拉下菜单〔使电脑程序显示它可以做的事情〕**3** [**pull** sb **down**] *AmE* to make someone less healthy or successful【美】使〔某人〕虚弱; 使〔某人〕受挫: *Her problems over the last few months have really pulled her down.* 她几个月以来遇到的问题确实使她很受挫。

pull in *phr v* **1** [I] if a train pulls in, it arrives at a station〔火车〕到站, 进站 **2** [I] if a car or a driver pulls in they move to the side of the road and stop〔汽车或司机〕靠路边停下: *She pulled in to let the ambulance pass.* 她把车开到路边停下让救护车过去。—compare 比较 **pull over** (PULL[1]), —see also 另见 PULL-IN **3** [T **pull** sb ↔ **in**] if a police officer pulls someone in, they take them to a police station because they think they may have done something wrong〔警察〕把〔嫌疑犯〕带回警察局 **4** [T **pull** sth ↔ **in**] *informal* if you pull in a lot of money you earn it【非正式】挣〔钱〕, 赚〔钱〕 **5** [T **pull** sb/sth **in**] if an event, a show etc pulls in a lot of people they go to see it〔事件、演出等〕吸引〔观众〕: *'Les Miserables' has been pulling in huge crowds in New York.*《悲惨世界》在纽约一直吸引着大批的观众。

pull off *phr v* [T] *informal*【非正式】**1** to succeed in doing something difficult 成功〔做困难的事〕: **pull sth ↔ off** *They gave you the money! How did you pull that off?* 他们给了你钱! 你是如何得到的? **2** if a car pulls off a road it turns into a smaller road or entrance〔汽车〕驶离大路进入小路[入口]: **pull off sth** *We pulled off the road to get some food.* 我们驶离大路去找点食物。

pull out *phr v* **1** [I] if a train pulls out it leaves a station〔火车〕驶出车站, 离站 —compare 比较 **pull away** (PULL[1]) **2** [I] **a)** to drive onto a road from another road, or after you have stopped at the side〔从另一条路或从路边停靠的地方〕开到路上: *Don't pull out! There's something coming.* 别开出来! 有车过来。**b)** to drive over to a different part of the road, especially where the traffic is moving faster, in order to OVERTAKE (1) 并线超车: *That truck pulled straight out in front of me.* 那辆卡车直接超车跑到我前面。—see picture on page A3 参见 A3 页图 **3** [I,T **pull** sb/sth ↔ **out**] to get out of a bad situation or dangerous place, or order someone else to do so (使) 摆脱〔不好的局面〕; (使) 撤离〔危险的地方〕: *Jim saw that the firm was going to be ruined, so he pulled out.* 吉姆看到公司即将垮台, 于是就退了出来。| *Most of the troops have been pulled out.* 大部分部队已经撤离。—see also 另见 **pull out all the stops** (STOP[2] (6))

pull over *phr v* [I,T **pull** sth/sb **over**] to stop the vehicle you are driving at the side of the road, or order someone else to do

so (使)〔车辆〕停靠在路边: *The policeman signalled to him to pull over.* 警察示意他把车停靠在路边。

pull through also 又作 **pull round** *phr v* [I,T **pull** sb **through**] **1** to stay alive after you have been very ill or badly injured, or help someone do this〔从重病或重伤中〕恢复健康; 帮助某人康复: *His injuries are severe but he's expected to pull through.* 他的伤势很重, 但有望康复。—compare 比较 **bring through** (BRING) **2** to succeed even though you have had a lot of difficulties, or help someone do this (帮助) 克服困难, 渡过难关: *Margaret had real problems, but the teacher pulled her through.* 玛格丽特确实遇到了困难, 但老师帮她渡过了难关。

pull together *phr v* **1** [I] if a group of people pull together, they all work hard to achieve something〔一群人〕同心协力, 通力合作: *If we all pull together, we'll finish on time.* 如果我们同心协力去做, 就能按时完成。**2 pull yourself together** to force yourself to stop behaving in a nervous, frightened, or disorganized way 控制自己的感情: *Stop behaving like a baby! Pull yourself together.* 别像个孩子似的! 要控制住自己的感情。**3** [T **pull** sth **together**] to improve something by organizing it more effectively 整顿; 把…重新组织好: *We need an experienced manager to pull the department together.* 我们需要一位有经验的经理来整顿这个部门。

pull up *phr v* **1** [I] to stop the vehicle that you are driving〔使车〕停住[停下]: *Don pulled up at the red light and we stopped behind him.* 唐在红灯处停下车, 而我们停在他后面。—see picture on page A3 参见 A3 页图 **2 pull up a chair/stool etc** to get a chair and sit down next to someone who is already sitting 拿把椅子/凳子等〔坐在某人旁边〕**3** [T **pull** sb **up**] to stop someone who is doing something wrong and tell them you do not approve 制止〔正在做错事的人〕; 责备, 斥责: [+**on**] *I felt I had to pull her up on her lateness.* 我觉得我必须制止她迟到。**4 pull sb up short/pull sb up with a jerk** if something pulls you up short it makes you stop and think about whether you are doing the right thing 使某人停下来思考〔自己是否做得对〕: *Jan's unexpected criticism pulled me up short.* 简那出乎意料的批评使我停下来考虑自己是否做得对。

pull² *n*

1 ▶ACT OF PULLING 拉的动作◀ [C] an act of using force to move something towards you or in the same direction that you are moving 拉, 拔, 拖: *Give the rope a good pull.* 使劲拉一下绳子。—compare 比较 TUG¹

2 ▶FORCE 力◀ [C usually singular 一般用单数] a strong force such as GRAVITY, that makes things move in a particular direction 拉力, 引力: *gravitational pull of the moon* 月球的引力

3 ▶EMOTIONAL 感情的◀ [C usually singular 一般用单数] a strong feeling that you want to go to a particular place or person〔想去某处或去见某人的〕强烈感情, 吸引(力): *The old sailor still felt the pull of the sea.* 老水手仍感到海上生活的吸引力。

4 ▶CLIMB 攀登◀ [singular] *BrE old-fashioned* a difficult climb up a steep road【英, 过时】费力攀登: *It was a long pull up that hill.* 登山的路又长又陡。

5 ▶INFLUENCE 影响◀ [singular, U] *informal* special influence that gives you an unfair advantage【非正式】〔特殊的〕影响力; 〔不公正的〕照顾, 优待: *His family's name gives him a lot of pull in this town.* 他家族的名望使他在镇上受到很多优待。

6 ▶SMOKE 烟◀ [C] an act of taking the smoke from a cigarette, pipe etc into your lungs 抽一口烟: *She took a long pull on her cigarette.* 她吸了一大口烟。

7 ▶DRINK 饮料◀ [C] an act of taking a long drink of something 喝一大口: *Brett took a good pull at his beer.* 布雷特喝了一大口啤酒。

8 ▶HANDLE 把手◀ [C] a rope or handle that you use to pull something〔用以拉动某物的〕拉绳; 把手: *a bell-pull* 拉铃索

9 ▶CRICKET/GOLF 板球/高尔夫球◀ [C] a way of hitting the ball in CRICKET (2) or GOLF so that it does not go straight, but moves to one side 向侧边的一击

pul·let /ˈpʊlɪt; ˈpʊlɪ̥t/ *n* [C] a young chicken during its first year of laying eggs〔第一年下蛋的〕小母鸡

pul·ley /ˈpʊli; ˈpʊli/ *n* [C] a piece of equipment consisting of a wheel over which a rope or chain is pulled to lift heavy things〔用来提起重物的〕滑车, 滑轮

pull-in /ˈ· ·/ *n* [C] *BrE informal* a place by the side of a road where vehicles can stop and drivers can buy food and drinks【英, 非正式】〔供司机停车休息并供应饮食的〕路旁停车处

Pull·man /ˈpʊlmən; ˈpʊlmən/ *n* [C] a very comfortable train carriage, especially one that you can sleep in, or a train made up of these carriages〔设备特别舒适的〕普尔曼式火车车厢, 〔尤指〕卧车车厢; 普尔曼式卧铺列车

pull-on /ˈ· ·/ *adj* [only before noun 仅用于名词前] a pull-on shirt, dress etc does not have any buttons, so you pull it on over your head〔无扣的衬衫、裙子等〕套穿的, 套头的

pull-out /ˈ· ·/ *n* [C] **1** part of a book or magazine that can be removed and is like a separate small book〔书刊中可单独取出的〕插页, 活页: *a 16-page pull-out on cake decorating* 有关蛋糕装饰的16页插页 **2** the act of an army, business, etc leaving a particular place or area of activity〔军队、公司等的〕撤离, 撤出: *The pull-out of troops will begin after the treaty is signed.* 和约签订后部队即开始撤离。

pull-o·ver /ˈpʊlˌovə; ˈpʊlˌəʊvə/ *n* [C] a piece of WOOLLEN clothing without buttons that you wear on the top half of your body 套头毛衣; SWEATER, JUMPER (1) *BrE*【英】

pull-up /ˈ· ·/ *n* [C] *AmE* an exercise in which you use your arms to pull yourself up towards a bar above your head【美】拉单杠(运动), 引体向上

pul·mo·na·ry /ˈpʌlməˌnɛri; ˈpʊlmənəri/ *adj technical* connected with the lungs or having an effect on the lungs【术语】肺的; 对肺有影响的

pulp¹ /pʌlp; pʌlp/ *n* [U] **1** a very soft substance that is almost liquid 浆状物: **boil/cook sth to a pulp** *First, boil the vegetables to a pulp.* 首先, 把蔬菜煮成糊状。**2** the soft inside part of a fruit or vegetable 果肉; 菜心: *Halve the melon and scoop out the seeds and pulp.* 把瓜切成两半, 挖出里面的籽和瓤。**3** wood or other substances from plants that are used for making paper 纸浆 **4** books, magazines, films etc that are of poor quality or are badly written 劣质书刊, 低级书刊; 庸俗电影 **5 beat sb to a pulp** *informal* to hit someone until they are seriously injured【非正式】狠揍[痛打]某人 **6** part of the inside of a tooth 牙髓 —**pulpy** *adj*

pulp² *adj* [only before noun 仅用于名词前] pulp magazines, stories etc are of poor quality and are often about sex and violence〔杂志、故事等〕纸张和内容很差的; 庸俗的, 低级趣味的: *pulp novels* 庸俗小说 | *pulp fiction* 庸俗小说

pulp³ *v* [T] **1** to beat or crush something until it becomes so soft that it is almost liquid 把…捣成[压成]浆状: *pulped apples* 捣成浆状的苹果 **2** to make books or newspapers into paper 把〔书或报纸〕化成纸浆

Pulp Fic·tion /ˌ· ˈ··/ (1994) a humorous and very violent US film, made by Quentin Tarantino《低俗小说》〔(1994), 美国暴力喜剧片, 由昆廷·塔伦蒂诺执导〕

pul·pit /ˈpʊlpɪt; ˈpʊlpɪt/ *n* [C] a raised, box-like structure at the front of a church, from which the priest speaks〔教堂中的〕讲坛, 布道坛

pulp·wood /ˈpʌlpwʊd; ˈpʌlpwʊd/ *n* [U] crushed wood that is used to make paper〔造纸用的〕木浆

pul·sar /ˈpʌlsɑr; ˈpʌlsɑː/ *n* [C] an object that is far away in space and like a star, that produces a regular radio signal 脉冲星〔发出周期性电波的星球〕

pul·sate /ˈpʌlset; pʌlˈseɪt/ *v* [I] **1** to make sounds or movements that are strong and regular like a heart beating 有规律地振动, 脉动: *The thumping, pulsating music shook the kitchen walls.* 砰砰的音乐声振动着厨房的墙壁。**2** *literary* to be strongly affected by a powerful emotion or feeling【文】受震动; 激动: [+**with**] *The whole city seemed to be pulsating with excitement.* 整个城市好像都激动不已。

pul·sa·tion /pʌlˈseʃən; pʌlˈseɪʃən/ *n* **1** [C] *especially technical* a beat of the heart or any regular beat that can be measured【尤术语】〔心脏或其他有规律能测量的〕搏动, 脉动 **2** [U] pulsating movement 有节奏的跳动

pulse¹ /pʌls; pʌls/ *n* **1** [C usually singular 一般用单数] **a)** the regular beat that can be felt, for example at your wrist, as your heart pumps blood around your body 脉搏: *I checked his pulse – he was still alive.* 我检查了他的脉搏——他还活着。**b)** also 又作 **pulse rate** the number of these beats per minute 脉率〔每分钟的心跳数〕: **take/feel sb's pulse** (=to count how many times someone's heart beats in a minute, usually by feeling their wrist) 量某人的脉搏, 给某人把脉 *The nurse took my pulse – it was faster than normal.* 护士给我量了脉搏——我的脉搏比正常的跳得快。| **your pulse quickens/races** (=it gets faster because you are excited, nervous etc) 脉搏加快 **2** [C] an amount of sound, light, or electricity that continues for a very short time〔声波、光波、电流等的〕脉冲: *emitting pulses of sound at around 200 cycles per second* 发出每秒钟大约200周的声波脉冲 **3 pulses** [plural] seeds such as beans, PEAS, and LENTILs that can be eaten 豆类植物的种子, 〔豌豆、扁豆等可食用的〕豆子 **4** [C,U] a strong regular beat as in music, or on a drum〔音乐、鼓等的〕拍子; 节奏, 律动 —see also 另见 **have/keep your finger on the pulse** (FINGER¹ (12))

pulse² *v* [I] **1** to move or flow with a steady rapid beat or sound 〔以稳定、迅速的节拍或声音〕移动, 流动; 搏动; 跳动: *the blood pulsing through his veins* 在他的血管中奔涌的血液 | *coloured lights pulsing in time with the music* 随着音乐闪动的彩灯 **2** if a feeling or emotion pulses through someone, they feel it very strongly 〔感情等〕被强烈地感觉到: *excitement pulsing through the crowd* 传遍人群的兴奋情绪

pul·ver·ize also 又作 **-ise** *BrE*【英】/ˈpʌlvəˌraɪz; ˈpʌlvəraɪz/ *v* [T usually passive 一般用被动态] **1** to crush something into a powder 把…磨成粉 **2** *informal* to completely defeat someone【非正式】彻底打败 —**pulverization** /ˌpʌlvəraɪˈzeʃən; ˌpʌlvəraɪˈzeɪʃən/ *n* [U]

pu·ma /ˈpjumə; ˈpjuːmə/ *n* [C] a COUGAR 美洲狮

pum·ice /ˈpʌmɪs; ˈpʌmɪ̱s/ also 又作 **pumice stone** /ˈ·· ·/ *n* **1** [U] very light silver-grey rock that has come from a VOLCANO, and is used as a powder for cleaning 浮石, 轻石〔用作清洁粉〕 **2** [C] a piece of this stone used for rubbing your skin to clean it or make it soft 〔一块〕浮石, 轻石〔用于清理皮肤或磨擦皮肤使其柔软〕

pum·mel /ˈpʌml; ˈpʌməl/ **pummelled, pummelling** *BrE*【英】, **pummeled, pummeling** *AmE*【美】*v* [T] **1** to hit someone or something many times quickly with your FISTS (=closed hands) 用双拳接连地捶打: *She flew at him and pummelled his chest.* 她冲向他并用拳头捶打他的胸膛。**2** *informal* to completely defeat someone at a sport【非正式】〔在运动中〕彻底击败

pump¹ /pʌmp; pʌmp/ *n* **1** [C] a machine for forcing liquid or gas into or out of something 泵; 唧筒; 抽水机; 打气筒〔将气体或液体注入或吸出某物的机器〕: **water/air/beer etc pump** (=for moving water/air etc) 抽水机/抽气机/啤酒泵等 | **hand/foot pump** (=operated by your hand or foot) 手压[摇]泵/脚踏泵 —see picture at 参见 BICYCLE¹ 图 | **petrol pump/gas pump** (=for putting petrol or gas into cars) 汽油加油泵 —see also 另见 STOMACH PUMP —see picture at 参见 BICYCLE¹ 图 **2** [C usually plural 一般用复数] *BrE* a flat light shoe for dancing, exercise etc【英】〔跳舞、锻炼等用的〕平底轻便鞋, 轻便舞鞋: *a pair of ballet pumps* 一双芭蕾舞鞋 **3** [C usually plural 一般用复数] *especially AmE* a woman's plain shoe that does not fasten【尤美】无带女便鞋 —see picture at 参见 SHOE¹ 图 **4** [C usually plural 一般用复数] *BrE* a shoe made of CANVAS (=thick cloth) with rubber on the bottom, used for sports【英】〔橡胶底帆布面的〕运动鞋: *Don't forget your pumps for PE.* 别忘了体育课穿的运动鞋。**5** [C] an act of pumping 抽吸; 泵送; 抽运 **6 all hands to the pumps** used to say that everyone must work hard because a very difficult job has to be done 〔为了完成困难的任务〕人人都要努力工作 —see also 另见 HEAT PUMP, **prime the pump** (PRIME³ (4)), PARISH PUMP

pump² *v* **1** [T always+adv/prep] to make liquid or gas move in a particular direction with a pump 〔用泵〕抽出, 注入〔液体、气体等〕: **pump sth into/out of/through etc** *The fire department are still pumping floodwater out of the cellars.* 消防员仍在用泵抽吸地下室里的洪水。| **pump gas** *AmE* (=put petrol into your car at a petrol station)【美】〔给汽车〕加油 **2** also 又作 **pump away** [I] to move very quickly in and out or up and down 快速地进进出出; 迅速地上下移动: *My heart was pumping fast.* 我的心脏跳得很快。**3** also 又作 **pump away** [I] to operate a pump 操作泵: *He pumped away furiously.* 他拼命地用泵抽吸。**4** [T] to bring a supply of water, oil etc to the surface from under the ground 从地下抽出〔水、油等〕 **5** [I always+adv/prep] when a liquid pumps from somewhere, it comes out in sudden small amounts 〔液体〕间歇地喷出: **[+from/out of etc]** *The blood was pumping from the wound in his thigh.* 血从他大腿的伤口处喷出。**6** [T] *informal* to ask someone a lot of questions, in order to find out something【非正式】盘问, 套问: **pump sb for sth** *I tried to pump him for information about their other contacts.* 我想方设法从他嘴里套出有关他们的其他联系人的情况。**7 pump sb full of sth** to put a lot of drugs into someone's body 把大量的〔药物〕注入某人的身体: *athletes pumped full of steroids* 注射了大量类固醇的运动员 **8 pump iron** *informal* to do exercises by lifting heavy weights【非正式】举重 **9 have your stomach pumped** to have the contents of your stomach removed by a pump, after swallowing something harmful 〔吞食有害的东西后〕洗胃

pump sth **into** sb/sth *phr v* [T] **pump bullets into sb/sth** *informal* to shoot someone several times【非正式】将多发子弹射入某人身体[某物]

pump out *phr v* **1** [I,T] if something such as music, information, or a supply of products is pumped out or pumps out, a lot of it is produced 〔音乐、信息、产品等〕大量提供, 大量供应; 连续播放: *There's a huge amount of propaganda pumped out by the food industry.* 食品工业进行了大张旗鼓的宣传。| *Music pumped out from the loudspeakers overhead.* 音乐连续不断地在头顶的喇叭里播放。**2** [T **pump** sth **↔ out**] to remove liquid from something using a pump 用泵抽出〔某物中的液体〕: *You'll have to pump the boat out.* 你得用泵把船里的水抽干。

pump sth **↔ up** *phr v* [T] **1** to fill a tyre, AIRBED etc with air until it is correctly filled; INFLATE (1) 给〔轮胎、充气床垫等〕充满气 **2** to increase the value, amount etc of something 增加〔某物的价值、数量等〕: *The US was able to pump up exports.* 美国能够增加出口量。**3 pump up the music/volume etc** *slang* to play music louder【俚】放大音乐声/音量等

pump sb **↔ up** *phr v* [T] to increase someone's excitement, interest etc 给〔某人〕打气; 使兴奋; 使更感兴趣: *He was really pumped up before the game.* 比赛前他劲头十足。

pump-ac·tion /ˈ· ,··/ *adj* **a pump-action shotgun/hairspray etc** a SHOTGUN etc that is operated by pulling or pressing part of it in or out 滑杆式猎枪/压出式头发定型喷剂等

pum·per·nick·el /ˈpʌmpɚˌnɪk]; ˈpʌmpənɪkəl/ *n* [U] a heavy dark brown bread 粗制裸麦黑面包

pump·kin /ˈpʌmpkɪn; ˈpʌmpkɪ̱n/ *n* **1** [C,U] a very large orange fruit that grows on the ground, or the inside of this fruit 南瓜: *pumpkin pie* 南瓜饼 —see picture on page A9 参见 A9 页图 **2** [singular] *AmE* a way of addressing someone you love【美】一种称呼所爱的人的方式

> **CULTURAL NOTE 文化注释**
>
> In the US, **pumpkin pie** is usually eaten as part of Thanksgiving Day dinner. In the story of Cinderella, the Fairy Godmother changes a pumpkin into a COACH to take Cinderella to the BALL, but she warns Cinderella that it will change back into a pumpkin after midnight. People who are out late at night, enjoying themselves, sometimes make jokes about turning into a pumpkin if they stay out until after midnight. 在美国, 吃南瓜饼通常是感恩节宴席的一部分。在《灰姑娘》的故事中, 仙姑将一个南瓜点化成一辆马车载着灰姑娘去参加舞会, 但是她也告诫灰姑娘说午夜过后马车会变回南瓜。深夜在外的人, 有时自娱自乐地开玩笑说待过午夜自己就会变成一个大南瓜。

pump room /ˈ· ·/ *n* [C] a room at a SPA where you can go to drink the water 〔温泉疗养地的〕矿泉水饮用室

pun¹ /pʌn; pʌn/ *n* [C] an amusing use of a word or phrase that has two meanings, or of words with the same sound but different meanings, for example 〔利用有两重含义的词或同音异义词的〕双关语, 语义双关的俏皮话: *Seven days without water make one weak.* (=1 week) 七天不喝水使人虚弱。〔weak 和 week 同音, 读音也可理解为七天不喝水为一周〕

pun² *v* **punned, punning** [I+on] to make a pun 使用双关语

Punch¹ /pʌntʃ; pʌntʃ/ also 又作 **Mr Punch** the main character in a Punch and Judy Show 潘趣先生〔夫妻打架木偶戏中的主角〕

Punch² *trademark* a British weekly magazine which was started in 1841 and is still produced today. It consists mainly of humorous articles and CARTOONS.【商标】《笨拙》〔一本英国周刊, 1841 年创刊, 现仍在刊印, 主要内容包括幽默文章和搞笑漫画〕

punch¹ *v* [T] **1** to hit someone or something hard with your FIST (=closed hand) 用拳猛击〔某人或某物〕: **punch sb in/on sth** *Gallacher swung round and punched me hard in the stomach.* 加拉赫猛转身朝我的腹部重击一拳。| **punch sb/sth** *I punched the wall in anger.* 我生气地用拳猛击墙壁。| **punch the air** (=to make a movement like a punch, to show that you are very pleased about something) 朝空中打一拳〔表示非常高兴〕 —see picture on page A20 参见 A20 页图 **2** to make a hole in something using a metal tool or other sharp object 〔用金属工具或其他利器〕在〔某物〕上打孔: **punch a ticket/card etc** *The guard punched my ticket.* 列车员在我的车票上打了孔。| **punch a hole in/through sth** *These bullets can punch a hole through 20mm steel plate.* 这些子弹可以穿透 20 毫米厚的钢板。**3** [T] to push a button or key on a machine 按〔按钮或键〕: *Sally punched the eighth floor button and the doors shut.* 萨莉按下八楼的按钮, 门关上了。**4** *AmE* [T] to move cattle from one place to another【美】赶〔牲口〕 **5 punch holes in an argument/idea etc** *BrE* to disagree with someone's idea or plan and show what is wrong with it【英】不同意某人的观点[计划]并指出其毛病 **6 punch the clock** *AmE informal* to record the time that you start or finish work by putting a card into a special machine【美, 非正式】打考勤卡记录上下班时间, 打卡上下班 **7 punch sb's lights out** *AmE informal* to hit someone hard in the face【美, 非正式】猛击某人的脸

punch in *phr v* **1** [I] *AmE* to record the time that you arrive at work, by putting a card into a special machine; CLOCK IN【美】打卡记录上班时间，打上班卡 **2** [T **punch** sth ↔ **in**] to put information into a computer by pressing buttons or keys〔按下按钮或键〕往电脑里输入信息

punch out *phr v AmE*【美】**1** to record the time that you leave work, by putting a card into a special machine; CLOCK OUT 打卡记录下班时间，打下班卡 **2** [T **punch** sb **out**] to hit someone so hard that they fall over 把某人打倒

punch² *n* **1** [C] a quick strong hit made with your FIST (=closed hand) 用拳打，殴打: **punch in/on etc** *a punch in the kidneys* 打在肾上的一拳 | **throw a punch** (=aim a punch at someone) 用拳头往某人身上打 **2** [U] a strong, effective quality in the way that you express things that makes people interested〔语言文字的〕力量，感染力: *The speech was O.K. but it had no real punch.* 那演讲还行，但没有真正的感染力。**3** [C] a metal tool for cutting holes or for pushing something into a small hole 打孔器: *a hole punch* 打孔器 **4** [C,U] a drink made from fruit juice, sugar, water, and usually some alcohol〔用果汁、糖、水制成并常搀酒的〕宾治，潘趣酒: *a bowl of rum punch* 一碗潘趣酒 **5 as pleased as Punch** very happy 非常快乐，十分开心: *He's as pleased as Punch about the baby.* 宝宝使他感到十分开心。**6 beat sb/sth to the punch** *informal* to do or get something before someone else【非正式】先发制人；抢先做某事 **7 not pull any punches** *informal* to express your disapproval very clearly, without trying to hide what you feel【非正式】〔批评时〕毫不留情: *He wasn't pulling any punches! He said my work was 'pathetic'.* 他毫不留情地说我干得"很差劲"。—see also 另见 **pack a (hard) punch** (PACK¹ (10))

Punch and Ju·dy show /ˈpʌntʃ ən ˈdʒuːdɪ ʃoː; ˌpʌntʃ ən ˈdʒuːdi ʃəʊ/ *n* [C] a traditional type of entertainment for children, especially at British SEASIDE towns, that uses PUPPETS 庞奇和朱迪木偶戏，夫妻打闹木偶戏〔一种传统儿童娱乐形式，尤指英国海滨城市供儿童看的木偶节目〕

punch-bag /ˈpʌntʃbæg; ˈpʌntʃbæg/ *BrE*【英】, **punching bag** *AmE*【美】/ˈ· · ·/ *n* [C] **1** a heavy leather bag hung from a rope, that is punched for exercise〔锻炼用的〕皮吊袋 **2 use sb as a punchbag** *BrE informal* to hit or punch someone【英，非正式】打某人，用拳猛打某人

punch ball /ˈ· ·/ *n* [C] a large leather ball that is fixed on a spring and is punched for exercise〔练习拳击用的〕皮吊球

punch bowl /ˈ· ·/ *n* [C] a large bowl in which punch (=a mixed drink) is served 盛潘趣[宾治]酒的大碗

punch-drunk /ˈ· ·/ *adj* **1** *informal* very confused, especially because you have had continuous bad luck or have been treated badly【非正式】〔尤指因连遭不幸或受虐待而〕神志恍惚的 **2** a BOXER who is punch-drunk is suffering brain damage from being hit too much〔拳击手〕被打得头晕眼花的

punched card /ˌ· ˈ·/ also 又作 **punch card** /ˈ· ·/ *n* [C] a card with a pattern of holes in it that was used in the past for putting information into a computer〔过去用于往电脑中输入信息的〕穿孔卡片

punch line /ˈ· ·/ *n* [C] the last few words of a joke or story, that make it funny or surprising〔笑话、故事中最后几句点题或抛出笑料等的〕妙语，画龙点睛的结尾语

punch-up /ˈ· ·/ *n* [C] *BrE informal* a fight【英，非正式】打斗，斗殴: *Two people are to appear in court after a punch-up at their London home.* 两个人在他们伦敦的家中打架之后将对簿公堂。

punch·y /ˈpʌntʃɪ; ˈpʌntʃi/ *adj* a punchy piece of writing or speech is very effective because it expresses ideas clearly in only a few words〔文章、演讲〕简短有力的；简洁的，简练的: *a punchy article* 一篇简洁有力的文章 —**punchiness** *n* [U]

punc·til·i·ous /pʌŋkˈtɪlɪəs; pʌŋkˈtɪliəs/ *adj formal* being very careful to behave correctly and keep exactly to rules【正式】〔行为〕拘谨的，一丝不苟的: *Jimmy was always most punctilious about repaying any loans.* 吉米总是格外谨慎地偿还贷款。—**punctiliously** *adv* —**punctiliousness** *n* [U]

punc·tu·al /ˈpʌŋktʃʊəl; ˈpʌŋktʃuəl/ *adj* arriving, happening etc at exactly the time that has been arranged 准时的，守时的，如期的: *She's always very punctual for appointments.* 她总是准时赴约。| *the punctual payment of invoices* 准时支付发票上的金额 —**punctually** *adv*: *The meeting began punctually at nine o'clock.* 会议于9点钟准时开始。—**punctuality** /ˌpʌŋktʃʊˈælətɪ; ˌpʌŋktʃuˈæləti/ *n* [U]

punc·tu·ate /ˈpʌŋktʃʊˌet; ˈpʌŋktʃueɪt/ *v* **1** [T] to divide written work into sentences, phrases etc using COMMAS, FULL STOPS etc 在…中加标点 **2 be punctuated by/with sth** to be interrupted many times with something such as a noise 不时被某事物打断: *silence occasionally punctuated by laughter* 偶尔被笑声打破的寂静

punc·tu·a·tion /ˌpʌŋktʃʊˈeʃən; ˌpʌŋktʃuˈeɪʃən/ *n* [U] the marks used in dividing a piece of writing into sentences, phrases etc 标点符号〔总称〕

punctuation mark /ˌ· ·ˈ· ·/ *n* [C] a sign, such as a COMMA or QUESTION MARK, that is used in dividing a piece of writing into sentences, phrases etc 标点符号〔如逗号、问号〕

punctuation marks 标点符号	
.	full stop *BrE*【英】/ period *AmE*【美】句号
,	comma 逗号
;	semi-colon 分号
:	colon 冒号
?	question mark 问号
!	exclamation mark *BrE*【英】/exclamation point *AmE*【美】感叹号
( )	brackets 括号
" "	quotation marks 引号

punc·ture¹ /ˈpʌŋktʃɚ; ˈpʌŋktʃə/ *n* [C] **1** *BrE* a hole made accidentally in a tyre, so that air comes out of it【英】〔轮胎上的〕刺孔；FLAT² (2) *AmE*【美】: *I'm sorry I'm late; I had a puncture.* 对不起我来晚了，我的车胎给扎了个洞。| *to mend a puncture* 修补车胎刺孔 **2** a small hole made by a sharp point〔尖物刺穿的〕小孔

puncture² *v* **1** [T] to make a small hole through the surface of something, especially in a tyre 刺破，刺穿〔尤指轮胎〕: *A nail on the road punctured one of my tyres.* 路上的一根钉子把我的轮胎刺破了。| *Puncture some holes in the cover.* 在盖子上刺几个孔。**2** [I] if a ball, tyre etc punctures, it gets a small hole in it so that gas or air comes out〔球、轮胎等〕刺破，戳破: *The ball punctured on the holly bush.* 那球落在冬青丛上刺破了。**3** [T] to suddenly destroy a feeling or belief, making someone feel unhappy, silly, or confused 突然破坏〔某人的感觉〕；摧毁〔信念〕；使感到不快[愚蠢，迷惑]: *The shocking news finally punctured his smug complacency.* 那个令人震惊的消息最终使他自满的情绪受挫。

pun·dit /ˈpʌndɪt; ˈpʌndɨt/ *n* [C] someone who knows a lot about a particular subject, and is often asked for their opinions on it〔经常接受咨询的〕权威，专家: *political pundits* 政治（问题）专家

pun·gent /ˈpʌndʒənt; ˈpʌndʒənt/ *adj* **1** a pungent taste or smell is strong and sharp〔味道、气味〕强烈的，刺激性的，刺鼻的: *the pungent aroma of garlic* 大蒜的刺鼻气味 **2** pungent remarks or writing criticize something in a very direct and clever way〔话语、文章〕辛辣的，尖锐的: *a few typically pungent remarks from Senator Moynihan* 参议员莫伊尼汉的几句典型的辛辣评论 —**pungently** *adv* —**pungency** *n* [U]

pun·ish /ˈpʌnɪʃ; ˈpʌnɪʃ/ *v* [T] **1** to make someone suffer because they have done something wrong or broken the law 处罚，惩罚〔做错事或犯法的人〕: *Some people believe that smacking is not an acceptable way to punish a child.* 一些人认为动手打孩子不是一种可以接受的惩罚方式。| *In some countries women who have abortions can be punished by imprisonment.* 在有些国家，堕胎的妇女会受到监禁的处罚。| **punish sb for (doing) sth** *Ewing was hauled before the Football Association to be punished for misconduct.* 尤因因行为不端而被传到足协接受处罚。**2** if you punish a crime you punish anyone who is guilty of it 惩处〔犯罪行为〕: *Vandalism will be severely punished.* 蓄意破坏行为将严惩不贷。**3 punish yourself (for sth/for doing sth)** to blame yourself for something 因为某事/做某事而责备自己: *The accident wasn't your fault; stop punishing yourself.* 这次事故不是你的错，别再怪罪自己了。

pun·ish·a·ble /ˈpʌnɪʃəbl; ˈpʌnɪʃəbəl/ *adj* a punishable act may be punished by law, especially in a particular way〔尤指以某种方式〕可依法惩处的: *a punishable offence* 应予惩罚的违例 | **[+by]** *Murder is punishable by death.* 犯谋杀罪可处以死刑。

pun·ish·ing¹ /ˈpʌnɪʃɪŋ; ˈpʌnɪʃɪŋ/ *adj* **punishing schedule/workload/journey etc** a SCHEDULE etc that is so long or difficult that it makes you tired and weak 累人的日程安排/繁重的工作负担/使人疲惫不堪的旅行等: *a punishing regime of exercise and diet* 艰苦的锻炼与节食 —**punishingly** *adv*

punishing² *n* **take a punishing** *informal* to suffer rough or damaging treatment【非正式】遭到粗暴对待；受到损坏: *The car took a real punishing on the journey.* 这辆汽车在旅行中饱受折腾。

pun·ish·ment /ˈpʌnɪʃmənt; ˈpʌnɪʃmənt/ *n* **1** [C] a way in which someone or something is punished 惩罚手段；处罚: **[+for]** *I sent Alex to bed early as a punishment for breaking the window.* 因为亚历克斯打破了窗玻璃，我罚他早上床睡觉。| *You know the punishment for treason, don't you?* 你知道叛国罪会受到什么

样的惩罚, 是吧? | **a harsh/severe punishment** (=one that makes someone suffer a lot) 严厉的惩罚 **2** [U] the act of punishing someone or the process of being punished 惩罚, 处罚; 受罚: *We are determined that the terrorists will not escape punishment.* 我们决心不让那些恐怖分子逍遥法外。 **3** [U] *informal* rough treatment; damage【非正式】粗暴对待; 损坏, 糟踏: *With five children in the house, the furniture has to take a lot of punishment.* 因家里有五个孩子, 家具免不了要受到糟蹋。—see also 另见 CAPITAL PUNISHMENT, CORPORAL PUNISHMENT

pu·ni·tive /ˈpjunətɪv; ˈpjuːnɪ̣tɪv/ *adj* **1 punitive taxes/price increases etc** taxes etc that are so severe that people find it very difficult to pay 重税/价格的急剧上涨等: *The new Bill enables people to sue and win punitive damages for discrimination.* 新的法案使人们可以因受到歧视而提出诉讼并获得高额补偿金。 **2 punitive actions/measures/damages etc** actions etc that are intended to punish someone 惩罚(性)行动/措施/赔偿费等: *plans to take punitive action against terrorists* 对恐怖分子采取惩罚行动的计划 —**punitively** *adv*

Pun·jab, the /ˈpʌndʒab; ˈpʌndʒɑːb/ a large area in eastern Pakistan and northwestern India. The Punjab was a single PROVINCE in the period of British rule, but it is now two states: one in Pakistan, which contains the city of Lahore, and one in India, which contains the city of Amritsar, a holy place for followers of the Sikh religion. Many of the people who live in the Indian Punjab are Sikhs, and some of them would like to become independent from India. 旁遮普〔巴基斯坦东部、印度西北部一广大地区。英国统治时期, 旁遮普是一个统一的行省, 如今划分为两个邦, 一个在巴基斯坦, 包括拉合尔市在内; 另一个在印度, 包括锡克教教徒的圣地阿姆利则市。住在印度旁遮普邦的居民大多为锡克教信徒, 其中有些人希望能从印度独立出去〕

punk /pʌŋk; pʌŋk/ *n* **1** also 又作 **punk-rock** /ˌ· ˈ·/ [U] a type of loud violent music popular in the late 1970s and the 1980s 朋克摇滚乐〔一种20世纪70年代末期和80年代流行的音乐〕: *great punk bands like the Sex Pistols and X-Ray spex* 如"性手枪"和"透视器"之类伟大的朋克摇滚乐队 **2** also 又作 **punk-rocker** [C] someone who dresses like people who follow punk rock, with brightly-coloured hair, chains and pins and torn clothing 朋克摇滚乐迷; 追随朋克风格者〔模仿朋克摇滚乐师的衣着、将头发染成鲜艳的颜色、佩戴链子和饰针、穿褴褛衣衫〕: *Marilyn was a punk in '79.* 1979年, 玛丽莲是个朋克摇滚乐迷。| *punk hairstyles* 朋克发型 **3** [C] *AmE slang* a young man or a boy who fights and breaks the law【美俚】小流氓, 阿飞: *You little punk!* 你这个小流氓! **4** [U] *AmE* a substance that burns without a flame and is used to light FIREWORK*s* etc【美】〔用于点焰火的〕火绒

pun·kah /ˈpʌŋkə; ˈpʌŋkə/ *n* [C] *especially IndE, PakE* a FAN¹ (2) hung across a room and swung backwards and forwards by pulling a rope, especially in the past【尤印和巴】〔尤指旧时用绳索拉动的〕布(屏)风扇

pun·kin /ˈpʌŋkɪn; ˈpʌŋkɪ̣n/ *n* [C] *AmE* another spelling of PUMPKIN (2)【美】pumpkin (2) 的另一种拼法

pun·net /ˈpʌnɪt; ˈpʌnɪ̣t/ *n* [C] *BrE* a small square basket in which soft fruits such as strawberries (STRAWBERRY) are sold, or the amount contained in one of these【英】〔出售草莓等软水果的〕小方篮[篓]; 一小篮[篓]之量

pun·ster /ˈpʌnstɚ; ˈpʌnstə/ *n* [C] someone who makes PUN*s* (=jokes involving two words that sound similar) 好用双关语的人

punt¹ /pʌnt; pʌnt/ *n* **1** [C] a long narrow river-boat with a flat bottom and square ends, that is moved by pushing a long pole against the bottom of the river〔用篙撑行的〕方头平底船 **2** [singular] the act of going out in a punt 撑方头平底船: *Let's go for a punt.* 我们去撑船吧。 **3** [C] in American football, a long kick that you make after dropping the ball from your hands〔美式橄榄球中〕踢悬空球 **4** [C] *BrE informal* money that you risk on the result of something such as a race; a BET【英, 非正式】赌注 **5 take a punt** *informal* to make a guess when you do not have full enough information to make a proper decision【非正式】〔在没有足够的信息帮助作出正确决定时〕猜测

punt² *v* **1** [I,T] in American football, to drop the ball from your hands and kick it〔美式橄榄球中〕踢(悬空球): *He punted the ball forty yards.* 他把球踢出40码。—see picture on page A22 参见A22页图 **2** [I,T] to go or take someone on a river by punt 乘方头平底船; 用方头平底船载运: *We were punting up the river.* 我们正撑着方头平底船溯河而上。

punt·er /ˈpʌntɚ; ˈpʌntə/ *n* [C] **1** *BrE informal* someone who makes a BET (=risks money) on the result of a horse race etc【英, 非正式】〔赛马等的〕赌徒: *a regular punter* 一个经常赌博的人 **2** *BrE informal* someone who uses a product or a service; customer【英, 非正式】顾客: *You've got to try to please the punters.* 你得尽量让顾客满意。 **3** the player who punts the ball in American football〔美式橄榄球中的〕踢悬空球的队员

pu·ny /ˈpjunɪ; ˈpjuːni/ *adj* **1** small, thin, and weak 弱小的, 瘦小的: *a puny little guy* 瘦小的人 **2** unimpressive and ineffective 质量差的; 微薄的; 无效的: *my own puny attempts at humour* 我收效甚微的幽默 —**puniness** *n* [U]

pup¹ /pʌp; pʌp/ *n* [C] **1** a young dog; a PUPPY 小狗, 幼犬: *a spaniel pup* 西班牙猎犬幼崽 **2** a young SEAL¹ (1) or OTTER 小海豹; 小水獭: *seal pups* 小海豹 **3** *old-fashioned* an insulting word for a young man who is rude or too confident【过时】小崽子〔侮辱性词语〕: *Don't you threaten me, you young pup!* 你别威胁我, 你这小兔崽子! **4 be sold a pup** *BrE old-fashioned* to be tricked into buying something that is worthless or useless【英, 过时】被欺骗购买了无价值[无用]的东西

pup² *v* [I] *technical* to give birth to pups【术语】〔狗等〕生幼崽

pu·pa /ˈpjupə; ˈpjuːpə/ *n plural* **pupas** or **pupae** /-pi; -piː/ [C] an insect in the middle stages of its development when it is protected inside a special cover〔昆虫的〕蛹 —**pupal** *adj*: *in the pupal stage* 在蛹的阶段

pu·pate /ˈpjupet; pjuːˈpeɪt/ *v* [I] *technical* to become a pupa【术语】化蛹, 变成蛹

pu·pil /ˈpjupḷ; ˈpjuːpəl/ *n* [C] **1** *especially BrE* someone who is being taught, especially a child【尤英】学生, 〔尤指〕小学生: *This school has about 500 pupils.* 这所学校大约有500名学生。| *I teach private pupils on Wednesdays.* 我星期三去当家庭教师。 **2** the small black round area in the middle of your eye 瞳孔 —see picture at 参见 EYE¹ 图 [2] [1]

pup·pet /ˈpʌpɪt; ˈpʌpɪ̣t/ *n* [C] **1** a model of a person or animal that you can move by pulling wires or strings, or by putting your hand inside it〔牵线〕木偶; 〔套在手上操纵的〕布袋木偶, 手套式木偶: *a puppet show* 木偶戏 **2** a person or organization that has lost their independent position and allows someone else to control them 受他人操纵的人[组织]; 傀儡: *She's just a puppet of the management.* 她只是资方的傀儡。| **puppet government/regime** (=a government controlled by a more powerful country or organization) 傀儡政府/政权

puppet〔牵线〕木偶

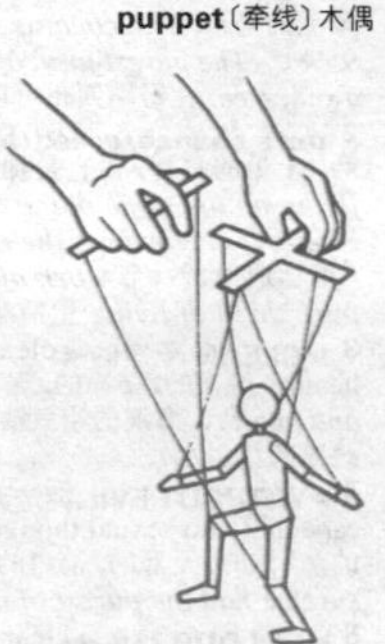

pup·pe·teer /ˌpʌpɪˈtɪr; ˌpʌpɪ̣ˈtɪə/ *n* [C] someone who performs with puppets 演木偶戏的人; 操纵木偶的人

pup·py /ˈpʌpɪ; ˈpʌpi/ *n* [C] **1** a young dog 小狗, 幼犬 **2** *old-fashioned* a young man who is rude or too confident【过时】无礼的年轻男人, 自负的年轻男子 [3]

puppy fat /ˈ·· ·/ *n* [U] *BrE informal* fat that children have on their bodies that they usually lose as they get older【英, 非正式】〔长大后通常消失的〕少年期肥胖

puppy love /ˈ·· ·/ *n* [U] a young boy's or girl's love for someone, which people do not regard as serious〔少男、少女的〕幼稚的迷恋, 不成熟的爱, 少年初恋: *It's only puppy love; he'll grow out of it.* 那只是少年初恋; 他长大后会清醒的。

pur·blind /ˈpɝˌblaɪnd; ˈpɜːblaɪnd/ *adj formal or literary* stupid or dull【正式或文】愚蠢的, 迟钝的; 笨的

Pur·cell /ˈpɝsḷ; ˈpɜːsəl/, **Henry** (1659-95) an English COMPOSER who wrote the OPERA *Dido and Aeneas* 普赛尔〔(1659-1695), 英国作曲家。作品有歌剧《狄朵与埃涅阿斯》〕

pur·chase¹ /ˈpɝtʃəs; ˈpɜːtʃɪ̣s/ *v* [T] **1** *formal* to buy something, especially something big or expensive【正式】购买, 采购〔尤指大或贵的物品〕: *a loan to purchase a new car* 购买一辆新汽车的贷款 **2** *literary* to gain something but only by losing something else【文】〔以某种代价〕换得: *They purchased life at the expense of honour.* 他们以牺牲名誉为代价换得了生命。—**purchasable** *adj* [3] [3]

purchase² *n* **1** [C,U] *formal* the act of buying something【正式】购买, 采购: *Fill in the date of purchase.* 填上购买日期。| *The company spent a lot on expansion including the purchase of a large warehouse.* 这家公司为扩大规模花费了很多, 其中包括购买了一个大型仓库。| **make a purchase** (=buy something) 购买 —see also 另见 HIRE PURCHASE —see graph at 参见 BUY¹ 图表 **2** [C usually plural 一般用复数] *formal* something that has been bought【正式】购买的物品, 购得物: *Do you wish us to deliver your purchases?* 您买的东西要我们送货吗? **3 on special** [3] [3]

purchase being sold at a cheaper price than usual 特价出售: *These boots are on special purchase.* 这些靴子特价出售。**4** [singular,U] *formal* a firm hold with your hands or feet【正式】〔手或脚的〕抓拿处, 搭脚处, 支点: *I tried to gain a purchase on the narrow ledge.* 我力图在狭窄的边缘处找到一个落脚点。

purchase price /ˈ·· ·/ *n* [singular] *formal* the price that has to be paid if you want to buy something【正式】购买价: *We need to borrow 80% of the purchase price.* 我们需要借贷购买价的八成。

pur·chas·er /ˈpɝtʃəsɚ; ˈpɜːtʃɪ̣sə/ *n* [C] *formal* the person who buys something【正式】购买者, 买主

purchasing pow·er /ˈ··· ˌ··/ *n* [U] **1** the amount of money that a person or group has available to spend compared to other people〔个人或集团的〕购买力: *Widespread wage rises result in increased purchasing power.* 工资的普遍上涨导致了购买力的增加。**2** the value of a unit of money considered in terms of how much you can buy with it〔货币的〕购买力: *The purchasing power of the dollar has declined.* 美元的购买力下降了。

pur·dah /ˈpɝdə; ˈpɜːdə/ *n* [U] **1** the custom, especially among Muslim people, according to which women stay in their home or cover their faces so that they cannot be seen by men〔尤指穆斯林的〕深闺制度〔妇女闭门不出或以面纱蒙脸不让男人窥见容貌〕**2 in purdah a)** women who are in purdah live according to this custom〔妇女〕按深闺制度生活的 **b)** staying away from other people 不与人交往的

S3 W3 **pure** /pjʊr; pjʊə/ *adj*

1 ►NOT MIXED 非混合的◄ not mixed with anything else 纯的, 纯净的: *Is this sweater made of pure wool?* 这件毛线衫是纯羊毛的吗? | *The cocaine was 95% pure.* 这种可卡因的纯度是95%。| *The purest form of the southern accent can be heard in Tennessee.* 在田纳西州可以听到最纯正的南方口音。

2 pure chance/greed/hell etc complete chance etc 纯属碰巧/十足的贪婪/简直是地狱等: *By pure chance my boss was flying on the same plane as me.* 我老板和我乘坐同一架飞机纯属碰巧。| *"How was the exam?" "Pure hell!"* "考试怎么样?" "糟糕透顶!" | *a work of pure genius* 完全是天才之作 | *the pure thrill of living* 生活激动人心的精粹之处

3 ►CLEAN 干净的◄ clean, without anything harmful or unhealthy 纯净的, 洁净的, 无有害物质的: *The air by the sea is pure and healthy.* 海滨的空气洁净, 有益健康。| *pure drinking water* 纯净的饮用水

4 ►WITHOUT EVIL 纯洁无邪的◄ having no evil ideas or plans, especially no sexual thoughts or experience; INNOCENT[1] (4) 纯洁的, 贞洁的, 无邪的, 清白的: *a pure young girl* 纯洁的少女 | *I'm sure he had the purest of motives.* 我相信他的动机非常单纯。

5 ►COLOUR 颜色◄ clear and not mixed with other colours 纯正的, 无杂色的: *a cloudless sky of the purest blue* 碧蓝无云的天空

6 ►SOUND 声音◄ very clear and beautiful to hear 纯正的, 清晰而优美的: *a pure note* 纯音 | *a lovely pure soprano* 优美而纯正的女高音

7 ►ART 艺术◄ a pure form of art is done exactly according to an accepted standard or pattern〔艺术〕精纯的

8 as pure as the driven snow an expression meaning morally perfect, often used jokingly to describe someone who is not like this at all 像白雪一样纯洁; 〔道德上〕完美无瑕〔常谑指与此根本不符的人〕

9 pure and simple *especially spoken* used to say that there is only one reason for something【尤口】完全是, 不折不扣的〔用来指某事只有唯一的原因〕: *The mistake was due to carelessness, pure and simple.* 这个错误完全是出于粗心造成的。

10 pure science/mathematics etc work done in science etc in order to increase our knowledge of it rather than to make practical use of it 纯科学/理论数学等: *pure and applied research* 理论和应用研究 —compare 比较 APPLIED —see also 另见 IMPURE, PURELY, PURIFY, PURITY —**pureness** *n* [U]

pure·blood·ed /ˌpjʊrˈblʌdɪd; ˌpjʊəˈblʌdɪ̣d◄/ *adj* with parents, grandparents etc from only one group or race of people, with no mixture of other groups 纯血统的

pure·bred /ˈpjʊrˌbrɛd; ˈpjʊəbred/ *adj* coming from only one breed of animal with no mixture of other breeds〔动物〕纯种的: *purebred Irish wolfhounds* 纯种爱尔兰猎狼犬 —compare 比较 PEDIGREE[2], THOROUGHBRED (1) —**purebred** *n* [C]

pu·ree **purée** /pjʊˈre; ˈpjʊəreɪ/ *n* [C,U] food that is boiled or crushed until it is a soft mass that is almost liquid〔经烹煮捣压制成的〕酱, 泥, 糊: *apple puree* 苹果泥 | *tomato puree* 番茄酱 —**puree, purée** *v* [T]

S2 W3 **pure·ly** /ˈpjʊrlɪ; ˈpjʊəli/ *adv* **1** completely and only, without anything else being involved 完全地, 纯粹地, 仅仅: *a decision that was taken for purely political reasons* 纯粹出于政治原因而作出的决定 | *I bumped into Sally purely by chance.* 我碰到萨莉纯属偶然。**2 purely and simply** used to emphasize that only one reason or purpose is involved in a situation or decision 完全是〔为了〕; 纯粹是〔因为〕: *I can tell you now, I'm doing it purely and simply for the money.* 我现在可以告诉你, 我做这件事完全是为了钱。

pur·ga·tive /ˈpɝgətɪv; ˈpɜːgətɪv/ *n* [C] a medicine or food that makes your BOWELS empty themselves 泻药, 能通便的食物 —**purgative** *adj*: *Figs often have a purgative effect.* 无花果通常有通便的效用。

pur·ga·tory /ˈpɝgəˌtɔrɪ; ˈpɜːgətəri/ *n* [U] **1 Purgatory** a place where, according to Roman Catholic beliefs, the souls of dead people must suffer for the bad things they did, until they are pure enough to enter heaven〔罗马天主教教义中的〕涤罪所, 炼狱 **2** *humorous* a place, situation, or time when you suffer a lot【幽默】受苦受难〔的地方〕: *It's purgatory listening to Ben trying to play the violin!* 听本练习拉小提琴简直是活受罪! —**purgatorial** /ˌpɝgəˈtɔrɪəl; ˌpɜːgəˈtɔːriəl◄/ *adj*

purge[1] /pɝdʒ; pɜːdʒ/ *v* [T] **1** to force your opponents or people who disagree with you to leave an organization or place, often by using violence 清除, 清洗, 肃清〔对手或反对者〕: **purge sth of sb/sth** *an attempt to purge the region of ethnic minorities* 把少数民族清除出这一地区的企图 | **purge sb/sth from sth** *purging dissidents from the party* 把不同政见者清除出党 **2** *literary* to get rid of your bad feelings such as hatred【文】消除, 涤除〔仇恨等不良情绪〕: **purge sb/sth of sth** *It took her months to purge herself of her feelings of guilt.* 她花了好几个月才消除自己的内疚感。| **purge sth from sth** *You must purge this hatred from your soul.* 你必须涤除灵魂中的这种仇恨。**3** *old-fashioned* to take a medicine to clear all the waste from your BOWELS【过时】〔服药〕使〔肠〕泻清, 使通便

purge[2] *n* [C] **1** an action to remove your opponents or people who disagree with you from an organization or place, often using violence〔通常使用暴力的〕清洗行动; 整肃: *The new president carried out a purge of disloyal army officers.* 新总统对不忠心的军官进行了清洗。| *the Stalinist purges of the 1930s* 20世纪30年代斯大林的清洗行动 **2** *old-fashioned* a medicine that clears all the waste from your BOWELS【过时】泻药

pu·ri·fi·ca·tion /ˌpjʊrəfəˈkeʃən; ˌpjʊərɪ̣fɪ̣ˈkeɪʃən/ *n* [U] **1** a process that removes the dirty or unwanted parts from something 净化; 提纯: *a water purification plant* 水净化厂 **2** acts or ceremonies to remove evil from someone 涤罪〔仪式〕: *ritual purification* 涤罪仪式

pu·ri·fy /ˈpjʊrəˌfaɪ; ˈpjʊərɪ̣faɪ/ *v* **purified, purifying** [T] **1** to remove the dirty or unwanted parts from something 使纯净, 净化: *The liquid is purified by passing it through charcoal.* 这种液体经由炭过滤后得到了净化。**2** to get rid of evil from your soul 净化〔灵魂〕 —**purifier** *n* [C] *a water purifier* 水净化器

Pu·rim /ˈpʊrɪm; ˈpʊərɪm/ a Jewish religious holiday which celebrates the time when Esther saved the Jewish people from being killed by their Persian rulers in the 5th century BC. 普珥节, 普林节〔一犹太宗教节日, 纪念公元前5世纪以斯帖从波斯统治者手中拯救犹太同胞这一事迹〕

pur·ist /ˈpjʊrɪst; ˈpjʊərɪ̣st/ *n* [C] someone who has very strong ideas about what is correct, for example in matters of grammar, art, or music〔在语法、艺术、音乐上〕力求纯正者, 纯粹主义者: *The purists won't like it but opera on TV certainly brings in the audiences.* 纯粹派不会喜欢这么做, 但电视上播出歌剧的确吸引了观众。—**purism** *n* [U]

pu·ri·tan /ˈpjʊrətn; ˈpjʊərɪ̣tən/ *n* [C] **1** someone who has very strict moral standards and thinks that pleasure is unnecessary or wrong 主张过清教徒式生活的人〔道德标准严格, 认为享乐没有必要或是错误的〕**2 Puritan** a member of a Protestant religious group in the 16th and 17th centuries, who wanted to make religion simpler 清教徒〔16世纪和17世纪新教一教派成员, 主张简化宗教仪式〕 —**puritan** also 又作 **Puritan** *adj*: *a Puritan background* 清教徒出身背景 | *puritan beliefs* 清教徒式的信仰

pu·ri·tan·i·cal /ˌpjʊrəˈtænɪkl; ˌpjʊərɪ̣ˈtænɪkəl/ *adj* having extreme attitudes about religion and moral behaviour 对宗教和道德行为持极端态度的, 清教徒式的: *a puritanical father who wouldn't let his children watch television* 不让孩子看电视的清教徒式的父亲 —**puritanically** /-klɪ; -kli/ *adv*

pu·ri·tan·is·m /ˈpjʊrətnɪzəm; ˈpjʊərɪ̣tənɪzəm/ *n* [U] **1** a way of living according to very strict rules, especially concerning religion and moral behaviour〔尤指在宗教或道德行为上〕非常拘谨的生活方式, 清教徒式的生活方式 **2 Puritanism** the beliefs and practices of the Puritans 清教主义〔指清教徒的教义和行为〕

pu·ri·ty /ˈpjurətɪ; ˈpjʊərɪ̥ti/ *n* [U] the quality or state of being pure 纯; 纯洁; 纯正; 纯粹: *Strict controls are needed to ensure the purity of herbal drugs.* 需要严格的控制手段来保证草药的纯度。—opposite 反义词 IMPURITY

purl¹ /pɝl; pɜːl/ *v* [I,T] to use the purl stitch when you KNIT (=make clothes from wool) 用反针编织

purl² *n* [U] one of the types of stitches that you use when you KNIT (=make clothes from wool) 〔编织中的〕反针, 倒针

pur·lieus /ˈpɝluz; ˈpɜːljuːz/ *n* [plural] *literary* the area in and around a place【文】邻近地区; 〔某处的〕周围

pur·loin /pɝˋlɔɪn; pɜːˈlɔɪn/ *v* [T] *formal or houmorous* to steal or borrow something without permission【正式或幽默】偷窃; 未经允许借〔某物〕: *Marek managed to purloin a copy of the house key.* 马雷克设法偷配了一把那房子的钥匙。

pur·ple /ˈpɝpl̩; ˈpɜːpəl/ *n* [U] **1** a dark colour that is a mixture of red and blue 紫色 —see picture on page A5 参见 A5 页图 **2 purple with rage/purple in the face etc** very red in the face as a result of being angry or embarrassed 由于生气[尴尬]而脸红 **3 purple passage/prose/patch** a piece of writing that has a grander style 辞藻华丽的段落/风格华丽的散文/华而不实的章句 **4 born to the purple** *literary* born into a high social class or position【文】生于帝王之家, 生于显贵之家 —**purple** *adj*

Purple Heart /ˌ·· ˈ·/ *n* [C] a special MEDAL given to US soldiers who have been wounded in battle 〔美国授予作战中负伤者的〕紫心勋章

purple heart *n* [C] *informal* a PILL containing an illegal drug that gives you a feeling of energy and excitement【非正式】紫心丸〔一种兴奋药丸〕

pur·plish /ˈpɝplɪʃ; ˈpɜːplɪʃ/ *adj* slightly purple 略带紫色的: *purplish blue* 略带紫色的蓝色

pur·port¹ /pɝˋpɔrt; pɜːˈpɔːt/ *v* [I,T] **purport to be/be purported to be** *formal* to claim to be something, and give the impression that it is true, even if it is not【正式】声称是…, 据称是…; 像是…: *The letter is purported to be a secret agreement between the president and the general.* 这封信据称是总统和将军之间的秘密协议。

pur·port² /ˈpɝpɔrt; ˈpɜːpɔːt/ *n* [U] *formal* the general meaning of what someone says【正式】〔某人言论的〕大意, 主旨: **[+of]** *The purport of her remarks was clear.* 她的话意思很清楚。

[S] 1 [W] 1 **pur·pose¹** /ˈpɝpəs; ˈpɜːpəs/ *n*

1 ▶WHAT STH IS SUPPOSED TO DO 目的; 用途◀ [C] the thing that an event, process, or activity is supposed to achieve, or the job that something is supposed to do 目的; 用途 —see 见 REASON¹ (USAGE): **[+of]** *The purpose of this meeting is to elect a new committee.* 这次会议的目的是选举新的委员会。| *What is the purpose of the little red button?* 这个小红按钮的用途是什么? | **the purpose of doing sth** *The sole purpose of conducting a business is to make money.* 做生意的唯一目的是赚钱。| **serve a purpose** (=have a particular purpose, or help you achieve a purpose) 起到某种作用; 帮助达到某个目的 *The discussion serves a twin purpose – instruction and feedback.* 这次讨论有双重的作用——指导和反馈。| *No useful purpose will be served by reopening the murder enquiry.* 对这次谋杀重新进行调查没什么用处。

2 on purpose deliberately 故意(地), 有意(地): *Jack's been really annoying me and I think he's doing it on purpose.* 杰克一直让我很烦, 我想他是故意那样干的。

3 ▶PLAN 计划◀ [C] *formal* an intention or a plan【正式】意图, 目的; 计划: *Tom went for a walk, with no definite purpose in mind.* 汤姆漫无目的地出去走走。| **purpose in doing sth** *My main purpose in setting up the experiment was to obtain fresh data.* 我设立该项实验的主要目的是获取新的数据。

4 ▶AIM 目标◀ [U] the feeling of having an aim in life 生活目标: *I need to find meaning and purpose in my life.* 我需要找出我生活的意义和目的。

5 for all practical purposes also 又作 **for all intents and purposes** used to say that something may not exactly be true but it is true in general 实际上; 大体上: *She became for all practical purposes, a director of the company.* 她实际上成了这个公司的董事。

6 for the purposes of used to say that someone or something will be considered in a particular way in a discussion, document etc 出于…目的, 为了…: *For tax purposes you will be treated as a married couple.* 报税时你们将被当作夫妻对待。

7 serve its purpose if something serves its purpose, it does what you intended it to do 起到应有的作用: *Our holiday had served its purpose; we both felt thoroughly relaxed.* 我们的假期已起到了它应有的作用, 我们两个都感到十分轻松自在。

8 to good purpose/to no purpose *formal* with good results or with no results【正式】大有效果/毫无效果: *Clara has used her musical talents to good purpose.* 克拉拉充分发挥了她的音乐天赋。

9 to the purpose *old-fashioned*【过时】useful or helpful 有用的, 有益的, 有帮助的 —see also 另见 **accidentally on purpose** (ACCIDENTALLY (2)), PURPOSELY, CROSS-PURPOSES

purpose² *v* [T] *old use* to intend to do something【旧】意欲, 打算: *Drake purposed to voyage around the globe.* 德雷克打算进行环球航行。

purpose-built /ˌ·· ˈ·◂/ *adj BrE* designed and made for a particular purpose【英】为某用途特制的, 特别为某一目的设计的: *purpose-built toilets for disabled people* 专为残疾人设计的厕所

pur·pose·ful /ˈpɝpəsfəl; ˈpɜːpəsfəl/ *adj* having a clear aim or purpose; determined 有目的的, 有明确目标的; 坚决的, 果断的: *a purposeful man who wouldn't worry about who he hurt* 一个不会因伤害了谁而烦忧的、志在必得的人 —**purposefully** *adv* —**purposefulness** *n* [U]

pur·pose·less /ˈpɝpəslɪs; ˈpɜːpəsləs/ *adj* not having a clear aim or purpose 无目的的, 无目标的: *a purposeless existence on the streets of London* 在伦敦街头毫无目标的生活 —**purposelessly** *adv* —**purposelessness** *n* [U]

pur·pose·ly /ˈpɝpəslɪ; ˈpɜːpəsli/ *adv formal* deliberately【正式】故意地: *a purposely provocative comment* 故意挑衅的评论

purr /pɝ; pɜː/ *v* **1** [I] if a cat purrs, it makes a soft, low sound in its throat to show that it is pleased 〔猫愉快时〕发出呜呜声: *A big grey tomcat sat in his lap purring contentedly.* 一只灰色的雄性大猫坐在他腿上, 满足地呜呜叫着。**2** [I] if the engine of a vehicle or machine purrs, it works perfectly and makes a quiet smooth sound 〔车辆或机器的发动机顺利运作时〕发出低沉的声音, 发出隆隆声: *The big Bentley purred along the wide road.* 那辆大宾利车行驶在宽阔的公路上, 发出低沉的震颤声。**3** [I,T] if someone purrs, they speak in a soft, low, and SEXY voice 〔人〕以轻柔低沉的声音说: *"Are you doing anything tonight?" she purred.* "你今晚有什么事吗?" 她娇声说。—**purr** *n* [C]

purses 钱包

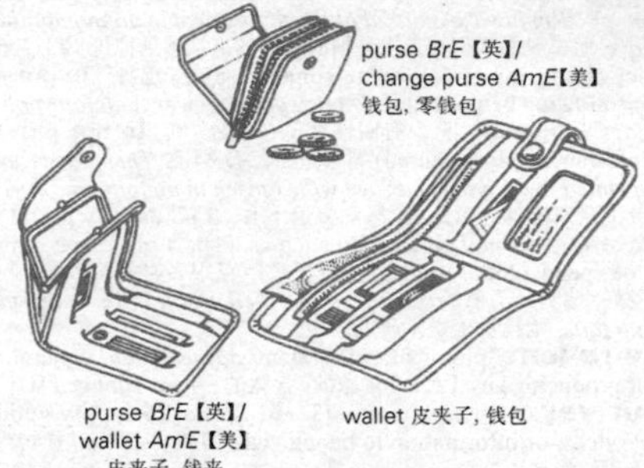

purse¹ /pɝs; pɜːs/ *n* **1** [C] *BrE* a small container for keeping coins in, made of leather, cloth, plastic etc, used especially by women【英】〔装零钱的〕钱包〔尤指女式钱包〕; CHANGE PURSE *AmE*【美】: *She took a pound coin out of her purse.* 她从钱包里拿出一枚一英镑的硬币。| *Hayley snapped her purse shut.* 海利啪嗒一声合上钱包。**2** [C] *BrE* a small flat leather container divided into parts for keeping paper money, cards, coins etc in, and used especially by women【英】〔装钞票、卡片、零钱等用的〕皮夹子, 钱夹〔尤指女式钱夹〕; WALLET *AmE*【美】: *Check my purse. I think I've only got a twenty pound note.* 查看一下我的钱夹, 我想我只有一张 20 镑的钞票。**3** [C] *AmE* a bag, often made of leather, in which a woman carries her money and personal things【美】〔女用〕手提包, 手袋; HANDBAG *BrE*【英】: *She reached in her purse and took out a mirror.* 她把手伸进手提包内取出一面镜子。—see picture at 参见 BAG¹ 图 **4** [singular] *formal* the amount of money that a person, organization, or country has available to spend【正式】〔个人、组织或国家的〕备用金, 可以使用的资金, 财力: *It was an expense that my purse could not afford.* 我支付不起那项费用。| **the public purse** (=money controlled by a government) 国库 *These defence commitments are a continuing drain on the public purse.* 这些防御义务使国库资金不断流失。**5** [C] the amount of money given to someone who [S] 3

wins a BOXING match〔给予拳击赛获胜者的〕奖金 **6 hold/control the purse strings** to control the money in a family, company etc 控制〔家庭、公司等的〕开支; 掌管钱财: *Maureen definitely holds the purse strings.* 莫琳毫无疑问掌管着开支。

purse² *v* **purse your lips** to bring your lips together tightly into a small circle, especially to show disapproval or doubt 撅起〔嘴唇〕: *Mrs Biddell pursed her lips and stared.* 比德尔夫人撅起嘴瞪眼看着。

purs·er /ˈpɝsɚ; ˈpɜːsə/ *n* [C] an officer who is responsible for the money on a ship and is also in charge of the passengers' rooms, comfort etc〔客轮上掌管账目、管理旅客房间等的〕事务长

P

pur·su·ance /pɚˈsuəns; pəˈsjuːəns/ *n* **in pursuance of** *formal*【正式】**a)** with the aim of doing or achieving something 为了做…; 为了取得…: *Staff voted to take industrial action in pursuance of a better deal.* 全体职工投票决定采取劳工行动以期得到更好的待遇。**b)** during the process of doing or achieving something 在做某事的过程中, 在完成某事时

S3 W2 **pur·sue** /pɚˈsu; pəˈsjuː/ *v* [T] **1** to continue doing an activity or trying to achieve something over a long period of time 追求; 继续进行: *Kristin pursued her acting career with great determination.* 克里斯汀意志坚定地追求她的表演事业。**2 pursue the matter/argument/question** to continue trying to ask about, find out about, or persuade someone about a particular subject 追究某件事/继续争论/追查某问题: *Janet did not dare pursue the matter too far.* 珍妮特不敢深入追查那件事。**3** to chase or follow someone or something, in order to catch them, attack them etc〔尤指为抓捕、袭击等而〕紧随…之后; 追捕, 追击: *Briggs ran across the field with one officer pursuing him.* 布里格斯跑过田地, 一名警官正在追捕他。**4** to keep trying to persuade someone to have a relationship with you 追求〔某人〕

pur·su·er /pɚˈsuɚ; pəˈsjuːə/ *n* [C] someone or something that is chasing you 追赶者, 追捕者〔指人或物〕: *Luckily, Joey managed to outrun his pursuers.* 幸运的是, 乔伊比追赶他的人跑得快, 逃脱了。

pur·suit /pɚˈsut; pəˈsjuːt/ *n* **1** [singular] the act of trying to achieve something in a determined way 追求: [**+of**] *the right of all people to the pursuit of liberty and happiness* 所有人追求自由和幸福的权利 | **in pursuit of** (=while trying to get) 在追求…时 *I'm always amazed at the things people do in pursuit of love.* 我总是为人们在追求爱情时所做的事情感到惊讶。**2** [U] the act of chasing or following someone 追赶, 追踪: **in pursuit** (=following behind) 追赶 *There were no fewer than four police cars in pursuit.* 至少有四辆警车在追赶。| **in hot pursuit** (=following close behind) 紧紧追赶, 穷追不舍 *The quarterback sprinted toward the end zone with Jansen in hot pursuit.* 那名四分卫全速向球门区跑去, 詹森穷追不舍。**3** [C usually plural 一般用复数] *formal* an activity such as a sport or HOBBY, which you spend a lot of time doing【正式】〔花很多时间从事的〕业余爱好, 嗜好; 消遣活动: *She immersed herself in academic pursuits.* 她投身于学术研究之中。

pu·ru·lent /ˈpjurələnt; ˈpjʊərələnt/ *adj technical* containing or producing PUS【术语】化脓的; 含脓的 —**purulence** *n* [U]

pur·vey /pɚˈve; pɜːˈveɪ/ *v* [T **+to**] *formal* to supply goods, services, or information to people【正式】提供, 供应〔货物、服务或信息〕

pur·vey·or /pɚˈveɚ; pɜːˈveɪə/ *n* [C usually plural 一般用复数] *formal* someone who supplies information, goods, or services to people, especially as a business【正式】承办商, 供应者, 提供者: *purveyors of farmyard fresh poultry* 农场鲜禽肉供应商

pur·view /ˈpɝvju; ˈpɜːvjuː/ *n* **within/outside the purview of** *formal* within or outside the limits of someone's job, activity, or knowledge【正式】〔工作、活动、知识等的〕范围[权限]之内/之外: *This matter comes within the purview of the Department of Health.* 这件事属于卫生部的管辖范围。

pus /pʌs; pʌs/ *n* [U] a thick yellowish liquid produced in an infected part of your body 脓: *Pus was oozing out of the wound.* 脓正从伤口渗出。

S1 W2 **push¹** /puʃ; pʊʃ/ *v*

1 ►MOVE 移动◄ [I,T] to make someone or something move by using your hands, arms, shoulders etc to put pressure on them 推; 推动: *It's still stuck – you'll have to push harder.* 那东西还卡着 —— 你得使劲推。| *When I give the signal, I want you all to push.* 我发出信号时, 你们就一起推。| **push sb/sth** *Johnson was penalised for pushing another player.* 约翰逊因推人犯规而被判罚。| **push sb/sth up/across/away etc** *They were trying to push me into the water.* 他们正试图把我推入水中。| *He pushed away his plate when he had finished.* 他吃完后把盘子推开。| **push the door open/shut** *I slowly pushed the door open.* 我慢慢推开门。—see picture on page A21 参见 A21 页图

2 ►BUTTON/SWITCH 按钮/开关◄ [I,T] to press a button, SWITCH etc, especially in order to make a piece of equipment start working 按下〔按钮、开关等〕: *You just push that button there, and the coffee comes out here.* 你只需按一下那边的开关, 咖啡就会从这里出来。

3 ►TRY TO GET PAST SB 设法从某人旁边经过◄ [I, T always+adv/prep] to use your hands, arms, shoulders etc to make someone move, especially so that you can get past them 挤, 推挤: *There's no need to push. There are enough tickets for everyone.* 没有必要推挤 —— 有足够的票给每个人。| **push past/through** *Jackson pushed past the journalists and escaped in his limousine.* 杰克逊从记者群中挤出来, 坐上他的高级轿车逃走了。| **push your way towards/across etc** *She pushed her way to the front of the crowd.* 她挤到人群的前面。

4 ►ENCOURAGE/PERSUADE 鼓励/劝说◄ [T] to encourage or persuade someone to do something that they do not want to do 鼓励, 力劝〔某人做其不想做的事〕: **push sb to do sth** *Her husband keeps pushing her to accept the job.* 她丈夫一直劝她接受这份工作。| **push sb into doing sth** *My parents pushed me into going to college.* 我父母力劝我上大学。

5 ►WORK HARD 努力工作◄ [T] to make someone work very hard 使〔某人〕努力工作: *The teachers don't seem to push these kids very hard.* 老师们好像对这些孩子督促不够。| **push yourself** *He's been pushing himself too much.* 他一直在卖命工作。

6 ►DRUGS 毒品◄ [T] *informal* to sell illegal drugs【非正式】贩卖〔毒品〕—see also 另见 PUSHER

7 ►ADVERTISE 做广告◄ [T] *informal* to try to sell more of a product by advertising it a lot【非正式】〔通过大量广告〕推销〔商品〕

8 ►IDEAS/OPINIONS 观点/意见◄ [T] to try to make people accept your ideas or opinions, especially by talking about them a lot 竭力使别人接受〔自己的观点或意见〕; 推销, 兜售〔观点或意见〕: *I wish you'd stop pushing all this political rubbish.* 我希望你不要再兜售这种政治垃圾了。

9 push the boat out *BrE informal* to spend a lot of money on something because you want to make sure that it is enjoyable, successful etc【英, 非正式】不惜费用地享乐[庆祝]

10 push your luck/push it *informal* to stupidly do something again, taking a risk that you will avoid problems because you have done it successfully before【非正式】〔因曾经成功而〕再次冒险; 得寸进尺; 想再交好运: *Look, just don't push it! I've had about enough of your criticism!* 哎, 别再得寸进尺了! 我已经受够了你的批评!

11 push sth to the back of your mind to try to forget about an unpleasant feeling or situation 把某事抛在脑后, 忘记〔不愉快的感觉或情况〕: *I think you should push all these doubts to the back of your mind.* 我认为你应该把这些疑虑通通抛在脑后。

12 push the point *old-fashioned* to keep trying to make someone accept your opinion in a way that they find annoying【过时】〔令人讨厌地〕拼命劝说某人接受自己的观点 —see also 另见 PULL¹, PUSHED, PUSHING

push ahead *phr v* [I] to continue with a plan or activity, especially in a determined way〔尤指坚定地〕继续进行〔计划或活动〕, 大力推进: [**+with**] *After careful consideration they decided to push ahead with the deal.* 经过仔细考虑他们决定大力推动这项交易的实现。

push along *phr v* [I] *spoken* to leave a place【口】离开: *It's getting late, I think we should be pushing along.* 天晚了, 我们该走啦。—see also 另见 **push off** (PUSH¹)

push sb **around** also 又作 **push** sb **about** *BrE*【英】*phr v* [T] to give someone orders in a rude or threatening way 对〔某人〕发号施令; 摆布〔某人〕: *Who do you think you're pushing around? Do it yourself.* 你以为你在对谁发号施令? 你自己做吧。

push sth ↔ **aside** *phr v* [T] to try to forget about something, especially something unpleasant, so that you can give your attention to what you are doing 忘掉〔尤指不愉快的事情〕: *You just have to try and push these negative thoughts aside.* 你必须尽量抛开这些消极的想法。

push (sb) **for** sth *phr v* [T] to keep asking for something or trying to persuade people to do something, because you believe it is important or necessary 一再地要求〔某事物〕; 敦促〔某人〕做某事: *People living near the airport are pushing for new restrictions on night flights.* 住在机场附近的人们正强烈要求订立限制夜航班机的新规定。| *I'll have to push you for a decision.* 我将不得不敦促你作出决定。

push forward *phr v* **1** [I] to continue moving towards a place,

in spite of difficulties〔不顾困难〕继续前进: *As the army pushed forward, the death toll mounted.* 随着部队的推进, 死亡人数在增加。**2 push yourself forward** to try to make other people notice you 使他人注意到自己; 出风头: *If she's going to do well at school, she'll have to push herself forward more.* 要是她想在学校干得好, 她就得尽量让别人注意到自己。

push in 插队

queue *BrE*【英】/
line *AmE*【美】队

push in *phr v* [I] **1** to give advice, join in a conversation etc when you are not really involved〔在不相干的情况下〕给人劝告; 插话; 干预: *No, it didn't seem like you were pushing in or anything, just trying to help.* 不, 你这并不是好像在干预什么, 只是试图帮忙而已。**2** *BrE informal* to rudely and unfairly join a line of people, in front of other people who were already waiting【英, 非正式】插队, 挤到等候的队伍前面

push off *phr v* [I] **1** *spoken, especially BrE used to* tell someone rudely to go away【口, 尤英】走开〔用作不礼貌的命令语〕**2** *old-fashioned* to leave a place【过时】离开 —see also 另见 **push along** (PUSH[1]) **3** if a boat pushes off from the shore, it moves away from it〔船〕离岸

push on *phr v* [I] **1** to continue travelling somewhere, especially after you have had a rest〔尤指休息之后〕继续前行: *It was getting dark but we decided to push on a little further.* 天越来越黑了, 但我们决定继续往前走一段。**2** to continue doing an activity 继续〔做某事〕: [+with] *I'd better push on with my homework.* 我最好继续做我的作业。

push sb/sth ↔**over** *phr v* [T] to make someone or something fall to the ground by pushing them 把〔某人或某物〕推倒: *Several people had been pushed over in the rush for bargains.* 在抢购便宜货时有几个人被推倒了。

push sth ↔**through** *phr v* [T] to get a new law officially accepted 使〔新法律〕获得通过: *The White House made every effort to push the policy through Congress.* 白宫尽力使这项政策获得国会通过。

push sth ↔**up** *phr v* [T] **1** to make the amount, number, or value of something increase 使〔某物的数量、价值〕增加, 使上涨: *The war has pushed up oil prices.* 战争使石油价格上涨。**2** **be pushing up (the) daisies** *humorous* to be dead【幽默】死, 入土, 一命呜呼

push[2] *n*

1 ▶PUSHING MOVEMENT 推的动作◀ [C] the act of pushing or pressing something 推; 按: *With a gentle push, the car started moving down the slope.* 轻轻一推, 这辆车开始顺坡而下。| **give sb/sth a push** *He gave her a push to see if she was awake.* 他推了她一下, 看她是否醒着。| *If the door's stuck, just give it a push.* 如果门卡住, 推一下就行了。| **at the push of a button** (=used to emphasize how easy a machine is to use) 按一下按钮就行了〔用于强调机器容易操作〕*The liquidizer is marvellous, creating tasty soups at the push of a button.* 这种榨汁机非常棒, 只需按一下按钮就能做出美味的汤来。

2 ▶ENCOURAGEMENT 鼓励◀ [singular] a small amount of encouragement, persuasion, or help from someone else〔少许〕激励, 劝导, 帮助: *It looked like she would never go, but all she needed was a gentle push.* 她看起来好像决不会去, 其实只需稍稍一劝她也就去了。

3 ▶ATTACK/ATTEMPT 进攻/攻势◀ a) [C] a planned military attack into the area where the enemy is〔有计划的军事上的〕攻击, 推进: *The army has made another big push into enemy territory.* 大军对敌占区进行了又一次大规模进攻。**b)** [C] a determined and well-planned attempt to gain an advantage over your opponents in business, advertising etc〔生意、广告等方面为赢得优势而进行的〕努力: *The company has recently made a big push into the Japanese market.* 该公司最近大举向日本市场推进。

4 give sb the push *BrE informal*【英, 非正式】**a)** to make someone leave their job, especially because they have done something wrong〔尤指因犯了错误而〕解雇 **b)** to tell someone that you no longer want to have a loving or sexual relationship with them 与情人分手, 断绝关系

5 at a push *informal, especially BrE* if you can do something at a push, it will be difficult, but you will be able to do it【非正式, 尤英】真有必要时, 不得已时: *We have room for five people, maybe six at a push.* 我们有容纳五个人的空间, 万不得已的情况下或许可容纳六个人。

6 it'll be a push *spoken* used to say that something will be difficult because you do not have enough time to do it【口】因为没有足够的时间做而觉得某事困难: *I'll do my best, but it'll be a bit of a push.* 我会尽我所能, 但时间会有点紧迫。

7 if it comes to the push also 又作 **when push comes to shove** *spoken* used to say what you can do if you are forced to make a decision or take action【口】一旦情况紧急时; 当必须采取行动时; 当必须作出决定时: *When push comes to shove you can always borrow the extra money from the bank.* 如有急用, 你总能从银行借到额外的钱。

push-bike /ˈ· ·/ *n* [C] *BrE informal* a BICYCLE【英, 非正式】自行车, 脚踏车, 单车

push-but·ton /ˈ· ˌ··/ *adj* [only before noun 仅用于名词前] **1** operated by pressing a button with your finger 按钮式的: *The old car had a push-button starter.* 这辆旧汽车有个按钮式的启动装置。**2** using computers or electronic equipment rather than traditional methods 使用电脑的; 使用电子设备的: *push-button warfare* 电子化战争 | *the push-button piloting of a ship* 轮船的电子化领航

push-cart /ˈpʊʃˌkɑrt; ˈpʊʃkɑːt/ *n* [C] a large flat container like a box with wheels, used especially by people who sell goods in the street〔尤指街头小贩使用的〕手推车

push-chair /ˈpʊʃˌtʃɛr; ˈpʊʃ-tʃeə/ *n* [C] *BrE* a small folding seat on wheels, in which a young child sits and is pushed along【英】(折叠式) 轻便婴儿手推车; STROLLER *AmE*【美】—compare 比较 BABY CARRIAGE —see picture at 参见 PRAM 图

pushed /pʊʃt; pʊʃt/ *adj* [not before noun 不用于名词前] *informal*【非正式】**1 be pushed for** to have difficulty finding enough time, money etc〔时间或金钱等〕不足, 拮据: *I'm always rather pushed for money at the end of the month.* 每当月底, 我总是手头很紧。**2** too busy 太忙的: *I'd love to help, but I'm a bit pushed at the moment.* 我很愿意帮忙, 但我现在有点忙。**3 be (hard) pushed to do sth** to have a lot of difficulty doing something 做某事有很多困难: *You'll be hard pushed to find someone to type your essay for you now.* 现在你很难找到人为你打论文。

push·er /ˈpʊʃɚ; ˈpʊʃə/ *n* [C] *informal* someone who sells illegal drugs【非正式】毒品贩子 —compare 比较 PEDDLER (2) —see also 另见 PENPUSHER

push·ing /ˈpʊʃɪŋ; ˈpʊʃɪŋ/ *prep* **be pushing 18/30/60 etc** *usually spoken* to be nearly 18,30,60 years old etc【一般口】将近18/30/60岁等: *Sheila must be pushing 40 by now.* 希拉现在一定将近40岁了。

Push·kin /ˈpʊʃkɪn; ˈpʊʃkɪn/, **Al·ek·san·dr** /ˌælɪgˈzændɚ; ˌælɪgˈzɑːndə/ (1799-1837) one of Russia's greatest writers who wrote NOVELS, plays, and poetry, and greatly influenced the development of Russian literature. His best-known works are *Eugene Onegin* and *Boris Godunov.* 普希金〔(1799-1837), 俄国最伟大的作家之一。作品有小说、戏剧和诗歌, 对俄国文学的发展产生了重大影响。最著名的作品有《叶甫盖尼·奥涅金》和《鲍里斯·戈都诺夫》〕

push·o·ver /ˈpʊʃˌovɚ; ˈpʊʃˌəʊvə/ *n informal*【非正式】**be a pushover a)** to be easy to persuade, influence, or defeat 易被劝服[影响, 击败]的: *Duncan will soon see that I'm no pushover.* 邓肯将很快看到我不是容易对付的人。| [+for] *Mr Wasco is a pushover for blondes with green eyes.* 瓦斯科先生很容易被金发碧眼的女人迷住。**b)** to be very easy to do or win 容易做的, 容易取胜的: *The exam was a pushover.* 这次考试很容易。

push-start /ˈ· ·/ *v* [T] to push a vehicle in order to make the engine start 推车发动〔引擎〕—**push-start** *n* [C]

push-up /ˈ· ·/ *n* [C] *AmE* an exercise in which you lie on the floor on your front and push yourself up with your arms【美】俯卧撑; PRESS-UP *BrE*【英】

push·y /ˈpʊʃɪ; ˈpʊʃi/ *adj* so determined to succeed and to get what you want that you behave in a way that seems rude 急于求成的, 咄咄逼人的: *a pushy salesman* 拼命劝别人买东西的推销员—**pushily** *adv*—**pushiness** *n* [U]

pu·sil·lan·i·mous /ˌpjusl̩ˋænəməs; ˌpjuːsɪ̩ˈlænɪ̩məs/ *adj formal* frightened of taking even small risks【正式】怯懦的, 胆小的 —**pusillanimously** *adv* —**pusillanimity** /pjusləˋnɪmətɪ; ˌpjuːsɪ̩ləˈnɪmɪ̩ti/ *n* [U]

puss /pʊs; pʊs/ *n* [usually singular 一般用单数] **1** *informal* a name for a cat, or a way of calling a cat【非正式】猫咪〔猫的名字或唤猫语〕: *Come here, puss, puss, puss!* 过来, 猫咪! **2** *AmE slang* face【美俚】脸: *a smack in the puss* 打一个耳光

Puss in Boots /ˌ· · ˈ·/ a FAIRY TALE about a clever cat who wore boots and did many tricks in order to make his owner rich《穿靴子的猫》,《长靴猫》〔一童话故事。故事中有一只穿着靴子的猫咪, 十分聪明, 为了让主人富有起来, 施用了不少计谋〕

pus·sy /ˋpʊsɪ; ˈpʊsi/ *n* [C] **1** also 又作 **pussy cat** /ˈ·· ·/ an informal word for a cat, used especially by or to children 猫咪〔儿语〕 **2** *taboo* a woman's sex organs【讳】女性(外)生殖器 **3** *AmE informal* an insulting word for a man who is weak or not brave【美, 非正式】懦夫, 脓包〔对于怯懦男人的侮辱性说法〕

pus·sy·foot /ˋpʊsɪˌfʊt; ˈpʊsifʊt/ also 又作 **pussyfoot around/about** *v* [I] *informal* to be too careful and frightened to do something, such as taking firm decisions or telling someone exactly what you think【非正式】缩手缩脚, 畏首畏尾; 优柔寡断: *Stop pussyfooting around, and tell me what he said!* 别再吞吞吐吐的, 告诉我他说了些什么!

pussy wil·low /ˈ·· ,··/ *n* [C,U] a tree with white flowers that are soft like fur 褪色柳

pus·tule /ˋpʌstʃʊl; ˈpʌstjuːl/ *n* [C] *technical* a small raised spot on your skin containing PUS (=a thick yellow liquid)【术语】小脓疱

put /pʊt; pʊt/ *v past tense* put *present participle* putting

① MOVE STH 移动某物
② CHANGE SB'S SITUATION 改变某人的境况
③ SAY/EXPRESS 说/表达
④ ASK FOR AN ANSWER/DECISION 要求答复/决定
⑤ ADD STH 加上某物
⑥ SEND SB SOMEWHERE 派某人到某处
⑦ PUT RIGHT/STRAIGHT 纠正/改正
⑧ STOP/END STH 停止/结束某事
⑨ IN ORDER OF IMPORTANCE/QUALITY 按重要性/质量的顺序
⑩ OTHER MEANINGS 其他意思
⑪ WRITE 写

① MOVE STH 移动某物

1 [T always+adv/prep] to move something from one place or position into another, especially using your hands 放; 放置: **put sth in/on/there etc** *Put those bags on the table.* 把那些包放在桌子上。| *You should put your hand over your mouth when you cough.* 你咳嗽时应用手捂住嘴。| *I can't remember where I put my keys.* 我记不起来把钥匙放在哪里。

② CHANGE SB'S SITUATION 改变某人的境况

2 [T always+adv/prep] to change someone's situation 改变〔某人〕的状态[境地, 局面]: *This was the shot that put Sampras into the semifinal.* 这是使桑普拉斯进入半决赛的一次抽球。| **put sb in an awkward position** (=make someone's situation difficult or embarrassing) 使某人处境困难[尴尬] *Paul's resignation has put us in an awkward position.* 保罗的辞职使我们处境困难。| **put sb out of a job/out of work** (=make them lose their job) 使某人失业 *Pit closures have put thousands of miners out of a job.* 煤矿关闭使成千上万的矿工失去了工作。| **put sb in a bad mood** (=make them feel annoyed) 使某人心情不好 *The long delay had put us all in a bad mood.* 长时间的延误使我们大家心情都不好。

3 put sb in command/charge/control to give someone authority over a group, activity, organization etc 使某人主管[负责]…: *Tom Pendlebury has been put in charge of the project.* 汤姆·彭德尔伯里奉命负责这项工程。

③ SAY/EXPRESS 说/表达

4 [T always+adv/prep] to express something using words in a particular way 说, 表达: **put sth well/cleverly/succinctly etc** *I thought her arguments were quite cleverly put.* 我认为她巧妙地表达了自己的论点。| *Well, since you put it like that, I can't really refuse.* 好, 既然你那么说, 我确实无法拒绝。| **as sb puts it** (=used to repeat what someone else has said) 正如某人所说 *Long-term planning is a waste of time because – as Keynes puts it – in the long term we're all dead.* 长期规划是浪费时间, 因为正如凯恩斯所说, 从长远来看, 我们总有一死。| **put sth into words** (=express a feeling or idea) 用语言表达某感觉[思想]

5 to put it bluntly *spoken* used to tell someone that you are going to say exactly what you think【口】坦率地说: *To put it bluntly, Robert's just not good enough for the job.* 坦率地说, 罗伯特不能胜任这份工作。

6 to put it mildly *spoken* used to say that a situation is actually worse than the way you are describing it【口】往轻处说: *We are, to put it mildly, in a mess.* 说得轻点, 我们正身处困境。

7 How can I put it? *spoken* used when what you are going to say might sound unpleasant or impolite【口】我该怎么说呢〔用于表示你要说的话可能听起来令人不愉快或不礼貌〕: *Derek's – how shall I put it – not very attractive.* 德里克 —— 我该怎么说呢 —— 不怎么有吸引力。

8 to put it another way used when trying to explain something in a different way and make it clearer 用另一种方式说, 换句话说: *Money makes money. To put it another way, the greater the investment, the greater the profit.* 钱能生钱, 换句话说, 投资越大, 利润越大。

④ ASK FOR AN ANSWER/DECISION 要求答复/决定

9 [T] to ask a question, especially when you want to get someone's opinion about something〔尤指为征求某人意见时〕提出〔问题〕: *After the break, you will be able to put your questions to the panel.* 短暂休息之后, 你们就可以向专题小组提问了。| **put it to sb** *I put it to you, Mr President, that these measures will not solve the problem of violent crime.* 总统先生请您考虑, 这些措施不能解决暴力犯罪问题。

10 put a proposition/proposal/case to to tell someone or a group of people about something and ask them to agree to it or make a decision about it 向…提出建议; 将提议交给…

⑤ ADD STH 加上某物

11 [T] to add something 加, 增加: *Put a little romance into your life.* 给你的生活增添一点浪漫。| *Just put a little more expression into it.* 对它再多投入些感情。

12 [T] to make money available to be used in a business, or add it to something such as a bank account 投资于; 投入; 加进; 存入〔银行账户〕

⑥ SEND SB SOMEWHERE 派某人到某处

13 [T always+adv/prep] to arrange for or order someone to go to a place for a particular purpose 安排[命令]某人去某处: **put sb in/on etc** *Putting troops into Rwanda is not an option.* 派部队进入卢旺达不是一个选择。

14 put sb on a train/plane etc to take someone to a plane, train etc to start a journey 把某人带上[送上]火车/飞机等

⑦ PUT RIGHT/STRAIGHT 纠正/改正

15 put sb straight/right to tell someone the true facts when they have made a mistake that annoys you 纠正[改正]某人的错误: *Let me put you straight on one thing, Andy's not a thief.* 让我纠正你一个错误, 安迪不是贼。

16 put sth straight to make something look clean and tidy 使某物看上去干净整洁, 把某物收拾[整理]好: *It took us all weekend to put the garden straight.* 我们花了一整个周末才收拾好花园。

17 put sth right to make a situation better, especially after

someone has made a mistake or behaved badly 改正, 纠正: *I'll put it right at once.* 我立即改过来。

⑧ STOP/END STH 停止/结束某事

18 put a stop to/put an end to to stop an activity that is harmful or unacceptable 结束, 终止〔有害或不能容忍的事〕; 使…停止: *There's too much money being wasted, and it's time we put a stop to it.* 浪费太多钱了, 是我们结束这种活动的时候了。
19 put paid to *BrE* to spoil and end your hopes or plans completely【英】使〔希望或计划〕成为泡影: *A car accident put paid to his chances of taking part in the race.* 一次汽车事故使他参加赛跑的机会成了泡影。

⑨ IN ORDER OF IMPORTANCE/QUALITY 按重要性/质量的顺序

20 [T always+adv/prep] to consider something as having a particular level of importance or quality 认为某事物具有某种重要性[品质]; 将某物看作[列为]: **put sb as/among/in etc** *I'd put Porto amongst the top ten European teams.* 我把波尔图队看作是欧洲十大强队之一。| **put sth first/before** *The job's important to him, but he puts his family first.* 这份工作对他来说很重要, 但他把自己的家庭放在首位。

⑩ OTHER MEANINGS 其他意思

21 put sth into action/effect/practice to start using a plan, idea, knowledge etc 把…付诸实践, 实施: *James was keen to put some of the things he had learned into practice.* 詹姆斯渴望把他学到的一些东西运用到实践中去。
22 put pressure on a) to make someone's situation difficult 使某人处境困难 **b)** to try to make someone do something 对某人施加压力
23 put energy/work/enthusiasm etc into to use a lot of energy etc when you are doing an activity 投入[付出]精力/劳动/热情等: *I hope the show's a success – they've put so much work into it.* 我希望这次演出成功——他们为之付出了很多心血。
24 put sth behind you to try to forget about an unpleasant event or experience and think about the future 忘掉〔不愉快的事情或经历〕, 把某事物抛诸脑后: *The team must put Saturday's defeat behind them and concentrate on tonight's game.* 全体队员必须忘掉星期六的失败而把心思集中在今晚的比赛上。
25 ►THROW 扔, 投◄ to throw a SHOT (=a heavy metal ball) in a sports competition 推〔铅球〕
26 put it there *spoken* used to tell someone to put their hand in yours, either as a greeting or after making an agreement with them【口】请跟我握手〔用于问候或达成协议时〕: *$500? OK, it's a deal. Put it there!* 500美元? 好吧, 成交。握手吧!

⑪ WRITE 写

27 [T] to write something or to make a mark with a pen or pencil 写下; 标上〔记号〕: **put sth in/on/under** *Put your name at the top of each answer sheet.* 把你的名字写在每张答题纸的上端。—see also 另见 **put your finger on** (FINGER[1] (4)), **put your foot down** (FOOT[1] (10)), **put your foot in it** (FOOT[1] (12)), **put sth to good use** (USE[2] (4)), **put your back into it** (BACK[2] (19))

put about *phr v* **1** [T **put** sth ↔ **about**] *BrE informal* to give other people news or information, especially when it is unpleasant or untrue【英, 非正式】散布〔尤指令人不愉快或不真实的消息或信息〕: **put it about that** *Someone's been putting it about that she's splitting up with her husband.* 有人在散布消息说她正和丈夫闹离婚。**2 put yourself about** *BrE informal* to have sexual relationships with a lot of different people【英, 非正式】与很多人有性关系 **3** [I,T] *technical* if a ship puts about or if you put it about, it changes direction【术语】〔船〕改变方向; 使〔船〕改变方向

put across *phr v* [T] **1** [**put** sth ↔ **across**] to explain your ideas, beliefs, policies etc in a way that people can understand 表达清楚, 解释清楚〔自己的想法等〕: *The union representative put her argument across very effectively.* 工会代表非常清楚有力地表达了自己的论点。**2 put yourself across** to communicate effectively, so that people have a clear idea of your character, your ideas etc 有效地传达自己的想法; 清楚地表达自己的意思: *Sue's never been very good at putting herself across at interviews.* 休一向不善于在面试时把自己的意思讲清楚。

put sth ↔ **aside** *phr v* [T] **1** to try to stop thinking about a problem, quarrel, or disagreement, because you want to achieve something 把…撇开不理, 不考虑: *The UN has called on the warring factions to put aside their differences.* 联合国呼吁交战各方抛开分歧。**2** to save money regularly, usually for a particular purpose 储存〔钱〕备用: *We're trying to put aside a few hundred dollars every month toward our vacation.* 我们尽量每月存几百美元供度假用。**3** to put down something you are reading or working with, in order to start doing something else 放下〔正在读的东西或正在干的活〕: *Charles put aside his newspaper and got up to answer the door.* 查尔斯放下报纸起身去开门。**4** to keep a period of time free in order to be able to do something 留出〔一段时间〕: *Try to put aside an hour each day for exercise.* 每天尽量腾出一个小时锻炼身体。

put sth **at** sth *phr v* [T] to calculate and state an amount, someone's age etc, without trying to be very exact 推测〔某物〕是…; 估计〔数量、年龄等〕是…: *Official estimates put the damage at over $10 million.* 官方估计损失大约为一千多万美元。

put sb/sth **away** *phr v* [T] **1** [**put** sth ↔ **away**] to put something in the place where it is usually kept 把〔某物〕收拾起来〔放回原处〕: *Let me just put these files away.* 让我把这些文件收拾好。**2** [**put** sb **away**] *informal* to put someone in a prison or in a mental hospital【非正式】把〔某人〕送入监狱[精神病院]: *He was put away for five years for armed robbery.* 他因持械抢劫而被关入监狱五年。**3** [**put** sth ↔ **away**] *informal* to eat or drink a lot【非正式】吃[喝]很多: *It's amazing the amount that child can put away.* 那孩子的食量真是惊人。**4** [**put** sth ↔ **away**] to save money 储存〔钱〕: *My Grandfather had put away over £50,000.* 我祖父已存了五万多英镑。

put back *phr v* **1** [T **put** sth ↔ **back**] to arrange for an event to start at a later time or date; POSTPONE 使〔某活动〕延期, 推迟: *The meeting has been put back to next Thursday.* 会议延期到下周四举行。**2** [T **put** sth ↔ **back**] to delay a process or activity by a number of weeks, months etc 使〔某过程或活动〕延迟〔几周、几个月等〕: *This fire could put back the opening date by several weeks.* 这场火灾会使开业日期延迟几个星期。**3 put a clock/a watch back** to make a clock or watch show an earlier time 把〔钟、表〕拨慢 —see also 另见 **put the clock back** (CLOCK[1] (2))

put sth ↔ **by** *phr v* [T] to save money regularly in order to use it later 储存〔钱〕备用: *We're trying to put a little by each month for a new car.* 我们正尽量每月存一点钱以备买辆新汽车用。

put down *phr v*
1 ►CRITICIZE 批评◄ [T **put** sb ↔ **down**] to keep criticizing someone in front of other people 一再当众批评某人: *I hate the way Dave puts me down the whole time.* 我很讨厌戴夫老是当众批评我。| **put yourself down** *"I don't stand a chance of getting the job." "Don't be silly, you mustn't put yourself down."* "我没有机会得到那份工作。""别傻了, 你不应贬低自己。"
2 ►PAY 付款◄ [T **put** sth ↔ **down**] to pay part of the total cost of something, so that you can pay the rest later 付〔订金〕: *How much could you afford to put down on a house?* 你付得起多少订金买一所房子?
3 ►WRITE 写◄ [T **put** sth ↔ **down**] *BrE* to write something, especially a name or number on a piece of paper or on a list【英】写下, 记下: *I'll just put your phone number down in my book.* 我这就把你的电话号码记在我的电话簿里。
4 ►KILL 杀死◄ [T **put** sth ↔ **down**] to kill an animal without causing it pain, usually because it is old or ill 杀死〔老、病动物以免除其痛苦〕: *We had to have the dog put down.* 我们不得不让人杀死这条狗。
5 put the phone down to put the RECEIVER back onto the telephone when you have finished speaking to someone 放下电话: **put the phone down on sb** (=to suddenly end a telephone conversation) 突然挂断某人的电话
6 put down a revolution/revolt/rebellion etc to stop a REVOLUTION (2) etc by using force 镇压[平息]革命/起义/叛乱等: *Military police were called in to put down the riot.* 宪兵被召来平定暴乱。
7 ►STOP A VEHICLE 使车辆停下◄ [T **put** sb **down**] *BrE* to stop a vehicle so that passengers can get off at a particular place【英】停车让〔乘客〕下来: *Just put me down at the gate.* 在大门口停车让我下来就行了。
8 ►AIRCRAFT 飞机◄ [I,T] if an aircraft puts down or if a pilot puts it down, it lands〔飞机〕着陆; 使〔飞机〕着陆: *The engine failed and the plane put down in the sea.* 发动机失灵, 飞机在海上降落了。
9 ►BABY 婴儿◄ [T **put** sb **down**] to put a baby in its bed 把〔婴儿〕放在他的床上: *We try to put Amy down at six every evening.* 我们尽量每晚6点把埃米放在床上让她睡觉。

10 I couldn't put it down *spoken* used to say that you found a book, game etc extremely interesting【口】我不能放下它〔用于表示你认为某本书或游戏极其有趣〕: *Once I'd started reading it I just couldn't put it down.* 我一开始读就爱不释手。
11 put down a motion/an amendment to suggest a subject, plan, change in the law etc for a parliament or committee to consider 提出一项动议/修正案〔供议会或委员会考虑〕

put sb **down as** sth *phr v* [T] to guess what someone is like or what they do, without having much information about them〔没充分根据就〕认为〔某人〕是…, 把〔某人〕看作是…: *They'd already put me down as a good-for-nothing young artist.* 他们已经把我当作一个无用的年轻艺术家。

put sb **down for** sth *phr v* [T] **1** to put someone's name on a list so that they can take part in an activity, join an organization etc 把〔某人的名字〕登记在参加者的名单上, 为〔某人〕报名参加某活动[加入某组织]: *We've put Simon's name down for nursery school.* 我们已给西蒙报名准备上幼儿园。**2 put sb down for £5/£20 etc** *especially BrE* to write someone's name on a list with an amount of money that they have promised to give【尤英】把〔某人的名字〕登记在认捐名单上并记录5英镑/20英镑等捐款数额

put sth **down to** sth *phr v* [T] **1** to explain the reason for something, especially when you are only guessing 把〔某事〕归因于: *I put Jane's moodiness down to the stress she was under.* 我把简的喜怒无常归因于她所承受的压力。**2 put it down to experience** used to tell someone not to feel too upset by failure, but to learn something useful from it 把它当作一次经验教训: *Everyone gets rejected from time to time; put it down to experience.* 每个人偶尔都会被拒绝, 把它当作一次经验教训吧。

put sth ↔**forth** *phr v* [T] **put forth leaves/shoots/roots etc** *literary* if a tree or bush puts forth leaves etc it begins to grow them【文】〔树或灌木〕长出叶子/新芽/根等

put sb/sth ↔**forward** *phr v* [T] **1** to suggest a plan, proposal etc, especially in order to start discussions about something that needs to be decided 提出〔计划、建议等〕: *The working party has put forward a good case for moving to a new site.* 特别工作组提出了一条很好的迁往新址的理由。| *the theories put forward by Dr. Kesner* 凯斯纳博士提出的理论 **2** to arrange for an event to start at an earlier time or date 将…提前: *The men's final has been put forward to 1:30.* 男子决赛提前到1点半举行。**3 put a clock/watch forward** to make a clock or watch show a later time 把〔钟、表〕拨快 **4 put yourself/sb's name forward** to suggest formally that you or someone else should be considered for a particular job, membership of an organization etc 提名〔推荐〕某人做某工作[成为某组织成员]: *We put Joe's name forward to serve on the local council.* 我们推举乔为地方议会成员。

put in *phr v*
1 ▶EQUIPMENT 设备◀ [T **put** sth ↔**in**] to fix a piece of equipment into your home so that it is ready to be used 安装〔设备〕: *We decided to have a new bathroom put in.* 我们决定安装一套新的盥洗设备。
2 ▶TIME/ENERGY 时间/能量◀ [T **put** sth ↔**in**] to spend time or use energy working or practising something 花费〔时间或精力〕做某事[练习某事]: *You have to put in a lot of effort to learn a new language.* 要学一门新的语言需要付出很大的努力。
3 ▶SAY STH 说某事◀ [T **put** sth ↔**in**] to interrupt someone in order to say something 插话: *"I'm sure Daniel's the best man for the job." Mrs Weevers put in.* "我相信丹尼尔是这项工作最合适的人选。"威弗斯夫人插话说。
4 put in a claim/request to officially make a claim or request 提出要求/请求: *She put in a claim for damage to the photographs.* 她为照片的损坏提出索赔。
5 ▶ELECT 选举◀ [T **put** sb ↔**in**] to elect a politician or political party 选举〔政治家或政党〕
6 put in an appearance to go to a social event, meeting etc for a short time〔在社交活动或会议上〕露面: *I don't really want to go to the party, but I'd better put in an appearance.* 我不大想去参加那个聚会, 但我最好露一下面。
7 ▶SHIP 船◀ [I] if a ship puts in, it enters a port〔船〕进港

put in for sth *phr v* [T] to make a formal request for something 正式要求, 申请: *It's time you put in for a pay increase.* 是你申请加薪水的时候了。

put sb/sth ↔**off** *phr v* [T] **1** to arrange to do something at a later time or date, especially because there is a problem, difficulty etc 推迟某事, 使某事延期: *The meeting's been put off till next week.* 会议已推迟到下星期了。| **put off doing sth** *We'll have to put off going on vacation until you're better.* 我们得推迟去度假, 直到你好些为止。**2** to delay meeting someone, paying someone etc because you do not want to do it until later 推迟〔与某人会面或付钱给某人〕, 搪塞〔某人〕, 敷衍〔某人〕: *I just don't have the money right now – I'll have to put him off for another week.* 我现在就是没钱——我得再拖一个星期还他。| *I managed to put Ron off with a promise to pay him next week.* 我答应罗恩说下星期付给他钱, 把他设法应付过去了。**3** to delay doing something until later because you do not want to do it now 拖延: *You really ought to write to her. You can't just keep putting it off.* 你确实应该给她写信, 你不能再拖了。**4** to make you dislike something or not want to do something 使不喜欢做某事, 使不想做某事: *The job sounded interesting but the idea of moving house again put me off.* 那份工作听起来很有趣, 但是一想起要再次搬家, 我就不乐意了。| *Don't be put off by the title – it's a really good book.* 别让书名给倒了胃口——它确实是一本好书。| **put sb off (doing) sth** *This lousy weather is enough to put anyone off camping.* 这种糟糕的天气足以让任何人打消野营的念头。**5** to make it difficult for someone to do something, by preventing them from thinking clearly about what they are doing 影响某人做某事; 使分心: *The photographers put McEnroe off his game.* 那些摄影师影响了麦肯罗比赛。| *Stop giggling! You're putting me off.* 别再咯咯笑啦! 你让我分心了。**6** to let someone leave a vehicle at a particular place 让〔某人〕下车: *I'll put you off at the bottom of the street.* 我会在这条街的尽头停车让你下来。

put sth ↔**on** *phr v* [T]
1 ▶CLOTHES 衣服◀ [**put** sth ↔**on**] to put a piece of clothing on your body 穿上, 戴上: *Put your coat on before you go outside.* 你出去之前把外套穿上。| *I'll have to put my glasses on; I can't read the sign from here.* 我得戴上我的眼镜; 从这里我看不清那个标志。
2 ▶ON SKIN 在皮肤上◀ [**put** sth ↔**on**] to put MAKE-UP, cream etc on your skin 在皮肤上涂[擦]〔化妆品、乳液等〕: *It takes Julie about half an hour to put her make-up on every morning.* 朱莉每天早上花大约半小时化妆。
3 ▶LIGHT/HEAT ETC 光/热等◀ [**put** sth ↔**on**] to make a light or a piece of electrical or gas equipment start working by pressing or turning a button 打开〔灯、电器或煤气装置〕: *Shall I put the kettle on?* 我要把水壶的开关打开吗?
4 ▶MUSIC 音乐◀ to put a record, TAPE or CD into a machine and start playing it 播放〔唱片、磁带或激光唱片〕
5 ▶PRETEND 假装◀ [**put** sth ↔**on**] to pretend to have a certain feeling, opinion, way of speaking etc especially in order to get attention 假装有…, 装出: *Sheila's not really that upset; she's just putting it on.* 希拉其实并没有那么难过, 她只是假装那样。| *He always puts on that posh voice when he's on the phone.* 他打电话时总是装出上流社会的腔调。
6 put on weight/12 lbs/4 kg etc to become fatter and heavier 增加体重/12磅/4公斤等: *Rosie's put on five kilos since she quit smoking.* 罗茜戒烟以来体重已增加了五公斤。
7 ▶PLAY/SHOW ETC 戏剧/节目等◀ [**put** sth ↔**on**] to arrange or perform a show, concert, play etc 上演〔戏剧等〕; 举行〔音乐会等〕; 表演〔节目〕: *We're putting on a concert to raise money for famine victims.* 我们将举行一场音乐会为饥民筹钱。
8 ▶COOK 烹调◀ [**put** sth ↔**on**] to start cooking something 开始烹调…: *Robbie will be home in ten minutes; I'd better put the potatoes on.* 罗比10分钟后到家, 我该开始做马铃薯了。
9 put on a bus/train/coach *BrE* to provide a bus or train in order to take people somewhere【英】提供公共汽车/火车/长途汽车: *British Rail will be putting on extra trains for football fans.* 英国铁路公司将为足球迷加开火车。
10 you're putting me on! *spoken, especially AmE* used to tell someone that you think they are joking【口, 尤美】你在愚弄[欺骗]我! 〔用于告诉某人你认为他们在开玩笑〕: *"They offered me a raise at work." "You're putting me on! How much?"* "他们提出给我加薪水。""你在骗我! 多少?"
11 ▶ADD 增加◀ [**put** sth **on** sth] to add an amount of money or tax onto the cost of something 增加某物的价格; 对某物征税: *The new tax could put another ten cents on the price of gas.* 新增的税收会使汽油价格再上涨10美分。
12 ▶RISK MONEY 赌钱◀ [**put** sth **on** sth] to risk an amount of money on the result of a game, race etc 下赌注于〔比赛结果等〕: *We put £50 on Brazil to win the Cup.* 我们以50镑赌巴西赢得世界杯。
13 put on a brake to make a vehicle stop or slow down by pressing a PEDAL or handle 刹车

put sb **onto** sb/sth *phr v* [T] *informal* to give someone information about something interesting or useful that they did not

know about【非正式】向某人提供〔有趣或有用事物的〕信息，向某人介绍某事: *Barbara put us onto this fantastic French restaurant in Baltimore.* 我们从芭芭拉那里知道了这家位于巴尔的摩的极好的法国餐馆。

put out 扑灭；熄灭

Joan put the fire out. 琼扑灭了火。

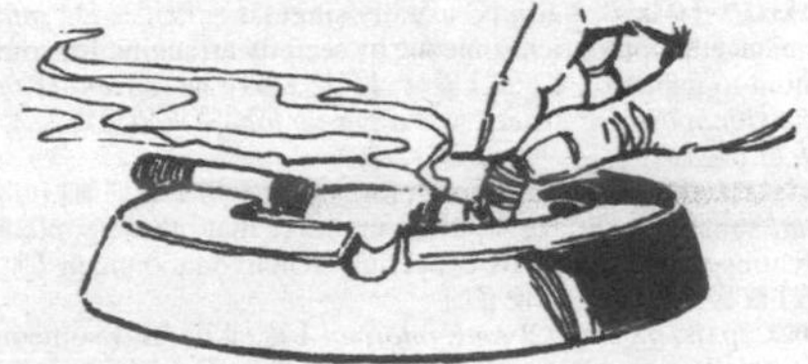

He put out his cigarette. 他熄灭了香烟。

put out *phr v*

1 put out a fire/cigarette etc to make a fire etc stop burning 扑灭火；熄灭香烟 —see 见 FIRE[1] (USAGE)

2 put out a light/lamp to make a light stop working by pressing or turning a button 关灯

3 feel/be put out to feel upset or offended 感到烦乱〔恼火〕: *We were a little put out at not being invited to the wedding.* 我们为没有被邀请参加婚礼感到有点恼火。

4 ▶MAKE WORK 麻烦◀[T **put** sb ↔ **out**] to make extra work or cause problems for someone 给〔某人〕添麻烦: *Will it put you out if I bring another guest?* 我要是多带一位客人来会不会给你添麻烦?

5 put yourself out to make an effort to do something that will help someone 努力做某事以帮助某人: *Fred rarely puts himself out on other people's behalf.* 弗雷德很少费心去帮助别人。

6 [T **put** sth ↔ **out**] to put something outside the house 将某物置于门外: *Remember to put the cat out before you go to bed.* 你睡觉前别忘了把猫赶出去。| **put the rubbish/garbage out** (=put dirty or unwanted things outside your house to be taken away) 把垃圾放在外面 | **put the washing out** (=put clothes outside to dry) 把衣服晾在外面

7 put your tongue out to push your tongue out of your mouth, especially as a rude sign to someone 伸出舌头〔尤作为不礼貌的表示〕

8 put your back/knee/shoulder etc out to injure part of your body, especially by stretching it too much 扭伤背/膝关节脱臼/肩关节脱臼等: *I put my knee out playing tennis yesterday.* 我昨天打网球膝关节脱臼了。

9 put your hand/foot/arm out to stretch your hand etc forward 伸出手/脚/胳膊: *Jimmy put his foot out and tripped me up.* 吉米伸出脚把我绊倒了。

10 ▶MAKE UNCONSCIOUS 使失去知觉◀[T **put** sb **out**] to make someone unconscious before a medical operation 使失去知觉；对…实施麻醉

11 put out information/statistics/a statement etc to produce information etc for people to read or listen to 发布消息/公布统计数字/发表声明等: *The police department has put out a statement apologizing for its officers' conduct.* 警察局发表了一项声明为警员的行为道歉。

12 ▶PRODUCE STH 制作某物◀ to produce radio signals, print magazines, broadcast programmes etc 发出〔无线电信号〕；出版；播出

13 put out feelers/antennae to try to discover information or opinions by listening to people or watching what is happening 伸出触角；通过倾听[观察]发现信息[了解观点]: *It might be worth putting feelers out to see if there are any jobs going in Paul's school.* 或许值得打听一下，看保罗的学校有没有什么工作可干。

14 ▶SHIP 船◀[I] if a ship puts out, it starts to sail〔船〕出航

15 ▶HAVE SEX 发生性关系◀[I] *AmE slang* if a woman puts out, she has sex with a man【美俚】〔女人〕与男人发生性关系

16 [T **put** sb **out**] to end a BATTER'S innings in BASEBALL by, for example, catching the ball that they have hit 使〔棒球的击球手〕出局

put sth ↔ **over** *phr v* [T] **1** to communicate an idea or feeling 传达〔想法或感情〕: *The course is designed to help you put over your ideas more effectively.* 该课程是为帮助你更有效地传达自己的观点而设计的。**2 put one over on** *informal* to deceive someone into believing something untrue or accepting something that is useless【非正式】欺骗某人使之相信虚假的事情[接受无价值的事物]: *They think they've found a way to put one over on the welfare office.* 他们以为他们已经找到了欺骗福利部门的方法。

put through *phr v* [T] **1** [**put** sb/sth ↔ **through**] to connect someone to someone else on the telephone 为某人接通电话: *One moment please, I'm just trying to put you through.* 请等一下，我这就给你接通电话。**2 put sb through school/college/university** to pay for someone to study at school or college 供某人上学/上大学: *Andrew's parents insisted on putting him through medical school.* 安德鲁的父母坚持让他上医科大学。**3** [**put** sb **through** sth] to make someone do something unpleasant or difficult 使某人做〔不愉快或困难的事〕: *We put all new recruits through a rigorous week-long training programme.* 我们让所有的新成员参加一套为期一个星期的严格的训练课程。| **put sb through it** *They really put me through it at that job interview.* 在那次工作面试中，他们确实使我经受了严格的考验。**4** [**put** sth ↔ **through**] to do what is necessary in order to get a plan or suggestion accepted or approved〔通过计划或建议的准备等〕完成，达成: *Production will start up again when these changes have been put through.* 这些改动顺利完成后，生产就将重新恢复。

put sth **to** sb *phr v* [T] **1** to ask someone a question or make a suggestion to them 向〔某人〕提〔问题或建议〕: *Can I put a question to the speaker?* 我能向演讲人提个问题吗? **2** to offer a group of people something such as a proposal or plan which they can accept or reject 提出〔建议或计划〕供考虑: *The latest offer will be put to the negotiating committee this afternoon.* 最新的出价将于今天下午提交谈判委员会考虑。| **put sth to the vote** (=get people to vote on it) 投票表决某事 *Let's put the motion to the vote.* 让我们投票表决这项动议。**3 put sb to trouble/inconvenience etc** [usually in questions and negatives 一般用于疑问句和否定句] to make someone do something that will cause them trouble or inconvenience 使某人为难/感到不便等 **4 put your name/signature to** to sign a letter, document etc saying that you agree with what is written in it 签名表示同意

put sth ↔ **together** *phr v* [T] **1** to prepare or produce something by collecting pieces of information, ideas etc〔通过收集资料、观点等〕整理出，拼凑，凑成: *We're putting together an anthology of war poetry.* 我们正在编一本战争诗集。| *It took all morning to put the proposal together.* 凑成这份提案花了一整个上午。**2** to make a machine, model etc by joining all the different parts 装配，组装〔机器、模型等〕: *I can't work out how to put this table together.* 我搞不清楚如何把这张桌子拼在一起。**3 more...than the rest put together** used when comparing two sets of people or things to say that one set contains more than the total of all the other sets …比其他合在一起还多: *Italy scored more points than the rest of the group put together.* 意大利的得分比同组其他队的得分加起来还多。

put up *phr v*

1 ▶BUILD 建造◀[T **put** sth ↔ **up**] to build a wall, fence, or tall building 建造〔墙、篱笆或高楼〕: *They're putting up several new office blocks in the centre of town.* 他们正在市中心建造几幢新办公楼。

2 ▶ON A WALL 在墙上◀[T **put** sth ↔ **up**] to put a picture, notice etc on a wall so that people can see it〔在墙上〕张贴〔图片、布告等〕: *The exam results will be put up on Friday afternoon.* 这次考试结果将于星期五下午公布。

3 ▶INCREASE 增加◀[T **put** sth ↔ **up**] to increase the cost or value of something 提高〔价钱等〕: *Our landlord keeps threatening to put the rent up.* 我们的房东老是威胁说要提高房租。

4 ▶LET SB STAY 让某人留下◀[T **put** sb ↔ **up**] to let someone stay in your house and give them meals 为〔某人〕提供膳

宿: *They agreed to put two foreign students up over the summer.* 他们同意夏季为两个留学生提供膳宿。

5 ▶STAY SOMEWHERE 在某处住宿◀ [I always+adv/prep] *especially BrE* to stay in a place for a short time【尤英】短期住宿: [**+at/in/with**] *We can put up at a hotel for the night.* 我们可以在旅馆住一夜。

6 put up a fight/struggle/resistance to show great determination to oppose something or get out of a difficult situation 奋勇战斗/斗争/抵抗: *Gina put up a real fight to overcome the disease.* 吉娜为战胜疾病进行了顽强的斗争。

7 put up money/$3 million/£50 to give an amount of money for a particular purpose 捐款/捐300万美元/捐50万英镑: *An anonymous donor put up $50,000 for the new science lab.* 一位不知名的捐赠者为新的科学实验室捐了5万美元。

8 ▶ELECTIONS 选举◀ [T **put** sb ↔ **up**] to suggest someone as a suitable person to be elected to a position 推举, 提名〔某人担任某职〕: *They're putting Tom Sackville up as a candidate in the next elections.* 他们要推举汤姆·萨克维尔为下次选举的候选人。

9 put up a proposal/argument/case etc to explain a suggestion or idea so that other people can think about it or discuss it 提出建议/论点/理由等: *If you can put up a good enough case, the board will provide the finance.* 如果你能提出足够好的理由, 董事会将提供资金。

put sb **up to** sth *phr v* [T] to encourage someone to do something stupid or dangerous 唆使〔某人〕做〔愚蠢或危险的事〕: *It's not like Martha to play practical jokes; someone must have put her up to it.* 玛莎不是玩恶作剧的人, 一定是有人唆使她这么干的。

put up with sb/sth *phr v* [T] to accept an unpleasant situation or person without complaining 忍受, 忍耐: *I don't know how you put up with their constant quarrelling.* 我不知道你是如何忍受他们无休止的争吵的。| *You see what I have to put up with!* 你看到我不得不忍受些什么了吧!

pu·ta·tive /ˈpjutətɪv; ˈpjuːtətɪv/ *adj* [only before noun 仅用于名词前] *formal* believed or accepted by most people【正式】公认的, 被普遍认为是的: *the putative father of her child* 被认为是她孩子的父亲的那个人

put-down /ˈ· ·/ *n* [C usually singular 一般用单数] something you say that is intended to make someone feel stupid or unimportant; SNUB[2] 贬损的话, 奚落的话: *Some feminists see the put-downs girls experience as the means by which men control women.* 一些女权主义者认为女孩所经受的奚落是男人控制女人的手段。—see also 另见 **put down** (PUT)

put-on /ˈ· ·/ *n* [C usually singular 一般用单数] *AmE informal* something you say or do to try to make someone believe something that is not true【美, 非正式】欺骗, 愚弄的话

pu·tre·fac·tion /ˌpjutrəˈfækʃən; ˌpjuːtrɪ̇ˈfækʃən/ *n* [U] *formal* the process of decay in a dead animal or plant, especially when it smells very bad【正式】〔死去动物或植物的〕腐烂(作用)

pu·tre·fy /ˈpjutrəˌfaɪ; ˈpjuːtrɪ̇faɪ/ *v* [I,T] *formal* if a dead animal or plant putrefies, it decays and smells very bad【正式】〔死去动植物等〕腐烂

pu·tres·cent /pjuˈtrɛsn̩t; pjuːˈtresənt/ *adj formal* beginning to decay and smell very bad【正式】开始腐烂的, 腐臭的: *putrescent fish* 腐臭的鱼 —**putrescence** *n* [U]

pu·trid /ˈpjutrɪd; ˈpjuːtrɪ̇d/ *adj* **1** dead animals, plants, or parts of the body that are putrid are decaying and smell very bad〔死去动物、植物或身体部位〕腐烂的, 腐臭的 **2** *informal* very unpleasant【非正式】令人非常不愉快的: *a putrid smell* 难闻的气味

putsch /pʊtʃ; pʊtʃ/ *n* [C] a secretly planned attempt to remove a government by force〔武装〕政变, 武力颠覆政府的秘密企图: *the military putsch of 1948* 1948年的军事政变

putt /pʌt; pʌt/ *n* [C] a light hit intended to move a GOLF BALL a short distance along the ground towards the hole〔高尔夫球赛中向球洞〕轻击球 —**putt** *v* [I,T] —see picture on page A23 参见A23页图

put·tee /pʌˈti; ˈpʌti/ *n* [C usually plural 一般用复数] a long piece of cloth that is wrapped arond the leg from the knee down, worn as part of an army uniform in the past〔旧时军人的〕绑腿

put·ter¹ /ˈpʌtɚ; ˈpʌtə/ *n* a kind of GOLF CLUB (=stick) to hit the ball a short distance towards or into the hole〔高尔夫球的〕轻击杆 —see picture on page A23 参见A23页图

putter² *v* [I always+adv/prep] **1** *AmE* to spend time doing things that are not very important in a relaxed way【美】放松地做〔不重要的事〕; POTTER[2] *BrE*【英】: *I puttered around for a while, tidying up the kitchen.* 我瞎忙了一会儿, 打扫了一下厨房。**2** *AmE* to walk or move slowly and without hurrying【美】闲逛; POTTER[2] *BrE*【英】**3** *informal* to make the low repeating sound that a vehicle makes when it is moving slowly【非正式】〔车辆缓慢移动时〕发出重复低沉的声音

put·ting /ˈpʌtɪŋ; ˈpʌtɪŋ/ *n* [U] a simple game of GOLF played on putting greens in Britain〔英国在高尔夫球轻击区玩的〕简易高尔夫球游戏, 推杆游戏

putting green /ˈ·· ·/ *n* [C] **1** one of the smaller smooth areas of grass on a GOLF COURSE where you hit the ball into the hole〔高尔夫球的〕轻击区, 果岭 **2** *BrE* a smooth area of grass with many holes in it for playing a simple type of GOLF【英】球洞草坪区〔用于玩简易高尔夫球游戏〕, 推杆草坪

put·ty /ˈpʌtɪ; ˈpʌti/ *n* [U] **1** a soft substance that dries hard and is used to fix glass into window frames 油灰, 腻子 **2 be putty in sb's hands** to be easily controlled or influenced by someone 易受某人摆布的, 易受某人影响的

put-up job /ˈ· ˌ· ·/ *n* [C usually singular 一般用单数] *informal* an attempt to trick someone by secretly arranging for something to happen【非正式】骗局, 奸计: *There were rumors that the kidnapping of Miletti was a put-up job.* 有谣传说绑架米勒蒂是个骗局。

put-up·on /ˈ· · ˌ·/ *adj* [not before noun 不用于名词前] *informal* someone who feels put-upon thinks that other people are treating them unfairly by expecting them to do too much【非正式】被利用的, 被占了便宜的

putz /pʌts; pʌts/ *n* [C] *AmE informal*【美, 非正式】**1** someone, especially a man, who is stupid, annoying, and unpleasant 愚蠢的人, 令人讨厌的人〔尤指男人〕**2** *taboo* a PENIS【讳】阴茎

puz·zle¹ /ˈpʌzl̩; ˈpʌzəl/ *v* [T] **1** to confuse someone or make them feel slightly anxious because they do not understand something 使困惑, 使迷惑: *What puzzles me is how the burglar got into the house without setting off the alarm.* 这个窃贼如何进入房子而没触动警报器, 使我大惑不解。**2** [I,T] to think for a long time about something because you cannot understand or solve it (为…)绞尽脑汁, 苦思冥想: [**+over/about**] *I've been sitting here puzzling about what to do.* 我一直坐在这里苦苦思索该怎么办。| **puzzle your head over** *I've been puzzling my head over this problem for weeks.* 好几个星期我都在琢磨这个问题。

puzzle sth ↔ **out** *phr v* [T] to solve a confusing or difficult problem by thinking about it carefully 仔细考虑解决〔难题等〕, 设法想出: *I've been trying to puzzle out why she's so upset.* 我一直想搞清楚她为什么如此烦恼。

puzzle² *n* [C] **1** [usually singular 一般用单数] something that is difficult to understand or explain 难题, 难解之事, 谜: *These computers are a puzzle to me.* 我搞不懂这些电脑。**2** a game or toy that has a lot of pieces that you have to fit together 拼图游戏, 拼图玩具 —see also 另见 JIGSAW (1) **3** a game in which you have to think hard to solve a difficult question or problem〔需要动脑筋的〕益智游戏: *a crossword puzzle* 填字游戏 **4 a piece of the puzzle** a piece of information that helps you to understand part of a difficult question, mystery etc〔有助于理解难题、神秘事物等的〕信息, 线索

puz·zled /ˈpʌzl̩d; ˈpʌzəld/ *adj* confused and unable to understand something 困惑的, 无法理解的, 迷惑的: *I'm still slightly puzzled as to why she never called us.* 她为什么从不给我们打电话, 我还感到有点困惑。| **puzzled look/expression** *Alice read the letter with a puzzled expression on her face.* 艾丽斯脸上带着迷惑的表情读了那封信。

puz·zle·ment /ˈpʌzl̩mənt; ˈpʌzəlmənt/ *n* [U] *formal* a feeling of being confused and unable to understand something【正式】迷惑, 困惑

puz·zler /ˈpʌzlɚ; ˈpʌzlə/ *n* [C] *informal* something that is difficult to understand or explain【非正式】难解的事, 难题

puz·zling /ˈpʌzlɪŋ; ˈpʌzlɪŋ/ *adj* confusing and difficult to understand or explain 令人迷惑的, 令人费解的: *The children showed a puzzling lack of curiosity about the new baby.* 孩子们对新生儿显得缺乏好奇心, 这很令人费解。

PVC /ˌpi vi ˈsi; ˌpiː viː ˈsiː◂/ *n* [U] a type of plastic 聚氯乙烯

pvt *AmE* the written abbreviation of 缩写= PRIVATE, the lowest military rank in the army【美】二等兵; PTE *BrE*【英】

pw the written abbreviation of 缩写= per week: *Rent is £55 pw.* 租金为每周55镑。

PWA /ˌpi dʌbl̩ju ˈe; ˌpiː dʌbəljuː ˈeɪ/ *n* [C] person with AIDS; someone who has the disease AIDS 艾滋病患者

PWR /ˌpi dʌbḷju ˋɑr; ˌpiː dʌbəljuː ˈɑː/ *n* [C] pressurized water reactor; a type of NUCLEAR REACTOR for producing electricity 压水反应堆〔一种发电的核反应堆〕

PX /ˌpi ˋɛks; ˌpiː ˈeks/ *n* [C] a special shop for food and other supplies on a US military base〔美国的〕军人消费合作社, 军队商店 —compare 比较 NAAFI

Pyg·ma·li·on /pɪgˋmelɪən; pɪgˈmeɪliən/ (1913) a play by George Bernard Shaw in which Professor Henry Higgins teaches a poor Cockney woman, Eliza Doolittle, how to speak and behave like an UPPER CLASS lady. The play was made into a MUSICAL (=a play that uses singing and dancing to tell a story) in 1956 and a successful film musical in 1964, both called *My Fair Lady*.《皮格马利翁》, 又译《卖花女》〔(1913), 萧伯纳的一部剧本。剧中人物亨利·希金斯教授教伦敦东区的穷姑娘伊莱扎·杜利特尔言谈举止如何像上流社会的淑女一样。该剧于1956年被改编成音乐剧, 1964年又被改拍成音乐片, 均取名《窈窕淑女》〕

pyg·my, pigmy /ˋpɪgmɪ; ˈpɪgmi/ *n* [C] **1** also 又作 **Pygmy** a person belonging to a race of very small people, especially one of the tribes of central Africa 俾格米人〔身材非常矮小的一个种族, 尤指中非一些部族〕 **2 pygmy rabbit/hippo/elephant etc** a very small type of rabbit, HIPPO etc〔体形特别小的〕小兔/小河马/小象等

py·ja·mas *especially BrE*【尤英】also 又作 **pajamas** *especially AmE*【尤美】/pəˋdʒæməz; pəˈdʒɑːməz/ *n* [plural] **1** a soft, loose pair of trousers and a top that you wear in bed〔一套〕睡衣裤: *a pair of striped pyjamas* 一套有条纹的睡衣裤 **2 pyjama party** a party where all the guests are asked to wear pyjamas 穿睡衣的聚会 **3** loose trousers that are tied around the waist, worn by Muslim men or women〔穆斯林男女穿的〕束腰宽松裤 —**pyjama** *adj*: *pyjama bottoms* 睡裤

py·lon /ˋpaɪlɑn; ˈpaɪlən/ *n* [C] **1** one of the tall metal structures that supports wires carrying electricity across the country 高压电线架, 电缆塔 **2** *AmE* one of a set of plastic CONES placed on a road to control traffic and protect people working there【美】〔放置在公路上控制交通并保护路上工作人员的〕圆锥形塑料指示标 **3** a tall structure or post used to support something heavy or to help guide aircraft to land〔用于支撑重物的〕高架, 高柱;〔机场的〕标塔, 指示塔

PYO *BrE* the abbreviation of 缩写= 'pick your own', used by farms that let people pick their own fruit and vegetables【英】水果[蔬菜]自摘

Pyongyang/ˋpjʌŋˋjɑŋ; ˈpjʌŋˈjɑːŋ/ the capital of North Korea, on the Taedong River, in the southwest of the country. It is Korea's oldest city. 平壤〔朝鲜首都, 位于该国西南部的大同江沿岸。它是朝鲜半岛历史最悠久的城市〕

py·or·rho·ea *BrE*【英】also 又作 **pyorrhea** *especially AmE*【尤美】/ˌpaɪəˋriə; ˌpaɪəˈriːə/ *n* [U] a DISEASE of your GUMS that makes your teeth become loose 牙槽脓溢

pyr·a·mid /ˋpɪrəmɪd; ˈpɪrəmɪd/ *n* [C] **1** a large stone building with four TRIANGULAR (=3 sided) walls that slope in to a point at the top, especially in Egypt and Central America〔尤指埃及和中美的〕金字塔 **2** [usually singular 一般用单数] a system or organization in which a small number of people have power or influence over a much larger number of people 金字塔式组织[体系]: *different levels of the management pyramid* 金字塔式管理中的不同等级 **3** a pile of objects that have been put into the shape of a pyramid 摆成金字塔形的一堆东西: **[+of]** *a pyramid of oranges* 一堆摆成金字塔形的橙子 **4** a pyramidshaped object 金字塔形物 —**pyramidal** /pɪˋræmɪdḷ; pɪˈræmɪdl/ *adj* —see picture at 参见 SHAPE[1] 图

Pyr·a·mids, the /ˋpɪrəmɪdz; ˈpɪrəmɪdz/ the ancient Egyptian PYRAMIDS, which were built to contain the bodies and possessions of the dead PHARAOHS (=kings of ancient Egypt). The most famous of these are the three pyramids at El Giza, near Cairo, which include the **Great Pyramid** and which are one of the Seven Wonders of the World. 金字塔群〔古埃及的一群金字塔。里面有法老的遗体及其陪葬品。最有名的是位于开罗附近吉萨的三座金字塔, 其中包括大金字塔, 是世界七大奇迹之一〕

pyramid sel·ling /ˈ··· ˌ··/ *n* [U] a system of selling things in which someone buys the right to sell a particular kind of goods and then sells these goods to lots of other people, who sell them to others, especially in their houses 金字塔式销售, 层压式推销〔一种商品销售体系, 某人先买下某商品的经销权, 然后将这些商品再卖给许多其他人, 其他人再转售〕

Pyr·a·mus and This·be /ˌpɪrəməs ənd ˋθɪzbɪ; ˌpɪrəməs ənd ˈθɪzbi/ in ancient Roman stories, a pair of lovers who killed themselves because each thought the other one was dead. They are best known from the play about them which Bottom and his friends perform in *A MidSummer Night's Dream* by William Shakespeare. 皮拉姆斯和西斯贝〔古罗马神话中的一对恋人。他俩都误以为对方已死而自杀。博顿及其朋友在威廉·莎士比亚的《仲夏夜之梦》中扮演了这两个角色, 从而使这对恋人的形象广为人知〕

pyre /paɪr; paɪə/ *n* [C] a high pile of wood on which a dead body is placed to be burned in a funeral ceremony 火葬柴堆

Pyr·e·nees, the /ˋpɪrəniz; ˌpɪrəˈniːz/ a range of mountains between France and Spain, which goes from the Bay of Biscay to the Mediterranean Sea 比利牛斯山脉〔法国与西班牙之间的一条山脉, 由比斯开湾绵延至地中海〕

Py·rex /ˋpaɪrɛks; ˈpaɪreks/ *n* [U] *trademark* a special type of strong glass that does not break at high temperatures and is used for making cooking dishes【商标】派热克斯玻璃, 耐热玻璃〔用于制造炊具〕

py·ri·tes /pəˋraɪtiz; paɪˈraɪtiːz/ *n* [U] a compound of SULPHUR with a type of metal, usually iron, or iron and COPPER 硫化矿物; 黄铁矿; 黄铜矿: *iron pyrites* 黄铁矿 —see also 另见 FOOL'S GOLD

py·ro·ma·ni·a /ˌpaɪrəˋmenɪə; ˌpaɪrəʊˈmeɪniə/ *n* [U] *technical* a mental illness that gives you a strong desire to start fires【术语】纵火狂症

py·ro·ma·ni·ac /ˌpaɪrəˋmenɪˌæk; ˌpaɪrəʊˈmeɪniæk/ *n* [C] **1** *technical* someone who suffers from the mental illness of pyromania【术语】纵火狂症患者 **2** *informal humorous* someone who enjoys making and watching fires【非正式, 幽默】爱玩火者

py·ro·tech·nics /ˌpaɪrəˋtɛknɪks; ˌpaɪrəʊˈteknɪks/ *n* **1** [plural] *formal or technical* a public show of FIREWORKS【正式或术语】烟火[花]表演; 放烟火[花] **2** [U] *technical* the skill or business of making FIREWORKS【术语】烟火制造术; 烟火制造业 **3** [plural] an impressive show of someone's skill as a public speaker, musician etc〔演说家、音乐家等的〕高超技巧的展示 —**pyrotechnic** *adj*

Pyr·rhic vic·to·ry /ˌpɪrɪk ˋvɪktərɪ; ˌpɪrɪk ˈvɪktəri/ *n* [C] a victory in which the person who wins suffers so much that the victory was hardly worth winning 以极大代价换取的胜利, 得不偿失的胜利

Py·thag·o·ras /paɪˋθægrəs; paɪˈθægərəs/ (?582-?507BC) a Greek PHILOSOPHER and MATHEMATICIAN who developed **Pythagoras' Theorem**, a way of calculating the length of one side of a TRIANGLE which has one angle of 90°, when you already know the length of the other two sides 毕达哥拉斯〔(公元前?582-前?507), 希腊哲学家、数学家, 以毕达哥拉斯定理[勾股定理]著称, 即在已知一个直角三角形两条边长的条件下, 可求出第三条边长〕

py·thon /ˋpaɪθɑn; ˈpaɪθən/ *n* [C] a large tropical snake that kills animals for food by winding itself around them and crushing them〔热带地区的〕大蟒

pyx /pɪks; pɪks/ *n* [C] a small container in which the holy bread used for the Christian ceremony of COMMUNION (2) is kept〔基督教圣餐仪式中的〕圣饼盒

Q,q

Q, q /kju; kjuː/ *plural* **Q's, q's** or **Qs, qs** *n* [C] the 17th letter of the English alphabet 英语字母表中的第十七个字母

q the written abbreviation of 缩写= QUESTION

Qad·daf·i, Qadhafi —see 见 Colonel Moamar al GADDAFI

QALY *technical* Quality Adjusted Life Year; a way of measuring how much improvement in their health someone is likely to get as a result of having a particular type of medical treatment in the National Health Service in Britain【术语】质量调整生命年〔一种测量方法，用以反映患者通过英国国民保健署的一定治疗后身体状况的改善程度〕

Qa·tar /ˋkatɑr; kʌˈtɑː/ a country in the Middle East, east of Saudi Arabia, which is ruled by an EMIR (=a type of king). Population: 769,152(2001). Capital: Doha. Qatar is mostly desert, but it produces a lot of oil. 卡塔尔〔中东一国家，位于沙特阿拉伯以东，由埃米尔统治。人口：769,152（2001），首都：多哈。卡塔尔境内大部分为沙漠，盛产石油〕

QC /ˌkju ˋsi; ˌkjuː ˈsiː/ *n* [C] Queen's Counsel; a BARRISTER (=type of lawyer) of high rank in the British legal system 王室法律顾问

QE2, the /ˌkju i ˋtu; ˌkjuː iː ˈtuː/ a large passenger ship which sails between Southampton in southern England and New York, and also takes passengers on CRUISES (=sea journeys for pleasure) all over the world "伊丽莎白二世女王"号〔一艘大型客轮，往返于英格兰南部的南安普顿与纽约之间，并为游客提供环球航行服务〕

QED /ˌkju i ˋdi; ˌkjuː iː ˈdiː/ the abbreviation of the Latin phrase quod erat demonstrandum, used to say that a fact, event etc proves that what you say is true 证毕，证讫〔拉丁文quod erat demonstrandum 的缩写〕

qr the written abbreviation of 缩写= QUARTER

qt the written abbreviation of 缩写= QUART

q.t. /ˋkju ˋti; ˌkjuː ˈtiː/ **on the q.t.** *informal* secret or secretly【非正式】秘密地，悄悄地

Q-tip /ˋkju tɪp; ˈkjuː tɪp/ *n* [C] *AmE trademark* a COTTON BUD【美，商标】Q牌棉签

qua /kwe; kweɪ/ *prep Latin formal* used to show you are talking about the main character or the general idea of something【拉丁，正式】作为；以…的资格[身份]：*Money, qua money, cannot provide happiness.* 钱本身不能给人带来快乐。

quack¹ /kwæk; kwæk/ *v* [I] to make the sound that ducks make 作鸭叫声，发出〔鸭子般的〕嘎嘎声

quack² *n* [C] *informal*【非正式】**1** someone who pretends to have medical knowledge or skills 冒牌医生；江湖医生，庸医：*a quack doctor* 庸医 **2** *BrE* a doctor【英】医生：*You'd better go and see the quack with that burn.* 你最好去找医生看看那处烧伤。**3** [C] a word used especially by or to children to mean the sound a duck makes 鸭叫声，嘎嘎声〔尤儿语〕

quack·er·y /ˋkwækərɪ; ˈkwækəri/ *n* [U] the activities of someone who pretends to have medical knowledge or skills 庸医的医术；江湖冒牌医生的骗术

quad /kwɑd; kwɒd/ *n* [C] **1** a square open area with buildings all around it, especially in a school or college〔尤指中小学或大学中周围有建筑物的〕四方院子；四方广场 **2** a short form of 缩略式= QUADRUPLET

quadr- /kwɑdr; kwɒdr/ *prefix* another form of the prefix QUADRI- 前缀 quadri- 的另一种拼法

Quad·ra·ges·i·ma /ˌkwɑdrəˋdʒɛsəmə; ˌkwɒdrəˈdʒesɪ̣mə/ the first Sunday in Lent. The name comes from the Latin word quadraginta, meaning 40, since Quadragesima is about 40 days before Easter. 四旬节〔四旬斋的第一个星期日。源自拉丁语 quadraginta，意为"40"。四旬斋的第一个星期日大约在复活节前的40天左右〕

quad·ran·gle /ˋkwɑdræŋgl; ˈkwɒdræŋgəl/ *n* [C] **1** a square open area with buildings all around it〔周围有建筑物的〕四方院子，四方广场 **2** *technical* a flat shape that has four straight sides【术语】四边形，四角形

quad·rant /ˋkwɑdrənt; ˈkwɒdrənt/ *n* [C] **1** a quarter of a circle 四分之一圆（周）；九十度弧；扇形体 —see picture at 参见 SHAPE¹ 图 **2** an instrument for measuring angles, used when sailing or when looking at the stars〔航海或观星时用的〕象限仪

quad·ra·phon·ic, quadrophonic /ˌkwɑdrəˋfɑnɪk; ˌkwɒdrəˈfɒnɪk◂/ *adj* using a system of sound recording, broadcasting etc in which sound comes from four different SPEAKERS at the same time 四声道（立体声）的 —compare 比较 MONO², STEREO²

quad·rat·ic e·qua·tion /kwɑdˋrætɪk ɪˋkweʒən; kwɒˌdrætɪk ɪˈkweɪʒən/ *n* [C] *technical* an EQUATION such as $ax^2+bx+c=y$, which includes numbers or quantities multiplied by themselves【术语】二次方程（式）

quadri- /kwɑdrɪ; kwɒdrɪ̣/ *prefix* also 又作 **quadru-** /kwɑdrə; kwɒdrʊ̣/, **quadr-** /kwɑdr; kwɒdr/ four; four times 四；四倍：*quadrilateral* (=with four straight sides) 四边的 | *a quadruped* (=an animal with four legs) 四足动物

quad·ri·lat·er·al /ˌkwɑdrəˋlætərəl; ˌkwɒdrɪ̣ˈlætərəl◂/ *n* [C] a flat shape with four straight sides 四边形—**quadrilateral** *adj*

qua·drille /kwəˋdrɪl; kwəˈdrɪl/ *n* [C] a dance, popular especially in the 19th century, in which the dancers form a square 夸德里尔舞〔一种由四对男女表演的方阵舞，尤在19世纪流行〕

qua·dril·lion /kwɑdˋrɪljən; kwɒˈdrɪljən/ *number* **1** *BrE* the number one followed by 24 zeros【英】一百万的四次幂 (10^{24})〔1后有24个零〕**2** *AmE* the number one followed by 15 zeros【美】一千的五次幂，千万亿 (10^{15})〔1后有15个零〕

quad·ro·phon·ic /ˌkwɑdrəˋfɑnɪk; ˌkwɒdrəˈfɒnɪk◂/ *adj* another spelling of QUADRAPHONIC quadraphonic 的另一种拼法

quadru- /kwɑdrə; kwɒdrʊ̣/ *prefix* another form of the prefix QUADRI- 前缀 quadri- 的另一种拼法

quad·ru·ped /ˋkwɑdrəˌpɛd; ˈkwɒdrʊped/ *n* [C] *technical* an animal that has four legs【术语】四足动物 —compare 比较 BIPED

quad·ru·ple¹ /kwɑdˋrupḷ; ˈkwɒdrʊpəl/ *v* [I,T] to increase and become four times as big or as high or make something increase in this way（使）成四倍，（使）翻两番：*Food prices quadrupled during the war.* 战争期间食品价格翻了两番。| *The company has quadrupled its profits in just three years.* 该公司仅仅三年时间就将其利润增加至四倍。

quadruple² *adj, predeterminer* **1** four times as big or as many 四倍的：*The subjects were given quadruple the normal dosage of the drug.* 让实验对象服用了四倍于正常剂量的药物。**2** having four parts 由四部分组成的—**quadruple** *adj*

quad·ru·plet /kwɑdˋruplɪt; ˈkwɒdrʊplɪ̣t/ *n* [C] one of four babies born at the same time to the same mother 四胞胎之一

quaff /kwæf; kwɒf/ *v* [T] *literary* to drink a lot of something quickly【文】痛饮，狂饮：*wedding guests quaffing champagne* 婚礼上痛饮香槟酒的客人们

quag·mire /ˋkwægˌmaɪr; ˈkwægmaɪə/ *n* [C usually singular 一般用单数] **1** an area of soft wet muddy ground 沼泽地；泥潭，泥泞地：*In the rainy season the roads become a quagmire.* 在雨季，道路变得一片泥泞。**2** a difficult or complicated situation 困难[复杂]的局势，困境：*Public housing regulations are a legislative quagmire.* 公共房屋管理是立法的一大难题。

quail¹ /kwel; kweɪl/ *n* **1** [C] a small bird like a PARTRIDGE 鹑，鹌鹑 **2** [U] the meat of a quail 鹌鹑肉

quail² *v* [I] *literary* to be afraid; TREMBLE【文】害怕；发抖：[+at] *She quailed visibly at the sight of the grim prison walls.* 看到阴森森的监狱围墙，她害怕得直发抖。

quaint /kwent; kweɪnt/ *adj* unusual and attractive, especially in an old-fashioned way 奇特的；老式而别致的；古色古香的：*one of those quaint British traditions* 那些奇特的英国传统之一

quake¹ /kwek; kweɪk/ *v* [I] **1** to shake or tremble, usually because you are very frightened〔通常指因恐惧而〕颤抖，哆嗦：[+with] *Quaking with fear, I reached for the phone to call the police.* 我伸手打电话报警，害怕得抖个不停。**2 quake in your boots** *informal* to feel very afraid【非正式】怕得发抖 **3** if the earth, a building etc quakes, it shakes violently〔大地、建筑物等〕剧烈颤动，震动：*The explosion made the whole house quake.* 爆炸使整座房子都晃动起来。

quake² *n* [C] an EARTHQUAKE 地震

Quak·er /ˋkwekə; ˈkweɪkə/ *n* [C] a member of the Society of Friends, a Christian religious group that opposes all violence, has no priests or ceremonies, and holds its religious meetings in silence〔基督教〕贵格会教徒，公谊会教徒，教友会教徒 —**Quaker** *adj*

qual·i·fi·ca·tion /ˌkwaləfəˋkeʃən; ˌkwɒlɪ̣fɪ̣ˈkeɪʃən/ *n* **1** [C usually plural 一般用复数] an examination that you have passed, especially at school or university 合格证明：*Eva had excellent*

academic qualifications, but no work experience. 伊娃有不错的学历，但没有工作经验。| a teaching qualification 教学资格证书 | **paper qualifications** (=official qualifications rather than experience or personal qualities) 书面资格证明 **2** [C] a skill, personal quality, or type of experience that makes you suitable for a particular job or position 资历，资格；技能条件：[+for] *The status of barrister provides a qualification for various public appointments.* 大律师的地位为担任各种公职提供了条件。| **qualification to do sth** *Isobel has all the right qualifications to become a good manager.* 伊索贝尔具有成为一个称职经理的所有条件。**3** [C,U] something that you add to a statement to limit its effect or meaning 限制；限定性条件：*The committee expressed support for our plans but with certain qualifications.* 委员会表示支持我们的计划，但提出若干条件。**4** [U] the achievement of reaching the necessary standard to enter a sports competition, or passing examinations for a particular job 取得〔参赛或就业〕资格：*On qualification you can expect to find work abroad.* 取得资格之后，你就可以在国外找工作了。| *We need to beat Poland to ensure qualification for the World Cup finals.* 我们需要打败波兰队以确保获得参加世界杯决赛的资格。

3 **qual·i·fied** /ˈkwɑləˌfaɪd; ˈkwɒlɪ̵faɪd/ *adj* **1** having suitable knowledge, experience, or qualifications, especially for a particular job 〔尤指对某项工作〕有资格的；合格的，胜任的：*a qualified accountant* 合格的会计师 | *highly qualified engineering staff* 非常胜任的工程人员 | **qualified to do sth** *He's qualified to teach in elementary school, but not in high school.* 他有资格教小学，但还不够教中学。| *It's a complex legal matter and I don't feel qualified to give an opinion.* 这是个复杂的法律问题，我觉得没资格提出看法。**2** qualified agreement, approval etc is limited in some way, because you do not completely agree or approve 有限制的，有保留的：*The Gann Report received qualified approval from the colleges.* 甘恩报告得到了那些学院有保留的赞同。

qual·i·fi·er /ˈkwɑləˌfaɪɚ; ˈkwɒlɪ̵faɪə/ *n* [C] **1** someone who has reached the necessary standard for entering a competition 取得参赛资格的人；合格者 **2** a game that you have to win in order to be able to take part in a competition 资格赛，预选赛：*Rosenthal looks set to miss tomorrow's World Cup qualifier in Helsinki.* 看来罗森塔尔参加不了明天在赫尔辛基举行的世界杯预选赛了。**3** *technical* a word or phrase that limits or adds to the meaning of another word or phrase 【术语】〔语法中的〕限定语，修饰语

2 3 **qual·i·fy** /ˈkwɑləˌfaɪ; ˈkwɒlɪ̵faɪ/ *v*

1 ▶PASS EXAMS 通过考试◀ [I] to pass an examination or reach the standard of knowledge or skill that you need in order to do something 取得资格；达到标准：[+as] *Olga recently qualified as a pilot.* 奥尔佳最近取得了飞行员资格。| *After qualifying, doctors spend at least two years working in hospitals.* 在取得行医资格后，医生至少要在医院工作两年。

2 ▶HAVE A RIGHT 有权◀ [I] to have the right to claim something 有资格，有权要求〔某物〕：[+for] *You may be able to qualify for unemployment benefit.* 你也许有资格获得失业救济金。

3 ▶MAKE SB SUITABLE 使某人合适◀ [T] if your knowledge or ability qualifies you to do something, it makes you a suitable person to do it 使具有资格，使合格：**qualify sb for sth** *Fluency in three languages qualifies her for work in the European Parliament.* 她能流利地说三种语言，这使她能胜任在欧洲议会的工作。| **qualify sb to do sth** *Our four-week course will qualify you to teach English overseas.* 我们为期四周的课程将使你有资格在国外教英语。

4 ▶HAVE THE RIGHT QUALITIES 具有符合要求的特征◀ [I] to have all the necessary qualities to be considered to be a particular thing 可被认为是，可算作：[+as] *I don't think that really qualifies as an answer.* 我认为那确实算不上一个答案。| *Does photography qualify as an art form?* 摄影算得上一种艺术形式吗？

5 ▶SPORT 体育◀ [I] to reach the necessary standard to enter or continue in a competition or sports event 取得参赛[下一轮比赛]的资格；预赛及格：*If the French team wins, it will qualify for a place in the finals.* 如果法国队获胜，它将取得参加决赛的资格。

6 ▶ADD SOMETHING 增加某事物◀ [T] to add to something that has already been said, in order to limit its effect or meaning; MODIFY 限定，限制，修饰：*Could I just qualify that last statement?* 我可以修正一下最后那句话吗？

qual·i·ta·tive /ˈkwɑləˌtetɪv; ˈkwɒlɪ̵tətɪv/ *adj* connected with the quality or nature of something 性质(上)的；质量的，定性的：*a qualitative study of educational services* 对教育服务的定性研究 —compare 比较 QUANTITATIVE

1 1 **qual·i·ty**¹ /ˈkwɑlətɪ; ˈkwɒlɪ̵ti/ *n* **1** [C] something such as courage, intelligence, or loyalty that people may have as part of their character 品德，品性：*You need special personal qualities to work as a nurse.* 你需要具备特殊的个人品德才能当护士。| *Bravery was never a quality that I noticed in Gerald.* 我从未在杰拉尔德身上发现勇敢的品性。**2** [C] something such as size, colour, feel or weight that makes one thing different from other things 性质；特性：*The analysis looks at the physical and chemical qualities of the sample.* 该分析测定样品的物理和化学特性。**3** [C,U] the degree to which something is good or bad 质，质量，品质：*The higher the price, the better the quality.* 价钱越高，质量越好。| *The recent hot, humid weather is affecting air quality.* 近来炎热、潮湿的天气影响了空气的质量。| **high quality** (=very good) 高质量的，优质的 *high quality ingredients* 优质配料 **4** [U] a high standard 优质：*Remember, it's quality we're aiming for, so don't rush the job.* 记住，我们追求的是质量，所以工作不要匆忙。| **of quality** *an actor of real quality* 非常优秀的演员 **5** **quality of life** the satisfaction in your life that comes from having good health, comfort, good relationships etc, rather than from money 生活质量 **6** **a man/lady of quality** *old-fashioned* a man or woman of high social rank 【过时】上流社会的男士/女士

quality² *adj* [only before noun 仅用于名词前] **1** *especially BrE* a word meaning very good, used especially by people who are trying to sell something 【尤英】优质的，非常好的〔尤为推销某物的人所用〕：*We provide quality rented accommodation for professional people.* 我们为专业人士提供优质租房。| *quality childcare at prices people can afford* 以人们能负担的价钱提供的优质儿童照管服务 | *quality double glazing* 优质的双层玻璃 **2** **quality newspapers/press/journalism** *BrE* newspapers etc aimed at educated readers 【英】内容严肃的报纸/新闻报道/新闻工作

quality as·sur·ance /ˈ··· ˌ·ˈ·/ *n* [U] management of the quality of goods or services so that they stay at a good standard 质量保证

quality con·trol /ˈ··· ·ˌ·/ *n* [U] the practice of checking goods as they are produced to make sure that their quality is good enough 质量控制，质量管理 —**quality controller** *n* [C]

quality time /ˈ··· ˌ·/ *n* [U] the time that you spend giving someone your full attention, especially time spent with your children after work 〔用于全心照顾某人，尤指下班后与孩子一起度过的〕宝贵时光

qualm /kwɑm; kwɑːm/ *n* [C usually plural 一般用复数] a feeling of slight worry because you are not sure that what you are doing is right 疑虑，不安，担忧：*Despite my qualms, I took the job.* 尽管有些疑虑，我还是接受了那份工作。| **have no qualms about** (=not be worried) 对…没有感到不安 *He seemed to have no qualms about breaking the speed limit.* 他对超速好像并没有感到不安。

quan·da·ry /ˈkwɑndrɪ; ˈkwɒndəri/ *n* **be in a quandary (about/over)** to be unable to decide what to do about a difficult problem or situation 不知所措，陷入窘境，左右为难：*The city council is in a quandary over whether to raise taxes or not.* 市政会对是否提高税收一事左右为难。

quan·go /ˈkwæŋgo; ˈkwæŋgəʊ/ *n plural* **quangos** [C] an independent organization in Britain, started by the government but with its own legal powers 〔英国的〕准自治管理机构；半官方机构

quan·ta /ˈkwɑntə; ˈkwɒntə/ the plural of QUANTUM

quan·ti·fi·er /ˈkwɑntəˌfaɪɚ; ˈkwɒntɪ̵faɪə/ *n* [C] *technical* a word or phrase such as 'much', 'few' or 'a lot of' that is used with a noun to show quantity 【术语】数量词

quan·ti·fy /ˈkwɑntəˌfaɪ; ˈkwɒntɪ̵faɪ/ *v* [T] to measure something and express it as a number, especially something that is difficult to measure 测定…的数量；用数量表示，量化：*Life has got worse for a lot of people, but in ways that are hard to quantify.* 对许多人来说，生活已变得更糟糕了，但其变化方式却难以量化。—**quantifiable** *adj*: *The damage caused by pollution is not easily quantifiable.* 污染造成的损害是难以估量的。—**quantification** /ˌkwɑntəfɪˈkeʃən; ˌkwɒntɪ̵fɪ̵ˈkeɪʃən/ *n* [U]

quan·ti·ta·tive /ˈkwɑntəˌtetɪv; ˈkwɒntɪ̵tətɪv/ *adj* connected with amounts rather than with the quality or nature of something (数)量的；与数量有关的；定量的：*quantitative estimates* 数量估计 | *quantitative chemical analysis* 定量化学分析 —compare 比较 QUALITATIVE —**quantitatively** *adv*

3 2 **quan·ti·ty** /ˈkwɑntətɪ; ˈkwɒntɪ̵ti/ *n* **1** [C] also 又作 **quantities** [plural] an amount of something that can be counted or measured 若干数量：[+of] *microscopic quantities of heroin* 极少量的海洛因 **2** [U] amount 量，数量：[+in] *Your work has im-*

proved in quantity and quality this term. 这个学期你的工作在数量上和质量上都有了改善。**3** also 又作 **quantities** [plural] a large amount or number 大量, 许多: [+of] *Quantities of arms were discovered hidden in the trucks.* 卡车上发现藏有大量武器。| **in quantity** (=in large amounts) 大量地 *It's a lot cheaper if you buy it in quantity.* 大批量购买要便宜得多。—see also 另见 **be an unknown quantity** (UNKNOWN[1] (4))

quantity sur·vey·or /ˈ‧‧‧‧, ‧ˈ/ *n* [C] someone whose job is to calculate the amount of materials that will be needed to build something, how long it will take to build and what it will cost〔估算建筑材料的用量、所需工时、成本等的〕估算员, 建筑工料测量师

Quan·tocks, the /ˈkwɑntɑks; ˈkwɒntɒks/ also 又作 **the Quantock Hills** a range of hills in Somerset, southwest England 匡托克山脉〔英格兰西南部萨默塞特郡一山脉〕

quan·tum /ˈkwɑntəm; ˈkwɒntəm/ *n plural* **quanta** /-tə; -tə/ *technical* an amount of energy in NUCLEAR PHYSICS, which varies from the next possible smaller or larger amount by a specific degree【术语】量子

quantum leap /‚‧‧ ˈ‧/ also 又作 **quantum jump** *AmE*【美】*n* [C] a very large and important improvement 长足的重大进展, 飞跃, 突飞猛进: *This discovery is a quantum leap for medical science.* 这一发现是医学上的重大突破。

quantum me·chan·ics /‚‧‧ ‧ˈ‧‧/ *n* [U] the study of the way that atoms and smaller pieces of MATTER[1] (30) behave 量子力学

quantum the·o·ry /ˈ‧‧, ‧‧/ *n* [singular] the idea that energy, especially light, travels in separate pieces and not in a continuous form 量子论

quar·an·tine[1] /ˈkwɔrən‚tin; ˈkwɒrəntiːn/ *n* [U] a period of time when a person or animal is kept apart from others in case they are carrying a disease 检疫隔离期: **in quarantine** (=being kept somewhere in a period of quarantine) 被隔离

quarantine[2] *v* **quarantined, quarantining** [T often passive 常用被动态] to put a person or animal in quarantine 对…进行检疫隔离

quark /kwɑrk; kwɑːk/ *n* [C] **1** *technical* one of the smallest known amounts of MATTER[1] (30) that forms part of an atom【术语】夸克〔构成原子的已知最小粒子〕**2** [U] a type of German soft cheese 凝乳, 夸克干酪〔一种德国乳酪〕

QuarkXPress /‚kwɑrkɪkˈsprɛs; ‚kwɑːkɪkˈspres/ *trademark* a type of computer software used for DESKTOP publishing【商标】QuarkXPress 桌面印刷软件〔一种电脑软件, 用于桌面排版〕

quar·rel[1] /ˈkwɔrəl; ˈkwɒrəl/ *n* [C] **1** an angry argument, often about something that is not important 争吵, 吵架, 争执: [+with] *She got into a silly quarrel with the other children.* 她傻乎乎地与其他孩子吵了起来。| [+about/over] *What was the quarrel all about?* 到底为了什么吵架? | **pick a quarrel (with)** (=deliberately start a quarrel) (向…)寻衅, 故意找碴 *He seems to enjoy picking a quarrel with everyone he meets.* 他好像喜欢跟他遇到的每个人找碴吵架。**2** a reason or subject for disagreement 不同意的原因; 争执的缘由: *Is there any quarrel between those two that I should know about?* 那两个人是否有什么不和, 我应该有所了解? **3 have no quarrel with** *formal* to have no reason to dislike someone or disagree with an idea, decision etc【正式】没有理由厌恶〔某人〕; 没有理由不同意〔某一想法、决定等〕: *We have no quarrel with the court's verdict.* 我们没有理由不同意法庭的裁决。

quarrel[2] *v* **quarrelled, quarrelling** *BrE*【英】, **quarreled, quarreling** *AmE*【美】[I] to have an argument 争吵, 吵架, 争执: *I wish you two would stop quarrelling.* 我希望你们两个别再争吵了。| [+with] *They're forever bickering and quarrelling with each other.* 他们总是争吵不休。| [+about] *We're not going to quarrel about a few dollars.* 我们不想为了几美元而吵架。

quarrel with sth *phr v* [T] to disagree with something or complain about something 不同意; 抱怨: *Few of us can quarrel with the idea of more choice and more competition.* 我们中几乎没人会反对更多选择、更多竞争的想法。

quar·rel·some /ˈkwɔrəlsəm; ˈkwɒrəlsəm/ *adj* someone who is quarrelsome seems to like quarrelling 喜欢争吵的; 好争论的: *a quarrelsome tone in his voice* 他声音中的火药味 —**quarrelsomeness** *n* [U]

quar·ry[1] /ˈkwɔrɪ; ˈkwɒri/ *n* [C] **1** a place where large amounts of stone, sand etc are dug out of the ground 采石场: *a slate quarry* 板岩采石场 —compare 比较 MINE[2] (1) **2** [singular] the person or animal that you are hunting or chasing 猎取的目标; 猎物: *The police saw the empty room and knew their quarry had escaped.* 警察看到空荡荡的房间, 明白他们追踪的疑犯已经逃走了。

quarry[2] *v* [T] to dig out stone, sand etc from a quarry〔在采石场〕采〔石〕; 挖〔沙〕: [+from] *It was built with stones quarried from Portland.* 这是用从波特兰开采的石头建成的。

quart /kwɔrt; kwɔːt/ *n* [C] **1** a unit used for measuring liquids and some dry goods 夸脱〔液体或固体的容积单位〕—see table on page C4 参见 C4 页附录 **2 put a quart into a pint pot** *BrE informal* to try to do more than you have time or space for【英, 非正式】以小容大; 做不可能做到的事

quar·ter[1] /ˈkwɔrtə; ˈkwɔːtə/ *n*

1 ▶AMOUNT 数量◀ [C] one of four equal or almost equal parts into which something can be divided 四分之一: *Cut it into quarters.* 把它切成四份。| [+of] *a quarter of a mile* 四分之一英里 | *in the last quarter of the 19th century* 在 19 世纪最后二十五年里 | *They're firing almost a quarter of the workforce.* 他们要解雇将近四分之一的劳动力。| *It's about a page and a quarter.* 约一又四分之一页。

2 ▶PART OF AN HOUR 一小时的一部分◀ [C] one of the four periods of 15 minutes into which each hour can be divided 一刻钟, 十五分钟: *I'll meet you in three-quarters of an hour.* (=in 45 minutes) 我 45 分钟后见你。| **quarter to** *BrE*【英】**/quarter of** *AmE*【美】(=15 minutes before the hour) 差一刻钟到…点 *It's a quarter of two.* (=1:45) 现在差一刻钟两点。| **quarter past** *BrE*【英】**/quarter after** *AmE*【美】(=15 minutes after the hour) …点过一刻钟 *a quarter past ten* (=10:15) 十点一刻

3 ▶MONEY 钱◀ [C] a coin in the US and Canada, worth 25 cents〔美国和加拿大〕二角五分的硬币

4 ▶THREE MONTHS 三个月◀ [C] a period of three months, used especially in connection with bills, wages, and income 季度, 三个月: *The company's profits rose by 11% in the first quarter of the year.* 公司的利润第一季度增长了11%。—see also 另见 QUARTERLY[1]

5 ▶PART OF A CITY 城市的一部分◀ [C] an area of a town or city where a particular kind of people typically live or work 区, 地区: *the student quarter* 学生(居住)区 | *We took a rented house in the Creole quarter of New Orleans.* 我们在新奥尔良市的克里奥尔人居住区租了一幢房子。

6 ▶HOME 家◀ quarters [plural] a house or rooms where you can live, especially in the army〔尤指军队的〕营房; 住房, 宿舍: *staff quarters* 职工宿舍 | **married quarters** (=where soldiers with wives live) 已婚军人宿舍

7 in/from ... quarters in or from different groups of people 在/来自…团体: *Offers of financial help came from the most unexpected quarters.* 财政援助是由那些最意想不到的团体提供的。| *There were doubts in many quarters about the country's ability to repay the debt.* 许多团体对那个国家偿还债务的能力表示怀疑。

8 all quarters of the Earth/globe *literary* everywhere in the world【文】世界各地

9 give no quarter *old use* to show no pity towards someone, especially an enemy whom you have defeated【旧】不怜悯〔某人, 尤指被打败的敌人〕: *It was a fight to the death, with no quarter given.* 那是一场殊死的搏斗, 谁也不心慈手软。

10 ▶WEIGHT 重量◀ [C] *BrE* a unit for measuring weight, equal to 28 pounds or about 13 kilos【英】夸特〔等于 28 磅, 约 13 公斤〕

11 ▶AT COLLEGE 在大学里◀ [C] *AmE* a period of 10 to 12 weeks into which a teaching year is divided in some American colleges and universities【美】学季〔10 至 12 周〕: *What classes are you taking this quarter?* 这个学季你要上什么课?

12 ▶SPORT 体育◀ [C] one of the four equal periods of time into which games of some sports are divided〔某些分四节进行的体育比赛的〕一节, 四分之一场

13 ▶MOON 月亮◀ [C] the period of time twice a month when you can see a quarter of the moon's surface 上弦; 下弦; 太阴月的四分之一

14 ▶MEAT 肉◀ [C] a large piece of meat from a large animal, including one of its legs〔从大型动物身上切下的〕包括整条腿的一大块肉: *a quarter of beef* 包括整条腿的一大块牛肉 —see also 另见 **at close quarters** (CLOSE[2] (2))

quarter[2] *v* [T] **1** to cut or divide something into four parts 把〔某物〕切成四部分, 把〔某物〕四等分: *Quarter the tomatoes and place them round the dish.* 把这些番茄切成四瓣, 排放在盘子里。**2** *old use* to provide soldiers, workers etc with a place to sleep and eat【旧】为…提供食宿: *Our forces were quartered in tents on the edge of the woods.* 我们的部队被安排住在林边的帐篷里。

quar·ter·back[1] /ˈkwɔrtə‚bæk; ˈkwɔːtəbæk/ *n* [C] **1** the player in AMERICAN FOOTBALL who directs the team's attacking play and passes the ball to the other players at the start of each attacking move〔美式橄榄球中组织进攻的〕四分卫, 枢纽前卫 **2 Monday**

morning quarterback *AmE* someone who gives advice on something only after it has happened【美】放马后炮的人, 事后孔明

quarterback² *v AmE*【美】**1** [I] to play in the position of quarterback in AMERICAN FOOTBALL〔在美式橄榄球中〕担任四分卫[枢纽前卫] **2** [T] *informal* to organize or direct an activity, event etc【非正式】组织, 指挥: *She quarterbacked the new sales campaign.* 她组织了那次新的促销活动。

quarter day /ˈ·· ·/ *n* [C] *BrE* a day which officially begins a three-month period of the year, and on which payments are made, for example at the STOCK EXCHANGE【英】季度结账日

quar·ter·deck /ˈkwɔrtɚˌdɛk; ˈkwɔːtədek/ *n* [C] the back part of the upper DECK (=floor level) of a ship, used mainly by officers〔主要供高级船员使用的〕上层后甲板区

quar·ter·fi·nal /ˌkwɔrtɚˈfaɪnl; ˌkwɔːtəˈfaɪnl/ *n* [C] one of the set of four games near the end of a competition, whose winners play in the two SEMIFINALS 四分之一决赛, 半准决赛

quarter horse /ˈ·· ,·/ *n* [C] a strong horse in the US, bred to run short races, usually of a quarter of a mile〔美国的〕夸特马〔用于短距离比赛, 一般跑四分之一英里〕

quar·ter·ly¹ /ˈkwɔrtɚlɪ; ˈkwɔːtəli/ *adj, adv* produced or happening four times a year 一年四次的[地], 每季度的[地]: *quarterly accounts* 季度账 | *a quarterly newsletter* 按季度出版的新闻简报

quarterly² *n* [C] a magazine that is produced four times a year 季刊

quar·ter·mas·ter /ˈkwɔrtɚˌmæstɚ; ˈkwɔːtəˌmɑːstə/ *n* [C] **1** a military officer in charge of providing food, uniforms etc 军需官 **2** a ship's officer in charge of signals and guiding the ship on the right course 舵手

quarter note /ˈ·· ·/ *n* [C] *AmE* a musical note which continues for a quarter of the length of a WHOLE NOTE【美】四分音符; CROTCHET *BrE*【英】—see picture at 参见 MUSIC 图

quarter ses·sions /ˈ·· ,··/ *n* [plural] an English law court in former times, which has been replaced by the Crown Court〔英国旧时的〕季审法院〔现已被刑事法庭取代〕

quar·ter·staff /ˈkwɔrtɚˌstæf; ˈkwɔːtəstɑːf/ *n* [C] a long wooden pole used as a weapon, especially in former times〔尤指旧时作武器用的〕铁头木棍

quar·tet /kwɔrˈtɛt; kwɔːˈtet/ *n* [C] **1** four singers or musicians who perform together 四重唱; 四重奏; 四重唱[奏]表演小组: *He's the trombonist in a jazz quartet.* 他是一个爵士乐四重奏小组中的长号手。**2** a piece of music written for four performers 四重唱曲; 四重奏曲 **3** four people or things of the same type 同类的四个[人/物]; 四人一组; 四个一套: *The same quartet of characters appears in another of her novels.* 同样的四个人物出现在她的另一部小说中。—compare 比较 QUINTET, TRIO

quar·to /ˈkwɔrto; ˈkwɔːtəʊ/ *n* [C] *technical*【术语】**1** the size of paper, or the paper itself, produced by folding a large sheet of paper twice, to produce four sheets 四开; 四开的纸: *quarto sheets of paper* 一些四开的纸 **2** a book with pages of quarto size 四开本(的书)

quartz /kwɔrts; kwɔːts/ *n* [U] a hard mineral substance, used in making electronic watches and clocks 石英: *a quartz gold watch* 石英金表

qua·sar /ˈkwezɑr; ˈkweɪzɑː/ *n* [C] *technical* a very bright, very distant object similar to a star【术语】类星体

quash /kwɑʃ; kwɒʃ/ *v* [T] *formal*【正式】**1** to officially state that a judgement or decision is no longer legal or correct 宣布〔判决、决定〕不再有效; 废除, 撤销: *The judge quashed the decision of the lower court.* 法官撤销了下级法院的裁决。**2** to use force to end protests or disobedience 镇压, 以武力平息; 压服: *quash a rebellion* 镇压叛乱

quasi- /kwezaɪ, kwɑzɪ; ˈkweɪzaɪ, kwɑːzi/ *prefix* **1** in some ways; partly 一定程度上; 部分地; 类似, 半, 准: *the chairman's quasi-judicial role* (=acting in some ways like a judge) 主席的准司法角色 **2** false or pretended 假的; 假装的: *quasi-scientific ideas* 伪科学思想

Qua·si·mo·do /ˌkwɑzɪˈmodo; ˌkwɑːzɪˈməʊdəʊ/ the main character in the book *The Hunchback of Notre Dame* (1831) by Victor Hugo. He is an ugly HUNCHBACK (=someone whose back has a large raised part at the top) whose job is to ring the bells in the Cathedral of Notre Dame in Paris. 卡西莫多〔维克多·雨果的小说《巴黎圣母院》(1831) 中的主人公。他是一个相貌奇丑的驼背的巴黎圣母院里的敲钟人〕

quat·er·cen·te·na·ry /ˌkwɑtɚˈsɛntəˌnɛrɪ; ˌkwætəsenˈtiːnəri/ *n* [C] the day or year exactly 400 years after a particular event 四百周年(纪念): *the quatercentenary of Shakespeare's birth* 莎士比亚诞生四百周年纪念

Quatermain /ˈkwɔrtɚˌmen; ˈkwɔrtɚˌmeɪn/, **Allan** /ˈælən; ˈælən/ the main character in several popular adventure NOVELS by Sir Henry Rider Haggard (1865-1925), especially *King Solomon's Mines* (1885) and *Allan Quatermain* (1887). 夸特曼〔亨利·赖德·哈格德爵士 (1865-1925) 的数部著名冒险小说中的主人公, 尤见于《所罗门王的宝藏》(1885) 和《艾伦·夸特曼》(1887)〕

quat·rain /ˈkwɑtren; ˈkwɒtreɪn/ *n* [C] a group of four lines in a poem 四行诗; 四行的诗节

qua·ver¹ /ˈkwevɚ; ˈkweɪvə/ *v* [I,T] if your voice quavers, it shakes as you speak, especially because you are nervous〔尤指因紧张令说话声〕颤抖; 用颤抖的声音说: *"Please help me," he quavered.* 他颤抖着说: "请帮帮我。" —**quavery** *adj*

quaver² *n* [C] **1** *BrE* a musical note which continues for an eighth of the length of a SEMIBREVE【英】〔音乐中的〕八分音符; EIGHTH NOTE *AmE*【美】— see picture at 参见 MUSIC 图 **2** a shaking sound in your voice 颤音

quay /ki; kiː/ *n* [C] a place where boats can be tied up or can stop to load and UNLOAD 码头: *a quay lined with fishing boats* 泊有许多渔船的码头

quay·side /ˈkiˌsaɪd; ˈkiːsaɪd/ *n* [C] the area next to a quay 码头边, 码头前沿地带, 码头区: *people strolling along the quayside* 沿码头漫步的人们 | *a quayside restaurant* 码头边上的餐厅

quea·sy /ˈkwizɪ; ˈkwiːzi/ *adj* feeling that you are going to VOMIT (感到) 恶心的, 想呕吐的: *The sea got rougher, and I began to feel a little queasy.* 海上风浪更猛了, 我开始感到有点恶心想吐。—**queasiness** *n* [U]

Que·bec /kwɪˈbɛk; kwɪˈbek/ **1** a PROVINCE in eastern Canada, whose capital city is also called Quebec, and whose largest city is Montreal. Quebec is the centre of French Canadian culture. Most of the population speak French as their first language, and there are laws forbidding the official use of English, for example in public signs. Many people in Quebec think that it should separate from the rest of Canada and become an independent country. People from Quebec are called **Québécois**, or sometimes **Quebeckers**. 魁北克省〔加拿大东部一省, 首府亦名魁北克, 最大城市为蒙特利尔。魁北克省是加拿大法语文化中心, 大部分居民把法语作为第一语言。该省制定有相关条例, 禁止在某些正式场合使用英语, 如公共指示牌。许多魁北克人认为魁北克应脱离加拿大并且成为一个独立国家。魁北克人称作 Québécois, 有时也称Quebecker〕**2** the capital city of Quebec province, and the centre of French Canadian nationalism 魁北克市〔魁北克省首府, 是加拿大法语民族文化中心〕

queen¹ /kwin; kwiːn/ *n* [C] S2 W2

1 ►**RULER** 统治者◄ also 又作 **Queen** **a)** the female ruler of a country 女王: *Elizabeth II became Queen of England in 1952.* 伊丽莎白二世于1952年成为英格兰女王。**b)** the wife of a king 王后

2 ►**CARD** 纸牌◄ a playing card with a picture of a queen on it 王后, Q(牌): *the queen of hearts* 红桃王后

3 ►**HOMOSEXUAL** 同性恋◄ *informal* an insulting word for a male HOMOSEXUAL, especially one who behaves like a woman【非正式】〔侮辱性用语, 尤指举止像女人的〕男同性恋者

4 **queen bee** a woman who behaves as if she is the most important person in a place〔在某场合〕举止宛若重要人物的女子, 领导社交活动的妇女

5 **the queen of** a woman who is regarded as the best at a particular activity or in a particular field〔指在某一活动或领域中〕最优秀的女子, 最出类拔萃的女子: *Tammy Wynette, the queen of country music* 乡村音乐王后塔米·怀尼特

6 ►**INSECT** 昆虫◄ a large female BEE, ANT etc, which lays the eggs for a whole group〔蜂、蚁等的〕后

7 ►**CHESS** 国际象棋◄ the most powerful piece in the game of CHESS 王后 —see also 另见 BEAUTY QUEEN, DRAG QUEEN, MAY QUEEN

queen² *v* [T] **1** **queen it over** *informal* to behave in an annoying way as if you are more important than other people【非正式】大摆架子, 盛气凌人 **2** *technical* to change a PAWN[1] (1) into a queen in the game of CHESS【术语】〔国际象棋中〕将卒子变为王后

Queen, the Her Majesty the Queen; the official title of the queen of the United Kingdom of Great Britain and Northern Ireland. The Queen is the official head of state of Britain and of other countries in the COMMONWEALTH, but has little real political power. She has to give her official agreement (Royal Assent) to all new laws before they can actually become laws but in fact she does not have the right to refuse this agreement. 女王〔也称女王陛下, 大不列颠及北爱尔兰联合王国女王的官方头衔。女王是英国及英联邦国家的元首, 但并不拥有真正的政治权力。所有新法律, 女王必须御准, 才可付诸实施, 但实际上她无权表示反对〕

Queen Anne /. ˈ ˈ/ **1** a style of furniture, popular in the UK in the 18th century. Queen Anne tables and chairs typically have curving legs. 安妮女王时期的家具风格〔18世纪流行于英国的一种家具风格。桌椅腿为典型的曲线形〕**2** a plain style of building using red brick, popular in the UK during the time of Queen Anne 安妮女王时期的建筑风格〔一种以红砖为材料的简朴建筑风格，流行于安妮女王统治时期的英国〕

Queen E·liz·a·beth Hall, the /. . . . ˈ ˈ/ a concert hall at the South Bank in London, which usually has performances of CLASSICAL music 伊丽莎白女王音乐厅〔伦敦南岸一音乐厅，通常演奏古典音乐〕

Queen Elizabeth II, the /. . . . ˈ . ˈ/ the full name of the QE2 "伊丽莎白二世女王"号〔QE2的全称〕

Queen E·liz·a·beth Is·lands, the /. . ˈ . . . ˈ/ a group of islands in the Arctic Ocean that are part of Canada 伊丽莎白女王群岛〔北冰洋一群岛，属加拿大领土〕

queen·ly /ˈkwinlɪ; ˈkwiːnli/ *adj* suitable for or like a queen 适合女王的；女王般的：*She gave a queenly wave as she rode past.* 她骑马经过时女王般地挥了挥手。

Queen Mab /ˌkwin ˋmæb; ˌkwiːn ˈmæb/ the queen of the fairies (FAIRY) in old stories and in literature 玛柏王后〔古老传说及文学作品中的仙后〕

Queen Moth·er /. ˈ . ./ *n* [singular] the mother of the ruling king or queen（王）太后

Queen Mother, the /. ˈ . ./ (1900-2002) the mother of the British Queen Elizabeth II, whose official title was **Queen Elizabeth the Queen Mother**. She was one of the most popular members of the royal family, and she was often called 'the Queen Mum' in British popular newspapers. 王太后〔（1900-2002），英国女王伊丽莎白二世的母亲，正式头衔为王太后伊丽莎白女王。她是最受人爱戴的英国王室成员之一，大众报纸常称她为the Queen Mum（女王妈妈）〕

Queen of Hearts, the /. . . ˈ/ **1** a character in the book *Alice's Adventures in Wonderland* by Lewis Carroll, who orders people's heads to be cut off, by saying "Off with his head!" 红桃王后〔路易斯·卡罗尔创作的《艾丽丝漫游奇境记》中的一个人物。她常说"砍下他的脑袋"来下令将人的头砍掉〕—see also 另见 ALICE IN WONDERLAND **2** a character from a NURSERY RHYME (=an old song or poem for young children) 红桃王后，红心王后〔一首童谣中的人物〕：*The Queen of Hearts, she baked some tarts, /All on a summer's day; / The Knave of Hearts, he stole the tarts, /And took them clean away.* 红桃皇后可真行，/亲自烤起果馅饼，夏日整天忙不停；/红桃杰克可真馋，/顺手牵羊不畏难，/一个没剩全偷完。

Queen of She·ba, the /ˌkwin əv ˋʃibə; ˌkwiːn əv ˈʃiːbə/ **1** someone who is very rich or who spends money as if they were very rich, from a story in the Old Testament of the Bible about the wealth of the Queen of Sheba 赛伯伊女王〔借指富人或花钱如流水的人。源自《圣经·旧约》中赛伯伊女王的财富故事〕**2 and I'm the Queen of Sheba** *humorous* used as a reply when someone claims that they are famous or that they have done something impressive, but you do not believe them【幽】那么我就是赛伯伊女王啦〔有人自称有名气或者做了一件了不起的事情，你却不信以为真。此时，你就可借用这一说法〕：*"I'd like to reserve a table for tonight – this is Demi Moore." "Oh yeah, and I'm the Queen of Sheba."* "我要订一张今晚的桌子 —— 我是黛米·摩尔。""噢，可以，那我就是赛伯伊女王啦。"

Queen of the May /. . . ˈ/ —see 见 MAY QUEEN

Queens /ˋkwinz; ˈkwiːnz/ one of the five BOROUGHs of New York City, at the western end of Long Island, where a lot of poorer people live 昆斯区〔纽约市五大行政区之一，位于长岛西端，是著名的贫民集居地〕

Queen's Bench, the /. ˈ ./ also 又作 **the Queen's Bench Division** /. ˈ . ˈ . . ./ a division of the High Court of Justice in England and Wales. This name is used when a queen is ruling, and it changes to the King's Bench when a king is ruling. 女王座分庭〔英格兰与威尔士高等法院的一分庭。女王统治时期用此名，国王统治时期改称the King's Bench（王座分庭）〕—see also 另见 HIGH COURT

Queens·ber·ry rules, the /ˌkwinzbɛrɪ ˋrulz; ˌkwiːnzbəri ˈruːlz/ the rules of fair fighting in the sport of boxing, which were established in 1867 by a British lord, the Marquess of Queensberry 昆斯伯里侯爵规则〔一套在拳击运动中公平竞赛的规则。该规则是英国的昆斯伯里侯爵1867年制订的〕

Queen's Coun·sel /. ˈ . ./ *n* a QC 王室法律顾问

Queen's En·glish /. ˈ . ./ *n BrE*【英】**speak the Queen's English** to speak very correctly and in a way that is typical of people who belong to the highest social class 说标准英语 —see also 另见 KING'S ENGLISH

Queen's ev·i·dence /. ˈ . . ./ *n BrE*【英】**turn Queen's evidence** if a criminal turns Queen's evidence, they agree to help the police, law courts etc to catch other criminals by giving them information 提供对同案犯不利的证据，〔罪犯〕作为污点证人指控同党 —see also 另见 EVIDENCE[1], KING'S EVIDENCE, STATE'S EVIDENCE

queen-size /ˈ . ./ *adj especially AmE* a queen-size bed, sheet etc is larger than the standard size for a bed for two people【尤美】〔床、床单等〕大号的，大于标准尺寸的 —compare 比较 DOUBLE BED, KING-SIZE, SINGLE[1] (4)

Queens·land /ˋkwinzlənd; ˈkwiːnzlənd/ a state in northeast Australia, whose capital and largest city is Brisbane. Its products include sugar, wool, and many types of minerals, including coal. Queensland is a popular place for tourists because of its warm weather, its beaches on the Gold Coast, and the Great Barrier Reef. 昆士兰州〔澳大利亚东北部一州。首府和最大城市是布里斯班，出产糖、羊毛以及包括煤在内的多种矿产。该州气候宜人，有黄金海岸和大堡礁，是著名的旅游区〕

Queens-Mid·town Tun·nel, the /. . ˈ . . ˈ ./ a TUNNEL for traffic in New York City, which goes under the East River and connects Manhattan and Queens 昆斯-市中心隧道〔纽约市区一交通隧道，从东河河底穿越而过，连接曼哈顿与昆斯区〕

Queen's speech, the /. . ˈ/ a speech given by the Queen at the official opening of the British Parliament each year, usually in October. The speech is actually written by the government, and it gives details of the government's plans for the next year, including the new laws it intends to make. When a king is ruling instead of a queen, it is called the 'King's Speech'. 女王敕语〔英国女王每年在国会开幕式上的讲话，通常在10月。文稿由政府拟定，详细介绍政府来年的规划，包括拟制定的新法律等。国王当政时则称为the King's Speech（国王敕语）〕

queer[1] /kwɪr; kwɪə/ *adj* **1** *old-fashioned* strange or difficult to explain【过时】奇怪的；难以解释的：*This orange tastes queer.* 这个橘子吃起来有怪味。| *She gave a queer laugh.* 她古怪地笑了笑。**2** *informal* a word meaning HOMOSEXUAL, considered offensive when used by people who are not homosexual【非正式】同性恋的〔冒犯用语〕**3** *BrE* ill or sick【英】不舒服的；想呕吐的：*I'm feeling a little queer – I think I'll go and lie down.* 我感觉有些不舒服 —— 我想我要去躺一下。**4 queer in the head** *old-fashioned* talking or behaving strangely; crazy【过时】言谈[举止]古怪的；精神不正常的 **5 be in queer street** *BrE old-fashioned* to owe people money【英，过时】负债 —**queerly** *adv*: *queerly shaped* 形状怪异的 —**queerness** *n* [U]

queer[2] *n* [C] *informal* an insulting word for a HOMOSEXUAL【非正式】同性恋者〔侮辱性用语〕

queer[3] *v* **queer sb's pitch** *BrE informal* to spoil someone's plans or chance to do something【英，非正式】破坏某人〔做某事〕的计划[机会]

queer bash·ing /ˈ . . ./ *n* [U] *informal* physical violence against people because they are HOMOSEXUAL【非正式】对同性恋者的暴力攻击[无故殴打]

quell /kwɛl; kwel/ *v* [T] *formal*【正式】**1** to bring an end to a violent situation especially when people are protesting 平息，镇压，制止〔暴乱局面〕：**quell a riot/revolt/disturbance etc** *They needed more troops to quell the ever-rising tide of rioting.* 他们需要更多的军队以平息不断上涨的暴乱潮。**2** to reduce unpleasant feelings, especially of doubt or worry 减轻，消除〔疑虑〕：*I thought about the advantages of the deal, trying to quell a growing sense of unease.* 我考虑了一下那笔交易的好处，设法消除内心越来越强烈的不安。

quench /kwɛntʃ; kwentʃ/ *v* [T] **1 quench your thirst** to stop yourself from feeling thirsty 止渴，解渴：*Iced tea really quenches your thirst.* 冰茶真解渴。**2 quench a fire** to make a fire stop burning 灭火

quer·u·lous /ˋkwɛrələs; ˈkwerʊləs/ *adj formal* complaining all the time in an annoying way【正式】老是抱怨的，好发牢骚的：*"But why can't I go?" he said in a querulous tone.* "但为什么我不能去？"他以抱怨的口气问道。—**querulously** *adv* —**querulousness** *n* [U]

que·ry[1] /ˋkwɪrɪ; ˈkwɪəri/ *n* [C] a question you ask to get information, or to check that something is true or correct 问题；疑问：*We will answer any queries by letter.* 我们将通过信函回答一切问题。

query[2] *v* [T] **1** to express doubt that something is true or correct 质疑，对…表示疑问：[**+whether**] *I'd query whether these figures are reliable.* 我想问一下这些数字是否可靠。**2** [T] to ask a question 提〔问题〕：*"What time are we leaving?" queried Mrs Evans.* "我们什么时候离开？"埃文斯夫人问道。

quest /kwɛst; kwest/ *n* [C] *especially literary* a long search for something such as truth or knowledge【尤文】〔长期的〕寻求，探求: [+for] *the quest for enlightenment* 对文明的追求 —**quest** *v* [I]: *to quest after the truth* 寻求真理

S1 W1 **ques·tion¹** /ˈkwɛstʃən; ˈkwestʃən/ *n* [C]

1 ▶ASKING FOR INFORMATION 要求得到信息◀ a sentence or phrase that asks for information 问题: **ask (sb) a question** *They asked me a lot of questions about my work experience.* 他们问了我许多有关我工作经验的问题。| *May I ask a question?* 我可以问一个问题吗？| **answer a question** *Answer three out of five questions on the exam paper.* 从试卷上五道问题中选答三道。| *Does anyone have any questions?* 谁有问题吗？ —see 见 ASK (USAGE)

2 ▶SUBJECT/PROBLEM 议题/难题◀ a subject or problem that needs to be settled, discussed, or dealt with; ISSUE¹ (1) 需要解决[处理]的事; 问题: *Several questions had still not been resolved.* 好几个问题仍然没有得到解决。| *This brings us to the question of government funding.* 这给我们提出了政府资助的问题。| **the question is** *The question is, do I take the job in Japan, or stay here?* 问题是，我是接受日本那份工作，还是留在这儿呢?

3 ▶DOUBT 疑问◀ a feeling of doubt about something 疑问，不确定的事情: **raise questions about** *This incident raises further questions about the effectiveness of airport security.* 这个事件使人们对机场保安的有效性提出了进一步的疑问。| **there is no question** (=there is no doubt) 毫无疑问 *He's by far the best, there's no question about it.* 他是最好的，这毫无疑问。| **open to question** (=likely or able to be doubted) 值得怀疑，有待论证 *The wisdom of this policy is open to question.* 这一政策是否明智尚难定论。

4 without question a) without any doubt 毫无疑问: *Marilyn was, without question, a very beautiful woman.* 毫无疑问，玛丽莲是一个非常漂亮的女子。**b)** if you obey an order without question, you obey immediately and do not complain at all 毫无异议地〔服从命令〕

5 there's no question of used to say that there is no possibility of something happening …是不可能的: *There is no question of the government holding talks with terrorists.* 政府不可能与恐怖分子进行谈判。

6 in question the things, people etc in question are the ones that are being discussed or talked about 正被讨论的; 谈论中的: *The goods in question had been stolen.* 所说的那些货物已经被盗。

7 be a question of used when you are giving the most important fact, part, or feature or something 问题在于，是一个…的问题: *Dance is a question of control and creative expression.* 舞蹈在于动作控制和创造性表现。| *I would love to come, but it's a question of time.* 我倒是想来，但问题是要看有没有时间。

8 out of the question not possible or not allowed 不可能的; 不允许的: *You can't go to the wedding in that old shirt – it's quite out of the question.* 你不能穿着那件旧衬衫去参加婚礼——这是绝对不行的。

9 it's just a question of *spoken* used to say that something is easy or not complicated【口】只是个…的问题: *It's just a question of putting in a couple of screws.* 只要拧上两颗螺丝钉问题就解决了。

10 pop the question *informal humorous* to ask someone to marry you【非正式，幽默】求婚: *Simon finally plucked up the courage to pop the question.* 西蒙终于鼓起了勇气求婚。

11 good question! *spoken* used to show that you do not know the answer to a question【口】好一个难题！问得好!〔用以表示不知道某问题的答案〕: *"How can we afford this?" "Good question!"* "我们怎么才能买得起这个呢?" "问得好!" —see also 另见 **leading question** (LEADING¹ (4)), **rhetorical question** (RHETORICAL (1)), **beg the question** (BEG (5)), **call into question** (CALL¹ (21))

S2 W3 **question²** *v* [T] **1** to ask someone questions to find out what they know about something, especially about a crime 询问; 盘问; 审问: *We're taking them in for questioning.* 我们要把他们带走审问。| **question sb about** *The police questioned him about the missing $10,000.* 警方就那丢失了的一万美元盘问他。| **question sb closely** (=ask them a lot of difficult questions to find out exactly what they know) 仔细盘问某人 **2** to have doubts about something or tell someone about these doubts 怀疑，对…提出质疑[异议]: *Are you questioning the truth of what I'm saying?* 你在怀疑我所讲的话的真实性吗？| *It makes me question the whole basis of the research.* 这使我对该研究的整个基础产生了疑问。

ques·tion·a·ble /ˈkwɛstʃənəbl̩; ˈkwestʃənəbəl/ *adj* **1** not definitely true or correct 不确定的; 有问题的: *The report's conclusions are questionable because the sample used was very small.* 那个报告的结论有问题，因为取样太少了。**2** behaviour or actions that are questionable seem likely to be dishonest or wrong〔行为〕不诚实的，可疑的: *business deals of a rather questionable kind* 非常可疑的交易

ques·tion·er /ˈkwɛstʃənɚ; ˈkwestʃənə/ *n* [C] someone who is asking a question, for example in a public discussion 问问题的人，提问者

ques·tion·ing /ˈkwɛstʃənɪŋ; ˈkwestʃənɪŋ/ *adj* a questioning look or expression shows that you have doubts about something or need some information 怀疑的; 询问的: *the questioning eyes of a child* 孩子那探询的目光 —**questioningly** *adv*

question mark /ˈ· · ·/ *n* [C] **1** the mark (?) that is used at the end of a sentence to show that it asks a question 问号 —see picture at 参见 PUNCTUATION MARK 图 **2 a question mark over** if there is a question mark over something, there is a possibility that it will not be successful or will not continue to exist 不确定性: *A big question mark hangs over the company's future.* 这家公司将来如何还是个大问号。

question mas·ter /ˈ· · ,· ·/ *n* [C] *BrE* the person who asks the questions in a QUIZ game【英】问答游戏的主持人

ques·tion·naire /ˌkwɛstʃənˈɛr; ˌkwestʃəˈneə/ *n* [C] a written set of questions which you give to a large number of people in order to collect information〔收集信息用的〕问卷，问题单，调查表: **fill in/complete a questionnaire** (=answer all the questions in it) 填妥问卷

question tag /ˈ· · ·/ *n* [C] *technical* a phrase such as 'isn't it?', 'won't it?', or 'does she?' that you add to the end of a statement to make it a question or to check that someone agrees with you【术语】疑问尾句，附加疑问句: *You're from Hamburg, aren't you?* 你来自汉堡，对吧?

question time /ˈ· · ·/ *n* [U] the period of time in a parliament when ministers answer questions from members of the parliament〔议会中的〕质询时间

Quet·zal·co·at·l /ˌkɛtsl̩koˈætl̩; ˌketsəlkəʊˈætl/ a Native American god of central America, shown as a snake with feathers on its head and thought of as the god of air and water 魁扎尔科亚特尔，羽蛇〔中美洲印第安人尊崇的神，状似头上有羽毛的蛇，被奉为空气与水之神〕

queue¹ /kju; kjuː/ *n* [C] *BrE*【英】**1** a line of people waiting to enter a building, buy something etc, or a line of vehicles waiting to move〔人或车辆为等候而排的〕队，行列; LINE¹ (22) *AmE*【美】: *The queue for the cinema went right round the building.* 为看电影而排的队拐过了那幢大楼。| *We were stuck in a queue for half an hour.* 我们在车流中被困了半个小时。| **jump a queue** (=go unfairly to the front of a queue instead of waiting) 插队，不按次序排队，加塞儿 —see picture at 参见 PUSH IN 图 **2** *technical* a list of jobs that a computer has to do in a particular order【术语】队列〔电脑必须按一定顺序处理的一系列工作〕; ORDER¹ (26) *AmE*【美】: *the print queue* 打印队列 —see also 另见 **the dole queue** (DOLE¹ (2))

queue² *past tense and past participle* **queued** *present participle* **queuing** or **queueing** also 又作 **queue up** [I] *BrE* to form or join a line of people or vehicles waiting to do something or go somewhere【英】排队〔等候〕; **line up** (LINE²) *AmE*【美】: *The post office was really busy – we had to queue for ages to get served.* 邮局非常忙——我们不得不排了好长时间的队等候。| [+for] *people queuing for tickets* 排队买票的人 S3

queue-jump /ˈ· ·/ *v* [I] *BrE informal* to go unfairly to the front of a queue, instead of waiting【英，非正式】插队，加塞儿

quib·ble¹ /ˈkwɪbl̩; ˈkwɪbəl/ *v* [I+over/about] to argue about small points or details that are completely unimportant〔为了细枝末节或琐事而〕争吵，吹毛求疵: *Don't quibble about the money – just pay what she asks.* 别为钱争执了——她要多少就给她多少好了。

quibble² *n* [C] a small complaint or criticism about something very unimportant 小小的不满[批评]; 吹毛求疵: *I have just one quibble – there's a spelling mistake here.* 我只有一点小意见——这儿有一处拼写错误。

quiche /kiʃ; kiːʃ/ *n* [C,U] a flat open piece of PASTRY (1) filled with a mixture of eggs, cheese, vegetables etc 什锦烘饼，蛋奶火腿馅饼

CULTURAL NOTE 文化注释

In Britain and the US, quiche is often humorously associated with weakness if it is being eaten by a man, and people sometimes make a joke by saying "Real men don't eat quiche". 在英国和美国，男人吃什锦烘饼常被戏称为软蛋。人们有时也因此逗乐说"好汉不吃什锦烘饼"。

quick¹ /kwɪk; kwɪk/ *adj*
1 ►SHORT TIME 短时间◄ continuing or existing for only a short time 短时间的, 短暂的; 匆匆的: *I just have to make a quick phone call.* 我得打一个简短的电话。| *John had a quick meal and then went out again.* 约翰匆匆吃了饭, 然后又出去了。| *That was quick! I thought you'd be another hour.* 真是太快了! 我原以为你还要一个小时呢。
2 ►FAST 快的◄ moving or happening fast 快速的, 迅速的: *She walked with short, quick steps.* 她迈着碎步急速走着。| *A series of quick changes take place as the chemicals bond.* 不同的化学品结合时会发生一连串快速的变化。
3 ►SOON 不久◄ happening very soon, without any delay 马上的, 即刻的: *We've put the house on the market and we're hoping for a quick sale.* 我们已把房子投放到市场上, 希望马上就卖出去。
4 ►CLEVER 聪明的◄ able to learn and understand things fast 聪敏的, 敏锐的, 脑子反应快的: *That child's a really quick learner.* 那个孩子确实学得快。| **a quick study** *AmE slang* (=a student who is clever and learns quickly)【美俚】聪明而学得快的学生
5 be quick to hurry 快点, 抓紧时间: *If you want to come with me you'll have to be quick – I'm leaving in ten minutes.* 如果你想和我一块去, 你就得抓紧点 —— 我 10 分钟后走。| **be quick about it** *Just bring me that book, and be quick about it.* 请把那本书给我拿来, 快一点。
6 be quick to do sth to react quickly to what someone says or does 性急地做某事: *You're always very quick to criticize my ideas – let's hear yours!* 你总是急不可耐地批评我的想法 —— 让我们听听你的!
7 be quick on the draw/uptake to quickly understand a situation or what someone tells you, so that you know what you have to do 理解力强, 领悟快
8 a quick one/half/pint *especially BrE informal* a drink that you have in a hurry 【尤英, 非正式】匆匆饮下的酒: *Let's stop for a quick one before the train comes.* 在火车到来之前, 让我们停下抓紧喝一杯。
9 have a quick temper to get angry very easily 易怒, 性情急躁
10 a quick fix *informal* a repair to something or an answer to a problem that will work only for a short time【非正式】应急解决办法, 权宜之计 —see also 另见 QUICKLY —**quickness** *n* [U]

quick² *interjection* used to tell someone to hurry or come quickly 快, 快点: *Quick! We'll miss the bus!* 快点! 我们赶不上公共汽车了! | *Come on! Quick!* 来吧! 快点!

quick³ *adv* quickly; fast 快速地, 迅速地: *Come back quick – something terrible has happened!* 赶快回来, 发生了可怕的事! | **quick as a flash** *informal* (=very quickly)【非正式】快如闪电 *Quick as a flash she replied "That's not what I've heard!"* 她迅速答道: "我听到的不是那样!"

quick⁴ *n* [U] **1 cut sb to the quick** if a remark or criticism cuts you to the quick, it makes you very upset〔用言语或批评〕刺痛某人, 使某人很不痛快 **2 the quick** the sensitive flesh under your fingernails and toenails〔手指甲或脚趾甲下的〕活肉: *Her nails were bitten to the quick.* 她的指甲被咬到肉里了。**3 the quick and the dead** *old use* all people, including those who are alive and those who are dead【旧】〔包括活人和死人的〕所有人

quick-change ar·tist /ˌ.ˈ. ˈ..ˌ./ *n* [C] an entertainer who can change their clothes or appearance very quickly 能迅速换服装[扮相]的演员

quick·en /ˈkwɪkən; ˈkwɪkən/ *v* [I,T] **1** to become quicker or make something quicker (使) 变快, 加快: *the quickening pace of technological change* 技术改革上加快的步伐 | **quicken your pace** (=walk faster) 加快步伐 *Ray glanced at his watch and quickened his pace.* 雷看了一眼手表, 加快了步伐。| **your heart/pulse quickens** (=your heart beats faster because you are afraid, excited etc)〔因害怕、激动等〕心脏/脉搏跳动加快 *Val caught sight of Rob and felt her heart quicken.* 瓦尔看见了罗布, 感到心跳加快了。**2** *formal* if a feeling quickens, or if something quickens it, it becomes stronger or more active【正式】(使)〔情绪〕变得更强烈[更活跃]: *This policy served only to quicken antigovernment feeling.* 这一政策只能加剧人们的反政府情绪。**3** *old use or literary* to come alive or make something come alive【旧或文】(使) 复活; (使) 有生气

quick·en·ing /ˈkwɪkənɪŋ; ˈkwɪkənɪŋ/ *n* [U] the first movements of a baby that has not been born yet〔胎儿最初的〕蠕动

quick·fire /ˈkwɪkˌfaɪr; ˈkwɪkfaɪə/ *adj* quickfire conversation, speech etc is very fast and full of clever or amusing remarks〔谈话、演说等〕像连珠炮似的; 快速且睿智风趣的: *He's full of quickfire patter and smooth gestures.* 他妙语如珠, 还有丰富的肢体语言。

quick-freeze /ˈkwɪkfriz; ˈkwɪkfriːz/ *v* [T] to freeze food very quickly so that it keeps all its taste 将〔食物〕速冻; FLASHFREEZE *AmE*【美】

quick·ie /ˈkwɪkɪ; ˈkwɪki/ *n* [C] *informal*【非正式】**1** something done or made quickly and easily 匆匆而做的事: *This recipe is a favourite quickie for when I'm in a hurry.* 这是我赶时间时喜欢用的快捷烹饪法。**2** *humorous* a sexual act done in a hurry【幽默】匆匆完事的性交 —**quickie** *adj*: *a quickie divorce* 草率的离婚

quick·lime /ˈkwɪkˌlaɪm; ˈkwɪk-laɪm/ *n* [U] a white substance obtained by burning LIMESTONE 生石灰

quick·ly /ˈkwɪklɪ; ˈkwɪkli/ *adv* **1** fast 快速地: *She checked nothing was coming and walked quickly across the road.* 她确信没有什么 (车辆) 过来, 便快速穿过马路。| *Quickly, John, we don't have much time.* 快点, 约翰, 我们时间不多了。**2** after only a very short time 很快, 马上: *I realized fairly quickly that this wasn't going to be easy.* 我马上就认识到这事没那么容易。**3** for a short time 短暂地, 片刻地: *I'll just quickly nip into that shop.* 我只是去那家商店很快看一下。

quick march /ˌ. ˈ./ *interjection* used as a command to tell a group of soldiers to march quickly〔口令〕齐步行进, 快步走

quick·sand /ˈkwɪkˌsænd; ˈkwɪksænd/ also 又作 **quicksands** *plural n* [C,U] wet sand that is dangerous because it pulls you down into it if you try to walk on it 流沙

quick·sil·ver /ˈkwɪkˌsɪlvə; ˈkwɪkˌsɪlvə/ *n* [U] *old use* MERCURY (=a metal that is liquid at normal temperatures)【旧】水银, 汞

quick·step /ˈkwɪkˌstɛp; ˈkwɪkstep/ *n* [C] a dance with fast movements of the feet, or the music for this dance 快步舞; 快步舞曲

quick-tem·pered /ˌ. ˈ..◂/ *adj* easily becoming angry 急躁的, 易怒的: *Our young men were quick-tempered and likely to do rash things.* 我们的年轻小伙子性情急躁, 有可能做出一些鲁莽的事情。

quick-wit·ted /ˌ. ˈ..◂/ *adj* able to understand things quickly and give quick, clever replies 聪明的; 机灵的; 敏捷的 —**quickwittedness** *n* [U]

quid /kwɪd; kwɪd/ *n plural* **quid** [C] *BrE informal*【英, 非正式】**1** one pound in money; £1 一英镑: *She earns at least 600 quid a week.* 她每周至少挣 600 英镑。**2 be quids in** to make a profit, especially a good profit 赚钱〔尤指赚大钱〕: *We'll be quids in if we get this contract.* 如果得到这份合同我们将赚大钱。

quid pro quo /ˈkwɪd pro ˈkwo; ˌkwɪd prəʊ ˈkwəʊ/ *n* [C] something that you give or do in exchange for something else, especially when this arrangement is not official 补偿物; 交换物: [+for] *The quid pro quo is that we pay them a very low rent.* 交换条件是我们支付他们很低的租金。

qui·es·cent /kwaɪˈɛsn̩t; kwiˈesənt/ *adj formal* not developing or doing anything, especially when this is only a temporary state【正式】静止的, 不活动的; 休眠的 —**quiescently** *adv* —**quiescence** *n* [U]

qui·et¹ /ˈkwaɪət; ˈkwaɪət/ *adj*
1 ►NO NOISE 没有声音的◄ not making much noise 轻声的; 安静的: *We'll have to be quiet so as not to wake the baby.* 我们得保持安静, 以免吵醒宝宝。| *The engine is 20% quieter than its nearest rival's.* 该发动机比性能最接近它的同类产品噪音低 20%。| **(as) quiet as a mouse** (=very quiet) 悄无声息; 非常安静
2 quiet!/be quiet! *spoken* used to tell someone, rather rudely, to stop talking or making noise【口】安静! 别作声!
3 ►PEACEFUL 平静的◄ a quiet place or time is one where there is not much activity and there are not many people 平静的, 宁静的, 寂静的: *I'd love to go on holiday somewhere where it's nice and quiet.* 我很想去一个既宜人又清静的地方度假。| **quiet day/weekend** *a quiet weekend at home* 一个在家里度过的清静的周末
4 ►NOT SPEAKING 不说话的◄ a) not saying much or not saying anything 不大说话的, 沉默的: *You're very quiet, Mom – is anything the matter?* 妈, 你话很少, 出什么事了吗? **b)** someone who is quiet does not usually talk very much 话不多的, 沉默寡言的; 文静的: *"What's she like?" "Oh, quiet – but friendly enough."* "她人怎么样?" "噢, 话不多 —— 但对人很友好。"
5 ►NOT BUSY 不忙碌的◄ if business is quiet, there are not many customers〔生意〕清闲的, 清淡的: *August is a quiet time of year for the retail trade.* 8 月是一年中零售业的淡季。
6 keep quiet to not say anything, because you do not know anything or because you do not want to tell a secret 保持沉默;

不声张: *I didn't know anything about it so I just kept quiet.* 我对那事一无所知, 所以只好保持沉默。

7 keep sth quiet/keep quiet about sth to keep information secret 对某事保密: *You're getting married? You kept that quiet!* 你要结婚了?这事你一直没说啊!

8 keep sb quiet to stop someone from talking, complaining, or causing trouble 使某人安静: *I gave the children some candy to keep them quiet.* 我给了孩子们一些糖果, 让他们安静下来。

9 have a quiet word (with) *especially BrE* to talk to someone privately when you want to criticize them or tell them about something serious【尤英】(与…)私下谈谈: *I'll have a quiet word with Brian about his behaviour.* 我将就布赖恩的行为和他私下谈谈。—see also 另见 QUIETLY **—quietness** *n* [U]

quiet² *n* [U] **1** quietness; calmness 宁静, 寂静, 平静: *the quiet of the churchyard* 教堂墓地的宁静 | **peace and quiet** *I've had an awful day – now I just want some peace and quiet.* 我今天过得糟透了 — 现在只想清静清静。**2** silence 沉默, 安静: *Can I have quiet please!* 请安静! **3 on the quiet** *informal* without telling anyone; secretly【非正式】秘密地, 私下地: *We found out he'd been doing some freelance work on the quiet.* 我们发现他私下里一直在做一些自由职业类的工作。

qui·et·en /ˈkwaɪətn̩; ˈkwaɪətn/ also 又作 **quiet** *AmE*【美】*v* **1** also 又作 **quieten down** [I,T] to become less noisy or less active, or to make someone or something do this (使)平静; (使)安静: *The chatter quietened briefly when she came into the room.* 她走进房间时, 喋喋不休的说话声暂时平静下来。| *Things tend to quieten down after the Christmas rush.* 圣诞节购物热潮过去之后, 一切便会平静下来。**2** [T] to make someone feel less frightened or worried 使〔某人〕减少〔恐惧或忧虑〕, 使缓解, 使减轻

qui·et·is·m /ˈkwaɪətɪzm̩; ˈkwaɪətɪzəm/ *n* [U] *formal* a calm state in which you accept situations and do not have any desire to change them【正式】淡泊; 清静无为; 消极接受

3 3 **qui·et·ly** /ˈkwaɪətlɪ; ˈkwaɪətli/ *adv* **1** without making much noise 轻声地, 悄声地; 静静地: *Peter spoke so quietly I could hardly hear him.* 彼得声音很轻, 我几乎听不见他的话。**2** in a way that does not attract attention 秘密地; 不张扬地: *They have quietly gathered enough support to challenge the leadership.* 他们已悄悄地争取到足够的支持来挑战领导层。**3 quietly confident/optimistic** *especially BrE* fairly confident of success, but without talking proudly about it【尤英】〔对成功〕暗中有信心/持乐观态度

qui·e·tude /ˈkwaɪəˌtjud; ˈkwaɪətjuːd/ *n* [U] *formal* calmness, peace, and quiet【正式】安静; 平静; 寂静; 宁静

qui·e·tus /kwaɪˈitəs; kwaɪˈiːtəs/ *n* [singular] *formal*【正式】**1** death 死亡 **2** the end of something 结束, 制止, 平息

quiff /kwɪf; kwɪf/ *n* [C] *BrE* a part of a man's hair style where the hair stands up at the front above his forehead【英】〔男子〕额前向上梳的一绺头发, 额发

quill /kwɪl; kwɪl/ *n* [C] **1** a bird's feather, especially a large one, including the stiff, hard part at the base which joins to the bird's body 羽毛管, 翮 **2** also 又作 **quill pen** a pen made from a large bird's feather, used in past times 羽毛笔, 羽管笔, 翮笔 **3** a thing like a thin, sharp stick that grows on some animals such as a PORCUPINE, in order to protect them〔豪猪等的〕刺

Quilp /kwɪlp; kwɪlp/, **Daniel** /ˈdænjəl; ˈdænjəl/ a character in *The Old Curiosity Shop* (1841) by Charles Dickens. He is a MONEYLENDER who cheats people and is cruel to his wife. 奎尔普〔查尔斯·狄更斯创作的小说《老古玩店》(1841)中的人物。他是一个高利贷商人, 经常欺骗他人, 虐待妻子〕

quilt /kwɪlt; kwɪlt/ *n* [C] **1** a warm thick cover for a bed, made of cloth filled with something such as feathers 被子, 被褥 **2** *especially AmE* a thin cloth cover used on a bed to make it look attractive【尤美】床罩

quilt·ed /ˈkwɪltɪd; ˈkwɪltɪ̣d/ *adj* quilted cloth or clothing has been made thicker and warmer by having a special layer of material stitched into it 绗有衬料的, 夹层的: *a quilted bath robe* 中间有衬里的浴袍

quilt·ing /ˈkwɪltɪŋ; ˈkwɪltɪŋ/ *n* [U] the work of making a quilt, or the material and stitches that you use 被子绗缝; 被子料

quin /kwɪn; kwɪn/ *n* [C] *BrE informal* a QUINTUPLET【英, 非正式】五胞胎之一

quince /kwɪns; kwɪns/ *n* [C,U] a hard, yellowish fruit like a large apple, used for making JELLY 榅桲〔用以制作果冻〕—see picture on page A8 参见 A8 页图

quin·ine /ˈkwaɪnaɪn; ˈkwɪniːn/ *n* [U] a drug used for treating fevers, especially MALARIA 奎宁, 金鸡纳霜

quinine wa·ter /ˈ··ˌ··/ *n* [U] *AmE* a bitter-tasting drink often mixed with strong alcoholic drinks such as GIN【美】奎宁水

Quin·qua·ges·i·ma /ˌkwɪnkwəˈdʒɛsəmə; ˌkwɪŋkwəˈdʒesɪ̣mə/ the Sunday before Lent. The word comes from the Latin word quinquaginta, meaning 50, since Quinquagesima is about 50 days before Easter. 四旬斋前的星期日〔源于拉丁语 quinquaginta, 意指"50"。四旬斋前的星期日大约在复活节前的50天左右〕

quint /kwɪnt; kwɪnt/ *n* [C] *AmE informal* a QUINTUPLET【美, 非正式】五胞胎之一

quin·tes·sence /kwɪnˈtɛsn̩s; kwɪnˈtesəns/ *n* **the quintessence of sth** *formal* a perfect type or example of something【正式】某事物的典范: *John is the quintessence of good manners.* 约翰是彬彬有礼的典范。

quin·tes·sen·tial /ˌkwɪntəˈsɛnʃəl; ˌkwɪntɪ̣ˈsenʃəl◂/ *adj* being a perfect example of a particular type of person or thing 典型的; 典范的: *'Guys and Dolls' is the quintessential American musical.*《少男少女》是典型的美国音乐剧。**—quintessentially** *adv*: *a quintessentially English rural scene* 典型的英国乡村景色

quin·tet /kwɪnˈtɛt; kwɪnˈtet/ *n* [C] **1** five singers or musicians who perform together 五重唱; 五重奏; 五重唱小组; 五重奏小组 **2** a piece of music written for five performers 五重唱曲; 五重奏曲 —compare 比较 QUARTET, SEXTET, TRIO

quin·tu·plet /kwɪnˈtuplɪt; ˈkwɪntjʊplɪ̣t/ *n* [C] one of five babies born to the same mother at the same time 五胞胎之一 —compare 比较 QUADRUPLET, SEXTUPLET

quip *v* [I] to say something short clever and amusing 说俏皮话, 说妙语: *"Practice makes perfect," quipped Peter when he saw Janet trying to ski.* "熟能生巧。"彼得看见珍妮特在尝试滑雪时风趣地说。**—quip** *n* [C]

quire /kwaɪr; kwaɪə/ *n* [C] *technical* 24 sheets of paper【术语】〔纸的〕一刀〔24张〕

quirk /kwɝk; kwɜːk/ *n* [C] **1** something strange that happens by chance〔偶然发生的〕奇事, 巧合: **quirk of fate/history etc** (=something that happens by chance and influences later events) 命运/历史等的巧合 *By a quirk of fate, he left just before the bomb exploded.* 由于命运的巧合, 他在炸弹爆炸前一刻离开了。**2** a strange habit or feature of someone's character 古怪; 怪癖: *one of her many annoying little quirks* 她许多烦人的怪癖之一

quirk·y /ˈkwɝkɪ; ˈkwɜːki/ *adj* strange and unusual, in an unexpected way 离奇的, 古怪的; 奇特的: *The music was a quirky mixture of jazz and classical violins.* 该乐曲是爵士乐和古典小提琴曲的奇妙组合。**—quirkily** *adv* **—quirkiness** *n* [U]

quis·ling /ˈkwɪzlɪŋ; ˈkwɪzlɪŋ/ *n* [C] someone who helps an army or enemy country that has taken control of his own country〔与占领本国的敌人合作的〕卖国贼, 内奸

quit /kwɪt; kwɪt/ *v past tense and past participle* **quit** also 又作 **quitted** *BrE*【英】*present participle* **quitting** **1** [I,T] *informal, especially AmE* to leave a job, school etc, especially because you are annoyed or unhappy【非正式, 尤美】〔尤因烦恼或愉快而〕辞去〔工作〕; 辍学: *I'm tired of being treated like this. I quit.* 我厌倦了别人这样对待我, 我不干了。| *Her husband had to quit because of ill health.* 她丈夫由于身体不好, 不得不辞去了工作。| **quit school/your job etc** *She quit school at 17 and left home.* 她17岁辍学后离开了家。**2** [T] *informal, especially AmE* to stop doing something bad or annoying【非正式, 尤美】停止〔做坏事或令人厌烦的事〕: *Quit it Robby, or I'll tell mom!* 住手, 罗比, 否则我告诉妈妈! | **quit doing sth** *I wish you'd all quit complaining.* 我希望你们都别抱怨了。**3 be quit of** *formal* to be finished with something that was causing you problems【正式】了结, 摆脱〔麻烦、难题等〕**4** [T] *old use* to leave a place【旧】离开〔某处〕

quite /kwaɪt; kwaɪt/ *predeterminer, adv* **1** [+adj/adv] *especially* 1 1
BrE fairly【尤英】很, 相当: **quite big/tall etc** *The restaurant does great food and the prices are quite reasonable.* 那家餐馆烹制的食物味道很好, 而且价钱相当合理。| *I got a letter from Sylvia quite recently.* 前不久我收到了西尔维娅的一封信。| **quite a big sth/a tall sth etc** *He's quite a good soccer player really.* 他确实是一个相当不错的足球运动员。| **quite a lot/a few etc** *We managed to get quite a lot of information for the survey.* 我们设法收集到了大量的调查资料。—see 见 RATHER (USAGE) **2 quite good/funny etc** *AmE* very good, funny etc【美】非常好/有趣等: *The food was quite good!* 食物好极了! **3 quite a lot/bit/few** large number or amount 许多, 大量: *She must have left here, oh, quite a few years ago.* 她一定是离开这儿了, 噢, 许多年以前就离开了。**4 not quite why/what/where etc** not exactly why, what, where etc 不完全是因为/是…那样/是某地等: *I must admit, the play wasn't quite what we expected.* 我必须承认, 那出戏剧并不完全如我们所期望。**5 not quite** not completely 没有完全地: *They weren't quite ready so we waited in the car.* 他们没有完全准备好, 所以我们在车里等着。**6 quite a/**

quite some used to describe something that is unusually good, long, interesting etc 不寻常的; 出众的; 相当的〔用以表示某事物非常好、长、有趣等〕: *That was quite a party you had last night.* 昨天晚上你们举行的晚会很特别。| *That makes quite a noise, doesn't it?* 会发出相当大的响声, 是吗? | *He ran quite some distance before he found a public telephone.* 他跑了老远的路才找到一部公用电话。**7** [+adj/adv] *BrE* very or completely【英】完全; 非常, 十分: *It's one thing driving a car but a lorry is quite different.* 开小汽车是一回事, 开大卡车又完全是另外一回事。| *That's quite ridiculous!* 真荒唐! | **quite the best/the worst etc** *It was quite the most interesting museum I've ever visited.* 这绝对是我参观过的最有趣的博物馆。**8 I'm not quite sure** used to say that you are not certain about something 我不十分肯定, 我拿不太准: *I'm not quite sure what her second name is.* 我说不太准她姓什么。

Frequencies of the adverb **quite** in spoken and written English 副词 quite 在英语口语和书面语中的使用频率

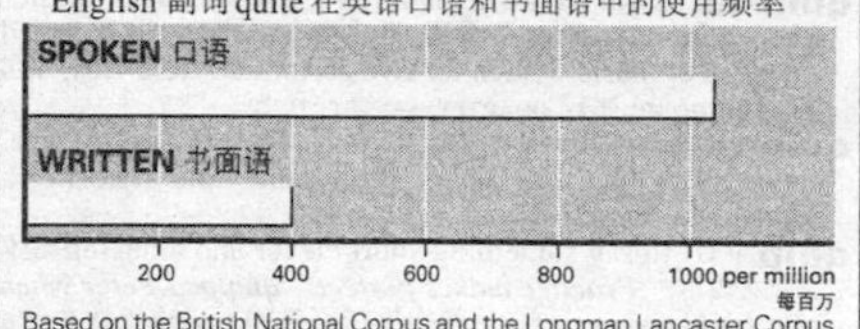

Based on the British National Corpus and the Longman Lancaster Corpus
据英国国家语料库和朗文兰开斯特语料库

This graph shows that the adverb **quite** is much more common in spoken English than in written English. This is because it is used a lot in spoken English to emphasize amounts, sizes etc or to emphasize how good, bad etc something is. It is also used in a lot of common spoken phrases. 本图表显示, 副词quite在英语口语中的使用频率远远高于书面语, 因为它经常用于口语中强调数量、大小、好坏等。口语中很多常用短语也是由quite构成的。

quite (*predeterminer, adv*) **SPOKEN PHRASES**
含 quite 的口语短语

9 quite right *BrE* used to show that you strongly agree with someone【英】完全正确: *"Why should they get paid more than us?" "Quite right, it's completely unfair."* "为什么他们的报酬就该比我们高呢?" "问得非常好, 这完全不公平。" **10 quite like** *BrE* to like something, but not very much【英】有些喜欢, 相当喜欢: *Well, I quite like maths, but I don't like the teacher.* 嗯, 我相当喜欢数学, 但我不喜欢数学老师。| *It's funny, but he quite likes it after all.* 虽然很可笑, 但他毕竟还是相当喜欢它。**11 that's quite all right** used to reply to someone that you do not mind what they are doing 一点都没关系: *"I hope I'm not disturbing you." "That's quite all right."* "我希望没有打扰你。" "一点都没关系。" **12 I'm quite happy to do something** *BrE* used to say that you are very willing to do something【英】我很乐意做某事: *If they want to come in and discuss it, I'd be quite happy to meet them.* 如果他们想进来讨论此事, 我很乐意见他们。**13 quite frankly/honestly** *BrE* used when you are giving a very direct or honest opinion【英】坦率地说/说老实话: *Well, quite frankly, I've never heard such rubbish in all my life!* 嗯, 坦率地说, 我这一辈子还从来没听说过这样的胡话! **14 quite/quite so** *BrE formal* used to show that you agree with what someone is saying【英, 正式】正是这样, 不错, 的确如此: *"They really should have thought of this before." "Yes, quite."* "他们以前确实该想到这一点。" "可不是嘛。" **15 quite enough** *especially BrE* used when you are annoyed with what someone is saying or doing and you want them to stop【尤英】够了〔表示恼怒〕: *I've heard quite enough about your problems. What about mine?* 你的困难我已听得够多了。我的困难怎么办? **16 quite something** *especially BrE* used to say that someone or something is very impressive【尤英】令人难忘的人[事]; 不寻常的人[事]: *You should have come to the Carnival, it was quite something, I can tell you.* 你真该去参加狂欢节, 告诉你吧, 真不错呢。

Quito /ˈkito; ˈkiːtəʊ/ the capital city of Ecuador 基多〔厄瓜多尔首都〕

quits /kwɪts; kwɪts/ *adj informal*【非正式】**1 be quits (with)** to be in an equal situation with someone again, especially because you have paid them what you owed (与…) 两相抵消; (与…) 互不相欠: *You pay for the taxi, and that'll make us quits.* 你付计程车车费, 我们就谁也不欠谁了。| *If I win the next game, we'll be quits.* 如果我赢了下一场比赛, 我们就平了。**2 call it quits a)** to agree that a debt or argument is settled 彼此两清; (同意) 结束争论: *Just give me $20 and we'll call it quits.* 给我20美元, 我们就两清了。**b)** to agree to stop doing something (同意) 停止做某事: *Let's just paint this door then call it quits for the day.* 我们且把这扇门漆完, 然后今天就收工吧。

quit·tance /ˈkwɪtn̩s; ˈkwɪtəns/ *n* [C] *law* a statement saying that someone no longer has to do something such as paying back money that they owe【法律】〔债务等的〕免除; 免除证书

quit·ter /ˈkwɪtɚ; ˈkwɪtə/ *n* [C] *informal* someone who does not have the determination or courage to finish something that is difficult【非正式】遇困难就放弃的人, 半途而废的人

quiv·er[1] /ˈkwɪvɚ; ˈkwɪvə/ *v* [I] to tremble slightly, especially because you feel angry, excited, or upset〔尤指因气愤、激动或伤心而轻微地〕颤抖, 发抖: *Suddenly the child's mouth began to quiver, and he burst into tears.* 突然孩子的嘴巴微微发颤, 然后就放声大哭。| [**+with**] *quivering with rage* 气得直发抖

quiver[2] *n* [C] **1** a slight trembling〔轻微的〕颤抖, 抖动: *I felt a quiver of excitement run through me.* 我全身感到了一阵兴奋的颤抖。**2** a long case for carrying ARROWS 箭筒, 箭囊, 箭袋

qui vive /ˌki ˋviv; ˌkiː ˈviːv/ *n* **on the qui vive** taking special care to notice things; watching closely 警戒着, 警惕着

quix·ot·ic /kwɪksˋɑtɪk; kwɪkˈsɒtɪk/ *adj* having ideas that are not practical and plans based on unreasonable hopes of improving the world 唐吉诃德式的, 愚侠(式)的; 不切实际的, 空想的: *a silly quixotic proposal* 愚蠢的不切实际的建议

quiz[1] /kwɪz; kwɪz/ *n plural* **quizzes** [C] **1** a competition in which you have to answer questions 问答比赛, 智力竞赛: **sports/news/general knowledge etc quiz** (=a quiz about sports, news etc) 体育知识/新闻知识/一般知识等问答比赛 *a quiz show on TV* 电视上的一个问答比赛节目 **2** a short test that a teacher gives to a class 小测验, 小考: *a biology quiz* 生物测验 —see also 另见 POP QUIZ

quiz[2] *v* **quizzed, quizzing** [T] to ask someone a lot of questions 查问, 盘问: *They kept quizzing me about my new boyfriend.* 他们不停地问我有关我新男友的问题。

quiz-mas·ter /ˈ· ˌ··/ *n* [C] *BrE* a QUESTION-MASTER【英】问答游戏的主持人

quiz·zi·cal /ˈkwɪzɪkl̩; ˈkwɪzɪkəl/ *adj* **a quizzical look/smile/expression** a look, smile etc that seems to ask a question, often in an amused way 探询[嘲弄]的目光/微笑/表情 —**quizzically** /-kl̩ɪ; -kli/ *adv*

quod /kwɑd; kwɒd/ *n* **in quod** *BrE old-fashioned* in prison【英, 过时】坐牢

quoit /kwɔɪt; kwɔɪt/ *n* **1 quoits** [U] a game in which you throw rings over a small upright post 套圈游戏 **2** [C] a ring used in the game of quoits〔套圈用的〕环, 圈

quon·dam /ˈkwɑndəm; ˈkwɒndəm/ *adj formal* connected with an earlier time【正式】曾经的, 昔日的, 以前的: *my quondam tutor* 我过去的导师

Quon·set hut /ˈkwɑnsɛt ˋhʌt; ˈkwɒnset ˌhʌt/ *n* [C] *AmE trademark* a building that is shaped like half a tube and is made of iron sheets【美, 商标】匡西特活动房屋

quo·rate /ˈkwɔrət; ˈkwɔːrɪ̈t/ *adj technical* a meeting that is quorate has a quorum present【术语】〔会议〕有法定人数出席的 —opposite 反义词 INQUORATE

Quorn /kwɔrn; kwɔːn/ *n* [U] *BrE trademark* a vegetable substance that can be used in cooking instead of meat【英, 商标】夸恩牌素肉[人造肉]

quo·rum /ˈkwɔrəm; ˈkwɔːrəm/ *n* [C usually singular 一般用单数] the smallest number of people who must be present at a meeting for official decisions to be made〔会议的〕法定人数

quo·ta /ˈkwotə; ˈkwəʊtə/ *n* [C] **1** the amount or share of something that you think is normal or that is officially expected 定额, 定量: *Salesmen selling over the quota receive a $1,000 bonus.* 超额完成销售任务的推销人员可获得一千美元奖金。**2** a limit, especially an official limit, on the number or amount of something that is allowed in a particular period 限额; 配额: *Most countries have an immigration quota.* 大多数国家都有外来移民限额。| *a strict quota on imports* 严格的进口限额 | *I think I've had my quota of coffee for the day.* 我想我今天喝的咖啡已经够多了。

quo·ta·ble /ˈkwotəbl̩; ˈkwəʊtəbəl/ *adj* a quotable remark or statement is interesting and noticeable, especially because it is clever or amusing 值得引用的

quo·ta·tion /kwoˋteʃən; kwəʊˈteɪʃən/ *n* **1** [C] a sentence or phrase, from a book, speech etc which you repeat in a speech or piece of writing because it is interesting, amusing etc 引语, 引文, 语录: *a quotation from the Bible* 引自《圣经》的话 | *a dic-*

tionary of quotations 引语词典，语录汇编 **2** [C] a written statement of exactly how much money a piece of work will cost 报价；行情：*Could you give us a quotation for fixing the roof?* 你能给我们一个修理屋顶的报价吗？—compare 比较 ESTIMATE[1] (2) **3** [U] the act of quoting something that someone else has written or said 引用，引述

quotation mark/ˈ· ˈ·· ˌ·/ *n* [C usually plural 一般用复数] one of a pair of marks (" ") or (' ') that show the beginning and end of reported speech or of a quoted word or phrase 引号；INVERTED COMMA *BrE*【英】—see picture at 参见 PUNCTUATION MARK 图

S2 W3 **quote**[1]/kwot; kwəʊt/ *v* **1** [I,T] to repeat exactly what someone else has said or written 引用，引述：**quote (sth) from sth** *She quoted from a newspaper article.* 她引用了报纸上一篇文章的内容。| **quote sb as saying sth** *The President himself was quoted as saying he would veto the bill.* 报道引述总统本人的话，说他要否决那个法案。| **don't quote me (on this)** (=used to show that what you are saying is not an official statement)〔这话〕别说是我说的，不要引用我的话 *Don't quote me on this, but the company is in deep trouble.* 这话别说是我说的，这家公司已深陷困境。| **quote sb/sth** *To quote an old saying, every dog has his day.* 用句老话来说，人人都有得意时。**2** [T] to mention an example of something to support what you are saying〔为支持论点〕举例，举证，引证 **3** [T] to tell a customer the price you will charge them for a service or product 报〔价〕，开〔价〕：*They quoted us $800 for car repairs.* 他们向我们开出了800美元的汽车修理价。—compare 比较 ESTIMATE[2] **4 quote ... unquote** *spoken* used at the beginning and end of a quoted word or phrase to emphasize that it is exactly correct【口】引文开始…引文结束〔用于所引话语的前后〕

quote[2] *n* [C] *informal*【非正式】**1** a QUOTATION 引语，引文；引用 **2 in quotes** words that are in quotes are between a pair of QUOTATION MARKS 在引号中 

quoth/kwoθ; kwəʊθ/ *v* [T] *old use*【旧】**quoth I/he/she etc** a way of saying 'I said', 'he said' etc 我/他/她等说过

quo·tid·i·an/kwoˈtɪdɪən; kwəʊˈtɪdiən/ *adj old use* daily; ordinary【旧】每日的；日常的；平常的

quo·tient/ˈkwoʃənt; ˈkwəʊʃənt/ *n* [C] *technical* the number which is obtained when one number is divided by another【术语】商，商数

Qu·r'an, the/kəˈræn; kɔːˈrɑːn/ *n* another spelling of KORAN (=the holy book of Islam)《古兰经》，《可兰经》〔Koran 的另一种拼法〕

q.v. *Latin* quod vide; used to tell readers to look in another place in the same book for a piece of information【拉丁】参见，参照该条

qwert·y/ˈkwɜtɪ; ˈkwɜːti/ *adj BrE* a qwerty KEYBOARD on a computer or TYPEWRITER has the keys arranged in the usual way, with Q, W, E, R, T, and Y on the top row【英】〔电脑或打字机的键盘〕标准型的〔键盘的上行通常排列着 Q, W, E, R, T 和 Y 六个字母〕

Q

R,r

R¹, r /ɑr; ɑː/ *plural* **R's, r's** the 18th letter of the English alphabet 英语字母表的第十八个字母 —see also 另见 **the three R's** (THREE (2))

R² **1** *AmE* the written abbreviation of 缩写= Republican Party【美】共和党: *Steve Gunderson (R)* 史蒂夫·冈德森(共和党) **2** the written abbreviation of 缩写= REX OR REGINA; the Latin words for king or queen〔拉丁文〕国王; 女王: *Elizabeth R* 伊丽莎白女王 **3** the written abbreviation of 缩写= river, used especially on maps 河, 江〔尤用于地图上〕 **4** *AmE* used to show that a film may not be watched by children under 17【美】R 级电影〔17 岁以下儿童不宜观看〕

RA /ˌɑr ˋe; ˌɑːr ˈeɪ/ **1** the abbreviation of 缩写= ROYAL ACADEMY **2** the abbreviation of 缩写= REAR ADMIRAL **3** *AmE* Regular Army; another name for the US Army【美】正规军〔美国陆军的别称〕

RAA /ˌɑr e ˋe; ˌɑːr eɪ ˈeɪ/ the abbreviation of 缩写= ROYAL ACADEMY OF ARTS

Rabat /rəˋbɑt; ræˈbæt/ the capital city of Morocco 拉巴特〔摩洛哥首都〕

rab·bi /ˋræbaɪ; ˈræbaɪ/ *n* [C] a Jewish priest 拉比〔犹太教教士〕

rab·bin·i·cal /rəˋbɪnɪkḷ; rəˈbɪnɪkəl/ *adj* connected with the writings or teaching of rabbis 拉比(的著作或教义)的

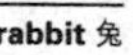
rabbit 兔

rabbit 兔　　hare 野兔

3 **rab·bit¹** /ˋræbɪt; ˈræbɪ̵t/ *n* **1** [C] a common small animal with long ears and soft fur, that lives in a hole in the ground 兔 **2** [U] the fur or meat of a rabbit 兔子的毛皮, 兔肉

rabbit² *v* **rabbited, rabbiting** **1 rabbit on** [I] *informal, especially BrE* to talk continuously, especially in an uninteresting or annoying way【非正式, 尤英】唠叨, 喋喋不休 **2 go rabbiting** to hunt or shoot rabbits 猎兔, 打兔子

rabbit hutch /ˋ‥ ˌ/ *n* [C] a wooden CAGE for pet rabbits 兔棚, 兔笼

rabbit punch /ˋ‥ ˌ/ *n* [C] a quick hit on the back of the neck, made with the side of the hand〔用手的侧面〕对着后颈项的一下猛击

rabbit war·ren /ˋ‥ ˌ‥/ *n* [C] **1** an area under the ground where wild rabbits live in their holes 野兔群居地, 野兔洞穴多的地方 **2** a building or place with a lot of narrow passages or streets where you can easily get lost 迷宫般的建筑[地方]

rab·ble /ˋræbḷ; ˈræbəl/ *n* [singular] **1** a noisy crowd of people who are likely to cause trouble 乌合之众; 暴民: *Their army was nothing more than an undisciplined rabble.* 他们的军队只不过是无纪律的乌合之众。**2** used about a group of people that you do not respect 无赖, 一帮痞子: *How can you hang out with that rabble in the bar each night?* 你怎么可以每天晚上都和那群无赖在酒吧里瞎混?

rabble-rous·er /ˋ‥ ˌ‥/ *n* [C] someone who tries to make a crowd of people angry and violent, especially in order to achieve political aims〔尤指抱有政治目的的〕煽动者, 蛊惑人心者 —**rabble-rousing** *adj*: *a rabble-rousing speech* 蛊惑人心的演说 —**rabble-rousing** *n* [U]

Rab·e·lais /ˋræbəle; ˈræbəleɪ/, **Fran·çois** /frɑnˋswɑ; ˈfrɒnswɑː/ (?1494-1553) a French writer whose book *Gargantua and Pantagruel* is a SATIRE (=a way of writing about society or powerful people that makes them seem funny in order to show their faults) with many jokes about sex 拉伯雷〔(?1494-1553) 法国作家, 著有讽刺小说《巨人传》, 其中不乏与性有关的笑料〕

rab·id /ˋræbɪd; ˈræbɪ̵d/ *adj* **1** having very extreme and unreasonable opinions, especially about politics; FANATICAL〔尤指在政治上〕过激的; 狂热的: *rabid right-wingers* 极端右翼分子 **2** suffering from rabies 患狂犬病的: *a rabid dog* 疯狗

ra·bies /ˋrebiz; ˈreɪbiːz/ *n* [U] a disease that kills animals and people, that you can catch if you are bitten by an infected dog etc 狂犬病

Rabin /ræˋbin; ræˈbiːn/, **Yitzhak** /ˋjɪtsɑk; ˈjɪtsɑːk/ (1922-95) an Israeli politician of the Labour Party, who was prime minister from 1974-77 and again from 1992 to 1995. In 1994 he shared the Nobel Peace Prize with Shimon Peres and Yasser Arafat. He was ASSASSINATED in 1995 when he was at a public meeting for peace. 拉宾〔(1922-1995), 以色列工党政治家, 1974-1977年、1992-1995年两度出任总理。1994 年, 他与佩雷斯和阿拉法特一起获得诺贝尔和平奖。1995年, 在出席和平集会时遇害〕

RAC, the /ˌɑr e ˋsi; ˌɑːr eɪ ˈsiː/ *n* the Royal Automobile Club; a British organization that helps its members when their cars break down during a journey 皇家汽车俱乐部〔英国一组织。会员行车中途抛锚时可获得该组织的帮助〕—COMPARE 比较 AA

rac·coon, racoon /ræˋkun; rəˈkuːn/ *n* **1** [C] a small North American animal that lives in trees, and has a long tail with black and white rings on it 浣熊〔产于北美, 生活在树上, 长尾上有黑白相间的环〕 **2** [U] the thick fur of a raccoon 浣熊的毛皮

race¹ /res; reɪs/ *n*

1 ►**SPORT 运动**◄ [C] a competition in which each competitor tries to run, drive etc fastest and finish first 赛跑; 赛车; 速度比赛: *She came fifth in the race.* 她在赛跑中获第五名。| *a swimming race* 游泳比赛 2 2

2 ►**PEOPLE 民族**◄ **a)** [C] one of the main groups that humans can be divided into according to the colour of their skin and other physical features 人种, 种族: *people of all races and creeds* 各种族和宗教的人 **b)** [U] the fact of belonging to one of these groups 种族区别: *The law forbids discrimination on the grounds of race or religion.* 法律禁止以种族或宗教为理由实行歧视。| *a person of mixed race* 混血儿 **c)** [C] a group of people with the same customs, history, language etc 民族: *the Nordic races* 北欧民族 —see also 另见 HUMAN RACE

3 ►**GET/DO STH FIRST 抢先得到/做某事**◄ [C usually singular 一般用单数] a situation in which one group of people tries to obtain or achieve something before another group does 竞赛, 争夺, 抢先: **race to do sth** *the race to develop a nuclear bomb* 抢先发展核弹 | **[+for]** *an international race for power and prestige* 国际间权力与声誉的争夺 | **the race is on** (=people are competing to do something) 正在竞争 *The race is on to find a cure for AIDS.* 正在争相寻找治疗艾滋病的方法。

4 ►**HORSE RACE 赛马**◄ **the races** an occasion when horse races are held 赛马的日子: *a day out at the races* 看赛马的一天 | *Doncaster Races* 唐克斯特赛马

5 a race against time an attempt to finish doing something very important fast 和时间赛跑, 争分夺秒

6 ►**ANIMAL/PLANT 动/植物**◄ [C] *technical* a type of animal or plant【术语】〔动植物的〕族, 小种 —see also 另见 ARMS RACE

> **USAGE NOTE 用法说明: RACE**
>
> WORD CHOICE 词语辨析: **race, nation, people, state, tribe**
>
> A **race** is a very large group of human beings of the same colour and/or physical type. race (种族) 指的是具有相同的肤色和/或体型的较大的人类集团: *different races and nationalities* 不同的种族和民族
>
> A **nation** is a group of people who share the same history and usually a language, and often live in the same area or independent country. nation (民族) 指的是这样一群人, 他们具有共同的历史, 一般也使用共同的语言, 通常居住在同一地区或独立国家中: *the Indian nations of North America* 北美洲诸印第安族 | *the Scottish nation* 苏格兰民族
>
> A **race** or a **nation** may also be called a **people** [C]. This is sometimes considered to be a more acceptable word than

race. race或nation也可叫做people。与race相比, people有时更能为人们接受: *the peoples of Asia* 亚洲各民族 | *the Jewish people* 犹太民族

A **state** is either a politically independent country, or one of the political parts that makes up a country. state指政治上独立的国家, 或组成一个国家的邦或州: *the Polish state* 波兰国家 | *the state of California* 加利福尼亚州 States can often contain people of different races or nations. 国家经常包括不同种族和民族的人。

A **tribe** is a social group, smaller than a nation, that shares the same customs and usually the same language, and often follows an ancient or traditional way of life. tribe(部落)是比nation(民族)小的集团, 有共同的风俗习惯, 一般使用相同的语言, 并通常遵循某种古老或传统的生活方式: *the tribes living in the Amazon region* 居住在亚马孙地区的部落

race² *v*

1 ▶**SPORT** 运动◀ **a)** [I,T] to compete against someone or something in a race (和…) 比赛: [**+against**] *She'll be racing against some of the world's top athletes.* 她将与一些世界顶尖运动员进行比赛。| **race sb to/back/there** *I'll race you to the end of the road.* 我和你赛跑, 看谁先跑到路的尽头。**b)** [T] to use an animal or a vehicle to compete in a race 使〔动物或车辆〕参加比赛: *Prouteau was racing a Ferrari in the Formula One championships.* 普鲁托驾驶一辆法拉利参加一级方程式锦标赛。| *young horses that had never been raced* 从未参加过比赛的马驹

2 ▶**MOVE QUICKLY** 迅速移动◀ [I always+adv/prep, T always+adv/prep] to move very quickly or make someone or something move very quickly (使) 快速移动, (使) 疾走[驰]: [**+out/home/into**] *I had to race back home for my umbrella.* 我不得不奔回家去取雨伞。| *I watched as her eyes raced over the page.* 我看着她很快地扫了一眼那一页。| **race sb to/back/there** *The sick woman was raced to the hospital.* 患病的妇女被迅速送往医院。

3 ▶**TIME** 时间◀ **race by/past** if time races by, it passes very quickly〔时间〕飞逝: *The seconds went racing past.* 几秒钟很快过去了。

4 ▶**HEART/MIND ETC** 心脏/大脑等◀ [I] if your heart, PULSE¹ (1), or mind races, it works harder and faster than usual, especially because you are ill or anxious〔尤指因生病或焦虑而心脏〕狂跳;〔大脑〕快速转动念头: *My heart started racing at the sound of approaching footsteps.* 听到越来越近的脚步声, 我的心脏开始剧烈跳动。

5 ▶**ENGINE** 发动机◀ [I] if an engine races, it runs too fast〔发动机〕转动速度太高

race car /ˈ· ·/ *n* [C] *AmE* a RACING CAR【美】赛车, 跑车

race·card /ˈresˌkɑrd; ˈreɪskɑːd/ *n* [C] *BrE* a programme giving the races, times, and horses at a horse racing event【英】〔赛马用的〕比赛程序单

race·course /ˈresˌkɔrs; ˈreɪs-kɔːs/ *n* [C] **1** *BrE* a track, usually covered with grass, around which horses race【英】赛马跑道, 赛马场; RACETRACK (2) *AmE*【美】**2** *AmE* a track around which runners, cars etc race【美】〔赛跑、赛车等用的〕跑道

race·go·er /ˈresˌgoɚ; ˈreɪsgəʊə/ *n* [C] someone who goes regularly to horse races 爱看赛马的人

race·horse /ˈresˌhɔrs; ˈreɪshɔːs/ *n* [C] a horse specially bred and trained for racing〔专门培育的〕比赛用的马

race meet·ing /ˈ· ˌ··/ *n* [C] *BrE* an occasion when horse races are held at a particular place【英】赛马会

race re·la·tions /ˈ· ·ˌ··/ *n* [plural] the relationship that exists between people from different countries, religions etc who are living in the same place 种族关系: *The result of the trial could have a damaging effect on race relations in the city.* 审判结果可能对该市的种族关系产生不利的影响。

Race Re·la·tions Act, the /ˌ· ·ˈ·· ˌ·/ a law passed in the UK in 1976 to protect the legal rights especially of black and Asian people, and to make sure that people of all races are treated fairly and equally《种族关系法》〔1976年英国通过的一项法案。该法旨在特别保护黑人和亚裔民众的合法权利, 不论种族确保所有公民均可得到公正和平等待遇〕

race ri·ot /ˈ· ˌ··/ *n* [C] violent behaviour, such as fighting and attacks on property, caused by hatred between people of different races 种族骚乱

race·track /ˈresˌtræk; ˈreɪs-træk/ *n* [C] **1** a track around which runners, cars etc race〔赛跑、赛车等用的〕跑道 **2** *AmE* a track, usually covered with grass, around which horses race【美】赛马跑道; RACECOURSE (1) *BrE*【英】

Rach·man·i·noff /rɑkˈmɑnɪnɔf; rækˈmænɪnɒf/, **Ser·gei** /sɛrˈge; ˈseəgeɪ/ (1873-1943) a Russian COMPOSER and pianist whose best known works are his piano CONCERTOs, symphonies (SYMPHONY), and his *Rhapsody on a Theme of Paganini* 拉赫玛尼诺夫〔(1873-1943), 俄国作曲家、钢琴家。其最著名的作品有钢琴协奏曲、交响曲和《帕格尼尼主题狂想曲》〕

ra·cial /ˈreʃəl; ˈreɪʃəl/ *adj* **1** [only before noun 仅用于名词前] connected with the relationships between different races of people 种族(关系)的: *an appeal for racial and religious tolerance* 呼吁不同种族和宗教间的宽容 | *racial conflict* 种族冲突 | **racial discrimination** (=unfair treatment of people because of their race) 种族歧视 | **racial prejudice** (=the belief that other races are not as good or as intelligent as your own race) 种族偏见 | **racial harassment** (=insulting or annoying someone because of their race) 种族骚扰 **2** connected with the various races that humans can be divided into 种族的: *a broad range of racial and ethnic groups* 多种多样的种族和民族群体 | *people of different racial origin* 不同种族背景的人 —**racially** *adv*: *Police officers believe the attack was racially motivated.* 警察认定攻击是出于种族原因。

ra·cial·is·m /ˈreʃəlˌɪzəm; ˈreɪʃəlɪzəm/ *n* [U] *BrE old-fashioned* RACISM【英, 过时】种族歧视; 种族暴力; 种族主义 —**racialist** *n, adj*

Ra·cine /ræˈsin; ræˈsiːn/, **Jean** /ʒɑn; ʒɒn/ (1639-99) a French writer of plays, whose work was based mainly on ancient Greek TRAGEDY and used many of the same subjects as Greek plays 拉辛〔(1639-1699), 法国剧作家。作品主要取材于古希腊悲剧故事, 借鉴了希腊戏剧作品的许多主题〕

rac·ing¹ /ˈresɪŋ; ˈreɪsɪŋ/ *n* [U] **1** the sport of racing horses 赛马: *watching the racing on television* 在电视上看赛马 | **racing results/tips/paper etc** *today's racing results* 今天的赛马结果 **2** **car/bicycle/greyhound etc racing** the sport of racing cars etc 汽车/自行车/灵猩等比赛

racing² *adj* [only before noun 仅用于名词前] designed or bred for racing 专为比赛设计[饲养]的: *racing pigeons* 赛鸽 | *a racing yacht* 赛艇

racing car /ˈ· · ·/ *n* [C] *BrE* a car that is specially designed for car races【英】赛车; RACE CAR *AmE*【美】

ra·cis·m /ˈresɪzəm; ˈreɪsɪzəm/ *n* [U] **1** unfair treatment of people, or violence against them, because they belong to a different race from your own 种族歧视; 种族暴力: *the ugly face of racism rearing its head again in Europe* 正在欧洲重新抬头的种族歧视的丑恶嘴脸 **2** the belief that different races of people have different characters and abilities, and that the qualities of your own race are the best 种族主义

rac·ist /ˈresɪst; ˈreɪsɪ̈st/ *n* [C] someone who believes that people of their own race are better than others, and who treats people from other races unfairly and sometimes violently 种族主义者: *white racists* 白人种族主义者 —**racist** *adj*: *racist attitudes* 种族主义态度

racks 搁物架

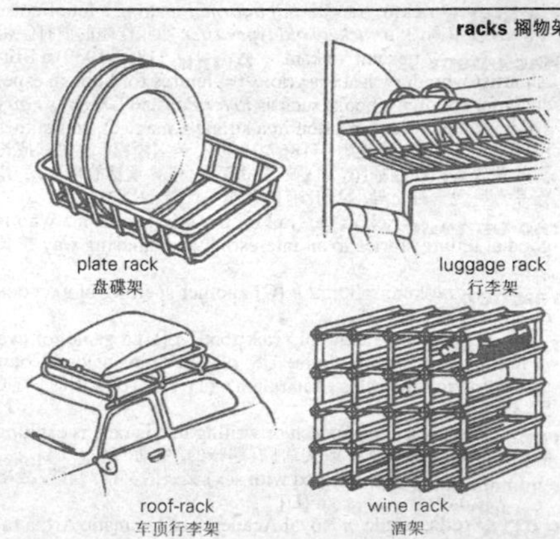

rack¹ /ræk; ræk/ *n* [C] **1** a frame or shelf, usually with bars or hooks, for holding things on〔通常带有横档或钩子的〕架子, 搁物架: *The dishes are on the plate rack.* 盘子在盘子架上。| *a magazine rack* 杂志架 —see also 另见 LUGGAGE RACK, ROOF-RACK **2** **the rack** a piece of equipment used in the past to make people

suffer severe pain by stretching their bodies 拉肢刑架〔旧时的一种酷刑刑具〕 3 **on the rack** suffering severe pain or anxiety 十分痛苦, 极度焦虑 4 **go to rack and ruin** to gradually get into a very bad condition as a result of not being looked after〔因缺乏照料所致的〕破损, 毁坏: *The old farmhouse had gone to rack and ruin.* 那间旧农舍已经破败不堪了。5 *AmE* a three-sided frame used for arranging the balls at the start of a game of SNOOKER[1] or POOL[1] (3)【美】〔用于台球或撞球比赛开球时放置球的〕三角框 6 **a rack of lamb/pork** *BrE* a fairly large piece of meat from the side of an animal【英】羊/猪胸腹两侧较大块的肉

rack² *v* 1 [T usually passive 一般用被动态] to make someone suffer great mental or physical pain 使受巨大〔精神或肉体〕痛苦: **be racked by/with** *She was racked by feelings of guilt.* 她深受负罪感的折磨。| *He lay on the ground racked with pain.* 他万分痛苦地躺在地上。2 **rack your brain(s)** to think very hard or for a long time 绞尽脑汁: *I really had to rack my brains to remember his name.* 我真的得绞尽脑汁, 才能记起他的名字。

rack sth ↔ **up** *phr v* [T] *informal*【非正式】1 *AmE* to gradually get points, votes etc, especially in a competition or election【美】〔尤指在竞赛或竞选中逐渐〕得〔分〕, 赢得〔选票〕: *The team racked up enough points to win the NFL title.* 该队累积了足够的得分获得〔美国〕全国橄榄球联盟冠军。2 *AmE* to damage or ruin something【美】破坏, 毁坏: *That motorcycle accident really racked up his leg.* 那场摩托车车祸确实毁了他的腿。3 to make the value, amount, or level of something go up 使增值, 增加, 提高: *High interest rates have racked up the pound.* 高利率造成英镑升值。

rack·et¹ /ˈrækɪt; ˈrækɨt/ *n* 1 [singular] *informal* a loud noise【非正式】吵闹(声), 喧嚣: *They're making a hell of a racket downstairs.* 他们正在楼下大吵大闹。—see 见 NOISE[1] (USAGE) 2 [C] *informal* a dishonest way of obtaining money, such as by threatening people or selling them illegal goods【非正式】敲诈, 勒索; 非法勾当〔销售违禁品〕: **drugs/gambling/smuggling etc racket** *He runs a numbers racket on the side.* 他私下经营非法彩票赌博。—see also 另见 PROTECTION RACKET 3 also 又作 **racquet** [C] a BAT[1] (2b) used for hitting the ball in games such as tennis 球拍: *a tennis racket* 网球拍 —see pictures at 参见 SQUASH and 和 TENNIS 图 4 **rackets** also 又作 **racquets** [U] a fast ball game for two or four players, played with rackets and a hard ball on an indoor court 硬球壁球〔运动〕

racket² *v* [I always+adv/prep] to make a lot of noise as you move around〔走动时〕发出大响声: [**+around/about etc**] *racketing about upstairs* 在楼上弄出很大响声

rack·e·teer /ˌrækɪˈtɪr; ˌrækɨˈtɪə/ *n* [C] someone who is involved in a dishonest method of obtaining money 敲诈[勒索]钱财者, 非法经营者

rack·e·teer·ing /ˌrækɪˈtɪrɪŋ; ˌrækɨˈtɪərɪŋ/ *n* [U] obtaining money dishonestly by means of a carefully planned system 敲诈, 勒索: *Keating is awaiting trial on fraud and racketeering charges.* 基廷被指控欺诈和勒索正听候审判。

rack·et·y /ˈrækɪtɪ; ˈrækɨti/ *adj informal* making a lot of noise【非正式】喧闹的: *a rackety old typewriter* 咔咔作响的旧打字机

Rack·ham /ˈrækəm; ˈrækəm/**, Arthur** (1867-1939) a British artist who drew ILLUSTRATIONS (=pictures for books), especially for children's books such as *Peter Pan* and *Grimm's Fairy Tales.* His pictures are often in a strange, magical, sometimes frightening style. 拉克姆〔(1867-1939), 英国画家。他尤其擅长为儿童故事书绘制插图, 如《彼得·潘》和《格林童话故事集》。其作品常呈现一种奇异、魔幻, 有时甚至是恐怖的风格〕

rac·on·teur /ˌrækɑnˈtɝ; ˌrækɒnˈtɜː/ *n* [C] someone who is good at telling stories in an interesting and amusing way 擅长讲故事的人

ra·coon /ræˈkun; rəˈkuːn/ *n* [C] another spelling of RACCOON raccoon 的另一种拼法

rac·quet·ball /ˈrækɪtˌbɔl; ˈrækɨtbɔːl/ *n* [U] a game for two or four players, popular in the US, played in an enclosed court and following the rules of HANDBALL (1)〔流行于美国的〕短拍壁球〔运动〕

rac·y /ˈresɪ; ˈreɪsi/ *adj* speech or writing that is racy is exciting and entertaining〔演讲或文章〕有趣味的, 生动的: **racy jokes/humour/stories** (=connected with sex) 猥亵的笑话/幽默/故事 —**racily** *adv* —**raciness** *n* [U]

RADA /ˈrɑdə; ˈrɑːdə/ *n* Royal Academy of Dramatic Art; a famous school in London for people who want to become actors 皇家戏剧艺术学院〔伦敦一所培养专业演员的著名学校〕

ra·dar /ˈredɑr; ˈreɪdɑː/ *n* [C,U] a method of finding the position of things such as planes or MISSILES by sending out radio waves 雷达: *The missile was identified using radar.* 导弹已被雷达识别出来。| *a radar screen* 雷达屏幕

radar trap /ˈ· · ·/ *n* [C] a method or set of equipment that uses radar to catch drivers who are going faster than the legal speed〔捕获超速行驶司机用的〕雷达监控法[器]

rad·dled /ˈrædḷd; ˈrædld/ *adj* 1 *BrE* looking old or tired【英】苍老的; 疲惫的 2 *AmE* confused or anxious【美】茫然的; 焦虑的

ra·di- /redɪ; reɪdi/ *prefix* another form of the prefix RADIO- 前缀 radio- 的另一种形式

ra·di·al¹ /ˈredɪəl; ˈreɪdiəl/ *adj* arranged in a circular shape with bars, lines etc coming from the centre 辐射状的: *radial street patterns* 辐射状的街道布局

radial² *n* [C] *informal* a RADIAL TYRE【非正式】辐射状[子午线]轮胎

radial tyre *BrE*【英】, **radial tire** *AmE*【美】/ˌ··· ˈ·/ *n* [C] a car tyre with wires inside the rubber that go completely around the wheel to make it stronger and safer 辐射状[子午线]轮胎

ra·di·ance /ˈredɪəns; ˈreɪdiəns/ *n* [U] 1 great happiness, or energy that shows in the way someone looks〔人或其外表的〕喜气洋洋, 容光焕发: *the unmistakeable radiance of youth* 显而易见的青春朝气 2 a soft light that shines from or onto something 光彩

ra·di·ant /ˈredɪənt; ˈreɪdiənt/ *adj* 1 full of happiness and love, in a way that shows in your face, eyes etc 喜悦的, 容光焕发的, 光彩照人的: *a radiant smile* 粲然一笑 | [**+with**] *radiant with joy* 满面春风 2 [only before noun 仅用于名词前] very bright 灿烂的, 明亮的: *a radiant blue sky* 湛蓝的天空 3 [only before noun 仅用于名词前] *technical* radiant heat, energy etc is sent out by radiation【术语】〔热、能等〕辐射的 —**radiantly** *adv*: *radiantly beautiful* 美得光彩照人

ra·di·ate /ˈredɪˌet; ˈreɪdieɪt/ *v* **radiated, radiating** 1 [I always+adv/prep,T] if something radiates light or heat, or if light or heat radiates from something, it is sent out in all directions 辐射〔光或热〕;〔向四面八方〕发射: *The log fire radiated a warm cosy glow.* 燃烧的圆木发出温暖舒适的光。| [**+down/from/away etc**] *Warmth radiated down from the tin roof.* 暖流从白铁屋顶散发下来。2 [I,T] if someone radiates a feeling or quality, or if it radiates from them, they show it or feel it in a way that is easy to notice 流露, 显示〔感情、态度等〕: *She radiated energy and self-confidence.* 她洋溢着活力与自信。| [**+from**] *Sexual magnetism radiated from him.* 他散发着性感。3 to spread out from a central point 从中心散开: [**+from/to**] *A system of roads radiates from the town centre.* 一组公路从市中心向四面八方伸展出去。

ra·di·a·tion /ˌredɪˈeʃən; ˌreɪdiˈeɪʃən/ *n* [U] 1 a form of energy that comes especially from NUCLEAR reactions, which is very harmful to living things if present in large amounts〔核〕辐射〔尤指核反应产生的能源形式, 如量大对生物非常危险〕: *an escape of low-level radiation from the nuclear power plant* 从核电厂泄漏的低度辐射 | *lethal doses of radiation* 致命的辐射剂量 2 energy in the form of heat or light sent out as beams that you cannot see〔热或光的能量〕辐射: *electromagnetic radiation* 电磁辐射 | *sun cream that filters out harmful ultraviolet radiation* 能滤去有害紫外线辐射的防晒霜 3 the radiating of heat, light etc 发热; 发光

radiation sick·ness /·ˈ·· ˌ··/ *n* [U] an illness caused by your body receiving too much radiation 辐射病, 放射病

ra·di·a·tor /ˈredɪˌetə; ˈreɪdieɪtə/ *n* [C] 1 a thing used for heating a room, consisting of a flat hollow metal container fixed to a wall, through which hot water passes〔指借热水循环供热的〕暖气装置 2 the part of a car or aircraft which stops the engine from getting too hot〔冷却汽车、飞机发动机的〕散热器 —see picture at 参见 ENGINE (1) 图

rad·i·cal¹ /ˈrædɪkḷ; ˈrædɪkəl/ *adj* 1 a radical change has a lot of important effects〔变革等〕重大的, 根本的: *radical alterations to the original script* 对原稿进行的重大修改 | *a radical reform of the tax system* 税收制度的彻底改革 2 radical opinions, ideas, leaders etc support thorough and complete social or political change〔人、观点、领导人等〕激进的, 极端的: *the radical views of the left wing of the party* 党内左翼的激进观点 3 related to the central or most important qualities of something; FUNDAMENTAL 根本的, 基本的: *a radical questioning of basic chauvinistic tenets* 对沙文主义基本信念提出的根本性怀疑 | *radical differences between the two groups* 两派间的根本分歧 4 *AmE slang* very good or enjoyable【美俚】顶呱呱的, 好玩的: *That was one radical party last night!* 昨晚的聚会太棒了! —**radically** /-klɪ; -kli/ *adv* 3

radical² *n* [C] someone who wants thorough and complete social and political change〔主张对社会和政治作彻底变革的〕激进分子 —**radicalism** *n* [U]

rad·i·i /ˈredɪ,aɪ; ˈreɪdiaɪ/ *n* the plural of RADIUS

ra·di·o- /redɪo; reɪdiəʊ/ *prefix* also 又作 **radi- 1** *technical*【术语】**a)** concerning waves of force, e.g. light, sound, or radio waves〔光、声、无线电波〕辐射: *radiopaque* (=which waves will not pass through) 辐射穿不透的 **b)** using radio waves 使用无线电波的: *a radiotelephone* (=working without wires) 无线电话(机) | *radiopaging* (=calling people by radio) 无线电传呼 **2** concerning RADIOACTIVITY 与放射有关的: *radiochemistry* (=the study of RADIOACTIVE chemicals) 放射化学

ra·di·o¹ /ˈredɪ,o; ˈreɪdiəʊ/ *n* **1 a)** [C] a piece of electronic equipment which you use to listen to programmes that are broadcast, such as music and news 收音机: *turn on the radio* 打开收音机 | *listening to the radio in the car* 在汽车里听收音机 | **on the radio** (=broadcast on a radio) 广播 *an interesting program on the radio this morning* 今晨广播里一个有趣的节目 **b) the radio** programmes that are broadcast on the radio, considered in general〔泛指〕广播节目: *I don't really listen to the radio much.* 我不怎么听广播。**c)** [U] the sending or receiving of programmes by radio 广播: *Radio was a powerful medium during the war years, keeping up people's morale.* 战争年代里，广播是一种很有力的媒介，激励着人们的士气。**2** [U] the activity of making and broadcasting programmes which can be heard on a radio (无线电)广播业: *David Jason worked in radio before TV.* 戴维·贾森到电视台工作前在电台工作过。| **local/national radio** (=programmes or companies broadcasting for a local area, or for the whole country) 地方/全国广播节目[公司] | **radio programme/show/drama etc** *John Peel's late-night radio show* 约翰·皮尔的深夜广播节目 **3 a)** [C] a piece of electronic equipment, for example on a plane or ship, which can send and receive spoken messages〔飞机、船上的〕无线电收发设备 **b)** [U] the sending or receiving of these messages 无线电通讯: *We've lost radio contact.* 我们失去了无线电联系。

radio² *v* [I,T] to send a message using a radio 用无线电发送(信息): *The ship radioed for help.* 这条船用无线电发出求救信号。| *Radio London for permission to land.* 用无线电请求伦敦准予降落。

Radio 1 /ˌredɪo ˈwʌn; ˌreɪdiəʊ ˈwʌn/ a BBC radio station which broadcasts mostly POP music and is listened to mostly by young people 广播一台〔英国广播公司一电台，主要播放流行音乐，听众多为青少年〕

Radio 2 /ˌredɪo ˈtu; ˌreɪdiəʊ ˈtuː/ a BBC radio station which broadcasts popular music and entertainment programmes. Unlike Radio 1, Radio 2 does not play the most recent music, and it is listened to especially by older people. 广播二台〔英国广播公司一电台，主要播放通俗流行音乐和娱乐节目。与广播一台不同的是，广播二台不播放最新推出的音乐，听众多为较年长的人群〕

Radio 3 /ˌredɪo ˈθri; ˌreɪdiəʊ ˈθriː/ a BBC radio station which broadcasts mostly CLASSICAL music 广播三台〔英国广播公司一电台，主要播放古典音乐〕

Radio 4 /ˌredɪo ˈfor; ˌreɪdiəʊ ˈfɔː/ a BBC radio station which broadcasts programmes on news and politics, as well as plays and arts programmes 广播四台〔英国广播公司一电台，主要播放新闻和时政节目，也播送戏剧和艺术节目〕

Radio 5 Live /ˌredɪo faɪv ˈlaɪv; ˌreɪdiəʊ faɪv ˈlaɪv/ a BBC radio station which broadcasts news and sports programmes 24 hours a day 广播五台〔英国广播公司一电台，每天24小时播送新闻和体育节目〕

ra·di·o·ac·tive /ˌredɪoˈæktɪv; ˌreɪdiəʊˈæktɪv◂/ *adj* containing RADIATION (=a form of energy that can harm living things) 具有放射性的: ***a highly radioactive material*** 高放射性物质 | *radioactive contamination* 放射性污染

radioactive dat·ing /ˌ······ˈ··/ *n* [U] *AmE* a scientific method of calculating the age of a very old object by measuring the amount of a certain substance in it【美】放射性年代测定(法)，碳年代测定(法); CARBON DATING *BrE*【英】

radioactive waste /ˌ·····ˈ·/ *n* [U] harmful radioactive substances that remain after energy has been produced in a NUCLEAR REACTOR〔核反应堆产生的〕放射性废料

ra·di·o·ac·tiv·i·ty /ˈredɪ,oækˈtɪvətɪ; ˌreɪdiəʊækˈtɪvəti/ *n* [U] **1** a quality that certain substances have which makes them send out RADIATION (=a form of energy that can harm living things) 放射(性) **2** the energy which is produced in this way 辐射能: *Workers were exposed to high levels of radioactivity.* 工人接触到高强度辐射。

radio bea·con /ˈ···, ·ˈ·/ *n* [C] a tower that sends out radio signals to help aircraft stay on the correct course 无线电导航塔

ra·di·o·car·bon dat·ing /ˌredɪokɑrbən ˈdetɪŋ; ˌreɪdiəʊkɑːbən ˈdeɪtɪŋ/ *n* [U] *formal* CARBON DATING【正式】碳年代测定(法)

radio-cas·sette play·er /ˌ··· ·ˈ· ˌ··/ *n* [C] a piece of electronic equipment that contains both a radio and a CASSETTE PLAYER 收录机

Radio Cit·y Mu·sic Hall /ˌ··· ·· ˈ·· ·/ a large theatre in New York City, where concerts, film FESTIVALs, the Tony Awards ceremony, and shows with lots of singing and dancing take place 广播城音乐厅〔纽约市一大剧院。在此举办的文艺活动有音乐会、电影节、托尼奖颁奖典礼和歌舞表演〕

radio-con·trolled /ˌ··· ·ˈ·◂/ *adj* **a radio-controlled aircraft/vehicle/vessel** controlled from far away using radio signals 无线电遥控飞机/车辆/船

ra·di·o·gram /ˈredɪə,græm; ˈreɪdiəʊgræm/ *n* [C] **1** *BrE* a piece of furniture, popular in the 1950s, which contained a radio and a record player【英】〔20世纪50年代流行的〕收音电唱两用机 **2** a message sent by radio 无线电报

ra·di·og·ra·pher /ˌredɪˈɑgrəfɚ; ˌreɪdiˈɒgrəfə/ *n* [C] someone whose job is to take X-RAY photographs of the inside of someone's body, or who treats people for illnesses using an X-RAY machine X射线照相师; 放射科医师

ra·di·og·ra·phy /ˌredɪˈɑgrəfɪ; ˌreɪdiˈɒgrəfi/ *n* [U] the taking of X-RAY photographs of the inside of someone's body for medical purposes〔医用〕X射线照相术

ra·di·ol·o·gist /ˌredɪˈɑlədʒɪst; ˌreɪdiˈɒlədʒɪst/ *n* [C] a hospital doctor who is trained in the use of RADIATION to treat people 放射科医师

ra·di·ol·o·gy /ˌredɪˈɑlədʒɪ; ˌreɪdiˈɒlədʒi/ *n* [U] the study and medical use of RADIATION〔医用〕放射学

radio-tel·e·phone /ˌ···ˈ···/ *n* [C] a telephone, used especially in cars, that works by sending and receiving radio signals〔尤指汽车的〕无线电话(机)

radio tel·e·scope /ˌ···ˈ···/ *n* [C] a very large piece of equipment that collects the RADIO WAVEs that come from stars and other objects in space 无线电望远镜

ra·di·o·ther·a·py /ˈredɪoˈθɛrəpɪ; ˌreɪdiəʊˈθerəpi/ *n* [U] the treatment of illnesses using RADIATION 放射治疗 —**radiotherapist** *n* [C]

Radio Times, The /ˌ···ˈ·/ a British weekly magazine that gives the times and details of television and radio programmes, as well as articles about programmes, actors, etc《广播时代》〔英国一周刊，刊载广播、电视节目的播出时间及内容简介，也刊登关涉节目、演员等内容的文章〕—see also 另见 TV GUIDE, TV TIMES

radio wave /ˈ···, ·/ *n* [C usually plural 一般用复数] a form of electric energy that can move through air or space 无线电波

rad·ish /ˈrædɪʃ; ˈrædɪʃ/ *n* [C] a small vegetable whose red or white root is eaten raw and has a strong SPICY taste〔可生吃、有辣味的红或白色的〕小萝卜 —see picture on page A9 参见A9页图

ra·di·um /ˈredɪəm; ˈreɪdiəm/ *n* [U] a rare metal that is RADIOACTIVE and is used in the treatment of diseases such as CANCER 镭

ra·di·us /ˈredɪəs; ˈreɪdiəs/ *n plural* **radii** /-dɪ,aɪ; -diaɪ/ [C] **1** the distance from the centre to the edge of a circle〔圆的〕半径: *The radius of the throwing circle should be 1.5 metres.* 投掷圈的半径应为1.5米。**2 within a 10 mile/200 metre etc radius** within a distance of 10 miles, 200 metres in all directions from a particular place 在10英里/200米等的半径范围内: *All vegetation was destroyed within a 2km radius of the volcano.* 火山方圆2公里内所有的植被都毁了。**3** a line drawn straight out from the centre of a circle to its edge 半径(线) —see picture at 参见 CIRCLE¹ 图 **4** *technical* the outer bone of the lower part of your arm【术语】桡骨 —see picture at 参见 SKELETON 图

Radley /ˈrædlɪ; ˈrædli/, **Boo** /bu; buː/ a character in the book *To Kill a Mockingbird* (1960) by Harper Lee. He is locked in the house by his father as a punishment, and is never allowed out. Because the people in the town never see him, they believe many strange stories about him, and think that he comes out at night to hunt and eat SQUIRRELs. 拉德利〔哈珀·李的小说《杀死一只知更鸟》(1960)中的人物。父亲惩罚他，把他锁在家里，绝不准他出来。镇上的人谁也没有见过他，所以对他的许多奇闻怪事都信以为真，认为他一到晚上就会出来捕捉松鼠，吃松鼠的肉〕

ra·don /ˈredɑn; ˈreɪdɒn/ *n* [U] a RADIOACTIVE gas that can be dangerous in large amounts 氡

rad·waste /ˈræd,west; ˈrædweɪst/ *n* [U] *AmE* RADIOACTIVE WASTE【美】放射性废料

RAF /ˌɑr e ˈɛf; ˌɑːr eɪ ˈef/ *n* the Royal Air Force; the British AIRFORCE〔英国〕皇家空军

raf·fi·a /ˈræfɪə; ˈræfiə/ *n* [U] a soft substance like string that comes from the leaves of a PALM tree and is used for making baskets, hats, MATs etc〔编织篮子、帽子、席子等用的〕酒椰叶纤维

raf·fish /ˈræfɪʃ; ˈræfɪʃ/ *adj literary* behaving or dressing in a confident and cheerful way that shows no concern for what other people think but is still attractive【文】〔人的行为或装束〕大胆脱俗的，落拓不羁的：*a raffish air about him which some women found appealing* 他让一些女人着迷的洒脱风度 —**raffishly** *adv* —**raffishness** *n* [U]

3 **raf·fle¹** /ˈræfl; ˈræfəl/ *n* [C] a kind of competition or game in which people buy numbered tickets and can win prizes 对奖售物（活动）

raffle² also 又作 **raffle off** *v* [T] to offer something as a prize in a raffle 在对奖售物活动中以…作奖品

Raf·fles /ˈræflz; ˈræfəlz/ a jewel thief who was also a gentleman in the book *The Amateur Cracksman* (1899). Raffles also played CRICKET for England. 莱佛士〔小说《业余神偷莱佛士》(1899) 中的绅士兼珠宝大盗。他也是英格兰板球队的队员〕

Raf·fles Ho·tel /ˌræflz hoˈtɛl; ˌræfəlz həʊˈtel/ a famous old hotel in Singapore, in a beautiful 19th century building. It is a popular place for wealthy people to stay, and is named after Sir Stamford Raffles, who brought Singapore under British control in 1819. 莱佛士酒店〔新加坡一著名老字号酒店，为一幢19世纪的漂亮建筑，是有钱人喜欢下榻的地方。1819年，斯坦福德·莱佛士爵士将新加坡置于英国统治之下。该酒店就是以他的姓氏命名的〕

raft¹ /ræft; rɑːft/ *n* [C] **1** a flat floating structure, usually made of pieces of wood tied together, used as a boat 木排，木筏 **2** a flat floating structure that you can sit on, jump from etc when you are swimming〔游泳时可坐或跳水的〕浮台 **3 a (whole) raft of** *spoken, especially AmE* a large number of things or large amount of something【口，尤美】许多，大量：*He has a whole raft of camera equipment.* 他有一大堆照相器材。**4** a small flat rubber boat filled with air, used if a boat sinks or a plane crashes into the sea 充气救生（橡皮）筏

raft² *v* [I,T] to travel by raft or carry things by raft 乘筏子；用筏子运送

raf·ter /ˈræftɚ; ˈrɑːftə/ *n* [C usually plural 一般用复数] one of the large sloping pieces of wood that form the structure of a roof 椽

rag¹ /ræg; ræg/ *n*

1 ▶CLOTH 布◀ [C,U] a small piece of old cloth, for example one used for cleaning things 一小块旧布；抹布：*Can I use this piece of rag for the car?* 我能用这块布擦车吗？| *an oily old rag* 沾满油污的旧抹布

2 in rags wearing old torn clothes 衣衫褴褛：*an old beggar dressed in rags* 衣衫褴褛的老乞丐

3 go from rags to riches to become very rich after starting your life very poor 白手起家

4 ▶NEWSPAPER 报纸◀ [C] *informal* a newspaper that you think is of low quality【非正式】粗制滥造的报纸：*The Evening News is just a provincial rag.*《晚报》不过是一份差劲的地方小报。

5 ▶MUSIC 音乐◀ [C] a piece of RAGTIME music 拉格泰姆乐曲：*Georgia Rag* 佐治亚州雷格泰姆音乐

6 ▶STUDENTS' EVENT 学生活动◀ [C] *BrE* an event organized by students every year in order to make money for people who are poor, sick etc【英】〔学生每年为穷人、病人等举行的〕慈善募捐活动：*rag week* 慈善募捐周

7 ▶TRICK 花招◀ [C] *BrE old-fashioned* a trick played on someone as a joke【英，过时】戏弄，恶作剧：*They did it as a rag.* 他们这样做只是为了寻开心。—see also 另见 **glad rags** (GLAD (6)), **like a red rag to a bull** (RED¹ (6))

rag² *v* **ragged, ragging** [T] *BrE old-fashioned* to laugh at someone or play tricks on them【英，过时】戏弄，对…搞恶作剧

ra·ga /ˈrɑgə; ˈrɑːgə/ *n* [C] **1** a piece of Indian music based on an ancient pattern of notes 拉加乐曲〔一种印度音乐〕**2** one of the ancient patterns of notes that are used in Indian music 拉加曲调

rag·a·muf·fin /ˈrægəˌmʌfɪn; ˈrægəˌmʌfɪn/ *n* [C] *literary* a dirty young child wearing torn clothes【文】衣衫褴褛的脏孩子

rag-and-bone-man /ˌ· · ˈ· ˌ/ *n* [C] *BrE* a man who goes around the streets buying and collecting old clothes and other things that people no longer want【英】〔沿街收购旧衣物的〕流动旧货商

rag·bag /ˈrægˌbæg; ˈrægbæg/ *n* **a ragbag of** a confused mixture of things that do not seem to go together or make sense …杂乱无章的东西，…的大杂烩：*a ragbag of ill-thought-out measures to help the homeless* 帮助无家可归者的计划不周的措施

rag doll /ˈ· ˌ·/ *n* [C] a soft DOLL¹ (1) made of cloth 布娃娃

rag doll 布娃娃

rage¹ /redʒ; reɪdʒ/ *n* [C,U] **1** a strong feeling of uncontrollable anger 盛怒，狂怒：*His letter had filled her with rage and disappointment.* 他的信使她盛怒而且失望。| **in a rage** *She stormed out of the room in a rage.* 她狂怒之下冲出房间。| **fly into a rage** (=suddenly become very angry) 勃然大怒 *Major Sanderson instantly flew into a terrible rage.* 桑德森少校立即大发雷霆。| **shaking/trembling/quivering with rage** *Blake sprang to his feet, his face trembling with rage.* 布莱克一跃而起，气得脸直抽搐。**2 be (all) the rage** *informal* to be very popular and fashionable【非正式】流行，时髦：*Platform shoes were all the rage then.* 厚底鞋当时风靡一时。**3 a rage for** *old-fashioned* a very popular fashion【过时】最时髦的东西，时新式样，时尚：*There was a great rage for open sports cars at that time.* 当时敞篷跑车非常流行。

rage² *v* [I] **1** if something rages, such as a battle, a disagreement, or a storm, it continues with great violence or strong emotions〔战斗、争论〕激烈进行，〔风暴〕狂吹：*Controversy over the scandal is still raging.* 有关该丑闻的争论仍然激烈。| *Outside a great storm was raging.* 屋外狂风大作。**2** [+at/about/against] to feel very angry about something and show this in the way you behave or speak 大怒，发脾气：*Margo raged against the unfairness of the situation.* 马戈对不公正的情况勃然大怒。

rag·ga /ˈrægə; ˈrægə/ *n* [U] a form of popular music from the West Indies 拉加〔西印度群岛的一种流行音乐〕

rag·ged /ˈrægɪd; ˈrægɪ̈d/ *adj*

1 ▶CLOTHES 衣服◀ also 又作 **raggedy** *especially AmE* torn and in bad condition【尤美】破旧的：*A beggar was dozing on a pile of ragged blankets.* 一个乞丐正坐在一堆破毯子上打瞌睡。| *piles of ragged old books* 成堆的破旧书籍

2 ▶PEOPLE 人◀ wearing clothes that are old and torn 衣衫褴褛的：*a group of ragged children* 一群穿得破破烂烂的孩子

3 ▶UNEVEN 不平的◀ also 又作 **raggedy** not straight or neat, but with rough uneven edges〔边缘〕参差不齐的：*a ragged hedge* 参差不齐的树篱

4 ▶TIRED 疲倦的◀ *informal* tired after using a lot of effort【非正式】疲乏的：*The walkers looked pretty ragged by the end of the day.* 一天结束时，行人都显得疲惫不堪。| **run sb ragged** (=make them do a lot of work) 使某人精疲力竭

5 ▶PERFORMANCE 表演◀ a ragged performance, shout etc is one that people are not doing together or properly〔表演、呼喊声等〕不协调的，不齐的：*He gave a somewhat ragged performance, I thought.* 我觉得他的表演很差劲。| *a ragged cheer* 不整齐的欢呼声

6 be on the ragged edge *AmE informal* to be feeling very tired or upset【美，非正式】极度疲惫；惴惴不安 —**raggedly** *adv*: *raggedly dressed* 衣衫褴褛的 —**raggedness** *n* [U]

Rag·ged·y Ann /ˌrægɪdɪ ˈæn; ˌrægɪ̈di ˈæn/ *trademark* a type of RAG DOLL (=doll made from cloth) which is a popular children's toy in the US. She has a large round face, red circles on her cheeks, and hair made from pieces of red wool. The male doll that looks like this is her brother, Raggedy Andy.【商标】碎布娃娃安妮〔美国儿童喜爱的一种布娃娃玩具。她有一张大圆脸，脸颊有红晕，头发用红色羊毛做成。与之相似的男娃娃是她的弟弟，名叫碎布娃娃安迪〕

rag·ing /ˈredʒɪŋ; ˈreɪdʒɪŋ/ *adj* **1** [only before noun 仅用于名词前] raging feelings and emotions are extremely strong〔感情〕强烈的：*a raging thirst* 极度干渴 | *raging jealousy* 强烈的嫉妒心 **2 a raging headache/toothache etc** a very bad pain in your head etc 剧烈的头痛/牙痛等 **3 raging stream/torrent/waters** water that flows fast and violently 湍急的溪流/激流/河水

rag·lan /ˈræglən; ˈræglən/ *adj* **1 raglan coat/sweater etc** a coat etc which has arms that are joined in a sideways line from the arm to the neck〔袖缝由臂部直至领部的〕连肩袖大衣/毛

衣等 **2 raglan sleeve** an arm of a coat etc joined in this way 连肩袖

ra·gout /ræ`gu; ræ'guː/ *n* [C,U] *French* a mixture of vegetables and meat boiled together; STEW[1] (1)【法】蔬菜炖肉

rag·tag /ˈræg,tæg; 'rægtæg/ *adj* **1** *informal* looking untidy, poor, and dirty【非正式】邋遢的, 肮脏的: *a ragtag bunch of kids* 一群肮脏的小孩 **2 ragtag and bobtail** *old-fashioned* a crowd of untidy, poor people【过时】一群邋遢的穷人

rag·time /ˈræg,taɪm; 'rægtaɪm/ *n* [U] a type of music and dancing that has a strong beat and was popular in the US in the early part of the 20th century 拉格泰姆〔一种节奏强劲的音乐, 20 世纪初流行于美国〕

rag trade, the /ˈ· ·/ *n BrE* the business of making and selling clothes, especially women's clothes【英】〔尤指女装的〕服装业

rag·weed /ˈræg,wid; 'rægwiːd/ *n* [U] a North American plant that produces a substance which causes HAY FEVER〔北美洲植物, 可引起花粉病的〕豚草

rag·wort /ˈræg,wɝt; 'rægwɜːt/ *n* [U] a common plant with yellow flowers, and leaves with uneven edges 千里光

raid¹ /red; reɪd/ *n* [C] **1** a short attack on a place by soldiers, planes, or ships, intended to cause damage but not take control 突袭, 袭击: **[+on]** *a bombing raid on the railway line* 对铁路线进行的轰炸 | *cross border raids* 越境突袭 | **carry out/launch/make a raid** *Aircraft are carrying out raids on enemy ships.* 飞机正对敌舰进行空袭。**2** a sudden visit by the police searching for something illegal〔警察进行的〕突击搜查: *Following this morning's raid, three people have been charged with possessing illegal drugs.* 在今天早上的突击搜查之后, 三个人被控持有违禁药品。| **police raid** *a police raid on a club* 警方对一家俱乐部进行的突然搜查 | **dawn raid** (=carried out very early in the morning) 拂晓搜查 **3** an attack by criminals on a bank or similar place〔对银行等处的〕抢劫, 打劫: *a bank raid* 银行劫案 | **[+on]** *raids on post offices in the area* 抢劫本区邮局 | **carry out a raid** *Armed robbers carried out a raid on the Gateway Bank last night.* 昨夜, 持枪劫匪抢劫了盖特威银行。**4** *technical* an attempt by a company to buy enough SHARES in another company to take control of it【术语】〔某公司〕大量购买另一家公司的股票以获得其控制权的企图 —see also 另见 AIR RAID

raid² *v* [T] **1** if police raid a place, they go there suddenly to search for something illegal〔警察〕突然搜查: *Suspected drug dealers' homes were raided.* 贩毒嫌疑分子的家被突然搜查。**2** to make a sudden armed attack on a place 武装突袭: *Vikings raided settlements on the east coast.* 维京人袭击了东海岸的村落。| **a raiding party** (=group taking part in an attack) 袭击队 **3** to take or steal a lot of things from a place 抢劫, 洗劫: *She raided Jim's cash box.* 她洗劫了吉姆的钱箱。| *Animal-rights activists got in and raided the laboratories.* 动物权利保护者洗劫了实验室。| **raid the larder/refrigerator** *humorous* (=take food from your family's kitchen because you are hungry)【幽默】〔因饥饿而〕扫荡食物橱/冰箱 —see also 另见 RAM-RAIDING —**raider** *n* [C]

2 2 **rail¹** /rel; reɪl/ *n* **1** [C] a bar that is fixed along or around something, especially to stop you from falling 栏杆, 扶手: *Mrs Kellow held tightly onto the rail as she climbed the stairs.* 凯罗太太上楼梯时紧紧抓着栏杆。**2** [C] a bar that you use to hang things on〔挂东西用的〕横杆: *a clothes rail* 晾衣杆 | *a towel rail fixed to the bathroom door* 固定在浴室门上的毛巾杆 **3** [C] one of the two long metal tracks fixed to the ground that trains move along 铁路路轨 **4** [U] travelling by train 乘火车旅行: *I prefer to go by rail.* 我喜欢乘火车去。| *rail travel* 乘火车旅行 **5 go off the rails** *informal* to start behaving in a strange or socially unacceptable way【非正式】〔行为〕越轨, 不正常: *At 17 he suddenly went off the rails and started stealing.* 17岁时, 他突然走上歪路, 开始偷窃。

rail² *v* **1** [T] to enclose or separate an area with rails 用栏杆把…围起; 把…隔开: **[+off/in]** *The police railed off the area where the accident happened.* 警察用围栏把事故现场隔开。**2** [I] *formal* to complain angrily about something, especially something that you think is very unfair【正式】谴责, 抱怨: **[+against/at]** *railing against injustice* 对不公正行为表示强烈不满

rail·ing /ˈrelɪŋ; 'reɪlɪŋ/ *n* [C usually plural 一般用复数] one of the metal bars in a fence that is made of a series of upright bars 栏杆: *Jimmy somehow got his head stuck in the railings.* 吉米不知怎的把头卡在栏杆中间。

rail·le·ry /ˈrelərɪ; 'reɪləri/ *n* [U] *formal* friendly joking about someone【正式】善意的嘲弄, 逗弄: *affectionate raillery* 亲热的逗弄

rail·road¹ /ˈrel,rod; 'reɪlrəʊd/ *n AmE*【美】**1** [C] a railway 铁路: *The supplies were sent on the railroad.* 补给是由铁路运送的。**2 the railroad** all the work, equipment etc connected with a train system 铁路系统: *He had taken a job as a ticket agent on the railroad.* 他在铁路部门任售票员。

railroad² *v* [T] to force or persuade someone do something without giving them enough time to think about it 迫使〔某人〕仓促行事: **railroad sb into doing sth** *The workers were railroaded into signing the agreement.* 工人们被迫草草地签了这个协议。

rail·way /ˈrel,we; 'reɪlweɪ/ *n BrE*【英】**1** [C] a method of travelling or moving things around by train 乘火车旅行, 经铁路运送; RAILROAD[1] (1) *AmE*【美】**2 the railway/the railways** all the work, equipment etc connected with a train system 铁路系统; the RAILROAD[1] (2) *AmE*【美】: *working on the railways* 在铁路系统工作 2 2

Railway Chil·dren, The /ˈ· ·, ·ˈ/ (1970) a British film, based on the book by E. Nesbit, about three children at the beginning of the 20th century and the adventures they have around the railway near their home《铁路儿童》〔(1970), 英国一影片, 根据E.内斯比特的同名小说改编, 讲述20世纪初的三个孩子在他们家附近的铁路线上的冒险经历〕

railway line /ˈ· · ·/ *n* [C] *BrE*【英】**1** one of the two metal tracks fixed to the ground that trains move along 铁路路轨 **2** a part of the railway system that connects two places 铁路线: *an old disused railway line* 废弃的旧铁路

railway sta·tion /ˈ· ·, ·ˈ/ *n* [C] *BrE* the place where trains stop for passengers to get on and off【英】火车站; RAILROAD STATION *AmE*【美】

rai·ment /ˈremənt; 'reɪmənt/ *n* [U] *literary* clothes【文】衣服, 服装

rain¹ /ren; reɪn/ *n* **1** [U] water that falls in small drops from clouds in the sky 雨: *Rain is forecast for tomorrow.* 预报明天有雨。| *We've had 5 inches of rain in two days!* 两天里下了五英寸的雨! | *We got caught in the rain and I'm soaked through.* 我们给雨淋了, 我浑身都湿透了。| **it looks like rain** *spoken* (=it is probably going to rain)【口】天好像要下雨 *It looks like rain, so let's go inside.* 天好像要下雨了, 我们进屋去吧。| **heavy/light rain** (=a large or small amount) 大雨/小雨 *There will be heavy rain in most parts of the country.* 全国大部分地区将下大雨。| **pour with rain** *BrE* (=to rain very hard)【英】下大雨 *It was pouring with rain as we set off.* 我们动身的时候, 正下着倾盆大雨。—see picture on page A13 参见 A13 页图 **2 the rains** a period in the year when there is a lot of rain in tropical countries; MONSOON〔热带国家的〕雨季: *The rains have started early this year.* 今年的雨季来得早。**3 be (as) right as rain** *spoken* to be healthy, especially after you have been ill or had a bad experience【口】健康; 状态良好〔尤指病后康复或经历困难后〕**4 (come) rain or shine** *spoken* whatever happens or whatever the weather is like【口】在任何情况下; 不论天气好坏: *Don't worry. We'll be there – rain or shine.* 别担心, 不管情况如何, 我们都会到那里去的。**5 under a rain of arrows/blows etc** being hit by many arrows etc at the same time 箭如雨下/拳如雨下等 —see also 另见 ACID RAIN —**rainless** *adj* 2 2

rain² *v* **1** [I] if it rains, drops of water fall from clouds in the sky 下雨: *Oh no! It's raining again!* 糟糕! 又下雨了! | *It was raining hard.* 正下着大雨。**2 be rained off** *BrE*【英】**/be rained out** *AmE*【美】if an event or activity is rained off or rained out, it has to stop because there is too much rain〔活动〕因雨暂停: *We were supposed to go to a double header but it was rained out.* 我们本来要去看接连举行的两场比赛, 但因下雨取消了。**3 it never rains but it pours** *spoken* used to say that as soon as one thing goes wrong, a lot of other things go wrong as well【口】祸不单行 **4 it's raining cats and dogs** *spoken* it is raining very hard【口】下着倾盆大雨

rain down *phr v* [I,T] if something rains down, or is rained down, it falls in large quantities 雨点般落下, 倾盆而下: *Tears rained down her cheeks.* 泪水如雨般顺着她的面颊流下。| *The falling chimney rained down dust and stones.* 灰尘和石块从正在倒塌的烟囱上如雨点般落下。

rain·bow /ˈren,bo; 'reɪnbəʊ/ *n* [C] a large curve of different colours that can appear in the sky when there is both sun and rain 彩虹, 虹

Rainbow War·ri·or /,· · ˈ· · ·/ a ship belonging to the organization Greenpeace, used for getting information about activities harmful to the environment and trying to prevent them "彩虹斗士"号〔绿色和平组织的一艘轮船。该船用于收集信息, 了解危害环境的各种活动, 并力图予以阻止〕

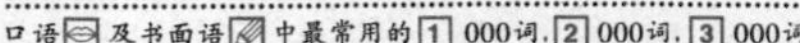

rain check /ˈ· ˌ·/ *n* **1 take a rain check (on)** *informal, especially AmE* used to say that you will do something in the future but not now【非正式，尤美】答应将来做（某事）: *"Care for a drink?" "I'll take a rain check – I figure you'd like to be alone."* "想喝点什么吗?" "改天吧，我猜你想独个儿静一下。" **2** [C] *AmE* a ticket for an outdoor event, such as a sports game, that you can use again if it rains and the action stops【美】〔球赛等户外活动因下雨而中止后〕可以再次使用的票根

rain·coat /ˈ· ·/ *n* [C] a coat that you wear when it is raining 雨衣 —see picture at 参见 COAT[1] 图

rain drop /ˈ· ·/ *n* [C] a single drop of rain 雨点，雨滴

rain·fall /ˈrenˌfɔl; ˈreɪnfɔːl/ *n* [C,U] the amount of rain that falls on an area in a particular period of time 雨量: *an area with very low rainfall* 雨量稀少的地区

rain for·est /ˈ· ˌ··/ *n* [C] a tropical forest with tall trees that are very close together, growing in an area where it rains a lot 热带雨林: *environmental groups campaigning against the destruction of the rain forest* 开展运动反对破坏热带雨林的环保团体

rain gauge /ˈ· ·/ *n* [C] an instrument that is used for measuring the amount of rain 雨量计，雨量器

Rai·ni·er /rəˈnɪr; ˈreɪniə/ **, Mount** a mountain in the west of the state of Washington, US, the highest mountain in the Cascade Range 雷尼尔山〔位于美国华盛顿州西部，为喀斯喀特山脉的最高峰〕

rain·proof /ˈrenˌpruf; ˈreɪnpruːf/ *adj* able to keep rain out 防雨的: *a rainproof jacket* 防雨短上衣

rain·storm /ˈrenˌstɔrm; ˈreɪnstɔːm/ *n* [C] a sudden heavy fall of rain 暴风雨

rain·wa·ter /ˈrenˌwɔtɚ; ˈreɪnwɔːtə/ *n* [U] water that has fallen as rain 雨水

rain·y /ˈrenɪ; ˈreɪni/ *adj* **1 rainy day/afternoon/weather etc** a day etc when it rains a lot 多雨的日子/下午/天气等 **2 save it for a rainy day** to save something, especially money, for a time when you will need it 留着以备不时之需〔尤指钱〕；未雨绸缪

raise[1] /rez; reɪz/ *v* [T]

1 ►MOVE 移动◄ a) to move or lift something to a higher position, place, or level 举起，提起，抬起；使升高: *Can you raise your arm above your head?* 你能把胳膊举过头顶吗? | *They're thinking of raising the ceiling in the kitchen.* 他们正在考虑升高厨房的天花板。| *The teacher raised his finger to his lips for silence.* 老师把手指放到唇边，示意安静。**b)** to move or lift something into an upright position 竖起，扶起，使直立: *The bridge can be raised in the middle to allow ships through.* 这桥的中部可以抬升让船只通过。**c)** to move your eyes or face so that you are looking upwards 抬起〔眼睛〕；仰起〔脸〕: *She raised her eyes from the newspaper when he came in.* 他进来的时候，她把视线从报纸上抬起来。**d)** also 又作 **raise up** to lift the upper part of your body from a lying position 支起上半身: *She raised herself up on her arms and looked around sleepily.* 她用胳膊把上半身撑起来，睡眼惺忪地环顾四周。

2 ►INCREASE 增加◄ to increase an amount, number, or level 增加，提高〔数量、数字或水平〕: *We have no plans to raise taxes at present.* 目前我们没有提高税收的计划。| *The reaction is started by raising the temperature to 140°C.* 把温度提高到140摄氏度，反应便会开始。

3 ►IMPROVE 改善◄ to improve the quality or standard of something 提高，改善〔质量、标准〕: *Better training will raise the efficiency of the workforce.* 更好的培训将提高劳动力的效率。

4 ►CHILDREN 孩子◄ *especially AmE* to look after your children and help them grow【尤美】抚养，养育；抚养〔孩子〕成人；BRING UP *BrE*【英】: *Many women return to work after raising their families.* 许多妇女在子女长大后重新就业。| **raise sb (as) a Catholic/Muslim etc** *His parents raised him as a Protestant.* 他的父母以新教徒的标准培养他。| **born and raised** *She was born and raised a country girl.* 她是一个在农村出生和长大的姑娘。| **be raised on** *These kids are raised on a diet of junk food.* 这些孩子是吃垃圾食品长大的。

5 ►FARMING 饲养，种植◄ to grow plants or keep cows, pigs etc so that they can be used as food 种植；饲养: *raise wheat/pigs* 种小麦/养猪

6 raise hopes/consciousness/awareness etc to make people more hopeful etc 唤起希望/觉悟/认识等: *The peace talks have raised hopes for the hostages' release.* 和谈增加了人质获释的希望。| *The conference is intended to raise people's awareness of AIDS.* 会议的目的是唤起人们对艾滋病的警觉。

7 ►EMOTION/REACTION 情感/反应◄ a) to cause a particular emotion or reaction 引起，激起〔某种情感或反应〕: *His long absence is beginning to raise fears for his safety.* 他很久未露面，人们为他的安全担心起来。| *His jokes barely raised a laugh.* 他的笑话几乎没有引起笑声。**b)** to try to show a particular feeling or emotion although you do not really feel it 设法显露出〔某种感觉、感情〕: *She felt so sad, she couldn't even raise a smile.* 她非常伤心，根本笑不出来。

8 raise a question/objection/point etc to begin to talk or write about a question etc that you want to be considered 提出问题/反对/观点等: *A number of objections were raised at the meeting.* 会上提出了许多反对意见。| *This raises important issues about security.* 此事提出了关于安保措施的重要问题。

9 ►COLLECT MONEY/PEOPLE 筹款/征集人员◄ a) to collect money, support etc so that you can use it to help people 筹集: *We are raising money to pay for a new hospital ward.* 我们正在筹集资金建一个新病房。**b)** *old-fashioned* to collect together a group of people, especially soldiers【过时】召集〔尤指士兵〕: *The king raised a vast army.* 国王召集起一支庞大的军队。

10 a) raise your eyebrows (at) to show surprise, doubt, disapproval etc by moving your EYEBROWS upwards （朝…）扬起眉毛〔表示吃惊、疑虑、反对等〕: *Chuck raised his eyebrows at her, not knowing what to say.* 查克朝她扬起眉毛，不知道说什么好。**b) raise eyebrows** if something raises eyebrows it surprises people 使…吃惊: *The story raised a few eyebrows in the media world.* 这篇报道引起媒体圈一些人惊奇。

11 ►VOICE 声音◄ raise your voice to speak loudly or shout because you are angry〔因生气而〕提高嗓门，高声说话: *Don't raise your voice to me, young man!* 别冲着我叫嚷，年轻人! | **raised voices** *We could hear raised voices coming from the bar.* 我们能够听到有人在酒吧高声说话。

12 raise your glasses *spoken* used to tell a group of people to celebrate something by holding up their glasses and drinking from them【口】〔邀某人〕为…举杯庆祝: *Ladies and gentlemen, will you raise your glasses to the bride and groom.* 各位女士、先生，请大家举杯，祝贺新娘和新郎。

13 raise the spectre of sth *literary* to make you aware of something frightening【文】使人感到某事的恐怖: *The continuing violence has raised the spectre of civil war.* 持续不断的暴力事件使人担心会爆发内战。

14 ►DEAD PERSON 死者◄ *biblical* to make someone who has died live again【圣经】使…起死回生，使…复活: *Jesus raised Lazarus from the grave.* 耶稣使拉撒路复活。

15 ►WAKE SB 唤醒某人◄ *literary* to wake someone who is difficult to wake【文】叫醒: *Try as he might he could not raise her.* 他想尽办法，却仍然无法叫醒她。

16 raise the alarm to warn people about danger 发出警报: *A passerby raised the alarm before the fire got out of control.* 一位过路人在火势尚未失控时发出了警报。

17 raise a siege/embargo *formal* to allow goods to go in and out of a place again after they have been stopped by force or by a law【正式】解除包围/禁运

18 ►CARD GAME 纸牌游戏◄ to make a higher BID than an opponent in a card game 比〔对手〕多下赌注: *I'll raise you $100.* 我再加100美元。

19 ►SPEAK TO SB 对某人说话◄ to speak to someone on a piece of radio equipment 用无线电与…通话: *They finally managed to raise him at Miller's sheep farm.* 他们终于通过无线电在米勒的养羊场上与他取得了联系。

20 ►BUILD 建造◄ *formal* to build something such as a MONUMENT【正式】建造〔纪念碑等〕

21 raise hell/Cain a) *informal* to behave in an angry and threatening way【非正式】非常生气/愤怒: *I'll raise hell with whoever is responsible for this mess.* 不管是谁惹的麻烦，我都会跟他没完。**b)** *especially AmE* to behave in a wild, noisy way that upsets other people【尤美】喧闹: *The kids next door were raising hell last night.* 隔壁的孩子昨晚闹翻了天。

22 raise the roof to make a very loud noise when singing, celebrating etc〔唱歌、欢庆作乐时〕高声吵闹

23 raise your hand *especially AmE* to put your arm in the air to show that you want something【尤美】举手: *Raise your hand if you know the answer.* 如果知道答案就请举手。

24 raise 2/4/10 etc to the power of 2/3/4 etc *technical* to multiply a number by itself a particular number of times【术语】使2/4/10等自乘2/3/4等次: *2 raised to the power of 3 (=2^3) is 8.* 2的3次方是8。

USAGE NOTE 用法说明: RAISE

WORD CHOICE 词语辨析: **raise, lift, increase, rise, bring up, rear, grow, improve**

People or other forces **raise** things to a higher position, though in informal language **lift** is usually used. 人或其

他力量把东西提/抬/举到高处时用raise，在非正式语言中通常用lift: *The crane raised/lifted the whole house.* 起重机吊起了整座房子。In a court of law you may hear 在法庭上可以听到: *Raise the book in your right hand.* 用右手把书举起。

People, governments etc **raise** or **increase** the price, cost, or amount of something. 人或政府等提高某物的价格、费用或数量时用raise或increase: *The government is raising the tax on cigarettes again.* 政府准备再次提高香烟税。| *Heavy traffic is raising/increasing the level of pollution in the town.* 拥挤的交通正在加重城里的污染程度。

When things or prices move upwards on their own, they **rise**. 东西或价格自己升高时用rise: *The balloon rose slowly from the ground.* 气球缓缓地从地面升起。| *the problem of rising inflation* 通货膨胀加剧的问题 | *Industrial production looks set to rise in the new year.* 工业生产看来在新的一年里很可能会增加。

You can also **raise** children, meaning you look after them as they grow up. This sense is more common in American English than in British English, where **bring up** is the more usual expression. 抚养孩子可用raise。此义多用于美国英语，英国英语更常用的表达方式是bring up。

In both British and American English it is common either to **raise** or **bring up** a point, question etc in a discussion. 在英国英语和美国英语中，raise或bring up均可表达在讨论中提出观点、问题等。

Again, especially in American English you may **raise** cattle or wheat on a farm. More generally, and in British English, you **rear** cattle and **grow** wheat, flowers or vegetables. 尤其在美国英语中，可以用 raise表示养牛，种植麦子。在英国英语中，则经常用rear表示养牛，用grow表示种植麦子、花或蔬菜。

When you are talking about making something better, people often use either **raise** or **improve**. 表示"将某事做得更好"或"改进"，人们经常用raise或improve: *I'm working hard to raise/improve my TOEFL score.* 我正在努力提高我的托福成绩。| *Women still need to raise/improve their position in society* (NOT 不用 *raise up*). 妇女仍然需要提高她们的社会地位。

When something gets better on its own you can use **rise** or **improve**. 事物改善时可用rise或improve: *Standards are rising/improving.* 水准正在提高。

The noun **raise** means a pay increase and is American English. 名词raise的意思在美国英语中是"加薪"。In British English you say 在英国英语中用: *He got a (pay) rise.* 他获得加薪。

Otherwise the noun is always **rise**. 在其他情况下rise总是名词: *a rise in house prices/standards* 房屋价格/标准的提高 | *the rise of the Roman Empire* 罗马帝国的兴起

GRAMMAR 语法

The past tense of **rise** is **rose**, the perfect tense is **have risen** (NOT 不用 *raised*). rise 的过去式是 rose，完成式是 have risen。

raise² *n* [C] *AmE* an increase in the money you earn【美】加薪; RISE² (2) *BrE*【英】

rai·sin /ˈrezn; ˈreɪzən/ *n* [C] a dried GRAPE (=the fruit that wine is made from) 葡萄干

rai·son d'êt·re /ˈrezɔn ˈdɛt; ˌreɪzɒn ˈdetrə/ *n* [C] *French* the reason something exists, why someone does something etc【法】存在的理由；做某事的目的: *Commerce was the main raison d'être of the town.* 商业是这个镇存在的主要原因。

Raj /rɑdʒ; rɑːdʒ/ *n* [singular] **the (British) Raj** the rule of the British government in India before India became independent in 1947〔1947年印度独立前〕英国在印度的统治(时期)

ra·jah, raja /ˈrɑdʒə; ˈrɑːdʒə/ *n* [C] the king or ruler of an Indian state〔印度的〕王公，邦主 —see also 另见 RANEE

rake¹ /rek; reɪk/ *n* **1** [C] a gardening tool with a row of metal teeth at the end of a long handle, used for making soil level, gathering up dead leaves etc〔长柄〕耙子 **2** [C] *old-fashioned* a man who behaves in an unacceptable way, having many sexual relationships, drinking too much alcohol etc【过时】酒色之徒，浪荡子 **3** [C] a tool used by a CROUPIER for gathering in the money at a table where games are played for money〔赌台上用的〕钱耙子 **4** [singular] the angle of a slope 坡度，倾角: *the rake of the stage* 舞台的坡度

rake² *v* **1** [I,T] to move a rake across a surface in order to make the soil level, gather dead leaves etc〔用耙子〕耙，耙平: [+**over/up**] *She raked over the soil to loosen the weeds.* 她用耙子平地，除掉杂草。**2** [I always+adv/prep] to search a place very carefully for something 仔细搜寻: [+**through/around/about**] *I've been raking through my drawers looking for those tickets.* 我一直在抽屉里仔细翻找那些票。**3** [T] to point something such as a gun, camera, or strong light, so that it covers a wide area, by slowly moving it from one side to another〔用枪、照相机或强光〕扫射: *The searchlight raked the open ground around the prison.* 探照灯在监狱周围的空地上来回扫射。**4 rake a fire/ashes/coals** to push a stick backwards and forwards in a fire in order to remove ashes 拨弄火/灰/煤块 **5 rake your fingers/nails** to pull your fingers or nails through something or across a surface〔用手指或指甲〕拢，刮: *Ken raked his fingers through his hair.* 肯用手指拢头发。

rake sth ↔**in** *phr v* [T] *informal* to earn a lot of money without trying very hard【非正式】轻易赚得〔许多钱〕: *Lou's been raking in the dollars since he opened his business.* 自从生意开张以来，卢赚到了大把的美元。| **rake it in** *If someone opened a burger bar, they'd really rake it in.* 如果有人开一家汉堡包快餐店，一定会发大财的。

rake sth ↔**up** *phr v* [T] *informal*【非正式】**1** also 又作 **rake together** to collect things or people together for a purpose, but with difficulty 勉强拼凑: *Karen has had real problems raking up enough players for the volleyball game.* 卡伦遇上了麻烦，她凑不够参加排球比赛的队员。| *Between them they could only rake together $300.* 他俩总共只凑到300美元。**2** to talk about something from the past that people would prefer you not to mention 重提〔别人不愿提起的往事〕: *Don't rake up that old quarrel again!* 别再提那次吵架的旧账了！

rake-off /ˈ· ·/ *n* [C] *informal* a dishonest share of profits【非正式】〔非法取得的〕回扣: *The taxi driver gets a rake-off from the hotel.* 这个出租车司机从该旅馆拿到回扣。

rak·ish /ˈrekɪʃ; ˈreɪkɪʃ/ *adj* **1 at a rakish angle** if you wear a hat at a rakish angle, you do not wear it straight, and this makes you look relaxed and confident 潇洒地〔歪戴帽子〕 **2** *old-fashioned* a rakish man behaves in an unacceptable way, having many sexual relationships, wasting money, drinking too much alcohol etc【过时】放荡的，挥霍的，纵情酒色的 —**rakishly** *adv* —**rakishness** *n* [U]

Raleigh /ˈrɑlɪ; ˈrɑːli/ the capital city of the US state of North Carolina 罗利〔美国北卡罗来纳州首府〕

Raleigh, Sir Wal·ter /ˈwɔltɚ; ˈwɔːltə/ (?1552-1618) an English explorer who made several journeys to North and South America and later wrote books about them. He is the person who first brought potatoes and tobacco to Britain. 雷利〔(?1552-1618)，英国探险家。他曾数次奔赴北美和南美，写有数部游记。他最早将马铃薯和烟草带回英国〕

Sir Walter Raleigh 沃尔特·雷利爵士

ral·ly¹ /ˈrælɪ; ˈræli/ *v* **rallied, rallying 1** [I,T] to come together or bring people together to support an idea, a political party etc〔为支持某种信念或政党等而〕集合；召集: *Margaret Thatcher's speech had the effect of rallying the party faithful.* 玛格丽特·撒切尔的讲话起到了团结忠实党员的作用。| [+**to**] *Fellow Republicans rallied to the President's defense.* 共和党党员都团结起来为总统辩护。| **rallying point** (=an idea, event etc that makes people come together to support something they believe in) 聚集点，号召因素 *The demonstration was a rallying point for students fighting for lower rents.* 那次示威游行使争取降低房租的学生团结了起来。| **rallying cry** (=a word or phrase used to unite people in support of an idea) 使人们团结起来的口号 **2** [I] to become stronger again after a period of weakness or defeat〔在虚弱、受挫后〕振作，恢复: *Towards the end of the race, Cram rallied and won in style.* 比赛接近尾声时，克拉姆重新振作起来，给人印象深刻地获胜。| *Stock prices rallied this afternoon after earlier falls.* 股票价格在早时下跌之后，今天下午回升。

rally round *phr v* [I,T] *informal* if a group of people rally round, they all try to help you in a difficult situation【非正式】〔一群人〕扶持，支持(处于困境的人): *Her friends all rallied round when she was ill.* 在她患病期间，她的朋友都来帮助她。

rally² *n* [C] **1** a large public meeting, especially one that is held outdoors to support a political idea, protest etc〔大型群众〕集会〔尤指为支持某政治观点、抗议等在户外举行的集会〕: *a big anti-abortion rally* 反堕胎的大型群众集会 **2** a car race on public roads〔在公路上举行的〕赛车, 汽车拉力赛: *the Monte Carlo Rally* 蒙特卡洛汽车拉力赛 **3** a series of hits of the ball between players in games like tennis〔网球等比赛中的〕持续对打, 拉锯战

RAM /ræm; ræm/ *n* [C,U] Random Access Memory; the memory in a computer system that is used as a temporary store for information, usually the software that organizes the DATA 内存, 随机存取存储器〔电脑中短期存储信息的存储器〕

ram¹ /ræm; ræm/ *v* **rammed, ramming** [T] **1** to run or drive into something very hard 猛撞: *I was waiting at the traffic lights when a car rammed me from behind.* 我正在等绿灯的时候, 一辆汽车从后面撞了我。**2** [always+ adv/prep] to push something into a position using great force 压入, 硬塞, 压实: **ram sth into/down** *First, you'll have to ram the posts into the ground.* 首先, 你必须把桩打进地里。**3 ram sth down sb's throat** to try to make someone accept an idea or opinion by continually repeating it, especially when they are not interested 向某人反复灌输〔使其接受不感兴趣的观点或意见〕

ram sth ↔ **home** *phr v* [T] to make sure someone fully understands something by emphasizing it and by providing a lot of examples, proof etc〔通过强调和援引大量例证等〕使〔某事〕令人信服, 充分说明: *He rammed his points home with graphic pictures of neglect.* 他绘影绘声地描述了种种玩忽职守的情况, 充分说明了自己的观点。

ram² *n* [C] **1** an adult male sheep 公羊 —compare 比较 EWE **2** a BATTERING RAM 破城槌 **3** *technical* a machine that hits something again and again to force it into a position【术语】冲压机, 撞锤

Ram·a·dan /ˌræmə`dɑn; 'ræmədæn/ *n* [U] the ninth month of the Muslim year, during which Muslims are not allowed to eat or drink during the day while it is light 斋月〔伊斯兰历的第九个月, 教徒白天禁饮食〕

Ra·ma·krish·na /ˌrɑmə`krɪʃnə; ˌrɑːmə'krɪʃnə/ (1834-86) an Indian Hindu religious man who said that all religions are of equal value because they are all different ways of understanding the same God 罗摩克希纳〔(1834-1886), 印度教人士。他曾认为, 所有宗教是对同一上帝的不同理解, 因而具有同等价值〕

Ram·bert Dance Com·pa·ny, the /rɑmˌbɛr `dæns ˌkʌmpənɪ; ˌrɒmbeə 'dɑːns ˌkʌmpəni/ also 又作 **the Ballet Rambert** a BALLET company based in London, which usually performs modern ballet. It is named after Marie Rambert, the dancer and teacher who started the company in 1930. 兰伯特芭蕾舞团〔伦敦一芭蕾舞团, 通常表演现代芭蕾舞。团名取自芭蕾舞演员兼教师玛丽·兰伯特的姓氏。该团是兰伯特 1930 年创建的〕

ram·ble¹ /`ræmbḷ; 'ræmbəl/ *v* [I] **1** [always+adv/prep] to go on a walk for pleasure 漫步, 闲逛: [**+through/along etc**] *We rambled through the woods.* 我们漫步穿过小树林。**2** to talk in a very confused way so that other people find it hard to understand you 语无伦次地闲扯, 漫谈; 说胡话: *The fever was getting worse and he was starting to ramble.* 他发烧越来越厉害, 开始说胡话。**3** a plant that rambles grows in all directions〔植物〕蔓生

ramble on *phr v* [I] to talk or write for a long time in a way that other people find boring 啰嗦地说[写]: *He rambled on about his trip to Paris.* 他喋喋不休地谈他的巴黎之行。

ramble² *n* [C] a long walk for pleasure 漫步, 闲逛: *We went on a ramble in the Peak District.* 我们在峰区漫步。

Rambler /`ræmblɚ; 'ræmblə/ *trademark* a popular type of small car once made by the American Motor Company【商标】兰豹〔过去曾流行一时的一款小汽车, 由美国汽车公司制造〕

ram·bler /`ræmblɚ; 'ræmblə/ *n* [C] **1** *BrE* someone who goes on rambles【英】喋喋不休的人 **2** a rose bush that rambles 蔓生蔷薇

Ramblers' As·so·ci·a·tion, the /'·· ···,··/ a British organization which supports people who want to walk for pleasure, and makes sure that public footpaths are kept open and in good repair 漫步者协会〔英国一组织, 旨在为喜欢漫步休闲的人士提供支持, 确保公用小径畅通无阻, 养护到位〕

ram·bling /`ræmblɪŋ; 'ræmblɪŋ/ *adj* **1** a building that is rambling has an irregular shape and covers a large area〔房子〕大而杂乱无章的: *a large rambling house on the hillside* 山坡上一座巨大而布局零乱的房子 **2** speech or writing that is rambling is very long and does not seem to have any clear organization or purpose〔言语、文章〕杂乱无章的, 漫无边际的: *a long and rambling letter* 东拉西扯的长信

Ram·bo /`ræmbo; 'ræmbəʊ/ a character played by Sylvester Stallone in several US films, called *First Blood, Rambo: First Blood II* etc. Rambo was a strong, very violent soldier who fought against the US's enemies. His name is often used to describe anyone who thinks fighting and violence are the only ways of settling disagreements. 兰博〔史泰龙在《第一滴血》、《第一滴血续集》等数部美国影片中扮演的角色。兰博是一名坚强勇猛的战士, 专门抗击美国的敌人。人们常借用他的名字指称认为打斗和暴力是解决分歧的唯一途径的人〕

ram·bunc·tious /ræm`bʌŋkʃəs; ræm'bʌŋkʃəs/ *adj AmE humorous* full of energy, fun, and noise【美, 幽默】喧闹的, 欢快的: *a weekend with three rambunctious kids* 与三个喧闹的小孩共度的周末 —**rambunctiously** *adv* —**rambunctiousness** *n* [U]

ram·e·kin /`ræməkɪn; 'ræmɨkɨn/ *n* [C] a small dish in which food for one person can be baked and served 一人用烤盘

ram·ie /`ræmɪ; 'ræmi/ *n* [C,U] a plant from which cloth is made 苎麻

ram·i·fi·ca·tion /ˌræməfə`keʃən; ˌræmɨfɨ'keɪʃən/ *n* [C usually plural 一般用复数] *formal*【正式】**1** an additional result of something you do, which may not have been clear when you first decided to do it 额外的后果, 派生的影响: *The environmental ramifications of the road-building program had not been considered.* 没有考虑筑路工程对环境造成的影响。**2** a part of a system or structure that has many parts 分支

ram·i·fy /`ræməˌfaɪ; 'ræmɨfaɪ/ *v* [I] *rare* to spread outwards and to form a system or network【罕】分支, 形成系统, 形成网络

ramp /ræmp; ræmp/ *n* [C] **1** *AmE* a road for driving onto or off a large main road【美】支路, 岔道; SLIP ROAD *BrE*【英】: *Take the Lake Drive ramp at Charles Street.* 在查尔斯街雷克车道的支路。**2** a slope that has been built to connect two places that are at different levels〔连接高低不同的两个点的〕人造斜坡; 坡道: *Ramps are needed at exits and entrances for wheelchair users.* 出入口处要有乘轮椅者使用的坡道。**3** *BrE* a change in the level between two parts of a road where repairs are being done【英】〔修路时〕路面高出部分 **4** a raised part on some roads, designed to make traffic drive more slowly; HUMP〔路上使车辆减速的〕小凸面

ram·page¹ /`ræmpedʒ; ræm'peɪdʒ/ *v* [I] to rush about in groups wildly or violently 横冲直撞: [**+about/through**] *football fans rampaging through the streets* 在街上横冲直撞的足球迷

rampage² *n* **on the rampage** rushing about in a wild and violent way, often causing damage 横冲直撞: *gangs of youths on the rampage* 成群结队横冲直撞的年轻人

ram·pant /`ræmpənt; 'ræmpənt/ *adj* **1** something bad that is rampant, such as crime or disease, is widespread and difficult to control〔犯罪、疾病〕猖獗的, 肆虐的, 失控的: *The country faces famine and rampant disease.* 这个国家面临饥荒, 疾病肆虐。| *rampant inflation* 失控的通货膨胀 **2** a plant that is rampant grows and spreads uncontrollably〔植物〕过于繁茂的, 蔓延的: *rampant garden weeds* 繁芜的园中杂草 **3** *technical* an animal drawn in HERALDRY that is rampant is standing on its two back legs【术语】〔纹章上所绘的动物〕用后腿站立的 —**rampantly** *adv*

ram·part /`ræmpɑrt; 'ræmpɑːt/ *n* [C usually plural 一般用复数] a wide pile of earth or a stone wall built to protect a castle or city in the past〔旧时城堡或城市周围的〕护城墙, 土垒

Ramp·ton /`ræmptən; 'ræmptən/ a special British hospital for people who are considered to be violent and extremely dangerous. It is not actually a prison, but its patients are guarded very strictly. 兰普顿医院〔英国一特殊医院。入院者具有暴力倾向, 极度危险。兰普顿虽然不是监狱, 但对住院病人的看管却非常严格〕

ram-raid·ing /'· ,··/ *n* [U] *BrE informal* the crime of driving a car into a shop window in order to steal goods from the shop【英, 非正式】飞车抢劫商店 —**ram-raider** *n* [C]

ram·rod /`ræmˌrɑd; 'ræmrɒd/ *n* [C] **1 stiff/straight as a ramrod** sitting or standing with your back straight and your body stiff〔坐立时〕背部笔直的, 僵直的 **2** a stick for pushing GUNPOWDER into an old-fashioned gun, or for cleaning a small gun〔旧时枪的〕推弹杆, 〔擦枪的〕通条

Ram·sey /`ræmzɪ; 'ræmzi/, **Sir Alf** /ælf; ælf/ (1922-99) an English football player and team manager, who was the manager of the English national team that won the World Cup in 1966 拉姆齐〔(1922-1999), 英国足球运动员、球队主教练。1966年, 英格兰足球队获世界杯时, 他任该球队的主教练〕

ram·shack·le /`ræmʃækḷ; 'ræmʃækəl/ *adj* a ramshackle building or vehicle is in bad condition and in need of repair〔建筑物、汽车等〕破旧的, 要散架似的, 需要维修的: *a ramshackle old farmhouse* 摇摇欲坠的旧农舍

ran /ræn; ræn/ the past tense of RUN

ranch /ræntʃ; rɑːntʃ/ *n* [C] **1** a very large farm in the western US and Canada where sheep, cattle, or horses are bred〔美国西部和加拿大的〕大牧场 **2** *AmE* a farm that produces a particular product【美】〔专门出产某种产品的〕农场: *a fruit ranch* 果园 **3** a RANCH HOUSE 平房; 农牧场主住宅

ranch·er /ˈræntʃə; ˈrɑːntʃə/ *n* [C] someone who owns or works on a ranch 牧场[农场]主; 牧场[农场]工人: *a cattle rancher* 养牛场场主[工人]

ranch house /ˈ· ·/ *n* [C] *AmE*【美】**1** a house built on one level, usually with a roof that does not slope much〔一般屋顶坡度不大的〕平房, 牧场式住宅 —see picture on page A4 参见 A4 页图 **2** a house on a ranch in which the rancher lives〔农牧场主居住的〕场内住宅

ranch·ing /ˈræntʃɪŋ; ˈrɑːntʃɪŋ/ *n* [U] work on a ranch (从事)农牧场工作

ran·cid /ˈrænsɪd; ˈrænsɨd/ *adj* oily or fatty food that is rancid smells or tastes unpleasant because it is no longer fresh〔油脂食物的气味、味道〕不新鲜的, 腐臭的, 酸臭的: *rancid butter* 变质黄油 —**rancidity** /rænˋsɪdətɪ; rænˈsɪdɨti/ *n* [U]

ran·cour *BrE*【英】, **rancor** *AmE*【美】/ˈræŋkə; ˈræŋkə/ *n* [U] *formal* a feeling of hatred, especially when you cannot forgive someone【正式】积怨, 深仇: *He spoke openly about the war without a trace of rancour.* 他不记前仇坦率地谈论了这场战争。—**rancorous** *adj* —**rancorously** *adv*

rand /rænd; rænd/ *n plural* **rand** [C] the standard unit of money in South Africa 兰特〔南非的货币单位〕

R and A, the /ˌɑr ənd ˋe; ˌɑːr ənd ˈeɪ/ the abbreviation of 缩写= the ROYAL AND ANCIENT

R and B /ˌɑr ən ˋbi; ˌɑːr ən ˈbiː/ *n* [U] rhythm and blues; a style of popular music that is a mixture of BLUES and JAZZ 节奏怨曲, 节奏布鲁斯〔一种布鲁斯与爵士乐结合的流行音乐〕

R and D /ˌɑr ən ˋdi; ˌɑːr ən ˈdiː/ *n* [U] research and development; the part of a business concerned with studying new ideas and planning new products 研究与开发(部)

ran·dom /ˈrændəm; ˈrændəm/ *adj* **1** happening or chosen without any definite plan, aim, or pattern 随意的, 任意的, 随机的: *a random sample* 随机的抽样 | *random drug testing of athletes* 对运动员进行的随机药物检测 | *A few random shots were fired.* 胡乱放了几枪。**2 at random** in a random way 任意地, 随便地: *The killer appears to have selected his victims at random.* 凶手似乎是胡乱选择被害人。—**randomly** *adv*: *7 randomly chosen numbers* 七个随机选择的数字 —**randomness** *n* [U]

random ac·cess mem·o·ry /ˌ·· ˈ·· ˌ···/ *n* [C,U] RAM 随机存取记忆器

R and R /ˌɑr ənd ˋɑr; ˌɑːr ənd ˈɑː/ *n* [U] *AmE* rest and relaxation; a holiday given to people in the army, navy, etc after a long period of hard work or during a war【美】〔官兵长期执勤或战时的〕休整假期

rand·y /ˈrændɪ; ˈrændi/ *adj BrE informal* full of sexual desire【英, 非正式】性欲冲动的: *She was feeling very randy.* 她感觉性欲强烈。—**randiness** *n* [U]

ra·nee, rani /ˈrɑnɪ; ˈrɑːni/ *n* [C] the queen or princess of an Indian state〔印度〕女邦主; 邦主妃 —see also 另见 RAJAH

rang /ræŋ; ræŋ/ the past tense of RING

range¹ /rendʒ; reɪndʒ/ *n*

1 ►GROUP 组◄ [singular] a number of things which are all different but of the same general type 批, 组, 类: **[+of]** *an interesting range of books and videos* 一批有趣的书籍和录像带 | *The drug is effective against a range of bacteria.* 这种药品对一类细菌有效。| *We teach the full range of ballroom dances.* 我们教授全套交际舞。| **wide/broad/whole range of** *We have students from a wide range of backgrounds.* 我们的学生来自各种不同的背景。

2 ►LIMITS/AMOUNTS 范围/数量◄ [singular] the limits within which amounts, quantities, ages etc can vary〔数、量、年龄等的〕范围, 界限: **age/price etc range** *toys suitable for children in the pre-school age range* 适合学龄前儿童的玩具 | **in the range (of)** *I would expect a salary in the range of $25,000 to $30,000.* 我希望得到一份在两万五千到三万美元之间的工资。| **beyond/out of sb's range** (=more than someone's limit on price, age etc) 超出某人〔关于价格、年龄等〕的范围 *The price of the house is well beyond our range.* 这所房子的价格远远超出我们的预算。

3 ►POWER/RESPONSIBILITY ETC 权力/责任等◄ [singular] the area of power, responsibility, or activities that a person or organization has; SCOPE〔人或组织的权力、责任或活动的〕范围: **the range of** *The range of his power was immense.* 他权势巨大。| **within/outside the range of** *These issues fall outside the range of the enquiry.* 这些问题不在调查范围之内。

4 ►PRODUCTS 产品◄ [C] a set of similar products made by a particular company or available in a particular shop〔某公司生产或某商店出售的〕成套产品; 系列商品: *The coconut shampoo is the best in the range.* 椰子洗发剂是此类产品中最好的。| **[+of]** *a new range of kitchenware* 一系列新的厨房用具 | **top of the range** (=best) 最好的 *a new top of the range racing bike* 新的顶尖比赛用自行车

5 ►DISTANCE 距离◄ **a)** [singular,U] the distance within which something can be seen or heard〔视觉、听觉的〕范围: **[+of]** *The transmitter has a range of 10,000 miles.* 发报机的发射范围是10,000英里。| **within range** (=near enough to reach, hear etc) 在〔可拿到、可听到等的〕范围内 *By now the ship was within range of enemy radar.* 该船现已进入敌人雷达的范围。| **out of range** (=too far away to reach, hear etc) 在〔可拿到、可听到等的〕范围外 *He was relieved that the others were out of range of his mother's penetrating voice.* 其他人听不到他妈妈刺耳的声音, 使他松了口气。| **at close range** (=very near) 很近地 *You can see the animals at very close range.* 你可以在极近的距离看那些动物。**b)** [singular,U] the distance over which a particular weapon can hit things 射程: *the gun's range* 枪的射程 | **[+of]** *missiles with a range of 500 miles* 射程为500英里的导弹 | **within range** (=near enough to hit) 在射程内 | **out of range** (=too far away to hit) 在射程外 *I ducked down to get out of range of the gunshots.* 我低下头避开枪弹。| **at close/short/point-blank range** (=from very close) 很近地 *Both men had been shot at point-blank range.* 两个人都是在近距离被射杀的。| **long/short range missile** *The destroyer was equipped with short range missiles.* 这艘驱逐舰装备了短程导弹。**c)** [C] the distance which a vehicle such as an aircraft can travel before it needs more petrol etc〔飞机等交通工具的〕续航距离: **[+of]** *The VR126 has a range of 2,000 miles.* VR126的续航距离达2000英里。

6 ►MUSIC 音乐◄ [C usually singular 一般用单数] all the musical notes that a particular singer or musical instrument can make 音域: *As the child grew older, his vocal range changed.* 随着孩子年龄的增长, 他的音域改变了。

7 ►MOUNTAINS 山峦◄ [C] a group of mountains or hills, usually in a line 山脉: *a village in the foothills of the Karakoram range* 位于哈喇昆仑山脉丘陵地带的村庄

8 ►WEAPONS TESTING 武器试验◄ [C] an area of land where you can test weapons or practise using them 射击场, 靶场: *a rifle range* 步枪射击场 | *a missile testing range* 导弹试验场

9 ►GRASS LAND 草地◄ [C,U] *AmE* a large area of grass land used by cattle【美】牧场, 牧区

10 ►COOKING 烹调◄ [C,U] **a)** *especially AmE* a COOKER【尤美】灶具 **b)** *BrE* a place in a kitchen where there is a fire for cooking, used in the past【英】〔旧时用火烹饪的〕炉灶 —see also 另见 FREE-RANGE

range² *v*

1 ►INCLUDE 包括◄ **a)** [I always+adv/prep] if prices, levels, temperatures etc range from one amount to another, they include both those amounts and anything in between〔价格、水平、温度等〕处于某范围内〔包括这个范围的上下限〕: **range from sth to sth** *There were 120 students whose ages ranged from 10 to 18.* 有120名学生, 年龄在10至18岁之间。| **range between sth and sth** *The population of these cities ranges between 3 and 5 million inhabitants.* 这些城市的人口在三百万到五百万之间。| **range in age/size etc** (include many different ages, sizes etc) 年龄/大小等的范围在… *The shoes range in price from $25 to $100.* 这些鞋的价格在25美元至100美元不等。**b)** [I always+adv/prep] to include a range of different feelings, actions etc〔感情、行动等〕在某范围内变化: **range from sth to sth** *Their reactions ranged from anger to humiliation.* 他们反应不一, 有的愤怒, 有的感到丢脸。| *US intervention has taken many forms, ranging from supplying medicines to full-scale air strikes.* 美国以多种形式进行干预, 从提供药品到全面空袭。

2 ►INCLUDE MANY SUBJECTS 包括许多话题◄ [I] to deal with a wide range of subjects or ideas in a book, speech, conversation etc〔在书籍、演讲、交谈等中〕涉及广泛的内容: **range (widely) over** *His lectures ranged widely over a variety of topics.* 他的讲座广泛涉及了各种各样的话题。—see also 另见 WIDE-RANGING

3 range yourself with/against to publicly state your agreement with, or opposition to, a particular group's beliefs and ideas 公开赞同/反对〔某种信念和思想〕: *Police rounded up any individuals who had ranged themselves against the authorities.* 警察拘捕了所有公开反对当局的人。

4 ►ARRANGE 安排◄ [T always+adv/prep] to put things in a particular order or position 排列: **range sth on/along/against**

etc *Cups and plates were neatly ranged on her shelves.* 杯子和盘子整齐地排列在她的架子上。

5►MOVE AROUND 四处移动◄ [I always+adv/prep] to move around in an area of land; wander 漫游, 闲逛: [+over/through] *Cattle ranged over the pastures in search of food.* 牛在牧场上走来走去觅食。

range·find·er /ˈrendʒˌfaɪndɚ; ˈreɪndʒˌfaɪndə/ *n* [C] an instrument for finding the distance of an object when firing a weapon or taking photographs〔射击或摄影用的〕测距仪

rang·er /ˈrendʒɚ; ˈreɪndʒə/ *n* [C] **1** someone whose job is to look after a forest or area of countryside 护林员: *a wildlife ranger* 野生动物管理员 **2** a police officer in North America in past times, who rode through country areas〔旧时北美的〕巡逻骑警 **3** a COMMANDO (=a specially trained soldier) 突击队员, 特别行动队队员 **4** a girl who belongs to a part of the Guide Association in Britain, for girls between the ages of 14 and 19 英国高年级女童军队员〔14至19岁〕—compare 比较 GUIDE[1] (4)

Range Rov·er /ˈ·, ·ˈ··/ *trademark* a type of large car made in the UK. Range Rovers are strongly built, like Land Rovers, so they can be driven on rough ground, but they are more comfortable.【商标】揽胜〔英国生产的一款大型轿车。"揽胜"和其他"路虎"汽车一样坚固耐用, 能在崎岖的地面上行驶, 但舒适度更高〕

Ran·gers /ˈrendʒɚz; ˈreɪndʒəz/ a Scottish football team based in Glasgow, officially called Glasgow Rangers, whose supporters are mainly Protestant. There is much competition between Rangers and Celtic, the other main Glasgow football team, whose supporters are mainly Roman Catholic. 流浪者队〔主场设在格拉斯哥的一支苏格兰足球队, 正式名称为"格拉斯哥流浪者队", 支持者大多为新教徒。流浪者队和凯尔特人队之间竞争激烈, 凯尔特人队的支持者主要为天主教徒〕

Ran·goon —see 见 YANGON

ra·ni /ˈrɑni; ˈrɑːni/ *n* a RANEE〔印度〕女邦主; 邦主妃

3 **rank¹** /ræŋk; ræŋk/ *n*

1►POSITION IN ARMY/ORGANIZATION 军队/组织中的职位◄ [C,U] the position or level that someone holds in an organization, especially in the police or armed forces 等级; 军阶, 军衔: *promotion to the rank of General* 晋升为将军 | **high/senior/low/junior rank** *Bates is very young to hold such a senior rank.* 贝茨年纪很轻便担任如此要职。

2the ranks a) all the members of the armed forces who are not officers 普通士兵:**be reduced to the ranks** (=be punished by no longer being an officer) 降为士兵 | **rise from the ranks** (=become an officer after being an ordinary soldier) 从士兵升为军官 **b)** the people who belong to an organization or to a group〔组织或团体的〕成员: *The pay freeze led to a lot of discontent in the ranks.* 工资冻结导致职员牢骚满腹。| *The Christian Democrats now face opposition from within their own ranks.* 基督教民主党目前面临党内的反对。| **join the ranks of** (=become a member of a group) 加入…的行列 *She was forced to join the ranks of the self-employed.* 她被迫加入了自由职业者的行列。

3close ranks if the people in a group close ranks, they join together to support each other against other people〔一群人〕团结一致〔以对付他人〕: *At the first hint of trouble their family closes ranks.* 刚有麻烦的迹象, 他们全家便团结一致了。

4break ranks a) to stop supporting a group that you are a member of 不再支持〔所属团体〕 **b)** if soldiers break ranks, they do not stay in line〔士兵〕打乱队形: *The police broke ranks and used their batons indiscriminately.* 警察散开队形, 用警棍乱打。

5pull rank (on) *informal* to use your authority over someone to make them do what you want, especially unfairly【非正式】〔尤指不公正地〕运用权势: *You may just have to pull rank and tell them they have to do it.* 也许你只需运用权势, 告诉他们必须这样做。

6►LINE 行, 列◄ [C] **a)** a line of people or things〔人或物的〕行, 列:**rank after rank/rank upon rank** *On the shelves were rank after rank of liquor bottles.* 架子上是一排排的酒瓶。**b)** a line of soldiers, police officers etc, standing side by side〔士兵、警察等的〕队列, 排

7of the first rank of the highest quality 一流的: *Emily Dickinson is a poet of the first rank.* 埃米莉·狄金森是一流诗人。

8►SOCIAL CLASS 社会阶层◄ [C,U] someone's position in society 社会阶层: *people of all ranks in society* 社会各阶层的人

9►TAXI 出租车◄ [C] a place where taxis wait in a line to be hired; TAXI RANK 出租车站

rank² *v* **1 a)** [I always+adv/prep, not in progressive 不用进行时] to have a particular position in a list of people or things that are put in order of quality or importance 具有…等级[地位]: [+among/as/with] *This recession ranks as one of the worst in recent times.* 近年来的经济衰退, 此次为最严重之一。**b)** [T often passive 常用被动态] to decide the position of someone or something on a list based on quality or importance 确定…的地位[等级]:**be ranked fourth/number one etc** *Agassi was at that time ranked sixth in the world.* 阿加西当时排名世界第六。| **rank sb/sth in order** *Rank them in order of ability.* 按能力把他们顺序排列。**2** [T] *AmE* to have a higher rank than someone else; OUTRANK【美】级别高于: *A general ranks a captain.* 将军的级别比上尉高。**3** [T often passive 常用被动态] to arrange things in a regular order 排列: *There were several pairs of riding boots ranked neatly in the hall.* 大厅里整齐地排列着几双马靴。

rank³ *adj* **1** having a very strong and unpleasant smell or taste 难闻的; 难吃的: *rank tobacco* 难闻的烟草 **2** [only before noun 仅用于名词前] complete; total 完全的, 十足的: *a rank beginner at the job* 工作上十足的新手 | *rank disobedience* 根本的违抗 | **rank outsider** (=person or animal that is not expected to win) 不被看好的比赛者 *The Olympic champion was beaten by a rank outsider.* 奥运会冠军败给冷门选手。**3** a plant that is rank is too thick and has spread everywhere〔植物〕过于茂盛的, 蔓生的—**rankly** *adv*—**rankness** *n* [U]

rank and file /ˌ· · ˈ·/ *n* **the rank and file** the ordinary members of an organization rather than the leaders〔组织中相对领袖而言的〕普通成员: *The rank and file of the party had lost confidence in the leadership.* 广大党员对领导人失去了信任。

rank·ing¹ /ˈræŋkɪŋ; ˈræŋkɪŋ/ *n* [C] a position on a scale that shows how good someone or something is when compared with others 排行, 名次: *In the last two years, she has moved steadily up the world rankings.* 在过去两年里, 她的世界排名不断上升。

ranking² *adj* [only before noun 仅用于名词前] a ranking person has a high position in an organization or is one of the best at an activity 地位高的; 最出色的: *a ranking member of the department* 部门里级别高的成员

ranking of·fi·cer /ˈ·· ,···/ *n* [singular] the officer in a group who has the highest rank〔一组军人中〕级别最高的军官

ran·kle /ˈræŋkl; ˈræŋkəl/ *v* [I] if something rankles, you still remember it angrily because it upset you or annoyed you a lot 令人怀恨: *a bitter dispute that still rankled months afterwards* 数月之后仍让人耿耿于怀的激烈辩论

ran·sack /ˈrænsæk; ˈrænsæk/ *v* [T] **1** to search a place very thoroughly 彻底搜索〔某地〕: *She's ransacking the desk drawers for old family photos.* 她把抽屉翻了个底朝天, 寻找家人的老照片。**2** to go through a place stealing things and causing damage 洗劫〔某处〕: *Houses were wrecked and ransacked by wandering gangs of soldiers.* 房屋遭到成群结队的散兵游勇的破坏和洗劫。

ran·som¹ /ˈrænsəm; ˈrænsəm/ *n* [C] **1** an amount of money paid to free someone who is held as a prisoner〔为使被绑架者获释而支付的〕赎金: *The kidnappers were demanding a ransom of $25,000.* 绑匪索取25,000美元的赎金。**2hold sb to ransom a)** to put someone in a situation where they are forced to agree to your demands 要挟某人: *The management will not allow the strikers to hold them to ransom.* 管理层不容许罢工者要挟他们。**b)** to keep someone prisoner until money is paid 劫持某人以索取赎金

ransom² *v* [T] to set someone free by paying a ransom〔付钱〕赎〔人〕

Ran·some /ˈrænsəm; ˈrænsəm/, **Arthur** (1884-1967) a British writer who wrote adventure stories about sailing for children, especially *Swallows and Amazons* 兰塞姆〔(1884-1967), 英国作家。他以创作儿童海上冒险故事见长, 尤以《燕子和亚马孙人》最为著名〕

rant /rænt; rænt/ *v* [I] to talk or complain in a loud, excited, and rather confused way because you feel strongly about something 怒气冲冲地叫嚷[抱怨]: *ranting on about the way his boss treats him* 怒气冲冲地抱怨老板对待他的方式 | **rant and rave** (=rant continuously) 大叫大嚷 *I see the tabloids are all ranting and raving about Fergie's skiing trip.* 我看到各家小报都在大叫大嚷, 批评弗吉的滑雪旅行。

rap¹ /ræp; ræp/ **rapped, rapping** *v*

1►HIT 敲, 打◄ [I,T] to hit or knock something quickly and lightly 轻敲, 急拍: *She rapped the table with her pen and called for silence.* 她用笔轻敲桌子, 要求安静。| [+at/on] *rapping loudly on the door* 大声敲门

2►SAY 说, 讲◄ also 又作 **rap out** [T] to say something loudly,

suddenly, and in a way that sounds angry 厉声地说: *Captain Blake rapped out an order.* 布莱克上尉厉声发出命令。
3 ►CRITICIZE 批评◄[T] a word meaning to criticize someone angrily used in newspapers〔在报纸上〕对…严厉指责: *a film rapped by critics for its excessive violence* 因过分渲染暴力而遭评论家严厉谴责的电影
4 ►MUSIC 音乐◄[I] to say the words of a RAP[2] (2) 表演说唱乐
5 ►CONVERSATION 谈话◄[I] *old-fashioned* to talk in an informal way to friends; CHAT【过时】聊天, 闲谈
6 rap sb over the knuckles to criticize someone, often officially, for something they have done wrong 谴责某人, 正式批评某人: *schools rapped over the knuckles for their failure to improve examination results* 因未能提高考试成绩而受到正式批评的学校

rap² *n*
1 ►KNOCK 敲◄[C] a quick light hit or knock 轻敲: *We heard a sharp rap on the door.* 我们听到急促的敲门声。
2 ►MUSIC 音乐◄[C,U] a type of popular music in which the words of a song are not sung, but spoken in time to music with a steady beat 说唱乐〔按固定的音乐节奏念出歌词的流行音乐〕
3 ►CRIME 犯罪◄*AmE informal*【美, 非正式】**a)** a statement by the state that someone is responsible for a serious crime; CHARGE[1] (4) 指控: **murder rap/drunk driving rap** *He's in police custody facing a murder rap.* 他被警察拘留, 面临谋杀指控。 **b)** time spent in prison as punishment for a crime 服刑的时间: **beat the rap**(=escape punishment) 逃避惩罚
4 take the rap (for sth) to be blamed or punished for a mistake or crime, especially unfairly〔尤指不公正地〕(因某事) 受到责罚: *It didn't worry him that someone else would have to take the rap for his greed.* 其他人会因为他的贪婪而代他受过, 这并不使他担心。
5 ►CRITICISM 批评◄ a rap on/over the knuckles *informal* strong criticism for something you have done wrong【非正式】严厉的指责: *The New York Post received an official rap over the knuckles for the way it reported the story.*《纽约邮报》因报道该事件的方式而受到正式的严厉指责。
6 ►NOT FAIR 不公正◄ a bum rap *AmE slang* unfair treatment or punishment【美俚】不公正的对待, 不公正的惩罚

ra·pa·cious/rə`peʃəs; rə'peɪʃəs/ *adj formal* taking everything that you can, especially by using violence【正式】掠夺的, 强取的: *a rapacious band of robbers* 一伙穷凶极恶的强盗 —**rapaciously** *adv* —**rapaciousness** *n* [U] —**rapacity**/rə`pæsətɪ; rə'pæsəti/ *n* [U]

rape¹/rep; reɪp/ *v* [T] to force someone to have sex, especially by using violence 强奸: *Burgess will be in court today, accused of raping a fifteen-year old girl.* 伯吉斯今天出庭, 他被控强奸了一名十五岁的女孩。

rape² *n* **1** [C,U] the crime of forcing someone to have sex, especially by using violence 强奸 (罪): *He was charged with the attempted rape of a female colleague.* 他被控企图强奸一位女同事。| *a rape victim* 遭强奸者 —see also 另见 DATE RAPE, RAPIST **2** [singular] sudden unnecessary destruction, especially of the environment〔尤指对环境的〕突然、不必要的破坏: *The timber companies are carrying out a systematic rape of our forests.* 这些木材公司正在有组织地毁坏我们的森林。**3** [U] a European plant with yellow flowers, grown as animal food and for its oil 油菜

Raph·a·el¹/`ræfɪəl; 'ræfeɪəl/ in the Christian religion, an ARCHANGEL (=a spirit of the highest rank who lives with God in Heaven) 拉斐尔〔基督教中的天使长〕—see also 另见 GABRIEL, MICHAEL

Raph·a·el²(1483-1520) an Italian painter and ARCHITECT (=someone who designs buildings), and one of the most important artists of the Renaissance, who painted mostly religious subjects. His full name in Italian is **Raffaello Sanzio** 拉斐尔〔(1483-1520), 意大利画家、建筑师, 文艺复兴时期最重要的艺术家之一。其绘画作品多以宗教为主题。他的意大利语全名为拉法埃洛·圣齐奥〕

[3] **rap·id**/`ræpɪd; 'ræpɨd/ *adj* done or happening very quickly and in a very short time 快的, 迅速的: *The patient made a rapid recovery.* 病人迅速康复。| *a period of rapid population growth* 人口快速增长期 —**rapidly** *adv*: *the rapidly changing world of computer technology* 迅速变化的电脑技术领域 —**rapidity**/rə`pɪdətɪ; rə'pɪdɨti/ *n* [U]: *Their debts mounted with alarming rapidity.* 他们的债务以惊人的速度增加。

rapid-fire/'‥·/ *adj* **1** rapid-fire questions, jokes etc are said quickly one after another〔问题、笑话等〕连珠炮地说出的 **2** a rapid-fire gun can fire shots quickly one after another〔枪〕速射的

rap·ids/`ræpɪdz; 'ræpɨdz/ *n* [plural] part of a river where the water looks white because it is moving very fast over rocks 急流, 湍流; WHITEWATER *AmE*【美】

rapid tran·sit sys·tem/,‥'‥,‥/ also 又作 **rapid transit** *n* [C] *AmE* a system for moving people quickly around a city using trains; SUBWAY【美】城市高速铁路系统; 地铁

ra·pi·er/`repɪə; 'reɪpiə/ *n* [C] a long thin sword with two sharp edges 轻剑 —see picture at 参见 SWORD 图

rap·ine/`ræpɪn; 'ræpaɪn/ *n* [U] *literary* the taking away of property by force; PLUNDER[2] (2)【文】劫掠, 抢夺

rap·ist/`repɪst; 'reɪpɨst/ *n* [C] a man who has forced someone to have sex, especially by using violence 强奸犯

rap·pel/ræ`pɛl; ræ'pel/ *v* [I] *AmE* to ABSEIL【美】〔用绳索〕下陡坡 —**rappel** *n* [C]

rap·per/`ræpə; 'ræpə/ *n* [C] someone who speaks the words of a RAP[2] (2) (=type of popular music) 说唱乐表演者: *world-famous rapper, Ice T* 世界著名说唱乐歌手艾斯提

rap·port/ræ`pɔrt; ræ'pɔː/ *n* [singular,U] friendly agreement and understanding between people 融洽, 和睦的关系: [**+between/with**] *She's established a good rapport with her new colleagues.* 她与新同事们建立了良好的关系。

rap·proche·ment/,ræproʃ`mã; ræ'prɒʃmɒŋ/ *n* [singular, U] *formal* the establishment of a good relationship between two countries or groups of people, after a period of unfriendly relations【正式】友好关系的重建: *the signs of a rapprochement between the two countries* 两国关系重新修好的迹象

rap·scal·lion/ræp`skæljən; ræp'skæljən/ *n* [C] *old use* someone who behaves badly, but whom you still like【旧】讨人喜欢的无赖

rap sheet/'‥/ *n* [C] *AmE informal* a list kept by the police of someone's criminal activities【美, 非正式】〔警方保存的〕犯罪记录

rapt/ræpt; ræpt/ *adj* **1** *AustrE informal* very pleased and happy【澳, 非正式】欣喜若狂的 **2** *literary* so interested in something that you do not notice anything else【文】全神贯注的, 出神的: *looks of rapt attention* 全神贯注的表情

rap·ture/`ræptʃə; 'ræptʃə/ *n* [U] **1** great excitement and happiness 狂喜: *He stared with rapture at his baby son.* 他欣喜若狂地凝视着他刚出生的儿子。**2 go into raptures** to express great pleasure and happiness about something〔因…〕欣喜若狂: [**+over/about/at**] *She went into raptures about the climate, the food, the spring flowers.* 她对这天气、食物和春天的花朵着迷。

rap·tu·rous/`ræptʃərəs; 'ræptʃərəs/ *adj formal* expressing great happiness or admiration【正式】狂喜的, 狂热的: *The audience leapt to their feet in rapturous applause.* 观众一跃而起, 狂热地鼓掌。| *A rapturous reception awaited the winning team.* 狂热的欢迎等待着获胜的球队。—**rapturously** *adv*

Ra·pun·zel /rə`pʌnzl; rə'pʌnzəl/ a character in a FAIRY TALE who is kept prisoner at the top of a high tower. She is set free when she lets her very long hair hang down the side of the tower and a handsome prince climbs up her hair, using it like a rope, and saves her. 长发公主〔童话故事中的一个人物。她被关押在一座高耸的塔楼顶部。于是, 她把自己的长发顺着塔楼的外墙垂下, 一位英俊王子手握发辫攀缘而上, 最终把她解救出来〕

Rapunzel 长发公主

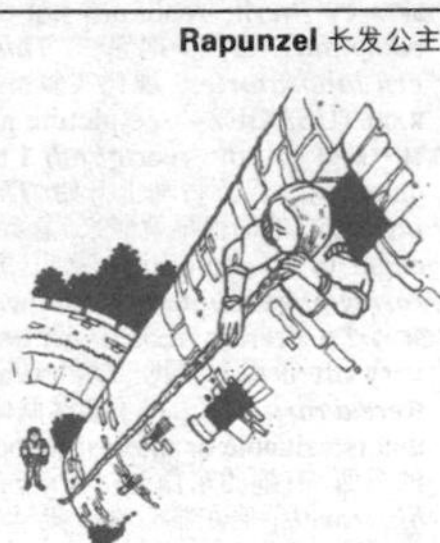

rare/rɛr; reə/ *adj* **1** not seen or found very often, or not happening very often 稀有的, 罕见的, 不常发生的: *This species of plant is becoming increasingly rare.* 这种植物越来越罕见。| *We only went to the cinema on very rare occasions.* 我们难得去看电影。| **it is rare to do sth** *It is rare to find such an interesting group of people.* 难得发现这样一群有趣的人。| **it is rare for sb/sth to do sth** *It's very rare for her to miss a day at school.* 她很少有不上学的日子。**2** meat that is rare has only been cooked for a short time and is still red〔肉〕煮得半熟的: *I like my steak rare.* 我喜欢半熟的牛排。**3** [only before noun 仅用于名词前] *BrE old-fashioned* unusually good or extreme【英, 过时】极好的; 极度的: *We had a rare old time at the party.* 我们在聚会中玩得高兴极了。**4** air that is rare has less oxygen than usual because it is in a high place〔空气〕稀薄的 —see also 另见 RARELY, RARITY —**rareness** *n* [U] [3] [2]

USAGE NOTE 用法说明: RARE

WORD CHOICE 词语辨析: **rare, uncommon, scarce, infrequent, unusual, rarely, scarcely**

Things that do not exist in large numbers or amounts, are **uncommon**. uncommon 指罕见的、不寻常的东西: *an uncommon name/species of birds* 不寻常的名字/罕见的鸟类。**Rare** things are uncommon, and often valuable. rare 指罕见而多半珍贵的东西: *a rare hand-crafted book cover* 手工制作的珍贵书封面 | *He collects rare coins.* 他收藏珍稀的硬币。

Things that you need and are difficult to find or get, though they may at other times be available, are **scarce**. scarce 指需要而又缺乏或不足的东西: *Food is scarce in the refugee camps.* 难民营里食品短缺。| *Parking spaces are scarce on Saturdays.* 星期六停车位不够用。

Events that do not happen often are **infrequent** or **rare**. infrequent 和 rare 指不经常(发生)的、难得的事件或情况: *Opportunities for promotion are rare/infrequent in this company.* 这家公司晋升的机会极少。| *the infrequent letters from her son* 她儿子偶尔来的信 | *the rare sight of a deer grazing* 鹿吃草的难得景象

It is unusual and rather formal to say 不常用且较正式的说法: *It is not rare to...* …并非偶然。People usually say **uncommon** or **unusual** or try to avoid using two negatives completely. For example, this sentence is perfectly acceptable. 人们常用 uncommon 或 unusual, 或完全避免使用两个否定词。如以下句子就是完全可以接受的: *It's not unusual to see tears at a wedding.* 婚礼上有人流泪并非不常见。But you could say instead 但也可以说: *You often see tears at a wedding.* 在婚礼上常会看到有人流泪。

Rarely means 'not often' but **scarcely** means 'hardly', or only 'just'. rarely 的意思是"不经常", scarcely 的意思是"几乎不"或"仅仅": *I rarely visit Houston* (NOT 不用 *scarcely*, though you could say 但可以说 *'scarcely ever'*). 我很少去休斯顿。| *The train leaves in an hour – we've scarcely got time to pack.* 火车再过一小时就开, 我们几乎没有时间整理行装。

R

rare earth /ˌ· ˈ·/ *n* [C] one of a group of rare metal substances 稀土元素

rar·e·fied /ˈrɛrəfaɪd; ˈreərɨfaɪd/ *adj* **1** *often humorous* rarefied ideas, opinions etc can only be understood by, or only involve, one small group of people【常幽默】〔想法、观点等〕只限于小圈子内的: *the rarefied atmosphere of international diplomacy* 国际外交的玄妙气氛 **2** rarefied air is the air in high places, which has less oxygen than usual〔空气〕稀薄的, 缺氧的

2 **rare·ly** /ˈrɛrlɪ; ˈreəli/ *adv* not often 很少, 难得: *She very rarely complains.* 她极少抱怨。| *This method is rarely used in modern laboratories.* 现代实验室里很少使用这种方法。—see 见 RARE (USAGE) —see picture at 参见 FREQUENCY 图

rar·ing /ˈrɛrɪŋ; ˈreərɪŋ/ *adj* **1 raring to go** very eager to start an activity 巴不得马上开始: *They woke up early and were raring to go.* 他们很早就醒来, 急着开始干。**2 raring to do sth** very eager to do something 急想[渴望]做某事: *The children were raring to get out into the snow.* 孩子们急着要到外面雪地里去。

rar·i·ty /ˈrɛrətɪ; ˈreərɨti/ *n* **1 be a rarity** to not happen or exist very often 极为罕见: *The village was so remote that visitors were a rarity.* 那个村子非常偏僻, 来客很罕见。**2** [C] something that is valuable or interesting because it is rare〔因稀罕而〕珍贵的东西; 有趣的东西: *He had picked up all kinds of rarities on his travels.* 他在旅行中收集了各种各样的珍奇物品。**3** [U] the quality of being rare 稀有, 罕见: *Such stamps are expensive because of their rarity.* 这种邮票由于罕见而价格昂贵。

ras·cal /ˈræskl; ˈrɑːskəl/ *n* [C] **1** *humorous* a child who behaves badly but whom you still like【幽默】小淘气: *You little rascal! Where have you hidden my shoes?* 你这个小调皮鬼! 你把我的鞋子藏到哪里去了? **2** *old-fashioned* a dishonest man【过时】恶棍, 无赖 —**rascally** *adj old use*【旧】: *a rascally trick* 卑鄙的伎俩

rash¹ /ræʃ; ræʃ/ *adj* doing something too quickly, without thinking carefully about whether it is sensible or not 急躁的, 鲁莽的, 草率的: *Don't go making any rash decisions about your future!* 不要对你的未来作任何草率的决定! | *It was rather rash of you to lend them your car.* 你把汽车借给他们, 真是太轻率了。—**rashly** *adv*: *I rashly agreed to look after the children.* 我草率地答应照看那些孩子。—**rashness** *n* [U]: *Strangely, it was his rashness which attracted me.* 奇怪的是, 正是他的鲁莽吸引了我。

rash² *n* [C] **1** a lot of red spots on someone's skin, caused by an illness 皮疹: *She had a nasty rash on her arms.* 她的胳膊上起了严重的皮疹。| **come/break out in a rash** *My mother comes out in a rash if she eats seafood.* 我母亲一吃海鲜就起疹子。| **heat rash/nettle rash/nappy rash etc** (=a rash caused by heat etc) 痱子/风疹/尿裤疹等 *The baby's got nappy rash again.* 宝宝又出尿裤疹了。**2 a rash of** *informal* a large number of unpleasant events, changes etc within a short time【非正式】大量的〔一下子出现的令人不快的事件、变化等〕: *a sudden rash of unofficial strikes* 突然出现的大量未经批准的罢工

rash·er /ˈræʃɚ; ˈræʃə/ *n* [C] *BrE* a thin piece of BACON or HAM¹ (1)【英】熏肉片; 火腿片: *a rasher of streaky bacon* 一片五花咸肉 —see picture on page A7 参见 A7 页图

rasp¹ /ræsp; rɑːsp/ *v* **1** [I,T] to make a rough unpleasant sound, like that of two surfaces rubbing together 发出刺耳的声音: *metal rasping against stone* 摩擦石头发出刺耳声音的金属 | *They could hear Peter's rasping breath as he fell to the ground.* 他们可以听到彼得摔到地上时粗重的喘气声。**2** [T] to rub a surface with something rough〔用粗糙地〕擦刮, 粗锉 —**raspingly** *adv*

rasp² *n* **1** [singular] an unpleasant noise, like the sound of two rough surfaces rubbing together 锉磨声音, 刺耳声: *With a rasp of steel, they drew their swords.* 他们铮地一声拔出了剑。| *the rasp of a saw* 锯子发出的刺耳声音 **2** [C] a metal tool with a rough surface, like a FILE¹ (5), used for shaping wood or metal 锉, 粗锉刀

rasp·ber·ry /ˈræzbɛrɪ; ˈrɑːzbəri/ *n* [C] **1** a soft sweet red berry, or the bush that this berry grows on 悬钩子, 覆盆子, 山莓: *raspberry jam* 山莓酱 —see picture on page A8 参见 A8 页图 **2** *informal* a rude sound made by putting your tongue out and blowing【非正式】〔吐舌爆气发出无礼的〕呸呸声: **blow a raspberry** *BrE*【英】/**give a raspberry** *AmE*【美】(=to make this sound) 发出呸呸声

Ras·pu·tin /ræˈspjutɪn; ræˈspjuːtɪn/, **Gri·go·ri** /grɪˈgɔrɪ; grɪˈgɔːri/ (1872-1916) a Russian who claimed to be a holy man, and who had a lot of power in the Russian government because of his influence over Alexandra, the wife of the Tsar (=ruler) Nicholas II. He was famous especially for the fact that, when he was murdered by his enemies, they had great difficulty in killing him. 拉斯普廷〔(1872-1916), 俄国人, 自称圣人。由于他对沙皇尼古拉二世之妻亚历山德拉的影响力, 他在俄国政府拥有很大权力。政敌谋杀他时颇费周折, 这给他的声名增益不少〕

Ras·ta /ˈræstə; ˈræstə/ *n* [C] *informal* a Rastafarian【非正式】拉斯塔法里教派成员

Ras·ta·fa·ri·an /ˌræstəˈfɛrɪən; ˌræstəˈfeəriən◂/ *n* [C] someone who believes in a religion that is popular in Jamaica, which has Haile Selassie as its religious leader, and has the belief that black West Indians will return to Africa 拉斯塔法里教派成员〔牙买加一教派成员, 该教派尊崇海尔·塞拉西为其领袖, 相信西印度群岛的黑人将返回非洲〕—**Rastafarian** *adj* —**Rastafarianism** *n* [U]

Ras·ta·man /ˈræstəmæn; ˈræstəmæn/ *n* [C] *informal* a male Rastafarian【非正式】拉斯塔法里教派男性成员

rat¹ /ræt; ræt/ *n* [C] **1** an animal that looks like a large mouse with a long tail 大老鼠: *rat poison* 灭鼠药 **2** *spoken* someone who has been disloyal to you or deceived you【口】卑鄙小人, 骗子: *But you promised to help us, you rat!* 可是你答应过帮助我们, 你这言而无信的小人! **3 look like a drowned rat** to look very wet and uncomfortable 看上去像只落水老鼠 **4 like rats deserting the sinking ship** used to describe people who leave a company, organization etc when it is in trouble 就像老鼠逃离沉船一样〔描写人们在公司、组织等出现困难的时候纷纷离去〕—see also 另见 RAT RACE, RATS, RAT TRAP, **smell a rat** (SMELL² (7))

rat² *v* **ratted, ratting** [I] *informal* to be disloyal to someone, especially by telling someone in authority about something wrong that person has done【非正式】告密, 背信弃义: **[+on]** *They'll kill you if they find out you've ratted on them!* 假如他们发现是你告发他们, 他们会杀掉你的!

rat-arsed /ˈræt ˌɑrst; ˈræt ˌɑːst/ *adj BrE slang* extremely drunk【英俚】烂醉如泥的

rat-a-tat /ˌræt ə ˈtæt; ˌræt ə ˈtæt/ also 又作 **rat-a-tat-tat** /ˌ· · · ˈ·/ *n* [singular] the sound of knocking, especially on a door 敲击声; 〔尤指敲门的〕砰砰声

rat·bag /ˈrætˌbæg; ˈrætbæg/ *n* [C] *BrE, AustrE informal* an unpleasant person【英, 澳, 非正式】讨厌的人

ratch·et /ˈrætʃɪt; ˈrætʃɨt/ *n* [U] a machine part consisting of a wheel or bar with teeth on it, which allows movement in only one direction 棘轮, 单向齿轮

ratchet 棘轮

rate¹ /ret; reɪt/ *n* [C]
1 ►SPEED 速度◄ the speed at which something happens over a period of time 速率: *Our money was running out at an alarming rate.* 我们的钱正以惊人的速度减少。| *Children learn at different rates.* 儿童学东西有快有慢。| [+of] *the rate of economic growth* 经济增长的速度
2 ►AMOUNT 数量◄ the number of times something happens or the number of examples of something within a certain period 比率, 率: **birth/unemployment/divorce/crime rate** *The divorce rate rose from 20,000 in 1961 to 150,000 in 1985.* 离婚率从1961年的2万例增加到1985年的15万例。| **high/low rate of** *high rates of unemployment* 高失业率 | **success/failure rate** (=the number of times that something succeeds or fails) 成功/失败率 *Penicillin has a high success rate in bacterial infections.* 青霉素治疗细菌感染的成功率很高。
3 ►MONEY 钱◄ a charge or payment fixed according to a standard scale 费用; 价格: *The sports centre has reduced rates for students.* 运动中心降低了对学生的收费。| *Nurses are demanding higher rates of pay.* 护士们正在要求提高工资。| **hourly/weekly rate** (=the amount paid per hour/week) 按小时/周付费 *What's the hourly rate for cleaning?* 打扫卫生每小时收费是多少? | **the going rate** (=the usual amount paid for work) 一般的收费 *I'm told $20 an hour is the going rate for private tuition.* 我听说家教的一般收费是每小时20美元。
4 at this rate *spoken* used to say what will happen if things continue to happen in the same way as now【口】照这种情况继续下去: *At this rate we won't even be able to afford a holiday.* 照这样下去, 我们就连度假都度不起了。
5 at any rate *spoken* used when you are stating one definite fact in a situation that is uncertain or unsatisfactory【口】无论如何, 不管怎样: *Well, at any rate, we won't starve!* 唉, 不管怎样, 我们不会挨饿的! | *They've had technical problems – at any rate that's what they told me.* 他们遇到了技术问题 —— 反正他们是这么跟我说的。
6 first-rate/second-rate/third-rate of good, bad, or very bad quality 一流/二流/三流的: *a cheap third-rate motel* 便宜的三流汽车旅馆
7 at a rate of knots *BrE informal* very quickly【英, 非正式】飞快地: *Jack's getting through the ironing at a rate of knots!* 杰克熨衣服熨得飞快!
8 rates [plural] a local tax, paid before 1990 by owners of buildings in Britain〔英国1990年前向房产主征收的〕房地产税 —see also 另见 BASE RATE, EXCHANGE RATE, INTEREST RATE

rate² *v*
1 ►JUDGE THE QUALITY 判断质量◄ a) [T] to think that someone or something has a particular quality, value, or standard 对…作评估, 评价: **be rated (as) sth** *Lewis is currently rated the world's No. 1 athlete.* 刘易斯目前被认为是世界排名第一的田径运动员。| *She is generally rated as one of the best modern poets.* 她被公认为最杰出的现代诗人之一。| **rate sb/sth highly** (=think they are very good or important) 对某人/某物评价高 *The company seems to rate him very highly.* 该公司似乎对他评价很高。**b)** [I] to be considered as having a particular quality, value, or standard 被认为, 被评价为: [+as] *Becker rates as one of the finest players of his generation.* 贝克尔被认为是那一代人中最优秀的球员之一。
2 ►THINK SB/STH IS GOOD 对某人/某物评价高◄ [T] *BrE informal* to think that someone or something is very good【英, 非正式】对…评价高: *I know they're your favourite team, but I just don't rate them.* 我知道他们是你喜欢的球队, 可我却认为他们不怎么样。
3 ►DESERVE 值得◄ [T] *informal, especially AmE* to deserve【非正式, 尤美】值得, 应得: *They rate a big thank-you for all their hard work.* 他们的辛勤工作值得好好感谢。| **rate a mention** (=be important enough to be in the news) 值得提及, 值得报道 *a local incident that didn't rate a mention in the national press* 不值得全国报纸报道的地方事件
4 ►FILMS 电影◄ be rated G/U/PG/X if a film is rated G, U etc it is officially judged to be suitable or unsuitable for children〔影片〕定为G/U/PG/X级〔即老少咸宜(美)/老少咸宜(英)/家长指导/只允许18岁以上者观看级〕—see also 另见 X-RATED
5 ►ANGRY 生气的◄ [I,T] *old use* to speak angrily to someone; BERATE【旧】责骂, 训斥

rate·a·ble val·ue, ratable value /ˌretəbl̩ ˈvælju; ˌreɪtəbəl ˈvælju:/ *n* [C] a value given to buildings in Britain before 1990 in order to calculate how much local tax the owner should be charged〔英国1990年前对房地产的〕征税估定价值

rate of ex·change /ˌ· · ˈ· ·/ *n* [C] the EXCHANGE RATE 外汇汇率, 兑换率

rate of re·turn /ˌ· · ˈ· ·/ *n* [singular] a company's profit for a year, expressed as a PERCENTAGE of the money that the company has spent during the year 收益率, 回报率

rate·pay·er /ˈretˌpeə; ˈreɪtpeɪə/ *n* [C] *BrE* someone who pays taxes that are used to provide local services【英】地方税纳税人

rat fink /ˈ· ·/ *n* [C] *AmE informal* someone who you trusted who has given information to the police or done something else wrong【美, 非正式】告密者; 卑鄙小人

ra·ther /ˈræðə; ˈrɑ:ðə/ *predeterminer, adv* **1** [+adj/adv] quite; fairly 相当, 颇: *I was rather surprised to see him with his ex-wife.* 看到他与前妻在一起我相当吃惊。| *He was limping rather badly as he walked off the field.* 他走出运动场时, 腿跛得厉害。| *It's not too big for you at all. I rather like the way it fits you.* 这对你来说根本不太大, 看来很合身, 我挺喜欢。| **rather a big hat/a tall man etc** *Simon's always been rather a difficult person to get along with.* 西蒙一直是个相当难相处的人。| **rather too big/too tall etc** *They spoke rather too quietly to be heard at the back of the hall.* 他们讲话的声音太轻, 在大厅的后面听不见。
2 would rather if you would rather do or have something, you would prefer to do it or have it 宁愿, 宁可: *I suppose I could lend it to them but I'd rather not.* 我想我是可以把它借给他们的, 但我还是不借的好。| *To be honest, I'd rather have a quiet night in front of the TV.* 老实说, 晚上我宁愿静静地看看电视。| **would rather do sth than do sth** *I'd rather die than ask him for his autograph.* 我宁死也不会去求他签名。| **would rather sb did sth** *We'd rather you didn't smoke in our home.* 我们希望你不要在我们家里抽烟。**3 rather than a)** more than or to a greater degree than someone or something else 在更大程度上: *The parents should be blamed rather than the children.* 应该受到责备的是父母而不是孩子。| *I think you'd call it a lecture rather than a talk.* 我认为, 与其说这是演说, 不如说是讲课。**b)** instead of someone or something else 而不是…: *Rather than squeezing your own oranges, have you tried buying packs of orange juice?* 你是否试过买包装橙汁, 而不是自己榨橙汁? **4 or rather** used to correct something that you have said, or give more specific information 更确切地说: *You have to be sixteen for cheap tickets – or rather under sixteen.* 你必须是16岁才能买便宜票 —— 更确切地说是不满16岁。**5 not...but rather...** used to say that someone does not do something but does something else instead 不是…而是…〔用以指某人不做某事, 而做另外的事〕: *The committee does not deal with individual correspondence, but rather discusses issues in its newsletter.* 该委员会不处理个人信件, 而是在定期通讯中讨论问题。**6 Rather!** *spoken BrE old-fashioned* used to agree with someone【口, 英, 过时】当然! 的确!

USAGE NOTE 用法说明: RATHER
WORD CHOICE 词语辨析: **fairly, quite, pretty, rather**
You use **fairly** or **quite** to describe something that is neither good nor bad. 表示某物既不好也不坏时用 fairly 或 quite: *The weather was fairly cold* (=more than a little cold, but not extremely cold). 天气相当冷〔有些冷, 但不十分冷〕。| *The movie was quite good* (=more than a little good). 那部电影相当好。
Rather is fairly formal, and is especially used in British English. It often suggests that something is bad or unsuitable. rather 较正式, 尤用于英国英语, 常表示不好的或不恰当的性质: *It's rather cold* (=colder than I would like). 天挺冷的。| *I was driving rather fast* (=a little too fast). 当时我的车开得相当快。
British English speakers often use **rather** about things they like very much. 英国人用 rather 来表示他们非常喜欢的事物: *Yes I painted it myself – I'm rather pleased with it.* 对, 是我自己刷的漆, 我挺满意的。
Pretty is the most usual way of saying 'fairly' or 'very' in American English, and is used in British English as well. It is more common in spoken English than in writing. 美国英语中一般用 pretty 来表示"相当"或"非常", 英国英语中也使用, 口语用得比书面多: *Charlie's Restaurant is pretty good, especially if you want somewhere cheap.* 查利餐厅非常好, 尤其是如果你想找个便宜的地方。| *You'd better wear a coat – it's pretty cold out.* 你最好穿件外衣吧, 外面很冷。
GRAMMAR 语法
Note that you say 注意, 可以说: *a rather/fairly/pretty long road* 一条相当长的路, but 但要说 *quite a long road* 一条相当长的路
Of these four words, only **rather** can be used with com-

parative forms. 上述四个词中，只有 rather 可以和比较级连用: *I'd prefer a rather shorter hairstyle.* 我想要理短一些的发型。

Rather is not used before *than* when you are comparing people or things. 比较人或事物时，rather 不用在 than 之前: *Books are more interesting than TV* (NOT 不用 *Books are interesting rather than TV*). 书籍比电视更有意思。But it is used when you are using adjectives to compare. 但用形容词进行比较时要用 rather: *TV is relaxing rather than interesting.* 电视使人放松，而不是有意思。

Rather can only be used to mean **prefer** in the phrase **I/he would rather** followed by the base form of a verb or a clause. 在短语 I/he would rather 中，rather 只用于表示喜欢、宁愿，并后接动词原形或从句: *They'd rather walk* (NOT 不用 *they rather to walk/walking/a walk*). 他们宁愿步行。| *I'd rather not answer that question.* 我不想回答那个问题。

rat·i·fy /ˈrætəˌfaɪ; ˈrætɪ̣faɪ/ *v* [T] to make a written agreement official by signing it 批准，正式签署: *The government delayed ratifying the treaty.* 政府推迟签署条约。—**ratification** /ˌrætəfəˈkeʃən; ˌrætɪ̣fɪ̣ˈkeɪʃən/ *n* [U]: *an attempt to delay ratification of the treaty* 推迟批准条约的企图

rat·ing /ˈretɪŋ; ˈreɪtɪŋ/ *n* **1** [C] a level on a scale that shows how good, important, popular etc someone or something is 等级，程度: *The President's popularity rating is low according to recent opinion polls.* 根据最近的民意测验，总统的民众支持率很低。**2 the ratings** a list that shows which films, television programmes etc are the most popular〔电影、电视节目等的〕排行榜: *The new comedy series shot up to the top of the ratings in the first week.* 这部新喜剧在第一周里就跃居排行榜首位。**3** [singular] a letter that shows whether or not a film is suitable for children〔电影是否适合儿童的〕级别: *The Godfather had an X-rating when it was first shown in 1972.*《教父》在 1972 年首映时定为 X 级。**4** [C] a SAILOR in the British navy who is not an officer〔英国海军〕水兵，水手 **5** [C] the class in which a ship or machine is placed, according to its size〔船舶、机器依其大小所定的〕等级，级别 —see also 另见 CREDIT RATING

ra·ti·o /ˈreʃo; ˈreɪʃiəʊ/ *n* [C] *plural* **ratios** a relationship between two amounts that is represented by a pair of numbers showing how much greater one amount is than the other〔两个数量之间的〕比，比例，比率: **the ratio of sth to sth** *The ratio of nursing staff to doctors is 2:1.* 护理人员与医生的比例为二比一。—compare 比较 PROPORTION[1]

ra·tion[1] /ˈræʃən; ˈræʃən/ *n* **1** [C] a fixed amount of something such as food or petrol that you are allowed to have, when there is not much available〔食品或汽油等在短缺时的〕配给量，定量配给: *the weekly meat ration* 肉类的每周配给量 **2 rations** [plural] the food that is given to a soldier or member of a group each day〔每日的〕口粮配给，口粮定量: *The expedition had sufficient rations to last them another five days.* 探险队有足够的给养再维持五天。**3 have had your ration of** to have had as much of something as you would expect or consider to be fair 得到想要[应得]的东西: *We've had more than our ration of bad luck this year.* 我们今年运气不佳。

ration[2] *v* [T] **1** to control the supply of something such as food or petrol by allowing people to have only a fixed amount of it 对…实行配给，定量供应: *Petrol was rationed during the war.* 战争期间，汽油实行定量供应。**2** to allow someone to have only a small amount of something because there is not enough〔因不够而〕实行定量供给，配给: **ration sb to sth** *We were rationed to two eggs a week.* 每周配给我们两个鸡蛋。—**rationing** *n* [U]

ration sth ↔ **out** *phr v* [T] to give out supplies of something in small amounts 少量配给〔供应品〕: *They rationed out the remaining water as fairly as they could.* 他们尽可能公平地按量分配剩下的水。

ra·tion·al /ˈræʃənl; ˈræʃənəl/ *adj* **1** based on clear, practical or scientific reasons〔原因〕合理的，基于理性的: *It can't have just disappeared! There must be a perfectly rational explanation.* 不可能就这么消失了！一定有某种非常合理的原因。**2** sensible and able to make decisions based on intelligent thinking rather than on emotion 有理性的，懂道理的: *rational behaviour* 合理的行为 | *We should be able to sort this out like rational human beings!* 我们应该像有理性的人那样处理这件事！—**rationally** *adv*: *Scientific training makes you think rationally.* 科学的训练能使人理性思考。—**rationality** /ˌræʃəˈnælətɪ; ˌræʃəˈnælɪ̣ti/ *n* [U] —opposite 反义词 IRRATIONAL

ra·tio·nale /ˌræʃəˈnæl; ˌræʃəˈnɑːl/ *n* [C,U] *formal* the reasons and principles on which a decision, plan, belief etc is based【正式】〔决定、计划、信念等的〕理据，基本原因，依据: *The rationale behind introducing this technique is that it will substantially speed up our work.* 引进这项技术的依据是它将大大加快我们的工作。

ra·tion·al·ist /ˈræʃənḷɪst; ˈræʃənəlɪ̣st/ *n* [C] someone who bases their opinions and actions on intelligent thinking, rather than on emotion or religious belief 理性主义者，唯理论者 —**rationalism** *n* [U] —**rationalist, rationalistic** /ˌræʃənḷˈɪstɪk; ˌræʃənəˈlɪstɪk◂/ *adj*

ra·tion·al·ize also 又作 **-ise** *BrE*【英】/ˈræʃənḷˌaɪz; ˈræʃənəlaɪz/ *v* [I,T] **1** to find or invent a reasonable explanation for your behaviour or attitudes 合理地解释，为…找出辩解的理由: *Tony was still trying to rationalize his decision to leave his wife and children.* 托尼仍在试图为他离开妻子儿女的决定辩解。**2** *especially BrE* to make a business system more effective by getting rid of unnecessary staff, equipment etc【尤英】(对…)进行合理化改革〔指裁减冗员、处理闲置设备等〕—**rationalization** /ˌræʃənələˈzeʃən; ˌræʃənəlaɪˈzeɪʃən/ *n* [C,U]: *Rationalization is a word management use when they are sacking people.* 管理层在解雇员工时总是用使机构合理化的说法。

rat race, the /ˈ· ·/ *n* [U] the unpleasant situation in business, politics etc in which people are continuously competing against each other for success〔商业、政治等中〕永无休止的竞争: *Paul went off to a Greek island to escape from the rat race.* 保罗跑到希腊的一个岛上去躲避永无休止的竞争。

rats /ræts; ræts/ *spoken* used as an expression of annoyance【口】讨厌〔用于表示恼怒〕: *Oh rats! I've left my purse at home.* 真讨厌！我把钱包留在家里了。

rat·tan /ræˈtæn; rəˈtæn/ *n* [U] the plant from which wicker furniture is made 藤属植物，藤

rat-tat /ˌræt ˈtæt; ˌræt ˈtæt/ *n* [singular] RAT-A-TAT 敲击声〔尤指敲门声〕

rat·ted *v* **get ratted** *BrE slang* to get extremely drunk【英俚】喝得烂醉

Rat·ti·gan /ˈrætɪgən; ˈrætɪ̣gən/, **Sir Ter·ence** /ˈtɛrəns; ˈterəns/ (1911-77) a British writer of plays including *The Winslow Boy*, *The Browning Version*, and *Separate Tables* 拉蒂根〔(1911-1977)，英国剧作家。作品有《温斯洛男孩》、《勃朗宁独特表现》和《分开的餐桌》〕

rat·tle[1] /ˈrætl; ˈrætl/ *v* **1** [I,T] to shake, or make something shake, with quick repeated knocking noises (使) 咯咯作响: *The windows rattled in the wind.* 窗户被风吹得咯咯作响。| *The beggar was rattling coins in an old mug.* 那个乞丐把旧杯子里的硬币摇得哗哗响。**2** [I] to move quickly, making a rattling noise 嘎拉嘎拉地快速移动: [**+along/past/over etc**] *The cart rattled along the stony road.* 那辆马车嘎拉嘎拉地沿着碎石路快速驶过。**3** [T] *informal* to make someone lose confidence or become nervous【非正式】使慌乱，使紧张: *Keep calm – don't let yourself get rattled.* 沉住气，别紧张。| *It was an old trick of his – rattling people by getting their names wrong.* 这是他惯用的伎俩 —— 把人们的姓名搞错使他们慌乱不安。**4 rattle sb's cage** *spoken humorous* to make someone feel angry or annoyed【口，幽默】使某人生气[恼怒]: *Who rattled your cage?* 是谁惹你了？—see also 另见 SABRE-RATTLING

rattle around *phr v* [I] *informal* to be in a house, office etc that is bigger than you need it to be【非正式】〔房子、办公室等〕过大: *We rattle around a bit now that the children have all left.* 孩子们都离开了家，屋子里现在有点空荡荡的。

rattle sth ↔ **off** *phr v* [T] to say something quickly and easily, from memory 迅速地背诵: *He rattled off the poem.* 他一口气背出了那首诗。

rattle on *phr v* [T] *informal* to talk quickly for a long time, about things that are not interesting【非正式】喋喋不休地说: *Nancy would rattle on for hours about her grandchildren.* 南希能几个小时喋喋不休地谈论她的孙儿孙女们。

rattle through sth *phr v* [T] *informal* to do something very quickly because you want to finish it as soon as possible【非正式】迅速完成: *She rattled through her speech in five minutes.* 她匆匆忙忙在五分钟内完成了演讲。

rattle[2] *n* **1** [singular] the noise that you hear when the parts of something knock against each other〔碰撞而发出的〕咯咯声，嘎嘎声: [**+of**] *the rattle of chains* 铁链相互撞击时发出的嘎嘎声 **2** [C] a baby's toy that makes this noise 拨浪鼓〔一种幼儿玩具〕**3** [C] a wooden instrument that makes a loud knocking noise, used by people watching football games〔观众在看足球比赛时使用的〕发出咯咯响声的木器具 —see also 另见 DEATH RATTLE

rat·tler /ˈrætlɚ; ˈrætlə/ *n* [C] *informal* a rattlesnake【非正式】响尾蛇

rattle·snake /ˈrætl̩ˌsnek; ˈrætlsneɪk/ *n* [C] a poisonous American snake that makes a noise like a rattle with its tail 响尾蛇

rat·tling /ˈrætlɪŋ; ˈrætlɪŋ/ *adj, adv old-fashioned* **a rattling good yarn/story** a very good or interesting story【过时】非常好[有趣]的故事: *He tells a rattling good story.* 他讲述一个非常有趣的故事。

rat trap /ˈ· ·/ *n* [C] *AmE informal* a dirty old building that is in very bad condition【美, 非正式】又脏又破的老房子

rat·ty /ˈrætɪ; ˈræti/ *adj* **1** *BrE informal* bad-tempered; IRRITABLE【英, 非正式】爱发脾气的, 易怒的 **2** *AmE informal* in bad condition; SHABBY【美, 非正式】破旧的, 褴褛的: *a ratty old sofa* 一张破旧的沙发 **3** like a rat 像老鼠的

rau·cous /ˈrɔkəs; ˈrɔːkəs/ *adj* a raucous voice is unpleasantly loud 沙哑的, 粗嘎的: *raucous shouts from the street* 街上传来的沙哑的叫喊声 **—raucously** *adv*: *They laughed raucously.* 他们粗声粗气地笑。**—raucousness** *n* [U]

raunch·y /ˈrɔntʃɪ; ˈrɔːntʃi/ *adj informal* sexually exciting or intended to make you think about sex【非正式】色情的, 淫秽的: *a raunchy dance* 色情舞蹈 **—raunchily** *adv* **—raunchiness** *n* [U]

Rauschenberg /ˈraʊʃənbɝg; ˈraʊʃənbɜːg/**, Robert** (1925-2008) a US painter who is one of the most famous painters in POP art. 劳森伯格〔(1925-2008), 美国画家, 著名波普艺术家之一〕

rav·age /ˈrævɪdʒ; ˈrævɪdʒ/ *v* [T often passive 常用被动态] to destroy, ruin, or damage something very badly; DEVASTATE (1) 严重破坏, 摧毁: **be ravaged by sth** *The population was ravaged by cholera.* 霍乱使许多人死去。

rav·ag·es /ˈrævɪdʒɪz; ˈrævɪdʒɪz/ *n* **the ravages of war/time/disease etc** the damage or destruction caused by something such as war, disease, storms etc 战争/时间/疾病等造成的破坏性后果: *The ravages of drink were clear in the dark rings under his eyes.* 他的黑眼圈证明了酗酒的恶果。

rave[1] /rev; reɪv/ *v* [I] **1** to talk in an angry, uncontrolled way 怒骂, 痛斥: **[+at]** *Dad raved at me for hours about how irresponsible I'd been.* 父亲一连几小时痛骂我不负责任。**2** to talk in a crazy way that is impossible to understand, especially because you are very ill〔尤指因病重〕胡言乱语 **3 rave about/over** to talk in a very excited way about something, saying how much you admire or enjoy it 极力赞美: *After the game people raved about Tommy Craig's performance.* 比赛后, 人们极力夸奖汤米·克雷格的表现。—see also 另见 **rant and rave** (RANT), RAVING

rave[2] *adj* **rave reviews/notices** newspaper articles that praise something a lot, for example a play or film〔报纸对某部戏剧或电影〕大加赞美的评论: *His last film got rave reviews in the British press.* 他的最后一部电影得到英国报刊的高度评价。

rave[3] *n* [C] **1** a very large party held in an empty building in Britain, at which young people dance and sometimes take illegal drugs〔英国年轻人在无人居住的房子里跳舞、吸毒的〕狂欢聚会: **rave scene/band/culture etc** (=a scene etc that is connected with raves) 狂欢的场面/狂欢聚会的乐队/狂欢聚会的文化等 **2** *especially AmE* a piece of writing in a newspaper, magazine etc that praises a film, play, or performance very much【尤美】〔报纸、杂志等上〕吹捧〔电影、戏剧、表演〕的文章 —see also 另见 RAVE-UP

rav·el /ˈrævl̩; ˈrævəl/ *v* **ravelled, ravelling** *BrE*【英】, **raveled, raveling** *AmE*【美】[I] **1** if something made from wool or cloth ravels, the threads in it become separated from one another〔织物〕开线, 散开 **2** if threads ravel, they become knotted and twisted〔线〕打结, 缠绕 —compare 比较 UNRAVEL

Ra·vel /ræˈvɛl; ræˈvel/**, Mau·rice** /moˈris; mɒˈriːs/ (1875-1937) a French COMPOSER whose most famous work is *Boléro* 拉威尔〔(1875-1937), 法国作曲家。代表作为《波莱罗》〕

ra·ven[1] /ˈrevən; ˈreɪvən/ *n* [C] a large shiny black bird with a large black beak 渡鸦

raven[2] *adj* [only before noun 仅用于名词前] raven hair is black and shiny〔头发〕乌黑发亮的

raven-haired /ˌ·· ˈ·◂/ *adj literary* having shiny black hair【文】长着一头乌黑发亮的头发的

rav·e·ning /ˈrævənɪŋ; ˈrævənɪŋ/ *adj literary* ravening animals are extremely hungry【文】〔动物〕饿极了的: *a ravening beast* 极其饥饿的野兽

rav·e·nous /ˈrævənəs; ˈrævənəs/ *adj* extremely hungry 饿极了的: *Have a sandwich – you must be ravenous!* 吃块三明治吧——你一定饿极了! **—ravenously** *adv*

rav·er /ˈrevɚ; ˈreɪvə/ *n* [C] *BrE informal* someone who goes to a lot of parties and has many sexual partners【英, 非正式】〔经常参加聚会、有许多性伙伴的〕放荡不羁的人

rave-up /ˈ· ·/ *n* [C] *BrE informal* a noisy party where people drink and dance a lot【英, 非正式】喧闹的聚会

ra·vine /rəˈvin; rəˈviːn/ *n* [C] a deep narrow valley with steep sides 沟壑, 峡谷: *21 killed as bus swerves into ravine* 公共汽车突然转向坠入深谷, 致使21人死亡

rav·ing /ˈrevɪŋ; ˈreɪvɪŋ/ *adj informal*【非正式】**1** talking or behaving in a crazy way 语无伦次的, 疯疯癫癫的: *a raving lunatic* 胡言乱语的疯子 | **raving mad** *informal especially BrE* (=completely crazy)【非正式, 尤英】完全丧失理智的 **2 raving beauty/success** someone who is very beautiful or something that is very successful 绝色美人/巨大成功

rav·ings /ˈrevɪŋz; ˈreɪvɪŋz/ *n* [plural] things someone says that are crazy and have no meaning 胡言乱语, 疯话: *Sometimes in his ravings he talks about a super-intelligent pig.* 有时候他会疯言疯语, 说有一头猪具有超级智能。

rav·i·o·li /ˌrævɪˈolɪ; ˌræviˈəʊli/ *n* [U] small squares of PASTA filled with meat 小方形饺 —see picture at 参见 PASTA 图

rav·ish /ˈrævɪʃ; ˈrævɪʃ/ *v* [T] *literary*【文】**1** to RAPE a woman 强奸 **2 be ravished** to feel great pleasure when you look at or listen to something 狂喜, 陶醉, 销魂: *I was ravished by her beauty.* 她的美貌使我倾倒。

rav·ish·ing /ˈrævɪʃɪŋ; ˈrævɪʃɪŋ/ *adj* very beautiful 非常美丽的, 十分标致的: *ravishing good looks* 令人倾倒的美貌 **—ravishingly** *adv*: *a ravishingly pretty young woman* 美艳绝伦的年轻女子

raw[1] /rɔ; rɔː/ *adj* 3

1 ▶FOOD 食品◀ not cooked 生的, 未烧煮的: *raw meat* 生肉 | *raw carrot* 生胡萝卜

2 ▶INFORMATION 信息◀ raw data/statistics etc information that has not been arranged, checked, or prepared for use 原始数据/统计数字等

3 ▶SKIN 皮肤◀ a part of your body that is raw is red and sore 又红又痛的, 刺痛的: *My hands were raw with cold.* 我的手冻得发痛。

4 ▶MATERIALS 材料◀ raw cotton, sugar, wool etc are in their natural state and have not yet been prepared for use〔棉、糖、羊毛等〕天然状态的, 未经过处理加工的 —see also 另见 RAW MATERIALS

5 ▶NOT EXPERIENCED 没有经验的◀ not experienced or not yet fully trained 没有经验的, 未经过充足训练的: *Most of our soldiers were raw recruits.* 我们大多数的士兵都是新兵。

6 touch/hit a raw nerve to upset someone by something you say〔说话〕触及某人痛处: *In mentioning his departure I knew I had touched a raw nerve.* 说到他的离去, 我知道我触及了对方的伤心处。

7 get a raw deal to be unfairly treated 受到不公正的待遇: *Women tend to get a raw deal when it comes to pay.* 妇女常常在工资方面受到不公正的待遇。

8 ▶WEATHER 天气◀ very cold and wet 湿冷的: *A raw wind chilled him to the bone.* 湿冷的风让他感到寒气刺骨。

9 ▶EMOTIONS/QUALITIES 情感/素质◀ raw emotions or qualities are strong and natural, but not completely developed or controlled 强烈的, 自然的〔但未经充分琢磨或约束的〕: *Katie was surprised by her own raw courage and endurance.* 凯蒂对自己原始的勇气和忍耐力吃了一惊。| *the singer's raw, husky voice* 那位歌手本色的沙哑嗓音

10 ▶LANGUAGE 语言◀ *AmE informal* containing a lot of sexual details【美, 非正式】下流的, 粗俗的

11 ▶DESCRIPTIONS 描述◀ giving the unpleasant facts, without trying to make them seem more acceptable 不加掩饰的: *a raw account of poverty in the cities* 对城市中的贫困状况毫不掩饰的叙述 **—rawness** *n* [U]

raw[2] *n* **1 life/nature in the raw** the way humans or animals live in their natural state including all the violence and cruelty 未开化的生活/原始的自然状态: *Her films portray nature in the raw.* 她的电影描绘了原始的自然状态。**2 in the raw** *AmE informal* not wearing any clothes【美, 非正式】裸体的: *She sunbathes in the raw.* 她裸着身子沐日光浴。**3 catch/touch sb on the raw** *BrE* to say or do something that upsets someone【英】〔说话或做事〕触及某人的痛处

raw·hide /ˈrɔˌhaɪd; ˈrɔːhaɪd/ *n* [U] natural leather that has not been specially treated 生皮

raw ma·te·ri·als /ˌ· ·ˈ···/ *n* [plural] materials such as coal, oil etc, in their natural state, before being treated in order to make things 原材料

ray /re; reɪ/ *n* [C] **1** [often plural 常用复数] a narrow beam of light from the sun or from something such as a lamp 光线, 光

束: *the sun's rays* 太阳光 | [+of] *Rays of light filtered through the pine trees.* 一束束光线透过松树。**2** *technical* a beam of heat, electricity, or other form of ENERGY (2)【术语】〔热、电或其他能源的〕束: *a gun that fires invisible rays* 一支射出隐形射线的枪 —see also 另见 COSMIC RAY, GAMMA RAY, X-RAY **3 ray of hope/light/comfort etc** something that provides a small amount of hope or happiness in a difficult situation 一线希望/光亮/一丝安慰等: *If only I could see some ray of hope for the future.* 但愿我能看到未来的一线希望。**4 ray of sunshine** *informal* an expression meaning someone or something that makes a situation seem better【非正式】安慰, 希望: *Little Annie was an unexpected ray of sunshine in her life.* 小安妮是她生活中一线意外的阳光。**5** a large flat sea fish with a long pointed tail 魟; 鳐〔一种体大而扁的海鱼, 尾长而尖〕

Ray, James Earl (1928-98) a US man accused of killing Rev. Martin Luther King in 1968 and sentenced to 99 years in prison 雷〔(1928-1998), 美国一男子。他被控于1968年刺杀马丁·路德·金牧师, 被判处99年监禁〕

Ray, Man (1890-1976) a US artist and photographer, who was one of the leaders of the Dada and SURREALIST movements 雷〔(1890-1976), 美国画家、摄影家, 达达派及超现实主义运动的领袖人物之一〕

Ray /raɪ; raɪ/, **Sat·ya·jit** /ˋsætjədʒɪt; ˈsætjədʒɪt/ (1921-92) an Indian film DIRECTOR whose work is well-known and respected all over the world. His films include *Pather Panchali* (1955) and *The Chess Players* (1977). 雷〔(1921-1992), 印度电影导演。他的作品全球闻名, 备受推崇, 其中有《大路之歌》(1955) 和《棋手》(1977)〕

Ray-Ban /ˈ· ·/ *trademark* a type of SUNGLASSES. The most typical Ray-Bans have fairly thick black frames and very dark lenses.【商标】雷朋太阳镜〔一款墨镜。其典型特征是, 镜框呈黑色, 质地厚实、镜片颜色很深〕

ray gun /ˈ· ·/ *n* [C] an imaginary gun in SCIENCE FICTION stories that fires rays which kill people 〔科幻故事里的〕光束枪, 射线枪, 激光枪

ray·on /ˋreɑn; ˈreɪɒn/ *n* [U] a smooth material used for making clothes 人造丝, 嫘萦

raze /rez; reɪz/ *v* [T] to completely destroy a town or building 把〔城镇、建筑物〕夷为平地: **raze sth to the ground** (=destroy it so that nothing is left) 夷为平地; 彻底破坏 *houses that had been razed to the ground in the war* 在战争中被夷为平地的房屋

razors 剃须刀

razor blade
安全剃刀刀片

razor blade
安全剃刀刀片

safety razor
安全剃刀

cut-throat razor *BrE*【英】/
straight razor *AmE*【美】
(直柄) 剃刀

electric razor/
electric shaver
电动剃须刀

ra·zor /ˋrezɚ; ˈreɪzə/ *n* [C] **1** a sharp instrument used for removing hair, especially from a man's face 剃刀, 刮胡刀: *an electric razor* 电动剃须刀 **2 be on a razor edge** to be in a dangerous position where a mistake could be very dangerous 处于险境: *Politically we are on a razor edge. Whatever judgment we make could have dire consequences.* 我们在政治上处于险境——无论我们作出什么样的决定, 都有可能造成可怕的后果。

razor blade /ˈ· · ·/ *n* [C] a small flat blade with a very sharp cutting edge used in a SAFETY RAZOR 安全剃刀刀片 —see picture at 参见 RAZOR 图

ra·zor-sharp /ˌ·· ˈ·◂/ *adj* **1** very sharp 锋利的, 锐利的: *a razor-sharp hunting knife* 一把非常锋利的猎刀 **2** very intelligent 非常敏锐的: *his razor-sharp wit* 他非常敏锐的才智

razz /ræz; ræz/ *v* [T] *AmE spoken* to make a joke about someone that is insulting or makes them feel embarrassed; TEASE[1] (1)【美口】嘲笑, 讥讽: *The kids were razzing Tom about Jenny.* 孩子们戏弄汤姆说他和珍妮的事。

raz·zle /ˋræzl; ˈræzəl/ *n* **go on the razzle** *BrE slang* to go somewhere such as to a party to enjoy yourself【英俚】狂欢, 作乐

razzle-daz·zle /ˌ·· ˈ··/ *n* [U] *informal*【非正式】**1** a lot of activity that is intended to be impressive and excite people 起哄, 欢闹 **2** *AmE informal* a complicated series of actions intended to confuse your opponent, especially in American football【美, 非正式】〔尤指美式橄榄球中〕障眼的假动作

razz·ma·tazz /ˌræzməˋtæz; ˌræzməˈtæz/ also 又作 **raz·za·ma·tazz** /ˌræzəməˋtæz; ˌræzəməˈtæz/ *n* [U] *informal* busy or noisy activity that is intended to attract people's attention【非正式】〔为了吸引人的〕令人眼花缭乱的活动: *all the razzmatazz surrounding presidential elections* 围绕总统选举的种种热闹喧嚣

RC /ˌɑr ˋsi; ˌɑː ˈsiː/ the abbreviation of 缩写= Roman Catholic 罗马天主教

RCA, the /ˌɑr ˋsi ˋe; ˌɑː ˈsiː ˈeɪ/ the abbreviation of 缩写= the ROYAL COLLEGE OF ART

RCM, the /ˌɑr ˋsi ˋɛm; ˌɑː ˈsiː ˈem/ the abbreviation of 缩写= the ROYAL COLLEGE OF MUSIC

RCMP /ˌɑr si ɛm ˋpi; ˌɑː siː em ˈpiː/ Royal Canadian Mounted Police; the national police force of Canada 加拿大皇家骑警队 —see also 另见 MOUNTIE

RD /ˌɑr ˋdi; ˌɑː ˈdiː/ *n* rural delivery; a postal service that delivers the mail in country areas in the US. The letters 'RD' are part of someone's address. 乡村递送〔美国乡村地区递送邮件的服务。RD是地址的一部分〕

Rd the written abbreviation of 缩写= Road, used in addresses 路〔用于地址〕

-rd /rd; d/ *suffix* forms written ORDINAL numbers with 3〔以3结尾的序数词写法〕: *the 3rd* (=third) *of June* 6月3日 | *his 53rd birthday* 他的53岁生日

RDA /ˌɑr di ˋe; ˌɑː diː ˈeɪ/ *n* [singular] Recommended Daily Allowance; the amount of substances such as VITAMINs or MINERALs that you should have each day〔维生素、矿物质等的〕建议每日摄入量

're /ɚ, ə/ the short form of 缩略式= are: *We're ready to go but they're not.* 我们已经准备好出发了, 但他们还没有。

RE /ˌɑr ˋi; ˌɑːr ˈiː/ *n* [U] Religious Education; a school subject in Britain 宗教教育〔英国的学校课程〕

re- /ri; riː/ *prefix* **1** again 再, 重新: *They're rebroadcasting the play.* 他们正在重播这出戏。**2** again in a new and better way 改进重来: *You'd better rewrite that letter.* 你最好重写那封信。**3** back to a former state 回复原状, (重) 又: *After years of separation they were finally reunited.* 经过多年的离别, 他们终于团聚了。

re[1] /ri; riː/ *prep* used especially in business letters to introduce the subject that you are going to write 'about' 关于〔尤用于商业信函中〕: *re your enquiry of the 19th October* 关于你10月19日的询问

re[2] /re; reɪ/ *n* [singular] the second note in a musical SCALE[1] (8) according to the SOL-FA system 全音阶的第二音

reach[1] /ritʃ; riːtʃ/ *v*

1 ►ARRIVE 到达◄ [T] to arrive at a particular place, especially when it has taken a long time or a lot of effort to get there 到达, 抵达〔尤指经过长时间或花费大气力以后〕: *It was a relief to reach the safety of our home at last.* 终于到家了, 这下安全了, 我们松了一口气。| *Your letter reached me yesterday.* 我昨天收到了你的信。

2 ►WITH YOUR HAND 用手◄ a) [I always+adv/prep, T always+adv/prep] to move your hand or arm in order to touch, hold, or pick up something 伸出〔手、臂来碰、拿或捡起〕: **[+for/in/over etc]** *I saw Kelly reach for the gun.* 我看到凯利伸手去拿枪。| **reach out a hand** *One of the men suddenly reached out a hand and grabbed my arm.* 其中一个人突然伸手抓住我的胳膊。**b)** [I,T not in progressive 不用进行时] to succeed in touching something by stretching out your hand or arm, especially something that is above your head 伸手触及〔尤指高于头顶的东西〕: *Even when I stood on tiptoe I couldn't reach the*

top shelf. 即使我踮起脚尖也够不到架子最高处。| *We picked all the fruit we could reach.* 我们摘了所有够得着的果实。**c)** ▶**TAKE STH/PICK STH UP** 拿起/举起某物◀ [T] to take or pick up something by stretching your arm, especially over your head 伸手去拿〔高处的东西〕: **reach sth down** *She reached down a can of peaches from the top shelf.* 她从架子顶格拿下一罐桃子。

3 ▶**LEVEL/STANDARD** 水平/标准◀ [T] to increase, improve, or develop to a particular level or standard over a period of time 达到: *These plants take a long time to reach maturity.* 这些植物要过很长时间才成熟。| *wind speeds reaching over 100 mph* 风速达到每小时一百多英里

4 ▶**ACHIEVE AN AIM** 实现目标◀ [T] to succeed in doing what you were trying to do 实现, 达到: **reach a decision/agreement/result etc** *After two years of negotiations, the warring parties have finally reached a settlement.* 经过两年的谈判, 交战各方最终达成和解协议。

5 ▶**LENGTH/HEIGHT** 长度/高度◀ [I always+adv/prep, T not in progressive 不用进行式] to be big enough, long enough, or high enough to get to a particular point or level 大得[长得, 高得]足以到达: *The flood waters reached the lower floor of the houses.* 洪水水位涨到房屋的下层。| **reach as far as/down to** *Her skirt reaches down to her ankles.* 她的裙子长及脚踝。

6 ▶**SPEAK TO SB** 对某人说话◀ [T] to speak to someone or leave a message for them, especially by telephone; CONTACT[2] 〔尤指通过电话〕联系: *Here's my phone number, in case you need to reach me.* 如果你需要与我联系, 这是我的电话号码。

7 ▶**BE SEEN/HEARD BY SB** 被某人看到/听到◀ [T] if a message, television programme etc reaches a lot of people, they hear it or see it 收听, 收看〔信息、电视节目等〕: *The sales campaign reached a target audience of 12,000 women.* 促销活动以〔某些〕女性为对象, 惠及了12,000人。

8 reach for the stars to aim for something that is very difficult to achieve 想摘天上的星星〔追求难以实现的东西〕

USAGE NOTE 用法说明: REACH

WORD CHOICE 词语辨析: **reach, arrive, get to, achieve, catch**

To **arrive** somewhere is to come to it after travelling. arrive 指从一地到达另一地: *Sam usually arrives home from work at 5.15.* 萨姆通常在5点15分下班回到家。| *What time does the train arrive?* 这班火车何时到达?

Reach suggests more time or effort is involved. reach 指用了较多时间、付出较大努力后到达: *At last we reached the base camp.* 我们终于到达了大本营。

In spoken English people usually use **get to**. 口语中通常使用 get to: *You can easily get to the city centre from here.* 从这里你可以方便地到达市中心。If a train, bus, plane etc arrives, you say **get in**. 火车、公共汽车、飞机等到达用 get in: *The bus gets in at four-thirty.* 这班公共汽车四点半到达。Note that you **get/arrive/reach etc home** (NOT 不用 **to home**). 请注意, 到家是 get/arrive/reach home。

You may **reach** a standard or level, especially through your own efforts, but **achieve** is often a better word. 达到某种标准或水平, 尤指通过自身努力时可用 reach, 但achieve往往更为恰当: *I want to reach/achieve a good level of English.* 我希望达到好的英语水平。| *He achieved his aim in life – to write a book* (NOT 不用 *reached*). 他实现了毕生的目标 —— 写一本书。

If you get to a bus, train etc just in time, you **catch** it. catch 指赶上公共汽车、火车等: *You'd better hurry if you want to catch that bus.* 你要是想赶上那班公共汽车就最好快点。

GRAMMAR 语法

You **reach** a place (NOT 不用 **reach at** or **reach to** it) 到达某地用 reach: *He reached Tokyo at 5 am.* 他早上5点到达了东京。

You **arrive at** a particular place, town, or building. 到达某个具体地点、城镇、房屋用 arrive at: *We arrived at the station at midnight.* 我们午夜时到达车站。| *What time will they arrive at his house?* 他们什么时候能到他家?

You **arrive in** a country or a big city. 到达某国家、大城市用 arrive in: *arrive in London/Tokyo/France* 到达伦敦/东京/法国

Sometimes you do not need a preposition at all. 有时不需要使用介词: *When will they arrive there/here/home?* 他们什么时候到那里/这里/家?

reach[2] *n* **1** [singular,U] the distance that you can stretch out your arm to touch something 伸手可及的距离: *a boxer with a long reach* 一名长臂拳击手 | **out of reach/beyond reach** *The cat jumped away, out of his reach.* 那只猫跳开了, 他够不着。| **within reach** *Adjust the car seat so that all the controls are within reach.* 把汽车座位调整一下, 以便所有的控制装置伸手可及。**2** [singular,U] the limit to which someone or something can have a power or influence 〔权力、影响〕能及的范围: **beyond the reach of** *He lives in Paraguay, beyond the reach of the British authorities.* 他住在巴拉圭, 英国当局鞭长莫及。**3 within (easy) reach of** within a distance that you can easily travel 在…可(容易)到达的地方: *All the main tourist attractions are within easy reach of the hotel.* 这家旅馆离所有的主要旅游景点都很近。**4** [C] a straight part of a river between two bends 〔两个弯道之间的〕笔直河段

reach 伸手可及的距离

The oranges are out of Tim's reach/beyond Tim's reach.
这些橙子蒂姆够不着。

re·act /rɪˋækt; riˈækt/ *v* [I] **1** to behave in a particular way because of something that has happened or something that has been said to you 反应: **[+to]** *How did Wilson react to your idea?* 威尔逊对你的想法有什么反应? | *He reacted angrily to accusations of disloyalty.* 有人指责他不忠, 他非常气愤。| **react by doing sth** *Ellie reacted by marching out of the room.* 埃利的反应是大步走出房间。—see also 另见 OVERREACT **2** *technical* if a chemical substance reacts, it changes when it is mixed with another chemical substance【术语】产生化学反应: **[+with/on]** *An acid reacts with a base to form a salt.* 酸与碱产生化学反应形成盐。**3** to become ill when you take a particular drug, eat a particular kind of food etc 〔因服某种药品、食用某种食物而〕产生不良反应: **[+to]** *The patient reacted badly to penicillin.* 病人对青霉素有不良反应。—compare 比较 RESPOND S3 W3

react against sth *phr v* [T] to show that you dislike someone else's rules or way of doing something by deliberately doing the opposite 反抗: *Feminists reacted against the limitations of women's traditional roles.* 女权主义者反抗妇女传统角色的局限。

re·ac·tion /rɪˋækʃən; riˈækʃən/ *n* S2 W2

1 ▶**TO A SITUATION/EVENT** 对情形/事件◀ [C,U] something that you feel or do that is a result of something that has happened to you or been said to you 反应: *What was Jeff's reaction when you told him about the job?* 你把那份工作的情况告诉杰夫的时候, 他是什么反应? | **[+to]** *Her parents' reaction to the news was surprisingly calm.* 她父母对那消息的反应平静得出乎意料。| **mixed reaction** (=people react in different ways) 各种不同的反应 *The pay offer brought a mixed reaction from union members.* 薪酬方案引起工会会员不同的反应。| **gut reaction** (=what you immediately feel before you have time to think) 直觉反应 *My gut reaction to her story was disbelief!* 听到她的故事, 我的直觉反应是不相信!

2 ▶**ABILITY** 能力◀ **reactions** [plural] your ability to move quickly when something dangerous happens suddenly 〔突发危险时的〕反应能力: **quick/slow reactions** *In motor racing the drivers need to have very quick reactions.* 赛车时, 车手需要具备非常迅速的反应能力。

3 ▶**TO FOOD/DRUGS** 对食品/药品◀ [C] a bad effect, such as illness, caused by food that you have eaten or a drug that you have taken 不良反应: *an allergic reaction* 过敏反应 | **[+to]** *Some people experience a mild reaction to the drug.* 有些人对这种药会有轻微不良反应。

4 ▶**SCIENCE** 科学◀ [C,U] **a)** a chemical change that happens when two or more chemical substances are mixed together; CHEMICAL REACTION 化学反应 **b)** a physical force that is the result of an equally strong physical force in the opposite direction 反作用力 —see also 另见 NUCLEAR REACTION

5 ▶**CHANGE** 变化◀ [singular] a change in people's attitudes, behaviour, fashions etc that happens because they disapprove of what was done in the past 〔态度、行为、时尚等的〕变化〔以示对过去的不满〕: **[+against]** *The attitudes of this generation are a reaction against the selfish values of the 1980s.* 这一代人的态度是对20世纪80年代自私价值观的不满。

6 ▶TIRED/SAD 疲惫/悲伤◀ [singular] a sudden feeling of weakness, tiredness, or unhappiness that you sometimes get after a lot of activity〔大量活动后引起的〕无力, 疲乏, 情绪低落: *Bridget seems depressed; I think she's suffering a reaction after all the excitement.* 布丽奇特似乎闷闷不乐; 我认为她是在极度兴奋之后感到疲乏无力。
7 ▶AGAINST CHANGE 反对变革◀ [U] *formal* strong and unreasonable opposition to all social and political changes【正式】反动: *The revolution was defeated by the forces of reaction.* 这场革命被反动势力打败了。—see also 另见 CHAIN REACTION

re·ac·tion·a·ry /rɪˋækʃən,ɛrɪ; riˈækʃənəri/ *adj* strongly and unreasonably opposed to social or political change 反动的: *The new measures were opposed by reactionary elements within the party.* 新措施遭到党内反动分子的反对。—**reactionary** *n* [C]

re·ac·ti·vate /rɪˋæktɪ,vet; riˈæktɪveɪt/ *v* [T] to make something start working again, or to start a process again 使重新开始工作; 使重新启动程序

re·ac·tive /rɪˋæktɪv; riˈæktɪv/ *adj* **1** reacting to events or situations rather than starting something new 反应的, 反对的〔而不是创新的〕: *Many businesses follow a reactive strategy rather than initiating new products.* 很多商家采取的是对市场环境作出应对的策略, 而不是研制新产品。**2** *technical* a reactive chemical substance changes when it is mixed with another chemical substance【术语】〔化学物质〕能起化学作用的

re·ac·tor /rɪˋæktɚ; riˈæktə/ *n* [C] a NUCLEAR REACTOR 核反应堆

R

read out 宣读

The teacher is reading out the list of successful students.
老师在宣读优秀学生名单。

read¹ /rid; riːd/ *v past tense and past participle* **read** /rɛd; red/
1 ▶WORDS/BOOKS 文字/书籍◀ [I;T] to look at written words and understand what they mean 阅读, 看懂: *Tom could read by the time he was four.* 汤姆四岁时就能阅读了。| **read sth** *Read the instructions carefully before you start.* 开始之前, 请仔细阅读操作指南。| *I'm sorry, I can't read your handwriting.* 对不起, 我看不懂你的字。| *I can read Spanish but I can't speak it very well.* 我能看懂西班牙文, 但说得不太好。| *I've read a lot of Agatha Christie.* 我读过许多阿加莎·克里斯蒂的著作。| *reading the paper* 看报纸
2 ▶INFORMATION 信息◀ [I,T not in progressive 不用进行时] to find out information from books, newspapers etc〔从书籍、报纸等中〕找到: *You can't believe everything you read in the papers.* 你不能完全相信报纸上看到的一切。| **[+about/of]** *Did you read about that terrible car crash?* 你在报上看到那起严重的撞车事件了吗? | *I read of his death in the local newspaper.* 我在地方报纸上看到了他去世的消息。| **read (that)** *Simon was amazed when he read that Sally had won a literary prize.* 在报纸上看到萨莉获得一项文学奖, 西蒙感到吃惊。
3 ▶READ AND SPEAK 朗读◀ [I,T] to say the written words in a book, newspaper etc so that people can hear them 读出, 朗读: **read sb sth** *Daddy, will you read me a story?* 爸爸, 给我念个故事好吗? | **read to sb** *Our mother reads to us every evening.* 妈妈每天晚上都给我们朗读(故事)。| **read (sth) aloud** *He glanced at the letter and began to read it aloud.* 他看了一下信, 便开始大声读。
4 ▶MUSIC/MAPS/SIGNS ETC 乐谱/地图/符号等◀ [T] to look at signs, pictures etc and understand what they mean 读懂: *He plays the flute well but can't actually read music.* 他长笛吹得很好, 但其实他看不懂乐谱。| *map reading* 查阅地图
5 ▶UNDERSTAND STH IN A PARTICULAR WAY 理解◀ [T] to choose to understand a situation, remark etc in one of several possible ways 理解, 洞察: **read sth as** *I read her reply as a refusal.* 我把她的答复理解为拒绝。| *The poem can be read as a protest against war.* 这首诗可以理解为对战争的抗议。| **read sth well/accurately** (=understand something correctly) 正确理解某事 *Reagan's speech showed that he had accurately read the mood of Congress.* 里根的讲话表明他正确把握了国会的情绪。
6 ▶HAVE A PARTICULAR FORM/MEANING 具有某种形式/含义◀ [I not in progressive 不用进行时] if words read in a particular way, they have a particular form, or produce a particular effect when you read them 读作: *The first sentence read: "If I should die before you receive this letter..."* 第一句的内容是: "假如我在你接到此信前离开人世…" | *The name should read 'Benson', not 'Fenton'.* 这个名字是 Benson, 而不是 Fenton。| **read well/awkwardly etc** (=be easy or difficult to read and understand) 易懂/难懂 *The report reads well, but it doesn't cover the most important points.* 报告虽然易懂, 但并未谈到最重要的问题。
7 read sth as sth/for sth read sth used to tell someone to replace a wrong number or word with the correct one 换用, 改作〔用于订正讹误〕: *Please read £50 as £15.* 请把 50 英镑改为 15 英镑。| *For 'November'* (=instead of November) *on line 6, read 'September'.* 第六行的 November 应作 September。
8 ▶MEASURING 度量◀ [T] **a)** to look at the number or amount shown on a measuring instrument 读〔度量仪器显示的数字〕: *Read the meter and tell me how much electricity we've used.* 请查看一下电表, 然后告诉一下我们用了多少电。**b)** if a measuring instrument reads a particular number, it shows that number〔度量仪器〕显示, 指示: *The thermometer read 46 degrees.* 温度计显示 46 度。
9 ▶AT UNIVERSITY 上大学◀ [T] *BrE* to study a subject at a university【英】攻读, 念〔某课程〕: *I read history at Cambridge.* 我在剑桥大学攻读历史。
10 take it as read (that) a) *especially BrE* to feel certain that something is true without having proof; ASSUME【尤英】可以认为是正确的, 假定: *You can take it as read that the press will support our opponents.* 你可以假定新闻界会支持我们的对手。**b)** to accept a report, statement etc as correct and complete without reading or hearing it 没有见[听见]就视…为正确和全面的: *We'll have to take the secretary's report as read.* 我们得认为秘书的报告不会有错。
11 read between the lines to guess someone's real feelings from something they say or write 看出字里行间的意思; 听出真实意思: *Reading between the lines, I'd say Robert's got a lot of problems.* 听言外之意, 我看罗伯特遇上了许多麻烦。
12 read sb's mind/thoughts to guess what someone else is thinking 猜测某人的心思: *As if he had read her mind, he stood up and offered her his seat.* 他仿佛猜透了她的心思, 站起身来把座位让给她。
13 read sb like a book to know someone so well that you immediately know what they are thinking or feeling 把某人琢磨透, 对某人了如指掌
14 read sb's palm to look carefully at someone's hand, in order to find out about their future 为某人看手相: *Have you ever had your palm read?* 你请人看过手相吗?
15 read sb's lips to understand what someone is saying by watching the way their lips move 唇读, 观唇辨意 —see also 另见 LIP-READ
16 ▶COMPUTER 电脑◀ [T] *technical* if the DISK DRIVE of a computer reads information from a disk, it takes the information and puts it into the computer's memory【术语】读取〔磁盘中的信息并调入电脑的内存〕
17 do you read me? *spoken* used to ask someone whether they fully understand what you are saying【口】明白吗?: *I do not want this to happen again! Do you read me?* 我不希望再发生这种事! 明白吗?
18 well-read/widely-read having read a lot of books and gained a lot of knowledge 博览群书的, 博学的: *She is an intelligent, well-read human being.* 她是个聪明、博学的人。
19 widely-read/little-read etc read by a lot of people, few people etc 读者众多的/不多的等: *Jon Naughton's widely-read column in the Observer* 乔恩·诺顿在《观察家报》上读者众多的专栏 —see also 另见 READING, **read (sb) the riot act** (RIOT¹ (4))

read for sth *phr v* [T] **1** *BrE old-fashioned* to study a subject in order to get a university degree【英, 过时】攻读〔学位〕: *She's reading for a degree in physics.* 她正在攻读物理学学位。**2** to perform the part of a particular character from a play, as a test of your ability to act in the play; AUDITION² 试演, 试镜

read sth **into** sth *phr v* [T] to think that a situation, action etc has a meaning or importance that it does not really have〔错误地〕认为〔某事〕含有某种意思: *It was only a casual remark. I think you're reading too much into it.* 那不过是随便说说, 我觉得你多心了。

read sth ↔ **out** *phr v* [T] to say the words that are written in a message, list etc, so that people can hear 朗读, 宣读: *He opened the envelope and read out the name of the winner.* 他打开信封, 宣读获胜者的姓名。

read sth ↔ **through/over** *phr v* [T] to read something carefully from beginning to end in order to check details or find mistakes 通读, 从头到尾细读: *Read the contract over carefully before you sign it.* 仔细读合同之后再签字。

read sth ↔ **up** also 又作 **read up on** sth *phr v* [T] *informal* to read a lot about something because you will need to know about it【非正式】攻读, 对…作大量阅读: *I'll have to read up on the tax laws before the meeting tomorrow.* 在参加明天的会议之前, 我必须好好地研究一下税法。

read² *n* [singular] **1** *BrE informal* an act of reading something, or time spent doing this【英, 非正式】阅读; 阅读时间: *have a nice quiet read* 安静地看一会儿书 **2 a good read** something that you enjoy reading 喜欢的读物: *It's not great literature, but it's a good read.* 这不是文学巨著, 但读起来引人入胜。

rea·da·ble /ˈridəbḷ; ˈriːdəbəl/ *adj* **1** interesting or enjoyable to read, and easy to understand 读起来有趣的, 易懂的: *a very readable account of their research into genetics* 有关他们对遗传学研究的非常有趣的叙述 **2** writing or print that is readable is clear and easy to read; LEGIBLE〔文章、印刷物〕清晰的, 易读的 —**readibility** /ˌridəˈbɪlətɪ; ˌriːdəˈbɪlɪ̣ti/ *n* [U] —opposite 反义词 UNREADABLE —see also 另见 MACHINE-READABLE

re·ad·dress /ˌriəˈdrɛs; ˌriːəˈdres/ *v* [T] *BrE* to FORWARD³ (1)【英】转寄

[3] [2] **read·er** /ˈridɚ; ˈriːdə/ *n* [C] **1** someone who reads a particular book, newspaper etc 读者: *At this point in the novel, the reader still does not know the hero's true identity.* 小说读到这里, 读者依然不知道主人公的真实身份。| *a Guardian reader*《卫报》的一名读者 **2** someone who reads a lot, or reads in a particular way 读书人; 以某种方式阅读的人: *an avid reader* 废寝忘食的读者 | *Susan isn't much of a reader* (=does not read a lot). 苏珊不太爱读书。| **a fast/slow reader** *I'm not a very fast reader, but I do like novels.* 我阅读的速度不快, 但我真的喜欢小说。**3** an easy book to help children learn to read, to help people learn a foreign language etc (初级) 读本, (初级) 读物 **4 Reader** a teacher in a British university who has the rank just below PROFESSOR〔英国大学的〕教授〔仅次于讲座教授级〕*Reader in Sociology at Bristol* 布里斯托尔大学社会学教授 —see also 另见 MIND READER —see 见 PROFESSOR (USAGE)

Reader, The a weekly US newspaper printed in Chicago, containing news about many subjects, but especially about entertainment《读者》〔美国芝加哥市印行的周报。其新闻涵盖多类主题, 尤以娱乐新闻居多〕

Reader's Di·gest /ˌ·· ˈ··/ a magazine containing short articles and stories on many different subjects, which is produced in many different languages and in separate editions in the UK and the US《读者文摘》〔一种以多语种出版的杂志。有英、美版本, 内容为短文和短篇小说, 涉及多类主题〕

read·er·ship /ˈridɚʃɪp; ˈriːdəʃɪp/ *n* [C,U] **1** the people who read a particular newspaper or magazine〔某报纸、杂志的〕全体读者: *The magazine has a readership of 60,000.* 这份杂志拥有六万名读者。**2** the job that a Reader has in a British university〔英国大学的〕教授职位: *a readership in linguistics* 语言学教授职位

[3] **read·i·ly** /ˈrɛdɪlɪ; ˈredɪ̣li/ *adv* **1** quickly and easily 迅速地, 容易地: *Computers make data readily available to users.* 电脑使用户得以很容易地查到数据。**2** quickly, willingly, and without complaining 迅速地, 愿意地, 心甘情愿地: *He readily obeyed.* 他很乐意地服从了。

read·i·ness /ˈrɛdɪnɪs; ˈredinɪ̣s/ *n* **1** [U] a state of being prepared and ready for what is going to happen 准备就绪: **in readiness (for)** *They stacked the firewood in readiness for the evening campfire.* 他们堆起了木柴, 准备傍晚生营火。**2** [singular,U] willingness to do something 愿意: **readiness to do sth** *the UN's readiness to intervene in the civil war* 联合国愿意干预这场内战

[2] **read·ing** /ˈridɪŋ; ˈriːdɪŋ/ *n*

1 ▶THE ACTIVITY/SKILL 活动/技能◀ [U] the activity of understanding written words 读, 阅读: *Children are taught reading and writing in their first years at school.* 孩子们在上学的最初几年里学习阅读和书写。

2 ▶UNDERSTANDING 理解◀ [C] your opinion of what a particular statement, situation, event etc means; INTERPRETATION 理解, 解释: *What's your reading of this response?* 你怎么看这样的回应?

3 ▶BOOKS 书籍◀ [U] the books, articles etc that you read 读物: *Her main reading seems to be mystery novels.* 她主要阅读的书似乎是悬疑小说。| **light reading** (=books that are easy and enjoyable) 轻松读物

4 ▶TO A GROUP 对一群人◀ [C] **a)** an occasion when a piece of literature is read to a group of people 文学作品朗诵会: *a poetry reading* 诗歌朗诵会 **b)** a piece of literature or part of the Bible that is read to a group of people〔文学作品、《圣经》章节的〕朗读内容: *The first reading is from Corinthians I, Chapter 3.* 朗读的第一篇选自《圣经·新约·哥林多前书》第三章。

5 ▶MEASUREMENT 度量◀ [C] a number or amount shown on a measuring instrument〔度量仪器上的〕读数: **take a reading** *Thermometer readings were taken every two hours.* 每两个小时记录一遍温度计的读数。

6 ▶THE ACT OF READING STH 阅读◀ [singular] the act of reading something 读, 阅读: *Even a casual reading of the text gives you an idea of the theme.* 即使是随意读一下文章也会使你对主题有所了解。

7 ▶IN PARLIAMENT 在议会中◀ [C] one of the three occasions in the British Parliament or the US Congress, when a BILL (=suggested new law) is read and discussed〔英国议会或美国国会〕宣读议案, 一项议案三读过程中的任何一读: *the second reading of the Industrial Relations Bill*《劳资关系议案》的二读

8 make good/interesting/boring etc reading to be enjoyable, interesting etc to read 读起来有趣/乏味等: *Your report made fascinating reading.* 你的报告读起来很吸引人。

re·ad·just /ˌriəˈdʒʌst; ˌriːəˈdʒʌst/ *v* **1** [I] to get used to a new situation, job or way of life 适应: [**+to**] *Soldiers struggled to readjust to life outside the army.* 士兵们努力适应部队以外的生活。**2** [T] to make a small change to something or to its position 调整: *The unemployment figures need to be readjusted to allow for people on training programmes.* 失业数字需要调整, 以便把参加培训项目的人考虑进去。—**readjustment** *n* [C,U]

R

read-only mem·o·ry /ˌ· · ˈ···/ *n* [C,U] ROM 只读存储器

read-out /ˈ· ·/ *n* [C] a record of information that has been produced by a computer, shown on a SCREEN or in print〔电脑屏幕上显示或打印出的〕信息读出: *This program gives you a readout of all the areas where sales have increased.* 这种程序能使你得到销售额增长地区的信息。—compare 比较 PRINTOUT

read·y¹ /ˈrɛdɪ; ˈredi/ *adj*

1 ▶PREPARED 有准备的◀ [not before noun 不用于名词前] prepared for what you are going to do 准备好的, 有准备的: *Come on. Aren't you ready yet?* 快来! 你还没准备好吗? | **ready to do sth** *Everything's packed, and we're ready to leave.* 所有的东西都装好了, 我们准备动身。| [**+for**] *I don't want to take the test yet; I'm not ready for it.* 我现在还不想考试, 我还没有准备好。| **get ready** *I need about half an hour to get ready, so I'll see you at six.* 我需要大约半小时做准备, 那我就在6点见你吧。| **make ready** *formal* (=prepare to start doing something)【正式】做好准备 | **ready for anything** *I felt strong, fit, and ready for anything.* 我觉得精力充沛, 身体健康, 干什么都行。| **ready and waiting** *When the right opportunity came, she was ready and waiting.* 当合适的机会到来时, 她已准备就绪。| **ready for (the) off** *spoken* (=ready to go somewhere)【口】准备动身: *Right, I'm ready for the off.* 对, 我马上可以动身。| **when you're ready** *spoken* (=used to tell someone that you are ready for them to start doing something)【口】当你一切就绪的时候〔告诉对方已经准备好, 等他开始做某事〕| **ready when you are** *spoken* (=used to tell someone that you are ready to do what you have arranged to do together)【口】当你一切就绪的时候〔告诉对方自己随时可以做安排了一起做的事〕| **ready to roll** *spoken* (=ready to start an activity, journey etc)【口】准备动手, 准备动身 —see graph at 参见 PREPARE 图表

2 ▶FOR IMMEDIATE USE 可立即使用◀ [not before noun 不用于名词前] something that is ready can be used or eaten immediately 现成的;〔食物〕已做好的: *When will supper be ready?* 晚饭何时做好? | *The peaches are ripe and ready to eat.* 桃子熟了, 可以吃了。| [**+for**] *Is everything ready for the exhibition?* 展览会一切就绪了吗? | **get sth ready** *We must get the house ready for the new tenants.* 我们必须给新房客把房子准备好。| **have sth ready** *Next time, I had my answer ready.* 下一次, 我把我的答案准备好。| **ready cooked/mixed etc** (=already cooked or mixed, and ready to be eaten or used) 已做好/配好等

3 be ready for a drink/meal/holiday etc *spoken* to need or want a drink, meal etc as soon as possible【口】想喝饮料/吃饭/度假等: *You must be ready for a drink after all that hard work.* 干了那么费力的工作, 你一定想喝点什么。

4 be ready to cry/drop etc *informal* to be so upset or tired that you feel you will cry, fall down etc【非正式】〔心烦意乱, 疲惫得〕想哭/快要瘫倒等: *By the end of that walk, we were ready to drop.* 步行完时, 我们都累得要倒下来。

5 ►WILLING 愿意的◄ willing and quick to do or give something 愿意〔做某事〕的；乐意〔给某物〕的：**[+with]** *She's always ready with an excuse.* 她总能找到借口。| **ready to do sth** *You're too ready to criticize.* 你太爱批评人了。| *They were wonderful neighbours – always ready to help in a crisis.* 他们真是好邻居，关键时刻总乐意帮忙。
6 ►QUICK 快的◄ [only before noun 仅用于名词前] quick or without delay 快的，迅速的：*a ready answer* 脱口而出的回答 | *This system gives readier access to the data.* 这种系统能更迅速地提取数据。| **a ready wit** (=the ability to think quickly of clever, amusing things to say) 机智
7 ready money/cash money that can be spent at once in coins or notes 现金：*He was only willing to sell it for ready cash.* 他只收现钱才卖。
8 ready, steady, go! *BrE spoken* used to tell people to start a race【英口】各就各位，预备，跑！〔用于赛跑发令时〕—see also 另见 READILY, READINESS, **rough and ready** (ROUGH¹ (13))

ready² *n* **1 at the ready** *especially BrE* available to be used immediately【尤英】处于准备好的状态，可随时使用：*The crowd stood around, cameras at the ready.* 人群站在四周，照相机随时准备拍照。**2 the readies** *BrE slang* money that is available to be used immediately【英俚】现钱：*I'm trying to scrape together the readies to pay for a trip to Hong Kong.* 我正在努力攒现钱支付去香港旅行的费用。

ready³ *v* [T] *formal* to make something ready【正式】预备，准备

ready-made /ˌ‥ ˈ‥◄/ *adj* [only before noun 仅用于名词前] **1** already prepared, and ready to be used immediately 现成的，预先做好的：*ready-made bolognese sauce* 调制好的博洛尼亚调味汁 **2** convenient and immediately available for you to use 方便的，现成的：*The rain gave us a ready-made excuse to stay at home.* 这场雨给了我们一个待在家里的现成借口。**3** ready-made opinions or ideas have been copied from someone else〔观点、思想〕老一套的，照搬他人的 **4** READY-TO-WEAR〔衣服〕现成的

ready-to-wear /ˌ‥ · ˈ·◄/ *adj old-fashioned* ready-to-wear clothes are made in standard sizes, not made specially to fit one person【过时】〔衣服〕现成的，预先做好的

re·af·firm /ˌriəˈfɝm; ˌriːəˈfɜːm/ *v* [T] to formally state an intention, belief etc again, especially as an answer to a question or doubt 重申，再次肯定：*The conference overwhelmingly reaffirmed its commitment to nuclear disarmament.* 会议以压倒多数重申它对裁减核武器所承担的义务。| **[+that]** *The statement reaffirmed that the government would never make concessions to terrorists.* 该声明重申，政府决不向恐怖分子让步。—**reaffirmation** /ˌriæfɚˈmeʃən; ˌriːæfəˈmeɪʃən/ *n* [C,U]

re·af·for·es·ta·tion /ˌriəfɔrəsˈteʃən; ˌriːəfɒrɪ̩ˈsteɪʃən/ *n* [U] *BrE technical* REFORESTATION【英，术语】重新造林

Reagan /ˈregən; ˈreɪgən/, **Ron·ald** /ˈrɑnḷd; ˈrɒnəld/ (1911-2004) a US politician in the Republican Party who was President of the US from 1981 to 1989. He reduced taxes, increased military spending, and improved the US's political relationship with the USSR by meeting President Gorbachev. He was called 'The Great Communicator' because of his ability to make speeches in a friendly and sincere way that made people trust him. Before Reagan became president he was a film actor and the Governor of California from 1967 to 1975. 里根（(1911-2004），美国共和党政治家，1981至1989年任美国总统。任职期间，他减低税赋，增加军备开支，与戈尔巴乔夫总统会晤，改善美苏政治关系。他讲话友好、真诚，赢得人民的信任，有"杰出交际家"之称。就任总统前，他曾当过电影演员，1967至1975年任加利福尼亚州州长）

Rea·gan·om·ics /ˌregəˈnɑmɪks; ˌreɪgəˈnɒmɪks/ the economic policies of the US government during the time when Ronald Reagan was president (1981-89), especially the POLICY of reducing taxes and reducing government spending on WELFARE (=help for poor people, people without jobs etc) 里根经济学〔罗纳德·里根任总统期间（1981-1989）美国政府采取的经济政策，尤指政府减低税赋和减少福利开支的政策〕

re·a·gent /riˈedʒənt; riˈeɪdʒənt/ *n* [C] *technical* a substance that shows that another substance in a compound exists, by causing a chemical REACTION (4a)【术语】试剂，试药

real¹ /ˈriəl; rɪəl/ *adj*
1 ►NOT ARTIFICIAL 非人造的◄ something that is real is actually what it seems to be and not false, artificial or pretended 真的，真正的，真实的：*Is that ring made of real gold?* 那枚戒指是真金的吗？| *He calls himself Peter Jones, but it's not his real name.* 他说自己叫彼得·琼斯，但那不是他的真实姓名。| *He's never shown any real regret.* 他从未表示出真心的歉意。| **the real thing/the real McCoy** *I don't like reproductions. It has to be the real thing or nothing.* 我不喜欢复制品，要就要真货。| *This is the real McCoy – genuine malt whisky.* 这是货真价实的东西——纯正的麦芽威士忌。
2 ►NOT IMAGINARY 非幻想的◄ actually existing and not just imagined 实际存在的，非想象的：*The children know that Santa Claus isn't a real person.* 孩子们知道圣诞老人不是真实的人物。| **very real danger/possibility/risk etc** *There is a very real danger of an explosion.* 确实存在爆炸的危险。| **in real life** *That kind of thing only happens in films, not in real life.* 那种事只发生在电影里，而不是现实生活中。| **in the real world** (=in actual situations where people have to deal with practical problems) 在现实世界里 *idealistic theories that don't work in the real world* 在现实世界里行不通的理想主义理论
3 ►TRUE 真的◄ actual and true, not what people think or say 真正的，真实的：*John later told me the real reason for his absence.* 约翰后来告诉我他缺席的真正原因。
4 ►PROPER 适当的◄ [only before noun 仅用于名词前] having all the right qualities that you expect a particular kind of thing or person to have 真正的，地道的：*Now he's what I'd call a real man.* 他就是我所说的真正的男人。| *The next day we had our first real meeting.* 第二天我们开了第一次真正的会议。
5 a real idiot/beauty/disaster etc *spoken* used to emphasize how stupid, beautiful, terrible etc someone or something is【口】十足的傻瓜/绝色美女/巨大的灾难等〔用于加强语气〕：*You're a real idiot!* 你是个十足的傻瓜！| *Our marriage was a real disaster!* 我们的婚姻真是一场灾难！| *Thanks – you've been a real help.* 谢谢，你帮了我大忙。
6 no real chance/hope/reason etc if there is no real chance etc, there is almost no chance 几乎没有机会/希望/理由等：*There's no real hope of Rod passing this examination.* 罗德通过这次考试的希望渺茫。
7 ►MOST IMPORTANT 最重要的◄ the real questions, problems etc are the most important ones 最重要的：*The government has failed to deal with the real issues.* 政府没能解决最重要的问题。
8 real income/costs/value etc income etc that is calculated after including in the calculation the general decrease in the value of money〔已把货币贬值计算在内的〕实际收入/成本/价值等：*a 2% annual growth in real income* 实际收入年增长两个百分点 | **in real terms** (=calculated in this way) 按照实际价值 *In real terms, the value of their wages has fallen.* 他们工资的实际价值减少了。
9 for real *spoken, especially AmE* seriously, not pretending【口，尤美】真正地，确实地，认真地：*After two trial runs we did it for real.* 经过两次试验，我们真正干了起来。
10 get real! *spoken, especially AmE* used to tell someone that they are being very silly or unreasonable【口，尤美】别傻了！别犯浑了！
11 are you for real? *AmE spoken* used when you are very surprised by or disapprove of what someone has done or said【美口】你是认真的？〔表示吃惊或不赞同〕

real² *adv AmE spoken* very【美口】非常：*I'm real sorry!* 我非常抱歉！| *He's real smart.* 他非常精明。

real es·tate /ˈ· ·ˌ·/ *n* [U] *especially AmE*【尤美】**1** property in the form of land or houses 房地产，不动产 **2** the business of selling houses or land 房地产业

real estate a·gent /ˈ· ·ˌ·, ·ˈ·/ *n* [C] *AmE* someone whose job is to sell houses or land for other people; ESTATE AGENT【美】房地产经纪人

re·a·lign /ˌriəˈlaɪn; ˌriːəˈlaɪn/ *v* [T] **1** to arrange something differently in relation to something else 重新排列：*You'll have to realign your text columns if you change the typeface.* 你如果要改动字体，就必须重新排列正文各栏。**2** to change the aims and relationships that a political party or other organization has 重新组合，调整〔政党或其他组织的目标和关系等〕：*an attempt to realign the relationship between the state and private business* 调整国家与私营企业之间关系的尝试

re·a·lign·ment /ˌriəˈlaɪnmənt; ˌriːəˈlaɪnmənt/ *n* [C,U] **1** a change in the way two or more things are organized, so that they have a different relationship to each other 重新组合：**[+of]** *a realignment of political parties* 政治党派之间的重新组合 **2** the process of arranging parts of something so that they return to their correct positions in relation to each other 复位：*the realignment of broken bones* 断骨的复位

Real IRA, the /ˌ· ˈ· ·/ a group that in 1998 exploded a bomb in the town of Omagh in Northern Ireland, which killed 28 people and injured more than 200. The Real IRA was formed in 1997 by members of the IRA who disagreed with the peace process. 真爱尔兰共和军〔该组织策划了1998年的北爱尔兰奥马炸弹袭击

事件，造成28人死亡，200多人受伤。真爱尔兰共和军成立于1997年，成员为反对和平进程的爱尔兰共和军分子）

re·al·is·m /ˈriəlˌɪzəm; ˈrɪəlɪzəm/ *n* [U] **1** the ability to accept and deal with situations in a practical way, without being influenced by feelings or false ideas 现实主义 **2** also 又作 **Realism** the style of art and literature in which everything is shown or described as it really is in life 现实主义，写实主义〔艺术、文学上的风格〕—**realist** *n* [C]

S3 **re·al·is·tic** /ˌriəˈlɪstɪk; rɪəˈlɪstɪk/ *adj* **1** judging and dealing with situations in a practical way according to what is actually possible 现实的，实际的：*It's just not realistic to expect a promotion so soon.* 这么快就想升职根本不现实。| *a realistic estimate of the costs* 对费用的现实估计 | **be realistic** (=think in a sensible, practical way) 持现实的态度 *Come on, be realistic – you can't just afford it!* 得啦！现实点，你根本花费不起！—opposite 反义词 UNREALISTIC **2** pictures, models, plays etc that are realistic show things as they are in real life〔图画、模型、戏剧等〕逼真的，栩栩如生的：*Her drawings aren't very realistic.* 她的画不太逼真。| *a realistic television drama* 一部写实的电视剧

re·al·is·tic·ally /ˌriəˈlɪstɪkl̩ɪ; rɪəˈlɪstɪkli/ *adv* **1** in a practical way and according to what is actually possible 现实地，实际地：*You have to look realistically at the options available.* 你必须现实地对待现有的选择。| [sentence adverb 句子副词] *Realistically, we can't expect things to improve before the end of next year.* 说实在的，我们不能指望情况在明年年底之前有改善。**2** in a way that shows or describes things as they are in real life 逼真地，栩栩如生地：*She told the ghost story so realistically that they were terrified.* 她把鬼故事讲得活灵活现，他们都感到害怕。

S2 W2 **re·al·i·ty** /rɪˈæləti; riˈælətɪ/ *n* **1** [U] things that actually happen or are true, not things that are imagined or thought about 真实，现实：*She can't tell the difference between fantasy and reality.* 她无法区分幻想与现实。| *Books can be an escape from reality.* 读书可以逃避现实。**2 in reality** used to say something is different from what people think 实际上：*Henry always seems so self-confident, but in reality he's extremely shy.* 亨利看来总是很自信，实际上他极为腼腆。**3 become a reality** to actually happen 成为现实：*Marilyn's dream of being a film star became a reality.* 玛丽莲想当电影明星的梦想成为了现实。**4 the reality/realities of** what actually happens in a situation, rather than what you think might happen …的实际情况：*They were unprepared for the reality of city life.* 他们对城市生活的现实情况毫无准备。| **harsh realities** *the harsh realities of unemployment* 失业的严酷现实 **5 the reality is that** used to say that the truth about a situation is very different from what people say 实际情况是…：*They keep saying we'll get the money, but the reality is that there's none left.* 他们再三说我们会得到钱的，但实际情况是没有钱剩下来。

rea·liz·a·ble also 又作 **realisable** *BrE*【英】/ˈriəˌlaɪzəbl; ˈrɪəlaɪzəbəl/ *adj* **1** possible to achieve 可实现的：*realizable goals* 可实现的目标 **2** in a form that can be changed into money 可换为现款的：*realizable value* 可变现价值

re·a·li·za·tion also 又作 **realisation** *BrE*【英】/ˌriələˈzeʃən; ˌrɪəlaɪˈzeɪʃən/ *n* [singular,U] **1** the act of understanding something that you had not noticed before 认识，领悟，意识：**[+that]** *the realization that changes were needed in the organization* 对组织需要有改变的认识 **2** the act of achieving what you had planned, hoped, or aimed for〔计划、希望、目标的〕实现：**[+of]** *the realization of happiness* 幸福的实现 **3 [+of]** the act of changing something into money by selling it 变卖，变现

S1 W1 **rea·lize** also 又作 **-ise** *BrE*【英】/ˈriəˌlaɪz; ˈrɪəlaɪz/ *v* [T not usually in progressive 一般不用进行时]

1 ▶KNOW STH'S IMPORTANCE 知道某事物的重要性◀ to know and understand the importance of something 知道，了解，认识到〔某事物的重要性〕：**realize (that)** *Do you realize that you're an hour late?* 你知道你迟到了一小时吗？| **realize who/what/how etc** *I realize how much she means to you.* 我知道她对你有多么重要。| **realize sth** *None of us realized the danger we were in.* 我们当中谁也没有意识到我们所处的险境。

2 ▶KNOW STH NEW 认识新事物◀ to start to know something that you had not noticed before 开始认识，领悟，意识到〔以前没有注意的事物〕：**realize (that)** *I suddenly realized he was crying.* 我突然发现他在哭。| *Later, we realized that we'd met before in Paris.* 我们后来才想起我们曾在巴黎见过面。| **realize who/what/how etc** *I realized then how hungry I was.* 那时我才意识到我有多么饿。| **realize sth** *Tim didn't realize his mistake until the next day.* 蒂姆直到第二天才知道他的错误。

3 realize an ambition/hope/goal etc *formal* to achieve something that you were hoping to achieve【正式】实现抱负/愿望/目标等：*She has finally realized her ambition of becoming a teacher.* 她终于实现了当教师的抱负。

4 sb's worst fears were realized used to say that the thing that you were afraid of actually happened 某人最害怕的事情发生了：*My worst fears were realized when I saw the exam questions.* 我一看到考题，就知道我最害怕的事情发生了。

5 ▶MONEY 金钱◀ a) to obtain an amount of money, especially by selling something〔通过出售而〕获得：*The initial campaign has realized $5000 in cash and pledges.* 初次活动就筹到了5000美元，包括现金和承诺捐款。| **realize a profit on sth** *We realized a profit on the house.* 我们卖房子赚了一笔钱。**b)** to change something that you own into money, especially by selling it 变卖：*We were obliged to realize most of our assets.* 我们不得不变卖我们的大部分资产。

real·ly /ˈriəli; ˈrɪəli/ *adv* S1 W1

1 ▶THE REAL SITUATION 真实情形◀ used when you are saying what is actually the truth of a situation, rather than what people might wrongly think 真实地，真正地：*What really happened?* 究竟发生了什么事？| *Oliver was not really her cousin.* 奥利弗其实不是她的表兄弟。| *You are pretending to be annoyed, but you're not really.* 你在装出生气的样子，其实你并不生气。

2 ▶DEFINITELY 确实地◀ *especially spoken* used to emphasize something you are saying【尤口】确实地，的确〔用于加强语气〕：*You ought really to have asked me first.* 你真该事先问问我的。| *I really don't mind.* 我真的不介意。| *I'm absolutely fine, Dad – really.* 我绝对没事，爸爸，真的。

3 ▶VERY MUCH 非常◀ very much; extremely 非常，极其：*really nice* 非常好 | *His letter really irritated her.* 他的信着实激怒了她。| *It doesn't really matter, does it?* 这不太要紧，对不对？

Frequencies of the adverb **really** in spoken and written English 副词 really 在英语口语和书面语中的使用频率

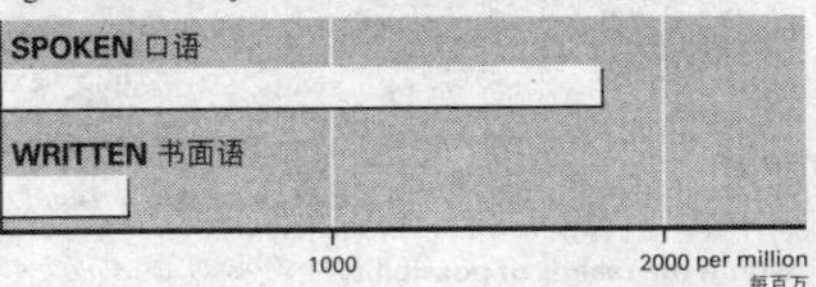

Based on the British National Corpus and the Longman Lancaster Corpus
据英国国家语料库和朗文兰开斯特语料库

This graph shows that the adverb **really** is much more common in spoken English than in written English. This is because it is used a lot in spoken English to emphasize what you are saying. It also has some special uses as a reply in conversation and is used in some common spoken phrases. 本图表显示，副词 really 在英语口语中的使用频率远远高于书面语，因为口语中经常用它来强调所说的话。really 还有一些特殊的用法，在对话中用于回答对方所说的话，而且口语中一些常用短语是由 really 构成的。

really (*adv*) **SPOKEN PHRASES**
含 really 的口语短语

4 really? a) used to show that you are surprised by what someone has said 是吗？真的？〔用于对某人的话表示吃惊〕：*"There are something like 87 McDonalds in Hong Kong." "Really?"* "香港有大约87家麦当劳快餐店。""是吗？" **b)** used in conversation to show that you are listening to or interested in what the other person is saying 真的？〔表示正在倾听或对对方的话感兴趣〕：*"I think we might go to the Grand Canyon in June." "Oh, really?"* "我看我们可以在六月份去大峡谷。""噢，真的吗？" **c)** *AmE* used to express agreement【美】是啊〔表示赞同〕：*"It's a pain having to get here so early." "Yeah, really!"* "必须这么早就到，可真让人痛苦。""可不是吗！" **d)** *especially BrE* used to express disapproval【尤英】真是的〔表示不赞成〕：*Really, Larry, you might have told me!* 真是的，拉里，你本该告诉我的！

5 not really used to say 'no' or 'not completely' 不是；不全是：*"Do you want to come along?" "Not really."* "你想一起去吗？""不太想。"

6 I don't really know used to say that you are not certain about something 我不太清楚〔表示没有把握〕：*I don't really know what he's up to. I haven't heard from him for ages.* 我不太清楚他在干什么，已经好久没听到他的消息了。

7 I really don't know used to say that you definitely do not know something, especially when someone has asked you about it 我确实不知道：*I can't answer that, I really don't know.* 我无法回答这个问题，我真的不知道。

8 **really and truly** used to emphasize a statement or opinion 真的〔用于加强语气〕: *Really and truly, I think you should tell him.* 真的, 我认为你应该告诉他。

USAGE NOTE 用法说明: REALLY

UK-US DIFFERENCE 英国英语－美国英语的区别

Really with an adjective or adverb meaning 'very' is common in British English, and is the usual word in American English. 在英国英语中, 用 really 修饰形容词或副词, 意为"非常"是很普通的, 在美国英语中则是最常用的词: *I'm really fed up with this job.* 我对这份工作厌倦透了。

In informal spoken American English **real** is often used. 在非正式美国口语中常用 real: *That's a real nice car.* 那是一辆很棒的汽车。

GRAMMAR 语法

Really meaning 'very' must go immediately before the adjective it strengthens. really 指"非常"时, 一定要紧接在所强调的形容词前面: *He's a really nice man* (=a very nice man). 他是一个非常好的人。| *I think she's really stupid.* 我觉得她非常愚蠢。

Really in other positions usually emphasises that what you are saying is true even though it might not seem to fit. really 在其他位置时强调所说是事实, 尽管表面上不一定对: *He's really a nice man* (=he is nice, though you might not think so). 他的确是个好人。| *She uses lots of long words, but really she's pretty stupid.* 她爱用大字眼, 其实她非常愚蠢。

Really is usually used before a verb but not immediately after it (except after the verb **to be**). really 通常用在动词前而不是紧接其后 (除动词 to be 外): *It's really cold in here.* 这里面的确很冷。| *She doesn't really know what to do.* 她不清楚该做些什么。

SPELLING 拼法

Remember there are two 'l's in **really**. 记住 really 有两个 l。

realm /rɛlm; relm/ *n* [C] **1** a general area of knowledge, interest, or thought〔知识、兴趣、思想的〕领域, 范围: *the spiritual realm* 精神领域 | [+of] *the realm of human history* 人类历史范畴 **2** **within the realms of possibility** possible 可能的: *Such a thing is not within the realms of possibility.* 这种事是不可能的。**3** *literary* a country ruled over by a king or queen【文】王国 **4** **the Realm** *formal* the United Kingdom【正式】联合王国: *the defence of the Realm* 联合王国的防务

Real Madrid /ˌ· ˌ·ˈ·/ a Spanish football club which was started in 1902. It is the most successful club in Europe, and has won the European Cup nine times, the UEFA Cup twice, and the World Club Cup twice. Among its famous players were Alfredo Di Stefano and Ferenc Puskas. 皇家马德里〔西班牙一足球俱乐部, 创建于 1902 年, 是欧洲最成功的俱乐部, 九次夺得欧洲冠军杯冠军, 两次夺得欧洲联盟杯冠军, 两次捧走世俱杯。著名足球运动员有阿尔弗雷多·迪·斯蒂法诺和费雷克·普斯卡什〕

re·al·pol·i·tik /reˈɑlˌpolɪˌtik; reɪˈɑːlpɒlɪtiːk/ *n* [U] politics based on practical situations and needs rather than on moral principles or ideas 现实政治〔基于现实情况和需要而不是道德原则或思想的政治〕

real prop·er·ty /ˌ· ˈ···/ *n* [U] *law* REAL ESTATE (1)【法律】房地产, 不动产

real-time /ˈ· ·/ *adj* [only before noun 仅用于名词前] *technical* a real-time computer system deals with information as fast as it receives it【术语】〔电脑〕即时处理的, 实时的 —**real time** *n* [U]: *Airline booking systems need to work in real time.* 航空公司的订票系统需要实时工作。

real·tor /ˈriəltɚ; ˈrɪəltə/ *n* [C] *AmE* a REAL ESTATE AGENT【美】房地产经纪人

ream[1] /rim; riːm/ *n* [C] **1** **reams** [plural] *informal* a large amount of writing on paper【非正式】〔写作的〕大量: [+of] *reams of notes* 大量的笔记 **2** *AmE* 500 pieces of paper【美】令〔纸张的计数单位, 在美国为 500 张〕 **3** *BrE* 480 pieces of paper【英】令〔纸张的计数单位, 在英国为480 张〕

ream[2] *v* [T] **1** *AmE informal* to treat someone badly, especially by cheating【美, 非正式】〔尤指通过欺骗而〕亏待; 欺诈 **2** *technical* to make a hole larger【术语】把〔孔〕扩大

re·an·i·mate /riˈænəˌmet; riːˈænɪmeɪt/ *v* [T] *formal* to give someone or something new strength or the energy to start again【正式】重振, 使重新获得力量

reap /rip; riːp/ *v* [I,T] **1** to cut and gather a crop of grain 收割 **2** **reap the benefit/reward/profit (of)** to get something good as a result of what you have done 受益/得到回报/获利: *Don't let others reap the benefits of your research.* 不要让别人坐享你的研究成果。—**reaper** *n* [C] —compare 比较 HARVEST[2]

re·ap·pear /ˌriəˈpɪr; ˌriːəˈpɪə/ *v* [I] to appear again after not being seen for some time 再现, 再出现: *They felt tense, knowing that he might reappear at any time.* 他们感到紧张, 因为知道他随时可能再次出现。—**reappearance** *n* [C,U]

re·ap·praise /ˌriəˈprez; ˌriːəˈpreɪz/ *v* [T] to examine something again in order to consider whether you should change your opinion of it 重新估计, 重新评价: *The time had come to reappraise their economic strategy.* 应该重新评价他们的经济策略了。—**reappraisal** *n* [C,U]

rear[1] /rɪr; rɪə/ *n* **1** **the rear** the back part of an object, vehicle or building, or a position at the back of an object or area 后部, 后面, 背部: *a garden at the rear of the house* 屋后的花园 | *The engine is in the rear.* 发动机在后边。—compare 比较 FRONT[1] (2) **2** [C] *informal* the part of your body which you sit on; BOTTOM[1] (7)【非正式】臀部 **3** **bring up the rear** to be at the back of a line of people or in a race 处在最后; 殿后: *Bringing up the rear is the smallest yacht in the race.* 最后到终点的是本次比赛中最小的快艇。

rear[2] *v* **1** [T] to look after a person or animal until they are fully grown 养育, 抚养; 饲养: *She's reared a large family.* 她抚养一大群孩子。| *cattle rearing* 养牛 —see 见 RAISE[1] (USAGE) **2** also 又作 **rear up** [I] if an animal rears, it rises upright on its back legs〔动物〕用后腿站起: *The horse reared and threw me off.* 那匹马后腿直立, 把我摔了下来。—compare 比较 BUCK[2] (1) **3** **be reared on** to be given a particular kind of food, books, entertainment etc regularly while you are a child〔小时候〕总是吃〔某种食物〕; 看〔某类书〕; 玩〔某类游戏〕: *reared on a diet of potatoes* 吃马铃薯长大的 **4** **rear its ugly head** if a problem or difficult situation rears its ugly head, it appears and is impossible to ignore〔问题、困境〕冒头, 出现: *Scandal rears its ugly head again.* 丑闻再次冒出来了。

rear[3] *adj* [only before noun 仅用于名词前] at or near the back of something 后部的, 后面的: *the rear door of the car* 汽车的后门 | *knock at the rear entrance* 敲后门

rear ad·mi·ral /ˌ· ˈ···◂/ *n* [C] a high rank in the navy 海军少将 —see table on page C6 参见 C6 页附录

rear·guard /ˈrɪrˌgɑrd; ˈrɪəgɑːd/ *n* **fight a rearguard action** **a)** to make a determined effort to prevent a change that you think is bad, although it seems too late to stop it 竭尽全力〔防止…〕: *A rearguard action is being fought against the sale of the land for business development.* 正在竭尽全力地反对出售这块地作商业开发。**b)** if an army fights a rearguard action, it defends itself at the back against an enemy that is chasing it 殿后作战, 后卫战斗〔由后卫部队阻击追兵〕

re·arm /riˈɑrm; riːˈɑːm/ *v* [I,T] to obtain weapons again or provide someone else with new weapons 重新武装: *If we're going to fight we must rearm.* 假如我们要打仗, 必须重新武装。| **rearm sb with sth** *They rearmed their allies with modern missiles.* 他们用现代化导弹重新装备了他们的盟国。—**rearmament** *n* [U]

rear·most /ˈrɪrˌmost; ˈrɪəməʊst/ *adj* [only before noun 仅用于名词前] furthest back; last 最后 (面) 的: *the rearmost carriage of the train* 火车的最后一节车厢

re·ar·range /ˌriəˈrendʒ; ˌriːəˈreɪndʒ/ *v* [T] **1** to change the position or order of things 重新安排, 重新布置: *Let's rearrange the furniture and have the desk by the window.* 我们来把家具重新布置一下, 把书桌靠窗放。**2** to change the time of a meeting etc 重新安排〔会期等〕 —**rearrangement** *n* [C,U]

rear·view mir·ror /ˌrɪrvju ˈmɪrɚ; ˌrɪəvjuː ˈmɪrə/ *n* [C] a mirror in a car etc that lets the driver see the area behind〔汽车〕后视镜 —see picture on page A2 参见 A2 页图

rear·ward /ˈrɪrwɚd; ˈrɪəwəd/ *adj* in or towards the back of something 在后面的, 在后部的; 向后面的 —**rearwards** also 又作 **rearward** *adv*

rea·son[1] /ˈrizn̩; ˈriːzən/ *n*

1 ►**CAUSE** 原因◄ [C] the cause or explanation for something that has happened or that someone has done 原因, 理由: *The reason I bought one was that it was so cheap.* 我买了一个, 因为价钱很便宜。| **reason (that)** *The only reason I went was that I wanted to meet your friends.* 我去的唯一理由是想见见你的朋友们。| **reason why** *We'd like to know the reason why she didn't accept the job.* 我们希望知道她不接受这份工作的理由是什么。| [+for] *I can see no reason for their behaviour.* 我不明白他们为何要这样做。| **give a reason** (=explain) 解释 *She just left without giving any reason.* 她没作任何解释就离开了。| **for personal/health etc reasons** *She wants to change her job for purely personal reasons.* 她想换工作纯属个人原因。| **for reasons of** *The main tower has been closed for reasons of safety.* 主塔由于

安全原因已经关闭。| **by reason of** *formal*【正式】*He was found not guilty by reason of insanity.* 他因为精神失常而被判无罪。| **for some reason** *especially spoken* (=for a reason that you do not know or cannot understand)【尤口】由于某种原因 *They've decided to change all our job titles, for some reason.* 由于某种原因，他们已决定更改我们所有人的职位名称。| **have your reasons** *spoken* (=have a secret reason for doing something)【口】有自己的理由 *"Why did you tell him?" "Oh, I had my reasons."* "你为什么要告诉他？""噢，我有我的道理。" | **for reasons best known to yourself** (=for reasons that other people do not understand) 由于别人不知道的原因 *For reasons best known to herself, she's sold the house and left the country.* 她已经卖掉房子离开了这个国家，没有人知道原因。—see 见 EXCUSE[2] (USAGE)

2 ▶GOOD OR FAIR REASON 好的或充分的理由◀ [U] a fact that makes it right or fair for someone to do something〔正确或充分的〕理由：**reason to do sth** *I have no reason to believe that Grant's death was not an accident.* 我没有理由相信格兰特的死不是意外事故。| *There is no reason to panic.* 没有理由惊慌失措。| **have every reason to do sth** (=have very good reasons for doing something) 完全有理由做某事 *Under the circumstances we had every reason to be suspicious.* 在这种情况下，我们有充分的理由表示怀疑。| **be no reason to do sth** *I know I'm late, but that's no reason to shout at me.* 我知道我迟到了，但也没理由对我大喊大叫。| **with (good) reason** (=not stupidly or unnecessarily)（完全）合乎情理 *Natalie was alarmed by the news, and with reason.* 纳塔莉听到消息很惊慌，这是合乎情理的。

3 all the more reason to do sth *spoken* used to say that what has just been mentioned is an additional reason for doing what you have suggested【口】更有理由做某事：*"She's going on holiday soon." "All the more reason to ask her today."* "她就要去度假了。""那更有理由今天去问她。"

4 ▶GOOD JUDGMENT 好的判断力◀ sensible judgment and understanding 道理：*There's reason in what he says.* 他说的话有道理。| **listen to reason** (=be persuaded by someone's sensible advice) 听取意见 *We keep telling her why it won't work, but she just won't listen to reason.* 我们一再告诉她这样做为什么不行，可是她怎么也不听劝告。| **see reason** (=accept advice and make a sensible decision) 明白事理；接受劝告 *They tried to make him see reason.* 他们试图使他明白道理。

5 within reason within sensible limits 有道理，合乎情理：*You can go anywhere you want, within reason.* 你可以想去哪里就去哪里，不过要有分寸。

6 go/be beyond all reason to be more than is acceptable or reasonable 不合理：*Their demands go beyond all reason.* 他们的要求太不合理了。

7 ▶ABILITY TO THINK 思考能力◀ [U] the ability to think, understand and form judgments that are based on facts 思考能力，判断力，理智：*The power of reason separates us from other animals.* 理性使我们不同于其他的动物。| **lose your reason** *old-fashioned* (=become mentally ill)【过时】失去理智；患精神病

8 no reason *spoken* used when someone asks you why you are doing something and you do not want to tell them【口】不为什么〔用于不想解释自己为什么做某事〕：*"Why d'you want to go that way?" "Oh, no reason."* "你为什么想走那条路？""噢，不为什么。" —see also 另见 **without rhyme or reason** (RHYME[1] (4)), **it stands to reason** (STAND[1] (40))

USAGE NOTE 用法说明：REASON

WORD CHOICE 词语辨析：**cause, reason, purpose**

A **cause** is anything that produces a result, often not a person. cause 指会产生结果的原因，一般不用于人：*the causes of inflation* 通货膨胀的原因 | *the cause of the accident* 事故的原因

A **reason** explains something, often after it has happened or been done. reason 是某件事情的解释，往往是它发生以后才提出的理由：*There was no reason for the attack.* 袭击是没有道理的。| *There are several reasons why the plan won't work.* 计划行不通有几个理由。| *Give me one good reason.* 给我一个好的理由吧。

A **purpose** is what you hope to achieve by something you do, and is intentional. purpose 是指通过努力想要实现的目标，是有意识的：*Their purpose is to attract attention to environmental issues.* 他们的目的是引起对环境问题的关注。

GRAMMAR 语法

Reason is often followed by **for, that,** or **why**. reason 后面常接 for, that, why: *What's the reason for all this noise?* (NOT 不用 the reason **of** or 或 **to**) 为什么这么吵？| *the reason that/why he left* (NOT 不用 *the reason because/how he left...*) 他离开的原因 It is also possible to leave out **that**. that 也可省略：*the reason he left* 他离开的原因

The nature of a **reason** is usually described in a *that* clause. reason 后一般用 that 引导的从句说明原因：*The reason for the party was that it was Sue's birthday.* 这次聚会的理由是庆祝休的生日。In spoken English you may also hear *because* used, though this is considered to be incorrect by many speakers. 英语口语中也有人使用 because，但不少人认为这种用法有误：*The reason for the party is because it's Sue's birthday.* 这次聚会是为了庆祝休的生日。

Purpose is often followed by **of** or **in**. purpose 常与 of 或 in 连用：*The purpose of the trip/of my coming is to see the President* (NOT 不用 *the purpose why I'm coming*). 此次旅行/我来的目的是见总统。| *My purpose in coming is to see the President* (NOT 不用 *of/for coming...*). 我来的目的是见总统。

People usually say 人们通常说 *For this reason/purpose...* (NOT 不用 *from/because of this reason..., in/on this purpose* or 或 *for this cause*) 为此原因/目的

reason[2] *v* **1** [T] to form a particular judgment about a situation after carefully considering the facts 论证，推断，分析：**reason (that)** *We reasoned that the terrorists would not negotiate unless we made some concessions.* 我们推断，除非我们作出某些让步，否则恐怖分子是不会谈判的。**2** [I] to think and make judgments 推理，判断，思考：*the ability to reason* 推理的能力

reason sth **out** *phr v* [T] to find an explanation or solution to a problem, by thinking of all the possibilities〔通过推理〕解释，解决：*Let's reason this out instead of quarrelling.* 我们不要争吵了，还是想想其中的道理吧。

reason with sb *phr v* [T] to talk to someone in order to try to persuade them to be more sensible 与…讲道理：*I tried to reason with her but she locked herself in the bathroom, crying.* 我想和她讲道理，她却把自己锁在浴室里哭。

rea·son·a·ble /ˈriznəbl̩; ˈriːzənəbəl/ *adj* **1** fair and sensible 讲道理的，合情理的：*Be reasonable – you can't expect her to do all the work on her own!* 要讲道理，你不能指望她一个人干所有的工作！| *a reasonable request* 合情合理的要求 | **it is reasonable to do sth** *It's reasonable to suppose that prices will come down soon.* 认为价格很快会下降是有道理的。—opposite 反义词 UNREASONABLE **2** fairly good, but not especially good 相当好的，不错的：*She has a reasonable chance of doing well in the exam.* 她考试考得好的可能性相当大。**3** a reasonable amount is not too much or too many 适度的：*They let a reasonable amount of time pass before visiting him again.* 他们适当过了一段时间之后才再次去看他。**4** prices that are reasonable seem fair because they are not too high〔价格〕公道的：*good quality furniture at reasonable prices* 价格公道的优质家具 —see 见 CHEAP[1] (USAGE) **5 beyond reasonable doubt** *law* if something is proved beyond reasonable doubt, it is shown to be almost certainly true【法律】无疑 —**reasonableness** *n* [U]

rea·son·a·bly /ˈriznəblɪ; ˈriːzənəbli/ *adv* **1** [+adj/adv] to a satisfactory degree, although not completely 相当地：*The car is in reasonably good condition.* 这车的车况相当好。| *I was reasonably happy with the results.* 我对结果相当满意。**2** in a way that is right or fair 合情理地，公允地：*He can't reasonably be expected to have known that.* 按照情理，他不应该知道情况。**3** in a sensible and reasonable way 理性地，有理智地：*Despite her anger, she had behaved very reasonably.* 她虽然生气，但表现得很理智。

rea·soned /ˈriznd; ˈriːzənd/ *adj* [only before noun 仅用于名词前] based on careful thought, and therefore sensible 经过缜密思考的，理智的：*a reasoned approach to the problem* 经过缜密思考的解决问题的办法

rea·son·ing /ˈriznɪŋ; ˈriːzənɪŋ/ *n* [U] a process of thinking carefully about something in order to make a judgment 推理，推论：*logical reasoning* 逻辑推理 | **the reasoning behind** *What is the reasoning behind this proposal?* 这项建议有什么道理？

re·as·sur·ance /ˌriəˈʃʊrəns; ˌriːəˈʃʊərəns/ *n* **1** [U] help or advice that makes you feel less worried or frightened about a problem 安慰，慰藉：*Martin always looked to his sister for reassurance.* 马丁总是指望姐姐来安慰他。**2** [C] a remark or statement that makes someone feel calmer about something that is worrying them 安慰，宽慰（的话）：*The patient needed repeated reassurances.* 病人需要反复安慰。

re·as·sure /ˌriəˈʃʊr; ˌriːəˈʃʊə/ *v* [T] to make someone feel calmer and less worried or frightened about a problem or situation 使安心，使放心，安慰：*I was reassured by their offer of*

support. 他们表示支持，使我感到安慰。| **reassure sb (that)** *They apologized and reassured us that the matter would be dealt with immediately.* 他们表示歉意，并向我们保证问题会立即得到处理。—see 见 INSURE (USAGE)

re·as·sur·ing /ˌriəˈʃʊrɪŋ; ˌriːəˈʃʊərɪŋ◂/ *adj* making you feel less worried or frightened 使人安心的，使人放心的，安慰的：*It's reassuring to know that there's always someone around to help.* 知道时刻会有人来帮忙，叫你感到放心。—**reassuringly** *adv: She smiled reassuringly at the newcomers.* 她微笑着让新来的人放心。

re·bar·ba·tive /rɪˈbɑrbətɪv; rɪˈbɑːbətɪv/ *adj formal* very unattractive or offensive【正式】令人讨厌的；唐突的：*Karajan has been subject to rebarbative questioning and criticism.* 卡拉扬一直受到令人讨厌的质询和批评。

re·bate /ˈribet; ˈriːbeɪt/ *n* [C] an amount of money that is paid back to you when you have paid too much tax, rent etc〔税、租金等的〕回扣；部分退款：*In the end I managed to claim a tax rebate.* 最后我设法取得退税。

reb·el¹ /ˈrɛbl̩; ˈrebəl/ *n* [C] **1** someone who opposes or fights against people in authority 造反者；反叛者：*Anti-government rebels have seized the radio station.* 反政府的叛乱分子占领了电台。| *rebel soldiers* 叛乱的士兵 **2** someone who refuses to do things in the normal way, or the way that other people want them to〔拒绝按常规办事、我行我素的〕反叛者，叛逆者：*Tom has always been the rebel of the family.* 汤姆始终是家庭的叛逆者。| *a teenage rebel* 叛逆少年

R

re·bel² /rɪˈbɛl; rɪˈbel/ *v* **rebelled, rebelling** [I] to oppose or fight against someone in a position of authority 造反；反叛：[**+against**] *the story of a teenager who rebels against his father* 少年反抗父亲的故事 | *those who had rebelled against the government* 那些反抗政府的人

re·bel·lion /rɪˈbɛljən; rɪˈbeljən/ *n* [C,U] **1** an organised attempt to change the government, or other authority, using violence 造反；叛乱；起义：*an armed rebellion* 武装叛乱 | [**+against**] *a rebellion against the military regime* 反抗军事政权的起义 | **put down/crush a rebellion** (=use violence to stop it) 镇压叛乱 **2** active opposition to someone in authority 反抗；抗争：*a rebellion by right-wing members of the party* 党内右翼党员的反抗 | [**+against**] *a clear rebellion against parental control* 对家长控制的明确反抗 —compare 比较 REVOLUTION (2)

re·bel·lious /rɪˈbɛljəs; rɪˈbeljəs/ *adj* **1** deliberately disobeying 叛逆的；反抗的：*rebellious teenagers* 叛逆的青少年 | *rebellious behaviour* 反叛行为 **2** fighting against the government of your country 造反的；起义的：*rebellious warlords* 造反的军阀 —**rebelliously** *adv* —**rebelliousness** *n* [U]

Rebel With·out a Cause /ˌ.. ..ˈ. ˈ./ (1955) a US film in which James Dean appeared as a TEENAGER from a middle class family who gets into trouble with the police. As a result of this performance Dean became the most typical example of a young REBEL (=someone who refuses to behave in the way that society expects).《无因的反叛》〔(1955)，美国一影片。詹姆斯·迪安在片中饰演一名少年，他出身中产阶级家庭，老是找警察的麻烦。迪安因为此片中的表演而成为反叛少年的典型〕

re·birth /riˈbɝθ; ˌriːˈbɜːθ/ *n* [singular] *formal* a change by which an important idea, feeling, or organization becomes active again【正式】〔思想、感情、组织的〕再生，复兴：*The 1980s saw a rebirth of conservative thinking.* 20 世纪 80 年代见证了保守主义思想的复兴。| *spiritual rebirth* 精神上的再生

re·boot /riˈbut; ˌriːˈbuːt/ *v* [I,T] if you reboot a computer, or if it reboots, you start it up again after it has stopped working〔电脑死机后〕重新启动：*Try rebooting the machine and see what happens.* 试试重新启动电脑，看会出现什么情况。

re·born /riˈbɔrn; ˌriːˈbɔːn/ *adj* [not before noun 不用于名词前] *literary*【文】**1** having become active again after being inactive 再生的；复兴的：*Our hopes of success were reborn when we received thousands of letters of support.* 收到数以千计的支持信，我们又有了成功的希望。**2 be reborn** to be born again, especially according to some beliefs, ancient stories etc〔信仰、传说等中的〕再生，转世

re·bound¹ /rɪˈbaund; rɪˈbaʊnd/ *v* **1** [I] if a ball or other moving object rebounds, it moves quickly back through the air, after hitting something〔球或其他运动物体〕弹回，跳回：[**+off**] *The ball rebounded off the wall and I caught it.* 球从墙上反弹回来，我把它接住了。**2** [I] if prices, values etc rebound, they increase again after decreasing〔价格、价值等下跌后的〕回升；反弹：*Share prices rebounded today after last week's losses.* 股票价格在上周下跌之后，今天反弹了。**3** [I,T] *technical* to catch a BASKETBALL after a player has tried unsuccessfully to get a point【术语】抢〔篮板球〕

rebound on/upon sb *phr v* [T not in passive 不用被动态] if a harmful action rebounds on someone, it has a bad effect on the person who did it 使自作自受

re·bound² /ˈriˌbaund; ˈriːbaʊnd/ *n* **1 on the rebound a)** someone who is on the rebound is upset or confused because a romantic relationship they had has ended〔因失恋而〕处于情绪波动的状态：*He married Victoria on the rebound, after Louise left him.* 路易丝离开他之后，他心灰意冷，与维多利亚结婚了。**b)** a ball that rebounds is moving back through the air after hitting something〔球〕在弹回时：*I caught the ball on the rebound.* 我接住了弹回的球。**2** [C] *technical* an act of catching a BASKETBALL after a player has tried unsuccessfully to get a point【术语】抢篮板球

re·buff /rɪˈbʌf; rɪˈbʌf/ *n* [C] *formal* an unkind or unfriendly answer to a friendly suggestion or offer of help; SNUB²【正式】回绝，断然拒绝：*Every attempt Yves made to befriend her met with a rebuff.* 伊夫每次向她表示友好都碰了一鼻子灰。—**rebuff** *v* [T]: *Brady rebuffed all her suggestions.* 布雷迪断然拒绝了她所有的建议。

re·build /riˈbɪld; ˌriːˈbɪld/ *past tense and past participle* **rebuilt** /-ˈbɪlt; -ˈbɪlt/ *v* [T] **1** to build something again, after it has been damaged or destroyed 重建：*Most of the houses you see were rebuilt after the Great Fire.* 你现在看到的房屋大多数都是伦敦大火之后重建的。**2** to make something strong and successful again 使复原，恢复：*The first priority is to rebuild the area's manufacturing industry.* 当务之急是恢复该地区的制造业。

re·buke /rɪˈbjuk; rɪˈbjuːk/ *v* [T] *formal* to speak to someone severely, about something they have done wrong【正式】斥责，指责：**rebuke sb for doing sth** *Father Cary rebuked her for using bad language.* 卡里神父指责她言语粗俗。—**rebuke** *n* [C, U]: *a stern rebuke* 严厉的斥责

re·but /rɪˈbʌt; rɪˈbʌt/ *v* **rebutted, rebutting** [T] *formal* to prove that a statement or a charge made against you is false; REFUTE【正式】驳斥，反驳 —**rebuttal** *n* [C]

re·cal·ci·trant /rɪˈkælsɪtrənt; rɪˈkælsɪ̵trənt/ *adj formal* refusing to do what you are told to do, even after you have been punished【正式】不顺从的，桀骜不驯的：*recalcitrant children* 难管束的孩子 —**recalcitrantly** *adv* —**recalcitrance** *n* [U]

re·call¹ /rɪˈkɔl; rɪˈkɔːl/ *v* [T]

1 ▶REMEMBER STH 记起某事◀ [not in progressive 不用进行时] to deliberately remember a particular fact, event, or situation from the past, especially in order to tell someone about it 回忆，回想：**recall that** *I seem to recall that Barry was with us at the time.* 我好像记得巴里当时是和我们在一起的。| **recall doing sth** *I don't recall ever meeting her.* 我想不起来曾经见过她。| **recall what/how/where etc** *Afterwards Olivia could not recall what they had talked about.* 之后，奥利维娅回想不起他们谈了些什么。| **as I recall** *spoken* (=used when you are telling someone what you remember about a past situation)【口】据我回忆 *As I recall, it was you who suggested this idea in the first place.* 据我回忆，是你首先提出这个想法的。

2 ▶PERSON 人◀ to officially tell someone to come back from a place where they have been sent 召回：[**+from**] *The Ambassador was recalled from Washington.* 大使被从华盛顿召回。

3 ▶PRODUCT 产品◀ if a company recalls one of its products, it asks you to return it because there may be something wrong with it 召回，收回〔有问题的产品〕：*The B Series cars have been recalled to the manufacturers due to an engine fault.* 由于发动机有问题，B 系列汽车已被制造商召回。

4 ▶ON A COMPUTER 在电脑上◀ to bring information back onto the screen of a computer〔在电脑屏幕上〕重新调出〔信息〕，检索

5 ▶BE SIMILAR TO 相似◀ if something recalls something else, it makes you think of it because it is very similar〔由于酷似而〕使回忆起：*a style of film-making that recalls Alfred Hitchcock* 一种使人想起希区柯克的电影摄制风格 —**recallable** *adj*

re·call² /ˈriˌkɔl; rɪˈkɔːl/ *n* **1** [U] the ability to remember something that you have learned or experienced 记忆力：**powers of recall** (=ability to remember) 记忆力 | **total recall** (=the ability to remember everything) 完整的记忆力 | **instant recall** (=the ability to remember a fact immediately) 瞬时记忆〔立刻记住一个事实的能力〕**2** [singular,U] a command telling someone to return from a place where they have been officially sent 召回：[**+of**] *the recall of all Allied seamen to their own countries* 将所有的盟军水兵召回本国 **3 beyond/past recall** impossible to bring back or remember 无法回忆的，记不起来的

re·cant /rɪˈkænt; rɪˈkænt/ *v* [I,T] *formal* to say publicly that you no longer have a political or religious belief that you had

before【正式】公开宣布放弃(以前的政治观点或宗教信仰): *Galileo was forced to recant his belief in the Copernican theory.* 伽俐略被迫公开宣布放弃他对哥白尼理论的信仰。—**recantation** /ˌrikænˋteʃən; ˌriːkænˈteɪʃən/ *n* [C,U]

re·cap /ˋrikæp; ˈriːkæp/ *v* **recapped, recapping** [I,T] to repeat the main points of something that has just been said; short for RECAPITULATE 扼要重述, 摘要说明: *Let me just recap what's been said so far.* 让我把已经谈到的内容简要复述一遍。—**recap** /ˋrikæp; ˈriːkæp/ *n* [C]

re·ca·pit·u·late /ˌrikəˋpɪtʃəˌlet; ˌriːkəˈpɪtʃʊleɪt/ *v* [I,T] *formal* to repeat the main points of something that has just been said【正式】扼要重述 —**recapitulation** /ˌrikəˌpɪtʃəˋleʃən; ˌriːkəpɪtʃʊˈleɪʃən/ *n* [C,U]

re·cap·ture /riˋkæptʃɚ; riːˈkæptʃə/ *v* [T] **1** to bring back the same feelings or qualities that you experienced in the past 使再现; 使再次经历: *an attempt to recapture our childhood innocence* 重新体验我们孩提时代天真无邪的尝试 **2** to catch a prisoner or animal that has escaped 重新抓获: *They travelled only at night, to avoid being recaptured by the enemy.* 为了避免被敌人重新抓获, 他们只在夜间行进。**3** to take control of a piece of land again by fighting for it 收复〔失地〕—**recapture** *n* [U]

re·cast /riˋkæst; ˌriːˈkɑːst/ *v past tense and past participle* **recast** [T] **1** to give something a new shape or a new form of organization 重铸; 重塑; 重组: *an attempt to recast the statement in less formal language* 用不太正式的语言改写声明的尝试 **2** to give parts in a play or film to different actors 更换〔戏剧、电影中〕的演员 —**recasting** *n* [C,U]

rec·ce /ˋrɛkɪ; ˈreki/ *n* [C,U] *informal* RECONNAISSANCE【非正式】侦察

recd the written abbreviation of 缩写= received (RECEIVE)

re·cede /rɪˋsid; rɪˈsiːd/ *v* [I] **1** if something you can see or hear recedes, it gets further and further away until it disappears〔景物、声音〕逐渐远去以至消失: [**+into**] *footsteps receding into the distance* 渐渐远去的脚步声 **2** if a memory, feeling, or possibility recedes, it gradually goes away〔记忆〕变模糊;〔感情〕逐渐淡漠;〔可能性〕逐渐消失: *As the threat of attack receded, village life returned to normal.* 随着袭击的威胁渐渐消失, 村里的生活恢复了正常。**3** if water recedes, it moves back from an area that it was covering〔水〕退, 退去: *Flood waters finally began to recede in November.* 洪水终于在十一月间开始退去。**4** if your hair recedes, you gradually lose the hair at the front of your head〔头发〕从前额开始向后脱落: **receding hairline** *Ian is getting self-conscious about his receding hairline.* 伊恩对自己不断后移的发际线感到越来越不自在。—see picture on page A6 参见 A6 页图 **5 receding chin** a chin that slopes backwards 向后收缩的下巴

S2 **re·ceipt** /rɪˋsit; rɪˈsiːt/ *n* **1** [C] a written statement that you give to someone, showing that you have received money or goods from them 收据, 收条: *Keep all your receipts for work-related expenses.* 保留你所有与工作相关的开支收据。| **make out a receipt** (=write a receipt) 开收据 **2** [U] *formal* the act or fact of receiving something【正式】收到: [**+of**] *Receipt of benefits is permitted for up to 12 months.* 允许领取救济金的时间最长为 12 个月。| **be in receipt of** *formal* (=to have received something)【正式】收讫 *We are now in receipt of your letter of the 17th.* 17 日大函敬悉。| **on/upon receipt of** *formal* (=when you have received something)【正式】收到…后 *On receipt of your instructions, we will dispatch the goods.* 收到你的指示后, 我们将发货。**3 receipts** [plural] *technical* the money that a business, bank, or government receives【术语】〔企业、银行、政府的〕收款, 进款; 收入: *total revenue receipts of $18.4 million* 总收入 1840 万美元

S1 W1 **re·ceive** /rɪˋsiv; rɪˈsiːv/ *v* [T]

1 ▶BE GIVEN STH 得到某物◀ to be officially given something 正式得到; 收到: *We have received numerous complaints about the airport noise.* 我们收到许多对机场噪音的投诉。| **receive sth from sb** *In 1962 she received an honorary doctorate from Harvard.* 1962 年, 她获得哈佛大学荣誉博士学位。| *You may be entitled to receive assistance from the state.* 你可能有资格领取国家的补助。—see 见 OBTAIN (USAGE)

2 ▶BE SENT STH 接到, 收到某物◀ *formal* to get a letter, message, telephone call etc【正式】接到〔信件、消息、电话等〕: *Yes, Anne received your letter Monday.* 对, 安妮星期一收到了你的信。| *By the time the police received the call it was too late.* 等警察接到电话, 已经太晚了。

3 ▶TREATMENT 待遇◀ *formal* if you receive a particular type of treatment, an injury etc, it is done to you or it happens to you【正式】受到〔某种待遇、伤害等〕; 接受〔治疗〕: *The victim received injuries from which he has since died.* 受害者多处受伤, 并因此死亡。| *a cancer patient receiving radiation therapy* 一个接受放射治疗的癌症患者

4 ▶IDEAS/INFORMATION 想法/信息◀ [usually passive 一般用被动态] to react in a particular way to a suggestion, idea, or piece of information 对〔建议、想法或消息〕作出反应; 回应: *Edith's plans were very well received by the board.* 董事会对伊迪丝的计划反应很好。| *He did not receive the news very cheerfully.* 听到这个消息他并不太开心。

5 be on the receiving end (of) to be the person who is most affected by someone else's actions, usually in an unpleasant way 遭受, 承受: *I'm the one who's always on the receiving end of his bad moods.* 他闹情绪, 我总要受罪。

6 ▶PEOPLE 人◀ *formal* to officially accept someone as a guest or member of a group【正式】接待, 招待; 接受〔为成员〕: *She only receives guests on Sundays.* 她只在星期天会客。| **receive sb into sth** *Tessa was later received into the Church.* 特莎后来被这个教会接纳为教友。

7 ▶BY RADIO 用无线电◀ a) if a radio or television receives radio waves or other signals, it makes them become sounds or pictures〔收音机、电视〕接收〔无线电或电视信号〕 **b)** to be able to hear a radio message that someone is sending 收听到〔无线电信号〕: *"Are you receiving me?" "Receiving you loud and clear!"* "你收到我的信号没有?" "你的信号又响又清楚!"

Frequencies of the verbs **receive** and **get** in spoken and written English 动词 receive 和 get 在英语口语和书面语中的使用频率

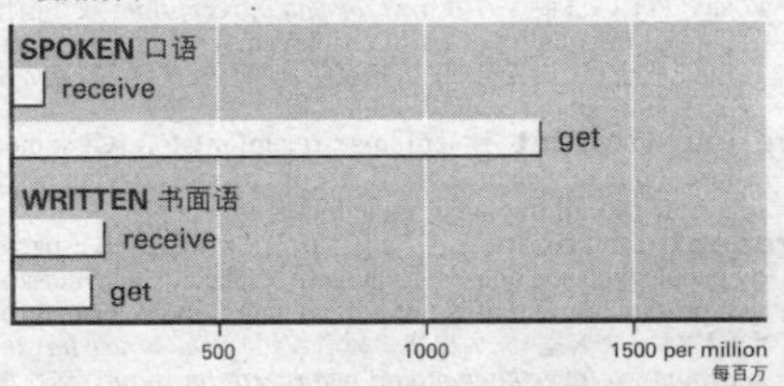

Based on the British National Corpus and the Longman Lancaster Corpus 据英国国家语料库和朗文兰开斯特语料库

This graph shows that it is much more usual in spoken English to use **get** rather than **receive**, which is more formal and is therefore more common in written English. 本图表显示, 英语口语中 get 的使用频率远远高于 receive; receive 比较正式, 因而更多的是在书面语中使用。

re·ceived /rɪˋsivd; rɪˈsiːvd/ *adj* [only before noun 仅用于名词前] *formal* accepted or considered to be correct by most people【正式】被普遍接受的; 公认的: *Sonntag's articles challenged received notions about photography.* 桑塔格的这些文章对公认的摄影概念提出了异议。| **received wisdom** (=the opinions most people have about what is true) 多数人的看法 *The received wisdom in Washington is that the Defense Secretary will resign.* 华盛顿的普遍看法是国防部长将辞职。

Received Pro·nun·ci·a·tion /ˌ·, ··ˈ··/ *n* [U] RP 标准发音

re·ceiv·er /rɪˋsivɚ; rɪˈsiːvə/ *n* [C]

1 ▶TELEPHONE 电话◀ the part of a telephone that you hold next to your mouth and ear〔电话〕听筒: *Cory slammed down the receiver and stormed out of the room.* 科里砰地一声摔下电话, 怒气冲冲地走出房间。

2 ▶BUSINESS 公司◀ someone who is officially in charge of a business or company that is BANKRUPT (=has no money)〔破产企业、公司的〕管理人, 接管人: *The business is in the hands of the receivers.* 公司现在由破产管理人接管。

3 ▶STOLEN PROPERTY 赃物◀ someone who buys and sells stolen property 买卖赃物者

4 ▶RADIO 无线电◀ *formal* a radio or television【正式】无线电接收机; 收音机; 电视机

5 ▶AMERICAN FOOTBALL 美式橄榄球◀ a player in American football who is in a position to catch the ball 接球手

re·ceiv·er·ship /rɪˋsivɚˌʃɪp; rɪˈsiːvəʃɪp/ *n* [U] **go into receivership** if a person or business goes into receivership, they are controlled by the official receiver (RECEIVER (2)) because they have no money〔破产者或公司〕由破产管理人看管

re·ceiv·ing /rɪˋsivɪŋ; rɪˈsiːvɪŋ/ *n* [U] the crime of buying and selling stolen goods 买卖赃物罪

re·cent /ˋrisn̩t; ˈriːsənt/ *adj* having happened or begun to exist only a short time ago 最近的, 不久前的, 近代的: *recent devel-* S2 W1

opments in medicine 医学领域的最新发展 | *my recent visit to China* 我最近去中国的旅行 | *In recent years, terrorism has become a greater threat.* 近年来，恐怖主义已经成为更大的威胁。—**recentness** *n* [U]

1 1 **re·cent·ly** /ˈrisn̩tli; ˈriːsəntli/ *adv* not long ago 最近，不久前，近来: *I've only recently started learning French.* 我只是最近才开始学法语的。| *Jerry lived in Cairo until quite recently.* 杰里住在开罗直至不久之前。| *a recently published biography* 一部最近出版的传记

re·cep·ta·cle /rɪˈsɛptəkl̩; rɪˈseptəkəl/ *n formal* a container for putting things in【正式】容器: *Please dispose of waste in the appropriate receptacle.* 请将废物投进适当的容器。

3 **re·cep·tion** /rɪˈsɛpʃən; rɪˈsepʃən/ *n* **1** [C usually singular 一般用单数] a particular type of welcome for someone, or a particular type of reaction to their ideas, work etc 接待，欢迎；接纳，承认: *If you spoke their language you'd get a friendlier reception.* 假如你能讲他们的语言，你就会受到更友好的接待。| *Vaughan's play met with a mixed reception from the critics.* 评论家对沃恩的剧作褒贬不一。**2** [C] a large formal party to celebrate an event or to welcome someone 欢迎会，招待会: *a wedding reception* 婚宴 | *A champagne reception will be held in honour of the ambassador's visit.* 为欢迎大使来访将举行香槟酒招待会。**3** [U] **a)** the desk or office where visitors arriving in a hotel or large organization go first〔旅店、大机构的〕接待处: *Please leave your key at the reception desk.* 请将你的钥匙留在接待处。**b)** *BrE* the area around or in front of this desk or office; LOBBY[1] (1)【英】前厅: *I'll wait for you in reception.* 我在前厅等你。**4** [U] the quality of radio or television signals that you receive〔收音机、电视机的〕接收性能，收听[收视]质量: *listeners complaining about poor reception* 抱怨收听质量太差的听众

re·cep·tion·ist /rɪˈsɛpʃənɪst; rɪˈsepʃənɪst/ *n* [C] someone whose job is to welcome and deal with people arriving in a hotel or office building, visiting a doctor etc 接待员

reception room /-ˈ.. ./ *n* [C] *BrE* a word, used especially by people who sell houses, for a room, especially a LIVING-ROOM, in a private house that is not a kitchen, bedroom, or bathroom【英】客厅；会客室〔尤为出售房屋者使用〕: *The house has three bedrooms, a large kitchen and two reception rooms.* 这所房子有三间卧室、一个大厨房和两间客厅。

re·cep·tive /rɪˈsɛptɪv; rɪˈseptɪv/ *adj* willing to consider new ideas or listen to someone else's opinions〔对新思想、别人的意见等〕乐于接受的: *You might find them in a more receptive mood tomorrow.* 也许他们明天更乐于接受意见。| **[+to]** *receptive to new ideas and values* 善于接受新思想和新价值观 —**receptively** *adv* —**receptiveness** also 又作 **receptivity** /ˌrisɛpˈtɪvətɪ; ˌriːsepˈtɪvɪti/ *n* [U]

re·cess[1] /ˈrisɛs; rɪˈses/ *n* **1** [C,U] a time for rest during the working day or year, especially in parliament, law courts etc 暂停；休息；休会；休庭: *Parliament's summer recess* 议会的夏季休会期 | *After Slater's testimony, the judge called a recess.* 斯莱特作证后，法官宣布休庭。**2** [U] *AmE* a short period of time between lessons at a school when children can go outdoors and play【美】课间休息；BREAK[2] (1c) *BrE*【英】: *The older kids were picking on Richie at recess.* 课间休息时，大一点的孩子们欺负里奇。**3** [C] a space in the wall of a room for shelves, cupboards etc〔墙壁上装架、柜等的〕凹进处；壁龛 **4 the recesses of** the inner hidden parts of something …的隐秘处，幽深处: *the deep recesses of the cave* 洞穴的深处

re·cess[2] *v* [I] *especially AmE* to take a recess (RECESS[1] (1))【尤美】休假；休会；休庭

re·cessed /ˈrisɛst; rɪˈsest/ *adj* fitted into a part of a wall that is further back than the rest of the wall 装入墙壁凹进处的: *a recessed bookshelf* 嵌进墙壁内的书架

2 3 **re·ces·sion** /rɪˈsɛʃən; rɪˈseʃən/ *n* [C] a period of time during which there is less trade, business activity, and wealth than usual〔经济〕衰退期

re·ces·sive /rɪˈsɛsɪv; rɪˈsesɪv/ *adj technical* a recessive physical feature is passed to children from their parents only if both parents have this feature in their GENES【术语】〔遗传基因〕隐性的

re·charge /riˈtʃɑrdʒ; ˌriːˈtʃɑːdʒ/ *v* [T] **1** to put a new supply of electricity into a BATTERY (1) 给〔电池〕重新充电 **2 recharge your batteries** to get back your strength and energy again 使自己恢复精力: *I'm going to spend a week in the mountains to recharge my batteries.* 我准备留在山里一个星期，以恢复精力。—**rechargeable** *adj* —**recharge** /ˈritʃɑrdʒ; ˈriːtʃɑːdʒ/ *n* [C]

re·cher·ché /rəˈʃɛrʃe; rəˈʃeəʃeɪ/ *adj formal* a recherché subject, idea, word etc is uncommon and has been chosen to make people admire your knowledge【正式】〔主题、思想、字眼等〕罕见的〔选来炫耀知识〕

re·cid·i·vist /rɪˈsɪdəvɪst; rɪˈsɪdɪvɪst/ *n* [C] *technical* a criminal who keeps doing things that are illegal, even after they have been punished【术语】惯犯 —**recidivism** *n* [U]

re·ci·pe /ˈrɛsəpɪ; ˈresɪpi/ *n* [C] **1** a set of instructions for cooking a particular type of food 烹饪法；食谱: **[+for]** *a recipe for tomato soup* 番茄汤的做法 | *a recipe book* 一本烹饪书 **2 be a recipe for** to be likely to cause a particular result 是…的秘诀[窍门]；很可能是造成…的原因: *The fact that four different companies are writing the software sounds like a recipe for disaster to me.* 四家不同的公司在编写这种软件，我觉得这很可能酿成灾祸。 3

re·cip·i·ent /rɪˈsɪpɪənt; rɪˈsɪpiənt/ *n formal* someone who receives something【正式】接受者，领受者: **[+of]** *the recipient of the Nobel Peace Prize* 诺贝尔和平奖得主

re·cip·ro·cal /rɪˈsɪprəkl̩; rɪˈsɪprəkəl/ *adj formal* a reciprocal arrangement or relationship is one in which two people or groups do or give the same things to each other【正式】相互的；交互的；互惠的: *Such treaties provide reciprocal rights and obligations.* 这种协议提供了互惠的权利与义务。—compare 比较 MUTUAL —**reciprocally** /-kl̩ɪ; -kli/ *adv*

re·cip·ro·cate /rɪˈsɪprəˌket; rɪˈsɪprəkeɪt/ *v* **1** [I,T] to do or give something, because something similar has been done or given to you 报答，酬答；互给: *I cannot accept his generosity – I am not in a position to reciprocate.* 我不能接受他的慷慨—我无法回报他。**2** [T] to feel the same about someone as they feel about you 回报以〔相同的感情〕: *Kara had fallen in love with Dan, but her affection was not reciprocated.* 卡拉爱上了丹，但她的爱没有得到回报。—**reciprocation** /rɪˌsɪprəˈkeʃən; rɪˌsɪprəˈkeɪʃən/ *n* [U]

re·ci·pro·ci·ty /ˌrɛsəˈprɑsətɪ; ˌresɪˈprɒsɪti/ *n* [U] *formal* a situation in which two people, groups, or countries give each other similar kinds of help or special rights【正式】互惠

re·cit·al /rɪˈsaɪtl̩; rɪˈsaɪtl/ *n* [C] **1** a performance of music or poetry, usually given by one performer 演奏会；演唱会；朗诵会〔一般由一个人表演〕: *a piano recital* 钢琴独奏会 | **[+of]** *a recital of operatic arias* 歌剧唱段演唱会 **2** *formal* a spoken description of a series of events【正式】〔一连串事件的〕叙述，口头描述: **[+of]** *Fred launched into a long recital of his adventures.* 弗雷德开始大谈特谈他的奇遇。

re·ci·ta·tion /ˌrɛsəˈteʃən; ˌresɪˈteɪʃən/ *n* [C,U] an act of saying a poem, piece of literature etc that you have learned, for people to listen to 背诵: *recitations from Shakespeare* 背诵莎士比亚的作品

re·ci·ta·tive /ˌrɛsətəˈtiv; ˌresɪtəˈtiːv/ *n* [C,U] *technical* a speech set to music sung by one person that continues the story of an OPERA (=musical play) between the songs【术语】〔歌剧中的〕宣叙部

re·cite /rɪˈsaɪt; rɪˈsaɪt/ *v* **1** [I,T] to say a poem, piece of literature etc that you have learned, for people to listen to 背诵: *a poem I had to recite at school* 我上学时必须背诵的一首诗 **2** [T] to tell someone a series or list of things 详述；列举: *Don't encourage him, or he'll recite the whole family history!* 别鼓励他，不然他会把整部家族史从头到尾讲一遍。—**reciter** *n* [C]

reck·less /ˈrɛklɪs; ˈrekləs/ *adj* not caring or worrying about the possible bad or dangerous results of your actions 轻率的；鲁莽的；不顾后果的: *reckless driving* 莽撞的驾驶 | *a reckless adventurer* 无所畏惧的冒险家 | *a reckless waste of money* 胡乱花钱 —**recklessly** *adv* —**recklessness** *n* [U]

reck·on /ˈrɛkən; ˈrekən/ *v* [T not in progressive 不用进行时] **1** *spoken especially BrE* to think that something is a fact, or have a particular opinion about something【口，尤英】认为，以为: **reckon (that)** *Wayne reckons we ought to call her.* 韦恩认为我们应该给她打个电话。| *Do you reckon they'll get married?* 你认为他们会结婚吗？**2** to guess a number or amount, without calculating it exactly 估算，估计: **reckon how much/how many etc** *How much do you reckon she earns?* 你估计她挣多少钱？| **reckon sth to be sth** *The likely cost of the system is reckoned to be about £10,000.* 估计这系统的成本可能在10,000英镑左右。| **be reckoned in thousands/millions** *Her personal fortune is reckoned in millions.* 估计她的个人财产达数百万。**3** *formal* to think that someone or something is a particular kind of person or thing【正式】认为〔某人或物〕是…: **be reckoned to be sth** *Julia is often reckoned to be the most beautiful woman in Hollywood.* 朱莉娅常被认为是好莱坞最漂亮的女人。| **reckon sb among/as** *I reckon him among my friends.* 我把他看做我的朋友。**4** *formal* to calculate an amount【正式】计算: *My pay is reckoned from the first of the month.* 我的工资从每月的第一天算起。 2 3

reckon sth ↔ **in** *phr v* [T] to include something when you are calculating 把…计算在内: *Have you reckoned in the cost of postage?* 你是否把邮费计算在内了?

reckon on sth *phr v* [T] to expect something to happen when you are making plans 指望: **reckon on doing sth** *We didn't reckon on spending so much on repairs.* 我们没有想到维修要花这么多钱。

reckon sth ↔ **up** *phr v* [T] *old-fashioned* to add up an amount, cost etc, in order to get a total【过时】把…加起来, 计算…的总数: *Can you reckon up the money we've made?* 你能不能把我们挣的钱加起来?

reckon with sb/sth *phr v* [T] **1 not reckon with** to not consider a possible problem when you are making plans 没有考虑到: *We hadn't reckoned with the possibility that it might rain.* 我们没有考虑到可能下雨。**2 sb/sth to be reckoned with** something or someone that is powerful and must be regarded seriously as a possible opponent, competitor, danger etc 必须认真考虑[对待]的某人/某事: *The principal was certainly a woman to be reckoned with.* 校长无疑是一个必须认真对付的女人。**3 have sb/sth to reckon with** to have to deal with someone or something powerful 必须对付某人/某事: *Any invader would have the military might of NATO to reckon with.* 任何入侵者都必须对付北约的军事力量。

reckon without sb/sth *phr v* [T] *BrE* to not consider a possible problem when you are making plans【英】没有考虑到; 对…不加考虑: *We had reckoned without the difficulty of selling the house.* 我们没有考虑到出售房子的困难。

reck·on·ing /ˈrɛkənɪŋ; ˈrekənɪŋ/ *n* **1** [U] calculation that is based on a careful guess rather than on exact knowledge 估算, 估计: *By my reckoning it must be 60 km from here to the coast.* 据我估计, 从这里到海边应该有60公里。**2** [C] *old use* a bill【旧】账单: *We paid our reckoning and left.* 我们付完账便走了。**3 day of reckoning** the time when the results of your actions or behaviour become clear and start to affect you, especially in a bad way 报应来到的日子; 算总账的日子 —see also 另见 DEAD RECKONING

re·claim /rɪˋklem; rɪˈkleɪm/ *v* [T] **1** to officially ask for something to be given back to you 要求收回; 要求恢复: *You may be entitled to reclaim some tax.* 你可以要求退回部分税款。**2** to make an area of desert, MARSH (=wet land) etc suitable for farming or building 开垦, 开拓 **3** to obtain useful products from waste material 自废料中回收〔有用材料〕: *metal reclaimed from old cars in junkyards* 从垃圾场的旧汽车上回收的金属 **—reclamation** /ˌrɛkləˋmeʃən; ˌrekləˈmeɪʃən/ *n* [U]: *land reclamation* 垦荒

re·cline /rɪˋklaɪn; rɪˈklaɪn/ *v* **1** [I] *formal* to lie or lean back in a relaxed way【正式】躺, 斜倚: **[+in/on]** *a girl reclining on a deck chair* 躺在帆布椅上的女孩 **2** [I,T] if you recline a seat or if it reclines, the back of the seat is lowered, so that you can lean back in it (使)〔椅背〕向后靠: *reclining seats* 躺椅

re·cluse /ˋrɛklus; rɪˈkluːs/ *n* [C] someone who chooses to live alone, and does not like seeing or talking to other people 隐居者, 隐士; 遁世者: *The guy was a recluse – a defrocked priest, so people said.* 那人是位隐士——一位被解除圣职的神父, 人们说。**—reclusive** /rɪˋklusɪv; rɪˈkluːsɪv/ *adj*

3 2 **rec·og·ni·tion** /ˌrɛkəgˋnɪʃən; ˌrekəgˈnɪʃən/ *n* **1** [U] the act of knowing someone or something because you have known or learned about them in the past 认识, 认出; 识别: *Years later, she passed me in the street without even the smallest sign of recognition.* 若干年后, 她在街上从我身边走过, 丝毫没有认识我的迹象。| **beyond/out of all recognition** (=having become impossible to recognize) 认不出来 *His face was bruised and swollen almost beyond recognition.* 他的脸又青又肿, 几乎认不出来了。**2** [singular,U] public admiration and thanks for someone's work or achievements 公开的赞扬, 表扬, 表彰: *Despite a life devoted to helping the poor, she never won any recognition before her death.* 尽管半生致力于救助穷人, 但她在生前从未得到任何表扬。| **in recognition of** (=show public thanks and admiration for something) 表彰… *This medal is awarded in recognition of outstanding courage.* 颁发这枚奖章以嘉奖非凡的勇气。**3** [singular,U] the act of realizing and accepting that something is true or that something is important 意识到, 承认; 接受: **[+of]** *There is a growing recognition among doctors of the need for more preventative treatment.* 越来越多的医生意识到需要更多的预防性治疗。**4** [U] the act of officially accepting that an organization, government, document etc has legal or official authority 正式承认: **[+of]** *the recognition of Latvia as an independent state* 承认拉脱维亚为一个独立国家 **5 speech/voice/image etc recognition** the ability of a computer to recognize voices, shapes etc〔电脑的〕语音/图像等识别能力

rec·og·nize also 又作 **-ise** *BrE*【英】/ˋrɛkəgˌnaɪz; ˈrekəgnaɪz/ 1 1
v **1** [T not in progressive 不用进行时] to know who someone is or what something is, because you have seen, heard, experienced, or learned about them in the past 认出, 认识; 辨认出: *She was humming a tune I didn't recognize.* 她正在哼一首我叫不上名来的曲子。| *Saleha came home so thin and weak her own children hardly recognized her.* 赛莉娅回家时又瘦又弱, 连她自己的孩子都几乎认不出她来了。| *You shouldn't go yourself. You'll be recognized.* 你不应该亲自去, 你会被人认出来的。| *It was malaria, but Dr Lee hadn't recognized the symptoms.* 患的是疟疾, 但李医生没有诊断出来。**2** [T] to officially accept that an organization, government, document etc has legal or official authority 正式承认, 认可: *The management recognizes three main trade unions.* 资方承认三个主要的工会。| *British medical qualifications are recognized in Canada.* 英国的行医资格在加拿大可得到认可。| **recognize sth as** *The US has not recognized the Cuban government since 1961.* 自从1961年以来, 美国一直不承认古巴政府。**3 be recognized as** to be thought of as being important or very good by a lot of people 得到承认, 被公认为: *Lawrence's novel was eventually recognized as a work of genius.* 劳伦斯的小说最终被公认为天才之作。| **recognized expert/authority** *a recognized authority on the teaching of English* 公认的英语教学权威 **4** [T] to accept and admit, often unwillingly, that something is true〔往往勉强地〕接受, 承认; 明白: **recognize (that)** *We recognize that this is an unpleasant choice to have to make.* 我们承认这是不得已而作出的令人不快的决定。| **recognize what/how/who etc** *Do you think he recognized how foolish he looks?* 你觉得他明白自己显得有多蠢吗? **5** [T] to officially and publicly thank someone for something they have done, by giving them a special honour 表扬; 表彰; 嘉奖 **—recognizable** /ˋrɛkəgˌnaɪzəbḷ; ˈrekəgnaɪzəbl/ *adj* **—recognizably** *adv*

re·coil¹ /rɪˋkɔɪl; rɪˈkɔɪl/ *v* [I] **1** to move back suddenly and quickly from something you dislike or are frightened of 退缩; 畏缩: **[+from]** *She recoiled from his touch as if she had been slapped.* 他一碰她, 她便往后缩, 仿佛被打了一巴掌。**2** to feel such a strong dislike of a particular situation that you want to avoid it〔因厌恶某情形而〕拖拉, 踌躇不前: **[+from]** *Rigby tends to recoil from making difficult decisions.* 里格比在难以作出决定时往往踌躇不前。**3** if a gun recoils, it suddenly moves backwards after it has been fired〔枪炮〕反冲; 产生后坐力

re·coil² /ˋrikɔɪl; ˈriːkɔɪl/ *n* [singular,U] the sudden backward movement of a gun after being fired〔枪炮的〕反冲, 后坐

rec·ol·lect /ˌrɛkəˋlɛkt; ˌrekəˈlekt/ *v* [T] *old-fashioned* to be able to remember something, especially by deliberately trying to remember【过时】记起; 想起: *As far as I recollect, I have never owned a black suit.* 在我的记忆里, 我从未有过一套黑色西服。| **recollect how/when/what etc** *Davenport tried to recollect when he had last used his car.* 达文波特努力回想最后一次使用他的汽车是在什么时候。| **recollect that** *One witness recollected that the visitor had arrived by the side door.* 一位证人记得来客是从边门进来的。| **recollect doing sth** *I recollect seeing Ryder some years ago in Bonn.* 我记得几年前曾经在波恩见过赖德。

rec·ol·lec·tion /ˌrɛkəˋlɛkʃən; ˌrekəˈlekʃən/ *n formal*【正式】**1** [U] an act of remembering something, especially something you try to remember 想起, 记起: **have no recollection** (=not remember) 不记得 *I have no recollection of ever having received the money.* 我不记得收到过这笔钱。| **to the best of my recollection** (=used when you are unsure if you remember correctly) 如果我没有记错的话 *To the best of my recollection, she drives a Mercedes.* 如果我没有记错的话, 她开的是一辆梅塞德斯。**2** [C] something from the past that you remember 记忆中的往事: *His earliest recollection was a great branch of lilac hanging outside the window.* 他最早的记忆是窗外悬着的一根很大的丁香树枝。

rec·om·mend /ˌrɛkəˋmɛnd; ˌrekəˈmend/ *v* [T] **1** to advise someone to do something, especially because you have special knowledge of a situation or subject 劝告; 建议: *The Senate Foreign Relations Committee recommended ratification of the treaty despite public opinion.* 尽管公众舆论反对, 参议院外交关系委员会建议批准这项条约。| **recommend that** *Doctors recommend that all children should be immunized against measles.* 医生们建议所有儿童都应该接种麻疹疫苗。| **recommend doing sth** *The manufacturers recommend changing the oil after 500 km.* 制造商建议在行驶500公里之后更换机油。| **strongly recommend** *Graham's father strongly recommended sending the boy to school in England.* 格雷厄姆的父亲极力建议把孩子送到英国上学。| **recommended limit/dosage/allowance etc** *It is dan-* 3 2

gerous to exceed the recommended dosage. 超过建议的服用剂量是危险的。**2** to praise something or someone, or suggest them for a particular purpose or job 推荐, 介绍: *I recommend the butter chicken – it's delicious.* 我推荐奶油鸡, 非常好吃。| *Can you recommend a good lawyer?* 你能不能介绍一位好律师? | **recommend sth to sb** *Oh, that book? Karen recommended it to me.* 噢, 那本书吗? 是卡伦推荐给我的。| **recommend sth for** *My mother always recommends the market for fresh fruit and veg.* 我母亲总是推荐去那个市场买新鲜水果和蔬菜。| **recommend sb for** *I would recommend Mr Bryant for the position of Assistant Manager.* 我想推荐布赖恩特先生担任助理经理。| **highly/thoroughly recommend** *That new restaurant in town is highly recommended.* 人们极力推荐镇上那家新餐馆。**3 sth has much/little/nothing to recommend it** used to say that something has many, few, or no good qualities 某物有很多/少有/没有可取之处: *As a tourist resort the place doesn't have anything to recommend it.* 这个地方游客众多, 但没有可取之处。

rec·om·men·da·tion /ˌrɛkəmɛnˋdeʃən; ˌrekəmenˈdeɪʃən/ *n* **1** [C] official advice given to someone, especially about what to do 正式建议; 意见: **make a recommendation** *The committee made a number of recommendations for improving safety standards.* 委员会提出了若干项提高安全标准的建议。**2** [U] the action of suggesting to someone that they should choose a particular thing or person that you think is very good 建议; 推荐: **on sb's recommendation** *On Hawley's recommendation five officers were court martialled.* 根据霍利的建议, 五名军官被送上军事法庭受审。**3** [C] *especially AmE* a formal letter or statement saying that someone would be a suitable person to do a job, take a course of study etc【尤美】推荐信

rec·om·pense¹ /ˋrɛkəmˌpɛns; ˈrekəmpens/ *v* [T] *formal* to give someone a payment for trouble or losses that you have caused them, or a reward for their efforts to help you【正式】补偿; 赔偿; 酬谢: **recompense sb for sth** *We hope this payment will go some way to recompense you for any inconvenience we may have caused.* 我们可能已经给您造成不便, 希望这笔款项可以作出些许补偿。—compare 比较 COMPENSATE (2)

recompense² *n* [singular,U] *formal* something that you give to someone for trouble or losses that you have caused them, or as a reward for their help【正式】补偿; 赔偿; 报酬: [**+for**] *£1,000 isn't really much recompense for all they've been through.* 他们经历了那么多波折, 1000 英镑其实算不了什么补偿。—compare 比较 COMPENSATION (1)

rec·on·cile /ˋrɛkənˌsaɪl; ˈrekənsaɪl/ *v* **1** [T] if you reconcile two ideas, situations, or facts you accept or show that they can exist together and are not directly opposed to each other 调和; 调解: **reconcile sth with sth** *She could never reconcile his violent temper with his pacifist ideals.* 她无论如何也看不出他暴躁的脾气同他的和平主义理想有什么相符的地方。| **reconcile accounts** (=to make two sets of figures add up to the same) 平账 **2 be reconciled (with)** to have a good relationship again with someone after you have quarrelled with them (与…)和解, 和好: *After 20 years of silence, he was finally reconciled with his family.* 经过20年的沉默后, 他终于与家人言归于好。

reconcile sb **to** sth *phr v* [T] to make someone able to accept a difficult or unpleasant situation 使接受〔困难或不愉快的情况〕: **reconcile yourself to sth** *We watch the character as he tries to reconcile himself to the idea of his own death.* 我们看到这个人物设法坦然面对自己的死亡。

rec·on·cil·i·a·tion /ˌrɛkənˌsɪlɪˋeʃən; ˌrekənsɪliˈeɪʃən/ *n* [singular,U] a situation in which two people, countries etc become friendly with each other again after quarrelling 和解, 修好: *All our attempts at reconciliation have failed.* 我们为和解所作的一切努力都失败了。| [**+between**] *There seemed little hope of reconciliation between the two superpowers.* 两个超级大国之间几乎没有什么修好的希望。| **spirit of reconciliation** *a new spirit of reconciliation in the negotiations* 谈判中表现出的新的和解精神

rec·on·dite /ˋrɛkənˌdaɪt; ˈrekəndaɪt/ *adj* [only before noun 仅用于名词前] *formal* recondite information, knowledge etc is not known about or understood by many people【正式】〔信息、知识等〕玄妙的; 深奥的

re·con·di·tion /ˌrikənˋdɪʃən; ˌriːkənˈdɪʃən/ *v* [T] to repair something, especially an old machine, so that it works like a new one 修理, 修复, 修整〔尤指旧机器〕—**reconditioned** *adj*: *a reconditioned engine* 修复的发动机

re·con·nais·sance /rɪˋkɑnəsəns; rɪˈkɒnɪ̵səns/ *n* [C,U] the military activity of sending soldiers and aircraft to find out about the enemy's forces 侦察: *a reconnaissance mission* 侦察任务

re·con·noi·tre *BrE*【英】, **reconnoiter** *AmE*【美】/ˌrikəˋnɔɪtɚ; ˌrekəˈnɔɪtə/ *v* [I,T] to try to find out the position and size of your enemy's army, for example by flying planes over land where their soldiers are 侦察

re·con·sid·er /ˌrikənˋsɪdɚ; ˌriːkənˈsɪdə/ *v* [I,T] to think again about something you have decided, with the possibility that you might change your mind 重新考虑: *I have received your letter of resignation but I want you to reconsider your decision.* 我收到了你的辞职信, 但我希望你重新考虑你的决定。—**reconsideration** /ˌrikənˌsɪdəˋreʃən; ˌriːkənsɪdəˈreɪʃən/ *n* [U]

re·con·sti·tute /riˋkɑnstəˌtut; riːˈkɒnstɪ̵tjuːt/ *v* **1** [T] to bring something, especially an organization, back into existence in a different form 重组, 重建, 改编: **reconstitute sth as** *remnants of the old regiments reconstituted as the New Model Army* 把以前那几个团的残余部队重组为"新模范军" **2 reconstituted milk/eggs etc** milk powder etc to which water has been added in order to change it back into the form it was in before it was dried 复水牛奶/鸡蛋等 —**reconstitution** /riˌkɑnstəˋtuʃən; ˌriːkɒnstɪ̵ˈtjuːʃən/ *n* [U]

re·con·struct /ˌrikənˋstrʌkt; ˌriːkənˈstrʌkt/ *v* [T] **1** to produce a complete description or copy of something that happened by collecting together pieces of information 〔由零碎的信息〕构想出…的全貌, 使〔完整的情景〕再现: *Police are trying to reconstruct the events of last Friday.* 警察在设法再现上星期五发生的那些事情。**2** to build something again after it has been destroyed or damaged 重建, 再建

Re·con·struc·tion /ˌrikənˋstrʌkʃən; ˌriːkənˈstrʌkʃən/ (1865-77) the period of American history after the Civil War when the southern states, under government and military control, rejoined the US. SLAVERY was ended, black people were given the right to vote, and a few universities were established for black people. Many white southerners strongly opposed these measures and some formed the Ku Klux Klan. (南方)重建时期〔(1865-1877), 指美国内战结束之后的一段历史时期。当时, 南部诸州在美国政府和军队的管制下重新加入美国联邦, 奴隶制被废除, 黑人被赋予了选举权, 还为黑人建立了几所大学。许多南方白人极力反对这些措施, 其中一些人还组成三K党〕

reconstruction *n* **1** [U] the work that is done after a war to repair the damage that was caused to a country's buildings, industry etc 〔战争后的〕重建: *Reconstruction of the town began in 1948.* 该镇的重建始于1948年。**2** [C usually singular 一般用单数] a copy of something that does not exist any more 复原物, 模型: [**+of**] *a reconstruction of a Native American village* 美洲印第安人村落的模型 **3** [C] a short film made using actors that tries to show how a real event happened 重现某真实事件的短片: *Police are broadcasting a reconstruction of the crime.* 警方正在播放一部再现犯罪经过的短片。

rec·ord¹ /ˋrɛkɚd; ˈrekɔːd/ *n*

1 ▶INFORMATION 信息◀ [C] information about an event or series of events that is written down or stored on computer, film etc so that it can be looked at in the future 录音; 录像; 记录: *medical records* 病历 | [**+of**] *records of births, marriages, and deaths* 出生、婚姻和死亡记录 | **keep a record** (=write down details of things as they happen) 做记录 *Keep a record of any money you pay out.* 把你支出的每一笔钱都做个记录。| **the biggest/lowest/highest etc on record** (=the biggest etc that has ever been recorded) 记载中最大/最低/最高等的 *Today saw some of the hottest temperatures on record.* 今天出现了几次有记载以来最高的温度。| **place/put sth on record** (=include something in the official records) 把某事记录在案 *I ask the court to place on record the fact that my client cooperated with the police.* 我要求法庭将我的当事人与警方合作这一事实记录在案。

2 ▶HIGHEST/BEST EVER 最高/最好◀ [C] the fastest speed, longest distance, highest or lowest level etc that has ever been reached, especially in sport 〔尤指体育运动的〕纪录: **break a record** (=do something faster, better etc than the previous record) 打破纪录 *Kenoco Oil's half-yearly profits broke all records.* 克诺科石油公司的半年度利润打破了所有的纪录。| **hold a record** (=be the person who has achieved the fastest speed, the greatest distance etc) 保持一项纪录 | **set a record** (=achieve a new record) 创纪录 *The Americans set a new world record in the sprint relay.* 美国运动员在短跑接力赛中创造了一项新的世界纪录。| **record level/figure/sales etc** (=the highest level etc that has ever been reached) 创纪录的水平/数字/销售额等 *a record level of unemployment* 创纪录的失业水平 | **an all-time record** (=the best that has ever been achieved) 有史以来最佳的纪录

3 ▶MUSIC 音乐◀ a round flat piece of plastic with a hole in the middle that music and sound is stored on 唱片: *the disc jockey*

who plays your favourite records 播放你最喜欢的唱片的音乐节目主持人

4 ▶SB'S PAST BEHAVIOUR 某人过去的行为◀ [singular] the known facts about someone's past behaviour and how successful, good, or bad they have been 履历, 经历: *Laporte's service record in Indochina* 拉波特在印度支那服役的履历 | **good/bad record** *The country has a fairly good record on human rights.* 该国有相当好的人权记录。| **sb's record on** *Senator Donegan asked the President to justify his record on welfare.* 多尼根参议员要求总统为他以往在福利方面的表现辩护。| **criminal record** (=a list made by the police of someone's crimes) 犯罪记录 *He'll never get a job if they find out about his criminal record.* 假如他们发现他的犯罪记录, 他永远也别想找到工作。| **sb's track record** (=how successful someone has been up to now) 某人的成绩记录 *The company has a good track record in the export trade.* 该公司在出口贸易方面一直业绩出色。

5 off the record if what you are telling someone is off the record, it is unofficial 私下说的, 不得引用的: *I'd like to emphasize that anything said here is strictly off the record.* 我想强调, 在这里所说的任何话都严禁发表。

6 be/go on record as saying to be known to have said something publicly or officially 公开/正式说过: *She's on record as saying she thinks men and women should live separate lives.* 她公开说过, 她认为男人和女人应该有各自不同的生活。

7 for the record *spoken* used to mean that you want people to remember what you are now saying【口】为了记录在案〔用于提起注意〕: *Let me just state for the record, that until yesterday my client had never seen Mr Rigati before.* 我必须郑重声明, 直到昨天之前, 我的当事人从未见过里加蒂先生。

8 put/set the record straight to tell people the truth about something, because you want to make it very clear that what they believe is not true 说明事实真相: *The director gave an interview to the newspapers to set the record straight.* 为澄清事实, 主管接受了报社记者的采访。

re·cord² /rɪˋkɔrd; rɪˈkɔːd/ *v* **1** [T] to write information down or store it in a computer or on film so that it can be looked at in the future 记录: *The expedition recorded over 500 new species of plants.* 探险队记录了五百多种新植物种类。| *Make sure you record the numbers of tickets you sell.* 一定要把你售出的票的号码记录下来。| **record that** *An official report records that at least half the nation's monuments are in need of repair.* 据一份官方报告记录, 这个国家至少一半的纪念碑需要维修。**2** [I,T] to store music, sound, television programmes etc on TAPE or DISCs so that people can listen to them or watch them again 录(音); 录(像): *Are you going to record tonight's concert?* 今晚的音乐会你打算录音吗? | *The group has just recorded a new album.* 该组合刚录制了一张新唱片。| *Is the machine still recording?* 机器还在录音吗? | *recording their conversation* 录下他们的谈话 **3** [T] if an instrument records the size, speed, temperature etc of something, it measures it and keeps that information 〔仪器〕显示, 记录: *Wind speeds of up to 100 kph have been recorded.* 已经记录到高达每小时100公里的风速。

record-break·ing /ˈ· ·, ·ˌ/ *adj* [only before noun 仅用于名词前] higher, faster etc than anything similar ever achieved 破纪录的: *his record-breaking flight across the Atlantic* 他跨越大西洋的破纪录飞行

re·cord·er /rɪˋkɔrdɚ; rɪˈkɔːdə/ *n* **1** [C] **cassette recorder/tape recorder/video recorder etc** a piece of electrical equipment that records music, films etc 卡式录音机/磁带录音机/录像机等 **2** [C] a simple musical instrument that you play by blowing straight down it 竖笛, 直笛 **3** a judge in a city court, in some areas of Britain and the US 〔英美某些地区市法院的〕法官

record-hold·er /ˈ· ·, ·ˌ/ *n* [C] the person who has achieved the fastest speed, the longest distance etc in a sport 纪录保持者: *the current world record-holder for the discus throw* 目前掷铁饼的世界纪录保持者

re·cord·ing /rɪˋkɔrdɪŋ; rɪˈkɔːdɪŋ/ *n* [C] **1** a piece of music or speech or a broadcast that has been recorded 录制品; 录音; 唱片: [+of] *Have you heard the new recording of Mozart's Requiem?* 你听过莫扎特《安魂曲》的新唱片吗? **2 recording studio/equipment etc** a studio etc used for recording music or sounds 录音室/设备等

record li·bra·ry /ˈ· ·, ·ˌ/ *n* [C] a place where lots of musical recordings are stored for people to borrow 唱片租借馆

record play·er /ˈ· ·, ·ˌ/ *n* [C] a piece of equipment for playing records or music 唱机 —compare 比较 STEREO¹

re·count¹ /rɪˋkaʊnt; rɪˈkaʊnt/ *v.* [T] *formal* to tell someone a story or describe a series of events【正式】叙述, 描述

re·count² /ˋriˌkaʊnt; ˈriːkaʊnt/ *n* [C] a process of counting votes again 重新计算选票, 重点选票: *I demand a recount!* 我要求重新计票! —**recount** /ˌriˋkaʊnt; riːˈkaʊnt/ *v* [T]

re·coup /rɪˋkup; rɪˈkuːp/ *v* [T] to get back an amount of money you have lost or spent 重新获得〔失去或花掉的钱〕, 收回: *Finance companies have managed to recoup some of the losses they made during the recession.* 金融公司挽回了经济衰退期间蒙受的部分损失。| **recoup yourself** (=to get money for yourself after you have lost some) 为自己挽回损失 *Landlords recouped themselves by charging higher rents for their other properties.* 房东以提高其他房子的租金来补偿自己的损失。

re·course /rɪˋkɔrs; rɪˈkɔːs/ *n formal* **have recourse to** to use something to help you when you are in a difficult situation【正式】求助于: **without recourse to** (=without having to use something) 无需 *We hope to solve this problem without recourse to further borrowing.* 我们希望不必依靠再借款来解决这个问题。

re·cov·er /rɪˋkʌvɚ; rɪˈkʌvə/ *v*

1 ▶GET BETTER 好转◀ [I] **a)** to get better after an illness, accident, shock etc 恢复健康: *After a few days of fever, he began to recover.* 发了几天烧之后, 他开始恢复健康。| [+from] *My boss is recovering from a heart attack.* 我的老板心脏病发作, 正在复原中。**b)** if something recovers after a period of trouble or difficulty, it returns to its normal condition 恢复(正常): *After this war, the country will take a long time to recover.* 经过这场战争, 这个国家将需要很长的时间才能恢复正常。

2 ▶STH STOLEN/LOST ETC 被窃/丢失等的物品◀ [T] to get back something that was taken from you, lost, or almost destroyed 重新获得; 找回: *Police have so far failed to recover the stolen jewellery.* 警方尚未找回被盗的珠宝。| *A number of bodies were recovered from the wreckage.* 从残骸中找出了若干具尸体。

3 ▶MONEY 金钱◀ [T] to get back the same amount of money that you have spent or lost; RECOUP 重新获得; 收回: *The company hopes to recover the cost of developing their new product.* 公司希望能够收回开发新产品的成本。

4 ▶ABILITIES/SENSES 能力/知觉◀ [T] to get back an ability, a sense, or control over your feelings, movements etc 恢复〔能力、知觉、对情绪的控制、活动能力等〕: *It was some hours before she recovered consciousness.* 过了几个小时她才恢复知觉。| **recover yourself** (=control yourself again after being upset, embarrassed etc) 使自己恢复到正常状态 *It took Mom a few minutes to recover herself, but then she was back in control again.* 妈妈过了几分钟才镇静下来, 然后又恢复了常态。| **recover your balance** (=stop yourself from falling) 恢复(身体)平衡 —**recoverable** *adj*

re·cov·er /ri ˋkʌvɚ; ˌriː ˈkʌvə/ *v* [T] to put a new cover on a piece of furniture 给〔家具〕换上新面子

re·cov·er·y /rɪˋkʌvərɪ; rɪˈkʌvəri/ *n* **1** [singular,U] a process of getting better after an illness, injury etc 恢复健康, 康复: [+from] *She made a quick recovery from the flu.* 流感后她很快恢复了健康。**2** [singular,U] the process of becoming stronger or more successful again after a difficult period 恢复, 复苏: *Hopes of economic recovery are fading.* 经济复苏的希望越来越渺茫。**3** [U] the act of getting something back 重新获得; 找回: [+of] *The recovery of the car from the lake took two hours.* 从湖里打捞出汽车用了两个小时。

recovery pro·gram /ˈ·ˈ· ·, ·ˌ/ *n* [C] *AmE* a course of treatment for people who are addicted (ADDICT (1)) to drugs or alcohol【美】〔戒毒、戒酒的〕康复计划

recovery room /ˈ·ˈ· · ·ˌ/ *n* [C] a room in a hospital where people first wake up after their operation 〔手术后的〕护理病房, 疗养室

rec·re·ant /ˋrɛkrɪənt; ˈrekriənt/ *n* [C] *old use* someone who is disloyal and lacks courage【旧】怯懦的叛徒, 变节者

re·cre·ate /ˌrikrɪˋet; ˌriːkriˈeɪt/ *v* [T] to make something from the past exist again or seem to exist again 使再现: *Scientists are trying to recreate these conditions.* 科学家们正在试图重新创造这些条件。

rec·re·a·tion /ˌrɛkrɪˋeʃən; ˌrekriˈeɪʃən/ *n* [C,U] an activity that you do for pleasure or amusement 娱乐, 消遣: *His only recreations are drinking beer and watching football.* 他仅有的消遣就是喝啤酒和观看足球比赛。| *a recreation center* 娱乐中心 —**recreational** *adj*: *recreational facilities* 娱乐设施

recreational ve·hi·cle /·ˌ· · ˈ· ·ˌ/ *n* [C] *AmE* an RV【美】活动房屋式旅游车, 房车

recreation ground /ˈ·ˈ· · ·ˌ/ *n* [C] *BrE* an area of public land used for sports and games【英】公共游乐场

recreation room /ˈ·ˈ· · ·ˌ/ *n* [C] **1** a public room, for example in a hospital, used for social activities or games〔医院等

处的)娱乐活动室 **2** *AmE* a room in a private house, where you can relax, play games etc【美】(家中的)娱乐室

re·crim·i·na·tion /rɪ͵krɪmə`neʃən; rɪ͵krɪmɪ̈ˈneɪʃən/ *n* [C, usually plural 一般用复数,U] a situation in which people blame each other, or what they say when they are blaming each other 互相指责: *Bitter accusations and recriminations followed the disaster.* 灾难过后, 严厉的指控和相互归咎随之而来。

rec room /ˈrɛk rum; ˈrek ruːm/ *n* [C] *AmE informal* a RECREATION ROOM (2)【美,非正式】(家中的)娱乐室

re·cru·des·cence /͵rikru`dɛsn̩s; ͵riːkruːˈdesəns/ *n* [usually singular 一般用单数] *formal* a sudden return or reappearance of something, especially something bad or unpleasant【正式】(尤指坏事或令人不快之事的)再次突然出现; 再发作: [+of] *a worrying recrudescence of urban violence* 都市暴力令人担忧的再度爆发

re·cruit¹ /rɪ`krut; rɪˈkruːt/ *v* **1** [I,T] to find new people to work in a company, join an organization, do a job etc 招聘, 吸收(新成员): *We're having difficulty recruiting enough properly qualified staff.* 我们难以招聘到足够的合格职员。**2 a)** [I,T] to get people to join the army or navy 招募(新兵): *Most of the men in the village were recruited that day.* 村里的大多数男子在那一天志愿参军。**b)** [T] to form a new army in this way (通过招募)组建(新部队) **3** [T] *informal* to persuade someone to do something for you【非正式】劝说, 说服: **recruit sb to do sth** *I recruited three of my friends to help me move everything to the new apartment.* 我动员了三个朋友帮我把所有的东西搬入新公寓。—**recruitment** *n* [U]

recruit² *n* [C] **1** someone who has just joined the army, navy, or air force 新兵: **raw recruit** (=one who is completely untrained) 未经任何训练的新兵 **2** someone who has recently joined an organization, group of people etc (机构、团体的)新成员: *The society was always trying to find ways of attracting new recruits.* 该社团总是在想方设法吸引新成员。

rec·tal /ˈrɛktl̩; ˈrektəl/ *adj technical* related to the RECTUM【术语】直肠的

rec·tan·gle /ˈrɛktæŋgl̩; ˈrektæŋgəl/ *n* [C] a shape that has four straight sides and four 90° angles at the corners. Usually two of the sides are longer than the other two. 长方形, 矩形 —compare 比较 SQUARE² (1) —see picture at 参见 SHAPE¹ 图

rec·tan·gu·lar /rɛk`tæŋgjələ; rekˈtæŋgjɪ̈lə/ *adj* having the shape of a rectangle 长方形的, 矩形的

rec·ti·fi·er /ˈrɛktə͵faɪə; ˈrektɪ̈faɪə/ *n* [C] *technical* an instrument that changes the flow of an electrical current in a wire【术语】整流器 —see also 另见 RECTIFY

rec·ti·fy /ˈrɛktə͵faɪ; ˈrektɪ̈faɪ/ *v* **rectified, rectifying** [T] **1** *formal* to correct something that is wrong【正式】纠正, 矫正: *I did my best to rectify the situation, but the damage was already done.* 我竭尽全力整顿局面, 但损失已经造成。| *Please rectify the mistake at once.* 请立即纠正错误。**2** *technical* to make alcohol pure【术语】精馏(酒精) **3** *technical* to change an ALTERNATING CURRENT (=flow of electricity backwards and forwards along a wire) to a DIRECT CURRENT (=flow in only one direction)【术语】整流(把电流由交流变成直流) —**rectifiable** *adj* —**rectification** /͵rɛktəfə`keʃən; ͵rektɪ̈fɪ̈ˈkeɪʃən/ *n* [C,U] —see also 另见 RECTIFIER

rec·ti·lin·e·ar /͵rɛktə`lɪnɪə; ͵rektɪ̈ˈlɪniə◂/ *adj technical* formed or moving in a straight line or consisting of straight lines【术语】成直线的; 直线运动的; 由直线组成的

rec·ti·tude /ˈrɛktə͵tud; ˈrektɪ̈tjuːd/ *n* [U] *formal* honesty and moral correctness【正式】诚实; 正直

rec·to /ˈrɛkto; ˈrektəʊ/ *n* [C] *technical* a page on the right-hand side of a book【术语】(书的)右页 —**recto** *adj* —opposite 反义词 VERSO

rec·tor /ˈrɛktə; ˈrektə/ *n* [C] **1** a priest in the Church of England or the Episcopal Church who is responsible for an area from which he receives his income directly (英国国教会或美国新教圣公会的)教区长 —compare 比较 VICAR **2** the person in charge of certain colleges and schools, especially in Scotland (尤指苏格兰的)学院院长; 学校校长

rec·to·ry /ˈrɛktərɪ; ˈrektəri/ *n* [C] a house where the rector of the local church lives, or used to live 教区长(曾住过)的住宅

rec·tum /ˈrɛktəm; ˈrektəm/ *n* [C] *technical* the lowest part of your BOWELS【术语】直肠 —see picture at 参见 DIGESTIVE SYSTEM 图

re·cum·bent /rɪ`kʌmbənt; rɪˈkʌmbənt/ *adj formal* lying down on your back or side【正式】躺着的, 仰卧的; 侧卧的: *a full-length portrait of the recumbent warrior* 一幅侧卧武士的全身肖像

re·cu·pe·rate /rɪ`kjupə͵ret; rɪˈkjuːpəreɪt/ *v* **1** [T] to get better again after an illness or injury 恢复, 复原: *The doctor sent her to the Sea View Rest Home to recuperate.* 医生让她去海景疗养院休养。| [+from] *A good night's sleep was all I needed to recuperate from the stresses of the day.* 我只需好好睡上一晚, 就可从一天的紧张中恢复过来。**2** [T] to get back money that you have spent or lost in business 重新获得; 弥补: *We've recuperated our losses.* 我们的损失已经得到补偿 —**recuperation** /rɪ͵kjupə`reʃən; rɪ͵kjuːpəˈreɪʃən/ *n* [U]

re·cu·pe·ra·tive /rɪ`kjupə͵retɪv; rɪˈkjuːpərətɪv/ *adj* helping you to get better again after an illness 有助康复的: *a recuperative vacation* 有助恢复健康的假日

re·cur /rɪ`kɜ; rɪˈkɜː/ *v* [I] **recurred, recurring** **1** if something, especially something bad or unpleasant, recurs, it happens again (尤指坏事或令人不快的事)再次发生: *There is a danger that the disease may recur in later life.* 年纪大了之后这种病有复发的危险。| *a recurring nightmare* 一再出现的恶梦 **2** *technical* if a number or numbers after a DECIMAL POINT recur, they are repeated forever in the same order【术语】(小数)循环

re·cur·rence /rɪ`kɜəns; rɪˈkʌrəns/ *n* [C,U] *formal* an occasion when something that has happened before, happens again【正式】再发生, 再现: [+of] *Measures must be taken to stop a recurrence of last night's violence.* 必须采取措施防止昨晚的暴力事件再次发生。

re·cur·rent /rɪ`kɜənt; rɪˈkʌrənt/ *adj* happening or appearing repeatedly 一再发生的, 反复出现的: *recurrent minor illnesses* 不断反复的小疾病 | *a recurrent theme in Eliot's poetry* 艾略特的诗歌中一再出现的主题 —**recurrently** *adv*

re·cy·cla·ble /ri`saɪkləbl̩; riːˈsaɪkləbəl/ *adj* used materials or substances that are recyclable can be recycled 可回收利用的 —**recyclable** *n* [usually plural 一般用复数] *AmE*【美】

re·cy·cle /ri`saɪkl̩; ͵riːˈsaɪkəl/ *v* [I,T] to put used objects or materials through a special process, so that they can be used again 再利用, 回收利用: *We take all our bottles and newspapers to be recycled.* 我们把所有的瓶子和报纸都送去回收利用。—**recycled** *adj*: *recycled paper* 再生纸

re·cy·cling /ri`saɪklɪŋ; ͵riːˈsaɪklɪŋ/ *n* [U] the process of treating things such as paper or steel so that they can be used again 回收利用: *Recycling is important to help protect our environment.* 回收利用对帮助保护我们的环境很重要。

red¹ /rɛd; red/ *adj* **redder, reddest**

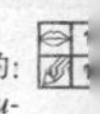

1 ▶COLOUR 颜色◀ having the colour of blood or fire 红色的: *We painted the door bright red.* 我们把门漆成鲜红色。| *a beautiful red rose* 一朵美丽的红玫瑰

2 ▶HAIR 头发◀ hair that is red has an orange-brown colour 褐红色的

3 ▶SKIN 皮肤◀ skin that is red is a bright pink colour, usually only for a short time 粉红色的: *Her cheeks were red with excitement.* 她兴奋得面颊红红的。

4 ▶POLITICS 政治◀ *informal* COMMUNIST or extremely LEFT-WING【非正式】共产主义的; 极左的

5 be as red as a beetroot *BrE*【英】**/beet** *AmE*【美】to have a very red face, usually because you are embarrassed (因尴尬而)满脸通红

6 like a red rag to a bull *BrE* very likely to make someone angry or upset【英】容易使人愤怒; 容易使人苦恼的: *Just mentioning his ex-wife's name was like a red rag to a bull.* 只要提到他前妻的名字他就会怒不可遏。

7 roll out the red carpet/give sb the red carpet treatment to give special treatment to someone important who is visiting you 隆重欢迎: *He's our best customer, so make sure you give him the red carpet treatment.* 他是我们最好的客户, 你们务必要隆重接待他。

8 a red cent [usually in negatives 一般用否定式] *AmE informal* a very small amount of money【美,非正式】极少量的钱: *They'll never be able to pay that – they don't have a red cent!* 他们永远也付不起这笔钱—他们身无分文! | *not worth a red cent* 一文不值的 —**redness** *n* [U] —see also 另见 **paint the town (red)** (PAINT² (6))

red² *n* **1** [C,U] the colour of blood or fire 红色: *Red is often used as a danger sign.* 红色经常被用作危险的信号。| *the reds and yellows of the fall trees* 秋天树木呈现的各种红色和黄色 | *The corrections were marked in red.* (=in red ink) 修改的部分用红笔标出。—see picture on page A5 参见 A5 页图 **2** [C,U] red wine 红葡萄酒: *a nice bottle of red* 一瓶香醇的红葡萄酒 **3** [C] *informal* a slightly insulting word for someone who has COMMUNIST or very LEFT-WING ideas or opinions【非正式】赤色分子; 共产主义者; 激进左翼分子(带有轻微侮辱意味) **4 see red** to become very angry 发怒: *The way he treated that dog just made me see red.* 他对待那条狗的方式使我愤怒。**5 in the red** *informal* owing more money than you have【非正式】亏欠; 有赤字:

These car payments are going to put me into the red again. 这几笔买车的付款让我再次出现赤字。—compare 比较 **be in the black** (BLACK² (4))

red ad·mi·ral /ˌ· ˈ···/ *n* [C] a type of BUTTERFLY that has black wings with bright red marks on them 红纹蝶

red a·lert /ˌ· ·ˈ·/ *n* [C usually singular 一般用单数] a warning of sudden very great danger 紧急警报, 红色警报: *Evacuate the building – this is a red alert!* 请撤离大楼, 这是紧急警报! | **be on red alert** (=be ready to deal with a danger) 处于紧急待命状态 *All the hospitals have been put on red alert.* 所有的医院已处于紧急待命状态。

Red Ar·my, the /ˌ· ˈ··/ the army of the former Soviet Union. This was its official name from 1918 until 1946, but people still used the name Red Army after that. 红军〔前苏联的军队, 1918至1946年的正式名称。此后人们仍沿用这一名称〕

Red Ar·rows, the /ˌ· ˈ··/ a team of specially trained pilots in the British air force, who fly small fighter planes and do AEROBATICS (=special tricks and movements in the air) to entertain people 红箭特技飞行队〔英国空军一支经过特殊训练的飞行队, 专门驾驶小型战斗机为观众做特技飞行表演〕

Red Bar·on, the /ˌ· ˈ··/ the NICKNAME of Baron von Richtofen 红色男爵〔冯·里希特霍芬男爵的绰号〕

Red Ber·ets, the /ˌ· ˈ··/ a popular name for the PARACHUTE division of the British army. They are called this because of the red BERETS (=soft hats) that are part of their uniform. 红色贝雷帽〔英军伞兵部队俗称。红色贝雷帽是他们统一着装的部分体现, 故名〕

red blood cell /ˌ· ˈ· ·/ also 又作 **red cor·pus·cle** /ˌ· ˈ···/ *n* [C] one of the cells in your blood that carry oxygen to every part of your body 红细胞, 红血球 —compare 比较 WHITE BLOOD CELL

red-blood·ed /ˌ· ˈ··◂/ *adj* a red-blooded man is strong and full of sexual energy 强有力的; 精力充沛的

red·breast /ˈrɛdˌbrɛst; ˈredbrest/ *n* [C] *poetic* a ROBIN【诗】(欧洲) 鸲, 知更鸟

red·brick /ˈrɛdˌbrɪk; ˈredbrɪk/ *adj* a redbrick university is one of the British universities built in the late 19th or early 20th century〔19世纪末、20世纪初在英国建成的〕红砖大学的 —compare 比较 OXBRIDGE

red card /ˌ· ˈ·/ *n* [C] a piece of red card held up by the REFEREE in a football match, to show that a player has done something against the rules and will not be allowed to play for the rest of the game〔足球〕红牌 —see picture on page A23 参见 A23 页图

Red Chi·na /ˌ· ˈ··/ *old-fashioned* a name for the People's Republic of China, used especially by western politicians when talking about its Communist government【过时】红色中国〔指中华人民共和国。西方政治家以前谈到中国共产党领导的政府时多用这一说法〕

red·coat /ˈrɛdˌkot; ˈredkəʊt/ *n* [C] a British soldier during the 18th and 19th centuries〔18、19世纪的〕英国士兵

Red Cres·cent /ˌ· ˈ··/ *n* [singular] an organization in Muslim countries that helps people who are suffering as a result of war, floods, disease etc 红新月会〔穆斯林国家中相当于红十字会的组织〕

Red Cross /ˌ· ˈ·/ *n* [singular] an international organization that helps people who are suffering as a result of war, floods, disease etc 红十字会

red·cur·rant /ˌrɛdˈkɝənt; ˌredˈkʌrənt◂/ *n* [C] a very small red fruit that grows on bushes in northern Europe〔北欧产的〕红醋栗 —compare 比较 BLACKCURRANT

red·den /ˈrɛdn̩; ˈredn/ *v* [I,T] to become red, or make something red (使) 变红: *Lynn's face reddened at this description of herself.* 听到对自己这样的描述, 林恩涨红了脸。

Red Dev·ils, the /ˌ· ˈ··/ a special British army team who give public performances of SKYDIVING (=jumping from an aircraft and making patterns in the air before the parachutes open) 红魔跳伞队〔英国军队的一支特技小队, 专门为观众表演高空跳伞〕

Red·ding, O·tis /ˈrɛdɪŋ, ˈotɪs; ˈredɪŋ, ˈəʊtɪs/ (1941-67) a US soul singer and songwriter, who died in a plane crash. His songs include *My Girl* and *(Sittin' On) The Dock of the Bay.* 雷丁 (1941-1967), 美国灵乐歌手、歌曲作家, 死于飞机失事。他的歌曲有《我的姑娘》和《海湾码头》等〕

red·dish /ˈrɛdɪʃ; ˈredɪʃ/ *adj* slightly red 微红的, 淡红的: *reddish-brown lipstick* 红褐色的口红

re·dec·o·rate /riˈdɛkəˌret; riːˈdekəreɪt/ *v* [I,T] *BrE* to put new paint or paper on the walls of a room【英】(给…) 重新粉刷墙壁; (给…) 重新贴上壁纸 —**redecoration** /riˌdɛkəˈreʃən; riːˌdekəˈreɪʃən/ *n* [U]

re·deem /rɪˈdim; rɪˈdiːm/ *v* [T] *formal*【正式】

1 ▶IMPROVE STH 改善某事物◀ to make something less bad 补救, 补偿: *Olivier's performance redeemed what was otherwise a second-rate play.* 要不是奥利维尔的表演, 这就是一出二流的戏。| **redeeming feature** (=the one good thing about someone or something that is unpleasant) 起弥补作用的特点 *a brutal man, whose one redeeming feature was his honesty* 一个残忍的人, 他的唯一可取之处是诚实

2 ▶FREE SB 解放某人◀ to free someone from the power or evil, especially in the Christian religion〔尤指基督教中〕救赎, 为…赎罪; 解救: *Christ came to Earth to redeem us from our sins.* 基督来到人间为我们赎罪。—see also 另见 REDEEMER

3 redeem yourself to do something that will improve what other people think of you, after you have behaved badly or failed 使自己免受责难; 挽回声誉: *She was trying desperately to redeem herself after last week's embarrassing mistake.* 在犯了上星期那个令人难堪的错误之后, 她拼命想挽回自己的声誉。

4 redeem a promise/pledge/obligation etc *formal* to do what you promised to do【正式】履行诺言/承诺/义务等: *The government found itself unable to redeem its election pledges.* 政府无法履行选举中所作的承诺。

5 ▶GET MONEY FOR STH 以某物兑换钱◀ to exchange a piece of paper representing an amount of money for the money that it is worth 把…兑换成现金: *Redeem this coupon for 20p off your next jar of coffee.* 你再买一瓶咖啡时, 用这张优惠券可省20便士。| *Bonus shares can be redeemed until 31st July.* 分红的股份可以在7月31日之前兑换成现金。

6 ▶GET STH BACK 重新获得某物◀ to buy something back which you had left with someone in order to borrow money from them 赎回: *I was finally able to redeem my watch from the pawnbrokers.* 我最终得以从当铺里赎回手表。—**redeemable** *adj*

Re·deem·er, the /rɪˈdimɚ; rɪˈdiːmə/ *n* [singular] *literary* Jesus Christ【文】救世主〔指耶稣基督〕

re·demp·tion /rɪˈdɛmpʃən; rɪˈdempʃən/ *n* [U] **1** the state of being freed from the power of evil, believed by Christians to be made possible by Jesus Christ〔基督教指耶稣的〕救赎, 赎罪 **2 past/beyond redemption** too bad to be saved, repaired, or improved 不可救药的, 无可挽回的 **3** *technical* the exchange of shares (SHARE² (5)), bonds (BOND¹ (1)) etc for money【术语】〔将股票、证券〕兑换现款; 赎回 —**redemptive** /-tɪv; -tɪv/ *adj*

Red En·sign, the /ˌ· ˈ··/ the flag of the British Merchant Navy, a red flag with the Union Jack in the top left corner 英国商船旗〔英国商船队的旗帜。底色为红色, 左上角有英国国旗图案〕

re·de·ploy /ˌridɪˈplɔɪ; ˌriːdɪˈplɔɪ/ *v* [T] to move someone or something to a different place or job 重新部署, 调遣〔人员〕, 调配〔物资〕: *Army tanks were redeployed elsewhere in the region.* 陆军坦克被重新部署在该地区的其他地方。—**redeployment** *n* [U]

re·de·vel·op /ˌridɪˈvɛləp; ˌriːdɪˈveləp/ *v* [T] to make an area more modern by putting in new buildings or changing the old ones 重建, 重新开发, 改建: *The old docks are being redeveloped as a business park.* 旧船坞正在被改建成商业园区。—**redevelopment** *n* [C,U]

red eye /ˈ· ·/ *n* [U] *AmE informal*【美, 非正式】**1** a plane that makes a journey at night 夜间航班, 红眼航班: *I took the red eye to LA.* 我乘坐夜间航班去洛杉矶。**2** cheap WHISKY 廉价威士忌酒

red-faced /ˌ· ˈ·◂/ *adj* embarrassed or ashamed 尴尬的; 羞愧的: *The election result left them rather red-faced.* 选举结果使他们相当尴尬。

red gi·ant /ˌ· ˈ··/ *n* [singular] a star that is near the middle of its life, and is larger and less solid than the sun 红巨星

Red Guard /ˌ· ˈ·/ a member of the group of young people, mostly students, who supported Mao Zedong's Cultural Revolution in China between 1966 and 1976. 红卫兵〔1966至1976年支持毛泽东发动"文化大革命"的青年组织成员, 多为学生〕

red-hand·ed /ˌ· ˈ··◂/ *adj* **catch sb red-handed** to catch someone at the moment when they are doing something wrong 当场抓住某人: *Earl was caught red-handed taking money from the register.* 厄尔从现金出纳机中拿钱时被当场抓获。

red·head /ˈrɛdˌhɛd; ˈredhed/ *n* [C] someone who has red hair 有红头发的人

red her·ring /ˌ· ˈ··/ *n* [C] a fact or idea that is not important but is introduced to take your attention away from the points that are important 转移注意力的事[想法]

red-hot /ˌ· ˈ·◂/ *adj* **1** metal that is red-hot is so hot that it shines red〔金属〕赤热的, 热得通红的: *The poker glowed red-hot in the fire.* 拨火棍在火里闪着赤热的光。**2** *informal* very hot【非

正式】非常热的, 烫的: *Be careful with those plates – they're red-hot.* 小心那些盘子, 烫极了。**3** *informal* extremely active or exciting【非正式】极富活力的; 令人十分激动的: *a red-hot news story* 令人兴奋的新闻报道 | *red-hot enthusiasm* 高涨的热情

re·dial /ˌriˋdaɪəl; ˌriːˈdaɪəl/ *v* [I,T] to DIAL a telephone number again 重拨(电话号码)

Red In·di·an /ˌ· ˈ···/ *n* [C] a word for a Native American, that is now usually considered offensive 美洲土著居民, 印第安人〔这词现在一般被认为是冒犯用语〕

re·di·rect, re-direct /ˌridəˋrɛkt; ˌriːdaɪˈrekt/ *v* [T] **1** to send something in a different direction, or use something for a different purpose 改向; 改用: *She was good at redirecting the children's energy into something useful.* 她善于把孩子们的精力转移到做有用的事情上。| *redirecting funds to other departments* 将资金转拨到其他部门 **2** *BrE* to send someone's letters to their new address from an address that they have left; FORWARD[3] (1)【英】改寄〔信件〕

re·dis·trib·ute /ˌridɪˋstrɪbjut; ˌriːdɪˈstrɪbjuːt/ *v* [T] to give something to each member of a group so that it is divided up in a different way than it was before 再分配, 再分发: *an attempt to redistribute the country's wealth more fairly* 更公平地重新分配国家财富的尝试 **—redistribution** /ˌridɪstrɪˋbjuʃən; ˌriːdɪstrɪˈbjuːʃən/ *n* [U]

Red Leices·ter /ˌrɛd ˋlɛstɚ; ˌred ˈlestə/ a type of Orange-coloured English cheese 莱斯特红酪〔英国一种橙色干酪〕

red-let·ter day /ˌ·ˈ·· ˌ·/ *n* [C] *informal* a day when something special happens that makes you very happy【非正式】喜庆的日子

red-light dis·trict /ˌ·ˈ· ˌ··/ *n* [C] the area of a town or city where there are many PROSTITUTES (=women who have sex for money) 红灯区

red meat /ˌ·ˈ·/ *n* [U] dark coloured meat such as BEEF or LAMB 红色肉类〈如牛肉、羊肉〉—compare 比较 WHITE MEAT

red·neck /ˋrɛdˌnɛk; ˈrednek/ *n* [C] *AmE informal* a man who lives in a country area of the US, is uneducated, and may have strong unreasonable opinions【美, 非正式】〔尤指顽固的〕乡巴佬 **—redneck** *adj*

Red Nose Day /ˌ·ˈ· ˌ·/ a day every year on which a lot of money is collected in Britain for people who need help in the UK and other countries. Red Nose Day is organized by the CHARITY organization Comic Relief, and people often wear plastic red noses or put them on the front of their cars to show their support. 红鼻子日〔英国一年一度的募捐活动日, 为该国和其他国家需要救济的人筹集资金。"红鼻子日"由慈善机构"喜剧演员济贫会"组织。人们戴着塑料红鼻子或将其放在汽车前部, 以示支持〕

re·do /riˋdu; riːˈduː/ *v* [T] *past tense* **redid** /-ˋdɪd; -ˈdɪd/ *past participle* **redone** /-ˋdʌn; -ˈdʌn/ to do something again 重做, 再做: *You'll have to redo this piece of work.* 你必须重新做这项工作。| *We're having the kitchen redone* (=decorated again) *professionally.* 我们正在请专业人员重新装修厨房。

red·o·lent /ˋrɛdl̩ənt; ˈredəl-ənt/ *adj formal*【正式】**1 redolent of** making you think of something 使人联想起…的: *a style redolent of the sixties* 使人联想起60年代的风格 **2** smelling strongly of something 散发出…强烈气味的: *The air was redolent with roses.* 空气中散发着玫瑰的芳香。**—redolence** *n* [U]

re·doub·le /riˋdʌbl̩; riːˈdʌbəl/ *v* [T] **redouble your efforts** to greatly increase your effort as you try to do something 加倍努力: *The musicians laughed and redoubled their efforts to keep up with the singer.* 乐师们笑了起来, 加倍努力跟上歌手的速度。

re·doub·ta·ble /rɪˋdautəbl̩; rɪˈdaʊtəbəl/ *adj literary* someone who is redoubtable is a person you respect or fear【文】令人敬畏的: *He was not looking forward to facing the redoubtable Mrs Macclesfield.* 他不希望面对令人敬畏的麦克尔斯菲尔德太太。

re·dound /rɪˋdaund; rɪˈdaʊnd/ *v* **redounded to sb's fame/credit/honour etc** *formal* to make someone more famous, more respected etc【正式】提高某人的声誉/信誉/荣誉等: *glorious deeds that redound to the honour of our country* 提高我国声誉的光荣事迹

red pep·per /ˌ·ˈ··/ *n* **1** [C] a red vegetable which you can eat raw or use in cooking; CAPSICUM 红辣椒: *stuffed red peppers* 酿红辣椒 **2** [U] a hot tasting red powder used in cooking; CAYENNE 辣椒粉

re·dress¹ /rɪˋdrɛs; rɪˈdres/ *v* [T] *formal*【正式】**1** to correct something that is wrong or unfair 修正, 改正; 矫正: *redressing the racial inequalities of society today* 纠正目前社会上种族不平等的现象 **2 redress the balance** to make a situation fair or equal when it has been unfair or unequal 调整; 使重新平衡: *If one species breeds too much, the theory says a new epidemic will arise to redress the balance.* 该理论称, 如果某一物种繁殖过多, 一种新的流行性传染病就会出现以重新达到平衡。

re·dress² /ˋridrɛs; rɪˈdres/ *n* [U] *formal* money that someone pays you because they have caused you harm, or damaged your property; COMPENSATION (1)【正式】〔对伤害或财产损坏的〕赔偿: *The only hope of redress is in a lawsuit.* 获得赔偿的唯一希望就是提出诉讼。

Red Riding Hood —see 见 LITTLE RED RIDING HOOD

Red River, the /ˌ· ˈ··/ a long river in the south of the US, which forms part of the border between the states of Oklahoma and Texas 红河〔美国南部一河流, 为俄克拉何马州和得克萨斯州的部分边界〕

Red Scare, the /ˈ· ˌ·/ a series of actions by the US government in 1919-20, against people who were believed to be Communists. Many US workers went on STRIKE (=stopped working to protest about their conditions) and the government was worried that there might be a revolution. Because of this, many people were arrested and many foreigners were forced to leave the country. 红色恐慌〔美国政府1919至1920年对被怀疑为共产党的公民所采取的一系列行动。当时, 美国有许多工人举行罢工, 政府担心会爆发一场革命。结果许多人被捕, 不少外国人被迫离境〕

Red Sea, the /ˌ· ˈ·/ a sea which separates Egypt, the Sudan, and Ethiopia from Saudi Arabia and Yemen. It is joined to the Mediterranean Sea by the Suez Canal, and is used by many ships. According to the story in the Old Testament of the Bible, God made a path for Moses and the Israelites through the Red Sea, by separating it into two parts, so that they could walk across the ground and escape from Egypt, where they had been prisoners. 红海〔将埃及、苏丹、埃塞俄比亚同沙特阿拉伯、也门分开的海域。红海通过苏伊士运河与地中海相连, 有许多船只经过。据《圣经·旧约》记载, 上帝将红海海水一分为二, 让摩西和他带领的以色列人步行穿过, 逃离埃及, 以摆脱被奴役的命运〕

red·skin /ˋrɛdˌskɪn; ˈredˌskɪn/ *n* [C] *old use* a word for a Native American, that is now considered to be offensive【旧】美洲土著居民, 印第安人〔这词现在一般被认为是冒犯用语〕

Red Square /ˌ· ˈ·/ the large square (=a broad, open area in a town) in the centre of Moscow, famous especially for the military processions that took place there on May Day when Moscow was the capital of the Soviet Union. The buildings in Red Square include St Basil's Cathedral and the Tomb of Lenin. 红场〔莫斯科市中心的大型广场。莫斯科为苏联首都时期, 每年五一节红场上都要举行阅兵仪式。红场上的著名建筑物有圣瓦西里大教堂和列宁墓〕

red tape /ˌ· ˈ·/ *n* [U] official rules that seem unnecessary and prevent things from being done quickly and easily 繁琐费时的手续; 繁文缛节: *a procedure surrounded by bureaucracy and red tape* 充斥着官僚作风和繁文缛节的程序

re·duce /rɪˋdus; rɪˈdjuːs/ *v* **1** [T] to make something smaller or less in size, amount, or price 缩小; 减少; 降低: *We were hoping that they would reduce the rent a little.* 我们希望他们会把租金降低一点。| **reduce sth by half/ten percent etc** *The workforce has been reduced by half.* 劳动力已经减少一半。| **[+to]** *All the shirts were reduced to £10.* 所有衬衫都减价至十英镑。—see also 另见 REDUCTION **2** [I] *especially AmE* to become thinner by losing weight【尤美】减肥 **3** [T] if you reduce a liquid or it reduces, you boil it or it boils until there is less of it〔煮沸液体以〕使浓缩 **4 in reduced circumstances** *old-fashioned* poorer than you were before【过时】更贫穷, 更潦倒 **5** [T] *old use* to take control of a place by using military force【旧】〔用武力〕攻克, 攻占

reduce sb/sth **to** sth *phr v* [T] **1 reduce sb to tears/silence etc** to make someone cry, be silent etc 使某人流泪/沉默等: *David's extraordinary reply reduced me to silence.* 戴维不寻常的回答使我无言以对。**2 reduce sb to doing sth** to force someone into a particular kind of behaviour or way of life 迫使某人做某事; 使不得不做某事: *Eventually Charlotte was reduced to begging on the streets.* 最后夏洛特被迫沦落到沿街乞讨。**3** to change something into a shorter simpler form 缩短, 简化: *The report can be reduced to three main points.* 报告可以归纳为三个要点。**4 reduce sth to rubble/ashes etc** to destroy something, especially a building, completely 把某物〔尤指建筑物〕夷为废墟/化为灰烬等 **5 reduce sb to the ranks** to make an army officer an ordinary soldier 把某人〔指军官〕降级为士兵

re·duc·tion /rɪˋdʌkʃən; rɪˈdʌkʃən/ *n* **1** [C,U] the fact of something becoming or being made smaller 缩小; 减少: **[+in]** *a slight reduction in the price of oil* 油价略有下降 | *strategies for noise reduction* 减少噪音的对策 | **make a reduction** (=sell some-

thing more cheaply) 减价 *We can make a reduction if you buy in bulk.* 如果你大批购买, 我们可以降低价格。**2** [C] a smaller copy of a photograph, map, or picture〔照片、地图或图画的〕缩版 —opposite 反义词 ENLARGEMENT (1)

2 **re·dun·dan·cy** /rɪˋdʌndənsɪ; rɪˈdʌndənsi/ *n* **1** [C,U] *BrE* a situation in which someone has to leave their job, because they are no longer needed【英】失业, 裁员, 解雇: *The closure of the export department resulted in over 100 redundancies.* 出口部的关闭导致一百多人被解雇。| *2,000 workers now face redundancy.* 2000 名工人目前面临着失业。**2** [U] a situation in which something is not used because something similar or the same already exists 重复; 多余; 累赘 **3** [C,U] *technical* the quality of containing additional parts that will make a system work if other parts fail【术语】〔部件的〕冗余〔确保即使有部件失灵, 系统依然正常工作〕

redundancy pay /ˈ· ·· , ·/ *n* [U] *BrE* money you get from your employer when you are made redundant【英】解雇津贴, 遣散费; SEVERANCE PAY *AmE*【美】

re·dun·dant /rɪˋdʌndənt; rɪˈdʌndənt/ *adj* **1** *BrE* if you are redundant your employer no longer has a job for you【英】失业的, 被解雇的: **make sb redundant** *Seventy factory workers were made redundant in the resulting cuts.* 在继而发生的裁员中七十名工人被解雇。**2** not necessary because something else does the same thing 多余的, 累赘的: *The word gradually became redundant and dropped out of the language.* 这个词逐渐变得累赘, 并从该语言中消失了。**—redundantly** *adv*

re·du·pli·cate /rɪˋdupləˌket; rɪˈdjuːplɪ̩keɪt/ *v* [T] *formal* to repeat a part of something, especially part of a word【正式】重复〔尤指词的某部分〕**—reduplication** /rɪˌdupləˋkeʃən; rɪˌdjuːplɪ̩ˈkeɪʃən/ *n* [C,U]

red·wood /ˋrɛdˌwʊd; ˈredwʊd/ *n* [C,U] a very tall tree that grows in California, or the wood from this tree〔生长在美国加利福尼亚的〕红杉(木)

reed /rid; riːd/ *n* [C] **1** a type of tall plant like grass that grows in wet places 芦苇: *Reeds grew in clumps all along the river bank.* 沿着河岸长着一丛丛芦苇。**2** a thin piece of wood that is fixed into a musical instrument such as an OBOE or CLARINET, and produces a sound when you blow over it〔管乐器的〕簧片

Reed, Sir Carol (1906-76) a British film DIRECTOR, whose films include *The Third Man* (1949), *Our Man in Havana* (1959), and the musical film *Oliver!* (1968) 里德〔(1906-1976), 英国电影导演。作品包括《第三个人》(1949)、《哈瓦纳特派员》(1959) 和音乐片《奥利弗!》(1968)〕

re·ed·u·cate /riˋɛdʒəˌket; riːˈedjʊkeɪt/ *v* [T] to teach someone to think or behave in a different way 再教育, 重新教育: *Young criminals must above all be re-educated.* 最重要的是必须对青少年罪犯进行再教育。

reed·y /ˋridɪ; ˈriːdi/ *adj* **1** a voice that is reedy is high and unpleasant to listen to〔声音〕尖的, 刺耳的 **2** a place that is reedy has a lot of reeds growing there 芦苇丛生的

reef¹ /rif; riːf/ *n* [C] a line of sharp rocks, often made of CORAL, or a raised area of sand near the surface of the sea 礁; 礁脉: *The ship was wrecked on a reef.* 这条船触礁失事了。| *the Great Barrier Reef* 大堡礁

reef² also 又作 **reef in** *v* [T] *technical* to tie up part of a sail in order to make it smaller【术语】缩〔帆〕

ree·fer /ˋrifɚ; ˈriːfə/ *n* [C] *old-fashioned* a cigarette containing the drug MARIJUANA【过时】大麻香烟

reef knot /ˈ· ·/ *n* [C] *especially BrE* a double knot that cannot come undone easily【尤英】缩帆结, 方结, 平结; SQUARE KNOT *AmE*【美】

reek¹ /rik; riːk/ *v* [I] **1** to smell strongly and unpleasantly of something 有臭味, 发出臭气: *This room absolutely reeks.* 这个房间真的臭极了。| **[+of]** *His breath reeked of garlic.* 他的呼吸带着蒜味。**2** to seem to be strongly connected with something bad or unpleasant 具有…的强烈气息: **[+of]** *The whole business reeks of dishonesty.* 整个交易充满欺诈的意味。

reek² *n* [singular] a strong unpleasant smell 浓烈的臭味, 恶臭: *a reek of tobacco and beer* 一股强烈的烟和啤酒的臭味

reel¹ /ril; riːl/ *n* [C] **1 a)** *BrE* a round object onto which thread, wire, fishing line, cinema film etc can be wound【英】卷轴, 卷筒; 卷盘; 绕线轮: *a cotton reel* 棉线团 —compare 比较 BOBBIN **b)** the amount that one of these objects will hold 一卷(之量): *Have you got another reel of film?* 你是否还有一卷胶卷? **2** one of the parts of a cinema film that is contained on a reel〔一部影片的〕一盘: *a scene from the final reel of 'High Noon'* 电影《正午》最后一盘中的一个场面 **3** a quick and cheerful Scottish or Irish dance, or the music for this 里尔舞〔一种轻快的苏格兰或爱尔兰舞〕; 里尔舞曲

reel² *v* **1** also 又作 **reel back** [I] to step backwards suddenly and almost fall over, especially after being hit or getting a shock〔尤指遭受打击或震惊而〕站立不稳: *Diane reeled back in amazement.* 黛安娜吃惊得朝后打了一个趔趄。| *A punch in his stomach sent him reeling.* 他的肚子上重重地挨了一拳, 人打了个趔趄。**2** [I] to feel very shocked or confused 震惊; 迷惑: *All these statistics make my head reel.* 所有这些数字搞得我头昏脑胀。| **[+from]** *The party is still reeling from its recent election defeat.* 该党由于最近选举的失败仍然惊魂未定。**3** [I] to seem to go around and around〔感觉〕晕眩, 天旋地转: *The room reeled before my eyes and I fainted.* 房间在我眼前旋转起来, 随即我就失去了知觉。**4** [T always+adv/prep] to make something move on or off a reel by winding it 卷, 绕: *He reeled in his fishing line.* 他绕着收回鱼线。**5** [I always+adv/prep] to walk in an unsteady way, moving from side to side as if you are drunk 蹒跚: *Captain Banks came reeling up the street.* 班克斯上校步履蹒跚地沿街走来。

reel sth ↔ **off** *phr v* [T] *informal* to repeat a lot of information quickly and easily【非正式】滔滔不绝地重复: *Jack reeled off a list of names.* 杰克一口气说出了一长串名字。

re·e·lect /ˌri əˋlɛkt; ˌriː ɪˈlekt/ *v* [T] to elect someone again 再次选, 重选 **—re-election** /-ˋlɛkʃən; -ˈlekʃən/ *n* [C,U]: *Barnes is seeking re-election.* 巴恩斯正在寻求连任。

re·en·try /riˋɛntrɪ; riˈentri/ *n* [C,U] an act of entering a place again 再进入: *The shuttle made a successful re-entry into the Earth's atmosphere.* 宇宙飞船成功地重返地球大气层。

reeve /riv; riːv/ *n* [C] **1** the president of a modern Canadian town council〔加拿大的〕市镇议会主席 **2** an English law officer in former times〔英国旧时的〕地方治安法官

ref¹ /rɛf; ref/ *n* [C] *BrE informal* a REFEREE【英, 非正式】裁判员

ref² the written abbreviation of 缩写= REFERENCE 2

re·fec·to·ry /rɪˋfɛktərɪ; rɪˈfektəri/ *n* [C] *BrE* a large room in a school, college etc where meals are served and eaten【英】〔学校、学院等的〕食堂, 餐厅; CAFETERIA *AmE*【美】

re·fer /rɪˋfɝ; rɪˈfɜː/ *v* **referred, referring** 1 1

refer to *phr v* [T] **1** **[refer to** sb/sth] to mention or speak about someone or something 提到, 谈到: *We agreed never to refer to the matter again.* 我们同意永远不再提这件事。| *Although she didn't mention any names, everyone knew who she was referring to.* 尽管她没有提名字, 但大家都知道她指的是谁。| **refer to sth/sb as** *Johnson referred to the discovery as a major breakthrough in medical science.* 约翰逊称这项发现是医学领域里的一个重大突破。**2** **[refer to** sth] to look at a book, map, piece of paper etc, for information 参考, 查看, 查阅: *Complete the exercise without referring to a dictionary.* 请不要查阅辞典完成这个练习。| *Let me just refer to my notes for the exact figures.* 让我查看笔记, 找出确切的数字。**3** **[refer to** sth/sb] if a statement, number etc refers to someone or something, it is about that person or thing 涉及, 关于: *The figures in the left-hand column refer to our sales abroad.* 左栏里的数字是关于我们的海外销售额的。**4** **[refer** sb/sth **to** sb/sth] to send someone or something to another place or person for information, advice, or a decision 让…去查询; 提交…作决定: *My complaint was referred to the manufacturers.* 我的投诉已转交给制造商。| *Professor Watson referred me to an article she had written on the subject.* 沃森教授要我去查阅她写的关于这个题目的一篇文章。| *My doctor is referring me* (=is sending me for treatment) *to a dermatologist.* 我的医生介绍我去看皮肤科医生。—see also 另见 CROSS-REFER

re·fer·a·ble /rɪˋfɝəbḷ; rɪˈfɜːrəbəl/ *adj* **[+to]** *formal* something that is referable to something else can be related to it【正式】与…有关的

ref·er·ee¹ /ˌrɛfəˋri; ˌrefəˈriː/ *n* [C] **1** someone who is in charge of a game in sports such as football, BASKETBALL, or BOXING〔体育比赛的〕裁判员 —compare 比较 UMPIRE¹ —see picture on page A22 参见 A22 页图 **2** *BrE* someone who provides information about you when you are trying to get a job【英】证明人, 介绍人, 推荐人: *His headmaster agreed to act as his referee.* 校长同意做他的推荐人。**3** someone who is asked to settle a disagreement 仲裁者, 公断者: *an independent referee* 一位独立仲裁人

referee² *v* **refereed, refereeing** [I,T] to be the referee for a game 当裁判; 为…担任裁判

ref·er·ence /ˋrɛfərəns; ˈrefərəns/ *n* **1** [C,U] something you say or write that mentions another person or thing 提及, 谈到: 3 
[+to] *There is no direct reference to her own childhood in the novel.* 小说里没有直接提及她的童年。| **make reference to** *Winston made no reference to what had happened.* 温斯顿没有提及所发生的事情。| **a passing reference (to)** (=a quick mention) 顺便提及 *a speech about the economy without even a*

passing reference to the problem of unemployment 丝毫没有提及失业的有关经济问题的讲话 **2** [C,U] the act of looking at something for information 查阅, 查看: *Use this dictionary for easy reference.* 为了查阅方便, 请使用这本辞典。| **for future reference** (=to have information in the future) 以供将来参考 *Keep their price list on file for future reference.* 请将他们的价目表存档, 以供日后参考。**3 with reference to** *formal* used to say what you are writing or talking about, especially in business letters 【正式】关于〔尤用于公函〕: *With reference to your recent advertisement, I am writing to request further details.* 关于贵方最近的广告, 现特函查询详情。**4** [C] **a)** a letter written by someone who knows you well, usually to a new employer, giving information about you 推荐信, 介绍信: **take up references** (=get references) 得到推荐信 *We will need references from your former employers.* 我们需要你前雇主的推荐信。**b)** a person who provides information about your character and abilities 推荐人, 介绍人: *Ask your teacher to act as one of your references.* 请你的老师做你的推荐人之一。**5** [C] **a)** a note that tells you where the information that is used in a book, article etc comes from 出处; 参考书目: *a list of references at the end of the article* 文章结尾处的参考书目 **b)** a number that tells you where you can find the information you want in a book, on a map etc 〔书籍或地图等中的〕参照号, 参照符号: *map reference SG49* 地图参照号 SG49 —see also 另见 CROSS-REFERENCE, FRAME OF REFERENCE, **terms of reference** (TERM[1] (18))

reference book /ˈ··· ·/ *n* [C] a book such as a dictionary or ENCYCLOPAEDIA that you look at to find information 工具书, 参考书

reference li·bra·ry /ˈ··· ,···/ *n* [C] a public place where books are stored, where you can use the books but cannot take them away 工具书阅览室

ref·e·ren·dum /ˌrɛfəˈrɛndəm; ˌrefəˈrendəm/ *n* [C, U] *plural* **referenda** or **referendums** an occasion when everyone in a country votes in order to make a decision about a particular subject 〔为表决某问题的〕全民投票: **hold a referendum** *A referendum was held on whether abortion should be made legal.* 就堕胎是否应该合法化进行了全民投票。

re·fer·ral /rɪˋfɜəl; rɪˈfɜːrəl/ *n* [C,U] *formal* an act of sending someone or something to another place for help, information, a decision etc 【正式】提交; 介绍: *the referral of the case to the Court of Appeal* 把案件提交给上诉法庭

re·fill[1] /riˋfɪl; ˌriːˈfɪl/ *v* [T] to fill something again 再填充, 再注满: *I'll just refill the coffee pot.* 我要把咖啡壶再灌满。—**refillable** *adj*: *a refillable lighter* 可再充气的打火机

re·fill[2] /ˋriˌfɪl; ˈriːfɪl/ *n* [C] **1** a container filled with something such as ink or petrol that you use to fill or replace the empty container in your pen, CIGARETTE LIGHTER etc 〔笔、打火机等的〕添补物; 〔笔芯等的〕替换物: *I must buy some refills for my pen.* 我必须给我的笔买些笔芯。**2** *spoken* another drink to refill your glass 【口】再倒 (一杯饮料): *Would you like a refill?* 你想再来一杯吗?

re·fine /rɪˋfaɪn; rɪˈfaɪn/ *v* [T] **1** to improve a method, plan, system etc by gradually making slight changes to it 〔慢慢地、微小地〕改进; 完善: *The current structure will be retained and refined.* 现有结构将予以保留并且不断完善。**2** to make a substance pure using an industrial process 净化; 提炼: *the petroleum refining industry* 炼油业

re·fined /rɪˋfaɪnd; rɪˈfaɪnd/ *adj* **1** [no comparative 无比较级] a substance that is refined has been made pure by an industrial process 精炼的; 精制的: *refined oil* 精炼油 | *refined white sugar* 精制白糖 **2** someone who is refined is polite and seems to be well-educated or to belong to a high social class 优雅的, 有教养的: *a refined way of speaking* 优雅的谈吐 **3** a method or process that is refined has been improved to make it more effective 精妙的; 完善的 —opposite 反义词 UNREFINED

re·fine·ment /rɪˋfaɪnmənt; rɪˈfaɪnmənt/ *n* **1** [C] an addition or improvement to an existing product, system etc 精巧的附加装置; 改良品: *The new car has a number of refinements such as an air bag and a catalytic converter.* 这款新车有许多改良的设备, 如气囊和催化转化器。**2** [U] the quality of being polite and well-educated, in a way that is typical of someone from a high social class 优雅, 高雅, 有教养: *a woman of great refinement* 非常文雅的女士 **3** [U] the process of improving something 完善, 改进: [+of] *the continued refinement of existing systems* 现行体制的不断完善 **4** [U+of] the process of making a substance pure 精炼; 提纯

re·fin·e·ry /rɪˋfaɪnərɪ; rɪˈfaɪnəri/ *n* [C] a factory where something such as metal, sugar, or oil is refined 〔金属、糖或石油的〕提炼厂, 精炼厂: *an oil refinery* 炼油厂

re·fit /riˋfɪt; ˌriːˈfɪt/ *v* **refitted, refitting** [I,T] to make a ship ready to be used again, by doing repairs and putting in new machinery 整修; 重新装备 (船只): *We sailed into port to refit.* 我们驶入港口整修船只。—**refit** /ˋriˌfɪt; ˈriːfɪt/ *n* [C,U]: *The yacht needs a refit.* 这艘游艇需要整修。

re·flate /riˋflet; riːˈfleɪt/ *v* [I,T] *technical* to increase the supply of money in a country or system, in order to encourage trade 【术语】(使) 通货增加以鼓励贸易: *measures to reflate the economy* 增加通货使经济复苏的措施

re·fla·tion /riˋfleʃən; riːˈfleɪʃən/ *n* [U] *technical* the process of increasing the amount of money being used in a country in order to increase trade 【术语】通货再膨胀 —**reflationary** *adj* —compare 比较 DEFLATION, INFLATION (1)

re·flect /rɪˋflɛkt; rɪˈflekt/ *v* **1** [T] if a surface reflects light, heat, sound, or an image, it throws back the light etc that hits it 反射〔光、热、声或影像等〕: *White clothes are cooler because they reflect the heat.* 白色的衣服比较凉快, 因为它们能反射热气。| *The moon reflects the sun's rays.* 月亮反射太阳光。| **be reflected in** *She could see her face reflected in the water.* 她看见自己的脸倒映在水中。**2** [T not usually in progressive 一般不用进行时] to show or be a sign of a particular situation or feeling 显示, 反映: *The low value of the dollar reflects growing concern about the US economy.* 美元币值低反映出人们对美国经济的忧虑日益增加。| **be reflected in** *The growing conflict has been reflected in the paper's editorial section.* 日益严重的冲突反映在该报的社论栏里。| **reflect who/what/how etc** *Does this letter reflect how you really feel?* 这封信是否反映了你的真实感受? **3** [I,T] to think carefully about something, or to express your thoughts 仔细思考; 表达意见: [+on] *Take some time to reflect on your future plans.* 抽点时间仔细考虑你未来的计划。| **reflect that** *I reflected that there wasn't much point in continuing with my plans now that Al was gone.* 我考虑过, 既然阿尔走了, 继续我的计划也就没有多大意义了。

reflect on/upon *phr v* [T] to influence people's opinion of someone or something, especially in a bad way 给某人对…的评价造成〔尤指不利的〕影响: **reflect on sb/sth** *an economic record that reflects badly on government policy* 使政府政策引起非议的经济记录 | *If my children are rude, that reflects on me as a parent.* 假如我的孩子没有礼貌, 那会使我这个做家长的丢脸。

reflecting tel·e·scope /·ˈ·· ,···/ *n* [C] an instrument for seeing distant objects that reflects an image in a mirror to make it bigger 反射 (式) 望远镜 —compare 比较 REFRACTING TELESCOPE

reflection 倒影

re·flec·tion /rɪˋflɛkʃən; rɪˈflekʃən/ *n* **1** [C] an image reflected in a mirror or similar surface 〔镜子或类似表面反射出来的〕影像: *We looked at our reflections in the lake.* 我们看着自己在湖中的倒影。**2** [C,U] careful thought, or an idea or opinion based on this 深思, 考虑; 〔经过仔细考虑形成的〕想法, 见解: *A moment's reflection will show the stupidity of this argument.* 只需认真思考一会儿便可看出这种观点多么愚蠢。| [+on] *It was interesting to hear her reflections on the situation in the Far East.* 听她发表对远东局势的看法十分有意思。| **on reflection** (=used to say that you have thought more about something, and changed your opinion) 经考虑之后〔改变看法〕 *At first I thought her ideas were crazy, but on reflection, I realized there was some truth in what she said.* 起初我觉得她的想法很荒唐, 但经过一番考虑, 我认识到她说的话有些道理。**3** [C] something that shows the effects of, or is a sign of, a particular situation 反映: [+of] *The rising crime rate is a reflection of an unstable society.* 犯罪率上升是社会不稳定的反映。| *His speech was an accu-*

rate reflection of the public mood. 他的讲话确切反映了公众的情绪。**4 be a reflection on** to show someone's character, abilities, work etc in an unfavourable way 使人们对…产生恶劣的评价: *The students' bad grades are no reflection on the teachers, but they do say something about the tests.* 学生成绩差并不说明老师不好, 但的确反映出测验的一些问题。**5** [U] the fact of light, heat, sound or an image being reflected〔光、热、声音或影像的〕反射

re·flec·tive /rɪˋflɛktɪv; rɪˈflektɪv/ *adj* **1** thinking quietly 沉思的: *in a reflective mood* 思潮起伏 **2** a reflective surface reflects (REFLECT (1)) the light〔表面〕反射的

re·flec·tor /rɪˋflɛktɚ; rɪˈflektə/ *n* [C] **1** a small piece of plastic that is fastened to a bicycle or piece of clothing, so that it can be seen more easily at night〔为夜间容易辨认而固定在自行车或衣服上的〕反光板; 反射物 —see picture at 参见 BICYCLE 图 **2** a surface that reflects light 反射器; 反射镜; 反射物

re·flex /ˋriflɛks; ˈriːfleks/ *n* [C] **1** a sudden movement that your muscles make as a natural reaction to a physical effect〔生理的〕反射(作用): *The doctor checked my reflexes.* 医生检查了我的反射能力。**2 reflexes** [plural] the natural ability to react quickly and well to sudden situations 反应能力: *A tennis player needs to have good reflexes.* 网球运动员需要有良好的反应能力。**3** also 又作 **reflex action** something that you do when you react to a situation without thinking 反射动作, 本能反应: *His hand went to his gun in a reflex action.* 他本能地去摸枪。

re·flex·ive /rɪˋflɛksɪv; rɪˈfleksɪv/ *adj technical* a reflexive verb or PRONOUN shows that the action in a sentence affects the person or thing that does the action【术语】〔动词或代词〕反身的 —**reflexive** *n* [C]

re·flex·ol·o·gy /ˌriflɛkˋsɑlədʒi; ˌriːflekˈsɒlədʒi/ *n* [U] a kind of ALTERNATIVE MEDICINE in which areas of the feet are touched or rubbed in order to cure a medical problem 反射疗法〔按摩足部某些部位来治病的一种替代疗法〕

re·for·est·a·tion /ˌriforɪsˋteʃən; riːˌfɒrɪ̵ˈsteɪʃən/ *n* [U] the practice of planting trees in order to grow a forest for industrial use or to improve the environment 植树造林 —**reforest** /riˋfɔrɪst; riːˈfɒrɪ̵st/ *v* [I,T]

re-form /ˌriˋfɔrm; ˌriːˈfɔːm/ *v* [I,T] **1** to start to exist again or to make something start to exist again 重新组成; 重建: *At the end of the year the company re-formed, and began trading again.* 该公司在年底重组后又开始了经营。**2** to form into lines again, or to make soldiers do this (使)重新编队: *The platoon re-formed, ready to attack.* 该排经过重新编队, 准备进攻。

re·form¹ /rɪˋfɔrm; rɪˈfɔːm/ *v* **1** [T] to change a system, law, organization etc so that it operates in a fairer or more effective way 改进, 改革: *plans to reform the tax system* 改革税收制度的计划 **2** [I,T] to change your behaviour and become a better person, or to make someone do this 改过, 改造: **be a reformed character** *Harry's a reformed character since he stopped taking drugs.* 戒毒以后, 哈里已经改过自新。| **reformed criminal/sinner/alcoholic etc** (=someone who is no longer a criminal etc) 改过自新的犯人/罪人/酗酒者等

2 **reform²** *n* [C,U] a change made to a system or organization, in order to improve it, remove unfairness etc 改进, 改革: *educational reform* 教育改革 | [+of] *a radical reform of the legal system* 法律制度的彻底改革

ref·or·ma·tion /ˌrɛfɚˋmeʃən; ˌrefəˈmeɪʃən/ *n* **1** [C,U] an improvement made by changing something a lot 改进; 改善; 改革 **2 the Reformation** the religious changes in Europe in the 16th century, that resulted in the Protestant churches being established〔欧洲16世纪的导致产生新教的〕宗教改革

re·for·ma·to·ry /rɪˋfɔrməˌtorɪ; rɪˈfɔːmətəri/ *n* [C] *AmE or old use* a special school where young people who have broken the law are sent【美或旧】少年管教所

re·form·er /rɪˋfɔrmɚ; rɪˈfɔːmə/ *n* [C] someone who tries to improve a system, law, or society 改革者, 革新者, 改良者: *a great social reformer* 伟大的社会改革者

re·form·ist /rɪˋfɔrmɪst; rɪˈfɔːmɪ̵st/ *adj* wanting to change systems or situations, especially in politics〔尤指政治上〕改革主义的 —**reformist** *n* [C]

reform school /ˑˈˑ ˑ/ *n* [C] *AmE* a REFORMATORY【美】少年管教所

re·fract /rɪˋfrækt; rɪˈfrækt/ *v* [T] *technical* to make light change direction when passing through glass or water【术语】使〔光〕折射 —**refraction** /rɪˋfrækʃən; rɪˈfrækʃən/ *n* [U]

refracting tel·e·scope /ˑˈˑ ˑˑˑ/ *n* [C] an instrument for seeing distant objects that refracts images by passing them through a LENS (=a piece of glass) 折射望远镜

re·frac·to·ry /rɪˋfræktərɪ; rɪˈfræktəri/ *adj formal* disobedient and difficult to deal with or control【正式】难驾驭的, 不服管教的

re·frain¹ /rɪˋfren; rɪˈfreɪn/ *v formal* to not do something that you want to do【正式】克制, 节制, 忍住: [+from] *Kindly refrain from smoking.* 请勿抽烟。

refrain² *n* [C] **1** part of a song that is repeated, especially at the end of each VERSE〔歌曲中, 尤指每小节末尾的〕反复句, 叠句, 副歌 **2** *formal* a remark or idea that is often repeated【正式】经常重复的话[想法]: *Our proposal met with the constant refrain that the company could not afford it.* 我们的建议一再得到的答复是公司负担不起。

re·fresh /rɪˋfrɛʃ; rɪˈfreʃ/ *v* **1** [T] to make someone feel less tired or less hot 使恢复精力, 提神; 使清凉: *He refreshed himself with a glass of beer.* 他喝了杯啤酒提提神。| *A shower will refresh you.* 洗个淋浴你就会精神一爽。**2 refresh sb's memory** to make someone remember something 使某人想起; 唤起某人的记忆: *I looked at the map to refresh my memory of the route.* 我看地图以唤起自己对这条路线的记忆。**3 refresh sb's drink** *AmE spoken* to add more of an alcoholic drink to someone's glass【美口】给某人添酒精饮料: *Can I refresh your drink?* 我给你再加点酒好吗? **4** [I,T] *technical* to provide computer OUTPUT again; UPDATE¹ (1)【术语】〔电脑输出〕刷新, 更新: *This display will not refresh until you repeat the command.* 你要重复指令, 显示的内容才会更新。—**refreshed** *adj*: *After a good sleep he awoke refreshed.* 好好睡了一觉后, 他醒来时恢复了精神。

re·fresh·er course /ˑˈˑˑ ˑ/ *n* [C] a training course that teaches you about new developments in a particular subject or skill, especially one that you need for your job〔职业的〕进修课程

re·fresh·ing /rɪˋfrɛʃɪŋ; rɪˈfreʃɪŋ/ *adj* **1** making you feel less tired or less hot 消除疲劳的, 提神的; 清凉的: *a long refreshing drink* 一大杯提神的饮料 | *The breeze was refreshing after the stuffy classroom.* 从闷热的教室出来后, 微风使人感到凉爽。**2** pleasantly different from what is familiar and boring 令人耳目一新的: *It made a refreshing change to talk to someone new.* 换个人谈话让人感觉很新奇。—**refreshingly** *adv*

re·fresh·ment /rɪˋfrɛʃmənt; rɪˈfreʃmənt/ *n* **1 refreshments** [plural] small amounts of food and drink that are provided at a meeting, sports event etc 茶点; 点心和饮料: *Refreshments will be served after the meeting.* 会后有茶点招待。**2** [U] food and drink in general 食物和饮料: *We worked all day without refreshment.* 我们不吃不喝地工作了一整天。| **liquid refreshment** *humorous* (=alcoholic drink)【幽默】酒 **3** [U] the experience of being made to feel less tired or hot 恢复精力; 凉爽

re·fri·ge·rant /rɪˋfrɪdʒərənt; rɪˈfrɪdʒərənt/ *n* [C] *technical* a substance used in refrigeration systems【术语】制冷剂, 冷冻剂

re·fri·ge·rate /rɪˋfrɪdʒəˌret; rɪˈfrɪdʒəreɪt/ *v* [T] to make something such as food or liquid cold in order to preserve it 冷冻, 冷藏: *refrigerate the mixture overnight* 把混合物冷藏过夜 —**refrigeration** /rɪˌfrɪdʒəˋreʃən; rɪˌfrɪdʒəˈreɪʃən/ *n* [U]: *Meat must be kept under refrigeration.* 肉类必须冷藏。

re·fri·ge·ra·tor /rɪˋfrɪdʒəˌretɚ; rɪˈfrɪdʒəreɪtə/ *n* [C] *BrE formal or AmE* a special cupboard kept cold by electricity, in which you store food and drink; FRIDGE【英, 正式或美】冰箱 —see picture on page A10 参见 A10 页图

re·fuel /riˋfjuəl; ˌriːˈfjʊəl/ *v* **refuelled, refuelling** *BrE*【英】, **refueled, refueling** *AmE*【美】**1** [I,T] to fill a vehicle or plane with FUEL before continuing a journey (给)加油, (给)加燃料: *We stopped in Dubai to refuel.* 我们在迪拜停下来加油。**2** [T] to make feelings, emotions, or ideas stronger 使〔感情、情绪或想法〕更强烈: *The news has refuelled speculation about whether there might be something illegal going on.* 这消息增添了人们对是否存在非法勾当的揣测。

ref·uge /ˋrɛfjudʒ; ˈrefjuːdʒ/ *n* [C] a place that provides protection or shelter from danger 庇护所, 避难处: *a refuge for battered wives* 受虐待妻子的庇护所 | [+from] *a refuge from the storm* 躲避风暴的地方 | **take/seek refuge in sth** (=look for or find safety somewhere) 在…寻求庇护 *During the frequent air raids people take refuge in their cellars.* 在频繁的空袭中, 人们躲在地下室里。

ref·u·gee /ˌrɛfjuˋdʒi; ˌrefjʊˈdʒiː/ *n* [C] someone who has been forced to leave their country, especially during a war〔尤指战争中的〕难民, 避难者: *Refugees were streaming across the border.* 难民涌过边界。| *a refugee camp* 难民营 3

re·ful·gent /rɪˋfʌldʒənt; rɪˈfʌldʒənt/ *adj literary* very bright【文】光辉的, 灿烂的 —**refulgence** *n* [U]

re·fund¹ /ˋriˌfʌnd; ˈriːfʌnd/ *n* [C] a sum of money that is given back to you 退款: *You can apply for a refund of your travel costs.* 你可以申请退还旅费。

re·fund² /rɪˋfʌnd; rɪˈfʌnd/ *v* [T] to give someone their money back, especially because they are not satisfied with the goods or services they have paid for 退还; 偿还〔尤指因对所购货物或服务不满意〕: *I took the radio back, and they refunded my money.* 我把收音机送回去，他们给我退款。—compare 比较 REIMBURSE

re·fur·bish /riˋfɝbɪʃ; ˌriːˈfɜːbɪʃ/ *v* [T] **1** to thoroughly repair and improve a building by painting and cleaning it 翻修，整修〔房子〕 **2** to change and improve a plan, idea or skill 修改，完善〔计划、思想或技术〕—**refurbishment** *n* [C,U]

re·fus·al /rɪˋfjuzḷ; rɪˈfjuːzəl/ *n* [C,U] **1** an act of saying or showing that you will not do something that someone has asked you to do 拒绝: **refusal to do sth** *His refusal to pay the fine got him into trouble.* 他拒绝付罚款，因而给自己惹了麻烦。| **point-blank refusal** (=an immediate direct refusal) 断然拒绝 **2** an act of not accepting something that is being offered to you 拒绝接受，谢绝: [+of] *They couldn't understand Raymond's refusal of a scholarship to Yale.* 他们无法理解雷蒙德为什么拒绝接受耶鲁大学的奖学金。**3 give sb first refusal** to let someone decide whether they want to buy a house, car etc that you are selling before you offer it to other people 给某人优先权〔购房屋、汽车等〕

S2 W1 **re·fuse¹** /rɪˋfjuz; rɪˈfjuːz/ *v* **1** [I] to say or show that you will not do something that someone has asked you to do 拒绝〔做某事〕: *I'm sure if you ask her to help you, she won't refuse.* 我肯定，如果你向她求助，她不会拒绝。| **refuse to do sth** *I refuse to take part in anything that's illegal.* 我拒绝参与任何违法的事情。| **flatly refuse/refuse point blank** (=refuse very firmly and directly) 断然拒绝 *Mother flatly refused to go back into the hospital.* 母亲断然拒绝再进医院。**2** [I,T] to say no to something that you have been offered; DECLINE² (4) 不接受，谢绝〔别人给的东西〕: *Mrs Sutton refused a second piece of cake.* 萨顿太太谢绝了第二块蛋糕。| *Their offer is too good to refuse.* 他们的开价好得无法抗拒。**3** [T] to not give or allow someone something that they want 拒绝把…给…: **refuse sb sth** *The US authorities refused him a visa.* 美国当局拒绝给他签证。

USAGE NOTE 用法说明: REFUSE

WORD CHOICE 词语辨析: **agree to, accept, refuse, reject, decline, turn down, deny**

Refuse, reject, decline, turn down all mean that you do not do something that someone has asked you to do (opposite: **agree to**), or do not take something that you are **offered** (opposite: **accept**). refuse, reject, decline, turn down 都表示拒绝，指不去做别人要求你做的某事〔反义词是 agree to〕或不接受别人提供的某物〔反义词是 accept〕。

You can **refuse** an invitation, application, offer, permission, or you can **refuse to** say or do something. 拒绝邀请、申请、建议，批准或拒绝讲或做某事，可用 refuse: *She refused to come with us.* 她拒绝和我们一道来。

More strongly, you **reject** an application, idea, proposal, offer, improvement, or plan. reject 语气更坚决，用于拒绝申请、想法、建议、提议、改进或计划: *The Greens rejected the proposals for the new road.* 格林夫妇拒绝了修建新路的建议。| *Her first novel was rejected by over 30 publishers.* 她的第一部小说遭到30多家出版商的拒绝。

You **decline** an invitation, offer, or to give permission by saying or writing something rather than doing something. This word is less strong but more formal and polite. 以口头或书面方式拒绝邀请、建议或拒绝同意，可用 decline，该词语气不太强，但更正式和客气: *The Senator has declined all our invitations to an open debate on the matter.* 我们多次邀请那位参议员公开辩论这个问题，他全都拒绝了。

Less formally, you can **turn down** an invitation, application, suggestion, offer, or plan. turn down 的语气不太正式，用于拒绝邀请、申请、建议、提议或计划等: *He turns down all offers of help.* 他拒绝了所有提出帮助的建议。

You can also **deny** someone permission, an opportunity, or their rights. But usually if you **deny** something especially something wrong that someone has said you have done, you say it is not true. 不予准许、拒绝给予机会或权利，可用 deny。但 deny 较常见的意思是"否认"，尤其是当 deny 的宾语是别人指责你做错事的时候: The sentence 这句 *She denied working for the enemy,* means 意思是 *She said she was not working for the enemy.* 她否认在为敌人工作。(NOT 不用 *She refused to work for the enemy.* 她拒绝为敌人工作。)

ref·use² /ˋrɛfjus; ˈrefjuːs/ *n* [U] *formal* waste material; RUBBISH¹ (1)【正式】废料；废物: *a refuse dump* 垃圾场 | *declining standards in housing maintenance, refuse collection and street lighting* 住房维修、垃圾收集和街道照明水平的下降

re·fute /rɪˋfjut; rɪˈfjuːt/ *v* [T] *formal*【正式】**1** to prove that a statement or idea is not correct 证明〔陈述或观点〕不对；反驳: *an attempt to refute Moore's theories* 企图驳斥摩尔的理论 **2** to say that a statement is wrong or unfair 驳斥: *She refuted the allegations of malpractice.* 她驳斥了有关她失职的指控。—**refutable** *adj* —**refutation** /ˌrɛfjuˋteʃən; ˌrefjʊˈteɪʃən/ *n* [C,U]

reg. /rɛdʒ; redʒ/ an abbreviation of 缩写= REGISTRATION: **L reg./M reg. etc** *BrE* (=to say what the age of a car is according to the year when it was registered)【英】〔表示汽车注册年数的〕注册类别

re·gain /rɪˋgen; rɪˈgeɪn/ *v* [T] **1** to get something back, especially an ability or quality that you have lost 收回，复得，恢复: *The family never quite regained its former influence.* 这个家族再也没有恢复往昔的影响力。| **regain consciousness** (=wake up after being unconscious) 恢复知觉 | **regain control (of)** *Government forces have regained control of some areas.* 政府军队重新控制了一些地区。| **regain your balance** (=stop yourself from falling) 恢复平衡 **2** *literary* to reach a place again【文】再到〔某地〕，重回

re·gal /ˋrigḷ; ˈriːgəl/ *adj formal* typical of a king or queen and therefore usually impressive【正式】帝王〔般〕的: *a regal manner* 王者风范 | *a ceremony of regal splendour* 富丽堂皇的仪式 —**regally** *adv*: *She held out her hand regally.* 她高贵地伸出手来。

re·gale /rɪˋgel; rɪˈgeɪl/ *v*

regale sb **with** sth *phr v* to entertain someone with something, especially stories 以…款待；〔尤指以故事〕使…愉悦: *Bailey regaled the customers with tales of our exploits.* 贝利给顾客讲我们的事迹，让他们听得津津有味。

re·ga·li·a /rɪˋgelɪə; rɪˈgeɪliə/ *n* [U] traditional clothes and decorations, used at official ceremonies〔正式场合穿的〕盛装，华服: *the royal regalia* 皇家的礼服

Re·gan /ˋrigən; ˈriːgən/ one of King Lear's daughters in the play *King Lear* by William Shakespeare. She and her sister Goneril pretend to love their father to make him give them his land, but then treat him very cruelly. Goneril finally kills her with poison. 里根〔威廉·莎士比亚的剧本《李尔王》中李尔王的女儿。她与姐姐高纳里尔假装爱自己的父亲，好让他把土地分给她俩，但之后却对他非常狠毒。高纳里尔最后又把里根毒死〕—see also 另见 CORDELIA, GONERIL

re·gard¹ /rɪˋgɑrd; rɪˈgɑːd/ *n formal*【正式】 S3

1 ►RESPECT 尊敬◄ [U] respect for someone or something 尊敬: [+for] *She has so little regard for him, she is unlikely to follow his advice.* 她很不尊重他，不太可能听从他的劝告。| **hold sb/sth in high regard** (=admire and respect them very much) 对某人/某物怀有敬意 *a teacher who is held in high regard by his colleagues* 备受同事尊敬的老师

2 ►ATTENTION 关注◄ [U] *formal* attention or consideration that is shown towards someone or something【正式】关注，关心: [+for] *He has no regard for her feelings.* 他无视她的感情。| [+to] *a report that pays scant regard to the facts of the case* 一份忽视案件事实的报告

3 as regards used to introduce the subject you are going to talk or write about 至于，关于: *As regards environmental issues, the government will enforce existing regulations.* 关于环境问题，政府将实施现行条例。

4 in this regard *formal* used to connect what you are going to say with something you have just mentioned【正式】关于此事〔用于承上启下〕: *Progress is slow. In this regard, lack of funds is a factor.* 就进展缓慢而言，缺乏资金是一个因素。

5 with/in regard to *formal* used to say what particular subject you are talking or writing about【正式】关于〔用于点题〕: *With regard to future oil supplies, the situation is uncertain.* 关于未来石油供应问题，情况尚不确定。

6 ►GREETING 问候◄ **regards** [plural] good wishes 问候；致意: *My husband sends his regards.* 我丈夫表示问候。| **with kind/best/warm regards** (=used to end a letter in a friendly but rather formal way) 谨致问候〔友善并相当正式的问候，用于信的末尾〕

7 ►LOOK 看◄ [singular] *literary* a long look without moving your eyes【文】注视

regard² *v* [T] **1** [not in progressive 不用进行时] to think about someone or something in a particular way 认为，看作: **regard sb/sth as sth** *Paul seems to regard sex as sinful and immoral.* 保罗好像把性看作是罪恶和不道德的。| *Edith wore strange* S2 W1

clothes and was widely regarded as eccentric. 伊迪丝穿着古怪，被大家视为怪人。| **regard sb with admiration/fear/concern etc** *Sue regarded the others with fear and jealousy.* 休对其他人既害怕又嫉妒。| **regard sb well/badly etc** *a work of art that is highly regarded by the experts* 一件为专家们高度评价的艺术品 **2** *formal* to look at someone or something, especially in a particular way【正式】注视: *I stood back a little and regarded him coldly.* 我往后站了一点，冷冷地注视着他。**3** *formal* to pay attention to something【正式】注意，重视: *You must regard the safety regulations.* 你必须重视安全规则。

3 **re·gard·ing** /rɪˋgɑrdɪŋ; rɪˈgɑːdɪŋ/ *prep formal* a word used especially in business letters to introduce the subject you are writing about【正式】关于〔尤用于公函中〕: *Regarding your recent inquiry...* 关于你最近的询问…

re·gard·less /rɪˋgɑrdlɪs; rɪˈgɑːdləs/ *adv* **1** if you continue doing something regardless, you do it in spite of difficulties or opposition 不管怎样，无论如何: *You get a lot of criticism but you just have to carry on regardless.* 你受到许多批评，但无论如何你必须坚持下去。**2 regardless of** without being affected by different situations, problems etc 不管，不顾: *equal treatment for all, regardless of race, religion, or sex* 不分种族、宗教或性别，对所有人一视同仁 | *All our proposals were rejected regardless of their merits.* 我们所有的建议都遭到拒绝，不管它们的可取之处。

re·gat·ta /rɪˋgætə; rɪˈgætə/ *n* [C] a sports event at which there are races for rowing boats or sailing boats〔划船或帆船比赛的〕赛船会

re·gen·cy /ˋridʒənsɪ; ˈriːdʒənsi/ *n* [C,U] a period of government by a REGENT (=person who governs instead of a king or queen) 摄政（期）

Regency *adj* Regency buildings, furniture etc are from or in the style of the period 1811-1820 in Britain 英国摄政时期〔1811–1820〕（风格）的

re·gen·e·rate /rɪˋdʒɛnə͵ret; rɪˈdʒenəreɪt/ *v* [T] *formal* to make something develop and grow strong again【正式】使再生；使恢复: *Given time the forest will regenerate itself.* 过一段时间后森林会自行再生。| *The Marshall Plan sought to regenerate the shattered Europe of 1947.* 马歇尔计划试图重建1947年千疮百孔的欧洲。—**regenerative** /-nə͵retɪv; -nərətɪv/ *adj*: *a regenerative process* 复兴的过程 —**regeneration** /rɪ͵dʒɛnəˋreʃən; rɪ͵dʒenəˈreɪʃən/ *n* [U]: *a new strategy for urban regeneration* 城市复兴的新策略

re·gent /ˋridʒənt; ˈriːdʒənt/ *n* [C] someone who governs instead of a king or queen ruling who is ill, absent, or still a child 摄政者 —**regent** *adj* [only after noun 仅用于名词后]: *the Prince Regent* 摄政王

Regent's Park /͵‥ ˈ‧/ a park in northwest London. It is the home of London Zoo and has an open-air theatre where plays by Shakespeare are performed in the summer. 摄政公园〔伦敦市西北部一公园。园内有伦敦动物园和一个露天剧场。夏季时节，该剧场经常上演莎士比亚的戏剧〕

Regent Street /ˈ‥ ͵‧/ a street in central London that runs from Regent's Park to Piccadilly Circus and crosses Oxford Street, and is a popular place for shopping 摄政街〔伦敦市中心一街道。该街道从摄政公园延伸至皮卡迪利广场，与牛津街相交，是著名的商业街〕

reg·gae /ˋrɛge; ˈregeɪ/ *n* [U] a kind of popular music from the West Indies with a strong regular beat 雷盖〔西印度群岛的一种节奏强劲的流行音乐〕

re·gi·cide /ˋrɛdʒə͵saɪd; ˈredʒɪsaɪd/ *n formal*【正式】**1** [U] the crime of killing a king or queen 弑君（罪）**2** [C] someone who does this 弑君者

2 **re·gime** /rɪˋʒim; reɪˈʒiːm/ *n* [C] **1** a government that has not been elected in fair elections〔未经公平选举而掌权的〕政府，政权: *The regime has liquidated all its opponents.* 该政权清除了所有的反对者。**2** a particular system of government or management, especially one you disapprove of 政体，政权〔尤含贬义〕: **the old/new regime** (=the previous or present system of government) 旧／新政权 | **the Thatcher/Eisenhower/Faulkner etc regime** (=the government of Thatcher etc) 撒切尔／艾森豪威尔／福克纳等政府 **3** a regimen 养生之道，摄生法

re·gi·men /ˋrɛdʒə͵mɛn; ˈredʒɪmɪn/ *n* [C] *formal* a special plan of food, exercise etc that is intended to improve your health【正式】养生之道，摄生法

re·gi·ment¹ /ˋrɛdʒəmənt; ˈredʒɪmənt/ *n* [C] **1** a large military group usually consisting of several BATTALIONS〔军队的〕团: *the Royal Sussex Regiment* 皇家萨塞克斯团 **2** a large number of people, animals, or things〔人、动物、物的〕大群，大量: *a whole regiment of ants* 一大群蚂蚁

re·gi·ment² /ˋrɛdʒə͵mɛnt; ˈredʒɪment/ *v* [T usually passive 一般用被动态] to organize and control people firmly and usually too strictly 严格控制: *the regimented routine of boarding school* 寄宿学校严格的常规 —**regimentation** /͵rɛdʒəmɛnˋteʃən; ͵redʒɪmenˈteɪʃən/ *n* [U]: *institutional regimentation* 大机构的严格管理

re·gi·ment·al /͵rɛdʒəˋmɛntl; ͵redʒɪˈmentl◂/ *adj* connected with a regiment 团的: *the regimental band* 团的乐队

Re·gi·na /rɪˋdʒaɪnə; rɪˈdʒaɪnə/ *n Latin*【拉丁】**1** used as a title in official writing after the name of the ruling British queen 女王〔公文中用于在位英国女王名字之后的称谓〕: *Elizabeth Regina* 伊丽莎白女王 **2** used to mean the governing power of the state in the title of a British law case when a queen is ruling 王国政府〔女王在位时用于诉案的名称中〕: *the case of Frankland v. Regina* (=Frankland against the government) 弗兰克兰诉王国政府案 —compare 比较 REX

re·gion /ˋridʒən; ˈriːdʒən/ *n* [C] **1** a fairly large area of a country or of the world, usually without exact limits〔无确定界线的〕地区，区域: 1 1 *oil fields in the Appalachian region of the US* 美国阿巴拉契亚地区的油田 | *The invaders occupied important coastal regions.* 入侵者占领了重要的沿海地区。| *America's main ally in this region* 美国在这个地区的主要盟国 —see 见 AREA (USAGE) **2** a particular part of someone's body〔人体的〕部，部位: *a pain in the lower back region* 后腰部疼痛 **3 (somewhere) in the region of** used to describe an amount of time, money, etc without being exact 大约，…左右: *The school received a grant somewhere in the region of £2,500.* 学校收到一笔大约2500英镑的补助金。**4 the regions** the parts of a country that are away from the capital city〔首都以外的〕各地区: *Government policy is to relocate jobs from the capital to the regions.* 政府的政策是将就业机会从首都转移到其他地区。

re·gion·al /ˋridʒənl̩; ˈriːdʒənəl/ *adj* connected with a particular region 地区的，区域的: 1 2 *regional cooking* 地方特色的烹饪 | *regional alliances such as NATO* 北约等区域性联盟

re·gion·al·is·m /ˋridʒənl̩͵ɪzəm; ˈriːdʒənəlɪzəm/ *n* [U] loyalty to a particular region of a country and the desire for it to be more politically independent 地方主义

re·gis·ter¹ /ˋrɛdʒɪstɚ; ˈredʒɪstə/ *n* 3 3

1 ▶OFFICIAL LIST 正式名单◀ [C] an official list containing the names of all the people, organizations, or things of one particular type 登记，注册: *a civil register of births, deaths and marriages* 出生、死亡、婚姻的民政登记 | *children on the 'at risk' register* "危险"名册上的儿童

2 ▶OFFICIAL BOOK 正式的簿/册◀ [C] a book kept for a special purpose, such as in a church or REGISTRY OFFICE, which a man and woman sign after their marriage ceremony 登记簿: *the school attendance register* 学校点名册

3 ▶MUSIC 音乐◀ [C] *technical* the range of musical notes that someone's voice or a musical instrument can reach【术语】〔人声或乐器的〕音域

4 ▶LANGUAGE STYLE 语言风格◀ [C,U] *technical* the words, style, and grammar used by speakers and writers in a particular situation or in a particular type of writing【术语】语域: *the correct register for a formal social situation* 正式社交场合的正确语言风格

5 ▶BUSINESS MACHINE 商用机器◀ [C] a CASH REGISTER 现金出纳机

6 ▶HEATING CONTROL 加热控制装置◀ [C] *AmE* a movable metal plate that controls the flow of air in a HEATING OR COOLING system【美】〔加热或冷却系统中控制气流的〕调风器，节气门

register² *v* 3

1 ▶ON A LIST 记入名单◀ a) [T] to record a name or details about someone or something in an official list 记录，登记: *We are registering the baby's birth this morning.* 我们今天上午要给刚出生的孩子登记。| *The tanker is registered in Rotterdam.* 这艘油轮是在鹿特丹注册的。| **be registered (as) unemployed/disabled etc** (=be on an official list of a particular group) 登记的失业者／残疾人等 **b)** [I] to put your name on an official list, for example when you arrive at a hotel, join a course of study etc〔旅馆入住〕登记;〔课程〕注册: [**+for**] *How many students have registered for English classes?* 有多少学生注册了英语课?

2 ▶SHOW A FEELING 表示感情◀ [T] to show or express a feeling 流露[表达]〔感情〕: *Her face registered shock and anger.* 她脸上流露出震惊和愤怒。

3 ▶STATE YOUR OPINION 发表意见◀ [T] *formal* to officially state your opinion about something so that everyone knows what you think or feel【正式】正式表达，说明: *The delegation regis-*

tered their protests at the White House meeting. 在白宫会议上，代表团正式表达了他们的抗议。
4 ▶REALIZE 意识到◀ [I usually in negatives 一般用否定式, T] if something registers, or if you register it, you notice it or realize it and then remember it 受到注意；注意到，意识到：*She must have told me her name, but it just didn't register.* 她一定告诉过我她的名字，不过我没记住。| *I'd been standing there for several minutes before he registered my presence.* 我在那儿站了几分钟之后他才注意到我。
5 ▶MEASUREMENT 度量◀ [I,T] if an instrument registers an amount or if an amount registers on it, the instrument shows or records that amount〔仪器〕显示，记录：*The thermometer registered 98.6°.* 温度计显示为98.6度。
6 ▶MAIL 邮件◀ [T] to send a parcel, letter etc by REGISTERED POST 以挂号邮寄：*Did you register the parcel?* 那包裹你是用挂号寄的吗？

registered nurse /, ··· ' ·/ also 又作 **RN** *n* [C] someone who has been trained and is officially allowed to work as a nurse 注册护士

registered of·fice /, ··· ' ·/ *n* [C] the office of a company in Britain, to which all letters and official documents must be sent〔英国公司接收信件和正式文件的〕注册办事处

registered post /, ··· ' ·/ *n* [U] *BrE* a way of insuring something that you send by post in case it gets lost or damaged【英】挂号邮寄；REGISTERED MAIL *AmE*【美】

register of·fice /' ··· , ·/ *n* [C] a REGISTRY OFFICE〔英国的〕户籍登记处

re·gis·trar /ˈrɛdʒɪˌstrɑr; ˌredʒɪˈstrɑː◂/ *n* [C] **1** someone who is in charge of official records, for example in a REGISTRY OFFICE or in a college〔登记处的〕注册主管，记录员，登记员；〔大学的〕注册主任，教务主任 **2** a British hospital doctor who has finished their training but is of a lower rank than a CONSULTANT (2)〔英国的〕专科住院医生

3 **re·gis·tra·tion** /ˌrɛdʒɪˈstreʃən; ˌredʒɪˈstreɪʃən/ *n* **1** [U] the act of recording names and details on an official list 登记，注册：*Student registration is the first week in September.* 学生注册是在9月的第一个星期。| [+of] *the registration of motor vehicles* 机动车的注册 **2** [C] *AmE* an official piece of paper containing details about a motor vehicle and the name of its owner【美】〔汽车的〕执照

registration doc·u·ment /··' ·· , ···/ *n* [C] *BrE* an official piece of paper containing details about a motor vehicle and its owner【英】〔汽车的〕执照

registration num·ber /··' ·· , ··/ *n* [C] *BrE* the official set of numbers and letters shown on the front and back of a motor vehicle on the NUMBER PLATE【英】〔汽车的〕牌照号码

registration plate /··' ·· , ·/ *n* [C] *AustrE, NZE* the metal plate on the front and back of a motor vehicle, which has a special number on it【澳，新西兰】〔汽车的〕号码牌；NUMBER PLATE *BrE*【英】，LICENSE PLATE *AmE*【美】

re·gis·try /ˈrɛdʒɪstrɪ; ˈredʒɪstri/ *n* [C] a place where all the information used by an organization is kept 档案处，档案室

registry of·fice /' ··· , ··/ *n* [C] a local government building in Britain where you can get married, and where births, marriages, and deaths are officially recorded〔英国办理出生、结婚、死亡登记的〕户籍登记处

re·gress /rɪˈgrɛs; rɪˈgres/ *v* [I] *technical* to go back to an earlier and worse condition, or to a less developed way of behaving【术语】退步，退化；倒退：*The patient had regressed to a state of childish dependency.* 病人退回到像小孩一样依赖他人的状态。—**regression** /rɪˈgrɛʃən; rɪˈgreʃən/ *n* [U] —**regressive** *adj*

regressive tax /·' ·· , ·/ *n* [C] a tax that has less effect on the rich than on the poor 递减税

re·gret[1] /rɪˈgrɛt; rɪˈgret/ *v* [T] **1** to feel sorry about something you have done and wish you had not done it 懊悔，悔恨；遗憾，惋惜：**regret doing sth** *She deeply regretted losing her temper.* 她为自己发了脾气而深感后悔。| [+that] *He regrets that he never went to college.* 他遗憾自己从未上过大学。| **regret sth** *It's a great opportunity, Mr Jarvis – you'll never regret it.* 这是个非常好的机会，贾维斯先生，你绝不会后悔的。| **bitterly/deeply regret** (=regret something very much) 深感遗憾[懊悔] *It was a stupid decision and I bitterly regret it.* 这是个愚蠢的决定，我非常遗憾。| **live to regret sth** (=regret something later) 日后为某事感到后悔 *I'm afraid this is a decision that he'll live to regret.* 恐怕这是一个他将来会感到后悔的决定。| **you'll regret it** *spoken* (=used when threatening someone)【口】你会后悔的〔表示威胁〕*You'd better not tell the police, or you'll regret it.* 你最好别报警，否则你会后悔的。**2** [not in progressive 不用进行时] *formal* to be sorry and sad about a situation【正式】对…感到抱歉：*The management regrets any inconvenience caused to its customers.* 店主对给顾客造成的不便表示歉意。| **I regret that** *formal* (=used to politely say that you cannot do something)【正式】很遗憾〔委婉地表示你不能做某事〕*I regret that I will be unable to attend.* 很遗憾，我不能参加。| **I regret to say/inform/tell** (=used when you are going to give someone bad news) 我遗憾地说/通知/告诉〔坏消息〕*I regret to inform you that your contract will not be renewed.* 我很遗憾地通知你，你的合同不能续签。

> **USAGE NOTE 用法说明：REGRET**
> GRAMMAR 语法
> **Regret** is often followed by an *ing* form of a verb, not often by the *to* form unless it is related to something that is about to be said. regret 后面常用动词 ing 形式，只有在对将要谈到的事情表示遗憾时用动词不定式。So if you say 因此如果说：*I regret to tell you this, but I just crashed the car,* you mean 是指 *I'm sorry, but I crashed the car.* 我很遗憾，我撞了车。Compare this with 比较：*I regret telling you I crashed the car.* This means 是指 *I'm sorry I told you I crashed the car.* 我后悔把撞车的事告诉了你。
> You **regret** something (NOT 不用 **regret about/for something**). regret 后紧接感到抱歉的事。

regret[2] *n* [C,U] **1** sadness that you feel about something because you wish it had not happened or that you had not done it. 懊悔，悔恨；遗憾，惋惜：[+at] *The company expressed deep regret at the accident.* 公司对这次事故深表遗憾。| *Jason detected a note of regret in her voice.* 贾森听出她有懊悔的口气。| **with (great/deep) regret** *With great regret they abandoned the idea of rebuilding the kitchen.* 他们非常遗憾地放弃了重建厨房的想法。| **have no/few regrets** (=not feel sorry about something that you have done) 不后悔，没有遗憾 *Hetty felt no regrets about her decision to leave home.* 对自己离开家的决定，赫蒂毫不后悔。**2 much to my regret** *formal* used to say that you are sorry about something【正式】非常遗憾：*Much to our regret, we will be unable to attend your wedding.* 非常遗憾，我们不能参加你们的婚礼。**3 give/send your regrets** *formal* to say that you are unable to go to a meeting, accept an invitation etc【正式】〔因不能赴会、接受邀请等〕表示歉意：*My father was ill and had to send his regrets.* 家父因病缺席，故此深表歉意！

re·gret·ful·ly /rɪˈgrɛtfəlɪ; rɪˈgretfəli/ *adv* **1** feeling sad because you do not want to do what you are doing 遗憾地；惋惜地：*She looked at her watch and turned regretfully towards home.* 她看了看表，惋惜地转身回家去了。**2** [sentence adverb 句子副词] used to talk about a situation that you wish was different or that you are sorry about 懊悔地；抱歉地：*Regretfully we cannot cater for small children or pets.* 对不起，我们不能接待幼童或宠物。—**regretful** *adj*

re·gret·ta·ble /rɪˈgrɛtəbl; rɪˈgretəbəl/ *adj* something that is regrettable makes you feel sorry or sad because it has unpleasant results 令人遗憾的，令人懊悔的：*Most workers regarded the strike as a regrettable necessity.* 大多数工人认为这次罢工虽然令人遗憾，但十分必要。| *It is a regrettable fact that our hearing fails as we grow old.* 随着年龄的增长，我们的听力会减退，这是一个令人遗憾的事实。

re·gret·ta·bly /rɪˈgrɛtəblɪ; rɪˈgretəbli/ *adv* [sentence adverb 句子副词] used when you consider the existing situation to be unsatisfactory 令人遗憾(地)：*Regrettably, the patients weren't asked for their opinion.* 很遗憾，没有征求病人的意见。| [+adj/adv] *Some of the students are regrettably ignorant of contraception.* 一些学生对避孕问题的无知，令人叹息。

re·group /riˈgrup; ˌriːˈgruːp/ *v* [I,T] to form new groups or form groups again, or to make people do this (使)重组：*The Russians retreated, needing to regroup their forces.* 俄国人需要重组军队，于是撤退了。

reg·u·lar[1] /ˈrɛgjələ; ˈregjʊlə/ *adj* 2 2
1 ▶EQUAL SPACES 均等的空间◀ a regular series of things has the same amount of time or space between each thing and the next 规则的，有规律的：*His breathing was slow and regular.* 他的呼吸缓慢而有规律。| **at regular intervals** *Plant the seeds at regular intervals.* 在固定的间隔距离内播种。
2 ▶EVERY DAY/WEEK ETC 每天/周等◀ [usually before noun 一般用于名词前] happening or doing something many times and often at the same times every day, month, year etc 定期的，固定的：*I really miss the security of a regular pay cheque.* 我实在怀念定期领取工资支票的安全感。| **on a regular basis** *It has always been our policy to review staff productivity on a regular*

basis. 我们的政策一贯是定期考核员工的生产效率。| **regular as clockwork** (=at exactly the same time every day, week etc) 准时（地）*He phones us every Sunday at six, regular as clockwork.* 他每星期天6点准时给我们打电话。

3 ▶OFTEN 经常◀ [only before noun 仅用于名词前] happening or doing something very often 频繁的, 经常的: **regular customer/visitor** *Old Joe is one of the bar's regular customers.* 老乔是这家酒吧的常客之一。

4 ▶USUAL 通常的◀ [only before noun 仅用于名词前] normal or usual 平常的, 惯常的: *Driving the van was a change from his regular duties.* 驾驶小货车不是他平时的工作。

5 ▶SHAPE 形状◀ evenly shaped with parts or sides of equal size 等边的, 匀称的: *a regular hexagon* 正六边形 | *He had strong, regular teeth.* 他的牙齿坚固整齐。| *regular features* (=an evenly shaped face) 端正的五官

6 ▶NORMAL 正常的◀ [only before noun 仅用于名词前] *especially AmE* of a normal or standard size【尤美】通常的; 标准的: *a regular coke* 标准容量的可乐

7 ▶ORDINARY 平常的◀ *especially AmE* ordinary, without any special feature or qualities【尤美】普通的, 一般的: *Regular teachers just don't have the training to deal with problem children.* 一般的教师都没有接受过应付问题儿童的训练。

8 ▶FRIENDLY 友好的◀ *AmE* nice and friendly【美】可亲的, 友好的: *a regular guy* 好人

9 be/keep regular *informal*【非正式】**a)** to get rid of waste from your BOWELs often enough to be healthy 大便正常的 **b)** a woman who is regular has her MENSTRUAL PERIOD at the same time each month〔妇女〕月经正常的

10 ▶GRAMMAR 语法◀ *technical* a regular verb or noun changes its forms in the same way as most verbs or nouns; the verb 'dance' is regular but 'be' is not【术语】〔动词、名词的变化〕规则的〈如 dance 是规则动词, 但 be 不是〉

11 ▶EMPHASIZING 强调◀ [only before noun 仅用于名词前] *informal* used to emphasize what you think someone is like【非正式】十足的, 完全的: *The child's so bossy – a regular little dictator!* 这小孩这么爱发号施令, 是个十足的小独裁者!

12 regular soldier/army/troops etc having a permanent job in the army 正规兵/军/部队等 —**regularity** *n* [U]

regular² *n* **1** [C] *informal BrE* a customer who goes to the same shop, bar etc very often【非正式, 英】常客, 老主顾: *The barman knows all the regulars by name.* 这位酒吧男招待员叫得出所有常客的名字。**2** [C] a soldier whose permanent job is in the army 正规兵 **3** [U] *AmE* petrol that contains LEAD【美】含铅汽油 —compare 比较 UNLEADED

reg·u·lar·ize also 又作 **-ise** *BrE*【英】/ˈrɛgjələˌraɪz; ˈregjʊləraɪz/ *v* [T] to make a situation that has existed for some time legal or official 使合法化; 使正规化 —**regularization** /ˌrɛgjələrəˈzeʃən; ˈregjʊlərаɪˈzeɪʃən/ *n* [U]

S3 W3 **reg·u·lar·ly** /ˈrɛgjələlɪ; ˈregjʊləli/ *adv* **1** at regular times, for example every day, week, or month 定期地: *The club meets regularly once a fortnight.* 俱乐部每两星期开一次例会。**2** often 经常: *I am regularly invited to give talks about my time in Nepal.* 我经常被邀请去介绍我在尼泊尔时的情况。**3** evenly arranged or shaped 匀称地, 整齐地: *a fence with regularly spaced vertical posts* 竖桩距离均等的围栏

reg·u·late /ˈrɛgjəˌlet; ˈregjʊleɪt/ *v* [T] **1** to control an activity or process, especially by rules〔尤指以规则〕控制, 管理: *There are strict rules regulating the use of chemicals in food.* 对食品中使用化学品有严格的规定。**2** to make a machine work at a particular speed, temperature etc; ADJUST 调拨, 校准, 调节: *You can regulate the thermostat by turning this little dial.* 转动这个小控制盘就可以调节恒温器。

S2 W2 **reg·u·la·tion¹** /ˌrɛgjəˈleʃən; ˌregjʊˈleɪʃən/ *n* **1** [C] an official rule or order 规则; 条例; 法令: **building/planning/safety etc regulations** *The company is very strict on enforcing health and safety regulations.* 该公司严格执行健康和安全规定。| **rules and regulations** *There are too many rules and regulations governing small businesses.* 约束小企业的规章制度太多。**2** [U] control over something, especially by rules 管制; 管理: *the regulation of public spending* 公共开支的管理

regulation² *adj* [only before noun 仅用于名词前] used or worn because of a rule or custom 规定要求的, 正规的: *regulation uniforms* 标准的制服

reg·u·la·tor /ˈrɛgjəˌletə; ˈregjʊleɪtə/ *n* [C] **1** an instrument for controlling the temperature, speed etc of something 调节器; 校准器 **2** someone who makes sure that, or makes it possible for, a system to operate properly or fairly 管理者, 调控者: *Oftel, the official telecommunications regulator*〔英国〕电信管制局, 官方的电信业监管机构

reg·u·la·to·ry /ˈrɛgjələˌtorɪ; ˌregjʊˈleɪtəri/ *adj formal* having the purpose of controlling an activity or process, especially by rules【正式】调整的; 管理的, 控制的

re·gur·gi·tate /rɪˈgɝdʒəˌtet; rɪˈgɜːdʒɪteɪt/ *v formal*【正式】**1** [I,T] to bring food that you have already swallowed back into your mouth 回吐; 反刍: *Some birds and animals regurgitate food to feed their young.* 有些鸟类和动物回吐已吞下的食物来喂养自己的幼儿。**2** [T] to repeat facts, ideas etc that you have read or heard without thinking about them yourself〔不假思考地〕重复 —**regurgitation** /riˌgɝdʒəˈteʃən; rɪˌgɜːdʒɪˈteɪʃən/ *n* [U]

re·hab /ˈrihæb; ˈriːhæb/ *n* [U] *AmE* the process of curing someone who has an alcohol or drugs problem【美】〔酗酒、吸毒者的〕康复治疗: *a rehab program* 康复治疗计划 | **in rehab** *She's been in rehab for a week.* 她接受康复治疗一星期了。—**rehab** *v* [T]

re·ha·bil·i·tate /ˌrihəˈbɪləˌtet; ˌriːhəˈbɪlɪteɪt/ *v* [T] **1** to help someone to live a healthy, useful, or active life again after they have been seriously ill or in prison〔重病或坐牢后〕使恢复正常生活: *a special unit for rehabilitating stroke patients* 协助中风患者康复的特殊病房 **2** to improve a building or area so that it returns to the good condition it was in before 使恢复原状, 修复〔建筑或地区〕**3** to make people think that someone is good again after a period when they thought that person was bad 恢复…的名誉: *President Nixon seems to have been rehabilitated in the US.* 尼克松总统似乎已经在美国恢复了名誉。—**rehabilitation** /ˌrihəˌbɪləˈteʃən; ˌriːhəbɪlɪˈteɪʃən/ *n* [U]

re·hash /riˈhæʃ; riːˈhæʃ/ *n* [C] something such as a piece of writing or a film which is really a copy of an earlier one, although some things have been changed to make it seem new〔略加变动的〕改写, 改编; 重拍; 改头换面: *just a rehash of the original 1959 version* 只不过是1959年原作的翻版 —**rehash** /riˈhæʃ; riːˈhæʃ/ *v* [T]: *He keeps rehashing the same old speech.* 他不断用改头换面的手法发表内容相同的演说。

re·hears·al /rɪˈhɝsḷ; rɪˈhɜːsəl/ *n* [C,U] a period or a particular occasion when all the people in a play, concert etc practise it before a public performance 排练, 排演 —see also 另见 DRESS REHEARSAL

re·hearse /rɪˈhɝs; rɪˈhɜːs/ *v* **1** [I,T] to practise or make people practise something such as a play or concert in order to prepare for a public performance（使）排练〔戏剧或音乐会〕, 排演, 预演: *The musicians were rehearsing until 2 o'clock in the morning.* 乐师一直排练到凌晨两点。**2** [T] to practise something that you plan to say to someone 练习, 演练: *Sandy rehearsed her resignation speech.* 桑迪演练她的辞职演说。**3** [T] *formal* to repeat an opinion that has often been expressed before【正式】反复讲〔过去经常有人表达的意见〕

re·heat /riˈhit; ˌriːˈhiːt/ *v* [T] to make a meal or drink hot again 重新加热

re·house /riˈhauz; ˌriːˈhaʊz/ *v* [T] to put someone in a new or better home 为〔某人〕提供新住房: *All flood victims will be rehoused as soon as possible.* 将尽快为所有遭受水灾的灾民提供新住房。

Reich /raɪk; raɪk/ *n German* **the Third Reich** the German state between 1933 and 1945【德】第三帝国〔1933年至1945年间的德国〕

reign¹ /ren; reɪn/ *n* [C] **1** the period of time during which someone is king or queen 某君主的统治时期: *the reign of Queen Victoria* 维多利亚女王统治时期 **2** a period during which something is the most powerful or most important feature of a place 主宰期, 支配期, 极盛期: *the reign of Stalinism in Russia* 斯大林主义在苏联占统治地位时期 | **reign of terror** (=when a government kills many of its political opponents) 恐怖统治时期

reign² *v* [I] **1** to be the king or queen 为王, 为君: *George VI reigned from 1936 to 1952.* 乔治六世于1936至1952年在位。**2** *literary* to be the most important feature of a place at a particular time【文】支配, 盛行: *Anarchy reigned for many months.* 无政府状态猖獗了好几个月。**3 the reigning champion** the most recent winner of a competition 现任冠军, 本届冠军: *the reigning Wimbledon champion* 本届温布尔登网球赛冠军

re·im·burse /ˌriɪmˈbɝs; ˌriːɪmˈbɜːs/ *v* [T] *formal* to pay money back to someone who has had to spend the money because of their work【正式】偿还, 付还: **reimburse sb for sth** *The company will reimburse you for any costs incurred on the course.* 你上课的全部费用可以向公司报销。—**reimbursement** *n* [C,U]

rein¹ /ren; reɪn/ *n* [C] **1** also 又作 **reins** [plural] a long narrow band of leather that is fastened around a horse's head in order to control it〔马〕缰绳 —see picture at 参见 HORSE¹ 图 **2 give (full/free) rein to** to allow an emotion or feeling to be expressed freely 放任, 对…不加约束: *He gave free rein to his imagina-*

R

tion and produced a brilliant piece of writing. 他充分发挥自己的想象力，写出了一篇佳作。**3 give sb (a) free rein** to give someone complete freedom to do a job in whatever way they choose〔工作上〕给予某人绝对自由 **4 keep a tight rein on sb/sth** to control something strictly 对某人/某事严加控制: *The finance director keeps a tight rein on spending.* 财务主管对开销严加控制。**5 take/hand over the reins** to take or give someone control over an organization or country 掌权; 交给〔某人〕掌管: *Who'll take over the reins while the boss is in hospital?* 老板住院期间将由谁负责管理?

rein² *v*

rein sth ↔ **in** *phr v* [T] **1** to start to control a situation more strictly 开始严加控制: *The government is reining in public expenditure.* 政府正严格控制公共开支。**2** to make a horse go more slowly by pulling on the reins 用缰绳勒住〔马〕

re·in·car·nate /ˌrinˋkɑrnet; ˌriːɪnˈkɑːneɪt/ *v* **be reincarnated** to be born again in another body after you have died〔灵魂〕被赋予新的肉体; 再生; 转世

re·in·car·na·tion /ˌrinkɑrˋneʃən; ˌriːɪnkɑːˈneɪʃən/ *n* **1** [U] the belief that after someone dies their soul lives again 再生, 转世: *Hindus believe in reincarnation.* 印度教徒相信人会转世投胎。**2** [C] the person or animal that a reincarnated person has become 转世化身: *She thinks she is a reincarnation of Cleopatra.* 她认为自己是〔古埃及女王〕克娄巴特拉转世。

rein·deer /ˋrenˌdɪr; ˈreɪndɪə/ *n plural* **reindeer** [C] a large DEER with long wide horns 驯鹿: *Herds of reindeer graze on the tundra.* 成群的驯鹿在冻原上吃草。

re·in·force /ˌriɪnˋfɔrs; ˌriːɪnˈfɔːs/ *v* [T] **1** to give support to an opinion, idea, or feeling, and make it stronger 加强〔信心、信念、感觉等〕: *Conclusions from the report have been reinforced by more recent studies.* 更多的最新研究证实了报告的结论。**2** to make part of a building, structure, piece of clothing etc stronger 加强, 加固〔建筑、结构、衣物等〕: *The sea wall is being reinforced with tons of cement.* 正在用成吨的水泥加固防波堤。**3** to make a group of people, especially an army, stronger by adding people, equipment etc 增援, 加强…的力量〔尤指军队〕

reinforced con·crete /ˌ···ˈ··/ *n* [U] CONCRETE with metal RODS in it, used to make buildings stronger 钢筋混凝土

re·in·force·ment /ˌriɪnˋfɔrsmənt; ˌriːɪnˈfɔːsmənt/ *n* **1** [U] the act of making something stronger 加强, 加固 **2 reinforcements** [plural] more soldiers who are sent to an army to make it stronger 援兵, 增援部队: *The Spanish soon returned with reinforcements and firearms.* 西班牙人很快就带着援兵和火器回来了。

Rein·hardt, Djan·go /ˋraɪnhɑrt, ˋdʒæŋgo; ˈraɪnhɑːt, ˈdʒæŋgəʊ/ (1910-53) a Belgian JAZZ musician and GUITAR player 莱因哈特〔(1910-1953), 比利时爵士音乐家和吉他演奏家〕

re·in·state /ˌriɪnˋstet; ˌriːɪnˈsteɪt/ *v* [T] to put someone back into a job or position of authority that they had before 使恢复原职: *The manager had been unfairly dismissed, and he was duly reinstated.* 经理被蒙冤解职, 后来还他清白, 予以复职。—**reinstatement** *n* [C,U]

re·in·sure /ˌriɪnˋʃur; ˌriːɪnˈʃʊə/ *v* [T] *technical* to share the insurance of something between two or more companies, so that there is less risk for each【术语】分保, 给…再保险〔由至少两家公司承保, 以分担风险〕—**reinsurance** *n* [U]

re·invent /ˌriɪnˋvɛnt; ˌriːɪnˈvent/ *v* [T] **1** to produce an idea that is based on something that existed in the past 在已有事物的基础上发明 **2 reinvent the wheel** *informal* to waste time trying to find a way of doing something when someone else has already discovered the best way to do it【非正式】徒劳, 白费功夫〔因为别人早已发现做此事的最好方法〕

re·is·sue /riˋɪʃu; ˌriːˈɪʃuː/ *v* [T] to produce a record, book etc again, after it has not been available for some time 再发行, 重印: *CBS reissued 'Lady in Satin'.* 哥伦比亚唱片公司重新发行了《身穿缎子服的女人》。—**reissue** *n* [C]

re·it·e·rate /riˋɪtəˌret; riːˈɪtəreɪt/ *v* [T] *formal* to repeat a statement or opinion in order to make your meaning as clear as possible【正式】反复地说, 重申: **reiterate that** *Let me reiterate that we have absolutely no plans to increase taxation.* 我重申, 我们绝对没有增加税收的计划。—**reiteration** /riˌɪtəˋreʃən; riːˌɪtəˈreɪʃən/ *n* [C,U]

Reith /riθ; riːθ/, **Lord** (1889-1971) a British administrator who was the first general manager of the BBC (1922-27) and its first director-general (1927-38). He had a great influence on the development of broadcasting in the UK, expected high standards, and believed that radio and television should 'educate, inform and entertain'. 里思〔(1889-1971), 英国一管理者, 曾任英国广播公司首任总经理(1922-1927)及首任董事长(1927-1938)。他对英国广播事业的发展产生了重要影响, 对节目品质要求很高, 认为广播与电视应履行"教育、提供信息和娱乐"三大职能〕

Reith lec·tures, the /ˌ·ˈ··/ *n* [plural] a yearly set of talks broadcast on the BBC, given by a person who is very knowledgeable about an important subject 里思讲座〔英国广播公司每年播出的专题系列讲座, 由专家主讲〕

re·ject¹ /rɪˋdʒɛkt; rɪˈdʒekt/ *v* [T]

1 ▶OFFER/SUGGESTION 提议/建议◀ to refuse to accept an offer, suggestion, or request 拒绝(接受): *Sarah rejected her brother's offer of help.* 莎拉拒绝了她弟弟的帮忙。—see 见 REFUSE¹ (USAGE)

2 ▶NOT EMPLOY 不雇用◀ to refuse to accept someone for a job, course of study etc 拒绝〔雇用、录取〕: *Ian was rejected by the army because of his bad eyesight.* 伊恩因为视力不好而被拒绝入伍。

3 ▶PRODUCT 产品◀ to throw away something that has just been made, because its quality is not good enough〔因质量不好而〕废弃: *We have very strict quality control, so anything that is imperfect is rejected.* 我们实行非常严格的质量检查, 凡是有缺陷的一概剔除。

4 ▶BELIEF 信念◀ to decide that you do not believe in something 摒弃: *The present generation has largely rejected the beliefs of its parents.* 现在这一代人在很大程度上摒弃了父母的观念。

5 ▶ORGAN 器官◀ if your body rejects an organ, such as a heart, after a TRANSPLANT operation, it produces substances that attack that organ 排斥〔移植器官〕

6 ▶NOT LOVED 不受关爱的◀ to refuse to give someone any love or attention 冷落: *She was six months pregnant and feeling fat and rejected.* 她怀着六个月的身孕, 觉得自己又胖又遭嫌弃。—**rejection** /-ˋdʒɛkʃən; -ˈdʒekʃən/ *n* [C,U]: *Above all, Phillips feared rejection and loneliness.* 最重要的是, 菲利普斯惧怕受冷落和孤独。| *China's rejection of the 1987 proposals* 中国对1987年建议的拒绝

re·ject² /ˋridʒɛkt; ˈriːdʒekt/ *n* [C] a product that has been rejected because there is something wrong with it 次品, 废品

re·jig /riˋdʒɪg; riːˈdʒɪg/ *BrE*【英】, **re·jig·ger** /riˋdʒɪgɚ; riːˈdʒɪgə/ *AmE*【美】*v* **rejigged, rejigging** [T] *informal* to arrange or organize something in a different way, especially in order to make it better, more suitable, more useful etc【非正式】重新安排, 调整: *Many of his songs are rejigged versions of old Hooker numbers.* 他的许多歌都是由老胡克的乐曲改编的。—**rejig** /ˋridʒɪg; ˈriːdʒɪg/ *n* [singular]

re·joice /rɪˋdʒɔɪs; rɪˈdʒɔɪs/ *v* [I] *literary* to feel or show that you are very happy【文】喜悦: **[+at/over]** *His family rejoiced at the news.* 听到这个消息他全家都很高兴。

rejoice in sth *phr v* [T] **1** to be very happy about something 因…而高兴: *We rejoiced in our good fortune.* 我们为自己的好运而感到高兴。**2** *BrE humorous* to have a name or title that is silly or amusing【英, 幽默】拥有〔某个可笑的名字或称号〕: *He rejoices in the name of Pigg.* 他有个有趣的姓氏, 叫Pigg〔与pig谐音〕。

re·joic·ing /rɪˋdʒɔɪsɪŋ; rɪˈdʒɔɪsɪŋ/ also 又作 **rejoicings** [plural] *n* [U] *literary* a situation in which a lot of people behave in a very happy way because they have had good news【文】欢庆, 庆祝: **[+at/over]** *There was great rejoicing over the victory.* 人们热烈庆祝胜利。

re·join¹ /ˌriˋdʒɔɪn; ˌriːˈdʒɔɪn/ *v* [T] **1** to go back to a group of people that you were with before 重返, 回到〔某一群人身边〕: *Crystal went to rejoin her friends in the lounge.* 克莉斯特尔回到休息室和她的朋友们在一起。**2** to join an organization again 重新加入: *In 1938 he rejoined the Socialists.* 1938年他重新加入社会党。**3** to join two things together again 使再连接: *The cables need to be rejoined.* 电缆需要重新连接。

re·join² /rɪˋdʒɔɪn; rɪˈdʒɔɪn/ *v* [T] *formal* to say something in reply, especially rudely or angrily【正式】〔尤指粗鲁或愤怒地〕回答

re·join·der /rɪˋdʒɔɪndɚ; rɪˈdʒɔɪndə/ *n* [C] *formal* a reply, especially a rude one【正式】〔尤指粗鲁的〕回答: *A smart rejoinder only occurred to me later.* 我只是在后来才想到一个巧妙的回答。

re·ju·ve·nate /rɪˋdʒuvəˌnet; rɪˈdʒuːvəneɪt/ *v* [T] **1** to make an organization effective again, for example by bringing in new ideas 使〔组织〕恢复活力: *The Party was rejuvenated by an influx of younger members.* 由于大量吸收较年轻的党员, 党恢复了活力。**2** [usually passive 一般用被动态] to make someone look or feel young and strong again 使变得年轻, 使恢复活力 —**rejuvenation** /rɪˌdʒuvəˋneʃən; rɪˌdʒuːvəˈneɪʃən/ *n* [singular,U]

re·kin·dle /riˋkɪndl; riːˈkɪndl/ *v* [T] **1** to make someone have a particular feeling, thought etc again 重新激起，重新引起: *a chance to rekindle an old friendship* 重修旧好的机会 **2** to light a fire or flame again 再点燃

re·laid /ˌriˋled; ˌriːˈleɪd/ past tense and past participle of RELAY[3]

re·lapse /rɪˋlæps; rɪˈlæps/ *v* [I] **1** to become ill again after you have seemed to improve〔旧病〕复发 **2** to start to behave badly again or become less active 故态复萌: **[+into]** *Clara relapsed into her usual sulky manner.* 克拉拉又像以前一样闷闷不乐。—**relapse** /ˋrilæps; rɪˈlæps/ *n* [C,U]: *She's had an unexpected relapse.* 没想到她旧病复发了。

Re·late /rɪˋlet; rɪˈleɪt/ a British organization which helps those who have problems with relationships, especially marriage. It used to be called the Marriage Guidance Council. 关系协调委员会〔英国一机构，旨在帮助人们解决人际关系矛盾，尤其是婚姻问题。旧称"婚姻指导委员会"〕

S2 W1 **relate** *v* **1** [I,T] to show or prove a connection between two or more things 把…联系起来，证明…有关联；有关联: *The police are still trying to relate the two pieces of evidence.* 警方还在试图找出这两个证据之间的联系。| **relate sth to** *The report seeks to relate the rise in crime to an increase in unemployment.* 报告想把犯罪率上升与失业率增加联系起来。**2** [T] *formal* to tell someone about events that have happened to you or to someone else【正式】讲述: *Witnesses to the same crime related the events completely differently.* 目击者对同一桩罪案经过的叙述完全不同。**3** [I] *AmE spoken* to feel that you understand someone's problem, situation etc【美口】认同，理解〔别人的问题、处境等〕: *"I'm just swamped with work right now." "Yeah, I can relate."* "我现在工作应接不暇。""是的，我可以理解。"

relate to sb/sth *phr v* [T] **1** to be concerned with or be about a particular subject 有关，涉及: *This relates to something I mentioned earlier.* 这与我早先提到的某件事有关。**2** to be directly connected with and affected by something 与…直接相关: *The cost relates directly to the amount of time spent on the project.* 这个项目的成本与所费的时间有直接关系。**3** to be able to have a good relationship with people because you understand their feelings and behaviour 和睦相处；认同: *Laurie finds it difficult to relate to children.* 劳丽发现很难和孩子相处得好。**4** *informal* to feel that you understand or sympathize with a particular idea or situation【非正式】认同，产生共鸣: *I can really relate to that song.* 我完全能够理解那首歌。

S2 W3 **re·lat·ed** /rɪˋletɪd; rɪˈleɪtɪ̈d/ *adj* **1** connected in some way 有关系的: *drug abuse and other related issues* 吸毒及其他相关的问题 | **[+to]** *The heart attack could be related to his car crash last year.* 心脏病发作可能与他去年的车祸有关。| **drug/stress-related** *stress-related illness* 与压力有关的疾病 **2** [not before noun 不用于名词前] connected by a family relationship 与…有亲戚关系的: *Catriona and I are related.* 卡特里奥娜和我有亲戚关系。| **[+to]** *I am related to Simon by marriage.* 西蒙是我的姻亲。**3** animals, plants, languages etc that are related belong to the same group 同类的，同族的，同系的 —**relatedness** *n* [U]

re·la·ting to /rɪˋletɪŋ tu; rɪˈleɪtɪŋ tuː/ *prep* about; relating 有关，涉及: *documents relating to immigration laws* 与移民法相关的文件

S2 W1 **re·la·tion** /rɪˋleʃən; rɪˈleɪʃən/ *n*

1 ▶FAMILY 家人◀ [C] a member of your family; relative 家人；亲戚: *We have relations in Canada and Scotland.* 我们在加拿大和苏格兰有亲戚。| **close/distant relation** *Diane's a distant relation of mine – a third cousin, I think.* 黛安娜是我的远亲，我想是隔三代的表姐。| **no relation** (=not a relative) 没有亲戚关系 *His name's Johnson too – no relation.* 他也姓约翰逊，但与我没有亲戚关系。—see also 另见 BLOOD RELATION, **poor relation** (POOR (12)) —see 见 RELATIONSHIP (USAGE)

2 ▶BETWEEN PEOPLE/COUNTRIES 人民/国家之间◀ relations [plural] **a)** official connections between companies, countries etc（正式）关系: *Canada and Italy established diplomatic relations in 1970.* 加拿大与意大利在1970年建立外交关系。**b)** the way in which people or groups of people behave towards each other（人际）关系: **[+between]** *Relations between workers and management have improved recently.* 劳资关系最近有所改善。

3 in relation to used to talk about something that is connected with or compared with the thing you are talking about 关于；与…相比: *Women's earnings are still very low in relation to men's.* 女性的收入相比于男性仍然很低。

4 ▶CONNECTION 联系◀ [C,U] a connection between two or more things〔事物间的〕联系: **bear no relation to** (=have no connection with and be completely different from something) 与…无关；与…完全不同 *The retail price bears no relation to the price the farmer receives.* 零售价格与农民得到的价格完全不相符。

5 have (sexual) relations (with) *old-fashioned* to have sex with someone【过时】(与…) 发生性关系

re·la·tion·al /rɪˋleʃənḷ; rɪˈleɪʃənəl/ *adj technical* a relational word is used as part of a sentence but without a meaning of its own, for example the word 'have' in 'I have gone'【术语】〔词〕表示关系的〈如 I have gone 中的 have〉—compare 比较 NOTIONAL

relational da·ta·base /ˌ·,···ˈ···/ *n* [C] *technical* a computer DATABASE that allows a user to find and work with the same information in many different ways【术语】〔电脑的〕相关数据库

re·la·tion·ship /rɪˋleʃən,ʃɪp; rɪˈleɪʃənʃɪp/ *n* **1** [C] the way in which two people or two groups behave towards each other 关系: **[+between]** *an improved relationship between the police and local people* 警方与当地居民之间已改善的关系 | **[+with]** *We have a good working relationship with the managers.* 我们与管理人员有良好的工作关系。**2** [C,U] the way in which two or more things are connected and affect each other 联系，关联: **[+between]** *the relationship between poor housing and health problems* 恶劣的住房与健康问题之间的联系 **3** [C] a situation in which two people spend time together or live together, and have romantic or sexual feelings for each other 男女关系: *I just don't feel I'm ready for a relationship right now.* 我就是觉得现在不想谈恋爱。**4** [U] the way in which you are related to someone in your family 亲属关系 S1 W1

USAGE NOTE 用法说明: RELATIONSHIP

WORD CHOICE 词语辨析: **relationship, relations, relation, connection**

A **relationship with** someone or something is usually close, and may involve strong feelings. relationship with 通常是指密切的关系，可能涉及强烈的感情: *Jane's stormy relationship with her husband* 简与她丈夫之间一波三折的关系 | *What kind of relationship does she have with her mother?* 她与她母亲的关系怎么样？

Relations between people, groups, countries etc are often about working together or communicating. relations 用于人、团体、国家等时，往往指共事或者交往的关系: *Relations between industrialists and environmentalists have improved recently.* 工业家与环境保护者之间的关系近来有所改善。Relations is a more official word. relations 这个词更为正式: *friendly relations in the workplace/between East and West* 工作场所里的友好关系/东西方之间的关系

A **relation** or **relationship to** someone or something, like a **connection**, is usually about a simple fact. relation 或 relationship to，如同 connection，通常表示一个简单的事实: *Jane's relationship to/connection with Jeff is that he is her uncle/boss.* 简与杰夫的关系是他是她的叔叔/上司。| *What relation has temperature to humidity?* 温度与湿度有什么联系？

A **relationship between** people and other people or things may be either close and full of emotion, or simply a matter of fact. relationship between 既可以表示人们或事情之间关系非常亲密或涉及强烈的情感，也可以仅仅表示一个事实: *the relationship between bosses and workers* 老板与工人的关系 | *What's the relationship between temperature and humidity?* 温度与湿度有什么联系？

rel·a·tive¹ /ˋrɛlətɪv; ˈrelətɪv/ *n* [C] a member of your family; RELATION (1) 家人；亲属，亲戚: *visit from friends and relatives at Christmas* 圣诞节时朋友与家人的来访 S3 W3

relative² *adj* **1** having a particular quality when compared with something else 比较的，相对的: **relative peace/comfort/safety etc** *an atmosphere of relative calm after the riots* 骚乱之后相对平静的气氛 | **relative merits/costs/values etc** (=the advantages, costs etc of two or more things that are compared with each other) 相对优点/成本/价值等 *discussing the relative merits of various sports cars* 讨论各种跑车的相对优点 | **it's all relative** (=used to mean it cannot be judged on its own but must be compared with others) 一切都是相对的〔表示事情必须透过比较来评价〕*You think you're poor, but look at people in really poor countries – it's all relative.* 你以为你很穷，可是你看看真正贫穷国家的人吧 —— 一切都是相对的。**2 relative to** connected with a particular subject 与…有关: *facts relative to this issue* 与这个问题有关的事实 W2

relative clause /ˌ···ˈ·/ *n* [C] *technical* a part of a sentence that has a verb in it, and is joined to the rest of the sentence by

'who', 'which', 'where' etc, for example, the phrase 'who lives next door', in the sentence 'The man who lives next door is a doctor'.【术语】关系从句〈如在 The man who lives next door is a doctor 一句中, who lives next door 是关系从句〉

rel·a·tive·ly /ˈrɛlətɪvlɪ; ˈrelətɪvli/ *adv* **1 relatively easy/few/cheap** fairly easy etc compared with other things 比较容易／少／便宜: *The drug has relatively few known side effects.* 这种药已知的副作用比较少。**2 relatively speaking** used when comparing something with all similar things 相对来说: *Relatively speaking, it's not important.* 相对而言, 这并不重要。

relative pro·noun /ˌ··· ˈ··/ *n* [C] *technical* a PRONOUN such as 'who', 'which', or 'that' by which a relative clause is connected to the rest of the sentence【术语】关系代词

rel·a·tiv·i·ty /ˌrɛləˈtɪvətɪ; ˌreləˈtɪvəti/ *n* [U] the relationship in PHYSICS between time, space, and MOTION (=movement) according to Einstein's THEORY〔爱因斯坦理论中的〕相对论

re·launch /ˈrilɔntʃ; ˈriːlɔːntʃ/ *n* [C] a new effort to sell a product that is already on sale 再次促销 —**relaunch** /riˈlɔntʃ; riːˈlɔːntʃ/ *v* [T]

re·lax /rɪˈlæks; rɪˈlæks/ *v*

1 ►REST 休息◄ [I,T] to feel calm and comfortable and stop worrying, or to make someone do this (使)放松, (使)轻松: *After a hard day's work, relax in the swimming pool.* 在一天的辛勤工作后, 到游泳池里去放松一下。| *Relax – I'm sure the kids will be back any minute.* 别紧张, 孩子们肯定马上就会回来。| **relax sth/sb** *A nice hot bath should help to relax you.* 好好洗个热水澡肯定会帮助你放松。

2 ►LOOSEN 放松◄ [I,T] if you relax a part of your body or it relaxes, it becomes less stiff or less tight (使)〔身体部位〕松弛, 放松: *Gentle exercise can relax stiff shoulder muscles.* 轻柔的运动可以放松僵硬的肩部肌肉。

3 relax your hold/grip a) to hold something less tightly than before 松开手: *Molassi relaxed his grip on my arm.* 莫莱西松开了抓着我胳膊的手。**b)** to become less strict in the way you control something 放宽: *It seemed unlikely that Britain would willingly relax her grip on the territories.* 看来英国不可能主动放松对领土的控制。

4 relax rules/controls/regulations etc to make rules etc less strict 放宽规定／控制／管制等: *Hughes believes that immigration controls should not be relaxed.* 休斯认为对移民的限制不能放宽。

5 relax your vigilance/concentration etc to reduce the amount of attention you give to something 放松警惕／使注意力松懈等

re·lax·a·tion /ˌrilæksˈeʃən; ˌriːlækˈseɪʃən/ *n* **1** [C,U] a way of resting and enjoying yourself 消遣, 娱乐: *I play the piano for relaxation.* 我弹钢琴自娱。| *Playing golf is one of Bruce's favorite relaxations.* 打高尔夫球是布鲁斯最喜欢的消遣之一。**2** [U] the process of making rules on the control of something less strict 放宽, 放松: **[+of]** *a relaxation of government controls* 政府控制的放宽

re·laxed /rɪˈlækst; rɪˈlækst/ *adj* **1** feeling calm and comfortable and not worried 轻松的, 无拘无束的: *Gail was lying in the sun looking very relaxed and happy.* 盖尔躺在阳光下, 看上去十分轻松愉快。**2** a situation that is relaxed is comfortable and informal 舒适的, 随便的, 轻松的: *a relaxed atmosphere* 轻松的气氛

re·lax·ing /rɪˈlæksɪŋ; rɪˈlæksɪŋ/ *adj* making you feel relaxed 使人放松的, 使人懒洋洋的: *a relaxing afternoon in the garden* 在花园中度过一个懒洋洋的下午

re·lay¹ /ˈrile; ˈriːleɪ/ *n* **1 in relays** if people do something in relays, several small groups of them do it, one group after another, so that the activity is continuous 轮班, 轮换 **2** [C] a relay race 接力赛跑 **3** [C,U] a piece of electrical equipment that receives radio or television signals and sends them on 中继设备, 转播设备

re·lay² /ˈrile; ˈriːleɪ/ *v past tense and past participle* **relayed** [T] **1** to pass a message from one person or place to another 传达, 传递: **relay sth to sb** *He quickly relayed this news to the other members of staff.* 他迅速地将消息传达给其他工作人员。**2** to send out radio or television signals by relay 转播: *The concert will be relayed at 9 pm.* 音乐会将于晚上 9 点转播。

re·lay³ /ˌriˈle; ˌriːˈleɪ/ *v past tense and past participle* **relaid** /-ˈled; -ˈleɪd/ [T] to lay something such as a CARPET¹ (1) again 再铺设〔地毯等〕

relay race /ˈ·· ˌ·/ *n* [C] a running or swimming race between two or more teams in which each member of the team takes part one after another 接力赛

re·lease¹ /rɪˈlis; rɪˈliːs/ *v* [T]

1 ►LET SB FREE 释放某人◄ to let someone go free 释放, 放出: *The hostages were released in November 1988.* 人质于1988年11月获释。| **release sb from** *They decided to release the bird from its cage.* 他们决定把鸟从笼子里放出来。

2 ►STOP HOLDING 松手◄ to stop holding something that you have been holding tightly or carefully 松开, 放开〔某物〕: *The man finally released her arm.* 那个人最终松开了她的手臂。| **release your grasp/grip/hold (on)** *The noise made him release his grasp.* 嘈杂声使他松开了紧握的手。

3 ►MAKE PUBLIC 公布◄ to let news or official information be known and printed 公开发表, 发布: *The new trade figures have just been released.* 新的贸易数字刚刚公布。

4 ►MACHINERY 机器◄ to allow part of a piece of machinery or equipment to move from the position in which it is fixed 放开, 松开: *Don't forget to release the handbrake.* 别忘了松开手刹。

5 ►FEELINGS 感情◄ to express or get rid of feelings such as anger or worry 表达; 发泄: *Physical exercise is a good way of releasing tension.* 体育锻炼是释放压力的好方法。

6 ►FILM/RECORD 电影/唱片◄ to make a record or film available for people to buy or see 发行; 上映

7 ►CHEMICAL 化学品◄ to let a substance flow out 释放: *Adrenalin is released in moments of danger.* 危急时肾上腺素会释放出来。

8 ►FROM A DUTY 从职务中◄ to allow someone not to do their duty or work 解除〔职务或工作〕; 解脱: **release sb from** *She was released from her teaching duties to attend the funeral.* 她获准不教课而去参加葬礼。

9 ►WEAPON 武器◄ to make a weapon fly or fall 发射, 投〔弹〕: *The missiles were released from a height of four thousand metres.* 导弹从4000米高空发射出去。

release² *n* 

1 ►FROM PRISON 从狱中◄ [singular,U] the act of allowing someone to go free or being allowed to go free 释放: *She went to the Governor to beg for her son's release.* 她去恳求州长释放她儿子。| **[+from]** *Simon has obtained early release from prison.* 西蒙获准提早出狱。

2 ►FEELINGS 感情◄ [U] **a)** freedom to show or express your feelings 流露, 表达: *Music has always provided me with a form of emotional release.* 音乐总给我某种形式的感情宣泄。**b)** a feeling that you are free from the worry or pain that you have been suffering 解脱, 摆脱: *that wonderful feeling of release when the examinations are over* 考完试之后那种如释重负的美妙感觉

3 ►RECORD/FILM 唱片/电影◄ [C] a new record or film 新唱片; 新电影: *the band's latest release* 该乐队最新发行的唱片

4 on (general) release if a film, record etc is on release it has recently become possible to see or buy it〔电影、唱片等〕已经上映[发行]

5 ►OFFICIAL STATEMENT 正式声明◄ [C] an official statement that is made available to be printed or broadcast〔发布的〕正式声明 —see also 另见 PRESS RELEASE

6 ►CHEMICALS 化学品◄ [U] the act of letting a chemical, gas etc flow out of its usual container 释放: *the slow release of toxic waste into the rivers* 有毒废料向河流的缓慢排放

7 ►MAKING STH AVAILABLE 提供某物◄ [U] the act of making something available 发布, 发行: *October 22nd is the date set for the report's release.* 定于10月22日发布该报告。

8 ►ON A MACHINE 在机器上◄ [C] a handle, button etc that can be pressed to allow part of a machine to move 释放装置; 松脱装置

rel·e·gate /ˈrɛləˌget; ˈreləgeɪt/ *v* [T] **1** *formal* to give someone or something a less important position than before【正式】将…置于次要地位; 贬低: *Academic excellence seems to have been relegated to a role of secondary importance.* 优异的学术成绩似乎已经被置于次要地位。**2 be relegated (to)** *especially BrE* if a sports team is relegated, it is moved into a lower DIVISION【尤英】〔运动队〕被降级(到…) —**relegation** /ˌrɛləˈgeʃən; ˌreləˈgeɪʃən/ *n* [U]

re·lent /rɪˈlɛnt; rɪˈlent/ *v* [I] to change your attitude and become less severe or cruel towards someone 变宽容, 变温和: *She finally relented and let him borrow the car.* 最后她态度缓和下来, 让他借用了车。

re·lent·less /rɪˈlɛntlɪs; rɪˈlentləs/ *adj* **1** someone who is relentless never stops being strict, cruel, or determined 严格的; 无情的; 坚决的: **[+in]** *a regime that was relentless in its persecution of dissidents* 一个残酷镇压持不同政见者的政权 **2** something unpleasant that is relentless continues without ever stopping or getting less severe〔不愉快的事物〕不间断的: *the relentless fury of the waves* 滚滚恶浪 | *a relentless struggle for power* 永无休止的权力斗争 —**relentlessly** *adv*: *Kate listened*

to the rain beating relentlessly against the window. 凯特听着雨点在不停地敲打窗户。

rel·e·vant /ˈrɛləvənt; ˈreləvənt/ *adj* directly connected with the subject or problem being discussed or considered 有关的, 切题的: *For further information see the relevant chapters in the users' manual.* 详情请查阅使用说明中的相关章节。| **[+to]** *These issues are directly relevant to the needs of slow learners.* 这些问题与迟钝的学习者的需要有直接关系。—opposite 反义词 IRRELEVANT —**relevance** also 又作 **relevancy** *n* [U]: *What you say has no relevance to the subject.* 你所说的与主题无关。—**relevantly** *adv*

re·li·a·ble /rɪˈlaɪəbl; rɪˈlaɪəbəl/ *adj* someone or something that is reliable can be trusted or depended on 可信赖的, 可靠的: *She may forget – she's not very reliable.* 她可能会忘记 — 她不太靠得住。| *a reliable source of information* 可靠的信息来源 —opposite 反义词 UNRELIABLE —**reliably** *adv*: *We are reliably informed that fighting has broken out between the two factions.* 我们获得可靠情报, 两派已经开战。—**reliability** /rɪˌlaɪəˈbɪlətɪ; rɪˌlaɪəˈbɪləti/ *n* [U]

re·li·ance /rɪˈlaɪəns; rɪˈlaɪəns/ *n* **1** [singular,U] the state of being dependent on something 依赖, 依靠: **[+on]** *our country's reliance on imported oil* 我国对进口石油的依赖 **2 place reliance on** *formal* to trust someone or something【正式】信赖…

re·li·ant /rɪˈlaɪənt; rɪˈlaɪənt/ *adj* **be reliant on/upon** to depend on someone or something 依赖于…: *In my view she's far too reliant on her parents for financial support.* 我认为, 她过于依赖父母提供的经济资助。—see also 另见 SELF-RELIANT

rel·ic /ˈrɛlɪk; ˈrelɪk/ *n* **1** [C] an old object or custom that reminds people of the past 遗迹; 遗物; 遗俗: *their crisp white uniforms, a relic of British colonial rule* 他们那挺括的白色制服, 是英国殖民统治的遗俗 | *She cleared up the glasses, the only relics of the previous night's party.* 她收拾了玻璃杯 — 前一天晚上聚会唯一遗留下来的东西。**2** [C] a part of the body or clothing of a holy person which is kept after their death because it is thought to be holy 圣骨, 圣物: *the sacred relics of John the Baptist* 施洗约翰的圣物 **3 relics** [plural] *old use* someone's dead body【旧】遗骸

re·lief /rɪˈlif; rɪˈliːf/ *n*

1 ▶COMFORT 安慰◀ [singular,U] a feeling of comfort when something frightening, worrying, or painful has ended or has not happened〔因恐惧、忧虑或痛苦的解除而感到的〕安慰: *I felt a huge surge of relief and happiness.* 我如释重负, 感到一阵欣慰。| **be a relief** *In a way it was a relief to know exactly what we were up against.* 确切了解我们面临的局面在一定程度上使人宽慰。| **to your relief** (=making you feel relief) 令人感到宽慰 *To our great relief the children all arrived home safely.* 孩子都安全到家, 使我们大大松了一口气。| **what a relief!** *"The boss didn't realize you were late." "What a relief!"* "老板不知道你迟到了。" "谢天谢地!" | **a sigh of relief** *The men went away and she heaved a sigh of relief.* 男人都走了, 她如释重负地松了一口气。

2 ▶REDUCTION OF PAIN 减少疼痛◀ [U] the reduction of pain or unhappy feelings〔疼痛或不快的〕减轻; 缓解: **pain relief** *the various methods of pain relief available to women in labor* 产妇分娩时减轻疼痛的各种方法 | **[+of]** *the relief of suffering* 减轻痛苦 | **[+from]** *Tranquillizers provide only temporary relief from depression.* 镇静剂只能暂时缓解抑郁的情绪。

3 ▶HELP 帮助◀ [U] money, food, clothes etc given to people who are poor or hungry 救济品: *a relief fund for refugees* 难民救济基金

4 ▶MONEY 金钱◀ [U] *especially AmE* money given by the government to help people who are poor, old, unemployed etc【尤美】救济金; BENEFIT[1] (2) *BrE*【英】

5 ▶REPLACE SB 替换某人◀ [C] a person or group of people that replaces another one and does their duty after they have finished 接班[替班]的人: *the relief for the military guard* 接班的卫兵 | *a relief driver* 换班司机

6 the relief of the act of freeing a town when it has been surrounded by an enemy …的解围, …的解救: *the relief of Mafeking*〔南非城市〕马弗京的解围

7 ▶DECORATION 装饰◀ [C] a shape or decoration that is raised above the surface it is on 浮雕, 浮雕品

8 ▶STICKING OUT 凸出◀ in relief a shape or decoration that is in relief sticks out above the rest of the surface it is on 凸出: **in high/low relief** (=sticking out a lot or a little) 深/浅浮雕的

9 stand out in bold/stark/sharp relief to be very different from everything around and therefore very easy to notice 与周围形成鲜明的反差; 非常突出: *The tree stood out in stark relief against the snow.* 树在雪的衬托下显得格外醒目。

10 light/comic relief a funny moment during a serious film, book, or situation〔严肃的电影、书或情景中作为调剂的〕轻松/滑稽场面: *There wasn't much in the way of light relief on the radio.* 广播里轻松的场面不多。

11 ▶MAP 地图◀ in relief if you show a part of the Earth's surface in relief, you show the differences in height between different parts of it 用地势图表示 —see also 另见 TAX RELIEF

relief map /·ˈ· ·/ *n* [C] a map with the mountains and high parts shown differently from the low parts, especially by being printed in a different colour〔用不同颜色表示地势高低的〕地势图, 地形图

re·lieve /rɪˈliv; rɪˈliːv/ *v* [T]

1 ▶PAIN/PROBLEM 疼痛/问题◀ to make a pain, problem, unpleasant feeling less severe 减轻, 缓解〔疼痛、麻烦或忧虑〕: *Drugs helped to relieve the pain.* 药物帮助舒缓疼痛。| *Volunteers were recruited to relieve the acute labour shortage.* 志愿者被招募来缓解严重的劳动力短缺。| *Adults often swear in order to relieve their feelings.* 成年人经常说粗话以发泄情绪。—see graph at 参见 PAIN[1] 图表

2 relieve the boredom/monotony etc to make something less dull and boring 排遣无聊/枯燥等: *I went for a walk to relieve the boredom of the day.* 一天下来无聊得很, 我去散步调剂一下。

3 relieve yourself a polite expression meaning to URINATE 小便〔礼貌的说法〕

4 ▶REPLACE SB 替换某人◀ to replace someone when they have completed their duty or when they need a rest 换…的班, 替换: *The guard will be relieved at midnight.* 哨兵在午夜时换班。

5 ▶A TOWN 城镇◀ to free a town which an enemy has surrounded 给…解围, 解救

relieve sb **of** sth *phr v* [T] **1** *formal* to help someone by taking something from them, especially a job they do not want to do or something heavy that they are carrying【正式】解除〔某人〕的负担: *Jessie could relieve you of some of the chores.* 杰西可以帮你做一些日常杂活。| *A tall gentleman kindly offered to relieve her of her suitcase.* 一位高个子男士好心地表示要帮她提箱子。**2 relieve sb of their post/duties/command etc** *formal* to take away someone's job because they have done something wrong【正式】免除某人的职务/职责/指挥权等: *After the defeat General Meyer was relieved of his command.* 战败之后, 迈耶将军被免除了指挥权。**3** *humorous* to steal something from someone【幽默】偷窃: *A couple of guys I met in the bar relieved me of my wallet.* 我在酒吧遇到的两个家伙偷了我的钱包。

re·lieved /rɪˈlivd; rɪˈliːvd/ *adj* feeling happy because you are no longer worried about something 宽慰的, 不再忧虑的: *She looked immensely relieved when she heard this news.* 她听说这个消息后, 流露出十分宽慰的神情。| **relieved to see/hear/know sth** *His mother was relieved to see him eating properly again.* 看到他吃饭又恢复正常, 他妈妈放心了。| **[+that]** *I feel so relieved that I haven't got to take that wretched exam again.* 我不必再参加那个讨厌的考试了, 感到很轻松。

re·li·gion /rɪˈlɪdʒən; rɪˈlɪdʒən/ *n* **1** [U] people's belief in the life of the spirit and usually in one or more gods 宗教信仰: *The theme was the relationship between religion and literature.* 主题是宗教信仰与文学之间的关系。| **get religion** *informal* (=suddenly become interested in religion in a way that seems strange to other people)【非正式】〔突然〕皈依 *He got religion in a big way when he was at college.* 他在上大学时突然信教了。**2** [C] a particular system of this belief and all the ways of expressing your love for your god, ceremonies, and duties that are connected with it 宗教: *Islam and Buddhism are two of the great religions of the world.* 伊斯兰教和佛教是世界上的两大宗教。| *the Christian religion* 基督教 | **practise a religion** (=take part in the ceremonies and obey the rules of a religion) 信仰某种宗教〔参加仪式并遵守教规〕**3** [singular] an activity or area of interest which is extremely or unreasonably important in your life 狂热的活动[爱好]: *Football was a religion in my family.* 足球是我们一家人狂热的爱好。

re·li·gious /rɪˈlɪdʒəs; rɪˈlɪdʒəs/ *adj* **1** connected with religion in general or with a particular religion 宗教的: *I don't go along with her religious beliefs.* 我不赞同她的宗教信仰。| *a religious ceremony* 宗教仪式 **2** believing strongly in your religion and obeying its rules carefully 笃信宗教的; 虔诚的: *a deeply religious person* 非常虔诚的信徒

re·li·gious·ly /rɪˈlɪdʒəslɪ; rɪˈlɪdʒəsli/ *adv* **1** if you do something religiously, you are always very careful to do it 认真地, 严谨地: *I was religiously following all the instructions.* 我一丝不苟地遵循所有指示。**2** in a way that is connected with religion 与宗教信仰有关地

re·lin·quish /rɪˋlɪŋkwɪʃ; rɪˈlɪŋkwɪʃ/ *v* [T] *formal* to let someone else have your position, power, or rights, especially unwillingly【正式】〔尤指不情愿地〕放弃，交出〔权力、职位等〕: *The Duke was obliged to relinquish all rights and claims to the territory.* 公爵被迫放弃了所有的权利和对领地的所有权。| **relinquish sth to sb** *He refused to relinquish sovereignty to his son.* 他拒绝把统治权交给他的儿子。| **relinquish your hold/grip on sth** *Richard stubbornly refused to relinquish his hold on the family business.* 理查德固执地拒绝交出管理家族生意的权力。

rel·i·qua·ry /ˋrɛlə,kwɛrɪ; ˈrelɪkwəri/ *n* [C] a container for religious objects that are connected with holy people 圣骨盒; 圣物盒

rel·ish[1] /ˋrɛlɪʃ; ˈrelɪʃ/ *v* [T] to enjoy an experience or the thought of something that is going to happen 喜爱，喜欢: *Peter didn't really relish the thought of spending Christmas at his in-laws.* 其实彼得并不喜欢在岳父母家过圣诞节。| *He spoke calmly, relishing the chance to infuriate his boss.* 他心平气和地说话，享受着激怒老板的机会。

relish[2] *n* **1** [U] great enjoyment of something 享受: *There was a certain relish in his voice as he announced the news.* 他宣布该消息时语气中有点得意。| **with (great) relish** *She looked forward with relish to the prospect of going abroad for the first time.* 她饶有兴趣地期待着第一次出国。**2** [C,U] a SAUCE eaten with food which adds taste to it 佐料，调味品: *tomato relish* 番茄调味汁

R

re·live /riˋlɪv; ˌriːˈlɪv/ *v* [T] to experience something again that happened in the past, or to remember or imagine it very clearly 重新体验，重温: *We often find ourselves reliving our schooldays when we meet up.* 我们聚会时经常重温我们的学生时代。

rel·lo /ˋrɛlo; ˈreləʊ/ *n* [C] *AustrE spoken* a relative【澳口】亲戚，亲属: *We're having the rellos over.* 有亲戚要来我们这里做客。

re·load /riˋlod; ˌriːˈləʊd/ *v* [I,T] to put another bullet into a gun, film into a camera, or PROGRAM into a computer 再装填〔子弹或胶卷〕; 再输入〔程序〕: *Reload the pistol, quick!* 再给手枪装上子弹，快!

re·lo·cate /riˋloket; ˌriːləʊˈkeɪt/ *v* [I,T] if a group of people or a business relocates, or is relocated, they move to a different place 重新安置; 移迁; 搬迁: [+to] *A lot of firms are relocating to the North of England.* 许多公司正在迁往英格兰北部。| **relocate sb/sth to** *The residents were relocated to temporary accommodation.* 居民被迁到临时住处。—**relocation** /ˌriloˋkeʃən; ˌriːləʊˈkeɪʃən/ *n* [U]

re·luc·tant /rɪˋlʌktənt; rɪˈlʌktənt/ *adj* slow and unwilling 勉强的，不愿的: *She gave a reluctant smile.* 她勉强笑了笑。| **reluctant to do sth** *She seemed reluctant to join in the discussion.* 她似乎不愿意参加讨论。—**reluctance** *n* [singular,U]: *He answered these questions with a certain reluctance.* 他有些不情愿地回答了这些问题。—**reluctantly** *adv*: *Reluctantly, he agreed.* 他答应了，但是很勉强。

2 2 **re·ly** /rɪˋlaɪ; rɪˈlaɪ/ *v*

rely on/upon sb/sth *phr v* [T] **1** to trust someone or something to do what you need or expect them to do 信任，信赖: **rely on sb/sth to do sth** *I think we can rely on Derek not to tell anyone.* 我认为我们可以信赖德里克，他不会告诉任何人。| **rely on sb/sth doing sth** *You can't just rely on your parents lending you the money.* 你不能只指望父母借钱给你。| **rely on sb/sth for sth** *Tim always relies on his wife for advice on clothes.* 在穿着方面，蒂姆一直靠他妻子指点。**2** to depend on something in order to continue to live or exist〔为生活或生存〕依赖: **rely on sth/sb for** *They have to rely on the river for their water.* 他们用水只能依靠这条河。

R.E.M /ˌar iˋɛm; ˌɑːr iː ˈem/ a US ROCK band popular in the 1980s and 1990s. Their ALBUMS include *Automatic for the People* and *Monster*. R.E.M 乐队〔美国一摇滚乐队，流行于20世纪80、90年代。其专辑包括《人民的自动武器》和《怪物》〕

1 1 **re·main** /rɪˋmen; rɪˈmeɪn/ *v* **1** [I always+adv/prep, linking verb 连系动词] to continue to be in the same state or condition 继续，依然: *Would the audience please remain seated?* 请观众不要站起来! | *'La Strada' remains one of Fellini's best films.* 《道路》依然是费利尼最好的电影之一。| *The Government remained in power for twelve years.* 该政府执政了12年。**2** [I] *formal* to stay in the same place without moving away【正式】停留，留下: [+at/in/with etc] *She remained at home to look after the children.* 她留在家里照顾孩子。**3** [I] to continue to exist, after others have gone or been destroyed 剩下，留存: *Little of the original architecture remains.* 原来的建筑留存下来的为数极少。| *What remains of the original art collection is now in the city museum.* 原来的艺术收藏品剩下来的现在都在市博物馆里。**4** [I] to be left after other things have been dealt with 留下，剩余: **remain to be done** *Several points remain to be settled.* 还剩几个问题要解决。| **it only remains for me to say/thank etc** (=used to introduce the last remark in a speech or meeting) 最后我想说/要感谢等 *It only remains for me to thank our hosts.* 最后我要感谢我们的主人。| **the fact remains** (=used to say that a particular fact cannot be ignored) 不能忽略的是 *I know Benson has a PhD but the fact remains he has no practical experience.* 我知道本森有博士学位，但不要忘记，他没有实践经验。**5 it remains to be seen** *spoken* used to say that it is still uncertain whether something will happen or is true【口】尚不确定，说不准: *It remains to be seen whether or not the operation was successful.* 手术是否成功，还有待观察。—see also 另见 REMAINING

Frequencies of the verbs **remain** and **stay** in spoken and written English 动词 remain 和 stay 在英语口语和书面语中的使用频率

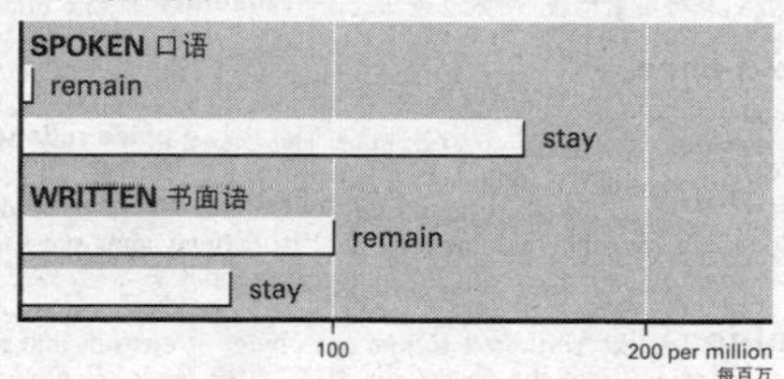

Based on the British National Corpus and the Longman Lancaster Corpus
据英国国家语料库和朗文兰开斯特语料库

This graph shows that it is much more usual in spoken English to use **stay** rather than **remain**, which is formal when used in this meaning and is therefore more common in written English.
本图表显示，在英语口语中 stay 的使用频率远远高于 remain，remain 表示这个意思时比较正式，因而更多的是用于书面语中。

re·main·der /rɪˋmendə; rɪˈmeɪndə/ *n* **the remainder** the part of something that is left after everything else has gone or been dealt with 剩余物，剩余部分: *Please pay half the money now and the remainder when you receive the goods.* 现在请付一半款，余款等你们收到货后再付。| [+of] *The remainder of the class should use this time for study.* 班里其余的人要用这段时间来学习。

re·main·ing /rɪˋmenɪŋ; rɪˈmeɪnɪŋ/ *adj* [only before noun 仅用于名词前] the remaining people or things are those that are left when the others have gone, been used, or been dealt with 留下的; 剩余的，其余的: *The few remaining guests were in the kitchen finishing off the wine.* 还没走的几位客人在厨房里把酒喝完。| *The only remaining question is whether we can raise the money.* 唯一剩下的问题是我们能否筹到这笔钱。 2

re·mains /rɪˋmenz; rɪˈmeɪnz/ *n* [plural] **1 the remains (of)** the parts of something that are left after the rest has been destroyed or has disappeared 剩下的东西[部分]; 遗迹: *He ate the remains of the casserole hungrily.* 他狼吞虎咽地吃掉剩下的炖菜。| *the extensive Roman remains* (=of ancient buildings) *at Arles* 在阿尔勒大片的古罗马遗迹 **2** the body of someone who has died 遗体: *Her remains are buried in Westminster.* 她的遗体葬在威斯敏斯特〔教堂〕。 3

re·make[1] /riˋmek; ˌriːˈmeɪk/ *v past tense and past participle* **remade** /-ˋmed; -ˈmeɪd/ [T] **1** to film a story or record a tune again 重新摄制; 重新录制: *The band has just remade an old Frank Sinatra hit.* 乐队刚刚重新录制了弗兰克·西纳特拉一首红极一时的旧歌。**2** to build or make something again 再建; 再制

re·make[2] /ˋri,mek; ˈriːmeɪk/ *n* [C] a record or film that has the same music or story as one that was made before 重新录制的唱片; 重新摄制的电影

re·mand[1] /rɪˋmænd; rɪˈmɑːnd/ *v* [T usually passive 一般用被动态] *BrE* to send someone back from a court of law, to wait for their TRIAL[1] (1)【英】将…还押[保释]候审: **be remanded in custody** (=be kept in prison until your TRIAL[1] (1)) 在押候审

remand[2] *n* [U] the period of time that someone spends in prison before their TRIAL[1] (1)〔审前〕在押期: *remand prisoners* 在押犯 | *a remand centre* 拘留中心 | **be on remand** (=in prison waiting for your TRIAL[1] (1)) 在押候审: *Evans committed suicide while on remand in Parkhurst prison.* 埃文斯在帕克赫斯特监狱在押候审期间自杀了。

remand home /ˋ· · ˏ·/ also 又作 **remand cen·tre** /ˋ· ˏ· ·/ *n* [C] *BrE* a place where young criminals are kept while waiting for a TRIAL[1] (1)【英】青少年犯拘留所

S3 W3 **re·mark¹** /rɪˋmɑrk; rɪˈmɑːk/ *n* **1** [C] something that you say when you express an opinion or say what you have noticed 意见，评论: **make/pass a remark** *She could hear the other girls making rude remarks about her.* 她可以听见其他女孩在说她的坏话。**2 (worthy) of remark** *old use* important enough to be noticed【旧】值得注意的: *Nothing of remark has happened since you left.* 你走后没有发生任何值得一提的事。

remark² *v* [T+that] to say something, especially about something you have just noticed 谈到，说起〔尤指刚察觉的事〕: *"That's a lovely shirt you're wearing," she remarked.* "你穿的衬衫真漂亮。"她说。| **remark that** *Her father remarked that it was time to leave.* 她的父亲说该走了。

remark on/upon sth *phr v* [T] to notice that something has happened and say something about it 谈论，评论: *Everyone remarked on his absence.* 大家对他的缺席议论纷纷。

W3 **re·mar·ka·ble** /rɪˋmɑrkəbḷ; rɪˈmɑːkəbəl/ *adj* unusual or surprising and therefore deserving attention or praise 值得注意的; 不寻常的，奇特的: *She has made remarkable progress.* 她取得了不起的进步。| *a remarkable coincidence* 奇特的巧合 | **[+about]** *There's nothing particularly remarkable about the landscape.* 这片景色没有什么特别之处。| **[+for]** *Finland is remarkable for its large number of lakes.* 芬兰以湖泊众多而著称。

re·mar·ka·bly /rɪˋmɑrkəblɪ; rɪˈmɑːkəbli/ *adv* unusually; noticeably 不寻常地; 突出地: [+adj/adv] *She plays the violin remarkably well for a child of her age.* 就她年龄来说，她的小提琴拉得特别好。| [sentence adverb 句子副词] *Remarkably, all of the passengers survived the crash.* 奇怪的是，所有的乘客在事故中都活下来了。

re·mar·ry /riˋmærɪ; ˌriːˈmæri/ *v* [I,T] to marry again 再婚; 再娶; 再嫁: *Widowed in 1949, Mrs Hayes never remarried.* 1949年丧夫后，海斯太太一直没有再婚。—**remarriage** /riˋmærɪdʒ; riːˈmærɪdʒ/ *n* [C]

re·mas·ter /riˋmæstɚ; riːˈmɑːstə/ *v* [T] *technical* to use a computer to make a better musical recording from the original【术语】〔用电脑提高唱片原本音质〕翻录: *digital remastering* 数码翻录

Rem·brandt /ˋrɛmbrænt; ˈrembrænt/ (1606-69) a Dutch artist, **Rembrandt van Rijn**, who is one of the greatest European painters. He painted many PORTRAITS (=pictures of people and of himself), as well as many pictures of religious subjects. He is admired especially for his use of light and shade. 伦勃朗〔(1606-1669)，荷兰画家，全名伦勃朗·范·赖恩，欧洲最伟大的画家之一。他创作有许多宗教主题的绘画作品和肖像画。他处理光线和阴影的手法尤其为人推崇〕

re·me·di·a·ble /rɪˋmidɪəbḷ; rɪˈmiːdiəbəl/ *adj formal* able to be put right or cured【正式】可纠正的; 可医治的

re·me·di·al /rɪˋmidɪəl; rɪˈmiːdiəl/ *adj* **1** aimed at correcting a fault in something, or curing a problem with someone's health 补救的; 纠正的; 治疗(上)的: *Some remedial work needs to be done on the foundations.* 需要对基础部分做一些补救工作。| *remedial care for head injuries* 头部受伤的治疗护理 **2 remedial course/class/teacher etc** a special course etc that helps students who have more difficulty in learning than others 补习课程/班/老师等: *a remedial program for helping teenagers with basic communication skills* 帮助青少年培养基本沟通技巧的辅助计划

W3 **rem·e·dy¹** /ˋrɛmədɪ; ˈremədi/ *n* [C] **1** a way of dealing with a problem or making an unsatisfactory situation better 补救(法): *Is Government intervention the appropriate remedy?* 政府干预是恰当的补救方法吗? | **[+for]** *The law doesn't provide a remedy for this kind of injustice.* 现行法律纠正不了这种不公正。**2** a medicine to cure an illness or pain that is not very serious 药物; 治疗物: *an excellent remedy for period pains* 治疗痛经的良药 **3 beyond/past/without remedy** *formal* if a situation is beyond remedy nothing can be done to make it better【正式】不可救药的; 无法挽回的: *She felt as if her marital problems were beyond remedy.* 她觉得她的婚姻问题已无法挽回。

remedy² *v* [T] to deal with a problem or improve a bad situation 补救; 纠正; 改善: *The company should act quickly to remedy these grievances.* 公司应该迅速采取行动消除这些不满情绪。

S1 W1 **re·mem·ber** /rɪˋmɛmbɚ; rɪˈmembə/ *v*

1 ►THE PAST 过去◄ [I,T] to have a picture in your mind of people, events, places etc from the past 记得: **remember sb/sth** *Do you remember Rosa Davies?* 你记得罗莎·戴维斯吗? | *Mr Wilson has lived on our street for as long as I can remember.* 威尔逊先生自我记事起就住在我们这条街上。| **remember (that)** *I remember you two couldn't stand each other at first!* 我记得你们俩开始时互不相容! | **remember sb doing sth** *I remember my father bringing home a huge Christmas tree.* 我记得父亲带回家一棵巨大的圣诞树。| **remember sb as sth** *I remember Clive as an irritable but tremendously creative man.* 我记得克莱夫是个容易激动但极富创造力的人。| **remember doing sth** *I remember meeting her at a party once.* 我记得曾在一次聚会上见过她。| **remember well/clearly** *"Do you remember a guy called Casey?" "Sure, I remember him well."* "你记得一个名叫凯西的人吗?" "当然啦，我清楚地记得他。" | **vaguely/dimly/scarcely remember** (=not remember well) 模糊地/隐约地/几乎不记得 *I vaguely remember reading something about her husband in the paper.* 我依稀记得在报纸上看到过有关她丈夫的情况。| **remember correctly/rightly** *They had three children, if I remember rightly.* 如果我没记错，他们有三个孩子。| **distinctly/vividly remember** *I distinctly remember telling you to be home by 10 o'clock.* 我清楚地记得告诉过你要在10点前回家。

2 ►INFORMATION/FACTS 信息/事实◄ [I,T] to bring information or facts that you know into your mind 想起; 回忆起: *What did I do with my car keys? Oh, I remember, I left them on the kitchen table.* 我把车钥匙放在哪儿了?噢，想起来了，我把它搁在餐桌上了。| *I can't remember her phone number.* 我想不起来她的电话号码。| **[+that]** *I suddenly remembered that I'd left the stove on.* 我突然想起我没有关炉子。| **remember what/how/why etc** *I'm trying to remember whether I said six or seven o'clock.* 我正在设法回忆我说的是6点还是7点。

3 ►TO DO/GET SOMETHING 要做/获得某事物◄ [I,T] to remember something that you must do, get, or bring 记住; 牢记: **remember to do sth** *Did you remember to get the bread?* 你记得要买面包吗? | *Remember to close the windows before you go out.* 出门之前别忘了关窗。| **remember sth** *I do hope he remembered the wine.* 我非常希望他没忘记那些酒。| *The thing to remember is to keep stirring the sauce.* 需要记住的是不停地搅拌酱汁。

4 ►KEEP STH IN MIND 记住某事◄ to keep a particular fact about a situation in your mind 记住; 牢记: **[+that]** *You must remember that we didn't have cars in those days.* 你肯定记得，那时我们没有汽车。

5 ►HONOUR THE DEAD 纪念死者◄ to think about someone who has died with special respect, often in a ceremony 纪念; 悼念: *On this day we remember the dead of two world wars.* 我们在这一天纪念两次世界大战的死难者。

6 be remembered for sth/as sth to be famous for something important that you once did 因…而著名: *Bobby Moore will always be remembered as captain of the England squad in 1966.* 博比·穆尔因身为1966年英格兰队队长而名垂后世。

7 ►GIVE SB A PRESENT 给某人送礼物◄ [T] to give someone a present on a particular occasion 给〔某人〕送礼物: *She always remembers me at Christmas.* 每逢圣诞节她总送礼物给我。| **remember sb in your will** (=arrange for someone to have something of yours after you die) 在遗嘱中把部分财产赠予某人

8 remember me to sb used to ask someone to give a greeting from you to someone else 代我向某人问好

This graph shows some of the words most commonly used with the verb **remember**. 本图表所示为含有动词remember的一些最常用词组。

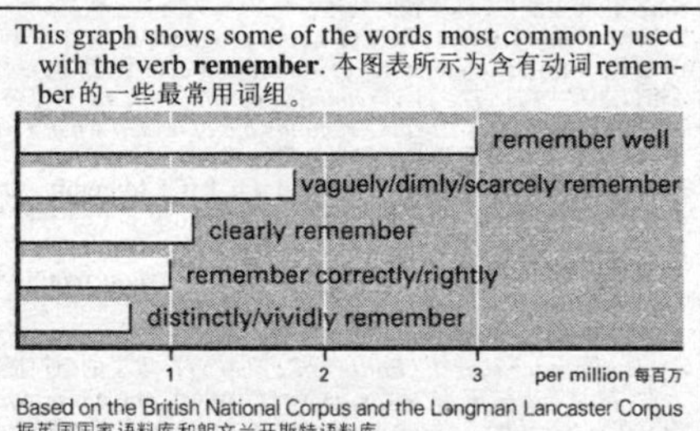

Based on the British National Corpus and the Longman Lancaster Corpus 据英国国家语料库和朗文兰开斯特语料库

re·mem·brance /rɪˋmɛmbrəns; rɪˈmembrəns/ *n* **1 in remembrance of sb** in order to remember and give honour to someone who has died 为了悼念某人: *a service in remembrance of those killed in the war* 悼念战争死难者的仪式 **2** [C,U] *formal* a memory that you have of a person or event【正式】记忆; 回忆: *fond remembrances* 深情的回忆

Remembrance Day /ˈ· ˈ·· ˌ·/ also 又作 **Remembrance Sunday** /ˌ·, ·· ˈ ·ˌ·/ *n* the Sunday nearest to November 11th, when a ceremony is held in Britain to remember people who were killed in the two world wars〔英国在最接近11月11日的星期日悼念两次世界大战中阵亡者的〕阵亡将士纪念日

CULTURAL NOTE 文化注释

Each year, on every Remembrance Sunday, there are special church services all over the UK, and special ceremonies at WAR MEMORIALS. In London, there is a ceremony in which the Queen and the leaders of the main political parties place a WREATH (=a circular arrangement of flowers) on the Cenotaph (=a large war memorial). Most people wear a red paper POPPY (=a type of flower) on their coats, and the money collected by selling these poppies is given to CHARITY organizations that help people who suffered in the wars. There is a similar occasion in the US and Canada called 'Veterans Day'. 在每年的阵亡将士纪念日这一天，全英国都会有特别的教堂礼拜仪式，此外在战争纪念碑前还举行特别的仪式。在伦敦的仪式上，女王和主要政党的领袖会向两次世界大战死难者纪念碑敬献花圈。很多人把纸制的红色罂粟花别在上衣上，而卖花的收入会捐献给慈善组织，慈善组织向在两次世界大战中受过伤害的人们提供帮助。美国和加拿大也有类似的纪念日，叫做"退伍军人节"。

re·mind /rɪˋmaɪnd; rɪˈmaɪnd/ *v* [T] **1** to make someone remember something that they must do 使想起；提醒：*I must pay the gas bill. I'll put it here to remind me.* 我得付煤气费了。我把账单放在这里提醒自己。| **remind sb about sth** *Will you remind me about that appointment?* 请你提醒我那个约会好吗？| **remind sb to do sth** *"Remind me to buy stamps." "OK."* "请提醒我买邮票。""好的。" | **remind sb (that)** *I'll just call Sylvia to remind her that we are meeting at 8.* 我要给西尔维娅打电话，提醒她我们在8点见面。| **that reminds me** *spoken* (=used when something has just made you remember something you were going to say or do)【口】那使我想起〔用于某事刚使你想起要说或做的事情〕*Oh, that reminds me, I saw Jenny in town today.* 噢，那让我记起来，我今天在城里看见了珍妮。| **remind sb what/how/when etc** *Remind me what to do, I haven't used this machine for ages.* 请提醒我该怎么做，我已经很久没用过这台机器了。| **remind yourself (to do sth)** *Find some way of reminding yourself to answer letters.* 想个办法提醒你自己写回信。**2** to make someone remember someone that they knew or something that happened in the past 使〔某人〕想起：**remind sb of sth** *Hearing that song always reminds me of a certain night in Santa Cruz.* 听到那首歌总使我想起在圣克鲁斯的某个夜晚。| **remind sb what/how etc** *The letter reminded me what a jerk Jim could be.* 这封信使我想起吉姆是个多么愚蠢的人。**3 Don't remind me** *spoken* used in a joking way when someone has mentioned something that embarrasses or annoys you【口】别跟我提这事〔某人提到使你尴尬或不快的事情时诙谐的说法〕：*"We've got a test tomorrow." "Don't remind me!"* "我们明天有考试。""别跟我提这事！" **4 let me remind you/may I remind you** *spoken formal* used to add force to a warning or criticism【口，正式】让我提醒你〔用于加强警告或批评的语气〕：[+that] *Let me remind you that you are expected to arrive on time.* 让我提醒你，你要按时到达。

remind sb **of** sb/sth *phr v* [T not in progressive 不用进行时] to seem similar to someone or something else 使〔某人〕想起〔相似之人或物〕：*The view reminded her of Scotland.* 这景色使她想起了苏格兰。| *Corinne reminds me of myself when I was her age.* 科莉娜使我想起了我自己像她那么大时的样子。

re·mind·er /rɪˋmaɪndɚ; rɪˈmaɪndə/ *n* **1** [C] something that makes you notice something or understand it better 提醒物：[+of] *a reminder of the dangers of drinking and driving* 对酒后驾车的危险警告 | [+about] *Kids need constant reminders about crossing roads safely.* 小孩子需要不断提醒他们要安全地过马路。| **be a reminder that** *Occasional bursts of gunfire are a reminder that the battle isn't over yet.* 零星的炮声提醒人们，战斗尚未结束。| **serve as a reminder** (=be a reminder) 提醒 *The President's bodyguards serve as a reminder that he's no ordinary guy out for a walk.* 总统的保镖们让人们意识到，他可不是一个出来散步的普通人。**2** [C] something that reminds you of something that happened or existed in the past 提醒人记忆之物：[+of] *Her disability remains as a perpetual reminder of the war years.* 她的残疾使人永远不会忘记战争的年代。**3** something, for example a letter, that reminds you to do something which you might have forgotten 起提醒作用的东西〈如信件〉

rem·i·nisce /ˌrɛməˋnɪs; ˌremɪ̆ˈnɪs/ *v* [I] to talk or think about pleasant events in your past 追忆往事，缅怀往事：[+about] *We walked on, reminiscing about the old days.* 我们向前走着，追忆着过去的日子。

rem·i·nis·cence /ˌrɛməˋnɪsn̩s; ˌremɪ̆ˈnɪsəns/ *n* [C,U often plural 常用复数] a spoken or written story about events that you remember 回忆往事的谈话；回忆录：[+of/about] *reminiscences of the war* 战争回忆录 —compare 比较 MEMOIR

rem·i·nis·cent /ˌrɛməˋnɪsn̩t; ˌremɪ̆ˈnɪsənt/ *adj* **1 reminiscent of** reminding you of something 使人想起…的：*written in a style strongly reminiscent of Virginia Woolf's novels* 写作风格酷似弗吉尼亚·吴尔夫的小说 **2** [only before noun 仅用于名词前] thinking about the past 回忆往事的，怀旧的：*"Those were the days," agreed Barrow with a reminiscent sigh.* "就是那些日子，"巴罗叹了口气附和着，流露出对往事的怀念。

re·miss /rɪˋmɪs; rɪˈmɪs/ *adj* [not before noun 不用于名词前] *formal* careless about doing something that you ought to do【正式】玩忽职守的，粗心的：**it is remiss of sb to do sth** *It was very remiss of me not to answer your letter.* 没有给你回信是我的疏忽。—**remissness** *n* [U]

re·mis·sion /rɪˋmɪʃən; rɪˈmɪʃən/ *n* **1** [C,U] *BrE* a reduction of the time that someone has to spend in prison【英】缩短刑期：*He was given six months' remission for good behaviour.* 他因为行为好而减刑六个月。**2** [C,U] a period when an illness improves for a time〔疾病的〕减轻；缓解（期）：**go into remission** *The cancer has gone into remission.* 癌症已经有所好转。**3** [U] *formal* the act of allowing someone to keep the money they owe you【正式】〔债务的〕免除 **4 the remission of sins** *formal* forgiveness from God for the bad things that you have done【正式】〔上帝〕饶恕罪恶

re·mit[1] /rɪˋmɪt; rɪˈmɪt/ *v formal*【正式】**1** [I,T] to send a payment by post 汇（款）：*Please remit payment by cheque.* 请用支票汇出付款。**2** [T] to free someone from a debt or punishment 免除〔债务或处罚〕—compare 比较 UNREMITTING

remit sth **to** sb/sth *phr v* [T] *formal* to send a proposal, plan, or problem back to someone for them to make a decision about【正式】把〔建议、计划或问题〕发回…〔以作出决定〕

re·mit[2] /ˋrimɪt; ˈriːmɪt/ *n* [singular,U] *BrE formal* the particular piece of work that someone has been officially asked to deal with【英，正式】职权范围：*It is not part of our remit to criticize government policy.* 批评政府的政策不在我们的职权范围之内。

re·mit·tance /rɪˋmɪtn̩s; rɪˈmɪtəns/ *n* **1** [C] *formal* an amount of money that you send by post to pay for something【正式】汇款额 **2** [U] the act of sending money by post 汇款：**on remittance of** (=when the money has been sent) 汇款收讫 *We will forward the goods on remittance of £10.* 10英镑汇到后即行发货。

re·mit·tent /rɪˋmɪtn̩t; rɪˈmɪtənt/ *adj formal* a remittent fever or illness is severe for short periods but improves between those times【正式】〔发烧、疾病〕弛张的，时重时轻的

rem·nant /ˋrɛmnənt; ˈremnənt/ *n* [C] **1** [usually plural 一般用复数] a small part of something that remains after the rest of it has been used, destroyed, or eaten 残余；剩余：*The remnants of a meal stood on the table.* 吃剩的饭菜摆在桌上。**2** a small piece of cloth left from a larger piece and sold cheap 零头布料

re·mod·el /ˌriˋmɑdl̩; ˌriːˈmɒdl/ **remodelled, remodelling** *BrE*【英】**remodeled, remodeling** *AmE*【美】*v* [T] to change the shape or appearance of something 改变…的形状[外观]；重新塑造：*He was in a terrible accident, and had to have his jaw remodelled.* 他遭遇了严重事故，颌部必须接受整形。

re·mon·strance /rɪˋmɑnstrəns; rɪˈmɒnstrəns/ *n* [C,U] *formal* a complaint or protest【正式】抱怨；抗议：*loud cries of remonstrance* 大声的抗议

rem·on·strate /rɪˋmɑnstret; ˈremənstreɪt/ *v* [I] *formal* to tell someone that you strongly disapprove of something they have said or done【正式】抗议：[+with/against] *They only stopped teasing after Evans remonstrated with them.* 直到埃文斯提出抗议，他们才停止捉弄他。—**remonstrative** /rɪˋmɑnstrətɪv; rɪˈmɒnstrətɪv/ *adj*

re·morse /rɪˋmɔrs; rɪˈmɔːs/ *n* [U] a strong feeling of being sorry that you have done something very bad 懊悔，悔恨：*When he saw tears in her eyes, he was full of remorse for what he had said.* 看到她眼泪汪汪，他对自己说的话悔恨不已。—**remorseful** *adj* —**remorsefully** *adv*

re·morse·less /rɪˋmɔrslɪs; rɪˈmɔːsləs/ *adj* **1** something unpleasant or threatening that is remorseless continues to happen and seems impossible to stop〔令人不快或威胁人的事〕无休止的：*Their coats gave little protection against the remorseless Baltic winds.* 他们的外衣基本无法抵御波罗的海持续不断的大风。**2** cruel, and not caring how much other people are hurt 冷酷的，无情的：*Within a few years, our country had been taken over by remorseless European settlers.* 在几年里，我们国家被冷酷无情的欧洲移民接管了。—**remorselessly** *adv*: *Stray sol-*

diers were remorselessly hunted down and shot. 掉队的士兵遭到无情的追捕和枪杀。—**remorselessness** *n* [U]

re·mort·gage /ˌriˈmɔrgɪdʒ; ˌriːˈmɔːgɪdʒ/ *v* [T] to borrow money by having a second MORTGAGE¹ (1) on your house, or increasing the one you have 再抵押，转抵押〔房子〕

3 **re·mote¹** /rɪˈmot; rɪˈməʊt/ *adj* **1** far away in space or time 遥远的: *remote stars* 遥远的星星 | *something from the remote past, dimly remembered* 依稀记得的久远的事物 | **a remote ancestor** (=someone related to you, who lived a long time ago) 远祖 **2** far from towns 偏僻的，偏远的: *As a westerner I was a strange sight in this remote spot.* 作为一个西方人，我成了这个偏远地方的奇观。**3** very different from something 很不相同的: **[+from]** *It was so alien, so remote from anything he had ever known.* 这东西很古怪，与他知道的所有东西都不一样。**4 a remote chance/possibility** a very slight chance or possibility 渺茫的希望/微乎其微的可能性: **[+that]** *There's a remote chance that you will catch him before he leaves.* 你不大可能在他离开前抓住他。**5** unfriendly, and not interested in people 不友善的，冷淡的: *She was quiet and remote, and had an annoying air of superiority.* 她话不多，对人冷淡，而且摆出高人一等的臭架子。**6 not have the remotest idea** used to emphasize the fact that you know nothing about something 一无所知: **[+what/where/who etc]** *Miranda hasn't the remotest idea where he's gone.* 米兰达一点儿也不知道他去哪儿了。—**remoteness** *n* [C]

remote² *n* [C] *spoken* REMOTE CONTROL【口】遥控

remote con·trol /ˌ· ·ˈ·/ *n* **1** [C] a thing you use for controlling a piece of electrical or electronic equipment without having to touch it, for example for turning a television on or off 遥控器 **2** [U] the process of controlling equipment from a distance, using radio or electronic signals〔用无线电或电子信号的〕遥控 —**remote-controlled** *adj*

re·mote·ly /rɪˈmotlɪ; rɪˈməʊtli/ *adv* **not remotely interested/similar/possible etc** not at all interested, similar etc 毫无兴趣/毫不相似/毫无可能等

remote sens·ing /ˌ·ˌ ˈ··/ *n* [U] the use of SATELLITEs to obtain pictures and information about the Earth 遥感〔用人造卫星向地球拍照并获取信息〕

re·mould¹ /ˈriˌmold; ˈriːməʊld/ *n* [C] an old tyre with a new surface, that you can use again 翻新的轮胎

re·mould² /riˈmold; ˌriːˈməʊld/ *v* [T] *formal* to change an idea, system, way of thinking etc【正式】改造，重新塑造: *They don't want to destroy the EC, but remould it in a more appropriate form.* 他们并不想毁掉欧共体，而只是想以更合适的形式对其加以改造。

re·mount /ˌriˈmaunt; ˌriːˈmaʊnt/ *v* [I,T] to get onto a horse, bicycle etc again 再次骑上〔马、自行车等〕

re·mov·a·ble /rɪˈmuvəbl; rɪˈmuːvəbəl/ *adj* easy to remove 可移动的；可拆装的: *The chair has a removable cover for easy cleaning.* 这椅子的椅套可拆装，清洗很方便。

3 **re·mov·al** /rɪˈmuvl; rɪˈmuːvəl/ *n* [C,U] **1** the act of taking something away 移动，搬动；去掉: *We'll arrange for the removal of this rubbish as soon as possible.* 我们将尽快安排人把这堆垃圾运走。| *stain removal* 去污 **2** the process of taking furniture from your old house to your new one 搬迁: **removal company/man etc** *The removal men have been in and out all day.* 搬运工一整天都在进进出出。

removal van /ˈ·ˈ·· ˌ·/ *n* [C] *BrE* a large VAN used for moving furniture from one house to another【英】搬家车，家具搬运车；MOVING VAN *AmE*【美】

2
1 **re·move** /rɪˈmuv; rɪˈmuːv/ *v*

1 ►TAKE AWAY 移走◄ [T] to take something away from the place where it is 移动，搬动，拿开: *Do not remove this notice.* 别取下这个布告。| **remove sth from** *Reference books may not be removed from the library.* 不得把参考书带出图书馆。

2 ►CLOTHES 衣服◄ [T] to take off a piece of clothing 脱掉；摘掉: *He removed his hat and gloves.* 他摘掉了帽子和手套。

3 ►GET RID OF 排除◄ [T] to get rid of something 清除；除去: *an operation to remove a tumour* 切除肿瘤的手术 | *These reforms will not remove poverty and injustice.* 这些改革消除不了贫穷和不公正。

4 be far removed from to be very different from something 与…迥然不同: *Life in the army was far removed from the comfort of his parents' home.* 军旅生活与在父母家的舒适相去甚远。

5 removed from *old use* hidden from someone or something【旧】隐藏的

6 ►FROM A JOB 免职◄ [T] to force someone out of an important position or dismiss them from a job 开除；把…免职: **[+from]** *The governor was removed from office, pending an investigation.* 州长被免职，等待调查。

7 ►PLACE 地点◄ [I] *old use* to go to live or work in another place【旧】迁移，移居: **[+from/to]** *Our office has removed from Boston to New York.* 我们的办事处已经从波士顿迁至纽约。

8 cousin once/twice etc removed the child, GRANDCHILD etc of your COUSIN, or your cousin's father, grandfather etc 隔一代/两代等的堂[表]亲戚

re·mov·er /rɪˈmuvə; rɪˈmuːvə/ *n* [C,U] **paint/nail-varnish/stain etc remover** a substance that removes paint marks etc 脱漆剂/去光水/去污剂等

REM sleep /ˈrɛm ˌslip; ˈrem sliːp/ *n* [U] a period during sleep when there is rapid movement of the eyes, thought to be a sign that you are dreaming 快速眼动睡眠〔据信是做梦的迹象〕

re·mu·ne·rate /rɪˈmjunəˌret; rɪˈmjuːnəreɪt/ *v* [T] *formal* to pay someone for something they have done for you【正式】酬报 —**remuneration** /rɪˌmjunəˈreʃən; rɪˌmjuːnəˈreɪʃən/ *n* [C,U]: *Our company offers a competitive remuneration package, including a company car.* 本公司提供一套具有竞争力的报酬组合，包括一辆汽车。

re·mu·ne·ra·tive /rɪˈmjunəˌretɪv; rɪˈmjuːnərətɪv/ *adj formal* making a lot of money【正式】赚钱多的；报酬高的 —**remuneratively** *adv*

Remus —see 见 ROMULUS AND REMUS

Re·nais·sance¹ /ˌrɛnəˈsɑns; rɪˈneɪsəns/ *n* **1 the Renaissance** the period of time in Europe between the 14th and 17th centuries when the art, literature, and ideas of ancient Greece were discovered again, examined, and developed〔欧洲 14 世纪至 17 世纪的〕文艺复兴时期 **2 Renaissance art/furniture/architecture etc** art, furniture etc belonging to the Renaissance period 文艺复兴时期的艺术/家具/建筑等

renaissance² *n* [singular] a new interest in a particular form of art, music etc, that has not been fashionable〔艺术、音乐等某一领域的〕复兴

re·nal /ˈrinl; ˈriːnl/ *adj* [only before noun 仅用于名词前] *technical* concerning the kidneys (KIDNEY (1))【术语】肾(脏)的: *acute renal failure* 急性肾衰竭

re·name /riˈnem; riːˈneɪm/ *v* [T] [usually passive 一般用被动态] to give something a new name 给…重新命名: **rename sth sth** *Myddleton Way was renamed Allende Avenue.* 米德尔顿路已重新命名为阿连德大街。

re·nas·cent /rɪˈnæsn̩t; rɪˈnæsənt/ *adj* [only before noun 仅用于名词前] *formal* becoming popular, strong, or important again【正式】复兴的，再生的: *Voters are flooding back to the renascent Labour Party.* 大批选民正重新支持东山再起的工党。

rend /rɛnd; rend/ *past tense and past participle* **rent** /rɛnt; rent/ *v* [T] *literary* to tear or break something violently into pieces【文】猛力撕碎；把…打碎

ren·der /ˈrɛndə; ˈrendə/ *v* **1 render sth useless/render sb harmless etc** to make someone or something useless etc 使某物变得无用/使某人变得无害等: *New laws have rendered this kind of assistance virtually impossible.* 新法律使这类援助几乎不可能。**2 render an apology/an explanation/a service etc** *formal* to say sorry to someone, give someone an explanation, etc【正式】道歉/解释/提供服务等: **for services rendered** (=in payment for something you have done) 支付所提供的服务 **3** [T] to express or present something in a particular way 表达；表现: **render sth as sth** *Through her art, she attempts to render feelings as colors.* 通过她的艺术作品，她试图将情感描绘成不同的色彩。| **render sth in sth** *Children soon learn to render their thoughts in speech.* 儿童很快学会用语言表达自己的思想。**4 render sth into English/Russian/Chinese etc** *old use* to translate something into English, Russian etc【旧】将某物译成英语/俄语/汉语等 **5** [T] *technical* to spread PLASTER¹ (1) or CEMENT on the surface of a wall【术语】往〔墙面〕抹灰泥[水泥]

render sth ↔ **down** *phr v* [T] to melt fat until it is pure 熬炼〔脂肪〕

render sth ↔ **up** *phr v* [T] *old use* to give something to someone, especially to a ruler or enemy【旧】给予〔尤指进贡〕

ren·der·ing /ˈrɛndərɪŋ; ˈrendərɪŋ/ *n* [U] **1** *BrE* the way a play or piece of music is performed; RENDITION (1)【英】表演；演奏: *her passionate rendering of Elgar's cello concerto* 她充满激情地演奏〔英国作曲家〕埃尔加的大提琴协奏曲 **2** a material made mainly of CEMENT and sand, used to protect the outside walls of buildings〔水泥和沙搅拌而成，用于保护外墙的〕灰泥

ren·dez·vous¹ /ˈrɑndəˌvu; ˈrɒndʒvuː/ *n plural* **rendezvous** **1** [C] an arrangement to meet at a particular time and place 约会，会面: **[+with]** *a midnight rendezvous with Jose* 与乔斯的午夜约会 **2** [C usually singular 一般用单数] a place where two

or more people have arranged to meet 约会地点: *We arrived early at the rendezvous.* 我们早早到达约会地点。**3** [C] a popular place for people to meet〔经常的〕聚会处: *The bar is a regular rendezvous for media people.* 这酒吧是传媒界人士经常聚会的地点。

rendezvous² *v* [I+with] to meet someone as you have arranged〔与…〕会合; 聚会; 见面

ren·di·tion /rɛnˋdɪʃən; renˈdɪʃən/ *n* **1** [U] the way a play or piece of music is performed 表演, 演奏; RENDERING (1) *BrE*【英】**2** [C] a TRANSLATION of a piece of writing 翻译, 译文: *an English rendition of a Greek poem* 一首希腊诗歌的英译

ren·e·gade /ˋrɛnɪˌged; ˈrenɪgeɪd/ *n especially literary* someone who joins an opposing side in a war, in politics etc【尤文】叛徒, 变节者: *a renegade, who had once been a leader of the Party* 曾经是该党领袖的叛徒 | **renegade soldiers/troops etc** *At the meeting were several renegade Communists.* 有几位变节的共产党人出席了会议。

re·nege /rɪˋnig; rɪˈniːg/ *v* [I] *formal*【正式】**renege on an agreement/a deal etc** to not do something you have promised or agreed to do 违背诺言/协议等: *Why has the government reneged on its commitment to the welfare program?* 政府为何违背了自己对该福利计划的承诺?

re·new /rɪˋnju; rɪˈnjuː/ *v* [T] **1** to arrange for a contract, membership of a club etc to continue 延长〔合同的期限或会员资格等〕, 使续期: *I must remember to renew the car insurance.* 我必须记得续办汽车的保险。**2** to replace something that is old or broken with something new 更换; 更新: *The window frames will have to be renewed.* 窗框得换新的了。**3** to begin to do something again, after a period of rest〔休止一段时间后〕重新开始: **renew an attack** *The naval attack was renewed the next morning.* 第二天早晨海军再次发起进攻。| **renew a friendship/acquaintance etc** (=start a relationship again) 恢复友谊/交往等 **4 renew a book** to arrange to borrow a library book for a further period of time 续借图书 —see also 另见 RENEWED

re·new·a·ble /rɪˋnuəbḷ; rɪˈnjuːəbəl/ *adj* **1** a renewable contract, ticket etc can be made to continue after the date on which it ends〔合同、票证等〕可延期的, 可续期的: *The permit is renewable after 12 months.* 许可证在12个月后可再续期。**2** something that is renewable can be replaced by natural processes or good management, so that it is never used up〔由于自然循环或管理有方〕可再生的: **renewable energy/resources** *Sun, wind and waves provide renewable sources of energy.* 太阳、风和浪提供用之不竭的能源。

re·new·al /rɪˋnuəl; rɪˈnjuːəl/ *n* **1** [singular,U] an act of renewing something 更新; 恢复; 更换: [+of] *a renewal of interest in late Victorian culture* 对维多利亚时代后期文化恢复兴趣 **2 inner city/urban renewal** the process of bringing new jobs, industry, homes etc to the poor areas of large towns 旧城区/市区重建

re·newed /rɪˋnud; rɪˈnjuːd/ *adj* **1 renewed interest/vigour/enthusiasm etc** interest etc that increases again after not being very strong 重新产生的兴趣/活力/热情等: *renewed concern about the effects of acid rain* 重新关注酸雨的影响 **2** [not before noun 不用于名词前] feeling healthy and relaxed again, after feeling ill or tired 体力恢复的; 重新振作的

ren·net /ˋrɛnɪt; ˈrenɪt/ *n* [U] a substance used for making milk thicker in order to make cheese 粗制凝乳酶〔用于制干酪〕

Re·no /ˋrino; ˈriːnəʊ/ a city in Nevada, US, which is a popular place for people to go in order to GAMBLE. PROSTITUTION is also legal there, and people can get a divorce more quickly and easily than in other places. 里诺〔美国内华达州一城市, 著名赌城。卖淫在当地是合法的, 办理离婚手续也十分便捷〕

Reno, Jan·et /ˋdʒænɪt; ˈdʒænɪt/ (1938-) a US lawyer who was the Attorney General from 1993 until 2001. She was the first woman to have this job. 雷诺〔(1938-), 美国律师, 1993至2001年任美国司法部长, 是美国历史上任该职的首位女性〕

Ren·oir /rənˋwɑr; ˈrenwɑː/, **Au·guste** /ɔˋgjust; ɔːˈgjuːst/ (1841-1919) a French artist who was one of the first impressionists, and had a bright, colourful style of painting. He is famous especially for his paintings of women. 雷诺阿〔(1841-1919), 法国画家, 印象派画家的先驱之一。其作品光线明亮、色彩饱满, 尤以女性题材的绘画作品闻名〕

re·nounce /rɪˋnauns; rɪˈnaʊns/ *v* **1** [T] to publicly say that you will no longer keep something, or stay in an important position, because you no longer have the right to it 宣布放弃〔职位等〕: *The only course left to Nixon was to renounce the presidency.* 尼克松唯一能做的就是宣布辞去总统职位。| **renounce a claim** *James II renounced all claims to the English throne.* 詹姆斯二世宣布放弃继承英国王位的全部权利。**2** [T] to publicly say that you no longer believe in or support something 宣布放弃〔信仰、支持〕: *Writers and artists were called upon to renounce all bourgeois values.* 号召作家和艺术家公开宣布放弃所有的资产阶级价值观。—see also 另见 RENUNCIATION

ren·o·vate /ˋrɛnəˌvet; ˈrenəveɪt/ *v* [T] to repair and paint a building so that it is in good condition again 修复; 装修; 整修: *They are living in temporary accommodation while their apartment is being renovated.* 公寓修整期间他们临时住在别处。—**renovation** /ˌrɛnəˋveʃən; ˌrenəˈveɪʃən/ *n* [U]

re·nown /rɪˋnaun; rɪˈnaʊn/ *n* [U] fame and admiration, that you get because of some special skill or something that you have done 名望, 声誉: [+as] *At college, I'd acquired some renown as a football player.* 上大学的时候, 我因为足球踢得好而小有名气。| **win renown** *She eventually won international renown with her film 'Dispute'.* 她最终以她的电影《争辩》而赢得国际声誉。

re·nowned /rɪˋnaund; rɪˈnaʊnd/ *adj* known and admired by a lot of people, especially for some special skill, achievement, or quality 有名望的, 著名的: **be renowned for** *The region is renowned for its fine Persian rugs.* 该地区以其精美的波斯地毯而著称。| **be renowned as** *Goldman was renowned as a journalist and author.* 戈德曼是位著名的记者和作家。| **renowned footballer/statesman/architect etc** *The lecture will be delivered by renowned Marxist historian, Jeff Davies.* 讲课的是著名马克思主义历史学家杰夫·戴维斯。—see 见 FAMOUS (USAGE)

rent¹ /rɛnt; rent/ *v* **1** [I,T] to regularly pay money to live in a house or room that belongs to someone else, or to use something that belongs to someone else 租房; 租用, 租借: **rent sth from sb** *We rent our apartment from an old retired couple.* 我们的公寓是向一对退休老夫妇租的。| *Nick's been renting for five years now, and he can't afford to buy.* 尼克已经租了五年房, 他买不起。| *a rented video recorder* 租用的录像机 —see 见 HIRE¹ (USAGE) **2** [T] also 又作 **rent ↔ out** to let someone live in a house, room etc that you own, in return for money 出租: *If you can't sell your house, why don't you think about renting it?* 如果你不能出售你的房子, 为何不考虑将它出租? | **rent sth out to sb** *She rents out her flat to students.* 她把公寓出租给学生。**3** [T] *especially AmE* to pay money for the use of something for a short period of time【尤美】租用; HIRE¹ (1) *BrE*【英】: *Why don't we rent a boat for the afternoon?* 我们下午为什么不租一条船呢? **4** [I+at/for] if a house rents at or rents for a particular amount of money, that is how much someone pays in order to use it 收取的租金为… **5 rent-a-crowd/mob etc** people who are willing to take part in a protest about something, even if they do not feel strongly about it〔花钱〕动员来的人群

rent² *n* **1** [C,U] the money that someone pays for the use of a room, a house etc that belongs to someone else 租金: **high/low rent** *Office rents are extremely high in this part of London.* 伦敦这个地区的办公室租金非常昂贵。| **pay the rent** *I don't earn enough to pay the rent, let alone run a car.* 我的收入不够交房租, 更不用说买汽车了。| **raise the rent/raise rents** (=make someone pay more rent) 提高租金 —see 见 COST¹ (USAGE) **2** [C,U] *especially AmE* an amount of money paid for the use of a car, boat etc that belongs to someone else【尤美】〔汽车、船等的〕租金 **3** [C] a large tear in cloth, or a hole shaped like a tear in something〔织物等的〕裂缝: *There were huge rents all down the side of the sofa.* 沙发侧面从上到下有几处大裂缝。

rent³ the past tense and past participle of REND

rent·al /ˋrɛntḷ; ˈrentl/ *n* **1** [C usually singular 一般用单数] the money that you pay to use a car, television, tools etc over a period of time〔汽车、电视、工具等的〕租金: *£20 of this telephone bill is for line rental.* 这份电话账单上有20英镑是线路租用费。**2** [C,U] an arrangement by which you rent something 租借, 租赁: *TV rentals* 电视租用 | *rental costs* 租金 | *a video rental shop* 录像带租借商店 **3** [C] *AmE* the act of renting something such as a car or house【美】〔汽车、房子等的〕租借: *Car rental is expensive in Ohio.* 在俄亥俄州租车非常贵。| **rental car** *We had a rental car when we were on vacation.* 我们度假时租了一辆车。| **rentals** (=houses for renting) 出租的房屋 *Are there any summer rentals in this area?* 这个地区有没有在夏季出租的房屋?

rent book /ˋ· ·/ *n* [C] a small book used to record the amounts and dates of someone's rent payments 租金登记簿

rent boy /ˋ· ·/ *n* [C] *BrE* a young man who has sex with other men in return for money; a male PROSTITUTE【英】〔年轻的〕男妓

rent·ed /ˋrɛntɪd; ˈrentɪd/ *adj* **rented accommodation/housing/apartment etc** houses etc that people pay rent for 租用的住房等: *financial aid for families living in rented accommodation* 为租房居住的家庭提供的经济资助

rent-free /ˌ· ˈ·◄/ *adj, adv* without payment of rent 不付租金的〔地〕: *He lives there rent-free.* 他免费住在那里。| *rent-free accommodation* 免收租金的住宿

rent re·bate /ˈ· ˌ·· / *n* [C] *BrE* money that some people get from local government to help them pay their rent【英】〔地方政府提供的〕房租补贴

rent strike /ˈ· ·/ *n* [C] a time when all the people living in a group of houses or apartments refuse to pay their rent, as a protest against something〔住户的〕集体抗租

re·nun·ci·a·tion /rɪˌnʌnsɪˈeʃən; rɪˌnʌnsiˈeɪʃən/ *n* [C,U] *formal* a decision not to keep a particular set of beliefs, way of life, power, or object【正式】〔对信仰、生活方式、权力或目标的〕放弃, 抛弃: [+of] *Eastern Europe's renunciation of communism* 东欧抛弃共产主义 | *The life of a monk is one of renunciation.* 僧侣过的是弃绝俗欲的生活。

re·o·pen /riˈopən; riːˈəʊpən/ *v* **1** [I,T] if a theatre, restaurant etc reopens or is reopened, it opens again after being closed (使)〔剧场、餐厅等〕重新开张 **2** [I,T] if you reopen a discussion or law case, or if it reopens, you begin it again after it has stopped 恢复〔谈判〕; 续审: *A report from medical scientists has reopened the debate on tobacco advertising.* 医学家的一份报告再次引发有关烟草广告的辩论。**3** [T] if a government reopens the border of their country, they allow people to pass through it again after it has been closed 重新开放〔边界〕

re·or·der /riˈɔrdɚ; riˈɔːdə/ *v* [I,T] **1** to order a product again 再订购: *Stock levels are getting low – we need to reorder.* 库存在减少, 我们需要再订货。**2** to change things or put them in a more suitable order 重新整理; 重新排列: *The whole system needs reordering.* 整个系统需要重新整理。

re·or·gan·ize also 又作 **-ise** *BrE*【英】/riˈɔrgəˌnaɪz; riːˈɔːgənaɪz/ *v* [I,T] to arrange or organize something in a new way 改组; 改编: *I've reorganized my room so there's space for my new bookcase.* 我重新布置房间, 这样就有地方摆我的新书架了。—**reorganization** /ˌriɔrgənəˈzeʃən; riːˌɔːgənaɪˈzeɪʃən/ *n* [U]

rep /rɛp; rep/ *n* **1** [C] *informal* a SALES REPRESENTATIVE【非正式】推销员 **2** [C] *informal* someone who speaks officially for a company or organization; REPRESENTATIVE² (1)【非正式】〔公司、组织的〕代表: *You need to speak to the union rep.* 你需要和工会代表谈谈。**3** [C] *informal* a REPERTORY theatre or company【非正式】〔轮演选定剧目的〕剧院, 剧团 **4** [U] *informal* REPERTORY【非正式】轮流演出选定的剧目 **5** [C] *AmE informal* a REPUTATION【美, 非正式】名声, 名誉 **6 Rep a)** the written abbreviation of 缩写= REPUBLICAN **b)** the written abbreviation of 缩写= REPRESENTATIVE

re·paid /rɪˈped; rɪˈpeɪd/ *v* the past tense and past participle of REPAY

S3 **re·pair¹** /rɪˈpɛr; rɪˈpeə/ *v* [T] **1** to fix something that is damaged, broken, or not working properly 修理, 修补: *I'll have to get the car repaired.* 我得把车修理一下。| *to repair a broken fence* 修补破损的栅栏 **2** *formal* to do something to remove the harm that your mistake or wrong action has caused【正式】纠正, 补救: *How can I repair the wrong I have done her?* 我冤枉了她, 怎样才能补救呢? —see also 另见 IRREPARABLE

repair to sth *phr v* [T] *old-fashioned* to go to a place【过时】去, 赴: *Shall we repair to the drawing room?* 我们去客厅好吗?

S3 W3 **repair²** *n* **1** [C,U] an act of repairing something 修理, 修补: *The garage is carrying out repairs on my car.* 汽车修理厂正在修理我的车。| **be in need of repair** *The church roof was badly in need of repair.* 教堂的屋顶急需修理。| **under repair** (=being repaired) 在修理 *The road is under repair.* 这条路正在修补。| **beyond repair** (=so damaged that it cannot be mended) 无法修理 *My watch was crushed beyond repair.* 我的手表被压得没法修理了。| **repair work** (=work to repair something) 修理(工作) **2 in good/bad/poor repair** in good or bad condition 维修良好/糟糕: *Many of our major roads are in bad repair.* 我们的许多主要道路都失修。**3** [C] place on something that has been repaired 修补处: *The repair on the table top can hardly be seen.* 桌面上修补的地方几乎看不出来。—**repairer** *n* [C]

re·pair·a·ble /rɪˈpɛrəbl; rɪˈpeərəbəl/ *adj* able to be repaired 能修补的

rep·a·ra·ble /ˈrɛpərəbl; ˈrepərəbəl/ *adj formal* a reparable loss is one that you can get back in some way【正式】可补救的, 可挽回的 —opposite 反义词 IRREPARABLE

rep·a·ra·tion /ˌrɛpəˈreʃən; ˌrepəˈreɪʃən/ *n* **1 reparations** [plural] money paid by a defeated country after a war, for all the deaths, injuries, and damage it has caused〔战败国偿付的〕赔款 **2** [C,U] *formal* payment made to someone for damage, loss, or injury that you have caused them in the past【正式】赔偿, 补偿: **make reparation (to sb) for sth** *No reparation has been made to African countries for the damage of the slave trade.* 没有向非洲国家赔偿因贩卖奴隶而造成的损害。

rep·ar·tee /ˌrɛpɚˈti; ˌrepɑːˈtiː/ *n* [U] conversation which is very fast and full of clever amusing remarks 机智敏捷、妙语连珠的谈话

re·past /rɪˈpæst; rɪˈpɑːst/ *n* [C] *formal or humorous* a meal【正式或幽默】餐

re·pat·ri·ate /riˈpetrɪˌet; riːˈpætrieɪt/ *v* [T] **1** to send someone back to their own country 遣送〔某人〕回国, 遣返: *At the end of the war, prisoners were repatriated.* 战争结束时, 俘虏被遣送回国。**2** to send profits or money you have earned back to your own country 把〔利润、钱〕汇回国内

re·pay /rɪˈpe; rɪˈpeɪ/ *v* **repaid** /-ˈped; -ˈpeɪd/, **repaying** [T] **1** to pay back money that you have borrowed 付还, 偿还: *The loan must be repaid with interest.* 贷款须与利息一起偿还。| **repay sb sth** *Jenny repaid her parents the £1000 they lent her.* 珍妮还给父母借给她的1000英镑。**2** to reward someone for helping you 报答, 回报: **repay sb for sth** *How can I ever repay you for what you've done?* 我怎么才能报答你为我所做的一切? | **repay sb's kindness/generosity etc** *He wanted to repay their kindness, and took them out for a meal.* 他想报答他们的好意, 就请他们出去吃了一顿饭。**3 repay your effort** to seem worth the time you have spent 付出的努力值得

re·pay·a·ble /rɪˈpeəbl; rɪˈpeɪəbəl/ *adj* money that is repayable at a certain time has to be repaid by that time 应偿还的: *Mortgages are usually repayable over 25 years.* 抵押借款的偿还期通常为25年。

re·pay·ment /rɪˈpemənt; rɪˈpeɪmənt/ *n* **1** [U] the act of paying back money 付还, 偿还: *The rate of repayment is based on your income.* 还款率根据你的收入而定。**2** [C] an amount of money that you pay back 还款(额): *mortgage repayments of about £330 per month* 每月约330英镑的抵押还款

re·peal /rɪˈpil; rɪˈpiːl/ *v* [T] if a government repeals a law it officially ends that law 废除〔法律〕: *It's high time this grossly unfair law was repealed.* 这项极不公正的法令该废除了。—**repeal** *n* [U]: *the repeal of the prohibition laws* 禁酒法令的废除

re·peat¹ /rɪˈpit; rɪˈpiːt/ *v* S2 W2

1 ▶STATE AGAIN 再次陈述◀ [T] to say or write something again 重说; 重写: *Can you repeat your question?* 你能重复一遍你的问题吗? | **repeat that** *Steven repeated patiently that he was busy.* 史蒂文耐心地重复说他很忙。—see 见 SAY¹ (USAGE)

2 ▶DO AGAIN 再做◀ [T] to do something again 重做: *Repeat the treatment twice a day if necessary.* 如有必要请每天重复两次这项治疗。| *Anyone who gets less than 45% will have to repeat the test.* 凡得分低于45分者须补考。

3 ▶ACHIEVE STH AGAIN 再次获得某事物◀ [T] to achieve the same results or the same high level of performance 重获, 再次达到: *Other scientists are trying to repeat these results.* 另一些科学家正在设法再次获得这些结果。| *Can he repeat his success of 1993?* 他能否重复自己1993年的成功呢?

4 ▶LEARN 记住◀ [T] to say something you have learned 背诵: *Sandra repeated the poem hesitantly.* 桑德拉结结巴巴地背诵了那首诗。| **repeat after sb** *Repeat after me: amo, amas, amat...* 请跟我读: amo, amas, amat...

5 ▶TELL STH YOU HEAR 讲述所听说的事物◀ [T] to say something that you have heard someone else saying 重复〔听说的东西〕: *Don't repeat this to anyone but I think Derek's got a new girlfriend.* 别告诉任何人, 我觉得德里克有新的女朋友了。

6 repeat yourself to say something that you have already said without realizing that you have done it〔不自觉地〕重复自己说过的话: *Mrs Fardell repeats herself a bit, but she's very good for 85.* 法德尔太太说话有点重复, 但作为85岁的人她头脑非常清楚。

7 ▶BROADCAST 播放◀ [T often passive 常用被动态] to broadcast a television or radio programme again 重播: *'Omnibus' will be repeated at 10 o'clock on Tuesday.* "荟萃"将于星期二10点钟重播。

8 ▶FOOD 食物◀ [I+on] *informal* if food repeats on you, its taste keeps coming back into your mouth after you have eaten it【非正式】〔食物吃后〕在口中留有余味

9 sth doesn't bear repeating used to say that you do not want to repeat what someone has said, especially because it is rude〔话〕粗鲁得不堪重复: *Her comments about her ex-husband just don't bear repeating!* 她对前夫的评论真是不堪重复!

10 history repeats itself used to say that an event is like something that happened before 历史重演

repeat² *n* [C] **1** a television or radio programme that has been broadcast before 重播(的节目): *There's nothing but repeats on the TV tonight.* 今晚电视上只有重播节目。**2** an event very like

something that happened before 〔事件的〕重演, 重现: **[+of]** *The England-Holland match was basically a repeat of last year's game at Wembley.* 英格兰队与荷兰队的比赛基本上是去年在文布利比赛的重演。| **repeat performance** (=something bad that happens again) 〔坏事〕再度发生 *Last year's holiday was a disaster – we don't want a repeat performance this year.* 去年的假期搞得一塌糊涂, 我们不希望今年重蹈覆辙。**3 repeat order** a supply of the same products to a customer who has ordered them before 相同货品的订单 **4 repeat prescription** *BrE* an order for medicine that you have had before, which you can get without seeing your doctor【英】〔不用看医生而取同样药物的〕相同处方 **5** *technical* the sign at the end of a line of written music that tells the performer to play the music again, or the act of playing the music again【术语】〔乐谱的〕反复记号

re·peat·ed /rɪ`pitɪd; rɪ'piːtɨd/ *adj* [only before noun 仅用于名词前] done or happening again and again 反复的, 再三的: *repeated calls for change* 再三呼吁变革 | *repeated failure* 一再失败

re·peat·ed·ly /rɪ`pitɪdlɪ; rɪ'piːtɨdli/ *adv* many times 一再; 多次: *Graham was repeatedly warned by the doctors to not work so hard.* 医生一再告诫格雷厄姆工作不要这么拼命。

re·peat·er /rɪ`pitɚ; rɪ'piːtə/ *n* [C] *technical* a repeating gun or clock【术语】连发枪; 打簧表[钟]

re·peat·ing /rɪ`pitɪŋ; rɪ'piːtɪŋ/ *adj* **1** a repeating gun can be fired several times without being loaded again〔枪〕可连发的 **2** a repeating watch or clock can be made to repeat the last STRIKE (=sound made at an hour or quarter of an hour)〔钟、表〕自鸣的, 打簧的

re·pel /rɪ`pɛl; rɪ'pel/ *v* **repelled, repelling 1** [T] if something repels you, you want to avoid it because you do not like it 使厌恶, 使反感: *Her heavy make-up and cheap scent repelled him.* 她的浓妆和廉价香水使他厌恶。**2** [T] to fight a group or military force and make them stop attacking you 击退: *repel invaders* 击退入侵者 | *repel an attack* 击退进攻 **3** [T] to keep something or someone away from you 驱除: *Fire repels wild animals.* 火能驱走野兽。**4** [I,T] *technical* if two things repel each other they push each other away with an electrical force【术语】排斥

re·pel·lent¹ /rɪ`pɛlənt; rɪ'pelənt/ *adj* **1** nasty or very unpleasant 令人厌恶的, 让人反感的: *Stories about famous villains can be both repellent and fascinating.* 著名的恶棍的故事既令人不快又引人入胜。**2 water repellent** water repellent material does not let water pass through it〔材料〕不透水的

repellent², repellant *n* [C,U] a substance that keeps insects away 驱虫剂: *mosquito repellent* 驱蚊剂

re·pent /rɪ`pɛnt; rɪ'pent/ *v* [I,T] **1** a word meaning to be sorry for something you have done, used especially in a religious context 忏悔〔尤用于宗教场合〕: **[+of]** *Repent of your sins and you will be forgiven.* 忏悔你的罪恶, 你将得到宽恕。**2** *formal* to be sorry for something and to wish you had not done it【正式】懊悔, 后悔: **repent doing sth** *I began to repent parting with you.* 我开始后悔与你分手。| **repent sth** *He repented his decision.* 他对自己的决定感到后悔。

re·pen·tance /rɪ`pɛntəns; rɪ'pentəns/ *n* [U] the state of being sorry for something you have done 懊悔, 后悔; 忏悔

re·pen·tant /rɪ`pɛntənt; rɪ'pentənt/ *adj formal* sorry for something wrong that you have done【正式】后悔的, 懊悔的; 忏悔的 —opposite 反义词 UNREPENTANT —**repentantly** *adv*

re·per·cus·sion /ˌripɚ`kʌʃən; ˌriːpə'kʌʃən/ *n* **1 repercussions** [plural] the results of an action or event, especially a bad one, that continue to have an effect for some time, in complicated and unexpected ways〔尤指不好的行动或事件的〕持续影响;〔复杂而出乎意料的〕反响: *The break-up of the USSR has had world-wide repercussions.* 苏联的解体造成了世界性的影响。**2** [C] *technical* a sound or force coming back after it hits something【术语】回声; 反冲; 反射

rep·er·toire /`rɛpɚˌtwar; 'repətwɑː/ *n* [C usually singular 一般用单数] **1** all of the plays, pieces of music etc, that a performer or group has learned and can perform〔演员、剧团的〕全部剧目, 常备节目 **2** the total number of things that someone or something is able to do 全部技能: *the behavioral repertoire of newborn infants* 新生儿的全部行为

rep·er·to·ry /`rɛpɚˌtorɪ; 'repətəri/ *n* **1** [U] a type of theatre work in which actors perform different plays on different days, instead of doing the same play for a long time 轮流演出选定的节目: *a repertory company* 轮流剧目剧团 **2** [C] a repertoire 保留剧目

rep·e·ti·tion /ˌrɛpɪ`tɪʃən; ˌrepɨ'tɪʃən/ *n* **1** [U] doing the same thing many times 重复: **[+of]** *his constant repetition of the same old jokes* 他那些翻过来调过去的老笑话 | *In my day, everything was learned by repetition.* 在我那个时代, 所有东西都是通过不断重复学会的。**2** [C] something that is done again 重复的事: **[+of]** *I don't want a repetition of this incident.* 我不希望这事重演。

rep·e·ti·tious /ˌrɛpɪ`tɪʃəs; ˌrepɨ'tɪʃəs◂/ *adj* saying the same thing several times〔说话〕重复的: *a boring, repetitious style* 乏味、叠床架屋的风格

re·pet·i·tive /rɪ`pɛtɪtɪv; rɪ'petɨtɪv/ *adj* done many times in the same way〔做事〕重复的, 反复的: *She hated the tedious, repetitive household tasks.* 她讨厌那些枯燥乏味、日复一日的家务工作。—**repetitively** *adv*

repetitive strain in·ju·ry /·ˌ··· ˈ· ˌ···/ *n* [U] *technical* RSI; pains in your hands, arms etc caused by doing the same hand movements very many times【术语】〔手掌、手臂等的〕重复性劳损

re·phrase /ri`frez; ˌriː'freɪz/ *v* [T] to express something in different words so that its meaning is clearer or more acceptable 重新措辞: *OK. Let me rephrase the question.* 好吧, 让我换个说法来提这个问题。

re·place /rɪ`ples; rɪ'pleɪs/ *v* [T] **1** to start doing something instead of another person, or being used instead of another thing 取代, 接替: *I'm replacing Sue on the team.* 我接替队里的休。| *These PCs replace the old system network.* 这些个人电脑替代了陈旧的系统网络。**2** to remove someone from their job or something from its place, and put a different person or thing there 替换, 调换: *Well, if he can't manage he'll have to be replaced.* 如果他应付不了, 就得找人替换他。| **replace sth with sth** *They're replacing the old windows with double glazing.* 他们正在用双层玻璃替换旧窗户。**3** to get something new to put in the place of something that has been broken, stolen etc 更换: *I'll replace the vase I broke as soon as possible.* 我会尽快更换我打破的花瓶。**4** to put something back in its correct place 把…放回原处: *He replaced the book on the shelf.* 他把书放回架子上。—**replaceable** *adj*

re·place·ment /rɪ`plesmənt; rɪ'pleɪsmənt/ *n* [U] **1** the act of replacing something, often with something newer, better etc 更换: *Those tyres are badly in need of replacement.* 那些轮胎急需更换。**2** [C] someone or something that replaces another person or thing 替换的人[物]: **[+for]** *It will be difficult to find a replacement for Ted.* 很难找到接替特德的人。| **replacement car/bulb/battery** *We'll need a replacement bulb for the hall light.* 我们需要给门廊里的灯换一个灯泡。

re·play¹ /ri`ple; ˌriː'pleɪ/ *v* [T] **1** to play a game of sport again 重新举行〔比赛〕: *The game ended in a draw and will be replayed on Wednesday.* 比赛结果不分胜负, 所以星期三要再赛一次。**2** to play something again that has been recorded 重放〔录音、录像〕: *We replayed all the romantic bits of the video.* 我们重放了录像中所有的浪漫片段。

re·play² /`riˌple; 'riːpleɪ/ *n* [C] **1** a game of sport that is played again 重赛: *Milan won the semi-final replay 3-0.* 米兰队在半决赛的重赛中以三比零取胜。**2** a piece of action in a game of sport seen on television, that is immediately shown again〔电视中比赛镜头的〕重播, 回放: *You can see on the replay that the goalkeeper was clearly fouled.* 你可以在重播的镜头中看到, 明显有人对守门员犯规。**3** *informal* something that is done exactly as it was before【非正式】重复: *a replay of the same mistakes* 重复相同的错误

re·plen·ish /rɪ`plɛnɪʃ; rɪ'plenɪʃ/ *v* [T+with] *formal* to fill something again or put new supplies into something【正式】再装满; 补充 —**replenishment** *n* [U]

re·plete /rɪ`plit; rɪ'pliːt/ *adj* [not before noun 不用于名词前] **1** *formal* fully supplied with something【正式】充分供应的, 充足的: **[+with]** *a book replete with diagrams* 一本有许多图表的书 **2** *old-fashioned* so full of food or drink that you want no more【过时】饱足的 —**repletion** /rɪ`pliʃən; rɪ'pliːʃən/ *n* [U]

rep·li·ca /`rɛplɪkə; 'replɪkə/ *n* [C] a very good copy, especially of a painting or other work of art〔尤指艺术〕复制品: **[+of]** *The model was an exact replica of the Taj Mahal.* 该模型是跟泰姬陵一模一样的复制品。

rep·li·cate /`rɛplɪˌket; 'replɨkeɪt/ *v* [T] *formal* to do or make something again, so that you get the same result or make an exact copy【正式】重做, 重制 —**replication** /ˌrɛplə`keʃən; ˌreplɨ'keɪʃən/ *n* [C,U]

re·ply¹ /rɪ`plaɪ; rɪ'plaɪ/ *v* **1** [I,T] to answer someone by saying or writing something 回答, 答复: *I asked Clive where he was going but he didn't reply.* 我问克莱夫他到哪儿去, 但他没有回答。| **[+to]** *You must reply to Dennis's letter soon.* 你必须及早给丹尼斯回信。| **reply that** *I can only reply that I did not realise what was happening.* 我只能回复说我不知道发生了什么事。|

"That's what I expected," replied Mandy. "那是我所期待的。"曼迪回答说。—see 见 ANSWER[2] (USAGE) **2** [I] to react to an action by doing something else 回应: [+to/with] *The terrorists replied to their threats with violence.* 恐怖分子以暴力回应他们的威胁。

S2 W3 **reply**[2] *n* [C] **1** something that is said, written, or done as a way of replying 回答, 答复; 回应: [+to] *We've had 60 replies to our advertisement so far.* 到目前为止, 我们已经收到60份对我们广告的回应。| **make no reply** (=not reply) 不回答 *I asked him if I could help, but he made no reply.* 我问他要不要帮忙, 但他没有回答。| *The only reply was a burst of gunfire.* 唯一的回答是一阵枪声。**2 in reply to** *formal* as a way of replying to something【正式】答复: *I am writing in reply to your letter of 1st June.* 我写此信回复你6月1日的来信。**3 without reply** if a sports team gets a number of points or goals (GOAL (2)) without reply, their opponents get no points〔比赛〕己方得分[进球]但对方未得分[进球]

reply-paid /ˌ·ˈ·◂/ *adj* a reply-paid envelope has had the cost of a stamp already paid by the person who sent it 回邮邮资已付的

re·po man /ˈripo mæn; ˈriːpəʊ mæn/ *n* [C] *informal* someone whose job is to REPOSSESS (=take away) cars that have not been paid for【非正式】〔赊购款汽车的〕回收员

S2 W1 **re·port**[1] /rɪˈport; rɪˈpɔːt/ *n* **1** [C] a written or spoken description of a situation or event, giving people the information they need 报告: *the chairman's report* 主席的报告 | [+on/of] *police reports of the accident* 警方关于事故的报告 **2** [C] a piece of writing in a newspaper about something that is happening, or part of a television or radio news programme 报道: *We're getting reports from the scene of the fighting.* 我们不断得到发自交战现场的报道。| *a weather report* 天气预报 **3** [C] an official piece of writing that carefully considers a particular subject, and is often written by a group of people〔正式的〕研究报告: [+on/of] *a recent report on child abuse* 新近一份关于虐待儿童的报告 —see graph at 参见 NEWS 图表 **4** [C,U] things people say that may or may not be true; RUMOUR 传闻, 传说: *According to reports he's not coming back.* 根据传闻, 他不会回来了。**5** [C] *BrE* a written statement by teachers about a child's work at school, sent to their parents【英】(学生)成绩报告单; REPORT CARD *AmE*【美】: *Dad promised me a new bike if I got a good report.* 爸爸答应我, 如果成绩报告单令人满意就送我一辆新自行车。**6** [C] *formal* the noise of an explosion or shot【正式】爆炸声; 枪声: *a loud report* 巨响

S3 W1 **report**[2] *v*

1 ▶NEWS 新闻◀ [I,T] to give people information about recent events, especially in newspapers and on television and radio 报道: *This is Gavin Williams, reporting from the United Nations in New York.* 我是加文·威廉斯, 从纽约联合国进行报道。| **report sth** *We aim to report the news as fairly as possible.* 我们的目标是尽量公正地报道新闻。| [+on] *The Post sent her to Bangladesh to report on the floods.*《邮报》派她去孟加拉报道水灾的情况。| **report that** *The newspapers reported that he had died in a car accident.* 报纸报道说他死于车祸。| **report doing sth** *They reported having seen the remains of the body.* 他们报道说看到了尸体残骸。| **be reported to be** *He is reported to have been driving whilst drunk.* 据报道, 他是酒后开车。

2 ▶JOB/WORK 工作◀ [I,T] to tell someone about what has been happening, or what you are doing as part of your job 报告, 汇报: **report (to sb) on** *Come back next week to report on your progress.* 下星期回来报告你的进展情况。| *Anything to report, Sergeant?* 有什么要报告吗, 中士?

3 ▶PUBLIC STATEMENT 公开声明◀ [T] to officially give information to the public 公告: *Scientists are due to report the first step towards the development of an AIDS vaccine.* 科学家将公布研制艾滋病疫苗的第一步情况。

4 ▶CRIME/ACCIDENT 犯罪/事故◀ [T] to tell the police or someone in authority that an accident or crime has happened 报告: *I'd like to report a theft.* 我要报告一桩偷窃案。| **report sth to sb** *All accidents must be reported to the safety officer.* 所有事故都必须向安全主任报告。| **report sb/sth missing** *The plane was reported missing in heavy fog.* 据报告, 那架飞机在大雾中失踪了。

5 ▶COMPLAIN 投诉◀ [T] to complain about someone to people in authority 告发, 检举: *Robert reported Guy for smoking in school.* 罗伯特告发了盖伊在学校里抽烟。| **report sb to sb** *Kevin was eventually reported to the police.* 凯文最终被人向警方举报了。

6 ▶ARRIVAL 到达◀ [I] to go somewhere and officially state that you have arrived 报到: [+to] *All visitors must report to the site office.* 所有来访者必须向现场办公室报到。

7 report sick to officially tell your employers that you cannot come to work because you are ill 请病假

report back *phr v* [I,T] to bring or send back an account of something 汇报: [+to] *Find out and report back to me quickly.* 搞清楚, 然后迅速向我汇报。| **report back that** *The soldiers reported back that enemy forces were moving towards the border.* 士兵汇报说, 敌军正在向边境移动。

report to sb *phr v* [T] to be responsible to someone at work and be managed by them 向…负责, 向…报告: *The accountants report to the Deputy Financial Director.* 会计们向财务副总监负责。

re·port·age /rɪˈportɪdʒ; rɪˈpɔːtɪdʒ/ *n* [U] **1** the particular style of reporting used in newspapers, radio or television 报告文学, 报道体裁 **2** the act of reporting news 报道(新闻)

report card /·ˈ· ·/ *n AmE* a written statement by teachers about a child's work at school, sent to their parents【美】(学生)成绩报告单; REPORT *BrE*【英】

re·port·ed·ly /rɪˈportɪdlɪ; rɪˈpɔːtɪdli/ *adv* [sentence adverb 句子副词] according to what people say 据报道, 据传说: *He is reportedly not intending to return to this country.* 据说, 他不打算返回这个国家。

reported speech /·,·· ˈ·/ *n* [U] the style of speech or writing used to report what someone says without repeating their actual words; INDIRECT SPEECH 间接引语 —compare 比较 DIRECT SPEECH

re·port·er /rɪˈportə; rɪˈpɔːtə/ *n* [C] someone who writes about events for a newspaper, radio, or television 记者 —compare 比较 JOURNALIST —see also 另见 COURT REPORTER S3

re·pose[1] /rɪˈpoz; rɪˈpəʊz/ *n* [U] *formal* a state of calm or comfortable rest【正式】平静; 憩息 —**reposeful** *adj*

repose[2] *v formal*【正式】**1** [I] if something reposes in a place it is put there 安置: [+on] *Two small glasses reposed on the tray.* 两只小玻璃杯安放在托盘上。**2** [I] if someone reposes somewhere they rest there 休息, 安息 **3 repose your trust/hope etc in sb** to trust someone to help you 信赖/寄希望于某人

re·pos·i·to·ry /rɪˈpɑzəˌtorɪ; rɪˈpɒzɪtəri/ *n* [C] **1** a place where things are stored in large quantities 贮藏室, 仓库: *a furniture repository* 家具仓库 **2** *formal or humorous* a person or book that gives a lot of information【正式或幽默】博学者; 包括大量信息的书: *Matthew is a repository of football statistics.* 马修是各种足球统计数字的宝库。

re·pos·sess /ˌripəˈzɛs; ˌriːpəˈzes/ *v* [T] to take back cars, furniture, or property from people who cannot pay for them as they had arranged 收回〔因赊购者未能按计划付款的货物〕: *Eventually the bailiffs came to repossess the flat.* 最终, 查封官收回了那个公寓。—**repossession** /-ˈzɛʃən; -ˈzeʃən/ *n* [C,U]

rep·re·hend /ˌrɛprɪˈhɛnd; ˌreprɪˈhend/ *v* [T] *formal* to express disapproval of a person or an action【正式】谴责, 申斥

rep·re·hen·si·ble /ˌrɛprɪˈhɛnsəbl; ˌreprɪˈhensɪbəl/ *adj formal* reprehensible behaviour is bad and deserves criticism【正式】〔行为〕应受斥责的: [+of] *It was really reprehensible of you to leave such young children alone.* 你把这么小的孩子撇下不管, 的确应该受批评。

rep·re·sent /ˌrɛprɪˈzɛnt; ˌreprɪˈzent/ *v* S2 W1

1 ▶SPEAK FOR SB 代表某人说话◀ [T] **a)** to speak officially for another person or group of people, giving their opinions and taking action for them 代表: *Mr Kobayashi was chosen to represent the company at the conference.* 小林先生被选为该公司出席会议的代表。| *He was represented in court by a famous criminal lawyer.* 在法庭上代表他的是一位著名的刑法律师。**b)** to say or do something that expresses the feelings, opinions etc of a group of people 表达〔某团体的情感、意见等〕: *The protesters represented only a small section of public opinion.* 抗议者仅陈述了一小部分民意。

2 be represented to have sent someone from your group to a meeting, ceremony etc〔某团体〕由〔某人〕代表出席: *All the local societies and clubs were represented in the parade.* 当地所有的社团和俱乐部都有代表参加游行。

3 represent an improvement/an obstacle/a challenge etc *formal* used to say that something should be thought of as a particular thing【正式】应视为进步/障碍/挑战等〔用于表示某事有某些特质〕: *This essay represents a considerable improvement on your recent work.* 这篇短论说明你最近的工作大有进步。

4 ▶GOVERNMENT 政府◀ [T] to be the member of a parliament or other law making institution, such as the Congress, for a particular area 当〔某地区〕的议员[其他立法机构的成员]: *Does Kathryn Walker still represent Worcester?* 凯瑟琳·沃克还是代表伍斯特的议员吗? | *He represents the 8th Congressional District of Illinois.* 他是代表伊利诺伊州第八国会选区的议员。

5 ▶A SIGN 标志◀ [T] to be a sign or mark that shows the position of a particular thing, especially on a map or plan; SYMBOLIZE〔尤指在地图上或平面图里〕象征, 表示: *The red lines on the map represent railways.* 地图上的红线表示铁路。
6 ▶SHOW STH 展现某物◀ [T] to be a picture or STATUE of something 用图画[雕塑]表示, 描绘, 雕出: *This painting represents the first settlers arriving in America.* 这幅画描绘了首批移民到达美洲时的情景。
7 represent yourself as to say that you are something that you are not 佯称自己是…: *They represented themselves as the party of low taxation.* 他们佯称自己是主张低税率的党。
8 represent sb as to describe someone in a particular way, so that people have a particular opinion of them 把某人描写为: *Shakespeare represents Richard III as a black-hearted villain.* 莎士比亚将理查三世描写成一个心肠狠毒的反派角色。

re·pre·sent /ˌri prɪˋzɛnt; ˌriː prɪˈzent/ *v* [T] to give, offer, or send something again, especially an official document〔尤指正式文件〕再送给; 再提出; 再递上: *The phone company re-presented the bill for payment.* 电话公司再度寄来账单要求付款。

rep·re·sen·ta·tion /ˌrɛprɪzɛnˋteʃən; ˌreprɪzenˈteɪʃən/ *n* **1** [U] the state of having representatives to speak, vote, or make decisions for you 代理, 代表; 代议权: *Minority groups need more effective parliamentary representation.* 少数派团体需要有更具实效的议会代表权。| *Paul appeared in court without any representation.* 保罗出庭时没有代理律师。—see also 另见 PROPORTIONAL REPRESENTATION **2** [U] the act of representing someone or something 代表, 代理 **3** [C] a painting, sign etc that shows or describes something else 描绘, 表现: *This painting is a representation of a storm at sea.* 这幅画描绘的是海上的暴风雨。**4 representations** [plural] *especially BrE* official complaints made in a formal way【尤英】〔正式〕投诉; 抗议: **make representations about/to** *A group of students made representations to the college about bad accommodation.* 一群学生就恶劣的住宿环境向校方提出抗议。

rep·re·sen·ta·tion·al /ˌrɛprɪzɛnˋteʃənḷ; ˌreprɪzenˈteɪʃənəl/ *adj* a representational painting or style of art shows things as they actually appear in real life〔绘画或艺术风格〕具象的; 写实的 —compare 比较 ABSTRACT[1] (3)

Rep·re·sen·ta·tive /ˌrɛprɪˋzɛntətɪv; ˌreprɪˈzentətɪv◂/ *n* [C] a member of the House of Representatives, the Lower House of Congress in the United States〔美国〕众议院议员

representative[1] *adj* **1** like other members of the same group; typical 代表性的; 代表…的; 典型的: [+of] *Are your opinions representative of the views of all the students?* 你们的意见代表全体学生的观点吗? **2** a representative system of government allows everyone to express their opinions by voting for representatives〔政制〕代表制的, 代议制的: *Change is needed if we are to have a fully representative democracy.* 如果我们想拥有一种完全代议制的民主, 那就需要改革。

representative[2] *n* [C] **1** a person who has been chosen to speak, vote, or make decisions for someone else 代表, 代理人: [+of] *an elected representative of the people* 民选代表 **2 Representative** a member of the House of Representatives, the Lower House of Congress in the United States 美国众议院议员 —see also 另见 SALES REPRESENTATIVE

re·press /rɪˋprɛs; rɪˈpres/ *v* [T] **1** to stop yourself expressing a feeling 压抑, 抑制〔感情〕: *I could hardly repress my laughter.* 我忍不住笑起来。**2** to control a group of people by force 镇压 —compare 比较 SUPPRESS (1)

re·pressed /rɪˋprɛst; rɪˈprest/ *adj* having feelings or desires that you do not allow yourself to express 受约束的; 被压抑的: *a repressed child* 一个被管得太死的孩子 | *I was boiling over with repressed anger.* 压抑着的愤怒在我心里翻腾。

re·pres·sion /rɪˋprɛʃən; rɪˈpreʃən/ *n* **1** [U] very strong control of feelings or desires which you are ashamed of, until you no longer know that you have them〔对感到羞耻的感情或欲望的〕压抑, 抑制: *years of sexual repression* 多年的性压抑 **2** [U] cruel and severe control of a large group of people 镇压: *fleeing from repression* 逃避镇压 **3** [C] an act of repressing people, or a feeling that is repressed 镇压行为; 受压抑的感情

re·pres·sive /rɪˋprɛsɪv; rɪˈpresɪv/ *adj* a repressive system of government or law is severe and cruel〔政制或法律〕残酷的; 严苛的: *a repressive regime, which imprisoned thousands* 一个关押了数千人的残酷政权 | *an old-fashioned and repressive education system* 一种压抑人的守旧教育制度 —**repressively** *adv* —**repressiveness** *n* [U]

re·prieve[1] /rɪˋpriv; rɪˈpriːv/ *v* [T usually passive 一般用被动态] to officially stop a prisoner from being killed as a punishment 撤销执行…的死刑

reprieve[2] *n* [C] an official order stopping the killing of a prisoner as a punishment 死刑撤销令; 死刑暂缓令: *A last minute reprieve saved him.* 最后一分钟的死刑撤销令救了他的命。

rep·ri·mand /ˋrɛprəˌmænd; ˈreprɪ̈mɑːnd/ *v* [T] to tell someone officially that something they have done is very wrong 训斥, 谴责: *The military court reprimanded him for failing to do his duty.* 军事法庭谴责他失职。—**reprimand** *n* [C]: *a severe reprimand* 严厉的斥责

re·print[1] /riˋprɪnt; ˌriːˈprɪnt/ *v* [I,T] if a book is reprinted or reprints, more copies are printed because the first ones have been sold 再版, 重印

re·print[2] /ˋriˌprɪnt; ˈriːprɪnt/ *n* [C] an act of printing a book again because all the copies of it have been sold 再版, 重印

re·pri·sal /rɪˋpraɪzḷ; rɪˈpraɪzəl/ *n* [C,U] also 又作 **repri·sals** [plural] an act of violence or other strong reaction, to punish your enemies or opponents for something they have done 报复行为: *They didn't tell the police for fear of reprisal.* 由于害怕报复, 他们没有报告警方。| **in reprisal (for)** *prisoners killed in reprisal for the raid* 为了对袭击进行报复而被杀的囚犯

re·prise /rɪˋpriz; rɪˈpriːz/ *n* [C] the repeating of all or part of a piece of music, film etc〔乐章的〕重复, 再现;〔电影的〕重演, 重放

re·proach[1] /rɪˋprotʃ; rɪˈprəʊtʃ/ *n formal*【正式】**1** [U] blame or disapproval for the things you have done 责备, 指责, 责怪: *"Are you going already?" he cried, his voice full of reproach.* "你这就要走?"他喊道, 声音中充满责备。| **beyond/above reproach** *formal* (=impossible to criticize; perfect)【正式】无可非议; 十全十美 *His behaviour throughout this affair has been beyond reproach.* 他在整个事件中的行为无懈可击。**2** [C] a remark that expresses criticism or disapproval 责备的话: *Her question was clearly a reproach.* 她的问题显然是在责备。**3 a reproach to** something that makes a person, society etc feel bad or ashamed; DISGRACE[1] …的耻辱: *These derelict houses are a reproach to the city.* 这些弃置的破房是该市的耻辱。

reproach[2] *v* [T] **1** *formal* to blame or criticize someone in a way that shows you are disappointed, but not angry【正式】责备, 怪责〔表示失望但不含怒气〕: **reproach sb for/with sth** *She reproached me for my lack of foresight.* 她责备我缺乏先见之明。| **reproach sb for doing sth** *Jake reproached her bitterly for abandoning him.* 杰克伤心地指责她抛弃了他。**2 reproach yourself** to feel guilty about something that you think you are responsible for 自责: *You've got nothing to reproach yourself for – it was his own decision.* 你没有什么可自责的, 那是他自己的决定。

re·proach·ful /rɪˋprotʃfl; rɪˈprəʊtʃfəl/ *adj* a reproachful look, remark etc shows that you are criticizing someone or blaming them〔眼神、话语等〕责备的, 谴责的: *She shot me a reproachful glance.* 她向我投来责备的目光。—**reproachfully** *adv*

rep·ro·bate /ˋrɛprəˌbet; ˈreprəbeɪt/ *n* [C] *formal or humorous* someone who behaves in an immoral way【正式或幽默】堕落者, 放荡者, 行为不检者: *an old reprobate who spent all his money on gin* 一个把所有钱都花在杜松子酒上的老无赖

re·pro·cess /riˋprɑsɛs; riːˈprəʊses/ *v* [T] to treat a waste substance so that it can be used again 对〔废弃物〕进行再加工, 再处理

re·pro·duce /ˌriprəˋdus; ˌriːprəˈdjuːs/ *v* **1** [I,T] if a plant or animal reproduces, or reproduces itself, it produces young plants or animals 生殖, 繁殖: *Fish reproduce by laying eggs.* 鱼类产卵繁殖。**2** [T] to make a photograph or printed copy of something 复制; 翻印: *This edition reproduces the original text in full.* 这个版本全文刊登了原文。**3** [T] to make something that is just like something else, or make something happen again in the same way as it happened the first time 重演; 重现: *British scientists have so far been unable to reproduce these results.* 迄今为止, 英国科学家仍未能再次得出这些结果。| *They try to reproduce the exact sounds of early music.* 他们设法如实再现早期音乐的声音。—**reproducible** *adj*

re·pro·duc·tion /ˌriprəˋdʌkʃən; ˌriːprəˈdʌkʃən◂/ *n* **1** [U] the act or process of producing young animals or plants 生殖, 繁殖: *Reproduction may not take place in poor conditions.* 在恶劣的条件下也许不能进行繁殖。**2** [U] the act of producing a copy of a book, picture, piece of music etc 复制; 再版; 翻印: *Unauthorized reproduction of this publication is strictly forbidden.* 未经许可严禁翻印本出版物。| *high quality sound reproduction* 高质量声响复制 **3** [C] a copy of a work of art, piece of furniture etc〔艺术品、家具等的〕复制品: *a cheap reproduction of a famous painting* 一幅名画的廉价复制品 | **reproduction furniture/chairs etc** *a reproduction Louis XIV table* 路易十四时期餐桌的复制品

re·pro·duc·tive /ˌriprəˋdʌktɪv; ˌriːprəˈdʌktɪv◂/ *adj* [only before noun 仅用于名词前] **1** connected with the process of producing young animals or plants 生殖的, 繁殖的: *the human reproductive system* 人类生殖系统 **2** connected with the copying of books, pictures, music etc 翻印的, 复制的: *the reproductive quality of audio tape* 录音磁带的复制质量

re·proof /rɪˈpruf; rɪˈpruːf/ *n formal*【正式】**1** [U] blame or disapproval 责备, 斥责, 责怪: *She felt the reproof of her father's gaze.* 她感觉到父亲的凝视里带着责备。**2** [C] a remark that blames or criticizes someone 责备之言: *a sharp reproof* 严厉的责备

re·prove /rɪˈpruv; rɪˈpruːv/ *v* [T] *formal* to criticize someone for something that they have done【正式】责备, 斥责: **reprove sb for doing sth** *I was reproved for wasting good paper.* 我因为浪费好纸而受到斥责。

re·prov·ing /rɪˈpruvɪŋ; rɪˈpruːvɪŋ/ *adj formal* expressing criticism of something that someone has done【正式】责备的, 责怪的: *There was a reproving tone in her voice.* 她的声音里带着责备的语气。—**reprovingly** *adv*

rep·tile /ˈrɛptḷ; ˈreptaɪl/ *n* [C] **1** a type of animal such as a snake or LIZARD whose blood changes according to the temperature around it, and that usually lays eggs 爬行动物 **2** *informal* someone who is unpleasant or cannot be trusted【非正式】可卑的人; 不可信赖的人: *That reptile must have told the police!* 那个卑鄙的家伙肯定告诉了警察!

rep·til·i·an¹ /rɛpˈtɪlɪən; repˈtɪliən/ *adj* like a reptile or connected with reptiles 爬行动物(似)的

reptilian² *n* [C] *technical* a reptile【术语】爬行动物

2 **re·pub·lic** /rɪˈpʌblɪk; rɪˈpʌblɪk/ *n* [C] a country governed by elected representatives of the people, and led by a president, not a king or queen 共和国; 共和政体 —compare 比较 MONARCHY

re·pub·li·can¹ /rɪˈpʌblɪkən; rɪˈpʌblɪkən/ *adj* **1** connected with or supporting a system of government that is not led by a king or queen and is elected by the people 共和国的, 共和政体的 **2 Republican** connected with or supporting the Republican Party (=one of the two main political parties in the US)〔美国〕共和党的; 支持共和党的 **3 Republican** connected with or supporting political parties that want Northern Ireland to become part of the Republic of Ireland, not part of the United Kingdom〔北爱尔兰〕共和派的〔主张北爱尔兰脱离联合王国而并入爱尔兰共和国〕; 支持共和派的 —**republicanism** *n* [U]

republican² *n* [C] **1** someone who believes in government by elected representatives only, with no king or queen 共和主义者; 拥护共和政体者 **2 Republican** a member or supporter of the Republican Party in the US〔美国〕共和党人; 共和党的支持者 **3 Republican** someone from Northern Ireland who believes that Northern Ireland should become part of the Republic of Ireland, not the United Kingdom〔北爱尔兰〕共和派人士

Re·pub·li·can·is·m /rɪˈpʌblɪkənˌɪzəm; rɪˈpʌblɪkənɪzəm/ *n* [U] **1** the principles and policies (POLICY) of the US Republican Party 共和主义〔美国共和党的政纲〕**2** the principles and policies of those groups in Northern Ireland, especially the political party Sinn Fein, who want Northern Ireland to leave the UK and become part of the Republic of Ireland 共和主义〔北爱尔兰共和派、尤其是新芬党的政治纲领。这些政治团体要求北爱尔兰脱离英国, 加入爱尔兰共和国〕

Republic of Ire·land, the /ˌ.. . ˈ../ also 又作 **Ireland, the Irish Republic, Eire, Southern Ireland** a country that forms the larger part of the island of Ireland, and which is a member of the EU. Population: 3,841,000 (2001). Capital: Dublin. It was formerly ruled by the British, but it became an independent country in 1921, when Ireland was divided into Northern Ireland (which remained as part of the UK) and the **Irish Free State**, which later became the Republic of Ireland. Ireland is mainly a Roman Catholic country. Its official languages are Irish Gaelic and English. Traditionally, Ireland's main industry was farming, but it has developed new industries. 爱尔兰共和国〔占爱尔兰岛大部分面积的一个国家, 为欧盟成员国。人口: 3,841,000 (2001), 首都: 都柏林。该国先前受英国统治, 1921年独立。当时, 爱尔兰被分为北爱尔兰和爱尔兰自由邦, 爱尔兰自由邦后来成为爱尔兰共和国。爱尔兰是一个以罗马天主教为主的国家, 官方语言为爱尔兰盖尔语和英语。从传统上来看, 爱尔兰以农业为主, 但现在也发展起了一些新兴产业〕—see also 另见 IRELAND, NORTHERN IRELAND

re·pu·di·ate /rɪˈpjudɪˌet; rɪˈpjuːdieɪt/ *v* [T] *formal*【正式】**1** to refuse to accept something; REJECT¹ (1) 拒绝: *He repudiated all offers of friendship.* 他拒绝一切友好的表示。**2** to state formally that something is untrue or incorrect〔正式〕否认; 驳斥: *I repudiate emphatically any suggestion that I have acted dishonourably.* 有人指桑骂槐, 指我行径可耻, 对此我郑重否认。**3** *old-fashioned* to state that you no longer have any connection with someone, especially a relative; DISOWN【过时】声明与…断绝关系〔尤指亲戚关系〕**4** to refuse to pay a debt 拒付〔债款〕—**repudiation** /rɪˌpjudɪˈeʃən; rɪˌpjuːdiˈeɪʃən/ *n* [U]

re·pug·nance /rɪˈpʌgnəns; rɪˈpʌgnəns/ *n* [U] *formal* a strong feeling of dislike for something very unpleasant or morally wrong【正式】厌恶; 强烈的反感: *They shrank back from what they saw, with looks of repugnance etched on their faces.* 看到那个场面, 他们往后退了退, 脸上充满极度的厌恶。

re·pug·nant /rɪˈpʌgnənt; rɪˈpʌgnənt/ *adj formal* very unpleasant and offensive【正式】令人厌恶的, 使人反感的: *I find his political beliefs completely repugnant.* 我认为他的政治信仰十分令人反感。

re·pulse¹ /rɪˈpʌls; rɪˈpʌls/ *v* [T] *formal*【正式】**1** to defeat a military attack 击退〔进攻〕: *They attacked with cavalry but were repulsed.* 他们以骑兵进攻但被击退。**2** if something or someone repulses you, you feel they are very unpleasant 使人厌恶, 使反感: *The very thought of his cold clammy hands repulsed me.* 一想到他那双湿冷黏糊的手我就感到厌恶。—see also 另见 REPULSIVE (1) **3** to refuse an offer of friendship or help in a way that is rude〔无礼地〕拒绝

repulse² *n* [singular] **1** *formal* the act of rudely refusing when someone offers to help you or be your friend【正式】〔粗暴的〕拒绝 **2** *technical* the defeat of a military attack【术语】击退

re·pul·sion /rɪˈpʌlʃən; rɪˈpʌlʃən/ *n* **1** [singular,U] a feeling that you want to avoid something or move away from it, because it is very unpleasant 厌恶, 反感 **2** [U] *technical* the electric or MAGNETIC force by which one object pushes another one away from it【术语】排斥力 —opposite 反义词 ATTRACTION

re·pul·sive /rɪˈpʌlsɪv; rɪˈpʌlsɪv/ *adj* **1** very unpleasant 令人厌恶的, 使人反感的: *What a repulsive man!* 多么讨厌的人! **2** *technical* repulsive forces push objects away from each other【术语】排斥的; 相斥的 —**repulsively** *adv* —**repulsiveness** *n* [U]

rep·u·ta·ble /ˈrɛpjətəbḷ; ˈrepjʊ̈təbəl/ *adj* respected for being honest or for doing good work 声誉好的, 有声望的; 有信誉的: *a very reputable firm* 一家信誉卓著的公司 —**reputably** *adv*

rep·u·ta·tion /ˌrɛpjəˈteʃən; ˌrepjʊ̈ˈteɪʃən/ *n* [C] **1** the opinion that people have about a particular person or thing because of what has happened in the past 名誉, 名望: [+for] *a reputation for honesty and efficiency* 以诚实和高效率著称 | [+as] *She had already begun to establish a reputation as a writer.* 身为作家, 她已经小有名声。| **a good/bad reputation** *This restaurant has a very good reputation.* 这家饭店名声很好。| **win/earn/establish a reputation as** *His approach had won him a reputation as a tough manager.* 作为经理, 他的办事方法使他以强硬著称。**2 live up to your reputation** to behave in the way that people expect 名不虚传, 不负盛名: *Martin lived up to his reputation and arrived late.* 马丁果然名不虚传, 姗姗来迟。**3 live up to its reputation** to be at least as bad or good as people had thought〔行为〕与名声相符: *a mountain that lived up to its fearsome reputation* 与其令人生畏之名声相符的山 3

re·pute /rɪˈpjut; rɪˈpjuːt/ *n* [U] *formal*【正式】**1** reputation 名誉, 名声: **of good/evil/international etc repute** *a man of good repute* 名声好的人 **2** a good reputation 好名声: *a hotel of some repute* 一家声誉相当好的旅馆

re·put·ed /rɪˈpjutɪd; rɪˈpjuːtʃd/ *adj* [only before noun 仅用于名词前] according to what most people say or think, but not definitely 据说的; 普遍认为的; 号称的: *the reputed billionaire Pablo Escobar* 号称亿万富翁的巴布罗·埃斯科巴尔 | **be reputed to be/do sth** *She is reputed to be extremely wealthy.* 据说她极为富有。

re·put·ed·ly /rɪˈpjutɪdlɪ; rɪˈpjuːtʃdli/ *adv* [sentence adverb 句子副词] according to what most people say or think 据说; 一般认为: *The committee had reputedly spent over $3000 on 'business entertainment'.* 据说, 委员会在"业务接待"上花了三千多美元。

re·quest¹ /rɪˈkwɛst; rɪˈkwest/ *n* **1** [C] a polite or formal demand for something 要求, 请求: [+for] *They have made an urgent request for international aid.* 他们紧急要求国际援助。| 2 2
request that *He ignored the neighbours' requests that he should make less noise.* 他无视邻居要他别那样吵闹的要求。| **at sb's request** (=because they asked you to) 应某人的要求 *I telephoned her in Paris, at Staunton's request.* 我应斯汤顿的要求, 在巴黎打了电话给她。| **on request** (=when you ask for it) 一经要求 *Further detail will be sent on request.* 详情承索即寄。| **by request** (=because someone has especially asked for it) 应…的要求[请求] *There were no flowers at the funeral, by request.* 按照要求, 葬礼上没有摆花。| **any requests?** *spoken* (=used to ask

people if they want anything)【口】要什么东西吗? *I'm going to the bar – any requests?* 我去酒吧——要什么吗? **2** [C] a piece of music that is played on the radio because someone has asked for it 点播的乐曲

3 **request**[2] *v* [T] **1** *formal* to ask for something politely or formally【正式】要求, 请求: *I wrote them a letter, officially requesting permission to proceed.* 我写信给他们, 正式请求允许我着手进行。| **request that** *The staff immediately requested that he reconsider his decision.* 员工立即要求他重新考虑他的决定。| **request sb to do sth** *All club members are requested to attend the annual meeting.* 请全体俱乐部会员出席年会。**2** to ask for a particular piece of music to be played on the radio 点播: *This song was requested by Mrs Simpson of Potters Bar.* 这首歌是波特斯酒吧的辛普森夫人点播的。

USAGE NOTE 用法说明: REQUEST

WORD CHOICE 词语辨析: **ask (for), request, demand**

Ask is the usual word for speaking or writing to someone in order to get something done. 为了完成某事而口头或书面向某人提出要求的最常用词是 ask: *I asked one of my friends to help me.* 我请求我的一个朋友帮助我。You use **ask for** when you are trying to get something. ask for 则表示设法得到某物: *I asked for help.* 我请求帮助。

Request is more formal and official. Also if you **request** something, often you have the right to get what you are asking for. request 比较正式, 通常用于要求你有权得到的事物: *The letter politely requested that Miss Willis present herself for interview the next day.* 那封信很有礼貌地要求威利斯小姐第二天去参加面试。| *The government has requested a meeting with community leaders.* 政府已要求与社区领袖会面。

Demand is even stronger. If you **demand** something, you feel strongly that you have the right to it. demand 的语气更强, 用于要求你强烈认为自己有权得到的事物: *I demand to see the manager!* 我要求见经理!

GRAMMAR 语法

You **request** something (NOT **request for** sth). But you do use **for** with the noun. 动词 request 后不用 for, 但名词 request 后需用 for: *requests for money* 要求金钱 (NOT 不用 *requests of money*)

req·ui·em /ˋrɛkwɪəm; ˈrekwiəm/ also 又作 **requiem mass** /ˌ··· ˈ·/ *n* [C] **1** a Christian religious ceremony of prayers for someone who has died 安魂弥撒 **2** a piece of music written for this ceremony 安魂曲

1 1 **re·quire** /rɪˋkwaɪr; rɪˈkwaɪə/ *v* [T not in progressive 不用进行时] **1** if a problem, or situation requires particular action it makes it necessary 需要〔某种行动〕: *It's a matter that requires very careful handling.* 这件事情需要谨慎处理。| *What's required is a complete reorganization of the system.* 需要彻底重组整个系统。**2** to need something 需要〔某物〕: *These plants require moist soil at all times.* 这些植物一直需要潮湿的土壤。**3** [usually passive 一般用被动态] to officially demand that people do something, because of a law or rule〔根据法规〕要求, 规定: **require sb to do sth** *You are required by law to wear seat belts.* 法律规定你要系安全带。| [**+that**] *Regulations require that students attend at least 90% of the lectures.* 规定要求学生至少听 90% 的课。| **the required standard/level/period etc** *You have not yet reached the required standard to pass grade 3.* 你还没有达到通过三年级考试要求的标准。**4** *formal* used to ask someone what they need【正式】需要〔用于询问〕: *Is there anything further you require, sir?* 先生, 您还需要什么吗?

Frequencies of the verbs **require** and **need** in spoken and written English 动词 require 和 need 在英语口语和书面语中的使用频率

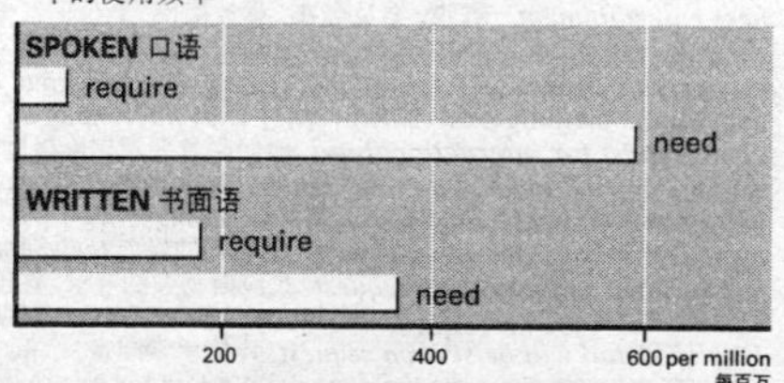

Based on the British National Corpus and the Longman Lancaster Corpus 据英国国家语料库和朗文兰开斯特语料库

This graph shows that **need** is much more common than **require** in both spoken and written English. **Require** is more formal than **need** and is therefore more common in written English than in spoken English. 本图表显示, 在英语口语和书面语中都是 need 比 require 常用得多。require 比 need 正式, 因而它在书面语中的使用频率要高于口语。

re·quire·ment /rɪˋkwaɪrmənt; rɪˈkwaɪəmənt/ *n* [C] **1** something that is needed or asked for 必需品; 需要的事物: *The refugees' main requirements are food and shelter.* 难民的主要需求是食物和住所。| **meet a requirement** (=have what is necessary) 符合要求 *The new computer system will meet all our requirements.* 新电脑系统将满足我们的全部要求。**2** something that a college, employer etc says you must have〔大学、雇主等的〕要求, 条件: *The minimum requirement was a degree in engineering.* 最低要求是具有工程学的学位。 2 2

req·ui·site /ˋrɛkwəzɪt; ˈrekwɨ̵zɨ̵t/ *adj formal* needed for a particular purpose【正式】需要的, 必要的: *He lacks the requisite qualifications.* 他不符合资格要求。

req·ui·sites /ˋrɛkwəzɪts; ˈrekwɨ̵zɨ̵ts/ *n* [plural] *formal* a word meaning things that are needed for a particular purpose, used especially in shops【正式】必备品〔该词尤在商店内使用〕: *The airport shop sells toilet requisites.* 机场商店出售梳洗必需品。

req·ui·si·tion[1] /ˌrɛkwəˋzɪʃən; ˌrekwɨ̵ˈzɪʃən/ *v* [T] to officially demand to have something, especially so that it can be used by an army〔尤指军队〕正式要求, 征用: *Troops had requisitioned houses in the town.* 部队征用了镇上的房屋。

requisition[2] *n* [C,U] an official demand to have something, usually made by an army or military authority〔军队的〕征用令

re·quit·al /rɪˋkwaɪtl; rɪˈkwaɪtl/ *n* [U] *formal*【正式】**1** payment for something done or given 报酬 **2** something that you do to harm someone who has harmed you 报复

re·quite /rɪˋkwaɪt; rɪˈkwaɪt/ *v* [T] *formal* to give or do something in return for something done or given to you in the past【正式】报答; 回报

re·re·lease /ˌri rɪˋlis; ˌriː rɪˈliːs/ *v* [T] if a record or film is re-released, it is produced and sold for a second time, usually with small changes〔唱片或电影通常略加改动后〕再发行; 再上演 — **re-release** /ˋri rɪˌlis; ˈriː rɪliːs/ *n* [C]

re·route /ˌriˋrut; ˌriːˈruːt/ *v* [T] to send vehicles in a different direction from the normal one 使〔车辆〕改变路线

re·run[1] /ˋriˌrʌn; ˈriːrʌn/ *n* [C] **1** a film or old television programme that is being shown again 重映影片; 重播的电视节目 **2** something that happens in the same way as something that happened before〔旧事的〕重演: *The government wants to avoid a rerun of last year's currency crisis.* 政府希望避免去年货币危机的重演。**3** a race or competition that is held again 重赛

re·run[2] /riˋrʌn; riːˈrʌn/ *v* [T] **1** to show a film or recorded television programme again 重映, 重播 **2** to arrange for a race or competition to be held again 使重赛

re·sched·ule /riˋskɛdʒʊl; ˌriːˈʃedjuːl/ *v* [T] **1** to arrange for something to happen at a different time, because the time you had planned is no longer convenient 重新安排…的时间: *The press conference had to be rescheduled for March 19.* 记者招待会的时间不得不改在 3 月 19 日。**2** *technical* to arrange for a debt to be paid back later than was originally agreed【术语】重新安排债务偿还时间

re·scind /rɪˋsɪnd; rɪˈsɪnd/ *v* [T] to officially end a law, decision, or agreement that has been made in the past〔正式〕废除, 取消〔法规、决定、合同〕

rescue 救援

res·cue[1] /ˋrɛskju; ˈreskjuː/ *v* [T] to save someone or something from a situation of danger or harm 拯救, 解救; 救援: *Hundreds are still in the water, waiting to be rescued.* 数以百计的人仍在水中, 等待着救援。| **rescue sb/sth from** *She died trying to rescue her children from the blaze.* 她在设法从大火中救出自

己的孩子时身亡。| *a final attempt to rescue the company from ruin* 拯救公司使之免于破产的最后尝试 —**rescuer** *n* [C]

rescue² *n* [C] an occasion when someone or something is rescued from danger 救援, 营救: *a daring rescue at sea* 在海上英勇的营救工作 | **rescue team/attempt/bid etc** *A rescue team is trying to reach the trapped miners.* 营救队正设法到达矿工被困的位置。| **come to the rescue** (=help someone in danger or difficulty) 救援 *His father came to his rescue and lent him the money.* 他的父亲借钱给他, 因而救了他。

S2 W1 **re·search¹** /ˈrisɚtʃ; rɪˈsɜːtʃ/ *n* [U] also 又作 **researches** [plural] **1** serious study of a subject, that is intended to discover new facts or test new ideas 研究; 探讨: **[+into/on]** *research into the causes of cancer* 癌症起因的研究 | **research project/student/grant etc** *Alison is a research student in our lab.* 艾莉森是我们实验室的研究生。**2** the activity of finding information about something that you are interested in or need to know about 研究(工作): **do research** *I'm doing some research for an article about student life.* 我正在为一篇关于学生生活的文章作一些研究。| *I've done some research – it looks as if the train will be fastest.* 我搜集了一些资料, 看来乘火车是最快的。—see also 另见 MARKET RESEARCH, R AND D

re·search² /rɪˈsɝtʃ; rɪˈsɜːtʃ/ *v* [T] **1** to study a subject in detail, especially in order to discover new facts or test new ideas 研究, 探索: *He's researching the effects of aerosols on the environment.* 他正在研究悬浮微粒对环境的影响。**2** to supply all the necessary facts and information for something 为…进行研究, 搜集资料: *This book has been very well researched.* 这本书是经过大量的研究写成的。—**researcher** *n* [C]

research and de·vel·op·ment /ˌ· ˌ· ˈ··/ *n* [U] R AND D 研究与开发

re·sell /ˌriˈsɛl; ˌriːˈsel/ *v past tense and past participle* **resold** /-ˈsold; -ˈsəʊld/ [T] to sell something that you have bought 转卖: *The retailer resells the goods at a higher price.* 零售商以高于进货的价格转卖商品。

re·sem·blance /rɪˈzɛmbləns; rɪˈzembləns/ *n* [C,U] a SIMILARITY between two things, especially in the way they look 〔尤指样子〕相似, 类似: **[+between]** *You can see the resemblance between Susan and her sister.* 你可以看出苏珊与她的妹妹很像。| **bear a resemblance to** (=look like) 像… *He bears a remarkable resemblance to Kurt Russell.* 他相貌酷似库尔特·拉塞尔。

re·sem·ble /rɪˈzɛmbḷ; rɪˈzembəl/ *v* [T not in progressive or passive 不用进行时或被动态] to look like, or be similar to, someone or something 像; 与…类似, 与…相似: **closely resemble** *Mick closely resembled his father.* 米克长得酷似他的父亲。

re·sent /rɪˈzɛnt; rɪˈzent/ *v* [T] to feel angry or upset about a situation or about something that someone has done, especially because you think that it is not fair 〔因受委屈而〕对…感到愤恨, 不满; 憎恶: **resent doing sth** *He resents having to get my permission first.* 他因为要先得到我的允许而忿忿不平。| **greatly/strongly/bitterly resent** *She greatly resented her brother's refusal to help.* 她对她哥哥拒绝帮助极为不满。

re·sent·ful /rɪˈzɛntfl; rɪˈzentfəl/ *adj* feeling angry and upset about something that you think is unfair 〔对不公平的事物〕感到愤怒的, 不满的, 憎恶的: **[+of/at/about etc]** *His daughters became increasingly resentful of his authority.* 他的女儿们对被他支配越来越憎恶。—**resentfully** *adv*: *"You should have told me," said Marion resentfully.* "你应该告诉我的。"玛丽昂不满地说。—**resentfulness** *n* [U]

re·sent·ment /rɪˈzɛntmənt; rɪˈzentmənt/ *n* [U] a feeling of anger because something has happened that you think is unfair 愤恨, 不满, 憎恶

S3 **res·er·va·tion** /ˌrɛzɚˈveʃən; ˌrezəˈveɪʃən/ *n* **1** [C] an arrangement made so that a place is kept for you in a hotel, restaurant, plane etc; BOOKING (1) 〔房间、座位等的〕预订: | **make a reservation** *Customers are advised to make seat reservations well in advance.* 建议顾客尽量提前订座。**2** [C,U] a feeling of doubt because you do not agree completely with a plan, idea, or suggestion 存疑; 保留(意见): **have/express reservations (about)** *I had serious reservations about his appointment as captain.* 我对任命他为船长郑重地持保留态度。| **without reservation** (=completely) 毫无保留 *We condemn their actions without reservation.* 我们毫无保留地谴责他们的行为。**3** [C] an area of land in the US kept separate for Native Americans to live on 〔美国印第安人的〕居留地, 保留地: *a Navajo reservation* 纳瓦霍印第安人居留地 **4** [C] *especially AmE* an area of land where wild animals can live without being hunted; RESERVE【尤美】〔野生动物的〕保护区: *a game reservation* 野生动物保护区, 禁猎区 —see also 另见 CENTRAL RESERVATION

re·serve¹ /rɪˈzɝv; rɪˈzɜːv/ *v* [T] **1** to arrange for a place in a hotel, restaurant, plane etc to be kept for you 预订: *Do you have to reserve tickets in advance?* 你需要预先订票吗? | *I'd like to reserve a table for two.* 我想预订一张两人的餐桌。**2** to keep something so that it can be used by a particular person or for a particular purpose 保留: **reserve sth for sb** *These seats are reserved for the elderly and disabled.* 这些座位是留给老人和残疾人的。| *Reserve a little of the mixture to sprinkle over the top of the pie.* 留一些配好的作料撒在馅饼上。**3** to use or show something only in one particular situation 留作, 用于〔特定场合〕: **reserve sth for** *a tone of voice she usually reserved for dealing with officials* 她通常在与官员打交道时才用的语气 **4 reserve the right to do sth** *formal* an expression meaning that you will do something if you think it is necessary, used especially in notices or official documents【正式】保留做某事的权利〔尤用于通知或官方文件〕: *The management reserves the right to refuse admission.* 管理部门保留谢绝入场的权利。 W3

reserve² *n* **1** [C] also 又作 **reserves** *plural* an amount of something kept for future use, especially for difficult or dangerous situations 贮藏(物); 储备: **[+of]** *reserves of food* 食物的储备 | *an inner reserve of strength* 体力蕴藏 **2 in reserve** ready to be used if needed unexpectedly 备用: *We always keep some money in reserve, just in case.* 我们总是存一些钱以防万一。**3** [U] a quality in someone's character that makes them not like expressing their emotions or talking about their problems 含蓄; 寡言: *His characteristic detachment and reserve made it difficult to guess his thoughts.* 他一贯的超然和寡言使人难以猜测他的心思。**4** [C] someone who will play in a sports team if one of the other players is injured or ill 替补队员, 后备队员 **5** [C] a price limit below which something will not be sold, especially in an AUCTION 〔尤指拍卖时的〕底价 **6** [U] also 又作 **reserves** a military force that a country has in addition to its usual army 后备军, 后备部队

R

re·served /rɪˈzɝvd; rɪˈzɜːvd/ *adj* **1** unwilling to express your emotions or talk about your problems 沉默寡言的; 含蓄的; 矜持的: *Ellen was a shy, reserved girl.* 埃伦是个腼腆、沉默寡言的姑娘。**2** kept specially to be used by one particular person 保留的, 预订的: *I'm sorry, but this seat's reserved.* 对不起, 这个座位已经有人预订了。| *reserved parking spaces* 专用停车处 | **[+for]** *The front row is reserved for the family of the bride.* 前排座位留给新娘的家人。**3 all rights reserved** used at the end of printed or recorded material to show that it is illegal to copy it without special permission 版权所有, 不得翻版〔用于印刷品或音像制品的结尾部分〕—**reservedly** /rɪˈzɝvɪdlɪ; rɪˈzɜːvɪ̈dli/ *adv* —**reservedness** *n* [U] —see also 另见 UNRESERVED

Reserve Of·fi·cer Train·ing Corps, the /ˌ· ˌ··· ˈ·· ˌ·/ *AmE*【美】—see 见 ROTC

reserve price /·ˈ· ·/ RESERVE² (5) 底价

re·serv·ist /rɪˈzɝvɪst; rɪˈzɜːvɪ̈st/ *n* [C] a soldier in the reserve (RESERVE² (6)), who is trained to fight and may join the professional army during a war 后备役军人

res·er·voir /ˈrɛzɚˌvwɑr; ˈrezəvwɑː/ *n* [C] **1** a lake, especially an artificial one, where water is stored before it is supplied to people's houses 水库; 蓄水池 **2** a large amount of something that has not yet been used 储藏, 积蓄: *She found she had reservoirs of unexpected strength.* 她发现自己积蓄着意想不到的力量。**3** *technical* a place where something, such as liquid, is kept before it is used【术语】储液器 —see picture at 参见 ENGINE 图

re·set¹ /riˈsɛt; ˌriːˈset/ *v past tense and past participle* **reset** *present participle* **resetting** [T] **1** to change a clock, control etc so that it shows a different time or number 校正, 调整〔钟表、控制装置等〕**2** to put a broken bone back into its correct place 重接〔断骨〕; 正〔骨〕: *The doctor reset the fracture.* 医生重接了骨折部位。**3** to load an OPERATING SYSTEM for a small computer from a DISK into the computer's memory; BOOT² (2) 重新启动〔电脑〕**4** to put a jewel into a new piece of jewellery 重镶〔宝石〕**5** to write a new set of questions for an examination 重出〔试题〕**6** *technical* to make new pages from which to print a book【术语】给…重新排版: *The book had to be reset because there were so many mistakes in the first printing.* 这本书首次印刷时错误太多, 必须重排。—**reset** *n* [C,U]

re·set² /ˈriˌsɛt; ˈriːset/ *adj* a reset button is used to make a machine or instrument ready to work again 〔按钮、键〕复位的, 重新启动的

re·set·tle /riˈsɛtl; riːˈsetl/ *v* **1** [I,T] to go to live in a new country or area, or help people to do this (协助人)在新的国家[地区]定居: *Many Ugandan Asian families resettled in Canada.* 许多乌干达的亚裔家庭迁居加拿大。| *tribesmen who were forcibly resettled by the government* 被政府强迫搬迁的部落人 **2** [T] to

start using an area again as a place to live 再〔在某地区〕定居: *The area was resettled in the latter half of the century.* 该世纪下半叶，人们重新到这个地区定居。—**resettlement** *n* [U]

re·shuf·fle¹ /ri`ʃʌfl; riːˈʃʌfəl/ *v* [T] *BrE* to change around the jobs of the people who work in an organization, especially in government【英】人事调整; 改组〔机构，尤指政府〕: *The Prime Minister reshuffled his cabinet.* 首相改组了内阁。

reshuffle² *n* [C] *BrE* the act of changing around the jobs of people who work in an organization, especially in a government【英】〔机构内的〕人事调整; 〔尤指政府的〕改组: *a Cabinet reshuffle* 内阁改组

re·side /rɪ`zaɪd; rɪˈzaɪd/ *v* [I always+adv/prep] *formal* to live in a particular place【正式】居住

reside in sth/sb *phr v* [T not in passive 不用被动态] *formal*【正式】**1** to be present in something 存在于: *For Fellini, the poetry of cinema resides primarily in movement.* 〔意大利导演〕费利尼认为，电影的诗意首先存在于运动之中。**2** also 又作 **reside within** sth/sb if a power, right etc resides in something or someone, it belongs to them 〔权力、权利等〕属于

res·i·dence /`rɛzədəns; ˈrezɪ̇dəns/ *n* **1** [C] *formal*【正式】**a)** a house, especially a large one 住宅, 住所, 公馆 **b)** the place where an AMBASSADOR (=important representative from a foreign country) lives 大使官邸 **2** [U] **a)** the state of living in a place 〔在某地〕居住〔的状态〕 **b)** permission to live somewhere permanently 永久居住许可 **3 in residence a)** *formal* living in a place or present there【正式】(住) 在某地的 **b)** a student who is in residence is at their university 〔大学生〕住校的 **4 artist/poet/playwright etc in residence** an artist etc who has been officially chosen by a college or other institution to work there and to help the students 〔大学等正式聘用工作和辅导学生的〕驻校艺术家/诗人/剧作家等 **5 take up residence** *formal* to start to live in a place【正式】开始居住: *He's taken up residence in an old castle.* 他在一座旧城堡里住下来。—see also 另见 HALL OF RESIDENCE

res·i·dent¹ /`rɛzədənt; ˈrezɪ̇dənt/ *adj* **1** *formal* living in a place【正式】居住的, 居留的: [+in] *Many retired British people are now resident in Spain.* 许多退休的英国人现在住在西班牙。**2** [only before noun 仅用于名词前] living or working in a particular place or institution 〔在某处、某机构〕居住[工作]的: *a resident tutor* 住校辅导老师 **3** [only before noun 仅用于名词前] *humorous* belonging to a particular group【幽默】属于…的: *He's our resident expert on computer games.* 他是我们当中的电脑游戏高手。

2 3 **resident²** *n* [C] **1** someone who lives or stays in a place such as a house or hotel 居民; 住客: *Only residents can drink in the hotel bar.* 只有住客才能在旅馆酒吧饮酒。**2** *AmE* a doctor working at a hospital where he is being trained【美】住院医生; REGISTRAR (2) *BrE*【英】

3 **res·i·den·tial** /ˌrɛzə`dɛnʃəl; ˌrezɪ̇ˈdenʃəl◂/ *adj* **1** a residential part of a town consists of private houses, with no offices or factories 住宅区的: *a quiet residential street* 一条安静的住宅区街道 **2** living at a place while you are doing something, or in order to do something 〔为做某事而〕在某处居住的: **a residential job/course/patient etc** *a residential school for the deaf* 聋人住宿学校 | *a weekend residential course* 周末住校课程

residential care /ˌ···· ˈ·/ *n* [U] a system of professional care for people who are too old or ill to look after themselves at home 〔为不能自理的老人或病人提供的〕上门护理

residential treat·ment fa·cil·i·ty /ˌ···· ˈ·· ·ˌ···/ *n* [C] *AmE technical* an expression meaning a MENTAL HOSPITAL, used because you want to avoid saying this directly【美, 术语】精神疗养所〔委婉用语，指精神病医院〕

resident phy·si·cian /ˌ··· ·ˈ··/ *n AmE* a RESIDENT² (2)【美】住院医生

residents' as·so·ci·a·tion /ˈ··· ·ˌ····/ *n* [C] an association of people who meet to discuss the problems and needs of the area where they live 居民协会

re·sid·u·al /rɪ`zɪdʒuəl; rɪˈzɪdʒuəl/ *adj* [only before noun 仅用于名词前] *formal* remaining after a process, event etc is finished【正式】残余的, 剩余的: *There was still some residual unrest after the rebellion had been crushed.* 叛乱被粉碎以后仍然余波未平。| **residual income** (=the money left from what you earn after you have paid your taxes) 税后收入

res·i·due /`rɛzəˌdu; ˈrezɪ̇djuː/ *n* [C] **1** *technical* a substance that is left after a chemical process【术语】〔化学过程的〕残余物, 渣滓: *a sticky residue in the bottom of the test tube* 试管底部黏稠的残余物 **2** the part of something that is left after the rest has gone or been taken away 剩余, 残余: [+of] *The residue of his estate goes to his daughter.* 他的剩余遗产归其女儿所有。

re·sign /rɪ`zaɪn; rɪˈzaɪn/ *v* [I,T] **1** to officially and permanently leave your job or position because you want to 辞职, 放弃〔工作、职位〕: [+from] *She's just resigned from the committee.* 她刚辞去了委员会的职务。| **resign your post/position** *The manager was forced to resign his post after allegations of corruption.* 在涉嫌贪污后，经理被迫辞职。**2 resign yourself to sth/to doing sth** to make yourself accept something that is unpleasant but cannot be changed 使自己安于某事/做某物〔无法避免的不愉快事〕, 听任, 顺从于…: *You must resign yourselves to waiting a bit longer.* 你们要耐心多等一会儿。—see also 另见 RESIGNED 3

res·ig·na·tion /ˌrɛzɪg`neʃən; ˌrezɪgˈneɪʃən/ *n* **1** [C,U] the act of resigning, or a written statement to say you are doing this 辞职; 辞呈: *You have the choice between resignation and dismissal.* 辞职还是开除由你自己选择。| **hand in your resignation/tender your resignation** (=resign) 递交辞呈 *Guess what? Roy's handed in his resignation.* 你猜得着吗? 罗伊递交了辞职书。**2** [U] the act of calmly accepting a situation that cannot be changed though it is unpleasant 听从, 顺从: *She accepted her fate with resignation.* 她听天由命。 3

re·signed /rɪ`zaɪnd; rɪˈzaɪnd/ *adj* **1** a resigned look, sound etc shows that you are making yourself accept something that you do not like 屈从的, 顺从的: *a resigned look on her face* 她脸上逆来顺受的表情 | *He sounded resigned and dejected.* 他的语气流露出无可奈何和沮丧的情绪。**2 be resigned to sth/to doing sth** to accept a situation that you do not like, but cannot change 安于某事/做某事: *Isabelle seems resigned to the fact that she's dying.* 伊莎贝尔似乎接受了她已来日无多的事实。—**resignedly** /rɪ`zaɪnədlɪ; rɪˈzaɪnɪ̇dli/ *adv*

re·sil·i·ence /rɪ`zɪlɪəns; rɪˈzɪliəns/ also 又作 **re·sil·i·en·cy** /-lɪənsɪ; -liənsi/ *n* [U] **1** the ability to return quickly to your usual health or state of mind after suffering an illness, difficulties etc 恢复力, 复原力: *resilience of character* 性格坚韧 **2** the ability of a substance to return to its former shape when pressure is removed; FLEXIBILITY 弹性

re·sil·i·ent /rɪ`zɪlɪənt; rɪˈzɪliənt/ *adj* **1** someone who is resilient quickly becomes healthy or happy again after an illness, difficulty, change etc 能恢复活力的; 坚韧的; 适应力强的: *I wouldn't worry – kids are very resilient.* 我不担心，孩子的适应力很强。**2** a resilient substance returns to its former shape when pressure is removed 〔物质〕有弹性的 —**resiliently** *adv*

res·in /`rɛzn; ˈrezɪ̇n/ *n* **1** [T] a thick sticky liquid that comes out of some trees 树脂 **2** [C] an artificial plastic substance that is produced chemically and used in industry 合成树脂, 人造树脂 —**resinous** *adj*

re·sist /rɪ`zɪst; rɪˈzɪst/ *v* **1** [T] to try to prevent change or prevent yourself being forced to do something 抗拒, 对抗: *Demonstrators today violently resisted attempts to evict them from the building.* 示威者今天强烈地抗拒要他们离开大楼的企图。| *I was in their power, and knew it was pointless to resist.* 我在他们股掌之中，知道反抗毫无意义。**2** [I,T] to oppose or fight someone or something 反抗, 抵抗: *The city resisted the enemy onslaught for two weeks.* 这座城市抵御敌人的猛攻达两个星期之久。**3** [I, T usually in negatives 一般用于否定句] to stop yourself having something that you like very much or doing something that you want to do 忍住〔拥有某东西的欲望〕, 按捺: **cannot resist sth/doing sth** *I just can't resist chocolates.* 我无法拒绝巧克力的诱惑。| *I couldn't resist sneaking a look at her diary.* 我忍不住偷看了一眼她的日记。| **hard/impossible to resist** *It's hard to resist an invitation like that.* 难以拒绝那样的邀请。| **resist the temptation/impulse etc** *She resisted the temptation to tell him what she really thought.* 她克制住自己，没有把真实想法告诉他。**4** [T] to not be changed or harmed by something 抵挡; 保持原状; 不受…的损害: *A balanced diet will increase your ability to resist infection.* 饮食均衡会增强你抗感染的能力。**5 resist arrest** to try to prevent the police from taking you to the police station 拒捕 —**resistable** *adj* 3

re·sist·ance /rɪ`zɪstəns; rɪˈzɪstəns/ *n* 2 3

1 ►AGAINST CHANGE 反对变化◄ [singular,U] a refusal to accept new ideas or changes 〔对新观念或改变的〕反对, 抗拒: *When you introduced computerized billing, was there much resistance from consumers?* 你们采用电脑打印账单时，有顾客反对吗? | [+to] *There has been a lot of resistance to this new law.* 对这项新法律有很大的反感。

2 ►FIGHTING 战斗◄ [singular,U] fighting against someone or something that is attacking you 反抗, 抵抗: **put up/offer resistance** (=resist) 反抗, 抵抗 *The defenders put up strong resistance.* 守军顽强抵抗。

3 ►AGAINST INFECTION/ILLNESS 抗感染/疾病◄ [singular, U] the natural ability of an animal or plant to stop diseases from

harming it 抗病能力: *Vitamins can build up your resistance to colds and flu.* 维生素可以增强抵抗感冒和流感的能力。
4 wind resistance/air resistance etc the degree to which a moving object, such as a car or plane, is made to move more slowly by the air it moves through 风的阻力/空气阻力等
5 ►ELECTRICITY 电◄ [U] the degree to which a substance can stop an electric current passing through 电阻
6 the resistance an organization that secretly fights against an enemy that now controls their country 抵抗组织: *Mitterand was in the French Resistance during the war.* 在战争期间, 密特朗是法国抵抗运动的成员。
7 take the line of least resistance to do the easiest thing in a difficult situation 〔在困境中〕采取最简便的方法
8 ►EQUIPMENT 设备◄ [C] a RESISTOR 电阻器 —see also 另见 PASSIVE RESISTANCE

re·sis·tant /rɪˋzɪstənt; rɪˈzɪstənt/ *adj* **1** not damaged or affected by something 有抵抗力的, 抵抗…的: [+to] *This type of flu is resistant to antibiotics.* 这种流感对抗生素有抗药力。**2** opposed to something and wanting to prevent it happening 抵制的, 反抗的, 抗拒的: [+to] *The Club is resistant to any form of change.* 该俱乐部反对任何形式的变革。**3 heat-resistant/fire-resistant** something that is heat-resistant etc will not be damaged by heat etc 耐热的/耐火的

re·sis·tor /rɪˋzɪstɚ; rɪˈzɪstə/ *n* [C] a piece of wire or other material used for increasing electrical resistance 电阻器

re·sit /ˌriˋsɪt; ˌriːˈsɪt/ *v past tense and past participle* **resat**, *present participle* **resitting** [T] *especially BrE* to take an examination again 【尤英】重新参加考试, 补考 —**resit** /ˋrisɪt; ˈriːsɪt/ *n* [C]

re·skill·ing /ˌriˋskɪlɪŋ; ˌriˈskɪlɪŋ/ *n* [U] *BrE* the teaching of new work skills, especially to unemployed people 【英】〔尤指对失业者的〕再培训

res·o·lute /ˋrɛzəˌlut; ˈrezəluːt/ *adj* doing something in a very determined way because you have very strong beliefs, aims etc 坚决的, 坚定的 —opposite 反义词 IRRESOLUTE —**resolutely** *adv*: *She resolutely resisted his amorous advances.* 她坚决拒绝了他的追求。—**resoluteness** *n*

res·o·lu·tion /ˌrɛzəˋluʃən; ˌrezəˈluːʃən/ *n*
1 ►DECISION 决定◄ [C] a formal decision or statement agreed on by a group of people, especially after a vote 决议, 决定: *The resolution was passed by a two-thirds majority.* 该决议得到三分之二多数通过。
2 ►SOLUTION 解决◄ [singular,U] the act of finding a way to deal with a difficulty 解决: *The lawyer's advice led to the resolution of this problem.* 律师的忠告使这个问题得以解决。
3 ►DETERMINATION 决心◄ [U] *approving* the quality of having strong beliefs and determination 【褒】坚决, 坚定, 决心
4 ►PROMISE 诺言◄ [C] a promise to yourself to do something 〔做事的〕决心: **make a resolution** *Carol made a resolution to work hard at school this year.* 卡罗尔下决心今年要用功学习。| **New Year's resolution** (=a resolution made on January 1st) 新年时下的决心 *a New Year's resolution to stop smoking* 新年时下决心戒烟 —compare 比较 RESOLVE[2]
5 ►CLEARNESS 清晰◄ [C,U] the power of a television, camera, MICROSCOPE etc to give a clear picture of things, or a measure of this 〔电视、照相机、显微镜的〕清晰度, 分辨率: *a high resolution microscope* 高分辨率显微镜

re·solve[1] /rɪˋzɑlv; rɪˈzɒlv/ *v* **1** [T] to find a satisfactory way of dealing with a problem or difficulty; settle 解决: *negotiations to resolve the dispute* 解决争端的谈判 | *There weren't enough beds, but the matter was resolved by George sleeping on the sofa.* 床不够用, 但乔治睡到沙发上问题就解决了。**2** [I,T] to make a definite decision to do something 下决心, 决定: **resolve to do sth** *After the divorce she resolved never to marry again.* 离婚以后, 她下决心永不再嫁。| **resolve that** *Mary resolved that she would try to work harder.* 玛丽决心更加努力工作。**3** [I,T] to make a formal decision, especially by voting 〔尤指投票〕作出决议: **resolve to do sth** *The Senate resolved to accept the President's budget proposals by 70 votes to 30.* 参议院以70票对30票通过决议, 同意总统的预算草案。**4** [T] to separate something into its different parts 分解, 使解体
resolve sth **into** sth *phr v* [T] **1** *technical* to separate or become separated into parts 【术语】把…分解为…: *This mixture will resolve into two separate compounds.* 这个混合物将分解成两种不同的化合物。**2 resolve itself into** to gradually change into something else; become 演变成: *The argument resolved itself into an uneasy truce.* 辩论停息了, 但很可能再次爆发。

resolve[2] *n* [U] *formal* strong determination to succeed in doing something 【正式】决心, 决意: *His encouragement and support strengthened our resolve.* 他的鼓励和支持增强了我们的决心。

res·o·nance /ˋrɛznəns; ˈrezənəns/ *n* **1** [U] the deep, loud, continuing quality of a sound 嘹亮; 洪亮: *the resonance of his voice* 他洪亮的嗓音 **2** [C,U] *formal* the special meaning that something has for you because it is connected with your own experiences 【正式】〔亲身经历引起的〕共鸣 **3** [C,U] *technical* sound that is produced or increased in an object by sound waves from another object 【术语】共鸣, 共振, 谐振

res·o·nant /ˋrɛznənt; ˈrezənənt/ *adj* **1** a resonant sound is deep, loud, clear, and continues for a long time 〔声音〕洪亮的, 回荡的 **2 resonant with** filled with a particular sound 充满…声音的: *The air was resonant with the shouts of children.* 空中回响着孩子们的叫喊声。**3** *technical* resonant materials increase any sound produced inside them 【术语】共鸣的, 共振的 —**resonantly** *adv*

res·o·nate /ˋrɛzəˌnet; ˈrezəneɪt/ *v* [I] **1** to make a deep, loud, clear sound that continues for a long time 发出洪亮的声音 **2** to make a sound that is produced as a reaction to another sound 产生共鸣, 共振
resonate with sth *phr v* [T] **1** *formal* to be full of a particular meaning or feeling 【正式】充满〔含义或感觉〕: *literature that resonates with biblical imagery* 充满圣经意象的文学作品 **2** to be full of a sound 回响着: *a hall resonating with laughter* 笑声荡漾的大厅

res·o·na·tor /ˋrɛzəˌnetɚ; ˈrezəneɪtə/ *n* [C] a piece of equipment for making the sound louder in a musical instrument 共鸣器, 共振器

re·sort[1] /rɪˋzɔrt; rɪˈzɔːt/ *n* **1** [C] a place where people often go for holidays 度假胜地: **seaside/beach/mountain etc resort** *a seaside resort south of Tokyo* 东京以南的一个海滨度假胜地 | **resort hotel/beach/town** *Jan and Matt run a small resort hotel in Vermont.* 简和马特在佛蒙特州经营一家小型度假旅馆。**2 as a last resort/in the last resort** used to say what you will do if everything else fails 〔一切都失败后〕作为最后的手段: *As a last resort we could borrow more money on the house.* 实在没有别的办法, 我们可以用房子抵押多借些钱。| **of last resort** (=used when everything else has failed) 最后一招 *a weapon of last resort* 最后使出的武器, 撒手锏 **3 have resort to** *formal* to do something bad or extreme because you cannot think of any other solution 【正式】〔不得已时〕诉诸〔坏的或极端的办法〕: *It may be necessary to have resort to force.* 诉诸武力可能是必要的。**4** [C] *AmE* a hotel for people on holiday 【美】度假旅馆

resort[2] *v*
resort to sth *phr v* [T] to use something or do something that is bad, in order to succeed or deal with a problem 采取, 诉诸〔不好的事物〕: *When polite requests failed Paul resorted to threats.* 当好言相求不起作用时, 保罗便耍起横来。| **resort to doing sth** *Sally resorted to stealing when her money ran out.* 萨利的钱用完了就去偷窃。

re·sound /rɪˋzaund; rɪˈzaʊnd/ *v* [I] **1** if a place resounds with a sound it is full of it; ECHO[1] (2) 〔地方〕回荡着声音, 回响: [+with/to] *The hall resounded with laughter and cheering.* 大厅里充满了笑声和欢呼声。**2** if a sound such as a musical note resounds, it continues loudly and clearly for quite a long time 〔声音〕鸣响, 回荡: [+through/around etc] *a horn resounding through the forest* 响彻森林的号角声

re·sound·ing /rɪˋzaundɪŋ; rɪˈzaʊndɪŋ/ *adj* **1** [only before noun 仅用于名词前] a resounding noise is so loud that it seems to continue for a few seconds 洪亮的, 回响的: *The vase fell to the floor with a resounding crash.* 花瓶掉到地板上, 铿然一声摔碎了。**2 resounding success/victory/defeat etc** a very great or complete success etc, that many people know about 巨大的成功/胜利/失败等: *The show, Five Guys Named Moe, was a resounding success.* 《五个名叫莫的人》这出戏取得巨大成功。—**resoundingly** *adv*

re·source[1] /ˋrisors; rɪˈzɔːs/ *n*
1 ►OIL/COAL ETC 石油/煤等◄ [C often plural 常用复数] something such as land, minerals, or natural energy that exists in a country and can be used to increase its wealth 资源: *Canada's vast mineral resources* 加拿大丰富的矿产资源 | **natural resources** *a country rich in natural resources* 自然资源丰富的国家
2 ►MONEY/PROPERTY ETC 钱/财产等◄ **resources** [plural] all the money, property, skills etc that you have available 物力, 财力; 资源: *We must make the best possible use of our limited financial resources.* 我们必须尽可能充分地利用有限的财力。| *resources for research and development* 研究与开发的资源 | **pool your resources** (=put together all the resources that each of you can provide) 集中所有资源
3 ►PERSONAL QUALITIES 个人素质◄ **resources** [plural] personal qualities, such as courage and a strong mind, that you

need to deal with a difficult situation〔对付困境所需的〕个人素质: **inner resources** *Martin has inner resources that will see him through this crisis.* 马丁是有内涵的人, 能渡过这次危机。—see also 另见 HUMAN RESOURCES

4 ▶EDUCATIONAL 教育的◀ [C] something such as a book, film, or picture used by teachers or students to provide information 资料;〔教学的〕资源: *resources for learning* 学习资料 | *a valuable new computer resource* 有价值的新的电脑资料 | **resource room/centre etc** (=a room, building etc where resources are kept) 资料室/中心等

5 ▶PRACTICAL ABILITY 实际能力◀ [U] *formal* ability in dealing with practical problems; RESOURCEFULNESS【正式】机智, 应变能力: *a man of great resource* 足智多谋的人

re·source² /rɪˋsɔrs; rɪˈzɔːs/ *v* [T] *technical* to provide money or other resources for something【术语】向…提供资源: *The program failed because it wasn't adequately resourced.* 由于资源不足, 计划失败了。

re·source·ful /rɪˋsɔrsfəl; rɪˈzɔːsfəl/ *adj approving* good at finding ways of dealing with practical problems【褒】足智多谋的, 机智的: *a resourceful woman who could cope in almost any circumstances* 几乎任何局面都能够应付的足智多谋的女人 —**resourcefully** *adv* —**resourcefulness** *n* [U]

re·spect¹ /rɪˋspɛkt; rɪˈspekt/ *n*

1 ▶ADMIRATION 钦佩◀ [U] admiration for someone, especially because of their personal qualities, knowledge or skill 尊敬, 敬重: **[+for]** *I have the greatest respect for Jane's judgment.* 我非常钦佩简的眼光。| **win/earn/gain the respect of** *With his decisive handling of the dispute, he had won the respect of everyone.* 由于果断处理了纠纷, 他赢得了大家的尊敬。| **command the respect of** (=have and deserve someone's respect) 受到并值得尊敬 *Dr Weiss commands the respect of all who know him.* 所有认识韦斯博士的人都对他非常尊敬。—opposite 反义词 DISRESPECT

2 with (the greatest) respect/with (all) due respect *spoken formal* used to politely introduce an expression of disagreement【口, 正式】尽管我尊敬你〔用于礼貌地表示不同意见〕: *With respect, sir, I think you're quite wrong.* 先生, 我认为您完全错了, 这样说并无不敬之意。

3 ▶CONSIDERATION 考虑◀ [U] an attitude of regarding something or someone as important so that you are careful not to harm them, treat them rudely etc 考虑; 顾及; 重视: **[+for]** *Out of respect for the wishes of her family, the affair was not reported in the newspapers.* 考虑到她家人的意愿, 此事没有在报上披露。| *children who show no respect for authority* 不尊重权威的孩子 | **treat sb/sth with respect** *Old people deserve to be treated with more respect.* 尊老敬老, 理所当然。

4 ▶FOR DANGER 对于危险◀ [U] a careful attitude towards something or someone that is dangerous 谨慎, 小心: **[+for]** *People should have a healthy respect for alcohol* (=a sensible careful attitude towards it). 人们应慎重对待酒精。

5 in one respect/in some respects/in every respect used to say that something is true in one way, in some ways, or in every way 在某个/某些/所有方面: *In many respects the new version is not so good as the old one.* 新版本在许多方面不如旧版本。| *Aunt Arabella is very stubborn. Kim takes after her in that respect.* 阿拉贝拉姨妈非常固执。金在这方面很像她。

6 ▶GREETINGS 问候◀ **respects** [plural] *formal* polite greetings【正式】敬意; 问候: **give/send your respects** *Give my respects to your wife.* 请代我问候嫂夫人。| **pay your respects** (=make a polite visit) 拜访 *I've come to pay my respects to the countess.* 我来向伯爵夫人请安。

7 pay your last respects (to) to go to someone's funeral 向〔死者〕告别, 参加…的丧礼

8 in respect of *formal*【正式】**a)** concerning or in relation to 关于, 有关: *This is especially true in respect of the United Kingdom.* 英国的情况尤其如此。**b)** an expression meaning in payment for, used in business letters 作为…的报酬〔尤用于商业信函中〕: *The builder will be paid £300 in respect of the work already done.* 将付给建筑商300英镑, 作为对已完成工程的报酬。

9 with respect to *formal* used to introduce a new subject, or to return to one that has already been mentioned【正式】关于, 谈到〔用于另起一个话题或回到谈过的话题〕: *With respect to your other proposals, I am not yet able to give you our decision.* 至于你的其他建议, 我现在还无法告诉你我们的决定。—see also 另见 SELF-RESPECT

respect² *v* [T] **1** [not in progressive 不用进行时] to admire someone because they have high standards and good personal qualities such as fairness and honesty 尊敬, 敬佩, 敬重: *He's not the most popular teacher, but the students respect him.* 他不是最受欢迎的老师, 但学生都尊敬他。| *John had always respected Matthew's opinion.* 约翰一向尊重马修的意见。| **respect sb for** *Molly always told us exactly what she thought, and we respected her for that.* 莫莉总是与我们坦诚相见, 我们为此敬佩她。**2** to be careful not to do anything against someone's wishes, rights etc 尊重; 顾及〔某人的意愿、权利等〕: *I promise to respect your wishes.* 我保证尊重你的意愿。| *The President is expected to respect the constitution.* 人们期望总统尊重宪法。

re·spec·ta·bil·i·ty /rɪˌspɛktəˋbɪlətɪ; rɪˌspektəˈbɪlɪti/ *n* [U] the quality of being considered morally correct and socially acceptable 可敬的品格, 得体, 体面: *The couple exuded an air of quiet respectability.* 这对夫妇神态沉静, 举止优雅得体。

re·spec·ta·ble /rɪˋspɛktəbl; rɪˈspektəbəl/ *adj* **1** having standards of behaviour, appearance etc that are socially acceptable and approved of〔行为、外观等〕体面的, 可敬的; 正派的: *a respectable married woman* 一位正经的已婚妇人 | *nice children from respectable homes* 来自正派家庭的好孩子 | *Let's make you look a bit more respectable before you go out.* 让我们把你打扮得更体面些你再出去。**2** *informal* good or satisfactory【非正式】好的; 令人满意的: *a respectable income* 不错的收入 | *Her exam results were respectable, although not brilliant.* 她的考试成绩不错, 尽管不优秀。—**respectably** *adv* —**respectableness** *n* [U]

re·spect·ed /rɪˋspɛktɪd; rɪˈspektɪd/ *adj* admired by many people because of your work, achievements etc 受尊敬的, 受敬重的: *a highly respected journalist* 深受尊敬的记者

re·spect·er /rɪˋspɛktə; rɪˈspektə/ *n* [C] **be no respecter of persons** to be equally harmful towards all people whether they are rich or poor, important or ordinary 对所有人一样有害: *Disease is no respecter of persons.* 疾病面前人人平等。

re·spect·ful /rɪˋspɛktfəl; rɪˈspektfəl/ *adj* feeling or showing respect 有礼貌的, 恭敬的: *The soldiers bowed their heads in respectful silence as the funeral procession went by.* 葬礼队伍经过时, 士兵都低头默哀。—opposite 反义词 DISRESPECTFUL —**respectfully** *adv* —**respectfulness** *n* [U]

re·spec·tive /rɪˋspɛktɪv; rɪˈspektɪv/ *adj* [only before noun 仅用于名词前] people's respective jobs, houses, families etc are the various ones that each of them has 各自的: *The two friends said goodbye and went their respective ways.* 两个朋友互相道别后分道而去。

re·spec·tive·ly /rɪˋspɛktɪvlɪ; rɪˈspektɪvli/ *adv* each separately in the order mentioned 各自地, 依次地: *My two sons, Adam and Alexander, are five and nine respectively.* 我的两个儿子亚当和亚历山大, 分别是5岁和9岁。

res·pi·ra·tion /ˌrɛspəˋreʃən; ˌrespɪˈreɪʃən/ *n* [U] *technical* the process of breathing【术语】呼吸 —see also 另见 ARTIFICIAL RESPIRATION

res·pi·ra·tor /ˋrɛspəˌretə; ˈrespɪreɪtə/ *n* [C] a piece of equipment that you wear over your nose and mouth to help you breathe in a place where there is gas, smoke etc 口罩; 防毒面具; 呼吸器

the human respiratory system 人体呼吸系统

nasal cavity 鼻腔
tonsils 扁桃体
epiglottis 会厌
glottis 声门
vocal cords 声带
windpipe/trachea 气管
bronchial tube 支气管
rib 肋骨
heart 心脏
right lung 右肺
left lung 左肺
oesophagus *BrE*【英】/ esophagus *AmE*【美】食道

re·spi·ra·to·ry /rɪˋspaɪrəˌtɔrɪ; rɪˈspɪrətəri/ *adj formal or technical* connected with breathing【正式或术语】与呼吸有关的; 呼吸道的: *respiratory diseases* 呼吸道疾病 | *the respiratory system* 呼吸系统

res·pite /ˈrɛspɪt; ˈrespɪt/ *n* [singular,U] **1** a short time when something unpleasant stops happening, so that the situation is temporarily better〔令人讨厌的事情的〕暂息; 缓解: **[+from]** *a welcome respite from the constant pressure of work* 持续的工作压力期间受欢迎的短暂休息 | **without respite** *The noise went on all night without even a moment's respite.* 吵闹声一刻不停地持续了一整夜。**2** a short period of delay before you have to do something that is unpleasant 暂缓: *We have a few days' respite before we need to pay the rent.* 我们还可以延迟几天才交租金。

re·splen·dent /rɪˈsplɛndənt; rɪˈsplendənt/ *adj formal* very beautiful, bright and shining in appearance【正式】华丽的; 辉煌的; 灿烂的: *the resplendent colours of the New England woods in the fall* 秋季新英格兰树林的瑰丽色彩 —**resplendence** *n* [U] —**resplendently** *adv*: *resplendently dressed in shimmering silk robes* 身着闪闪发光的华丽绸袍

re·spond /rɪˈspɑnd; rɪˈspɒnd/ *v* **1** [I] to react to something that has been said or done 反应, 回应: **[+to]** *Clive responded to my suggestion with a laugh.* 克莱夫对我提的建议报以一笑。| **respond by doing sth** *The US responded by sending troops into Laos.* 美国的反应是派遣军队进入老挝。—see 见 ANSWER² (USAGE) **2** [I,T **+that**] to say or write something as a reply 答复: *He responded that he would be pleased to attend.* 他回答说, 他很高兴出席。| **[+to]** *No one has yet responded to our complaints.* 还没有人对我们的投诉作出回复。**3** [I] to improve as a result of a particular kind of treatment 有良好反应: **[+to]** *Her cancer failed to respond to treatment.* 治疗对她的癌症没起作用。| *Most children respond well to individual attention in class.* 在课堂上照顾到每个孩子, 这种做法大多数儿童都反应良好。

re·spon·dent /rɪˈspɑndənt; rɪˈspɒndənt/ *n* [C] **1** *formal* someone who answers questions【正式】回答者, 答复者 **2** *law* someone who has to defend their own case in a law court, especially in a DIVORCE case【法律】〔尤指离婚案的〕被告 —compare 比较 CO-RESPONDENT

re·sponse /rɪˈspɑns; rɪˈspɒns/ *n* **1** [C,U] something that is done as a reaction to something that has happened or been said 反应: *The attack provoked an angry response.* 攻击引起愤怒的反应。| **[+to]** *a sympathetic response to our appeal for help* 对我们要求帮助的呼吁的积极反应 | **in response to** (=as a response to) 作为…的回应 *The law was passed in response to public pressure.* 在公众压力下该法规获得通过。**2** [C] something that is said or written as a reply 回答: *His question failed to get a response from any of the students.* 没有学生回答他提的问题。**3** [C] a part of a religious service that is spoken or sung by the people as an answer to a part that is spoken or sung by the priest〔宗教仪式上会众同牧师的〕轮流应答[吟唱]的祈祷文

re·spon·si·bil·i·ty /rɪˌspɑnsəˈbɪləti; rɪˌspɒnsəˈbɪləti/ *n*

1 ►**IN CHARGE** 负责◄ [U] a duty to be in charge of or look after something, so that you make decisions and can be blamed if something bad happens 责任, 负责: *She was given promotion and more responsibility.* 她晋升了, 所负的责任也增加了。| **have responsibility for** *The Health Minister has overall responsibility for Britain's hospitals.* 卫生大臣全面负责英国的医院。| **take responsibility for** (=agree to be in charge of something or someone) 对…负责 *My husband took full responsibility for organizing the trip.* 我丈夫全权负责组织这次旅行。| **assume responsibility for** (=agree to be in charge of) *formal*【正式】承担…的责任 *Richard assumed responsibility for his brother's children.* 理查德承担起照顾侄子侄女的责任。| **accept responsibility for** *The management accepts no responsibility for cars left in the car park.* 管理部门对留在停车场内的汽车不承担责任。

2 ►**DUTY** 责任, 义务◄ [C] a duty that you have, especially because you are in charge of something 任务, 职责: *The head of a large company has many responsibilities.* 大公司的领导人负有很多责任。| **have a responsibility to do sth** *Every citizen has a responsibility to vote.* 每位公民都有投票的义务。| **it is sb's responsibility to do sth** *It is your responsibility to check that all doors and windows are locked.* 你的任务是查看所有的门窗是否都锁好了。| **moral responsibility** (=a duty to do something because it is morally right) 道义责任

3 ►**BLAME** 责备◄ [U] blame for something bad that has happened〔对不良事件负的〕责任: **accept/take responsibility** *We refuse to accept responsibility for the breakdown of negotiations.* 我们拒绝承担谈判破裂的责任。

4 sense of responsibility an ability to behave sensibly so that you can be trusted to do the right thing 责任感: *Parents need to encourage a sense of responsibility in their children.* 家长必须培养孩子的责任感。

5 a responsibility to sb a duty to help or serve someone because of your work, position in society etc 对某人负有责任: *A doctor's first responsibility is to her patients.* 医生首先要对病人负责。

6 do sth on your own responsibility to do something without being told to do it or officially allowed to do it 自行负责地做某事

7 claim responsibility (for) to officially state that you are the person or organization that did something, especially an act of TERRORISM (=violence in order to get political power) 声称〔对某事, 尤指恐怖行为〕负责

re·spon·si·ble /rɪˈspɑnsəbl; rɪˈspɒnsəbəl/ *adj*

1 ►**GUILTY** 有罪的◄ [not before noun 不用于名词前] if someone is responsible for an accident, mistake, crime etc, it is their fault or they can be blamed〔对事故、错误、罪行等〕负有责任的, 应承担责任的: **[+for]** *The police arrested those responsible for the burglaries.* 警察逮捕了那些盗窃犯。| *When he loses his temper, he isn't responsible for his actions.* 他发脾气时不顾自己行为的后果。| *If any of the children got hurt, I should feel responsible.* 要是哪个孩子受了伤, 应该由我承担责任。| **hold sb responsible (for)** (=blame someone for something)〔因…〕怪罪某人 *I shall hold you personally responsible for anything that goes wrong.* 如果出什么差错的话, 我将唯你是问。

2 ►**IN CHARGE OF** 负责◄ [not before noun 不用于名词前] having a duty to be in charge of or to look after someone or something〔对某人、某事〕负责的: **[+for]** *Each commissioner is responsible for a department.* 每位委员负责一个部门。| *They're not my children, but I still feel responsible for them.* 他们不是我的孩子, 但我仍然觉得应对他们负责。

3 responsible job/position/post a job in which the ability to make good judgments and decisions is needed 要职

4 ►**SENSIBLE** 明智的◄ sensible and able to make good judgments so that you can be trusted 可信赖的, 可靠的: *You can leave the children with Stuart – he's very responsible.* 你可以把孩子交给斯图尔特, 他非常可靠。—opposite 反义词 IRRESPONSIBLE

5 be responsible to if you are responsible to someone, that person is in charge of your work and you must explain your actions to them 对〔某人〕负责: *In the US, cabinet members are directly responsible to the president.* 在美国, 内阁成员直接对总统负责。

6 ►**CAUSE** 起因◄ if something is responsible for a change, problem, event etc, it causes it 作为原由的: **[+for]** *Social changes are responsible for many of our modern problems.* 社会变革是引起我们许多现代问题的原因。

re·spon·si·bly /rɪˈspɑnsəblɪ; rɪˈspɒnsəbli/ *adv* in a sensible way which makes people trust you 负责地, 可靠地: *Can I rely on you to behave responsibly while I'm away?* 我外出时你要规规矩矩, 我可以信赖你吗?

re·spon·sive /rɪˈspɑnsɪv; rɪˈspɒnsɪv/ *adj* **1** ready to react in a useful or helpful way 关心的; 积极的: **[+to]** *We try to be responsive to the needs of the customer.* 我们努力去满足顾客的需求。**2** easily controlled, and reacting quickly in the way that you want 易操纵的; 反应快的; 灵敏的: *a car with very responsive steering* 方向盘操纵灵活的汽车 | *The disease is not proving responsive to treatment.* 这种病的疗法都不奏效。**3** willing to give answers or show your feelings about something 积极回应的: *I tried to get him talking but he wasn't very responsive.* 我试图让他讲话, 但他不太愿意发表意见。—**responsively** *adv* —**responsiveness** *n* [U] —opposite 反义词 UNRESPONSIVE

re·spray /ˌriˈspre; ˌriːˈspreɪ/ *v* [T] to change the colour of a car by putting new paint on it 给〔汽车〕重喷油漆 —**respray** /ˈrispre; ˈriːspreɪ/ *n* [C]

rest¹ /rɛst; rest/ *n*

1 the rest what is left after everything else has been used, dealt with, killed etc 剩余部分; 余下的人[物]: *I got half way through reciting the poem and couldn't remember the rest.* 我背诗背到一半, 余下的部分想不起来了。| *At least four of the enemy were killed and the rest fled.* 至少四个敌人被击毙, 其余的逃跑了。| **[+of]** *He'll be in a wheelchair for the rest of his life.* 他的余生将在轮椅上度过。

2 ►**RELAXING** 放松◄ [C,U] a period of time when you are not doing anything tiring and you can relax or sleep 休息(时间): *The doctor says I need complete rest.* 医生说我需要彻底休息。| *You'll feel much better after a good night's rest.* 好好睡上一晚后你会感觉好得多。| **have/take a rest** *You must be tired. Why don't you take a rest?* 你一定累了, 为什么不休息一下? | **well-earned rest** (=rest that you deserve because you have been working hard)〔辛勤劳动后〕应该享受的休息

3 put/set sb's mind at rest to make someone feel less anxious or worried 使某人放心: *I managed to set his mind at rest about my safety.* 我终于让他不再为我的安全担心。

4 come to rest a) to stop moving 停住: *The car braked sharply, coming to rest on the edge of the cliff.* 汽车猛地刹住，停在悬崖边上。**b)** if your eyes come to rest on something, you stop looking around and look at that one thing〔目光〕停留

5 give it a rest! *BrE spoken* used to tell someone to stop talking about something because they are annoying you【英口】别说啦!〔用于因受到烦扰而叫对方停止说话〕: *Oh, give it a rest! I don't want to hear about your job!* 好啦，别烦了！我不想听你谈你的工作！

6 at rest a) *technical* not moving【术语】静止的: *Measure the mass of an object at rest.* 测量物体在静止时的质量。**b)** an expression meaning dead, used to avoid upsetting someone 安息〔委婉语〕: *He now lies at rest in the churchyard.* 他现在长眠在教堂墓地里。

7 lay/put sth to rest to get rid of a false idea or belief by showing that it is not true 揭穿真相从而制止某事〔谬误等〕: *At last these dangerous rumours have been put to rest.* 这些危险的谣传终于被制止了。

8 and all the rest of it *BrE spoken* used at the end of a short list to mean other things of a similar type【英口】诸如此类，不一而足: *They accused me of being unreliable, irresponsible, and all the rest of it.* 他们指责我不可靠、不负责任等等。

9 for the rest *BrE* used to introduce a short final remark at the end of a speech or piece of writing【英】至于其他，至于其余的〔情况〕: *For the rest, we can only guess the effect of these changes.* 除此之外，我们只能猜测这些变革产生的影响。

10 and the rest! *BrE spoken* used to emphasize in a humorous way that a number or amount is really much higher than someone thinks【英口】不止吧!: *"I'd say she's about 40." "Yeah, and the rest!"* "我说她40岁上下。""噢，不止吧!"

11 lay sb to rest an expression meaning to bury someone, used when you want to avoid saying this directly 安葬某人〔委婉语〕: *She was laid to rest in the graveyard behind the church.* 她被安葬在教堂后面的墓地中。

12 ►IN MUSIC 音乐◄ [C] **a)** a period of silence of a particular length in a piece of music〔音乐作品中的〕休止 **b)** a written sign that shows how long the period of silence should be 休止符

13 ►SUPPORT 支撑物◄ [C] a support that you can rest your arm, head etc on〔可供搁放胳膊、头等的〕撑架，托，垫

S3 W3 **rest²** *v*

1 ►RELAX 放松◄ [I] to stop working or doing an activity for a time and sit down or lie down to relax 休息，歇息: *If you're tired, we'll stop and rest for a while.* 如果你累了，我们就停下来歇一会儿。

2 rest your feet/legs/eyes etc to stop using a part of your body because it is feeling sore or tired 歇歇脚/腿/眼睛等

3 ►GIVE SUPPORT 给予支撑◄ [T always+adv/prep] to support an object or part of your body by putting it on or against something 使依靠，使得到支撑: **rest sth against/on etc** *Rest your head on my shoulder.* 把你的头靠在我肩上。

4 ►LIE/LEAN ON 倚靠◄ [I always+adv/prep] to lie or lean on something for support 搁；倚，靠: **[+against/on etc]** *The ladder rested against the wall.* 梯子靠着墙。| *She sat with her elbows resting on the table.* 她坐着，双肘放在桌上。

5 let the matter rest also 又作 **let it rest** to stop discussing or dealing with something 不再讨论[办理]某事: *We could go on arguing but I think we'd better let the matter rest.* 我们可以争论下去，但我认为我们最好别再讨论这个问题了。

6 rest assured (that) *formal* used to tell someone not to worry, because what you say about a situation is true【正式】请放心: *You can rest assured that I will never tell anyone.* 你尽管放心，我绝不会告诉任何人。

7 will not rest until if you will not rest until something happens, you will not be satisfied until it happens 直到…才罢休: *We will not rest until the murderer is found.* 找不到凶手我们决不罢休。

8 ►LIE BURIED 安葬◄ [I always+adv/prep] a word meaning to lie buried, used when you do not want to say this directly 长眠〔委婉用语〕: *My mother rests beside my father in the family graveyard.* 我母亲在家族墓地里长眠在我父亲身边。| **last/final resting place** (=the place where someone is buried) 长眠之处 *He decided Rome, where he had been so happy, would be his final resting place.* 他选择罗马这个他曾经度过快乐时光的地方作为自己日后的长眠之地。| **rest in peace** (=often written on a grave) 安息〔常刻在墓碑上〕

9 rest on your laurels to be satisfied with what you have done, so that you do not make any further effort 满足于既得的成就；吃老本；不再求进步

10 I rest my case *spoken*【口】**a)** *formal* used by a lawyer when they have finished trying to prove something in a court of law【正式】本人停止举证；本人对案情陈述完毕〔律师出庭用语〕**b)** *humorous* used when something happens or is said which proves that you were right【幽默】我讲够了；还用我多说吗〔表示发生的事或所说的话证明是正确的〕

rest on/upon sth *phr v* [T not in progressive 不用进行时] **1** *formal* to depend on or be based on something【正式】依赖；以…为依据: *Success in management ultimately rests on good judgment.* 管理的成功最终依靠正确的判断。**2** if your eyes rest on something, you look at it〔目光〕落在…上

rest with sb *phr v* [T not in progressive 不用进行时] if a decision rests with someone, they are responsible for it 由〔某人〕负责: *The final decision rests with the President.* 得由总统作最后的决定。

rest a·rea /ˈ· ,··/ *n* [C] *especially AmE* a place near a road where you can stop and rest, go to the toilet etc【尤美】〔公路旁的〕休息站

re·state /riˋstet; ˌriːˈsteɪt/ *v* [T] to say something again in a different way, so that it is clearer or more strongly expressed〔换一种方式〕重说: *He restated the question.* 他换个方式把问题重说了一遍。—**restatement** *n* [C,U]

res·tau·rant /ˋrɛstərənt; ˈrestərɒnt/ *n* [C] a place where you can buy and eat a meal 饭店，餐馆: *an expensive fish restaurant* 价格昂贵的鱼肴餐馆 S3 W2

restaurant car /ˈ··· ·/ *n* [C] a carriage on a train where meals are served; DINING CAR〔火车的〕餐车

res·tau·ra·teur /ˌrɛstərəˋtɝ; ˌrestərəˈtɜː/ also 又作 **res·tau·ran·teur** /ˌrɛstərɑnˋtɝ; ˌrestərɒnˈtɜː/ *n* [C] someone who owns and manages a restaurant〔亲自管理餐馆的〕餐馆老板，饭店主人

rest·ed /ˋrɛstɪd; ˈrestɪ̣d/ *adj* [not before noun 不用于名词前] feeling healthier, stronger, or calmer because you have had time to relax〔休息之后感到〕精神的；有精力的；清醒的: *We came back feeling rested and ready for work.* 我们回来时感到精力充沛，准备随时投入工作。

rest·ful /ˋrɛstfəl; ˈrestfəl/ *adj* peaceful and quiet, making you feel relaxed 平静的，悠闲的: *restful music* 悠闲的音乐 —**restfully** *adv*

rest home /ˈ· ·/ *n* [C] a place where old or sick people can live and be looked after〔老人或病人的〕疗养所

res·ti·tu·tion /ˌrɛstəˋtuʃən; ˌrestɪ̣ˈtjuːʃən/ *n* [U] *formal* the act of giving back something that was lost or stolen to its owner, or of paying for damage【正式】归还，赔偿: **make restitution** *The court ordered him to make full restitution to the family.* 法院命令他全数赔偿给那家人。

res·tive /ˋrɛstɪv; ˈrestɪv/ *adj* unable to keep still, especially because you are impatient or bored 不安宁的，焦躁不安的，烦躁的: *The children were becoming restive from sitting at the dinner table so long.* 孩子们在饭桌边坐得太久，开始坐不住了。—**restively** *adv* —**restiveness** *n* [U]

rest·less /ˋrɛstlɪs; ˈrestləs/ *adj* **1** unable or unwilling to keep still, especially because you are nervous or bored〔尤指因紧张或沉闷〕烦躁的，不耐烦的: *The children had been indoors all day and were getting restless.* 孩子们在屋内待了一整天，开始烦躁不安。**2** unwilling to stay in one place, and always wanting new experiences 待不住的，求变的: *After a few weeks in Marseille, I grew restless and decided to take a ship to Corsica.* 在马赛待了几周后，我开始待不住了，决定乘船去科西嘉。**3 restless night** a night during which you cannot sleep or rest 不眠之夜 —**restlessly** *adv* —**restlessness** *n* [U]

re·stock /riˋstɑk; ˌriːˈstɒk/ *v* [I,T+**with**] to bring in more supplies to replace those that have been used（为…）补充货物；备办新货

res·to·ra·tion /ˌrɛstəˋreʃən; ˌrestəˈreɪʃən/ *n* [C,U] **1** the act of thoroughly repairing something such as an old building or a piece of furniture so that it looks the same as it did when it was first made〔旧建筑、家具的〕修复: *a fund for the restoration of historic buildings* 历史建筑的修复基金 **2** the act of bringing back a law, tax, or system of government〔法律、税收、政体的〕重新采用，恢复: **[+of]** *They're fighting for the restoration of democratic rights.* 他们正在为恢复民主权利而斗争。| *the restoration of the monarchy in Spain* 西班牙君主政体的复辟 **3 the Restoration** the return of Charles II to become King of England in 1660, and the period afterwards 王政复辟（时期）〔1660 年英王查理二世复辟及其后的一段时期〕: **Restoration comedy/drama**

(=plays written during this time in England) 王政复辟时期的喜剧/戏剧 **4** the act of officially giving something back to its former owner (正式) 归还: *an attempt to secure the restoration of their lands* 使他们的土地得以归还的努力

Restoration com·e·dy /ˌ····ˈ···/ a humorous type of play that was popular in England during the time of the Restoration, which includes a lot of SATIRE and jokes about people's social and sexual behaviour. Plays by Oliver Goldsmith and William Congreve are typical examples of Restoration COMEDY. 王政复辟时期的喜剧〔指王政复辟时期英国流行的一种滑稽剧。剧中有不少针对人的社会行为和性行为的插科打诨。奥利佛·戈德史密斯和威廉·康格里夫的作品是这一时期喜剧的典范〕

re·sto·ra·tive[1] /rɪˈstɔrətɪv; rɪˈstɔːrətɪv/ *adj formal* making you feel healthier or stronger【正式】恢复健康[体力]的: *the restorative power of long walks* 长距离步行使人恢复健康的效力

restorative[2] *n* [C] *humorous* a drink, especially an alcoholic one, that makes you feel better【幽默】饮料〔尤指酒等令人感觉舒畅的饮料〕

3 **re·store** /rɪˈstor; rɪˈstɔː/ *v* [T]

1 ▶FORMER SITUATION 以前的状态◀ to make something return to its former level or condition 恢复: *So far all attempts to restore normal relations between the two countries have failed.* 迄今为止, 所有试图恢复两国正常关系的努力都失败了。| **restore sth to sth** *The government promises to restore the economy to full strength.* 政府承诺使经济完全恢复。

2 restore hope/confidence/calm etc to make a person or group feel hopeful, confident, calm etc again 恢复希望/信心/镇静等: *a victory that restored the team's confidence* 使球队恢复了信心的一场胜利

3 restore order to make people stop fighting and breaking the law 恢复秩序: *Police were called in to restore order.* 警察被召来恢复秩序。

4 ▶REPAIR 修理◀ to repair an old building, piece of furniture, or painting etc so that it is in its original condition 修复: *The church was carefully restored after the war.* 战后这座教堂得到精心修复。

5 ▶GIVE STH BACK 归还某物◀ *formal* to give back to someone something that was lost or taken from them【正式】归还: **restore sth to sb** *In 1972 a treaty restored Okinawa to Japan.* 1972年, 冲绳根据一份条约归还给日本。

6 restore sb's sight/hearing etc to make someone able to see, hear etc again 恢复某人的视力/听力等: *an operation to restore his hearing* 使他恢复听力的手术

7 ▶BRING BACK A LAW 恢复法律◀ to bring back a law, tax, right etc 恢复, 重新采用〔法律、税收、权利等〕: *a campaign to restore the death penalty* 鼓吹恢复死刑的运动

8 restore sb to power/the throne *formal* to give back power to a king, queen, or president【正式】使某人重新掌权/恢复王位

re·stored /rɪˈstord; rɪˈstɔːd/ *adj* [not before noun 不用于名词前] feeling better and healthier 精神得到恢复的: *restored by the mountain freshness* 呼吸山间的清新空气, 令人心旷神怡

re·strain /rɪˈstren; rɪˈstreɪn/ *v* [T] **1** to prevent someone from doing something harmful or stupid 阻止, 抑制〔某人做有害或愚蠢的事〕: **restrain sb from doing sth** *I had to restrain her from running out into the street after him.* 我不得不阻止她跑到街上去追他。| **restrain yourself (from)** *She could hardly restrain herself from hitting Walt.* 她几乎克制不住自己, 要去揍沃尔特。**2** to control or limit something that is tending to increase 控制, 限制〔趋于增长的东西〕: *Price rises restrain consumer spending.* 价格上涨限制了消费开支。

re·strained /rɪˈstrend; rɪˈsteɪnd/ *adj* **1** behaviour that is restrained is calm and controlled and does not show your real feelings〔行为〕克制的, 有节制的: *a restrained and cool-headed response to their unfair criticisms* 对他们那些不公正的批评所作的克制而又冷静的反应 **2** not too brightly coloured or decorated〔颜色或装饰〕淡雅的, 朴素的: *The decor was subtle and restrained.* 布置精巧而素雅。

re·straint /rɪˈstrent; rɪˈstreɪnt/ *n* **1** [U] the ability not to do something that you very much want to do, because you know it is more sensible not to do it 克制, 抑制〔指理智地抑制做某事的冲动〕: *The police were commended for their restraint in handling the disturbances.* 警方因为在处理骚乱事件中表现出的克制而受到嘉奖。| **show/exercise restraint** *I think he showed great restraint, considering how she treated him.* 考虑到她对待他的态度, 我认为他表现出极大的克制。**2** [C usually plural 一般用复数, U] a rule or principle that limits people's activity or behaviour 限制, 制约, 约束: [+on] *restraints on public spending* 对公共开支的限制 | *moral restraints on sexual behaviour* 对性行为的道德约束 | **impose restraints** (=make rules to control something) 加以限制 *The government imposed restraints on the export of military hardware.* 政府对军事装备出口实施限制。| **wage restraint** (=agreement not to demand or pay large wage increases) 工资增长限制 **3** [U] *formal* physical force used to stop someone from moving freely, especially because they are likely to be violent【正式】管制, 管束: *the proper use of physical restraint to control dangerous prisoners* 适当使用人身管制以控制危险囚犯 **4** [C] a SEAT BELT〔汽车座椅上的〕安全带

3 3 **re·strict** /rɪˈstrɪkt; rɪˈstrɪkt/ *v* [T]

1 ▶SIZE/AMOUNT/RANGE 体积/数量/范围◀ to limit or control the size, amount, or range of something 限制; 控制: *The new law restricts the sale of hand guns.* 新法规限制了手枪的销售。| **restrict sth to** *The speaker restricted her remarks to* (=only talked about) *the health care proposals.* 发言者只谈了有关医疗保健的一些建议。

2 ▶MOVEMENT/ACTIVITY 运动/活动◀ to limit someone's actions or movements 约束, 限制〔行动、活动〕: *The cramped living conditions severely restricted the children's opportunities for play.* 拥挤的居住条件严重限制了孩子游戏的机会。

3 restrict yourself to to allow yourself to have only a particular amount of something, or do only a particular type of activity 限制自己…: *I'm restricting myself to two cigarettes a day.* 我限制自己每天只抽两支烟。| *Journalists should restrict themselves to reporting the facts.* 记者应该只报道事实真相。

re·strict·ed /rɪˈstrɪktɪd; rɪˈstrɪktǝd/ *adj* **1** small or limited in size, area, or amount 狭小的; 有限的: *It's difficult trying to work in such a restricted space.* 要在这么狭窄的空间干活很困难。**2** limited or controlled, especially by laws or rules〔尤指在法律或规则上〕受限制的, 受约束的: *Press freedom is severely restricted.* 新闻自由受到严重限制。| [+to] *The sale of alcohol is restricted to* (=can only be sold to) *people over the age of 18.* 酒类仅限出售给18岁以上的人。| *restricted access for large vehicles* 大型车辆禁止入内 **3** limited in what you can do, or in your movements〔活动、行动〕受限制的: *A stroke left her with restricted movement in her right leg.* 中风使她的右腿行动不便。| **restricted life** (=limited in your experiences) 生活范围狭窄 *Many women lead very restricted lives, staying at home and bringing up children.* 许多妇女待在家里抚养子女, 生活圈子很小。**4** a restricted area or document can only be seen or used by a particular group of people because it is secret or dangerous〔地区或文件〕限某一类人使用[传阅]的: *No Entry – restricted area for army personnel only.* 非军事人员不得入内。**5 be restricted to** to only affect a limited area, group etc 仅限于…: *The damage is restricted to the left side of the brain.* 损伤仅限于大脑左侧。

2 3 **re·stric·tion** /rɪˈstrɪkʃən; rɪˈstrɪkʃən/ *n* **1** [C often plural 常用复数] a rule or system that limits or controls what you can do or what is allowed to happen 限制, 约束: [+on] *restrictions on immigration from Mexico into the US* 对从墨西哥移居美国实施的限制 | **impose/place restrictions on sth** *The 1986 law imposed new financial restrictions on private companies.* 1986年的法律对私营公司规定了新的财务限制。| **raise/lift a restriction** (=remove a restriction) 解除限制 *Speed restrictions were lifted once the roadworks were completed.* 道路施工一竣工便取消了(行车)速度限制。**2** [U] the act of restricting the size, amount, or range of something〔对大小、数量或范围的〕限制

re·stric·tive /rɪˈstrɪktɪv; rɪˈstrɪktɪv/ *adj* tending to restrict your activity too much 限制(性)的, 约束(性)的: *restrictive trade legislation* 限制性贸易立法 | *Rimbaud found life in Charleville too restrictive.* 兰波认为在沙勒维尔生活受到太多限制。

restrictive clause /·ˌ··ˈ·/ also 又作 **restrictive rel·a·tive clause** /·ˌ··ˌ···ˈ·/ *n* [C] *technical* a part of a sentence that says which person or thing is meant. For example in 'the man who came to dinner', the phrase 'who came to dinner' is a restrictive clause.【术语】限定性从句〔又称限制性关系从句。例如在the man who came to dinner中, who came to dinner是个限定性从句〕

restrictive prac·ti·ces /·ˌ··ˈ···/ *n* [plural] **1** unreasonable limits that one TRADE UNION puts on the kind of work that members of other trade unions are allowed to do〔工会实行的〕排他限制 **2** an unfair trade agreement between companies that limits the amount of competition there is〔公司之间不公平的〕限制竞争协议

rest room /ˈ··/ *n* [C] *AmE* a room with a toilet, in a place such as a restaurant or cinema【美】〔餐馆、电影院等中的〕洗手间

re·struc·ture /ˌriˋstrʌktʃɚ; ˌriːˈstrʌktʃə/ *v* [T] to change the way in which something such as a government, business, or system is organized 重新组织，调整，改组: *The school curriculum has been restructured to include more science.* 学校课程进行了调整，加进更多自然科学的内容。

re·sult[1] /rɪˋzʌlt; rɪˈzʌlt/ *n*

1 ▶HAPPENING BECAUSE OF STH 因为某事而发生◀ [C,U] something that happens or exists because of something that happened before 结果，后果: [+of] *One result of the cold weather has been a sharp increase in our heating bill.* 寒冷天气的结果之一是我们的暖气费用大大增加了。| *Ken's illness is the result of an accident at work.* 肯的病是一次工伤事故造成的。| **as a result (of)** (=because of something that has happened) 作为…的结果；由于 *As a result of the pilots' strike, all flights have had to be cancelled.* 由于飞行员罢工，所有航班都取消了。| **with the result that** *Sara wasn't at school last week, with the result that she missed an important test.* 萨拉上星期没上学，结果错过了一次重要考试。| **be a direct result (of)** (=caused by one thing only) 是…的直接结果 *High unemployment is a direct result of the recession.* 高失业率是经济衰退的直接后果。| **end/final/net result** (=the result at the end of a long process) 最终结果 *The net result of all these changes is that people will pay more tax.* 所有这些变化的最后结果是人们将交更多的税。—see 见 THUS (USAGE)

2 ▶SPORTS/ELECTIONS 体育运动/选举◀ [C] the final number of points, votes etc at the end of a competition, game, or election〔比赛〕成绩，比分；〔选举的〕结果: *The election results were announced at midnight.* 选举结果已于午夜宣布。| *the football results* 足球比赛的结果

3 ▶SCIENTIFIC TESTS 科学测试◀ [C] the answers that are produced by a scientific study or test〔科学研究、测试的〕结果: *Results show that men are twice as likely to suffer from stress as women.* 结果显示男性受压力影响的可能性比女性高出一倍。| *We should have the result of your blood test tomorrow.* 明天我们该有你验血的结果了。

4 ▶EXAMINATIONS 考试◀ [C] *BrE* the mark you get in an examination【英】成绩: *When do we get our exam results?* 我们什么时候知道考试成绩？

5 ▶SUCCESS 成功◀ results [plural] things that happen successfully because of your efforts 成效: **get results** (=succeed in getting what you want) 取得成效 *If the program doesn't get results, it should be dropped.* 如果这计划不见成效就应该放弃。

6 ▶BUSINESS 生意◀ results [plural] a company's results are the accounts that show how successful it has been over a period of time, usually a year〔年度〕业绩

7 get a result *BrE informal* to win a victory in a sports match【英，非正式】〔在体育比赛中〕赢，取胜: *We didn't play well but at least we got a result.* 我们打得不好，但至少我们赢了。

result[2] *v* [I] to happen or exist as a result of something〔因…〕产生，发生；〔由…而〕造成: [+from] *problems resulting from past errors* 由于以往的过失而造成的问题

result in sth *phr v* [T not in passive 不用被动态] to make something happen; cause 导致，造成: *an accident that resulted in the death of two passengers* 导致两名乘客死亡的事故

re·sul·tant /rɪˋzʌltənt; rɪˈzʌltənt/ *adj* [only before noun 仅用于名词前] *formal* happening or existing as a result of something【正式】作为…的后果而发生[存在]的: *a growing economy and its resultant benefits* 增长中的经济以及由此带来的效益

re·sume[1] /rɪˋzum; rɪˈzjuːm/ *v* **1** [I,T] *formal* to start doing something again after a pause or interruption【正式】〔中断之后〕继续: *They were silent, then Billy resumed his story.* 他们都静下来，然后比利继续讲故事。| *Let us resume where we left off.* 让我们从中断的地方继续下去。**2** if an activity or process resumes, it starts again after a pause〔活动或过程〕重新开始: *Work resumed on the following day.* 工作在第二天重新开始。**3 resume your seat/place/position** *formal* to go back to the seat, place, or position where you were before【正式】回到座位/原地/原职位: *Everyone resumed their seats for the second half of the performance.* 大家都回到座位上看下半场演出。

re·su·me[2], **résumé** /ˌrɛzuˋme; ˈrezjʊmeɪ/ *n* [C] **1** [+of] a short account of something such as an article or speech, that gives the main points but not details〔文章或讲话等的〕梗概，摘要 **2** *AmE* a short written account of your education and your previous jobs that you send to an employer when you are looking for a new job【美】个人简历; cv *BrE*【英】

re·sump·tion /rɪˋzʌmpʃən; rɪˈzʌmpʃən/ *n* [singular,U] *formal* the act of starting an activity again after a pause【正式】重新开始: [+of] *the resumption of underground nuclear testing* 地下核试验的恢复

re·sur·face /riˋsɝfɪs; ˌriːˈsɜːfɪ̣s/ *v* **1** [I] to appear again 重新出现: *Old rivalries began to resurface.* 昔日的竞争又重新开始了。**2** [I] to come back up to the surface of the water 重新露出水面 **3** [T] to put a new surface on a road 给…重铺路面

re·sur·gence /rɪˋsɝdʒəns; rɪˈsɜːdʒəns/ *n* [singular,U] the appearance again and growth of a belief or activity, especially one that is harmful or undesirable〔尤指有害、不良的信仰或活动的〕复苏，再起: [+of] *a resurgence of racial violence* 种族暴力的再起 | [+in] *a resurgence in the popularity of 60s music* 20世纪60年代音乐的再次流行 —**resurgent** *adj*

res·ur·rect /ˌrɛzəˋrɛkt; ˌrezəˈrekt/ *v* [T] to start an old practice, custom, belief etc again after it has not existed for a long time 使〔久已中断的传统、消亡的信仰等〕复活，恢复: *Old theories about the origin of the universe have been resurrected.* 昔日关于宇宙起源的种种理论复活了。

res·ur·rec·tion /ˌrɛzəˋrɛkʃən; ˌrezəˈrekʃən/ *n* [U] **1** also 又作 **Resurrection** the return of Jesus Christ to life after his death after being crucified (CRUCIFY), which is one of the main beliefs of the Christian religion 耶稣复活 **2** also 又作 **Resurrection** the return of all dead people to life at the end of the world〔世界末日时所有死者的〕复活 **3** a situation in which an idea, custom, feeling etc is brought back into existence〔思想、传统、感觉等的〕复活，复兴；恢复: *a resurrection of old jealousies* 昔日嫉妒心的再次出现

re·sus·ci·tate /rɪˋsʌsəˌtet; rɪˈsʌsɪ̣teɪt/ *v* [T] to make someone breathe again or become conscious after they have almost died 使恢复呼吸，使苏醒 —**resuscitation** /rɪˌsʌsəˋteʃən; rɪˌsʌsɪ̣ˈteɪʃən/ *n* [U] —see also 另见 CPR

re·tail[1] /ˋritel; ˈriːteɪl/ *n* [U] the sale of goods in shops to customers, for their own use and not for selling to anyone else 零售，零卖: *goods for retail only* 仅供零售的商品 | **retail trade/business etc** *workers in the retail trade* 零售业工人 | **retail outlet** (=a shop) 零售店 —compare 比较 WHOLESALE[1]

retail[2] /ˋritel; rɪˈteɪl/ *v* **1** [I,T] *technical* to sell goods in a shop【术语】零售，零卖: *The product is retailed through a big chain of furniture stores.* 该产品通过一家大型连锁家具商店零售。**2 retail at $5/£20 etc** *technical* to be sold at a particular price in shops【术语】以5美元/20英镑等的价格零售: *This wine retails at £6.95 a bottle.* 这种酒的零售价格是每瓶6.95英镑。**3** [T] *formal* to tell people about something, especially about other people's private affairs【正式】散布〔尤指关于别人私事的流言飞语〕: *Who is responsible for retailing these rumours?* 是谁散布这些流言飞语？

retail[3] *adv* from a shop 从商店里: *We bought it retail.* 我们从商店里买来的。

re·tail·er /ˋritelɚ; ˈriːteɪlə/ *n* [C] someone who sells things in a shop; SHOPKEEPER 零售商

re·tail·ing /ˋritelɪŋ; ˈriːteɪlɪŋ/ *n* [U] the business of selling goods to the public in shops 零售业: *People who work in retailing are often badly paid.* 从事零售业的人收入往往很低。| *retailing organizations* 零售业组织

retail park /ˈ‥ ˌ/ *n* [C] *BrE* a special area outside a town with many large shops and space for cars to park【英】购物中心〔在镇以外的地区，有很多大型商店和停车位〕

retail price in·dex /ˌ‥ ˈ‥ ˌ‥/ abbreviation 缩写为 **RPI** *n* [singular] an official system of numbers that shows changes in the cost of living in Britain each month, based on the price of goods and services bought by an average person 零售价格指数 —see also 另见 CONSUMER PRICE INDEX

re·tain /rɪˋten; rɪˈteɪn/ *v* [T] *formal*【正式】**1** to keep something or continue to have something 保留，保有: *A copy of the invoice should be retained by the Accounts Department.* 发票的副本须由财务部保留。| *It's important that the elderly should retain a sense of dignity.* 老年人保持尊严感很重要。| *a heavy soil that retains water* 能保持水分的黏质土 —see also 另见 RETENTION (1) **2** to keep facts in your memory 记住 **3** to make sure that you will have someone's help or services, by paying for them before you actually have them 付订金聘请: *They decided to retain their lawyer at their own expense.* 他们决定自己花钱付订金聘请律师。| **retaining fee** (=money paid to keep someone working for you) 聘金

re·tain·er /rɪˋtenɚ; rɪˈteɪnə/ *n* [C] **1** an amount of money paid to someone, especially a lawyer, for work that they are going to do〔尤指付给律师的〕律师费，聘用订金 **2** a reduced amount of rent that you pay for a room, flat etc when you are not there, so that it will still be available when you return〔外出期间为

保留房间、公寓等支付的〕订金 **3** *old use* a servant, especially one who has always worked for a particular person or family【旧】〔服务多年的〕仆人: *an old and trusted family retainer* 可靠的老家仆

re·take¹ /riˋtek; ˌriːˈteɪk/ *v* [T] **1** to get control of an area again in a war〔在战争中〕收复, 夺回〔失地〕: *Rebels have retaken the city.* 叛军夺回了该城市。**2** to take an examination again because you have previously failed it〔由于不及格〕重新参加〔考试〕**3** to film or photograph something again 重拍, 重摄

re·take² /ˋriˌtek; ˈriːteɪk/ *n* [C] **1** an act of filming or photographing something again 重拍, 重摄: *They had to do several retakes before the director was satisfied.* 他们重拍了几次导演才满意。**2** *BrE* an examination or test that you take again because you failed it【英】补考

re·tal·i·ate /rɪˋtælɪˌet; rɪˈtælieɪt/ *v* [I] to do something bad to someone because they have done something bad to you 报复, 反击: **retaliate by doing sth** *When the police started to arrest people, some of the demonstrators retaliated by throwing stones.* 当警察开始逮捕人时, 一些示威者投掷石块以示报复。

re·tal·i·a·tion /rɪˌtælɪˋeʃən; rɪˌtæliˈeɪʃən/ *n* [U] action against someone who has done something bad to you 报复, 反击: *the threat of retaliation* 要报复的威胁 | **in retaliation for** *Union leaders are threatening strike action in retaliation for the recent pay cuts.* 工会领袖威胁以罢工行动来报复最近的减薪。

re·tal·i·a·to·ry /rɪˋtælɪəˌtorɪ; rɪˈtæliətəri/ *adj formal* done against someone because they have harmed you【正式】报复(性)的: *retaliatory raids* 报复性袭击

re·tard¹ /rɪˋtɑrd; rɪˈtɑːd/ *v* [T] *formal* to delay the development of something, or to make something happen more slowly than expected【正式】减缓, 阻碍: *Cold weather retards the growth of many plants.* 寒冷的天气使许多植物生长放缓。—**retardation** /ˌritɑrˋdeʃən; ˌriːtɑːˈdeɪʃən/ *n* [U]

re·tard² /ˋritɑrd; ˈriːtɑːd/ *n* [C] *slang* an offensive word meaning a stupid person【俚】笨蛋〔冒犯用语〕

re·tard·ed /rɪˋtɑrdɪd; rɪˈtɑːdɪ̣d/ *adj* less intelligent than other people because of slower mental development 智力发育迟缓的, 弱智的: *a special programme for retarded children* 为弱智儿童制定的特殊计划 | *mentally retarded* 智力迟钝的

retch /rɛtʃ; retʃ/ *v* [I] to try to VOMIT, or feel as if you are going to vomit when you do not 恶心, 干呕: *Like someone drowning, she fought for air, gasping and retching.* 就像溺水的人一样, 她拼命呼吸, 大口喘气和干呕。

retd the written abbreviation for 缩写= RETIRED; used after the name of a former military officer 退伍的〔用于退役军官的姓名之后〕

re·tell /riˋtɛl; ˌriːˈtel/ *v* [T] *past tense and past participle* **retold** /-ˋtold; -ˈtəʊld/ to tell a story again, often in a different way or in a different language〔以不同的方式或语言〕重讲, 复述

re·ten·tion /rɪˋtɛnʃən; rɪˈtenʃən/ *n* [U] **1** *formal* the act of keeping something【正式】保持, 保留: **[+of]** *Committee members voted for the retention of the existing voting system.* 委员会成员投票赞成保留现有的投票制度。**2** *technical* the ability or tendency of something to hold liquid, heat etc within itself【术语】〔液体〕潴留; 〔热〕滞留 **3** the ability to keep something in your memory 记忆力: *powers of retention* 记忆力

re·ten·tive /rɪˋtɛntɪv; rɪˈtentɪv/ *adj* a retentive memory or mind is able to hold facts and remember them 记忆力强的 —**retentively** *adv* —**retentiveness** *n* [U]

re·think /riˋθɪŋk; ˌriːˈθɪŋk/ *v past tense and past participle* **rethought** /-ˋθɔt; -ˈθɔːt/ [I,T] to think about a plan or idea again in order to decide if any changes should be made 再思考, 重新考虑: *an opportunity to rethink our campaign strategy* 重新思考我们的竞选战略的机会 —**rethink** /ˋriˌθɪŋk; ˈriːθɪŋk/ *n* [singular]

ret·i·cent /ˋrɛtəsn̩t; ˈretɪ̣sənt/ *adj* unwilling to talk about what you feel or what you know 沉默的, 不愿意谈的: *She's naturally reticent, even with some of her closest friends.* 她素来寡言少语, 即使和一些最亲密的朋友在一起也是一样。| **[+about]** *Mr Jamieson was very reticent about the reasons for his decision.* 贾米森先生对他所作决定的原因不肯多谈。—**reticence** *n* [U] —**reticently** *adv*

re·tic·u·la·ted /rɪˋtɪkjəˌletɪd; rɪˈtɪkjʊ̈leɪtɪ̣d/ *adj technical* forming or covered with a pattern of squares and lines that looks like a net【术语】网状的 —**reticulation** /rɪˌtɪkjəˋleʃən; rɪˌtɪkjʊ̈ˈleɪʃən/ *n* [C,U]

ret·i·na /ˋrɛtn̩ə; ˈretɪ̣nə/ *n* [C] the area at the back of your eye that receives light and sends an image of what you see to your brain 视网膜 —see picture at 参见 EYE¹ 图

ret·i·nue /ˋrɛtn̩ju; ˈretɪnjuː/ *n* [C] a group of helpers or supporters who are travelling with an important person〔重要人物的〕随从, 随员: *visiting Congressmen and all their retinue* 来访的国会议员及他们的全部随员

re·tire /rɪˋtaɪr; rɪˈtaɪə/ *v* 

1 ►FROM WORK 离开工作◄ a) [I] to stop work at the end of your working life 退休: *He retired when he was 65.* 他 65 岁时退休了。| **[+from]** *After retiring from the army it took William a long time to adjust to civilian life.* 从军队退役后, 威廉花了很长时间才适应平民的生活。| **retire early** (=retire before the usual age) 提前退休 **b)** [T usually passive 一般用被动态] to dismiss someone and pay them a PENSION, especially because of illness 使退职〔尤指因病〕: *The manager was retired on half salary.* 经理半薪退职了。

2 ►TO A QUIET PLACE 到僻静处◄ [I] *formal* to go away to a quiet place【正式】去安静的地方: *He often retires to his country home to work on his book.* 他经常躲到乡间家中写书。| *The jury has retired to consider its verdict.* 陪审团退庭去考虑其裁决。

3 ►FROM A GAME 从比赛中◄ [I] to stop competing in a game or race because you are losing or injured〔因失利或受伤〕退出比赛: *He was forced to retire from the competition due to a leg injury.* 因为腿部受伤, 他不得不退出比赛。

4 ►TO BED 上床◄ [I] *literary* to go to bed【文】就寝

5 ►ARMY 部队◄ [I] to move back from a battle after being defeated 撤退: *The army retired to regroup for a fresh attack.* 军队撤下来进行整编, 准备发起新的攻击。—compare 比较 RETREAT¹ (2)

re·tired /rɪˋtaɪrd; rɪˈtaɪəd/ *adj* having stopped working, usually because of your age 退休的: *a retired teacher* 退休教师 | *Both my parents are retired now.* 我父母现在都已退休。

re·tir·ee /rɪˌtaɪˋri; rɪˌtaɪəˈriː/ *n* [C] *AmE* someone who has stopped working, usually because of their age【美】退休者

re·tire·ment /rɪˋtaɪrmənt; rɪˈtaɪəmənt/ *n* **1** [C,U] the act of retiring from your job, or the time when you do this 退休: *June's colleagues arranged a surprise party for her retirement.* 琼的同事为她的退休安排了一个令她惊喜的聚会。| **retirement present/party etc** (=a present, party etc for someone who is retiring) 退休礼物/聚会等 | **on retirement** (=from the time when you retire) 从退休起 *On retirement you will receive a small pension.* 退休后你将得到小额的退休金。| **take early retirement** (=retire at an earlier age than usual) 提前退休 | **retirement age** (=the age when people usually stop working) 退休年龄 **2** [singular,U] the period after you have retired 退休期间: *a long and happy retirement* 漫长而幸福的退休生活 | *a retirement pension* 退休金

retirement plan /ˈ· ˌ·· ˌ·/ *n* [C] *AmE* a system for saving money for your retirement, especially if you will not receive money from your employer【美】退休金计划〔尤指雇主不付养老金, 而是本人为养老金储蓄的制度〕—compare 比较 PENSION PLAN

re·tir·ing /rɪˋtaɪrɪŋ; rɪˈtaɪərɪŋ/ *adj* **1** not wanting to be with other people, especially people you do not know; SHY¹ (1) 离群的; 害羞的: *As a child, Elizabeth was very retiring.* 小时候的伊丽莎白非常怯生。**2 the retiring president/manager/director etc** a president etc who is soon going to leave their job 即将卸任的总裁/经理/董事等

re·tool /riˋtul; ˌriːˈtuːl/ *v* **1** [T] *AmE informal* to organize something in a new way【美, 非正式】重新组织; 改组: *The College Board has retooled the admission exams.* 大学委员会重新组织了入学考试。**2** [I,T] to change or replace the machines or tools in a factory〔工厂〕更换机器[工具]

re·tort¹ /rɪˋtɔrt; rɪˈtɔːt/ *v* [T] to reply quickly, in an angry or humorous way〔立即愤怒或幽默地〕反驳, 回嘴: *"It's all your fault!" he retorted.* "那都是你的过错!"他反驳说。

retort² *n* [C] **1** a short and angry or humorous reply〔简短的, 愤怒或幽默的〕反驳, 回嘴: *He was about to make a jovial retort, but stopped.* 他刚想友善地反驳, 但又止住了。**2** a bottle with a long narrow bent neck, used for heating chemicals 曲颈甑, 蒸馏甑, 蒸馏器

re·touch /riˋtʌtʃ; ˌriːˈtʌtʃ/ *v* [T] to improve a picture or photograph by painting over marks or making other small changes 修描, 润色〔图画、照片〕: *postcards that have been retouched to cover the grey skies* 为遮盖灰色天空而修描过的明信片

re·trace /rɪˋtres; rɪˈtreɪs/ *v* [T] **1** to go back the way you have come 顺原路返回, 折返: **retrace your steps** *After about fifty paces, he turned around and began to retrace his steps.* 走了大约 50 步之后, 他转过身开始顺着原路返回。**2** to repeat exactly the same journey that someone else has made 重走〔别人走过的路〕: *We shall be retracing the route taken by Marco Polo.* 我们将重走马可波罗走过的路。**3** to find out about a series of past

actions or events 追查: *Detectives are hoping to retrace her movements.* 侦探们希望追查她的行踪。

re·tract /rɪˋtrækt; rɪˈtrækt/ *v* **1** [T] to make an official statement saying that something which you said previously is not true; WITHDRAW (3) 正式收回〔声明〕: *He confessed to the murder but later retracted his statement.* 他承认犯有谋杀罪但后来又翻供了。**2** [I,T] if part of a machine or an animal's body retracts or is retracted, it moves back into the main part (使)缩回, (使)缩入: *Cats can retract their claws.* 猫能把爪子缩进去。

re·tract·a·ble /rɪˋtræktəbl; rɪˈtræktəbəl/ *adj* **1** a retractable part of something can be pulled back into the main part 可收起的, 可缩回的: *a knife with a retractable blade* 刀片可收起的刀 **2** having a retractable part 有可缩回[收进]部分的: *a retractable ball-point pen* 可缩回式圆珠笔

re·trac·tion /rɪˋtrækʃən; rɪˈtrækʃən/ *n* **1** [C] an official statement saying that something which you said previously is not true 正式收回〔以前所说的不真实的话〕: *The newspaper was forced to publish a retraction of all its allegations.* 这家报纸被迫发表声明收回它的所有指控。**2** [U] the act of retracting something 收回, 撤回

re·train /riˋtren; ˌriːˈtreɪn/ *v* [I,T] to learn or to teach someone the skills that are needed to do a different job (对…)再训练; 接受再培训: *Staff are being retrained to use the new machinery.* 工作人员正在接受使用新机器的再培训。—**retraining** *n* [U]: *a retraining programme for unemployed miners* 对失业矿工的再培训计划

re·tread¹ /ˋriˌtrɛd; ˈriːtred/ *n* [C] **1** a retreaded tyre 翻新的轮胎 **2** *AmE informal* something that is made or done again, with a few changes added【美, 非正式】〔只作少量变化的〕翻版: *retreads of old TV shows* 新瓶旧酒的电视节目 **3** *AmE informal* someone who has been trained to do work which is different from what they did before【美, 非正式】接受过再培训的人员

re·tread² /riˋtrɛd; ˌriːˈtred/ *v* [T] to put a new rubber surface on an old tyre 给〔旧轮胎〕装新胎面, 翻新〔轮胎〕

re·treat¹ /rɪˋtrit; rɪˈtriːt/ *v* [I]

1 ►**MOVE BACK** 后退◄ **a)** to walk back and away from someone or something because you are afraid or embarrassed〔因恐惧或尴尬而〕后退, 退却: *He saw her and retreated, too shy to speak to her.* 他看见她便往后退, 不好意思跟她讲话。| [+to/from etc] *Perry lit the fuse and retreated to a safe distance.* 佩里点燃导火线, 然后退至安全距离。**b)** if an area of water, snow or land retreats, it gradually gets smaller〔水、雪、土地〕范围缩小: *The flood waters are slowly retreating.* 洪水正在慢慢退却。

2 ►**OF AN ARMY** 军队◄ to move away from the enemy after being defeated in battle 撤退: *The rebels retreated, pursued by government troops.* 叛军撤退了, 政府军在后面追赶。

3 ►**CHANGE YOUR MIND** 改变主意◄ to change your mind about a promise you have publicly made or about a principle you have stated, because the situation has become too difficult〔承诺、立场等〕撤回: [+from] *Current economic problems have forced the government to retreat from its pledge to cut taxes.* 目前的经济问题迫使政府撤回对削减税收的承诺。

4 ►**TO A QUIET PLACE** 到僻静处◄ to go away to a place that is quiet or safe 去宁静、安全的地方: [+from/into/to] *After the noise of the city he was glad to retreat to his hotel room.* 经历了城市的喧嚣之后, 他很高兴躲进自己的旅店房间。

5 retreat into yourself/your thoughts etc to ignore what is happening around you and give all your attention to your private thoughts 陷入沉思

retreat² *n*

1 ►**MOVEMENT BACK** 后退◄ [singular,U] a movement back and away from someone or something, because you are afraid, embarrassed etc 后退, 退却, 躲避: **beat a retreat** (=walk away quickly) 匆匆离开 *Jim beat a hasty retreat when he saw his wife's mother at the door.* 吉姆看到岳母在门口便赶紧跑掉。

2 ►**CHANGE OF INTENTION** 改变意图◄ [singular,U] an act of changing your mind about a promise you publicly made or a principle you stated, because the situation has become too difficult〔承诺的〕撤回;〔立场的〕改变, 放弃: *a retreat from hard-line policies* 放弃强硬政策

3 ►**OF AN ARMY** 军队◄ [C,U] a movement away from the enemy after a defeat in battle 撤退: *Napoleon's retreat from Moscow* 拿破仑从莫斯科的撤退 —opposite 反义词 ADVANCE¹ (3) | **be in full retreat** (=be retreating fast and continuously) 全线溃退 | **sound the retreat** (=give a loud signal for retreat) 吹号收兵, 鸣金收兵

4 ►**PLACE** 地方◄ [C] a place you can go to that is quiet or safe 静养所, 静居所: *von Mulne's retreat in the mountains* 冯·慕尼在山里的静居所

5 ►**THOUGHT AND PRAYER** 冥想与祈祷◄ [C,U] a period of time that you spend praying or studying religion in a quiet place〔宗教的〕静修(期): *They go on retreat twice a year.* 他们每年静修两次。

re·trench /rɪˋtrɛntʃ; rɪˈtrentʃ/ *v* [I] if a government or organization retrenches, it spends less money〔开支〕紧缩 —**retrenchment** *n* [C,U]: *a government policy of retrenchment* 政府的紧缩政策

re·tri·al /riˋtraɪəl; ˌriːˈtraɪəl/ *n* [C] a process of judging a law case in court again 再审, 复审: *The jury was dismissed and the judge ordered a retrial.* 陪审团被解散, 法官下令对案件复审。

ret·ri·bu·tion /ˌrɛtrəˋbjuʃən; ˌretrɪˈbjuːʃən/ *n* [singular, U] severe punishment that is deserved 应得的惩罚: [+for] *retribution for terrorist attacks* 恐怖袭击应得的严惩 | **divine retribution** (=punishment from God) 上帝的惩罚 | **mete out retribution** (=give retribution) 予以严惩 —**retributive** /rɪˋtrɪbjətɪv; rɪˈtrɪbjətɪv/ *adj*: *retributive justice* 报应

re·triev·al /rɪˋtrivl; rɪˈtriːvəl/ *n* [U] **1** *technical* the process of getting back information from a computer system【术语】〔电脑系统信息的〕检索: *information retrieval* 信息检索 | *a retrieval system* 检索系统 **2** [U] the act of getting back something you have lost or left somewhere 找回, 取回 **3 be beyond/past retrieval** if a situation is beyond retrieval, it has become so bad that it cannot be made right again 无可挽回, 无可补救

re·trieve /rɪˋtriv; rɪˈtriːv/ *v* **1** [T] *formal* to find something and bring it back【正式】找回; 收回, 取回: **retrieve sth from** *I went back to the locker room to retrieve my jacket.* 我回更衣室取回我的上衣。| *The wreckage of the crashed plane was retrieved from the ocean.* 从海中打捞到了失事飞机的残骸。**2 retrieve your losses** get back money equal to what you lost 抵偿某人损失 **3** [T] *technical* to get back information that has been stored in the memory of a computer【术语】检索〔储存于电脑的信息〕**4 retrieve a situation** to make a situation satisfactory again after there has been a serious mistake or problem 挽回局面: *She tried to apologise but it was already too late to retrieve the situation.* 她企图道歉, 想挽回局面, 但已经太迟。**5** [I,T] if a dog retrieves, it finds and brings back birds and small animals its owner has shot〔狗〕衔回(主人击中的猎物) —**retrievable** *adj*

re·triev·er /rɪˋtrivə; rɪˈtriːvə/ *n* [C] a type of dog that can be trained to retrieve birds that its owner has shot 拾猎〔经训练会衔回猎物的猎犬〕

retro- /rɛtro; retrəʊ/ *prefix* **1** back towards the past 追溯的: *retroactive legislation* (=which has an effect on things already done) 有追溯效力的立法 | *in retrospect* (=looking back at what has happened) 回顾, 回想 **2** back towards an earlier and worse state 倒退的: *a retrograde step* 倒退 | *to retrogress* 倒退, 退化 **3** backwards 向后: *a retrorocket* (=that fires backwards, opposite to the direction of travel) 反向火箭, 制动火箭, 减速火箭

ret·ro¹ /ˋrɛtro; ˈretrəʊ/ *adj* deliberately using styles of fashion or design from the recent past〔时装、设计〕复旧的,〔早年式样〕重新流行的: *retro clothing stores* 怀旧时装店

retro² *n* [C] *AmE informal* a RETROSPECTIVE【美, 非正式】回顾展

ret·ro·ac·tive /ˌrɛtroˋæktɪv; ˌretrəʊˈæktɪv◂/ *adj formal* a law or decision that is retroactive is effective from a particular date in the past【正式】〔法律、决定〕有追溯效力的: *a retroactive pay increase* 应追溯补发的增薪 —see also 另见 RETROSPECTIVE¹ —**retroactively** *adv*

ret·ro·flex /ˋrɛtrəˌflɛks; ˈretrəfleks/ *adj technical* a retroflex speech sound is made with the end of your togue pointing backwards and upwards【术语】卷舌(音)的

ret·ro·grade /ˋrɛtrəˌgred; ˈretrəgreɪd/ *adj formal* involving a return to an earlier and worse situation【正式】倒退的, 后退的: **a retrograde step** *Privatisation is seen as a retrograde step.* 私有化被认为是倒退。

ret·ro·gress /ˋrɛtrəˌgrɛs; ˌretrəˈgres/ *v* [I+to] *formal* to go back to an earlier and worse state【正式】倒退, 衰退, 退化 —**retrogression** /-ˋgrɛʃən; -ˈgreʃən/ *n* [U]

ret·ro·gres·sive /ˌrɛtrəˋgrɛsɪv; ˌretrəˈgresɪv◂/ *adj formal* returning to an earlier and worse situation【正式】倒退的, 衰退的, 退化的: *a retrogressive idea* 倒退的想法 | *retrogressive change* 倒退的变化 —**retrogressively** *adv*

ret·ro·spect /ˈrɛtrəˌspɛkt; ˈretrəspekt/ *n* [U] **in retrospect** thinking back to a time in the past, especially with the advantage of knowing more now than you did then 回顾，回想：*In retrospect, it was the wrong time to set up a new company.* 回想起来，那时建立新公司的时机不对。| *My teenage years seem happier in retrospect than they were.* 我的青少年时代回忆起来似乎比实际情况更快乐。

ret·ro·spec·tion /ˌrɛtrəˋspɛkʃən; ˌretrəˈspekʃən/ *n* [U] *formal* thought about the past【正式】回顾，回想

ret·ro·spec·tive¹ /ˌrɛtrəˋspɛktɪv; ˌretrəˈspektɪv◂/ *adj* **1** a law or decision that is retrospective is effective from a particular date in the past; RETROACTIVE〔法律、决定〕有追溯效力的：*retrospective legislation* 有追溯效力的立法 **2** concerned with or thinking about the past 回顾的，追忆的：*in a retrospective mood* 沉浸在回忆之中

retrospective² *n* [C] a show of the work of an ARTIST, that includes all the kinds of work they have done〔一个艺术家各种作品的〕回顾展

re·try /riˋtraɪ; ˌriːˈtraɪ/ *v* [I] to judge a law case again in court 重审，复审

ret·si·na /rɛtˋsinə; retˈsiːnə/ *n* [U] a Greek wine that tastes of the RESIN (=juice) of certain trees 一种带树脂香味的希腊葡萄酒

S2 W1 **re·turn¹** /rɪˋtɝn; rɪˈtɜːn/ *v*

1 ▶GO BACK 返回◀ [I] to go back to a place where you were before, or come back from a place where you have just been 返回，回来：[+to] *Conor did not return to Ireland until 1937.* 直到1937年康纳才回到爱尔兰。| [+from] *When Alice returned from university, she was a changed person.* 艾丽斯从大学回来时变了个人。| **return home** *We got lost, returning home well after midnight.* 我们迷了路，午夜后很久才回到家。| **never to return** *formal*【正式】*500 airmen flew from these airfields, never to return.* 500名空军士兵从这些机场起飞，一去不复返。

2 ▶GIVE BACK 归还◀ [T] to give something back to its owner, or put something back in its place 归还，退还，放归原处：*We lent them our lawnmower and they never returned it!* 我们把割草机借给他们，他们始终没有还给我们！| **return sth to sb/sth** *I have to return some books to the library.* 我得去图书馆还一些书。

3 ▶FEELING/PROBLEM 感觉/问题◀ [I] if a feeling, problem, quality etc returns, it starts to exist again or to have an effect again 重新出现：*If the pain returns, take two of the tablets every four hours.* 如果又出现疼痛的话，每四小时服两片药。| [+to] *Stability will only return to the region when the civil war ends.* 只有结束内战，这个地区才能恢复稳定。

4 ▶START AGAIN 重新开始◀ [I] to go back to an activity, job etc that you were doing before you stopped or were interrupted; RESUME¹ (1) 重新开始，继续 [+to] *Nicholas looked up, grinned, then returned to his newspaper.* 尼古拉斯抬起头，咧嘴笑了笑，又接着看他的报纸。| **return to work** *Most mothers return to full-time work within twelve months.* 大多数母亲在12个月内重新开始全职工作。

5 ▶DISCUSS AGAIN 再讨论◀ [I] to start discussing or dealing with a subject that you have already mentioned, especially in a piece of writing〔某个主题〕再讨论，重新处理：[+to] *I shall return to the subject of inflation in chapter five.* 我将在第五章再谈通货膨胀这个题目。| *Returning to sanctions, do you think they will really be effective?* 回到制裁问题，你认为制裁真的有效吗？

6 ▶REACT 作出反应◀ [T] to do something or give something to someone because they have given the same thing to you〔以相同的东西〕回报：*I smiled at her but she refused to return my smile.* 我朝她微笑，但她拒绝还以微笑。| *You never returned my call!* 你从没给我回电话！| **return fire** (=shoot back at someone shooting at you) 还击 *The enemy returned our fire.* 敌人向我们还击。

7 ▶BALL 球类◀ [T] to send the ball back to your opponent in a game such as tennis〔网球等〕回击〔球〕

8 ▶ELECT 选举◀ [T usually passive 一般用被动态] *BrE* to elect someone to a political position, especially to represent you in parliament【英】选举，选出〔尤指议会议员〕：*Durrant was returned with an increased majority.* 达兰特当选了，得票比例比以往更大。

9 return a verdict if a jury return their VERDICT, they say whether someone is guilty or not〔陪审团〕宣布裁决

10 ▶PROFIT 利润◀ [T] if an INVESTMENT returns a particular amount of money, that is how much profit it produces 产生，获得〔利润〕：*Government bonds return around 10%.* 政府债券的利润在10%左右。

11 ▶TAX 税收◀ [T] *formal* to give a particular amount as the answer to an official question concerning tax【正式】申报

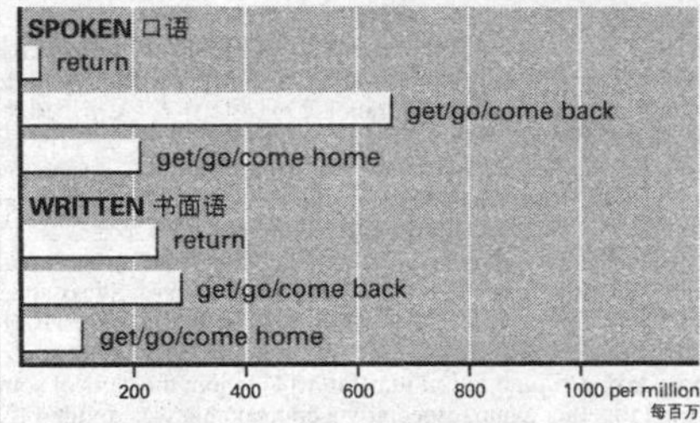

This graph shows that it is much more usual in spoken English to use **get/go/come back** or **get/go/come home** rather than **return**. **Return** is much more common in written English than in spoken English. 本图表显示，在英语口语中get/go/come back和get/go/come home要比return常用得多。return在书面语中的使用频率远远高于口语。

S2 W2 **return²** *n*

1 ▶GOING BACK 返回◀ [singular,U] the act of returning from somewhere, or your arrival back in the place where you started from 返回，回来：*We're all looking forward to your return!* 我们都盼着你回来！| **on/upon your return** (=when you return) 一回来（就…） *On his return from Germany he was promoted to Colonel.* 他从德国一回来就被晋升为上校。

2 ▶OF A FEELING/PROBLEM 感觉/问题◀ [U] the fact of something such as a problem, feeling, or activity starting to happen or exist again 再发生，重新出现：[+of] *the return of nationalism to Eastern Europe* 民族主义在东欧的重新出现

3 ▶GIVING BACK 归还◀ [U] the act of giving, putting, or sending something back 归还，送还，放回：*The family are demanding the return of the dowry.* 这家人要求退还嫁妆。| *a return of prisoners* 遣返犯人

4 ▶TO AN ACTIVITY 回到某种活动◀ [singular] returning to an activity, job, or way of life〔某种活动、工作、生活方式的〕恢复：[+to] *the idea of a return to a simpler, more natural way of life* 回归一种更简朴、更自然的生活方式的想法 | **a return to work** (=after stopping work as a protest)〔罢工后〕复工 *an end to the strike and an immediate return to work* 结束罢工，立即复工

5 ▶PROFIT 利润◀ [U] also 又作 **returns** [plural] the amount of profit that you get from something 利润（率），收益：*The company returns over the last three years have been spectacular.* 过去三年公司的利润可观。| **return on investment/capital/sales** *£10,000! That's not a bad return on our investment, is it?* 10,000英镑！我们投资的回报不错嘛，对不对？

6 in return (for) in exchange for, or as payment for something 作为…的交换，作为…的回报：*I'd like to buy you a meal in return for all your hospitality.* 我想请你吃饭来回报你的盛情好客。| *She gave us food and clothing and asked for nothing in return.* 她给了我们食物和衣服，没有要求任何回报。

7 ▶STATEMENT 声明◀ [C] a statement giving information in reply to an official question 申报（书），汇报：**tax return** *Have you sent in your tax return yet?* 你交所得税申报表了吗？

8 by return (of post) *BrE* if you reply to a letter by return, you send your reply almost immediately【英】〔接到信后〕立即回复

9 ▶TICKET 票◀ [C] *BrE* a ticket for a trip from one place to another and back again【英】往返票，来回票；ROUND TRIP *AmE*【美】—compare 比较 SINGLE² (4) —see also 另见 DAY RETURN

10 many happy returns *BrE* used to greet someone on their birthday【英】生日快乐〔生日贺词〕

11 ▶COMPUTER 电脑◀ [U] the control that you press on a computer or TYPEWRITER after you have finished the line you are writing〔电脑、打字机的〕回车键：*Key in your file name and press return.* 请键入文档名称并按回车键。—see also 另见 **the point of no return** (POINT¹ (7))

return³ *adj* **return ticket/fare** a ticket for, or the price charged for, a trip from one place to another and back again 往返票/票价；ROUND-TRIP *AmE*【美】—compare 比较 SINGLE¹ (6)

re·turn·a·ble /rɪˋtɝnəbl; rɪˈtɜːnəbəl/ *adj* **1** returnable bottles, containers etc can be given back to the shop, often to be used again〔瓶子、容器等〕可退还的 **2** *formal* something such as money or an official paper that is returnable must be given or sent back【正式】必须归还的, 必须退回的: *a returnable deposit* 必须退还的押金

re·turn·er /rɪˋtɝnɚ; rɪˈtɜːnə/ *n* [C] *BrE* someone who goes back to work after a long time away, especially a woman who left work to look after her children【英】重返工作者〔尤指因照顾子女而离职的妇女〕

returning of·fi·cer /ˈ·ˈ·· ,··ˈ/ *n* [C] the official in each town or area of Britain who arranges an election to Parliament and announces the result〔英国市镇、地区的〕议会选举监察官

Reu·ben sand·wich /ˌrubin ˋsændwɪtʃ; ˌruːbɪ̥n ˈsænwɪdʒ/ *n* [C] an American SANDWICH made with SALT BEEF, Swiss cheese and SAUERKRAUT 鲁宾三明治〔用腌牛肉、瑞士干酪和德国式泡菜制作的美式三明治〕

re·u·nify /riˋjunəˌfaɪ; riːˈjuːnɪ̥faɪ/ *v* [T] to join the parts of something together again, especially a country that was divided 使重新统一〔尤指曾分裂的国家〕—compare 比较 REUNITE —**reunification** /riˌjunəfəˋkeʃən; riːˌjuːnɪ̥fɪ̥ˈkeɪʃən/ *n* [U]: *the reunification of Germany* 德国的重新统一

Réunion /riˋjunjən; riːˈjuːnjən/ an island in the western Indian Ocean east of Madagascar, which is a dependency of France. Population: 732,570 (2001). Capital: Saint-Denis. 留尼汪岛〔马达加斯加以东印度洋西部一岛屿, 法国属地。人口: 732,570 (2001), 首府: 圣但尼〕

R

re·u·nion /riˋjunjən; riːˈjuːnjən/ *n* **1** [C] the state of being brought together again after a period of being separated 重聚: **[+with]** *Joseph's eventual reunion with his brother* 约瑟夫最终与他兄弟的重逢 **2** [C] a social meeting of people who have not met for a long time, especially people who were at school or college together〔尤指同学久别后的〕聚会, 联谊活动: *our college reunion* 我们大学同学的联谊聚会

re·u·nite /ˌrijuˋnaɪt; ˌriːjuːˈnaɪt/ *v* [I,T usually passive 一般用被动态] to come together again or bring people together again (使)再联合, (使)重新结合; (使)重聚: **be reunited with** *reunited with his family* 与他的家人团聚

re·use /riˋjuz; ˌriːˈjuːz/ *v* [T] to use something again 再使用, 再利用: *Disposable syringes are not to be reused.* 用后即弃的注射器不得再次使用。—**reusable** *adj* —**reuse** /ˌriˋjus; ˌriːˈjuːs/ *n* [U]: *the reuse of derelict urban land* 城市弃荒地的再利用

Reu·ters /ˋrɔɪtɚz; ˈrɔɪtəz/ *trademark* a British company which employs JOURNALISTS in many different countries to send it news from all over the world so that it can sell these reports to many different newspapers and radio and television stations.【商标】路透社〔英国一通讯社。该公司聘用世界各国记者为其提供国际新闻, 然后再将记者的新闻报道转售给不同的报刊、电台和电视台〕

Rev also 又作 **Revd** *BrE*【英】the written abbreviation of 缩写= Reverend; a title used before the name of a minister of the Christian church〔基督教的〕牧师〔一种称谓, 放在姓名前〕: *the Rev D Macleod* D.麦克劳德牧师

rev[1] /rɛv; rev/ *n* [C] *informal* a complete turn of a wheel or engine part, used as a unit for measuring the speed of an engine; REVOLUTION (4)【非正式】〔轮子等的〕旋转一周〔转速单位〕

rev[2] also 又作 **rev up** *v* **revved, revving** [I,T] if you rev an engine, or if an engine revs, you make it work faster 加快(发动机)转速: *the sound of a car revving up in the driveway* 汽车发动机在车道上加速的声音

re·val·ue /riˋvælju; riːˈvæljuː/ *v* [T] **1** to examine something again in order to calculate its present value 对…再估价, 对…重新估价: *I'm having all my grandmother's jewelry revalued to see if I need to insure it.* 我正请人对我祖母的全部首饰重新估价, 看是否需要买保险。**2** to increase the value of a country's money in relation to that of other countries 使〔货币〕升值: *The dollar has just been revalued.* 美元刚刚升值。—compare 比较 DEVALUE —**revaluation** /ˌrivæljuˋeʃən; riːˌvæljuːˈeɪʃən/ *n* [C,U]

re·vamp /riˋvæmp; riːˈvæmp/ *v* [T] *informal* to arrange something in a new way so that it appears to be better although often there is no real improvement【非正式】修改, 翻新: *They've revamped the whole exam system.* 他们修改了整个考试制度。—**revamp** /ˋriˌvæmp; ˈriːvæmp/ *n* [C]: *an amazing revamp of her stage personality* 她的舞台个性的惊人变化

Revd *BrE* a British spelling of REV【英】Rev 的英式拼法

3 1 **re·veal** /rɪˋvil; rɪˈviːl/ *v* [T] **1** to show something that was previously hidden 展现, 显露: *The curtains opened to reveal a darkened stage.* 大幕拉开, 露出一个漆黑的舞台。**2** to make known something that was previously secret or unknown 揭示, 揭露, 泄露: *The newspaper story revealed a cover-up of huge proportions.* 报纸的报道揭露了一件掩饰真相的事件, 此事牵连甚广。| **reveal (that)** *He revealed that he had been in prison twice before.* 他透露自己以前曾两次入狱。

re·veal·ing /rɪˋvilɪŋ; rɪˈviːlɪŋ/ *adj* **1** a remark or event that is revealing shows you something interesting or surprising about a situation or someone else's character 揭露性的, 揭示内情的: *Some of her comments during the interview were very revealing.* 她在采访中作的一些评论揭示了许多鲜为人知的情况。**2** revealing clothes allow parts of your body to be seen which are usually kept covered〔衣服〕暴露的: *a very revealing dress* 非常暴露的连衣裙

re·veil·le /ˋrɛvlɪ; rɪˈvæli/ *n* [singular,U] a special tune played as a signal to wake soldiers in the morning, or the time at which it is played 起床号; 吹起床号的时间

rev·el /ˋrɛvl; ˈrevəl/ *v* **revelled, revelling** *BrE*【英】, **reveled, reveling** *AmE*【美】[I] *old use* to spend time dancing, eating, drinking etc, especially at a party【旧】狂欢, 纵酒, 作乐 —**revel** *n* [C usually plural 一般用复数]: *their drunken revels* 他们纵酒狂欢

revel in sth *phr v* [T] to enjoy something very much, especially praise, popularity, or something that other people do not expect you to enjoy 陶醉于, 沉湎于: *He seems to be revelling in all the attention he's getting.* 他似乎因自己引起别人注意而飘飘然起来。| *revelling in their embarrassment* 对他们的尴尬幸灾乐祸

rev·e·la·tion /ˌrɛvlˋeʃən; ˌrevəˈleɪʃən/ *n* **1** [C] a surprising fact about someone or something that is made known and was previously secret 揭露/披露的(惊人)事实: *revelations in the papers about a government scandal* 报纸对一桩政府丑闻的揭露 **2** **be a revelation** *informal* to be surprisingly good, enjoyable, or useful【非正式】出乎意料的〔乐趣、用处等〕: *Alice Walker's novel was a real revelation to me.* 艾丽斯·沃克的小说使我大开眼界。**3** [U] the act of suddenly making known a surprising fact that had previously been secret 揭露, 披露〔秘密的事〕 **4** [C,U] an event, experience etc that is considered to be a message from God〔上帝的〕启示

Rev·e·la·tions /ˌrɛvlˋeʃən; ˌrevəˈleɪʃən/ the last book of the New Testament of the Bible, in which the story of the end of the world is told. It is thought to have been written by Saint John and is sometimes also called *The Book of Revelation* or *The Apocalypse*.《启示录》(《圣经·新约》之末卷, 描写世界末日的情形。《启示录》的作者据认为是圣约翰。该书有时也称作 The Book of Revelation 或 The Apocalypse)

rev·el·ler *BrE*【英】, **reveler** *AmE*【美】/ˋrɛvlɚ; ˈrevələ/ *n* [C usually plural 一般用复数] someone who is having fun singing, dancing etc in a noisy way 狂欢者, 寻欢作乐者: *drunken revellers in Trafalgar Square on New Year's Eve* 除夕夜特拉法尔加广场上醉醺醺的狂欢者

rev·el·ry /ˋrɛvlrɪ; ˈrevəlri/ *n plural* **revelries** [U] wild noisy dancing, eating, drinking etc 狂欢, 欢宴作乐

re·venge[1] /rɪˋvɛndʒ; rɪˈvendʒ/ *n* [U] **1** something you do in order to punish someone who has harmed or offended you 报复, 报仇: **[+for]** *Hamlet was seeking revenge for his father's murder.* 哈姆雷特设法报杀父之仇。| **get/take revenge (on)** *He took revenge on his employers by setting fire to the factory.* 他对雇主进行报复, 放火烧了工厂。| **be out for revenge** (=be trying to get your revenge) 企图报复 | **in revenge** (=to punish someone) 作为报复 *a bomb attack in revenge for the imprisonment of the terrorists* 为报复恐怖分子被抓而进行的炸弹袭击 **2** **get your revenge** to defeat someone who has previously defeated you in a sport 雪耻〔指在比赛中战胜曾击败自己的对手〕—**revengeful** *adj*

revenge[2] *v* [T] **revenge yourself on/be revenged on** *formal* to punish someone who has harmed you【正式】向…报仇: *his unconscious desire to be revenged on her for her disloyalty* 他潜意识中因她不忠而产生的复仇欲望

rev·e·nue /ˋrɛvəˌnu; ˈrevɪ̥njuː/ also 又作 **revenues** *plural n* 2
[U] **1** money that a business or organization receives over a period of time, especially from selling goods or services 收益, 收入: *advertising revenue* 广告收入 **2** money that the government receives from tax〔政府的〕税收 —see also 另见 INLAND REVENUE, INTERNAL REVENUE SERVICE

re·ver·be·rate /rɪˋvɝbəˌret; rɪˈvɜːbəreɪt/ *v* [I] **1** if a loud sound reverberates, it is heard many times as it is sent back from different surfaces, so that the room or building where it is seems to shake〔声音〕回荡, 回响: **[+through/around/along etc]** *The sound of a train passing reverberated through the house.* 火车经过的声音在整个房子里回荡。**2** if an event, action, or idea reverberates, it has a strong effect over a wide area〔事件、活

动、思想〕反响: *His death shocked the whole country and reverberated far beyond its boundaries.* 他的去世举国震惊，其反响远远超出了国界。

re·ver·be·ra·tion /rɪˌvɜbəˋreʃən; rɪˌvɜːbəˈreɪʃən/ *n* **1** [C usually plural 一般用复数] a severe effect that is caused by a particular event 反响，巨大影响: *The reverberations of the energy crisis are felt especially by the car industry.* 能源危机的巨大影响在汽车业感受最强。**2** [C,U] a loud sound that hits a surface and is heard again and again 回荡，回响: *the deep reverberation of the bass drum* 低音鼓发出的深沉回响

re·vere /rɪˋvɪr; rɪˈvɪə/ *v* [T] *formal* to respect and admire someone or something very much【正式】尊敬，崇敬: *a much revered teacher* 非常受尊敬的老师

Revere, Paul (1735-1818) an American FOLK HERO who rode at night on the 18th April 1775 to the town of Concord in Massachusetts, in order to warn the people there that the British soldiers were coming. The next day the American Revolutionary War started. His brave action is described in Longfellow's poem *Paul Revere's Ride*.里维尔〔(1735-1818)，美国民族英雄。1775年4月18日，他骑马星夜兼程赶到马萨诸塞州康科德镇，把英军正在赶来的消息通报给当地居民。次日，美国独立战争爆发。他的英勇行为在朗费罗的诗篇《英勇骑士》中有所描述〕

rev·e·rence[1] /ˋrɛvərəns; ˈrevərəns/ *n* **1** [U] *formal* great respect and admiration for someone or something【正式】尊敬，崇敬: [+for] *You should show proper reverence for the national flag.* 你对国旗必须表现出应有的崇敬。**2 your/his reverence** *old use* used when speaking to or about a priest【旧】尊敬的阁下〔对神职人员的尊称〕: *The visitors have arrived, your reverence.* 来访者已经到了，牧师阁下。

reverence[2] *v* [T] *old use* to revere someone or something【旧】尊敬，崇敬

Rev·e·rend[1] /ˋrɛvərənd; ˈrevərənd/ *n* a title of respect used before the name of a minister of the Christian church 牧师〔基督教教士的尊称，用于姓名前〕: *the Reverend John Graham* 约翰·格雷厄姆牧师

reverend[2] *adj* [only before noun 仅用于名词前] *old use* deserving respect【旧】值得尊敬的

Reverend Moth·er /ˌ···ˈ··/ *n* [C] a title of respect for the woman in charge of a CONVENT; MOTHER SUPERIOR 女院长〔对女修道院主管的尊称〕

rev·e·rent /ˋrɛvərənt; ˈrevərənt/ *adj formal* showing respect and admiration【正式】恭敬的，虔诚的: *They sat in reverent silence.* 他们肃然坐着，默默无声。—**reverently** *adv*: *He kissed her hand reverently.* 他恭敬地吻了她的手。

rev·e·ren·tial /ˌrɛvəˋrɛnʃəl; ˌrevəˈrenʃəl◂/ *adj formal* showing respect【正式】恭敬的，表示敬意的: *He spoke of the dead man in reverential tones.* 他以恭敬的口气提及死者。—**reverentially** *adv*: *They treated him reverentially.* 他们对他毕恭毕敬。

rev·e·rie /ˋrɛvərɪ; ˈrevəri/ *n* [C,U] a state of imagining or thinking about pleasant things, that is like dreaming 幻想，梦想: *She was startled out of her reverie by the door bell.* 门铃声将她从梦幻中惊醒。

re·vers·al /rɪˋvɜsl; rɪˈvɜːsəl/ *n* [C,U] **1** a change to an opposite arrangement, process or course of action 反向；反转；倒转: *There has been a dramatic reversal of government policy.* 政府政策发生了巨大转变。**2** [C] a failure or other problem that prevents you from being able to do what you want 逆转，倒退〔指阻止人达到目标的失败等〕: *In spite of setbacks and reversals, his business was at last making money.* 尽管遭遇挫折和失败，他的生意最后还是赚钱了。

re·verse[1] /rɪˋvɜs; rɪˈvɜːs/ *v*

1 ▶CHANGE STH 改变某事物◀ [T] to change something, such as a decision, judgment, or process so that it is the opposite of what it was before 推翻，撤销: *The court of appeal reversed the original verdict and set the prisoner free.* 上诉法院撤销了原判，释放了那个犯人。| *What can we do to reverse the present trend of falling sales?* 我们能做些什么来扭转目前销售额下降的趋势?

2 ▶CAR 汽车◀ [I,T] if a car or its driver reverses, they go backwards 倒车: [+out/into etc] *a car reversing out of a driveway* 正在倒出车道的车 | *Before you reverse, make sure there are no pedestrians behind you.* 要确定后面没有行人才倒车。| **reverse a car/bus etc** (=make it reverse) 倒车 —see picture on page A3 参见A3页图

3 ▶CHANGE THE ORDER 改变顺序◀ [T] to change round the usual order of the parts of something 颠倒〔通常的次序〕: *They reversed the normal order for the ceremony and started with prayers.* 他们改变了仪式的常规顺序，以祈祷开始。

4 ▶TURN STH OVER 翻转某物◀ [T] to turn something over, so as to show the back of it 翻转: *Reverse the paper in the printer.* 请把打印机中的纸翻过来。

5 reverse the charges *BrE* to make a telephone call which is paid for by the person you are telephoning【英】〔电话〕由受话方付款; CALL COLLECT *AmE*【美】—**reversible** *adj*: *This coat is reversible, you can wear it inside out.* 这件上衣双面式的，里子能朝外翻过来穿。—**reversibility** *n* [U]

reverse[2] *n*

1 ▶THE OPPOSITE 相反◀ the reverse the exact opposite of what has just been mentioned 正相反: *The economic situation is certainly improving, although recent trade figures suggest the reverse.* 经济形势无疑在好转，尽管最近的贸易数字说明的情况正相反。| **quite the reverse** (=completely the opposite) 完全相反 *I was not happy – quite the reverse, I was seething with anger.* 我并不高兴，恰恰相反，我气极了。

2 go into reverse if a trend or process goes into reverse, it starts to happen in the opposite way 逆转: *a danger that the movement towards democracy will go into reverse* 民主运动发生逆转的危险

3 ▶IN A CAR 在汽车里◀ [U] the control in a vehicle that makes it go backwards; REVERSE GEAR 倒车挡 | **into/in reverse** *Put the car into reverse.* 挂上倒挡倒车。

4 ▶A DEFEAT 失败◀ [C] *formal* a defeat or a problem that delays your plans; SETBACK【正式】失败；挫折: *Losing the Senate vote was a serious reverse for the President.* 被参议院投票否决对总统来说是个严重的挫折。

5 ▶OTHER SIDE 另一面◀ [singular] the less important side or the back of an object that has two sides 背面: *Is there a pattern on the reverse of the cloth?* 布的背面有图案吗?

6 ▶OF A COIN 硬币◀ [singular] the side of a coin that does not show a person's head 背面: *The British ten-pence piece has a lion on the reverse.* 英国10便士硬币反面的图案是一头狮子。

reverse[3] *adj* [only before noun 仅用于名词前] **1 reverse order/procedure/process etc** the opposite order etc to what is usual or to what has just been stated 相反的顺序/程序/过程等: **in reverse order** *Reassemble the parts in reverse order.* 按相反顺序重新组装零件。**2 the reverse side** the back of something 反面，背面: *Sign the check on the reverse side.* 请在支票上背书。

reverse di·scrim·i·na·tion /·ˌ· ···ˈ··/ *n* [U] the practice of giving unfair treatment to a group of people who usually have advantages, in order to be fair to the group of people who were unfairly treated in the past 逆向歧视〔以不公平的方式对待通常占优势的团体，从而公平地对待过去受歧视的团体〕—compare 比较 POSITIVE DISCRIMINATION

reverse gear /·ˌ·ˈ·/ *n* [U] the control in a vehicle that makes it go backwards 倒车挡

reversing light /·ˈ··ˌ·/ *n* [C] a light on the back of a car which comes on when the car is going backwards 倒车灯 —see picture on page A2 参见A2页图

re·ver·sion /rɪˋvɜʒən; rɪˈvɜːʃən/ *n* [singular,U] *formal*【正式】**1** a return to a former, usually bad, condition or habit〔以前的情况或习惯，一般是恶劣情况或不良习惯的〕恢复，回复: [+to] *the danger of a reversion to tribal warfare in the region* 该地区再次爆发部族战争的危险 **2** *law* the return of property to a former owner【法律】〔财产的〕归还

re·vert /rɪˋvɜt; rɪˈvɜːt/ *v*

revert to sb/sth *phr v* [T] **1** to go back to a former condition or habit, especially one that was bad 恢复，回复〔尤指不好的情况或习惯〕: *As soon as they stopped farming, the land reverted to wilderness.* 他们一停止耕种，土地又变成一片荒芜。| *He had reverted to lazing in bed and coming in late to work.* 他故态复萌，贪睡赖床，上班迟到。| **revert to type** (=return to your former type of behaviour) 故态复萌 **2** to return to an earlier subject of conversation 回到〔先前的话题〕: *I'd like to revert to the first point you made.* 我想回到你提出的第一点上。**3** *law* if land or a building reverts to someone, it becomes the property of its former owner again【法律】归还〔地产、房屋等〕

re·vet·ment /rɪˋvɛtmənt; rɪˈvetmənt/ *n* [C] *technical* a surface of stone or other building material added for strength to a wall that holds back loose earth, water etc【术语】铺面，砌面；护墙；护坡，护带

re·view[1] /rɪˋvju; rɪˈvjuː/ *n* **1** [C,U] an act of carefully examining and considering a situation or process 回顾，检查，检讨: *The Department of Agriculture ordered an urgent review of pesticide safety.* 农业部命令对杀虫剂的安全性进行紧急审查。| *a review of progress in computer science over the last 20 years* 对过去20年计算机科学所取得的进步的回顾 | **under review** S3 W2

R

(=being examined and considered) 在审查中 *Nuclear weapons systems are currently under review.* 核武器系统目前正接受审查。| **come up for review** (=come to the time when there is supposed to be a review) 到提交审查的时间 *The ban on whaling came up for review in 1990.* 捕鲸的禁令在1990年应该进行审查。**2** [C] an article in a newspaper or magazine that gives an opinion about a new book, play, film etc〔报纸、杂志上的〕评论〔文章〕; 书评, 剧评, 影评: *Her latest novel got good reviews in the press.* 她的最新小说得到了报界的好评。**3** [U] the work of writing these 评论〔的写作〕: *He sent her an offprint of the article for review.* 他寄给她该文章的印样, 请她写评论。| **review copy** (=a copy of a book etc sent to a magazine or newspaper for review) 书评用赠阅本 **4** [C] an official show of the army, navy etc in the presence of a king, president, or officer of high rank〔军队的〕检阅, 阅兵式: *a naval review* 海军检阅 **5** [C] a REVUE〔穿插歌舞和时事讽刺的〕表演剧

review² *v* **1** [T] to examine, consider and judge a situation or process carefully 仔细审度〔情况或程序〕; 详查; 回顾, 检讨: *Government spending has been reviewed to try and reduce the budget deficit.* 对政府开支进行了审核, 以争取减少预算赤字。**2** [I,T] to write an article judging a new book, play, film etc〔为…〕写书评[影评等]: *Bernstein sometimes reviewed classical music in the 'Post'.* 伯恩斯坦有时在《邮报》上发表评论古典音乐的文章。| **be well reviewed** (=be praised by reviewers) 受到好评 **3** [T] to officially examine a group of soldiers, ships etc at a military show 检阅〔军队〕: *The President will review the soldiers on parade.* 总统将在阅兵式中检阅部队。**4** [T] *AmE* to look again at something quickly, such as school work, notes of lessons, or a report etc【美】复习, 温习〔功课、笔记、报告等〕—compare 比较 REVISE (2)

re·view·er /rɪˋvjuɚ; rɪˈvjuːə/ *n* [C] someone who writes about new books, plays etc in a newspaper or magazine〔评论新书、戏剧等的〕评论家

re·vile /rɪˋvaɪl; rɪˈvaɪl/ *v* [T] to express hatred of someone or something 谩骂, 辱骂: *The President was now reviled by the very Party he had helped to lead.* 总统目前受到了他曾协助领导的政党的痛斥。—**reviler** *n* [C]

re·vise /rɪˋvaɪz; rɪˈvaɪz/ *v* **1** [T] to change your opinions, plans etc because of new information or ideas 改变〔意见、计划等〕, 修正: *I've revised my opinion of Bill – he's much more intelligent than I thought.* 我改变了对比尔的看法, 他比我原来认为的要聪明得多。| *Our original forecast of this year's profits has now been revised upwards.* (=we think profits will be higher) 我们对本年度利润的原先预测现在已经向上调整。| **revised estimate** (=a calculation that has been changed to make it more accurate) 修正的估计 *Are there any questions on the revised estimates of the budget?* 对财政预算的修订估计还有什么问题吗? **2** [I,T] *BrE* to study lessons or notes again, in order to learn them before an examination【英】复习: *She's still got a lot of revising to do before the exam.* 她在考试前还有许多东西要复习。**3** [T] to change a piece of writing by adding new information, making improvements, or correcting mistakes 审订; 修订, 校订〔文稿〕: *Eliot revised his American lectures for publication.* 艾略特对他的美国讲座文稿进行修正, 准备出版。| **revised edition** (=a new and improved form or copy of a book) 修订版 *a revised edition of the encyclopedia* 百科全书的修订版 —compare 比较 REVIEW² —**reviser** *n* [C]

Revised Stan·dard Ver·sion, the /ˌ· ˈ·· ˈ·· ·/ abbreviation 缩写为 **the RSV** an improved and corrected translation of the Bible produced by US SCHOLARS in 1952《圣经》标准译本修订版〔美国学者1952年推出的《圣经》勘校版〕

Revised Ver·sion, the /ˌ· ˈ·· ·/ an improved and corrected edition of the Authorized Version of the Bible, produced in the late 19th century《圣经》钦定本修订版〔19世纪末完成的《圣经》钦定本勘校版〕

re·vi·sion /rɪˋvɪʒən; rɪˈvɪʒən/ *n* **1** [C,U] the process of changing something, especially a piece of writing, in order to improve it by correcting it or including new information or ideas〔尤指文稿的〕修改, 修订, 校订: *His lecture needs a lot of revision.* 他的演讲需要大加修改。| **be subject to revision** (=be considered for possible change) 可能需要修订 *The department budget is subject to monthly revision.* 部门的预算须每月审查修订。**2** [C] a piece of writing that has been improved and corrected 修订稿 **3** [U] *BrE* the work of studying lessons, notes etc again in order to learn them【英】复习, 温习: *I'll have to do some revision before my exam.* 考试前我得温习功课。

re·vi·sion·is·m /rɪˋvɪʒənɪzəm; rɪˈvɪʒənɪzəm/ *n* [U] ideas which are changing away from the main beliefs of a political system, especially a Marxist system 修正主义〔尤指对马克思主义的修改〕—**revisionist** *adj* —**revisionist** *n* [C]: *revisionist writings* 修正主义的著作

re·vis·it /riˋvɪzɪt; ˌriːˈvɪzɪt/ *v* [T] **1** to return to a place you once knew well 重游, 再访: *They revisited the town where he grew up.* 他们重游了那个镇, 他是在那里长大的。**2** to come back to in order to discuss again 回到〔某问题以重新讨论〕: *OK, so we need to revisit this proposal as soon as the budget position is clearer.* 好, 预算的情况更明朗时, 我们就需要立即重新讨论这项建议。**3 revisited** an event, fashion etc revisited is something else very like it that reminds you of it〔事件、时尚的〕翻版: *a music festival that was essentially Woodstock revisited* 基本上是伍德·斯托克音乐节的翻版

re·vi·tal·ize also 又作 -ise *BrE*【英】/riˋvaɪtḷˌaɪz; riːˈvaɪtəlaɪz/ *v* [T] to put new strength or power into something 使恢复元气; 注入新的活力: *They hope to revitalize the neighborhood by providing better housing.* 他们希望通过提供更好的住房条件使住宅区恢复活力。—**revitalization** /riˌvaɪtḷəˋzeʃən; riːˌvaɪtəlaɪˈzeɪʃən/ *n* [U]

re·vi·val /rɪˋvaɪv; rɪˈvaɪvəl/ *n* **1** [C,U] a process of something becoming active or strong again 复兴, 复活: *The Roosevelt administration wanted to stimulate an economic revival.* 罗斯福政府希望刺激经济复苏。| [+of] *the revival of old fears and jealousies* 昔日的恐惧和嫉妒的复现 **2** [C,U] the fact of something becoming popular again 再流行: [+of] *the revival of Buddhism in China* 佛教在中国的复兴 | *Opera is enjoying a revival.* 歌剧又流行起来。**3** [C] a new production of a play that has not been recently performed〔旧剧的〕重新上演: *a revival of 'West Side Story'*〔音乐剧〕《西城故事》的重新上演 **4** [C] a REVIVAL MEETING〔基督教的〕复兴〔信仰〕布道会

re·vi·val·is·m /rɪˋvaɪvḷɪzəm; rɪˈvaɪvəlɪzəm/ *n* [U] an organized attempt to make a religion more popular 宗教复兴运动 —**revivalist** *adj*

revival meet·ing /ˈ·ˈ·· ˌ··/ *n* [C] a public religious meeting with music, famous speakers etc, that is intended to make people interested in Christianity〔基督教的〕复兴〔信仰〕布道会

re·vive /rɪˋvaɪv; rɪˈvaɪv/ *v* **1** [I,T] to become or make someone conscious, healthy, or strong again〔使〕苏醒, 复原: *The doctors revived her with injections of glucose.* 医生给她注射葡萄糖使她苏醒过来。| *The plant will revive if you water it.* 如果给那株植物浇水, 它就会再活过来。**2** [T] to come back or bring something back into existence or popularity 使再兴起, 使再流行: *Helen's trip home has revived memories of her childhood.* 海伦的故乡之旅唤起了她对童年的回忆。| *reviving old customs* 复兴旧习俗

re·viv·i·fy /riˋvɪvəˌfaɪ; riːˈvɪvɨfaɪ/ *v* [T] *formal* to give new life and health to someone or something【正式】使恢复活力, 使恢复生气: *The aim was to strengthen, revivify and revitalise the Labour Party.* 目的是加强、恢复和振兴工党。

rev·o·ca·tion /ˌrɛvəˋkeʃən; ˌrevəˈkeɪʃən/ *n* [C,U] the act of revoking a law, decision etc〔法律、决定等的〕废除, 撤销, 取消

re·voke /rɪˋvok; rɪˈvəʊk/ *v* [T] to officially state that a law, decision, contract etc is no longer effective; CANCEL【正式】废除, 取消〔法律、决定、合同等〕: *Their work permits have been revoked.* 他们的工作许可证被吊销了。

re·volt¹ /rɪˋvolt; rɪˈvəʊlt/ *v* **1** [I] if a group of people revolt, they take strong and often violent action against the government, usually with the aim of taking power away from them; REBEL² 造反, 起义; 反叛: *George III's repressive measures forced the Colonies to revolt.* 乔治三世的高压手段迫使各殖民地起义。**2** [I] to refuse to accept someone's authority or obey rules, laws etc〔对权威、规章、法律等〕反抗, 拒绝服从: [+against] *Public opinion will revolt against any further increase in taxes.* 公众舆论将反对进一步增加税收。**3** [T] if something revolts you, it is so unpleasant that it makes you feel sick and shocked 使作呕, 使反感, 使憎恶; 使震惊: **be revolted by/at** *We were revolted by their cruelty.* 我们对他们的残忍感到震惊。—see also 另见 REVULSION

revolt² *n* **1** a refusal to accept someone's authority or obey rules, laws etc 反抗, 反对: *The President faces a Senate revolt.* 总统面临参议院的反对。| *a child's revolt against rigid, oppressive parents* 孩子对固执、霸道的父母的反抗 **2** strong and often violent action by a lot of people against their ruler or government 造反, 起义; 反叛: [+against] *an armed revolt against a tyrannical regime* 反对暴政的武装起义 | **in revolt** *The peasants rose up in armed revolt.* 农民发动了武装起义。**3** a feeling of being sick and very shocked at something unpleasant 作呕, 反感: *a sense of revolt at the bloody scenes* 看到血腥场面后想吐的感觉

re·volt·ing /rɪˋvoltɪŋ; rɪˈvəʊltɪŋ/ *adj* extremely unpleasant; DISGUSTING 使人厌恶的，令人作呕的: *the revolting taste of sour milk* 变酸的牛奶极难闻的味道 | *His leering glances were revolting to her.* 他色迷迷的目光令她反感。—**revoltingly** *adv*: *Your socks are revoltingly dirty.* 你的袜子脏得叫人恶心。

S3 W2 **rev·o·lu·tion** /ˌrɛvəˋluʃən; ˌrevəˈluːʃən/ *n* **1** [C] a complete change in ways of thinking, methods of working etc〔思想、工作方式等的〕彻底变革: *Computer technology has caused a revolution in business practices.* 电脑技术引起了商务活动的巨大改变。—see also 另见 INDUSTRIAL REVOLUTION **2** [C,U] a time of great, usually sudden, social and political change, especially the changing of a ruler or political system by force 革命: *the French Revolution* 法国大革命 | *social inequalities that led to revolution* 导致革命的社会不平等 —see also 另见 COUNTER-REVOLUTION **3** [C,U] one complete circular movement, or continued circular movement, around a fixed point 旋转一周; 循环（运动）: [+round/around] *The Earth makes one revolution round the sun each year.* 地球每年绕太阳公转一圈。**4** one complete circular spinning movement, made by something such as a wheel fixed on a central point 旋转一周: *a speed of 100 revolutions per minute* 每分钟 100 转的转速 —see also 另见 REVOLVE

rev·o·lu·tion·a·ry[1] /ˌrɛvəˋluʃənˌɛrɪ; ˌrevəˈluːʃənəri◂/ *n* [C] someone who joins in or supports a political or social revolution 革命者，革命家: *socialist revolutionaries* 社会主义革命者

revolutionary[2] *adj* **1** completely new and different, especially in a way that leads to great improvements 革命性的，创新的: *The new cancer drug is a revolutionary breakthrough.* 这种新抗癌药是革命性的突破。**2** [only before noun 仅用于名词前] connected with a political or social revolution 革命的: *a revolutionary leader* 革命领袖

Revolutionary War, the /ˌ…… ˈ ·/ —see 见 the AMERICAN REVOLUTIONARY WAR

rev·o·lu·tion·ize also 又作 **-ise** *BrE*【英】/ˌrɛvəˋluʃənˌaɪz; ˌrevəˈluːʃənaɪz/ *v* [T] to completely change the way people think or do things, especially because of a new idea or invention 使彻底变革: *New metal alloys have revolutionized car manufacture.* 新金属合金使汽车制造业发生了根本变革。

re·volve /rɪˋvɑlv; rɪˈvɒlv/ *v* [I,T] to spin around or make something spin around, on a central point; ROTATE (1)（使）旋转: *The metal disc revolves at high speed.* 那个金属盘以高速旋转。| **revolve sth** *Revolve the drum to get all the clothes out of the dryer.* 转动滚筒把所有衣服从烘干机中取出。

revolve around sth *phr v* [T not in passive 不用被动态] **1** [not in progressive 不用进行时] to have something as a main subject or purpose 以…为主题[目的]，围绕: *The story revolves around a young girl who runs away from home.* 故事围绕着一个离家出走的年轻姑娘展开。| *Her life seems to revolve around her career.* 她的生活似乎以她的事业为中心。| **think the world revolves around you** *informal* (=think that you are more important than anyone or anything else)【非正式】认为自己比谁都重要 **2** to move in circles around something 围绕…旋转: *The moon revolves around the Earth.* 月球围绕地球旋转。

re·volv·er /rɪˋvɑlvɚ; rɪˈvɒlvə/ *n* [C] a small gun which has a revolving container for bullets, so that several shots can be fired without having to put more bullets in 左轮手枪

re·volv·ing /rɪˋvɑlvɪŋ; rɪˈvɒlvɪŋ/ *adj* a revolving object is designed so that it turns with a circular movement 旋转的: *a revolving stage in the theatre* 剧场的旋转舞台

revolving door /·ˌ·· ˈ·/ *n* [C] a type of door in the entrance of a large building, that goes round and round as people go through it 旋转门

re·vue /rɪˋvju; rɪˈvjuː/ *n* [C] a show in a theatre, that includes songs, dances, and jokes about recent events〔穿插歌舞和时事讽刺的〕表演剧

re·vul·sion /rɪˋvʌlʃən; rɪˈvʌlʃən/ *n* [U] a strong feeling of shock and very strong dislike 厌恶，憎恶，强烈的反感: *News of the atrocities produced a wave of anger and revulsion.* 暴行的消息激起一阵愤怒和反感。

W3 **re·ward**[1] /rɪˋwɔrd; rɪˈwɔːd/ *n* **1** [C,U] something that you receive because you have done something good or helpful 报答，报偿，酬谢，奖赏: [+for] *She received a crystal decanter as a reward for her services.* 作为对她服务的酬谢，她得到一只水晶盛酒瓶。| *$100 was a poor reward for all my work!* 我做了那么多工作，100 美元的报酬太少了！**2** [C] an amount of money that is offered to someone who finds something that was lost or gives the police information 赏金: *A reward was offered for the return of the jewels.* 为找回珠宝而悬赏。**3 be its own reward** if something that you do is its own reward, it makes you feel happy and satisfied 本身就是奖赏: *Working for a good cause can be its own reward.* 为有意义的事业工作本身就是奖赏。

reward[2] *v* [T] to give something to someone because they have done something good or helpful 酬谢，报答，奖赏: *How can I reward your kindness?* 对你的好意，我怎么来报答呢？| **reward sb with sth** *Larry complimented her and was rewarded with a smile.* 拉里恭维她，她报以微笑。| **reward sb for sth** *She was generously rewarded for her work.* 她的工作得到了慷慨的报酬。

re·ward·ing /rɪˋwɔrdɪŋ; rɪˈwɔːdɪŋ/ *adj* making you feel happy and satisfied because you feel you are doing something useful or important, even if you do not earn much money 值得做的，有益的，有意义的: *Teaching can be a very rewarding career.* 教书可以是一种很有意义的职业。

re·wind /riˋwaɪnd; riːˈwaɪnd/ *v* to make a CASSETTE TAPE or VIDEO go backwards so as to see or hear it again 倒回〔录音带或录像带〕

re·wire /riˋwaɪr; ˌriːˈwaɪə/ *v* [T] to put new electric wires in a building, machine, light etc 更换…的电线

re·word /riˋwɝd; ˌriːˈwɜːd/ *v* [T] to say or write something again in different words, in order to make it easier to understand or more suitable 重述，改写，改变…的措辞: *Let me reword my question.* 让我换个说法来提问。

re·work /riˋwɝk; ˌriːˈwɜːk/ *v* [T] to make changes in music or a piece of writing, in order to use it again 改编〔乐曲、作品〕

re·write /riˋraɪt; ˌriːˈraɪt/ *v past tense* **rewrote** /-ˋrot; -ˈrəʊt/ *past participle* **rewritten** /-ˋrɪtn; -ˈrɪtn/ [T] to change something that has been written, especially in order to improve it, or because new information is available〔尤指为改进或有新资料〕重写，改写: *Rewrite the passage in your own words.* 用你自己的话改写这段。—**rewrite** /ˋriˌraɪt; ˈriːraɪt/ *n* [C]: *Software packages may need complete rewrites to match new hardware.* 套装软件可能需要全部改写以便与新的硬件相配。

Rex /rɛks; reks/ *n Latin*【拉丁】**1** a title used in official writing after the name of a king, when the king's name has been written in Latin 王，君王，国王〔公文中用于以拉丁文写成的君王名字之后的称谓〕: *Henricus Rex* 亨利国王 **2** *law* a word meaning the state, used in the names of law cases in Britain when a king is ruling【法律】王国政府〔英国国王在位时用于讼案的名称中，代表国家〕: *Rex v Jones* 王国政府诉琼斯案

Rey·kja·vik /ˋrekjəvɪk; ˈreɪkjəvɪk/ the capital city and main port of Iceland, which is the centre of the country's fishing industry 雷克雅未克〔冰岛首都和主要港口，是冰岛的捕鱼业中心〕

Rey·nard the Fox /ˌrɛnɑrd ðə ˋfɑks; ˌrenɑːd ðə ˈfɒks/ a FOX in old European stories, who often behaves badly but always escapes punishment by his cleverness 列那狐〔欧洲传说故事中的一只狐狸。它经常惹是生非，但总会凭着聪明劲儿逃避惩罚〕

Reynolds /ˋrɛnḷdz; ˈrenəldz/, **Sir Joshua** /sɚ ˋdʒɑʃuə; sə ˈdʒɒʃjuːə/ (1723-92) a British painter who became the first president of the Royal Academy. His best known works are his PORTRAITS (=paintings of people). 雷诺兹〔(1723-1792)，英国画家。他曾为皇家艺术学院首任院长，以肖像画最为著名〕

rhap·so·dize also 又作 **-ise** *BrE*【英】/ˋræpsəˌdaɪz; ˈræpsədaɪz/ *v* [I] to talk about something in an eager, excited, and approving way 热烈地赞美，称颂: [+about/over] *rhapsodizing about the aroma of the mountain forests* 赞美山林的芳香

rhap·so·dy /ˋræpsədɪ; ˈræpsədi/ *n* [C] **1** a piece of music that is written to express emotion, and does not have a regular form 狂想曲 **2** an expression of eager and excited approval 赞美之辞，热情赞颂: *listening to Miss Duval's rhapsodies about Venice* 听杜瓦尔小姐对威尼斯的赞美之辞

rhe·o·stat /ˋriəˌstæt; ˈriːəstæt/ *n* [C] a piece of equipment that controls the loudness of a radio or the brightness of an electric light, by limiting the flow of electric current 变阻器

Rhe·sus fac·tor /ˋrisəs ˌfæktɚ; ˈriːsəs ˌfæktə/ *n* [singular] *technical* a substance whose PRESENCE (RHESUS POSITIVE) or absence (RHESUS NEGATIVE) in the red blood cells may have dangerous effects for some babies or when a person receives blood from another person【术语】猕因子，Rh 因子〔红血球中含有此种物质（即 Rh 阳性），或缺乏此种物质（即 Rh 阴性）都有可能对某些婴儿或接受输血的人造成危险的后果〕

rhesus mon·key /ˋrisəs ˌmʌŋkɪ; ˈriːsəs ˌmʌŋki/ *n* [C] a small monkey from northern India that is often used in medical tests〔产于印度北部的〕恒河猴

rhet·o·ric /ˋrɛtərɪk; ˈretərɪk/ *n* [U] **1** language used to persuade or influence people, especially by politicians〔尤指政治家使用的〕雄辩言辞，煽动性语言: *the rhetoric of their political rallies* 他们在政治集会上使用的煽动性语言 **2** speech or writing that

sounds impressive, but is not actually sincere or very useful 巧辩, 浮夸之词: *Positive action is better than rhetoric.* 积极的行动胜过浮华的词藻。**3** the art of speaking or writing to persuade or influence people 修辞学

rhe·tor·i·cal /rɪˋtɔrɪkḷ; rɪˈtɒrɪkəl/ *adj* **1** **rhetorical question** a question that you ask as a way of making a statement, without expecting an answer, such as 'Who knows what might happen?' 修辞性疑问句 **2** using speech or writing in special ways in order to persuade people or to produce an impressive effect 修辞的, 与修辞有关的: *impassioned rhetorical phrases* 慷慨激昂的巧辩华辞 —**rhetorically** /-kḷɪ; -kli/ *adv*

rhet·o·ri·cian /ˌrɛtəˋrɪʃən; ˌretəˈrɪʃən/ *n* [C] *formal* someone who is trained or skilful in the art of persuading or influencing people through speech or writing【正式】修辞学家

rheu·mat·ic /ruˋmætɪk; ruːˈmætɪk/ *adj* **1** connected with rheumatism 风湿病的, 风湿性的: *a rheumatic condition of the joints* 关节风湿 **2** suffering from rheumatism 患风湿病的

rheumatic fe·ver /ˌ·ˌ··ˋ··/ *n* [U] a serious infectious disease that causes fever, swelling in your joints, and sometimes damage to your heart 风湿热

rheu·mat·ick·y /ruˋmætəkɪ; ruːˈmætɪki/ *adj informal* rheumatic【非正式】风湿病的, 风湿性的

rheu·mat·ics /ruˋmætɪks; ruːˈmætɪks/ *n* [plural] *informal especially BrE* rheumatism【非正式, 尤英】风湿病

rheu·ma·tis·m /ˋrumәˌtɪzәm; ˈruːmәtɪzәm/ *n* [U] a disease that makes your joints or muscles painful and stiff 风湿病

R

rheu·ma·toid ar·thri·tis /ˌrumətɔɪd ɑrˋθraɪtɪs; ˌruːmətɔɪd ɑːˈθraɪtḷs/ *n* [U] a disease that continues for many years, and makes your joints painful and stiff, and often makes them lose their proper shape 类风湿性关节炎

RH fac·tor /ˌɑr ˋɛtʃ ˌfæktɚ; ˌɑːr ˈeɪtʃ ˌfæktə/ *n* [C] the RHESUS FACTOR 猕因子, Rh因子

Rhine, the /raɪn; raɪn/ an important river in western Europe, which goes from Switzerland through Germany to the Netherlands and into the North Sea, and is used for carrying goods by boat 莱茵河〔西欧一重要河流, 发源于瑞士, 流经德国和荷兰, 最后注入北海。河上常有往来的货船〕

rhine·stone /ˋraɪnˌston; ˈraɪnstəʊn/ *n* [C,U] a jewel made from glass or a transparent rock that is intended to look like a diamond 莱茵 (水晶) 石

Rhine wine /ˌ·ˈ·/ any of several white wines produced in the Rhine valley 莱茵酒〔产于莱茵河流域的任何一款白葡萄酒〕

rhi·no /ˋraɪno; ˈraɪnəʊ/ *n plural* **rhinos** [C] *informal* a rhinoceros【非正式】犀牛

rhi·no·ce·ros /raɪˋnɑsərəs; raɪˈnɒsərəs/ *n* [C] a large heavy African or Asian animal with thick skin and either one or two horns on its nose 犀牛

rhi·no·plas·ty /ˋraɪnoˌplæstɪ; ˈraɪnəʊˌplæsti/ *n* [U] PLASTIC SURGERY on your nose 鼻整形手术 —**rhinoplastic** /ˌraɪnəˋplæstɪk; ˌraɪnəʊˈplæstɪk◂/ *adj*

rhi·zome /ˋraɪzom; ˈraɪzəʊm/ *n* [C] *technical* the thick stem of some plants such as the IRIS, which lies flat along the ground with roots and leaves growing from it【术语】根茎, 根状茎

Rhode Is·land /ˋrod ˌaɪlənd; ˈrəʊd ˌaɪlənd/ abbreviation 缩写为 **RI** the smallest of the US states, in New England in the northeastern US. It was one of the 13 original states of the US, and its capital and largest city is Providence. 罗得岛州〔美国最小的一个州。位于美国东北部新英格兰地区, 是美国最早的13个州之一。首府和最大的城市是普罗维登斯〕

Rhodes /rodz; rəʊdz/ a large Greek island near the coast of Turkey. In ancient times Rhodes was famous because of the Colossus of Rhodes, and now it is a popular place for tourists. 罗得岛〔希腊一大岛, 濒临土耳其海岸。古时该岛以罗得岛巨像闻名, 如今是著名旅游胜地〕

Rhodes, Ce·cil /ˋsɛsɪl; ˈsesḷl/ (1853-1902) a South African politician, born in the UK, who was Prime Minister of Cape Colony (1890-96) and is famous for his IMPERIALISM (=the policy by which rich and powerful countries gain political and economic control over poorer countries). He also made a lot of money from DIAMOND mines, and he used some of this to set up the Rhodes Scholarships. 罗得斯〔(1853-1902), 南非政治家, 生于英国, 曾任开普殖民地总理 (1890-1896), 以其帝国主义政策而知名。他从钻石矿上赚了不少钱, 用部分资金设立了罗得斯奖学金〕

Rho·de·si·a /roˋdiʒə; rəʊˈdiːʃə/ a former name for Zimbabwe. During the period of British rule, Zimbabwe was known as **Southern Rhodesia** and Zambia was known as **Northern Rhodesia**. 罗得西亚〔津巴布韦旧称。英国统治期间, 津巴布韦和赞比亚分别被称为南罗得西亚和北罗得西亚〕—**Rhodesian** *n, adj*

Rhodes Schol·ar·ship /ˌ·ˈ···/ a sum of money given to some students from the US, the British Commonwealth, and Germany to allow them to study at Oxford University. The money for these SCHOLARSHIPS was originally provided by Cecil Rhodes. A student receiving one of these scholarships is called a Rhodes Scholar. 罗得斯奖学金〔授予美国、英联邦国家以及德国学生的一种奖学金, 使其可在牛津大学就读。奖学金最初由塞西尔·罗得斯设立。获此奖学金的学生被称为罗得斯学者〕

rho·do·den·dron /ˌrodəˋdɛndrən; ˌrəʊdəˈdendrən/ *n* [C] a bush with bright flowers which keeps its leaves in winter 杜鹃花属植物

rhom·boid[1] /ˋrɑmbɔɪd; ˈrɒmbɔɪd/ *n* [C] *technical* a shape with four sides whose opposite sides are equal; PARALLELOGRAM【术语】长菱形, 长斜方形, 平行四边形 —see picture at 参见 SHAPE[1] 图

rhomboid[2] also 又作 **rhom·boid·al** /rɑmˋbɔɪdḷ; rɒmˈbɔɪdl/ *adj technical* shaped like a rhombus【术语】菱形的

rhom·bus /ˋrɑmbəs; ˈrɒmbəs/ *n* [C] *technical* a shape with four equal straight sides, especially one that is not a square【术语】菱形 —see picture at 参见 SHAPE[1] 图

Rhon·dda, the /ˋrɑndə; ˈrɒndə/ also 又作 **the Rhondda Valley** an area in South Wales, UK. The Rhondda was traditionally an important coal-mining area, but by 1990 all the coal mines had closed down. 朗达〔英国南威尔士一地区。过去, 该区为一重要产煤区, 但到了1990年当地所有煤矿均已关闭〕

Rhône, the /ron; rəʊn/ a river that goes from southern Switzerland to France and into the Mediterranean Sea. In southern France, the Rhône goes through an important wine-producing area. 罗讷河〔源于瑞士南部, 流经法国, 最后注入地中海的一条河流。该河还流经法国南部一重要酿酒区〕

RHS Royal Horticultural Society; a society founded in the UK in 1804 for the improvement of HORTICULTURE, and that is responsible for the Chelsea Flower Show. 皇家园艺协会〔1804年成立于英国一协会, 旨在促进园艺发展, 负责主办切尔西花展〕

rhu·barb /ˋrubɑrb; ˈruːbɑːb/ *n* **1** [U] a plant with broad leaves and a thick red stem that can be eaten (食用的) 大黄 **2** [U] *spoken* a word used by actors to make a sound like many people talking【口】演员模仿人声嘈杂时使用的词 **3** [C] *AmE old-fashioned* a noisy argument【美, 过时】激烈的争吵

rhyme[1] /raɪm; raɪm/ *n* **1** [C] a short poem or song, especially for children, using words that rhyme 押韵诗;〔押韵的〕儿歌 —see also 另见 NURSERY RHYME **2** [C] a word that rhymes with another word, for example 'fold' and 'cold' 同韵词: [+for] *I can't find a rhyme for 'orange'.* 我找不到和 orange 同韵的词。**3** [U] the use of words that rhyme in poetry, especially at the ends of lines 在诗中同韵词的使用, 押韵: *Shakespeare sometimes wrote in rhyme.* 莎士比亚有时写韵文。**4** **without rhyme or reason** in a way that cannot be reasonably explained 无缘无故, 毫无道理: *Joe's moods change without rhyme or reason.* 乔的情绪会无缘无故地变化。

rhyme[2] *v* [not in progressive 不用进行时] **1** [I] if two words or lines of poetry rhyme, they end with the same sounds, including a vowel 押韵, 成韵: [+with] *'House' rhymes with 'mouse'.* house 和 mouse 押韵。| **rhyming couplet** (=two lines of poetry that end in words that rhyme) 押韵的两行诗 **2** [T] to put two or more words together to make them rhyme 用…押韵, 使成韵: [+with] *You can't rhyme 'box' with 'backs'.* box 和 backs 不押韵。

rhyming slang /ˌ··ˈ·/ *n* [U] a way of talking, used especially by COCKNEYS (=people from east London), in which you use words or phrases that rhyme with the words you mean, instead of using the normal words. For example, 'plates of meat' is rhyming slang for 'feet' 同韵俚语〔尤在伦敦东区方言中常用, 如plates of meat表示feet〕

Rhys-Jones /ris ˋdʒonz; riːs ˈdʒəʊnz/, **Sophie** /ˋsofɪ; ˈsəʊfi/ (1965-) the wife of Prince Edward. She met the prince in 1993 and they got married in 1999. After the marriage, she became the Countess of Wessex. 里斯－琼斯〔(1965-), 爱德华王子之妻。她与爱德华王子1993年相识, 1999年结婚, 婚后成为威塞克斯女伯爵〕

rhyth·m /ˋrɪðəm; ˈrɪðəm/ *n* [C,U] **1** a regular repeated pattern of sounds or movements 节律, 节奏; 律动: *the exciting rhythms of African drum beats* 非洲鼓声那激动人心的节拍 | *the rhythm of your heartbeat* 你的心跳节律 **2** a regular pattern of changes 规则变化 (模式): *the rhythm of the seasons* 四季的交替

rhythm and blues /ˌ···ˈ·/ *n* [U] R AND B (=a type of music) 节奏布鲁斯

rhyth·mic /ˋrɪðmɪk; ˈrɪðmɪk/ also 又作 **rhyth·mic·al** /-ɪk]; -ɪkəl/ *adj* having rhythm 有节奏的: *the rhythmic thud of the bass*

drum 低音鼓有节奏的重击声 **—rhythmically** /-klɪ; -kli/ *adv*: *tapping rhythmically on the table* 有节奏地敲击桌子

rhythm meth·od /'· ·, ·/ *n* [singular] a method of BIRTH CONTROL which depends on having sex only at a time when the woman is not likely to become PREGNANT 安全期避孕法

rhythm sec·tion /'· ·, ·/ *n* [C] the part of a band that provides a strong RHYTHM with drums and other similar instruments〔乐团的〕节奏乐器组

RI /ˌɑr 'aɪ; ˌɑːr 'aɪ/ **1** the written abbreviation of 缩写= RHODE ISLAND **2** religious instruction; the study of religion in school 宗教教育

ri·al /rɪ'ɑl; ri'ɑːl/ *n* [C] a RIYAL 里亚尔〔沙特阿拉伯及其他许多阿拉伯国家的货币单位〕

rib[1] /rɪb; rɪb/ *n* [C] **1** one of the 12 pairs of curved bones that surround your chest 肋骨: *He broke a rib in the accident.* 他在事故中折断了一根肋骨。—see picture at 参见 RESPIRATORY 图 **2** a piece of meat that includes an animal's rib 肋条（肉）: *barbecued ribs* 烤肋条 **3** a curved piece of wood, metal etc that is used as part of the structure of something such as a boat or building〔木制或金属的〕肋条, 肋材 —see also 另见 PRIME RIB, SPARERIBS, **dig sb in the ribs** (DIG[1] (5))

rib[2] *v* **ribbed, ribbing** [T] *informal* to make jokes and laugh at someone so that you embarrass them, but in a friendly way【非正式】〔友善地〕开…的玩笑, 取笑: *Tony's always ribbing me about my accent.* 托尼总是取笑我的口音。

rib·ald /'rɪbḷd; 'rɪbəld/ *adj* ribald songs, remarks, riddles, or jokes are humorous, rude and usually about sex〔歌曲、玩笑等〕粗俗的, 下流的

rib·ald·ry /'rɪbḷdrɪ; 'rɪbəldri/ *n* [U] ribald songs, remarks, or jokes 粗俗下流的歌曲; 猥亵的笑话

ribbed /rɪbd; rɪbd/ *adj* having a pattern of raised lines 有棱线的, 有凸起条纹的, 有罗纹的: *ribbed stockings* 罗纹长袜

Rib·ben·trop /'rɪbəntrɑp; 'rɪbəntrɒp/, **Jo·a·chim von** /'joəkɪm vɑn; 'jəʊəkɪm vɒn/ (1893-1946) a German Nazi official who became Hitler's foreign minister and advised him on foreign POLICY. After World War II Ribbentrop was found guilty of war crimes, and was hanged. 里宾特洛甫〔(1893-1946), 德国纳粹官员, 希特勒的外交部长和外交顾问。二战之后, 他被控犯有战争罪并处以绞刑〕

rib·bing /'rɪbɪŋ; 'rɪbɪŋ/ *n* [U] **1** friendly jokes and laughter about someone that embarrasses them〔友善的〕开玩笑, 取笑, 戏弄: *Jake always took some ribbing about his lack of hair.* 杰克总是因为头发少而被取笑。**2** a pattern of raised lines in knitting (KNIT (1))〔编织中的〕棱线, 罗纹, 凸条

rib·bon /'rɪbən; 'rɪbən/ *n*

1 ▶SILK 丝绸◀ [C,U] a long narrow piece of cloth used to tie things or as a decoration 丝带, 缎带: *a red ribbon in her hair* 她头发上系的红缎带

2 ▶STH NARROW 窄的东西◀ [singular] something that is long and narrow 狭长的东西; 条, 带: *a ribbon of shining water* 一条波光粼粼的狭长水道

3 be cut/torn to ribbons to be very badly damaged by being cut or torn in many places 割烂/撕烂: *Her feet were cut to ribbons on the rocks.* 她的脚在岩石上磨烂了。| **be in ribbons** (=be badly torn in many places) 多处撕裂 *His coat was in ribbons.* 他的外衣破烂不堪。

4 ▶PRIZE 奖品◀ [C] *AmE* a small arrangement of coloured ribbon in the form of a flat flower, that is given as a prize in a competition; ROSETTE【美】〔作为比赛奖品的〕绶带: **blue ribbon** (=the first prize) 蓝色绶带〔一等奖〕

5 ▶MILITARY HONOUR 军队的荣誉◀ [C] a piece of ribbon with a special pattern or colours on it, worn to show that you have received a military honour〔军功的〕勋章, 勋带

6 ▶INK 墨汁◀ a long narrow piece of cloth or plastic with ink on it that is used in a TYPEWRITER〔打字机用的〕色带

ribbon de·vel·op·ment /'· ··, ··/ *n* [U] *BrE* long lines of houses along the side of the main roads leading out of a city, or the practice of arranging houses in this way【英】〔城市沿着干道两侧向郊外建房的〕带状发展

rib cage /'· ·/ *n* [C] the structure of RIBS around your lungs, heart, and other organs 胸廓, 胸腔

Ri·be·na /raɪ'binə; raɪ'biːnə/ *trademark* a type of sweet drink made from BLACKCURRANTS, sold in the UK and drunk especially by children【商标】利宾纳〔英国一种甜味饮料, 用黑加仑子制成, 尤为儿童喜爱〕

ri·bo·fla·vin /ˌraɪbə'flevɪn; ˌraɪbəʊ'fleɪvɪn/ *n* [U] *technical* VITAMIN B2, a substance that exists in meat, milk, and some vegetables, and that is important for your health【术语】核黄素, 维生素 B2

rice /raɪs; raɪs/ *n* [U] **1** a food that consists of small white or brown grains that you boil in water until they become soft enough to eat 米; 米饭: *a tasty sauce served with rice or pasta* 与米饭或面食一起上的美味酱汁 **2** the plant that produces this grain（水）稻

rice pad·dy /'· ,··/ *n* [C] a field in which rice is grown 稻田

rice pa·per /'· ,··/ *n* [U] **1** a thin paper made especially in China and used by painters there〔中国的〕宣纸 **2** a similar type of thin paper that can be eaten, which is used in cooking〔用于烹饪、可以吃的〕米纸

rice pud·ding /ˌ· '··/ *n* [U] a sweet dish made of rice, milk, and sugar cooked together 大米布丁〔用大米、牛奶、糖一起做成的甜食〕

rich /rɪtʃ; rɪtʃ/ *adj* ②②

1 ▶WEALTHY 富的◀ a) having a lot of money or valuable possessions 有钱的, 富有的: *one of the richest women in America* 美国最富有的女性之一 | *He got rich by making money on the stock market.* 他在股票市场上赚钱致富。| *a rich and powerful nation* 富有的强国 **b) the rich** people who have a lot of money and possessions 富人: *tax laws that benefit the rich* 使富人受益的税法

2 ▶LARGE AMOUNT 大量◀ having or containing a lot of something 富含…的: **[+in]** *Citrus fruits are rich in vitamin C.* 柑橘类水果富含维生素 C。| **oxygen-rich/nutrient-rich/protein-rich etc** (=containing a lot of oxygen etc) 富含氧气/营养/蛋白质等的 *Pregnant women should eat protein-rich foods.* 孕妇应该吃富含蛋白质的食物。

3 ▶FULL OF INTEREST 非常有趣的◀ full of interesting or important events, ideas etc 丰富的: *the rich literary tradition of England* 英格兰丰富的文学传统 | **[+in]** *a story that was rich in detail* 充满细节描述的故事

4 ▶SMELL 气味◀ having a strong pleasant smell〔气味〕浓郁的: *The rich scent of the pine trees was heavy in the air.* 空气中散发着松树的浓郁芳香。

5 ▶COLOUR 颜色◀ having a beautiful strong colour〔色彩〕浓艳的: *stained glass dyed a rich blue* 染成鲜艳的蓝色的彩色玻璃

6 ▶FOOD 食物◀ containing foods such as butter, cream, and eggs, which make you feel full very quickly〔含黄油、奶油、鸡蛋等〕容易让人感到饱的; 油腻的: *a rich fruit cake* 脂肪含量高的水果蛋糕

7 ▶MUSIC/SOUNDS 音乐/声音◀ having a pleasant low sound〔声音〕低沉浑厚的: *the rich tone of a cello* 大提琴低沉浑厚的音色

8 ▶SOIL/LAND 土壤/土地◀ good for growing plants in; FERTILE (1) 肥沃的, 富饶的: *Cotton grew well in the rich, black soil.* 棉花在肥沃的黑土地里生长得很好。

9 ▶CLOTH/JEWELLERY ETC 衣物/珠宝等◀ expensive and beautiful 昂贵的, 华丽的: *She stroked the rich velvet of the dress enviously.* 她羡慕地抚摸着连衣裙华贵的天鹅绒。

10 that's rich (coming from him/you etc) used to say that what someone has said is unreasonable and that they are criticizing you for doing something that they do themselves（他/你等说的话）不合情理[真荒谬]: *Ron told me I was disloyal. That's pretty rich coming from a married man.* 罗恩说我不忠诚。这话出自一个有妇之夫实在可笑。

11 ▶PETROL 汽油◀ having too much petrol mixed with the air, so that a car's engine does not operate smoothly〔汽车的内燃机里汽油与空气的混合物中〕汽油成分过高的

Richard /'rɪtʃəd; 'rɪtʃəd/, **Maurice** /'mɔrɪs; 'mɔːrɪs/ (1921-2000) a Canadian ICE HOCKEY player, who some people think was the best in the history of the sport. He was known as 'Rocket', and played for the Montreal Canadiens. He scored more goals than any other player in the National Hockey League (NHL) in 1945, 1947, 1950, 1954, and 1955. In 1945 he became the first player to score 50 goals in a 50-game season. 理查德〔(1921-2000), 加拿大冰球运动员, 被认为是有史以来最优秀的球员。他享有"火箭得分手"的美誉, 曾效力于蒙特利尔加拿大人队。他在 1945、1947、1950、1954 和 1955 年的（美加）国家冰上曲棍球联盟比赛中成为进球最多的运动员。1945 年, 他成为首位 50 场比赛攻进 50 球的运动员〕

Richard I /ˌrɪtʃəd ðə 'fɜst; ˌrɪtʃəd ðə 'fɜːst/, **King** (1157-99) the king of England from 1189 until his death. During his period as king, he was almost never in England, because he spent a lot of time fighting in the CRUSADES and in France. He was a popular king and regarded as very brave, and for this reason he is often called Richard the Lionheart or Richard Coeur de Lion. 理查一世〔(1157-1199), 1189 年任英格兰国王直至去世。在位期间, 他长期在国外征战, 参加了十字军东征, 后来还在

法国作战。他是位大名鼎鼎的国王，以勇敢无畏著称。鉴于此，他有“狮心王理查”之称〕

Richard II /ˌrɪtʃɚd ðə ˋsɛkənd; ˌrɪtʃəd ðə ˈsekənd/, **King** (1367-1400) the king of England from 1377 to 1399. He became very unpopular by ordering many of his opponents to be killed, and he was removed from power by his COUSIN, who then became King Henry IV. Richard was put in prison in 1399, and died or was murdered the next year. These events are described in Shakespeare's play *Richard II*. 理查二世〔(1367-1400)，1377至1399年任英格兰国王。他曾下令杀死许多异己，因而很不得民心。后来，他被其表兄（即后来的国王亨利四世）赶下台。1399年，理查二世被投入狱中，次年死亡或被谋害。这些事件在莎士比亚的剧本《理查二世》中有所描述〕

Richard III /ˌrɪtʃɚd ðə ˋθɝd; ˌrɪtʃəd ðə ˈθɜːd/, **King** (1452-85) the king of England from 1483 until his death. When his brother, King Edward IV, died in 1483, Richard had the job of taking care of Edward's sons, who were still boys. But he put the boys in prison in the Tower of London (the Princes in the Tower). They disappeared and he took the position of king for himself. He was later killed at the Battle of Bosworth Field. In Shakespeare's play *Richard III*, Richard is shown as a cruel and ugly man, but some writers now believe that he was in fact an effective king and a brave military leader, who was not responsible for the deaths of the princes. 理查三世〔(1452-1485)，1483年起任英格兰国王，直至去世。其兄爱德华四世1483年去世后，他照顾起了兄长的两个遗孤。然而，他却把两个孩子关进伦敦塔的牢房里。两个孩子失踪之后，他自立为王，后来在博斯沃思原野战役中被杀。莎士比亚的剧本《理查三世》把他描绘成一个残暴、丑陋之人。现代的一些作家则认为理查三世事实上是一位卓有成效的国王，也是一位勇敢善战的将领。两个王子之死与他无关〕

Rich·ard·son /ˋrɪtʃɚdsn̩; ˈrɪtʃədsən/, **Sam·u·el** /ˋsæmjuəl; ˈsæmjuəl/ (1689-1761) an English writer who influenced the development of the modern NOVEL with his novels *Pamela* and *Clarissa*, which are written in the form of letters 理查森〔(1689-1761)，英国作家。他的书信体小说《帕美勒》和《克拉丽莎》对现代小说的发展具有一定影响〕

Riche·lieu /ˋriʃəlu; ˈriːʃljɜː/, **Cardinal** (1585-1642) a French CARDINAL (=a Roman Catholic priest of the highest rank) who was also the chief minister of France and had a lot of influence with King Louis XIII. He destroyed the political power of the Huguenots, and is thought of as a typical example of someone who uses his influence with a ruler to achieve great power. 黎塞留〔(1585-1642)，法国红衣主教、法国首席大臣，对国王路易十三的影响颇大。他曾挫败胡格诺派的政治力量，被认为是利用对统治者的影响力获取巨大权力的范例〕

rich·es /ˋrɪtʃɪz; ˈrɪtʃɨz/ *n* [plural] *especially literary* expensive or beautiful possessions and large amounts of money【尤文】财富，财宝：*the riches he had brought back from his travels* 他出门旅行带回来的财宝

rich·ly /ˋrɪtʃlɪ; ˈrɪtʃli/ *adv* **1 richly decorated/embroidered etc** beautifully and expensively decorated etc 装饰华丽的／刺绣精美的等：*a cloak richly embroidered with gold thread* 用金线刺绣的华丽披风 **2 richly coloured** having beautiful strong colours 色彩浓艳的：*the richly coloured mosaic* 色彩浓艳的镶嵌工艺品 **3 richly deserve** to completely deserve something such as success or punishment 完全应该得到〔成功或惩罚〕：*They got the punishment they so richly deserved.* 他们真是罪有应得。**4** in large amounts 大量（地）：*He was richly rewarded for his services.* 他的服务得到了丰厚的报酬。

Rich·mond /ˋrɪtʃmənd; ˈrɪtʃmənd/ **1** the capital city of the state of Virginia, in the eastern US, which has an important tobacco industry. It was also the capital of the Confederacy during the American Civil War. 里士满〔美国弗吉尼亚州首府，位于美国东部，烟草业在该市具有重要地位。里士满也是美国内战时期南方邦联的首府〕 **2** a COUNTY of New York City which includes Staten Island 里士满〔纽约市一县，包括斯塔滕岛〕 **3** a market town in North Yorkshire, England 里士满〔英格兰北约克郡一集镇〕 **4** Richmond-upon-Thames 泰晤士河畔里士满

Richmond-u·pon-Thames /ˌ‥ ‥ ˈ·/ also 又作 **Richmond** an area of southwest London that includes Kew Gardens, Hampton Court, and Richmond Park, a very large park 泰晤士河畔里士满〔伦敦西南部一地区。那里有基尤植物园、汉普顿宫和占地面积很大的里士满公园〕

Richt·ho·fen, Baron von /ˋrɪkthofən, ˋbærən vɑn; ˈrɪkthəʊfən, ˈbærən vɒn/ (1892-1918) a German aircraft pilot known as the **Red Baron**, who commanded a group of fighter planes in World War I known as Richthofen's **Flying Circus**. He shot down 80 aircraft during the war, which was more than any other pilot, before being killed. 里希特霍芬〔(1892-1918)，德国飞行员，有“红色男爵”之称。一战时期，他曾指挥“里希特霍芬飞行杂技团”的一批战斗机，在战斗中击落80架敌机，战绩无人可及，最后在战场阵亡〕

rick[1] /rɪk; rɪk/ *n* [C] a large pile of STRAW or grass that is kept in a field until it is needed 禾堆；干草堆[垛]

rick[2] *v* [T] *BrE* to twist and slightly injure your back, neck, ANKLE etc【英】扭伤：*He whirled around so quickly he ricked his neck.* 他转身太快，扭伤了脖子。

rick·ets /ˋrɪkɪts; ˈrɪkɨts/ *n* [U] a disease that children get in which their bones become soft and bent, caused by a lack of VITAMIN D〔儿童由于缺乏维生素D而患的〕佝偻病

rick·et·y /ˋrɪkətɪ; ˈrɪkɨti/ *adj* a rickety piece of furniture or part of a building is in such bad condition that it looks as if it will break if you use it 快要散架的，摇摇晃晃的：*an old rickety wooden chair* 一把快要散架的旧木椅 —see picture on page A18 参见A18页图

rick·shaw /ˋrɪkʃɔ; ˈrɪkʃɔː/ *n* [C] a small vehicle used in South East Asia for carrying one or two passengers, that is pulled by someone walking or riding a bicycle 人力车，黄包车

ric·o·chet[1] /ˋrɪkʃe; ˈrɪkəʃeɪ/ *v* [I] if a moving object, such as a bullet or stone, ricochets, it changes direction when it hits a surface at an angle〔子弹、石块等运动物体〕回跳，反弹：[+off] *Bullets ricocheted off the boulders around him.* 子弹从他周围的巨石上飞窜。

ricochet[2] *n* [C] **1** something such as a bullet or a stone that has ricocheted 弹飞的物体 **2** an act of ricocheting 弹飞，反弹

rid[1] /rɪd; rɪd/ *adj* **1 get rid of a)** to throw away something you do not want or use any more 丢弃，扔掉：*It's time we got rid of all these old toys.* 该是我们把这些旧玩具全部丢掉的时候了。**b)** to take action so that you no longer have something unpleasant that you do not want 摆脱，除去：*I can't get rid of this cough.* 我咳嗽老是不好。| *He opened the windows to get rid of the smell of stale tobacco.* 他打开窗户想排除污浊的烟草味。**c)** to make someone leave because you do not like them or because they are causing problems 赶走〔某人〕：*I had to get rid of my assistant because he was habitually late.* 我不得不把我的助手开除，因为他总是迟到。**2 be rid of** to have got rid of something or someone so that they are not there to worry or annoy you 摆脱，除掉，除去：*The clerical part of his job was tedious, and he was glad to be rid of it.* 他的那部分文书工作枯燥乏味，摆脱了之后他很高兴。| **be well rid of** *especially spoken* (=be lucky to be rid of)【尤口】有幸摆脱了… *You're well rid of her, she's nothing but trouble.* 你幸亏摆脱了她，她只会给人添麻烦。

rid[2] *v past tense* **rid** or **ridded** *past participle* **rid** *present participle* **ridding**

rid sb/sth **of** sth *v* [T] **1** to remove something or someone that is bad or harmful from a place, organization etc 使摆脱，使除掉〔不好或有害的人或东西〕：*A huge vaccination program rid the world of smallpox.* 庞大的疫苗接种计划使天花在世界上绝迹。**2 rid yourself of sth** to take action so that you do not have a feeling, thought, or problem that was causing you trouble any more 使自己摆脱某事物：*She's trying to rid herself of a dependence on drugs.* 她正在努力戒除毒瘾。

rid·dance /ˋrɪdn̩s; ˈrɪdns/ *n* [U] **good riddance** *spoken* a rude way of saying you are glad someone has left【口】总算摆脱了〔庆幸某人走后说的不礼貌的话〕：*"Jim's left." "Well, good riddance," said Faye. "I never liked him."* “吉姆走了。”“哦，谢天谢地，”费伊说，“我压根儿就不喜欢他。”

-ridden /rɪdn̩; rɪdn/ *suffix* [in adjectives 构成形容词] **1** feeling too much of a strong emotion 为…所苦的：*her guilt-ridden dreams* 她那充满内疚感的梦 **2** too full of something 充斥…的，全是…的：*mosquito-ridden swamps* 蚊虫为患的沼泽

rid·dle[1] /ˋrɪdl̩; ˈrɪdl/ *n* [C] **1** a question that is deliberately very confusing and usually has a humorous or clever answer 谜，谜语：*Solve this riddle – What is black and white and red all over? Answer – An embarrassed zebra.* 猜猜这个谜语：什么东西黑白相间却全身通红？谜底是：一匹难为情的斑马。**2** a mysterious action, event, or situation that you do not understand and cannot explain 奥秘，费解之事：*The origins of the Basque language remain a riddle.* 巴斯克语的起源仍是个谜。| *the riddle of the universe* 宇宙的奥秘 **3** a large wire container with holes in it used to separate earth from stones〔筛分土石的〕粗筛

riddle[2] *v* [T] **1** to shake the coal etc in a fire or push it about with a stick, in order to remove ashes 摇动〔炉栅〕；用〔拨火棍〕使灰落下 **2** to make a lot of small holes in something 在…上弄许多小洞

rid·dled /ˋrɪdl̩d; ˈrɪdld/ *adj* **1 riddled with** very full of something, especially something bad or unpleasant 充斥，布满：

awful concrete apartment blocks, riddled with damp 令人讨厌的、潮湿的混凝土公寓住宅区 | *an isolated village community, riddled with prejudice* 一个与世隔绝、充满偏见的村落 **2 riddled with holes** full of small holes 到处是小洞的: *The wall of the fort was riddled with bullet holes.* 城堡的墙壁上到处是子弹洞。| *streets riddled with potholes* 到处坑坑洼洼的街道

ride¹ /raɪd; raɪd/ *v past tense* **rode** /rod; rəʊd/ *past participle* **ridden** /ˈrɪdn̩; ˈrɪdn/

1 ▶ANIMAL 动物◀ [I,T] to sit on an animal, especially a horse, and make it move along 骑（马等）: *She learnt to ride when she was seven.* 她7岁时学会了骑马。| **ride away/across/back etc** *He rode away across the marshes.* 他骑马穿过沼泽离去。| **ride sth** *I've never ridden a horse.* 我从未骑过马。| **ride on sth** *She arrived riding on a white horse.* 她骑着一匹白马到来。| **go riding** *I go riding every Saturday.* 我每个星期六都去骑马。| **ride a race** *I rode a good number of races last season.* 上个赛季我参加了许多次赛马。| **ride a winner** (=ride a horse that wins a race) 赛马获胜 *I rode my first winner last year.* 去年我第一次在赛马中获胜。| **ride the countryside/range** *AmE* (=to travel on a horse across the countryside) 【美】骑马穿过乡间 *They rode the countryside in search of her.* 他们骑马穿过乡间寻找她。

2 ▶BICYCLE/MOTORBIKE 自行车/摩托车◀ [I always+ adv/prep,T] to travel on a bicycle or MOTORBIKE 骑（自行车或摩托车）**ride away/down/to etc** *They mounted their bikes and rode off.* 他们骑上自行车离开了。| **ride sth** *She rode her bicycle to school every day.* 她每天骑自行车上学。| **ride on sth** *Can I ride on your bike?* 我能骑你的自行车吗?

3 ▶VEHICLE 车辆◀ [I always+adv/prep,T] *especially AmE* to travel in a bus, car, or other vehicle 【尤美】乘坐（车辆）: **ride in/on sth** *It was the first time they had ridden in a train.* 这是他们第一次坐火车。| *I ride in cabs whenever I can.* 只要可能我总是坐计程车。| **ride to/into/back etc** *We got onto the bus and rode into San Francisco.* 我们上了公共汽车，到圣弗朗西斯科去。| **ride a bus** *AmE* 【美】: *Ann rode a bus for the rest of the distance.* 剩下的路程安乘了公共汽车。

4 ride on sb's shoulders/back if a child rides on someone's shoulders or back, they are carried in that way〔小孩〕骑在某人肩上/背在某人背上: *He was tired so he rode on his father's shoulders.* 他累了，于是骑在父亲的肩上。

5 ▶IN A LIFT 在电梯里◀ [I always+adv/prep,T] *especially AmE* to travel up or down in a lift 【尤美】乘坐（电梯）: **ride up/down** *I walked to the elevator and rode back down.* 我走过去乘电梯回到楼下。| **ride sth** *When the elevator arrived he rode it down to his floor.* 电梯来了，他乘电梯下到他那层。

6 ▶IN WATER 在水里◀ **a)** [I always+adv/prep] to move or float on the water 航行; 漂浮: *The smaller boat was lighter and rode higher in the water.* 那条较小的船比较轻，在水里浮得比较高。| **ride at anchor** *There was a large ship riding at anchor in the bay.* 一艘大船抛锚停泊在海湾。**b) ride a wave** to float on a wave and move forward with it 随浪漂浮（前进）: *The sea was full of surfboarders riding the waves.* 海里到处是踏浪而行的冲浪者。

7 be riding high to feel very happy and confident 春风得意，扬扬自得: *They were riding high on their election victory.* 他们因在选举中获胜而春风得意。

8 let sth ride *spoken* to take no action about something that is wrong or unpleasant 【口】听之任之，放任自流: *He made a derogatory remark, but I let it ride.* 他说了无礼的话，不过我并没有计较。

9 ride roughshod over to ignore someone else's feelings or ideas because you have the power or authority to do this 忽视〔别人的感受或意见〕: *He was accused of riding roughshod over his colleagues' proposals.* 他被指责无视同事的建议。

10 ▶ANNOY SB 惹恼某人◀ [T] *AmE spoken* to annoy someone by repeatedly criticizing them or asking them to do things 【美口】数落，缠住: *Stop riding her – she's doing her best.* 不要缠着她不放，她正在尽全力。

11 ride a punch/blow to move back slightly when someone hits you, so that you are not hit with so much force〔稍微后退以〕躲闪拳击/重击: *He managed to ride the punch.* 他往后一闪，虽然中了一拳，但力量减轻了。

12 be riding for a fall *informal* to be doing something unwise which could result in failure 【非正式】〔不顾后果地〕蛮干，鲁莽行事: *I had a feeling he was riding for a fall, and tried to tell him so.* 我感觉他在蛮干，于是设法告诉他这一点。

ride sb ↔ **down** *phr v* [T] to knock someone down when you are riding on a horse 骑马撞倒〔某人〕: *They were almost ridden down by the cavalry.* 他们差一点儿被骑兵撞倒。

ride on sth *phr v* [T] if someone's success or the respect that they get is riding on something, it depends on it〔成功、名誉等〕取决于: *He knew he had to win – his reputation was riding on it.* 他知道自己必须取胜，他的名声都系于此。

ride sth ↔ **out** *phr v* **1** [T] if a ship rides out a storm, it manages to keep floating until the storm has ended〔船只〕平安度过〔风暴〕**2** [T] if you ride out a difficult situation, you are not badly harmed by it 安然渡过〔难关〕: *The company was deeply involved in the scandal, but managed to ride it out successfully.* 该公司深陷丑闻中，但还是成功地渡过了难关。

ride up *phr v* [I] if a skirt rides up, it moves upwards so that it is no longer covering your body properly〔衣服等〕向上拱，往上缩

ride² *n* [C]

1 ▶JOURNEY 旅行◀ a journey on a horse or bicycle, or in a vehicle〔骑马、骑自行车或乘车的〕旅行，旅程: *It was a lovely morning for a ride.* 那天早上天气很好，适合出去兜风。| [+in/on] *a ride in the director's personal car* 乘坐主任的私人汽车 | **go for a ride** *Let's go for a ride in the countryside.* 让我们乘车到郊外去兜一圈吧。| **have a ride** *Can I have a ride on your motorbike?* 我能不能搭你的摩托车? | **take sb for a ride** *Shall I take you for a ride in my car?* 我带你坐我的车去兜一圈好吗? | **give sb a ride** *A man gave me a ride back to Harrisburg.* 一位男士让我搭车回到哈里斯堡。| **a car/lorry/train etc ride** *He was exhausted after the coach ride from Manchester.* 他从曼彻斯特乘长途汽车来，非常疲劳。| **get a (free) ride** *I managed to get a free ride down to the station.* 我设法免费搭车到了车站。| **hitch a ride** *She hitched a ride into town.* 她搭便车进了城。

2 give sb a rough ride *informal* to make a situation difficult or unpleasant for someone in authority 【非正式】使某人难受，给某人出难题: *The journalists gave the Prime Minister a pretty rough ride.* 记者们让首相下不了台。

3 take sb for a ride *spoken* to trick someone, especially in order to get money from them 【口】欺骗某人〔尤指骗钱〕: *I'd just begun to realise he was taking me for a ride.* 我才开始意识到他在骗我。

4 come/go along for the ride *spoken* to join what other people are doing just for pleasure, not because you are seriously interested in it 【口】凑热闹: *I had nothing better to do, so I thought I'd go along for the ride.* 我没有什么事可做，因此想去凑凑热闹。

5 have/be in for a bumpy ride *informal* to have or be likely to have difficulties or problems 【非正式】会有麻烦

6 ▶MACHINE 机器◀ a large machine that people ride on for pleasure at a FAIR〔游乐场中〕供人乘坐娱乐的装置: *The rides are exciting, but very expensive.* 乘坐那些玩意儿令人兴奋，可是很贵。

7 ▶PATH 小路◀ a path that is suitable for horses but not for cars〔供马走的〕小道: *a grassy ride* 长满草的小道

Ride a Cock-Horse /, · · · ˈ · / a NURSERY RHYME (=an old song or poem for children).《骑木马》〔一童谣名〕: *Ride a cock-horse to Banbury Cross, /To see a fine lady ride on a white horse, /With rings on her fingers and bells on her toes, /She shall have music wherever she goes.* 班伯里十字架，跨木马观一下，/举头见摩登女，骑白马一同去，/纤细手指环绕，饰银铃脚趾俏，/随兴致策马行，脚铃声响不停。

Ride of the Valkyries, the /, · · · ˈ · · / an exciting piece of music from the OPERA *The Valkyries* by Richard Wagner, played when the Valkyries, female messengers of the god Odin, ride into battle on their flying horses and take the souls of dead soldiers to Valhalla. The music is often used in films and advertisements.《女武神在飞翔》〔理查德·瓦格纳的歌剧《女武神》中的一段感人的旋律。天神奥丁的女信使即女武神骑着飞马奔向战场，把阵亡将士的灵魂带到瓦尔哈拉英灵殿时演奏的就是这段音乐。这段音乐也常用于电影和广告〕

rid·er /ˈraɪdɚ; ˈraɪdə/ *n* [C] **1** someone who rides a horse, bicycle etc 骑师; 骑车者 **2** a statement that is added, especially to an official decision or judgment〔尤指正式决议或裁决的〕附文，附件; 附加条款: *The rider stated that paragraph 27 applied only to foreign imports.* 附件说第27段仅适用于外国进口货物。

ridge¹ /rɪdʒ; rɪdʒ/ *n* [C] **1** a long area of high land, especially at the top of a mountain 山脊: *a windswept ridge* 当风的山脊 — see picture on page A12 参见A12页图 **2 a)** a line of something that rises above a surface 一列隆起物: *a ridge of boulders* 一列隆起的巨石 | *a sandy ridge* 沙脊 **b)** a long narrow raised part of a surface 狭长的隆起部分: *The ridges on the soles give the shoes a better grip.* 鞋底上隆起的棱可以更好地防滑。**3 a ridge of high pressure** *technical* a long area of high ATMOSPHERIC pressure 【术语】高压脊

ridge² *v* [T] to make a ridge or ridges in something 使成脊状，使隆起

ridged /rɪdʒd; rɪdʒd/ *adj* something that is ridged has ridges on its surface 隆起的，皱起的: *gnarled, ridged bark* 扭曲起皱的树皮

rid·i·cule¹ /ˈrɪdɪkjul; ˈrɪdʒkjuːl/ *n* [U] unkind laughter or remarks intended to make someone or something seem stupid 嘲笑，奚落: **be held up to ridicule** (=be publicly made to look stupid) 成为笑话 | **an object of ridicule** (=a person or thing that everyone laughs at and regards as stupid) 被取笑[嘲笑]的对象 *In 'The Lord of the Flies', Piggy had become an object of ridicule, ignored by the other boys.* 在《蝇王》中，佩奇成了众人取笑的对象，其他男孩都不把他放在眼里。

ridicule² *v* [T] to laugh at a person, idea, institution etc 嘲笑，嘲弄，奚落: *My ideas were ridiculed by the rest of the team.* 我的想法受到其他队员的嘲笑。| *He used his acute brain and mischievous wit to ridicule Tory MPs.* 他用自己敏锐的头脑和顽皮的机智来嘲笑保守党的议员。

S2 **ri·dic·u·lous** /rɪˈdɪkjələs; rɪˈdɪkjᵊləs/ *adj* silly or unreasonable 愚蠢的；荒唐的，可笑的: *She looked absolutely ridiculous in those trousers.* 她穿着那条裤子显得非常可笑。| *"I'm too scared to go on my own." "Oh, don't be ridiculous!"* "我很害怕，不敢自己一个人去。" "噢，别傻啦！" | **it is ridiculous that** *It's ridiculous that we have to wait six weeks.* 我们得等六个星期，这太荒唐了。—**ridiculously** *adv* —**ridiculousness** *n* [U]

rid·ing /ˈraɪdɪn; ˈraɪdɪŋ/ *n* [U] the sport or activity of riding horses 骑马（运动）

Ries·ling /ˈrizlɪn; ˈriːzlɪŋ/ a type of white wine, made especially in Germany, that has a light flowery taste 雷斯令〔尤指产于德国的一款白葡萄酒，有淡淡的花香味〕

rife /raɪf; raɪf/ *adj* **1** [not before noun 不用于名词前] if something bad or unpleasant is rife, it is very common 〔坏事或讨厌的事〕普遍存在的，流行的: *Violent crime is rife in our inner cities.* 暴力犯罪在我们的贫民区非常普遍。—see also 另见 **run rife** (RUN¹ (37)) **2 rife with** full of something bad or unpleasant 充斥着…: *The streets were rife with rumors of the President's resignation.* 大街小巷都充斥着总统辞职的谣传。

riff /rɪf; rɪf/ *n* [C] a repeated series of notes in popular or JAZZ music 〔流行音乐或爵士乐中的〕重复乐段: *whistling a Scott Joplin riff* 用口哨吹奏〔美国作曲家〕斯科特·乔普林一首乐曲的重复乐段

rif·fle /ˈrɪfl; ˈrɪfəl/ also 又作 **riffle through** *v* [T] *informal* to quickly turn over the pages of a book, magazine etc 【非正式】快速翻阅〔书、杂志等〕

riff-raff /ˈrɪf ˌræf; ˈrɪf ræf/ *n* [U] an insulting word for people who are noisy, badly-behaved, or of low social class 地痞流氓；乌合之众〔含侮辱之意〕: *She seemed to have invited most of the local riff-raff.* 她似乎邀请了当地大部分不三不四的人。

ri·fle¹ /ˈraɪfl; ˈraɪfəl/ *n* [C] a gun with a long BARREL (=tubeshaped part) which you hold up to your shoulder 来复枪，步枪

rifle² *v* [T] **1** also 又作 **rifle through** to search quickly through a cupboard, drawer etc 迅速翻遍〔柜子、抽屉等〕: *He rifled through his pockets for a coin.* 他为找一枚硬币翻遍了口袋。**2** to steal things from a place 偷窃: *The warehouse's entire stock was rifled.* 仓库的全部存货都被偷走了。

rifle range /ˈ· · ·/ *n* [C] a place where people practise shooting with rifles 步枪射击场

rift /rɪft; rɪft/ *n* [C] **1** a situation in which two people or groups have begun to dislike or distrust each other, usually caused by a serious disagreement 分裂，不和: *The government has been weakened by internal rifts.* 内部不和把政府削弱了。**2** a crack or narrow opening in a large mass of rock, cloud etc 〔岩石、云等的〕裂缝，裂口

rift val·ley /ˈ· ˌ· ·/ *n* [C] a valley with very steep sides, formed by the cracking and moving of the Earth's surface 裂谷

rig¹ /rɪg; rɪg/ *v* **rigged, rigging** [T] **1** to arrange or influence an election, competition etc in a dishonest way so that you get the result that you want 〔以不正当手段〕操纵〔选举、比赛等〕；在〔选举、比赛等〕中做手脚: *She claimed the election was rigged.* 她声称这次选举被人操纵。**2** [usually passive 一般用被动态] to provide a ship with ropes, sails etc 给〔船〕配备索具、帆具等: *a fully-rigged vessel* 一艘配备齐全的船

rig sb ↔ **out** *phr v* [T] *informal* to dress someone in special or unusual clothes 【非正式】给〔某人〕穿上特别[奇异]的衣服: *They had rigged the little boy out in a sailor suit.* 他们给那个小男孩穿上了水手服。

rig sth ↔ **up** *phr v* [T] *informal* to make equipment, furniture etc quickly from objects that you find around you 【非正式】仓促拼凑: *We rigged up a simple shower at the back of the cabin.* 我们在小木屋的后面匆匆装了一个简单的淋浴器。

rig² *n* [C] **1** a large structure in the sea used for getting oil from the ground under the sea 〔油田的〕海上钻台 **2** the way in which a ship's sails and MASTS are arranged 帆桅的装配〔方式〕 **3** *informal* a large TRUCK 【非正式】大型卡车: *driving the rig down to Baltimore* 将这辆大卡车开到巴尔的摩 **4** *AmE informal* a set of equipment for a special purpose 【美，非正式】成套设备: *the photographer's camera and all the rest of his rig* 摄影师的照相机和他其余的设备 **5** *old-fashioned* a set of clothes 【过时】套装

Ri·ga /ˈrigə; ˈriːgə/ the capital city of Latvia on the coast of the Baltic Sea 里加〔拉脱维亚首都，位于波罗的海沿岸〕

rig·a·ma·role /ˈrɪgəmərol; ˈrɪgəmərəʊl/ *n* [C] an American spelling of RIGMAROLE rigmarole 的美式拼法

rig·a·to·ni /ˌrɪgəˈtonɪ; ˌrɪgəˈtəʊni/ *n* [U] a type of PASTA in the shape of short tubes 波纹管状通心粉 —see picture at 参见 PASTA 图

rig·ging /ˈrɪgɪn; ˈrɪgɪŋ/ *n* [U] all the ropes, chains etc that hold up a ship's sails 船上的全部帆缆，索具 —see picture at 参见 YACHT 图

right¹ /raɪt; raɪt/ *adj* S1 W1

1 ►TRUE/CORRECT 真实的/正确的◄ based on true facts; correct 如实的；正确的: *Is that the right time?* 那时间对吗？| *Yes. $6.47 is the right answer.* 对，6.47美元是正确答案。| *New research has proved their theories right.* 新的研究证明他们的理论是正确的。| **be right about** *You were right about the party – it was awful.* 聚会的事你说对了 —— 非常糟糕。| **half right** (=partly but not completely right) 对了一半 *Well, you're half right – he's not actually an actor, but he does work in the theatre.* 啊，你说对了一半——他其实不是演员，但确实在剧院工作。

2 ►CORRECT/NORMAL 正确的/正常的◄ in the position, order or state which is correct or where something works best 正确的；正常的: *This diagram's not right!* 这张图表不对！| **put sth right** (=change something so that it is correct or works properly) 纠正某事 *You'll have to call a plumber to put the machine right.* 你得请管子工来把机器修理好。

3 that's right *spoken* 【口】 **a)** used to agree with what someone says or to answer 'yes' to a question 没错；对: *"Is this Piccadilly Circus?" "That's right, mate."* "这里是皮卡迪利广场吗？" "是的，老兄。" | *"...and before you know it, it's too late." "That's right, that's right."* "…再等就太晚了。" "是的，是的。" **b)** used when you are telling someone that you are angry about what they are doing 行啦；够啦〔用于对别人所做的事感到愤怒时〕: *That's right! Just go out and leave me to do the dishes as usual!* 行啦！你出去算了，还是跟平时一样让我来洗碗吧！

4 ►SIDE 侧面◄ [only before noun 仅用于名词前] **a)** concerning or belonging to the right side of your body, which has the hand that most people write with 右边的，右侧的: *Raise your right arm.* 请举起右手。| *My right shoe pinches.* 我右脚的鞋夹脚。—opposite 反义词 LEFT¹ (1) **b)** on the same side of something as your right side 右方的，靠右的: *Take the next right turn.* 在下一个路口往右拐。| *the right bank of the river* 河的右岸 —opposite 反义词 LEFT¹ (2)

5 ►SUITABLE 合适的◄ most suitable for a particular occasion or purpose 恰当的: *This is definitely the right decision for the company.* 这对于公司来说肯定是正确的决定。| **be right for/be the right person for** *Floella is the right person for that job.* 佛罗埃拉是那份工作的恰当人选。| **be right for sb/be the right person for sb** (=to be a suitable partner for someone) 对某人是合适的/是合适的搭档 *Elaine and Stu are so right for each other!* 伊莱恩和斯图如此般配！

6 ►MORALLY 道义上◄ an action that is right is morally correct 符合道德的，正当的: **right to do sth** *Do you think I was right to report them to the police?* 你觉得我向警方检举他们做得对吗？| *It can't be right to keep lying to your husband.* 老是欺骗你的丈夫是不对的。| **it's only right** (=anything else would not be right) 唯一正确的 *It's only right that the children get an equal share.* 只有平均分给孩子们才是正确的。| **it is right that** *I think it's right that the people who work hardest should earn the most.* 我认为工作最努力的人报酬最高是合理的。—opposite 反义词 WRONG¹ (4)

7 ►TOTAL 完全的◄ [only before noun 仅用于名词前] *BrE spoken* used to emphasize how bad someone or something is 【英口】完全的，地道的〔强调某人或某事坏的程度〕: *He sounds like a right idiot!* 他听起来像个十足的白痴！| *Don't go in there, it's a right rip-off.* 别进去，那简直是敲竹杠。| **right royal** (=extremely special in a way that is suitable for a king, queen etc) 皇家气派的 *a right royal welcome* 非常隆重的欢迎

8 things are not right used to say that there are problems connected with a relationship or situation 〔关系或情况〕不对头，有

问题: *Things haven't been right between Carl and me for a while now.* 卡尔和我之间的关系不好已经有段时间了。

9 be in the right place at the right time to seem to always be in the place where something useful becomes available or is being offered 在恰当的时间出现在恰当的地方: *Being a news photographer is all about being in the right place at the right time.* 当新闻摄影师，就是要在恰当的时间出现在恰当的地点。

10▶HEALTHY 健康的◀ *spoken* healthy【口】健康的: *I haven't been feeling right all day.* 我一整天都觉得不舒服。| **put sb right** (=make someone feel healthy again) 让某人恢复健康 *A week's rest will put you right again.* 休息一个星期，你就没事了。—see also 另见 **put sb straight/right** (PUT (15))

11 not right in the head/not in your right mind *usually humorous* crazy【一般幽默】疯了: *If he thinks he can get to the Olympics, he's not in his right mind!* 他如果以为自己可以参加奥运会，那真是疯了！

12 (as) right as rain *informal* completely healthy, especially after an illness【非正式】〔尤指病后〕完全健康: *The doctor says I'll be as right as rain in a couple of days.* 医生说我过两天就会完全恢复正常。

13▶SOCIALLY 社交上◀ *BrE* the right people, places, schools etc are considered to be the best or most important【英】〔人、地方、学校等〕最优秀的，地位最高的: *Sonia's always careful to be seen with the right people.* 索尼娅交朋友很谨慎，总是让人看见她和有社会地位的人在一起。

14 right you are/righto/righty ho *BrE spoken* used to agree with what someone is saying or telling you to do【英口】没错；好的: *"Shut the door, will you?" "Righto."* "把门关上好吗?" "好的。"

15 am I right in thinking (that) *spoken* used when you think that something is true, but you are not completely sure【口】我认为…对吗: *Am I right in thinking that you come from Australia?* 我觉得你是澳大利亚人，对不对?

Frequencies of the word **right** in spoken and written English 单词 right 在英语口语和书面语中的使用频率

Based on the British National Corpus and the Longman Lancaster Corpus 据英国国家语料库和朗文兰开斯特语料库

This graph shows that the word **right** is much more common in spoken English than in written English. This is because it has several uses as an interjection in conversations. 本图表显示，单词 right 在英语口语中的使用频率远远高于书面语，因为它有些用法是在对话中用作感叹语。

right (*adj*) **SPOKEN USES**
right 的口语用法

16 *BrE* used to get someone's attention so that you can tell them something【英】好〔用来引起注意〕: *Right! Open your books on page 16.* 好！将书翻到第 16 页。

17 *BrE* used to say you are ready to do something【英】好〔表示准备就绪〕: *Right, let's go!* 好，我们走吧！

18 *especially BrE* used to say 'yes' to a suggestion or order【尤英】是的，好的〔用于对建议或命令的回答〕: *"Come over tomorrow." "Right, OK, see you then."* "请明天过来。" "好的，好，明天见。"

19 used to agree with what someone says 对，是〔表示同意〕: *"I mean, why shouldn't she go out with him if she wants to?" "Yeah, right."* "我的意思是，如果她愿意，为什么不跟他谈恋爱?" "对，就是。"

20 used as a question to ask if what you have said is correct 对不对〔询问自己所说的是否正确〕: *We're leaving at 10.30, right?* 我们 10 点 30 分走，对不对?

21 used to check that someone is understanding what you are saying 对不对〔问对方明不明白你说的话〕: *So I went into the bar, right, and I saw the manager, right, and I said...* 于是我走进酒吧，对不对，我看见了经理，对不对，我说…

right² *adv* [1] [1]

1 right at/behind/in front of exactly in a particular position or place 就在…/…后面/…前面: *She was standing right in the middle of the room.* 她就站在屋子的正中间。| *There's the house, right in front of you.* 就是那所房子，就在你面前。

2▶IMMEDIATELY 立刻◀ immediately and without any delay 立刻，立即: **right now/away/after** *I'll find the address for you right away.* 我马上就给你找到地址。| *It's on right after the 6:30 news.* 6 点 30 分的新闻之后马上播出。| **right off the bat** *AmE* (=without much thought)【美】立即，不假思索 *Kay wrote the answers down right off the bat.* 凯立刻就写下了答案。

3▶CORRECTLY 正确地◀ correctly 正确地: *We guessed right – they'd already gone.* 我们猜对了—他们已经走了。

4▶DIRECTION/SIDE 方向/侧面◀ towards the direction or side that is on the right 向右，朝右: *Turn right at the crossroads.* 在十字路口向右拐。—opposite 反义词 LEFT²

5 right along/through/into/around etc all the way along, through etc 一直沿着/穿过/进入/围绕等: *Go right to the end of the road.* 一直走到路的尽头。| *I haven't read the book right through yet.* 我还没看完这本书。

6 be right behind sb *spoken* to completely support someone in their ideas or in what they are trying to achieve【口】完全支持某人

7 I'll be right with you/right there *spoken* used to ask someone to wait because you are coming very soon【口】我马上就来/到: *"Lunch is ready!" "I'll be right there."* "吃午饭啦!" "我马上就到。"

8 be right up there (with) *informal* to be as good or as important as the very best【非正式】(与…) 不相上下；(与…) 同等重要: *As far as I'm concerned he's right up there with Bob Dylan.* 依我看，他与鲍勃·迪伦不相上下。

9 right, left and centre *BrE*【英】, **right and left** *AmE*【美】everywhere or in every way 到处，处处: *We're losing money right, left and centre.* 我们处处都在亏本。

R

right³ *n* [2] [1]

1▶ALLOWED 允许的◀ [C usually singular 一般用单数] if you have the right to do something you are morally, legally, or officially allowed to do it 权利: **right to do sth** *We have a constitutional right to defend ourselves.* 宪法赋予我们自卫的权利。| *Everyone should have the right to live in peace.* 每个人都应该拥有和平生活的权利。| **be within your rights (to do sth)** (=be morally or legally allowed to do something)〔在道德或法律上〕(做某事)是正当的 *You'd be well within your rights to take him to court.* 你完全有权控告他。| **as of right** *formal* (=because it is their right)【正式】有权 *Every shareholder will receive an invitation as of right.* 每一位股东都将接到邀请，这是他们的权利。

2 have a right to be annoyed/upset/angry to have a good or understandable reason for being annoyed, upset etc 感到烦恼/不快/生气是有道理的: *You had every right to be angry with them.* 你有充分理由生他们的气。

3 have no right to do sth used to say that someone's actions are completely unreasonable or unfair 没有权利做某事: *You have no right to treat us like this – we are innocent.* 你没有权利这样对待我们，我们是无辜的。

4 the right a) the side of your body that has the hand that most people write with, or this side of anything else 右边，右方，右侧: *Take the first turning on the right.* 在右边第一个路口转弯。| *On your right, you can see the Houses of Parliament.* 在你的右侧你可以看到议会大厦。| *Take two steps to the right.* 向右走两步。**b)** also 又作 **the Right** [singular] political parties or groups such as the CONSERVATIVES in Britain or the REPUBLICANS in the US, which strongly support the CAPITALIST economic system 右翼政党〈如英国的保守党、美国的共和党等〉

5 rights [plural] the freedom and advantages that everyone should be allowed to have〔人人应有的〕权利，权益: *We must stand up and fight for our rights!* 我们必须起来为我们的权利而斗争！| *a denial of basic human rights* 剥夺基本人权 | **women's/workers' rights etc** *New legislation is gradually taking away workers' rights.* 新的立法正在逐渐削减工人的权利。| **equal rights** (=the same rights for everyone, whatever their sex, race, or social position) 平等的权利 —see also 另见 CIVIL RIGHTS, HUMAN RIGHTS

6▶CORRECT BEHAVIOUR 恰当的行为◀ [U] behaviour that is generally agreed to be morally correct〔道德上〕正确，对: *You're old enough to know what's right.* 你已经长大了，该知道什么是对的。| *Some of these kids don't seem to know the difference between right and wrong.* 这些孩子当中有的似乎不能分辨是非。

7 be in the right to have the best reasons, arguments etc in a disagreement with someone else〔在与别人的争论中〕有理: *Both sides are convinced that they are in the right.* 双方都相信自己有理。

8 by rights *spoken* used to describe what should happen if things are done fairly or correctly【口】按理(说): *By rights Jenkins should have had a promotion by now.* 按理说，詹金斯现在应该提升了。

9 in your own right without depending on anyone or anything else 依靠自己的能力，根据自己的权利〔而不依赖于其他因素〕: *Elizabeth II is Queen in her own right.* 伊丽莎白二世是名正言顺地继承王位的。

10 put sth/sb to rights to make a place, person, or situation return to normal again 使某事/某人恢复正常，纠正某事/某人: *This medicine will soon put you to rights.* 这药会很快使你痊愈的。| *It took ages to put the room to rights again.* 把房间收拾好花了很长时间。

11 the rights and wrongs of all the different reasons for and against something …的是非曲直: *I'm not interested in the rights and wrongs of the system, I just want my money back!* 我对这个制度的是与非不感兴趣，我只是想取回我的钱!

12 do right by *old-fashioned* to do what is morally correct for someone【过时】公正对待〔某人〕: *I mean to do right by her.* 我打算公正待她。

13 ►HIT 击打◄ [C] a hit using your right hand 右手打出的一击，右手拳: *He got me with a right on the jaw.* 他一个右拳打在我的下巴上。—**rightness** *n* [U] —see also 另见 **two wrongs don't make a right** (WRONG³ (5))

right⁴ *v* [T] **1 right a wrong** to do something to prevent an unjust situation from continuing 矫枉; 平反 **2** to put something back into the state or situation that it should be in 矫正，纠正: *We must try to right the balance between taxation and government spending.* 我们必须设法恢复税收与政府开支之间的平衡。**3** to put something, especially a boat, back into its correct upright position 把〔尤指小船〕扶正，摆止; 扭转: *I finally managed to right the canoe.* 我终于把独木舟翻过来了。

right an·gle /ˈ· ˌ··/ *n* [C] **1** an angle of 90°, like the angles at the corners of a square 直角 —see picture at 参见 ANGLE¹ 图 **2 be at right angles (to sth)** if two things are at right angles, they make a 90° angle where they touch (与某物) 成直角 —**right-angled** *adj*: *a right-angled triangle* 直角三角形

right·eous /ˈraɪtʃəs; ˈraɪtʃəs/ *adj* **1 righteous indignation/anger etc** strong feelings of anger when you think a situation is not morally right or fair 义愤: *"You should have asked me first," said Corrine, full of righteous indignation.* "你应该先问问我的。"科林义愤填膺地说。**2** *formal* morally good and fair【正式】正派的，正直的: *a righteous and loving God* 正义、慈爱的上帝 —see also 另见 SELF-RIGHTEOUS —**righteously** *adv* —**righteousness** *n* [U]

right field /ˈ· ·/ *n* **1** [C] one of the main areas of the playing field in BASEBALL〔棒球的〕右外场 —opposite 反义词 LEFT FIELD **2** [U] the position of someone who plays in this area 右外场手

right·ful /ˈraɪtfəl; ˈraɪtfəl/ *adj* [only before noun 仅用于名词前] *formal* according to what is legally and morally correct【正式】合法的; 正义的，公正的: *Every effort was made to return the purse to its rightful owner.* 尽了一切努力把钱包还给它的合法主人。| *the rightful heir to the throne* 王位的合法继承人 —**rightfully** *adv*: *the lands that are rightfully yours* 理应属于你的土地 —**rightfulness** *n* [U]

right-hand /ˈ· ·/ *adj* [only before noun 仅用于名词前] on the right side of something 右边的，右侧的: *Get into the right-hand lane.* 进右边的车道。| *It's on the right-hand side.* 在右边。—opposite 反义词 LEFT-HAND

right-hand drive /ˌ· · ˈ·/ *adj* [only before noun 仅用于名词前] a right-hand drive vehicle is one in which the driver sits on the right〔交通工具〕右御的，右座驾驶的 —opposite 反义词 LEFT-HAND DRIVE

right-hand·ed /ˌ· ˈ··◄/ *adj* **1** a right-handed person uses their right hand for writing, throwing etc〔写字、投掷等〕惯用右手的 **2** a right-handed tool is designed for right-handed people〔工具〕为惯用右手的人设计的: *right-handed scissors* 供右手用的剪子 —opposite 反义词 LEFT-HANDED —**right-handed** *adv*

right-hand·er /ˌ· ˈ··/ *n* [C] **1** someone who uses their right hand for writing, throwing etc 惯用右手的人 **2** a hit with your right hand 右手打出的一击，右手拳 —opposite 反义词 LEFT-HANDER

right-hand man /ˌ· · ˈ·/ *n* [singular] the person who supports and helps you the most, especially in your job〔尤指工作中的〕得力助手

Right Hon the written abbreviation of 缩写= RIGHT HONOURABLE

Right Hon·our·a·ble /ˈ· ˌ····/ *adj* used when formally announcing or talking about lords or important government ministers in Britain 阁下〔对英国贵族或政府大臣的尊称〕: *the Right Honourable Giles Williams MP* 贾尔斯·威廉斯议员阁下

right·ist /ˈraɪtɪst; ˈraɪtɪst/ *adj* supporting RIGHT-WING ideas or groups 右派的，右倾的 —opposite 反义词 LEFTIST —**rightist** *n* [C] —**rightism** *n* [U]

right·ly /ˈraɪtlɪ; ˈraɪtli/ *adv* **1** for a good or sensible reason 有道理地，有充分理由地: *The audience was rightly outraged at this suggestion.* 听众对这个建议感到愤慨是有道理的。| **quite rightly** *BrE*【英】*She insisted, quite rightly, that we all put our seat belts on.* 她坚持要我们全都系好安全带，这很有道理。**2** correctly 正确地: *As she rightly pointed out, this will do nothing to solve the problem.* 如她正确指出的那样，这丝毫无助于解决问题。| **if I remember rightly** *spoken*【口】*If I remember rightly, Ray's parents emigrated shortly after the war.* 如果我没记错，雷的父母战后不久就移居国外了。**3 rightly or wrongly** used to say that whatever you think of someone's action, this is what they did 不管怎样，不问对不对: *Rightly or wrongly, the Italians decided to withdraw from the competition.* 无论如何，意大利队决定退出比赛。**4 and rightly so** *spoken* used to say that a decision or action you have just described is fair and morally right【口】应该的〔指决定或行动公正且合乎道德〕: *Bryan was punished, and rightly so.* 布赖恩受到了惩罚，这是罪有应得。**5 I can't rightly say/don't rightly know** *spoken* used to say that you are not sure whether something is correct or not【口】我无法肯定

right-mind·ed /ˌ· ˈ··◄/ *adj* a right-minded person has opinions, principles, or standards of behaviour that you approve of 有正义感的，正直的: *All right-minded people will support us.* 所有有正义感的人都会支持我们。—**right-mindedness** *n* [U]

right of ap·peal /ˌ· · ·ˈ·/ *n plural* **rights of appeal** [C] *law* the legal right to ask for a court's decision to be changed【法律】上诉权

right-of-cen·tre /ˌ· · ˈ··◄/ *adj* supporting ideas and aims that are between the centre and the right in politics〔政治上〕中间偏右的 —opposite 反义词 LEFT-OF-CENTRE

right of way /ˌ· · ˈ·/ *n* **1** [U] the right to drive into or across a road before other vehicles〔车辆的〕先行权: *I never know who has right of way at this junction.* 我从来搞不清这个交叉路口谁有先行权。**2** [C] *plural* **rights of way a)** the right to walk across someone else's land〔穿过他人土地的〕穿行权: *We have a right of way across his field to our house.* 我们有穿过他的田地回家的穿行权。**b)** a path that people have the right to use 有权通行的小路: *Private property – no right of way.* 私人土地 —— 禁止穿行。

right on /ˌ· ˈ·◄/ *adj* **1** *BrE* someone who is right on or has right on opinions, supports social justice, equal rights etc【英】伸张正义的，主张平等的: *It's one of those annoyingly right on magazines about the environment.* 这是那些极力主张环保，以致让人厌烦的杂志之一。**2** *AmE* someone is right on when they say something that is correct or that you completely agree with【美】〔某人〕完全正确的: *Jodie was right on with that remark.* 乔迪那样说是完全正确的。

rights is·sue /ˈ· ˌ··/ *n* [C] *technical* an offer of company SHARES (=part of the company you can own) at a cheaper price than usual, to people who own some already【术语】股权股发行，权利股发行〔公司以优惠价向原股东出售新股〕

right-think·ing /ˌ· ˈ··◄/ *adj* a right-thinking person has opinions, principles or standards of behaviour that you approve of 有正义感的，正直的: *Any right-thinking woman would agree.* 任何有正义感的女人都会赞同。

right·ward /ˈraɪtwəd; ˈraɪtwəd/ *adj* on or towards the right 在右的; 向右的: *a rightward glance* 向右一瞥 —opposite 反义词 LEFTWARD

right·wards /ˈraɪtwədz; ˈraɪtwədz/ *especially BrE*【尤英】, usually 一般作 **rightward** *AmE*【美】*adv* on or towards the right 在右侧; 向右 —opposite 反义词 LEFTWARDS

right wing, the /ˌ· ˈ·◄/ *n* political groups that believe very strongly in the CAPITALIST economic system〔政治上的〕右翼，右派: *The party is dominated by its right wing.* 该党为右翼所控制。—**right-wing** *adj*: *right-wing views* 右翼观点 —**right-winger** *n* [C]: *a prominent right-winger in the party* 党内著名的右翼人士 —opposite 反义词 LEFT WING

ri·gid /ˈrɪdʒɪd; ˈrɪdʒɪd/ *adj* **1** rigid methods, systems etc are very strict and difficult to change〔方法、体制等〕严格的，不易改变的: *Betty's finding it hard to keep to the school's rigid rules.* 贝蒂认为很难遵守学校各项严格的规定。| *the rigid discipline of army life* 军旅生活严格的纪律 **2** someone who is rigid is very unwilling to change their ideas〔人〕不愿改变的，顽固的: *He's very rigid and old fashioned.* 他非常顽固，而且老派。| *rigid*

attitudes 固执的态度 **3** stiff and not moving or bending 僵硬的; 不动的; 不能弯曲的: *a tent supported on a rigid framework* 由坚固的骨架支撑的帐篷 | *The rabbit stopped, rigid with fear.* 那只兔子停下来, 吓得一动不动。**4 bore sb rigid** to make someone very bored 使某人感到极度厌烦 —**rigidly** *adv*: *rigidly opposed to all new ideas* 顽固地反对一切新思想 —**rigidity** /rɪˈdʒɪdətɪ; rɪˈdʒɪdɪ̥ti/ *n* [U] —**rigidify** /rɪˈdʒɪdəˌfaɪ; rɪˈdʒɪdɪ̥faɪ/ *AmE*【美】*v* [I,T]

rig·ma·role /ˈrɪgməˌrol; ˈrɪgmərəʊl/ also 又作 **rigamarole** *AmE*【美】*n* **1** [singular,U] a long confusing process or description 漫长纷乱的过程; 冗长杂乱的话: *Omar went into this rigmarole about how he lost his passport.* 奥马尔拉拉杂杂讲了半天, 说他如何丢失了护照。**2** [U] a long confusing series of actions that seems silly 一长串混乱而愚蠢的举动: *I had to go through the whole rigmarole of kissing the Bible and swearing to tell the truth.* 我不得不完成吻《圣经》和宣誓保证讲实话这一长串烦琐的程序。

rig·or /ˈrɪgɚ; ˈrɪgə/ *n* [U] the American spelling of RIGOUR rigour 的美式拼法

rig·or mor·tis /ˌrɪgɚˋmɔrtɪs; ˌrɪgə ˈmɔːtɪ̥s/ *n* [U] *Latin* the condition in which someone's body becomes stiff after they die【拉丁】尸僵, 死后强直

rig·or·ous /ˈrɪgərəs; ˈrɪgərəs/ *adj* **1** careful, thorough, and exact 严密的, 缜密的; 精确的: *rigorous safety checks* 仔细彻底的安全检查 **2** very severe or strict 严酷的, 严厉的: *rigorous army training* 严苛的军训 —**rigorously** *adv*

rig·our *BrE*【英】, **rigor** *AmE*【美】/ˈrɪgɚ; ˈrɪgə/ *n* [U] **1 the rigours of** the problems and unpleasant conditions of a difficult situation〔环境的〕严酷[艰苦]: *all the rigours of a Canadian winter* 加拿大冬天的严寒 **2** *BrE formal* strictness or severity of a punishment【英, 正式】〔惩罚的〕严厉, 严格: *He deserves to be punished with the full rigour of the law.* 他应该受到法律最严厉的惩罚。**3** great care and thoroughness in making sure that something is correct 严密, 缜密, 严谨: *Their research seems to me to be lacking in rigour.* 他们的研究在我看来不够严谨。

rig-out /ˈ· ·/ *n* [C] *BrE informal* a set of clothes【英, 非正式】一套衣服: *You can't go out in that rig-out!* 你不能穿着那身衣服出去! —see also 另见 **rig out** (RIG¹)

Rig-Ve·da /ˌrɪg ˋvedə; ˌrɪg ˈveɪdə/ the first of the four holy books of the *Veda*, which contains prayers and HYMNs to gods in the Hindu religion《梨俱吠陀》〔《吠陀》汇集印度教赞美神灵的祈祷文和颂歌, 由四部圣书构成,《梨俱吠陀》为首部〕

rile /raɪl; raɪl/ *v* [T] *informal* to make someone extremely angry【非正式】激怒, 使非常生气: *It really riled her to think that Henry was lying.* 想到亨利在说谎, 她非常生气。

Ri·ley /ˈraɪlɪ; ˈraɪli/ *n* **lead the life of Riley** *BrE informal* to have enough money to do what you like【英, 非正式】过着无忧无虑的生活: *Barbara's been leading the life of Riley since that lottery win.* 中彩之后芭芭拉一直过着无忧无虑的生活。

rim¹ /rɪm; rɪm/ *n* [C] **1** the outside edge of something circular〔圆形物的〕外缘, 边缘, 边: *the rim of a glass* 玻璃杯口 | *Fit the tyre round the rim of the wheel.* 把轮胎安在辋圈上。**2 gold-rimmed/red-rimmed etc** with a gold, red etc rim 金框/红框的等: *gold-rimmed spectacles* 金边眼镜 —**rimless** *adj*: *Annie wore rimless glasses.* 安妮戴着无边眼镜。

rim² **rimmed, rimming** *v* [T] *literary* to be around the edge of something【文】环绕〔边缘〕: *Trees rimmed the lake.* 湖周围树木环绕。

Rim·baud /ræmˋbo; ˈræmbəʊ/, **Arthur** (1854-91) a French poet whose works include *Les Illuminations* 兰波〔(1854-1891), 法国诗人。其诗集包括《灵光篇》〕

rime /raɪm; raɪm/ *n* [U] *literary* FROST (=powdery ice)【文】(白)霜

Rime of the Ancient Mariner, the —see 见 ANCIENT MARINER

Rim·i·ni /ˈrɪmɪnɪ; ˈrɪmɪni/ a city on the Adriatic coast of north-east Italy. It is an industrial port and a tourist centre. 里米尼〔意大利东北部一城市。该市濒临亚得里亚海, 为一工业港口和旅游中心〕

Rim·sky-Kor·sa·kov /ˌrɪmskɪ ˋkɔrsəkɔf; ˌrɪmski ˈkɔːsəkɒf/, **Nik·o·lai** /ˈnɪkəlaɪ; ˈnɪkəlaɪ/ (1844-1908) a Russian COMPOSER whose most famous work is *Scheherezade*. He also ORCHESTRATed works by other Russian composers. 里姆斯基-科萨科夫〔(1844-1908), 俄国作曲家。最著名的作品为《天方夜谭》, 他还把俄国其他作曲家的作品编成管弦乐曲〕

rind /raɪnd; raɪnd/ *n* [C,U] **1** the thick outer skin of some types of fruit, such as oranges〔某些果实的〕外皮: *grated lemon rind* 磨碎了的柠檬皮 —compare 比较 PEEL² **2** the thick outer skin of some foods, such as BACON or cheese〔熏猪肉、干酪等的〕外皮

ring¹ /rɪŋ; rɪŋ/ *n* [S1] [W2]

1 ▶JEWELLERY 首饰◀ [C] a piece of jewellery that you wear on your finger 戒指, 指环: *a diamond ring* (=decorated with diamonds) 钻戒 —see also 另见 ENGAGEMENT RING, WEDDING RING —see picture at 参见 JEWELLERY 图

2 ▶CIRCLE 环状物◀ [C] **a)** a circular line or mark 环状线; 环形记号: *Martha had dark rings round her eyes from too many sleepless nights.* 玛莎好多夜没睡, 眼睛周围都有黑圈了。**b)** an object in the shape of a circle 环, 圆圈: *curtain rings* 窗帘吊环 | *piston rings* 活塞环 | *Slice the onions into rings.* 把洋葱切成薄圈。**c)** a group of people or things arranged in a circle〔人或物的〕环形排列: *A ring of armed troops surrounded the building.* 一圈武装士兵包围了该建筑。

3 ▶BELLS 钟; 铃◀ [C] the sound made by a bell or the act of making this sound 钟[铃]声; 敲钟; 按铃: *He gave several loud rings at the door.* 他在门口使劲摇了几下铃。—see picture on page A19 参见 A19 页图

4 give sb a ring *BrE informal* to make a telephone call to someone【英, 非正式】给某人打电话: *I'll give you a ring later in the week.* 我会在本周晚些时候给你打电话。

5 ▶CRIMINALS 罪犯◀ [C] a group of people who illegally control a business or criminal activity〔非法交易或犯罪的〕团伙, 帮派: **drugs/spy ring** *Police suspect a drug ring may be operating in the area.* 警察怀疑有一个贩毒团伙在该地区活动。| *revelations of a massive spy ring* 一个庞大间谍团伙的揭露

6 have a ring of truth to seem likely to be true 看来是真的: *Mrs Datchet's story had a ring of truth about it.* 达切特夫人所讲的情况似乎是真实的。

7 have a familiar ring if something has a familiar ring, you feel that you have heard it before 听起来耳熟: *Jerry's excuse had a strangely familiar ring.* 杰里的借口听起来有点耳熟。

8 run rings around *informal* to be able to do something much better than someone else can【非正式】大大胜过: *My five-year-old can run rings around me on the computer.* 我五岁的孩子用电脑比我强得多。

9 ▶COOKING 烹调◀ [C] *especially BrE* one of the circular areas on top of a COOKER that is heated by gas or electricity【尤英】环形灶盘 —see picture on page A10 参见 A10 页图

10 ▶SPORT/ENTERTAINMENT 体育/娱乐◀ a) a small square area surrounded by ropes, where people BOX or WRESTLE〔用绳子围起来的〕拳击台; 摔跤台 **b)** a large circular area surrounded by seats at a CIRCUS〔马戏团的〕圆形表演场 **c) the ring** the sport of BOXING 拳击运动: *He retired from the ring at 34.* 他 34 岁结束了拳击生涯。

ring² *v past tense* **rang** /ræŋ; ræŋ/ *past participle* **rung** /rʌŋ; rʌŋ/ [S1] [W2]

1 ▶BELL 钟, 铃◀ a) [T] to make a bell make a sound 使鸣响〔钟、铃〕: *I rang the doorbell but no one came.* 我按了门铃, 但没有人来。**b)** [I] if a bell rings, it makes a noise〔钟、铃〕鸣响: *At that moment, the bell rang for lunch.* 就在那时, 午餐铃响了。**c)** [I] to ring a bell to call someone to serve you 摇[按]铃呼唤: [+for] *Ring for service.* 请按铃叫人。

2 ▶SOUNDS 声音◀ [I] **a)** to make a high continuous sound 发出连续的嗡嗡声: *Tap the glass gently, and you'll hear it ring.* 轻轻地敲玻璃杯, 就会听到嗡嗡的声音。**b)** your ears ring after you have been somewhere very noisy or heard a loud sound〔耳〕鸣: *The explosion made our ears ring.* 爆炸声使我们耳鸣。**c)** *literary* if a place rings with a sound it is full of that sound【文】回响, 响彻: *The courtyard rang with the sound of horses' hooves.* 院子里回响着马蹄声。

3 ▶TELEPHONE 电话◀ a) [I,T] *BrE* to make a telephone call to someone【英】(给…)打电话; CALL¹ (7) *especially AmE*【尤美】: *I rang you yesterday but you weren't in.* 我昨天给你打了电话, 但是你不在。| *Ring 192 for information.* 查询请拨打 192。| [+for] *Sally rang for a taxi.* 萨莉打电话叫出租车。—see 见 TELEPHONE (USAGE) **b)** [I] if a telephone rings, it makes a sound to show that someone is phoning you〔电话铃〕鸣响: *The phone hasn't stopped ringing all day.* 电话铃整天响个不停。

4 ring a bell *informal* if something rings a bell, you think you have heard it before【非正式】听起来耳熟: *Her name rings a bell but I can't remember her face.* 她的名字好像很熟, 但是我记不起她的面孔。

5 not ring true if something does not ring true, you do not believe it, even though you are not sure why 听起来不真实: *It was a clever excuse but it didn't really ring true.* 这是个巧妙的托词, 但是听起来不真实。

6 ring the changes to make changes to something, not because it needs changing but just in order to make it more interesting, more attractive etc〔为了装饰或增加趣味而〕推出

新花样，作出不同的安排：*It's easy to ring the changes in your living room with some new cushion covers.* 用一些新的座垫套就很容易给你的客厅画龙点睛。

7 ring hollow if words ring hollow, you do not feel that they are true or sincere 听起来不真实[无诚意]：*Their expressions of sympathy rang hollow.* 他们的同情显得很虚伪。

8 ring in your ears if a sound or remark rings in your ears, you seem to continue to hear it after it has finished 在耳际回响：*She went out, his cruel laughter ringing in her ears.* 她走了出去，他那冷酷的笑声在她耳际回响。

ring back *phr v* [I,T **ring** sb **back**] *BrE* to telephone someone again, for example because you were not available when they telephoned you【英】回(…的)电话：*John rang, and he wants you to ring him back.* 约翰给你打过电话，他要你给他回电话。

ring in *phr v* **1** [I] *BrE* to telephone the place where you work【英】给办公室打电话：*Jane's rung in to say she'll be late.* 简来电话说她要晚到一会儿。**2 ring in the New Year** to celebrate the beginning of the New Year by ringing church bells 教堂鸣钟迎接新年

ring off *phr v* [I] *BrE* to end a telephone call【英】挂断电话：*He rang off without giving his name.* 他没留下姓名就挂了电话。

ring out *phr v* **1** [U] a voice, bell etc that rings out is loud and clear〔嗓音、钟声等〕响亮：*The sound of a shot rang out.* 传来一声响亮的枪声。**2 ring out the Old Year** to celebrate the end of the year by ringing church bells 教堂鸣钟辞别旧岁

R

ring round *phr v* [I,T] *BrE* to make telephone calls to a group of people, in order to organize something, find out information etc【英】(给…)遍打电话：*I'll ring round to see whether anyone's interested in coming with us.* 我会给朋友打电话，看谁有兴趣和我们一起来。

ring sth/sb ↔ **up** *phr v* **1** [I,T **ring** sb ↔ **up**] *BrE* to telephone someone【英】(给…)打电话：*I'll ring the manager up tomorrow.* 明天我会给经理打电话。**2** [T **ring** sth ↔ **up**] to press buttons on a CASH REGISTER to record how much money is being put inside 把〔收进的钱〕计入收银机：*The cashier rang up $300 by mistake.* 出纳员误计了收进300美元。

ring³ *v past tense and past participle* **ringed** [T] **1** to surround something 包围，环绕：*Police marksmen ringed the office block.* 警察狙击手包围了办公大楼。| **ring sth with** *Her fair hair was ringed with light.* 她的金发光闪闪的。**2** to draw a circular mark around something 把…圈起来：*Ring the mistakes in red.* 用红笔把错误圈出来。**3** to put a metal ring around a bird's leg 给〔鸟腿〕系环

Ring, The a set of four OPERAS by Richard Wagner, known also as *The Ring of the Nibelung* or *The Ring Cycle*. They are based on stories from German MYTHOLOGY.《指环》〔理查德·瓦格纳创作的一套四部歌剧，又称《尼贝龙根的指环》或《指环套曲》。故事情节根据德国神话故事改编而成〕

Ring a ring o'ros·es *BrE*【英】; **Ring-around-the-rosy** *AmE*【美】/ˌ· · ˈ· ·, · · ˈ· ·/ a children's singing game in which the children join hands and dance round in a circle singing 边唱边跳绕圈转〔儿童游戏。大家手拉手，一边绕圈而舞，一边唱道〕：*Ring a ring o'roses,/A pocket full of posies /A-tishoo! A-tishoo! /We all fall down.* 围绕玫瑰花环跳起舞，/满口袋的花束圆鼓鼓，/阿嚏！阿嚏！/我们齐倒地。People believe it comes from the time when there was a PLAGUE in London (=a very serious infectious disease, quickly causing death to large numbers of people), because when people coughed and SNEEZEd, saying 'atishoo', it was a sign that they had caught the plague.〔据说歌词源于伦敦发生瘟疫的年代。当时，谁要是又咳嗽又打喷嚏，那谁就染上了瘟疫〕

Ring-a·round-the-ros·y /ˌ· · ˈ· ·, · · ˈ· ·/ —see 见 RING A RING O'ROSES

ring·er /ˈrɪŋɚ; ˈrɪŋə/ *n* [C] someone who rings church bells or hand bells〔教堂的〕打钟人；摇手铃的人 —see also 另见 **dead ringer** (DEAD¹ (28))

ring·fence /ˈrɪŋˌfɛns; ˈrɪŋfens/ *v* [T] to decide officially that something, especially money, can only be used for a particular purpose〔尤指钱〕指定用于…：*Ok, so this £20,000 is ringfenced as the training budget.* 好吧，这20,000英镑指定作为培训预算。

ring fin·ger /ˈ· ˌ· ·/ *n* [C] the finger that you traditionally wear your WEDDING RING on 无名指

ring·ing /ˈrɪŋɪŋ; ˈrɪŋɪŋ/ *adj* a ringing sound or voice is loud and clear 洪亮的，响亮的；清脆的：*"Come here!" he commanded, in ringing tones.* "过来！"他声音洪亮地命令道。

ring·lead·er /ˈrɪŋˌlidɚ; ˈrɪŋˌliːdə/ *n* [C] someone who leads a group that is doing something illegal or wrong〔匪徒的〕头目，首恶，魁首：*Police arrested the ringleaders but let the others go free.* 警察逮捕了那些头目，但把其他人都放了。

ring·let /ˈrɪŋlɪt; ˈrɪŋlɪ̣t/ *n* [C] a long curl of hair that hangs down〔下垂的〕长鬈发

ring-pull /ˈ· ·/ *n* [C] the ring on the top of a can of drink that you pull to open it〔易拉罐上的〕拉环

ring road /ˈ· ·/ *n* [C] *BrE* a road that goes around a large town to keep the traffic away from the centre【英】环城公路；BELTWAY *AmE*【美】

ring·side /ˈrɪŋˌsaɪd; ˈrɪŋsaɪd/ *n* [singular] **1** the area nearest to the performance in a CIRCUS, BOXING match etc〔马戏团表演、拳击比赛等的〕台边区 **2 ringside seat** a seat very near to the performers in a CIRCUS, BOXING match etc 台边区前排座位

ring span·ner /ˈ· ˌ· ·/ *n* [C] *BrE* a tool with a circular end that fits over a NUT to make it tighter or looser【英】套筒扳手，梅花扳手；BOX END WRENCH *AmE*【美】—see picture at 参见 TOOL¹ 图

ring·worm /ˈrɪŋˌwɝm; ˈrɪŋwɜːm/ *n* [U] a skin infection that causes red rings, especially on your head〔尤指头上的〕癣

rink /rɪŋk; rɪŋk/ *n* [C] **1** a specially prepared area of ice for skating (SKATE²) 溜冰场 **2** a special area with a smooth surface where you can go around on ROLLER SKATEs 旱冰场

rink·y-dink /ˈrɪŋkɪˌdɪŋk; ˈrɪŋki dɪŋk/ *adj AmE informal* cheap and of bad quality【美，非正式】廉价的，劣质的

rinse¹ /rɪns; rɪns/ *v* [T] **1** to wash clothes, dishes etc quickly with water, especially running water, and without soap 冲洗，〔用流动的水〕清洗：*Let me just rinse my hands.* 让我把手冲洗一下。| *Rinse the vegetables under a cold tap.* 在冷水龙头下面冲洗这些蔬菜。**2** to wash something in clean water in order to remove soap from it〔用干净的水〕把〔肥皂〕从…上冲洗掉：*Rinse your hair thoroughly to get all the shampoo out.* 把你头发上的洗发剂彻底冲干净。**3** to remove soap, dirt etc from something by washing it quickly with water 把〔肥皂、污垢等〕冲洗掉：**rinse sth out/away/off etc** *I tried to rinse the mud off under the tap.* 我努力在水龙头下面把泥巴冲掉。**4** to put colour into your hair 染〔发〕

rinse sth ↔ **out** *phr v* [T] to wash something in clean water, especially to remove soap from it〔用清水〕漂洗〔尤指冲掉肥皂〕：*Don't forget to rinse out your swimsuit.* 别忘记用清水漂洗干净你的游泳衣。

rinse² *n* **1 give sth a rinse** to rinse something 漂洗[冲洗]某物：*I'll just give this shirt a quick rinse.* 我要把这件衬衣很快地漂洗一下。**2** [C,U] a product you use to change the colour of your hair or to make it more shiny 染发液：*a blue rinse for grey hair* 染灰白头发用的蓝色染发液

Ri·o de Ja·nei·ro /ˌrio de ʒəˈnɛro; ˌriːəʊ də ʒəˈnɪərəʊ/ also 又作 **Rio** a large city and port in East Brazil. Rio was the capital of Brazil until the new city of Brasilia was built in 1960. It is famous for its beaches, such as the Copacabana, its CARNIVAL, and for Sugarloaf Mountain, on which there is a very large STATUE of Jesus Christ. 里约热内卢〔巴西东部一大城市和港口，1960年新城巴西利亚建成之前为巴西首都。该市以科帕卡巴纳等海滩、狂欢节和糖峰著称。糖峰上有耶稣基督的巨型雕像〕

Ri·o Grande, the /ˌrio ˈgrænd; ˌriːəʊ ˈgrænd/ a river in the south of the US which forms a border between the US and Mexico. The Mexican name for it is Rio Bravo. 格兰德河〔美国与墨西哥之间的一条界河，位于美国南部。在墨西哥，其西班牙语名为 Rio Bravo (布拉沃河)〕

Rio Sum·mit, the /ˈrio ˌsʌmɪt; ˈriːəʊ ˌsʌmɪ̣t/ —see 见 EARTH SUMMIT

ri·ot¹ /ˈraɪət; ˈraɪət/ *n* **1** [C] a situation in which a large crowd of people are behaving in a violent and uncontrolled way especially when they are protesting about something 骚乱，暴乱，暴动：*The army were called in to put down the riot.* 军队奉命前来平息暴乱。| **race riot** (=between people of different races) 种族骚乱 *Ethnic tensions led to a massive race riot.* 种族之间的紧张关系导致了大规模的种族骚乱。**2 a riot of colour** something with many different bright colours 五颜六色，色彩缤纷：*The garden is a riot of colour in May.* 在5月，花园色彩缤纷，美不胜收。**3 run riot a)** if people run riot, they behave in a violent, noisy, and uncontrolled way 狂暴，无法无天：*Demonstrators are running riot through the town.* 示威者发疯似地在城里到处闹事。**b)** if your imagination, thoughts etc run riot, you cannot control them〔想象、思绪等〕无法控制 **c)** if a plant runs riot, it grows very quickly〔植物〕疯长 **4 read (sb) the riot act** *often humorous* to give someone a strong warning that they must stop causing trouble【常幽默】严厉警告(某人)必须停止闹事：*If the kids don't settle down soon, I'll go up and read them the riot act.* 如果孩子不马上安静下来，我就上去严厉警告他们。**5** [singular] *old-fashioned* someone or something that is very funny or enjoyable【过时】有趣的人[事]：*Sally's a riot when she's had a*

few drinks! 几杯酒下肚，萨莉就变得非常有趣！| **have a riot** (=have a lot of fun) 有趣，好玩 *"How was the party?" "Oh, we had a riot!"* "聚会怎么样？""噢，我们玩得很痛快！"

riot² *v* [I] if a crowd of people riot, they behave in a violent and uncontrolled way, for example by fighting the police and damaging cars or buildings 骚乱，闹事: *Students were rioting in the streets.* 学生们在街上闹事。—**rioting** *n* [U] —**rioter** *n* [C]

ri·ot·ous /ˈraɪətəs; ˈraɪətəs/ *adj* **1** wild, exciting, and uncontrolled 狂暴的，兴奋的，无法控制的: *riotous drinking and singing* 狂饮高歌 **2** uncontrolled, noisy, and perhaps dangerous 放纵的，喧闹的: **riotous behaviour** *BrE*【英】*Steve was arrested for riotous behaviour the night before his wedding.* 史蒂夫在婚礼前一天晚上因行为放纵而被捕。—**riotously** *adv* —**riotousness** *n* [U]

riot po·lice /ˈ· · ·, ·ˈ/ *n* [U] police whose job is to stop riots 防暴警察: *The riot police used tear gas to control the mob.* 防暴警察使用了催泪弹来控制暴徒。

RIP /ˌɑr aɪ ˈpi; ˌɑːr aɪ ˈpiː/ the written abbreviation of 缩写= Rest in Peace (=words written on a stone over a grave) 安息〔墓碑上的铭文〕

rip¹ /rɪp; rɪp/ **ripped, ripping** *v* **1** [I,T] to tear something or be torn quickly and violently 撕，扯，撕裂，扯开: *I've ripped my skirt on a nail.* 我的裙子被钉子划破了。| *The sails ripped under the force of the wind.* 强劲的风把帆扯破了。| **rip sth open** (=open something by tearing it) 把某物撕开 *Impatiently, Sue ripped the letter open.* 休急不可待地撕开信封。—see picture on page A18 参见 A18 页图 **2** [T always+adv/prep] to remove something quickly and violently, using your hands〔迅速而粗暴地用手〕移去〔某物〕: **rip sth out/off/away/down** *We've had to rip down all the old wallpaper.* 我们得把所有的旧墙纸都扯下来。**3 rip sth/sb to shreds a)** to destroy something or damage it badly by tearing it in many pieces 扯碎；撕碎: *Jill's kitten is ripping her sofa to shreds.* 吉尔的小猫把她的沙发抓扯得稀烂。**b)** to strongly criticize someone, or their opinions, remarks, behaviour etc 严厉批评，抨击: *My argument was ripped to shreds at once.* 我的论点立即被批驳得体无完肤。**4 let rip** *informal* to speak or behave violently or emotionally【非正式】说话[行为]激烈的，强烈的: **[+at/about]** *Mom really let rip about the state of my room.* 妈妈果真对我房间的状况大发雷霆。**5 let sth rip** *informal* to make a car, boat etc go as fast as it can【非正式】让〔车、船等〕全速前进: *Put your foot on the gas and let her rip!* 踩着油门，让车子飞驰吧！

rip off *phr v* [T] *spoken*【口】**1** [**rip** sb ↔ **off**] to charge someone too much money for something 对〔某人〕索价过高[敲竹杠]: *They really ripped us off at that hotel!* 那家旅馆着实敲了我们一下竹杠！**2** [**rip off** sth] to steal something 偷窃: *Somebody's ripped off my bike!* 有人偷了我的自行车！—see also 另见 RIP-OFF

rip through sth *phr v* [T] to move through a place quickly and with violent force 迅猛地冲过: *A huge explosion ripped through the courthouse.* 猛烈的爆炸严重损毁了法院。

rip sth ↔ **up** *phr v* [T] to tear something into several pieces 把…撕成碎片: *Pru ripped his photo up into tiny bits.* 普鲁把他的相片撕得粉碎。

rip² *n* [C] a long tear or cut 长的裂口[裂缝]: *There was a rip in the tire caused by a sharp stone.* 轮胎上有一长条被尖石划破的口子。

rip·cord /ˈrɪpkɔrd; ˈrɪpkɔːd/ *n* [C] **1** the string that you pull to open a PARACHUTE〔降落伞的〕开伞索 **2** the string that you pull to let gas out of a BALLOON〔气球放气用的〕拉索

ripe /raɪp; raɪp/ *adj* **1** ripe fruit or crops are fully grown and ready to eat〔水果、庄稼〕成熟的: *Those apples aren't ripe yet.* 那些苹果还没熟。—opposite 反义词 UNRIPE **2 be ripe for** to be in a suitable condition for something, especially for some kind of change 适宜…，〔尤指变革等〕条件成熟: *The land was ripe for industrial development.* 这个国家已经具备了发展工业的条件。**3 the time is ripe (for)** used to say it is a very suitable time for something to happen（…的）时机已经成熟: *The time was ripe for a challenge to the government.* 向政府挑战的时机已经成熟。**4 ripe old age** if you live to a ripe old age, you are very old when you die 很大年纪: *Grandad lived to the ripe old age of 94.* 爷爷活到94岁高龄。**5** ripe cheese has developed a strong taste and is ready to eat〔干酪〕熟透的 **6** a ripe smell is strong and unpleasant〔气味〕浓烈难闻的: *The office was so hot that we all smelled rather ripe by the end of the day.* 办公室非常热，下班时我们个个身上都散发着难闻的气味。**7** *BrE informal* rude but amusing【英，非正式】〔语言〕粗俗有趣的: *I thought his language was a bit ripe.* 我认为他的语言有些粗俗，但不乏幽默。—**ripeness** *n* [U]

rip·en /ˈraɪpən; ˈraɪpən/ *v* [I,T] to become ripe or to make something ripe（使）成熟: *The tomatoes quickly ripened in the hot weather.* 天气炎热，番茄很快就熟了。

rip-off /ˈ· ·/ *n* [C] *informal* something that is unreasonably expensive【非正式】〔某物〕价格太高，要价不合理: *Five pounds for a coffee? What a rip-off!* 一杯咖啡就要五英镑？真是敲竹杠啊！—see also 另见 **rip off** (RIP¹)

ri·poste¹ /rɪˈpost; rɪˈpɒst/ *n* [C] **1** *formal* a quick, clever, and amusing reply【正式】迅速而巧妙的回答: *a suitably witty riposte* 恰如其分的机敏的答复 **2** *technical* a quick return stroke with a sword in FENCING (=the sport of fighting with swords)【术语】〔击剑〕敏捷的还击

riposte² *v* **1** [I,T] *formal* to reply quickly and cleverly【正式】机敏地答复[反驳] **2** [I] *technical* to make a riposte in FENCING【术语】〔击剑〕敏捷地还击

rip·ple¹ /ˈrɪpl; ˈrɪpəl/ *v* **1** [I,T] to move in small waves, or to make something move in this way（使）起涟漪，（使）起细浪: *Arnie's muscles rippled as he carried the huge crates.* 阿尼搬大板条箱时，肌肉一起一伏。| *Look how the breeze is rippling the long grass.* 看微风吹拂着长长的草，泛起阵阵细浪。**2** [I always+adv/prep] to pass from one person to another like a wave〔在人群中〕传开: **ripple around/through etc** *Excitement rippled around the courtroom.* 法庭里人人心潮澎湃。| *A thrill of pleasure rippled through me.* 一阵快感传遍我全身。**3** [I] to make a noise like water that is flowing gently 发出潺潺声: *The water rippled over the stones.* 石头上流水潺潺。| *a rippling brook* 潺潺的小溪

ripple² *n* **1** [C] a small low wave on the surface of a liquid 细浪，涟漪: *The wind made ripples on the surface of the pond.* 风吹皱池水。—see picture at 参见 REFLECTION 图 **2 a ripple of applause/laughter etc** a sound that gets gradually louder and softer 此起彼伏的掌声/笑声等: *A ripple of laughter ran through the audience.* 听众发出阵阵笑声。**3 a ripple of shock/unease/nervousness etc** a feeling that spreads through a person or a group because of something that has happened 一阵震惊/不安/紧张等: *A ripple of shock ran around the meeting.* 与会者都感到震惊。**4** [C] a shape or pattern that looks like a wave 波痕，波纹: *ripples on the sand* 沙上的波痕 **5 raspberry ripple/chocolate ripple etc** a type of ICE CREAM that has different coloured bands of fruit, chocolate etc in it 山莓/巧克力等彩条冰淇淋 **6 ripple effect** a situation in which one action causes another, which then causes a third, etc 涟漪作用，连锁反应

rip-roar·ing /ˌ· ˈ· ·◂/ *adj informal*【非正式】**1 rip-roaring success** a very big success 巨大成功: *The new musical looks set to become a rip-roaring success.* 那部新音乐剧看来注定会非常卖座。**2** noisy, exciting, and uncontrolled 喧闹的；欢腾的: *Micky had a rip-roaring time spending his first wage packet.* 米基第一次拿到工资，痛快地玩了个够。| **rip-roaring drunk** (=very drunk) 烂醉如泥

rip·snort·er /ˌrɪpˈsnɔrtɚ; ˌrɪpˈsnɔːtə/ *n* [C] *old-fashioned* something very exciting【过时】非常刺激的事物: *The roller coasters there are real ripsnorters.* 那里的过山车真够刺激的。

Rip van Win·kle /ˌ· · ˈ· ·/ the main character in a story by Washington Irving, who sleeps for 20 years and finds that the world has changed a lot when he wakes up 瑞普·范·温克尔〔华盛顿·欧文一部小说中的主人公。他一觉睡了20年，醒来发觉周围的世界已经大变样了〕

rise¹ /raɪz; raɪz/ *v past tense* **rose** /roz; rəʊz/ *past participle* **risen** /ˈrɪzn; ˈrɪzən/ [I] S2 W1

1 ▶INCREASE 增加◀ to increase in number, amount or value〔数、量或价值的〕增加，增长: *House prices are likely to rise towards the end of this year.* 今年年底房价可能会上涨。| **rise by 10%/$3/a large amount etc** *Sales rose by 20% over the Christmas period.* 圣诞节期间销售量增加了20%。| **rise dramatically/sharply** (=increase greatly) 急剧增长 *The number of people seeking asylum in the United Kingdom has risen sharply from five thousand a year in 1988 to over thirty thousand in 1990.* 在英国寻求政治庇护的人数从1988年的每年五千人，猛增到1990年的三万多人。| **rise steadily** (=increase slowly but continuously) 持续增长 *The divorce rate has risen steadily since the 1950s.* 20世纪50年代以来，离婚率不断上升。| **rising prices/unemployment etc** *Rising crime has driven many families out of down-town areas.* 上升的犯罪率迫使许多家庭离开了市中心。| **rise and fall** *Populations rise and fall in response to the availability of food.* 人口数目随粮食的供应量而增减。| **... and rising** *The unemployment level is twelve percent and rising.* 失业水平是20%并且在上升。—see 见 RAISE¹ (USAGE)

2 ►GO UPWARDS 上升◄ to go upwards 升高，上升: *The polar ice caps will melt and the sea level will rise.* 极地的冰盖将融化，海平面将升高。| *Smoke rose from the chimney.* 烟从烟囱中冉冉升起。| *The road rises steeply from the village.* 公路从那个村子起突然变得陡峭。

3 ►STAND 站立◄ *especially written* to stand up【尤书面】站起；起立: *Mick McGrath rose and shouted, "Right, lads! Five minutes to finish your beer and then let's go."* 米克·麦格拉思站起来喊道："好吧，小伙子们！给你们五分钟喝完啤酒，然后我们就走。" | **rise from the table/your chair etc** *Charlotte rose from the table and went over to the window.* 夏洛特从桌旁站起身走到了窗边。| **rise to your feet** *He rose to his feet and tapped on the table as if he was going to speak.* 他站起身轻轻敲打桌子，仿佛要发言似的。

4 ►BECOME SUCCESSFUL 取得成就◄ to become important, powerful, successful or rich 地位提高；发迹: [+from] *Damascus had risen from a provincial centre of commerce to the capital of the world's greatest empire.* 大马士革从一个地方贸易中心变成世界上最大帝国的首都。| [+to] *He had entered the army as a boy and risen to the rank of colonel by 1914.* 他参军时还是个少年，到1914年已经升到上校。| **rise to the top** *The people who rise to the top in politics are usually the most ruthless.* 政坛巨头通常都是最无情的。| **rise to fame** *The Beatles rose to fame in the early 60s.* 甲壳虫乐队在60年代初声名大噪。| **rise to power** *Mussolini rose to power in Italy in 1922.* 1922年墨索里尼在意大利夺取政权。

5 ►VOICE/SOUND 嗓音/声音◄ **a)** to be heard〔声音〕发出: [+from] *The sound of children playing rose from the street.* 孩子们玩耍的声音从街上传来。| **rise above sth** (=be louder than something) 比…响亮 *He could hear the rhythm of chanting voices rising above the sound of the traffic.* 他听到有节奏的呼喊声盖过了来往车辆的声音。**b)** to become louder or higher〔声音〕变响，提高: *Her voice rose with anger and emotion: "I trusted you!"* 她怒气冲冲，提高嗓门叫道："我居然相信了你！"

6 ►SUN/MOON/STAR 太阳/月亮/星星◄ to appear in the sky 升起，在天空出现: *The sun rose and the sea turned gold.* 太阳升起来，大海变成了金色。

7 ►EMOTION 感情◄ if a feeling or emotion rises, you feel it more and more strongly〔感情或情绪〕变得强烈. *I felt panic rising, and my heart banged loudly in my chest.* 我感到越来越恐慌，我的心在胸膛里怦怦地跳。| *rising excitement* 越来越激动 | **sb's spirits rise** (=they become much happier) 某人的情绪高涨 *Our spirits rose when we heard of the ship's safe return.* 我们听说船安全返航，精神大振。

8 ►BE TALL 高◄ to be very tall 耸立，矗立: *Snow-capped mountains rose in the distance.* 白雪覆盖的山峰耸立在远方。| **rise above** (=be much taller than) 大大高于 *The tower rose above the surrounding trees.* 那座塔高高地耸出周围的树木。

9 rise from if something tall rises from a place, its base is in that place 从…升起: *Spiro was pointing at a gentle curve of hillside that rose from the glittering sea.* 斯皮罗正指着从波光粼粼的大海中升起的缓缓山坡。

10 ►BREAD/CAKES ETC 面包/蛋糕等◄ if bread, cakes etc rise they become bigger because they contain YEAST or as they are baked〔面包、蛋糕等〕因发酵[被烘烤]而胀大，膨松

11 ►BED 床◄ *literary* to get out of bed in the morning【文】起床

12 ►AGAINST A GOVERNMENT/ARMY 反抗政府/军队◄ also 又作 **rise up** if a large group of people in a country rise, they try to defeat the government or army that is controlling them 反抗，造反: *The Russian people rose in rebellion in 1917.* 俄国人民于1917年起义。

13 rise to the occasion/challenge to deal successfully with a difficult situation or problem 成功应付困难局面/挑战

14 rise to sth if you rise to a remark, you reply to it rather than ignoring it, especially because it has made you angry 对某事〔尤指令人气愤的评论〕反应强烈: *She refused to rise to his sexist remarks.* 她对他的性别歧视的话置之不理。

15 rise from the dead/grave to come alive after having died 复活: *On the third day Jesus rose from the dead.* 耶稣在第三天复活。

16 rise through the ranks to start working for an organization in a low-paid job, and to gradually improve your position, until you get a very important, well-paid job〔在一家机构中工作〕由低职位开始晋升高位: *She had risen through the ranks, having joined the company as a secretary after she graduated from high school.* 高中毕业后她到这家公司当秘书，一步步升到了重要的职位。

17 rise from the ranks to become an officer in the army after having been an ordinary soldier〔军官〕士兵出身

18 rise out of sth to be caused by sth or begin with sth 起因于…，由…引起: *The quarrel had risen out of a misunderstanding.* 这场争吵是由误会引起的。| *All this fuss and extravagance rose out of a sudden whim to please his small, first-born son.* 所有的小题大做和铺张浪费都是因为他突发奇想要取悦他年幼的长子。

19 ►COURT/PARLIAMENT 法庭/议会◄ if court etc rises, that particular meeting is formally finished 休庭；休会

20 all rise *spoken formal* used to tell people to stand up at the beginning of a meeting of a court of law【口，正式】全体起立〔用于法庭开庭前〕

21 rise and shine *spoken humorous* used to tell someone to wake up and get out of bed【口，幽默】快起床〔用于叫醒某人〕

22 ►RIVER 河流◄ if a river rises somewhere, it begins there〔河流〕发源: *The River Rhine rises in Switzerland.* 莱茵河发源于瑞士。

23 ►WIND 风◄ if the wind rises, it becomes stronger〔风力〕增强: *battling against the rising gale* 与越来越强的大风搏斗

rise above *phr v* [T] **1** to deal with an insult or unpleasant situation without letting yourself become upset by it 超脱，不计较: *Her name was splashed across the newspapers every day, but somehow she managed to rise above it.* 她的名字每天都出现在报纸的显著位置，但她总能泰然处之。**2** to be morally good or wise enough to be able to avoid something that you should not do 克服，摆脱: *We must rise above the desire for power, personal advancement and material gain.* 我们必须摆脱对权力、个人升迁和物质利益的欲望。**3** to be of a higher standard than other things that are similar〔水平〕超过〔相似的东西〕；优于: *The novel is spirited and witty, but rarely rises above the level of pulp fiction.* 这部小说充满生气和情趣，但总的来说没有超出庸俗小说的水平。**4** to have the knowledge and wisdom to understand and realize things that other people do not notice〔知识和智慧〕超越〔他人〕: *A true historian seeks the truth: he rises above his own race and writes for mankind.* 真正的历史学家追求的是真理：他超越自己的种族，为人类撰写历史。**5** to improve your situation by becoming more successful, rich or important〔通过成功、致富或势力〕改善〔境遇〕: *I was ambitious and wanted to rise above such a life.* 我雄心勃勃，不安于这种生活。

rise against *phr v* [T] **1** if a group of people rise against the government, king etc they try to defeat them so that they can control the country 起义；反抗: *Rebels rose in discontent against the government and began killing people indiscriminately.* 叛乱分子因不满而起来反抗政府，并滥杀无辜。**2** *literary* to be very angry and upset by something【文】对…反感: *His whole heart rose against this.* 他对此深恶痛绝。

rise² *n* 2

1 ►INCREASE 增加◄ [C] an increase in number, amount or value〔数、量、值的〕增加: *We have sold 120,000 cars this year, a 20% rise on 1988.* 今年我们已售出12万辆汽车，比1988年增加了20%。| [+in] *In the last ten years we have seen a three percent rise in serious and fatal accidents on our roads.* 过去10年里，公路上的严重致命事故增加了3%。| **rise in costs/prices/taxes etc** *A rise in taxes will be necessary if we are to improve our education system.* 我们要改善教育制度，就需要增加税收。| **rent/price rise** *Tenants face a 20% rent rise.* 房客们面临房租上涨20%的局面。| **rise and fall** *the rise and fall of the temperature during the day* 一天当中温度的升降

2 ►WAGES 工资◄ [C] *BrE* an increase in wages【英】加薪；RAISE² *AmE*【美】: *After you've worked here for one year you get a rise.* 你在这里工作一年后就会加薪。| **pay rise** *The railworkers were offered a 3% pay rise.* 铁路工人获得了3%的加薪。

3 ►SUCCESS/POWER 成功/权力◄ [singular] the achievement of importance, success or power 升迁；成功，兴起: [+of] *The fifteenth century saw the rise of a new social class – the merchant class.* 15世纪见证了一个新的社会阶级——商人阶级的兴起。| *the rise of fascism in Italy* 法西斯主义在意大利的兴起 | **rise to power** *Thatcher's rise to power in the late 1970s* 撒切尔夫人在20世纪70年代末掌权 | **rise to fame** *The band's sudden rise to fame took everyone by surprise.* 这乐队突然走红让所有人都感到意外。| **rise and fall** *the rise and fall of the Roman Empire* 罗马帝国的兴亡

4 give rise to sth *especially written* to be the reason why something, especially something bad or unpleasant happens【尤书面】引起[导致]某事〔尤指坏事〕: *Two phenomena are giving rise to world-wide concern – mass unemployment and mass migration into cities.* 有两个现象——大规模失业和向城市大规模移民——正引起全球关注。| *The President's absence has given rise to speculation about his health.* 总统的缺席引发了对他健康状况的猜测。

5 ►SLOPE 坡◄ [C] an upward slope 斜坡: *There's a slight rise in the road just before our house.* 就在我们房子前的路有一个小斜坡。

6 **get a rise out of sb** to make someone become annoyed or embarrassed by making a joke about them〔开玩笑〕激怒某人; 使某人尴尬: *You can always get a rise out of Peter by teasing him about his age.* 拿彼得的年龄开玩笑, 准能把他惹恼。—see also 另见 HIGH RISE

ris·er /ˈraɪzə; ˈraɪzə/ *n* [C] **1 early/late riser** someone who usually gets out of bed very early or very late 早起/晚起的人 **2** *technical* the upright part of a step on a set of stairs【术语】〔楼梯的〕竖板

ris·i·ble /ˈrɪzəbl; ˈrɪzʒbəl/ *adj formal* something that is risible is so stupid that it deserves to be laughed at【正式】令人发笑的, 滑稽的: *a risible suggestion* 可笑的建议 —**risibility** /ˌrɪzəˈbɪlətɪ; ˌrɪzʒˈbɪlʒti/ *n* [U]

ris·ing[1] /ˈraɪzɪŋ; ˈraɪzɪŋ/ *n* [C] a sudden attempt by a large group of people to violently remove a government or ruler 造反, 起义

rising[2] *adj* **1** [only before noun 仅用于名词前] becoming more important or famous〔重要性或名望〕上升的, 兴起的: *a rising young actor* 崭露头角的年轻演员 **2 rising five/six etc** nearly five, six etc years old 将近五/六岁等 **3 the rising generation** young people who will soon be old enough to vote, have jobs etc 即将成年的一代

rising damp /ˌ‥ ˈ‥/ *n* [U] *BrE* a condition where water comes up from the ground and gets into the walls of a building【英】〔由地面渗入墙壁的〕上升潮气

S2 W1 **risk**[1] /rɪsk; rɪsk/ *n*

1 ►POSSIBILITY OF BAD RESULT 不良后果的可能性◄ [C, U] the possibility that something bad, unpleasant, or dangerous may happen 危险性, 风险: *If you're considering starting a business, think carefully about the risks involved.* 如果你在考虑创办公司, 要认真地想想所涉及的各种风险。| [+of] *the risk of serious injury* 严重受伤的危险 | **reduce/increase the risk of** *Wear rubber gloves to reduce the risk of infection.* 戴上橡皮手套以减少感染的危险。| [+that] *There was some risk that fire would break out again.* 大火有死灰复燃的危险。| **a calculated risk** (=a risk you think will have a good result) 利大于弊的风险 *It was a calculated risk to appoint a man without management experience to such a senior post.* 委任一个没有管理经验的人担任这样高的职位得冒风险, 但应该利大于弊。| **an element of risk** (=some risk, but not much) 略有风险 *There's an element of risk in any kind of investment.* 任何种类的投资都存在一定的风险。| **it's worth the risk** *I never walk home alone at night – it's not worth the risk.* 我从不在夜里独自步行回家——不值得冒这个险。

2 **take a risk** to decide to do something even though you know it may have bad results 冒险: *The fuel tank could blow up, but that's a risk we'll have to take.* 燃料罐有可能爆炸, 但我们必须冒这个险。

3 **at risk** be in a situation where you may be harmed 处境危险: *We must stop these rumours; the firm's reputation is at risk.* 我们必须制止这些谣传; 公司的名誉有受损的危险。| **be at risk of** *People with fair skins are more at risk of skin cancer.* 皮肤白的人患皮肤癌的危险较大。| **put sb/sth at risk** *I've no respect for a man who would put his children at risk like that.* 我鄙视一个像那样使自己的孩子遭受危险的人。

4 **run a risk** to be in a situation where there is a risk of something bad happening to you 冒险: *Anyone travelling without a passport runs the risk of being arrested.* 任何不带护照旅行的人都有被逮捕的危险。

5 **at the risk of doing sth** used when you think that what you are going to say or do may have a bad result, may offend or annoy people etc 冒着…的危险: *At the risk of sounding stupid, can I ask a simple question?* 恕在下愚昧, 我能否问一个简单的问题?

6 **at your own risk** if you do something at your own risk, you do it even though you understand the possible dangers and have been warned about them 自担风险, 责任自负: *You leave valuables in the classroom at your own risk.* 将贵重物品留在教室里, 责任自负。

7 ►CAUSE OF DANGER 危险的起因◄ [C] something or someone that is likely to cause harm or danger 可能造成伤害[危险]的事[人]: [+to] *Polluted water supplies are a risk to public health.* 受到污染的供水会危害公众健康。| **health risk** (=something likely to harm people's health) 对健康的威胁 *Meat from the infected animals is regarded as a serious health risk.* 受感染动物的肉被视为对健康的严重威胁。| **fire risk** (=something that could cause a dangerous fire) 火灾隐患 *The tyre dump is a major fire risk.* 那堆车胎是一个重大的火灾隐患。| **security risk** (=someone who may tell important secrets to an enemy country) 危险分子〔有可能向敌对国家提供重要机密的人〕

8 ►INSURANCE/BUSINESS 保险/商业◄ [C] a person or business judged according to the danger involved in giving them insurance or lending them money〔按其风险评估的〕保险对象; 贷款对象: **a good/bad/poor risk** *a good credit risk* 信誉好的贷款对象 | *Drivers under 21 are regarded as poor risks by insurance companies.* 21岁以下的驾车者被保险公司看成是风险较高的保险对象。

This graph shows some of the words most commonly used with the noun **risk**. 本图表所示为含有名词 risk 的一些最常用词组。

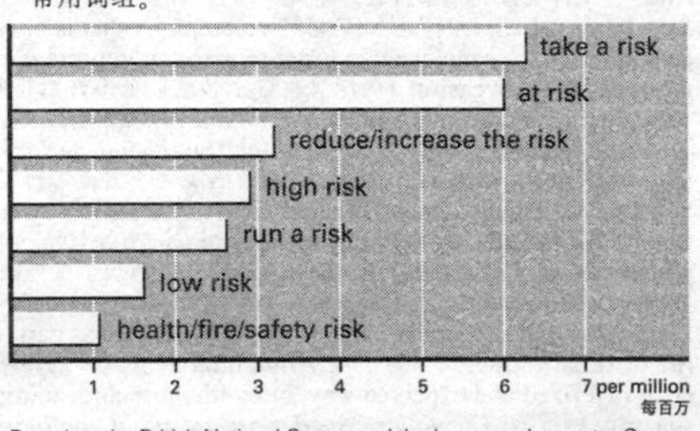

Based on the British National Corpus and the Longman Lancaster Corpus
据英国国家语料库和朗文兰开斯特语料库

risk[2] *v* [T] **1** to put something in a situation in which it could be lost, destroyed, or harmed 使遭受〔失去、毁坏或伤害〕的危险: *When children start smoking, they don't realize that they're risking their health.* 儿童开始抽烟时, 并没有意识到是拿自己的健康去冒险。| **risk sth on sth** *You'd be crazy to risk your money on an investment like that!* 把钱冒险用于那样的投资, 你简直疯了! | **risk your life** *Martina risked her life to save her dog from the fire.* 马丁娜冒着生命危险从火场中救出她的狗。| **risk your neck** *informal* (=do something very dangerous in order to help someone)【非正式】冒极大的危险〔帮助别人〕*I'm not going to risk my neck just to save a common criminal.* 我不会拼了命去救一个普通的犯人。| **risk life and limb** (=do something very dangerous) 冒极大的危险 *Why risk life and limb jumping out of a plane without a parachute on your back?* 为什么要冒着巨大的危险不背降落伞跳出飞机? **2** to get into a situation where something unpleasant may happen to you 担…风险, 冒…的危险: **risk defeat/death/dismissal etc** *The government risks an embarrassing defeat if it calls an election now.* 政府如果现在进行选举, 就有遭受令人尴尬的失败的危险。| **risk being defeated/killed/dismissed etc** *Workers who broke the strike risked being attacked when they left the factory.* 破坏罢工的工人在离开工厂时有遭受攻击的危险。**3** to do something that you know may have dangerous or unpleasant results 冒险做〔某事, 其结果是危险或令人讨厌的〕: **risk doing sth** *Are you prepared to risk traveling without an armed guard?* 你准备冒险不带武装警卫出行吗? | **risk it** *spoken*【口】*You could slip out of school between classes, but I wouldn't risk it.* 你可以在课间溜出学校, 但我不会冒险这样干。

risk man·age·ment /ˈ· ˌ···/ *n* [U] a system to prevent or reduce dangerous accidents or mistakes 风险管理

risk-tak·ing /ˈ· ˌ··/ *n* [U] the practice of doing things that involve risks in order to achieve something 冒险 —**risk-taker** *n* [C]

risk·y /ˈrɪskɪ; ˈrɪski/ *adj* involving a risk that something bad will happen; rather dangerous 冒险的; 非常危险的: *It's risky to go out so soon after being ill.* 病后这么快就外出, 太危险啦。| *a risky investment* 有风险的投资 | **a risky business** (=a dangerous action or situation) 危险的事 *Buying a secondhand car is a risky business.* 买二手汽车是有风险的事。—**riskily** *adv* —**riskiness** *n* [U]

ri·sot·to /rɪˈsɔto; rɪˈzɒtəʊ/ *n plural* **risottos** [C,U] a hot meal made from rice mixed with cheese, vegetables, or pieces of meat〔用干酪、蔬菜或肉等烹制的〕煨饭

ris·qué /rɪsˋke; ˈrɪskeɪ/ *adj* a joke, remark etc that is risqué is slightly shocking, especially because it is about sex〔笑话、评论等〕粗野的, 近乎淫秽的

ris·sole /ˈrɪsol; ˈrɪsəʊl/ *n* [C] cooked meat cut into very small pieces mixed with potato or bread, and cooked in hot fat〔加进马铃薯或面包的〕炸肉饼, 炸肉丸

Ritalin *trademark* a drug that is used to treat Attention Deficit Hyperactivity Disorder (=a condition that causes people, especially children, to be too active and not able to pay attention for very long)【商标】利他林〔一种药物, 用于治疗注意力缺陷多动症〕

rite /raɪt; raɪt/ *n* [C] **1** a ceremony that is always performed in the same way, usually for religious purposes〔常指宗教〕仪式, 典礼: *funeral rites* 葬礼 | *satanic rites* 撒旦崇拜仪式 | **perform a rite** *a traditional rite that was performed at harvest time* 收获期举行的传统仪式 **2 rite of passage** a special ceremony or action that is a sign of a new stage in someone's life, especially when a boy starts to become a man "人生新阶段"仪式〔标志着人生进入新阶段, 尤其是男孩成年的特殊仪式〕, 成人仪式 **3 last rites** final prayers or religious ceremonies for someone who is dying 临终圣礼: *A priest came to give him the last rites.* 一位神父来为他举行临终圣礼。

rit·u·al[1] /ˈrɪtʃuəl; ˈrɪtʃuəl/ *n* [C,U] **1** a ceremony that is always performed in the same way, in order to mark an important religious or social occasion〔为纪念重要宗教或社会事件举行的〕仪式, 典礼: *the ritual of communion in the Christian Church* 基督教教会的圣餐仪式 | **perform a ritual** *The shaman performed the ritual on the young boy.* 那位萨满教巫医为小男孩举行了仪式。**2** something that you do regularly and in the same way each time 惯例, 老规矩, 例行公事: *The children performed the bedtime ritual of washing and brushing their teeth.* 孩子按照惯例在睡觉前洗脸刷牙。

ritual[2] *adj* [only before noun 仅用于名词前] **1** done as part of a rite or ritual 作为仪式一部分的: *ritual dances* 仪式中的舞蹈 **2** done in a fixed and expected way, but without real meaning or sincerity 例行的: *The police issued the usual ritual apology.* 警方发表了官样文章式的道歉。—**ritually** *adv*

rit·u·al·is·tic /ˌrɪtʃuəlˈɪstɪk; ˌrɪtʃuəˈlɪstɪk◂/ *adj* ritualistic words, types of behaviour etc always follow the same pattern, especially because they form part of a ritual〔话语、行为等〕惯常的, 例行的; (遵守) 仪式的: *ritualistic incantations* 举行仪式时说的咒语 | *I got tired with the boring, almost ritualistic weekly meeting.* 我厌倦了无聊的、几乎是例行公事的周会。—**ritualistically** /-klɪ; -kli/ *adv*

Ritz, the /rɪts; rɪts/ a famous large hotel, named after the original Swiss owner, César Ritz. Several large cities, including London and Paris, have Ritz hotels. 里茨饭店〔一家著名大酒店, 以创始人瑞士老板塞萨尔·里茨的名字命名。伦敦、巴黎等几个大城市都有里茨饭店〕

Ritz crack·ers /ˌ· ˈ·· ·/ *trademark* a type of small round salty CRACKER (=thin biscuit) sold in boxes in the US and the UK【商标】乐之饼干〔一种又小又圆的咸味薄脆饼, 在英美以盒装销售〕

ritz·y /ˈrɪtsɪ; ˈrɪtsi/ *adj informal* fashionable and expensive【非正式】时髦而豪华的: *a ritzy restaurant* 时髦而豪华的饭店

ri·val[1] /ˈraɪvl; ˈraɪvəl/ *n* [C] **1** a person, group, or organization that you compete with in sport, business, a fight etc 对手, 竞争者: *He left the government to become her most formidable rival.* 他离开政府, 成了她最难以应付的对手。| [+for] *The two girls were rivals for Jack's attention.* 这两个女孩为获得杰克的青睐而争风吃醋。| **rival company/nation/team etc** *Sheena left her job and went to work for a rival company.* 希娜辞了职, 转到一家对头公司工作。| **arch-rival** (=main rival) 最主要的对手 *Hanover High School was our arch-rival in football.* 汉诺威中学队是我们最主要的足球对手。**2** something that is equally as good or important as something else 匹敌者, 可相比的东西: **rival claim/explanation/argument etc** *The court listened to the rival explanations in turn.* 法庭逐一听取控辩双方针锋相对的辩解。| **have no/few rivals** (=be better than all others or most others) 没有/鲜有敌手

rival[2] *v* **rivalled, rivalling** *BrE*【英】, **rivaled, rivaling** *AmE*【美】[T] to be as good or important as someone or something else 与…匹敌[媲美]: *The college's facilities rival those of Harvard and Yale.* 这所学院的设施可以同哈佛和耶鲁的媲美。—see also 另见 UNRIVALLED

ri·val·ry /ˈraɪvlrɪ; ˈraɪvəlri/ *n* [C,U] continuous competition 不断的竞争: *a fierce rivalry between the two basketball teams* 这两支篮球队之间的激烈竞争

Ri·vals, The /ˈraɪvlz; ˈraɪvəlz/ (1775) a humorous play by Richard Brinsley Sheridan, whose best-known character is Mrs Malaprop《情敌》〔(1775), 理查德·谢里丹的幽默戏剧。剧中最著名的人物是梅拉普洛普夫人〕

riv·en /ˈrɪvən; ˈrɪvən/ *adj formal* split violently apart【正式】撕裂的, 分裂的: *a community riven by religious differences* 因宗教分歧而分裂的社区

riv·er /ˈrɪvə; ˈrɪvə/ *n* [C] **1** a natural and continuous flow of water in a long line across a country into the sea 江, 河: *the Mississippi River* 密西西比河 | *We swam to a large rock in the middle of the river.* 我们游到河心的一块大石头那里。| **river bank** (=the land at the side of a river) 河岸 *We ate our lunch on the river bank.* 我们在河边吃了午餐。| **mouth of the river** (=where a river joins the sea) 河口 | **up river** (=in the opposite direction from the way the river is flowing) 向上游, 逆流 *a ship sailing up river* 逆流而上的船 | **down river** (=in the same direction as the way the river is flowing) 向下游, 顺流 **2** a large amount of moving liquid 巨流; 大量流动液体: [+of] *a river of hot lava flowing from the volcano* 从火山涌出的炽热熔岩流 —see also 另见 **sell sb down the river** (SELL[1] (12))

Rivera /rɪˈvɛrə; rɪˈveərə/, **Diego** /dɪˈego; dɪˈeɪgəʊ/ (1886-1957) a Mexican painter of MURALS which expressed his socialist political ideas 里维拉〔(1886-1957), 墨西哥画家。他以壁画表达自己的社会主义政治思想〕

river ba·sin /ˈ·· ˌ··/ *n* [C] an area from which all the water flows into the same river〔江、河的〕流域, 河流盆地

river bed /ˈ·· ·/ *n* [C] the ground over which a river flows 河床

riv·er·side /ˈrɪvəˌsaɪd; ˈrɪvəsaɪd/ *n* [singular] the land on the banks of a river 河边, 河畔: *We had a picnic by the riverside.* 我们在河边野餐。| **riverside path/cottage etc** *a riverside inn* 河畔小旅馆

riv·et[1] /ˈrɪvɪt; ˈrɪvɪt/ *v* **1 be riveted on/to** if your attention is riveted on something, you are so frightened or so interested that you keep looking at it 目不转睛, 紧盯在…上: *Barnes watched in terror, his eyes riveted on the huge tiger.* 巴恩斯恐惧地注视着, 眼睛紧盯着那只大老虎。**2 be riveted to the spot** to be so shocked or frightened that you cannot move〔惊吓得〕动弹不得 **3** [T] to fasten something with rivets〔用铆钉〕固定, 铆接

rivet[2] *n* [C] a metal pin used to fasten pieces of metal together 铆钉

riv·et·ing /ˈrɪvɪtɪŋ; ˈrɪvɪtɪŋ/ *adj* **1** something that is riveting is so interesting or exciting that you cannot stop watching it or listening to it 令人着迷的; 非常精彩的; 引人入胜的: *a riveting performance* 非常精彩的演出 **2** *humorous* used when you do not really think something is interesting at all【幽默】有趣的〔反话〕: *What a riveting conversation!* 多么有趣的谈话!

ri·vi·e·ra /ˌrɪvɪˈɛrə; ˌrɪviˈeərə/ *n* **the Riviera** a warm coast that is popular with people who are on holiday, especially the Mediterranean coast of France 气候温暖的海滨度假胜地〔尤指法国的地中海沿岸地区里维埃拉〕

> **CULTURAL NOTE 文化注释**
>
> People think of the Riviera as being fashionable and expensive, and a place where rich and famous people go. 人们认为里维埃拉是个时尚、花费很高的地方, 吸引着不少富豪名流前去光顾。— see also 另见 SOUTH OF FRANCE

riv·u·let /ˈrɪvjəlɪt; ˈrɪvjələt/ *n* [C] a very small stream of liquid, especially water 小溪, 小河: *Rivulets of sweat ran down his face.* 津津汗水顺着他的脸流淌下来。

Riy·adh /ˈriæd; ˈriːæd/ the capital city of Saudi Arabia 利雅得〔沙特阿拉伯首都〕

ri·yal, rial /riˈɔl; riˈɑːl/ *n* [C] the standard unit of money in Saudi Arabia and other Arab countries 里亚尔〔沙特阿拉伯及其他阿拉伯国家的货币单位〕

RN /ˌɑr ˈɛn; ˌɑːr ˈen/ **1** Royal Navy; the British navy 英国皇家海军: *Captain Anstruther, RN* 皇家海军安斯特拉瑟上校 **2** REGISTERED NURSE 注册护士

RNA /ˌɑr ɛn ˈe; ˌɑːr en ˈeɪ/ *n* [U] an important chemical that exists in all living cells 核糖核酸

RNIB, the /ˌɑr ɛn aɪ ˈbi; ˌɑːr en aɪ ˈbiː/ the abbreviation of 缩写= Royal National Institute for the Blind〔英国〕皇家全国盲人协会

RNLI, the /ˌɑr ɛn ɛl ˈaɪ; ˌɑːr en el ˈaɪ/ the Royal National Lifeboat Institution; a British CHARITY organization that raises money to pay for the lifeboat service, which saves people who are in trouble at sea around the coast of the UK 皇家全国救生艇协会〔英国一慈善机构, 专为救生服务筹款, 用于营救英国沿海一带的遇险者〕

> **CULTURAL NOTE 文化注释**
>
> The British lifeboat service is not paid for by the government, and the sailors who go in the lifeboats are VOLUNTEERS (=they work for no money). In the US, this job is done by the COASTGUARD, a government organization. 英国的救生艇服务不依靠政府拨款, 而且其救生员也全是志愿者。在美国从事此类服务的是海岸警卫队, 它是一个政府组织。

roach /rotʃ; rəʊtʃ/ *n* **1** *AmE informal* a COCKROACH【美，非正式】蟑螂 **2** a European fish similar to a CARP 拟鲤，斜齿鳊〔欧洲产的鱼，类似鲤鱼〕**3** *slang* the part of a MARIJUANA cigarette that you suck smoke through【俚】大麻烟卷的烟蒂

1 1 **road** /rod; rəʊd/ *n* **1** [C,U] a specially prepared hard surface for cars, buses, bicycles etc to travel on 路，道路，公路：*a busy road* 交通繁忙的马路 | *at the end of the road* 在路的尽头 | **up/down/along the road** (=further along the road) 沿着路 *We live just down the road.* 我们就住在这条路上不远处。| **by road** (=driving) 开车 *It takes three hours by road.* 开车去要花三个小时。| **main road** *Take the main road out of town and turn left at the first light.* 走干道出城，在第一个有交通灯的路口向左拐。| **side road** (=a small road that is not used much) 支路，小路 | **dirt road** *especially AmE* (=a road without a hard surface)【尤美】未铺平的土路 | **road accident/repairs/user etc** *He was killed in a road accident.* 他死于道路交通事故。| **road sense** (=knowledge about how to behave sensibly near traffic) 开车[走路]时注意安全的意识 *Kids of that age have no road sense.* 那个年龄的孩子走路时没有注意安全的意识。| **road safety** (=how to be safe when driving or walking on roads) 道路交通安全 *a road safety campaign* 道路交通安全运动 —see 见 STREET (USAGE) **2 Road** written abbreviation 缩写为 **Rd** used in addresses after the names of roads 路〔用在地址中街道名称之后〕：*65 Maple Road* 枫树路65号 **3 on the road a)** travelling in a car, especially for long distances〔尤指长途〕乘车[开车]旅行：*I've been on the road since 5.00 a.m. this morning.* 我从今早5点起就一直在路上行驶。**b)** if a group of actors or musicians is on the road they are travelling from place to place giving performances 巡回演出 **c)** if your car is on the road, you have paid for the repairs, tax etc necessary for you to legally drive it〔汽车〕可以合法行驶〔指维修好、已交税等〕：*It costs a lot of money to keep these old cars on the road.* 开这些旧汽车很费钱。**4 on the road to success/recovery/peace etc** developing in a way that will result in success etc 向成功/复原/和平等迈进：*It was this deal that set him on the road to his first million.* 正是这笔交易使他赚到迈向100万的第一桶金。**5 go down a road** *informal* to follow a particular course of action【非正式】按某方法做事：*You could move your pension to a private scheme, but I wouldn't advise going down that road.* 你可以把你的养老金转到私人计划中，不过我建议你不要这样做。**6 one for the road** *spoken* a last alcoholic drink before you leave a party, PUB etc【口】〔离开聚会、酒吧等前喝的〕最后一杯酒 **7 get out of the road!** *BrE spoken* a rude way of telling someone to move【英口】〔无礼地叫人〕走开！—see also 另见 **the end of the road** (END[1] (18)), **hit the road** (HIT[1] (16))

road·block /ˈrodˌblɑk; ˈrəʊdblɒk/ *n* [C] **1** a place where the police are stopping traffic〔警察设置的〕路障：*Roadblocks were set up after two prisoners escaped from the county jail.* 两名犯人从县监狱越狱后，路障已经设置起来。**2** *AmE* something that stops the progress of a plan【美】障碍：*mental roadblocks that get in the way of success* 妨碍成功的心理障碍

road hog /ˈ· ·/ *n* [C] *informal* someone who drives too fast without thinking about other people's safety【非正式】〔开快车而不顾他人安全的〕莽撞驾车者

road·house /ˈrodˌhaus; ˈrəʊdhaʊs/ *n* [C] *AmE* a restaurant or bar on a main road outside a city【美】〔城外公路边的〕路旁餐馆，路旁酒吧

road·ie /ˈrodɪ; ˈrəʊdi/ *n* [C] *informal* someone whose job is moving equipment for musicians【非正式】为〔巡回演出的〕乐师搬运设备的人

road man·a·ger /ˈ· ˌ· · ·/ *n* [C] someone who makes arrangements for entertainers when they are travelling 巡回演出表演者的经纪人

road rage /ˈ· ·/ *n* [U] violence and angry behaviour by car drivers towards other car drivers 当路暴怒〔指路上的驾驶者对其他驾驶者所表现的暴力和愤怒行为〕：*a road rage attack* 因当路暴怒引发的攻击行为

road·run·ner /ˈrodˌrʌnɚ; ˈrəʊdrʌnə/ *n* [C] a small bird that runs very fast 走鹃

road·show /ˈrodˌʃo; ˈrəʊdʃəʊ/ *n* [C] *BrE* a group that travels around the country giving performances for entertainment or advertising【英】巡回演出队；巡回宣传团

road·side /ˈrodˌsaɪd; ˈrəʊdsaɪd/ *n* [singular] the edge of the road 路边，路旁：**roadside cafe/pub etc** (=next to a road) 路边小餐馆/酒吧等

road·sign /ˈrodˌsaɪn; ˈrəʊdsaɪn/ *n* [C] a sign next to a road, that gives information to drivers 路标

road tax /ˈ· ·/ *n* [C,U] a tax in Britain that the owner of a vehicle must pay in order to drive it on the roads〔在英国对车主征收的〕道路税，通行税

road test /ˈ· ·/ *n* [C] a test to check that a vehicle is in good condition and safe to drive〔检查车辆性能的〕道路试车 —**roadtest** *v* [T]

road·way /ˈrodˌwe; ˈrəʊdweɪ/ *n* [singular] the part of the road used by vehicles 车行道

road·work /ˈrodˌwɝk; ˈrəʊdwɜːk/ *n* **roadworks** [plural] *BrE* repairs that are being done to a road【英】道路施工

road·wor·thy /ˈrodˌwɝðɪ; ˈrəʊdˌwɜːði/ *adj* a vehicle that is roadworthy is in good condition and safe enough to drive〔车辆〕适于行驶的 —**roadworthiness** *n* [U]

roam /rom; rəʊm/ *v* **1** [I,T] to walk or travel, usually for a long time, with no clear purpose or direction 闲逛，漫步；漫游：[**+over/around/about etc**] *herds of wild deer roaming freely over the hills* 在小山上自由漫步的野鹿群 | **roam the streets/hills etc** *You shouldn't let your children roam the streets.* 你不应该让孩子在街上游荡。**2** [I **+over**] if your eyes roam over something, you look slowly at all parts of it〔目光缓慢地〕端详：*His eyes roamed over the bookshelves.* 他仔细端详书架上一排排的书，从一个书架看到另一个书架。

roan /ron; rəʊn/ *n* [C] a horse of a particular colour, especially light brown〔尤指〕栗色马 —**roan** *adj*

roar[1] /rɔr; rɔː/ *v* **1** [I] to make a deep, very loud noise 吼叫，呼啸：*We heard a lion roar.* 我们听到一声狮吼。**2** [T] to say or shout something in a deep, powerful voice 咆哮，大声喊叫：*"Get out of my house!" he roared.* "滚出我的房子！"他大声吼道。**3** [I] also 又作 **roar with laughter** *especially BrE* to laugh loudly and continuously【尤英】哄笑，大笑，狂笑：*When Charlie's trousers fell down, the audience roared.* 查利的裤子掉下来时，观众哄堂大笑。**4** [I always+adv/prep] if a vehicle roars somewhere, it moves very quickly and noisily〔车辆〕轰鸣着疾驶：[**+past/down etc**] *There was a cloud of dust as a truck roared past.* 一辆卡车轰鸣着疾驶而过，扬起一大团灰尘。

roar[2] *n* [C] **1** a deep, loud noise made by an animal such as a LION, or by someone's voice 吼叫声，咆哮声：*A roar of approval came from the crowd.* 人群大声叫喊表示同意。**2** a continuous loud noise, especially made by a machine or a strong wind〔机器的〕轰鸣声；〔风的〕呼啸声：*the roar of the traffic* 来往车辆的轰鸣声

roar·ing /ˈrɔrɪŋ; ˈrɔːrɪŋ/ *adj* **1** [only before noun 仅用于名词前] making a deep, very loud, continuous noise 发出吼声的，咆哮的，呼啸的：*the roaring wind and waves* 咆哮的风浪 **2 roaring fire** a roaring fire burns with a lot of flames and heat 熊熊烈火 **3 do a roaring trade (in)** *BrE informal* to sell a lot of something very quickly【英，非正式】生意兴隆 **4 be a roaring success** *BrE* to be extremely successful【英】获得极大成功：*The new musical has been a roaring success.* 这部新音乐剧非常卖座。**5 roaring drunk** *BrE* very drunk and noisy【英】酩酊大醉

Roaring Twen·ties, the /ˌ· ˌ· ˈ· ·/ a name sometimes used to describe the 1920s, especially in the US, where life was thought to be very exciting and interesting, partly because of Prohibition (=the law that made alcohol illegal) and the criminal activity that this caused, and partly because of the development of more modern styles in music, dancing, women's clothes etc. 兴旺的20年代〔有时尤其用来指代美国20世纪20年代这一时期。这十年的生活激动人心、十分有趣，一方面因为当时实施的《禁酒令》及其引发的犯罪活动，另一方面因为当时的音乐、舞蹈、女士服饰等日新月异，风格空前摩登〕

roast[1] /rost; rəʊst/ *v* **1** [I,T] to cook something, such as meat, in an OVEN or over a fire 烤（肉等）—see picture on page A10 参见A10页图 **2** [I,T] to heat nuts, coffee, beans etc quickly in order to dry them and give them a particular taste 烘，焙（坚果、咖啡、豆类等）：*dry-roasted peanuts* 干烘的花生 **3** [T] *informal* to strongly criticize or make insulting remarks about someone or something【非正式】严厉地批评；嘲讽：*Her first play got roasted by the critics.* 她的第一部剧被评论家批评得一无是处。

roast[2] *n* [C] **1** a large piece of roasted meat 大块烤肉 —see also 另见 POT ROAST **2** *AmE* an occasion at which people celebrate a special event in someone's life by telling funny stories or giving speeches about them【美】庆祝聚会：*We're going to have a roast for Jack when he retires.* 杰克退休时，我们要为他举行一个庆祝会。**3 hot dog roast/oyster roast etc** *AmE* an outdoor party at which food is cooked on an open fire【美】户外烧烤热狗/牡蛎等野餐会

roast[3] *adj* [only before noun 仅用于名词前] roasted 烤好的，烤制的：*roast chicken* 烤鸡

CULTURAL NOTE 文化注释

Roast beef, especially served with Yorkshire pudding for Sunday lunch, is thought of as the most typical English food. 烤牛肉，特别是与约克郡布丁一起用作周日午餐的烤牛肉，被认为是最典型的英国饭菜。

roast·ing[1] /ˈrostɪŋ; ˈrəʊstɪŋ/ also 又作 **roasting hot** /,.. ˈ. ◂/ *adj informal* very hot, especially so that you feel uncomfortable【非正式】灼热的〔尤指令人感到不舒服〕: *a roasting hot day* 酷热的一天 | *I'm absolutely roasting in this suit.* 穿着这套衣服，我着实热死了。

roasting[2] *n* **give sb a roasting** *informal especially BrE* to talk angrily to someone in order to tell them that you disapprove of their behaviour【非正式，尤英】申斥，非难

S3 **rob** /rɑb; rɒb/ *v* **robbed, robbing** [T] **1** to steal money or property from a person, bank etc 抢劫，抢夺，打劫: *The gang tried to rob a bank using a sawn-off shotgun.* 那伙罪犯企图用一支截短的猎枪抢劫一家银行。| **rob sb of sth** *Mrs Clegg was severely beaten and robbed of all her possessions.* 克莱格太太遭到毒打，并被抢去全部财物。| *The company director robbed pensioners of millions.* 这家公司董事侵吞了养老金领取者数以百万计的钱。—see 见 STEAL[1] (USAGE) —see picture at 参见 STEAL[1] 图 **2 rob sb/sth of sth** to take away an important quality, ability etc from someone or something 使…丧失…: *Being bullied has robbed Duane of his self-confidence.* 杜安受到欺侮，这使他丧失了自信。**3 rob Peter to pay Paul** to take money away from someone or something that needs it in order to pay someone else or use it for something else 拆东墙补西墙；剜肉补疮 **4 I was robbed!** *spoken* used when you think that you were beaten unfairly in a sport【口】我输得很冤枉!〔用于体育比赛中〕**5 rob the cradle** *AmE humorous* to have a sexual relationship with someone who is a lot younger than you【美，幽默】与比自己年龄小很多的人发生性关系; CRADLE-SNATCH *BrE*【英】

rob·ber /ˈrɑbɚ; ˈrɒbə/ *n* [C] someone who steals money or property 强盗，盗贼，抢劫者: *a bank robber* 银行抢劫犯

robber bar·on /,.. ˈ.. / *n* [C] a powerful man who used force to get money, land etc, for example a businessman in US in the 19th century who made a lot of money in a dishonest way 强盗贵族〈如19世纪靠不正当手段发财的美国商人〉

rob·ber·y /ˈrɑbərɪ; ˈrɒbəri/ *n* [C,U] the crime of stealing things from a bank, shop etc, especially using violence 抢劫，劫夺: *Police are investigating a series of bank robberies in South Wales.* 警方正在调查南威尔士发生的一连串银行抢劫案。| **armed robbery** (=robbery using a gun) 持枪抢劫 *a 10 year prison sentence for armed robbery* 因持枪抢劫被判10年监禁 —see also 另见 **daylight robbery** (DAYLIGHT (2))

robe[1] /rob; rəʊb/ *n* [C] **1** also 又作 **robes** a long loose piece of clothing, especially one worn for official ceremonies〔尤指正式典礼时穿的〕长袍，礼服: *a priest's robes* 牧师的长袍 **2** *especially AmE* a long loose piece of clothing that you wear over your night clothes or after a bath【尤美】睡袍；浴衣; DRESSING GOWN *especially BrE*【尤英】—see also 另见 BATHROBE

robe[2] *v formal*【正式】**1 be robed in** to be dressed in a particular way 穿着…: *The hostess looked very glamorous, robed in emerald velvet.* 女主人身穿翠绿色天鹅绒衣服，看上去非常迷人。**2 robe yourself** *literary* to put on your clothes【文】穿上衣服

Rob·erts /ˈrɑbɚts; ˈrɒbəts/, **Oral** (1918-) a US Christian TELEVANGELIST (=someone who talks about religion on television), who has a weekly television programme and his own radio station, and who also started a university in Oklahoma called Oral Roberts University 罗伯茨〔(1918-)，美国一基督教电视布道人。他主持一档电视节目，每周播出一次。他有自己的电台，还在俄克拉何马州开办了一所大学，名为奥拉尔·罗伯茨大学〕

Robertson /ˈrɑbɚtsn̩; ˈrɒbətsən/, **Pat** (1930-) a US Christian leader and TELEVANGELIST (=someone who talks about religion on television) who owns a television company called The Christian Broadcasting Network Inc. He started the Christian Coalition, a RIGHT WING Christian political group, in 1989. He is also a politician in the Republican Party. 罗伯逊〔(1930-)，美国基督教领袖、电视布道人。他拥有一家电视公司，名为"基督教广播网"，曾于1989年创立了右翼基督教政治团体"基督教联合会"。他还是一位共和党政治家〕

Robert the Bruce —see 见 Robert (the) BRUCE

Robe·son /ˈrobsn̩; ˈrəʊbsən/, **Paul** (1898-1976) a US singer and actor, famous for his beautiful, deep singing voice and for his Communist beliefs and his work to achieve civil rights for black people in the US. He sang the song *Ol' Man River* in the film *Showboat* (1936). 罗伯逊〔(1898-1976)，美国著名歌唱家、演员。他的嗓音浑厚动听。他怀有共产主义信念，致力于为美国黑人争取民权的事业。影片《演艺船》(1936) 的插曲《老人河》就是由他演唱的〕

Robes·pierre /ˈrobspɪr; ˈrəʊbspɪə/, **Max·i·mil·i·en** /ˌmæksɪˈmɪlɪən; ˌmæksəˈmɪliən/ (1758-94) one of the leaders of the French Revolution, famous for starting the 'reign of terror' (1793-94) during which thousands of people were executed because they were believed to be enemies of the Revolution. He was later removed from power and killed by the GUILLOTINE. 罗伯斯庇尔〔(1758-1794)，法国大革命的著名领袖人物之一。他开启了"恐怖统治"时期(1793-1794)，数千人被认定为大革命的敌人而遭到处决。后来他失势并被送上了断头台〕

Rob·in /ˈrɑbɪn; ˈrɒbən/ a character in stories and films about Batman. Robin is a young man who helps Batman to fight criminals, and is also called the Boy Wonder 罗宾〔蝙蝠侠故事和电影中的一个人物。他是个年轻人，协助蝙蝠侠与罪犯作斗争。他还被称作"神童"〕

robin *n* [C] **1** a common small European bird with a red breast and brown back〔欧洲〕鸲，知更鸟 **2** a North American bird like a European robin, but larger〔北美〕鸫

Robin, Christopher —see 见 CHRISTOPHER ROBIN

Robin Hood 罗宾汉

Robin Hood /,.. ˈ. / in old English stories, a man who lived as an OUTLAW (=someone who does not obey the law and is hiding from the authorities) in Sherwood Forest in central England, with his followers, known as his 'Merry Men'. These include Friar Tuck, Little John, and Maid Marian. His enemy is the evil Sheriff of Nottingham, who is always trying to catch him. Robin Hood is usually shown dressed in green clothes, known as Lincoln green, and holding a BOW. There have been many stories, films, and television programmes about his life and adventures. He is famous especially for robbing the rich and giving to the poor, and people use his name to describe a situation in which money is taken from rich people and given to poor people. 罗宾汉〔英国古代传说故事中的绿林好汉。他身居英格兰中部的舍伍德森林，手下有一班人马，叫做"快乐伙伴"，其中包括修士塔克、小约翰和少女玛丽安。他的敌人是邪恶的诺丁汉郡郡长，此人总是想方设法要抓到他。故事中的罗宾汉通常身着"林肯绿呢"，手执一把弓箭。他的生平和冒险经历被改编成许多故事、电影和电视节目。罗宾汉尤以劫富济贫闻名，人们常借用他的名字描写劫富济贫的情形〕: *a new higher-rate tax that will have a 'Robin Hood effect' on income distribution* 对收入分配具有"劫富济贫效果"的高税率新税制

Robinson /ˈrɑbɪnsn̩; ˈrɒbənsən/, **Edward G.** (1893-1973) a US film actor who appeared as a GANGSTER (=members of a group of violent criminals) in films such as *Little Caesar* (1930) and *Key Largo* (1948). 鲁宾逊〔(1893-1973)，美国电影演员。他曾在《小凯撒》(1930) 和《盖世枭雄》(1948) 等影片中扮演一名匪徒〕

Robinson, Jackie (1919-72) a US BASEBALL player who was the first black person to be allowed to play in the Major Leagues 鲁宾逊〔(1919-1972)，美国棒球运动员。他是首位获准参加美国职业棒球大联盟赛事的黑人球员〕

Robinson, Smok·ey /ˈsmokɪ; ˈsməʊki/ (1940-) a US soul singer and record producer for the record company Motown, of which he later became a DIRECTOR. He started working with his

group The Miracles in 1957 and their songs include *The Tracks of My Tears*, and *I Second That Emotion*. 罗宾逊〔(1940-)，美国灵歌歌手、汽车城唱片公司唱片制作人。他后来成为该公司的一名董事，1957年开始运作他的“奇迹”乐队，作品有《我的泪痕》和《同感》等〕

Robinson, Sugar Ray (1921-89) a very successful US BOXER who was world CHAMPION in the 1940s and 1950s, first as a WELTERWEIGHT (=boxer weighing between 63.5 and 66.5 kilos), and then as a MIDDLEWEIGHT (=boxer weighing between 70 and 72.5 kilos) 罗宾逊〔(1921-1989)，美国杰出拳击手。20世纪40、50年代的世界冠军。他的竞技生涯始于次中量级，后来成为次重量级拳击手〕

Robinson Cru·soe /ˌrɑbɪnsn̩ ˈkruso; ˌrɒbɪ̇nsən ˈkruːsəʊ/ the main character in the book *Robinson Crusoe* by Daniel Defoe. When Robinson Crusoe's ship sinks, he manages to reach a desert island (=a small tropical island with no people living on it) where he builds a home. Later he meets a black man whom he calls Man Friday, who becomes his servant and friend. They are both finally discovered by a British ship and taken home. 鲁滨逊·克鲁索〔丹尼尔·笛福的小说《鲁滨逊漂流记》中的主人公。鲁滨逊·克鲁索在乘坐的船只沉没之际，费了一番周折才登上一座荒岛，然后在岛上搭建了一个安身之处。后来，他遇到一个黑人，管他叫“星期五”。那个黑人于是成了他的仆人和朋友，最后，有一艘英国船发现了他们，并把他们带回家乡〕

ro·bot /ˈrobət; ˈrəʊbɒt/ *n* [C] **1** a machine that can move and do some of the work of a person, and is usually controlled by a computer 机器人: *cars built by robots* 机器人制造的汽车 **2** someone who works or behaves like a machine, without having thoughts or feelings 机器一般的人 —**robotic** /roˈbɑtɪk; rəʊˈbɒtɪk/ *adj*

ro·bo·tics /roˈbɑtɪks; rəʊˈbɒtɪks/ *n* [U] the study of how robots are made and used 机器人学

Rob Roy /ˌrɑb ˈrɔɪ; ˌrɒb ˈrɔɪ/ (1671-1734) a Scottish OUTLAW who lived mostly by stealing cows and making people pay for protection against thieves. He is the subject of a famous NOVEL by Sir Walter Scott. 罗布·罗伊〔(1671-1734)，苏格兰一不法分子。他主要以偷窃奶牛和向乡民收取防盗保护费为生，是瓦尔特·司各特爵士的一部著名小说的主人公〕

ro·bust /roˈbʌst; rəˈbʌst/ *adj* **1** a robust person is strong and healthy 强健的，健壮的: *a robust 85-year-old* 一位健壮的85岁老人 **2** a robust object is strong and not likely to break〔东西〕结实的，坚固的: *a six-foot giant who seemed likely to flatten even the most robust of deckchairs* 一个看来可能会把最结实的帆布躺椅坐塌的六英尺高的大汉 **3** a robust system, organization etc is strong and not likely to have problems〔系统、组织等〕健全的，稳固的: *The US economy is now much more robust.* 美国经济目前稳固多了。**4** behaving or speaking in a strong and determined way〔行为或说话〕强硬的，坚定的: *a typically robust performance by the former Prime Minister* 前首相一如既往的坚定表现 —**robustly** *adv* —**robustness** *n* [U]

Roc, the /rɑk; rɒk/ in ancient Eastern stories, a bird of great size and strength which, in the story of *Sindbad the Sailor*, carried Sindbad out of the valley of DIAMONDS 大鹏〔东方古代传说故事中的一种具有神力的巨鸟。在《辛巴达历险记》中，正是这只巨鸟把辛巴达从钻石谷带了出来〕

Roch·es·ter /ˈrɑtʃɪstɚ; ˈrɒtʃɪ̇stə/, **Mrs** a character in the book *Jane Eyre* (1847) by Charlotte Brontë. Mrs Rochester is mentally ill and kept locked in the ATTIC (=a room under the roof) of the house so that no one can see her. She finally destroys the house by setting it on fire. 罗彻斯特夫人〔夏洛蒂·勃朗特的小说《简爱》(1847)中的一个人物。她有精神病，被锁在屋顶的阁楼里，免得别人看见。最后，她放火焚烧了整幢房屋〕

S2 W2 **rock¹** /rɑk; rɒk/ *n*

1 ▶**STONE** 石头◀ **a)** [U] stone, or a type of stone that forms part of the Earth's surface 岩石: *To build the tunnel, they had to cut through 500 feet of solid rock.* 为了建造这条隧道，他们必须凿穿500英尺的坚硬岩石。| **rock formation** (=a shape made naturally from rock) 岩层，岩石 *the rock formations of the Arizona desert* 亚利桑那沙漠的岩层 **b)** [C] a piece of stone, especially a large one 岩块，石块: *Kim sat down on a rock.* 金坐在一块大石头上。**c) rocks** [plural] a line of rock under or next to the sea 礁石: *A ship had been driven onto the rocks during the storm.* 一条船在暴风雨中触礁。

2 ▶**MUSIC** 音乐◀ [U] also 又作 **rock music** a type of popular modern music with a strong loud beat, played using GUITARS and drums 摇滚乐: *a rock concert* 摇滚乐音乐会 | *rock veteran, Eric Clapton* 摇滚乐老牌歌星埃里克·克拉普顿

3 as solid/steady as a rock a) very strongly built or well supported and not likely to break or fall 坚如磐石/稳如磐石的 **b)** someone who is as solid or steady as a rock is very strong and calm in difficult situations and you can depend on them〔指人面对困难时〕坚定的，镇定的，可靠的 —see also 另见 ROCK-SOLID

4 be on the rocks *informal* a relationship or business that is on the rocks is having a lot of problems and is likely to fail soon【非正式】困难重重，濒临失败: *Tim's marriage is on the rocks.* 蒂姆的婚姻濒临破裂。

5 scotch/vodka etc on the rocks an alcoholic drink that is served with ice but no water 加冰块的苏格兰威士忌/伏特加酒等

6 ▶**SWEET FOOD** 甜食◀ [U] *BrE* a hard sweet food made in long round pieces【英】棒形硬糖: *a stick of Blackpool rock* 一条布莱克浦硬棒糖

7 ▶**JEWEL** 首饰◀ [C usually plural 一般用复数] *informal* a DIAMOND or other jewel【非正式】钻石；宝石

8 be (stuck) between a rock and a hard place to have a choice between two things, both of which are unpleasant 左右为难，进退维谷

9 get your rocks off *slang* if a man gets his rocks off, he has sex【俚】〔男人〕发生性行为

rock² *v* **1** [I,T] to move gently backwards and forwards or from side to side, or to make something do this (使)来回摆动，(使)摇摆: *Paul sat gently rocking the child in his arms.* 保罗坐着，把孩子抱在怀里轻轻摇晃。| *The waves made the boat rock from side to side.* 波浪使那条船摇来摇去。| **rock with laughter** *Jim rocked with laughter when he heard what had happened.* 吉姆听了发生的事情后笑得前仰后合。**2** [T] to make the people in a place or organization feel very shocked or surprised 使震惊，使震动: *In 1970, the city of Newark was rocked by a major scandal.* 1970年，一宗重大的丑闻震撼了纽瓦克市。**3 rock the boat** *informal* to cause problems for other members of a group by criticizing something or trying to change the way something is done【非正式】捣乱；改变做事的方式〔从而给别人惹麻烦〕: *A lot of people didn't really agree with the policy, but they didn't want to rock the boat.* 许多人事实上都不赞成这项政策，但他们不想惹是生非。**4** [T] if an explosion, or EARTHQUAKE (=violent movement of the earth) rocks an area, it makes it shake〔爆炸或地震〕使剧烈震动

rock and roll /ˌ· · ˈ·/ *n* [U] ROCK 'N' ROLL 摇滚乐

Rock A·round the Clock /ˌ· · · · ˈ·/ a song by Bill Haley and his Comets. It is one of the first songs that made ROCK 'N' ROLL popular in 1955.《昼夜摇滚》〔比尔·哈利和他的“彗星”乐队演唱的一首歌曲，也是1955年使摇滚乐得以流行的最早歌曲之一〕

rock bot·tom /ˌ· ˈ· ·◂/ *n* **hit/reach rock bottom** *informal* to become as unhappy or unpleasant as it is possible to be【非正式】极不愉快: *My personal life had hit rock bottom.* 我的私生活糟透了。

rock-bottom *adj* a rock-bottom price is as low as it can possibly be〔价格〕最低的，不能再低的: *bargain holidays at rock-bottom prices* 特价旅行团，折扣价无可再低

rock cake /ˈ· ·/ also 又作 **rock bun** *n* [C] *BrE* a small hard cake with a rough surface that has dried fruit in it【英】岩皮饼〔一种表面粗硬有干果的小甜饼〕

rock climb·ing /ˈ· ˌ··/ *n* [U] the sport of climbing up very steep rock surfaces such as the sides of mountains 攀岩(运动) —**rock climber** *n* [C]

rock-crys·tal /ˈ· ˌ··/ *n* [U] pure natural QUARTZ (=a very hard mineral) that is transparent 水晶

Rock·e·fel·ler /ˈrɑkəfɛlɚ; ˈrɒkəfelə/, **John D.** (1839-1937) a US businessman and PHILANTHROPIST, famous for being extremely rich, who started the Standard Oil Company in 1870. He used part of his great wealth to start the University of Chicago in 1892, the Rockefeller Institute for Medical Research (which is now Rockefeller University) in 1901, and the Rockefeller Foundation in 1913. His son, John D. Rockefeller II (1874-1960), gave the UN the land for its HEADQUARTERS, and built the Rockefeller Center, a large group of buildings in New York City, which includes offices, concert halls, shops, and works of art. 洛克菲勒〔(1839-1937)，美国实业家、慈善家，以巨富闻名。1870年创建美孚石油公司，1892年捐资创立芝加哥大学，1901年成立洛克菲勒医学研究院(现为洛克菲勒大学)，1913年设立洛克菲勒基金。儿子约翰·D.洛克菲勒二世(1874-1960)向联合国捐赠土地兴建联合国总部，并在纽约市建立了洛克菲勒中心。该中心为一大型建筑群，内有写字楼、音乐厅、商店以及各种艺术品〕

rock·er /ˈrɑkɚ; ˈrɒkə/ *n* [C] **1** one of the curved pieces of wood fixed to the bottom of a ROCKING CHAIR, that allows it to move backwards and forwards if you push it〔摇椅底部的〕弧形摇板 **2 be off your rocker** *spoken* to be crazy【口】发疯 **3** a member of a group of young people in Britain in the 1960s who wore

leather JACKETS, rode MOTORCYCLES, and listened to ROCK 'N' ROLL music 摇滚青年〔20世纪60年代英国穿皮短上衣、骑摩托车、听摇滚乐的年轻人〕—compare 比较 MOD **4** a ROCKING CHAIR 摇椅

rock·e·ry /ˈrɑkərɪ; ˈrɒkəri/ *n* [C] part of a garden where there are rocks with small plants growing between them 岩石庭园〔园林中陈设岩石、有花草生长的部分〕; 假山

rock·et[1] /ˈrɑkɪt; ˈrɒkɪ̠t/ *n* [C] **1** a vehicle used for travelling or carrying things into space, which is shaped like a big tube 火箭 **2** a similar object used as a weapon, especially one that carries a bomb 火箭式投射器, 火箭弹: *anti-tank rockets* 反坦克火箭 **3** a small tube fixed to a stick, that contains explosive powder and is used as a FIREWORK 流星烟火, 火箭式烟火 **4 give sb a rocket** *BrE informal* to criticize someone angrily because they have done something wrong【英, 非正式】斥责某人

rocket[2] *v* [I] **1** also 又作 **rocket up** if a price or amount rockets, it increases quickly and suddenly〔价格、数量〕迅速上升, 猛涨: *Interest rates rocketed.* 利率急速上升。**2** [always+adv/prep] to move somewhere very fast 急速移动: [+through/along etc] *The train rocketed through the tunnel.* 火车高速驶过隧道。**3** [always+adv/prep] to achieve a successful position very quickly 迅速取得成功地位; 一跃成名: [+to] *Their new album rocketed to number one in the charts.* 他们的新唱片迅速攀升到排行榜榜首。

rocket launch·er /ˈ·· ,··/ *n* [C] a weapon like a tube used for firing military rockets into the air 火箭发射装置, 火箭发射筒

Rock·ettes, the /rɑˈkɛts; rɒˈkets/ a group of women entertainers at Radio City Music Hall in New York City, who sing and dance, usually while standing in a line across the stage 洛克慈女郎舞团〔纽约无线电城音乐厅的歌舞女演员。她们通常在舞台上站成一排唱歌, 跳舞〕

rock·fall /ˈrɑk,fɔl; ˈrɒk,fɔːl/ *n* [C] a pile of rocks that are falling or have fallen 岩崩; 塌方

rock gar·den /ˈ· ,··/ *n* [C] a ROCKERY 岩石庭院; 假山

rock-hard /,· ˈ·◂/ *adj* **1** extremely hard 非常坚硬的: *The bread was stale and rock-hard.* 这个面包既不新鲜又很硬。**2** *BrE humorous* strong and not afraid of anyone【英, 幽默】坚强的; 谁也不怕的

Rock·ies, the /ˈrɑkɪz; ˈrɒkiz/ another name for the Rocky Mountains 落基山脉〔Rocky Mountains 的别称〕

rock·ing chair /ˈ·· ·/ *n* [C] a chair that has two curved pieces of wood fixed under it, so that it moves backwards and forwards 摇椅 —see picture at 参见 CHAIR[1] 图

rocking horse /ˈ·· ·/ *n* [C] a wooden horse for children that moves backwards and forwards when you sit on it〔小孩骑的〕摇动木马

rock mu·sic /ˈ· ,··/ *n* [U] a type of popular modern music with a strong loud beat, played using GUITARS and drums 摇滚乐

Rock·ne /ˈrɑknɪ; ˈrɒkni/, **Knute** /nut; nuːt/ (1888-1931) a US football COACH (=someone who trains a team) at the University of Notre Dame in Indiana, who developed new methods of playing that made his team extremely successful. According to a well-known story, when one of his players was ill, Rockne told his team to win the game they were going to play for "the Gipper". Ronald Reagan appeared as an actor in a film about Rockne, and later, when he became US president, he often used the phrase "do it for the Gipper". 罗克尼〔(1888-1931), 美国印第安纳州圣母大学美式橄榄球教练。他首创了新颖的打球方法, 令球队战绩格外突出。关于罗克尼, 有一则广为人知的趣闻。有一次, 他手下的队员吉佩尔病了, 他就对即将参赛的其他队员说: "要为吉佩尔打赢这场比赛"。罗纳德·里根出演过一部描写罗克尼的影片, 后来成为美国总统后, 他经常也喜欢说"要为吉佩尔打赢这场比赛"〕

rock 'n' roll /,rɑk ən ˈrol; ,rɒk ən ˈrəʊl/ *n* [U] a style of music that was very popular in the 1950s, and has a strong loud beat〔流行于20世纪50年代的〕摇滚乐: *Elvis, the king of rock 'n' roll* 摇滚乐之王埃尔维斯

Rock of Gi·bral·tar, the /,· · ·ˈ··/ a narrow mountain area on a PENINSULA (=piece of land surrounded on three sides by water) in the south of Spain, at the western end of the Mediterranean Sea. The state of Gibraltar is there. 直布罗陀岩山〔地中海最西端西班牙南部一半岛上的狭窄山区, 也是英国属地直布罗陀所在地〕

CULTURAL NOTE 文化注释

British people sometimes use the phrase 'like the Rock of Gibraltar' to talk about something that is so solid and permanent that it will never break or be destroyed. 英国人有时用 like the Rock of Gibraltar (像直布罗陀岩一样) 来形容某物坚固耐用, 不易破损。

rock pool /ˈ· ·/ *n* [C] *BrE* a small pool of water between rocks by the sea【英】〔海边岩石间的〕小水潭; TIDE POOL *AmE*【美】

rock salt /ˈ· ·/ *n* [U] a kind of salt which is obtained from under the ground 岩盐

rock-sol·id /,· ˈ··◂/ *adj* **1** very strong so that you can depend on it 稳健的, 可靠的 **2** very hard and not likely to break 坚硬的; 结实的, 牢固的

rock-stead·y /,· ˈ··◂/ *adj* very strong or very calm 坚如磐石的; 极镇定的: *rock-steady nerves* 极坚强的勇气

Rock·well /ˈrɑkwəl; ˈrɒkwəl/, **Norman** (1894-1978) a US artist famous for his pictures which appeared on the cover of *The Saturday Evening Post*. His pictures often show children and families in ordinary places such as at home, in the countryside, or in small shops. 洛克威尔〔(1894-1978), 美国著名画家。以刊载于《星期六晚邮报》的画作而闻名。他常在作品中表现日常生活场景中的儿童和家庭, 如在家中、乡村或小店铺中〕

Rock·y /ˈrɑkɪ; ˈrɒki/ (1976) the first of a series of films in which Sylvester Stallone appears as a determined BOXER called Rocky. Four more films, called *Rocky II*, *Rocky III* etc, were made about the same character. 《洛奇》〔(1976), 西尔维斯特·史泰龙演出的系列影片中的第一集。史泰龙在影片中扮演一位不屈不挠的拳击手洛奇。其他四部影片为《洛奇第二集》、《洛奇第三集》等, 讲述的是同一个人的故事〕

rocky *adj* **1** covered with rocks or made of rock 多岩石的; 由岩石形成的: *the rocky hills of New England* 新英格兰满是岩石的丘陵 **2** *informal* a relationship or situation that is rocky is difficult and may not continue or be successful【非正式】〔关系或环境〕难以维持的, 可能失败的: *The company faces a rocky road ahead.* 这家公司面临着一条坎坷的道路。—**rockiness** *n* [U]

Rocky Moun·tains, the /,·· ˈ··/ also 又作 **the Rockies** a long range of high mountains in North America which go from Alaska down to New Mexico, and separate the Midwest of the US from the West Coast 落基山脉〔北美洲一大型山系, 从阿拉斯加州绵延至新墨西哥州, 将美国的中西部与西海岸隔开〕

CULTURAL NOTE 文化注释

The Rocky Mountains is a very popular place for tourists to visit for camping, walking, climbing, and SKIing. There are several NATIONAL PARKS in the Rockies, including Yellowstone National Park and Glacier National Park. There are also some famous ski RESORTS, such as Vail in Colorado and Banff in Alberta, Canada. 落基山脉是旅游胜地, 深受游客欢迎, 他们去那里露营、步行、爬山和滑雪。落基山脉有几处国家公园, 例如黄石国家公园和冰河国家公园。那里还有一些著名的滑雪旅游胜地, 像科罗拉多州的韦尔和加拿大艾伯塔省的班夫。

People in the US think of the Rockies as mainly being in Canada and the states of Montana, Idaho, Wyoming, Utah, and Colorado. 美国人认为落基山主要在加拿大和美国的蒙大拿、爱达荷、怀俄明、犹他和科罗拉多几个州境内。

ro·co·co /rəˈkoko; rəˈkəʊkəʊ/ *adj* rococo buildings and furniture have a lot of curly decoration and were fashionable in Europe in the 18th century〔建筑、家具〕洛可可式的〔18世纪流行于欧洲, 多用弯曲形装饰的风格〕

rod /rɑd; rɒd/ *n* [C] **1** a long thin pole or bar 竿, 棒: *The walls are reinforced with steel rods.* 这些墙是用钢筋加固的。**2** a long thin pole used with a line and hook for catching fish 钓竿: *a fishing rod* 钓鱼竿 **3 make a rod for your own back** to do something that will cause trouble for you in the future 自讨苦吃, 自找麻烦 —see also 另见 HOT ROD, **rule sb/sth with a rod of iron** (RULE[2] (6))

rode /rod; rəʊd/ the past tense of RIDE[1]

ro·dent /ˈrodnt; ˈrəʊdənt/ *n* [C] one of a group or small animals with long sharp front teeth, such as rats or rabbits 啮齿动物〈如老鼠、兔子〉

ro·de·o /ˈrodɪ,o; ˈrəʊdiəʊ/ *n plural* **rodeos** [C] a type of entertainment in which COWBOYS ride wild horses, and catch cattle with ropes 牛仔竞技表演〔驯服烈马、用绳圈套牛〕

Ro·de·o Drive /ro,deo ˈdraɪv; rəʊ,deɪəʊ ˈdraɪv/ a street in Beverly Hills, California, which has many expensive shops 罗德奥大道〔加利福尼亚州贝弗利山庄一街道。沿街有许多高档精品店〕

Rod·gers /ˈrɑdʒɚz; ˈrɒdʒəz/, **Richard** (1902-79) a US COMPOSER who wrote the music for many MUSICALS (=films or plays that use singing and dancing to tell a story) with the songwriters Lorenz Hart and Oscar Hammerstein. The musicals that Rodgers and Hart wrote together include *Babes in Arms*

and *Pal Joey*, and those that Rodgers and Hammerstein wrote together include *Oklahoma!*, *The King and I*, *South Pacific*, and *The Sound of Music*. 罗杰斯〔(1902-1979),美国作曲家。他与词作家洛伦茨·哈特和奥斯卡·哈默斯坦一起合作为许多音乐剧创作音乐。他与哈特合写的音乐剧有《怀中佳丽》和《好伙伴雷伊》,与哈默斯坦合作的作品有《俄克拉何马!》、《国王与我》、《南太平洋》和《音乐之声》〕

Ro·din /ro`dæn; 'rəʊdæn/, **Au·guste** /o`gjust; əʊ'gjuːst/ (1840-1917) a French SCULPTOR (=an artist who makes solid objects out of stone, metal, clay etc) who many people think was the greatest sculptor of his time. His most famous works are *The Thinker* and *The Kiss*. 罗丹〔(1840-1917),法国雕塑家,被认为是同时代最伟大的雕塑家。最著名的作品是《思想者》和《吻》〕

roe /ro; rəʊ/ *n* [C,U] fish eggs eaten as a food〔供食用的〕鱼子

Roe·dean /`rodin; 'rəʊdiːn/ a private school for girls in the south of England 罗迪安私立女子学校〔英国南部一私立女子学校〕

roe deer /'· ·/ *n* [C] a small European and Asian DEER that lives in forests 狍(子)〔产于欧亚森林的小鹿〕

roent·gen, röntgen /`rɛntgən; 'rɒntgən/ *n technical* the international measure for X-RAYS【术语】伦琴〔X光的国际放射量单位〕

Roe v. Wade /,· ·· '·/ a court case decided by the US Supreme Court in 1973 which said that the states cannot prevent a woman from having an ABORTION 罗诉韦德案〔1973年美国联邦最高法院判决的一宗诉讼案。该案判决结果是,美国各州无权阻止女性堕胎〕

Ro·ger /`rɑdʒə; 'rɒdʒə/ —see 见 JOLLY ROGER

roger[1] *interjection* used in radio conversations to say that a message has been understood 已收到,明白〔无线电对话用语〕

roger[2] *v* [T] *BrE slang taboo* to have sex with someone【英俚,讳】与…性交

Ro·gers /`rɑdʒəz; 'rɒdʒəz/, **Buck** the main character in a US COMIC who has many adventures in other parts of the universe. The character has also been used in films and television programmes. 罗杰斯〔美国一喜剧片中的主角,在宇宙其他地方历经许多冒险奇遇。该角色也可见于电影和电视节目之中〕

Rogers, Ginger (1911-95) a US dancer and film actress who made many musical films, often with the dancer Fred Astaire. Her films include *42nd Street* (1933) and *Top Hat* (1935). 罗杰斯〔(1911-1995),美国舞蹈演员、电影演员。她拍过许多音乐片,常与弗莱德·阿斯泰尔合舞。演出的影片有《第四十二街》(1933)和《高礼帽》(1935)〕

Rogers, Richard (1933-) a British ARCHITECT (=someone who designs buildings), born in Italy. His buildings are very modern, and are famous for having pipes etc on the outside. He is especially known for his work on the Pompidou Centre in Paris and for buildings in London, especially the Lloyd's Building. 罗杰斯〔(1933-),英国建筑师,生于意大利。他设计的建筑十分现代,以使用管道等配套设施装点建筑物外部而闻名。他设计的巴黎蓬皮杜中心和伦敦劳埃德大厦等建筑尤为著名〕

Rogers, Roy /rɔɪ; rɔɪ/ (1912-98) a US film and television actor and singer who usually appeared as a COWBOY. He is best known for the 1950s television programme *The Roy Rogers Show*, in which he appeared with his wife Dale Evans (1912-2001) and his horse Trigger. At the end of the programme they always sang the song *Happy Trails to You*. 罗杰斯〔(1912-1998),美国影视演员、歌手,常扮演牛仔。他以20世纪50年代的电视节目《罗伊·罗杰斯》最为知名,与妻子戴尔·埃文斯(1912-2001)和他那匹名叫"扳机"的马一起演出。每次节目结束时,他们总要唱《祝你旅途愉快》这首歌〕

Rogers, Will (1879-1935) a US humorous writer and performer. Rogers sometimes told jokes while spinning a LASSO (=a rope with one end tied in a circle) and often used jokes to criticize politicians. He was known for his short, clever, funny sayings, such as "I don't make jokes – I just watch the government and report the facts." 罗杰斯〔(1879-1935),美国幽默作家、表演艺术家。他有时一边讲笑话,一边甩动一个套索,还常借笑话批评政客。他以简短睿智的妙语著称,比如:"我可不跟你们开玩笑——我只不过是看着政府,讲讲实话罢了。"〕

Ro·get's The·sau·rus /ro,ʒez θɪ`sɔrəs; ,rɒʒeɪz θɪ'sɔːrəs/ *trademark* (1852) the first English thesaurus (=a book in which words and phrases are put into groups with other words and phrases that have similar meanings) written by Peter Mark Roget (1779-1869)【商标】《罗氏同义词词典》〔(1852),第一部英语同义词词典,由彼得·马克·罗热(1779-1869)编纂〕

rogue[1] /rog; rəʊg/ *n* [C] **1** *often humorous* a man or boy who behaves badly or causes trouble, but who you like in spite of this【常幽默】坏蛋,淘气鬼〔指男人或男孩〕: *What's the little rogue done now, I wonder?* 不知道那个小淘气鬼干什么啦? | *a lovable rogue* 可爱的捣蛋鬼 **2** *old-fashioned* a man who is dishonest and has a bad character【过时】无赖,流氓: **rogues' gallery** (=a group of bad people) 一群无赖 —**roguery** *n* [U]

rogue[2] *adj* [only before noun 仅用于名词前] **1** a rogue person or organization does not follow the usual rules or methods and often causes trouble 不循常规的;常制造麻烦的 **2** a rogue wild animal lives apart from the main group and is often dangerous〔野兽〕离群而危险的

rogu·ish /`rogɪʃ; 'rəʊgɪʃ/ *adj* someone with a roguish expression or smile looks amused, especially because they have done something slightly dishonest or wrong〔表情或笑容〕淘气的,调皮的 —**roguishly** *adv* —**roguishness** *n* [U]

rois·ter /`rɔɪstə; 'rɔɪstə/ *v* [I] *old-fashioned* to behave in a cheerful, rough, noisy way【过时】喧闹作乐 —**roisterer** *n* [C]

Ro·laids /`roledz; 'rəʊleɪdz/ *trademark* a type of ANTACID (=medicine for your stomach), which is sold in the US【商标】罗雷兹〔在美国出售的一种抗酸剂,用于治疗胃病〕

role /rol; rəʊl/ *n* [C] **1** the way in which someone or something is involved in an activity or situation, and how much influence they have on it 作用: **play a leading/major/key role** (=be important in making changes happen) 起最重要/主要/关键作用 *Mandela played a leading role in ending apartheid in South Africa.* 曼德拉在结束南非种族隔离的运动中起了主要作用。| *the growing role of China's mainland in Hong Kong's economy* 中国内地在香港经济中所起的越来越重要的作用 | *the role of diet in the prevention of diseases such as cancer* 饮食对预防癌症等疾病的作用 **2** the character played by an actor in a play or film〔戏剧、电影中的〕角色: **play a role** (=act a role) 担任一个角色 *Matthews plays the role of a young doctor suspected of murder.* 马修斯扮演一位涉嫌谋杀的年轻医生。| **the lead/leading role** (=the most important role) 主角 | **minor role** (=an unimportant role) 配角 **3** the position that someone has in society, in an organization etc, or the way they are expected to behave in a relationship with someone else〔社会、组织等中的〕地位,职责;〔关系中的〕角色: *Women are often forced into a supportive role.* 妇女往往被迫在社会中处于从属地位。| **role reversal** (=a situation in which two people, especially a man and a woman, take each other's roles)〔尤指男、女角色的〕反串,角色倒转

role mod·el /'· ,··/ *n* [C] someone whose behaviour, attitudes etc people try to copy because they admire them 模范,榜样

role-play /'· ·/ *n* [C,U] an exercise in which you behave in the way that someone else would behave in a particular situation, especially to help you learn something〔尤指协助学习某事物的〕角色扮演: *the use of role-play in the classroom* 在教室里使用角色扮演的方法 —**role-play** *v* [I,T]

Ro·lex /`rolɛks; 'rəʊleks/ *trademark* a type of very high quality watch【商标】劳力士〔一款十分高档的手表〕

roll[1] /rol; rəʊl/ *v*

1 ►**ROUND OBJECT** 圆形物件◄ [I always+adv/prep, T] if something that is round rolls or if you roll it, it moves along a surface by turning over and over (使)滚动: *The ball rolled into the street.* 球滚到了街上。| **roll sth** *Maybe we can roll the log to the middle of the campsite.* 也许我们可以把这根原木滚到营地中央。

2 ►**PERSON/ANIMAL** 人/动物◄ [I always+adv/prep] to turn your body over one or more times while lying down 打滚,翻身: *The dog had been rolling in mud puddles.* 那条狗一直在泥坑里打滚。| *Ralph rolled onto his stomach.* 拉尔夫翻身趴下。

3 ►**STH WITH WHEELS** 有轮子的东西◄ [I always+ adv/prep, T always+adv/prep] to move on wheels, or make something that has wheels move 开动,行驶: **[+into/forwards/past etc]** *We watched as the bus rolled slowly backwards down the hill.* 我们望着那辆公共汽车缓缓地倒着下山。| **roll sth to/around/by etc** *The waitress rolled the dessert cart over to our table.* 女服务员把甜点车推到我们桌子跟前。

4 ►**PAPER/STRING ETC** 纸/绳等◄ [T] also 又作 **roll up** to bend or wind something such as paper, string etc into the shape of a tube or ball 卷,绕,把〔纸、绳等〕卷成筒[球状]: *Harry rolled the newspaper and put a rubber band around it.* 哈里把报纸卷起来,再套上一根橡皮筋。| *Roll the yarn into a ball.* 把线绕成团。

5 ►**DROP OF LIQUID** 液滴◄ [I always+adv/prep] to move over a surface smoothly without stopping〔平稳地〕滚动: **[+down/onto]** *Tears rolled down her cheeks.* 眼泪顺着她的面颊滚滚流下。

6 ►**WAVES/CLOUDS** 浪/云◄ [I always+adv/prep] to move in a particular direction〔朝着特定方向〕滚动,飘移: **[+into/towards etc]** *Mist rolled in from the sea.* 雾从海上滚滚而来。| *waves rolling onto the beach* 海浪涌上沙滩

7 roll your eyes to move your eyes round and upwards, especially in order to show that you are annoyed 骨碌碌地转动眼睛，翻白眼〔尤表示不快〕: *Marta rolled her eyes as Will started to tell another stupid joke.* 威尔开始讲另一个愚蠢的笑话时，玛尔塔翻了个白眼。

8 ▶GAME 游戏◀ [I,T] if you roll DICE, you throw them as part of a game 掷（色子）

9 ▶SHIP/PLANE 船/飞机◀ [I] if a ship or plane rolls, it leans one way and then another with the motion of the water or air 〔随着水流或气流〕左右摇晃，摇摆

10 ▶MAKE STH FLAT 弄平某物◀ [T] to make something flat by moving something heavy over it 把…碾平: *Roll the pie crust flat with a rolling pin.* 用擀面杖把馅饼的油酥皮擀平。

11 ▶WALK 行走◀ [I always+adv/prep] to walk in a rather uncontrolled way, moving your body from side to side, usually because you are drunk 摇摇晃晃地走〔一般指喝醉酒〕: *We rolled out of the bar at about 3.00 that morning.* 那天清晨大约3点钟我们摇摇晃晃地走出酒吧。

12 ▶SOUND 声音◀ [I] if drums or THUNDER[1] (1) roll, they make a long low series of sounds〔鼓或雷〕隆隆作响

13 ▶MACHINE/CAMERA 机器/照相机◀ [I] if a machine such as a film camera or a PRINTING PRESS rolls, it operates 运转: *Quiet! The cameras are rolling!* 肃静！正拍摄呢！

14 (all) rolled into one if something is several different things rolled into one, it includes qualities of all those things 合为一体: *Mum was cook, chauffeur, nurse, and entertainer all rolled into one.* 妈妈集厨师、司机、护士和演员于一身。

15 get rolling if a plan, business etc gets rolling, it starts operating〔计划、企业等〕开始实施; 开始运作: *When the business gets rolling, we'll have more time to think about other things.* 企业开始运作后，我们将有更多时间思考其他事情。

16 roll a cigarette to make your own cigarette, using loose tobacco and special paper 卷烟: **roll your own** (=make your own cigarettes) 自己卷烟 *It's cheaper to roll your own.* 自己动手卷烟比较便宜。

17 roll out of bed *informal* to get out of bed【非正式】起床: *I finally rolled out of bed about noon.* 中午前后我终于起床了。

18 be rolling in the aisles if people in a theatre, cinema etc are rolling in the aisles, they are laughing a lot〔剧院、戏院观众〕笑得东倒西歪

19 be ready to roll *spoken especially AmE* used to say you are ready to do something【口，尤美】准备就绪: *OK, everything's in the car. Is everybody ready to roll?* 好，所有东西都装进了汽车。大家准备好了吗？

20 roll on *BrE* used to say that you wish a time or event would come quickly【英】但愿…早日来到: *Roll on the weekend!* 但愿周末早点儿来到！

21 ▶ATTACK 攻击◀ [T] *AmE* to rob someone, especially when they are drunk and asleep【美】〔趁人醉酒和睡着时〕抢劫: *punks on the streets rolling drunks for small change* 抢劫醉汉零钱的街头小流氓

22 roll your r's to pronounce the sound /r/ using your tongue in a way that makes the sound very long 用舌尖颤音发 r 音

23 a rolling stone gathers no moss used to say that someone who often changes jobs, etc does not have any real relationships or responsibilities 滚石不生苔〔形容经常转换工作等的人没有实在的关系或责任〕—see also 另见 **set/start the ball rolling** (BALL[1] (9)), **heads will roll** (HEAD[1] (52)), **be rolling in it** (ROLLING (3))

roll around/round *phr v* [I] if something that happens regularly rolls around, it happens again 周而复始，循环: *By the time autumn rolled around, we still hadn't finished painting the house.* 当秋天又来临时，我们还没有粉刷完房子。

roll away *phr v* [I always+adv/prep] if countryside rolls away, it is full of small hills as far as you can see 延绵起伏: *green pastures rolling away into the distance* 绿油油的牧场延绵起伏，伸向远方

roll sth ↔ **back** *phr v* [T] **1** to force your opponents in a war to move back from their position 使〔敌方〕退却，击退 **2** to reduce the influence or power of a system, government etc, especially because it has too much power 降低〔影响或权力〕，削减: *Dulles saw communism as something evil to be rolled back, not just contained.* 杜勒斯认为共产主义是邪恶的，应该加以削弱而不仅仅是抵制。**3** *AmE* to reduce the price of something【美】降低〔价格〕: *the administration's promise to roll back taxes* 政府关于减税的承诺

roll sth ↔ **down** *phr v* [T] **roll a window down** to open a car window 摇下车窗

roll in *phr v* [I] **1** to happen or arrive in large numbers or quantities 大量发生[涌来]: *Pleas for help were made to the public, and the money came rolling in.* 呼吁公众提供帮助后，钱源源不断地涌来。**2** to arrive later than usual or expected without seeming to be worried〔心安理得地〕迟到: *Chris finally rolled in at about 4.00 am.* 克里斯终于若无其事地在凌晨4点左右回来了。**3** if clouds, mist etc roll in, they begin to cover an area of the sky or land〔云、雾等〕滚滚而来: *Fog rolled in from the sea.* 雾从海上滚滚而来。

roll sth ↔ **out** *phr v* [T] **1** to make something flat and thin by pushing a special tube shaped object over it 把…碾平，把…擀薄: *Roll out the pastry.* 把面团擀薄。—see picture on page A11 参见 A11 页图 **2** to make something flat and straight on the ground, after it has been rolled into a tube shape 把…铺开: *Roll out your sleeping bag inside the tent.* 在帐篷里把你的睡袋铺开。**3 roll out the red carpet** to make special preparations for an important visitor 铺开红地毯〔隆重欢迎〕

roll over *phr v* **1** [I] to turn your body round once so that you are lying in a different position 翻身: *Ben rolled over and kissed her.* 本翻过身来吻了吻她。**2** [T] **roll** sb/sth **over** to turn someone's body over on the ground 把某人翻身/把某物翻过来: **roll sb onto** *The guards rolled him over onto his front.* 卫兵们把他翻过身来脸朝下。

roll up *phr v* **1 roll your sleeves/trousers up** to turn the ends of your sleeves etc over several times so that they are shorter 卷起衣袖/裤腿 **2 roll your sleeves up** to start doing a job even though it is difficult or unpleasant 卷起袖子〔准备苦干〕: *We're just going to have to roll our sleeves up and get on with it.* 我们正准备动手继续干呢。**3 roll a window up** to close the window of a car 摇上车窗 **4** [I] to arrive somewhere, especially late or unexpectedly 姗姗来迟; 意外到来: *Brad and Debbie rolled up in their new convertible at about 9.00.* 布拉德和黛比大约9点才开着新敞篷车姗姗而来。**5 roll up!** *BrE spoken* used to call people to come and watch or buy things at a CIRCUS (1), FAIR[3] (2) etc【英口】快来呀！快来看！〔尤用于招呼人们进去看马戏或在集市上购物〕

roll[2] *n*

1 ▶PAPER/FILM/MONEY ETC 纸/胶片/钱等◀ [C] a piece of paper, film, money that has been rolled into the shape of a tube〔纸、胶片、钱的〕一卷: [+of] *a roll of film* 胶卷 | *8 rolls of toilet paper for $1.99* 1.99 美元八卷卫生纸 | *Dusty pulled a huge roll of $100 bills from his pocket.* 达斯蒂从口袋里抽出一大卷100美元的钞票。

2 ▶BREAD 面包◀ [C] a small round LOAF of bread for one person 面包卷，小圆面包: *Put the rolls on the table.* 把面包卷放在桌上。| **ham/cheese etc roll** *BrE* (=one that is filled with ham, cheese etc)【英】火腿/干酪等面包卷

3 ▶PHYSICAL MOVEMENT 身体动作◀ [C] **a)** the action of moving by rolling your body 滚动: *a young horse having a roll in the field* 在田野里打滚儿的马驹 **b)** a movement done, often as part of a sport, by rolling on the ground in a controlled way with your body curled 打滚儿，翻筋斗: *tumblers doing rolls and handstands at the circus* 在马戏团里翻筋斗和倒立的杂技演员

4 ▶SHIP/PLANE 船/飞机◀ [C] the movement of a ship or plane when it leans from side to side with the motion of the water or air 摇晃

5 ▶SKIN/FAT 皮肤/脂肪◀ [C+of] a thick layer of skin or fat, usually just below your waist〔通常指腰部以下的〕赘皮; 肥肉

6 roll of drums/guns/thunder a long low fairly loud sound made by drums etc 隆隆的鼓/炮/雷声

7 be on a roll *informal* to be having a lot of success with what you are trying to do【非正式】取得接二连三的巨大成就

8 ▶GAME 游戏◀ [C] the action of throwing DICE as part of a game 掷色子: *It's your roll, Rob.* 该你掷了，罗布。

9 ▶LIST OF NAMES 名单◀ an official list of names, especially of people at a meeting, in a class etc〔尤指参加会议、上课等的〕名单，名册: **call/take the roll** (=say the list of names to check that everyone on it is there) 点名

10 roll in the hay *informal* an act of having sex with someone【非正式】做爱

roll bar /ˈ· ·/ *n* [C] a strong metal bar over the top of a car, intended to protect the people inside if the car turns over〔汽车顶盖上的〕翻车保护杆

roll-call /ˈ· ·/ *n* [C,U] the act of reading out an official list of names to check who is there 点名

rolled gold /ˌ· ˈ·/ *n* [U] a thin layer of gold on the surface of another metal 金箔，包金; FILLED GOLD *AmE*【美】

rolled oats /ˌ· ˈ·/ *n* [plural] *especially BrE* a kind of oats (OATS (1)), used for making PORRIDGE【尤英】燕麦片

roll·er /ˈrolɚ; ˈrəʊlə/ *n* [C] **1** a tube-shaped piece of wood, metal etc that can be rolled over and over, used in a machine for

crushing, printing etc〔用于辗压、印刷等的〕轧辊, 滚筒, 滚轴 **2** a large tube-shaped piece of stone, metal etc that you roll over the surface of grass or roads to make them smooth 碾压机, 轧路机: *a garden roller* 碾草坪机 **3** a long, powerful wave 巨浪: *great Atlantic rollers* 大西洋的巨浪 **4** a tube-shaped piece of metal or wood, used for moving heavy things that have no wheels〔用于移动无轮重物的〕滚棒, 滚杆, 滚柱 **5** a small tube-shaped piece of metal or plastic that you wrap your hair around to make it curl 卷发夹 **6** a ROLLS-ROYCE 劳斯莱斯汽车

Rollerblade /ˈ· · ˌ/ *n trademark* special boots with a single row of wheels fixed under it【商标】一字轮旱冰鞋 —compare 比较 ROLLER SKATE

roller blind /ˈ· · ˌ/ *n* [C] *BrE* a piece of cloth or other material that can be rolled up and down to cover a window【英】〔窗户的〕卷帘 —see picture at 参见 BLIND³ 图

roller coaster 过山车

roller coast·er /ˈ· · ˌ· ·/ *n* [C] **1** a track with sudden steep slopes and curves, which people ride on for excitement in special small carriages 过山车, 云霄飞车 **2** a situation that is impossible to control, because it keeps changing very quickly〔因为情况一直在快速变化而〕无法控制的局面, 急转突变: *Their relationship was a continual emotional roller coaster.* 他们的感情时好时坏。

roller skate /ˈ· · ˌ/ *n* [C] a special boot with four wheels fixed under it 四轮旱冰鞋 —**roller-skate** *v* [I] —**roller skating** *n* [U]

roller tow·el /ˈ· ·, ˌ· ·/ *n* [C] a cloth you use for drying your hands, which is joined together at the ends and wound around a bar of wood or metal〔两头缝结、套在木制或金属棒上的〕环状擦手毛巾

rol·lick·ing¹ /ˈrɑlɪkɪŋ; ˈrɒlɪkɪŋ/ *adj* [only before noun 仅用于名词前] *old-fashioned* noisy and cheerful【过时】喧闹的, 欢闹的: *a rollicking song* 欢乐喧闹的歌

rollicking² *n* **give sb a rollicking** *BrE informal* to criticize someone angrily for something they have done【英, 非正式】斥责某人

roll·ing /ˈrolɪŋ; ˈrəʊlɪŋ/ *adj* **1** [only before noun 仅用于名词前] rolling hills have many long gentle slopes 绵延起伏的 **2** if you have a rolling walk, you move from side to side as you walk〔走路的样子〕摇晃的, 摇摆的 **3 be rolling in it** *informal* to be extremely rich【非正式】非常有钱, 十分富有: *If James can afford that car, he must be rolling in it!* 如果詹姆斯能买得起那辆车, 他必定非常有钱!

rolling mill /ˈ· · ˌ/ *n* [C] a factory or machine in which metal is rolled into large, flat, thin pieces 轧钢厂; 轧钢机

rolling pin /ˈ· · ˌ/ *n* [C] a long tube-shaped piece of wood used for making PASTRY flat and thin before you cook it 擀面杖

> **CULTURAL NOTE 文化注释**
> In old CARTOONS, women are sometimes shown holding a rolling pin while chasing their husbands or a mouse. 以前的漫画中有时会出现妇女手持擀面杖追打丈夫或者追赶老鼠的形象。

rolling stock /ˈ· · ˌ/ *n* [U] all the trains, carriages etc that are used on a railway 铁路上使用的所有车辆〈如火车、客车车厢等〉

Rolling Stone /ˌ· · ˈ·/ a US magazine that contains articles on people and events involved in ROCK and POP music《滚石》〔美国一音乐杂志。登载的文章关涉摇滚、流行音乐界的人物和活动〕

Rolling Stones, The /ˌ· · ˈ·/ also 又作 **The Stones** a British ROCK group who first became popular in 1963 and became one of the most successful groups ever. Their songs include *(I Can't Get No) Satisfaction*, *Jumping Jack Flash* and *Honky Tonk Woman*. Most of their songs are written by Keith Richards, who also plays the GUITAR, and Mick Jagger, their main singer. 滚石乐队〔英国一摇滚乐队。1963 年开始走红, 成为有史以来最成功的乐队之一。演唱的歌曲包括《满足》、《闪跳杰克》和《酒吧女郎》。大部分歌曲由吉他手凯西·理查兹和主唱米克·贾格尔创作〕

roll·mop /ˈrolˌmɑp; ˈrɒlmɒp/ *n* [C] a HERRING that has been rolled up and preserved in VINEGAR 醋腌鲱鱼卷

roll of hon·our /ˌ· · ˈ· ·/ *n* [C] *BrE* a list of the names of people who are officially praised, especially because they were brave in battle【英】荣誉名册〔尤用于表扬在战争中表现英勇者〕; HONOR ROLL *AmE*【美】

roll-on /ˈ· ˌ/ *n* [C] **1** also 又作 **roll-on de·o·dor·ant** /ˌ· · ˈ· · ·/ a bottle which contains liquid that you rub under your arms in order to stop your SWEAT² (1) from smelling unpleasant 滚抹除臭剂 **2** a woman's GIRDLE (=type of underwear) that you pull on in one piece, worn in the past〔旧时女子穿的〕束腹

roll-on roll-off /ˈ· ·, ˌ· ˌ/ *adj* [only before noun 仅用于名词前] *BrE* a roll-on roll-off ship is one that vehicles can drive straight on and off【英】〔船〕车辆可开上开下的: *a roll-on roll-off car ferry* 汽车渡轮

Rolls-Royce /ˌrolz ˈrɔɪs; ˌrəʊlz ˈrɔɪs◂/ *n* [C] **1** *trademark* a very expensive and comfortable car made by a British company【商标】劳斯莱斯汽车〔英国生产的一种极昂贵和舒适的汽车〕 **2** *BrE informal* something that is regarded as the highest quality example of a particular type of product【英, 非正式】〔同类中〕最优良的产品; CADILLAC *AmE*【美】: *the Rolls-Royce of video recorders* 录像机中的极品

roll-top desk /ˌ· · ˈ· ˌ/ *n* [C] a desk that has a cover that you roll back when you open it 卷盖式书桌

roll-up /ˈ· ˌ/ *n* [C] *BrE* a cigarette that you make yourself【英】自卷香烟

ro·ly-po·ly¹ /ˈrolɪ ˌpolɪ; ˌrəʊli ˈpəʊli◂/ *adj* a roly-poly person is round and fat〔人〕圆圆胖胖的

roly-poly² *n* [C,U] a British sweet food made of JAM¹ (1) that is rolled up inside PASTRY〔英国的〕果酱布丁卷

ROM /rɑm; rɒm/ *n* [U] read-only memory; the part of a computer where permanent instructions and information are stored 只读存储器 —compare 比较 RAM

Ro·man /ˈromən; ˈrəʊmən/ *adj* **1** connected with ancient Rome or the Roman Empire 古罗马的, 罗马帝国的 **2** connected with the city of Rome 罗马城的 —**Roman** *n* [C]

roman *n* [U] *technical* the ordinary style of printing that uses small upright letters, like the style used for printing these words【术语】罗马字体, 正体字 —compare 比较 ITALICS

Roman al·pha·bet /ˌ· · ˈ· · ·/ *n* [singular] the alphabet used in English and many other European languages, which begins with the letters A, B, C 罗马字母表〔以 A, B, C 等字母开始, 用于英语和许多其他欧洲语言中〕

Roman Cath·o·lic /ˌ· · ˈ· · ·◂/ *adj* belonging to or connected with the part of the Christian religion whose leader is the Pope 罗马天主教的 —**Roman Catholic** *n* [C] —**Roman Catholicism** /ˌ· · ˈ· · · ·/ *n* [U]

ro·mance¹ /roˈmæns; rəʊˈmæns/ *n* **1** [C] an exciting and often short relationship between two people who love each other 罗曼史, 艳事: **a whirlwind romance** (=one that happens very suddenly and quickly) 闪电式的风流韵事 **2** [U] love, or a feeling of being in love 浪漫, 爱情: *The romance had gone out of their relationship.* 他们的关系已经失去了浪漫。**3** [U] the feeling of excitement and adventure that is connected with a particular place, activity etc 传奇色彩, 浪漫色彩: *the romance of life in the Wild West* 西大荒生活的浪漫色彩 **4** [C] a story about the love between two people 爱情故事 **5** [C] a story that has brave characters and exciting events 传奇故事: *a Medieval romance* 中世纪的传奇故事

> **CULTURAL NOTE 文化注释**
> In Britain and the US, romance is typically represented by boxes of chocolates, red roses, dinners by CANDLELIGHT, love letters, and walks by the light of the moon. 在英国和美国, 表现浪漫的方式一般有送盒装巧克力或一束玫瑰花、共进烛光晚餐、写情书、在月光下漫步等。

romance² *v* [I] to describe things that have happened in a way that makes them seem better or more important than they really were 夸张, 渲染: [+about] *an old man romancing about the past* 一位夸张地大谈往事的老人

Romance lan·guage /ˈ· · ˌ· ·/ *n* [C] a language that comes from Latin, for example French or Spanish〔由拉丁语演变而成的〕罗曼语〈如法语或西班牙语〉

Roman Em·pire, the /ˌ··ˈ··/ the countries of Europe, north Africa, and western Asia that were ruled by the ancient Romans from around 44 BC until AD 395, when the empire was divided into two parts. The Western Roman Empire continued until 476, and the Eastern Roman Empire continued until the 15th century.罗马帝国〔约公元前44年至公元395年古罗马人统治的欧洲、北非与西亚诸国。之后, 罗马帝国分裂为两部分。西罗马帝国延续到公元476年, 东罗马帝国一直延续到15世纪〕— see also 另见 the HOLY ROMAN EMPIRE

Ro·man·esque /ˌromənˋɛsk; ˌrəʊməˈnesk◂/ *adj* in the style of building that was popular in Western Europe in the 11th and 12th centuries, and had many round ARCH*es* and thick PILLAR*s* 罗马式的〔多用圆拱顶和粗圆柱的建筑风格, 流行于11和12世纪的西欧〕

Ro·ma·ni·a /roˋmenjə; rəʊˈmeɪniə/ also 又作 **Rumania, Roumania** a country in southeast Europe, east of Hungary and west of the Black Sea. Population: 22,364,000 (2001). Capital: Bucharest. From the end of World War II it was a Communist country, but after 1989 the political situation changed and Romania is a member of the European Union now. 罗马尼亚〔欧洲东南部一国家, 位于匈牙利以东, 黑海以西。人口: 22,364,000 (2001), 首都: 布加勒斯特。自二战结束之后, 该国一直由共产党领导, 1989年以后政治情况有所改变, 现已加入欧盟〕—**Romanian** *n, adj*

Roman law /ˌ··ˈ·/ *n* [U] *law* CIVIL LAW【法律】民法, 民事法

Roman nose /ˌ··ˈ·/ *n* [C] a nose that curves out near the top 高鼻梁, 鹰钩鼻 —see picture on page A6 参见A6页图

roman nu·mer·al /ˌ··ˈ···/ *n* [C] a number in a system first used in ancient Rome that uses the combinations of the letters I, V, X, L, C, D, and M 罗马数字

Romano- /rəmɑno; rəmɑːnəʊ/ *prefix* **1** connected with ancient Rome; Roman 古罗马的; 罗马的 **2** ancient Roman and 古罗马和…的: *Romano-British art* 古罗马－不列颠艺术

ro·man·tic¹ /roˋmæntɪk; rəʊˈmæntɪk/ *adj*

1 ▶SHOWING LOVE 表现感情的◀ showing strong feelings of love 多情的: *"Tom always sends me red roses on my birthday." "How romantic!"* "我过生日时汤姆总给我送红玫瑰。" "真是多情啊!"

2 ▶CONNECTED WITH LOVE 与爱情有关的◀ connected with feelings of love or with a loving relationship 浪漫的, 风流的: *It's not a romantic relationship – they're just business partners.* 这不是什么浪漫关系——他们只是生意上的伙伴。

3 ▶BEAUTIFUL 美丽的◀ beautiful in a way that affects your emotions and makes you think of love or adventure 富于浪漫色彩的; 充满传奇色彩的: *a romantic village nestling at the foot of the mountains* 一个坐落在山脚下富有浪漫气息的村庄

4 ▶NOT PRACTICAL 不实际的◀ not practical, and basing your actions too much on an imagined idea of the world 不切实际的, 耽于幻想的, 空想的: *romantic notions about becoming a famous actress* 希望成为著名女演员的幻想

5 ▶STORY/FILM 故事/电影◀ a romantic story or film is about love 关于爱情的, 浪漫的: *a romantic comedy* 爱情喜剧

6 Romantic art/literature etc art or literature that is based on the ideas of romanticism 浪漫主义的艺术/文学等 —**romantically** /-klɪ; -kli/ *adv*

romantic² *n* [C] **1** someone who shows strong feelings of love and likes doing things that are connected with love such as buying flowers, presents etc 富于浪漫气息的人: *Oh, Andy, you're such a romantic!* 噢, 安迪, 你是如此浪漫的人! **2** someone who is not practical, and bases their ideas too much on an imagined idea of the world 爱幻想的人, 浪漫主义者: *an incurable romantic* 不可救药的幻想家 **3** also 又作 **Romantic** a writer, painter etc, whose work is based on romanticism 浪漫主义作家〔画家等〕

ro·man·ti·cis·m, Romanticism /roˋmæntəˌsɪzəm; rəʊˈmæntɪ̵sɪzəm/ *n* [U] a way of writing or painting that was popular in the late 18th and early 19th century, in which feelings and wild natural beauty were considered more important than anything else 浪漫主义〔18世纪末至19世纪初流行的写作或绘画风格〕

ro·man·ti·cize also 又作 **-ise** *BrE*【英】/roˋmæntəˌsaɪz; rəʊˈmæntɪ̵saɪz/ *v* [T] to talk or think about things in a way that makes them seem more romantic or attractive than they really are 使浪漫化, 使具有浪漫色彩: *a rather romanticized picture of life in the war* 对战时生活浪漫的描绘

Romantic Movement, the /·ˈ··ˌ··/ a group of writers, artists etc in English and Euorpean literature, art, and music, who followed their feelings and emotions rather than logical thought or reason, and who preferred wild, natural beauty to things made by people. It first became popular in the late 18th century. 浪漫主义运动〔欧洲作家和艺术家在文学、艺术和音乐领域发起的一场文艺运动。他们主张按照个人的情感, 而不是逻辑思维或理性进行创作。相对人造之物而言, 他们偏爱野性之美和自然之美。该运动最早盛行于18世纪后期〕

Ro·ma·ny /ˈrɑmənɪ; ˈrəʊməni/ *n* **1** [C] a GIPSY 吉卜赛人 **2** [U] the language of the GIPSY people 吉卜赛语

Rome /rom; rəʊm/ **1** the capital city of Italy, which is famous for its art, its history, and its many public and religious buildings from ancient times and the Renaissance. It also contains the Vatican City, a separate state where the Pope lives.罗马〔意大利首都。罗马的艺术、历史以及古代和文艺复兴时期的许多公共建筑和宗教建筑闻名于世。位于意大利罗马城内的梵蒂冈是罗马教皇统治的一个独立国家〕**2 Rome wasn't built in a day** a phrase meaning that it takes time to achieve something important, and you should not expect to succeed immediately 罗马非一日建成; 伟业非朝夕之功 **3 When in Rome (do as the Romans do)** a phrase meaning that when you are in a different place you should behave like the people who live there 入国问禁; 入乡随俗

Ro·me·o /ˈromɪo; ˈrəʊmiəʊ/ *n* the main male character in the play *Romeo and Juliet* by William Shakespeare 罗密欧〔威廉·莎士比亚的戏剧《罗密欧与朱丽叶》中的男主人公〕

ro·me·o, Romeo /ˈromɪˌo; ˈrəʊmiəʊ/ *n* [C] *often humorous* a man who tries to attract all the women he meets in a ROMANTIC¹ (1) or sexual way【常幽默】罗密欧式的男人〔浪漫多情的男子〕: *the office Romeo* 办公室的罗密欧

Romeo and Ju·li·et /ˌ··· ··ˈ···/ one of William Shakespeare's best-known plays, a sad romantic story about two young people, Romeo and Juliet, who fall in love although their families are great enemies. They marry secretly, but are prevented from being together, and finally they both kill themselves. Many phrases from the play are well known, especially "Romeo, Romeo, wherefore art thou Romeo?", which Juliet says while she is standing on a BALCONY and Romeo is below her in the garden.《罗密欧与朱丽叶》〔威廉·莎士比亚最著名的戏剧之一, 讲述罗密欧与朱丽叶这一对青年男女凄婉的爱情故事。他们不顾两家的世仇, 真心相爱, 并私自成婚, 但却无法在一起, 最后双双殉情。剧中的许多语句十分有名, 尤其是"罗密欧, 罗密欧, 为何偏偏你姓罗密欧呢?"这一句。朱丽叶说这句话时站在阳台上, 罗密欧则站在下面的花园里〕

Rom·mel /ˈrɑml; ˈrɒməl/, **Field Marshal** (1891-1944) a German military leader in World War II who was called the Desert Fox, and who won important battles in North Africa and Egypt, but was defeated by Montgomery at El Alamein in 1942. He was part of a secret plan to kill Hitler, and when this failed he killed himself. 隆美尔〔(1891-1944), 二战时期的德军将领, 以"沙漠之狐"著称。他在北非和埃及打赢过数场重要战役, 但1942年在阿拉曼战役中败给蒙哥马利。他还参与了刺杀希特勒的秘密计划, 但刺杀未遂, 自尽而亡〕

romp¹ /rɑmp; rɒmp/ *v* [I] **1** [always+adv/prep] to play in a noisy way, especially by running, jumping etc〔尤指又跑又跳地〕嬉闹: **[+around/about]** *They could hear the children romping around upstairs.* 他们听得到孩子们在楼上蹦跳打闹的声音。**2 romp home** if someone or something, especially a horse in a race, romps home, they win the race or competition easily〔尤指赛马〕轻松取胜

romp through sth *phr v* [T] *BrE informal* to succeed in doing or finishing something quickly and easily【英, 非正式】轻易获得成功, 轻易完成

romp² *n* [C] **1** *informal* a piece of amusing entertainment which has a lot of exciting scenes【非正式】打闹逗笑的表演节目: *Branagh's new film is an enjoyable romp.* 布拉纳的新片子是一部有趣的闹剧。**2** *BrE humorous* a word for sexual activity, used especially by newspapers【英, 幽默】调情〔尤用于报纸上〕**3** an occasion when people play noisily and roughly 嬉闹

Romp·er Room /ˈ··ˌ·/ a television programme for young children in the US in the 1960s. It involves a group of children who play and learn things from a woman whose name always begins with 'Miss', such as 'Miss Nancy' or 'Miss Sharon'.《游戏屋》〔美国20世纪60年代的一档少儿电视节目。节目中一群儿童跟着女主持人边玩边学。女主持人总是被称作"某某小姐", 如"南希小姐"或"莎伦小姐"〕

romp·ers /ˈrɑmpɚz; ˈrɒmpəz/ *n* [plural] a piece of clothing for babies, made like a top and trousers joined together〔婴儿穿的〕连衫裤

Rom·u·lus and Re·mus /ˌrɑmjələs ənd ˋriməs; ˌrɒmjʊ̵ləs ənd ˈriːməs/ in ancient Roman stories, the two brothers who established the city of Rome. Romulus and Remus were TWINS (=two children born at the same time) who were left to die when

they were babies. They were taken care of by a WOLF (=a wild animal like a large dog), who fed them with her milk. Later, when they had started to build the city of Rome, Romulus killed Remus after a quarrel. 罗慕路斯和雷穆斯〔古罗马传说故事中兴建罗马城的两兄弟。他们是一对双胞胎，幼时遭人遗弃，巧遇一只母狼照顾，母狼用奶哺育他们。他俩开始兴建罗马城不久有过一次争吵，结果罗慕路斯杀了雷穆斯〕

ron·do /ˈrɑndo; ˈrɒndəʊ/ *n plural* **rondos** [C] a piece of music in which the main tune is repeated several times 回旋曲

Ron·nie Scott's /ˌrɑnɪ ˋskɑts; ˌrɒni ˈskɒts/ a JAZZ club in London which was started by Ronnie Scott in 1959, and is famous because many popular and well-known jazz musicians perform there 龙尼·斯科特俱乐部〔伦敦一爵士乐俱乐部。由龙尼·斯科特于1959年创立，以许多爵士音乐名家在此表演而闻名〕

rönt·gen /ˈrɛntgən; ˈrɒntgən/ *n* [C] another spelling of ROENTGEN roentgen的另一种拼法

rood /rud; ruːd/ *n* [C] *old use or technical* a Christian cross, usually in a church【旧或术语】〔常指基督教教堂中的〕耶稣受难像十字架

rood screen /ˈ· ·/ *n* [C] a decorated wooden or stone wall in a Christian church, that divides the part where the CHOIR (=singers) sit from the part where other people sit〔基督教教堂里把唱诗班与会众隔开的〕圣坛隔屏

S3 W2 **roof¹** /ruf; ruːf/ *n* [C]

1 ▶OF A BUILDING 建筑的◀ the outside surface or structure on top of a building, vehicle, tent etc 屋顶；车顶；帐篷顶：*Our roof used to leak whenever it rained.* 以前，只要下雨我们的屋顶就会漏水。| *We can probably strap the cases to the roof of her car.* 我们也许可以把箱子捆在她的车顶上。—see picture on page A4 参见 A4 页图

2 ▶OF A PASSAGE 通道的◀ the top of passage under the ground; CEILING (1)〔地下通道的〕顶部；天花板：*Soon, the whole tunnel roof was collapsing on top of the miners.* 很快，整个坑道顶部开始塌陷，落到矿工们身上。

3 a roof over your head somewhere to live 住处：*I may not have a job, but at least I've got a roof over my head.* 我可能没有工作，但我至少有家可回。

4 go through the roof *informal*【非正式】**a)** also 又作 **hit the roof** to suddenly become very angry〔突然〕暴跳如雷，火冒三丈：*Put that back before Dad sees you and hits the roof!* 趁早放回去，省得爸爸看见时大发雷霆！**b)** if a price, cost etc goes through the roof, it increases to a very high level〔价格〕飞涨

5 ▶OF YOUR MOUTH 嘴的◀ the hard upper part of the inside of your mouth 上腭

6 under the same roof/under one roof in the same building or home 在同一个屋檐下：*We enjoy each other's company, but we can't live under the same roof or we argue all the time.* 我们在一起非常愉快，但不能住在一起，否则会吵个不停。

7 under my/her etc roof in your home 在我/她等的家里：*As long as you live under this roof, young man, you'll do as your mother says.* 只要你住在这个家里，年轻人，你就必须照你妈妈说的办。

8 the roof falls in/caves in *AmE informal* if the roof falls in or caves in, something bad suddenly happens to you when you do not expect it【美，非正式】飞来横祸；突遭不幸

9 red-roofed/slate-roofed etc having a roof that is red, made of SLATE¹ (2) etc 红顶/石板瓦顶等的 —see also 另见 **raise the roof** (RAISE¹ (22)), SUNROOF

roof² *v* [T usually passive 一般用被动态] to put a roof on a building 给〔建筑物〕盖屋顶：**be roofed with** *a cottage, roofed with the local slate* 用当地的石板瓦做房顶的小屋

roof sth ↔ **in/over** *phr v* [T] to cover an open space by putting a roof over it 在〔空地上〕加盖顶：*We're going to roof in the yard to make a garage.* 我们打算给院子加上顶盖做个车库。

roof·ing /ˈrufɪŋ; ˈruːfɪŋ/ *n* [U] stones, tiles (TILE¹ (2)) etc for making or covering roofs〔石、瓦等〕盖屋顶的材料

roof-rack /ˈ· ·/ *n* [C] *BrE* a metal frame fixed on top of a car and used for carrying bags, cases etc【英】〔汽车的〕车顶行李架；LUGGAGE RACK *AmE*【美】—see picture at 参见 RACK¹ 图

roof·top /ˈrufˌtɑp; ˈruːftɒp/ *n* [C] the upper surface of a roof 屋顶：*the view across the rooftops* 屋顶上看到的景色 —see also 另见 **shout sth from the rooftops** (SHOUT¹ (3))

rook¹ /rʊk; rʊk/ *n* [C] **1** a large black European bird like a CROW¹ (1) 秃鼻乌鸦，白嘴鸦 **2** one of the pieces in a game of CHESS; CASTLE〔国际象棋中的〕车

rook² *v* [T] *old-fashioned* to cheat someone, especially to get their money【过时】诈骗〔尤指金钱〕

rook·e·ry /ˈrʊkərɪ; ˈrʊkəri/ *n* [C] a group of NESTs made by rooks 连成一片的秃鼻乌鸦巢

rook·ie /ˈrʊkɪ; ˈrʊki/ *n* [C] **1** *especially AmE* someone who has just started doing a job and has little experience【尤美】新手：*rookie cops* 警察新手 **2** *AmE* someone who is in their first year of playing a professional sport【美】〔第一年参加某项职业体育比赛的〕新队员：*a rookie out of Georgia Tech* 来自佐治亚理工大学的新队员

S1 W1 **room¹** /rum; ruːm/ *n*

1 ▶IN A BUILDING 在建筑物里◀ [C] a part of the inside of a building that has its own walls, floor and ceiling 房间，室：**bathroom/dining room/meeting room etc** (=a room used for washing, eating etc) 浴室/饭厅/会议室等 *The meeting room's upstairs on your right.* 会议室在楼上右侧。| *We could hear someone laughing in the next room.* 我们听得见隔壁有人在笑。| *It's bedtime – you'd better go up to your room.* 该睡觉了——你最好到楼上自己的房间去。| *I'm staying at the Arosa Hotel – Room 348.* 我住在阿罗莎酒店348号房间。| **single/double room** (=a room in a hotel for one person or for two) 单人/双人房间 —see 见 PLACE¹ (USAGE)

2 ▶SPACE 空间◀ [U] enough space for a particular purpose〔足够的〕空间，空地：**there's room in** *I'd like to bring the children if there's room in the car.* 如果车子坐得下，我想带孩子去。| **there's room for** *There's not enough room in the fridge for all this food.* 冰箱里装不下所有这些食物。| **there's room to do sth** *There wasn't really room to lie down comfortably.* 地方实在太小，无法舒服地躺下。| **have room (for sth)** *Do you have room for another book in your bag?* 你的包里能再装下一本书吗？| *Have you got room for some dessert?* (=can you eat some?) 你还吃得下甜点吗？| **make room (for sth)** *I'll just clear out the cupboard to make room for your stuff.* 我这就把橱柜清理一下给你腾出地方放东西。| **leave room (for sth)** (=make sure there is enough room for something)〔为某物〕留出〔足够〕地方 *Leave room for people to get past.* 留出地方给人们通过。| **take up room** (=use a lot of space) 占地方 *That old wardrobe takes up too much room.* 那个旧衣柜太占地方。| **leg-room/head-room** (=space for your legs or head in a vehicle)〔交通工具内〕腿/头可以活动的空间 *You have more leg-room if you travel first class.* 如果你坐头等舱，腿的活动空间就较多。| **there's not enough room to swing a cat** *informal* (=used to say that there is very little space in a room)【非正式】〔房间里〕空间狭窄得无法转身 —see also 另见 ELBOW-ROOM

3 ▶OPPORTUNITY 机会◀ [U] the chance to do the things that you want to do or need to do 机会；余地：[+for] *There's little room for innovation.* 没有多少创新的空间。| **room to do sth** *Children need to have room to develop their natural creativity.* 儿童需要发挥他们天生创造力的空间。| **room for manoeuvre** (=freedom to change your plans or decisions) 回旋余地 *The strict export regulations left us no room for manoeuvre.* 严格的出口规定使我们没有回旋余地。

4 ▶POSSIBILITY 可能性◀ [U] the possibility that something may exist or will happen〔某事物存在或发生的〕可能性：**room for doubt** *The evidence left no room for doubt – Brooks was guilty.* 证据确凿——布鲁克斯有罪。

5 there's room for improvement used to say that someone's work or performance is not perfect and needs to be improved 有改进的余地

6 one-roomed/two-roomed etc having one room, two rooms etc 有一个/两个等房间的

7 ▶APARTMENT 公寓◀ rooms [plural] *old-fashioned especially BrE* two or more rooms that you rent in a building, or stay in at a college【过时，尤英】一套房间；寓所 —see also 另见 FRONT ROOM, LIVING ROOM, SITTING ROOM

room² *v* [I] *AmE*【美】**1 room with sb** to share a room with someone at college〔大学〕与某人同住一室 **2** [+in] to rent and live in a room somewhere 租住一个房间

room and board /ˌ· · ˈ·/ *n* [U] *AmE* a room to sleep in and food【美】食宿：*I pay $1200 a quarter for room and board.* 我一个季度交1200美元食宿费。

room·er /ˈrumɚ; ˈruːmə/ *n* [C] *AmE* someone who pays rent to live in a house with its owner【美】房客，寄宿者；LODGER *BrE*【英】

room·ful /ˈrumful; ˈruːmfʊl/ *n* [C] a large number of things or people that are all together in one room 一屋子的物[人]：[+of] *It's too intimidating to read my poetry to a roomful of strangers.* 向一屋子陌生人朗读我的诗太令人恐惧了。

rooming house /ˈ· · ·/ *n* [C] *AmE* a house where you can rent a room to live in【美】〔出租房间的〕公寓；LODGING HOUSE *BrE*【英】

room·mate /ˈrumˌmet; ˈruːmˌmeɪt/ *n* [C] **1** someone who you share a room with, especially at college〔尤指大学的〕室友，住

在同室的人: *Ben and I were roommates at university.* 本和我是大学的室友。**2** *AmE* someone you share a room, apartment, or house with【美】同住一室[一套公寓，一所房子]的人; FLATMATE *BrE*【英】: *I hate the way my roommate never does the dishes.* 我讨厌我的室友从不洗碗。

room ser·vice /ˈ· ,··/ *n* [U] a service provided by a hotel, by which food, drink etc can be sent to a guest's room〔旅馆提供的〕客房用餐服务

room tem·pe·ra·ture /ˈ· ,····/ *n* [U] the normal temperature inside a house 室温，室内温度

Room with a View, A /,· · ·ˈ·/ (1908) a NOVEL by E.M. Forster about a group of English people who meet while staying at a small hotel in Florence in Italy《看得见风景的房间》〔(1908)，E.M.福斯特创作的一部小说。书中描述一群英国人在意大利佛罗伦萨一家旅馆邂逅的故事〕

room·y /ˈrumɪ; ˈruːmi/ *adj* a house, car etc that is roomy is large and has a lot of space inside it〔房子、汽车等里面〕宽敞的 —**roominess** *n* [U]

Roo·se·velt /ˈrozəvɛlt; ˈrəʊzəvelt/, **El·ea·nor** /ˈɛlɪnɚ; ˈelɪnə/ (1884-1962) a US writer and politician who was the wife of President Franklin D. Roosevelt. She actively supported improvements in the social and economic conditions of ordinary people, and many people think that she influenced the 'New Deal' policy of her husband's government. She was also interested in human rights, and was part of the group that produced the *UN (United Nations) Declaration of Human Rights* in 1945. 埃莉诺·罗斯福〔(1884-1962)，美国作家、政治家，富兰克林·D.罗斯福总统的夫人。她积极支持改善普通百姓的社会和经济状况的举措，许多人认为她对富兰克林政府实施的"新政"起到了一定作用。她还关心人权问题，是1945年《联合国人权宣言》起草小组的成员之一〕

R

Roosevelt, Franklin D. /ˈfræŋklɪn di; ˈfræŋklɪn diː/ (1882-1945) also 又作 **FDR** a US politician in the Democratic Party, who was the President of the US from 1933 to 1945. He helped to end the Great Depression by starting a programme of social and economic changes called the New Deal. He also tried to give support to the Allies without getting the US involved in World War II, but when Japan attacked the US in 1941 he was forced to join the war. 罗斯福〔(1882-1945)，美国民主党政治家。1933至1945年任美国总统，实施"新政"，启动社会和经济改革计划，以结束"大萧条"。他还试图在美国不介入二战的前提下帮助同盟国，但当1941年日本袭击美国本土时，他被迫参战〕

CULTURAL NOTE 文化注释

Roosevelt is the only person who has ever been elected President of the US four times. In 1921 he had POLIO (=a serious illness which affects your nerves) and was unable to walk afterwards, so he used a WHEELCHAIR. He was extremely popular when he was president, and many people listened to his fireside chats on the radio, in which he explained his plans and policies. His wife was Eleanor Roosevelt. 罗斯福是唯一一位连任了四届的美国总统。1921年他得了脊髓灰质炎，从此双腿不能行走，只能靠轮椅代步。他任总统期间受到人民的热烈拥戴。很多人通过收音机收听他的炉边谈话节目，节目中他阐述自己的计划和政策。他夫人名叫埃莉诺·罗斯福。

Roosevelt, The·o·dore /ˈθiədɔr; ˈθiːədɔː/ (1858-1919) a US politician in the Republican Party who was the 26th president of the US, from 1901 to 1909. He became famous for his military achievements during the Spanish-American War of 1898, when he formed and led a group of soldiers called the Rough Riders in Cuba. During his period as president, the US organized the building of the Panama Canal, and Roosevelt described US foreign POLICY using the phrase "Speak softly and carry a big stick". He was informally called Teddy Roosevelt, and the TEDDY BEAR (=a soft toy bear) is named after him. 罗斯福〔(1858-1919)，美国共和党政治家，1901至1909年任美国第26届总统。1898年美西战争期间，他在古巴建立并指挥一支叫"莽骑兵"的部队，因战绩显赫而闻名。执政期间，美国政府组织修建了巴拿马运河。罗斯福在形容美国外交政策时用了这样的话："说话温和，大棒紧握。"人们在非正式场合称他"泰迪·罗斯福"。"泰迪熊"即取自他的名字〕

roost¹ /rust; ruːst/ *n* [C] a place where birds rest and sleep〔鸟的〕栖息处 —see also 另见 **rule the roost** (RULE² (5))

roost² *v* [I] **1** if a bird roosts, it rests or sleeps somewhere〔鸟类〕栖息 **2** **sb's chickens come home to roost** used to say that someone's past mistakes are causing problems for them now 恶有恶报

roost·er /ˈrustɚ; ˈruːstə/ *n* [C] *especially AmE* a male chicken【尤美】公鸡; COCK¹ (1) *BrE*【英】

root¹ /rut; ruːt/ *n* [C]

1 ▸PLANT 植物◂ the part of a plant or tree that grows under the ground and gets water from the soil 根: *Be careful not to damage the roots when repotting.* 换盆时小心别伤了根。| *tree roots* 树根 —see picture at 参见 GERMINATE 图

2 ▸CAUSE OF A PROBLEM 问题的起因◂ the main cause of a problem〔问题的〕根源，起因: *Money is the root of all evil.* 金钱是万恶之源。| **be/lie at the root of** (=be the cause of a problem) 是…的根本原因 *Often allergies are at the root of a lot of the problems.* 过敏往往是许多问题的根源。| **get to the root of** (=find out the cause of a problem) 探本溯源 | **root cause** (=the main reason for a problem) 根本原因

3 ▸OF A CUSTOM/TRADITION 风俗/传统的◂ roots the origins of a custom or TRADITION that has continued for a long time 根源，起源: **has its roots in** *Jazz has its roots in the folk songs of the southern states of the US.* 爵士乐起源于美国南部诸州的民歌。

4 ▸OF AN IDEA/BELIEF 思想/信仰的◂ the main part of an idea or belief which all the other parts come from 根本，基础: **has its roots in** *The revival of the Gaelic language has its roots in 19th century nationalism.* 盖尔语复兴的基础是19世纪的民族主义。

5 ▸FAMILY CONNECTION 家族联系◂ sb's roots your connection with a place because you were born there, or your family used to live there 某人的出生地，老家: *Naita has come to Ghana in search of her roots.* 内塔来到加纳寻找她的根。

6 put down roots if you put down roots somewhere, you start to feel that this place is your home and to have relationships with the people there 扎根〔某地〕

7 ▸TOOTH/HAIR ETC 牙齿/头发等◂ the part of a tooth, hair etc that fixes it to the rest of your body 根部

8 take root a) if an idea takes root, people begin to accept or believe it〔思想〕深入人心: *The concepts of democracy and free trade are finally beginning to take root.* 民主和自由贸易的概念终于开始深入人心。**b)** if a plant takes root, it starts to grow where you have planted it〔植物〕生根

9 have a (good) root round *informal especially BrE* to search for something by moving other things around【非正式，尤英】翻找

10 root and branch if you destroy something root and branch, you get rid of it completely and permanently because it is bad 彻底地，永久地〔把坏事物消除〕

11 ▸LANGUAGE 语言◂ *technical* the basic part of a word which shows its main meaning, to which other parts can be added【术语】词根: *The suffix 'ness' can be added to the root 'cold' to form the word 'coldness'.* 后缀ness可以加在词根cold上构成coldness一词。—compare 比较 STEM¹ (4)

12 ▸MATHEMATICS 数学◂ *technical* a number that when multiplied by itself a certain number of times, equals the number that you have【术语】根: *2 is the fourth root of 16.* 2是16的4次方根。—see also 另见 CUBE ROOT, SQUARE ROOT, GRASS ROOTS

root² *v*

1 ▸SEARCH 寻找◂ [I always+adv/prep] to search for something by moving things around 翻找: [+through/in/around] *"Hang on a second," said Leila, rooting through her handbag for a pen.* "请稍等。"莉拉说着，一边在手提包里翻找钢笔。| [+for] *pigs rooting for food* 拱土寻觅食物的猪

2 ▸PLANT 植物◂ a) [I] to grow roots 生根: *New shrubs will root easily in summer.* 新灌木在夏季容易生根。**b)** [T usually passive 一般用被动态] to fix a plant firmly by its roots 使〔植物〕牢牢扎根: *The bush was too firmly rooted in the hard earth to dig up easily.* 这灌木在坚实的土壤里牢牢扎根，不容易挖出来。| **root itself** *Clumps of thyme had rooted themselves between the rocks.* 一丛丛百里香在岩石中间扎了根。—see also 另见 **deeply rooted** (DEEPLY (5))

3 be rooted in to have developed from something and be strongly influenced by it 起源于: *policies that are rooted in Marxist economic theory* 源于马克思主义经济学理论的政策

4 be rooted to the spot to be so shocked, surprised, or frightened that you cannot move〔震惊、惊讶或害怕得〕呆若木鸡

root for sb *phr v* [T] *informal*【非正式】**1** to give support and encouragement to someone in a competition, test or difficult situation, because you want them to succeed 给〔参赛者、应试者或面对困难的人〕支持，鼓励，声援: *Good luck – we'll all be rooting for you!* 祝你好运，我们都支持你! **2** *especially AmE* to support a sports team or player by shouting and cheering【尤美】为〔参赛队或运动员〕欢呼，喝彩，加油: *We'll all be rooting*

for the Dallas Cowboys in the Superbowl. 在超级碗赛中我们都为达拉斯牛仔队欢呼。

root sth ↔ **out** *phr v* [T] **1** to find out where a particular kind of problem exists and get rid of it 把〔问题〕根除, 杜绝: *Racism cannot be rooted out without strong government action.* 如果政府不采取有力行动, 种族主义是无法根除的。**2** *informal* to find something by searching for it【非正式】搜寻: *I'll try and root out something suitable for you to wear.* 我会设法找出一些合适的衣服给你穿。

root sth ↔ **up** *phr v* [T] to dig or pull a plant up with its roots 将〔植物〕连根拔起

root beer /ˈ· ·/ *n* [C,U] a sweet, non-alcoholic drink made from the roots of some plants, drunk especially in the US 根啤, 根汁汽水〔尤在美国饮用一种由某些植物根制成的不含酒精的饮料〕

root·bound /ˈrut,baund; ˈruːtbaʊnd/ *adj AmE* a plant that is rootbound cannot grow any more because its roots have filled the pot it is growing in【美】〔植物〕根长满盆后不能再生长的, 盆缚的; POTBOUND *BrE*【英】

root crop /ˈ· ·/ *n* [C] a vegetable or plant that is grown so that its root parts can be used 根用植物

root·le /ˈrutl; ˈruːtl/ also 又作 **rootle around/about** *v* [I] *BrE informal* to search for something by moving many other things around【英, 非正式】翻找, 搜寻

root·less /ˈrutlɪs; ˈruːtləs/ *adj* having nowhere that you feel is really your home 无家可归的, 无归属的: *a rootless existence on the street* 流浪街头, 无家可归 —**rootlessness** *n* [U]

Roots (1976) a NOVEL by the US writer Alex Haley (1921-92) which was also made into a television programme. It tells the story of several generations of an African-American family, and it is partly based on stories told in Haley's own family. The story starts with Kunta Kinte, a man from West Africa who is caught and taken to the US as a SLAVE, and then describes what happens to him there and to his children and grandchildren until the time of the Civil War. The book and television programme encouraged many African-Americans to try to find out more about their own family origins.《根》〔(1976), 亚历克斯·黑利(1921-1992) 创作的小说, 后被改编成电视剧。小说讲述一个非洲裔美国人家庭几代人的故事, 其中部分内容取材于黑利自己家族的传说。故事从一个西非男子昆塔·金特的遭遇开始, 他在非洲遭人抓捕, 被当作奴隶运到美国, 接着描述他自己及其后人的经历, 一直写到美国内战。该书和改编的电视剧激发了许多非洲裔美国人去寻找自己家族的根〕

root vege·ta·ble /ˈ·, ···/ *n* [C] a vegetable such as a potato or CARROT that grows under the ground〔可食用的〕块根植物 —see picture on page A9 参见 A9 页图

S3 W3 **rope**[1] /rop; rəʊp/ *n* **1** [C,U] very strong, thick string, made by twisting together many threads of NYLON or other material 粗绳, 绳索, 缆: *They tied up the prisoner with rope.* 他们用绳子把犯人捆起来。| *a bell rope* 钟绳 **2 know the ropes** to know how to do all the parts of a job, deal with a system etc, because you have a lot of experience of it 精通, 在行 **3 show sb the ropes** to teach someone how to do a job or deal with a system 教某人〔做某项工作的〕方法, 给某人指点窍门: *This is Shirley's first day, so will you show her the ropes?* 这是雪莉第一天上班, 你能教教她这里的规矩吗? **4 be on the ropes** *informal* to be in a very bad situation, in which you are likely to be defeated【非正式】处境十分困难〔可能被击败〕 **5 give sb plenty of rope** to give someone a lot of freedom to do something in the way they want to do it 给某人许多自由 **6 give sb enough rope to hang themselves** to give someone freedom to do what they want to do, because you think they will cause problems for themselves 任由某人自作自受, 听任某人自取灭亡 **7 be at the end of your rope** *especially AmE* to have no more PATIENCE or strength left to deal with a problem or a difficult situation【尤美】忍无可忍, 计穷力竭〔无法解决困难〕 **8 the rope** *old-fashioned* HANGING as a punishment【过时】绞刑 **9 the ropes** the rope fence that surrounds an area used for BOXING or WRESTLING〔拳击、摔跤场地的〕栏索 **10 a rope of pearls** PEARLS on a string, worn around your neck as jewellery〔用作项链的〕一串珍珠 —see also 另见 JUMP ROPE, **money for old rope** (MONEY (16))

rope[2] *v* **1** [T always+adv/prep] to tie things together using rope〔用绳索〕捆, 绑: **rope sth to sth** *Harvey roped his horse to a nearby tree.* 哈维把马拴在附近的一棵树上。| **rope sb/sth together** *Two firemen roped themselves together and plunged into the lake.* 两名消防员用绳索把自己系在一起, 跳入湖中。**2** [T] *AmE* to catch an animal using a circle of rope【美】用绳套捕捉〔动物〕

rope sb ↔ **in** *phr v* [T] *informal* to persuade someone to help you in a job, or to join in an activity, especially when they do not want to【非正式】劝说〔尤指不愿意者〕帮忙[参加]: **rope sb in to do sth** *I've roped Dad in to help with the entertainment.* 我把爸爸拉来帮忙招待。| **rope sb into doing sth** *Have you been roped into selling tickets?* 你是被拉来帮忙卖票的吗?

rope sth ↔ **off** *phr v* [T] to surround an area with ropes, especially in order to separate it from another area 用绳把〔某一区域〕围起来, 用绳分隔: *Last night police roped off the area of the find.* 昨晚警察用绳把发现的现场隔开了。

rope lad·der /ˈ·, ·ˈ·/ *n* [C] a LADDER made of two long ropes connected by wooden pieces that you stand on 绳梯

rop·ey, ropy /ˈropɪ; ˈrəʊpi/ *adj BrE informal*【英, 非正式】**1** in bad condition or of bad quality 破旧的; 劣质的: *We stayed in a really ropey hotel.* 我们住在一家非常蹩脚的旅馆里。**2** slightly ill 轻微不舒服的: *I'm feeling a bit ropey this morning.* 今天早上我觉得有些不舒服。

Roque·fort /ˈrokfət; ˈrɒkfɔː/ a strong-tasting French cheese with blue lines in it, made from sheep's milk 罗克福尔干酪〔一种由羊奶制成的带蓝色纹理、味道较重的法国干酪〕

ro-ro /ˈro ˌro; ˈrəʊ rəʊ/ *n* [C] *BrE informal* a ROLL-ON ROLL-OFF ship【英, 非正式】容许车辆开上开下的船

Ror·schach test /ˈrɔrʃɑk tɛst; ˈrɔːʃɑːk test/ *n* [C] a method of testing someone's character, by making them say what spots of ink with various shapes look like 罗夏测验〔让测试对象解释不同的墨迹图形, 以判断其性格的一种测试方法〕

ro·sa·ry /ˈrozərɪ; ˈrəʊzəri/ *n* **1** [C] a string of BEADS used by Roman Catholics for counting prayers〔罗马天主教徒用的〕念珠 **2 the Rosary** the set of prayers that are said by Roman Catholics while counting rosary BEADS〔罗马天主教的〕玫瑰经

ro·sé /roˈze; ˈrəʊzeɪ/ *n* [U] pink wine 玫瑰葡萄酒

rose[1] /roz; rəʊz/ *n*

1 ▶**FLOWER** 花◀ [C] a flower that has a pleasant smell, and is usually red, pink, white, or yellow, or the bush that this grows on 玫瑰; 蔷薇

2 ▶**COLOUR** 颜色◀ [U] a pink colour 玫瑰〔红〕色 —see picture on page A5 参见 A5 页图

3 not all roses also 又作 **not a bed of roses** *informal* if a job or situation is not all roses, it is not always pleasant and there are often difficult things to deal with【非正式】不尽如人意, 并非事事顺利

4 put the roses back in sb's cheeks *informal* to make someone look healthy again【非正式】使某人恢复健康的容貌

5 be coming up roses *informal* be happening or developing in the best possible way【非正式】一帆风顺

6 not come out of sth smelling of roses *informal* to have been involved in a situation that makes you seem dishonest, so that people stop trusting you【非正式】显得不诚实〔因而失去人们的信任〕

7 ▶**FOR WATER** 供水◀ [C] a circular piece of metal with holes in it, that is fitted to the end of a pipe or WATERING CAN so that liquid comes out in several thin streams〔水管或洒水壶上的〕莲蓬式喷嘴

8 ▶**LIGHT** 灯◀ [C] *technical* the circular object from which an electric CEILING light hangs【术语】〔天花板上的〕灯线盒

rose[2] *adj* having a pink colour 玫瑰色的, 粉红色的

rose[3] the past tense of RISE[1]

ro·se·ate /ˈrozɪ-ɪt; ˈrəʊzi-ɪt/ *adj poetic* pink【诗】玫瑰色的, 粉红色的

Roseau /roˈzo; rəʊˈzəʊ/ the capital city of Dominica, in the southwest of the country on the Roseau River, formerly called Charlotte Town 罗索〔多米尼加首都, 位于该国西南部的罗索河沿岸, 旧称夏洛特镇〕

Rose Bowl /ˈ· ,·/ an American football game held on January 1st every year in Pasadena, California, between the winners of the two main college conferences, the Big Ten and the Pac 10 玫瑰碗体育馆橄榄球赛, 玫瑰杯〔每年1月1日在加利福尼亚州帕萨迪纳举行的美式橄榄球赛。参赛球队为两大橄榄球联合会的"十强"和"太平洋十强"〕

rose·bud /ˈroz,bʌd; ˈrəʊzbʌd/ *n* [C] the flower of a rose before it opens 玫瑰花苞

rose bush /ˈ· ·/ *n* [C] the plant that roses grow on 蔷薇丛, 玫瑰丛

rose-col·oured *BrE*【英】, **rose-colored** *AmE*【美】/ˈ· ,··/ *adj* **1** having a pink colour 玫瑰色的, 粉红色的 **2** a rose-coloured idea of what something is like shows that you think something is more pleasant than it really is, because you do not notice anything unpleasant〔对事物的看法〕过于乐观的, 想得比实际更

美好的: **see sth through rose-coloured/rose-tinted spectacles** (=never notice bad things) 盲目乐观的看法

rose hip /ˈ· ·/ *n* [C] the small red fruit of some kinds of rose bush, used in medicines and juices 玫瑰果: *rose hip syrup* 玫瑰果糖浆

rose·ma·ry /ˈrozˌmɛrɪ; ˈrəʊzməri/ *n* [U] leaves that have a strong, pleasant smell and are used in cooking, or the bush that these come from 迷迭香叶〔可用作调味料〕; 迷迭香

Rose Pa·rade, the /ˈ· ·ˌ·/ a PARADE held every year in Pasadena, California, on January 1st, that has many large vehicles covered with flowers, marching bands, and horse riders. The parade is shown on television all over the US. 玫瑰花车游行〔每年1月1日在加利福尼亚州帕萨迪纳举行的游行。游行队列中有玫瑰装饰的大型花车、行进乐队和骑兵队等。游行盛况由电视台面向全美直播〕

Roses, War of the —see 见 the WARS OF THE ROSES

rose-tint·ed /ˈ· ·ˌ·/ *adj especially BrE* ROSE-COLOURED【尤英】玫瑰色的; (过分) 乐观的

Ro·set·ta Stone, the /roˈzɛtə ˌston; rəʊˈzetə ˌstəʊn/ a large, ancient stone that was found in Egypt in 1799, which had the same piece of writing on it in three different writing systems: Greek letters, Egyptian letters, and ancient Egyptian HIEROGLYPHICS. This important discovery made it possible for people to translate hieroglyphics for the first time. The stone is now kept in the British Museum. 罗塞塔石碑〔1799年在埃及发现的一块巨型古石碑。同一碑文分别用希腊文字、埃及文字和古埃及象形文字刻成。这一重要发现使现代人首次得以解读古埃及象形文字。罗塞塔石碑现存于大英博物馆〕

ro·sette /roˈzɛt; rəʊˈzet/ *n* [C] **1** a circular BADGE made of coloured RIBBON that is given to the winner of a competition or that people in Britain wear to show support for a particular football team or political party 玫瑰花结〔授予比赛的胜利者; 英国人佩戴以示对某足球队或政党的支持〕 **2** a shape like a round flat flower that has been made in stone or wood 玫瑰花形石[木]雕

rose·wa·ter /ˈrozˌwɔtɚ; ˈrəʊzˌwɔːtə/ *n* [U] a liquid made from roses, used for its pleasant smell 玫瑰香水

rose·wood /ˈrozˌwʊd; ˈrəʊzwʊd/ *n* [U] a hard dark red wood, used for making expensive furniture 花梨木, 黄檀木

Rosh Ha·sha·nah, Rosh Hashana /ˌroʃ hɑˈʃɔnə; ˌrɒʃ həˈʃɑːnə/ an important Jewish religious holiday, which celebrates the beginning of the Jewish new year and continues for two days. It is usually in September. 岁首节〔犹太人一重要宗教节日, 庆祝犹太新年, 为时两天, 一般在公历9月〕

Ro·si·cru·cians, the /ˌrozɪˈkruʃənz; ˌrəʊzɪˈkruːʃənz/ *n* [plural] an international secret society of men, begun in the 17th century, who were involved in mysterious practices involving magic and spirits. There are also modern groups with the same name, especially in the US, who claim to be related to the original Rosicrucians. 玫瑰十字会〔起源于17世纪的一个国际性男子秘密社团, 从事魔术、招魂术之类的神秘活动。也有一些现代团体使用同一名称, 尤其是在美国, 他们自称与最早的玫瑰十字会有承袭关系〕

Rosie the Riv·et·er /ˌrozɪ ðə ˈrɪvɪtɚ; ˌrəʊzi ðə ˈrɪvɪ̣tə/ a NICKNAME given to any US woman who worked in factories making weapons or aircraft during World War II. Rosie the Riveter was a character who appeared in US government films and POSTERS about the work that women did during the war. 铆工罗茜〔二战期间在兵工厂或飞机制造厂工作的美国妇女的绰号。铆工罗茜是美国政府制作的宣传影片和招贴画上的一个人物, 以此反映二战时期的美国妇女承担的工作〕

ros·in /ˈrɑzɪn; ˈrɒzɪ̣n/ *n* [U] a solid, slightly sticky substance that you rub on the BOW of a VIOLIN etc, to keep it moving correctly on the strings 松香 —**rosin** *v* [T]

Ross /rɔs; rɒs/, **Bet·sy** /ˈbɛtsɪ; ˈbetsi/ (1752-1836) the woman who is believed to have made the first US flag 罗斯〔(1752-1836), 被认为是制作第一面美国国旗的妇女〕

Ros·set·ti /roˈzɛtɪ; rəʊˈzeti/, **Chris·ti·na Geor·gi·na** /krɪˈstinə dʒɔrˈdʒinə; krɪˈstiːnə dʒɔːˈdʒiːnə/ (1830-94) a British poet known for her religious poems, some of which are used as HYMNS. She was the sister of Dante Gabriel Rossetti. 罗塞蒂〔(1830-1894), 英国诗人, 以宗教诗闻名。她的一些诗歌被用作赞美诗。她是但丁·加布里埃尔·罗塞蒂的妹妹〕

Rossetti, Dante Gabriel /ˈdɑnte ˈgebrɪəl; ˈdænti ˈgeɪbriəl/ (1828-82) a British artist and poet who helped to start the Pre-Raphaelite movement. His paintings were mostly based on religious subjects or old stories about King Arthur. He was the brother of Christina Georgina Rossetti. 罗塞蒂〔(1828-1882), 英国画家、诗人。他参与发起了拉斐尔前派运动, 画作大多以宗教或亚瑟王传奇为题材。他是克莉丝蒂娜·乔治娜·罗塞蒂的哥哥〕

Ros·si·ni /roˈsinɪ; rɒˈsiːni/, **Gio·ac·chi·no** /ˌdʒoəˈkino; ˌdʒəʊəˈkiːnəʊ/ (1792-1868) an Italian COMPOSER most famous for writing many OPERAS, especially *The Barber of Seville* (1816). The OVERTURE to his opera *William Tell* (1829) is very well known. 罗西尼〔(1792-1868), 意大利著名作曲家。他创作有多部歌剧, 以《塞维利亚的理发师》(1816) 尤为著名。歌剧《威廉·退尔》(1829) 的序曲也非常有名〕

ros·ter[1] /ˈrɑstɚ; ˈrɒstə/ *n* [C] a list of people's names showing the jobs they must do and the times when they must do them 值勤表, 勤务表: *a duty roster* 值勤表

roster[2] *v* [T] to put someone's name on a roster 把〔某人的名字〕列入值勤表

ros·trum /ˈrɑstrəm; ˈrɒstrəm/ *n* [C] a small PLATFORM (=raised area) that you stand on when you are making a speech or conducting (CONDUCT[1] (2)) musicians 讲坛; 〔乐队指挥站的〕指挥台

ros·y /ˈrozɪ; ˈrəʊzi/ *adj* **1** pink 粉红色的: *rosy cheeks* 红润的面颊 **2** seeming to offer hope of success or happiness 充满成功希望的, 美好的: *The future is beginning to look much rosier.* 未来开始显得有希望多了。| *rosy optimism* 充满希望的乐观主义 | **paint a rosy picture of** (=describe a situation in a way that makes it seem much better than it really is) 对…作不切实际的乐观描绘 —**rosiness** *n* [U]

rot[1] /rɑt; rɒt/ *v* **1** [I,T] to decay by a gradual natural process, or to make something do this (使) 腐败, 腐烂: *Sugar rots your teeth.* 糖会蛀蚀牙齿。| *the stench of rotting eggs* 坏鸡蛋的臭气 **2 rot in jail/prison etc** to get into a bad mental or physical condition because you have been forced to stay in a place such as a prison 在监狱等处逐渐憔悴[衰弱]: *As far as they're concerned we can rot in jail.* 我们会在监狱中慢慢死去, 他们才不管呢。

rot away *phr v* [I,T] to decay completely and disappear or break into small pieces, or to make something do this (使) 彻底腐烂: *In places the timbers have rotted away.* 有些木材腐朽了。

rot[2] *n* [U] **1 stop the rot** *informal* to stop a bad situation from getting worse and worse【非正式】使坏情况不再恶化: *If Leeds don't stop the rot soon they can say goodbye to a top eight team ranking.* 如果利兹队无法阻止这种走下坡的势头, 他们将与八强排名无缘。**2 the rot set in** *informal* used to say that a situation starts to get worse, and nothing could stop this process【非正式】〔情况〕开始恶化并无可挽回 **3** the natural process of decaying or the part of something that has decayed 腐败, 腐烂; 腐烂物 **4** *BrE old-fashioned* nonsense【英, 过时】废话, 愚蠢的话: *You do talk rot!* 你尽说蠢话! —see also 另见 DRY ROT

ro·ta /ˈrotə; ˈrəʊtə/ *n* [C] *BrE* a list that shows when each person in a group must do a particular job【英】勤务轮值表: *a cleaning rota* 打扫值勤表

ro·ta·ry[1] /ˈrotərɪ; ˈrəʊtəri/ *adj* **1** turning in a circle around a fixed point, like a wheel 旋转的, 转动的: *the rotary movement of the helicopter blades* 直升机桨叶的旋转运动 **2** having a main part that does this〔机器〕有旋转部件的: *a rotary engine* 旋转式发动机

rotary[2] *n* [C] *AmE* a ROUNDABOUT【美】环岛

Rotary Club, the /ˈ· ··, ·/ *n* an organization of business people in a town who work together to raise money for people who are poor or sick 扶轮社〔城市里商界人士为贫困者和病人筹款的组织〕

ro·tate /ˈrotet; rəʊˈteɪt/ *v* **1** [I,T] to turn around a fixed point, or to make something do this (使) 旋转, 转动: *a rotating blade* 旋转的叶片 **2** [I,T] if a job rotates, or if people rotate jobs, they each do the jobs for a fixed period of time, one after the other (使) 轮流做…, 轮换: *The chairmanship of the committee rotates annually.* 委员会主席的职位每年轮换一次。| *We usually rotate the worst jobs, so that no one gets stuck with them.* 我们通常轮流做最难堪的工作, 这样谁都不至于老干那种活儿。**3** [T] *technical* to regularly change the crops grown on a piece of land, in order to preserve the quality of the soil【术语】轮种, 轮作

ro·ta·tion /roˈteʃən; rəʊˈteɪʃən/ *n* **1** [U] the action of turning around a fixed point 旋转: [+about/around/on] *the rotation of the Earth on its axis* 地球的自转 **2** [C] one complete turn around a fixed point 旋转一周: *The blades spin at 100 rotations per minute.* 叶片每分钟旋转100圈。**3 in rotation a)** if a group of people do something in rotation they do it one after the other in a regular order〔按一定顺序的〕循环, 轮换: *The four were Area Board chairmen, serving in rotation.* 这四个人轮流担任地区董事会主席。**b)** if a group of things are used in rotation they are used one after the other in a regular order〔按一定顺序的〕交替使用: *It's good practice to use three balls in rotation in cold weather.* 在寒冷的天气里, 轮流使用三个球是个好办法。**4** [U] the

practice of changing regularly from one thing to another, or regularly changing the person who does a particular job 轮换, 交替 **5 crop rotation** *technical* the practice of regularly changing the crops that are grown on a piece of land, in order to preserve the quality of the soil【术语】轮作制 —**rotational** *adj*

ROTC, the /ˈrɑtsɪ; ˈrɒtsi/ Reserve Officer Training Corps; a programme run by the US army to train college students in military leadership 后备军官训练队〔美国军方培训在校大学生军事指挥能力的一个项目〕

rote /rot; rəʊt/ *n* [U] *formal* a method of learning that involves repeating something until you remember it, without having to understand it【正式】死记硬背: **learn (sth) by rote** *old-fashioned grammar teaching and learning by rote* 旧式的语法讲授和死记硬背的学习方法

rot·gut /ˈrɑtˌgʌt; ˈrɒtgʌt/ *n* [U] *informal* strong cheap low-quality alcohol【非正式】廉价的劣质烈酒

Roth /rɔθ; rɒθ/, **Philip** (1933-) a US writer whose best known book is *Portnoy's Complaint*, which deals humorously with middle class Jewish life in the US 罗斯〔(1933-), 美国作家。最著名的作品为《波特诺伊的抱怨》, 以幽默的笔调描述美国中产阶级犹太人的生活〕

Roth·ko /ˈrɑθko; ˈrɒθkəʊ/, **Mark** (1903-70) a US artist, born in Russia, known especially for his large paintings of squares and RECTANGLES in different colours 罗思科〔(1903-1970), 美国画家, 生于俄国。他创作的巨幅作品由不同颜色的正方形和长方形色块组成, 并因此闻名于世〕

Rothschild /ˈrɔθstʃaɪld; ˈrɒθstʃaɪld/ a family of Jewish bankers in Europe who had a lot of influence over two hundred years. 罗思柴尔德家族〔欧洲一犹太人银行世家, 其影响力长达200余年〕

ro·tis·ser·ie /roˈtɪsərɪ; rəʊˈtɪsəri/ *n* [C] a piece of equipment for cooking meat by turning it around and around on a metal rod 旋转式烤肉架

ro·tor /ˈrotə; ˈrəʊtə/ *n* [C] *technical*【术语】**1** a part of a machine that turns around on a fixed point〔机器的〕旋转部分, 转子 **2** also 又作 **rotor blade** the long flat part on top of a HELICOPTER that turns around and around〔直升机的〕(水平) 旋翼

rot·ten¹ /ˈrɑtn; ˈrɒtn/ *adj* **1** badly decayed 腐烂的, 变质的: *rotten fruit* 腐烂的水果 | *the smell of rotten eggs* 变质鸡蛋的气味 | *The wood was completely rotten.* 这木头完全腐朽了。**2** *informal* very nasty or unpleasant【非正式】非常糟糕的, 非常讨厌的: *What rotten weather!* 多么糟糕的天气! | *It's a rotten thing to do.* 干这件事非常讨厌。**3** *informal* a word meaning very bad at doing something, or very badly done, used especially when you feel annoyed about this【非正式】极差的, 糟糕透了的〔尤用于表示恼怒〕: *He's a rotten driver.* 他是个糟糕的司机。**4 feel rotten a)** to feel ill 感到不舒服 **b)** to feel unhappy and guilty about something 感到不高兴, 感到内疚: **[+about]** *I felt rotten about having to fire him.* 不得不解雇他我感到很遗憾。**5 a rotten apple** one bad person who has a bad effect on all the others in a group 害群之马 —**rottenly** *adv* —**rottenness** *n* [U]

rotten² *adv informal*【非正式】**1 spoil sb rotten** to treat someone too well or too kindly, especially a child 溺爱, 宠坏某人〔尤指小孩〕: *Melanie's beautiful, wilful, and she's been spoiled rotten all her life.* 梅拉妮漂亮、任性, 她一生都被宠坏了。**2 fancy sb rotten** *BrE humorous* to be extremely attracted to someone in a sexual way【英, 幽默】对某人神魂颠倒[极为迷恋]

rot·ter /ˈrɑtə; ˈrɒtə/ *n* [C] *BrE old-fashioned* an unpleasant person who treats other people badly【英, 过时】无赖, 恶棍

rott·wei·ler /ˈrɑtˌwaɪlə; ˈrɒtwaɪlə/ *n* [C] **1** a type of strong and dangerous dog, often used as a guard dog 罗威纳犬, 罗特韦尔狗〔一种强壮凶猛的看门狗〕**2 rottweiler politics/tendencies etc** *humorous* politics etc in which politicians attack each other in a very determined way【幽默】政客相互猛烈攻击的政治手腕/倾向等

CULTURAL NOTE 文化注释

Rottweilers became feared by many people after a series of violent attacks on adults and children in the late 1980s and early 1990s. In Britain, rottweilers must now be REGISTERed and wear a MUZZLE (=a covering around the dog's mouth to prevent it from biting) when they are in a public place. 20世纪80年代晚期和90年代早期发生了一系列罗威纳犬恶意伤人的严重事件, 人们因此对这种狗充满恐惧。在英国, 现在喂养这种狗必须登记, 在公共场合必须给狗戴上口套。

ro·tund /roˈtʌnd; rəʊˈtʌnd/ *adj humorous* having a fat round body【幽默】〔身体〕圆胖的 —**rotundity** *n* [U]

ro·tun·da /roˈtʌndə; rəʊˈtʌndə/ *n* [C] a round building or hall, especially one with a DOME (=a round bowl-shaped roof)〔尤指有圆顶的〕圆形建筑; 圆形大厅

rou·ble, ruble /ˈrubl; ˈruːbəl/ *n* [C] the standard unit of money in Russia and Belarus 卢布〔俄罗斯和白俄罗斯的货币单位〕

rouge /ruʒ; ruːʒ/ *n* [U] *old-fashioned* pink or red powder or cream that women put on their cheeks【过时】胭脂 —**rouge** *v* [T]

rough¹ /rʌf; rʌf/ *adj* 2 3

1 ▶NOT SMOOTH 不平的◀ having an uneven surface〔表面〕粗糙的, 不平的: *Her hands were rough from hard work.* 她的双手因干重活儿而变得粗糙。| *A rough track led to the farm.* 一条崎岖的小路通向那个农场。| *rough grass* 高矮不齐的草 —opposite 反义词 SMOOTH¹ (1)

2 ▶NOT EXACT 不精确的◀ not exact or not containing many details; APPROXIMATE 粗略的, 大致的: *This is just a rough sketch but it gives you the idea.* 这只是个草图, 但能给你一个大概意思。| *a rough translation* 粗略的翻译 | **a rough idea** *Could you give me a rough idea what time you'll be home?* 你能告诉我你大概什么时候回家吗? | **at a rough guess** *spoken* (=without being at all certain or exact)【口】粗略地猜测 *At a rough guess, I'd say he was about 45.* 大致猜猜, 我看他在45岁上下。| **a rough estimate** *I can only give you a rough estimate of the cost at this stage.* 目前我只能给你粗略估计一下费用。—see graph at 参见 IDEA 图表

3 ▶NOT GENTLE 不温柔的◀ using force or violence 粗野的, 粗暴的: *Rugby is a very rough game.* (英式) 橄榄球是一项非常粗野的运动。| *A stroller should be easy to fold and capable of withstanding rough treatment.* 轻便婴儿手推车应该容易折叠, 并且坚固耐用。

4 ▶TOWN/AREA ETC 城镇/地区等◀ a rough area is a place where there is a lot of violence or crime〔地方〕多暴力的, 犯罪率高的: *a rough part of town* 城市里犯罪率高的地区

5 ▶HAVING A LOT OF PROBLEMS/DIFFICULTIES 有许多问题/困难◀ [usually before noun 一般用于名词前] a rough period is one in which you have a lot of problems or difficulties〔时期〕艰难的: *Don't be too angry with her – she's had a very rough time of it lately.* 不要太生她的气, 最近她的日子很艰难。| *I've had a really rough day.* 今天我很不走运。| **go through a rough patch** (=experience problems or difficulties) 历经磨难, 日子不好过 | **give sb/sth a rough ride** (=a very difficult time) 使某人/某事遇到麻烦 *The bill may have gotten through the House but it's in for a rough ride in the Senate.* 提案获得了众议院通过, 但在参议院会有麻烦。

6 ▶UNFAIR/UNLUCKY 不公平的/不幸的◀ unfair or unlucky 不公平的; 倒霉的: **it's rough on sb** *It's rough on him, losing his job like that.* 他就那样丢掉了工作, 真倒霉。| *Two burglaries in one week? That's a bit rough!* 一周遭受两次入室盗窃? 太倒霉了!

7 ▶WEATHER/SEA 天气/海◀ with strong wind or storms 狂暴的: *In the evening we were sick, it was a very rough crossing.* 晚上我们晕船了, (因为) 渡海时碰上了暴风雨。

8 ▶NOT COMFORTABLE 不舒服的◀ uncomfortable, with difficult conditions 不舒服的, 条件艰苦的: *a rough, pioneering way of life* 艰苦的、拓荒者的生活方式

9 ▶VOICE/SOUND 嗓音/声音◀ **a)** not sounding soft or gentle, and often rather unpleasant or angry〔声音〕不悦耳的, 粗声粗气的: *the rough voices of the workmen* 工匠们沙哑的说话声 **b)** having an unpleasant sound, especially because there is something wrong with a machine〔尤指机器出故障时发出的声音〕刺耳的, 难听的: *The clutch sounds rough, better get it checked.* 离合器的声音听起来不对头, 最好请人检查一下。

10 ▶SIMPLE/NOT WELL MADE 简单的/做得不好的◀ simple and often not very well made 简单的, 粗糙的: *We constructed a rough shelter using whatever materials we could find.* 我们用能找到的材料搭了一个简陋的棚子。

11 feel rough *informal* to feel ill【非正式】感觉生病: *I think I'd better go to bed – I'm feeling pretty rough.* 我想我最好去睡觉, 我很不舒服。

12 look rough *informal* to look untidy, dirty, or unhealthy【非正式】看上去不整洁[脏乱, 不健康]: *We had been travelling for two days, and must have looked pretty rough.* 我们已经旅行了两天, 看上去肯定很邋遢。

13 rough and ready simple, but just good enough for a particular purpose 简单[不讲究]但实用的

14 rough justice punishment that is severe or unfair 严厉[不公平]的惩罚

15 a rough night a night when you did not sleep well 不眠之夜, 辗转反侧的一夜

16 rough stuff *spoken* violent behaviour【口】粗野的行为
17 a bit of rough *BrE humorous* someone from a lower social class than you, with whom you have a sexual relationship【英, 幽默】〔社会地位低于自己的〕性伙伴
18 give sb the rough side of your tongue *BrE old-fashioned* to speak angrily to someone【英, 过时】严斥某人 —**roughness** *n* [U] —see also 另见 ROUGH DIAMOND, ROUGH PARER, ROUGHLY

rough² *n* **1 take the rough with the smooth** to accept the bad things in life as well as the good ones 既能享乐也能吃苦; 好坏都能接受 **2** [C] a picture drawn very quickly, not showing all the details 草图, 略图 **3 the rough** uneven ground with long grass on a GOLF course〔高尔夫球场的〕生有长草的起伏地面, 长草区 —see picture on page A23 参见 A23 页图 **4 in rough** *BrE* if you write or draw something in rough, you do it without paying attention to details or tidiness【英】粗略地, 马虎地: *It's best to work in rough first, and then write it out neatly.* 最好先打一个草稿, 然后再工整地誊写出来。—see also 另见 DIAMOND IN THE ROUGH

rough³ *v* **rough it** *informal* to live for a short time in conditions that are not very comfortable【非正式】〔短时期〕过不很舒适的生活: *Let's just take the tent – I don't mind roughing it for a bit.* 我们只带帐篷就行, 我不在乎过点儿简陋的生活。

rough sth ↔ **in** *phr v* [T] to add something to a picture, without showing all the exact details 勾勒, 画…的轮廓: *If you look here you can see another angle for the arm roughed in.* 如果你从这儿看, 可以从另一个角度看到画上去的胳膊轮廓。

rough sth ↔ **out** *phr v* [T] to draw or write something, without showing all the exact details 草拟〔某事物〕; 画…的草图: *Iain was peering at a diagram the engineer had roughed out on his notepad.* 伊恩凝视着工程师在便笺簿上画的一幅草图。

rough sb ↔ **up** *phr v* [T] *informal* to attack someone and hurt them by hitting them【非正式】揍, 向〔某人〕动粗

rough⁴ *adv* **1 sleep rough** *BrE* to sleep outside with nothing to protect you from the weather【英】露宿: *sleeping rough on the street* 露宿街头 **2 play rough** to play in a fairly violent way 玩得粗野 —see also 另见 **cut up rough** (CUT¹)

rough·age /ˈrʌfɪdʒ; ˈrʌfɪdʒ/ *n* [U] a substance contained in some foods that helps your BOWELS to work; DIETARY FIBRE 食物中的粗纤维: *Wholemeal bread is a valuable source of roughage.* 全麦面包含有丰富的粗纤维。

rough-and-tum·ble /ˌ· · ˈ· ·/ *n* **1** [singular,U] noisy rough behaviour when playing or fighting, especially by children〔尤指孩子的〕喧闹, 打闹, 粗野的举止 **2** [U] the usual busy, noisy, or rough way in which a particular activity takes place〔某事发生时的〕喧闹, 混乱, 斗争: *the rough-and-tumble of politics* 政治的众声喧哗, 争强好胜

rough·cast /ˈrʌfˌkæst; ˈrʌfkɑːst/ *n* [U] a rough surface on the outside of a building, made of PLASTER¹ (1) mixed with little stones or broken shells〔建筑物外墙用石灰混合石子或碎贝壳打的〕底子, 粗灰泥 —**roughcast** *adj*

rough di·a·mond /ˌ· ˈ· · ·/ *n* [C] *informal* someone who seems rude, rough, or unfriendly, but is actually kind and generous【非正式】外粗内秀的人; DIAMOND IN THE ROUGH *AmE*【美】

rough·en /ˈrʌfən; ˈrʌfən/ *v* [I,T] to become rough, or to make something rough (使)变得粗糙, (使)变得不平

rough-hewn /ˌ· ˈ·◂/ *adj* rough-hewn wood or stone has been roughly cut and its surface is not yet smooth〔木材或石头〕粗砍成的, 粗凿成的, 不光滑的

rough·house¹ /ˈ· ·/ *n* [singular] *BrE old-fashioned* a noisy fight, usually without weapons【英, 过时】〔一般指徒手的〕打斗, 殴斗

roughhouse² *v* [I] *AmE* to play roughly or fight; WRESTLE (1)【美】打闹; 扭打: *Either stop roughhousing or play outside!* 要么停止打闹, 要么到外面去玩!

rough·ly /ˈrʌflɪ; ˈrʌfli/ *adv* **1** not exactly; about 粗略地, 大致上: *There were roughly 200 people there.* 那儿大约有200人。| *How much have you got, roughly?* 你大约有多少钱? | *Azaleas flower at roughly the same time each year.* 杜鹃花每年大致在相同的时间开放。| **roughly speaking** (=used when saying something without giving exact details or information) 粗略地说 *Roughly speaking, I'd say we need about $500.* 粗略地说, 我认为我们大约需要500美元。—see graph at 参见 APPROXIMATELY 图表 **2** not gently or carefully 粗暴地, 粗野地, 粗鲁地: *Alan dropped the cat roughly to the floor.* 阿伦粗暴地把猫摔到地上。

rough·neck /ˈrʌfˌnɛk; ˈrʌfnek/ *n* [C] **1** a member of a team of people who make or operate an OIL-WELL 油井工人 **2** *informal especially AmE* someone who usually behaves in a rough, rude, or angry way【非正式, 尤美】粗暴的人, 脾气暴躁的人

rough pa·per /ˌ· ˈ· ·/ *n* [U] *BrE* paper that is used for writing or drawing things that will later be changed or copied more neatly【英】草稿纸

Rough Rid·ers, the /ˈ· ˌ· ·/ a group of US COWBOYS and farmers who were trained to fight against the Spanish in Cuba in the Spanish-American War (1898). They were led by Theodore Roosevelt, who later became the US president. 莽骑兵〔由美国牧工和牧场主组成的一支军队。美西战争(1898)期间, 他们在古巴与西班牙人作战, 率领他们作战的是西奥多·罗斯福, 即后来的美国总统〕

rough·shod /ˈrʌfˈʃɑd; ˈrʌfʃɒd/ *adj* **ride roughshod over** to behave in a way that ignores other people's feelings or opinions 轻蔑地对待, 对…横行霸道

rou·lette /ruˈlɛt; ruːˈlet/ *n* [U] a game in which a small ball is spun around on a moving wheel, and people try to win money by guessing which hole it will fall into 轮盘赌 —see also 另见 RUSSIAN ROULETTE

round¹ /raʊnd; raʊnd/ *adj* **1** shaped like a circle 圆(形)的: *a round table* 圆桌 | *Jamie's eyes grew round with delight.* 杰米高兴得眼睛睁得滚圆。**2** shaped like a ball 球形的: *a plant with small round berries* 长着小圆浆果的植物 **3** fat and curved 滚圆的, 丰满的: *Charlie had a chubby face and round cheeks.* 查利的脸很丰满, 双颊圆滚滚的。**4** a round number is a whole number, often ending in 0 整数的〔常指10的倍数〕: *Let's make it a round £50 I owe you.* 我就欠你整50英镑吧。| **a round hundred/dozen etc** (=a complete hundred etc) 整一百/一打等 **5 in round figures** not expressed as an exact number but as the nearest 10, 100, 1000 etc 以约整数表示〈如10, 100, 1000等〉: *In round figures, the expected profit is about £600 million.* 以整数计, 预期利润约为6亿英镑。—see also 另见 ROUNDLY, **a square peg in a round hole** (SQUARE¹ (11)) —**roundness** *n* [U]

round² *adv* [only after verb 仅用于动词后] *especially BrE*【尤英】**1** if something moves round, it moves in a circular movement 绕圈子, 围绕地: *It is water moving through the mechanism which pushes the wheel round.* 水流过机械装置推动轮子转动。| **round and round** *He stared at the washing machine, just watching the clothes go round and round.* 他盯着洗衣机, 看着衣物一圈圈地转。**2** if something such as a group of people or things are round something, they surround that thing 在周围: *If you'll all gather round we'll begin the experiment.* 请大家围成一圈, 我们将开始实验。| **all round** *The garden had a fence all round to keep out dogs.* 花园四周圈着篱笆防止狗进入。**3** to many people or in many parts of a place, a room etc 挨个地, 逐一地; 到处: *Please, come in, let me show you round.* 请进, 让我带你到处看看。| *Would someone hand the drinks round please.* 请哪位把饮料递给所有在场的人好吗? | **all round** *It was a beautiful room, with cushions scattered all round.* 这是个漂亮的房间, 到处摆着靠垫。| **enough to go round** (=enough for everyone) 足够分配 *Do you think there are enough seats to go round?* 你看座位够不够? **4** in the opposite direction 朝相反方向, 转过来: *When he turned round I recognised him immediately.* 他转过身来, 我立即认出了他。**5** if you go round, you do not go the most direct way to get somewhere 绕道地, 迂回地: *I don't mind driving round by the market on my way to the station.* 我不介意在开车去车站的路上绕道去市场。**6 the wrong/the other/the opposite etc way round a)** facing the wrong, other, opposite etc direction 方向相反: *You're wearing your T-shirt the wrong way round.* 你把T恤衫穿反了。**b)** in the wrong, other, opposite etc order 顺序颠倒: *You got it the wrong way round. She left him, he didn't walk out on her!* 你搞错了。是她离开了他, 而不是他扔下了她! **7 round about** about a particular time or amount 大约: *It's a coincidence that all his grandparents died round about the same time.* 他的祖父母和外祖父母差不多同时去世, 这是个巧合。**8 change/switch etc round** to change the position that things are in so that they are in each other's places 交换位置: *The dartboard was at the back, but they've changed things round.* 飞镖的圆靶原来在后面, 但他们把东西的位置调换了。**9** *informal* to or in someone's house【非正式】去[在]〔某人〕家: *I'm inviting the neighbours round for a drink.* 我打算请邻居到我家来喝酒。| *Sally left a note saying she'd be round at her cousin's house.* 萨莉留下便条, 说她去了她表姐家。**10 (just) round the corner** not very far away at all 在附近, (就)在拐角上: *She could walk, it's only round the corner.* 她可以步行去, 就在附近。**11 go round the shops/pub etc** to go to the shops etc 到商店/酒吧等去: *I could go round the village and see if something's still open.* 我可以去村里转转, 看还有什么地方开门。**12 go round (and round) in circles** to not make progress at something such as trying to solve a problem〔解决问题等〕原地打转, 没有进展 **13 2 metres/12 feet etc round**

having a CIRCUMFERENCE of 2 metres, 12 feet etc 周长2米/12英尺等 **14 the first/second etc time round** the first, second etc time that you do something 第一次/第二次等〔做某事〕: *Who says marriage is better the second time round?* 谁说第二次婚姻较美满? —see also 另见 ALL-ROUND —compare 比较 AROUND

round³ *prep especially BrE*【尤英】**1** if something moves round something, it moves around it in a circular movement 围绕, 环绕: *The earth goes round the sun.* 地球围绕着太阳旋转。| *The lions slowly circled round the gazelle, waiting to pounce.* 那些狮子围着瞪羚慢慢转, 等待着猛扑上去。—see picture on page A1 参见A1页图 **2** surrounding or covering something 围着〔某物〕; 覆盖着〔某物〕: *sitting round the table* 围着桌子坐 | *Why have you got a bandage round your wrist?* 你的手腕上为什么缠着绷带? **3** if you go round something you do not go the most direct way to get somewhere 绕过: *You'll have to go right round the roadworks to get there.* 你必须绕过道路施工处才能到那里去。**4** at or to the other side of something 在[向]…另一侧: *Suddenly the thief disappeared round the corner.* 突然, 小偷在拐角处消失了。| *There must be another entrance round the back of the house.* 房子后面肯定还有一个入口。**5** to or in all parts of a place 到处, 在各处: *Let me show you round the castle.* 我带你到城堡里四下看看。| *travelling round Europe* 游历欧洲各国 **6** a way round a difficult situation or problem is a way to solve it or avoid it 解决〔问题〕; 绕过〔问题〕: *We'll have to leave earlier – there's no other way round it!* 我们得早点儿走, 没有别的办法! **7 round here** in the place, area of a town etc where you are now 在此地, 在附近: *Do you live round here?* 你在附近住吗? | *There must be a pen round here somewhere.* 这里的什么地方肯定有支钢笔。**8** at about a particular time〔时间〕大约: *It must have been round midnight when I heard the scream.* 我听到尖叫声时一定是午夜前后。—compare 比较 AROUND —see also 另见 **round the clock** (CLOCK¹ (6))

USAGE NOTE 用法说明: ROUND

WORD CHOICE 词语辨析: **round, around, about** In many contexts, **round** and **around** have the same meaning in British English, though American speakers do not use **round** in this way. 在许多语境中, round和around在英国英语中意义相同, 但讲美国英语的人则不会这样使用round: *The price was somewhere round three thousand* (*BrE* 英). 价格在三千左右。| *The price was somewhere around three thousand.* 价格在三千左右。

In British English, you can use **round** for describing a circular movement. 在英国英语里, 可以用round来描述"旋转": *The satellite travelled right round the Earth.* 卫星围绕着地球运转。Americans would always use **around** in this meaning. 美国人总是用around表达这个意思: *The satellite traveled right around the Earth.* 卫星围绕着地球运转。The same is true when you use **around** and **round** to mean moving to different places. 用around和round表示"到各处"时也是如此: *He's travelling round the world for a few years* (*BrE* 英). 几年来他周游世界各地。| *He's traveling around the world for a few years.* 几年来他周游世界各地。Both **round** and **around** are correct in British English, although **round** is slightly less formal. 在英国英语里, round和around都正确, 不过round稍微不那么正式。

British English speakers often use **about** instead of **around** in some meanings. 在表达某些意义时, 讲英国英语的人经常使用about而不用around: *Stop fooling about, you two.* 别再瞎混了, 你们俩。| *"Where's my bag?" "It must be about somewhere."* "我的包呢?" "肯定就在附近某个地方。"

Both British and American speakers use **about** to mean 'approximately'. 讲英国英语和美国英语的人都用about来表示"大约": *He's about six feet tall.* 他大约六英尺高。

round⁴ *n* [C]

1 ►SERIES 系列◄ a number or set of events that are connected 一连串相关的事件: [+of] *For Jodie, life was a continual round of parties.* 对于乔迪来说, 生活是一连串的宴会, 玩乐不断。| *the next round of arms talks* 下一轮军备谈判

2 ►FOOD/NEWSPAPERS/LETTERS ETC 食品/报纸/信件等◄ a regular visit to a number of houses, offices etc to deliver or sell things 例行路线〔有规律地到住宅、办公室等递送或售卖东西〕: **paper/milk round etc** (=a job in which you deliver newspapers, milk etc to people's houses) 按固定路线送报纸/牛奶等

3 ►VISITS 探访◄ rounds the usual visits that someone, especially a doctor, regularly makes as part of their job 巡访, 〔尤指医生的〕定期巡诊: **be (out) on your rounds** *I'm sorry; the doctor is out on her rounds till 3 o'clock.* 对不起, 医生出去巡诊, 3点以后才回来。

4 do the rounds of to go around from one place to another, often looking for work 在…到处转〔常指寻找工作〕: *Daniela's doing the rounds of the theatrical agents.* 丹妮拉正在到一个个剧院经纪人那儿找工作。

5 do the rounds *informal*【非正式】also 又作 **go the rounds** *BrE*【英】if an illness or piece of news does the rounds, it is passed on from one person to another〔疾病、新闻〕传播: *There's a nasty kind of flu doing the rounds this winter.* 今年冬天一种非常厉害的流感正在蔓延。

6 ►ALCOHOL 酒◄ if you buy a round of drinks in a bar, you buy drinks for all the people in your group〔在酒吧为同伴买的〕每人一份〔饮料〕: **it's my/your etc round** (=used to say that you or another person should buy drinks for all the other people in your group) 我/你等请客 *What are you having? It's my round.* 你们想喝什么? 我请客。

7 round of applause a period when people are clapping (CLAP¹ (1)) to show that they enjoyed a performance 一阵掌声

8 round of sandwiches *especially BrE* SANDWICHES made from two whole pieces of bread【尤英】〔用两个整片面包做成的〕三明治

9 round of toast *especially BrE* one whole piece of bread that has been toasted (TOAST² (2))【尤英】一整片烤面包

10 ►GOLF 高尔夫球◄ a complete game of GOLF 一场〔指打完球场中所有的洞〕

11 ►BOXING 拳击◄ one of the periods of fighting in a boxing (BOX² (1)) or wrestling (WRESTLE (1)) match that are separated by short rests 拳击[摔跤]比赛的一个回合: *Bruno was knocked out in the second round.* 布鲁诺在第二个回合中被击倒。

12 ►COMPETITION 比赛◄ one of the stages in a sports competition, especially in tennis or football〔尤指网球或足球比赛的〕轮, 阶段: *Did Sampras get through to the third round?* 桑普拉斯进入第三轮比赛了吗?

13 ►GUN SHOT 枪弹发射◄ a single shot from a gun, or a bullet for one shot 一发, 一枪: *I've only got ten rounds of ammunition left.* 我就剩10发子弹了。

14 ►CIRCLE 圆◄ something that has a circular shape 圆形物: *Slice the potatoes into rounds.* 把马铃薯切成圆形薄片。

15 ►SONG 歌曲◄ a song for three or four singers, in which each one sings the same tune, starting at different times 轮唱(曲)

16 the daily round the things that you have to do every day 每天的例行工作: *the daily round of cooking and cleaning* 每日的做饭和打扫工作

17 in the round a play that is performed in the round is performed on a central stage surrounded by the people watching it 舞台设在中央〔观众围绕着舞台四周〕

round⁵ *v* [T] **1** to go round something such as a bend or the corner of a building 环绕…而行, 拐〔弯〕: *The Ferrari rounded the bend at top speed.* 那辆法拉利车全速拐过弯道。**2** to make something into a round shape 使成圆形: *Jenny rounded her lips and blew him a kiss.* 珍妮撮起嘴唇给了他一个飞吻。

round sth ↔ **down** *phr v* [T] to reduce an exact figure to the nearest whole number 把〔数〕下舍入〔取仅比某数小的整数为其近似值〕—compare 比较 **round up**

round sth ↔ **off** *phr v* [I,T] **1** to do something as a way of ending an event, performance etc in a suitable or satisfactory way (使)〔活动、表演等〕圆满完成: **round sth ↔ off with** *Fresh strawberries would round the meal off nicely.* 最后来些新鲜草莓, 这顿饭就吃得心满意足了。**2** [T] to take the sharp edges off something 去掉〔某物〕的锋利边缘: *Round off the corners with a pair of scissors.* 用剪刀把角剪圆。**3** to change an exact figure to the nearest whole number 四舍五入成整数

round on sb/sth *phr v* [T] to suddenly turn and attack someone when they do not expect it, physically or with words 突然攻击; 突然责骂: *Then, for no reason at all, she rounded on me and started screaming.* 这时她毫无理由地突然冲着我尖声大叫大嚷起来。

round out *phr v* [T] to make an experience more thorough or complete 彻底完成: **round sth ↔ out** *Denise decided to round out her education with a year in Paris.* 丹尼丝决定在巴黎花一年时间完成学业。

round sb/sth ↔ **up** *phr v* [T] **1** to find a particular group of people and force them to go to prison 逮捕; 肃清: *The government's opponents are being rounded up and thrown in jail.* 反对政府的人遭到逮捕, 被投入监狱。**2** to find and gather together a group of people or things 集拢〔人或物〕: *See if you can round up a few friends to help you!* 看你能否找几个朋友帮

R

你忙！—see also 另见 ROUND-UP (1) **3** to increase an exact figure to the next highest whole number 把〔数〕上舍入〔取仅比某数大的整数为其近似值〕—compare 比较 **round down** **4** to finish a meeting or other event by doing something 以…结束〔会议或其他活动〕: *Frances likes to round up a speech with a joke.* 弗朗西丝喜欢以笑话来结束演讲。

round·a·bout[1] /ˈraʊndəˌbaʊt; ˈraʊndəbaʊt/ *n* [C] *BrE*【英】**1** a raised circular area which cars drive around, used where three or more roads join 环岛, 环形交叉路口; TRAFFIC CIRCLE *AmE*【美】**2** round structure which children sit on while people push it around and around〔儿童坐的〕旋转椅; MERRY-GO-ROUND *AmE*【美】**3** a MERRY-GO-ROUND (1)〔游乐场里的〕旋转木马 —see also 另见 **swings and roundabouts** (SWING[2] (8))

roundabout[2] *adj* not done in the shortest, most direct way possible 绕弯子的; 不直截了当的, 转弯抹角的: *a roundabout route to avoid the worst of the traffic* 绕道避开交通最拥挤的地段 | *It was a roundabout way of telling us to leave.* 这是在转弯抹角地要我们离开。

round·ed /ˈraʊndɪd; ˈraʊndɨd/ *adj* having a round shape; curved 圆形的; 弯曲的 —see also 另见 WELL-ROUNDED

roun·ders /ˈraʊndəz; ˈraʊndəz/ *n* [singular] a British ball game, similar to BASEBALL, in which players hit the ball and then run around the edge of an area 圆场棒球

Round·head /ˈraʊndˌhɛd; ˈraʊndhed/ *n* [C] someone who supported Parliament against the King in the English Civil War in the 17th century〔17世纪英国内战时支持议会反对国王的〕圆颅党人 —compare 比较 CAVALIER

round·ly /ˈraʊndlɪ; ˈraʊndli/ *adj* **roundly condemn/criticize etc** (=criticize someone strongly and severely) 强烈谴责/严厉批评等 *All the major parties roundly condemned the attack.* 所有主要政党都强烈谴责这次袭击。

round rob·in /ˌ· ˈ··/ *n* [C] **1** a competition in which every player or team plays against each of the other players or teams 循环赛 **2** a letter expressing opinions or complaints, signed by many people and sent as a form of protest〔由很多人签名的〕圆形签名请愿[抗议]书

round-shoul·dered /ˌ· ˈ··◂/ *adj* having shoulders that are bent forwards or slope downwards 圆肩的, 拱背曲肩的

round-ta·ble /ˌ· ˈ··◂/ *adj* [only before noun 仅用于名词前] a roundtable discussion or meeting is one in which everyone can talk about things in an equal way 圆桌的〔讨论或会议, 指与会者不分主次参与讨论〕

Round Ta·ble, the /ˌ· ˈ··/ **1** the table at which King Arthur and his knights sat, according to old stories. As it was round, all the places at it were equal. 圆桌〔指传说故事中亚瑟王与骑士围坐的那张桌子。桌子呈圆形, 座位不分主次〕**2** a CHARITY organization for men under 40, who hold meetings and do work for their local areas. It is related to the Rotary Club, whose members are usually a little older. 青年圆桌协会〔40岁以下男士参加的一个慈善组织。会员定期举行会议, 为当地社区做慈善工作。该协会与扶轮社有一定关系, 扶轮社的成员通常年龄稍大一些〕

round-the-clock /ˌ· · ˈ·◂/ *adj* [only before noun 仅用于名词前] all the time, both day and night 二十四小时不间断的, 不分昼夜的: *He'll need round-the-clock hospital care.* 他需要不分昼夜的住院照顾。—see also 另见 **round the clock** (CLOCK[1] (6))

round trip /ˌ· ˈ·/ *n* [C] a journey to a place and back again 往返旅程: *The round trip took just over an hour.* 往返旅程需要一个小时多一点。

round-trip /ˌ· ˈ·◂/ *adj AmE* a round-trip ticket includes the journey to a place and back again【美】〔票〕往返的; RETURN[2] (9) *BrE*【英】

round-up /ˈ· ·/ *n* [C] **1** an occasion when people, or animals, of a particular type are all brought together, often using force〔把某类人或动物强行的〕集拢, 聚集: *a round-up of suspected drug-dealers* 搜捕涉嫌毒品贩子 **2** a short description of the main parts of the news, on the radio or on televison〔广播或电视里的〕新闻简报 —see also 另见 **round up** (ROUND[5])

rouse /raʊz; raʊz/ *v* **1** **rouse sb (from their sleep/slumbers)** to wake someone up with difficulty because they are sleeping deeply〔艰难地把某人从熟睡中〕唤醒 **2** [T] to make someone start doing something, especially when they have been too tired or unwilling to do it 激励〔某人做某事, 尤其在他很疲倦或不愿意做时〕; 使振奋: **rouse sb into action** *The commander tried to rouse them all into action.* 指挥官设法激励他们都行动起来。| **rouse yourself** *When Alice finally roused herself, she realized Harold was already home.* 等到艾丽斯终于振作起来的时候, 她才知道哈罗德已经到家了。**3** [T] to make someone feel a particular emotion, such as hope or fear 激起〔希望、恐惧等〕—compare 比较 AROUSE

roused /raʊzd; raʊzd/ *adj* [not before noun 不用于名词前] angry 发怒的: **when roused** *When roused, he could be quite violent.* 一旦被激怒, 他会变得相当粗暴。

rous·ing /ˈraʊzɪŋ; ˈraʊzɪŋ/ *adj* a rousing song, speech etc makes people feel excited and eager to do something〔歌曲、讲演等〕激动人心的; 鼓励人〔行动〕的

Rous·seau /ruˈso; ˈruːsəʊ/**, Henri** /ˈhɛnrɪ; ˈhenri/ (1844-1910) a French artist who painted using bright colours and often had EXOTIC (=unusual and foreign) subjects 卢梭〔(1844-1910), 法国画家。画作色彩鲜艳, 主题常具有异国情调〕

Rous·seau, Jean-Jacques /ʒɑn ʒɑk; ʒɒn ʒæk/ (1712-78) a French writer and PHILOSOPHER, born in Switzerland, whose book *The Social Contract* developed the idea that governments must always work according to the wishes of the people. His work had a great influence on the French Revolution, and he invented the phrase, "Liberty, Equality, Fraternity", which was later used by people who supported the Revolution. He also wrote about the NOBLE SAVAGE. 卢梭〔(1712-1778), 法国作家、哲学家, 生于瑞士。他在《社会契约论》中提出了政府行为必须始终符合人民的意志这一观点, 对法国大革命产生了重大影响。他还首次提出了"自由、平等、博爱"的口号, 后来为支持大革命的人所采用。他还写有以"高尚的野蛮人"为主题的论著〕

roust /raʊst; raʊst/ *v* [T] *AmE* to make someone move from a place【美】撵出, 驱逐: *Go roust the kids, it's time we went.* 去把孩子赶出来, 我们该走了。

rous·ta·bout /ˈraʊstəˌbaʊt; ˈraʊstəbaʊt/ *n* [C] *especially AmE* a man who does work for which he needs to be strong but not skilled, especially in a port, an OILFIELD, or a CIRCUS (1)【尤美】〔尤指在港口、油田或马戏团干重活儿的〕非熟练工, 普通工; 场地工

rout[1] /raʊt; raʊt/ *v* [T] to defeat someone completely in a battle, competition, or election〔在战斗、竞赛或选举中〕击溃, 彻底击败

rout[2] *n* [singular] a complete defeat in a battle, competition or election〔在战斗、竞赛或选举中〕溃败, 彻底失败: **put sb to rout** *literary* (=defeat them completely in a battle)【文】彻底击败某人

route[1] /rut; ruːt/ *n* [C] **1** the way from one place to another, especially a way that is regularly used and can be shown on a map〔尤指经常使用, 可在地图上显示的〕路线: **[+to/from]** *What's the best route to Cambridge?* 到剑桥的最佳路线怎么走? | **take/follow a route** (=use a route) 沿某路线走 *We weren't sure about which route we should take.* 我们拿不准应该走哪条路线。**2** a road, railway, or imaginary line along which vehicles often travel〔交通工具常用的〕路线: *The London-New York route is the busiest.* 伦敦至纽约的航线是最繁忙的。| *Is your office on a bus route?* 你的办公室在公共汽车路线上吗? **3** a way of doing something or achieving a particular result〔做事或达到特定结果的〕途径, 方法: *the surest route to disaster* 必定会引向灾难的途径 | *his route to fame and fortune* 他的成名发财之路 **4** **Route 66, 54 etc** used to show the number of a main road in the US〔美国〕66[54]号等公路: *Take Route 95 through Connecticut.* 走95号公路穿过康涅狄格州。—see also 另见 EN ROUTE, SNOW ROUTE, TRADE ROUTE

route[2] *v* [T] to send something or someone using a particular route 按特定路线发送〔东西或人〕: **[+through/by]** *They had to route the goods through Germany.* 他们必须经由德国运送货物。—see also 另见 RE-ROUTE

Route 66 /ˌrut sɪkstɪ ˈsɪks; ˌruːt sɪksti ˈsɪks/ a famous road in the US that is mentioned in books, films, and songs. It was built in the early 1930s, and was the first road to go a long distance across the US, from Chicago to Los Angeles. 66号公路〔美国一著名公路, 图书、影片和歌曲中都曾提到过。该公路修成于20世纪30年代初期, 从芝加哥延伸至洛杉矶, 是横贯全美的首条公路〕

route march /ˈ· ·/ *n* [C] a long march done by soldiers when they are training〔士兵训练时的〕长途行军

rou·tine[1] /ruˈtin; ruːˈtiːn/ *n* **1** [C,U] the usual or normal way in which you do things 惯例, 常规: *John's departure had upset their daily routine.* 约翰的离去打乱了他们每日的常规。| *Mark longed to escape from the same old familiar routine.* 马克渴望摆脱千篇一律的老套。| **a break in the routine** (=a change from what you normally do) 打破常规 **2** [C] a set of steps learned and practised by a dancer for a public performance〔表演的〕一套固定舞步, 舞蹈动作 **3** [C] *technical* a set of instructions given to a computer so that it will do a particular operation【术语】〔输入电脑的〕程序 —**routinize** /ruˈtinaɪz, ruːˈtiːnaɪz/ *v* [T] *AmE*【美】

rou·tine[2] /ruˈtin; ˌruːˈtiːn◂/ *adj* **1** **routine questions/examination/visit etc** (=usual questions etc that are not concerned with any kind of serious problem) 例行问题/检查/访问等 *It's just a routine medical examination, nothing to get worried about.* 这只是例行的体格检查, 没有什么好担心的。| *a routine visit to*

the dentist 例行看牙医 **2** ordinary and boring 一般的, 平淡的, 乏味的: **routine jobs/tasks** *What's more, routine jobs make people less motivated.* 此外, 枯燥乏味的工作会减少人们的动力。

rou·tine·ly /ruˋtinlı; ruːˈtiːnli/ *adv* if something is routinely done, it is usually done as part of the normal process of working, doing a job etc 惯常地, 例行地

roux /ru; ruː/ *plural* **roux** /ruz; ruːz/ *n* [C,U] a mixture of flour, butter, and milk that is used for making SAUCES〔做调味汁用的〕黄油牛奶面粉糊

rove /rov; rəʊv/ *v* [I] **1** to travel from one place to another 漫游, 流浪: **roving reporter** (=someone who works for a newspaper or television company, and moves from place to place) 流动记者 **2** if someone's eyes rove, they look continuously from one part of something to another 扫视: [+around/over] *Benedict's eyes roved boldly over her sleeping body.* 本尼迪克特的眼睛放肆地扫视着熟睡中的她的身躯。**3** **have a roving eye** *old-fashioned* to be always looking for a chance to have romantic relationships【过时】好色

rov·er /ˋrovɚ; ˈrəʊvə/ *n* [C] *literary* someone who travels around from place to place【文】流浪者, 漂泊者

Rover's Re·turn, the /,‥ ·ˈ·/ the PUB in the British television SOAP OPERA *Coronation Street*, where many of the characters often meet 浪子回头酒馆〔英国电视肥皂剧《加冕街》中的一个小酒馆。剧中人物经常在此聚会〕

row¹ /ro; rəʊ/ *n* [C] **1** a line of things or people next to each other 一排, 一行, 一列: [+of] *a row of houses* 一排房子 | *rows of trees* 成排的树 | *Plant the seedlings in parallel rows.* 把这些秧苗插成平行的几行。| **in a row** (=next to each other) 成一行 *On a long table, place the containers in a row.* 在长桌上把这些容器摆成一排。| *The children were asked to stand in a row.* 孩子们被要求站成一排。| **row upon row** (=many rows) 一排又一排 *row upon row of shelves stacked with books* 一排排堆满书的架子 **2** a line of seats in a theatre or cinema〔剧院或电影院里的〕一排座位: *We sat in the front row.* 我们坐在前排。**3** **three/four etc times in a row** happening a number of times in exactly the same way or with the same result 连续三/四次等: *She won four times in a row.* 她连续四次获胜。**4** **go for a row** to take a short journey in a ROWING BOAT 去划船

row² /rau; raʊ/ *n BrE*【英】**1** [C] an angry argument that lasts a short time, especially between people who know each other well〔尤指互相熟悉的人之间的〕争吵, 吵架: *The news caused a terrible family row.* 这消息使全家人激烈争吵。| **have a row (with sb)** *Those two are always having rows.* 那两个人老是吵架。**2** [C] a situation in which people disagree strongly about important public matters; CONTROVERSY 争辩, 争论: [+about/over] *The Prime Minister is at the centre of a new row over government secrecy.* 在有关政府机密的新争论中, 首相成了中心人物。**3** [singular] a loud unpleasant noise that continues for a long time〔持续时间长的〕喧闹声, 吵嚷声: *Stop that row – I'm trying to get to sleep!* 别吵啦, 我要睡觉了!

row³ /ro; rəʊ/ *v* **1** [I,T] to make a boat move across water using OARS (=long poles that are flat at the end) 划(船): [+away/towards/across] *She rowed across the lake.* 她划船到湖对岸。**2** [I] to be able to make a boat move in this way, or to do this as a sport 划船; 参加划船比赛: *Jenny used to row at college.* 珍妮以前在大学里经常参加划船比赛。

row⁴ /rau; raʊ/ *v* [I+about] *BrE* to argue in an angry way【英】争吵, 吵架

row·an /ˋroən; ˈrəʊən/ *n* [C] a small tree that has bright red berries 花楸树

row·boat /ˋro,bot; ˈrəʊbəʊt/ *n* [C] *AmE* a small boat that you move through the water with OARS (=long poles that are flat at the end)【美】划艇, 用桨划的小船; ROWING BOAT *BrE*【英】

row·dy¹ /ˋraudı; ˈraʊdi/ *adj* behaving in a noisy, rough way that is likely to cause arguments and fighting 吵闹的, 粗暴的: *a rowdy group of soccer fans* 一群粗野的足球迷 —**rowdily** *adv* —**rowdiness** *n* [U]

rowdy² *n* [C, usually plural 一般用复数] *old-fashioned* someone who behaves in a rough noisy way【过时】吵闹的人, 粗野的人

row house /ˋro haus; ˈrəʊ haʊs/ *n* [C] *AmE* a house that is part of a line of houses that are joined to each other【美】排屋〔互相连接的一排房屋之一幢〕; TERRACED HOUSE *BrE*【英】—see picture on page A4 参见 A4 页图

row·ing /ˋroıŋ; ˈrəʊıŋ/ *n* [U] the sport or activity of making a boat move through water with OARS 划船运动

rowing boat /ˋroıŋ bot; ˈrəʊıŋ bəʊt/ *n* [C] *BrE* a small boat that you move through the water with OARS (=long poles that are flat at the end)【英】划艇, 用桨划的小船; ROWBOAT *AmE*【美】

Rowling /raulıŋ; raʊlıŋ/, **J.K. (Joanne)** (1965-) a British writer whose books for children about Harry Potter, a boy MAGICIAN (=person who can use magic), are very successful 罗琳〔(1965-), 英国作家。她创作的有关哈利·波特的系列儿童小说十分成功。哈利·波特是个通晓魔法的男孩〕

row·lock /ˋro,lak; ˈrɒlək; *technical* 术语 ˋro,lak; ˈrəʊlɒk/ *n* [C] *BrE* one of the U-shaped pieces of metal that holds the oars of a rowing boat【英】桨架; OARLOCK *AmE*【美】

roy·al¹ /ˋrɔıəl; ˈrɔıəl/ *adj* [only before noun 仅用于名词前] **1** connected with or belonging to a king or queen 国王的, 女王的, 王室的: *the royal chapel at Versailles* 凡尔赛宫的教堂 —compare 比较 REGAL **2** very impressive, as if done for a king or queen 盛大的, 隆重的: *a royal welcome* 隆重的欢迎 —see also 另见 **right royal** (RIGHT¹ (7)) **3** *informal* used to emphasize how bad something or someone is【非正式】极度的〔用以强调某物或某人的坏处〕: *She's a royal pain in the neck!* 她是个极其讨厌的人! **4** **the royal 'we'** *BrE* the use of the word 'we' instead of 'I', by the Queen or King【英】御用"我们"〔女王或国王自称时使用 we 而不用 I〕—**royally** *adv*

royal² *n* [C] *informal* a member of a royal family【非正式】王室成员

Royal A·cad·e·my /,‥ ·ˈ‥/ also 又作 **the Royal Academy of Arts** **1** an important British society of artists, whose members use the letters RA after their names. It has a school for artists, and it organizes many EXHIBITIONS (=public shows of paintings etc), including its well-known Summer Exhibition, which takes place every year and shows new paintings by British artists, including work by ordinary people who are not professional artists.皇家艺术学会〔英国一重要美术家学会, 会员姓名后面加有字母 RA。该学会拥有一所美术学院, 定期组织展览会, 包括一年一度著名的夏季展览会, 展出英国画家的新作, 其中也有业余画家的作品〕 **2** the building in Piccadilly, central London, where the Royal Academy's exhibitions take place 皇家艺术学会大厦〔位于伦敦市中心的皮卡迪利广场, 皇家艺术学会在此举办美术展览〕

Royal Academy of Mu·sic, the /,‥ ·,‥ ·ˈ·/ an important London music college〔英国〕皇家音乐学院

Royal Air Force /,‥ ·ˈ·/ —see 见 RAF

Royal Al·bert Hall /,‥ ,‥ ˈ·/ —see 见 ALBERT HALL

Royal and An·cient, the /,‥ · ˈ‥/ also 又作 **the R and A** the Royal and Ancient Golf Club of St Andrews; an important old GOLF club based in St Andrews, Scotland, which is responsible for the rules of golf for most countries except the US 皇家古老高尔夫球俱乐部〔苏格兰圣安德鲁斯的一家历史悠久、举足轻重的高尔夫球俱乐部。负责制订除美国以外大部分国家的高尔夫球赛规则〕

Royal As·cot /,‥ ˈ‥/ a four-day horse-racing event at Ascot, England, every June 皇家阿斯科特赛马会〔每年6月在英格兰阿斯科特举行的为期四天的赛马会〕

> **CULTURAL NOTE 文化注释**
>
> Royal Ascot is one of the most important race meetings in Britain and members of the royal family always attend. One of the days is called Ladies' Day and some of the women like to wear unusual and usually big hats. It is popular especially with UPPER-CLASS people. 皇家阿斯科特赛马会是英国最重要的赛马会之一, 而且王室成员也会参加。其中的一天称为"女士日", 一些女性会穿上非同寻常的服装, 通常还戴上大帽子。这个赛马会特别受上层阶级的欢迎。

royal as·sent /,‥ ·ˈ·/ *n* [U] the signing of a law by the British king or queen after it has been decided by Parliament, so that it officially becomes law 御准〔英国国王或女王签署议会通过的法令〕

Royal Bal·let, the /,‥ ·ˈ‥/ the UK's national BALLET company, which includes many dancers of international quality, and has its base at Covent Garden in London 皇家芭蕾舞团〔英国国家芭蕾舞团。该团由许多国际顶级舞蹈演员组成, 总部设在伦敦的科文特加登〕

royal blue /,‥ ˈ·◂/ *n* [U] a strong, bright blue colour 品蓝色, 红光蓝色 —**royal blue** *adj* —see picture on page A5 参见 A5 页图

Royal Brit·ish Le·gion, the /,‥ ,‥ ˈ‥/ —see 见 BRITISH LEGION

Royal Ca·na·di·an Mount·ed Police, the /,‥ ·,‥ ,‥ ·ˈ·/ abbreviation 缩写为 **RCMP** the national police force of Canada, whose officers are called 'Mounties' 加拿大皇家骑警队〔加拿大国家警察部队。骑警被称为 Mountie〕

Royal Col·lege of Art, the/ˌ··ˌ··ˈ·/ abbreviation 缩写为 **the RCA** an important art school in London 皇家艺术学院〔英国伦敦一所颇具影响力的艺术学院〕

Royal College of Mu·sic, the/ˌ··ˌ··ˈ·/ abbreviation 缩写为 **the RCM** a school in London for young musicians who have great ability, and who come from all over the world 皇家音乐学院〔伦敦一所音乐学院。学员为有音乐天赋的青年人,他们来自世界各地〕

Royal College of Nurs·es, the/ˌ··ˌ··ˈ·/ abbreviation 缩写为 **the RCN** an organization that represents nurses in the UK, and provides higher education for them in its institute 皇家护士协会〔英国一护士团体。其附设的学院培养高等护理专业人才〕

royal com·mis·sion/ˌ··ˈ··/ *n* [C] a group of people who make suggestions about a subject that the British government thinks may need new laws 皇家专门调查委员会〔负责就英国政府认为可能需要制定新法律的事项提出建议〕

Royal Court, the/ˌ··ˈ·/ also 又作 **the Royal Court Theatre** a theatre in London which shows mainly serious new plays 皇家宫廷剧院〔伦敦一座剧院,主要上演严肃类新剧〕

Royal En·clos·ure, the/ˌ··ˈ··/ a special area of the Ascot horse-racing track in the south of England, which can only be used by the British royal family and by people who have special tickets 皇家专用看台〔英格兰南部皇家阿斯科特赛马会赛道旁的特别席位区,仅供英国王室成员和持有贵宾入场券的人士使用〕

Royal Fes·ti·val Hall/ˌ··ˌ···ˈ·/ —see 见 the FESTIVAL HALL

royal flush/ˌ··ˈ·/ *n* [C usually singular 一般用单数] a set of cards that someone has in a card game, which are the five most important cards in a SUIT (=one of the four different types of card) (纸牌游戏中的)同花大顺

Royal Green Jackets, the/ˌ··ˈ·ˌ·/ also 又作 **the Green Jackets** a REGIMENT (=a large division of men) in the British army 皇家绿衣军〔英国军队一个军团〕

Royal Green·wich Ob·ser·va·to·ry, the/ˌ··ˌ···ˈ····/ the British national OBSERVATORY (=a place where scientists study the stars), which was established in the 17th century, in Greenwich, South London, although it was moved away from there after World War II and it is now in Cambridge. The 0° MERIDIAN (=an imaginary line that divides the east part of the world from the west) passes through the building in Greenwich. 皇家格林尼治天文台〔英国国家天文台,17 世纪建于南伦敦的格林尼治,二战后迁至剑桥。本初子午线从天文台位于格林尼治的旧址经过〕—see also 另见 GREENWICH MEAN TIME

Royal High·ness/ˌ··ˈ··/ *n* [C] **your/his/her royal Highness** used when speaking about or to a royal person, especially a prince or princess 殿下〔用于间接提及或当面称呼王室成员,尤指王子或公主〕

Royal Horse Guards, the/ˌ··ˈ·ˌ·/ also 又作 **The Blues** a former REGIMENT (=large division of men) of the British army, called The Blues because of their blue uniform, which joined with the Royal Dragoons in 1969 to form the Blues and Royals 皇家骑兵卫队〔原为英国陆军一个军团。因身穿蓝色制服,故又称"蓝色军团"。1969 年与皇家龙骑兵团合并组成皇家禁卫骑兵团〕

roy·al·ist/ˈrɔɪəlɪst; ˈrɔɪəlɪst/ *n* [C] someone who supports a king or queen, or believes that a country should be ruled by kings or queens 君主主义者, 保皇主义者 —**royalist** *adj*

Royal Mail, the/ˌ··ˈ·/ the part of the British Post Office that deals with the collection and delivery of letters 皇家邮政〔隶属英国邮政总局,主要负责信件收发业务〕

Royal Ma·rines, the/ˌ··ˈ·/ a British military group whose members are trained to fight both on land and at sea. There is a similar force in the US called the Marine Corps. 皇家海军陆战队〔英国一海陆两栖作战部队。美国也有一类似部队,称作 Marine Corps (海军陆战队)〕

Royal Mile, the/ˌ··ˈ·/ a line of old streets in Edinburgh which runs from the Castle to Holyrood Palace 皇家英里街〔英国爱丁堡市几条老街的总称,从古城堡延伸至霍利鲁德宫〕

Royal Mil·i·ta·ry A·cad·e·my, the/ˌ··ˌ····ˈ····/ —see 见 SANDHURST

Royal Mint, the/ˌ··ˈ·/ **1** a British government department which is responsible for producing paper money and coins 皇家铸币局〔英国一政府部门,负责印制纸币和铸造硬币〕 **2** the building where this work is done 皇家铸币厂

Royal Na·tion·al Thea·tre, the/ˌ··ˌ···ˈ··/ the official name of the National Theatre in London 皇家国立剧院〔伦敦国家剧院的正式名称〕

Royal Na·val Col·lege, the/ˌ··ˈ··ˌ··/ a training college at Dartmouth, southwest England, where young people in the Royal Navy learn to be officers 皇家海军学院〔位于英格兰西南部达特茅斯,专为英国皇家海军培训青年军官〕

Royal Na·vy, the/ˌ··ˈ··/ the part of the UK's military groups that operates at sea in ships and SUBMARINES 皇家海军〔英国军种之一,驾驶军舰和潜艇在海上作业〕

Royal Op·e·ra House, the/ˌ··ˈ···/ a theatre in Covent Garden in London where the members of the Royal Opera and the Royal Ballet are based, which is often simply called Covent Garden. 皇家歌剧院〔伦敦科文特加登一剧院,为皇家歌剧院和皇家芭蕾舞团所在地。该剧院常简称为"科文特加登"〕

> **CULTURAL NOTE 文化注释**
>
> The Royal Opera House is the most important opera house in the UK, and many of the greatest opera singers in the world come to perform there. It is sometimes criticized for being ELITIST (=only intended for a small part of the population who have special advantages) and the cost of tickets is known to be very high. It received a lot of money from the National Lottery to help with its programme of rebuilding. Some people believed this was an unsuitable use of Lottery money. 皇家歌剧院是英国最重要的歌剧院,有很多世界最著名的歌剧演唱家在此献唱。也有不少批评声音说它太过精英化,而且票价高昂。皇家歌剧院的重建计划接受了国家彩票的很多钱,不少人认为这是彩票资金的非正当使用。

Royal Pa·vil·ion, the/ˌ··ˈ···/ a building in an original and unusual ORIENTAL style built in Brighton, southern England, in 1817 for the Prince of Wales, who later became George IV 皇家亭阁〔一幢具有东方风格的独特建筑,位于英格兰南部布里奇顿。1817 年,为威尔士亲王即后来的乔治四世而建〕

Royal Phil·har·mon·ic Or·ches·tra, the/ˌ···ˈ·····/ also 又作 **the Royal Philharmonic, the RPO** a leading British ORCHESTRA, based in London 皇家爱乐乐团〔英国最重要的管弦乐团,总部设在伦敦〕

royal pre·rog·a·tive/ˌ··ˈ···/ *n* [singular,U] the special rights that a king or queen has 国王[女王]的特权

Royal Shakes·peare Com·pa·ny, the/ˌ··ˈ··ˌ··/ abbreviation 缩写为 **the RSC** a British theatre company that performs plays by Shakespeare and other writers. It performs mainly in the Barbican (in London) and in Stratford-upon-Avon. 皇家莎士比亚剧团〔英国一剧团,专门上演莎士比亚等剧作家的作品。演出活动主要集中在伦敦巴比肯文化中心和埃文河畔的斯特拉特福〕

Royal So·ci·e·ty, the/ˌ··ˈ···/ the oldest and most respected scientific society in the UK, started in the 17th century. Its members are called 'Fellows' and they are elected if they have done high-quality work in any area of science. There is a similar society for people working in the humanities (HUMMANITY=subjects such as language, literature, and history), called the British Academy. 皇家学会〔英国历史最悠久、最有名望的科学团体,成立于 17 世纪。其会员称作"研究员",从已取得高品质科研成果的人士当中选拔产生。英国还有一类似学会,由人文学科的专业人士组成,名为"英国学会"或"不列颠学会"〕

Royal Tour·na·ment, the/ˌ··ˈ···/ a yearly public show produced by the British army, air force, and navy in which they show their skills with displays of GYMNASTICS etc 皇家军队表演〔英国皇家陆、海、空三军一年一度的技能和技艺大汇演〕

roy·al·ty/ˈrɔɪəltɪ; ˈrɔɪəlti/ *n* **1** [U] members of a royal family 王室[皇族]成员 **2 royalties** [plural] payments made to the writer of a book or piece of music〔付给作家、作曲家的〕版税

Royal Ul·ster Con·stab·u·la·ry, the/ˌ··ˌ··ˈ·····/ *n* the RUC

Roy Ro·gers/ˌrɔɪ ˈrɑdʒəz; ˌrɔɪ ˈrɒdʒəz/ a drink for children in the US, made from LEMONADE and GRENADINE (=a sweet red liquid), and served with a CHERRY. Roy Rogers are usually served in restaurants, and they are sometimes called Shirley Temples if they are served to girls. 罗伊·罗杰斯饮料〔美国一款儿童饮料,由柠檬和石榴糖浆调制而成,并用一粒樱桃作点缀。饭店经常出售这种饮料,卖给女孩子的话,有时称"秀兰·邓波儿"〕

RP/ˌɑr ˈpi; ˌɑː ˈpiː/ *n* [U] Received Pronunciation; the form of British pronunciation that many educated people in Britain use, and that is thought of as the standard form 英语标准发音〔在英国,很多接受过教育的人使用的英语发音形式,被视为发音的标准〕

CULTURAL NOTE 文化注释

RP is used by MIDDLE-CLASS and UPPER-CLASS people from all over the UK, especially in the south of England, and it is the form of pronunciation shown in British dictionaries. RP was traditionally the ACCENT that was most respected, and it was also the accent used by most people on radio and television, especially people who read the news or WEATHER FORECAST and people who introduced programmes. For this reason it is sometimes called 'BBC English'. However, it is no longer regarded as the only 'correct' form of British pronunciation, and many other accents can be heard on British radio and television. 英语标准发音是全英国，特别是英国南部的中产阶级和上层阶级的发音，同时它也是英国词典中标注的发音。标准发音传统上最受人推崇，它也是广播电视上大多数人所操的发音，特别是新闻播报员、天气预报员和节目预告员的发音。因为这个缘故，标准发音有时也被称为"英国广播公司英语"。然而，标准发音现在已经不再被视为唯一"正确的"英国发音，其他口音也可以在英国的广播电视中听到。—see Cultural Note at ACCENT 见 ACCENT 文化注释

rpm /ˌɑr pi ˋɛm; ˌɑː piː ˈem/ revolutions per minute; a measurement of the speed at which an engine or RECORD PLAYER turns〔发动机或唱机的〕每分钟转数，转/分

RPO, the /ˌɑ pi ˋo; ˌɑː piː ˈəʊ/ the abbreviation of 缩写= the ROYAL PHILHARMONIC ORCHESTRA

RR /ˌɑr ˋɑr; ˌɑːr ˈɑː/ rural route; used in addresses in country areas of the US, to show which mail delivery area a letter should go to 乡村投递路线〔在美国乡村地区的通信地址中使用〕

RSA, the /ˌɑr ɛs ˋe; ˌɑːr es ˈeɪ/ the Royal Society of Arts; a British organization that encourages education in arts (=languages, history, literature etc) subjects and for business. It organizes examinations in many different subjects, including English as a Foreign Language. 皇家人文协会〔英国促进文科和商科教育的一个组织。该机构经常组织人文学科的考试，其中包括以英语作为外语的考试〕

RSC, the /ˌɑr ɛs ˋsi; ˌɑːr es ˈsiː/ the abbreviation of 缩写= the ROYAL SHAKESPEARE COMPANY

RSI /ˌɑr ɛs ˋaɪ; ˌɑːr es ˈaɪ/ *n* [U] repetitive strain injury; pain in your hands, arms etc caused by doing the same movements very many times, especially when typing (TYPE[2] (2)) 重复性劳损〔手掌、手臂等重复做相同动作，尤其是打字，而引致的疼痛〕

RSPB, the /ˌɑr ɛs pi ˋbi; ˌɑːr es piː ˈbiː/ the Royal Society for the Protection of Birds; a British CHARITY organization which looks after wild birds, and educates the public about them. There is a similar organization in the US called the Audubon Society. 皇家鸟类保护协会〔英国一慈善机构，旨在保护野生鸟类，普及鸟类知识。美国也有一类似机构，名为"奥杜邦协会"〕

RSPCA, the /ˌɑː ɛs pi si ˋe; ˌɑːr es piː siː ˈeɪ/ the Royal Society for the Prevention of Cruelty to Animals; a British CHARITY organization which aims to protect animals from cruel treatment, and can bring a legal case to court if someone is cruel to an animal. The RSPCA looks after animals with no homes, and sells them to people who want them. There is a similar organization in the US called the ASPCA. 皇家防止虐待动物协会〔英国一慈善机构，旨在防止虐待动物的行为，并会把施虐者告上法庭。该机构还照管无家可归的动物，或把它们卖给想养动物的人家。美国也有一类似机构，名为 ASPCA（美国防止虐待动物协会）〕

RSV /ˌɑr ɛs ˋvi; ˌɑːr es ˈviː/ the abbreviation of 缩写= REVISED STANDARD VERSION

RSVP /ˌɑr ɛs vi ˋpi; ˌɑːr es viː ˈpiː/ *French* used on invitations to ask someone to reply【法】敬请赐复〔请柬用语〕

Rt Hon the written abbreviation of 缩写= RIGHT HONOURABLE

3 **rub**[1] /rʌb; rʌb/ **rubbed, rubbing** *v* **1** [I,T] to move your hand, a cloth etc over a surface while pressing against it 擦，磨擦：*Kolchinsky nodded and then rubbed his eyes wearily.* 科尔琴斯基点了点头，然后疲倦地揉了揉眼睛。| *She began rubbing her hair with a towel.* 她开始用毛巾擦头发。| *You'll have to rub harder if you want to get it clean.* 如果想使它干净，你就要更用劲地擦。—see picture on page A20 参见 A20 页图 **2** [T] to make something press against something else and move it around 使…相互磨擦，揉搓：**rub sth against/on** *Celia's cat purred loudly, rubbing against her legs.* 西莉亚的猫咕噜咕噜地大声叫着，在她的腿上蹭来蹭去。| **rub sth together** *We tried to make a fire by rubbing two pieces of wood together.* 我们尝试用两块木头相互磨擦来生火。**3** [I] to move around while pressing against another surface, often causing pain, damage etc〔在另一表面上〕磨擦引致疼痛，磨损：[+**against/on**] *These shoes are too tight – they keep rubbing on my heels.* 这双鞋子太紧，老是磨我的脚跟。**4** [T always+adv/prep] to put a substance into or onto the surface of something by pressing it and moving it about with your hand, a cloth etc 把…涂擦在表面；〔揉搓〕使渗入，搽：**rub sth on/into/over/etc** *Can you rub some sun cream on my back for me, please?* 请给我的背上涂些防晒霜好吗？**5 rub it in** *informal* to remind someone about something they want to forget, especially because they are embarrassed about it【非正式】提起某人的痛处：*Look, I know I should have been more careful, but there's no need to keep rubbing it in.* 听我说，我知道我本应该更小心一点儿，但也没有必要老提那件事。**6 rub shoulders with** *informal* to spend time with rich or famous people【非正式】与〔富人、名人〕交往：*As a reporter he gets to rub shoulders with all the big names in politics and the media.* 作为记者，他有机会与政界和媒体的大人物打交道。**7 rub salt into the wound** *informal* to make a bad situation even worse for someone【非正式】加深伤害[痛楚] **8 rub sb's nose in it/in the dirt** *informal* to keep reminding someone about something they did wrong or failed to do, especially in order to punish them【非正式】不断提起某人以前的过失；揭某人的疮疤〔尤指为惩罚某人〕**9 rub sb up the wrong way** *informal* to annoy someone by the way you behave towards them【非正式】惹恼某人，触犯某人：*I don't know what it is about Paula, but she really rubs me up the wrong way.* 我不清楚葆拉是怎么回事，但她的确惹得我很不高兴。**10 be rubbing your hands** *informal* to be pleased because something has happened which gives you an advantage, especially because something bad has happened to someone else【非正式】〔某事发生带给你好处而〕高兴得两手搓来搓去〔尤因坏事发生在他人身上〕**11 not have two pennies/halfpennies to rub together** *BrE humorous* to not have any money【英，幽默】身无分文

rub along *phr v* [I+**with/together**] *BrE* to have a friendly relationship with someone【英】与…保持友好关系

rub down *phr v* [T] **1** [**rub** sth ↔ **down**] to make a surface dry or smooth by rubbing it with a cloth or SANDPAPER〔用布〕把〔表面〕擦干；〔用砂纸〕把〔表面〕擦平滑 **2** [**rub** sb **down**] **a)** to MASSAGE (=rub their muscles) someone, especially after hard exercise 按摩〔尤在剧烈运动后〕**b)** [**rub** sb/sth **down**] to dry a person or animal by rubbing them with a cloth, TOWEL etc〔用布、毛巾等〕擦干〔人或动物〕全身 —see also 另见 RUBDOWN

rub off *phr v* [**rub** (sth ↔) **off**] **1** [I,T] to remove something from a surface by rubbing it, or to come off a surface because of being rubbed 擦掉，磨去：*Be careful not to rub off the paint.* 小心，别把油漆擦掉。**2** [I] if a feeling, quality, or habit rubs off on someone, they start to have it because they are with another person who has it〔感情、特质、习惯等〕影响〔某人〕：[+**on**] *His enthusiasm shines through and seems to rub off on everyone else.* 他热情洋溢，似乎感染了每一个人。

rub sb/sth **out** *phr v* [T] **1** *BrE* to remove writing, a picture etc from a surface by rubbing it with a piece of rubber, a cloth etc【英】〔用橡皮、布等〕把〔字迹、图等〕擦掉；ERASE (2) *especially AmE*【尤美】：*You might as well rub the whole thing out and start over.* 你不妨把所有东西都擦掉重新开始。**2** *AmE old-fashioned* to murder someone【美，过时】杀掉〔某人〕

rub[2] *n* **1 give sb/sth a rub** to rub something or MASSAGE[2] (1) someone for a short time〔短时间〕擦某个东西；给某人按摩：*Give the table a good rub with a damp cloth.* 用湿布好好擦一擦桌子。**2 there's/here's the rub** used when saying that a particular problem is the reason why a situation is so difficult 困难就在那儿/这儿

rub·ber /ˋrʌbɚ; ˈrʌbə/ *n*

1 ▶MATERIAL 材料◀ [U] a substance used to make tyres, gloves, boots etc, which is made from the juice of a tropical tree or artificially 橡胶；合成橡胶：*a rubber ball* 橡皮球

2 ▶FOR REMOVING MARKS 用于擦去痕迹◀ *BrE*【英】**a)** a thing you use for removing pencil marks; ERASER 橡皮 **b)** a thing you use for cleaning marks from a BLACKBOARD; ERASER 黑板擦

3 ▶SEX 性◀ [C] *AmE informal* a CONDOM【美，非正式】避孕套

4 ▶SHOE 鞋◀ [C usually plural 一般用复数] *AmE old-fashioned* a rubber shoe that you wear over an ordinary shoe when it rains or snows【美，过时】雨[雪]天用的橡胶鞋套；GALOSH *BrE*【英】

5 ▶SERIES OF GAMES 连续的比赛◀ [C] a series of games of BRIDGE (=a card game) or CRICKET (2)〔桥牌或板球的〕一盘〔规定先胜多少局才赢得一盘〕

6 ▶FOR STANDING ON/IN 供站立用◀ [C] the piece of white rubber where the PITCHER (=person who throws the ball) stands in a BASEBALL game〔棒球比赛中的〕投手板

rubber band /ˌ‥ ˈ‥/ *n* [C] a thin circular piece of rubber used for fastening things together 橡皮筋，橡皮圈；ELASTIC BAND *BrE*【英】

rubber boot /ˈ· · ˌ/ *n* [C] a tall boot made of rubber that keeps your feet and the lower part of your legs dry 防水橡胶靴, 长统橡胶雨靴; WELLINGTON *BrE*【英】—see picture at 参见 BOOT[1] 图

rubber bul·let /ˌ· · ˈ· ·/ *n* [C] a bullet made of rubber that is not intended to seriously hurt or kill people, but is used to control violent crowds 橡胶子弹

rubber check /ˌ· · ˈ·/ *n* [C] *AmE informal* a cheque that the bank refuses to accept because the person who wrote it does not have enough money【美, 非正式】空头支票

rubber din·ghy /ˌ· · ˈ· ·/ *n* [C] a small rubber boat that is filled with air 橡皮艇, 橡皮船

rub·ber·neck /ˈrʌbɚˌnɛk; ˈrʌbənek/ *v* [I] *informal especially AmE* to look around at something, especially something such as an accident while you are driving past【非正式, 尤美】〔尤指开车经过发生意外事故等地方时〕回头看热闹: *tourists rubbernecking at the White House* 在白宫东张西望的游客 —**rubbernecker** *n* [C]

rubber plant /ˈ· · ˌ/ *n* [C] a plant with large, shiny, dark green leaves that is often grown indoors 橡胶植物〔一种室内生长的植物, 叶子大、深绿而有光泽〕

rubber stamp /ˌ· · ˈ·/ *n* [C] a small piece of rubber with a handle, used for printing dates or names on paper 橡皮图章

rubber-stamp /ˌ· · ˈ·/ *v* [T] to give official approval to something without really thinking about it 不加思考就照例批准: *Democrats in Congress refused to rubber-stamp the Reagan program.* 国会的民主党议员拒绝例行公事式地批准里根的计划。

rub·ber·y /ˈrʌbərɪ; ˈrʌbəri/ *adj* **1** looking or feeling like rubber 橡皮似的: *The meat was rather rubbery.* 这肉太老了。**2** if your legs or knees are rubbery, they feel weak or unsteady〔腿或膝〕软[不稳]的

rub·bing /ˈrʌbɪŋ; ˈrʌbɪŋ/ *n* [C] a copy of a shape or pattern made by rubbing wax, CHALK etc onto a piece of paper laid over it〔用蜡、粉笔等的〕拓印: *a brass rubbing* 铜像拓印

rubbing al·co·hol /ˈ· · ˌ· · ·/ *n* [U] *AmE* a type of alcohol used for cleaning wounds or skin【美】消毒用酒精; SURGICAL SPIRIT *BrE*【英】

S3 **rub·bish**[1] /ˈrʌbɪʃ; ˈrʌbɪʃ/ *n* [U] *especially BrE*【尤英】**1** food, paper etc that is no longer needed and has been thrown away 垃圾, 废弃物; GARBAGE (1) *AmE*【美】: *The dustmen collect the rubbish on Thursdays.* 垃圾工每星期四收垃圾。**2** *informal* objects, papers etc that you no longer use and should throw away【非正式】没用的东西, 该扔掉的东西: *I must clear some of the rubbish from my desk.* 我必须把桌上一些没用的东西清理掉。**3** *informal* an idea, statement etc that is rubbish is silly or wrong and does not deserve serious attention; nonsense【非正式】胡说八道, 废话: *Oh, don't talk such rubbish!* 噢, 别说这种废话! | **a load of (old) rubbish** *I reckon all this stuff about reincarnation is a load of rubbish.* 我认为关于转世投胎的种种说法都是无稽之谈。| **rubbish!** *spoken* (=used to tell someone that what they have just said is completely wrong)【口】胡说八道!〔指对方说的话完全错误〕**4** *informal* a film, book etc that is rubbish is very bad【非正式】水平低劣的/粗制滥造的电影[书等]: *the usual Hollywood rubbish* 好莱坞惯常的低劣电影

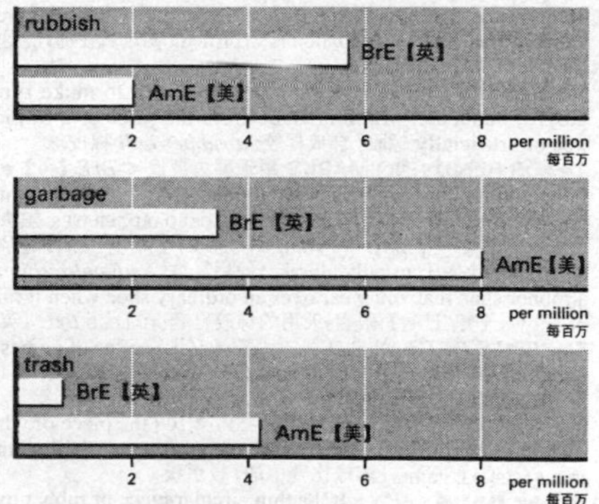

In British English **rubbish** is commonly used to mean something that is no longer needed and has been thrown away, or something that is very bad in quality or does not deserve serious attention. In American English **garbage** and **trash** are commonly used for these meanings. **Trash** is only used in British English to mean something, especially a book, film etc that is of very bad quality. 在英国英语中, rubbish 经常用来指不再需要而被扔掉的垃圾, 或品质极差、无须重视的东西。在美国英语中则常用 garbage 和 trash 来表示这些意思。英国英语中的 trash 只用来指品质很差的东西, 尤指书、电影等。

rubbish[2] *v* [T] *BrE* to say something is bad or useless【英】把〔某物〕说得一无是处

rubbish[3] *adj BrE informal* not skilful at a particular activity【英, 非正式】技术差劲的: *They're a rubbish football team.* 他们是一支末流的足球队。

rub·bish·y /ˈrʌbɪʃɪ; ˈrʌbɪʃi/ *adj BrE informal* silly or of a very low quality; TRASHY【英, 非正式】愚蠢的, 低劣的, 毫无价值的: *rubbishy magazines* 垃圾杂志

rub·ble /ˈrʌbl; ˈrʌbəl/ *n* [U] broken stones or bricks from a building or wall that has been destroyed〔被毁的建筑物或墙壁的〕碎石, 碎砖, 瓦砾

rub·down /ˈrʌbˌdaun; ˈrʌbdaʊn/ *n* [C] **1** *especially AmE* if you give someone a rubdown, you rub their body to make them relaxed, especially after exercise; MASSAGE[1]【尤美】〔尤指运动后的〕按摩 **2** if you give a surface a rubdown, you rub it to make it smooth or clean〔表面的〕磨平滑; 擦干净 —see also 另见 **rub down** (RUB[1])

rube /rub; ruːb/ *n* [C] *AmE slang* someone, usually from the country, who has no experience of other places and thinks in a simple way【美俚】乡巴佬, 土包子

Rube Gold·berg /ˌrub ˋgoldbɚg; ˌruːb ˈgəʊldbɜːg/ *adj AmE* a Rube Goldberg machine etc is very complicated and impractical, in an amusing way【美】〔机器等〕复杂却可笑而不实用的; HEATH ROBINSON *BrE*【英】

ru·bel·la /ruˋbɛlə; ruːˈbelə/ *n* [U] *technical* an infectious disease that causes red spots on your body, and can damage an unborn child; GERMAN MEASLES【术语】风疹; 德国麻疹

Ru·bens /ˈrubənz; ˈruːbɪnz/**, Peter Paul** (1577-1640) a Flemish artist, one of the greatest European painters, who produced several thousand paintings, especially based on religious subjects and scenes from ancient Greek and Roman stories. The women in his paintings usually have attractively large, rather fat bodies, and a woman who looks like this is sometimes called Rubenesque or is compared to a Rubens painting. 鲁本斯〔(1577-1640), 佛兰德斯画家, 也是欧洲最伟大的画家之一。他一生创作了数千幅作品, 主要取材于宗教和古希腊、古罗马的神话场景。他笔下的女性通常体态丰盈, 十分迷人。此类身材的女性有时被称为鲁本斯风格的女性, 或然可与鲁本斯的画作相提并论〕

Ru·bi·con /ˈrubɪˌkɑn; ˈruːbɪkən/ *n* **cross the Rubicon** to do something that will have extremely important effects in the future and that you cannot change 破釜沉舟; 采取断然行动

ru·bi·cund /ˈrubəˌkʌnd; ˈruːbɪkənd/ *adj literary* someone who is rubicund is fat and has a red face【文】〔人〕肥胖而面色红润的

ru·ble /ˈrubl; ˈruːbəl/ *n* [C] another spelling of ROUBLE rouble 的另一种拼法

ru·bric /ˈrubrɪk; ˈruːbrɪk/ *n* [C] *formal* a set of instructions or an explanation in a book, examination paper etc【正式】〔书、考卷等中的〕指示, 说明

ru·by /ˈrubɪ; ˈruːbi/ *n* **1** [C] a red jewel 红宝石 **2** [U] the colour of this jewel 红宝石色, 深红色

Ruby, Jack (1911-67) the man who killed Lee Harvey Oswald two days after Oswald was charged with killing President John F. Kennedy. Some people believed that these actions were part of a CONSPIRACY (=secret plan) to kill the President, and that Ruby shot Oswald to prevent him from giving any information about it. 鲁比〔(1911-1967), 杀死李·哈威·奥斯瓦德的凶手。奥斯瓦德刺杀了约翰·F.肯尼迪总统, 在被起诉的两天后遭到杀害的。有些人认为, 这些行动是刺杀总统阴谋的组成部分, 鲁比枪击奥斯瓦德是为了杀人灭口〕

RUC, the /ˌɑ ju ˋsi; ˌɑː juː ˈsiː/ the Royal Ulster CONSTABULARY; the former name of the Police Service of Northern Ireland 北爱尔兰皇家警察部队的旧称

ruck[1] /rʌk; rʌk/ *n* [C] **1** **the ruck** ordinary events or people, which seem rather boring compared to the lives of rich or famous people 普通的事件[人]〔与富人或名人比较〕: *She dreamed of getting out of the ruck and becoming a famous singer.* 她梦

想出人头地，成为著名的歌星。**2** a group of RUGBY players trying to get the ball when it is lying on the ground〔橄榄球赛中的〕逼攻争球的一群球员

ruck² *v*

ruck (sth) ↔ **up** *phr v* [I,T] if a piece of cloth rucks up, or if you ruck it up, it forms folds in an untidy way (使)〔布〕起皱，起褶: *Your coat's all rucked up at the back.* 你的外套后背全起皱了。

ruck·sack /ˈrʌkˌsæk; ˈrʌksæk/ *n* [C] *especially BrE* a bag used for carrying things on your back, especially by people on long walks; BACKPACK[1]【尤英】〔尤指长途步行用的〕背包，背囊

ruck·us /ˈrʌkəs; ˈrʌkəs/ *n* [singular] *informal especially AmE* a noisy argument or confused situation; RUMPUS【非正式，尤美】高声争吵，喧闹，骚乱: *drunken fraternity boys raising a ruckus at 3 in the morning* 喝醉酒的大学生联谊会的小伙子在凌晨3点大吵大闹

ruc·tions /ˈrʌkʃənz; ˈrʌkʃənz/ *n* [plural] *informal especially BrE* complaints and comments because many people are annoyed about a situation【非正式，尤英】大吵大闹

rud·der /ˈrʌdɚ; ˈrʌdə/ *n* [C] a flat part at the back of a ship or aircraft that can be turned in order to control the direction in which it moves〔船或飞机的〕方向舵 —see picture at 参见 YACHT 图

rud·der·less /ˈrʌdɚlɪs; ˈrʌdələs/ *adj* without a leader who can make decisions 无人领导的: *a company left rudderless by the resignation of its CEO* 因首席执行官辞职而处于无人领导状态的公司

rud·dy /ˈrʌdɪ; ˈrʌdi/ *adj* **1** a ruddy face looks pink and healthy〔脸色〕红润的，健康的: *ruddy cheeks* 红润的面颊 **2** a word used instead of BLOODY when saying strongly that you are annoyed with someone or something 可恶的，讨厌的，该死的，十足的〔用于代替 bloody，加强语气，表示愤怒〕: *I wish that ruddy dog would stop barking!* 我希望那只该死的狗不要再吠了! **3** *literary* red【文】红色的: *The fire cast a ruddy glow over the room.* 火把房间映得通红。—**ruddiness** *n* [U] —**ruddy** *adv*

rude /rud; ruːd/ *adj* **1** speaking or behaving in a way that is not polite and is likely to offend or annoy people〔说话或行为〕不礼貌的，粗鲁的，讨厌的: *Don't be so rude to your father!* 不要对你爸爸这么没礼貌! | *a rude remark* 粗鲁的话 | *I didn't mean to be rude, but I had to leave early.* 我并不想不讲礼貌，但我必须早走。| **it is rude to do sth** *It's rude to stare.* 盯着人看是不礼貌的。**2** rude jokes, words, songs etc are about sex〔玩笑、话语、歌曲等〕粗俗的，下流的 **3 a rude awakening** a situation in which you suddenly realize something unpleasant 突然察觉〔不愉快的事〕 **4 in rude health** *BrE* very healthy【英】十分健壮的 **5** *literary* made in a simple, basic way【文】简单的，粗制的: *a rude wooden hut* 简陋的小木屋 —**rudely** *adv* —**rudeness** *n* [U]

ru·di·men·ta·ry /ˌrudəˋmɛntərɪ; ˌruːdʒˈmentəri◂/ *adj* **1** a rudimentary knowledge or understanding of a subject is very simple and basic〔对某学科的知识或理解〕基本的，初步的，粗浅的: *a rudimentary knowledge of Japanese* 略懂日语 **2** rudimentary equipment, methods, systems etc are very basic and not advanced〔设备、方法、系统等〕简陋的，不先进的: *The classroom equipment is pretty rudimentary.* 教室里的设备相当简陋。**3 a rudimentary tail/wing/eye** a part of an animal that has only developed into a very simple form 雏形的尾巴/翅膀/眼睛

ru·di·ments /ˈrudəmənts; ˈruːdʒmənts/ *n* [plural] *formal* the most basic parts of a subject, which you learn first【正式】〔某学科的〕基础(部分)，入门: **[+of]** *the rudiments of tennis* 网球入门

Ru·dolph, the Red-nosed Rein·deer /ˌrudɑlf ðə ˌrɛd nozd ˋrendɪr; ˌruːdɒlf ðə ˌred nəʊzd ˈreɪndɪə/ a character in a children's Christmas song. Rudolph is a REINDEER (=a large grass-eating wild animal with large horns) who has a shiny red nose. The other reindeer think his nose looks silly, but Santa Claus asks him to help the other reindeer to pull his SLEIGH on a FOGGY night, because his bright nose helps them to see where they are going. 红鼻驯鹿鲁道夫〔儿童圣诞歌曲中的一个角色。鲁道夫是一头驯鹿，长着一只光亮的红鼻子。别的驯鹿都觉得它的鼻子看上去挺可笑，但圣诞老人却让它帮着其他驯鹿在大雾弥漫的夜晚拉雪橇，因为它那光亮的鼻子可给大家指路〕

rue /ru; ruː/ *v* [T] *literary* to wish that you had not done something; REGRET[1] (1)【文】后悔，遗憾: **rue the day (that)** *She learned to rue the day she had met Henri.* 不快的经历使她后悔认识亨利。

rue·ful /ˈrufəl; ˈruːfəl/ *adj* feeling or showing that you wish you had not done something 后悔的，悔恨的: *a rueful smile* 悔恨的苦笑 —**ruefully** *adv*

ruff /rʌf; rʌf/ *n* [C] **1** a stiff circular white collar, worn in Europe in the 16th century〔16世纪欧洲人服饰的〕白色轮状硬领 **2** a circle of feathers or fur around the neck of an animal or bird〔野兽的〕颈毛;〔鸟的〕颈羽

ruf·fi·an /ˈrʌfɪən; ˈrʌfiən/ *n* [C] *old-fashioned* a violent man, involved in crime【过时】流氓，暴徒: *a gang of ruffians* 一伙流氓 —**ruffianly** *adj*

ruf·fle¹ /ˈrʌfl; ˈrʌfəl/ *v* [T] **1** also 又作 **ruffle up** to make a smooth surface uneven 把〔平整的表面〕弄乱，弄皱，使起伏不平: *Birds ruffle up their feathers for warmth.* 鸟把羽毛竖起来保暖。**2** to offend or upset someone slightly 使稍微生气，使有点不快: **ruffle sb's feelings/pride etc** *Louise's sharp comments had ruffled his pride.* 路易斯的尖锐评论打击了他的自尊心。| **get ruffled** *Some of the audience were shouting, and the speaker began to get ruffled.* 一些观众在大喊大叫，演讲者开始有点生气了。| **ruffle sb's feathers** (=upset or annoy someone slightly) 使某人稍微不高兴，惹恼

ruffle² *n* [C] a band of thin cloth sewn in folds as a decoration around the edge of something such as a collar〔衣领等的〕褶边，饰边；褶饰

rug /rʌg; rʌg/ *n* [C] **1** a piece of thick cloth or wool that is smaller than a CARPET and is put on the floor as decoration 小地毯 —compare 比较 MAT[1] **2** *BrE* a large piece of material that you can wrap around yourself, especially when you are travelling【英】〔尤指旅行用的〕大毛毯 **3 pull the rug (out) from under sb's feet** *informal* to suddenly take away something that someone was depending on to achieve what they wanted【非正式】突然停止对某人的支持 **4** *humorous especially AmE* a TOUPÉE【幽默，尤美】(男用的)假发

R

Rug·by /ˈrʌgbɪ; ˈrʌgbi/ a town in central England best known for the PUBLIC SCHOOL (=expensive private school) there called Rugby School, where the game of RUGBY was first played 拉格比〔英格兰中部一城镇，以拉格比公学最为闻名。该校也是最早开展英式橄榄球运动的地方〕

rugby (英式) 橄榄球

rugby also 又作 **rugby foot·ball** /ˌ.. ˈ.. / *n* [U] a type of football played with an OVAL (=egg-shaped) ball that you can catch and carry in your hands (英式) 橄榄球 S3 W3

CULTURAL NOTE 文化注释

There are two forms of rugby: Rugby Union and Rugby League. (英式) 橄榄球运动共分两种: 橄榄球联盟运动和橄榄球联合会运动。

Rugby Union Rugby Union used to be played only by AMATEURS (=people who are not paid), but in 1995 the rules were changed to allow players to be paid, and the most successful clubs formed a professional LEAGUE (=a group of clubs that play against each other). There are 15 players in each team. Rugby Union is played internationally in many countries including Australia, Fiji, France, Italy, South Africa, Argentina, England, Ireland, Wales, Scotland, and New Zealand. Teams from these countries sometimes play against each other. In England it is played

especially in PUBLIC SCHOOLS (=expensive private schools), and it is thought of as a mainly MIDDLE-CLASS game. 橄榄球联盟运动: 过去橄榄球联盟运动都是业余选手参加的, 但是1995年修改了规则, 允许选手获取报酬, 由此最成功的俱乐部组建了一个职业联合会。每队有15名队员。橄榄球联盟运动是国际性的运动, 在澳大利亚、斐济、法国、意大利、南非、阿根廷、英格兰、爱尔兰、威尔士、苏格兰和新西兰等地开展比赛。来自这些地区的球队常捉对厮杀。在英国, 这项运动在公学尤其盛行, 被认为是主要是中产阶级的运动。

Rugby League Rugby League is a professional game played mainly in the north of England and also in Australia. There are 13 players on each team, and the rules are slightly different from Rugby Union. In the UK it is thought of as a mainly WORKING-CLASS game. Both types of rugby are rough hard games in which players often get injured, and rugby players are typically large strong-looking men. 橄榄球联合会运动: 橄榄球联合会运动是一项职业运动, 主要在英格兰北部和澳大利亚开展。每队有13名队员, 规则和橄榄球联盟运动有些微区别。在英国它被认为是主要是劳动阶层的运动。两种橄榄球运动都很粗野, 队员很容易受伤, 而橄榄球运动员通常都是膀大腰圆的壮汉。

Rug·by League /,·· '·/ *n* [U] a type of rugby played by teams of players who are usually paid for playing 橄榄球联合会运动

Rug·by U·nion /,·· '··/ *n* [U] a type of rugby played by teams of 15 players 橄榄球联盟运动

rug·ged /ˈrʌgɪd; ˈrʌgᵻd/ *adj* **1** land that is rugged is rough and uneven 不平的, 崎岖的, 起伏的: *rugged terrain* 起伏的地形 | *a rugged coastline* 崎岖不平的海岸线 **2** a rugged car or piece of equipment etc is strongly built and not likely to break easily; STURDY〔汽车、设备等〕坚固的, 结实的 **3** a man who is rugged is good-looking and has strong features which are often not perfect〔人〕相貌粗犷的: *Ann admired his rugged good looks.* 安喜欢他粗犷而英俊的容貌。**4** rugged behaviour is confident and determined but not always polite〔行为举止〕自信而坚决的〔但有时有点粗鲁的〕—**ruggedly** *adv* —**ruggedness** *n* [U]

rug·ger /ˈrʌgə; ˈrʌgə/ *n* [U] *BrE informal* Rugby Union【英, 非正式】橄榄球联盟运动

Rug·rats /ˈrʌgræt; ˈrʌgræt/ a children's CARTOON shown on television, about a group of very young children in the US. They all play together, and they always imagine they are involved in exciting adventures, even though they are really doing ordinary activities.《原野小兵兵》, 又译《小毛孩》〔一儿童电视卡通片, 讲述美国一群儿童的故事。他们常在一起玩耍, 总以为自己在做刺激而冒险的事情, 即使他们所做的只不过是些平凡之事〕

ru·in[1] /ˈruɪn; ˈruːᵻn/ *v* [T] **1** to spoil or destroy something completely〔完全地〕毁坏, 毁掉: *The rain ruined our holiday.* 这场雨把我们的假期毁了。| *My new white dress was totally ruined!* 我那件白色的新裙子全给毁了! —see 见 DESTROY (USAGE) **2** to make someone lose all their money 使破产: *Jefferson was ruined by the law suit.* 杰斐逊因那场官司而倾家荡产。—**ruined** *adj* [only before noun 仅用于名词前]: *ruined houses* 颓垣败瓦的房屋

ruin[2] *n* **1** [U] a situation in which you have lost all your money, your social position, or the good opinion that people had about you 破产; 垮台; 身败名裂: **lead to sb's ruin** *Joe's rashness led ultimately to his ruin.* 乔的鲁莽轻率最终葬送了自己。| **be on the road to ruin** (=be doing something that will make you lose your money, position etc) 正在走向毁灭〔做某事将会使自己破产、垮台等〕| **be on the brink of ruin** (=be about to lose all your money or your position) 濒临破产[垮台] *With the collapse of grain prices, small farmers are on the brink of financial ruin.* 谷物价格的暴跌使小农场主们陷于破产的边缘。**2 be the ruin of** *humorous* to make someone lose all their money, their good health, the good opinion that other people have about them etc【幽默】使…破产[身体垮掉, 名誉扫地等]: *Drinking was the ruin of him.* 酗酒毁了他。**3** [C] also 又作 **ruins** [plural] the part of a building that is left after the rest has been destroyed 倒塌的建筑物, 废墟: *an interesting old ruin* 很有意思的古老废墟 | *the ruins of a bombed-out office block* 被炸毁的办公楼的废墟 **4 the ruins of** the parts of something such as an organization, system, or set of ideas that remain after the rest have been destroyed〔组织、体制或思想的〕残余部分: *the ruins of the Welfare State in post Thatcher Britain* 英国后撒切尔时期福利国家残存的制度 **5 be/lie in ruins a)** if a building is in ruins it has fallen down or been badly damaged〔建筑物〕倾塌了的, 破败不堪的: *The castle now lies in ruins.* 那座城堡现在已成一片废墟了。**b)** if someone's life, hopes, plans, or an organization is in ruins, they are having great problems and cannot continue〔人的生命、希望、计划或组织有严重困难, 无法继续而〕垮掉: *After the war the Japanese economy lay in ruins.* 战后日本的经济完全崩溃。**6 go to ruin** also 又作 **fall into ruin** if something goes to ruin it becomes damaged or destroyed because no one is taking care of it〔某物因缺乏照料而〕衰落, 败落: *His brother had let the farm go to ruin.* 他的弟弟使农场走向破败。—see also 另见 MOTHER'S RUIN, **go to rack and ruin** (RACK[1] (4))

ru·in·a·tion /ˌruɪnˈeʃən; ˌruːᵻˈneɪʃən/ *n* [U] *old-fashioned or humorous* a situation in which someone or something is ruined, or the cause of this【过时或幽默】毁灭; 毁坏; 崩溃; 毁灭之原因, 祸根

ru·in·ous /ˈruɪnəs; ˈruːᵻnəs/ *adj* **1** costing much more than you can afford 导致破产的, 极昂贵的 **2** causing great destruction 招致极大破坏的: *ruinous civil war* 毁灭性的内战 —**ruinously** *adv*: *ruinously expensive* 极其昂贵的

rule[1] /rul; ruːl/ *n*

1 ▶INSTRUCTION 指示◀ [C] an official instruction that says how things must be done or what is allowed, especially in a game, organization, or job〔正式的〕规则; 章程; 条例〔尤用于游戏、团体或工作〕: *the school rules* 校规 | **against the rules** *You can't come in if you're not a member – it's against the rules.* 非会员不得入内——这样做违反规定。| **break the rules** (=disobey) 犯规 *There's a penalty if you break the rules.* 违反规则的话, 就要受到惩罚。| **stick to the rules** (=obey) 遵守规则 *I'm not going to play if you won't stick to the rules!* 如果你不遵守规则我就不玩了! | **bend/stretch the rules** (=say that on this occasion someone does not have to obey a particular rule) 变通执行规则, 通融 *We might be able to bend the rules just this one time.* 我们或许可以通融这一次。| **the rules that govern sth** (=the rules that say how something should be done) 行事规则 *changes to the rules governing international athletics* 国际田径运动规则的变更 | **rules and regulations** *I'm sick of all their petty rules and regulations.* 我讨厌他们那些琐碎的规章制度。| **hard and fast rule** (=clear and definite rule) 清楚严格的规定 *There are no hard and fast rules about what to wear to classes.* 对于上课时的穿着没有清楚严格的规定。| **unwritten rule** (=something that people usually expect you to do) 不成文规定 *an unwritten rule concerning being late for work* 关于上班迟到的不成文规定 | **rules are rules** *spoken* (=used to tell someone that rules must be obeyed)【口】规定就是规定〔告诉某人要遵守规则〕

2 ▶BEHAVIOUR 行为◀ [C] the way of behaving that is accepted as right by most people 习惯, 惯例: *the rules of etiquette* 礼仪习惯

3 ▶OF GRAMMAR/OF A SYSTEM 语法/系统的◀ [C] a statement about what is usually allowed in the grammar of a language, or according to a particular system 语法规则: *English grammar has very few rules that cannot be broken.* 英语语法很少有不能打破的规则。

4 ▶GOVERNMENT 政府◀ [U] the government of a country by a particular group of people or using a particular system 统治: *an end to over 200 years of French rule* 结束二百多年的法国统治 | *rule by a social elite* 社会精英的统治 | **under sb's rule** (=when someone is the leader of a country) 在…的统治下 *Britain prospered under Elizabeth's rule.* 英国在伊丽莎白女王的统治下繁荣昌盛。| **foreign rule** (=government by foreigners) 外国人的统治 | **majority rule** (=government by the political party that most people have voted for) 多数党执政 *majority rule in South Africa* 南非的多数党统治 | **the rule of law** (=a situation in which the people in a country obey the laws) 法治 *The rule of law had broken down and the army was sent in to restore order.* 法治崩溃后, 军队奉命恢复秩序。

5 ▶CONTROL 控制◀ [U] a system for controlling a group of people〔支配一群人的〕体系: [+by] *rule by the gun* 军人统治

6 as a (general) rule used to say that something usually happens or is usually true 通常, 一般来说: *As a rule most students finish their coursework by the end of May.* 一般来说, 大多数学生在5月底结束课程。

7 be the rule used to say that something is the usual situation 普遍情况: *It tends to be the rule that boys are more interested in cars than girls.* 普遍情况是, 男孩比女孩对汽车更有兴趣。

8 sth is the exception, not the rule used to say that something is unusual 某事是例外, 不是常见的: *You do get some women in managerial positions, but it's the exception rather than the rule.* 的确有一些妇女担任管理职务, 但这是例外, 不是常见的。

9 rule of thumb a rough method of calculation, based on practical experience〔根据实际经验的〕粗略的计算方法: *As a rule*

of thumb, you'll pay £10 a month for each £100 you borrow. 据经验估计，你所借的每100英镑每月要偿还10英镑。

10 the rule is *spoken* used when advising someone what to do in a particular situation【口】惯例是…〔用于对人提出忠告〕: *The rule is: if you feel any pain you should stop exercising immediately.* 一般来说，如果你感到疼痛，就应立即停止锻炼。

11 make it a rule (to do sth) to try to make sure that you always do something 有(做某事)的习惯: *I generally make it a rule to be up by 7.* 我通常7点前起床。

12 ►FOR MEASURING 供度量用◄ [C] *old-fashioned* RULER (2)【过时】尺子，直尺 —see also 另见 GOLDEN RULE, GROUND RULES, HOME RULE, SLIDE RULE, **work to rule** (WORK[1] (29))

rule[2] *v*

1 ►GOVERNMENT 政府◄ [I,T] to have the official power to control a country and the people who live there 统治，治理: *Queen Victoria ruled England for 64 years.* 维多利亚女王统治英国64年。| [+over] *Alexander the Great ruled over a large empire.* 亚历山大大帝统治着一个庞大的帝国。

2 ►CONTROL/INFLUENCE 控制/影响◄ [T] if a feeling or desire rules someone it has a powerful and controlling influence on their actions〔情感或欲望〕控制，支配: *the passion for power and success which rules her life* 对权力和成功的欲望控制着她的一生

3 ►COURT/LAW 法庭/法律◄ [I always+adv/prep,T] to make an official decision about something, especially a legal problem〔尤指对法律问题〕判定，裁定: **rule that** *The judge ruled that she should have custody.* 法官判定她有监护权。| [+on] *The Supreme Court has yet to rule on the case.* 最高法院尚未裁定此案。| **rule in favour of** *The tribunal ruled in her favour.* 审理委员会作出了有利于她的裁决。—see also 另见 RULING[1]

4 let your heart rule your head to make decisions based on what you feel not what you think 感情用事

5 rule the roost *informal* to be the most powerful person in a group【非正式】当家作主，支配一切: *It's his wife who rules the roost in their house.* 他们家里他妻子说了算。

6 rule sb with a rod of iron to control a group of people in a very severe way 实行严酷的高压统治

7 sb rules an expression, often written on walls, used to say that the team, GANG etc mentioned is better than anyone else …必胜〔写在墙上的标语，表示某队等比其他优秀〕: *Arsenal rules OK.* 阿森纳队必胜。| *Midland High rules!* 米德兰高中必胜!

8 ►DRAW A LINE 划线◄ [T] to draw a line using a ruler or other straight edge〔用尺子等〕划线: *Rule a line under each answer.* 请在每一个答案下面划一条线。

9 be ruled by sb *old-fashioned* to do what someone else tells you to do【过时】听人摆布 —see also 另见 OVERRULE

rule sth/sb ↔ **out** *phr v* [T] **1** to decide that something is not possible or suitable 排除，拒绝考虑: *The police have ruled out suicide.* 警方已经排除了自杀的可能。**2** to make it impossible for something to happen 使〔某事〕不可能发生: *The mountainous terrain rules out most forms of agriculture.* 多山的地形使大多数形式的农业耕作无法进行。

rule·book /ˈrulˌbʊk; ˈruːlbʊk/ *n* **1 go by the rulebook** *informal* to obey exactly the rules about how something should be done【非正式】按规则行事: *If we went by the rulebook I'd have to report this conversation.* 如果我们按照规则行事，我就必须汇报这次谈话。**2** [C] a book of rules, especially one that is given to workers in a job〔尤指给工人的〕规则手册

Rule Bri·tan·nia /ˌ· ·ˈ··/ a song about the power Britain used to have at sea because of its navy, which people sing on PATRIOTIC occasions, such as the Last Night of the Proms. Some of the words are: *Rule Britannia, Britannia rule the waves,/ Britons never, never, never shall be slaves.*《统治吧，不列颠!》〔一首歌颂大英帝国依仗海军而掌握海上控制权的歌曲。逍遥音乐会终场之夜等爱国主义场合经常演唱这首歌曲。部分歌词是: 英国，英国，挽住那狂涛骇浪，/英国人绝不、绝不、绝不做奴隶〕

ruled /ruld; ruːld/ *adj* ruled paper has parallel lines printed across it〔纸张〕有平行线条的

rul·er /ˈrulɚ; ˈruːlə/ *n* [C] **1** someone such as a King or Queen who has official power over a country or area 统治者 **2** a flat narrow piece of plastic, metal etc with straight edges, that you use for measuring things or drawing straight lines 尺子，直尺: *a 12-inch ruler* 12英寸长的尺子

rul·ing[1] /ˈrulɪŋ; ˈruːlɪŋ/ *n* [C+on] an official decision, especially one made by a court〔尤指法庭的〕裁决，裁定

ruling[2] *adj* [only before noun 仅用于名词前] **1** the ruling group in a country or organization is the group that controls it〔在国家中〕执政的;〔在组织中〕起领导作用的 **2 sb's ruling passion** the thing that interests someone more than anything else 某人的最大乐趣: *The martial arts are Sandy's ruling passion.* 武术是桑迪最大的爱好。

rum[1] /rʌm; rʌm/ *n* [C,U] a strong alcoholic drink made from sugar, or a glass of this drink 朗姆酒〔一种由糖制成的酒精浓度高的酒〕; 一杯朗姆酒

CULTURAL NOTE 文化注释

Rum is the TRADITIONAL drink of sailors, and is associated especially with PIRATES, who are often shown drinking rum in stories. 朗姆酒是水手的传统饮用酒，特别是与海盗有关，故事中常描述海盗喝朗姆酒。

rum[2] *adj old-fashioned* unusual or strange【过时】古怪的，离奇的

Ru·ma·ni·a /ruˋmenɪə; ruːˈmeɪniə/ another spelling of ROMANIA Romania 的另一拼法

rum·ba /ˈrʌmbə; ˈrʌmbə/ *n* [C,U] a popular dance from Cuba, or the music for this dance〔源于古巴的〕伦巴舞(曲)

rum·ble[1] /ˈrʌmbḷ; ˈrʌmbəl/ *v* **1** [I] to make a series of long low sounds, especially a long distance away from you 发出隆隆声〔尤指来自远处〕: *We could hear thunder rumbling in the distance.* 我们听得见远处雷声轰鸣。**2** [I always+adv/prep] to move slowly while making this sound 缓慢而隆隆地行进: [+along/past etc] *A tank rumbled past.* 一辆坦克隆隆驶过。**3** if your stomach rumbles, it makes a noise, especially because you are hungry〔肚子因饥饿〕发出辘辘声 **4** [T] *informal especially BrE* to find out what someone is secretly intending to do【非正式，尤英】发现〔某人秘密的企图〕: *We've been rumbled; someone must have told the police.* 我们已经被发现了，一定是有人告诉了警察。

rumble[2] *n* [singular] a series of long low sounds 隆隆声，轰轰声: *the rumble of distant gunfire* 远处隆隆的炮声

rum·bling /ˈrʌmblɪŋ; ˈrʌmblɪŋ/ *n* **1 rumblings** comments that show that people are starting to become annoyed, or that a difficult situation is developing 不满的言论，抱怨: *rumblings of discontent* 怨声载道 **2** [C usually singular 一般用单数] a rumbling noise 隆隆声，轰轰声

ru·mi·nant /ˈrumənənt; ˈruːmɪ̣nənt/ *n* [C] *technical* an animal such as a cow that has several stomachs and eats grass【术语】反刍动物〈例如牛〉

ru·mi·nate /ˈruməˌnet; ˈruːmɪ̣neɪt/ *v* [I] **1** *formal* to think for a long time about something【正式】沉思，反复思考: [+about/on etc] *He sat ruminating on the answer he'd been given.* 他坐在那里，反复思考得到的答案。**2** *technical* if animals such as cows ruminate, they bring food back into their mouths from their stomachs and CHEW it again【术语】〔动物〕反刍 —**rumination** /ˌruməˋneʃən; ˌruːmɪ̣ˈneɪʃən/ *n* [C,U]

rum·mage[1] /ˈrʌmɪdʒ; ˈrʌmɪdʒ/ *v* [I always+adv/prep] also 又作 **rummage around** to search for something by moving things around in a careless way 翻找，乱翻: [+in/through etc] *Looks like someone's been rummaging around in my desk.* 看来有人翻过我的书桌。

rummage[2] *n* **1 have a rummage** *informal* to rummage【非正式】翻找，乱翻 **2** [U] *especially AmE* old clothes, toys etc that you no longer want【尤美】〔旧衣物、旧玩具等〕无用的东西; JUMBLE[1] (2) *BrE*【英】

rummage sale /ˈ·· ·/ *n* [C] *AmE* an event at which old clothes, toys etc are sold as a way of getting money, for example to help a school or church【美】旧杂物的义卖〔如为资助学校或教堂〕; JUMBLE SALE *BrE*【英】

rum·my /ˈrʌmɪ; ˈrʌmi/ *n* [U] a simple card game 拉米纸牌游戏

ru·mour *BrE*【英】, **rumor** *AmE*【美】/ˈrumɚ; ˈruːmə/ *n* [U] information that is passed from one person to another and which may or may not be true, especially about someone's personal life or about an official decision 流言，谣言，谣传: [+about/of] *I've heard all sorts of rumors about him and his secretary.* 我听说了有关他和他的秘书的各种传闻。| [+that] *There's a rumour going around that Eddie's bankrupt.* 埃迪破产的谣言正四处流传。| **rumour has it (that)** (=there is a rumour that) 据谣传 *Rumour has it that Jean's getting married again.* 传说琼又要结婚了。

ru·moured *BrE*【英】, **rumored** *AmE*【美】/ˈrumɚd; ˈruːməd/ *adj* if something is rumoured to be true, people are saying secretly or unofficially that it may be true 传闻的，谣传的: **it is rumoured that** *It was rumoured that Johnson had been poisoned.* 谣传约翰逊被毒死了。| **be rumoured to be sth** *She was rumoured to be a millionaire.* 据说她家财百万。| **widely rumoured** *a young man widely rumoured to be her lover* 小伙子是她情人的盛传

R

ru·mour·mon·ger *BrE*【英】, **rumormonger** *AmE*【美】 /ˈruməˌmʌŋgə; ˈruːməˌmʌŋgə/ *n* [C] someone who tells other people rumours 散布谣言者, 造谣的人

rump /rʌmp; rʌmp/ *n* **1** [C] the part of an animal's back that is just above its legs〔动物的〕臀部 **2 rump steak** meat that comes from this part of a cow 后腿肉牛排 **3** [C] *humorous* the part of your body that you sit on; BOTTOM[1] (7)【幽默】〔人的〕臀部 **4** *BrE* [singular] the part of a group or government that remains after most of the other members have left【英】残余分子, 余党

Rum·pel·stilt·skin /ˌrʌmpl̩ˋstɪltskɪn; ˌrʌmpəlˈstɪltskɪn/ the main character in a story called *Rumpelstiltskin* by Jacob and Wilhelm Grimm. Rumpelstiltskin is an ugly DWARF (=a creature like a very small man) who teaches a young girl how to make STRAW into gold thread by using a SPINNING WHEEL. As a reward for teaching her this, he says she must give him her first child. She becomes queen and has a child, but Rumpelstiltskin says he will not take her child if she can discover what his name is within three days. By chance a servant hears him saying his name, and when the girl tells him what it is, he gets so angry that he dies. 侏儒妖〔雅各·格林和威廉·格林两兄弟创作的故事《侏儒妖》中的主人公。侏儒妖是个长相丑陋的小矮人, 他教一个女孩用纺车把干草纺成金线。为此, 他要求女孩将来把她的头胎孩子送给他, 以回报他的教育之恩。后来, 女孩成了王后, 生了个孩子。侏儒妖说只要她能在三天内说出他的名字, 他就可以不要孩子。碰巧有个仆人以前听到侏儒妖说过自己的名字。王后最后说出了他的名字, 他气过了头, 一命呜呼〕

rum·ple /ˈrʌmpl̩; ˈrʌmpəl/ *v* [T] to make hair, clothes etc less tidy 把〔头发、衣服等〕弄乱, 弄皱 —**rumpled** *adj*: *rumpled sheets* 皱了的床单

rum·pus /ˈrʌmpəs; ˈrʌmpəs/ *n* [singular] *informal* a lot of noise, especially made by people quarrelling【非正式】争吵, 喧闹: *There's a real rumpus going on upstairs.* 楼上正吵得不可开交。

rumpus room /ˈ··· ·/ *n* [C] *AmE* a room in a house that is used by the family for games, parties etc【美】〔家庭的〕聚会室, 游艺室, 娱乐室

rump·y pump·y /ˌrʌmpɪ ˋpʌmpɪ; ˌrʌmpi ˈpʌmpi/ *n* [U] *BrE humorous* sexual activity【英, 幽默】性行为

run[1] /rʌn; rʌn/ *v past tense* ran /ræn; ræn/ *past participle* run *present participle* running

① MOVE QUICKLY ON FOOT 奔跑
② CONTROL/BE IN CHARGE OF 控制/掌管
③ MACHINES/SYSTEMS 机器/系统
④ CARS/TRAINS/BOATS ETC 汽车/火车/船等
⑤ WATER/LIQUIDS 水/液体
⑥ CONTINUE 继续
⑦ HAPPEN/TAKE PLACE 发生
⑧ TOUCH/RUB A SURFACE 接触/磨擦表面
⑨ THOUGHTS/FEELINGS 思想/感情
⑩ ROADS/FENCES ETC 道路/篱笆等
⑪ COLOUR/PAINT 颜色/油漆
⑫ NOT ENOUGH/NONE LEFT 不足/没有剩余
⑬ BECOME UNCONTROLLED 失去控制
⑭ DO/ARRANGE STH 做/安排某事
⑮ OTHER MEANINGS 其他意思

① MOVE QUICKLY ON FOOT 奔跑

1 [I] to move quickly on foot by moving your legs more quickly than when you are walking 跑, 奔跑: *I had to run to catch the bus.* 我不得不跑着去赶那辆公共汽车。| *Two youths were killed when running to help people injured in the bomb blast.* 两个年轻人跑过去救助被炸弹炸伤的人时丧生。| [+adv/prep] *Each morning we ran down to the harbour to see the previous night's catch.* 每天早晨我们都跑去港口观看前一天夜里的鱼获。| **run for cover** (=run in order to find shelter or protection) 跑着找掩蔽物 *Suddenly shots rang out, and we had to run for cover.* 突然响起了枪声, 我们不得不跑着寻找躲避之处。| **run for your life** (=in order to avoid being killed) 逃命 *Hundreds ran for their lives from the burning building.* 数以百计的人从着火的大楼里跑出来逃命。

2 ►IN A RACE 赛跑中◄ a) [I,T] to take part in a running race 参加〔赛跑〕: *I'd never run a marathon before.* 我以前从未参加过马拉松比赛。| [+in] *Are you running in the 100 metres?* 你参加100米赛跑吗? **b)** [T] to hold a race 举行〔比赛〕: *The Derby will be run at 3 o'clock.* 德比马赛将于3点钟举行。

3 run for it *spoken* to run as quickly as possible in order to escape【口】赶快逃跑: *Police – quick, run for it!* 警察——快跑!

4 run and fetch/get/do sth *spoken* used to ask a child to get or do something quickly for you【口】快去取/拿/干某事〔用于要求孩子给你做事〕: *Run and tell your father supper's ready.* 快去告诉你爸爸晚饭好啦。

5 run along *spoken* used to tell a child to go away【口】走开〔用于要求孩子〕: *Run along now, all of you, I'm busy.* 你们都走开, 我忙着呢。

② CONTROL/BE IN CHARGE OF 控制/掌管

6 [T] to control or be in charge of a company, an organization, or system 控制〔一个公司、机构或系统〕; 支配, 管理, 经营: *For a while, she ran a restaurant in Boston.* 她在波士顿开了一段时间餐馆。| *Many people belong to a pension scheme run by their employers.* 许多人参加了由雇主管理的养老金计划。| **well/badly run** (=organized efficiently/inefficiently) 经营良好/不好 *A well-run company should not have problems of this kind.* 一家经营良好的公司不应该有这种问题。| **state-run** (=controlled and paid for by the state) 国营的 *a state-run airline* 国营航空公司 —see 见 CONTROL[2] (USAGE)

7 run sb's life *informal* to keep telling someone what they should do all the time, in a way that they find annoying【非正式】不断指使某人〔令对方讨厌〕: *Don't try to run my life!* 不要试图主宰我的生活!

③ MACHINES/SYSTEMS 机器/系统

8 ►MACHINES 机器◄ [I] if a machine runs, it operates 运转, 开动: *Don't touch the engine while it's running.* 发动机运转的时候不要去碰它。| **run on electricity/gas/unleaded petrol etc** (=get its power from electricity etc) 以电/天然气/无铅汽油等为动力 | **run smoothly** (=operate with all its parts working exactly as they should) 运转正常 *My car's not running too smoothly at the moment.* 我的汽车现在开起来有点不顺畅。

9 ►COMPUTERS 电脑◄ [I,T] to operate a computer PROGRAM[1] (1) (使)〔电脑程序〕运行: *The RS8 system runs both Unix and MPX-32.* RS8系统运行Unix和MPX-32。

10 up and running working fully and correctly 全面而正确地展开工作: *The new system won't be up and running until next week.* 新的系统要到下周才能完全投入使用。

④ CARS/TRAINS/BOATS ETC 汽车/火车/船等

11 ►PUBLIC TRANSPORT 公共交通◄ a) [I] if a bus, train etc service runs, it takes people from one place to another at fixed times of the day〔公共汽车、火车等〕定时行驶: *The buses don't run on Sundays.* 公共汽车星期天停驶。**b)** [T] if someone runs a bus, train etc service, they make it operate 经营〔公共汽车、火车等〕: *They're running special trains to and from the exhibition.* 他们经营去展览会的往返火车专线。

12 ►FAST/OUT OF CONTROL 快速/失控◄ [I always+ adv/prep] to move too fast or in an uncontrolled way 过于快速移动, 失控: [+into/down/through etc] *The truck ran downhill at a frightening speed.* 卡车以惊人的速度向山下冲去。| *Her car ran into a tree.* 她的汽车撞到了树上。

13 run aground/ashore if a ship runs aground, it cannot move because the water is not deep enough〔船只〕搁浅: *An oil tanker*

has run aground near the Valdez oil terminal. 一艘油轮在瓦尔迪兹石油集散码头附近搁浅。
14 run a car to pay for all the things that are needed to keep a car working 养车〔指为保持一辆汽车处于工作状态而支付所有必要费用〕: *I can't really afford to run a car.* 我的确养不起车。
15 run sb home/to the station etc *informal* to take someone somewhere in your car【非正式】用汽车把某人送到家/车站等: *Shall I run you home?* 要我开车送你回家吗?

⑤ WATER/LIQUIDS 水/液体

16 [I always+adv/prep] to flow in a particular direction or place〔向特定方向或地方〕流动: [**+down/along etc**] *Big tears ran down Stephanie's face.* 大颗的眼泪顺着斯蒂芬妮的脸颊往下流。| *A stream ran through the garden.* 一条小溪流过花园。
17 ►TAP 龙头◄ [I] if a TAP (=thing for controlling the supply of water) is running, there is water coming out of it〔水从龙头〕流出: *Did you leave the kitchen faucet running?* 你是不是忘了关厨房的水龙头?
18 run a bath to fill a bath with water 把〔浴缸〕放满水: **run sb a bath** *Could you run me a nice hot bath while I finish my meal?* 你能不能在我吃饭时给我放上一浴缸热水?
19 ►SB'S NOSE 某人的鼻子◄ [I] if someone's nose is running, liquid is flowing out of it 流鼻涕

⑥ CONTINUE 继续

20 ►OFFICIAL PAPERS 官方文件◄ [I] to continue to be officially able to be used for a particular period of time 有效, 可以合法使用: *The contract runs for a year.* 合同有效期为一年。| *My car insurance only has another month to run.* 我的汽车保险期只剩一个月了。
21 ►PLAY/FILM 戏剧/电影◄ [I] to continue being performed regularly in one place〔在某处〕定期上演: *The play ran for two years.* 该剧连续演了两年。
22 ►STORY/ACCOUNT ETC 故事/叙述等◄ [I] to continue in a particular way〔以特有的方式〕继续: *I forget now how the story runs.* 我现在不记得故事怎么发展的了。
23 run its course to continue in the expected way until finished 听其自然发展〔直至结束〕: *Wait until the illness has run its course.* 等到病自己好吧。
24 this one will run and run *BrE humorous* used to say that you think a problem, joke etc will continue for a long time【英, 幽默】〔问题、玩笑等〕将持续很长时间

⑦ HAPPEN/TAKE PLACE 发生

25 [I] to happen or take place, especially in the way that was intended〔尤指按照预想计划〕发生: **run according to plan** (=happen in the way that you had planned) 按计划进行 *So far, it had all run exactly according to plan.* 到目前为止, 一切都完全按照计划进行。| **run smoothly** (=happen with no unexpected problems) 运作顺利 *Her job is to ensure university catering runs smoothly.* 她的职责是确保办好大学的伙食供应服务。

⑧ TOUCH/RUB A SURFACE 接触/磨擦表面

26 [T always+adv/prep] to move or rub something lightly along a surface〔在表面〕轻轻移动, 轻擦: **run sth down/through/along** *Charles ran his fingers through her hair.* 查尔斯用手指拢了拢她的头发。

⑨ THOUGHTS/FEELINGS 思想/感情

27 [I always+adv/prep] if thoughts or feelings run through you, you experience them suddenly 突然而来, 掠过: [**+through/down etc**] *The same thought kept running through his mind.* 同一想法一直在他脑海里萦回。| *I felt a sharp pain run down my leg.* 我感到一阵剧痛传遍我的腿。
28 be running high if feelings are running high, people are becoming angry or upset about something〔情绪〕激动, 不安: *Feelings at the game were running high.* 比赛场上情绪激动。

⑩ ROADS/FENCES ETC 道路/篱笆等

29 [I always+adv/prep] to exist in a particular place or continue in a particular direction 存在于某处; 朝某方向延伸: [**+along/through etc**] *The road runs along a valley.* 这条路沿着山谷延伸。

⑪ COLOUR/PAINT 颜色/油漆

30 [I] if colour runs, it spreads from one area of cloth to another, when the cloth is wet〔湿织物上的颜色〕掉色: *The colour ran when I washed your red shirt, and now all your socks are pink!* 你的红衬衣洗的时候掉色了, 现在你的袜子全都成了粉红色!
31 [I] if paint runs, it moves onto an area where you did not intend it to go〔油漆〕流到别处, 扩散

⑫ NOT ENOUGH/NONE LEFT 不足/没有剩余

32 be running short (of sth) to have very little of something left (某物) 没剩多少; (某物) 快用完: *I'm running short of cash – do you think you could lend me some?* 我的现金快用完了——你能否借给我一些?
33 time is running short used to say that there is little time left 时间不多了: *Time was already running short.* 剩下的时间已经不多了。
34 be running low (on sth) to have very little left of something that you normally keep a supply of〔正常的供应〕快用完, 不足: *We're running low on fuel again.* 我们的燃料又快用完了。
35 run dry if a river or WELL (=hole in the ground for getting water) runs dry, there is no water left in it〔河流或水井〕干涸: *The drought was so severe that even the well ran dry.* 干旱十分严重, 连井都干涸了。

⑬ BECOME UNCONTROLLED 失去控制

36 run wild to behave in an uncontrolled way 放肆, 撒野: *Since their mother left, those children have been running wild.* 妈妈出门后, 那些孩子一直在撒野。
37 run rife to spread quickly in an uncontrolled way 迅速蔓延: *Disease is running rife in the shanty towns.* 疾病在贫民区迅速蔓延。
38 run riot a) if people run riot, they start to behave in a violent or uncontrolled way 粗暴, 不受控制: *Angry demonstrators ran riot through the town.* 愤怒的示威者发疯似地在市区到处闹事。**b)** if feelings run riot, they increase quickly in a way that you cannot control〔感情〕约束不住: *Let your imagination run riot.* 让你的想象力自由驰骋吧。

⑭ DO/ARRANGE STH 做/安排某事

39 run a check/test on to arrange for something or someone to be checked or tested 安排对…的检查/测试: *A check had to be run on all participants, for security reasons.* 出于安全理由, 需要对所有参与者进行检查。| *We'd better run a test on all the equipment before we begin.* 开始前我们最好测试一下所有设备。
40 run an errand a) to go to a shop, office etc in order to buy, do, or get something for someone else〔给某人〕跑腿: *a boy running errands for his mother* 一个给妈妈跑腿的男孩 **b)** *AmE* to go to a shop, office etc to buy or get something that you need【美】〔去商店、办公室等〕采购, 办事: *I have a few errands to run downtown.* 我在城里有几件事要办。

⑮ OTHER MEANINGS 其他意思

41 ►IN AN ELECTION 选举中◄ [I] to try to be elected in an election; STAND¹ (41) 竞选: [**+for**] *Bob Dole's running for President.* 鲍勃·多尔在竞选总统。| [**+against**] *The Democrats chose Mondale to run against Reagan.* 民主党人选派蒙代尔与里根竞选。
42 ►HOLE IN CLOTHES 衣物上的洞◄ [I] if a hole in TIGHTS, STOCKINGS etc runs, it gets bigger in a straight line〔裤袜、长统袜等〕脱线, 抽丝
43 run drugs/guns to bring drugs or guns into a country illegally in order to sell them 走私毒品/枪支 —see also 另见 DRUG RUNNER, GUN-RUNNING
44 run a story/feature/article to print a story etc in a newspaper or magazine〔在报纸或杂志上〕刊登报道/特写/文章: *The editor decided at the last minute not to run the story.* 在最后一刻编辑决定不登这则报道。
45 run in the family if something such as a quality, disease, or skill runs in the family, many people in that family have it 家族遗传, 具有家族特征: *Karen's very good at music too – it runs in the family.* 卡伦也非常擅长音乐, 这是家族遗传。
46 run a temperature/fever to have a body temperature that is higher than normal, because you are ill 发烧: *She's running a temperature of a 102°F.* 她发烧102华氏度。
47 run a mile *informal* to try very hard to avoid a situation, person, or place, because you find them frightening or embarrassing【非正式】〔对令人惊慌或尴尬的情况、人或地方〕尽量避而远之: *She's so shy that if a man ever spoke to her I think she'd run a mile!* 她很害羞, 如果有男人和她说话, 我看她一定会躲得远远的!

48 be running late to be doing everything later than planned or expected 比计划[预期]的晚: *They were running late, so I didn't get interviewed until nearly 4 o'clock.* 他们晚了，所以我差不多4点才面试。
49 be running scared to have become worried about the power of an enemy or opponent 担心〔敌人或对手的力量〕; 烦恼: *Their new software has the competition running scared.* 他们的新软件使竞争对手坐立不安。
50 come running a) *informal* to respond in a very eager way when someone asks or tells you to do something【非正式】热心〔做别人要自己做的事〕: *He thinks he's only got to crook his finger and I'll come running.* 他以为他只要弯弯手指，我就会迫不及待地给他干。**b)** *especially spoken* to ask someone for help, advice, or sympathy when you have a problem【尤口】请求帮助[指点，同情]: [+to] *Well I warned you, so don't come running to me when it all goes wrong!* 我警告过你的，所以出了问题别来求我！
51 run your eyes over *informal* to look quickly at something【非正式】扫视，浏览: *Could you run your eyes over my report before I turn it in?* 我把报告交上去之前，你能看一下吗？
52 run that by me again *spoken* used to ask someone to explain something again, because you did not completely understand【口】请再解释一下 —see also 另见 RUNNING, **run amok** (AMOK), **make your blood run cold** (BLOOD¹ (5)), **run counter to** (COUNTER³), **cut and run** (CUT¹ (30)), **run deep** (DEEP¹ (5)), **run sb/sth to earth** (EARTH¹ (13)), **run to fat** (FAT² (6)), **run the gauntlet** (GAUNTLET (5)), **run sb to ground** (GROUND¹ (22)), **run rings around** (RING¹ (8)), **run to seed** (SEED¹ (3))

run across sb/sth *phr v* [T] to meet or find someone or something by chance 与…不期而遇，偶然碰见: *I ran across an old friend last week.* 上星期我偶然碰见了一个老朋友。

run after sb/sth *phr v* [T] **1** to chase someone or something 追逐，追赶: *Her dog was running after a rabbit.* 她的狗在追赶一只兔子。**2** *informal* to try to get someone's attention, especially because you are sexually attracted to them【非正式】〔因爱慕而〕追求 **3** *spoken* to do many small jobs for someone, like a servant【口】伺候，服侍: *I can't keep running after you all day!* 我不能整天跟着伺候你！

run around *phr v* [I] **1** to run in an area, without a definite direction or purpose 到处跑: *The children were running around in the garden.* 孩子们在花园里跑来跑去。**2 run around with sb** to spend a lot of time with someone, especially in a way that other people disapprove of 常与某人混在一起，厮混: *Is it true that she's been running around with an older man?* 她和一个岁数较大的男人混在一起，这是真的吗？**3** *informal* to be very busy doing many small jobs【非正式】忙于琐事: *At fifty, I didn't want to be running around making bottles and changing diapers.* 50岁时，我不想再忙忙碌碌地冲牛奶和换尿布了。—see also 另见 RUN-AROUND

run away *phr v* [I] **1** to leave a place, especially secretly, in order to escape from someone or something〔秘密地〕逃跑: [+from] *Toby ran away from home at the age of 14.* 托比14岁时离家出走。| *They ran away together to get married.* 他们私奔结了婚。—see also 另见 RUNAWAY **2** to try to avoid a problem or difficult situation because it is unpleasant or embarrassing 逃避问题[困局]: *You've got to stop running away, and learn to face your problems.* 你不能再逃避了，要学会面对问题。

run away with sb/sth *phr v* [T] **1 run away with you** if your feelings, ideas etc run away with you, they start to control how you behave because you can no longer think in a sensible way〔感情、思想等〕控制住〔某人〕，使按捺不住: *Don't let your imagination run away with you!* 不要想入非非！**2** to leave a place secretly or illegally with someone else 带着〔某人〕潜逃；和〔某人〕私奔: *He ran away with the boss's wife.* 他和老板的妻子私奔了。**3 run away with the idea/impression that** *spoken* to think that something is true when it is not【口】误有…想法/印象: *Don't run away with the idea that this is going to be easy!* 别以为这会是轻而易举的事。**4** *informal* to win a competition or sports game very easily【非正式】轻易赢得〔比赛〕: *The Reds ran away with the championship.* 红人队轻易地夺得冠军。**5** to steal something 偷窃: *They found that the treasurer had run away with the proceeds.* 他们发现财务主管卷款逃走了。

run down *phr v* **1** [T **run** sb/sth ↔ **down**] to drive into a person or animal and kill or injure them〔开车〕撞死[撞伤]: *Their daughter was run down by a car just outside their house.* 他们的女儿就在他们的房子外面被车撞倒。**2** [T **run** sb/sth ↔ **down**] *informal* to say things that are rude, unpleasant, or unfair about someone or something【非正式】指责，非难: *Paula's jealous of you – that's why she keeps running you down.* 葆拉妒忌你，所以她老说你的不是。| *Don't run yourself down!* 不要自咎！**3** [I] if a clock, machine, BATTERY etc runs down, it has no more power and stops working〔钟、机器因缺乏动力〕停了；〔电池〕用完了 **4** [T **run** sth ↔ **down**] to let a company, organization etc gradually become smaller or stop working 使〔公司、机构等的规模〕逐渐缩减，使逐渐停办: *The coal industry is being slowly run down.* 煤炭工业在慢慢衰退。**5** [T **run** sb/sth ↔ **down**] to find someone or something after searching for a long time〔经过长时间寻找而〕发现；找到: *I finally ran him down at his new office in Glendale.* 最后我是在格伦代尔他的新办公室里找到他的。—see also 另见 RUNDOWN, RUN-DOWN

run sb/sth ↔ **in** *phr v* [T] **1** *old-fashioned* if the police run a criminal in, they catch them; ARREST¹ (1)【过时】〔警察〕抓获〔罪犯〕，逮捕 **2** if you run in a new car, you drive it slowly and carefully at first〔小心地、慢慢地〕试开〔新车〕

run into sb/sth *phr v* [T] **1** to hit someone or something with a car or other vehicle〔汽车〕撞上: *His car skidded and ran into a lamp-post.* 他的车打滑，撞到一根路灯柱上。**2** *informal* to meet someone by chance【非正式】偶然遇见: *Guess who I ran into in town today!* 猜猜今天我在城里碰见了谁！**3 run into difficulties/problems/debt etc** to start to experience difficulties 遇到困难/问题；负债等: *After a promising start, the company ran into trouble.* 公司起初很有生气，但之后便陷入了困境。**4 run into hundreds/thousands etc** to reach an amount of several hundred, several thousand etc 累计达到数百/数千等: *By now they had debts running into thousands of pounds.* 目前他们的债务达到了几千英镑。**5** if something such as a word, colour etc runs into another word, colour etc, it joins it or mixes with it so that it is difficult to separate them〔词、颜色等〕混合在一起〔难以分辨〕**6 run sth into the ground a)** to use something so much that you destroy it〔因使用太多〕把某物用坏: *We ran that Chevrolet right into the ground.* 我们把那辆雪佛兰汽车一直用到报废。**b)** to talk about a subject so much that there is nothing more left to say 把〔某个话题的〕话都谈尽

run off *phr v* **1** [I] to leave a place or person in a way that people disapprove of 逃跑，离弃: *Amy's husband had run off and left her with two children to bring up.* 埃米的丈夫弃家而去，留下她抚养两个孩子。**2** [T **run** sth ↔ **off**] to quickly print several copies of something 快速印出: *Shall I run off some more of those notices for you on the photocopier?* 要不要我用复印机给你再复印几份通知？**3** [T **run** sth **off**] to write a speech, poem, piece of music etc quickly and easily 迅速地写出〔演讲稿、诗、乐谱等〕: *He could run off a comedy monologue in half an hour.* 他可以在半小时内很快写出一篇喜剧独白。**4 be run off your feet** to be so busy that you do not have time to stop or rest 忙得脚不沾地，疲于奔命 **5 run off at the mouth** *AmE informal* to talk too much【美，非正式】话多，喋喋不休 **6** [T **run** sth ↔ **off**] to get rid of weight by running 通过跑步减轻〔体重〕: *I'm trying to run off some of my excess fat!* 我正努力跑步减肥！

run off with sth/sb *phr v* [T] *informal*【非正式】**1** to go away somewhere with someone, because you are having a sexual relationship that people do not approve of 与…私奔: *Liz shocked us all by running off with a married man.* 莉兹与一个有妇之夫私奔了，使我们都感到震惊。**2** to take something without permission 偷走，拐走: *Then I found that he had run off with all my savings.* 这时我才发现，他已带着我的全部积蓄逃走了。

run on *phr v* [I] to continue happening for longer than expected or planned 持续〔超出预定的时间〕: *The lecture ran on until 11 o'clock.* 讲座一直持续到11点。

run out *phr v* **1** [I] to use all of something and not have any of it left〔某东西〕用完，耗尽: [+of] *The truck's run out of gas again.* 卡车的汽油又用完了。**2** [I] if food, money etc runs out, there is none left〔食物、金钱等〕用完，没有了: *Our supplies soon ran out.* 我们的补给很快就用尽了。| *My patience was running out.* 我有点忍无可忍了。**3** [I] if an agreement, official document etc runs out, it reaches the end of the period when it is officially allowed to continue; EXPIRE (1)〔协议、正式文件等〕期满，到期: *My contract runs out in September.* 我的合同9月份期满。**4 run out on** to leave someone, when you should not 离开〔某人〕，遗弃: *He ran out on his*

run out 用完

second wife two years later. 两年以后他遗弃了他第二任妻子。**5 run out of steam** *informal*【非正式】also 又作 **run out of gas** *AmE*【美】to have no energy or eagerness left for something that you are trying to do 泄气, 对…提不起劲[失去热情]: *The whole team seemed to have run out of gas.* 全队似乎都失去了热情。**6 run sb out of town** *old-fashioned* to force someone to leave a place, because they have done something wrong【过时】(把做错事的人)赶走, 逐出 **7** [T **run** sb ↔ **out**] to end a player's INNINGS in CRICKET (2) by hitting the stumps (STUMP[1] (4)) with the ball while they are running〔板球比赛中以球触三门柱〕使〔正在奔跑的击球手〕出局

run over *phr v* **1** [T **run** sb/sth ↔ **over**] to hit someone or something with a car or other vehicle, and drive over them〔开车〕辗过, 轧过: *He was run over by a bus and killed.* 他被公共汽车辗死了。**2** [T **run over** sth] to explain or practise something again 反复解释, 练习, 排练: *Could we just run over the section on verbs again?* 我们把有关动词的部分再练习一遍好吗? **3** [T **run over** sth] to think about a series of events, possibilities etc 思考〔一连串事件、可能等〕: *I ran over the options in my mind.* 我对各种选择一一作了考虑。**4** [I] also 又作 **run over time** to continue past the arranged time 超过时间: *The meeting ran over, and I was late for lunch.* 会议散得晚, 我吃午饭迟了。**5** [I] if a container runs over, there is so much liquid inside that some flows out; OVERFLOW〔容器〕满溢; 〔液体〕溢出

run through *phr v* [T] **1** [**run through** sth] to repeat something so that you remember it or get better at it 复习; 反复练习, 排练: *Let's run through the first scene again.* 让我们再排练一遍第一场。**2** [**run through** sth] to read, look at, or explain something quickly 匆匆阅读[浏览, 解释]: *I'll just run through the figures with you.* 我将很快地把这些数字看一遍。**3** [**run through** sth] to be present in many parts of something or continue through it, for example in an artist's work or in a society 贯穿于…之中: *This theme runs through the whole book.* 该主题贯穿全书。| *a fundamental problem running right through our society* 我们社会普遍存在的根本问题 **4** [**run** sb **through**] *literary* to push a sword completely through someone【文】(用剑)把〔某人〕刺穿 —see also 另见 RUN-THROUGH

run to sth *phr v* [T] **1** to reach a particular amount 达到〔一定数量〕: *The damages awarded by the court could easily run to one billion pounds.* 法院判付的赔偿费很可能达到10亿英镑。**2** *BrE* to be enough money to pay for something, or have enough money for it【英】〔钱〕足够做某事: *My wages won't run to a new car.* 我的工资买不起一辆新车。

run sth ↔ **up** *phr v* [T] **1 run up a bill/expenses/debts** to use a lot of something or borrow a lot of money, so that you will have to pay a lot of money 积欠大量账款/花费/债务: *She ran up an enormous phone bill.* 她积欠下很多电话费。**2** to make something, especially clothes, very quickly 赶制〔尤指衣服〕: *I ran this dress up in a single evening.* 我用了一个晚上赶做出这件衣服。**3** to raise a flag on a pole 升旗

run up against sth/sb *phr v* [T] to have to deal with unexpected problems or a difficult opponent 碰到〔突如其来的问题或难应付的对手〕: *We ran up against some unexpected opposition.* 我们遭到了意想不到的反对。

R

run[2] *n*

1 ▶ON FOOT 跑, 跑步◀ [C] a period of time spent running, or a distance that you run 跑步的时间[距离]: *a 5-mile run* 五英里跑 | **go for a run** (=for exercise or pleasure) 跑步 *She usually goes for a run before breakfast.* 她通常在早饭前跑步。| **break into a run** (=start running) 开始跑 *He was still following me, and in a panic I broke into a run.* 他仍然尾随着我, 慌乱中我拔腿就跑。| **at a run** (=running) 跑着 *Sarah left the house at a run.* 萨拉跑着离开了房子。

2 be on the run a) to be trying to escape or hide, especially from the police〔尤指为逃避警察而〕逃跑, 躲藏: *A dangerous criminal is on the run in the bay area of the city.* 一名危险的罪犯潜逃在该市的海湾区。**b)** if an army or an opponent is on the run, they may soon be defeated〔军队或对手〕行将失败

3 make a run for it to suddenly start running, in order to escape 突然逃跑: *One of the prisoners made a run for it.* 一名囚犯突然逃跑。

4 in the long run later in the future, not immediately 从长远来看, 终究: *The less you rely on painkillers now, the better it will be for your health in the long run.* 从长远来看, 你现在越少依赖止痛片, 对你的健康越有益。

5 in the short run in the near future 从短期来看, 不久: *Economies like these save money in the short run, but in the end you'll be no better off.* 像这样节省从短期来看能省钱, 但到头来你不会更富有。

6 a run of good/bad luck several lucky or unlucky things happening quickly after each other 一连串的好运/倒霉事: *Losing my job was the start of a run of bad luck that year.* 那一年, 失业是我碰到的一连串倒霉事的开始。

7 a run of failures/wins/strikes etc a series of failures, wins etc 一连串的失败/胜利/打击等: *The company has had a run of spectacularly successful years.* 这家公司一连几年业绩辉煌。

8 a run on a situation in which lots of people suddenly buy a particular product 抢购: *There's been a big run on ice-cream during this hot weather.* 天气炎热, 冰淇淋销量激增。

9 have the run of to be allowed to use a place when and how you want 可以随意使用〔某地方〕: *I had the run of the house for the afternoon.* 下午我可以随意使用那所房子。

10 in the normal run of events used when saying what usually happens 按照一般情况, 通常: *In the normal run of events, I would never have gone there.* 按照一般情况, 我是决不会去那里的。

11 have a (good) run for your money *informal* if you have a good run for your money, you have succeeded in doing something for an unusually long time or you have been unusually successful【非正式】该满足了〔用于表示某人的成功比一般长久或巨大〕: *He lived to be 92, so I think he had a good run for his money.* 他活到92岁, 我想他应该满足了。

12 give sb a good run for their money to play well in a competition or sports game, so that your opponent has to use all their skill and effort to defeat you 让对手竭尽全力才获胜: *They beat us, but we certainly gave them a good run for their money.* 他们打败了我们, 不过是费尽九牛二虎之力才赢的。

13 ▶ILLNESS 疾病◀ the runs *informal* DIARRHOEA (=an illness that makes you need to go to the toilet often)【非正式】腹泻, 拉肚子

14 ▶PLAY/FILM 戏剧/电影◀ [C] a continuous series of performances of a play, film etc in the same place (在相同地方)连续演出: *His first play had a three-month run in the West End.* 他的第一部戏在伦敦西区连续上演了三个月。

15 ▶JOURNEY 旅程◀ [singular] **a)** a journey by train, ship, TRUCK etc, made regularly between two places〔火车、船、卡车等的〕固定行程[航程]: *It's only a 55-minute run from London to Brighton.* 从伦敦到布赖顿只是55分钟的车程。**b)** *informal* a short journey in a car, for pleasure【非正式】〔乘车〕兜风: *Let's take the car out for a run.* 我们开车兜兜风去。

16 ▶FOR ANIMALS 动物使用的◀ [C] an enclosed area where animals such as chickens or rabbits are kept〔鸡、兔子等的〕饲养场

17 ▶SPORT 体育◀ [C] a point won in CRICKET or BASEBALL〔板球或棒球比赛中的〕一分

18 ▶SKIING 滑雪◀ [C] a sloping area of land that you can SKI down 滑雪斜坡: *They don't let beginners go on the higher runs.* 他们不允许初学者使用高坡滑道。

19 ▶IN CLOTHES 在衣物上◀ [C] *AmE* a line of torn stitches in TIGHTS, STOCKINGS etc【美】〔裤袜、长统袜等的〕脱线, 抽丝; LADDER[1] (3) *BrE*【英】

20 ▶BANK 银行◀ [singular] an occasion when lots of people all take their money out of a bank at the same time 挤提存款, 挤兑

21 run on the dollar/pound etc a situation in which a lot of people sell dollars etc and the value goes down〔很多人〕抛售美元/英镑等

22 ▶MUSIC 音乐◀ [C] a set of notes played or sung quickly up or down a SCALE in a piece of music〔按音阶顺序的〕速奏; 速唱

23 ▶CARD GAMES 纸牌游戏◀ [C] a set of cards with numbers in a series, held by one player 顺子 —see also 另见 DRY RUN, DUMMY RUN, FUN RUN, MILK RUN, TRIAL RUN

run-a-bout /ˈrʌnəˌbaʊt; ˈrʌnəbaʊt/ *n* [C] *informal* a small car used for short journeys【非正式】轻便小汽车

run-a-round /ˈ· · ˌ·/ *n* **give sb the run-around** *informal* to deliberately avoid giving someone a definite answer, especially when they are asking you to do something【非正式】〔尤指别人要你做事时〕搪塞, 顾左右而言他: *Every time we ask the landlord about fixing the roof, he gives us the run-around.* 每次我们要求房主修理屋顶时, 他总是搪塞。—see also 另见 **run around** (RUN[1])

run-a-way[1] /ˈrʌnəˌwe; ˈrʌnəweɪ/ *adj* [only before noun 仅用于名词前] **1** a runaway vehicle or animal has gone out of con-

trol〔车辆或动物〕失控的 **2 runaway success/inflation etc** success, INFLATION etc that happens quickly or uncontrollably 迅速的成功; 失控的通货膨胀: *The film was a runaway success.* 这部电影一炮打响。**3** a runaway person has left the place where they are supposed to be 逃跑的: *a runaway child* 一个离家出走的孩子

runaway² *n* [C] someone, especially a child, who has left home without telling anyone and does not intend to come back 离家出走者〔尤指小孩〕—see also 另见 **run away** (RUN¹)

run·down /ˈrʌnˋdaʊn; ˈrʌndaʊn/ *n* [C usually singular 一般用单数] **1** a quick report or explanation of an idea, situation etc〔关于某构想、情况等的〕简要报告, 扼要说明, 梗概: **give sb a rundown on** *Someone give Charlie a quick rundown on what we've done so far.* 请谁给查利简要报告一下到目前为止我们所做的工作。**2** [singular] the process of making a business or industry smaller and less important〔公司、工业等的规模或重要性的〕缩减

run-down /ˌ· ˈ·◂/ *adj* **1** a building or area that is rundown is in very bad condition〔建筑物或地区〕破旧的, 失修的: *a run-down inner-city area* 破败的旧城区 **2** [not before noun 不用于名词前] someone who is run-down is tired and not healthy〔人〕精疲力竭的, 衰弱的: *You look a bit run-down – maybe you need a rest.* 你看来有点儿累, 也许你需要休息。

rune /run; ruːn/ *n* [C] *technical*【术语】**1** one of the letters of the alphabet used in the past by people in Northern Europe 如尼字母〔古代北欧的一种字母〕**2** a magic song or written sign 神秘的歌; 神秘的符号 —**runic** *adj*

R

rung¹ /rʌŋ; rʌŋ/ the past tense of RING²

rung² *n* [C] **1** one of the bars that form the steps of a ladder 梯子的横档, 梯级 **2** *informal* a particular level or position in an organization or system【非正式】〔组织或体制中的〕等级, 地位: *on the highest rung of the salary scale* 薪金级别最高的一级 **3** a bar between two legs of a chair〔椅子腿间的〕横档

run-in /ˈ· ·/ *n* [C] an argument or disagreement, especially with someone in an official position〔尤指与公务人员的〕争吵, 争执: **have a run-in with** *Michael got drunk and had a run-in with the police.* 迈克尔喝醉了, 跟警察发生了争执。

run·ner /ˈrʌnə; ˈrʌnə/ *n* [C] **1** someone who runs as a sport 参加赛跑的人: *a long-distance runner* 长跑运动员 **2** someone who walks or runs from place to place carrying messages, especially in former times〔尤指旧时的〕送信者 **3 do a runner** *BrE* to leave somewhere quickly in order to avoid paying for something or having to meet someone【英】〔为避免付款或逃避某人而〕迅速逃离, 溜掉: *By the time the police got there, the boys had done a runner.* 警察到达那里的时候, 那些男孩子已经溜掉了。**4** one of the two thin pieces of metal that a SLEDGE has, or the single piece of metal under a SKATE¹ (1)〔雪橇的〕滑板;〔冰鞋的〕冰刀 **5** the bar of wood or metal that a drawer or curtain slides along〔抽屉或帘子的〕滑槽, 滑道 **6** *technical* a stem with which a plant such as a STRAWBERRY spreads itself along the ground【术语】长匐茎, 匍匐茎 **7** a long narrow piece of cloth or CARPET 狭长的布[地毯] —see also 另见 DRUG RUNNER, FRONT-RUNNER

runner-bean /ˌ·· ˈ·/ *n* [C] *BrE* a vegetable that grows as a long green POD (=seed container) on a climbing plant【英】红花菜豆 —see picture on page A9 参见 A9 页图

runner-up /ˌ·· ˈ·/ *n plural* **runners-up** [C] the person or team that comes second in a race or competition〔比赛中的〕第二名, 亚军

run·ning¹ /ˈrʌnɪŋ; ˈrʌnɪŋ/ *n* [U] **1** the act or sport of running 跑步, 赛跑: **running shoes/track etc** *new facilities including a pool and a running track* 包括一个游泳池和一条跑道的新设施 **2 the running of** the way in which a business, home, organization etc is managed or organized 管理, 经营: *Brian took over the running of the company while his father was away.* 父亲不在期间, 布赖恩接手公司的管理。**3 be in the running/out of the running** to have some hope or no hope of winning a race or competition〔在比赛中〕有/没有希望取胜: *Bruno is still in the running for the world title.* 布鲁诺仍有希望获得世界冠军。**4 make (all) the running** *BrE informal*【英, 非正式】**a)** to be the person who makes most of the suggestions in a relationship, plan, activity etc〔在关系、计划、活动等中〕主动; 带头 **b)** to be the leader in a competition, race, election etc〔在比赛、竞选等中〕领先

running² *adj* [only before noun 仅用于名词前] **1 running water a)** water that comes from a TAP¹ (1) 自来水: *Disease spreads fast in villages where there is no running water.* 疾病在没有自来水的村庄里迅速传播。**b)** water that is flowing or moving 流动的水: *Many fish prefer running water.* 许多鱼喜欢流动的水。**2 running repairs** small repairs that you do to a machine to keep it working〔维持机器继续运作的〕小修理 **3 running total** a total that is continually increased as new costs, amounts etc are added 不断增加的总数: *Keep a running total of your expenses as you go along.* 你一面干, 一面记下开支的总数。**4 running commentary** a spoken description of an event, especially a race or game, made while the event is happening〔比赛或体育运动的〕现场实况报道: *a running commentary on the basketball game* 篮球比赛的现场实况报道 **5 running battle/argument** an argument that continues or is repeated over a long period of time 争执不下, 持续的争论 **6 running sore** a sore area on your skin, that has liquid coming out of it 流脓的创口 **7 in running order** a machine that is in running order is working correctly〔机器〕运转正常的 **8 the running order** the order in which the different parts of an event have been arranged to take place 日程表, 安排: *changes in the running order for the teachers' conference* 教师大会日程表的变更

running³ *adv* **three years/five times etc running** for three years etc without a change or interruption 连续三年/五次等: *Sylvie has won the poetry prize for the fourth year running.* 西尔维已经连续四年获得诗歌奖。

running costs /ˈ·· ·/ *n* [plural] the amount of money that is needed to operate an organization, system etc〔组织等的〕经营成本

running jump /ˌ·· ˈ·/ *n* [C] **1** a jump made by running up to the point at which you leave the ground 跑跳, 跑步跳远 **2 take a running jump** *spoken* used to tell someone to go away and stop annoying you【口】走开〔用于斥退讨厌的人〕: *If he hassles you again tell him to take a running jump!* 如果他再打搅你, 就叫他滚开!

running mate /ˈ·· ·/ *n* [C usually singular 一般用单数] the person who someone who is trying to become president, leader etc chooses to help them in an election〔总统候选人等的〕竞选伙伴: *Al Gore was Bill Clinton's running mate in the 1992 election.* 在1992年的选举中, 阿尔·戈尔是比尔·克林顿的竞选伙伴。

run·ny /ˈrʌnɪ; ˈrʌni/ *adj informal*【非正式】**1** something, especially a food, that is runny is not solid or thick enough〔尤指食物〕稀的, 黏软的: **go runny** (=become runny) 融化 *The butter had gone runny in the heat.* 黄油遇热融化了。**2** a runny nose, runny eyes etc have liquid coming out of them, usually because you have a cold〔尤指因感冒而〕流鼻涕的; 流泪的

Run·ny·mede /ˈrʌnɪmid; ˈrʌnimiːd/ a field near the River Thames at Egham, southern England, where it is believed that King John signed the Magna Carta in 1215. There is also a small area of land there which was given to the American people in 1965, and which contains a MEMORIAL to President John F. Kennedy. 兰尼米德〔英格兰南部埃格姆境内一地区, 靠近泰晤士河, 据说, 国王约翰1215年在此签署了《大宪章》。1965年, 英国把兰尼米德的一小块地送给了美国人民, 现立有约翰·F.肯尼迪总统纪念碑〕

run-off /ˈ· ·/ *n* **1** [C] a second competition or election that is arranged to decide the winner when two competitors get an equal number of points or votes the first time〔比赛打平手后的〕重赛;〔得票相同者之间的〕决胜选举 —compare 比较 PLAY-OFF —see also 另见 **run off** (RUN¹) **2** [U] *technical* rain or other liquid that flows off the land into rivers【术语】径流, 溢流〔指流入河流中的雨水或其他液体〕: *nitrogen-rich run-off from agricultural land* 从农田流出的高含氮量溢流

run-of-the-mill /ˌ· · · ˈ·◂/ *adj* not special or interesting in any way; ordinary 普通的, 一般的, 不突出的: *a run-of-the-mill performance* 平平的表现

run-on sen·tence /ˈ· · ,· ·/ *n* [C] *especially AmE* a sentence that has two main CLAUSES without connecting words or correct PUNCTUATION【尤美】连写句〔含有两个主句, 但没有连接词或正确的标点符号〕

runt /rʌnt; rʌnt/ *n* [C] **1** the smallest and least developed baby animal of a group born at the same time〔一胎中的〕最小且发育不全的小动物: *the runt of the litter* 一窝中最小的一个 **2** *informal* a small, unpleasant or unimportant person【非正式】矮小[讨厌, 无足轻重]的人

run-through /ˈ· ·/ *n* [C] a short practice before a performance, test etc〔时间短的〕排练, 预演; 预习: *a final run-through of the play* 这场戏的最后一次排练

run-up /ˈ· ·/ *n* **1 the run-up to** the period of time just before an important event〔重要事件的〕前奏期, 预备期间: *the run-up to the 1992 election* 1992年选举的竞选阶段 **2** [C] the act of running, or the distance that you run, before you kick a ball, jump over a pole etc〔踢球、跳高等之前的〕助跑; 助跑距离

run·way /ˈrʌnˌwe; ˈrʌnweɪ/ *n* [C] **1** a long specially prepared hard surface like a road on which aircraft land and take off〔机场的〕跑道 **2** *AmE* a long narrow part of a stage that stretches out into the area where the AUDIENCE sits【美】伸入观众席的延伸舞台

Run·yon /ˈrʌnjən; ˈrʌnjən/, **Da·mon** /ˈdemən; ˈdeɪmən/ (1884-1946) a US writer of humorous short stories about GANGSTERS (=members of violent criminal groups) and people who worked on Broadway in New York City. His characters use a lot of SLANG and unusual expressions. His most famous collection of stories, *Guys and Dolls*, was later made into a successful musical show.鲁尼恩〔(1884-1946)，美国幽默短篇小说家。笔下的人物为匪徒和纽约市百老汇的上班族，言谈中多俚语和怪词。最有名的作品是短篇小说集《少男少女》，后来被改编成一部优秀音乐剧〕

ru·pee /ruˈpi; ruːˈpiː/ *n* [C] the standard unit of money in India, Pakistan, and some other countries 卢比〔印度、巴基斯坦等国家的货币单位〕

Ru·pert Bear /ˌrupɚt ˈbɛr; ˌruːpət ˈbeə/ a little bear who wears a red SWEATER, yellow checked trousers, and a SCARF. He is the main character of popular stories for children invented by the British writer and artist Mary Tourtel. 鲁珀特熊〔一只穿红色套衫、黄色格子裤、围一条围巾的小熊。它是一些流行儿童读物中的主人公，由英国作家和画家玛丽·图泰尔塑造〕

rup·ture[1] /ˈrʌptʃɚ; ˈrʌptʃə/ *n* **1** [C,U] an occasion when something suddenly breaks apart or bursts〔突然的〕破裂，裂开: *the rupture of a blood vessel* 血管的突然破裂 **2** [C] a situation in which two countries or groups of people suddenly disagree and often end their relationship with each other〔两个国家或团体之间关系的〕突然决裂，断绝: *the rupture between the two religious communities* 两个宗教团体之间关系的突然决裂 **3** [C,U] a medical condition in which an organ of the body sticks out through the wall of muscle that normally surrounds it; HERNIA 疝

rupture[2] *v* **1** [I,T] to break or burst, or make something break or burst (使)破裂，爆裂: *A pipeline carrying crude oil has ruptured.* 一条输送原油的管道破裂了。**2 rupture yourself** to cause a RUPTURE[1] (3) in your body 使〔自己〕发疝气

W2 **ru·ral** /ˈrʊrəl; ˈrʊərəl/ *adj* **1** happening in or connected with the countryside, not the city 农村的，乡村的，田园的: *a peaceful rural setting* 平静的乡村景象 | *rural bus routes* 农村的公共汽车路线 **2** like the countryside or reminding you of the countryside 像农村的; 使人想起农村的: *It's very rural round here, isn't it?* 这周围很像农村，对不对？—opposite 反义词 URBAN

rural de·liv·er·y /ˌ‥ ·ˈ‥·/ *n* RD 乡村递送

rural route /ˈ‥ ·/ *n* RR 乡村投递路线

Rur·i·ta·ni·a /ˌrurɪˈteniə; ˌrʊərɪˈteɪniə/ an imaginary small European country, where many exciting and romantic adventures happen in the NOVEL *The Prisoner of Zenda* by Anthony Hope 卢里坦尼亚王国〔一虚构的欧洲小国。据安东尼·霍普的小说《曾达的囚徒》所述，这里有过不少令人激动的浪漫奇遇〕—**Ruritanian** *n, adj*

ruse /ruz; ruːz/ *n* [C] a clever trick used to deceive someone 诡计，计策: *It dawned on me that this was only a ruse, done to gain time.* 我猛然醒悟，这不过是缓兵之计。

S2 W3 **rush**[1] /rʌʃ; rʌʃ/ *v*

1 ►MOVE QUICKLY 快速移动◄ [I always+adv/prep] to move very quickly, especially because you need to be somewhere very soon〔尤因为要很快到某处而〕急速行进，猛冲: [**+out/past/through/along etc**] *We rushed home to find out what had happened to Julie.* 我们急速赶回家去看朱莉出了什么事。| *One of the pipes burst and water came rushing out.* 有一条管道破裂了，水不断涌出来。

2 ►DO STH QUICKLY 急速做某事◄ [I,T] to do something too quickly, especially so that you do not have time to do it carefully or well 仓促行事，仓促完成: *There's plenty of time – we don't need to rush.* 时间充足，我们不必匆忙。| **rush sth** *You shouldn't rush this sort of work.* 这种工作你不应匆匆忙忙地做。

3 rush to do sth to do something eagerly and without delay 抢着做某事，赶紧做某事: *Fans rushed to buy tickets as soon as they went on sale.* 一开始售票，支持者就抢着去买。

4 ►TAKE/SEND URGENTLY 急忙地送◄ [T always+ adv/prep] to take or send something somewhere very quickly, especially because of an unexpected problem〔尤指因意外事件而〕急送〔某物到某地〕: *The Red Cross rushed medical supplies to the war zone.* 红十字会火速将医疗供应品送往作战地区。| **rush sb somewhere** *Dan was rushed to the hospital with serious head injuries.* 丹因头部受重伤被迅速送往医院。

5 ►MAKE SB HURRY 催促某人◄ [T] to try to make someone do something more quickly than they want to 催促〔某人做某事〕: *I'm sorry to rush you, but we need a decision by Friday.* 很抱歉催你，不过我们在星期五之前需要作出决定。| **rush sb into doing sth** *Don't let them rush you into signing the contract.* 别让他们催你签合同。

6 ►ATTACK 攻击◄ [T] to attack someone suddenly and in a group〔一伙人〕突然袭击: *They rushed the guard and stole his keys.* 他们突然袭击守卫，偷了他的钥匙。

7 ►AMERICAN UNIVERSITIES 美国大学◄ *AmE*【美】**a)** [T] to give parties for students, have meetings etc, in order to decide whether to let them join a FRATERNITY or SORORITY (=type of club) 招待〔大学生联谊会用舞会、聚会等来吸收新会员〕**b)** [I,T] to go through the process of trying to be accepted into these clubs 争取加入(大学生联谊会)

8 ►AMERICAN FOOTBALL 美式橄榄球◄ [I,T] to carry the ball forward 带(球)跑动 —see also 另见 RUSHED

rush about/around *phr v* [I] to try to do a lot of things in a short period of time 匆匆忙忙: *I was rushing around all morning trying to get everything ready for the trip.* 整个上午我都在忙忙碌碌地为旅行做准备。

rush into sth *phr v* [T] to get involved in something without taking enough time to think carefully about it 仓促做，急忙做: **rush into things** *spoken*【口】: *He's asked me to marry him, but I don't want to rush into things.* 他要我嫁给他，但是我不想太仓促。

rush sth ↔ **out** *phr v* [T] to make a new product, book etc available for sale very quickly 赶制〔新产品〕; 赶印〔书〕

rush sth ↔ **through** *phr v* [T] to deal with official or government business, more quickly than usual 加急处理〔公务〕: *The legislation was rushed through Parliament.* 议会仓促通过了法律。

R

rush[2] *n*

1 ►FAST MOVEMENT 急速行动◄ [singular] a sudden fast movement of things or people 冲，奔: *Someone shouted 'fire!', and there was a rush towards the door.* 有人大声叫喊"失火啦!"，人们都朝门口涌去。| **in a rush** *Her words came out in a rush.* 她急急忙忙地说。| *a sudden rush of wind* 突然刮起的风

2 ►HURRY 赶紧◄ [singular,U] a situation in which you need to hurry 匆忙，赶紧: *There's always such a rush to get things done.* 做事总是这么匆忙。| **there's no rush** *spoken* (=there is no need to hurry)【口】不必着急 *There's no rush. We don't have to leave till 10.30.* 不必着急，我们到10:30分才走。| **do sth in a rush** (=do something quickly, especially so that it is not done well) 匆忙做某事〔尤指事情因而做得不好〕*It all seems to have been decided in such a rush.* 决定似乎非常仓促。| **be in a rush** *I'm sorry, I can't talk now – I'm in kind of a rush.* 对不起，我现在不能聊，我得赶时间。

3 ►BUSY PERIOD 繁忙时期◄ **the rush** the time in the day, month, year etc when a place or group of people are particularly busy〔一天、一月、一年中，某地或某些人〕特别忙碌的时期: *The café is quiet until the lunchtime rush begins.* 在最忙碌的午饭时间前，小餐馆很宁静。| *the Christmas rush* 圣诞节购物热潮 —see also 另见 RUSH HOUR

4 ►PEOPLE WANTING STH 人们需要某物◄ [singular] a situation in which a lot of people suddenly try to do or get something〔很多人〕争做，急需: [**+on**] *a rush on swimsuits in the hot weather* 天气炎热，泳衣的需求激增 | **rush to do sth** *There was a big rush to get tickets for the football game.* 人们抢购那场足球赛的门票。—see also 另见 GOLD RUSH

5 ►PLANT 植物◄ [C] a type of tall grass that grows in water, often used for making baskets, mats etc 灯芯草〔常用来编筐、垫等〕

6 ►FEELING 感觉 **a)** [C] *informal* a strong, usually pleasant feeling that you get from taking a drug or from doing something exciting【非正式】〔服用药物或做了令人兴奋的事而得到〕快感: *Playing in front of a packed house was a real rush.* 在满座的剧场表演真带劲。**b) rush of excitement/panic etc** a sudden very strong feeling of excitement etc 一阵激动/慌乱等: *I felt a rush of excitement as she walked through the door.* 她走进门时我感到一阵激动。

7 ►FILM 电影◄ **rushes** [plural] the first prints of a film before it has been edited (EDIT (1)) 拍摄后未经剪辑的影片; DAILY[3] (3) *AmE*【美】

8 ►AMERICAN STUDENTS 美国学生◄ [singular] *AmE* the time when students in American universities who want to join a FRATERNITY or SORORITY (=type of club) go to a lot of parties【美】〔大学生联谊会为吸收新会员而举办的〕一连串活动期间: *rush week* (大学生联谊会吸收新会员的)活动周 | *a rush party* (大学生联谊会吸收新会员举行的)聚会

Rush·die /ˈrʊʃdɪ; ˈrʊʃdi/, **Sal·man** /sælˈmɑn; sælˈmɑːn/ (1947-) a British writer born in India, who won the Booker

Prize for his NOVEL *Midnight's Children*. In 1988 his novel *The Satanic Verses* offended Muslims because they said that it was insulting to their religion, with the result that Ayatollah Khomeini in Iran gave a FATWA, an order that Rushdie should be killed. He had to live in a secret place for many years. 拉什迪〔(1947-),生于印度的英国作家。他曾以《午夜之子》获布克奖。1988年,他的小说《撒旦诗篇》冒犯了穆斯林,按穆斯林的说法,该书是对伊斯兰教的侮辱,结果阿亚图拉霍梅尼在伊朗下了一道追杀令,要求把拉什迪处死。多年来,拉什迪只好躲藏起来生活〕

rushed /rʌʃt; rʌʃt/ *adj* **1** done very quickly or too quickly, because there was not enough time 匆忙的, 仓促的: *a rather rushed meeting* 非常匆忙的会议 **2 be rushed off your feet** *especially BrE* to be so busy that you do not have time to stop or rest【尤英】忙得不可开交

rush hour /ˈ· ·/ *n* [C,U] the time of day when the roads, buses, trains etc are most crowded, because people are travelling to or from work〔上下班的〕高峰时间, 交通拥挤时间: *heavy rush hour traffic* 高峰时间拥挤的交通

CULTURAL NOTE 文化注释

The images people have of rush hour is of a lot of tired unsmiling faces crowded into buses and trains and long lines of cars trying to get to or from work as fast as possible. 在上下班高峰时间,人们急着上下班,多是满脸困倦、毫无笑意地挤在公交车和火车上,而汽车也排起长龙。

R

Rush·more /ˈrʌʃmɔr; ˈrʌʃmɔː/, **Mount** also 又作 **Mount Rushmore National Memorial** a mountain in South Dakota, US, where the rock has been cut into the shape of the faces of four US presidents: Washington, Jefferson, Lincoln, and Theodore Roosevelt 拉什穆尔山〔美国南达科他州的一座山。山岩上雕刻有四位美国总统的头像,分别是华盛顿、杰弗逊、林肯和西奥多·罗斯福〕

rusk /rʌsk; rʌsk/ *n* [C] *especially BrE* a hard sweet dry bread for babies to eat【尤英】〔婴儿食用的〕甜面包干, 脆饼干

Ruskin /ˈrʌskɪn; ˈrʌskɪn/, **John** (1819-1900) a British art CRITIC and social critic, who wrote many essays including *Modern Painters* 罗斯金〔(1819-1900),英国艺术评论家、社会评论家。他写过许多著作,其中包括《现代画家》〕

Rus·sell /ˈrʌsl; ˈrʌsəl/, **Ber·trand** /ˈbɜtrənd; ˈbɜːtrənd/ (1872-1970) a British PHILOSOPHER and MATHEMATICIAN who developed new ideas connecting mathematics and LOGIC. He was also known for being a PACIFIST (=someone who believes that all wars are wrong), and he was one of the leading members of the opposition to NUCLEAR weapons. He received the Nobel Prize for Literature in 1950. 罗素〔(1872-1970),英国哲学家、数学家。他曾提出将数学与逻辑相联系的新观点。他是一位著名的和平运动者,也是反对核武器的领袖人物之一。1950年获诺贝尔文学奖〕

Russell, Charles (1864-1926) a popular US artist who painted scenes of COWBOYS and Native Americans 拉塞尔〔(1864-1926),美国著名画家,专画牛仔与印第安人〕

rus·set /ˈrʌsɪt; ˈrʌsɨt/ *n* [U] *especially literary* a reddish-brown colour【尤文】赤褐色 —**russet** *adj* —see picture on page A5 参见 A5 页图

Rus·sia /ˈrʌʃə; ˈrʌʃə/ a very large country in Eastern Europe and northern Asia, officially called the Russian Federation. It consists of the land from the Arctic Ocean in the north to the Black Sea in the south, and from the borders of Belarus and Ukraine in the west to the Pacific Ocean in the east. Population: 145,470,197 (2001). Capital: Moscow. Before 1917, Russia was a large, powerful country, ruled by a king called the tsar. After 1917, it formed the largest part of the Soviet Union, and people often used the name 'Russia' when they meant the whole Soviet Union and its Communist government. Since 1991, Russia has had a new government. 俄罗斯〔欧洲东部和亚洲北部一个地域辽阔的国家,正式名称为俄罗斯联邦。北起北冰洋,南至黑海,西起白俄罗斯和乌克兰边境,东至太平洋。人口: 145,470,197 (2001),首都: 莫斯科。1917年前的俄罗斯在沙皇统治下是一个幅员辽阔的强国。1917年后俄罗斯并入苏联,并成为面积最大的加盟共和国。过去,人们常用Russia指称苏联及其共产党领导的政府。1991年,俄罗斯建立了一个新政府〕

Rus·sian[1] /ˈrʌʃən; ˈrʌʃən/ *n* **1** [U] the language of Russia 俄语 **2** [C] someone from Russia 俄罗斯人; 俄国人

Russian[2] *adj* from or connected with Russia 俄国的, 俄罗斯的

Russian Or·tho·dox Church, the /,·· ,··· ˈ·/ the main religious group of Russia. It is a Christian church that began in the 11th century by separating from the Catholic Church. The Orthodox Church has very complicated religious ceremonies in which the words are mostly sung rather than spoken, and it is closely related to the Greek Orthodox Church. 俄罗斯正教会〔俄罗斯的主要宗教团体,是11世纪脱离天主教而另行成立的一个基督教教派。正教会的宗教礼仪非常复杂,经文主要是吟唱而并非诵读。俄罗斯正教会与希腊正教会有着密切联系〕—**Russian Orthodox** *adj*

Russian Rev·o·lu·tion, the /,·· ···ˈ··/ the events of 1917, when the Russian people overthrew (OVERTHROW) their TSAR before the communists took over under the leadership of Lenin 俄国革命〔1917年的一系列事件。当时,俄国人推翻了沙皇统治,共产党人在列宁的领导下夺取了政权〕

Russian rou·lette /,·· ·ˈ·/ *n* [U] a game in which you risk killing yourself by shooting at your head with a gun that has a bullet in only one of six CHAMBER*s* 俄罗斯轮盘赌〔一种玩命的游戏。在有六个弹位的左轮手枪内仅装一颗子弹,然后旋转弹膛,举枪对准自己的头部扣动扳机〕

rust[1] /rʌst; rʌst/ *n* [U] **1** the reddish-brown substance that forms on iron and steel when they get wet 锈, 铁锈: *There were large patches of rust on the car.* 汽车上有大块的锈斑。**2** a plant disease that causes reddish-brown spots〔植物的〕锈病 —see also 另见 RUSTPROOF, RUSTY

rust[2] *v* [I,T] to become covered with rust or make something become covered in rust (使)生锈: *a rusted old basketball hoop* 一个生锈的旧篮圈

rust away *phr v* [I] to be gradually destroyed by rust 因生锈而慢慢烂掉

Rust Belt, the /ˈ· ·/ *AmE* an area in the northern US, including parts of the states of Illinois, Michigan, Indiana, Ohio, and Wisconsin, where many large, older industries, especially the steel and car industries, have become less successful and many factories have closed down【美】铁锈地带, 夕阳工业带, 经济衰退带〔美国北部一区域,包括伊利诺伊、密歇根、印第安纳、俄亥俄和威斯康星诸州的部分地区。许多大型传统工业,尤其是钢铁和汽车工业每况愈下,许多工厂关闭〕

rus·tic[1] /ˈrʌstɪk; ˈrʌstɪk/ *adj* **1** simple, old-fashioned, and not spoiled by modern developments, in a way that is typical of the countryside 质朴的, 乡村的, 农村风味的: *The village had a certain rustic charm.* 这个村庄有一种迷人的田园风情。**2** [only before noun 仅用于名词前] roughly made from wood 用木头粗制的: *a rustic chair* 一把木头粗制而成的椅子 —**rusticity** *n* [U]

rustic[2] *n* [C] *literary or humorous* someone from the country, especially a farm worker【文或幽默】乡下人, 庄稼人, 乡巴佬

rus·tle[1] /ˈrʌsl; ˈrʌsəl/ *v* **1** [I,T] if leaves, papers, clothes etc rustle, or if you rustle them, they make a noise as they rub against each other (使)〔树叶、纸、衣物等〕沙沙作响: *Stop rustling that newspaper!* 别把报纸弄得沙沙响! **2** [T] to steal farm animals such as cattle, horses, or sheep 偷〔牧场的牲畜, 如牛、马、羊〕

rustle sth ↔ **up** *phr v* [T] *informal* to find or make something quickly, especially food or a meal【非正式】迅速弄到, 仓促拼凑〔尤指食物或一顿饭〕: *I'll rustle up a couple of steaks on the barbecue.* 我要在烤肉架上赶紧烤两块牛排。

rustle[2] *n* [singular] the noise made when something rustles 沙沙声, 窸窣声: *a rustle of leaves* 树叶的沙沙声 —see picture on page A19 参见 A19 页图

rus·tler /ˈrʌslɚ; ˈrʌslə/ *n* [C] someone who steals farm animals such as cattle, horses, or sheep 偷牲畜的贼

rust·proof /ˈrʌst,pruf; ˈrʌstpruːf/ *adj* metal that is rustproof will not RUST〔金属〕防锈的, 抗锈的

rust·y /ˈrʌstɪ; ˈrʌsti/ *adj* **1** metal that is rusty is covered in RUST[1] (1) 生锈的: *a rusty nail* 生锈的铁钉 —see picture on page A18 参见 A18 页图 **2** if someone's skill in a particular activity or subject is rusty, it is not as good as it used to be, because they have not practised it for a long time〔技术等〕荒疏的, 荒废的: *My French is very rusty these days.* 近来我的法语相当生疏了。—**rustiness** *n* [U]

rut /rʌt; rʌt/ *n* **1** [C] a deep narrow track left in soft ground by a wheel 车辙 **2 in a rut** living or working in a situation that never changes, so that you feel bored〔生活或工作〕固定又乏味, 一成不变: **be stuck in a rut** *I was stuck in a rut, and decided to look for a new job.* 我干的都是老一套, 所以决定找一份新工作。**3 the rut** *technical* the period of the year when some male animals, especially DEER, are sexually active【术语】〔雄性动物, 尤指鹿的〕发情期

ru·ta·ba·ga /,rutəˈbegə; ,ruːtəˈbeɪgə/ *n* [C] *AmE* a large round yellow vegetable【美】芜菁甘蓝〔一种圆形黄色的蔬菜〕; SWEDE *BrE*【英】—see picture on page A9 参见 A9 页图

Ruth /ruθ; ruːθ/, **Babe** (1895-1948) a US BASEBALL player, the most famous ever, who played mainly for the New York

Yankees team, and got more HOME RUNS than anyone before him. He was called the Sultan of Swat. 鲁思〔(1895-1948)，美国有史以来最伟大的棒球运动员。他曾主要效力于纽约扬基队，击出有史以来最多的本垒打，有"安打王"之称〕

Rutherford /ˈrʌðəfəd; ˈrʌðəfəd/, **Er·nest** /ˈɜnɪst; ˈɜːnɪst/ (1871-1937) a British scientist, born in New Zealand, who discovered the structure of the atom, and discovered that there are three types of RADIATION – alpha, beta, and gamma rays. He is most famous for being the first person to 'split the atom', when he split the NUCLEUS (=central part) of an atom in 1919. 卢瑟福〔(1871-1937)，英国科学家，生于新西兰。他发现了原子结构和三种辐射，即α、β、γ射线。最为著名的是，1919年他将原子核分裂开来，从而成为"分裂原子"的第一人〕

ruth·less /ˈruθlɪs; ˈruːθləs/ *adj* **1** so determined to get what you want that you do not care if you have to hurt other people in order to do it 无情的，冷酷的，残忍的: *a ruthless dictator* 残忍的独裁者 | *a ruthless disregard for basic human rights* 对基本人权无情的蔑视 **2** determined and firm when taking unpleasant decision〔作出令人不快的决定时〕坚决的: *We'll have to be ruthless if we want to eliminate this kind of time-wasting.* 如果我们想杜绝这种对时间的浪费就必须坚决果断。—**ruthlessly** *adv* —**ruthlessness** *n* [U]

Rut·land /ˈrʌtlənd; ˈrʌtlənd/ a local government area and former COUNTY in central England. It used to be England's smallest county. 拉特兰〔旧时英格兰中部一郡和地方政府所在地，也曾是英格兰最小一郡〕

rut·ted /ˈrʌtɪd; ˈrʌtɪd/ *adj* a surface that is rutted has deep narrow tracks in it left by the wheels of vehicles 留有车辙的: *a rutted dirt road* 留有车辙的土路

RV /ˌɑr ˈvi; ˌɑː ˈviː/ *n* [C] *AmE* recreational vehicle; a large vehicle, usually with cooking equipment and beds in it, that a family can use for travelling or camping【美】活动房屋式旅游车，房车〔通常有炊具和床，供家庭旅行、露营时使用〕

Rw·an·da /ruˈɑndə; ruˈændə/ a country in east central Africa between Tanzania and Zaïre. Population: 7,810,056 (2003). Capital: Kigali. In 1994 there was a civil war between two tribes, the Hutus and the Tutsis. 卢旺达〔中非东部一国家，位于坦桑尼亚和赞比亚之间。人口: 7,810,056 (2003)，首都: 基加里。1994年，胡图族与图西族之间爆发了一场内战〕—**Rwandan** *n, adj*

Rx. *AmE*【美】the written abbreviation of 缩写= PRESCRIPTION (1)

Ryan /ˈraɪən; ˈraɪən/, **No·lan** /ˈnolən; ˈnəʊlən/ (1947-) a US BASEBALL player who was a PITCHER, and is famous for a type of PITCH called a 'flamethrower' because it was so fast. He is one of the best baseball players ever, and he established more than 50 records. 瑞安〔(1947-)，美国著名棒球投手，以一种名为"喷火机"的快速投法而著名。他是有史以来最优秀的棒球运动员之一，创造了50多项纪录〕

Ryder Cup, the /ˌraɪdə ˈkʌp; ˌraɪdə ˈkʌp/ an important GOLF competition held every two years, in which two teams compete, one representing Europe and the other the US 赖德杯〔每两年一次的重要高尔夫球赛事。欧洲和美国各派一支球队参赛〕

rye /raɪ; raɪ/ *n* [U] **1** a type of grain that is used for making bread and WHISKY 黑麦，裸麦: *rye bread* 黑麦面包 **2** also 又作 **rye whis·key** /ˌ· ˈ··/ *AmE* a type of American WHISKY made from rye【美】黑麦威士忌酒: *rye and Coke* 黑麦威士忌酒加可口可乐

rye·grass /ˈraɪˌgræs; ˈraɪgrɑːs/ *n* [U] a type of grass that is grown as food for animals 黑麦草〔一种作动物饲料的草〕

R

S,s

S, s /ɛs; es/ *plural* **S's, s's** *n* [C] **1** the 19th letter of the English alphabet 英语字母表的第十九个字母 **2** the written abbreviation of 缩写= south or southern

-s /z, s; z, s/ *suffix* **1** forms the plural of nouns〔构成名词的复数〕: *a cat and two dogs* 一只猫和两条狗 **2** forms the third person singular of the present tense of most verbs〔构成大多数动词的第三人称单数现在式〕: *he plays* 他玩 | *she sits* 她坐 **3** *especially AmE* forms adverbs meaning during a particular time【尤美】〔构成副词表示"在某一段特定时间"〕: *Do you work Sundays?* (=regularly each Sunday) 你星期天工作吗? | *Summers we go to the seaside.* 我们每年夏天都去海滨。

-s' /z, s; z, s/ *suffix* forms the possessive case of plural nouns〔构成复数名词的所有格〕: *the girls' dresses* (=the dresses belong to the girls) 姑娘们的连衣裙

-'s¹ /z, s; z, s/ **1** the short form of 缩略式= 'is': *John's here.* 约翰在这儿。| *What's that?* 那是什么? | *She's writing a letter.* 她在写信。**2** the short form of 缩略式= 'has': *Polly's gone out.* 波莉出去了。| *A spider's got eight legs.* 蜘蛛有八条腿。**3** a short form of 缩略式= 'does' used in questions after who, what etc and that many people think is incorrect〔用于疑问句中的 who, what 等词后, 但许多人认为这种用法不正确〕: *How's he plan to do it?* 他计划怎样去做这件事? —compare 比较 -'D **4** a short form of 缩略式= 'us' used only in 'let's'〔只用于 let's 一词〕

-'s² *suffix* **1** forms the possessive case of singular nouns, and of plural nouns that do not end in -s〔构成单数名词和非 -s 结尾的复数名词的所有格〕: *my sister's husband* 我的妹[姐]夫 | *Mary's generosity* 玛丽的慷慨 | *yesterday's lesson* 昨天的功课 | *the children's bedroom* 孩子们的卧室 | *the man in the corner's coat* (=the coat belonging to the man in the corner) 角落里那个男子的上衣 **2** *BrE* the shop or home of someone【英】〔某人的〕店, 家: *I bought it at the baker's.* (=at the baker's shop) 这是我在面包店买的。| *I met him at Mary's.* (=at Mary's house) 我是在玛丽家遇见他的。

S4C /ˌɛs for ˋsi; ˌes fɔː ˈsiː/ a television station in Wales, which broadcasts programmes in the Welsh language as well as many programmes in English, provided by Channel 4 威尔士第四频道〔威尔士一电视台, 播出威尔士语节目和由第四频道电视台提供的英语节目〕

S & L /ˌɛs ənd ˋɛl; ˌes ənd ˈel/ *n* [C] *informal* SAVINGS AND LOAN ASSOCIATION【非正式】购房互助协会

Saba /ˋsɑbə; ˈsɑːbə/ a mountainous island, five miles square in size, in the Dutch Antilles in the Caribbean. It has the world's shortest commercial RUNWAY for aircraft. 萨巴岛〔位于加勒比海荷属安的列斯群岛的一个多山岛屿, 方圆五英里。该岛有世界上最短的商用飞机跑道〕

Sa·bah /ˋsɑbɑ; ˈsɑːbɑː/ one of the states that form the country of Malaysia. Sabah is on the island of Borneo. 沙巴〔马来西亚一州, 位于婆罗洲岛〕

sab·ba·tar·i·an /ˌsæbəˋtɛrɪən; ˌsæbəˈteəriən◂/ *n* [C] someone who strongly believes that the Sabbath should be a holy day on which people do not work 严守安息日的人 —**sabbatarian** *adj*

Sab·bath /ˋsæbəθ; ˈsæbəθ/ *n* **1 the Sabbath a)** Sunday, considered as a day of rest and prayer by most Christian churches 安息日〔星期日, 大多数基督徒认为应当休息和祈祷的日子〕 **b)** Saturday, considered as a day of rest and prayer in the Jewish religion 安息日〔星期六, 犹太教认为应当休息和祈祷的日子〕 **2 keep/break the Sabbath** to obey or not obey the religious rules of this day 守/不守安息日

sab·bat·i·cal /səˋbætɪkl; səˈbætɪkəl/ *n* [C,U] a period when someone, especially someone in a university job, stops doing their usual work in order to study or travel 休假〔尤指大学教师暂停平时的工作去进行研究或旅行的假期〕: **be on sabbatical** *Dr. Watson's not here at the moment, she's on sabbatical.* 沃森博士目前不在这里, 她正在休假。—**sabbatical** *adj*: *a sabbatical year* 休假年

sa·ber /ˋsebɚ; ˈseɪbə/ *n* [C] the usual American spelling of SABRE sabre 的一般美式拼法

sa·ble¹ /ˋsebl; ˈseɪbəl/ *n* [C,U] an expensive fur used to make coats etc, or the small animal that this fur comes from 貂皮; 貂

sable² *adj poetic* black or very dark【诗】黑色的; 深色的

sab·o·tage¹ /ˋsæbəˌtɑʒ; ˈsæbətɑːʒ/ *v* [T] **1** to secretly damage or destroy equipment, vehicles etc that belong to an enemy or opponent, so that they cannot be used 暗中破坏〔敌人或对手的设备、车辆等〕: *Every single fighter plane had been sabotaged.* 每架战斗机都遭到了破坏。**2** to deliberately spoil someone's plans because you do not want them to succeed 故意破坏〔某人的计划〕: *Her father sabotaged her acting ambitions by refusing to pay for her to go to drama school.* 她父亲有意挫伤她学演艺的抱负, 拒绝供她上戏剧学校。

sabotage² *n* [U] damage that has been done deliberately to equipment, vehicles etc in order to prevent an enemy or opponent from using them〔对敌人或对手的设备、车辆等的〕蓄意破坏: *This is no accident – it's a deliberate act of sabotage.* 这不是什么事故——这是一次蓄意破坏行为。

sab·o·teur /ˌsæbəˋtɝ; ˌsæbəˈtɜː/ *n* [C] someone who deliberately damages, destroys, or spoils someone else's property or activities, in order to prevent them from doing something 蓄意破坏者 —see also 另见 HUNT SABOTEUR

sa·bre *BrE*【英】, **saber** *AmE*【美】/ˋsebɚ; ˈseɪbə/ *n* [C] **1** a light pointed sword with one sharp edge used in FENCING〔击剑用的〕佩剑 **2** a heavy sword with a curved blade, used in more former times 军刀, 马刀 —see picture at 参见 SWORD 图

sabre-rat·tling /ˈ·· ,··/ *n* [U] threats to use military force, especially when you do not think they are very frightening or serious 炫耀武力, 武力恫吓

sac /sæk; sæk/ *n* [C] *technical* a part inside a plant or animal that is shaped like a bag and contains liquid or air【术语】〔动物、植物的〕囊, 液囊

Sac·a·ja·we·a /ˌsækədʒəˋwiə; ˌsækədʒəˈwiːə/ (?-1812) a Native American woman who acted as a guide on Lewis and Clark's travels from St. Louis to the Pacific Ocean 萨卡加维亚〔(?-1812), 北美印第安妇女。她是刘易斯和克拉克的旅行向导, 随同他们从圣路易斯到达太平洋沿岸〕

sac·cha·rin /ˋsækərɪn; ˈsækərɪn/ *n* [U] a chemical substance that tastes sweet and is used instead of sugar in drinks 糖精

sac·cha·rine /ˋsækəˌrin; ˈsækəriːn/ *adj formal* too romantic in a way that seems silly and insincere【正式】故作多情的; 过分甜蜜的: *a saccharine love story* 过于缠绵的爱情故事

sac·er·do·tal /ˌsæsɚˋdotl; ˌsæsəˈdəʊtl◂/ *adj technical* connected with or belonging to a priest【术语】牧师的, 神甫的

sach·et /sæˋʃe; ˈsæʃeɪ/ *n* [C] a small plastic or paper package containing a liquid or powder〔装有液体或粉末的〕小袋: *a sachet of shampoo* 一小袋洗发剂 —see picture at 参见 CONTAINER 图

sack¹ /sæk; sæk/ *n* **1** [C] **a)** a large bag made of strong rough cloth or strong paper, used for storing or carrying flour, coal, vegetables etc〔装面粉、煤、蔬菜等用的〕麻袋; 粗布袋; 厚纸袋; 大口袋: *a sack of potatoes* 一大袋马铃薯 **b)** also 又作 **sackful** the amount that a sack can contain 一(大)袋 **2 get the sack/give sb the sack** *BrE informal* to be dismissed from your job or to dismiss someone from their job【英, 非正式】被解雇/开除某人: *He got the sack for stealing.* 他因偷东西而被解雇。| *They've never actually given anyone the sack.* 他们实际上从未辞退过任何人。**3 hit the sack** *spoken* to go to bed【口】上床睡觉: *It's one o'clock – time to hit the sack I think.* 一点钟了——我想该上床睡觉了。**4 in the sack** *informal* in bed【非正式】(躺)在床上

sack² *v* [T] **1** *BrE informal* to dismiss someone from their job【英, 非正式】解雇〔某人〕; FIRE² (2) *especially AmE*【尤美】: *She was sacked for organizing a union.* 她因组织工会而被解雇。**2** to knock down the QUARTERBACK¹ (1) in American football〔在美式橄榄球中〕擒抱〔四分卫〕 **3** if an army sacks a place they go through it destroying or stealing things, and attacking people〔军队〕劫掠, 洗劫〔所到之处〕

sack out *phr v* [I] *AmE informal* to go to sleep【美, 非正式】上床睡觉: *He sacked out on the sofa.* 他在沙发上睡觉。

sack·cloth /ˋsækˌklɔθ; ˈsæk-klɒθ/ also 又作 **sacking** /ˋsækɪŋ; ˈsækɪŋ/ *n* [U] **1** rough cloth for making sacks 麻袋布, 粗麻布 **2 wear sackcloth and ashes** to behave in a way that shows everyone you are sorry about something you have done wrong 表示懊悔, 悔恨

sack race /ˈ· ·/ *n* [C] a race in which the competitors, usually children, have to jump forwards with both legs inside a SACK[1] (1a) 套袋赛跑〔通常为儿童玩的、双脚套上袋子的跳跃式赛跑〕

sac·ra·ment /ˈsækrəmənt; ˈsækrəmənt/ *n* [C] **1 the Sacrament** the bread and wine that is eaten at Christian ceremonies 〔基督教的〕圣餐 **2** one of the important Christian ceremonies, such as marriage or COMMUNION (2) 圣事, 圣礼〈如婚礼、圣餐等〉 —**sacramental** /ˌsækrəˈmɛntl; ˌsækrəˈmentl◂/ *adj*

Sac·ra·men·to /ˌsækrəˈmɛnto; ˌsækrəˈmentəʊ/ a city which is the capital city of the US state of California 萨克拉门托〔美国加利福尼亚州首府〕

sa·cred /ˈsekrɪd; ˈseɪkrɪ̈d/ *adj* **1** connected with a god or religion 神的, 宗教(性)的: *sacred painting* 圣画 | *a sacred vow* 庄严的誓言 **2** greatly respected, or believed to be holy 受崇敬的, 神圣的: *Cows are sacred to Hindus.* 对印度教徒来说, 牛是神圣的。| *Human life is sacred.* 人的生命是神圣的。**3** extremely important to you, especially in a way that other people think is silly or annoying 极重要的〔尤指在他人看来有点愚蠢〕: *He thinks his parking space is sacred.* 他认为他的停车位不容侵犯。 **4 is nothing sacred?** *spoken* used to express shock when something you think is valuable or important is being changed or harmed【口】怎么能这样呢?〔表示在贵重物品或重要事物受到损害时的惊讶〕: *They're putting a tax on books – is nothing sacred?* 他们要对图书征税——怎么能这样为所欲为? —**sacredly** *adv* —**sacredness** *n* [U]

sacred cow /ˌ·· ˈ·/ *n* [C] a belief that is so important to some people that they will not let anyone criticize it 不容置疑的信念

sac·ri·fice[1] /ˈsækrəˌfaɪs; ˈsækrɪ̈faɪs/ *n* **1** [C,U] something valuable that you decide not to have, in order to get something that is more important 牺牲: *the need for economic sacrifice* 在经济上作出牺牲的必要性 | **make sacrifices** *My parents were forever reminding me of the sacrifices they made to give me an education.* 我父母不断提醒我, 他们为了供我受教育所作出的牺牲。**2** [C,U] the act of offering something to a god, especially in former times by killing an animal or a person in a religious ceremony 献祭〔尤指从前在宗教仪式中把动物或人杀死作祭品〕: **make a sacrifice** *It was common to make sacrifices to the gods to ensure a good harvest.* 为了保丰收而祭神是很普通的事。**3** [C] an object or animal that is offered to a god in a ceremony of sacrifice 祭品, 供品: **human sacrifice** (=a person killed as a sacrifice) 杀死后用作祭品的人 **4** *literary* **the final/supreme sacrifice** the act of dying while you are fighting for a principle【文】牺牲自己的生命, 捐躯

sacrifice[2] *v* **1** [T] to willingly stop having something you want or doing something you like in order to get something more important 牺牲, 献出: **sacrifice sth for** *It's not worth sacrificing your health for your career.* 你为事业而牺牲健康是不值得的。| **sacrifice sth to do sth** *He sacrificed a promising career to look after his handicapped daughter.* 他为了照顾残疾女儿牺牲了有前途的事业。**2** [I,T] to offer something or someone to a god as a sacrifice 献祭; 以…作祭品

sac·ri·fi·cial /ˌsækrəˈfɪʃəl; ˌsækrɪ̈ˈfɪʃəl◂/ *adj* connected with or offered as a sacrifice (用于)献祭的; (作为)牺牲的: *a sacrificial gift* 供品, 祭品 —**sacrificially** *adv*

sac·ri·lege /ˈsækrəlɪdʒ; ˈsækrɪ̈lɪdʒ/ *n* [C,U] **1** the act of treating something holy in a way that does not show respect 渎圣行为 **2** *spoken* the act of treating something badly when someone else thinks it is very important【口】不敬: *You recorded over his Jimi Hendrix tapes? That's sacrilege!* 你拿他的吉米·亨德里克斯的磁带来录音? 真是太不敬了! —**sacrilegious** /ˌsækrɪˈlɪdʒəs; ˌsækrɪ̈ˈlɪdʒəs◂/ *adj* —**sacrilegiously** *adv*

sac·ris·tan /ˈsækrɪstən; ˈsækrɪ̈stən/ *n* [C] *technical* someone whose job is to take care of the holy objects in a church【术语】〔教堂的〕圣器保管员, 司事

sac·ris·ty /ˈsækrɪstɪ; ˈsækrɪ̈sti/ *n* [C] *technical* a small room in a church where holy cups and plates are kept, and where priests put on their ceremonial clothes; VESTRY【术语】〔教堂的〕圣器室

sac·ro·sanct /ˈsækroˌsæŋkt; ˈsækrəʊsæŋkt/ *adj* something that is sacrosanct is considered to be so important that no one is allowed to criticize or change it 神圣不可侵犯的: *Weekends are sacrosanct in our family so I never take any work home.* 我们家的周末时间是神圣不可侵犯的, 所以我从来不把工作带回家里去做。

S2 W3 **sad** /sæd; sæd/ *adj*

1 ▶UNHAPPY 不愉快的◀ unhappy, but especially because something unpleasant has happened to you or someone else 不愉快的, 伤心的, 难过的: *What's the matter with him? He looks so sad.* 他怎么啦? 看上去愁容满面的样子。| **be sad to do sth** *I was sad to see them go in the end.* 看到他们终于要走, 我心里很难过。| **[+about]** *I was glad to be going home, but sad about the friends I was leaving behind.* 快要回家让我高兴, 但要离开朋友却又使我难过。| **sad smile/face/ expression etc** *There was such a sad look in her eyes.* 她的眼神很是忧伤。—opposite 反义词 HAPPY (1)

2 ▶STH THAT MAKES YOU SAD 伤心的事◀ a sad event, situation etc makes you feel unhappy 令人伤心的, 使人难过的: *A special meeting was called to announce the sad news of his death.* 召开了特别会议宣布他去世的噩耗。| **sad book/song/film etc** *What a sad movie! I cried all the way through.* 多么令人悲伤的电影! 我从头到尾都在哭。| **it is sad that** *It's sad that James can't be with us.* 詹姆斯不能和我们在一起, 真令人难过。| **it is sad to see/hear etc** *It was sad to see all that food going to waste.* 看到要浪费那么多食物真让人痛心。| **sad time/day/moment etc** *This is a sad day for all of us.* 这是使我们大家都感到伤心的一个日子。

3 ▶NOT SATISFACTORY 不能令人满意的◀ [only before noun 仅用于名词前] a sad situation is very bad or unacceptable〔状况〕糟糕的, 不能令人接受的: **sad state of affairs** (=bad situation) 糟糕的状况 *It's a sad state of affairs when you can't go out at night for fear of being attacked.* 晚上怕被袭击而不敢出门, 这种状况真糟糕。| **the sad fact is (that)** *spoken*【口】: *The sad fact is that prejudice and discrimination still exist.* 可悲的是, 偏见和歧视依然存在。| **sad to say** *spoken*【口】: *Sad to say, we never found them.* 很遗憾, 我们从未找到他们。

4 ▶LONELY 孤独的◀ a sad person or someone who has a sad life seems lonely and unhappy and you feel sorry for them 寂寞的, 可怜的: *She's a sad character – I don't think she has any friends at all.* 她是个孤独的人——我认为她没有什么朋友。| **sad case** (=someone you feel sorry for) 可怜的人

5 ▶BORING 令人厌烦的◀ *spoken slang* used to say that someone or something is boring and unfashionable【口, 俚】乏味的, 不流行的, 不受欢迎的: *I think Carole's a bit of a sad name. Oh, sorry, is your mum called Carole?* 我觉得"卡萝尔"是个有点乏味的名字。啊, 对不起, 你妈妈是叫"卡萝尔"吗? | **sad bastard** *Get a life, you sad bastard.* 别再烦人了, 你这个讨厌鬼。

6 sadder but wiser having learned something from an unpleasant experience 因吃过苦头而变得聪明: *He came out of the relationship sadder but wiser.* 他摆脱了那种关系, 吃了苦头也学精了。—**sadness** *n* [singular,U] —see also 另见 SADLY

Sa·dat /səˈdæt; səˈdæt/, **An·war al-** /ˈænwar ˌæl; ˈænwɑː æl/ (1918-81) the President of Egypt from 1970 to 1981, who tried to bring peace between the Arabs and Israelis. He shared the Nobel Peace Prize with Menachem Begin in 1978 and they signed the Camp David agreement in the following year. He was ASSASSINATED in 1981. 萨达特〔(1918-1981), 1970至1981年任埃及总统。他致力于阿拉伯人与以色列人的和平事业, 1978年与梅纳赫姆·贝京分享诺贝尔和平奖。次年, 他们签署了《戴维营协议》。1981年, 萨达特遇刺身亡〕

Sad·dam /sæˈdæm; sæˈdæm/ **Hussein** (1937-2006) the President of Iraq since 1979. He led Iraq in a long war against Iran (1980-88), and in 1990 he tried to take control of Kuwait. This caused the Gulf War, and Saddam's armies were forced to leave Kuwait by United Nations forces, led by the US. 萨达姆〔(1937-2006), 1979年起任伊拉克总统。他领导伊拉克同伊朗进行了一场旷日持久的战争(1980-1988)。1990年, 他企图占领科威特, 从而引发了海湾战争。在以美国为首的联合国军队的打击下, 最后被迫从科威特撤军〕

sad·den /ˈsædn̩; ˈsædn/ *v* [T often passive 常用被动态] *formal* to make someone feel sad or disappointed【正式】使伤心, 使难过: *Dorothea was saddened by his sudden change of heart.* 他突然变心, 这使多罗西娅很难过。| **it saddens sb** *It saddened him to think that the others no longer trusted him.* 一想起大家不再信任他了, 他就很伤心。

sad·dle[1] /ˈsædl̩; ˈsædl/ *n* **1** [C] a seat made of leather that is put on a horse's back so that someone can ride it (马)鞍 —see picture at 参见 HORSE[1] 图 **2** [C] a seat on a bicycle or a MOTORCYCLE〔自行车、摩托车等的〕车座 —see picture at 参见 BICYCLE[1] 图 **3 be in the saddle** *informal*【非正式】**a)** to be in a position in which you have power or authority 在位, 掌权: *He's been in the saddle for 30 years now, and it's time he retired.* 他已经在位30年, 也该退休了。**b)** to be riding a horse 骑着马: *They were weary after many hours in the saddle.* 他们骑了几个小时的马之后都很疲倦。

saddle[2] *v* [T] to put a saddle on a horse 给(马)装上鞍

saddle up *phr v* [I,T] to put a saddle on a horse 给(马)装上鞍: *We saddled up and rode quickly back to the farm.* 我们装上马鞍, 骑马迅速回到农场。

saddle sb **with** sth *phr v* [T] to give someone a difficult or boring job 使〔某人〕承担〔苦差事〕: *It's his party, but I've been saddled with organizing the whole thing!* 这是他举行的聚会，但一切却都是我来张罗的！

saddle bag /ˈ‥ ˌ/ *n* [C] a bag for carrying things that is fixed to the saddle on a horse or bicycle 鞍囊，马褡裢；〔自行车车座后的〕挂包

sad·dler /ˈsædlə; ˈsædlə/ *n* [C] someone who makes saddles and other leather products, or a shop where these are sold 鞍匠，马具工；马具店

sad·dler·y /ˈsædlərɪ; ˈsædləri/ *n* [U] **1** goods made by a saddler 鞍具，马具 **2** the art of making saddles and other leather goods 鞍具制造(术)

saddle shoe /ˈ‥ ˌ/ *n* [C] *AmE* a shoe that has a toe and heel of one colour, with a different colour in the middle【美】鞍脊鞋〔一种鞋面中部与鞋头、鞋跟颜色不同的鞋〕

saddle-sore /ˈ‥ ˌ/ *adj* [not before noun 不用于名词前] feeling stiff and sore after riding a horse or bicycle〔骑马或骑自行车后〕疼痛并发僵的，胯疼腿僵的

Sade /sɑd; sɑːd/, **Mar·quis de** /ˈmɑrkɪ də; ˈmɑːki də/ (1740-1814) a French writer who was put in prison for his violent sexual actions. He wrote NOVELs and plays about the sexual pleasure he got from hurting other people, and sadism, the word for this type of sexual pleasure, is based on his name. 萨德〔(1740-1814)，法国作家。曾因暴力性行为入狱。他创作的小说和戏剧描述自己对他人实施性虐待而获得的性快感。特指此类性快感的名词 sadism (性虐待狂) 即源于其姓氏〕

sa·dhu /ˈsɑdu; ˈsɑːduː/ *n* [C] a Hindu holy man who lives a very simple life〔印度教的〕圣人，苦行高僧

Sa·die Haw·kins Day /ˌsedɪ ˈhɔkɪnz ˌde; ˌseɪdi ˈhɔːkɪnz ˌdeɪ/ a day when, according to an old US custom, women can ask men to go out with them to start a romantic relationship, or women can ask men to dance with them at an event called a Sadie Hawkins dance. Sadie Hawkins Day is usually in November, and it is based on an imaginary character who first appeared in the US CARTOON STRIP (=a set of drawings that tell a funny story in a newspaper or magazine) *L'il Abner* in the 1930s. 萨迪·霍金斯节〔根据美国的旧习俗，女性可在这一天邀请男士约会并开始恋爱关系，或在一项名为萨迪·霍金斯舞会的活动中邀请男士跳舞。该节日通常在11月，最早可追溯至20世纪30年代美国连环画《利尔·阿布纳》中的一个虚构人物〕

sa·dis·m /ˈsedɪzəm; ˈseɪdɪzəm/ *n* [U] **1** the practice of getting pleasure from being cruel to someone 施虐狂: *New recruits were treated with ruthless sadism.* 新兵受到施虐狂般的残酷对待。**2** the practice of getting sexual pleasure from hurting someone 性虐待狂

sa·dist /ˈsedɪst; ˈseɪdɪst/ *n* [C] someone who enjoys being cruel to other people 施虐狂者

sa·dis·tic /səˈdɪstɪk; səˈdɪstɪk/ *adj* cruel and enjoying making other people suffer 施虐狂的: *He took a sadistic delight in humiliating her.* 他通过羞辱她获取施虐的快感。—**sadistically** /-klɪ; -kli/ *adv*

Sad·ler's Wells /ˌsædləz ˈwɛlz; ˌsædləz ˈwelz/ a theatre in London where many famous dancers performed, and where the Royal Ballet was based for many years. It was rebuilt in the 1990s and is used for OPERA, BALLET, and modern dance performances. 萨德勒威尔斯剧院〔伦敦一剧院。许多著名舞蹈演员曾在此献艺，也是皇家芭蕾舞团多年的大本营。20世纪90年代重建后，该剧院上演歌剧、芭蕾舞及现代舞〕

sad·ly /ˈsædlɪ; ˈsædli/ *adv* **1** in a way that shows that you are sad 伤心地，悲伤地: *Peter shook his head sadly and turned away.* 彼得难过地摇摇头走开了。**2** [sentence adverb 句子副词] unfortunately 不幸地；说来遗憾: *Sadly, they just can't be trusted.* 遗憾的是，他们就是不可信任。**3** in a way that makes you sad 令人伤心地: *He was a popular man and will be sadly missed.* 他的人缘很好，大家都会忧伤地怀念他。| *We were sadly disappointed.* 我们万分失望。**4 sadly lacking/neglected etc** in a way that seems bad or wrong 严重地缺乏／受忽视等: *The garden was beautiful once, but it has been sadly neglected.* 这个花园曾经很漂亮，但现在已经完全荒芜了。
5 be sadly mistaken to be completely wrong about something 完全弄错: *If you think you'll get any money from him, you're sadly mistaken.* 如果你以为可以从他那儿弄到钱，那你就完全搞错了。

sa·do·mas·o·chis·m /ˌsedoˈmæsəkɪzm; ˌseɪdəʊˈmæsəkɪzəm/ *n* [U] the practice of getting sexual pleasure from hurting someone or being hurt (性) 施虐狂；受虐狂 —**sadomasochist** *n* [C] —**sadomasochistic** /ˌsedomæsəˈkɪstɪk; ˌseɪdəʊmæsəˈkɪstɪk◂/ *adj*

sae /ˌɛs e ˈi; ˌes eɪ ˈiː/ *BrE*【英】**1** stamped addressed envelope; an envelope that you put your name, address, and a stamp on, so that someone else can send you something〔贴足邮票并写有自己姓名地址的〕回邮信封 **2** self-addressed envelope; an envelope that you put your own name and address on 写有自己姓名地址的信封 —see also 另见 SASE

sa·fa·ri[1] /səˈfɑrɪ; səˈfɑːri/ *n* [C] a trip through countryside in Africa, that you go on to watch wild animals〔在非洲的〕野外观兽旅行，游猎: **go/be on safari** *They spent their vacation on safari in Kenya.* 他们假期在肯尼亚进行野外观兽旅行。

safari[2] *adj* **safari suit/jacket** a suit or JACKET (1) that is made of light-coloured material, usually with a belt and two pockets on the chest 轻便猎装／猎装夹克〔用浅色衣料做成，通常有腰带和两个胸袋〕

safari park /ˈ‥ ˌ/ *n* [C] an enclosed area of land where wild animals are kept, so that people can drive round and look at them〔可以驾车游览的〕野生动物园

safe[1] /sef; seɪf/ *adj*

1 ▶NOT CAUSING HARM 不会引起伤害◀ not likely to cause any physical injury or harm 安全的: *Flying is one of the safest forms of travel.* 乘飞机是最安全的旅行方式之一。| *the safe disposal of radioactive waste* 放射性废物的安全处理 | *Don't go too near the edge – it isn't safe.* 不要太靠近边缘 —— 那样不安全。| **it is safe to do sth** *Is it safe to swim here?* 在这儿游泳安全吗？| **[+for]** *Parents want play-areas that are safe for their children.* 家长希望自己的孩子有安全的游戏场地。

2 ▶NOT IN DANGER 没有危险◀ [not before noun 不用于名词前] not in danger of being lost, harmed, or stolen 安全的，保险的: *Will you feel safe in the house on your own?* 你一个人待在房子里感到安全吗？| **[+from]** *We were safe from attack in the shelter.* 我们在掩蔽所里很安全，不会受到袭击。| **keep sth safe** *I'm trusting you with these documents – so make sure you keep them safe.* 我把这些文件托付给你 —— 你一定要保管好。| **safe and sound** (=unharmed, especially after being in danger) 平安无恙 *The missing children were found safe and sound.* 失踪的孩子们都安然无恙。

3 ▶PLACE 地方◀ a safe place is one where something is not likely to be stolen or lost 保险的，安全的. *Keep the receipt in a safe place.* 把收据放在安全的地方。

4 safe journey/arrival/return etc a journey etc that ends safely 平安的旅行／到达／归来等: *They prayed for their father's safe return.* 他们祈求父亲平安归来。| **safe journey** *spoken* (=what you say to someone when they start a long journey)【口】一路平安

5 ▶NO RISK 没有风险◀ not involving any risk and very likely to succeed 没有风险的: *a safe investment* 没有风险的投资 | *a safe method of contraception* 安全的避孕方法 | **(as) safe as houses** (=completely safe) 绝对安全

6 ▶SUBJECT 话题◀ a subject of conversation that is safe is not likely to upset anyone or make people argue 不会令人不快的，不会引起争议的. *I kept to safe subjects, like the weather.* 我只谈一些无关痛痒的话题，例如天气。

7 better (to be) safe than sorry *spoken* used to say that it is better to be careful now, even if this takes time, effort etc, so that nothing bad will happen later【口】宁愿稳妥免致后悔: *I've checked all the safety harnesses – better safe than sorry!* 我检查过所有的安全带了 —— 但求稳妥以免后悔呀！

8 to be on the safe side *spoken* to do something especially carefully in order to avoid an unpleasant situation【口】为安全起见，为了稳妥: *I'd take an umbrella, just to be on the safe side.* 为稳妥起见，我还是带把伞好。

9 be in safe hands to be with someone who will look after you very well 受到妥善照顾: *I've needed to know my kids were in safe hands.* 我必须知道我的孩子都得到妥善的照顾。

10 a safe pair of hands someone you can trust to do a difficult job without making mistakes 信得过的人 —**safely** *adv*: *Drive safely!* 安全驾驶！| *I think we can safely assume that she will pass the exam.* 我想我们可以有把握地假定她会通过考试。—see also 另见 **play (it) safe** (PLAY[1] (11)), **a safe bet/a sure bet that** (BET[2] (6)), **a safe seat** (SEAT[1] (5))

safe[2] *n* [C] a strong metal box or cupboard with special locks where you keep money and valuable things 保险柜，保险箱

safe con·duct /ˌ· ˈ· ˌ/ *n* [C,U] official protection for someone when they are passing through a dangerous area 安全通行(权): *This letter should guarantee you safe conduct through the war zone.* 这封信应能保证你安全通过战区。

safe-de·pos·it box /ˈ· ·ˌ·· ˌ/ *n* [C] a SAFETY-DEPOSIT BOX 贵重物品存放箱

safe·guard[1] /ˈsefˌgɑrd; ˈseɪfgɑːd/ *v* [T] to protect something from harm or damage 保护，保卫〔某物〕: *New regulations were*

introduced to safeguard the environment. 制定了新条例以保护环境。| **safeguard sth against** *a program for safeguarding the computer system against viruses* 电脑防病毒程序

safeguard² *n* [C] a rule, agreement etc that is intended to protect someone or something from possible dangers or problems 保障条款; 保护措施: *The law contains important safeguards to protect housebuyers.* 该法律包含了保护购房者利益的重要条款。| **[+against]** *safeguards against the exploitation of children* 避免儿童受剥削的保护措施

safe ha·ven /,· ˈ· ·/ *n* [C] a place where someone can go to in order to escape from possible danger or attack 庇护所, 避难所

safe house /,· ˈ·/ *n* [C] a house where someone can hide when their enemies are looking for them〔躲避敌人搜寻的〕安全房, 安全藏身处

safe·keep·ing /ˈsefˋkipɪŋ; ˌseɪfˈkiːpɪŋ/ *n* [U] **1 for safekeeping** if you put something somewhere for safekeeping, you put it in a place where it will not get damaged, lost, or stolen 为了安全保管 **2 be in sb's safekeeping** to be in a position or situation where someone is looking after you 受到某人的妥善照顾

safe sex /,· ˈ·/ *n* [U] ways of having sex that reduce the risk of the spread of AIDS and other sexual diseases, especially by using a CONDOM〔尤指使用避孕套的〕安全性交

S3 W2 **safe·ty** /ˈseftɪ; ˈseɪfti/ *n*

1 ▶NOT IN DANGER 没有危险◀ [U] the state of being safe from danger or harm 安全: *The company seemed totally unconcerned about the safety of its workers.* 这家公司好像完全不关心自己员工的安全。| **in safety** (=without any danger) 毫无危险 *Spectators could watch the launch in complete safety.* 观众可以绝对安全地观看发射。| **for safety's sake** (=in order to be safe) 为了安全起见 *We travelled in pairs, for safety's sake.* 为了安全起见, 我们两人一组结伴旅行。

2 sb's safety how safe someone is in a particular situation 某人的安全(问题): *The boy has now been missing for 5 days and there are fears for his safety.* 男孩失踪已经五天了, 大家都担心他会遇到不测。| **for sb's own safety** *For your own safety please do not smoke inside the plane.* 为了您自身的安全, 请勿在飞机内抽烟。

3 ▶NOT DANGEROUS 不危险◀ [U] the state of not being dangerous or likely to cause harm or injury 安全, 无害: *Some scientists expressed concern over the safety of the test.* 一些科学家对这次试验是否安全表示担心。| **safety measures/precautions/checks** (=things that are done in order to make sure that something is safe) 安全措施/防范措施/安全检查 *The accident would never have happened if the correct safety procedures had been followed.* 如果正确的安全程序得以遵循的话, 这次事故根本不会发生。| **road safety** (=safety of people using the roads) 交通安全 *Police are visiting schools as part of their latest road safety campaign.* 作为他们最近开展的交通安全运动的一部分, 警察正在巡视各个学校。

4 ▶SAFE PLACE 安全的地方◀ [U] a place where you are safe from danger 没有危险的地方: **the safety of** *When the shelling began people fled to the safety of the city.* 炮轰开始时, 人们逃往城里安全的地方。| **lead/take sb to safety** *Fire fighters led the children to safety.* 消防人员把孩子们带到安全的地方。| **reach safety** *We were relieved to reach dry land and safety.* 我们到了岸上安全的地方后, 全都松了一口气。

5 safety in numbers *spoken* used to say that a dangerous or unpleasant situation is better if there are a lot of people with you【口】人多势众, 人多保险

6 ▶SPORT 体育运动◀ [C] *technical* a way of getting two points in American football by making the other team put the ball down in its own GOAL (3)【术语】安全得分〔美式橄榄球中迫使对方在自己球门区内将球放下的得分方式〕

safety belt /ˈ· · ·/ *n* [C] a SEAT BELT 安全带

safety catch /ˈ· · ·/ *n* [C] a lock on a gun that stops it from being fired accidentally〔枪支的〕保险机, 保险栓

safety cur·tain /ˈ· ·, · ·/ *n* [C] a thick curtain at the front of a theatre stage that prevents fire from spreading〔舞台上的〕防火幕, 安全幕

safety-de·pos·it box /ˈ· · ·, · · ˈ·/ *n* [C] a small box used for storing valuable objects, usually kept in a special room in a bank〔银行里的〕贵重物品存放箱, 出租保险箱

safety glass /ˈ· · ·/ *n* [U] strong glass that breaks into very small pieces that are not sharp, used for example in car windows〔用于车窗等的〕安全玻璃

safety is·land /ˈ· ·, · ·/ *n* [C] *AmE* a TRAFFIC ISLAND【美】安全岛

safety lamp /ˈ· · ·/ *n* [C] a special lamp used by MINERs, that has a flame which will not make underground gases explode〔矿工用的〕安全灯

safety match /ˈ· · ·/ *n* [C] a match that can only be lit by rubbing it along a special surface on the side of its box 安全火柴〔只有在火柴盒侧面特定的地方才能划着〕

safety net /ˈ· · ·/ *n* [C] **1** a large net used to catch someone who is performing high above the ground if they fall〔高空杂技表演等用的〕安全网 **2** a system or arrangement that exists to help you if you have serious problems or get into a difficult situation〔一种帮助遇到严重问题或陷入困境者的〕安全保障措施[系统]: *a safety net of welfare payments for the poor* 穷人福利金支付安全系统

safety pin /ˈ· · ·/ *n* [C] a wire pin with a cover that its point fits into so that it cannot hurt you 安全别针 —see picture at 参见 PIN¹ 图

safety ra·zor /ˈ· ·, · ·/ *n* [C] a RAZOR that has a cover over part of the blade to protect your skin〔刀片上有盖的〕安全剃刀 —see picture at 参见 RAZOR 图

safety valve /ˈ· · ·/ *n* [C] **1** something you do that allows you to express strong feelings such as anger without doing any harm〔无害的〕用以发泄情绪的途径: *Exercise provided him with a good safety valve from pressure at work.* 运动成了他消除工作压力的一种良好方式。**2** a part of a machine that allows gas, steam etc to be let out when the pressure becomes too great〔机器的〕安全阀

saf·fron /ˈsæfrən; ˈsæfrən/ *n* [U] **1** bright orange powder that is used in cooking to give food a special taste and colour 番红花粉〔用于调味〕: *saffron rice* 番红花米饭 **2** a bright orange-yellow colour 番红花色, 橘黄色

SAG /sæg; sæg/ Screen Actors' Guild; a TRADE UNION in the US for actors and actresses who perform in films for the cinema or television 银幕演员协会〔美国一影视演员行会〕—compare 比较 AFTRA, EQUITY

sag¹ /sæg; sæg/ **sagged, sagging** *v* [I] **1** to sink or bend downwards and away from the usual position 下垂; 下陷; 下弯: *The branch sagged under the weight of the apples.* 树枝因苹果的重压弯下来了。| *His shoulders sagged dejectedly.* 他沮丧地垂着肩。**2** to become weaker or less valuable 下降; 萧条: *attempts to revive the sagging economy* 为了使衰退中的经济复苏所作的努力 | *My morale sagged still further.* 我越发意志消沉了。

sag² *n* [singular,U] a downward bending or sinking movement or position 下垂; 下陷: *a sag in a mattress* 褥垫陷下的部位

sa·ga /ˈsɑgə; ˈsɑːgə/ *n* [C] **1** a long story, especially one that continues over a period of many years 长篇故事, 家世小说: *an absorbing family saga* 吸引人的家世小说 **2** *informal* a long and complicated series of events or a description of this【非正式】一长串的事件; 长篇的描述: *I had to listen to a great long saga about her medical problems.* 我不得不听关于她的医疗问题的一番冗长不堪的叙述。**3** one of the stories written about the Vikings of Norway and Iceland 萨迦〔关于挪威和冰岛地区海盗的传说〕

sa·ga·cious /səˋgeʃəs; səˈgeɪʃəs/ *adj formal* able to understand and judge things very well; WISE¹ (2)【正式】聪慧的, 明智的 —**sagaciously** *adv*

sa·ga·ci·ty /səˋgæsətɪ; səˈgæsəti/ *n* [U] *formal* good judgment and understanding; WISDOM【正式】聪慧, 明智

Sa·gan /ˈsegən; ˈseɪgən/, **Carl** (1934-96) a US ASTRONOMER (=a scientist who studies the stars), who was especially interested in discovering whether there were living creatures in other parts of the universe. He made a popular series of television programmes about the universe, called *Cosmos.* 萨根〔(1934-1996), 美国天文学家。其研究兴趣侧重于探寻宇宙中的其他地方是否存在生命。他制作了介绍宇宙奥秘的大众电视系列节目, 名为《宇宙》〕

sage¹ /sedʒ; seɪdʒ/ *n* **1** [U] a plant with grey-green leaves that are used in cooking 鼠尾草, 洋苏草〔其灰绿色叶子可用于烹调〕**2** [C] *literary* someone, especially an old man, who is very wise【文】圣人, 哲人

sage² *adj literary* very wise, especially as a result of a lot of experience【文】睿智的, 贤明的: *sage advice* 明智的忠告 —**sagely** *adv*

sage·brush /ˈsedʒˌbrʌʃ; ˈseɪdʒbrʌʃ/ *n* [U] a small plant that is very common in the western US〔美国西部常见的〕灌木蒿

sag·gy /ˈsægɪ; ˈsægi/ *adj informal* having a shape that sinks or drops downwards【非正式】下垂的; 下陷的: *The mattress was rather saggy in the middle.* 床垫中间下陷得相当深。

Sa·git·tar·i·us /ˌsædʒɪˋtɛrɪəs; ˌsædʒəˈteəriəs/ *n* **1** [singular] the ninth sign of the ZODIAC, represented by an animal that is half-horse and half-human, and believed to affect the character and life of people born between November 22 and December 21 人马宫[座]〔黄道十二宫的第九宫〕**2** [C] someone who was born between November 22 and December 21 出生于人马宫时段〔即11月22日至12月21日〕的人

sa·go /ˈsego; ˈseɪgəʊ/ *n* [U] a white food substance used to make sweet dishes with milk 西谷米, 西米

Sa·ha·ra, the /səˈhærə; səˈhɑːrə/ also 又作 **the Sahara Desert** the world's largest desert, which covers a very large area of North Africa 撒哈拉沙漠〔世界上面积最大的沙漠, 覆盖北非大部分地区〕

sahib /ˈsɑ ɪb; sɑːb/ *n* [C] *IndE & PakE* used as a title of respect for a man in India, especially in former times【印和巴】先生, 老爷〔过去印度对男子的一种尊称〕: *Good morning, sahib!* 早上好, 先生!

said[1] /sɛd; sed/ the past tense and past participle of SAY[1]

said[2] *adj* [only before noun 仅用于名词前] *law or humorous* used when giving more information about someone or something that has just been mentioned【法律或幽默】该…, 上述的: *The said weapon was later found in the defendant's home.* 该武器后来在被告家中发现。

Sai·gon /ˌsaɪˈgɑn; ˌsaɪˈgɒn/ the former name of Ho Chi Minh City in southern Vietnam. It was the capital of South Vietnam when the country was divided in two, and it was badly damaged during the Vietnam War. 西贡〔越南南方城市胡志明市旧称。越南南北分裂期间, 西贡为南越首都, 越战期间遭到严重破坏〕

S3 **sail**[1] /sel; seɪl/ *v* **1** [I always+adv/prep] to travel across an area of water in a boat or ship (乘船) 航行: *the first Europeans to sail across the Atlantic* 乘船横渡大西洋的首批欧洲人 | *Three tall ships sailed past.* 三艘大船驶了过去。**2** [I,T] to direct or control the movement of a boat or ship 驾驶 (船只): *The captain sailed his ship safely through the narrow passage.* 船长驾船安全通过狭窄的航道。| *My father taught me to sail when I was 14.* 我 14 岁时父亲就教我驾船。**3** [I] to start a journey by boat or ship 起航: *We sail at dawn.* 我们在黎明时起航。| [+for] *They're sailing for Antigua next week.* 他们下星期要起航前往安提瓜岛。**4** [I always+adv/prep] to move quickly and smoothly through the air 飘过; 飞过: *At that moment a ball came sailing over the fence and landed in my lap.* 就在那时, 一个球飞过篱笆, 落在我的膝上。**5** [I always+adv/prep] to move forwards gracefully and confidently 优雅而自信地走: *Penelope sailed into the room, her dress billowing behind her.* 佩内洛普婀娜地步入房间, 裙子在身后飘起。**6 sail close to the wind** to do or say something that is nearly wrong, illegal, or dishonest 接近非法, 几乎逾规, 近乎说谎: *You're sailing a bit close to the wind with that remark.* 你那样说未免有点冒失。—see also 另见 **sail/fly under false colours** (FALSE (10))

sail through *phr v* [I,T] to succeed very easily in a test, examination etc 顺利通过 (考试等)

sail[2] *n* [C] **1** a large piece of strong cloth fixed onto a boat, so that the wind will push the boat along 帆: *a yacht with white sails* 扬着白帆的小艇 | **hoist/lower the sails** (=put the sails up or down) 扬/下帆 **2 set sail** to begin a journey by boat or ship 起航: *The following week the 'Queen Elizabeth' set sail for Jamaica.* "伊丽莎白女王号"于下星期起航前往牙买加。**3 under sail** *literary* moving along on a ship or boat that has sails【文】扬帆航行

sail·board /ˈselbɔrd; ˈseɪlbɔːd/ *n* [C] a flat board with a sail, that you stand on in the sport of WIND-SURFING〔风帆滑浪用的〕帆板

sail·boat /ˈselˌbot; ˈseɪlbəʊt/ *n* [C] *AmE* a small boat with one or more sails【美】小帆船

sail·ing /ˈselɪŋ; ˈseɪlɪŋ/ *n* **1** [U] the sport or activity of travelling in or directing a small boat with sails 帆船运动: *Sylvia had always enjoyed sailing.* 西尔维娅向来喜欢帆船运动。**2** [C] a time when a ship leaves a port 起航时间; 〔船的〕航班: *Luckily, there was another sailing at 2 o'clock.* 幸好两点钟还有一班船。—see also 另见 PLAIN SAILING

sailing boat /ˈ· · ·/ *n* [C] *BrE* a small boat with one or more sails【英】小帆船

sailing ship /ˈ· · ·/ *n* [C] a large ship with sails 大帆船

sail·or /ˈselɚ; ˈseɪlə/ *n* [C] **1** someone who works on a ship 水手, 海员 **2** someone who travels in a boat 乘船者: **bad/good sailor** (=someone who does or does not feel sick when they are in a boat) 晕船的/不晕船的人

CULTURAL NOTE 文化注释

The STEREOTYPE of a sailor is a man who has a strong desire for sex when he returns to land, and people sometimes joke that sailors have a different woman waiting for them in every port that they visit. 水手的典型形象是, 他们每次踏上陆地都迫不及待地搜寻性目标发泄; 因此人们有时候开玩笑说, 在水手到达的每个港口都有一个新欢等着他们。

sailor suit /ˈ· · ·/ *n* [C] a blue and white suit that looks like an old-fashioned sailor's uniform, worn by children〔儿童穿的〕水手装

Sainsbury Wing, the /ˈ· · · ˌ ·/ a new part that was added to the National Gallery in London in 1991 塞恩斯伯里展厅〔伦敦国家美术馆 1991 年扩建的部分〕

saint /sent; seɪnt/ *n* [C] **1** someone who is given a special honour by the Christian church after they have died, because they were very good or holy〔死后由基督教会追封的〕圣徒, 圣人: *Saint Patrick* 圣帕特里克 **2** *informal* someone who is extremely good, kind, or patient【非正式】道德高尚的人; 极为慈爱的人; 极有耐心的人: *His wife must have been a saint to put up with him for all those years.* 他妻子容忍了他那么多年, 一定是个极有耐心的人了。**3 the patience of a saint** a very large amount of patience 极大的耐心: *You need the patience of a saint for this job.* 做这份工作你要有极大的耐心。

Saint Bernadette —see 见 Saint BERNADETTE

saint·ed /ˈsentɪd; ˈseɪntɪ̣d/ *adj* **1** having been made a saint by the Christian church 被 (基督教会) 追封为圣徒的 **2** *old-fashioned* used when talking about a dead person【过时】已进天国的, 已升天的 **3 my sainted aunt!** *old-fashioned spoken* used to express surprise or shock【过时, 口】我的妈呀! 〔用于表示惊讶或震惊〕

Saint George —see 见 Saint GEORGE

Saint George's /sent ˋdʒɔrdʒɪz; sənt ˋdʒɔːdʒɪz/ the capital city of Grenada 圣乔治〔格林纳达首都〕

saint·hood /ˈsentˌhʊd; ˈseɪnthʊd/ *n* [U] the state of being a saint 圣徒的身份

Saint Joan —see 见 JOAN OF ARC

Saint John the Bap·tist /ˌ· ˌ · ˈ · ·/ (about 12 BC-28 AD) a religious teacher in the New Testament of the Bible who BAPTIZEd Jesus in the river Jordan 施洗者圣约翰〔(公元前约 12－公元 28),《圣经·新约》中在约旦河为耶稣行洗礼的传教士〕

Saint Leger —see 见 the ST LEGER

saint·ly /ˈsentlɪ; ˈseɪntli/ *adj* seeming to be completely good and honest, with no faults 圣贤似的; 圣洁的: *a doctor who had led a saintly and blameless life* 生平道德高尚无可指摘的医生 —**saintliness** *n* [U]

Saint Pat·rick —see 见 Saint PATRICK

Saint Patrick's Cathedral /ˈ· ˌ · · ˈ · ·/ the largest Roman Catholic church in the US. It is in New York City on Fifth Avenue and was built between 1858 and 1879 圣帕特里克大教堂〔美国最大的天主教堂。位于纽约市第五大道, 建于 1858 至 1879 年间〕

Saint Paul's Cathedral /ˈ· ˌ · · ˈ · ·/ a CATHEDRAL in central London, which is the largest Protestant church in the UK and one of the best-known buildings in London. It was designed by Sir Christopher Wren and built between 1676 and 1710. A previous cathedral in the same place was destroyed in the Great Fire of London (1666). 圣保罗大教堂〔伦敦市中心的一座大教堂。英国最大的新教教堂和最著名的建筑之一。由克里斯托弗·雷恩爵士设计, 1676 至 1710 年间建成。该处原有另一座大教堂, 但毁于1666年的伦敦大火〕

Saint Peter —see 见 Saint PETER

Saint Peter's /ˌ· ˈ · ·/ the largest Christian church in the western world, in the Vatican City in Rome, built in the 16th century. It is the most important church in the Roman Catholic religion, and the artist Michelangelo was one of its main designers. 圣彼得大教堂〔西方世界最大的基督教教堂。位于罗马梵蒂冈城, 始建于16世纪, 为天主教最重要的教堂。画家米开朗琪罗是主要设计者之一〕

Saint Petersburg —see 见 ST PETERSBURG

Saint Peter's Square /ˌ· ˌ · · ˈ ·/ the very large square outside Saint Peter's in Rome, where thousands of people gather to hear the Pope give special messages at Christmas and Easter 圣彼得广场〔罗马圣彼得大教堂外的大型广场。每逢圣诞节、复活节, 成千上万的民众聚集在此聆听教皇发表特别文告〕

Saint-Saëns /ˌsæn ˋsɑns; ˌsæn ˈsɒns/, **Ca·mille** /kæˈmil; kæˈmiːl/ (1835-1921) a French COMPOSER whose works include *Carnival of the Animals*, *the Organ Symphony*, and the OPERA *Samson and Delilah* 圣桑〔(1835-1921), 法国作曲家。作品包括《动物狂欢节》、《管风琴交响曲》及歌剧《参孙与达利拉》〕

saint's day /ˈ· ·/ *n* [C] the day of the year when the Christian church remembers a particular saint〔基督教纪念某一圣徒的〕圣徒节

Saint Swith·in's Day /sent ˋswɪðɪnz de; sənt ˈswɪðɪ̣nz deɪ/ July 15th. According to an old British tradition, if it rains on Saint Swithin's Day it will rain for the next 40 days. 圣斯威

逊节〔7月15日。根据英国的传说，如果圣斯威逊节这天下雨，那么未来40天都会有雨〕

Saint Val·en·tine's Day /˙ˈ···, ˌ/ also 又作 **Valentine's Day** February 14th, when traditionally people send a VALENTINE (=special card) to someone they love, often without saying who the card is from. They may also send flowers, especially red roses, or other presents as a sign of love. 圣瓦伦丁节，情人节〔2月14日。这一天，人们按照惯例给自己所爱的人寄一张情人卡，但不写明寄卡人姓名。人们还会给情人送花，尤以送红玫瑰为最多，或送其他礼物以示爱意〕

saith /sɛθ; seθ/ *biblical* says【圣经】说

sake¹ /sek; seɪk/ *n* [U] **1 for the sake of** in order to help, improve, or please someone or something 由于，为了〔…的缘故〕: *He moved to the seaside for the sake of his health.* 他为了健康而迁居海滨。| *I only went for Kay's sake.* 我只是为了凯才去的。| **for sb's own sake** (=because it will be good for them) 为了自己的利益 *I hope he's told her the truth for his own sake.* 为了他自己好，我希望他已经把真相告诉了她。**2 for the sake of it** if you do something for the sake of it, you do it because you want to and not for any particular reason 只想那样做〔没有特殊的原因〕: *I'm sure she agrees with you really – she just likes arguing for the sake of it.* 我肯定她其实是同意你的 —— 她只是为争论而争论罢了。**3 for the sake of argument** *spoken* if you say something for the sake of argument, what you say may not be true but it will help you to have a discussion【口】为了便于讨论: *Let's say, just for the sake of argument, that you've got £200 to invest.* 为了便于讨论，比方说吧，你有200英镑，打算进行投资。**4 for God's/Christ's/goodness'/Heaven's etc sake** *spoken*【口】**a)** used when you are telling someone how important it is to do something or not to do something 看在上帝的份上，行行好吧〔表示某事很重要〕: *For goodness' sake, don't tell him that!* 行行好，千万别把这事告诉他! **b)** used to show that you are angry or annoyed 天哪〔表示生气或厌烦〕: *What's the matter now, for God's sake?* 天哪，到底出了什么事? —see 见 GOD (USAGE)

sa·ke² /ˈsɑkɪ; ˈsɑːki/ *n* [U] a Japanese alcoholic drink made from rice, served in small cups, usually warm 日本清酒〔一种米酒〕

Sak·ha·rov /ˈsækərɔf; ˈsækərɒf/, **An·drei** /ˈɑndre; ˈɑːndreɪ/ (1921-89) a Russian physicist who helped to develop the Soviet HYDROGEN BOMB and who was also a DISSIDENT (=someone who criticizes his country's government and is badly treated because of his beliefs). He won the Nobel Peace Prize in 1975, but the Soviet government would not allow him to travel to Norway to receive it. He was sent away from Moscow as a punishment, until Mikhail Gorbachev became Soviet president and allowed him to return. 萨哈罗夫〔(1921-1989)，前苏联物理学家。参与过苏联第一枚氢弹的研制工作，他也是一位持不同政见者。1975年获诺贝尔和平奖，但苏联政府不允许其前往挪威领奖，并将其逐出莫斯科以示惩罚。戈尔巴乔夫就任苏联总统后，才允许他返回莫斯科〕

Sa·ki /ˈsɑkɪ; ˈsɑːki/ the name used by the British writer H.H. Munro (1870-1916), who wrote amusing short stories which often had unexpected endings 萨基〔英国作家H.H.芒罗(1870-1916)的笔名。他创作的幽默短篇小说结局往往出人意料〕

sa·laam /səˈlɑm; səˈlɑːm/ *v* [I] to bend forwards and put your hand against your forehead, as a polite greeting in some Eastern countries 行额手礼〔右手掌置额前，深弯腰; 某些东方国家的行礼方式〕 —**salaam** *n* [C]

sal·a·ble /ˈseləbl; ˈseɪləbəl/ *adj* another spelling of SALEABLE saleable 的另一种拼法

sa·la·cious /səˈleʃəs; səˈleɪʃəs/ *adj formal* expressing too much unpleasant sexual detail【正式】淫秽的，诲淫的: *salacious jokes* 黄色笑话 —**salaciously** *adv* —**salaciousness** *n* [U]

sal·ad /ˈsæləd; ˈsæləd/ *n* [C,U] **1** a mixture of raw vegetables, especially LETTUCE, CUCUMBER, and TOMATO 色拉，沙拉，沙律〔用生菜、黄瓜、番茄等生的蔬菜作原料的凉拌菜〕: *a cheese salad* 乳酪沙拉 | *Would you like some salad with your pasta?* 你的通心粉要放些沙拉吗? | *a salad bowl* 沙拉碗 | **toss a salad** (=mix it all together, usually with a DRESSING) 拌沙拉 **2** raw or cooked food cut into small pieces and served cold〔用生或熟的食物切成小块做的〕凉拌菜: *potato salad* 马铃薯沙拉

salad cream /ˈ·· ˌ/ *n* [U] *BrE* a thick light-coloured liquid, similar to MAYONNAISE, that you put on salad【英】〔奶油状的〕沙拉酱

salad days /ˈ·· ˌ/ *n* [plural] *old-fashioned* the time of your life when you are young and not very experienced【过时】经验不足的青年时代，初出茅庐的时期

salad dress·ing /ˈ··, ··/ *n* [C,U] a liquid mixture made from oil and VINEGAR, for putting on salads 沙拉调味料

sal·a·man·der /ˈsæləˌmændɚ; ˈsæləmændə/ *n* [C] a small animal similar to a LIZARD 蝾螈〔一种形似蜥蜴的小动物〕

sa·la·mi /səˈlɑmɪ; səˈlɑːmi/ *n* [C,U] a large SAUSAGE with a strong taste, that is eaten cold 萨拉米香肠

sal·a·ried /ˈsælərɪd; ˈsælərid/ *adj* receiving money every month for the work you do, rather than for every week or every hour (按月)领薪水的: *salaried workers* 领薪水的员工

sal·a·ry /ˈsælərɪ; ˈsæləri/ *n* [C,U] money that you receive as payment from the organization you work for, usually paid to you every month〔通常按月发的〕薪水: **be on a salary of** (=be earning a particular amount) 薪水为… *She's on a salary of £16,000.* 她的薪水为16,000英镑。—compare 比较 WAGE¹ (1) —see 见 PAY² (USAGE)

sale /sel; seɪl/ *n*

1 ►ACT OF SELLING 卖◄ [C,U] the act of giving property, food, or other goods to someone in exchange for money 出售，贩卖: **[+of]** *The use and sale of marijuana remains illegal.* 吸食和贩卖大麻仍然是非法的。| *The house sale was completed in two weeks.* 那栋房子的出售是在两周内完成的。| **make a sale** (=sell something) 卖出，做成一笔买卖 *Every time Harvey makes a sale he gets $50 commission.* 哈维每做成一笔生意，都得到50美元的佣金。| **lose a sale** (=not sell something that you were going to sell) 未卖成，做不成某笔生意 *Rather than lose a sale, car salesmen will often bring down the price.* 汽车推销员往往宁愿降价也不想让一笔生意落空。

2 for sale available to be bought 待售: *Excuse me, are these for sale?* 请问，这些要出售吗? | *There was a "for sale" sign in the yard.* 院子里有一块写着"待售"字样的牌子。| **put sth up for sale** (=to make something, especially a house, available to be bought) 将〔房子等〕出售 *Reluctantly, they put the family home up for sale.* 他们很不情愿地着手卖掉自己的家庭住宅。

3 ►LOWER PRICES 降价◄ a period of time when shops sell their goods at lower prices than usual 大减价，贱卖: *Marsdon's department store is having a sale this week.* 马斯顿百货店本周大减价。| **the sales** *BrE* (=when all the shops have a sale)【英】〔各商店的〕大减价期间 | **the January/summer/autumn etc sales** *I picked up some real bargains in the January sales this year.* 我在今年1月份大减价时买了一些真正的便宜货。

4 ►EVENT 事件◄ [C] an event at which things are sold to the person who offers the highest price; AUCTION¹ 拍卖: *a sale of 17th century paintings* 17世纪绘画拍卖会

5 sales a) [plural] the total number of products that a company sells during a particular period of time 总销售量: *We grossed more than $500,000 in sales last year.* 我们去年的销售总额超过50万美元。| **sales figures/targets etc** *We've already reached our sales targets for this year.* 我们已经达到了今年的销售指标。**b)** [U] the part of a company that deals with selling products 销售部，营业部: *She found a job in sales.* 她找到了一份销售部的工作。| *a sales manager* 销售部经理

6 sales drive/campaign an effort made by a company to try to increase the number of products it sells 促销行动/推销运动

7 sales pitch/talk the things that someone says when they are trying to persuade you to buy something 推销游说/宣传

8 on sale a) available to be bought in a shop 上市，出售: *Stephen King's new novel will go on sale next week.* 斯蒂芬·金的新小说将于下星期出售。**b)** *especially AmE* available to be bought at a lower price than usual【尤美】廉价出售: *I could only afford to buy the CD player because it was on sale.* 只是因为大减价我才买得起这台激光唱机。

9 (on) sale or return if a shop buys something on sale or return, it can return the goods that it is unable to sell 剩货包退〔零售商可以把卖不完的货物退还给批发商〕—see also 另见 BILL OF SALE, JUMBLE SALE, POINT OF SALE

sale·a·ble, salable /ˈseləbl; ˈseɪləbəl/ *adj* something that is saleable can be sold, or is easy to sell 可出售的; 易于销售的: *a saleable commodity* 有销路的商品 —**saleability** /ˌseləˈbɪlətɪ; ˌseɪləˈbɪləti/ *n* [U]

Sa·lem /ˈseləm; ˈseɪləm/ a town in Massachusetts in the eastern US, famous for the Salem Witch Trials in 1692, when many women were taken to a court of law and then officially killed because they were thought to be WITCHes (=women who use magic powers to do bad things). People sometimes use the word 'witch-hunt' to describe situations in which INNOCENT people are punished for things they did not do or for having opinions that other people do not approve of, especially the situation in the US when the HUAC punished people who were believed to be Communists. 塞勒姆〔美国东部马萨诸塞州一城镇，以1692年的塞勒姆女巫审判案闻名。当时，很多妇女被视为女巫而受到法

庭审判并遭到处决。人们有时借用 witch-hunt 一词形容某人无辜或因持有异议而受到惩罚的境遇，尤指美国众议院非美活动调查委员会对那些被认为是共产党的人士进行迫害一事〕

sale of work /ˌ· · ˈ·/ *n* [C] *BrE* an event at which people sell things they have made, especially in order to get money for a good purpose【英】自制品售卖；〔尤指〕义卖

sale·room /ˈselˌrum; ˈseɪlrʊm/ *n* [C] *BrE* a room where things are sold by AUCTION[1]【英】拍卖厅，拍卖行

sales·clerk /ˈselzˌklɝk; ˈseɪlzklɑːk/ *n* [C] *AmE* someone who sells things in a shop【美】售货员，店员，营业员；SHOP ASSISTANT *BrE*【英】

sales·girl /ˈselzˌgɝl; ˈseɪlzgɜːl/ *n* [C] *old-fashioned* a young woman who sells things in a shop【过时】女售货员，女店员，女营业员

sales·man /ˈselzmən; ˈseɪlzmən/ *n plural* **salesmen** /-mən; -mən/ [C] a man whose job is to persuade people to buy his company's products 男推销员

> CULTURAL NOTE 文化注释
>
> **Used car salesmen** In the US and the UK, the STEREOTYPE of a salesman who sells used cars is someone you cannot trust because he is dishonest and has clever ways of hiding a car's faults. 二手车销售员：在美国和英国，人们对二手车销售员的典型看法是不值得信任，因为他们不诚实并且用巧妙的手法掩饰汽车的缺陷来欺诈顾客。

sales·per·son /ˈselzˌpɝsn̩; ˈseɪlzpɜːsən/ *n* [C] someone whose job is selling things 售货员

sales rep·re·sen·ta·tive /ˈ· ·,· · ·/ also 又作 **sales rep** /ˈ· ·/ *n* [C] someone who travels around, usually within a particular area, selling their company's products〔公司的〕销售代表

sales slip /ˈ· ·/ *n* [C] *AmE* a small piece of paper that you are given in a shop when you buy something; RECEIPT (1)【美】售货单据，售货收据

sales tax /ˈ· ·/ *n* [C,U] *AmE* a tax that you have to pay in addition to the cost of something you are buying【美】〔顾客购物时付的〕销售税 —compare 比较 VAT

sales·wom·an /ˈselzˌwumən; ˈseɪlzˌwʊmən/ *n plural* **saleswomen** /-ˌwɪmɪn; -ˌwɪmɪn/ [C] a woman whose job is selling things 女售货员

Sal·ford /ˈsɔlfɚd; ˈsɔːlfəd/ an industrial city in northwest England, near to Manchester 索尔福德〔英格兰西北部一工业城市，临近曼彻斯特〕

sa·li·ent /ˈselɪənt; ˈseɪliənt/ *adj formal* the salient points or features of something are the most important or most noticeable parts of it【正式】显著的，突出的：*The salient features of his plan are summarized in this report.* 他那个计划的显著特点已经概括在这份报告中了。—**salience** *n* [U]

sa·line[1] /ˈselaɪn; ˈseɪlaɪn/ *adj* containing or consisting of salt (含)盐的：*saline solution* 盐溶液 —**salinity** /səˈlɪnətɪ; səˈlɪnɪ̈ti/ *n* [U]

saline[2] *n* [U] a special mixture of water and salt 生理盐水

Sal·in·ger /ˈsælɪndʒɚ; ˈsælɪndʒə/, **J. D.** (1919-2010) a US writer who wrote *The Catcher in the Rye*, one of the most famous and popular US NOVELS ever written 塞林格〔(1919-2010)，美国作家。其作品《麦田里的守望者》是美国历史上最著名、最受读者喜爱的小说之一〕

Salis·bu·ry /ˈsɔlzbɛrɪ; ˈsɔːlzbəri/ a city in southern England famous for its large 13th century CATHEDRAL, which attracts many tourists 索尔兹伯里〔英格兰南部一城市。该市以其13世纪的大教堂闻名，前去观赏的游人众多〕

Salisbury Plain /ˌ· · · ˈ·/ a large piece of open country in southern England, used by the army as a training area. Stonehenge, a structure of stone circles from 2500-1500 BC, is on Salisbury Plain. 索尔兹伯里平原〔英格兰南部一空旷原野，为陆军训练场。巨石阵即位于该平原，由多圈石柱组成，建于公元前2500年至公元前1500年间〕

sa·li·va /səˈlaɪvə; səˈlaɪvə/ *n* [U] the liquid that is produced naturally in your mouth 涎，唾液

salivary gland /ˈ· · · ·, ·/ *n* [C] a part of your mouth that produces saliva 唾液腺

sal·i·vate /ˈsæləˌvet; ˈsælɪ̈veɪt/ *v* [I] to produce more saliva in your mouth than usual, especially because you see or smell food〔因见到或闻到食物而〕流口水，分泌唾液 —**salivation** /ˌsæləˈveʃən; ˌsælɪ̈ˈveɪʃən/ *n* [U]

Salk /sɔlk, sɔːlk/, **Jo·nas** /ˈdʒonəs; ˈdʒəʊnəs/ (1914-95) a US scientist who produced the first successful VACCINE (=a substance that is put into a person's body to protect them from a disease) against POLIO (=a serious disease that damages muscles permanently) 索尔克〔(1914-1995)，美国科学家，最早成功研制出骨髓灰质炎疫苗〕

sal·low /ˈsælo; ˈsæləʊ/ *adj* sallow skin looks slightly yellow and unhealthy〔皮肤〕灰黄色的，土色的：*a sallow complexion* 灰黄的脸色 —**sallowness** *n* [U]

sal·ly[1] /ˈsælɪ; ˈsæli/ *n* [C] **1** an amusing clever remark 俏皮话，妙语 **2** a sudden quick attack and return to a position of defence 突击

sally[2] *v*

sally forth *phr v* [I] *old-fashioned* to leave somewhere that is safe in order to do something that you expect to be difficult or dangerous【过时】出发；出来〔指从安全处出来面对困难或危险〕：*Each morning they sallied forth in search of jobs.* 他们每天早上外出找工作。

Sally Ar·my, the /ˌ· · ˈ· ·/ *BrE* an informal name for the Salvation Army【英】救世军〔Salvation Army俗称〕

salm·on /ˈsæmən; ˈsæmən/ *n* **1** [C] *plural* **salmon** a large fish with silver skin and pink flesh that lives in the sea but swims up rivers to lay its eggs 鲑鱼，三文鱼，大麻哈鱼 **2** [U] this fish eaten as food〔食用〕鲑肉

sal·mo·nel·la /ˌsælməˈnɛlə; ˌsælməˈnelə/ *n* [U] a kind of BACTERIA in food that makes you ill 沙门氏菌属

Sa·lo·me /səˈlomɪ; səˈləʊmi/ in the New Testament of the Bible, the stepdaughter of King Herod who performed a dance called the dance of the seven veils. Her dancing pleased Herod so much that he said she could have anything she wanted. She asked him to give her the head of John the Baptist on a plate, which he did. 莎乐美，又译撒罗米〔《圣经·新约》中希律王的继女。她表演的"七重纱之舞"使龙心大悦。希律王许诺说，她想要什么，就可以得到什么。于是，她请求国王令人用盘子把施洗者约翰的头颅端给她，希律王满足了她的要求〕

sal·on /səˈlɑn; ˈsælɒn/ *n* [C] **1** a shop where you can get your hair cut etc〔提供理发等服务的〕厅，院，廊：*a beauty salon* 美容院 **2** a shop where fashionable and expensive clothes are sold 高级服装店；时装店 **3** a room in a very large house where people can meet and talk〔大宅中的〕客厅 **4** a regular meeting of famous people at which they talk about art, literature, or music, popular in 18th century France 沙龙〔18世纪法国名流定期谈论文艺的社交集会〕

sa·loon /səˈlun; səˈluːn/ *n* [C] **1** a public place where alcoholic drinks were sold and drunk in the western US in the 19th century〔19世纪美国西部的〕酒馆 **2** *BrE* a car that has a separate enclosed space for your bags etc【英】〔可装行李的〕箱式小客车；大轿车；SEDAN *AmE*【美】**3** a large comfortable room where passengers on a ship can sit and relax〔客轮上的〕交谊厅

saloon bar /ˈ· · ˈ·/ *n* [C] *BrE* a comfortable room in a PUB【英】〔酒馆中的〕雅座酒吧

Sal·op /ˈsæləp; ˈsæləp/ a former name for the English COUNTY of Shropshire 萨洛普〔英国什罗普郡旧称〕

sal·sa /ˈsælsə; ˈsælsə/ *n* [U] **1** a type of Latin American dance music〔拉丁美洲的〕萨尔萨舞曲 **2** a SAUCE (1) made from onions, tomatoes (TOMATO) and chillies (CHILLI (2)) that you put on Spanish or Mexican food 辣酱〔一种用洋葱、番茄和辣椒做的西班牙或墨西哥调味辣汁〕

SALT /sɔlt; sɔːlt/ Strategic Arms Limitation Talks; talks between the US and the former Soviet Union, which aimed to reach agreement about limiting the number of NUCLEAR weapons that each country kept. Two SALT Treaties (=official agreements) were signed: SALT I (1972) and SALT II (1979). 限制战略武器会谈〔美苏双方协议制定核武器保有量上限的会谈。先后共签署过两个限制战略武器条约，即《第一次限制战略武器谈判协定》(1972年)和《第二次限制战略武器谈判协定》(1979年)〕

salt[1] /sɔlt; sɔːlt/ *n* **1** [U] a natural white mineral that is added to food to make it taste better or to preserve it; SODIUM CHLORIDE *technical* 盐，食盐；【术语】氯化钠：*Try to reduce the amount of salt you use.* 你要尽量少吃些盐。| *a pinch of salt* 一撮盐 | **table salt** (=very small grains of salt you use in cooking) 精制食盐，佐餐盐 | **sea salt** (=large grains of salt made by drying sea water)〔粗粒〕海盐，粗盐 | **rock salt** (=salt in a solid form rather than in grains)〔块状〕岩盐 **2 the salt of the earth** someone who is ordinary, but good and honest 普通但诚实的好人 **3 take sth with a pinch/grain of salt** *informal* to not completely believe what someone tells you because you know that they do not always tell the truth【非正式】〔因某人老是不说实话而〕对某事半信半疑 **4** [C] *technical* a type of chemical substance【术语】盐类〔一种化学物质〕—see also 另见 BATH SALTS, EPSOM SALTS, SMELLING SALTS, OLD SALT, **rub salt into the wound** (RUB[1] (7)), **worth his/her salt** (WORTH[1] (10))

2 3

S

salt² *v* [T] **1** to add salt to food to make it taste better 给食物放盐（调味）**2** also 又作 **salt down** to add salt to food to preserve it 用盐腌制〔食物〕**3** to put salt on the roads to prevent them from becoming icy〔为融化冰雪〕撒盐于〔道路〕上

salt sth ↔ **away** *phr v* [T] to save money for the future, especially dishonestly by hiding it 储蓄〔尤指把钱私存起来〕

salt³ *adj* [only before noun 仅用于名词前] **1** preserved by salt 用盐腌制的: *salt pork* 腌猪肉 **2** **salt water** water that contains salt, especially naturally in the sea 海水，咸水；盐水 **3** consisting of salt water 咸水的，由咸水形成的: *a salt lake* 盐湖

salt cel·lar /ˈ·ˌ··/ *n* [C] *BrE* a small container for salt【英】小盐瓶；SALT SHAKER *AmE*【美】

Salt Lake Cit·y /ˌ·ˈ··/ the capital city of Utah in the western US. It is the centre of the Mormon religion. 盐湖城〔犹他州首府，位于美国西部，摩门教中心〕

salt·pe·tre *BrE*【英】, **saltpeter** *AmE*【美】/ˈsɔltˈpitɚ; ˌsɔːltˈpiːtə/ *n* [U] a substance used in making GUNPOWDER (=powder that causes explosions) and matches 硝石，硝酸钾

salt shak·er /ˈ·ˌ··/ *n* [C] *AmE* a small container for salt【美】小盐瓶

salt truck /ˈ··/ *n* [C] *AmE* a large vehicle that puts salt or sand on the roads in winter to make them less icy【美】撒盐车；撒沙车〔冬季在路面撒盐或沙以融化冰雪的卡车〕；GRITTER *BrE*【英】

salt·wa·ter /ˈsɔltˈwɔtɚ; ˈsɔːltˌwɔːtə/ *adj* [only before noun 仅用于名词前] living in salty water or in the sea 海生的，生活于咸水的: *saltwater fish* 咸水鱼

salt·y /ˈsɔltɪ; ˈsɔːlti/ *adj* **1** tasting of or containing salt 含盐的，咸的 **2** *old-fashioned* a story, joke, or conversation that is salty is amusing and often about sex【过时】〔故事、玩笑或谈话〕不正经的；下流的

sa·lu·bri·ous /səˈlubrɪəs; səˈluːbriəs/ *adj formal* a place that is salubrious is pleasant and healthy to be in【正式】〔场所〕有益于健康的: *They've moved to a more salubrious part of town.* 他们已经搬到城里更清洁宜人的地方去了。

sal·u·ta·ry /ˈsæljəˌtɛrɪ; ˈsæljətəri/ *adj* a salutary experience is unpleasant but teaches you something〔不愉快但〕有教益的

sal·u·ta·tion /ˌsæljəˈteʃən; ˌsæljəˈteɪʃən/ *n formal*【正式】**1** [C] a word or phrase used at the beginning of a letter or speech, such as "Dear Mr. Smith"〔书信、演讲等开头的〕称呼语 **2** [C, U] something you say or do when greeting someone 问候，致意

sa·lute¹ /səˈlut; səˈluːt/ *v* **1** [I,T] to move your right hand to your head in order to show respect to an officer in the army, navy etc（向…）行军礼；（向…）致敬 **2** [T] *formal* to praise someone for the things they have achieved, especially publicly【正式】〔尤指公开地〕赞扬，颂扬: **salute sb as** *James Joyce was saluted as the greatest writer of the 20th century.* 詹姆斯·乔伊斯被颂扬为 20 世纪最伟大的作家。**3** [T] *old-fashioned* to greet someone in a polite way, especially by moving your hand or body【过时】〔以挥手等〕向〔某人〕打招呼，致意

salute² *n* **1** [C] an act of raising your right hand to your head as a sign of respect, usually done by a soldier to an officer〔通常指士兵向军官的〕敬礼，致敬 **2** [C] an occasion when guns are fired into the air in order to show respect for someone important〔向要人致敬的〕鸣礼炮（仪式）: *a 21-gun salute* 鸣礼炮 21 响 **3** [C,U] *formal* a movement made to greet someone with your hand or head【正式】〔以挥手、点头等动作表示的〕打招呼，致意

sal·vage¹ /ˈsælvɪdʒ; ˈsælvɪdʒ/ *v* [T] **1** to save something from a situation in which other things have already been damaged, destroyed, or lost〔在火灾、洪水等灾难中〕抢救出〔某物〕: **salvage sth from** *We managed to salvage a few photo albums from the fire.* 我们设法从大火中抢救出几本相册。**2** to do something to make sure that you do not fail completely or lose something completely 挽救，挽回〔某物〕: *They brought on Christiansen in a last-minute attempt to salvage the game.* 他们在最后一分钟换克里斯琴森上场，试图挽回败局。| *Is there still a chance of salvaging their marriage?* 他们的婚姻还有望挽救吗？| **salvage your reputation** (=do something so that you do not lose people's respect) 挽回声誉

salvage² *n* [U] **1** the act of saving things from a situation in which other things have already been damaged, destroyed, or lost 抢救，救援: *a salvage operation* 抢救行动 **2** things that have been saved in this way 抢救出的财物

[S3] **sal·va·tion** /sælˈveʃən; sælˈveɪʃən/ *n* [U] **1** the state of being saved from evil or death in the Christian religion〔基督教中对灵魂的〕得救，救世 **2** something that prevents danger, loss, or failure 解救物；救星，救助者: **be the salvation of** *The recent rain will be the salvation of this year's wheat crop.* 最近这场雨会成为今年小麦作物的救星。

Salvation Ar·my, the /·ˌ··ˈ··/ *n* a Christian organization that tries to help poor people 救世军〔指基督教慈善组织〕

salve¹ /sæv; sælv/ *n* [C,U] a substance that you put on sore skin to make it less painful〔缓解疼痛的〕药膏，软膏

salve² *v* [T] *formal*【正式】**salve your conscience** if you do something to salve your conscience, you do it to make yourself feel less guilty 使良心得到宽慰: *Buying his wife flowers helped to salve his conscience.* 他给妻子买花，以使自己的良心得到宽慰。

sal·ver /ˈsælvɚ; ˈsælvə/ *n* [C] a large metal plate used for serving food or drink at a formal meal〔端饭菜或饮料用的〕金属托盘: *a silver salver* 银托盘

sal·vo /ˈsælvo; ˈsælvəʊ/ *n* [C usually singular 一般用单数] *formal*【正式】**1** [+of] the firing of several guns during a battle or as part of a ceremony〔火炮的〕齐放；〔礼炮的〕齐鸣 **2** **opening salvo** the first in a series of questions, statements etc that you use to try to win an argument〔在争论中提出的〕第一个问题，头一炮: *In his opening salvo against the education practices of the 1960s, Stein mentioned several important studies.* 在向 20 世纪 60 年代教育实践开第一炮时，斯坦提到几项重要的研究。**3** sudden laughter, APPLAUSE etc from many people at the same time〔突如其来的〕一阵，一片〔笑声、掌声等〕

Sal·zburg /ˈsɔlzbɝg; ˈsæltsbɜːg/ a city in Austria famous for the music FESTIVAL that takes place there every year, and for being the place where Mozart was born 萨尔茨堡〔奥地利一城市。该市以每年举办的音乐节和莫扎特的出生地而闻名〕

Sa·mar·i·tan /səˈmærətn̩; səˈmærətən/ also 又作 **good samaritan** *n* [C] someone who helps you when you have problems 助人为乐者

Sa·mar·i·tans, the /səˈmærɪtn̩z; səˈmærətənz/ a British organization that offers a free telephone service that people who are very sad, worried, or confused can call to talk to someone. The Samaritans listen to people who feel uncomfortable talking to someone they know about their problems, or who feel so unhappy that they want to kill themselves. 撒马利亚会〔英国一组织，专为情绪消沉、心情焦虑或迷惘的人提供免费热线电话服务。打电话到撒马利亚会的人，有的是不愿意向熟人倾吐心事，有的则因抑郁产生了轻生的念头〕

sam·ba /ˈsæmbə; ˈsæmbə/ *n* [C,U] a fast dance from Brazil, or the type of music played for this dance〔巴西的〕桑巴舞；桑巴舞曲

same¹ /sem; seɪm/ *adj* [only before a noun 仅用于名词前] **1** **the same person/place/thing etc** **a)** one particular person, thing etc and not a different one 同一人/地方/物品等: *He is in the same chair every evening.* 他每晚都坐在同一张椅子上。| *I'll never make the same mistake again.* 我再也不会犯同样的错误了。| [+as] *It's hard to believe she's the same age as Brian.* 真难相信她和布赖恩同龄。| **this same person/that same thing etc** *It is those same people who voted for the Democrats who now complain about their policies.* 正是那些投了民主党票的人，现在却抱怨起民主党的政策。**b)** used to say two or more people, things etc are exactly like each other; IDENTICAL 同样的人/地方/物品等: *It was so embarrassing! Both women were wearing the same dress.* 真尴尬，两位女士穿着一模一样的连衣裙。| *It's the same kind of work, just a different department.* 还是同样的工作，只是换了个部门。| [+as] *He gets the same pay as me but he gets his own office.* 他和我拿同样的工资，但他有自己专用的办公室。| **just/exactly the same** *If you can ride a pushbike then riding a motorbike is exactly the same thing. It's a question of balance.* 如果你会骑自行车，那么骑摩托车也完全一样。只要保持平衡就行。| **much the same** (=almost the same) 大致相同 *The furniture is made in much the same way as it was over 200 years ago.* 这家具的制作工艺和两百多年前的大致一样。**2** used to say that a particular person or thing does not change 没有变化的，一成不变的: *Her perfume has always had the same effect on me.* 她身上的香水味一直对我起着同样的作用。| *He's the same old Peter, moody and irritable.* 他还是以前那个老样子的彼得 —— 喜怒无常，动不动就发火。**3** **at the same time** if two things happen at the same time they both happen together 同时: *Kate and I both went to live in Spain at the same time.* 我和凯特在同时间移居西班牙。**4** **the very same/the self same** used when you are surprised that someone or something is the same person or thing and not a different one 正是这一个/就是原来那个〔用于表示惊奇〕: *It is hard to believe it was in the very same house that Shakespeare wrote his plays.* 真难相信，莎士比亚正是在这所房子里写出了他的剧作。**5** **amount/come to the same thing** to have the same result or effect 结果[效果]都一样: *It doesn't matter whether she was happy to leave or not – it amounts to the same thing. We need a new secretary.* 她是否

S

乐意走并没有什么关系，反正我们需要换个秘书。**6 the same old story/excuse etc** *informal* something that you have heard many times before【非正式】老一套/老借口〔指听过多次的话〕: *It's the same old story – his wife didn't really love him.* 还是那一套 —— 他老婆并不真正爱他。**7 same difference** *spoken especially AmE* used to say that different actions, behaviour etc have the same result or effect【口，尤美】都一样，反正一个样〔用于表示行为或表现等不同但效果一样〕: *"I could mail the letter tomorrow morning or send a fax." "Same difference, it'll still not get there on time."* "我可以在明天上午发封信或发个传真。""都一样，反正都来不及。" **8 by the same token** in the same way, or for the same reasons 同样地；由于同样的原因: *I realise that he hasn't come up with any new ideas, but by the same token we haven't needed any.* 我知道他没有提出什么新的想法，不过我们也并不需要。**9 be in the same boat** to be in the same difficult situation that someone else is in 处于同样的困境

USAGE NOTE 用法说明: SAME

GRAMMAR 语法

Remember that **same** almost always has *the* or *this/that* etc before it. 切记，same 几乎总用在 the, this, that 等词之后: *They wear the same clothes every day* (NOT 不用 *They wear same clothes*). 他们每天都穿同样的衣服。| *People are the same all over the world.* 全世界的人都一样。| *That very same day, Trisha phoned him.* 就在同一天，特丽莎给他打了个电话。

In informal spoken English you will hear **same** used with *the* left out, but this is not considered correct in writing. 在非正式口语中有时与 same 连用的 the 被省略，但在书面语中则认为是不正确的: *"I thought the game was really good." "Same here."* "我认为这场比赛打得很精彩。""我也有同感。" | *"What would you like?" "Same again please."* "你想要些什么?""请再来一杯同样的。"

When you are comparing, you always say that one things is **the same as** another. 进行比较时，the same as 表示一物与另一物相同: *Bob dresses just the same as his father did.* 鲍勃的衣着跟他父亲当年的完全一样。| *I go to the same college as you* (NOT 不用 *...to the same college with*). 我和你上的是同一所大学。

same² *pron* **1 the same a)** used to say that two or more people or things are exactly like each other 同样的〔人或事物〕: *The coins may look the same but one's a forgery.* 这些硬币看起来也许一样，但其中有一个是假的。| *Thanks for your help – I'll do the same for you one day.* 谢谢你的帮助 —— 有一天我会报答你的。**b)** used to say that a particular person or thing does not change 没有变化: *"How's your wife?" "About the same, thanks."* "你太太好吗?""还是老样子，谢谢。" | *Now that Sam's retired, things just won't be the same.* 既然萨姆已经退休，情况就会不一样了。**2 (and the) same to you!** *spoken* used as a reply to a greeting or as an angry reply to a rude remark【口】你也一样！〔用于对问候语或粗鲁话的回答〕: *"Happy Christmas!" "And the same to you, Ben."* "圣诞快乐！""也祝你圣诞快乐，本。" **3 just/all the same** in spite of a particular situation, opinion etc 仍然，还是，照样: *I realise she can be very annoying, but I think you should apologise all the same.* 我知道她可能很讨厌，但我认为你还是应当向她道歉。**4 same here** *spoken* used to say that you feel the same way as someone else【口】我也一样〔用于表示与别人有同感〕: *"I'm absolutely exhausted." "Same here!"* "真累死我了。""我也一样。" **5 (the) same again** used to ask for another drink of the same kind 再来一杯〔用于吩咐要同样的饮料〕 **6 more of the same** used to mean a person, thing etc like the one just mentioned 也是一样[相同]的〔用于指人或事物与刚才提及的那个一样〕: *He has produced a string of thrillers, and this movie is just more of the same.* 他制作了一连串的惊悚片，这部电影又属这一类。—see also 另见 **it's all the same to me** (ALL² (10)), **one and the same** (ONE³ (7))

same³ *adv* **1 the same (as)** in the same way 相同地，一样地: *"Rain" and "reign" are pronounced the same even though they are spelt differently.* rain 和 reign 发音相同，尽管拼法不一样。| *Everyone had to dress the same as a well known historical figure.* 每个人都必须装扮成一位历史名人。**2 same as sb** *spoken* just like someone else【口】和某人一样: *I have my pride, same as anyone else.* 和别人一样，我有自尊心。

same·ness /ˈsemnɪs; ˈseɪmnɪs/ *n* [U] a boring lack of variety, or the quality of being very similar to something else 千篇一律，单调；相同性，共同之处

same·y /ˈsemɪ; ˈseɪmi/ *adj informal* boring and having very little variety【非正式】单调的，无变化的: *His novels tend to be very samey.* 他的小说往往单调乏味。

Samoa /səˈmoə; səˈməʊə/ a group of islands in the South Pacific, including Savai'i and Upolu. Until 1997, it was called Western Samoa. Population: 179,058 (2001). Capital: Apia. 萨摩亚〔南太平洋一群岛，包括萨瓦伊和乌波卢。1997 年以前称西萨摩亚。人口: 179,058 (2001)，首都: 阿皮亚〕—**Samoan** *n, adj*

sa·mo·sa /səˈmosə; sæˈməʊsə/ *n* [C] a type of Indian food made from meat or vegetables covered in thin PASTRY (1) and cooked in hot oil 油炸三角饺〔印度的一种肉馅或菜馅饺〕

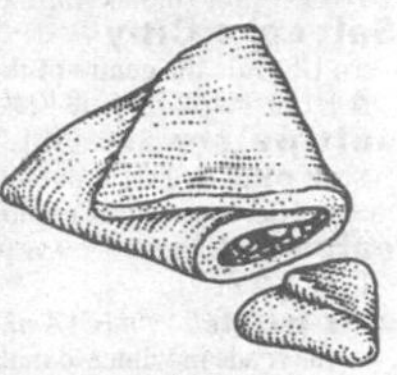

samosa 油炸三角饺

sam·o·var /ˈsæməˌvɑr; ˈsæməvɑː/ *n* [C] a large metal container used in Russia to boil water for making tea 俄式茶炊

sam·pan /ˈsæmpæn; ˈsæmpæn/ *n* [C] a small boat used in China and Southeast Asia〔中国和东南亚用的〕舢舨

sam·ple¹ /ˈsæmpl; ˈsɑːmpəl/ *n* [C] **1** a small part or amount of something that is examined in order to find out something about the whole 样品，标本，试样: *They took a blood sample to test for hepatitis.* 他们取了血样以检查有无肝炎。| **[+of]** *I'd like to see some samples of your work.* 我想看看你作品的一些样品。**2** a small amount of a product that people can try in order to find out what it is like 试用产品，货样: **[+of]** *samples of a new shampoo* 新型洗发剂的货样 **3** a group of people who have been chosen to give information or answers to questions〔抽样调查时〕被抽选的一组人: *The sample consisted of 344 elementary and secondary school teachers.* 这次调查的抽样包括 344 位中小学教师。| **random sample** (=one in which you choose people without knowing anything about them) 随机抽样 *Out of a random sample of drivers, 21% had been involved in an accident in the previous year.* 在随机抽样调查的驾驶员中，有 21% 曾在上一年发生过事故。| **representative sample** (=one that is planned to include several different types of people) 代表性抽样 *a nationally representative sample of over 4500 elderly persons* 抽选 4500 余位老人的全国代表性抽样

sample² *v* [T] **1** to taste food or drink in order to see what it is like 品尝，尝试〔食品、饮料等〕—see 见 TASTE² (USAGE) **2** [often passive 常用被动态] to choose some people from a larger group in order to ask them questions or get information from them 对〔人群〕作抽样调查: *18% of the adults sampled admitted having had problems with alcohol abuse.* 在接受抽样调查的成年人中有 18% 承认有酗酒问题。**3** to try an activity, go to a place etc in order to see what it is like 体验: *Here's your chance to sample the delights of country life.* 你去体验乡村生活乐趣的机会来了。

sam·pler /ˈsæmplɚ; ˈsɑːmplə/ *n* [C] a piece of cloth with different stitches on it, made to show how good someone is at sewing 刺绣样品

Sam·son /ˈsæmsn; ˈsæmsən/ in the Old Testament of the Bible, a very strong man who is a great fighter. A woman called Delilah finds out that his strength comes from his long hair, and she uses her sexual power to trick Samson into having his hair cut off. This allows his enemies, the Philistines, to make him a prisoner and blind him. His strength returns when his hair grows again, and he destroys the Philistines' TEMPLE by pulling down the PILLARS that hold the roof up, killing himself and his enemies. 参孙〔《圣经·旧约》中一位善战的大力士。一个名叫大利拉的女人发现他的力气来自他的长发，于是利用自己的肉体魅力，施诡计剪去他的头发。如此一来，参孙就沦为敌人非利士人的阶下囚，并被剜去双眼。后来，他的头发又长了出来，使他恢复了体力。他把支撑非利士人大殿屋顶的立柱推倒，结果殿塌人亡，参孙与敌人同归于尽〕

sam·u·rai /ˈsæmʊˌraɪ; ˈsæmʊraɪ/ *n* [C] *plural* **samurai** a member of a powerful military class in Japan in former times〔日本从前的〕武士 —**samurai** *adj*: *a samurai sword* 武士刀

Sana /sɑˈnɑ; sɑːˈnɑː/ also 又作 **San'a, Sanaa** the capital of Yemen, formerly the capital of North Yemen 萨那〔也门首都。曾为北也门首都〕

San An·dre·as fault, the /ˌsæn ændreəs ˈfɔlt; ˌsæn ændreɪəs ˈfɔːlt/ a crack in the Earth's surface which goes from the north to the south of California in the western US. The large areas of rock on either side of this crack are slowly moving in different directions, and this sometimes causes EARTHQUAKES.

圣安德烈亚斯断层〔地壳上的一个断层。位于美国西部，纵贯加利福尼亚州南北。断层两边的大面积岩层向不同方向缓慢移动，因此有时会引发地震〕

San An·to·ni·o /ˌsæn ænˋtonɪo; ˌsæn ænˈtəʊniəʊ/ a city in southern Texas which has large numbers of Mexican-Americans and the Alamo 圣安东尼奥〔得克萨斯州南部一城市，大量墨西哥裔美国人及阿拉莫人聚居于此〕

san·a·to·ri·um /ˌsænəˋtorɪəm; ˌsænəˈtɔːriəm/ *n* [C] a kind of hospital for sick people who are getting better but still need rest and a lot of care 疗养院

San·cho Pan·za /ˌsæntʃo ˋpænzə; ˌsæntʃəʊ ˈpænzə/ the servant of DON QUIXOTE in the book by Miguel de Cervantes 桑丘〔米盖尔·德·塞万提斯的小说《堂吉诃德》中堂吉诃德的仆人〕

sanc·ti·fy /ˋsæŋktəˌfaɪ; ˈsæŋktɪ̣faɪ/ *v* [T] **1** to make something socially or religiously acceptable or to give something official approval 正式认可，批准；使成为可接受的：*sexual roles that are sanctified by marriage* 为婚姻所认可的两性角色 **2** to make something holy 使神圣化，使圣洁化 —**sanctification** /ˌsæŋktəfəˋkeʃən; ˌsæŋktɪ̣fɪ̣ˈkeɪʃən/ *n* [U]

sanc·ti·mo·ni·ous /ˌsæŋktəˋmonɪəs; ˌsæŋktɪ̣ˈməʊniəs◂/ *adj formal* behaving as if you are morally better than other people, in a way that is annoying【正式】假装圣洁的，伪善的，自认为道德高尚的：*sanctimonious politicians preaching to everyone about family values* 逢人便大谈家庭价值观的虚伪政客 —**sanctimoniously** *adv* —**sanctimoniousness** *n* [U]

sanc·tion¹ /ˋsæŋkʃən; ˈsæŋkʃən/ *n* **1 sanctions** [plural] official orders or laws stopping trade, communication etc with another country, as a way of forcing its leaders to make political changes〔对某国的〕制裁：[**+against**] *US sanctions against Cuba* 美国对古巴的制裁 | **impose sanctions on** (=start using sanctions) 实施制裁 | **lift sanctions** (=stop using sanctions) 解除制裁 **2** [U] official permission, approval, or acceptance 正式许可，批准；接受：*It emerged that the aide had acted without White House sanction.* 真相暴露，原来该助理的行动并未经过白宫批准。**3** [C] a form of punishment that can be used if someone disobeys a rule or law 处罚，惩罚

sanction² *v* [T] *formal*【正式】**1** to officially accept or allow something 批准，准许：*The church refused to sanction the king's second marriage.* 教会拒绝批准国王的第二次婚姻。**2 be sanctioned by** to be made acceptable by something 为…所认可：*a barbaric custom, but one sanctioned by long usage* 一种野蛮但由来已久的风俗

sanc·ti·ty /ˋsæŋktətɪ; ˈsæŋktɪ̣ti/ *n* [U] **1 the sanctity of life/marriage etc** the quality that makes life, marriage etc so important that it must be respected and preserved 生命/婚姻等的神圣：*the sanctity of the Constitution* 宪法的无上尊严 **2** *formal* the holy or religious character of a person or place【正式】神圣，圣洁：*an aura of sanctity* 神圣的气氛

sanc·tu·a·ry /ˋsæŋktʃʊˌɛrɪ; ˈsæŋktʃuəri/ *n* **1** [C,U] a peaceful place that is safe and provides protection, especially for people who are in danger 庇护所，避难所：**find/seek sanctuary** *Refugees fleeing from the advancing army found sanctuary in Geneva.* 大军逼近，难民们逃到日内瓦避难。**2** [C] an area for birds or animals where they are protected and cannot be hunted 禁猎区，鸟兽保护区：**bird/wildlife etc sanctuary** *The park is the largest wildlife sanctuary in the US.* 这个公园是美国最大的野生动物保护区。**3** [U] the right that people had under Christian law, especially in former times, to be protected from police, soldiers etc by staying in a church〔从前教堂的〕庇护权〔指根据基督教教规，在教堂的人有权不受警察或军人的逮捕〕**4** [C] the part of a religious building that is considered to be the most holy〔教堂内的〕圣坛 **5** [C] *AmE* the room where religious services take place【美】〔进行宗教活动的〕殿堂，圣所

sanc·tum /ˋsæŋktəm; ˈsæŋktəm/ *n* [C] **1 inner sanctum** *often humorous* a place or room that only a few important people are allowed to enter【常幽默】〔只允许少数要人入内的〕私室，密室 **2** a holy place inside a temple〔庙宇中的〕圣所，内殿

Sanc·tus, the /ˋsæŋktəs; ˈsæŋktəs/ a prayer or HYMN (=song of praise to God) which is said or sung as part of the mass in Christian churches《圣哉经》〔基督教弥撒中使用的祷告词或赞美诗〕

3 **sand¹** /sænd; sænd/ *n* [U] **1 a)** a substance consisting of very small pieces of rocks and minerals, that forms beaches and deserts 沙，沙子：*footprints in the sand* 沙子上的脚印 **b)** this substance when it is found in soil, used in building etc〔建筑用的〕砂；沙子：*a mixture of sand and cement* 砂和水泥的混合物 **2 sands** [plural] *BrE* an area of beach【英】沙滩：*miles of golden sands* 绵延几英里的金色沙滩 **3 the sands of time** *literary* moments of time that pass quickly【文】光阴，时光

sand² *v* **1** [I,T] also 又作 **sand down** to make a surface smooth by rubbing it with SANDPAPER or using a special piece of equipment〔用砂纸等〕把…磨光，擦净 **2** [T] to put sand on a frozen road to make it safer〔为防滑〕撒沙于〔结冰的路面〕

Sand /sɑnd; sɒnd/, **George** /ʒɔrʒ; ʒɔːʒ/ (1804-76) a French female writer of NOVELs, whose real name was Amandine Aurore Dupin. She is famous for her long relationship with the COMPOSER Chopin, and for wearing men's clothes to show her belief that women should have the same rights as men. 乔治·桑〔(1804-1876)，法国女小说家，真名为阿芒丁·奥罗尔·迪潘。她与作曲家肖邦有过长期恋爱关系，还常穿男装，以此彰显她坚信的男女同权的观念。这一切是她成名的缘由所在〕

san·dal /ˋsændḷ; ˈsændl/ *n* [C] a light shoe that is fastened onto your foot by leather bands and worn in warm weather 凉鞋 —see picture at 参见 SHOE¹ 图

san·dal·wood /ˋsændḷˌwʊd; ˈsændlwʊd/ *n* [U] pleasant-smelling wood from a Southern Asian tree, or the oil from this wood 檀香木；檀香油

sand·bag /ˋsændˌbæg; ˈsændbæg/ *n* [C] a bag filled with sand used for protection against floods, explosions etc〔用于防洪、防爆炸等的〕沙包，沙袋

sand·bank /ˋsændˌbæŋk; ˈsændbæŋk/ *n* [C] a raised area of sand in a river, ocean etc〔河川、海洋中的〕沙坝

sand bar /ˋ· ·/ *n* [C] a long pile of sand in a river or the ocean formed by the movement of the water 河口沙洲〔河流或海洋中由水流形成的长条形沙洲〕

sand·blast /ˋsændˌblæst; ˈsændblɑːst/ *v* [T] to clean or polish metal, stone, glass etc with a machine that sends out a powerful stream of sand 对…喷砂〔以清洗或研磨金属、石头、玻璃等〕

sand·box /ˋsændˌbɑks; ˈsændbɒks/ *n* [C] *especially AmE* a special area of sand for children to play in【尤美】〔供儿童玩的〕沙坑，沙盒；SANDPIT *BrE*【英】

Sand·burg /ˋsændbɝg; ˈsændbɜːg/, **Carl** (1878-1967) a US writer and poet who won Pulitzer Prizes for his books about the life of Abraham Lincoln and for his poetry, which is typically about cities and industry 桑德堡〔(1878-1967)，美国作家、诗人。他为亚伯拉罕·林肯撰写传记，还创作了以城市与工业为题材的诗歌，并因此获普利策奖〕

sand·cas·tle /ˋsændˌkæsḷ; ˈsændˌkɑːsəl/ *n* [C] a small model of a castle made out of sand by children playing on a beach〔儿童在海滩堆成的〕沙堡

sand dune /ˋ· ·/ *n* [C] a hill formed of sand in a desert or near the sea〔沙漠或海边的〕沙丘 —see picture on page A12 参见 A12 页图

sand·er /ˋsændɚ; ˈsændə/ also 又作 **sanding ma·chine** /ˋ· · ˌ·/ *n* [C] an electric tool with a rough surface that moves very quickly, used for making surfaces smooth 打磨机

sand fly /ˋ· ·/ *n* [C] a small fly that bites people and lives on beaches 白蛉

Sand·hurst /ˋsændhɝst; ˈsændhɜːst/ the Royal Military Academy in the village of Sandhurst in southern England, which trains officers for the British army. Sandhurst is the best known and most respected military college in the UK. 桑德赫斯特皇家军事学院〔位于英格兰南部的桑德赫斯特村，为英国陆军培养军官。桑德赫斯特是英国最为著名、最受推崇的军事院校〕：*The senior officers were mostly Sandhurst men.* 高级军官大多毕业于桑德赫斯特。

San Di·e·go /sæn dɪˋego; sæn diˈeɪgəʊ/ a city in southern California, US, which is a port, an industrial centre, and a base for the US navy 圣迭戈〔美国加利福尼亚州南部一城市。该市为一港口城市，也是一工业中心和美国海军基地〕

San·di·nis·tas, the /ˌsændɪˋnistə; ˌsændɪ̣ˈniːstə◂/ *n* [plural] a LEFT-WING political organization in Nicaragua in central America, who gained power in 1979 and got rid of the DICTATOR Somoza. They were the government of Nicaragua until they were defeated in elections in 1990. The Sandinistas were strongly opposed by the US, which provided money, weapons, and military training to a RIGHT-WING opposition group called the Contras. 桑地诺民族解放阵线〔中美洲尼加拉瓜一左翼政治组织。1979年推翻了独裁统治者索摩查，掌握政权。组成尼加拉瓜政府，直至1990年大选失利。该组织遭到美国的强烈反对，美国给右翼反对派孔特拉斯集团提供资金、武器及军事训练等援助〕

sand·man /ˋsændmæn; ˈsændmæn/ *n* [singular] an imaginary man who is supposed to make children go to sleep〔童话中能使儿童入睡的〕睡魔

sand·pa·per¹ /ˋsændˌpepɚ; ˈsændˌpeɪpə/ *n* [U] strong paper covered on one side with sand or a similar substance, used for rubbing wood in order to make the surface smooth 砂纸

sandpaper² *v* [T] to rub something with sandpaper 用砂纸擦[磨]

sand·pip·er /ˈsændˌpaɪpɚ; ˈsændˌpaɪpə/ *n* [C] a small bird with long legs and a long beak that lives around muddy or sandy shores 鹬〔一种生活在泥岸或沙滩的腿和喙较长的小鸟〕

sand·pit /ˈsændˌpɪt; ˈsændˌpɪt/ *n* [C] *BrE* a special area of sand for children to play in【英】〔供儿童玩的〕沙坑, 沙盒; SANDBOX *AmE*【美】

San·dring·ham /ˈsændrɪŋəm; ˈsændrɪŋəm/ also 又作 **Sandringham House** a large house in Norfolk in the east of England, where the British royal family lives for part of the year, especially around Christmas 桑德灵厄姆〔英格兰东部诺福克郡一幢大宅。英国皇室成员每年在此居住一段时间, 尤其是在圣诞节前后〕

sand·stone /ˈsændˌston; ˈsændstəʊn/ *n* [U] a type of soft yellow or red rock often used in buildings 砂岩

sand·storm /ˈsændˌstɔrm; ˈsændstɔːm/ *n* [C] a storm in the desert in which sand is blown around by strong winds 沙暴

sand·trap /ˈsændˌtræp; ˈsændtræp/ *n* [C] *AmE* a hollow place on a GOLF course, filled with sand, from which it is difficult to hit the ball【美】〔高尔夫球场作为障碍的〕沙坑; BUNKER (3) *BrE*【英】—see picture on page A23 参见 A23 页图

S2 **sand·wich¹** /ˈsændwɪtʃ; ˈsænwɪdʒ/ *n* **1** [C] two pieces of bread with cheese, meat, egg etc between them 夹心面包片, 三明治: *I've brought sandwiches for lunch today.* 我今天带了三明治作午餐。| *a ham sandwich* 火腿三明治 **2** [C] *BrE* a cake consisting of two layers with JAM¹ (1) and cream between them【英】果酱奶油夹心蛋糕 —see also 另见 CLUB SANDWICH, OPEN SANDWICH

sandwich² *v* [T] **be sandwiched between** to be in a very small space between two other things 被夹在…中间: *The car was sandwiched between two big trucks.* 小汽车被夹在两辆大货车中间。

sandwich board /ˈ‥ ‥/ *n* [C] two boards with advertisements on them that hang in front and behind someone who is paid to walk around in public〔在公共场所到处走动做广告者胸前和背后所挂的〕人身悬挂夹板广告牌, 三明治广告牌

sandwich course /ˈ‥ ‥/ *n* [C] *BrE* a course of study at a college or university that includes periods spent working in industry or business【英】〔学院或大学的〕工读交替制课程

sand·y /ˈsændɪ; ˈsændi/ *adj* **1** covered with sand 被沙覆盖的: *My towel's all sandy!* 我的毛巾上全是沙子! | **sandy beach** *BrE* (=one that is made of sand not stones)【英】沙滩 **2** hair that is sandy is a yellowish-brown〔头发等〕沙色的, 浅黄灰色的, 浅黄棕色的 —**sandiness** *n* [U] —see picture on page A12 参见 A12 页图

sane /sen; seɪn/ *adj* **1** able to think in a normal and reasonable way 心智健全的, 神智正常的 —opposite 反义词 INSANE **2** reasonable and based on sensible thinking 明智的, 清醒的: *a sane solution to a delicate problem* 解决微妙问题的明智方法 **3 keep sb sane** to stop someone from thinking about their problems and becoming upset 不让某人担忧 —**sanely** *adv* —see also 另见 SANITY

San Fran·cis·co /ˌsæn frənˈsɪsko; ˌsæn frənˈsɪskəʊ/ a city and port in California, US. It is a very beautiful city, built on hills next to a BAY (=an area of sea that curves inwards towards the land) on the Pacific Ocean. Its famous areas include Chinatown, where many people live whose families originally came from China, the Golden Gate Bridge, and the prison island of Alcatraz. The city is close to the San Andreas Fault, and was almost destroyed by the great earthquake and fire of 1906. 圣弗朗西斯科, 又译旧金山〔美国加利福尼亚州一港口城市。建于太平洋一处海湾附近的山丘上, 风光旖旎。市内著名景点有唐人街华人聚居区、金门大桥、阿尔卡特拉兹岛监狱等。旧金山临近圣安德烈亚斯断层, 在1906年的一场大地震和大火中几乎毁于一旦〕

sang /sæŋ; sæŋ/ the past tense of SING

Sanger /ˈsæŋɚ; ˈsæŋə/, **Margaret** /ˈmɑrgrət; ˈmɑːgrət/ (1883-1966) a US woman who started the first birth control center in the US, to help women control the number of children they had 山额夫人, 又译桑格夫人〔一美国妇女。她创立了美国第一个节育中心, 帮助妇女控制生育〕

sang-froid /sɑŋ ˈfrwɑ; ˌsɒŋ ˈfrwɑː/ *n* [U] courage and the ability to keep calm in dangerous or difficult situations 镇定, 沉着, 冷静: *The British, once renowned for their stiff upper lip and sang-froid, were now regarded as a nation of hooligans.* 曾经以顽强不屈和沉着冷静著称的英国人, 后来却被看成是一个无赖民族。

san·gri·a /sæŋˈgrɪə; sæŋˈgriːə/ *n* [U] a Spanish drink made from red wine, fruit, and fruit juice 桑格利亚汽酒〔一种由红葡萄酒、水果和果汁配成的西班牙饮料〕

san·gui·na·ry /ˈsæŋgwɪnˌɛrɪ; ˈsæŋgwɪ̈nəri/ *adj formal* involving violence and killing【正式】血腥的, 残暴的: *a bitter and sanguinary war* 惨烈的血战

san·guine /ˈsæŋgwɪn; ˈsæŋgwɪ̈n/ *adj formal*【正式】**1** cheerful and hopeful about the future; CONFIDENT 乐观的; 充满自信的: *We are less sanguine about the prospects for peace since the row at the UN.* 自从在联合国发生那场争吵以后, 我们对和平的前景就不那么乐观了。**2** red and healthy looking 有血色的, 红润的: *a sanguine complexion* 红润的肤色 —**sanguinely** *adv*

san·i·tar·i·um /ˌsænəˈtɛrɪəm; ˌsænɪ̈ˈteəriəm/ *n* [C] an American spelling of SANATORIUM sanatorium 的美式拼法

san·i·ta·ry /ˈsænəˌtɛrɪ; ˈsænɪ̈təri/ *adj* **1** [only before noun 仅用于名词前] connected with health, especially with the removal of dirt, infection, or human waste 有关卫生的, 与健康有关的: *After examining the sanitary arrangements, they ordered the whole place to be disinfected.* 检查过公共卫生的安排之后, 他们下令整个地方都要消毒。**2** clean and not involving any danger to your health 清洁的; 于健康无害的 —opposite 反义词 INSANITARY

sanitary pad /ˈ‥‥ ˌ‧/ also 又作 **sanitary tow·el** /ˈ‥‥ ˌ‥/ *BrE*【英】, also 又作 **sanitary napkin** *AmE*【美】*n* [C] a piece of soft material that a woman wears between her legs during her PERIOD¹ (4) 卫生巾, 月经带

san·i·ta·tion /ˌsænəˈteʃən; ˌsænɪ̈ˈteɪʃən/ *n* [U] the protection of public health by removing and treating waste, dirty water etc 公共卫生, 环境卫生

sanitation work·er /ˌ‥ˈ‥ ˌ‥/ *n* [C] *AmE formal* someone who removes waste material that people put outside their houses【美, 正式】垃圾工, 清洁工〔挨家挨户收垃圾的工人〕

san·i·tize also 又作 -ise *BrE*【英】/ˈsænəˌtaɪz; ˈsænɪ̈taɪz/ *v* [T] **1** to make news, literature etc less offensive by taking out anything unpleasant, with the result that it is not complete or interesting 删除…的令人不快内容, 净化〔以减少冒犯性, 因而使作品不完整或乏味〕: *The film is a highly sanitized version of his life, making no mention of his many affairs.* 这部传记影片经过了大量删节, 没有提到他的许多风流韵事。**2** to clean something thoroughly, removing dirt and BACTERIA 对…作卫生处理, 使…卫生, 给…消毒

san·i·ty /ˈsænətɪ; ˈsænɪ̈ti/ *n* [U] **1** the ability to think in a normal and sensible way 神智清楚, 心智健全: *I took a vacation by myself to try to regain my sanity.* 我独自去休假, 想让自己清醒一下。**2** the condition of being mentally healthy 明智, 清醒: *The man's story became stranger and stranger, and I began to doubt his sanity.* 那个人的话越说越离奇, 我开始怀疑他是否神智正常。—opposite 反义词 INSANITY

San José /sæn hoˈze; sæn həʊˈzeɪ/ the capital of Costa Rica, in the centre of the country, on the Pan-American Highway 圣何塞〔哥斯达黎加首都。位于该国中部, 泛美公路经过该城〕

sank /sæŋk; sæŋk/ the past tense of SINK

San Ma·ri·no /sæn məˈrino; sæn məˈriːnəʊ/ a very small country in northeast Italy. Population: 27,336 (2001). Capital: San Marino. 圣马力诺〔意大利东北部一小国。人口: 27,336 (2001), 首都: 圣马力诺〕

San Quent·in /sæn ˈkwɛntɪn; sæn ˈkwentɪ̈n/ a large prison in the town of San Quentin, in California, US 圣昆廷监狱〔美国加利福尼亚州圣昆廷镇一座大型监狱〕

San Salvador /sæn ˈsælvədɔr; sæ ˈsælvədɔː/ the capital city of El Salvador 圣萨尔瓦多〔萨尔瓦多首都〕

San·skrit /ˈsænskrɪt; ˈsænskrɪt/ *n* [U] an ancient language of India 梵文, 梵语〔印度古代的语言〕

sans ser·if /sæn ˈsɛrɪf; , sæn ˈserɪ̈f/ *n* [U] *technical* a style of printing in which letters have no SERIF【术语】〔印刷中的〕无衬线字体

San·ta Claus /ˈsæntɪ ˌklɔz; ˈsæntə klɔːz/ also 又作 **Santa** *n* [singular] an imaginary old man with red clothes and a long white BEARD who, children believe, brings them presents at Christmas 圣诞老人; FATHER CHRISTMAS *BrE*【英】

CULTURAL NOTE 文化注释

In the US and the UK, parents tell their young children that Santa Claus (who is also called Father Christmas in the UK), will come down the chimney to put presents in their CHRISTMAS STOCKINGs or, in the US, under the CHRISTMAS TREE, if they have been good. If they have been bad, they are told they will get coal or ASHes. Before Christmas, children usually write a letter to Santa to tell him what things they would like to be given for Christmas. Then on Christmas Eve they leave something for him to eat or drink. When the children are asleep, their parents put the

presents out. Parents say that Santa lives at the North Pole, where he and his elves (ELF) make toys for children during the year. On Christmas Eve he flies to the houses of all the good children in the world in a SLEIGH that is pulled by REINDEER who can fly. Children usually stop believing in Santa Claus when they are about eight or nine years old. People think of Santa Claus as a very kind happy character who laughs a lot, saying "Ho ho ho!" He is often used to represent Christmas, and cards, Christmas tree decorations, toys etc are often designed to look like him. 在美国和英国，父母对小孩子们说，如果他们一直很乖，圣诞老人会顺着烟囱爬进屋子里，然后把礼物装到圣诞袜里，或者（在美国）放到圣诞树下面；不乖的孩子只能得到煤块和灰烬。圣诞节之前，孩子们经常给圣诞老人写信告诉他自己想要什么样的圣诞礼物。圣诞节前夜（平安夜）他们会给圣诞老人留些吃的和喝的。等孩子们睡着后，父母就会把圣诞礼物拿出来。父母说圣诞老人住在北极，一年的其他时候他和他的小精灵们都在为孩子们赶制玩具。在圣诞节前夜，会飞的驯鹿拉着圣诞老人乘坐的雪橇飞到全世界所有乖孩子的家里。到了八九岁，孩子们就不再相信有什么圣诞老人了。人们认为圣诞老人非常和蔼，又很快活，不住地"呵！呵！呵！"地笑着。圣诞老人常被用作圣诞节的象征，贺卡、圣诞树装饰品和玩具等都常被设计成圣诞老人的样子。— see also Cultural Note at CHRISTMAS 另见 CHRISTMAS文化注释

San·ta Fe /ˌsæntə ˋfe; ˌsæntə ˈfeɪ/ the capital city of New Mexico, which is a popular place for tourists to visit. Mexicans and Native Americans played an important part in its history and culture 圣菲〔新墨西哥州首府，旅游胜地。墨西哥人与印第安人在该州历史与文化发展中曾发挥过重要作用〕

Santa Fe Trail, the /ˌ··· ˈ·/ an important road in the West of the US, starting in Missouri and ending in Santa Fe, which was used in the 19th century by American settlers 圣菲小道〔美国西部一要道。始于密苏里州，终于圣菲，为19世纪的美国移民所使用〕

Santa Ma·ri·a /ˌsæntə məˋriə; ˌsæntə məˈriːə/ one of the three ships which sailed to America with Christopher Columbus in 1492. The other two ships were The Niña and The Pinta "圣马利亚"号〔1492年随克里斯托弗·哥伦布驶往美洲的三艘船之一。另外两艘分别为"尼娜"号和"平塔"号〕

Santa Monica /ˌsæntə ˋmɑnɪkə; ˌsæntə ˈmɒnɪkə/ a city close to Los Angeles in southwest California in the US. It has a beautiful beach that people like to visit, and has many art galleries (GALLERY) and artists' STUDIOs 圣莫尼卡〔美国加利福尼亚州西南部一城市，临近洛杉矶。境内有一处海滩颇受游人青睐。该市还有许多美术馆和画家工作室〕

San·ti·a·go /ˌsæntiˋɑgo; ˌsæntiˈɑːgəʊ/ the capital and largest city of Chile, in South America, which is the country's industrial and financial centre 圣地亚哥〔南美洲国家智利首都，为智利最大城市，也是该国工业与金融中心〕

Santiago de Com·po·stel·a /sæntɪˌɑgo də kɑmpəˋstɛlə; sæntiˌɑːgəʊ də kɒmpəˈstelə/ a city in northwest Spain, where the body of St James, one of Jesus Christ's DISCIPLEs is supposed to be buried. It is famous as a place which PILGRIMs (=people making a religious journey) have visited for hundreds of years. 圣地亚哥－德孔波斯特拉〔西班牙西北部一城市。据说耶稣基督的门徒雅各安葬于此。几百年来一直是朝圣者瞻仰的圣地〕

San·to Do·min·go /ˌsænto dəˋmɪŋgo; ˌsæntəʊ dəˈmɪŋgəʊ/ the capital city of the Dominican Republic, in the Caribbean Sea 圣多明各〔加勒比海国家多米尼加共和国首都〕

São Pau·lo /saʊm ˋpaʊlo; saʊm ˈpaʊləʊ/ the largest city in southeast Brazil, in South America, and Brazil's financial and industrial centre 圣保罗〔南美洲最大城市。位于巴西东南部，为该国金融与工业中心〕

São To·mé and Prín·ci·pe /saʊn təˌme ənd ˋprɪnsɪpə; saʊn təˌmeɪ ənd ˈprɪnsɪpə/ a small country made up of a group of islands off West Africa in the Gulf of Guinea. Population: 165,034 (2001). Capital: São Tomé. 圣多美和普林西比岛〔西非一小国。由一群岛屿组成，位于几内亚湾。人口：165,034（2001），首都：圣多美〕

sap[1] /sæp; sæp/ *n* **1** [U] the watery substance that carries food through a plant〔植物的〕液，汁 **2** [C] *AmE informal* a stupid person who is easy to deceive or treat badly【美，非正式】傻瓜，容易上当的人 **3 feel the sap rising** *humorous* to begin to feel full of energy, especially in a sexual way【幽默】觉得精力〔尤指性欲〕旺盛起来，觉得元气旺盛

sap[2] *v* **sapped, sapping** [T] to gradually weaken or destroy something〔逐渐〕削弱；〔逐渐〕破坏：**sap sb's courage/energy/strength** *Her long illness was gradually sapping Charlotte's strength.* 长期生病正逐渐消耗着夏洛特的元气。

sa·pi·ent /ˋsepɪənt; ˈseɪpiənt/ *adj literary* very wise【文】睿智的，贤明的 —**sapiently** *adv* —**sapience** *n* [U]

sap·ling /ˋsæplɪŋ; ˈsæplɪŋ/ *n* [C] a young tree 幼树，树苗

sap·per /ˋsæpɚ; ˈsæpə/ *n* [C] *BrE* a soldier whose job involves digging and building【英】工兵，工程兵

sap·phic /ˋsæfɪk; ˈsæfɪk/ *adj literary* LESBIAN【文】女性同性恋的

sap·phire /ˋsæfaɪr; ˈsæfaɪə/ *n* [C,U] a transparent bright blue jewel 蓝宝石

Sap·pho /ˋsæfo; ˈsæfəʊ/ (6th century BC) an ancient Greek poet who lived on the island of Lesbos. Her poems are mostly about love and personal feelings, including love between women, and she is especially admired by LESBIANs. 萨福〔(公元前6世纪)，古希腊诗人，生活在莱斯沃斯岛上。她的诗作大多涉及爱情及个人感触，包括女性之间的恋情。萨福颇受女同性恋者仰慕〕

sap·py /ˋsæpɪ; ˈsæpi/ *adj* **1** *AmE* expressing love and emotions in a way that seems silly【美】多情得傻乎乎的；SOPPY (1) *BrE*【英】：*a sappy song* 伤感的歌曲 **2** full of SAP (=liquid in a plant)〔植物〕多汁液的

sap·ro·phyte /ˋsæproˌfaɪt; ˈsæprəfaɪt/ *n* [C] a kind of plant that eats substances that were once living 腐生植物 —**saprophytic** /ˌsæproˋfɪtɪk; ˌsæprəˈfɪtɪk/ *adj*

sap·wood /ˋsæpˌwʊd; ˈsæpwʊd/ *n* [U] the younger outer wood in a tree, that is paler and softer than the wood in the middle〔树皮和心材之间较轻软的〕边材

sar·a·band /ˋsærəˌbænd; ˈsærəbænd/ *n* [C] a slow piece of music based on a type of 17th century dance 萨拉班德舞曲〔源自17世纪的一种缓慢的舞曲〕

Sar·a·cen /ˋsærəsn̩; ˈsærəsən/ *n* [C] *old use* a word for a Muslim, used in the Middle Ages【旧】萨拉森人〔中世纪时对穆斯林的称呼〕

Sar·a·je·vo /ˌsærəˋjevo; ˌsærəˈjeɪvəʊ/ the capital city of Bosnia Herzegovina. Many battles between Serbs and Bosnian Muslims were fought there in the 1990s during the Bosnian War, and much of the city was destroyed. During the war, Sarajevo was under SIEGE by the Bosnian Serb army who surrounded it and would not let any people out or any food or goods in. It is also the place where the Archduke Franz Ferdinand was murdered in 1914, an event which led to the start of World War I. 萨拉热窝〔波斯尼亚和黑塞哥维那首都。20世纪90年代的波黑战争中，塞族人和波斯尼亚穆斯林在此进行过多次战役，城市的大部分遭到残毁。战争期间，萨拉热窝被波斯尼亚塞族军队包围，城内的人出不去，城外的食品和物资运不进来。1914年，法兰西斯·斐迪南大公在萨拉热窝遇刺身亡，成为第一次世界大战的导火索〕

Sa·ran Wrap /səˋræn ræp; səˈræn ræp/ *n* [U] *AmE trademark* thin transparent plastic used for wrapping food【美，商标】塞纶（食物）保鲜膜；CLINGFILM *BrE*【英】

Sa·ra·wak /səˋrɑwək; səˈrɑːwək/ one of the states that form the country of Malaysia. Sarawak is on the island of Borneo 沙捞越〔马来西亚一州，位于婆罗洲〕

sar·cas·m /ˋsɑrkæzəm; ˈsɑːkæzəm/ *n* [U] a way of speaking or writing that involves saying the opposite of what you really mean in order to make an unkind joke or to show that you are annoyed 讽刺，挖苦：**heavy sarcasm** (=very clear sarcasm) 尖刻的讽刺 *She was an hour late. "Good of you to arrive on time," George said, with heavy sarcasm.* 她迟到一个钟头。"你准时到达，真难得，"乔治以尖刻的讽刺口吻说。

sar·cas·tic /sɑrˋkæstɪk; sɑːˈkæstɪk/ *adj* saying things that are the opposite of what you mean in order to make an unkind joke or to show that you are annoyed 挖苦的，嘲讽的：*a sarcastic remark* 讽刺的话 —**sarcastically** /-klɪ; -kli/ *adv*

sar·coph·a·gus /sɑrˋkɑfəgəs; sɑːˈkɒfəgəs/ *n* [C] a decorated stone box for a dead body, used in ancient times〔古代有装饰的〕石棺

sar·dine /sɑrˋdin; sɑːˈdiːn◂/ *n* **1** [C] a small young fish that is often packed in flat metal boxes〔罐头〕沙丁鱼 **2 be packed like sardines** to be crowded tightly together in a small space 挤得像沙丁鱼一样，拥挤不堪：*commuters packed like sardines on the evening train* 晚班火车上挤得像沙丁鱼一样的乘客

Sar·din·i·a /sɑrˋdɪnɪə; sɑːˈdɪniə/ a large island which is part of Italy, south of Corsica and west of Italy in the Mediterranean Sea 萨丁岛〔意大利一大岛，位于地中海科西嘉岛以南、意大利半岛以西〕

sar·don·ic /sɑrˋdɑnɪk; sɑːˈdɒnɪk/ *adj* speaking or smiling in an unpleasant way, that shows you do not have a good opinion

of someone or something 嘲讽的，讥讽的: *Brett raised a sardonic eyebrow.* 布雷特嘲讽地扬起一道眉毛。—**sardonically** /-klɪ; -kli/ *adv*

sa·ree /ˈsari; ˈsɑːri/ *n* [C] another spelling of SARI sari的另一种拼法

sarge /sardʒ; sɑːdʒ/ *n* [singular] *spoken* SERGEANT【口】中士；巡佐

Sar·gent /ˈsardʒənt; ˈsɑːdʒənt/, **John Singer** (1856-1925) a US artist who lived and worked mainly in London and who painted many paintings of rich and important people 萨金特〔(1856-1925)，美国画家。主要在伦敦工作和生活，画了不少富豪、权贵的肖像画〕

sa·ri /ˈsari; ˈsɑːri/ *n* [C]a long piece of cloth that you wrap around your body, worn especially by women from India〔印度妇女用以裹身的〕莎丽(服)

sari 莎丽(服)

Sark /sark; sɑːk/ one of the Channel Islands between England and France. It is politically part of the UK, but it also has its own parliament. There are no cars on Sark. 萨克岛〔海峡群岛的岛屿之一，位于英格兰与法国之间。政治上隶属于英国，但有自己的议会。岛上没有汽车〕

sar·ky /ˈsarkɪ; ˈsɑːki/ *adj BrE informal* SARCASTIC【英，非正式】嘲讽的

sar·nie /ˈsarnɪ; ˈsɑːni/ *n* [C] *BrE informal* a SANDWICH【英，非正式】三明治

sa·rong /səˈrɔŋ; səˈrɒŋ/ *n* [C] a loose skirt consisting of a long piece of cloth wrapped around your waist 莎笼〔裹在腰部的一种宽松服装〕

sar·sa·pa·ril·la /ˌsæspəˈrɪlə; ˌsɑːspəˈrɪlə/ *n* [U] a sweet non-alcoholic drink made from the root of the SASSAFRAS plant 菝葜汽水

sar·to·ri·al /sarˈtɔrɪəl; sɑːˈtɔːriəl/ *adj formal* connected with men's clothes or how they are made【正式】男装的；关于男装缝制的: **sartorial elegance** *a man of great sartorial elegance* 着装极其讲究的男子 —**sartorially** *adv*

Sar·tre /ˈsartrə; ˈsɑːtrə/, **Jean-Paul** /ʒan pɔl; ʒɒn pɔːl/ (1905-80) a French PHILOSOPHER who also wrote novels, plays, and short stories. He was a leading influence in the development of EXISTENTIALISM, and is one of the best-known philosophers of the 20th century. His NOVELs include the TRILOGY (=a series of three books) *Les chemins de la liberté* (translated as *Roads to Freedom*). He is also famous for his long relationship with the feminist writer Simone de Beauvoir, and for his LEFT-WING political views and his support for student protests in France in 1968 萨特〔(1905-1980)，法国哲学家，也创作小说、剧本和短篇故事。是存在主义发展的主导人物，20世纪最著名的哲学家之一。创作的小说包括《自由之路》三步曲。与女权主义作家西蒙娜·波伏瓦保持长期情爱关系，以持有左翼政治观点并在1968年支持法国学生的抗议活动而闻名〕

SAS /ˌɛs e ˈɛs ˌes eɪ ˈes/ *n* [singular] Special Air Service; a British military force that is specially trained to do secret and dangerous work 特种空勤部队〔英国一支经特殊训练、执行秘密危险任务的特种部队〕

SASE /ˌɛs e ɛs ˈi; ˌes eɪ es ˈiː/ *n* [C] *AmE* self-addressed stamped envelope; an envelope that you put your name, address, and a stamp on, so that someone else can send you something【美】〔写有自己姓名地址并贴足邮票的〕回信信封

sash /sæʃ; sæʃ/ *n* [C] **1** a long piece of cloth that you wear around your waist like a belt 腰带: *a party dress with a blue sash* 有蓝色腰带的晚礼服 **2** a long piece of cloth that you wear over one shoulder and across your chest as a sign of a special honour〔斜挂在肩上标志荣誉的〕绶带，肩带: *a sash with the words Miss USA* 写着"美国小姐"字样的绶带 **3** a wooden frame that has a sheet of glass fixed into it to form part of a window 窗框，窗扇

sa·shay /sæˈʃe; sæˈʃeɪ/ *v* [I always+adv/prep] *informal* to walk in a confident way moving your body from side to side, especially so that people look at you【非正式】大摇大摆地走；轻快自信地走: *Olivia sashayed down the catwalk.* 奥利维娅轻快自如地走在T形台上。

sash win·dow /ˈ· ,·ˈ/ *n* [C] a window consisting of two frames that you open by sliding one up or down, behind or in front of the other 上下拉窗，框格窗

Sas·katch·e·wan /sæˈskætʃəwən; sæˈskætʃəwən/ a PROVINCE in central Canada, which has a border with the US states of Montana and North Dakota 萨斯喀彻温省〔加拿大中部一省，与美国蒙大拿州、北达科他州接壤〕

Sas·quatch /ˈsæskwɑtʃ; ˈsæskwætʃ/ another name for bigfoot, an animal like a human which some people claim to have seen in the northwestern US 大脚野人〔bigfoot的别称。一种形状类似人的动物。有人声称曾在美国西北部见过〕

sass /sæs; sæs/ *v* [T] *AmE informal* to talk in a rude way to someone you should respect【美，非正式】对…粗鲁无礼，与…顶嘴: *Don't you sass me young lady!* 你可别顶撞我，小姑奶奶!

sas·sa·fras /ˈsæsəˌfræs; ˈsæsəfræs/ *n* [C,U] a small Asian or North American tree, or the pleasant-smelling roots of this tree used in food and drink 檫树〔产于亚洲或北美的小乔木〕；檫树根〔用作食品和饮料的香料〕

Sas·se·nach /ˈsæsn̩ˌæk; ˈsæsənæk/ *n* [C] *ScotE* a word meaning an English person, used as a joke or to show disapproval【苏格兰】英格兰人〔戏谑或贬称用语〕

sas·sy /ˈsæsɪ; ˈsæsi/ *adj AmE*【美】**1** a child who is sassy is rude to someone they should respect〔小孩〕粗鲁的，无礼的 **2** a woman who is sassy behaves in a way that is intended to be attractive to men〔女人〕活泼的，轻佻的

Sat a written abbreviation 缩写= SATURDAY

sat /sæt; sæt/ the past tense and past participle of SIT

Sa·tan /ˈsetn̩; ˈseɪtn/ *n* [singular] the Devil, considered to be the main evil power and God's opponent 撒旦，魔鬼，恶魔

sa·tan·ic /seˈtænɪk; səˈtænɪk/ *adj* **1** connected with practices that treat the Devil like a god 崇拜恶魔的: *satanic rites* 撒旦崇拜仪式 **2** extremely cruel or evil 穷凶极恶的，极其邪恶的: *satanic laughter* 狰狞的笑 —**satanically** /-klɪ; -kli/ *adv*

Satanic Vers·es, The /·,··ˈ·/ (1988) a NOVEL by Salman Rushdie which caused great offence to people whose religion is Islam and caused the Ayatollah Khomeini to give a fatwa, which was an order that Rushdie should be killed《撒旦的诗篇》〔(1988)，萨尔曼·拉什迪的一部小说。此书极大地冒犯了伊斯兰教徒，为此，阿亚图拉霍梅尼下达追杀令，欲致拉什迪于死地〕

sat·an·is·m /ˈsetn̩ˌɪzəm; ˈseɪtənɪzəm/ *n* [U] the practice of respecting the Devil as if he were a god 撒旦崇拜，对恶魔的崇拜 —**satanist** *n* [C] —**satanist** *adj*

sat·ay sauce /ˌsate ˈsɔs; ˌsæteɪ ˈsɔːs/ *n* [U] a thick liquid made with PEANUTS and used to give a special taste to meat〔烹调用的〕花生酱，沙爹酱

satch·el /ˈsætʃəl; ˈsætʃəl/ *n* [C] a leather bag that you carry over your shoulder, used especially in the past by children for carrying books to school〔皮制的〕书包，小背包 —see picture at 参见 BAG[1] 图

sate /set; seɪt/ *v* [T] *literary* **be sated (with)** to have had enough or more than enough of something to satisfy you【文】充分满足于(…)；(对…)感到腻烦

sat·el·lite /ˈsætl̩ˌaɪt; ˈsætl̩aɪt/ *n* [C] **1** a machine that has been sent into space and goes around the Earth, moon etc, used for radio, television, and other electronic communication 人造卫星: *the launch of a communications and weather satellite* 气象通信卫星的发射 | **by satellite** (=using a satellite) 通过人造卫星 *This broadcast comes live by satellite from New York.* 本节目是通过人造卫星从纽约现场直播的。**2** a moon that moves around a PLANET 卫星. *The moon is a satellite of the Earth.* 月亮是地球的卫星。**3 a)** a country, town, or organization that is controlled by or is dependent on another larger one 卫星国；卫星城；附属机构: **satellite country/town/suburb** (=one that has developed next to a large city) 卫星国/卫星城/郊区

satellite dish /ˈ··· ,·/ *n* [C] a large circular piece of metal that receives special television signals so that you can watch satellite television 碟形卫星天线

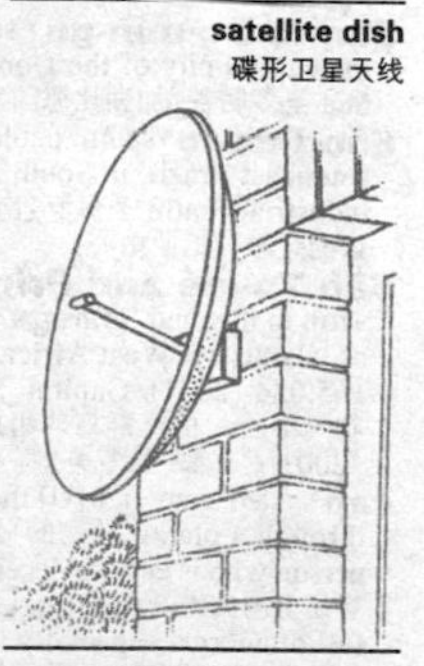

satellite dish 碟形卫星天线

satellite tel·e·vi·sion /,····ˈ···/ also 又作 **satellite TV** /,··· ·ˈ·/ *n* [U] television programmes that are broadcast using satellites in space 卫星电视

sa·ti·ate /ˈseʃɪˌet; ˈseɪʃieɪt/ *v* [T usually passive 一般用被动态] *literary* to satisfy a desire or need for something such as food or sex, especially so that you feel you have had too much【文】使充分满足，使过饱 —**satiated** *adj*: *Zeke lay on the couch, satiated after his meal.* 齐克吃饱饭后，在长沙发上躺着。—**satiety** /səˈtaɪətɪ; səˈtaɪəti/ *n* [U]

sat·in[1] /ˈsætn; ˈsætɪn/ *n* [U] a type of cloth that is very smooth and shiny 缎子

satin² *adj* having a smooth shiny surface 缎子般光滑的

sat·in·wood /ˈsætn̩ˌwʊd; ˈsætn̩wʊd/ *n* [C,U] an East Indian tree, or the hard smooth wood that comes from this tree〔产于印度东部的〕缎木;〔坚硬平滑的〕缎木木材

sat·in·y /ˈsætɪnɪ; ˈsætn̩i/ *adj* smooth, shiny, and soft 光滑的, 柔软的, 缎子似的

sat·ire /ˈsætaɪr; ˈsætaɪə/ *n* **1** [U] a way of talking or writing about something, for example politics and politicians, in which you deliberately make them seem funny so that people will see their faults 讽刺, 讥讽: *the characteristic use of satire in Jonson's work* 琼森作品中讽刺手法的典型运用 **2** [C] a play, book, story etc written in this way〔戏剧、书、故事等的〕讽刺作品: *a political satire* 政治讽刺作品 —**satirical** /səˈtɪrɪkl; səˈtɪrɪkəl/ *adj* —**satiric** *adj* —**satirically** /-klɪ; -kli/ *adv*

sat·i·rist /ˈsætərɪst; ˈsætərɪst/ *n* [C] someone who writes satire 讽刺作家, 讽刺作品创作者

sat·ir·ize also 又作 **-ise** *BrE*【英】/ˈsætəˌraɪz; ˈsætəraɪz/ *v* [T] to use satire to make people see someone or something's faults 讽刺: *a play satirizing the fashion industry* 一部讽刺时装业的戏剧

3 3 **sat·is·fac·tion** /ˌsætɪsˈfækʃən; ˌsætəsˈfækʃən/ *n* **1** [C,U] a feeling of happiness or pleasure because you have achieved something or got what you wanted 满足, 满意; 称心: *She got great satisfaction from helping people learn.* 她从帮助人们学习中得到很大的满足。| *a sigh of deep satisfaction* 深感满足地舒一口气 | **job satisfaction** (=enjoyment of your job) 从工作中得到的满足感 —opposite 反义词 DISSATISFACTION **2** [U] fulfilment of a need, demand, claim, desire etc〔需要、愿望等的〕满足, 实现: *the satisfaction of public demand* 对公众要求的满足 | *sexual satisfaction* 性欲的满足 **3** [U] *formal* a reply to a complaint that you have made【正式】〔对投诉的〕回应: **get satisfaction** *I got no satisfaction from the customer complaints department.* 我没有得到顾客投诉部的圆满答复。**4 have/get the satisfaction of doing sth** to get a small amount of pleasure from a situation that is unsatisfactory in other ways 得到做某事的补偿: *Well, at least you'll get the satisfaction of knowing you were right.* 哎, 你至少可以知道自己没有错并感到欣慰吧。**5 to sb's/sth's satisfaction a)** if something is explained, proved etc to someone's satisfaction, they now accept and believe it 让…相信和接受 **b)** if a situation, arrangement etc is to someone's satisfaction, they are pleased with it 使…感到满意: *Finally we got the furniture arranged to her satisfaction.* 我们终于把家具布置得令她满意。

sat·is·fac·to·ry /ˌsætɪsˈfæktərɪ; ˌsætəsˈfæktəri◂/ *adj* **1** good enough for a particular situation or purpose 合适的, 满足要求的: *Reicher could not provide a satisfactory excuse for his absence.* 赖歇尔对自己的缺席给不出一个言之成理的解释。| *None of the solutions was entirely satisfactory.* 这些解决办法没有一个是完美的。**2** making you feel pleased and happy 令人满意的, 令人高兴的: *a satisfactory conclusion* 令人满意的结论 —**satisfactorily** *adv* —opposite 反义词 UNSATISFACTORY

3 **sat·is·fied** /ˈsætɪsˌfaɪd; ˈsætəsfaɪd/ *adj* **1** pleased because something has happened in the way that you want, or because you have achieved something 满意的, 满足的: *a satisfied smile* 满意的微笑 | [+with] *I'm not really satisfied with the way he cut my hair.* 我对他给我理的发型不太满意。—opposite 反义词 DISSATISFIED **2** feeling sure that something is right or true 确信的: [+that] *The police weren't satisfied that Boyet was telling the truth.* 警方不相信博伊特讲的是真话。**3 satisfied?** *spoken* used to show that someone has annoyed you by asking too many questions or making too many demands【口】该满意了吧?〔对提出过多的问题或要求表示不耐烦〕: *Okay, okay, I'll go over there and ask him this afternoon. Satisfied?* 好吧, 好吧, 我今天下午就过去问他。该满意了吧? —see also 另见 SELF-SATISFIED

2 2 **sat·is·fy** /ˈsætɪsˌfaɪ; ˈsætəsfaɪ/ *v* [T] **1** to please someone by providing enough of what they want 使〔某人〕满意: *Nick felt that nothing he did would satisfy his boss.* 尼克觉得他做的工作没有一件能使老板满意。**2 satisfy a request/desire/need etc** to provide what someone has asked for, what they need etc 满足要求/欲望/需要等: *Just to satisfy my curiosity, how much did it cost?* 我只是出于好奇心, 这花了多少钱? | *The salad just didn't satisfy her hunger.* 那份沙拉她根本吃不饱。**3** *formal* to make someone feel sure that something is right or true; CONVINCE【正式】使〔某人〕确信[信服]: **satisfy sb of sth** *Jackson tried to satisfy me of his innocence.* 杰克逊尽量让我相信他的清白无辜。**4** *formal* to be good enough for a particular purpose, standard etc【正式】符合〔要求、标准等〕: *You have not yet satisfied all the conditions for admission.* 你尚未达到所有的录取条件。**5** *formal* to FULFIL an EQUATION (1) in mathematics, etc【正式】满足〔方程〕

sat·is·fy·ing /ˈsætɪsˌfaɪ·ɪŋ; ˈsætəsfaɪ-ɪŋ/ *adj* **1** making you feel pleased and happy, especially because you have got what you wanted 令人高兴的, 令人满意的: **it is satisfying to do sth** *After all he'd put me through, it was very satisfying to see him begging for once.* 吃了他那么多苦头之后, 我终于看到他有一次向人求乞, 这真是大快人心。**2** food that is satisfying makes you feel that you have eaten enough〔饭菜〕丰足的: *a satisfying meal* 丰盛的一餐 —**satisfyingly** *adv*

sat·su·ma /sætˈsumə; sætˈsuːmə/ *n* [C] a fruit that looks like a small orange, and has no seeds 无籽小蜜橘

sat·u·rate /ˈsætʃəˌret; ˈsætʃəreɪt/ *v* [T] **1** *formal* to make something very wet; SOAK¹ (2)【正式】浸湿, 使湿透: *Water poured through the hole, saturating the carpet.* 水从洞里流出来, 浸湿了地毯。**2** to put a large number of people or things into a particular place, especially so that you could not add any more 使充满, 使充斥: *The area was saturated with police to prevent further trouble.* 那个地区到处都部署了警察, 以防进一步的骚乱。**3 saturate the market** to offer so much of a product for sale that there is more than people want to buy 使市场饱和 **4** *technical* to mix as much of a solid into a chemical mixture as possible【术语】使〔化学溶液〕饱和

sat·u·rat·ed /ˈsætʃəˌretɪd; ˈsætʃəreɪtəd/ *adj* **1** extremely wet 湿透的, 浸透的: *By the time I arrived home, I was completely saturated.* 回到家时, 我全身都湿透了。| [+with] *saturated with sweat* 被汗水湿透的 **2** *technical* if a chemical mixture is saturated, it has had as much of a solid mixed into it as possible【术语】饱和的

saturated fat /ˌ···· ˈ·/ *n* [C,U] a kind of fat from meat and milk products that is thought to be less healthy than other kinds of fat from vegetables or fish 饱和脂肪

sat·u·ra·tion /ˌsætʃəˈreʃən; ˌsætʃəˈreɪʃən/ *n* [U] **1** the act or result of making something completely wet 浸透, 湿透 **2 saturation bombing** a military attack in which a whole area is bombed 饱和轰炸 **3 saturation coverage** a situation in which a particular event is given so much attention by newspapers, television etc that everyone has heard about it 饱和报道: *The trial was given saturation coverage by the press.* 新闻界对这次审讯进行了饱和报道。**4** *technical* the state of a chemical mixture that has reached its SATURATION POINT (2)【术语】饱和〔状态〕

saturation point /··ˈ·· ·/ *n* [C usually singular 一般用单数] **1** a situation in which no more people or things can be added because there are already too many 饱和点; 极限: *The number of summer tourists in the area has now reached saturation point.* 这一地区的夏季旅游者人数已趋饱和。**2** *technical* the state that a chemical mixture reaches when it has had as much of a solid substance mixed into it as possible【术语】〔化学溶液的〕饱和点

Sat·ur·day /ˈsætədɪ; ˈsætədi/ *n* [C,U] the day between Friday and Sunday. In Britain, Saturday is considered the sixth day of the week, and in the US it is considered the seventh day of the week 星期六〔在英国, 星期六被看作是一周中的第六天; 而在美国, 它是一周中的第七天〕: **on Saturday** *We went for a picnic on Saturday.* 我们星期六去野餐。| *Deats always goes home on Saturdays.* 迪茨每个星期六都回家。| **last/next Saturday** *I saw Sally last Saturday at the Mall.* 我上星期六在购物中心见到了萨莉。| **on a Saturday** *My birthday is on a Saturday this year.* 我今年的生日是个星期六。

Saturday Eve·ning Post, The /ˌ···ˌ··ˈ·/ a popular US family magazine that started in 1821 and continued until 1969. It contained news, short stories, humorous CARTOONS and reviews. Pictures by Norman Rockwell often appeared on its cover.《星期六晚邮报》〔美国一大众家庭杂志。1821 年创刊, 1969 年停刊。内容包括新闻、短篇小说、漫画、评论。常用诺曼·罗克韦尔创作的图画作为封面〕

Saturday Night and Sunday Morning /ˌ···ˌ··ˌ·· ˈ··/ (1958) a novel by British writer Alan Sillitoe, about a young man Arthur Seaton, who works in a factory. On Saturday nights he goes out, drinking a lot in PUBS and has an affair with the wife of one of his friends. He was considered an example of the Angry Young Man of that time.《星期六晚上与星期天早晨》, 又译《年少莫轻狂》〔(1958), 英国作家艾伦·西利托的一部小说。讲述的是在工厂上班的年轻人亚瑟·西顿的故事。他每逢周六晚上都要去酒吧喝不少酒, 还要和某个朋友的妻子幽会。被认为是当时"愤怒的年轻人"的典型代表〕

Saturday Night Fe·ver /ˌ··· ˈ··/ (1977) a US film in which John Travolta appears as a young man who is very good at DISCO dancing. The music, played by the Bee Gees, and the clothes in the film, are typical of the 1970s.《周末的狂热》〔(1977), 美国电影。约翰·特拉沃尔塔在影片中扮演一位青年迪

斯科舞高手。片中"比吉"乐队演奏的音乐和人物的服饰被认为是20世纪70年代的典型风格〕

Saturday Night Live /ˌsætədɪ naɪt ˈlaɪv; ˌsætədi naɪt ˈlaɪv/ a humorous US television programme which started in the 1970s, on which many well-known COMEDIANs first appeared《星期六夜生活》〔美国20世纪70年代一部幽默电视剧。许多著名喜剧演员都通过这部电视剧首次亮相〕

Sat·urn /ˈsætən; ˈsætən/ *n* [singular] the PLANET that is sixth in order from the sun and is surrounded by large rings 土星 —see picture at 参见 SOLAR SYSTEM 图

sat·ur·na·li·a /ˌsætəˈneliə; ˌsætəˈneɪliə/ *n* [C] *literary* an occasion when people enjoy themselves in a very wild and uncontrolled way【文】纵情欢乐, 狂欢

sat·ur·nine /ˈsætəˌnaɪn; ˈsætənaɪn/ *adj literary* looking sad and serious, especially in a threatening way【文】忧郁的, 阴沉的: *Goebbel's lean saturnine face had the hypnotic power of a swaying cobra.* 戈培尔那副瘦削阴郁的面孔具有眼镜蛇昂首摆动时的催眠力。

sat·yr /ˈsætə; ˈsætə/ *n* [C] a god in ancient Greek literature, represented as half human and half goat 萨堤尔〔古希腊神话中半人半羊的神〕

sauce /sɔs; sɔːs/ *n* **1** [C,U] a thick cooked liquid that is served with food to give it a particular taste（浓）调味汁, 酱汁, 沙司: **tomato/chocolate etc sauce** *pasta with tomato sauce* 浇了番茄酱的意大利面条 **2** [U] *BrE old-fashioned* rude remarks made to someone that you should respect【英, 过时】无礼的话, 顶撞的话: *Less of your sauce, my girl!* 不得无礼, 女孩子!

sauce boat /ˈ· ·/ *n* [C] a container that has a handle and is shaped like a boat, used for serving sauce with a meal〔有柄的〕船形调味汁碟[碗]

sauce·pan /ˈsɔsˌpæn; ˈsɔːspæn/ *n* [C] a deep round metal container with a handle that is used for cooking〔有柄的〕深平底锅 —see picture at 参见 PAN[1] 图

sau·cer /ˈsɔsə; ˈsɔːsə/ *n* [C] a small round plate that curves up at the edges that you put a cup on 茶托 —see also 另见 FLYING SAUCER

sauc·y /ˈsɔsɪ; ˈsɔːsi/ *adj* **1** *especially BrE* saucy pictures, jokes etc are about sex in a way that is amusing but not shocking【尤英】讲无伤大雅的性笑话的: *saucy postcards* 印有性笑话图画的明信片 **2** slightly rude, in a way that is amusing 戏谑的, 没大没小的: *a saucy remark* 莽撞的话语 —**saucily** *adv* —**sauciness** *n* [U] —see also 另见 SAUCE (2)

Saudi A·ra·bi·a /ˌ· · ˈ· · ·/ an oil-producing country in the Middle East, ruled by a king. Population: 22,757,000 (2001). Capital: Riyadh. The city of Mecca, the holiest place in the religion of Islam, is in Saudi Arabia. 沙特阿拉伯〔中东一产油国, 由国王统治。人口: 22,757,000 (2001), 首都: 利雅得。伊斯兰教圣城麦加位于该国境内〕 —**Saudi Arabian** *n, adj*

sau·er·kraut /ˈsaʊrˌkraʊt; ˈsaʊəkraʊt/ *n* [U] a German food made from CABBAGE (=a round green vegetable) that has been left in salt so that it tastes sour（德国式）泡菜

sau·na /ˈsaʊnə; ˈsaʊnə/ *n* [C] **1** a room that is heated to a very high temperature by hot air, where people sit because it is considered healthy 蒸汽浴室, 桑拿浴室 **2** a period of time when you sit or lie in a room like this 蒸汽浴, 桑拿浴: **have/take a sauna** *I have a sauna and massage every week.* 我每星期洗一次桑拿浴并做一次按摩。

saun·ter /ˈsɔntə; ˈsɔːntə/ *v* [I always+adv/prep] to walk in a slow unhurried way, that makes you look confident or proud〔自信或傲慢地〕漫步: *Will came sauntering down the road with his hands in his pockets.* 威尔两手插在衣袋里大摇大摆地沿路漫步。—**saunter** *n* [singular]

3 **saus·age** /ˈsɔsɪdʒ; ˈsɒsɪdʒ/ *n* [C,U] **1** [C] a small tube of skin filled with a mixture of meat, SPICEs etc, eaten hot or cold 香肠: *pork sausages* 猪肉香肠 **2 not a sausage!** *BrE old-fashioned, informal* nothing at all【英, 过时, 非正式】一点也没有!: *"Have you heard from Tom yet?" "No, not a sausage!"* "你有没有汤姆的消息?" "没有, 毫无音讯!"

sausage dog /ˈ· · ·/ *n* [C] *BrE informal* a DACHSHUND【英, 非正式】腊肠犬〔即达克斯猎狗〕

sausage meat /ˈ· · ·/ *n* [U] the soft meat mixture that is used to make sausages 灌香肠用的碎肉, 香肠肉馅

sausage roll /ˌ· · ˈ·/ *n* [C] *BrE* a piece of sausage meat inside a tube of PASTRY【英】〔外包面皮的〕香肠肉卷

sau·té /soˈte; ˈsəʊteɪ/ *v* [T] to cook something quickly in a little hot oil or fat〔用少量油〕快炸; 快煎; 快炒: *Sauté the potatoes for 5 minutes.* 把马铃薯炸上五分钟。

Sau·ternes *especially BrE*【尤英】; **Sauterne** *AmE*【美】/soˈtɜn; səʊˈtɜːn/ a sweet gold-coloured French wine 苏特恩〔法国生产的一种金色甜葡萄酒〕

sav·age[1] /ˈsævɪdʒ; ˈsævɪdʒ/ *adj* **1** very cruel and violent 凶猛的, 残暴的: *a savage dog* 恶狗 | *The punishment seemed too savage.* 这种惩罚似乎太凶残了。**2** criticizing someone or something very severely〔批评〕猛烈的, 恶狠狠的: **savage attack/criticism etc** *an unexpectedly savage attack on the President's record* 对总统政绩出其不意的猛烈抨击 **3** very severe and harmful 极严重的; 有害的: *savage pay cuts* 大幅度减薪 **4** [only before noun 仅用于名词前] *old-fashioned* an insulting way of describing a person or group from a country where the way of living seems very simple and undeveloped; PRIMITIVE[1] (1)【过时】未开化的, 原始的, 野蛮的〔侮辱性说法〕—**savagely** *adv* —**savageness** *n* [U]

savage[2] *n* [C] *old-fashioned* an insulting word for someone from a country where the way of living seems very simple and undeveloped【过时】未开化的人, 野蛮人〔侮辱性用词〕: *This culture flourished while Europeans were still savages living in caves.* 当欧洲人还是穴居的野蛮人时, 这个地方的文化早已十分发达了。

savage[3] *v* [T] **1** if an animal savages someone, it attacks and bites them, causing serious injuries〔动物〕乱咬, 凶猛地攻击: *savaged by a mad dog* 被疯狗咬了 **2** to criticize someone or something very severely 激烈地批评: *The play was savaged by the critics.* 这出戏受到评论家的猛烈批评。

sav·ag·e·ry /ˈsævɪdʒrɪ; ˈsævɪdʒəri/ *n* [C,U] extremely cruel and violent behaviour 野蛮, 残暴（行为）: *He used to beat the boy with great savagery.* 他过去常常极其残暴地殴打那个男孩。

sa·van·na, savannah /səˈvænə; səˈvænə/ *n* [C,U] a large flat area of grassy land in a warm part of the world〔热带或亚热带的〕稀树草原

sav·ant /səˈvɑnt; ˈsævənt/ *n* [C] *literary* someone who knows a lot about a particular subject【文】博学之士, 专家, 学者

save[1] /sev; seɪv/ *v* 1 1

1 ►FROM HARM/DANGER 免除伤害/危险◄ [T] to make someone or something safe from danger, harm, or destruction 救, 拯救, 挽救: *Thousands of lives have been saved by this drug.* 这种药挽救了成千上万人的生命。| **save sb/sth from** *He saved his friend from drowning.* 他救起了他那位溺水的朋友。| *The sudden fall in interest rates saved the company from bankruptcy.* 利率的突然下降救了这家公司, 使其免于破产。

2 ►MONEY IN A BANK 银行存款◄ also 又作 **save up** [I,T] to keep money so that you can use it later, especially when you gradually add more money over a period of time 储蓄, 积攒: [+for] *I'm saving up for a new car.* 我正在攒钱准备买辆新车。| *So far, I've saved about £500.* 到目前为止, 我已储蓄了大约500英镑。—see also 另见 SAVER

3 ►NOT WASTE 不浪费◄ [T] to use less money, time, energy etc so that you do not waste any 节省, 节约, 避免〔金钱、时间、精力等的〕浪费: *We'll save a lot of time if we go by car.* 我们要是乘汽车去可以节省很多时间。| *modern energy-saving devices* 现代化的节能装置 | **save sb sth** *Reserving a seat in advance could save you $10.* 提前订座可以让你节省10美元。

4 ►TO USE LATER 以备后用◄ [T] to keep something so that you can use or enjoy it in the future 保留, 保存: *Let's save the rest of the cake for later.* 我们把剩下的蛋糕留着以后吃吧。| *He saved his strength for the end of the race.* 他保存体力准备在赛跑的最后关头冲刺。

5 ►COLLECT 收集◄ also 又作 **save** sth ↔ **up** [T] to keep all the objects of a particular kind that you can find, so that they can be used for a special purpose 收集〔以备后用〕, 积存: *She always saved foreign stamps for her grandson's album.* 她经常为孙子的集邮簿收集外国邮票。| *I'm saving up tokens for a free set of wine glasses.* 我正在积存礼品券, 以免费换取一套酒具。

6 ►HELP TO AVOID 使避免◄ [T] to help someone by making it unnecessary for them to do something unpleasant or inconvenient 使…免除〔不愉快或不方便的事情〕: **save sb sth** *If you could lend me £5, it would save me a trip to the bank.* 如果你能借我五英镑, 我就省得去一趟银行了。| **save sb doing sth** *A brush with a long handle will save you having to bend down.* 用长柄刷子, 你就不必弯腰了。| **save sb the trouble/bother (of doing sth)** *I'll wash up and save you the trouble of doing it later.* 我来洗碗吧, 省得你待一会儿还得洗。

7 ►KEEP FOR SB 替某人保留◄ [T] to stop people from using something so that it is available for someone else〔为某人〕保留: **save sb sth** *Will you save me a seat on the bus?* 请在公共汽车上给我留个座位好吗? | **save sth for sb** *We'll save some dinner for you if you're late.* 你要是回来晚了, 我们会给你留饭的。

8 save sb's life to prevent someone from dying 救某人的命: *Surgeons operated in an attempt to save her life.* 外科医生给她动了手术, 试图挽救她的生命。

9 you saved my life *spoken* used to thank someone who has got you out of a difficult situation or solved a problem for you【口】你帮了我的大忙: *Thanks again for the loan – you really saved my life.* 再一次谢谢你那笔贷款, 你真是帮了我大忙了。
10 save sb's skin/neck/bacon etc *informal* to make it possible for someone to escape from an extremely difficult or dangerous situation【非正式】逃脱危险; 免遭伤害: *He lied in court to save his skin.* 他为了保命在法庭上撒了谎。
11 save the day to make a situation end successfully when it seemed likely to end badly 扭转局面; 挽回败局; 解围: *Frank saved the day by offering to drive us all there.* 弗兰克提出要开车送我们大家去, 使问题迎刃而解。
12 save face to do something that will stop you looking stupid or feeling embarrassed 保全面子 —see also 另见 FACE-SAVING
13 saving grace the one good thing that makes someone or something acceptable〔弥补不足的〕可取之处: *Beautiful photography was the saving grace of an otherwise awful film.* 这部电影拍得很糟糕, 但优美的摄影弥补了它的不足。
14 not be able to do sth to save your life *informal* to be completely unable to do something【非正式】完全不会做某事: *He couldn't paint to save his life!* 他无论如何也不会画画!
15 save your breath *spoken* used to tell someone that it is not worth saying anything, because nothing they say will make any difference to the situation【口】用不着白费唇舌, 说也没有用
16 save sb from themselves to prevent someone from doing something that is likely to harm them in the end 阻止某人做某事以免自尝苦果
17 ►SPORT 体育运动◄ [T] to stop the other side from getting a GOAL (2) in a sport such as football, HOCKEY etc〔足球、曲棍球等〕阻碍对方得分, 救〔球〕—see picture on page A23 参见 A23 页图
18 ►COMPUTER 电脑◄ [I,T] to make a computer keep the work that you have done on it 保存〔输入的资料〕: *Don't forget to save before you close the file.* 在关闭文件之前, 不要忘记保存。
19 ►RELIGION 宗教◄ [I,T] in the Christian church, to free someone from the power of evil and SIN〔基督教〕拯救〔某人〕; 使摆脱罪孽: *Jesus came to save sinners.* 基督降世以拯救罪人。

save on sth *phr v* [T] to avoid wasting something by using as little as possible of it 节省, 避免浪费: *We use a wood stove to save on electricity.* 我们使用烧柴的炉子以节省电力。

save[2] *n* [C] an action by the GOALKEEPER in football, HOCKEY etc that prevents the other team from getting a GOAL (2)〔足球、曲棍球等守门员的〕救球, 阻碍对方得分

save[3] also 又作 **saving** *prep formal* except for【正式】除…(之)外: *She answered all the questions save one.* 除了一个问题以外, 她回答了所有问题。| [+that] *I agree with you, save that you've got one or two details wrong.* 除了你有一两处细节弄错以外, 我同意你的看法。

sav·er /ˈseɪvə; ˈseɪvə/ *n* [C] *especially BrE* someone who saves money in a bank or BUILDING SOCIETY【尤英】〔存款于银行或购房互助会等的〕储蓄者: **regular saver** (=someone who usually saves money with a particular bank etc) 固定储户, 老储户 *Regular savers can benefit from a 3% annual bonus.* 固定储户每年可获得3%的红利。

Save the Child·ren Fund, the /ˌ· · ˈ· · ˌ· ·/ also 又作 **Save the Children** an international CHARITY organization which helps children all over the world, especially in poorer countries. Its president is Princess Anne. 拯救儿童基金会〔一国际慈善机构, 为全世界儿童尤其是贫困国家的儿童提供帮助。现任主席为英国的安妮公主〕

Savile Row /ˌsævɪl ˈrəʊ; ˌsævɪl ˈrəʊ◂/ a street in London where there are many clothes shops for men. They sell traditional, often hand-made suits, which are considered to be of high quality. 萨韦尔街〔伦敦市一街道。有许多男士服装店, 出售传统套装, 常为手工制作, 品质上乘〕: *a Savile Row suit* 一套萨韦尔街出售的西装

W3 **sav·ing** /ˈseɪvɪŋ; ˈseɪvɪŋ/ *n* **1 savings** [plural] all the money that you have saved, especially in a bank 银行存款, 储蓄金, 积蓄 **2** [C usually singular 一般用单数] an amount of something that you have not used or spent 未使用[消耗]的量: *This amount represents a considerable saving over last year's expenditure.* 这个数额表示去年的开支有相当大的节余。**3** [U] the act of keeping money so that you can use it later 存钱〔以备后用〕—see also 另见 SAVE[1] (2)

savings ac·count /ˈ· · ˌ·/ *n* [C] a bank account that pays INTEREST[1] (4) on the money you have in it〔可获利息的〕储蓄账户

savings and loan as·so·ci·a·tion /ˌ· · ˈ· · · ·, · ˈ·/ *n* [C] *AmE* a business that lends money, usually so that you can buy a house, and into which you pay money to be saved【美】购房互助协会, 储蓄贷款协会〔贷款给会员作购房用, 会员也可在其中储蓄的商业机构〕; BUILDING SOCIETY *BrE*【英】

savings bank /ˈ· · ·/ *n* [C] a bank that encourages people to save small amounts of money〔鼓励小额存款的〕储蓄银行

savings bond /ˈ· · ·/ *n* [C] *technical* a BOND[1] (1) sold by the US government that cannot be sold from one person to another【术语】〔美国政府发行的不能转卖给他人的〕储蓄公债

sa·viour *BrE*【英】, **savior** *AmE*【美】/ˈseVjə; ˈseɪvjə/ *n* **1** [C usually singular 一般用单数] someone or something that saves you from a difficult or dangerous situation 救助者, 挽救者, 救星 **2** [singular] in the Christian religion, a word for Jesus Christ〔基督教的〕耶稣基督, 救世主

sav·oir-faire /ˌsævwɑr ˈfɛr; ˌsævwɑː ˈfeə/ *n* [U] the ability to do or say the right things, especially in social situations 机敏处事的才干, 随机应变的能力: *famous in diplomatic circles for his savoir-faire* 在外交界以他灵活应变的能力而闻名

sa·vo·ry /ˈsevərɪ; ˈseɪvəri/ *n* **1** [U] a plant used in cooking to add taste to meat, beans etc〔烹调用的〕香薄荷 **2** [C] the American spelling of SAVOURY savoury 的美式拼法

sa·vour[1] *BrE*【英】, **savor** *AmE*【美】/ˈsevə; ˈseɪvə/ *v* [T] to make an activity or experience last as long as you can, because you are enjoying every moment of it 品尝; 欣赏: *She sipped her wine, savouring every drop.* 她慢慢地啜着酒, 细细品尝每一滴的滋味。—see 见 TASTE (USAGE)

savour of sth *phr v* [T] *formal* to seem to have a small amount of a quality that people do not like【正式】具有〔少量令人们讨厌〕的性质, 带有…的意味: *radical ideas savouring of revolution* 带有革命意味的激进思想

savour[2] *BrE*【英】, **savor** *AmE*【美】*n* [singular,U] *formal*【正式】**1** a taste or smell, especially one that is pleasant 滋味, 气味, 〔尤指令人愉快的〕味道 **2** interest and enjoyment 趣味, 乐趣, 吸引力: *Life seemed to have lost its savour for him.* 对他来说, 生活似乎已经失去了乐趣。

sa·vour·y[1] *BrE*【英】, **savory** *AmE*【美】/ˈsevərɪ; ˈseɪvəri/ *adj* **1** *BrE* having a taste that is not sweet【英】咸味的; 辛辣的 **2** having a pleasant and attractive smell or taste 味道可口的, 美味的: *A savoury smell of stew came from the kitchen.* 从厨房飘出一阵炖肉的香味。**3 not very savoury/none too savoury etc** something that is not savoury seems unpleasant or morally unacceptable 令人不快的, 名声不好的: *This hotel doesn't have a very savoury reputation.* 这家旅馆的名声可不大好。

savoury[2] *BrE*【英】, **savory** *AmE*【美】*n* [C] a small amount of salty food, sometimes served at the end of a formal meal〔最后上的〕咸味小菜

sa·voy /səˈvɔɪ; səˈvɔɪ/ *n* [C] a type of CABBAGE (=round green vegetable) with curled leaves 皱叶甘蓝, 皱叶卷心菜

Savoy, the *trademark* a very famous hotel in central London, next to the River Thames【商标】萨伏依酒店〔伦敦市中心泰晤士河畔一著名酒店〕

sav·vy /ˈsævɪ; ˈsævi/ *n* [U] *informal* practical knowledge and ability【非正式】实际知识和能力 —**savvy** *adj AmE*【美】: *I just wasn't savvy enough in high school to keep up.* 我读高中时水平不够, 总是跟不上。

saw[1] /sɔ; sɔː/ the past tense of SEE

saw[2] *n* [C] **1** a tool that has a flat blade with a row of V-shaped metal pieces, used for cutting wood 锯 —see picture at 参见 TOOL[1] 图 **2** *old use* a well-known wise statement; PROVERB【旧】格言, 谚语

saw[3] *v past tense* **sawed** *past participle* **sawn** /sɔn; sɔːn/ *especially BrE*【尤英】, **sawed** *especially AmE*【尤美】[I,T] to cut something using a saw〔用锯子〕锯, 锯开: *We had to saw the board in half.* 我们不得不把那块板锯成两半。| [+through] *He sawed through a power cable by mistake.* 他误把电缆给锯断了。

saw at sth *phr v* [T] to cut something with a repeated backwards and forwards movement 拉锯似地来回切: *He sawed at the loaf with a blunt knife.* 他用钝刀拉锯似地切那条面包。

saw sth ↔ **off** *phr v* [T] to remove something by cutting it off with a saw 锯掉〔某物〕: *One branch was dead and needed to be sawn off.* 有根树枝枯死了, 需要锯掉。

saw sth ↔ **up** *phr v* [T] to cut something into many pieces, using a saw 把〔某物〕锯成小块: *I sawed up the tree for firewood.* 我把那棵树锯成一段段作木柴用。

saw·bones /ˈsɔˌbonz; ˈsɔːbəʊnz/ *n* [C] *AmE informal* a doctor or SURGEON【美, 非正式】医生; 外科医生

saw·buck /ˈsɔˌbʌk; ˈsɔːbʌk/ *n* [C] *AmE old-fashioned* a $10 note【美, 过时】面额 10 美元的钞票

saw·dust /ˈsɔˌdʌst; ˈsɔːdʌst/ *n* [U] very small pieces of wood that are left when you cut wood with a SAW² (1) 锯末，锯（木）屑

saw·mill /ˈsɔˌmɪl; ˈsɔːmɪl/ *n* [C] a factory where logs are cut into boards using a machine〔把木材锯成木板的〕锯木厂

sawn-off shot·gun /ˌ. . ˈ. ./ *BrE*【英】, **sawed-off shot·gun** *AmE*【美】*n* [C] a SHOTGUN that has had its BARREL (=long thin part) cut short 枪管锯短的猎枪

saw·yer /ˈsɔjɚ; ˈsɔːjə/ *n* [C] *old use* someone whose job is sawing wood【旧】锯工，锯材手，操锯手

Saw·yer /ˈsɔjɚ; ˈsɔːjə/, **Tom** the main character in the book *The Adventures of Tom Sawyer* (1876) by Mark Twain, who is a brave and clever boy, but often gets into difficult or dangerous situations. His best friend is Huckleberry Finn. 汤姆·索耶〔马克·吐温创作的《汤姆·索耶历险记》(1876) 中的主人公。他是个聪明勇敢的男孩，却常常陷入困境或险境。他最好的朋友是哈克贝里·费恩〕

Sax·on /ˈsæksn̩; ˈsæksən/ *n* [C] a member of the German race that came to live in England in the 5th century 撒克逊人〔在 5 世纪定居于英格兰的日耳曼人〕—**Saxon** *adj*

sax·o·phone /ˈsæksəˌfon; ˈsæksəfəʊn/ *n* [C] also 又作 **sax** /sæks; sæks/ *informal*【非正式】a metal musical instrument with a single REED (2), used mostly in JAZZ and dance music 萨克斯管〔一种铜管乐器〕

sax·oph·o·nist /ˈsæksəˌfonɪst; sækˈsɒfənɪst/ *n* [C] someone who plays the saxophone 萨克斯管吹奏者

say¹ /se; seɪ/ *v past tense and past participle* **said** /sɛd; sed/ *3rd person singular present tense* **says** /sɛz; sez/

① USE WORDS 运用词语
② WRITING/NUMBERS 文字/数字
③ MEAN/SHOW 表示/表明
④ GENERAL OPINION 普遍观点
⑤ SUGGEST/SUPPOSE 认为/假定
⑥ SPOKEN PHRASES 口语短语
⑦ OTHER MEANINGS 其他意思

① USE WORDS 运用词语

1 ►WORD/SOUND 词/声音◄ [T] to pronounce a word or sound 说，讲: *"What did you say?"* "你说什么?" | *"I'm so tired," she said.* "我很累，"她说。| **say hello/goodbye etc** *She left without even saying goodbye.* 她连一声再见也没说就走了。—see 见 SPEAK (USAGE)

2 ►THOUGHT/OPINION 思想/意见◄ [I only in questions and negatives 仅用于疑问句和否定句,T] to express a thought, opinion, explanation etc in words〔用言语〕表达〔思想、意见等〕: *Don't believe anything he says.* 他说的你都不要相信。| *"Why did she leave?" "I don't know – she didn't say."* "她为什么走了?" "我不知道 —— 她没有说。" | **thing to say** *What a ridiculous thing to say!* 说这样的话真荒唐! | **say (that)** *Adam says he's thirsty.* 亚当说他口渴。| *I always said that you'd do okay in the end, didn't I?* 我总是说你一定会有好结局的，我没这样说吗? | **say how/why/who etc** *Did she say what happened?* 她有没有说发生了什么事? | *The doctor couldn't say how long it would take.* 医生没有说清楚这需要多长时间。| **say yes/no (to)** (=agree or refuse) 同意/拒绝 *Can I go, Mum? Oh please say yes!* 妈，我可以去吗? 求求你让我去吧! | **say so/not** *"Do you think they're happy?" "I wouldn't say so."* "你认为他们快乐吗?" "我可不这么认为。" | **sth to say** *Does anyone else have anything to say?* 还有谁要说什么吗? | *I couldn't think of anything to say to him.* 我想不出有什么话要对他说。| **say (you're) sorry** *Look, I've said I'm sorry – what more do you want?* 哎，我都已经道歉了，你还想怎么样? | **say a few words** (=make a short speech) 说几句话，作简短的发言 *I'd just like to say a few words about the schedule.* 我只想简单谈谈关于时间安排的问题。| **say your piece** (=say what you want to say) 畅所欲言，说自己想说的话 *OK, you've said your piece – now shut up.* 行了，你要说的话都说了，现在该闭嘴了。

3 say to yourself to think something 心里想，自忖，暗自思量: *So I said to myself "It's time I left."* 于是我心里想，"我该走了。"

4 ►TELL SB TO DO STH 吩咐某人做某事◄ [T not in progressive 不用进行时] to tell someone to do something 叫某人去做某事: **say to do sth** *Nina said to meet her at 4.30.* 尼娜吩咐 4 点 30 分去见她。

5 ►RULES 规则◄ [T] to state what people are allowed to do 规定，要求: **say (that)** *The law says you can't sell alcohol on a Sunday afternoon.* 法律规定星期日下午不能出售酒类。| *Mom says we're not allowed to talk to strangers.* 妈妈吩咐我们不要和陌生人说话。

6 say your prayers/say grace etc [T] to speak the fixed set of words that form a prayer etc 祈祷: *Have you said your prayers?* 你祈祷了吗?

7 say sth to sb's face *informal* to make an unpleasant or criticizing remark to the person that the remark is about【非正式】当着某人的面直说[直接批评]: *If you're going to make comments about my work, at least have the courage to say them to my face!* 你如果要对我的工作评头品足，至少要有勇气当着我的面说!

8 say sth you shouldn't *informal* to say something that is embarrassing or secret【非正式】说不该说的话: *Oh dear, have I said something I shouldn't again?* 噢，亲爱的，我又说了什么不该说的话了吗? —see also 另见 **say a mouthful** (MOUTHFUL (4))

② WRITING/NUMBERS 文字/数字

9 [T not in passive 不用被动态] to give information in written words, numbers, or pictures〔用文字、数字、图画等〕表示〔信息〕，说明: *The clock in the hall said it was 7.30.* 大厅的钟是 7 点 30 分。| *What does this word say?* 这个词是什么意思? | *Well that's what Sue said in her letter.* 唔，那就是休在她信中所说的意思了。| **say (that)** *It said in the paper that there were no survivors.* 报上说没有生还者。| **say to do sth** *The label says to take one before meals.* 标签上说要在饭前服一片。| **say who/what/how etc** *Does it say in the instructions how much you should use?* 说明书上有没有说明该用多少?

③ MEAN/SHOW 表示/表明

10 ►NOT DIRECTLY 非直接地◄ [T] to suggest what you mean in an indirect way 间接表示，表达: *What do you think the writer is saying in this passage?* 你认为作者在这一段要表达什么意思? | *So what you're saying is, there's none left.* 那么你的意思是说，一个都没剩下? | **say (that)** *Are you saying I'm fat?* 你的意思是说我胖吗?

11 ►SHOW CHARACTER/QUALITIES 表明特性/性质◄ [T] to show what someone or something's real character or qualities are 表明〔某人的性格或某物的特质〕是…: **say a lot about** (=show something very clearly) 清楚地表明 *The fact that he returned the money says a lot about his character.* 他退还那笔钱这件事清楚地表明了他的品格。| **say a lot for** (=show that someone or something has a lot of good qualities) 表明〔某人或某物〕有许多优点 *It says a lot for Jayne that she had the sense not to tell them.* 杰恩懂得不该告诉他们，这表明她品德很好。| **not say much for** (=show that something is not of a high standard or quality) 表明〔某事物〕质量不高 *These results don't say much for the quality of the teaching.* 这些成绩表明教学的质量不高。

12 ►HAVE MEANING 有意义◄ [T] to have or show a meaning that someone can understand 表达〔某种意义〕: *Most modern art doesn't say much to me.* 大部分现代艺术在我看来没有多大意思。

④ GENERAL OPINION 普遍观点

13 [T] to express an opinion that a lot of people have 多数人认为: *Well, you know what they say – blood's thicker than water.* 噢，你知道，常言说: 血浓于水。| **they say (that)** (=people think that) 人们认为 *They say he's been all round the world.* 大家都说他周游过全世界。| **(be) said to do sth** *She's said to be the richest woman in the world.* 据说她是世界上最富有的女人。| **it is said (that)** *It is said that he was a spy during the war.* 据说在战争时期他是个间谍。

⑤ **SUGGEST/SUPPOSE** 认为/假定

14 [T usually in imperative 一般用于祈使句] to suggest or suppose that something might happen or might be true 认为; 假定, 比方说: *I say we should forget the whole thing.* 我认为我们应该把整件事情都忘掉。| **let's/just say (that)** *Let's say your plan fails, then what?* 假定你的计划失败了, 那时候怎么办? | *Just say you won the lottery – what would you do?* 假定你的彩票中了奖, 你将会做什么?

Frequencies of the verb **say** in spoken and written English
动词 say 在英语口语和书面语中的使用频率

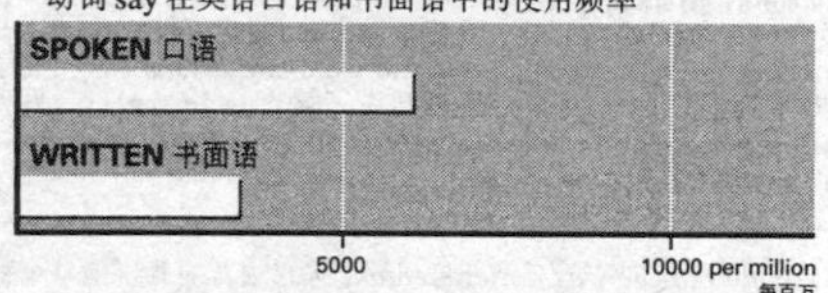

Based on the British National Corpus and the Longman Lancaster Corpus
据英国国家语料库和朗文兰开斯特语料库

This graph shows that the verb **say** is much more common in spoken English than in written English. This is because it is used in a lot of common spoken phrases. 本图表显示, 动词 say 在英语口语中的使用频率远远高于书面语, 因为口语中很多常用短语是由 say 构成的。

⑥ **SPOKEN PHRASES** 口语短语

15 I must say used when you want to emphasize what you are saying 我得说〔用以表示强调〕: *Well, that's clever, I must say!* 这个, 我得说那可真聪明! | *I must say it made me jump.* 我跟你说, 它吓了我一跳。

16 I can't say (that) used to say that you definitely do not think or feel something 我绝不认为: *I can't say I envy her being married to him!* 我绝对不会羡慕她能嫁给他!

17 having said that used before saying something that makes the opinion you have just given seem less strong 尽管如此, 话虽如此: *Hannah didn't do a very good job, but having said that, I don't think I could have done any better.* 汉娜干得不太好, 但尽管如此, 我想我也不见得会干得更好。

18 say no more used to show that you understand what someone means, although it has not been said directly 不用再说了〔用以表示明白了某人的意思〕: *"I saw him leaving her flat at 6.30 this morning." "Say no more!"* "我看见他今天早晨6点30分离开她的住处。" "不用再说了!"

19 enough said used to say that something is clear, and does not need to be explained any further 无须再作解释〔用以表示某事已经清楚〕

20 I'd rather not say used when you do not want to tell someone something 我最好还是不说〔表示不想把某事告诉某人〕: *"So what are your plans now?" "I'd rather not say at the moment."* "你现在有什么打算?" "眼下我最好不去谈它。"

21 you can say that again! used to say that you completely agree with someone 你说得真对〔用以表示完全同意某人的意见〕: *"Gosh, it's hot today." "You can say that again!"* "哎呀, 今天真热。" "你说得真对!"

22 say when used to ask someone to tell you when to stop doing something, especially pouring them a drink 够了就请说一声〔尤用于斟酒时〕

23 who says? used to say that you do not agree with a statement, opinion etc 谁说的?〔用以表示不同意别人的说法〕: *Who says I have to retire at 60?* 谁说我 60 岁一定要退休?

24 who can say? used to say that nobody knows the answer to a question 谁能说得准?〔用以表示没有人知道问题的答案〕: *Who can say whether they'll ever find a cure?* 谁也不能肯定他们能否找到一种治疗的办法。

25 who's to say? used to say that your judgment of a situation might not be correct, because you can never be sure what will happen in the future 谁能断定?〔用以表示对将来发生的事没有把握〕: *But who's to say that she won't do better than him in the end?* 谁能断定她最终不会干得比他好?

26 what do you say? used to ask someone if they agree with a suggestion 你觉得怎样? 你看行吗?〔用以询问某人是否同意所提的建议〕: *We could go into partnership; what do you say?* 我们可以合伙做生意, 你觉得怎样? | **what do you say we do sth?** *What do you say we all go to a movie?* 我们大家一起去看电影, 你看怎么样? | **what do/would you say to (doing) sth?** *What would you say to a meal out?* 我们出去吃饭, 你说好吗?

27 you don't say! used to show that you are not at all surprised by what someone has just told you 你用不着说!〔用以表示对某人告诉你的事一点也不觉得惊讶〕

28 say the word used to tell someone they have only to ask and you will do what they want 只要你说一声〔用以表示愿意做某人要求的事〕: *Just say the word and I'll get rid of her.* 只要你开口, 我就叫她走人。

29 I'll say this for him/her etc used when you want to mention something good about someone, especially when you have been criticizing them 我也要为他/她等说句(公道)话〔尤用在批评过某人之后〕: *I will say this for Tom – at least he's consistent.* 我要为汤姆说句公道话, 他至少能始终如一。

30 say what you like *especially BrE* used when giving an opinion that you are sure is correct, even if the person you are talking to might disagree with you【尤英】即使你不同意, 不管你怎么认为〔用以强调自己的看法没错〕: *Say what you like, she's a very good mother.* 不管你怎么认为, 她就是个好母亲。

31 whatever you say used to tell someone that you agree to do what they want, accept their opinion etc, especially because you do not want an argument 不管你怎么说我都同意〔尤用于不想争论时〕

32 can't say fairer than that *BrE* used to say that you have given the best offer that you can【英】不能给更优厚的条件了, 不能出更高的价格了: *I'll give you £25 for it; I can't say fairer than that.* 我给你 25 英镑买它, 不能出更高的价了。

33 you said it! **a)** used when someone says something that you agree with, although you would not have actually said it yourself 正是如此!〔表示同意对方的话, 但自己不会那么说〕: *"I was always stubborn as a kid." "You said it!"* "我小时候总是很固执。" "这话你可说对了。" **b)** *AmE* used to say that you agree with someone【美】我同意! 你说得对!: *"Let's go home." "You said it! I'm tired."* "我们回家去吧。" "同意! 我也累了。"

34 what have you got to say for yourself? used to ask someone for an explanation when they have done something wrong 你还有什么理由可说?: *Late again? What have you got to say for yourself?* 又迟到了吧? 这回你怎么解释?

35 that's not saying much used to emphasize that something is not very strange or unusual 没什么奇怪的, 没什么不寻常的〔用以强调〕: *She's taller than me, but I'm only 5 foot 2, so that isn't saying much.* 她比我高, 不过我才五英尺二英寸, 所以那也没什么奇怪的。

36 when all's said and done used to remind someone about an important point that they should remember 说到底, 毕竟〔用以提醒某人记住某个重要情况〕: *When all is said and done, he's only nine years old – don't expect too much.* 他毕竟才九岁, 不能对他期望过高。

37 I wouldn't say no (to) used to say that you would like something, and would accept if you were offered it 我想(要)…: *I wouldn't say no to a cup of coffee.* 我不反对喝杯咖啡。

38 I say *old-fashioned*【过时】**a)** *BrE* used to get someone's attention【英】喂; 我说呀〔用以引起他人的注意〕: *I say, could you pass me that book?* 喂, 请把那本书递给我好吗? **b)** used to show you are slightly interested, angry etc 啊, 嘿〔用以表示略感兴趣或生气等〕: *"My husband's ill today." "I say! I'm sorry to hear that."* "我丈夫今天病了。" "啊! 听到这事我很难过。"

⑦ **OTHER MEANINGS** 其他意思

39 go without saying used to say that something is so clear that it does not really need to be stated 显然; 不言而喻: *It goes without saying that I'll return the money afterwards.* 用不着说, 我以后会把钱归还的。

40 to say the least used to say that you could have described something, criticized someone etc a lot more severely than you have 至少可以说: *Jane could have been more considerate, to say the least.* 简本来应当考虑得更周到一点, 至少可以这么说。

41 that is to say used before describing what you mean in more detail 那就是说; 换句话说; 更具体地说: *Let's do as he suggested, that is to say, you fly down and I'll bring the car.* 我们就按他的建议做吧, 也就是说, 你乘飞机去, 我则开汽车过去。

42 that's not to say used to make it clear that something is not true, when you think someone might think that it is 那并不是说, 那并不表示: *That's not to say that I agree with what you're doing, of course.* 当然, 这并不是说我赞同你在做的事。

43 not to say *especially BrE* used to show that you could have used a stronger word to describe something【尤英】近乎, 甚至可以说: *It would be silly, not to say mad, to sell your car.* 你要是把汽车卖掉那就太蠢了, 简直是疯了。

44 say £45/100 years/Tuesday etc used to suggest a pos-

S

sible example, amount etc when discussing something 比方说45英镑/100年/星期二等〔用于在商讨时提出一个可能的例子、数量等〕: *They must owe say $2,000 in rent.* 他们一定欠了比方说2000美元的租金。| *Can you come to dinner? Say, 7.30?* 你能来吃晚饭吗? 7点30分怎么样?

45 there's no saying how/what/when etc used to say that it is impossible to know something 说不准怎样/什么/什么时候等: *There's no saying what he'll do next.* 不可能知道他下一步要做什么。

46 nothing/something/not much etc to be said for used to say that there are a lot of, not many etc good reasons for doing something 〔某种做法〕没有/有些/没有多少道理: *There's a lot to be said for taking a few days off now and then.* 偶尔休假几天是大有好处的。| *It was a strange plan, with very little to be said for it.* 那是一份很奇怪的计划, 看不出它有什么道理。

47 to say nothing of used to say that you have described only some of the bad points about something 更不用说; 何况〔用以表示对某事物的坏处只提及了其中的几点〕: *It was a complete waste of time, to say nothing of all the stress and bother!* 这完全是浪费时间, 紧张和麻烦就更不用说了!

48 have something to say about to be angry about something 为…不高兴, 对…生气: *If you don't do your homework your father will have something to say about it!* 你要是不做作业, 你父亲就会生气了!

49 have a lot to say for yourself someone who has a lot to say for themselves talks all the time 有许多话要说, 说个没完

50 what sb says goes used to emphasize who is in control in a situation 某人说了算; 照某人说的办〔用于强调〕: *My wife wants to go to Italy this year, and what she says goes!* 我妻子想今年去意大利, 而去哪里是她说了算! —see also 另见 **wouldn't say boo to a goose** (BOO² (3)), **easier said than done** (EASY² (6)), **no sooner said than done** (SOON (4))

USAGE NOTE 用法说明: SAY

WORD CHOICE 词语辨析: **say, tell, repeat, give, tell sb about/of, talk about/of, speak about/of**

In general, you **say** words **to** someone, but what you **tell** someone is facts, information etc. 一般地说, say ... to 是对别人说话, 而 tell 表示把事实、信息等告诉别人: *I said hello/sorry/thanks/a few words to her* (NOT 不用 *told her 'Hello'*). 我向她问好/道歉/道谢/说了几句话。| *I told her the reason/the truth/a lie/a story/a joke* (NOT 不用 *said*). 我告诉她原因/告诉她真相/对她撒谎/给她讲了个故事/给她讲了个笑话。

You usually only use **say** with the actual words that are spoken. 在表达某人所说的原话时通常只能用 say: *He said, "Open the door."* "开门。"他说。Only **tell** can be used to report commands. 而引述命令时只能用 tell: *He told me to open the door.* 他叫我开门。

There are special verbs for **say**ing certain things. 说某些事要用某些特殊动词: *I asked "Where is it?"* (less often 较少用 *I said...*). 我问道:"在什么地方?" | *I'd like to welcome you* (NOT usually 一般不用 *say welcome*). 我欢迎你。| *He congratulated her* (=said 'Congratulations!'). 他向她表示祝贺。| *She explained why she had done it* (=said why she had done it). 她说明她为什么要那样做。If you **say** something **again**, you **repeat** it. 如果你把某事再说 (say) 一遍, 你就用 repeat (重复)。

With some kinds of information **give** is more usual than **tell**. 表示"提供"某些信息时, 较常用动词 give, 而少用 tell: *He gave (us) his opinion/some advice/the details/a lot of information/an order/a message.* 他(向我们)谈了他的意见/提了一些忠告/谈了具体的细节/提供了许多信息/发布了一道命令/传达了一条信息。

You usually **tell** someone **about**, **talk about** or **speak about** (formal) people, things etc that are not themselves information. 表示"向某人谈及某人某事"或"谈及某人、某事"时, 通常用 tell someone about, talk about 或 speak about 〔正式〕, 这里所传达的信息不是某人、某事本身 (而是与其有关的情况): *He told us about Harvey/the accident* (NOT 不用 *said the accident to us*). 他向我们谈及哈维/那起事故的情况。| *I'm here to talk about the school/the school fair on Friday* (NOT 不用 *tell you the fair*). 我来这里是想谈谈学校/星期五学校义卖会的情况。

Of can be used instead of **about** with these verbs, but this can sound old-fashioned or literary. 上面的几个动词也可以不与 about 连用, 而和 of 连用, 但这样就会显得过时或文雅了: *a story that tells of a frog* (you would usually just say 通常只说 *a story about a frog*) 关于一只青蛙的故事。

GRAMMAR 语法

Say cannot have a person as its object. The person you are speaking to can be mentioned as well, but only after *to*. 动词 say 不能以人作宾语, 除非在人的前面加介词 to: *She said goodbye to her parents.* (NOT 不用 *She said her parents goodbye.*) 她向父母说再见。| *I said to them 'What do you need?'* 我对他们说:"你们需要些什么?" | *Celia once said to me that her husband tended to be violent.* 西莉亚有一次对我说, 她丈夫有暴力倾向。

However, where the object is a *that* clause, and you want to mention the person you are talking to as well, people often use **tell**, which can have a person as object. 但是, 当宾语是以 that 引导的从句, 而又要表达这是对谁说的, 那就常用动词 tell〔因为它可以用人作宾语〕: *You used to tell me that he was a nice person.* 你过去常对我说他是个好人。With a *wh-* clause in indirect speech **tell** is far more common. 在带有 wh- 从句的间接引语中, tell 要常用得多: *Tell me what you need* (NOT 不用 *Say to me what you need*). 告诉我你需要什么。

Where the object is a clause and you do not want to mention the person you are talking to it is usual to use **say**. 当宾语是个从句, 又不希望提到是对谁说的时, 则动词常用 say: *Call us to say when you'll arrive* (NOT 不用 *to tell when*). 给我们打电话说你将在什么时候到达。

In spoken English *that* is often left out of the *that* clause. 在英语口语中, 引导从句的 that 常被省略: *Tell me it's not true!* 告诉我那不是真的! | *I said I was sorry.* 我说我很抱歉。

Tell (but not **say**) can be followed by *to* forms of verbs. tell (而不是 say) 后面可以接带 to 的动词不定式: *He told us to do it* (NOT 不用 *said to us to do it*). 他叫我们去做。However, there must be an object noun as well (NOT 不用 *He told to do it*). 不过, 在 tell 之后必须有个宾语。

Tell (unlike **say**) is not usually followed immediately by *to* and a noun. tell (不同于 say) 后面通常不能直接带介词 to 加名词: *I'll tell my parents the truth/tell the truth to my parents* (NOT 不用 *...tell to my parents the truth*). 我会把真相告诉我父母。

Say and **tell** can both be used with **about**, but usually you use it with an object as well. say 和 tell 都可以和 about 连用, 但通常也要有宾语: *Let me say something about my family.* 让我谈谈我的家庭情况吧! | *Sally was telling us all about the party.* 萨莉在给我们讲晚会的情况。In informal spoken English you will quite often hear things like 在非正式口语中, 经常可以听到下面这类说法: *I've already said about that!* 这个问题我已经说过了! | *You were saying about Harvey?* 你是在谈哈维的情况吗? But some people would consider these to be incorrect. More often people use other verbs here. 不过, 有些人认为这类说法不正确。在这种句子中, 人们常用其他动词: *I've already talked about my family.* 我已经谈过我的家庭情况了。

say² *n* [singular,U] **1** the right to take part in deciding something (参与) 决定权; 发言权: [+in] *The workers had no say in how the factory was run.* 工人们在工厂管理方面没有发言权。| *Don't I have any say in the matter?* 难道我对这件事情没有发言权了吗? **2 have/say your say** *informal* to have the opportunity to give your opinion about something【非正式】有发表意见的机会: *Mark always has to have his say, even if he knows nothing about the subject.* 马克即使对该问题一无所知, 也总是非发表自己的意见不可。

say³ *interjection AmE informal* used to express surprise, or to introduce an idea you have just had【美, 非正式】哎呀〔用于表示惊讶、突然想到的主意等〕: *Say, haven't I seen you before somewhere?* 哎呀, 我以前是不是在什么地方见过你?

Say·ers /ˈseəz; ˈseɪəz/, **Dor·o·thy** /ˈdɔrəθɪ; ˈdɔrəθi/ **L.** (1893-1957) a British writer who wrote DETECTIVE NOVELS (=books about crime and murder) in which the main characters are Lord Peter Wimsey and Harriet Vane 塞耶斯 (1893-1957), 英国侦探小说家。创作的小说中的主角是彼得·温姆西勋爵和哈丽雅特·文

say·ing /ˈseɪŋ; ˈseɪ-ɪŋ/ *n* [C] **1** a well-known short statement that expresses an idea most people believe is true and wise 格言, 谚语, 警句 —compare 比较 PROVERB **2 as the saying goes** used to introduce a particular phrase that people often say 常言 3

道，正如俗话所说：*One thing led to another as the saying goes.* 常言道：一事牵出另一事。

say-so *n* [singular] *informal*【非正式】**1** someone's permission 允许，许可：*Without his say-so, you can't leave the hospital.* 没有他的许可，你不能离开医院。**2 on sb's say-so** based on someone's personal statement without any proof 根据某人的个人意见〔而不是凭实据〕：*Why should I believe it on your say-so?* 为什么你随便说说我就要相信它？

S-bend /ˈɛs ˌbɛnd; ˈes bend/ *n* [C] *BrE*【英】**1** a bend in a road in the shape of an 'S' that can be dangerous to drivers〔道路的〕S 形弯道；S-CURVE *AmE*【美】**2** part of a waste pipe in the shape of an 'S' that keeps bad smells out of a building〔建筑为防止臭气溢出的〕S 型曲管

SC the written abbreviation of 缩写= SOUTH CAROLINA

scab /skæb; skæb/ *n* [C] **1** a hard layer of dried blood that forms over a cut or wound while it is getting better〔伤口上结的〕痂 **2** an insulting word for someone who works while the other people in the same factory, office etc are on STRIKE[2] (1) 拒不参加罢工的人；破坏罢工者，工贼〔侮辱性用词〕—**scab** *v* [I]

scab·bard /ˈskæbɚd; ˈskæbəd/ *n* [C] a metal or leather cover for the blade of a knife or sword; SHEATH (1)〔刀、剑的〕鞘

scab·by /ˈskæbɪ; ˈskæbi/ *adj* **1** scabby skin is covered with scabs 结（满）痂的：*scabby knees* 结满痂的膝盖 **2** *BrE* a word meaning nasty or unpleasant, used especially by children【英】卑鄙的，讨厌的〔尤为儿语〕

sca·bies /ˈskebɪˌiz; ˈskeɪbiz/ *n* [U] a skin disease caused by very small insects 疥疮，疥螨病

sca·brous /ˈskebrəs; ˈskeɪbrəs/ *adj literary* rude or shocking, especially in a sexual way【文】猥亵的，淫猥的；粗俗的：*The film is a joy – hilariously funny and unremittingly scabrous.* 看这部电影是乐事——它滑稽逗笑、荤镜头源源不绝。

scads /skædz; skædz/ *n* [plural] *informal* large numbers or quantities of something【非正式】大量，大批：*scads of money* 大批的钱

Sca·fell Pike /ˌskɔfɛl ˈpaɪk; ˌskɔːfel ˈpaɪk/ a mountain in the Lake District, northwest England, which is the highest mountain in England 斯科费尔峰〔英格兰西北部湖区一山峰，为英格兰最高峰〕

scaf·fold /ˈskæfḷd; ˈskæfəld/ *n* [C] **1** a structure built next to a building or high wall, for workmen to stand on while they build, repair, or paint the building〔建筑工人用的〕脚手架 **2** a structure with a raised stage used for killing criminals by hanging them or cutting off their heads 绞刑架；〔行斩首刑的〕刑台 **3** *AmE* a structure that can be moved up and down to help people work on high buildings【美】〔建筑工人用的〕升降吊架，吊篮；CRADLE[1] (5) *BrE*【英】

scaf·fold·ing /ˈskæfḷdɪŋ; ˈskæfəldɪŋ/ *n* [U] poles and boards that are built into a structure for workmen to stand on when they are working next to a high wall on the outside of a building 搭脚手架（的材料）

scal·a·wag /ˈskæləˌwæg; ˈskæləwæg/ *n* [C] the usual American spelling of SCALLYWAG scallywag 的一般美式拼法

scald[1] /skɔld; skɔːld/ *v* [T] to burn your skin with hot liquid or steam〔沸腾的液体或蒸汽等〕烫伤〔皮肤〕：*Mind you don't scald yourself with that kettle!* 小心别让水壶烫着你！

scald[2] *n* [C] a burn caused by hot liquid or steam〔沸腾的液体或蒸汽造成的〕烫伤

scald·ing /ˈskɔldɪŋ; ˈskɔːldɪŋ/ *adj* **1** extremely hot 滚烫的；灼热的：*a cup of scalding tea* 一杯滚烫的茶 **2** scalding criticism is very severe〔批评〕严厉的，尖锐的

scale[1] /skel; skeɪl/ *n* (S3, W2)

1 ►SIZE/LEVEL 大小/程度◄ [singular,U] the size or level of something, or the amount that something is happening or being done 规模，范围，程度：**[+of]** *The scale of the pollution problem was much worse than scientists had predicted.* 污染问题的程度比科学家所预言的还严重。| **large/small etc scale** *There has been development on a massive scale since 1980.* 自 1980 年以来一直在大规模地发展。| *a large-scale research project* 大规模的研究项目

2 ►RANGE 范围◄ [C usually singular 一般用单数] the whole range of different types of people, things, ideas etc, from the lowest level to the highest 等级，级别：*At the other end of the scale are the super-rich.* 在这个等级范围的另一端是那些超级富翁。| *Fish are lower down the evolutionary scale.* 鱼类在进化等级中属于较低的。

3 ►MEASURING INSTRUMENT 计量器具◄ scales [plural] also 又作 **scale** *AmE*【美】**a)** a machine for weighing people or objects 磅秤：*the bathroom scales* 浴室磅秤 —see picture on page A10 参见 A10 页图 **b)** a piece of equipment with two dishes used especially in the past for weighing things by comparing them to a known weight 天平 —see also 另见 **tip the balance/scales** (TIP[2] (8))

4 ►MEASURING SYSTEM 计量制◄ [C] a system for measuring the force, speed, amount etc of something〔用于计量强度、速度、数量等的〕标准，级别：*Earthquakes are measured on the Richter scale.* 地震强度是按里氏震级测定的。| *the company pay scale* 公司的工资级别

5 on a scale of 1 to 10 *spoken* used when you are asking someone to say how good they think something is【口】按照 1 到 10 的等级〔用于征询别人对某事物的评价〕：*On a scale of 1 to 10, how do you rate his performance?* 按照 1 到 10 的等级，你怎样评价他的表现？

6 ►MEASURING MARKS 计量标度◄ [C] a set of marks with regular spaces between them on a tool or instrument used for measuring 刻度，标度：*a ruler with a metric scale* 有公制刻度的尺子 | *the scale on a thermometer* 温度计上的刻度

7 ►MAP/MODEL 地图/模型◄ [C,U] the relationship between the size of a map, drawing, or model and the actual size of the place or thing that it represents〔实物与图表、模型之间的〕比例（尺），比率：*a scale of 1:250,000* 1:250,000 的比例尺 | *What's the scale of this map?* 这张地图的比例尺是多少？

8 ►MUSIC 音乐◄ [C] a series of musical notes moving upwards or downwards in PITCH[1] (3) with fixed distances between each note 音阶

9 ►FISH 鱼类◄ [C usually plural 一般用复数] one of the small flat pieces of skin that cover the bodies of fish, snakes etc〔鱼、蛇等的〕鳞 —see picture at 参见 FISH 图

10 ►TEETH 牙齿◄ [U] a white substance that forms on your teeth 牙垢

11 ►WATER PIPES 水管◄ [U] a white substance that forms around the inside of hot water pipes or containers in which water is boiled〔热水管、容器内的〕水垢，水锈

12 the scales fell from my eyes *literary* used to say that you suddenly realized what had been clear to other people【文】恍然大悟，突然看清真相 —see also 另见 FULL-SCALE

scale[2] *v* [T] **1** to climb to the top of something that is high and difficult to climb 攀登：*Rescuers had to scale a 300m cliff to reach the injured climber.* 救援人员要登上 300 米的悬崖才能到达受伤的登山者身旁。**2** to remove the SCALES (=skin) from a fish 刮去〔鱼鳞〕—compare 比较 DESCALE

scale sth ↔ **down** *phr v* [T] *BrE*【英】, **scale** sth ↔ **back** *AmE*【美】to reduce the size of an organization, plan etc so that it operates at a lower level 缩减，缩小〔组织、计划等的规模〕：*Both companies have announced plans to scale back auto production next year.* 两家公司都宣布了明年缩减汽车生产的计划。

sca·lene tri·an·gle /ˌskelin ˈtraɪæŋgl; ˌskeɪliːn ˈtraɪæŋgəl/ *n* [C] a flat shape with three angles and three sides of unequal length 不等边三角形 —see picture at 参见 SHAPE[1] 图

scal·lion /ˈskæljən; ˈskæljən/ *n* [C] *AmE* a young onion with a small round end and a long green stem【美】大葱；SPRING ONION *BrE*【英】

scal·lop[1] /ˈskɑləp; ˈskɒləp/ *n* [C] **1** a small sea creature that has a hard flat shell made of two parts that fit together 扇贝〔一种贝壳类海产动物〕**2** [usually plural 一般用复数] one of a row of small curves decorating the edge of clothes, curtains etc 扇形饰边

scallop[2] also 又作 **scollop** *v* [T] **1** to decorate something by making the edge into a row of small curves 在〔边缘〕装饰扇形饰边 **2** to bake something in a cream or cheese SAUCE (1)〔浇上奶油或干酪等调味汁〕烤制，烘焙：*scalloped potatoes* 烤马铃薯

scal·ly·wag /ˈskælɪˌwæg; ˈskæliwæg/ *especially BrE*【尤英】, also 又作 **scalawag** *AmE*【美】*n* [C] *humorous* someone, especially a child, who causes trouble but not in a serious way【幽默】调皮鬼，小坏蛋〔尤指小孩〕

scalp[1] /skælp; skælp/ *n* [C] **1** the skin on your head 头皮 **2** *informal* a clear sign that you have completely defeated someone else【非正式】〔表明击败他人的〕标志，战利品：*The public were calling for his scalp.* 公众要置他于死地而后快。

scalp[2] *v* [T] **1** *AmE informal* to buy tickets for an event and sell them again at a much higher price【美，非正式】倒卖，炒卖〔戏票、球票等〕**2** to cut off a dead enemy's scalp as a sign of victory 割下〔敌人〕的头皮作为战利品

scal·pel /ˈskælpəl; ˈskælpəl/ *n* [C] a small very sharp knife used by doctors in operations 手术刀，解剖刀 —see picture at 参见 KNIFE[1] 图

scal·per /ˈskælpɚ; ˈskælpə/ *n* [C] *AmE* a person who makes money by buying tickets for an event and selling them again at a very high price【美】〔戏票、球票等的〕倒卖者；TOUT[2] (1) *BrE*【英】

scal·y /ˈskelɪ; ˈskeɪli/ *adj* **1** an animal, such as a fish, that is scaly is covered with small flat pieces of hard skin 有鳞的 **2** scaly skin is dry and rough〔皮肤〕干涩粗糙的 —**scaliness** *n* [U]

scam /skæm; skæm/ *n* [C] *slang* a clever but dishonest plan, usually to get money【俚】骗局, 诡计, 欺诈

scamp /skæmp; skæmp/ *n* [C] *old-fashioned* a child who has fun by tricking people【过时】小淘气, 调皮鬼: *Come back here with my hat, you young scamp!* 快把我的帽子拿回来, 你这个小淘气!

scam·per /ˈskæmpɚ; ˈskæmpə/ *v* [I always+adv/prep] to run with quick short steps, like a child or small animal 跳跳蹦蹦地跑: [+**in/out/off etc**] *Giggling, the children scampered back to the house.* 孩子们咯咯地笑着, 蹦蹦跳跳地跑回屋里。

scam·pi /ˈskæmpɪ; ˈskæmpi/ *n BrE*【英】**1** [plural] large PRAWN*s* (=sea creature that can be eaten)〔海里的〕大虾 **2** [U] PRAWN*s* covered in BATTER and cooked in oil〔外裹面糊的〕油炸大虾: *scampi and chips* 炸大虾和马铃薯条

scan[1] /skæn; skæn/ *v* **scanned, scanning 1** [T] to examine an area carefully, because you are looking for a particular person or thing 细看, 审视, 查找: *He scanned the horizon ahead, but there was no sign of the convoy.* 他仔细瞭望前面的地平线, 但看不见车队的踪影。| [**+for**] *The police scanned the whole area but found no trace of her body.* 警察仔细搜查了这个地区, 但没有找到她尸体的踪迹。**2** also 又作 **scan through** [I,T] to read something quickly in order to understand its main meaning or to find some particular information 粗略地看, 浏览, 快读: *I scanned the page quickly for her name.* 我迅速浏览那一页找她的名字。**3** [T] if a machine scans an object or a part of your body, it passes an ELECTRICAL BEAM[1] (1) over it to produce a picture of what is inside〔用电磁波等〕扫描: *All luggage has to be scanned at the airport.* 所有行李在机场都得接受扫描检查。—see also 另见 SCANNER (1) **4** [T] if a machine or instrument scans an area it searches it with RADAR or SONAR〔用雷达或声呐〕搜索, 寻找, 探测: *The ship scanned the area ahead for enemy submarines.* 那艘船探测前面海域, 寻找敌军潜艇。**5** *technical*【术语】**a)** [I] poetry that scans has a correct regular pattern of beats〔诗〕符合格律 **b)** [T] to find or show a regular pattern of beats in a poem or line of poetry 找出[标出]〔诗或诗句的〕格律 —see also 另见 SCANSION

scan[2] *n* [C] **1** the act of scanning something 细查, 审视 **2** a test done by a SCANNER (=special machine for producing a picture) 扫描(检查): *a brain scan* 脑部扫描检查 **3** an image of an unborn baby, produced by a SCANNER〔胎儿的〕扫描影像: *The scan showed the baby was normal.* 扫描影像显示胎儿正常。

scan·dal /ˈskændl; ˈskændl/ *n* **1** [C,U] behaviour or events, often involving famous people, that are considered to be immoral or shocking〔常牵涉知名人士的〕丑闻, 丑事: *a sex scandal involving several government officials* 涉及几个政府官员的性丑闻 | *Some newspapers thrive on spreading gossip and scandal.* 一些报纸因传播流言飞语和丑闻而销量大增。| **a scandal breaks** (=becomes known to everyone) 丑闻广为传播 *They had already left the country when the scandal broke.* 丑闻传开时, 他们已经离境了。**2 be a scandal** *spoken* to be very shocking or unacceptable【口】令人震惊; 不能接受: *The price of beef these days is an absolute scandal!* 近日的牛肉价格高得简直让人不能接受!

scan·dal·ize also 又作 **-ise** *BrE*【英】/ˈskændḷˌaɪz; ˈskændəlaɪz/ *v* [T usually passive 一般用被动态] to do something that shocks people very much 使震惊, 使愤慨: *The entire village was scandalized by the affair.* 全村都为这起事件感到震惊。

scan·dal·mon·ger /ˈskændḷˌmʌŋgɚ; ˈskændəlˌmʌŋgə/ *n* [C] someone who tells people untrue and shocking things about someone else 散布流言飞语者, 搬弄是非者, 诽谤他人者 —**scandalmongering** *n* [U]

scan·dal·ous /ˈskændḷəs; ˈskændələs/ *adj* completely unfair and wrong 极不公正的, 令人反感的: *a scandalous waste of public money* 骇人听闻的公款浪费 | *It's scandalous that you still haven't been paid!* 你到现在还领不到钱, 这太不像话了! —**scandalously** *adv*

Scan·di·na·vi·a /ˌskændəˈnevɪə; ˌskændɪˈneɪviə/ an area of North Europe consisting of Norway, Sweden, Denmark, Finland, and Iceland 斯堪的纳维亚〔北欧一地区, 包括挪威、瑞典、丹麦、芬兰和冰岛〕

Scan·di·na·vi·an /ˌskændəˈnevɪən; ˌskændɪˈneɪviən◂/ *n* [C] someone from the area of Northern Europe that consists of Norway, Sweden, Denmark, and usually Finland and Iceland 斯堪的纳维亚人〔指北欧的挪威、瑞典、丹麦、芬兰和冰岛诸国的人〕—**Scandinavian** *adj*: *Scandinavian languages* 斯堪的纳维亚诸语言

scan·ner /ˈskænɚ; ˈskænə/ *n* [C] **1** a machine that passes an ELECTRICAL BEAM[1] (1) over something in order to produce a picture of what is inside 扫描器, 扫描检测仪: *An electronic scanner was passed over the package.* 电子扫描器扫描了这个包裹。—see picture on page A14 参见 A14 页图 **2** a piece of computer equipment that copies an image from paper onto a computer〔可把页面上的文字、图像等复制到电脑中的〕扫描装置, 扫描仪

scan·sion /ˈskænʃən; ˈskænʃən/ *n* [U] the pattern of regular beats in poetry, or the marks you write to represent this〔诗的〕韵律; 韵律分析〔划分音步、标出重音等〕

scant /skænt; skænt/ *adj* [only before noun 仅用于名词前] not enough 不足的, 缺乏的: **scant attention/regard/consideration** *I paid scant attention to all my father's warnings.* 我没怎么注意听父亲对我的种种告诫。

scant·y /ˈskæntɪ; ˈskænti/ *adj* not big enough for a particular purpose〔大小或数量〕不够的, 不足的: *a scanty bikini* 衣不蔽体的比基尼泳装 —**scantily** *adv*: *scantily clad models* 几乎全裸的模特儿

Sca·pa Flow /ˌskɑpə ˈflo; ˌskɑːpə ˈfləʊ/ an area of sea between two of the Orkney Islands in northern Scotland. It was an important base for the British navy during World War I, and 71 German warships which had SURRENDER*ed* were sunk there when the war ended. 斯卡帕湾〔苏格兰北部一海域, 位于奥克尼群岛的两个岛屿之间。一战期间是英国一处重要的海军基地。战争结束时, 缴获的71艘德国战舰在此被沉入海底〕

-scape /skep; skeɪp/ *suffix* (in nouns 构成名词) a wide view of a particular area, especially in a picture 景色, 图景: *the impressive cityscape of New York* 令人难忘的纽约市区景色 | *some old Dutch seascapes* (=pictures of the sea) 几幅古老的荷兰海景画

scape·goat /ˈskepˌgot; ˈskeɪpgəʊt/ *n* [C] someone who is blamed for something bad that happens, even if it is not their fault 代人受过的人, 替罪羊: *He claimed he had been made a scapegoat for the administration's failures.* 他声称自己成了行政失当的替罪羊。—**scapegoat** *v* [T]

scap·u·la /ˈskæpjələ; ˈskæpjʊlə/ *n* [C] *technical* one of the two flat bones on each side of your upper back; SHOULDER-BLADE【术语】肩胛骨 —see picture at 参见 SKELETON 图

scar[1] /skɑr; skɑː/ *n* [C] **1** a permanent mark that is left after you have had a cut or wound (伤)疤 —see picture on page A6 参见 A6 页图 **2** a permanent emotional or mental effect caused by an upleasant experience〔精神上的〕创伤: **leave scars** *The trauma of her mother's death had left deep scars.* 母亲的死给她留下了很深的精神创伤。**3** an ugly permanent mark on something 疤痕, 伤痕: *The old mines are a scar on the rural landscape.* 这些废矿井成了这一带乡村风景的丑陋疤痕。**4** *BrE* a cliff on the side of a mountain【英】悬崖, 峭壁, 陡岩坡

scar[2] *v* **1 be scarred** to have a permanent mark on your skin because of a cut or wound 留下伤痕[疤痕]: *His hands were badly scarred by the fire.* 他的双手满是那次失火中严重烧伤的疤痕。**2** [T] if an unpleasant experience scars you, it has a permanent effect on your character or feelings 使〔精神上〕受创伤: **be scarred for life** (=never completely recover from an unpleasant experience) 留下终身的精神创伤 *She's likely to be scarred for life by the attack.* 她很可能因那次遭袭击而留下终身的精神创伤。**3** [I] also 又作 **scar over** if a wound scars, it becomes healthy but leaves a permanent mark on your skin 留下伤疤

scar·ab /ˈskærəb; ˈskærəb/ also 又作 **scarab bee·tle** /ˈ‥ ˌ‥/ *n* [C] a large black BEETLE (=insect with a hard shell) or a representation of this 圣甲虫; 圣甲虫形护符[饰物]

scarce[1] /skɛrs; skeəs/ *adj* **1** if food, clothing, water etc is scarce, there is not enough of it available 不足的, 缺乏的: *Fruit was always scarce in winter, and cost a lot.* 冬天水果总是稀少, 而且价格昂贵。—see 见 RARE (USAGE) **2 make yourself scarce** *informal* to leave a place, especially in order to avoid an unpleasant situation【非正式】〔为避免麻烦等〕离开; 溜走

scarce[2] *adv literary* scarcely【文】几乎不[没有]; 仅仅

scarce·ly /ˈskɛrslɪ; ˈskeəsli/ *adv* **1** almost not or almost none at all 几乎不, 几乎没有: *Parts of the city had scarcely changed since we were last there.* 自从我们上次来过这个城市之后, 有些地方至今几乎没有什么改变。| **scarcely any/ever** *There's scarcely any coffee left.* 咖啡几乎没剩下多少了。| **can/could scarcely** *It was getting dark and she could scarcely see in front of her.* 天越来越黑, 她几乎看不见前面的东西。| **scarcely a word/moment/day etc** *Scarcely a day goes by when I don't think of him.* 我几乎没有一天不想起他。—see 见 RARE (USAGE) **2** only just 仅仅, 刚刚: **have scarcely done sth when** *Scarcely had I opened the door when the dog came running in.* 我一开门那条狗就跑进来了。—see 见 ALMOST (USAGE) **3** definitely not or almost certainly not 决不, 一定不: *This is scarcely the place*

S

to talk about your personal problems. 这决不是谈你个人问题的地方。

scar·ci·ty /ˈskɛrsətɪ; ˈskeəsɮti/ *n* [singular,U+**of**] a situation in which there is not enough of something 不足，短缺: *the present scarcity of labour* 当前劳工的短缺

scare¹ /skɛr; skeə/ *v* **1** [T] to make someone feel frightened 使〔某人〕惊恐，吓唬: *Ignore him, he's just trying to scare us.* 不要理他，他只是想吓唬我们罢了。| **scare the hell/life/shit out of sb** (=scare someone very much) 把某人吓得魂不附体/要命/屁滚尿流 *You scared the hell out of me jumping out like that!* 你这样跳出来，吓死我了。**2** [I] to become frightened 受惊吓，感到害怕: *I don't scare easily you know!* 你知道我不是那么容易给吓倒的！

scare sb ↔ **into** *phr v* [T] to make someone do something by frightening them or threatening them 恐吓〔某人去做某事〕: **scare sb into doing sth** *Some parents try to scare their children into behaving well.* 有些父母试图用吓唬的法子使孩子守规矩。

scare sb/sth ↔ **off/away** *phr v* [T] **1** to make someone or something go away by frightening them 把…吓跑: *We lit fires to scare away the wolves.* 我们点起火堆来把狼群吓跑。**2** to make someone uncertain or worried so that they do not do something they were going to do 把…吓得不敢…: *Rising prices are scaring off many potential customers.* 涨价把很多潜在的顾客都吓跑了。

scare up sth *phr v* [T] *AmE informal* to make something although you have very few things to make it from【美，非正式】〔在东西不够用时〕凑合做成: *Let me see if I can scare up something for you to eat.* 让我看看能不能凑合着做点东西给你吃。

scare² *n* **1** [singular] a sudden feeling of fear 惊恐，惊吓: **give sb a scare** *That car only just missed me – it gave me a real scare!* 那辆车差一点就撞着我，真把我吓了一大跳！**2** [C] a situation in which a lot of people become frightened about something 〔社会上的〕大恐慌: *a bomb scare* 炸弹恐吓 | *An escape of radioactive gas caused a major scare.* 一次放射性气体的泄漏造成了社会上的大恐慌。

scare·crow /ˈskɛrˌkro; ˈskeəkrəʊ/ *n* [C] an object made to look like a person that a farmer puts in a field to frighten birds 〔放在田里吓鸟用的〕稻草人，假人

S3 **scared** /skɛrd; skeəd/ *adj* frightened of or nervous about something 害怕…的；对…感到惊慌[恐惧]的: [+**of**] *I've always been scared of dogs.* 我一向都怕狗。| *Don't be scared of asking if you need any help.* 你要是需要什么帮助，不要怕开口。| **scared (that)** *I was scared that they might tell the police.* 我害怕他们可能向警方告发。| **scared to do sth** *Janice lay on the floor trembling, too scared to move.* 贾尼丝躺在地板上直发抖，吓得动都不敢动。| **scared stiff/scared to death/scared out of your wits** (=extremely frightened) 被吓呆了/被吓得要死/被吓傻了 *I was scared stiff at the thought of having to make a speech.* 我一想到要去演讲就吓得发呆。

scare·dy-cat /ˈskɛrdɪkæt; ˈskeədikæt/ *n* [C] *informal* an insulting word for someone who is easily frightened, used especially by children【非正式】胆小鬼〔尤为儿语〕

scare·mon·ger·ing /ˈskɛrˌmʌŋgərɪŋ; ˈskeəˌmʌŋgərɪŋ/ *n* [U] the practice of deliberately making people worried or nervous, especially in order to get a political or other advantage 〔为取得政治或其他优势而〕散播引起忧虑或恐慌的消息，危言耸听: *Jackson publicly accused the anti-nuclear lobby of scaremongering.* 杰克逊公开谴责反核团体在危言耸听。—**scaremonger** *n* [C]

scare sto·ry /ˈ·ˌ··/ *n* [C] a report, especially in a newspaper, that makes a situation seem more serious or worrying than it really is 〔尤指报纸上的〕夸大报道

scare tac·tics /ˈ·ˌ··/ *n* [plural] methods of persuading people to do something by frightening them 恐吓战术: *Employers had used scare tactics to force a return to work.* 雇主们已使用恐吓战术迫使雇员复工。

scare·y /ˈskɛrɪ; ˈskeəri/ *adj* another spelling of SCARY scary 的另一种拼法

scarf¹ /skɑrf; skɑːf/ *n* [C] *plural* **scarfs** *or* **scarves** /skɑrvz; skɑːvz/ **1** a long narrow piece of material that you wear around your neck to keep it warm 〔长的〕围巾 **2** a square piece of material that a woman wears over her head or around her neck 〔女用的方形〕头巾；领巾

scarf² also 又作 **scarf down/up** *v* [I,T] *AmE slang* to eat something very quickly and noisily【美俚】狼吞虎咽地吃；SCOFF (2) *BrE*【英】

Scar·face /ˈskɑrfes; ˈskɑːfeɪs/ —see 见 Al CAPONE

scar·i·fy /ˈskɛrəˌfaɪ; ˈskeərɮfaɪ/ *v* [T] **1** to break and make loose the surface of a road or field using a pointed tool 〔用尖锐的工具〕挖开，翻松〔路面等〕**2** *technical* to make small cuts on an area of skin using a sharp knife【术语】〔用利刃〕在皮肤上切〔小口〕**3** *literary* to criticize someone very severely【文】严厉地批评

Scar·lat·ti /skɑrˈlætɪ; skɑːˈlæti/, **Do·men·i·co** /doˈmɛnɪko; dɒˈmenɪkəʊ/ (1685-1757) an Italian COMPOSER who wrote over 500 pieces of music for the HARPSICHORD 斯卡拉蒂〔(1685-1757)，意大利作曲家，创作了500多首大键琴曲〕

scar·let /ˈskɑrlɪt; ˈskɑːlɮt/ *adj* bright red 绯红色的，猩红色的，鲜红色的 —**scarlet** *n* [U] —see picture on page A5 参见A5页图

scarlet fe·ver /ˌ·· ˈ··/ also 又作 **scar·la·ti·na** /ˌskɑrləˈtinə; ˌskɑːləˈtiːnə/ *n* [U] a serious infectious illness that causes a sore throat and red spots on your skin 猩红热

scarlet pim·per·nel /ˌ·· ˈ···/ *n* [C] a small wild plant with bright red flowers 〔开鲜红色花的〕海绿，海丝

Scarlet Pim·per·nel, The /ˌ·· ˈ···/ the main character in the adventure story *The Scarlet Pimpernel* (1905) by Baroness Orczy. The 'Scarlet Pimpernel' is the name used by Sir Percy Blakeney, an Englishman who uses many clever DISGUISES (=ways of changing your clothes and appearance so that people do not recognize you) in order to help French people from a high social class to escape from France, and from the possibility of having their heads cut off by the GUILLOTINE during the French Revolution. There is a well-known short poem about him, which begins with the words "They seek him here, they seek him there...", and is about how difficult it is to find the Scarlet Pimpernel. 红花侠〔奥切女男爵的冒险故事《红花侠》(1905)的主人公。"红花侠"是英国人帕西·布莱克尼爵士的化名。法国大革命期间，他使用各种巧妙的伪装术帮助法国上流社会人士逃离法国，以免被送上断头台。有一首描写他的著名短诗，说的是红花侠很难找到。诗的开头是这样的："他们这里寻他，他们那里找他…"〕

scarlet wom·an /ˌ·· ˈ··/ *n* [C] *old-fashioned* a woman who has sexual relationships with many different people【过时】淫妇，荡妇

scarp /skɑrp; skɑːp/ *n* [C] *technical* a line of natural cliffs【术语】断线崖

scar·per /ˈskɑrpɚ; ˈskɑːpə/ *v* [I] *BrE informal* to run away【英，非正式】逃跑，溜走: *Those kids scarpered without paying their bill!* 那些孩子不付钱就溜走了！

scarves /skɑrvz; skɑːvz/ the plural of SCARF¹

scar·y, scarey /ˈskɛrɪ; ˈskeəri/ *adj informal* frightening【非正式】可怕的，骇人的，恐怖的: *a scary movie* 恐怖电影

scat¹ /skæt; skæt/ *interjection* used to tell a child or an animal to go away 〔用于叫小孩或动物〕走开！: *Go on, scat! And don't come back!* 快点，走开！不要回来！

scat² *n* [U] a style of JAZZ¹ (1) singing, in which the voice is made to sound like a musical instrument 〔爵士音乐中模仿乐器声的〕拟声唱法

scath·ing /ˈskeðɪŋ; ˈskeɪðɪŋ/ *adj* scathing remarks, comments etc criticize someone or something very severely 〔批评等〕严厉的，尖刻的: *The newspapers were extremely scathing about him.* 报纸对他的批评极其严厉。| *scathing criticism* 尖刻的批评 —**scathingly** *adv*

scat·o·lo·gic·al /ˌskætəˈlɑdʒɪkḷ; ˌskætəˈlɒdʒɪkəl◂/ *adj formal* too interested in or connected with human waste, in a way that is unpleasant【正式】对粪便过分感兴趣的；关于粪便的: *scatological humor* 脏笑话 —**scatology** /skæˈtɑlədʒɪ; skæˈtɒlədʒi/ *n* [U]

scarves 围巾

scat·ter /ˈskætɚ; ˈskætə/ *v* **1** [T] to throw or drop a lot of things over a wide area in an irregular way 撒: **scatter sth over/on/around** *Books lay scattered all over the floor.* 地板上到处散放着书。| **scatter sth with sth** *The sky was scattered with stars.* 天上繁星点点。**2** [I,T] if a group of people scatter, or if something scatters them, everyone suddenly moves in different directions, especially to escape danger (使)分散, 驱散, (使)散开〔尤指为逃离危险〕: *There was a sudden crack of gunfire and the crowd scattered in all directions.* 突然一声枪响, 人群向四处逃散。**3 be scattered to the four winds** *literary* to be broken up or separated and lost【文】东零西散 —see also 另见 SCATTERED, SCATTERING

scat·ter·brain /ˈskætɚˌbren; ˈskætəbreɪn/ *n* [C] someone who often forgets or loses things because they do not think in a practical way 疏忽健忘的人, 心不在焉的人, 精神不集中的人: *Don't tell me you've lost your glasses again, you scatterbrain!* 不要跟我说你又把眼镜丢了, 你这个丢三落四的家伙! —**scatterbrained** *adj*

scat·tered /ˈskætɚd; ˈskætəd/ *adj* spread over a wide area or over a long period of time 分散的, 稀疏的: *houses scattered across the hillside* 稀稀落落地散布在小山坡上的房子 | **scattered showers** (=used in weather reports to say there will be some short periods of rain) 零星阵雨〔用于大气预报〕

scat·ter·ing /ˈskætərɪŋ; ˈskætərɪŋ/ *n* [C] a small number of things or people spread out over a large area 少量分散的人或物: **[+of]** *a largely Catholic country with a scattering of Protestant communities* 以天主教徒为主但亦有少量新教徒社区分布的国家

scat·ty /ˈskætɪ; ˈskæti/ *adj BrE informal* someone who is scatty often forgets or loses things because they are not sensible or practical【英, 非正式】心不在焉的, 丢三落四的, 没有头脑的 —**scattiness** *n* [U]

scav·enge /ˈskævɪndʒ; ˈskævɪ̈ndʒ/ *v* [I,T] **1** if an animal scavenges, it eats anything that it can find〔动物〕以〔垃圾、腐肉等〕为食: *dogs scavenging from the dustbins* 在垃圾桶里觅食的狗 **2** if someone scavenges, they search through things that other people do not want for food or useful objects〔人〕在废弃物中寻找〔可食或可用的东西〕: **[+for]** *a man scavenging for food in piles of garbage* 在垃圾堆里翻找食物的男人 —**scavenger** *n* [C]

SCE /ˌɛs si ˋi; ˌes siː ˈiː/ Scottish Certificate of Education; an examination taken by students in schools in Scotland. There are three levels of examination in many different subjects: SCE O grades are taken at the age of 15 or 16; SCE highers are taken a year later; and *Sixth Year Studies* are taken a year later in the last year of school 苏格兰教育证书考试〔苏格兰在校学生参加的一种考试。考试有多个科目, 分三个级别进行。15至16岁的学生参加普通级别SCE的考试, 一年以后参加高级SCE的考试, 再过一年, 即在校最后一年参加"第六年证书"考试〕

sce·na·ri·o /sɪˈnærɪˌo; sɪ̈ˈnɑːriəʊ/ *n plural* **scenarios** [C] **1** a situation that could possibly happen but has not happened yet 可能发生的事, 可能出现的情况: *Try to imagine a scenario where only 20% of people have a job.* 设想一下这个情况: 只有20%的人有工作。| **worst-case/nightmare scenario** (=the worst possible situation) 可能出现的最坏/噩梦般的情况 *the nightmare scenario of a radiation leak* 可能出现的放射物泄漏的可怕情况 **2** a written description of the characters, place, and things that will happen in a film, play etc〔电影、戏剧等的〕剧情概要

scene /sin; siːn/ *n*

1 ▶PLAY/FILM 戏剧/电影◀ [C] **a)** part of a play during which there is no change in time or place〔戏剧中的〕一场: *Hamlet, Act 5 Scene 2*《哈姆雷特》第五幕, 第二场 **b)** a single piece of action that happens in one place in a film, book etc〔电影、书等中的〕场景, 场面: *Some of the more violent scenes are very disturbing.* 一些暴力较多的场面着实令人不安。| *a love scene* 恋爱场面

2 ▶VIEW/PICTURE 风景/图画◀ [C] a view of a place as you see it, or as it appears in a picture〔某地方或图画中的〕景色: *a peaceful country scene* 宁静的乡村景色 | *a painter of street scenes* 画街景的画家

3 ▶ACCIDENT/CRIME 事故/罪行◀ [singular] the place where an accident, crime etc happened〔事故或罪行的〕发生地点, 现场: **[+of]** *the scene of the crime* 犯罪现场 | **on/at the scene** *Investigators are now at the scene, searching for clues to the cause of the explosion.* 调查人员正在出事现场, 寻找爆炸案的线索。| *Journalists were on the scene within minutes of the crash.* 新闻记者在发生撞车事故几分钟后就到达了出事现场。

4 the gay/fashion/political etc scene a particular set of activities and the people who are involved in them 同性恋者天地/时装界/政治等领域: *Keith is heavily involved in the London theatre scene.* 基思与伦敦的戏剧界关系甚为密切。| *the drugs scene* 毒品圈子

5 ▶ARGUMENT 争辩◀ [C] a loud angry argument, especially in a public place〔在公开场合的〕争吵, 吵嚷: *a terrible scene that ended with Rachel running out of the restaurant in tears* 一场最后以雷切尔哭着跑出餐馆而结束的激烈争吵 | *There were angry scenes in parliament today.* 议会今天出现了愤怒的争吵场面。| **make a scene** *If you don't sit down and stop making a scene, I'm leaving!* 你要是再不坐下来, 还继续大吵大闹, 那我就走了!

6 ▶SITUATION 情景◀ [C] all the things that are happening in a place, and the effect or situation that they cause 情景, 景象: **[+of]** *The burning building was a scene of panic as everyone ran to get out.* 人们从起火的大楼逃出来时, 真是一片慌乱的景象。| *a scene of perfect peace and harmony* 一片理想的宁静和谐的景象

7 bad scene *AmE informal* a difficult or unpleasant situation【美, 非正式】困境: *We realized by the looks on their faces that we had walked into a bad scene.* 根据他们脸上的表情, 我们知道已经陷入了困境。

8 not your scene *informal* not the type of thing you like【非正式】并非某人喜爱的事物, 不合口味的东西: *Loud discos aren't really my scene.* 喧闹的迪斯科并不合我的口味。

9 behind the scenes secretly, while other things are happening publicly 秘密地, 在幕后: *Most important political decisions are made behind the scenes.* 大多数的重要政治决定都是秘密作出的。

10 set the scene a) to provide the conditions in which an event can happen〔为…〕提供条件: *The government seems unaware that these policies are setting the scene for social unrest.* 政府似乎没有意识到这些政策为社会动乱提供了条件。**b)** to describe the situation before you begin to tell a story〔在讲故事前〕叙述背景

11 be/come on the scene to be or become involved in a situation, activity etc 出现, 到来; 参与, 卷进: *By then, there was a boyfriend on the scene.* 那时, 她已经有一位男朋友了。—see also 另见 **change of scenery/air etc** (CHANGE[2] (3)), **steal the show/limelight/scene** (STEAL[1] (3))

sce·ne·ry /ˈsinərɪ; ˈsiːnəri/ *n* [U] **1** the natural features of a particular part of a country, such as mountains, forests, deserts etc 风景, 景色: *The best part of the trip was the scenery. It was fantastic.* 这次旅行最精彩的部分就是自然景色, 那真是美极了。**2** the painted background, furniture etc used on a theatre stage 舞台布景

sce·nic /ˈsinɪk; ˈsiːnɪk/ *adj* surrounded by views of beautiful countryside 景色优美的: *Let's take the scenic route home.* 我们走这条风景优美的路回家吧。—**scenically** /-klɪ; -kli/ *adv*

scent[1] /sɛnt; sent/ *n* **1** [C] a pleasant smell that something has 香味: *the scent of roses* 玫瑰的芳香 **2** [C] the smell of a particular animal or person that some other animals, for example dogs, can follow〔动物或人的〕臭气, 臭迹: **on the scent** (=following this smell) 循着线索[气味] *The hounds were soon on the stag's scent.* 那群猎犬马上循着臭气追踪牡鹿。**3 throw/put sb off the scent** to give someone false information to prevent them from catching you or discovering something〔给某人错误信息〕使某人失去线索: *The gang changed car to throw the police off the scent.* 歹徒们换车以摆脱追捕他们的警察。**4** [C,U] *especially BrE* a liquid that you put on your skin to make it smell nice; PERFUME[1] (1)【尤英】香水

scent[2] *v* **1** [T] if an animal scents another animal or a person, it knows that they are near because it can smell them〔动物〕嗅出…的气味: *The deer scented our presence and ran back into the forest.* 那头鹿嗅出我们在那里, 便跑回树林里去了。**2 scent fear/danger/victory etc** *literary* to feel sure that something is going to happen【文】觉察到恐怖/危险/胜利等的气息: *We scented danger and decided to leave.* 我们觉察到有危险, 便决定离开。

scent·ed /ˈsɛntɪd; ˈsentɪ̈d/ *adj* having a particular smell, especially a pleasant one【文】芬芳的, 有香气的: **[+with]** *an air freshener scented with spring flowers* 一种散发春天花香的空气清新剂

scent·less /ˈsɛntləs; ˈsentləs/ *adj* without a smell 无气味的, 无香味的

scep·ter /ˈsɛptɚ; ˈseptə/ *n* [C] the American spelling of SCEPTRE sceptre的美式拼法

scep·tic *BrE*【英】, **skeptic** *AmE*【美】/ˈskɛptɪk; ˈskeptɪk/ *n* [C] someone who does not believe things unless they have definite proof 持怀疑态度的人: *A lot of my friends believe in astrology, but I'm a sceptic myself.* 我的许多朋友都相信占星术, 但我自己却持怀疑态度。

scep·ti·cal BrE【英】, **skeptical** AmE【美】/ˋskɛptɪkl; 'skeptɪkəl/ *adj* tending to doubt or not believe what other people tell you 持怀疑态度的, 不相信的: [+about] *Many scientists remain skeptical about the value of this research program.* 很多科学家对这个研究方案的价值仍持怀疑态度。—**sceptically** /-klɪ; -kli/ *adv*

scep·ti·cis·m BrE【英】, **skepticism** AmE【美】/ˋskɛptəˌsɪzəm; 'skeptɪsɪzəm/ *n* [U] a sceptical attitude 怀疑态度; 怀疑论: *The government's claim that the country is now coming out of recession is being treated with deep scepticism.* 政府声称国家正在摆脱经济衰退, 但这种说法受到极大的怀疑。

scep·tre BrE【英】, **scepter** AmE【美】/ˋsɛptɚ; 'septə/ *n* [C] a short decorated stick carried by kings or queens at ceremonies〔国王或女王在仪式中手持的表示权力的〕权杖

S3 W3 **sched·ule¹** /ˋskɛdʒul; 'ʃedju:l/ *n* [C] **1** a plan of what someone is going to do and when they are going to do it 计划表, 进度表, 日程表: **full schedule** (=busy schedule) 排得很满的日程表 *I've got a very full schedule today.* 我今天的日程表排得满满的。| **tight schedule** (=including a lot of things that must be done in a short time) 时间很紧的日程表 *Our production schedule is so tight that we may have to take on extra staff.* 我们的生产进度排得这样紧, 大概只能雇用临时工了。| **ahead of/on/behind schedule** (=before, at, after the planned time) 先于/按照/迟于预定时间 *We finished the project three weeks ahead of schedule.* 我们提前三个星期完成了这项工程。**2** *AmE* a list that shows the times that buses, trains etc leave or arrive at a particular place【美】〔公共汽车、火车等的〕时间表, 时刻表; TIMETABLE¹ (1) *BrE*【英】**3** a formal list of something, for example prices 一览表, 清单, 明细表: *a schedule of postal charges* 邮费价目表

schedule² *v* [T] [usually passive 一般用被动态] to plan that something will happen at a particular time 排定, 把…安排在, 预定: [+for] *The meeting has been scheduled for this afternoon.* 会议已定于今天下午举行。| **be scheduled to do sth** *The new airport is scheduled to open just before Christmas.* 新机场定于圣诞节前开始使用。| **scheduled flight** (=a plane service that flies at the same time every day or every week) 定期航班

Sche·her·a·zade, **Sheherezade** /ʃəˌhɛrəˋzad; ʃəˌherə'zɑ:d/ the woman who tells the stories in *The Arabian Nights*. Scheherazade marries a man who always kills his wife on the night after the wedding. To prevent him from killing her too, she tells him part of an interesting story and then says she will tell him the rest of the story the next night. Because he wants to hear the end of the story, he does not kill her. She does this every night for one thousand and one nights, and after this, he allows her to live. 山鲁佐德〔《天方夜谭》里讲故事的女子。山鲁佐德嫁给了一个男子, 这名男子总是在新婚之夜就把妻子杀死。为了免此厄运, 山鲁佐德就给他讲故事。每当一个有趣的故事刚讲了一半, 她就说第二天晚上接着再讲。他为了听到故事的结尾就暂不杀她。她就这样连续讲了一千零一个晚上, 最后男子决定不杀她了〕

sche·ma /ˋskimə; 'ski:mə/ also 又作 **sche·ma·ta** /ˋskimətə; 'ski:mətə/ *n* [C] *technical* a plan showing only the important parts of something; DIAGRAM【术语】纲要, 概要; 图解, 图表

sche·mat·ic /skiˋmætɪk; ski:'mætɪk/ *adj* in the form of a basic plan or arrangement 概要的, 计划的; 图解的: *a schematic outline* 计划纲要 | *a schematic diagram of DNA* 脱氧核糖核酸结构简图

sche·ma·tize also 又作 **-ise** BrE【英】/ˋskiməˌtaɪz; 'ski:mətaɪz/ *v* [T] to arrange something in a system 对…作系统性组合

W1 **scheme¹** /skim; ski:m/ *n* [C] **1** *BrE* an official plan that is intended to help people in some way, for example by providing education or training【英】计划, 规划, 方案〔指正式计划, 如教育、培训等〕: *a government training scheme for the unemployed* 政府对失业者的培训计划 | *a pension scheme* 养老金方案 **2** a clever plan, especially to do something bad or illegal 阴谋, 诡计: *another one of his dumb schemes for making money* 他的又一个愚蠢的挣钱诡计 **3** a system that you use to organize information, ideas etc〔用于组织资料等的〕系统, 体系, 组合: *classification scheme* 分类系统 | **colour scheme** (=the way the colours have been organized in a room) 色彩布局 **4 be in the scheme of things** to be part of the way things generally happen, or are organized 按事物的一般规律, 在一般格局中: *It was seen as a medium-sized company in the general scheme of things.* 在芸芸企业中, 它被视为一家中等规模的公司。

scheme² *v* [I] to secretly make clever and dishonest plans to get or achieve something 搞阴谋, 密谋, 策划: **scheme to do sth** *He spent the next two years bitterly scheming to get his revenge.* 他在随后的两年中苦苦策划如何报仇。| **scheme against sb** *She became convinced that her family was scheming against her.* 她已经确信她的全家都在处心积虑地反对她。—**schemer** *n* [C]

scher·zo /ˋskɛrtso; 'skeətsəʊ/ *n* [C] a cheerful piece of music played quickly and happily 诙谐曲, 谐谑曲 —**scherzo** *adj, adv*

Schil·ler /ˋʃɪlɚ; 'ʃɪlə/, **Frie·drich von** /ˋfridrɪk vɑn; 'fri:drɪk vɒn/ (1759-1805) a German writer of plays, poetry, and history, who wrote *Ode to Joy* which Beethoven set to music as part of his *Choral Symphony* 席勒〔(1759-1805), 德国剧作家、诗人、史传家。其作品《欢乐颂》由贝多芬谱曲, 成为《合唱交响曲》的一部分〕

Schind·ler's List /ˌʃɪndlɚz ˋlɪst; ʃɪndləz 'lɪst/ (1993) a US film, made by Steven Spielberg, about an Austrian businessman who saved many Jews from being killed by the Nazis during World War II. It is based on a book called *Schindler's Ark* by Thomas Keneally. 《辛德勒的名单》〔(1993), 美国电影。史蒂文·斯皮尔伯格执导。故事讲述的是, 二战期间一名奥地利商人营救了许多犹太人, 使他们免遭纳粹的屠杀。影片根据托马斯·基尼利的小说《辛德勒的方舟》改编而成〕

schis·m /ˋsɪzəm; 'sɪzəm/ *n* [C,U] the separation of a group into two groups, caused by a disagreement about its aims and beliefs, especially in the Christian church〔由于信仰、目标等分歧引起的〕分裂;〔尤指基督教的〕教会分裂

schis·mat·ic /sɪzˋmætɪk; sɪz'mætɪk/ *adj* related to or connected with schism 分裂的, 引起分裂的, 分裂教会的

schist /ʃɪst; ʃɪst/ *n* [U] *technical* a type of rock that naturally breaks apart into thin flat pieces【术语】片岩

schiz·o /ˋskɪtso; 'skɪtsəʊ/ *n* [C] *slang* a SCHIZOPHRENIC【俚】精神分裂症患者

schiz·oid /ˋskɪtsɔɪd; 'skɪtsɔɪd/ *adj* **1** *technical* typical of schizophrenia【术语】精神分裂症的 **2** *informal* quickly changing between opposite opinions or attitudes【非正式】〔意见、态度等〕反复无常的, 自相矛盾的

schiz·o·phre·ni·a /ˌskɪzəˋfrinɪə; ˌskɪtsəʊ'fri:niə/ *n* [U] a serious mental illness in which someone's thoughts and feelings become separated from what is really happening around them 精神分裂症

schiz·o·phren·ic¹ /ˌskɪzəˋfrɛnɪk; ˌskɪtsəʊ'frenɪk◂/ *adj* **1** *technical* typical of or connected with schizophrenia【术语】(患)精神分裂症的 **2** *informal* quickly changing from one opinion, attitude etc to another【非正式】〔意见、态度等〕反复无常的, 朝秦暮楚的

schizophrenic² *n* [C] someone who has schizophrenia 精神分裂症患者

schlep /ʃlɛp; ʃlep/ *v* [T] *AmE informal* to carry or pull something heavy【美, 非正式】携带〔重物〕; 拖拽: [+down/out/along etc] *I schlepped his bag all the way to the airport and he didn't even thank me.* 我把他的行李一直送到飞机场, 他竟然连谢谢也不说一声。

schlep around *phr v* [I] to spend your time lazily doing nothing useful 游手好闲, 无所事事

schmaltz·y /ˋʃmɔltsɪ; 'ʃmɔ:ltsi/ *adj informal especially AmE* a schmaltzy piece of music, book etc deals with emotions such as love and sadness in a way that seems silly and insincere【非正式, 尤美】〔音乐、书等〕煽情的, 情感浅薄的: *a schmaltzy love song* 造作的情歌—**schmaltz, schmalz** *n* [U]

schmooze /ʃmuz; ʃmu:z/ *v* [I] *AmE informal* to talk about unimportant things【美, 非正式】闲聊, 闲扯: *drinking and schmoozing after filming was done* 拍完电影后喝酒闲聊

schmuck /ʃmʌk; ʃmʌk/ *n* [C] *AmE informal* a stupid person【美, 非正式】蠢货, 笨蛋

Schna·bel /ˋʃnabl; 'ʃnɑ:bəl/, **Ar·tur** /ˋatuɚ; 'ɑ:tʊə/ (1882-1951) a US PIANIST (=someone who plays the piano), born in Austria, famous especially for playing music by Beethoven 施纳贝尔〔(1882-1951), 美国钢琴家。生于奥地利, 以擅长演奏贝多芬的钢琴曲闻名〕

schnapps /ʃnæps; ʃnæps/ *n* [U] a strong alcoholic drink 荷兰烈酒; 荷兰杜松子酒

schnit·zel /ˋʃnɪtsəl; 'ʃnɪtsəl/ *n* [C,U] a small piece of VEAL covered with small pieces of bread and cooked in oil〔裹面包屑的〕炸小牛肉片

schnook /ʃnʊk; ʃnʊk/ *n* [C] *AmE informal* a stupid person【美, 非正式】蠢家伙, 笨蛋

schnoz·zle /ˋʃnɑzəl; 'ʃnɒzəl/ *n* [C] *AmE humorous* a nose【美, 幽默】鼻子

Schoenberg /ˋʃonˌbɝg; 'ʃəʊnbɜ:g/, **Arnold** /ˋarnḷd; 'ɑ:nəld/ (1874-1951) an Austrian COMPOSER who went to the US in 1933. He invented the 'twelve-tone system' of writing modern music, in which music is written around a set of twelve

notes of a Chromatic scale. His system has influenced many modern composers. His works include *Transfigured Night*, *Pierrot Lunaire*, and an OPERA that he did not finish *Moses and Aaron*. 勋伯格〔(1874-1951)，奥地利作曲家。1933年赴美。他开创了现代音乐创作手法"十二音列作曲法"，采用半音音阶的十二个音符进行谱曲。这一作曲体系影响了许多现代作曲家。代表作有《升华之夜》、《月光下的彼埃罗》以及他去世时尚未完成的歌剧《摩西与亚伦》〕

schol·ar /ˈskɑlɚ; ˈskɒlə/ *n* [C] **1** someone who knows a lot about a particular subject, especially one that is not a science subject 学者〔尤指精于一门文科学问的人〕: *a Latin scholar* 研究拉丁语的学者 **2** *informal* a clever and well-educated person【非正式】聪明且受过良好教育的人，有学问的人: *I'm afraid I'm not much of a scholar.* 我恐怕是算不上有学问的人。**3** someone who has been given a SCHOLARSHIP (=money) to study at a school or college 大学奖学金获得者: *a Rhodes scholar* 罗得斯奖学金获得者 **4** *literary or BrE old use* a child who is at school【文或英，旧】小学生

schol·ar·ly /ˈskɑlɚlɪ; ˈskɒləli/ *adj* **1** concerned with serious study of a particular subject 学术性的: *a scholarly journal* 学术刊物 **2** someone who is scholarly spends a lot of time studying, and knows a lot about a particular subject 好学并〔对某一学科〕具有渊博学识的

schol·ar·ship /ˈskɑlɚˌʃɪp; ˈskɒləʃɪp/ *n* **1** [C] an amount of money that is given to someone by an educational organization to help pay for their education 奖学金 **2** [U] the knowledge, work, or methods involved in serious studying 学问，学识；学术研究: *Her latest publication is a fine piece of scholarship.* 她最新出版的书是一部优秀的学术著作。

scho·las·tic /skəˋlæstɪk; skəˈlæstɪk/ *adj* [only before noun 仅用于名词前] *formal*【正式】**1** connected with schools or teaching 学校的，教学的: *scholastic books* 教学用书 **2** connected with scholasticism 经院哲学的，烦琐哲学的

scho·las·ti·cis·m /skəˋlæstəˌsɪzəm; skəˈlæstɪsɪzəm/ *n* [U] a way of studying thought, especially religious thought, based on things written in ancient times〔古代的〕经院哲学，烦琐哲学

school¹ /skul; skuːl/ *n*

1 ►WHERE CHILDREN LEARN 供孩子学习的地方◄ [C] a place where children are taught 学校: *Which school do you go to?* 你上哪所学校？| *There are several good schools in the area.* 这个地区有几所好学校。| **school bus/building etc** *the school hall* 学校礼堂 | **to/from school** *Mum takes us to school every morning.* 妈妈每天早晨送我们上学。

2 ►TIME AT SCHOOL 在学校的时间◄ [U] **a)** a day's work at school〔在学校的〕上课，一天的课程: *School begins at 8.30.* 8点30分开始上课。| **before/after school** *I'll see you after school.* 下课后我来看你。**b)** the time during your life when you go to a school 受学校教育的时间，上学期间: *After two years of school, he still couldn't read.* 他上了两年学仍然不会阅读。| **start/leave school** *She started school when she was four.* 她四岁开始上学。| *I left school two years ago.* 我两年前就毕业离校了。

3 ►UNIVERSITY 大学◄ **a)** [C,U] *AmE* a university, or the time when you study there【美】大学；在大学学习期间: *Where did you go to school?* 你在哪儿上大学？| **law/medical/graduate etc school** *After two years of medical school, I thought I knew everything.* 在医学院学习两年后，我以为自己什么都懂了。**b)** [C] a department that teaches a particular subject at a university〔大学的〕学院: [+of] *the School of Oriental Languages* 东方语言学院

4 ►ONE SUBJECT 一门课程◄ [C] a place where a particular subject or skill is taught 专科学校: *a language school in Brighton* 布赖顿的一所语言学校 | *the Pastern Riding School* 帕斯顿骑术学校 | [+of] *Amwell School of Motoring* 阿姆韦尔汽车驾驶学校

5 at school a) in the school building 在学校里: *I can get some work done while the kids are at school.* 孩子上学以后我可以做一些工作。**b)** *BrE* attending a school, rather than being at college or university or having a job【英】在求学，在上学〔指中、小学〕: *We've got two children at school, and one at university.* 我们有两个孩子在读中学，一个在读大学。

6 in school a) in the school building 在学校里: *Sandra's not in school today – she's not well.* 桑德拉今天没上学 —— 她身体不舒服。**b)** *AmE* attending a school or university as opposed to having a job【美】在求学: *Are your boys still in school?* 你们的孩子还在学校念书吗？

7 ►ART 艺术◄ [C] a number of people who are considered as a group because of their style of work 学派，流派: *the Impressionist school* 印象派

8 school of thought an opinion or way of thinking about something that is shared by a group of people 学派，流派；有类似观点的一批人: *There are two schools of thought on drinking red wine with fish.* 关于红葡萄酒配鱼的问题，有两派不同的看法。

9 of the old school having old-fashioned values or qualities, especially good ones 老派的，老式的，具有传统观念的〔尤指好的传统〕: *an officer of the old school* 老派军官

10 ►SEA ANIMALS 海里的动物◄ [C] a large group of fish, WHALES¹ (1), DOLPHINS etc that are swimming together〔鱼、鲸、海豚等的〕群: [+of] *a school of whales* 一群鲸鱼

11 the school of hard knocks *old-fashioned* the difficult or unpleasant experiences you have in life【过时】艰难困苦的磨炼，不愉快的经历

school² *v* [T] *old-fashioned* to train or teach someone【过时】训练；教育: **be schooled in sth** *a young lady schooled in all the usual accomplishments* 受过各种普通技艺训练的年轻女子

school board /ˌ· ˈ·/ *n* [C] a group of people, including some parents, who are elected to govern a school or group of schools in the US〔美国的〕校董会，学校教育委员会

school·boy /ˈskulˌbɔɪ; ˈskuːlbɔɪ/ *n* [C] *especially BrE*【尤英】**1** a boy attending school〔中、小学的〕男生 **2 schoolboy humour** jokes that are silly and rude but not offensive 幼稚的玩笑，小恶作剧

school·child /ˈskulˌtʃaɪld; ˈskuːltʃaɪld/ *n plural* **schoolchildren** /ˈskulˌtʃɪldrən; ˈskuːltʃɪldrən/ [C] a child attending school 学童，中小学生

school·day /ˈskulˌde; ˈskuːldeɪ/ *n* [C] **1** a day of the week when children are usually at school 学校上课日 **2 schooldays** the time of your life when you go to school 学生时代

school dis·trict /ˈ· ˌ··/ *n* [C] an area in one state of the US that includes a number of schools which are governed together〔美国的〕学区

school friend /ˈ· ·/ *n* [C] *especially BrE* a friend who goes to the same school as you【尤英】校友；同学

school·girl /ˈskulˌgɝl; ˈskuːlgɜːl/ *n* [C] *especially BrE* a girl attending school【尤英】〔中、小学的〕女生

school gov·ern·or /ˌ· ˈ···/ *n* [C] a member of a group of people in Britain who are elected to make decisions about how a school should be managed〔英国的〕学校管理委员会委员

school·house /ˈskulˌhaʊs; ˈskuːlhaʊs/ *n* [C] a school building, especially for a small village school〔尤指乡村学校的〕校舍

school·ing /ˈskulɪŋ; ˈskuːlɪŋ/ *n* [U] school education 学校教育

school·kid /ˈskulˌkɪd; ˈskuːlkɪd/ *n* [C] *informal* a child attending school【非正式】学童

school-leav·er /ˈ· ˌ··/ *n* [C] *BrE* someone who leaves school, especially when they are looking for a job rather than going to college, university etc【英】〔中学的〕辍学学生；离校生: *a shortage of jobs for school-leavers* 中学离校生就业机会的不足

school·marm /ˈskulˌmɑrm; ˈskuːlmɑːm/ *n* [C] a woman who is considered to be old-fashioned, strict, and easily shocked 古板严厉、大惊小怪的女人 —**schoolmarmish** *adj*

school·mas·ter /ˈskulˌmæstɚ; ˈskuːlˌmɑːstə/ *n* [C] *especially BrE* a male teacher, especially in a PRIVATE SCHOOL (=one that parents pay to send their children to)【尤英】〔尤指私立中、小学的〕男教师

school·mate /ˈskulˌmet; ˈskuːlmeɪt/ *n* [C] someone who goes or went to the same school as you 同学

school mis·tress /ˈ· ˌ··/ *n* [C] *especially BrE* a female teacher, especially in a PRIVATE SCHOOL (=one that parents pay to send their children to)【尤英】〔尤指私立中、小学的〕女教师

school·room /ˈskulˌrum; ˈskuːlruːm/ *n* [C] a room used for teaching in a small school 教室

school·teach·er /ˈskulˌtitʃɚ; ˈskuːlˌtiːtʃə/ *n* [C] a TEACHER〔中、小学的〕教师

school tie /ˌ· ˈ·/ *n* [C] **1** a special tie with a particular colour or pattern that children wear at some schools in Britain〔英国某些中、小学的〕校服上的领带 **2 the old school tie** *BrE informal* the unofficial system by which people who went to the same school, especially an expensive one, help each other to gain important positions later in their lives【英，非正式】〔校友离校后相互扶持的〕校友关系网

school·work /ˈskulˌwɝk; ˈskuːlwɜːk/ *n* [U] work done for or during school classes 功课，〔课堂〕作业

schoo·ner /ˈskunɚ; ˈskuːnə/ *n* [C] **1** a fast sailing ship with two sails (斯库纳) 双桅纵帆船 **2** a large tall glass for SHERRY or beer 大玻璃酒杯〔尤指盛雪利酒或啤酒的杯子〕

Schu·bert /ˈʃubɚt; ˈʃuːbət/, **Franz** /frænts; frænts/ (1797-1828) an Austrian COMPOSER whose best-known works are his songs, known as **lieder**, his music for the piano, and his symphonies (SYMPHONY) 舒伯特〔(1797-1828)，奥地利作曲家。代表作有艺术歌曲、钢琴曲及交响曲〕

Schultz /ʃults; ʃʊlts/, **Charles** (1922-2000) a US newspaper CARTOONIST who was famous for his strip CARTOON *Peanuts* in which the characters Charlie Brown, Linus, Lucy, and Snoopy the dog appeared. The cartoon first appeared in eight US newspapers in 1950, but soon appeared in newspapers all over the world. 舒尔茨〔(1922-2000)，美国报纸漫画家。他以连环漫画《花生》著名，塑造了查利·布朗、莱纳斯、露西、小狗史努比等形象，1950年，其漫画首次被美国八家报纸刊载，并遂见于全球各大报纸〕

Schu·mann /ˈʃumæn; ˈʃuːmən/, **Rob·ert** (1810-56) a German COMPOSER who wrote symphonies and many songs, but is best known for the music he wrote for the piano. He was married to Clara Schumann (1819-96), who was also a pianist and composer. 舒曼〔(1810-1856)，德国作曲家。作品有交响曲和许多歌曲，以钢琴曲最为著名。其妻克拉拉·舒曼(1819-1896)同为钢琴家、作曲家〕

schwa /ʃwɑ; ʃwɑː/ *n* [C] *technical* a vowel typically heard in parts of a word that are spoken without STRESS[1] (4), such as the "a" in "about"【术语】非重读音节中的轻读元音〈如 about 中的 a〉

Schwar·zen·eg·ger /ˈʃwɔrtsənɛgɚ; ˈʃwɔːtsənegə/, **Arnold** (1947-) a US actor born in Austria, who was a famous BODYBUILDER (=someone who develops large muscles through physical exercise), and then became an actor in exciting, violent films such as *The Terminator* (1984) and *Total Recall* (1990). 施瓦辛格〔(1947-)，美国演员，生于奥地利。他曾是著名健美运动员，后成为惊险动作片演员，出演了《终结者》(1984)和《宇宙威龙》(1990)等影片〕

Schweit·zer /ˈʃwaɪtsɚ; ˈʃwaɪtsə/, **Albert** (1875-1965) a German doctor who went to Africa as a Christian MISSIONARY and started a hospital in 1913 in Gabon, where he worked until his death, especially treating people who were suffering from LEPROSY. He was also a musician and a PHILOSOPHER, and he was given the Nobel Peace Prize in 1952. 施韦策〔(1875-1965)，德国医生。他曾以基督教传教士身份前往非洲，于1913年在加蓬创办了一所医院，在此工作直至去世，以收治麻风病患者为主。他还是音乐家、哲学家，1952年获诺贝尔和平奖〕

sci·at·ic /saɪˈætɪk; saɪˈætɪk/ *adj technical* connected with the hips (HIP[1](1))【术语】坐骨的

sci·at·i·ca /saɪˈætɪkə; saɪˈætɪkə/ *n* [U] pain in the lower back, hips (HIP[1] (1)) and legs 坐骨神经痛

1 1 **sci·ence** /ˈsaɪəns; ˈsaɪəns/ *n* **1** [U] knowledge about the world, especially based on examination and testing, and on facts that can be proved 科学: *Science has taught us how atoms are made up.* 科学使我们明白原子是怎样构成的。| *The computer is one of the marvels of modern science.* 电脑是现代科学的奇迹之一。| *developments in science and technology* 科学技术的发展 **2** [U] the study of science 理科: *a degree in science* 理科学位 **3** [C] a particular part of science, for example BIOLOGY, CHEMISTRY, or PHYSICS 理科的一门学科〈如生物、化学、物理〉: *the physical sciences* 自然科学 —see also 另见 NATURAL SCIENCE, SOCIAL SCIENCE, **blind sb with science** (BLIND[2] (4))

science fic·tion /ˌ‥ ˈ‥/ *n* [U] a kind of writing in which imaginary future developments in science and their effect on life are described 科幻小说

Science Mu·se·um, the /ˈ‥ ‥ˌ‥/ a large MUSEUM in London containing many important scientific objects, which show the history and development of science and technology 科学博物馆〔伦敦一大型博物馆。馆藏反映科技发展史的大量重要实物〕

science park /ˈ‥ ‥/ *n* [C] an area where there are a lot of companies or organizations that do scientific work 科学园区，新技术(研究)开发区

3 2 **sci·en·tif·ic** /ˌsaɪənˈtɪfɪk; ˌsaɪənˈtɪfɪk◂/ *adj* **1** [no comparative 无比较级] about or connected with science, or using its methods 科学(上)的: *scientific discoveries* 科学发现 | *scientific proof* 科学证明 **2** *informal* done very carefully, using an organized system【非正式】精细的; 有系统的, 有条理的: *We do keep accounts for the business, but we're not very scientific about it.* 我们做生意确是有账目的，但我们做得不够精细有条理。—**scientifically** /-klɪ; -kli/ *adv*

Scientific A·mer·i·can /ˌ‥‥ ˈ‥‥/ a monthly magazine with articles about new discoveries and developments in all the sciences, written for educated readers《科学美国人》，又译《科学人》〔美国一月刊。刊载的文章反映各个科学领域的新发现和新发展，读者对象为知识分子〕—compare 比较 The NEW SCIENTIST

sci·en·tist /ˈsaɪəntɪst; ˈsaɪəntɪst/ *n* [C] someone who works or is trained in science 科学家 3 2

Sci·en·tol·o·gy /ˌsaɪənˈtɑlədʒɪ; ˌsaɪənˈtɒlədʒi/ *trademark* a religion that was started in the 1950s by the US writer L. Ron Hubbard, officially called the Church of Scientology. It aims to solve its members' problems in life and to improve their ability to achieve what they want.【商标】科学论派〔美国作家L.罗恩·哈巴德20世纪50年代创立的一种宗教，正式名称为"科学论教会"。该教派旨在解决信徒生活中遇到的问题，提高他们实现人生目标的能力〕—**Scientologist** *n.*

sci-fi /ˌsaɪ ˈfaɪ; ˌsaɪ ˈfaɪ◂/ *n* [U] *informal* SCIENCE FICTION【非正式】科幻小说

Scil·ly Isles, the /ˈsɪlɪ ˌaɪlz; ˈsɪli ˌaɪlz/ also 又作 **the Isles of Scilly** a group of about 140 small islands off southwest England, five of which have people living on them. The Scilly Isles are popular with tourists, and the weather there is warmer than in the rest of Britain. 锡利群岛〔与英格兰西南海岸隔海相望的一个群岛。由大约140个小岛组成，其中五个岛上有人居住。锡利群岛为旅游胜地，气候比英国其他地区温暖〕

scim·i·tar /ˈsɪmətɚ; ˈsɪmɪtə/ *n* [C] a sword with a curved blade 弯刀 —see picture at 参见 SWORD 图

scin·til·la /sɪnˈtɪlə; sɪnˈtɪlə/ *n* [singular] **not a scintilla of truth/evidence etc** not even the smallest amount of truth etc 毫无真实性/证据等: *There isn't a scintilla of evidence to prove it.* 没有丝毫的证据可以证明它。

scin·til·late /ˈsɪntḷˌet; ˈsɪntɪleɪt/ *v* [I] *literary* to shine with small quick flashes of light; SPARKLE[1] (1)【文】闪烁，闪闪发光 —**scintillation** /ˌsɪntəˈleʃən; ˌsɪntɪˈleɪʃən/ *n* [U]

scin·til·lat·ing /ˈsɪtḷˌetɪŋ; ˈsɪntɪleɪtɪŋ/ *adj* interesting, clever, and amusing 有趣的; 聪明灵巧的: *scintillating conversation* 妙趣横生的谈话

sci·on /ˈsaɪən; ˈsaɪən/ *n* [C] **1** *technical* a living part of a plant that is cut off, especially for fixing onto another plant【术语】〔尤指为接枝而剪下的〕幼枝，接穗 **2** *literary* a young member of a famous or important family【文】〔名门贵族的〕子孙，后裔: *scions of wealthy East coast families* 东海岸的富家子弟

scissors 剪刀

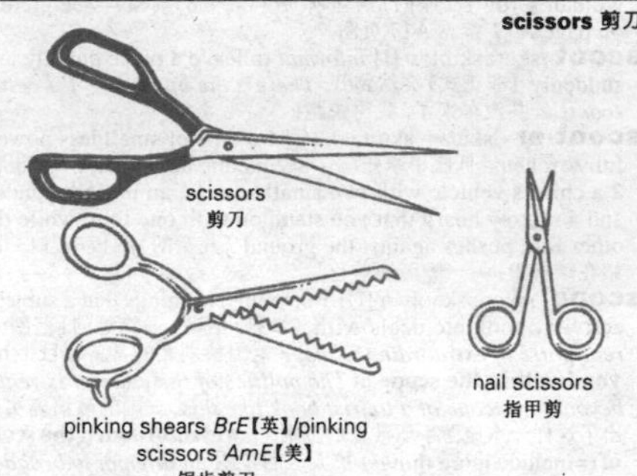

scis·sors /ˈsɪzɚz; ˈsɪzəz/ *n* [plural] a tool for cutting paper, made of two sharp blades and a handle with two holes for your fingers 剪刀: *a pair of scissors* 一把剪刀

scle·ro·sis /sklɪˈrosɪs; sklɪˈrəʊsɪs/ *n* [C,U] *technical* a disease that causes an organ or soft part of your body to become hard【术语】硬化(症) —**sclerotic** /sklɪˈrɑtɪk; sklɪˈrɒtɪk/ *adj* —see also 另见 MULTIPLE SCLEROSIS

scoff /skɔf; skɒf/ *v* **1** [I] to laugh at a person or idea, and talk about them in a way that shows you think they are stupid 嘲笑，讥笑，嘲弄: [+at] *They scoffed at the idea that anything could be changed.* 他们嘲笑那种认为任何事情都可以改变的想法。**2** [T] *BrE informal* to eat something very quickly【英，非正式】狼吞虎咽地吃: *Who's scoffed all the cake?* 是谁把蛋糕都吃光了?

scold[1] /skold; skəʊld/ *v* [T] to angrily criticize someone, especially a child, about something they have done 责骂，斥责〔某人，尤指小孩〕: *As kids we were always getting scolded by the local farmer.* 我们小时候经常被当地的农场主责骂。—**scolding** *n* [C,U]

scold[2] *n* [C] *old use* a woman who often complains or criticizes【旧】爱埋怨指责的妇人

scol·lop /ˈskɑləp; ˈskɒləp/ *n* [C] another spelling of SCALLOP scallop的另一种拼法

sconce /skɑns; skɒns/ *n* [C] an object that is fixed to a wall and holds CANDLES or electric lights 壁式烛台[灯台]

scone /skon; skɒn/ *n* [C] a small round, soft cake sometimes containing dried fruit 司康，(圆形)烤饼: *scones and cream* 烤饼涂奶油

Scone /skun; skuːn/, **the Stone of** —see 见 the STONE OF SCONE

scoop¹ /skup; skuːp/ *n* [C] **1** a round deep spoon for holding or serving food such as corn, flour, or ICE CREAM 勺，球形勺: *an icecream scoop* 冰淇淋勺 **2** also 又作 **scoopful** an amount of food removed with this kind of spoon 一勺之量: **[+of]** *three scoops of ice cream* 三勺冰淇淋 **3** an important or exciting news story that is printed in one newspaper before any of the others know about it〔抢先登出的〕独家新闻: *Royal Diary Scoop!* 王室日记的独家报道! **4** a very big profit that a company makes〔公司赚到的〕巨额利润 **5 what's the scoop?** *spoken especially AmE* used to ask someone for information or news about something【口，尤美】有什么消息吗?〔用以询问某人关于某事的情况〕

scoop² *v* [T] **1** to pick something up with a scoop, a spoon, or with your curved hand〔用勺或勺状物〕舀出，取出，铲出: **[+up/out/off etc]** *She scooped up a handful of sand.* 她舀起一把沙子。| *Scoop out the seeds from the melon.* 用勺挖出香瓜里的籽。**2** to be the first newspaper to print an important news report〔报纸〕首先报道重要新闻，抢先报道: *The Daily News scooped the other papers by revealing the prince's marriage plans.*《每日新闻》抢在别家报纸前面披露了王子的结婚计划。

scoop neck /ˌ· ˈ·◂/ *n* [C] a round, quite low neck on a woman's TOP〔女服的〕汤匙领，开得较低的圆领 —see picture on page A17 参见 A17 页图

scoot /skut; skuːt/ *v* [I] *informal* to leave a place quickly and suddenly【非正式】突然跑开: *There's the bus now – I'd better scoot!* 公共汽车来了，我得快跑!

scoot·er /ˈskutɚ; ˈskuːtə/ *n* [C] **1** a type of small less powerful MOTORBIKE 低座小摩托车 —see picture at 参见 MOTORBIKE 图 **2** a child's vehicle with two small wheels, an upright handle, and a narrow board that you stand on with one foot, while the other foot pushes against the ground〔儿童的〕踏板车〔以一脚站在踏板上，另一脚蹬地前行〕

2 **scope¹** /skop; skəʊp/ *n* [U] **1** the range of things that a subject, activity, book etc deals with〔学科、活动、书籍等的〕范围: *a repertoire of extraordinary scope* 范围特别大的常备剧目 | **beyond/within the scope of** *The politics of the country is really beyond the scope of a tourist book like this.* 一国的政情确实超出了这样一本旅游手册涉及的范围。| **widen/broaden the scope of** (=include more things) 扩大…的范围 *an attempt to broaden the scope of the inquiry* 扩大调查范围的尝试 **2** the opportunity to do or develop something〔发挥能力的〕机会，施展余地: **[+for]** *Is there much scope for initiative in this job?* 这份工作有没有机会让人施展才华?

scope² *v* [T]

scope sth/sb **out** *phr v* [T] *AmE old-fashioned* to look at something or someone to see what they are like【美，过时】了解，查清，探明: *Let's scope out that new club tonight.* 让我们今晚去看看那个新俱乐部是什么样的。

Scopes tri·al, the /ˈskops ˌtraɪəl; ˈskəʊps ˌtraɪəl/ also 又作 **the Monkey Trial** a famous US court case in which John Scopes, a biology teacher, was taken to a court of law in 1925 for teaching Darwin's theory of Evolution, because this was against the law in the state of Tennessee, where the story of the creation as told in the Old Testament of the Bible had to be taught in state schools. He was defended by the lawyer Clarence Darrow, but was found guilty. 斯科普斯审判案〔美国一宗著名庭审案。1925 年，生物教师约翰·斯科普斯因讲授达尔文的进化论而触犯了田纳西州的法律并遭到起诉。田纳西州的法律规定，州立学校必须讲授《圣经·旧约》的《创世记》故事。斯科普斯虽有克拉伦斯·达罗律师为其辩护，但仍被裁定为有罪〕

scorch¹ /skɔrtʃ; skɔːtʃ/ *v* **1** [I,T] if you scorch something, or if it scorches, its surface burns slightly and changes colour (使)烧焦，(使)烤焦: *The walls had been blackened and scorched by the fire.* 这些墙被大火烧黑了。| *I scorched my new shirt with the iron.* 我用熨斗把新衬衫给烫焦了。**2** [T] if strong heat scorches plants, it dries them and kills them〔炙热把植物〕灼伤，使枯萎: *All the grass had been scorched brown.* 所有的草都被晒得一片枯黄。**3** [T] if strong heat scorches you, it burns you 烫，烫伤: *The hot sand scorched our feet.* 炙热的沙子烫着我们的脚。**4** [I always+adv/prep] *BrE informal* to travel extremely fast【英，非正式】飞驰，高速行驶: **[+along/down/across etc]** *A car came scorching down the fast lane at 110 miles an hour.* 一辆汽车以每小时 110 英里的速度在快车道上疾驰。

scorch² *n* **1** [C] a mark made on something where its surface has been burnt 焦痕，烧焦或烤焦处 **2** [U] brown colouring on plants caused by some plant diseases〔植物因病害出现的〕枯萎

scorched earth pol·i·cy /ˌ· · ˈ· · ·/ *n* [C] the destruction by an army of everything useful in an area, especially crops, so that the land cannot be used by an enemy 焦土政策〔军队放弃某地区前实行的烧毁农作物等的彻底破坏行动〕

scorch·er /ˈskɔrtʃɚ; ˈskɔːtʃə/ *n* [C usually singular 一般用单数] *informal* an extremely hot day【非正式】大热天: *Phew, what a scorcher!* 啊，天气真热!

scorch·ing /ˈskɔrtʃɪŋ; ˈskɔːtʃɪŋ/ *adj* extremely hot 极热的，灼热的: *scorching sun* 烈日 | **scorching hot** *a scorching hot day* 极热的一天

score¹ /skɔr; skɔː/ *n* [C] 3 2

1 ▶IN A GAME 在比赛中◀ [C] the number of points that each team or player has won in a game or competition〔游戏、竞赛中得的〕分数，比分: **the score** *What's the score?* 比分是多少? | **keep (the) score** (=make a record of the score) 记分 *Is anybody keeping score?* 有没有人负责记分? | **final score** *The final score was Everton 2, Spurs 4.* 最后的比分是二比四，爱华顿队败给热刺队。

2 ▶MUSIC 音乐◀ [C] a written or printed copy of a piece of music, especially for a large group of performers 乐谱: *a vocal score* 声部乐谱 | *Who wrote the score for the movie?* 这部电影的配乐是谁谱写的?

3 ▶IN A TEST 考试◀ [C] *AmE* the number of points a student has earned for correct answers in a test【美】〔学生考试的〕分数

4 on that score *spoken* concerning the particular thing you have just mentioned【口】关于那一点，关于那个问题: *As for the cost, you don't need to worry on that score.* 至于费用，你不需要为这个问题操心。

5 know the score *informal* to know the real facts of a situation, including any unpleasant ones【非正式】知道事情真相，了解实情: *John won't do anything risky – he knows the score.* 约翰不会去做任何冒险的事——他心中有数。

6 settle a score to do something to harm or hurt someone who has harmed or hurt you in the past 报宿怨，算旧账: *Jack came back after five years to settle some old scores.* 杰克在五年之后回来报仇雪耻。

7 ▶MARK 记号◀ a mark that has been cut onto a surface with a sharp tool〔利器造成的〕刻痕，划痕: *deep scores in the wood* 木头上一道道很深的划痕

score² *v* 2

1 ▶WIN POINTS 得分◀ [I,T] to win a point in a sport, game, or competition〔在运动、游戏、比赛中〕得(分): *Arsenal scored in the final minute of the game.* 阿森纳队在比赛的最后一分钟进了球。| **score a goal/point/run** *Which player has scored the most runs this season?* 这个赛季哪个球员得分最多?

2 ▶RECORD POINTS 记分◀ [I] to record the number of points someone has in a game or competition as it is played〔在比赛中〕记分: *Will you score for us?* 你来给我们记分好吗?

3 ▶GIVE POINTS 评分◀ [T] **a)** to give someone a particular number of points in a game or competition〔在游戏、竞赛等中〕给〔某人〕评分，打分: **score sb 6/8 etc** *The Canadian judge scored her 15.* 加拿大裁判给她打了 15 分。**b)** to be worth a particular number of points in a game or competition〔在游戏、竞赛等中〕得分: *A bull's-eye scores 50 points.* 击中靶心可得 50 分。

4 score points also 又作 **score off sb** to argue with someone in order to prove that you are better than they are〔在辩论中〕驳倒对方

5 ▶SUCCEED 成功◀ [I,T] *informal* to be very successful in something you do【非正式】成就辉煌: *Atwood has scored again with another popular book.* 阿特伍德的另一部畅销书又获得很大成功。| **score a success** *The Green party scored some successes in the northwest.* 绿党在西北部获得了几次成功。

6 ▶HAVE SEX 做爱◀ [I] *slang* to have sex with someone you have just met【俚】〔与新认识的人〕发生性关系: *Did you score, then?* 那么你们有没有做爱?

7 ▶PAPER 纸张◀ [T] to mark a line on a piece of paper, using a sharp instrument〔用利器〕在〔纸上〕刻痕，划线: *Scoring the*

paper first makes it easier to fold. 先在上面划一道痕, 纸就比较容易折了。

8 ▶MUSIC 音乐◀ [usually passive 一般用被动态] to arrange a piece of music for a group of instruments or voices〔为一组乐器演奏或声部〕配乐, 谱曲

9 ▶GET DRUGS 弄到毒品◀ [I,T] *slang* to manage to buy or get illegal drugs【俚】非法买到[弄到]毒品

score sth ↔ **out/through** *phr v* [T] to draw a line through something that has been written 划掉, 删去〔文字〕

score[3] *number* **1** *old use* twenty【旧】二十 **2 scores of** a lot of 很多, 大量: *scores of people in line for food* 很多人在排队等候食物

score·board /ˈskɔrˌbɔrd; ˈskɔːbɔːd/ *n* [C] a board on which the points won in a game are recorded〔比赛中的〕记分牌

score·card /ˈskɔrˌkɑrd; ˈskɔːkɑːd/ *n* [C] a printed card used by someone watching a sports match or race to record what happens〔观赛者持的〕比赛成绩记录卡

scor·er /ˈskɔrɚ; ˈskɔːrə/ *n* [C] **1** also 又作 **scorekeeper** someone who keeps an official record of the points won in a sports game〔体育比赛的〕记分员 **2** a player who wins a point or GOAL (2) 得分[进球]的运动员 **3 high/low scorer** someone who gets a large or small number of points in a test 高/低分者〔在考试中获得高分或低分者〕

scorn[1] /skɔrn; skɔːn/ *n* [U] the feeling that someone or something is stupid, old-fashioned, or not as good as other people or things; CONTEMPT 鄙视, 蔑视, 轻视: **[+for]** *They had nothing but scorn for their working-class parents.* 他们对自己劳动阶级的父母完全看不起。| **pour scorn on** *Davis poured scorn on the proposal.* 戴维斯对那个提议嗤之以鼻。

scorn[2] *v* [T] to refuse to accept ideas, suggestions etc because you think they are stupid, old-fashioned, or unreasonable〔认为愚蠢、过时或不合理而〕拒绝接受〔思想、建议等〕; 鄙视: *Most young people today scorn the idea that virginity is important.* 当今大部分年轻人都对认为贞操很重要的看法不屑一顾。| **scorn to do sth** (=refuse to do something, because you think it is not good enough) 不屑做某事 *She scorned to hide away like a coward.* 她不屑像懦夫一样躲起来。

scorn·ful /ˈskɔrnfəl; ˈskɔːnfəl/ *adj* feeling or showing scorn 轻蔑的, 鄙视的: *a scornful look* 轻蔑的表情 | **[+of]** *They remained scornful of all our attempts to find a solution.* 他们对我们寻找解决办法的一切努力都持鄙视态度。—**scornfully** *adv*

Scor·pi·o /ˈskɔrpɪˌo; ˈskɔːpiəʊ/ *n* **1** [singular] the eighth sign of the ZODIAC, represented by a SCORPION, and believed to affect the character and life of people born between October 23 and November 21 天蝎宫[座]〔黄道第八宫〕 **2** [C] someone who was born between October 23 and November 21 出生于天蝎宫时段〔10月23日至11月21日〕的人

scor·pi·on /ˈskɔrpɪən; ˈskɔːpiən/ *n* [C] a tropical animal like an insect with a curving tail and a poisonous sting 蝎子

scorpion 蝎子

Scor·se·se /skɔrˈsezɪ; skɔːˈseɪzi/, **Martin** (1942-) a US film DIRECTOR whose films often deal with violent subjects. He has made many of his films with the actor Robert De Niro, including *Taxi Driver* (1976), *Raging Bull* (1980), *Goodfellas* (1990), and *Cape Fear* (1991). 斯科塞斯〔(1942-), 美国电影导演。作品常以暴力为题材, 执导的许多影片都由罗伯特·德尼罗担纲主演。 代表作有《出租车司机》(1976)、《愤怒的公牛》(1980)、《盗亦有道》(1990) 和《恐怖角》(1991) 等〕

Scot /skɑt; skɒt/ *n* [C] someone from Scotland 苏格兰人

scotch /skɑtʃ; skɒtʃ/ *v* [T] to stop something happening by firmly doing something to prevent it 遏止, 制止, 阻止: *British delegates soon scotched any idea of a deal.* 英国代表们很快就把任何想达成协议的意见压了下去。| **scotch a rumour** (=stop people saying something untrue) 制止谣言

Scotch[1] *n* [C,U] a strong alcoholic drink made in Scotland, or a glass of this (一杯) 苏格兰威士忌 (酒)

Scotch[2] *adj* SCOTTISH 苏格兰的

Scotch broth /ˌ· ˈ·/ *n* [U] thick soup made from vegetables, meat and BARLEY (=type of grain)〔用蔬菜、肉类、大麦等熬煮的〕苏格兰浓汤

Scotch egg /ˌ· ˈ·/ *n* [C] a cooked egg covered with meat and small pieces of bread〔外裹肉和面包屑的〕苏格兰式煮蛋

Scotch mist /ˌ· ˈ·/ *n* [C,U] thick mist with light rain 苏格兰雾〔一种带毛毛雨的浓雾〕

Scotch pan·cake /ˌ· ˈ· ·/ *n* [C] a small round flat cake 苏格兰烙饼〔一种小圆烙饼〕

Scotch tape /ˌ· ˈ·/ *n* [U] *AmE trademark* sticky thin transparent material used for sticking light things together【美, 商标】思高透明胶带; SELLOTAPE *BrE trademark*【英, 商标】

scotch tape *v* [T] *AmE* to stick things together with Scotch tape【美】用透明胶带粘贴; SELLOTAPE *BrE*【英】

scot-free /ˌskɑt ˈfri; ˌskɒt ˈfriː/ *adv* **get away/off scot-free** *informal* to avoid being punished although you deserve to be【非正式】逃脱惩罚

Scot·land /ˈskɑtlənd; ˈskɒtlənd/ a country in the United Kingdom, north of England. Population: 5,062,011 (2001). Capital: Edinburgh. Scotland was an independent country until the Scottish and English parliaments were united by the 'Act of Union' in 1707, and it still has a different legal system and a different education system from the rest of the UK. Since 1999, Scotland has had its own parliament, although it is part of the UK. Scottish Gaelic is still spoken by some people in the northwest of the country and in the islands off the west coast. Scotland is famous for its beautiful countryside and its many LOCH*s* (=lakes), islands, and mountains. The national symbol of Scotland is the THISTLE, and its PATRON SAINT is Saint Andrew. People from Scotland are called Scots. 苏格兰〔联合王国的组成部分, 位于英格兰以北。人口: 5,062,011 (2001), 首府: 爱丁堡。苏格兰曾是一个独立国家。1707年, 苏格兰议会与英格兰议会根据《合并法案》合二为一, 但其法律和教育体系至今仍与联合王国其他地区有所不同。苏格兰隶属于联合王国, 但1999年开始有了自己的议会。居住在西北部和西海岸附近岛屿的一些居民仍使用苏格兰盖尔语。苏格兰以美丽的乡村、众多的湖泊、小岛、山脉闻名。苏格兰的民族标志为蓟, 主保圣人是圣安德列。苏格兰人被称为 Scot〕

Scot·land Yard /ˌskɑtlənd ˈjɑrd; ˌskɒtlənd ˈjɑːd/ *n* [singular] *BrE* the part of the London police that deals with serious crimes, or their main office【英】苏格兰场〔伦敦警察厅的刑事侦缉部或总部〕

Scots /skɑts; skɒts/ *adj* Scottish 苏格兰的; 苏格兰人的; 苏格兰英语的

Scots law /ˌ· ˈ·/ —see 见 the SCOTTISH LEGAL SYSTEM

Scots·man /ˈskɑtsmən; ˈskɒtsmən/ *n* [C] a man who comes from Scotland 苏格兰男人

Scots·man, The /ˈskɑtsmən; ˈskɒtsmən/ a serious Scottish daily newspaper《苏格兰人》〔苏格兰一严肃类日报〕

Scots·wom·an /ˈskɑtsˌwʊmən; ˈskɒtsˌwʊmən/ *n* [C] a woman who comes from Scotland 苏格兰女人

Scott /skɑt; skɒt/, **Captain Rob·ert Fal·con** /ˈrɑbɚt ˈfɔlkən; ˈrɒbət ˈfɔːlkən/ (1868-1912) an officer in the British navy, who is often called Scott of the Antarctic. He made two journeys to the Antarctic to try to be the first person to reach the South Pole. He and his group reached the South Pole in 1912, shortly after the Norwegian EXPLORER Roald Amundsen, but Scott's group all died on the way back. His journal, in which he describes their terrible journey, was discovered a year later. 斯科特〔(1868-1912), 英国海军军官, 常被称为"南极的斯科特"。为了成为到达南极的第一人, 他曾两度远征南极。1912年, 他和他的远征队抵达南极, 但比挪威探险家罗阿尔·阿蒙森稍晚。在归途中, 斯科特及其队友全部遇难。一年之后, 他的探险日记被人发现, 其中记载了那场可怕的远征经历〕

Scott, Dred —see 见 DRED SCOTT CASE

Scott, Ron·nie /ˈrɑnɪ; ˈrɒni/ (1927-96) a British SAXOPHONE player who started the UK's most famous JAZZ club, Ronnie Scott's in London 斯科特〔(1927-1996), 英国萨克斯管演奏家。他在伦敦创办了英国最著名的爵士乐俱乐部, 名为"龙尼·斯科特俱乐部"〕

Scott, Sir Wal·ter /ˈwɔltɚ; ˈwɔːltə/ (1771-1832) a Scottish writer and poet who was one of the most popular British writers of the 19th century. He wrote many historical NOVEL*s* based on Scottish history, such as *Rob Roy*, and on old English stories, such as *Ivanhoe*. One of his best known poems is *The Lady of the Lake*. 司各特〔(1771-1832), 苏格兰作家、诗人, 19世纪最受欢迎的英国作家之一。他创作了多部苏格兰历史小说, 如《罗布·罗伊》, 有的小说还取材于英国的古老传说, 如《艾凡赫》。最著名的一篇诗作是《湖上夫人》〕

Scot·tish /ˈskɑtɪʃ; ˈskɒtɪʃ/ *adj* from or belonging to Scotland 苏格兰的; 苏格兰人的; 苏格兰英语的

Scottish Borders /ˌ·· ˈ··/ a COUNTY in southern Scotland, that has a border with northern England 苏格兰边区〔苏格兰南部一郡, 与英格兰北部接壤〕

Scottish High·lands, the /ˌ·· ˈ··/ an area with many mountains in the northern half of Scotland 苏格兰高地〔苏格兰北部群山连绵的一个地区〕

S

Scottish Le·gal System, the /,·· '··, ··/ also 又作 **Scots Law** the system of law in Scotland which is based on CIVIL LAW, and is different from that of England and Wales, although the highest court of law in all three countries is the House of Lords. When laws are made in the British parliament, they do not always become law in Scotland because the legal system is different there. 苏格兰法律体系〔以民法为基础的苏格兰法律体系，与英格兰、威尔士有所不同，虽然三地的最高法院同为上议院。英国议会通过的法律在苏格兰并不一定生效，因为苏格兰的法律体系不同〕

Scottish Na·tion·al Par·ty, the /,·· '···, ··/ the full name of the SNP 苏格兰民族党〔SNP 的全称〕

Scottish Of·fice /'·· ,··/ the British government department responsible for carrying out government policy in Scotland 苏格兰事务部〔英国一政府部门，负责落实政府的苏格兰政策〕

Scottish Parliament /'·· ,··/ the parliament for Scotland which was established in 1999 and has the power to make laws in Scotland. The leader of the parliament is the First Minister, and its 129 members are called MSPs, or Members of the Scottish Parliament. They are elected by a system of proportional representation. 苏格兰议会〔苏格兰地方议会，成立于1999年，在苏格兰具有立法权。议会领导人为首席大臣，议会的129名成员称为苏格兰议会议员，议员按比例代表制选举产生〕

Scottish Play, the /'·· ,·/ a name for Shakespeare's play *Macbeth*, used by actors because they believe that it is unlucky to say Macbeth 苏格兰剧〔演员对莎士比亚剧作《麦克白》的别称。他们认为直接说"麦克白"不吉利〕

Scot·ty /'skɒtɪ; 'skɒti/ also 又作 **Mr Scott** a character in the *Star Trek* films and television programmes, known especially for the phrase said to him by the other characters 'Beam me up, Scotty.' 斯科蒂〔电影、电视剧《星际旅行》中的一个角色。剧中的其他角色对斯科蒂说的"斯科蒂，快把我送走"这句台词非常有名〕

S

scoun·drel /'skaʊndrəl; 'skaʊndrəl/ *n* [C] *old-fashioned* a bad or dishonest man【过时】恶棍，无赖: *a charming scoundrel, without morals* 一个有魅力而无道德的无赖

scour /skaʊr; skaʊə/ *v* [T] **1** to search very carefully and thoroughly through an area, a document, etc〔彻底地〕搜查〔某地或某物〕: *A team of detectives is scouring the countryside.* 一队侦探正在搜查整个乡村地区。**2** also 又作 **scour out** to clean something very thoroughly by rubbing it with a rough material 擦净，擦亮: *The pans really needed to be scoured.* 这些锅真需要好好擦一擦了。—see picture at 参见 CLEAN[2] 图 **3** also 又作 **scour out** to form a hole by continuous movement over a long period〔长期不断地〕冲刷成〔洞〕: *Over the years, the stream had scoured out a round pool in the rock.* 溪水长年累月地在岩石上冲出了一个圆形水坑。—**scour** *n* [singular]

scour·er /'skaʊrə; 'skaʊərə/ *n* [C] a small ball of wire or rough plastic for cleaning cooking pots and pans 刷洗锅盘用的金属〔塑料〕团，百洁布

scourge[1] /skɜdʒ; skɜːdʒ/ *n* [C] **1** something that causes a lot of harm or suffering 祸根，祸害: [+of] *The scourge of apartheid has finally ended.* 种族隔离的祸害终于结束了。**2** a WHIP used to punish people in former times〔旧时用作刑具的〕鞭子

scourge[2] *v* [T] **1** to cause a lot of harm or suffering to a place or group of people 使遭受苦难，蹂躏: *a country scourged by disease and war* 饱受疾病和战火蹂躏的国家 **2** to hit someone with a whip as punishment in former times 鞭打〔旧时的一种刑罚〕

scouring pad /'·· ·/ *n* [C] a scourer 刷洗锅盘用的金属〔塑料〕团，百洁布

Scouse /skaus; skaʊs/ *n* [U] *BrE*【英】**1** the way of speaking that is typical of people from Liverpool 利物浦地区的方言 **2** a thick soup with meat, potatoes, and vegetables〔用肉、马铃薯、蔬菜等做的〕利物浦浓汤 —**Scouse** *adj*

Scous·er /'skausə; 'skaʊsə/ *n* [C] someone from Liverpool 利物浦人

scout[1] /skaut; skaʊt/ *n* [C] **1 a) the scouts** an organization for young boys that teaches them practical skills 童子军〔组织〕 **b)** also 又作 **boy scout** a boy who is a member of this organization 男童子军〔成员〕 **2** *AmE* also 又作 **girl scout** a girl who is a member of an organization for girls that teaches them practical skills【美】女童子军; GUIDE *BrE*【英】 **3** a soldier, plane etc that is sent to search the area in front of an army, get information about the enemy 侦察兵; 侦察机; 侦察艇: *He sent three scouts ahead to take a look at the bridge.* 他派遣三名侦察兵到前头侦察大桥的情况。**4** someone whose job is to look for good sports players, musicians etc in order to employ them 物色新秀者，人才发掘者〔尤指发掘运动员、音乐人才等〕，星探: *He was spotted by a scout at the age of 13.* 他在13岁时被星探发现。—see also 另见 TALENT SCOUT **5 a scout round/around** *BrE informal* a quick search of an area【英，非正式】搜索，到处寻找: *I'll have a scout round to see if I can find it.* 我要去四处找一下，看能否把它找出来。

scout[2] *v* **1** also 又作 **scout round/around** [I] to look for something in a particular area〔在某地区〕寻找: [+for] *I want you all to scout round for any wood you can find.* 我想要你们大家去尽量找点木柴回来。**2** also 又作 **scout out** [T] to examine a place or area in order to get information about it, especially in a military situation〔尤指军事上〕对〔某地〕进行侦察: *A group was sent off to scout out the area ahead.* 一队人被派去侦察前面的地区。**3** [T] *AmE* to find out about the abilities of sports players, musicians etc【美】弄清〔运动员、音乐人才等〕的才能

scout·ing /'skautɪŋ; 'skaʊtɪŋ/ *n* [U] the activities that scouts take part in 侦察活动; 童子军活动

scout·mas·ter /'skaut,mæstə; 'skaʊt,mɑːstə/ *n* [C] a man who is the leader of a group of scouts (SCOUT[1] (1a)) 童子军领队〔小队长〕

scowl[1] /skaul; skaʊl/ *v* [I+at] to look at someone in an angry way 怒视〔某人〕

scowl 怒视

scowl[2] *n* [C] an angry or disapproving expression on someone's face 怒容; 不悦之色

Scrab·ble /'skræbl; 'skræbəl/ *n* [U] *trademark* a game in which players try to make words from the separate letters they have【商标】〔用得到的若干字母组词的〕纵横拼字游戏

scrab·ble *v* [I always+adv+prep] to try to find something by feeling with your fingers, especially quickly among a lot of other things〔用手指〕扒找〔尤指在一堆物品中快速翻找〕: [+around/about etc] *She was scrabbling through her pockets for a cigarette.* 她用手在衣袋里摸索着找香烟。

scrag end /,· '·/ also 又作 **scrag** *n* [U] *BrE* the bony part of a sheep's neck, that is sometimes boiled for soup【英】〔有时用于熬汤的〕羊颈肉

scrag·gly /'skræglɪ; 'skrægəli/ *adj AmE informal* growing in a way that looks uneven and in bad condition【美，非正式】〔长得〕参差不齐的; 散乱的: *his scraggly unwashed hair* 他的又脏又乱的头发

scrag·gy /'skrægɪ; 'skrægi/ *adj* too thin and bony 骨瘦如柴的，皮包骨的: *scraggy wrists* 皮包骨的手腕

scram /skræm; skræm/ *v* [I usually in imperative 一般用于祈使句] *informal* to leave a place very quickly, especially so that you do not get caught【非正式】〔尤指为避免被抓住而〕迅速离开，跑开: *Scram, you two!* 快走开，你们两个!

scram·ble[1] /'skræmbl; 'skræmbəl/ *v*

1 ►CLIMB 攀爬◄ [I always+adv/prep] to climb up or over something with difficulty, using your hands to help you 爬，攀登: [+up/down/back etc] *We scrambled up a rocky slope.* 我们爬上一个岩石陡坡。

2 scramble to your feet to stand up quickly and awkwardly 狼狈地赶快爬起来: *He scrambled to his feet, blushing furiously.* 他狼狈地赶快站了起来，羞得满脸通红。

3 ►COMPETE 竞争◄ [I] to struggle or compete with other people to get or reach something 争夺，抢夺: [+for] *People were scrambling madly for shelter.* 人们发疯似地抢着奔向隐蔽所。

4 ►INFORMATION/MESSAGE 情报/消息◄ [T] *technical* to use special equipment to mix messages, radio signals etc into a different form, so that they cannot be understood by other people, especially an enemy【术语】加扰，扰乱〔用仪器把信息、无线电等加密使别人无法理解〕: *A magnetic field will scramble the information on a computer disk.* 磁场会扰乱储存在电脑磁盘上的信息。

5 scramble an egg to cook an egg by mixing the white and yellow parts together and heating it 炒蛋〔把蛋白和蛋黄搅拌后炒〕

6 scramble sb's brains *informal* to make someone unable to think clearly or reasonably【非正式】使某人头脑糊涂，使某人思维混乱: *This girl has taken enough drugs to completely scramble her brains.* 这个女孩吸了大量毒品，足以使她头脑一片混乱。

7 ▶AIRCRAFT 飞机◀ [I] *technical* if a military plane scrambles, it goes up into the air very quickly in order to escape or to attack an enemy【术语】〔军用飞机为逃跑或进攻敌人而〕紧急起飞

scramble² *n* **1** [singular] a difficult climb in which you have to use your hands to help you 攀爬, 爬行: *a rough scramble over boulders* 在巨石上艰难的攀爬 **2** [singular] a situation in which people compete with and push each other in order to get what they want〔互相推撞的〕争夺, 争抢: **[+for]** *a scramble for the best seats* 争抢最好的座位 | **a scramble to do sth** *a scramble to pick up the scattered coins* 争着去拾散落的硬币 **3** [singular] a situation in which something has to be done very quickly, with a lot of rushing around〔因赶任务出现的〕忙乱, 乱作一团: **mad scramble** *It was a mad scramble trying to get things ready in time.* 为了及时把东西准备好, 结果乱成了一团。**4** [C] a MOTORCYCLE race over rough ground 摩托车越野赛

scrambled egg /,.. '.'/ *n* [C,U] egg cooked in a pan after the white and yellow parts have been mixed together〔蛋黄和蛋白搅拌后的〕炒蛋

scram·bler /ˈskræmblɚ; ˈskræmblə/ *n* [C] a machine that mixes up a radio or telephone message so that it cannot be understood without special equipment 扰码器〔扰乱无线电、电话等信号, 使无特殊仪器者无法接收〕

scrap¹ /skræp; skræp/ *n*

1 ▶PAPER/CLOTH 纸/布◀ [C] a small piece of paper, cloth etc 小片, 小块; 碎屑: **[+of]** *He wrote his address on a scrap of paper and gave it to me.* 他把住址写在小纸片上交给了我。| *a quilt made out of scraps of old fabric* 用各种旧布片拼缀成的被子 —see picture on page A7 参见 A7 页图

2 ▶OLD OBJECTS 旧物◀ [U] materials or objects that are no longer used for the purpose they were made for, but can be used again in another way 废品, 废弃材料: *The car was eventually sold for scrap.* 那辆汽车最后被当作废铁卖掉了。| **scrap metal** (=metal from old cars, machines etc that is melted and used again) 废旧金属

3 ▶FOOD 食物◀ **scraps** [plural] pieces of food that are left after you have finished eating 吃剩的东西, 残羹剩饭: *They fed the dog on scraps.* 他们用吃剩的饭菜喂狗。

4 ▶INFORMATION 信息◀ [C] a small piece of information, truth etc〔消息、事实等的〕一点点, 点滴: **[+of]** *There wasn't a single scrap of evidence to connect him with the murder.* 没有丝毫证据说明他与这宗谋杀案有关。| *scraps of news* 零星的消息

5 not make a scrap of difference *informal* to not change a situation at all【非正式】〔对情况〕没有影响, 毫无作用: *Nothing I said made a scrap of difference.* 我说的话丝毫不起作用。

6 ▶FIGHT 打架◀ [C] *informal* a short fight or argument【非正式】争吵, 吵架; 打架: *The girls have scraps over their toys sometimes, but nothing serious.* 女孩子们有时会为了玩具争吵, 但不严重。

scrap² *v* **scrapped, scrapping 1** [T] to decide not to use a plan or system because it is not practical〔因不切实际而〕放弃, 抛弃〔计划、体系等〕: *We've decided to scrap the whole idea of renting a car.* 我们决定放弃租车的想法。**2** [T] to get rid of an old machine, vehicle etc, and use its parts in some other way 把〔旧机器、旧汽车等〕当作废料处理, 报废: *The navy's biggest aircraft carrier is being scrapped this year.* 海军最大的一艘航空母舰今年就要被当作废钢铁处理了。**3** [I] *informal* to have a short fight or argument【非正式】打架; 吵架

scrap·book /ˈskræpˌbʊk; ˈskræpbʊk/ *n* [C] a book with empty pages where you can stick pictures, newspaper articles, or other things you want to keep〔粘贴图片、剪报等的〕剪贴簿

scrape 刮除

scrape¹ /skrep; skreɪp/ *v* **1** [T] to remove something from a surface, using the edge of a knife, stick etc〔用小刀等〕刮除: *Scrape the carrots and slice them thinly.* 把这些胡萝卜刮皮并切成薄片。| **scrape sth away/off etc** *I tried to scrape some of the mud off my boots.* 我设法把靴子上的泥刮掉一些。| *We scraped away several layers of old varnish.* 我们把几层旧漆刮掉了。| **scrape sth clean** *The plates had all been scraped clean.* 这些盘子都已经擦干净了。**2** [I always+adv/prep,T] to rub against a rough surface in a way that causes slight damage or injury, or to make something do this (使) 摩擦, 擦伤; 刮坏: **[+on/against etc]** *The car exhaust was hanging down and scraping the ground.* 汽车的排气管垂了下来, 擦着了地面。| **scrape sth on/against etc** *I scraped my knee painfully on the concrete.* 我的膝盖在水泥地上擦得很痛。**3** [I,T] to make an unpleasant noise by rubbing roughly against a surface (使) 乱擦发出刺耳声: *Chairs scraped loudly as they stood up.* 他们站起来时椅子发出刺耳的响声。| **scrape (sth) on/down/against etc** *Her fingernails scraped down the blackboard.* 她的指甲在黑板上刮出了声音。**4 scrape home** *especially BrE* to win a race, election, or competition by a very small amount【尤英】〔在赛跑、选举、竞赛中〕险胜: *Johnson scraped home just milliseconds ahead of Lewis.* 约翰逊仅以千分之几秒领先刘易斯而获胜。**5 scrape a hole** to make a hole or hollow place in the ground by rubbing the surface〔在地上〕挖出窟窿, 刨成一个洞 **6 scrape (the bottom of) the barrel** *informal* to have to use something even though it is not very good because there is nothing better available【非正式】〔因为没有更好的选择而〕勉强使用某物; 把标准降到最低 —see also 另见 **bow and scrape** (BOW¹ (4)), **pinch and scrape** (PINCH¹ (5)), **scrape/scratch a living** (LIVING² (1))

scrape by *phr v* [I] **1** to have just enough money to live 收入仅够维持生活, 勉强糊口: *They just managed to scrape by on Fred's tiny salary.* 他们仅靠弗雷德的微薄工资勉强度日。**2** *especially AmE* to only just succeed in passing an examination or dealing with a difficult situation【尤美】勉强通过 (考试); 勉强克服 (困难)

scrape in/into *phr v* [I,T] to only just succeed in getting a job, place at university, position in government etc 勉强通过 (考试); 勉强获得 (一份工作或政府职位): *He just scraped into college.* 他勉强上了大学。| *Labour scraped in by a small majority.* 工党以微弱的优势上台执政。

scrape through *phr v* [I,T] to only just succeed in passing an examination or dealing with a difficult situation 勉强通过 (考试); 勉强克服 (困难): *Dani just scraped through her exams.* 丹妮勉强通过了考试。

scrape sth ↔ **together/up** *phr v* [T] to get enough money for a particular purpose, when this is difficult〔为某目的〕勉强筹集; 凑足〔款项〕: *She scraped together the last of her savings to buy the cottage.* 她动用了全部积蓄才凑够钱买那所小屋。

scrape² *n* **1** [singular] the unpleasant noise made when one surface rubs roughly against another 刮擦声: *We heard the scrape of a chair downstairs and then footsteps.* 我们听到楼下拖动椅子的声音, 接着是脚步声。**2** [C] a situation that is difficult or slightly dangerous 困境, 窘境; 麻烦: *He got himself into all sorts of scrapes as a boy.* 他在童年时惹出过各种麻烦事。**3** [C] a mark or slight injury caused by rubbing against a rough surface 擦伤, 擦痕: *We came away from the accident with only a few cuts and scrapes.* 我们在事故中安全脱险, 只是有几处划破和擦伤。

scrap·er /ˈskrepɚ; ˈskreɪpə/ *n* [C] a tool used to remove something from a surface by rubbing 刮削用具〈如刮刀、刮板等〉: *a paint scraper* 刮漆刀

scrap·heap /ˈskræpˌhip; ˈskræphiːp/ *n* **1 throw sb/sth on the scrapheap** *informal* to get rid of someone or something because you no longer think they are useful, in a way that seems unfair【非正式】把某人/某物扔到废物堆里, 抛弃某人/某物: *Twenty years of loyal service and they're throwing him on the scrapheap!* 他忠心耿耿地服务了 20 年, 而他们准备把他一脚踢开! **2** [C] a pile of unwanted things, especially pieces of metal 废料堆〔尤指废金属堆〕

scra·pie /ˈskrepɪ; ˈskreɪpi/ *n* [U] a serious disease that sheep get 痒病〔绵羊患的一种严重疾病〕

scrap·ings /ˈskrepɪŋz; ˈskreɪpɪŋz/ *n* [plural] small pieces that have been scraped from a surface 刮屑, 削片, 刮下的碎屑

scrap pa·per /'. ,../ *n* [U] *BrE* paper, often paper that has already been used on one side, that you use for making notes, lists etc【英】废纸〔常指一面已用过, 另一面可用于记琐事的废纸〕; SCRATCH PAPER *AmE*【美】

scrap·ple /ˈskræpl; ˈskræpl/ *n* [U] *AmE* food made from pieces of meat mixed together with CORNMEAL【美】碎肉玉米饼

scrap·py /ˈskræpɪ; ˈskræpi/ *adj* **1** untidy or badly organ-ized 不整洁的; 散乱的, 无条理的: *a scrappy, badly written report* 一篇杂乱无章、写得很差的报告 | *a scrappy bit of paper* 一些零碎的废纸 **2** *AmE informal* always wanting to argue or fight【美, 非正式】好争斗的; 爱吵架的

scratch[1] /skrætʃ; skrætʃ/ *v*

scratch 挠, 轻抓

1 ►RUB YOUR SKIN 挠皮肤◄ [I, T] to rub your skin with your nails, especially because it itches (ITCH[1] (1))〔用指甲〕挠, 搔, 轻抓: *Try not to scratch those mosquito bites.* 尽量别挠那些蚊子叮起的包。

2 ►MAKE A MARK 划痕◄ [T] to rub something sharp or rough against a hard surface so that it makes a thin mark〔用尖利或粗糙的东西〕刮出〔痕迹〕, 划伤: *Mind you don't scratch the table with those scissors!* 小心别用剪刀划坏桌面!

3 ►MAKE A CUT 割破◄ [I,T] to make a small cut by pulling something sharp against someone's skin〔利器把皮肤〕划伤, 割破: *I scratched my hand on a blackberry bush.* 我的手被黑莓树丛划破了。| *Be careful. That cat scratches.* 小心, 那只猫会抓伤人的。

4 ►MAKE A NOISE 发出声音◄ [I always+adv/prep] to make a noise by rubbing something with a sharp or pointed object〔用尖利物〕刮擦出声音: *The dog kept scratching at the door to be let in.* 狗在不断地抓门想进屋。

5 ►REMOVE STH 除去某物◄ [T always+adv/prep] to remove something from a surface by rubbing it with something sharp 刮掉, 划掉: **scratch sth off/away etc** *I scratched away a little of the paint with my fingernail.* 我用指甲把一点油漆刮掉了。

6 ►STOP PLANNING 停止计划◄ [T] to stop planning to do something because it is no longer possible or practical〔因不可能或不切实际而〕取消〔计划等〕: *I guess we can scratch that idea.* 我想我们可以打消那个念头。

7 scratch the surface to deal with only a very small part of a subject 仅触及问题的表面: *In this essay I can only hope to scratch the surface of the topic.* 在这篇文章里, 我只希望能对这个问题做个粗浅的探讨。

8 scratch your head *informal* to think hard about a difficult question or problem【非正式】动脑筋,〔对难题〕苦思冥想: *The last question really had us scratching our heads.* 最后那个问题真让我们伤脑筋。

9 ►REMOVE FROM RACE 取消比赛资格◄ [I,T] to remove someone from a race or competition before it begins (令…)退出比赛

10 you scratch my back, I'll scratch yours *spoken* used to say that you will help someone if they agree to help you【口】你帮我, 我也帮你 —see also 另见 **scrape/scratch a living** (LIVING[2] (1))

scratch sth ↔ **out** *phr v* [T] to draw a line through a word, in order to remove it 划掉〔文字〕, 删掉: *Philippa's name had been scratched out.* 菲莉帕的名字被划掉了。

scratch[2] *n*

1 ►MARK OR CUT 痕迹或破痕◄ [C] a thin mark or cut on the surface of something or on someone's skin〔物件或皮肤上的〕划痕, 刮痕, 划伤: *a scratch on the car door* 车门上的刮痕

2 from scratch if you do or start something from scratch, you begin it without using anything that existed or was prepared before 从零开始, 从头开始, 白手起家: *It was years since I'd learnt any German, and I really had to start again from scratch.* 多年前我学过一点德语, 现在只得再从头学起。

3 not come/be up to scratch to not be good enough for a particular standard 达不到标准: *His schoolwork really hasn't been up to scratch lately.* 他近来的功课确实达不到标准。

4 ►SOUND 声音◄ [C] a sound made by something sharp or rough being rubbed on a hard surface〔利器在硬物上刮的〕刮擦声: *I could hear the scratch of the dog's claws on the floor.* 我能听到狗爪子抓地板的声音。

5 have a scratch to rub part of your body with your nails〔用指甲在身上〕抓挠

6 it's only/just a scratch *spoken* used to say that you are not seriously hurt or injured【口】只是擦破一点皮罢了〔用以表示伤势不重〕

7 without a scratch if you escape from a dangerous situation without a scratch, you are not injured at all 安然无恙, 安然脱险

8 ►MUSIC 音乐◄ [U] a type of popular music produced by stopping a record while it is playing and moving it with your hands to make a sound 刮擦乐〔一种流行音乐, 在唱片播放时用手中断唱片并转动它使其发出声音〕

scratch[3] *adj* [no comparative 无比较级] **1** a scratch team, game, side etc is put together in a hurry, using anyone that is available〔球队等〕仓促拼凑的, 匆匆组成的 **2** a scratch player in a sport does not have a HANDICAP (=officially arranged disadvantage)〔体育比赛〕无让步优待的, 平等的

scratch·ings /ˈskrætʃɪŋz; ˈskrætʃɪŋz/ *n* [plural] *BrE* small pieces of pig's skin that have been cooked in hot fat and are eaten cold【英】炸猪皮片; PORK RINDS *AmE*【美】

scratch·pad /ˈskrætʃˌpæd; ˈskrætʃpæd/ *n* [C] *especially AmE* several sheets of cheap paper joined together at the top or side, used for writing notes or lists【尤美】拍纸簿

scratch pa·per /ˈ· ,··/ *n* [U] *AmE* paper, often paper that has already been used on one side, that you use for making notes, lists etc【美】便条纸〔常指一面已用过、另一面可用于记琐事的废纸〕; SCRAP PAPER *BrE*【英】

scratch test /ˈ· ·/ *n* [C] a medical test that involves cutting someone's skin slightly and putting a substance on it to see how their body reacts 划痕试验〔指在皮肤上划破一点后施用某种物质以观察身体的反应〕

scratch·y /ˈskrætʃɪ; ˈskrætʃi/ *adj* **1** scratchy clothes or materials feel rough and uncomfortable〔衣物等〕粗糙的, 扎人的, 使皮肤发痒的 **2** a scratchy record makes a lot of unpleasant noises because it is old or damaged〔旧唱片、录音带等〕发沙沙声的 —**scratchiness** *n* [U]

scrawl[1] /skrɔl; skrɔːl/ *v* [T] to write in a careless and untidy way, so that your words are not easy to read 潦草地写, 乱涂乱画

scrawl[2] *n* [singular] something written in an untidy careless way, or an untidy careless way of writing 潦草写成的东西; 潦草的笔迹

scraw·ny /ˈskrɔnɪ; ˈskrɔːni/ *adj* thin, unattractive, and looking weak 瘦弱的, 皮包骨的: *a scrawny kid in jeans and a T-shirt* 穿着牛仔裤和T恤衫的瘦弱孩子

scream[1] /skrim; skriːm/ *v* **1** [I] to make a loud high noise with your voice because you are hurt, frightened, excited etc〔因疼痛、惊恐、兴奋等〕尖声大叫: *Shots rang out, and people started screaming.* 枪声响起, 人们尖声大叫起来。| *a screaming baby* 尖声哭叫的婴儿 | **[+with/in]** *The woman lay there, screaming with pain.* 那个女人躺在那儿, 痛得直尖叫。| **scream with laughter** (=laugh very loudly in a high voice) 尖声大笑 **2** also 又作 **scream out** [I,T] to shout something in a very loud high voice because you are angry or frightened〔因愤怒或恐惧而〕高声喊叫: *"Get out!" she screamed.* "出去!"她高声叫道。| **[+for]** *I screamed for help.* 我高声呼救。| **[+at]** *Calm down and stop screaming at me!* 冷静点, 不要对我大声嚷嚷! | **scream insults/abuse etc** *Lola screamed insults at him as he left.* 在他离开时洛拉大声辱骂他。**3** [I] to make a very loud high noise 发出尖锐的叫声: *The police car approached, its siren screaming.* 警车驶近, 警报器尖声呼啸着。

scream (out) at sb *phr v* [I] *informal* if something such as a very bright colour or a mistake screams at you, it is very noticeable and annoying【非正式】〔颜色〕刺眼;〔错误〕触目惊心

scream[2] *n* [C] **1** a loud high sound made with your voice because you are very frightened, angry, hurt, or excited〔因恐惧、痛苦或兴奋而发出的〕尖叫声: *Her screams could be heard all down the block.* 整个街区都能听到她的尖叫声。| **scream of laughter/terror etc** *There were screams of excitement when he finally walked on stage.* 当他终于登台时, 观众报以激动的尖叫声。| **let out a scream** *He let out a scream of terror.* 他发出惊恐的尖叫声。**2** a very loud high sound 大而尖的声音, 尖锐刺耳的声音: *The scream of the jet taking off drowned Ryan's response.* 喷气式飞机起飞时的呼啸声淹没了瑞安的回答。**3 be a scream** *informal* used to describe someone or something that is very funny【非正式】是非常滑稽的人[事物]: *We went to the party dressed as twins. It was a scream!* 我们打扮成双胞胎去参加聚会, 真是滑稽!

scream·ing·ly /ˈskrimɪŋlɪ; ˈskriːmɪŋli/ *adv* **screamingly funny** extremely funny 极其滑稽可笑地

scree /skri; skriː/ *n* [C] an area of small loose broken rocks on the side of a mountain 山坡上的碎石地带, 岩屑堆: *a scree slope* 碎石斜坡 —see picture on page A12 参见 A12 页图

screech /skritʃ; skriːtʃ/ *v* **1** [I,T] to make a very unpleasant, high noise with your voice, especially because you are angry〔因生气等〕尖叫, 尖声喊叫: **[+at]** *She screeched at me to take off my muddy shoes.* 她尖声地叫我脱掉粘满泥污的鞋子。**2** [I] if a vehicle or its wheels screech, they make a high loud unpleasant noise〔车辆或轮子〕发出尖锐刺耳声: *The train's wheels screeched and clattered as it drew out of the station.* 火车开出车站时, 轮子发出尖锐刺耳的声音。**3 screech to a halt/stop/**

S

standstill if a vehicle screeches to a halt, it stops very suddenly, so that the wheels make a loud unpleasant noise〔车辆〕嘎的一声突然停住 —**screech** *n* [singular]: *a screech of tires* 轮胎发出的刺耳声音

screen¹ /skrin; skriːn/ *n*

1 ▶TELEVISION/COMPUTER 电视机/电脑◀ [C] the flat glass part of a television or computer 屏幕, 萤光屏: *This popular show will be back on your screens in the autumn.* 这个受欢迎的节目将在秋天再次和大家见面。| **on screen** (=on a computer screen) 在电脑屏幕上 *It's easy to change the text on screen before printing it.* 打印前在屏幕上作文字修改是很容易的。

2 ▶CINEMA 电影◀ **a)** [C] the large white surface that pictures are shown on in a cinema 银幕, 屏幕 **b)** [singular,U] films in general 电影〔总称〕: *The play was adapted for the screen.* 这部戏剧被改编成电影了。

3 ▶MOVABLE WALL 活动的墙◀ [C] a kind of wall that can be moved around, used to divide one part of a room from another 屏风: *The nurse put a screen around my bed.* 护士围着我的床竖起一道屏风。

4 ▶HIDE OR PROTECT 隐藏或保护◀ [C usually singular 一般用单数] something or someone that protects or hides someone or something else 掩蔽物, 屏障: *We planted these bushes as a screen, as the shed is so ugly.* 我们种这些灌木丛作屏障, 因为工具房太难看了。| *It turned out that the used car business was just a screen for his drug-dealing activities.* 原来他做旧车买卖只是为了掩护他的贩毒活动。

5 ▶DOOR/WINDOW 门/窗◀ [C] a wire net put in front of a window or door that allows air into the house but keeps insects out〔防蚊虫进入的〕纱门, 纱窗

6 ▶CHURCH 教堂◀ [C] a decorative wall in some churches 装饰性围屏

7 ▶SPORTS 体育运动◀ [C] *AmE* a player or group of players in a game who protect the player who has the ball【美】掩护〔动作〕—see also 另见 SMOKESCREEN, SUNSCREEN

screen² *v* [T]

1 ▶TEST FOR ILLNESS 检查疾病◀ to do tests on a lot of people to find out whether they have a particular illness 给〔很多人〕作检查〔以确定是否患有某种疾病〕: *Because of the higher risks, we try to screen all women over 50.* 50岁以上的妇女由于发病率较高, 我们尽量对她们进行普查。| **screen sb for** *We were all screened for hepatitis.* 我们都接受检查以确定是否患有肝炎。

2 ▶HIDE STH 隐藏某物◀ to hide or protect something by putting something in front of it〔在前面放置某物以〕隐藏, 遮蔽, 隐蔽: [+off] *A large hat screened her face.* 一顶大帽子遮住了她的脸。| *Part of the room was screened off as a reception area.* 房间的一部分被隔开作接待室用。| **screen sth (off) from** *The house is screened from the road by a row of trees.* 一排树木把那所房子和大路分隔开来。

3 ▶TEST EMPLOYEES 考查雇员◀ to examine or test people to make sure that they will be loyal to your company, organization etc〔为确保雇员的忠诚而进行〕审查, 甄别: *All applicants are screened for security.* 对所有申请人都要审查以确保安全。

4 ▶PROTECT SB 庇护某人◀ to protect someone who is involved in dishonest or illegal activities 包庇, 掩护, 袒护〔违法者〕: *He had been screening his business partner during the fraud investigation.* 在那宗诈骗案的调查中, 他一直在包庇他的生意合伙人。

5 ▶TELEVISION 电视◀ to show a film or television programme 放映〔影片〕; 播放〔电视节目〕

screen sth ↔ **out** *phr v* [T] **1** to prevent something harmful from entering or passing through 把〔有害东西〕挡住, 把…隔开: *Sun lotions screen out damaging ultraviolet light.* 防晒油把有害的紫外线挡住。**2** to decide that someone or something is not suitable for a job, position etc 剔除, 清除〔不符合条件者〕

Screen Ac·tors' Guild, the /ˈ· · ·, ·/ the full name of the SAG【美】银幕演员协会〔SAG的全称〕

screen door /ˈ· ·, ·/ *n* [C] *AmE* a door outside the main door, that will let air in but keep insects out【美】〔防止蚊虫等进入的〕纱门

screen·ing /ˈskrinɪŋ; ˈskriːnɪŋ/ *n* **1** [C,U] the showing of a film or television programme 放映电影, 播放电视节目: *a screening of Spielberg's new movie* 放映斯皮尔伯格的新影片 **2** [U] tests done to make sure that someone does not have a particular disease 检查〔以确定未患某种病〕: *screening for breast cancer* 检查是否患乳腺癌 **3** [U] tests or checks done to make sure that someone or something is suitable for a particular purpose 甄别, 审查〔是否符合要求〕

screen·play /ˈskrinˌple; ˈskriːnpleɪ/ *n* [C] a story written for film or television 电影[电视]剧本: *her first screenplay, an adaptation of Austen's 'Sense and Sensibility'* 她的第一个电影剧本改编自奥斯汀的《理智与情感》

screen print·ing /ˈ· , · ·/ *n* [U] a way of printing pictures by pushing paint or ink through a specially prepared cloth onto paper〔图画的〕丝网印刷法

screen test /ˈ· , ·/ *n* [C] an occasion when someone is filmed while performing, in order to see if they are suitable to act in a film 试镜头〔以挑选电影演员〕

screen·writ·er /ˈskrinˌraɪtɚ; ˈskriːnˌraɪtə/ *n* [C] someone who writes plays for film or television 影视剧本作家, 编剧

screws 带螺纹的物体

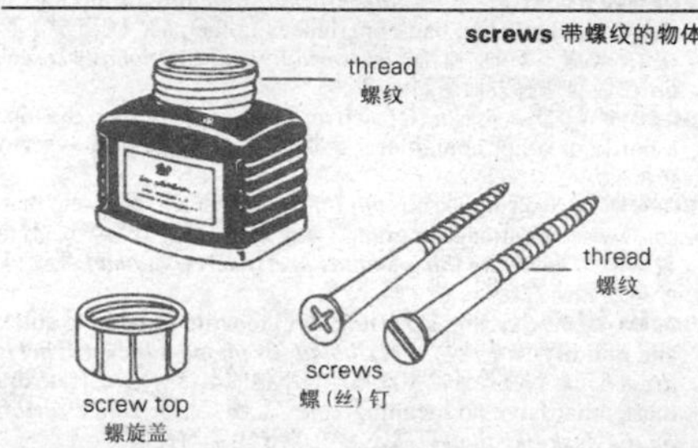

screw¹ /skru; skruː/ *n* **1** [C] a thin pointed piece of metal that you push and turn in order to fasten pieces of metal or wood together 螺丝, 螺(丝)钉: *Tighten the screws on the plug.* 把插座上的螺丝拧紧。**2** [C] *slang taboo* an act of having sex【俚, 讳】性交 **3 have a screw loose** *informal often humorous* to be slightly crazy【非正式, 常幽默】有点疯疯癫癫, 头脑有些不正常 **4 put/tighten the screws on sb** *informal* to force someone to do something by threatening them【非正式】威逼某人做某事 **5** [C] *BrE slang* a word for a prison officer, used especially by prisoners【英俚】监狱看守人〔尤为囚犯用语〕**6 a screw of tobacco/tea etc** *BrE old-fashioned* a small amount of tobacco, tea etc in a twisted paper packet【英, 过时】一小包烟草/茶叶等

screw² *v* **1** [T always+adv/prep] to fasten one object to another using a screw〔用螺丝〕将…固定: **screw sth into/onto/to sth** *Screw the socket into the wall.* 用螺丝把插座固定在墙上。| *The bar stools were screwed to the floor.* 酒吧的凳子是被螺钉固定在地板上的。**2** [T always+adv/prep] to fasten or close something by turning it until it cannot be turned anymore 拧紧, 旋紧: **screw sth on/together etc** *Don't forget to screw the cap back onto the toothpaste.* 不要忘记拧好牙膏的盖子。**3** [I,T] *taboo* to have sex with someone【讳】与〔某人〕发生性关系 **4 screw you/him/that etc** *spoken taboo* used to show that you are very angry with someone【口, 讳】让你/他/那等见鬼去〔对某人表示愤怒〕: *"Screw you!" he yelled.* "去你的!"他吼道。**5** [T always+adv/prep] to twist paper or cloth into a small round shape 把〔纸或布〕拧成小卷: **screw sth (up) into sth** *She screwed the letter up into a ball and threw it in the bin.* 她把信揉成一团扔进垃圾桶里。**6** [T often passive 常用被动态] *informal* to cheat someone or treat them in a dishonest way, especially to get money from them【非正式】欺骗〔尤指骗钱〕: *They really screwed you in that nightclub, charging £10 for a drink.* 他们的那个夜总会一杯饮料要收费10英镑, 这完全是诈骗。| **screw sb for** *They screwed us for $60 in the end.* 他们最后敲诈了我们60美元。—see also 另见 **have your head screwed on (straight)** (HEAD¹ (28))

screw around *phr v* [I] *taboo* to have sex with a lot of different people【讳】到处乱搞男女关系, 乱交

screw up *phr v* **1 screw your eyes/face up** to move the muscles in your face in a way that makes your eyes seem narrow 眯紧眼睛/扭歪脸: *He screwed up his eyes against the bright light.* 他对着强光眯起眼睛。**2** [I] *informal* to make a bad mistake or do something very stupid【非正式】犯大错, 做蠢事: *I really screwed up, didn't I?* 我的确做了蠢事, 不是吗? **3** [T **screw** sth ↔ **up**] *informal* to spoil something such as a plan, by doing something stupid【非正式】把〔计划等〕搞糟, 弄糟: *Breaking my ankle really screwed up our holiday plans!* 我摔断了脚踝, 完全打乱了我们的度假计划! **4** [T **screw** sb ↔ **up**] *informal* to make someone feel very unhappy, confused, or anxious, especially for a long time【非正式】〔尤指长时间〕使〔某人〕很不愉快[为难, 焦虑]: *It really screwed her up when her mother died.* 她母亲去世时, 她真是非常难过。—see also 另见 SCREWED UP **5 screw up your courage** to try to be brave enough to do something

you are very nervous about 鼓起勇气: *I screwed up my courage and went over to talk to her.* 我鼓起勇气走过去对她说话。

screw·ball /ˋskruˏbɔl; ˈskruːbɔːl/ *n* [C] *informal especially AmE* someone who seems very strange or crazy【非正式, 尤美】古怪的人; 疯子

screw·driv·er /ˋskruˏdraɪvɚ; ˈskruːˏdraɪvə/ *n* [C] **1** a tool with a narrow blade at one end that you use for turning screws 螺丝刀, 螺丝起子, 改锥 —see picture at 参见 TOOL[1] 图 **2** an alcoholic drink made from VODKA and orange juice 伏特加橙汁鸡尾酒

screwed up /ˏ· ˈ·◂/ *adj informal* unhappy or anxious because you have had bad experiences in the past【非正式】不愉快的, 焦虑不安的, 神经质的: *sexually and emotionally screwed up* 在性和情感方面受到困扰

screw top /ˏ· ˈ·◂/ *n* [C] a cover that you twist onto the top of a bottle or other container〔容器的〕螺旋盖, 螺旋塞 —**screw-top** *adj*

screw·y /ˋskruɪ; ˈskruːi/ *adj informal* an idea, plan, etc that is screwy seems strange or crazy【非正式】〔意见、计划等〕古怪的, 荒谬的: *The whole thing sounds pretty screwy to me!* 我觉得整个事情相当古怪!

scrib·ble[1] /ˋskrɪbḷ; ˈskrɪbəl/ *v* **1** [T] to write something quickly and untidily 潦草地写: *I scribbled his phone number in my address book.* 我在地址簿上潦草地写下他的电话号码。**2** [I] to draw marks that have no meaning 乱涂, 乱画, 乱写: *Don't scribble on the desk like that!* 不要这样在桌子上乱写乱画!

scribble[2] *n* **1** [U] also 又作 **scribbles** meaningless marks or pictures, especially done by children〔尤指小孩的〕乱涂的无意义的东西, 涂鸦 **2** [singular,U] untidy writing that is difficult to read 潦草的字

scrib·bler /ˋskrɪblɚ; ˈskrɪbələ/ *n* [C] *informal* a writer, especially an unimportant one【非正式】作家〔尤指无足轻重者〕

scribe /skraɪb; skraɪb/ *n* [C] someone employed to copy things in writing, especially before printing was invented〔尤指在印刷术发明之前的〕抄写员

scrim·mage /ˋskrɪmɪdʒ; ˈskrɪmɪdʒ/ *n* **1** [C] *informal* a fight【非正式】扭打, 打架 **2** [U] a practice game of football, BASKETBALL etc〔足球、篮球等的〕练习比赛, 队内分组比赛

scrimp /skrɪmp; skrɪmp/ *v* [I] to try to save as much money as you can even though you have very little 尽力攒钱, 尽量节省: **scrimp and save** *We had to scrimp and save to pay for the holiday.* 我们得拼命节省才能攒下度假的钱。

scrip /skrɪp; skrɪp/ *n* [U] an official piece of paper, especially a SHARE that is instead of money or a DIVIDEND 代股息的股份; 临时凭证: *scrip dividend* 股息凭证 | *scrip issue* 红股发行

script /skrɪpt; skrɪpt/ *n* **1** [C] the written form of a speech,play, film etc〔演讲的〕原稿, 讲稿; 戏剧[电影]剧本: *Galton and Simpson wrote some excellent comedy scripts.* 高尔顿和辛普森写了一些精彩的喜剧脚本。**2** [C,U] the set of letters used in writing a language; ALPHABET〔一种语言的〕全套字母, 字母表: *Arabic script* 阿拉伯语字母表 **3** [C] *BrE* a piece of work written by a student in an examination【英】〔考生的〕笔试答卷, 考卷 **4** [singular,U] *formal* writing done by hand, especially with the letters of the words joined【正式】笔迹, 手迹; 〔尤指〕英语中字母连写的手写体

script·ed /ˋskrɪptɪd; ˈskrɪptɪ̣d/ *adj* a speech or broadcast that is scripted has been written down before it is read〔演讲、广播〕照原稿宣读[广播]的

scrip·tur·al /ˋskrɪptʃərəl; ˈskrɪptʃərəl/ *adj* connected with or based on the Bible 根据[源出]《圣经》的

scrip·ture /ˋskrɪptʃɚ; ˈskrɪptʃə/ *n* **1** also 又作 **the (Holy) Scriptures** [U] the Bible《圣经》**2** [C,U] the holy books of a particular religion〔某一宗教的〕经文, 经典, 圣书: *Buddhist scriptures* 佛经 **3** [U] *old-fashioned* the study of the Bible, taught as a school subject【过时】〔学校课程中的〕《圣经》课

script·writ·er /ˋskrɪptˏraɪtɚ; ˈskrɪptˏraɪtə/ *n* [C] someone who writes SCRIPTS for films, television etc〔电影、电视等的〕剧本作者, 剧作家

scrof·u·la /ˋskrɔfjələ; ˈskrɒfjʊ̣lə/ *n* [U] a disease that makes the organs in your neck swell up 颈淋巴结结核, 瘰疬 —**scrofulous** *adj*

scroll[1] /skrol; skrəʊl/ *n* [C] **1** a long piece of paper that can be rolled up, and is used as an official document〔用于写正式文件的〕纸卷, 卷轴 **2** a decoration shaped like a roll of paper 涡卷形装饰

scroll[2] *v* [I,T] to move information on a computer screen up or down so that you can read it〔在电脑屏幕上〕将信息上下移动[滚动, 卷动]〔以便阅读〕: **[+up/down]** *Could you scroll down a few lines?* 请你往下移几行好吗?

scroll·work /ˋskrolˏwɝk; ˈskrəʊlwɜːk/ *n* [U] *technical* decoration in the shape of scrolls【术语】涡卷形装饰

scrooge /skrudʒ; skruːdʒ/ *n* [C] *informal* someone who hates spending money【非正式】吝啬鬼, 守财奴: *My landlord's a real scrooge.* 我的房东是个十足的吝啬鬼。

scro·tum /ˋskrotəm; ˈskrəʊtəm/ *n plural* **scrota** /-tə; -tə/ *or* **scrotums** [C] the bag of flesh that contains the TESTICLES of men and male animals 阴囊

scrounge[1] /skraʊndʒ; skraʊndʒ/ *v* [I,T] *informal* to get money or something you want by asking other people for it rather than by paying for it yourself【非正式】乞讨, 索取: **scrounge (sth) off/from sb** *I managed to scrounge some money off my dad.* 我设法从爸爸那儿要到了一点钱。—**scrounger** *n* [C]

scrounge[2] *n* **be on the scrounge** *BrE informal* to be trying to get money or things you want by asking other people for them【英, 非正式】向人伸手索要钱[物], 在索取钱物

scrub[1] /skrʌb; skrʌb/ *v* **1** [I,T] to rub something hard, especially with a stiff brush in order to clean it〔尤指用硬刷子〕擦洗, 擦净: *She was down on her hands and knees scrubbing the floor.* 她在趴着擦地板。| **[+at]** *Tom scrubbed at the stain but it wouldn't come out.* 汤姆擦洗污迹, 但是擦不掉。—see picture at 参见 CLEAN[2] 图 **2** [T] *informal* to decide not to do something that you had planned【非正式】取消〔计划等〕: *We had to scrub our plans for a party.* 我们不得不取消开晚会的计划。

scrub sth ↔ **out** *phr v* [T] to clean the inside of a place or object thoroughly 彻底擦洗〔某物内部〕: *Prisoners must scrub their cells out once a week.* 囚犯们每星期必须把牢房彻底擦洗一次。

scrub up *phr v* [I] to wash your hands and arms before doing a medical operation〔医生〕在手术前刷洗双手和手臂

scrub[2] *n* **1** [U] low bushes and trees that grow in very dry soil 矮树丛, 灌木丛 **2 give sth a scrub** *especially BrE* to clean something by rubbing it hard【尤英】把某物好好擦洗一番

scrub·ber /ˋskrʌbɚ; ˈskrʌbə/ *n* [C] **1** *BrE* an offensive word for PROSTITUTE (=a woman who has sex for money)【英】妓女, 卖淫妇〔冒犯用词〕**2** a plastic or metal object you use to clean pans〔塑料或金属制的〕刷子

scrubbing brush /ˈ·· ˏ/ *especially BrE*【尤英】, **scrub brush** /ˈ· ˏ/ *AmE*【美】—*n* [C] a stiff brush that you use for cleaning things 硬毛刷, 板刷 —see picture at 参见 BRUSH[1] 图

scrub·by /ˋskrʌbɪ; ˈskrʌbi/ *adj* **1** covered by low bushes 长满矮树丛的: *scrubby terrain* 灌木丛生的地带 **2** *informal* looking dirty and untidy【非正式】不整洁的, 脏乱的: *a scrubby schoolboy* 邋遢的小男生

scrub·land /ˋskrʌblənd; ˈskrʌblənd/ *n* [U] land that is covered with low bushes 灌木丛林地

Scrubs, The /skrʌbs; skrʌbs/ an informal name for Wormwood Scrubs prison 斯各拉伯斯监狱〔Wormwood Scrubs 监狱的非正式名称〕

scruff /skrʌf; skrʌf/ *n* **1 by the scruff of the neck** if you hold a person or animal by the scruff of their neck, you hold the flesh, fur, or clothes at the back of the neck 抓住〔动物的〕颈背; 抓住〔人的〕衣领 **2** [C] *BrE informal* someone who looks untidy or dirty【英, 非正式】不整洁的人, 肮脏的人

scruf·fy /ˋskrʌfɪ; ˈskrʌfi/ *adj* dirty and untidy 邋遢的, 不整洁的: *a scruffy old pair of jeans* 一条肮脏的旧牛仔裤 —**scruffily** *adv* —**scruffiness** *n* [U]

scrum[1] /skrʌm; skrʌm/ *n* **1** [C] a particular arrangement of players in the game of RUGBY 并列争球〔橄榄球赛中球员的一种队形排列〕**2** [singular] *BrE informal* a crowd of people who are all pushing each other to try and get something【英, 非正式】互相推挤着争夺某物的人群: *There was the usual scrum for tickets when the box office opened.* 售票处一开门, 照例出现了互相推挤抢先购票的混乱场面。

scrum[2] *v*

scrum down *phr v* [I] to form a scrum during a game of RUGBY〔橄榄球赛的〕并列争球, 混战

scrum-half /ˏskrʌmˋhæf; ˏskrʌmˈhɑːf/ *n* [C] a player in RUGBY who has to put the ball into the SCRUM[1] (1)〔橄榄球赛中的〕争球前卫

scrum·mage /ˋskrʌmɪdʒ; ˈskrʌmɪdʒ/ *n* [C] a SCRUM[1] (1) 并列争球〔橄榄球赛中球员的一种队形排列〕

scrump /skrʌmp; skrʌmp/ *v* [T] *BrE old-fashioned* to steal fruit, especially apples, from trees【英, 过时】偷摘〔水果, 尤指苹果〕

scrump·tious /ˋskrʌmpʃəs; ˈskrʌmpʃəs/ *adj informal* food that is scrumptious tastes very good【非正式】〔食物〕美味的, 可口的, 顶呱呱的: *a scrumptious chocolate dessert* 美味可口的巧克力甜食

scrum·py /ˈskrʌmpɪ; ˈskrʌmpi/ *n* [U] *BrE* a strong alcoholic drink made from apples【英】烈性苹果酒

scrunch /skrʌntʃ; skrʌntʃ/ *v* [I] *informal* if stones or other objects scrunch under your feet, they make a noisy sound when you walk on them【非正式】〔脚踩碎石等时〕发出咯吱声: *The pebbles scrunched as we walked along the beach.* 我们在海滩漫步时, 脚下的砾石咯吱咯吱地直响。

scrunch sth ↔ **up** *phr v* [T] to crush and twist something into a small round shape 把…揉成一团: *I scrunched up the letter and threw it in the bin.* 我把信揉成一团扔进垃圾桶。

scru·ple¹ /ˈskrupl; ˈskruːpəl/ *n* [C usually plural 一般用复数] a belief about right and wrong that prevents you from doing something bad 顾忌, 顾虑: *Atkins was a ruthless man with few moral scruples.* 阿特金斯这个人残酷无情, 对什么道德良心满不在乎。| **without scruple** (=without caring about the effects your actions may have on other people) 毫无顾忌 *They made thousands of families homeless without scruple.* 他们肆无忌惮地使成千上万个家庭流离失所。

scruple² *v* **not scruple to do sth** *literary* to be willing to do something even though it may have harmful or unpleasant effects【文】毫无顾忌地做某事: *I did not scruple to tell him what I thought.* 我毫无顾忌地把我的想法告诉了他。

scru·pu·lous /ˈskrupjələs; ˈskruːpjʊləs/ *adj* **1** careful to be honest and fair 力求诚实公平的, 正直的: *Mr Samuel has always been most scrupulous in his dealings with us.* 塞缪尔先生和我们进行交易向来是很诚实公平的。—opposite 反义词 UNSCRUPULOUS **2** done very carefully so that every detail is correct 极仔细认真的, 一丝不苟的: *scrupulous attention to detail* 对细节的一丝不苟 —**scrupulously** *adv*: *scrupulously clean* 极其清洁的 —**scrupulousness** *n* [U]

scru·ti·neer /ˌskrutəˈnɪr; ˌskruːtɪˈnɪə/ *n* [C] *BrE* an official who examines or counts votes in an election【英】〔选举中的〕监票人, 点票员

scru·ti·nize also 又作 **-ise** *BrE*【英】/ˈskrutn̩ˌaɪz; ˈskruːtɪnaɪz/ *v* [T] to examine someone or something very thoroughly and carefully 仔细彻底地检查, 详审: *James scrutinized the painting closely.* 詹姆斯认真审视那幅画。

scru·ti·ny /ˈskrutn̩ɪ; ˈskruːtɪni/ *n* [U] careful and thorough examination of someone or something 仔细的审视; 彻底的检查: **careful/close scrutiny** *Close scrutiny of the document showed it to be a forgery.* 经过仔细检查证明这份文件是伪造的。| **under scrutiny** *Diana resented her private life being under such public scrutiny.* 戴安娜对自己的私生活受到这样的公开监视非常反感。

scu·ba div·ing /ˈskubə ˌdaɪvɪŋ; ˈskuːbə ˌdaɪvɪŋ/ *n* [U] the sport of swimming under water while breathing through a tube connected to a container of air on your back 斯库巴潜泳, 水肺式潜泳〔戴自携式潜水呼吸器潜泳〕

scud /skʌd; skʌd/ *v* [I always+adv/prep] *literary* if clouds scud past, they move quickly across the sky【文】〔云〕飘过, 掠过

scuff /skʌf; skʌf/ *v* **1** [T often passive 常用被动态] to make a mark on a smooth surface by rubbing it against something rough 使磨损: *scuffed brown shoes* 磨损了的褐色皮鞋 **2 scuff your feet/heels** to walk in a slow lazy way, dragging your feet along the ground〔懒洋洋地〕拖着脚走路

scuf·fle¹ /ˈskʌfl; ˈskʌfəl/ *n* [C] a short fight between a few people that is not very violent 扭打〔不太猛烈的短时打斗〕: *a brief scuffle in a corner of the bar* 酒吧一角的短暂斗殴

scuffle² *v* [I] **1** to have a short fight with someone, in a way that is not very serious or violent〔与某人〕扭打, 厮打 **2** [always+adv/prep] to walk or move quickly in a way that makes a noise〔发出声响地〕匆匆急走: *a mouse scuffling in the leaves* 在树叶间匆匆地爬过的老鼠

scuff·mark /ˈskʌfˌmark; ˈskʌfmɑːk/ *n* [C] a mark made on something by scuffing 磨痕, 擦痕

scull¹ /skʌl; skʌl/ *n* [C] **1** a small light boat for only one person〔单人〕轻便小船 **2** one of the OARs that you use when you are sculling a boat 桨

scull² *v* [I,T] to ROW³ (1) a small light boat, especially a boat that is only for one person〔用桨〕划〔尤指单人轻便小船〕

scul·le·ry /ˈskʌlərɪ; ˈskʌləri/ *n* [C] a room next to the kitchen, especially in a large old house, where cleaning jobs are done〔尤指古老大宅中紧挨厨房的〕洗涤室

scul·lion /ˈskʌljən; ˈskʌljən/ *n* [C] *old use* a boy employed to work in a kitchen【旧】干粗活的男厨工, 厨师帮工

sculpt /skʌlpt; skʌlpt/ *v* [T often passive 常用被动态] **1** to make a solid object that represents someone or something, by shaping stone, wood, clay etc 雕刻, 雕塑 **2** to make something into a particular shape as a result of a natural process, for example the movement of a river〔自然进程如河水流动等〕刻蚀, 侵蚀

sculp·tor /ˈskʌlptə; ˈskʌlptə/ *n* [C] someone who makes sculptures 雕刻家, 雕塑家

sculp·ture /ˈskʌlptʃə; ˈskʌlptʃə/ *n* **1** [U] the art of making solid objects representing people or animals out of stone, wood, clay etc 雕刻[雕塑]艺术: *a talent for sculpture* 雕刻天才 **2** [C, U] the objects produced in this form of art 雕刻[雕塑]作品: *an interesting abstract sculpture* 有趣的抽象派雕塑作品

sculp·tured /ˈskʌlptʃəd; ˈskʌlptʃəd/ *adj* **1 sculptured features/beauty/muscles etc** features etc that have a clear shape as if they had been made by an artist 似雕塑成的面貌/美貌/肌肉等 **2** [only before noun 仅用于名词前] decorated with sculptures 有雕刻装饰的: *a sculptured pedestal* 有雕刻装饰的柱基

scum /skʌm; skʌm/ *n* **1** [singular,U] an unpleasant substance that forms on the surface of a liquid〔液体表面的〕浮渣, 浮垢: *The pond was covered with green scum.* 池塘水面盖满了绿色的浮藻。**2** [C] *plural* **scum** *spoken* an unpleasant nasty person【口】社会渣滓, 人渣: *Don't you ever dare say that again you scum!* 你还敢再说那样的话就有你好看的, 你这个人渣! | **scum of the earth** (=the worst people you can imagine) 世上的人渣, 败类 —**scummy** *adj*

scum·bag /ˈskʌmˌbæg; ˈskʌmbæg/ *n* [C] *spoken* an unpleasant person【口】卑鄙的人

scup·per¹ /ˈskʌpə; ˈskʌpə/ *v* [T] *BrE*【英】**1** [usually passive 一般用被动态] *informal* to ruin someone's plans or chances of success【非正式】破坏〔计划、机会等〕: *The recent terrorist attacks have scuppered any chance of a peace settlement.* 最近的恐怖分子袭击事件已经毁了和平解决的任何机会。**2** to deliberately sink your own ship 故意使〔自己的船〕沉没

scupper² *n* [C] *technical* a hole in the side of a ship that allows water to flow back into the sea【术语】〔船舷上的〕排水孔

scur·ri·lous /ˈskɜəələs; ˈskʌrɪləs/ *adj formal* scurrilous remarks, articles etc contain damaging and untrue statements about someone【正式】〔话语、文章等〕辱骂(性)的, 伤人的 —**scurrilously** *adv* —**scurrilousness** *n* [U]

scur·ry /ˈskɜɪ; ˈskʌri/ *v* [I always+adv/prep] to move quickly with short steps〔用小步〕急跑, 急走, 急赶: **[+along/past/across]** *A beetle scurried across the path.* 一只甲虫匆匆爬过小路。—**scurry** *n* [singular,U]

S-curve /ˈɛs ˌkɜv; ˈes kɜːv/ *n* [C] *AmE* a bend in the road in the shape of an 'S', that can be dangerous to drivers【美】S形弯道; S-BEND *BrE*【英】

scur·vy /ˈskɜvɪ; ˈskɜːvi/ *n* [U] a disease caused by not eating foods such as fruit and vegetables that contain VITAMIN C 坏血病〔因缺乏维生素C所致〕

scut·tle¹ /ˈskʌtl; ˈskʌtl/ *v* **1** [I always+adv/prep] to move quickly with short steps 小步急跑, 疾走: **[+along/past/down]** *I caught sight of Miss Rawlings scuttling down the corridor.* 我瞥见罗林斯小姐沿着走廊快步走过。**2** [T] to sink a ship by making holes in the bottom, especially in order to prevent it being used by an enemy 凿沉〔船只, 尤指不让敌人使用〕

scuttle² *n* [C] a container for carrying coal 煤斗, 煤筐

scut·tle·butt /ˈskʌtl̩ˌbʌt; ˈskʌtlbʌt/ *n* [U] *AmE informal* stories about other people's personal lives, especially containing things that are unkind and untrue about them【美, 非正式】〔对别人私生活的〕流言飞语

scuz·zy /ˈskʌzɪ; ˈskʌzi/ *adj informal* unpleasant and dirty【非正式】脏得令人难受[讨厌]的

Scyl·la and Cha·ryb·dis /ˌsɪlə ənd kəˈrɪbdɪs; ˌsɪlə ənd kəˈrɪbdɪs/ **between Scylla and Charybdis** in a situation where you have to choose between two possible actions, but both are dangerous or unpleasant. The phrase comes from the ancient Greek stories of Scylla, a MONSTER, and Charybdis, a WHIRLPOOL (=water that spins around and pulls things down into it), that killed sailors in the sea between Italy and Sicily. People sometimes also use the phrase 'between a rock and a hard place' to mean the same thing. 斯库拉与卡律布狄斯, 进退两难的境地〔此习语源自古希腊传说中斯库拉水怪和卡律布狄斯大漩涡的故事。它们吞没了来往于意大利和西西里两地的水手。人们有时也使用between a rock and a hard place 这一习语表达同一意思〕

scythe /saɪð; saɪð/ *n* [C] a farming tool that has a long curved blade fixed to a long wooden handle, and is used to cut grain or long grass 长柄大镰刀

SD the written abbreviation of 缩写= SOUTH DAKOTA

SDI /ˌɛs di ˈaɪ; ˌes diː ˈaɪ/ Strategic Defense Initiative; a military plan started in the US in 1983 for making special weapons that could destroy an enemy country's MISSILEs before they could reach the US. It was often called 'Star Wars' because the plan

was for a system of SATELLITES containing LASER weapons that would destroy missiles from space. Many scientists believed that the plan was impossible to achieve. 战略防御计划〔美国于1983年开始实施的一项军事计划。其目标是制造特种武器，能在敌国导弹到达美国之前将其摧毁。该计划拟建造的卫星系统配备有可摧毁空中导弹的激光武器，因此通常也称之为“星球大战计划”。许多科学家认为这一计划根本无法实现〕

SDLP, the /ˌɛs di ɛl ˈpi; ˌes diː el ˈpiː/ the Social Democrat and Labour Party; a political party in Northern Ireland, mostly supported by Catholics, which has fairly LEFT WING ideas. Although the SDLP wants Northern Ireland to become part of the Republic of Ireland, it is completely opposed to the use of violence to achieve this aim. The SDLP had an important part in the peace talks in Northern Ireland in the 1990s. 社会民主工党〔北爱尔兰一左翼政党。其政治主张相当左翼，支持者多为天主教徒。该政党要求北爱尔兰归属爱尔兰共和国，但完全反对使用暴力手段实现这一目标。20世纪90年代，该政党在北爱尔兰举行的和平谈判中发挥了重要作用〕

SE the written abbreviation of 缩写= SOUTHEAST or SOUTHEASTERN

sea /si; siː/ *n* **1** [singular] *especially BrE* the large area of salty water that covers much of the earth's surface; OCEAN【尤英】海，海洋: *You don't often get the chance to swim in the sea in England – it's too cold!* 在英格兰你不常有机会在海里游泳——因为太冷了！| **rough/calm sea** (=with or without large waves) 波涛汹涌/风平浪静 *The sea was calm and there was no breeze.* 海不扬波，没有一丝风。| **by sea** (=on a ship) 坐船，经由海路 *I sent my luggage ahead of me by sea.* 我先把行李经海路托运。| **by the sea** (=on the coast) 在海滨，在海边 *She lives in a little cottage by the sea.* 她住在海边的一间小屋里。| **at sea** *Life at sea was never easy and he was always pleased to be back home.* 海上生活从来都不轻松，他回到家里总是非常高兴。| **put to sea** (=start a journey on the sea) 出海，出航 | **the open sea** (=far away from land) 外海，外洋；公海 | **lost at sea** (=drowned) 在海里淹死[溺死] **2** [C] a large area of salty water that is mostly enclosed by land 内海: *the Mediterranean Sea* 地中海 **3 a sea of** a large number of something 大量，一大片: *A sea of faces stared up at me from the audience.* 数不清的观众仰起脸注视着我。**4 be (all) at sea** to be confused or not sure what to do 困惑，茫然不知所措: *I'm all at sea with this maths homework.* 我完全不知道这些数学作业怎么做。**5 the seas** *literary* the sea, used especially when you are not talking about a particular ocean【文】海，大海〔尤用于谈论非特定海洋时〕: **across the seas** (=far away) 遥远，远隔重洋 *She was born in a northern land far, far across the seas.* 她出生在一个遥远的北方国家。**6** [C] one of the broad plains on the moon and Mars 海〔指月球或火星表面的一片广阔平原〕

sea a·nem·o·ne /ˈ· ·ˌ···/ *n* [C] a brightly-coloured sea animal that sticks onto rocks and looks like a flower 海葵〔色泽鲜艳的海生动物〕

sea bed /ˈ· ·/ *n* [singular] the land at the bottom of the sea 海床，海底

Sea·bee /ˈsiˌbi; ˈsiːˌbiː/ a member of a part of the US Navy that builds landing areas for aircraft and other structures that are needed in places where there is fighting. The official name of this unit is the 'Construction Battalion', and the word Seabee comes from the first letters of this name. 海军工兵营士兵〔美国海军一支部队的成员。其任务是修筑战地停机坪和其他军用设施。该部队的正式名称为 Construction Battalion（工兵营），Seabee 是英文名称首字母 CB 的变体〕

sea·bird /ˈsiˌbɝd; ˈsiːbɜːd/ *n* [C] a bird that lives near the sea and finds food in it 海鸟

sea·board /ˈsiˌbɔrd; ˈsiːbɔːd/ *n* [C] the part of a country that is near the sea 海岸，海滨，沿海地区: *the eastern seaboard of the US* 美国的东海岸

sea·borne /ˈsiˌbɔrn; ˈsiːbɔːn/ *adj* carried on or arriving in ships 海运的，经由[来自]海上的: *the threat of a seaborne invasion* 从海上入侵的威胁

sea breeze /ˈ· ·/ *n* [C] a light wind that blows from the sea onto the land 吹向陆地的微风，海风

sea cap·tain /ˈ· ˌ··/ *n* [C] the CAPTAIN of a ship 船长

sea change /ˈ· ·/ *n* [singular] a very big change in something 巨变: *a sea change in public opinion* 公众舆论的巨大变化

sea dog /ˈ· ·/ *n* [C] *literary or humorous* someone with a lot of experience of ships and sailing【文或幽默】有经验的水手，老海员

sea·far·ing /ˈsiˌfɛrɪŋ; ˈsiːˌfeərɪŋ/ *adj* [only before noun 仅用于名词前] **1** connected with the life and activities of a sailor 航海的，水手生活的: *a story from my seafaring days* 我的航海岁月中的一件事 **2** having strong connections with ships and the sea, especially because of international trade 和航海有密切关系的，以航海为业的: **seafaring nation/country** *The Danes are an ancient seafaring nation.* 丹麦人是一个古老的航海民族。—**seafarer** *n* [C]

sea·food /ˈsiˌfud; ˈsiːfuːd/ *n* [U] animals from the sea that you can eat, especially SHELLFISH 海产食品，海味〔尤指贝类等〕

sea·front /ˈsiˌfrʌnt; ˈsiːfrʌnt/ *n* [C usually singular 一般用单数] *especially BrE* the part of a town where the shops, houses etc are next to the beach【尤英】〔城镇的〕滨海区: *a hotel right on the seafront* 滨海区旅馆

sea·go·ing /ˈsiˌgoɪŋ; ˈsiːˌgəʊɪŋ/ *adj* [only before noun 仅用于名词前] built to travel on the sea 〔船〕适于航海的: *a seagoing yacht* 航海帆船

sea·gull /ˈsiˌgʌl; ˈsiːgʌl/ *n* [C] a common grey and white bird that lives near the sea 海鸥

Sea Har·ri·er /ˈ· ˌ···/ —see 见 HARRIER JUMP JET

sea·horse /ˈsiˌhɔrs; ˈsiːhɔːs/ *n* [C] a small sea fish with a head and neck that look like those of a horse 海马〔海生小型鱼类〕

Sea King /ˈ· ·/ *trademark* a type of HELICOPTER【商标】海霸王〔一种直升机〕

seal[1] /sil; siːl/ *n* [C]

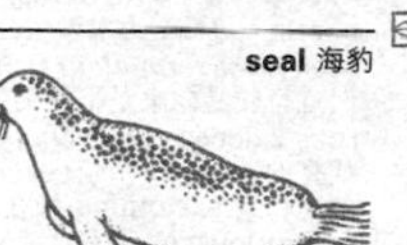
seal 海豹

1 ▶ANIMAL 动物◀ a large sea animal that eats fish and lives around coasts or on floating pieces of ice 海豹
2 ▶OFFICIAL MARK 正式印记◀ a mark that has a special design and shows the legal or official authority of a person or organization 印章，图章，印鉴: *a black book stamped with the Presidential Seal* 盖着总统印章的黑皮书
3 ▶ON CONTAINERS/PIPES 在容器/管子上◀ a) a piece of rubber or plastic that keeps air, water, dirt etc out of something 〔防止空气、水等渗入的〕密封条，密封纸: *Do not use this product if the inner seal is broken.* 如内部密封纸破损，请勿用此产品。**b)** a piece of WAX[1] (1), paper, wire etc that you have to break in order to open something 封蜡，封条，火漆
4 seal of approval if you give something your seal of approval, you say that you approve of it, especially officially （正式）认可[批准]: *All we need now is the chairman's seal of approval.* 我们现在所需要的就是主席的正式批准。
5 set the seal on to make something definite or complete 使确定，使成定局: *A last-minute goal set the seal on Tottenham's victory.* 最后一分钟的一个进球使托特纳姆队的胜利成为定局。
6 seal of friendship/success/victory etc something that makes your friendship stronger, your success more certain etc 友谊的缔造/成功的保证/胜利的保证等

seal[2] *v* **1** also 又作 **seal up** [T] to close an entrance or a container with something that stops air, water etc from coming in or out of it 〔为防止空气、水、污物渗入或渗出〕把…封住，封闭: *The windows have been sealed up for years.* 这些窗户已经封闭多年了。**2** [T] to close an envelope, pack etc by using something sticky to hold its edges in place 粘住〔信封等〕，封住: *Don't seal the envelope yet.* 先不要把这个信封封上。**3 my lips are sealed** *spoken* used to say that you are not going to tell someone something【口】我一定会守口如瓶〔表示决不把某事说出来〕 **4 seal sb's fate** to make something, especially something bad, sure to happen 决定某人的命运〔尤指厄运〕: *He was about to say the words that would seal my fate for ever.* 他即将说出决定我今后命运的那些话。**5 seal a friendship/promise/agreement etc** to do something that makes a friendship, promise etc more formal or definite 缔交/郑重承诺/正式达成协议等

seal sth ↔ **in** *phr v* [T] to stop what something contains from getting out 密藏〔某物〕，将〔某物〕封住: *Fry the meat quickly to seal in the flavor.* 把肉快速煎好以保持原味。

seal sth ↔ **off** *phr v* [T] to stop people entering an area or building, because it is dangerous 封闭，〔因有危险而〕封锁〔某地区或某幢建筑〕: *Following a bomb warning, police have sealed off the whole area.* 接到有炸弹的警报后，警方封锁了整个地区。

sea lane /ˈ· ·/ *n* [C] a fixed path across the sea that ships regularly use 海上航线[航路]

seal·ant /ˈsilənt; ˈsiːlənt/ *n* [C,U] a layer of paint, polish etc that is put on the surface of something to protect it from air, water etc 密封胶，密封剂，防渗漏剂

sealed /sild; siːld/ *adj* shut with something that prevents air, water etc from getting in or out 密封的，封闭的：*Keep all dressings in a sealed sterile pack.* 把各种包扎用品保存在一个消毒的密封袋里。

sea legs /ˈ· ·/ *n* [plural] **find/get your sea legs** to begin to be able to walk normally, not feel ill etc when you are travelling on a ship 开始能在颠簸的航船甲板上平稳走动，开始不晕船

seal·er /ˈsilə; ˈsiːlə/ *n* **1** [C,U] a layer of paint, polish etc put on the surface of something to protect it from air, water etc 密封剂，密封材料 **2** [C] a person or ship that hunts seals (SEAL[1] (1)) 捕猎海豹的人［船］

sea lev·el /ˈ· ˌ· ·/ *n* [U] the average height of the sea, used as a standard for measuring other heights and depths, such as the height of a mountain 海平面：**above/below sea level** *1,000m above sea level* 海拔1000米

seal·ing /ˈsilɪŋ; ˈsiːlɪŋ/ *n* [U] the hunting or catching of seals (SEAL[1] (1)) 捕猎海豹

sealing wax /ˈ· · ·/ *n* [U] a red substance that melts and becomes hard again quickly, used for sealing (SEAL[2] (2)) letters, documents etc 封蜡，火漆

sea li·on /ˈ· ˌ· ·/ *n* [C] a large type of SEAL[1] (1) 海狮〔大型海豹的一种〕

seal·skin /ˈsilˌskɪn; ˈsiːlˌskɪn/ *n* [U] the skin or fur of some types of SEAL[1] (1), used for making leather or clothes 海豹皮〔用于制作皮革或衣服〕

seam /sim; siːm/ *n* [C] **1** a line where two pieces of cloth, leather etc have been stitched together〔两块布、皮革等连接处的〕缝，线缝：*a split in the seam of his jeans* 他的牛仔裤绽开的线缝 —see picture on page A17 参见A17页图 **2** a layer of a mineral, especially coal, under the ground 矿层〔尤指煤层〕：**a rich seam** (=one that contains a lot of high quality coal) 优质的富煤层 **3** a line where two pieces of metal, wood etc have been joined together〔两块金属、木板等的〕接合处，接缝 **4 be coming/falling apart at the seams a)** if a plan, organization etc is coming or falling apart at the seams, so many things are going wrong with it that it will probably fail〔计划〕失败；〔组织〕分崩离析：*Her whole life was threatening to come apart at the seams.* 她的整个生活面临着崩溃的危险。**b)** if a piece of clothing etc is coming or falling apart at the seams, the stitches on it are coming unfastened〔衣服等的〕线缝裂开；缝口破裂 **5 be bursting at the seams** if a room or building is bursting at the seams, it is so full of people that hardly anyone else can fit into it〔房间等〕挤满，过于拥挤

sea·man /ˈsimən; ˈsiːmən/ *plural* **seamen** /-mən; -mən/ *n* [C] **1** a sailor on a ship or in the navy who is not an officer 水手，海员；水兵：*a merchant seaman* 商船船员 —see table on page C6 参见C6页附录 **2** someone who has a lot of experience of ships and the sea 航海老手

sea·man·ship /ˈsimənˌʃɪp; ˈsiːmənʃɪp/ *n* [U] the skills and knowledge that an experienced sailor has 航海术，航海技能，船舶驾驶术

seamed /simd; siːmd/ *adj* [only before noun 仅用于名词前] **1** having a seam 有缝的，缝合的：*seamed stockings* 有接缝的长袜 **2** a seamed surface has many deep lines on it 有皱纹的：*A gentle smile spread over her old, seamed face.* 慈祥的微笑展现在她那苍老的、有皱纹的脸上。

sea mile /ˈ· ·/ *n* [C] a unit for measuring distance at sea that is slightly longer than a land mile, and equals 1,853 metres; NAUTICAL MILE 海里〔较陆上英里略长的长度单位，等于1853米〕

sea mist /ˈ· ·/ *n* [U] a mist on land that comes in from the sea 海雾〔从海上漂到陆上的雾〕

seam·less /ˈsimləs; ˈsiːmləs/ *adj* **1** not having any seams (SEAM (1)) 无缝的：*seamless stockings* 无缝长统袜 **2** something seamless is done or happens so smoothly that you cannot tell where one thing stops and another begins 平滑的，浑然一体的：*I see the piece very much as a flowing, seamless whole.* 我觉得这件作品流畅自然，浑然一体。

seam·stress /ˈsimstrɪs; ˈsiːmstrɪs/ *n* [C] *old-fashioned* a woman whose job is SEWING and making clothes【过时】女缝纫工，女裁缝

seam·y /ˈsimɪ; ˈsiːmi/ *adj* involving unpleasant things such as crime, violence, poverty, or immorality〔犯罪、暴力、贫困、不道德行为等〕令人不快的，丑恶的：**seamy side (of sth)** *the seamy side of the film industry* 电影业的阴暗面

se·ance /ˈseɑns; ˈseɪɑːns/ *n* [C] a meeting where people try to talk to or receive messages from the spirits of dead people 降神会〔试图与亡灵对话的集会〕

CULTURAL NOTE 文化注释

The STEREOTYPE of a seance involves a group of people sitting around a table holding hands with each other in a dark room. One person is called a MEDIUM, which is someone (typically a woman) who claims that they can communicate with the dead friends and relatives of the people present. The medium claims to receive messages from the dead people and give them to the people at the seance, but many people think that seances are a trick and that the medium does not really communicate with the dead. Other people think seances are evil and dangerous. Many religions also believe that it is wrong, impossible, or immoral to hold seances. 典型的降神会有一群人参与其中，他们在黑暗的房间里相互拉着手围坐在一张桌子边。其中有一个充当灵媒的人（通常是女性），声称能与其他在座的人的已故亲朋进行交流。灵媒说从死人那里得到了口信，然后将口信传达给死人的亲朋。可是很多人认为降神会是一场骗局，灵媒也不是真的能和死人交流。还有人认为降神会既邪恶又危险。很多宗教也相信举行降神会是不对的，不可能成功的，也是不道德的。

Sea of Mar·ma·ra, the /ˌsi əv ˋmɑrmərə; ˌsiː əv ˈmɑːmərə/ an INLAND (=surrounded by land) sea in northwest Turkey, between the Bosphorus and the Dardanelles 马尔马拉海〔土耳其西北部一内陆海，位于博斯普鲁斯海峡和达达尼尔海峡之间〕

sea·plane /ˈsiˌplen; ˈsiːpleɪn/ *n* [C] a plane that can take off from and land on the surface of the sea 水上飞机

sea·port /ˈsiˌport; ˈsiːpɔːt/ *n* [C] a large town on or near a coast with a HARBOUR[1] that big ships can use 海港，海港市镇

sea pow·er /ˈ· ˌ· ·/ *n* **1** [U] the size and strength of a country's navy〔一国的〕海军力量，海上实力 **2** [C] a country with a powerful navy 海军强国

SEAQ /ˈsiæk; ˈsiːæk/ the computer system used in the London STOCK EXCHANGE, which gives information about the price of shares 证券自动报价系统〔伦敦证券交易所使用的计算机系统，提供股票价格信息〕

sear[1] /sɪr; sɪə/ *v* **1** [I always+adv/prep,T] to burn something with a sudden powerful heat 烙，烧灼：*The choking fumes seared their lungs.* 那些令人窒息的浓烟灼伤了他们的肺部。**2** [T] to cook the outside of a piece of meat, quickly at a high temperature, in order to keep its juices in 用快速高温烧烤〔肉的表层以保存其汁液〕 **3** [I always+adv/prep] to have a very strong sudden and unpleasant effect on you〔在思想上〕留下烙印，铭刻：**[+into/onto/on]** *The scene will be forever seared onto my memory.* 那景象将永远铭刻在我的记忆里。

sear[2] *adj literary* another spelling of SERE【文】sere 的另一种拼法

search[1] /sɝtʃ; sɜːtʃ/ *n* **1** [C usually singular 一般用单数] an attempt to find someone or something 寻找，查找；搜寻，搜查：**[+for]** *Bad weather is hampering the search for survivors.* 恶劣的天气妨碍了对幸存者的搜寻。| **in search of** (=looking for) *Mario went off in search of some matches.* 马里奥出去找火柴。| **call off a search** (=stop looking for someone or something) 终止寻找〔某人或某物〕，停止搜索 | **carry out a search** *Security guards will be carrying out a search of the premises.* 保安人员即将搜查这幢建筑物及其周围地带。| **house-to-house search** (=one that involves searching every house or building in an area) 挨家挨户的搜查 | **strip search** (=an official search in which you must take off all of your clothes)〔官方对疑犯的〕裸身搜查 **2** [singular] an attempt to find a solution to a problem or an explanation for something 探索，寻求：*the search for the meaning of life* 对生命意义的探索 **3 search and rescue** the process of searching for someone who is lost and who may need medical help, for example in the mountains or at sea〔在山中或海上对失踪者或遇险者的〕搜寻和营救 S3 W2

search[2] *v* W3

1 ▶LOOK FOR 找寻◀ [I,T] to spend time looking for someone or something 查找，搜查，搜寻：*Rescue workers searched all night in the hope of finding more survivors.* 营救人员彻夜搜寻，希望找到更多的幸存者。| **[+for]** *a mother bird searching for food* 觅食的母鸟 | **search sth for sth** *Detectives are out searching the yard for clues.* 侦探们出动在院子寻找线索。| **search through sth** (=look for something among papers in a drawer etc) 翻遍〔抽屉内的文件等〕以寻找某物 | **search in/under/around etc** *"Two beers, please," Patricia ordered, searching in her purse.* "两杯啤酒。"帕特里夏边吩咐边在钱包里摸索。

2 ▶PERSON 人◀ [T] to look in someone's pockets, clothes etc in order to find something, especially drugs or weapons 搜查

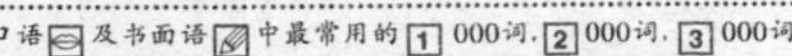
口语 S 及书面语 W 中最常用的 1 000词，2 000词，3 000词

〔口袋、衣服等看是否藏有毒品、武器等〕: *Visitors to the prison are thoroughly searched before they are allowed in.* 探监者要经彻底检查后才获准入内。

3 ▶SOLUTION/EXPLANATION ETC 解答/解释等◀ [I] to try to find a solution to a problem, an explanation for something etc 探索, 寻找解决办法: [+for] *Scientists are still searching for a cure for the disease.* 科学家仍在寻求治疗这种疾病的方法。

4 Search me! *spoken* used to tell someone that you do not know the answer to a question【口】我不知道!: *"So where's she gone tonight then?" "Search me!"* "她今晚上哪儿去了?" "我不知道!"

5 ▶EXAMINE 检查◀ [T] to examine something very carefully in order to find something out 细察, 细查: *Anya searched his face anxiously.* 阿妮娅焦虑不安地察看他脸上的表情。

search sth ↔ **out** *phr v* [T] to find or discover something by searching 找到, 找出, 查出, 搜寻出: *We were too tired to search out extra blankets.* 我们太累了, 不想再找出更多的毯子了。

Frequencies of **search, look for** and **try to find** in spoken and written English 英语口语和书面语中 search, look for 和 try to find 的使用频率

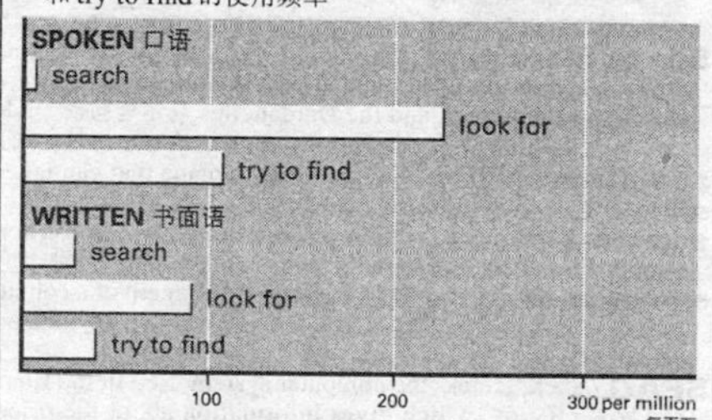

Based on the British National Corpus and the Longman Lancaster Corpus
据英国国家语料库和朗文兰开斯特语料库

This graph shows that the expressions **look for** and **try to find** are much more common in both spoken and written English than the verb **search**. **Look for** and **try to find** are used in a very general way. **Search** is used when someone, often a group of people, spends time looking for something or someone in a careful, organized way. It is more common in written English than in spoken English. 本图表显示, 短语 look for 和 try to find 在英语口语和书面语中的使用频率远远高于动词 search。look for 和 try to find 用于一般性的说法, 而 search 则用于表示某人〔通常是一组人〕细致而有序地去搜寻某物或某人, 它在书面语中的使用频率高于口语。

search·ing /ˈsɝtʃɪŋ; ˈsɜːtʃɪŋ/ *adj* [only before noun 仅用于名词前] **1 searching look/glance** a look from someone who is trying to find out as much as possible about someone's thoughts and feelings 探究的目光 **2 searching examination/investigation/analysis** an examination etc that looks thoroughly at all the facts 彻底的检查/调查/分析 —**searchingly** *adv*

search·light /ˈsɝtʃˌlaɪt; ˈsɜːtʃlaɪt/ *n* [C] a powerful light that can be turned in any direction, used for finding people, vehicles etc in the dark 探照灯

search par·ty /ˈ· ˌ··/ *n* [C] a group of people organized to look for someone who is missing or lost 搜索队, 救援队

search war·rant /ˈ· ˌ··/ *n* [C] a legal document that gives the police official permission to search a building, for example in order to look for stolen goods 搜查令, 搜查证

sear·ing /ˈsɪrɪŋ; ˈsɪərɪŋ/ *adj* **1** searing heat is extremely hot 炽热的, 灼热的 **2** searing pain is severe and feels like a burn 灼痛的, 剧痛的: *a searing pain behind the eyes* 眼底的灼痛 **3** searing words or attitudes are very severe and critical〔言语、态度〕严厉的, 苛刻的: *an expression of deep, searing contempt* 极其严厉而鄙视的表情

sea·scape /ˈsiˌskep; ˈsiːskeɪp/ *n* [C] a picture or painting of the sea 海景画

sea ser·pent /ˈ· ˌ··/ *n* [C] an imaginary large snake-like animal that people used to think lived in the sea〔传说中的〕海蛇怪

sea·shell /ˈsiˌʃɛl; ˈsiːʃel/ *n* [C] the shell of some types of sea animal 海贝壳

sea·shore, the /ˈsiˌʃɔr; ˈsiːʃɔː/ *n* the land along the edge of the sea, usually consisting of sand and rocks 海滨, 海岸, 海滩 —compare 比较 BEACH, SEASIDE

sea·sick /ˈsiˌsɪk; ˈsiːˌsɪk/ *adj* feeling very ill because of the movement of a boat or ship 晕船的 —**seasickness** *n* [U]

sea·side, the /ˈsiˌsaɪd; ˈsiːsaɪd/ *n especially BrE* an area or town along the edge of the sea, especially a place you go to have a holiday or to enjoy yourself【尤英】〔尤指作为度假地的〕海滨; 海滨城镇: **seaside resort** (=where a lot of people go for their holidays) 海滨度假胜地 —see 见 SHORE[1] (USAGE)

CULTURAL NOTE 文化注释

Although seaside holidays in the UK are not as popular as they used to be, many British people still go to a seaside town for their summer holidays. The STEREOTYPE is of a family who go to the beach for a PICNIC even if the weather is cold and windy. The parents sit in DECKCHAIRS and the children build SANDCASTLES, go for DONKEY rides, and eat ROCK (=a hard sticky sweet) or ICE CREAM. Many seaside towns have a PIER (=a long wooden structure that is built out over the sea for people to walk along), which usually has an AMUSEMENT ARCADE where people can play VIDEO GAMES or ONE-ARMED BANDITS (=a machine that you put money in to try and win more money). 尽管在英国去海边度假已经不像过去那样受人欢迎, 还是会有不少英国人去海滨城镇消暑。最典型的是, 一家人去海滩上野餐, 即便天气阴冷多风。父母坐在帆布躺椅上, 而孩子们堆沙堡, 骑毛驴, 吃硬棒糖和冰淇淋。很多海滨城市建有突堤, 上面常有游乐场, 人们可以玩电子游戏和吃角子老虎。— see Cultural Note at HOLIDAY 见 HOLIDAY 文化注释

sea·son¹ /ˈsizn; ˈsiːzən/ *n* S3 W1

1 ▶IN A YEAR 一年之中◀ [C] one of the four main periods in a year; spring, summer, autumn, or winter〔春、夏、秋、冬的〕季(节)

2 ▶USUAL TIME FOR STH 通常会发生某事的时期◀ [singular] a period of time in a year when something happens most often or when something is usually done〔每年某事发生最频繁的〕季节: **rainy/dry/wet etc season** (=when there is a lot of rain etc) 雨季/旱季/潮湿季节等 | **growing/raspberry/asparagus etc season** (=when particular plants are growing) 种植/悬钩子生长/芦笋等生长季节 | **hunting/shooting/fishing etc season** (=when you can do that sport) 狩猎/射猎/钓鱼等季节 | **mating/breeding season** (=when animals breed)〔动物的〕交配/繁殖季节 | **football/basketball etc season** (=when a sport is officially played) 足球/篮球等赛季 | **tourist season** *AmE*【美】, **holiday season** *BrE*【英】(=the time of year when people come to a particular place for a holiday) 度假旺季 | **high/peak season** (=the time of year when a place is most busy, especially a holiday place) 旺季, 极盛时期 | **low/off/slack season** (=the time of year when a place or company is not busy) 淡季 | **the holiday season** *AmE* (=Thanksgiving, Christmas, and New Year's)【美】〔感恩节、圣诞节、新年的〕节期

3 be in season a) if vegetables or fruit are in season, it is the time of year when they are ready to eat〔蔬菜、水果〕当令(的), 应时(的) **b)** if a female animal is in season, she is ready to MATE² (1)〔雌性动物〕在发情期

4 out of season a) if vegetables or fruit are out of season, it is not the time of year when they would normally become ready to eat〔蔬菜、水果〕不当令(的), 反季(的) **b)** if you travel or stay somewhere out of season, you do it at the time of year when most people do not〔旅游或度假的〕淡季

5 ▶FASHION 时装◀ [C] a time during which particular designs of clothes are produced and sold and are considered to be fashionable〔特殊设计的时髦服装展出和销售的〕时装季节: *The Paris season began in May.* 巴黎时装季节 5 月份开始。

6 ▶FILMS ETC 电影等◀ [singular] a time during which a series of films, television programmes etc is shown, especially ones made by the same person or about the same subject 电影节, 电影周〔尤指放映一系列同一制作者或同一主题的片子〕: *a new season of comedy on BBC1* 在英国广播公司电视一台播出的新喜剧系列

7 season's greetings used especially on greetings cards to say that you hope someone has a happy Christmas 圣诞快乐, 恭贺圣诞〔圣诞贺卡上的祝词〕

8 the season of good will the time around Christmas 圣诞节节期 —see also 另见 CLOSE SEASON, OPEN SEASON, SILLY SEASON

season² *v* [T] **1** to add salt, pepper etc to something you are cooking to make it taste better〔加盐、胡椒粉等〕给〔食品〕调味 **2** to make wood hard and ready to use by gradually drying it 使〔木材〕风干

sea·so·na·ble /ˈsizṇəbl; ˈsiːzənəbəl/ *adj formal*【正式】**1** suitable for the time of year 合时令的 **2** coming or happening at a suitable time 及时的, 正合时宜的 —**seasonably** *adv*

sea·son·al /ˈsizn̩l; ˈsiːzənəl/ *adj* **1** usually happening or available during a particular season 季节的，时令的，当令的：*a pie made with seasonal fruits* 用时令水果做的馅饼 | **seasonal norm** *BrE* (=the average weather conditions for a particular season)【英】某一季节的平均天气状况 **2** happening or needed only at a particular time of year 季节性的，随季节而变化的：**seasonal workers/labour/employment etc** *seasonal jobs in the tourist industry* 旅游业的季节性工作

sea·son·ally /ˈsiznəlɪ; ˈsiːzənəli/ *adv* according to what is usual for a particular season 季节性地，随季节地：**seasonally adjusted figures** *BrE* (=figures, especially about the number of unemployed people, that are changed according to what usually happens at a particular time of year)【英】随季节调整的数字〔尤指失业率〕

sea·soned /ˈsiznd; ˈsiːzənd/ *adj* **1 seasoned traveller/campaigner/veteran etc** a very experienced traveller etc 经验丰富的旅行者／竞选者／老兵等 **2** seasoned food has salt, pepper etc added 已调味的，调过味的：**well seasoned/highly-seasoned** (=with a strong taste) 调味得恰到好处的／佐料味浓的

sea·son·ing /ˈsiznɪŋ; ˈsiːzənɪŋ/ *n* [C,U] salt, pepper, spices (SPICE[1] (1)) etc that add a more interesting taste to food 调味品，佐料

season tick·et /ˈ‥ ˌ‥/ *n* [C] a ticket for several journeys, performances, games etc that costs less than you would pay altogether if you paid for each journey etc separately〔价格优惠的〕季票，定期车票，套票；〔观看表演、比赛的〕长期入场券：**season ticket holder** (=someone who owns a season ticket) 季票持有者

S2 W1 **seat¹** /sit; siːt/ *n*

1 ►PLACE TO SIT 坐的地方◄ [C] a place where you can sit, for example a chair 座，座位：*Excuse me, can you tell us where our seats are?* 劳驾，你能告诉我们座位在哪里吗？| *a 150-seat airliner* 有150个座位的客机 | **have/take a seat** *spoken* (=used to politely invite someone to sit down)【口】请坐 *If you'd like to take a seat, the doctor will see you shortly.* 你稍坐一会儿，医生很快就会给你看病的。| **back/front seat** (=the seats in the back or front of a car etc)〔汽车的〕后座／前座 | **passenger seat** (=the seat next to the driver in a car)〔汽车司机旁边的〕乘客座位 | **take your seat** (=sit down in your seat) 就座 *The judge hurried in and took his seat.* 法官匆匆进来并就座。| **reserve a seat** (=pay for a theatre seat before you go) 预订座位，订座 —see picture at 参见 THEATRE 图

2 ►PART OF A CHAIR 椅子的一部分◄ [C usually singular 一般用单数] the flat part of a chair etc that you sit on〔椅子等的〕座部：*Don't put your feet on the seat!* 不要把脚放在椅座上！

3 seat of your trousers/pants the part of your trousers that you sit on 裤子的臀部

4 two-seater/three-seater etc a vehicle or piece of furniture with two seats, three seats etc 两座位／三座位〔的车辆或家具〕等

5 ►OFFICIAL POSITION 正式职位◄ [C] a position as a member of a government or a group that makes official decisions 职位，席位，成员资格：*a seat on the board of directors* 董事会的一个席位 | **win/lose a seat** *The Tories won 419 seats in the last election.* 保守党在上届选举中获得419个席位。| **a safe seat** (=a position held by a political party that is not likely to be lost in an election)〔某政党在选举中〕能稳保的席位

6 seat of learning/government etc *formal* a place, usually a city, where a university or government is based【正式】学府／政府等所在地

7 take a back seat to let someone else make the important decisions 退居次要位置，让别人去作重要决定

8 be on the edge of your seat to be waiting excitedly to see what happens next 心情紧张地等待，兴奋地等待〔某事〕

9 do sth by the seat of your pants to do something by using only your own skill and experience, without any help from anyone or anything else 仅凭本人的技能和经验做某事

10 be in the driving seat *BrE*【英】also 又作 **be in the driver's seat** *especially AmE*【尤美】to control everything that happens in an organization, relationship, or situation 处于控制地位

11 be in the hot seat to be in a position in which you have to make important decisions or answer a lot of difficult questions 处于〔必须作出重大决定、回答很多难题的〕困难地位

12 ►ON A HORSE 骑马◄ [singular] *technical* the way someone sits on a horse【术语】〔骑马的〕坐姿，骑姿：*Sally's got a good seat.* 萨莉的骑姿很优美。

13 ►HOUSE 房子◄ [C] a home of a rich, important family in the countryside〔富人、要员在乡间的〕别墅，宅邸：**family/country seat** 家庭／乡间宅第 —see also 另见 **back seat driver** (BACK SEAT (2)), LOVESEAT, WINDOW SEAT

seat² *v* [T]

1 be seated a) to be sitting down 坐下：*Paul was seated at the head of the table with his wife next to him.* 保罗坐在饭桌的上首，他的妻子在旁边坐着。**b)** *spoken formal* used to politely invite people to sit down【口，正式】请（就）座〔礼貌用语〕：*Please be seated so we can begin the meeting.* 请坐下，我们的会议可以开始了。

2 remain/stay seated to stay in your seat 继续坐着：*Remain seated until the aircraft has come to a complete stop.* 请继续坐着，等飞机完全停下。

3 seat yourself beside/in/on etc *formal* to sit down somewhere【正式】坐在…旁边／里面／上面等

4 ►ARRANGE WHERE PEOPLE SIT 给人们安排座位◄ [always+adv/prep] to arrange for someone to sit somewhere 安排某人坐在…：**seat sb beside/on/near etc** *Whatever you do, make sure you don't seat Alan and Pat next to each other.* 不管你怎么做，千万不要把艾伦和帕特安排在相邻的座位。—see 见 SIT (USAGE) —see picture on page A15 参见 A15 页图

5 ►HOLD A NUMBER OF PEOPLE 容纳若干人◄ [not in progressive 不用进行时] if a room, vehicle, table etc seats a certain number of people, it has enough seats for that number〔房间、车辆、桌子等〕坐得下…人，能供给…座位：*The new stadium seats 60,000.* 新体育场能容纳 60,000 人。

6 ►FIT STH SOMEWHERE 将某物固定于某处◄ *technical* to fit something, tightly into a space that is specially made for it【术语】使牢牢地固定于〔某处〕

seat belt /ˈ‥ ˌ/ *n* [C] a strong belt fastened to the seat of a car or plane which you fasten around yourself to prevent yourself being thrown out of your seat in an accident〔汽车或飞机上的〕安全带 —see picture on page A2 参见 A2 页图

> **CULTURAL NOTE 文化注释**
> In Britain, a seat belt must always be worn by the driver of a car and any passenger in the front seat. They must also be worn by passengers in the back seat if they have been fitted in the car. In the US, seat belt laws vary from state to state. 在英国，司机和坐在汽车前座上的乘客必须系上安全带。如果汽车后座也装有安全带，那么后座乘客也必须系上。在美国，各州对系安全带与否有不同的规定。

seat·ing /ˈsitɪŋ; ˈsiːtɪŋ/ *n* [U] **1** all the seats in a theatre, cinema etc〔剧院、电影院等内的〕全部座位：**seating capacity** (=the number of people that can fit in a theatre, cinema etc) 座位数，可容纳人数 **2** a way of arranging seats, or a plan of who will sit in them〔某人坐某位置的〕座位安排，座位设置：**seating plan/arrangements etc** *Do you have a seating plan for the dinner guests?* 你有没有宴会宾客的座位示意图？

SEATO /ˈsito; ˈsiːtəʊ/ Southeast Asia Treaty Organization; an organization formed by Australia, the UK, France, New Zealand, the Philippines, Thailand, and the US for giving military help to each other in southeast Asia and the southwest Pacific area 东南亚条约组织〔一军事互助组织。成员国有澳大利亚、英国、法国、新西兰、菲律宾、泰国和美国。该组织旨在实现成员国在东南亚和太平洋西南地区的军事互助〕

Se·at·tle /siˈætl; siˈætl/ a city and port in Washington State, in the northwest of the US. It is an important business and cultural centre. 西雅图〔美国西北部华盛顿州一港口城市，也是一个重要的商业和文化中心〕

sea ur·chin /ˈ‥ ˌ‥/ *n* [C] a small round sea animal that has a hard shell, sometimes with sharp points 海胆

sea·wall /ˈsiˌwɔl; ˌsiːˈwɔːl/ *n* [C] a wall built along the edge of the sea to stop the water from flowing over an area of land 海堤，防波堤

sea·ward /ˈsiwəd; ˈsiːwəd/ *adj* facing or directed towards the sea 向海的，朝海的：*the seaward side of the town* 城镇的朝海一边 | **seaward wind/breeze** (=going towards the sea) 吹向大海的风／微风

sea·wards /ˈsiwədz; ˈsiːwədz/ also 又作 **seaward** *adv* towards the sea 向海，朝海

sea·way /ˈsiˌwe; ˈsiːweɪ/ *n* [C] **1** a line of travel regularly used by ships on the sea 海上航道 **2** a river or CANAL (1) used by ships to go from the sea to places that are not on the coast〔供轮船从海上进入内陆港的〕内河航道[运河]

sea·weed /ˈsiˌwid; ˈsiːwiːd/ *n* [U] a common plant that grows in the sea 海藻，海草

sea·wor·thy /ˈsiˌwɝðɪ; ˈsiːwɜːði/ *adj* a ship that is seaworthy is safe and in good condition〔船〕能安全行驶的，状况良好的，适于航行的 **—seaworthiness** *n* [U]

se·ba·ceous /sə`beʃəs; sə'beɪʃəs/ *adj technical* related to a part of the body which produces special oils【术语】分泌油脂的: *sebaceous glands* 皮脂腺

SEC /ˌɛs i `si; ˌes iː 'siː/ the abbreviation of 缩写= the SECURITIES AND EXCHANGE COMMISSION

sec /sɛk; sek/ *n* [C] *spoken*【口】**1** a very short time 一小会儿, 片刻: **hang on a sec/hold on a sec/just a sec etc** (=used to ask someone to wait a short time) 稍等一会儿 *"Is Clive there, please?" "Hold on a sec, I'll go and see."* "请问克莱夫在吗?" "请等一会儿, 我去看看。" | **in a sec** (=very soon) 不久, 很快 *I'll be with you in a sec.* 我一会儿就回来。**2** the written abbreviation of 缩写= SECRETARY

sec·a·teurs /ˌsɛkə`tɝz; 'sekətɜːz/ *n* [plural] *BrE* large, very strong sharp scissors that you use for cutting plant stems【英】修枝剪, 整枝剪; CLIPPERS (1) *AmE*【美】

se·cede /sɪ`sid; sɪ'siːd/ *v* [I] *formal* to formally leave an organization, especially because there has been a disagreement about its aims etc【正式】〔尤因意见分歧而〕退出〔团体、组织〕, 脱离: [+from] *By 1861, 11 states had seceded from the Union.* 到1861年, 已有11个州从联邦退出。—**secession** *n* [singular,U]

se·clude /sɪ`klud; sɪ'kluːd/ *v* [T] *formal* to keep yourself or someone else away from other people【正式】使〔自己或某人与其他人〕隔离

se·clud·ed /sɪ`kludɪd; sɪ'kluːdɨd/ *adj* **1** a secluded place is private and quiet because it is a long way from other places and people 僻静的, 偏僻的: *We eventually came to a secluded farmhouse.* 最后我们到了一间僻静的农舍。**2 a secluded life/existence** a way of living that is quiet and private because you do not see many people 隐居生活, 离群索居

se·clu·sion /sɪ`kluʒən; sɪ'kluːʒən/ *n* **1** [U] the state of being private and away from other people 与世隔绝, 隐居: **live/dwell/rest etc in seclusion** *The Emperor lived in utter seclusion behind the walls of the Forbidden City.* 皇帝生活在紫禁城的高墙之内完全与世隔绝。| **the seclusion of** *Writers are attracted to the peace and seclusion of the area.* 作家们被这个地方的安宁和僻静所吸引前来居住。**2** [singular,U] an act of keeping yourself or someone else alone and away from other people 深居简出; 隔离: **keep sb in seclusion** *In some societies, women are still kept in seclusion.* 在某些社会里, 妇女仍处于被隔离状态, 不许与人接触。| **be in seclusion** (=be in a situation where you will not or cannot see or speak to other people) 处于被隔离状态

S

sec·ond¹ /`sɛkənd; 'sekənd/ *number* **1** 2nd; the person, thing, event etc after the first one 第二的: *His second goal was from a penalty.* 他的第二次进球是罚点球得分。| *a second year student at University* 大学二年级学生 | *In the second of a series of programmes we look at the role of women in industry.* 在系列节目中的第二集, 我们可以看到妇女在工业中的作用。| **the second largest/biggest etc** (=the one after the largest, the biggest etc) 第二大的, 仅次于最大的 *Dalton is the second tallest boy in the class.* 多尔顿在班里是第二高的男孩。| **come/finish second** (=be the one after the winner of a race or competition)〔在比赛中〕获第二名 **2 second home/car etc** another home, car etc besides the one you use most of the time〔除了常用的第一个之外的〕另一个住所/另一辆汽车等 **3 be/come a poor second** to not be as good, interesting etc as something else 与第一名相差甚远的第二名: *Once you've tasted real vanilla, the artificial stuff is a poor second.* 一旦你尝过真正的香子兰精之后, 就知道人造香草精差多了。**4 every second year/person/thing etc** the second, then the fourth year etc 每隔一年/一人/一事等: *Only water the plants every second day.* 只要隔天给这些植物浇水就行了。**5 be second only to sth** to be the most important thing, the best thing etc, apart from one other particular thing 仅次于某物: *Colin's career was second only to his family.* 科林看重事业仅次于他的家庭。**6 be second to none** to be the best 不亚于任何人[事物], 首屈一指: *As a singer, Ella Fitzgerald was second to none.* 作为歌唱家, 埃拉·菲茨杰拉德是首屈一指的。

second² *n* **1** [C] a unit for measuring time that is equal to 1/60 of a minute 秒〔时间单位, 等于1/60分〕: **for 5/20/30 etc seconds** *Hold your breath for four seconds.* 请你屏气四秒钟。| **take 5/20/30 etc seconds** *The whole operation takes about twenty seconds.* 整个工作大概需要20秒钟。**2** [C] *especially spoken* a very short period of time【尤口】一会儿, 片刻, 瞬间: **a few seconds** *Just wait there for a few seconds.* 请在那里稍等一会儿。| **within seconds** (=after a few seconds) 立刻, 马上 *Within seconds Cassie called me back.* 凯西立刻给我回了电话。| **just a second** *spoken* (=wait a moment)【口】稍等一会 *Just a second and I'll come and help.* 稍等一会, 我就过来帮忙。| **in a matter of seconds** (=in a very short time) 片刻间 —see also 另见 SPLIT SECOND **3 seconds** [plural] **a)** *informal* another serving of the same food after you have eaten your first serving【非正式】添加的饭菜, 添菜: *Does anyone want seconds?* 有谁想添菜吗? **b)** clothes or other goods that are sold cheaply in shops because they are not perfect〔衣物等削价出售的〕次货, 次品 —compare 比较 SECOND-HAND **4** [C] someone who helped and supported someone who was fighting in a DUEL¹ (1) or other organized fight in former times〔旧时决斗者等的〕副手, 助手

second³ *adv* [sentence adverb 句子副词] used to add another piece of information to what you have already said or written; SECONDLY 第二, 其次: *Firstly the church is a place of worship and second, is somewhere the community can congregate.* 教堂首先是做礼拜的地方, 其次是社区大众的聚集地。

second⁴ *v* [T] to formally support a suggestion or plan made by another person in a meeting〔在会议上〕附议〔动议或计划〕: **second a motion/proposal/amendment etc** *Who'll second the motion?* 这项动议有谁附议?

second⁵ /sɪ`kand; sɪ'kɒnd/ *v* [T] *BrE* to send someone to do someone else's job for a short time【英】临时调派, 借调…: **second sb to** *Jill's been seconded to the marketing department while David's away.* 戴维不在的时候, 吉尔被临时调到市场部工作。—see also 另见 SECONDMENT

Second Ad·vent, the /ˌ·· `··/ another name for the Second Coming 基督复临〔Second Coming 的别称〕

sec·ond·a·ry /`sɛkənˌdɛrɪ; 'sekəndəri/ *adj* **1 secondary education/schooling/teaching etc** the education, teaching etc of children between the ages of 11 and 16 中等教育/教学〔指对11岁至16岁孩子的教育〕**2** not as important or urgent as something else 第二的, 次要的: *a secondary role* 次要角色 | **be of secondary importance/be a secondary consideration** *Getting there's the main thing – how we get there is a secondary consideration.* 要去那里是主要的 —— 至于怎样去, 那是第二位的考虑。| **be secondary to** *Social skills shouldn't necessarily be seen as secondary to academic achievement.* 社交技巧的重要性不应被看成一定逊于学术成就。**3** coming after or developing from something else of the same type 从属的, 继发(性)的: *The danger isn't from the disease itself, but from secondary infections that might occur.* 危险不在于这种病本身, 而在于可能发生的继发感染。—**secondarily** *adv* 2

secondary mod·ern /ˌ···· `··/ *n* [C] a type of school that existed in Britain until the 1960s, where children who were thought not to be the most intelligent were sent 中等学校〔英国20世纪60年代以前专为智力一般的儿童开设的学校〕—compare 比较 COMPREHENSIVE SCHOOL, GRAMMAR SCHOOL

secondary school /`···· ˌ·/ *n* [C] a school for children between the ages of 11 and 16 or 18〔为年龄在11至16或18岁之间的儿童开办的〕中等学校, 中学 —compare 比较 ELEMENTARY SCHOOL, PRIMARY SCHOOL

secondary stress /ˌ···· `·/ *n* [C,U] *technical* the second strongest STRESS¹ (4) given in speech to part of a word or sentence, and shown in this dictionary by the mark ˌ【术语】次重音

second base /ˌ·· `·/ *n* [singular] the second place you have to run to in games such as BASEBALL〔棒球〕二垒

second best¹ /ˌ·· `·◂/ *adj* not quite as good as the best thing of the same type 仅次于最好的, 居于第二位的: *Allie was the second best shooter on the team.* 阿莉是队里的二号射手。

second best² *n* [U] something that is not as good as the best 居第二位者, 次于最好的事物: *I've never been able to accept second best.* 我从来不接受第二好的东西。

second child·hood /ˌ·· `··/ *n* [U] **be in your second childhood** a polite expression meaning that an old person is behaving and thinking like a small child because their mental abilities are not as good as they used to be 处于老年昏聩期〔礼貌说法〕

second class /ˌ·· `·/ *n* **1** [U] a way of delivering mail in Britain that is cheaper and slower than sending things by FIRST CLASS (2) mail 二类邮件〔在英国指比一类邮件收费便宜但速度较慢的邮件〕: **send sth second class** *If you send it second class, it won't get there till the end of the week.* 假如你把它作为二类邮件寄出, 要在周末才能收到。**2** [U] the system in the US for delivering newspapers, magazines, advertisements etc 二类邮件〔在美国指寄递报纸、杂志、广告等〕**3** [U] a way of travelling, especially on a train, that is cheaper but not as comfortable as FIRST CLASS (1) travel〔尤指火车的〕二等(车): **travel second class** *Are you travelling first or second class?* 你此行准备坐头等车还是坐二等车? **4** [singular] a level of a university degree in Britain that is below the top level 二级荣誉学位〔英国大学的学士学位, 仅次于优等的一级〕

second-class /ˌ·· ˈ·◂/ *adj* **1** [only before noun 仅用于名词前] considered to be less important than other people or things 二等的，次等的，较差的: **second-class citizen** (=someone who is not as important as other people in society) 二等公民 *Why should children be treated like second-class citizens?* 为什么小孩就该受到二等公民的待遇? **2 second-class carriage/compartment/ticket etc** connected with cheaper and less comfortable travel on a train 二等车厢/(车厢)隔间/车票等: *Two second-class tickets, please.* 请给两张二等票。 **3 second-class mail/post/stamp etc** connected with posting things more cheaply and slowly 二类邮件/邮票等 —compare 比较 FIRST CLASS

second cous·in /ˌ·· ˈ··/ *n* [C] a child of a COUSIN (1) of one of your parents 父母的堂[表]兄弟姐妹的子女

second-de·gree /ˌ·· ·ˈ·◂/ *adj* **second-degree burn/burns** *technical* the second most serious form of burn 【术语】二度烧伤

second-guess /ˌ·· ˈ·/ *v* [T] **1** to try to say what will happen or what someone will do before they do it 猜测，预测，预言 **2** *AmE* to criticize something after it has already happened 【美】事后批评，放马后炮

second hand /ˈ·· ˌ·/ *n* [C] the pointer that shows seconds on a clock or watch〔钟表的〕秒针

second-hand /ˌ·· ˈ·/ *adj* not new, and used by someone else before you 旧的，用过的，第二手的: *When I was a kid I hated wearing second-hand clothes.* 我小时候最不喜欢穿别人穿过的衣服。| **get/buy sth second-hand** *They get all their furniture second-hand.* 他们全部家具都是二手货。

second-hand shop /ˌ·· ˈ· ·/ *n* [C] a shop where you can buy cheap second-hand goods, especially clothes〔尤指经营旧衣服的〕旧货店

second-in-com·mand /ˌ·· · ·ˈ·/ *n* [C] the person who has the next highest rank to the person who has the highest rank, especially in a military organization〔尤指军队的〕副司令员，第二把手

second lan·guage /ˌ·· ˈ··/ *n* [C usually singular 一般用单数] a language that you speak in addition to the language you learned as a child 第二语言〔母语以外所讲的另一种语言〕

second lieu·ten·ant /ˌ·· ·ˈ··/ *n* [C] a middle rank in several of the US and British military forces, or someone who has this rank 少尉〔美、英军队的军阶〕—see table on page C6 参见C6页附录

3 **sec·ond·ly** /ˈsɛkəndlɪ; ˈsekəndli/ *adv* [sentence adverb 句子副词] used to introduce the second fact, reason, subject etc that you want to talk about 第二，其次: *First we must establish exactly what happened. Secondly, we must try to find out why.* 首先我们必须确切查明出了什么事，其次我们要尽力找出原因。

se·cond·ment /sɪˈkɑndmənt; sɪˈkɒndmənt/ *n* [singular,U] *especially BrE* a period of time that you spend away from your usual job, either doing another job or studying 【尤英】临时调任，暂调，借调: **be on secondment from** *He's not at the university permanently – he's on secondment.* 他不是固定在这所大学工作，他只是临时借调来的。

second na·ture /ˌ·· ˈ··/ *n* [U] **be second nature (to sb)** something that is second nature to you is something you have done so often that you do it almost without thinking 是(某人的)第二天性，成为习性: *Wearing a seatbelt is second nature to most drivers.* 对大多数驾驶员来说，系安全带已经习以为常了。

second per·son /ˌ·· ˈ··/ *n technical* a form of a verb or PRONOUN that is used to show the person you are speaking to. For example, 'you' is a second person PRONOUN, and 'you are' is the second person singular and plural of the verb 'to be' 【术语】〔动词或代名词的〕第二人称〈例如 you 是第二人称代名词，而 you are 是动词 to be 的第二人称单数和复数〉—compare 比较 FIRST PERSON, THIRD PERSON

second-rate /ˌ·· ˈ·◂/ *adj* [usually before noun 一般用于名词前] not very good 二流的，较差的，次等的: *second-rate artists* 二流艺术家

second sight /ˌ·· ˈ·/ *n* [U] the ability to know what will happen in the future, or to know about things that are happening somewhere else 预见力，洞察力

second-string /ˌ·· ˈ·◂/ *adj* [only before noun 仅用于名词前] *AmE* not regularly part of a team, group etc, but sometimes taking someone else's place in it 【美】〔队、组等成员〕替补的，二线的

second thought /ˌ·· ˈ·/ *n* **1 on second thoughts** *BrE* 【英】, **on second thought** *AmE* 【美】 *spoken* used to say that you have changed your mind about something 【口】〔经过重新考虑之后〕改变主意: *I'll have a coffee please. Oh no, on second thought, make it a beer.* 请来杯咖啡。啊，不，想想还是换成啤酒吧。 **2 have second thoughts** to change your mind, or start having doubts about something 改变主意；开始怀疑: *You're not having second thoughts, are you?* 你不会改变主意吧，是吗?

second wind /ˌsɛkənd ˈwɪnd; ˌsekənd ˈwɪnd/ *n* [singular] a new feeling of energy that you get when you have been working or exercising very hard and had thought you were too tired to continue〔感到筋疲力尽以后的〕恢复精力，重振精神: **get your second wind** *OK, let's go – you should have got your second wind by now.* 好吧，我们走吧! 你现在应该已经恢复精力了。

Second World War, the /ˌ·· ˌ· ˈ·/ —see 见 WORLD WAR II

se·cre·cy /ˈsikrəsɪ; ˈsiːkrəsi/ *n* [U] **1** the process of keeping something secret, or the state of being kept a secret 保密，秘密状态: *I must stress the need for absolute secrecy about the project.* 我必须强调对这项计划绝对保密的必要。 **2 be sworn to secrecy** if you have been sworn to secrecy by someone, you have promised them that you will not repeat what they have told you 发过誓要保密: *I really can't tell you, I've been sworn to secrecy.* 我真的不能告诉你，我发过誓要保密的。

se·cret¹ /ˈsikrɪt; ˈsiːkr̩t/ *adj* **1** known about by only a few people and kept hidden from others 秘密的，隐秘的: **secret passage/hideout/hiding place etc** *Rosie took them to a secret hideout in the woods.* 罗西把他们带到树林里一个秘密的藏匿处。| **secret diplomacy/negotiations/meetings etc** *She's had secret meetings with him behind your back.* 她背着你和他秘密会面。| **keep sth secret** *They kept their marriage secret until last year.* 他们结了婚却秘而不宣，直到去年才公开。—see also 另见 TOP-SECRET **2** [only before a noun 仅用于名词前] secret feelings or actions are ones that you do not want other people to know about〔感情、行动〕不公开的，暗自的: *I still have my secret fears about his intentions.* 我内心里依然对他的意图感到害怕。| **a secret admirer** *Did you know you had a secret admirer?* 你知道有人在暗恋你吗? | **a secret drinker/smoker** *the watery eyes of a secret drinker* 秘密酗酒者一双湿润的眼睛 **3 secret about sth** liking to keep things secret; SECRETIVE 对某事严守秘密 —**secretly** *adv*: *They were secretly married last week.* 他们上周秘密结婚。

secret² *n* **1** something kept hidden or known about by only a few people 秘密: *Our plans must remain a secret.* 我们的计划必须保密。| **keep a secret** (=not tell a secret to anyone) 保守秘密 *Can you keep a secret?* 你能保守秘密吗? | **let sb in on the secret** (=tell someone a secret) 让某人知道某个秘密 | **closely-guarded secret** (=one that is carefully kept) 严守的秘密 **2 the secret of** a particular way of achieving a good result, that is the best or only way …的秘诀，…的诀窍: *the secret to making good bread* 制作上乘面包的秘诀 | **the secret of success** *What do you think is the secret of her success?* 你认为她成功的诀窍是什么? **3 in secret** in a private way or place that other people do not know about 秘密地，暗地里: *Lilian cried in secret, afraid to tell anyone.* 莉莲偷偷地哭，不敢告诉任何人。 **4 make no secret of** to make your opinions about something clear 不隐瞒〔意见〕: *Howard made no secret of his disappointment.* 霍华德毫不掩饰他的失望。 **5 the secrets of nature/the universe etc** the things no one yet knows about nature etc 大自然/宇宙等的奥秘

secret a·gent /ˌ·· ˈ··/ *n* [C] someone whose job is to find out and report on the military and political secrets of other countries 特工人员，特务〔收集他国军事和政治秘密的人〕

sec·re·tar·i·al /ˌsɛkrəˈtɛrɪəl; ˌsekr̩ˈteəriəl/ *adj* connected with the work of a secretary (有关)秘书工作的: *a secretarial course* 秘书课程

sec·re·tar·i·at /ˌsɛkrəˈtɛrɪət; ˌsekr̩ˈteəriət/ *n* [C] a government office or the office of an international organization with a SECRETARY (2) or SECRETARY GENERAL who is in charge 秘书处，书记处: *the United Nations Secretariat in New York* 设在纽约的联合国秘书处

sec·re·ta·ry /ˈsɛkrəˌtɛrɪ; ˈsekr̩təri/ *n* [C] **1** someone who works in an office typing (TYPE² (1)) letters, keeping records, arranging meetings etc 秘书: *Julie works as a secretary in a lawyer's office.* 朱莉在一个律师事务所当秘书。| *You can ring my secretary to make an appointment.* 你可以打电话给我的秘书预约时间。 **2 a)** a British government official, such as a minister or someone who has a high rank in a department〔英国的〕大臣，高级官员: *the Foreign Secretary* 外交大臣 | **Secretary of State** *the Secretary of State for Home Affairs* 内政大臣 | **Permanent Secretary** (=someone in charge of a government department) 政府部门主管 **b)** an official who is chosen by the president of the US, who is in charge of a large government department〔美国政府的〕部长: *the Secretary of the Treasury* 财政部长 | **Secretary of State** (=the person who deals with American relations with other countries) 国务卿 **c)** a British government representative, below the rank of AMBASSADOR

〔英国的〕大使馆秘书: *the First Secretary at the British Embassy* 英国大使馆的一等秘书 **3** an official of an organization who keeps records, writes official letters etc〔一个组织的〕书记员, 干事: *secretary of the Wilton Tennis Club* 威尔顿网球俱乐部干事

> **CULTURAL NOTE 文化注释**
> In the US and UK, secretaries are often women. The STEREOTYPE of a secretary is of a pretty young woman who is very concerned about her appearance, and who spends a lot of time talking to her friends on the telephone and filing (FILE[2]) her nails. People often joke about married male employers having sexual relationships with their secretaries. 在美国和英国, 秘书通常是女性。典型的秘书是年轻漂亮的女子, 她们过分关注自己的外表, 花很多时间给朋友打电话闲谈和修指甲。人们经常开玩笑说已婚男雇主同他们的秘书发生性关系。

secretary gen·e·ral /ˌ····ˈ···/ *n* [C] the most important official in charge of a large organization, especially an international organization〔主管大机构, 尤其是国际组织的〕秘书长, 书记长, 总干事: *the UN Secretary General* 联合国秘书长

se·crete /sɪˋkrit; sɪˈkriːt/ *v* [T] *technical*【术语】**1** if a part of an animal or plant secretes a substance, it produces it〔动物或植物的某一部分〕分泌〔某物质〕: *Hormones are secreted by various glands.* 激素是由各种腺体分泌的。—see also 另见 EXCRETE **2** *formal* to hide something【正式】隐藏, 藏匿〔某物〕: *McCready secreted the package inside his donkey-jacket.* 麦克里迪把包裹藏在他的厚外衣里面。

se·cre·tion /sɪˋkriʃən; sɪˈkriːʃən/ *n* **1 a)** [C,U] *technical* a substance, usually liquid, produced by part of a plant or animal【术语】〔动物或植物某一部分的〕分泌物 **b)** [U] the production of this material 分泌: *the secretion of enzymes* 酶的分泌 **2** [U] *formal* the act of hiding something【正式】藏匿

se·cre·tive /ˋsikrətɪv; ˈsiːkrətɪv/ *adj* someone who is secretive likes to keep their thoughts, intentions or actions hidden from others〔某人〕守口如瓶的, 遮遮掩掩的: *Everyone was very secretive about their earnings.* 每个人都闭口不谈自己的薪酬。—**secretively** *adv* —**secretiveness** *n* [U]

secret po·lice, the /ˌ··ˈ·/ *n* a police force controlled by a government, that secretly tries to defeat the political enemies of that government〔政府用以打击政敌的〕秘密警察

secret ser·vice /ˌ··ˈ··/ *n* [singular] **1** a British government organization that uses SECRET AGENTS to obtain secret information about other countries〔英国的〕特工部门, 特务机关 **2** a US government department dealing with special kinds of police work, especially protecting the President〔尤指保护美国总统的〕特工处

sect /sɛkt; sekt/ *n* [C] a group of people with their own particular set of beliefs and practices, especially within or separated from a larger religious group 派别, 宗派;〔尤指宗教的〕教派: *an early, ascetic Christian sect* 一个早期的基督教禁欲教派

sec·tar·i·an /sɛkˋtɛrɪən; sekˈteəriən/ *adj* **1 sectarian violence/conflict/murder etc** violence etc that is connected with the strong feelings between people of different religious groups 教派之间的暴力/冲突/谋杀等 **2** *especially AmE* supporting a particular religious group and its beliefs【尤美】宗派的, 教派的: *a sectarian journal* 教派的期刊 —**sectarianism** *n* [U]

sec·tion[1] /ˋsɛkʃən; ˈsekʃən/ *n*

1 ▶PLACE/OBJECT 地方/物品◀ [C] one of the parts that something, such as an object or place is divided into 部分: **[+of]** *The spoons go in the front section of the drawer.* 匙子放在抽屉内靠前的地方。| *one of the older sections of Philadelphia* 费城旧城区的一部分 | *Decorate the torte with orange sections.* 用一瓣瓣的橙子装饰这个大蛋糕。| *the back section of the plane* 飞机的后部

2 ▶GROUP OF PEOPLE 人群◀ [C] a separate group within a larger group of people〔大集体中的〕小团体, 小集团: **[+of]** *a large section of the American public* 美国公众的一大部分 | **all sections of the community** (=everyone in a particular place) 社区内的每一个人

3 ▶ORGANIZATION/INSTITUTION 组织/机构◀ [C] one of the parts of an organization, institution, department etc 部门; 处, 科, 组: *all the salespeople in my section* 我这个部门的全体销售人员 | *the reference section of the library* 图书馆的参考书阅览室 | **brass/woodwind etc section** (=the part of an orchestra that plays those instruments)〔交响乐队中的〕铜管/木管乐组等

4 ▶FITTING TOGETHER 装配◀ [C] one of the parts of something that you fit together 部件, 零件: *You buy the bookcase in sections and assemble it.* 你买书橱的部件, 然后自己把它组装起来。

5 ▶BOOK/NEWSPAPER/REPORT 书/报纸/报道◀ [C] a separate part of something that is written, such as a book or newspaper〔书、报等的〕节; 栏; 版: *Who has the sports section?* 谁拿走了报纸的体育版? | *in the final section of this chapter* 在这一章的最后一节

6 ▶SIDE/TOP VIEW 侧视/顶视图◀ [C,U] a picture that shows what a building, part of the body etc would look like if it were cut from top to bottom or side to side 纵剖面, 纵切面; 横切面, 断面: **in section** *Here's the outside view, and here are the floors in section.* 这是外视图, 而这是各楼层的剖面图。

7 ▶MEDICAL/SCIENTIFIC 医学的/科学的◀ *technical*【术语】**a)** [C,U] a medical operation that involves cutting〔医疗手术的〕切开, 开刀 **b)** [C] a very thin flat piece that is cut from skin, a plant etc to be looked at under a microscope〔放在显微镜下观察的皮肤、植物等的〕切片

8 ▶PART OF A TOWN 城镇的一部分◀ [C] *AmE* a part of a town in the western US that is one mile square【美】〔美国西部城镇〕一英里见方的面积

9 ▶MATHEMATICS 数学◀ [C] *technical* the shape that is made when a solid figure is cut by a flat surface in mathematics【术语】〔数学中的〕截面: *conic sections* 圆锥截面 —see also 另见 CROSS-SECTION

section[2] *v* [T] *technical*【术语】**1** to cut a SECTION from skin, a plant, or a shape in mathematics etc 做〔皮肤或植物〕的切片; 显示[做]〔数学图形〕的截面 **2** to draw a SECTION[1] (6) of something such as a house 画〔房子等的〕剖面图 **3** to cut a part of the body in a medical operation〔在医疗手术中〕把〔身体的某部分〕切开, 开刀

section sth ↔ off *phr v* [T] to divide an area into parts, by making a dividing line between them 将〔某物〕分成部分: *The vegetable plots were sectioned off by a low wall.* 菜地被矮墙分成一块一块的。

sec·tion·al /ˋsɛkʃənl; ˈsekʃənəl/ *adj* **1** made up of sections that can be put together or taken apart 拼合而成的, 可拆卸的; *a six-foot sectional sofa* 一张六英尺长的组合沙发 **2** limited to one particular group or area within a larger group 某一群体的, 局部的: *different sectional interests each seeking to represent working women* 寻求代表职业妇女的各个不同利益集团 **3** connected with a SECTION[1] (6) 断面的, 截面的: *a sectional view of the new building* 新大楼的断面图

sec·tion·al·is·m /ˋsɛkʃənḷˌɪzəm; ˈsekʃənəlɪzəm/ *n* [U] too much loyalty towards your own political or social group 宗派主义; 地方主义; 本位主义

Section Eight /ˌ··ˈ·/ *AmE* an order that someone should be dismissed from the US army because they are crazy【美】《美国陆军条例》第八款〔有关开除精神失常者军籍的条款〕

sec·tor /ˋsɛktɚ; ˈsektə/ *n* [C] **1** a part of an area of activity, especially of business, trade etc〔尤指商业、贸易等的〕部门; 行业: **[+of]** *the agricultural sector of the economy* 〔国民〕经济中的农业部门 | *understaffing in all sectors of the educational system* 教育系统各部门的人员不足问题 | **public/private sector** (=business controlled by the government or by private companies)〔商业的〕国营/私营部门 **2** one of the parts into which an area is divided for a purpose, especially for military reasons〔为某种目的设立的〕地区;〔尤指军事的〕防区, 战区: *Planes searched a broad sector of the Indian Ocean.* 飞机搜索了印度洋的一大片海域。**3** *technical* an area in a circle enclosed by two straight lines drawn from the centre to the edge【术语】扇形 —see picture at 参见 SHAPE[1] 图

sec·u·lar /ˋsɛkjəlɚ; ˈsekjʊlə/ *adj* **1** not connected with or controlled by a church or other religious authority 不与教会联系的, 不受教会管辖的: *secular education* 世俗教育 | *our modern secular society* 我们现代的世俗化社会 **2** a secular priest lives among ordinary people, rather than with other priests in a MONASTERY〔教士〕住在俗人之中的, 不住在修道院内的

sec·u·lar·is·m /ˋsɛkjələrˌɪzəm; ˈsekjʊlərɪzəm/ *n* [U] a system of social organization that keeps out all forms of religion 现世主义, 世俗化〔指拒绝一切宗教教义或活动的社会组织体系〕—**secularist** *n* [C]

sec·u·lar·ize also 又作 **-ise** *BrE*【英】/ˋsɛkjələˌraɪz; ˈsekjʊləraɪz/ *v* [T] to remove the control or influence of religious groups from a society or an institution 使世俗化, 使脱离宗教影响 —**secularization** /ˌsɛkjələrəˋzeʃən; ˌsekjʊləraɪˈzeɪʃən/ *n* [U]

[2] **se·cure¹** /sɪˈkjʊr; sɪˈkjʊə/ *v* [T] **1** to get or achieve something that will be permanent, especially after a lot of effort〔尤指经过努力而〕获得, 永久得到〔某物〕: *UN negotiators are still trying to secure the release of the hostages.* 联合国的谈判人员仍在努力争取人质获释。| *a deal to secure the company's future* 为保障公司前途的交易 **2** to make something safe from being attacked, harmed, or lost 使安全, 保护…〔免受攻击、伤害或损失〕: **[+against]** *Extra men will be needed to secure the camp against attack.* 需要增加兵力以保护兵营免遭攻击。**3** to fasten or tie something firmly in a particular position 缚牢, 系紧, 将〔某物〕固定: *a tent secured with heavy wooden pegs* 用粗大木桩牢牢固定的帐篷 | **secure sth to sth** *John secured the boat firmly to the jetty.* 约翰把小船牢牢地系在码头上。**4** to legally promise that if you cannot pay back money you have borrowed, you will give the lender goods or property of the same value instead 向〔债权人〕提供保证〔偿还债务〕, 为〔借款〕作保: *a secured loan* 有担保的贷款

[3] **secure²** *adj*

1 ▶PERMANENT/CERTAIN 永久的/确定的◀ a situation that is secure is one that you can depend on because it is not likely to change 稳固的, 可靠的, 稳定的: *There is no such thing as a secure job these days.* 近来已没有稳定的工作这种事情了。| *a secure source of funds* 可靠的资金来源 | **on secure ground** (=when you know exactly what to do or say) 有把握

2 ▶SAFE PLACE 安全的地方◀ **a)** locked or guarded so that people cannot get in or out, or steal anything 锁牢的; 关紧的: *Make sure the doors and windows are secure before you leave.* 出门之前一定要把门窗关好。**b)** safe from and protected against attacks 安全的, 受保护的: **[+from]** *The southern border is secure from enemy shelling.* 南部边境不会遭受敌人的炮轰。

3 ▶SAFE FEELING 安全感◀ feeling safe and protected from danger 安心的, 无恐惧的, 感到安全的: *I'll feel more secure with a burglar alarm.* 装了防盗警报器, 我就更加安心了。

4 ▶CONFIDENT 有信心的◀ **a)** feeling confident about yourself and your abilities〔对自己和自己的能力〕有自信的: *a secure and happy child* 自信而快乐的小孩 —opposite 反义词 INSECURE (1) **b)** feeling confident and certain about a situation and not worried that it might change 有保障的, 没有顾虑的: *We're waiting to have kids until we're financially secure.* 我们要等到经济上有保障时才生养孩子。| **secure in the knowledge that** *Myles relaxed, secure in the knowledge that they wouldn't find him.* 迈尔斯知道他们不会发现他, 因而放下心来。

5 ▶FIRMLY FIXED 牢固的◀ firmly fixed, tied, or fastened 固定住的, 系牢的, 缚紧的: *Are you sure that shelf is secure?* 你肯定那个架子牢固吗?

se·cure·ly /sɪˈkjʊrlɪ; sɪˈkjʊəli/ *adv* tied, fastened etc tightly, especially in order to make something safe 牢靠地: **securely locked/fastened/tied etc** *Make sure the saddle is securely buckled so it doesn't come loose.* 一定要把马鞍牢牢扣紧, 以免松开。

Securities and Ex·change Com·mis·sion, the /ˌ·ˌ··· ·ˈ· ·ˌ··/ abbreviation 缩写为 **SEC** a US government organization which makes sure that people and companies obey the laws about the sale of STOCKs and BONDs 证券交易委员会〔美国一政府机构。其职责是确保个人和公司遵守股票与债券交易的有关法规〕

Securities and In·vest·ments Board, the /ˌ·ˌ··· ·ˈ··ˌ ·/ abbreviation 缩写为 **SIB** a British organization that makes sure investment businesses in the UK work fairly and are not involved in dishonest business methods 证券与投资委员会〔英国一机构。其职责是确保英国投资公司公平交易, 不使用非正当经营手段〕

[1] **se·cu·ri·ty** /sɪˈkjʊrətɪ; sɪˈkjʊərɪ̣ti/ *n*

1 ▶PUBLIC/GOVERNMENT SAFETY 公众/政府的安全(保障)◀ [U] things that are done in order to keep someone or something safe 保安, 保安措施: *For reasons of security, all luggage must be searched.* 出于安全考虑, 所有行李必须接受检查。| **security measures/checks/procedures etc** *Strict security measures were in force during the President's visit.* 总统访问期间实行了严密的保安措施。| **national/state security** (=protection of a country from attack or harm) 国家的安全 | **tight security** (=careful protection using a lot of soldiers, police etc) 严密的保安(措施) | **security man/guard** (=someone employed to protect a person or building) 保安人员 | **security forces/operations etc** (=those whose job is to protect a country, sometimes used to avoid saying military) 保安部队/行动等 *the UN Security Forces* 联合国维和部队 | **security firm** (=a company that provides protection for other people's property, money etc)〔向别人提供对财产、金钱等保护的〕保安公司 | **maximum security prison** (=for very dangerous prisoners, from which it is very difficult to escape) 采取最严密警戒措施的监狱 | **high security** (=carefully protected or made safe) 严密保护

2 ▶PROTECTION FROM BAD SITUATIONS 对不良环境的抵御◀ [U] **a)** the state of being protected from the bad things that could happen to you 保障, 保护: **job security** (=not being in danger of losing your job) 工作保障 | **financial security** (=knowing you have enough money to pay for the things you need) 经济保障 *This plan can offer your family financial security in the event of your death.* 这个方案能在你一旦死亡时给你的家庭提供经济保障。**b)** something that protects you from the bad things that could happen to you 提供保障的东西, 防御物: **[+against]** *Does your insurance provide enough security against illness?* 你的保险对疾病的治疗能提供足够的保障吗? | **[+of]** *the security of a loving family* 相亲相爱的家庭所带来的安全感

3 ▶GUARDS 保安◀ [U] the department of a company which deals with the protection of its buildings and equipment〔公司的〕保安部门: *I'll have to report this to Security.* 我将不得不把此事报告保安部门。

4 ▶BORROWING MONEY 借钱◀ [U] something such as property that you promise to give someone if you cannot pay back money you have borrowed from them 抵押品: **put sth up as security** *She had to put up her house as security on the loan.* 她不得不以自己的房子作为那笔贷款的抵押。

5 ▶SAFETY FROM HARM 不受损害◀ [U] how safe something is from being lost, stolen, or damaged 安全: *If you're worried about their security, put your jewels in the hotel safe.* 要是你担心珠宝的安全, 那就存放在旅馆的保险柜里吧。

6 securities [plural] stocks (STOCK¹ (3)) or shares (SHARE² (5)) 证券

security blank·et /·ˈ··· ˌ··/ *n* [C] a BLANKET¹ (1), soft toy etc that a child likes to hold and touch to comfort themselves 安乐毯〔小孩喜欢抱着和抚摸而产生舒适感的小绒毯〕

security clear·ance /·ˈ··· ˌ··/ *n* [C,U] official permission for someone to see secret documents etc, or to enter a building, after a strict checking process 安全审查〔经严格审查后正式准予阅读机密文件或进入某处〕

Security Coun·cil, the /·ˈ··· ˌ··/ the most powerful part of the United Nations, which is responsible for making sure that countries behave peacefully towards each other, and for deciding what the United Nations should do if countries go to war. It is a committee of five permanent members (the US, the UK, Russia, France, and China) and ten other members who change every two years. 安全理事会, 安理会〔联合国权力最大的机构。其职责是确保各国和平相处, 如有国家交战, 决定联合国应采取何种行动。安全理事会有五个常任理事国(美国、英国、俄罗斯、法国、中国)和十个理事国, 理事国每两年改选一次〕

security guard /·ˈ··· ˌ·/ *n* [C] someone whose job is to guard a building or a vehicle carrying money 保安人员〈如门卫或押解运钞车者〉

security light /·ˈ··· ˌ·/ *n* [C] a light that turns on when someone tries to enter a dark building or area 智控安全灯〔当有人进入黑暗建筑物或地区时能自动启亮的灯〕—see picture on page A4 参见 A4 页图

security risk /·ˈ··· ˌ·/ *n* [C] someone who cannot be trusted by a government and who therefore is not allowed to do particular jobs〔不能担任涉及国家安全职务的〕不可靠分子, 政府不信任的人

security ser·vice /·ˈ··· ˌ··/ *n* [C] a government organization that protects a country's secrets against enemy countries or protects the government against attempts to take away its power〔政府的〕保安部门, 安全机构

se·dan /sɪˈdæn; sɪˈdæn/ *n* [C] *AmE and AustrE* a large car that has a separate enclosed space for your bags etc【美和澳】大轿车, 厢式轿车; SALOON (2) *BrE*【英】

sedan chair /·ˌ· ˈ·/ *n* [C] a seat on two poles with a cover around it on which an important person was carried in former times〔旧时的〕轿子

se·date¹ /sɪˈdet; sɪˈdeɪt/ *adj* **1** moving in a slow and rather formal way〔行进〕缓慢而庄重的: *a sedate procession* 缓慢而庄重的队伍 **2** peaceful, ordinary, and not very exciting 安静的, 安详的: *a sedate seaside town on the South Coast* 南部海岸宁静的海边小镇 —**sedately** *adv* —**sedateness** *n* [U]

sedate² *v* [T often passive 常用被动态] to make someone sleepy or calm by giving them drugs 给〔某人〕服镇静剂

se·da·tion /sɪˈdeʃən; sɪˈdeɪʃən/ *n* [U] the use of drugs to make someone sleepy or calm〔服镇静剂后的〕镇静〔状态〕: **under (heavy) sedation** *I couldn't speak to her as she was still under sedation.* 我不能同她说话, 因为她仍处于服药后的镇静状态。

S

sed·a·tive /ˋsɛdətɪv; ˈsedətɪv/ *n* [C] a drug used to make someone sleepy or calm 镇静药, 镇静剂

sed·en·ta·ry /ˋsɛdn̩ˌtɛrɪ; ˈsedəntəri/ *adj formal*【正式】**1** a sedentary job is done while sitting down, and without moving around very much〔工作〕坐着做的, 案头的 **2** a sedentary group of people tend always to live in the same place; SETTLED〔人群〕固定不迁移的, 定居的: *a sedentary population* 定居人口

Seder /ˋsedɚ; ˈseɪdə/ a special dinner which takes place on the first two nights of Passover and is held to remember the occasion when the Jewish people left Egypt 逾越节家宴〔逾越节前两个晚上的特殊餐宴。是纪念犹太人出埃及的日子〕

sedge /sɛdʒ; sedʒ/ *n* [U] a plant like grass that grows in groups on low wet ground〔生长于低洼湿地的〕苔草

sed·i·ment /ˋsɛdəmənt; ˈsedɪ̣mənt/ *n* [singular,U] solid matter that settles at the bottom of a liquid 沉淀物, 沉积物: *a brownish sediment at the bottom of the tank* 罐底的褐色沉淀物 —see picture on page A12 参见 A12 页图

sed·i·men·ta·ry /ˌsɛdəˋmɛntərɪ; ˌsedɪ̣ˈmentəri◂/ *adj* made of the solid matter that settles at the bottom of the sea, rivers, lakes etc〔在海、河、湖等的底部〕沉积的, 由沉淀物形成的: *sedimentary rock* 沉积岩 | *sedimentary deposits* 沉积矿床

sed·i·men·ta·tion /ˌsɛdəmɛnˋteʃən; ˌsedɪ̣menˈteɪʃən/ *n* [U] the natural process by which small pieces of rock, earth etc settle at the bottom of the sea etc and form a solid layer〔地质上的〕沉积(作用)

se·di·tion /sɪˋdɪʃən; sɪˈdɪʃən/ *n* [U] *formal* speech, writing, or actions intended to encourage people to disobey a government【正式】煽动反政府的言论[行动]: *Leading activists of their party were charged with sedition.* 他们党的主要活动分子被指控犯有煽动反政府罪。

se·di·tious /sɪˋdɪʃəs; sɪˈdɪʃəs/ *adj formal* intended to illegally encourage people to disobey the government【正式】〔非法〕煽动性的, 煽动反政府的: *a seditious speech* 煽动性的演说 —**seditiously** *adv*

se·duce /sɪˋdjus; sɪˈdjuːs/ *v* [T often passive 常用被动态] **1** to persuade someone to have sex with you, especially someone who is younger than you or in a weaker position than you〔尤指对比自己年轻或处于弱势的人的〕诱奸, 勾引: *The head lecturer here was sacked for seducing female students.* 这儿的首席讲师因诱奸女学生而被解雇。**2** to make someone want to do something by making it seem very attractive or interesting to them 引诱, 诱使: **seduce sb into doing sth** *Jim was seduced into leaving the company by the offer of higher pay.* 吉姆受了更优厚薪酬的诱惑而离开公司。—**seducer** *n* [C]

se·duc·tion /sɪˋdʌkʃən; sɪˈdʌkʃən/ *n* **1** [C,U] an act of persuading someone to have sex with you for the first time 引诱, 勾引: *the seduction scene in Act 2 of the Opera* 歌剧第二幕的诱奸戏 **2** [C usually plural 一般用复数] something that strongly attracts people, but often has a bad effect on their lives〔常指对人产生不良后果的〕诱惑物, 有魅力的东西: *the seduction of money* 金钱的诱惑

se·duc·tive /sɪˋdʌktɪv; sɪˈdʌktɪv/ *adj* **1** someone who is seductive is sexually attractive〔人〕性感的, 勾引人的: *She had a low, seductive voice.* 她有一种低沉而富有诱惑力的嗓音。**2** something that is seductive is very interesting or attractive to you, in a way that persuades you to do something you would not usually do〔某物〕有吸引力的, 有诱惑力的: *the seductive power of advertising* 广告的诱惑力 —**seductively** *adv*: *She smiled seductively at him across the table.* 她坐在桌子的对面向他展现诱人的微笑。—**seductiveness** *n* [U]

sed·u·lous /ˋsɛdʒələs; ˈsedjʊ̣ləs/ *adj formal* hard working and determined【正式】勤奋的, 孜孜不倦的: *a sedulous worker* 勤奋的工人 —**sedulously** *adv*

see 看(见)

Karen was blindfolded so she couldn't see anything.
卡伦被蒙住了眼睛, 什么也看不见。

They looked at the paintings.
他们看着画。

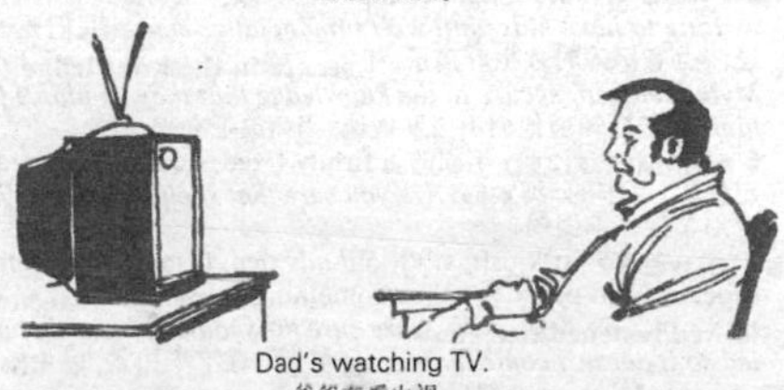

Dad's watching TV.
爸爸在看电视。

see¹ /si; siː/ *v past tense* **saw** /sɔ; sɔː/ *past participle* **seen** /sin; siːn/

① UNDERSTAND/REALIZE 理解/意识	⑦ FUTURE 将来
② WITH YOUR EYES 用眼睛	⑧ IMAGINE 想象
③ FIND OUT 发现	⑨ MAKE SURE 确保
④ GOODBYE 道别	⑩ EXPERIENCE 经验
⑤ VISIT/MEET 探访/见面	⑪ GO WITH SB 陪同某人
⑥ CONSIDER 考虑	⑫ OTHER MEANINGS 其他意思

① UNDERSTAND/REALIZE 理解/意识

1 [I,T] to understand or realize something 明白, 理解, 认识到: *I can see that you're not very happy with the situation.* 我能理解你对这种状况不太愉快。| *Seeing his distress, Louise put her arm around him.* 看到他苦恼, 路易丝伸出手臂搂住他。| [**+why/what/who etc**] *"Ann's really fed up." "I can see why!"* "安确实厌烦了。" "我知道为了什么!" | **see what sb means** *usually spoken* (=understand what someone is saying)【一般口】明白某人的意思 *Do you see what I mean?* 你明白我的意思吗? | **see the point** (=understand the reason for something) 认识〔某事的〕意义 *I can't see the point of learning Latin when you're never going to use it.* 既然你永远用不上拉丁文, 我就不明白你学习它有什么意义。| **see both sides** (=understand both opinions in a discussion or argument)〔在讨论或争辩中〕了解双方的观点 | **not see that it matters** (=not think something is important) 认为它无关紧要 *The recipe says to use fresh cream, but I can't see that it matters.* 食谱说要用新鲜奶油, 但我认为这无关紧要。| **not see the joke** (=not understand why something is funny) 听不懂那有什么好笑 *Ian laughed politely even though he couldn't see the joke.* 伊恩尽管听不懂那个笑话, 但还是礼貌地笑了笑。| **not see reason/sense** (=realize you are being silly or unreasonable) 不明白道理 *I've tried to explain that we can't afford it, but he just won't see reason.* 我已尽力解释过我们买不起, 但他就是不明白这个道理。

2 I see *spoken* used to show that you are listening to what someone is telling you and that you understand it【口】我明白了〔用于表示听懂别人所说的话〕: *"You turn this dial to control the central heating." "Oh, I see."* "你转动这个标度盘来控制中央暖气的温度。""噢，我明白了。"

3 you see *spoken* used when you are explaining something to someone【口】你瞧，你知道〔用于对别人解释某事〕: *The shop's open till 8 you see, so I can pick some stuff up after work.* 你知道，这商店一直要开到 8 点，所以我可以在下班后买点东西。| *You see the thing is I'm really busy right now.* 你瞧，事实上我此刻的确很忙。

4 see *spoken* used to check that someone is listening and understands what you are explaining to them【口】明白了吧〔用于弄清对方是否在听并理解所作的解释〕: *You mix the flour and eggs like this, see.* 你把面粉和鸡蛋这样混在一起，明白了吗？

5 see sth for what it is/see sb for what they are to realize that someone or something is not as good or pleasant as they seem 看透某事/识破某人

6 not see the wood for the trees also 又作 **not see the forest for the trees** *AmE*【美】to be unable to understand something because you are looking too much at small details rather than the whole thing 见木不见林，见小不见大，只见细节不见全面

② WITH YOUR EYES 用眼睛

7 ▶ABILITY TO SEE 视力◀ [I,T not in progressive 不用进行时] to be able to use your eyes to look at things and know what they are 看，看见，看到: *I can't see a thing without my glasses!* 我不戴眼镜什么也看不见！| **not see to do sth** *It's so dark I can hardly see to do my work.* 天太黑了，我几乎看不见，没法做我的工作。

8 ▶NOTICE/EXAMINE 注意/察看◀ [T not in progressive 不用进行时] to notice, examine, or recognize someone or something by looking 看出，留意（到），查看，认出: *Can I see your ticket, please?* 我可以查看一下你的票吗？| *You see a lot of men with long hair these days.* 如今你可以看到很多男人留着长头发。| **[+where/what/who]** *Can you see where I put my pen?* 你看到我把笔放在哪儿了吗？| **see (that)** *They could see that he had been crying.* 他们能看出他一直在哭。| **see sb/sth doing sth** *I see the neighbours are having a barbecue again.* 我看邻居们又在烧烤了。| *The suspect was seen entering the building at 15.00 hours.* 有人看到嫌疑犯在下午 3 点钟进入那幢大楼。| **see sb/sth do sth** *Pat thought he saw her drive off about an hour later.* 帕特认为自己看到她大约在一小时后驾车离去。| **[+if/whether]** *Nick went out to see if the pond had frozen over.* 尼克出去看看水塘是否结了冰。| **see sb around** (=notice someone regularly in places you go to without knowing them) 经常见到某人〔但并不认识〕 *I don't know his name but I've seen him around.* 我不知道他的姓名，但我常常在那儿见到他。

9 see a film/movie/play to watch a film etc 看电影/看戏: *I saw a really good movie last night.* 昨晚我看了一部很精彩的电影。

10 ▶TELEVISION 电视◀ [T not in progressive 不用进行时] to watch a particular programme on television 看〔电视节目〕: *Did you see the game last night?* 你昨晚看了球赛没有？

11 ▶FIND INFORMATION 发现信息◀ [T only in imperative 仅用于祈使句] used to tell you where you can find information 参阅，见: *See p.58.* 参阅第 58 页。| *See press for details.* 详情请阅报纸。| **see above/below** *The results are shown in Table 7a (see below).* 结果如表 7a 所示（见下文）。

12 be seen to look at or be noticed by people who are important in society〔重要人物〕露面; 受〔重要人物〕注意: *Royal Ascot is the place to be seen.* 皇家阿斯科特赛马会是要人露面的场所。

13 be seen to be doing sth to make sure that other people notice you working hard or doing something good 让他人注意到自己在努力做某事: *The government must be seen to be doing something about the rise in violent crime.* 政府必须向大家证明确实采取行动对付暴力犯罪的增加。

③ FIND OUT 发现

14 [T] to find out information or a fact 查看，发现〔信息或事实〕: **[+what/when/who/how etc]** *Can you see who's at the door?* 你去看看门外是谁来了，好吗？| **[+if/whether]** *Sharon! See if there's any beer in the fridge!* 莎伦！看看冰箱里还有没有啤酒！| *an experiment to see whether the new material melts at high temperatures* 观察这种新材料在高温下是否熔化的实验 | **see for yourself** (=used to tell someone to look at something so that they can find out if it is true) 亲眼看看 *If you don't believe me, see for yourself.* 你要是不相信我，那就亲自去看看吧。

15 see what sb/sth can do *spoken*【口】**a)** to find out if you can deal with a situation or problem 弄清楚某人/某物能做什么: **[+about]** *I'll see what I can do about speeding up the process.* 我会看看我能否做些什么来加快这个进程。**b)** to find out how good someone or something is at what they are supposed to be able to do 弄清某人/某物是否真能…: *Let's take the Porsche out to the racetrack and see what it can do!* 我们把这辆保时捷开到跑道上去，看看它到底能跑多快！

④ GOODBYE 道别

16 see you! *spoken* used to say goodbye when you know you will see someone again【口】再见: **see you tomorrow/at 3/Sunday etc** *See you Friday – your place at 8:30.* 星期五见——8 点 30 分在你家。| **see you in a bit** *BrE* (=see you soon)【英】待会儿见 | **see you in a while** (=see you soon) *AmE*【美】待会儿见 | **(I'll) be seeing you!** (=see you soon) 再见！待会儿再见！

17 see you around *spoken* used to say goodbye to someone when you have not made a definite arrangement to meet again【口】再见〔用于在分别时没有约定再见面的具体时间〕

18 see you later *spoken* used to say goodbye to someone when you are going to see them again soon or later in the same day【口】回头见〔用于在当天晚些时候或不久后还要再见面〕

⑤ VISIT/MEET 探访/见面

19 ▶VISIT/MEET SB 探访/会见某人◀ [T] to visit or meet someone 探访，会见: *We're going to see Lucy after work.* 我们下班后去探望露西。| **see you** (=I will meet you) 再见 *See you at 8 at Bear's Place.* 8 点在贝厄餐馆见。

20 ▶HAVE A MEETING 会见◀ [T] to have an arranged meeting with someone 约见，接待: *Mr Thomas is seeing a client at 2:30.* 托马斯先生两点半要接待一位客户。| **see sb about sth** (=see someone to discuss something) 会见某人讨论某事 *I have to see my teacher about my grades.* 我得去见老师谈我的分数问题。

21 ▶BY CHANCE 偶然地◀ [T, not in progressive 不用进行式] to meet someone by chance 偶遇，碰见: *I saw Penny in town today.* 今天我在城里遇见了彭妮。

22 ▶SPEND TIME WITH SB 与某人在一起◀ [T] to spend time with someone 与…来往，与…见面: *Do you still see any of your old college friends?* 你还和昔日的大学同学保持来往吗？| **see a lot of sb** (=see someone often) 常与某人见面 *She's been seeing a lot of John recently.* 她近来与约翰经常见面。| **see more/less of sb** (=see someone more or less often) 较多/较少见到某人 *They've seen much more of each other since Dan moved to London.* 自从丹搬到伦敦之后，他们彼此见面的机会就多得多了。

23 ▶HAVE A VISIT 接待来访◀ [T] to have a visit from someone 接待〔某人〕的造访，来访: *She's too sick to see anyone at the moment.* 她目前病得很重，不能见任何人。

24 be seeing sb to be having a romantic relationship with someone 与某人谈恋爱: *Is she seeing anyone at the moment?* 她这阵子是否正在和什么人谈恋爱？

⑥ CONSIDER 考虑

25 see sb/sth as sth to consider something to be a particular thing or to have a particular quality 把某人/某物看作…: *Jake saw any man who spoke to his wife as a potential threat.* 杰克认为任何一个与他妻子说话的男人都是一个潜在的威胁。| **be seen as sth** *America is seen as the land of opportunity.* 美国被认为是充满机遇的国家。

26 ▶CONSIDER STH IN A PARTICULAR WAY 以特定方式考虑某事◀ [T always+adv/prep] to regard or consider something in a particular way〔以特定方式〕考虑，看待〔问题〕: *He sees things differently now that he's in management.* 他既已进了管理层，看问题就不同了。| **as sb sees it** (=according to someone's opinion of a situation) 依某人的观点 *As they see it, I'm the one to blame.* 他们认为，我是难辞其咎的。| **the way I see it** *spoken*【口】*Well, the way I see it, nothing's really going to change around here.* 嗯，依我看，这儿不会有什么真正的改变。| **see fit (to do sth)** (=consider an action to be right and sensible) 认为〔某种做法〕妥当[合适] *You must do whatever you see fit.* 你必须做你认为合情合理的事情。

27 seeing that considering that 考虑到: *She writes very well seeing that English isn't her first language.* 考虑到英语不是她的第一语言，她写得算是够棒的了。

28 (be) seen against sth to be considered together with something else 与某事摆在一起来考虑: *The unemployment data must*

be seen against the backdrop of world recession. 失业数字一定要放在全球经济不景气的背景下来考虑。

⑦ **FUTURE** 将来

29 [I,T] to find out about something in the future〔将来〕见到: [**+if/whether**] *It will be interesting to see whether Glenn gets the job.* 看格伦能否得到这份工作将会是很有意思的。| [**+how/what/when etc**] *I might come – I'll see how I feel tomorrow.* 我也许会来，我要等明天看看身体如何。| **we'll see** *spoken* (=used when you do not want to make a decision immediately)【口】看看再说 *"Can we go to the zoo, Dad?" "We'll see."* "爸爸，我们可以去动物园吗?" "看看再说吧。" | **I'll/we'll have to see** (=used when you cannot make a decision immediately) 我/我们得看看再说 *I don't know if I can lend you that much – I'll have to see.* 我不知道能否借给你那么多钱——我得看看再说。| **wait and see** *spoken*【口】*We'll just have to wait and see.* 我们还得等着瞧。| **see how it goes/see how things go** *usually spoken* (=used when you are going to do something and will deal with problems as they appear)【一般口】看看情况怎样发展 | **you'll see** *spoken* (=used to tell someone that something will happen in the way you have described it)【口】将来你就知道 *I'll do better than any of them, you'll see.* 我会做得比他们任何人都好，你等着瞧吧。

30 **see sth coming** to realize that there is going to be a problem before it actually happens 预见会出现某事[问题]: *We should really have seen this mess coming.* 我们早该预料到会有这种麻烦的。

⑧ **IMAGINE** 想象

31 [T not in progressive 不用进行时] to form a picture of something or someone in your mind; IMAGINE (1) 想象，设想: *He could see a great future for her in music.* 他能看出她在音乐方面前途远大。| **can't see sth** (=think that something is unlikely to happen or be true) 无法想象某事 *Stuart thinks the car will go, but I can't see it myself.* 斯图尔特认为这辆车能走，但我自己认为这不可能。| **see sb as sth** (=be able to imagine someone being something) 能够想象某人就是… *I just can't see her as a ballet dancer.* 我简直无法想象她竟然是一位芭蕾舞演员。

32 **be seeing things** to imagine that you see something which is not really there 产生幻觉，见神见鬼: *There's no one there – you must have been seeing things.* 那里没有人——你大概是见鬼了。

⑨ **MAKE SURE** 确保

33 [T not in progressive 不用进行时] to make sure or check that something is done correctly 确保，查明: **see that** *It's up to you to see that the job's done properly.* 由你负责确保该项工作做得妥妥当当。| **see to it** (=make sure that something is done) 确保办妥某事 *Don't worry – I'll see to it.* 不用担心，我一定会办好的。

34 ▶**WARNING** 警告◀ [T, only in imperative 仅用于祈使句] used as a warning that something is important and must be done 务必注意，一定要做到〔用于提醒某事重要，必须办妥〕: **see (that)** *Please see that the room is straightened up before you leave.* 你离开之前务必要把房间整理好。

⑩ **EXPERIENCE** 经验

35 ▶**PERSON** 人◀ [T not in progressive 不用进行式] to have experience of something 有…的经验; 经历: *We've seen some good times together, Dave and I.* 戴夫和我，我们共同度过了一些美好的时光。| **have seen it all (before)** (=to have experienced something before, especially so that there is nothing else for you to learn about it)〔这一切〕早已经历过了 —see also 另见 **(been there), seen that, done that** (BEEN (3))

36 ▶**TIME/PLACE** 时间/地方◀ [T] if a time or place has seen a particular event or situation, it happened or existed in that time or place〔事件或情况在某时或某地〕发生，存在: *This year has seen a big increase in road accidents.* 今年道路交通事故大增。

⑪ **GO WITH SB** 陪同某人

37 **see sb across the road** to help someone to cross a road safely 陪伴[搀扶]某人过马路

38 **see sb home** to go with someone when they go home to make sure that they are safe 送某人回家: *Wait a minute! I'll get Nick to see you home.* 等一会儿！我叫尼克送你回家。

39 **see sb to the door** to go to the door with someone when they leave your house, to say goodbye to them 送某人到门口

⑫ **OTHER MEANINGS** 其他意思

40 **let me see/let's see** *spoken* used to show that you are trying to remember something【口】让我/我们想想: *Let me see…where did I put that letter?* 让我想想…我把信放在哪儿了?

41 **seeing as/how/that** *spoken* an expression meaning because, used especially when a situation makes you decide or suggest something that you had not intended【口】由于…，既然…〔尤用于表示临时的想法〕: *Seeing as you're going into town, can you get a few things for me?* 既然你要进城，能不能替我捎点东西回来? | **seeing (as) it's you** *humorous* (=used to say that you are treating someone especially well because you like them)【幽默】只因为是你〔表示因喜欢某人，所以对其特别好〕

42 **I don't see why not** *spoken* used to say yes in answer to a request【口】我认为没有什么不可以的，有何不可〔用于表示答应某人的请求〕: *"Can we go to the park?" "I don't see why not."* "我们可以去公园吗?" "我看没什么不可以的。"

43 **have seen better days** *informal* to be in a bad condition【非正式】已经破败，已经破旧: *This coat has seen better days.* 这件外套已经破旧了。

44 **see the back of sb** *spoken* used to say that you will be happy when someone leaves because you do not like them【口】摆脱某人〔因不喜欢与其打交道〕: *I can't wait to see the back of him.* 我巴不得他离开。

45 **see the last of sb/sth** to not see someone or something again because they have gone or are finished〔因某人已离开或某事已完成〕不再与某人/某事打交道: *By Friday we should be seeing the last of the rain for a while.* 到星期五雨就会停一段时间。

46 **see the light** **a)** to realize that something is true 明白，领悟 **b)** to have a special experience that makes you believe in a religion〔宗教上〕省悟，皈依 **c)** also 又作 **see the light of day** to exist or first appear 问世，首次出现: *The book that she had planned to write never saw the light of day.* 她计划写的书始终没有面世。

47 **I'll see what I can do** *spoken* used to say that you will try to help someone【口】我会尽量帮忙的: *Leave the ones you haven't done with me, and I'll see what I can do.* 把你还没有做完的留给我吧，我会尽力帮你忙的。

48 **see your way (clear) to** *spoken* to be able and willing to help someone【口】能够并愿意帮助人: *I think I could see my way to lending you a little.* 我想我能借点钱给你。

49 **see sb coming (a mile off)** *spoken* to recognize that someone will be easy to trick or deceive【口】看出某人容易上当受骗: *You paid £500 for that! They must have seen you coming!* 你花 500 英镑买这东西！他们肯定看出你会上当的！

50 **not see beyond the end of your nose** to be so concerned with yourself and what you are doing that you do not realize what is happening to other people around you 眼睛只能看到鼻子尖，目光短浅，没有远见

51 **see sb right** *BrE spoken* to make sure that someone is properly rewarded【英口】确保某人得到适当报酬: *Just do this for me and I'll see you right.* 你就替我做这个，我一定不会亏待你的。

52 ▶**GAME OF CARDS** 纸牌游戏◀ to risk the same amount of money as your opponent in a CARD¹ (7) game 与〔对方〕下同样的赌注

see about sth *phr v* [T] **1** to make arrangements or deal with something 安排，着手处理: *I'd better see about dinner.* 我还是去料理晚饭吧。| **see about doing sth** *Claire's gone to see about getting tickets for that concert.* 克莱尔已经去安排买音乐会门票的事了。**2** **we'll have to see about that** *spoken* used to say that you do not know if something will be possible【口】我们还得看看行不行: *"The school trip's really cheap and Dad says I can go." "We'll have to see about that!"* "学校组织的旅行真便宜，爸爸说我可以去。" "我们还得再看看！" **3** **we'll soon see about that** *spoken* used to say that you intend to stop someone doing something they are planning to do【口】我们等着瞧吧〔用于阻止某人计划要做的事〕

see around also 又作 **see round** *BrE*【英】*phr v* [T] to visit a place and walk around looking at it 四处[到处]看看: *Would you like to see around the old castle?* 你想看看那座古城堡吗?

see in *phr v* **1** [T **see** sth ↔ **in** sb/sth] to notice a particular quality in someone or something that makes you like them 注意到〔某人或某物有某种让人喜欢的特点〕: *He saw a gentleness in Susan.* 他觉得苏珊有一种温柔的气质。| **not know what sb sees in sb** *spoken* (=not know why someone likes someone)【口】不知道某人为何喜欢某人 *I really don't know what she*

sees in him! 我真不知道她看中他什么！**2** [T **see** sb **in**] to show a visitor the way when they arrive at a building 带领〔某人〕进入: *Will you see the guests in when they arrive?* 客人到达后，你把他们领进来好吗？**3** [I] to be able to see into someone's house 看到〔某人的〕室内: *Close the curtains so that no one can see in while I dress.* 把窗帘拉上，以免我穿衣服时让外面的人看见。**4 see in the new year** to celebrate the beginning of a new year 迎接新年的开始[来临]

see sb/sth **off** *phr v* [T] **1** to go to an airport, train station etc to say goodbye to someone〔到机场、火车站等〕给〔某人〕送行: *I think they've gone to the airport to see their daughter off.* 我想他们是去机场给女儿送行了。**2** to chase someone away, or make someone leave an area 赶走，逐出；使离开: *Security guards saw him off the premises.* 保安人员把他赶出门外。**3** to defend yourself successfully in a fight or battle, or beat an opponent in a game〔在战斗中〕抵挡住；〔在比赛中〕击败〔对手〕: **see off the competition** *They saw off the competition to become the nation's number one bestseller.* 它们在竞争中胜出，成为全国的第一畅销商品。**4** *BrE slang* to kill someone【英俚】杀死〔某人〕

see sb/sth **out** *phr v* [T] **1** to go to the door with someone to say goodbye to them when they leave 将〔某人〕送到门口: **I'll see myself out** *spoken* (=used to tell someone they do not have to come to the door with you)【口】我自己出去，不用送了 **2** to continue to do something until it finishes, even if you do not like doing it 坚持到〔某事〕结束，坚持把〔某事〕做完: *I don't enjoy the course but I'll see it out.* 我不喜欢这门课，但我会坚持上完它。

see over sth *phr v* [T] *BrE* to examine something large such as a house, especially when you are considering buying it【英】查看〔房屋等，尤指在考虑购买它时〕

see through *phr v* [T] **1** [**see through** sth] to recognize the truth about something that is intended to deceive you 看穿，识破〔骗局等〕: *I could see through his lies.* 我能识破他的谎言。**2** [**see through** sb] to know what someone is really like, especially what their bad qualities are 看透〔某人，尤指其恶劣品质〕 **3** [**see** sth **through**] to continue doing something, especially something difficult or unpleasant, until it is finished 把〔某事〕进行到底〔尤指某种困难或惹人讨厌的工作〕: *Martin felt sick with nerves, but was determined to see the thing through.* 马丁因神经紧张而感到不适，但还是决心把事情做完。**4** [**see** sb **through** sth] to give help and support to someone during a difficult time 帮助〔某人〕渡过〔难关〕: *I've given him a sedative; that should see him through the night.* 我已经给了他一服镇静剂；那应该能使他安度这一夜了。

see to sb/sth *phr v* [T] to deal with something or do something for someone 处理〔某事〕；照料，关照〔某人〕: *We'll have to see to that window – the wood's rotten.* 我们得修理那窗户了——木头已经朽了。| **have/get sth seen to** *You should get that tooth seen to by a dentist.* 你应该找牙医看看你那颗牙了。| **see to it that** *Will you see to it that this letter gets mailed today?* 请你务必今天把这封信寄出去，好吗？—see also 另见 **not see sb for dust** (DUST[1] (6)), **it remains to be seen** (REMAIN (5)), **see red** (RED[2] (4)), **see the colour of sb's money** (COLOUR[1] (12)), **I wouldn't be seen dead** (DEAD[1] (17))

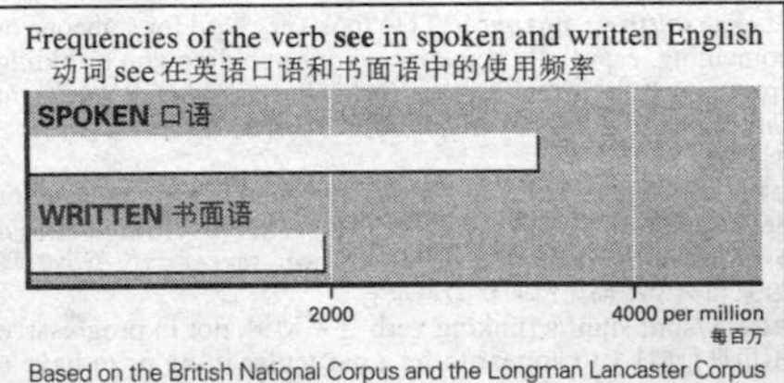

This graph shows that the verb **see** is much more common in spoken English than in written English. This is because it is used in a lot of common spoken phrases. 本图表显示，动词 see 在英语口语中的使用频率远远高于书面语，因为口语中很多常用短语是由 see 构成的。

see² *n* [C] *technical* an area governed by a BISHOP (1)【术语】主教教区

S3 W3 **seed¹** /sid; siːd/ *n plural* **seeds** or 或 **seed** **1 a)** [C,U] a small, hard object produced by plants, from which a new plant of the same kind grows 种子: *sunflower seeds* 葵花籽 | **plant/sow seeds** (=put them into the ground) 播种 *Plant the seeds in sandy soil, about 10 cm apart.* 把种子种在沙土里，每粒相隔约 10 厘米。| **grow sth from seed** (=grow a plant from a seed, rather than planting it when it is already partly grown) 用种子种〔某物〕 **b)** [U] a quantity of seeds〔若干〕种子，籽: *grass seed* 草籽 **2** *AmE* [C] one of the small hard objects in a fruit such as an apple or orange, from which new fruit trees grow【美】〔苹果、橙子等水果的〕果核; PIP[1] (1) *BrE*【英】**3 go/run to seed a)** if a plant or vegetable goes or runs to seed, it starts producing flowers and seeds as well as leaves〔植物或蔬菜〕开花结子 **b)** if a person goes or runs to seed, they become unattractive, fat, or unhealthy especially because of getting old or lazy〔人，尤指因渐老或懒惰而〕衰颓，颓废 **4 the seeds of sth** something that makes a new situation start to grow and develop 某物的起因[根源]: *the seeds of victory* 胜利的种子 | **sow (the) seeds of doubt/destruction/rebellion etc** (=do or say something which makes a bad feeling or situation develop and become a much more serious problem) 播下怀疑/毁灭/叛乱等的种子 *Sectarian agitators did much to sow the seeds of discontent among the people.* 宗派主义鼓动者在人民中间大力播下不满的种子。**5 number one/number three etc seed** [C] a tennis player who is given a particular position according to how likely they are to win a competition 头号/三号种子选手等〔在比赛中实力较强的网球选手，按其获胜的可能排序〕: *He's been top seed for the past two years.* 他在过去两年中一直是头号种子选手。**6** *biblical or humorous* SEMEN or SPERM【圣经或幽默】精液，精子 **7** [U] *biblical* the group of people who have a particular person as their father, grandfather etc, especially when they form a particular race【圣经】子孙，后裔

seed² *v* **1** [T] to remove seeds from fruit 给〔果实〕去籽[去核]: *seeded raisins* 无籽葡萄干 **2** [T usually passive 一般用被动态] to give a tennis player a particular position, according to how likely they are to win a competition〔根据网球运动员在比赛中获胜的可能〕挑选〔某人〕为种子选手: *seeded fourth at Wimbledon* 被定为温布尔登网球赛四号种子 **3** [T often passive 常用被动态] to plant seeds in the ground 在〔地里〕播种 **4** [I] to produce seeds 结籽

seed·bed /ˈsidˌbɛd; ˈsiːdbed/ *n* [C] **1** an area of ground where young plants are grown from seeds before they are planted somewhere else 苗床 **2** a place or condition that encourages something, especially a bad situation, to develop〔尤指容易滋生坏事的〕温床: [**+of**] *The city's slums were a seedbed of rebellion.* 这个城市的贫民窟是叛乱的温床。—see also 另见 HOTBED

seed cap·i·tal /ˈ· ˌ···/ *n* [U] the money you have to start a new business with 本钱，原始资本

seed·ling /ˈsidlɪŋ; ˈsiːdlɪŋ/ *n* [C] a young plant grown from seed 籽苗，种苗，幼苗

seed pearl /ˈ· ·/ *n* [C] a very small and often imperfect PEARL〔常有点瑕疵的〕小粒珍珠

seed·y /ˈsidɪ; ˈsiːdi/ *adj informal*【非正式】**1** a seedy person or place looks dirty or poor, and is often involved in or connected with illegal, immoral, or dishonest activities〔人或地方〕肮脏的；破旧的: *a bunch of seedy characters* 一群衣衫褴褛的人 **2** *old-fashioned informal* feeling slightly ill【过时，非正式】有点不舒服的，有小病的 —**seediness** *n* [U]

see·ing /ˈsiɪŋ; ˈsiːɪŋ/ *conjunction spoken* because a particular fact or situation is true【口】鉴于，由于: **seeing (that)** *We could have a joint party, seeing that your birthday is the same day as mine.* 既然你和我的生日是在同一天，我们可以一起开个生日派对。| **seeing as** *I won't stay long, seeing as you're busy.* 我不会待太久，因为你很忙。 S3

seeing eye dog /ˌ·· ˈ· ˌ·/ *n* [C] *AmE* a dog trained to guide blind people; GUIDE DOG【美】〔经过特殊训练能为盲人引路的〕领路犬，导盲犬

seek /sik; siːk/ *v past tense and past participle* **sought** /sɔt; sɔːt/ W1

1 ►LOOK FOR 寻找◄ [I,T] **a)** a word meaning to look for something that you need such as a job or friendship, used especially in newspapers and advertisements 寻求，寻找: *Virgo woman seeks Scorpio man.* 室女座女士寻找天蝎座男士。| *new graduates seeking employment* 正在求职的新毕业生 **b)** *formal* to look for the answer to a question or problem【正式】寻觅〔答案〕，探索

2 ►TRY TO GET 设法得到◄ [T] *formal* to try to achieve or get something【正式】设法获得，寻求: *Do you think the President*

will seek reelection? 你认为总统会竞选连任吗? | *We only seek justice, not revenge.* 我们只是寻求公正, 不是报复。| **seek to do sth** *We are always seeking to improve productivity.* 我们一直在设法提高生产力。| **attention-seeking/publicity-seeking** (=trying to attract people's attention) 追求别人注意/知名度的 *a publicity-seeking stunt* 为了出名的花招

3 ►ASK FOR 请求◄ **seek (sb's) advice/help/assistance etc** *formal* to ask someone for advice or help【正式】征求(某人的)意见/请求(某人的)帮助/援助等: *If the symptoms persist, seek medical advice.* 如症状持续下去, 便需求医诊治。

4 seek your fortune *literary* to go to another place hoping to gain success and wealth【文】寻找成功致富之路: *Young William went to America to seek his fortune.* 年轻的威廉到美国去闯天下。

5 ►MOVE TOWARDS 向…移动◄ [T] to move naturally towards something or into a particular position 自然地向…移动: *Water seeks its own level.* 水会自动地流成水平面。—see also 另见 HEAT-SEEKING, HIDE-AND-SEEK, SELF-SEEKING, SOUGHT-AFTER

seek sb/sth ↔ **out** *phr v* [T] to look very hard for someone or something, especially someone who is avoiding you or hiding from you 找出[找到]〔某人或某物〕: *Our mission is to seek out the enemy and destroy them.* 我们的任务是要找到敌人并把他们消灭。

seek·er /ˈsikɚ; ˈsiːkə/ *n* [C] someone who is trying to find or get something 找寻者, 追求者: **job-seeker/asylum-seeker** *a brilliant politician and a ruthless power-seeker* 一位杰出的政治家和一个冷酷无情的权力追求者

seem /sim; siːm/ *v* [linking verb 连系动词, not in progressive 不用进行时] **1** to appear to be a particular thing or to have a particular quality, feeling, or attitude 看来, 似乎, 好像: *Dinah didn't seem very sure.* 黛娜似乎不是很有把握。| **seem to sb** *Larry seemed pretty angry to me.* 我觉得拉里好像很生气。| *"How did she seem to you?" "Kind of upset."* "你觉得她怎么了?" "有点不高兴。" | **seem like** *Well, it seemed like a good idea at the time.* 这个嘛, 在当时似乎是个好主意。| **sb/sth seems a** *That seems a risky thing to try.* 那件事似乎做起来有风险。| **not be what he/she/it etc seems** *Things aren't always what they seem.* 事物并不总是与表象一致的。**2** to appear to exist or be true 似乎存在, 好像真实: **seem to** *I seem to have lost my car keys.* 我好像把汽车钥匙给丢了。| **it seems to sb (that)** *It seems to me you don't have much choice.* 在我看来你没有多少选择的余地。| **It seems (that)/it would seem (that)** *It would seem that someone left the building unlocked.* 似乎有人没锁大门就出去了。| **it seems like** *It seems like only yesterday that Tommy was born.* 汤米出生仿佛才是昨天的事。| **it seems as if/as though** *It seemed as though she didn't have a friend in the world.* 看起来她在这个世界上没有一个朋友。| **so it seems** (=it appears to be true) 好像是这样, 看起来是这样 *"So Bill's leaving her?" "So it seems."* "那么说, 比尔要离开她?" "好像是这样。" **3** to appear to be happening or to be doing something 好像正在发生, 似乎正在〔做某事〕: **seem to do sth** *The rainbow seemed to end on the hillside.* 彩虹好像一直延续到山坡为止。| **seem like** *It seemed like the whole town had come to the show.* 好像全镇的人都出来看演出。**4 can't/couldn't seem to do sth** used to say that you have tried to do something but cannot do it 似乎无法做某事〔用于表示某事已经试过但做不了〕: *I just can't seem to get it into his head that he has to plan things better.* 我好像根本没法使他明白他做事必须加强计划性。

seem·ing /ˈsimɪŋ; ˈsiːmɪŋ/ *adj* [only before noun 仅用于名词前] *formal* appearing to be something, especially when this is not actually true; APPARENTLY【正式】似是而非的, 表面上的: *It was a seeming piece of good luck which later led to all kinds of trouble.* 那件事看上去是个好运, 而后来却招致了各种各样的麻烦。

seem·ing·ly /ˈsimɪŋlɪ; ˈsiːmɪŋli/ *adv* **1** appearing to be something when this is not actually true; APPARENT 看上去, 表面上, 外观上: *The road was dusty and seemingly endless.* 路上尘土飞扬, 似乎没有尽头。**2** [sentence adverb 句子副词] according to the facts as you know them 从已知事实来看, 看样子: *There is seemingly nothing we can do to stop the plans going ahead.* 看样子我们无法阻止这些计划的实施。

seem·ly /ˈsimlɪ; ˈsiːmli/ *adj old-fashioned* suitable for a particular situation or social occasion, according to accepted standards of behaviour【过时】适宜的, 得体的, 合乎行为规范的: *It would be more seemly to keep quiet about it in front of the guests.* 在宾客面前对此事保持沉默会显得更加得体。—opposite 反义词 UNSEEMLY —**seemliness** *n* [U]

seen /sin; siːn/ the past participle of SEE

seep /sip; siːp/ *v* [I always+adv/prep] to flow slowly through small holes or spaces 渗漏: [**+in/into/through etc**] *Whenever it rained water started seeping in.* 每逢下雨, 水就渗漏进来。

seep·age /ˈsipɪdʒ; ˈsiːpɪdʒ/ *n* [singular,U] a gradual flow of liquid through small spaces or holes〔液体的〕渗漏: *Looks like a seepage problem in your basement.* 看来你的地下室有渗漏问题。

seer /sɪr; sɪə/ *n* [C] *especially literary* someone who can see into the future and say what will happen【尤文】预言者, 先知

seer·suck·er /ˈsɪrˌsʌkɚ; ˈsɪəˌsʌkə/ *n* [U] a light cotton cloth with an uneven surface and a pattern of lines 绉面薄织物, 泡泡纱

see·saw[1] /ˈsiˌsɔ; ˈsiːsɔː/ *n* [C] a piece of equipment that children play on, made of a board that is balanced in the middle, so that when one end goes up the other goes down 跷跷板

seesaw[2] *v* [I] to move repeatedly from one state or condition to another and back again 交替重复: *seesawing emotions* 时起时伏的情感

seethe /sið; siːð/ *v* [I] if a place is seething with people, insects etc there are a lot of them all moving quickly in different directions〔某地方〕充满〔人群、昆虫等〕,〔人、昆虫等〕密集(于): *seething with ants* 到处是乱爬的蚂蚁 | *a seething mass of people* 密密麻麻走向四面八方的人群

seeth·ing /ˈsiðɪŋ; ˈsiːðɪŋ/ *adj* extremely angry, but unable or unwilling to show it 内心极度愤怒的: *By the time we got home, David was seething.* 我们回到家时, 戴维气极了。

see-through /ˈ· ·/ *adj* a see-through piece of clothing is made of cloth that you can see through〔衣服〕透明的: *This dress is completely see-through when it's wet!* 这件连衣裙湿了以后完全是透明的。—compare 比较 TRANSPARENT (1)

seg·ment /ˈsɛgmənt; ˈsegmənt/ *n* [C] **1** a part of something that is in some way different from or affected differently from the whole 部分: *A large segment of the public is against the new tax.* 公众中一大部分人反对征收新税。**2** a part of a fruit, flower or insect that naturally divides into parts〔水果、花或自然形成的〕片, 块, 瓣;〔昆虫的〕节: *the segments of an orange* 橙子的瓣 —see picture on page A7 参见 A7 页图 **3** *technical* a part of a circle separated from the rest of the circle by a straight line across it【术语】弓形, 弦 —see picture at 参见 SHAPE[1] 图 **4** *technical* the part of a line between two points【术语】〔线的〕段

seg·men·ta·tion /ˌsɛgmɛnˈteʃən; ˌsegmenˈteɪʃən/ *n* [U] the act of dividing something or to be divided into smaller parts 分割(成部分)

seg·ment·ed /sɛgˈmɛntɪd; segˈmentɪd/ *adj* made up of separate parts that are connected to each other 分割的, 分段的

seg·re·gate /ˈsɛgrɪˌget; ˈsegrɪgeɪt/ *v* [T often passive 常用被动态] to separate one group of people from others, especially because they are of a different race, sex or religion〔尤指因种族、性别、宗教不同而〕使分开, 分离, 隔离: *Blacks were segregated from whites in churches, schools and colleges.* 那时在教堂、学校和大学里, 黑人都与白人隔离开。

seg·re·gat·ed /ˈsɛgrəˌgetɪd; ˈsegrɪgeɪtɪd/ *adj* a segregated school or other institution can only be attended by members of one sex, race etc〔男女〕分开的;〔种族〕隔离的: *a segregated audience* 清一色是女性[男性、某种族等]的听众 —compare 比较 INTEGRATED

seg·re·ga·tion /ˌsɛgrɪˈgeʃən; ˌsegrɪˈgeɪʃən/ *n* [U] the practice of keeping people of different races or religions apart and making them live, work, or study separately〔不同种族、宗教的〕分开, 隔离: *The US Supreme Court ruled in 1954 that segregation in schools was unconstitutional.* 美国最高法院于 1954 年裁定, 学校实行种族隔离是违反宪法的。—compare 比较 INTEGRATION

sei·gneur /sinˈjɝ; seˈnjɜː/ *n* [C] someone who owned land in a FEUDAL system〔封建社会的〕领主, 庄园主

Seine, the /sen; seɪn/ a river in northern France which flows through Paris and Rouen, and flows into the English Channel near Le Havre 塞纳河〔法国北部一河流, 流经巴黎和鲁昂, 在勒阿弗尔附近注入英吉利海峡〕

seis·mic /ˈsaɪzmɪk; ˈsaɪzmɪk/ *adj technical* connected with or caused by EARTHQUAKEs or powerful explosions【术语】地震[强烈爆炸]的, 地震[强烈爆炸]引起的: *an increase in seismic activity* 地震活动的增加

seis·mo·graph /ˈsaɪzməˌgræf; ˈsaɪzməgrɑːf/ *n* [C] an instrument that measures and records the movement of the earth during an EARTHQUAKE 地震仪

seis·mol·o·gy /saɪzˈmɑlədʒɪ; saɪzˈmɒlədʒi/ *n* [U] the scientific study of EARTHQUAKEs 地震学 —**seismologist** *n* [C]

seize /siz; si:z/ *v* **1** [T] to take hold of something suddenly and violently〔突然猛烈地〕抓取，攫取: *He seized my hand and dragged me away from the window.* 他抓住我的手，把我从窗户旁拉开。| **seize sth from sb** *Maggie seized the letter from her and began to read out loud.* 玛吉从她手上把信抢过去并开始大声朗读。**2** [T] to take control of a place suddenly and quickly, using military force〔用武力〕夺取，占领，抢去: **seize power/seize control (of)** *The rebels have seized power in a violent coup.* 叛乱分子已在暴力政变中夺取了政权。**3** [T] if the police or government officers seize something, they take away illegal goods such as drugs or guns 没收〔毒品、武器等非法物品〕，收缴〔物品〕**4 seize a chance/opportunity (with both hands)** to quickly and eagerly do something when you have the chance 抓住机会/机遇 **5 be seized with terror/desire etc** to suddenly be affected by an extremely strong feeling 突然感到恐惧/受到欲望支配等: *I was seized with a sudden desire to laugh out loud.* 我突然想要放声大笑。**6** [T] to suddenly catch someone and make sure they cannot get away 抓获，捕获: *The gunmen were seized in a military style operation.* 那些持枪歹徒在一场军事式的行动中被抓获。

seize on/upon sth *phr v* [T] to suddenly become very interested in an idea, excuse, what someone says etc 抓住，利用〔借口等〕: *Margot seized on the excuse to get out of choir practice.* 玛戈利用那个借口逃避合唱队的练习。

seize up *phr v* [I] **a)** if an engine or part of a machine seizes up, its moving parts stop working and can no longer move, for example because of lack of oil〔发动机或机器部件在运转中因缺油等〕卡住，停止运转 **b)** if a part of your body, such as your back, seizes up you suddenly cannot move it and it is very painful〔背等身体部位〕突然僵痛

sei·zure /ˈsiʒɚ; ˈsi:ʒə/ *n* **1** [U] the act of suddenly taking control or possession of something 夺取；没收: *the Fascist seizure of power in 1922* 1922年法西斯的夺取政权 **2** [C] a sudden attack of an illness, for example a HEART ATTACK〔心脏病等疾病的〕突然发作: *an epileptic seizure* 癫痫发作

Selassie —see 见 HAILE SELASSIE

sel·dom /ˈsɛldəm; ˈseldəm/ *adv* very rarely 很少，罕见，不常: *She seldom reads newspapers.* 她很少读报。—see picture at 参见 FREQUENCY 图

se·lect¹ /səˈlɛkt; sɪ̆ˈlekt/ *v* [T] to choose something by carefully thinking about which is the best, most suitable etc〔经过认真思考〕挑选，选择，选拔: *I selected four postcards and handed them to the cashier.* 我挑选了四张明信片，然后交给收银员。| **select sb to do sth** *Simon's been selected to represent us at the conference in Rio.* 西蒙已被推选出来代表我们出席里约热内卢的会议。

select² *adj formal*【正式】**1** a select group of people or things is a small special group that has been carefully chosen 挑选出的，精选的: *The information was only given to a select group of reporters.* 这条消息只提供给一组经过挑选的记者。| *select cuts of beef* 几块精选的牛肉 **2** only lived in, visited, or used by a small number of rich people; EXCLUSIVE¹ (1) 仅限于少数富人居住[参观，使用]的，专用的，高级的，奢华的: *a select apartment block* 高档的公寓大楼

select com·mit·tee /ˌ· ˈ··/ *n* [C] a small group of politicians and advisers from various parties that has been chosen to examine a particular subject〔从各党派选拔出来负责审查某一特殊问题的〕特别委员会

se·lec·tion /səˈlɛkʃən; sɪ̆ˈlekʃən/ *n* **1** [U] the careful choice of a particular person or thing from among a group of similar people or things 挑选，选择，选拔: *the process of jury selection* 陪审团（成员）的挑选过程 | **make a selection** *Please make your selections and move along.* 请作出选择并向前移动。**2** [C] something that has been chosen from among a group of things 挑选出来的东西: **[+from]** *a program of selections from Gilbert and Sullivan* 演奏吉尔伯特和沙利文的歌曲选的节目 **3** [C usually singular 一般用单数] a collection of things of a particular type, especially of things that are for sale; range 供选购的同类物品: **[+of]** *a fine selection of perfumes* 可供选购的各种精选香水 —see also 另见 NATURAL SELECTION

se·lec·tive /səˈlɛktɪv; sɪ̆ˈlektɪv/ *adj* **1** careful about what you choose to do, buy, allow etc〔做事、购物等〕认真选择[挑拣]的: **[+about]** *We're very selective about what we let the children watch on TV.* 我们对于让孩子们看哪些电视节目是经过慎重选择的。**2** affecting or concerning the best or most suitable people or things from a larger group 有选择的，选择性的，择优的: *the selective breeding of horses* 选择性的马种培育 —**selectively** *adv* —**selectivity** /səˌlɛkˈtɪvətɪ; sɪ̆ˌlekˈtɪvɪ̆ti/ *n* [U]

se·lec·tor /səˈlɛktɚ; sɪ̆ˈlektə/ *n* [C] **1** *BrE* a member of a committee that chooses the best people for something such as a sports team【英】〔运动队〕选拔委员会委员 **2** *technical* a piece of equipment that helps you find the right thing, for example the correct GEAR¹ (1) in a car【术语】选择器〔例如汽车的换挡器〕

se·le·ni·um /səˈlinɪəm; sɪ̆ˈli:niəm/ *n* [U] a poisonous ELEMENT (1) that is not a metal and is used in some electrical instruments to make them sensitive to light 硒〔一种非金属有毒元素，用于一些电子器材使其感光〕

self /sɛlf; self/ *n plural* **selves** /sɛlvz; selvz/ **1** [usually singular 一般用单数] the type of person you are, your character, your typical behaviour etc 自身，本身，自己，自我: **sb's usual/normal self** *Sid was not his usual smiling self.* 锡德不像往常那样笑容满面了。| **be/look/feel (like) your old self** (=be the way you usually are again, especially after having been ill, unhappy etc)〔尤指生病或不愉快等之后〕恢复老样子 *Howard was beginning to feel like his old self again.* 霍华德又开始感到自己和以前一样了。| **sb's true self** (=what someone is really like, rather than what they pretend to be like) 某人的真面目 **2** [U] **sb's sense of self** someone's consciousness of being a separate person, different from other people 某人的自我意识 **3 be a shadow/ghost of your former self** to not be at all like the cheerful, healthy, strong etc person that you used to be 判若两人〔已不再像从前那样开朗、健康、强壮了〕**4** [U] *spoken* your own desires and satisfaction rather than anyone else's【口】私利，私心，自私: *It's always self, self, self! You never think of anyone else!* 你总是自己，自己，自己！从不考虑一下别人！**5** [U] a word written in business letters, on cheques etc meaning yourself 本人〔用于商业函件、支票等〕

self- /sɛlf; self/ *prefix* **1** by yourself or by itself 由[靠]自己的: *He's self-taught.* (=he taught himself) 他是自学成材。| *self-propelled* 自行驱动的 **2** of, to, with, for, or in yourself or itself（对）自身的；为自己的；独自的: *a self-addressed envelope* (=which you address to yourself) 写给自己收的信封 | *a self-portrait* (=a picture that you have drawn or painted of yourself) 自画像 | *self-restraint* 自我克制

self-ab·ne·ga·tion /ˌ· ··ˈ··/ *n* [U] *formal* a lack of interest in your own needs and desires; ABNEGATION【正式】忘我，克己

self-ab·sorbed /ˌ· ·ˈ·◂/ *adj* concerned only with yourself and the things that affect you 只顾自己的，自我专注的: *I wouldn't worry – teenagers always seem totally self-absorbed.* 我不会担心——青少年总是显得完全只顾自己。—**self-absorption** *n* [U]

self-ad·dressed /ˌ· ·ˈ·◂/ *adj* a self-addressed envelope has the sender's address on it so that it can be sent back to them〔信封〕写上发信人自己地址的 —see also 另见 SAE, SASE

self-ad·he·sive /ˌ· ·ˈ··◂/ *adj* a self-adhesive envelope, BANDAGE etc has a sticky surface and does not need liquid or glue to make it stay closed〔信封等〕自粘贴的

self-ap·point·ed /ˌ· ·ˈ··◂/ *adj* thinking that you are the best person to lead other people or represent their wishes and opinions, especially when you are not 自命的，自封的: *a self-appointed guardian of morality* 一个自封的道德卫士

self-as·sem·bly /ˌ· ·ˈ··◂/ *adj* sold as separate parts that you put together yourself at home〔由顾客〕自行组装的

self-as·ser·tive /ˌ· ·ˈ··◂/ *adj* very confident and not shy about saying what you think or want 极自信的，勇于说出自己的想法或要求的 —**self-assertiveness** *n* [U] —**self-assertion** *n* [U]

self-as·sur·ance /ˌ· ·ˈ··/ *n* [U] confidence and the belief that you are able to deal with people and problems easily 自信

self-as·sured /ˌ· ·ˈ·◂/ *adj* calm and confident about what you are doing 自信的: *His air of self-assured confidence made him a born leader.* 他那种充满自信的气派使他成为一个天生的领袖。—**self-assurance** *n* [U]

self-a·ware·ness /ˌ· ·ˈ··/ *n* [U] knowledge and understanding of yourself 自知，自我了解，自我意识: *Personal doubts often serve to focus self-awareness.* 自我怀疑往往能有助于自我了解。

self-ca·ter·ing /ˌ· ˈ···/ *adj BrE* a self-catering holiday is one where you stay in a place where you can cook your own food【英】〔在度假住宿处〕自己做饭的，自办伙食的 —**self-catering** *n* [U]

self-cen·tred *BrE*【英】, **self-centered** *AmE*【美】/ˌ· ˈ··◂/ *adj* paying so much attention to yourself that you do not notice what is happening to other people; SELFISH 自我中心的，只顾自己的，自私的 —**self-centredness**

self-con·fessed /ˌ· ·ˈ·◂/ *adj* [only before noun 仅用于名词前] admitting that you have a particular quality, especially one that is bad 自己承认的，自动坦白的〔尤指坏事〕: *a self-confessed television addict* 自认的电视迷

self-con·fi·dent /,· '···/ *adj* sure that you can do things well, that people like you, that you are attractive etc, and not shy or nervous in social situations 自信的，对自己信心十足的 —**self-confidently** *adv* —**self-confidence** *n* [U]

self-con·gra·tu·la·tion /,· ····'··/ *n* [U] behaviour that shows in an annoying way that you think you have done very well at something 沾沾自喜，扬扬自得 —**self-congratulatory** /,· ····'··/ *adj*: *a smug, self-congratulatory smile* 沾沾自喜的笑容

self-con·scious /,· '··/ *adj* **1** worried and embarrassed about what you look like or what other people think of you〔因顾虑他人看法而〕忸怩（作态）的，害羞的，不自然的：*I hate wearing glasses – they make me feel self-conscious.* 我讨厌戴眼镜——它让我感到很不自然。| [+about] *Jerry's pretty self-conscious about his weight.* 杰里对自己的体重颇为敏感。**2** self-conscious art, writing etc shows that the artist etc is too aware of how the public will react to them〔艺术作品等〕过于重视公众反应的，强调社会效果的：*self-conscious art-house movies* 太重视观众反应的艺术影片 —**self-consciously** *adv* —**self-consciousness** *n* [U]

self-con·tained /,· '·◂/ *adj* **1** something that is self-contained is complete in itself, and does not need other things or help from somewhere else to make it work 配套齐全的，自成体系的：*a self-contained database package* 配套齐全的数据库软件包 **2** someone who is self-contained tends not to be friendly or show their feelings〔人〕不友善的，感情不外露的 **3** *BrE* a self-contained FLAT[2] (1) has its own kitchen and bathroom【英】〔公寓〕有独立厨房和浴室的

self-con·tra·dic·to·ry /,· ···'···/ *adj* containing two opposite statements or ideas that cannot both be true 自相矛盾的

self-con·trol /,· ·'·/ *n* [U] the ability to behave calmly and sensibly even when you feel very excited, angry etc 自制力，控制情感的能力：*Greater self-control is the simple answer to most people's eating problems.* 更好的自我克制就是解决大多数人饮食问题的简单答案。—**self-controlled** *adj*

self-de·cep·tion /,· ·'··/ *n* [U] the act of making yourself believe something is true when it is not 自欺：*He was unwilling to admit that the visionary idea was sheer self-deception.* 他不愿意承认那种不切实际的想法纯粹是自欺。—**self-deceptive** *adj*

self-de·feat·ing /,· ·'··◂/ *adj* causing exactly the same problems and difficulties that you are trying to prevent or deal with 适得其反的，弄巧成拙的

self-de·fence *BrE*【英】, **self-defense** *AmE*【美】/,· ·'·/ *n* [U] **1** something you do to protect yourself or your property 自卫，防身：**in self-defence** (=to protect yourself) 出于自卫 *I swear, I shot him in self-defense.* 我发誓，我开枪打他是出于自卫。**2** skills that you learn to protect yourself if you are attacked 自卫术，防身本领：*a self-defence class for women* 妇女自卫训练班

self-de·ni·al /,· ·'··/ *n* [U] the practice of not doing or having the things you enjoy, either because you cannot afford it, or for moral or religious reasons〔由于经济、道德原因〕克己；〔宗教的〕苦行 —**self-denying** *adj*

self-dep·re·cat·ing /,· '····/ *adj* trying to make your own abilities or achievements seem unimportant 自我贬低的，谦逊的：*self-deprecating humour* 自贬身价的幽默

self-des·truct /,sɛlf dɪ'strʌkt; ,self dɪ'strʌkt◂/ *v* [I] if something such as a bomb self-destructs, it destroys itself, usually by exploding〔炸弹等〕自爆，自毁 —**self-destruct** *adj*: *a self-destruct mechanism* 自爆装置

self-des·truc·tion /,· ·'··/ *n* [U] the practice of deliberately doing things that are likely to seriously damage or kill you 自残；自毁：**be bent on self-destruction** (=be determined to damage or destroy yourself) 一心要伤害[毁灭]自己 —**self-destructive** *adj*: *self-destructive behaviour* 自毁行为

self-de·ter·min·a·tion /,· ·,··'··/ *n* [U] the right of the people of a particular country to govern themselves and to choose the type of government they will have〔民族〕自决权，自决

self-dis·ci·pline /,· '···/ *n* [U] the ability to make yourself do the things you know you ought to do, without someone making you do them 自我约束，自律：*I just wonder if I've got enough self-discipline to finish the course.* 我只是怀疑自己是否有足够的自我约束能力去完成这个课程。—**self-disciplined** *adj*

self-doubt /,· '·/ *n* [U] the feeling that you and your abilities are not good enough 自我怀疑，缺乏自信心

self-drive /,· '·◂/ *adj* [only before noun 仅用于名词前] *BrE* a self-drive car is one that you have hired (=paid for) to drive yourself【英】〔汽车〕租来自己驾驶的

self-ed·u·cat·ed /,· '····◂/ *adj* having taught yourself by reading books etc, rather than learning things in school 自学〔而非由学校教育〕的，自修的

self-ef·fac·ing /,· ·'··◂/ *adj* not wanting to attract attention to yourself or your achievements, especially because you are not socially confident 避免引人注目的，不爱抛头露面的：*He was loved for his skill and also his self-effacing modesty.* 他受到爱戴是由于他有技术，还有他的谦逊。—**self-effacement** *n* [U]

self-em·ployed /,· ·'·◂/ *adj* working for yourself and not employed by a company 自己经营而不受雇于人的，自雇的，个体户的：**go self-employed** (=become self-employed) 做个体户 | **the self-employed** (=people who are self-employed) 自雇者，个体户 *pension plans for the self-employed* 为自雇者准备的养老金计划 —**self-employment** *n* [U]

self-es·teem /,· ·'·/ *n* [U] the feeling that you are someone who deserves to be liked, respected, and admired 自尊(心)：*Teachers need to help build up their students' sense of self-esteem.* 教师需要帮助学生建立起自尊心。| **low self-esteem** (=not much self-esteem) 不强的自尊心

self-ev·i·dent /,· '···◂/ *adj* clearly true and needing no more proof; OBVIOUS (1) 不证自明的，显而易见的：*self-evident truths* 不证自明的真理

self-ex·am·in·a·tion /,· ·,··'··/ *n* [U] **1** careful thought about whether your actions and your reasons for them are right or wrong 自省，〔对自己行为等的〕反省 **2** the practice of checking parts of your body for early signs of some illnesses〔对身体的〕自我检查

self-ex·plan·a·to·ry /,· ·'····/ *adj* clear and easy to understand without needing further explanation 无须解释的，不解自明的：*Messages displayed as a result of user error are self-explanatory.* 使用者操作有误时显示出的信息一看即明。

self-ex·pres·sion /,· ·'··/ *n* [U] the expression of your feelings, thoughts, ideas etc, especially through activities such as painting, writing, or acting etc〔尤指通过绘画、写作、演戏等的〕自我表现：*The curriculum needs room for creative self-expression.* 这套课程需要给创造性的自我表现留有余地。—**self-expressive** *adj*

self-ful·fil·ling /,· ·'··◂/ *adj* **self-fulfilling prophecy** a statement about what is likely to happen in the future that becomes true because you expected it to happen and therefore changed your behaviour 自我完成的预言〔指作出预言的人改变自己的行为因而使预言实现〕

self-gov·ern·ing /,· '···/ *adj* a country or organization that is self-governing is controlled by its own members rather than by someone from another country or organization〔国家、组织〕自治的，自己管理的：*a self-governing trust* 自己管理的信托机构

self-gov·ern·ment /,· '···/ *n* [U] the government of a country by its own citizens, without people from other countries having any control or influence 自治，独立自主

self-help /,· '·/ *n* [U] the use of your own efforts to deal with your problems instead of depending on other people 自助，自救：**self-help group** (=a group of people with a particular illness or problem who help each other)〔患同一种病或有相同问题者的〕自助小组

self·hood /'sɛlfhʊd; 'selfhʊd/ *n* [U] *technical* the knowledge of yourself as an independent person separate from others【术语】自我意识；个性

self-im·age /,· '··/ *n* [C] the idea you have of your own abilities, physical appearance, and character 自我形象〔指对自己的能力、外表、性格的自我感觉〕：*Bullies often have a poor self-image.* 恃强凌弱者往往自我形象不佳。

self-im·port·ance /,· ·'··/ *n* [U] the attitude that shows you think you are more important than other people 妄自尊大，自负，高傲

self-im·por·tant /,· ·'··◂/ *adj* behaving in a way that shows you think you are more important than other people 妄自尊大的，自负的，高傲的：*a self-important, pompous little man* 妄自尊大、自命不凡的小人物 —**self-importantly** *adv*

self-im·posed /,· ·'·◂/ *adj* a self-imposed rule, condition, responsibility etc is one that you have made yourself accept, and which no one has asked you to accept〔法规、条件等〕自愿遵守的，〔责任〕自己主动承担的：*five years of self-imposed exile in Bolivia* 在玻利维亚自我流放的五年

self-in·dul·gence /,· ·'··/ *n* [singular,U] the act of allowing yourself to have or do something that you enjoy but do not need 自我放纵，放任自己：*My one self-indulgence is expensive coffee.* 我对自己的一个放纵就是喝昂贵的咖啡。

self-in·dul·gent /,· ·'··◂/ *adj* allowing yourself to have or do things you enjoy but do not need, especially if you do this too much 放纵自己的，放任自己的 —**self-indulgently** *adv*

self-in·flict·ed /,· ·'··◂/ *adj* self-inflicted pain, problems, illnesses etc are those you have caused yourself〔痛苦、问题、

疾病等〕自己造成的，自己施加的：*It cannot be a self-inflicted blow, so it must be murder.* 这不可能是自己打的，因此必然是谋杀。

self-in·terest /ˌ· ˈ···/ *n* [U] consideration only of what is best for you rather than other people 自私自利，利己之心：*His offer was motivated solely by self-interest.* 他的提议仅仅是出于私利。—**self-interested** *adj*

self·ish /ˈsɛlfɪʃ; ˈselfɪʃ/ *adj* caring only about yourself and not about other people 自私的，自私自利的：*How can you be so selfish?* 你怎能这样自私？| *selfish motives* 自私的动机 —**selfishly** *adv* —**selfishness** *n* [U]

self-knowl·edge /ˌ· ˈ··/ *n* [U] an understanding of your own character, your reasons for doing things etc 自我认识，自知（之明）

self·less /ˈsɛlflɪs; ˈselfləs/ *adj* caring about other people more than about yourself 忘我的，无私的：*selfless devotion to their work* 他们对工作的无私奉献 —**selflessly** *adv* —**selflessness** *n* [U]

self-made /ˌ· ˈ·◂/ *adj* a self-made man or woman has become successful and rich by their own efforts, and did not have advantages like money or a high social position when they started 靠个人奋斗而成功的，白手起家的：*a self-made millionaire* 白手起家的百万富翁

self-o·pin·ion·at·ed /ˌ· ·ˈ····◂/ *adj* always believing that your own opinions and ideas are always right and that everyone else should always agree with you 自以为是的，固执己见的

self-pit·y /ˌ· ˈ··/ *n* [U] the feeling of being sorry for yourself because you have been unlucky or you think people have treated you badly 自怜：*Stop wallowing in your own self-pity and do something about it!* 不要再自叹自怜了，做点实事吧！—**self-pitying** *adj*

self-por·trait /ˌ· ˈ··/ *n* [C] a drawing, painting, or description that you do of yourself 自画像；自我描述

self-pos·sessed /ˌ· ·ˈ·◂/ *adj* calm, confident, and in control of your feelings, even in difficult or unexpected situations 〔在困难或意外情况下〕镇定的，沉着的，泰然自若的 —**self-possession** *n* [U]

self-pres·er·va·tion /ˌ· ··ˈ··/ *n* [U] protection of yourself in a threatening or dangerous situation 自我保存，自我保护：*the instinct for self-preservation* 自我保护的本能

self-pro·claimed /ˌ· ·ˈ·◂/ *adj* having given yourself a position or title without the approval of other people 自称的，自封的：*a self-proclaimed champion of the working class* 自封的工人阶级斗士

self-rais·ing flour /ˌ· ·· ˈ··/ *n* [U] *BrE* a type of flour that contains BAKING POWDER【英】〔掺有发酵粉的〕自发面粉；SELF-RISING FLOUR *AmE*【美】

self-reg·u·la·to·ry /ˌ· ˈ·····/ also 又作 **self-regulating** /ˌ· ˈ····/ *adj* a self-regulatory system, industry, or organization is one that controls itself, rather than having an independent organization or laws to make sure that rules are obeyed 〔系统、工业或组织〕自我调节的，自动控制的 —**self-regulation** /ˌ· ··ˈ··/ *n* [U]

self-re·li·ant /ˌ· ·ˈ··◂/ *adj* able to decide what to do by yourself, without depending on the help or advice of other people 依靠自己的，自力更生的：*In his famous essay, Emerson called on the US to be self-reliant.* 爱默生在他那篇著名的文章中号召美国（人）要自力更生。—**self-reliance** *n* [U]

self-re·spect /ˌ· ·ˈ·/ *n* [U] a feeling of being happy about what you are, what you do, and what you believe in 自尊，自重：*It's difficult to keep your self-respect when you have been unemployed for a long time.* 你在长时间失业之后，就很难保持自尊了。

self-re·spect·ing /ˌ· ·ˈ··◂/ *adj* [only before noun 仅用于名词前] having respect for yourself and your abilities and beliefs 自尊的，自重的，有自尊心的：**no self-respecting ... would do sth** *No self-respecting actor would appear in a porn movie.* 自重的演员是不演色情电影的。

self-re·straint /ˌ· ·ˈ·/ *n* [U] the ability not to do or say something you very much want to, because you know this is more sensible 自我克制，自我约束：**exercise self-restraint** *Police officers must learn to exercise self-restraint.* 警察必须学会自我克制。

self-right·eous /ˌ· ˈ··◂/ *adj* proudly sure that your beliefs, attitudes, and morals are good and right, in a way that annoys other people 自以为正直善良的；自以为是的：*That's the most unfair, self-righteous statement I've ever heard!* 那是我听过最不公正、最自以为是的声明。—**self-righteously** *adv* —**self-righteousness** *n* [U]

self-ris·ing flour /ˌ· ·· ˈ··/ *n* [U] *AmE* a type of flour that contains BAKING POWDER【美】〔掺有发酵粉的〕自发面粉；SELF-RAISING FLOUR *BrE*【英】

self-rule /ˌ· ˈ·/ *n* [U] the government of a country or part of a country by its own citizens 自治

self-sac·ri·fice /ˌ· ˈ···/ *n* [U] the act of doing without things you want, need, or care about in order to help someone else 自我牺牲，献身 —**self-sacrificing** *adj*

self-same /ˈ· ·/ *adj* [only before noun 仅用于名词前] *literary* exactly the same【文】完全相同的，同一的：*two great victories on the self-same day* 同一天内的两大胜利

self-sat·is·fied /ˌ· ˈ···/ *adj* too pleased with yourself and what you have done 沾沾自喜的，自鸣得意的：*He seemed as smug and self-satisfied as his father.* 他看来和他父亲一样自鸣得意。—**self-satisfaction** /ˌ· ··ˈ··/ *n* [U]

self-seek·ing /ˌ· ˈ··◂/ *adj* doing things only because they will give you an advantage that other people do not have 追逐私利的，为自己打算的：*a self-seeking politician* 追求私利的政客

self-serv·ice /ˌ· ˈ··◂/ *adj* a self-service restaurant, shop etc is one in which you get things for yourself and then pay for them 自助（式）的 —**self-service** *n* [U]

self-start·er /ˌ· ˈ··/ *n* [C] someone who is able to work successfully on their own without needing other people's help or a lot of instructions 有独立工作能力的人，工作主动积极的人

self-styled /ˈ· ·/ *adj* [only before noun 仅用于名词前] having given yourself a title or position without having a right to it 自封的，自称的：*a self-styled professor* 自封的教授

self-suf·fi·cient /ˌ· ·ˈ··◂/ *adj* providing all the things you need without help from outside 自给自足的：*In those days the farm was largely self-sufficient.* 在那些日子里，这个农场基本上能自给自足。—**self-sufficiency** *n* [U]

self-sup·port·ing /ˌ· ·ˈ··◂/ *adj* able to earn enough money to support yourself 自食其力的，自立的：*The business will soon become self-supporting.* 这家公司很快就能自力经营了。

self-taught /ˌ· ˈ·◂/ *adj* having learned a skill or subject by yourself, rather than in a school 自学而成的，自学成材的：*a self-taught accountant* 自学成材的会计

self-willed /ˌ· ˈ·◂/ *adj* very determined to do what you want, even when this is unreasonable 任性的，固执的，执拗的：*a wild and self-willed child* 野蛮任性的小孩 —**self-will** *n* [U]

self-wind·ing /ˌself ˋwaɪndɪŋ; ˌself ˈwaɪndɪŋ◂/ *adj* a self-winding watch is one that you do not have to WIND² (2) to make it work 〔手表〕自动上发条的

sell¹ /sɛl; sel/ *v past tense and past participle* **sold** /sold; səʊld/

1 ►GIVE STH FOR MONEY 把某物卖钱◄ [I,T] to give something to someone in exchange for money 卖，销售，把…卖给…：*If you offer them another thousand, I think they'll sell.* 如果你再给他们一千元钱，我想他们会卖的。| **sell sth for £100/$50/30p etc** *Toni's selling her car for £700.* 托妮准备以 700 英镑卖掉她的汽车。| **sell sb sth/sell sth to sb** *I'm not selling you my shares!* 我是不会把我的股份卖给你的！| *The vase was sold to an American buyer.* 那个花瓶卖给了一位美国买主。| **sell sth** *Now he regrets selling all his old records.* 他现在后悔卖掉了所有的旧唱片。| **sell sth at a profit/loss** (=making or losing money on a sale) 出售某物赚钱/以亏损出售 —opposite 反义词 BUY

2 ►MAKE STH AVAILABLE 有现货出售◄ [T] to offer something for people to buy 有…出售[卖]：*Do you sell cigarettes?* 你们有香烟卖吗？| *a job selling advertising space* 推销广告版面的工作

3 sell at/for £100/$50/30p to be offered for sale at a particular price 以 100 英镑/50 美元/30 便士出售：*Smoke alarms sell for as little as five pounds.* 烟雾警报器最低价仅五英镑。

4 ►MAKE STH ATTRACTIVE 使某物吸引人◄ [T] to make people want to buy something 使〔某物〕吸引顾客，使〔某物〕畅销：*Scandal sells newspapers.* 丑闻可使报纸畅销。| **sell sb sth/sell sth to sb** (=persuade someone that they want to buy something) 向某人推销某物 *You have to go out and really sell the stuff, Leo.* 你得走出去真正推销这东西才行，利奥！

5 ►SELL A LOT 销量大◄ [I] to be bought by people in large numbers 有销路，大量售出：*Tickets for the concert just aren't selling.* 这场音乐会的门票没有销路。| **sell well/badly** *Anti-age creams always sell well.* 抗衰老霜总是畅销的。

6 sell like hot cakes to sell quickly and in large amounts 非常畅销，抢手

7 ►IDEA/PLAN 主意/计划◄ [I,T] to try to make someone accept a new idea or plan, or to become accepted 〔意见或计划〕使（人）接受，被接受：*It's all right for Washington, but will it sell in small-town America?* 这在华盛顿没有问题，但在美国小城镇能被接受吗？| **sell sb sth/sell sth to sb** *Just try selling taxes*

to the voters. 试试去说服选民接受税收政策吧。| **be sold on (doing) sth/be sold on the idea** (=think an idea or plan is very good) 认为(做)某事极好/认为主意不错 *Joe's completely sold on the concept – he thinks it's brilliant.* 乔完全接受了这个想法,认为它非常棒。

8 **sell yourself** a) to be able to make yourself seem impressive to other people 自我宣传,自荐: *If you want a promotion, you've got to sell yourself better.* 你如果想晋升,就得更好地推销自己。 b) to do something that is against your principles in exchange for money or some other advantage 出卖自己(的原则)

9 **sell sb/sth short** to not give someone or something the praise, attention, or reward that they deserve 对某人/某事评价太低: *You're selling yourself short – tell them about all your qualifications.* 你委屈自己了,把你所有的资历都告诉他们。

10 **sell your body** to have sex with someone for money 卖淫,出卖肉体

11 **sell your soul (to the devil)** to do something bad in exchange for money, power etc 出卖灵魂〔以换取金钱、权力等〕

12 **sell sb down the river** to do something that harms a group of people who trusted you to help them, in order to gain money or power for yourself〔为个人利益或权力〕出卖[背叛]某一群人

13 **sell your support/vote** *AmE* to give your support or vote to the person who will give you the biggest financial advantage【美】谁给钱多就支持谁/投谁的票

sell off *phr v* [T] 1 **sell** sth ↔ **off** to try to get rid of things that no one seems to want to buy by selling them cheaply 廉价处理掉,削价卖掉〔某物〕: *Looks like they're trying to sell off a bunch of junk.* 看来他们好像在设法廉价处理掉一批废旧杂物。2 to sell something because you need the money〔因需要钱而〕把…卖掉: *After the war we were forced to sell off part of the farm.* 战争结束后,我们被迫卖掉农场的一部分。3 to sell all or part of an industry or company 卖掉〔部分或整个企业或公司〕

sell out *phr v* 1 **be/have sold out** if a shop sells out of something, it has no more of that particular thing left to sell〔货物〕已卖完: *Sorry, we're sold out.* 对不起,全卖完了。| **have sold out of sth** *We've completely sold out of those shirts in your size, sir.* 先生,您那个尺码的衬衫已经全部卖完了。2 [I] if a product, tickets, places at a concert etc sell out, they are all sold and there are none left〔产品、入场券等〕卖光,售完: *Wow! Those scarves sold out fast.* 哇!那些围巾很快就销售一空。| **be sold out** *Tonight's performance is completely sold out.* 今晚的演出门票全卖光了。3 [I,T] to not keep to your beliefs or principles in order to get more money, a comfortable life, or a political advantage〔为了钱财或政治利益〕出卖原则,放弃信仰: *ex-hippies who've sold out and become respectable businessmen* 放弃了原有宗旨而成了体面商人的前嬉皮士 4 [I+to] to sell your business or your share in a business 卖掉生意,出售股份: *Wyman says he'll sell out if business doesn't pick up.* 怀曼说如果生意没有起色,他就要把商店卖掉。

sell up *phr v* [I,T] *especially BrE* to sell most of what you own, especially your house or your business【尤英】卖掉(绝大部分财产)〔尤指住房或企业〕: *Liz decided to sell up and move abroad.* 莉兹决定卖掉房子移居外国。

sell² *n* [singular] *BrE informal* something you have been tricked into buying or doing that disappoints you【英,非正式】受骗所购之物;受骗所做之事. *What a sell! It's only plastic that looks like wood.* 真是骗人!这只是一件看似木制的塑料品。—see also 另见 HARD SELL, SOFT SELL

Sel·la·field /ˈsɛləfild; ˈseləfiːld/ a NUCLEAR power and nuclear reprocessing station in Cumbria, northwest England, which used to be called 'Windscale'. Sellafield produces electricity, and also treats waste from nuclear fuel so that it can be used again. 塞拉菲尔德〔英格兰西北部坎布里亚郡的一座核电站及核燃料后处理站,旧称温斯卡尔。该站不仅发电,而且还对核废料进行再利用处理〕

sell-by date /ˈ· · ,·/ *n* [C] *BrE*【英】1 the date stamped on a food product, after which it should not be sold〔印在食品包装上的〕销售期限,售出的截止日期; EXPIRATION DATE *AmE*【美】2 **be past its sell-by date** *informal* if an idea, method, system etc is past its sell-by date it has become no longer useful or interesting【非正式】〔思想、方法、体系等〕过时,无用;不再受关注

sell·er /ˈsɛlɚ; ˈselə/ *n* [C] 1 someone who sells something 卖方,卖者 —opposite 反义词 BUYER 2 **good/bad etc seller** a product that sells well, badly etc 畅销/滞销品等 —see also 另见 BEST-SELLER

Sel·lers /ˈsɛlɚz; ˈseləz/, **Peter** (1925-80) a British actor and COMEDIAN who appeared in the British radio programme *The Goon Show* (1951-59), and is known especially for appearing as the humorous character of Inspector Clouseau, a French police officer who keeps making stupid mistakes and causing accidents in films such as *The Pink Panther* (1963) and *The Return of the Pink Panther* (1975) 塞勒斯〔(1925-1980),英国喜剧演员。他曾出演英国广播剧《傻瓜秀》(1951-1959),尤以饰演《粉红豹》(1963)和《粉红豹归来》(1975)等片中的滑稽角色克卢索警官而闻名。克卢索是法国警官,总是犯愚蠢错误,惹出事端〕

seller's mar·ket /,·· ˈ··/ *n* [singular] a situation in which there is not much of a particular product available for sale, so prices tend to be high 卖方市场〔某种商品因供不应求而价格偏高,因而对卖方有利的市场状况〕—opposite 反义词 BUYER'S MARKET

sell·ing /ˈsɛlɪŋ; ˈselɪŋ/ *n* [U] the job and skill of persuading people to buy things; sales (SALE (5b)) 推销(术): *a career in selling* 推销工作

selling point /ˈ· · ·/ *n* [C] something about a product that will make people want to buy it〔吸引顾客的〕商品特色,销售特色,卖点: *The computer's two main selling points are that it's cheap and portable.* 这种电脑的两大卖点是价格便宜和便于携带。

selling price /ˈ· · ·/ *n* [C] the price at which something is actually sold〔实际的〕售价 —compare 比较 **asking price** (ASK (8))

sell-off /ˈ· ·/ *n* [C] *BrE* the act of selling an industry, especially one that the government owns, to private buyers【英】〔尤指政府所有的〕工业企业向私人的出售,私有化: *fears that services will be cut after the sell-off* 对私有化之后公共服务将会削减的担心

Sel·lo·tape /ˈsɛlə,tep; ˈseləteɪp/ *n* [U] *BrE trademark* sticky thin clear material in a long narrow length that is used for sticking things together【英,商标】〔用于粘贴东西的〕透明胶带; SCOTCH TAPE *AmE*【美】: *a roll of sellotape* 一卷透明胶带 — **sellotape** *v* [T]

sell-out /ˈ· ·/ *n* [singular] 1 a performance, sports game etc, for which all the tickets have been sold〔演出、体育比赛等〕爆满,满座 2 *informal* a situation in which someone has not done what they promised to do or were expected to do by the people who trusted them【非正式】违背诺言;出卖,背叛: *a political sell-out* 政治背叛

sel·vage, selvedge /ˈsɛlvɪdʒ; ˈselvɪdʒ/ *n* [C] the edge of a piece of cloth, made strong in such a way that the threads will not come out〔用于防脱线的布的〕织边

selves /sɛlvz; selvz/ the plural of SELF

Selznick /ˈsɛlznɪk; ˈselznɪk/, **David O.** (1902-65) a US film producer, famous for *Gone with the Wind* (1939), which he also helped to write and direct. He also produced *Rebecca* (1940), *Spellbound* (1945) and was co-producer of *The Third Man* (1949). 塞尔兹尼克〔(1902-1965),美国电影制片人。他以《乱世佳人》(1939)的制片成名,还参与了该片的编剧和导演工作。他还是《蝴蝶梦》(1940)和《爱德华大夫》(1945)的制片人、《第三者》(1949)的联合制片人〕

se·man·tic /səˈmæntɪk; sɪˈmæntɪk/ *adj* connected with the meanings of words 语义的 —**semantically** /-klɪ; -kli/ *adv*: *"Purchase" and "buy" are semantically the same.* (=they mean the same thing) purchase和buy语义相同。

se·man·tics /səˈmæntɪks; sɪˈmæntɪks/ *n* [U] 1 the study of the meaning of words and other parts of language 语义学 2 **the semantics of** *technical* the meaning of a word or piece of writing【术语】〔词或文章的〕语义

sem·a·phore /ˈsɛmə,for; ˈseməfɔː/ *n* [U] a system of sending messages using two flags, that you hold in different positions to represent letters and numbers 旗语

sem·blance /ˈsɛmbləns; ˈsembləns/ *n* 1 **semblance of** a condition or quality that is similar to another one〔情况或性质的〕相似,类似: *The herbs slow the heart and give the body a semblance of death.* 这些草药降低心率,使身体处于某种假死状态。2 a condition or quality that is at least slightly like another one 稍微相似,有点类似: **some semblance of** *The troops were called in to bring some semblance of order to the riot-torn city.* 这些部队被调来维持这个骚乱城市的起码秩序。

se·men /ˈsimən; ˈsiːmən/ *n* [U] the liquid produced by the male sex organs in humans and animals that contains SPERM 精液

se·mes·ter /səˈmɛstɚ; sɪˈmestə/ *n* [C] one of the two periods into which a year at high schools and universities is divided, especially in the US〔尤指美国中学和大学的〕一学期,半学年 —compare 比较 TERM¹ (9)

sem·i /ˈsɛmɪ; ˈsemi/ *plural* **semis** *n* [C] 1 *BrE informal* a house that is joined to the one next to it to form a pair【英,非正式】

〔一侧与他屋相连的〕联式房屋, 半独立式住宅; DUPLEX (1) *AmE*【美】: *a two-bedroomed semi* 一所两卧室的联式住宅 **2** *informal* a SEMIFINAL【非正式】半决赛 **3** *AmE* a very large heavy vehicle consisting of two connected parts, that carries goods over long distances【美】〔长途运输的〕铰接式重型卡车; JUGGERNAUT (1) *BrE*【英】

semi- /ˈsɛmɪ; semi/ *prefix* **1** exactly half〔一〕半: *a semicircle* 半圆 **2** partly but not completely 部分(地): *in the semidarkness* 在半明半暗之中 | *a semi-invalid* 半病弱者 | *semi-literate people* 半文盲 **3** happening, appearing etc twice in a particular period 〔在一段时间内〕出现两次的: *a semi-weekly visit* 一周两次的访问 | *a semi-annual publication* 半年一期的出版物 —compare 比较 BI-

semi-au·to·mat·ic /ˌ‥ˈ‥◂/ *adj* a semi-automatic weapon moves each new bullet into position ready for you to fire, so that you can fire the next shot very quickly〔武器〕半自动的 —**semi-automatic** *n* [C]

sem·i·breve /ˈsɛməˌbriv; ˈsemibriːv/ *n* [C] *BrE* a musical note which continues as long as two MINIMS【英】全音符; WHOLE NOTE *AmE*【美】—see picture at 参见 MUSIC 图

sem·i·cir·cle /ˈsɛməˌsɝkl; ˈsemiˌsɜːkəl/ *n* [C] **1** half a circle 半圆 —see picture at 参见 SHAPE[1] 图 **2** a group arranged in a curved line, as if on the edge of half a circle 半圆形排列: *Get the kids to sit in a semicircle.* 叫孩子们围成半圆形坐着。—**semicircular** /ˌsɛməˈsɝkjələ; ˌsemiˈsɜːkjələ◂/ *adj*

sem·i·co·lon /ˈsɛməˌkolən; ˌsemiˈkəʊlən/ *n* [C] a PUNCTUATION MARK (;) used to separate independent parts of a sentence or list 分号〔;〕—see picture at 参见 PUNCTUATION MARK 图

sem·i·con·duc·tor /ˌsɛməkənˈdʌktə; ˌsemikənˈdʌktə/ *n* [C] a substance, such as SILICON, that allows some electric currents to pass through it and is used in electronic equipment for this purpose 半导体 —compare 比较 CONDUCTOR (3)

sem·i-de·tached /ˌsɛmədɪˈtætʃt; ˌsemidɪˈtætʃt◂/ *adj BrE* a semi-detached house is joined to another house by one shared wall【英】〔房屋〕一侧与他屋相连的, 半独立式的 —compare 比较 DETACHED (2), TERRACED HOUSE —see picture on page A4 参见 A4 页图

sem·i·fi·nal /ˌsɛməˈfaɪnl; ˌsemiˈfaɪnl◂/ *n* [C] one of a pair of sports games, whose winners then compete against each other to decide who wins the whole competition 半决赛: *the world chess championship semifinal at Linares, Spain* 在西班牙利纳雷斯举行的世界国际象棋锦标赛半决赛

sem·i·fi·nal·ist /ˌsɛməˈfaɪnəlɪst; ˌsemiˈfaɪnəl-ɪst/ *n* [C] a person or team that competes in a semifinal 参加半决赛的选手[队]

sem·i·nal /ˈsɛmənl; ˈsemɪnəl/ *adj* **1** *formal* a seminal book, piece of music etc is new and important, and influences the way in which literature, music etc develops in the future【正式】〔书、乐曲等〕开创性的, 有重大影响的: *Barry Commoner's seminal 1970s book on ecology* 巴里·康芒纳20世纪70年代关于生态学的开创性著作 **2** [only before noun 仅用于名词前] *technical* producing or containing SEMEN【术语】(产生或含有)精液的: *seminal fluid* 精液

sem·i·nar /ˈsɛməˌnɑr; ˈsemɪnɑː/ *n* [C] a class in which a small group of students meet to study or talk about a particular subject〔学生分组对专题进行讨论的〕研讨班: *a Shakespeare seminar* 莎士比亚研讨班

sem·i·na·ry /ˈsɛməˌnɛrɪ; ˈsemɪnəri/ *n* [C] **1** a college for training priests or ministers〔培养神父、牧师的〕神学院 **2** *old-fashioned* a school【过时】学校

sem·i·ot·ics /ˌsɛmɪˈɑtɪks; ˌsemiˈɒtɪks/ also 又作 **sem·i·ol·o·gy** /ˌsɛmɪˈɑlədʒɪ; ˌsemiˈɒlədʒi/ *n* [U] *technical* the way in which people communicate through signs and images, or the study of this【术语】符号学 —**semiotician** /ˌsɛmɪəˈtɪʃən; ˌsemiəˈtɪʃən/, **semiologist** /ˌsɛmɪˈɑlədʒɪst; ˌsemiˈɒlədʒɪst/ *n* [C] —**semiotic** *adj*

sem·i-pre·cious /ˌsɛməˈprɛʃəs; ˌsemiˈpreʃəs◂/ *adj* a semi-precious jewel or stone is valuable, but not as valuable as a DIAMOND, RUBY etc〔宝石〕次贵重的, 〔仅次于钻石或红宝石等的〕半宝石的

semi-pro·fes·sion·al /ˌ‥ˈ‥‥◂/ *adj* **semi-professional player/footballer/musician etc** someone who is paid for doing a sport etc, but does not do it as their main job 半职业的球员/足球员/音乐家等

sem·i·qua·ver /ˈsɛməˌkwevə; ˈsemiˌkweɪvə/ *n* [C] *BrE* a musical note which continues for a sixteenth of the length of a SEMIBREVE【英】十六分音符; SIXTEENTH NOTE *AmE*【美】—see picture at 参见 MUSIC 图

semi-skilled /ˌ‥ˈ◂/ *adj* **a)** a semi-skilled worker is not highly skilled or professional, but needs some skills for the job they are doing〔工人〕半熟练的 **b)** a semi-skilled job is one that you need some skills to do, but you do not have to be highly skilled〔工作〕需半熟练工人做的

semi-skimmed /ˌ‥ˈ◂/ *n* [U] *BrE* milk that has had about half the fat removed【英】〔牛奶〕半脱脂的; TWO PERCENT MILK *AmE*【美】

Se·mite /ˈsɛmaɪt; ˈsiːmait/ *n* [C] someone who belongs to the race of people that includes Jews, Arabs and, in ancient times, Babylonians, Assyrians etc 闪米特人〔包括犹太人、阿拉伯人、古巴比伦人和古亚述人等〕—see also 另见 ANTI-SEMITISM

Se·mit·ic /səˈmɪtɪk; sɪˈmɪtɪk/ *adj* **1 a)** belonging to the race of people that includes Jews, Arabs and, in ancient times, Babylonians, Assyrians etc 闪米特人的〔包括犹太人、阿拉伯人、古巴比伦人和古亚述人等〕 **b)** belonging to or connected with any of the languages of these people 闪米特语的 **2** another word for JEWISH 犹太人的

sem·i·tone /ˈsɛməˌton; ˈsemitəʊn/ *n* [C] *BrE* the difference in PITCH[1] (3) between any two notes that are next to each other on a piano【英】半音; HALF STEP *AmE*【美】

sem·i·trop·i·cal /ˌsɛməˈtrɑpɪkl; ˌsemiˈtrɒpɪkəl◂/ *adj* SUBTROPICAL 亚热带的, 副热带的

semi-vo·wel /ˈ‥ˌ‥/ *n* [C] *technical* a sound made in speech that sounds like a vowel, but is in fact a consonant, like /w/【术语】半元音〈如 /w/〉

sem·i·week·ly /ˌsɛməˈwiklɪ; ˌsemiˈwiːkli◂/ *adj, adv* appearing or happening twice a week 每周两次的[地]: *a semiweekly paper* 每周出版两次的报纸

sem·o·li·na /ˌsɛməˈlinə; ˌseməˈliːnə/ *n* [U] **1** grains of crushed wheat, used especially in making sweet dishes and PASTA〔尤指用于做甜食和意大利面食的〕粗粒面粉 **2** a sweet dish made with these grains and milk 用粗粒面粉和牛奶做的甜食

Sem·tex /ˈsɛmtɛks; ˈsemteks/ *n* [U] *trademark* a powerful explosive often used illegally to make bombs【商标】森泰克斯塑胶炸药〔一种烈性炸药〕

S

sen·ate, Senate /ˈsɛnɪt; ˈsenɪt/ *n* **1** [singular] one of the two parts of the government that has the power to make laws, in countries such as the US, Australia, and France, which is smaller than the other part but has a higher rank〔美国、澳大利亚、法国等国家的〕参议院: *The Senate may veto this year's spending bill.* 参议院可能否决今年的开支议案。**2** [singular] the highest level of government in ancient Rome〔古罗马政府最高级别的〕元老院 **3** [C] the governing council at some universities〔某些大学的〕理事会, 评议会

sen·a·tor, Senator /ˈsɛnətə; ˈsenətə/ *n* [C] a member of a senate 参议员: *Senator Kennedy* 肯尼迪参议员 —**senatorial** /ˌsɛnəˈtɔrɪəl; ˌsenəˈtɔːriəl◂/ *adj*: *senatorial duties* 参议员的职责

send /sɛnd; send/ *v past tense and past participle* **sent** /sɛnt; sent/ S1 W1

1 ►BY POST/RADIO ETC 通过邮政/无线电等◄ [T] to arrange for something to go or be taken to another place, especially by post 送出, 发出, 〔尤指用邮政〕寄出: **send sb a letter/message/card** *Honestly, I get tired of sending Christmas cards.* 老实说, 我对寄圣诞贺卡已经厌倦了。| **send sth to** *Send your bill to the above address.* 把你的账单寄到上述地址。| **send sth by post/sea/air etc** *It will get there quicker if you send it by airmail.* 如果你寄航空, 它将较快到达。| **send a letter/message/card** *I sent her a message to say that I'd be late.* 我给她捎了口信说我会迟到。| **send a signal** *Radio signals were sent into deep space.* 无线电信号被发送到遥远的太空。| **send sth back/up/over etc** *I've ordered some coffee to be sent up here.* 我已经叫了一些咖啡并要他们送到这里来。

2 ►SEND SB TO DO STH 派某人做某事◄ [T] to tell someone to go somewhere, usually so that they can do something for you there 派〔某人〕往〔某处〕, 派遣: *Who sent you?* 谁派你来的? | *Richard couldn't come so he sent his sister instead.* 理查德不能来, 所以派了妹妹来代替他。| **send sb to** *The United Nations will send troops to the region.* 联合国将派遣部队到该地区。| **send sb around/over/home etc** *At noon the principal sent everyone home.* 中午校长把大家都打发回家了。| **send sb to do sth** *I sent Jean to go get some more butter.* 我叫琼去再买些黄油来。

3 ►SEND SB TO STAY SOMEWHERE 派送某人到某地停留◄ [T always+adv/prep] to arrange for someone to go somewhere and spend some time there 安排〔某人〕到〔某地〕, 将〔某人〕送往〔某地〕: **send sb to** *I'd never send my kids to boarding school.* 我永远也不会把孩子送去上寄宿学校。| *People get sent to jail for doing stuff like that!* 干那种勾当的人是要坐牢的! | **send sb on sth** *We want to send you on a short management course.* 我们想送你去参加短期管理课程。

4 send your love/regards/best wishes etc to ask someone to give your greetings, good wishes etc to someone else 请某人代为致意/问候/致良好祝愿等: *Mother sends her love.* 母亲向你问好。

5 ►AFFECT SOMEONE 影响某人◄ [T] to affect someone's feelings or condition 影响〔某人的感情或状态〕: **send sb to/into** *His boring speeches always send me to sleep.* 他那枯燥乏味的讲话总是使我昏昏入睡。| **send sb** (=make them feel extremely happy) 使人感到非常快乐 *Oh, doesn't his music just send you?* 啊, 他的音乐不是令你心旷神怡吗?

6 send sb/sth flying/sprawling/reeling etc to make someone or something move quickly through the air 使某人/某物乱飞/趴倒在地/摇晃等: *The explosion sent glass flying everywhere.* 爆炸使玻璃到处乱飞。

7 send out/up/forth etc to make something come out of itself 〔从自身〕发出等: *The fire was sending up thick clouds of smoke.* 大火中升起一股股浓烟。

8 send word to tell someone something by sending them a letter or message 捎信, 传话: **send word (to sb) that** *Somebody should send word that Rhoda's ill.* 应该找人将罗达生病的消息让大家知道。| **send word through sb** *Send word through Davies that we need more supplies.* 让戴维斯捎信说我们需要更多补给。

9 send sb packing also 又作 **send sb about their business** *informal*【非正式】to tell someone who is not wanted that they must leave at once 叫某人立即离开, 撵走某人

send away *phr v* **1** [T **send** sb ↔ **away**] to send someone to another place 把〔某人〕送往〔某处〕, 送走: *I was sent away to school at the age of seven.* 我七岁时就被送往别处上学。**2 send away for sth** to order something to be sent to you by post 邮购某物, 函索某物: *Send away for your free poster.* 请来信索取免费招贴画。

send sth ↔ **back** *phr v* to return something to where it came from 送回, 退还; 发送回来: *The steak was completely raw so I sent it straight back.* 牛排完全是生的, 所以我立刻把它退了回去。

send down *phr v* **1** [T **send** sth ↔ **down**] to make something lose value 使〔价格〕下降: *Reports of the company's bad trading figures sent its share prices down.* 关于该公司营业额差的报道使它的股票价格下跌了。**2** [T **send** sb **down**] *BrE informal* to send someone to prison【英, 非正式】送〔某人〕进监狱: *Do you think he'll be sent down for it?* 你认为他会因为这件事坐牢吗? **3 be sent down** *BrE* to be told to leave a university because of bad behaviour【英】〔大学生因行为不检而〕被开除, 被勒令退学

send for sb/sth *phr v* [T] **1** to ask or order someone to come to you by sending them a message 派人去叫[请]〔某人〕来: *Should I send for a doctor?* 要我派人去请医生吗? | **send for help** *Quick – go send for help.* 快——去请人来帮帮忙。**2** to ask or order that something be brought or sent to you 索取: *We'll have to send for the spare parts.* 我们必须派人把备用零件送来。

send sth ↔ **in** *phr v* [T] **1** to send something, usually by post, to a place where it can be dealt with 寄去, 〔邮寄〕递交: *I sent in a couple of job applications last week.* 上星期我寄出了几封求职信。**2** to send soldiers, police etc somewhere to deal with a very difficult or dangerous situation 派遣〔军队、警察等〕: *It's time to send in the troops.* 是应当出动军队的时候了。

send off *phr v* **1** [T **send** sth ↔ **off**] to send something somewhere by post 邮寄出〔某物〕, 发送: *I sent off the check this morning.* 我今天早上把支票寄出去了。**2 send off for sth** to order something to be sent to you by post 函购某物; 函索某物: *I'd better send off for an application form.* 我还是寄信去要份申请表吧。**3** [T **send** sb ↔ **off**] to send someone to another place 把〔某人〕送往〔另一地方〕: *We sent the kids off to their grandparents this morning.* 我们今天上午把孩子送到他们的 (外) 祖父母那里去了。**4** [T **send** sb ↔ **off**] *BrE* to order a sports player to leave the field because they have broken the rules【英】罚〔犯规的运动员〕出场 —see picture on page A23 参见 A23 页图

send sth ↔ **on** *phr v* [T] **1** *especially BrE* to send someone's letters or possessions to their new address from their old address【尤英】〔从旧地址〕把〔信件等〕转寄到新地址; FORWARD[3] (1) *AmE*【美】: *My flatmate said she'd send on all my post.* 曾和我合租公寓的朋友说她会把我的全部邮件转寄给我。**2** to send something that has been received to another place so that it can be dealt with 把〔收到的东西〕转送〔到另一处〕: *The data is then sent on to the Census Bureau.* 那些数据资料接着被转送到人口普查局。

send out *phr v* **1** [T **send** sth/sb ↔ **out**] to send something from a central point to various other places 发出〔某物〕; 送出〔某人〕: *Make sure you send out the invitations in good time.* 你务必及时把邀请信发出去。| *Search parties were sent out to look for survivors.* 搜索队被派出去寻找幸存者。**2** [**send** sth ↔ **out**] to broadcast or produce a signal, light, sound etc 广播[发射]〔信号等〕: *The ship is sending out an SOS signal.* 那艘船正在发出呼救信号。**3 send out for sth** to ask a restaurant or food shop to deliver food to you at home or at work 要餐馆[食品店]送食物上门: *Halfway through the meeting we sent out for sandwiches.* 会议开到一半时我们叫餐馆送三明治来。

send up *phr v* [T **send** sth/sb ↔ **up**] **1** to make something increase in value 使〔价格〕上升: *The shortage is bound to send prices up.* 供应短缺必将导致价格上涨。**2** *BrE informal* to show how silly something is by copying it in a very funny way【英, 非正式】〔通过滑稽模仿〕使显得可笑, 取笑, 嘲弄: *The film sends up all those Hollywood disaster movies.* 这部电影在嘲笑好莱坞所有那些灾难片。

send·er /ˈsɛndɚ; ˈsendə/ *n* [C] the person who sent a particular letter, package, message etc〔信件、包裹、信息等的〕发送者, 寄件人: **Return to Sender** (=stamped on a parcel when it could not reach the person it was sent to) 退回寄件人〔在无法投递的邮件上打上的戳〕

send-off /ˈ· ·/ *n* [C] *informal* a party or other occasion when people gather together to say goodbye to someone who is leaving【非正式】欢送会, 送别: **give sb a good send-off** *We gave her a really good send-off.* 我们非常热情地欢送她。

send-up /ˈ· ·/ *n* [C] *BrE informal* the act of copying someone or something in a way that makes them look funny or silly【英, 非正式】嘲弄性模仿: **[+of]** *a brilliant send-up of Clint Eastwood* 对克林特·伊斯特伍德妙惟肖的讽刺性模仿

Sen·e·ca /ˈsɛnɪkə; ˈsenɪkə/ (about 4 BC-65 AD) a Roman PHILOSOPHER, politician, and writer of plays. He was the teacher of Nero, the emperor, and had a lot of influence over him. But later, Nero believed Seneca was involved in a plan to kill him, and ordered him to kill himself. 塞内加〔(约公元前4年-公元65年), 古罗马哲学家、政治家、剧作家。他曾任尼禄皇帝的教师, 对其产生了不少影响。后来, 尼禄认为塞内加参与了谋杀他的一项计划, 于是赐令塞内加自尽〕

Sen·e·gal /ˌsɛnɪˈgɔl; ˌsenɪˈgɔːl/ a country in West Africa on the Atlantic coast. Population: 10,285,000 (2001). capital: Dakar. 塞内加尔〔西非一国家, 濒临大西洋。人口: 10,285,000 (2001), 首都: 达喀尔〕—**Senegalese** /ˌsɛnɪgəˈliz; ˌsenɪgəˈliːz◂/ *n, adj*

se·nes·cent /səˈnɛsnt; sɪˈnesənt/ *adj technical* becoming old and showing the effects of getting older【术语】变老的, 衰老的: *a senescent industry* 衰落的行业 —**senescence** *n* [U]

se·nile /ˈsinaɪl; ˈsiːnaɪl/ *adj not technical* mentally confused or behaving strangely, because of old age【非术语】因年老而糊涂的, 老迈的: *The poor old lady's getting senile: she hardly recognizes me now.* 那位可怜的老太太因年迈而糊涂了: 她现在几乎不认识我了。—**senility** /səˈnɪlətɪ; sɪˈnɪlɪti/ *n* [U]

senile de·men·tia /ˌ··ˈ··/ *n* [U] a medical condition that can affect the minds of old people 老年性痴呆 (症)

Se·ni·or /ˈsinjɚ; ˈsiːniə/ written abbreviation 缩写为 **Sr.** *AmE*【美】, **Snr** *BrE*【英】*adj* [only after noun 仅用于名词后] *especially AmE* used after a man's name to show that he is the older of two men who have the same name and come from the same family【尤美】年纪较大的, 年长的〔用于一个家庭里同名的两个男人中〕: *John J. Wallace, Sr.* 老约翰·J.华莱士

senior[1] *adj* **1** [only before noun 仅用于名词前] older 年长的: *Senior pupils have certain privileges.* 年纪较大的学生有一定的特权。**2** having a higher position or rank〔地位或级别〕较高的: *a very senior officer* 级别很高的军官 | **[+to]** *Only one manager is senior to me now.* 现在只有一位经理比我地位高。| **senior partner** (=the more important person in a business partnership)〔商行等合股公司的〕主要合伙人 —compare 比较 JUNIOR[1] 2

senior[2] *n* [C] **1 be two/five/ten etc years sb's senior** to be two, five, ten etc years older than someone 比某人大两岁/五岁/十岁: *Her husband was nine years her senior.* 她丈夫比她大九岁。—opposite 反义词 JUNIOR[2] (1) **2** *AmE* a student in their last year of HIGH SCHOOL or university【美】〔中学或大学〕最高年级的学生, 毕业班学生: *Jen will be a senior this year.* 珍今年是毕业班学生了。—compare 比较 FRESHMAN, JUNIOR[2] (4), SOPHOMORE **3** *CanE* a SENIOR CITIZEN【加】老年人

senior cit·i·zen /ˌ···ˈ···/ *n* [C] an old person, especially someone who is over 60, or who is RETIRED 老年人〔尤指 60 岁以上或已退休者〕—see 见 OLD (USAGE)

senior high school /ˌ···ˈ··/ also 又作 **senior high** /ˌ··ˈ·/ *n* [C] *AmE* a school in the US for students between 14 and 18【美】高级中学〔学生年龄为 14 岁至 18 岁〕—compare 比较 JUNIOR HIGH SCHOOL

se·ni·or·i·ty /sinˋjɔrətɪ; ˌsiːniˈɒrəti/ *n* [U] **1** the situation of being older or higher in rank than someone else 年长; 职位[级别]高: *Her seniority finally earned her some respect.* 她的老资格终于使她赢得了人们的几分尊敬。**2** official advantage that you have because of the length of time you have worked in a company or organization 年资, 资历: *Workers with less than 5 years' seniority may be laid off.* 资历不足五年的工人可能被解雇。

sen·na /ˋsɛnə; ˈsenə/ *n* [U] a tropical plant with a fruit that is often used to make a medicine to help your bowels (BOWEL (1)) work 番泻〔一种热带植物, 其果实常用作泻药〕

sen·sa·tion /sɛnˋseʃən; senˈseɪʃən/ *n* **1** [U] the ability to feel, especially through your sense of touch〔感官的〕感觉能力〔尤指触觉〕: *Jerry realized with alarm that he had no sensation in his legs.* 杰里吃惊地意识到他的双腿已经没有感觉了。**2** [C,U] a feeling that you get from one of your five senses, especially the sense of touch〔由感官得到的〕感觉〔尤指触觉〕: *a tingling sensation in the skin* 皮肤的刺痛感 | **[+of]** *a strange sensation of weightlessness* 一种失重的奇特感觉 **3** [C] a feeling that is hard to describe, caused by a particular event, experience, or memory〔由某一事件、经历或记忆引起的难以描述的〕感受: **sensation (that)** *The fog gave me the strange sensation that I was alone in the world.* 大雾使我产生一种世界上只有我孤零零一个人的奇异感觉。**4 a sensation** extreme excitement or interest, or someone or something that causes this 轰动, 激动; 引起轰动的人[事]: *News of their engagement created a great sensation.* 他们订婚的消息引起很大的轰动。

sen·sa·tion·al /sɛnˋseʃənḷ; senˈseɪʃənəl/ *adj* **1** very interesting and exciting 令人极度兴奋的, 轰动的: *The effect of the discovery was sensational.* 这个发现有轰动的效果。| *a sensational result* 令人兴奋不已的结果 **2** intended to interest, excite, or shock people, in a way that you disapprove of or find unpleasant 为了引起轰动的; 耸人听闻的: *sensational press coverage of the divorce* 新闻界对这起离婚大事渲染的报道 **3** *informal* very good or impressive【非正式】极好的, 令人难忘的: *You look sensational in that dress!* 你穿那件连衣裙漂亮极了。—**sensationally** *adv*

sen·sa·tion·al·is·m /sɛnˋseʃənḷˌɪzəm; senˈseɪʃənəlɪzəm/ *n* [U] a way of reporting events or stories that makes them seem as strange, exciting, or shocking as possible, and in a way that people disapprove of〔新闻报道、文艺作品中的〕追求轰动效应; 耸人听闻的手法 —**sensationalist** *adj*: *a sensationalist magazine article on teenage sex* 杂志上一篇采用耸人听闻的手法描写青少年性问题的文章

sen·sa·tion·al·ize also 又作 **-ise** *BrE*【英】/sɛnˋseʃənəˌlaɪz; senˈseɪʃənəlaɪz/ *v* [T] to deliberately make something seem as strange, exciting, or shocking as possible, in a way that people disapprove of 用追求轰动效应[耸人听闻]的手法处理〔某事〕: *a sensationalized account of the trial* 对这场审判耸人听闻的报道

sense¹ /sɛns; sens/ *n*

S1 W1

① JUDGMENT/UNDERSTANDING 判断/理解(力)
② A FEELING 感觉
③ MAKE SENSE 有意义
④ SEE/SMELL/TOUCH ETC 看见/嗅到/触摸等
⑤ SKILL/ABILITY 技能/能力
⑥ MEANING 意思
⑦ CRAZY/SILLY 疯狂的/愚蠢的
⑧ OTHER MEANINGS 其他意思

① JUDGMENT/UNDERSTANDING 判断/理解(力)

1 [U] good understanding and judgment, especially about practical things〔尤指对某具体事物的〕判断力, 辨别力: **have the sense to do sth** *You should have had the sense to turn off the electricity before touching the wires.* 你本该懂得在触摸电线之前先把电源切断。—see also 另见 COMMON SENSE

2 there is no sense in (doing) sth *spoken* used to say that it is not sensible to do something【口】(做)某事是没意义的: *There's no sense in getting upset about it now.* 现在为这件事苦恼是没有意义的。

3 talk sense *spoken* to say things that are reasonable or sensible【口】说话有道理: **talk sense!** (=used when you are annoyed with someone for saying something silly) 说话要头脑清楚!〔用于表示对某人的蠢话感到厌烦〕*Oh talk sense, Stuart, we couldn't possibly go without the car.* 斯图尔特, 说话得讲道理! 没有车我们根本走不了。

4 talk/knock some sense into sb to try to persuade someone to stop behaving in a way that you think is silly 说服某人改变愚蠢行为: *He says he's dropping out of school – will you try and talk some sense into him?* 他说他要退学 —— 你去试试说服他不要这么犯傻好吗?

5 see sense to realize that you are being silly and unreasonable 明白事理, 意识到自己犯傻: *I hope Jack sees sense before it's too late.* 我希望杰克尽快明白过来, 免得后悔莫及。

6 bring sb to their senses to make someone think or behave in a reasonable and sensible way 使某人醒悟, 使某人恢复理智: *I hope she fails. That'll bring her to her senses.* 我巴不得她失败, 那样才会让她醒悟过来。

7 come to your senses to realize that what you are doing is not sensible 恢复理智, 醒悟过来: *One day he'll come to his senses and see what a fool he's been.* 总有一天他会醒悟过来, 认识到自己是多么愚蠢。

② A FEELING 感觉

8 [C] a feeling about something〔对某物的〕感觉: **[+of]** *The whole affair left me with a sense of complete helplessness.* 整个事情让我产生一种完全无助的感觉。| *A new sense of urgency had entered into their negotiations.* 在他们的谈判中出现了一种新的紧迫感。| **have the sense that** *I don't know why, but I had the sense that he was lying.* 我不知道为什么, 但我觉得他是在撒谎。

③ MAKE SENSE 有意义

9 make sense a) to have a clear meaning that is easy to understand 有〔明确而容易理解的〕意义: *Read this and tell me if it makes sense.* 读读这篇东西, 告诉我它的意思是否明确。**b)** to have a good reason or explanation 有道理, 合乎情理: *It just doesn't make sense – why would she do a thing like that?* 这真是无法解释 —— 她为什么会做出这样的事情? **c)** to be a sensible thing to do 是明智的做法: *It makes sense to save money while you can.* 能省钱时就节省, 这是明智的。

10 make sense of sth to understand something, especially something difficult or complicated 了解某事的意义, 理解〔尤指困难或复杂的〕某事物: *Can you make any sense of this article at all?* 你究竟能不能理解这篇文章的意思?

④ SEE/SMELL/TOUCH ETC 看见/嗅到/触摸等

11 [C] one of the five natural powers of sight, hearing, feeling, taste, and smell, that give us information about the things around us 感觉官能; 视觉; 听觉; 触觉; 味觉; 嗅觉: **sense of smell/taste/touch etc** *a poor sense of smell* 嗅觉迟钝 | **the five senses** (=all of the senses) 五种官能 | **the senses** (=several or all of the five senses) 五种感觉官能〔或其中的几种〕*combinations of flavors, textures, and color to delight the senses* 使感官愉悦的风味、质地和颜色的组合 —see also 另见 SIXTH SENSE

⑤ SKILL/ABILITY 技能/能力

12 [singular] a natural ability to judge something 判断力, 辨别力: **sense of direction/rhythm/timing etc** *I'll probably get lost – I haven't got a very good sense of direction.* 我可能会迷路 —— 我的方向感不太好。| **dress/clothes sense** *He has no dress sense at all.* (=does not know what clothes look good) 他对服装毫无鉴赏力。

⑥ MEANING 意思

13 [C] the meaning of a word, phrase, sentence etc〔单词、短语、句子等的〕意义, 意思: *I'm using the word 'family' in its broadest sense.* 我是在最广义上用 family (家庭) 这个词。| *In this dictionary the different senses of a word are marked by numbers.* 本词典中每个词的不同义项用数码标明。| **in every sense of the word** (=using all possible meanings of this word)

从这个词的各种意义上说 *He's a gentleman in every sense of the word.* 从各方面来讲, 他都是个绅士。
14 the sense of sth the basic meaning of something 某事物的基本意义

⑦ CRAZY/SILLY 疯狂的/愚蠢的
15 take leave of your senses to start to behave in an unreasonable or silly way 发疯: *You're challenging him to a fight? Have you taken leave of your senses?* 你提出要和他打架? 你疯了吗?
16 be out of your senses to behave in a way that other people think is unreasonable and possibly risky 不明智, 愚蠢

⑧ OTHER MEANINGS 其他意思
17 sense of humour *BrE*【英】, **sense of humor** *AmE*【美】 the ability to understand or enjoy things that are funny, or to make people laugh 幽默感: *I like Michelle – she's got a really good sense of humour.* 我喜欢米歇尔 —— 她很有幽默感。
18 in no sense used to emphasize that something is definitely not true 决不〔用于强调〕: *In no sense does this excuse their actions.* 这决不能成为他们行为的托辞。
19 in a very real sense used to emphasize the fact that something is definitely true 确实地, 毫无疑问地〔用于强调〕: *In a very real sense, we can say that education is the most vital of all resources.* 毫无疑问, 我们可以说在所有资源中教育是最重要的。
20 sense of occasion a feeling or understanding that an event or occasion is very serious or important 对某重要事件或时刻的感觉或理解
21 in a sense/in one sense/in some senses etc in one particular way, but without considering all the other facts or possibilities 在某种意义上等: *In some senses this may be true, but it's not really relevant.* 从某些意义上说, 这也许是真实的, 但它并非真正至关重要。| *In a sense, I think he likes being responsible for everything.* 从某种意义上说, 我认为他喜欢包揽一切。
22 regain your senses *old-fashioned* to stop feeling FAINT¹ (3) or unwell【过时】恢复清醒的头脑, 恢复精神: *Out in the fresh air, she quickly regained her senses.* 她在室外呼吸点新鲜空气, 很快就恢复精神了。

sense² *v* [T] **1** if you sense something, you feel that it exists or is true, without being told or having proof 感觉到, 意识到: *The horse sensed danger and stopped.* 那匹马感到有危险, 于是停了下来。| *I could sense her growing irritation.* 我察觉到她越来越不耐烦。| **sense (that)** *I sensed that there was someone in the room with me.* 我感觉到有人和我一起在房间里。| **sense what/how/who etc** *Hugo had already sensed how unhappy she was.* 雨果已经察觉到她是多么的不开心。**2** if a machine senses something, it discovers and records it〔机器〕检测: *an electronic device used for sensing intruders* 自动检测闯入者的电子装置

Sense and Sen·si·bil·i·ty /ˌ· · ·ˌ·ˈ· · ·/ (1811) a book by Jane Austen about two sisters, Elinor, who is a very sensible person, and Marianne, who is a very romantic and emotional person, and the difficulties they face in finding suitable husbands《理智与情感》〔(1811), 简·奥斯汀的一部小说。讲述的是两姐妹的故事, 姐姐埃莉诺是一个极为理智的人, 妹妹玛丽安娜却非常浪漫, 充满激情。她们在寻觅如意郎君的过程中遭遇了种种波折〕

sense·less /ˈsɛnslɪs; ˈsensləs/ *adj* **1** happening or done for no good reason or with no purpose 无道理的, 无目的的, 无意义的: *the senseless death of a young girl* 一个少女毫无意义的死 | *senseless violence* 毫无意义的暴力行为 **2** unconscious 失去知觉的: *They beat him senseless, and left him for dead.* 他们把他打得失去知觉, 然后丢下他不管死活。—**senselessly** *adv* **senselessness** *n* [U]

sense or·gan /ˈ· ˌ··/ *n* [C] a part of your body through which you see, smell, hear, taste, or feel something〔用以看、嗅、听、品尝或触摸的〕感觉器官

sen·si·bil·i·ty /ˌsɛnsəˈbɪlətɪ; ˌsensɪ̵ˈbɪlɪ̵ti/ *n plural* **sensibilities 1 wound/offend sb's sensibilities** to offend someone by being rude or unpleasant etc 伤害/触犯某人的感情: *It wounded her delicate sensibilities to be addressed in such a vulgar manner.* 用这样粗俗的态度对她说话, 伤害了她脆弱的感情。**2** [U] the ability to understand feelings, especially those expressed in literature or art〔尤指对文学、艺术的〕感受力, 鉴赏力: *Basil was above all a person of sensibility and perception.* 巴兹尔尤其是一个有鉴赏力和洞察力的人。

3 3 **sen·si·ble** /ˈsɛnsəbl̩; ˈsensɪ̵bəl/ *adj* **1** *especially BrE* reasonable, practical, and able to judge things well【尤英】明智的, 合理的, 实际的: *I think that's a very sensible suggestion.* 我看这是一个非常合理的建议。| *Surely it would be sensible to get a second opinion.* 多听取一种意见肯定是明智的。| *Come now, be sensible.* 嗨, 明智点! **2 sensible clothes/shoes** *especially BrE* clothes or shoes that are practical, comfortable, and strong rather than attractive or fashionable【尤英】实用的衣服/鞋子 **3 sensible of sth** *old-fashioned* knowing or recognizing something【过时】感知某事, 察觉到某事: *He was sensible of the trouble he had caused.* 他意识到自己造成的麻烦。**4** *formal* noticeable【正式】可感觉到的, 明显的: *a sensible increase in temperature* 温度的明显上升 —**sensibly** *adv*: *Sensibly, Barbara had brought an umbrella.* 芭芭拉明智地带了一把雨伞。

3 3 **sen·si·tive** /ˈsɛnsətɪv; ˈsensɪ̵tɪv/ *adj*
1 ►UNDERSTANDING PEOPLE 理解别人◄ able to understand other people's feelings and problems 能理解〔别人的感情和问题〕的: *Underneath all that macho stuff, he's really a sensitive guy.* 在所有那些大男子气概下面, 他实际上是个体贴的人。| **[+to]** *We must be sensitive to the community's needs.* 我们必须善于体察大众的需要。—opposite 反义词 INSENSITIVE
2 ►EASILY OFFENDED 容易生气的◄ easily hurt, upset, or offended by things that people say〔感情〕易受伤害的, 神经过敏的: *Don't be so sensitive – I wasn't criticizing you!* 别那么神经过敏 —— 我不是在批评你! | **[+about]** *Lara's very sensitive about her figure.* 拉腊对她自己的体形非常敏感。| **sensitive soul** (=someone who is easily upset by small or unimportant things) 过度敏感的人 —see also 另见 HYPERSENSITIVE
3 ►COLD/PAIN ETC 冷/疼痛等◄ able to feel physical sensations, especially pain, more than usual〔尤对疼痛〕易感受的, 敏感的: *Make sure you protect sensitive areas of your skin with a good suncream.* 一定要用好的防晒霜保护你皮肤的敏感部分。| **be sensitive to sth** *Ruth is very sensitive to cold.* 鲁思对寒冷很敏感。
4 ►ART/MUSIC ETC 艺术/音乐等◄ able to understand or express yourself through art, music, literature etc〔对文学艺术〕感受力强的, 有表现能力的: *a sensitive musician* 表现力强的音乐家 | *a very sensitive performance* 非常细腻的演出
5 ►SITUATIONS/SUBJECTS 情况/问题◄ a situation or subject that is sensitive needs to be dealt with very carefully because it may offend people or make them angry〔情况、问题等〕需小心处理的, 敏感的, 可能触怒人的: *Sorry I didn't realize it was such a sensitive issue.* 对不起, 我没有认识到这是个如此敏感的问题。
6 ►HEAT/LIGHT ETC 热/光等◄ able to measure or react to very small changes in heat, light etc〔对光、热等的变化〕能准确计量的, 灵敏度高的: *We need a more sensitive thermometer for this.* 我们需要一个灵敏度高些的温度计来对此测量。| **highly sensitive** (=very sensitive) 高度敏感的 *a highly sensitive electronic camera* 高敏感度的电子摄像机 | **[+to]** *film that is sensitive to ultraviolet light* 对紫外光敏感的胶卷 | **light-sensitive/heat-sensitive etc** *light-sensitive photographic paper* 感光相纸 —**sensitively** *adv* —**sensitivity** /ˌsɛnsəˈtɪvətɪ; ˌsensɪ̵ˈtɪvɪ̵ti/ also 又作 **sensitiveness** /ˈsɛnsətɪvnəs; ˈsensɪ̵tɪvnɪ̵s/ *n* [U]

sen·si·tiv·i·ties /ˌsɛnsəˈtɪvətɪz; ˌsensɪ̵ˈtɪvɪ̵tiz/ *n* [plural] someone's feelings and the fact that they could be upset or offended〔感情上的〕敏感性, 易受伤害的特性: *The sensitivities of the black community were largely ignored.* 黑人社会心理上的敏感性在很大程度上被忽视了。

sen·si·tize also 又作 **-ise** *BrE*【英】/ˈsɛnsəˌtaɪz; ˈsensɪ̵taɪz/ *v* **1** [T usually passive 一般用被动态] to give someone some experience of a particular problem or situation so that they can notice it and understand it easily 使〔某人对某问题或情况〕敏感: **sensitize sb to sth** *Her upbringing had sensitized her to discrimination.* 她所受的教养使她对歧视很敏感。**2** [T] *technical* to treat a material or a piece of equipment so that it will react to physical or chemical changes【术语】使对物理[化学]变化有反应: *sensitized photographic paper* 感光相纸 —**sensitization** /ˌsɛnsətəˈzeʃən; ˌsensɪ̵taɪˈzeɪʃən/ *n* [U]

sen·sor /ˈsɛnsɚ; ˈsensə/ *n* [C] *technical* a piece of equipment used for discovering the presence of light, heat, sound etc, especially in small amounts【术语】〔探测光、热、声等的〕传感器, 感应装置

sen·so·ry /ˈsɛnsərɪ; ˈsensəri/ *adj* connected with or using your senses of sight, hearing, smell, taste or touch 感官的; 感觉上的: *sensory stimuli* 感官刺激 | *sensory deprivation* 感觉剥夺 —see also 另见 ESP (1)

sen·su·al /ˈsɛnʃuəl; ˈsenʃuəl/ *adj* **1** connected with the feelings of your body rather than your mind 肉体上的, 官能的:

purely sensual pleasures 纯粹肉体上的快乐 **2** interested in or making you think of physical pleasure, especially sexual pleasure 肉欲的; 刺激性欲的; 性感的: *sensual lips* 性感的嘴唇 | *a sensual woman* 性感的女人 —**sensuality** /ˌsɛnʃʊˈælətɪ; ˌsenʃuˈælɨti/ *n* [U] —**sensually** *adv*

sen·su·al·ist /ˈsɛnʃʊəlɪst; ˈsenʃuəlɨst/ *n* [C] someone who is only interested in physical pleasure 追求感官享受的人, 耽于声色的人

sen·su·ous /ˈsɛnʃʊəs; ˈsenʃuəs/ *adj* **1** pleasing to your senses 给感官以快乐的, 给人以快感的: *the sensuous feeling of silk on her skin* 丝绸给她皮肤带来的美妙感受 **2** full of powerful images or sounds that suggest physical pleasure 使人赏心悦目的, 使人愉悦的: *sensuous music* 动听悦耳的音乐—**sensuously** *adv* —**sensuousness** *n* [U]

sent /sɛnt; sent/ the past tense and past participle of SEND

sen·tence¹ /ˈsɛntəns; ˈsentəns/ *n* [C] **1** a group of words that usually contains a subject and a verb, expresses a complete idea or asks a question, and that, when written in English, begins with a capital letter and ends with a FULL STOP¹ (1) 句子, 句 **2** a punishment that a judge gives to someone who has been declared guilty of a crime 判决, 判刑: *a six year prison sentence* 六年徒刑 | **heavy/light sentence** (=long or short time in prison) 重判/轻判 | **life sentence** (=very long time in prison) 无期徒刑 *a life sentence for murder* 因谋杀罪被判无期徒刑 | **death sentence** (=punishment by death) 死刑 | **serve a sentence** (=spend time in prison as a punishment) 服刑 **3 pass/pronounce sentence** to officially state what a punishment will be 宣布判决, 宣判

sentence² *v* [T often passive 常用被动态] if a judge sentences someone found guilty of a crime, they officially and legally give them a punishment〔法官〕判决, 宣判: [+to] *Sanchez was sentenced to three years in prison for his part in the crime.* 桑切斯因参与犯罪被判处三年徒刑。

sentence ad·verb /ˈ· ·, · ·/ *n* [C] an adverb that expresses an opinion about the whole sentence that contains it 句子副词

sen·ten·tious /sɛnˋtɛnʃəs; senˈtenʃəs/ *adj formal* saying clever things about morality or the way people should behave【正式】说教的, 劝诫的: *sententious remarks* 说教式的言语 —**sententiously** *adv*

sen·tient /ˈsɛnʃənt; ˈsenʃənt/ *adj formal or technical* having feelings and knowing that you exist【正式或术语】有感知力的: *Man is a sentient being.* 人是有感知的生物。

sen·ti·ment /ˈsɛntəmənt; ˈsentɨmənt/ *n* **1** [C,U] *formal* an opinion or feeling you have about something【正式】意见, 观点, 感想: *It is my sentiment that we should vote against the motion.* 我的意见是我们应该对这个动议投反对票。| **popular sentiment** (=what most people think) 民意 | **my/your sentiments** *I share your sentiments entirely.* 我和你的看法完全相同。**2** [U] feelings of pity, love, sadness etc that are often considered to be too strong or not suitable for a particular situation 多愁善感: *There's no place for sentiment in business!* 做生意容不得感情用事。

sen·ti·ment·al /ˌsɛntəˋmɛntḷ; ˌsentɨˈmentl◂/ *adj* **1** someone who is sentimental is too easily affected by emotions such as love, sympathy, sadness etc 多愁善感的, 感情用事的: *There's nothing wrong with being a little sentimental!* 有点多愁善感没什么不对! **2** based on or connected with your feelings rather than on practical reasons 感情上的, 情绪上的, 非理性的: **for sentimental reasons/purposes** *I only keep these old photos for sentimental reasons.* 我只是因感情上的原因才保存这些旧照片。**3 sentimental value** if something has sentimental value, it is not worth much money, but it is important to you because it reminds you of someone you love or a happy time in the past 感情价值: *The stolen rings were of great sentimental value to the owner.* 那些被盗的戒指对失主是有很大感情价值的。**4** a story, film, book etc that is sentimental deals with emotions such as love and sadness in a way that seems silly and insincere〔故事、电影、书等〕感伤的; 感情轻浮虚伪的: *I enjoyed the movie but the ending was too sentimental.* 我喜欢这部电影, 但它的结局太伤感了。—**sentimentally** *adv*

sen·ti·men·tal·ist /ˌsɛntəˋmɛntḷɪst; ˌsentɨˈmentlɨst/ *n* [C] someone who behaves or writes in a sentimental way 多愁善感的人, 伤感主义者 —**sentimentalism** *n* [U]

sen·ti·men·tal·i·ty /ˌsɛntəmɛnˋtælətɪ; ˌsentɨmenˈtælɨti/ *n* [U] the quality of being sentimental 多愁善感, 感情用事

sen·ti·ment·al·ize also 又作 **-ise** *BrE*【英】/ˌsɛntəˋmɛntḷˌaɪz; ˌsentɨˈmentlaɪz/ *v* [I,T] to speak, write or think about something in a way that mentions only the good or happy things about something, but not the bad things 只谈[思考]某事美好的一面: *a sentimentalized account of life during the war* 对战争时期生活的美化 | [+about/over] *Listen to Albert sentimentalizing about his childhood again.* 你再听听艾伯特把他的童年说成多么浪漫美好吧。

sen·ti·nel /ˈsɛntənḷ; ˈsentɪnəl/ *n* [C] *old-fashioned* a sentry【过时】哨兵, 卫兵, 岗哨

sen·try /ˈsɛntrɪ; ˈsentri/ *n* [C] a soldier standing outside a building as a guard〔守卫于建筑物外面的〕哨兵, 卫兵, 岗哨

sentry box /ˈ· · ·/ *n* [C] a tall narrow shelter with an open front where a soldier can stand while guarding a building 岗亭

Seoul /sol; səʊl/ the capital city of South Korea, a business, industrial, and cultural centre 首尔〔韩国首都, 也是一个商业、工业和文化中心〕

se·pal /ˈsɛpḷ; ˈsepəl/ *n* [C] *technical* one of the small leaves directly under a flower【术语】〔花的〕萼片

sep·a·ra·ble /ˈsɛpərəbḷ; ˈsepərəbəl/ *adj* two things that are separable can be separated or considered separately 可分开[分隔, 分离]的: *Supply and demand are not easily separable.* 供给和需求不易分开。—opposite 反义词 INSEPARABLE—**separably** *adv*—**separability** /ˌsɛpərəˈbɪlətɪ; ˌsepərəˈbɪlɨti/ *n* [U]

sep·a·rate¹ /ˈsɛpərɪt; ˈsepərɨt/ *adj* **1** things, places, buildings etc that are separate are not joined to each other or touching each other〔事物、地方、建筑物等〕分开的; 不相连的; 独立的: *separate bedrooms* 不相连[独立]的卧室 | *The poor travelled in a separate carriage.* 过去穷人外出时乘坐分开的车厢。| [+from] *Keep the fish separate from the other food.* 把鱼和其他食物分开存放。**2** ideas, information, activities etc that are separate are not connected or do not affect each other in any way〔主意、信息、活动等〕互不相关的, 各自的: *two separate problems* 两个互不相关的问题 | [+from] *He tries to keep his professional life completely separate from his private life.* 他尽量把他的职业生活和私人生活完全分开。**3** different 不同的, 不一样的: *This word has 3 separate meanings.* 这个词有三个不同的意思。| *She's been warned on three separate occasions that her work is not good enough.* 她已受到三次警告, 被指出工作不够好。**4 go your separate ways a)** to finish a relationship with someone, especially a romantic relationship 结束(与某人的)关系〔尤指恋爱关系〕; 不再交往 **b)** to start travelling in a different direction from someone you have been travelling with 分手, 分道而行—**separately** *adv*: *They did arrive together, but I think they left separately.* 他们确实是一起到达的, 但我想他们是各自离开的。

sep·a·rate² /ˈsɛpəˌret; ˈsepəreɪt/ *v*

1 ▶BE BETWEEN 在…之间◀ [T often passive 常用被动态] if something separates two places or two things, it is between them so that they are not touching each other or connected with each other 把…隔开: *The two towns are separated by a river.* 这两个城镇被一条河隔开。| *Seventeen years had separated them.* 他们离别已有17年了。

2 ▶DIVIDE 分开◀ [I,T] to divide or split into different parts, or layers, or to make something do this (把…)分成不同部分; (使)分离: *Here's a trick to keep your salad dressing from separating.* 这里有个能使色拉调味汁不沉淀的诀窍。| [+from] *At this point the satellite separates from its launcher.* 在这个时候, 卫星就脱离发射器。| **separate sth into** *It would help if we separated this stuff into three different piles.* 要是我们把这东西分成三堆, 也许会有帮助。| **separate eggs** (=divide the white part from the yellow part) 把蛋白和蛋黄分开

3 ▶STOP LIVING TOGETHER 停止同居◀ [I] to start to live apart from your husband, wife or sexual partner〔夫妻〕分居;〔性伴侣〕分手: *It's the children who suffer when their parents separate.* 父母分居时受罪的是子女。

4 ▶RECOGNIZE DIFFERENCE 识别差异◀ [T] to recognize that one idea is different from another, and to deal with each idea alone 识别〔思想的〕差别; 分别处理: [+from] *It's not always easy to separate cause from effect.* 因果关系并不总是容易区分的。

5 ▶MOVE APART 分开◀ [I,T] to move apart, or make people move apart (使)分开, 把〔人〕隔开: [+from] *We had to separate Philip and Jason because they were talking all the time.* 我们不得不把菲利普和贾森分开, 因为他们老在讲话。

6 ▶MAKE SB/STH DIFFERENT 使某人/某事物不同◀ [T+from] to be the thing that makes someone or something different from other similar people or things 使区别于, 使与众不同: *What is it that you think separates her from the other applicants?* 你认为是什么使她不同于其他申请人?

7 separate the men from the boys *informal* to do something that makes it clear which people are brave or strong and which are not【非正式】区分强者与弱者; 识别勇敢者与懦弱者: *The climb through the mountains will definitely separate the men from the boys.* 这次登山肯定会把强者和弱者区分开来。

8 separate the sheep from the goats also 又作 **separate the wheat from the chaff** to separate the good things from the bad things 区分好的和坏的; 区别优劣

separate sth ↔ **out** *phr v* [I,T] if part of something separates out or is separated out, it becomes separate from the other parts (使) 分离, 析出

sep·a·rat·ed /ˋsɛpəˏretɪd; ˈsepəreɪtɪ̵d/ *adj* not living with your husband, wife or sexual partner any more 〔夫妻〕分居的; 〔性伴侣〕不再同居的: *David and I have been separated for six months but we're not divorced yet.* 我和戴维已经分居六个月了, 但还没有离婚。

sep·a·rates /ˋsɛpərɪts; ˈsepərɪ̵ts/ *n* [plural] women's clothing, such as skirts, shirts, and trousers, that can be worn in different combinations 可以任意配套穿的女服〈如裙子、衬衫、裤子等〉

sep·a·ra·tion /ˏsɛpəˋreʃən; ˌsepəˈreɪʃən/ *n* **1** [C,U] a period of time that two or more people spend apart from each other 分开的时期: *Their separation lasted over 20 years.* 他们分离已逾 20 年。**2** [C] a situation in which a husband and wife agree to live apart even though they are still married 夫妇分居 —compare 比较 DIVORCE[1] (1) **3** [U] the act of separating or the state of being separate 分开, 分离; 分居

sep·a·ra·tist /ˋsɛpəˏretɪst; ˈsepərətɪ̵st/ *n* [C] a member of a group in a country that wants to establish a new separate country with its own government 〔企图另组建独立国家的〕分离主义者 —**separatism** *n* [U]

sep·a·ra·tor /ˋsɛpəˏretɚ; ˈsepəreɪtə/ *n* [C] a machine for separating liquids from solids, or cream from milk 分离器, 离析器; 脱脂器

se·pi·a /ˋsipɪə; ˈsiːpiə/ *n* [U] **1** a dark reddish brown colour 深褐色 **2 sepia photograph/print** a photograph, picture etc, especially an old one, that is this colour 〔尤指旧的〕深褐色照片/图画 **3** an ink used for drawing which has this colour 深褐色墨汁

sep·sis /ˋsɛpsɪs; ˈsepsɪ̵s/ *n* [U] *technical* an infection in part of the body, in which PUS is produced【术语】脓毒病[症]

Sep·tem·ber /sɛpˋtɛmbɚ; sepˈtembə/ written abbreviation 缩写为 **Sept** *n* [C,U] the ninth month of the year, between August and October 九月: **in September (1998/2000 etc)** *The project is due to finish in September.* 工程预定在 9 月完成。| **last/next September** *We haven't seen each other since last September.* 我们自从 (去年) 9 月就没有见过面了。| **on September 6th** (also 又作 **on 6th September** *BrE* 英): *The meeting will be on September 6th.* 会议将于 9 月 6 日举行。(spoken as 读作: *on the sixth of September* or 或 on *September the sixth* or 或 (*AmE* 美) *on September sixth*)

sep·tet /sɛpˋtɛt; sepˈtet/ *n* [C] **1** a group of seven singers or musicians who perform together 七重唱; 七重奏 **2** a piece of music written for seven performers 七重唱[奏]曲

sep·tic /ˋsɛptɪk; ˈseptɪk/ *adj especially BrE* a wound or part of your body that is septic is infected with BACTERIA【尤英】〔伤口等〕脓毒性的, 受感染的: *a septic finger* 感染化脓的手指

sep·ti·cae·mi·a *BrE*【英】, **septicemia** *AmE*【美】/ˏsɛptəˋsimɪə; ˌseptɪ̵ˈsiːmiə/ *n* [U] *technical* a serious condition in which infection spreads from a small area of your body through your blood; BLOOD POISONING【术语】败血症

septic tank /ˋ‥ ˏ/ *n* [C] a large container kept under ground used for putting human body waste into 化粪池

sep·tu·a·ge·nar·i·an /ˏsɛptʃuədʒəˋnɛrɪən; ˌseptʃuədʒɪ̵ˈneəriən/ *n* [C] someone who is between 70 and 79 years old 70 至 79 岁的人

Sep·tu·a·ges·i·ma /ˏsɛptʃuəˋdʒɛsəmə; ˌseptʃuəˈdʒesɪ̵mə/ in the Christian religion, the third Sunday before Lent 七旬斋〔基督教大斋节前的第三个星期日〕

se·pul·chral /səˋpʌlkrəl; sɪ̵ˈpʌlkrəl/ *adj* **1** *literary* sad, serious and slightly frightening【文】忧伤的, 阴沉的, 阴森森的: *a sepulchral voice* 低沉忧郁的嗓音 **2** *technical* related to burying dead people【术语】埋葬死人的, 丧葬的

sep·ul·chre *BrE*【英】, **sepulcher** *AmE*【美】/ˋsɛpl̩kɚ; ˈsepəlkə/ *n* [C] *old use* a small room or building in which the bodies of dead people were put【旧】墓室, 冢

se·quel /ˋsikwəl; ˈsiːkwəl/ *n* **1** [C] a book, film, play etc that continues the story of an earlier one, usually written or made by the same person 〔书、电影、戏剧等的〕续集, 续篇 **2** [C usually singular 一般用单数] an event that happens as a result of something that happened before 随之而来的事; 后果; 后续; 余波

se·quence /ˋsikwəns; ˈsiːkwəns/ *n* [C,U] **1** a series of related events, actions etc which have a fixed order and usually lead to a particular result 〔通常导致某种结果的〕一连串相关事件[行动]: **sequence of events** *the sequence of events leading up to the war* 导致那次战争的一连串事件 **2** [C,U] the order that events or actions happen in, or are supposed to happen in 〔事件或行动发生的〕顺序, 次序: **in/out of sequence** (=in or out of order) 按顺序/不按顺序 *Please check that the page numbers are in sequence.* 请检查这些页码是否按顺序排列。**3** [C] one part of a story, film etc that deals with a single subject or action 〔电影中描述同一主题或动作的〕连续镜头; 一段情节; 〔故事的〕片段: *the dream sequence at the beginning of Ryder's film* 赖德影片开始时的连续梦境镜头

se·quenc·ing /ˋsikwənsɪŋ; ˈsiːkwənsɪŋ/ *n* [U] *formal* the arrangement of things into an order, especially events or actions【正式】〔尤指事件或动作的〕先后安排; 编排顺序

se·quen·tial /sɪˋkwɛnʃəl; sɪˈkwenʃəl/ *adj formal* connected with or happening in a sequence【正式】连续的; 相继的; 顺序的; 序列的 —**sequentially** *adv*

se·ques·ter /sɪˋkwɛstɚ; sɪˈkwestə/ *v* [T] **1** to force a group of people, such as a JURY, to stay away from other people 使〔陪审团等〕与他人隔离; 使隔绝 **2** to sequestrate 扣押〔债务人的财产〕

se·ques·tered /sɪˋkwɛstɚd; sɪˈkwestəd/ *adj literary* a sequestered place is quiet and far away from people【文】〔地方〕僻静的, 与世隔绝的

se·ques·trate /sɪˋkwɛstret; sɪˈkwestreɪt/ *v* [T usually passive 一般用被动态] to take property away from the person it belongs to because they have not paid their debts 扣押〔债务人的财产〕 —**sequestration** /ˏsikwɛsˋtreʃən; ˌsiːkwɪ̵ˈstreɪʃən/ *n* [C,U]

se·quin /ˋsikwɪn; ˈsiːkwɪ̵n/ *n* [C] a small shiny round flat piece of metal that you SEW onto clothing for decoration 〔装饰衣服用的〕闪光金属装饰圆片 —**sequined, sequinned** *adj*

se·quoi·a /sɪˋkwɔɪə; sɪˈkwɔɪə/ *n* [C] a tree from the western US that can grow to be 100 metres in height 红杉〔产于美国西部, 树高可达 100 米〕

Sequoia Na·tion·al Park /ˏ‥ ˏ‥ ‥ˈ/ a US national park in the Sierra Nevada mountains in California, famous for its extremely large Sequoia trees, especially the General Sherman Tree, which is the largest living thing in the world 红杉国家公园〔美国一国家公园。位于加利福尼亚州境内的内华达山脉, 以巨型杉树闻名。园内的谢尔曼将军树是世界上最大的生物活体〕

Se·quoy·ah /sɪˋkwɔɪə; sɪˈkwɔɪə/ (1760?-1843) a Native American of the Cherokee tribe, who invented a way of writing the Cherokee language, so that he could record his people's way of life 塞阔雅〔(1760?-1843), 美国切罗基族印第安人。他发明了切罗基语书写体, 以记录本族人的生活方式〕

se·ra·glio /sɪˋrɑljo; sɪ̵ˈrɑːljəʊ/ *n* [C] a HAREM 〔伊斯兰教徒的〕女眷居住的内室

ser·aph /ˋsɛrəf; ˈserəf/ *plural* **seraphs** also 又作 **seraphim** /-rəfɪm; -rəfɪm/ *n* [C] one of the ANGELS that protects the seat of God, according to the Bible 撒拉弗, 炽天使〔《圣经》中守护上帝宝座的天使〕

se·raph·ic /səˋræfɪk; sɪ̵ˈræfɪk/ *adj literary* extremely beautiful or pure, like an ANGEL【文】天使般的, 美丽纯洁的

Serb·i·a /ˋsɝbɪə; ˈsɜːbiə/ a country of Eastern Europe, which became part of Yugoslavia at the end of World War II. In 1992 when the old Yugoslavia broke up, it remained with Montenegro to form the Federal Republic of Yugoslavia. In 2006, Serbia became a country, called The Republic of Serbia 塞尔维亚〔东欧一国家, 二战结束时成为南斯拉夫的一部分。1992 年, 原南斯拉夫解体, 塞尔维亚与黑山组成了南斯拉夫联盟共和国。2006 年, 塞尔维亚独立, 称塞尔维亚共和国〕

Serbia and Mon·te·ne·gro /ˏ‥‥ ˏ‥ˈ‥/ another name for the Federal Republic of Yugoslavia 塞尔维亚和黑山〔南斯拉夫联盟共和国的别称〕

sere /sɪr; sɪə/ *adj literary* very dry【文】极干的, 干枯的

ser·e·nade[1] /ˏsɛrəˋned; ˌserɪ̵ˈneɪd/ *n* [C] **1** a song that a man performs for the woman he loves, especially standing below her window at night 〔尤指男子晚上站在其意中人窗外唱或奏的〕小夜曲 **2** a piece of gentle music 柔和的乐曲

serenade[2] *v* [T] if you serenade someone, you sing or play music to them to show them that you love them 〔为表爱慕之情而〕对…唱[奏]乐曲

ser·en·dip·i·ty /ˏsɛrənˋdɪpətɪ; ˌserənˈdɪpɪ̵ti/ *n* [U] *literary* the natural ability to make interesting or valuable discoveries by accident【文】善于无意中发现有趣或珍奇事物的天赋

se·rene /səˋrin; sɪ̵ˈriːn/ *adj* **1** someone who is serene is very calm and relaxed 安详的, 宁静的: *Mother sat in the evening sunlight, serene and beautiful.* 母亲坐在夕阳下, 安详而美丽。**2** a place or situation that is serene is very peaceful 〔地方或环境〕宁静的, 安宁的, 平静的: *a serene summer night* 宁静的夏夜 —**serenely** *adv* —**serenity** /səˋrɛnətɪ; sɪ̵ˈrenɪ̵ti/ *n* [U]

serf /sɝf; sɜːf/ *n* [C] someone in former times who lived and worked on land that they did not own and who had to obey the owner of this land 〔旧时的〕农奴 —compare 比较 SLAVE[1] (1)

serf·dom /ˈsɜfdəm; ˈsɜːfdəm/ *n* [U] the state of being a serf 农奴身份; 农奴制

serge /sɜdʒ; sɜːdʒ/ *n* [U] strong, usually WOOLLEN cloth 哔叽〔衣料〕

ser·geant /ˈsɑrdʒənt; ˈsɑːdʒənt/ *n* [C] a low rank in the army, air force, police etc, or someone who has this rank 军士〔一种低级军阶〕; 中士; 〔警察的〕巡佐, 警佐 —see table on page C6 参见 C6 页附录

sergeant-at-arms /ˌ· · · ˈ·/ *n* [C] a SERJEANT-AT-ARMS〔在英国法庭、议会等维持秩序的〕警卫官

sergeant ma·jor /ˌ· · ˈ· ·/ *n* [C] a military rank 军士长 —see table on page C6 参见 C6 页附录

se·ri·al[1] /ˈsɪriəl; ˈsɪəriəl/ *n* [C] a story that is broadcast or printed in several separate parts on television, in a newspaper etc〔报纸上的〕连载小说; 电视连续剧: *a six-part serial* 六集连续剧[连载小说]

serial[2] *adj* [only before noun 仅用于名词前] **1** arranged or happening one after the other in the correct order 顺序排列的, 连续的; 一连串[系列]的: *placed in serial order* 按顺序放置的 | *serial processing on a computer* 电脑上的串行处理 **2 serial killings/murders** killings or murders that are done in the same way one after the other〔手法相同的〕连环杀人/谋杀(案) —**serially** *adv*

se·ri·al·ize also 又作 **-ise** *BrE*【英】/ˈsɪrɪəlˌaɪz; ˈsɪəriəlaɪz/ *v* [T often passive 常用被动态] to print or broadcast a story in several separate parts〔小说等〕连载; 连播: *His book was first serialized in The New Yorker.* 他的书首先是在《纽约人》杂志上连载的。—**serialization** /ˌsɪrɪələˈzeʃən; ˌsɪəriəlaɪˈzeɪʃən/ *n* [U]

serial kill·er /ˈ· · ·, ˌ· ˈ· ·/ *n* [C] someone who has killed several people, one after the other and in the same way 连环杀手

serial num·ber /ˈ· · ·, ˌ· ˈ· ·/ *n* [C] a number put on things that are produced in large quantities so that each one is slightly different〔同类物的〕连续编号, 顺序号码: *serial numbers on dollar bills* 美钞上的顺序号码

2 1 **se·ries** /ˈsɪriz; ˈsɪəriːz/ *n plural* **series** [C] **1** [singular] several events or actions of the same kind that happen one after the other but that are not connected 连续发生的同类事件; 系列: [+of] *There's been a whole series of accidents on this stretch of road recently.* 近来在这一路段发生了一连串事故。**2** a group of events that are connected and have a particular result〔相互联系并有特定结果的〕系列(事件): *a strange series of events that led to his death* 导致他死亡的一连串怪事 **3** a set of television or radio programmes in which each one tells the next part of a story or deals with the same kind of subject〔电视、广播等的〕系列片; 系列节目: *a new comedy series* 新的喜剧系列片 **4** a group of events or actions of the same kind that are planned to happen one after another in order to achieve something〔有计划的〕系列活动: *It'll have to undergo a series of tests.* 这必须经过一系列的试验。| *a series of lectures on the subject of biotechnology* 以生物工艺学为主题的系列讲座 **5 in series** *technical* being connected so that electricity passes through the parts of something electrical in the correct order【术语】〔电器的〕串联

ser·if /ˈsɛrɪf; ˈserɪf/ *n* [C] a short flat line at the top or bottom of some printed letters 衬线〔某些印刷体字母顶部或底部的短线〕—see also 另见 SANS SERIF

1 1 **se·ri·ous** /ˈsɪriəs; ˈsɪəriəs/ *adj*

1 ▶SITUATION/PROBLEM 情况/问题◀ a serious situation, problem, accident etc is extremely bad or dangerous〔情况、问题等〕严重的, 危险的: *a serious illness* 重病 | *How serious do you think the situation is?* 你认为情况有多严重? | **serious crime** *The number of serious crimes has increased dramatically in the last year.* 重大罪案数字在去年急剧上升。

2 be serious a) if someone is serious about something, they say what they really mean and are not joking or pretending 认真的, 并非开玩笑的; 非假装的: [+about] *I stopped laughing when I realized Jen was serious about it.* 当我意识到珍并非开玩笑时, 我就不再笑了。| **I'm serious!** *spoken* (=used to emphasize that something is important)【口】我是当真的!〔用于强调某事很重要〕*I'm serious, Kerry. You'd better listen!* 我是认真的, 克里。你最好听着! | **deadly serious** (=extremely serious) 极为认真的 **b)** *spoken* used to tell someone that what they have just said is silly or impossible【口】你别开玩笑了〔用于告诉对方他所说的是蠢话或办不到的〕: *"We could make it from here to Florida if we drove all night." "Be serious! It's a three day drive."* "我们要是通宵开车, 可以从这里到达佛罗里达州。""别瞎扯了! 那是要开三天车才行的。" | **you can't be serious!** *"I thought I'd try to fix the car myself." "You can't be serious!"* "我想过要设法自己修理这辆汽车。""你真会开玩笑!"

3 ▶CAREFUL 仔细的◀ careful and thorough 细心缜密的, 细致的: *I think this matter needs serious consideration.* 我想这件事需要深思熟虑。| *a serious article* 发人深省的文章

4 ▶ROMANTIC RELATIONSHIP 浪漫关系◀ a serious romantic relationship is intended to continue for a long time 严肃认真的, 真诚的: *Oo, sounds like it's serious!* 啊, 听起来像是认真的! | [+about] *Are you really serious about her then?* 那你对她是真心实意的吗? | **serious boyfriend/girlfriend** *Don't even think about Peter. He has a serious girlfriend.* 不用考虑彼得了, 他已经有了一个真心相爱的女朋友。

5 ▶PERSON 人◀ someone who is serious is always very sensible and quiet 明智的; 严肃的; 庄重的: *He's a nice guy, but very serious.* 他是个好人, 但很严肃。

6 ▶IMPORTANT 重要的◀ important 重要的, 重大的: *They agreed to have lunch before starting on the serious business.* 他们同意先吃午饭, 然后开始办正事。

7 serious money/exercise etc *informal* a large amount of money etc【非正式】大量的钱/运动等: *I'll have to do some serious exercise before I can fit into that dress.* 我得做相当多的运动才能穿上那套连衣裙。

8 ▶VERY GOOD 非常好的◀ [only before noun 仅用于名词前] *informal* very good and often expensive【非正式】很好的, 质优价高的: *He's got some serious stereo equipment!* 他有些高档的立体声音响设备!

9 ▶SPORT/ACTIVITY 体育运动/活动◀ [only before noun 仅用于名词前] someone very interested in something, and spending a lot of time doing it 极感兴趣的, 热衷的: *a serious golfer* 热衷于打高尔夫球者 | *Any serious student of psychology should read this article.* 凡是对心理学真正感兴趣的学生都应该读读这篇文章。

10 ▶WORRIED/UNHAPPY 忧虑的/不愉快的◀ seeming slightly worried or unhappy 担心的, 不愉快的: *You look serious. What's wrong?* 你显得心事重重, 出了什么事? —**seriousness** *n* [U]

Serious Fraud Of·fice, the /ˌ· · · ˈ· ·, ˌ· ˈ·/ abbreviation 缩写为 **SFO** a British government department whose job is to examine complicated cases of FRAUD (=dishonest business practices) to find out whether businesses have cheated or made money in illegal ways. The SFO has the right to ask the police to charge people if it thinks they are guilty of fraud 重大诈骗案调查处〔英国一政府机构。其职责是调查复杂诈骗案件, 查明商业机构是否有欺诈或非法牟利的行为。一旦该调查处认为某人犯有欺诈罪, 就有权要求警方对其提起诉讼〕

se·ri·ous·ly /ˈsɪriəslɪ; ˈsɪəriəsli/ *adv* **1** in a serious way 认真地; 严肃地; 严重地: *I think it's about time we talked seriously about our relationship.* 我想现在该是认真严肃地谈谈我们之间关系的时候了。| *Is she seriously ill?* 她病得很重吗? | *I'm seriously concerned about Ben.* 我对本真的很担心。**2 take sb/sth seriously** to believe that someone or something is worth paying attention to or should be respected 认真对待某人/某事: *No-one's likely to take Laurie seriously.* 恐怕没有人会把劳丽当回事的。| *Don't joke with Linda, she takes everything far too seriously.* 不要和琳达开玩笑, 她对待每件事都过于认真。| **never take anything seriously** *It's infuriating that he never takes anything seriously.* 他对任何事从来都不认真, 很让人恼火。**3 seriously?** *spoken* used to ask someone if they really mean what they have just said【口】真的?〔用于弄清对方的话是否当真〕: *Quit your job? Seriously?* 你要辞职, 真的吗? **4 seriously** *spoken* [sentence adverb 句子副词] used to show that what you say next is not a joke【口】说正经的〔用于表示将要说的话并非开玩笑〕: *Seriously though, I really think Toby likes you!* 说正经的, 我真的认为托比喜欢你。 2 2

ser·jeant-at-arms, sergeant-at-arms /ˌsɑrdʒənt ət ˈɑrmz; ˌsɑːdʒənt ət ˈɑːmz/ *n* [C] an officer of a British law court or parliament whose job is to keep meetings quiet enough to be useful〔英国法庭、议会等维持秩序的〕警卫官

ser·mon /ˈsɜmən; ˈsɜːmən/ *n* [C] **1** a religious talk given as part of a Christian church service, usually based on a part of the Bible〔基督教的〕布道, 讲道: **preach a sermon** *Pastor Grisson preached a sermon on evangelism.* 格里森牧师以传福音为题进行讲道。**2** *informal* a talk in which someone tries to give you unwanted moral advice; LECTURE[1] (2)【非正式】说教, 训诫

ser·mon·ize also 又作 **-ise** *BrE*【英】/ˈsɜmənˌaɪz; ˈsɜːmənaɪz/ *v* [I] to give a lot of unwanted moral advice in a serious way〔喋喋不休地〕训诫, 〔不中听地〕说教

Sermon on the Mount, the /ˌ· · · · ˈ·/ a SERMON given by Jesus in which he explains his religious ideas. It is one of the best-known parts of the New Testament of the Bible, and it includes a set of statements called the **beatitudes**, in which Jesus names the types of people who are 'blessed' (=specially loved by God). 登山宝训〔耶稣的一次布道。他在布道中阐释了自己的宗教思想。此次布道是《圣经·新约》中最著名的片段之一, 内容包括"八福词", 其中列举了八类"有福"之人〕

ser·pent /ˈsɝpənt; ˈsɜːpənt/ *n* [C] **1** *literary* a snake, especially a large one【文】蛇〔尤指大蛇〕**2 the Serpent** the evil snake in the Garden of Eden according to the Bible〔《圣经》所载〕伊甸园中邪恶的蛇

ser·pen·tine /ˈsɝpənˌtin; ˈsɜːpəntaɪn/ *adj* twisting or winding like a snake 曲折的，蜿蜒的: *the serpentine course of the river* 弯弯曲曲的河道

Serpentine, the a lake in Hyde Park in London 瑟彭泰恩湖，蛇形湖〔伦敦海德公园一湖泊〕

SERPS /sɝps; sɜːps/ State Earnings-Related Pension Scheme; a British government system which pays a regular income to people who have stopped working because they are old, based on the amount that they earned while they were working 国家工薪收入关联型养老金计划〔英国政府的一项制度。政府根据退休人员在职时的收入水准定期给其发放养老金〕

ser·rat·ed /ˈsɛretɪd; sɪ̵ˈreɪtɪ̵d/ *adj* **serrated knife/edge** with a sharp edge made of a row of connected V shapes like teeth 锯齿状刀子/边缘 —**serration** /-ˈreʃən; -ˈreɪʃən/ *n* [C,U]

ser·ried /ˈsɛrɪd; ˈserid/ *adj* [no comparative 无比较级] *literary* pressed closely together; CROWDED【文】排紧的，靠拢的，密集的

se·rum /ˈsɪrəm; ˈsɪərəm/ *n* [C,U] **1** a liquid containing substances that fight infection, that is put into a sick person's blood〔用于治疗的〕免疫血清 —compare 比较 VACCINE **2** *technical* the watery part of blood or the liquid from a plant【术语】血清；〔植物的〕浆液，树液 —**serous** *adj*

ser·vant /ˈsɝvənt; ˈsɜːvənt/ *n* [C] **1** someone who is paid to clean someone's house, cook for them, answer the door etc 仆人，佣人 **2 servant of sth/sb** someone who is controlled by someone or something 受某人/某物支配的人: *Are we the masters or the servants of computers?* 我们是电脑的主人还是奴仆? —see also 另见 CIVIL SERVANT

serve[1] /sɝv; sɜːv/

1 ►FOOD/DRINK 食物/饮料◄ [I,T] to give someone food or drink as part of a meal 送上〔食物或饮料〕，端上〔饭菜等〕；侍候〔某人进餐〕: *What kind of wine should we serve?* 请问要上什么酒? | **serve sth with sth** *Serve the dish with rice and a green salad.* 用米饭和蔬菜沙拉配这道菜。| **serve sb** *Why aren't you out there serving the guests?* 你为什么不出去侍候客人? | **serve sth hot/cold etc** *delicious served hot or cold* 冷热均可，味美可口 | **serve breakfast/lunch/dinner** *Breakfast is served between 7 and 9 a.m.* 早上7点至9点供应早餐。| **serving spoon/dish** (=one used to serve food) 分菜肴用的大匙/上菜用的盘子 —see picture on page A15 参见A15页图

2 serve two/three/four etc if food serves two, three etc people, there is enough for that number of people〔食品〕足够供二人/三人/四人等吃: *One large fish should serve two to three people.* 一条大鱼应够两个至三个人吃。

3 ►BE USEFUL/HELPFUL 有用/有帮助◄ [I,T] to be useful or helpful for a particular purpose or reason 适合作…用: **serve as sth** *The old couch had to serve as a guest bed.* 这张旧的长沙发只好用作客人的床了。| **serve sb well** *Her talent for selling will serve her well in the future.* 她的推销本领将来对她会很有用。| **serve sb's needs** *We don't get enough aid to serve our needs.* 我们得不到足够的援助来满足我们的需要。| **serve a purpose** *If you haven't got a crate, a large cardboard box will serve the purpose.* 要是你没有板条箱，一只大的硬纸箱也行。| *Sure, you could phone her, but what purpose would that serve?* 当然，你可以给她打电话，但这又管什么用?

4 ►DO A HELPFUL JOB 做有益的工作◄ [I,T] to spend a period of time doing a job, especially one that helps the organization 为 工作；供职；服役: *The school board members serve a two-year term.* 学校董事会的董事任期两年。| **[+in]** *He returned to Greece to serve in the army.* 他回到希腊服役。| **[+on]** *Annette serves on various local committees.* 安妮特担任当地多个委员会的委员。| **[+as]** *Martin served as ambassador to Burma in the '60s.* 马丁在60年代担任驻缅甸大使。| **serve sb/sth** *And let's not forget the women who served their country in the war.* 让我们不要忘记那些在战争中为国尽职的妇女。

5 ►HAVE AN EFFECT 产生效果◄ [I,T] to have a particular effect or result 起作用，产生效果: **serve to do sth** *Let that serve to demonstrate what happens if you don't pay attention.* 让这件事向你证明，如果你粗心大意会出什么样的问题。| **serve (sb) as sth** *The pictures only served as a reminder of happier times.* 这些照片只能令人忆及过去的美好时光。

6 ►SHOP/RESTAURANT 商店/餐馆◄ [I,T] to help the customers in a shop, restaurant etc, especially by bringing them the things that they want 接待（顾客）〔尤指为他们取来所需之物〕，为（顾客）服务: *The waitress doesn't seem to want to serve us.* 那个女服务员似乎不想接待我们。| *Are you being served?* 有人接待您了吗?

7 ►PROVIDE STH 供应某物◄ [T] to provide a group of people with something that is necessary or useful 向〔某群体〕供应必须[有用]的东西，供给: *water mains to serve the new homes in the area* 给这个地区新建住宅供水的总水管

8 ►PRISON 监狱◄ [T] to spend a particular period of time in prison 服刑，坐牢: **serve a sentence** *Fox had served an eighteen-month sentence for burglary.* 福克斯因入室盗窃罪坐了18个月的牢。| **serve time** (=spend time in prison) 服刑，坐牢

9 it serves sb right *spoken* used to say that you think someone deserves it if something unpleasant happens to them, because they have been stupid or unkind【口】〔某人〕活该！这是某人应得的惩罚: *"Ouch! She pinched me!" "Serves you right, teasing her like that."* "哎唷！她掐我！""活该！谁叫你那样取笑她。"

10 ►SPORT 体育运动◄ [I,T] to start playing in a game such as tennis or VOLLEYBALL by throwing the ball up in the air and hitting it to your opponent〔网球、排球等〕发球，开球 —see picture on page A23 参见A23页图

11 serve an apprenticeship to learn a job or skill by working for a fixed period of time for someone who has a lot of experience 当学徒

12 serve a summons/writ etc to officially send or give someone a written order to appear in a court of law 发传票〔传某人出庭〕

13 ►CHURCH 教堂◄ [I] to help a priest during the EUCHARIST〔做弥撒时〕充当助祭 —see also 另见 **If my memory serves me (well/correctly)** (MEMORY (4))

serve sth ↔ **out** *phr v* [T] **1** to continue doing something until the end of a fixed period of time 继续做到期满: *Dillon's served out nearly all his sentence.* 狄龙服刑快要期满了。**2** *BrE* to put food onto plates【英】把食物盛到各人盘子里: *Serve out the rice, will you?* 你来给大家盛饭，好吗?

serve sth ↔ **up** *phr v* [T] to put food onto plates so that people can eat it 把〔食物〕分到大家的盘子里

serve[2] *n* [C] the action in a game such as tennis or VOLLEYBALL in which you throw the ball in the air and hit it to your opponent〔网球、排球等的〕发球

serv·er /ˈsɝvɚ; ˈsɜːvə/ *n* [C] **1** a special spoon or tool for putting a particular kind of food onto a plate 分菜肴用具〈如匙、叉、勺等〉: *salad servers* 盛取沙拉用的叉匙 **2** a player who hits a ball to begin a game in tennis, VOLLEYBALL etc〔网球、排球等的〕发球者 **3 a)** the main computer on a NETWORK[1] (4), that controls all the others〔电脑网络的〕主机 **b)** one of the computers on a network that provides a special service〔电脑网络中的〕服务器: **file/print/mail server** *All important data is stored on a central file server.* 所有的重要数据资料都储存在中央档案服务器内。**4** someone who helps a priest during the EUCHARIST〔做弥撒时的〕助祭（者）

ser·ve·ry /ˈsɝvərɪ; ˈsɜːvəri/ *n* [C] *BrE* the part of a restaurant where people get food to take back to their tables【英】〔餐厅里摆放做好的食物供客人自己选取的〕供餐处，取餐处

ser·vice[1] /ˈsɝvɪs; ˈsɜːvɪ̵s/ *n*

① FOR THE PUBLIC 为公众
② HELP 帮助

③ WORK DONE FOR SB 为某人做的工作
④ ARMY/NAVY ETC 陆军/海军等
⑤ OTHER MEANINGS 其他意思

① FOR THE PUBLIC 为公众

1 public services [C often plural 常用复数] things such as education, hospitals, banks etc that are provided for the public to use〔教育、医院、银行等的〕公共服务: *the decline in public services in recent times* 近期公共服务的减少 | **the welfare/medical/social etc service** (=services provided especially by

the government)〔尤指政府提供的〕福利/医疗/社会等服务 | **police/fire/ambulance etc service** *He joined the police service at the age of 18.* 他18岁就进入警察部门。

2 jury/military/community etc service something that ordinary people can be asked to do for the public as a public duty or as a punishment 陪审团工作/兵役/社区服务等: *You're lucky you were only sentenced to community service.* 你算走运的了，只判你社区服务。

② HELP 帮助

3 [singular,U] help that you give to someone〔对别人的〕帮助，效劳: **be of service** (=help someone) 有用，能帮忙 *Don't thank me – I'm glad to be of service.* 不用谢，我很高兴能帮点忙。| **do sb a service** (=do something to help someone) 帮某人的忙 *Oh, thanks, it'll be doing me a service.* 噢，谢谢，这就帮了我的忙了。| **provide a service** (=provide help for someone) 提供帮助，给予帮忙 | **for services rendered** *formal* (=for help that you have given)【正式】为了所给予的帮助

4 ▶SHOP/HOTEL ETC 商店/旅馆等◀ [U] the help that people who work in a shop, restaurant, bar etc give you 服务，接待，侍候: *What was the service in that new restaurant like?* 那家新饭馆的服务如何？| **customer service** *For refunds, please go to the customer service counter.* 退货请到顾客服务柜台。

5 ▶ORGANIZATION 机构◀ [C] an organization that provides advice and help, for example with legal or personal problems〔提供咨询、帮助等的〕服务机构: *a careers information service* 职业信息服务机构

6 be at your service *formal or humorous* if someone or something is at your service, they are available to help you in some way if you need them【正式或幽默】愿为您效劳，听候您的吩咐: *My secretary and library are at your service.* 我的秘书和藏书都随时为您效劳。

7 press sb/sth into service to persuade someone to help you, or use something to help you do something 说服某人帮忙/使用某物协助做某事: *We pressed Georgie's old bike into service.* 我们临时拿乔吉的旧自行车来用。

③ WORK DONE FOR SB 为某人做的工作

8 ▶EMPLOYMENT 雇用◀ [plural,U] the work you do for a person or organization 为某人[某机构]做的工作: **20/30 years etc of service** *Brian's retiring after 25 years of loyal service to the company.* 布赖恩为公司忠心耿耿地效力25年后就要退休了。| **services to sb** (=work, especially successful work, you have done for someone) 为某人做的工作〔尤指成功的工作〕 *an award for services to the printing industry* 因对印刷业所作贡献而获得的奖赏 | **public service** (=work done for the public or the government) 公益服务

9 ▶SERVANT 佣人◀ [U] the job of working as a servant in someone's house, especially in former times〔尤指旧时的〕帮佣的工作: **be in service** (=be working as a servant in someone's house) 当佣人 | **domestic service** (=the job of working for someone in their house) 家庭帮佣的工作

10 ▶BUSINESS 商业◀ [C] a business that provides help or does jobs for people rather than producing things 服务性行业，非生产性行业: *the export of both manufactured goods and services* 成品和劳务的输出 | **a baby-sitting/press-cutting/ironing etc service** *She's set up a dog-walking service in her local area.* 她在本地区开了一家遛狗服务中心。—see also 另见 SERVICE INDUSTRY

11 ▶GOVERNMENT 政府◀ [C usually singular 一般用单数] an organization that works directly for a government 政府机构，政府部门: *the diplomatic service* 外交部门 | *the foreign service* 外交机构

④ ARMY/NAVY ETC 陆军/海军等

12 the services a country's military forces, especially considered as a job 各军种〔尤用于把参军作为职业时〕: *I'm not sure what I'll do, maybe join the services.* 我还说不定要干什么，也许去参军。

13 (be on) active service to be actually fighting in a battle or war while you are in the army, navy etc 正在参战

⑤ OTHER MEANINGS 其他意思

14 ▶RELIGION 宗教◀ [C] a formal religious ceremony, for example in church 正式的宗教仪式，礼拜: **hold/conduct a service** (=be the person in charge of a service) 主持宗教仪式 *The Reverend James Wilkins will conduct the service.* 詹姆斯·威尔金斯牧师将主持礼拜仪式。| **marriage/funeral/christening etc service** *memorial service for the disaster victims* 为罹难者举行的追悼仪式

15 ▶SPORT 体育运动◀ [C] an act of hitting a ball through the air in order to start a game, for example in tennis〔网球等的〕发球: *It's your service.* 该你发球了。

16 services *BrE* a place near a MOTORWAY where you can stop and have a meal or drink, or buy food, petrol etc【英】服务区，路边服务站〔高速公路上的服务设施，有餐饮、加油站等〕: *How far is it to the next services?* 这里距下一个服务站有多远？—see also 另见 SERVICE STATION

17 ▶CAR/MACHINE 汽车/机器◀ [C] an examination and repair of a machine or car to keep it working properly 检修，保养: *I'm getting the bus home – my car's in for a service.* 我要坐公共汽车回家——我的汽车送去检修了。

18 ▶PLATES ETC 盘子等◀ dinner/tea service a set of matching plates, bowls, cups etc〔整套〕餐具/茶具等

19 ▶BUS/TRAIN 公共汽车/火车◀ [C usually singular 一般用单数] a regular journey made by a bus, train, boat etc to a particular place or at a particular time〔车、船等的〕交通服务，班次: *the 8:15 service to Cambridge* 8点15分开往剑桥的班次 —see also 另见 LIP SERVICE

service² *v* [T] **1** to examine a machine or vehicle and fix it if necessary 检修，维修〔机器或车辆〕: *I'm having the car serviced next week.* 我的汽车下星期检修。**2** to provide people with something they need or want 为…提供服务: *city departments that service the local communities* 向地方社区提供服务的市政部门 **3** *technical* to pay the INTEREST[1] (4) on a debt【术语】支付〔借款〕利息

service³ *adj* **service stairs/elevator etc** stairs etc that are only for the use of people working in a place, rather than the public〔员工的〕专用楼梯/电梯等

ser·vice·a·ble /ˈsɝvɪsəbl̩; ˈsɜːvɪ̣səbəl/ *adj* ready or suitable to be used for a particular purpose 可供使用的，宜用的: *serviceable shoes* 适穿的鞋子 —**serviceability** /ˌsɝvɪsəˈbɪlətɪ; ˌsɜːvɪ̣səˈbɪlɪ̣ti/ *n* [U]

service a·re·a /ˈ‥ ˌ‥/ *n* [C] *BrE* a place where you can stop on a MOTORWAY that has petrol, food, toilets etc【英】〔高速公路旁的〕服务区〔有餐馆、加油站、厕所等〕

service charge /ˈ‥ ˌ/ *n* [C] **1** *BrE* an amount of money that is added to a bill in a restaurant and given to the waiters【英】〔加在餐馆账单上的〕服务费，小费 **2** an amount of money paid to the owner of a block of FLATs for services such as cleaning the stairs〔付给公寓房东的〕清洁卫生等服务费

service club /ˈ‥ ˌ/ *n* [C] *AmE* a usually national organization made of smaller local groups in which members do things to help their COMMUNITY【美】〔由全国各地方团体组成的〕服务社〔成员为社区做好事或谋福利〕

service in·dus·try /ˈ‥ ˌ‥/ *n* [C,U] an industry that provides a service such as insurance, bank accounts, or advertising rather than a product 服务性行业，服务业〈如保险、银行、广告等〉

ser·vice·man /ˈsɝvɪsˌmæn; ˈsɜːvɪ̣smən/ *n plural* **servicemen** /-ˌmɛn; -mən/ [C] a man who is a member of the military 军人

service sta·tion /ˈ‥ ˌ/ *n* [C] a place that sells petrol, food, etc〔有餐饮等出售的〕汽车加油站

ser·vice·wom·an /ˈsɝvɪsˌwʊmən; ˈsɜːvɪ̣sˌwʊmən/ *n plural* **servicewomen** /-ˌwɪmɪn; -ˌwɪmɪn/ [C] a woman who is a member of the military 女军人

ser·vi·ette /ˌsɝvɪˈɛt; ˌsɜːviˈet/ *n* [C] *BrE & CanE* a NAPKIN【英和加】餐巾 —see picture on page A15 参见A15页图

ser·vile /ˈsɝvl̩; ˈsɜːvaɪl/ *adj* **1** too eager to obey someone without questioning them 过分屈从的，卑躬屈膝的: *a servile attitude* 卑躬屈膝的态度 **2** connected with SLAVES or with being a slave 奴隶的；有关奴隶的 —**servilely** *adv* —**servility** /sɝˈvɪlətɪ; sɜːˈvɪlɪ̣ti/ *n* [U]

serv·ing /ˈsɝvɪŋ; ˈsɜːvɪŋ/ *n* [C] an amount of food that is enough for one person; HELPING〔供一人食用的〕一份食物: *How many servings does the recipe make?* 这个食谱的量够多少人吃？

ser·vi·tor /ˈsɝvətɚ; ˈsɜːvɪ̣tə/ *n* [C] *old use* a male servant【旧】男仆，男侍从

ser·vi·tude /ˈsɝvəˌtud; ˈsɜːvɪ̣tjuːd/ *n* [U] the condition of being a SLAVE or being forced to obey someone else 奴役；苦役，劳役: *The legislation of 1781 abolished penal servitude in Bohemia.* 1781年的立法废除了波希米亚的劳役监禁。—see also 另见 **penal servitude** (PENAL (1))

ses·a·me /ˈsɛsəmɪ; ˈsesəmi/ *n* [U] a tropical plant grown for its seeds and oil and used in cooking 芝麻 —see also 另见 OPEN SESAME

Sesame Street /ˈ··· ,·/ one of the most popular and admired television programmes for young children, made in the US and also shown in the UK and other countries. It teaches children about numbers, letters etc in an amusing way, and it also deals with social questions such as RACISM and attitudes to people who are disabled. The characters who appear in the programme include Big Bird, Kermit the Frog, Oscar the Grouch, and the Cookie Monster.《芝麻街》〔美国摄制的最受欢迎、最受推崇的儿童电视节目之一，也在英国和其他国家播出。该节目寓教于乐，让儿童学习数字、字母等内容，还触及种族歧视、对待残疾人的态度等诸多社会问题。剧中角色有大鸟、青蛙克米特、牢骚大王奥斯卡和曲奇怪物〕

ses·sion /ˈsɛʃən; ˈseʃən/ *n* [C] **1** a meeting or period of time used for a particular purpose, especially by a group of people 会期；〔某团体从事某项活动的〕集会〔时间〕: *a drinking session* 饮酒聚会 | *question-and-answer sessions* 问答时间 | *a jazz session* 爵士乐演奏会 **2** a formal meeting or group of meetings of an organisation, especially a court or parliament 正式会议；〔法院的〕〔一次〕开庭；〔议会的〕一次会议: **in session** *the noise of Parliament in session* 英国议会开会时的喧闹声 **3 sessions a)** petty sessions 简易法庭 **b)** QUARTER SESSIONS 季审法庭

set¹ /sɛt; set/ *v past tense and past participle* **set**

① PUT DOWN 放下
② START STH HAPPENING 引发某事
③ DECIDE/ESTABLISH 决定/确立
④ JOB/STH TO DO 工作/要做的事
⑤ MAKE READY 作好准备
⑥ MUSIC/BOOKS 音乐/书籍
⑦ WANT/NOT WANT 想要/不想要
⑧ OTHER MEANINGS 其他意思

① PUT DOWN 放下

1 ►PUT 放◄ [T always+adv/prep] to carefully put something down somewhere, especially something that is difficult to carry 放置，放下〔尤指不便携带的物件〕: **set sth down/on etc** *She set the tray down on a table next to his bed.* 她把盘子放在他床边的桌子上。

② START STH HAPPENING 引发某事

2 set sth on fire/alight/ablaze to make something start burning 点燃某物；放火烧某物；把某物付之一炬: *Crowds of youths started overturning cars and setting them on fire.* 一群群年轻人开始把汽车推翻并放火将其点燃。

3 set the pattern/tone/trend to happen or do something in a particular way that is then repeated many times or which continues for a long time 定模式/定调子/领潮流: *Gabriel's style set the trend for the scores of rock videos that followed.* 加布里埃尔的风格为后来的许多摇滚乐录像开了先河。

4 set in motion/progress/train to make something start happening, especially by means of an official order 使开始运作[产生影响]〔尤指用正式命令〕: *The government is to set in motion a wide-ranging review of defence spending.* 政府要着手进行一次对国防开支的大范围检查。

③ DECIDE/ESTABLISH 决定/确立

5 set a time/date/price etc to decide that something should happen at a particular time, cost a particular amount of money etc 确定时间/日期/价格等: *Have you set a date for the wedding?* 你们确定了婚礼的日期没有?

6 set guidelines/standards/conditions/limits etc to officially establish rules, standards etc for doing something 制定方针/标准/条件/界限等: *standards of hygiene set by the Health Department* 卫生部制定的卫生标准

7 set a precedent if an event or action sets a precedent, it shows people a way of doing something which they can use or copy 开创先例: *If her claim against her employers is successful, it could set a legal precedent.* 她向雇主提出的索赔如果得到满足，这将开创一个法律上的先例。

④ JOB/STH TO DO 工作/要做的事

8 set sb a task/challenge/goal etc to decide that someone should try and achieve something, especially something that needs a lot of effort 向某人提出任务/挑战/目标等: *Wilkins then set himself the task of tagging all the birds on the island.* 威尔金斯于是给自己定下任务，要给岛上所有的鸟带上标签。| **set yourself to do sth** *She had set herself to write a novel.* 她已下了决心去写一部长篇小说。

9 ►GIVE SB A PIECE OF WORK 给某人规定任务◄ [T] *BrE* to give someone a piece of work to do, especially a student in your class or someone who works for you【英】〔给学生〕布置作业；〔给下属〕指派任务: **set sb sth** *Mr. Phipps set us an essay on the origins of the French Revolution.* 菲普斯老师给我们布置了作业，要写一篇关于法国大革命起因的论文。

10 ►EXAMINATION 考试◄ [T] *BrE* to invent questions for students to answer, especially in an examination【英】出〔题目〕〔尤指出考题〕: *Whoever set the questions obviously didn't know much about physics.* 出考题的人显然对物理学懂得不多。

11 set to work to start doing something in a determined way, especially something that is difficult and needs a lot of effort 坚决地着手做某事〔尤指困难的需要努力去做的工作〕: **set to work to do sth** *They set to work to paint the outside of the building.* 他们着手给大楼的外墙刷油漆。| **[+on]** *Davies is about to set work on a second book.* 戴维斯即将开始写第二本书了。

12 set sb to work to make someone start doing a particular kind of work for you 使某人着手干活: **set sb to work doing sth** *Before dawn Harry had set them to work collecting firewood for breakfast.* 天亮之前哈里已布置他们去拾柴做早餐。

13 set sb/sth doing sth to make someone start doing something or make something start happening 使某人开始做某事/某事开始发生: *Her last remark had set me thinking.* 她最后的话引起了我的思考。| *The wind set the trees rustling.* 风吹得树木沙沙作响。

⑤ MAKE READY 作好准备

14 ►MOVE PART OF A MACHINE/CLOCK ETC 调整仪器/拨准钟表◄ [T] to move part of a machine, clock etc so that it is in a particular position and is ready to be used 调整〔仪器〕至所需位置；拨正〔钟表〕；拨〔闹钟〕至指定时间: *Have you set the alarm?* 你拨好闹钟了吗? | **set sth to/at** *Just set the dial to 'hot wash' and press the 'on' button.* 把刻度盘调到"热洗"位置，再按"开始"按钮。

15 set the table to arrange plates, knives, cups etc on a table so that it is ready for a meal 摆好餐桌[准备开饭]

16 set a trap a) to make a trap ready to catch an animal 设陷阱〔以捕捉动物〕 **b)** to invent a plan to show that someone is doing something wrong 布下圈套〔以诱人自我暴露〕: *The FBI set a trap for the Congressmen it believed were taking bribes.* 联邦调查局对认为受贿的国会议员布下了圈套。

⑥ MUSIC/BOOKS 音乐/书籍

17 ►FILM/PLAY/STORY 电影/戏剧/故事◄ [T usually passive 一般用被动态] if a film, play, story etc is set in a place or period, it happens there or at that time 为〔电影、戏剧、小说等〕设定发生的地点和时间；设置〔电影、戏剧、小说等的〕背景: *The novel is set in France in the early 19th century.* 这部小说以19世纪初的法国为背景。

18 ►PRINTING 印刷◄ to make the words and letters of a book, newspaper etc ready to be printed 为〔书、报等〕排字，排版: *In those days books had to be set by hand.* 在那时，书籍得用手工排版。

19 set sth to music to write music for a story or a poem, so that it can be sung 为〔故事或诗歌等〕谱曲

⑦ WANT/NOT WANT 想要/不想要

20 set your mind/sights/heart on sth to be determined to achieve something or decide that you definitely want to have it 一心想达成某目标[得到某物]: *Once Sharon sets her mind on something, she usually gets what she wants.* 莎伦一旦决心想得到某样东西，她通常都会如愿以偿。

21 set yourself against to be determined that you do not want something to happen or you do not want to take part in some-

thing 坚决反对; 坚决不参加: *Angie seems to have set herself against the idea completely.* 安吉似乎完全反对这个主意。

⑧ **OTHER MEANINGS** 其他意思

22 set a record to run a race in a faster time than anyone else, jump further than anyone else, win a competition more times than anyone else etc〔在体育竞赛中〕创造纪录: *The Kenyan runner set a new Olympic Record in the 3000 metres.* 肯尼亚选手创下了3000米赛跑的奥林匹克新纪录。

23 ▶SUN 太阳◀ [I] if the sun sets, it moves close to the horizon and then goes below it〔日〕落,〔太阳〕下山

24 set an example to behave in a way that shows other people how to behave 树立榜样: *Teachers should set an example for their students.* 教师应给学生树立榜样。

25 set sb straight/right to tell someone the right way to do something or the true facts about something 纠正某人的做法[想法]: **[+on]** *I set him right on one or two points of procedure.* 我帮助他纠正了一两处程序上的问题。—see also 另见 **set the record straight** (STRAIGHT² (7))

26 set sth right to deal with any problems, mistakes etc 解决问题, 改正错误: *I wish you'd been here – you could easily have set things right.* 我真希望你当时在这里, 那样很容易就可以把问题解决了。

27 set sb free/loose to allow someone to be free, or to allow a dangerous person to escape 释放某人; 把〔危险人物〕放走: *Brian Keenan and the other hostages were finally set free.* 布赖恩·基南和其他人质终于获释。

28 set great store by/set a high value on to consider something to be very important 认为〔某物〕非常重要: *At my old school they set great store by athletic achievements.* 我以前那所学校极其重视体育成绩。

29 ▶LIQUID/GLUE/CEMENT ETC 液体/胶水/水泥等◀ [I] to become hard and solid 凝结, 凝固: *How long does it take for the glue to set?* 这种胶需要多长时间才能凝固?

30 ▶BONE 骨头◀ a) [T] if you set a broken bone, you move the broken ends so that they are in the right place to grow together again 将〔断骨〕复位〔以便愈合〕 **b)** [I] if a broken bone sets, it joins together again〔断骨〕愈合

31 ▶HAIR 头发◀ [T] to arrange someone's hair while it is wet so that it has a particular style when it dries〔趁头发潮湿时〕把〔某人的头发〕梳理成某种发型, 做〔头发〕

32 be set into to be fixed into the surface of something 被嵌入: *a large brick fireplace which was set into the wall* 嵌在墙里建的宽大砖砌壁炉

33 be set with gems etc to be decorated with jewels 镶嵌着宝石的: *a gold bracelet set with rubies* 镶有红宝石的金手镯

set about *phr v* [T] **1** to start doing something, especially something that needs a lot of time and effort 开始[着手]做某事〔尤指费时费劲的事〕: **set about doing sth** *She set about clearing up after the party.* 聚会之后, 她开始收拾东西打扫卫生。**2** to deal with something in a particular way 处理: *I think you're setting about the problem in the wrong way.* 我认为你处理这个问题的方法错了。**3** *especially literary* to attack someone by hitting and kicking them【尤文】攻击; 对…拳打脚踢: *They set about him with their fists.* 他们挥拳打他。

set against *phr v* [T] **1** [**set** sb **against** sb] to make someone start to fight or quarrel with another person, especially a person who they had friendly relations with before 使与〔某人〕对立, 敌对; 使与〔朋友等〕打[吵]架: *The bitter civil war has set brother against brother.* 激烈的内战使兄弟反目成仇。**2** [**set** sth **off against** sth] to consider something in relation to another thing, especially when that other thing is very important 将…与…联系起来考虑: *The recent improvement in output has to be set against increased labour costs.* 最近的产量提高必须与人工成本的增加联系起来考虑。**3 set sth (off) against tax** to make an official record of the money you have spent on something connected with your job, in order to reduce the amount of tax you have to pay 将与工作相关的开支列入以减少应纳税款

set apart *phr v* [T] **1** [**set** sb/sth **apart**] to make someone or something different and often better than other people or things 使〔某人或某物〕与众不同, 使优于〔他人或他物〕: *It is man's ability to think which sets him apart from other animals.* 具有思维能力使人类有别于其他动物。**2** [**set** sth **apart**] to keep something for a special purpose and only use it for that purpose 留出…〔作某种用途〕, 拨出: *Regular times should be set apart for seeing patients.* 应该留出查看病人的固定时间。

set sth **↔ aside** *phr v* [T] **1** to keep something, especially money or time, for a special purpose and only use it for that purpose〔为某种目的〕留出, 拨出〔金钱或时间等〕: **[+for]** *Try to set aside at least an hour each day for learning new vocabulary.* 争取每天至少抽出一个小时学习新词汇。| *a room that had been set aside for visitors* 留给客人用的房间 **2** to decide that you will not be influenced by a particular feeling, belief, or principle, because something else is more important 不受〔某种感情、信仰、原则等的〕影响, 不顾; 把…置之不理: *Congress ought to set aside its political differences to pass a health care bill.* 国会应当抛开政治分歧, 通过一项关于卫生保健的议案。**3** to declare that a previous legal decision or agreement no longer has any effect 宣布〔以前的法律决定或协议〕无效, 撤销, 驳回: *The judge set aside the verdict of the lower court.* 法官宣布下级法院的判决无效。

set back *phr v* [T] **1** [**set** sb/sth **↔ back**] to delay the progress or development of something, or delay someone from finishing something 延缓〔某事的进展〕; 阻碍〔某人完成某事〕; 拖…后腿: *The Cultural Revolution set back the modernization of China by many years.* "文化大革命"使中国的现代化延缓了许多年。**2** [**set** sb **back**] *informal* to cost someone a lot of money【非正式】使〔某人〕花费大笔钱: *The new laptop from Toshiba will set you back a cool $2,000.* 这台东芝牌笔记本电脑得花费你整整2000美元。

set down *phr v* [T] **1** [**set** sth **↔ down**] to write about something so that you have a record of it 写下, 记下: *I wanted to set my feelings down on paper.* 我想把我的感想写下来。**2** [**set** sth **↔ down**] to establish how something should be done in an official set of rules or an official document〔在正式文件中〕制定, 规定: *The club rules are set down in its constitution.* 俱乐部的规则都写在其章程里。**3** [**set** sb **↔ down**] *BrE* to stop a car, bus etc and allow someone to get out【英】将〔汽车、公共汽车等〕停下让〔乘客〕下车: *The driver set her down at the station.* 司机在车站停下车让她下去。

set forth *phr v* **1** [T **set** sth **↔ forth**] *formal* to write or talk about an idea, argument, or set of figures【正式】〔书面或口头〕陈述〔观点等〕, 阐明: *Rousseau set forth his theories on education in his book "Emile".* 卢梭在他的小说《爱弥儿》中阐述了他的教育理论。**2** [I] *literary* to begin a journey【文】出发, 启程: *They were about to set forth on a voyage into the unknown.* 他们即将启航前往一个未知的世界。

set in *phr v* [I] if something sets in, especially something unpleasant, it begins and seems likely to continue for a long time〔尤指不愉快的事情〕开始, 来临: *Winter seems to be setting in early this year.* 今年的冬天似乎来得早。| *A period of further economic decline set in during the 1930s.* 20世纪30年代出现了一段经济进一步衰退的时期。

set off *phr v* **1** [I] to start to go somewhere 出发, 启程, 动身: *I wanted to set off early in order to avoid the traffic.* 我想早点

set off 出发; 触发

She set off early in the morning.
她一大早就出发了。

The burglar set the alarm off.
小偷触动了警报器。

S

出发以避开交通拥堵。| *The old man set off down the path towards the river.* 老人开始沿着小路向河边走去。**2** [T **set** sth ↔ **off**] to make something start happening or make people suddenly start doing something, especially when you do not intend to do so 引起, 激发〔尤指意外事件〕: *The incident set off a chain of events which resulted in the outbreak of World War I.* 这一事件引起了连锁事件, 从而导致第一次世界大战的爆发。| *News of the deal set off a flurry of activity on Wall Street.* 那宗交易的消息引起了华尔街一阵骚动。**3** [T **set** sth ↔ **off**] to make something such as an alarm system start operating, especially when you do not intend to do so〔尤指无意中〕引起某事〈如触响警报系统〉; 触发: *The high winds set off a lot of car alarms.* 强风使很多汽车的报警器响了起来。**4** [T **set** sth ↔ **off**] to make a bomb explode, or cause an explosion 使〔炸弹等〕爆炸; 引发〔爆炸〕: *The slightest movement would have set off the device and blown us all sky high.* 最轻微的动作都会使这个炸弹爆炸, 把我们炸得血肉横飞。**5** [T **set** sth ↔ **off**] if a piece of clothing, colour, decoration etc sets something off, it makes it look attractive〔衣服、颜色、装饰等〕将〔某物〕衬托得很漂亮; 使更具吸引力: *a stylish beige dress, set off by a blue jacket and scarf* 用蓝色外套和围巾衬托的一套时髦的米色连衣裙 **6** [T **set** sb **off**] to make someone start laughing, crying, or talking about something 激起〔某人的某种情感〕; 引起〔某人笑、哭、谈论某事等〕: *Don't mention anything about weddings – you'll only set her off again.* 不要提任何有关婚礼的事, 否则你又会使她喋喋不休了。

set on *phr v* [T] [**set** sb **on/onto** sb] to make people or animals attack someone 使〔人或动物〕攻击〔某人〕: *The farmer threatened to set his dogs on them if they didn't get off his land.* 农场主威吓说, 如果他们不离开他的土地, 就要放狗咬他们。| **be set on/upon by sb** (=be suddenly attacked by people or animals) 突然遇袭, 突然被〔某人或动物〕袭击 *He was set on by a gang of hooligans as he was leaving the bar.* 他离开酒吧时突然遭到一伙流氓的袭击。

set out *phr v* **1** [I] to start a journey, especially a long journey 动身踏上〔漫长的旅途〕: *Columbus and his crew set out from Europe in 1492.* 哥伦布和他的船员在 1492 年从欧洲启航。| [+**for**] *We packed our rucksacks and set out for the hills.* 我们收拾好背包向群山进发。**2 set out to do sth** to start doing something or making plans to do something in order to achieve a particular result〔为达到某个结果而〕开始做某事, 着手进行: *She deliberately set out to poison her husband.* 她蓄意着手毒杀她的丈夫。| **set out with the intention of doing sth** *They set out with the intention of becoming the number one team in the league.* 他们决意争取成为球赛联合会中最强的球队。**3** [T **set** sth ↔ **out**] to write or talk about something such as a group of facts, ideas, or reasons, especially in a clearly organized way〔清楚而系统地用书面或口头〕陈述, 阐明: *He set out the reasons for his decision in his report.* 他在报告中陈述了他作出这个决定的理由。| *The guidelines are set out in paragraph two.* 第二段阐述了指导原则。**4** [T **set** sth ↔ **out**] to put a group of things down and arrange them in order 摆放, 安排, 陈列: *Auntie Lou set out the dinner on the table.* 卢阿姨在桌上摆好了晚餐。**5 set out on a career/course of action** to start a particular kind of job or start doing something in a particular way 开始从事某种职业/开始采取某种行动: *My nephew is just setting out on a career in journalism.* 我的侄儿刚开始从事新闻工作。

set to *phr v* [I] *BrE* to start doing something eagerly and with a lot of effort and determination【英】开始积极做某事, 决心努力做某事: *If we all set to, we can finish the cleaning in half an hour.* 如果我们大家都努力干, 半个小时就可以完成打扫工作。

set up *phr v*

1 ►**COMPANY/ORGANIZATION ETC** 公司/机构等◄ [I,T] to start a company, organization, committee etc; ESTABLISH 建立, 设立, 创立〔公司、机构等〕: **set sth ↔ up** *The Race Relations Board was originally set up in 1965.* 种族关系委员会最初成立于 1965 年。| *They want to set up their own import-export business.* 他们想创办自己的进出口公司。| **set up as** (=start your own business as) 当上…, 开业做… *John used his inheritance to set up as a graphic designer.* 约翰用他获得的遗产开业, 当上了平面造型设计师。| **set up shop/set up in business** (=begin operating a business) 开业, 开始经营〔生意〕*We mortgaged our house and set up shop with the money from that.* 我们用自己的房子抵押贷款并用这笔钱来创业。

2 ►**ARRANGE/ORGANIZE** 安排/组织◄ [T **set** sth ↔ **up**] to make the necessary arrangements so that something can happen, such as a meeting, an event, or a system for doing something 安排〔会议等〕; 建立〔制度等〕: *I'll get my secretary to set up a working lunch for us.* 我去吩咐秘书给大家安排工作午餐。| *There was a lot of work involved in setting up the festival.* 安排好这个节日活动需要做很多工作。| *We need to set up emergency procedures to deal with this sort of problem.* 我们需要建立应急程序来处理这类问题。

3 ►**EQUIPMENT** 设备◄ [I,T] to prepare the equipment that will be needed for an activity so that it is ready to be used 安装; 架设: *The next band was already setting up on the other stage.* 下一支乐队已经开始在另一个舞台架设装备了。| **set** sth ↔ **up** *Does anyone know how to set up this generator?* 有谁懂得怎样安装这台发电机吗? | *Why don't you set up the Monopoly game while I finish washing the dishes?* 你为什么不趁我洗盘子的时候先摆好"大富翁"游戏棋呢?

4 ►**BUILD/PUT UP** 建立/竖立◄ [T **set** sth ↔ **up**] to place or build something such as a sign or STATUE somewhere 建起, 竖起〔标志牌、塑像等〕: *The army has set up road blocks round the city.* 军队已在城市四周设置了路障。

5 set up home/house to start living in your own home, especially with someone else, instead of living with your parents〔尤指离开父母〕成家, 过独立生活: *Lucy and Paul are thinking of setting up house together.* 露西和保罗正在考虑成家的事。

6 set up camp a) to put up a tent or group of tents in a place so that you can stay there 搭帐篷: *We set up camp near the shore of the lake.* 我们在湖边搭起了帐篷。**b)** *informal* to move all your things to a place so that you can start to live or work there【非正式】搬迁到某地〔工作或生活〕: *She's set up camp in my office.* 她已经搬到我的办公室工作了。

7 ►**MAKE SB SEEM GUILTY** 使某人似乎有罪◄ [T **set** sb ↔ **up**] *informal* to deliberately make other people think that someone has done something wrong, or illegal【非正式】诬陷, 陷害〔某人〕: *The four terrorists claimed they had been set up by the police.* 那四名恐怖分子声称他们是被警方诬陷的。

8 ►**HEALTHY/FULL OF ENERGY** 健康/精力充沛◄ [T **set** sb **up**] to make you feel healthy and full of energy 使〔某人〕觉得健康, 使〔某人〕精力旺盛: **set sb up for the day** *A good breakfast will set you up for the day.* 一顿丰盛的早餐可以使你整人都精力充沛。

9 set sb up for life *informal* if something sets you up for life, it provides you with enough money for the rest of your life【非正式】使某人一生有足够的钱: *In a few more years you should be set up for life.* 再过几年, 你就该拥有终生够用的钱了。

10 ►**START HAPPENING** 引发◄ [T **set up** sth] *especially technical* to make a condition or a process start happening【尤术语】使〔某种情况〕产生; 引起, 造成: *If one reactor has a meltdown, it could set up a chain reaction.* 假如一个核反应堆的堆芯熔毁, 就会引发连锁反应。| *Stimulation of the sensory receptors sets up neural activity.* 对感官感受器的刺激会引起神经的活动。

11 ►**NOISE** 噪声◄ **set up a commotion/din/racket etc** to stark making a loud, unpleasant noise 发出喧闹声/嘈杂声/吵闹声: *At this, the two babies set up a tremendous howling.* 那两个婴儿随即都哇哇大哭起来。

set² *n*

1 ►**GROUP OF THINGS** 一组事物◄ [C] a group of things that form a whole〔物品的〕一套, 一副, 一组: *a chess set* 一副棋 | [+**of**] *a set of tools* 一套工具 | *We are now facing a whole new set of problems.* 我们现在面临着一大堆新问题。

2 ►**TELEVISION/RADIO** 电视/无线电◄ [C] a television, or a piece of equipment for receiving radio signals 电视机, 收音机: *a colour television set* 彩色电视机 —see also 另见 CRYSTAL SET

3 ►**STAGE** 舞台◄ [C] the scenery, furniture etc that is put on a stage to represent where the action of the play is taking place〔舞台的〕布景, 场景〈如自然景色、家具布置等〉: *The play wasn't that good but the set was impressive.* 这出戏并不怎么好, 但布景倒是给人印象很深。

4 ►**FILM** 影片◄ [C] a place where a film or television programme is acted and filmed〔拍摄电影或电视节目的〕拍摄场地, 摄影场: *Everyone must be on the set to start filming at eight o'clock.* 大家都必须准时到达拍摄现场, 8 点钟开拍。

5 ►**SPORT** 体育运动◄ [C] one part of a game such as tennis or VOLLEYBALL〔网球或排球等的〕一盘: *Agassi won the second set 6–4.* 阿加西以 6 比 4 赢了第二盘。

6 ►**MUSIC** 音乐◄ [C] a series of songs performed by one band or singer as part of a concert〔音乐会中由某个乐队或歌手演出的〕一组乐曲[歌曲]

7 ▶HAIR 头发◀ [singular] an act of arranging your hair in a particular style when it is wet 做发型，做头发: **a shampoo and set** (=washing the hair and arranging it in a style) 洗头和做发型

8 ▶PEOPLE 人群◀ [singular] a group of people with similar interests〔趣味相投的〕一群人: *Joanna got in with a rather wild set at college.* 乔安娜在大学时和一伙相当放荡的人厮混。—see also 另见 JET SET

9 ▶FIRMNESS 结实◀ [singular] the state of becoming firm or solid 凝结，凝固: *You'll get a better set if you use gelatine.* 如果你用明胶，就会凝结得好些。

10 ▶PART OF BODY 身体某个部分◀ [C] the way in which you are sitting, standing etc, especially when you look stiff〔坐或站的〕姿态，姿势: [+of] *From the set of her shoulders it was obvious that Sue was exhausted.* 从她肩膀的姿势来看，休显然是精疲力竭了。

11 ▶STUDENTS 学生◀ [C] *BrE* a group of children who have the same level of ability in a subject at school【英】〔在某个科目上能力相似的〕一组学生，一班学生: *Adam's in the top set for maths.* 亚当属于数学成绩最好的一组学生。

12 ▶MATHS 数学◀ [C] *technical* a collection of numbers etc in MATHEMATICS【术语】〔数学中的〕集: *The set (x, y) has two members.* (x, y) 这个集有两个项。

13 ▶ONION 洋葱◀ [C] a small brown root planted in order to grow onions〔种植用的〕球茎: *onion sets* 洋葱球茎

set³ *adj*

1 ▶PLACED 位于某处的◀ being in the position that is mentioned 在…位置的，位于…的: *a town set on a hill* 山丘上的市镇 | *Diane had very deep-set eyes.* 黛安娜的眼窝很深。| *a house set back from the road* 离公路有一段距离的房子

2 ▶WAGE/TIME 工资/时间◀ a set time, amount etc is fixed and cannot be changed〔时间、数目等〕固定的，不变的: *We pay a set amount each week.* 我们每星期支付一笔固定的钱。

3 **a set book/text etc** *BrE* a book that must be studied for an examination【英】考试必读的书/课本等 —see also 另见 SET¹ (10)

4 **a set menu/meal** *BrE* a set meal has a fixed price and includes a combination of foods that the restaurant suggests【英】〔固定价格和菜式的〕套菜/套餐

5 **be set on/upon/against** to be very determined about something 决心要…/坚决反对…: *Nina's very set on going to this party.* 尼娜决心要去参加这个聚会。| **be dead set on/upon/against** *The government's dead set against the plan.* 政府坚决反对这项计划。

6 **have your heart set on sth** to be determined to do something 决心做某事: *She's got her heart set on going to France this summer.* 她下决心要在今年夏天去法国。

7 ▶READY 准备好的◀ [only after noun 仅用于名词后] *informal* someone who is set for something is prepared for it【非正式】准备就绪的: **set for sth** *Are you all set for the journey?* 你们都为旅行作好准备了吗? | **set to do sth** *I was all set to leave when the phone rang.* 我正准备离开时，电话铃响了。| **get set** (=get ready) 预备，作好准备 *"On your marks – get set – go!" said the starter.* "各就各位 — 预备 — 跑!"发令员喊道。| **all set** *Okay, I'm all set, let's get going.* 好了，我一切都准备停当了，咱们走吧。

8 **set smile/teeth/jaw** a set smile etc shows that you are not happy about something or are determined to do something 假笑/咬紧牙关〔表示不悦或坚决〕: *Gloria greeted her guests with a set smile.* 格洛丽亚面带假笑迎接客人。

9 **set opinions/beliefs etc** set opinions or beliefs are ones you are not likely to change 执着的主张/信念等

10 **be set in your ways** to be used to doing the same things every day 积习难改，习惯根深蒂固: *Uncle's 80 now and very set in his ways.* 叔叔80岁了，种种习惯都根深蒂固。

11 **set to (do sth)** likely to do something 很可能(做某事): *The temperature is set to drop very low tonight.* 今晚的气温很可能会降得很低。| *This issue is set to cause the government serious embarrassment.* 这个问题很可能给政府造成非常尴尬的局面。

set·back /ˈsɛtˌbæk; ˈsetbæk/ *n* [C] something that delays or prevents progress, or makes things worse than they were 阻碍发展的事物；挫折: *The recent crime figures are a major setback for the law and order reforms.* 最近的犯罪率使治安法规改革严重受挫。—see also 另见 **set back** (SET¹)

set piece /ˌ· ˈ·◂/ *n* [C] part of a play, piece of music, painting etc that follows a well-known formal pattern or style, and is often very impressive〔戏剧、音乐、绘画等遵循著名的固定模式或风格的〕精彩部分: *The trial scene at the end of the play is a classic set piece.* 这出戏结尾的一场审判是经典的场景。

set-square /ˈsɛtˋskwɛr; ˈsetskweə/ *n* [C] a flat piece of plastic or metal with three sides and one right angle, used for drawing or testing angles; TRIANGLE (4)〔绘图和测量直角用的〕三角板

set·tee /sɛˋti; seˈtiː/ *n* [C] a long seat with a back and usually with arms, for more than one person to sit on; SOFA 长沙发，长靠椅

set·ter /ˋsɛtɚ; ˈsetə/ *n* [C] **1** a long-haired dog often trained to find where animals or birds are so they can be shot 塞特种猎犬，蹲伏猎狗〔一种长毛狗，被训练去发现猎物位置以助猎〕 **2** someone who does a particular job, or who does things that other people copy 制定者；倡导者: **exam setter/trap setter/fashion setter etc** (=someone who gives exams, puts out traps etc) 考试命题者/陷阱设置者/时尚倡导者 —see also 另见 **set the pattern/tone/trend** (SET¹ (3)), TRENDSETTER

set·ting /ˋsɛtɪŋ; ˈsetɪŋ/ *n* [C usually singular 一般用单数] **1 a)** all the things that surround someone or something at a particular time, including the events that happen, their environment, or the people they are with 背景，环境〔指周围的人与事物〕: *an old farm house in a beautiful setting* 环境优美的古老农舍 | *children brought up in a privileged setting* 在优越环境中长大的小孩 **2** the place or time that the action of a book, film etc happens〔书、影片等中情节发生的〕地点[时间]: *Canberra is the setting for his latest novel.* 他的最新小说以堪培拉为背景。**3** [C] the position in which you fix the controls on a machine or instrument〔机器、仪器等调控装置的〕设定位置: *The freezer's already on its highest setting.* 冷冻室已经调到最底一档了。**4** [C] the metal that holds a stone in a piece of jewellery, or the way the stone is fixed〔宝石的〕镶嵌底座[式样]: *a diamond ring in a gold setting* 黄金钻戒 **5** [C] music that is written to go with a poem, prayer etc〔为诗、祷文等谱写的〕乐曲 **6 the setting of the sun** *literary* the time when the sun goes down【文】日落 —see also 另见 PLACE SETTING

set·tle¹ /ˈsɛtl; ˈsetl/ *v*

1 ▶MAKE COMFORTABLE/SAFE 使舒适/安全◀ **a)** [I always+adv/prep, T always+adv/prep] to put yourself or someone else in a comfortable position (使)处于舒适的位置: [+back/into/down] *Mel settled back in his chair and closed his eyes.* 梅尔舒舒服服地坐在椅子上，闭着眼睛。| **settle yourself** *Kari had already settled herself in a corner where she could watch.* 卡丽早已在一个方便观察的小角落里舒服地坐下来了。**b)** to put something carefully in a particular place so that it stays there 放置，安放〔某物〕: *Lee settled the cup on the saucer.* 李把杯子放在茶碟上。

2 ▶MOVE DOWN/STAY 落下/停留◀ [I] **a)** if dust, snow etc settles it comes down and stays in one place〔灰尘、雪等〕降落；落下；沉降: [+on/in] *snow settling on the roofs* 房顶上的积雪 | *The sediment will settle in the bottle after a few days.* 沉淀物过几天就会沉积到瓶底。**b)** if a bird, insect etc settles it flies down and rests on something〔鸟、昆虫等〕停下，落下，栖息于: [+on] *A fly settled on the plate of cookies.* 一只苍蝇落在那盘小甜饼上。

3 ▶END AN ARGUMENT 结束争辩◀ [I,T] to end an argument by agreeing on something〔通过取得一致意见而〕结束(争论): [+with] *It looks like they're finally going to settle with the railroad.* 看来他们终于要和铁路部门结束争端了。| **settle a quarrel/argument/dispute etc** *There's only one way to settle the dispute, and they know it.* 要解决争端只有一种方法，他们是知道的。| **settle out of court** (=come to an agreement to avoid going to a court of law) 庭外和解 | **settle your differences** (=agree to stop arguing with someone) 解决分歧

4 ▶DECIDE 决定◀ [T] to decide on something, especially so that you can make definite arrangements 确定，决定: **settled (that)** *It was settled that Jim would visit us on the weekend.* 已经确定，吉姆周末将来探访我们。| **It is settled** (=it is now decided) 现在决定 *It's settled then. I'll go back to the States in June.* 那么现在就定下来，我6月份回美国。| **That settles it!** (=this is enough information for a decision to be made) 那就解决了!；那就可以决定了! *Carol's only 15? That settles it. We are not taking her with us.* 卡罗尔只有15岁? 那就定了，我们不带她一起去。

5 ▶PAY MONEY 付钱◀ [T] to pay money that is owed 支付〔欠债、账目〕，结算: **settle a bill/account/claim** *We expect you to settle your account in full each month.* 我们要求你每月结清全部账目。| *These insurance companies take forever to settle a claim.* 这些保险公司要拖很久才支付赔偿金。

6 ▶TAKE CARE OF DETAILS 处理细节◀ [T] to put all the details of a piece of business into order and deal with them, for example before you travel or because you may die soon〔在旅行前或临终前〕安排好某事的细节: **settle the details** (=deal with the details of a plan, agreement etc) 安排细节 | **settle your af-**

fairs (=put your personal business in order) 安排好自己的事 | **settle an estate** (=deal with the way someone's property is divided after they die) 办理遗产分配

7 ►QUIET/CALM 平静/安定◄ [I,T] to become quiet or calm, or to make someone or something quiet or calm (使)平静, (使)安定: *When the children had settled, Miss Brown gave out the new reading books.* 孩子们静下来后, 布朗小姐分发新的读本。| **settle your nerves/stomach** (=stop your nerves or stomach from being upset) 使神经镇静; 缓解胃部不适 *A little soda should settle your tummy.* 喝点苏打水, 肚子就不会难受了。

8 ►LIVE IN A PLACE 住在某地◄ **a)** [I] to go to live in a new place, and stay there 〔到新的地方〕定居: *After returning from abroad they settled in Chicago.* 从国外回来以后他们就在芝加哥定居。**b)** [T] to go to a new place where there are few people and start to live there 〔到人口稀少的地方〕定居: *Jamestown was already settled when the Pilgrims came to America.* 当英国的清教徒来到美洲时, 詹姆斯敦已经有人定居了。

9 ►A FEELING/QUALITY 感觉/特质◄ [I always+adv/prep] if a quality or feeling settles over a place or on someone it has a strong effect 围绕; 充满; 强烈影响着: **[+over/on]** *Despair seemed to settle on him and he could hardly work.* 绝望情绪好像老在困扰着他, 使他无法工作。| *A velvety silence settled over the room.* 房间里一片宁静。

10 settle a score/account to do something to hurt or cause trouble for someone because they have harmed or offended you 清算积怨, 报宿仇: *She's got a few old scores to settle with him.* 她有几笔旧账要跟他算。

11 ►SINK 沉降◄ [I] if something such as a building or the ground settles it sinks slowly to a lower level 下陷, 下沉: *The crack in the wall is caused by the ground settling.* 墙壁的裂缝是地面沉降造成的。

12 ►LOOK 看◄[I] if your eyes settle on someone or something you look at them carefully for a period of time 〔目光〕停留, 凝视: **[+on]** *The teacher's steely eyes settled on Bobby.* 老师冷峻的目光注视着博比。

13 ►EXPRESSION 表情◄ [I] if a particular expression settles on your face, it stays there 〔某种表情在脸上〕固定下来: *His face settled into a severe frown.* 他双眉紧锁, 神色凝重。

14 ►FOOD 食物◄ [I] if something you eat settles, it is digested (DIGEST[1] (1)) well 〔食物〕被消化: *Give your lunch a chance to settle.* 吃午饭后要让它消化一下。

settle down *phr v* **1** [I,T **settle** sb **down**] to stop talking or behaving in an excited way, or to make someone do this (使)安静下来, (使)停止讲话: *Everybody settle down so we can hear the story.* 大家安静下来, 好让我们听故事。| *Sheila seems to have settled down more since school started.* 自开学以来, 希拉似乎已经踏实多了。**2** [I] to start living in a place with the intention of staying there, especially after you have travelled a lot 〔尤指四处奔波之后〕安顿下来, 定居: *They'd like to see her daughter settle down, get married, and have kids.* 他们想看到女儿安顿下来, 结婚生子。**3** [I,T] to start giving all of your attention to a job, activity etc 开始专心于〔工作、活动等〕, 着手认真做〔某事〕: **[+to]** *They settled down to a serious discussion over coffee.* 他们喝着咖啡, 开始认真讨论问题。| **settle yourself down** *Sally sighed, and settled herself down to listen.* 萨莉叹了口气, 静下心来听。

settle for sth *phr v* [T not in passive 不用被动态] to accept or agree to something, especially something that is less than what you want 〔勉强〕接受, 〔将就着〕同意: *We've no TV and have had to settle for hearing the news on the radio.* 我们没有电视机, 只好用收音机收听新闻。| *They want $3,000 for their car and won't settle for anything less.* 他们的汽车要卖3000美元, 少于此数就不行。| *You'll have to settle for a cheaper car.* 你只好买辆便宜些的车算了。

settle in/into *phr v* **1** [I,T **settle** sb **in**] to become used to a new home, job, surroundings etc or to help someone do this (使)适应〔新的家、工作、环境等〕: *Are you settling in OK?* 你已经逐渐适应了吗? | *It takes a few months to settle into life at college.* 要经过几个月才能习惯大学生活。**2** [I] to make yourself comfortable and prepare to stay somewhere for a period of time 安定下来, 安心下来: **[+for]** *They settled in for a long wait in the airport lounge.* 他们在机场大厅安顿下来, 准备长时间等候。

settle on/upon *phr v* [T] **1** [**settle on** sth/sb] to decide or agree on something 决定, 同意〔某事〕: *They haven't settled yet on a name for the baby.* 他们还没有决定给婴儿取什么名字。**2** [**settle** sth **on** sb] *BrE formal* to make a formal arrangement to give money or property to someone 【英, 正式】〔正式〕授予, 赠与〔金钱或财产〕: *She settled a small yearly sum on each of her children.* 她办了手续, 确定每年给每个孩子一小笔钱。

settle up *phr v* **1** [I] to pay what you owe on an account or bill 付清欠账, 结清账单: **[+with]** *I'll settle up with the bartender and we can leave.* 我先和酒吧侍者结账, 然后我们就可以走了。**2** [I] if two or more people settle up, they agree on a final arrangement for paying money, dividing property etc 协议清账; 还清债务; 分清财产: *It's time we settled up. What do I owe you?* 我们现在该清清账了, 我欠你多少钱?

settle² *n* [C] a long wooden seat with a high back that usually has a hollow place for storing things under the seat 高背木制长椅〔座位下有空柜放东西〕

set·tled /ˈsetḷd; ˈsetld/ *adj* **1** unlikely to change; fixed 不大可能改变的, 固定的: *They lead a settled life.* 他们过着稳定的生活。| *The community has firm and settled ideas on this question.* 公众对这个问题有固定不变的看法。**2 feel/be settled** to feel comfortable about living or working in a particular place 〔对某地的生活或工作〕感到舒适惬意: *I'd work better if I felt more settled in my job.* 如果我对自己的工作感到惬意, 就会工作得更好。

set·tle·ment /ˈsɛtḷmənt; ˈsetlmənt/ *n* 2

1 ►OFFICIAL AGREEMENT 正式协议◄ [C,U] an official agreement or decision that ends an argument between two sides 〔解决双方争端的〕正式协议, 和解: **reach/achieve a settlement** *failure to reach a settlement in the trade war* 在贸易战中未能达成协议 | **negotiated/political/peaceful etc settlement** (=made after discussions are held, political decisions taken etc) 谈判/政治/和平等协定 | **divorce/peace/financial etc settlement** (=the agreement about what the two sides will do after a divorce, after fighting stops etc) 离婚/和平/经济等协议 *Martin lost the house in their divorce settlement.* 马丁在他们的离婚协议中失去了房子。| **out-of-court settlement** (=money you pay or things you agree to do to prevent someone going to court) 庭外和解〔指用付钱等办法使对方不向法院起诉〕

2 ►GROUP OF HOUSES 住宅群◄ [C] a group of houses and buildings where people live, in an area where no group lived before 〔人口稀少地区的〕拓居群, 小村落: *a Bronze Age settlement* 青铜器时代的村落 | *Wrangell is Alaska's second oldest settlement.* 兰格尔是阿拉斯加第二古老的拓居地。

3 ►NEW AREA/PLACES 新的地区/地方◄ [U] the movement of a new population into a place to live there 殖民, 移民, 拓居: **[+of]** *the settlement of the American West* 向美国西部的移民

4 ►PAYMENT 支付◄ [C,U] the payment of money that you owe someone 〔欠款的〕清偿: **in settlement** *a $1,000 check in settlement* 用以清偿账目的1000美元支票

5 ►GIFT 礼物◄ [C,U] a formal gift of money or property 〔金钱或财产的〕正式授予, 赠与: **on/upon** *He made a handsome settlement on his daughter when she married.* 他女儿结婚时, 他赠与她一笔可观的财产。

6 ►SINKING 下沉◄ [U] the slow sinking of a building, the ground under it etc; SUBSIDENCE 〔建筑物、地基等的〕沉降, 下陷

set·tler /ˈsɛtlə; ˈsetlə/ *n* [C] someone who goes to live in a new place where there are few people 〔到人口稀少的新地区定居的〕移民, 殖民者: *early settlers in Australia* 澳大利亚的早期移民

set-to /ˈ· ·/ *n* [C usually singular 一般用单数+**with**] *informal* a short fight or quarrel 【非正式】〔短时间的〕打斗〔争吵〕—see also 另见 **set to** (SET[1])

set-up /ˈ· ·/ *n* [usually singular 一般用单数] **1** a way of organizing or arranging something 组织机构; 〔事物的〕安排, 布局: *a less traditional classroom se-tup* 不太传统的教室座位安排 | *He has a nice little set-up, with a studio at the back and gallery space at the front.* 他的安排相当精巧, 工作室在后面, 艺术品陈列在前面。**2** all the parts that work together in a system, for example in a computer system 〔电脑等的〕装配; 调试 **3** *informal* a dishonest plan that tricks you 【非正式】圈套, 骗局, 诡计: *How do I know this isn't a set-up?* 我怎么才知道这不是个骗局? —see also 另见 **set up** (SET[1])

Seu·rat /suˋrɑ; ˈsɜːrɑː/, **Georges** /ʒɔrʒ; ʒɔːʒ/ (1859-91) a French artist who developed the method of painting known as POINTILLISM (=using many small spots of pure colour, rather than longer lines made with the brush) 修拉〔(1859-1891), 法国画家。他首创点彩派画法〕

Seuss /zjus; zjuːs/, **Dr** (1904-91) a US children's writer whose funny stories, poems, and pictures are very popular with young children, and include *The Cat in the Hat*, *Green Eggs and Ham*, and *How the Grinch Stole Christmas* 索伊斯博士〔(1904-1991), 美国儿童作家。其滑稽故事、诗歌和插图深受儿童喜爱。作品包括《帽中猫》、《绿鸡蛋和火腿》及《圣诞怪杰》〕

sev·en /ˈsɛvən; ˈsevən/ *number* **1** 7 七 **2 the seven year itch** *humorous* the idea that after seven years of being married, people

feel less satisfied with their relationship【幽默】七年之痒〔指结婚七年后对婚姻关系感到不够满意〕 —**seventh** *number* —see also 另见 **at sixes and sevens** (SIX (3))

Seven Dead·ly Sins, the /ˌ· · ˌ· · ˈ·/ according to the Christian church in the Middle Ages, the seven most serious types of bad behaviour. The SINs are pride (=thinking you are better than other people), lechery (=too much desire for sex), envy (=disliking someone because they have things that you want and do not have), anger, covetousness (=wanting someone else's wealth or possessions), gluttony (=eating too much), and sloth (=laziness). 七宗罪〔中世纪基督教会规定的七种最为严重的恶行，即傲慢、淫欲、嫉妒、暴怒、贪婪、贪食、懒惰〕

Seven Dwarfs, the /ˌ· · ˈ·/ a group of seven very small men in the fairy tale *Snow White*. In the Walt Disney film of the story their names are Doc, Grumpy, Sleepy, Bashful, Happy, Sneezy, and Dopey. 七个小矮人〔童话故事《白雪公主》中的七个小矮人。在迪斯尼改编的影片中，他们的名字分别是博士、牢骚鬼、瞌睡虫、害羞鬼、开心鬼、喷嚏虫和糊涂虫〕

7-E·le·ven /ˌsɛvən ɪˋlɛvən; ˌsevən ɪˈlevən/ *trademark* a shop that sells food, drinks, magazines, cleaning products etc. 7-Elevens are smaller than supermarkets. They are usually in busy parts of a city and they are open from early in the morning until very late at night. 7-Elevens are very common in the US, and there are also some in the UK, especially in London.【商标】711便民店〔经销食品、饮料、杂志、清洁用品等商品的店家，规模比超市小，通常位于闹市区，清早开始营业，深夜打烊。711便民店在美国十分常见，英国，尤其是伦敦也有这样的商店〕

747 /ˌsɛvən for ˋsɛvən; ˌsevən fɔː ˈsevən/ *n* [C] a large passenger plane made by the US Boeing Corporation. The 747 was the first JUMBO JET and it can carry over 400 passengers. These planes are used all over the world, especially for long-distance flights. 波音747〔美国波音公司生产的一款大型客机。747是首款巨型喷气式客机，可载客400余人，在世界各地均有使用，尤其适用于长途航班〕

Seventeen a US magazine for teenage girls, containing pictures and articles about fashion, health, popular music, boys, etc, and answers to readers' questions about personal problems. In the UK there is a similar magazine called *J-17*.《十七岁年华》〔美国一少女杂志。刊载的图片和文章涉及时装、健康、流行音乐、男孩等主题，解答读者提出的个人问题。英国也有一类似杂志，名为J-17（《刚满十七》）〕

sev·en·teen /ˌsɛvənˋtin; ˌsevənˈtiːn◂/ *number* 17 十七

sev·enth /ˋsɛvənθ; ˈsevənθ/ *n* **1** [C] one of seven equal parts of something 七分之一 (¹/₇) **2 be in seventh heaven** *informal* to be extremely happy【非正式】感到非常快活，非常幸福: *He's in seventh heaven when he's watching football.* 他一看足球比赛就快活似神仙。

Seventh-Day Ad·vent·ist /ˌ· · · ˈ· · ·/ *n* [C] a member of a Christian religious group that believes that Christ will return to Earth in the near future. Unlike most Christian groups, Seventh-Day Adventists have a religious day of rest on Saturday instead of Sunday. 基督复临安息日会教友〔基督教一教派的教徒。他们相信基督在不久的将来会复临人世。与其他基督教派不同的是，他们的礼拜日是星期六，而非星期天〕

737 /ˌsɛvən θri ˋsɛvən; ˌsevən θriː ˈsevən/ *n* [C] a medium-sized passenger plane made by the Boeing Corporation 波音737〔美国波音公司生产的一款中型客机〕

sev·en·ty /ˋsɛvəntɪ; ˈsevənti/ *number* **1** 70 七十 **2 the seventies** the years from 1970 to 1979 70年代〔从1970年至1979年〕 **3 in your seventies** aged between 70 and 79 从70岁至79岁: **in your early/late seventies** (=below or above 75) 70（岁）开外〔不到75〕/年将80〔75岁以上〕 **4 in the seventies** if the temperature is in the seventies, it is between 70° and 79° FAHRENHEIT〔温度〕在70至79华氏度之间 —**seventieth** *adj*

seventy-eight /ˌ· · · ˈ·/ *n* [C] an old-fashioned record that is played by being turned 78 times a minute 每分钟78转的旧式唱片

7-Up /ˌsɛvən ˋʌp; ˌsevən ˈʌp/ *trademark* a type of popular non-alcoholic drink with BUBBLEs, which tastes of LEMON and LIME【商标】七喜汽水〔指不含酒精，含有气泡，带有柠檬和酸橙味道的一种畅销饮品〕

Seven Won·ders of the World, the /ˌ· · ˌ· · · · · ˈ·/ seven ancient structures which were considered to be the most interesting and impressive things in the world made by ancient peoples. These were the Pyramids of Egypt, the Hanging Gardens of Babylon, the statue of Zeus at Olympia, the Temple of Artemis at Ephesus, the mausoleum (=building where people are buried) at Halicarnassus, the Colossus of Rhodes, and the Pharos (a lighthouse) at Alexandria. 世界七大奇观〔七大古建筑。它们被认为是古代各民族创造的最为别致壮观的伟迹，包括埃及金字塔、巴比伦空中花园、奥林匹亚的宙斯神像、以弗所的阿耳忒弥斯神庙、哈利卡纳苏斯的摩索拉斯陵墓、罗德岛巨人像、亚历山大城的法罗斯岛灯塔〕

Seven Years' War, the /ˌ· · · ˈ·/ a war fought in Europe, North America, and India between 1756 and 1763. The war was about French and English colonies (COLONY), and also Austria and Prussia wanting to control Europe. As a result of the war, France lost most of its land in India and North America to Britain, and Prussia became a leading European power under Frederick II. 七年战争〔1756至1763年在欧洲、北美和印度爆发的一场战争。这是英法争夺殖民地的战争，也是奥地利和普鲁士企图控制欧洲的战争。结果法国战败，英国获得了法国在印度和北美的大部分殖民地，普鲁士在腓特烈二世的领导下成为欧洲的主要大国〕

sev·er /ˋsɛvɚ; ˈsevə/ *v formal*【正式】**1** [I,T] to cut through something, separating it into two parts, or to become severed in this way 切断，割断: *Martin's hand was severed in the accident.* 马丁的一只手在事故中被切断了。| *a severed rope* 切断的绳子 **2** to end a relationship with someone, or a connection with something 与…断绝（关系）: *severing family ties* 断绝家庭关系 —see also 另见 SEVERANCE PAY —**severance** *n* [U]

sev·er·al¹ /ˋsɛvərəl; ˈsevərəl/ *quantifier* a number of people or things that is more than a few, but not a lot 几个，数个，一些: *I visited him in Kansas several times.* 我曾几次去堪萨斯拜会他。| *several million dollars* 数百万美元 | *Several people have volunteered to go.* 有几个人自愿前往。| [+**of**] *Several of us think it's a bad idea.* 我们当中好几个人认为这个主意不好。 S1 W1

several² *adj* [only before noun 仅用于名词前, no comparative 无比较级] *formal or literary* different and separate; RESPECTIVE【正式或文】不同的，各自的，各别的: *They shook hands and went their several ways.* 他们握手后便各自走了。—**severally** *adv*: *These issues can be considered severally, or as a whole.* 这些问题可以分开考虑，也可以作为一个整体来考虑。

sev·er·ance pay /ˈ· · · · ˌ·/ *n* [U] money you get when you leave a company because your employer no longer has a job for you 遣散费；解雇费；离职金

se·vere /səˋvɪr; sɪ̰ˈvɪə/ *adj* S3 W2

1 ►**VERY BAD** 非常糟◄ very bad, or serious enough for you to worry about 严重的，剧烈的: *severe injuries to the head and neck* 头部和颈部的重伤 | *severe depression* 严重抑郁 | *a severe setback to hopes of peace* 对和平希望的严重挫折 —see graph at 参见 PAIN¹ 图表

2 ►**WEATHER** 天气◄ severe weather conditions are extremely hot, cold, dry etc and are unpleasant or dangerous 严酷的；恶劣的；极热[冷，干]的: *the severest winter since 1948* 自1948年以来最寒冷的冬天 | *severe flooding* 严重的水灾

3 ►**STRICT** 严格的◄ someone who is severe is very strict and demands that rules of behaviour are obeyed or standards are followed〔人〕严格的，严厉的，苛刻的: *Don't be so severe with the children.* 对小孩不要这么严厉。

4 ►**EXTREME** 极度的◄ criticism or punishment that is severe is extreme, and intended to prevent more crimes or bad behaviour〔批评、惩罚等〕极其严厉的: *Drug smuggling continues to flourish despite the severe sentences of the courts.* 尽管法院的判决极为严厉，毒品走私仍然十分猖獗。| *a report containing severe criticism of the company's actions* 包含对这家公司行为的尖锐批评的报告

5 ►**UNFRIENDLY** 不友好的◄ disapproving or unfriendly 不赞成的；不友好的: *a severe expression* 严厉的表情

6 ►**PLAIN** 朴素的◄ plain and simple in style with little or no decoration; AUSTERE 朴素的；简洁的；不加装饰的: *The town hall of Bruges is less severe but equally imposing.* 布鲁日的市政大厅不那么简朴，但同样显得庄严。—**severity** *n* [C,U]: *We didn't realize the severity of her illness.* 我们没有意识到她病得如此严重。| *"You can't leave now," he said with some severity.* "你现在不能走。"他用略带严厉的口吻说。

se·vere·ly /səˋvɪrlɪ; sɪ̰ˈvɪəli/ *adv* **1** very badly or to a great degree 严重地: *a severely damaged building* 严重毁坏的建筑物 | *severely disabled* 有严重残疾的 | *His movements are severely restricted.* 他的活动被严加限制。**2** in a strict way 严厉地，严格地: *Parents don't punish their children so severely these days.* 如今父母不再那么严厉地惩罚孩子了。**3** in a way that shows you disapprove greatly 严肃地〔表示很不赞成〕: *"Stop behaving like a fool!" she said severely.* "别再像个傻瓜一样！"她严肃地说。**4** in a plain simple style with little or no decoration 朴素地，朴实无华地: *severely dressed* 穿着朴素的

Sev·ern, the /ˋsɛvɚn; ˈsevən/ a river in South Wales and southwest England which flows from the Welsh mountains to

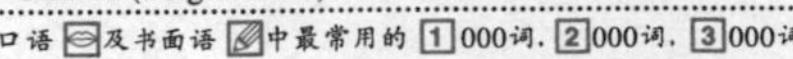
口语 S 及书面语 W 中最常用的 1 000词，2 000词，3 000词

the Bristol Channel 塞文河〔威尔士南部和英格兰西南部一河流。源于威尔士山脉，注入布里斯托尔湾〕

Severn Bridge, the /ˌ· · ˈ·/ a SUSPENSION bridge over the River Severn, which joins southwest England with South Wales 塞文河吊桥〔横跨塞文河的一座吊桥，连接英格兰西南与威尔士南部〕

Se·ville /səˈvɪl; səˈvɪl/ a city in southwest Spain, which has many beautiful and historical buildings, especially the ALCAZAR (=castle) built by the Moors who ruled Seville between 712 and 1248 塞维利亚〔西班牙西南部一城市。该市拥有众多漂亮的历史建筑，尤以摩尔人建造的宫殿式城堡著称。摩尔人公元712至1248年曾统治塞维利亚〕

sew /so; səʊ/ *v past tense* **sewed** *past participle* **sewn** /son; səʊn/ also 又作 **sewed** *AmE*【美】[I,T] to use a needle and thread to join pieces of cloth together to make or repair clothes or fasten something such as a button to them 缝，缝纫；缝制；缝补：*I learned to sew at school.* 我在学校学过缝纫。| **sew sth on sth** *Can you sew a patch on my jeans?* 你能帮我给这条牛仔裤缝块补丁吗？

sew sth ↔ **up** *phr v* [T] **1** to close or repair something by sewing it 缝合；缝补：*Could you sew up this hole in my trousers?* 你能补好我裤子上这个洞吗？**2** [usually passive 一般用被动态] *informal* to finish a business agreement or plan and get the result you want【非正式】顺利完成〔协议或计划〕；解决；决定：*Bob reckons the deal should be sewn up in a week.* 鲍勃估计那宗交易一周之内可谈妥。**3** [usually passive 一般用被动态] to gain control over a situation so that you are sure to win or gain something 控制〔局势〕；确保〔胜利、利益等〕：*It seems like the Democrats have the election all sewn up.* 看来民主党这次选举稳操胜券了。

sew·age /ˈsuɪdʒ; ˈsjuːɪdʒ/ *n* [U] the mixture of waste from the human body and used water that is carried away from houses by sewers 下水道的污水，污物：*Chlorine is used in sewage treatment.* 氯被用于污水处理。

sewage farm /ˈ· · ˌ·/ *BrE*【英】, **sewage plant** *AmE*【美】*n* [C] a place where sewage is treated to stop it being harmful 污水处理场

Sew·ard /ˈsjuəd; ˈsjuːəd/, **William Henry** (1801-72) a US politician in the Republican Party who was Secretary of State from 1861 to 1869. He helped to arrange the deal in which the US bought Alaska from Russia in 1867. At the time, many people thought Alaska was a bad piece of land to buy, and they called it 'Seward's Folly'. 西沃德〔(1801-1872)，美国共和党政治家。1861至1869年任国务卿。经他安排，美国1867年从俄国买下阿拉斯加。然而，当时的许多人认为阿拉斯加是一块一文不值的贫瘠土地，把买地一事称作"西沃德的蠢事"〕

sew·er /ˈsuə; ˈsjuːə/ *n* [C] a pipe or passage under the ground that carries away waste material and used water from houses and factories 下水道；阴沟；污水管

sew·er·age /ˈsuərɪdʒ; ˈsjuːərɪdʒ/ *n* [U] the system by which waste material and water is carried away in sewers and then treated to stop it being harmful 污水处理系统；下水道系统

sew·ing /ˈsoɪŋ; ˈsəʊɪŋ/ *n* [U] **1** the activity or skill of making or repairing clothes or decorating cloth with a needle and thread〔用针线的〕缝纫（技巧）**2** something you have sewn or are going to sew〔缝好或未缝好的〕缝制品：*Imogen sighed and picked up her sewing.* 伊莫金叹了口气，拿起了她的针线活。

sewing ma·chine /ˈ· · ·ˌ·/ *n* [C] a machine for stitching cloth or clothes together 缝纫机

S1 W2 **sex¹** /sɛks; seks/ *n* **1** the activity in which a male and female join their sexual organs in order to create babies, or for pleasure 性活动，性行为：*All you see on TV is sex and violence these days.* 这些日子在电视上看到的尽是性行为和暴力的镜头。**2 have sex** when two people have sex they take part in an activity that involves contact between their sexual organs 做爱，性交：*Would you have sex with someone on your first date?* 你会和初次约会的人做爱吗？**3** the male or female nature of a person, animal, or plant〔人、动物、植物的〕性别：*Please put your name, age, and sex at the top of the form.* 请在表格上方填上你的姓名、年龄和性别。| *You can now tell the sex of a baby before it is born.* 现在婴儿出生前就能知道性别了。**4** the two sexes are the two groups of male and female people, animals etc 男性或女性；雌性或雄性：**the opposite sex** (=the group that you are not in) 异性 *He's terrified of the opposite sex.* 他对异性怕得要命。| **sex discrimination** (=unfair treatment because of which sex you are) 性别歧视 *She's prosecuting the company for sex discrimination.* 她起诉该公司性别歧视。**5 single-sex school/college etc** *BrE* a school etc for either males or females, but not for both together【英】单一性别的学校/学院等

CULTURAL NOTE 文化注释

Sex is one of the subjects that many people in the UK and US do not really talk much about, even with their friends, because it is considered private. (Death and religion are the other subjects that people usually avoid talking about.) Despite this, many magazines, television programmes, and films talk about sex or show sexual situations a lot. Some people disapprove of this, and think that films etc show too much sex. 性是英美人实际上不愿多谈的话题之一，即便朋友之间亦如此，因为性被认为是一种隐私。（人们通常回避的话题还有死亡和宗教。）尽管如此，还是有很多杂志、电视节目和电影屡屡谈及性话题或暴露性场面。有人对此持否定态度，认为电影等展露了太多的性。

In the UK and in most states of the US, people must be at least 16 before they can legally have sex. This is known as the 'age of consent'. However, people are not usually ARREST*ed* by the police for having sex unless one of the two people is younger than sixteen and the other is very much older. Many people worry that teenagers are having sex when they are really too young, so that young girls are having babies when they are still children themselves. In the US, there is an organization, called True Love Waits, which encourages young people to wait until they are married before they have sex for the first time. 在英国和美国的大多数州，法律规定只有年满16岁才可以发生性行为，这就是所谓的"同意年龄"。但是，除非一方年龄低于16岁而且另一方年龄远大于16岁时，即便人们发生了性关系警察通常也不会逮捕他们。很多人担心的是年龄很小的少男少女的性行为，这导致了很多小女孩怀孕，而她们自己还是个孩子。在美国有一个叫"真爱等待"的组织，鼓励年轻人等到婚后再发生性行为。— see also Cultural Note at HOMOSEXUAL 另见 HOMOSEXUAL 文化注释

sex² *v* [T] *technical* to find out whether an animal is male or female【术语】鉴别〔动物的〕性别

sex·a·ge·na·ri·an /ˌsɛksədʒəˈnɛrɪən; ˌseksədʒəˈneəriən/ *n* [C] *formal* someone who is between 60 and 69 years old【正式】60到69岁之间的人—**sexaganarian** *adj*

Sex·a·ges·i·ma /ˌsɛksəˈdʒɛsəmə; ˌseksəˈdʒesəmə/ in the Christian religion, the second Sunday before Lent 六旬斋〔基督教大斋节前第二个星期日〕

sex ap·peal /ˈ· ·ˌ·/ *n* [U] the quality of being sexually attractive 性感，性魅力：*He's a nice guy – but he's got no sex appeal!* 他这人挺不错，就是不性感！

sex change /ˈ· ˌ·/ *n* [C usually singular 一般用单数] a medical operation or treatment which changes someone's body so that they look like someone of the other sex〔通过外科手术等手段达到的〕性别改变，变性

Sex Di·scrim·i·na·tion Act, the /ˌ· ·ˌ· · ˈ· · ˌ·/ a British law passed in 1975 to prevent sex DISCRIMINATION (=unfair treatment of someone because of their sex), especially in employment and education《性别歧视法案》〔英国一法律。该法于1975年通过，旨在禁止就业和教育领域的性别歧视〕

sex drive /ˈ· ˌ·/ *n* [C usually singular 一般用单数] someone's ability or need to have sex regularly 性欲

sex ed·u·ca·tion /ˈ· ·ˌ· ·/ *n* [U] education in schools about the physical processes and emotions involved in sex〔学校中的〕性教育

sex·is·m /ˈsɛksɪzəm; ˈseksɪzəm/ *n* [U] the belief that women are weaker, less intelligent, and less important than men〔对女性的〕性别偏见[歧视]：*The book gives a range of examples of sexism in education.* 这本书列举了一系列在教育领域歧视女性的事例。

sex·ist /ˈsɛksɪst; ˈseksɪst/ *adj* **1** believing that women are weaker, less intelligent, and less important than men 歧视妇女的，性别歧视的 **2** resulting from or connected with this belief 由于性别歧视的；与性别歧视有关的：*sexist attitudes* 性别歧视的态度—**sexist** *n* [C]

sex·less /ˈsɛkslɪs; ˈseksləs/ *adj* **1** not sexually attractive; not SEXY 缺乏性魅力的，不性感的 **2** neither male nor female; NEUTER¹ (1) 无性（别）的，无雌雄特征的；中性的

sex life /ˈ· ˌ·/ *n* [C] someone's sexual activities 性生活：*Jim's too busy to have much of a sex life.* 吉姆太忙，没有多少性生活。

sex-linked /ˈ· ˌ·/ *adj technical* an illness or medical condition that is sex-linked is caused by the GENES of only one sex and so is passed to children by parents of that sex【术语】性连锁的，伴性（遗传）的

sex ma·ni·ac /ˈ·,··/ *n* [C] someone who always wants to have sex, thinks about it all the time, and is unable to control these feelings 性欲狂者

sex ob·ject /ˈ·,··/ *n* [C] someone you consider only as a means of satisfying your sexual desire rather than as a whole person 发泄性欲的对象, 性玩物

sex of·fend·er /ˈ·,·,··/ *n* [C] someone who is guilty of a crime related to sex 性侵犯者, 性犯罪者

sex·ol·o·gy /sɛksˈɑlədʒɪ; sekˈsɒlədʒi/ *n* [U] the study of sexual behaviour, especially among humans〔尤指人类的〕性(行为)学 —**sexologist** *n* [C]

sex or·gan /ˈ·,··/ *n* [C] a part of the body concerned with the production of children, such as the PENIS or VAGINA 性器官, 生殖器官

Sex Pis·tols, The /ˈ·,··/ a British PUNK band who were popular in the mid-1970s and greatly influenced the punk style of clothes and music. Their members included Johnny Rotten and Sid Vicious. They deliberately shocked people with their violent behaviour, swearing, and lack of respect for the British royal family. Their records include *Anarchy in the UK*, and the ALBUM *Never Mind the Bollocks – Here's the Sex Pistols.* 性手枪乐队〔英国一支朋克乐队。该乐队流行于20世纪70年代中叶, 对朋克服饰和音乐风格产生了重大影响。成员中有约翰尼·罗顿和锡德·维舍斯。他们举止粗野, 口出不逊, 对王室不恭, 故做惊人之举。作品包括歌曲《英国的无政府主义》和专辑《别在乎那些废话 — 性手枪在此》〕

sex·ploi·ta·tion /ˌsɛksplɔɪˈteʃən; ˌseksplɔɪˈteɪʃən/ *n* [U] *informal* a word meaning the use of sex in films and magazines in order to make money, used by people who think this is wrong【非正式】〔在电影、杂志中为赚钱的〕色情利用

sex·pot /ˈsɛkspɑt; ˈsekspɒt/ *n* [C] *informal* a word meaning a sexually attractive woman, that many women think is offensive【非正式】性感的女人〔被多数女性视为是冒犯语〕

sex shop /ˈ··/ *n* [C] *BrE* a shop selling goods, magazines etc related to sex and sexual activities【英】〔出售色情杂志、性用具等的〕性用品商店

sex sym·bol /ˈ·,··/ *n* [C] someone who represents society's idea of what is sexually attractive 性感偶像: *sex symbols such as Madonna and Tom Cruise* 像麦当娜和汤姆·克鲁斯那样的性感偶像

sex·tant /ˈsɛkstənt; ˈsekstənt/ *n* [C] a tool for measuring angles between stars in order to calculate the position of your ship or aircraft 六分仪〔用于测量星与星之间的角度以计算船或飞机的位置〕

sex·tet /sɛksˈtɛt; seksˈtet/ *n* [C] **1** a group of six singers or musicians performing together 六重唱; 六重奏 **2** a piece of music for six performers: *Brahms' sextet in B flat* 勃拉姆斯的降B调六重奏曲

sex·ton /ˈsɛkstən; ˈsekstən/ *n* [C] someone who takes care of a church building, and sometimes rings the bells and digs graves 教堂司事〔负责管理教堂房屋、敲钟、挖掘墓穴等工作〕

sex·tu·plet /sɛkˈstʌplɪt; sekˈstjuːplɪ̈t/ *n* [C] one of six people who are born at the same time and have the same mother 六胞胎之一

[2] [2] **sex·u·al** /ˈsɛkʃuəl; ˈsekʃuəl/ *adj* **1** connected with sex 性的; 与性(生活)有关的: *a disease passed on by sexual contact* 由性接触传染的疾病 | *sexual relationships* 性关系 | *sexual desire* 性欲 **2** connected with the social relationships between men and women 性别的, 两性社会关系的: *sexual politics* 性别政治 **3** connected with the way people or animals have babies 生殖的: *sexual reproduction* 有性繁殖 —**sexually** *adv*: *sexually experienced* 性经验丰富的 | *sexually attractive* 具有性吸引力的

sexual har·ass·ment /···ˈ···/ *n* [U] unwelcome touching or remarks about sex from someone, especially if you are expected to accept this to make progress in your job〔尤指利用工作之便的〕性骚扰

sexual in·ter·course /,···ˈ···/ *n* [U] *formal* the act of two people having sex with each other【正式】性交

sex·u·al·i·ty /ˌsɛkʃuˈælətɪ; ˌsekʃuˈælɪ̈ti/ *n* [U] the things people do and feel that are connected with their desire or ability to have sex 性欲; 性能力; 性行为: *Sexuality was never discussed.* 性的问题从未讨论过。| **male/female sexuality** *a study of male sexuality* 对男性性行为的研究

sex·u·al·ly trans·mit·ted dis·ease /,····,··ˈ·/ *n* [C,U] STD; a disease that is passed on through sexual intercourse, such as AIDS, HERPES etc 性传播疾病〈如艾滋病、疱疹等〉

sex·y /ˈsɛksɪ; ˈseksi/ *adj* **sexier, sexiest 1** sexually exciting or attractive 引起情欲的, 性感的: *Oh, don't you think he's sexy?* 啊, 难道你不认为他性感吗? | *a sexy picture* 性感的图片 **2** *informal* exciting to think about or use【非正式】吸引人的; 令人兴奋的: *Constitutional change is not a sexy issue.* 宪法的修改不是一个令人兴奋的问题。| *sexy computer software* 诱人的电脑软件 —**sexily** *adv* —**sexiness** *n* [U] —see 见 BEAUTIFUL (USAGE)

Seychelles, the /seˈʃɛlz; seɪˈʃelz/ a country which is consists of about 85 small islands in the Indian Ocean, to the east of Kenya. Population: 79,715 (2001). Capital: Victoria. It is popular with tourists. 塞舌尔〔印度洋一国家。由大约85个小岛组成, 位于肯尼亚以东。人口: 79,715 (2001), 首都: 维多利亚。该国为旅游胜地〕—**Seychellois** /seʃɛlˈwɑ; ˌseɪʃelˈwɑː◂/ *n, adj*

SF /ˌɛs ˈɛf; ˌes ˈef/ *adj* the abbreviation of 缩写= SCIENCE FICTION

Sgt the written abbreviation of 缩写= SERGEANT

sh /ʃ; ʃ/ *interjection* used to tell someone to be quiet 嘘!别作声!〔用于要求某人安静〕: *Sh! I'm trying to sleep.* 嘘, 安静点! 我要睡觉了。 [3]

Shabbat Saturday /ʃəˌbɑt ˈsætədɪ; ʃəˌbɑːt ˈsætədi/ considered as a day of rest and prayer in the Jewish religion 安息日〔犹太教的休息日和祈祷日〕

shab·by /ˈʃæbɪ; ˈʃæbi/ *adj* **1** untidy and in a bad condition from being used for a long time 肮脏破旧的: *a shabby suit* 又脏又旧的套服 | *shabby hotel rooms* 破旧的旅馆房间 **2** wearing clothes that are old and worn 衣衫褴褛的, 衣着寒酸的: *a shabby tramp* 衣衫褴褛的流浪汉 **3** unfair and unkind 不公平的; 不仁慈的: *That's a shabby way to treat someone.* 这样待人是不公正的。| *a shabby trick* 卑鄙的花招 —**shabbily** *adv* —**shabbiness** *n* [U]

Sha·bu·oth /ʃəˈvot; ʃəˈvuːəs/ —see 见 PENTECOST

shack¹ /ʃæk; ʃæk/ *n* [C] a small building that has not been built very well 简陋的小屋, 棚屋: *a tin shack* 铁皮棚屋

shack² *v*

shack up *phr v* [I] *informal* to start living with someone who you have sex with but are not married to【非正式】〔未婚者〕同居: **shack up together/with** *Last I heard, they were shacked up together in Croydon.* 最近一次我听说, 他们在克罗伊登同居。

shack·le¹ /ˈʃækl; ˈʃækəl/ *n* [C] **1 the shackles of slavery/convention etc** *literary* the limits put on your freedom and happiness by SLAVERY etc【文】奴隶制/传统等的枷锁 **2** one of a pair of metal rings joined by a chain that are used for fastening together a prisoner's hands or feet 镣铐; 手镣; 脚镣

shackle² *v* [T] **1** to put many limits on what someone can do 束缚, 羁绊: *Industrial progress is being shackled by a mass of regulations.* 工业的进步正受到诸多规定的束缚。**2** to put shackles on someone 给〔某人〕戴上镣铐

Shackleton /ˈʃækltən; ˈʃækəltən/**, Ernest** /ˈɝnɪst; ˈɜːnɪ̈st/ (1874-1922) a British EXPLORER of the Antarctic. He was a member of the EXPEDITION led by Robert Scott, and then led three more expeditions himself. He found the south MAGNETIC POLE in 1908-09, and died on his fourth expedition. 沙克尔顿〔(1874-1922), 英国南极探险家, 罗伯特·斯科特领导的探险队成员之一。后来, 他自己率队三次前往南极探险, 1908至1909年发现了南极磁场, 在第四次探险途中遇难〕

shad /ʃæd; ʃæd/ *n* [C,U] a north Atlantic fish used for food 西鲱〔产于北大西洋的食用鱼〕

shade 荫

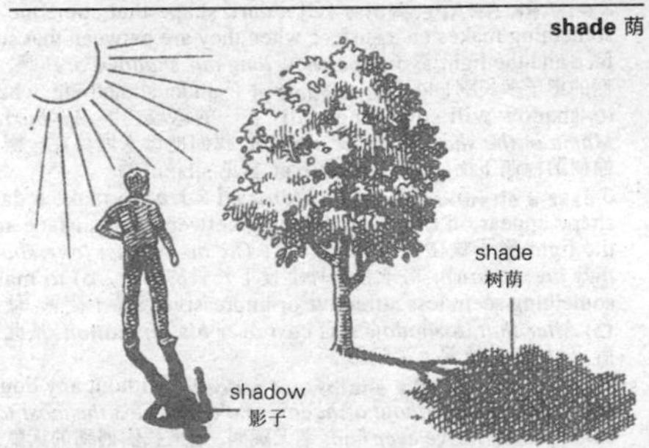

shade¹ /ʃed; ʃeɪd/ *n*

1 ►SLIGHT DARKNESS 阴暗◄[U] slight darkness or shelter from the direct light of the sun made by something blocking it 荫, 背阴处: *a plant that likes a lot of shade* 喜阴的植物 | **in the shade** *Let's find a table in the shade.* 我们在阴凉处找张桌子吧。| *It's 35°C in the shade.* 背阴处的气温为35°C。| **in the shade of a tree/wall etc** *sitting in the shade of a large oak tree* 坐在一棵大橡树的树荫下 —compare 比较 SHADOW¹ (1)

2 ►FOR BLOCKING LIGHT 用于遮光◄[C] **a)** something you

use to reduce or block light 遮光物: **lampshade/eyeshade** (=over a lamp, or above your eyes) 灯罩/遮光帽檐[眼罩] **b)** *AmE* a BLIND³ (1)【美】〔能上下卷叠的〕窗帘, 百叶窗

3 shades [plural] *informal* SUNGLASSES【非正式】太阳镜, 墨镜

4 ▶IN A PICTURE 在图画中◀ [U] the dark places in a picture 〔图画等中的〕阴影, 阴暗部分: **light and shade** *using light and shade to mould figures* 用明暗来勾画图形

5 ▶COLOUR 颜色◀ [C] a particular kind of red, green, blue etc 〔某一色彩的〕浓淡, 深浅, 色度: **[+of]** *a wonderful shade of pink* 一种浓淡恰到好处的粉红色

6 shade of meaning/opinion/feeling etc a meaning etc that is slightly different from other ones; NUANCE 有细微差别的含义/意见/情感等: *various shades of opinion in the party* 党内各种不同的意见

7 a shade *formal* very slightly【正式】有点, 略为: *Ken was just a shade too honest about his feelings.* 肯对待感情未免有点太老实了。

8 shades of used to say that something reminds you of someone or something else, especially when you would rather forget 使人联想起〔尤指宁愿忘却的人或事〕: *Huh. Shades of my poorer days.* 嘿, 这又使我想起那些穷日子。

9 put sth in the shade to be so good or impressive that other similar things or people seem much less important or interesting 使某事物逊色: *Well Arthur, your choir puts our little town chorus in the shade.* 噢, 阿瑟, 你们的合唱队使我们这个小镇的歌咏队黯然失色了。

10 *literary* the spirit of a dead person; GHOST¹ (1)【文】幽灵, 鬼魂

11 have it made in the shade *AmE informal* to be extremely rich【美, 非正式】极其富有

shade² *v* [T] **1** to protect something from direct light 为…遮阳[挡光], 遮蔽〔光线〕: *See, the yucca plant's being shaded by that tree.* 看, 这株丝兰被那棵树挡住阳光了。| **shade your eyes/face etc** *Shading her eyes, Anita scanned the horizon.* 安妮塔用手挡住阳光, 仔细眺望地平线。**2** also 又作 **shade in** to make part of a picture or drawing darker 将〔图画某部分的〕颜色加深; 画阴影于〔图画的某部分〕: *You still need to shade in that bit there.* 你还要把那一小块画得暗些。

shade into sth *phr v* [T] if one thing shades into another, it is impossible to tell where one stops and another starts 渐渐与分辨不清, 逐渐融合于: *Sea shades into sky at the horizon.* 在地平线处, 海天融为一体。| *Right and wrong often shade into each other.* 正确和错误之间常常无明确界限。

shad·ing /ˈʃedɪŋ; ˈʃeɪdɪŋ/ *n* **1** [U] the areas of a drawing or painting that have been made to look darker 〔图画中〕较暗的部分 **2 shadings** [plural] slight differences between things, situations, or ideas 〔事物、情况、意见等的〕细微差别

shad·ow¹ /ˈʃædo; ˈʃædəʊ/ *n*

1 ▶DARKNESS 黑暗◀ [U] also 又作 **shadows** *plural* darkness caused by something preventing light from entering a place 阴影, 暗影, 阴暗区: **in shadow** *The room was half in shadow.* 这房间有一半是暗的。| **in the shadows** *a thief lurking in the shadows* 潜伏在阴暗处的小偷

2 ▶DARK SHAPE 黑影◀ [C] a dark shape that someone or something makes on a surface when they are between that surface and the light 影子: *Look how long our shadows are!* 瞧, 我们的影子多长啊! | **in the shadow of** (=under something, where its shadow will sometimes fall) 在…的遮蔽之下 *We buried Mama in the shadow of the old elm.* 我们把母亲埋葬在一棵老榆树的树荫下面。—see picture at 参见 SHADE¹ 图

3 cast a shadow over/on *literary*【文】**a)** to make a dark shape appear on a surface by being between that surface and the light 影了映在…, 投影于…上: *The house cast long shadows on the lawn.* 房子在草坪上投下长长的影子。**b)** to make something seem less attractive or impressive 使蒙上阴影; 使逊色: *After that, a shadow was cast over his reputation.* 从此以后, 他的声誉便蒙上了阴影。

4 without/beyond a shadow of a doubt without any doubt at all 毫无疑问: *Without a shadow of a doubt he's the most talented player we've ever had.* 毫无疑问, 他是我们遇到的天赋最高的选手。

5 be in sb's shadow to be less happy and successful than you could be because someone else gets noticed much more 在某人的盛名之下〔显得逊色〕: *Kate grew up in the shadow of her film star sister.* 凯特在她那位影星姐姐的盛名笼罩之下长大。

6 be a shadow of your former self to be so unhappy that you seem like a different person 因很不愉快而前后判若两人

7 shadows under sb's eyes small dark areas under someone's eyes that show they are tired 眼睛下面的黑圈〔表示疲劳〕

8 sb's shadow someone who follows someone else everywhere they go 形影不离的人; 某人的跟随者 —see also 另见 **afraid of your own shadow** (AFRAID (4)), FIVE O'CLOCK SHADOW

shadow² *v* [T] **1** to follow someone closely in order to watch what they are doing 跟踪, 尾随, 盯…的梢: *Detectives shadowed them for weeks, collecting evidence.* 侦探跟踪他们好几个星期收集证据。**2** [usually passive 一般用被动态] *literary* to cover something with a shadow, or make it dark【文】投阴影于; 遮蔽: *a shadowed alley* 阴暗的小巷

shadow³ *adj* **1 shadow chancellor/foreign secretary etc** the politician in the main opposition party in the British parliament who would become CHANCELLOR (1) etc if their party was in government, and who is responsible for speaking on the same subjects 影子财政大臣/外交大臣〔指英国议会中, 主要反对党若执政时成为财政大臣等的人〕**2 shadow cabinet** the group of politicians in the British parliament who would become ministers if their party was in government 影子内阁〔指英国议会中, 若其政党执政则会成为部长的一群政治家〕

shadow box·ing /ˈ· ·, ·ˈ/ *n* [U] fighting with an imaginary opponent, especially as training for BOXING〔尤指拳击训练时〕与假想对手的拳击, 假想拳

shadow pup·pet /ˈ· ·, ·ˈ/ *n* [C] a flat PUPPET that makes special shapes on a wall when you shine a light behind it 影偶

shad·ow·y /ˈʃædəwɪ; ˈʃædəʊi/ *adj* **1** mysterious and difficult to know anything about 神秘的, 难以捉摸的: **shadowy figure** *Anastasia Romanov is a shadowy figure.* 阿纳斯塔西娅·罗曼诺娃是个神秘的人物。**2** full of shadows, or difficult to see because of shadows 多阴影的; 幽暗的; 模糊的: *a shadowy room* 幽暗的房间

shad·y /ˈʃedɪ; ˈʃeɪdi/ *adj* **1** protected from the sun or producing shade 遮阳的; 背阴的, 成荫的: *the shady side of the street* 街道背阴的一边 | *shady trees* 多荫的树木 **2** probably dishonest or illegal 可能不诚实的, 可疑的; 不正当的: *a shady character* 可疑的人物 | *She's been involved in some shady deals.* 她卷进了一些不正当的交易。

shaft¹ /ʃæft; ʃɑːft/ *n*

1 ▶HANDLE 柄◀ [C] a long handle on a tool, SPEAR etc 〔工具的〕长柄; 矛杆 —see picture on page A23 参见A23页图

2 ▶PASSAGE 通道◀ [C] a passage which goes up through a building or down into the ground, so that someone or something can get in or out 竖井: **mine/elevator/ventilation shaft** *a 300-foot elevator shaft* 一个300英尺的电梯井

3 shaft of light/sunlight [C] a narrow beam of light 一道光线/阳光

4 ▶ENGINE PART 引擎部件◀ [C] a thin long piece of metal in an engine or machine that turns and passes on power or movement to another part of the machine 〔机器的〕轴; 传动轴

5 ▶FOR A HORSE 马用的◀ [C usually plural 一般用复数] one of a pair of poles between which a horse is tied to pull a vehicle 〔马车的〕辕

6 shaft of wit [C] *literary* a clever amusing remark, especially an unkind one【文】机智风趣的话〔尤指挖苦话〕

7 ▶ARROW 箭◀ [C] *literary* an ARROW (1)【文】(一枝)箭

8 give sb the shaft *AmE slang* to treat someone unfairly, for example by dismissing them from their job without a good reason【美俚】不公正地对待某人, 亏待某人〈如无理辞退〉

shaft² *v* [T] *slang* to treat someone unfairly, especially by dishonestly getting money from them【俚】不公正地对待〔尤指骗钱〕: *We really got shafted in that computer deal.* 我们在那宗电脑交易中的确吃了亏。

Shaftes·bu·ry Av·e·nue /ˌʃæftsbɛrɪ ˈævɪnu; ˌʃɑːftsbəri ˈævənjuː/ a street in central London where there are many theatres 沙夫茨伯里大道〔伦敦市中心一大街。沿街有许多剧院〕

shag¹ /ʃæg; ʃæg/ *adj* **shag carpet/rug** a CARPET¹ (1) or RUG (1) with a rough surface made from long threads of wool 长绒地毯

shag² *n* **1** [C] *BrE taboo* an act of having sex with someone【英讳】性交 **2** [C] a large black sea bird 长鼻鸬鹚 **3** [U] strong-tasting TOBACCO with thick leaves cut into small thin pieces 浓味烟丝

shag³ *v* [I,T] *BrE taboo* to have sex with someone【英讳】(与某人)性交

shagged /ʃægd; ʃægd/ also 又作 **shagged out** /ˌ· ˈ·/ *adj BrE slang taboo* very tired【英俚, 讳】疲惫不堪的, 精疲力竭的: *I'm not going – I'm too shagged!* 我不去了, 太累了!

shag·gy /ˈʃægɪ; ˈʃægi/ *adj* **1** shaggy hair or fur is long and untidy〔头发、毛等〕又长又乱的, 蓬乱的: *a shaggy black beard* 蓬乱的黑胡子 **2** having shaggy hair 有乱蓬蓬毛发的: *a shaggy sheepskin coat* 表面粗糙的羊皮外套 —**shagginess** *n* [U]

shaggy dog sto·ry /ˌ· ˈ· ˌ·, ·ˈ/ *n* [C] a long joke that often ends in a silly or disappointing way 冗长的笑话〔其结尾通常很无聊, 令人失望〕

Shah /ʃɑ; ʃɑː/ *n* [C] the title of the kings of Iran, used in the past 沙〔旧时伊朗国王的称号〕

Shah Ja·han /ˌʃɑ dʒəˋhɑn; ˌʃɑː dʒəˈhɑːn/ (1592-1666) an EMPEROR (=ruler) of northern India from 1628 to 1658, who many people consider the greatest of the Mogul family of Indian emperors. Shah Jahan built the Taj Mahal and many other impressive buildings. 沙·贾汗〔(1592-1666)，北印度王朝一皇帝。1628至1658年在位，被认为是印度莫卧儿王朝最伟大的皇帝。他下令建造了泰姬陵等许多宏伟建筑〕

S3 W2 **shake**[1] /ʃek; ʃeɪk/ *past tense* **shook** /ʃuk; ʃʊk/ *past participle* **shaken** /ˋʃekən; ˈʃeɪkən/ *v*

shake 摇动

1 ►MOVEMENT 动作◄ [I] to move up and down or from side to side with quick repeated movements〔上下或左右〕摇动，摇撼；颤抖: *His hand shook as he signed the paper.* 他在文件上签名时手在发颤。| *The ground was shaking beneath their feet.* 大地在他们脚下颤动。| **shake with anger/fear/laughter etc** (=be so angry, frightened etc that you cannot stop shaking) 气得/怕得/笑得浑身发抖 | **shake like a leaf** (=shake a lot, especially because you are very nervous or frightened)〔因紧张、害怕而〕全身发抖 *What's the matter? You're shaking like a leaf.* 怎么回事？你浑身在发抖。

2 ►SHAKE STH 摇动某物◄ [T] to make something or someone move up and down or from side to side with quick repeated movements 抖；使摇动；使颤抖: *The blast shook windows five miles away.* 爆炸使五英里以外的窗户都颤动了。| **shake sth onto/out/over etc** *Shake the sand out of your shoes.* 把你鞋里的沙子抖掉。

3 ►SHAKE SB 摇晃某人◄ [T] to hold someone by their shoulders and push and pull them backwards and fowards roughly, especially because you are angry with them〔尤指生气时抓住某人的肩膀〕摇晃，猛摇: *She was being such a brat, I felt like shaking her.* 她那样淘气，我真想揪住她晃几下。

4 shake your head to move your head from side to side as a way of saying no 摇头〔表示"不"〕: *He didn't reply, but just shook his head.* 他不回答，只是摇头。

5 shake hands (with) also 又作 **shake sb's hand/shake sb by the hand** to move someone's hand up and down with your own hand as a greeting or as a sign you have agreed something (与某人) 握手: *Wilkinson shook my hand warmly.* 威尔金森热情地和我握手。

6 shake on it *spoken* to agree on a decision or business agreement by shaking hands【口】握手为定: *Let's shake on it.* 让我们握手为定吧。

7 be shaken to feel very shocked and upset 感到震惊；受到惊吓；被弄得心烦意乱: *Kerrie was so shaken by the attack that she still won't go out alone.* 凯利被那次袭击吓坏了，现在还不愿意单独外出。

8 shake sb's confidence/faith/belief to make someone feel less confident, less sure about their beliefs etc 动摇某人的信心/信仰/信念

9 shake your fist to show that you are angry by holding up and shaking your tightly closed hand 挥动拳头〔表示愤怒〕

10 ►VOICE 声音◄ [I] if your voice shakes it sounds nervous or uncertain〔因精神紧张等而〕声音发颤: *Reg's voice shook with rage.* 雷吉气得声音发颤。

11 shake a leg *spoken* used to tell someone to start doing something now【口】赶忙，赶紧，快点儿〔用以催促别人开始做某事〕: *C'mon you guys, shake a leg! We haven't got all day.* 喂，你们这些家伙，快点啦！我们没有多少时间了。

12 shake in your shoes/boots *informal* to be very nervous【非正式】非常紧张: *I was shaking in my shoes – I thought he'd give me the sack.* 我紧张得要命，以为他要解雇我了。

shake down *phr v* **1** [I] *BrE informal* to get used to a new situation that you are working or living in【英，非正式】适应新环境，安顿下来 **2** [T **shake** sb **down**] *AmE informal* to get money from someone by using threats【美，非正式】敲诈，勒索〔某人〕 **3** [T **shake** sb/sth ↔ **down**] *AmE informal* to search a person or place thoroughly【美，非正式】彻底搜查 **4** [T **shake** sth ↔ **down**] *BrE* to test a ship or plane under real conditions【英】对〔船或飞机〕进行试航 —see 见 SHAKEDOWN **5** [I **+in/on etc**] *BrE informal* to sleep on the floor, on a seat etc, instead of in a proper bed【英，非正式】在没有床的地方凑合着睡〈如睡地板、椅子等〉

shake sb/sth ↔ **off** *phr v* **1** [T **shake** sth ↔ **off**] to get rid of an illness, problem etc 治好〔疾病〕；摆脱〔问题〕: *I can't seem to shake off this cold.* 我好像就是没法治好这感冒。**2** [T] to escape from someone who is chasing you 甩掉〔跟踪者〕，摆脱〔追赶者〕

shake sth ↔ **out** *phr v* [T] to shake a cloth, a bag, a sheet etc so that any small pieces of dirt, dust etc come off 把…抖落干净: *Shake the crumbs out of the tablecloth.* 把桌布上的面包屑抖干净。

shake sb/sth ↔ **up** *phr v* [T] **1** [T **shake** sb ↔ **up**] to give someone a very unpleasant shock, so that they feel very upset and frightened 使震惊；使震动；使不安: *Seeing that accident really shook me up.* 目睹那次事故，我真的被吓坏了。—see also 另见 SHAKEN **2** [T] to make changes to an organization in order to make it more effective 改组〔机构〕，整顿 —see also 另见 SHAKEUP

shake[2] *n* **1** [C] an act of shaking 摇动，摇晃: **give sth a shake** *Give the bottle a good shake before you pour.* 倒出前先把瓶子好好摇一摇。| **shake of the head** (=a movement of the head from side to side to say no) 摇头 *She just refuses with a smile and a shake of the head.* 她微笑着摇头拒绝。**2 the shakes** *not technical* a nervous shaking of your body caused by illness, fear, too much alcohol etc【非术语】〔因生病、恐惧、喝酒过多等而〕哆嗦: **get the shakes** *As soon as they left I started getting the shakes.* 他们一走，我就开始打哆嗦。**3 in a couple of shakes/two shakes** *informal* very soon【非正式】一刹那，立刻，马上: *We'll be back in a couple of shakes.* 我们马上就回来。**4 no great shakes** *spoken* not very skilful【口】技术并不高明的，不大出色的: *He's no great shakes, but he's better than the last chef they had.* 他算不上厨艺高超，但比他们上次雇的那位厨师长要强些。**5** [C] *AmE* a cold drink made from milk that tastes of fruit, chocolate etc; MILK SHAKE【美】泡沫牛奶，奶昔〔牛奶与水果、巧克力等搅打而成的饮料〕 **6 fair shake** *AmE informal* fair treatment【美，非正式】公正的对待，公平的待遇: *Dave didn't get his fair shake – everyone else had the chance of an interview.* 戴夫没有得到公平的待遇——其他人个个都有一次面试的机会。

shake·down /ˋʃekˌdaun; ˈʃeɪkdaʊn/ *n* **1** [C] *AmE informal* the act of getting money from someone by using threats【美，非正式】敲诈，勒索 **2** [C] *AmE informal* a thorough search of a place or a person【美，非正式】彻底搜查 **3** [C] a final test of a boat, plane etc before it is put into general use〔船、飞机等的〕最后测试，试航: *a shakedown flight* 试飞 **4** [singular] *BrE informal* a place prepared as a bed on the floor, on a seat etc【英，非正式】〔地板、椅子等上的〕临时床铺

shak·en /ˋʃekən; ˈʃeɪkən/ also 又作 **shaken up** *adj* [not usually before noun 一般不用于名词前] upset, shocked, or frightened 心烦的；震惊的；受惊的: *"How's Jacob?" "Pretty shaken up, but nothing's broken."* "雅各布怎么样?" "几乎吓坏了，不过有惊无险。"

shake·out /ˋʃekˌaut; ˈʃeɪkaʊt/ *n* **1** [C usually singular 一般用单数] a situation in which several companies fail because they cannot compete with stronger companies in difficult economic conditions〔在困难的经济条件下〕某些公司无法与大公司竞争而被淘汰 **2** [C] a SHAKEUP 改组，重新组合

shak·er /ˋʃekɚ; ˈʃeɪkə/ *n* [C] **1** a container with holes in the lid, used to shake sugar etc onto food〔盖上有小孔的〕佐料瓶: *a salt shaker* 盐瓶 **2** also 又作 **cocktail shaker** a container in which drinks are mixed 鸡尾酒调酒器 **3** a small container for shaking DICE[1] (1) 色子盒 —see also 另见 **movers and shakers** (MOVER (4))

Shakes·peare /ˋʃekspɪr; ˈʃeɪkspɪə/, **William** (1564-1616) an English writer of plays and poems, born in Stratford-on-Avon in England, who most people regard as the greatest of all English writers. His many famous plays include the tragedies (TRAGEDY) *Romeo and Juliet*, *Julius Caesar*, *Hamlet*, *Macbeth*, *Othello*, and *King Lear*; the comedies (COMEDY) *A Midsummer Night's Dream*, *Twelfth Night*, and *As You Like It*; and the historical plays *Richard III* and *Henry V*. Many well-known English sayings come from Shakespeare's work, and he had a great influence on the English language and English literature. Shakespeare also wrote poetry, including the Sonnets, and worked as an actor at the Globe Theatre in London. 莎士比亚〔(1564-1616)，英国剧作家、诗人。生于英格兰埃文河畔的斯特拉特福，被认为是英国最伟大的作家。他

William Shakespeare 威廉·莎士比亚

创作了大量著名剧作，包括《罗密欧与朱丽叶》、《尤利乌斯·凯撒》、《哈姆雷特》、《麦克白》、《奥塞罗》、《李尔王》等悲剧，《仲夏夜之梦》、《第十二夜》、《皆大欢喜》等喜剧，以及《理查三世》、《亨利五世》等历史剧。英语中的许多名言佳句均出自于莎士比亚的剧本。他对英国语言文字和英国文学产生了巨大影响。莎士比亚还创作诗歌，其中包括十四行诗。他还在伦敦环球剧院当过演员〕

Shakes·pea·re·an /ʃekˋspɪrɪən; ʃeɪkˈspɪəriən/ *adj* [only before noun 仅用于名词前] **1** in the style of Shakespeare 莎士比亚风格的: *an almost Shakespearean richness of language* 近乎莎士比亚那样丰富多彩的语言 **2** connected with the work of Shakespeare (涉及) 莎士比亚作品的: *a famous Shakespearean actor* 莎士比亚戏剧的著名演员

shake·up /ˋʃek,ʌp; ˈʃeɪkʌp/ *n* [C] a process by which an organization makes a lot of big changes in a short time to improve its effectiveness 改组，重新组合: *a huge shakeup of the education system* 教育体制的大改组

shak·y /ˋʃekɪ; ˈʃeɪki/ *adj* **1** weak and unsteady because of old age, illness or shock〔因年迈、疾病、惊吓而〕摇晃的; 颤抖的; 衰弱的: *shaky voice* 颤抖的声音 | **be shaky on your feet** (=not able to walk very well) 步履不稳 *Grandad was a little shaky on his feet after the accident.* 爷爷在那次事故之后走路有点不稳。**2** not thorough, complete, or certain 不全面的; 不完整的; 没有把握的: *My knowledge of history is a little shaky.* 我的历史知识不够全面。| *shaky evidence* 不可靠的证据 **3** not firm or steady 不牢的，不稳固的: *shaky foundations* 不牢固的基础 —**shakily** *adv* —**shakiness** *n* [U]

shale /ʃel; ʃeɪl/ *n* [U] a smooth soft rock which breaks easily into thin flat pieces 页岩

S3 W1 **shall** /ʃəl; ʃəl *strong* 强读 ʃæl; ʃæl/ *modal verb negative short form* 否定缩略式= **shan't** **1 I/we shall** used to express what you will do in the future 我/我们将要〔用于表示未来要做的事〕: *We shall be away next week.* 我们下周不在这里。| *I shall have finished it by Friday.* 到星期五我就做完了。**2 shall I/we?** *BrE* used to make a suggestion, or ask a question that you want the other person to decide about【英】…好吗? 要不要…?〔用于提建议或要求他人作决定的问句中〕: *Shall I open the window?* 我要开窗吗? | *What shall I get for dinner?* 我弄些什么来作晚餐? | *Shall we say 6 o'clock, then?* 那么，我们就定在6点钟好吗? **3 you/he/she/they shall** *formal or old-fashioned* used to describe what will happen to someone, especially when you are saying that it is very definite【正式或过时】你(们)/他/她/他们一定会[一定要]〔用于表示必然性和必要性〕: *They shall be judged only by God.* 他们一定只会受到上帝的审判。| *I said you could go, and so you shall.* 我说过你能去，所以你一定要去。**4 we shall see** *spoken* used when you do not know what will happen in the future, or when you do not want to give someone a definite answer【口】我们看看再说〔用于不清楚将会发生何事或不想给某人明确答复之时〕 **5** *formal* used in official documents to show a law, command, promise etc【正式】应该，必须〔用于正式文件中，表示法律、命令、允诺等〕: *All payments shall be made by the end of the month.* 所有款项必须在月底前付清。

shal·lot /ʃəˋlɑt; ʃəˈlɒt/ *n* [C] a vegetable like a small onion 青葱

shal·low¹ /ˋʃælo; ˈʃæləʊ/ *adj* **1** something that is shallow has only a short distance from the bottom to the surface 浅的，不深的: *a shallow river* 浅河 | *the shallow end of the swimming pool* 游泳池的浅水区 | *a shallow grave* 埋得浅的坟墓 —see picture at 参见 LOW¹ 图 **2** not interested in or showing any understanding of important or serious matters〔对问题的理解等〕肤浅的，浅薄的: *a shallow argument* 肤浅的论点 | *If he's only interested in your looks, that just shows how shallow he is.* 如果他只是对你的外貌感兴趣，那正好说明他多么浅薄。**3 shallow breathing** breathing that only takes in small amounts of air 浅呼吸〔吸入少量空气〕 —**shallowly** *adv* —**shallowness** *n* [U]

shallow² *v* [I] to become shallow 变浅

shal·lows, the /ˋʃæloz; ˈʃæləʊz/ *n* an area of shallow water 浅水区，浅滩: *We could see fish darting about in the shallows.* 我们可以看见鱼儿在浅水区游来游去。

Sha·lom /ʃæˋlom; ʃæˈlɒm/ *interjection* a Jewish word used to say hello or goodbye 喂，你好; 再见〔犹太人打招呼或告别用语〕

shalt /ʃəlt; ʃəlt; *strong* 强读 ʃælt; ʃælt/ *v* **thou shalt** *old use*【旧】= you shall

sham¹ /ʃæm; ʃæm/ *n* **1** [singular] an attempt to deceive people by pretending something is true or good, especially when it is easy to see that it is not 虚伪，伪善; 假象: *These so-called democratic reforms are a complete sham.* 这些所谓的民主改革全是假象。**2** [singular] someone who pretends to be something they are not, especially to gain an advantage or sympathy〔尤指要得到好处或同情的〕假冒者，假装者: *He was bogus, a sham, an imposter!* 他是伪装的，一个假冒者，一个骗子! **3** [U] behaviour or actions intended to deceive people by pretending that something is true or good 虚假行为; 假冒; 假装

sham² *adj* [only before noun 仅用于名词前] made to appear real in order to deceive people; false 假的; 仿制的; 伪造的; 冒充的: *sham jewellery* 假珠宝

sham³ *v* [I,T] to pretend to be upset, ill etc to gain sympathy or an advantage 假装，佯装〔苦恼、生病等〕: *She's not ill, she's only shamming.* 她没有病，只不过是装病罢了。

sha·man /ˋʃɑmən; ˈʃɑːmən/ *n* [C] someone with religious authority in some tribes, who is believed to be able to talk to spirits, cure illnesses etc 萨满 (教巫师) —**shamanism** *n* [U]

sham·ble /ˋʃæmbḷ; ˈʃæmbəl/ *v* [I always+adv/prep] to walk slowly and awkwardly, dragging your feet in a tired, weak, or lazy way〔疲倦地或懒洋洋地〕拖着脚走; 蹒跚而行: [**+along/past/out etc**] *The old man shambled out of the room muttering to himself.* 那个老人蹒跚着走出房间，口中喃喃自语。| **shambling gait** (=a shambling way of walking) 步履蹒跚

sham·bles /ˋʃæmbḷz; ˈʃæmbəlz/ *n informal*【非正式】**a shambles a)** an event or situation that is a complete failure because it has not been organized or planned properly〔因缺乏组织或计划而造成事情的〕失败; 一团糟; 混乱场面: **be (in) a shambles** *By 1985 the economy was in a shambles.* 到1985年，经济已经变得一团糟。| **make a shambles of sth** *Potts, you made a complete shambles of that speech.* 波茨，你的演讲杂乱无章。**b)** a place where there is a lot of damage, destruction, and confusion 遭严重破坏的地方; 凌乱的景象: *This kitchen is a shambles!* 这个厨房凌乱不堪!

sham·bol·ic /ʃæmˋbɑlɪk; ʃæmˈbɒlɪk/ *adj informal* lacking organization or planning【非正式】混乱的，凌乱的: *The way they run this place is totally shambolic.* 他们对这个地方的管理完全杂乱无章。

shame¹ /ʃem; ʃeɪm/ *n* **1 it's a shame (that)/what a shame!** S2 *spoken* used to say that a situation is disappointing, and you wish things had happened differently【口】…真遗憾! 多可惜啊!: *It's a shame you have to leave so soon.* 真遗憾，你们那么快就得走了。| *Oh it's raining. What a shame!* 啊，下雨了，真糟糕! **2** [U] the uncomfortable feeling of being guilty and embarrassed that you have when you have done something wrong〔因做错事感到的〕羞愧，羞耻，惭愧: *a deep sense of shame* 深深的羞愧感 | **to your shame** (=making you feel ashamed) 使你感到惭愧 *She realized to her shame that she had forgotten Nina's birthday.* 她感到不好意思，居然忘了尼娜的生日。| **hang/bow your head in shame** (=look downwards and avoid looking at other people because you feel ashamed) 惭愧地低下头来 **3 Shame on you!** *spoken* used to tell someone that they should feel shame because of something they have done【口】你应该感到羞耻! **4** [U only in questions and negatives 仅用于疑问句和否定句] the ability to feel shame 羞愧感，羞耻之心: *How could you do such a thing? Have you no shame?* 你怎么能做出这种事? 你难道就不知道羞耻吗? **5 put sb/sth to shame** *informal* to be so much better than someone or something else that it makes the other thing seem very bad or ordinary【非正式】使某人/某物黯然失色，使某人/某物相形见绌: *His cooking puts mine to shame.* 与他的烹饪技术相比，我大为逊色。**6** [U] loss of honour and respect 耻辱，丢脸: **there is no shame in sth** (=it should not make you feel ashamed) 某事并非耻辱 *There's no shame in being poor.* 贫穷并不是耻辱。| **bring shame on sb** *You've brought shame on this family.* 你已经使这个家庭蒙羞了。

USAGE NOTE 用法说明: SHAME

WORD CHOICE 词语辨析: **shame, embarrassment, ashamed, feel silly, embarrassed**

Shame is an uncomfortable feeling you have when you have done something wrong, and you feel that people will no longer respect you. If you make a mistake this may cause **embarrassment**, but not usually **shame** because **shame** is much stronger. shame (羞耻，羞愧) 指做了错事，担心自己不再受人尊重，因而产生的一种不自在的感觉。如果犯了一般性错误或有失误，那就可能感到 embarrassment (不好意思)，但通常不用 shame，因为它的意思要强得多。

Ashamed (adj) is not quite so strong, but still not usually used about unimportant or accidental things. 形容词 ashamed (惭愧的) 的意思不那么强，但也不用于小事或偶然的失误上: *I couldn't think of anything to say and felt silly/embarrassed* (NOT 不用 *ashamed*). 我想不出该说些什么，觉得有点不好意思。However, someone might be **ashamed** if they are caught cheating in test, for example, because they have done something morally wrong. 不过，做了有损道德的错事，例如在考试中作弊被抓住，那就可能感到 ashamed (羞愧) 了。

shame² *v* **1** [T] **shame sb** to make someone feel ashamed 使某人感到羞耻: *It shames me to say it, but I lied.* 说出来令我羞愧，但我是撒了谎。**2 shame sb into doing sth** to force someone to do something by making them feel ashamed 使某人因羞愧而不得不做某事: *His wife shamed him into handing the money back.* 他的妻子使他羞愧得只好把钱交回去。**3** to be so much better than someone else that you make them seem bad or feel embarrassed 使黯然失色，使相形见绌: *They have a training record that would shame most other companies.* 他们的培训记录很好，足以使其他大多数公司相形见绌。**4** make someone feel that they have lost honour and respect 使蒙羞，玷辱: **shame sb** *Your cowardice has shamed us all.* 你的懦弱行为使我们大家蒙羞。

shame·faced /ˋʃem͵fest; ͵ʃeɪmˈfeɪst◂/ *adj* looking ashamed or embarrassed about having behaved badly 羞怯的，惭愧的: *"You really blew it, Ian." He nodded, shamefaced.* "你确实把事情搞糟了，伊恩。"他点了点头，面带愧色。—**shamefacedly** /-͵fesɪdlɪ; -ˈfeɪsɨdli/ *adv*

shame·ful /ˋʃemfəl; ˈʃeɪmfəl/ *adj* shameful behaviour is so bad that people think you should be ashamed of it〔行为〕可耻的，丢脸的: *It's shameful the way some people treat their pets.* 有些人如此对待他们的宠物，真是可耻。| *a shameful family secret* 家丑 —**shamefully** *adv* —**shamefulness** *n* [U]

shame·less /ˋʃemlɪs; ˈʃeɪmləs/ *adj* not seeming to be ashamed of your bad behaviour 无耻的，不知羞耻的，不要脸的: *a shameless liar* 无耻的说谎者 —**shamelessly** *adv* —**shamelessness** *n* [U]

sham·my /ˋʃæmɪ; ˈʃæmi/ *n* [C] a piece of soft leather used for cleaning and polishing glass or metal; CHAMOIS (2) 羚羊皮软革〔用于擦拭玻璃、金属等〕

sham·poo¹ /ʃæmˋpu; ʃæmˈpuː/ *n* **1** [C,U] a liquid soap for washing your hair 洗发剂，香波 **2** [C,U] a liquid used for cleaning carpets (CARPET¹ (1))〔清洁地毯用的〕洗涤剂 **3** [C] an act of shampooing or having your hair shampooed 洗头，洗发: *$21 for a shampoo, cut, and blow-dry* 洗剪吹共21美元

shampoo² *v* [T] to wash something with shampoo 用洗发剂洗；用洗涤剂洗

sham·rock /ˋʃæmrɑk; ˈʃæmrɒk/ *n* [C] a small plant with three green leaves on each stem that is the national EMBLEM of Ireland 三叶草，白花酢浆草〔爱尔兰的国花〕

shamrock 三叶草，白花酢浆草

shan·dy /ˋʃændɪ; ˈʃændi/ *n* [C, U] a drink made of beer mixed with LEMONADE (2), or a glass of this drink（一杯）香迪酒〔啤酒与柠檬水混合的饮料〕

Shane /ʃen; ʃeɪn/ a Western film which many people consider to be one of the best ever made. Shane is a mysterious gunfighter who wants a different kind of life. But when he rides into a Wyoming valley in 1889 he is forced to use his gun to protect a group of farmers against a rich and powerful man who wants to take their land.《原野奇侠》〔一西部影片，被视为最优秀的西部片之一。主人公沙恩是一名神秘枪手，内心却向往另一种生活。然而，1889年当骑马来到怀俄明峡谷时，他又不得不拿出自己的枪保护一群农民，对付一个想霸占他们土地的有钱有势的恶人〕

Shanghai a MUNICIPALITY in East China. Shanghai is China's largest city, its most important port and a major business centre. 上海〔中国东部一直辖市，中国最大城市、最重要港口和主要商业中心〕

shang·hai /ʃæŋˋhaɪ; ʃæŋˈhaɪ/ *v* [T_{+into}] to trick or force someone into doing something unwillingly 诱骗；强迫〔某人做某事〕: *I got shanghaied into organizing the kids' party.* 我被骗去组织孩子们的聚会。

Shan·gri-La /͵ʃæŋgrɪ ˋlɑ; ͵ʃæŋgri ˈlɑː/ a distant, beautiful, imaginary place where everyone is happy. The name comes from the book *Lost Horizon* by James Hilton, about an imaginary valley in Tibet. 香格里拉〔一个遥远而美丽的虚拟之地。那里的居民怡然自得。该词出自詹姆斯·希尔顿的小说《失去的地平线》，描写西藏境内一片虚构的河谷〕

shank /ʃæŋk; ʃæŋk/ *n* **1** [C] a straight narrow part of a tool or object that connects the two ends〔工具或物件的〕柄，杆: *the shank of a key* 钥匙柄 **2** [C,U] a piece of meat cut from the leg of an animal〔动物的〕一块腿肉 **3** [C usually plural 一般用复数] *old use* the part of a person's or animal's leg between the knee and ANKLE【旧】〔人或动物的〕胫〔膝盖至脚踝的部分〕—see picture at 参见 HORSE¹ 图

Shan·khill Road, the /ˋʃæŋkɪl ˋrod; ͵ʃæŋkɪl ˈrəʊd/ a street in the Protestant part of Belfast in Northern Ireland, where a lot of violence has taken place since the 1960s 香基尔路〔北爱尔兰贝尔法斯特新教徒居住区的一条街道。20世纪60年代起成为暴力事件多发地〕—compare 比较 FALLS ROAD

Shan·non, the /ˋʃænən; ˈʃænən/ a river in the Republic of Ireland, flowing into the Atlantic Ocean near Limerick 香农河〔爱尔兰共和国一河流，在利默里克附近注入大西洋〕

shan't /ʃænt; ʃɑːnt/ *especially BrE*【尤英】the short form of 缩略式 = shall not: *I shan't see you again.* 我不会再见到你了。

shan·ty /ˋʃæntɪ; ˈʃænti/ *n* [C] **1** a small, roughly built hut made from thin sheets of wood, TIN¹ (1), plastic etc that very poor people live in〔穷人居住的〕简陋小木屋，铁皮[塑料板]棚屋 **2 sea shanty** a song sung by sailors in former times, as they did their work〔昔日水手工作时唱的〕号子，船夫号子，船歌

shan·ty·town /ˋʃæntɪ͵taʊn; ˈʃænti͵taʊn/ *n* [C] an area in or near a town where people live in shanties〔城镇或其附近的〕贫民区，棚户区

SHAPE /ʃep; ʃeɪp/ Supreme Headquarters Allied Powers Europe; the place in Belgium where the Supreme Allied Commander of Europe, one of the military commanders of NATO, is based 欧洲盟军最高司令部〔北约欧洲盟军最高司令部驻地，位于比利时〕

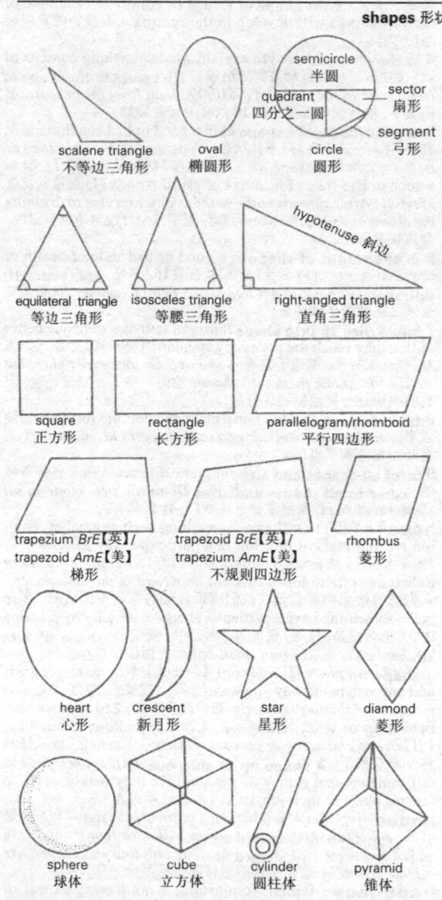

shape¹ /ʃep; ʃeɪp/ *n*

1 ▶OUTER FORM 外形◀ **a)** [C,U] the outer form of something, that you see or feel 形，形状，外形: *What shape is the table – round or oval?* 那张桌子是什么形状的 —— 圆形还是椭圆形？| *You can recognize a tree by the shape of its leaves.* 你可以根据

树叶的形状辨认出是什么树。| **round/square etc in shape** *The eyeball is almost spherical in shape.* 眼球几乎是球形的。| **lose its shape** (=become the wrong shape) 变形 *His battered old hat had completely lost its shape.* 他那顶破旧的帽子完全变形了。| **out of shape** (having become the wrong shape) 变形,走样 *Meryl's sweater had stretched completely out of shape.* 梅里尔的毛衣撑得完全走样了。| **in the shape of** (=having the same shape as something) 某种形状的 *She was wearing a pin in the shape of a bird.* 她佩戴着一枚鸟状的饰针。**b)** [C] a particular shape, or thing that is that shape 某种形状; 某形状之物: *OK Katie, which of these shapes are triangles?* 好,凯蒂,你看这些形状中哪几个是三角形?

2 ►THING NOT SEEN CLEARLY 看不清楚的东西◄ [C] a thing or person that you cannot see clearly enough to recognize〔物或人〕朦胧的形状,看不清的东西: *A large shape loomed up out of the mist.* 雾中隐约出现一个很大的影像。

3 ►CHARACTER OF STH 某物的特色◄ [singular] a particular combination of qualities and features that something has 形态; 形式; 方式: **the shape of** *the shape of British politics today* 今日英国的政治形态 | *Dr Singh was responsible for the final shape of the report.* 辛格博士负责这份报告的定稿。| **in any shape or form** (=of any kind) 任何形式的 *We will not tolerate racism in any shape or form.* 我们不会容忍任何形式的种族主义。| **the shape of things to come** (=an example of the way things will develop in the future) 未来事物的发展状态[方向]

4 in the shape of used to explain what something consists of 以…的形式〔用以解释某物的组成〕: **sth comes in the shape of** *Help came in the shape of a $10,000 loan from his parents.* 帮助来了,他从父母那里得到 10,000 美元的贷款。

5 in good/bad/poor shape a) in a good or bad condition 情况良好/不好; 处于良好/不佳状态: *Considering how old the car is, it's not in bad shape.* 这么老的汽车,状况就算不错了。**b)** in a good or bad state of health or physical FITNESS (1) 健康状况良好/不好: *After three months without any exercise or training the champion's in poor shape.* 那位冠军三个月没运动也不训练,身体状况很差。

6 in shape/out of shape in a good or bad state of health or physical FITNESS (1) 健康[身体]状况良好/不好: **get (yourself) into shape** *I've got to get into shape before summer.* 我必须在夏天之前把身体锻炼好。

7 knock/lick sb into shape *informal* to make someone better so that they reach the necessary standard【非正式】把某人训练好,使达到标准,使趋于完善: *Some of them lack experience, but we'll soon knock them into shape.* 他们有些人还缺乏经验,但我们很快就会把他们训练好的。

8 take shape to develop into a clear and definite form 形成,使成形: *An idea was beginning to take shape in his mind.* 一个主意开始在他脑子里形成。

9 in/of all shapes and sizes of many different types 各种各样的: **come in all shapes and sizes** *Domestic pets come in all shapes and sizes.* 家庭宠物五花八门,什么都有。

S3 **shape²** *v* **1** [T] to influence something such as a belief, opinion etc and make it develop in a particular way 形成〔某种信仰、看法等〕,决定〔某事物的发展方向等〕: *People's political beliefs are often shaped by what they read in the newspapers.* 人们的政治信仰常常是在他们所读报纸的影响下形成的。**2** to make something have a particular shape, especially by pressing it〔尤指通过挤、压等〕使成为某种形状,使成形: **shape sth into sth** *Shape the dough into small balls.* 把面团搓成小圆球。

shape up *phr v* [I] *informal*【非正式】**1** to make progress and improve in the way you want 进展;〔按要求〕发展: *The new recruits are shaping up nicely.* 新兵进步很快。**2** to improve your behaviour or work 改进〔行为、工作〕: *If you don't shape up, I'll have to contact your parents.* 假如你不上进的话,我只好和你父母联系了。**3 shape up or ship out** *AmE spoken* used to tell someone that if they do not improve they will be made to leave a place or their job【美口】不改进就走人

shaped /ʃept; ʃeɪpt/ *adj* having a particular shape 具有某种形状的: **egg-shaped/V-shaped etc** *an L-shaped living room* 一间呈L形的起居室 | **be shaped like** *The building was shaped like a giant pyramid.* 这幢大楼的形状像座巨型金字塔。

shape·less /ˈʃeplɪs; ˈʃeɪpləs/ *adj* **1** not having a clear or definite shape 无[不成]形状的: *Why should fat women have to wear baggy, shapeless dresses?* 为什么肥胖的女人就得穿宽松、没形的衣服? **2** something such as a book or a plan that is shapeless does not seem to have a clear structure〔书、计划等〕没有条理的,结构凌乱的 —**shapelessly** *adv* —**shapelessness** *n* [U]

shape·ly /ˈʃeplɪ; ˈʃeɪpli/ *adj* having a body that has an attractive shape 身材好的,匀称的: *shapely curved legs* 线条优美的腿 —**shapeliness** *n* [U]

shard /ʃɑrd; ʃɑːd/ also 又作 **sherd** *n* [C] a sharp piece of broken glass, metal etc〔玻璃、金属等的〕锋利碎片

share¹ /ʃɛr; ʃeə/ *v* S1 W1

1 ►USE EQUALLY 共同使用◄ [I,T] to have or use something that other people also have or use at the same time〔与他人〕共有〔某物〕,共享; 共用: *We don't have enough books for everyone, so you'll have to share.* 我们的书不够每人一本,所以大家要合着用。| **share sth** *The last bus had gone, so the three of us shared a taxi.* 最后一班公共汽车已经开走,所以我们三人合乘一辆出租车。| **share sth with sb** *I shared a room with her at college.* 我上大学时和她共住一个房间。| **shared house/flat** *BrE* (=with people not related to each other living in it)【英】共住的房子/公寓 —see 见 BETWEEN (USAGE)

2 ►LET SB USE STH 让某人用某物◄ [T] to let someone have or use something that belongs to you 让别人分享〔自己的东西〕: *Even as a kid he'd never share his toys.* 即使在小时候他也从不让别的孩子玩他的玩具。| **share sth with** *I shared my lunch with a few hungry pigeons.* 我和几只饥饿的鸽子分享我的午餐。

3 ►DIVIDE 划分◄ also 又作 **share** sth ↔ **out** [T] to divide something between two or more people〔在若干人之间〕分配: **share sth between/among sb** *At his death, his property was shared out between his children.* 他死后财产分给了子女们。

4 ►SAME INTEREST/OPINION ETC 相同的兴趣/看法等◄ [T] to have the same opinion, experience, feeling etc as someone else 与某人有共同的〔看法、经历、感受等〕: *I share your concern about this.* 我和你一样为这件事担心。| **share in sth** *His daughters did not share in his happiness.* 他的女儿们没有分享过他的快乐。| **share sth with sb** *Stubbornness was a characteristic he shared with his mother.* 固执是他和他母亲共有的一个特征。| **share an interest** (=have the same interest in something as someone else) 兴趣相同

5 ►RESPONSIBILITY 责任◄ [T] to be equally responsible for doing something, paying for something etc 分担〔责任〕,分摊〔费用〕: *I own the house, but we share the bills.* 我拥有这所房子,但我们分担各项开支。| *We all share some blame for the mess-up.* 弄得这样糟,我们大家都有一定责任。

6 ►TELL SB STH 将某事告诉某人◄ [I,T] to tell other people about an idea, secret, problem etc 把〔想法、秘密、问题等〕向别人诉说: *It's always better to share your worries.* 向别人倾诉你的忧虑总比憋在心里要好。| **share sth with sb** *Are you going to share the joke with us?* 你要把笑话讲给我们听吗? | **share** *especially AmE*【尤美】: *If you feel the need to share we're all listening.* 你如果觉得有必要讲出来,我们都将洗耳恭听。

7 share and share alike *spoken* used to say that you should share things fairly and equally between everyone【口】应均分[平均分担,平均分享]

share² *n* 

1 ►PART OF STH 某事物的一部分◄ [singular] the part of something that belongs to you, or that should be paid for or done by you〔某人应得或应负担的〕一份: **[+of/in]** *I gave them my share of the bill and left.* 我把账单上我该付的那份钱交给他们就走了。| *a share in the profits* 一份利润 | **do your share** (=do your part of a job, duty etc that you share with other people) 做你那一份〔分担的工作、义务等〕*I do my share of the housework.* 我做我那份家务活。

2 flat/house share *BrE* a situation in which people who are not related to each other live together【英】公寓/房子共用

3 your (fair) share a) as much or more of something as you could reasonably expect to have 应得的一份: *She's had more than her fair share of bad luck this year.* 她今年倒霉事特别多。| *You've sure had your share of problems, haven't you?* 你肯定也有过你自己的问题,是吗? **b)** as much as everyone else 和每个人一样多的一份: *Don't worry – you'll get your fair share.* 不用担心,你会得到同样多的一份。| *I've made my share of mistakes.* 我自己也犯了不少错误。

4 share in your part in an activity, event etc〔活动、事件等的〕参与: *Employees are always given a share in decision-making.* 雇员始终有参与决策的权利。

5 ►FINANCIAL 经济的◄ [C] one of the equal parts into which the ownership of a company is divided 股,股份: **[+in]** *He decided to sell his shares in Allied Chemicals.* 他决定出售他在联合化工公司的股份。| **share offer/issue** (=a time when shares in a company are sold or begin to be sold) 股票发行 —compare 比较 STOCK¹ (3)

6 ►FARM TOOL 农具◄ [C] *old-fashioned* a PLOUGHSHARE【过

时】犁铧 —see also 另见 **the lion's share** (LION (3)), TIMESHARE —**sharing** *n* [U]

share·crop·per /ˈ· ,··/ *n* [C] *especially AmE* a farmer who uses someone else's land, and gives the owner half the crop in return【尤美】收益分成的佃农〔耕种他人的土地, 收获各分一半〕

share·hold·er /ˈʃɛr,holdɚ; ˈʃeə,həʊldə/ *n* [C] *especially BrE* someone who owns shares in a business【尤英】股东, 股票持有者; STOCKHOLDER *especially AmE*【尤美】: *Shareholders have been told to expect an even lower result for 1995.* 股东们被告知, 1995 年业绩预计会更差。

share in·dex /ˈ· ,··/ *n* [C] *technical* an official and public list of SHARE[2] (5) prices【术语】股票指数

share·ware /ˈʃɛr,wɛr; ˈʃeəweə/ *n* [U] free or cheap computer SOFTWARE that is produced by small companies 共享软件〔小公司生产的免费或廉价电脑软件〕

sha·ri·a, sheria /ʃəˈriə; ʃəˈriːə/ *n* [U] a system of religious laws followed by Muslims 伊斯兰教法

shark /ʃɑrk; ʃɑːk/ *n* [C] **1** *plural* **shark** or **sharks** a large fish with several rows of very sharp teeth that is sometimes considered to be dangerous to humans 鲨(鱼) **2** *informal* someone who cheats other people out of money【非正式】诈骗(钱财)者 —see also 另见 LOAN SHARK

sharp 锋利的; 尖的

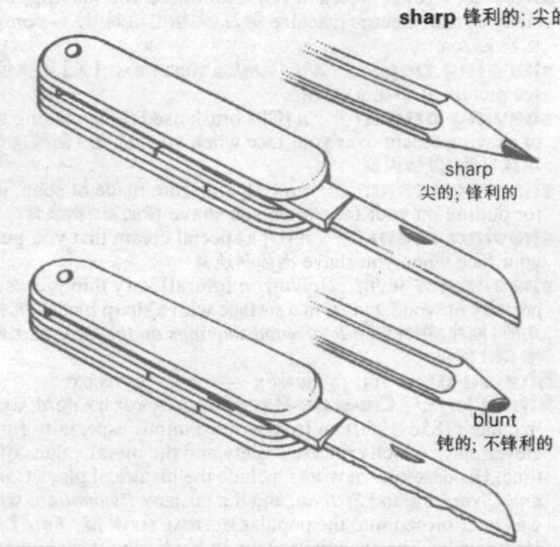

sharp[1] /ʃɑrp; ʃɑːp/ *adj*

1 ►ABLE TO CUT 能切割的◄ having a very thin edge or point that can cut things easily 锋利的, 锐利的, 尖的: *Peel the apples using a sharp knife.* 用锋利的刀子削苹果。| *The metal was jagged with lots of sharp edges.* 这块金属表面粗糙, 有很多锋利的边缘。| **razor sharp** (=very sharp) 非常锋利的 —opposite 反义词 BLUNT[1] (1)

2 ►SOUNDS 声音◄ loud, short, and sudden 刺耳的, 短促的, 突如其来的: *The branch broke with a sharp crack.* 树枝折断, 发出刺耳的劈啪声。| *a sharp cry of pain* 痛苦的尖叫声

3 ►TASTE 味道◄ having a slightly bitter taste 辛辣的: *Add mustard to give the dressing a sharper taste.* 加些芥末使调料带点辛辣味。

4 ►DIRECTION 方向◄ a sudden extreme change of direction 急转弯的, 方向突变的: **sharp bend/turn** *We came to a sharp bend in the road.* 我们到了公路的一个急转弯处。| **sharp left/right** *Take a sharp left after the church.* 过了教堂之后, 向左急转弯。

5 ►PAIN 疼痛◄ sudden and severe 急剧的, 剧烈的: *I felt a sharp pain in my back.* 我感到背部一阵剧痛。—see graph at 参见 PAIN[1] 图表

6 ►REMARK 话语◄ severe, angry, and criticizing 尖锐的, 严厉的, 愤怒的, 责备的: *a sharp rebuke* 严厉的斥责 | *John's tone was sharp.* 约翰语气尖刻。| **be sharp with sb** *The boss can be very sharp with people when she's busy.* 老板忙起来会训斥人。

7 have a sharp tongue to often talk to people in an angry, unkind, or criticizing way 说话尖酸刻薄

8 ►PEOPLE 人◄ able to think and understand things very quickly, and not easily deceived 敏锐的, 机灵的: *a journalist with an extremely sharp mind* 头脑极其敏锐的新闻记者

9 ►EYES 眼睛◄ able to see and notice details very well 灵敏的, 锐利的: **a sharp eye for detail** (=the ability to notice and deal with details) 观察入微的眼力

10 keep a sharp eye on sb to watch someone very carefully, especially because you do not trust them 密切注意某人〔尤指因对其不信任〕: *Keep a sharp eye on the kids at all times!* 任何时候都要睁大眼睛盯住这些孩子!

11 ►PENCIL 铅笔◄ having a very thin point, that can draw an exact line〔笔芯〕很尖的 —opposite 反义词 BLUNT[1] (1)

12 ►SHAPE 形状◄ not rounded or curved; ANGULAR 尖突的, 有突边的, 线条分明的: *Janice had the same sharp features as her mother.* 贾尼丝像她母亲, 五官轮廓也很分明。

13 ►CHANGE 变化◄ a sharp increase, rise etc is very sudden and very big〔增长、上升等〕急剧的, 猛烈的: *a sharp increase in prices* 价格的急剧上涨

14 ►DIFFERENCE 差别◄ clear and definite, so that there is no doubt 明显的, 清楚的: *The distinction between public and private services is much less sharp here.* 公共服务和私人服务的差别在这里远没有那样明显。| **in sharp contrast** (=very different from someone or something else) 形成鲜明的对照 *Keele wore a smart suit, in sharp contrast to everyone's else's casual attire.* 基尔穿着一套帅气的西装, 与其他人的便装形成鲜明对照。

15 ►PICTURE/IMAGES 图画/影像◄ having a shape that is clear and detailed 轮廓清晰的, 线条分明的: *The outlines of the cypress trees were sharp and clear.* 那些柏树轮廓清晰, 枝条挺拔。

16 a) F sharp/D sharp/C sharp etc a musical note that is sharp has been raised by one SEMITONE from the note F, D, C etc 升 F(调)/D(调)/C(调)〔指音符升半音〕—see picture at 参见 MUSIC 图 **b)** if music or singing is sharp, it is played or sung at a slightly higher PITCH[1] (3) than it should be〔比准确音调〕略偏高的

17 ►MOVEMENT 动作◄ quick and sudden 急促的, 突然的: *The wind blew across the lake in sharp gusts.* 一阵阵急风刮过湖面。| *a sharp intake of breath* 猛吸一口气

18 ►FEELINGS 感情◄ very strong and unexpected 非常强烈的, 意料不到的: *I was left with a sharp sense of disappointment.* 我泛起一股强烈的失望感。

19 sharp practice behaviour, especially in business, that is dishonest but not illegal〔尤指商业中合法但〕不诚实的交易手段

20 a sharp frost a very cold severe FROST[1] (1) 刺骨的寒霜

21 be on the sharp end of sth to experience the worst effects of something 经历某事的最坏情况: *We were always on the sharp end of clients' complaints.* 处理顾客投诉的压力总是由我们来承受。

22 sb looks sharp *AmE* if someone looks sharp, they are dressed well and attractively【美】〔人〕衣着时髦的, 漂亮的, 吸引人的; SMART[1] (2) *especially BrE*【尤英】: *Tod looked really sharp in his tux.* 托德穿着晚礼服看上去挺帅。—**sharpness** *n* [U] —see also 另见 SHARPLY

sharp[2] *adv* **1 at ten-thirty/2 o'clock etc sharp** at exactly 10.30, 2.00 etc 在 10 点 30 分/两点整: *We're meeting at 10 o'clock sharp.* 我们将在 10 时整会面。**2 sharp left/right** if you turn sharp left or right, you make a sudden change of direction to the left or right 向左转/向右急转弯: *You turn sharp right at the crossroads.* 在十字路口向右急转弯。**3 look sharp** *spoken*【口】**a)** *BrE* used to tell someone to do something quickly【英】〔用于叫别人〕赶快, 赶紧: *If you look sharp you might catch him before he leaves for London.* 你如果赶紧去, 也许能在他出发去伦敦前见到他。**b)** *especially AmE* used to warn someone about something【尤美】留神, 注意〔用于提醒别人〕: *Look sharp, the boss is coming!* 留心, 老板来了! **4** played or sung at a slightly higher PITCH[1] (3) than is correct〔演奏或演唱得比正确的音调〕略为偏高

sharp[3] *n* [C] **1** a musical note that has been raised one SEMITONE above the note written〔音符的〕升半音 **2** the sign (*#*) in a line of written music used to show this 升号〔#, 表示升半音〕—see picture at 参见 MUSIC 图

Sharp, Beck·y /ˈbɛkɪ; ˈbeki/ the main character in the book *Vanity Fair* (1847-48) by William Thackeray. She is a clever, attractive, and ambitious young woman (=someone who wants very much to become rich and successful), who treats people cruelly and unfairly to get what she wants. 夏普〔威廉·萨克雷的小说《名利场》(1847-1848) 中的女主角。她是一个聪明漂亮、野心勃勃的女人, 为了自己的所求不惜对人使用无情、不公的手段〕

sharp-eared /,· ˈ·◄/ *adj* able to hear very well 听觉灵敏的, 耳灵的

sharp·en /ˈʃɑrpən; ˈʃɑːpən/ *v* **1** [I,T] to become sharper or make something sharper (使)变锋利[尖锐, 清晰]: *Sharpen all your pencils before the test.* 考试前把你所有的铅笔削尖。| *The light grew brighter and the shadows sharpened.* 灯光变得更加明亮, 阴影也更清晰。**2** [T] to make a feeling stronger and more

urgent 使〔某种感觉〕增强，使感到迫切：*These latest moves have sharpened fears of a military conflict.* 最近的这些行动增加了人们对发生军事冲突的担心。

sharpen sth ↔ **up** *phr v* [T] to improve something so that it is up to the necessary standard, quality etc 使达到标准；使符合质量要求：*We need more rehearsals to sharpen up the dance routine.* 我们需要更多的排练使舞步更加完美。

sharp·en·er /ˈʃɑrpənə; ˈʃɑːpənə/ *n* [C] a tool or machine for sharpening pencils, knives etc 磨削的工具〈如铅笔刀、磨刀器等〉

sharp·er /ˈʃɑrpə; ˈʃɑːpə/ *n* [C] *old-fashioned* someone who cheats or is dishonest【过时】骗子，诈骗者

Sharpe·ville /ˈʃɑrpvɪl; ˈʃɑːpvɪl/ a town near Johannesburg, South Africa, where, on 21 March 1960, police shot dead 69 black people who were protesting against the system of APARTHEID. 沙佩维尔〔南非约翰内斯堡附近一城镇。1960年3月21日，警察在此开枪打死了69名抗议种族隔离制度的黑人〕

sharp-eyed /ˌ· ˈ·◂/ *adj* able to see very well and notice small details 目光敏锐的：*My sharp-eyed mother had already spotted him.* 我那目光敏锐的母亲已经认出他了。

sharp·ish /ˈʃɑrpɪʃ; ˈʃɑːpɪʃ/ *adv BrE spoken* quickly【英口】迅速地：*We'd better leave pretty sharpish if we want to catch that bus.* 如果我们想赶上那趟公共汽车，就最好快点动身。

3 **sharp·ly** /ˈʃɑrplɪ; ˈʃɑːpli/ *adv*

1 ▶**SPEAK/LOOK** 说/看◀ in a severe and disapproving way 严厉地，毫不客气地：*"What do you mean by that?" Paul asked sharply.* "你那样说是什么意思？"保罗厉声问道。| *I glanced at her sharply, but said nothing.* 我严厉地看了她一眼，但没有说话。| **sharply critical** (=very critical and disapproving) 非常苛刻[挑剔]的

2 ▶**CHANGE** 变化◀ if something rises, falls etc sharply, it rises or falls quickly and suddenly 急剧地；急〔升〕，骤〔降〕，暴〔跌〕：*Prices have risen sharply over the last few months.* 过去几个月里价格一直在急剧上涨。

3 ▶**MOVE** 移动◀ quickly and suddenly 迅速地，突然地：*She heard a noise behind her and turned around sharply.* 她听到背后有声音，便迅速地转过身来。

4 ▶**SHOW DIFFERENCES** 出现分歧◀ clearly and definitely 明显地，确切地：*Opinion is sharply divided.* 意见分歧明显。

5 sharply contrasted/contrasting very different 呈鲜明的对照，截然不同：*His aggressive behaviour contrasted sharply with the mild manners of his brother.* 他咄咄逼人的行为跟他兄弟的温和举止形成鲜明的对照。

sharp-wit·ted /ˌ· ˈ··◂/ *adj* able to think and react very quickly〔思维和反应〕敏捷的，敏锐的，机智的

shat /ʃæt; ʃæt/ the past tense and past participle of SHIT[2]

shat·ter /ˈʃætə; ˈʃætə/ *v* **1** [I,T] to break suddenly into very small pieces, or to make something break in this way（使）粉碎，（使）破碎：[**+into**] *The plate hit the floor, and shattered into tiny bits.* 盘子砸在地板上，摔得粉碎。| **shatter sth** *A stone shattered the window.* 一块石头把窗户玻璃打碎了。**2** [T] to make someone feel disappointed by showing or proving that someone's hopes or beliefs are impossible or wrong 使〔希望、信念〕破灭，粉碎：*Hopes of a peace agreement were shattered today when talks broke down again.* 今天谈判再次失败，达成和平协议的希望破灭了。| **shatter sb's illusions** *A few weeks in a tiny damp room soon shattered his illusions about university life.* 在狭小潮湿的房间里住了几个星期后，他对大学生活的幻想破灭了。

shat·tered /ˈʃætəd; ˈʃætəd/ *adj* [not before noun 不用于名词前] **1** very shocked and upset 感到震惊的；难过的；心烦意乱的：*I wasn't just disappointed, I was absolutely shattered.* 我不仅是失望，简直是十分难过。**2** *BrE informal* very tired; EXHAUSTED (1)【英，非正式】精疲力竭的，极度疲劳的：*By the time we got home we were both shattered.* 回到家时，我们两人都精疲力竭了。

shat·ter·ing /ˈʃætərɪŋ; ˈʃætərɪŋ/ *adj* **1** very shocking and upsetting 令人震惊的；使人心烦意乱的：*shattering news from home* 从家乡传来的令人震惊的消息 **2** *BrE informal* making you very tired【英，非正式】使人疲倦的，使人精疲力竭的

shat·ter·proof /ˈʃætəˌpruf; ˈʃætəpruːf/ *adj* glass that is shatterproof is specially designed so that it will not form sharp dangerous pieces if it is broken〔玻璃〕防碎的〔经特殊设计的一种玻璃，即使打破也不会形成锋利的碎片〕

3 **shave**[1] /ʃev; ʃeɪv/ *v* **1** [I,T] to cut off hair very close to the skin, especially from the face 刮（胡子）；刮（脸），剃（须）：*I washed and shaved, then hurried out of the house.* 我洗脸，刮胡子，然后匆匆出了门。| *His hands shake so badly his wife has to shave him.* 他的手颤抖得很厉害，他妻子只好给他刮胡子。| **shave your head/legs/armpits etc** *Once Jenni shaved her head for a bet.* 珍妮有一次为打赌剃了光头。**2** [T] to touch something slightly as you pass it; SCRAPE[1] (2) 轻轻擦过：*The car just shaved the wall as we went round the corner.* 我们转弯时汽车轻轻擦到了墙壁。

shave sth ↔ **off** *phr v* [T] **1** to remove hair by shaving 剃掉〔毛发〕：*They made me shave off my beard when I joined the army.* 我参军时，他们要我把胡子刮掉。**2** to remove very thin pieces from the surface of something, using a knife or other cutting tool〔用刀或刨等〕刮去〔表层〕，把…刨去〔一层〕：*I had to shave a few millimetres off the bottom of the door to make it shut.* 我不得不把门的底部刨掉几毫米使它能够关上。**3** to reduce an amount or number very slightly 略减，削减：*She's shaved half a second off the world record.* 她把世界纪录缩短了半秒。

shave[2] *n* [C usually singular 一般用单数] **1** an act of shaving your face 刮脸，刮胡子：*He looked as if he needed a shave.* 他看上去似乎需要刮刮胡子。| **have a shave** *I'll just have a shave before we go.* 我们走之前我要去刮刮胡子。**2 a close shave a)** a situation in which you only just avoid an accident or something 幸免，侥幸脱险 **b)** a shave that cuts the hair very close to your face 把胡子剃得干净

shav·en /ˈʃevən; ˈʃeɪvən/ *adj* with all the hair shaved off 剃光毛发的：*his shaven head* 他那剃光了的头 —see also 另见 CLEAN-SHAVEN, UNSHAVEN

shav·er /ˈʃevə; ˈʃeɪvə/ *n* [C] a tool used for shaving, especially a small electric machine 剃刀〔尤指电动剃刀〕—compare 比较 RAZOR

shav·ing bag /ˈ·· ˌ·/ *n* [C] *AmE* a TOILET BAG【美】化妆包 —see picture at 参见 BAG[1] 图

shaving brush /ˈ·· ˌ·/ *n* [C] a brush used for spreading soap or shaving cream over your face when you shave〔刮须前用以涂抹皂液的〕修面刷

shaving cream /ˈ·· ˌ·/ *n* [U] a mixture made of soap, used for putting on your face when you shave 修面霜，剃须膏

shaving foam /ˈ·· ˌ·/ *n* [U] a special cream that you put on your face when you shave 泡沫剃须膏

shav·ings /ˈʃevɪŋz; ˈʃeɪvɪŋz/ *n* [plural] very thin pieces, especially of wood, cut from a surface with a sharp blade〔尤指木头的〕刨片，削片：*a pile of wood shavings on the floor* 地上的一堆（木）刨花

Sha·vu·ot /ʃəˋvot; ʃəˈvuːəs/ *n* —see 见 PENTECOST

Shaw /ʃɔ; ʃɔː/, **George Ber·nard** /dʒɔrdʒ bəˋnɑrd; dʒɔːdʒ ˈbɜːnəd/ (1856-1950) an Irish writer famous especially for his clever plays which criticize society and the moral values of the time. His best known works include the historical plays *Caesar and Cleopatra* and *St Joan*, and the COMEDY *Pygmalion*, which was later turned into the popular MUSICAL SHOW *My Fair Lady*. He was a leading socialist and wrote books about socialism. 萧伯纳〔(1856-1950)，爱尔兰作家，尤以抨击现实社会和道德观念的工巧之作著称。代表作包括历史剧《恺撒和克娄巴特拉》、《圣女贞德》及喜剧《皮格马利翁》。《皮格马利翁》后来被改编成一部颇受欢迎的音乐剧，名为《窈窕淑女》。他是一位杰出的社会主义者，撰有关于社会主义的著作〕

shawl /ʃɔl; ʃɔːl/ *n* [C] a piece of soft cloth, in a square or TRIANGULAR shape, that is worn around the shoulders or head, especially by women〔尤指女用的〕披巾，披肩大围巾：*an embroidered shawl* 刺绣披肩

she- /ʃi; ʃiː/ *prefix* female 雌（性），女（性）：*a she-goat* 母山羊 | *a she-devil* (=evil woman) 女魔

she[1] /ʃɪ; ʃi *strong* 强读 ʃi; ʃiː/ *pron* [used as the subject of a verb 用作动词的主词] **1 a)** a woman or girl who has been mentioned already, or who the person you are talking to already knows about 她〔指人〕：*What did she say when you told her?* 你告诉她之后，她说了些什么？| *Why don't you ask Beth – she's got plenty of money.* 你为什么不问贝丝，她很有钱。| *I saw you talking to that girl. Who is she?* 我看见你和那个女孩子说话，她是谁？**b)** a female animal who has been mentioned already 她〔指提及过的雌性动物〕**2 a)** used to talk about a boat or ship 她〔指船舶〕：*The QE2 docked at Portsmouth Harbour where she will spend the next few months being refurbished.* "女王伊丽莎白二世号"邮轮停靠在朴次茅斯港，她将要在那里花几个月重新整修。**b)** used to talk about a country 她〔指一个国家〕**c)** used to talk about a vehicle or machine that you are very fond of 她〔指非常喜爱的车辆、机器〕 1 1

she[2] /ʃi; ʃiː/ *n* [singular] *informal* a female【非正式】女性，雌性：*What a beautiful child! Is it a he or a she?* 多漂亮的孩子！是男孩还是女孩？

sheaf /ʃif; ʃiːf/ *plural* **sheaves** /ʃivz; ʃiːvz/ *n* [C **+of**] **1** a bunch of wheat, corn etc tied together after it has been cut〔谷物等收割后捆成的〕束，捆 **2** several pieces of paper held or tied together〔纸张等的〕扎，叠，捆

shear /ʃɪr; ʃɪə/ *v past tense* **sheared** *past participle* **sheared** *or* **shorn** /ʃɔrn; ʃɔːn/ **1** [T] to cut the wool off a sheep 给〔羊〕剪羊毛 **2 be shorn of** to have something valuable or important taken away from you 被剥夺，被除去: *Shorn of all real power by the new laws, the deputy soon resigned.* 实权被新法律剥夺净尽，议员不久就辞职了。 **3** also 又作 **shear off, shear away** [I,T] *technical* to break apart because of a sideways or twisting force【术语】折断，扭断；剪断 **4** [T] *literary* to cut off someone's hair【文】给〔某人〕剪〔头发〕

shear·er /ˈʃɪrə; ˈʃɪərə/ also 又作 **sheep shearer** *n* [C] someone who cuts the wool off sheep 剪羊毛的人

shears /ʃɪrz; ʃɪəz/ *n* [plural] a heavy tool for cutting, like a big pair of scissors 大剪刀: **a pair of shears** *Sam was trimming the hedge with a pair of garden shears.* 萨姆在用园艺剪刀修剪树篱。

sheath /ʃiθ; ʃiːθ/ *plural* **sheaths** /ʃiðz; ʃiːðz/ *n* [C] **1** a cover for the blade of a knife or sword〔刀、剑的〕套，鞘 **2** *BrE* CONDOM【英】避孕套，保险套，安全套 **3** a close-fitting part of a plant or animal that acts as a protective covering〔植物或动物包覆的起保护作用的〕鞘状物

sheathe /ʃið; ʃiːð/ *v* **1** [T] to put a knife or sword into a sheath 将〔刀、剑〕插入鞘中: *He sheathed his sword.* 他把剑插入鞘内。 **2** to be enclosed in a protective outer cover〔用鞘、护套等〕包覆: **be sheathed in/with** *The nuclear reactor is sheathed with lead.* 核反应堆是用铅包封住的。

sheath·ing /ˈʃiðɪŋ; ˈʃiːðɪŋ/ *n* [C usually singular 一般用单数] a protective outer cover, for example for a building or a ship〔建筑物的〕保护性外层，包覆材料；〔船的〕船底包板

sheath knife /ˈ· ·/ *n* [C] a knife with a fixed blade that does not fold, that is carried in a sheath 鞘刀〔刀身固定且有刀鞘的非折合式刀〕

sheaves /ʃivz; ʃiːvz/ the plural of SHEAF

She·ba /ˈʃibə; ˈʃiːbə/, **Queen of**—see 见 the QUEEN OF SHEBA

she·bang /ʃəˈbæŋ; ʃɪˈbæŋ/ *n* **the whole shebang** *informal, especially AmE* the whole thing【非正式，尤美】全部事情: *It's a big project, and she's in charge of the whole shebang.* 这是项大工程，而她负责全部事务。

she·been /ʃɪˈbin; ʃɪˈbiːn/ *n* [C] *informal, especially IrishE* a place where alcoholic drinks are sold illegally【非正式，尤爱尔兰】非法经营的酒馆

she'd /ʃɪd; ʃid *strong* 强读 ʃid; ʃiːd/ **1** the short form of 缩略式= she had: *She'd already gone when we got there.* 我们到达那里时她已经走了。 **2** the short form of 缩略式= she would: *She'd like to come with us.* 她想和我们一起来。

W3 **shed**[1] /ʃɛd; ʃed/ *n* [C] **1** a small building, often made of wood, used especially for storing things 棚屋，小屋，小库房〔通常为简陋小木房，尤用于存放杂物〕: *We had a tool shed in our back yard.* 我们后院有一间工具房。| *a cattle shed* 牲口棚 | *a garden shed* 园子里的棚屋 **2** a large industrial building where work is done, large vehicles are kept or machinery is stored etc〔用作车间、停放大型车辆或存放机器等的〕棚式建筑物

shed[2] *v* [T] *past tense and past participle* **shed** *present participle* **shedding**

1 ►LIGHT 光线◄ if something sheds light, it lights the area around it〔灯〕发出〔光线〕；照亮，照射: *The lamp shed a yellow glow onto the desk.* 灯的黄色光线照射在书桌上。

2 ►DROP/FALL OFF 落下◄ a) to drop something or allow it to fall 落下，使〔某物〕脱落: *He strode across the bathroom, shedding wet clothes as he went.* 他大步走过浴室，边走边把湿衣服脱下来。 **b)** if an animal sheds skin or hair or a plant sheds leaves etc, they fall off as part of a natural process〔动物或植物〕使〔外皮、毛发、叶子等〕蜕下，脱落，剥落: *Deciduous trees shed their leaves in autumn.* 落叶树在秋天落叶。| *As it grows, a snake will regularly shed its skin.* 蛇在成长时定期蜕皮。

3 ►GET RID OF 去掉◄ to get rid of something that you no longer need or want 去掉〔不需要或不想要的东西〕: *The company is planning to shed about a quarter of its workforce.* 这家公司正在计划削减四分之一的员工。| *I shed my inhibitions and joined the dancing.* 我丢开思想顾虑，和大家一起跳舞。| **shed pounds/stones** (=get thinner by losing several pounds etc) 减轻体重 *I'd like to shed a few pounds.* 我希望减掉几磅体重。

4 shed light on to make something easier to understand, by providing new or better information〔通过提供新信息等〕使〔某事物〕清楚些〔易于理解〕: *We're hoping his letter will shed some light on the mystery.* 我们希望他的信将有助于解开这个疑团。

5 ►WATER 水◄ if something sheds water, the water flows off its surface, instead of sinking into it〔表面〕排掉，不沾〔水〕

6 shed blood to kill or injure people, especially during a war or a fight 流血〔尤指战争或打斗中的杀戮或伤害〕: *Too much blood has already been shed in this conflict.* 这次冲突已造成太多的流血牺牲了。—see also 另见 BLOODSHED

7 shed tears *especially literary* to cry【尤文】流泪: *She had not shed a single tear during the funeral.* 在葬礼上她一滴泪也没有流。

8 shed its load *BrE* if a vehicle sheds its load, the goods it is carrying accidentally fall off【英】〔车辆不经意〕掉落〔所载货物〕

sheen /ʃin; ʃiːn/ *n* [singular,U] a soft smooth shiny appearance; LUSTRE (1)〔外表的〕光泽，光彩: *Her hair had a lovely coppery sheen.* 她的头发有一种美丽的古铜色光泽。

W2 S3 **sheep** /ʃip; ʃiːp/ *n* [C] *plural* **sheep** **1** a grass-eating farm animal that is kept for its wool and its meat 羊，绵羊: *Sheep were grazing on the hillside.* 羊群在山坡上吃草。| *a sheep farmer* 养羊者 | **a flock of sheep** (=a group of sheep) 一群羊 —see also 另见 LAMB **2** [often plural 常用复数] someone who does not think independently, but follows what everyone else does or thinks 没有主见的人，任人摆布的人，随大流的人 **3 separate the sheep from the goats** to find out which people are intelligent, skilful, successful etc, and which are not 分出优劣，辨明好坏: *This test should really separate the sheep from the goats.* 这次考试应能真正分出考生的优劣。 **4 make sheep's eyes at** *old-fashioned* to look at someone in a way that shows you love them【过时】用充满爱意的眼神看某人，向某人送秋波 —see also 另见 **black sheep, count sheep** (COUNT[1] (2)), **a wolf in sheep's clothing** (WOLF[1] (2))

CULTURAL NOTE 文化注释

Sheep are generally considered to be stupid animals that follow each other without thinking about where they are going. People are sometimes called sheep if they do what someone tells them to do without thinking about it first. 羊一般被认为是一种愚蠢的动物，它们只会互相追随而不知自己的去向。那些别人让干什么就干什么、对事情不作考量的人有时也被称作"羊"。

sheep-dip /ˈ· ·/ *n* [C,U] a chemical used to kill insects that live in sheep's wool, or a special bath in which this chemical is used 浴羊药液〔一种用以杀死羊毛中的昆虫的消毒液〕;〔使用该药液的〕灭虫浴

sheep dog /ˈ· ·/ *n* [C] **1** a dog that is trained to control sheep 牧羊犬 **2** *informal* a dog of a type that is often used for this, usually a COLLIE【非正式】一种常用作牧羊犬的狗〔通常为柯利犬〕—see also 另见 OLD ENGLISH SHEEPDOG

sheep·fold /ˈʃipˌfold; ˈʃiːpfəʊld/ *n* [C] an area of land with a fence or wall around it, used for keeping sheep in 羊栏，羊圈，羊舍

sheep·ish /ˈʃipɪʃ; ˈʃiːpɪʃ/ *adj* uncomfortable or embarrassed because you know that you have done something silly or wrong 局促不安的，腼腆的，困窘的: *Richard was looking sheepish.* 理查德看上去有点局促不安。—**sheepishly** *adv*: *She grinned sheepishly.* 她腼腆地笑了一笑。—**sheepishness** *n* [U]

sheep·pen /ˈ· ·/ *n* [C] a small area of ground with a fence around it, used for keeping sheep together for a short time 羊栏，羊圈，羊舍

sheep·skin /ˈʃipˌskɪn; ˈʃiːpˌskɪn/ *n* [C,U] the skin of a sheep with the wool still on it 带毛的羊皮: *a sheepskin coat* 羊皮大衣

sheer[1] /ʃɪr; ʃɪə/ *adj* **1 sheer luck/happiness/stupidity etc** luck, happiness etc with no other feeling or quality mixed with it 十足的运气/快乐/愚蠢等: *It was sheer bliss not having to get up.* 不用起床真幸福。| *sheer hypocrisy* 十足的虚伪 **2 the sheer weight/size etc of** used to emphasize how heavy, big etc something is〔某物〕之重/之大等〔用于强调〕: *The sheer size of the country makes communications difficult.* 该国幅员辽阔，造成了通讯的困难。 **3** a sheer drop, cliff, slope etc is very steep and almost VERTICAL[1] (1)〔悬崖、斜坡等〕垂直的，陡峭的: *There was a sheer drop to the sea 200 feet below.* 悬崖与海面垂直距离200英尺。 **4** sheer NYLON, silk etc is very thin and fine, so that it is almost transparent〔尼龙、丝绸等〕很薄的，几乎透明的: *sheer stockings* 透明的长统袜

sheer[2] *adv* straight up or down in an almost VERTICAL[1] (1) line 陡峭地，垂直地: *The mountains rise sheer from the sea.* 群山从海面峭拔而起。

sheer[3] *v* [I] **sheer off/away** to change direction suddenly, especially in order to avoid something 突然转向〔尤指为了避开

S

某物): *The boat sheered away and headed out to sea again.* 这艘船突然调头,又驶向大海。

sheet /ʃit; ʃiːt/ *n* [C] **1** a large piece of thin cotton or NYLON cloth that you put on a bed to lie on or lie under 床单,被单: **change the sheets** (=put clean sheets on a bed) 换上干净的床单 **2** a thin flat piece of something such as paper, glass, or metal, that usually has four sides〔纸、玻璃、金属等的〕片,块,张: [+of] *I picked up a clean sheet of paper and began to write.* 我拿起一张空白纸写了起来。| *a sheet of glass* 一块玻璃 —see picture on page A7 参见 A7 页图 **3** a large flat area of something such as ice or water spread over a surface〔冰、水等的〕一大片: *A sheet of ice covered the lake.* 湖面上覆盖着一大片冰。**4** a sheet of rain or fire is a very large moving mass of it〔大雨、火的〕一团,一片,一层: *The rain was coming down in sheets.* 大雨倾盆而下。**5** *technical* a rope or chain that controls the angle between a sail and the wind on a ship【术语】〔帆船的〕帆脚索 —see also 另见 BAKING SHEET, BALANCE SHEET, **white as a sheet** (WHITE[1] (2)), **a clean sheet** (CLEAN[1] (10))

sheet an·chor /ˈ· ˌ··/ *n* [C] **1** a ship's largest ANCHOR[1] (1), used only in times of danger 备用大锚〔船上最大的锚,只在危险时用〕**2** someone or something that you depend on very much in a difficult or dangerous situation 在困难[危险]时主要依靠的人[物]

sheet·ing /ˈʃitɪŋ; ˈʃiːtɪŋ/ *n* [U] cloth or other material that is made into sheets, or used in the form of a sheet〔用作床单、被单等的〕布料; 薄板材料: *The roof was covered in plastic sheeting.* 房顶是用塑料薄板盖的。| *cotton sheeting* 棉质床单布料

sheet light·ning /ˌ· ˈ··/ *n* [U] a type of LIGHTNING that appears as a sudden flash of brightness covering a large area of sky 片状闪电 —compare 比较 FORKED LIGHTNING

sheet met·al /ˈ· ˌ··/ *n* [U] metal in the form of thin sheets 金属薄板

sheet mu·sic /ˈ· ˌ··/ *n* [U] music that is printed on single sheets and not fastened together inside a cover 活页乐谱,印在散页上的乐谱

Shef·field /ˈʃɛfild; ˈʃefiːld/ a city in South Yorkshire in the north of England, famous for making tools, steel, and CUTLERY (=knives, forks, and spoons), although most of its old industry has now closed down. Sheffield is the home of the National Centre for Popular Music. 设菲尔德〔英格兰北部南约克郡一城市,以生产工具、钢铁、餐具闻名。不过,这些传统行业大部分现已关闭。该市是国家流行音乐中心的所在地〕

She·her·a·zade /ʃəˌhɛrəˈzɑd; ʃəˌherəˈzɑːd/ —see 见 SCHEHERAZADE

sheikh, sheik /ʃik; ʃeɪk/ *n* [C] **1** an Arab chief or prince〔阿拉伯的〕酋长,族长,首领; 王子 **2** a Muslim religious leader or teacher 伊斯兰教的领袖,教士,教长

sheikh·dom, sheikdom /ˈʃikdəm; ˈʃeɪkdəm/ *n* [C] a place that is governed by an Arab chief or prince〔阿拉伯〕酋长统治的领土,酋长国

shei·la /ˈʃilə; ˈʃiːlə/ *n* [C] *AustrE or NZE slang* a young woman【澳或纽西兰,俚】少妇,少女,女郎

shek·el /ˈʃɛkl; ˈʃekəl/ *n* [C] **1** the standard unit of money in Israel 谢克尔〔以色列的货币单位〕**2 shekels** [plural] *humorous* money【幽默】钱

shelf /ʃɛlf; ʃelf/ *n plural* **shelves** /ʃɛlvz; ʃelvz/ **1** [C] a long flat narrow board fixed onto a wall or in a frame or cupboard, used for putting things on or storing things on〔靠墙架设可存放东西的〕架子;〔书橱、柜子的〕搁板: *Put it back on the top shelf.* 把它放回到顶层的搁板上。| *shelves of books* 几架子书 | *supermarket shelves* 超级市场的货架 **2** [C] a narrow surface of rock shaped like a shelf, especially underwater 搁板状岩石;〔尤指海底的〕暗礁,大陆架 **3 off the shelf** available to be bought immediately without having to be specially designed or ordered 现货供应: *off-the-shelf computer software packages* 现货供应的电脑软件组件 —compare 比较 OFF-THE-PEG **4 be (left) on the shelf a)** *old-fashioned* considered to be too old to get married【过时】因年龄太大而找不到对象结婚 **b)** if a plan, idea etc is left on the shelf it is not used or considered〔计划、主意等〕不被考虑,搁置不用 —see also 另见 SHELVE

shelf life /ˈ· ·/ *n* [singular] the length of time that food, chemicals etc can be kept in a shop before they become too old to sell〔食品、药品等的〕保存期限,在商店的存货期限: *Chocolate has a shelf life of 9 months.* 巧克力的保存期限为九个月。

she'll /ʃɪl; ʃil *strong* 强读 ʃil; ʃiːl/ the short form of 缩略式= she will: *She'll be back in a minute.* 她过一会就回来。

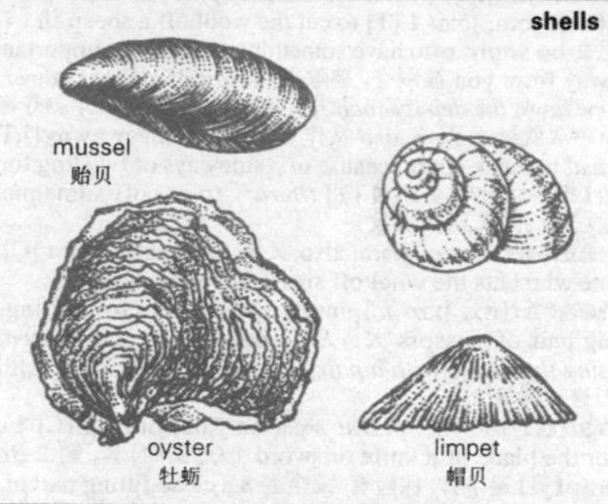

shell[1] /ʃɛl; ʃel/ *n* **1** [C] **a)** a hard outer part that covers or protects a nut, egg, or seed and some types of animal〔坚果、禽蛋、种子或某些动物的〕壳: *a snail shell* 蜗牛壳 **b)** the shell of a small sea animal such as a COCKLE or MUSSEL especially one that is lying on a beach〔鸟蛤、贻贝等的〕壳;〔尤指海滩上的〕贝壳 **2** [C] a metal container, like a large bullet, which is full of an explosive substance and is fired from a large gun 炮弹: *We ran for cover as shells dropped all around us.* 炮弹落在我们周围,我们都跑着找地方掩蔽。**3** [C] *especially AmE* a metal tube containing a bullet and an explosive substance used in a gun; CARTRIDGE (1)【尤美】子弹; 弹药筒 **4** [C] the outside structure of something, especially the part of a building that remains when the rest of it has been destroyed〔尤指建筑物等遭破坏后剩下的〕框架,骨架 **5 come out of your shell** to become less shy and more confident and willing to talk to people 不再羞怯,愿意与人攀谈,开始活跃起来: *She's really come out of her shell since she went to college.* 她自从上了大学后,的确变得开朗大方了。

shell[2] *v* [T] **1** to fire shells at something 炮轰: *Opposition forces have been shelling the town since yesterday.* 反政府部队从昨天起一直在炮轰该城镇。**2** to remove something such as beans or nuts from a shell or a POD[1] (1) 剥去〔豆荚或坚果等〕的壳: *Josie was shelling peas on the verandah.* 乔西在走廊里剥豌豆荚。

shell out *phr v* [T] *informal* to pay a lot of money for something, especially unwillingly【非正式】〔尤指不情愿地〕花大笔钱,付款: *If you want the repairs done right, you'll have to shell out at least $800.* 假如你想修妥当,至少得花 800 美元。

shel·lac /ʃəˈlæk; ʃəˈlæk/ *n* [U] a kind of transparent paint for protecting or hardening surfaces〔用于保护表面或使表面坚硬的〕虫胶(清漆)

shel·lack·ing /ʃəˈlækɪŋ; ʃəˈlækɪŋ/ *n* [singular] *AmE informal* a situation in which you are severely defeated or criticized【美,非正式】彻底失败,惨败; 受到严厉批评: *The Chargers got a shellacking in the Superbowl.* 电光队在超级杯赛中惨败。

Shel·ley /ˈʃɛlɪ; ˈʃeli/, **Ma·ry Woll·stone·craft** /ˈmɛrɪ ˈwʊlstənkræft; ˈmeəri ˈwʊlstənkrɑːft/ (1797-1851) a British writer, whose best-known NOVEL is *Frankenstein*. She was married to Percy Bysshe Shelley, and was the daughter of the FEMINIST writer Mary Wollstonecraft. 雪莱〔(1797-1851),英国作家。最著名的作品是《弗兰肯斯坦》。丈夫为珀西·比希·雪莱,她是女权主义作家玛丽·沃斯通克拉夫特的女儿〕

Shelley, Per·cy Bysshe /ˈpɝsɪ bɪʃ; ˈpɜːsi bɪʃ/ (1792-1822) a British poet of the Romantic Movement, who disliked religion and believed strongly in political freedom. His most famous works were written after 1818 when he went to live in Italy with his wife Mary Shelley, and they include *Adonais*, written in memory of the poet John Keats, *Prometheus Unbound*, and *To a Skylark*. 雪莱〔(1792-1822),英国浪漫主义诗人。他不喜欢宗教,极力主张政治自由。1818 年携妻子玛丽·雪莱定居意大利,写下了他最为知名的作品,如纪念诗人约翰·济慈的《阿多尼斯》、《解放了的普罗米修斯》和《致云雀》〕

shell·fire /ˈʃɛlˌfaɪr; ˈʃelfaɪə/ also 又作 **shell·ing** /ˈʃɛlɪŋ; ˈʃelɪŋ/ *n* [U] the firing of large guns at a place 炮轰: **come under shellfire** (=have these guns fired at you) 遭到炮轰 *The city came under heavy shellfire.* 这城市遭到猛烈的炮轰。

shell·fish /ˈʃɛlˌfɪʃ; ˈʃelˌfɪʃ/ *plural* **shellfish** *n* **1** [C,U] a sea or water animal that does not have a BACKBONE, but has a shell〔无脊但有壳的〕水生贝类动物: *Lobsters and oysters are shellfish.* 龙虾和牡蛎都是水生贝类动物。**2** [U] such animals as a type of food 可食的水生贝类动物: *Do you like shellfish?* 你喜欢吃水生贝类动物吗?

shell shock /'· ·/ *n* [U] *old-fashioned* a type of mental illness caused by the shock of fighting in a war or battle【过时】炮弹休克〔因曾参加战争而产生的一种精神异常〕

shell shocked /'· ·/ *adj* **1** *informal* feeling tired, confused or anxious because of a recent difficult experience【非正式】疲劳的；慌乱的，焦虑的：*I think she's a bit shell-shocked after her exams.* 我想她考完试后有点头脑发昏。**2** mentally ill because of the terrible experiences of war〔因战争的可怕经历而精神异常的〕患炮弹休克的

shell suit /'· ·/ *n* [C] *BrE* a light brightly-coloured piece of clothing consisting of trousers and a JACKET (1), that fit tightly at the wrists and at the bottom of the legs【英】紧身便装〔包括夹克和长裤，其袖口和裤腿束紧〕

Shelter a British CHARITY organization that helps people who are HOMELESS (=do not have a home to live in) 收容所〔英国一慈善机构，专门帮助无家可归者〕

shel·ter¹ /'ʃɛltɚ; 'ʃeltə/ *n* **1** [U] a place to live, considered as one of the basic needs of life 栖身之地，住处：*They are in desperate need of food, clothing and shelter.* 他们急需食物、衣服和住处。**2** [U] protection, from danger or from wind, rain, hot sun etc 庇护；掩蔽，遮蔽：**the shelter of** *We eventually reached the shelter of the caves.* 我们终于到了可供掩蔽的山洞里。| *They grow well in the shelter of big oak trees.* 它们在大橡树的遮蔽下生长得很好。| **take shelter** *The men took shelter in a bombed-out farmhouse.* 那些男人躲在一间被炸毁的农舍里。| **run for shelter** *All around me, people were running for shelter.* 我周围的人都在急忙找地方躲避。| **give sb shelter** (=protect them, especially from the weather or from danger) 庇护某人〔尤指使之避开恶劣天气或危险〕—see also 另见 TAX SHELTER **3** [C] a building or an area with a roof over it that protects you from the weather or from danger 庇护所；避难所；遮蔽物：*a shelter for the homeless* 无家可归者的收容所 | *We tried to fix up a shelter from the rain.* 我们设法搭起一个遮雨的地方。| **air-raid shelter** (=to protect people from bombs dropped by planes) 防空洞 | **bus shelter** (=a small structure with a roof where you wait for a bus) 公共汽车站的候车亭

shelter² *v* **1** [T] to provide a place where someone or something is protected, especially from the weather or from danger 为…提供庇护处〔使之避开恶劣天气或危险〕；收容：*Collins was arrested for sheltering enemy soldiers.* 柯林斯因窝藏敌兵而被逮捕。| **shelter sb/sth from** *Plant herbs next to a wall to shelter them from the wind.* 把药草种在墙边以免风吹。**2** [I] to stay in or under a place where you are protected from the weather or from danger 躲避；避难：**[+from]** *We sat in the shade, sheltering from the sun.* 我们坐在背阴处免受太阳暴晒。

shel·tered /'ʃɛltɚd; 'ʃeltəd/ *adj* **1 a sheltered life/childhood/existence etc** a life etc in which someone has been too protected from difficult or unpleasant experience 受到庇护的生活/童年/生存等：*Marian's sheltered upbringing had left her unprepared for such extreme poverty.* 玛丽安在优越的环境中长大，这使她对如此极度的贫困毫无准备。**2** a place that is sheltered is protected from extreme weather conditions〔地方〕受掩护的，免遭恶劣天气影响的：*a sheltered valley* 不受暴风雨侵袭的山谷 **3 sheltered accommodation/housing** *BrE* a place for people to live who cannot fully look after themselves where help is provided if they need it【英】收容所；救济院：*sheltered accommodation for the elderly* 老人收容所

shelve /ʃɛlv; ʃelv/ *v* **1** [T] to decide not to continue with a plan, idea etc, although you might continue with it at a later time 将〔计划、意见等〕搁置：*We had to shelve the new building plans due to lack of funding.* 由于缺乏资金，我们不得不把建新楼的计划搁置起来。**2** [I always+ adv/prep] land that shelves is at a slight angle〔地面〕轻微倾斜：**[+up/down/towards etc]** *The garden shelves gently towards the sea.* 这个花园稍微向海面倾斜。**3** [T] to put something on a shelf, especially books 将〔书等〕放在架子上，上架

shelves /ʃɛlvz; ʃelvz/ the plural of SHELF

shelv·ing /'ʃɛlvɪŋ; 'ʃelvɪŋ/ *n* **1** [U] wood, metal etc used for shelves 搁板材料〈如木头、金属等〉**2** a set of shelves fixed to a wall〔安在墙上的〕架子；一组搁板

Shen·an·do·ah /,ʃɛnən'doə; ,ʃenən'dəʊə/ a river and a valley in northwest Virginia in the eastern US. Shenandoah National Park, in the Blue Ridge Mountains, covers about 300 square miles, and includes forests and Skyline Drive, from which the Shenandoah Valley can be seen. 谢南多厄河谷〔美国东部弗吉尼亚州西北部一河谷。蓝领山脉谢南多厄国家公园占地约300平方英里，园内有森林和山景公路，从那里可俯瞰谢南多厄河谷〕

she·nan·i·gans /ʃə'nænəgənz; ʃɪ'nænɪgənz/ *n* [plural] *informal*【非正式】**1** bad behaviour that is not very serious; MISCHIEF 恶作剧，胡闹，淘气 **2** slightly dishonest activities 诡计，欺骗行为

Shepard, Alan (1923-98), a US ASTRONAUT, who was the second man in space and later the fifth man to walk on the moon 谢泼德〔(1923-1998)，美国宇航员。他是进入太空的第二人，后来还成为月面行走的第五人〕

shep·herd¹ /'ʃɛpɚd; 'ʃepəd/ *n* [C] someone whose job is to take care of sheep 牧羊人，羊倌

shepherd² *v* [T always+adv/prep] to lead or guide a group of people somewhere, making sure that they go where you want them to go 带领〔一群人〕，引导〔人群〕：**shepherd sb into/out/towards etc** *I don't enjoy those tours where you're always being shepherded around some old ruins.* 我不喜欢那些老是被人带去看古老废墟的旅游。

shep·herd·ess /'ʃɛpɚdɪs; 'ʃepədes/ *n* [C] a woman or girl whose job is to take care of sheep 牧羊女

shepherd's pie /,·· '·/ *n* [U] a baked dish made of small pieces of cooked meat covered with cooked potato 肉馅马铃薯饼

sher·bet /'ʃɝbɪt; 'ʃɜːbət/ *n* **1** [C] *AmE* a frozen sweet made with water, fruit, milk and the white part of an egg【美】果汁冰糕〔一种用水、水果、牛奶、蛋白等制成的冷冻甜食〕**2** [U] *BrE* a powder that is eaten as a sweet【英】甜味果味粉〔一种甜食〕

sherd /ʃɝd; ʃɜːd/ *n* [C] another spelling of SHARD shard的另一种拼法

sher·iff /'ʃɛrɪf; 'ʃerɪ̣f/ *n* [C] **1** an elected law officer of a COUNTY in the US〔美国的〕县治安官〔由选举产生的县级司法长官〕**2** also 又作 **High Sheriff** the chief officer of the King or Queen in a COUNTY of England and Wales, who has mostly ceremonial duties〔英格兰和威尔士的〕郡长〔一种礼仪性职务〕**3** the chief judge in a DISTRICT (2) or COUNTY in Scotland〔苏格兰的〕区[郡]法官

Sheriff of Not·ting·ham, the /,·· ··'··/ an evil man who is the main enemy of Robin Hood in old English stories 诺丁汉郡长〔英国传说中的一个邪恶男子，他是罗宾汉的头号敌手〕

sheriff's court /'·· ,·/ *n* [C] the lower court of law in Scotland, dealing with CIVIL (3) and criminal cases〔苏格兰的〕郡法院，初等法院〔兼管民事和刑事案件〕

Sherlock Holmes —see 见 Sherlock HOLMES

Sher·pa /'ʃɝpə; 'ʃɜːpə/ *n* [C] a Himalayan person who is often employed to guide people through mountains 夏尔巴人〔喜马拉雅人，常受雇当登山者向导〕

sher·ry /'ʃɛrɪ; 'ʃeri/ *n* [C, U] a pale or dark brown strong wine, originally from Spain 雪利酒〔原产于西班牙的一种白色或深褐色烈性酒〕

Sher·wood For·est /,ʃɝwʊd 'fɔrɪst; ,ʃɜːwʊd 'fɒrɪ̣st/ a forest in central England, mainly in Nottinghamshire, which is famous as the place where Robin Hood lived in old English stories 舍伍德森林〔英格兰中部一林区，大部分在诺丁汉郡境内。据古老的英国传说，罗宾汉即居于此〕

she's /ʃɪz; ʃiz *strong* 强读 ʃiz; ʃiːz/ **1** the short form of 'she is' 缩略式= she is **2** the short form of 'she has' 缩略式= she has

Shet·land Is·lands, the /,ʃɛtlənd 'aɪləndz; ,ʃetlənd 'aɪləndz/ also 又作 **Shetland, the Shetlands** a group of about 100 small islands off the north coast of Scotland, further north than the Orkneys. The main industries of the islands are fishing, farming, producing woollen clothes, and, more recently, dealing with the oil which is taken from nearby areas of the North Sea. People from the Shetland Islands are called Shetlanders. 设得兰群岛〔与苏格兰北部海岸隔海相望的一群岛。位于奥克尼群岛以北，由大约100座小岛组成。该地的主要产业有渔业、畜牧业、羊毛服装加工业等，近年来开始冶炼北海临近地区的石油。设得兰群岛居民称为Shetlander〕

Shet·land po·ny /,ʃɛtlənd 'ponɪ; ,ʃetlənd 'pəʊni/ *n* [C] a small strong horse with long rough hair 设得兰矮种马〔一种体小毛粗但强壮耐劳的马〕

shew /ʃo; ʃəʊ/ *v* [I,T] an old spelling of SHOW show的旧式拼法

shh /ʃ; ʃ/ *interjection* used to tell people to be quiet 嘘，别作声〔用以叫别人安静下来〕：*Shh! I can't hear what he's saying.* 嘘！我听不见他在说什么了。

Shi·a, Shiah /'ʃiə; 'ʃiːə/ *n* **1 the Shiah** the Shiite branch of the Muslim religion 什叶派〔伊斯兰教的一派〕**2** [C] a Shiite 什叶派教徒

shi·a·tsu /ʃɪ'ɑtsu; ʃi'ɑːtsuː/ *n* [U] a Japanese form of MASSAGE (=pressing and rubbing someone's body) used to prevent or treat physical or emotional problems 日式按摩，指压按摩

shib·bo·leth /'ʃɪbəlɪθ; 'ʃɪbəleθ/ *n* [C] *formal* an old idea, custom or principle you think is no longer important or suitable

S

for modern times【正式】〔认为已不重要或已过时的〕陈旧思想，陈规陋习

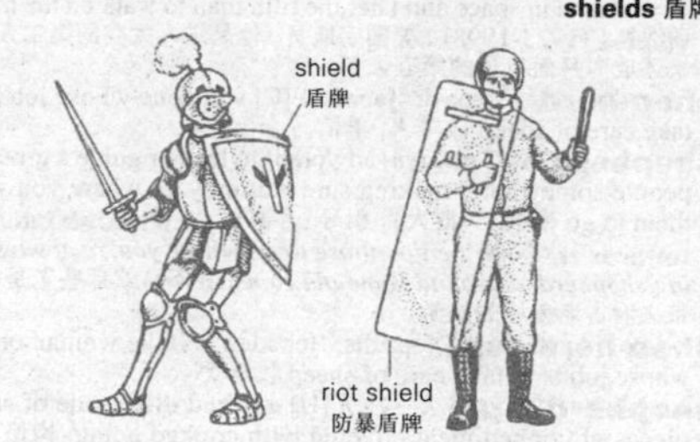

shield¹ /ʃild; ʃiːld/ *n* [C] **1 a)** a thing that soldiers used consisting of a broad piece of metal or leather 盾，盾牌 **b)** also 又作 **riot shield** a piece of equipment made of strong plastic, used by the police to protect themselves against angry crowds〔警察用来保护自己的〕防暴盾牌 **2** something in the shape of a shield, wide at the top and curving to a point at the bottom, that is used for a COAT OF ARMS, a prize in sport etc 盾形纹[徽]章，〔体育比赛中的〕盾形奖牌 **3** something that protects a person or thing against harm or damage 护盖，护罩；保护[防御]物：*the ozone layer, the shield that protects the Earth from the Sun's harmful rays* 臭氧层，使地球免受太阳有害射线辐射的保护层

shield² *v* [T] to protect someone or something from being harmed, or damaged 保护，保卫：*Women will often lie to shield even the most abusive partner.* 妇女常会撒谎以保护哪怕是对她最粗暴的伙伴。| **shield sb/sth from sth** *He held up his hands, shielding his eyes from the sun.* 他举起双手，遮住眼睛免受阳光照射。| *import tariffs that shield firms from foreign competition* 保护企业免受外国竞争的进口关税

S

3 **shift¹** /ʃɪft; ʃɪft/ *v*

1 ▶MOVE 移动◀ a) [I,T] to move from one place or position to another, or make something do this（使）移动〔地点、位置〕，（使）转移：*Jonas stood and listened, shifting uncomfortably from one foot to another.* 乔纳斯站着听，不自在地把重心从一只脚转移到另一只脚。| *The sun had shifted around to the west.* 太阳已经转到西边了。| *She shifted her gaze from me to Bobby with a look of suspicion.* 她用怀疑的目光凝视着我，然后又转向博比。**b)** [T] *informal* to move something, especially by picking it up and carrying it【非正式】移动；搬动〔尤指提起来搬〕：*Give me a hand to shift these chairs.* 请帮我挪一挪这几把椅子。

2 shift attention/emphasis/focus to change a situation, discussion etc by giving special attention to one idea or subject instead of to a previous one 转移注意力/重点/中心：*The president is shifting the focus of the debate to foreign policy issues.* 总统正在把辩论的焦点转移到外交政策问题上。| **attention/emphasis/focus shifts** *Under these new arrangements, the emphasis has shifted from state provision to personal responsibility.* 在这些新的安排下，重点已经从国家供应转移到个人责任上来。

3 ▶COSTS/SPENDING 费用/开支◀ [T always+adv/prep] to change the way that money is paid or spent 转嫁，转给：*This simply shifts the cost of medical insurance from employer to employee.* 这不过是把医疗保险费从雇主转嫁给雇员了。| *the need to shift more resources towards the alleviation of poverty* 把更多财力物力转向缓解贫困的需要

4 ▶OPINIONS 意见◀ [I,T] to change your opinions or beliefs, especially about political matters 改变〔意见、信仰，尤指政治方面〕：*Opinion in the country was beginning to shift to the right.* 国内舆论开始向右转变。| *shifting attitudes towards marriage* 改变对待婚姻的态度 | **shift your ground** (=change your opinion) 改变立场[看法] *The government shifted its ground, and gradually lent its support to African nationalism.* 政府改变了立场，对非洲民族主义逐渐采取支持的态度。

5 shift the blame/responsibility to make someone else responsible for something, especially for something bad that has happened 推卸责任：*It was a blatant attempt to shift the responsibility for the crime on to the victim.* 这是个无耻的企图，想把犯罪的责任转嫁给受害者。

6 ▶DIRT/MARKS 污垢/痕迹◀ [T] *BrE* to remove dirt or marks from a surface or piece of clothing【英】除去〔表面或衣服上的污迹〕：*a new washing powder that will shift any stain* 一种能洗掉任何污迹的新洗衣粉

7 ▶IN A CAR 在汽车中◀ [I,T] *especially AmE* to change the gears (GEAR¹ (1)) when you are driving【尤美】换挡，调挡：*I shifted into second gear.* 我把车速调到第二挡。

shift² *n* [C] **1** a change in the way people think about something, in the way something is done etc〔想法、做法等的〕改变：[**+from/to**] *a major shift from manufacturing to service industries* 从制造业到服务业的重大改变 | [**+in**] *a shift in emphasis from defense spending to civilian spending* 从国防开支到民用开支的重心转移 | **a marked shift** (=a very noticeable change) 明显的改变 *There has been a marked shift in attitudes towards homosexuality.* 人们对同性恋的态度有了明显的改变。**2 a)** one of the periods during each day and night when workers in a factory, hospital etc are at work〔工作人员在工厂、医院等轮值工作的〕当班时间：**do/work a shift** *I usually work the night shift, which is from 10 at night till 6 in the morning.* 我通常上夜班，从晚上10点到早上6点。| *Do you do shift work?* 你们是不是轮班工作？**b)** the workers who work during one of these periods 轮班工人 **3 a)** a simple straight loose-fitting woman's dress 宽松直筒式家常女服 **b)** *old use* a similar piece of clothing worn as underwear【旧】裙式女内衣 **4** the KEY² (3) on a computer or TYPEWRITER that you press to print a capital letter〔电脑、打字机上的〕大写字母转换键：*To run the spellchecker, press SHIFT and F7.* 要使用拼写检查程序，按转换键和F7。**5** *old use* a clever trick or method【旧】手段，计谋

shift key /'· ·/ *n* [C] the KEY² (3) on a KEYBOARD that you press to make a capital letter〔键盘上的〕大写字母转换键

shift·less /'ʃɪftlɪs; 'ʃɪftləs/ *adj* lazy and seeming to have no interest in working hard or trying to succeed 懒惰的，不求上进的，得过且过的：*my shiftless nephew, who was never any good* 我那个不求上进、一无是处的侄儿 —**shiftlessly** *adv* —**shiftlessness** *n*

shift·y /'ʃɪfti; 'ʃɪfti/ *adj informal* looking dishonest and slightly nervous【非正式】狡诈的，躲躲闪闪的，鬼鬼祟祟的：*a shifty-looking little man* 模样诡诈的矮小男子 | *shifty eyes* 一双贼眼 —**shiftily** *adv* —**shiftiness** *n* [U]

Shi·ite /'ʃiaɪt; 'ʃiː-aɪt/ *n* a member of one of the two main branches of the Muslim religion〔伊斯兰教两大分支之一的〕什叶派教徒 —compare 比较 SUNNI —**Shiite** *adj*

Shi·ko·ku /'ʃikoku; 'ʃiːkəʊkuː/ the smallest of Japan's four main islands 四国〔日本四大岛中最小的岛屿〕

shil·ling /'ʃɪlɪŋ; 'ʃɪlɪŋ/ *n* [C] **1** a coin used in Britain until 1971, worth 12 old pence and 1/20 of £1 先令〔1971年之前英国的货币单位，等于12旧便士或1/20英镑〕**2** a unit of money used in Tanzania, Kenya, Uganda, and Somalia 先令〔坦桑尼亚、肯尼亚、乌干达和索马里的货币单位〕

shil·ly-shal·ly /'ʃɪlɪ,ʃælɪ; 'ʃɪli ,ʃæli/ *v* [I] *informal* to waste time or take too long to make a decision【非正式】〔作决定时〕犹豫不决，踌躇

shim·mer /'ʃɪmɚ; 'ʃɪmə/ *v* [I] to shine with a soft light that looks as if it shakes slightly 发微光，闪闪发亮：*The lake shimmered in the moonlight.* 湖水在月色下闪闪发光。—**shimmer** *n* [U]: *the shimmer of the desert air in the midday heat* 中午酷热时分沙漠热气中发出的闪光

shin¹ /ʃɪn; ʃɪn/ *n* [C] the front part of your leg between your knee and your foot（外）胫，胫部 —see picture at 参见 BODY 图

shin² *v* [I] **shin up/shin down** to climb up or down a tree, pole etc by using your hands and legs, especially quickly 爬上/爬下〔尤指快速地用手和腿爬树或杆等〕；SHINNY *AmE*【美】：*to shin up the drainpipe* 沿着排水管往上爬

shin·bone /'· ·/ *n* [C] the front bone in your leg below your knee; TIBIA 胫骨 —see picture at 参见 SKELETON 图

shin·dig /'ʃɪndɪg; 'ʃɪndɪg/ *n* [C] *old-fashioned* a noisy party【过时】喧闹的聚会

shine¹ /ʃaɪn; ʃaɪn/ *v past tense and past participle* **shone** /ʃon; 3
ʃɒn/ **1** [I] to produce light 发光，发亮：*At last the sun was shining after weeks of rain.* 下了几个星期的雨，太阳终于出来了。| [**+in/on**] *That lamp's shining in my eyes.* 那盏灯的光直刺我的眼。**2** [I] to look bright and shiny〔看上去〕光亮，闪光，发亮：*a big basket of shining fish of every shape and size* 一大筐各种各样闪闪发亮的鱼 | *I want you to clean this kitchen until it shines.* 我要你把厨房收拾得干干净净。**3** [T] to hold or point a lamp, light etc so that the light from it goes in a particular direction 使〔灯光等〕向…照射：**shine sth into/across/onto etc** *Shine the flashlight over here so that I can see what I'm doing.* 把手电筒照到这边，好让我看清我干的活。**4** [I] if your eyes shine, or your face shines, you have an expression of happiness〔眼睛、脸上〕流露出快乐的表情：*"I passed!" exclaimed Rufus, his eyes shining.* "我及格了！"鲁弗斯喊道，高兴得两眼放光。**5** [I not in progressive 不用进行时] to be very good at something 表现突

出, 出众: [+in/at] *He really shines in history.* 他在历史方面确有特长。

shine through *phr v* [I] if a quality that someone has shines through, you can easily see that they have it〔某种特质〕显而易见, 表现明显: *What shines through in all her work is her enthusiasm for life.* 她的所有作品都显示出她对生活的热情。

shine² *past tense and past participle* **shined** *v* [T] to make something bright by rubbing it; polish 擦亮, 磨光

shine³ *n* **1** [singular,U] the brightness that something has when light shines on it 光泽; 光亮: *The old table has a beautiful shine.* 这张旧桌子闪着漂亮的光泽。**2** [singular] an act of making something bright by polishing it 擦亮: **give sth a shine** *Give your shoes a good shine before you go.* 你走之前要把鞋子好好地擦擦。**3 take a shine to** *informal* to like someone very much when you have only just met them【非正式】一眼就喜欢上〔某人〕—see also 另见 **(come) rain or shine** (RAIN¹ (4))

shin·gle /ˈʃɪŋgl; ˈʃɪŋgəl/ *n* **1** [C,U] one of many small thin pieces of building material, especially wood, used to cover a roof or wall〔盖房顶或墙用的〕木瓦; 屋面板, 墙面板 **2** [U] small round pieces of stone on a beach〔海滩上的〕小圆石: *shingle glistening with broken shells* 夹杂着碎贝壳的闪闪发光的小圆石 —see picture on page A12 参见 A12 页图 **3 hang out your shingle** *AmE* to start your own business, especially as a doctor or lawyer【美】〔尤指医生或律师〕挂牌开业

shin·gles /ˈʃɪŋglz; ˈʃɪŋgəlz/ *n* [U] a disease caused by an infection of the nerve endings, which produces painful red spots 带状疱疹

shin·ing /ˈʃaɪnɪŋ; ˈʃaɪnɪŋ/ *adj* [only before noun 仅用于名词前] excellent in a way that is easy to see 杰出的, 出众的: **a shining example of** *O'Reilly was a shining example of courage on the battlefield.* 奥赖利在战场上是英勇作战的光辉典范。

shin·ny /ˈʃɪnɪ; ˈʃɪni/ *v* [I] *AmE*【美】**shinny up/down** to SHIN² 爬上/爬下

Shin·to /ˈʃɪnto; ˈʃɪntəʊ/ also 又作 **Shin·to·is·m** /ˈʃɪntoɪzm; ˈʃɪntəʊɪzəm/ *n* [U] the ancient religion of Japan that has gods who represent various parts of nature, and gives great importance to people who died in the past〔日本的〕神道教

shin·ty /ˈʃɪntɪ; ˈʃɪnti/ *n* [U] a game played in Scotland, similar to HOCKEY (1) 简化曲棍球戏〔一种苏格兰人玩的类似曲棍球的运动〕

shin·y /ˈʃaɪnɪ; ˈʃaɪni/ *adj* smooth and bright 光滑发亮的, 闪光的: *a shiny polished table* 擦得闪闪发亮的桌子 | *shiny hair* 光滑发亮的头发 | *a big shiny limousine* 闪闪发亮的豪华大轿车 —**shininess** *n* [U] —see picture at 参见 SLIP¹ 图

-ship /ʃɪp; ʃɪp/ *suffix* (in nouns 构成名词) **1 a)** the state of having a particular position or job 身份, 地位, 资格: *Full membership* (=being a full member) *of the club costs $35.* 该俱乐部的正式会员需交会费 35 美元。| *professorship* (=the job of PROFESSOR) 教授职位 **b)** the time during which this lasts (…期间的) 状况: *their long friendship* 他们的长久友谊 | *during his premiership* 在他担任总理期间 **2** the art or skill of a particular person〔某人的〕技能, 技巧: *her peerless musicianship* 她无与伦比的音乐才华 | *a work of great scholarship* 一部学术巨著 —see also 另见 -MANSHIP **3** the whole group of a particular group 某群体的全部: *a magazine with a readership of 9,000* (=with 9,000 readers) 拥有 9000 名读者的杂志 **4** forms part of certain title 构成某种头衔或身份: *your ladyship* 夫人

ship¹ /ʃɪp; ʃɪp/ *n* [C] **1** a large boat used for carrying people or goods across the sea 大船; 海轮, 舰: *a cruise ship* 海上游船 | *a merchant ship* 商船 | **by ship** *Most of the island's supplies are brought in by ship.* 这个海岛的大部分给养都是由船只运来的。**2** a large SPACECRAFT or aircraft 宇宙飞船, 太空船; 飞船 **3 ships that pass in the night** people who meet for a short time and then never meet again 萍水相逢的人〔以后不再相遇〕 **4 when your ship comes in** used when you are wishing that something will suddenly happen to make you rich 有朝一日发大财[发迹]的时候: *When my ship comes in, I'll quit work and travel around the world.* 等我发了财, 我就辞掉工作并周游世界。

ship² *past tense* **shipped** *present participle* **shipping** *v* [T] **1** to send or carry something by ship 用船运送: **ship sth out/to etc** *I'm flying over to the States and having my car shipped out later.* 我坐飞机前往美国, 会安排我的汽车稍后经海运送去。**2** to deliver goods or make them available for people to buy 发货; 供货; 使〔商品〕上市: *The new Windows software was announced in April and they're planning to ship it in October.* 这种新视窗软件在 4 月宣布推出, 并计划于 10 月供货。**3** to order someone to go somewhere 遣送〔某人〕, 将〔某人〕送往…: **ship sb off/out etc** *As soon as the doctor saw her, he shipped her straight off to the hospital.* 医生给她检查以后, 立即把她送往医院。| *I was in Heidelberg at the time, about to be shipped out to Vietnam.* 我当时在海德堡, 即将被送往越南。**4 ship water** if a boat ships water, water comes into it over its sides〔船〕在舷侧进水 **5 ship oars** to stop rowing and to bring the OARs into the boat〔停止划桨〕把桨收进船内 —see also 另见 **shape up or ship out** (SHAPE UP (3))

ship·board /ˈʃɪpˌbɔrd; ˈʃɪpbɔːd/ *n* [U] **on shipboard** on a ship 在船上

ship·build·er /ˈʃɪpˌbɪldɚ; ˈʃɪpˌbɪldə/ *n* [C] a company that makes ships 造船公司 —**shipbuilding** *n* [U]: *an old shipbuilding town* 古老的造船业城镇

ship·load /ˈʃɪpˌlod; ˈʃɪpləʊd/ *n* [C] the amount of goods or people a ship can carry 一艘船的装货量; 载人量: [+of] *A shipload of new cars has just arrived.* 一船新汽车刚刚运到。

ship·mate /ˈʃɪpˌmet; ˈʃɪpmeɪt/ *n* [C] a SAILOR's shipmate is another sailor who is working on the same ship 同船的水手[船员]

ship·ment /ˈʃɪpmənt; ˈʃɪpmənt/ *n* [C,U] a load of goods sent by sea, road, or air, or the act of sending them〔经海路、陆路或航空运送的〕货物;〔货物的〕装运, 运送: [+of] *The goods are now ready for shipment.* 这批货物现已准备好, 可以装运了。| *a large shipment of grain* 一大批装运的谷物

ship·per /ˈʃɪpɚ; ˈʃɪpə/ *n* [C] a company that sends goods to places by ship 承办货运的轮船公司, 航运商

ship·ping /ˈʃɪpɪŋ; ˈʃɪpɪŋ/ *n* [U] **1** ships considered as a group 船舶〔总称〕: *The port is closed to all shipping.* 这个港口已封港。**2** all the ships belonging to a particular country〔一国的〕船舶总数: *Israeli shipping was excluded from the Straits of Tiran.* 以色列船只不得进入蒂朗海峡。**3** the delivery of goods, especially by ship〔货物的〕运输〔尤指船运〕

shipping fore·cast /ˈ‥, ‥/ *n* [C] *BrE* a radio broadcast that says what the weather will be like at sea【英】海洋天气预报

shipping lane /ˈ‥, ·/ *n* [C] an officially approved path of travel that ships must follow〔官方规定的〕海上航道, 商船航线

ship's chand·ler /ˌ· ˈ‥/ *n* [C] someone who sells equipment for ships 船具供应商

ship·shape /ˈʃɪpˌʃep; ˈʃɪpʃeɪp/ *adj* [not before noun 不用于名词前] neat and clean 整齐清洁的, 井井有条的: *Let's get this house shipshape.* 让我们把这所房子收拾干净。

ship-to-shore /ˌ· · ˈ·◂/ *adj* providing communication between a ship and people on land〔通讯〕船与岸之间的: *ship-to-shore radio* 船与岸之间的无线电

ship·wreck¹ /ˈʃɪpˌrɛk; ˈʃɪp-rek/ *n* [U] the destruction of a ship in an accident 海难, 船只失事: *The survivors of the shipwreck were flown to land by helicopter.* 海难的生还者被直升机送上了岸。

shipwreck² *v* **be shipwrecked** to have been sailing in a ship that has had a serious accident and can no longer sail 遭遇海难: *Beatty was shipwrecked off the coast of Africa.* 贝蒂在非洲海岸附近遭遇了海难。

ship·wright /ˈʃɪpˌraɪt; ˈʃɪp-raɪt/ *n* [C] someone who builds or repairs ships 造船者; 修船工

ship·yard /ˈʃɪpˌjɑrd; ˈʃɪp-jɑːd/ *n* [C] a place where ships are built or repaired 造[修]船厂, 船坞

Shir·az /ʃɪəˈrɑz; ʃɪəˈrɑːz/ a type of red wine made from the Shiraz GRAPE. Shiraz is made especially in Australia and South Africa. 希拉兹〔一种用希拉兹葡萄酿造的红葡萄酒, 主产区位于澳大利亚和南非〕

shire /ʃaɪr; ʃaɪə/ *n* [C] **1 the shires** the country areas in the central part of England 英格兰中部的农村地区 **2** *BrE old use* a COUNTY【英旧】郡

shire horse /ˈ· ·/ *n* [C] a type of large powerful horse used for pulling large loads〔一种高大强壮的〕拉车马, 重挽马

shirk /ʃɝk; ʃɜːk/ *v* [I,T] to deliberately avoid doing something you should do, because you are lazy〔因懒惰而〕逃避〔工作、责任等〕: *a salesman who was fired for shirking* 由于逃避工作而被解雇的推销员 | **shirk your responsibilities/duties/obligations** *Are you accusing me of shirking my responsibilities?* 你是在指责我逃避责任吗? —**shirker** *n* [C]

Shir·ley Tem·ple /ˌʃɝlɪ ˋtɛmpl; ˌʃɜːli ˈtempəl/ a popular drink for children in the US, made from LEMONADE and GRENADINE (=a sweet red liquid), and served with a CHERRY. Shirley Temples are usually served in restaurants, and they are sometimes called Roy Rogers if they are served to boys. 秀兰·邓波儿〔美国一种儿童饮料。用柠檬汽水和石榴糖浆调制而成, 饮用时加一颗樱桃, 常在餐厅里出售。如果男孩饮用, 则称为罗依·罗杰斯〕

shirt /ʃɝt; ʃɜːt/ *n* [C] **1** a piece of clothing that covers the upper part of your body and your arms, usually has a collar, and is fastened at the front by buttons 衬衫, 恤衫: *I have to wear a*

shirt and tie to work. 我上班要穿衬衫，系领带。—see picture on page A17 参见 A17 页图 **2 keep your shirt on** *spoken* used to tell someone who is becoming angry that they should stay calm【口】请保持冷静，请不要发火〔用以劝告正在发火的人〕**3 have the shirt off someone's back** *informal* to take everything that someone owes you, without showing any sympathy【非正式】拿走某人所欠的一切东西，冷酷无情地讨债 **4 put your shirt on sth** *BrE* to risk all your money on something【英】对…孤注一掷，把所有钱财押在…上 —see also 另见 STUFFED SHIRT

shirt·front /ˈʃɝtˌfrʌnt; ˈʃɜːtfrʌnt/ *n* [C] the part of a shirt that covers your chest 衬衫的前胸

shirt·sleeves /ˈʃɝtˌslivz; ˈʃɜːtsliːvz/ *n* **in (your) shirtsleeves** wearing a shirt but no JACKET (1) 只穿衬衣〔不穿外套〕: *It was 90° and the men were in their shirtsleeves.* 气温达到 90 华氏度，男士都只穿衬衣，不穿外套。

shirt tail /ˈ· ·/ *n* [C] the part of a shirt that is below your waist and is usually inside your trousers 衬衫的下摆

shirt·waist·er /ˈʃɝtˌwestɚ; ˈʃɜːtˌweɪstə/ *BrE*【英】, **shirtwaist** /ˈʃɝtˌwest; ˈʃɜːtweɪst/ *AmE*【美】*n* [C] a woman's dress in the style of a long shirt 衬衫式连衣裙

shirt·y /ˈʃɝtɪ; ˈʃɜːti/ *adj BrE informal* bad-tempered, angry, and rude【英，非正式】脾气坏的，动辄发怒的，粗暴的: *Phil got a bit shirty when I tried to tell him he was wrong.* 我向菲尔指出他不对时，他有点生气。

shish ke·bab /ˈʃɪʃ kɪˌbɑb; ˈʃɪʃ kəˌbæb/ *n* [C] small pieces of meat that are put on a long thin metal stick and cooked 烤肉串

[2] **shit¹** /ʃɪt; ʃɪt/ *n taboo, especially spoken*【讳，尤口】

1 shit!/oh shit! used to express anger, fear, or disappointment 呸！放屁！〔表示愤怒、恐惧或失望〕: *Shit! I've left my purse at home.* 妈的！我把钱包忘在家里了。

2 ▶BODY WASTE 身体排泄物◀ [U] solid waste that comes out of your body from your BOWELs 粪，大便: *Mind that dog shit!* 当心那些狗屎！

3 have/get the shits to have or get DIARRHOEA 腹泻，泻肚

4 ▶STH UNPLEASANT/BAD QUALITY 讨厌/劣质的东西◀ [U] something that is useless or very bad quality 无用之物，劣质品: *Their apartment is full of cheap modern shit.* 他们公寓里尽是些廉价劣质的时髦货。| *What's that shit you're reading?* 你在读什么屁东西?

5 ▶STUPID/UNTRUE TALK 蠢话/假话◀ [U] something that you think is stupid or untrue 胡说八道，谎言: *You expect me to believe that shit?* 你以为我会相信那种屁话? | **full of shit** (=saying things that are stupid or not true) 全是胡说八道，胡扯 *You're full of shit, Rudy. All this stuff about money and cars is just to impress the girls.* 鲁迪，你尽胡扯，说一些关于钱财名车的谎话来哄女孩子。

6 ▶PERSON 人◀ [C] someone who is very unpleasant and treats other people badly 讨厌的人，卑鄙的人: *You don't want to get involved with Colin – he's a complete shit.* 你别和科林打交道，他是个十足的混蛋。

7 in deep shit also 又作 **in the shit** *BrE*【英】in a lot of trouble 遇到大麻烦，陷入困境: *Pete's in deep shit because his wife's found out that he lied to her.* 皮特这回可遇上大麻烦了，他老婆发现他对她撒了谎。

8 not give/care a shit to not care at all about something 毫不在乎，毫不关心: *I don't give a shit what you think!* 我才不在乎你是怎么想的！

9 feel like shit to feel very ill 感到很不舒服: *I woke up with a hangover, and felt like shit for the rest of the day.* 我醒来后宿酒未消，一整天都觉得很难受。

10 beat/kick the shit out of to beat or kick someone very violently 把〔某人〕打得屁滚尿流: *I'll beat the shit out of you!* 我要狠狠地揍你！

11 give sb shit to insult someone or criticize them 侮辱某人；批评某人: *She's always giving me shit about my clothes and stuff.* 她总是把我的衣服等说得一钱不值。

12 the shit will hit the fan used to say that there will be a lot of trouble when someone finds out about something 大麻烦到来，灾难临头: *He'll be back this afternoon, and that's when the shit will really hit the fan.* 他今天下午就回来，到那时可就麻烦了。—see also 另见 **scare the shit out of** (SCARE¹ (1)), **tough shit** (TOUGH¹ (7))

shit² *v past tense and past participle* **shit** or **shat** /ʃæt; ʃæt/ *taboo, especially spoken*【讳，尤口】**1** [I] to pass solid waste out of your body from your BOWELs 拉屎，排便 **2 shit yourself** to feel very worried or frightened 极其担忧[害怕]: *I'm absolutely shitting myself about the test next week.* 我对下星期的考试真是怕得要命。**3** [T] *AmE* to tell someone something that is untrue【美】撒谎，胡说: *Are you shitting me?* 你在对我撒谎?

shit³ *adj taboo, spoken*【讳，口】**1** *especially BrE* very bad【尤英】极坏的，极差的: *Jim is shit at football.* 吉姆足球踢得蹩脚透了。| *It's a really shit job.* 这种工作真是糟透了。**2 be up shit creek** to be in a very difficult or dangerous situation 处境十分困难[危险]

shite /ʃaɪt; ʃaɪt/ *n BrE, spoken* another word for SHIT¹ (1)【英口】呸，放屁〔shit¹ 的另一说法〕

shit-faced /ˈ· ·/ *adj taboo, spoken* very drunk【讳，口】大醉的，烂醉如泥的

shit-for-brains /ˌ· · ˈ·/ *n* [C] *taboo* someone who is very stupid【讳】笨蛋，白痴

shit hole /ˈ· ·/ *n* [C] *taboo, spoken* a place that is very dirty and unpleasant【讳，口】极肮脏的地方；令人极不愉快的地方: *They live in a total shit hole.* 他们住在一个肮脏透顶的地方。

shit-hot /ˌ· ˈ·◂/ *adj taboo, spoken* extremely good【讳，口】极好的

shit·less /ˈʃɪtlɪs; ˈʃɪtləs/ *adj* **scare sb shitless** *taboo, spoken* to make someone feel very frightened【讳，口】吓得某人魂不附体

shit stir·rer /ˈ· ˌ·· / *n taboo, especially BrE*【讳，尤英】[C] someone who deliberately makes trouble for other people 故意捣乱者，制造麻烦者

shit·ty /ˈʃɪtɪ; ˈʃɪti/ *adj taboo, spoken* very bad, unpleasant, or nasty【讳，口】令人不愉快的；极坏的: *Dave's been in a shitty mood all morning.* 戴夫整个上午情绪都不好。

Shi·va /ˈʃivə; ˈʃiːvə/ —see 见 SIVA

shiv·er¹ /ˈʃɪvɚ; ˈʃɪvə/ *v* [I] to shake slightly because you are cold or frightened〔因寒冷或害怕而〕颤抖，哆嗦，发抖: *The children stood outside shivering.* 孩子们站在外面直发抖。| [+with] *Juanita was shivering with cold.* 朱厄妮塔冻得直发抖。

shiver 发抖

shiver² *n* [C] **1** a slight shaking movement of your body caused by cold or fear〔因寒冷或恐惧引起身体的〕颤抖，发抖: *A shiver ran through her at the thought of Worrel's ugly face.* 她想起沃雷尔那张丑陋的脸就毛骨悚然。**2 give you the shivers** *informal* to make you feel afraid【非正式】使人打寒颤[害怕]: *Snakes give me the shivers.* 蛇令我颤栗。**3 send shivers (up and) down your spine** *informal* to make you feel very frightened or excited【非正式】使人脊骨发凉，令人毛骨悚然；令人兴奋: *A sudden scream from outside sent shivers down his spine.* 外边突然传来一声尖叫，令他毛骨悚然。**4 shivers** [plural] *literary* one of the very small pieces into which something breaks when it is hit or dropped【文】碎片，破片

shiv·er·y /ˈʃɪvərɪ; ˈʃɪvəri/ *adj* trembling or shaking because of cold, fear, or illness〔因寒冷、恐惧或疾病〕颤抖的，发抖的: *He felt shivery and nauseous.* 他感到颤抖和恶心。

shoal /ʃol; ʃəʊl/ *n* [C] **1** a large group of fish swimming together 鱼群，一大群游鱼 **2** a small hill of sand just below the surface of water that makes it dangerous for boats 浅滩，沙洲

shock¹ /ʃɑk; ʃɒk/ *n* 2 2

1 ▶SHOCKING EVENT/SITUATION 令人震惊的事件/情况◀ [C usually singular 一般用单数] an unexpected and unpleasant event, situation, or piece of news that surprises and upsets you 令人震惊的事件[情况，消息]: *It was a real shock to hear that the factory would have to close.* 听到工厂将不得不倒闭的消息，真是令人震惊。| **come as a shock** (=be a shock) 令人震惊 *We knew Rob had cancer, but it still came as a shock when he died.* 我们早知道罗布患了癌症，但他的死仍然令人震惊。

2 ▶UNEXPECTED UNPLEASANT FEELING 意外的不愉快感觉◀ [singular U] the feeling of surprise and disbelief you have when something very unpleasant happens unexpectedly 吃惊，震惊，惊愕: *I was numb with shock when I found out Graham was having an affair.* 我发现格雷厄姆和别人私通时真是惊呆了。| **get a shock** *They'll get a shock when they get this bill.* 他们收到这份账单时必定会大吃一惊。| **in a state of shock** (=extremely shocked by something and unable to think or react normally) 大为震惊 *Several hours after we had heard that Cobain was dead, we were still in a state of shock.* 我们听到柯本去世的噩耗后，好几小时后都还感到震惊。

3 ▶MEDICAL 医学的◀ [U] a medical condition in which someone looks pale and their hearts and lungs are not working correctly, usually after a sudden very unpleasant experience 休

克: **suffer from shock** *Several witnesses were taken to hospital suffering from shock.* 好几位目击者因休克被送进医院。| **in (a state of) shock** *Paul's in shock, but otherwise his injuries are not serious.* 保罗处于休克状态，但他的伤势不算严重。

4 ▶ELECTRICITY 电◀ also 又作 **electric shock** [C] a sharp, painful feeling caused by a dangerous flow of electricity passing through your body 电震，电击: **get a shock** *I got a shock off the toaster this morning.* 今天早上我在碰到烤面包机时被电击了一下。

5 ▶SHAKING 震动◀ [C,U] violent shaking caused for example by an explosion or EARTHQUAKE etc〔爆炸、地震等引起的〕剧烈震动: *The shock of the explosion was felt miles away.* 爆炸引起的震动在好几英里以外都能感觉到。—see also 另见 SHOCK WAVE

6 a shock of hair a very thick mass of hair 一头浓密的头发 —see also 另见 SHOCKED, SHELL SHOCK, TOXIC SHOCK SYNDROME

USAGE NOTE 用法说明: SHOCK

WORD CHOICE 词语辨析: **shock, surprise, shocking**

Shock and **shocking** are both fairly strong words and you may have to think whether they are the words you really need to express your meaning. shock 和 shocking 的含义都相当强，因此在使用时必须考虑它们是否恰当地表达了自己的意思。

If something **is, comes as**, or **gives you a shock** it is unexpected and often very bad. 如果某事 is, comes as, 或 gives you a shock, 即表示其来得突然，而且常指不好的事情: *It came as a great shock to hear she was leaving home.* 她要离家的消息听了令人大吃一惊。| *He'll be OK once he gets over the shock.* 等他从震惊中恢复过来就没事了。

A **surprise** is something that is unexpected, but is not necessarily bad. surprise 也表示意外的事，但不一定是不好的: *What a nice surprise! I didn't even think you were in the country!* 多令人惊喜呀！我压根没想到你在国内。| *It was quite a surprise to know I was actually good at drawing.* 我发现自己原来很会画画，真叫人大感意外。

Something that is **shocking** is extremely bad, often in an offensive or immoral way. 说某事 shocking, 则表示此事极其不好，而且常指令人反感，在道德上不好: *shocking violence* 令人震惊的暴力。So you would not use **shocking** to describe, for example, your first day at school, or something that was simply an unpleasant surprise. 因此，如果是第一天上学，或仅是一件不太愉快的意外之事，就不该用 shocking 去形容。

shock² *v* **1** [T] to make someone feel very surprised and upset, and unable to believe what has happened 使震惊，使惊愕，使难以置信: *The murder of such a young child deeply shocked the whole community.* 杀害这样年幼的孩子使整个社区极度震惊。| **it shocks sb to do sth** *It shocked me to think how close we had come to being killed.* 想到我们差一点丧命，我就非常害怕。**2** [I, T] to make someone feel very offended, by talking or behaving in an immoral or socially unacceptable way〔言语或行为〕(使)愤慨，(使)生气，(使)不快: *He seems to enjoy shocking people.* 他好像喜欢得罪人。| *Just ignore all their bad language – they only do it to shock.* 不要管他们的污言秽语——他们只是想气人罢了。**3** [T] to give an electric shock to someone 使受电击，使触电

shock³ *adj* [only before noun 仅用于名词前] a word meaning very surprising, used especially in newspapers 令人吃惊的，令人大感意外的〔尤用于报纸〕: *England's shock defeat by Luxembourg in last night's game* 昨晚英格兰队对卢森堡队的意外败北

shock ab·sorb·er /ˈ· ·,·/ *n* [C] a piece of equipment connected to each wheel of a vehicle to make travelling more comfortable〔车辆的〕减震器，缓冲装置

S3 **shocked** /ʃɑkt; ʃɒkt/ *adj* **1** feeling surprised and upset by something very unexpected and unpleasant 惊愕的，受震惊的: [+at] *We were shocked at their terrible working conditions.* 我们看到他们如此恶劣的工作条件感到大为吃惊。| **shocked to see/hear/learn etc** *I was very shocked to hear of Brian's death.* 听到布赖恩去世的噩耗我感到非常震惊。**2 a shocked silence** a situation in which no one speaks because they are all very shocked 惊愕得一片沉默: *A shocked silence greeted Helen's announcement that she was pregnant.* 海伦宣布她怀孕后，大家惊愕得一片沉默。

shock·er /ˈʃɑkɚ; ˈʃɒkə/ *n* [C] *informal* a film, news story etc that shocks you【非正式】〔影片、新闻等〕引起震惊的东西: *TV star in drugs shocker!* 电视明星吸毒的惊人大新闻！

S3 **shock·ing** /ˈʃɑkɪŋ; ˈʃɒkɪŋ/ *adj* **1** very offensive or upsetting 令人讨厌的；令人恼怒的: *The book was originally thought to be too shocking to publish.* 这本书原先被认为过于离谱，不能出版。**2** *BrE informal* very bad【英，非正式】极坏的，很糟的: *It's shocking, the way he treats his wife.* 他那样对待自己的妻子，真是太糟糕了。—**shockingly** *adv*

shocking pink /,· ·ˈ·/ *n* [U] a very bright pink colour 鲜艳的粉红色 —**shocking pink** *adj*

shock·proof /ˈʃɑk,pruf; ˈʃɒkpruːf/ *adj* a watch, machine etc that is shockproof is designed so that it is not easily damaged if it is dropped or hit〔手表、机器等〕防震的

shock tac·tics /ˈ· ,··/ *n* [plural] methods of achieving what you want by deliberately shocking someone〔为达到某个目的而采取的〕惊人举动

shock treat·ment /ˈ· ,··/ also 又作 **shock ther·a·py** /ˈ· ,···/ *n* [U] treatment of mental illness using powerful electric shocks〔治疗精神病的〕休克疗法

shock wave /ˈ· ·/ *n* [plural] **1 shock waves** strong feelings of shock that people feel when something bad happens unexpectedly〔对发生意外坏事的〕激烈反应: *The stock market crash sent shock waves through the financial community.* 股市暴跌在金融界引起强烈反应。**2** [C,U] a very strong wave of air pressure or heat from an explosion, EARTHQUAKE etc〔爆炸、地震等引起的〕冲击波

shod /ʃɑd; ʃɒd/ the past tense and past participle of SHOE²

shod·dy /ˈʃɑdɪ; ˈʃɒdi/ *adj* **1** made or done cheaply or carelessly 劣质的，粗制滥造的: *shoddy workmanship* 低劣的工艺 **2** unfair and dishonest 不正当的，卑鄙的: *a shoddy trick* 卑鄙的伎俩 —**shoddily** *adv* —**shoddiness** *n* [U]

shoes 鞋

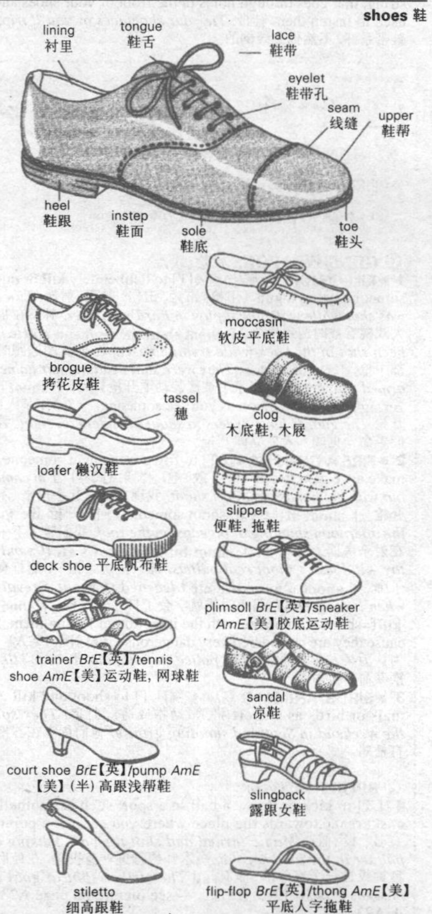

S2 W3 **shoe¹** /ʃu; ʃuː/ *n* [C] **1** something that you wear to cover your feet, made of leather or some other strong material 鞋: *Children*

grow out of shoes very quickly. 小孩长得快，鞋子很快就小了。| *high-heeled shoes* 高跟鞋 | *a pair of tennis shoes* 一双网球鞋 —compare 比较 BOOT[1] (1), SANDAL, SLIPPER **2** a curved piece of iron that is nailed onto a horse's foot; HORSESHOE〔马的〕蹄铁，马掌 **3 be in sb's shoes** to be in someone else's situation, especially a bad one 处于某人的境地〔尤指恶劣处境〕: *I'm glad I'm not in his shoes with all those debts to pay off.* 我很庆幸自己不是处在他那种境况，有那么多的债要还。| *If I were in your shoes, I'd tell Jan to get lost!* 我要是处在你的位置，我会叫简滚开的！**4 step into/fill sb's shoes** to do a job that someone else used to do, and do it as well as they did 接替某人的工作[职位]: *It'll be hard to find someone to fill Pete's shoes.* 很难找到合适的人接替皮特的工作。**5 if the shoe fits (, wear it)** *AmE spoken* used to say that if a remark that has been made about you is true, then you should accept it【美口】如果批评得对〔那就应当接受〕: *"Are you saying I'm a fool?" "If the shoe fits..."* "你说我是个笨蛋?" "如果说得对…"

shoe² *v* [T] *past tense* **shod** /ʃɑd; ʃɒd/ *present participle* **shoeing 1 well/badly/elegantly etc shod** *especially literary* wearing good, bad etc shoes【尤文】穿着很好/破旧/漂亮的鞋子 **2** to put a shoe on a horse 给〔马〕钉蹄铁

shoe·horn, shoe-horn /ˈʃuˌhɔrn; ˈʃuːhɔːn/ *n* [C] a curved piece of metal or plastic that you can put inside the back of a shoe when you put it on, to help your heel go in easily 鞋拔

shoe·lace /ˈʃuˌles; ˈʃuːleɪs/ *n* [C] a thin piece of material, like string, that goes through holes in the front of your shoes and is used to fasten them 鞋带: *Tie your shoelaces or you'll trip.* 把鞋带系好，不然你会绊倒的。

shoe·mak·er /ˈʃuˌmekə; ˈʃuːmeɪkə/ *n* [C] someone who makes shoes and boots; COBBLER (2) 制鞋匠

shoe·shine stand /ˈ· · ˌ·/ *n AmE* a place, often in the street, where you pay to have your shoes polished【美】擦鞋亭，擦鞋摊位

shoe·string /ˈʃuˌstrɪŋ; ˈʃuːˌstrɪŋ/ *n* **1 on a shoestring** *informal* if you do something on a shoestring, you do it without spending much money【非正式】以极少的钱: *The program was run on a shoestring for years until they found a sponsor.* 这个计划靠极少的资金支撑了几年之后才找到了赞助者。| *a movie that was made on a shoestring budget* 一部以很小的预算拍摄的电影 **2** *AmE* a shoelace【美】鞋带

shoe·tree /ˈʃuˌtri; ˈʃuːtriː/ *n* [C] an object shaped like a shoe that you put inside a shoe so that it keeps its shape 鞋楦

sho·gun /ˈʃoˌgun; ˈʃəʊgʌn/ *n* [C] a military leader in Japan until the middle of the 19th century 幕府将军〔19世纪中叶前统治日本的军事领袖〕

shone /ʃon; ʃɒn/ the past tense and past participle of SHINE

shoo¹ /ʃu; ʃuː/ *interjection* used to tell a child or an animal to go away 嘘!〔用以叫小孩走开或将动物赶走〕

shoo² *v* [T always+adv/prep] to make a child or animal go away, especially because they are annoying you〔尤因受到小孩或动物烦扰时〕发嘘声把…赶走: **shoo sb out/away etc** *He shooed the kids out of the kitchen.* 他发出嘘声把孩子们赶出厨房。

shoo-in /ˈ· ·/ *n* [C] *AmE informal* someone who is expected to win a race, election etc easily【美，非正式】〔比赛、选举中〕预期会轻易取胜的人，稳操胜券者

shook /ʃuk; ʃʊk/ the past tense of SHAKE

S2 W2

shoot¹ /ʃut; ʃuːt/ *v past tense and past participle* shot /ʃɑt; ʃɒt/

① GUNS/WEAPONS 枪炮/武器
② SPORT 体育运动
③ SPEAK/TALK/ASK 说话/交谈/询问
④ QUICK/SUDDEN 迅速/突然
⑤ OTHER MEANINGS 其他意思

① GUNS/WEAPONS 枪炮/武器

1 ▶KILL/INJURE 杀死/伤害◀ [T] to deliberately kill or injure someone using a gun〔用枪〕击毙，击伤；射死，射伤: *Lincoln was shot while watching a play in Ford's Theater.* 林肯在福特大戏院看戏时遭到枪杀。| **shoot sb in the leg/head etc** *He had been shot in the back while trying to escape.* 他试图逃跑时背部中枪。| **shoot sb dead** *They were shot dead in their home by armed robbers.* 他们在家中被武装劫匪开枪打死。| **shoot (sb) on sight** (=shoot as soon as you see someone) 一看到（某人）就开枪 *The guards have orders to shoot intruders on sight.* 警卫们奉命一见闯入者就立即开枪。

2 ▶FIRE A GUN 开枪◀ [I,T] to fire a weapon at someone, or make a weapon fire 开（枪）；放（炮），发射（武器）: *I'm coming out with my hands up, don't shoot.* 我现在就举起手出来，不要开枪。| **shoot at** (=try to shoot someone) 向…开枪 *We spent the afternoon shooting at pigeons on the roof.* 我们整个下午都在射杀房顶上的鸽子。| **shoot bullets/arrows etc** *It's only a toy – it doesn't shoot real bullets.* 那只是玩具枪，不能打真的子弹。| **shoot a gun/rifle etc** *I learned to shoot a revolver when I was a child.* 我小时候就学会了打左轮手枪。| **shoot to kill** (=shoot at someone with the intention of killing them, because they are considered very dangerous) 开枪射杀（某人）〔因为认为某人非常危险〕*The police were told to shoot to kill.* 警察奉命开枪射杀。

3 ▶BIRDS/ANIMALS 鸟/兽类◀ [I,T] to shoot and kill animals or birds as a sport 猎杀〔动物或鸟〕，打猎: *They spent the weekend in Scotland shooting grouse.* 他们周末在苏格兰打松鸡。

② SPORT 体育运动

4 [I,T] to kick or throw a ball in a sport such as football or BASKETBALL towards the place where you can get a point 射（门）；投（篮）: *Magic turned and shot the ball, making a 3 pointer in the final second.* 魔术师约翰逊转身投篮，在最后一秒钟投进一个三分球。| [**+at**] *The striker shot at goal but missed.* 前锋射门但没有射中。—see picture on page A23 参见 A23 页图

5 shoot pool/billiards etc *AmE informal* to play a game such as POOL[1] (3) or BILLIARDS【美，非正式】打撞球/台球

③ SPEAK/TALK/ASK 说话/交谈/询问

6 shoot questions at to ask someone a lot of questions very quickly〔连珠炮似地〕急促提问: *The lawyer shot a series of rapid questions at Hendrickson.* 律师连珠炮似地向亨德里克森提了一连串问题。

7 shoot your mouth off *informal* to talk about something that you should not talk about or that you know nothing about【非正式】信口开河，瞎说一通: *Don't go shooting your mouth off, now.* 行了，不懂就不要瞎说了。

8 shoot the bull/shoot the breeze *AmE informal* to have an informal conversation about unimportant things【美，非正式】谈天，闲聊，闲扯: *Cal and I were sitting on the porch shooting the breeze.* 卡尔和我坐在门廊里闲聊。

9 ▶SHOOT! 说吧!◀ *AmE spoken* used to tell someone to start speaking【美口】开始讲: *"Shoot, Ward," Richards said, "ask anything you want."* "沃德，说吧，"理查兹说，"随便问吧。"

④ QUICK/SUDDEN 迅速/突然

10 ▶MOVE QUICKLY 迅速移动◀ [I always+adv/prep, T always+adv/prep] to move quickly in a particular direction, or to make something move in this way（使）疾驰: [**+past/along etc**] *She shot past me and ran into the house.* 她从我身边飞奔过去，跑进屋里。| *Flames were shooting skyward.* 火焰直冲高空。| **shoot sth up/in/along etc** *The fountains shoot water at the walls of the pool.* 喷泉把水喷到池壁上。

11 shoot to fame/stardom etc to suddenly become very successful 一举成名/跃为明星: *Their new album shot straight to the top of the album charts.* 他们的新专辑迅速跃居唱片排行榜的榜首。

12 ▶PAIN 疼痛◀ [I always+adv/prep] if pain shoots through your body, you feel it going quickly through it 刺痛，剧痛: [**+through/along**] *A spasm of pain suddenly shot along his arm.* 他的手臂突然感到一阵剧痛。| **shooting pains** (=continuous short pains passing through your body) 一阵阵的剧痛 *shooting pains in your back* 你背部的阵阵剧痛

13 shoot a look/glance (at) to look at someone quickly, especially so that other people do not see, to show them how you feel 迅速地向…看一眼: *Jack shot an anxious look at his mother.* 杰克焦急地看了母亲一眼。

⑤ **OTHER MEANINGS** 其他意思

14▶PHOTOGRAPH 照片◀ [I,T] to take photographs or make a film of something 拍摄（照片）；拍（电影）：*When one of the actors died, they had to shoot the final scene again.* 一名演员死了，他们只好重拍最后的镜头。

15▶PLANTS 植物◀ [I] if a plant shoots, a new part of it starts to grow, especially a new stem and leaves 发芽，长出新枝[新叶]

16▶LOCK ON A DOOR 门闩◀ to move the BOLT on a door so that it is in the locked or unlocked position 拉上，打开〔门闩〕

17 shoot! *AmE spoken* used to show that you are annoyed or disappointed about something【美口】呸！什么！〔表示不耐烦、失望等〕：*Shoot! I knew this would happen.* 呸！我早知道这种事一定会发生。

18 shoot yourself in the foot to say or do something stupid that will cause you a lot of trouble〔因说错话或做错事而〕自找麻烦，自寻烦恼：*Glen really shot himself in the foot shouting at his boss like that.* 格伦对老板这样大吵大嚷，真是自找麻烦。

19 shoot the lights *BrE informal* to keep driving even though the traffic lights say you should stop【英，非正式】〔开车〕闯红灯

20 shoot your bolt *BrE*【英】also 又作 **shoot your wad** *AmE*【美】*informal* to have used all of your money, power, energy etc【非正式】竭尽全力；用尽了财力[能力，精力等] —see also 另见 SHOT¹, **blame/shoot the messenger** (MESSENGER (2))

shoot sb/sth ↔ **down** *phr v* [T] **1** to destroy an enemy plane while it is flying 击落〔敌机〕，击毁：*Rhodes's plane was shot down over France.* 罗兹的飞机是在法国上空被击落的。**2** to kill someone with a gun, especially someone who cannot defend themselves 击毙〔尤指无法自卫者〕：*They are accused of shooting down unarmed demonstrators.* 他们因开枪打死手无寸铁的示威者而受到指控。**3 shoot sb/sth down (in flames)** *informal* to tell someone that what they are saying or suggesting is wrong or stupid【非正式】否决，驳倒：*Another of my great ideas shot down in flames!* 我的又一个好主意被否定了。

shoot for/at sth *phr v* [T] *informal, especially AmE* to try to achieve a particular aim, especially one that is very difficult【非正式，尤美】试图达到〔尤指困难的目标〕，为…而努力：*Management is shooting for a 50% increase in sales in the next financial year.* 管理层正在争取下一财政年度的销售额增加50%。

shoot off *phr v* [I] *BrE informal* to leave quickly or suddenly【英，非正式】迅速走开，突然离开：*Sorry, but I'll have to shoot off before the end of the meeting.* 对不起，我得在会议结束前先走了。

shoot through *phr v* [I] *informal especially AustrE*【非正式，尤澳】**1** to leave a place, especially very quickly〔尤指迅速地〕离开 **2** to die 死去

shoot up *phr v* **1** [I] to quickly increase in number or amount〔数字或数量〕猛增：*Prices have certainly shot up recently.* 最近价格确实在猛涨。| *Supermarkets are shooting up all over the area.* 这个地区超级市场的数量正在猛增。**2** [I] to grow taller very quickly 迅速长高：*Your son's really shot up since we last saw him.* 我们上次见过你儿子后，他真是长高了许多。**3** [T **shoot** sb/sth ↔ **up**] to injure or damage someone or something by shooting them with bullets 开枪击伤〔某人〕，击坏〔某物〕：*The building was so badly shot up it was unrecognizable.* 这幢大楼遭到严重枪击，已经面目全非了。**4** [I,T] *slang* to take illegal drugs by using a needle【俚】注射毒品

shoot down 击落

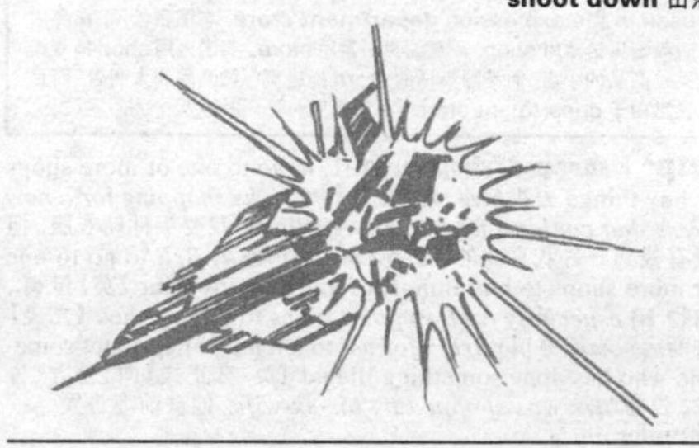

shoot² *n* [C] **1** the part of a plant that comes up above the ground when it is just beginning to grow〔植物的〕芽，苗，嫩枝 —see picture at 参见 GERMINATE 图 **2** an occasion when someone takes photographs or makes a film〔照片、电影的〕拍摄：*One of the models is on a shoot for that new perfume Passion.* 一位模特儿正在为"激情"牌新香水拍广告。**3** an occasion when people shoot birds or animals for sport, or the area of land where they do this 打猎，狩猎；狩猎区

shoot·er /ˈʃutɚ; ˈʃuːtə/ *n* [C] *informal* a word meaning a gun, used especially in films about COWBOYS or criminals【非正式】枪〔尤用于有关牛仔或罪犯的电影里〕

shoot·ing /ˈʃutɪŋ; ˈʃuːtɪŋ/ *n* **1** [C] a situation in which someone is injured or killed by a gun 枪击；枪杀：*politically-motivated shootings* 有政治动机的枪杀事件 **2** [U] the sport of shooting animals and birds 打猎，射猎：*the shooting season* 狩猎季节

shooting gal·le·ry /ˈ.. ,.../ *n* [C] **1** a place where people shoot guns at objects to win prizes 打靶场，射击场 **2** *AmE slang* a large empty building in a city, where people buy drugs and INJECT (1) them【美俚】〔城市中〕人们购买及注射毒品的荒废的大楼

shooting match /ˈ.. ./ *n* **the whole shooting match** *spoken* the whole of a situation, or an event that is the best or most complete of its kind【口】全部的人[事物]，有关的全部东西；最好[最完备]的事：*We're having a big church wedding with bridesmaids, a pageboy – the whole shooting match.* 我们将在教堂举行盛大的婚礼，有女傧相、小男傧相 —— 一应俱全。

shooting star /,.. ˈ./ *n* [C] a small piece of rock or metal from space, that burns brightly as it falls towards the Earth; METEOR 流星

shooting stick /ˈ.. ./ *n* [C] a pointed stick with a top that opens out to form a seat that you use when doing outdoor sports〔顶端可以打开作坐凳的〕折叠座手杖 —see picture at 参见 STICK² 图

shoot-out /ˈ. ./ *n* [C] **1** a fight using guns to settle an argument〔为解决争执的〕开枪格斗，枪战 **2** a PENALTY SHOOT-OUT 点球大战

shop¹ /ʃɑp; ʃɒp/ *n* S1 W1

1▶PLACE WHERE YOU BUY THINGS 购物处所◀ [C] **a)** *BrE* a building or part of a building where things are sold to the public【英】商店；STORE *AmE*【美】：*The shops in town close at 5:30.* 城里的商店5点30分关门。| **toy shop/pet shop etc** *Have you seen that new shoe shop?* 你去过那家新开的鞋店没有？**b)** a small shop that sells one particular type of thing 专卖（某种商品的）店，专柜：*a candle shop* 蜡烛店 —see also 另见 BUCKET SHOP, CORNER SHOP, COFFEE SHOP

2▶MAKING/REPAIRING THINGS 制造/修理物件◀ [C] a place where things are made or repaired 制造厂，修配店：*After assembly, the cars go to the paint shop to be painted.* 这些汽车装配后就送到喷漆车间去喷漆。| *a repair shop* 修配厂 —see also 另见 SHOP FLOOR, SHOP STEWARD

3▶SCHOOL SUBJECT 学校科目◀ [U] *AmE* a subject taught in schools that shows students how to use tools and machinery to make things out of wood and metal【美】〔学校开设的教学生使用工具和机器做木制品或金属制品的〕工艺课

4 set up shop *informal* to start a business【非正式】开业

5 shut up shop *informal* to close a shop or business, either temporarily or permanently【非正式】〔暂时或永久性地〕停止营业，关店

6 talk shop *informal* to talk about things that are connected to your work, especially in a way that other people find boring【非正式】谈与业务有关的事，谈公事，谈工作：*I'm fed up with you two talking shop.* 你们两人老谈业务，我都听腻了。

7 all over the shop *BrE spoken*【英口】**a)** scattered around untidily 凌乱放置，到处散置：*There were bits of paper all over the shop.* 小纸片撒得到处都是。**b)** confused and disorganized 混乱的，杂乱无章的：*I'm all over the shop this morning.* 我今天早上真是乱得一团糟。

8▶GO SHOPPING 去购物◀ [singular] *BrE spoken* an occasion when you go shopping, especially for food and other things you need regularly【英口】去买东西〔尤指买食品或日常必需品〕：*doing the weekly shop* 进行每周的购物

Frequencies of the nouns **shop** and **store** in British and American English 名词shop和store在英国英语和美国英语中的使用频率

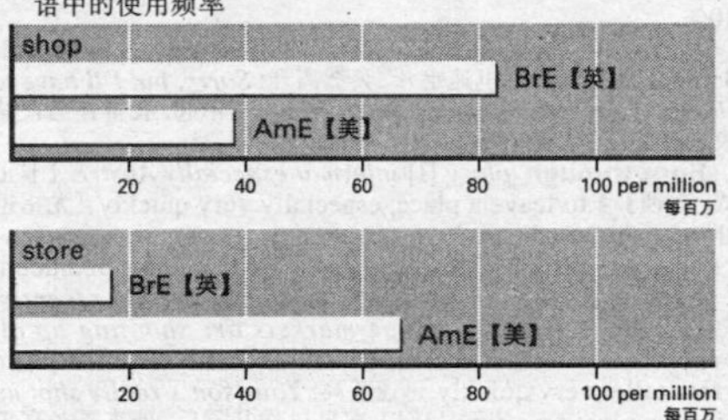

Based on the British National Corpus and the Longman Lancaster Corpus
据英国国家语料库和朗文兰开斯特语料库

This graph shows that when talking about a building where things are sold, **shop** is the usual word in British English and **store** is the usual word in American English. Americans use **shop** to mean a small shop where one particular type of thing is sold. In British English **store** is used to mean a very large shop that sells many different types of things, and is usually used in the expression **department store**. 本图表显示，指商店时英国英语常用 shop，而美国英语常用 store。美国人用 shop 指专卖某种商品的小店，而英国英语的 store 指售卖各种商品的大商店，而且通常用于 department store〔百货商店〕这一说法中。

2 **shop[2]** *v* **shopped, shopping 1** [I] to go to one or more shops to buy things 去买东西，购物：**[+for]** *I was shopping for a new dress, but couldn't find anything I liked.* 我要买件新衣服，但没有找到一件我喜欢的。**2 go shopping a)** *BrE* to go to one or more shops to buy things, often for enjoyment【英】逛街，购物 **b)** *especially AmE* to go to shops to buy clothes【尤美】去商店买衣服 **3** [T] *BrE informal* to tell the police about someone who has done something illegal【英，非正式】向〔警方〕告发，告密：*He was shopped by his ex-wife.* 他被前妻告发。—**shopper** *n* [C]

shop around *phr v* [I] to compare the price and quality of different things before you decide which to buy〔买前〕比较各种商品价格与质量，逐店比较地选购：*Shop around before you decide which insurance policy to take out.* 你在决定买保险之前，要把各家保险公司作个比较。

shop as·sis·tant /ˈ· ·,··/ *BrE n* [C] someone whose job is to help customers in a shop【英】售货员，店员；SALESCLERK *AmE*【美】

shop·fit·ting /ˈʃɑp,fɪtɪŋ; ˈʃɒp,fɪtɪŋ/ *n* [U] *BrE* the business of putting equipment in shops such as shelves, containers etc【英】商店的内部装修或安装〔业务〕—**shopfitter** *n* [C]

shop floor, the /,· ˈ·◂/ *n BrE*【英】**1** the area in a factory where the ordinary workers do their work 工厂的生产区，工作车间：*The chairwoman started her working life on the shop floor.* 这位主席是从生产车间开始她的工作生涯的。**2** the ordinary workers in a factory, not the managers〔工厂的〕普通工人，〔与资方相对的〕劳方

shop front /ˈ· ·/ *n* [C] the outside part of a shop that faces the street〔向街的〕店面，铺面；STOREFRONT *AmE*【美】

shop·keep·er /ˈʃɑp,kipɚ; ˈʃɒp,kiːpə/ *n* [C] *especially BrE* someone who owns or is in charge of a small shop【尤英】〔小店的〕店主，店老板；STOREKEEPER *AmE*【美】

shop·lift /ˈʃɑp,lɪft; ˈʃɒp,lɪft/ *v* [I] to take something from a shop without paying for it 在商店内偷窃商品，在商店顺手牵羊—**shoplifter** *n* [C]: *Shoplifters will be prosecuted.* 顺手牵羊者必究。

shop·lift·ing /ˈʃɑp,lɪftɪŋ; ˈʃɒp,lɪftɪŋ/ *n* [U] the crime of stealing things from shops, for example by hiding them in your bag, or under your clothes 商品偷窃

shop·per /ˈʃɑpɚ; ˈʃɒpə/ *n* [C] someone who buys things in shops〔商店的〕顾客，购物者：*The streets were crowded with shoppers.* 街上挤满了购物者。

2 3 **shop·ping** /ˈʃɑpɪŋ; ˈʃɒpɪŋ/ *n* [U] **1** the activity of going to shops to buy things 买东西，购物：*Shopping is now a major leisure industry.* 购物现在是一种重要的休闲产业。—see also 另见 WINDOW-SHOPPING **2 do the shopping** *BrE* to go shopping to buy food and other things you need regularly【英】买食品和日常必需品：*We always do our shopping on Fridays.* 我们总是在星期五去买日常需要的东西。**3** *BrE* the things that you have just bought from a shop【英】刚买的东西：*Do you need some help carrying your shopping?* 要不要帮你提这些刚买的东西？

CULTURAL NOTE 文化注释

In the US, when people go shopping, they usually go to a MALL which has many different stores. For food, people go to large SUPERMARKET*s*. Very large stores such as WAL-MART often have food and many other types of goods for sale at low prices. Some people shop at WAREHOUSE STORE*s*, which sell things packaged in large amounts at low prices. OUTLET STORE*s* sell clothes and other goods at low prices, by selling things that ordinary stores could not sell or that factories made too many of. 在美国，人们通常去购物中心购物，里面有各种各样的商店。人们采购食品就去大型超市，像沃尔玛这样的大商场既有食品又有各种其他商品出售，而且价格低廉。有些人去仓储店购物，那里低价批量出售成包的货品。折扣店低价销售服装和其他物品，他们销售的是一般商店不销售或者是工厂生产过剩的商品。

In the UK, there are some big shopping centres, especially in big cities, but most people shop in the HIGH STREET in their town. Many towns have big shops on the edge of the town, especially shops that sell electrical goods or DIY products. People shop for food at large supermarkets or CORNER SHOP*s*, or at a MARKET. Markets are usually outdoors and sell food, especially fruit and vegetables, and some other goods at low prices. 在英国，特别是在大城市，有一些很大的购物中心；但是大多数人是去本地的商业大街购物。很多城镇的周边有一些大商店，特别是电器店和DIY产品店。人们在大型超市、街头便利店或市场上采购食品。市场通常是露天的，出售食品，特别是水果和蔬菜，还有其他货品，价格都较低。

Many people in both the US and the UK shop ONLINE at stores such as Amazon or on Ebay. Some people, especially in the US, buy things they see on special shopping CHANNEL*s* on CABLE TELEVISION. 很多英美人在Amazon或eBay这样的网站上购物。有些人，特别是美国人会购买在有线电视的特别购物频道上看到的商品。

shopping cen·tre *BrE*【英】, **shopping center** *AmE*【美】/ˈ·· ,··/ *n* [C] a group of shops built together in one area, often under one roof 购物中心

shopping mall /ˈ·· ·/ *n* [C] *AmE* a large, specially built covered area where there are a lot of shops; MALL【美】〔有顶盖的〕大型购物商场

shopping pre·cinct /ˈ·· ,··/ *n* [C] *BrE* an area in a town where there are a lot of shops and where cars are not allowed【英】〔城内禁止车辆通行的〕购物区，商业步行街

shop-soiled /ˈ· ·/ *adj BrE*【英】**1** something that is shop-soiled is slightly damaged or dirty because it has been in a shop for a long time〔商品在商店陈列过久而〕残旧的，弄脏了的；SHOP-WORN *AmE*【美】**2** an idea that is shop-soiled is no longer interesting because it has been discussed many times before〔主意因谈论过多次〕不再令人感兴趣的，陈旧的：*the same old shop-soiled arguments* 还是那老一套陈词滥调

shop stew·ard /,· ˈ··/ *n* [C] a worker who is elected by members of a TRADE UNION in a factory or other business to represent them in dealing with managers〔由工会会员选出与资方打交道的〕工会代表

shop·walk·er /ˈʃɑp,wɔkɚ; ˈʃɒpwɔːkə/ *n* [C] *especially BrE* someone who is employed in a large shop to help the customers and watch the other workers to make sure they are working properly【尤英】〔大商店中协助顾客、监督店员的〕店〔铺〕面巡视员

shop·worn /ˈʃɑp,wɔrn; ˈʃɒpwɔːn/ *adj AmE*【美】= SHOP-SOILED

shore[1] /ʃɔr; ʃɔː/ *n* **1** [C,U] the land along the edge of a large area of water, such as an ocean or lake〔海、湖等大水域的〕岸，滨：*We could see a boat about a mile from shore.* 我们能看见离岸约一英里处有一艘船。| *the shores of the Mediterranean* 地中海海岸 | **on shore** (=away from a ship) 在岸上 *We had a couple of hours on shore.* 我们有几个小时可以上岸。**2 these shores/British shores/our shores etc** *especially literary* a particular country that has a border on the sea【尤文】这个国家/英国/我们的国家〔指沿海的国家〕：*Millions of immigrants flocked to these shores in the 19th century.* 数百万移民在19世纪蜂拥到这个国家。—see also 另见 ASHORE, OFFSHORE, ON-SHORE

USAGE NOTE 用法说明: SHORE
WORD CHOICE 词语辨析: **shore, bank, coast, seaside, beach**

The usual word for the land at the edge of a sea or lake is **shore**. 表示海或湖的岸边通常用 shore: *At night he would stand on the shore and gaze out to sea.* 晚上，他常会站在岸边凝视远处的海面。| *There was a little cabin on the opposite shore.* 对岸有间小屋。

The edges of a river are its **banks**. 河流的两岸则称 banks。

When you are talking about a country, or a large area of a country, you call the land next to the sea the **coast**. 一个国家或其一大片土地的沿海陆地称为 coast: *the Atlantic coast of Spain* 西班牙的大西洋海岸 | *I could tell from his clothes that he was from the West Coast.* 我从他穿的衣服可以断定他来自西海岸。

In British English the **seaside** is the area by the sea considered as a place of enjoyment. 在英国英语中，seaside（海滨）是指可供游乐的场所: *a holiday at the seaside* 在海滨度假。In American English you are more likely to use **beach**. 但在美国英语中，人们更多使用 beach（海滩）: *In summer, my mother used to take me to the beach.* 以前在夏天，我母亲经常带我去海滩玩。But you can also use **beach** in both British and American English for the flat land right at the edge of the sea, that is covered by water some of the time. 不过，在英国英语和美国英语中都可以用 beach 表示海滩: *They walked hand in hand along the beach.* 他们手挽手沿着海滩走。

shore² *v*

shore sth ↔ **up** *phr v* [T] **1** to support a wall with large pieces of wood, metal etc to stop it from falling down〔用木头、金属等支柱〕支撑〔墙〕: *The roof had been shored up with old timbers.* 这房顶一直用旧木柱支撑着。**2** to help or support something that is likely to fail or is not working well 帮助，支持〔可能失败或运转失常的事〕: *attempts to shore up the struggling economy* 为支撑摇摇欲坠的经济而作的努力

shorn /ʃɔrn; ʃɔːn/ *v* the past participle of SHEAR

short¹ /ʃɔrt; ʃɔːt/ *adj*

S1 W1

① LENGTH/HEIGHT/DISTANCE 长度/高度/距离
② TIME 时间
③ NOT ENOUGH 不足
④ AMOUNT 数量
⑤ BOOK/SPEECH ETC 书/演说等
⑥ SHORT FORM OF …的缩略形式
⑦ PRONUNCIATION 发音
⑧ OTHER MEANINGS 其他意思

① LENGTH/HEIGHT/DISTANCE 长度/高度/距离

1 measuring a small amount in distance or length〔距离或长度〕短的: *a short corridor with two rooms on each side* 每边两个房间的短过道 | *a short skirt* 一条短裙 | *It's a short drive from the airport.* 从飞机场到这里车程不长。| *Anita had her hair cut short.* 安妮塔把头发剪短了。—see picture on page A6 参见 A6 页图

2 ▶PERSON 人◀ someone who is short is of less than average height 矮的: *a short plump woman* 一个又矮又胖的女人

3 be 3 feet/10 miles/2 metres short of to have not quite reached a place you are trying to get to 距离…还差三英尺/十英里/两米: *Our car broke down two miles short of the town.* 我们的车在离城镇两英里处抛锚了。

② TIME 时间

4 happening or continuing for only a little time or for less time than usual 短(暂)的: *a short meeting* 一个短会 | *I'm afraid there will be a short delay.* 怕是要耽搁一会儿。| *Morris gave a short laugh.* 莫里斯笑了一声。| *I've only been living in Brisbane a short time.* 我在布里斯班才住了很短的一段时间。| *Some people have short memories, don't they?* 有些人记忆力很差，不是吗？| **a short space of time** *Both her parents died within a short space of time.* 她的双亲在很短时间内相继去世。

5 at short notice *BrE*【英】also 又作 **on short notice** *AmE*【美】with very little warning that something is going to happen 没有提前多少时间的通知，很迟才通知: *The party was arranged at very short notice.* 聚会是接到通知后匆忙筹备的。| *I can't make it Friday. It's a bit short notice I'm afraid.* 我无法在星期五去，通知得恐怕有点太迟了。

6 in the short term during the period of time that is not very far into the future 在短期内: *Interest rates are unlikely to fall in the short term.* 利率在短期内不太可能下降。—see also 另见 SHORT-TERM

7 in short order in a short time and without delay 迅速地，在短时间内；毫不拖延地: *All the tents were put up in short order.* 所有的帐篷很快就搭起来了。

8 make short work of *informal* to finish something quickly and easily, especially a meal or a job【非正式】迅速完成，轻易解决〔尤指一顿饭或一项工作〕: *The kids made short work of the sandwiches.* 孩子们很快就把三明治都吃光了。

9 short and sweet *spoken* not taking a long time and less boring or unpleasant than you expected【口】简短扼要: *They won't listen to a long lecture, so just keep it short and sweet.* 他们不愿听冗长的演讲，所以要讲得简短扼要。

③ NOT ENOUGH 不足

10 a) not having enough of something you need 短缺的，不足的: **be short of** *I'm a little short of money at the moment.* 目前我的钱不大够。| *Your little girl's not short of confidence, is she?* 你的小女儿不缺乏自信，是吗？| **be 5p/$10 etc short** *Have you all paid me? I'm still about $9 short.* 你们全都付钱给我了吗？我这里还差大约九美元。**b) be short** if time, money etc is short, there is not as much of it as you need〔时间、金钱等〕不够的，不足的: *Money was short in those days. We had to get by on $30 a week.* 那些日子钱不够用，我们只能靠每周30美元度日。| *It'll be difficult – time and resources are short.* 会很难，时间和资源都不够。

11 be in short supply if something is in short supply, there is not enough of it available 供应不足: *Gasoline was in short supply just after the war.* 战争刚结束时汽油供应不足。

12 be (a bit/rather) short *BrE* to not have much money【英】缺钱，钱不够: *Could you lend me £5? I'm a bit short tonight.* 你能借给我五英镑吗？今晚我的钱有点不大够。

13 be short on *informal* to have less of something than you should have【非正式】欠缺: *Sometimes I think he's a little short on common sense.* 有时候我觉得他有点缺乏常识。

14 give sb short measure to give someone less than the correct amount of something, especially in a shop〔尤指商店售货〕少给分量，分量不足，缺斤短两

④ AMOUNT 数量

15 just short of/a little short of etc not quite as much as; a little less than 差不多达到/只差一点就达到〔某数目〕: *The total cost will be just short of $17 million.* 全部费用差不多达到1700万美元。| *Her time was only 2 seconds short of the world record.* 她的成绩比世界纪录只差两秒钟。

⑤ BOOK/SPEECH ETC 书/演说等

16 a book, letter, speech etc that is short does not have many words or pages〔书、信、演说等〕简短的: *a short article on energy conservation* 一篇关于节省能量的短文 —see also 另见 SHORT STORY

⑥ SHORT FORM OF …的缩略形式

17 be short for to be a shorter way of saying a name 简称: *Her name is Alex, short for Alexandra.* 她名叫 Alex（亚力克丝），是 Alexandra（亚力山德拉）的简称。

18 for short as a shorter way of saying a name 简略为；缩写；简称: *the Reformed Electoral System (or the RES for short)* 新的选举制度（简称 RES）

⑦ **PRONUNCIATION** 发音

19 *technical* a short vowel is pronounced quickly and without being emphasized【术语】〔元音〕发短音的: */æ/, as in 'cat', is a short vowel.* 如在cat一词中的/æ/音是个短元音。

⑧ **OTHER MEANINGS** 其他意思

20 **be short with** to speak to someone using very few words, in a way that seems rude or unfriendly〔对人说话〕简短得像无礼的; 简慢的: *Sorry I was short with you on the phone this morning – I was being hassled by the kids.* 对不起, 我今天上午和你通话时对你简慢无礼 —— 我被孩子们弄烦了。

21 **give sb/sth short shrift** to not give much attention or sympathy to someone 对某人/某事怠慢[冷淡]: *Her suggestions were given short shrift by the chairman.* 她的建议受到主席的冷落。| **get short shrift** *My warnings, as usual, got short shrift.* 我的告诫照例无人理睬。

22 **have a short temper** to get angry very easily 脾气暴躁

23 **nothing/little short of** used to emphasize that something is very good, very surprising etc 毫不逊于: *Brigitte's recovery seemed nothing short of a miracle.* 布丽吉特的康复简直是个奇迹。

24 **draw/get the short straw** to be given something difficult or unpleasant to do, especially when other people have been given something better 得个苦差事; 比别人吃亏

25 **life's too short** *spoken* used to say that something is too unimportant to worry about or spend time on【口】人生太短暂〔表示没必要为琐事浪费时间〕—**shortness** *n* [U]

short² *adv* **1** **be running short** if you are running short of something, or if something is running short, it is being used up and there will soon not be enough left 使用殆尽, 几乎用完: *We're running short of coffee again.* 我们的咖啡又快用完了。| *Our supplies of beer were running short.* 我们的啤酒存货不多了。| *Let's go – time's running short.* 我们走吧, 时间不多了。**2** **stop short** to suddenly stop speaking or stop what you are doing, for example because something has surprised you or you have just thought of something〔在说话或工作时〕突然停下 **3** **stop short of doing sth** to almost do something but decide against actually doing it 将要做某事时突然罢手, 险些做某事: *Paula stopped just short of accusing me of lying.* 葆拉差点儿要说我撒谎。**4** **pull/bring sb up short** to make someone suddenly stop moving or stop what they are doing 使某人突然停止移动或做某事: *The sight of the gun in her hand pulled me up short.* 我一看见她手里拿着枪就愣住了。**5** **cut sb short** to stop someone before they have finished speaking, by interrupting them 打断某人的话: *I was halfway through my explanation when Walter cut me short.* 我才解释了一半, 沃尔特就打断了我的话。**6** **cut sth short** to suddenly bring something to an end before it has properly finished 突然中断某事: *His death at the age of 38 cut short a brilliant career.* 他38岁英年早逝, 使其辉煌事业未竟全功。**7** **fall short of** to be less than the result, level, or standard that you expect or to fail to achieve something you are hoping for 达不到〔目的、水平、标准〕: *The appeal for money has fallen well short of its target.* 筹集的资金远未达到目标。| *I'm afraid the results fell short of our expectations.* 这些结果怕是达不到我们的预期目的。**8** **go short (of)** to have less food, money etc than you need〔食品、钱等〕不够, 欠缺: *She made sure that her children never went short.* 她保证自己的孩子什么都不缺。**9** **short of (doing) sth** without actually doing something 除非; 除了〔某种做法〕外: *Short of locking her in her room, he couldn't really stop her from seeing Jack.* 除非把她锁在房间里, 否则他无法真正制止她和杰克会面。**10** **be taken short/be caught short** *BrE informal* to have a sudden strong need to go to the toilet【英, 非正式】突然要上厕所

short³ *n* **1** **in short** used when you want to say, in just a few words, what is the most important point about a situation 总而言之, 简单地说: *In short, he is a liar.* 总而言之, 他是个骗子。**2** **shorts** [plural] **a)** short trousers ending at or above the knees 短裤: *a pair of tennis shorts* 一条网球短裤 **b)** *especially AmE* men's UNDERPANTS【尤美】男短内裤 **3** [C] *BrE informal* a strong alcoholic drink, drunk in a small glass【英, 非正式】〔用小酒杯喝的〕烈性酒 **4** [C] *informal* a short film shown before the main film at a cinema【非正式】〔在电影正片前放映的〕短片 **5** [C] *informal* a SHORT CIRCUIT【非正式】短路: *a short in the system* 系统短路

short⁴ *v* [I,T] *informal* to SHORT-CIRCUIT, or make something do this【非正式】(使) 短路: *Maybe the battery has shorted.* 可能电池短路了。

short·age /ˈʃɔrtɪdʒ; ˈʃɔːtɪdʒ/ *n* [C,U] a situation in which there is not enough of something that people need 短缺, 不足, 缺乏: [+of] *a shortage of skilled labour* 缺乏熟练工 | **water/gasoline/bread etc shortage** *water shortages in the summer* 夏季供水不足

short back and sides /ˌ· · · ˈ·/ *n* [singular] *BrE* a way of cutting a man's hair so that it is very short at the back and sides of his head and slightly longer on top【英】男子盖式发型〔后面和两边剪得很短, 顶部略长〕

short·bread /ˈʃɔrtˌbrɛd; ˈʃɔːtbred/ *n* [U] a hard, sweet BISCUIT made with a lot of butter 牛油甜酥饼干

short·cake /ˈʃɔrtˌkek; ˈʃɔːtkeɪk/ *n* [U] **1** *BrE* thick SHORTBREAD【英】〔较厚的〕牛油甜酥饼 **2** *AmE* cake over which a sweet fruit mixture is poured【美】〔上面覆有水果混合物的〕蛋糕

short-change /ˌ· ˈ·/ *v* [T often passive 常用被动态] **1** to treat someone unfairly by not giving them what they deserve 欺诈, 欺骗, 少给〔某人〕应得的东西: *When the band only played for 15 minutes the fans felt they had been short-changed.* 乐队只演奏了15分钟, 歌迷们觉得受了欺骗。**2** to give back too little money to someone who has paid for something by giving more than the exact price 少找钱给〔顾客〕

short cir·cuit /ˌ· ˈ· ·/ *n* [C] the failure of an electrical system caused by bad wires or a fault in a connection in the wires 短路

short-circuit *v* **1** [I, T] to have a short circuit or cause a short circuit in something (使) 短路 **2** [T] to get something done without going through the usual long methods 使〔某事〕简化; 绕过; 避开: *I short-circuited the whole process by a simple telephone call.* 我把整个程序给简化了, 只简单打了个电话。

short·com·ing /ˈʃɔrtˌkʌmɪŋ; ˈʃɔːtˌkʌmɪŋ/ *n* [C usually plural 一般用复数] a fault in someone's character or abilities, or in a product, system etc, that makes something less successful or effective than it should be〔性格、能力、产品、制度等的〕缺点, 短处: *In spite of all her shortcomings, she's still the best teacher the school has.* 她尽管有些缺点, 但仍然是该校最好的教师。| *The present system, whatever its shortcomings, has worked well for several years.* 目前的制度尽管有缺点, 几年来还一直运行得很好。| [+in] *The inspection revealed some serious shortcomings in our safety procedures.* 这次检查暴露出我们在安全程序上的一些严重缺陷。

short·crust pas·try /ˌʃɔrtkrʌst ˈpestrɪ; ˌʃɔːtkrʌst ˈpeɪstri/ *n* [U] a kind of PASTRY (1) made with half as much fat as flour 起酥饼, 酥 (皮) 点心

short cut /ˌ· ˈ·/ *n* [C] **1** a quicker, more direct way of going somewhere than the usual one 捷径, 近路: *We were late for the game, but found a short cut through the fields.* 我们看球赛出发迟了, 但找到了一条穿过田野的近路。| **take a short cut** *Carlos decided to take a short cut home.* 卡洛斯决定抄近路回家。**2** a quicker way of doing something〔做事情的〕快捷办法, 捷径: [+to] *There aren't really any short cuts to learning English.* 学英语实在没有什么捷径可走。

short·en /ˈʃɔrtn̩; ˈʃɔːtn/ *v* [I,T] to become shorter or make something shorter (使) 变短, 缩短: *The days are shortening now.* 现在白天变得越来越短了。| **shorten sth** *They're talking about shortening the working week.* 他们在谈论有关缩短工作周的问题。—opposite 反义词 LENGTHEN

short·en·ing /ˈʃɔrtn̩ɪŋ; ˈʃɔːtnɪŋ/ *n* [U] fat made from vegetable oil that you mix with flour when making PASTRY (1)〔用植物油做的〕起酥油〔用于和面做糕点〕

short·fall /ˈʃɔrtˌfɔl; ˈʃɔːtfɔːl/ *n* [C] the difference between the amount you have and the amount you need or expect 不足之数, 差额: *severe crop shortfalls* 严重的农作物歉收 | [+in/of] *a shortfall in staffing levels* 人员配备不足 | *a shortfall of about £1 million* 约一百万英镑的差额

short·hand /ˈʃɔrtˌhænd; ˈʃɔːthænd/ *n* [U] **1** a fast method of writing using special signs or shorter forms to represent letters, words, and phrases 速记 (法): **in shorthand** *The reporter took notes in shorthand.* 记者用速记作记录。—compare 比较 LONGHAND **2** **be shorthand for** to be a shorter but less clear way of saying something 简短而意思隐晦的说法: *He's been 'relocated', which is shorthand for 'given a worse job a long way away'.* 他已经被"调职", 这个说法的实际意义是"被派到很远的地方做一份更差的工作"。

short·hand·ed /ˈʃɔrtˈhændɪd; ˌʃɔːtˈhændɪd◂/ *adj* having fewer helpers or workers than you need 人手不够的: *We'll be shorthanded next month as five of my staff will be on holiday.* 我们下个月将会人手不足, 因为我的员工中有五人要休假。

shorthand typ·ist /ˌ· · ˈ· ·/ *n* [C] *BrE* someone whose job is to use shorthand to write down what someone else says and

then TYPE[2] (1) a copy of it【英】速记(打字)员〔其工作是速记后用打字机打出来〕; STENOGRAPHER *especially AmE*【尤美】

short-haul /ˈʃɔrtˋhɔl; ˈʃɔːthɔːl/ *adj* a shorthaul aircraft or flight travels a fairly short distance〔飞机航程〕短距离的, 短途的

short·ie /ˈʃɔrtɪ; ˈʃɔːti/ *adj* [only before noun 仅用于名词前] *informal* a shortie coat or JACKET (1) etc is one that is shorter than the usual size【非正式】〔外套、夹克等〕较通常尺码短的 —see also 另见 SHORTY

short list[1] /ˈ· ·/ *n* [C] *BrE* a list of the most suitable people for a job, chosen from all the people who were first considered【英】〔从初选名单筛选出的〕决选名单

short-list[2] *v* [T usually passive 一般用被动态] *BrE* to put someone on a short list for a job【英】把〔某人〕列入决选名单: **short-list sb for** *She's been shortlisted for the sales director's job.* 她已被列入销售经理职务的决选名单。

short-lived /ˈʃɔrt ˋlaɪvd; ˌʃɔːt ˈlɪvd◂/ *adj* lasting only a short time 短暂的: *Our happiness was short-lived.* 我们的快乐是短暂的。

3 **short·ly** /ˈʃɔrtlɪ; ˈʃɔːtli/ *adv* **1** soon 不久, 很快, 立刻: *Ms Jones will be back shortly.* 琼斯小姐很快就会回来。| **shortly before/after** *The accident happened shortly before midday.* 事故是在正午前不久发生的。**2** speaking impatiently〔说话〕不耐烦地: *"I've explained that already," Rod said shortly.* "那个问题我已经解释过了。"罗德不耐烦地说。

short-or·der cook /ˌ· ··ˈ ·/ *n* [C] *AmE* someone in a restaurant kitchen who makes the food that can be prepared easily or quickly【美】快餐厨师

short-range /ˌ· ˈ·◂/ *adj* **1** designed to travel or operate only within a short distance 短程的: *a shortrange missile* 短程导弹 **2** **shortrange plan/goal/forecast etc** concerned only with the period that is not very far into the future 短期计划/目标/预测等: *shortrange plans* 短期计划

short-sheet /ˈ· ·/ *v* [T] *AmE* to fold the top sheet on a bed so that no one can get into it, as a trick; APPLE PIE BED【美】把…的床单叠短〔为了捉弄别人, 把床单折叠成两层, 使床单看似已经铺好, 但人钻进被窝时双腿却不能伸直〕

short-sight·ed /ˌ· ˈ··◂/ *adj* **1** *especially BrE* unable to see objects clearly unless they are very close【尤英】近视的; NEARSIGHTED *especially AmE*【尤美】—opposite 反义词 LONGSIGHTED **2** not considering the possible effects of something that seems to save time, money, or effort at the moment 目光短浅的, 无远见的: *a short-sighted policy of stopping investment in training* 一项停止在培训上投入资金的目光短浅的政策 —opposite 反义词 FARSIGHTED —**short-sightedly** *adv* —**short-sightedness** *n* [U]

short-staffed /ˌ· ˈ·◂/ *adj* having fewer than the usual or necessary number of workers 人员不足的: *We'll try to get the order through by Monday, but we're very short-staffed at the moment.* 我们将设法在星期一前交货, 但目前我们人手非常不足。

short·stop /ˈʃɔrtˌstɑp; ˈʃɔːtstɒp/ *n* [C] a player in BASE-BALL who tries to stop any balls that are hit between second and third BASE[2] (8)〔棒球第二垒与第三垒之间的〕游击手

short sto·ry /ˌ· ˈ··/ *n* [C] a short written story about imaginary situations, usually containing only a few characters 短篇小说

short-tem·pered /ˌ· ˈ··◂/ *adj* **1** easily becoming angry or impatient 脾气暴躁的, 易怒的: *Roger's back pain is making him pretty short-tempered these days.* 罗杰这几天背疼, 弄得他脾气相当暴躁。**2** angry and impatient 气冲冲的, 不耐烦的: *a short-tempered reply* 不耐烦的回答

short-term /ˌ· ˈ·◂/ *adj* [usually before noun 一般用于名词前] continuing for only a short time, or concerned only with the period that is not very far into the future 短期的: *The treatment may bring short-term benefits to Aids sufferers.* 这种疗法对艾滋病患者会有短期的好处。| *Most of the staff are on short-term contracts.* 大部分职员都是订的短期合同。—opposite 反义词 LONG-TERM —**short-term** *adv*

short-term·is·m /ˌ· ˈ···/ *n* [U] a way of planning or thinking that is concerned only with what gives you advantage now, rather than what might happen in the future 短期效益主义〔只考虑目前利益的做法〕: *short-termism in the banking world* 银行界的短期效益主义 —**short-termist** *adj*

short time /ˌ· ˈ·◂/ *n* **be on short time** *BrE* a factory or office that is on short time is operating for less than the usual number of hours or days【英】〔工厂、办公室的〕缩短工作时间, 实行短工时: *Workers were put on short time because raw materials were scarce.* 由于原料短缺, 工人的工时都减少了。

short wave /ˌ· ˈ·◂/ *n* [U] radio broadcasting on waves of less than 60 metres in length, which can be sent around the world 短波〔波长在60米以下, 可在全球范围内传送的无线电波〕—see also 另见 LONG WAVE, MEDIUM WAVE

short·y /ˈʃɔrtɪ; ˈʃɔːti/ *n* [C] an insulting name for someone who is not very tall 矮子, 矬子〔侮辱性称谓〕

Shos·ta·ko·vich /ˌʃɑstəˋkovɪtʃ; ˌʃɒstəˈkəʊvɪtʃ/, **Di·mi·tri** /dɪˋmitrɪ; dɪˈmiːtri/ (1906-75) a Russian COMPOSER whose best-known works are his symphonies (SYMPHONY) and his OPERA, *Lady Macbeth of Mtsensk*. The Soviet government sometimes disapproved of his music because they considered that it did not express Soviet principles. 肖斯塔科维奇(1906-1975), 俄罗斯作曲家。最著名的作品是其交响曲和歌剧《姆钦斯克县的麦克白夫人》。苏联政府有时不认同其作品, 认为没有体现政府的原则〕

shot[1] /ʃɑt; ʃɒt/

① GUNS/SHOOTING 枪/射击
② SPORT 体育运动
③ FILM/PHOTOGRAPHS 电影/照片
④ ATTEMPT/GUESS 尝试/猜测
⑤ OTHER MEANINGS 其他意思

① GUNS/SHOOTING 枪/射击

1 **fire a shot** to fire a gun 开枪: *He pulled out his rifle and fired three shots.* 他掏出来复枪开了三枪。

2 **take a shot at** to try to kill or injure someone by firing a gun at them 向…开枪: *Someone took a shot at him as he was getting out of his car.* 他下车时有人向他开枪。

3 ▶**SOUND** 声音◀ [C] the sound of a gun being fired 枪声: *Where were you when you heard the shot?* 听到枪声时你在什么地方?

4 ▶**BULLETS** 子弹◀ [U] **a)** small metal balls for shooting from a SHOTGUN〔猎枪用的〕弹丸 **b)** *old use* large metal balls for shooting from a CANNON[1]【旧】炮弹

5 **a good shot/bad shot** someone who can shoot a gun well, badly etc 优秀的/差劲的射手: *Sergeant Cooper is an excellent shot.* 库珀中士是一位优秀的枪手。

② SPORT 体育运动

6 [C] an attempt to throw, kick, or hit the ball towards the place where you can get a point〔为得分的〕投球, 射球, 击球: *Shaw made the shot and turned to run down the court.* 肖投篮得分后转身跑向球场的另一头。| *Good shot!* 好球!

7 [C] a heavy metal ball that competitors try to throw as far as possible in the sport of SHOT PUT〔推铅球用的〕铅球

8 **a 10 to 1 shot/50 to 1 shot etc** a horse, dog etc in a race, whose chances of winning are expressed as numbers that show the ODDS〔赛马、赛狗等的〕10比1/50比1的获胜机会

③ FILM/PHOTOGRAPHS 电影/照片

9 [C] a photograph 一张照片: *I managed to get some good shots of the carnival.* 我总算拍到几张狂欢节的精彩照片。

10 [C] the view of something in a film, television programme, or photograph that is produced by having the camera in a particular position〔电影、电视节目或照片的〕镜头: *In the opening shot we see Garfield at his desk reading.* 在开始的镜头中, 我们看到加菲尔德坐在书桌旁看书。

④ ATTEMPT/GUESS 尝试/猜测

11 [C] *informal* an attempt to do something or achieve something【非正式】尝试, 试图, 设法: [+at] *This will be his second shot at the championship.* 这将是他第二次尝试夺取冠军。| **have a shot (at sth)** *I decided to have a shot at decorating the house myself.* 我决定试试自己动手装修房子。

12 **a long shot** an attempt or guess at something that is not very likely to be successful, but is still worth trying〔成功希望不大但值得作的〕尝试[猜测]: *It's a long shot, but if we hurry*

we might still find her. 看来希望不大，但我们如果赶紧行动，也许还能找到她。
13 a shot in the dark an attempt to guess something without having any facts or definite ideas 瞎猜，乱猜：*My answer to the last question was a complete shot in the dark.* 我最后一道题的答案完全是瞎猜的。

⑤ OTHER MEANINGS 其他意思
14 ►DRINK 饮料◄ [C] a small amount of a strong alcoholic drink〔烈酒的〕少量，一小口：[+of] *He poured himself another shot of whiskey.* 他又给自己斟了一点威士忌。
15 ►DRUG 药物◄ [C] *AmE* an INJECTION of a drug (when it is put into the body with a needle)【美】一次注射，一针：*Have you had your typhoid and cholera shots?* 你打过伤寒和霍乱的预防针吗？
16 ►REMARK 话语◄ [C] an angry remark 愤怒的话，尖锐的话：**a parting shot** (=something you say as you are leaving) 分手时说的气话，临别恶语 *Carl turned for one parting shot: "You marry him, then!"* 卡尔在分手时转身说了句气话："那你就嫁给他好了。" | **a cheap shot** (=an unnecessarily rude remark) 多余的粗话，不必要的气话
17 big shot an important or powerful person, especially in business〔尤指商界的〕要人，权势人物：*a big shot in the record business* 唱片业的大腕
18 like a shot if you do something like a shot, you do it very quickly and eagerly〔做事〕飞快地，毫不迟疑地，立刻：*If he asked me to go to Africa with him, I'd go like a shot!* 如果他叫我和他一起去非洲，我会毫不迟疑地去！
19 a shot in the arm something that makes you more confident or more successful 令人增强信心的事物，令人鼓舞的事物：*The latest opinion poll has given the Socialists a much needed shot in the arm.* 最近的民意调查给社会党人打了一针他们急需的兴奋剂。
20 a shot across the bows *especially BrE* something you say or do to warn someone about what might happen if they fail to do what you want them to do【尤英】警告〔表示如不服从将有严重后果〕—see also 另见 **call the tune shots** (CALL¹ (25)), MUGSHOT, **not by a long chalk/shot** (LONG¹ (16))

shot² *adj* [not before noun 不用于名词前] **1 be shot** to be in bad condition because of being used too much or treated badly 用坏的；耗尽的；破旧的：*My back tires are shot. I'll have to get new ones before we go.* 我车子的后胎已经磨坏了，我得换上新的才能动身。| **shot to pieces** *After a long day of exams, my nerves were shot to pieces.* 考试了一整天，我已经筋疲力尽了。**2 be/get shot of** *informal* to get rid of someone or something【非正式】摆脱…，把…处理掉：*I don't care how nice the house is any more. I just want to be shot of it.* 我已不在乎房子有多漂亮了，只想把它处理掉。**3 be shot through with** *formal*【正式】**a)** if a piece of cloth is shot through with a colour, it has very small threads of that colour woven into it〔布料等〕闪色的，颜色闪变的〔因织入了这种颜色的细线〕：*a fine silk shot through with gold threads* 一块闪着金色丝线的精美丝绸 **b)** to have a lot of a particular quality or feeling 充满〔某种特质或情感〕的：*a charming collection of stories, shot through with a gentle humour* 一本妙趣横生引人入胜的小说集

shot³ *v* the past tense and past participle of SHOOT

shot·gun /ˈʃɑtˌgʌn; ˈʃɒtgʌn/ *n* [C] a long gun fired from the shoulder, especially one used for killing birds or animals 猎枪

shotgun wed·ding /ˌ‥ ˈ‥/ *n* [C] a wedding that has to take place immediately because the woman is going to have a baby〔因女方已怀孕〕不得不立即举行的婚礼

CULTURAL NOTE 文化注释
In CARTOONS the man and woman are often shown with the woman's father holding a shotgun to force the man to marry his daughter. 漫画中常有女方父亲手持猎枪逼着一个男的娶他闺女的画面。

shot put /ˈ· ·/ *n* [singular] a sporting competition in which you throw a heavy metal ball as far as you can 推铅球 —**shot putter** *n* [C]: *an Olympic shot putter* 奥运铅球选手

S1 W1 **should** /ʃəd; ʃəd *strong* 强读 ʃud; ʃʊd/ *modal verb* [negative short form 否定缩略式= **shouldn't**] **1** used to show that something is the best thing to do because it is morally right, fair, honest etc 应当，应该〔表示这样做是最好的，因为体现道德、公正、诚实等〕：*He should learn to be more polite.* 他应该学会更有礼貌。| *What you should have done is call the police.* 你本该叫警察来。| *I have no sympathy for him. He shouldn't accept bribes.* 我一点也不同情他，他不应该接受贿赂。| *"I don't care what people think." "Well, you should."* "我才不在乎人们怎么想。""啊，你应该在乎。" **2** used to show that something is the best thing to do because it helps you, is good for you etc 应当，应该〔表示这样做是最好的，因为对自己有好处〕：*The leaflet tells you what you should do if the power fails.* 这份传单告诉你万一停电应该怎样做。| *Why shouldn't I smoke if I want to?* 如果我想吸烟，为什么不？| *I think he should have tried to get some more qualifications before applying for the job.* 我认为他在申请这份工作之前应努力取得更多的资历。**3** used to show what the correct or expected amount, situation etc is, especially when it is not correct or not what is expected 应当，应该〔表示某数量或事应当是怎样的，尤用于表示原来并非如此〕：*Eat noodles the way they should be eaten, with chopsticks.* 吃面条要像那么回事——用筷子。| *What do you mean there are only ten tickets? There should be twelve.* 只有10张票，你这是什么意思？应该有12张才对。**4** used to say that something will probably be good, bad, interesting etc 应，应当〔表示推测〕：*It should be a good movie – its reviews were very good.* 这应当是一部好电影，各种评论都很肯定。| *With her talent and experience, she should do well for herself.* 凭着她的才能和经验，她自己应能做得很好。**5** used after 'that' in some expressions showing an opinion or feeling〔用在that之后，表示某种意见或感情〕：*It's odd that he should react in this way.* 很奇怪，他竟然作出这样的反应。| *The residents demanded that there should be an official inquiry.* 居民要求进行一次正式调查。**6 should it rain/should there be a problem etc** if it rains, if there is a problem etc 要是下雨/有问题的话：*Should anyone phone, tell them I'm in conference.* 要是有人来电话，告诉他我在开会。**7** *formal, especially BrE*【正式，尤英】used after 'I' or 'WE' in conditional sentences〔用于条件句中，置于I或we之后〕：*I should stay in bed if I were you.* 我要是你就卧床休息。| *I should be surprised if he came.* 他要是来，我会感到意外。**8** *formal especially BrE* used after IF, to emphasize that something might or might not happen【正式，尤英】〔用在"if"之后，强调某事有可能发生〕：*If the wound should become inflamed do not hesitate to call me.* 万一伤口发炎，请随时打电话给我。**9** used in reported speech to mean SHALL 将会〔用于间接引语中，表示shall〕：*I promised I should be back by midnight.* 我保证会在午夜之前回来。**10 what should happen but/who should appear but etc** *especially humorous* used to show that you were surprised when something happened, a particular person appeared etc【尤幽默】〔用以表示惊讶〕你猜发生了什么，你猜谁来了：*Just at that moment who should walk in but old Jim himself.* 就在那时，你猜是谁进来了？是老吉姆亲自来了。**11 I should worry/he should care etc** *humorous* used to mean the opposite of what you seem to be saying【幽默】〔表示相反的意思〕我用不着担心/他不会计较的：*With all his money, he should worry about giving the waiter a tip!* 他那么有钱，还会计较给服务员那点小费吗！**12 I should have thought** *spoken especially BrE* used as a polite or joking way of showing that you disagree with what someone has said【口，尤英】我想〔用于礼貌地或开玩笑地表示不同意对方的话〕：*"Why isn't it working?" "I should have thought that was obvious."* "为什么它不运转？""我想那是再明显不过的了。" **13 I should like** *formal, especially BrE* used to say politely that you want something【正式，尤英】我想要…〔用于礼貌地表示想要某物〕：*"Will you require anything else?" "Yes, I should like a dry martini."* "您还需要其他什么吗？""是的，我想要一杯干马蒂尼酒。" **14 I should think** used to say what you believe or expect to be true 我相信，我估计：*I shouldn't think there'll be a problem parking at that time of night.* 我想晚上这个时间停车不会成问题的。**15 I should think so/not** *spoken* used to strongly agree with what someone has said【口】〔表示强调〕当然！当然不！：*"I'm not going out tonight." "I should think not, with so much work to do!"* "我今晚不准备外出了。""当然不出去啦，还有那么多工作要做！"

shoul·der¹ /ˈʃoldə; ˈʃəʊldə/ *n* [C] S2 W2
1 ►BODY PART 身体的一部分◄ one of the two parts of the body at each side of the neck where the arm is connected 肩膀：*Put a shawl around your shoulders in case you get cold.* 如果你觉得冷就披一条披肩。| **shrug your shoulders** (=raise them to show that you do not know something or do not care) 耸耸肩〔表示不知道或不在乎〕*Keith just shrugged his shoulders and said it wasn't his problem.* 基思只是耸耸肩，并说这不是他的问题。—see pictures at 参见 BODY, HORSE¹ 图

2 ►CLOTHES 衣服◄ the part of a piece of clothing that covers your shoulders 衣服的肩部，衣肩: *a jacket with padded shoulders* 一件有垫肩的夹克（衫）

3 ►MEAT 肉类◄ the upper part of the front leg of an animal that is used for meat〔动物前腿上半部的〕肩肘肉，前腿肉: *a shoulder of pork* 猪肘子

4 **a shoulder to cry on** someone who gives you sympathy 给予同情[安慰]的人: *Ben is always there when I need a shoulder to cry on.* 我需要人安慰时，本总是在我身边。

5 **shoulder to shoulder** working together to achieve the same thing 肩并肩地: *We worked shoulder to shoulder for five years in that hell-hole.* 我们在那个地狱般的地方肩并肩工作了五年。

6 **stand shoulder to shoulder with** to completely share someone's opinions about something and support them in what they are doing 和〔某人〕肩并肩地站在一起，完全同意并支持〔某人〕

7 **on sb's shoulders** if a difficult or unpleasant responsibility is on someone's shoulders, they are the person that has that responsibility〔任务〕落在某人肩上，〔责任〕由某人承担: *The duty of informing the children's parents fell on the shoulders of Sergeant Flynn.* 通知小孩家长的责任落在弗林警佐的肩上。| *The blame rests squarely on Jim's shoulders.* 过失的责任无疑该由吉姆承担。

8 **put your shoulder to the wheel** to start to work with great effort and determination 开始奋力工作

9 ►ROAD-SIDE 路边◄ *AmE* an area of ground beside a road where drivers can stop their cars if they are having trouble【美】路肩，〔公路两旁的〕紧急停车道 —see also 另见 HARD SHOULDER, SOFT SHOULDER —see picture on page A3 参见 A3 页图

10 ►MOUNTAIN 山◄ a rounded part of a mountain just below the top 山肩〔山顶以下的圆形部分〕—see also 另见 **cry on sb's shoulder** (CRY¹ (4)), **give sb the cold shoulder** (COLD¹ (8)), **have a chip on your shoulder** (CHIP¹ (5)), **rub shoulders with** (RUB¹ (6)), **head and shoulders above the rest** (HEAD¹ (50)), **straight from the shoulder** (STRAIGHT¹ (9))

shoulder² *v* 1 [T] **shoulder a responsibility/duty/cost etc** to accept a difficult or unpleasant responsibility, duty etc 承担责任/职责/费用等: *The residents are being asked to shoulder the costs of the repairs.* 居民们被要求承担这笔修理费。2 [T] to lift something onto your shoulder to carry it〔用肩〕挑，扛，掮: *They shouldered the boat and took it down to the river.* 他们把船扛在肩上抬到河里。3 **shoulder your way through/into etc** to move through a large crowd of people by pushing with your shoulder 用肩膀挤着过去/进去: *She shouldered her way through the onlookers.* 她用肩膀挤着穿过围观的人群。4 **shoulder arms** an order given to a soldier telling him to hold his weapon against his shoulder〔命令士兵〕枪上肩

shoulder bag /ˈ·· ·/ *n* [C] a bag that hangs from your shoulder〔有肩带的〕背包式手提包

shoulder blade /ˈ·· ·/ *n* [C] one of the two flat bones on each side of your back SCAPULA 肩胛骨 —see picture at 参见 SKELETON 图

shoulder-high /,·· ˈ·◄/ *adj, adv* as high as your shoulder 齐肩高的[地]: *shoulder-high grass* 齐肩高的草

shoulder-length /ˈ·· ,·/ *adj* shoulder-length hair hangs down to your shoulders〔头发〕长至肩部的 —see picture on page A6 参见 A6 页图

shoulder pad /ˈ·· ·/ *n* [C] a thick flat piece of material that is fixed under the shoulders of a piece of clothing to make your shoulders look bigger〔缝在衣肩内的〕垫肩

shoulder strap /ˈ·· ·/ *n* [C] 1 a long narrow piece of material on a piece of women's clothing that goes over the shoulder 女服的肩带 2 a long narrow piece of material fixed to a bag etc so that you can carry it over your shoulder 手提包的肩带

should-n't /ˈʃʊdn̩t; ˈʃʊdnt/ *v* the short form of 'should not' 缩略式= should not

shouldst /ʃədst; ʃədst *strong* 强读 ʃʊdst; ʃʊdst/ *v old use* the second person singular form of the verb SHOULD【旧】动词 should 的第二人称单数形式

shout¹ /ʃaʊt; ʃaʊt/ *v* 1 [I, T] to say something very loudly 大声说，喊叫，呼喊: *There's no need to shout, I'm not deaf!* 用不着这样大声喊叫，我又不是聋子！| *We could hear them shouting for help.* 我们能听到他们大声呼救。| *"Watch out!" she shouted, as the car started to move.* "小心！"汽车开动时她大声喊道。| **shout at sb** *I wish you'd stop shouting at the children.* 我希望你别再对孩子们大喊大叫。| **shout sth at sb** *He was shouting insults at the lorry driver.* 他对那个货车司机破口大骂。| **shout yourself hoarse** (=make your voice rough and weak by shouting a lot) 喊得嗓子沙哑 2 to call out loudly, for example because you are angry or in pain〔因愤怒或疼痛等〕大叫: *My brother shouted in pain as the ball hit him.* 我弟弟被球击中时痛得大叫了起来。3 **shout sth from the rooftops** to tell everyone about something because you want everyone to know about it 使尽人皆知，使某事家喻户晓: *But she was in love, and she wanted to shout the fact from the rooftops.* 她在谈恋爱，而且希望所有的人都知道。4 **be all over bar the shouting** *BrE spoken* used to say that something is almost finished and there is no doubt what the result will be【英口】〔事情快要结束而且〕大局已定: *The kids were arrested and pleaded guilty. It was all over bar the shouting.* 孩子们被逮捕并已服罪，一切已成定局。

shout sb ↔ **down** *phr v* [T] to shout in order to prevent someone from being heard 用喊叫压倒某人[淹没某人的声音]: *Unpopular speakers were shouted down by the crowd.* 听众向不受欢迎的演讲者大喝倒彩。

shout out *phr v* [I **shout** sth ↔ **out**] to say something suddenly in a loud voice 突然大声地说: *Don't shout out the answer in class, put up your hand.* 上课时不要大声喊着回答问题，要先举手。

shout² *n* 1 [C] a loud call expressing anger, pain, excitement etc〔表示生气、疼痛、兴奋等的〕喊叫（声），呼叫（声）: *a warning shout* 表示警告的呼喊声 | *shouts of delight from the football crowd* 足球观众的欢呼声 | **give a shout** *Tom gave a shout of triumph as he realized he'd won.* 汤姆知道自己获胜时发出了胜利的欢呼。2 **give sb a shout** *spoken* to go and find someone and tell them something【口】去告诉某人某事: *Give me a shout when you're ready to go.* 你准备好动身时告诉我一声。3 **sb's shout** *AustrE or BrE informal* someone's turn to buy drinks【澳或英，非正式】轮到某人请喝饮料: *It's my shout. Same again?* 轮到我负责买饮料了，还要上次那种吗？

shove¹ /ʃʌv; ʃʌv/ *v* 1 [I,T] to push someone or something, in a rough or careless way, using your hands or shoulders〔用手或肩〕推，推挤，推撞: **shove sb aside/into etc** *Secret Service men shoved people aside to make way for the President.* 特工人员把人群推到一旁为总统开路。| **shove sb/sth** *Stop shoving me or I'll tell the teacher!* 不要再推我，否则我要告诉老师了。| **pushing and shoving** (=pushing with your body, especially in a crowd)〔尤指在人群中〕推推搡搡 *There was no trouble at the rally apart from a little pushing and shoving.* 在群众集会上除了有点推推搡搡之外，没有出现麻烦事。—see picture on page A21 参见 A21 页图 2 [T always+adv/prep] to put something somewhere carelessly or without thinking much 随意地放〔东西〕，漫不经心地乱放: **shove sth into/under etc** *Let's shove everything into the closet just for now.* 我们暂时把所有东西都放进壁橱里吧。3 **shove up/over** *spoken, especially BrE* to move along on a seat to make space for someone else【口，尤英】移动身子〔腾出位置〕: *Shove up mate, there's no room to sit down here.* 老兄，挪过去一点，这里没地方坐了。—see also 另见 **when push comes to shove** (PUSH² (7))

shove off *phr v* [I] 1 *spoken* used to tell someone rudely or angrily to go away【口】〔粗暴地或生气地叫人〕走开，离开: *Shove off! I'm busy.* 走开！我忙得很。2 to push a boat away from the land, usually with a pole〔用篙〕把船撑离岸

shove² *n* [C] a strong push 猛推: **give sth a shove** *We gave the door one good shove and it came open.* 我们用力一推，门就开了。

shov·el¹ /ˈʃʌvl̩; ˈʃʌvəl/ *n* [C] 1 a tool with a rounded blade and a long handle used for moving earth, stones etc 铲子，铁锹 —compare 比较 SPADE (1) 2 a part of a large vehicle or machine used for moving or digging earth 推土机[挖土机]前面的铲形部分

shovel² *v* **shovelled, shovelling** *BrE*【英】, **shoveled, shoveling** *AmE*【美】[I,T] 1 to lift and move earth, stones etc with a shovel〔用铲子〕铲起: *The workmen shovelled loads of gravel onto the road.* 工人们把大量的碎石铲到路面上。| **shovel the driveway/sidewalk etc** *AmE* (=shovel snow from a road or path)【美】铲去车道/人行道上的积雪 *Chris, I asked you two days ago to shovel the front path.* 克里斯，两天前我就叫你把门前路上的积雪铲掉。2 **shovel sth into/onto etc** to put something into a place quickly 迅速将某物放进/放上…: *He was shovelling spaghetti into his mouth.* 他大口大口地吃意大利面条。

shov·el·ful /ˈʃʌvl̩fʊl; ˈʃʌvəlfʊl/ *n* [C] the amount of coal, snow, earth etc that you can carry on a shovel〔煤、雪、泥等〕一满铲的量

show¹ /ʃo; ʃəʊ/ *v past tense* **showed** *past participle* **shown** /ʃon; ʃəʊn/

1 ►PROVE 证明◄ [T] to provide facts or information that make it clear that something is true or that something exists〔提供事实、信息〕证明，证实: **show (that)** *The latest poll clearly shows that most voters are unaware of this.* 最新的民意调查清楚地说

明, 大部分选民都不知道这件事。| *As her record plainly shows, Wyler is one of the world's all-time great players.* 怀勒的记录清楚表明, 她是世界上空前卓越的一位球员。| **show how/what** *Her experience shows how easily young women can get into trouble abroad.* 她的经历证明, 年轻女子在国外是多么容易遇到麻烦。| **show sth** *Recent events in Somalia show the futility of war.* 最近在索马里发生的事件证明战争无济于事。| *Statistics show a marked rise in nitrogen levels at this point.* 统计数字说明氮的浓度在此刻显著升高。| **show sb/sth to be** *formal*【正式】: *He later showed himself to be an excellent chess player.* 他后来证明自己是一名优秀的棋手。| **it just shows/it just goes to show** *spoken* (=when a bad experience you have been talking about proves something)【口】〔某经验教训〕恰恰证明 *And he took everything she had. It just goes to show, you should never trust a stranger.* 他竟然拿走了她所有的东西, 这恰恰证明你绝对不可以相信陌生人。—see graph at 参见 INDICATE 图表

2▶SHOW YOUR FEELINGS ETC 流露感情等◀ [T] to let your feelings, attitudes, or personal qualities be clearly seen in the way you behave, the way you look etc 表现出, 流露出〔感情、态度、个人品质〕: *She's never shown much interest in my work.* 她从未对我的工作表示出多大的兴趣。| *I think it shows great determination on her part.* 我认为这表现出她的巨大决心。| *He showed his agreement by a slight nod.* 他轻轻地点了一下头表示同意。| **show how/what etc** *I was determined not to show how upset I was.* 我决心不流露出我是多么难过。

3▶INFORMATION/MEASUREMENTS ETC 信息/计量等◀ [T not usually in progressive 一般不用进行时] **a)** if a picture, map etc shows something, you can see it on the picture, map etc〔图片、地图等〕标示, 标明: *This diagram shows the correct position of the gear lever.* 此图标出了变速杆的正确位置。| *a useful chart showing all the flights coming into and out of Paris* 一张很有用的、标明进出巴黎的所有航班的一览表 **b)** if a clock or other measuring instrument shows a time, a number etc, you can see that time etc on it〔时钟〕指示〔时间〕;〔计量仪等〕读数, 指示数目: *The victim's watch showed five minutes past two.* 遇难者的手表指针指着两点零五分。

4▶LET SB SEE 向某人出示◀ [T] to let someone see something, for example by holding it out so that they can look at it 把…指给别人看, 出示: **show sb sth** *Jackie showed the official her passport.* 杰姬向那位官员出示了护照。| **show sth to sb** *Show your ticket to the man at the entrance.* 向入口处的那个人出示你的门票。| **show sth** *All passes must be shown on entering the building.* 进入这幢大楼必须出示通行证。

5▶TELL/EXPLAIN STH 说/解释某事◀ [T] **a)** to tell someone how to do something, by explaining it to them, often by doing it yourself so that they can see you〔通过示范〕解释, 说明: **show sb how to do sth** *I showed him how to work the coffee machine.* 我给他示范如何使用这台咖啡机。| **show sb sth** *Show her the right way to do it.* 向她解释做这件事的正确方法。**b)** to tell someone where a place or thing is, for example by pointing to it 向…指出…在何处: **show sb sth** *I'll show you the exact spot where it happened.* 我会告诉你事情发生的确切地点。| **show sb where** *Could you show me where I can put my coat?* 告诉我我的大衣该放在哪儿好吗?

6▶GUIDE SB 指引某人◀ [T always+adv/prep] to go with someone and guide them to a place 带领, 指引: **show sb to/in/out/around** *Goodbye, Mrs Davies. My secretary will show you out.* (=out of the office or building) 再见, 戴维斯太太, 我的秘书会送你出去的。| **show sb sth** *Come on out, and I'll show you the garden.* 出来, 我带你去看看花园。—see also 另见 **show sb ↔ around, show sb over sth** —see 见 LEAD¹ (USAGE)

7▶CAN BE SEEN 可被看见◀ a) [I] if something shows it is easy to see 看得见, 显露: *His happiness showed in his face.* 他喜形于色。| *Don't worry about that tiny stain; it won't show.* 不用担心那点小小的污迹, 看不出来的。**b)** [T] if material shows dirt or a mark, it is easy to see the dirt or mark on it〔材料容易〕显露〔污迹或痕迹〕: *That light jacket will show the slightest crease.* 那件浅色夹克稍有一点折痕都会看得出来。

8▶FILM 电影◀ a) [I] if a film is showing at a cinema, you can see it there〔电影〕放映 **b)** [T] if a cinema shows a film, it makes it available for people to see〔电影院〕上映〔影片〕: *The local movie theater is showing Tom Cruise's latest picture.* 当地的电影院正在上映汤姆·克鲁斯的最新影片。—see also 另见 SHOWING

9 have something/nothing etc to show for if you have something to show for your efforts, hard work etc, you have achieved something as a result of them 在…方面的努力有成绩/没有成绩: *Is that all you've got to show for a whole week's work?* 这就是你整整一周工作所取得的全部成绩吗?

10 show a profit/loss if a company shows a profit or loss, it makes a financial profit or loss〔公司〕赢利/亏本

11 show your hand to make your true power or intentions clear, especially after you have been keeping them secret〔尤指保密一段时间后〕显露实力; 表明意图和打算: *She needed to be cautious, and not show her hand too soon.* 她需要谨慎行事, 不急于表明意图。

12 show your face if you will not show your face somewhere, you will not go there because you have a good reason to feel ashamed or embarrassed about being there 露面, 出现: *He wouldn't dare show his face here after the way he behaved last week!* 他经过上星期那番表现之后不敢再在这儿露面了!

13▶ART/PICTURES 艺术/图画◀ [T often passive 常用被动态] to put a collection of paintings or other works of art in one place so that people can come and see them 展览, 展出: *Her recent sculptures are being shown at the Hayward Gallery.* 她最近的雕塑作品正在海沃德画廊展出。

14▶ANIMAL 动物◀ [T] to put an animal into a competition with other animals 参赛展示〔动物〕

15▶ARRIVE 抵达◀ [I] *informal, especially AmE* to arrive at the place where someone is waiting for you; show up【非正式, 尤美】到场, 出席, 露面: *I came to meet Hank, but he never showed.* 我来见汉克, 但他始终没有露面。

16 ... and it shows *spoken* used to say that something, especially something bad, is very clear to see【口】〔尤指不好的东西〕显而易见, 完全看得出来: *"I did the whole report in only two days!" "And it shows!"* "我写整份报告只花了两天时间。" "这看得出来!"

17 I'll show him/them etc *spoken* used to say that you will prove to someone that you are better, more effective etc than they think you are【口】我要让他/他们看看〔证明自己比别人想得更好, 更高效等〕: *They're convinced I'm going to fail, but I'll show them!* 他们相信我会失败, 但我要干给他们看看。

18 show sb in a good/bad etc light if an action shows you in a good or bad light, it makes people have a good or bad opinion about you 提高/降低人们对某人的评价: *a decision which does not show Roosevelt in a particularly favourable light* 一项并不显示罗斯福有多高明的决策

19 show sb the door to make it clear that someone is not welcome and should leave 撵某人出去, 对某人下逐客令

20 show sb who's boss *informal* to prove to someone who is threatening your authority that you are more powerful than they are【非正式】让某人明白该听谁的, 要某人服从指挥: *Don't let your horse pull his head down – show him who's boss.* 不要让马耷拉着头, 要让它听你的。

21 show the way if you show the way for other people, you do something new that others then try to copy 指出路子, 做出榜样: *In the 70s Panderm showed the way with its revolutionary new techniques.* (20世纪) 70年代, 潘德姆公司以其创新的技术闯出条新路子。

22 show a leg! *BrE spoken* used to tell someone to get out of bed【英口】〔用于叫某人〕起床

23 show a clean pair of heels *BrE old-fashioned informal* to run away very fast【英, 过时, 非正式】迅速逃脱, 逃之夭夭

show sb **↔ around** (sth) *phr v* [T] to go around a place with someone when they first arrive there, to show them what is interesting, useful etc 为新到的客人作向导, 带某人参观: *Pat will show you around the building so you can meet everyone.* 帕特会带你到楼里各处看看, 让你和大家见个面。| *We were shown around by an elderly guide.* 我们由一位年长的向导带着四处参观。

show off *phr v* **1** [I] to try to impress people and make them admire your abilities, achievements, or possessions〔自我〕炫耀, 卖弄[表现]自己: *Pay no attention to Susan – she's just showing off.* 不要理苏珊, 她不过是在卖弄。**2** [T **show** sth **↔ off**] to show something to a lot of people because you are very proud of it 夸耀〔引以自豪的东西〕, 炫耀〔某物〕: *Peter was keen to show off his new car.* 彼得很喜欢炫耀他的新汽车。**3** [T **show** sth **↔ off**] if one thing shows off something else, it makes the other thing look especially attractive 使〔某物〕更具吸引力, 使夺目: *The white dress showed off her dark skin beautifully.* 白色的裙子把她那黝黑的皮肤衬托得很漂亮。

show sb **over** sth *phr v* [T] *especially BrE* to guide someone through an interesting building or a house that is for sale【尤英】带领某人参观〔有趣的建筑物或待售的房子〕: *Our company chairman showed the Prime Minister over the new plant.* 我们公司的董事长陪同首相参观新工厂。

show sb **↔ round** (sth) *phr v BrE* to SHOW AROUND【英】带某人参观

show up *phr v* **1** [I] *informal* to arrive, especially at the place where someone is waiting for you【非正式】到达〔尤指有人在等候之处〕: *I was almost asleep when Chris finally showed up.* 克里斯最终来到时，我几乎睡着了。**2** [T **show** sth ↔ **up**] to make it possible to see or notice something that was not clear before 使〔某物〕显现出来: *The sunlight showed up the cracks in the wall.* 阳光使墙上的裂缝显现出来。| *These riots show up the deficiencies in police training.* 这些骚乱暴露出警察训练不足。**3** [I] to be easy to see or notice 显露，显现出来: *The subtitles won't show up against such a light background.* 字幕在这样浅色的背景下太不显眼。| *A lot of bugs showed up when I ran the program.* 我在运行这个程序时，出现了许多故障。**4** [T **show** sb ↔ **up**] to make someone feel embarrassed by behaving in a stupid or unacceptable way when you are with them〔因举止失当〕使某人羞于与之为伍，使别人难堪: *Why must you always show me up at these occasions?* 你为什么总是在这些场合令我难堪呢？

show² *n*

1 ►PERFORMANCE 表演◄ [C] an entertaining performance, especially one that includes singing, dancing, or jokes〔尤指包括唱歌、舞蹈、笑话的〕娱乐表演，演出: *She is appearing in a show on Broadway.* 她正在百老汇参加演出。| *Cowan's one-man show opens on April 16th.* 考恩的个人表演从4月16日开始。—see also 另见 FLOOR SHOW

2 ►TV/RADIO 电视/无线电◄ a programme on television or on the radio〔电视或无线电广播的〕节目: *She's been in a lot of popular TV shows.* 她出演过很多流行电视节目。| *comedy shows* 喜剧节目 | **chat/talk show** (=a show on which well-known people talk about their lives, work etc) 谈话[漫谈]节目;〔由知名人士谈他们的生活、工作等〕脱口秀 | **game show** (=a show in which people play games for prizes) 游戏节目〔一种有奖游戏〕| **quiz show** (=a show in which people compete to answer questions) 问答游戏节目〔要参赛者回答问题的竞赛节目〕

3 ►A COLLECTION OF THINGS 收集物◄ [C] an occasion when a lot of similar things are brought together in one place so that people can come and look at them, or so that they can compete against each other; EXHIBITION〔供参观或进行评比的〕展览会，展评（会）: **flower/dog etc show** *The annual pet show takes place in August.* 一年一度的宠物展览在8月份举行。| *Are you entering your pony in the show?* 你准备为你的小马报名参展吗？| **fashion/air etc show** *We have a stand at the 1996 travel show.* 我们在1996年旅游展览会上设有一个摊位。| *exhibits at the Motor Show* 汽车展览会上的展品 | **hold/put on/stage a show** *The gallery is holding a major show of her work next month.* 该画廊将在下月举办一个她作品的大型展览会。

4 be on show to be shown to the public 在陈列，在展出: *The painting will be on show until the end of the month.* 这幅画将展出到这个月底。| *Frink's works will go on show next week.* 弗林克的作品将在下星期开始展出。

5 ►FEELINGS/QUALITIES 感情/质量◄ a show of [C] something that shows what something is like, how someone feels etc; DISPLAY OF 显示，表示: *a little show of bad temper* 发点小脾气 | **a show of strength/force** *Their army staged a big military parade as a show of strength.* 他们的军队举行盛大阅兵式以显示其军力。

6 [singular,U] something you do to pretend to other people that something is true; PRETENCE 假装，假象: **[+of]** *"Oh, no. I don't mind," she said, with a show of cheerfulness.* "啊，不，我不介意。"她装出高兴的样子说。| **make a show of/put on a show of** *I made a show of interest, but I didn't really care what happened.* 我表面上装作感兴趣，其实发生了什么我并不在乎。| **for show** *We went through a marriage ceremony, but it was all for show, to convince the authorities.* 我们举行了婚礼，但这只是做给别人看的，以便取得当局的信任。

7 ►EVENT/SITUATION 事件/情况◄ *informal singular* a place or situation where something is being done or organized【非正式】事情，活动: **run the show** (=be in charge of something) 负责某事，主管 *Who's running this show, you or me?* 谁负责这次活动，是你还是我？

8 put up a good/poor etc show *informal* to perform, play etc well or badly【非正式】表现得好/差: *Our team put up a pretty good show, but we lost in the end.* 我们队发挥得相当好，但最后还是输了。

9 let's get this show on the road *spoken* used to tell people it is time to start working or start a journey【口】咱们干起来吧；咱们出发吧

10 (jolly) good show *BrE old-fashioned spoken* used to express your approval of something【英，过时，口】干得好！真棒！真不错！〔用以表示赞赏〕—see also 另见 **steal the show** (STEAL¹ (3))

show³ *adj* **show-house/-flat** *BrE* a house or apartment that has been built and filled with furniture to show buyers what similar new houses or apartments look like【英】〔配有家具向顾客展示的〕样板房；样板公寓，示范单位

show and tell /ˌ· · ˈ·/ *n* [U] an activity for school children in which they bring an object to school and tell the other children about it "展示和讲述"课〔小学教学的一种课堂练习形式，学生带一件实物到班上向同学展示并讲述与该物有关的事〕: *Ramona brought in a fossil for show and tell.* 拉蒙娜带了一块化石去上"展示和讲述"课。

show·biz /ˈʃoˌbɪz; ˈʃəʊbɪz/ *n* [U] *informal* SHOW BUSINESS【非正式】演艺界

show busi·ness /ˈ· ˌ··/ also 又作 **showbiz** *informal*【非正式】*n* [U] the entertainment industry, for example television, films, popular theatre etc 娱乐界，演艺界，娱乐性行业〈如电视、电影等〉: *Some of the biggest names in show business will be at the gala.* 娱乐界的一些名人将出席这次盛会。

show·case /ˈʃoˌkes; ˈʃəʊkeɪs/ *n* [C] **1** an event or situation that is designed to show the good qualities of a person, organization, product etc 显示优点的地方[机会]: **[+for]** *The new musical is a good showcase for her talents.* 这出新的音乐剧是她展示才华的好机会。**2** a glass box containing objects for people to look at in a shop, at an art show etc 玻璃陈列柜，橱窗 — **showcase** *v* [T]

show·down /ˈʃoˌdaun; ˈʃəʊdaʊn/ *n* [C usually singular 一般用单数] a meeting, argument, fight etc that will settle a disagreement or competition that has continued for a long time 摊牌，决一雌雄: *Sunday's game will be a showdown between the two leading teams.* 星期天的比赛将是这两支积分领先球队决一雌雄的一战。| **[+with]** *a showdown with the striking auto workers* 与罢工的汽车工人摊牌

show·er¹ /ˈʃauɚ; ˈʃaʊə/ *n* [C]

1 ►FOR WASHING IN 洗澡用◄ a thing that you stand under to wash your whole body 淋浴用的喷头，淋浴器: *Why does the phone always ring when I'm in the shower?* 为什么电话铃总在我淋浴时响？

2 ►ACT OF WASHING 洗澡◄ an act of washing your body while standing under a shower 淋浴: *I need a shower.* 我需要洗个淋浴。| **take a shower** *especially AmE*【尤美】**have a shower** *especially BrE*【尤英】: *Nick rolled out of bed, took a shower and got dressed.* 尼克翻身起床，洗个淋浴，然后穿上衣服。

3 ►RAIN 雨◄ a short period of rain or snow〔短时间的〕降雨，阵雨；降雪: *Heavy showers are forecast in the hills tomorrow.* 预报明天山区有强阵雨。| *a snow shower* 短时间的降雪

4 ►THINGS IN THE AIR 空中的东西◄ a lot of small, light things falling or appearing together〔许多细小而轻的东西〕大量洒落或出现: **[+of]** *Peter kicked the fire and sent up a shower of sparks.* 彼得抬脚去踢那堆火，扬起了很多火星。

5 ►PARTY 聚会◄ *especially AmE* a party at which presents are given to a woman who is going to get married or have a baby【尤美】〔为将要结婚或分娩的女子举行的〕送礼会: *We're having a shower for Sherri on Friday.* 我们星期五要为谢丽举行送礼会。| *a baby shower* 分娩送礼会

> **CULTURAL NOTE 文化注释**
>
> In the US, showers are traditionally only for women and are usually held at someone's house, although baby showers are sometimes held at work. Bridal showers (=for a woman who is getting married) are organized by the woman's friends or her MAID OF HONOUR. The women play silly games, and the presents are usually either things for the home or sexy underwear. At a baby shower, the presents are typically toys, clothes, and equipment for the new baby. 在美国，传统上只为女性举行送礼会，而且通常会在某人家中进行；尽管有时也在办公场所为婴儿举行送礼会。新娘送礼会是由新娘的朋友或伴娘组织的。她们玩些傻里傻气的游戏，送的礼物通常是家庭用品或性感内衣等。婴儿送礼会上的礼物一般是玩具、衣服和新生儿用品等。— compare 比较 HEN NIGHT

6 ►PEOPLE 人◄ *BrE informal* a group of stupid or lazy people【英，非正式】一群笨[懒]人

shower² *v* **1** [I] to wash your whole body while standing under a shower 洗淋浴 **2** [I always+adv/prep, T] to scatter a lot of small light things onto a person or place, or to be scattered in this way（使）〔大量细而轻的东西〕洒落: **[+down/over/upon]** *Volcanic dust showered down on the onlookers.* 火山灰洒落在观看者身上。| **shower sb/sth with** *The branches of the trees showered me with snow.* 树枝上的雪花洒落在我身上。| **shower**

sth down/over/on *Thousands of leaflets were showered over occupied France.* 成千上万张传单撒在被占的法国领土上。**3** to generously give someone a lot of things 给〔某人〕大量东西: **shower sb with sth** *They were set on by a mob that showered them with stones.* 他们突然被一群暴徒用石头袭击。| **shower sth on/upon sb** *Childless herself, she'd shower my kids with toys.* 她自己没有子女, 常送很多玩具给我的孩子。

shower cap /ˈ·· ·/ *n* [C] a plastic hat that keeps your hair dry in a shower〔防止头发被淋湿的〕浴帽

shower gel /ˈ·· ·/ *n* [U] *BrE* a type of liquid soap that you use to wash yourself in a shower【英】浴液

show·er·proof /ˈʃauɚˌpruf; ˈʃauəpruːf/ *adj* showerproof clothes keep you dry in light rain but not in heavy rain〔只能防小雨的〕防雨服

show·er·y /ˈʃaurɪ; ˈʃauəri/ *adj* raining frequently for short periods 多阵雨的: *a showery day* 阵雨频繁的一天

show·girl /ˈʃogɝl; ˈʃəugɜːl/ *n* [C] one of a group of women who sing or dance in a musical show〔音乐剧中的〕歌舞女演员

show·ing /ˈʃoɪŋ; ˈʃəuɪŋ/ *n* **1** [C] an occasion when a film, art show etc can be seen or looked at, especially a special occasion that people are invited to〔电影的〕放映;〔艺术品的〕展览, 陈列: *a private showing of the film 'King Kong'* 电影《金刚》的私人专场放映 **2** [singular] something that shows how well or how badly you are doing 成绩, 表现: **a good/poor showing** *Their poor showing in the mid-term elections is being blamed on the President.* 他们在中期选举中的欠佳表现被归咎于总统。| **on sb's present/current showing** (=judging by the way they are performing now) 根据某人目前的表现 *On our present showing, we're unlikely to get into the finals.* 根据我们目前的表现, 我们不大可能进入决赛。

show jump·ing /ˈ· ˌ··/ *n* [U] a sport in which horses with riders have to jump a series of fences as quickly and skilfully as possible 骑马跳越障碍运动 —**show jumper** *n* [C]

show·man /ˈʃomən; ˈʃəumən/ *n plural* **showmen** /-mən; -mən/ [C] someone who is good at entertaining people and getting a lot of public attention 善于卖弄并引起公众注意的人物, 爱出风头的人物: *In politics it helps to be a bit of a showman.* 出点风头在政治上不失为一种有用的手段。

show·man·ship /ˈʃomənˌʃɪp; ˈʃəumənʃɪp/ *n* [U] skill at entertaining people and getting public attention 引起公众注意的技巧

shown /ʃon; ʃəun/ the past participle of SHOW

show-off /ˈ· ·/ *n* [C] *informal* someone who always tries to show how clever or skilled they are so that other people will admire them【非正式】喜欢卖弄的人, 爱炫耀自己的人: *Don't be such a show-off!* 不要这样炫耀自己!

show of hands /ˌ· · ˈ·/ *n* [singular] a vote taken by counting the raised hands of the people at a meeting〔会议上的〕举手表决: *The dispute was settled with a show of hands.* 这次争论以举手表决的方式解决。

show·piece /ˈʃoˌpis; ˈʃəupiːs/ *n* [C usually singular 一般用单数] something that an organization, government etc wants people to see, because it is a very good or successful example 成功的典范, 样板: *The modern languages department is the showpiece of the university.* 现代语言系是这所大学的模范系。| *a showpiece factory* 模范工厂

show·place /ˈʃoˌples; ˈʃəupleɪs/ *n* [C] a place which is open to the public because of its beauty, historical interest etc 供参观的地方, 游览胜地

show·room /ˈʃoˌrum; ˈʃəurum/ *n* [C] a large room where you can look at things that are for sale such as cars or electrical goods〔商品的〕陈列室: *a car showroom* 汽车展厅

show-stop·ping /ˈ· ˌ··/ *adj* a show-stopping performance is extremely good or impressive〔表演〕极精彩的, 令人难忘的: *his show-stopping performance as Stanley Kowalski* 他扮演斯坦利·科瓦尔斯基的精彩表演 —**showstopper** *n* [C]

show tri·al /ˈ· ˌ··/ *n* [C] an unfair TRIAL[1] (1) that is organized by a government for political reasons, not in order to find out whether someone is guilty〔政府为政治宣传而举行的〕警戒式公审: *inadequacies of the Soviet system that made such show trials necessary* 苏维埃制度的缺陷使得有必要实施这种警戒式公审

show·y /ˈʃoɪ; ˈʃəui/ *adj* something that is showy is very colourful, big, expensive etc, especially in a way that attracts people's attention 花哨的, 华丽的; 引人注目的: *a showy car* 引人瞩目的汽车 —**showily** *adv* —**showiness** *n* [U]

shrank /ʃræŋk; ʃræŋk/ the past tense of SHRINK

shrap·nel /ˈʃræpnəl; ˈʃræpnəl/ *n* [U] small pieces of metal from a bomb, bullet etc that are scattered when it explodes〔炸弹、子弹等炸开后的〕弹片, 榴霰弹(弹片): *Robert suffers from an old shrapnel wound.* 罗伯特经常感到旧弹伤的疼痛。

shred[1] /ʃrɛd; ʃred/ *n* **1** [C] a small thin piece that is torn or cut roughly from something〔撕下或切下的〕细条, 碎片, 薄片: **[+of]** *a shred of cloth* 碎布条 | *shreds of dried coconut* 干椰丝 | **tear/rip/cut sth to shreds** *Jackie was so mad with Tom she tore all his letters to shreds.* 杰姬对汤姆非常恼火, 把他所有的信都撕得粉碎。—see picture on page A7 参见 A7 页图 **2 in shreds a)** torn in many places 撕破多处的, 破成碎片的: *My scarf was in shreds after the dog had played with it.* 我的围巾被狗扯得破烂不堪。**b)** completely ruined 彻底毁掉: *Simon went home with his career in shreds.* 西蒙回家去了, 他的事业一败涂地。**3** [singular] a very small amount 少量, 些微: **not a shred of proof/evidence/doubt** (=not at all) 没有丝毫证明/证据/怀疑 | *There's not a shred of evidence to convict him.* 没有丝毫证据可以给他定罪。

shred[2] *v* **shredded, shredding** [T] **1** to cut or tear something into small thin pieces 把…切成碎片, 把…撕成细条: *Coleslaw is made with shredded cabbage.* 凉拌卷心菜丝是用切成细丝的卷心菜做的。**2** to put a document into a shredder 把〔文件〕放进碎纸机切碎: *By the time the police got there the files had all been shredded.* 警察到达那里时, 档案已被碎纸机切碎了。

shred·der /ˈʃrɛdɚ; ˈʃredə/ *n* [C] a machine that cuts documents into small pieces so that no one can read them 碎纸机

shrew /ʃru; ʃruː/ *n* [C] **1** a very small animal like a mouse with a long pointed nose 鼩鼱〔鼻子长而尖的鼠状动物〕**2** *old use* an unpleasant woman who always argues and disagrees with people【旧】泼妇, 悍妇

shrewd /ʃrud; ʃruːd/ *adj* **1** good at judging what people or situations are really like, especially in a way that makes you successful in business, politics etc〔尤指在生意、政治等方面〕善于判断的, 精明的, 敏锐的: *Martin's a shrewd judge of character.* 马丁能敏锐地判断人的性格。| *a shrewd businesswoman* 精明的女商人 **2** well judged and likely to be right 判断准确的, 有把握的: *At a shrewd guess, I'd say Henry is going to leave his job.* 我猜亨利十有八九要辞去他的工作。| **have a shrewd idea** (=have an opinion about something that is probably correct) 持有高见 —**shrewdly** *adv*: *"Were you jealous of her?" asked Sara shrewdly.* "你忌妒她吗?"萨拉尖锐地问道。—**shrewdness** *n* [U]

shrew·ish /ˈʃruɪʃ; ˈʃruːɪʃ/ *adj old use* a shrewish woman is one who always argues and disagrees with people【旧】泼妇般的, 爱骂街的

Shrews·bu·ry /ˈʃrozbɛrɪ; ˈʃrəuzbəri/ a town in western England, near the border with Wales 什鲁斯伯里〔英格兰西部一镇, 靠近威尔士边境〕

shriek[1] /ʃrik; ʃriːk/ *v* [I] **1** to make a very high, loud sound 尖叫, 尖声喊叫: *Judith suddenly shrieked and looked to see what had bitten her.* 朱迪丝突然尖叫起来, 看看是什么东西咬了她。| **shriek with joy/pain/fright etc** *Everyone was shrieking with laughter in the bar.* 酒吧里每个人都在开怀大笑。**2** [T] to say something in a high, loud voice because you are excited, afraid, or angry〔由于激动、害怕或愤怒〕大叫大嚷: *Anne stood in the doorway shrieking abuse at him.* 安妮站在门口对他高声漫骂。

shriek[2] *n* [C] a loud high sound made because you are frightened, excited, angry etc〔由于受惊、兴奋、愤怒等的〕尖叫声: **[+of]** *a shriek of terror* 一声恐惧的尖叫 | **with a shriek** *Miss Lavish, with a shriek of dismay, dragged her backwards.* 拉维施小姐惊慌地尖叫了一声, 忙把她往后拖。

shrill[1] /ʃrɪl; ʃrɪl/ *adj* **1** a shrill sound is very high and unpleasant; PIERCING (1)〔声音〕尖锐的, 刺耳的: *He heard the shrill voice of a woman in the next room.* 他听到隔壁房间一个女人刺耳的声音。| *a shrill whistle* 刺耳的汽笛声 **2** shrill words express repeated, often unreasonable complaints or criticism〔话语等〕反反复复而不讲道理的; 不断埋怨的: *We use quiet persuasion rather than shrill denunciation.* 我们采取平心静气的说服而不是尖刻粗暴的谴责。—**shrillness** *n* [U] —**shrilly** /ˈʃrɪl·lɪ; ˈʃrɪl-li/ *adv*

shrill[2] *v* **1** *especially literary* [I] to produce a very high and unpleasant sound【尤文】发出尖锐刺耳的声音: *The telephone shrilled twice.* 刺耳的电话铃响了两下。**2** [T] to say something in a very high voice 尖声说: *"Shame!" she shrilled.* "真可耻!"她尖声叫道。

shrimp /ʃrɪmp; ʃrɪmp/ *n* [C] **1 a)** *BrE* a small pink sea creature that you can eat, with ten legs and with a soft shell【英】(小)虾 **b)** *AmE* a creature like this, but bigger【美】虾, 大虾; PRAWN *BrE*【英】**2** *humorous* someone who is very small【幽默】小个子, 矮子

shrimp cock·tail /ˌ· ˈ· ˌ·/ *n* [C,U] *AmE* shrimps without their shells in a red sauce, eaten before the main part of a meal【美】大虾冷盘〔一道开胃菜〕; PRAWN COCKTAIL *BrE*【英】

shrimp·ing /ˈʃrɪmpɪŋ; ˈʃrɪmpɪŋ/ *n* [U] the activity of fishing for shrimps 捕(小)虾

shrine /ʃraɪn; ʃraɪn/ *n* [C] **1** a place that is connected with a holy event or holy person, and that people visit to pray 圣坛, 神殿 **2** a place that people visit and respect because it is connected with a famous person or event 圣地: *Elvis's home has become a shrine for his fans.* 猫王的故居成了他的歌迷的圣地。

Shrin·er /ˈʃraɪnɚ; ˈʃraɪnə/ a member of a US organization whose members are MASONS of high rank. Shriners are known especially for doing CHARITY work for children and for their travelling CIRCUS. 圣地兄弟会会员〔美国一组织的成员, 为高级别共济会会员。他们尤以儿童慈善工作和巡回演出的马戏团闻名〕

shrink[1] /ʃrɪŋk; ʃrɪŋk/ *v past tense* **shrank** /ʃræŋk; ʃræŋk/ *past participle* **shrunk** /ʃrʌŋk; ʃrʌŋk/ **1** [I,T] to become smaller or to make something smaller through the effects of heat or water (使)缩小, (使)收缩: *Hot water shrinks woollen clothes.* 热水会使羊毛衣服缩水。| *Will it shrink if I wash it?* 它会缩水吗? —see also 另见 PRE-SHRUNK, SHRUNKEN **2** [I,T] to become smaller in amount, size or value〔数量、体积或价值〕变小, 减少, 缩小: *The number of students has shrunk from 120 to 70.* 学生人数已从120人减至70人。| *The shrinking pound damages the tourist trade.* 日益贬值的英镑使旅游业遭受损失。**3** [I always+adv/prep] *especially literary* to move back and away from something, especially because you are frightened【尤文】〔因恐惧而〕退缩, 畏缩: **[+back/away/from]** *Jenny shrank back against the wall in horror.* 珍妮害怕地退后, 靠着墙。

shrink from sth *phr v* [T] to avoid doing something difficult or unpleasant 避免做, 不愿做〔困难或不愉快的事〕: *I will not shrink from my duties.* 我不会逃避责任。| **shrink from doing sth** *The Prime Minister is unlikely to shrink from making tough decisions.* 首相不大可能优柔寡断。

shrink[2] *n* [C] *informal humorous* a PSYCHOANALYST or PSYCHIATRIST【非正式, 幽默】精神分析学家; 精神科医生

shrink·age /ˈʃrɪŋkɪdʒ; ˈʃrɪŋkɪdʒ/ *n* [C] the act of shrinking, or the amount that something shrinks 缩小; 减少(量); 收缩(程度): *a further shrinkage in the size of the workforce* 劳工人数的进一步减少

shrink·ing vi·o·let /ˌ·· ˈ···/ *n* [C] *humorous* someone who is very shy【幽默】羞怯的人

shrink-wrapped /ˌ· ˈ·◂/ *adj* goods that are shrink-wrapped are wrapped tightly in plastic〔用塑料薄膜〕收缩包装的 —**shrink-wrap** *n* [U]

shriv·el /ˈʃrɪvl̩; ˈʃrɪvəl/ also 又作 **shrivel up** *v* **shrivelled, shrivelling** *BrE*【英】, **shriveled, shriveling** *AmE*【美】[I,T] if something shrivels or is shrivelled, it becomes smaller and its surface is covered in lines because it is very dry or old (使)皱缩; (使)干枯; (使)干瘪: *The grapes are left out in the sun to shrivel up and become raisins.* 葡萄被放在太阳下晒成葡萄干。—**shrivelled** *adj*: *Mrs Carey was a tiny, shrivelled old lady.* 凯里太太是一位矮小干瘪的老太太。

Shrop·shire /ˈʃrɑpʃɚ; ˈʃrɒpʃə/ a COUNTY in western England near the border with Wales. Its local government is based at Shrewsbury. 什罗普郡〔英格兰西部一郡, 靠近威尔士边境, 其地方政府设在什鲁斯伯里〕

shroud[1] /ʃraud; ʃraʊd/ *n* [C] **1** a cloth that is wrapped around a dead person's body before it is buried 寿衣, 裹尸布 **2** something that hides or covers something 覆盖物, 遮蔽物: *The fog rolled in, and a grey shroud covered the city.* 大雾滚滚而来, 一张灰色的天幕笼罩着这个城市。| **[+of]** *A shroud of silence surrounded the general's death.* 将军之死笼罩在一片静默中。

shroud[2] *v* **1 be shrouded in mist/smoke etc** to be covered and hidden by mist, smoke etc 被雾/烟等笼罩着: *The black streets were shrouded in fog.* 大雾笼罩着黑沉沉的街道。**2 be shrouded in mystery/secrecy etc** to be mysterious, secret etc 笼罩在神秘/秘密之中: *The origins of this ritual are shrouded in mystery.* 这种仪式的起源被蒙上了神秘的色彩。

Shrove Tues·day /ˌʃrov ˈtjuzdɪ; ˌʃrəʊv ˈtjuːzdi/ *n* [C,U] the day before the first day of the Christian period of Lent, when people traditionally eat PANCAKES〔基督教的〕忏悔星期二,〔基督教〕大斋首日的前一天

shrub /ʃrʌb; ʃrʌb/ *n* [C] a small bush with several woody stems 灌木(丛)

shrub·be·ry /ˈʃrʌbərɪ; ˈʃrʌbəri/ *n* [C,U] shrubs planted close together in a group, or a part of a garden where shrubs grow 灌木丛;〔花园里的〕灌木栽植地

shrug[1] /ʃrʌg; ʃrʌg/ *v* [I,T] to raise and then lower your shoulders in order to show that you do not know something or do not care about something 耸(肩)〔表示不知道或不感兴趣〕

shrug ↔ sth **off** *phr v* [T] to treat something as unimportant and not worry about it〔认为不重要而〕不予理会, 对…不屑一顾: *We can't just shrug these objections off.* 我们不能不理会这些反对意见呀。

shrug[2] *n* [C usually singular 一般用单数] a movement of your shoulders upwards and then downwards again 耸肩

shrunk /ʃrʌŋk; ʃrʌŋk/ the past tense and past participle of SHRINK

shrunk·en /ˈʃrʌŋkən; ˈʃrʌŋkən/ *adj* [usually before noun 一般用于名词前] having become smaller or been made smaller 萎缩的, 收缩的, 干瘪的: *a shrunken old woman* 干瘪的老太太

shtick, schtick /ʃtɪk; ʃtɪk/ *n* [U] *AmE* the style of humour that a particular actor or COMEDIAN typically uses【美】滑稽逗笑风格

shuck /ʃʌk; ʃʌk/ *v* [T] *AmE* to remove the outer cover of a vegetable such as corn or PEAS, or the shell of OYSTERS or CLAMS【美】剥去〔谷物、豆类的〕外壳, 去荚; 剥去〔牡蛎或蛤蜊〕壳

shuck off *phr v* [T] *AmE informal* to take off a piece of clothing【美, 非正式】脱掉〔一件衣服〕: *She shucked off her jacket and ran upstairs.* 她脱掉夹克, 跑上楼去。

shucks /ʃʌks; ʃʌks/ *interjection AmE old-fashioned* used to show you are a little disappointed about something【美, 过时】唉! 糟了!〔表示有点失望〕

shud·der[1] /ˈʃʌdɚ; ˈʃʌdə/ *v* [I] **1** to shake uncontrollably for a short time because you are frightened, or cold, or because you think something is very unpleasant〔因恐惧、寒冷等而短暂地〕打颤, 颤抖: **[+at]** *He touched Ralph's bare shoulder and Ralph shuddered at the human contact.* 他一摸拉尔夫赤裸的肩膀, 拉尔夫吓得颤了一下。**2** if a vehicle or machine shudders, it shakes violently〔车辆或机器〕剧烈震动, 颤动: *The train shuddered to a halt.* 火车剧烈震动了一下便停住了。**3 I shudder to think** used to say that you do not want to think about something because it is too unpleasant 一想到…就颤抖〔用于表示想到不愿想的某种不愉快之事〕: *I shudder to think what they'll say when they see the mess the house is in.* 一想到他们看见房子这样脏乱会说些什么, 我就心里打颤。

shudder at *phr v* [T] to think that something is very bad or unpleasant 对…感到恐惧: *Modern doctors shudder at treatments such as bleeding people with leeches.* 现代医生对用水蛭给病人放血之类的疗法感到恐惧。

shudder[2] *n* [C usually singular 一般用单数] a shaking movement 战栗, 发抖: *The building gave a sudden shudder.* 这幢大楼突然颤动了一下。

shuf·fle[1] /ˈʃʌfl̩; ˈʃʌfəl/ *v* **1** [I always+adv/prep] to walk very slowly and noisily, without lifting your feet off the ground 拖着脚步走, 缓慢地走: **[+along/towards/down etc]** *The old man shuffled along the sidewalk.* 那位老人拖着步子慢慢地走在人行道上。| *The class came shuffling in from the playground.* 全班学生从操场慢吞吞地走了进来。—see picture on page A24 参见A24页图 **2** [T] to move something such as papers into a different order or into different positions 把〔文件等〕移来移去, 反复改变…的顺序[位置]: *Jack sat nervously shuffling the papers around on his desk.* 杰克紧张地坐在那里, 不停地乱翻桌子上的文件。**3** [I,T] to mix PLAYING CARDS around into a different order before playing a game with them 洗(牌): *Is it my turn to shuffle?* 轮到我洗牌了吗? **4 shuffle your feet** to move your feet slightly, especially because you are bored or embarrassed〔尤指因厌烦或尴尬而〕移动双足: *Malcolm shuffled his feet and apologized again.* 马尔科姆尴尬地来回移动着双脚, 再一次表示歉意。—**shuffler** *n* [C] —see also 另见 RESHUFFLE[1]

shuffle[2] *n* **1** [singular] a slow walk in which you do not lift your feet off the ground 拖着脚步走 **2** [C] the act of mixing cards into a different order before playing a game 洗牌

shuf·fle·board /ˈʃʌfl̩ˌbɔrd; ˈʃʌfəlbɔːd/ *n* [U] a game played in the US in which you use a long stick to push a flat round object towards an area with numbers on it〔美国的〕推移板游戏〔用长的推杆把圆盘推入标有号码的得分区〕

shuf·ti /ˈʃʊftɪ; ˈʃʊfti/ *n* **have a shufti** *BrE spoken* to have a quick look at something【英口】瞥上一眼, 瞥视

shun /ʃʌn; ʃʌn/ *v* [T] to avoid someone or something deliberately〔故意〕避开〔某人或某物〕，躲开：*a shy woman who shunned publicity* 避免惹人注意的羞怯女子 | *Victims of the disease found themselves shunned by society.* 这种病的患者发现社会上的人都躲着他们。

shunt¹ /ʃʌnt; ʃʌnt/ *v* [T] **1** to move a train or railway carriage onto a different track 使〔火车〕转轨 **2** to move someone or something to another place, especially in a way that seems unfair 将〔某人或某物〕转移至另一地方〔尤指带有不公正的意味〕：**shunt sb off/around/aside etc** *Smith was shunted off to one of the company's smaller offices.* 史密斯被调到公司下属的一个较小办事处。

shunt² *n* [C] an act of moving a train or railway carriage to a different track 调轨，转轨

shush /ʃʌʃ; ʃʊʃ/ *v* **1 shush!** *spoken* used to tell someone, especially a child, to be quiet【口】嘘！安静！〔尤指叫小孩安静〕："*Shush!" said Jerry, "Not so loud."* "嘘！"杰里说，"别这么大声。" **2** [T] to tell someone to be very quiet, especially by putting your fingers against your lips or by saying 'shush' 使安静，使肃静〔尤指以手指抵住双唇或发"嘘"声表示〕：*He started to cry and Francesca shushed him.* 他哭了起来，弗朗西丝卡发出"嘘"声，要他安静。

shut¹ /ʃʌt; ʃʌt/ *v past tense and past participle* **shut** *present participle* **shutting** **1** [I,T] to close something, or to become closed（使）关[合]上，（使）关闭：*The door shut with a bang.* 门砰的一声关上了。| *She lay down on her bed and shut her eyes.* 她在床上躺下，闭上眼睛。| *Laruelle put the jewels back and shut the lid of the box.* 拉吕埃勒把珠宝放回盒子里，合上盖子。—see 见 OPEN² (USAGE) **2 shut sth in the door/drawer etc** to shut a door etc against something so that it gets trapped there 把…夹在门缝里/抽屉缝里：*Watch out! You're going to get the cat's tail shut in the door.* 小心！你要把猫尾巴夹在门缝里了。**3 shut your mouth/trap/face!** *spoken* used to rudely and angrily tell someone to stop talking【口】闭嘴！住嘴！〔用于粗暴、生气地制止别人讲话〕**4 shut it!** *BrE spoken* used to tell someone rudely and angrily to stop talking【英口】住嘴〔用于粗暴地、生气地制止别人讲话〕**5** [I,T] *especially BrE* to stop being open to the public for a short time or permanently; CLOSE¹ (3)【尤英】（使）〔暂时或永久地〕关门，停止营业：*The post office shuts at 5 o'clock.* 邮局5点钟关门。| *He lost his job when they shut the factory.* 他们把工厂关闭以后，他就失业了。**6 shut your eyes/ears to** to refuse deliberately to notice or pay attention to something〔故意地〕闭眼不看；不愿考虑；拒不理会：*You simply can't shut your eyes to the truth of the matter.* 你不能对真相置之不理呀。**7 shut your ears to** to deliberately not listen to something 故意不听某事，拒不听某事：*He could not shut his ears to the cries and groans coming from inside the room.* 对房里传出的喊叫声和呻吟声，他无法置若罔闻。

shut sb/sth ↔ **away** *phr v* [T] **a)** to put someone or something in a place away from other people where they cannot be seen 把…关起来，把…藏起来，使…与人隔开 **b) shut yourself away** to stay at home or go somewhere quiet, so that you can be alone 把自己关起来，使自己与别人隔开：*She shut herself away in her room to work on her novel.* 她把自己关在房间里写小说。

shut down *phr v* **1** [I,T] if a company, factory, large machine etc shuts down or is shut down, it stops operating（使）〔公司、工厂等〕关闭；（使）〔机器〕停止运转：*There's a rumor going around that the plant is shutting down next year.* 有传闻说这个工厂明年要关闭。| *The printing press had been shut down for servicing.* 这台印刷机已被关掉进行维修。**2** [T **shut** sb ↔ **down**] *AmE informal* to prevent an opposing team or player from playing well or getting points【美，非正式】〔在比赛中〕阻止对方得分[正常发挥]：*We all knew that if we wanted to win we'd have to shut down Bobby Mitchell.* 我们都知道，如果要赢，就一定不能让博比·米切尔得分。

shut sb **in** *phr v* [T] to put or keep someone in a room and stop them from getting out 将〔某人〕关在房内：*The children would be shut in the dormitory at night.* 孩子们晚上都会被关在宿舍里。

shut off *phr v* **1** [I,T] if a machine, tool etc shuts off or if you shut it off, it stops operating（把）〔机器等〕关掉：*The machine shuts off automatically if it gets too hot.* 这台机器在温度过高时会自动关掉。| **shut sth ↔ off** *I let the engine run for a minute and then shut it off.* 我让发动机运转一分钟，然后把它关掉。**2** [T **shut** sth ↔ **off**] to prevent goods or supplies from being available or being delivered 切断〔商品、物资等的〕供应：*a strike that closed the mines and shut off coal supplies* 一次使矿井关闭和煤供应中断的罢工 **3 shut yourself off** to avoid meeting and talking to other people 使自己与…隔绝：**[+from]** *After her last movie, Garbo shut herself off from the world.* 拍完最后一部电影，嘉宝便退隐了。**4 be shut off from** to be separated from other people or things, especially so that you are not influenced by them〔尤指为了不受别人影响而〕与…隔绝：*The valley is completely shut off from the modern world by a range of high mountains.* 连绵的高山使这个山谷与现代世界完全隔绝。

shut sb/sth **out** *phr v* [T] **1** [**shut** sb ↔ **out**] to deliberately not let someone join you in an activity or share your thoughts and feelings〔故意〕把某人排斥在外：*I felt I was being shut out from all the family's affairs.* 我觉得我正被排斥在一切家庭事务之外。| *How can I help you if you just keep shutting me out all the time?* 如果你总是把我排除在外，我又怎么能帮你？**2** [**shut** sb/sth ↔ **out**] to prevent someone or something from entering a place 不让…进入，挡住：*Paula packed the bottom of the doors with blankets to shut out the draught.* 葆拉用毛毯塞住门底的空隙，把风堵在门外。| *heavy curtains that shut out the sunlight* 挡住阳光的厚窗帘 **3** [**shut** sth ↔ **out**] to stop yourself from thinking about or noticing something, so that you are not affected by it 不去想〔某事〕，排除〔干扰〕，使自己不受…影响：*When she's reading, she seems to be able to shut out the rest of the world.* 她在读书时似乎能够完全不受外界的干扰。**4** [**shut out** sb] *AmE* to defeat an opposing team and prevent them from getting any points【美】〔在比赛中〕获胜并使〔对方〕不能得分：*The Chicago Bears shut out the Broncos.* 野马队被芝加哥熊队打得一败涂地，一分未得。

shut up *phr v* **1 shut up!** *spoken* used to tell someone rudely to stop talking【口】闭嘴！住嘴！别说了！：*Oh, shut up! I don't want to hear your excuses.* 噢，别说了！我不想听你的借口。| **[+about]** *We know you won, but just shut up about it, okay!* 我们知道你赢了，不要再讲了，行不行！**2** [T **shut** sb **up**] to make someone stop talking or be quiet 使〔某人〕停止讲话，堵住〔某人〕的嘴：*The only way to shut Philippa up was to give her something to eat.* 要菲莉帕不讲话，唯一的办法就是拿吃的堵上她的嘴。**3** [T **shut up** sb] to keep someone in a place away from other people, and prevent them from leaving 把〔某人〕隔离：*I've had a terrible cold and been shut up in my room for a week.* 我患了重感冒，只好在房间里关了一个星期。**4** [T **shut** sth ↔ **up**] to close a shop, room etc so that people cannot get into it 关闭〔商店、房间等〕：*Bernadette cleaned the attic and then shut it up for another year.* 伯尔纳黛特把阁楼打扫干净，然后又把它关了一年。**5 shut up shop** *informal BrE* to close a business or stop working, at the end of the day or permanently【非正式，英】〔商店在一天营业结束后〕关门，打烊；〔永久地〕停业；〔工作暂时或永久〕停止

shut² *adj* [not usually before noun 一般不用于名词前] **1** not open; closed 关闭的，关上的：*Is the door shut properly?* 门关好了吗？| *He sat with his eyes shut.* 他闭上眼睛坐着。| **blow/slam/bang shut** *The door slammed shut behind him.* 门在他身后砰的一声关上了。| **pull/kick/slide etc sth shut** *Jenny pulled the window shut.* 珍妮把窗户拉上。**2** *BrE* not open for business【英】〔商店〕停止营业的，关门的；closed *AmE*【美】：*It's 6.30 pm and the banks are shut.* 现在是下午6点30分，银行已经关门了。| **[+for]** *The first four hotels we tried were shut for the winter.* 我们最早联系过的四家旅馆冬季都停止营业。

shut·down /ˈʃʌt,daʊn; ˈʃʌtdaʊn/ *n* [C] the closing of a factory, business, or piece of machinery〔工厂、生意的〕停止，停业，关闭；〔机器的〕停止运转：*the shutdown of several power stations* 几家电厂的关闭

Shute /ʃut; ʃuːt/, **Nev·il** /ˈnɛvl; ˈnevəl/ (1899-1960) a British writer who went to live in Australia, and whose best-known NOVELs are *A Town Like Alice* and *On the Beach*. 舒特〔(1899-1960)，英国作家，旅居澳大利亚。最著名的小说有《像艾丽斯一样的城市》和《在沙滩上》〕

shut-eye /ˈ· ·/ *n* [U] *informal* sleep【非正式】睡觉：*I've got to get some shut-eye.* 我得眯一会儿眼睛。

shut-in /ˈ· ·/ *n* [C] *AmE* someone who is ill or DISABLED and cannot leave their house very easily【美】〔因病、残而〕不能随意外出的人：*visiting the sick and shut-ins* 探访卧病在家不便出门的人

shut-out /ˈ· ·/ *n* [C] *AmE* a game in which one team is prevented by the other from getting any points【美】不让对方得分的比赛

shut·ter /ˈʃʌtə; ˈʃʌtə/ *n* [C] **1** [usually plural 一般用复数] one of a pair of wooden or metal covers on the outside of a window that can be closed to keep light out or prevent thieves from coming in 百叶窗；窗板 —see picture on page A4 参见A4页图 **2** a part of a camera that opens for a very short time to let light onto the film〔照相机的〕快门，遮光器 **3 put up the shutters** *BrE*

informal to close a business at the end of the day or permanently【英，非正式】〔暂时或永久性地〕停止营业；打烊；关门

shut·ter·bug /ˈʃʌtɚˌbʌg; ˈʃʌtəbʌg/ *n* [C] *AmE informal* someone who likes to take a lot of photographs【美，非正式】摄影爱好者，摄影迷

shut·tered /ˈʃʌtɚd; ˈʃʌtəd/ *adj* with closed shutters, or having shutters 关上百叶窗的；装有百叶窗的：*A gust of wind shook the shuttered windows.* 一阵狂风吹得百叶窗摇摇晃晃。

shut·tle¹ /ˈʃʌtl; ˈʃʌtl/ *n* [C] **1** a plane, bus, or train that makes regular short journeys between two places〔飞机、公共汽车或火车的〕短程穿梭运行：*He took the Washington-New York shuttle.* 他乘坐华盛顿—纽约的穿梭客机。**2** a SPACECRAFT that can fly into space and return to Earth, and can be used more than once; SPACE SHUTTLE 航天飞机 **3 shuttle service** a plane, bus, or train service that goes regularly between two places that are fairly near each other〔飞机、公共汽车、火车的〕短程穿梭服务，往返运输业务：*There's a shuttle service from the city center to the airport.* 市中心和飞机场之间有往返的班车。**4** a pointed tool used in weaving, to pass a thread over and under the threads that form the cloth〔织布机的〕梭子 **5 shuttle diplomacy** international talks, for example to make a peace agreement, carried out by someone who travels between countries and talks to members of the governments 穿梭外交（活动）

shuttle² *v* **1** [I always+adv/prep] to travel frequently between two places 穿梭往返，频繁往返（两地）：**[+between/back and forth]** *Susan shuttles between Rotterdam and London for her job.* 苏珊因工作关系经常往返于鹿特丹和伦敦两地。**2** [T] to move people from one place to another place that is fairly near 短程穿梭运送〔人〕：*The passengers were shuttled to the hotel by bus.* 旅客由班车送到酒店。

shut·tle·cock /ˈʃʌtlˌkɑk; ˈʃʌtlkɒk/ *n* [C] a small light object that you hit over the net in the game of BADMINTON 羽毛球；BIRDIE¹ (3) *AmE*【美】—see picture on page A23 参见 A23 页图

shy¹ /ʃaɪ; ʃaɪ/ *adj* **1** nervous and embarrassed about talking to other people, especially people you do not know〔尤指在陌生人面前〕羞怯的，腼腆的：*Billy's very shy with adults, but he's fine with other children.* 比利在大人面前很害羞，但和其他孩子在一起时就不这样。| *a shy smile* 腼腆的微笑 | **painfully shy** (=extremely shy) 极其羞怯的 *At 15, I was painfully shy.* 我在15岁时腼腆得很。| **be too shy to do sth** *I needed a ride home but was too shy to ask anyone.* 我想搭便车回家，但不好意思向别人提出来。| **go all shy** *spoken* (=suddenly become very shy)【口】突然变得很害羞 *Look, she's gone all shy – stop teasing her!* 你看，她已经很难为情了，不要再拿她开玩笑了！**2** unwilling to do something or get involved in something 不愿意的：**[+about/of]** *Men are often shy about sharing their problems.* 男人常常不愿意把自己的问题告诉别人。| *Madonna is certainly not shy of publicity.* 麦当娜绝对不怕出名。**3** [not before noun 不用于名词前] *especially AmE* less than the amount needed【尤美】不足的，未达到所需数量的：**[+of]** *He was only 30 votes shy of the number he needed for the nomination.* 他只差30票就达到提名所需的票数。**4 fight shy of (doing) sth** to avoid doing something or getting involved in something 避免做某事，避免介入某事：*He fought shy of an open quarrel.* 他避免公开争吵。**5** shy animals get frightened easily and are unwilling to come near people〔动物〕易受惊的，不愿近人的，胆怯的 —see also 另见 **once bitten twice shy** (BITE¹ (13)), CAMERA-SHY —**shyly** *adv*: *"I have a question," she said, shyly stroking Ralph's arm.* "我有个问题。"她说，羞怯地抚着拉尔夫的手臂。—**shyness** *n* [U]

shy² *v* **1** if a horse shies, it makes a sudden movement away from something because it is frightened〔马〕惊退，惊跳 **2** [T] *old-fashioned* to throw a ball or other object at something【过时】向…投，掷，扔〔球等〕

shy away from sth *phr v* [T] to avoid doing something because you are not confident enough or you are worried or nervous about it〔因缺乏信心，或因担心或紧张而〕回避，避开：*They criticized the leadership, but shied away from a direct challenge.* 他们批评领导层，但避免正面质疑。

Shy·lock /ˈʃaɪlɑk; ˈʃaɪlɒk/ a character in the play *The Merchant of Venice* by William Shakespeare. He is a Jewish MONEYLENDER who lends money to Antonio, and when Antonio is unable to pay the money back, Shylock says he has the right to cut a pound of flesh from Antonio's body. In some ways Shylock is shown in a negative way as someone who is only interested in money, but he also makes a famous speech in which he states that he is like any other human being ("If you prick me, do I not bleed...") and describes how he and other Jewish people are unfairly treated. 夏洛克〔威廉·莎士比亚戏剧《威尼斯商人》中的一个角色。他是个犹太人，以放债为业。他将钱借给了安东尼奥，当安东尼奥无力偿还时，他便声称自己有权从安东尼奥身上割一磅肉。从某些角度来讲，夏洛克在剧中被塑造成反面角色，代表只认金钱的一类人。但他讲过的一段话却十分有名，声明自己与别的人是一样的（"如果你戳我一下，难道我不会流血吗…"），还提及自己与其他犹太人受到的不公待遇〕

shys·ter /ˈʃaɪstɚ; ˈʃaɪstə/ *n* [C] *AmE informal* a dishonest person, especially a lawyer or politician【美，非正式】奸诈的人〔尤指律师或政客〕

Si·am /ˌsaɪˈæm; ˌsaɪˈæm/ a former name for Thailand 暹罗〔泰国的旧称〕

Si·a·mese cat /ˌsaɪəmiz ˈkæt; ˌsaɪəmiːz ˈkæt/ *n* [C] a type of cat that has blue eyes, short grey or brown fur, and a dark face 暹罗猫

Siamese twin /ˌ··· ˈ·/ *n* [C usually plural 一般用复数] one of two people who are born joined to each other 连体双胞胎，暹罗孪生子

SIB, the /ˌɛs aɪ ˈbi; ˌes aɪ ˈbiː/ the abbreviation of 缩写= the SECURITIES AND INVESTMENTS BOARD

Si·be·li·us /sɪˈbeliəs; sɪˈbeɪliəs/, **Jean** /ʒæn; ʒæn/ (1865-1957) a Finnish COMPOSER whose music is about nature and old Finnish stories and literature. His best-known works are *Finlandia*, *The Karelia Suite*, and his symphonies (SYMPHONY). 西贝柳斯〔(1865-1957)，芬兰作曲家。作品或歌颂大自然或取材于芬兰的古老传说和文学作品。最为著名的作品有《芬兰颂》、《卡列拉组曲》及交响曲〕

Si·be·r·ia /saɪˈbɪrɪə; saɪˈbɪəriə/ a very large area in Russia, between the Ural Mountains and the Pacific Ocean, where there are many minerals but very few people. It is extremely cold, and the Soviet governments used to send people there who disagreed with them. 西伯利亚〔俄罗斯一片广袤的土地。位于乌拉尔山脉与太平洋之间，矿藏异常丰富，人口非常稀少。那里的气候极为寒冷。前苏联政府过去常将持不同政见者流放于此〕—**Siberian** *adj*

sib·ilant¹ /ˈsɪbl̩ənt; ˈsɪbl̩ənt/ *adj formal* making or being an "s" or "sh" sound【正式】发出咝咝声的：*a sibilant, fluttering voice* 颤动的咝咝声

sibilant² *n* [C] *technical* a sibilant sound such as /ʃ/ in English【术语】〔英语中的〕咝音〈如 /ʃ/〉

sib·ling /ˈsɪblɪŋ; ˈsɪblɪŋ/ *n* [C] **1** *formal* a brother or sister【正式】兄弟；姊妹 **2 sibling rivalry** competition between brothers and sisters for their parents' attention or love 同胞竞争，手足相争〔指兄弟姐妹为得到父母的关注或爱而产生的竞争〕

sib·yl /ˈsɪbl̩; ˈsɪbɪl/ *n* [C] one of a group of women in the ancient world who were thought to know the future〔古代的〕女预言家，女先知

sic¹ /sɪk; sɪk/ *adv Latin* used after a word that you have copied in order to show that you know it was not spelled or used correctly【拉丁】原文如此〔置于所引用文字之后，表示虽知该词有错误，却是原文〕：*We had seen several signs that said 'ORANGE'S (sic) FOR SALE'.* 我们看到几个牌子写着ORANGE'S〔原文如此〕FOR SALE。

sic² *v* [T] *AmE informal*【美，非正式】**1** to tell a dog to attack someone 嗾使〔狗〕去攻击：*He sicced his dog on me.* 他嗾使他的狗来攻击我。**2 sic 'em!** *spoken* used to tell a dog to attack someone【口】咬他！追他！〔嗾使狗攻击某人〕

Si·ci·ly /ˈsɪsɪlɪ; ˈsɪsəli/ an island in the Mediterranean Sea, which is part of Italy and is close to the country's southwest coast. Many people think of it as the home of the Mafia. Capital: Palermo. 西西里岛〔地中海一岛屿，属于意大利，毗邻意大利西南海岸。很多人认为该岛是黑手党的老巢。首府：巴勒莫〕—**Sicillian** /sɪˈsɪlɪən; səˈsɪliən/ *n, adj*

sick¹ /sɪk; sɪk/ *adj*

1 ▶ILL 生病的◀ suffering from a disease or illness 有病的，患病的：*Where's Sheila – is she sick?* 希拉在哪儿？她病了吗？| *a sick child* 病孩 | **get sick** *AmE* (=become ill)【美】生病，患病 *At the last minute I got sick and couldn't go.* 我在最后一刻病倒，结果不能去。| **sick as a dog** (=very sick) 病得很重 *Pete's at home in bed, sick as a dog.* 皮特在家卧床不起，病得很重。| **be off sick** (=be away from work or school because you are ill) 因病缺勤[缺课] *I was off sick for four days with the flu.* 我因患流感休了四天病假。| **call in sick** (=telephone to say you are not coming to work because you are ill) 打电话请假 *You have to call in sick before 9.30.* 必须在9点30分之前打电话请病假。| **take sick** *old-fashioned* (=become ill)【过时】生病 *He took sick and died a week later.* 他得了病，一星期后死了。—see graph at 参见 ILL¹ 图表

2 be sick to bring food up from your stomach through your mouth; VOMIT 呕吐：*The cat's been sick on the carpet.* 猫吐在地毯上了。| *You'll be sick if you eat any more of that chocolate!*

S

S1 W3

你如果再吃那些巧克力，你会呕吐的。| **violently sick** (=suddenly and severely sick) 突然呕吐得厉害 *I was violently sick the last time I ate prawns.* 我上次吃了大虾以后，吐得很厉害。
3 feel sick also 又作 **be/feel sick to your stomach** to feel as if you are going to VOMIT 反胃的，恶心的，作呕的：*As soon as the ship started moving I began to feel sick.* 轮船一开动，我就开始想吐了。—see also 另见 CARSICK, SEASICK, TRAVEL-SICK
4 be sick (and tired) of also 又作 **be sick to death of** to be angry and bored with something that has been happening for a long time 对…感到厌烦的，腻烦的，厌倦的：*I'm really sick of housework!* 我对家务活厌倦透了。| *We're getting sick and tired of listening to them argue all the time.* 听他们一直争论不休，我们都感到腻烦得很。
5 be worried sick/be sick with worry to be extremely worried 极为担心：*Why didn't you tell me you were coming home late? I've been worried sick!* 你为什么不早说你要晚归？我都担心死了！
6 make me/you sick *spoken*【口】**a)** to make you feel very angry 令我/你非常气愤：*People like you make me sick!* 像你这样的人真叫我生气。**b)** *spoken humorous* to make someone feel jealous【口，幽默】令人眼红：*You make me sick with your 'expenses paid' holidays!* 你享受"费用由他人支付"的度假待遇，真叫我眼红。
7 ►STRANGE/CRUEL 反常的/残酷的◄ a) someone who is sick does things that are strange and cruel, and seems mentally ill 变态的，〔心理〕不正常的，精神有病的：*I keep getting obscene phone calls from some sick pervert.* 我不断收到一个性变态者打来的下流电话。| *a sick mind* 病态的心理 **b)** sick stories, jokes etc deal with death and suffering in a cruel or unpleasant way〔故事、笑话等〕残忍的，残酷的，可怖的：*Did you see that film 'Brain Dead'? Sick, isn't it?* 你看过那部叫《新空房禁地》的电影没有？真恐怖，是吗？| *Has he told you his sick joke about the undertaker?* 他给你讲过他那个关于殡仪工人的恐怖笑话没有？
8 sick as a parrot *BrE spoken humorous* extremely disappointed【英口，幽默】极为失望的：*"How did you feel when you missed that penalty?" "Sick as a parrot."* "你那次射失点球有什么感觉？""失望极了。"
9 sick at heart *literary* very unhappy, upset, or disappointed about something【文】很不愉快，很失望：*I was sick at heart to think that I would never see the place again.* 我想到再也看不到这个地方时，心里非常难过。

USAGE NOTE 用法说明：SICK
WOLD CHOICE 词语辨析：**sick, vomit, throw up, ill, not well, unwell, something wrong with**
In spoken British English to **be sick** is more often used to mean 'to throw up the contents of the stomach through the mouth' than 'to be generally ill'. 在英国英语口语中，be sick 较多用于表示"呕吐"，而较少用于表示"生病"：*If you eat too many sweets you'll be sick.* 如果你吃太多的糖果，你会呕吐的。The more formal word in British and American English is **vomit**, and a less formal word is **throw up**. 在英国英语和美国英语中表示"呕吐"时，动词 vomit 的用法比较正式，而 throw up 则比较口语化。
If you are talking about general illness, especially when you do not say exactly what illness it is, you would usually use **ill** in British English, and **sick** in American English. 表示"生病"但不必具体说明什么病时，英国英语通常用 ill，而美国英语用 sick：*She's been ill for several days now.* 她生病已有好几天了。| *You'll end up getting sick if you don't get more rest.* 如果你不多休息，你最终会生病的。In British and American English you can also use **not well**. 在英国英语和美国英语中都可以用 not well：*Diana hasn't been feeling very well lately.* 黛安娜近来身体一直不大好。
Ill usually has a stronger meaning than **not well**. You may be **not well** because of a bad cold but **ill** with cancer. **Unwell** is a more formal word for **not well** or **ill**. ill 的含义通常要比 not well 强。得了重感冒时可以说是 not well，但患了癌症则使用 ill。与 not well 或 ill 相比，unwell 是比较正式的用法。
Before a noun **sick** always means 'generally not well' (**ill** and **unwell** are not usually used before a noun). 用于名词前时，sick 表示"生病的"〔但 ill 和 unwell 通常不用于名词之前〕：*He's gone to visit his sick mother.* 他已去探望他生病的母亲了。
When you want to talk about a particular part of the body that is hurt or has a disease you can say there is **something wrong with…**. 要表示身体某部分受了伤或有病时，可以用 there is something wrong with…：*Tommy can't play today – there's something wrong with his knee.* (NOT 不用 *He has a sick knee* | *he is sick with his knee*). 汤米今天不能打球了，他膝部有点不适。
SPELLING 拼写
Note that **homesick** is written as one word. 注意 homesick 需拼作一个单词。

sick² *n* **1 the sick** people who are ill 病人，生病的人：*The sick and wounded were allowed to go free.* 伤病员获得释放。**2** [U] *BrE informal* VOMIT【英，非正式】呕吐物
sick³ *v*
sick sth ↔ **up** *phr v* [T] *BrE informal* to bring up food from your stomach; VOMIT¹【英，非正式】呕吐
sick·bay /ˈsɪkˌbe; ˈsɪkbeɪ/ *n* [C] a room on a ship, in a school etc where there are beds for people who are sick〔船上、学校等的〕医务室
sick·bed /ˈsɪkˌbɛd; ˈsɪkbed/ *n* [C usually singular 一般用单数] the bed where a sick person is lying 病床：*The president carried on working from his sickbed.* 总裁卧病在床还继续工作。
sick·en /ˈsɪkən; ˈsɪkən/ *v* **1** [T] to make you feel shocked and angry, especially because you strongly disapprove of something 使厌恶；使气愤：*The idea of organized dog fights sickens me.* 组织斗狗的主意使我恶心。| *All decent people should be sickened by such a pointless waste of lives.* 一切正直的人都应对这种毫无意义的浪费生命感到愤慨。**2 be sickening for something** *spoken especially BrE* to start to have an illness and show signs of having it【口，尤英】开始生病，有生病的症状：*I think Tommy must be sickening for something, the way he's been moping around.* 看汤米那副无精打采到处晃的样子，我想他可能得什么病了。**3** [I] *old-fashioned* to gradually become very ill【过时】逐渐患上重病：*The older people just sickened and died as food supplies ran low.* 随着食品供应的减少，老人们相继患病而死。
sicken of sth *phr v* [T] to lose your desire for something or your interest in it 对…感到厌烦，对…失去兴趣：*He finally sickened of the endless round of parties and idle conversation.* 他终于对那一连串无休止的聚会和闲聊感到厌烦了。
sick·en·ing /ˈsɪkənɪŋ; ˈsɪkənɪŋ/ *adj* **1** very shocking, annoying, or upsetting; DISGUSTING 令人震惊的，令人厌恶的，令人作呕的：*Local police said it was one of the most sickening attacks they had come across.* 当地警方说这是他们所遇到过的最令人震惊的袭击之一。| *their sickening hypocrisy* 他们那令人恶心的虚伪嘴脸 **2 a sickening thud/crash** an unpleasant sound that makes you think someone has been injured or something has been broken 可怕的重击声/碰撞声：*His head hit the floor with a sickening thud.* 他的头砰的一声撞在地板上。**3** *BrE spoken* making you feel jealous【英口】令人羡慕的；令人妒忌的：*"Helen's just bought herself a new BMW." "God, how sickening!"* "海伦刚刚买了一辆新宝马汽车。""啊，真叫人羡慕！" —**sickeningly** *adv*
sick·ie /ˈsɪkɪ; ˈsɪki/ *n* [C] *AustrE & BrE informal* a day when you say that you are ill and do not go to work, even though you are not really ill【澳和英，非正式】托病休息的一天
sick·le /ˈsɪkl̩; ˈsɪkəl/ *n* [C] a tool with a blade in the shape of a hook, used for cutting wheat or long grass 镰刀
sickle-cell a·nae·mi·a *BrE*【英】, **sickle-cell anemia** *AmE*【美】/ˌ‥ ·ˈ‥/ *n* [U] a serious illness that mainly affects black people, in which the blood cells change shape, causing weakness and fever 镰状细胞贫血〔患此病者多为黑人〕
sick·ly /ˈsɪklɪ; ˈsɪkli/ *adj* **1** weak, unhealthy, and often ill 虚弱的，不健康的，常生病的：*a sickly child* 体质差的孩子 | *a sickly pallor to his face* 他脸色病态的苍白 **2** a sickly smell, taste etc is unpleasant and makes you feel sick〔气味等〕令人恶心的：*the sickly odor of rotting garbage* 令人恶心的腐烂垃圾味
sick·ness /ˈsɪknɪs; ˈsɪknəs/ *n* **1** [U] the state of being ill; ILLNESS 患病：*an insurance policy against long-term sickness and injury* 对长期患病和受伤的保险 | *working days lost due to sickness* 因病损失的工作日 **2** [U] the feeling that you are about to bring up food from your stomach; NAUSEA 呕吐，恶心：*A wave of sickness came over him.* 他感到一阵恶心。| **morning sickness** (=sickness that some women get when they are going to have a baby)〔孕妇〕晨吐 | **travel/car/sea/air sickness** (=sickness that some people get while travelling) 旅行眩晕/晕车/晕船/晕机 **3** [C] a particular illness〔某种〕疾病：*They died within a few days of each other, probably from a sickness like the plague.* 他俩在几天内相继死去，也许是死于鼠疫之类的疾病。**4** [U] the serious problems and weaknesses of a social,

political, or economic system〔社会、政治、经济制度的〕弊病，不健全状态: *He said the idea of 'success' was part of the sickness of Western cultures.* 他说，对"成功"的理解是西方文化弊端的一部分。

sickness ben·e·fit /ˈ··,··/ *n* [U] *BrE* money paid by the government to someone who is too sick to work【英】〔政府发给因病不能工作的人的〕疾病补助金

sick note /ˈ··/ *n* [C] *BrE* a note written by your doctor or your parents saying that you were too sick to go to work or school【英】〔医生开的〕病假单;〔父母为子女写的〕因病请假便条; EXCUSE[2] (5) *AmE*【美】

sick·o /ˈsɪko; ˈsɪkəʊ/ *n* [C] *slang especially AmE* someone who gets pleasure from things that most people find unpleasant or upsetting【俚，尤美】有精神病的人，心理变态的人: *There's plenty of twisted sickos out there who are into kiddie porn.* 有很多心理变态的人沉迷于儿童色情。

sick-out /ˈ··/ *n* [C] *AmE* a STRIKE (=protest about pay or working conditions) in which all the workers at a company say they are sick and stay home on the same day【美】集体托病罢工

sick pay /ˈ··/ *n* [U] money paid by an employer to a worker who cannot work because of illness 病假工资

sick·room /ˈsɪkˌrum; ˈsɪkrʊm/ *n* [C] a room where someone who is sick can go to lie down 病房

S1 W1

side[1] /saɪd; saɪd/ *n* [C]

① PLACE/AREA/POSITION 地方/区域/位置
② DIRECTION 方向
③ SUBJECT/SITUATION 主题/形势
④ IN A QUARREL/WAR/SPORT 在吵架/战争/体育运动中
⑤ PEOPLE 人们
⑥ SUPPORT 支持
⑦ OTHER MEANINGS 其他意思

① PLACE/AREA/POSITION 地方/区域/位置

1 ▶PART OF AN AREA 区域的一部分◀ one of the two areas that are on either the left or the right of an imaginary line, or on either the left or the right of a border, wall, river etc〔想象中的分界线的左或右的〕部分，地带，半边;〔边界、墙、河等的左或右的〕边，面，侧: *Drive on the left-hand side of the road.* 靠道路左侧行驶。| *a scar on the right side of his face* 他右边脸上的伤疤 | *Fuel is cheaper on the French side of the border.* 燃料在法国境内便宜些。| *The south side of town is pretty run-down.* 这个城镇的南边相当破旧。| the far/other side (=the area furthest from you or opposite you) 另一边[头]，那一边[头] *I could just see Rita on the far side of the square.* 我勉强能看见在广场那一边的丽塔。| to one side (of) *Off to one side was a small wooden shed.* 在那边有间小木屋。

2 ▶NEXT TO 在旁边，挨着◀ [usually singular 一般用单数] the place or area directly next to someone or something, on the right or the left 身边，身旁，旁边: *Put the table on the left side of the couch.* 把桌子放在长沙发的左侧。| *Stand on this side of me so Dad can get a photo.* 站在我这一侧，好让爸爸给照张相。| **by/at sb's side** (=beside them) 在某人身旁 *Tyler's daughter walked at his side.* 泰勒的女儿走在他身旁。| **side by side** (=next to each other) 并排地，肩并肩地 *Two bottles stood side by side on the shelf.* 两个瓶子并排放在架子上。| *We walked along the beach, side by side.* 我们并肩沿着海滨走。| **on either side** (=on the left side and the right) 在两边，在两旁 *On either side of the front gates stood a tall tree.* 前门两旁各有一棵大树。

3 ▶EDGE 边缘◀ the part of an object or area that is furthest from the middle, at or near the edge〔物体或范围的〕边，边缘: *a little store by the side of the highway* 公路边上的小店 | *a triangle with unequal sides* 不等边三角形 | *Jack sat down heavily on the side of the bed.* 杰克在床边重重地坐了下来。| **roadside/lakeside etc** *a charming hotel on the riverside* 河边漂亮的旅店 —see also 另见 SEASIDE

4 ▶OF A BUILDING/OBJECT/VEHICLE ETC 属于建筑物/物体/车辆等的◀ a surface of something that is not its front, back, top, or bottom 侧面，旁边: *There's an entrance at the side of the building.* 大楼旁边有个入口。| *The lifeboat was lowered over the ship's side.* 救生艇从船舷放下。| *Someone ran into the side of my car.* 有人撞到我汽车的侧面。| *Scrape the batter from the sides of the bowl.* 把碗边上的面糊刮掉。

5 ▶MOUNTAIN/VALLEY ETC 大山/山谷等◀ one of the sloping areas of a hill, mountain etc 山坡: *an old cave in the side of the valley* 山坡上的古老洞穴 | **hillside/mountainside etc** *sheep grazing on the steep hillside* 在陡峭的山坡上吃草的羊群

6 ▶FLAT SURFACE 平面◀ one of the flat surfaces of something〔物体的〕(一个) 平面: *Which side of the box do you put the label on?* 你把标签贴在箱子的哪一面? | *A cube has six sides.* 立方体有六个面。

7 ▶OF A THIN OBJECT 薄物体的◀ one of the two surfaces of a thin flat object 扁平物体两面中的任何一面: *Write only on one side of the paper.* 请只在纸的一面上写。| *I'll paint the other side of the fence tomorrow.* 我明天要漆篱笆的另一面。| *Try playing side A of the tape.* 试试放磁带的A面。

8 three-sided/four-sided etc with three sides, four sides etc 三/四边的: *a five-sided shape* 五边形 —see also 另见 ONE-SIDED

9 steep-sided/bare-sided etc with a particular type of side 山坡陡峭的/边上光秃秃的〔用于表示某种类型的坡、边、面等〕: *a sheer-sided gorge* 两边都是悬崖峭壁的峡谷 | *a huge flat-sided rock* 表面平整的巨石

10 ▶PAGE 页◀ *BrE* a page of writing on one side of a piece of paper【英】〔写上文字的〕一页;〔纸张的〕一面: *How many sides have we got to write?* 我们要写多少页?

② DIRECTION 方向

11 from side to side moving continuously, first in one direction then in the other 从一边到另一边: *The rope bridge swung from side to side in a terrifying manner.* 索桥左右摇晃，十分吓人。

12 from all sides from every direction 从各个方向，从四面八方: *Planes were attacking us from all sides.* 飞机从四面八方向我们发起攻击。

13 on all sides/on every side in every direction 在各方面，到处: *We were surrounded on all sides by a wall of flames.* 我们四面八方都被火墙包围了。| *Gunfire erupted on every side.* 四面八方响起了炮火的轰鸣声。

③ SUBJECT/SITUATION 主题/形势

14 one part or feature of a subject, problem, or situation, especially when compared with another part〔主题、问题、形势的〕一个方面〔尤指与其他方面相比时〕: *Tell me your side of the story.* 请把你对情况的看法告诉我。| *We expect you to keep your side of the bargain.* 我们期望你方信守在这项交易中所作的承诺。| **all/both sides** *Try to look at all sides of the issue.* 要从各个方面考虑这个问题。| **technical/financial/social etc side** *She takes care of the financial side of the business.* 她负责公司财务方面的工作。| **serious/funny etc side** *Can't you see the funny side of all this?* 难道你看不出这件事滑稽的一面吗?

④ IN A QUARREL/WAR/SPORT 在吵架/战争/体育运动中

15 one of the people, groups, or countries opposing each other in a quarrel, war etc〔吵架、交战等双方的〕一方: *fighting on the Bosnian side in the civil war* 在内战中为波斯尼亚一方而战 | *My sympathy lay on the side of the rebels.* 我同情叛乱者一方。| **take sides** (=choose to support a particular person or opinion) 支持一方，偏袒一方 *I'm sorry, but I'm not taking sides on this one.* 很抱歉，但在这个问题上我不能支持一方。| **be on sb's side** (=agree with someone and support them) 站在某人一边 *Thank God at least you're on my side.* 谢天谢地，至少你是站在我一边的。| **whose side are you on?** *spoken* (=used when someone is arguing against you when they should be supporting you)【口】你究竟站在哪一边?〔用于表示某人本应支持你但却发表了反对你的意见〕

16 ►IN SPORT 在体育运动方面◄ [also+plural verb *BrE*] *BrE* a sports team【英】运动队, 球队: *He plays for the Welsh side.* 他是威尔士队球员。

⑤ PEOPLE 人们

17 ►PART OF SB'S CHARACTER 某人性格的一部分◄ [usually singular 一般用单数] one part of someone's character, especially when compared with another part〔某人性格的〕一面〔尤指相对于另一面而言〕: *One side of me is cautious, and another side says go ahead and do it!* 我性格的一面是谨慎, 但另一面却说"干吧, 动手干!" | *It was a side of Shari I hadn't seen before.* 我以前从没见过莎丽性格的这一面。| **emotional/romantic/funny etc side** *Jeff does have his romantic side, honestly!* 一点不假, 杰夫确有他浪漫的一面。

18 ►PART OF YOUR BODY 身体的一部分◄ the part of your body from your shoulder to the top of your leg〔肩膀以下至大腿上端的〕身体的侧边: *He had a scar running right the way down his side.* 他肋部有一条从上到下的大伤疤。

19 ►OF A FAMILY 家庭的◄ the parents, grandparents etc of your mother or your father 血统, 家系, 父[母]系: *Ken is Scottish on his mother's side.* 肯的母系是苏格兰血统。

⑥ SUPPORT 支持

20 not leave sb's side to always be with someone and look after them 永远照顾某人: *Promise me you'll never leave her side.* 答应我你会永远照顾她。

21 side by side closely together with each other and helping each other 并排地, 肩并肩地: *We've worked side by side for years.* 我们肩并肩一道工作好多年了。

⑦ OTHER MEANINGS 其他意思

22 on the high side/the heavy side etc *spoken* a little too high, too heavy etc【口】偏高/偏重等: *Ooh, the price is a bit on the high side, isn't it?* 噢, 这个价钱有点偏高, 不是吗? | *The sheets are still a little on the damp side.* 这些被单还是有点潮。

23 on the side: a) in addition to your regular job 作为副业, 作为兼职: *Freelancing can help you make a little money on the side.* 当自由撰稿人可以帮助你业余挣点小钱。—see also 另见 SIDELINE¹ (1) **b)** dishonestly or illegally 暗地里, 非法地: *Simms didn't seem the type to have a lover on the side.* 西姆斯不像是背地里有情妇的那种人。—see also 另见 **a bit on the side** (BIT¹ (21)) **c)** food that is served on the side is ordered with the main dish in a restaurant, but is not usually part of that dish〔与主菜同时点的〕配菜: *Could I have waffles with an egg on the side?* 我可以要一份华夫饼加鸡蛋作配菜吗?

24 have sth on your side to have an advantage that increases your chances of success 有…方面的优势, …对某人有利: *Greg has youth on his side, he'll recover.* 格雷格年轻, 他会恢复健康的。| *We've got the law on our side.* 我们有法律的支持。

25 get on the right/wrong side of sb *informal* to make someone very pleased with you or very angry with you【非正式】使某人很高兴/生气: *Be careful not to get on the wrong side of her.* 你要小心别惹她生气。

26 let the side down *BrE informal* to behave in a way that makes things difficult for your family, team etc, or makes them embarrassed【英, 非正式】使自己的家人或队友等难堪, 辱没自己一方: *I'm disappointed in you, Alex, you've really let the side down.* 我对你太失望了, 亚历克斯, 你真叫大家难堪。

27 ►TV STATION 电视台◄ [usually singular 一般用单数] *BrE informal* a television station; CHANNEL¹ (1)【英, 非正式】电视频道: *What's on the other side?* 其他频道有什么节目?

28 a side of beef/bacon one half of an animal's body, cut along the BACKBONE and bought for food 牛肋肉/腌熏猪肋肉〔沿脊骨切开供食用的动物的半边躯体或肋肉〕

29 put/leave/set sth to one side to save something to be dealt with or used later 将…留到以后再用/处理: *Let's leave that question to one side for now.* 咱们暂时把那个问题放在一边吧。| *Put a little money to one side each week.* 你要每星期都存一点钱。

30 on the right/wrong side of 30, 40 etc *spoken* younger or older than 30, 40 etc【口】不到/已过30岁、40岁等

31 take etc sb to one side to take someone away from other people for a short time for a private talk 把某人拉到一旁〔私下交谈〕: *Maybe you can quietly take Pam to one side and ask about Henry.* 也许你可以把帕姆悄悄地拉到一旁, 问他关于亨利的事。

32 on the wrong/right side of the law *informal* breaking/not breaking the law【非正式】犯法/不犯法: *OK, do it, but keep on the right side of the law!* 好, 干吧, 可别犯法!

33 this side of without going as far as 不去…那么远: *It's the best Chinese food this side of Beijing.* 除非跑到北京, 否则这就是最好的中国菜了。

34 criticize/scold/curse sb up one side and down the other *AmE spoken* criticize someone, treat them unkindly etc without worrying about how they feel【美口】狠狠地批评/责骂/诅咒某人 —see also 另见 FLIP SIDE, **to be on the safe side** (SAFE¹ (8)), **split your sides** (SPLIT¹ (9)), **two sides of the same coin** (COIN¹ (4)), **the other side of the coin** (COIN¹ (3)), **get out of bed (on) the wrong side** (BED¹ (9)), **err on the side of caution** (ERR (1))

side² *adj* [only before noun 仅用于名词前] **1** in or on the side of something 旁边的, 侧面的: **a side door/panel etc** *Hannah slipped out through a side exit.* 汉纳从侧门溜了出去。**2** from the side of something 从一侧的, 从侧面来的: *Can you get a side view?* 你能看到侧景吗? **3 side street/road etc** a street, road etc that is smaller than a main street but is often connected to it〔与大街相连的〕小街, 小巷;〔与干线相连的〕支路, 岔路, 小路: *He'd found a nice quiet side street off San Vincente.* 他在圣维森特大街旁找到一条安静的小街。

side³ *v* [I] to support or argue against a person or group in a quarrel, fight etc 站在…一边, 偏袒…: [**+with/against**] *Frank sided with David against their mother.* 弗兰克站在戴维一边反对妈妈。

side·arm /ˈsaɪdˌɑrm; ˈsaɪd-ɑːm/ *n* [C often plural 常用复数] a weapon carried or worn at someone's side, for example a gun or sword〔佩带在腰间的〕随身武器〈如手枪或佩剑〉

side·board /ˈsaɪdˌbɔrd; ˈsaɪdbɔːd/ *n* **1** [C] a long low piece of furniture usually in a DINING ROOM, used for storing plates, glasses etc〔餐厅里的〕餐具柜 **2 sideboards** *BrE* sideburns【英】〔男子的〕鬓角

side·burns /ˈsaɪdˌbɝnz; ˈsaɪdbɜːnz/ *n* [plural] hair grown down the sides of a man's face in front of his ears〔男子的〕鬓角 —see picture on page A6 参见A6页图

side·car /ˈsaɪdˌkɑr; ˈsaɪdkɑː/ *n* [C] a seat, often enclosed, that is joined to the side of a MOTORCYCLE and has a separate wheel〔附在摩托车旁的〕边车, 跨斗

side dish /ˈ· ·/ *n* [C] a small amount of food such as a SALAD that you eat with a main meal〔正菜以外的〕小菜, 配菜〈如沙拉〉

side ef·fect /ˈ· ·ˌ·/ *n* [C] **1** an effect that a drug has on your body in addition to curing pain or illness〔药物的〕副作用: *a natural remedy with no harmful side effects* 一种没有副作用的天然药物 **2** an unexpected or unplanned result of a situation or event〔事态发展等的〕意外后果; 意想不到的效果: *These policy changes could have beneficial side effects for the whole economy.* 政策的这些变化可能对整个经济产生良好的效果。

side is·sue /ˈ· ˌ··/ *n* [C] *especially BrE* a subject or problem that is not as important as the main one, and may take people's attention away from the main subject【尤英】〔可能分散注意力的〕次要问题: *We mustn't let the meeting get bogged down in side issues.* 我们绝对不要在会上就次要问题纠缠不清。

side·kick /ˈsaɪdˌkɪk; ˈsaɪdˌkɪk/ *n* [C] *informal* someone who spends time with or helps another person, especially when that person is more important than they are【非正式】助手,〔次要的〕伙伴: *He starred as Sherlock Holmes' bumbling sidekick Watson.* 他在影片中扮演歇洛克·福尔摩斯笨手笨脚的助手华生。

side·light /ˈsaɪdˌlaɪt; ˈsaɪdlaɪt/ *n* [C] *BrE* one of the two small lights next to the main front lights on a car【英】〔汽车的〕侧灯〔前灯旁的小灯〕; PARKING LIGHT *AmE*【美】—see picture on page A2 参见A2页图

side·line¹ /ˈsaɪdˌlaɪn; ˈsaɪdlaɪn/ *n* **1** [C] an activity that you do as well as your main job or business in order to earn more money 副业, 兼职: *Zoe does a bit of freelance photography as a sideline.* 佐伊搞一点自由摄影作为副业。**2 on the sidelines** not taking part in an activity even though you want to or should do 旁观, 不直接参与: *A severe knee injury put him on the sidelines for the rest of the season.* 膝部严重受伤使他不能参加本赛季其余的比赛了。| *You can't stay on the sidelines for ever; it's time you got involved.* 你总不能永远旁观呀, 这是你亲身体验的时候了。**3 sidelines** [plural] the area just outside the lines that form the edge of a sports field〔球场等的〕界外地区, 场外: *Beckenbauer stood on the sidelines shouting instructions to his team.* 贝肯鲍尔站在场边向他的队员们高喊指令。**4** [C] a line at

the side of a sports field, which shows where the players are allowed to play〔球场的〕边线—see picture at 参见 TENNIS 图

sideline² *v* **be sidelined** to be unable to play in a game because you are injured, or unable to take part in something because you are not as good as someone else〔因伤病或水平不够而〕不让〔运动员〕参加比赛; 使不能参加〔活动〕, 使靠边: *Baggio was once again sidelined through injury.* 巴乔又一次因伤无法参赛。

side·long /ˈsaɪd,lɔn; ˈsaɪdlɒŋ/ *adj* **1 a sidelong look/glance** a way of looking at someone by moving your eyes to the side, especially so that it seems secret, dishonest, or disapproving〔看人时眼睛〕斜向的, 横向的〔表示有秘密、不诚实或不以为然等〕: *He stole a sidelong glance at the woman sitting next to him.* 他斜着眼瞥了一下坐在身旁的女子。**2 a sidelong look at** an unusual and often humorous way of considering a subject 以不平常[幽默]的眼光看待: *The book takes a sidelong look at life in Hollywood.* 这本书以与众不同的眼光来看好莱坞的生活。—**sidelong** *adv*

side-on /ˌ· ˈ·◂/ *adj* coming from one side rather than from in front or behind 从侧面的, 从一侧的: *a side-on collision* 从侧面的碰撞 —**side-on** *adv*

side or·der /ˈ· ,··/ *n* [C] a small amount of food ordered in a restaurant to be eaten with a main meal but served on a separate dish〔餐馆中〕主菜之外另点的小菜: *a side order of onion rings* 另点的洋葱圈

si·der·e·al /saɪˈdɪrɪəl; saɪˈdɪəriəl/ *adj technical* related to or calculated using the stars【术语】恒星的, 以恒星为计算标准的: *the sidereal day* 恒星日

side·sad·dle /ˈ· ,··/ *adv* **ride/sit side-saddle** to ride or sit on a horse with both legs on the same side of the horse 偏坐在马鞍上, 侧坐在马鞍上〔双腿在同侧〕

side·show /ˈsaɪd,ʃo; ˈsaɪdʃəʊ/ *n* [C] **1** a separate small part of a FAIR³ (1) or CIRCUS (1), where you pay to play games or watch a performance〔游乐场或马戏中的〕杂耍, 主场以外的游乐节目 **2** an event that is much less important or serious than another one 次要的事件, 附带的活动: *The initial conflict was a mere sideshow compared with the World War that followed.* 起初的冲突同随后发生的世界大战相比, 只是一个次要的事件。

side·split·ting /ˈsaɪd,splɪtɪŋ; ˈsaɪd,splɪtɪŋ/ *adj* extremely funny 令人捧腹大笑的, 极其滑稽的: *He told some sidesplitting jokes.* 他讲了一些令人捧腹的笑话。

side·step /ˈsaɪd,stɛp; ˈsaɪdstep/ *v* **1 sidestep a problem/issue/question** to avoid doing something that will cause you difficulty or inconvenience, such as dealing with a difficult problem 回避问题: *The report simply sidesteps the environmental issues.* 报告干脆回避了环境问题。**2** [I,T] to step quickly sideways to avoid being hit or walking into someone 横跨一步以避免〔被打击或撞到人〕—**sidestep** *n* [C]

side·swipe¹ /ˈsaɪd,swaɪp; ˈsaɪdswaɪp/ *n* **take a sideswipe at** to criticize someone or something while you are talking about something different 旁敲侧击, 指桑骂槐, 附带批评: *At the end of the speech he couldn't resist taking a sideswipe at his former boss.* 讲话结束时, 他忍不住对他的前任老板指桑骂槐地说了几句。

sideswipe² *v* [T] *AmE* to hit the side of a car with another car so that the two sides touch quickly【美】〔驾车时〕擦边撞击〔另一车〕: *She was going too fast and sideswiped a parked car.* 她车开得太快, 刮擦到一辆停着的汽车。

side·track¹ /ˈsaɪd,træk; ˈsaɪdtræk/ *v* [T usually passive 一般用被动态] to make someone stop doing what they should be doing, or stop talking about what they started talking about, by making them interested in something else 岔开…的思路, 使离题, 使转移目标: **get sidetracked** *Don't get too sidetracked by the audience's questions.* 不要因听众的提问而离题太远了。

sidetrack² *n* [C] *AmE* a short railway track connected to a main track【美】〔铁路的〕侧线

side·walk /ˈsaɪd,wɔk; ˈsaɪdwɔːk/ *n* [C] *AmE* a hard surface or path at the side of a street for people to walk on【美】人行道; PAVEMENT *BrE*【英】—see graph at 参见 PAVEMENT 图表 —see picture on page A4 参见 A4 页图

sidewalk art·ist /ˈ·· ,··/ *n* [C] *AmE* someone who draws pictures on a sidewalk, hoping that people will give them money【美】街头画家〔在人行道上画画, 以此向行人讨钱的人〕; PAVEMENT ARTIST *BrE*【英】

side·ways /ˈsaɪd,wez; ˈsaɪdweɪz/ *adv* **1** to or towards one side 向一边地, 横着地: *A strong gust of wind blew the car sideways into the ditch.* 一阵狂风把汽车横着刮进了沟里。**2** with the side, rather than the front or back, facing forwards 侧面朝前地: *They brought the piano sideways through the front door.* 他们把钢琴侧面朝前地抬着通过前门。—**sideways** *adj*: *a furtive sideways glance* 偷偷侧目一瞥

side-wheel·er /ˈsaɪd ,hwilə; ˈsaɪd ˌwiːlə/ *n* [C] *AmE* an old-fashioned type of ship which is pushed forward by a pair of large wheels at the sides【美】明轮船〔两舷有轮子推动船前进的旧式船船〕; PADDLE STEAMER *BrE*【英】

sid·ing /ˈsaɪdɪŋ; ˈsaɪdɪŋ/ *n* [C] a short railway track connected to a main track, where trains are kept when they are not being used〔铁路的〕侧线, 旁轨

si·dle /ˈsaɪdl; ˈsaɪdl/ *v* [I always+adv/prep] to walk towards something or someone slowly and quietly, as if you do not want to be noticed 悄悄地慢慢走近, 鬼鬼祟祟地走向某人[某物]: **[+up/towards/along]** *A woman in dark glasses sidled up to us and asked if we wanted to buy a watch.* 一个戴墨镜的女人鬼鬼祟祟地走近我们, 问我们要不要买手表。

siege /sidʒ; siːdʒ/ *n* [C,U] **1** a military operation during which an army surrounds a place and tries to gain control of it by stopping supplies of food, weapons etc from reaching it〔军队的〕包围, 围困, 围攻: *The siege lasted almost four months.* 这次围困历时近四个月。| **lay siege to** (=start a siege) 实施包围 *In June 1176 King Richard laid siege to Limoges.* 理查一世国王于 1176 年 6 月对利摩日实施包围。| **raise a siege** (=end it) 解除包围, 解围 **2** a situation in which the police surround a building to try and force the people inside to come out〔警察对建筑物的〕包围: **lay siege to** *When the scandal broke, dozens of journalists laid seige to Mellor's apartment.* 爆出丑闻后, 数十名记者包围了梅勒的公寓。**3 be under siege a)** to be surrounded by an army in a seige 被军队包围 **b)** to be continually criticized, or attacked by questions, problems, threats etc 不断受到批评[质问, 威胁等], 受到围攻: *The TV station has been under siege from irate viewers phoning in to complain.* 电视台受到愤怒观众的围攻, 他们不断打电话来投诉。**4 siege mentality** the feeling among a group of people that they are surrounded by enemies and must do everything they can to protect themselves 受围心态, 被围困时必须奋力自卫的心态

Sie·gel /ˈsigl; ˈsiːgəl/, **Bug·sy** /ˈbʌgzɪ; ˈbʌgzi/ (1906-47) a New York GANGSTER (=member of a violent group of criminals), who built the first large hotel and CASINO in Las Vegas in 1947, and made Las Vegas the most popular place for GAMBLING (=playing games to win money) in the US 西格尔〔(1906-1947), 纽约一黑帮成员。1947 年建成拉斯韦加斯第一座大饭店和赌场, 使拉斯韦加斯成为美国赫赫有名的赌城〕

Sieg·fried Line, the /ˈsigfrid ,laɪn; ˈsiːgfriːd ˌlaɪn/ a line of military defences that the German armies built on the Western Front during World War I and before and during World War II 齐格菲防线〔一道军事防线。一战期间、二战战前和战时, 德国军队在西部战线修筑而成〕

si·en·na /sɪˈɛnə; siˈenə/ *n* [U] a type of earth that is dark yellow, used to make paint〔用作颜料的〕浓黄土, 赭石

si·er·ra /sɪˈɛrə; siˈerə/ *n* [C] a row or area of sharply pointed mountains 锯齿山脊, 峰峦起伏的山脉

Si·er·ra Club, the /ˌ·ˈ·· ,·/ a US organization that tries to protect the environment, especially natural areas such as forests, mountains, and rivers. The Sierra Club is also a social club for people who like to HIKE. 峰峦俱乐部〔美国一环境保护组织, 尤侧重保护森林、山川和河流等自然资源。该俱乐部也是徒步旅行爱好者的一个社交俱乐部〕

Sierra Le·one /sɪ,ɛrə lɪˈonɪ; si,erə liˈəʊn/ a country in West Africa between Liberia and Guinea. Population: 5,500,000 (2001). Capital: Freetown. 塞拉利昂〔西非一国家。位于利比里亚与几内亚之间。人口: 5,500,000 (2001), 首都: 弗里敦〕—**Sierra Leonean** *n, adj*

Sierra Ma·dre, the /sɪ,ɛrə ˈmɑdre; si,erə ˈmɑːdreɪ/ a group of mountain ranges in Mexico 马德雷山脉〔墨西哥境内一山脉〕

Sierra Ne·va·da, the /ˌ·,·· ˈ··/ **1** also 又作 **the Sierras** a mountain range in California 内华达山脉〔加利福尼亚州一山脉〕**2** a mountain range in southern Spain 内华达山脉〔西班牙南部一山脉〕

si·es·ta /sɪˈɛstə; siˈestə/ *n* [C] a short sleep in the afternoon, especially in warm countries〔尤指炎热国家的〕午后小睡, 午睡: **take/have a siesta** *The stores all close after lunch when everyone takes a siesta.* 午饭后所有商店都关门, 这段时间人人都在睡午觉。

sieve¹ /sɪv; sɪv/ *n* [C] **1 a)** a round wire kitchen tool with a lot of small holes, used for separating solid food from liquid or small pieces of food from large pieces〔厨具中的〕漏勺 **b)** a round wire tool for separating small objects from large objects 筛子, 细筛 **2 have a memory like a sieve** *informal* to forget things easily【非正式】记性很差

S

sieve² *v* [T] to put flour or other food through a sieve 筛; 滤

sieve sth ↔ **out** *phr v* [T] to separate solid objects from liquid or smaller objects from larger ones by using a sieve 筛出; 滤出: *sieve out the seeds from the raspberry jam* 把籽从山莓果酱中滤出来 —see picture on page A11 参见 A11 页图

sift /sɪft; sɪft/ *v* [T] **1** to put flour, sugar etc through a sieve or similar container in order to remove large pieces 筛〔面粉、白糖等〕 **2** also 又作 **sift through** to examine information, documents etc carefully in order to find something out or decide what is important and what is not 细查, 详查, 严密检查〔信息、文件等〕: *Police are sifting through the evidence in the hope of finding more clues.* 警方正在对证据作详细审查, 希望能找出更多的线索。

sift sth ↔ **out** *phr v* [T] to separate something from other things 挑选出, 筛选: [+from] *It's hard to sift out the truth from the lies in this case.* 在这个案件中, 不容易把事实和谎言区分出来。

sift·er /ˈsɪftɚ; ˈsɪftə/ *n* [C] a container with a lot of small holes in the top used for shaking flour, sugar etc onto things〔盖上有小孔、用于筛撒面粉、白糖等的〕撒粉瓶

sigh¹ /saɪ; saɪ/ *v* [I] **1** to breathe in and out making a long sound, especially because you are bored, disappointed, tired etc〔尤指因厌烦、失望、疲倦等〕叹气, 叹息: *"Well, there's nothing we can do about it now," she sighed.* "唉, 我们现在已经无能为力了。" 她叹口气说。| **sigh heavily/deeply** *Frankie stared out of the window and sighed deeply.* 弗朗姬凝望着窗外, 深深地叹了口气。| [+with] *He sighed with despair at the thought of all the opportunities he had missed.* 他想到自己失去的许多机会, 绝望地叹了口气。 **2** if the wind sighs, it makes a long sound like someone sighing〔风〕呼啸, 呜咽: *The wind sighed in the trees.* 风在树丛中呼啸。 **3** **sigh for sth** to be sad because you are thinking about a pleasant time in the past 思念, 惋惜: *Emilia sighed for her lost youth.* 埃米莉亚惋惜逝去的青春。

S

sigh² *n* [C] an act or sound of sighing 叹气[叹息]: [+of] *She settled down in her chair with a long sigh of relief.* 她坐在扶手椅上, 长长地舒了一口气。| **breathe/give/heave/let out a sigh of relief** *We all heaved a sigh of relief when we heard they were safe.* 我们听到他们平安无事时, 大家都松了一口气。

S2 W2 **sight¹** /saɪt; saɪt/ *n*

1 ▶**ABILITY TO SEE** 视力◀ [U] the physical ability to see 视力, 视觉: *Anne's sight is very good for someone of her age.* 在安妮这种年龄, 她的视力算是很好的了。| *He has no sight in his right eye, but his left eye is fine.* 他的右眼已经没有视力了, 但左眼还很好。| **lose your sight** (=become blind) 失明 *She had lost her sight in a riding accident.* 她在一次骑马事故中失明了。

2 ▶**ACT OF SEEING** 看见◀ [singular,U] the act of seeing something 看, 看到, 看见: *The crowd was waiting for a sight of the Queen.* 人群在等着一睹女王的风采。| **at the sight of** *I always faint at the sight of blood.* 我一看见血就犯晕。| **catch sight of** (=suddenly see or notice something) 突然看到[瞥见、注意到] *Sheila caught sight of her own face in one of the shop windows.* 希拉在一扇橱窗里瞥见了自己的脸。| **be hidden from sight** *The house is hidden from sight behind trees.* 这座房子隐藏在树丛后面, 人们看不见。| **on sight** (=as soon as you see someone) 一看见就… *soldiers trained to shoot on sight* 受过训练一看到目标就能立即开枪的士兵 | *Jo disliked him on sight.* 乔一见到他就讨厌。| **at first sight** (=the first time you see someone) 初见; 乍看 *We fell in love with the cottage at first sight.* 我们一见到那个小屋就爱上它了。

3 ▶**THING YOU SEE** 所见之物◀ [C] **a)** something you can see, especially something unusual, beautiful etc 景物, 景象: *Tourists are a familiar sight in this part of the city.* 在城里这一带地方, 游客是人们熟悉的景象了。| *the rare sight of a fox* 难得一见的狐狸 | *all the sounds and sights of the forest* 森林中的种种声音和景象 | **a sorry sight** *often humorous* (=something you see that makes you feel sad or sympathetic)【常幽默】一副可怜相 *Fiona was a sorry sight in her wet clothes.* 菲奥娜浑身湿透, 一副可怜兮兮的样子。 **b)** **the sights** [plural] famous or interesting places that tourists visit 名胜, 风景, 奇观: *In the afternoon, you'll have a chance to relax or to go and see the sights.* 大家下午可以休息, 也可以去参观风景名胜。—see also 另见 SIGHTSEEING

4 **in/within sight** **a)** inside the area that you can see 在视野内, 看得见: *When we got to the beach, there wasn't a soul in sight.* 我们到达海滩时一个人也见不到。| *If you don't lock up the food, they'll eat everything in sight.* 如果你不把食物锁起来, 他们看见就会吃光的。 **b)** likely to happen soon 可能即将发生: *Six months from the start of the strike, there is still no end in sight.* 罢工开始至今六个月了, 眼下还看不出结束的迹象。| *Peace is now in sight.* 和平在望了。

5 **out of sight** **a)** outside the area that you can see 在视野外, 看不见: *Karen waved until the car was out of sight.* 卡伦不断挥手, 直到汽车看不见为止。 **b)** *old-fashioned slang* extremely good【过时, 俚】极好的: *The skiing there is out of sight!* 那里滑雪棒极了!

6 **be within sight of** **a)** to be in the area where you can see something 在…视野内, 看得见…: *We camped within sight of the lake.* 我们在看得见湖的地方露营。 **b)** to be in a position where you will soon be able to get something or achieve something 眼看就能得到[成功]: *Dan was now within sight of the championship.* 丹现在眼看就要拿到锦标赛冠军了。

7 **lose sight of** **a)** to forget to think about or deal with something important 忘记考虑[处理]某要事: *It's easy to lose sight of the real issue.* 真正的问题倒是容易忘掉的。| *Never lose sight of the fact that you have a lot of talent.* 永远不要忘记你是很有才华的。 **b)** to stop being able to see something or someone 不再看得见…: *I lost sight of him in the crowd.* 在人群中, 我再也看不到他了。

8 **come into sight/disappear from sight etc** to appear or disappear 出现/消失: *Soon the train came into sight.* 很快, 火车便出现了。

9 **not let sb out of your sight** to make sure that someone stays near you 让某人留在自己眼皮下: *Since the accident, Donna hasn't let the children out of her sight.* 那次事故之后, 唐娜从未让孩子离开过自己半步。

10 **be sick of/hate/can't stand the sight of** to dislike someone or something very much 非常不喜欢…: *Alan and Sam can't stand the sight of each other.* 艾伦和萨姆都非常讨厌对方。

11 **a sight for sore eyes** *spoken*【口】**a)** someone or something that you feel very happy to see 使人看着高兴的人; 赏心悦目的东西 **b)** *BrE* someone or something that is very unattractive or very funny to look at【英】难看[样子滑稽]的人[物]

12 **set your sights on** to decide that you want something and will make a determined effort to achieve it 决心要做到: *I was still young then, and my sights were set on an acting career.* 我当时还年轻, 决心要从事演艺事业。

13 **come in sight of** to arrive at a position from which you can see a particular place, building etc 来到看得见…的地方: *At last they came in sight of the city.* 他们终于看见那座城市了。

14 **at first sight** when you first start considering something 乍看起来, 开始考虑时: *The results of the tests were, at first sight, surprising.* 乍看起来, 测试的结果是惊人的。

15 **a sight more/a sight better etc** *spoken* a lot more etc【口】多得多/好得多等: *You'd earn a damn sight more if you got a proper qualification.* 如果你有张合适的资格证书, 你挣的钱就会多得多。

16 **be a sight/look a sight** to look very funny or stupid, or very untidy or unpleasant 样子滑稽[愚蠢、脏乱、难看]: *We'd had an all-night party, and the place looked a bit of a sight.* 我们开了个通宵晚会, 那地方看起来有点不像样子了。

17 ▶**GUN** 枪◀ [C often plural 常用复数] the part of a gun or other weapon that guides your eye when you are aiming at something〔步枪等武器的〕瞄准器, 准星 —see picture at 参见 GUN¹ 图

18 **out of sight, out of mind** used to say that you will soon forget someone if you do not see them for a while 眼不见, 心不想: *I pestered him continuously: I wasn't going to allow myself to become a case of out of sight, out of mind.* 我不断去缠着他, 我可不想让自己成为"眼不见, 心不想"的实例。—see also 另见 **know sb by sight** (KNOW¹ (16))

sight² *v* [T] to see something from a long distance away, or see something you have been looking for〔从很远处或经过一番寻找后〕看见, 发现: *The sailors gave a shout of joy when they sighted land.* 水手们看到陆地时高声地欢呼了起来。| *Several rare birds have been sighted in the area.* 这个地区已经发现了好几种珍稀的鸟类。

sight·ed /ˈsaɪtɪd; ˈsaɪtɨd/ *adj* someone who is sighted can see, and is not blind〔人〕看得见的, 有视力的, 不盲的: **partially sighted** (=having limited ability to see) 视力受限制的 —see also 另见 CLEAR-SIGHTED, FAR-SIGHTED, LONG-SIGHTED, SHORT-SIGHTED

sight·ing /ˈsaɪtɪŋ; ˈsaɪtɪŋ/ *n* [C] an occasion on which something is seen, especially something rare or something that people are hoping to see 看见, 发现〔尤指见到少见的或希望见到的事物〕: *Several people in the area have reported sightings of UFOs.* 这个地区有好几个人都曾报告发现过不明飞行物。

sight·less /ˈsaɪtlɪs; ˈsaɪtləs/ *adj literary* blind【文】看不见的, 失明的, 盲的

sight-read /ˈsaɪt ˌrid; ˈsaɪt riːd/ *v past tense and past participle* **sight-read** /-ˌrɛd; -red/ [I,T] to play or sing written music

when you look at it for the first time, without practising it first 〔不经准备〕随看〔乐谱〕随奏, 看谱即唱 —**sight-reader** *n* [C]— **sight-reading** *n* [U]

sight-see-ing /ˈsaɪtˌsiɪŋ; ˈsaɪtˌsiːɪŋ/ *n* [U] the act of visiting famous or interesting places, especially as tourists 〔尤指旅客的〕观光, 游览: **go sightseeing** *We bought souvenirs and then went sightseeing.* 我们买了纪念品, 然后就去参观游览。

sight-se-er /ˈsaɪtˌsiɚ; ˈsaɪtˌsiːə/ *n* [C] someone, especially a tourist, who is visiting a famous or interesting place 观光者, 游览者

signs 标记

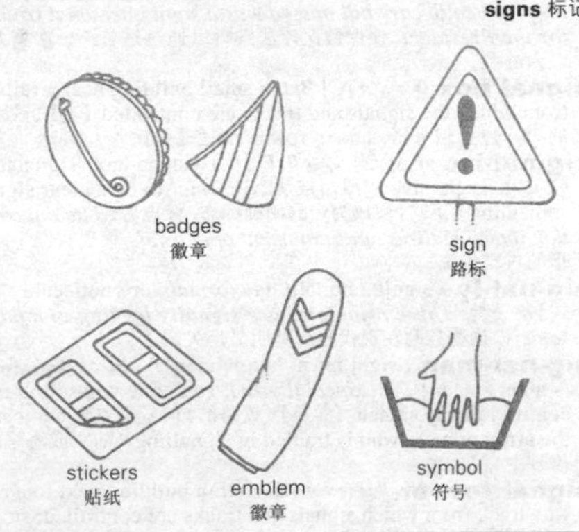

sign¹ /saɪn; saɪn/ *n*

1 ►STH THAT PROVES STH 证明◄ [C] an event, fact etc that shows that something is happening or that something is true; INDICATION 迹象, 痕迹, 征兆: **sign of** *The tests can detect early signs of disease.* 这些检查可以发现疾病的早期征兆。| **sign that** *Exports have risen by 20%, a sign that the economy is improving.* 出口增长了 20%, 这是经济增长的迹象。| **a sure sign** (=clear proof) 明显的证据 *You know Eric, if he won't eat, it's a sure sign that he's in love again!* 你是了解埃里克的, 如果他不想吃饭, 那就表明他一定又在谈恋爱了! | **telltale sign** (=a sign that is easy to recognize, usually of something bad) 〔常为坏事的〕明显迹象 *telltale signs of drug abuse* 滥用毒品的明显迹象 | **show signs of** *For the first time she was beginning to show signs of her age.* 她头一次开始显露青春不再的痕迹。| **every sign of** (=clear signs of) …的明显迹象 *They showed every sign of being willing to cooperate.* 他们表现出种种愿意合作的迹象。—see graph at 参见 INDICATE 图表

2 there's no sign of a) if there is no sign of something, you cannot see anything which shows that it exists or has happened 没有…的迹象: *The police looked all around the house, but there was no sign of a struggle.* 警察搜查了整幢房子, 但没有发现打斗过的迹象。**b)** if there is no sign of someone, you cannot see them anywhere, or they have not arrived when you expected them to 不见〔某人的〕踪影, 踪影全无: *Jerry kept looking out of the window, but there was still no sign of her.* 杰里不断往窗外看, 但还是不见她的踪影。

3 ►MOVEMENT OR SOUND 动作或声音◄ [C] a movement, sound etc that you make in order to tell someone to do something or give them information; GESTURE¹ (1) 手势, 姿势, 信号: **give/make a sign** *Nobody move until I give the sign.* 在我发出信号之前, 谁也不许动。| **[+that]** *Bruce made a sign that he was ready to leave.* 布鲁斯作了一个姿势, 表示他准备走了。| **sign for sb to do sth** *Three short blasts on the whistle was the sign for us to begin.* 三下短哨声就是我们开始的信号。

4 ►GIVES INFORMATION 传达信息◄ [C] a piece of paper, metal etc in a public place, with words or drawings on it that give people information, warn them not to do something etc 标记, 指示牌, 标牌: *road signs* 路标 | *a no smoking sign* 不准抽烟的告示牌

5 ►PICTURE/SYMBOL 图画/符号◄ [C] a picture, shape etc that has a particular meaning; SYMBOL 图形, 符号, 记号: *For some reason the computer can't display the dollar sign.* 由于某种原因, 这台电脑不能显示元的符号。

6 ►STAR SIGN 星座◄ [C] also 又作 **star sign** a group of stars, representing one of 12 parts of the year, that some people believe influences your behaviour and your life 宫〔黄道十二宫之一〕, 星座: *I'm a Scorpio – what sign are you?* 我是天蝎座的, 你是什么星座?

7 ►LANGUAGE 语言◄ [U] a language that uses hand movements instead of spoken words, used by people who cannot hear; SIGN LANGUAGE 〔聋哑人的〕手语

8 sign of life a movement that shows that someone is alive, or something that shows that there are people in a particular place 〔人〕活着的迹象; 有人的迹象; 生命迹象: *We entered the building with caution but strangely there was no sign of life.* 我们小心翼翼地进入那栋楼房, 但是很奇怪, 里面见不到有人待过的迹象。

9 sign of the times something that shows how bad society has become 〔坏的〕时尚, 潮流, 时代特征: *So many houses have burglar alarms nowadays. It's a sign of the times I suppose.* 如今那么多家庭都安装了防盗报警器, 我想这就是世风日下的特征吧。

10 the sign of the Cross the hand movement that some Christians make in the shape of a cross, to show respect for God or to protect themselves from evil 〔基督徒在祝福等时在胸前〕画十字的手势

sign² *v* **1** [I,T] to write your SIGNATURE on a letter or document to show that you wrote it, agree with it 签(名), 署(名); 〔在文件等上〕签字: *Sign here please.* 请在这里签字。| **sign sth** *You forgot to sign the check!* 你忘了在支票上签字! | *Over a hundred people have signed the petition.* 已有一百多人在请愿书上签了名。| *a signed photo of Paul McCartney* 一张保罗·麦卡特尼的签名照片 | **sign your name** *The artist had signed his name in the corner of the painting.* 画家在画的角上署了名。**2 sign an agreement/treaty etc** to show formally that you agree to do something, by signing a legal document 签署协议书/条约等: *Both presidents signed the treaty as part of the new peace plan.* 两位总统签署了那个条约作为新和平计划的一部分。| **sign sth with sb** *France has just signed a new trade deal with Japan.* 法国和日本刚刚签订了一项贸易协定。**3** [T] if an organization such as a football team or music company signs someone, that person signs a contract agreeing to work for it 签约聘请, 签约雇用: *CBS Records had signed her back in 1988 on a three-album contract.* 哥伦比亚唱片公司早在 1988 年就和她签订了发行三张专辑的合同。**4** [I] to try to tell someone something or ask them to do something by using signs and movements 做手势〔示意〕: **sign to sb to do sth** *He was desperately signing to me to not mention anything about Jack.* 他拼命地向我打手势, 叫我不要提起杰克的任何事。| **sign for sb to do sth** *She signed for us to go inside.* 她打手势让我们进去。**5 all signed and sealed** with all the necessary legal documents agreed and signed 手续完备: *It'll all be signed and sealed by Friday, you can move in then.* 星期五之前所有手续都会办完, 你也就可以搬进来了。**6** [I,T] to use SIGN LANGUAGE 用手语表达, 把…译成手语: *The whole performance was signed* (=translated into sign language) *by a local interpreter.* 整场演出都由一位当地译员译成手语。—**signer** *n* [C]

sign 签字

sign sth ↔ **away** *phr v* [T] to sign a document that gives your property or legal right to someone else 签字放弃[让与]〔财产或法定权利〕: *She had signed away all claims to the house.* 她已签字放弃对该房子的一切权利。

sign for sth *phr v* [T] **1** to sign a document to prove that you have received something 签收: *This is a registered letter, someone will have to sign for it.* 这是一封挂号信, 必须有人签收才行。**2 sign for Liverpool/Arsenal etc** *BrE* to sign a contract agreeing to play for a particular football team 【英】签约于利物浦足球队/阿森纳足球队

sign in *phr v* **1** [I] to write your name on a form, in a book etc when you enter a place such as a hotel, office or club 签到: *Remember to sign in at reception.* 记住要在接待处签到。**2** [T **sign** sb ↔ **in**] to write someone else's name in a book so that they are allowed to enter a club that you are a member of 〔会员〕为〔某人〕登记使其得以进入俱乐部[会所等]

sign off *phr v* [I] **1** *informal* to end a radio or television programme by saying goodbye 【非正式】〔以告别〕结束广播[电视节目] **2** to finish an informal letter by writing your name at

the end of it〔写非正式信件时以签名〕结束写信: *It's getting late so I'll sign off now. Love, John.* 时间不早了, 我就此搁笔。爱你的约翰。

sign on *phr v* **1** [I,T] to sign a document agreeing to work for someone, especially as a soldier, sailor etc, or to persuade someone to do this (使) 签约受雇〔尤指当兵、当水手等〕, 受聘: *He signed on as a soldier in the US army.* 他报名参加美国军队当士兵。| **sign sb ↔ on** *I went to the local recruiting office and was signed on for three years.* 我到当地新兵征募办事处去, 签约当兵三年。**2** [I] *BrE* to state officially that you are unemployed by signing a form, so that you can get money from the government【英】登记失业〔以便领取政府的救济款〕

sign out *phr v* **1** [I] to write your name in a book when you leave a place such as a hotel, office or club〔在离开旅馆、办公室、俱乐部等时〕签名登记离开 **2** [T **sign** sth ↔ **out**] to write your name on a form or in a book to show that you have taken or borrowed something 登记拿走[借走]: *Bernstein signed out a company car and drove to the meeting.* 伯恩斯坦登记借用公司的一辆汽车去参加会议。

sign sth ↔ **over** *phr v* [T] to sign an official document that gives your property or rights to someone else 签字将〔财产、权利等〕转让[给与]〔某人〕: **[+to]** *When he became ill, he signed his property in France over to his son.* 他生病后便签字把在法国的财产给了他儿子。

sign up *phr v* **1** [T usually passive 一般用被动态] if someone is signed up by an organization, they sign a contract agreeing to work for that organization 使签约受雇, 签约雇用: *Several well-established researchers have been signed up for the project.* 好几名很有声望的研究人员都已签约参加这个项目了。**2** [I] to arrange to take part in a course of study 经报名参加〔课程学习〕: **[+for]** *I'm thinking of signing up for the philosophy course this term.* 我在考虑报名参加这个学期的哲学课。| **sign up to do sth** *Over half the people who signed up to do engineering were women.* 报名读工程学的人过半都是女性。

sign with sth *phr v* [T] **1** *AmE* to sign a contract agreeing to play for a particular sports team【美】签约受雇参加〔某球队〕**2** to sign a contract agreeing that a particular company has the right to record and sell your music 与〔唱片公司〕签约

sig·nal¹ /ˈsɪgnl; ˈsɪgnəl/ *n* [C] **1** a sound or action that you make in order to give information to someone or tell them to do something 信号, 暗号: **signal (for sb) to do sth** *A bell began to ring, the 8 o'clock signal to start work.* 铃声响起, 这是8点钟开工的信号。| *When he closes his book, it's a signal for everyone to stand up.* 当他把书合上时, 这就表示该全体起立了。| **give a signal** *Don't start yet – wait for me to give the signal.* 先别开始——等我发信号。| **at a signal (from sb)** *At a signal from their leader the worshippers knelt to pray.* 礼拜者依照领头人的示意下跪祷告。| **danger signal/warning signal etc** *A red flag is often used as a danger signal.* 红色的旗子常被用作危险的信号。—see also 另见 SMOKE SIGNAL **2** an event or action that shows what someone feels or what is likely to happen 暗示, 预示: **signal that** *Gorbachev's speech was a signal that major changes were on the way.* 戈尔巴乔夫的演说暗示即将发生重大的变化。| **a clear signal** *The opinion poll is a clear signal that voters do not support the President's foreign policy.* 民意测验清楚地表明选民不支持总统的对外政策。| **danger signal/warning signal** *Rapid breathing is a danger signal and you should call your doctor.* 呼吸急促是个危险的征兆, 该去请医生了。| **send/give a signal** *This will send the wrong signal to potential investors.* 这会给潜在的投资者发出错误的信号。**3** a series of light waves, sound waves etc that carry an image, sound, or message, such as is used in radio or television〔无线电或电视的〕信号, 讯息, 图像: **send out/transmit a signal (to)** *The signal was sent out to our troops immediately.* 信号被马上发送到我们的部队。| **receive/pick up a signal** *Astronomers have been picking up faint signals that may be from a distant planet.* 天文学家一直在接收可能来自遥远行星的微弱信号。**4** a piece of equipment with coloured lights, used on a railway to tell train drivers whether they can continue or must stop 铁路信号: **signal failure** (=when these lights do not work) 信号灯故障 *The report confirmed that signal failure had been the cause of the accident.* 报告确定信号灯失灵是这次事故的原因。

signal² *v* **signalled, signalling** *BrE*【英】, **signaled, signaling** *AmE*【美】**1** [I,T] to give a signal in order to give information or tell someone to do something 发信号, 打信号: **[+at]** *Mary was signalling wildly at us, but we didn't even notice.* 玛丽拼命向我们打信号, 但我们根本没有注意。| **[+to]** *The judge signaled to a police officer and the man was led away.* 法官向一位警察示意, 随即那个人被带走了。| **[+for]** *He pushed his plate away and signaled for coffee.* 他把盘子推开, 并示意要杯咖啡。| **signal (to) sb to do sth** *She was signalling to the children to stay outside.* 她在向孩子们打手势, 要他们留在外面。—see picture on page A3 参见 A3 页图 **2** [T] to make something clear by what you say or do〔用语言或行动〕表明, 表示: *Both sides have signaled their willingness to start negotiations.* 双方都表明了他们谈判的意愿。**3** [T] to be a sign or proof of something 标志, 证明: *the lengthening days that signal the end of winter* 白天变长标志着冬天的结束

signal³ *adj* [only before noun 仅用于名词前] *formal* important【正式】重要的: **signal achievement/success/failure etc** *Getting the health care bill passed was a signal personal triumph for the President.* 使保健医疗法案得以通过是总统一次重大的个人胜利。

signal box /ˈ‥ ·/ *n* [C] *BrE* a small building near a railway from which the signals and tracks are controlled【英】〔铁路旁的〕信号房, 信号塔; SIGNAL TOWER *AmE*【美】

sig·nal·ize also 又作 **-ise** *BrE*【英】/ˈsɪgnəˌlaɪz; ˈsɪgnəlaɪz/ *v* [T usually passive 一般用被动态] *formal* to be a clear sign of something【正式】使成为…的明确标志, 标志着: *a quaint tradition that signalizes our attainment of learning* 代表我们学问造诣的古雅传统

sig·nal·ly /ˈsɪgnḷɪ; ˈsɪgnəli/ *adv formal* very noticeably【正式】显著地: *These principles are signally lacking in modern society.* 这些准则在现代社会是明显地欠缺了。

sig·nal·man /ˈsɪgnḷˌmæn; ˈsɪgnəlmən/ *n plural* **signalmen** /-ˌmən; -mən/ [C] **1** *especially BrE* someone whose job is to control railway signals【尤英】〔铁路的〕信号员 **2** a member of the army or navy who is trained in signalling〔陆军或海军的〕信号手, 信号兵

signal tow·er /ˈ‥ ˌ‥/ *n* [C] *AmE* a building next to a railway track from which signals and tracks are controlled; SIGNAL BOX【美】信号塔, 信号房

sig·na·to·ry /ˈsɪgnəˌtorɪ; ˈsɪgnətəri/ *n* [C] one of the people or countries that sign an official agreement, especially an international one〔尤指国际条约的〕签署者; 签约国: **[+to/of]** *Most Western countries are signatories of this treaty.* 大多数西方国家都是这个条约的签约国。

sig·na·ture /ˈsɪgnətʃə; ˈsɪgnətʃə/ *n* [C] your name written in the way you usually write it, for example at the end of a letter or contract or on a cheque〔书信、合同、支票等结尾处的〕签字, 签名: *I couldn't read his signature.* 我认不出他的签字。| *a petition with four thousand signatures* 一份有四千人签名的请愿书 | **put your signature to/on** (=sign something to show that you agree with it) 在…上签字〔表示同意〕—see picture at 参见 SIGN² 图

signature tune /ˈ‥‥ ˌ·/ *n* [C] a short piece of music used at the beginning and end of a television or radio programme〔一项电视或广播节目开始和结束时的〕信号曲, 主题曲

sig·net /ˈsɪgnɪt; ˈsɪgnḷt/ *n* [C] a metal object used for printing a small pattern in WAX¹ (1) as an official SEAL 图章, 私章

signet ring /ˈ‥ ·/ *n* [C] a ring that has a signet on it 图章戒指

sig·nif·i·cance /sɪgˈnɪfəkəns; sɪgˈnɪfɪkəns/ *n* [singular,U] **1** the meaning of a word, sign, action etc, especially when this is not immediately clear〔尤指尚未清楚的〕意义, 含义: **[+of]** *Could you explain the significance of this part of the contract?* 请你解释一下合同中这一部分的意思好吗? | **the full/real/true significance** *It was only later that we realized the true significance of his remark.* 后来我们才领会到他那些话的真正意义。**2** the importance of an event, action etc, especially because of the effects or influence it will have in the future〔事件、行动等的〕重要性, 重大意义: **[+of]** *It is impossible to overestimate the significance of this major discovery.* 对这次重大发现的意义怎样高估都不过分。| **[+for]** *a judgment that has long-term significance for the rights of disabled people* 对残疾人权益有长远重大意义的判决 | **be of great/major/little significance** *So far, research has not produced anything of very great significance.* 迄今为止, 研究尚未产生任何具有重大意义的结果。

sig·nif·i·cant /sɪgˈnɪfəkənt; sɪgˈnɪfɪkənt/ *adj* **1** having an important effect or influence, especially on what will happen in the future 重要的, 重大的, 影响深远的: *His most significant political achievement was the abolition of the death penalty.* 他最重大的政治成就是废除了死刑。| *Please inform us if there are any significant changes in your plans.* 如果你们的计划有什么重大改变, 请通知我们。| **highly significant** (=very significant) 非常重要的 *a highly significant discovery that might eventually lead to a vaccine* 一项可能最终导致一种新疫苗研制成功的重大发现 | **[+for]** *The result is highly significant for the future of the province.* 这一结果对该省的未来极为重要。| **it is**

significant that *Police believed it was significant that he had recently opened a bank account abroad.* 警方认为，他最近在国外银行开账户的事很重要。**2** large enough to be noticeable or have noticeable effects 相当数量的，影响明显的: *A significant number of drivers fail to keep to speed limits.* 有相当多的司机不遵守车速限制。| *A background in computing will give you a significant advantage.* 计算机专业的背景将是你的一大优越条件。**3** a significant look, smile etc has a special meaning that is not known to everyone〔眼神、微笑等〕表示某种意义的，有特殊含义的: *They exchanged significant glances.* 他们彼此交换了意味深长的目光。

S3 W2 **sig·nif·i·cant·ly** /sɪgˋnɪfəkəntlɪ; sɪgˈnɪfɪkəntli/ *adv* **1** in an important way or to an important degree 重大地，可观地: *Health problems can be significantly reduced by careful diet.* 通过注意饮食可以大大减少健康方面的问题。| **[+from]** *Methods used by younger teachers differ significantly from those used by older ones.* 年轻教师所用的方法与老教师的方法有重大差别。| **significantly better/greater/worse etc** *Delia's work has been significantly better since her training course.* 自从参加培训班之后，迪莉娅的工作做得好多了。| [sentence adverb 句子副词] *Significantly, no newspaper has dared to print this shocking story.* 值得注意的是，没有一份报纸敢发表这个骇人听闻的消息。**2** in a way that seems to have a special meaning 意味深长地，含义深远地: *Tom nodded significantly at the suggestion, but did not comment.* 听了这个建议以后，汤姆意味深长地点了点头，但是没有发表意见。

sig·nif·i·ca·tion / sɪgˌnɪfəˋkeʃən; ˌsɪgnɪfɪˈkeɪʃən/ *n* [C] *formal* the intended meaning of a word【正式】〔词的〕含义，意义

sig·ni·fy /ˋsɪgnəˌfaɪ; ˈsɪgnɪfaɪ/ *v* [not in progressive 不用进行时] **1** [T] to represent, mean, or be a sign of something 代表，表示，象征，意味着: *Some tribes use special facial markings to signify status.* 有些部落的人用特殊的面部符号代表他们的地位。| **signify that** *Recent changes in climate may signify that global warming is starting to have an effect.* 最近的气候变化可能表示全球变暖正在开始产生影响。**2** [T] *formal* to make a wish, feeling, or opinion known by doing something【正式】〔用动作〕表示〔愿望、感觉或意见〕: **signify that** *With a gesture Mr Bosch signified that the three representatives could depart.* 博施先生做了个手势，表示三位代表可以走了。| **signify sth (to sb)** *He turned away from her slightly to signify his indifference.* 他稍稍背过脸以表示对她的冷淡。**3** [I] to be important enough to have an effect on something 要紧，有关系，有重要性: *These figures don't really signify in the overall results.* 这些数字对于总体结果没有实际重要意义。

sign·ing /ˋsaɪnɪŋ; ˈsaɪnɪŋ/ *n* **1** [U] the act of signing something such as an agreement or contract〔协议或合约的〕签字，签署: *The club was excited about the signing of these two Argentinian football stars.* 俱乐部全体成员对这两位阿根廷足球明星的签约感到兴奋。**2** [C] *BrE* someone who has just signed a contract to join a sports team【英】已签约参加球队的运动员: *United's latest signing will make his debut for the club on Saturday.* 联队的最新签约球员将于星期六代表俱乐部首次出场。

sign lan·guage /ˋ· ,··/ *n* [C,U] a language that uses hand movements instead of spoken words, used by people who cannot hear〔聋人的〕手语，手势语

sign·post¹ /ˋsaɪnˌpost; ˈsaɪnpəʊst/ *n* [C] a sign on a road showing directions and distances 路标: *The signpost said 'Bedford 3 miles'.* 路标上写着"距贝德福德三英里"。| **[+to]** *Just follow the signposts to Padua.* 只要跟着去往博杜瓦的路标走就行了。

signpost² *v* [T] *BrE*【英】**1 be well/badly signposted** to be clearly or unclearly marked by signposts 给/未给…设置明显的路标: *The village isn't very well signposted so it's quite hard to find.* 这个村子没有设置明显的路标，所以很难找。**2** to show something clearly so that everyone will notice and understand it 清楚地表明: *They have signposted their conclusions in the report.* 他们已在报告中清楚地表明了自己的结论。

Sikes /saɪks; saɪks/, **Bill** a character in the book *Oliver Twist* by Charles Dickens. He is a violent thief who murders his girlfriend, Nancy. 赛克斯〔查尔斯·狄更斯小说《雾都孤儿》中的一个人物。他是一名凶狠的窃贼，杀害了自己的女友南希〕

Sikh /sik; siːk/ *n* [C] a member of an Indian religious group that developed from Hinduism in the 16th century 锡克教教徒〔16世纪从印度教分出的一支教派的信徒〕—**Sikh** *adj*

Sikh·is·m /ˋsikɪzṃ; ˈsiːkɪzəm/ *n* [U] the religion of the Sikhs 锡克教

si·lage /ˋsaɪlɪdʒ; ˈsaɪlɪdʒ/ *n* [U] grass or other plants cut and stored so that they can be used as winter food for cattle 青贮饲料

si·lence¹ /ˋsaɪləns; ˈsaɪləns/ *n* W2

1 ▶NO NOISE 没有响声◀ [U] complete absence of sound or noise 无声，寂静: *In the silence he heard a faint clicking noise.* 寂静中他听到一声微弱的咔嗒声。| **[+of]** *Nothing disturbed the silence of the night.* 没有什么打破这夜晚的寂静。| **silence falls (on/upon)** (=it begins to be completely quiet) 变得完全寂静 *After the explosion, an eerie silence fell upon the scene.* 爆炸之后，现场陷入一片可怕的寂静。| **break/shatter the silence** *The silence was suddenly broken by a loud scream.* 一声刺耳的尖叫突然打破了沉寂。| **absolute/complete/dead silence** *the complete silence of the forest at night* 夜间森林的绝对寂静

2 ▶NO TALKING 不说话◀ a) [C,U] complete quiet because no one is talking, or a period of complete quiet 静默，缄默，默不作声: *There was a long silence before anyone answered.* 长时间的静默以后才有人回答。| *She raised her hand and waited for silence.* 她举起手，等待大家静下来。| *"Silence!" thundered the judge.* "安静！"法官大声叫道。| **in silence** (=not saying anything) 什么话也不说 *We walked back to the house in silence.* 我们默不作声地走回房子去。| **embarrassed/awkward/stunned etc silence** *There was a moment's embarrassed silence.* 有一阵子大家都尴尬地默不作声。| **stony silence** (=when someone has said something very shocking or unreasonable)〔当有人说了一些非常令人震惊或不合理的话时〕无任何反应 *Their suggestion was met with a stony silence.* 他们的建议没有引起任何反应。**b)** [U] failure or refusal to discuss something or answer questions about something 只字不提，保持沉默: **[+on]** *The government's silence on such an important issue seems very strange.* 政府对如此重大的问题保持沉默，显得非常奇怪。| **take sb's silence for/as** (=think that someone's silence has a particular meaning) 认为某人的沉默有特殊的含义 *She took his silence as an agreement.* 她把他的沉默视作同意。

3 ▶NO COMMUNICATION 没有交流◀ [C,U] failure to write a letter to someone, telephone them etc 无音信，失去联系: *After two years of silence he suddenly got in touch with us again.* 两年杳无音信之后，他突然又跟我们取得了联系。

4 reduce sb to silence to speak to someone so angrily, rudely etc that they are too shocked or upset to reply〔因说话粗暴等〕使某人不能回答[作声]: *This stinging criticism reduced me to silence for the rest of the meeting.* 这种尖刻的批评使我噤若寒蝉直到会议结束。

5 a one-minute silence/two-minute silence etc a period of time in which everyone stops talking as a sign of honour and respect towards someone who has died 静默一分钟/两分钟等〔对死者表示敬意〕

silence² *v* [T] **1** to make someone stop talking, or stoˋ something making a noise 使安静，使缄默: *"Just a minute," she snapped, silencing him with a look of hatred.* "你等一等。"她厉声地说，用带着仇恨的眼神使他静了下来。**2** to make someone stop expressing opposition or criticisms 压制〔反对意见或批评〕: *Opponents of the regime were silenced by threats of violence.* 政权的反对者因受到暴力威胁而不敢发表意见。| *a brilliant new book that silenced her critics* 她的一部使批评家无话可说的出色新书

Silence of the Lambs, The /ˌ· · · ˈ·/ (1990) an extremely frightening US film about a young policewoman and a man called Hannibal Lecter who kills people and then eats them. 《沉默的羔羊》〔(1990)，一部极恐怖的美国影片，讲述一名年轻女警和一个名叫汉尼拔·雷克特的杀人狂的故事，他先把人杀死然后再吃掉〕

si·lenc·er /ˋsaɪlənsɚ; ˈsaɪlənsə/ *n* [C] **1** a thing that is put on the end of a gun so that it makes less noise when it is fired〔手枪末端的〕消声器 **2** *BrE* a piece of equipment that is connected to the EXHAUST² (1) of a vehicle to make its engine quieter【英】〔与车辆内燃机排气管装置相连的〕消声器; MUFFLER (2) *AmE*【美】

si·lent /ˋsaɪlənt; ˈsaɪlənt/ *adj* W3

1 ▶NOT SPEAKING 不说话◀ a) not saying anything 不语的，缄默的，默默的: *Phil was silent for a moment as he thought about his reply.* 菲尔在考虑如何答复前沉默了一会儿。| **fall silent** (=become quiet) 安静下来 *The crowd fell silent when the President appeared.* 总统出现时，人群安静了下来。**b)** not talking much to other people 沉默寡言的: *Nate was in his late teens, a silent and self-contained boy.* 内特将近20岁，是个安静而矜持的男孩。| **the strong silent type** (=a man who looks strong and does not talk very much) 坚强而沉默寡言的人

2 ▶NOT COMMUNICATING 不交流◀ failing or refusing to talk about something or express an opinion 不表态的，只字不提的: **[+on/about]** *The company is suspiciously silent about its plans for cutting costs.* 公司对于削减开支的计划只字不提，令

人疑惑。| **remain silent** *The prisoner remained silent when questioned.* 犯人被讯问时保持缄默。

3 ▶QUIET 安静的◀ without any sound, or not making any sound 无声的, 寂静的: *In the early morning the village was completely silent.* 村子在清晨一片寂静。| *At last the guns were silent.* 枪声终于沉寂下来了。

4 ▶FILMS 影片◀ a silent film is a cinema film with no sound, of the type made before about 1927〔约在 1927 年前摄制的电影〕无声的: *silent movies* 无声电影

CULTURAL NOTE 文化注释

Silent films starred (STAR) people such as Charlie CHAPLIN, Buster Keaton, and Rudolph Valentino. People's movements in them appear sudden and not at all smooth. A few words appeared on the screen to help people follow the story, and a piano was usually played in the cinema when they were shown. 无声电影的明星包括查理·卓别林、巴斯特·基顿和鲁道夫·瓦伦蒂诺等。电影中人们的动作显得突兀而不顺畅。屏幕上会出现几个词来帮助人们理顺故事情节。无声电影在电影院中播放时通常会有钢琴伴奏。

5 ▶LETTER 字母◀ a silent letter in a word is not pronounced and does not have a sound 不发音的: *The 'w' in 'wreck' is silent.* 单词 wreck 中的字母 w 是不发音的。

6 silent as the grave completely silent, often in a way that seems mysterious 寂静无声的, 像坟墓一样寂静的 —**silently** *adv*

silent ma·jor·i·ty, the /,‥'‥‥/ *n* all the people in a country who are not politically active, whose opinions are believed to represent the ideas that most ordinary people have 沉默的大多数〔指一个国家在政治上不积极的人们, 其意见被认为代表了大多数普通人的观点〕

Silent Night /,‥'‥/ a well-known Christmas CAROL (=a traditional religious song), which was originally written in German《平安夜》〔一首著名的圣诞颂歌, 最初用德语写成〕

silent part·ner /,‥'‥/ *n* [C] *AmE* someone who owns part of a business but is not actively involved in the way it operates【美】不参与经营的合伙人; SLEEPING PARTNER *BrE*【英】

sil·hou·ette /,sɪluˋɛt; ,sɪluˈet/ *n* [C] a dark image, shadow, or shape, seen against a light background 侧面影像, 黑色轮廓像, 剪影: *The silhouette of the cathedral could be seen against the dawn sky.* 在黎明的天空映衬下可以看见大教堂的轮廓。—**silhouetted** *adj*: *tall chimney stacks silhouetted against the orange flames* 在橙色火焰映衬下高大烟囱的轮廓

sil·i·ca /ˋsɪlɪkə; ˈsɪlɪkə/ *n* [U] a chemical compound that exists naturally as sand, QUARTZ, and FLINT, used in making glass 硅石, 二氧化硅〔制造玻璃的原料〕

sil·i·cate /ˋsɪlɪ,ket; ˈsɪlɪkeɪt/ *n* [C,U] *technical* one of a group of common solid mineral substances【术语】硅酸盐

sil·i·con /ˋsɪlɪkən; ˈsɪlɪkən/ *n* [U] *technical* a simple substance that is not a metal, and exists naturally in large quantities combined with other metals, minerals etc【术语】硅

silicon chip /,‥'‥/ *n* [C] a CHIP[1] (4) (=in a computer)〔用于电脑的〕硅片

sil·i·cone /ˋsɪlə,kon; ˈsɪlɪkəʊn/ *n* [U] one of a group of chemicals that are not changed by heat or cold and are used in making types of rubber, oil, and RESIN (2) 硅酮〔一种不因冷热而变化的化学物质, 用于制造各种橡胶、石油、树脂等产品〕

silicone im·plant /,‥'‥/ *n* [C] a piece of silicone that is put into the body, especially into a woman's breasts to make them larger〔尤指女子隆胸用的〕硅酮植入物

Silicon Glen /,‥'‥/ a humorous name for an area of central Scotland where there are many companies producing computer products. Its name is based on Silicon Valley, because "glen" is a Scottish word for a valley. 小硅谷〔苏格兰中部一地区的谑称。该地有许多生产电脑产品的公司。名称源于 Silicon Valley (硅谷)。苏格兰语的 glen 就是 valley (谷) 的意思〕

Silicon Val·ley /,‥'‥/ a part of California in the area between San Francisco and San José, which is a centre of the computer industry. Many important inventions were made in this area, and many large and small companies producing computer SOFTWARE and HARDWARE are based there. It is called Silicon Valley because the computer industry is based on the SILICON chip. 硅谷〔加利福尼亚州一地区。位于旧金山和圣何塞之间, 为计算机工业中心。不同规模的电脑软硬件公司云集此地, 诞生了一大批重大发明。因硅片为计算机工业基础, 故名〕

sil·i·co·sis /,sɪlɪˋkosɪs; ,sɪlɪˈkəʊsɪs/ *n* [U] an illness of the lungs caused by breathing SILICA, common among people who work in mines etc 石末沉着病, 硅肺〔常见于矿工〕

silk /sɪlk; sɪlk/ *n* **1** [U] a thin, smooth, soft cloth made from very thin thread which is produced by a silkworm 丝绸: *a silk shirt* 丝绸衬衣 | *a dress made of the finest silk* 用最好的丝绸做的连衣裙 **2** [C] *BrE law* a KC or QC (=type of important lawyer)【英, 法律】英国王室法律顾问, 御用大律师 | **take silk** (=become a KC or QC) 成为御用大律师 **3 silks** *technical* the coloured shirts worn by JOCKEYS (=people who ride horses in races)【术语】〔骑士在赛马时穿的〕彩色丝绸赛马服

silk·en /ˋsɪlkən; ˈsɪlkən/ *adj literary*【文】**1** soft, smooth, and shiny like silk〔丝绸般〕柔软光滑的: *her silken hair* 她那柔软光滑的头发 **2** made of silk 丝绸制的: *a silken handkerchief* 丝绸手绢

Silk Road, the /'‥/ an ancient route along which silk was carried from China and across central Asia to the Eastern Mediterranean and Europe 丝绸之路〔指将丝绸从中国经中亚运至地中海以东地区及欧洲的一条古道〕

silk screen /'‥/ also 又作 **silk screen print·ing** /,‥'‥/ *n* [U] a way of printing by forcing paint or ink onto a surface through a stretched piece of cloth 丝网印刷(术)

silk·worm /ˋsɪlk,wɝm; ˈsɪlkwɜːm/ *n* [C] a type of MOTH whose young produces silk thread 蚕

silk·y /ˋsɪlkɪ; ˈsɪlki/ *adj* **1** soft, smooth and shiny, like silk〔丝绸般〕柔软光滑的: *silky fur* 柔滑的皮毛 **2** a silky voice is gentle, and is used especially when someone is trying to persuade you to do something〔声音〕柔和的〔尤指在试图说服别人做某事时的话音〕—**silkily** *adv* —**silkiness** *n* [U]

sill /sɪl; sɪl/ *n* [C] **1** the narrow shelf at the base of a window frame 窗台 **2** the part of a car frame at the bottom of the doors 底梁〔指汽车的框架在车门以下的部分〕: *You've got a lot of rust on your sills.* 你汽车的底梁已经锈得很厉害了。

sil·la·bub /ˋsɪlə,bʌb; ˈsɪləbʌb/ *n* [C,U] SYLLABUB 乳酒冻

sil·ly[1] /ˋsɪlɪ; ˈsɪli/ *adj* **1** not sensible, showing bad judgment 蠢 3
的, 愚昧的: *This may sound like a silly question, but what is the point of this exercise?* 也许我这个问题很傻, 可是, 这种运动有什么意思? | **a silly thing to do/say** *I left my keys at home, which was a pretty silly thing to do.* 我把钥匙落在家里了, 干了件没脑子的事。—see 见 SHAME[1] (USAGE) **2** stupid in a childish or embarrassing way 傻的, 可笑的: *I wish you kids would stop being so silly.* 我希望你们这些小家伙不要这么傻了。| *a silly hat* 一顶可笑的帽子 | *I hate their parties – we always end up playing silly games.* 我讨厌他们的聚会 — 最后总是玩一些愚蠢的游戏。**3** *spoken* not serious or practical【口】随便的; 不切实际的; 不实用的: *They served us coffee in these silly little cups.* 他们竟然用这种不实用的小杯子给我们上咖啡。| *Try making a silly offer – they might just accept it.* 随便开个价 — 他们也许就会接受的。**4 bore sb silly** *informal* to make someone extremely bored【非正式】令某人极为厌烦 **5 drink yourself silly** *informal* to get very drunk【非正式】喝得烂醉 —**silliness** *n* [U]

silly[2] *n* [singular] *spoken* used to tell someone that you think they are being stupid【口】傻瓜, 笨蛋: *No, silly, I didn't mean that!* 不, 傻瓜, 我不是那个意思!

silly bil·ly /'‥,‥/ *n* [C] *spoken* used to tell someone, especially a child, that they are behaving in a silly way【口】〔尤指小孩〕笨蛋, 小傻瓜

silly sea·son, the /'‥,‥/ *n BrE informal* a period in the summer when newspapers print stories that are not very serious because there is not much political news【英, 非正式】〔新闻界的〕无聊季节〔在夏季, 报上因政治新闻不多而登载一些不很严肃的内容〕; 新闻淡季

si·lo /ˋsaɪlo; ˈsaɪləʊ/ *n* [C] **1** a tall structure like a tower that is used for storing grain, winter food for farm animals etc〔贮藏牲畜冬季用饲料等的〕青贮塔 **2** a large structure under the ground from which a large MISSILE can be fired 导弹地下发射井

silt[1] /sɪlt; sɪlt/ *n* [U] moving sand, mud, soil etc that is carried in water and then settles at a bend in a river, an entrance to a port etc 淤泥,〔沉积的〕泥沙

silt[2] *v*

silt up *phr v* [I,T] to fill or become filled with silt (使) 淤塞; (被) 淤塞: *The old harbour silted up years ago.* 这个老港湾在许多年前就淤塞了。

sil·van /ˋsɪlvən; ˈsɪlvən/ *adj* SYLVAN (在) 森林和乡村中的

sil·ver[1] /ˋsɪlvɚ; ˈsɪlvə/ *n* **1** [U] a shiny, whitish, valuable metal 3
that is used to make jewellery, knives, coins etc, and is a chemical ELEMENT 银 **2** [U] spoons, forks, dishes etc that are made of silver or a similar metal 银餐具〈如汤匙、叉子、碟子等〉: *As kitchen-maid, it was my job to polish the silver.* 作为帮厨女佣, 我的工作是擦亮银餐具。**3** [U] the colour of silver 银(白)色 **4** [C] *informal* a SILVER MEDAL【非正式】银奖牌 **5** [U] *BrE old-fashioned* coins that are made partly or completely of silver【英,

过时】银币 —see also 另见 **be born with a silver spoon in your mouth** (BORN[2] (11)), **every cloud has a silver lining** (CLOUD[1] (7))

silver[2] *adj* **1** made of silver 银制的, 银质的: *a silver teapot* 银茶壶 **2** coloured silver 银(白)色的: *a silver Mercedes* 银白色的奔驰汽车

silver[3] *v* [T] *technical* to cover a surface with a thin shiny silver coloured surface in order to make a mirror【术语】给…包银, 在…上镀银〔或银色物质以制作镜子〕

Silver, Long John —see 见 LONG JOHN SILVER

silver an·ni·ver·sa·ry /ˌ‥ ˈ··/ *n* [C] SILVER WEDDING ANNIVERSARY 银婚

silver birch /ˌ‥ ˈ·/ *n* [C,U] a type of BIRCH tree that has a silvery-white TRUNK and branches 纸皮桦, 银桦(树)

silver dol·lar /ˌ‥ ˈ·/ *n* [C] a former US one dollar coin, that is now very valuable〔美国过去的〕银元, 一元银币〔现已很珍贵〕

sil·ver·fish /ˈsɪlvəˌfɪʃ; ˈsɪlvəfɪʃ/ *n plural* **silverfish** or **silverfishes** [C] a small silver-coloured insect that is found in houses and sometimes damages paper or cloth 蠹鱼〔一种蛀蚀纸和布的银色小昆虫〕

silver foil /ˌ‥ ˈ·/ *n* [U] *BrE* FOIL (=very thin sheets of metal)【英】箔; 金属薄片

silver ju·bi·lee /ˌ‥ ˈ···/ *n* [C] *especially BrE* the date that is exactly 25 years after the date of an important public event, especially a CORONATION【尤英】25周年纪念〔尤指加冕纪念〕: *the Queen's Silver Jubilee* 女王加冕25周年纪念

silver med·al /ˌ‥ ˈ·/ *n* [C] a MEDAL made of silver that is given to the person who finishes second in a race or competition〔奖给亚军的〕银奖牌

silver pa·per /ˌ‥ ˈ··◂/ *n* [U] *BrE* paper that is shiny like metal on one side, used especially for wrapping food【英】锡纸, 银箔纸〔尤用于包装食物〕

silver plate /ˌ‥ ˈ·◂/ *n* [U] metal with a thin covering of silver 外层镀银的金属 —**silver-plated** *adj*: *a silver-plated candlestick* 镀银的烛台

silver screen, the /ˌ‥ ˈ·/ *n old-fashioned* the film industry, especially of Hollywood【过时】电影业〔尤指好莱坞〕: *stars of the silver screen* 电影明星

sil·ver·smith /ˈsɪlvəˌsmɪθ; ˈsɪlvəˌsmɪθ/ *n* [C] someone who makes things out of silver 银(器)匠

silver-tongued /ˌ‥ ˈ·◂/ *adj especially literary* good at talking to people and persuading them【尤文】讲话有说服力的, 雄辩的

sil·ver·ware /ˈsɪlvəˌwɛr; ˈsɪlvəweə/ *n* [U] **1** objects made of silver, especially knives, spoons, dishes etc 银器; 银餐具 **2** *AmE* knives, spoons and forks made of any metal【美】金属餐具〔刀子、汤匙、叉子等〕—see picture on page A15 参见A15页图

silver wed·ding an·ni·ver·sa·ry /ˌ‥ ˈ·· ‥ˌ··/ *n* [C] the date that is exactly 25 years after the date of a wedding 银婚纪念日〔结婚25周年纪念日〕

sil·ver·y /ˈsɪlvərɪ; ˈsɪlvəri/ *adj* **1** shiny and silver in colour 光亮如银的, 银白色的: *the silvery light of the moon* 银色的月光 **2** *especially literary* having a pleasant, light, musical sound【尤文】〔声音〕银铃般的, 清脆悦耳的: *peals of silvery laughter* 一阵阵银铃般的笑声

sim·i·an /ˈsɪmɪən; ˈsimiən/ *adj technical* connected with or similar to a monkey or APE[1] (1)【术语】(像)猿[猴]的 —**simian** *n* [C]

S1 W1 **sim·i·lar** /ˈsɪmələ; ˈsɪmələ/ *adj* **1** almost the same but not exactly the same 相似的, 近似的, 类似的: *We have similar tastes in music.* 我们对音乐的品味相近。| *students of roughly similar abilities* 能力大致相当的学生 | *These two signatures are so similar it's very difficult to tell them apart.* 这两个签名非常相似, 很难区别。| *I saw something similar in yesterday's 'Times'.* 我在昨天的《泰晤士报》上看到类似的内容。| [+to] *My opinions on the matter are similar to Kay's.* 我对这件事的见解和凯的差不多。**2** [no comparative 无比较级] *technical* exactly the same in shape but not size【术语】相似的〔形状相同但大小有异的〕: *Similar triangles have equal angles.* 相似三角形的各个角都相等。—see also 另见 SIMILARLY

W2 **sim·i·lar·i·ty** /ˌsɪməˈlærətɪ; ˌsɪmḷˈlærḷti/ *n* **1** [U] the fact of being similar to something else, or the degree to which two or more things are similar to each other; RESEMBLANCE 类似, 相似: [+between] *a striking similarity between the two designs* 这两项设计之间惊人的相似 | [+to] *What I like about his poetry is its similarity to Wordsworth's.* 我喜欢他的诗是它跟华兹华斯的很相似。| *The stories show some similarity to parts of the Old Testament.* 这些故事与《旧约全书》的若干部分有些近似。**2** [C] a way in which things or people are similar 类似之点, 相似之处: *The police say there are some similarities between the two attacks.* 警方说这两次袭击之间有些相似之处。| [+in] *When studying children and other young animals we can see similarities in their behaviour.* 在研究小孩和动物幼崽时, 我们可以看到两者在行为上的一些类似之处。

sim·i·lar·ly /ˈsɪmələlɪ; ˈsɪmḷləli/ *adv* in a similar way 差不多, 相似地; 同样地, 相同地: **similarly situated/expressed/inclined etc** *This idea is similarly expressed in his most recent book.* 这一观点在他最近出版的新书中也有类似的表达。| [sentence adverb 句子副词] *Men must wear a jacket and tie. Similarly, women must wear a skirt or dress and not trousers.* 男士必须穿外套并打领带。同样, 女士必须穿裙子或连衣裙, 不能穿裤子。

sim·i·le /ˈsɪməlɪ; ˈsɪmḷli/ *n* **1** [C] an expression that describes something by comparing it with something else, using the words 'as' or 'like', for example 'as white as snow' 明喻〔用as或like将两件事物作比较, 如"像雪一样白"〕**2** [U] the use of expressions like this 明喻的运用

sim·mer[1] /ˈsɪmə; ˈsɪmə/ *v* **1** [I,T] to cook something slowly in water that is gently boiling〔用文火〕慢慢地煮, 煨, 炖: *A pot was simmering on the stove.* 一只锅在炉子上煨着。**2** [I] if you are simmering or your emotions are simmering, you feel anger, hate, love etc very strongly, and can only just prevent yourself from expressing it 内心充满某种强烈的感情〈如怒火、仇恨、爱等〉;〔怒火、仇恨、爱等〕即将爆发: *Passions were simmering underneath the surface.* 激情正在内心涌动。| [+with] *The crowd was simmering with rage by the time the defendant arrived in court.* 当被告到达法庭时, 人群怒火中烧。**3 simmer down!** *spoken* used to tell someone to be less excited, angry etc【口】冷静下来! 请息怒!: *Simmer down, Holly – it won't help to lose your temper.* 冷静点, 霍莉——发脾气是无济于事的。

simmer[2] *n* [singular] the condition of simmering 慢慢沸腾的状态, 将沸未沸状态, 小沸: *Bring the vegetables to a simmer.* 用文火煮这些菜。

sim·nel cake /ˈsɪmnəl ˌkek; ˈsɪmnəl ˌkeɪk/ *n* [C] *BrE* a cake made with dried fruit, that is traditionally eaten at Easter【英】水果蛋糕〔复活节传统食品〕

Simon, Paul —see 见 SIMON AND GARFUNKEL

Simon and Gar·fun·kel /ˌsaɪmən ənd gɑˈfʌŋkḷ; ˌsaɪmən ənd gɑːˈfʌŋkəl/ two US singers, Paul Simon and Art Garfunkel, who started playing together during the 1960s and became very famous when some of their songs were used in the film *The Graduate* (1967). Their songs, most of which were written by Paul Simon, include *The Sound of Silence*, *Mrs Robinson* and *Bridge Over Troubled Water*. Paul Simon later became successful in singing and playing by himself. 西蒙与加丰克尔〔美国歌手保罗·西蒙和阿特·加丰尔克。二人20世纪60年代开始联袂演出, 一些歌曲被选用作为电影《毕业生》(1967) 插曲之后, 他们名声大振。大部分歌曲出自于保罗·西蒙之手, 包括《寂静之声》、《鲁宾逊太太》和《忧愁河上的金桥》。此后, 保罗·西蒙的个人演艺事业也颇为成功〕

Si·mone /sɪˈmon; sɪˈməʊn/**, Ni·na** /ˈninə; ˈniːnə/ (1933-2003) a US JAZZ and blues singer who also plays the piano. As well as being a musician, she was involved in the Civil Rights Movement in the US in the 1960s 西蒙〔(1933-2003), 美国爵士乐及布鲁斯音乐歌手。她还弹奏钢琴。除此之外, 她还参加了20世纪60年代美国的民权运动〕

sim·pat·i·co /sɪmˈpætɪko; sɪmˈpætɪkəʊ/ *adj AmE informal*【美, 非正式】**1** someone who is simpatico is easy to like 可爱的, 讨人喜欢的 **2** in agreement 一致的, 和谐的: *He and I are simpatico about a lot of things.* 我和他对许多问题的看法都很一致。

sim·per /ˈsɪmpə; ˈsɪmpə/ *v* [I] to smile in a silly, annoying way 傻笑, 假笑: *Betsy simpered coyly at him as she spoke.* 贝齐说话时对他腼腆地傻笑。—**simper** *n* [C] —**simperingly** *adv*

sim·ple /ˈsɪmpḷ; ˈsɪmpəl/ *adj* S1 W1

1 ►PLAIN 朴素◄ without a lot of decoration or unnecessary things added 无装饰的; 简朴的, 朴素的: *a simple dress* 朴素的连衣裙 | *simple but delicious food* 简单美味的食物 | *a building constructed in a simple, classic style* 建筑风格朴实无华的传统式楼房

2 ►EASY 容易◄ not difficult or complicated 简单的, 简易的, 容易的: *I'm sure there's a perfectly simple explanation.* 我敢肯定会有一个十分简单的解释。| *a simple but effective solution to the problem* 对这个问题简单而有效的解决办法 | **it's not as simple as that** *spoken* (=used to say that something is not as easy as someone thinks it is)【口】没有〔某人〕所想的那么容易 *I wish we could offer you more money but I'm afraid it's not as simple as that.* 我希望我们能多给你一点钱, 但事情并没有那么简单。

3 ▶ONLY 仅仅◀ [only before noun 仅用于名词前] not complicated or involving anything else 单纯的, 纯粹的; 不复杂的: *Completing the race is not just a simple matter of physical fitness.* 要跑完全程不仅是具备强健体格的问题。| *We can't do it, for the simple reason that we don't have enough time.* 我们做不了, 这纯粹是因为我们没有足够的时间。| **the simple truth/fact is** (=used to emphasize the truth about something) 事实就是〔用于强调事实〕*The simple truth is, he isn't good enough for the job.* 坦白地说, 他不能胜任这份工作。| **pure and simple** (=without any other reason or feature) 仅仅如此; 没有其他原因 *Their motive was greed, pure and simple.* 他们的动机就是贪婪, 就是这样。

4 ▶NOT HAVING MANY PARTS 没有许多部分◀ consisting of only a few necessary parts 结构简单的: *Bacteria are simple forms of life.* 细菌是简单的生命形式。| *A knife is a simple tool.* 刀子是一种简单的工具。

5 ▶ORDINARY 普通◀ honest and ordinary and not special in any way 朴实的; 普通的: *Joe was just a simple farmer.* 乔只是一个普普通通的农民。

6 the simple life *informal* life without all the problems of the modern world, especially life in the countryside, without too many possessions, or modern machines【非正式】简朴的生活〔尤指乡村生活〕

7 ▶UNINTELLIGENT 不聪明◀ [not before noun 不用于名词前] not intelligent 头脑简单的, 愚蠢的: *I'm afraid old Luke's a bit simple.* 我觉得老卢克似乎有点傻。

simple frac·ture /ˌ.. ˈ../ *n* [C] *technical* a broken or cracked bone that does not cut through the flesh that surrounds it【术语】单纯骨折 —compare 比较 COMPOUND FRACTURE

simple in·terest /ˌ.. ˈ.../ *n* [U] INTEREST[1] (4) that is calculated on the sum of money that you first invested (INVEST (1)), and does not include the interest it has already earned 单利〔首笔投资产生的利息〕—compare 比较 COMPOUND INTEREST

S

simple-mind·ed /ˌ.. ˈ..◂/ *adj* unable to understand complicated things, and not showing much understanding of the world 头脑简单的, 愚钝的, 不懂事的: *a simple-minded desire for a return to the past* 一种想要回到过去的愚蠢的想法

Simple Si·mon /ˌ.. ˈ../ a stupid person who believes everything he is told, from the name of a stupid young man in a NURSERY RHYME (=an old song or poem for young children). The rhyme goes: *Simple Simon met a pieman/Going to the fair;/Says Simple Simon to the pieman/ "Let me taste your ware."* 傻瓜西蒙〔轻信他人的傻瓜。源于一首童谣: 傻瓜西蒙路上走, /有人赶集去卖饼; /傻瓜西蒙把口开, /"让我尝尝你的饼"〕

sim·ple·ton /ˈsɪmpl̩tən; ˈsɪmpəltən/ *n* [C] *old-fashioned* someone who has a very low level of intelligence【过时】智能低下的人, 傻子, 蠢人

sim·pli·ci·ty /sɪmˈplɪsətɪ; sɪmˈplɪsɪ̈ti/ *n* [U] the quality of being simple, especially when this is attractive or useful 朴素, 简朴, 简单: *Mona wrote with a beautiful simplicity of style.* 莫娜的文笔优美而质朴。| *For the sake of simplicity, the tax form is divided into three sections.* 为简单明了起见, 税务表格分成三个部分。| **be simplicity itself** (=be very simple) 十分简单 *The plan was simplicity itself – how could she have misunderstood?* 这个计划简单得很, 她怎么可能误解了?

sim·pli·fy /ˈsɪmpləˌfaɪ; ˈsɪmplɪ̈faɪ/ *past tense and past participle* **simplified** *v* [T] to make something easier or less complicated 使简易, 使简明, 简化: *an attempt to simplify the tax laws* 简化税收法的尝试 | *Try to simplify your explanation for the children.* 设法解释得简明一些, 好让孩子们听懂。—see also 另见 OVERSIMPLIFY —**simplified** *adj*: *a simplified version of Chinese script* 简化版汉字 —**simplification** /ˌsɪmpləfəˈkeʃən; ˌsɪmplɪ̈fɪ̈ˈkeɪʃən/ *n* [C,U]

sim·plis·tic /sɪmˈplɪstɪk; sɪmˈplɪstɪk/ *adj* treating difficult subjects in a way that is too simple 过分简单化的: *a naive and simplistic approach to economic policy* 对经济政策问题幼稚而简单化的处理方法 —**simplistically** /-klɪ; -kli/ *adv*

S1 W1 **sim·ply** /ˈsɪmplɪ; ˈsɪmpli/ *adv* **1** only 仅仅, 只不过: *Some students lose marks simply because they don't read the question properly.* 有些学生失分只是因为没有把题目看清楚。| *Simply fill in the coupon and take it to your local store.* 只要把这张优惠券填好交给当地的商店就行。| *It isn't simply a question of money.* 这不仅仅是钱的问题。**2** in a way that is easy to understand 简易地, 简单明了地; 清楚地: *Try to express yourself more simply.* 把你的意思尽量表达得更简单明了。| **to put it simply** (=to explain things in a simple way) 简单地说 *To put it simply, the tax cuts mean the average worker will be about 3% better off.* 简单地说, 减税意味着每个普通工人的工资大约增加3%。**3** used to emphasize what you are saying 简直, 完全, 实在〔用以强调所说的话〕: *What a simply wonderful idea!* 一个多么精彩的想法啊! | *This piece of work simply isn't good enough.* 这项工作做得实在不够好。| **quite simply** *It is, quite simply, the most ridiculous idea I've ever heard.* 这简直是我所听到过的最荒谬的想法。**4** in a plain and ordinary way, without spending much money 朴素地, 简朴地: *We had to live very simply on my father's small salary.* 我们只能依靠父亲微薄的工资简朴地过日子。

Simp·son /ˈsɪmpsn̩; ˈsɪmpsən/, **O.J.** (1947-) a US football player, one of the most successful players of the 1970s, who later became an actor. In 1994 he was charged with murdering his wife, Nicole Brown Simpson, and her friend, Ronald Goldman. The jury decided that he did not kill her. Later, relatives of the murdered people won a civil court case against him and he was ordered to pay them $8.5 million. 辛普森〔(1947-), 美国橄榄球运动员。他是20世纪70年代最为成功的球员之一, 后来成为电影演员。1994年, 他被指控谋杀妻子尼科尔·布朗·辛普森和妻子的朋友罗奈尔得·戈德曼, 结果陪审团裁定他无罪。后来, 受害人亲属通过民事法庭打赢了官司, 法庭判他赔偿850万美元〕

Simpson, Wal·lis /ˈwalɪs; ˈwɒlɪs/ (1896-1986) a US woman, often known simply as Mrs Simpson, who had a relationship with the British king Edward VIII. Because she had already been married twice before, Edward was not allowed to marry her. In 1938, he decided to ABDICATE (=give up his position as king) so that he could marry her. She then became the Duchess of Windsor. 辛普森〔(1896-1986), 美国一女子, 常简称辛普森夫人。她与英王爱德华八世相爱。由于她此前结过两次婚, 根据规定, 爱德华不得与她结婚。1938年, 爱德华决定退位以便与她结婚。婚后, 她成了温莎公爵夫人〕

Simp·sons, The /ˈsɪmpsn̩s; ˈsɪmpsənz/ a humorous US television CARTOON programme about a family called Simpson. The children argue and fight a lot. Their father loves his children but spends a lot of time watching TV, eating, and drinking beer. Many people think it shows the problems and worries that real families experience, which the 'perfect' families in some other television shows do not. 《辛普森家庭》〔美国一滑稽卡通电视剧, 讲述辛普森一家的故事。这家的孩子经常打打闹闹, 父亲喜欢他们, 但却把大量时间用在看电视、吃东西、喝啤酒上。许多人认为这部电视剧反映了现实家庭存在的问题和忧虑, 而这在其他电视节目中所谓的"完美"家庭里是得不到反映的〕

sim·u·la·crum /ˌsɪmjəˈlekrəm; ˌsɪmjʊ̈ˈleɪkrəm/ *n* [C+of] *formal* an image of something【正式】像, 影像

sim·u·late /ˈsɪmjuˌlet; ˈsɪmjʊ̈leɪt/ *v* [T] **1** to make or produce something that is not real but has the appearance of being real 模仿, 模拟: *a machine that simulates conditions in space* 一台模拟太空状况的机器 | *A sheet of metal can be shaken to simulate thunder.* 抖动金属片可以模仿雷声。**2** *formal* to pretend to have a feeling; FEIGN【正式】假装, 伪装: *We tried to simulate surprise.* 我们假装吃惊。

sim·u·lat·ed /ˈsɪmjəˌletɪd; ˈsɪmjʊ̈leɪtɪ̈d/ *adj* not real, but made to look, feel etc like a real thing, situation, or feeling 模仿的, 模拟的, 仿制的; 假装的: *simulated leather* 仿皮革 | *a simulated nuclear explosion* 模拟的核爆炸

sim·u·la·tion /ˌsɪmjəˈleʃən; ˌsɪmjʊ̈ˈleɪʃən/ *n* **1** [C,U] an activity or situation that produces conditions which are not real, but have the appearance of being real, used especially for testing something〔用于试验的〕模拟操作; 模拟研究: *a computer simulation used to train airline pilots* 用于训练飞行员的电脑模拟程序 | **[+of]** *an audio-visual simulation of the beginning of the universe* 对宇宙诞生情景的一次视听模拟试验 **2** [U] the act or process of simulating something 模拟, 模仿

sim·u·la·tor /ˈsɪmjəˌletɚ; ˈsɪmjʊ̈leɪtə/ *n* [C] a piece of equipment used for training people by letting them feel what real conditions are like, for example in an aircraft〔用于人员训练的〕模拟装置, 模拟器: *a flight simulator* 飞行模拟装置

sim·ul·cast /ˈsɪməlˌkæst; ˈsɪməlkɑːst/ *v* [T usually passive 一般用被动态] *AmE* to broadcast a programme on television and radio at the same time【美】〔无线电和电视〕联播〔节目〕—**simulcast** *n* [C]

sim·ul·ta·ne·ous /ˌsaɪmlˈtenɪəs; ˌsɪməlˈteɪniəs◂/ *adj* happening or done at exactly the same time 同时〔发生或做出〕的: *a simultaneous broadcast of the concert on TV and radio* 电视和电台对音乐会的联播 | **simultaneous translation** (=immediate translation of what someone is saying as they are speaking) 同声传译, 同声翻译 —**simultaneously** *adv*: *two pictures taken simultaneously from different camera angles* 同时从两个不同摄影角度拍下的两张照片 —**simultaneity** /ˌsaɪmltəˈniətɪ; ˌsɪməltəˈniːɪ̈ti/ *n* [U]

sin¹ /sɪn; sɪn/ *n* **1** [C,U] disobedience to God, or an offence against God or religious laws〔冒犯上帝或宗教法规的〕罪，罪恶，罪孽：*The Bible says adultery is a sin.*《圣经》说通奸是一种罪。| *the sin of pride* 傲慢之罪 | *the Christian concept of sin* 基督教对罪的概念 | **commit a sin** (=do something that breaks a religious law) 造孽 **2** [singular] *informal* something that you strongly disapprove of【非正式】过错，罪过：*It's a sin the way they waste all this money.* 他们浪费那么多钱，真是罪过。| **commit a sin** *I had committed the unforgivable sin of forgetting her birthday.* 我忘记了她的生日，犯了不可饶恕的过错。| **it's a sin to do sth** *It'd be a sin to evict them just because they haven't paid their rent.* 仅仅因为没有交房租就把他们赶出去，这是很不对的。**3 live in sin** *old-fashioned* if two people live in sin they live together in a sexual relationship without being married【过时】〔未婚男女〕同居，姘居 **4 as miserable/ugly/guilty as sin** *spoken* very unhappy, ugly, guilty etc【口】非常不愉快/难看/内疚 **5 for my sins** *spoken especially BrE* an expression used to suggest jokingly that something is like a punishment【口，尤英】自作自受，活该，该死：*I'm the local party organizer, for my sins.* 我是当地聚会的组织者，真是自讨苦吃。—see also 另见 SINFUL, **cover/hide a multitude of sins** (MULTITUDE (3)), ORIGINAL SIN —**sinless** *adj*

sin² *v* **sinned, sinning** [I] **1** to break God's laws 违反上帝的戒律，违犯教规：**[+against]** *He has sinned against God.* 他得罪了上帝。**2 be more sinned against than sinning** *old-fashioned* used to say that someone should not be blamed for what they have done wrong, because they have been badly treated by other people【过时】人负我甚于我负人；受到超过应得的惩罚

sin³ *technical*【术语】the written abbreviation of 缩写= SINE

Si·nai /ˈsaɪnaɪ; ˈsaɪnaɪ/ the part of northeast Egypt to the east of the Gulf of Suez and the Suez Canal 西奈半岛〔埃及东北部地区，位于苏伊士湾和苏伊士运河以东〕

Sinai, Mount a mountain in Sinai in northeast Egypt on which, according to the Old Testament of the Bible, Moses received the Ten Commandments from God 西奈山〔埃及东北部西奈半岛上的一座山。据《圣经·旧约》记载，摩西在西奈山上领受了上帝的十诫〕

Si·na·tra /sɪˈnɑtrə; sɪˈnɑːtrə/, **Frank** (1915-98) a US singer and film actor, who first became successful in the 1940s, and is famous especially for the song *My Way*. He is one of the most famous and successful singers of the 20th century. 西纳特拉〔(1915-1998)，美国歌手、电影演员。最早成名于20世纪40年代，尤以歌曲《我的路》著称。他是20世纪最著名、最成功的歌手之一〕

Sin·bad, Sindbad /ˈsɪnbæd; ˈsɪnbæd/ the main character in the story of Sinbad the Sailor from *The Arabian Nights*, who has many adventures at sea 辛巴达〔《天方夜谭》里"辛巴达历险记"故事中的主要人物。他在海上有过不少冒险经历〕—see also 另见 the ROC, The OLD MAN OF THE SEA

since¹ /sɪns; sɪns/ *conjunction* [used with the present perfect and the past perfect tenses 与现在完成时及过去完成时连用] **1** at a time after a particular time or event in the past 自从…以来，自从…以后：*In the 12 months since I last wrote to you a lot has happened to me.* 自从上次我给你写信以后的12个月里，我经历了许多事。| *I can't have seen him since 1983.* 自1983年以来，我不可能见过他。| *It's been years since I enjoyed myself so much.* 我已有很多年没有那样痛快过了。**2** during the period of time after a particular time or event in the past 从…以后〔的一段时间里〕，自从…以来就一直…：*Since he started that diet he's lost over 20 lbs in weight.* 自从开始节食以来，他体重已减了二十多磅。| **ever since** *We've been friends ever since we met at school.* 我们自从在学校认识以来一直是朋友。**3** used to give the reason for something 因为，既然：*I'll be forty next month, since you ask.* 既然你问起，我下个月就满40岁了。| *Since you are unable to answer perhaps we should ask someone else.* 既然你不能回答，我们也许该问问别人。

since² *prep* [used with the present perfect and the past perfect tenses 与现在完成时及过去完成时连用] **1** at a time in the past after a particular time or event 自从…以来，自从…之后：*They haven't met since the wedding last year.* 自从去年那个婚礼之后，他们就再没有见过面了。| *Since the end of the war over a dozen hostages have been released.* 自从战争结束以来，已有超过12名人质获释了。—compare 比较 FOR¹ (8) **2** for the whole of a long period of time after a particular time or event in the past 自从…以后（的整段时间里），从…以后一直…：*Since the day we met I have known he was not to be trusted.* 从我们认识那天起，我就知道他不可靠。| **ever since** *Ever since the war she's been able to feed a whole family with a few potatoes and eggs.* 自从战争以来，她只能一直用几个马铃薯和鸡蛋养活全家。**3 since when?** *spoken* used in questions to show surprise, anger etc【口】自从什么时候起…?〔用于问句表示惊讶、气愤等〕：*Have you checked this bill? Since when does £42 plus £5 service charge come to £48?* 你检查过这张账单没有？什么时候起42英镑加5英镑服务费等于48英镑？

since³ *adv* [used with the present perfect and the past perfect tenses 与现在完成时及过去完成时连用] **1** at a time in the past after a particular time or event 从那时以来，后来：*Her husband died over ten years ago but she has since remarried.* 她丈夫于十多年前去世，但她后来又结婚了。| *I've since forgotten what our argument was about.* 我后来就忘掉我们为什么争吵了。| *He walked out of that door last Tuesday and no one's seen him since.* 他上星期二从那个门口走了出去，以后就再没有人见过他了。**2** for the whole of a long period of time after a particular time or event in the past 从那时至今〔的整段时间里〕，从那时起一直…：*The accident happened four years ago and she has hardly spoken since.* 四年前发生了事故，从那以后她几乎一直没有说过话。| **ever since** *We came to the UK in 1974 and have lived here ever since.* 我们于1974年来英国，自此便一直住在这里。**3 long since** if something has long since happened, it happened a long time ago 很久以前，早已…：*I've long since forgiven her for what she did.* 我早已原谅她的所作所为了。

USAGE NOTE 用法说明：SINCE

WORD CHOICE 词语辨析：since (*prep/conj*), from, after, from...to/till/until, for

Since is mainly used where you want to talk about a state or activity that started at some time in the past and has continued to the time when you are speaking. since 主要用于表示在过去某个时间发生并持续至说话时的情况或活动：*I've been here since ten o'clock this morning.* 我今天上午10点以后一直都在这里。| *The place had completely changed since I went there three years ago* (NOT 不用 *It has changed since three years/three years before*). 自从我三年前去过那里以后，那个地方已经完全变样了。

From or **after** may be used to show the starting points of periods of time where you do not use **since**. 表示某段时间的起点用 from 或 after 而不用 since。For example 例如：*I hope they'll be friends from now on* (NOT 不用 *since now on*)（我希望他们从现在起成为朋友）means I hope they will be friends from now and into the future. 这表示我希望他们从现在到将来都是朋友。*She was very unhappy for a while after leaving home* (NOT 不用 *since*)（她离家以后有一段时间很不愉快）means that she was unhappy from a period of time in the past until a later time in the past. 这表示她这一段不愉快的时间是从过去某个时间开始，到后来某个时间结束。

From...to/until/till is used where you want to give both ends of a period of time during which some state existed or some activity was being done. This construction can go with most tenses of the verb. from…to/until/till 用于表示某种状态或活动所持续时段的起止，并可与大多数时态连用：*I was here from ten till two.* 我从10点到两点都在这里。| *From 1990 to the present he's had no regular job* (NOT 不用 *since 1990 to the present*). 从1990年到现在，他一直没有固定的工作。| *She works from sunrise until sunset.* 她从日出工作到日落。

For is used where you want to give the length of a period of time, but do not need to say exactly when it started or finished. It goes with all tenses of verbs. for 用于表示时段的长度，但不必准确说明起止的时间。它可与动词各种时态连用：*We lived there for a long time.* 我们在那里住了很长时间。| *She's only staying for a week.* 她只准备逗留一个星期。When you use **for** with the present perfect tense, it gives a period of time that ends at the time of speaking. 当 for 与现在完成式连用时，所指时段在说话之时结束：*I've been waiting for two hours* (NOT 不用 *since two hours*). 我已等了两小时了。

In spoken English the **for** is often left out 在英语口语中 for 常被省略：*I've been here two hours.* 我在这里已有两小时了。| *She's only staying a week.* 她只准备逗留一星期。

GRAMMAR 语法

The point of time with **since** may be shown by a clause, which may contain a verb in the simple past. since 所指的时间起点可以用从句表示，从句中的时态可以用一般过去式：*He's been ill ever since he arrived.* 他到了以后就一直在生病。

The point of time with **since** may also be shown less exactly, by mentioning a period of time that ended in the past.

since 所指的时间起点也可以不甚明确，而只用一个在过去结束的时段来表示: *He's been working here since last week/the 60s* (=he started at some time during the 60s). 他自从上个星期以来／从60年代以来一直在这里工作。| *Since I was a kid I've always wanted to visit Disney World.* 从我的孩提时代起，我就一直想去迪斯尼乐园。

A **since** clause may also itself cover the whole period from a point in the past to the time of speaking. since 所引导的从句本身也可以覆盖从过去的时间起点直至说话之时的整个时段: *Since she's been living here she's made a lot of friends.* 自从她住在这里以来，她已经结交了许多朋友。

However, as in all the above examples, the main verb in any clause with **since** usually has to be in one of the perfect tenses. 但是，正如以上各例所示，凡用 since 的句子，其主动词通常得用其中一种完成时态。Compare also 还请比较: *Yesterday Bobby told me he hadn't eaten since Tuesday.* (=between Tuesday and yesterday he did not eat anything) 昨天博比告诉我，他从星期二起就没吃什么东西了。

Non-perfect tenses are used only in particular situations, for example where you are talking about the length of time itself. 非完成时态只用于特殊情况，例如谈的是时段本身的长度: *It's two weeks since I've seen you* (NOT 不用 *...since I haven't seen you*). 从我上次见你到现在已有两星期了。| *It seems like months since you last paid me.* 从你上次给我发工资到现在，好像有几个月了。Note also 另请注意: *Since the car accident she can't walk properly.* (=she hasn't been able to walk properly) 自从出了车祸以后，她一直不能正常走路。

S

sin·cere /sɪn`sɪr; sɪn'sɪə/ *adj* **1** a feeling, belief, statement etc that is sincere is honest and true, and based on what you really feel and believe; GENUINE (1)〔感情等〕由衷的，真诚的，真心实意的: *sincere admiration* 由衷的钦佩 | *a sincere desire to find out the truth* 弄清真相的真诚愿望 **2** someone who is sincere is honest and says what they really feel or believe〔人〕真诚的，不虚伪的，诚恳的: *He was gentle and sincere by nature.* 他本性温和正直。| [+in] *They were completely sincere in their beliefs.* 他们对自己的信仰是完全真诚的。—opposite 反义词 INSINCERE

sin·cere·ly /sɪn`sɪrlɪ; sɪn'sɪəli/ *adv* **1** in a sincere way 由衷地，真诚地；真挚地: *I sincerely hope I'll see her again.* 我衷心希望再见到她。| *a sincerely held belief* 虔诚的信仰 **2** **sincerely/yours sincerely** an expression used to end a formal letter that you have begun by addressing someone by name 谨上，敬上，谨启〔写在正式信件末尾的客套话〕

sin·cer·i·ty /sɪn`serətɪ; sɪn'serɨti/ *n* [U] **1** the quality of honestly believing something or really meaning what you say 真诚，真挚: *I don't doubt her sincerity, but I think she's got her facts wrong.* 我不怀疑她的诚意，但我认为她没弄清楚事实。**2** **in all sincerity** *formal* very sincerely【正式】十分真诚地: *May I say in all sincerity that your support has been most valuable.* 请让我由衷地说，你的支持极为宝贵。

Sinclair /`sɪŋkler; 'sɪŋkleə/, **Up·ton** /`ʌptən; 'ʌptən/ (1878-1968) a US writer who wrote *The Jungle*, a NOVEL about the meat-packing industry in Chicago, which showed that the workers were badly treated and the food was not clean and was likely to cause disease 辛克莱（1878-1968），美国作家。其小说《屠场》涉及芝加哥肉食品包装行业，揭露工人备受虐待，食品不干净可能引发疾病等弊端〕

Sind·bad /`sɪnbæd; 'sɪnbæd/ another spelling of SINBAD 辛巴达〔Sinbad 的另一拼法〕

sine /saɪn; saɪn/ *n* [C] *technical* the FRACTION (2) calculated for an angle by dividing the length of the side opposite it in a TRIANGLE with a RIGHT ANGLE by the length of the side opposite the RIGHT ANGLE【术语】〔数学上的〕正弦 —compare 比较 COSINE, TANGENT (3)

si·ne·cure /`saɪnɪ,kjʊr; 'saɪnɪkjʊə/ *n* [C] a job which you get paid for even though you do not have to do very much〔有薪酬而工作不多的〕闲职，挂名职务，领干薪的职位

si·ne qua non /`saɪnɪ kwe `nɑn; ,sɪni kwɑː 'nəʊn/ *n* [singular] *Latin formal* something that you must have, or which must exist, for something else to be possible【拉丁，正式】必要的条件，必需的东西，必具的资格: [+for/of] *The control of inflation is a sine qua non for economic stability.* 控制通货膨胀是经济稳定的必要条件。

sin·ew /`sɪnju; 'sɪnjuː/ *n* [C,U] **1** *not technical* a long strong piece of TISSUE (3) in your body that connects a muscle to a bone【非术语】腱〔连接骨与肌肉的索状组织〕**2** [usually plural 一般用复数] *literary* a means of strength or support【文】力量的源泉；支柱: *the sinews of our national defense* 我国国防的中流砥柱

sin·ew·y /`sɪnjəwɪ; 'sɪnjuːi/ *adj* having strong muscles 肌肉发达的，强壮的: *a big man with long, sinewy arms* 胳膊又长又壮的高个男子

sin·ful /`sɪnful; 'sɪnfəl/ *adj* **1** *literary or biblical* morally wrong or guilty of doing something morally wrong【文或圣经】有罪过的: *a sinful man* 罪孽深重的男子 | *Even within marriage they believed it was sinful to seek pleasure in sex.* 他们认为，即使在婚姻生活中追求性愉悦也是罪过。**2** very wrong or bad 有严重过错的；极不应该的: *a sinful waste of taxpayers' money* 对纳税人钱款极不应该的浪费 —**sinfully** *adv*

sing /sɪŋ; sɪŋ/ *v past tense* **sang** /sæŋ; sæŋ/ *past participle* **sung** /sʌŋ; sʌŋ/ **1** [I,T] to produce musical sounds, songs etc with your voice 唱，歌唱: *Sophie's been singing in the church choir for years.* 索菲参加教会合唱团唱歌已经多年了。| **sing a song/tune etc** *We all enjoy singing carols at Christmas.* 我们都喜欢在圣诞节唱颂歌。| **sing sb a song/tune etc** *Come on, sing us a song!* 来吧，给我们唱支歌！| **sing to sb** *She walked along, singing to herself.* 她边走边唱。**2** **sing sb to sleep** to sing to a baby or child until they go to sleep 唱歌哄〔婴儿或小孩〕入睡 **3** [I] if birds sing, they produce high musical sounds〔鸟〕啼，啭: *I awoke to hear the birds singing outside my window.* 我醒来听到鸟儿在窗外啼啭。**4** [I always+adv/prep] to make a high, continuous, ringing sound 呜呜作响，发嗡嗡[嗖嗖]声: [+on] *A kettle was singing on the stove.* 炉上的水壶在呜呜作响。| [+past/by etc] *An enemy bullet sang past my ear.* 敌人的一颗子弹从我耳边嗖的一声飞过。**5** **sing sb's praise(s)** to praise someone very much 高度赞扬某人: *Diane really admires you – she's always singing your praises.* 黛安娜的确很佩服你，她总是高度赞扬你。**6** [I] *slang* to tell someone or the police everything you know about a crime, especially a crime you were involved in yourself【俚】招供，交待罪行: *We'll soon make him sing.* 我们很快就会让他老实交待了。**7** [I+of,T] *literary* to praise someone in poetry【文】用诗歌赞美，〔用诗〕歌颂，吟咏

sing along *phr v* [I] to sing with someone else who is already singing 跟着〔某人〕一起唱: *Sing along if you know the words.* 如果你们知道歌词，就跟着一起唱吧。

sing out *phr v* [I,T] *informal* to sing or shout out clearly and loudly【非正式】大声唱；高声叫喊: *If you see anything that looks interesting, sing out.* 如果你们看到什么有趣的东西就喊出来。

sing up *phr v* [I] to sing more loudly 放声[大声]唱: *Sing up, boys, I can't hear you!* 唱大声些，孩子们，我听不见呢！

sing·a·long /`sɪŋə,lɔŋ; 'sɪŋəlɒŋ/ *n* [C] *AmE* an informal occasion when people sing songs together【美】〔非正式的大家一起唱的〕唱歌聚会; SINGSONG *BrE*【英】

Sing·a·pore /`sɪŋgə,por; ,sɪŋə'pɔː◂/ a small country on an island in southeast Asia, between Malaysia and Indonesia. Population: 4,300,000 (2001). Capital: Singapore City. Singapore is an important business, industrial, and financial centre. 新加坡〔东南亚一小国，位于马来西亚与印度尼西亚之间的一座小岛上。人口: 4,300,000 (2001)，首都: 新加坡城。新加坡是重要的商业、工业和金融中心〕—**Singaporean** /,sɪŋgə`porɪən; ,sɪŋə'pɔːriən◂/ *n, adj*

Sing a song of six·pence /,· · ·, · `· ·/ a NURSERY RHYME (=an old song or poem for young children) which starts: *Sing a song of sixpence,/A pocket full of rye;/Four-and-twenty blackbirds/Baked in a pie./When the pie was opened,/The birds began to sing,/Wasn't that a dainty dish/To set before the King?* 《六便士之歌》〔一首童谣，开首为: 六便士歌唱一首，／黑麦满满装一袋；／二十四只黑鹂鸟，／放入馅饼一同烤。／馅饼打开品品，／鸟儿齐声把歌唱，／放在国王御宴前，／岂不一道美佳肴?〕

singe[1] /sɪndʒ; sɪndʒ/ *v* [I,T] to burn something slightly on its surface or edge, or to be burned in this way（把）〔表面或边上〕略微烧焦: *If the iron's too hot it'll singe your shirt.* 如果熨斗太热，它会把你的衬衣烫焦。

singe[2] *n* [C] a mark made by burning something slightly 轻微烧焦的痕迹

sing·er /`sɪŋɚ; 'sɪŋə/ *n* [C] someone who sings, especially as a profession〔尤指职业的〕歌手，歌唱家: *an opera singer* 歌剧演唱家 | *a pop singer* 流行歌手

Singer, I·saac Ba·shev·is /`aɪzək bɑ`ʃevɪs; 'aɪzək bɑː'ʃevɨs/ (1904-91) a Jewish-American writer, born in Poland, who won the Nobel Prize for Literature in 1978, and who is best known for his short stories and for his NOVEL *The Slave*. He wrote in Yiddish and his work has been translated into many languages. 辛格（1904-1991），犹太裔美国作家，生于波兰。1978年获诺贝尔文学奖，以短篇小说和长篇小说《奴隶》最为著名。他用意第绪语创作，作品被译成多种文字〕

singer-song·writ·er /ˌ‥'‥/ *n* [C] someone who writes songs and sings them 创作型歌手, 歌手兼歌曲作者

sing·ha·lese /sɪŋgəˈliːz; ˌsɪŋgəˈliːz◂/ *n, adj* SINHALESE 僧伽罗人; 僧伽罗语

Sing·in' in the Rain /ˈ‥‥ˈ/ (1952) a very famous and popular US MUSICAL (=a film that uses singing and dancing to tell a story) in which Gene Kelly and Debbie Reynolds appear. The film contains a famous scene in which Gene Kelly dances in the street while it is raining, and sings 'Singin' in the Rain'. 《雨中曲》〔(1952), 美国一部非常有名、广受欢迎的音乐片。由吉恩·凯利和戴比·雷诺兹联袂主演。片中有一段场景十分有名, 吉恩·凯利冒雨在街头一边跳舞, 一边唱着《雨中曲》〕

S2 W1 **sin·gle¹** /ˈsɪŋgl; ˈsɪŋgəl/ *adj*

1 ▶ONE 一（个）◀ [only before noun 仅用于名词前] only one 单一的, 唯一的, 仅一个的: *A single tree gave shade from the sun.* 仅有的一棵树挡住了太阳, 给我们提供了阴凉处。| *They won the game by a single point.* 他们仅以一分赢了这场比赛。| *Write your answer on a single sheet of paper.* 只用一张纸写上你的答案。| **not a single** (=not even one) 一个也没有 *We didn't get a single reply to our advertisement.* 我们的广告连一个回应也没有。

2 ▶SEPARATE 分别的◀ [only before noun 仅用于名词前] considered on its own 个别的, 单独的: *the highest price ever paid for a single work of art* 为单件艺术品所支付的最高价格 | **the single most/biggest/greatest etc** *Cigarette smoking is the single most important cause of lung cancer.* 吸烟是导致肺癌的一个最重要的原因。| *The single biggest problem we face is apathy.* 我们面临的一个最大问题就是冷漠。| **every single word/day etc** *There's no need to write down every single word I say.* 没有必要把我说的每一个字都记下来。

3 ▶PEOPLE 人们◀ a) not married 未婚的, 单身的: *changes in the tax rate for single people* 适用于单身人士的税率调整 **b)** not involved in a romantic relationship 没有男[女]朋友的, 没有情侣关系的: *I never meet any attractive single men!* 我从来没有遇见过没有女朋友的英俊男子! —see also 另见 SINGLE PARENT

4 single bed/room etc meant for or used by one person only 单人床/房间等: *You have to pay extra for a single room.* 你要住单人房就得额外付费。—compare 比较 DOUBLE¹ (4) —see picture at 参见 BED¹ 图

5 ▶NOT DOUBLE 不是双重的◀ having only one part, quality etc, as opposed to having two or more 单一的, 单个的; 非双重或多重的: *Use double, not single, thread to reinforce the seams.* 要用双线而不是单线加固缝口。| *A single flower has only one set of petals.* 单瓣花只有一层花瓣。| *a single-sex school* (=either for boys or for girls, but not both) 单性别学校〔指男校或女校〕

6 ▶TICKET 票◀ *BrE* a single ticket etc is for a trip from one place to another but not back again; ONE-WAY【英】〔车票等〕单程的 —compare 比较 RETURN³ —see also 另见 SINGLY

single² *n* [C] **1** a musical record that has only one short song on each side 单曲唱片〔每面只有一首歌曲的唱片〕: *Have you heard their latest single?* 你听过他们最新的单曲唱片没有? **2 a)** a single RUN² (17) in CRICKET (2)〔板球中击球后完成一次交换位置的跑动而得的〕一分 **b)** a hit that allows the person who is hitting the ball to reach first BASE¹ (8) in BASEBALL〔棒球的〕一垒打, 安全打〔使击球手能上第一垒的击球〕**3 singles** a game, especially in tennis, played by one person against another〔尤指网球的〕单打比赛: *I prefer singles – you get more exercise.* 我更喜欢单打, 这样运动量比较大。| *Who won the women's singles?* 女子单打谁赢了? —compare 比较 **doubles** (DOUBLE² (5)) | **singles bar/club/night** (=a bar, club etc intended for people who are not married or involved in a romantic relationship) 独身者酒吧/俱乐部/晚会 **4** *BrE* a ticket for a trip from one place to another but not back again【英】单程票: *A single to Oxford, please.* 请给我一张到牛津的单程票。—compare 比较 RETURN² (9) **5** *AmE* a one dollar BILL¹ (3)【美】一美元纸币: *Anybody have five singles?* 谁有五张一元的钞票?

single³ *v*

single sb/sth ↔ **out** *phr v* [T] to choose someone or something from among a group of similar people or things, especially in order to praise them or criticize them 挑出, 选出〔人或事物以进行表扬或批评〕: *His article starts by singling out the five key goals of US foreign policy.* 他的文章一开头就突出了美国对外政策的五个重要目标。| **single sb out for praise/blame etc** *The report singles out Mr Clarke and Mr Heseltine for special criticism.* 这份报告挑出克拉克先生和赫塞尔廷先生给予特别的批评。

single-breast·ed /ˌ‥'‥◂/ *adj* a single-breasted suit has a JACKET with only one set of buttons at the front〔上衣〕单排（纽）扣的, 单襟的 —compare 比较 DOUBLE-BREASTED —see picture on page A17 参见 A17 页图

single cream /ˌ‥'ˈ/ *n* [U] thin cream that can be poured〔可以倒出的〕稀奶油 —compare 比较 DOUBLE CREAM *BrE*【英】; HEAVY CREAM *AmE*【美】

single cur·ren·cy /ˌ‥'‥/ *n* [C] a unit of money that is shared by several different countries 统一[单一]货币〔多国共用的货币单位〕: *paving the way for monetary union and a single currency in Europe* 为欧洲的币制联合和单一货币铺平道路

Single Eu·ro·pe·an Mar·ket /ˌ‥ˌ‥‥'‥/ also 又作 **the Single Market** *n* [singular] the unrestricted movement of goods and services between the countries of the European Union 欧洲单一市场〔指欧盟国家之间货物和服务行业工作的自由流动〕

single fig·ures /ˌ‥'‥/ *n* **in single figures** any number below 10 单位数, 个位数字: *Interest rates have stayed in single figures for over a year now.* 利率保持在个位数字已有一年多了。

single file /ˌ‥'ˈ/ *n* [U] moving in a line, with one behind another（成）一路纵队,（成）单行: *We walked in single file across the narrow bridge.* 我们排成一行走过狭窄的桥。—**single file** *adv*: *kids shuffling single file down the hall* 成单行沿着走廊慢慢走去的孩子

single-hand·ed /ˌ‥'‥◂/ *adj* [only before noun 仅用于名词前] done by one person without help from anyone else 单人完成的, 独力的: *a single-handed voyage across the Atlantic* 横渡大西洋的单人航行 —**single-handed, single-handedly** *adv*: *She rebuilt the house single-handed.* 她独自一人重建了这所房子。

single hon·ours /ˌ‥'‥/ *n* [U] a university degree course in Britain in which only one main subject is studied〔英国只修一门主课的〕单科学位课程 —compare 比较 JOINT HONOURS

single lane road /ˌ‥ˌ‥'ˈ/ *n* [C] *AmE* a road that is only wide enough for one car to go along it【美】单行车道

single mar·ket /ˌ‥'‥/ *n* [singular] the SINGLE EUROPEAN MARKET 欧洲单一市场

single-mind·ed /ˌ‥'‥◂/ *adj* someone who is single-minded has one clear aim and works very hard to achieve it 目的专一的, 一心一意的, 专心致志的: *Molly worked with single-minded determination, letting nothing distract her.* 莫莉对工作专心致志, 不让任何事情分心。—**single-mindedly** *adv* —**single-mindedness** *n* [U]

sin·gle·ness /ˈsɪŋglnɪs; ˈsɪŋgəlnəs/ *n* [U] *formal* **singleness of purpose** great determination when you are working to achieve something【正式】专一; 坚定不移

single par·ent /ˌ‥'‥/ *n* [C] a mother or father who looks after their children on their own, without a partner 单亲

sin·glet /ˈsɪŋglɪt; ˈsɪŋglət/ *n* [C] *BrE* a piece of clothing without SLEEVES that is worn as underwear or as a light shirt when playing some sports【英】无袖汗衫, 运动背心

single track road /ˌ‥ˌ‥'ˈ/ *n* [C] *BrE* a road that is only wide enough for one car to go along it【英】单行车道

sin·gly /ˈsɪŋglɪ; ˈsɪŋgli/ *adv* one at a time; separately 一个一个地, 各自地, 单独地: *The children walked along the beach singly or in groups of two or three.* 孩子们各自或三两成群地沿着海滩走。

Sing Sing /ˈ‥ˈ/ a prison in New York State, famous in the past for controlling prisoners very strictly 辛辛监狱〔纽约一监狱, 曾因对囚犯管教严苛闻名〕

sing·song /ˈsɪŋˌsɒŋ; ˈsɪŋsɒŋ/ *n* **1** [C] *BrE* an informal occasion when people sing songs together【英】〔非正式的〕唱歌聚会, "大家唱"; SINGALONG *AmE*【美】: *There was a bit of a singsong at the pub.* 有些人在酒馆里唱歌自娱。**2** [singular] a way of speaking in which your voice repeatedly rises and falls 说话时声音的抑扬顿挫: *She talked in a strange singsong.* 她说话时怪声怪调的。—**singsong** *adj*: *a singsong voice* 有起伏节奏的声音

sin·gu·lar¹ /ˈsɪŋgjələ; ˈsɪŋgjələ/ *adj* **1** a singular noun, verb, form etc is used when writing or speaking about one person or thing〔名词、动词等〕单数的: *If the subject is singular, use a singular verb.* 如果主语是单数, 就用动词的单数形式。**2** *formal* very great or very noticeable【正式】极大的; 突出的; 非凡的: *a woman of singular beauty* 美貌超群的女子 | *He showed a singular lack of tact in the way he handled the situation.* 他处理这件事情的方式显得极不机敏。**3** *literary* very unusual or strange【文】异常的, 奇异的: *a singular novel by an eccentric writer* 一位特立独行的作家写的怪异小说

singular² *n* [C] the form of a word used when writing or speaking about one person or thing〔词的〕单数形式

sin·gu·lar·i·ty /ˌsɪŋgjəˈlærətɪ; ˌsɪŋgjəˈlærəti/ *n* **1** [C] *technical*【术语】**a)** another word for a BLACK HOLE black hole 的另一种说法 **b)** a set of events that do not obey the usual laws of nature, especially the events that happened at the BIG BANG

(=beginning of the universe)〔宇宙开端时的〕奇点〔指不遵循已知自然规律而发生的事件〕**2** [U] *old-fashioned* strangeness【过时】异常, 奇怪, 奇特

sin·gu·lar·ly /ˈsɪŋgjələ˞lɪ; ˈsɪŋgjʊləli/ *adv formal*【正式】**1** very noticeably 突出地; 异常地: *a singularly beautiful woman* 非常漂亮的女子 | *a singularly unsuccessful attempt to gain publicity* 一次为博得名声的极不成功的尝试 **2** *old-fashioned* in an unusual way; strangely【过时】奇异地, 奇特地

Sin·ha·lese /ˌsɪnhəˈliz; ˌsɪnhəˈliːz◂/ *n* [C] **1** a person from one of the groups of people who live in Sri Lanka〔斯里兰卡的〕僧伽罗人 **2** one of the languages of Sri Lanka 僧伽罗语 —**Sinhalese** *adj*

sin·is·ter /ˈsɪnɪstə˞; ˈsɪnɪ̀stə/ *adj* making you feel that something evil, wrong, or illegal is happening or will happen 不祥的, 凶兆的; 阴险的, 邪恶的: *a sinister figure lurking in the shadows* 埋伏在阴影中的邪恶身影 | *a sinister looking mask* 样子凶恶的面具 | *Was it all a cover-up for more sinister activities?* 那是不是为了掩盖更加险恶的阴谋活动?

W3 **sink**[1] /sɪŋk; sɪŋk/ *v past tense* **sank** /sæŋk; sæŋk/ or **sunk** /sʌŋk; sʌŋk/ *past participle* **sunk**

1 ►IN WATER 在水里◄ a) [I] to go down below the surface of water, mud etc 沉, 下沉, 沉没: *The Titanic sank after hitting an iceberg.* "泰坦尼克"号撞到冰山后沉没。| *If you put it in water, will it float or sink?* 如果你把它放在水中, 它会浮起来还是沉下去? | *The heavy guns sank up to their barrels in the mud.* 这些沉重的枪支在泥里直陷到枪管。**b)** [T] to damage a ship so badly that it sinks 使〔船〕沉没: *Three ships were sunk that night by enemy torpedoes.* 那天夜里有三艘船被敌人的鱼雷击沉。

2 ►MOVE LOWER 降低◄ [I] **a)** to move downwards to a lower level 下降〔至某一高度〕, 降低: *It was several days before the flood waters sank and life returned to normal.* 几天之后洪水才退去, 生活于是恢复了正常。| *Her head sank onto her chest as she dozed off in her chair.* 她在椅子上打瞌睡, 脑袋垂到胸前。**b)** to fall down or sit down heavily, especially because you are very tired and weak〔尤指因疲倦或无力〕倒下, 颓然坐下: **[+into/on/down etc]** *Sinking down on the bed, she tried to collect her thoughts.* 她倒在床上, 努力集中思绪。| **sink to your knees** (=fall into a kneeling position) 下跪 *The prisoner sank to his knees, begging for mercy.* 那个囚犯跪下乞求宽恕。

3 ►SUN/MOON 太阳/月亮◄ [I] to move downwards in the sky, and disappear from sight 落下, 下沉: *The sun was sinking behind the coconut palms.* 太阳在椰子树后渐渐落下。

4 ►CHANGE/GET WORSE 改变/变坏◄ [I always+adv/prep] to gradually pass into a different state, especially one that is worse 衰退, 恶化: **sink into crisis/despair/decay etc** *The Soviet economy was sinking deeper and deeper into crisis.* 苏联经济陷入越来越深的危机。| *neglected buildings sinking into decay* 日渐衰败、无人管理的楼房 | **be sinking fast** (=getting weaker and about to die) 越来越虚弱, 濒临死亡 *By this time, she was sinking fast and there was little we could do for her.* 到这时, 她的病情急剧恶化, 我们也回天乏术。

5 ►LOWER AMOUNT/VALUE 数量减少/价值降低◄ [I] to go down in amount or value〔数量、价值等〕减少, 降低: *The population had sunk to a few dozen families.* 那里的人口已经减到几十户了。| *efforts by the central banks to prop up the sinking dollar* 各中央银行为支撑正在贬值的美元所作的努力

6 ►QUIET 安静◄ [I] if your voice sinks you start talking more quietly〔声音〕降低: *Holmes's voice sank as he revealed the truth about the murders.* 福尔摩斯在揭露那些谋杀案的真相时说话声音很低。| **sink into silence** *moaning and crying out in pain, and finally sinking into silence* 痛苦地呻吟和喊叫, 后来终于陷入寂静

7 your heart sinks/your spirits sink to lose hope or confidence, especially when you feel unable to do everything that you have to do 心情沉重/情绪低落〔失去信心或希望〕: *The journey seemed never-ending, and her spirits sank lower.* 旅程好像没完没了, 她的情绪更加低落了。| *I realized, with a sinking heart, that I had forgotten to post that vital letter.* 我发现我竟忘了寄出那封重要的信件, 我的心直往下沉。

8 that sinking feeling *informal* the unpleasant feeling that you get when you suddenly realize that something bad is going to happen【非正式】不安的感觉: *I had that sinking feeling you get when you know you've made a huge mistake.* 我当时心乱如麻, 那就是当一个人意识到自己犯了大错时的感觉。

9 be sunk a) *informal* to be in a situation when you are certain to fail or have a lot of problems【非正式】陷入麻烦: *If we can't find a taxi we'll really be sunk.* 如果我们找不到出租车, 那就真的麻烦了。**b) be sunk in gloom/misery/apathy etc** to be so unhappy, tired etc that you feel completely unable to improve your situation 陷于忧愁/痛苦/麻木不仁等: *He wandered around aimlessly all day, then returned home sunk in gloom.* 他整天漫无目的地到处闲逛, 然后心情一片灰暗地回到家里。

10 sink without trace a) if a ship sinks without trace, it sinks and no one knows where it has sunk〔船〕沉没后无影无踪 **b)** if someone sinks without trace, they disappear mysteriously and you never hear about them again〔人〕神秘地消失, 销声匿迹: *Actors who quarrelled with their studios just seemed to sink without trace.* 一些影星跟制片公司争吵后好像就消失得无影无踪了。

11 sink so low/sink to doing sth to be dishonest enough or selfish enough to do something very bad or unfair 不老实[自私]到这种地步/干出这种事来: *Cheating his own sister – how could he have sunk so low?* 骗他自己的妹妹, 他怎能干出这种事来?

12 sink your teeth/claws/knife etc into sth to put your teeth or something sharp into someone's flesh, into food etc 用牙咬/用爪子抓/用刀子捅等: *The dog sank its teeth into my arm.* 那条狗狠狠地咬了我的手臂。

13 sink a well/hole/mine etc to dig a deep hole in the ground 挖井/挖洞/开矿等

14 ►MONEY 钱◄ [T] to lend or spend a lot of money on a business, in the hope of making more money in the future; INVEST 投入, 投下〔资金〕: **sink sth in/into** *They had sunk most of their savings into a property venture.* 他们把大部分积蓄投资于房地产生意。

15 ►BALL 球类◄ [T] to hit a ball into a hole in games such as GOLF or SNOOKER〔高尔夫球、斯诺克等〕将〔球〕击入洞中[袋中]

16 sink your differences to agree to stop arguing and forget about your disagreements, especially in order to unite and oppose someone else 摒弃分歧, 摒除歧见〔尤指为了联合对付别人〕

17 sink or swim to suceed or fail without help from anyone else 沉浮全凭自己, 无论成功或失败也无人援手: *They don't give you a lot of guidance – you're just left to sink or swim, really.* 他们不会给你很多指导。你失败或成功只能靠你自己, 真的。

18 ►DRINK 喝酒◄ [T] *BrE informal* to drink alcohol, especially in large quantities【英, 非正式】喝〔酒, 尤指痛饮〕: *We sank a few pints at the pub first.* 我们先在酒馆里痛饮了几品脱的啤酒。

sink in *phr v* [I] if information, facts etc sink in, you gradually understand them or realize their full meaning 逐渐被充分理解: *For a moment her words didn't sink in.* 有一会儿, 她的话不能被人们完全理解。| *The stupidity of what I had done began to sink in with an awful finality.* 等我开始意识到了自己所做的蠢事之后, 坏事已成定局。

sink[2] *n* [C] **1** *BrE* a large open container, especially in a kitchen, that you fill with water and use for washing dishes etc【英】〔尤指厨房的〕洗涤槽: *Dirty plates were piled high in the sink.* 脏盘子在洗涤槽里堆得很高。—see picture on page A10 参见 A10 页图 **2** *AmE* an open container in a kitchen or bathroom that you can fill with water and use for washing yourself, washing dishes etc【美】〔厨房的〕洗涤槽; 〔浴室的〕洗脸池 —see also 另见 **everything but the kitchen sink** (EVERYTHING (6))

sinker —see 见 **hook, line and sinker** (HOOK[1] (7))

sinking fund /ˈ·· ,·/ *n* [C] *technical* money saved regularly by a business to pay for something in the future【术语】〔公司储备的〕偿债基金

sin·ner /ˈsɪnə˞; ˈsɪnə/ *n* [C] *especially biblical* someone who has sinned (SIN) by not obeying God's laws【尤圣经】〔违犯上帝律法的〕罪人, 有罪过者

Sinn Féin /ˌʃɪn ˋfen; ˌʃɪn ˈfeɪn/ *n* [singular] an Irish political party, active especially in Northern Ireland, which wants Northern Ireland to become part of the Republic of Ireland. It is sometimes called the 'political wing of the IRA'. From the mid-1990s, Sinn Fein had an active part in the 'peace process' (=the attempts to achieve a peaceful solution to the problems of Northern Ireland) under its president Gerry Adams. 新芬党〔爱尔兰一政党, 尤其在北爱尔兰较为活跃。该党要求北爱尔兰加入爱尔兰共和国。新芬党有时被称为"爱尔兰共和军的政治组织"。20世纪90年代中期起, 新芬党在格里·亚当斯主席的领导下在"和平进程"中发挥了积极作用〕

Sino- /ˈsaɪno; ˈsaɪnəʊ/ *prefix* **1** of China; Chinese 中国的; 中国人的 **2** Chinese and 中国与…的: *Sino-Japanese trade* 中日贸易

si·nol·o·gy /saɪˋnɑlədʒɪ; saɪˈnɒlədʒi/ *n* [U] *technical* the study of Chinese language, history, literature etc【术语】汉学〔对中国的语言、历史、文学等的研究〕

sin·u·ous /ˈsɪnjuəs; ˈsɪnjuəs/ *adj* smoothly curving and twisting, like the movements of a snake 蜿蜒的, 弯弯曲曲的, 迂回的: *a dance with sinuous movements* 婀娜多姿的舞蹈 | *the river's sinuous course* 河流的迂回

si·nus /ˈsaɪnəs; ˈsaɪnəs/ *n* [C] one of the hollow spaces filled with air in the bones of your face that have an opening in your nose 窦〔颅骨中与鼻孔相通的空穴〕

sip¹ /sɪp; sɪp/ *v* [I,T] to drink something slowly, taking very small mouthfuls 小口地喝,〔慢慢地〕饮, 啜, 呷: *She was sitting at the bar sipping a Martini.* 她坐在吧台旁啜着马蒂尼酒。| [+at] *Kruger sipped at his whisky thoughtfully.* 克鲁格若有所思地啜着威士忌酒。

sip² *n* [C] a very small amount of a drink 一小口〔饮料〕, 一啜之量: **take a sip (of)** *George took another sip of coffee.* 乔治又啜了一口咖啡。

si·phon¹, syphon /ˈsaɪfən; ˈsaɪfən/ *n* [C] **1** a bent tube used for getting liquid out of a container, by holding the other end of the tube at a lower level than the container 虹吸管 **2** also 又作 **soda siphon** *BrE* a kind of bottle for holding SODA WATER that is forced out of the bottle using gas pressure【英】〔以气体压力压出苏打水的〕苏打水瓶

siphon², syphon *v* [T always+adv/prep] **1** to remove liquid from a container by using a siphon 用虹吸管吸出: **siphon sth off/out/into etc** *I siphoned some gasoline out of the tank.* 我用虹吸管从油箱中吸出一些汽油。**2** to dishonestly take money from a business, account etc to use it for a purpose for which it was not intended〔非法地〕抽调〔资金等〕, 挪用: **siphon sth off/from etc** *Corrupt officials had been siphoning off public funds for private business ventures.* 贪官污吏一直在挪用公款进行私人商业投资。| *I later found she had siphoned thousands of dollars from our bank account.* 我后来发现她私自从我们的银行账户调走了数千美元。

3 **sir** /sə; sə strong 强读 sɜ; sɜː/ *n* **1** *spoken* a way of addressing a man, for example a male customer in a shop or a military officer that shows respect【口】先生, 阁下; 长官〔对男子的敬称, 例如店员对顾客, 士兵对长官等〕: *"Report back to me in an hour, sergeant." "Yes, sir."* "一小时后向我报告, 中士。" "是, 长官。" | *Can I help you, sir?* 我能为你效劳吗, 先生? —compare 比较 MADAM (1) *BrE*【英】; MA'AM *AmE*【美】 **2** *AmE spoken* used to get the attention of a man whose name you do not know【美口】先生〔用于引起一个不知其名的男子的注意〕: *Sir! You dropped your wallet!* 先生! 你的钱包掉了! —compare 比较 MA'AM **3** **Dear Sir** used at the beginning of a formal letter to a man 敬启者〔对男子的称呼, 用于正式信函的开头〕**4** **Sir** a title used before the first name of a KNIGHT or BARONET 爵士〔冠于爵士或准男爵名字之前的尊称〕: *Sir James Wilson* 詹姆斯·威尔逊爵士 | *Sir Jasper* 贾斯珀爵士 **5** *BrE spoken* used by children at school as a way of addressing or talking about a male teacher【英口】老师〔中小学生对男教师的直接或间接称呼〕: *Sir, I've forgotten my homework.* 老师, 我忘了做家庭作业。| *Look out – sir's coming back!* 当心, 老师回来了! —compare 比较 MISS² (2) **6** **no sir!** also 又作 **no siree!** *AmE old-fashioned spoken* used to emphasize that you do not want something, will not accept something etc【美, 过时, 口】绝不接受, 绝不: *I will not have that man in my home, no sir!* 我不要那个人待在我家里, 绝对不行!

sire¹ /saɪr; saɪə/ *n* **1** *old use* a way of addressing a king【旧】陛下〔对国王的尊称〕: *The people await you, sire.* 臣民在恭候您, 陛下。**2** [C usually singular 一般用单数] *technical* the father of a four-legged animal, especially a horse【术语】〔马等四足动物的〕雄性种兽, 种马

sire² *v* [T] **1** to be the father of an animal, especially a horse〔尤指雄马〕生殖, 繁殖: *a stallion that has sired several race winners* 繁殖了好几匹赛马冠军的雄种马 **2** *old-fashioned or humorous* to be the father of a person【过时或幽默】为〔人〕之父

si·ren /ˈsaɪrən; ˈsaɪərən/ *n* [C] **1** a piece of equipment that makes very loud warning sounds, used on police cars, fire engines etc〔警车、消防车等的〕汽笛, 警报器: *police sirens wailing in the distance* 警车的警报器在远处呜呜地响 **2** **siren voices/call/song** *literary* encouragement to do something that sounds very attractive, but will have bad results【文】诱人犯错的声音/号召/歌声: *The government must ignore the siren voices calling for a cut in interest rates.* 政府绝不能听信那些要求降低利率的谗言。**3** a word used especially in newspapers meaning a woman who is very attractive but also dangerous to men 妖艳而危险的女人, 妖妇〔尤用于报刊〕: *Hollywood sirens like Marilyn Monroe* 像玛丽莲·梦露一样的好莱坞性感女星 **4** **the Sirens** a group of women in ancient Greek stories, whose beautiful singing made sailors sail towards them into dangerous water 塞壬〔古希腊故事中用美妙歌声引诱水手进入危险水域的一群女海妖〕

Sir Ga·wain and the Green Knight /sə ˌgɑwen ənd ðə ˌgrin ˈnaɪt; sə ˌgɑːweɪn ənd ðə ˌgriːn ˈnaɪt/ a long English poem written in the 14th century by an unknown poet. It is about Gawain, a brave knight in the time of King Arthur, and his adventures with a mysterious green knight.《高文爵士和绿衣骑士》〔14世纪一首英文长诗, 作者佚名。讲述的是亚瑟王时期一位名叫高文的勇敢骑士与一位神秘的绿衣骑士的冒险经历〕—see also 另见 ARTHURIAN LEGEND

Sir·han Sir·han /sɚˌhæn sɚˈhæn; sɜːˌhɑːn sɜːˈhɑːn/ (1944-) a man from Jordan who murdered the US politician Robert F. Kennedy, the brother of President John F. Kennedy, in 1968, when Robert Kennedy was trying to become president 西尔汉〔(1944-), 约旦人。他于1968年刺杀了约翰·F.肯尼迪的弟弟罗伯特·F.肯尼迪〕

sir·loin /ˈsɚlɔɪn; ˈsɜːlɔɪn/ also 又作 **sirloin steak** /ˌ‥ ˈ·/ *n* [C, U] expensive meat cut from a cow's lower back 牛腰肉, 牛里脊肉; 西冷牛扒

si·roc·co /səˈrɑko; sɪ̣ˈrɒkəʊ/ *n* [C] a hot wind blowing from the desert of North Africa across to southern Europe 西罗科风〔由北非沙漠吹向南欧的一种热风〕

sir·rah /ˈsɪrə; ˈsɪrə/ *n old use* an angry and disrespectful way of addressing a man【旧】小子, 家伙〔对男子表示生气或轻蔑的称呼〕

sis /sɪs; sɪs/ *n spoken especially AmE* used when speaking to your sister【口, 尤美】姐姐; 妹妹〔用于称呼自己的姊妹〕

Sis·sing·hurst /ˈsɪsɪŋhɚst; ˈsɪsɪŋhɜːst/ a castle in Kent, southern England, with beautiful gardens, which were designed by its owner, the writer Vita Sackville-West 锡辛赫斯特堡〔英格兰南部肯特郡一城堡, 以身为作家的主人维塔·萨克维尔－韦斯特设计的美丽花园闻名〕

sis·sy, cissy /ˈsɪsɪ; ˈsɪsi/ *n* [C] *informal* a boy that other boys dislike because he prefers doing things that girls enjoy【非正式】女孩子气的男孩〔为其他男孩所看不起〕: *David played with dolls and used to get called a sissy by the other kids.* 戴维喜欢玩洋娃娃, 所以曾被其他小孩叫做娘娘腔的男孩。—**sissy** *adj*

sis·ter /ˈsɪstɚ; ˈsɪstə/ *n* [C] **1** a girl or woman who has the same 1 1
parents as you 姊妹; 姐姐; 妹妹: *Janet and Abigail are sisters.* 珍妮特和阿比盖尔是两姐妹。| *He has three sisters and two brothers.* 他有三个姊妹和两个兄弟。—see picture at 参见 FAMILY 图 **2** also 又作 **Sister** *BrE* a nurse in charge of a hospital WARD¹ (1)【英】护士长: *I'm feeling a bit better today, Sister.* 我今天觉得好些了, 护士长。| *the night sister* 夜班护士 **3** also 又作 **Sister** a NUN 修女: *Good morning, Sister Mary.* 早上好, 玛丽修女。**4** **sister company/organization/ship etc** a company etc that belongs to the same group or organization 姊妹公司/组织/船等: *the Daily Express and its sister paper the Daily Star* 《每日快报》及其姊妹报《每日星报》**5** *AmE spoken* a way of addressing a woman, used especially by African Americans【美口】〔尤指美国黑人对女子的称呼〕大姐, 小妹, 小姐 **6** a word used by women to talk about other women and to show that they have feelings of friendship and support towards them 姊妹〔妇女对其他妇女表示友好和支持时的用语〕: *We have to support our sisters in southern Africa.* 我们一定要支持我们在南非的姐妹们。

sis·ter·hood /ˈsɪstɚhud; ˈsɪstəhʊd/ *n* **1** [U] a special, loyal relationship among women who share the same ideas and aims, especially among FEMINISTS〔尤指女权主义者之间的〕姐妹关系[情谊] **2** [C] a group of women who live a religious life together 修女会, 女修道会

sister-in-law /ˈ· · · ˌ·/ *plural* **sisters-in-law** or **sister-in-laws** *n* [C] **1** the sister of your husband or wife 姑子, 姨子〔夫或妻的姊妹〕**2** your brother's wife 嫂子, 弟媳〔兄或弟的妻子〕**3** the wife of the brother of your husband or wife 妯娌〔配偶的兄弟之妻〕—see picture at 参见 FAMILY 图

sis·ter·ly /ˈsɪstɚlɪ; ˈsɪstəli/ *adj* typical of a loving sister 姊妹的, 亲如姊妹的: *sisterly affection* 姊妹般的爱 —**sisterliness** *n* [U]

Sis·tine Chap·el, the /ˌsɪstin ˈtʃæpl; ˌsɪstiːn ˈtʃæpəl/ a chapel in the Vatican, Rome, famous for the paintings on its ceiling done by Michaelangelo, which many people consider one of the most impressive works of art in Europe 西斯廷礼拜堂〔罗马梵蒂冈一礼拜堂, 以天顶上米开朗琪罗的绘画作品闻名, 这些画被认为是欧洲最引人入胜的艺术作品〕

Si·su·lu /sɪˈsulu; sɪ̣ˈsuːluː/, **Wal·ter** /ˈwɔltɚ; ˈwɔːltə/ (1912-2003) a South African civil rights worker and the first full-time Secretary General of the African National Congress. He was in prison for 25 years for his opposition to APARTHEID. 席苏鲁〔(1912-2003), 南非民权工作者, 非洲人国民大会第一位全职秘书长。他因反对种族隔离制度而被监禁25年〕

Sis·y·phus /ˈsɪsɪfəs; ˈsɪsɪ̣fəs/ in ancient Greek stories, an evil king whose punishment after death was to roll a very large stone to the top of a steep hill. Each time he got near to the top of the hill, the stone rolled down to the bottom, and he had to start again, and he had to continue doing this forever. A very difficult job that seems impossible to finish is sometimes de-

scribed as a ‘Sisyphean task’. 西绪福斯〔古希腊神话中的邪恶国王。他死后所受的惩罚是将一块巨石推上陡峭的山顶。每次将达到山顶时，巨石又滚回到山脚下，他只得从头再来，如此重复永无止境。人们有时把一件看似无法完成的艰难任务称为“西绪福斯的任务”〕

sit 坐

sitting on a chair 坐在椅子上

sitting at a desk 坐在书桌旁

sitting in an armchair 坐在扶手椅里

sit /sɪt; sɪt/ *v past tense and past participle* **sat** /sæt; sæt/ *present participle* **sitting**

1 ▶IN A CHAIR ETC 在椅子上等◀ **a)** [I] to be on a chair or seat, or on the ground, with the top half of your body upright and your weight resting on your BUTTOCKS 坐: **[+on/in/by etc]** *sitting in a comfortable armchair* 坐在一张舒适的扶手椅里 | *We all sat around the campfire and sang songs.* 我们大家围坐在营火边唱歌。| *She's the girl that sits next to me in my math class.* 她是在数学课上坐我旁边的女同学。| **sit at a desk/table etc** (=sit facing it) 面向桌子坐 *Harry sat at his desk and stared out of the window.* 哈里坐在书桌前，凝望着窗外。| **sit doing sth** *We sat watching TV for a while.* 我们坐着看了一会儿电视。| **sit still** *I wish you children would sit still for 5 minutes.* 我希望你们这些孩子能安静地坐五分钟。**b)** [I always+adv/prep] to get to a sitting position after you have been standing up 坐下: *Jim walked over and sat beside her.* 吉姆走过来，在她身旁坐下。**c)** [T always+adv/prep] to make someone sit down or help them to sit down 使坐下，使就座: **sit sb down/on/in etc** *I sat him down in the armchair by his bed.* 我让他坐在床边的扶手椅里。

2 ▶OBJECTS/BUILDINGS ETC 物件/楼房等◀ [I always+adv/prep] to lie or be placed in a particular position 在某位置，位于，坐落在: **[+on/in etc]** *"Where's my coat?" "It was sitting on the bottom of the stairs last time I saw it."* “我的上衣在哪里?”“我上次见到它是在楼梯脚上。” | *a village sitting on the side of a hill* 坐落在山腰处的村庄 | *When I got to work I found a huge bunch of flowers sitting on my desk.* 我上班时发现一大束花摆在我的桌子上。

3 ▶DO NOTHING 不干事◀ [I always+adv/prep] to stay in one place for a long time, especially sitting down, doing nothing useful or helpful 闲(坐)着: *I spent half the morning sitting in a traffic jam.* 我遇上塞车，在车里待了半个上午。| *Well, I can't sit here chatting all day.* 好了，我可不能整天坐在这儿闲扯。| *She just sits there complaining all day.* 她就会整天坐在那里发牢骚。

4 ▶COMMITTEE/PARLIAMENT ETC 委员会/议会等◀ [I] **a)** to be a member of a committee, parliament, or other official group 占议席；当委员；担任职务: **[+in/on]** *She sits on several government committees.* 她担任政府里好几个委员会的委员。| *Their father sits in the National Assembly.* 他们的父亲在国民议会任职。**b)** to have a meeting in order to carry out official business〔官方机构〕开会；开庭: *The council only sits once a month.* 该委员会每月只开一次会。| *The court will sit until all the evidence has been heard.* 法院将一直开庭到所有证词都陈述完毕为止。

5 sit tight a) to stay where you are and not move 留在原处，(稳坐)不动: *If your car breaks down, just sit tight and wait for the police.* 如果你的汽车抛锚，你就留在原地等待警察到来。**b)** to stay in the same situation, and not change your mind and do anything new 坚持立场；不改变主意: *We're advising all our investors to sit tight till the market improves.* 我们奉劝所有投资者不要动摇，等待市场复苏。

6 be sitting pretty to be in a very good or favourable position 处于有利地位: *With profits up by over 80%, the company is sitting pretty.* 这家公司利润增长超过80%，生意很好。

7 sit in judgment on/over to give your opinion about whether someone has done something wrong, especially when you have no right to do this 对…进行评论〔尤指妄加评论〕，指手画脚

8 sit on sb's tail to drive very close behind a car, especially because you are waiting for a chance to pass it 紧跟在一辆汽车后面〔尤指因等待机会超车〕

9 ▶ANIMAL/BIRD 兽类/鸟类◀ [I always+adv/prep] **a)** to be in, or get into, a resting position, with the tail end of the body resting on a surface〔兽或鸟〕尾巴着地而坐，栖息: *The cat likes to sit on the wall outside the kitchen.* 这只猫喜欢坐在厨房外的墙头上。**b)** if a bird sits on its eggs, it covers them with its body to make the eggs HATCH〔鸟类〕孵蛋

10 ▶PICTURE/PHOTO 画像/照片◀ **[I+for]** to sit somewhere so that you can be painted or photographed 坐着让人画像[照相]

11 ▶LOOK AFTER 照看◀ **[I+for]** to look after a baby or child while its parents are out; BABYSIT 代人临时照看孩子

12 ▶EXAMS 考试◀ **[I+for**,T] *BrE* to take an examination【英】参加〔考试〕，参加…的考试: *Tracy's sitting her GCSEs this year.* 特蕾西准备参加今年的普通中学教育证书考试。

sit around/about *phr v* [I] to spend a lot of time sitting and doing nothing very useful 闲坐，无所事事: *We used to just sit around for hours talking about the meaning of life.* 我们过去常常一坐几个小时，讨论生活的意义。

sit back *phr v* [I] **1** to settle yourself in a comfortable chair and relax 轻松地坐在椅子上: *You sit back and watch TV – I'll wash up.* 你去轻轻松松地坐下看电视，我来洗碗。**2** to relax and make no effort to get involved in something or influence what happens 不采取行动，袖手旁观: *Don't just sit back and wait for new business to come to you.* 你可不能只是悠闲地等待新业务来找你呀。| *All we have to do now is sit back and watch the checks roll in.* 我们现在只要舒舒服服地坐看支票滚滚而来就行了。

sit down *phr v* [I] **1** to be in a sitting position or get into a sitting position 坐着；坐下: *Come over here and sit down!* 到这边来坐下！| *If you work sitting down, you need to take plenty of exercise.* 如果你都是坐着工作，你就需要大量的体育锻炼。| **sit yourself down** *spoken*【口】*Come in Sally, sit yourself down.* 进来，萨莉，坐吧。**2 sit down and ...** to try to solve a problem or deal with something that needs to be done, by giving it all your attention 坐下来〔专心解决或认真研究〕: *I think we need to sit down and analyse these figures properly.* 我想我们有必要坐下来好好分析分析这些数字。| *Maybe if you sat down and talked it through you could reach an agreement.* 要是你们坐下来好好谈谈，也许就能达成一致的意见。

sit in *phr v* [I] **1** to be present at a meeting but not take an active part in it 列席，旁听: **[+on]** *Do you mind if I sit in on some of the interviews?* 如果我来旁听几场面试，你介意吗？**2** to do a job, go to a meeting etc instead of the person who usually does it 代理〔某人的〕工作；代表〔某人〕出席会议: **[+for]** *This is Alan James sitting in for Suzy Williams on the mid-morning show.* 我是艾伦·詹姆斯，代替苏齐·威廉斯主持今天上午10点钟的节目。**3** to take part in a SIT-IN (=kind of protest) 参加静坐示威

sit on sth *phr v* [T] *informal* to delay dealing with something【非正式】拖延不办，搁置: *I sent my application about six weeks ago and they've just been sitting on it.* 我大约六周前就把申请寄去了，可他们就是一直压着不办。

sit sth ↔ **out** *phr v* [T] to stay where you are until something finishes, especially something boring or unpleasant 坐到〔不快之事等〕结束，一直等到…过去: *We forced ourselves to sit the play out.* 我们逼着自己坐在那里，直到那出戏演完。| *rich businessmen who had sat the war out comfortably in South Africa* 舒适地住在南非等着战争结束的富商们

sit through sth *phr v* [T] to attend a meeting, performance etc, and stay until the end, even if it is very long and boring 一直坐到〔会议、演出等〕结束: *As a councillor, you have to sit through endless planning meetings.* 作为政务委员，你就非得待到那些没完没了的计划会议结束不可。

sit up *phr v* **1** [I] to be in a sitting position or get into a sitting position after you have been lying down 坐起来: *By the time I got there he was sitting up in bed and reading a book.* 我到那里时，他已经在床上坐着看书了。| *At this, Faye sat up and flung aside the bed covers.* 一听这话，费伊从床上坐了起来，把被子掀到一边。**2** [T **sit** sb **up**] to help someone to sit after they have been lying down 帮助〔某人〕坐起来 **3** [I] to sit in a chair with your back up straight 坐直，端坐: *Just sit up straight and stop*

slouching. 坐直身子, 别无精打采的了。**4** [I] to stay up very late 熬夜: *Sometimes we just sit up and watch videos all night.* 有时我们通宵熬夜看录像。**5 make sb sit up (and take notice)** to do something surprising or impressive that makes someone pay attention to you 使某人惊讶; 引起某人的注意: *a fantastic performance that made all the critics sit up and take notice* 使所有评论家都大感兴趣的精彩表演

USAGE NOTE 用法说明: SIT

WORD CHOICE 词语辨析: **sit, sit at/in front of/on/in, sit down, seat, be seated**

You **sit at** a table, piano, or desk (unless you choose to **sit on** them!), and also **at** a computer or the controls of a car or plane. However, you sit **in front of** the television or the fire (though you can also sit *by* or *around* a fire). 如果要说"坐在桌子、钢琴或书桌前"就用sit at ... (真的要说"坐在…上面", 那就用 sit on ...)。要说"坐在电脑前或汽车、飞机等的操纵器之前", 也用 sit at ...。但"坐在电视机或火炉前"要用sit in front of ...。表示"坐在火炉前"或"围炉而坐"还可以用 sit by ... 或 sit around...。

You **sit on** something that has a flat, level surface such as the floor, the grass, a simple chair or seat, a bench, or a bed. 表示坐在表面平坦的东西〈如地板、草地、椅子、长凳或床〉上面, 用 sit on ...。

You **sit in** a tree, long grass, a car, a room, a corner, an armchair, the driving seat of a car. 表示"坐在树上, 坐在长的草丛中, 坐在汽车、房间、角落、扶手椅里"或"坐在汽车驾驶座位上", 用 sit in ...。

When you are talking about the action of moving from standing to sitting, it is more common to use **sit down** rather than **sit** on its own. 如果谈的是从站姿到坐姿的动作变化, 比较普通的用语是 sit down 而不只是 sit: *They quietly sat down again.* (NOT usually 一般不用 *sat again*). 他们又安静地坐了下来。*Please sit down!* 请坐(下来)! You usually only say *Sit!* to a dog. Sit! 通常只在对狗发命令时说。

Note that **seat** as a verb is only transitive, is a little formal, and is used in these ways 注意 seat 作为动词只有及物的用法, 文体也比较正式, 其用法见下面例句: *This hall will seat 100 people* (=has seats for 100 people). 这个大厅可以容纳 100 人。| *They seated us at the front* (=put us in seats at the front). 他们请我们在前排就座。

Be seated is a formal expression for **sit down**. be seated 是 sit down 的正式表达法。At a formal dinner for example, you might hear 例如在正式晚宴上会听到: *Please be seated* (=please sit down). 请就座。

sit·com /ˈsɪtkɑm; ˈsɪtkɒm/ *n* [C,U] a popular type of television or radio entertainment consisting of a series of amusing stories about the same set of characters 情境喜剧, 连续单元喜剧〔一种以固定人物为中心, 故事相对独立的流行电视或广播喜剧〕

sit-down /ˈ· ·/ *adj* **1 sit-down meal/dinner/lunch etc** a meal served to people sitting at a table〔由服务员端上〕坐在饭桌边吃的一顿饭/晚餐/午餐等: *a sit-down meal for 20 people* 供 20 人吃的一顿饭 **2 sit-down strike/protest** a protest in which people sit down, especially to block a road or other public place, until their demands are listened to〔尤指在道路等公共场所举行的〕静坐罢工/静坐抗议

W2 **site**[1] /saɪt; saɪt/ *n* [C] **1** a place where something important or interesting happened〔重要事件发生的〕场所, 遗址, 地方: *an archaeological site* 考古现场 | [**+of**] *the site of the Battle of Waterloo* 滑铁卢战役遗址 **2** an area of ground where something is being built or will be built〔建筑的〕工地, 用地: *a construction site* 建筑工地 | [**+of**] *the site of a proposed missile base* 计划中的导弹基地 **3 camp/camping/caravan site** *especially BrE* a piece of ground where you can camp【尤英】露营场所/拖车式活动房屋停泊场地

site[2] *v* **be sited** be placed or built in a particular place 坐落于, 建于〔选定地点〕: [**+in/near etc**] *The new factory is to be sited in Fort Collins.* 按计划新工厂将建于柯林斯堡。

sit-in /ˈ· ·/ *n* [C] a type of protest in which people refuse to leave the place where they work or study until their demands are agreed to 静坐示威: **hold/stage a sit-in** *Students staged a sit-in to protest about experimentation on animals.* 学生们举行静坐示威, 抗议用动物进行实验。

sit·ter /ˈsɪtɚ; ˈsɪtə/ *n* [C] **1** someone who sits or stands somewhere so that someone else can paint them or take photographs of them 坐着供人画像[拍照]的人,〔供画家或摄影师画像或拍照的〕模特儿 **2** *especially AmE* a BABYSITTER【尤美】代人临时照看小孩的人

sit·ting /ˈsɪtɪŋ; ˈsɪtɪŋ/ *n* [C] **1** one of the times when a meal is served in a place where there is not enough space for everyone to eat at the same time〔分批接待用餐的其中〕一批: *The first sitting is at 12:30, and the second is at 1:30.* 第一轮的开饭时间为 12:30, 第二轮为 1:30。**2** an occasion when you have yourself painted or photographed (一次) 坐着供人画像或照相 (的时间) **3** a meeting of a law court or parliament〔法庭〕开庭;〔议会〕开会 **4 at/in one sitting** during one continuous period when you are sitting in a chair 持续坐着: *I sat down and read the whole book in one sitting.* 我坐下来, 一口气看完了这本书。

Sitting Bull /ˌ·· ˈ·/ (1834-90) a native American chief of the Sioux tribe who helped Crazy Horse to win a victory over General Custer's army of US soldiers in the battle at the Little Bighorn in 1876. He later performed in Buffalo Bill's Wild West Show. 坐牛〔(1834-1890), 印第安苏族酋长。1876 年, 他协助"疯马"与卡斯特将军领导的美军在小比格霍恩河作战, 并取得了一次胜利。后来, 他曾在"野牛比尔"的荒蛮西部演艺会上表演节目〕

sitting duck /ˌ·· ˈ·/ *n* [C] someone who is easy to attack or easy to cheat 易被击中的目标, 易被攻击者; 易上钩者: *Out in the open, the soldiers were sitting ducks for enemy fire.* 在毫无掩蔽的地方, 士兵容易被敌人的炮火击中。

sitting mem·ber /ˌ·· ˈ··/ *n* [C] *BrE* someone who is a member of a parliament at the present time【英】现任议员: *the sitting member for Newbury* 纽伯里的现任议员

sitting room /ˈ·· ·/ *n* [C] *especially BrE* the room in a house where you sit, relax, watch television etc; LIVING ROOM【尤英】起居室, 客厅

sitting ten·ant /ˌ·· ˈ··/ *n* [C] *BrE* someone who lives in a rented house or flat, especially when this gives them legal rights to stay there【英】〔房屋或公寓的〕承租人, 现住房客, 现任租户

sit·u·ate /ˈsɪtʃuˌet; ˈsɪtʃueɪt/ *v* [T] *formal* to describe or consider something as being part of something else or connected with something else【正式】认定…为…的部分; 说明[认为]…与…有联系; 将…置于某环境中: **situate sth in** *Freud situates the origins of these anxieties in the subconscious.* 弗洛伊德认为这些焦虑起源于潜意识。

sit·u·at·ed /ˈsɪtʃuˌetɪd; ˈsɪtʃueɪtɪd/ *adj* **1 be situated** to be in a particular place or position 位于…的, 坐落在…的: *a small town situated just south of Cleveland* 地处克利夫兰南边的小镇 | **beautifully/conveniently/pleasantly situated** *All the apartments are beautifully situated overlooking the beach.* 所有的公寓都环境优美, 俯瞰海滨。**2 be well/badly situated** to be in a particular situation 境况良好/处境困难: *Microsoft is well situated to exploit this new market.* 微软具备良好的条件开拓这个新市场。

sit·u·a·tion /ˌsɪtʃuˈeʃən; ˌsɪtʃuˈeɪʃən/ *n* [C] **1** a combination of all the things that are happening and all the conditions that exist at a particular time in a particular place 形势, 情况, 状况: *In the present situation, I wouldn't advise you to sell your house.* 在目前情况下, 我不建议你把房子卖掉。| *You're putting me in a very awkward situation.* 你使我陷于非常尴尬的境地。| *I'd better go and see the boss and explain the situation.* 我最好去见老板, 把情况向他解释一下。| *With no rain for three months and food supplies running out, the situation here is getting desperate.* 三个月无雨, 食品供应也将消耗殆尽, 这里的情况越来越危急了。| **the economic/political/financial situation** *In view of the company's financial situation, there will be no salary increases this year.* 鉴于公司的财务状况, 今年将不会加薪。| **fire situation/crisis situation etc** *especially spoken*【尤口】*We are unlikely to have a full-employment situation this year.* 今年不大可能出现全体就业的情况。| **no-win situation** (=a situation which will end badly, whichever choice you make) 必败的局面 **2** a word meaning the kind of area where a building is situated, used especially by people who sell or advertise buildings 环境, 位置〔尤用于房地产广告〕: *The house is in a charming situation, on a wooded hillside.* 这座房子位于林木茂密的山坡上, 环境优美迷人。**3** *old-fashioned* a job【过时】工作, 职位: *She managed to get a situation as a parlour maid.* 她设法找到了一份做女仆的工作。 S1 W1

situation com·e·dy /ˌ···· ˈ···/ *n* [C,U] *formal* a SITCOM【正式】情境喜剧, 连续单元喜剧

Situations Va·cant /ˌ···· ˈ··/ *n* [singular] *BrE* the title of the part of a newspaper where jobs are advertised【英】〔报刊的〕招聘广告栏, 招聘启事

sit-up /ˈ· ·/ *n* [C] an exercise in which you sit up from a lying position, while keeping your feet on the floor 仰卧起坐

Si·va /ˈsivə; ˈsiːvə/ also 又作 **Shiva** one of the three main gods in the Hindu religion. People see him as both 'the Destroyer'

and 'the Creator' of the universe 湿婆〔印度教三大主神之一。该神既是宇宙的毁灭者，又是宇宙的创造者〕—see also 另见 BRAHMA, VISHNU

six /sɪks; sɪks/ *number* **1** 6〔数字〕六 **2 it's six of one and half a dozen of the other** *spoken* used to say there is not much difference between two possible choices, situations etc【口】半斤八两，不相上下 **3 at sixes and sevens** *BrE informal* disorganized and confused【英，非正式】乱七八糟；七上八下；杂乱无章：*When the visitors arrived we were still at sixes and sevens.* 客人到来时我们这儿还是乱七八糟的。**4** a hit in the game of CRICKET, worth six runs (RUN² (17)), in which the ball goes beyond the edge of the playing area before touching the ground〔板球〕得六分的击球[安打]〔球落地前飞出球场〕—**sixth** *number*: *our sixth child* 我们的第六个孩子

six·fold /ˈsɪksˌfold; ˈsɪksfəʊld/ *adv* by six times as much or as many 六倍：*Burglaries have increased sixfold.* 入屋盗窃案已经增加了六倍。—**sixfold** *adj*: *a sixfold increase in teenage pregnancies* 青少年怀孕数字的六倍增加

six-foot·er /ˌ·ˈ··/ *n* [C] *informal* someone who is at least six feet (1.83 metres) tall【非正式】身高六英尺(1.83米)以上的人

six-pack /ˈ· ·/ *n* [C] six CANs or bottles of a drink, especially beer, sold together as a set〔尤指啤酒等饮料的〕六罐[瓶]包装，半打装：*There's a six-pack in the fridge.* 冰箱里还有一盒半打装的。

six·pence /ˈsɪkspəns; ˈsɪkspəns/ *n* [C,U] a small silver-coloured coin worth six old pennies (PENNY), used in Britain until 1971, or this amount of money〔1971年以前英国的〕六便士(硬币)

six-shoot·er /ˈ· ˌ··/ *n* [C] *old-fashioned, especially AmE* a small gun holding six bullets【过时，尤美】六发手枪，六响手枪

six·teen /sɪksˈtin; ˌsɪkˈstiːn◂/ *number* 16〔数字〕十六 —**sixteenth** *number*

six·teenth /sɪkˈstinθ; ˌsɪkˈstiːnθ◂/ *n* [C] one of sixteen equal parts of something 十六分之一

sixteenth note /ˈ·· ˌ·/ *n* [C] *AmE* a musical note which continues for a sixteenth of the length of a WHOLE NOTE【美】〔音乐的〕十六分音符；SEMIQUAVER *BrE*【英】—see picture at 参见 MUSIC 图

sixth /sɪksθ; sɪksθ/ *n* [C] one of six equal parts of something 六分之一：*About one sixth of the children admitted to taking drugs.* 大约六分之一的儿童承认吸毒。

sixth form /ˈ· ·/ *n* [C] the highest level in the British school system, for students, usually aged between 16 and 18, who are preparing to take A LEVELs (=the highest level of exams) 六年级，中六〔英国中学的最高年级，一般在16至18岁之间〕—**sixth former** *n* [C]

sixth form col·lege /ˈ· ·, ˌ··/ *n* [C] a type of school in Britain for students over the age of 16 六年级学校，预科学校〔英国为16岁以上学生开设的学校〕

sixth sense /ˌ·ˈ·/ *n* [singular] a special feeling or ability to know things without using any of your five ordinary senses such as your hearing or sight 第六感官，第六感，直觉：*A sixth sense told me that I was in danger.* 我凭直觉感到自己有危险。

six·ties /ˈsɪkstɪz; ˈsɪkstiz/ *n* [plural] **1 the sixties** also 又作 **the '60s** the years from 1960 to 1969 1960年至1969年期间，60年代 **2 in your sixties** aged from 60 to 69 60岁至69岁之间，六十多岁：**early/late sixties** *I'd say she was in her late sixties.* 我认为她已经年近70了。**3** the numbers from 60 to 69, especially when used to measure temperature〔尤指气温〕60度至69度之间，六十多度：**the low sixties/the upper sixties** *a fine spring day with the temperature in the upper sixties* (=about 68 or 69 degrees) 气温将近70度的一个晴朗春日

CULTURAL NOTE 文化注释

The sixties are remembered as being a time of great social change, when young people in many Western countries began developing a new set of values and opinions that were very different from the traditional ones their parents had. Young people, especially students, took part in political protests against the Vietnam War and against war in general. People began to become more concerned about equal rights for women and for people of different races. In the US and UK young people began using drugs for pleasure, and they also had much more sexual freedom than their parents, especially because of 'the pill' (see Cultural Note at PILL). The music and clothes of the period also expressed their new ways of thinking. The UK was an important centre of music and fashion and, because of this, people sometimes talk about the 'swinging sixties'. Some people, especially politicians, now criticize the sixties as a time when many traditional ideas, for example regarding marriage or education, were replaced by modern ideas, and these people blame the sixties for many of today's social problems. Other people see the sixties as a time of freedom, enjoyment, and social progress. 人们记忆中的20世纪60年代是社会发生翻天覆地变化的时代，在这一时期很多西方国家的年轻人开始形成一套新的价值观念体系，与他们父辈的传统观念差别很大。年轻人，尤其是学生，投入到反抗越南战争和其他一切战争的政治运动中。人们开始关注给予女性和不同种族人群平等的权利。在美国和英国，年轻人开始吸食毒品取乐寻欢。他们比起父辈也有了更多的性自由，特别是避孕药的使用更是起到推波助澜的作用(见 PILL 文化注释)。这一时期的音乐和着装也是年轻人新思维方式的表达。英国是音乐和时尚的重要中心，人们有时会因为这个而谈起"放浪多变的60年代"。现在有人，特别是政治家批判60年代是传统观念被现代观念颠覆的时代，例如在婚姻和教育方面。他们把当今社会的很多问题都归咎于60年代。也有人认为60年代是自由、享受和社会进步的时代。— see also HIPPIE, PERMISSIVE SOCIETY and see Feature on page F9 另见 HIPPIE, PERMISSIVE SOCIETY 并见 F9 页文化特写

six·ty /ˈsɪkstɪ; ˈsɪksti/ *number* 60〔数字〕六十 —**sixtieth** *number*

sixty-four-thou·sand-dol·lar ques·tion /ˌ·· ˌ·· ˌ·· ˈ··/ *n* [singular] *informal* the most important question, which you do not know the answer to【非正式】最重要的问题，关键问题：*But will they accept the offer? That's the sixty-four-thousand-dollar question.* 但是他们会接受这个建议吗？这可是关键问题。

CULTURAL NOTE 文化注释

This expression started to be used because of a television game show (=a show in which people play games or answer questions to win prizes). The PRESENTER (=person who asks the questions) used these words just before he asked the last and most difficult question. 这一表达法的使用源于电视有奖游戏或有奖问答节目。(负责提问的)主持人在问最后一个、也是最难的问题时会先说这句话。

Sixty Min·utes /ˌ·· ˈ··/ a US television news programme made by CBS, which deals with several subjects in detail in each programme《时事60分》〔美国一电视新闻节目。由哥伦比亚广播公司制作，每期节目详细报道几个时事主题〕

siz·a·ble /ˈsaɪzəbl̩; ˈsaɪzəbəl/ *adj* another spelling of SIZEABLE sizeable 的另一种拼法

size¹ /saɪz; saɪz/ *n*

1 ►HOW BIG 有多大◄ [C,U] how big or small something is 大小，尺寸，规模：*The American states vary enormously in size and population.* 美国各州的面积大小和人口数量悬殊很大。| *The firm underestimated the size of the market for their new product.* 公司低估了他们的新产品的市场。| **be the size of** (=be the same size as) 和…同样大小 *There were rats the size of cats.* 有些老鼠和猫一样大。| *He's a small boy, about John's size.* 他是个小个子男孩，个头和约翰差不多。| *Their apartment is half the size of ours.* 他们的公寓有我们的一半大。| **that size/this size** (=as big as that/this) 和那个/这个一样大 *In a class this size, there are bound to be a few trouble-makers.* 在一个这样大的班里，难免会有几个调皮捣蛋的学生。| **in all/different/various shapes and sizes** *They make these replacement windows in all shapes and sizes.* 他们所生产的这类替换窗备有各种形状和尺寸。| **full size** (=the biggest size that something usually is) 通常的最大尺寸 *He's quite a big dog, but he's still not full size yet.* 它是一只体形很大的狗，但它还没有完全长大。| **be a good/fair/nice size** (=be fairly big) 相当大的 *The garden's a pretty good size.* 这花园相当大。| *It's a nice size bedroom.* 这间卧室相当大。

2 ►VERY BIG 很大的◄ [U] the fact of being very big 大，巨大：*You should have seen the size of their car!* 你该看看他们的汽车有多大！| **sheer size** *What offends people is the sheer size of these pay increases.* 触怒人们的是这些巨额的工资增长。

3 ►CLOTHES/GOODS 衣服/商品◄ [C] one of a set of standard measures according to which clothes and other goods are produced and sold 尺码，型，号：*These shoes are one size too big.* 这双鞋子大了一码。| *The shirts come in three sizes, small, medium, and large.* 这些衬衣分三种尺码：小号，中号，大号。| **size 8/16 etc** *I take size 10 shoes.* 我穿10号鞋。

4 large-sized/medium-sized etc large in size etc 大号/中号等的：*a medium-sized car* 中型汽车 | **bite-sized** (=small enough

to be eaten easily) 一口一个的 *Cut the meat into bite-sized chunks.* 把肉切成一口一个的小块。
5 try sth for size to try something, especially clothing, to see if it is the right size for you 试穿, 试用〔尤指对衣物试穿以确定尺寸是否合适〕
6 to size if you cut, make, or prepare something to size, you make it the right size for a particular use 成为合适的尺寸: *Cut the tile to size and fix it to the wall with adhesive.* 把瓷砖切成合适的尺寸, 用黏合剂粘到墙上。
7 that's about the size of it *spoken* used to agree that what someone has said about a situation is a good or correct way of describing it【口】(大体) 就是这么一回事, 实际情况 (大致) 就是这样
8 ▶GLUE 胶◀ [U] a thick sticky liquid used for giving stiffness and a shiny surface to paper, cloth etc 胶料, 浆料〔用于使纸张、布料等挺直而有光泽〕—see also 另见 **cut sb down to size** (CUT DOWN (5))

size² *v* [T] **1** to sort things according to their size 按大小把…分类: *Shrimp are sized for canning into large, medium and small.* 虾被分成大、中、小三类来做罐头。**2** to cover or treat something with SIZE¹ (8) 给…上浆[上胶]
size sth/sb ↔ **up** *phr v* [T] to look at or consider a person or situation and make a judgment about them 估计, 估量, 判断: *It only took a few seconds for her to size up the situation.* 她只花了几秒钟就对情况作出判断。

size·a·ble, sizable /ˈsaɪzəbḷ; ˈsaɪzəbəl/ *adj* fairly large 相当大的: *a sizeable cash payment* 数目庞大的现金支付

Size·well /ˈsaɪzwɛl; ˈsaɪzwəl/ a NUCLEAR power station in Suffolk, eastern England. There are two power stations there, the older Sizewell A and the newer Sizewell B. 塞斯韦尔〔英格兰东部萨福克郡的一核电站。该地有两座核电站, 先建的称"塞斯韦尔 A", 后建的称"塞斯韦尔 B"〕

siz·zle /ˈsɪzḷ; ˈsɪzəl/ *v* [I] to make a sound like water falling on hot metal〔像水落在烧热的金属上〕发嗞嗞声: *The steak was sizzling on the barbecue.* 肉排在烤架上嗞嗞作响。—**sizzle** *n* [singular] —see picture on page A19 参见 A19 页图

siz·zler /ˈsɪzlɚ; ˈsɪzələ/ *n* [C] *informal* a very hot day【非正式】大热天: *Yesterday was a real sizzler!* 昨天真是个大热天!

siz·zling /ˈsɪzlɪŋ; ˈsɪzəlɪŋ/ *adj especially AmE* very hot【尤美】很热的: *It's sizzling in the sun.* 太阳底下非常热。

SJ a written abbreviation used after a priest's name, to show that he is a JESUIT 耶稣会〔用于神职人员的名字后, 表示他是耶稣会会士〕

ska /skɑ; skɑː/ *n* [U] a kind of popular music from the West Indies with a fast regular beat, similar to REGGAE 斯卡音乐〔一种源于西印度群岛的节奏明快的音乐, 与"雷盖"音乐相似〕

skag, scag /skæg; skæg/ *n* [U] *slang* HEROIN【俚】海洛因

skate¹ /sket; skeɪt/ *n* **1** [C] one of a pair of boots with metal blades on the bottom, for moving quickly on ice; ICE-SKATE² (溜) 冰鞋 **2** [C] one of a pair of boots or frames with small wheels on the bottom, for moving quickly on flat smooth surfaces; ROLLER SKATE 四轮旱冰鞋 **3** [C,U] *plural* **skate** *or* **skates** a large flat sea fish that can be eaten 鳐〔一种可食用的扁平大海鱼〕**4 get/put your skates on** *BrE spoken* used to tell someone to hurry【英口】〔用于催促别人〕赶快, 赶紧: *Put your skates on, or you'll be late for school.* 动作快点, 不然你上学要迟到了。

skate² *v* [I] **1** to move on skates 滑冰, 溜冰: *The children skated on the frozen pond.* 孩子们在结冰的池塘上滑冰。**2 be skating on thin ice** *informal* to be doing something that may get you into trouble【非正式】做冒险的事 —**skater** *n* [C]
skate over/around sth *phr v* [T] to avoid mentioning a problem or subject, or not give it enough attention 避免提起〔某问题等〕, 把〔问题等〕轻轻带过, 回避: *The President was accused of skating over the issue of the homeless.* 总统因在无家可归者的问题上轻描淡写而受到指责。

skate·board /ˈsket͵bɔrd; ˈskeɪtbɔːd/ *n* [C] a short board with two small wheels at each end, which you can stand on and ride as a sport 滑板 —**skateboarding** *n* [U]

skat·ing /ˈsketɪŋ; ˈskeɪtɪŋ/ *n* [U] the activity or sport of moving on skates 滑冰, 溜冰: **go skating** *Zelda's going skating in the afternoon.* 泽尔达准备下午去溜冰。

skating rink /ˈ‥ ͵·/ *n* [C] a place or building where you can SKATE² (1) 滑冰场, 溜冰场

ske·dad·dle /skɪˈdædḷ; skɪˈdædl/ *v* [I] *spoken humorous* to leave a place quickly, especially because you do not want to be caught【口, 幽默】逃跑, 仓皇逃窜

skeet shoo·ting /ˈskit ͵ʃutɪŋ; ˈskiːt ͵ʃuːtɪŋ/ *n* [U] *AmE* the sport of shooting at clay objects that have been thrown into the air【美】飞靶射击, 打飞靶; CLAY PIGEON SHOOTING *BrE*【英】

Skeg·ness /͵skɛgˈnɛs; ͵skegˈnes◂/ a town on the east coast of England which is a popular place especially for working class people from central England to go for a day or for their holidays 斯凯格内斯〔英格兰东海岸一镇。英格兰中部的工薪阶层尤其喜欢去那里消闲一日或度假〕

skein /sken; skeɪn/ *n* [C] a long loosely wound piece of thread, wool, or YARN (1)〔线、纱等的〕一束, 一绞

skel·e·tal /ˈskɛlətəl; ˈskelɨtəl/ *adj* like a skeleton or connected with a skeleton 骨骼的, 像骨骼的: *the skeletal bodies of the starving people* 饥民们骨瘦如柴的身躯

skeleton 骨骼

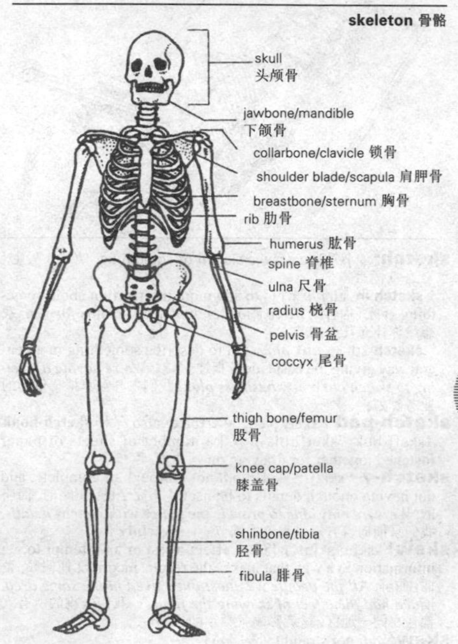

skel·e·ton /ˈskɛlətn̩; ˈskelɨtən/ *n* [C]
1 ▶BONES 骨◀ a) the structure consisting of all the bones in a human or animal body〔人体或动物的〕全副骨骼: *the human skeleton* 人体骨骼 **b)** a set of these bones or a model of them, fixed in their usual positions, used for example by medical students〔医学研究用的〕骷髅, 骨架; 骨架模型
2 ▶MAIN PART 主要部分◀ the most important parts of something, to which more detail can be added later 骨架, 框架; 梗概, 纲要: **[+of]** *It is just a skeleton of the report, showing the three basic points.* 这只是报告的梗概, 提出了三个要点。
3 ▶THIN 瘦的◀ *informal* an extremely thin person or animal【非正式】骨瘦如柴的人[动物]: *The prisoners were just skeletons.* 这些囚犯真是骨瘦如柴。
4 a skeleton in the cupboard/closet *informal* an embarrassing or unpleasant secret about something that happened to you in the past【非正式】不可外扬的家丑, 隐私, 秘密
5 skeleton staff/service only enough to keep an operation or organization running 最基本的人员 / 服务: *British Rail is operating a skeleton service on Christmas Day.* 英国铁路公司在圣诞节只提供最基本的服务。

skeleton key /ˈ‥‥ ͵·/ *n* [C] a key made to open a number of different locks 万能钥匙

skep·tic /ˈskɛptɪk; ˈskeptɪk/ *n* [C] the American spelling of SCEPTIC sceptic 的美式拼法

skep·ti·cal /ˈskɛptɪkəl; ˈskeptɪkəl/ *adj* the American spelling of SCEPTICAL sceptical 的美式拼法

skep·ti·cism /ˈskɛptə͵sɪzəm; ˈskeptɨsɪzəm/ *n* [C,U] the American spelling of SCEPTICISM scepticism 的美式拼法

sketch¹ /skɛtʃ; sketʃ/ *n* [C] **1** a simple, quickly-made drawing that does not show much detail 素描, 速写; 草图: *First she makes a sketch of a scene and then she paints it.* 她先画一幅风景素描, 然后上颜料。**2** a short humorous scene on stage, television

etc that is part of a larger show〔舞台、电视等上的〕滑稽短剧: *Her TV programme is made up of a series of comic sketches.* 她的电视节目是由一系列滑稽短剧组成的。**3** a short written or spoken description 短篇描写, 随笔; 简介, 梗概: *a brief sketch of the main weaknesses of the British economy* 对英国经济主要弱点的简述

sketch 素描

sketch² *v* [I,T] to draw a sketch of something〔给…〕写生,〔给…〕画素描

sketch in sth *phr v* [T] to add more information about something 补充〔内容〕: *I'd like to sketch in a few details for you.* 我想给你补充几点细节。

sketch sth ↔ **out** *phr v* [T] to describe something in a general way giving the basic ideas 概述; 草拟: *We're having a meeting to sketch out a new business plan.* 我们在开会草拟一份新的业务计划。

sketch·pad /ˈskɛtʃˌpæd; ˈsketʃpæd/ also 又作 **sketch·book** /ˈskɛtʃˌbʊk; ˈsketʃbʊk/ *n* [C] a number of sheets of paper fastened together for drawing on 写生簿, 素描簿

sketch·y /ˈskɛtʃɪ; ˈsketʃi/ *adj* not thorough or complete, and not having enough details to be useful 不完全的, 粗略的, 简略的: *We were only able to provide the police with sketchy details.* 我们只能向警方提供粗略的细节。—**sketchily** *adv*

skew¹ /skju; skjuː/ *v* [T] to affect a test or an attempt to get information in a way that makes the results incorrect 使偏颇; 歪曲, 曲解: *All the people we questioned lived in the same area, which had the effect of skewing the figures.* 我们查询的所有人都住在同一地区, 这就影响了数字的准确性。

skew² *adj* not straight〔歪〕斜的

skew·bald /ˈskjuˌbɔld; ˈskjuːbɔːld/ *n* [C] a horse with large white and brown shapes on it 有大片白色和棕色斑点的马, 杂色马, 花斑马 —**skewbald** *adj*

skewed /skjud; skjuːd/ *adj* **1** an opinion, piece of information, result etc that is skewed is incorrect, especially because you do not know all the facts〔看法等〕偏颇的, 不正确的〔尤因对事实掌握不全〕: *The results of a telephone poll will always be skewed since those who do not have phones are obviously excluded.* 电话民意调查的结果总会有偏颇, 因为没有电话的人明显地被排除在外。**2** something that is skewed is not straight and is higher on one side than the other 歪〔斜〕的, 倾斜的: *The picture on the wall was slightly skewed.* 墙上的画稍微有点歪。

skew·er¹ /ˈskjuɚ; ˈskjuːə/ *n* [C] a long metal or wooden stick for putting through pieces of meat while cooking them〔金属或木棍做的〕串肉扦, 烤肉叉

skewer² *v* [T] to make a hole through a piece of food, an object etc with a skewer or with something similar〔用烤肉叉或类似东西〕把…串起来: *Grant skewered bits of meat and put them on the barbecue.* 格兰特用烤肉叉把肉片串好放到烤架上。—see picture on page A11 参见 A11 页图

skew-whiff /ˌ· ˈ·◂/ *adj BrE informal* not straight【英, 非正式】不正的, 歪斜的: *The top of the bookcase is skew-whiff.* 书橱顶是歪的。

ski¹ /ski; skiː/ *n plural* **skis** [C] **1** one of a pair of long thin narrow pieces of wood or plastic that you fasten to your boots and use for moving on snow 滑雪板 **2** a piece of strong material shaped like a ski under a small vehicle so that it can travel on the snow〔滑雪车等的〕滑橇

ski² *v past tense and past participle* **skied** *present participle* **skiing** [I] to move on skis for sport or in order to travel on snow 滑雪: *I'm learning to ski.* 我在学滑雪。| **go skiing** *We went skiing in Colorado last winter.* 去年冬天我们去科罗拉多州滑雪了。—see also 另见 SKIER

CULTURAL NOTE 文化注释

In both the US and the UK, skiing holidays are popular in the winter. In the US people tend to buy or rent special homes in the mountains, and go skiing in places such as the Rocky Mountains or Vermont. In the UK people often buy a PACKAGE HOLIDAY (where the price includes travel, food, a place to stay etc), and go to France, Switzerland, or Austria. There are also some ski RESORT*s* in Scotland, such as Aviemore and Glencoe. 在美国和英国, 冬季的滑雪度假都很受人青睐。在美国, 人们会在山区购买或租赁特别的房屋, 然后到落基山或佛蒙特州等地去滑雪。在英国, 人们常选择去法国、瑞士和奥地利等地的包价度假游〔价格中包含游览、食宿等〕。苏格兰也有一些滑雪胜地, 例如阿维莫尔和格伦科。

ski·bob /ˈskiˌbab; ˈskiːbɒb/ *n* [C] a vehicle like a bicycle with skis instead of wheels〔形状像自行车的〕滑雪车, 雪车

ski boot /ˈ· ·/ *n* [C] a specially made boot that fastens onto a ski 滑雪鞋[靴]

skid¹ /skɪd; skɪd/ *v* **skidded, skidding** [I] if a vehicle or wheel skids, it suddenly slides sideways and you cannot control it〔车辆或车轮〕打滑, 失控滑向一侧: *The wheels of the truck skidded on the wet snow.* 货车的轮子在湿雪地上打滑。

skid² *n* **1** [C] a sudden uncontrollable sliding movement of a vehicle〔车辆的〕打滑: *She could hear the skid of the car as it went around the corner.* 她可以听到车子拐弯时打滑的声音。| **go into a skid** (=start skidding) 开始打滑 *He slammed on the brakes and we went into a long skid.* 他猛然煞车, 我们的车子向前滑了很远。| **skid marks** *The only sign of the crash were the skid marks on the road.* 撞车事故的唯一痕迹是路面上车轮的打滑印迹。**2 on the skids** *informal* being in a situation that is bad and getting worse【非正式】处境越来越坏的: *He's been on the skids since losing his job.* 他丢了工作以后境况越来越糟。**3 put the skids under** *informal* to make it likely or certain that something will fail【非正式】使…失败: *The recession put the skids under his plans for starting a new business.* 经济衰退使他难以实现开新店的计划。**4** [C] a part that is underneath some aircraft used in addition to wheels for landing on〔某种飞机的〕起落橇, 滑橇: *helicopter skids* 直升机起落橇 **5** [usually plural 一般用复数] a piece of wood that is put under a heavy object to lift or move it〔支承重物的〕垫木;〔使重物易于滑动的〕滑动垫木

skid·pan /ˈskɪdˌpæn; ˈskɪdpæn/ *n* [C] *BrE* a special slippery surface where drivers can practise controlling skidding cars【英】滑面试车场〔供驾驶者练习控制打滑车辆的特制路面〕

skid row /ˌskɪd ˈro; ˌskɪd ˈrəʊ/ *n* [U] **be on skid row** *informal* if someone is on skid row, they drink too much and have no job, nowhere to live etc【非正式】〔失业酒徒〕无家可归, 流落街头

ski·er /ˈskiɚ; ˈskiːə/ *n* [C] someone who skis (SKI²) 滑雪者

skies /skaɪz; skaɪz/ *n* the plural form of SKY

skiff /skɪf; skɪf/ *n* [C] a small light boat for one person〔单人划或驾驶的〕小艇, 轻舟

skif·fle /ˈskɪfəl; ˈskɪfəl/ *n* [U] *especially BrE* a type of popular music played in the 1950s and often using instruments made by

ski 滑雪

skiing 滑雪

snowboarding 单板滑雪

the players themselves【尤英】即兴演奏的爵士乐〔20世纪50年代的一种流行音乐, 其乐器常由演奏者自制〕

ski·ing /ˈskiːɪŋ; ˈskiːɪŋ/ *n* [U] the sport of moving down hills or across the countryside in the snow, wearing SKIs 滑雪运动

ski jump /ˈ· ·/ *n* [C] **1** a competition in which people wearing SKIs jump off a cliff at the bottom of a slope to see how far they can go through the air 跳台滑雪比赛 **2** a steep slope ending in a cliff, used for ski jump competitions 跳台滑雪助滑道

skil·ful *BrE*【英】, usually 一般作 **skillful** *AmE*【美】/ˈskɪlfəl; ˈskɪlfəl/ *adj* **1** good at doing something, especially something that needs special ability or training 有技术的, 熟练的, 灵巧的: *a skilful team player* 技巧娴熟的队员 **2** made or done very well and cleverly 显示技巧的; 制作精良的: *her skilful handling of a difficult problem* 她处理难题的熟练技巧 | *the skilful use of sound effects* 音响效果的巧妙运用 —**skilfully** *adv*

ski lift /ˈ· ·/ *n* [C] a piece of equipment that carries SKIERs up to the top of a slope〔运送滑雪者上到坡顶的〕滑雪索道, 滑雪缆车

[3] [1] **skill** /skɪl; skɪl/ *n* [C,U] an ability to do something well, especially because you have learned and practised it〔尤指经学习和实践而得到的〕技能, 技巧, 技艺: *Reading and writing are two different skills.* 阅读和写作是两种不同的技能。| *You need computing skills for that job.* 你必须掌握电脑技能以胜任那份工作。| **[+at/in]** *I admired his skill at driving.* 我佩服他的驾驶技术。| **with great skill/with a lot of skill** *The whole team played with great skill and determination.* 整支球队都表现出纯熟的技巧和争胜的决心。

skilled /skɪld; skɪld/ *adj* **1** someone who is skilled has the training and experience that is needed to do something well 有技巧的, 熟练的: *Skilled craftsmen, such as carpenters, bricklayers, etc, are in great demand.* 熟练工匠如木工、砖瓦匠等都很需要。| **highly skilled** *a highly skilled negotiator* 老练的谈判手 | **[+at/in]** *She's very skilled at dealing with members of the public.* 她和公众打交道很有一套。**2** work that is skilled needs special abilities or training in order to do it〔工作〕需要技能的, 要有熟练能力的: *Bricklaying is very skilled work.* 砌砖是一项需要高度技能的工作。—opposite 反义词 UNSKILLED

skil·let /ˈskɪlɪt; ˈskɪlɪ̱t/ *n* [C] a flat heavy cooking pan with a long handle 长柄平底煎锅 —see picture at 参见 PAN[1] 图

skill·ful /ˈskɪlfəl; ˈskɪlfəl/ *adj* an American spelling of SKILFUL skilful 的美式拼法

skim /skɪm; skɪm/ *v* **skimmed, skimming** **1** [T] to remove floating fat or solids from the surface of a liquid 从液体表面撇去〔漂浮的油脂或固体物质〕: **skim sth off/from** *After simmering the meat and vegetables skim the fat from the surface.* 把那些肉和蔬菜炖好后, 再撇去表面的油脂。**2** [I,T] to read something quickly to find the main facts or ideas in it〔为掌握大意的〕略读, 浏览: *She skimmed the sports page to find out who had won the game.* 她浏览体育新闻版, 想知道谁赢了那场比赛。| **skim through sth** *Just skim through the second section to save time.* 只略读第二部分以节省时间。**3** [T] to move along quickly, nearly touching a surface 飞快掠过, 擦过: *seagulls skimming the waves* 掠过浪尖的海鸥 **4 skim stones/pebbles etc** *BrE* to throw smooth, flat stones into a lake, river etc in a way that makes them jump across the surface【英】〔用扁石等在水面〕打水漂 —compare 比较 SKIP[1] (8) **5** [T] *AmE* to take money illegally, especially by not saying that you have made profits so that you do not have to pay tax【美】〔为逃税而〕瞒报〔收入〕; 非法捞到〔钱〕

skim sb ↔ **off** *phr v* [T] to take and keep for yourself the best people, the most money etc 挖走〔最优秀的人〕; 选取〔精华〕; 〔通过瞒报而〕捞走〔大部分的钱〕: *Professional sport skims off all the best players.* 职业体育运动会把最优秀的选手都挖走。

skimmed milk /ˌ· ˈ·/ *n* [U] milk that does not contain much fat because the cream has been removed from it 脱脂(牛)奶

skim·mer /ˈskɪmɚ; ˈskɪmə/ *n* [C] **1** a kitchen tool with holes in it, used for removing solids from the surface of a liquid 撇沫器, 漏勺 **2** a sea bird that flies low over the sea 掠水鸥, 剪嘴鸥〔在海面上低飞的海鸟〕

skimp /skɪmp; skɪmp/ *v* [I,T] to not spend enough money or time on something, or not use enough of something, so that what you do is unsuccessful or of bad quality 舍不得花〔足够的钱、时间等〕, 克扣, 少给: **[+on]** *It's vital not to skimp on staff training.* 对员工培训不能吝啬, 这点十分重要。

skimp·y /ˈskɪmpɪ; ˈskɪmpi/ *adj* **1** a skimpy dress or skirt etc is very short and does not cover very much of your body〔衣、裙等〕太短[小]的; 过分暴露的 **2** not providing enough of something 不足的; 吝啬的, 过分节省的: *a skimpy meal* 不够吃的一顿饭 —**skimpily** *adv* —**skimpiness** *n* [U]

skin[1] /skɪn; skɪn/ *n* [2] [2]

1 ▶BODY 身体◀ [C,U] **a)** the natural outer layer of a human or animal body〔人或动物的〕皮, 皮肤: *Babies have beautifully soft skin.* 婴儿皮肤细嫩。| *amphibians with their smooth, moist skins* 皮肤光滑湿润的两栖动物 | *a skin disease* 皮肤病 | **fair/dark skin** *Madhur was beautiful with her thick black hair and smooth dark skin.* 玛德赫有一头浓密的黑发, 皮肤光滑呈深色, 非常漂亮。**b)** the skin on your face 脸部的皮肤: *Some soaps just seem to dry my skin up.* 有几种香皂好像会使我脸上的皮肤变得干燥。| **bad skin** (=unhealthy-looking skin) 看起来不健康的皮肤 —see also 另见 SKINCARE

2 dark-skinned/fair-skinned/smooth-skinned etc having dark skin, smooth skin etc 皮肤黑的/白皙的/光滑的等: *If you are very fair-skinned you should avoid going in the sun too much.* 如果你肤色很白, 就不应过多地去晒太阳。—see also 另见 **have a thick skin** (THICK[1] (11))

3 ▶ANIMAL SKIN 兽皮◀ [C,U] the skin of an animal, used as leather, fur etc 皮革, 毛皮, 兽皮: *a tiger skin* 一张虎皮 | *a sheepskin jacket* 羊皮夹克

4 ▶FOOD 食物◀ [C,U] **a)** the natural outer cover of some fruits and vegetables〔某些水果和蔬菜的〕皮, 外皮: *banana skins* 香蕉皮 | *onion skin* 洋葱皮 **b)** the outer cover of a SAUSAGE〔香肠的〕肠衣 **c)** a thin solid layer that forms on the top of a liquid when it gets cold or is left uncovered〔液体冷却后或置于空气中时形成的〕薄层: *Cover the soup to stop a skin from forming.* 把汤盖上以免结一层皮。

5 by the skin of your teeth *informal* if you do something by the skin of your teeth, you only just succeed in doing it【非正式】好不容易才…, 差点就没…, 勉强: *We woke up late and caught the plane by the skin of our teeth.* 我们起床迟了, 差点没赶上飞机。

6 get under sb's skin *informal* if someone gets under your skin, they annoy you, especially by the way they behave【非正式】激怒某人: *What really gets under my skin is people who push straight to the front of the line.* 真正叫我恼火的是那些径直跑到前面去插队的人。

7 be skin and bone *informal* to be extremely thin in a way that is unattractive and unhealthy【非正式】瘦得皮包骨: *Tania was all skin and bone when she got back from her world tour.* 塔妮娅周游世界回来时瘦得皮包骨。

8 it's no skin off my nose *spoken* used to say that you do not care what someone else thinks or does because it does not affect you【口】我根本不在乎, 我才不管呢: *Well, I offered to help out, but if she doesn't want me to, it's no skin off my nose!* 我已经提出要帮助她, 但是她如果不想我帮助, 我才不在乎呢! —see also 另见 **save sb's skin** (SAVE[1] (10)), **jump out of your skin** (JUMP[1] (4))

skin[2] *v* **skinned, skinning** [T] **1** to remove the skin from an animal, fruit, or vegetable 剥去…的皮: *Add the tomatoes, skinned and sliced.* 把去了皮和切成片的番茄加进去。**2** to hurt yourself by rubbing off some skin 擦破…皮, 擦伤…的皮: *She skinned her knee when she fell off her bike.* 她从自行车上摔下来时擦破了膝盖。**3 skin sb alive** *humorous* to punish someone very severely【幽默】严厉惩罚某人, 活剥某人的皮: *I'll skin him alive if I get hold of him!* 如果我抓住他就活剥了他的皮! **4** *AmE informal* to completely defeat someone【美, 非正式】彻底击败: *The football team really skinned Watertown last year.* 该足球队去年彻底击败了沃特敦队。

skin up *phr v* [I] *BrE slang* to make a cigarette with MARIJUANA in it【英俚】制香烟时掺进大麻

skin·care /ˈskɪnˌkɛr; ˈskɪnkeə/ *adj* skincare products are intended to improve the condition of your skin, especially the skin on your face〔尤指对脸部皮肤〕护肤的, 润肤的 —**skincare** *n* [U]

skin-deep /ˌ· ˈ·◂/ *adj* [not before noun 不用于名词前] something that is skin-deep seems to be important or real, but in fact it is not because it only affects the way things appear 肤浅的, 表面的: *Beauty is only skin deep.* 美貌只是表面的。

skin-div·ing /ˈ· ˌ· ·/ *n* [U] the sport of swimming under water with light breathing equipment but without a protective suit〔不穿潜水衣的〕潜水[泳], 裸潜 —**skin-diver** *n* [C]

skin·flint /ˈskɪnˌflɪnt; ˈskɪnˌflɪnt/ *n* [C] *informal* someone who hates spending money or giving it away; MISER【非正式】吝啬鬼, 小气鬼

skin·ful /ˈskɪnˌfʊl; ˈskɪnfʊl/ *n* **have a skinful** *BrE spoken* to drink a lot of alcohol and become drunk【英口】醉酒

skin·graft /ˈskɪnˌgræft; ˈskɪngrɑːft/ *n* [C] a medical operation in which healthy skin is removed from one part of your body and used on another to replace burned or damaged skin 表皮移植(术), 植皮(术)

skin·head /ˈskɪn,hɛd; ˈskɪnhed/ *n* [C] a young man who has hair that is cut very short, especially one who behaves violently 光头青年; 光头暴徒: *a gang of noisy skinheads* 一帮吵吵嚷嚷的光头青年

Skin·ner /ˈskɪnɚ; ˈskɪnə/, **B.F.** (1904-90) a US PSYCHOLOGIST (=a scientist who studies the way the human mind works) who developed the ideas of behaviourism. He did a lot of experiments, especially with animals, to see how they behave in certain situations and how they can be trained to change their behaviour. He also invented 'programmed learning', a teaching method which influenced the way that languages and other subjects were taught in the 1970s, although most teachers now think that Skinner's method was wrong. 斯金纳〔(1904-1990), 美国心理学家, 提出了行为主义理论。他做过大量实验, 大多在动物身上进行, 以此观察实验对象在某些情景下的行为, 同时了解如何通过训练改变其行为。他还发明了"程式学习法", 对20世纪70年代的语言教学和其他课程的教学产生了影响, 不过现在的大多数教师认为这一方法是错误的〕

3 **skin·ny** /ˈskɪnɪ; ˈskɪni/ *adj informal* very thin, especially in a way that is unattractive【非正式】瘦削的, 皮包骨的: *Some supermodels are far too skinny.* 有些超级模特儿过于瘦骨嶙峋了。—see 见 THIN (USAGE)

skinny-dip·ping /ˈ· ·, · ·/ *n* [U] *informal* swimming with no clothes on【非正式】裸(体游)泳

skint /skɪnt; skɪnt/ *adj* [not before noun 不用于名词前] *BrE informal* having no money, especially for a short time【英, 非正式】〔暂时〕不名一文的: *I'm skint at the moment.* 我现在身无分文。

skin-tight /ˈ· ,· ◂/ *adj* clothes that are skin-tight fit tightly against your body〔衣服〕紧身的: *skin-tight jeans* 紧身牛仔裤

skip[1] /skɪp; skɪp/ *v*

1 ▶**MOVEMENT 移动**◀ [I] to move forwards with quick steps and jumps 蹦跳着走: **[+across/along etc]** *Maria skipped along at her mother's side.* 玛丽亚在她妈妈身旁蹦蹦跳跳地向前走。

2 ▶**NOT DO STH 不做某事**◀ [T] *informal* to not do something that you usually do or that you should do【非正式】不做〔本来常做或应做的事〕: *Children who skip breakfast often don't concentrate as well as others.* 不吃早饭的小孩常常没有其他小孩那样注意力集中。| *He skipped chemistry class three times last month.* 他上个月三次没上化学课。

3 ▶**NOT DEAL WITH 不处理**◀ [I,T] to leave something out, or not do something that would normally be the next thing you deal with 略过, 跳过, 遗漏: *I decided to skip the first two chapters.* 我决定跳过开头两章。| **[+to]** *Let's skip to the last item on the agenda.* 让我们跳到议程上的最后一项吧。| **[+over]** *I suggest we skip over the details and get to the main point.* 我建议我们略过细节, 就谈要点。

4 ▶**CHANGE SUBJECTS 换主题**◀ [I always+adv/prep] to go from one subject to another in no fixed order 不按次序地改变话题, 随意跳动: **[+about/around/to etc]** *It was a badly organized talk – he just kept skipping around from one idea to another.* 那次演讲条理很差, 他不断地随意变换话题。

5 also 又作 **skip rope** *AmE*【美】[I] to jump over a rope as you pass it over your head and under your feet as a game 跳绳

6 **skip town/skip the country** to leave a place suddenly and secretly, especially to avoid being punished or paying debts 逃出城/国境: *Martin skipped the country with £5,000.* 马丁带着5000英镑潜逃国外。

7 **skip it!** *spoken* used to say angrily that you do not want to talk about something【口】〔生气地说〕别再提这件事了!: *"Sorry, what were you saying?" "Oh, skip it!"* "对不起, 你说什么?" "噢, 别再提了!"

8 **skip rocks/stones** *AmE* to throw smooth, flat stones into a lake, river etc in a way that makes them jump across the surface【美】〔用扁平小石块〕打水漂 —compare 比较 SKIM (4)

9 **skip a year/grade** to start a new school year in a class that is one year ahead of the class you would normally enter〔在学校〕跳级

10 **sb's heart skips a beat** used to say that someone is very excited, surprised, or frightened 心跳停一下〔用于表示非常兴奋、惊讶或害怕〕: *His heart skipped a beat when he realized Mattie was there.* 当他发现玛蒂在那里时, 他吓得心跳都停了一下。

skip out also 又作 **skip off** *phr v* [I] to leave suddenly and secretly, especially in order to avoid being punished or paying money 偷偷离开, 秘密逃走: *Martha skipped out without paying her bill.* 玛莎没有付账就偷偷溜走了。| **skip out on** *AmE* (=leave someone when they need you)【美】抛弃〔某人〕 *Joel skipped out on his wife when she was 8 months pregnant.* 乔尔在妻子怀孕八个月时抛弃了她。

skip[2] *n* [C] **1** a quick light stepping and jumping movement 轻跳, 蹦跳 **2** *BrE* a large container for bricks, wood and similar heavy waste【英】〔用来清理砖、木等沉重废料的〕废料桶; DUMPSTER *AmE*【美】

ski pants /ˈ· ·/ *n* [plural] tight trousers with a band of cloth that goes under your foot, worn by women 滑雪裤; 女子紧身裤

ski plane /ˈ· ·/ *n* [C] an aircraft that has skis (SKI[1] (2)) for landing on snow, instead of wheels〔装有滑橇的〕雪上飞机

ski pole /ˈ· ·/ *n* [C] one of two pointed short poles used for balancing and for pushing against the snow when skiing (SKI[2]) 滑雪杖

skip·per[1] /ˈskɪpɚ; ˈskɪpə/ *n* [C] *informal*【非正式】**1** the person in charge of a ship 船长 **2** the leader of a sports team〔运动队的〕队长

skipper[2] *v* [T] *informal* to be in charge of a ship, sports team etc【非正式】当船长; 当〔运动队等的〕队长

skipping rope /ˈ· ·, ·/ *n* [C] *BrE* a long piece of rope with handles that children use for jumping over【英】〔带手柄的〕跳绳用的绳子, 跳绳; JUMP ROPE *AmE*【美】

Skip·py a name for any KANGAROO, named after the kangaroo in a British TV programme in the 1960s 斯奇皮, 又译跳跳鼠〔20世纪60年代一部英国电视剧中袋鼠的名字, 后来成为所有袋鼠的代名词〕

skirl /skɝl; skɜːl/ *v* [I] to make a high sharp sound 发出尖(叫)声: *A seagull skirled overhead.* 一只海鸥在头上鸣叫。—**skirl** *n* [singular]

skir·mish[1] /ˈskɝmɪʃ; ˈskɜːmɪʃ/ *n* [C] **1** a fight between small groups of soldiers, ships etc, especially one that happens away from the main part of a battle 小规模战斗, 小冲突 **2** a short argument, especially between political opponents〔尤指政治对手间的〕小争论, 小冲突, 口角: *Bates was sent off after a skirmish with the referee.* 贝茨和裁判冲突后被罚下场。

skirmish[2] *v* [I+with] to be involved in a short fight or argument 进行小规模战斗; 卷入小争论 —**skirmisher** *n* [C]

skirt[1] /skɝt; skɜːt/ *n* [C] **1** a piece of outer clothing worn by women and girls, which hangs down from the waist like the bottom part of a dress 裙子: *She wore a white blouse and a plain black skirt.* 她穿着白衬衣和朴素的黑裙子。—compare 比较 DRESS[1] (1) —see picture on page A17 参见 A17 页图 **2** also 又作 **skirts** [plural] the part of a dress or coat that hangs down from the waist〔连衣裙或大衣的〕下摆 **3 the skirts of a forest/hill/village etc** the outside edge of a forest etc 森林的边缘; 小山/村子等的周围 **4 a bit of skirt** *BrE informal* an offensive expression meaning an attractive woman【英, 非正式】有吸引力的女人〔冒犯说法〕

skirt[2] also 又作 **skirt around** *v* [T] **1** to go around the outside edge of a place or area 沿着…边缘走, 围绕着…: *The old footpath skirts around the village.* 那条古老的小径围绕着村庄。**2** to avoid talking about an important subject, especially because it is difficult or embarrassing 绕过, 避开〔重要话题〕: *a disappointing speech that skirted around all the main issues* 回避了所有主要问题的令人失望的演说

skirting board /ˈ· · ·/ *n* [C,U] *BrE* a long narrow piece of wood that is fixed along the bottom of the walls in a room【英】〔墙壁与地板相接处的〕壁脚板, 踢脚板; BASEBOARD *AmE*【美】—see picture on page A4 参见 A4 页图

ski run /ˈ· ·/ *n* [C] a marked track on a slope for skiing (SKI[2]) 滑雪坡, 滑雪道

skit /skɪt; skɪt/ *n* [C] a short humorous performance or piece of writing that shows how silly something is by copying it〔通过模仿进行讽刺的〕滑稽短剧; 讽刺短文: **[+on]** *They did a skit on beauty contests.* 他们演了一出讽刺选美的滑稽短剧。

skit·ter /ˈskɪtɚ; ˈskɪtə/ *v* [I] to run very quickly and lightly, like a small animal〔像小动物那样〕轻快地跑

skit·tish /ˈskɪtɪʃ; ˈskɪtɪʃ/ *adj* **1** a horse or other animal that is skittish easily gets excited or frightened〔马等动物〕易受惊的, 易激动的 **2** a person who is skittish is not very serious, and their feelings, behaviour, and opinions keep changing〔人〕轻浮的, 轻佻的; 善变的 —**skittishly** *adv* —**skittishness** *n* [U]

skit·tle /ˈskɪtl; ˈskɪtl/ *n* **1 skittles** [U] a British game in which a player tries to knock down objects shaped like bottles by rolling a ball at them〔英国的〕撞柱戏, 九柱戏〔沿球道以球击倒数根瓶状木柱的游戏〕 **2** [C] one of the objects you roll the ball at in the game of skittles〔撞柱戏用的〕瓶状小木柱 —see also 另见 **not all beer and skittles** (BEER (3))

skive /skaɪv; skaɪv/ also 又作 **skive off** *v* [I] *BrE informal* to avoid work or school by staying away or leaving without permission【英, 非正式】逃避工作, 旷工; 逃学, 旷课 —**skiver** *n* [C]

skiv·vies /ˈskɪvɪz; ˈskɪviz/ *n* [plural] *AmE* a man's underwear【美】男用内衣

skiv·vy¹ /ˈskɪvɪ; ˈskɪvi/ *n* [C] *BrE humorous* a servant who does only the dirty unpleasant jobs in a house【英, 幽默】〔专干脏活的〕用人, 仆人: *You iron your shirt – I'm not your skivvy.* 你自己熨衬衣吧, 我不是你的用人。

skivvy² *v* [I] *BrE* to do all the dirty unpleasant jobs in a house, as if you were a servant【英】〔像用人似地〕干脏[杂]活

Skopje /ˈskɔpje; ˈskɔːpjeɪ/ the capital city of the former Yugoslav Republic of Macedonia, in the north of the country on the River Vardar 斯科普里〔前南斯拉夫马其顿共和国首都, 位于该国北部的瓦尔达尔河畔〕

skul·dug·ge·ry /skʌlˋdʌgərɪ; ˌskʌlˈdʌgəri/ *n* [U] *often humorous* secretly dishonest or illegal activity【常幽默】弄虚作假, 诡计, 花招; 非法活动: *Some skulduggery no doubt went on during the election.* 肯定有人在选举过程中做了手脚。

skulk /skʌlk; skʌlk/ *v* [I always+adv/prep] to hide or move about secretly, trying not to be noticed, especially when you are intending to do something bad〔为了不良企图而〕躲藏; 鬼鬼祟祟地走动: **[+about/around/in etc]** *He was still skulking around outside when they left the building.* 他们离开大楼时他还在外面鬼鬼祟祟的。

skull /skʌl; skʌl/ *n* [C] **1** the bones of a person's or animal's head〔人或动物的〕头颅骨, 头骨 —see picture at 参见 SKELETON 图 **2 sb can't get it into their (thick) skull** *spoken* to be unable to understand something very simple【口】笨脑袋无法明白: *He can't seem to get it into his skull that I'm just not interested in him.* 他这个笨蛋好像无法明白我对他根本不感兴趣。

skull and cross·bones /ˌ· · ˈ· ·/ *n* [singular] **1** a picture of a human skull with two bones crossed below it, used in former times on the flags of PIRATE¹ (3) ships〔从前海盗船上的〕骷髅旗 **2** a picture of a human skull with two bones crossed below it, used on containers to show that what is inside is very dangerous〔画在装毒药的瓶子上表示危险的〕骷髅图标志

skull cap /ˈ· ·/ *n* [C] a simple close-fitting cap for the top of the head, worn sometimes by priests or Jewish men〔牧师或犹太男子有时戴的〕无檐便帽

skunk¹ /skʌŋk; skʌŋk/ *n* [C] a small black and white North American animal that produces a strong unpleasant smell if it is attacked 臭鼬〔一种北美产的黑白色动物, 受袭击时会放出恶臭自卫〕

skunk² *v* [T] *AmE informal* to defeat a player or team very easily【美, 非正式】轻易地击败对手[对方球队]

skunk cab·bage /ˈ· ˌ· ·/ *n* [C,U] a large North American plant similar to a CABBAGE, with an unpleasant smell〔北美产的〕臭鼬草, 臭菘

Sky /skaɪ; skaɪ/ —see 见 SKY TV

S2 W2 **sky** *n* [singular,U] **1** the space above the earth where clouds and the sun and stars appear 天, 天空: *The rocket shot up into the sky.* 火箭升上了天空。| *The sky turned dark just before the storm.* 暴风雨将至, 天色转暗。| **a patch/strip etc of sky** *There's a patch of blue sky between the clouds.* 乌云之间露出小片蓝天。| **a blue/cloudy etc sky** (=used to describe how the sky looks at a particular time) 蓝色的/多云的天空 *The sun blazed down from a clear blue sky.* 太阳在晴朗的蓝天发出耀眼的光芒。**2 skies** a word meaning sky, used especially when describing the weather 天空〔尤用于描写天气〕: *a land of blue skies and warm sunshine* 拥有蔚蓝色天空和温暖阳光的土地 | **the skies** *The skies were filled with scudding clouds.* 满天都是飞掠而过的云彩。| *the crowded skies above our major airports* 我国各大机场上往来航班繁忙的天空 **3 the sky's the limit** *spoken* used to say that there is no limit to what someone can achieve, spend, win etc【口】〔指对花钱、取得成绩等〕毫无限制, 没有上限 —see also 另见 **pie in the sky** (PIE (4)), **praise sb/sth to the skies** (PRAISE¹ (1))

sky-blue /ˌ· ˈ· ◂/ *n* [U] the bright blue colour of a clear sky 天蓝色 —**sky-blue** *adj* —see picture on page A5 参见 A5 页图

sky·cap /ˈskaɪˌkæp; ˈskaɪkæp/ *n* [C] *AmE* someone who carries passengers' cases at an airport【美】机场行李搬运工

sky·div·ing /ˈskaɪˌdaɪvɪŋ; ˈskaɪˌdaɪvɪŋ/ *n* [U] the sport of jumping from an aircraft and falling through the sky before opening a PARACHUTE〔延缓张伞的〕跳伞运动 —**skydiver** *n* [U]

Skye /skaɪ; skaɪ/ also 又作 **the Isle of Skye** an island off the northwest coast of Scotland. It is the largest island of the Inner Hebrides. 斯凯岛〔苏格兰西北海岸附近一岛屿, 是内赫布里底群岛的最大岛屿〕

sky-high /ˌ· ˈ· ◂/ *adj informal* extremely high【非正式】极高的, 高入云霄的: *If this thing explodes we'll be blown sky-high.* 这个东西如果发生爆炸, 我们就要给抛到半空中。—**sky-high** *adv* —see also 另见 **blow sth sky-high** (BLOW¹ (19))

sky·lark /ˈskaɪˌlɑrk; ˈskaɪlɑːk/ *n* [C] a small bird that sings while flying high in the sky 云雀

sky·light /ˈskaɪˌlaɪt; ˈskaɪlaɪt/ *n* [C] a window in the roof of a building〔屋顶的〕天窗

sky·line /ˈskaɪˌlaɪn; ˈskaɪlaɪn/ *n* [C] the shape made by hills or buildings against the sky〔山或建筑物在天空映衬下的〕轮廓(线)

sky·rock·et /ˈskaɪˌrɑkɪt; ˈskaɪˌrɒkɪt/ *v* [I] *informal* to increase suddenly and greatly【非正式】急升, 猛升, 剧增, 剧涨: *The trade deficit has skyrocketed.* 贸易逆差已经急剧增长。

sky·scrap·er /ˈskaɪˌskrepə; ˈskaɪˌskreɪpə/ *n* [C] a very tall modern city building 摩天大楼

Sky TV /ˌskaɪ ti ˋvi; ˌskaɪ tiː ˈviː/ also 又作 **Sky, BskyB** a television company owned by Rupert Murdoch's News Corporation, which operates several different SATELLITE television programmes in the UK 天空电视台, 天空电视〔鲁珀特·默多克新闻集团旗下的一英国电视公司, 经营若干不同卫星电视节目〕

Sky·walk·er /ˈskaɪwɔlkə; ˈskaɪwɔːlkə/, **Luke** one of the main characters in The Star Wars films, who leads the fight against the evil empire and Darth Vader, who is in fact Luke's father 天行者路克〔影片《星球大战》中的主角之一。他率领大家反抗邪恶帝国和黑武士达斯·韦德。实际上, 黑武士正是天行者路克的父亲〕

sky·wards /ˈskaɪwədz; ˈskaɪwədz/ *adv* up into the sky or towards the sky 向着天空; 朝向天空: *The bird soared skywards.* 鸟儿向高空翱翔。

slab /slæb; slæb/ *n* [C] **1** a thick flat four-sided piece of a hard material such as stone〔石头等四边形硬质材料的〕平板, 厚板: *The patio was made of stone slabs.* 露台是用石板铺砌的。—see picture on page A7 参见 A7 页图 **2 a slab of cake/chocolate etc** a large flat piece of cake etc 一大块蛋糕/巧克力等 **3 on the slab** *slang* lying dead in a hospital or MORTUARY【俚】停尸在医院[太平间]

slack¹ /slæk; slæk/ *adj* **1** not taking enough care or making enough effort to do things right 懒散的, 懈怠的, 马虎的: *Tollitt blundered with a slack header towards the goalkeeper.* 托利特朝向守门员顶出一记有气无力的头球, 犯了大错。| *The report criticized airport security as 'disgracefully slack'.* 那份报告批评机场的保安工作"松懈得令人颜面尽失"。**2** with less business activity than usual〔生意〕萧条的, 清淡的: *Business is slack just now.* 目前生意清淡。**3** hanging loosely, or not pulled tight〔绳子等〕不(拉)紧的, 松弛的: *The fan belt is a little slack.* 风扇皮带有点松了。| *a slack mouth* 没合拢的嘴 | *Keep the rope slack till I say 'pull'.* 让绳子松着, 等到我喊"拉"。—**slackly** *adv* —**slackness** *n* [U]

slack² *n* **1** [C] money, space, or people that an organization has, but does not need 闲置的资源〈如不需要的资金、场地、人力等〉: *There is very little slack in the training budget for this year.* 在今年的培训预算中没有多少闲置资金了。**2 take up the slack a)** to make a rope tighter 把绳子拉紧 **b)** to do something that needs to be done because someone else is no longer doing it 接替别人停下的工作: *We're relying on Walters to take up the slack while Gonzalez is gone.* 我们靠沃尔特斯来接替冈萨雷斯离开期间的工作。**3** [U] looseness in the way that something such as a rope hangs or is fastened〔绳子、绳结等的〕松弛, 不紧 **4 slacks** [plural] *old-fashioned* trousers【过时】宽松长裤, 便裤 **5** [U] coal in very small pieces 煤屑

slack³ also 又作 **slack off** *v* [I] to make less of an effort than usual or be lazy in your work 放松, 松劲, 懈怠

slack·en /ˈslækən; ˈslækən/ also 又作 **slacken off** *v* [I,T] **1** to gradually become slower, weaker, less active etc, or to make something do this (使) 减慢, (使) 放缓, (使) 减弱: *The heavy rain showed no signs of slackening off.* 大雨没有减弱的迹象。| **slacken your pace/speed** (=go or walk more slowly) 放慢脚步/速度 *Once outside the gates, I slackened my pace.* 一出大门, 我就放慢了脚步。**2** to make something looser or to become looser (使) 松弛, (使) 变松: *Just slacken the screws a little.* 把螺丝拧松一点。—opposite 反义词 TIGHTEN

slack·er /ˈslækə; ˈslækə/ *n* [C] someone who is lazy and does not do all the work they should 懒惰的人, 偷懒者

slag¹ /slæg; slæg/ *n* **1** [U] light waste material rather like glass, which is left when metal is obtained from rock 矿渣, 熔渣, 炉渣 **2** [C] *BrE slang* an insulting word for a woman, used to suggest that she has had a lot of sexual partners【英俚】淫妇, 荡妇〔此词具侮辱性〕—**slaggy** *adj*

slag²

slag sb ↔ **off** *phr v* [T] *BrE informal* to talk about someone in a very critical way, especially when they are not there【英, 非正式】〔尤指在背后〕诋毁; 责难; 批评: *He's always slagging her off behind her back.* 他老是在背后说她的坏话。

slag heap /ˈ· ·/ *n* [C] *especially BrE* a pile of waste material at a mine or factory【尤英】矿渣堆, 熔渣堆

slain /slen; sleɪn/ *v* the past participle of SLAY

slake /slek; sleɪk/ *v* [T] *literary*【文】**1 slake your thirst** to drink so that you are not THIRSTY any more 解渴 **2** to satisfy a desire 满足〔欲望〕

sla·lom /ˈslɑləm; ˈslɑːləm/ *n* [U] a race for people on SKIs or in CANOEs down a winding course marked by flags〔穿过插有旗杆的蜿蜒赛道进行的〕回转滑雪赛; 小划子[独木舟]回旋赛

slam¹ /slæm; slæm/ *v*

1 ▶DOOR/GATE 门/大门◀ [I,T] if a door, gate etc slams, or if someone slams it, it shuts with a loud noise (使) 砰地关上, 使劲关闭: *Please don't slam the door.* 请不要使劲关门。| *We could hear people shouting and doors slamming in the house next door.* 我们可以听到隔壁人家大声喊叫和用力关门的声音。| **slam shut** *A door slammed shut in the distance.* 远处有一扇门砰地关上了。

2 ▶PUT STH SOMEWHERE 放东西◀ [T always+adv/prep] to put something on or against a surface with a fast violent movement 砰地放下, 使劲放下: **slam sth on/down etc** *Henry slammed the phone down and walked angrily out of the room.* 亨利摔下电话筒, 怒气冲冲地走出了房间。

3 slam on the brakes to make a car stop very suddenly 猛踩煞车

4 ▶CRITICIZE STH 批评某事◀ [T] a word used especially in newspapers, meaning to criticize something strongly 猛烈抨击〔尤用于报刊〕: *The government's amnesty for tax-dodgers was slammed today by Opposition leaders.* 政府对逃税者的赦免今天遭到反对党领袖的猛烈抨击。| **slam sb for sth** *The television company was slammed by the media for its portrayal of a gang rape.* 这家电视台因为播出一段轮奸片段而受到媒体的猛烈抨击。

5 slam the door in sb's face a) to shut a door hard when someone is trying to come in 用力关门不让某人进入, 让某人吃闭门羹 **b)** to rudely refuse to meet someone or talk to them〔粗鲁地〕拒绝会见某人; 拒绝与某人谈话

slam into sth *phr v* [T] to drive or move very fast towards something and hit it〔驾驶等因速度太快而〕撞到…: *The car slammed into a lamp-post.* 那辆汽车撞上了灯柱。

slam² *n* [C usually singular 一般用单数] the noise or action of a door or gate slamming 砰的关门;〔门〕砰的关上 —see also 另见 GRAND SLAM

slam dunk /ˈ· ·/ *v* [I, T] to put a ball through the net in BASKETBALL using a lot of force〔篮球运动中〕扣篮, 灌篮 —**slam dunk** *n* [C]

slam·mer /ˈslæmɚ; ˈslæmə/ *n* **in the slammer** *slang* in prison【俚】坐牢: *He was thrown in the slammer.* 他被投进监狱。

slan·der¹ /ˈslændɚ; ˈslɑːndə/ *n* **1** [C] a false spoken statement about someone that is intended to damage the good opinion that people have 诽谤, 诋毁 **2** [U] the legal offence of making a statement of this kind〔法律上的〕诽谤罪: *The doctor was awarded record damages against her partners for slander.* 这位医生因合作伙伴对她犯了诽谤罪而获得创纪录的损害赔偿金。—compare 比较 LIBEL¹ —**slanderer** *n* [C]

slander² *v* [T] to say untrue things about someone in order to damage other people's good opinion of them 诽谤, 诋毁, 造谣中伤

slan·der·ous /ˈslændərəs; ˈslɑːndərəs/ *adj* a slanderous statement about someone is untrue, and is intended to damage other people's good opinion of them 诽谤的, 诋毁的, 造谣中伤的: *slanderous allegations* 诽谤性的指控

slang /slæŋ; slæŋ/ *n* [U] very informal language that includes new and sometimes rude words, especially words used only by particular groups of people such as criminals, schoolchildren, or people who take drugs 俚语: *schoolboy slang* 男生俚语 | **a slang word/expression/term** *'Screw' is a slang word used by prisoners to mean prison officer.* screw 是囚犯用以指监狱看守的俚语词。—**slangy** *adj*: *slangy expressions* 俚语表达法

slanging match /ˈ·· ,·/ *n* [C] *BrE informal* an angry argument in which people insult each other【英, 非正式】互相谩骂, 对骂, 辱骂: *They got into a bit of a slanging match in the pub.* 他们在酒馆里对骂了一阵子。

slant¹ /slænt; slɑːnt/ *v* [I] *especially literary* to slope or move in a sloping line【尤文】倾斜, 歪斜; 斜穿: *slanting handwriting* 倾斜的字迹 | *The sun's rays slanted through the trees.* 阳光斜射进树林。—**slantingly** *adv*

slant² *n* **1** a sloping position or angle 斜面; 斜线; 斜角: *a steep slant* 陡峭的斜面 | **at/on a slant** *Set the pole at a slant.* 把柱子斜着竖起来。**2** a way of writing about or thinking about a subject that shows strong support for a particular opinion or set of ideas〔有倾向性的〕观点, 看法, 意见; 偏见: *The editorial had an anti-union slant.* 这篇社论带有一种反工会的偏见。| *The report provides a new slant on important environmental issues.* 这份报告对重要的环境问题提出了一种新的见解。

slant·ed /ˈslæntɪd; ˈslɑːntɪ̡d/ *adj* **1** providing facts or information in a way that unfairly favours one opinion, one side of an argument etc; BIASED 有偏见的: **[+towards]** *The survey was heavily slanted towards the ruling party.* 这篇调查报告严重地偏向执政党。**2** sloping to one side 倾斜的, 歪斜的

slap¹ /slæp; slæp/ *v* **slapped, slapping 1** [T] to hit someone quickly with the flat part of your hand 用巴掌打, 掴; 拍: *Do you think it's OK to slap children if they're really rude?* 孩子要是真的粗鲁无礼, 你认为打他们耳光妥当吗? | **slap sb on the back** (=hit them on the back in a friendly way)〔友好地〕拍某人的肩膀 —see picture on page A20 参见 A20 页图 **2** [T always+adv/prep] to put something down noisily on a surface, especially when you are angry〔尤指生气时〕啪的一声放下, 掷下, 扔下: **slap sth on/down** *I slapped the report down on his desk and told him to do it again.* 我把那份报告扔在他桌上, 叫他重写。**3** [I] to hit a surface, making a sound like someone being slapped noisily 啪啪地撞击, 拍击: **[+against]** *Small waves slapped against the jetty.* 细浪拍击着防波堤。 2

slap sb **down** *phr v* [T] to unfairly and unkindly criticize someone so that they lose confidence 粗暴地批评, 压制

slap sth ↔ **on** *phr v* [T] *informal*【非正式】**1** to put or spread something quickly or carelessly onto a surface 匆匆地涂, 草草地抹: *She rushed upstairs and slapped on some make-up.* 她冲上楼, 匆匆上了点妆。**2** to suddenly announce a new charge, tax etc, especially unfairly or without warning〔尤指突然或强行地〕增加〔费用、税款等〕: *Many tour operators slap on supplements for single people.* 许多旅游公司对散客强行增收额外的费用。

slap² *n* [C] **1** a quick hit with the flat part of your hand 一巴掌; 一拍: **give sb a slap** *Julia gave Roy a friendly slap on the cheek.* 朱莉娅友好地拍了拍罗伊的脸颊。**2 a slap in the face** an action that seems to be deliberately intended to offend or upset someone, especially someone who has tried very hard to do something 侮辱; 打击: *When I wasn't promoted it felt like such a terrible slap in the face.* 我没得到晋升时, 觉得好像受了极大的打击。**3 a slap on the wrist** *informal* a punishment that is not very severe【非正式】轻微的处罚

slap³ /slæp; slæp/ also 又作 **slap-bang** /,· ˈ·/ *adv informal* hitting something very hard, especially when you are running, driving etc【非正式】〔尤指在跑着或开车时〕猛烈地, 重重地〔撞到某物〕: **[+into]** *I ran slap-bang into a lamp-post.* 我猛然撞在灯柱上。

slap·dash /ˈslæp,dæʃ; ˈslæpdæʃ/ *adj* careless and done too quickly 粗心的, 草率的, 仓促的: *a very slapdash piece of work* 非常仓促完成的工作

slap·hap·py /ˈslæp,hæpɪ; ˈslæp,hæpi/ *adj* cheerfully careless and likely to make mistakes 大大咧咧的, 满不在乎的; 粗心大意的

slap·per /ˈslæpɚ; ˈslæpə/ *n* [C] *BrE slang* a sexually immoral woman, or a woman who remains strong and cheerful in spite of a difficult life【英俚】淫荡的女人;〔在困境中仍〕坚强开朗的妇女

slap·stick /ˈslæp,stɪk; ˈslæp,stɪk/ *n* [U] humorous acting in which the performers fall over, throw things at each other etc 滑稽表演, 打闹剧

> **CULTURAL NOTE 文化注释**
>
> A typical slapstick scene might include someone being hit in the face with a CUSTARD PIE or people accidentally running into one another or hitting one another. 蛋奶馅饼正好砸到某人脸上, 偶然和别人撞个满怀, 或不经意间打中了别人, 所有这些都是打闹剧中可能出现的典型场景。

slap-up /ˈ· ·/ *adj* **slap-up meal/dinner etc** *BrE informal* a very large enjoyable meal【英, 非正式】美餐/精美大餐等

slash¹ /slæʃ; slæʃ/ *v* **1** [I always+adv/prep,T] to violently cut or try to cut something with a knife, sword etc〔用刀、剑、棒等〕猛削, 猛砍, 乱打: *Most of the seats on the train had been slashed by vandals.* 火车上大多数座位都被破坏公物者划破了。| **[+at/through]** *Alan was slashing at the snake with a huge stick.* 艾伦用大棒猛打那条蛇。| **slash your way through** (=make a path through something by slashing) 从…中劈出一条路 *They had to slash their way through thick undergrowth.* 他们得在茂密的灌木丛中劈出一条路。| **slash your wrists** (=deliberately cut your wrists with the intention of killing yourself) 割腕 (自杀) **2** [T

often passive 常用被动态] a word used especially in newspapers and advertising meaning to greatly reduce an amount, price etc 大幅度削减〔数量、价格等，尤用于报刊及广告中〕: *Over the last year the workforce has been slashed by 50%.* 去年劳动力已削减了50%。

slash² *n* [C] **1** a quick movement that you make with a sword, knife etc in order to cut someone or something〔用刀、剑等〕砍，劈，削 **2** also 又作 **slash mark** a line (/) used in writing to separate words, numbers, or letters 斜线符号〔用以分隔单词、数字或字母〕 **3** a long narrow wound or a long narrow cut in a piece of material〔长条的〕伤痕，砍痕；〔长条的〕切口，裂口: *He staggered into hospital with slashes across his face.* 他摇摇晃晃地走进医院，脸上伤痕累累。**4 have/take a slash** *BrE spoken* an impolite expression meaning to URINATE【英口】撒尿〔不雅的说法〕

slat /slæt; slæt/ *n* [C] a thin flat piece of wood, plastic etc used especially in furniture〔家具的〕细长板条 —**slatted** *adj*: *a slatted bench* 板条长凳

slate¹ /slet; sleɪt/ *n*

1 ▶ROCK 岩石◀ [U] a dark grey rock that can easily be split into flat thin pieces 板岩，板石: *a slate mine* 板石矿

2 ▶ON A ROOF 房顶上◀ [C] one of the small pieces of slate or similar material used for covering roofs 石板瓦: *There were several slates missing from the roof.* 房顶有几块石板瓦掉了。

3 slate blue/grey a dark grey or blue colour 深灰色；蓝灰色

4 ▶POLITICS 政治◀ [C] *especially AmE* a list of people that voters can choose in an election or that are being considered for an important job【尤美】候选人名单

5 put sth on the slate *BrE old-fashioned* to arrange to pay for something later, especially food or drink【英，过时】〔尤指对食物和饮料〕赊账，挂账: *Two whiskies, and could you put them on the slate!* 来两杯威士忌，请给挂账。

6 ▶FOR WRITING ON 写字用的◀ [C] a small board in a wooden frame used for writing on in schools in former times〔从前学校里写字用的〕石板 —see also 另见 **a clean slate** (CLEAN¹ (10)), **wipe the slate clean** (WIPE¹ (6))

slate² *v* [T] **1** *BrE informal* to criticize a book, film etc severely, especially in a newspaper【英，非正式】〔尤指在报纸上〕严厉批评〔书、电影等〕: *Donkin's most recent novel has been slated by the critics.* 唐金的最新小说受到评论家的严厉批评。**2 be slated** *especially AmE*【尤美】**a)** to be expected to succeed in getting a particular position or job 可望担任某职: **be slated to be/do sth** *Rogers is slated to be the Democratic candidate.* 罗杰斯被提名为民主党候选人。**b)** to be expected or planned to happen at a time in the future 预定〔举行〕，定于: **be slated for** *The office buildings are slated for demolition next June.* 这些办公大楼定于明年6月拆毁。—**slated** *adj*

slath·er /ˈslæðɚ; ˈslæðə/ *v* [T] *AmE* to cover something with a thick layer of a soft substance【美】给…厚厚地涂抹〔酱状物〕: *toast slathered with butter* 涂着厚厚一层黄油的烤面包

slat·tern /ˈslætɚn; ˈslætən/ *n* [C] *old-fashioned* a dirty untidy woman【过时】邋遢女人，懒婆娘 —**slatternly** *adj*

slaugh·ter¹ /ˈslɔtɚ; ˈslɔːtə/ *v* [T] **1** to kill large numbers of people in a cruel or violent way 屠杀，杀戮，残杀: *Hundreds of innocent civilians were slaughtered.* 数以百计的无辜平民遭到杀戮。—see 见 KILL¹ (USAGE) **2** to kill an animal for food 屠宰〔动物〕 **3** *informal* to defeat an opponent by a large number of points【非正式】〔在体育比赛中〕使惨败: *We got slaughtered 110–54.* 我们以54比110惨败。

slaughter² *n* [U] **1** the act of killing large numbers of people in a cruel or violent way 屠杀，杀戮，残杀 **2** the act of killing animals for food〔对动物的〕屠宰，宰杀

slaugh·ter·house /ˈslɔtɚˌhaus; ˈslɔːtəhaʊs/ *n* [C] a building where animals are killed 屠宰场

Slaughter of the In·no·cents, the /ˌ· · · · ˈ· · ·/ —see 见 the MASSACRE OF THE INNOCENTS

slave¹ /slev; sleɪv/ *n* [C] **1** someone who is legally owned by another person and works for them for no money 奴隶: *accusing her mother of treating her like a slave* 控告她母亲把她当奴隶对待 **2 be a slave to/of** to be completely influenced by something so that you cannot make your own decisions 完全受某物的控制: *A lot of kids nowadays are slaves of fashion.* 如今许多孩子都成了时尚的奴隶。**3 slave driver** *informal* someone who makes people work extremely hard【非正式】逼迫他人拼命干活的人，苛刻的工头: *She knew the girls called her a slave driver behind her back.* 她知道姑娘们在背后把她叫做无情的工头。

slave² *v* [I always+adv/prep] to work very hard with little time to rest 拼命干，苦干: **[+away/over/for]** *I've been slaving away for hours to get this report finished.* 为了完成这份报告，我已经苦干好几个钟头了。| **slaving away over a hot stove** (=a humorous way of saying you are cooking) 在火热的灶头拼命干〔下厨做饭的幽默说法〕

slave la·bour *BrE*【英】, **slave labor** *AmE*【美】/ˌ· ˈ· ·/ *n* [U] **1** *informal* work for which you are paid an unreasonably small amount of money【非正式】奴隶劳动，报酬极低的工作: *£2 an hour! That's slave labour!* 每小时两英镑！这是廉价劳动！**2** work done by SLAVEs or the people who do this work 奴隶做的苦工；做苦工的奴隶: *The Pyramids were largely built by slave labour.* 金字塔大部分是由做苦工的奴隶建成的。

slav·er¹ /ˈslævɚ; ˈslævə/ *v* [I] to let SALIVA (=liquid produced inside your mouth) come out of your mouth, especially because you are hungry 垂涎，淌口水: *The dog started slavering at the sight of the bone.* 那条狗看见骨头就流口水。

slaver over sth *phr v* [T] *informal* to be very excited about something, especially in an unpleasant or stupid way【非正式】渴望，对…垂涎: *slavering over the parked Ferrari out front* 对停在面前的法拉利轿车垂涎三尺

slav·er² /ˈslevɚ; ˈsleɪvə/ *n* [C] *old use*【旧】**1** someone who sells slaves 奴隶贩子 **2** a ship for slaves 奴隶贩运船

sla·ve·ry /ˈslevərɪ; ˈsleɪvəri/ *n* [U] **1** the system of having slaves 奴隶制度: *the abolition of slavery* 奴隶制的废除 **2** the condition of being a slave 奴隶身份: **sell sb into slavery** (=to sell someone as a SLAVE) 把某人卖去当奴隶

CULTURAL NOTE 文化注释

Both the US and UK were involved in the slave trade from the 17th century until the 19th century. Slaves were taken from Africa and usually sold in the colonies (COLONY) of European countries. Often this involved journeys in ships with terrible conditions for the slaves, many of whom died. Slaves were usually given no education, and families were often separated when children or parents were sold to different people. Some owners treated their slaves well, but many others treated them very badly. In the US, the northern states tried to end slavery, but the southern states strongly disagreed with this, because they were very dependent on using slaves on their farms. This disagreement was one of the main causes of the American Civil War. People in the US and UK who believed that slavery was wrong and wanted to ABOLISH it (=end it) were called 'abolitionists'. In his *Emancipation Proclamation*, President Lincoln announced officially that slavery would be abolished in the US on January 1, 1863. 英美两国都卷入了17至19世纪的奴隶贸易中。奴隶从非洲被贩卖到欧洲国家的殖民地。经常需要用船来运送奴隶，而船上的条件极差，这导致了很多奴隶死亡。奴隶通常接受不到教育，当父母和子女分别被卖给不同的奴隶主时，一个奴隶家庭就支离破碎了。尽管有善待奴隶的奴隶主，但更多的奴隶主对待奴隶的手段非常粗暴。美国北部诸州试图废除奴隶制，但南部诸州却坚决抵制，因为他们严重依赖奴隶在其种植园上劳动。在这个问题上的分歧是导致美国内战的主要原因之一。在英美，认为奴隶制是错误的并想废除它的人被称为"废奴主义者"。林肯总统在《解放宣言》中正式宣布奴隶制将于1863年1月1日在美国废除。— see Cultural Note at DEEP SOUTH 见 DEEP SOUTH 文化注释; see also 另见 AFRICAN AMERICAN, UNDERGROUND RAILROAD

slave trade /ˈ· ·/ *n* [singular] the buying and selling of slaves, especially Africans who were taken to America 奴隶贸易，奴隶买卖〔尤指过去对被抓到美洲的非洲人进行的买卖〕

slav·ish /ˈslevɪʃ; ˈsleɪvɪʃ/ *adj* **slavish imitation/devotion etc** behaviour or actions that show that you cannot make your own decisions about what you should do 一味的模仿/奴性的忠诚等: *a slavish devotion to duty* 奴性地忠于职守 —**slavishly** *adv* —**slavishness** *n* [U]

slaw /slɔ; slɔː/ *n* [U] *AmE* a cold dish made with CABBAGE, CARROTs, and onions; COLESLAW【美】〔用卷心菜、胡萝卜和洋葱做的〕生拌凉菜，凉拌卷心菜丝

slay /sle; sleɪ/ *v past tense* **slew** /slu; sluː/ *past participle* **slain** /slen; sleɪn/ [T] **1** *literary* a word meaning to kill someone, often used in newspaper reports; MURDER² (1)【文】杀害，残杀，谋杀〔常用于新闻报道〕: *Thousands were slain in the battle.* 数以千计的人在这场战役中被杀害。**2** *AmE informal* to amuse someone a lot【美，非正式】逗…乐[笑]，使笑倒: *That guy really slays me!* 那个人真把我逗乐了。—**slayer** *n* [C]

SLD, the /ˌɛs ɛl ˈdi; ˌes el ˈdiː/ the Social and Liberal Democrats; a British political party 社会自由民主党〔英国一政党〕—see also 另见 LIBERAL DEMOCRATS

sleaze /sliz; sliːz/ *n* **1** [U] immoral behaviour, especially involving sex or dishonesty 不道德; 不诚实; 卑劣〔尤涉及性或虚伪〕: *the sleaze factor in US politics* 美国政治中的不道德因素 **2** also 又作 **sleazebag** *slang especially AmE* someone who is immoral or cannot be trusted【俚, 尤美】卑劣的人, 卑鄙小人

slea·zy /ˈslizɪ; ˈsliːzi/ *adj* **1 sleazy hotel/bar etc** a hotel etc that looks dirty and cheap 肮脏的廉价旅馆/酒吧等 **2** someone who is sleazy is immoral or unpleasant〔人〕卑劣的, 讨厌的: *sleazy business associates* 卑劣的生意合伙人 **—sleaziness** *n* [U]

sledge¹ /slɛdʒ; sledʒ/ *BrE*【英】, **sled** /slɛd; sled/ *AmE*【美】—*n* [C] a vehicle for travelling over snow with two long narrow pieces of wood or metal fixed under it 雪橇

sledge² *BrE*【英】, **sled** *AmE*【美】—*v* [I] to travel or ride on a sledge 乘雪橇

sledge·ham·mer /ˈslɛdʒˌhæmɚ; ˈsledʒˌhæmə/ *n* [C] a large heavy hammer 大锤

sleek¹ /slik; sliːk/ *adj* **1** sleek hair or fur is straight, shiny, and healthy-looking〔头发、皮毛〕平直光滑的, 有光泽的, 健康的: *The cat had sleek black fur.* 这只猫有着光滑的黑毛。**2** a vehicle or other object that is sleek has a smooth attractive shape〔汽车等〕光洁漂亮的, 造型优美的: *the sleek lines of the new Mercedes* 新款梅赛德斯－奔驰汽车的优美外型 **3** someone who is sleek looks rich, but you feel that you cannot trust them〔人〕装扮得时髦阔气的: *sleek executive types in their expensive suits* 身穿华服的时髦的行政人员 **—sleekly** *adv* **—sleekness** *n* [U]

sleek² *v* [T always+adv/prep] to make hair or fur smooth and shiny by putting water or oil on it〔在头发或皮毛上抹水或油〕使平滑光亮: **sleek sth back/down etc** *His hair was sleeked back with oil.* 他的头发用油向后梳理得平滑光亮。

sleep¹ /slip; sliːp/ *v past tense and past participle* **slept** /slɛpt; slept/

1 ►REST 休息◄ [I] to rest your mind and body by being asleep 睡, 睡觉, 睡着: *I normally sleep on my back.* 我通常都仰卧着睡觉。| *You're welcome to stay if you don't mind sleeping on the floor.* 你如果不介意睡地板的话, 那就欢迎你住下来。| **sleep well/soundly** *Did you sleep well?* 你睡得好吗? | **sleep like a log/top** *informal* (=sleep very well)【非正式】睡得很熟/很死 | **sleep late** (=sleep until late in the morning) 睡到很晚才起床 *We usually sleep late on Sundays.* 我们通常在星期天早上睡懒觉。| **not sleep a wink** (=not sleep at all) 根本没有合眼, 完全没有睡着 *I didn't sleep a wink all night.* 我整夜都没合过眼。| **sleep the night** *BrE* (=sleep at someone else's house for the night)【英】在别人家里过夜 *We talked till late and then Bob ended up sleeping the night.* 我们谈到很晚, 结果鲍勃留下过夜。

2 sleep rough *BrE* to sleep outdoors in uncomfortable conditions, especially because you have no money【英】〔尤因没有钱而〕在户外随便找个地方睡觉, 露宿

3 sleep on it *informal* to not make a decision about something important until the next day【非正式】把某事留待第二天决定: *Why don't you sleep on it and give me your final reply tomorrow?* 你为什么不多考虑一个晚上, 明天再给我最后回复?

4 sleep tight *spoken* used especially to children before they go to bed to say that you hope they sleep well【口】睡个好觉〔尤对睡觉前的小孩子说〕: *Good night, sweet-heart. Sleep tight!* 晚安, 亲爱的。睡个好觉!

5 ►NUMBER OF PEOPLE 人数◄ [T] to have enough beds for a particular number of people〔有床〕可供〔若干人〕睡: **sleep two/four/six etc** *The villa will sleep four easily.* 这栋别墅足可以供四人住宿。

6 let sleeping dogs lie to deliberately avoid mentioning a problem or argument that you had in the past, so that you do not cause any problems 别惹是生非; 别自寻烦恼: *She decided to let sleeping dogs lie and not to ask her son about the missing money.* 她决定不去自寻烦恼, 不去问儿子关于丢钱的事。

7 ►BE QUIET AT NIGHT 夜里静悄悄◄ [I] *literary* if a village, house etc sleeps it is night time and very quiet【文】〔入夜后的房子、村庄等〕静寂, 保持安静: *While the house slept, he crept downstairs and out of the front door.* 等全家人进入梦乡之后, 他蹑手蹑脚地下了楼, 从前门溜了出去。

sleep around *phr v* [I] *informal* to be too willing to have sex with a lot of different people【非正式】到处和别人睡觉, 乱搞男女关系

sleep in *phr v* [I] to sleep later than usual in the morning〔早上〕睡懒觉: *They like to sleep in on Saturdays.* 他们喜欢在星期六早上睡懒觉。—compare 比较 OVERSLEEP

sleep sth **↔ off** *phr v* [T] to sleep until you do not feel ill any more, especially after drinking too much alcohol〔尤指在醉酒后〕用睡眠解除〔不适〕: *sleeping off the effects of last night's party* 用睡觉解除昨天晚会后的醉意

sleep over *phr v* [I] to sleep at someone's house for a night 在别人家里过夜, 借宿: *If you don't want to drive, you're welcome to sleep over.* 如果你不想开车, 欢迎你在我家过夜。

sleep through *phr v* **1** [T **sleep through** sth] to sleep while something is happening and not be woken by it 在…发生时未醒来: *How did you manage to sleep through that thunderstorm?* 雷雨那么大你怎么能睡得着? **2** [I] to sleep continuously for a long time 一直睡到…: *I slept right through till lunchtime.* 我一觉睡到吃午饭的时候。

sleep together *phr v* [I] *informal* to have sex【非正式】性交: *I'm sure those two are sleeping together.* 我敢肯定那两个人睡在一起了。

sleep with sb *phr v* [T] *informal* to have sex with someone, especially someone you are not married to【非正式】与某人〔尤指非配偶〕发生性关系: *It's common knowledge that he's sleeping with his secretary.* 大家都知道他和秘书有染。

sleep² *n*

1 ►AT NIGHT 在晚上◄ [U] the natural state of being asleep 睡眠, 睡觉: *I didn't get much sleep last night.* 我昨天晚上睡得不多。| *Try and get some sleep before the journey.* 去旅行之前尽量多睡点觉。| **get to sleep** (=succeed in sleeping) 入睡 *I had terrible trouble getting to sleep last night.* 我昨晚怎么也睡不着。| **in your sleep** (=while you are sleeping) 在(你)睡着时 *She sometimes talks in her sleep.* 她有时睡觉说梦话。| **send sb to sleep** (=make someone sleep) 使某人入睡 *The combination of warmth and music sent him to sleep.* 暖意和音乐伴他进入梦乡。| **sing/rock sb to sleep** (=sing to a baby until it sleeps or gently move it) 唱歌哄婴儿入睡/轻轻地摇婴儿入睡

2 ►PERIOD OF SLEEPING 睡眠时间◄ [singular] a period of sleeping (一段)睡眠时间: *I usually have a sleep after lunch.* 我通常在午饭后睡一会儿。| **a light/deep sleep** *She was woken from a deep sleep by a ring at the door.* 她在酣睡中被门铃声吵醒。| **a good night's sleep** (=a night when you sleep well and after which you feel healthy and active) 一夜的酣睡

3 go to sleep a) to start sleeping 入睡: *I went to sleep at 9 o'clock and woke up at 6.* 我9点钟入睡, 6点钟醒来。**b)** *informal* if a part of your body goes to sleep, you cannot feel it for a short time because it has not been getting enough blood【非正式】〔身体某部位〕麻木, 发麻〔因供血不足所致〕

4 don't lose sleep over it *spoken* used to tell someone not to worry about something【口】〔劝人〕不要为担心某事而失眠

5 put sb/sth to sleep a) to give drugs to a sick animal so that it dies without too much pain 使〔动物〕长眠; 人道毁灭〔动物〕〔指用药使有病痛的动物无痛苦地死去〕 **b)** *informal* to make someone unconscious before an operation by giving them drugs【非正式】〔手术前用麻醉药〕使〔某人〕失去知觉

6 can do sth in your sleep *informal* to be able to do something very easily, especially because you have done it many times before【非正式】〔尤指因已做过多次而能〕轻而易举地做; 闭上眼睛都能做

7 ►IN YOUR EYES 在眼睛内◄ [U] *informal* a substance that forms in the corners of your eyes while you are sleeping【非正式】眵, 眼眵, 眼屎

sleep·er /ˈslipɚ; ˈsliːpə/ *n* [C] **1 a) a heavy sleeper** someone who does not wake easily 睡得很死的人, 不易醒的人 **b) a light sleeper** someone who wakes easily 睡得不熟的人, 易醒的人 **2** someone who is asleep 睡着的人 **3** a train with carriages that have beds for passengers to sleep in, or a bed on this kind of train〔火车的〕卧铺车厢; 〔火车上的〕卧铺 **4** *especially BrE* a heavy piece of wood or CONCRETE supporting a railway track【尤英】〔铁路的〕枕木; TIE² (7) *AmE*【美】**5** *BrE* a small ring worn in your ear【英】小耳环, 耳环圈 —see picture at 参见 JEWELLERY 图 **6** *AmE* a film, book etc which is successful but not immediately【美】〔长期遭忽视后〕突然获得成功的影片[图书等]

sleeping bag 睡袋

sleeping bag /ˈ· · ·/ *n* [C] a large warm bag for sleeping in, especially when camping〔尤指露营用的〕睡袋

Sleeping Beauty 睡美人

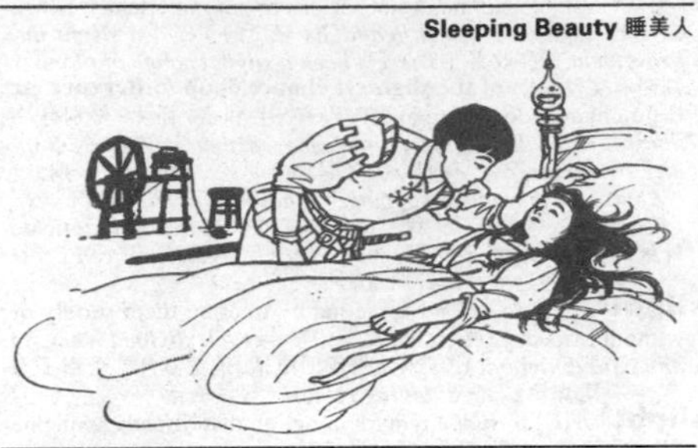

Sleeping Beau·ty /ˌ·· ˈ··/ **1** the main character in a FAIRY TALE called *Sleeping Beauty*, who is a princess who lives in a castle. An evil fairy makes the princess and everyone else in the castle fall asleep for ever. After a hundred years, a prince finds Sleeping Beauty and kisses her, and then she and everyone else in the castle wakes up. There is a BALLET with music by Tchaikovsky based on this story. 睡美人〔童话故事《睡美人》中的主人公。她是一位公主,居住在城堡中。一个邪恶的神仙施法术让公主和城堡中的人长眠不醒。一百年后,一位王子发现睡美人并亲吻了她,睡美人与城堡中的其他人都苏醒了。柴可夫斯基根据这一故事创作了一部芭蕾舞剧〕 **2** someone who seems to be sleeping peacefully 静静安睡者,沉睡的人: *Just look at Sleeping Beauty there!* 看那个人睡得真安稳!

sleeping car /ˈ·· ·/ *n* [C] a part of a train with beds for passengers〔火车的〕卧铺车厢,卧车

sleeping draught /ˈ·· ·/ *n* [C] *old use* a special drink which makes you sleep【旧】安眠药水

sleeping part·ner /ˌ·· ˈ··/ *n* [C] *BrE* someone who owns part of a business but is not actively involved in operating it【英】不参与经营的合伙人; SILENT PARTNER *AmE*【美】

sleeping pill /ˈ·· ·/ *n* [C] a PILL which helps you to sleep 安眠药(片)

sleeping po·lice·man /ˌ·· ·ˈ··/ *n* [C] *BrE* a narrow raised part in a road which makes traffic go slowly; SPEED BUMP【英】交通减速板,减速路埂〔为防止车速过快而横设于路面的隆起物〕

sleeping sick·ness /ˈ·· ˌ··/ *n* [U] a serious African disease that causes extreme tiredness, fever and makes you lose weight 昏睡病〔非洲一种使人极度疲倦、发烧和消瘦的严重疾病〕

sleep·less /ˈsliplɪs; ˈsliːpləs/ *adj* unable to sleep 失眠的,不眠的: **sleepless night** *David spent a sleepless night wondering what to do.* 戴维一夜未眠,想着该怎么办。—**sleeplessly** *adv* —**sleeplessness** *n* [U]

sleep·o·ver /ˈslipˌovɚ; ˈsliːpəʊvə/ *n* [C] *AmE* a party for children in which they stay the night at someone's house【美】不在自己家过夜的儿童晚会,睡衣晚会

sleep·walk·er /ˈslipˌwɔkɚ; ˈsliːpˌwɔːkə/ *n* [C] someone who walks while they are sleeping 梦游者 —**sleepwalk** *v* [I] —**sleepwalking** *n* [U]

sleep·y /ˈslipɪ; ˈsliːpi/ *adj* **1** tired 困乏的,想睡的: *The warmth from the fire made her feel sleepy.* 炉旁的温暖使她昏昏欲睡。**2** a sleepy town or village is very quiet and not much happens there〔城镇、乡村〕寂静的; 冷清的; 死气沉沉的 —**sleepily** *adv* —**sleepiness** *n* [U]

sleep·y·head /ˈslipɪˌhɛd; ˈsliːpihed/ *n* [C] *spoken* someone, especially a child, who looks as if they want to go to sleep【口】〔尤指孩子〕想睡的人,贪睡的人,懒虫: *Come on sleepyhead, wake up!* 好了,小懒虫,快醒醒!

sleet /slit; sliːt/ *n* [U] snow and rain which falls when it is very cold 冻雨,雨夹雪 —**sleet** *v* [I] —**sleety** *adj* —see picture on page A13 参见 A13 页图

sleeve /sliv; sliːv/ *n* [C] **1** the part of a piece of clothing which covers your arm or part of your arm 袖子: *a dress with long sleeves* 长袖连衣裙 —see picture on page A17 参见 A17 页图 **2** **long-sleeved/short-sleeved etc** having sleeves that are long or short 长袖/短袖等的 **3** **have something up your sleeve** *informal* to have a secret plan or idea that you are going to use later【非正式】暗中已有应急的打算[计划]; 有锦囊妙计: *Come on, what have you got up your sleeve?* 你说,你有什么锦囊妙计? **4** *especially BrE* a stiff envelope for keeping a record in【尤英】唱片套; JACKET (3) *AmE*【美】**5** *technical* a tube that surrounds a machine part【术语】〔机器部件的〕套筒,套管 —see also 另见 **laugh up your sleeve** (LAUGH[1] (13))

sleeve·less /ˈslivlɪs; ˈsliːvləs/ *adj* a sleeveless jacket, dress etc has no sleeves 无袖的

sleigh /sle; sleɪ/ *n* [C] a large vehicle pulled by animals, used for travelling over snow〔动物拉的〕雪橇,雪车

sleight of hand /ˌslaɪt əv ˈhænd; ˌslaɪt əv ˈhænd/ *n* [U] **1** the use of clever tricks and dishonesty to achieve something〔为达到某目的而使出的〕手腕,花招 **2** quick skilful movement with your hands, especially when performing magic tricks〔尤指变戏法中的〕巧妙手法

slen·der /ˈslɛndɚ; ˈslendə/ *adj* **1** thin and graceful 细长而优美的,修长的; 苗条的; 纤细的: *She had a long slender neck.* 她的脖子细长好看。| *a row of slender columns* 一排细长优美的柱子 —see 见 THIN (USAGE) **2** not enough to be useful, helpful, or effective 微少的,微薄的,不足的: **slender chance/hope** *The company now only has a slender hope of survival.* 这家公司现在很难维持下去了。| **by/with a slender majority** *The Republicans won by a slender majority.* 共和党人以微弱多数获胜。—**slenderness** *n* [U]

slept /slɛpt; slept/ the past tense and past participle of SLEEP

sleuth /sluθ; sluːθ/ *n* [C] *old-fashioned* someone who tries to find out information about a crime; DETECTIVE【过时】侦探

S lev·el /ˈɛs lɛvḷ; ˈes levəl/ an examination at a very high standard in the British GCE system, higher than an A level, usually taken at the age of 18 S 级考试,特级程度考试〔英国普通教育证书体系中较高级别的考试。高于 A 级,应试者多为 18 岁的学生〕

slew[1] /slu; sluː/ *v* [I,T always+adv/prep] to turn or swing suddenly and violently, or to make something do this (使)急转,(使)突然侧滑: **[+around/sideways]** *I lost control of the car and it slewed sideways into the ditch.* 我的车子突然失去控制,侧滑掉进了沟里。

slew[2] the past tense of SLAY

slew[3] *n* **a slew of** *informal* a large number of【非正式】大量,许多: *We've got a whole slew of difficulties.* 我们有一大堆的困难。

slice[1] /slaɪs; slaɪs/ *n* **1** [C] a flat piece of bread, meat etc cut from a larger piece 片,薄片,切片: *a slice of bread and butter* 一片(抹上)黄油(的)面包 | *Cut the pork into thin slices.* 把猪肉切成薄片。—see picture on page A7 参见 A7 页图 **2** [C] a part or share of something good〔指好东西的〕份儿,部分: *Everyone wanted a slice of the profits.* 这利润每个人都想占一份。**3** [C] a kitchen tool used for lifting and serving pieces of food〔用于分菜或铲起食物的〕小铲子,锅铲 —see also 另见 FISH SLICE **4 a)** [U] a spinning movement of the ball in sports such as tennis and golf, which makes it move to one side rather than straight ahead〔网球、高尔夫球等的〕削球,斜切球,侧旋球 **b)** [C] a way of hitting the ball which makes it do this 削球打法,斜切球打法 **5** **a slice of life** a description or image in a film, play, or book which shows life as it really is〔电影、书等中如实反映的〕生活的一个侧面,现实生活的片段 —see also 另见 **a slice of the cake** (CAKE[1] (7))

slice[2] *v* **1** also 又作 **slice up** [T] to cut meat, bread etc into thin flat pieces 把…切成薄片: *Could you slice the joint for me?* 你能替我把这一大块肉切成薄片吗? —see picture on page A11 参见 A11 页图 **2** [I always+adv/prep,T] to cut something easily with one long movement of a sharp knife or edge〔干净利落地〕切,割,切开,割破: **[+into/through]** *The blade's so sharp it could easily slice through your finger.* 这刀片锋利得很,一下就能割破你的手指。| **slice sth in two/in half etc** 把…切成两半 **3** [I always+adv/prep,T] to move quickly and easily through something such as water or air, or to make something do this (使)轻松迅速地划过〔水面等〕; (使)轻快地穿过〔空中等〕: **[+through/into]** *The speedboat sliced through the waters of the lake.* 快艇轻快地在湖水中前进。**4** [T] to hit the ball in sports such as tennis or golf so that it spins sideways instead of moving straight forward〔打网球、高尔夫球等时〕削〔球〕,斜切〔球〕,打〔侧旋球〕**5** **any way you slice it** *AmE spoken* whatever way you choose to consider the problem【美口】无论你怎样考虑这个问题

slice sth ↔ **off** *phr v* [T] to cut something with one long movement of a sharp knife etc so that it becomes separate〔一刀〕切下,〔一刀〕割去: *With one blow of his sword, Igor sliced off the man's head.* 伊戈尔把剑一挥,砍下了那个人的头。

sliced bread /ˌ· ˈ·/ *n* [U] **1** bread that is sold already cut into slices〔出售时已切好的〕切片面包 **2** **the best thing since sliced bread** *informal* to be new and very helpful, useful etc【非正式】新且非常有用的东西: *He reckons his new word processor is the best thing since sliced bread.* 他认为他那台新的文字处理机是最近问世的最好的产品。

S

slick¹ /slɪk; slɪk/ *adj* **1** using clever talk to persuade people but in a way that does not seem sincere or honest 圆滑的, 花言巧语的: *a slick salesman* 圆滑的推销员 **2** a slick film, programme etc is cleverly made and attractive but contains no important or interesting ideas〔电影等〕制作精巧而内容肤浅的; 华而不实的: *the usual slick Hollywood stuff* 那种技巧高明而内容肤浅的好莱坞常见货色 **3** *informal* working or moving very smoothly, skilfully and effectively【非正式】熟练的, 灵巧的: *a slick operation* 技巧纯熟的手术 | *He got round the defender using some slick footwork.* 他用灵巧的步伐突破了后卫的防守。**4** smooth and slippery 光滑的, 滑溜的: **[+with]** *He felt his hands grow slick with sweat.* 他觉得自己双手在出汗变滑。**5** *AmE old-fashioned* very good or attractive【美, 过时】很好的, 吸引人的 **—slickly** *adv* **—slickness** *n* [U]

slick² *n* [C] **1** an area of oil on the surface of water or on a road; OIL SLICK〔水面或路面的〕浮油, 油层, 油膜 **2** *AmE* a magazine printed on good quality paper with a shiny surface, usually with a lot of colour pictures【美】用优质有光纸印刷并带有大量彩色图片的杂志; glossy magazine (GLOSSY²(1)) *especially BrE*【尤英】**3** a smooth car tyre used for racing〔赛车的〕磨光轮胎

slick³ *v*

slick sth ↔ **down/back** *phr v* [T] to make hair or fur smooth and shiny by using oil, water etc〔用油、水等〕使〔头发等〕光滑发亮: *His hair was slicked back, as was the fashion then.* 他的头发用油向后梳理得光溜溜的, 那是当时的时尚。

slick·er /ˈslɪkɚ; ˈslɪkə/ *n* [C] *AmE* a coat made to keep out the rain【美】油布雨衣, 防水衣 —see also 另见 **city slicker**

slide¹ /slaɪd; slaɪd/ *v past tense and past participle* **slid** /slɪd; slɪd/ **1** [I,T] to move smoothly over a surface while continuing to touch it, or to make something move in this way (使)滑动: **[+along/across/down etc]** *The kids were sliding on the ice.* 孩子们在冰上滑行。| **slide sth across/along etc** *Peter slid his glass across the table.* 彼得推动玻璃杯使它滑到桌子对面。**2** [I,T always+adv/prep] to move somewhere quietly without being noticed, or to move something in this way (使)悄悄移动, 偷偷溜走: **[+into/out of etc]** *Daniel slid out of the room when no one was looking.* 丹尼尔趁没人看见, 偷偷溜出了房间。| **slide sth into/out of etc** *She slid a gun into her pocket.* 她悄悄地把手枪放进口袋。**3** [I] if prices etc slide, they become lower〔价格等〕下滑, 降低: *When will the government take action to support the sliding pound?* 政府什么时候才会采取行动支持正在下跌的英镑? **4 let sth slide** to let a situation get gradually worse, without trying to stop it〔对某事〕听其自然, 任其恶化, 放任不管: *Simon had really let things slide and the house was a mess.* 西蒙真的是不闻不问, 任由房子变得一团糟。

slide² *n*

1 ►FOR CHILDREN 儿童用的◄ [C] a large structure for children to slide down at a PLAYGROUND〔儿童游戏用的〕滑梯

2 ►FOR HAIR 用于头发◄ [C] a small metal or plastic object that holds your hair in place 小发夹

3 ►MOVEMENT 移动◄ [singular] a sliding movement across a surface 滑动, 打滑: *The car went into a slide on the surface.* 汽车在地面上打滑。

4 ►PICTURE 图片◄ [C] a small piece of film in a frame that shows a picture on a SCREEN¹ (2a) when you shine light through it 幻灯片: *Don't you want to see my slides of Korea?* 你不想看看我那介绍韩国的幻灯片吗?

5 ►PRICE/AMOUNT 价格/数量◄ [singular] a fall in prices, amounts etc 滑落, 跌落, 下降: *a slide in living standards* 生活水平的下降

6 ►IN SCIENCE 在科学上◄ [C] a small piece of thin glass used for holding something when you look at it under a MICROSCOPE〔显微镜用的〕载(物)玻(璃)片 —see picture at 参见 LABORATORY 图

7 ►MUSIC 音乐◄ [C] a part of a machine or musical instrument, such as the U-shaped tube of a TROMBONE〔机器或乐器的〕滑动部件〈如长号的U字形伸缩管〉

8 ►EARTH/SNOW 土/雪◄ [C] *AmE* a sudden fall of earth, stones, snow etc down a slope【美】〔土、石、雪等的〕崩落, 崩塌 —see also 另见 LANDSLIDE

slide rule /ˈ· ·/ *n* [C] an old-fashioned instrument that looks like a ruler with a middle part that slides, used for calculating 滑尺, 计算尺〔一种旧式计算工具〕

sliding door /ˌ·· ˈ·/ *n* [C] a door that slides open rather than swinging from one side 滑门, 拉门

sliding scale /ˌ·· ˈ·/ *n* [C] a system for paying tax, wages etc in which the rates that you pay VARY according to changing conditions〔工资、税额等随情况的变化而调整的〕滑动折算制, 浮动计算法, 比例相应增减制

slight¹ /slaɪt; slaɪt/ *adj* **1** not serious or not important 轻微的, 微小的, 少量的: *a slight headache* 轻微的头痛 | *a slight improvement* 些许改善 | *There's been a slight change of plan.* 计划略有变动。| **not the slightest chance/doubt/difference etc** (=no chance, doubt etc at all) 没有一点机会/怀疑/差别等 *It doesn't make the slightest difference whether we discuss it today or tomorrow.* 我们今天还是明天讨论, 没有任何区别。| *"What were they talking about?" "I haven't the slightest idea."* "他们当时在谈什么?" "我一点也不知道。" **2** thin and delicate 纤细的, 瘦小的; 纤弱的; 脆弱的: *a slight figure in a red dress* 一个穿着红色连衣裙的纤弱身影

slight² *v* [T] to offend someone by treating them rudely or without respect 轻视, 怠慢, 冷落: *Denver felt slighted when no one called him back.* 没人给丹佛回电话, 他觉得自己受到了冷落。**—slighting** *adj*: *slighting remarks* 轻蔑的话

slight³ *n* [C] *formal* a remark or action that offends someone【正式】轻蔑, 怠慢, 冷落: **[+on/to]** *Jane took your comment as a slight on her work.* 简把你的评论看作是对她工作的轻视。

slight·ly /ˈslaɪtlɪ; ˈslaɪtli/ *adv* **1 slightly different/older/worried etc** a little bit different, older etc 略为不同/年长了些/有点担心等: *a slightly different attitude* 略为不同的态度 | *Alison is slightly older than the others.* 艾利森比其他人略为年长。| *"Are you worried about him?" "Just slightly."* "你为他担心吗?" "稍微有一点。" **2 slightly-built** having a thin and delicate body 身材瘦小的

Sli·go /ˈslaɪgo; ˈslaɪgəʊ/ a COUNTY in the west of the Republic of Ireland 斯莱戈〔爱尔兰共和国西部一郡〕

slim¹ /slɪm; slɪm/ *comparative* 比较级 **slimmer** *superlative* 最高级 **slimmest** *adj* **1** someone who is slim is attractively thin 苗条的, 修长的: *a slim waist* 苗条的腰身 —see 见 THIN (USAGE) **2 slim chance/hopes etc** very little chance etc of getting what you want〔机会、希望等〕微小的, 渺茫的: *There's a slim chance someone may have survived.* 有人幸存下来的可能性不大。**3** thinner than usual or less than usual 非常薄[少]的: *a slim volume of poetry* 薄薄的一册诗歌集 | *the slimmest of majorities* 极微弱的多数

slim² *v* **slimmed, slimming 1** [I] to make yourself thinner by eating less, taking a lot of exercise etc〔通过节食、加强运动等〕减肥: *I'm going to start slimming after Christmas.* 我准备过了圣诞节就开始减肥。**2** [I,T] also 又作 **slim down** to reduce the size or number of something (使)减少, 缩小; 裁减: *It was decided to slim down the workforce.* 已经决定要裁减人员。**—slimmer** *n* [C]

slime /slaɪm; slaɪm/ *n* [U] **1** a thick slippery substance that looks or smells unpleasant〔令人不愉快的〕黏质物 **2** a slippery substance that comes from the bodies of SNAILS and slugs (SLUG¹ (1))〔蜗牛、鼻涕虫等的〕黏液

slim·line /ˈslɪmˌlaɪn; ˈslɪmlaɪn/ *adj* **1** a slimline drink has fewer CALORIES than the normal type〔饮料〕低卡路里的, 低热量的, 适于减肥的 **2** a slimline piece of equipment is smaller or thinner than others of the same type〔设备〕体型较小的, 小巧型的: *a slimline dishwasher* 小型洗碗机

slim·ming /ˈslɪmɪŋ; ˈslɪmɪŋ/ *n* [U] the activity of trying to make yourself thinner by eating less, taking exercise etc〔通过节食、运动等〕减轻体重, 减肥: **slimming club/magazine/foods etc** *I've found a good slimming plan.* 我发现了一个很好的减肥方案。

slim·y /ˈslaɪmɪ; ˈslaɪmi/ *adj* **1** covered with slime 有黏液的, 黏糊糊的: *slimy mud* 黏糊糊的泥巴 **2** *informal* unpleasantly friendly in order to get something for yourself【非正式】谄媚的, 讨好的: *a slimy manner* 谄媚的态度 **—sliminess** *n* [U]

sling¹ /slɪŋ; slɪŋ/ *v past tense and past participle* **slung** /slʌŋ; slʌŋ/ [T always+adv/prep] **1** to throw something roughly or with a lot of force 用力投, 掷, 抛〔某物〕: *Sling me the keys, will you?* 把钥匙抛给我, 好吗? | **sling sth across/into etc** *Fiona slung her bag across the room.* 菲奥娜把手提包扔到屋子那边。**2** to throw or put something somewhere so that it can hang 悬起, 使吊起, 使落在…上: **sling sth on/over etc** *He slung his coat over his shoulder.* 他把外衣搭在肩上。| *A line of flags was slung between the trees.* 一排旗子挂在两棵树之间。**3** *informal* to make someone leave or go to a place【非正式】把〔某人〕赶出…; 开除; 把〔某人〕投进…: **sling sb into/out of etc** *Sam was slung into jail for punching a cop.* 萨姆因出拳殴打警察而被投进监狱。| *Watch it, or you'll be slung out of school.* 当心点, 不然你会被学校开除的。**4 sling your hook** *BrE slang* to go away【英俚】走开, 离开 —see also 另见 MUDSLINGING

sling² *n* [C] **1** a piece of cloth tied around your neck to support your injured arm or hand〔用以固定断臂或断手的〕悬带, 吊带: *She had her arm in a sling for months.* 她的胳膊吊了几个月的

悬带。**2** a set of ropes or strong pieces of cloth that hold heavy objects to be lifted or carried〔用以提起或悬挂重物的〕吊索, 吊链 **3** a special cloth seat that fastens over your shoulders for carrying a baby〔背小孩的〕背带 **4** a cloth band on a weapon for carrying it〔枪的〕肩带, 背带 **5** a long, thin piece of rope with a piece of leather in the middle, used in the past as a weapon for throwing stones〔从前的〕投石器; 弹弓

sling·back /ˈslɪŋˌbæk; ˈslɪŋbæk/ *n* [C] a kind of woman's shoe that is open at the back and has a band going round the heel〔鞋后帮为一条带的〕露跟女鞋 —see picture at 参见 SHOE[1] 图

sling·shot /ˈslɪŋˌʃɑt; ˈslɪŋʃɒt/ *n* [C] *AmE* a small stick in the shape of a Y with a thin band of rubber, used by children to throw stones【美】〔儿童用以发射石子的〕弹弓; CATAPULT[1] (2) *BrE*【英】

slink /slɪŋk; slɪŋk/ *past tense and past participle* **slunk** /slʌŋk; slʌŋk/ *v* [I always+adv/prep] to move somewhere quietly and secretly, especially because you are afraid or ashamed 鬼鬼祟祟地走, 偷偷溜走: **[+away/off/back etc]** *I saw you slinking off early!* 我看见你一早就偷偷溜走!

slink·y /ˈslɪŋkɪ; ˈslɪŋki/ *adj* a slinky dress etc is smooth and tight and shows the shape of your body〔衣服等〕紧身的, 显出体形线条的: *a slinky black dress* 紧身的黑色连衣裙

slip[1] /slɪp; slɪp/ *v* **slipped, slipping** (S3, W2)

1 ►SLIDE 滑◄ [I] to accidentally slide a short distance quickly or to fall by sliding 滑; 滑倒, 失足: *Suddenly, Frank slipped and fell over the edge.* 弗兰克突然滑倒, 从边缘上掉了下去。| *My foot slipped and I nearly fell.* 我的脚一滑, 差点摔倒。—see also 另见 SLIPPERY

2 ►MOVE QUICKLY 快速移动◄ [I always+adv/prep] to move quickly, smoothly, or secretly 溜走, 悄悄地走: **slip out/through/by etc** *Nobody saw her slip silently out.* 没有人看到她悄悄地溜了出去。| *The weeks slipped slowly by.* 这几个星期在不知不觉中慢慢流逝了。| *The terrorists had slipped through the airport's security net.* 恐怖分子混过了机场的安全检查。

3 ►PUT STH SOMEWHERE 把某物置于某处◄ [T] to put something somewhere or give someone something quietly, secretly, or smoothly 把…悄悄放在[递给]…, 偷偷塞进[给]; 利落地放置: **slip sth around/into/through etc** *I slipped a note into his hand under the table.* 我偷偷从桌子底下塞给他一张条子。| *I slipped the Mercedes into gear.* 我利索地把梅赛德斯－奔驰汽车挂上挡。| **slip sb sth** *Jerry slipped the waiter £5 to get them a good table.* 杰里悄悄塞给侍者五英镑, 以便给他们安排个好桌位。

4 ►LOSE YOUR HOLD 松手◄ [I always+adv/prep] if something that you are holding slips, it falls because it is difficult to hold or was not held firmly 滑落, 滑掉, 滑跌: *The soap slipped out of my hand.* 肥皂从我手中滑落。| *The knife slipped and cut my finger.* 刀子一滑, 划破了我的手指。

5 ►GET WORSE 变坏◄ [I] to become worse or lower than before 变坏; 下降, 下跌: *Profits have slipped slightly this year.* 今年利润略有下降。| *You must be slipping – you never used to miss a shot like that.* 你肯定退步了, 你过去打枪从没有这样失过手。

6 slip your mind/memory if something slips your mind you forget to do something 被忽略/被遗忘: *I'm sorry I missed your birthday; it completely slipped my mind.* 我很抱歉错过了你的生日; 我完全忘了。

7 let sth slip (through your fingers) to not take an opportunity, offer etc 错过〔机会等〕: *You're not going to let a chance like that slip through your fingers, are you?* 你不会错过那样的好机会吧, 是吗?

8 slip a disc to suffer an injury when one of the connecting parts between the bones in your back moves out of place 椎间盘滑脱[突出]

9 ►GET FREE 获得自由◄ [T] to get free from something that was holding you 挣脱, 摆脱: *The dog slipped his collar and ran away.* 那条狗挣脱项圈跑掉了。

10 let (it) slip (that) to say something without meaning to, when you had wanted it to be a secret 无意中说出〔秘密〕: *Leila let slip that she's thinking about leaving the company.* 莉拉无意中说出她打算离开公司。

11 slip through the net if someone or something slips through the net, they are not caught or dealt with by the system that is supposed to catch them or deal with them 漏网; 未受到有关部门的抓捕[处理]: *homeless people slipping through the social security net* 社会福利制度未照顾到的无家可归者

slip into sth *phr v* [T] **1** to put clothes on quickly 迅速穿上〔衣服〕: *I'll just slip into something more comfortable.* 我要穿件舒服一点的衣服。**2 slip into sleep/unconsciousness etc** to gradually fall asleep, become unconscious etc 慢慢入睡/逐渐失去知觉等: *Granny slipped into a coma and died peacefully that night.* 奶奶那天晚上逐渐陷入昏迷, 安详辞世。

slip sth ↔ **off** *phr v* [T] to take clothes off quickly 迅速脱去〔衣服〕: *Slip off your shirt and I'll take your blood pressure.* 把衬衣脱掉, 我来给你量血压。

slip sth ↔ **on** *phr v* [T] to put clothes on quickly 迅速穿上〔衣服〕: *Amanda slipped her robe on.* 阿曼达匆忙地穿上了长袍。

slip out *phr v* [I] if something slips out, you say it without really intending to 被无意说出: *I'm sorry I spoilt your surprise. It just slipped out.* 很抱歉我泄露了你要给人的惊喜, 我不小心说漏了嘴。

slip out of sth *phr v* [T] to take clothes off quickly 迅速脱下〔衣服〕: *Keith slipped out of his jacket.* 基思迅速脱下夹克。

slip sth **over on** sb *phr v* [T] *informal, especially AmE* to play a clever trick on someone【非正式, 尤美】巧妙地捉弄某人, 欺骗某人

slip up *phr v* [I] to make a mistake 犯错误, 疏忽: *The office slipped up and the letter was never sent.* 办公室出了点差错, 根本没有发出那封信。—see also 另见 SLIP-UP

slip[2] *n*

1 ►PAPER 纸◄ [C] a small or narrow piece of paper 小纸片, 纸条: **[+of]** *Rosie marked her place with a slip of paper.* 罗西用纸条, 标出她(看书)看到了什么地方。

2 ►MISTAKE 错误◄ [C] a small mistake 小错误: *If you make a slip, rub it out neatly.* 如果你写错了, 那就擦干净。

3 a slip of the tongue/pen something that you say when you meant to say something else 口误/笔误: *"Jim" was a slip of the tongue; I meant to say 'John'.* Jim(吉姆)是口误, 我是想说 John(约翰)。—see also 另见 FREUDIAN SLIP

4 give sb the slip *informal* to manage to escape from someone who is chasing you【非正式】摆脱某人的追逐, 甩掉某人: *Bates gave the police the slip.* 贝茨摆脱了警察的追捕。

5 ►SLIDE 滑◄ [C] an act of sliding a short distance or of falling by sliding 滑动; 滑倒

6 ►WOMAN'S CLOTHES 女服◄ [C] a piece of clothing that a woman wears under her clothes, and which hangs from her shoulders or her waist〔背带式〕衬裙; 〔半截式〕衬裙

7 a slip of a girl/boy etc *old-fashioned* a small thin young person【过时】瘦小的女孩/男孩等: *He was only a slip of a lad.* 他只是一个瘦小的男孩。

8 ►CRICKET 板球◄ [C usually plural 一般用复数] a part of the field where players stand, trying to catch the ball in CRICKET〔板球运动中击球员右后方的〕防守位置

9 ►CLAY 黏土◄ [U] clay that is almost liquid and is used for making pots〔制陶器用的〕泥浆, 泥釉

slip case /ˈ· ·/ *n* [C] a hard cover for putting a book in〔厚纸做的〕书套

slip co·ver /ˈ· ˌ··/ *n* [C] *AmE*【美】**1** a paper cover for a book; DUST JACKET〔书的〕封套, 书套 **2** a loose cloth cover for furniture 家具套

slip·knot /ˈslɪpˌnɑt; ˈslɪpnɒt/ *n* [C] a knot that you can make tighter or looser by pulling one of its ends 活结, 滑结

slip-on /ˈ· ·/ *n* [plural] shoes without a fastening that you can slide onto your feet 无带扣的鞋子, 便鞋, 拖鞋 —**slip-on** *adj*: *slip-on shoes* 无带扣的便鞋

slip·page /ˈslɪpɪdʒ; ˈslɪpɪdʒ/ *n* [C,U] the amount by which something slips, or the act of slipping 滑动(量); 下降, 下跌

slipped disc /ˌ· ˈ·/ *n* [C usually singular 一般用单数] a painful injury caused when one of the connecting parts between the bones in your back moves out of place 椎间盘滑脱

slip·per /ˈslɪpɚ; ˈslɪpə/ *n* [C] a light soft shoe that you wear at home（室内）便鞋, 拖鞋 —see picture at 参见 SHOE[1] 图

slip·per·y /ˈslɪpərɪ; ˈslɪpəri/ *adj* **1** something that is slippery is difficult to hold, walk on etc because it is wet or GREASY〔因湿或有油脂〕滑的, 滑溜的: *Be careful! The floor's very slippery.* 小心！地板很滑。**2** *informal* someone who is slippery cannot be trusted and usually manages to avoid being punished【非正式】滑头的, 不可信赖的: **slippery customer** (=someone you cannot trust) 狡猾的家伙 *I wouldn't lend him any money, he's a real slippery customer.* 我一点钱也不会借给他, 他是个不折不扣的老滑头。**3 be on the slippery slope** *BrE informal* to have begun a process or habit which is hard to stop and which will develop into something extremely bad【英, 非正式】〔恶习等〕无法克制以至后果严重: *Once you start taking soft drugs you're on the slippery slope to becoming an addict.* 一旦开始吸食软性毒品, 你就会无法克制, 一定会变成个瘾君子。—**slipperiness** *n* [U]

slip·py /ˈslɪpɪ; ˈslɪpi/ *adj informal* a slippy surface or object is difficult to hold, walk on etc because it is wet or GREASY【非正式】〔因湿或有油脂〕滑的, 滑溜的

slip road /ˈ· ·/ *n* [C] *BrE* a road for driving onto or off a MOTORWAY【英】〔高速公路的〕支路, 叉道; RAMP (1) *AmE*【美】—see picture on page A3 参见 A3 页图

slip·shod /ˈslɪp͵ʃɑd; ˈslɪpʃɒd/ *adj* done too quickly and carelessly 马虎的, 随便的, 草率的: *a slipshod piece of work* 马虎完成的工作

slip·stream /ˈslɪp͵strim; ˈslɪpstriːm/ *n* [singular] the area of low air pressure just behind a fast-moving vehicle〔飞驰的赛车后面形成的〕低压气穴

slip-up /ˈ· ·/ *n* [C] a careless mistake that spoils a process or plan〔影响进程或计划的〕失误, 疏忽: *We should have informed you, I'm sorry for the slip-up.* 我们本该通知你们的, 对这一失误我表示歉意。

slip·way /ˈslɪp͵we; ˈslɪpweɪ/ *n* [C] a sloping track that is used for moving boats into or out of the water〔船的〕下水滑道, 滑台, 船台

slit[1] *v* /slɪt; slɪt/ *past tense and past participle* **slit** *present participle* **slitting** [T] to make a straight narrow cut in cloth, paper, skin etc 切开; 裁开; 撕开: **slit sth open** (=open it by slitting it) 撕开[裁开]某物 *Guy slit open the envelope.* 盖伊拆开信封。| **slit sb's throat** (=kill someone with a knife) 割开某人的喉咙

slit[2] *n* [C] a long straight narrow cut or hole 狭长的切口; 裂缝: *light shining through a slit in the door* 透过门缝照进来的光线 | *a skirt with a slit up the side* 侧边开叉的裙子

slith·er /ˈslɪðɚ; ˈslɪðə/ *v* [I always+adv/prep] to slide smoothly across a surface, twisting or moving from side to side 蜿蜒地滑动; 摇晃地滑行: **[+through/across etc]** *snakes slithering through the grass* 蜿蜒爬过草丛的蛇 | *He slithered down the muddy bank into the water.* 他摇摇晃晃地走下泥泞的堤岸踩入水里。

slith·er·y /ˈslɪðərɪ; ˈslɪðəri/ *adj* unpleasantly slippery〔令人不快地〕滑溜溜的

sliv·er /ˈslɪvɚ; ˈslɪvə/ *n* [C] a very small thin pointed piece of something that has been cut or broken off something〔切下或裂开的〕碎片, 裂片: *a sliver of glass* 一块玻璃碎片 | *a sliver of cake* 一小块蛋糕 —see picture on page A7 参见 A7 页图

sliv·o·vitz /ˈslɪvəvɪts; ˈslɪvəvɪts/ *n* [U] a strong alcoholic drink made in SE Europe from PLUMS 梅子白兰地〔产于东南欧的一种烈性酒〕

Sloane Square /͵slon ˋskwɛr; ͵sləʊn ˈskweə/ a fashionable, expensive part of central London with many expensive shops 斯隆广场〔伦敦市中心一处时尚豪华的地区, 有许多高档商店〕

slob /slɑb; slɒb/ *n* [C] *informal* someone who is lazy, dirty, untidy, or rude【非正式】懒虫; 脏鬼; 粗鲁汉: *Come on, get up and do something you big slob!* 来吧, 起来干点活, 你这条大懒虫!

slob around *phr v* [I] *BrE slang* to spend time doing nothing and being lazy【英俚】游手好闲, 无所事事

slob·ber /ˈslɑbɚ; ˈslɒbə/ *v* [I] to let SALIVA (=the liquid produced by your mouth) come out of your mouth and run down 流涎, 淌口水: *I hate dogs that slobber everywhere.* 我讨厌到处淌口水的狗。

slobber over sth/sb *phr v* [T] to keep saying how much you love someone in a way that embarrasses or annoys other people〔使他人难为情地〕对…表达爱慕, 肉麻地示爱: *They keep slobbering over each other.* 他俩老是肉麻地示爱。

slob·ber·y /ˈslɑbərɪ; ˈslɒbəri/ *adj* a slobbery kiss or mouth is unpleasantly wet〔嘴巴〕口水多的, 湿得讨厌的

sloe /slo; sləʊ/ *n* [C] a small bitter fruit like a PLUM 黑刺李

sloe gin /͵· ˈ·/ *n* [U] an alcoholic drink made with SLOEs, GIN, and sugar 黑刺李杜松子酒

slog[1] /slɑg; slɒg/ *v informal*【非正式】**1 slog (away) at** *especially BrE*【尤英】also 又作 **slog through** to work hard at something without stopping, especially when the work is boring or difficult 不停地卖力苦干: *I've been slogging away at this essay for days.* 为了这篇文章我已经埋头苦干了好几天了。| *all those books we had to slog through at school* 我们必须在学校啃完的那些书 | **slog your guts out** *informal* (=work extremely hard)【非正式】拼命干 *slogging their guts out to get it finished on time* 拼命干争取按时完成 **2** [I always+adv/prep] to make a long hard journey somewhere, especially on foot〔徒步〕长时间艰苦地行进: **[+down/up/through etc]** *We slogged up the hill with the wind blowing against us.* 我们顽强地顶着风爬上了山。**3 slog it out** *BrE* to fight or argue about something until one side wins【英】斗个胜负, 争出个高低

slog[2] *n* [singular] **1** *BrE informal* a piece of work that takes a lot of time and effort and is usually boring【英, 非正式】艰苦乏味的工作: *It was a bit of a slog addressing all those envelopes.* 给这么多信封写上姓名地址, 真是一件乏味的苦差事。**2** a long period of tiring walking 长途跋涉: *a long hard slog uphill* 长时间的艰苦爬山

slo·gan /ˈslogən; ˈsləʊgən/ *n* [C] a short easily-remembered phrase used by an advertiser, politician etc 口号, 标语: *demonstrators chanting anti-racist slogans* 齐声高呼着反种族歧视口号的示威者 | *We need an advertising slogan for the new campaign.* 我们这次新的促销活动需要一条广告标语。

sloop /slup; sluːp/ *n* [C] a small sailing ship with one central MAST (=pole for sails) 单桅小帆船

slop[1] /slɑp; slɒp/ *v* **slopped, slopping 1** [I always+adv/prep] if liquid in a container slops, it moves around or over the edge in an uncontrolled way〔液体〕晃荡; 溅出, 溢出: **[+around/about/over]** *The water slopped around in the bucket.* 水在桶里晃荡。**2** [T] to make liquid do this 使〔液体〕晃荡; 使溅出, 使溢出: **slop sth over/into etc** *He slopped his beer all over her skirt.* 他把啤酒溅了她一裙子。**3** [T] *AmE* to feed slop to pigs【美】用食物残渣喂〔猪〕

slop about *phr v* [I] *BrE informal*【英, 非正式】**1** to spend time being lazy 懒散地消磨时间: *We spent the day slopping about the house.* 我们在家里懒懒散散地过了一天。**2** to play or move around in mud, dirty water etc 在烂泥[脏水等]中玩耍[走动]

slop out *phr v* [I] when prisoners slop out, they empty their toilet buckets〔囚犯〕倒便桶 —**slopping-out** *n* [U]

slop[2] also 又作 **slops** *plural n* [U] **1** food waste that is used to feed animals〔喂动物的〕食物残渣, 残汤剩菜 **2** *BrE* liquid waste from food or drinks【英】〔食物或饮料的〕剩汁, 残汁, 泔水: *Empty all your slops into the bucket over there.* 请把你们的剩饭全部倒进那边的桶里。**3** *BrE* dirty water or URINE【英】脏水; 粪尿 **4** food that is too soft and tastes bad 稀软味差的流质食物: *They served up some kind of slop I just couldn't eat.* 他们端上一些我简直无法下咽的汤汤水水。

slope[1] /slop; sləʊp/ *n* **1** [C] a piece of ground or a surface that slopes 斜坡, 斜面: *walking slowly up a steep slope* 慢慢爬上陡峭的斜坡 | **a gentle slope** (=a slope that is not steep) 平缓的斜坡 **2** [singular] the angle at which something slopes in relation to a flat surface 斜度, 坡度: *a slope of 30 degrees* 30° 的斜坡 3

slope[2] *v* [I] if the ground or a surface slopes, it is higher at one end than the other 倾斜, 成斜坡: **[+up/down/away etc]** *The land slopes down to the sea.* 这块地向海边倾斜。

slope off *phr v* [I] *BrE informal* to leave somewhere quietly and secretly, especially when you are avoiding work【英, 非正式】〔尤指为了逃避工作〕悄悄走开, 溜掉: *Mike's always sloping off when it's time to do the dishes.* 到了洗碗的时候迈克总要溜掉。

slop·py /ˈslɑpɪ; ˈslɒpi/ *adj* **1** not done carefully or thoroughly 马虎的, 随便的, 草率的: *This piece of work is very sloppy.* 这件工作做得非常马虎。| *sloppy writing* 草率的写作 **2** sloppy clothes are loose-fitting, untidy, or dirty〔衣服〕太宽的, 不整洁的, 邋遢的: *a sloppy old sweater* 一件又脏又旧的毛衣 **3** expressing your feelings of love too strongly and in a silly way 痴情得可笑的: *He keeps sending me sloppy letters.* 他不断给我寄痴情可笑的求爱信。**4** not solid enough 太稀的; 不结实的: *sloppy jelly* 稀果冻 —**sloppily** *adv* —**sloppiness** *n* [U]

sloppy joe /͵slɑpɪ ˋdʒo; ͵slɒpi ˈdʒəʊ/ *n* [C] **1** *AmE* a kind of food, made from BEEF with SPICEs added and served on a BUN (2)【美】〔涂面包用的〕炒牛肉酱 **2** *BrE* a big loose-fitting SWEATER【英】宽松套衫; 宽松运动衣

slosh /slɑʃ; slɒʃ/ *v* **1** [I always+adv/prep] if a liquid in a container sloshes around, it moves against the sides of its container in an uncontrolled way〔容器中的液体〕摇动, 晃荡: **[+around/about]** *Water sloshed about in the bottom of the boat.* 水在船底

哗啦哗啦地晃荡。**2** [T always + adv/prep] to make a liquid do this 摇动〔液体〕，使晃荡：**slosh sth around/about** *Joe sloshed the whisky around in his glass.* 乔摇动着他杯子里的威士忌酒。**3** [I always+adv/prep] to walk through water or mud noisily 哗哗地涉水而行，在泥泞中走：**[+through/about]** *sloshing through the mud* 在泥泞中跋涉 **4** [T] *BrE slang* to hit someone; PUNCH[1] (1)【英俚】打，猛击〔某人〕

sloshed /slaʃt; slɒʃt/ *adj* [not before noun 不用于名词前] *informal* drunk【非正式】喝醉的：*He was already well sloshed when we got there.* 我们到那里时，他已经喝得烂醉了。

slot[1] /slat; slɒt/ *n* [C] **1** a long narrow hole made in a surface, especially for putting something into〔可放进东西的〕狭孔，狭缝；投币口：*Place your coins in the slot slowly.* 把你的硬币慢慢放进投币口。**2** a short period of time allowed for one particular event on a programme or timetable〔节目单或时间表上为某节目或事项排定的〕一段时间：*a regular ten-minute slot on the breakfast show* 早餐节目中定时的10分钟广播时间 | *landing slots at Heathrow Airport* 希思罗机场的规定降落时间

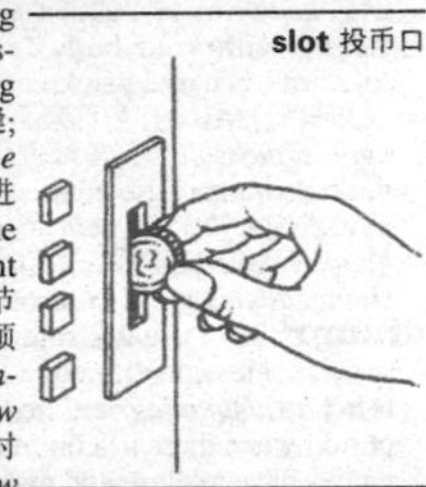

slot[2] *v* **slotted, slotting** [I,T always+adv/prep] to go into a slot, or to make something do this（把…）插进窄孔，插入狭缝：**[+in]** *The disc slots in at the front.* 磁盘是从前面插进去的。| **slot sth together** (=fit together) *You buy the bookshelf in pieces and then slot them together yourself.* 这种书橱你买的是组件，然后自己把组件组装起来。

slot in *phr v* [I,T] *informal* to find a time or a place for someone or something in a plan, organization etc【非正式】（给）定时间；（给）定位置：**slot sb/sth ↔ in** *We should be able to slot the meeting in before lunch.* 我们应该可以把会议安排在午饭之前。

sloth /sloθ; sləʊθ/ *n* **1** [C] an animal of Central and South America that moves very slowly, has grey fur, and lives in trees 树獭〔产于中、南美洲，有灰色的皮毛，在树上生活，动作迟缓〕**2** [U] *formal* laziness【正式】懒惰，懒散：*combination of sloth and boredom* 懒惰加上厌倦

sloth·ful /ˈsloθfəl; ˈsləʊθfəl/ *adj formal* lazy or not active【正式】懒惰的，懒散的，不活跃的 —**slothfully** *adv* —**slothfulness** *n* [U]

slot ma·chine /ˈ· ·,·/ *n* [C] **1** a machine used for playing a game that starts when you put money into it 吃角子老虎机，投币式自动赌博机 **2** *BrE* a machine that you buy cigarettes, food, or drink from; VENDING MACHINE【英】〔投币式〕自动售货机

slotted spat·u·la /,‥ˈ···/ *n AmE* a FISH SLICE【美】煎鱼铲，（长柄）锅铲

slotted spoon /,‥ˈ·/ *n* [C] a large spoon with holes in it 有孔的大勺

slouch[1] /slautʃ; slaʊtʃ/ *v* [I] to stand, sit, or walk with a slouch 低头垂肩地站[坐、走]，无精打采地站[坐、走]：*Stop slouching, it's not good for your back.* 不要低着头，这样对你的背不好。| *I slouched in my chair.* 我无精打采地坐在椅子上。—**slouchingly** *adv*

slouch[2] *n* **1** [singular] a way of standing, sitting, or walking with your shoulders bent forward that makes you look tired or lazy〔站、坐、走路时表现出来的〕无精打采，委靡不振 **2 be no slouch (at)** *informal* to be very good or skilful at something【非正式】善于做〔某事〕：*She's certainly no slouch where organization is concerned.* 在组织工作方面她的确是个能手。

slough[1] /slʌf; slʌf/ *v*

slough sth ↔ **off** *phr v* [T] **1** *technical* to get rid of a dead outer layer of skin【术语】蜕〔皮〕，脱〔皮〕**2** *literary* to get rid of a feeling, belief etc【文】抛弃，消除〔感觉、信念等〕：*He was unable to slough off the stigmatizing label of criminal.* 他无法消除那个耻辱的犯罪标签。

slough[2] /slau; slaʊ/ *n* **1** [C] an area of land covered in deep dirty water or mud 泥沼，沼泽地，泥坑 **2 a slough of despair/troubles etc** *literary* a bad situation or condition that you cannot get out of easily【文】绝望的境地/烦恼的深渊等：*He soon became the forgotten man and was able to return to his slough of despondency.* 他很快就成为被遗忘的人，又回到他绝望的深渊。

Slough of Des·pond, the /ˌslau əv dɪˈspand; ˌslaʊ əv dɪˈspɒnd/ *literary* a situation in which you are very unhappy and there seems to be no hope that things will improve. The expression comes from the name of a place in the book *The Pilgrim's Progress* by John Bunyan.【文】绝望的深渊，绝望的泥沼〔源自于约翰·班扬的作品《天路历程》〕

Slo·va·ki·a /sloˈvakɪə; sləʊˈvɑːkiə/ a country in Eastern Europe between the Ukraine and the Czech Republic, that was formed in 1993 when Czechoslovakia was divided. 斯洛伐克〔东欧一国家。位于乌克兰和捷克共和国之间，于1993年捷克斯洛伐克解体后成立〕—**Slovakian, Slovak** /ˈslovæk; ˈsləʊvæk/ *n, adj*

Slo·ve·ni·a /sloˈvinɪə; sləʊˈviːniə/ a country in southeast Europe, between Austria and Croatia, that was formerly part of Yugoslavia. Population: 1,930,000 (2001). Capital: Ljubljana. 斯洛文尼亚〔欧洲东南部一国家。位于奥地利和克罗地亚之间，原属南斯拉夫。人口：1,930,000（2001），首都：卢布尔雅那〕—**Slovenian** *n, adj*

slov·en·ly /ˈslʌvənlɪ; ˈslʌvənli/ *adj* lazy and untidy and not caring about your appearance 不整洁的，邋遢的，不修边幅的：*The landlady was fat and slovenly.* 女房东又胖又不修边幅。—**slovenliness** *n* [U]: *a man with shabby clothes and a general air of slovenliness* 衣着褴褛、一身邋遢相的男子

Slo·vo /ˈslovo; ˈsləʊvəʊ/, **Joe** /dʒo; dʒəʊ/ (1926-95) a white South African lawyer, born in Lithuania, who had an important part in opposing the system of APARTHEID in South Africa. He was the leader of the South African Communist Party, and a leading member of the ANC. In the last two years of his life he was a minister in Nelson Mandela's government. 斯洛沃〔(1926-1995)，南非白人律师，生于立陶宛。他在反对南非种族隔离制度的斗争中发挥了重要的作用。他是南非共产党领袖，也是非洲人国民大会的领导成员。他在去世前的两年里任纳尔逊·曼德拉政府的部长〕

slow[1] /slo; sləʊ/ *adj* 

1 ▶MOVE ETC 移动等◀ not moving, being done, or happening quickly 慢的，缓慢的：*a slow train* 缓慢的火车 | *a slow, smoochy dance at the end of the evening* 晚会快结束时搂抱着跳的慢舞 | *The computer's just so slow today, isn't it?* 电脑今天速度真慢，是吧？

2 ▶LONG TIME 长时间◀ a) taking a long time or a longer time than usual〔比平常〕缓慢的，费时长的，耗费时日的：*With the fog and ice, our journey was very slow.* 又有雾又结冰，我们的旅程非常缓慢。| *It's quite a slow process.* 进程相当慢。**b)** taking too long, especially because of someone being unwilling〔尤指因不愿意而〕慢吞吞的，不利索的，磨磨蹭蹭的：*a slow response to our requests for help* 对我们的求助反应迟缓 | **slow to recognize/see/follow etc** *Our companies have been very slow to react to foreign competition.* 我们各公司对外国竞争的反应一直都很迟缓。

3 ▶CLOCK 时钟◀ [not before noun 不用于名词前] if a clock is slow it is showing a time earlier than the correct time〔走得〕慢了的，慢了…的：**ten minutes/five minutes etc slow** *The station clock was five minutes slow.* 火车站的钟慢了五分钟。

4 ▶LARGE ROAD 大马路◀ [only before noun 仅用于名词前] the slow lane on a large road is not intended for fast-moving vehicles〔慢车道〕不容许快速行驶的

5 ▶BUSINESS 生意◀ if business or trade is slow, there are not many customers or not much is sold 停滞的，清淡的

6 ▶STUPID 愚蠢的◀ not good or quick at understanding things 迟钝的，愚笨的：*Sometimes he can be rather slow.* 有时他会相当迟钝。| *helping the slower pupils* 帮助学得比较慢的学生 | **slow off the mark/slow on the uptake** (=not good at understanding things) 理解能力不好 —**slowly** *adv*: *The time passed slowly.* 时间过得很慢。| *slowly gathering speed as we rolled downhill* 我们的车子下坡时渐渐加快的速度

slow[2] *v* [I,T] also 又作 **slow up** to become slower or make something slower（使）放慢，（使）减速：*The train slowed as it went around the bend.* 火车在拐弯时减速。| *Business slows up at this time of year.* 每年在这个时候生意渐趋清淡。—see picture on page A3 参见A3页图 

slow down *phr v* **1** [I,T **slow** sth ↔ **down**] to become slower or make something slower（使）慢下来，（使）减速：*Motorists should slow down and take extra care in foggy conditions.* 司机在雾天应减速行驶并特别小心。| *My aching knee was beginning to slow me down.* 膝盖的疼痛开始影响到我走路的速度。**2** [I] to become less active or busy than you usually are 减少活动[工作]：*You're sixty, it's time you slowed down a bit.* 你60岁了，到了该放松一下的时候了。

slow[3] *adv* slowly 慢慢地，缓慢地 —see also 另见 GO-SLOW

slow burn /,·ˈ·/ *n* **do a slow burn** *AmE informal* to slowly get angry【美，非正式】逐渐发火：*Tony fumbled the ball and I could see the coach do a slow burn.* 托尼漏接了球，我能看出教练的火气在渐渐上升。

slow·coach /ˈsloˌkotʃ; ˈsləʊkəʊtʃ/ *n* [C] *BrE informal* someone who moves or does things too slowly【英，非正式】慢性子的人，迟钝的人，行动缓慢的人; SLOWPOKE *AmE*【美】: *Come on slowcoach, hurry up!* 嘿，磨磨蹭蹭的家伙，快点！

slow·down /ˈsloˌdaʊn; ˈsləʊdaʊn/ *n* **1** [C usually singular 一般用单数] a reduction in activity or speed 减速;〔活动的〕减少，减慢; 减退: *a slowdown in the US economy* 美国经济发展的放缓 **2** [C] *AmE* a period when people deliberately work slowly in order to protest about something【美】〔工人表示抗议的〕怠工

slow mo·tion /ˌ· ˈ··/ *n* [U] movement on film shown at a slower speed than it really happened〔影片中的〕慢动作，慢镜头: **in slow motion** *Let's show that goal again in slow motion.* 让我们用慢动作重放这次进球得分的情况。

slow pitch /ˈ· ·/ *n* [U] *AmE* a game like SOFTBALL, played by mixed teams of men and women【美】慢投垒球〔一种男女混合对打的垒球〕

slow·poke /ˈsloˌpok; ˈsləʊpəʊk/ *n* [C] *AmE informal* SLOWCOACH【美，非正式】慢性子的人，迟钝的人

slow-wit·ted /ˌ· ˈ··◂/ *adj* not good at understanding things 头脑迟钝的，笨的: *He was a big, slow-witted man who would hurt no-one.* 他这个人身材高大但头脑迟钝，不会伤害任何人。

slow·worm /ˈ· ·/ *n* [C] a small European LIZARD with no legs, which looks like a small snake〔欧洲产的〕无足蛇蜥

sludge /slʌdʒ; slʌdʒ/ *n* [U] **1** soft thick mud, especially at the bottom of a liquid〔沉淀于液体下面的〕软泥，烂泥 **2** the solid substance that is left when SEWAGE (=the liquid waste from houses, factories etc) has been cleaned〔从下水道清理出的〕淤泥，污泥，污物 **3** thick dirty oil in an engine〔发动机中的〕油垢，油污，油泥 —**sludgy** *adj*

slug[1] /slʌg; slʌg/ *n* [C] **1** a small slow-moving creature with a soft body like a SNAIL but without a shell 鼻涕虫，蛞蝓 **2** *AmE informal* a bullet【美，非正式】子弹 **3** *informal* a small amount of a strong alcoholic drink【非正式】少量烈酒: *a slug of brandy* 一口白兰地 **4** *AmE informal* a piece of metal shaped like a coin used to illegally get a drink, ticket etc from a machine【美，非正式】〔用以开动自动售货机获取饮料、票券等的〕硬币状金属块，假硬币

slug[2] *v* [T] **1** *informal* to hit someone hard with your closed hand【非正式】用拳猛击: *I stood up and he slugged me again.* 我站了起来，他又用拳对我猛击。**2** to hit a ball hard〔对球〕重击，强打 **3 slug it out** if two people slug it out, they fight by hitting each other hard 狠斗，决一雌雄

slug·ger /ˈslʌgɚ; ˈslʌgə/ *n* [C] *informal AmE* a BASEBALL player who hits the ball very hard【非正式，美】〔棒球运动的〕强击手

slug·gish /ˈslʌgɪʃ; ˈslʌgɪʃ/ *adj* moving or reacting more slowly than normal 行动缓慢的，反应迟缓的: *I always feel sluggish first thing in the morning.* 我早上刚起床时总觉得提不起精神来。| *the company's sluggish sales performance* 公司的滞销状况 —**sluggishly** *adv*: *The stream flows sluggishly through the fields.* 小溪缓缓地流过田野。—**sluggishness** *n* [U]

sluice[1] /slus; sluːs/ *n* [C] a passage for water to flow through, with a special gate which can be opened or closed to control it 水闸，水门

sluice[2] *v* **1** [T] to wash something with a lot of water〔用大量的水〕冲洗: **sluice sth out/down** *Can you sluice out the cow shed?* 你把牛棚冲洗一下好吗？| **sluice sth over/into etc** *I sluiced water over the wound.* 我用水冲洗伤口。**2** [I+out/over] if water sluices somewhere, a large amount of it suddenly flows there〔水〕奔流，奔泻

slum[1] /slʌm; slʌm/ *n* **1** [C] a house or an area of a city that is in very bad condition, where very poor people live〔城市中的〕贫民窟，贫民区: **the slums** (=a slum area) 贫民区 *He grew up in the East London slums.* 他是在东伦敦的贫民区长大的。**2** [singular] *informal* a very untidy place【非正式】非常脏乱的地方

slum[2] *v* **slum it/be slumming** *informal often humorous* to spend time in conditions that are much worse than you are used to【非正式，常幽默】过简陋的生活: *If we're going to travel for 6 months we'll have to slum it most of the time.* 如果我们准备出去旅行六个月，大部分时间就得勒紧裤腰带了。

slum·ber[1] /ˈslʌmbɚ; ˈslʌmbə/ *v* [I] *literary* to sleep【文】入睡，安睡

slumber[2] *n* also 又作 **slumbers** [singular,U] *literary* sleep【文】睡眠: *He passed into a deep slumber.* 他酣然入梦。

slumber par·ty /ˈ·· ˌ··/ *n* [C] *AmE* a children's party when a group of children sleep at one child's house【美】睡衣晚会〔儿童的聚会，当晚都在一个孩子家里过夜〕

slum·lord /ˈslʌmlɔrd; ˈslʌmlɔːd/ *n* [C] *AmE* someone who owns houses in a very poor area and charges high rents for buildings that are in bad condition【美】〔出租简陋房屋收取高额租金的〕贫民区房东

slum·my /ˈslʌmɪ; ˈslʌmi/ *adj* a slummy area is one where very poor people live and the buildings are in bad condition 贫民区的，〔地方〕贫困的: *a little junk shop in the slummy quarter of the town* 城里贫民区的一家小旧货店

slump[1] /slʌmp; slʌmp/ *v* **1** [I] to suddenly go down in price, value, or number〔物价、价值等〕暴跌，剧降: *Sales slumped by 20% last year.* 去年的销售额暴跌了20%。**2 be slumped** to be sitting with your body leaning completely backwards or forwards, because you are tired or unconscious〔由于疲倦或失去知觉而〕倒伏的，后仰颓坐的: **[+in/against]** *a drunk slumped against the wall* 颓然靠墙倒伏的醉鬼 **3** [I] to suddenly fall down or sit down because you feel weak or become unconscious〔因乏力或失去知觉而〕颓然倒下，突然跌坐: **[+back/over/on]** *His head slumped on his chest.* 他的头无力地垂在胸前。| *Father slumped back in his chair.* 父亲颓然跌坐到椅子上。

slump[2] *n* [C usually singular 一般用单数] **1** a sudden fall in prices, sales, profits etc〔物价、销售额、利润等的〕突然下跌: **[+in]** *a slump in agricultural prices* 农产品价格的突然下降 **2** a period when there is a big reduction in trade so that many companies have to close and many people lose their jobs 贸易锐减，衰退，萧条（时期）: *the slump in the late 80s* 80年代后期的经济萧条 **3** *especially AmE* a period when a player or team does not play well【尤美】〔运动员或运动队〕竞技状态不佳的时期: *The Dodgers have been in a slump for the last three weeks.* 道奇队在过去三周竞技状态一直不佳。

slung /slʌŋ; slʌŋ/ *v* the past tense and past participle of SLING

slunk /slʌŋk; slʌŋk/ *v* the past tense and past participle of SLINK

slur[1] /slɝ; slɜː/ *v* **1** [I,T] to speak unclearly without separating your words or sounds correctly 含糊地说（话）: **slur your words/speech** *He was obviously drunk and slurring his words.* 他显然喝醉了，说话含糊不清。**2** [T] to criticize someone or something unfairly 诽谤，诋毁 **3** [T] to play a group of musical notes smoothly together〔圆润地〕连奏 —**slurred** *adj*: *slurred speech* 含糊不清的话

slur[2] *n* **1** [C] an unfair criticism that is intended to make people dislike someone or something 诋毁，诽谤: **[+on]** *a slur on my reputation* 对我名誉的中伤 **2** [singular] an unclear way of speaking in which the words are not separated 含糊不清的说话: *the slur in his voice* 他说话声音含糊不清 **3** [C] a curved line written over musical notes to show they must be played together smoothly 标于乐谱音符上的连（接）线

slurp /slɝp; slɜːp/ *v* [I,T] to drink a liquid while making a noisy sucking sound 出声地喝〔水等〕，咕嘟咕嘟地喝: *Don't slurp your soup!* 喝汤不要咕嘟咕嘟地出声。—**slurp** *n* [C usually singular 一般用单数]: *He drank his coffee with a slurp.* 他咕嘟咕嘟地喝咖啡。

Slur·pee /ˈslɝpɪ; ˈslɜːpi/ *trademark* a drink made with crushed ice and a sweet liquid, usually tasting of fruit【商标】思乐冰〔一种由碎冰加糖水制成的饮料，通常为水果味〕

slur·ry /ˈslɝɪ; ˈslʌri/ *n* [U] a mixture of water and mud, coal, or animal waste 泥浆，淤浆〔水和泥土、煤或牲畜粪的混合物〕

slush /slʌʃ; slʌʃ/ *n* **1** [U] partly melted snow 半融雪 **2** [U] *informal* feelings or stories that seem silly because they are too concerned with love and romantic subjects【非正式】庸俗的浪漫情调; 无聊的爱情故事: *And don't give us that slush about your children just to make us feel sorry for you!* 不要光为了博得我们的同情而大讲你儿女无聊的罗曼史！**3** [C,U] *especially AmE* a drink made with crushed ice and a sweet liquid【尤美】加碎冰的甜饮料，果冰: *cherry slush* 樱桃冷饮 —**slushy** *adj*: *a slushy movie* 无聊的爱情片

slush fund /ˈ· ·/ *n* [C] a sum of money kept for dishonest purposes, especially by a politician〔尤指政客的〕行贿基金，秘密收藏起来作不正当用途的基金

slut /slʌt; slʌt/ *n* [C] **1** an offensive word for a woman who has had many sexual partners 淫妇，荡妇: *Get out of here you slut!* 滚出去，你这个婊子！**2** an offensive word for a lazy untidy woman 懒婆娘，邋遢女人〔冒犯用语〕—**sluttish** *adj*: *a dress that was nasty and sluttish* 又脏又臭的连衣裙 —**sluttishness** *n* [U]

sly /slaɪ; slaɪ/ *adj* **1** very clever in the way that you use tricks and dishonesty to get what you want 狡猾的，狡诈的: *The way he did it was really sly.* 他的做法真够狡猾的。**2 sly smile/glance/wink etc** a smile, look etc shows that you are hiding something you know from other people 诡秘的微笑／一瞥／眼色等: *She gave me a sly look.* 她诡秘地看了我一眼。**3 on the sly** *informal* secretly, especially when you are doing something

that you should not do【非正式】秘密地, 偷偷地, 暗地里: *They'd been seeing each other on the sly for months.* 他们偷偷约会已有几个月了。 —**slyly** *adv* —**slyness** *n* [U]

smack[1] /smæk; smæk/ *v* [T] **1** to hit a child with your hand in order to punish them〔用手掌〕打, 掴, 拍〔小孩, 以示惩罚〕: *To bed now, or I'll smack your bottom!* 现在就上床睡觉, 不然我要打你的屁股! —see picture on page A20 参见 A20 页图 **2** to hit something against something else so that it makes a short loud noise〔用某物〕啪啪地打: **smack sth against/into etc** *He smacked his fist against his palm.* 他用拳头啪啪地击打掌心。**3 smack your lips** to make a short loud noise with your lips because you are hungry〔由于肚子饿〕出声地咂嘴唇 **4** *BrE informal* to hit someone hard with your closed hand; PUNCH[1] (1)【英, 非正式】用拳猛揍: *Say that again and I'll smack you!* 你再说一遍我就狠狠地揍你!

smack of sth *phr v* [T] if something smacks of dishonesty, desperation etc it seems to contain some of that quality 有…的含义, 含有…的意味: *I don't want to say anything that smacks of disloyalty.* 我不想说什么显得我不够忠诚的话。

smack[2] *n* **1** [C] **a)** a hit made with your hand held flat, especially to punish a child 打一巴掌〔尤指给小孩的惩罚〕: *Quiet, or I'll give you a smack!* 安静, 不然我就给你一巴掌! **b)** *BrE informal* a hard hit with your closed hand; PUNCH[2] (1)【英, 非正式】猛击一拳 **2** [C] a short loud noise caused especially when something hits something else 啪的一声〔尤指一物打着另一物的响声〕 **3 give sb a smack on the lips/cheek** *informal* to kiss someone【非正式】给某人的嘴唇/脸颊一个响吻 **4 have a smack at** *BrE informal* to try to do something【英, 非正式】尝试做 **5** [U] *slang* HEROIN (=a dangerous illegal drug)【俚】海洛因〔一种危险的毒品〕 **6** [C] a small fishing boat 小渔船

smack[3] *adv informal*【非正式】**1** exactly or directly in the middle or in front of something 恰好, 准确地, 不偏不倚地: **smack in the middle/in front of etc** *There was a hole smack in the middle of the floor.* 正好在地板的中央有一个洞。| **smack-bang** *BrE*【英】/**smack-dab** *AmE*【美】*The plane was stuck there, smack-dab in the middle of the lake!* 飞机就倒插在那儿, 正好在湖的中央! **2** if something moves smack into or against something, it hits it with a lot of force, making a loud noise 猛烈地; 砰的一声: *The car ran smack into the side of the bus.* 小轿车猛地撞在公共汽车的侧面。

smack·er /ˈsmækə; ˈsmækə/ *n* [C] *slang*【俚】**1** a pound or a dollar 一英镑; 一美元: *It cost me fifty smackers.* 这花了我 50 英镑[美元]。**2** also 又作 **smack·er·oo** /ˌsmækəˈru; ˌsmækəˈruː/ a loud kiss 响吻

small[1] /smɔl; smɔːl/ *adj*

1 ▶**SIZE** 尺寸◀ not large in size or amount〔体积、尺寸、数量等〕小的; 少的: *He's a small man, only five feet tall.* 他是个矮小的男子, 只有五英尺高。| *Luxembourg is one of the smallest countries in Europe.* 卢森堡是欧洲最小的国家之一。| *No, not that one – the small one with the red handle!* 不, 不是那个 —— 是那个红柄的小的! | *a smaller increase in the inflation rate than last year* 增幅小于去年的通胀率 —see 见 LITTLE[1] (USAGE)

2 ▶**UNIMPORTANT** 不重要的◀ a small problem, job, mistake etc is unimportant or easy to deal with〔问题、错误、工作等〕小的, 琐细的, 微不足道的, 容易对付的: *Your work is good, but I found a number of small mistakes.* 你的工作做得不错, 不过我也发现了一些小的差错。| *It's a small matter but worth mentioning.* 这是件小事, 不过值得一提。

3 ▶**YOUNG CHILD** 年幼小孩◀ a small child is young 幼小的, 年幼的: *She's married with three small children.* 她已经结婚, 有三个年幼的孩子。

4 small farmer/dealer/business a farmer, business etc that does not involve large amounts of money 小农/小生意人/小本生意: *Most of the land in this region belongs to small farmers.* 这个地区的大部分土地都归小农场主所有。

5 ▶**LETTER** 字母◀ small letters are the smaller of the two forms that we use, for example 'b' rather than 'B' 小写体的, 小写的

6 a conservative with a small 'c'/a pacifist with a small 'p' etc *informal* someone who believes in the principles you have mentioned, but not very strongly【非正式】温和的保守派/和平主义者

7 small fortune a lot of money 一大笔钱: *That dress must have cost you a small fortune.* 那件连衣裙一定花了你不少钱。

8 make sb feel small to do something to make someone feel stupid, unimportant, or ashamed 令人自觉渺小, 使人自惭形秽: *She was always laughing at me and making me feel small.* 她老是嘲笑我, 使我感到自卑。

9 in a/some small way if something helps, affects, influences etc in a small way it has an effect but not an important one 小规模地; 有点儿: *It was good to feel we had helped in some small way.* 知道我们能帮上一点小忙, 我们已觉得不错了。

10 ▶**VOICE** 声音◀ a small voice is quiet and soft 低的, 细弱的, 柔和的: *"I don't want to stay here." she said in a small voice.* "我不想待在这儿。" 她低声地说。

11 small beer *BrE*【英】/**small potatoes** *AmE*【美】someone or something that is not at all important 微不足道的人[东西]: *Parking fines? Pretty small beer compared with some of the things he's done in the past.* 违规停车罚款? 和他过去做过的一些事情相比算是小事一桩。

12 small fry *informal*【非正式】**a)** unimportant people or things 小人物; 小事情: *Of course no one bothers about small fry like us.* 当然, 谁也不会为我们这样的小人物操心。**b)** *AmE* children【美】孩子们: *I've sent the small fry out to play in the yard.* 我已经把孩子们打发到外面院子里去玩了。 —**small** *adv*: *He writes so small I can't read it.* 他写的字太小, 我没法看。—**smallness** *n* [U]

small[2] *n* **1 the small of your back** the lower part of your back where it curves 腰背部 **2 smalls** [plural] *BrE old-fashioned informal* underwear【英, 过时, 非正式】内衣裤

small ad /ˈ· ·/ *n* [C] *BrE* an advertisement put in a newspaper by someone who wants to buy or sell something【英】小广告, 分类广告〔出售或求购物品的短广告〕; WANT AD *AmE*【美】

small arms /ˈ· ·/ *n* [plural] guns that are held in one or both hands for firing 轻武器〔可用一只手或双手拿着射击的武器〕

small change /ˌ· ˈ·/ *n* [U] money in coins of low value 小额硬币, 零钱: *Do you have any small change?* 你有零钱吗?

small claims court /ˌ· ˈ· ˈ·/ *n* [C] a court where people can try to get back small amounts of money from other people or from companies when they think it has been taken unfairly 小额钱债(赔偿)法庭

smallest room /ˌ·· ˈ·/ *n* [singular] *BrE* the room where the toilet is, used to avoid the word toilet【英】厕所, 洗手间〔委婉的说法〕

small·hold·ing /ˈsmɔlˌholdɪŋ; ˈsmɔːlˌhəʊldɪŋ/ *n* [C] *BrE* a piece of land used for farming that is smaller than an ordinary farm【英】〔比普通农场小的〕小块农田 —**smallholder** *n* [C]

small hours, the /ˈ· ·/ *n* [plural] the early morning hours, between about one and four o'clock 凌晨时分〔约从一时至四时〕: *We stayed up talking into the small hours.* 我们没去睡觉, 而是一直谈到凌晨。

small in·tes·tine /ˌ· ·ˈ··/ *n* [singular] the long tube that food goes through after it has gone through your stomach 小肠 —see picture at 参见 DIGESTIVE SYSTEM 图

small·ish /ˈsmɔlɪʃ; ˈsmɔːlɪʃ/ *adj especially BrE* fairly small【尤英】略小的, 较小的: *a smallish town* 小镇 | *She's smallish with red hair.* 她个子略小, 一头红发。

small-mind·ed /ˌsmɔlˈmaɪndɪd; ˌsmɔːlˈmaɪndɪd◂/ *adj* too concerned with the small problems and details of your life, so that you do not think about what is really important; PETTY (1) 小气的, 心胸狭窄的, 目光短浅的: *a greedy, bigoted and small-minded man* 贪婪、固执、心胸狭窄的男人 —**small-mindedness** *n* [U] —compare 比较 NARROW-MINDED

small·pox /ˈsmɔlˌpɑks; ˈsmɔːlpɒks/ *n* [U] a serious disease that causes spots which leave marks on your skin 天花

small print /ˈ· ,·/ *n* [U] all the details in a contract or agreement which contain many rules and restrictions〔合约中包含种种限制性规定的〕细则: *Always read the small print before you sign anything.* 在签约之前, 一定要阅读合约细则。

small-scale /ˌ· ˈ·◂/ *adj* small in size 小规模的: *a small-scale study* 小规模的研究

small screen /ˈ· ,·/ *n* [singular] television 电视: *a film made for the small screen* 为电视拍摄的影片

small talk /ˈ· ·/ *n* [U] polite friendly conversation about unimportant subjects 闲谈, 聊天: *small talk about the weather* 关于天气情况的闲聊

small-time /ˌ· ˈ·◂/ *adj* **small-time crook/gangster etc** a criminal who is not very successful 轻罪犯/小流氓等 —**small-timer** *n* [C]

small-town /ˈ· ·/ *adj* [only before noun 仅用于名词前] **1** connected with a small town 小镇的, 乡镇的: *a small-town lawyer* 乡镇律师 **2** *especially AmE* not very interested in anything new or different【尤美】偏狭的; 对新事物不感兴趣的: *small-town attitudes* 狭隘的观点

CULTURAL NOTE 文化注释

The STEREOTYPE of someone who comes from a small town in the US is someone who is not very educated, and who gets married when they are young and has a lot of children.

They are also thought to have rather old-fashioned ideas and values, and to be easily tricked into believing something that is not true. They stay in the same town all their lives, and do not travel or know much about other places and CULTURES. 美国小城镇居民的典型形象是所受教育不多，结婚很早并且有一大群孩子。人们还认为这些人的观念和价值观比较过时，而且很容易上当。他们一辈子都待在小城镇里，很少出远门，对其他地方和其他文化知之甚少。
However, people also think of small towns as good, safe places to grow up in, because everyone knows one another and helps take care of anyone who needs help. 然而，人们也认为小城镇是一个人成长的好地方，又很安全，因为在那里人们都相互认识，互帮互助。

smarm·y /ˈsmɑrmɪ; ˈsmɑːmi/ *adj* polite in an insincere way that you think is unpleasant 奉承的，讨好的，假殷勤的: *He fooled us with his soft smarmy ways.* 他用甜言蜜语骗了我们。

S3 W2 **smart¹** /smɑrt; smɑːt/ *adj*
1 ►CLEVER 聪明的◄ *especially AmE*【尤美】**a)** intelligent 聪颖的，精明的，机灵的: *The smart kids get good grades and go off to college.* 聪明的孩子成绩好，可直升大学。| *Some smart lawyer got him out of jail.* 某位精明的律师帮他出了狱。**b)** trying to seem clever in a disrespectful way 自命不凡的，不恭的: *Don't get smart with me, young man.* 不要跟我耍小聪明，年轻人。
2 ►WELL-DRESSED 穿着考究的◄ *BrE* wearing neat attractive clothes and having a generally tidy appearance【英】衣着整洁漂亮的，帅气的: *Chris was looking very smart in his new grey suit.* 克里斯穿着一身灰色的新西服，看上去非常帅气。
3 ►FASHIONABLE 时髦的◄ *BrE* fashionable or used by fashionable people【英】时髦的，时髦人士用的: *one of Bonn's smartest restaurants* 波恩其中一家最时髦的餐馆
4 ►QUICK 迅速的◄ a smart movement is done quickly and with force〔动作〕迅猛的，厉害的: *a smart blow on the head* 在头上猛力的一击 | **at a smart pace** (=fairly fast) 轻快地 *The horse set off at a smart pace.* 马儿轻快地跑了起来。
5 ►EXCELLENT 优秀的◄ *BrE old-fashioned* excellent【英，过时】极好的，杰出的 —**smartly** *adv*: *smartly dressed women* 穿着时髦的妇女 | *He turned smartly and walked away.* 他轻快地转身走开了。—**smartness** *n* [U]

smart² *v* [I] **1** to be upset because someone has hurt your feelings or offended you 感到痛苦[伤心]: **be smarting from** *She was still smarting from the insult.* 她还在为那次受辱而感到伤心。**2** if a part of your body smarts, it hurts with a stinging pain 感到刺痛，感到剧痛: *My eyes were smarting from the smoke.* 我的眼睛被烟熏得刺痛。

smart³ *n* [singular] **1** a feeling that you have when you are upset and offended by something 伤心，痛苦，难受 **2** a stinging pain 刺痛 **3 smarts** [U] *AmE informal* intelligence【美，非正式】聪明，智慧: *If she had any smarts, she'd get rid of the guy.* 她如果有一点头脑，就该把那个家伙甩掉。

smart al·eck /ˌsmɑrt ˋælɪk; ˈsmɑːt ˌælɪk/ *n* [C] *informal* someone who always says clever things or always has the right answer in a way that is annoying【非正式】自作聪明的人，自以为是的人

smart arse /ˈ· ·/ *BrE*【英】, also 又作 **smart ass** *AmE*【美】*n* an impolite word for a smart aleck 自作聪明的人，自以为是的人: *He got in trouble with the teacher for being such a smart ass in class.* 他因在班上过分自以为是而受到老师的批评。—**smart-arse** also 又作 **smart-ass** *adj*: *smart-arse remarks* 自以为是的话

smart bomb /ˈ· ·/ *n* [C] a bomb that is fired from an aircraft and guided by a computer〔飞机发射并由电脑制导的〕聪明炸弹[导弹]

smart card /ˈ· ·/ *n* [C] a small plastic card with an electronic part that records and remembers information 智能卡

smart·en /ˈsmɑrtn̩; ˈsmɑːtn/ *v*
smarten up *phr v especially BrE*【尤英】**1** also 又作 **smarten yourself up** [I] to make yourself look neat and tidy 打扮得干净整齐: *You'd better smarten yourself up a bit before the interview.* 你参加面试前最好打扮得干净整齐一点。**2** [T] **smarten** sth ↔ **up** to make something look neater 使〔某物〕整洁: *a coat of paint to smarten the room up* 涂一层油漆使房间焕然一新

Smar·ties /ˈsmɑrtɪz; ˈsmɑːtiz/ *trademark* a type of small, round chocolate sweet with a hard sugar covering in various colours, sold in Britain【商标】聪明豆〔一种在英国出售的圆形小巧克力豆，外裹一层彩色糖衣〕

smart·y·pants /ˈsmɑrtɪˌpænts; ˈsmɑːtipænts/ *n* [C] *humorous* someone who always says clever things or always has the right answer, in a slightly annoying way【幽默】自以为是的人，自以为样样都懂的人

smash¹ /smæʃ; smæʃ/ *v* **1** [I,T] to break into many small pieces violently or noisily, or to make something do this by dropping, throwing, or hitting it 打破，打碎，(使) 粉碎: *I dropped the plate and it smashed.* 我失手把盘子掉在地上，摔得粉碎。| *He used a chair to smash the window.* 他用椅子把窗玻璃砸碎。**2** [I always+adv/prep, T always+ adv/prep] to hit an object or surface violently, or to make something do this (使) 猛撞，猛击，猛掷: **smash sth against/down/into** *Larry smashed his fist down on the table.* 拉里用拳头猛击桌子。**3** [T] to destroy something such as a political system or criminal organization 击溃，击毁；消灭: *The French police claim to have smashed a massive drugs racket.* 法国警方宣称已破获一大宗贩毒交易。**4** [T] to hit a high ball in tennis etc with a strong downward action〔在网球等运动中〕杀〔球〕，猛扣〔球〕—see picture on page A23 参见 A23 页图
smash sth ↔ **down** *phr v* [T] to hit a door, wall etc violently so that it falls to the ground 击倒〔门、墙等〕
smash sth ↔ **in** *phr v* [T] to hit something so violently that you break it and make a hole in it 将〔某物〕撞出窟窿: **smash sb's face/head in** *informal* (=hit someone hard in the face or head)【非正式】狠击某人的脸/头 *He had threatened to smash Jo's head in if he ever went there again.* 他曾威胁说，如果乔再去那儿他就砸碎他的脑袋。
smash sth ↔ **up** *phr v* [T] to deliberately damage or destroy something〔故意〕撞毁，打碎: *A gang of thugs came into the bar and smashed the place up.* 一帮暴徒闯进酒吧，把东西砸得粉碎。—see also 另见 SMASH-UP

smash² *n* **1** [singular] the loud sound of something breaking 撞碎声，破碎声: **[+of]** *We heard the smash of plates breaking in the kitchen.* 我们听到厨房里盘子的碎裂声。**2** [C] a hard downward shot in tennis or similar games〔网球等的〕杀球，扣球 **3** [C] *BrE* a serious road or railway accident【英】严重的交通事故，车祸

smash-and-grab /ˌ· · ˈ·/ *adj* **smash-and-grab raid** the act of robbing a shop by breaking the window and stealing valuable goods 砸破橱窗劫掠贵重商品的暴行 —**smash and grab** *n* [C]

smashed /smæʃt; smæʃt/ *adj* [not before noun 不用于名词前] *informal* very drunk or affected by a drug【非正式】喝醉酒的；吸毒后神魂恍惚的: *She's smashed out of her mind.* 她醉得神志不清。

smash·er /ˈsmæʃɚ; ˈsmæʃə/ *n* [C] *BrE old-fashioned* someone that you think is very attractive, or something that is very good【英，过时】非常漂亮的人；极好的东西: *It's a beautiful boat – a real smasher!* 非常漂亮的船，真是漂亮极了!

smash hit /ˌ· ˈ·/ *n* [C] a very successful new play, book, film etc 非常成功的新戏[新书、新影片等]: *This film is going to be a smash hit.* 这部电影将会大受欢迎。

Smash Hits /ˌ· ˈ·/ *trademark* a British music magazine for young people, with articles on popular music and the singers and bands who produce it【商标】《流行金曲排行榜》〔英国一音乐杂志。面向青年读者，介绍流行音乐及其歌手和乐队〕

smash·ing /ˈsmæʃɪŋ; ˈsmæʃɪŋ/ *adj BrE old-fashioned* very good【英，过时】非常好的，极佳的: *We had a smashing holiday.* 我们过了一个非常痛快的假日。

smash-up /ˈ· ·/ *n* [C] a serious road or railway accident〔公路或铁路上〕严重的撞车事故

smat·ter·ing /ˈsmætərɪŋ; ˈsmætərɪŋ/ *n* [C+of] **1** a small number or amount of something 少数，少量: *a smattering of rain* 一点点的雨 **2 have a smattering of** [not in progressive 不用进行时] to have a small amount of knowledge about a subject, especially a foreign language 略知，懂得一点点〔某门学科，尤指外语〕

smear¹ /smɪr; smɪə/ *n* [C] **1** a dirty or oily mark on something 污斑，油渍: *There were smears of chocolate on Charlie's shirt.* 查理的衬衣上有些巧克力污迹。**2** a SMEAR TEST 子宫颈刮片检查，涂片试验 **3** an attempt to harm someone by spreading untrue stories about them 诬蔑，诽谤 —**smeary** *adj*

smear² *v*
1 ►SPREAD 涂抹◄ [T always+adv/prep] to spread a liquid or soft substance over a surface, especially carelessly or untidily〔尤指胡乱地〕涂，抹〔液体或酱状物〕: **smear sth with** *The tablecloth was smeared with jam, crayon and berry juice.* 桌布上涂满了果酱、蜡笔颜料和浆果汁。| **smear sth on/over etc** *Elaine smeared sun tan lotion liberally on her body.* 伊莱恩往身上抹了很多防晒霜。
2 ►DIRTY 脏的◄ [T] to make something dirty or oily; SMUDGE 弄脏: *Careful! You'll smear my shirt!* 小心! 你会弄脏我的衬衣!

S

3 ▶UNCLEAR 不清楚的◀ [I,T] to become unclear or make something unclear by rubbing it (使)〔因擦拭而〕变模糊: *Several words were smeared and I couldn't read them.* 有几个字给擦得很模糊，我看不清。

4 ▶TELL LIES 说谎◀ [T] to spread an untrue story about someone in order to harm them 诬蔑，诽谤: *an attempt to smear the party leadership* 企图诬蔑党的领导

5 ▶PAINT 油漆◀ [I] if a substance such as paint smears when something touches it, it spreads over parts of a surface where it should not be〔油漆等〕沾染，涂污: *Don't lean on the wall or the paint will smear.* 不要靠在墙上，不然涂料会沾你一身。

smear cam·paign /ˈ· ·,·/ *n* [C] a deliberate plan to tell untrue stories about someone, especially a politician etc in order to harm them 有预谋的诽谤活动〔尤指针对政客〕

smear test /ˈ· ·/ *n* [C] a medical test in which cells from the entrance to a woman's WOMB (=the place where a baby grows) are examined under a microscope; CERVICAL SMEAR 子宫颈刮片检查，涂片试验〔一种探查子宫颈癌变的方法〕

S2 W3 **smell¹** /smɛl; smel/ *n* **1** [C] the quality that people and animals recognize by using their nose 气味: *Some flowers have a stronger smell than others.* 有些花的气味比别的花强烈。| *The wine has a light, lemony smell.* 这种酒有一种淡淡的柠檬香味。| **[+of]** *I opened the window to get rid of the smell of beer and cigarettes.* 我打开窗户把啤酒和香烟的味道放出去。—compare 比较 AROMA, FRAGRANCE **2** [C] an unpleasant smell 难闻的气味，臭味: *Pooh! What a smell!* 呸！多难闻的气味啊！—compare 比较 ODOUR, STINK² (1) **3** [U] the ability to notice or recognize smells 嗅觉: *A mole finds its food by smell alone.* 鼹鼠觅食全凭嗅觉。| **sense of smell** *Blind people often have an excellent sense of smell.* 盲人的嗅觉大多特别灵敏。**4** [C usually singular 一般用单数] an act of smelling something 闻，嗅: *Have a smell of this cheese; does it seem all right?* 你闻一闻这些乳酪，有问题吗？

S2 W3 **smell²** *v past tense and past participle* **smelled** *especially AmE*【尤美】, **smelt** /smɛlt; smelt/ *BrE*【英】

1 ▶A PARTICULAR SMELL 某种味道◀ [I always+adv/prep; linking verb+adj] to have a particular smell 有…气味，发出…气味: **smell nice/good/spicy etc** *That soup smells delicious!* 那汤闻起来真香！| *a sweet-smelling flower* 气味芬芳的花 | **[+of]** *The car smelled of leather and wood.* 这辆汽车发出皮革和木头的气味。| **smell like** *It smells like a hospital in here – has anyone been using disinfectant?* 这里闻起来好像医院似的 — 有谁用了消毒剂吗？

2 ▶UNPLEASANT 难闻的◀ [I] to have an unpleasant smell 发出臭气，气味难闻: *His breath smells.* 他有口臭。| *We must clean out the bird-cage – it's starting to smell.* 我们必须清洗鸟笼了 — 它开始发臭了。

3 ▶RECOGNIZE A SMELL 闻到味道◀ [T] to notice or recognize a particular smell 闻到，嗅到: *I think I smell gas!* 我觉得闻到了煤气味！| **smell that** *I could smell that the milk wasn't fresh.* 我闻得出这牛奶不新鲜。

4 ▶PUT YOUR NOSE NEAR STH 把鼻子靠近某物◀ [T] to put your nose near something to discover what kind of smell it has; SNIFF¹ (2) 闻一闻〔看有什么气味〕: *Diane smelled his breath to see if he'd been drinking.* 黛安娜闻了闻他呼出的气味，看他有没有喝过酒。

5 ▶ABILITY TO SMELL 闻到气味的能力◀ [I] to have the ability to notice and recognize smells 有嗅觉: *I've got a cold and I can't smell.* 我得了感冒，闻不出味道。

6 **smell trouble/danger etc** to feel that something bad is going to happen 感到有麻烦/有危险等: *He smelt trouble and got up to leave.* 他觉得会有麻烦，便站起来走了。

7 **smell a rat** *informal* to guess that something wrong or dishonest is happening【非正式】怀疑某事不对头，怀疑其中有诈: *They know we hate them and will smell a rat if we try to be nice to them.* 他们知道我们恨他们，所以如果我们试图对他们好，他们倒会产生怀疑了。

8 **smell fishy** if a story, excuse etc smells fishy, you think it is likely to be untrue〔说法、理由等〕可疑的，似乎是假的: *Max can't be working late again! It smells very fishy to me.* 马克斯不可能又工作到这么晚！我觉得非常可疑。

9 ▶SEEM 似乎◀ [linking verb 连系动词] *informal* to seem【非正式】好像，似乎: **smell wrong/odd/worrying etc** *Sarah's description of events didn't smell right to me.* 我觉得萨拉对事情的描述好像不大对头。

smell sb/sth ↔ **out** *phr v* [T] **1** to find something by smelling 闻出，嗅出: *The hounds smelt out a fox.* 猎犬嗅出有狐狸。**2** *informal* to find something such as trouble or violence because you have a natural ability to do this【非正式】感觉到，觉察到〔麻烦事等〕: *Wherever the fighting is, Sergeant Cooper can smell it out.* 无论哪里有殴斗，库珀警官都能觉察出来。**3** to make a place smell unpleasant 使〔某处〕充满难闻的气味: *That fish is smelling the kitchen out.* 那条鱼使厨房臭气熏天。

smelling salts /ˈ· · ·/ *n* [plural] a strong-smelling chemical that you hold under someone's nose to make them conscious again 嗅盐〔一种苏醒剂〕

smell·y /ˈsmɛlɪ; ˈsmeli/ *adj* **smellier, smelliest** having an unpleasant smell 有臭味的: *smelly socks* 臭袜子 —**smelliness** *n* [U]

smelt¹ /smɛlt; smelt/ *BrE*【英】a form of the past tense and past participle of SMELL

smelt² *v* [T] to melt a rock that contains metal in order to remove the metal 熔炼，提炼，炼取〔矿石〕

smelt³ *n* [C] a small fish 银白鱼〔胡瓜鱼科海鱼〕

smid·gin, smidgen /ˈsmɪdʒɪn; ˈsmɪdʒɪ̇n/ *n* [singular] *informal* a small amount of something, especially food【非正式】〔尤指食物〕少量，一点点: *"More cheese?" "Just a smidgin, please."* "再来点儿乳酪好吗？""那就再来一点儿吧。"

smile¹ /smaɪl; smaɪl/ *v* S3 W1

1 [I] to have or make a smile on your face 微笑: **smile at sb** *Joanna was smiling at us in a friendly way.* 乔安娜在友好地向我们微笑。| *Neil smiled to himself, thinking about how he had tricked them.* 尼尔在偷笑着，心里在想他是怎样捉弄了他们。

2 smile at sth to be amused by something, often without showing it 觉得某事好笑；嘲笑: *Graham smiled at his colleague's suggestion.* 格雷厄姆觉得他同事的建议很可笑。

3 [T] to say or express something with a smile 微笑着说；以微笑表示: *"So this is your secret weapon," he smiled.* "原来这就是你的秘密武器。"他笑道。| *She smiled a welcome.* 她微笑着表示欢迎。—compare 比较 GRIN¹ (1)

4 smile to think/see/remember etc to be amused when you think about something, see something etc 想起来/看见/回忆起来等就觉得好笑: *When I look back at my youth I smile to think how naive I was.* 我在回顾青年时代时，一想到自己有多么幼稚就觉得好笑。

5 ▶LUCK/FORTUNE 运气/幸运◀ [T] *especially literary* if luck or FORTUNE smiles on you, you have very good luck【尤文】〔幸运之神〕向…微笑，对…有利 —**smilingly** *adv*: *Melissa smilingly reached for a cigarette.* 梅利莎微笑着伸手拿烟。

smile² *n* [C] an expression on your face in which your mouth curves upwards to show that you are happy, amused, friendly, etc 微笑，笑容: *George had a big smile on his face.* 乔治笑容满面。| *"Hello," he said with a smile.* "你好。"他笑着说。| **give sb a smile** *Tracy gave the girl a warm smile.* 特蕾西对那女孩热情地一笑。| **be all smiles** (=to look very happy and to behave in a friendly way) 满面笑容，显得非常愉快 S2 W2

smirk /smɝk; smɜːk/ *v* **[I+at]** to smile in an unpleasant way that shows that you are pleased by someone else's bad luck 得意地笑，幸灾乐祸地笑: *They smirked knowingly at each other across the table.* 他们隔着桌子彼此会意地坏笑。—**smirk** *n* [C]: *Wipe that smirk off your face – there's nothing funny about it!* 收起你脸上的傻笑，没有什么好笑的！

smite /smaɪt; smaɪt/ *v past tense* **smote** /smot; sməʊt/ *past participle* **smitten** /ˈsmɪtn̩; ˈsmɪtn/ **[T+down]** **1** *old use* to hit something hard【旧】猛打，重击 **2** *biblical* to destroy, attack, or punish someone【圣经】摧毁；袭击；惩罚

smith /smɪθ; smɪθ/ *n* [C] **1** someone who makes and repairs things made of iron; BLACKSMITH 铁匠，锻工 **2 goldsmith/silversmith etc** someone who makes things from gold, silver etc 金匠/银匠等

-smith /smɪθ; smɪθ/ *suffix* [in nouns 构成名词] a maker of something 工匠；制作者: *a gunsmith* (=someone who makes guns) 枪炮工匠 | *a wordsmith* (=someone who works with words, for example a JOURNALIST) 耍笔杆子的人〈如新闻记者〉—see also 另见 -SMITH

Smith, Adam (1723-90) a Scottish ECONOMIST who strongly believed in FREE ENTERPRISE (=an economic system in which private businesses are free to make money, and there is not much government control). He developed his ideas in his book *The Wealth of Nations*, which has had an important influence on modern economic and political ideas 亚当·斯密〔(1723-1790)，苏格兰经济学家。他极力主张自由企业制，其著作《国富论》进一步阐发了这一思想。该书对现代经济思想和政治思想产生了重大影响〕

Smith, Bes·sie /ˈbɛsɪ; ˈbesi/ (1895-1937) a US BLUES singer who was very popular in the 1920s, and whose style influenced many later musicians. Many people know the story of how she died after a car crash, when she was not allowed to enter a hospital for white people because she was black. 史密斯〔(1895-

1937)，美国布鲁斯歌手，20世纪20年代非常著名。其演唱风格影响了后来的许多音乐家。不少人都知道她的经历，遭遇车祸后，一家白人医院因为她是黑人而拒绝收治，终于不治身亡〕

Smith, De·li·a /ˈdiliə; ˈdiːliə/ (1941-) a British woman who writes books and makes very popular television programmes that teach people how to cook. Her books are among the most popular books sold in the UK, and people often simply call her 'Delia' 史密斯〔(1941-)，英国一女性。著有烹饪书籍，居英国最畅销图书之列。她还主持烹饪电视节目。人们常常称呼她时只叫名字"迪莉娅"〕: *Have you tried Delia's fish pie recipe?* 你有没有试过按迪莉娅的菜谱做鱼肉馅饼吗？

Smith, I·an /ˈiən; ˈiːən/ (1919-2007) the Prime Minister of Rhodesia from 1964 to 1978. He made Rhodesia independent of the UK without British agreement, with a government of only white people, although most people in the country were black. 史密斯〔(1919-2007)，1964至1978年任罗得西亚总理。未经英国方面同意，他单方面宣布罗得西亚脱离英国独立。不顾该国人口以黑人为主的事实，建立了由清一色白人组成的政府〕—see also 另见 ZIMBABWE

Smith, Joseph (1805-44) a US religious leader who started the Mormon religion. He described how an angel showed him where two golden TABLETs (=flat pieces of metal with words cut into them) were buried in a hill in the state of New York. He translated the writing on the tablets and it became *The Book of Mormon*, the holy book of the Mormon religion 史密斯〔(1805-1844)，美国宗教领袖，创立了摩门教。他称曾有一位天使指点他，说在纽约州的一座小山丘埋有两块金匾。他将金匾上的经文译了出来，于是就有了摩门教的经典《摩门经》〕

Smith, Win·ston /ˈwɪnstən; ˈwɪnstən/ the main character in the book *1984* (1949) by George Orwell, who lives in a time when the government controls everything that people do. Smith is punished by the government because he tries to have a romantic relationship with a woman. 史密斯〔乔治·奥威尔的小说《一九八四》(1949)中的主人公。在史密斯生活的那个年代，政府对人民的一切行为实行控制。他因想与一名女子建立浪漫关系而受到政府的惩罚〕

S

Smith and Wes·son /ˌsmɪθ ənd ˈwɛsn; ˌsmɪθ ənd ˈwesən/ *trademark* a type of HANDGUN【商标】史密斯-韦森〔一种手枪〕

smith·e·reens /ˌsmɪðəˈrinz; ˌsmɪðəˈriːnz/ *n* [plural] **smash sth to smithereens** *informal* to completely destroy something by breaking it into very small pieces【非正式】把某物撞成碎片

Smith·so·ni·an In·sti·tu·tion /smɪθˌsonɪən ˌɪnstɪˈtuʃən; smɪθˌsəʊniən ˌɪnstɪˈtjuːʃən/ also 又作 **the Smithsonian** a large group of different MUSEUMs and scientific institutions in Washington, D.C., which was established in 1846 using money left by James Smithson, an English scientist 史密森学会〔一大型组织。由华盛顿特区众多不同主题的博物馆和科学协会组成，1846年用英国科学家詹姆斯·史密森的遗产建立〕

Smith Square /ˌ· ˈ·/ the place in London where Central Office, the HEADQUARTERS of the Conservative Party, is based 史密斯广场〔位于伦敦，英国保守党总部所在地〕

smith·y /ˈsmɪθɪ; ˈsmɪði/ *n plural* **smithies** [C] a place where iron objects such as HORSESHOEs were made and repaired in the past〔从前的〕铁匠铺

smit·ten /ˈsmɪtn; ˈsmɪtn/ *v* **1** the past participle of SMITE **2 be smitten (with sb/sth)** to suddenly feel that you love someone or like something very much〔一见钟情地〕爱上…的；〔突然〕迷上…的: *The young man was smitten with Miranda and her charms.* 那位年轻人对米兰达一见钟情，为她的魅力倾倒。| **be smitten with a desire to do sth** (=want to do it very much) 极想做某事 *She was smitten with a sudden desire to be rich like them.* 她突然产生一种要和他们一样富有的强烈欲望。

smock /smɑk; smɒk/ *n* [C] **1** a piece of clothing like a long, loose shirt, worn especially by women who are PREGNANT (=going to have a baby) 宽松上衣，孕妇服 **2** a piece of clothing like a coat, worn by artists, hospital workers etc〔画家、医生等穿的〕罩衣，工作服

smock·ing /ˈsmɑkɪŋ; ˈsmɒkɪŋ/ *n* [U] a type of decoration made on cloth by pulling the cloth into small regular folds held tightly with stitches〔衣服的〕褶子，褶饰

smog /smɑg; smɒg/ *n* [U] brown unhealthy air caused by smoke from cars and factories in cities〔由汽车和工厂废气所造成的褐色〕烟雾

3 3 **smoke¹** /smok; sməʊk/ *n* **1** [U] grey gas that is produced by something burning〔燃烧所产生的〕烟: *Clouds of black smoke belched from the building.* 一团团黑烟从大楼喷出。| *cigarette smoke* 香烟的烟雾 **2** [C usually singular 一般用单数] an act of smoking a cigarette etc 抽〔一支〕烟: *a cup of coffee and a smoke* 喝杯咖啡抽支烟 **3** [C] *slang* a cigarette or drugs that are smoked【俚】〔抽的〕香烟；〔吸的〕毒品 **4 the Smoke** *BrE, AustrE* London or any large town or city【英，澳】伦敦；〔类似的〕大城市〔城镇〕**5 go up in smoke** *informal* if your plans go up in smoke, you cannot do what you intended to do【非正式】〔计划等〕化为泡影，化为乌有 **6 there's no smoke without fire** *spoken* used to say that if something bad is being said about someone, it is probably partly true【口】无火不冒烟；无风不起浪；事出有因 —**smokeless** *adj*

smoke² *v* **1** [I,T] to suck or breathe in smoke from a cigarette, pipe etc 抽〔香烟或烟斗等〕，吸烟: *I haven't smoked for over two years.* 我已有两年多不抽烟了。**2** [T] to breathe in smoke from burning an illegal drug 吸〔毒品〕，抽〔麻醉品〕: *smoking dope* 吸毒 **3** [I] if something smokes it has smoke coming out of it 冒烟: *a smoking chimney* 冒烟的烟囱 **4** [I] if a fire smokes it lets too much smoke into a room〔室内的火炉〕冒浓烟 **5** [T] to give fish and meat a special taste by hanging it in smoke〔用烟〕熏制〔鱼、肉等〕

smoke sb/sth ↔ **out** *phr v* [T] **1** to fill a place with smoke to force someone or something to come out〔用烟〕把〔人、动物等〕熏出 **2** to discover who is causing a particular problem and force them to make themselves known 揭露，查出〔闹事者〕: *an attempt to smoke out and defeat the subversive forces in government* 揭露和挫败政府中颠覆势力的一次尝试

smoke a·larm /ˈ· ·ˌ·/ also 又作 **smoke detector** /ˈ· ·ˌ·/ *n* [C] a piece of electronic equipment which warns you when there is smoke or fire in a building 烟雾警报器 —see picture at 参见 ALARM¹ 图

smoke bomb /ˈ· ·/ *n* [C] something that you throw that lets out clouds of smoke, used by police to control crowds〔警察为驱散人群用的〕烟雾弹

smoked /smokt; sməʊkt/ *adj* **smoked salmon/bacon/sausage etc** fish, meat etc that has been left in smoke to give it a special taste 熏三文鱼/咸肉/香肠等

smoked glass /ˌ· ˈ·/ *n* [U] glass that is a dark grey colour 烟色玻璃，深灰色玻璃

smoke-free /ˌ· ˈ·◂/ *adj* **smoke-free area/zone etc** a place where you are not allowed to smoke 禁烟区/地带等

smok·er /ˈsmokɚ; ˈsməʊkə/ *n* [C] **1** someone who smokes cigarettes, CIGARs etc 吸烟者: **heavy smoker** (=someone who smokes a lot) 烟瘾很大的人，抽烟很多的人 **2** a railway carriage in which smoking is allowed〔火车上的〕吸烟车厢

smoke·screen /ˈsmokˌskrin; ˈsməʊkskriːn/ *n* [C] **1** something that you do or say to hide your real plans or actions 伪装，障眼法，〔用以掩盖真相的〕烟幕: *All that stuff about being a businessman was just a smokescreen to hide his criminal activities.* 什么商人身份，这些都是用以掩饰他犯罪活动的烟幕。**2** a cloud of smoke produced so that it hides soldiers, ships etc during a battle〔战役中用以掩蔽士兵、船只等的〕烟幕

smoke sig·nal /ˈ· ˌ··/ *n* [C] a message sent out to people who are far away, using the smoke from a fire 烟雾信号

smoke·stack /ˈsmokˌstæk; ˈsməʊkstæk/ *n* [C] a tall CHIMNEY at a factory or on a ship〔工厂或轮船的〕大烟囱

smokestack in·dus·try /ˈ· ·, ˈ···/ *n* [C usually plural 一般用复数] *especially AmE* a big traditional industry such as car-making or coal-mining【尤美】〔传统的〕重型制造业，有大烟囱的工业〈如汽车制造业，采煤业等〉

Smo·key the Bear /ˌsmokɪ ðə ˋbɛr; ˌsməʊki ðə ˈbeə/ a character used by the US Forest Service to warn people about the need to prevent forest fires. Smokey is a bear shown wearing a hat and saying 'Only you can prevent forest fires'. 斯莫基熊，烟熊〔美国林务局用来提醒人们防止森林火灾的一个形象。斯莫基是一只头戴帽子的熊，口中说"只有你能防止森林火灾"〕

smok·ing /ˈsmokɪŋ; ˈsməʊkɪŋ/ *n* [U] the habit or activity of breathing in tobacco smoke from a cigarette, pipe etc 吸烟，抽烟: *The sign says 'No Smoking'.* 牌子上写着"禁止吸烟"。| **give up smoking** (=stop) 戒烟，不再吸烟 *I gave up smoking nearly ten years ago.* 我差不多10年之前就戒烟了。—see also 另见 PASSIVE SMOKING 2

CULTURAL NOTE 文化注释

In both the US and the UK, there are more and more limits on where people can smoke in public places, because smoking is considered to be bad for your health. Some states in the US have laws that say you cannot smoke in any public place, even bars. Most office buildings in the US and the UK do not allow smoking except in outside areas and you cannot smoke on planes,

trains, or buses. 在美国和英国，对于在公共场合可以吸烟的地点有了越来越多的限制，因为吸烟被认为是有害健康的。美国的一些州颁布法律禁止在任何公共场合吸烟，甚至在酒吧也不允许吸烟。英国和美国的大多数办公楼都禁止吸烟，除非在室外；同样，在飞机、火车和汽车上也不准吸烟。

The governments of both countries demand that cigarette companies print a health warning on cigarette packets, and in the UK the warnings say things such as 'Smoking Kills'. Fewer people smoke now because of the health risks, although it is common for young people to try smoking. Many people who smoke regularly do actually want to stop, and some use things such as NICOTINE PATCH*es* to help them. 两国政府都要求卷烟公司在烟盒上印上警示语，例如在英国会印上"吸烟致死"等。因为担心对健康的危害，现在吸烟的人少了，尽管有不少年轻人尝试吸烟。很多经常吸烟的人真的很想戒掉，有些人使用尼古丁贴片之类的药物来戒烟。

There have been LAWSUIT*s* against tobacco companies, claiming that the companies knew their products could cause CANCER and other health problems. In 1998 US courts decided that tobacco companies should pay $206 billion in fines over 25 years in order to help states pay for the medical care of people who smoked. 一直就有人在起诉烟草公司，说这些公司知道他们的产品会致癌和导致其他健康问题。1998 年美国法院判决烟草公司在25年内支付2060亿美元的罚金，以偿付州政府为医治吸烟病人而花费的钱。

smoking jack·et /'‥‚‥/ *n* [C] a type of man's JACKET (1) 吸烟服〔男子在家穿的一种外衣〕

smoking room /'‥‥/ *n* [C] a room where smoking is allowed in a building such as a hotel or factory〔旅馆、工厂等的〕吸烟室

smok·y /ˈsmokɪ; ˈsməʊki/ *adj* **1** filled with smoke 多烟的，烟雾弥漫的：*a smoky room* 烟雾弥漫的房间 **2** producing too much smoke 冒烟的：*a smoky old diesel engine* 冒烟的旧柴油发动机 **3** having the taste, smell, or appearance of smoke 有烟熏味的；似烟的：*his smoky green eyes* 他那烟青色的眼睛 —**smokiness** *n* [U]

Smoky Moun·tains, the /‚‥'‥‥/ —see 见 GREAT SMOKY MOUNTAINS

smol·der /ˈsmoldɚ; ˈsməʊldə/ *v* [I] the American spelling of SMOULDER smoulder 的美式拼法

smooch /smutʃ; smuːtʃ/ *v* [I+with] *informal* if two people smooch, they kiss and hold each other in a romantic way【非正式】拥抱接吻

smooch·y /ˈsmutʃɪ; ˈsmuːtʃi/ *adj BrE informal* a smoochy song is slow and romantic【英，非正式】〔歌曲〕节奏缓慢而浪漫的

smooth¹ /smuð; smuːð/ *adj*

1 ▶**FLAT** 平的◀ a smooth surface is completely flat and even 平滑的；平坦的；平整的：*The stone steps had been worn smooth by centuries of visitors.* 这些石台阶已被几个世纪的参观者踩得很平滑了。—opposite 反义词 ROUGH¹ (1)

2 ▶**SOFT** 柔软的◀ skin or fur that is smooth is soft and pleasant to touch, and your hand moves easily over it 柔软的，光滑的：*Sheila stroked the cat's silky smooth fur.* 希拉抚摸着猫儿像丝一样柔软光滑的毛。| *as smooth as a baby's bottom* 像婴儿屁股一样光滑

3 ▶**LIQUID** 液体◀ a liquid mixture that is smooth is thick but with no big pieces in it〔液体混合物〕无结块的，均匀的，调匀的：*Beat the eggs and flour until they are smooth.* 把鸡蛋和面粉一直搅拌至均匀为止。—opposite 反义词 LUMPY

4 ▶**GRACEFUL** 优美的◀ [only before noun 仅用于名词前] a smooth movement, style, way of doing something etc is graceful and has no sudden awkward changes〔动作、风格等〕平稳的；流畅的；优美的：*Swing the tennis racquet in one smooth motion.* 用流畅优美的动作挥动网球拍。—opposite 反义词 JERKY¹

5 ▶**WITHOUT PROBLEMS** 没有问题的◀ a system, operation, or process that is smooth operates well and without problems 顺利的；无困难的，无问题的：*contributing to the smooth running of the company* 有助于公司的顺利经营 —see also 另见 **go smoothly** (SMOOTHLY (2))

6 ▶**PLEASANT TASTE** 美味的◀ a drink such as WHISKY or beer that is smooth is not bitter but tastes pleasant and is easy to swallow〔酒〕不苦的，味美的，醇和的

7 ▶**POLITE** 客气的◀ someone who is smooth is polite, confident, and relaxed, but does not seem sincere 圆滑的，八面玲珑的，迎合讨好的：*I never trust these smooth salesmen.* 我从不相信这些油腔滑调的推销员。

8 ▶**COMFORTABLE** 舒适的◀ a journey that is smooth is comfortable because the plane does not shake, or the sea is not rough〔旅途等〕平稳的，平静的，无颠簸的，顺畅的：*We had a smooth crossing on the boat.* 我们坐船平稳地渡了过去。| *a smooth flight* 平稳的飞行 —opposite 反义词 BUMPY —see also 另见 SMOOTHLY, SMOOTH-TALKING —**smoothness** *n* [U]

smooth² *v* [T] **1** also 又作 **smooth out** to make something such as paper or cloth flat by moving your hands across it〔用手〕弄平，抚平，使平滑：*They smoothed out the map on the table and planned their route.* 他们把地图在桌上铺平，定出要走的路线。**2** also 又作 **smooth down** to make something that is raised flat by moving your hands across it〔用手把凸起的东西〕抹平，捋平：*Angela smoothed her hair down neatly.* 安杰拉把头发捋得平顺整齐。**3** also 又作 **smooth down** to take away the roughness from the surface of wood, clay etc〔把粗糙表面等〕磨光，擦平：*You have to smooth it before you varnish it.* 在上清漆前先要把它打磨光滑。**4** [always+adv/prep] to rub a liquid, cream, etc gently over a surface or into a surface 轻轻地涂擦〔液体、面霜等〕：**smooth sth into/over** *She smoothed suntan lotion over her legs.* 她轻轻地给双腿抹上防晒霜。**5 smooth the way** to make it easier for something to happen, by dealing with any problems first〔为…〕铺平道路：*an agreement smoothing the way to an eventual merger* 为最终合并铺平道路的协议

smooth sth ↔ **away** *phr v* [T] to get rid of problems or difficulties easily〔顺利地〕摆脱〔困境〕，排除〔困难〕：*A few objections have to be smoothed away before we can start the project.* 我们在开展这个项目之前，先得排除几种反对意见。

smooth sth ↔ **over** *phr v* [T] to make problems or difficulties seem less important 缓和〔困难等〕；减轻；纾解：*Sally managed to smooth over the bad feelings between them.* 萨莉设法缓和了他们之间的对立情绪。

smooth·ie, smoothy /ˈsmuðɪ; ˈsmuːði/ *n* [C] *informal* someone who is good at persuading people, but does not seem to be sincere【非正式】圆滑的人：*Yuk! What a smoothie!* 呸！多圆滑的家伙！

smooth·ly /ˈsmuðlɪ; ˈsmuːðli/ *adv* **1** in a smooth way 平稳地，顺畅地，顺利地 **2 go smoothly** if a planned event, piece of work etc goes smoothly, there are no problems to spoil it 顺利进行：*It'll take about three hours, if everything goes smoothly.* 如果一切顺利的话，大约需要三小时。

smooth-talk·ing /'‥‚‥/ *adj* a smooth-talking person is good at persuading people and saying nice things but you do not trust them 油嘴滑舌的，花言巧语的：*a smooth-talking salesman* 花言巧语的推销员

smor·gas·bord /ˈsmɔrgəs‚bɔrd; ˈsmɔːgəsbɔːd/ *n* [C,U] a meal in which people serve themselves from a large number of different dishes〔有大量的各式精美食物的〕自助餐

smote /smot; sməʊt/ the past tense of SMITE

smoth·er /ˈsmʌðɚ; ˈsmʌðə/ *v* **1** [T always+adv/prep] **smother sth with/in** to cover the whole surface of something with something else 完全覆盖；笼罩：**smother sth with/in** *a delicious sponge cake smothered in chocolate* 裹着一层巧克力的美味松蛋糕 | *He smothered her with kisses.* 他吻得她透不过气来。**2 smother your anger/irritation** to hide your feelings 抑制愤怒/忍住怒气：*struggling to smother her jealousy* 拼命想掩盖她的妒忌心 **3 smother sb with love/kindness etc** to express your feelings for someone too strongly, so that your relationship with them cannot develop normally 爱得/体贴得过分使人受不了 **4** [T] to kill someone by putting something over their face to stop them breathing 使〔某人〕窒息，把〔某人〕闷死：*One night she took a pillow and smothered him.* 一天夜里，她用枕头把他闷死。**5** [T] to make a fire stop burning by preventing air from reaching it 把〔火〕闷熄 **6** [T] to get rid of anyone who opposes you 清除，压制〔对手〕：*They ruthlessly smother all opposition.* 他们无情地压制一切反对的声音。

smoul·der *BrE*【英】，**smolder** *AmE*【美】/ˈsmoldɚ; ˈsməʊldə/ *v* [I] **1** if something such as wood smoulders, it burns slowly without a flame 无火焰地慢慢烧，闷燃：*a smouldering log* 一块闷烧着的木头 **2** if someone smoulders or if their feelings smoulder, they have strong feelings that they do not express〔强烈的情绪〕闷在心里，郁积：*He sensed a smouldering hostility towards him.* 他觉察到别人压抑着对他的敌对情绪。| **smoulder with passion/anger** *The workforce were smouldering with discontent.* 劳工们压抑着不满的情绪。

smudge 弄脏

smudge¹ /smʌdʒ; smʌdʒ/ *n* [C] a dirty mark 污迹, 污斑, 污痕: *There's a smudge of grease on your chin.* 你下巴上沾了一点油渍。—**smudgy** *adj*

smudge² *v* **1** [T] to make writing, painting etc become unclear by touching or rubbing it 把〔字、画等〕弄脏, 使变脏: *Don't touch it! You'll smudge the ink.* 别碰它! 你会把墨水抹花的。**2** [I] if ink, writing etc smudges, its edges become unclear because it has been touched or rubbed〔墨迹、字迹等〕被抹脏, 被碰脏; 被擦模糊 **3** [T] to make a dirty mark on a surface 在…上留下污迹: *Someone had smudged the paper with their greasy hands.* 有人用油腻的手把这张纸弄脏了。

smug /smʌg; smʌg/ *adj* **smugger, smuggest** showing too much satisfaction with your own cleverness or success 自满的, 自鸣得意的, 沾沾自喜的: *"I knew I'd win," she said with a smug smile.* "我早知道我会赢的。" 她自鸣得意地笑着说。| *What are you looking so smug about?* 你为什么这样洋洋得意? —**smugly** *adv*: *Simon sat back smugly as Gould left the room.* 古尔德离开房间时, 西蒙得意地坐了回去。—**smugness** *n* [U]: *his unbearable smugness* 他那令人难以容忍的得意神气

smug·gle /ˈsmʌgl̩; ˈsmʌgəl/ *v* [T] **1** to take something or someone illegally from one country to another 走私, 偷运: **smuggle sth into/out of** *They caught her trying to smuggle drugs into France.* 他们发现她企图把毒品偷运进法国。| **smuggle sth through customs** (=to illegally take something past the officials who check what is being brought into the country) 走私某物混过海关 **2** *informal* to take something or someone secretly to a place where they are not allowed to be【非正式】偷偷携带, 夹带: *He managed to smuggle his notes into the examination.* 他设法把笔记偷偷带进了考场。

smug·gler /ˈsmʌglɚ; ˈsmʌglə/ *n* [C] someone who takes something illegally from one country to another 走私者: *a drug smuggler* 毒品走私者

smug·gling /ˈsmʌglɪŋ; ˈsmʌgəlɪŋ/ *n* [U] the crime of taking things illegally from one country to another 走私: *a diamond-smuggling operation* 钻石走私活动

smut /smʌt; smʌt/ *n* **1** [U] books, stories, talk etc that offend some people slightly because they are about sex 淫秽图书[故事], 淫言秽语: *I won't have smut like that in my house!* 我不准家里有那种淫秽东西! **2** [C,U] dirt or SOOT (=black powder produced by burning), or a piece of this (一小块) 污垢, 煤烟 (灰)

smut·ty /ˈsmʌtɪ; ˈsmʌti/ *adj* **smuttier, smuttiest 1** books, stories etc that are smutty offend some people slightly because they are about sex〔图书、作品等〕淫秽的, 黄色的: *smutty jokes* 黄色笑话 **2** marked with small pieces of dirt or SOOT 煤灰弄黑的, 弄脏的 —**smuttiness** *n* [U] —**smuttily** *adv*

snack /snæk; snæk/ *n* **1** [C] a small amount of food that is eaten between main meals or instead of a meal〔正餐以外的〕小吃, 点心: *I only had time to grab a quick snack.* 我只能匆匆地抓点零食吃。| **snack food** (=food, such as PEANUTS or POPCORN that is intended to be eaten as a snack) 小食, 零食〈如花生、爆玉米花等〉**2 snacks** [plural] small things to eat that are provided at a party, meeting etc〔开会、聚会等时的〕点心, 小食品

snack bar /ˈ· ·/ *n* [C] a place where you can buy snacks 点心店, 小吃店, 快餐部: *Let's get a chilli dog at the snack bar.* 我们到快餐部买个辣味热狗吧。

snaf·fle /ˈsnæfl; ˈsnæfəl/ *v* [T] *BrE informal* to take something quickly, especially when it is rude or unfair to do this【英, 非正式】扒取, 偷窃〔某物〕

sna·fu /snæˈfu; snæˈfuː/ *n* [singular] *AmE informal* a situation in which a plan does not happen in the way it should【美, 非正式】混乱, 一团糟: *What a snafu! Three of the contestants didn't even show up!* 真是一团糟! 有三名参赛者竟然没有露面!

snag¹ /snæg; snæg/ *n* [C] **1** a disadvantage or problem, especially one that is not very serious 小问题, 小障碍: *It's an interesting job. The only snag is that it's not very well paid.* 这是一份很有趣的工作, 唯一缺憾是工资不高。**2 a)** a sharp part of something that holds or cuts things that touch it〔会钩住或钩破东西的〕尖锐突出物 **b)** a tear in something made by getting it stuck on a snag〔衣物等的〕被钩破处, 被刮破的裂口

snag² *v* **snagged, snagging** [T] **1** to damage something such as a piece of clothing by getting it stuck on something 钩住; 撕破: *Oh damn! I've snagged my stockings.* 噢, 该死! 我把长筒袜钩破了。**2** *AmE informal* to try to get someone to notice you, especially when you want help【美, 非正式】〔尤指在需要帮助时〕引起〔某人的〕注意; 抓住: *I'll try to snag the waiter next time he comes by.* 下次服务员走过时我会叫住他的。

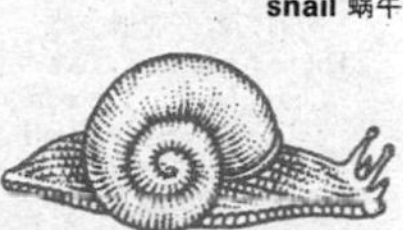

snail 蜗牛

snail /snel; sneɪl/ *n* [C] **1** a small soft creature that moves very slowly and has a hard shell on its back 蜗牛 **2 at a snail's pace** extremely slowly 极慢地, 慢吞吞地

snail mail /ˈ· ·/ *n* [U] *humorous* an expression meaning letters that are sent by post, used especially by people who send computer messages【幽默】蜗牛邮件, 普通邮件〔尤为使用电子邮件者用语〕

snake¹ /snek; sneɪk/ *n* [C] **1** an animal with a long thin body and no legs, that often has a poisonous bite 蛇 **2** an insulting word meaning someone who cannot be trusted 奸险的人, 狡猾的人 **3 snake in the grass** *informal* someone who pretends to be your friend but does something to harm you【非正式】伪装成朋友的阴险小人 3

CULTURAL NOTE 文化注释

Snakes are often used in stories to represent evil, and they are thought of as very dishonest and likely to trick people. Typical examples are the SERPENT that influences Eve in the Bible and the snake in *The Jungle Book*. In the *Harry Potter* books, the main evil character is described as having eyes like a snake. Snakes are also used in a lot of frightening and exciting films because many people are afraid of them. 故事中的蛇通常是邪恶的代表, 它们被认为很不诚实、喜欢骗人。典型的例子有《圣经》中诱惑夏娃的蛇和《丛林故事》中的蛇。在《哈里·波特》系列图书中, 邪恶的主角被描述成长着蛇一样的眼睛。在许多恐怖刺激的电影中蛇也是常客, 因为很多人对它们不寒而栗。— see also Cultural Note at SERPENT 另见 SERPENT 文化注释

snake² *v* [I always+adv/prep] if a river, road, train, or line snakes somewhere, it moves in long, twisting curves 弯弯曲曲地移动, 蜿蜒前进: **[+along/past/down etc]** *The road snaked along the valley far below.* 公路沿着谷底弯弯曲曲伸向远方。| **snake its way through/into etc** *The train was snaking its way through the mountains.* 火车在山区蜿蜒地向前行驶。

snake·bite /ˈsnekˌbaɪt; ˈsneɪkbaɪt/ *n* **1** [C,U] the bite of a poisonous snake 毒蛇咬伤 **2** [C] *BrE* an alcoholic drink that is half LAGER and half CIDER【英】淡啤酒和苹果酒各半的混合酒

snake charm·er /ˈ· ˌ··/ *n* [C] someone who entertains people by controlling snakes by playing music to them〔用音乐声使蛇起舞的〕玩蛇者, 弄蛇人

CULTURAL NOTE 文化注释

In pictures, especially CARTOONS, Indian snake charmers are often shown playing a pipe and making a snake rise out of a basket. 在图画、特别是漫画中, 常常画有印度耍蛇人吹奏笛子引蛇蠕动出篮的场景。

snakes and lad·ders /ˌ· · ˈ··/ *n* [U] *BrE* a children's game played on a board in which you can move forwards and upwards along pictures of LADDERS or go downwards and backwards along pictures of snakes【英】蛇梯棋〔一种儿童棋类游戏, 棋子沿梯形图前进, 沿蛇形图后退〕; CHUTES AND LADDERS *AmE*【美】

snake·skin /ˈsnekˌskɪn; ˈsneɪkˌskɪn/ *n* [U] the skin of a snake used to make shoes, bags etc 蛇皮 (革): *snakeskin shoes* 蛇皮鞋

snak·y /ˈsnekɪ; ˈsneɪki/ *adj* moving or lying in twisting curves 像蛇一样弯曲的, 弯曲地移动的: *a snaky road* 蜿蜒曲折的道路

3 **snap**[1] /snæp; snæp/ *v*

1 ▶BREAK 折断◀ [I,T] if something snaps, or if you snap it, it breaks with a sudden sharp noise (使)啪的一声折断, 断开: *Pablo felt the second blow on his collar bone and heard it snap.* 帕勃罗觉得锁骨受到第二次击打, 并听到它啪的一声断了。| *The impact must have snapped the cable.* 这次冲击一定把缆绳弄断了。| **snap sth off** *Patricia snapped a twig off.* 帕特里夏啪地折下一根小树枝。| **snap sth in two/in half etc** (=break it into two pieces) 折成两半 *The teacher snapped the chalk in two and gave me a piece.* 老师把粉笔折成两段, 给了我一段。

2 ▶MOVE (STH) SUDDENLY 突然移动◀ [I always+ adv/prep, T always+adv/prep] to move into a particular position suddenly, making a short sharp noise, or to make something move like this (使)突然啪地移动〔至某位置〕: **snap together/back etc** *The pieces just snap together like this.* 这两个部件就像这样啪的一声合在一起。| *The sails would be flat one minute, then snap and billow out with the wind the next.* 帆一会儿是平的, 一会儿又啪地迎风扬起。| **snap open/shut** *She snapped her briefcase shut.* 她啪的一声合上了公文包。

3 ▶SAY STH ANGRILY 怒气冲冲地说◀ [I,T] to say something quickly in an angry or annoyed way 急速地说; 厉声说: *He laughed. "What's so funny?" I snapped.* 他哈哈大笑。"有什么好笑的?"我厉声说。| [+at] *He was jumpy and aggressive, and snapped at Walter for no reason.* 他神经过敏又咄咄逼人, 无缘无故呵斥沃尔特。| **snap sb's head off** *BrE* (=say something in a very angry way) 【英】呵斥某人, 怒气冲冲地顶撞某人 *I told her I was going to be late and she nearly snapped my head off!* 我告诉她我会迟到一会儿, 她便火冒三丈地呵斥我!

4 ▶ANIMAL 动物◀ [I] if an animal such as a dog snaps, it tries to bite you〔狗等〕咬, 噬: [+at] *Boxer was snapping at his ankles.* 拳师狗正要咬他的脚踝。

5 ▶PHOTOGRAPH 摄影◀ [T] to take a photograph 给…拍快照, 拍摄〔照片〕: *wandering around Paris, snapping all the landmarks* 在巴黎到处逛, 拍摄所有的名胜古迹

6 snap your fingers to make a short, sharp noise by moving one of your fingers quickly against your thumb, for example in order to get someone's attention 打响指

7 ▶BECOME ANGRY/ANXIOUS ETC 变得生气/焦虑等◀ [I] to suddenly stop being able to control your anger, anxiety, or other feelings in a difficult situation〔精神等〕崩溃: *I was handling the stress OK but then suddenly I just snapped.* 正当我把紧张的压力调节得不错的时候, 我突然间却崩溃了。

8 ▶MIND 神志◀ *old-fashioned* if your mind snaps, you become mentally ill【过时】患上精神病

9 snap to it also 又作 **snap it up** *AmE spoken* used to tell someone to hurry and do something immediately【美口】赶快, 快干: *Come on, snap to it, get that room cleaned up!* 来吧, 赶快, 把那个房间打扫干净!

10 snap to attention if soldiers snap to attention, they suddenly stand very straight〔士兵们〕猛地立正, 啪的一声立正 —see also 另见 SNAP-ON

snap sth ↔ **on/off** *phr v* [T] to turn a light on or off 开/关〔灯〕

snap out of sth *phr v* [T not in passive 不用被动态] **snap out of it** to stop being sad or upset and make yourself feel better 克服悲伤或烦乱情绪, 打起精神, 振作起来: *Chantal's been depressed for days. I wish she'd snap out of it.* 钱塔尔情绪低落已经好几天了, 我希望她能振作起来。

snap sb/sth ↔ **up** *phr v* [T] **1** to buy something immediately, especially because it is very cheap 把…赶快弄到手, 抢购: *If you see one for under $100, you should snap it up.* 如果你看到某一款售价在 100 美元以下, 你就应当马上买下来。**2** to eagerly take an opportunity to have someone as part of your company, team etc 急于聘请〔某人〕: *They needed a good quarterback and would have snapped him up if they'd had a chance.* 他们需要一名优秀的四分卫, 一旦有机会, 就会把他抢到手。

snap[2] *n*

1 ▶SOUND 声音◀ [singular] a sudden loud sound, especially made by something breaking or closing 突然折断[闭上]的声音, 啪的一声: *I shut the book with a snap, and put it away.* 我啪地把书合上, 放到一旁 —see picture on page A19 参见 A19 页图

2 ▶PHOTOGRAPH 照片◀ [C] *informal especially BrE* a photograph taken by someone who is not a professional photographer【非正式, 尤英】〔由非专业摄影师拍的〕快照, 快相: *holiday snaps* 假日留影

3 be a snap *AmE informal* to be very easy to do【美, 非正式】轻而易举: *The test was a snap.* 这次测验容易得很。

4 a snap of your fingers a sudden sound made by quickly moving one of your fingers against your thumb 打响指的噼啪声

5 ▶GAME 游戏◀ [U] a card game in which players put down one card after another and try to be the first to shout 'snap' when there are two cards that are the same 呼"同"牌戏〔玩牌者将手中的牌一张张地发到桌上, 抢先认出两张相同者即呼"同"〕

6 ▶CLOTHES FASTENER 衣服扣子◀ [C] *AmE* a small metal fastener on clothes that works by pressing two parts together【美】〔金属的〕揿扣, 按扣, 子母扣 —see also 另见 BRANDY SNAP, COLD SNAP —see picture at 参见 FASTENER 图

snap[3] *adj* **snap judgment/decision** a judgment or decision made quickly and without enough thought or preparation 仓促的判断/匆忙的决定: *I hate making snap decisions.* 我不喜欢匆忙作出决定。

snap[4] *interjection* **1** *BrE spoken* used when you see two things that are exactly the same【英口】真巧啊! 一模一样!〔发现两件相同的物品时的惊叹语〕: *Hey, snap! I've got a dress just like that!* 嘿, 真巧! 我有一件和那件一模一样的连衣裙! **2** *spoken* said in the game of snap when two cards that are the same are put down【口】"同!"〔在呼"同"牌戏中发现两张相同的牌一起摆出时的呼喊〕

snap·drag·on /ˈsnæpˌdrægən; ˈsnæpˌdrægən/ *n* [C] a garden plant with white, red, or yellow flowers 金鱼草, 龙嘴花〔一种开白色、红色或黄色花朵的庭园花卉〕

snap-on /ˈ· ·/ *adj* [only before noun 仅用于名词前] a snap-on part of a toy or tool can be fastened on and removed easily〔玩具或工具部件〕容易拆下[装上]的, 可吧嗒一声合上的

snap·per /ˈsnæpə; ˈsnæpə/ *n* [C] a type of fish that lives in warm seas, often used as food 啮鱼〔产于热带海域的食用鱼〕

snap·pish /ˈsnæpɪʃ; ˈsnæpɪʃ/ *adj* bad-tempered 急躁的, 脾气暴躁的: *Children are often spiteful and snappish.* 小孩子常常故意刁难人而且急躁。—**snappishly** *adv* —**snappishness** *n* [U]

snap·py /ˈsnæpɪ; ˈsnæpi/ *adj* **1** quick to react in an angry way 反应快的, 易怒的 **2** a snappy title or phrase is easy to remember〔标题、词语等〕短小精悍的, 易记的 **3 make it snappy** also 又作 **look snappy** *informal* used to tell someone to hurry【非正式】快点! 赶快!: *Get me a drink and make it snappy.* 给我一杯饮料, 快一点。**4** *BrE informal* snappy clothes are attractive and fashionable【英, 非正式】〔衣服〕漂亮的, 时髦的: *a snappy suit* 一套时髦的西服 | **a snappy dresser** (=someone who wears fashionable clothes) 穿着入时的人 —**snappily** *adv* —**snappiness** *n* [U]

snap·shot /ˈsnæpˌʃɑt; ˈsnæpʃɒt/ *n* [C] **1** an informal photograph 快照, 快相: *holiday snapshots* 假日快照 **2** a piece of information that quickly gives you an idea of what the situation is like at a particular time 简讯, 简况: *The US balance sheet provides a snapshot of what Americans own and owe.* 这份美国资产负债表提供了美国人拥有的财富和负债的概况。

snare[1] /snɛr; sneə/ *n* [C] **1** a trap for catching an animal, especially one that uses a wire or rope to catch the animal by its foot 罗网, 套索, 陷阱〔尤指用绳索绊住兽类足部的捕兽器〕 **2** *literary* something that is intended to trick someone and get them into a difficult situation【文】〔诱人上当的〕圈套, 骗局, 陷阱

snare[2] *v* [T] **1** to catch an animal by using a snare〔用陷阱等〕捕捉, 诱捕〔兽类〕 **2** to deceive someone so that they cannot escape from a difficult situation 诱使〔某人〕上当, 设计陷害〔某人〕

snare drum /ˈ· ·/ *n* [C] a small flat drum that makes a hard continuous sound when you hit it〔扁形〕小鼓

snarl /snɑrl; snɑːl/ *v* **1** [I] if an animal snarls it makes a low angry sound and shows its teeth〔动物张牙露齿低声地〕咆哮, 吼: [+at] *The alsatian snarls at strangers.* 这只德国牧羊狗对陌生人总是龇牙咧嘴地低声咆哮。**2** [I,T] to speak or say something in a nasty angry way 咆哮着说, 怒吼: *"Shut up," he snarled.* "住口。"他怒吼道。**3** also 又作 **snarl up** [T usually passive 一般用被动态] to prevent traffic from moving 使〔交通〕堵塞: *The traffic was snarled up on both sides of the road.* 马路两边的交通都被堵塞了。—**snarl** *n* [C]

snarl-up /ˈ· ·/ *n* [C] **1** a confused situation that prevents work from continuing 混乱; 纠缠 **2** a situation in which traffic is prevented from moving 交通堵塞: *There was a big snarl-up on the M1.* 在 1 号高速公路上交通严重堵塞。

snatch[1] /snætʃ; snætʃ/ *v* [T] **1** to take something away from someone with a quick violent movement; GRAB[1] (1) 抢, 强夺, 攫取: *The thief snatched her purse and ran.* 小偷抢过她的钱包后拔腿便跑。**2** to quickly take the opportunity to do something for an hour etc because you do not have much time 抓住〔机会〕; 抓紧〔时间〕: *I managed to snatch an hour's sleep on the train.* 我在火车上抓紧时间睡了一小时。**3** to take someone or something away from a place by force 抓走, 抢去, 夺走: *Vargas*

was snatched from his home by two armed men. 瓦尔加斯被两名持枪男子从家中抓走。

snatch at sth *phr v* [T] to quickly put out your hand to try to take or hold something 伸手试图抓住[攫取]: *Jessie snatched at the bag but I pulled it away.* 杰西伸手想抓袋子，但我把它拉了过来。

snatch² *n* [C] **1 a snatch of conversation/music/song etc** a short and incomplete part of a conversation, song etc that you hear 谈话/音乐/歌曲等的片段 **2 in snatches** for short periods 断断续续地: *I only slept in snatches during the night.* 我夜里睡觉不时会醒。**3** [+with] a quick movement with your hand in order to take or hold something or someone 抓，抢，夺

snatch squad /'· ,·/ *n* [C] a group of policemen who go quickly into a crowd to ARREST¹ (1) people〔在人群中抓人的〕特别搜捕队

snaz·zy /ˈsnæzɪ; 'snæzi/ *adj informal* clothes that are snazzy are bright, fashionable, and attractive【非正式】〔衣服〕华丽的，时髦的，鲜艳夺目的: *a snazzy red jacket* 鲜艳的红外套 —**snazzily** *adv*

sneak¹ /snik; sniːk/ *v past tense and past participle* **sneaked** /snikt; sniːkt/ **snuck** /snʌk; snʌk/ *AmE*【美】**1** [I always+adv/prep] to go somewhere secretly and quietly in order to avoid being seen or heard 鬼鬼祟祟地行动，偷偷地走，潜行: [+in/past/around etc] *They managed to sneak past the guard on the gate.* 他们总算蹑手蹑脚躲着门卫溜了过去。**2** [T always+adv/prep] to hide something and take it somewhere secretly 偷偷携带: **sneak sth through/by/past etc** *I'm going to try and sneak these bottles of wine through Customs.* 我准备偷偷带这几瓶酒过海关。**3 sneak a look/glance at** to look at something quickly and secretly, especially something that you are not supposed to see 偷看一眼〔尤指不该看的东西〕**4** [T] *informal* to quickly and secretly steal something unimportant or of little value【非正式】偷窃〔不贵重的小东西〕: **sneak sth from** *We used to sneak cigarettes from Dad to smoke in the garden.* 我们过去常常偷爸爸的香烟到花园里抽。

sneak on sb *phr v* [T] *informal* to tell someone such as a parent or teacher about something that another person has done wrong, because you want to cause trouble for that person【非正式】〔向老师或同学的家长〕告密，打小报告: *Adrian's not popular because he's always sneaking on other kids.* 大家都不喜欢阿德里安，因为他总是给其他孩子打小报告。

sneak up *phr v* [I] to come near someone very quietly, so that they do not see you until you reach them 偷偷地走近，蹑手蹑脚地靠近: [+on/behind etc] *Don't sneak up on me like that! You gave me quite a shock.* 不要那样悄悄地走近我！你吓了我一跳。—see also 另见 **sneak preview** (PREVIEW (1))

sneak² *n* [C] *BrE informal* a child who is disliked because they tell adults about bad things that other children have done wrong【英，非正式】向大人告密的孩子

sneak·er /ˈsnikɚ; 'sniːkə/ *n* [C] *especially AmE* a type of light soft shoe with a rubber SOLE (=bottom) used for sports【尤美】胶底运动鞋 —see picture at 参见 SHOE¹ 图

sneak·ing /ˈsnikɪŋ; 'sniːkɪŋ/ *adj* **1 have a sneaking admiration/affection etc for** to have a secret feeling of admiration etc for someone 暗地钦佩/爱慕等 **2 have a sneaking suspicion/feeling (that)** to have a slight feeling that someone has done something wrong without being sure 暗自有点怀疑/隐隐觉得: *I have a sneaking suspicion he throws away my letters without even reading them.* 我心里有一种感觉，我的信他连看也不看就扔掉了。

sneak·y /ˈsnikɪ; 'sniːki/ *adj* doing things in a secret and dishonest or unfair way 偷偷摸摸的，鬼鬼祟祟的: *That was really sneaky, hiding his wallet!* 那样太不老实了，竟然把他的钱包藏了起来！—**sneakily** *adv*

sneer¹ /snɪr; snɪə/ *v* [I,T] to smile or speak in a very unkind way that shows you have no respect for someone or something 冷笑；讥笑，嘲笑: [+at] *Bob always sneers at my taste in clothes.* 鲍勃总是嘲笑我的衣着品味。—**sneering** *adj*: *a sneering letter* 冷言冷语的信 —**sneeringly** *adv*

sneer² *n* [C] an unkind smile or remark that shows you have no respect for something or someone 冷笑；讥笑，嘲笑；鄙视

sneeze¹ /sniz; sniːz/ *v* [I] **1** to have sudden uncontrolled burst of air out of your nose, for example when you have a cold 打喷嚏: *The baby keeps sneezing – she must be getting a cold.* 宝宝不停地打喷嚏，她一定是着凉了。**2 not to be sneezed at** *spoken* good enough to be considered carefully【口】不可轻视，值得认真考虑: *An offer of £900 is not to be sneezed at.* 900英镑的出价可是值得认真考虑的。

CULTURAL NOTE 文化注释

When a person sneezes, it is polite to say "Bless you!" or (especially in the US) "Gesundheit". The person who has sneezed usually replies "Thank you." 遇到人打喷嚏时，礼貌的话是"长命百岁!"或者(特别是在美国也可以说)"身体康健!"而打喷嚏的人会回答说:"谢谢。"

sneeze² *n* [C] an act or sound of sneezing 喷嚏(声)

snick /snɪk; snɪk/ *v* [T] *BrE* to make a small cut or mark on something; NICK² (1)【英】刻细痕于，留刻痕于 —**snick** *n* [C]

snick·er /ˈsnɪkɚ; 'snɪkə/ *v* [I] *AmE* to laugh quietly, and often unkindly, at something which is not supposed to be funny【美】暗笑，窃笑; SNIGGER *BrE*【英】—**snicker** *n* [C]

snide /snaɪd; snaɪd/ *adj informal* making unkind criticisms, often in a clever, indirect way【非正式】挖苦的，讽刺的: **snide remarks/comments** *She's always making snide remarks about Marco's pronunciation.* 她老是针对马科的发音说些挖苦的话。—**snidely** *adv*

sniff¹ /snɪf; snɪf/ *v*

1 ▶BREATHE NOISILY 有声地吸气◀ [I] to breathe air into your nose noisily, especially in short breaths〔短促有声地〕以鼻吸气: *Stop sniffing — why can't you blow your nose?* 别再哧哧地抽鼻子了，你为什么不能擤擤鼻涕？

2 ▶SMELL 闻◀ [I,T] to breathe air in through your nose in order to smell something〔出声地〕闻，嗅: *He opened the milk and sniffed it.* 他打开牛奶罐闻了一闻。| [+at] *The dog was sniffing at the dead bird.* 狗在嗅着那只死鸟。

3 [T] to say something in a proud complaining way 嗤之以鼻地说，轻蔑地说: *"I expected something much better," she sniffed.* "我还以为是什么好东西呢。"她不屑地说。

4 not to be sniffed at *spoken* good enough to be considered carefully【口】不可嗤之以鼻，值得认真考虑: *An 8% salary increase is not to be sniffed at.* 对8%的工资增长不该嗤之以鼻了。

5 [T] to take a harmful drug through your nose 用鼻子吸入〔有害药物〕: *sniffing cocaine* 吸可卡因 —see also 另见 GLUE SNIFFING

sniff out sth *phr v* [T] **1** to discover or find something by its smell 靠嗅觉发现，嗅出: *They've got dogs at the customs for sniffing out drugs.* 海关人员用狗嗅查毒品。**2** *informal* to find out something【非正式】找出，发现，察觉: *Vic's been asking questions, trying to sniff out where you went last night.* 维克一直在问这问那，想探出昨晚你去了什么地方。

sniff² *n* [C] an act or sound of sniffing 以鼻吸气(声)

sniffer dog /'·· ·/ *n* [C] a dog that has been trained to find drugs or explosives by using its sense of smell〔用于探查毒品和炸药的〕嗅探犬，嗅探警犬

snif·fle¹ /ˈsnɪfl; 'snɪfəl/ *v* [I] to sniff repeatedly to stop liquid from running out of your nose, especially when you are crying or you have a cold 反复抽鼻子〔尤指在哭或感冒时为了不让鼻涕流出〕: *For goodness sake, stop sniffling!* 看在老天爷面上，别再抽鼻子了！

sniffle² *n* an act or sound of sniffling 抽鼻子；抽鼻子声: **have the sniffles** (=keep sniffing) 不停地抽鼻子

sniff·y /ˈsnɪfɪ; 'snɪfi/ *adj BrE informal* having a disapproving attitude towards something or someone especially because you think they are not good enough for you【英，非正式】瞧不起人的，傲慢的: *Don't get sniffy, he's a friend of mine!* 别瞧不起人，他可是我的朋友啊！

snif·ter /ˈsnɪftɚ; 'snɪftə/ *n* [C] **1** *AmE* a special glass for drinking BRANDY【美】〔喝白兰地用的〕小口短脚酒杯 —see picture at 参见 GLASS¹ 图 **2** *BrE old fashioned* a small amount of an alcoholic drink【英，过时】少量的酒，一口酒

snig·ger /ˈsnɪgɚ; 'snɪgə/ *v* [I] *BrE* to laugh quietly, and often unkindly, at something which is not supposed to be funny【英】暗笑，窃笑; SNICKER *AmE*【美】: [+at] *What are you sniggering at? This is a serious poem.* 你偷笑什么？这是一首严肃的诗。—**snigger** *n* [C]

snip¹ /snɪp; snɪp/ *n* [C] **1** a quick small cut with scissors〔剪刀的〕一剪，剪口 **2 be a snip** *BrE informal* to be surprisingly cheap【英，非正式】极其廉价的: *At £20 for a dozen, they're a snip.* 20英镑一打，真便宜。—see 见 CHEAP (USAGE)

snip² *v* [I,T] to cut something by making quick cuts with scissors 用剪刀迅速地剪: *I hurriedly snipped the string and untied the parcel.* 我匆忙地把绳子剪断，将包裹解开。| **snip sth off** (=remove it by snipping) 剪掉某物 *Snip the ends of the beans off before you cook them.* 先把菜豆两头剪掉然后才煮。—see picture on page A11 参见 A11 页图

snipe¹ /snaɪp; snaɪp/ *v* [I] **1** to shoot from a hidden position at unprotected people 伏击，狙击，打冷枪 **2** to criticize someone in

a nasty way 诽谤, 中伤: [+at] *I wish you two would stop sniping at each other.* 我希望你们两个别再互相诽谤。—**sniping** *n* [U]

snipe² *n* [C] **1** a bird with a very long thin beak that lives in wet areas, and is often shot for sport 鹬, 沙锥〔嘴细长、居于湿地的一种鸟〕 **2** *AmE* someone who is strongly disliked【美】极讨厌的人

snip·er /ˈsnaɪpɚ; ˈsnaɪpə/ *n* [C] someone who shoots at unprotected people from a hidden position 狙击手: *Edwards was shot and killed by snipers.* 爱德华兹被几名狙击手枪杀。

snip·pet /ˈsnɪpɪt; ˈsnɪpʒt/ *n* [C] **snippet of information/news etc** a small piece of information etc 简短的消息/新闻等: *We'd welcome any odd snippets of information you might pick up.* 你能打听到的任何零星消息我们都要。

snip·py /ˈsnɪpɪ; ˈsnɪpi/ *adj AmE informal* quick to show that you are angry or offended, or that you will not obey someone【美, 非正式】脾气急躁的; 目中无人的

snit /snɪt; snɪt/ *n* **be in a snit** *AmE informal* to be unreasonably annoyed about something【美, 非正式】不合理地生气: *Martha's in a snit because I used her omelet pan.* 玛莎因我用过她的炒蛋锅而生气。

snitch¹ /snɪtʃ; snɪtʃ/ *v informal*【非正式】**1** [I+on] to tell someone such as a parent or teacher about something that another person has done wrong because you want to cause trouble for that person〔向家长或老师〕告密, 告发 **2** [T] to quickly steal something unimportant or of little value 偷, 扒窃〔不太值钱的东西〕

snitch² *n* [C] **1** *informal* someone who is disliked because he or she tells a parent or teacher about something wrong that another person has done【非正式】〔向家长或老师告密的〕告密者 **2** *BrE humorous* a nose【英, 幽默】鼻子

sniv·el /ˈsnɪvl; ˈsnɪvəl/ *v* **snivelled, snivelling** *BrE*【英】, **sniveled, sniveling** *AmE*【美】[I] to behave or speak in a weak complaining way, especially when you are crying 啜泣, 抽泣; 哭诉: *I warned you – so don't come snivelling back to me when it all goes wrong!* 我早已警告过你, 所以现在出问题, 你就不要哭哭啼啼回来找我! | *a snivelling coward* 哭哭啼啼的胆小鬼

snob /snɑb; snɒb/ *n* [C] **1** someone who thinks they are better than people from a lower social class and dislikes being with them or doing the things they do 势利的人; 自命不凡者: *John wouldn't go to a football match, he's too much of a snob.* 约翰不会去看足球赛, 他这个人太自命高雅了。**2 intellectual snob** someone who thinks they are too intelligent to enjoy ordinary forms of entertainment 自以为学识超群蔑视流行娱乐方式的人 **3 music/wine etc snob** someone who knows a lot about music, wine etc and thinks their opinions are better than other people's 自以为很懂音乐/很会品酒等的人 **4 snob value/appeal** something that has snob value is liked by people who think they are better than other people〔商品〕在势利者眼中的价值/对势利者的吸引力: *A Rolls-Royce has snob appeal.* 劳斯莱斯汽车对爱慕虚荣者颇具吸引力。

snob·be·ry /ˈsnɑbərɪ; ˈsnɒbəri/ *n* [U] **1** the feelings and behaviour of snobs 势利(行为), 谄上欺下 **2 inverted snobbery** a type of snobbery in which people of a low social class think they are better than people of a higher social class 反面势利(行为)〔社会地位低的人认为自己比社会地位高的人优秀〕

snob·bish /ˈsnɑbɪʃ; ˈsnɒbɪʃ/ also 又作 **snob·by** /ˈsnɑbɪ; ˈsnɒbi/ *adj* having attitudes, behaviour etc that are typical of a snob 势利眼的; 谄上欺下的 —**snobbishly** *adv* —**snobbishness** *n* [U]

snog /snɑg; snɒg/ *v* **snogged, snogging** [I,T] *BrE informal* if two young people snog, they kiss each other, especially for a long time【英, 非正式】〔长时间〕接吻 —**snog** *n* [C usually singular 一般用单数]

snook /snuk; snuːk/ *n* —see 见 **cock a snook** (COCK² (5))

snoo·ker¹ /ˈsnukɚ; ˈsnuːkə/ *n* [U] a game played on a special table covered in green cloth, in which two people hit coloured balls into holes at the sides and corners of the table with CUE*s* (=long sticks) 斯诺克(台球)

snooker² *v* [T, often passive 常用被动态] *BrE informal* to make it impossible for someone to do what they want to do【英, 非正式】使陷于困境: *If the council refuses our planning application, we're snookered.* 如果政务委员会不批准我们的规划申请, 我们就一筹莫展了。

snoop /snup; snuːp/ *v* [I] to try to find out about someone's private affairs by secretly looking in their house, examining their possessions etc 探听, 窥探, 窥视: [+around/about] *I caught him snooping around in my office.* 我发现他在我办公室里到处窥探。—**snoop** *n* [singular] **snooper** *n* [C]

Snoop·y /ˈsnupɪ; ˈsnuːpi/ *trademark* a dog who is one of the main characters in the popular US CARTOON STRIP (=a set of drawings that tell a story) *Peanuts*, which appears in many newspapers【商标】史努比〔美国著名连环漫画《花生》中的一条狗, 许多报纸予以登载〕

snoot /snut; snuːt/ *n* [C] *AmE informal* your nose【美, 非正式】鼻子

snoot·y /ˈsnutɪ; ˈsnuːti/ *adj informal* rude and unfriendly, because you think you are better than other people【非正式】傲慢的, 目中无人的, 妄自尊大的: *snooty neighbours* 傲慢的邻居 —**snootily** *adv* —**snootiness** *n* [U]

snooze /snuz; snuːz/ *v* [I] *informal* to have a short, light sleep【非正式】小睡, 打盹: *Dad was snoozing in a deckchair.* 爸爸在躺椅上打盹。—**snooze** *n* [C]

snore¹ /snor; snɔː/ *v* [I] to breathe noisily through your mouth and nose while you are asleep 打鼾, 打呼噜: *Bill's snoring is driving me nuts.* 比尔的呼噜真把我气坏了。

snore² *n* [C] the noise you make when you snore 打鼾声

snor·kel¹ /ˈsnorkl; ˈsnɔːkəl/ *n* [C] **1** a tube that allows a swimmer to breathe air under water〔潜水者的〕呼吸管 **2** a piece of equipment that allows a SUBMARINE to take in air when it is under water〔潜水艇的〕通气管

snorkel² *v* [I] to swim under water using a snorkel 使用呼吸管潜泳 —**snorkelling** *BrE*【英】, **snorkeling** *AmE*【美】—*n* [U]

snort¹ /snort; snɔːt/ *v* **1** [I,T] to express anger, impatience, or amusement by breathing air noisily through your nose 发哼声; 哼着鼻子〔表示生气、不耐烦、被逗乐〕: *"Certainly not," he snorted.* "肯定不是。"他哼了一声说。| [+with] *She snorted with contempt at the suggestion.* 她哼了一声表示对这个建议的轻蔑。**2** [I] to make a loud noise by forcing air out through your nose 从鼻子呼气作声, 喷鼻息: *The horse snorted and stamped its hoof impatiently.* 这匹马呼哧呼哧地喷着气, 不耐烦地跺着蹄。**3** [T] *slang* to take drugs by breathing them in through your nose【俚】用鼻吸入〔毒品〕: *snorting cocaine* 用鼻吸可卡因

snort² *n* [C] **1** a loud sound made by breathing through your nose, especially to show anger, impatience, or amusement 哼声, 喷鼻息声: *a snort of laughter* 扑哧一笑 **2** a small amount of a drug that is breathed in through the nose〔用鼻吸入的〕少量毒品: *a snort of cocaine* 用鼻吸入的一点可卡因

snot /snɑt; snɒt/ *n informal*【非正式】**1** [U] an impolite word for the thick MUCUS (=liquid) produced in your nose 鼻涕〔非礼貌用词〕**2** [C] someone who is SNOTTY (1) 高傲的人

snot-nosed /ˈ· ·/ *adj AmE informal* an impolite word used to describe children who are not very clean【美, 非正式】〔小孩〕脏兮兮的〔非礼貌用词〕: *that snot-nosed kid next door* 隔壁那个脏兮兮的孩子

snot·ty /ˈsnɑtɪ; ˈsnɒti/ *adj informal*【非正式】**1** thinking that you are more important than other people 高傲的, 妄自尊大的: *I won't be told what to do by some snotty little clerk!* 我不许一个妄自尊大的小职员来告诉我该干什么! **2** wet and dirty with MUCUS 被鼻涕弄得脏湿的

snotty-nosed /ˈ·· ·/ *adj BrE informal* SNOTTY (2)【英, 非正式】被鼻涕弄得脏湿的

snout /snaut; snaʊt/ *n* [C] **1** the long nose of some kinds of animals, such as pigs〔猪等动物的〕口鼻部, 长鼻子 **2** *BrE informal* a criminal who gives information about other criminals to the police【英, 非正式】向警方告发其同伙的罪犯

snow¹ /sno; snəʊ/ *n* **1** [U] water frozen into soft white FLAKE*s* (=pieces) that fall from the sky in cold weather and cover the ground 雪: *mountain peak covered with snow* 白雪覆盖的山峰 | *roads blocked by deep snow* 为厚厚的积雪所阻塞的道路 | *melting snow* 在融化的积雪 —see picture on page A13 参见 A13 页图 **2** [C] a period of time in which snow falls 降雪; 降雪期: *one of the heaviest snows this winter* 今年冬天最大的降雪之一 **3** [U] *slang* COCAINE【俚】可卡因 S3 W3

CULTURAL NOTE 文化注释

In northern and eastern parts of the US, it snows a lot all winter, but in the south and some western parts, it hardly snows at all. Northern cities are well-prepared for snow, and have people employed to keep roads clear. Many people enjoy winter sports such as SKIING, and children enjoy the snow by riding down slopes on SLEDGE*s*, building snowmen (SNOWMAN), and having SNOWBALL fights. People from cold parts of the US, especially RETIRED people, sometimes travel to warm states such as Arizona or Florida to stay there for the winter. These people are called SNOWBIRD*s*. 在美国北部和东部, 冬季会下很多雪; 但是在南部和西部的一些地区, 几乎不怎么下雪。北部的城市有很好的应对下雪的措施, 并雇有专人清扫道路上的雪。很多人喜欢滑雪之类的冬季运动, 而下了雪孩子

S

们也很喜欢，他们乘雪橇从高坡滑下，还玩堆雪人和打雪仗。美国寒冷地区的人，尤其是退了休的老人，有时旅行到亚利桑那和佛罗里达等温暖的州来躲避冬季，人们把他们称作"躲雪鸟"。

The UK usually does not get much snow, except in parts of Scotland, so it is often not very prepared for snow when it comes. When it does snow, it can cause problems on the roads and for trains even if there is only a small amount. But children like it when it snows, because schools usually close and they can go and play in the snow. 在英国，除了苏格兰的一些地区外，通常雪下得不多；因此一旦下雪了也不能很好地应对。下了雪，即便是很薄的雪也会对道路交通和火车运行造成影响。但是孩子们很喜欢下雪，因为学校通常要放假，他们也可以去雪地里玩。

snow² *v* **1** [I] **it snows** if it snows, snow falls from the sky 下雪: *It snowed all night.* 下了一整夜雪。| *Look! It's snowing!* 瞧！下雪了！ **2** [T] *AmE informal* to persuade someone to believe or support something, especially by lying to them【美，非正式】〔尤指靠说谎〕说服〔某人〕，赢得〔某人的〕信任[支持]: *I was completely snowed by his Southern charm.* 我完全被他那种南方人的魅力蒙骗了。 **3 be snowed in/up** to be unable to travel from a place because so much snow has fallen there〔人〕被雪困住/〔地方〕被雪封住: *We were snowed in for three days last winter.* 去年冬天我们被大雪困了三天。 **4 be snowed under (with sth)** to have more work than you can deal with 被…压得透不过气来，〔工作多得〕忙不过来，穷于应付

Snow·ball /ˈsnoˌbɔl; ˈsnəʊbɔːl/ a main character in *Animal Farm*, a SATIRE on the Soviet Union by George Orwell. Snowball is a pig who helps the animals to drive out the cruel farmer who owns them. But he is then chased away by another pig, Napoleon. Snowball represents Leon Trotsky, who was forced to leave the Soviet Union by Joseph Stalin. 斯诺博尔〔小说《动物农庄》中的主要形象。被认为是一部讽刺前苏联的作品，作者为乔治·奥威尔。斯诺博尔是一头猪，帮助动物们赶走了残酷的农场主，后来自己却被另一头名为拿破仑的猪赶出了庄园。斯诺博尔被认为象征的是被约瑟夫·斯大林赶出苏联的托洛斯基〕

S

snowball¹ *n* [C] **1** a ball of snow that children make and throw at each other 雪球: *a snowball fight* 打雪仗 **2 not have a snowball's chance in hell** *informal* to have no chance at all【非正式】毫无机会，机会渺茫

snowball² *v* [I] if a plan, problem, business etc snowballs it grows bigger at a faster and faster rate〔计划、问题、生意等〕滚雪球似地迅速增大: *Once the contest became popular, it quickly snowballed into an all-day event with TV coverage.* 这种比赛一流行起来，就迅速发展成为电视的全天播放节目。

snow·bird /ˈsnoˌbɝd; ˈsnəʊbɜːd/ *n* [C] *AmE informal* someone, especially an old person, who moves to a warmer place every winter【美，非正式】"躲雪鸟"〔每年迁往温暖地方过冬的人，尤指老人〕

snow blind·ness /ˈ· ˌ··/ *n* [U] eye pain and difficulty in seeing things, caused by looking at snow in bright sunlight 雪盲（症）〔由于雪地阳光反射刺激而引起的眼睛痛和暂时失明〕—**snow blind** *adj*

snow·blow·er /ˈ· ˌ··/ *n* [C] *especially AmE* a machine which clears snow from roads by blowing it away【尤美】〔清除路面积雪的〕吹雪机

snow·board /ˈsnoˌbɔrd; ˈsnəʊbɔːd/ *n* [C] a long wide board made of plastic, which people use to travel over snow for sport〔运动用的〕滑雪板 —**snowboarder** *n* [C] —**snowboarding** *n* [U] —see picture at 参见 SKI² 图

snow·bound /ˈsnoˌbaʊnd; ˈsnəʊbaʊnd/ *adj* blocked or prevented from leaving a place by large amounts of snow 被雪困住[封闭]的: *snowbound traffic* 被雪封闭的交通

snow-capped /ˈ· ·/ *adj literary* snow-capped mountains are covered in snow at the top【文】〔山〕顶部被雪覆盖的

snow chains /ˈ· ·/ *n* [plural] a set of chains that are fixed around the wheels of a car so that it can drive over snow without slipping〔汽车轮胎上的〕防滑链

Snow·don /ˈsnodn̩; ˈsnəʊdn/ the highest mountain in Wales, in the Snowdonia National Park 斯诺登山〔威尔士境内最高的山，位于斯诺多尼亚国家公园〕

Snow·do·ni·a /snoˋdonɪə; snəʊˈdəʊniə/ an area with many mountains in North Wales, which is a National Park and is a popular place for climbers and tourists 斯诺多尼亚〔威尔士北部一山区，为国家公园，是登山者和旅游者的好去处〕

snow·drift /ˈsnoˌdrɪft; ˈsnəʊˌdrɪft/ *n* [C] a deep mass of snow piled up by the wind〔风吹成的〕雪堆

snow·drop /ˈsnoˌdrɑp; ˈsnəʊdrɒp/ *n* [C] a European plant with a small white flower which appears in early spring〔欧洲产的〕雪花莲

snow·fall /ˈsnoˌfɔl; ˈsnəʊfɔːl/ *n* [C,U] the amount of snow that falls, or the amount that falls in a particular period of time 降雪；〔某一时期的〕降雪量: *an average snowfall of eight centimetres a year* 每年平均8厘米的降雪量 | *Heavy snowfalls are forecast.* 天气预报说将有几次大雪。

snow·field /ˈsnoˌfild; ˈsnəʊfiːld/ *n* [C] a wide area of land that is always covered in snow〔终年积雪的〕雪原，雪野

snow·flake /ˈsnoˌflek; ˈsnəʊfleɪk/ *n* [C] a small soft flat piece of frozen water that falls as snow 雪片，雪花

snow job /ˈ· ·/ *n* [singular] *AmE informal* an act of persuading someone to believe or support something, especially by lying to them【美，非正式】花言巧语的劝说

snow line, the /ˈsno,laɪn; ˈsnəʊlaɪn/ *n* the level above which snow on a mountain never melts 雪线〔高山上终年积雪的最低界线〕—see picture on page A12 参见 A12 页图

snow·man /ˈsnoˌmæn; ˈsnəʊmæn/ *n* [C] a figure of a person made of snow, made especially by children〔尤指儿童用雪堆成的〕雪人

snow·mo·bile /ˈsnomoˌbil; ˈsnəʊməbiːl/ *n* [C] a small vehicle with a motor that moves over snow or ice easily 雪地机动车，摩托雪橇

snow pea /ˈ· ·/ *n* [C] *AmE* a kind of PEA whose POD (=cover) and seeds you can eat【美】糖荚豌豆；MANGETOUT *BrE*【英】

snow plough *BrE*【英】, **snow plow** *AmE*【美】/ˈ· ·/ *n* [C] a vehicle or piece of equipment for pushing snow off roads, railways etc 雪犁，扫雪机

snow route /ˈ· ·/ *n* [C] *AmE* an important road in a city that cars must be removed from when it snows, so that it can be cleared of snow【美】雪道〔在下雪天不准停放车辆以便扫雪的交通要道〕

snow·shoe /ˈsnoˌʃu; ˈsnəʊʃuː/ *n* [C] one of a pair of wide flat frames which you attach to your shoes, so that you can walk on snow without sinking〔装在鞋底，用于在雪地上行走的〕雪鞋

snow·storm /ˈsnoˌstɔrm; ˈsnəʊstɔːm/ *n* [C] a storm with strong winds and a lot of snow 雪暴，暴风雪

snow·suit /ˈsnoˌsut; ˈsnəʊsuːt/ *n* [C] a warm piece of clothing that covers the whole of a child's body〔儿童〕风雪服

snow tire /ˈ· ·/ *n* [C] *AmE* a special car tyre used when driving on snow or ice【美】〔用于雪地、冰上的〕防滑轮胎

Snow White 白雪公主

Snow White /ˌ· ˈ·/ the main character in a FAIRY TALE called *Snow White*, who is a beautiful princess who has a jealous stepmother. The stepmother sends Snow White into the forest to be killed. Snow White does not die, but goes to live with seven DWARFS (=imaginary creatures like very small men). Her stepmother then tries to kill her with a poisoned apple, but instead of dying she goes to sleep until a prince kisses her and wakes her. There is a famous Walt Disney CARTOON film based on the story, made in the 1930s. 白雪公主〔童话故事《白雪公主》中的主人公。白雪公主是一位美丽的公主。她的继母嫉妒心很强，想把白雪公主带进森林杀掉。可是白雪公主并没有死，而与七个小矮人共同生活着。继母又企图用毒苹果害死她，但白雪公主还是没死，只是昏迷过去，直到有一天一个王子吻了她，她才醒了过来。20世纪30年代，沃尔特·迪斯尼公司将这一故事改编成动画片搬上银幕〕

snow-white /ˌ· ˈ·◂/ *adj* pure white 雪白的，纯白的

snow·y /ˈsnoɪ; ˈsnəʊi/ *adj* **1** full of snow or snowing 多雪的，积雪的；下雪的: *Today it will be snowy in many areas.* 今天许

多地区将下雪。**2** *literary* pure white【文】雪白的, 纯白的: *snowy hair* 雪白的头发 —**snowiness** *n* [U]

SNP, the /ˌɛs ɛn ˋpi; ˌes en ˈpiː/ the Scottish National Party; a political party in Scotland which wants Scotland to become an independent country in the EU (=European Union) 苏格兰民族党〔苏格兰一政党, 主张苏格兰成为欧盟的一个独立国家〕

Snr the written abbreviation of 缩写= SENIOR, used after someone's name 年纪较大的, 老〔用于名字之后〕: *James Taylor, Snr* 老詹姆斯·泰勒

snub¹ /snʌb; snʌb/ *v* **snubbed, snubbing** [T] to treat someone rudely, especially by intentionally ignoring them when you meet 冷落, 怠慢, 对…不予理睬: *Mayor Koch snubbed the Giants and refused to offer them a victory parade.* 科克市长对巨人队不予理睬, 拒绝给他们举行庆祝胜利的游行。

snub² *n* [C] an act of snubbing someone 冷落, 怠慢, 不理睬: *Still smarting from the snub, he stalked from the room.* 他受冷落后伤心不已, 大步走出了房间。

snub³ *adj* a snub nose is short and flat and points slightly upwards〔鼻子〕短扁微上翘的

snub-nosed /ˌ·ˈ·◂/ *adj* having a snub nose that points slightly upwards 翘鼻子的, 狮子鼻的

snuck /snʌk; snʌk/ *AmE*【美】past tense and past participle of SNEAK

snuff¹ /snʌf; snʌf/ *v* **1** also 又作 **snuff out** [T] to put out a CANDLE flame by pressing the burning part with your fingers or covering it with a snuffer 掐灭, 熄灭〔蜡烛〕 **2** [I,T] if an animal snuffs, it breathes air into its nose noisily in order to smell something; SNIFF¹ (2)〔动物〕出声地吸气, 闻〔味〕 **3 snuff it** *BrE informal* to die【英, 非正式】断气, 死

snuff sth **out** *phr v* [T] to suddenly end something, especially someone's life〔突然地〕结束〔生命〕, 扼杀: *a young life snuffed out* 突然结束的年轻生命

snuff² *n* [U] a type of tobacco in powder form, which people suck in through their noses 鼻烟: *a pinch of snuff* 一撮鼻烟

snuff·er /ˋsnʌfɚ; ˈsnʌfə/ *n* [C] a tool with a small bell-shaped end on a handle for putting out CANDLEs 烛剪

snuf·fle /ˋsnʌfl; ˈsnʌfəl/ *v* [I] to breathe noisily through your nose making low sounds 呼哧呼哧地呼吸, 抽鼻子: *pigs snuffling round* 到处嗅来嗅去的猪

snug¹ /snʌg; snʌg/ *adj* **snugger, snuggest 1** a room or space that is snug is small, warm, and comfortable and makes you feel protected〔房间或空间〕小而温暖舒适的, 安适的: *a snug little sitting-room with a log fire burning* 一间生着火、温暖舒适的小客厅 **2** someone who is snug feels comfortable, happy, and warm〔人〕舒服的, 快乐的, 温暖的: *The kids were soon tucked up snug in their beds.* 孩子们马上钻进被窝, 舒服地睡到床上。**3** clothes that are snug fit closely〔衣服〕贴身的, 紧身的 —**snugly** *adv* —**snugness** *n* [U]

snug² *n* [C] *BrE* a small comfortable room in a PUB【英】〔酒馆的〕舒适小房间

snug·gle /ˋsnʌgl; ˈsnʌgəl/ *v* [I always+adv/prep] *informal* to settle into a warm comfortable position【非正式】依偎, 〔舒服地〕蜷缩: **[+up/down/into etc]** *Let's snuggle up together and watch TV.* 我们靠在一起看电视吧。

Snyder /ˋsnaɪdɚ; ˈsnaɪdə/, **Ruth** /ruθ; ruːθ/ (1894-1928) a woman famous for being photographed while being killed in the electric chair in Sing Sing prison in the US 斯奈德〔(1894-1928), 美国一女性, 因其在美国辛辛监狱被用电椅处以极刑的照片而出名〕

1 1 **so¹** /so; səʊ/ *adv* **1 a) so big/tall etc** [+adj/adv] used to describe how big, tall etc something is, especially when it is very big or very tall 这么大/高等〔用于形容大或高等的程度〕: *Why does life have to be so complicated?* 为什么生活非得这样复杂不可? | *It was so embarrassing – everyone was standing there looking at us!* 多么尴尬 —— 人人都站在那儿望着我们! | *I've never seen so many people attend this church before.* 我以前从未见过有这么多人来这个教堂做礼拜。| **so tall a man/so high a mountain etc** *formal*【正式】*I've never seen so beautiful a baby before.* 我以前从未见过这么漂亮的小宝宝。**b) worry/talk etc so** *formal* to worry, talk etc a great deal【正式】非常担心/说得很多等: *I wish he wouldn't fuss so – it makes me feel nervous.* 我希望他不要那么大惊小怪, 这样会使我感到紧张。**2 so tall/big etc (that)** used when you mean that because someone or something is very tall, big etc, something happens or someone does something 这么高/大等(以致…): *He was so fat he couldn't get through the door.* 他胖得无法通过这扇门。| *You couldn't hear yourself think, the music was so loud.* 什么也听不清 —— 那音乐太响了。| **so tall etc as to be sth** *The statement was so ambiguous as to be totally meaningless.* 那句话这么含糊不清, 根本不知所云。**3** used to talk about an idea, suggestion, situation etc that has been mentioned before 如此, 如是〔用于提及已经提到过的想法、建议、情况等〕: *"Will I need my umbrella?" "I don't think so."* "我需要带雨伞吗?" "我认为不需要。" | *He seemed to be very understanding, more so than I expected.* 他好像非常理解, 超过了我的期望。**4 so would John/so do I/so is he etc** used to add a positive statement to one that has just been mentioned 约翰也会这样/我也这样/他也这样等: *If you're going to take the day off then so will I.* 如果你想那天休息, 那么我也一样。| *Frank adores dogs and so does his wife.* 弗兰克非常爱狗, 他妻子也一样。**5 not so tall/big etc as...** not as tall, big etc as something else 没有…那么高/大等, 不像…那样高/大等: *You know, Harry's not so clever as I first thought.* 你知道, 哈里不像我原先想的那么聪明。—see also 另见 **as far as** (FAR¹ (3)), **as/so long as** (LONG² (6)) **6 so as to do sth** in order to do something 以便做某事: *Credit has been arranged so as to spread the payments over a 10 month period.* 贷款已经安排好, 在10个月内分期偿还。| *So as not to cause offence many of the mourners stood at the back of the church.* 为了避免引起反感, 许多送葬者都站到教堂的后部。**7 so many/much a)** a particular amount, number, level, degree etc 这么多, 那么多〔指特定的数量、数目、程度等〕: *There's only so much you can do with hair this fine.* 头发这么细, 只能做到这个程度了。**b)** used to say that something is the same as something else that is worse 等于, 简直是〔用于指某物与另一物一样糟〕: *Teenage magazines are just so much wasted paper.* 青少年杂志完全就是浪费纸张。**8 (just) as...so...** used to compare two people or things, when they are the same 正如…, …也一样〔用于比较两个相同的人或东西〕: *Just as the French love their wine, so the English love their beer.* 正如法国人喜欢喝葡萄酒, 英国人则爱喝啤酒。**9** used when you are being polite to mean 'very' 很, 十分〔用于表示礼貌〕: *I'm so pleased to meet you at last.* 我非常高兴终于见到你了。| **ever so** *BrE*【英】*The children are ever so excited. It's the first time they've been to Disneyland.* 孩子们非常兴奋, 这是他们第一次来迪斯尼乐园。**10** *formal* therefore【正式】因此: *The passport was found to have passed its expiry date and so to be void.* 护照已经过期, 因而无效。—see 见 THUS (USAGE) —see also 另见 **and so forth** (FORTH), **even so** (EVEN¹ (4)), **so far** (FAR¹ (24)), **so far as possible** (FAR¹ (25)), **so much for** (MUCH² (12)), **just so** (JUST¹ (29))

Frequencies of the word **so** in spoken and written English
单词so在英语口语和书面语中的使用频率

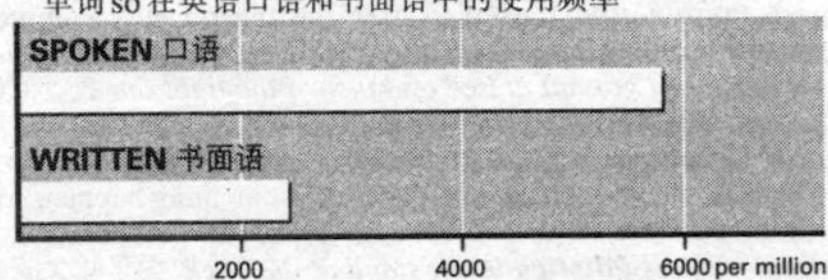

Based on the British National Corpus and the Longman Lancaster Corpus
据英国国家语料库和朗文兰开斯特语料库

This graph shows that the word **so** is much more common in spoken English than in written English. This is because it has special uses in spoken English and is used in some common spoken phrases. 本图表显示, 单词so在英语口语中的使用频率远远高于书面语, 因为它在英语口语中有特殊的用法, 而且口语中一些常用短语是由so构成的。

so (*adv*) **SPOKEN USES AND PHRASES**
含so的口语用法和短语

11 so a) used to get someone's attention, especially in order to ask them a question 那么〔尤在提问题前用于引起别人的注意〕: *So, how long do you think you'll be staying in England?* 那么, 你将在英国逗留多久? **b)** used to check that you have understood something 这么说〔用于核对自己已清楚某事〕: *So let me get this straight. You two aren't actually married then?* 这么说, 让我来弄清楚这一点吧。你们实际上并没有结婚? **c)** used to show that you do not think something is important 那又怎么样〔用于表示某事并不重要〕: *So, I lied. They can't put me in prison for that!* 我撒了谎, 那又怎么样, 他们总不能因此把我送进监狱去吧! **d)** used to show that you have found something out about someone 哦〔用于表示发现了某人的某事〕: *So! You've got a new girlfriend, huh?* 哦! 你有新的女朋友了, 嗯? **e)** used with a movement of your hand to show how big, high etc something or someone is 这么, 这样〔用于配合手势表示有多高、多大等〕: *Oh, he must be about so tall.* 哦, 他一定有差不多这么高。**f)** also

又作 **like so** used when you are showing someone how to do something using your hands, feet etc 像这样〔用于以手、脚等演示某事该如何做〕: *Fold the material, so, and push the needle through.* 把材料折起来，像这样，然后把针穿过去。**g)** used when asking a question about what has just been said 那么〔用于对某人刚说过的话发问〕: *"I've decided to leave." "So what are you going to do?"* "我决定要离开。""那么，你打算干什么？" **12 so she is/so they are etc** used to agree with something that has just been mentioned and that you had not noticed or had forgotten 她/他们是…的等〔用于表示同意某人刚提到的事，而自己未曾注意或已忘记了此事〕: *"Don't forget your brother is coming round for dinner." "So he is. I'd better get some food in."* "别忘记你弟弟会来吃晚饭。""对了，他要来的。我还是去买点吃的回来。" **13 so what?** used to show that you do not think that something that has been mentioned is important 那有什么关系？〔用于表示某事并不重要〕: *Yeah, I do smoke. So what?* 是啊，我是抽烟的。那又怎么样？ **14 so long!** *AmE* used to say goodbye【美】再见！ **15 so be it** used to show that you do not agree with someone's decision but you will accept it anyway 就那样吧，只好如此〔用于表示勉强同意某人的决定〕: *If you're sure you want to sell your car, then so be it!* 如果你确定要把汽车卖掉，那就随便吧。 **16 I do so/it is so etc** *AmE* used especially by children to say that something is true, can be done etc when someone else says that it is not, cannot etc【美】我会的/它是真的等〔尤指小孩否定别人的陈述时〕: *"You can't swim." "I can so."* "你不会游泳。""我会的。" **17 so I see** used to say that you know that what someone is telling you is true because you can see that it is 我看到是这样〔用于表示别人说的话是真的，因为可以看到〕: *"I broke my leg." "So I see. How did it happen?"* "我把腿给弄断了。""我看出来了。怎样发生的？" **18 so much the better** used to say that if something happens it will make the situation even better than it already is 那就更好了〔用于表示如果发生某事则情况会更好〕: *Katie's coming with us and if you join in too, so much the better.* 凯蒂准备和我们一起去。如果你也参加，那就更好了。 **19 so help me** used to say that you are determined to do something bad to someone, even though you know it is wrong 我发誓；上天作证〔用于表示明知故犯地伤害某人〕: *One more word and so help me I'll kill you!* 你再说一句，我发誓我会杀了你！

so² *conjunction* **1** used to give the reason why something happens, why someone does something etc 因此，所以: *I heard a noise so I got out of bed and turned the light on.* 我听到喧闹声，所以起床开灯。| *There was no food in the house so we rang out for a pizza.* 家里没有吃的东西，所以我们打电话叫了一个比萨饼。 **2 so (that) a)** in order to make something happen, something possible etc 为了，以便〔表示目的〕: *So that everyone can see, will the taller children stand at the back.* 为了让大家都看得见，请个子高的孩子站到后面去。| *The vase had been put on top of the cupboard so it wouldn't get broken.* 花瓶放在橱柜顶，以免打破。 **b)** used to say that something happens as a result of something else 结果；以致: *Many contestants later failed drug tests, so that the race had to be rerun.* 许多参赛者后来都没有通过药物测试，比赛只得重新进行。

so³ *adj* [not before noun 不用于名词前] **1 be so** *especially spoken* to be true or correct【尤口】是这样的，真的，对的: *The newspapers claim she killed him in self-defence but that just isn't so.* 报纸宣称她出于自卫杀死了他，但那根本不是真的。| *"Bill says that you appeared in court last week." "Is that so? Well let me tell you one or two things about Bill."* "比尔说，你上星期去法庭了。""真的吗？好吧，让我告诉你比尔的一两件事吧。" **2 more so/less so/too much so** phrases in which 'so' is used instead of repeating an adjective that you have mentioned before 更…/没那么…/太…〔用于避免重复刚才用的形容词〕: *Bill is very popular and Ted is even more so.* 比尔非常受欢迎，而特德更受欢迎。| *Jerry is very honest, maybe too much so.* 杰里很诚实，也许太诚实了。 **3 be just/exactly so** to be arranged tidily, with everything in the right place 安排妥帖，井井有条: *With Tim, if everything isn't just so he can't relax.* 对于蒂姆，如果每件事不是都安排得妥妥帖帖，他是不能放心的。—see also 另见 SO-SO

so⁴ *n* [singular] the fifth note in a musical SCALE¹ (8) according to the SOL-FA system 全音阶的第五音

S3 **soak¹** /sok; səʊk/ *v* **1** [I,T] if you soak something or let it soak, you keep it covered with a liquid for a period of time, especially in order to make it softer or easier to clean 浸，泡: *Soak the beans overnight.* 把豆子浸泡过夜。| **leave sth to soak** *Just leave the dishes to soak; I'll wash them later.* 盘子就放到水里泡着吧；我晚些再洗。| **soak sth off/out** (=remove it by soaking) 浸掉，浸除 *Soak the label off the jar.* 把罐子上的标签浸掉。 **2** [I always+adv/prep,T] to make something completely wet, or to become completely wet 把〔某物〕浸透；渗透，湿透: [**+through/into etc**] *If the ink soaks through the paper, it'll stain the table underneath.* 墨水如果渗透这张纸，就会把下面的桌子弄脏。| **soak sth** *The rain came suddenly and soaked all the washing.* 突然下雨，把所有晒的衣服都淋湿了。 **3** [I] to spend a long time taking a bath 长时间泡浴 **4** [T] *informal* to make someone pay too much money in prices or taxes【非正式】向…敲竹杠[征重税]: *the new President's supposed plans to soak the rich to give to the poor* 新总统的那些被认为是打富济贫的计划

soak sth ↔ **up** *phr v* [T] **1** if something soaks up a liquid, it takes the liquid into itself 吸收〔液体〕，吸干: *He used a towel to soak up the blood.* 他用毛巾把血吸掉。 **2** to learn something quickly and easily 很快学会〔某事物〕: *That child just soaks up information.* 那个小孩吸收知识很快。 **3 soak up the sun** to sit outside for a long time enjoying the sun 晒太阳，沐日光浴

soak² *n* [C] **1** a long and enjoyable time spent in the bath 〔在浴缸里的〕长时间泡浴: *a good long soak after shopping all day* 购物一整天后在浴缸里好好地泡一泡 **2** an act of soaking something 浸泡: **give sth a soak** *Give the towels a good soak, they're very dirty.* 把毛巾好好泡一泡，太脏了。 **3 an old soak** *BrE humorous* someone who is often drunk【英，幽默】酒鬼，经常喝醉的人

soaked /sokt; səʊkt/ *adj* [not before noun 不用于名词前] **1** very wet or wearing very wet clothes 很湿的；穿湿衣服的: *The rain's coming on heavier – we're going to get soaked.* 雨越下越大，我们快湿透了。| **soaked through** (=completely wet) 全湿的，湿透的 *Get those clothes off; they're soaked right through!* 把衣服脱掉，都湿透了。| **soaked to the skin** (=wearing clothes that are completely wet) 衣服湿透 **2 be soaked in** to be full of a particular quality 充满〔某种特质〕的: *a city soaked in history* 历史悠久的城市

soak·ing¹ /ˈsokɪŋ; ˈsəʊkɪŋ/ also 又作 **soaking wet** /ˌ· · ˈ·/ *adj* very wet 很湿的，湿透的: *You're soaking! Come in and dry off.* 你浑身都湿透了！快进来弄干。

soaking² *n* [C] a SOAK² (2) 浸泡

soaking sol·u·tion /ˈ· · ˌ· ·/ *n* [C,U] a liquid that you keep CONTACT LENS*es* in when you are not wearing them 隐形眼镜护理液

so-and-so /ˈ· · ˌ·/ *n plural* **so-and-sos 1** [U] an expression meaning a particular person or thing, used when you do not give their name 某某人；某某事: *They're always gossiping about so-and-so having an affair with so-and-so.* 他们老是说某男与某女关系暧昧的闲话。—compare 比较 SUCH AND SUCH **2** [C] a word meaning a very unpleasant or unreasonable person, used to avoid saying a stronger word, such as BASTARD 讨厌[无理]的人〔用以代替"狗杂种"一类强烈的字眼〕: *Peter can be a real so-and-so at times.* 彼得有时候讨厌得很。

soap¹ /sop; səʊp/ *n* **1** [U] the substance that you use to wash your body 肥皂: *Wash thoroughly with soap and water.* 用肥皂和水彻底洗一洗。| *a bar of soap* 一条肥皂 —compare 比较 DETERGENT **2** [C] *informal* a television or radio story about the daily lives of the same group of people, which is broadcast regularly; SOAP OPERA【非正式】肥皂剧〔一种以同一群人的日常生活为题材的电视或广播连续剧〕 S3

soap² *v* [T] to rub soap on or over someone or something 给…擦肥皂: *Will you soap my back for me?* 你给我背上擦点肥皂好吗？

soap·box /ˈsopˌbɑks; ˈsəʊpbɒks/ *n* **get on your soapbox** *informal* to tell people your own strong opinions about something loudly and forcefully【非正式】大发议论，高谈阔论: *Don't mention politics, or Burt will be back on his soapbox again.* 不要提政治，否则伯特又要大发议论一番。

soap·flakes /ˈsopˌfleks; ˈsəʊpfleɪks/ *n* [plural] small thin pieces of soap used for washing delicate clothes 〔洗精致衣服用的〕皂片

soap op·e·ra /ˈ· ˌ· · ·/ *n* [C] a SOAP¹ (2) 肥皂剧

CULTURAL NOTE 文化注释

In both the US and Britain there are soap operas that have been running for 20 years or more. Most people either like or strongly dislike soap operas. American soap operas are often about the lives of rich and GLAMOROUS people, but British soap operas are usually about more ordinary or WORKING-CLASS people, and often show the effects of various social problems on people's lives. Soap operas are normally based in a particular place or part of

the country, for example *EastEnders* takes place in the East End of London and *Coronation Street* is set in an industrial city in Northern England. Some British people also like watching Australian soap operas such as *Neighbours*. People who like soap operas try to see every EPISODE and talk about what happened with their friends or at work the next day. 在美国和英国都有长盛不衰地上演了20多年的肥皂剧。大多数人都是要么喜欢要么非常讨厌肥皂剧。美国的肥皂剧往往是讲述富有、显赫的人的生活, 而英国的肥皂剧通常关注更普通的人或者工人阶级, 展示各种社会问题对人们生活的影响。肥皂剧的故事一般发生在国内某个特定的地方或地区, 例如《东区人》取材于伦敦市的东区,《加冕街》以英格兰北部的一个工业城市为背景。有些英国人喜欢看澳大利亚的肥皂剧, 像《邻居》等。喜欢看肥皂剧的人希望一集不漏, 然后第二天这些就成了和朋友及同事谈论的话题。

soap pow·der /ˈ·,··/ *n* [U] *BrE* a powder that is made from soap and other chemicals, used for washing clothes【英】〔洗涤用的〕皂粉

soap·stone /ˈsop,ston; ˈsəʊpstəʊn/ *n* [U] a soft stone that feels like soap 皂石〔一种软岩石〕

soap·suds /ˈsop,sʌdz; ˈsəʊpsʌdz/ *n* [plural] the mass of small BUBBLES formed on top of soapy water 肥皂泡沫

soap·y /ˈsopɪ; ˈsəʊpi/ *adj* **1** containing soap 含有肥皂的: *warm soapy water* 温暖的肥皂水 **2** like soap 像肥皂的: *This cheese is kind of soapy-tasting.* 这种干酪味道有点像肥皂。**3** *BrE informal* so pleasant that it seems false【英, 非正式】油腔滑调的, 讨好的: *Joan reads those awful soapy romances.* 琼经常看那些讨厌的媚俗的浪漫故事。—**soapiness** *n* [U]

soar /sɔr; sɔː/ *v* [I]

1 ►AMOUNTS/PRICES ETC 数量/价格等◄ to increase quickly to a high level 猛增, 骤升: *The temperature soared to 90 degrees.* 温度骤升至90度。| *Health care costs continue to soar.* 卫生保健费用在继续猛增。

2 ►IN THE SKY 在天上◄ a) to fly, especially very high up in the sky, floating on air currents 高飞, 翱翔 **b)** to go quickly upwards to a great height 急速升高: *The rocket soared into orbit.* 火箭升空进入轨道。

3 ►SPIRITS/HOPES 情绪/希望◄ if your spirits or hopes soar, you begin to feel very happy or hopeful 高涨, 腾飞: *Adam's smile sent her spirits soaring.* 亚当的微笑使她神采飞扬。

4 ►LOOK TALL 显得很高◄ [not in progressive 不用进行时] if buildings, trees, towers etc soar they look very tall and impressive 耸立, 屹立: *Here the cliffs soar 500 feet above the sea.* 这里悬崖耸立, 高出海面500英尺。—**soaring** *adj*: *a soaring skyscraper* 高耸入云的摩天大厦 | *soaring crime figures* 猛升的犯罪数字

sob /sɑb; sɒb/ *v* **sobbed, sobbing 1** [I] to cry noisily while breathing in short, sudden bursts 啜泣, 呜咽, 抽噎: *Josie flung herself on the bed, sobbing.* 乔茜抽抽搭搭地扑倒在床上。**2** also 又作 **sob out** [T] to say something or tell someone something while you are sobbing 哭诉, 呜咽地说: *Joshua sobbed out the whole sad story.* 乔舒亚呜咽着诉说那个悲惨的故事。—**sob** *n* [C]: *loud sobs* 大声的啜泣 —**sobbingly** *adv*

so·ber[1] /ˈsobɚ; ˈsəʊbə/ *adj* **1** not drunk 未喝醉的, 清醒的: *I've never seen him sober.* 我从未见他有过不醉的时候。| **as sober as a judge** (=completely sober) 一点不醉的, 完全清醒的 **2** having a serious attitude to life 认真的, 严肃的: *a sober and intelligent young man* 认真而有才智的年轻人 **3** plain and not at all brightly coloured 素淡的, 朴素的: *a sober grey suit* 一套朴素的灰色衣服 —**soberly** *adv*

sober[2] *v* also 又作 **sober down** [I,T] to become or make someone become more serious in behaviour or attitude (使)变得严肃[谨慎; 持重]: *Diane sobered down a lot as she got older.* 随着年龄的增长, 黛安娜变得持重多了。

sober sb ↔ **up** *phr v* [I,T] to gradually become or make someone become less drunk (使)酒醉后清醒过来, (使)醒酒: *A cup of black coffee might sober you up.* 喝一杯黑咖啡也许可以使你醒酒。

so·ber·ing /ˈsobərɪŋ; ˈsəʊbərɪŋ/ *adj* making you feel very serious 使觉得严肃的; 使认真的: *a sobering thought* 严肃的思想 | *The news had a sobering effect.* 这消息是发人深省的。

so·bri·e·ty /səˈbraɪətɪ; səˈbraɪəti/ *n* [U] *formal* behaviour that shows a serious attitude to life【正式】严肃, 庄重

so·bri·quet /ˈsobrɪ,ke; ˈsəʊbrɪkeɪ/ also 又作 **soubriquet** *n* [C] *literary* an unofficial title or name; NICKNAME【文】绰号, 诨名

sob sto·ry /ˈ·,··/ *n* [C] *informal* a story, especially one that is untrue, that someone tells you in order to make you feel sorry for them【非正式】〔尤指不真实的〕为了博取同情的故事, 伤感故事: *She had some sob story about her cat getting run over.* 她有个她的猫被汽车碾死的所谓伤感故事。

Soc. the written abbreviation of 缩写= SOCIETY (3)

so-called /,·ˈ·◄/ *adj* [only before noun 仅用于名词前] a word used to describe someone or something that has been given a name that you think is wrong 所谓的: *The so-called expert on international affairs turned out to be a research student.* 这个所谓的国际事务专家原来是个研究生。 W3

soc·cer /ˈsɑkɚ; ˈsɒkə/ *n* [U] a word for the game of FOOTBALL (1) used so that it is not confused with AMERICAN FOOTBALL or RUGBY *BrE* 足球 —see picture on page A23 参见 A23 页图

so·cia·ble[1] /ˈsoʃəbl; ˈsəʊʃəbəl/ *adj* someone who is sociable enjoys being with other people 好交际的, 喜欢与人交往的: *a pleasant, sociable couple* 一对和善、喜欢与人交往的夫妇 —opposite 反义词 UNSOCIABLE —**sociably** *adv* —**sociability** /,soʃəˈbɪlətɪ; ,səʊʃəˈbɪləti/ *n* [U]

sociable[2] *n* [C] *AmE old-fashioned* a SOCIAL[2]【美, 过时】社交聚会

so·cial[1] /ˈsoʃəl; ˈsəʊʃəl/ *adj* S2 W1

1 ►SOCIETY 社会◄ concerning human society and its organization, or the quality of people's lives 社会的, 有关社会的: *Various social issues, such as unemployment and education, were discussed.* 讨论了各种社会问题, 如失业和教育等。| *social trends* 社会趋势 | *demands for social change* 对社会变革的要求

2 ►RANK 地位◄ related to the position in society that you have, according to your job, family, wealth etc 社会地位[阶层]的: *social status* 社会地位 | *a wide circle of friends from different social backgrounds* 广泛的社会背景各异的朋友圈子 | **social class** (=a group of people who have the same social position) 社会阶层 *every social class, from manual workers to aristocrats* 从劳工到贵族的各个社会阶层 | **social mobility** (=ability to move into a higher social class) 社会流动能力

3 ►MEETING PEOPLE 与人交往◄ related to the way you meet people and form relationships 社交的, 交际的: **social skills** (=ability to meet people easily and deal well with them) 社交技能 *College gives you an opportunity to develop your social skills.* 大学给你提供一个发展社交技能的机会。| **social contacts** (=people you meet outside work)〔工作以外的〕社交关系 | **social graces** (=attractive manners, behaviour etc when you meet people) 社交风度

4 ►WITH FRIENDS 和朋友在一起◄ related to the time you spend with your friends for enjoyment 交谊的, 联谊的: **social life** (=activities with your friends) 社交生活 *You sure seem to have a busy social life these days!* 你近来的社交生活好像的确很忙碌! | **social club/evening/gathering etc** (=a club or occasion at which people can enjoy being together) 联谊俱乐部/晚会/聚会等 | **social drinking** (=drinking alcohol with your friends) 与朋友相聚欢饮

5 ►ANIMALS 动物◄ forming groups or living together in their natural state 群居的, 合群的: *Elephants are social animals.* 大象是群居动物。—see also 另见 ANTI-SOCIAL, SOCIABLE, UNSOCIAL —**socially** *adv*: *socially acceptable behaviour* 在社会上可以接受的行为 | *Do you and your colleagues ever meet socially?* 你和同事们有社交聚会吗?

social[2] *n* [C] *old-fashioned* a planned informal party for the members of a group, club or church【过时】社交聚会; 联谊会; 教友联谊会

Social and Lib·e·ral Dem·o·crats, the /,··,···ˈ···/ the official name of the Liberal Democrats, a British political party 社会自由民主党〔英国一政党, 自由民主党的正式名称〕

Social Chap·ter, the /ˈ··,··/ also 又作 **European Social Chapter** a document produced by the EU (=European Union) and agreed upon by all the member countries, which contains details of the most important employment and social rights that should be available in these countries. The document includes rules about working hours, working conditions, payment for work, health and safety, equal treatment between men and women, and the protection of children and young people.《社会宪章》〔一份由欧盟制定、所有成员国一致通过的文件。内容涉及各成员国最重要的就业权利和社会权利的详情, 还包含有关工作时间、工作条件与报酬、健康与安全、男女同工同酬、保护儿童与青少年的规定〕

social climb·er /,··ˈ··/ *n* [C] someone who tries to get accepted into a higher social class by becoming friendly with people who belong to that class 结交权贵向上爬的人, 设法挤进上流社会的人

social de·moc·ra·cy /,··ˈ···/ *n* **1** [U] a political and economic system based on socialism combined with DEMOCRATIC

S

principles, such as personal freedom and government by elected representatives 社会民主主义 **2** [C] a country with a government based on this system 社会民主主义国家 —**social democrat** /ˌ· · ˈ· · ·/ *n* [C]

Social Dem·o·crat and La·bour Par·ty, the /ˌ· · ·, · · · ˈ· · ˌ· · ·/ the full name of the SDLP, a political party in Northern Ireland 社会民主工党〔北爱尔兰一政党。SDLP的全称〕

social di·sease /ˈ· · · ˌ· ·/ *n* [C] an expression meaning VENEREAL DISEASE, used to avoid saying this directly 社交病〔性病的一种委婉说法〕

social en·gi·neer·ing /ˌ· · · · ˈ· ·/ *n* [U] the practice of making changes in the law in order to change society according to a political idea 社会工程〔指根据一种政治思想来改革法律从而变革社会的做法〕

so·cial·is·m /ˈsoʃəlˌɪzəm; ˈsəʊʃəlɪzəm/ *n* [U] a system of political beliefs and principles whose main aims are that everyone should have an equal opportunity to share wealth and that industries should be owned by the government 社会主义 —compare 比较 CAPITALISM, COMMUNISM

so·cial·ist[1] /ˈsoʃəlɪst; ˈsəʊʃəlɪ̈st/ *adj* **1** based on socialism or connected with a political party that supports socialism 社会主义的; 社会党的: *socialist principles* 社会主义原则 | *the socialist manifesto* 社会党宣言 **2** a socialist country or government has a political system based on socialism 社会主义的〔国家或政府〕

socialist[2] *n* [C] someone who believes in socialism 社会主义者

Socialist Work·ers Par·ty, the /ˌ· · · ˈ· ·, · ·/ the full name of the SWP 社会主义工人党〔SWP的全称〕

so·cia·lite /ˈsoʃəˌlaɪt; ˈsəʊʃəlaɪt/ *n* [C] someone who is well-known for going to many fashionable parties 社交界名人, 社会名流: *He's married to some rich Miami socialite.* 他娶了迈阿密某位富有的社交名媛。

so·cial·i·za·tion /ˌsoʃələˈzeʃən; ˌsəʊʃəlaɪˈzeɪʃən/ *n* [U] the process by which people, especially children, are made to behave in a way that is acceptable in their society 社会化; 〔尤指儿童的〕合群: *the socialization of young offenders* 青少年罪犯回归社会的问题

so·cial·ize also 又作 **-ise** *BrE*【英】/ˈsoʃəˌlaɪz; ˈsəʊʃəlaɪz/ *v* **1** [I] to spend time with other people in a friendly way 社交往来; 交友, 交谊: **[+with]** *I enjoy socializing with my students after class.* 我喜欢在课后和学生交往。**2** [T] *technical* to train someone to behave in a way that is acceptable in the society they are living in【术语】使社会化; 使合群

socialized medi·cine /ˌ· · · ˈ· · ·/ *n* [U] *AmE* medical care provided by a government and paid for through taxes【美】〔由政府提供、靠税收支付的〕公费医疗

social sci·ence /ˌ· · ˈ· ·/ *n* **1** [U] the study of people in society, which includes history, politics, ECONOMICS, SOCIOLOGY and ANTHROPOLOGY 社会科学〔包括历史、政治、经济、社会学和人类学〕 **2** [C] one of these subjects 一门社会科学 —compare 比较 NATURAL SCIENCE —**social scientist** *n* [C]

social se·cu·ri·ty /ˌ· · · ˈ· · ·/ *n* [U] **1** *BrE* government money that is paid to people who are unemployed, old, ill etc【英】〔政府发给失业者、老人、病人等的〕救济金; WELFARE (3) *AmE*【美】: **be on social security** (=be receiving money from the government) 领取社会福利金 **2 Social Security** a system of insurance run by the American government, into which workers make regular payments, and which provides money when they are unable to work, especially because they are old 社会保障(制度)〔美国的社会保险制度, 工人定期交纳保险金, 退休后领取退休金〕—compare 比较 NATIONAL INSURANCE

social serv·ice /ˌ· · ˈ· ·/ *n* **1** [C] a service that is necessary for society to work properly and is provided by the government or supported by government money 〔由政府提供或资助的〕社会服务: *Should the railways make a profit or should they be run as a social service?* 铁路应当营利, 还是应当作为社会服务来管理? **2 social services** [plural] *especially BrE* the special services provided by a government or local council to help people who have particular problems【尤英】〔向有特殊问题者提供帮助的〕社会福利事业, 公益事业: *Cuts in social services have been widespread.* 削减公益事业的做法已经很普遍了。

social stud·ies /ˈ· · ˌ· ·/ *n* [plural] the study of people in society; SOCIAL SCIENCE 社会研究; 社会学

social work /ˈ· · ·/ *n* [U] work done by government or private organizations to improve bad social conditions and help people with particular social problems 社会福利工作〔由政府或私人机构进行, 旨在改善社会环境和帮助有特殊社会问题的人〕

social work·er /ˈ· · ˌ· ·/ *n* [C] someone who is employed in SOCIAL WORK 社会福利工作者

so·ci·e·tal /səˈsaɪətl̩; səˈsaɪətl/ *adj technical* related to a particular society【术语】社会的: *societal attitudes* 社会态度

so·ci·e·ty /səˈsaɪətɪ; səˈsaɪ̈ti/ *n*

1 ►PEOPLE IN GENERAL 整个社会◄ [U] people in general, considered in relation to the structure of laws, organizations etc that makes it possible for them to live together 社会, 群体: *Society has a right to expect people to obey the law.* 社会有权要求人们遵守法律。| **a danger to society** *He should be locked up; he's a danger to society!* 他应当被关起来; 他对社会是个祸害!

2 ►A PARTICULAR GROUP 某一群体◄ [C,U] a particular large group of people who share laws, organizations, customs etc〔有共同的法律、组织、习俗等的〕某类社会: *Britain is a multiracial society.* 英国是个多种族社会。| *Drug abuse is one of the problems confronting modern Western society.* 滥用药物是现代西方社会面临的问题之一。| **the consumer society** *Is greed a product of the consumer society?* 贪婪是不是消费型社会的一种产物? | **the affluent society** *Shopaholics are a new problem, born of the affluent society.* 购物成瘾是富足型社会所产生的一个新问题。| **polite society** (=people who think they have the highest standards of behaviour) 上流社会〔自认为有最高言行标准的人群〕

3 ►CLUB 社团◄ [C] an organization or a club with members who share similar interests, aims etc 社团, 协会, 学会: *the university film society* 大学的电影协会 | *the Law Society* 法律协会

4 ►UPPER CLASS 上等阶层◄ [U] the fashionable group of people who are rich and belong to the upper class 上层社会, 社交界: *a society wedding* 上层社会的婚礼 | **high society** (=the richest, most fashionable etc people) 上流社会 | **be introduced into society** (=to begin to attend the fashionable events organized by this group) 被介绍进入上流社会

5 ►COMPANY 交谊◄ [U] *formal* the companionship of other people【正式】交谊, 交际, 交往: *Jacob shunned the society of others, preferring to be alone.* 雅各布避免与人交往, 宁愿独个儿生活。—see also 另见 BUILDING SOCIETY, FRIENDLY SOCIETY

Society of Friends, the /·ˌ· · · · ˈ·/ the formal name of the Quakers 公谊会〔贵格会的正式名称〕

Society of Je·sus, the /·ˌ· · · · ˈ· ·/ the formal name of the Jesuits, a large and respected society of Roman Catholic priests, which was established in the 16th century by St Ignatius Loyola to do MISSIONARY work (=to spread the Catholic religion) and to set up Catholic universities in many parts of the world 耶稣会〔Jesuits的正式名称。耶稣会是一个受人尊敬的大型组织, 成员为罗马天主教牧师。由罗耀拉的圣依纳爵于16世纪创建, 旨在传播教义并在世界各地建立教会大学〕

socio- /sosɪo; səʊsiəʊ/ *prefix technical*【术语】**1** concerning society; social (关于)社会的: *sociology* (=study of society) 社会学 **2** social and 社会以及…的: *sociopolitical* 社会政治的

so·ci·o·ec·o·nom·ic /ˌsosɪoˌɛkəˈnɑmɪk; ˌsəʊsiəʊekəˈnɒmɪk/ *adj* based on a combination of social and economic conditions 社会经济的 —**socioeconomically** /-klɪ; -kli/ *adv*

so·ci·ol·o·gy /ˌsosɪˈɑlədʒɪ; ˌsəʊsiˈɒlədʒi/ *n* [U] the scientific study of societies and the behaviour of people in groups 社会学 —compare 比较 ANTHROPOLOGY, ETHNOLOGY, SOCIAL SCIENCE —**sociologist** *n* [C] —**sociological** /ˌsosɪəˈlɑdʒɪkl̩; ˌsəʊsiəˈlɒdʒɪkəl/ *adj*: *a sociological study of the working class* 对工人阶级的社会学研究 —**sociologically** /-klɪ; -kli/ *adv*

so·ci·o·path /ˈsosɪəˌpæθ; ˈsəʊsiəˌpæθ/ *n* [C] *technical* someone whose behaviour towards other people is considered unacceptable, strange, and possibly dangerous【术语】〔在行为上〕反社会者 —**sociopathic** /ˌsosɪəˈpæθɪk; ˌsəʊsiəˈpæθɪk◄/ *adj*

sock[1] /sɑk; sɒk/ *n* [C] **1** a piece of clothing made of soft material that you wear on your foot inside your shoe 短袜: *a pair of cotton socks* 一双棉线短袜 **2 give sb/sth a sock** *informal* to hit someone or something very hard, especially with your hand closed【非正式】狠击某人/某物一拳 **3 pull your socks up** *BrE informal* to make an effort to improve your behaviour or your work【英, 非正式】努力, 用功: *If you don't pull your socks up, you'll fail the exam.* 如果你不用功, 你考试会不及格的。**4 put a sock in it** *BrE informal* used to tell someone in a joking way to stop talking【英, 非正式】〔以玩笑的方式要某人〕闭嘴, 住口 **5 knock sb's socks off** *AmE informal* to surprise someone very much【美, 非正式】使某人大吃一惊: *When I saw all the people there, it knocked my socks off!* 看到所有人在那儿, 我大吃一惊!

sock[2] *v* [T] **1** *informal* to hit someone very hard【非正式】猛击, 狠打: *He socked the intruder on the jaw.* 他猛击闯入者的下巴。**2 sock it to sb** *old-fashioned* to tell someone something in

a direct and forceful way【过时】直截了当地对某人说: *Go on, sock it to him!* 去吧,直截了当地跟他说清楚!

sock in *phr v* [T] *AmE* **be socked in** if an airport, road, or area is socked in, it is very difficult to see far because of bad fog, snow, or rain【美】〔机场、道路或地方因大雾、大雪、大雨〕能见度很低, 看不清

sock·e·roo /ˌsakəˋru; ˌsɒkəˋruː/ *n* [singular] *AmE informal* something that is very successful and impressive【美, 非正式】非常成功的事物; 印象深刻的东西: *That was one sockeroo of a firework show!* 那次的烟火节目精彩极了!

sock·et /ˋsakɪt; ˋsɒkɪ̠t/ *n* [C] **1** a piece of plastic with holes in it, which is fixed into a wall and which you can connect electrical equipment to (电源)插座: *Don't let the baby stick her fingers in the socket.* 别让婴儿把她的手指伸进插座。**2** a hollow part of a structure into which something fits 窝, 臼, 槽, 穴: *Kendrick grabbed my arm, nearly pulling it out of its socket.* 肯德里克抓住我的胳膊, 差点把它拉脱了臼。

sock·ing /ˋsakɪŋ; ˋsɒkɪŋ/ *adv* **socking great** *BrE spoken* extremely big【英口】极大的: *a socking great hole in the floor* 地板上一个硕大无比的洞

sock·o /ˋsako; ˋsɒkəʊ/ *adj AmE informal* very impressive or strong【美, 非正式】给人以强烈印象的; 强壮的

Soc·ra·tes /ˋsakrətiz; ˋsɒkrətiːz/ (?470-399 BC) a Greek PHILOSOPHER from Athens, who was the teacher of Plato and whose ideas are known from Plato's writings. He encouraged people to think carefully about ideas before accepting them and developed a method of examining ideas according to a system of questions and answers in order to find out the truth. This is known as 'the Socratic method' or 'dialectic'. The Greek authorities disapproved of his ideas and methods, and said he was a bad influence on young people. They forced him to kill himself by drinking HEMLOCK, a powerful poison. 苏格拉底〔(公元前?470-公元前399), 古希腊哲学家, 雅典人, 柏拉图的老师。其观点主要见于柏拉图的著作。他鼓励人们在接受一种观点之前先要详加考究, 并提出了一种通过诘问和回答来寻求真理的观念验证法。这种方法被称为"苏格拉底法"或"辩证法"。希腊当局不赞同他的思想与方法, 认为他腐蚀青年, 下令让他服由毒芹提取的毒药自尽〕—**Socratic** /səˋkrætɪk; səˋkrætɪk/ *adj*

sod[1] /sad; sɒd/ *n* **1** [C] *BrE informal* an impolite word meaning a stupid or annoying person, especially a man【英, 非正式】笨蛋, 讨厌鬼〔尤指男人, 非礼貌用语〕: *Get up, you lazy sod!* 起来, 你这个懒鬼! **2** **be a sod** *BrE informal* an impolite expression meaning to be very difficult【英, 非正式】难对付的, 棘手的〔非礼貌说法〕: *That door's a sod to open.* 那扇讨厌的门真难开。**3** **poor sod** *BrE spoken* an impolite expression meaning someone you feel sorry for, or have no respect for【英口】可怜的家伙〔非礼貌说法〕: *The poor sod's wife left him.* 那个可怜的家伙被老婆甩了。**4** [C,U] a piece of earth or the layer of earth with grass and roots growing in it 草皮; 草地

sod[2] *v* [T only in imperative or infinitive 仅用于祈使句或不定式] *BrE spoken*【英口】**1** **sod it/that** used to rudely express anger or great annoyance at something or someone 该死, 真糟糕〔用于粗鲁地对某人或某事表示生气〕: *Sod it, I've missed the train.* 真糟糕, 我误了火车。| *"He thinks you should apologize." "Well, sod that!"* "他认为你应当道歉。""嘿, 见鬼去吧!" **2** used to say rudely that something is not important 去你的〔用于粗鲁地表示某事并不重要〕: *Sod the job, I'm going home.* 去你的工作, 我要回家啦。**3** **sod off** used to tell someone rudely to go away 走开, 滚蛋〔非礼貌说法〕: *Just tell him to sod off.* 叫他给我滚蛋。

so·da /ˋsodə; ˋsəʊdə/ *n* **1** [C,U] water containing bubbles (BUBBLE[1] (1)) of gas that is added to alcoholic drinks 苏打水: *Do you want soda in your Scotch?* 你的苏格兰威士忌要加苏打水吗? **2** [U] a sweet drink filled with gas 汽水: *a bottle of orange soda* 一瓶橘子汽水 **3** [C] *AmE* an ICE-CREAM SODA【美】冰淇淋苏打 **4** [U] a compound of SODIUM in powder form that is used for cooking or cleaning〔烹饪或清洁用的〕苏打; 碳酸钠: *baking soda* 小苏打

soda foun·tain /ˋ‥ ˌ‥/ *n* [C] *AmE old-fashioned* a place in a shop at which drinks, ice cream etc are served【美, 过时】〔商店中的〕冷饮柜台; 冷饮部

sod all /ˌ· ˋ·/ *n* [U] *BrE informal* an impolite expression meaning nothing at all【英, 非正式】什么也没有〔非礼貌说法〕: *I got sod all from the deal.* 这笔交易我什么也没有得到。

soda si·phon /ˋ‥ ˌ‥/ *n* [C] a special type of bottle from which SODA WATER is forced out in a fast stream by gas pressure 苏打水瓶, 汽水瓶

soda wa·ter /ˋ‥ ˌ‥/ *n* [U] water with bubbles (BUBBLE[1] (1)) of gas in it that is added to alcoholic drinks〔加进酒精饮料的〕苏打水

sod·den /ˋsadn̩; ˋsɒdn/ *adj* very wet and heavy 湿而重的, 湿透的, 湿淋淋的: *the sodden ground* 湿透的地面 | *sodden clothing* 湿淋淋的衣物

sod·ding /ˋsadɪŋ; ˋsɒdɪŋ/ *adj BrE informal* an impolite word used to emphasize that you are angry【英, 非正式】倒霉的, 他妈的〔用于强调愤怒, 非礼貌用词〕: *This sodding computer's crashed again!* 这台倒霉的电脑又坏了!

so·di·um /ˋsodɪəm; ˋsəʊdiəm/ *n* [U] a silver-white metal that is an ELEMENT (=simple substance) and only exists naturally in combination with other substances 钠

sodium bi·car·bo·nate /ˌ‥ ‥ˋ‥/ *n* [U] a white powder used in baking to make cakes etc lighter 碳酸氢钠, 小苏打

sodium chlo·ride /ˌ‥ ˋ‥/ *n* [U] *techincal* salt【术语】氯化钠, 食盐

Sod·om and Go·mor·rah /ˌsadəm ənd gəˋmɔrə; ˌsɒdəm ənd gəˋmɒrə/ two ancient cities in the Middle East which, according to the Old Testament of the Bible, were destroyed by God as a punishment for the immoral sexual behaviour of their people. The cities' names are sometimes used to describe a place or situation where people's sexual behaviour is regarded as very shocking. 所多玛和蛾摩拉, 罪恶之城〔中东两座古城。据《圣经·旧约》记载, 上帝为了惩罚当地居民的邪淫行为而将这两座城市毁灭。其名称有时用以指称性行为令人震惊的某一地方或场景〕

sod·o·mite /ˋsadəmˌaɪt; ˋsɒdəmaɪt/ *n* [C] *old use* a word meaning someone who practices sodomy【旧】鸡奸者

sod·o·my /ˋsadəmɪ; ˋsɒdəmi/ *n* [U] *old use or law* a sexual act in which a man puts his sex organ into someone's ANUS, especially that of another man【旧或法律】〔尤指男性间的〕鸡奸

Sod's law /ˌ· ˋ·/ *n* [U] *BrE humorous* the natural tendency for things to go wrong whenever possible【英, 幽默】墨菲定律〔一种认为凡有可能出差错的事终将出差错的论断〕: *It's Sod's law that the car breaks down when you need it most.* 在你最需要汽车的时候汽车就会坏掉 —— 这就是墨菲定律。

so·fa /ˋsofə; ˋsəʊfə/ *n* [C] a comfortable seat with raised arms and a back, wide enough for two or three people; SETTEE〔两人或三人坐的〕长沙发

sofa bed /ˋ‥ ˌ·/ *n* [C] a sofa which can be changed into a bed (坐卧)两用沙发, 沙发床

So·fi·a /ˋsofɪə; ˋsəʊfiə/ the capital city of Bulgaria 索非亚〔保加利亚首都〕

soft /sɔft; sɒft/ *adj*

1 ▶NOT HARD 不硬◀ a) not hard or firm, but easy to press (柔)软的, 松软的: *a soft pillow* 软枕头 | *My feet sank into the soft ground.* 我的双脚陷进了松软的地里。| **get/go soft** *Cook the onions until they go soft.* 把洋葱煮到变软为止。**b)** less hard than average 中等硬度以下的, 硬度低的: *a soft lead pencil* 软铅笔 | *a soft cheese* 软干酪

2 ▶NOT ROUGH 不粗糙的◀ having a surface that is smooth and pleasant to touch 柔滑的, 细嫩的: *a baby's soft skin* 婴儿细嫩的皮肤 | *The fur was soft to the touch.* 这皮毛摸起来很柔滑。

3 ▶NOT LOUD 不响亮的◀ a soft sound, voice, or music is quiet and pleasant to listen to 轻柔的, 低声的: *a whisper so soft that I could hardly hear it* 声音轻得我几乎听不见的耳语 | *a soft accent* 轻柔的音调

4 ▶NOT BRIGHT 不鲜艳的◀ [only before noun 仅用于名词前] soft colours or lights are pleasant and relaxing because they are not too bright〔颜色、灯光〕柔和的, 不刺眼的: *Soft lighting creates a romantic atmosphere.* 柔和的灯光营造出一种浪漫的气氛。| *The room was a soft peach colour.* 这个房间过去是淡淡的桃红色。

5 ▶GENTLE 温和的◀ gentle and without much force 轻轻的, 温和的: *a soft breeze* 和风

6 ▶TOO EASY 过于容易的◀ *informal* a soft job, life etc is too easy and does not involve much work or hard physical work【非正式】〔工作、生活等〕轻松的, 容易的: *Mike's landed himself a soft job in the stores.* 迈克在商店里谋到一份轻松的工作。| **soft option** (=a choice that allows you to avoid difficulties or hard work) 省事的选择[舍难求易] *The computer course isn't a soft option – it's pretty tough.* 电脑课程并不轻松 —— 是相当繁重的。| *If you agree, you're taking the soft option.* 如果你同意, 你就是在挑轻松的工作。

7 ▶NOT STRICT 不严厉的◀ someone who is soft seems weak because they are not strict enough with other people 软弱的, 过于温和的: *If you give way, the kids'll think you're soft.* 你如果让步的话, 孩子们就会以为你软弱可欺了。| **be soft on** *No politician wants to seem soft on crime.* 政治家都不想对犯罪行为显得心慈手软。| **take a soft line** (=not be strict enough) 态度温

和，不够严厉 *Courts have been taking too soft a line with young offenders.* 法庭对青少年罪犯过于宽容了。—opposite 反义词 TOUGH

8 ►WATER 水◄ not containing much LIME[1] (3) so that it forms bubbles (BUBBLE[1] (1)) from soap easily 不含石灰的，软性的〔肥皂容易起泡沫〕

9 ►PHYSICAL CONDITION 体质◄ *informal* having a body that is not in a strong physical condition, because you do not do enough exercise【非正式】〔由于运动不够而〕健康欠佳的，虚弱的: *He'd got soft after all those years in a desk job.* 他干了那么多年办公室工作之后，身体变得虚弱了。

10 have a soft spot for to be fond of someone even when they do not behave well 偏爱，对…有好感: *She's always had a soft spot for Grant.* 她一向对格兰特有好感。

11 a soft touch *informal* someone from whom you can easily get money, because they are kind or easy to deceive【非正式】轻易借钱给他人的人; 宽厚[容易受骗]的人: *The children regard their aunt as a bit of a soft touch.* 孩子们把姑母当作有点容易上当受骗的人。

12 ►STUPID 愚蠢的◄ *BrE* stupid or silly【英】笨的; 傻的: *You must be soft if you think I'll give you fifty quid!* 你如果以为我会给你50英镑，那你一定是傻了。

13 soft in the head *old-fashioned* very stupid or crazy【过时】很蠢的; 疯的

14 be soft on *old-fashioned* to be sexually attracted to someone【过时】受异性吸引 **—softly** *adv*: *She stroked his head softly.* 她轻轻地抚摸着他的头。| *Music played softly in the background.* 背景音乐轻柔地演奏着。**—softness** *n* [U]

soft·ball /ˈsɔftˌbɔl; ˈsɒftbɔːl/ *n* **1** [U] a game similar to BASEBALL but played on a smaller field with a slightly larger and softer ball 垒球(运动) **2** [C] a special ball used to play this game 垒球

soft-boiled /ˌ·ˈ·◄/ *adj* an egg that is soft-boiled is boiled long enough for the white part to become solid, but not the yellow part in the centre〔蛋〕煮得半熟的，溏心的 —compare 比较 HARD-BOILED

soft cop·y /ˈ· ˌ··/ *n* [U] *technical* information stored in a computer's memory or shown on a SCREEN[1] (1) rather than printed on paper【术语】〔电脑的〕软拷贝〔指储存于电脑中或显示在荧屏上而不是以纸张打印出的资料〕—compare 比较 HARD COPY

soft cur·ren·cy /ˌ·ˈ···/ *n* [C,U] money of a particular country that may fall in value and is difficult to exchange for the money of a country that is economically stronger 软通货，软货币〔指币值不够稳定、难以与经济实力较强国家的货币相兑换的通货〕

soft drink /ˈ· ·/ *n* [C] a cold drink that does not contain alcohol 软饮料〔指不含酒精的饮料〕

soft drug /ˌ·ˈ·/ *n* [C] an illegal drug such MARIJUANA that is not considered to be harmful 软性毒品〔指大麻等被认为无害的毒品〕

soft·en /ˈsɔfən; ˈsɒfən/ *v* [I,T] **1** to become softer or make something softer (使)变软，(使)变柔滑，(使)变轻柔: *Choose a good moisturizer to soften and protect your skin.* 选用一种好的润肤霜以保护你的皮肤，并使它变得柔滑。| *Cook until the onion has softened.* 把洋葱煮到变软为止。**2** if your attitude softens, or if something softens it, it becomes less strict and more sympathetic (使)〔态度等〕软化，(使)变温和: *The British position on textile imports is softening.* 英国对纺织品进口问题的立场正在软化。| *Local police have softened their attitude towards young people who live on the streets.* 地方警察对待流浪街头的年轻人的态度已经变温和了。**3 soften the blow/impact etc** to make the effect of something less severe 缓和打击/冲击等: *The minister may try to soften the blow of pay freezes by announcing a cut in interest rates.* 部长以宣布降低利率来企图缓和冻结工资的打击。**4** if your expression, or voice softens or if something softens it, you look or sound kinder and more gentle (使)〔表情、声音〕变轻柔，(使)变柔和: *His voice softened when he spoke to her.* 他对她说话时声音变轻柔了。—opposite 反义词 HARDEN (2)

soften sb/sth ↔ **up** *phr v* [T] **1** *informal* to be nice to someone before you ask them to do something so that they will be ready to help you【非正式】使…心软; 打动: *You'll have to soften Alison up before you ask to borrow her car.* 在向艾莉森借汽车之前，你必须先打动她。**2** to make an enemy's defences weaker so that they will be easier to attack, especially by bombing them〔尤指通过轰炸〕削弱〔敌人的防御设施以便进攻〕

soft·en·er /ˈsɔfənɚ; ˈsɒfənə/ *n* [C] a substance that you add to water to make clothes feel soft after washing〔衣物〕柔软剂，软化剂: *a fabric softener* 织物柔软剂 —see also 另见 WATER SOFTENER

soft fo·cus /ˌ·ˈ··◄/ *n* [U] the arrangement of a photographic LENS (2) in a camera so that the edge of the object that is being photographed is not clear〔摄影的〕软聚焦，模糊焦点〔使影像周边模糊不清的聚焦〕

soft fruit /ˌ·ˈ·/ *n* [C,U] *especially BrE* small fruit that you can eat that has no hard skin【尤英】〔无硬皮的〕无核小果: *Strawberries and raspberries are soft fruit.* 草莓和山莓都是无核小果。

soft fur·nish·ings /ˌ·ˈ···/ *n* [plural] *BrE* things such as curtains, chair covers etc that are made of cloth and are used in decorating a room【英】〔窗帘、椅子套等用布料做的〕室内陈设品

soft·heart·ed /ˈsɔftˌhɑrtɪd; ˌsɒftˈhɑːtɪd◄/ *adj* easily affected by feelings of pity or sympathy for other people 心肠软的，好心的，仁慈的: *Paul's really kind and softhearted.* 保罗确实很仁慈，富于同情心。

soft·ie /ˈsɔftɪ; ˈsɒfti/ *n* [C] another spelling of SOFTY softy 的另一种拼法

soft land·ing /ˌ·ˈ··/ *n* [C] a situation in which a SPACECRAFT comes down onto the ground gently and without any damage〔宇宙飞船的〕软着陆

softly-softly /ˌ··ˈ··/ *adj BrE* **softly-softly approach** a way of dealing with something or somone which involves being very patient and careful【英】耐心谨慎的方法: *I think we need to adopt a softly-softly approach with Mike.* 我认为我们对待迈克需要采取耐心谨慎的方法。

softly-spok·en /ˌ··ˈ··/ *adj* another form of the word SOFT-SPOKEN soft-spoken 的另一种形式

soft pal·ate /ˌ·ˈ··/ *n* [C] the soft part of the back of the top of your mouth〔口中的〕软腭

soft ped·al /ˌ·ˈ··/ *v* [T] *informal* to make something seem less important or less urgent than it really is【非正式】使…显得不那么重要[紧迫]; 淡化

soft porn /ˌ·ˈ·/ *n* [U] magazines, pictures etc that show sexual acts and images in a way that is intended to be sexually exciting, but which are not of the most offensive type 软性色情作品〔不太露骨的杂志、图片等〕—compare 比较 HARD PORN

soft sell /ˌ·ˈ·◄/ *n* [singular] a way of advertising or selling things that involves gently persuading people to buy something in a friendly and indirect way 软推销〔指用友好诱导的方法进行的广告宣传或推销〕—compare 比较 HARD SELL

soft shoul·der /ˌ·ˈ··/ *n* [C] ground at the edge of a road that is too soft to drive on〔不适宜车辆行驶的〕软质路肩 —compare 比较 HARD SHOULDER

soft-soap /ˈ· ·/ *v* [T] *informal* to say nice things to someone in order to persuade them to do something, change their mind etc【非正式】用甜言蜜语说服: *Don't think you can soft-soap me!* 别以为你能用好话来说服我！**—soft soap** *n* [U]

soft-spok·en /ˌ·ˈ··◄/ *adj* having a pleasant gentle voice 声音柔和悦耳的

soft toy /ˌ·ˈ·/ *n* [C] *BrE* a toy for young children made of cloth and filled with soft material【英】软玩具〔用布和软填塞物做成〕; STUFFED ANIMAL *AmE*【美】

soft·ware /ˈsɔftˌwɛr; ˈsɒftweə/ *n* [U] the sets of PROGRAMS (=instructions) that you put into a computer when you want it to do particular jobs〔电脑〕软件: *She loaded the new software.* 她给电脑装上新的软件。| *word processing software* 文字处理软件 —compare 比较 HARDWARE (1)

soft·wood /ˈsɔftˌwʊd; ˈsɒftwʊd/ *n* [C,U] wood from trees such as PINE[1] (1) and FIR that is cheap and easy to cut, or a tree with this type of wood 软(木)材，针叶树材〔如松木、冷杉木等价格低、易切割的木材〕; 针叶树 —compare 比较 HARDWOOD

soft·y, softie /ˈsɔftɪ; ˈsɒfti/ *n* [C] *informal* someone who is too easily affected by feelings of pity or sympathy, or who is too easily persuaded【非正式】心肠软的人; 极易被说服的人: *He's a big softy.* 他是个过分心软的人。

sog·gy /ˈsɑgɪ; ˈsɒgi/ *adj* unpleasantly wet and soft 湿透的，湿软的: *The ground was soggy from the rain.* 雨后地面湿透了。| *The bottom of the pie has gone all soggy.* 馅饼底部全都湿乎乎的。**—soggily** *adv* **—sogginess** *n* [U]

soh /so; səʊ/ *n* [singular,U] another spelling of SO[4] so[4] 的另一种拼法

So·Ho /ˈsoˌho; ˈsəʊˌhəʊ/ *n* Small Office; Home Office; an expression referring to electronic office systems, including especially E-MAIL 小型办公室; 家庭办公室〔是指包含电子邮件的电子办公室系统〕: *SoHo accounting software* 供家庭办公室使用的会计软件

So·ho /ˈsoho; ˈsəʊhəʊ/ **1** an area in central London famous for its sex shops and GAY bars, and also as a place where there are

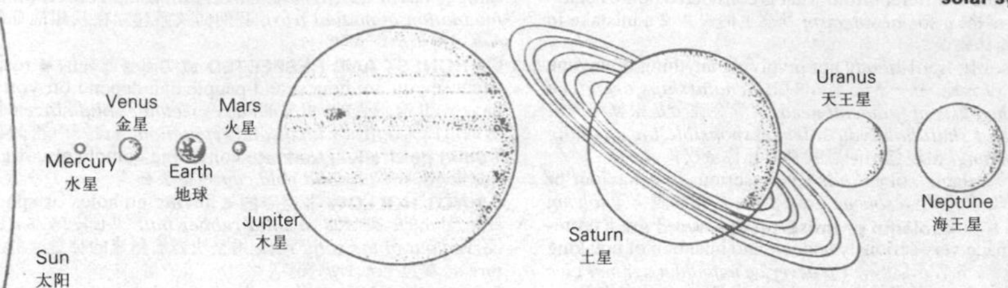

many shops and restaurants selling foreign food, especially Chinese and Italian food. 苏豪区〔伦敦市中心一区域，以性用品商店和同性恋酒吧闻名。许多商店和餐厅供应外国食品，尤其是中式和意大利式食品〕 **2** an area of Manhattan, New York City, south of Houston Street, where there are many art galleries (GALLARY), restaurants, and small fashionable shops 苏豪区〔纽约市曼哈顿一区域。位于休斯顿大街以南，有许多艺术馆、餐厅和时尚小店〕

soi·gné, **soignée** *fem*【阴性】/swɑˋnje; ˈswɑːnjeɪ/ *adj formal* dressed or arranged fashionably and with care【正式】衣着讲究的，时髦的: *a soignée divorcee in her forties* 一个四十多岁穿着入时的离婚女人

W2 **soil¹** /sɔɪl; sɔɪl/ *n* **1** [C,U] the top layer of the earth in which plants grow 土壤，土地，泥土: *an area of rich soil* 一片肥沃的土地 | *The bush grows well in a sandy soil.* 这种灌木在沙质土地里生长良好。—see 见 LAND¹ (USAGE) **2 the soil** *literary* farming as a job or way of life【文】务农，种地为生: *They make their living from the soil.* 他们以务农为生。**3 on British soil/French soil etc** *formal* in Britain, in France etc【正式】在英国/法国等（国土上）: *The crime was committed on American soil.* 这桩罪案是在美国犯下的。**4 sb's native soil** *literary* your own country【文】某人的故土[故乡，故国] —see also 另见 NIGHT SOIL

soil² *v* [T] **1** *formal* to make something dirty, especially with waste from your body【正式】〔尤指用人的排泄物〕弄脏，弄污 **2 not soil your hands** to not do something because you consider it too dirty, unpleasant, or dishonest 不玷污双手〔指不做卑污的事〕: *I wouldn't soil my hands with such a devious scheme.* 我不会让这个肮脏的计划玷污我的双手。—**soiled** *adj*: *soiled diapers* 脏尿布

Soil As·so·ci·a·tion, the /ˈ· ···,··/ an organization in the UK which establishes standards for ORGANIC foods, making sure that they really have been grown in a natural way that does not harm the environment. Foods that are approved of in this way can have a special Soil Association sign on the package. 土壤管理协会〔英国一组织。其职责是制定有机食品标准，确保这些食物是在对环境无害的自然条件下生产的。检验合格者可在包装上加盖该协会的特别标志〕

soi·ree, **soirée** /swɑˋre; ˈswɑːreɪ/ *n* [C] *old-fashioned* a formal evening party, often including a performance of music【过时】晚会〔常指有音乐表演的正式晚会〕

soj·ourn /ˋsodʒɝn; ˈsɒdʒɜːn/ *n* [C] *literary* a short period of time that you stay in a place that is not your home【文】逗留，暂住: *a brief sojourn in Europe* 在欧洲的小住 —**sojourn** *v* [I]

sol /sɑl; sɒl/ *n* [singular,U] so⁴ 全音阶的第五音

sol·ace¹ /ˋsɑlɪs; ˈsɒlɪs/ *n* **1** [U] *formal* a feeling of emotional comfort at a time of great sadness or disappointment【正式】安慰，慰藉: **seek/find solace in** *After the death of her son, Val found solace in the church.* 在儿子死后，瓦尔在教会找到了慰藉。**2 be a solace to** to bring a feeling of comfort and calmness to someone, when they are sad or disappointed 是…的安慰[慰藉]: *Mary was a great solace to me after Arthur died.* 阿瑟死后玛丽就是我最大的安慰。

solace² *v* [T] *literary* to give emotional comfort to someone; CONSOLE¹【文】安慰，抚慰

so·lar /ˋsolɚ; ˈsəʊlə/ *adj* **1** connected with the sun 太阳的，和太阳有关的 **2** using the power of the sun's light and heat 利用太阳光[能]的: *solar energy* 太阳能

solar cell /,·· ˈ·/ *n* [C] a piece of equipment for producing electric power from sunlight 太阳能电池

so·lar·i·um /soˋlɛrɪəm; səʊˈleəriəm/ *n* [C] **1** a place with SUNBEDS (=beds with special lamps) where you can get an artificial SUNTAN 日光浴室〔设有日光浴床，让人把皮肤晒黑〕: *The hotel has a solarium and sauna.* 这家旅店有日光浴室和蒸汽浴室。**2** a room, usually enclosed by glass, where you can sit in bright sunlight〔通常用玻璃建的〕日光室

solar pan·el /,·· ˈ··/ *n* [C] a piece of equipment, usually on a roof, that uses the heat of the sun to heat water or to make electricity〔通常放在房顶的〕太阳能电池板

solar plex·us /ˌsolɚ ˋplɛksəs; ˌsəʊlə ˈpleksəs/ *n* [singular] *not technical* the front part of your body below your chest【非术语】心窝，心口〔胸部靠下的部位〕

solar sys·tem /ˈ·· ,··/ *n* **1 the solar system** the sun and the PLANETS that go around it 太阳系〔太阳和绕太阳运行的所有行星〕 **2** [C] this kind of system around another star 绕其他星球运行的太阳系

solar year /,·· ˈ·/ *n* [C] the period of time which the Earth travels around the Sun, equal to just over 365 days 太阳年〔地球绕太阳运行一周的时间，稍稍超过365天〕

sold /sold; səʊld/ the past tense and past participle of SELL

sol·der¹ /ˋsɑdɚ; ˈsɒldə/ *n* [U] a soft metal, usually a mixture of lead and tin, which can be melted and used to join two metal sufaces, wires etc 焊料，焊锡〔通常为铅与锡的合金〕

solder² *v* [T] to join or repair metal surfaces with solder 焊接，焊合

soldering i·ron /ˈ··· ,··/ *n* [C] a tool which is heated, usually by electricity, for melting and putting on solder〔焊接用的〕烙铁

sol·dier¹ /ˋsoldʒɚ; ˈsəʊldʒə/ *n* [C] a member of the army of a country, especially someone who is not an officer 士兵，军人〔尤指不是军官的军队成员〕 S2 W2

soldier² *v*

soldier on *phr v* [I] *especially BrE* to continue working in spite of difficulties【尤英】〔不畏困难地〕继续干下去，坚持干下去: *He doesn't like the job, but he'll soldier on until they can find a replacement.* 他不喜欢这份工作，但他会坚持干下去，直到他们找到接替他的人为止。

sol·dier·ing /ˋsoldʒərɪŋ; ˈsəʊldʒərɪŋ/ *n* [U] the life or job of a soldier 军人的生活[工作]

sol·dier·ly /ˋsoldʒɚlɪ; ˈsəʊldʒəli/ *adj* typical of a good soldier 像军人的，有军人风度的

soldier of for·tune /,·· ·ˈ··/ *n* [C] *literary* someone who works as a soldier for anyone who will pay him; MERCENARY【文】雇佣兵

sol·dier·y /ˋsoldʒərɪ; ˈsəʊldʒəri/ *n* [singular,U] *literary* a group of soldiers of a particular, usually bad, kind【文】〔通常指坏的〕军人，军队

sold-out /ˈ·ˈ·◂/ *adj* a concert, performance etc that is sold-out has no more tickets left〔音乐会、表演等的门票〕已全部售完的，售罄的

sole¹ /sol; səʊl/ *adj* [only before noun 仅用于名词前] **1** the sole person, thing etc is the only one 唯一的，仅有的: *the sole American in the room* 房间里唯一的一位美国人 **2** a sole duty, right, responsibility etc is one that is not shared with anyone else 专有的，独占的，唯一的: *Derek has sole responsibility for sales in Eire.* 德里克独自负责在爱尔兰的销售业务。 W3

sole² *n* **1** [C] the bottom surface of your foot, especially the part you walk or stand on 脚掌，脚底（板）: *The soles of his feet were caked in mud.* 他的两只脚掌粘满泥巴。—see picture at 参见 FOOT¹ 图 **2** [C] flat bottom part of a shoe, not including the heel 鞋底〔不包括鞋跟〕—see picture at 参见 SHOE¹ 图 **3 thick-soled/leather-soled etc** having soles that are thick, made of leather etc〔鞋〕厚底/皮底的等 **4** [C,U] a flat fish that is often used for food 鳎（鱼）—see also 另见 LEMON SOLE

sole³ *v* [T usually passive 一般用被动态] to put a new sole on a shoe 给〔鞋〕配新底，给〔鞋〕换底

so·le·cis·m /ˈsɑləˌsɪzəm; ˈsɒlɪ̣sɪzəm/ *n* [C] *formal*【正式】**1** something that is different from what is considered polite behaviour 失礼，出格: *a social solecism* 社交上的失礼 **2** a mistake in grammar 语法错误

sole·ly /ˈsol·lɪ; ˈsəʊl-li/ *adv* not involving anything or anyone else; only 唯一地，独一无二地；仅仅: *Scholarships are given solely on the basis of financial need.* 奖学金完全是根据经济需要发放的。| *I shall hold you solely responsible for anything that goes wrong.* 出现任何问题我都要让你全权负责。

sol·emn /ˈsɑləm; ˈsɒləm/ *adj* **1** very serious in behaviour or style 严肃的，庄重的: *a solemn expression* 严肃的表情 | *solemn music* 严肃音乐 **2 solemn promise/pledge/word etc** a promise that is made very seriously and with no intention of breaking it 郑重的诺言／誓言／话语等: *I'll never be unfaithful again. I give you my solemn word.* 我再也不会对你不忠了，我郑重向你保证。**3** a solemn ceremony is performed in a very serious way〔仪式〕庄严的，隆重的 —**solemnly** *adv* —**solemness** *n* [U]

so·lem·ni·ty /səˈlɛmnətɪ; səˈlemnɪ̣ti/ *n* **1** [U] the quality of being serious in behaviour or manner 庄严，隆重；庄重，严肃: *the solemnity of a great religious occasion* 重大宗教场合的庄严肃穆 **2 solemnities** [plural] the ceremonies of an important and serious occasion 隆重的仪式: *He was buried with all the solemnities befitting a monarch.* 他以君主应有的隆重仪式安葬。

sol·em·nize also 又作 **-ise** *BrE*【英】/ˈsɑləmˌnaɪz; ˈsɒləmnaɪz/ *v* **solemnize a marriage** *formal* to perform a wedding ceremony in a church【正式】在教堂举行婚礼 —**solemnization** /ˌsɑləmnəˈzeʃən; ˌsɒləmnaɪˈzeɪʃən/ *n* [U]

So·lent, the /ˈsolənt; ˈsəʊlənt/ the narrow area of sea between the Isle of Wight and the south coast of England 索伦特海峡〔位于怀特岛与英格兰南部海岸之间的狭长海域〕

sol-fa /sol ˈfɑ; ˌsɒl ˈfɑː/ *n* [U] the system in which the notes of the musical SCALE[1] (8) are represented by seven short words DO, RE, MI etc, used especially in singing〔尤指声乐中的〕阶名唱法

so·li·cit /səˈlɪsɪt; səˈlɪsɪ̣t/ *v* **1** [I] to offer to have sex with someone in exchange for money〔卖淫者〕拉（客）: *She was arrested for soliciting.* 她因拉客而被逮捕。**2** [I,T] *formal* to ask someone for money, help, or information【正式】请求；恳求；乞求: **solicit sth from sb** *The governor sent two officials to Mexico City to solicit aid from the President.* 州长派出两名官员去墨西哥城向总统求助。**3** [T] *AmE* to sell something by taking orders for a product or service, usually by going to people's houses or businesses【美】〔上门〕招揽〔生意〕，兜销 —**solicitation** /səˌlɪsɪˈteʃən; səˌlɪsɪ̣ˈteɪʃən/ *n* [C,U]

S3 W2 **so·lic·i·tor** /səˈlɪsətɚ; səˈlɪsɪ̣tə/ *n* [C] a type of lawyer in Britain who gives advice, does the necessary work when property is bought and sold, and defends people, especially in the lower courts of law 事务律师〔英国的一种律师，其职责为提供咨询、办理房地产买卖手续、在下级法庭出庭替人辩护等〕—compare 比较 ADVOCATE[2] (2), BARRISTER —see 见 LAWYER (USAGE)

so·lic·i·tor gen·e·ral /ˌ···ˈ···/ *n* [C] the government law officer next in rank below the ATTORNEY GENERAL〔英国的〕副检察长

so·lic·i·tous /səˈlɪsɪtəs; səˈlɪsɪ̣təs/ *adj formal* anxiously caring about someone's safety, health, or comfort【正式】关怀的，关切的，操心的: **[+of/for/about]** *Mary was always solicitous of my health.* 玛丽总是为我的健康操心。—**solicitously** *adv* —**solicitousness** *n* [U]

so·lic·i·tude /səˈlɪsəˌtud; səˈlɪsɪ̣tjuːd/ *n* [U+**for**] *formal* anxious and eager care for someone's health, safety etc【正式】关怀，关切，牵挂

S3 W3 **sol·id¹** /ˈsɑlɪd; ˈsɒlɪ̣d/ *adj*

1 ▶**FIRM/HARD** 坚实/坚硬的◀ having a firm shape, and usually hard 固体的；坚硬的: *Even the milk was frozen solid.* 连牛奶也冻结了。| *After wading through the marshes we were glad to be on solid ground.* 我们跋涉过了沼泽之后，很高兴又踏上坚实的地面。| **solid food(s)** *The baby isn't old enough to eat solid foods yet.* 这个婴儿还太小，不能吃固体食物。

2 ▶**STRONGLY MADE** 做得坚固的◀ strong and well made 结实的，牢固的: *good, solid furniture* 结实的优质家具 | **as solid as a rock** (=very solid) 坚如磐石，非常坚固 *The frame looks quite flimsy, but in fact it's as solid as a rock.* 这个框架看起来不怎么结实，但其实非常坚固。

3 ▶**VALUABLE WORK** 有价值的工作◀ well done and of real practical value 出色的；扎实的: *five years of solid achievement* 五年的出色成绩 | *a good solid education* 良好扎实的教育

4 ▶**DEFINITE FACTS** 明确的事实◀ [only before noun 仅用于名词前] based on real facts; definite 实在的；明确的: *We need some solid evidence to prove our case.* 我们需要一些可靠的证据来证明我们的案例。

5 solid basis/foundation a strong principle on which something is based 坚实的基础: *Our relationship is built on a solid foundation of mutual trust.* 我们的关系建立在互相信任的坚实基础上。

6 ▶**HONEST AND RESPECTED** 诚实而受尊敬的◀ respected because you are honest and people can depend on you to behave well 有信誉的，可靠的: *a respectable solid citizen* 体面可敬的市民 | *a firm with a solid reputation* 有良好声誉的公司

7 solid gold/silver/oak etc consisting completely of gold 纯金／银／橡木等: *a solid gold cup* 纯金奖杯

8 ▶**NOT HOLLOW** 非空心的◀ having no holes or spaces inside 无孔的；实心的: *a solid rubber ball* 实心皮球 | *a shrine carved out of the solid rock* 用整块岩石凿成的神龛 —see picture at 参见 HOLLOW[1] 图

9 ▶**LOYAL** 忠诚的◀ giving loyal support that you can depend on 忠实可靠的: *a solid supporter of the Clinton administration* 克林顿政府的忠实支持者

10 ▶**CONTINUOUS** 连续不断的◀ *informal* without any pauses【非正式】不断的: *The lecture lasted two solid hours.* 那讲座持续了整整两个小时。| **five hours/two weeks solid** *On Saturday I went to bed and slept fourteen hours solid.* 我从星期六开始睡觉，连续睡了整整14个钟头。

11 ▶**CLOSE TOGETHER** 密集在一起的◀ very close together without any spaces in between 密密麻麻的，没有空隙的: *The road was blocked by a solid mass of protesters.* 公路被密密麻麻的抗议者堵塞了。| *a solid line of traffic stretching away into the distance* 延伸到很远的一辆接一辆的汽车

12 ▶**GEOMETRY** 几何图形◀ *technical* having length, width, and height; THREE-DIMENSIONAL【术语】立体的；三维的: *A sphere is a solid figure.* 球体是立体形状。

13 ▶**IN AGREEMENT** 一致◀ **be solid** *BrE* to be in complete agreement【英】全体一致: *The workers are 100% solid on this issue.* 工人们在这个问题上是百分之百地一致。| **[+for/against]** *The members were solid against the idea.* 全体成员一致反对这个意见。—**solidly** *adv*: *solidly built* 体格结实的 —**solidness** *n* [U]

solid² *n* **1** [C] a firm object or substance that has a fixed shape, unlike a gas or liquid 固体: *Water changes from a liquid to a solid when it freezes.* 水结冰时从液体变成固体。**2 solids a)** [plural] food that is not liquid 固体食物，非流质食物: *He's still too ill to eat solids.* 他仍病得很重，不能吃固体食物。**b)** [C] *technical* the part of a liquid which has the qualities of a solid when it is separated from the SOLVENT[2]【术语】〔液体中的〕固形物: *milk solids* 牛奶中的固体物质 **3** *technical* a shape which has length, width, and height【术语】立体

Sol·i·dar·i·ty /ˌsɑləˈdærətɪ; ˌsɒlɪ̣ˈdærɪ̣ti/ a TRADE UNION which was started in Poland in 1980 by Lech Walesa. Solidarity organized strikes in order to force Poland's Communist government to make political and economic changes. For a time it was an illegal organization and many of its leaders were put in prison. By the late 1980s it had become very powerful, and in 1989 it became the leading party in the new government. It later lost power. 团结工会〔一工会团体，由瓦文萨1980年在波兰发起。为迫使波兰共产党政府实行政治和经济改革，团结工会组织了数次罢工。它曾一度被列为非法组织，许多领导人被捕入狱。20世纪80年代末，团结工会的势力已极为强大，1989年成为新政府中的主要党派，后来失势〕

solidarity *n* [U] loyalty and general agreement between all the people in a group, or between different groups because they all have a shared aim 团结，一致: *an appeal for workers' solidarity* 呼吁工人们团结一致 | **[+with]** *The rail workers will strike to show their solidarity with the miners.* 铁路工人将举行罢工以显示与矿工间的团结一致。

solid fu·el /ˌ··ˈ··/ *n* [C] a solid substance such as coal that is burnt to produce heat or power 固体燃料〈如煤〉

so·lid·i·fy /səˈlɪdəˌfaɪ; səˈlɪdɪ̣faɪ/ *v* **1** [I,T] to become solid or make something solid（使）变成固体: *The volcanic lava solidifies as it cools.* 火山熔岩一冷却就变成固体。**2** [T] to make an agreement, plan, attitude etc firmer and less likely to change 使巩固；使坚固: *The two countries signed a treaty to solidify their alliance.* 这两个国家签订条约以巩固双方的联盟。—**solidification** /səˌlɪdəfəˈkeʃən; səˌlɪdɪ̣fɪ̣ˈkeɪʃən/ *n* [U]

so·lid·i·ty /səˈlɪdətɪ; səˈlɪdɪ̣ti/ *n* [U] **1** the strength or hardness of something 坚固，坚硬: *the solidity of the stone walls* 石墙的坚固性 **2** the quality of something that is permanent and can be depended on 稳固，可靠（性）: *the solidity and respectability of bourgeois institutions* 资产阶级制度的稳固与体面

solid-state /ˌ··ˈ·◂/ *adj* **1** a solid-state electrical system uses TRANSISTORS〔电子装置〕固态的，全晶体管的 **2** solid-state PHYS-

ICS is concerned with the qualities of solid substances, especially the way in which they CONDUCT[1] (3) electricity〔物理学〕固态的〔固态物理学研究固态物质的性质，尤指其导电方式〕

sol·i·dus /ˈsɑlɪdəs; ˈsɒlɪ̈dəs/ *n plural* **solidi** /-daɪ; -daɪ/ [C] an OBLIQUE[2] 斜线符号

so·lil·o·quy /səˈlɪləkwɪ; səˈlɪləkwi/ *n* [C,U] a speech in a play in which a character talks to himself or herself so that the audience knows their thoughts〔戏剧中的〕独白 —compare 比较 MONOLOGUE —**soliloquize** /-ˌkwaɪz; -kwaɪz/ *v* [I]

sol·ip·sis·m /ˈsɑlɪpsɪzm̩; ˈsɒlɪ̈psɪzəm/ *n* [U] the idea that only the SELF exists or can be known 唯我论〔认为只有自我存在或可知的思想〕

sol·i·taire /ˌsɑləˈtɛr; ˌsɒlɪ̈ˈteə/ *n* **1** [C] a single jewel or a piece of jewellery with a single jewel in it, especially a large diamond 独粒宝石〔尤指大粒的钻石〕；镶有独粒宝石的饰物 **2** [U] a game played by one person with small wooden or plastic pieces on a board 单人跳棋 **3** [U] *AmE* a game of cards for one person【美】单人纸牌戏；PATIENCE (4) *BrE*【英】

sol·i·ta·ry[1] /ˈsɑləˌtɛrɪ; ˈsɒlɪ̈təri/ *adj* **1** [only before noun 仅用于名词前] a solitary person or thing is the only one you can see in a place 单个的，唯一的：*a solitary tree in the middle of the field* 田野中孤零零的一棵树 **2** spending a lot of time alone, usually because they like being alone 喜欢独处的，不愿与人接触的：*a solitary man who never spoke to anyone* 一个喜欢独处、从不与人讲话的男子 —see 见 ALONE[1] (USAGE) **3** done or experienced without anyone else around 单独的，无伴的：*a long, solitary walk across the moors* 独自长途跋涉通过荒野 **4 not a solitary word/thing etc** if there is not a solitary thing or person, there is not even one 一言不发/空无一物等：*He followed her round without a solitary word.* 他跟着她到处走，一句话也不说。—**solitarily** *adv* —**solitariness** *n* [U]

solitary[2] *n* **1** [U] *informal* solitary confinement【非正式】单独监禁 **2** [C] someone who lives completely alone; HERMIT 隐士，隐居者

solitary con·fine·ment /ˌ···· ·ˈ··/ *n* [U] an additional punishment for a prisoner in which they are kept alone and are not allowed to see anyone else 单独监禁〔作为对囚犯的加重惩罚〕

sol·i·tude /ˈsɑləˌtud; ˈsɒlɪ̈tjuːd/ *n* [U] the state of being alone especially when this is what you enjoy 孤独，孤单，独居：*She wished for the solitude of her house on the lake.* 她向往她在湖边那所房子的独居生活。

so·lo[1] /ˈsolo; ˈsəʊləʊ/ *adj* **1** done alone without anyone else helping you 独自的，单独的：*Ridgeway's solo voyage across the Atlantic* 里奇韦横跨大西洋的单独航行｜**go solo** (=start doing something on your own) 独自干 **2** related to or played as a musical solo 独奏的；独唱的：*a solo passage for viola* 中提琴独奏的段落 —**solo** *adv*: *When did you first fly solo?* 你第一次单独飞行是什么时候？

solo[2] *n plural* **solos** [C] **1** a piece of music for one performer 独奏曲；独唱曲 —compare 比较 DUET **2** a job or performance that is done alone, especially an aircraft flight 单独表演〔尤指单人飞行〕

so·lo·ist /ˈsoˌlo-ɪst; ˈsəʊləʊɪ̈st/ *n* [C] a musician who performs a solo 独奏者；独唱者

Sol·o·mon /ˈsɑləmən; ˈsɒləmən/ **1** (10th century BC) a king of Israel, the son of King David, who built the temple in Jerusalem. He is famous for being extremely wise. 所罗门〔(公元前10世纪)，以色列国王，大卫王之子。曾在耶路撒冷建造神庙，以超凡的智慧闻名〕**2 the wisdom of Solomon** a very special ability to make the right decision in situations where it is extremely difficult to know what to do 所罗门的智慧〔能在极度困难的情况下作出正确选择的过人能力〕：*Whoever is chosen to chair the peace talks is going to need the wisdom of Solomon.* 无论选谁来主持和平会谈，都得具备所罗门的智慧才行。—see also 另见 the SONG OF SOLOMON

Solomon Is·lands, the /ˈ··· ˌ··/ a country made up of several islands in the southwest Pacific, to the east of Papua New Guinea. Population: 480,442 (2001). Capital: Honiara. 所罗门群岛〔太平洋西南部一国家。由数个小岛组成，位于巴布亚新几内亚以东。人口：480,442 (2001)，首都：霍尼亚拉〕

sol·stice /ˈsɑlstɪs; ˈsɒlstɪ̈s/ *n* [C] the time of either the longest or the shortest day of the year 至，至日〔一年中最长或最短的一天〕—compare 比较 EQUINOX

Sol·ti /ˈʃoltɪ; ˈʃɒlti/, **Sir Georg** /dʒɔrdʒ; dʒɔːdʒ/ (1912-97) a British CONDUCTOR, born in Hungary, who was the musical DIRECTOR of many important ORCHESTRAS and had a very energetic style as a conductor 索尔蒂〔(1912-1997)，英国指挥家，生于匈牙利。曾任许多重要交响乐团的音乐总监，以其充满活力的指挥风格闻名〕

sol·u·ble /ˈsɑljəbl̩; ˈsɒljɪ̈bəl/ *adj* **1** a soluble substance can be dissolved (DISSOLVE (1)) in a liquid 可溶的，易溶解的：*soluble aspirin* 可溶性阿斯匹林 **2** *formal* a problem that is soluble, can be solved【正式】〔问题〕可解决的，可解答的 —opposite 反义词 INSOLUBLE —**solubility** /ˌsɑljəˈbɪlətɪ; ˌsɒljɪ̈ˈbɪlɪ̈ti/ *n* [U]

so·lu·tion /səˈluʃən; səˈluːʃən/ *n* **1** [C] a way of solving a problem or dealing with a difficult situation〔对问题、困难局面的〕解决，解决办法：*The best solution would be for them to separate.* 最好的解决办法是他们分开。｜[**+to/for**] *There are no simple solutions to the problem of overpopulation.* 对人口过多的问题没有简单的解决办法。｜**find a solution** *Both sides are trying to find a peaceful solution.* 双方都在努力寻求和平的解决方案。**2** [C] the correct answer to a problem in an exercise or competition〔练习或比赛的〕解答，答案：[**+to**] *The solution to last week's puzzle is on page 12.* 上星期字谜的谜底在第12页。**3** [C,U] a liquid mixed with a solid or gas, usually without a chemical change 溶液〔液体与固体或气体的混合物，通常不产生化学反应〕：*a weak sugar solution* 稀淡的糖溶液

solve /sɑlv; sɒlv/ *v* [T] **1** to find or provide a way of dealing with a problem 解决〔问题〕：*Charlie thinks money will solve all his problems.* 查利认为金钱会解决他所有的问题。**2** to find the correct answer to a problem or the explanation for something that is difficult to understand 解答，解释〔难题〕：*solving a mathematical equation* 解一个数学方程式｜**solve a crime/mystery/case** *The police haven't been able to solve the murder yet.* 警方至今未能侦破这宗谋杀案。—**solvable** *adj*

sol·vent[1] /ˈsɑlvənt; ˈsɒlvənt/ *adj* having enough money to pay your debts 有还债[偿付]能力的：*I have to wait until my paycheck arrives before I'm solvent again.* 我要等拿到薪金支票才有钱还债。—opposite 反义词 INSOLVENT —**solvency** *n* [U]

solvent[2] *n* [C,U] a liquid that is able to turn a solid substance into liquid 溶剂

solvent a·buse /ˈ·· ·ˌ·/ *formal n* [U] the habit of breathing in gases from glues or similar substances in order to get a pleasant feeling; GLUE-SNIFFING【正式】吸胶毒〔可得到快感〕

Sol·zhe·nit·syn /ˌsolʒəˈnɪtsɪn; ˌsɒlʒəˈnɪtsɪn/, **Al·ex·an·der** /ˌælɪgˈzændɚ; ˌælɪgˈzɑːndə/ (1918-2008) a Russian writer who spent many years in prison because of his criticism of Stalinism and the system of government in the former Soviet Union. He was forced to leave the Soviet Union in 1974 and went to live in the US. His books include *One Day in the Life of Ivan Denisovich*, *Cancer Ward*, and *The Gulag Archipelago*. He was given the Nobel Prize for literature in 1970. 索尔仁尼琴〔(1918-2008)，俄罗斯作家。因批判斯大林主义及前苏联政体而被捕入狱多年。1974年被迫离开苏联移居美国。作品有《伊凡·杰尼索维奇的一天》、《癌症病房》和《古拉格群岛》等，1970年获诺贝尔文学奖〕

So·ma·li·a /səˈmɑlɪə; səˈmɑːliə/ a country in East Africa between Ethiopa, Kenya, and the Indian Ocean. Population: 7,489,000 (2001). Capital: Mogadishu. 索马里〔东非一国家。位于埃塞俄比亚、肯尼亚和印度洋之间。人口：7,489,000 (2001)，首都：摩加迪沙〕

som·bre *BrE*【英】, **somber** *AmE*【美】/ˈsɑmbɚ; ˈsɒmbə/ *adj* **1** sad and serious; GRAVE[2] (1) 忧郁的；严峻的：*They sat in sombre silence.* 他们默默地坐着，神情严肃。｜*a sombre expression* 忧郁的表情｜*on the sombre occasion of his mother's funeral* 在他母亲葬礼的忧伤场合 **2** dark and without any bright colours 昏暗的，阴沉的，暗淡的：*a suit of sombre grey* 一套暗灰色的衣服 —**sombrely** *adv* —**sombreness** *n* [U]

som·bre·ro /sɑmˈbrɛro; sɒmˈbreərəʊ/ *n plural* **sombreros** [C] a Mexican hat for men that is tall with a wide, round BRIM[1] (1) turned up at the edges〔墨西哥男子戴的〕阔边帽 —see picture at 参见 HAT 图

some[1] /səm; səm *strong* 强读 sʌm; sʌm/ *determiner* **1** a number of people or things or an amount of something, when the exact number or amount is not stated 一些，若干：*I need some apples for this recipe.* 我需要一些苹果来做这道菜。｜*My mother has inherited some land in western Australia.* 我母亲继承了一些在澳大利亚西部的土地。｜*They're looking for someone with some experience.* 他们在物色有一定经验的人。｜*The doctor gave her some medicine for her cough.* 医生给了她一些治咳嗽的药。**2** a number of people or things or an amount of something but not all 有些，一部分：*Some people believe in life after death.* 有些人相信有来世。｜*She's been so depressed that some days she can't get out of bed in the morning.* 她一直很消沉，有几天早上都无法起床。**3** used to mean a person or thing, when you do not know or say exactly which 有个，某个〔未知或不确指的人或物〕：*There must be some reason for her behaviour.* 她的行为一定是有某种理由的。｜*Some woman came up to me and told me we'd*

been to school together. 有个妇女走到我跟前告诉我，我们曾经一起上过学。| *Can you give me some idea of the cost?* 你能告诉我这大约要花多少钱吗？**4** a fairly large number of people or things or a fairly large amount of something 相当多(的)，不少(的)：*Some days later I read that he had died.* 许多天以后我才获悉他已经去世。| *It was some time before they managed to turn the alarm off.* 过了好长时间他们才关掉警报器。| *The donation went some way towards paying for the damage.* 这笔捐款支付了相当大的一部分损坏赔偿。**5 some friend/help! etc** *especially spoken* used, especially when you are annoyed, to mean someone has not been friendly, helpful etc【尤口】这算什么朋友/毫无帮助！〔尤用于生气之时〕：*"Surely you can have a day off soon?" "Some hope with this new boss!"* "你肯定很快就可以休假一天了吧？" "在这个新老板手下，根本没有希望！" **6** used to say that something was very good or very impressive 出色的，了不起的：*That was some party last night!* 昨晚的聚会好极了！| *Some speech you made last night Tom!* 汤姆，你昨晚做了一次精彩的演讲！**7 some...or other/another** *informal* used to show that you are not certain exactly which person, thing or place and do not think it matters【非正式】某个，某一；某几个，某些〔用于表示不确指何人、何物、何地等〕：*Just give him some excuse or other.* 就给他说个理由吧。| *I think he's staying with some friends or another in Wales.* 我想他正住在威尔斯的某些朋友家里。

some² /sʌm; sʌm/ *pron* **1** a number of people or things or an amount of something, when the exact number or amount is not stated 一些，若干：*I've made a pot of coffee. Would you like some?* 我冲了一壶咖啡，你想喝点吗？| *"Do you know where the screws are?" "Yes, there are some in the garage."* "你知道螺丝钉在哪儿吗？" "知道，车库里有一些。" | *People gave plenty of suggestions and we used some in the new show.* 人们提了许多建议，我们在新的演出中采用了一些。**2** a number of people or things or an amount of something but not all 有些，一部分：*Some say it was an accident but I don't believe it.* 有些人说那是一次事故，但我不相信。| *Many of the exhibits were damaged in the fire and some were totally destroyed.* 许多展品在那场大火中损坏了，一部分则被完全焚毁了。| **[+of]** *Some of his jokes were very rude indeed.* 他讲的笑话有一些真的很粗鲁。**3 and then some** *informal especially AmE* and more【非正式，尤美】更多，还不止这么多：*"They say he earns $40,000." "Yes, and then some!"* "他们说他一年挣四万美元。" "是的，而且还不止这些呢！"

some³ *adv* **1 some 10 people/50%/£100 etc** an expression meaning about 10 people, 50%, £100 etc 大约 50 人/50%/100 英镑等：*She gained some 25 pounds in weight during pregnancy.* 她在怀孕期间体重增加了大约 25 磅。**2** *AmE* a fairly or a little【美】有几分，稍微，有点：*"Are you feeling better today?" "Some, I guess."* "你今天觉得好些了吗？" "我想稍微好些吧。" **3 some little/some few** a fairly large number or amount of something 相当多：*We travelled some little way before noticing that Bradley wasn't with us.* 我们走了相当长的路程才注意到，布拉德利没跟我们在一起。**4 some more** an additional number or amount of something 再要一点：*Would you like some more cake?* 你再要一点蛋糕吗？

-some¹ /səm; səm/ *suffix* [in adjectives 构成形容词] **1** causing or producing something 引起[产生]…的：*a troublesome boy* (=who causes trouble) 烦人的孩子 **2** liking to do something 喜欢…的：*a quarrelsome woman* (=who likes to quarrel) 爱吵架的女人 | *frolicsome* 爱嬉戏的 **3** describes someone or something that can be treated in a particular way, or that you would like to treat in that way 可用某种方式〔对待〕的，想要…的：*a cuddle-some baby* (=that you would like to hold in your arms) 逗人喜爱的婴儿

-some² *suffix* [in nouns 构成名词] a group of a particular number, especially in a game〔尤指在体育活动中〕…人一组：*a golf foursome* (=four people playing GOLF together) 打高尔夫球的四个人

1 3 **some·bod·y¹** /ˈsʌmˌbɑdɪ; ˈsʌmbɒdi/ *pron* used to mean a person, when you do not know, or do not say who the person is 某人，有人：*There's somebody waiting to see you.* 有人在等着要见你。| *Somebody's car alarm kept me awake all night.* 不知谁的汽车警报器吵得我整晚都无法入睡。| **somebody new/different etc** *We need somebody neutral to sort this out.* 我们需要个中立的人来处理这件事。| **somebody else** (=a different person) 另一个人 *If you can't make it, we can always invite somebody else.* 如果你做不到，我们完全可以另请他人。| **or somebody** (=or someone similar) 诸如此类的人 *"Who was at the door?" "It was a priest or somebody wanting to talk about religion."* "谁在门外？" "是个牧师之类的人，想谈谈宗教方面的问题。"

somebody² *n* **be somebody** to be or feel important 很重要；感觉很重要：*She was the first teacher who'd made Paul feel like he was somebody.* 她是第一位使保罗觉得自己还有所作为的老师。

some·day /ˈsəmˌde; ˈsʌmdeɪ/ *adv* at an unknown time in the future especially a long time in the future 将来会有一天，有朝一日：*Maybe someday I'll be rich!* 也许有朝一日我会富起来的！

some·how /ˈsʌmˌhau; ˈsʌmhaʊ/ *adv* **1** in some way, or by some means, although you do not know how 用某种方法；不知怎么地：*Don't worry, we'll get the money back somehow.* 别担心，我们总会把那些钱拿回来的。| **somehow or other** *Maybe we could glue it together somehow or other.* 说不定我们总会有办法把它给粘起来。**2** for some reason that is not clear 由于某种不明原因，不知为什么：*Somehow, I just don't think it'll work.* 不知为什么，我就是觉得行不通。

Some Like It Hot /ˌ· · · ˈ·/ (1959) a humorous US film, directed by Billy Wilder, which is still very popular. The main actors are Marilyn Monroe, Jack Lemmon, and Tony Curtis. The film tells the story of two men who accidentally see GANGSTERS (=members of a group of violent criminals) murder people, and then try to escape from them by dressing as women and joining a band of women musicians.《热情如火》〔(1959)，美国滑稽电影，比利·怀德执导，至今仍广为人喜爱。影片主演为玛丽莲·梦露、杰克·莱蒙、托尼·寇蒂斯。影片讲述的是两名男子无意中撞见一帮匪徒杀人，为摆脱这帮匪徒，他们穿上女人的衣服混进一个女子音乐团体〕

some·one¹ /ˈsʌmˌwʌn; ˈsʌmwʌn/ *pron* used to mean a person, when you do not know, or do not say, who the person is 某人，有人：*What would you do if someone tried to rob you in the street?* 要是有人在街上抢劫你，你怎么办？| *Will someone please explain what's going on.* 谁来解释一下正在发生的事。| **someone new/different etc** *We'll make an appointment as soon as we find someone suitable.* 我们一找到合适的人，就会加以任命。| **someone else** (=a different person) 另一个人 *They noticed someone else in the water.* 他们注意到水中还有另外一个人。| **or someone** (=or someone similar) 诸如此类的人 *You have to get a doctor or someone to sign as a witness.* 你必须找一位医生之类的人签字作证。

someone² *n* **be someone** to be or feel important 很重要；感觉很重要

some·place /ˈsʌmples; ˈsʌmpleɪs/ *adv especially AmE* somewhere【尤美】某个地方，某处：*I must have left my jacket someplace.* 我一定是把外套遗忘在什么地方了。

som·er·sault /ˈsʌmɚˌsɔlt; ˈsʌməsɔːlt/ *n* [C] a movement in which someone rolls or jumps forwards or backwards so that their feet go over their head before they stand up again 跟头，斤斗；〔向前或向后的〕滚翻：**do/turn a somersault** *Lana turned a somersault in midair.* 拉娜在半空中翻了个斤斗。—**somersault** *v* [I]: *The car somersaulted twice before coming to a stop.* 那辆车翻滚了两下才停下来。

Som·er·set /ˈsʌmɚsɛt; ˈsʌməset/ a county in southwest England, famous for producing very good CIDER. Its local government is based in Taunton. 萨默塞特〔英格兰西南部一郡。以酿造优质苹果酒闻名。地方政府所在地为陶顿〕

Somerset House /ˌ··· ˈ·/ a building in the Strand in London where documents were kept containing information about British people, such as their names and their date and place of birth, etc. The office dealing with these documents is now at St Catherine's House in Kingsway in London, but people still often call it Somerset House. 萨默塞特大厦〔坐落在伦敦斯特兰德大街的一幢大楼，保存着英国国民的姓名、生日、出生地等个人信息。现在保存这些文件的机构蛉在伦敦金斯威的圣凯瑟琳大厦，但人们仍经常抉它称作萨默塞特大厦〕

Somerset Maugham, W. —see 见 Somerset MAUGHAM

some·thing /ˈsʌmθɪŋ; ˈsʌmθɪŋ/ *pron* [not usually in questions or negatives 一般不用于疑问句或否定句] **1** used to mean a particular thing when you do not know its name, do not know exactly what it is etc 某物，某事，某种东西：*There's something in my eye.* 我眼睛里有东西。| *Sarah said something about coming over later.* 萨拉说她等一会要来什么的。| **something new/old etc** *It's a good little car but I'm looking for something faster.* 这辆小车不错，不过我想找一辆跑得更快的。| **something else** (=something different) 另外的东西，别的东西 *The house was too small so they decided to look for something else.* 那栋房子太小，所以他们决定另外找一栋。**2 there is something about** used to say that a person, situation etc has a quality or feature that you recognize but you cannot say exactly what it is 具有某种难以言传的特点：*There's something about America that I find really exciting.* 美国有某种我觉得真正令人兴奋的东西。| **there**

is something unusual/strange etc about *There was always something a little sad about her.* 她总是带着一点忧伤(的样子)。**3 do something** to do something in order to deal with a problem or difficult situation 动手去解决问题, 做点什么: *Don't just stand there – do something!* 不要只是袖手旁观, 要动动手! | **do something about sth** *Can't you do something about that smell!* 难道你不能设法去除掉那味道! **4 it's (quite/really) something** used to say that something should be admired because it is impressive 真了不起, 真精彩: *Running your own company at age 21 is really something!* 你21岁就经营自己的公司, 真了不起。**5 something like 100/two thousand etc** approximately 100, two thousand etc 100/2000等左右: *Something like 80% of the population has no running water.* 大约80%的人口没有自来水用。**6 something of a** used like 'rather' to emphasize the effect of something, the seriousness of something etc 多少有点, 颇有几分〔用于强调某事的效果、严重性等〕: *He has made something of a name for himself in the world of tennis.* 他在网球界可以说是颇有名气。**7 be something of a gardener/an expert etc** to know a lot about something or to be very good at something 算得上是园艺家/专家等: *Charlie's always been something of an expert on architecture.* 查利一直可以算得上是建筑方面的专家。**8 have something of** to have a few of the same features or qualities that someone else has 有〔某人〕的某些特点: *It was clear that Jenkins had inherited something of his father's brilliance.* 很明显, 詹金斯继承了他父亲的某些聪明才智。**9 there's something in** used to admit that someone's words are true or their ideas are successful etc〔某人的话、主意等〕有道理: *They had to concede that there was something in his teaching methods.* 他们不得不承认他的教学方法有道理。**10 have/be something to do with** to be connected with or related to a particular person or thing, but you are not sure in what way 与…有联系, 和…有关系: *I don't know much about his work, but I know it's something to do with animals.* 我不太了解他的工作, 但我知道和动物有关。**11 thirty-something/forty-something etc** *especially humorous* used to say that someone is aged between 30 and 39, between 40 and 49 etc when you do not know exactly【尤幽默】三十多岁/四十多岁等 **12 a little something** a small or cheap gift 一件小[廉价]礼物: *I got you a little something from my holiday.* 我度假时给你买了一件小礼物。

Frequencies of the word **something** in spoken and written English 单词something在英语口语和书面语中的使用频率

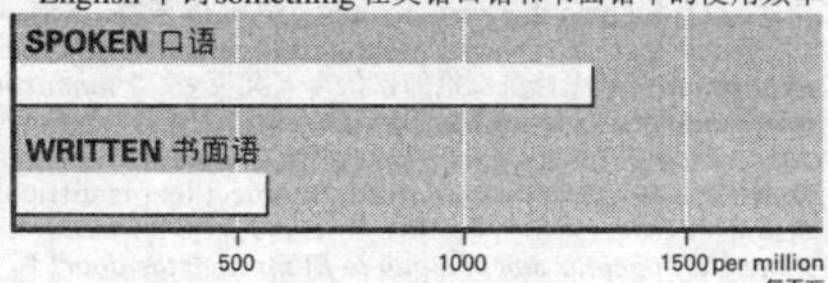

Based on the British National Corpus and the Longman Lancaster Corpus
据英国国家语料库和朗文兰开斯特语料库

This graph shows that the word **something** is much more common in spoken English than in written English. This is because it is used in a lot of common spoken phrases. 本图表显示, something在英语口语中的使用频率远远高于书面语, 因为口语中很多常用短语是由something构成的。

something (*pron*) **SPOKEN PHRASES**
含something的口语短语

13 or something used when you cannot remember or do not want to give another example of something you are mentioning 或者什么的, 诸如此类: *Here's some money. Get yourself a sandwich or something.* 这里有一点钱, 你给自己去买三明治之类的东西吃吧。| *Her name was Judith, or Julie or something.* 她的名字叫朱迪丝, 或者朱莉什么的。**14 something like that** used when you cannot remember or do not want to say something exactly 大致是那样: *She works in sales or promotion, something like that.* 她从事销售或推销, 大致是这一类工作。**15 there's something wrong with** used to say that something is not working properly …出了问题[故障]: *There's something wrong with my car so I had to get the bus.* 我的汽车坏了, 所以我不得不去坐公共汽车。**16 something to eat/drink** some food or a drink 吃的/喝的东西: *Would you like something to drink?* 你想喝点什么吗? | *We had something to eat after the show.* 表演结束后我们吃了一点东西。**17 something to do** an activity or task 活动; 任务: *If you're looking for something to do, why not clean up the kitchen?* 你如果想找点事情干, 为什么不把厨房打扫干净? **18 sixty something/John something etc** used when you cannot remember the rest of a number or name 六十多/约翰什么的〔表示记不清尾数或某人的全名等〕: *It cost over a hundred pounds. A hundred and twenty something it was.* 这花了一百多英镑, 大概有一百二十多英镑。**19 that's something** used to say that there is one thing that you should be glad about 那还算不错〔表示某事可以聊以自慰〕: *At least we have some money left. That's something, isn't it?* 至少我们还剩一点钱。还算不错, 是不是?

some·time[1] /ˋsʌmˌtaɪm; ˈsʌmtaɪm/ *adv* at a time in the future or in the past, although you do not know exactly when 在〔将来或过去的〕某个时候: *We'll take a vacation sometime in September.* 我们将在9月的某个时候休假。| *Our house was built sometime around 1900.* 我们的房子建于1900年左右。

sometime[2] *adj* [only before noun 仅用于名词前] *formal* former【正式】曾经的, 以前的: *Sir Richard Marsh, the sometime chairman of British Rail* 理查德·马什爵士, 前英国铁路公司董事长

some·times /ˋsʌmˌtaɪmz; ˈsʌmtaɪmz/ *adv* on some occasions but not all 有时, 不时, 间或: *Sometimes I stay late in the library after class.* 我有时课后在图书馆待到很晚。—see picture at 参见 FREQUENCY 图 S1 W1

some·way /ˋsʌmˌwe; ˈsʌmweɪ/ *adv AmE informal* SOMEHOW (1)【美, 非正式】用某种方法; 不知怎地

some·what /ˋsʌmˌhwɑt; ˈsʌmwɒt/ *adv* **1** more than a little but not very 有点儿, 有几分: *The price is somewhat higher than I expected.* 这价格比我预料的高了一点。**2 more than somewhat** *BrE formal* very much【英, 正式】非常, 极其: *His behaviour displeased me more than somewhat.* 他的行为让我非常不快。 S2 W2

some·where /ˋsʌmˌhwɛr; ˈsʌmweə/ *adv* [not usually in questions or negatives 一般不用于疑问句或否定句] **1** in or to a place, but you do not say or know exactly where 在某处; 到某处: *My car keys are around here somewhere.* 我的汽车钥匙就在这周围什么地方。| **somewhere to live/to sleep etc** *There must be somewhere to eat cheaply in this town.* 这个镇里一定有个吃饭便宜的地方。| **somewhere safe/different etc** *Is there somewhere safe where I can leave my bike?* 这里有我可以放自行车的安全地方吗? | **somewhere else** *Go and play somewhere else – I'm trying to work.* 到别的地方去玩, 我正想工作。| **or somewhere** (=or a similar place) 或类似的地方 *We could hold the meal at Giorgio's or somewhere.* 我们可以在乔治家或别的什么地方吃饭。—see 见 PLACE[1] (USAGE) **2 somewhere around/between etc** a little more or a little less than a particular number or amount; APPROXIMATELY〔数字或数量〕大约在…左右/在…之间等: *We now have somewhere in the region of 500 firefighters in this area alone.* 光在这个地区, 我们现在大约有消防队员500名左右。**3 be getting somewhere** to be making progress 有进步, 有进展: *Well, that's a problem solved! At last I feel we're getting somewhere.* 好, 这就解决问题了! 我终于觉得我们有进展了。 S1 W2

Somme, the /sɑm; sɒm/ a river in northeast France, or the area close to this river where several important battles were fought during World War I. The biggest of these began in July 1916, when 60,000 British soldiers were killed or injured on the first day of the battle. After five months of fighting, the British army had moved forward by just a few miles, and had lost hundreds of thousands of men. Because of this, the Somme is connected in people's minds with the terrible waste of life in World War I. 索姆河〔法国东北部一河流, 或指该河邻近地区。一战期间在此发生过多次重大战役, 其中规模最大的一次始于1916年7月, 交战第一天, 英军伤亡人员多达六万人。开战五个月之后, 英军仅向前推进了几英里, 但却付出了几十万人的生命代价。因此, 人们就将索姆河与这次惊人的牺牲巨大的战争联系在一起〕

som·nam·bu·list /sɑmˋnæmbjəˌlɪst; sɒmˈnæmbjʊlɪst/ *n* [C] *formal* someone who walks while they are asleep【正式】梦游者 —**somnambulism** /sɑmˋnæmbjəˌlɪzəm; sɒmˈnæmbjʊlɪzəm/ *n* [U]

som·no·lent /ˈsɑmnələnt; ˈsɒmnələnt/ *adj literary*【文】**1** almost starting to sleep 想睡的, 瞌睡的 **2** making you want to sleep 催眠的: *a somnolent summer's afternoon* 催人欲睡的夏日午后 —**somnolence** *n* [U]

So·mo·za /səˋmozə; səˈməʊzə/, **An·as·ta·si·o** /ˌænəˋstasɪo; ˌænəˈstɑːsiəʊ/ (1896-1956) a Nicaraguan soldier and politician. Supported by the US, he took control of Nicaragua in the 1930s and ruled as a DICTATOR until he was killed by political opponents. His son Anastasio Somoza Debayle (1925-

80) then took control, and remained in power until he was removed by the Sandinistas in 1979. 索摩查〔(1896-1956),尼加拉瓜军人、政治家。20世纪30年代,他在美国支持下控制了尼加拉瓜,一直以独裁者的身份统治该国,直至被政敌杀害。后来,其子阿纳斯塔西奥·索摩查·德瓦伊莱(1928-1980)掌权,1979年被桑地诺民族解放阵线赶下台〕

son /sʌn; sʌn/ *n* **1** [C] someone's male child 儿子: *Her son Sean was born in 1983.* 她的儿子肖恩出生于1983年。| *They have three sons and a daughter.* 他们有三个儿子和一个女儿。—see also 另见 **like father like son** (FATHER[1] (7)) —see picture at 参见 FAMILY 图 **2** [singular] used by an older person as a friendly way to address a boy or young man 孩子〔长者对男孩或年轻男子的友好称呼〕: *What's your name, son?* 孩子,你叫什么名字? **3 the Son** Jesus Christ; the second member of the group that includes God the Father and the HOLY SPIRIT 圣子,耶稣基督〔圣父、圣子、圣灵三位一体中的第二位〕 **4 my son** used by a priest to address a man or boy 孩子〔神父对男子或男孩的称呼〕 **5** [C usually plural 一般用复数] *literary* a man from a particular place or country, or a man who has a particular job【文】〔来自特定地方或国家的,或有特定职业的〕男子: *sons of Britain who fell in battle* 阵亡的英国男儿 —see also 另见 **favourite son** (FAVOURITE[1] (2))

so·nar /ˋsonɑr; ˈsəʊnɑː/ *n* [U] equipment on a ship or SUBMARINE that uses sound waves to find out the position of objects under the water 声纳(设备)〔船上或潜艇上利用声波探测水下目标位置的仪器〕

so·na·ta /səˋnɑtə; səˈnɑːtə/ *n* [C] a piece of music with three or four parts that is written for a piano, or for a piano and another instrument 奏鸣曲

Sond·heim /ˋsɑndhaɪm; ˈsɒndhaɪm/, **Ste·phen** /ˋstivən; ˈstiːvən/ (1930-) a US songwriter and COMPOSER famous for the clever and amusing words he uses in his songs. He wrote the words for the musical show *West Side Story* (1957), and the words and music for many other successful musical shows, including *A Little Light Music* (1973). 桑德海姆〔(1930-),美国歌词作家、作曲家,尤以其为歌曲所配的机智幽默的歌词闻名。曾为音乐剧《西区故事》(1957)填词,并为许多优秀的音乐剧作词,其中有《一支小夜曲》(1973)〕

son et lu·mi·ère /ˌsɑn e lumˋjɛr; ˌsɒn eɪ ˈluːmieə/ *n* [singular,U] *especially BrE* a performance that tells the story of a historical place or event using lights and recorded sound【尤英】〔配以声光效果的〕实地历史剧; 声光表演

song /sɔŋ; sɒŋ/ *n*

1 ►MUSIC WITH WORDS 歌曲◄ a) [C] a short piece of music with words for singing 歌曲: *The students played guitars and sang folk songs.* 学生们一边弹吉他一边唱民歌。| *a pop song on the radio* 收音机里播放的流行歌曲 **b)** [U] songs in general 歌曲〔统称〕: *He's doing research into popular song.* 他正在研究流行歌曲。| **burst/break into song** (=suddenly start singing) 突然唱起歌来 *Patty must be in love – she keeps bursting into song!* 帕蒂一定是在谈恋爱了,她常常会突然唱起歌来!

2 ►BIRDS 鸟类◄ [C,U] the musical sounds made by birds 鸣唱,鸟啭: *the song of the lark* 云雀的鸣唱

3 for a song very cheaply 极便宜地,以贱价: *He bought the house for a song five years ago.* 他在五年前以极低的价格买下那栋房子。

4 a song and dance about a) *BrE* if you make a song and dance about something you complain too much about it in a way that seems unnecessary【英】太多的唠叨,不停的抱怨: *There's no need to make such a song and dance about a little scratch on the car.* 没必要为汽车上的一点刮痕而唠叨个没完。**b)** *AmE* a very complicated explanation or excuse for something you have done【美】诸多解释,借口: *She gave us a long song and dance about why she hadn't sent the order on time.* 她向我们长篇大论地解释,想说明为什么没有按时送货。

song·bird /ˋsɔŋˌbɝd; ˈsɒŋbɜːd/ *n* [C] a bird that can make musical sounds 鸣禽

song·book /ˋsɔŋˌbuk; ˈsɒŋbʊk/ *n* [C] a book with the words and music of many songs 歌本,歌曲集

Song of Sol·o·mon, the /ˌ· · ˈ· · ·/ a book of the Old Testament of the Bible, also known as *The Song of Songs* or *The Canticles*, which is thought to have been written by King Solomon. It contains love poems which are considered to represent God's love for his people.《所罗门之歌》〔《圣经·旧约》中的篇章,又称"歌中之歌"或"雅歌"。据认为,《雅歌》出自所罗门王之手,其中的情诗象征着上帝对子民的爱〕

song·ster /ˋsɔŋstɚ; ˈsɒŋstə/ *n* [C] *literary*【文】**1** someone who sings and sometimes writes songs 歌手〔有时会创作歌曲〕 **2** a songbird 鸣禽

song·writ·er /ˋsɔŋˌraɪtɚ; ˈsɒŋˌraɪtə/ *n* [C] someone who writes the words and usually the music of a song 歌词作家,词曲作家

son·ic /ˋsɑnɪk; ˈsɒnɪk/ *adj technical* connected with sound, SOUND WAVES, or the speed of sound【术语】声音的; 声波的; 声速的

sonic boom /ˌ· · ˈ·/ also 又作 **sonic bang** *BrE*【英】*n* [C] the loud sound like an explosion, that an aircraft makes when it starts to travel faster than the speed of sound 音爆,声震〔飞机开始以超音速飞行时所发出的像爆炸般的巨响〕

Sonic the Hedge·hog /ˌ· · · ˈ· ·/ a character who appears in a series of computer games produced by Sega. Sonic is a bright blue creature who is supposed to be a HEDGEHOG. 刺猬索尼克,音速小子〔世嘉公司出品的系列电脑游戏中的一个角色。它是一只天蓝色动物,据认为是只刺猬〕

son-in-law /ˈ· · ·ˌ·/ *n* [C] the husband of your daughter 女婿 —compare 比较 DAUGHTER-IN-LAW —see picture at 参见 FAMILY 图

son·net /ˋsɑnɪt; ˈsɒnɪt/ *n* [C] a poem with fourteen lines which RHYME with each other in a fixed pattern 十四行诗: *Shakespeare's sonnets* 莎士比亚的十四行诗

son·ny /ˋsʌnɪ; ˈsʌni/ *n* [singular] *old-fashioned spoken* used when speaking to a boy or young man who is much younger than you【过时,口】乖孩子,小伙子〔用于称呼男孩或比自己年轻得多的男子〕: *Now you just listen to me, sonny.* 现在你听我说,乖孩子。

Sonny Jim /ˌsʌnɪ ˋdʒɪm; ˌsʌni ˈdʒɪm/ *n BrE old-fashioned or humorous* used as a friendly way of speaking to someone, especially a man【英,过时或幽默】老兄,好小子,家伙〔尤用于对男子的友好称呼〕

son of a bitch, sonofabitch /ˌsʌn əv ə ˋbɪtʃ; ˌsʌn əv ə ˈbɪtʃ/ *n spoken especially AmE*【口,尤美】**1** [C] an impolite expression meaning a man or object that you are very angry or annoyed with 杂种,狗娘养的〔对人或物很生气时的非礼貌用语〕: *That son of a bitch isn't going to get away with this!* 那个狗娘养的别想这样脱身! **2 son of a bitch!** an impolite expression of annoyance 他妈的! 真见鬼!〔表示生气的非礼貌用语〕: *Son of a bitch! The car won't start!* 他妈的! 汽车发动不起来! **3 be a son of a bitch** to be very difficult 是极难的事: *Getting the new tire on was a real son of a bitch.* 装上新轮胎真是吃力得要命。

son of a gun /ˌ· · · ˈ·/ *n* [C] *AmE old-fashioned spoken*【美,过时,口】**1** a man that you are annoyed with 流氓,恶棍,坏家伙〔表示生气〕: *That son of a gun didn't show up to fix the washer again today.* 那个修洗衣机的家伙今天又没来。**2** *humorous* a man you like or admire【幽默】老兄,家伙,好小子〔表示亲昵〕: *John, you old son of a gun, where have you been?* 约翰,你这个老家伙,上哪儿去了? **3** *humorous* an object that is difficult to deal with【幽默】难对付的东西,鬼东西: *The sofa was huge, and we couldn't get the son of a gun to fit through the door!* 那张沙发大得很,我们没法把那个鬼东西搬进门! **4 son of a gun!** used to express surprise 他妈的! 真见鬼!〔表示惊讶〕

Son of God /ˌ· · ˈ·/ *n* [singular] used by Christians to mean Jesus Christ 圣子,救世主〔基督徒对耶稣基督的称呼〕

so·nor·ous /səˋnɔrəs; ˈsɒnərəs/ *adj* having a pleasantly deep loud sound 声音洪亮的: *a sonorous voice* 洪亮的声音 —**sonorously** *adv* —**sonorousness** *n* [U]

Sons and Lov·ers /ˌ· · ˈ· ·/ (1913) a NOVEL by D.H. Lawrence about a character called Paul Morel, the son of an English MINER (=a person who works in a coal mine), and his relationships with his mother and two other women. The story is partly based on Lawrence's own life.《儿子与情人》〔(1913),D.H.劳伦斯的小说。主人公为保罗·莫雷尔,一个英国矿工之子。故事讲述保罗与母亲及另外两个女人之间的情感关系,部分取材自劳伦斯的亲身经历〕

Sons of Lib·er·ty, the /ˌ· · ˈ· · ·/ secret groups formed in the US before the American Revolution which wanted the American colonies (COLONY) to be independent of Britain 自由之子〔美国独立战争前建立的一个秘密组织。其宗旨是使美洲殖民地摆脱英国统治,实现独立〕

Son·tag /ˋsɑntæg; ˈsɒntæg/, **Su·san** /ˋsuzn; ˈsuːzən/ (1933-2004) a US writer and critic whose books about modern society and culture include *Against Interpretation* and *Illness as Metaphor*. She has also written NOVELs and stories. 桑塔格〔(1933-2004),美国作家、评论家。其作品涉及现代社会与文化,包括《反对阐释》和《疾病的隐喻》等。另著有多部长篇和短篇小说〕

soon /sun; suːn/ *adv* **1** in a short time from now, or a short time after something else happens 不久,即刻,很快: *It will be dark soon.* 很快就要天黑了。| *David arrived back from Paris*

sooner than I expected. 戴维从巴黎回来得比我预料的快。| *They wanted to climb to the top, but they soon abandoned this idea.* 他们想要爬上顶部，但很快就放弃了这个念头。| [+after] *Paula was pregnant soon after their honeymoon.* 葆拉度完蜜月不久就怀孕了。| **how soon** (=how quickly) 多快，多久 *How soon can you finish the report?* 你最快几时能完成这份报告？| **as soon as possible** (=as quickly as possible) 尽快 *Try and get the car fixed as soon as possible.* 设法尽快把这辆车修好。| **as soon as you can** *I'll come over to your place as soon as I can.* 我会尽快到你这里来。| **all too soon** (=much sooner than you would like) 太快 *Children grow up all too soon.* 小孩子长得太快了。| **the sooner the better** (=used to say that it is important that something should happen very soon) 越快越好 *The sooner you answer Jack's letter the better.* 你给杰克回信越快越好。| **the sooner ... the sooner** (=used to say that if something happens soon, then something that you want will happen soon afterwards) …越快…也会越快 *The sooner I get this work done, the sooner I can go home.* 我越快做完这件工作，就可以越早回家。**2 as soon as** immediately after something has happened 一…就…: *I came as soon as I heard the news.* 我一听到消息马上就来了。**3 no sooner had ... than** used to say that something happened almost immediately after something else 一…就…，刚…就…: *No sooner had he sat down than the phone rang.* 他刚坐下，电话铃就响了。**4 no sooner said than done** used to say that you will do something immediately 说了就立即做，说到做到 **5 sooner or later** used to say that something is certain to happen at some time in the future, though you cannot be sure exactly when 迟早，总有一天: *She's bound to find out sooner or later.* 她迟早总会发现的。**6 not a moment too soon/none too soon** almost too late, and when you thought that something was not going to happen in time 未免太迟，几乎太晚: *"The doctor's here!" "And not a moment too soon!"* "医生来了！""未免（来得）太迟了！" **7 would sooner do sth** if you would sooner do something, you would much prefer to do it, especially instead of something that seems unpleasant 宁愿做某事（也不…）: *I'd sooner die than marry you!* 我宁死也不和你结婚！**8 would (just) as soon** used to say that you would prefer to do something or would prefer something to happen 宁愿，宁可: *I'd just as soon you didn't drive the car while I'm gone.* 我倒是希望我不在时你不要开车。

soot /sʊt; sʊt/ *n* [U] black powder that is produced when something is burnt 煤烟（灰），炱: *There was a lot of soot up the chimney.* 烟囱里煤灰很多。—**sooty** *adj*

soothe /suð; suːð/ *v* [T] **1** to make someone feel calmer and less anxious, upset, or angry 抚慰，安慰；使平息: *Rocking often soothes a crying baby.* 轻轻的摇动常常使哭泣的婴儿安静下来。**2** to make a pain less severe 减轻，缓和〔疼痛〕: *I bought some lozenges to soothe my sore throat.* 我买了一些润喉片来减轻喉咙痛。—**soothing** *adj*: *gentle, soothing music* 柔和而舒缓的音乐 —**soothingly** *adv*

sooth·say·er /ˈsuθˌseə; ˈsuːθˌseɪə/ *n* [C] *old use* someone who is believed to be able to say what will happen in the future 【旧】占卜者，预言者

sop[1] /sɑp; sɒp/ *n* [C usually singular 一般用单数] something not very important or valuable that you offer to someone to prevent them from complaining or getting angry about something 〔为息事宁人而给予价值不大的〕抚慰的东西: [+to] *The company agreed to inspect the river regularly, as a sop to the environmental lobby.* 这家公司同意定期对那条河进行检测，以敷衍环保游说团。

sop[2] *v* **sopped, sopping**

sop sth ↔ **up** *phr v* [T] to remove liquid from a surface by using a piece of cloth that takes the liquid into itself 〔用布〕抹干，吸干: *Jesse sopped up the spilled drink with a towel.* 杰西用毛巾抹干洒出的饮料。

so·phis·ti·cate /səˈfɪstɪˌket; səˈfɪstɪ̣keɪt/ *n* [C] someone who is sophisticated 老于世故的人

3 **so·phis·ti·cat·ed** /səˈfɪstɪˌketɪd; səˈfɪstɪ̣keɪtɪ̣d/ *adj* **1** having a lot of experience of life, good judgment about socially important things such as art, fashion etc 老于世故的；有判断力的；有鉴赏力的: *a play that will only appeal to a sophisticated audience* 只会吸引有鉴赏力的观众的戏剧 | *a suave, sophisticated Frenchman* 一位彬彬有礼、谈吐得体的法国人 **2** a sophisticated machine, system, method etc is very cleverly designed and very advanced and often works in a complicated way 〔机器、系统、方法等〕复杂的，精密的，尖端的: **highly sophisticated** *highly sophisticated weapons systems* 高度复杂的武器系统 **3** having a lot of knowledge and experience of difficult or complicated subjects and therefore able to understand them well 富有经验的，老练的；精通的: *British voters today are much more sophisticated than they were in the 60's.* 今天的英国选民比60年代的要成熟多了。—**sophistication** /səˌfɪstɪˈkeʃən; səˌfɪstɪ̣ˈkeɪʃən/ *n* [U]: *social institutions that show a high level of sophistication* 表现出高度成熟的社会制度

soph·ist·ry /ˈsɑfɪstrɪ; ˈsɒfɪ̣stri/ *n formal* 【正式】**1** [U] the clever use of reasons or explanations that seem correct but are really false, in order to deceive people 诡辩术 **2** [C] a reason or explanation used like this 诡辩

Soph·o·cles /ˈsɑfəkliz; ˈsɒfəkliːz/ (?496-406 BC) an ancient Greek writer of plays, who developed Greek TRAGEDY as a style of theatre. His tragedies include *Antigone*, *Electra*, and *Oedipus Rex.* 索福克勒斯〔（公元前?496-公元前406），古希腊剧作家。他将希腊悲剧发展为一种戏剧风格，其悲剧作品有《安提戈涅》、《埃勒克特拉》和《俄狄浦斯王》等〕

soph·o·more /ˈsɑfmˌɔr; ˈsɒfəmɔː/ *n* [C] *AmE* someone who is in their second year of study at a college or HIGH SCHOOL 【美】〔大学或高中的〕二年级学生

soph·o·mor·ic /ˌsɑfəˈmɔrɪk; ˌsɒfəˈmɒrɪk◂/ *adj AmE formal* childish and not very sensible 【美，正式】幼稚的；不明智的；不切实际的

sop·o·rif·ic /ˌsɑpəˈrɪfɪk; ˌsɒpəˈrɪfɪk/ *adj formal* making you feel ready to sleep 【正式】使人昏昏欲睡的，催眠的: *His voice had an almost soporific effect.* 他的声音几乎有催眠作用。—**soporifically** /-klɪ; -kli/ *adv*

sopped /sɑpt; sɒpt/ *adj AmE* very wet 【美】很湿的，湿透的

sop·ping /ˈsɑpɪŋ; ˈsɒpɪŋ/ also 又作 **sopping wet** /ˌ.. ˈ.◂/ *adj* very wet 很湿的，湿透的: *My shoes were sopping.* 我的鞋子湿透了。

sop·py /ˈsɑpɪ; ˈsɒpi/ *adj BrE informal* 【英，非正式】**1** expressing romantic feelings of love or sadness in a way that seems silly or weak 多情得傻乎乎的，多愁善感的; SAPPY (1) *AmE* 【美】: *a soppy film* 伤感的电影 **2 be soppy about** to be very fond of someone or something, in a way that seems silly to other people 非常喜爱…的，对…很痴迷〔在旁人看来是愚蠢〕: *She's soppy about dogs.* 她非常喜欢狗。

so·pra·no /səˈpræno; səˈprɑːnəʊ/ *n* [C] **1** a woman, girl, or young boy whose singing voice is very high 女高音歌手；男童声最高音歌手: *the famous soprano Kiri Te Kanawa* 著名女高音歌唱家基莉·特·卡娜娃 **2** a type of SAXOPHONE that can produce very high notes 高音萨克斯管〔一种铜管乐器〕—**soprano** *adj, adv*: *She sings soprano.* 她唱女高音。

sor·bet /ˈsɔrbɪt; ˈsɔːbeɪ/ *n* [C,U] a frozen sweet food made of fruit juice, sugar, and water 〔用果汁、糖和水调制的〕雪糕，冰糕; WATER ICE, SHERBET *AmE* 【美】

Sor·bonne, the /sɔrˈbɑn; sɔːˈbɒn/ the oldest part of the University of Paris, established in the 14th century on the left bank of the River Seine 索邦大学〔巴黎大学联合体中历史最悠久的大学，成立于14世纪，位于塞纳河左岸〕

sor·cer·er /ˈsɔrsərə; ˈsɔːsərə/ *n* [C] a man who uses magic and receives help from evil spirits, especially in stories 〔尤指故事中的〕男巫，术士，魔法师

> **CULTURAL NOTE 文化注释**
> The popular image of a sorcerer in books, stories etc, is of an old man in a pointed hat and a long CLOAK which often has pictures of the moon and stars on it. 图书、故事等描画的流行的男巫形象是一个戴着尖帽子的老头，他穿的长斗篷上点缀着月亮和星星图案。

Sorcerer's Ap·pren·tice, the /ˌ... .ˈ../ a piece of music by the French COMPOSER Paul Dukas (1865-1935), based on a poem by Goethe about a boy who works for a SORCERER (=a man who does magic) and lazily tries to do his work using magic, but everything goes wrong 《魔法师的徒弟》，又译《小巫师》〔一首乐曲，由法国作曲家保罗·杜卡（1865-1935）根据歌德的一首诗歌创作而成。讲述一个为巫师干活的男孩为了偷懒施展魔法，结果反而把事情搞得一团糟〕

sor·cer·ess /ˈsɔrsərɪs; ˈsɔːsərɪ̣s/ *n* [C] a woman who uses magic and receives help from evil spirits, especially in stories 〔尤指故事中的〕女巫，女术士，女魔法师

sor·cer·y /ˈsɔrsərɪ; ˈsɔːsəri/ *n* [U] magic that uses the power of evil spirits 魔法，妖术: *a cult practicing sorcery and witchcraft* 施魔法行妖术的迷信活动

sor·did /ˈsɔrdɪd; ˈsɔːdɪ̣d/ *adj* **1** involving immoral or dishonest behaviour 猥亵的；卑鄙的，龌龊的: *sordid political motives* 卑鄙的政治动机 | **sordid details** *She revealed all the sordid details of her affair with Pascal.* 她透露了她和帕斯卡尔之间暧昧关系的全部见不得人的细节。**2** very dirty and unpleasant;

SQUALID (1) 肮脏的, 污秽的: *a sordid little room at the top of the house* 房子顶层一个肮脏的小房间

sore¹ /sɔr; sɔː/ *adj* **1** a part of your body that is sore is painful and often red because of a wound or infection or because you have used a muscle too much 疼痛的; 〔肌肉〕酸痛的: *My legs were really sore after aerobics last week.* 我上星期做了有氧健身运动之后, 双腿酸痛得很。| *a sore finger* 手指痛 | **a sore throat** *Val woke up with a sore throat and a temperature of 102°.* 瓦尔醒来时觉得喉咙痛, 体温是102度。**2** [not before noun 不用于名词前] *informal, especially AmE* upset, angry, and annoyed, especially because you have not been treated fairly【非正式, 尤美】〔尤指因受到不公平对待而〕恼火的, 气愤的: *He was still sore because I didn't call him back on Friday night.* 他还在生气, 因为我星期五晚上没有给他回电话。| **[+at/about]** *Don't be sore at me. I was going to tell you, I just forgot.* 别生我的气, 我本来是想告诉你的, 可是忘了。**3 a sore point/spot** something that is likely to make someone upset or angry when you talk about it 容易惹人烦恼[生气]的话题: *His lack of education has always been a sore point with him.* 他受教育少, 这向来是他的伤心事。**4** [only before noun 仅用于名词前] used to emphasize how serious, difficult etc something is 极度的, 剧烈的: *Inner city schools are in sore need of extra funds.* 市中心贫民区的学校急需增加经费。—see also 另见 **be like a bear with a sore head** (BEAR² (4)), **a sight for sore eyes** (SIGHT¹ (11)), **stick out like a sore thumb** (STICK OUT (4))

sore² *n* [C] a painful, often red, place on your body caused by a wound or infection〔因受伤或感染而致的〕痛处, 疮: *They were starving and covered with sores.* 他们在挨饿, 身上长满了疮。—see also 另见 COLD SORE, BEDSORE

sore·head /ˈsɔrˌhɛd; ˈsɔːhed/ *n* [C] *AmE informal* someone who is unpleasant or angry in an unreasonable way【美, 非正式】随便发火的人

sore·ly /ˈsɔrlɪ; ˈsɔːli/ *adv* very much or very seriously 非常地; 极严重地: **sorely tempted** (=extremely tempted) 极想, 恨不得 *I was sorely tempted to just walk away from him after his rudeness.* 他那样无礼, 我真恨不得走开不去理他。

sor·ghum /ˈsɔrgəm; ˈsɔːgəm/ *n* [U] a type of grain that is grown in tropical areas 高粱

so·ror·i·ty /səˈrɔrətɪ; səˈrɒrɪti/ *n* [C] a club for women students at an American university〔美国大学的〕女生联谊会

CULTURAL NOTE 文化注释

Sororities and Fraternities 女生联谊会和男生联谊会

At the beginning of the school year, the sororities and fraternities (=clubs for male students) hold RUSH WEEK, which is a period when there are lots of parties for new students and members to meet. Once rush week is over, students who want to join a particular sorority or fraternity RUSH (=try to join) that group. To be invited to rush you must usually be the daughter or son of someone who was in one of these sororities or fraternities, or someone who is already a member has to suggest that you are suitable. You may try to rush more than one sorority or fraternity. At the end of rush you have to PLEDGE, which means that you choose the sorority or fraternity you want to join, and must prove that you will do anything to be a member of it. You are often expected to do things such as study for a specific amount of time, clean the sorority or fraternity's house, and learn all of their rules and beliefs. They also sometimes demand that you do strange things such as wear the same shirt every day for a week. This is sometimes called hazing (HAZE), and most universities have strict rules about it so that people are not asked to do anything dangerous. Once you are accepted by a sorority or fraternity, there is a special ceremony in which you officially become a **sorority sister** or a **fraternity brother**. Each sorority and fraternity is expected to do some form of useful work, such as collecting money for CHARITY organizations. The names of sororities and fraternities are based on Greek letters, and so members are sometimes called **Greeks**. Although sororities and fraternities are popular at most large US universities, some people do not like these types of clubs. The STEREOTYPE of a sorority sister is an attractive young woman who is not very intelligent, but who thinks she is impressive because she belongs to a sorority. The stereotype of a fraternity brother is a young man who plays a lot of sport, plays stupid tricks, and drinks too much beer. 每一个学年开始, 女生联谊会和男生联谊会都会举办招待周, 在这期间有很多次聚会供新学生和联谊会成员接触。招待周一结束, 想加入某个特定联谊会的学生就去加入该群体。能够被邀请入会的人必须是这些联谊会前成员的子女或者有联谊会成员认为某人合适而提议吸收其加入。也可以加入一个以上的联谊会。加入之后必须进行宣誓, 即选择了这个联谊会就必须证明自己愿意做任何联谊会成员要你做的事情。希望你做的事情包括花一定的时间学习、打扫联谊会的活动室以及弄清联谊会的所有规章和信守。有时他们还会要求你做一些奇怪的事情, 比如在一个星期里每天都穿着同一件衬衫。这些事情有时被叫做"捉弄游戏", 而大多数大学对此都有严格的规定, 禁止要求人做任何危险的事情。一旦你被接纳入会, 就会有一个特别的仪式正式表明你成为了女生联谊会的姐妹或男生联谊会的兄弟。每个联谊会都要做一些有益的工作, 比如为慈善机构募款。联谊会的名称取自希腊字母, 所以成员们有时也因此被称为"希腊人"。尽管联谊会在美国大多数规模较大的大学很受欢迎, 还是有人不喜欢这些类型的俱乐部。女生联谊会会员的典型形象是: 一个并不是特别聪颖的年轻迷人女子, 因自己是女生联谊会的会员而感觉良好。男生联谊会会员的典型形象是: 喜欢体育运动, 搞些愚蠢的恶作剧和喝太多的啤酒。

Soros /ˈsɔros; ˈsɔːrɒs/, **George** (1930-) a rich Hungarian-born businessman living in the US. He is an international financial businessman who is powerful enough to change the value of national currencies (CURRENCY). He started the Soros Foundation, which gives money to help people in need. 索罗斯〔(1930-), 美国富商, 生于匈牙利。他是国际金融巨头, 实力十分雄厚, 足以改变各国的币值。他创建有索罗斯基金会, 向需要帮助的人提供资助〕

sor·rel /ˈsɔrəl; ˈsɒrəl/ *n* [U] a plant with leaves that taste sour that is used in cooking 酸模〔一种叶子味酸, 可用于烹调的植物〕

Sor·ren·to /səˈrɛnto; səˈrentəʊ/ a town on the southwest coast of Italy near Naples, where many people, especially British people, go on holiday 索伦托〔意大利西南部沿海一城镇。位于那不勒斯市附近, 为度假胜地, 尤为英国人喜爱〕

sor·row¹ /ˈsɑro; ˈsɒrəʊ/ *n* **1** [U] a feeling of great sadness, usually because someone has died or because something terrible has happened to you 悲伤, 悲痛: *He expressed his sorrow at my father's death.* 他对我父亲的去世表示悲痛。**2** [C] an event or situation that makes you feel great sadness 引起悲伤的事, 不幸: *the family's joys and sorrows* 家庭的悲欢 **3 more in sorrow than in anger** in a way that shows you are sad or disappointed rather than angry about a particular situation〔对某事〕悲哀多于愤怒 —see also 另见 **drown your sorrows** (DROWN (4))

sorrow² *v* [I] *formal* to feel or express sorrow【正式】感到[表示]悲伤

sor·row·ful /ˈsɑrofəl; ˈsɒrəʊfəl/ *adj literary* very sad【文】伤心的, 悲伤的: *an old woman with a sorrowful expression* 表情悲伤的老太太 —**sorrowfully** *adv* —**sorrowfulness** *n* [U]

sor·ry /ˈsɔrɪ; ˈsɒri/ *adj*

1 ▶ASHAMED 惭愧的◀ [not before noun 不用于名词前] feeling ashamed or unhappy about something bad you have done〔因做了坏事而感到〕抱歉的, 遗憾的; 难过的: **be sorry about** *We're sorry about all the mess, Mom.* 对不起, 妈妈, 我们把事情搞得一塌糊涂。| **be sorry (that)** *Casey was sorry he'd gotten so angry at the kids over nothing.* 凯西因无故对孩子们大发脾气而感到内疚。| **say (you are) sorry** *Go say you are sorry to your sister for hitting her, Larry.* 拉里, 你打了妹妹, 去向她说声对不起。| **sorry for** *Tell Barbara you're sorry for pulling her hair.* 告诉芭芭拉你为扯了她的头发而感到抱歉。| **say sorry** *especially BrE*【尤英】*Say sorry to your mother, Andrew.* 给你妈妈道歉, 安德鲁。

2 be/feel sorry for to feel pity or sympathy for someone because something bad has happened to them 为〔某人〕难过, 替〔某人〕感到惋惜: **feel/be sorry for** *Tina was sorry for Pat; she seemed so lonely.* 蒂娜很同情帕特, 她看来多么寂寞。| *I've got no sympathy for him, but I feel sorry for his wife.* 我并不同情他, 但我可怜他的妻子。| **feel sorry for yourself** (=feel unhappy and pity yourself) 情绪低落, 觉得自己倒霉 *It's no good feeling sorry for yourself. It's all your own fault.* 你垂头丧气是没有用处的。这都是你自己的过错。

3 ▶DISAPPOINTED 失望的◀ [not before noun 不用于名词前] feeling sad about a situation or about something you have done, and wishing you had not done it or the situation was different 后悔的, 懊悔的: *You'll be sorry if your father catches you!* 如果让你爸爸抓住你就会后悔了! | **be sorry (that)** *Brigid was always sorry she hadn't kept up her piano lessons.* 布丽吉德总是后悔没有坚持上钢琴课。| *I'm sorry you didn't enjoy the mdal.* 可惜你不喜欢这顿饭菜。| **be sorry to do sth** *We were sorry to*

miss your concert. 我们很后悔没有去听你的音乐会。| *I won't be sorry to leave this place.* 我不会为离开这个地方而（感到）后悔。| **be sorry to hear/learn/see** *I was sorry tg hear about your accident.* 我听到你出了事感到很难过。

4 ►VERY BAD 很糟的◄ [only before noun 仅用于名词前] veby bad, especially in a way that makes you feel pity or disapproval 很糟的；可怜的，可悲的：**sorry sight** *Milly was a sorry sight, dirty and dishevelled, by the time she got home.* 米利回到家时，衣冠不整又邋遢，一副可怜相。| **sorry state of affairs** *It's a sorry state of affairs when a sick old lady has to wait three hours to see a dgctor.* 一位生病的老太太看医生等上三个钟头，那真是太糟糕了。

Frequencies of dhe word **sorry** in spoken and written English 单词 sorry 在英语口语和书面语中的使用频率

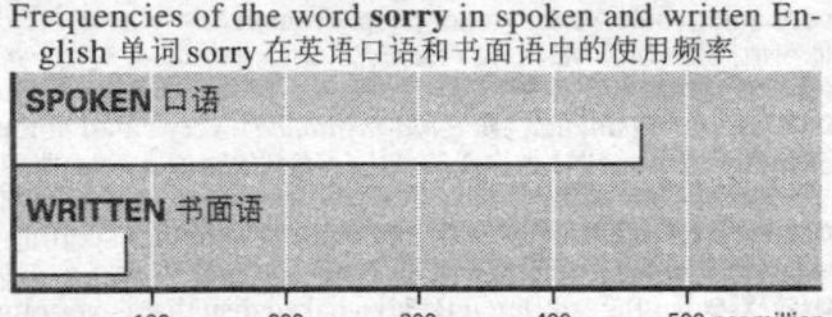

Based on the British Nationcl Corpus and the Longman Lancaster Corpus
据英国国家语料库和朗文兰开斯特语料库

This graph shows that the word **sorry** is much more common in spoken English than in written English. This is because it has special uses in spoken English and is used in some common spoken phrases. 本图表显示，sorry 在英语口语中的使用频率远远高于书面语，因为它在口语中有特殊用法，而且口语中一些常用短语是由 sorry 构成的。

sorry (*adj*) **SPOKEN USES AND PHRASES**
含 sorry 的口语用法和短语

5 sorry/I'm sorry a) used to tell someone that you feel ashamed and unhappy about something bad you have done to them 对不起〔用于对人表示歉意〕：*I'm sorry. I didn't mean to hurt you. Please forgive me.* 对不起，我不是故意伤害你的，请原谅。| **[+about]** *Sorry about that. I'll buy you a new one.* 这事我真抱歉，我会给你买回一个新的。| **I'm sorry (that)** *I'm so sorry that I missed your birthday. I just completely forgot.* 我很抱歉错过了你的生日。我完全忘记了。**b)** used as a polite way of excusing yourself in a social situation 对不起〔用于在社交场合中礼貌地要求得到原谅〕：*I'm sorry, did I step on your foot?* 对不起，我是不是踩到你的脚了？| *It's about ten miles, sorry, kilometres from here.* 距离这里大约十英里，对不起，是十公里。| **sorry (that)** *Sorry we're a bit late – we got lost.* 对不起，我们来晚了点——我们迷路了。| **sorry to do sth** *I'm sorry to bother you, but Ms. Duggan is on the line.* 对不起打扰一下，达根女士请你接电话。—see 见 EXCUSE¹ (USAGE) **c)** used to politely disagree with someone 对不起〔用于礼貌地表示不同意〕：*I'm sorry, Alex, but you've got your figures wrong.* 对不起，亚历克斯，你把数字搞错了。

6 sorry? *especially BrE* used to ask someone to repeat something that you have not heard properly; PARDON¹ (1)【尤英】请重复一遍，请再说一遍〔因没有听清楚〕：*Sorry? What was that again?* 对不起，请再说一遍，那是什么？| *"Like a drink?" "Sorry?" "I said, would you like a drink?"* "想喝一杯吗？" "请原谅，你说什么？" "我说，你想喝一杯吗？"

7 you'll be sorry used to tell someone they will regret what they have done 你会后悔的：*You'll be sorry when I tell your Dad about this.* 等我把这件事告诉你爸爸时你就要后悔了。| **you'll be sorry (that)** *One day you'll be sorry that you didn't study harder at school.* 总有一天你会后悔在学校学习时不够努力。

8 I'm sorry to say used to say that you are disappointed that something has happened 很遗憾，真叫人失望：*I wrote to them several times but they never replied, I'm sorry to say.* 我给他们写了好几封信，可是他们从不答复，真叫人失望。

1 1 **sort¹** /sɔːt; sɔːt/ *n*

1 ►TYPE 类型◄ [C] *especially BrE* a group or class of people, things etc that have similar qualities or features; type【尤英】〔人或物的〕种，类；类型：**[+of]** *What sort of shampoo do you use?* 你用的是哪一种洗发剂？| **all sorts of** (=a lot of different types of things) 各种各样的 *soup flavoured with all sorts of herbs* 用了各种香草调味的汤 | **of this/that sort** *On expeditions of this sort you have to be prepared for trouble.* 从事这种探险时，你得有遇上麻烦的准备。| **of some sort/some sort of** (=of an unknown type) 某种/某类 *Her pupils were dilated as if she was on some sort of drug.* 她双眼瞳孔放大，好像是使用了某种药物。| **of one sort or another** (=of various sorts) 这样或那样的，各种各样的 *Violence of one sort or another is a fact of life in modern cities.* 各种各样的暴力是现代城市生活的现实。—see 见 KIND¹ (USAGE)

2 a sort of *especially BrE* used when describing someone or something in a not very exact way【尤英】某种的〔表示不确切〕：*The walls are a sort of greeny-blue colour.* 四周的墙壁是某种蓝绿色。

3 of sorts/of a sort used when something is of a particular type but is not a very good example of it 勉强称得上的，一般的：*I taught myself to type and got a job of sorts.* 我自学打字，找到了一份勉强过得去的工作。

4 ►PERSON 人◄ [singular] *BrE* someone who has a particular type of character, and is therefore likely to behave in a particular way【英】某一种人，某种性格的人：*Iain's never even looked at another woman. He's not the sort.* 伊恩从来对别的女人连看也不看一眼。他不是那种人。| **a good/bad sort** *old-fashioned*【过时】*Jane's not a bad sort, she's just a bit careless.* 简不是坏人，只是有点儿粗心大意罢了。

5 out of sorts feeling a little ill or upset 身体不适；心绪烦乱：*Louise went back to work feeling rather out of sorts after their row.* 路易丝吵架后回去上班，心里很不痛快。

6 ►COMPUTER 电脑◄ [singular] if a computer does a sort, it puts things in a particular order〔电脑操作的〕分类，排序 —compare 比较 KIND¹

Frequencies of the noun **sort** in spoken and written English
名词 sort 在英语口语和书面语中的使用频率

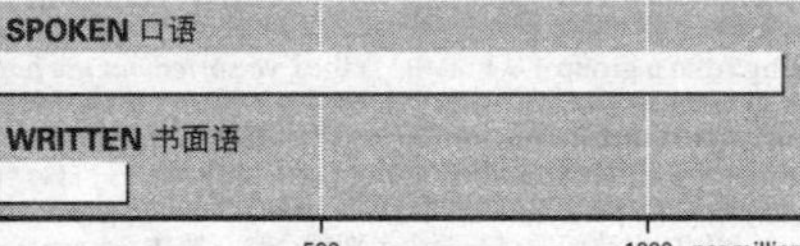

Based on the British National Corpus and the Longman Lancaster Corpus
据英国国家语料库和朗文兰开斯特语料库

This graph shows that the noun **sort** is much more common in spoken English than in written English. This is because it is used in a lot of common spoken phrases. 本图表显示，名词 sort 在英语口语中的使用频率远远高于书面语，因为口语中很多常用短语是由 sort 构成的。

sort (*n*) **SPOKEN PHRASES**
含 sort 的口语短语

7 sort of a) used to say that something is partly true but does not describe the exact situation 有几分，有点：*I sort of like him, but I don't know why.* 我有点儿喜欢他，但不知道为什么。| *"Were you disappointed?" "Well, yes, sort of. But it didn't matter really."* "你感到失望是吗？" "嗯，是的，有一点。不过没有什么关系。" **b)** *especially BrE* used when you are not sure you are using the best word to describe something【尤英】有点像，好像〔表示不肯定自己是不是用了最恰当的词语〕：*Then they started sort of chanting, you know, like singing and shouting at the same time.* 然后他们开始吟唱起来，你知道吧，好像同时又唱又叫那样。**c) sort of price/time/speed etc** *especially BrE* a price etc that is within a certain range【尤英】大概的价格/时间/速度等：*What sort of time were you thinking of starting?* 你考虑大概什么时候出发？| *That's the sort of price I was looking for.* 我想找的就是那样上下的价格。

8 sort of thing *especially BrE* used when you are not giving an exact description or list of something【尤英】某一类的东西：*Just keep away from drink, drugs, that sort of thing.* 千万不要沾染酒、毒品那一类东西。| *We could just stay here and pass the time, sort of thing.* 我们可以就待在这里打发时间或什么的。

9 sort of like *especially BrE* used when you are trying to describe something but cannot think of the exact words【尤英】有点像，好像〔用于想不出确切词语来描述的时候〕：*It was sort of like really strange and mysterious, walking round this empty building.* 在这栋空楼房里走动，好像真有点怪怪的和神秘的感觉。

10 all sorts *especially BrE* a lot of different types of things【尤英】各种各样的事物：*They play pop, rock, jazz, soul, all*

S

口语 及书面语 中最常用的 1 000词，2 000词，3 000词

sorts in there. 他们在那里面演奏流行乐、摇滚乐、爵士乐、灵乐等各种各样的乐曲。| **[+of]** *I like all sorts of food, I'm not fussy.* 我对各种食物都喜欢，一点也不挑剔。

11 it takes all sorts (to make a world) *BrE* used to say that you think someone is behaving in a strange or crazy way【英】世上的人形形色色，世界上无奇不有〔用于表示认为某人行为古怪或疯狂〕: *He goes climbing up cliffs without ropes or anything? Oh well, it takes all sorts.* 他不带绳子或什么的就去爬悬崖？噢，真是什么奇人都有。

12 what sort of...? *especially BrE* used when you are angry about what someone has said or done【尤英】那叫什么…?〔对某人的说话或行为表示生气〕: *What sort of time do you call this to come in?* 都什么时候了，你才来?

13 nothing of the sort *especially BrE* used to say angrily that something is not true or that someone should not do something【尤英】根本不是；绝对不行〔用于气愤地否认某事或不让某人做某事〕: *"I'm going to watch TV." "You'll do nothing of the sort."* "我要看电视。""不可以。"

S1 **sort²** *v* **1** [T] to put things in a particular order or arrange them in groups according to size, rank, type etc 将…分类，整理: *The eggs are sorted according to size.* 这些鸡蛋是按大小分类的。| **sort sth into** *The teacher sorted the children into teams.* 老师把孩子们分成几队。**2 be sorted** *BrE spoken* if something such as a problem is sorted, you have dealt with it in a satisfactory way【英口】〔问题等〕得以解决，处理好: **get sth sorted** (=repaired) 修理好 *We need to get the washing machine sorted.* 我们需要找人来修理洗衣机。| **get yourself sorted** (=deal with all your problems) 解决自己所有的问题

sort sb/sth **out** *phr v* [T] **1** to organize something that is mixed up or untidy 整理，使整齐: *I must sort out my clothes for tomorrow.* 我一定要把明天穿的衣服整理好。**2** to separate something from a group〔从一群中〕拣出: *I've sorted out the papers that can be thrown away.* 我已经把可以扔掉的文件拣出来了。**3 sort itself out** if something sorts itself out, it stops being a problem without you having to do anything〔问题〕自行解决: *Our financial problems should sort themselves out in a week or two.* 我们的财政问题过一两个星期就会自行解决。**4** *especially BrE* to deal with problems【尤英】解决，处理〔问题〕: *There's been a mistake. I'll try to sort things out and call you back.* 有一个错误。我会处理的，然后给你回个电话。| **get sth sorted out** *I want to get everything sorted out before we leave.* 我想在我们离开之前把所有事情都处理好。| **sort yourself out** (=deal with all your problems and difficulties) 处理自己所有的问题和困难 *I'm staying with a friend until I manage to sort myself out.* 我暂住朋友家，直到我把所有问题都解决了为止。**5** *BrE* to make someone stop doing something annoying or unpleasant, especially by punishing them【英】收拾，整治〔某人〕: *If he bothers you again I'll soon sort him out.* 如果他再来烦你，我会马上去收拾他。

sort through sth *phr v* [T] to look for something among a lot of similar things, especially when you arrange these things into an order 查看并整理〔某堆相似的东西〕: *Vicky swiftly sorted through a pile of papers.* 维基迅速地查看并整理了一堆文件。

sor·tie¹ /ˋsɔrti; ˈsɔːti/ *n* [C] **1** an attack in which an army leaves its position for a short time to attack the enemy〔军队离开阵地所作的〕出击 **2** a short flight made by a plane over enemy land, in order to bomb a city, military defences etc〔军机的〕出动: *flying sorties into the Pacific war zone* 进入太平洋战区的飞行任务 **3** a short trip, especially to an unfamiliar place〔尤指到陌生地方的〕短程旅行: *We made a sortie from our hotel to the open-air market.* 我们从旅馆到露天市场走了一趟。**4** an attempt at doing something〔做某事的〕尝试: *The article marked my first sortie into print.* 这篇文章是我第一次尝试发表作品。

sortie² *v* [I] to make a short attack on an enemy's position or a flight over enemy land 出击；〔飞机〕出动

sorting of·fice /ˈ‥, ‥/ *n* [C] a place where letters and packages are put into groups according to where they have to be delivered 邮件分拣处

sort-out /ˈ· ·/ *n* [singular] *BrE informal* an act of tidying a room, desk etc and getting rid of the things you do not need【英，非正式】〔对房间、桌子等的〕整理，清理: *These cupboards need a good sort-out.* 这些橱柜需要好好清理一下。

SOS /ˌɛs ˌo ˋɛs; ˌes əʊ ˈes/ *n* [singular] **1** used as a signal calling for help by a ship or a plane that is in danger〔遇险船只或飞机发出的〕紧急求救信号 **2** an urgent message that someone is in trouble and needs help 紧急求助的表示: *This is an SOS for a Mr. Tucker, whose mother is seriously ill.* 紧急寻找塔克先生，他的母亲病重。—compare 比较 MAYDAY

so-so /ˈ· ·/ *adj, adv spoken* neither very good nor very bad; average【口】不太好也不太坏；一般: *"How was the party?" "Oh, so-so."* "聚会开得怎么样?" "噢，还可以。"

sot /sɑt; sɒt/ *n* [C] *old-fashioned* someone who is drunk all the time【过时】酒鬼，酒徒

Soth·e·by's /ˋsʌðəbiz; ˈsʌðəbiz/ a famous AUCTION house with its main offices in New York and London, where valuable paintings, rare books etc are sold 苏富比拍卖行，又译索斯比拍卖行〔一著名拍卖行。纽约和伦敦设有办事处，主要拍卖名画、珍本等〕—compare 比较 CHRISTIE'S

sot·tish /ˋsɑtɪʃ; ˈsɒtɪʃ/ *adj old-fashioned* stupid and often drunk【过时】愚蠢的，常醉酒的 —**sottishness** *n* [U]

sot·to vo·ce /ˌsɑto ˋvotʃɪ; ˌsɒtəʊ ˈvəʊtʃi/ *adv formal* in a very quiet voice, so that other people cannot easily hear【正式】低声地，轻声地: *"No, it was Daniel," she continued, sotto voce.* "不，那是丹尼尔。"她接着低声说道。

sou /su; suː/ *n* [singular] *BrE old-fashioned* a very small amount of money【英，过时】极少量的钱: *He didn't have a sou.* 他一个子儿也没有。

sou·bri·quet /ˋsubrɪˌke; ˈsuːbrɪkeɪ/ *n* [C] another spelling of SOBRIQUET sobriquet的另一种拼法

souf·flé /suˋfle; ˈsuːfleɪ/ *n* [C,U] a baked dish that is very light and is made with egg whites and often cheese or fruit 蛋奶酥

sough /sʌf; sʌf/ *v* [I] *literary* if the wind soughs, it makes a soft sound when passing through trees【文】〔风吹过树时〕发出飒飒声 —**sough** *n* [U]

sought /sɔt; sɔːt/ the past tense and past participle of SEEK

sought-af·ter /ˈ· ,· ·/ *adj* wanted by a lot of people but rare or difficult to get 广受欢迎的，吃香的〔但罕有或难得到〕: **much/highly sought-after** *Bryce became a much sought-after defense lawyer.* 布赖斯成了大为吃香的辩护律师。

souk /suk; suːk/ *n* [C] a market in an Arab country〔阿拉伯国家的〕露天市场

soul /sol; səʊl/ *n* S3 W3 

1 ►SPIRIT 灵魂◄ [C] the SPIRITUAL part of a person that is believed to continue to exist after they die 灵魂: *A prayer was said for the souls of those who had died in the accident.* 为在事故中丧生者的灵魂作了祷告。

2 ►INNER CHARACTER 内心深处◄ [singular] the part of a person that contains their true character, where their deepest thoughts and feelings come from 心灵: *Deep down in her soul she knew she could never marry him.* 她在心灵深处知道自己绝对不会和他结婚。

3 ►PERSON 人◄ [C] a person〔一个〕人: *Betty's a happy soul with a ready smile.* 贝蒂是个快乐的人，脸上常带着笑容。| **not a (living) soul** (=no one) 没有人 *I won't tell a living soul.* 我不会告诉任何人。| **not a soul to be seen** *There wasn't a soul to be seen in the park.* 公园里一个人也没有。| **poor old soul** *The poor old soul had fallen and broken her hip.* 这位可怜的老太太跌了一跤，摔坏了髋部。

4 ►POPULATION 人口◄ souls [plural] *literary* people, considered as the population of a place【文】〔某地的〕人们，人口: *a village with a population of 300 souls* 有300人的一个村子

5 ►SENSE OF BEAUTY 审美观◄ [U] **a)** the ability to be emotionally affected by great art, music, or literature〔对艺术、音乐、文学等的〕审美能力: *My brother doesn't appreciate poetry – he has no soul.* 我的兄弟不会欣赏诗歌，他缺乏审美能力。**b)** the quality of sincere human feelings that makes a painting, piece of music, performance etc attractive 真情实感，热诚，内涵: *Her performance was technically perfect, but it lacked soul.* 她的表演在技巧上无懈可击，但缺乏内涵。

6 ►SPECIAL QUALITY 特质◄ [U] the special quality or part that gives something its true character 精神，精髓: **[+of]** *Basho's poems capture the true soul of old Japan.* 松尾芭蕉的诗歌抓住了古代日本的真正精神。

7 be the soul of discretion etc to always be extremely careful to keep secrets 是谨慎等的化身: *You can trust Leon, he's the very soul of discretion.* 你可以相信利昂，他是个极能严守秘密的人。

8 ►MUSIC 音乐◄ [U] SOUL MUSIC 灵乐

9 bless my soul/upon my soul *old-fashioned spoken* used to express surprise【过时，口】天哪/哎呀〔用于表示惊讶〕

10 be good for the soul *humorous* if something is good for the soul, it is good for you and you should do it, even though it may seem unpleasant【幽默】对人有好处[有益]: *They say that hardship is good for the soul.* 人们说艰难困苦对人有好处。

11 God rest his/her soul used when you mention the name of someone who is dead 愿上帝保佑他/她的灵魂安息〔在提到已故者的名字时说的话〕: *Your Uncle Edward, God rest his soul, loved cricket.* 你的伯父爱德华——愿上帝保佑他的灵魂安息——

喜欢打板球。—see also 另见 **bare your soul** (BARE² (2)), **be the life and soul of the party** (LIFE (32)), **keep body and soul together** (BODY (14)), **heart and soul** (HEART (2)), **sell your soul (to the devil)** (SELL¹ (11)), SOUL MUSIC

soul broth·er /ˈ· ,··/ *n* [C] *AmE informal* an expression meaning a black man, used especially by young black people in the 1960s and 1970s【美, 非正式】黑人兄弟〔尤为20世纪60、70年代黑人青年用语〕

soul-des·troy·ing /ˈ· ·,··/ *adj* something soul-destroying is extremely boring or makes you feel unhappy 极枯燥乏味的; 令人厌烦的: *the soul-destroying monotony of routine jobs* 单调乏味、消磨精神的日常事务

soul food /ˈ· ·/ *n* [U] *AmE* food that is typically cooked and eaten by black people in the Southern US【美】美国南方黑人常吃的食物

soul·ful /ˈsolfəl; ˈsəʊlfəl/ *adj* expressing deep, usually sad emotions 深情的, 〔常指〕伤感的: *a soulful look* 伤感的表情 —**soulfully** *adv* —**soulfulness** *n* [U]

soul·less /ˈsol·lɪs; ˈsəʊl-ləs/ *adj* lacking attractive qualities that make human beings happy 没有灵魂的, 没有生气的, 无情的: *a soulless city of grey concrete and steel* 一座毫无生气的灰色钢筋水泥城市 —**soullessly** *adv* —**soullessness** *n* [U]

soul mate /ˈ· ·/ *n* [C] someone you have a close relationship with because you share the same emotions and interests 知己, 挚友

soul mu·sic /ˈ· ,··/ *n* [U] a type of popular music that often expresses deep emotions, usually performed by black singers and musicians; SOUL (8) 灵乐〔一种通常由黑人演唱和演奏、表达强烈情感的通俗乐曲〕

soul-search·ing /ˈ· ,··/ *n* [U] careful examination of your thoughts and feelings because you are very worried about whether or not it is normally right to do something 深刻反省, 自省: *After much soul-searching, I decided to resign.* 经过一番自我反省之后, 我决定辞职。

soul sis·ter /ˈ· ,··/ *n* [C] *AmE informal* an expression meaning a black woman, used especially by young black people in the 1960s and 1970s【美, 非正式】黑人姊妹〔尤为20世纪60、70年代黑人青年用语〕

1 1 **sound¹** /saund; saʊnd/ *n*

1 ▶SENSATION 感觉◀ [U] something that you hear, or what can be heard 声, 声音: *strange sounds coming from the next room* 从隔壁房间传来的奇怪声音 | **[+of]** *the sound of voices* 谈话的声音 | **not make a sound** (=keep quiet) 别出声 *Don't make a sound, any of you!* 你们谁也别出声! | *Light travels faster than sound.* 光比声音传得快。| *a vowel sound* 母音 —see 见 NOISE¹ (USAGE)

2 ▶TV/RADIO 电视/无线电◀ [U] **a)** the sound produced by a television or radio broadcast, a film etc〔电视、广播、电影等的〕声音; 播音: *We apologize for the loss of sound during that report.* 对于刚才的报道节目声音中断我们很抱歉。| *a sound engineer* 一位音响工程师 **b)** the loudness of a television, radio, film etc〔电视、广播、电影等的〕音量: *Turn the sound down will you?* 请把音量调低一点好吗?

3 by the sound of it/things judging from what you have heard or read about something 听起来; 看来: *By the sound of it, her problems are worse than we thought.* 听起来, 她的问题比我们原来想的要严重。

4 not like the sound of to feel worried by something that you have heard or read 感觉〔某事〕不妙: *I don't like the sound of this. How long has she been missing?* 我感觉这事不妙。她失踪有多久了?

5 sounds [plural] *BrE spoken* music, especially on a record, CASSETTE etc【英口】〔尤指唱片、录音带中的〕音乐: *Have you got any sounds?* 你有什么盒带吗?

1 2 **sound²** *v*

1 ▶SEEM 好像◀ [linking verb 连系动词] if something or someone sounds good, bad, strange etc, that is how they seem to you when you hear or read about them 听起来, 看起来, 好像: **sound like** *Serge's idea sounds like fun.* 瑟奇的想法听起来很有趣。| **sound good/bad/awful etc** *Istanbul sounds really exciting.* 伊斯坦布尔听起来真够刺激的。| *Sue sounds a strange person.* 休这个人好像很怪。| *£50 sounds about right.* 50英镑好像差不多是对的。| **it sounds as if/as though** *It sounds to me as if he needs professional help.* 我觉得他似乎需要专业帮助。

2 ▶VOICE 话音◀ [linking verb 连系动词] to seem to show a particular quality with your voice 听起来: **sound tired/cheerful/awful etc** *Josie didn't sound very keen when I spoke to her.* 我跟乔茜讲话时, 她显得兴趣不大。| **sound as if/as though** *You sound as if you've got a cold.* 你听起来好像感冒了。

3 ▶MAKE A NOISE 发出响声◀ [I,T] if something sounds or if you sound it, it makes a noise 鸣响, (使) 发出响声: *The bell sounded for dinner.* 吃晚饭的铃声响了。| **sound sth** *Sound your horn to warn other drivers.* 按喇叭以提醒其他的司机。

4 sound the alarm to warn people of danger 按响警铃, 拉响警报〔以示有危险〕

5 ▶PRONOUNCE 发音◀ [T usually passive 一般用被动态] *technical* to make the sound of a letter in a word【术语】发音: *The 's' in 'island' is not sounded.* island 中的字母 s 是不发音的。

6 ▶MEASURE DEPTH 测量深度◀ [T] *technical* to measure the depth of the sea, a lake etc【术语】测量〔海、湖等的〕水深 —see also 另见 SOUNDINGS (2)

sound off *phr v* [I] **1** *informal* to express strong opinions about something especially when you are complaining angrily【非正式】大发议论〔表示强烈的不满〕: **sound off about** *Philip's always sounding off about the environment.* 菲利普总是对环境问题大发议论。**2** *AmE* if soldiers sound off they shout out their names to show that they are present【美】报数; 〔士兵〕大声报出姓名〔表示已到〕

sound sb/sth ↔ **out** *phr v* [T] to talk to someone in order to find out what they think about a plan or idea 试探…的意见, 探听…的意图, 探询: *I think I ought to sound him out about it before doing anything.* 我想, 在做任何事之前我都应当听听他的意见。| *We'd like to sound out your ideas on the new project.* 我们希望听听你对这项新计划的想法。

sound³ *adj* 3

1 ▶WELL-JUDGED 判断正确的◀ sensible and likely to produce the right results 明智的, 合理的, 正确的: **sound advice/judgement/reasons** *Ted'll always give you sound advice.* 特德总会给你提出明智的忠告。| *an environmentally sound policy* 有利于环境保护的政策 | *a sound investment* 合理的投资 —opposite 反义词 UNSOUND

2 ▶PERSON 人◀ someone who is sound can be depended on to make good decisions and give good advice 有判断力的, 见地高的: *a sound person to have on a committee* 委员会里需要的一位有见地的委员 | **[+on]** *Brown is not altogether sound on matters of finance.* 布朗在财务问题上并不总是判断正确。—opposite 反义词 UNSOUND

3 ▶THOROUGH 彻底的◀ complete and thorough 完全的, 彻底的: *a sound knowledge of the European market* 对欧洲市场的全面了解

4 ▶IN GOOD CONDITION 状况良好的◀ in good condition and not damaged in any way 完好的, 无损的: *The bodywork's sound but the engine needs replacing.* 汽车车身完好, 但引擎需要更换了。| **sound as a bell** (=in perfect condition) 完美无缺 (的)

5 ▶HEALTHY 健康的◀ physically or mentally healthy〔生理或心理上〕健康的: **sound as a bell** (=in perfect health) 十分健康的 | **of sound mind** *law* (=not mentally ill)【法律】心智健全的 *Dorothy contested the will, saying that Mr. Palmer had not been of sound mind when it was drawn up.* 多萝西对这份遗嘱提出质疑, 说在立遗嘱时帕尔默先生已经神智不健全了。

6 ▶SLEEP 睡觉◀ sound sleep is deep and peaceful 酣的, 深沉的, 平静的: **sound sleeper** (=someone who always sleeps well) 睡得香甜的人, 睡得酣畅的人

7 ▶PUNISHMENT 惩罚◀ severe and thorough 严厉的, 沉重的: *a sound beating* 一顿痛打 —**soundness** *n* [U]

sound⁴ *adv* **sound asleep** deeply asleep 熟睡

Sound and the Fury, The a NOVEL by US writer William Faulkner, which tells the story of the Compsons, a family who were once important in the American Deep South.《喧哗与骚动》〔美国作家威廉·福克纳的小说, 讲述曾在美国南方腹地显赫一时的康普生家族的故事〕

sound bar·ri·er, the /ˈ· ,···/ *n* the sudden increase in the pressure of air against an aircraft when it reaches the speed of sound 声障: **break the sound barrier** (=go faster than the speed of sound) 突破声障〔以超音速飞行〕 *Chuck Yeager flew the first jet to break the sound barrier.* 查克·耶格尔驾驶第一架喷气式飞机突破声障。

sound bite /ˈ· ·/ *n* [C] a very short part of a speech or statement, especially one made by a politician, that is broadcast on radio or television〔尤指广播或电视中政治人物的〕演说[声明]片断

sound check /ˈ· ·/ *n* [C] the process of checking that all the equipment needed for broadcasting or recording is working properly〔广播或录音前对音响设备的〕效果检查, 校音

sound ef·fects /ˈ· ·,·/ *n* [plural] sounds produced artificially for a radio or television broadcast, a film etc〔广播、电视、电影等的〕音响效果

sounding board /ˈ· · ·/ *n* **1** [C] someone you discuss your ideas with in order to try them out 被征询意见的人: **[+for]** *Ivan uses his secretary as a sounding board.* 伊万把秘书当作自己观点的咨询人。**2** [C] a board that is placed behind someone who is speaking to a large group of people so that they can be heard more easily〔置于演讲者后方以增加音响效果的〕增音板，响板

sound·ings /ˈsaundɪŋz; ˈsaʊndɪŋz/ *n* [plural] **1** careful or secret questions that you ask someone to find out what they think about something〔小心或秘密的〕试探，调查: **take soundings** *We're taking soundings to find out how people feel about the changes.* 我们正在调查，以找出人们怎样看待这些变化。**2** measurements you make to find out how deep water is 为测量水深而作的探测

sound·less /ˈsaundlɪs; ˈsaʊndləs/ *adj* without any sound 无声的，寂静的 —**soundlessly** *adv*: *Theo crept soundlessly into the room.* 西奥蹑手蹑脚地走进房间。—**soundlessness** *n* [U]

soundly /ˈsaundlɪ; ˈsaʊndli/ *adv* **1** if you sleep soundly, you sleep deeply and peacefully〔睡觉〕酣畅地，沉沉地: *The baby slept soundly all night.* 宝宝整晚睡得很香甜。**2 soundly beaten/whipped/defeated** completely defeated or severely punished 受到痛打/被彻底击败: *The Green candidate was soundly beaten.* 那位绿党候选人被彻底击败。

Sound of Mu·sic, The /ˌ· · ˈ· ·/ (1965) a very popular US MUSICAL (=a film that uses singing and dancing to tell a story) in which Julie Andrews appears as a NUN who goes to live in the mountains to take care of a large family of children whose mother has died. She teaches them to sing, has a romantic relationship with their father and marries him, and helps them to escape from the Nazis. Many of the songs in the film are very well known, including 'Climb Every Mountain' and the song of the title, which begins "The hills are alive with the sound of music".《音乐之声》〔(1965)，一部深受喜爱的美国音乐片。朱莉·安德鲁斯在影片中饰演一名修女。山中有一户人家，母亲去世了，留下一大群孩子。她帮助照顾孩子，教他们唱歌，后来与他们的父亲相恋成婚，并帮助全家逃脱了纳粹的魔掌。影片中的许多歌曲家喻户晓，如《攀山越岭》和片名曲，第一句歌词为"群山荡起音乐之声"〕

sound·proof[1] /ˈsaundˌpruf; ˈsaʊndpruːf/ *adj* a soundproof wall, room etc is one that sound cannot pass through or into 隔音的

soundproof[2] *v* [T] to make something soundproof 使隔音

sound sys·tem /ˈ· ˌ· ·/ *n* [C] a very large STEREO system, especially one that includes the equipment a band needs to control its sound at a performance 音响系统〔尤指乐队演出用的大型立体声音响设备〕

sound·track /ˈsaundˌtræk; ˈsaʊndtræk/ *n* [C] **1** the recorded music from a film 电影配乐 **2** the band near the edge of a piece of film where the sound is recorded〔电影胶片边上的〕声带，声迹

sound wave /ˈ· ·/ *n* [C] the form that sound takes when it travels 声波

3 **soup**[1] /sup; suːp/ *n* **1** liquid cooked food often containing small pieces of meat, fish, or vegetables 汤: *chicken noodle soup* 鸡汤面条 **2 be in the soup** *informal* to be in trouble【非正式】陷入困境: *If Dad catches you you'll be in the soup.* 要是被爸爸抓住，你就麻烦大了。

soup[2] *v*

soup sth ↔ up *phr v* [T] *informal* to improve something by making it bigger, more attractive, or more exciting【非正式】〔使增大、更有吸引力、更刺激〕以改善〔某物〕: *software programs to soup up the office E-mail* 能改进办公室电子邮件（系统）的软件程序

soup·çon /supˋsɔn; ˈsuːpsɒn/ *n* [singular] *French, formal or humorous* a small amount of something【法，正式或幽默】少量，一点点: *It needs a soupçon more salt.* 需要再加一点点盐。

souped-up /ˌ· ˈ·◂/ *adj* a souped-up car has been made more powerful, especially by adding special parts to the engine〔指汽车尤因引擎增加了特殊零件〕增大了马力的: *a souped-up Mustang* 加大了马力的野马牌汽车

soup kitch·en /ˈ· ˌ· ·/ *n* [C] a place where people with no money and no homes can get free food〔救济穷人的〕施粥所，施食处

soup spoon /ˈ· ·/ *n* [C] a round spoon that is used for eating soup 汤匙 —see picture at 参见 SPOON[1] 图

sour[1] /saur; saʊə/ *adj* **1** having a sharp acid taste that stings your tongue, like the taste of a LEMON 酸的，酸味的: *sour, tangy apples* 味道浓烈的酸苹果 | *Sprinkle a little sugar over the strawberries if they are sour.* 草莓如果酸，就撒上一点糖吧。—compare 比较 BITTER[1] (4), SWEET[1] (1) **2** milk or other food that is sour is not fresh and has an unpleasant taste because it has fermented (FERMENT[1]) 馊（味）的，酸臭的〔牛奶等发酵后的味道〕: **turn/go sour** (=become sour) 变酸 *In warm weather, milk can go sour in just a few hours.* 在热天，牛奶只要几小时就变酸了。**3** unfriendly or looking bad-tempered 不友善的，脾气坏的: *Rob gave me a sour look.* 罗布狠狠地瞪了我一眼。| **sour-faced** *a sour-faced old man* 绷着脸的老人 **4 sour grapes** the attitude of someone who pretends to dislike something that they really want, because they cannot have it 酸葡萄〔指某人其实想要某物，但因得不到而装作不喜欢聊以自慰的心态〕 **5 turn/go sour** *informal* if a relationship or plan turns or goes sour, it becomes less enjoyable, pleasant, or satisfactory【非正式】〔关系、计划等〕变坏，变得令人不快[不满意]: *As time went by their marriage turned sour.* 随着时间的推移，他们的婚姻关系变坏了。—**sourly** *adv* —**sourness** *n* [U]

sour[2] *v* [I,T] **1** if a relationship or someone's attitude sours, or if something sours it, it becomes unfriendly or unfavourable（使）〔关系、态度等〕变坏，变得不友善: *An unhappy childhood has soured her view of life.* 不幸的童年扭曲了她的人生观。**2** if milk sours or something sours it, it begins to have an unpleasant sharp taste（使）〔牛奶〕变酸，变馊

source[1] /sɔrs; sɔːs/ *n* [C] **1** a thing, place, activity etc that you get something from 来源，出处: *They get their money from various sources.* 他们从各种来源得到钱。| **[+of]** *Milk is a very good source of calcium.* 牛奶含有丰富的钙。| *For me, music is a great source of enjoyment.* 对我来说，音乐是乐趣的重大源泉。| **at source** *Is your pension taxed at source?* (=before it is paid to you) 你的养老金是不是在领取时就扣除了税金？**2** the cause of something, especially a problem, or the place where it starts〔问题等的〕原因，根源: **[+of]** *We've found the source of the trouble – a faulty connection.* 我们已找出故障的原因 —— 接触不好。| *Two players have the same name, which has been the source of some confusion.* 两位球员名字相同，这就是为什么会搞错。**3** a person, book, or document that supplies you with information 提供消息者；资料来源: *List all your sources at the end of the essay.* 请在文章末尾列出你所有资料的来源。| **reliable sources** *I've heard from reliable sources that the company is in trouble.* 我从可靠消息来源那里获悉，那家公司遇上了麻烦。**4** the place where a stream or river starts 溪流的发源地，水源 2 1

source[2] *v* [T] to find out where something can be obtained from 找出…的来源；找…的货源

source code /ˈ· ·/ *n* [U] *technical* a computer PROGRAM[1] that can be read by someone who knows the language it is written in【术语】〔电脑程序的〕源（代）码 —compare 比较 MACHINE CODE

sour cream /ˌ· ˈ·/ also 又作 **soured cream** *BrE*【英】*n* [U] cream which has been made sour by adding a kind of BACTERIA〔加细菌发酵致酸的〕酸奶油

sour·dough /ˈsaurˌdo; ˈsaʊədəʊ/ *n* [U] *AmE* uncooked DOUGH (=bread mixture) that is left to FERMENT[1] before being used to make bread【美】面肥，酵头: *sourdough bread* 用面肥发的面包

sour·puss /ˈsaurˌpʊs; ˈsaʊəpʊs/ *n* [C] *humorous* a BAD-TEMPERED person, who always complains and is never satisfied【幽默】脾气坏的人，满腹牢骚的人

Sou·sa /ˈsuzə; ˈsuːzə/, **John Philip** (1854-1932) a US COMPOSER and BAND leader, who wrote many famous MARCHes (=music for soldiers to walk to), including *The Stars and Stripes Forever* 苏萨〔(1854-1932)，美国作曲家、乐队领队。曾创作《星条旗永不落》等多部著名进行曲〕

sou·sa·phone /ˈsuzəˌfon; ˈsuːzəfəʊn/ *n* [C] a very large musical instrument made of metal, which you blow into, used especially in marching bands〔游行乐队用的〕大号，低音大喇叭

souse /saus; saʊs/ *v* [T] to put something in water or pour water over something, making it completely wet 把…浸入水中；倒水于…上；使湿透

soused /saust; saʊst/ *adj* **1** soused fish has been preserved in water, salt, and VINEGAR〔鱼〕腌渍的: *soused herrings* 腌鲱鱼 **2** *informal* drunk【非正式】喝醉酒的: *He was so soused he couldn't even write his name.* 他喝得烂醉，连自己的名字也写不了。

south[1], **South** /sauθ; saʊθ/ written abbreviation 缩写为 **S** *n* [singular,U] **1** the direction that is at the bottom of a map of the world, below the EQUATOR, and is on the right of someone facing the rising sun 南，南方，南面: *I'm lost; which direction is South?* 我迷失方向了，哪个方向是南？| **from/towards the south** *winds blowing from the south* 从南面吹来的风 | **to the south (of)** *Gatwick airport is a few miles to the south of London.* 盖特威克机场在伦敦以南数英里处。| **in the south** *A strange star appeared in the south.* 一颗奇怪的星星出现在南方。**2 the south** the southern part of a country〔一国的〕南部: *There'll be show-* 1 2

ers in the south tomorrow. 明天南部将有阵雨。| *the South of France* 法国南部 **3 the South** the southern states of the US 美国南部各州: *the cotton fields of the South* 美国南部各州的棉田

south² *adj* [only before noun 仅用于名词前] **1** in the south or facing the south 在南方的; 向南的: *The south side of the building gets a lot of sun.* 建筑物向南的那面阳光充足。| *South America* 南美洲 **2** a south wind comes from the south〔风〕来自南方的

south³ *adv* **1** towards the south 向南: *The swallows fly south in the winter.* 冬季燕子向南飞。| *The garden faces south so it gets a lot of sun.* 花园朝南, 所以阳光充足。**2 down south** *BrE informal* in or to the southern part of England【英, 非正式】在〔英格兰的〕南部, 向〔英格兰的〕南部: *We moved down south about five years ago.* 我们大约五年前迁居英格兰南部。**3 go south** *AmE informal* if a situation, organization, or set of standards goes south, it becomes very bad although it was once very good【美, 非正式】变坏; 下跌, 下降: *Seems like all our moral standards have just gone south.* 我们的道德准则好像都已下降。

South, the 1 the southeastern states of the US, used especially when talking about politics or history. When people in the US talk about the South, they mean the states that were originally part of the Confederacy during the Civil War. The economy of these states was based on SLAVERY, and after slavery was officially ended in 1863, most Southern states made laws that were unfair to black people or separated them from white people. Today, people think of the South as a place where people are more CONSERVATIVE (=not wanting changes) than in other parts of the US. 美国南方〔尤其在谈及美国政治或历史话题时使用。美国人多用南方一词指称内战时期的南部邦联诸州。这些州的经济基础是奴隶制, 1863年奴隶制正式废除后, 南方各州大多制定了歧视黑人的法律, 或对黑人实行种族隔离。现在, 人们认为南方人比其他地区居民更为保守。〕—see 见 DEEP SOUTH

CULTURAL NOTE 文化注释

When people in the US talk about the South, they mean the states that were originally part of the Confederacy during the American Civil War. The economy of these states depended on SLAVERY, and after slavery was officially ended in 1863, most Southern states made laws that were unfair to African-American people or separated them from white Americans. During the Civil Rights movement of the 1950s and 1960s, when African Americans demanded equal rights as citizens, many white people in the South refused to accept changes. There was also a lot of violence against African Americans, especially by members of the KU KLUX KLAN. Now, while there is still RACISM in many parts of the US, including the South, the situation is not as bad and the Ku Klux Klan is not as active. 美国人谈起南方时, 他们指的是美国内战时期属于南部邦联的那些州。这些州的经济依赖奴隶制, 而在1863年奴隶制正式废除之后, 南部的大多数州制定了一些对黑人很不公平的法律或者将他们与白人隔离开来。20世纪50、60年代的民权运动中, 黑人要求给予平等的公民权, 南部的白人依然拒绝变革。有很多针对黑人的暴力行为, 尤以三K党的行为为甚。现在尽管在包括南部在内的美国多个地区仍存在种族主义, 情况还是比过去好了很多, 三K党也不像以前那么猖獗了。

Attitudes Today the South is thought of as a place where people are more CONSERVATIVE (=not wanting to change) than in other parts of the US, and Southerners are generally considered to have more traditional ideas about the family, sex, and religion. People from the South are also known for their polite manners and for their 'Southern HOSPITALITY', because Southerners are generally considered to be very generous towards their guests, especially by feeding them good food made at home. 态度: 当今美国南部的居民被认为比美国其他地方的人更为保守, 并且他们对待家庭、性和宗教的观念也更加传统。南方人还以彬彬有礼和"南方式的好客"而广为人知, 因为一般认为南方人对待客人很大方, 特别是宴请他们到家中吃一顿丰盛的饭菜。

Religion The South is sometimes called the Bible Belt, meaning that there are many FUNDAMENTALIST Christian churches there, whose members believe that everything in the Bible is exactly true. There are also many BAPTISTS and ROMAN CATHOLICS in the South. 宗教: 南部有时被称为"圣经地带", 意思是那里有很多基要派教会, 教徒相信《圣经》所载的一切都千真万确。南部还有很多浸礼会教友和天主教教徒。

Way of Speaking People who live in the South tend to speak slowly with long vowel sounds and a strong ACCENT known as a Southern DRAWL. 说话方式: 南方人说话一般语速较慢, 元音拉得很长, 还带有"南方拖腔"的浓重口音。— see Cultural Note at DEEP SOUTH 见 DEEP SOUTH 文化注释

2 the southern part of England. The South of England, especially the area around London is generally considered to be richer than the rest of the UK, and a more expensive place to live. 英格兰南部〔人们一般认为, 英格兰南部, 尤其是伦敦周边地区比英国其他地区更为富裕, 生活费用也更高〕。

CULTURAL NOTE 文化注释

The South of England, especially London and the area around London, is generally considered to be richer than the rest of the UK, and a more expensive place to live. People from other parts of the country often think that people from the South are unfriendly and only interested in work and money. They also think that people in London are not interested in what is happening in the rest of the UK. Some people in the South joke that anywhere 'north of Watford' (=a town at the northern edge of London) is like a foreign country. 英格兰南部, 特别是伦敦及其周边地区, 一般被认为比英国的其他地方要富裕, 生活成本也相对高昂。在其他地方的人眼里, 南部人不够友好, 只知道工作和挣钱。他们还认为, 伦敦人对英国其他地方发生了什么没有一点兴趣。有些南部的人开玩笑说, "(伦敦北部边缘一小镇) 沃特福德以北"的任何地方就像是另一个国度。— see also 另见 HOME COUNTIES

3 the poorer countries of the southern parts of the world, including most of Africa, parts of Central and South America, and parts of southern Asia 南半球贫穷国家〔包括非洲大部分地区、中南美洲部分地区和南亚部分地区〕

South Af·ri·ca /ˌ· ˈ···/ also 又作 **the Republic of South Africa** a country in southern Africa south of Namibia, Botswana, and Zimbabwe. Population: 43,586,000 (2001). Capitals: Pretoria, Cape Town and Bloemfontein. Largest city: Johannesburg. Until the 1990s, the country was ruled by an all-white government using the system of APARTHEID, which separated people of different races and gave no political rights to black people. In 1994 the African National Congress (ANC), led by Nelson Mandela, won South Africa's first fully democratic election and became the government. South Africa's best-known products are gold and DIAMONDS. 南非〔非洲南部一国家。位于纳米比亚、博茨瓦纳、津巴布韦以南。人口: 43,586,000 (2001), 首都: 比勒陀利亚、开普敦和布隆方丹, 最大城市: 约翰内斯堡。1990年以前, 该国一直由清一色白人组成的政府统治, 实行种族隔离政策, 将不同种族的人分隔开来, 同时剥夺黑人的政治权利。1994年, 纳尔逊·曼德拉领导的非洲人国民大会在首次完全民主化的大选中获胜并成为执政党。该国以出产黄金和钻石著称〕

South·all /ˈsaʊθɔl; ˈsaʊθɔːl/ an area of West London close to Heathrow Airport, which has a large population of people whose families originally came from India and Pakistan. 绍索尔〔西伦敦靠近希思罗机场的一个区域, 居住着为数不少的印度和巴基斯坦移民的后裔〕

South A·mer·i·ca /ˌ· ·ˈ···/ the fourth-largest CONTINENT in the world, between the Atlantic and Pacific Oceans, which goes from the southern coast of the Caribbean Sea (in the north) to Tierra del Fuego (in the south). It includes the Andes Mountains, the Amazon River, and large areas of tropical RAINFOREST, as well as many large cities. Its largest country is Brazil. The main language in Brazil is Portuguese, but in all the other countries of South America, the main language is Spanish. 南美洲〔世界第四大洲, 位于大西洋和太平洋之间。北起加勒比海南岸, 南至火地岛, 包括安第斯山脉、亚马孙河和大片热带雨林, 同时拥有许多大型城市。南美洲面积最大的国家是巴西, 主要语言为葡萄牙语, 但南美其他各国主要使用西班牙语〕—**South American** *n, adj* —see also 另见 LATIN AMERICA

South·amp·ton /saʊθˈhæmptn̩; saʊθˈhæmptən/ a city on the English Channel coast in the south of England. It is an important port for both passengers and goods. 南安普敦〔英格兰南部英吉利海峡沿岸一城市, 是重要的客货两运港口〕

South Aus·tra·li·a /ˌ· ·ˈ···/ a state in central South Australia whose capital is Adelaide 南澳大利亚州〔澳大利亚中南部一州, 首府为阿德莱德〕

South Bank, the /ˈ· ˌ ·/ an important cultural centre on the south bank of the River Thames in London. The National Theatre, the National Film Theatre, the Royal Festival Hall, the Museum of the Moving Image, and the Hayward Gallery are all there. 南岸艺术中心〔伦敦市泰晤士河南岸一处重要的文化中心，建有国家剧院、国家电影院、皇家节庆厅、动态影像博物馆、海沃德美术馆等〕

south·bound /ˈsauθˌbaund; ˈsaʊθbaʊnd/ *adj* travelling or leading towards the south 向南行的: *southbound traffic* 南行的车辆

South Car·o·li·na /ˌsauθ kærəˈlaɪnə; ˌsaʊθ kærəˈlaɪnə/ abbreviation 缩写为 SC a state in the southeast US, between North Carolina and Georgia and with a border on the Atlantic Ocean. It was one of the 13 original states, and its capital and largest city is Columbia. In 1860, South Carolina was the first of the southern states to formally announce that it was leaving the Union, and this led to the US Civil War. Its products include tobacco, wood, paper, and TEXTILEs. 南卡罗莱纳州〔美国东南部一州。位于北卡罗莱纳州和佐治亚州之间，濒临大西洋，美国最早的13个州之一。哥伦比亚市为其首府和最大城市。1860年，南卡罗莱纳州成为南方正式宣布脱离联邦的第一个州，从而引发了美国内战。该州出产烟草、木材、纸张和纺织品等〕

South Chi·na Mor·ning Post, the /ˌ· ˌ· ·, ˌ· · ˈ· ·/ abbreviation 缩写为 SCMP a newspaper written in English in Hong Kong《南华早报》〔香港编印的一种英文报纸〕

South Da·ko·ta /ˌsauθ dəˈkotə; ˌsaʊθ dəˈkəʊtə/ abbreviation 缩写为 SD a state in the northern part of the central US, north of Nebraska and south of North Dakota. Its largest city is Sioux Falls. Its main industry is farming, and it produces a lot of meat and grain. 南达科他州〔美国中北部一州。位于内布拉斯加州以北，北达科他州以南。最大城市是苏福尔斯。该州以农业为主，盛产肉类和谷物〕

S

South Downs, the /ˌ· ˈ·/ a range of hills in the south of England, mostly in Sussex, where there are many sheep farms 南部丘陵〔大部分位于英格兰的萨塞克斯郡境内，当地有许多牧羊场〕

south·east[1] /ˌsauθˈist; ˌsaʊθˈiːst◂/ *n* [U] **1** the direction that is exactly between south and east 东南，东南方 **2 the southeast** the southeastern part of a country 〔一国的〕东南部 —southeast *adv*: *The road runs southeast.* 这条路通往东南方向。

southeast[2] *adj* [only before noun 仅用于名词前] **1** a southeast wind comes from the southeast 〔风〕来自东南方的 **2** in the southeast of a place 〔一地区的〕东南部的: *the southeast quarter of the city* 该市的东南部分

South East, the /ˌ· ˈ·/ **1** the southeastern part of England, including London, which has a high population and many industries and businesses 东南部〔包括伦敦在内的英格兰东南部地区。该地区人口稠密，工商业集中〕 **2** the southeastern part of the US, including the states of Alabama, Georgia, Florida, and South Carolina 东南部〔包括亚拉巴马州、佐治亚州、佛罗里达州和南卡罗莱纳州在内的美国东南部地区〕

Southeast A·sia /ˌ· ˌ· ˈ· ·/ the countries of Asia between India and Bangladesh in the West, and China and the Pacific Ocean in the East. Southeast Asia includes the following countries: Brunei, Cambodia, Indonesia, Laos, Malaysia, Myanmar (Burma), the Philippines, Singapore, Thailand, and Vietnam. 东南亚〔指位于印度、孟加拉国以东，中国和太平洋以西的亚洲国家。包括：文莱、柬埔寨、印度尼西亚、老挝、马来西亚、缅甸、菲律宾、新加坡、泰国和越南〕

south·east·er /ˌsauθˈistə; ˌsaʊθˈiːstə/ *n* [C] a strong wind or storm coming from the southeast 东南强风[风暴]

south·east·er·ly /ˌsauθˈistəlɪ; ˌsaʊθˈiːstəli/ *adj* **1** towards or in the southeast 向东南的；在东南的: *Snow will spread to southeasterly regions tonight.* 今晚降雪将蔓延到东南地区。 **2** a southeasterly wind comes from the southeast 〔风〕来自东南方的

south·east·ern /ˌsauθˈistən; ˌsaʊθˈiːstən/ *adj* in or from the southeast part of a country 位于[来自]〔一国〕东南部的

south·east·ward /ˌsauθˈistwəd; ˌsaʊθˈiːstwəd/ *adj* going towards the southeast 向东南方行进的: *in a southeastward direction* 朝东南的方向 —**southeastwards, southeastward** *adv*

South·end on Sea /ˌsauθɛnd ˌɑn ˈsi; ˌsaʊθend ˌɒn ˈsiː/ a town on the southeast coast of England, near London, which is a popular place for people from London, especially WORKING-CLASS people, to go for the day or for their holidays 滨海绍森德〔英格兰东南沿海一城镇，位于伦敦附近。是伦敦市民，尤其是伦敦工薪阶层休闲度假的好去处〕

south·er·ly /ˈsʌðəlɪ; ˈsʌðəli/ *adj* **1** in the south or towards the south 在南方的；向南的: *Tara walked in a southerly direction.* 塔拉朝南走去。 **2** a southerly wind comes from the south 〔风〕来自南方的

south·ern /ˈsʌðən; ˈsʌðən/ *adj* in or from the south part of the world or of a country 位于[来自]〔世界或一国之〕南方的: *southern Italy* 意大利南部 | *the southern hemisphere* 南半球 | *a strong southern accent* 浓重的南方口音 S2 W2

Southern Alps, the /ˌ· · ˈ·/ the mountain ranges on the South Island of New Zealand. Their highest point is Mount Cook, which is the highest point in New Zealand. 南阿尔卑斯山〔新西兰南岛一山脉。库克峰为其最高峰，也是新西兰海拔最高的地方〕

Southern Bap·tist /ˌ· · ˈ· ·/ a member of a Baptist religious group that was established in the Southern US in 1845. Southern Baptists often have FUNDAMENTALIST Christian beliefs, and they believe that everything in the Bible is exactly true. 南方浸礼联会教徒〔南方浸礼联会是1845年在美国南部成立的一个宗教团体。其教徒往往信仰基督教原教旨主义，认为《圣经》字字皆真言〕

Southern Com·fort /ˌ· · ˈ· ·/ *trademark* a type of strong, sweet alcoholic drink which is made in the American South【商标】金馥酒，南方安逸酒〔产于美国南方的一种烈性甜酒〕

South·ern·er /ˈsʌðənə; ˈsʌðənə/ *n* [C] someone who lives in or comes from the southern part of a country 〔一国的〕居住在南方的人，南方人

Southern Ire·land /ˌ· · ˈ· ·/ another name of the Republic of Ireland 南爱尔兰〔爱尔兰共和国的别称〕

Southern Lights, the /ˌ· · ˈ·/ *n* [plural] bands of coloured light in the night sky, seen in the most southern parts of the world 南极极光〔夜空中出现的彩色光带，见于地球最南端〕— see also 另见 NORTHERN LIGHTS

south·ern·most /ˈsʌðənˌmost; ˈsʌðənməʊst/ *adj* furthest south 极南的，最南端的: *the southernmost tip of the island* 海岛的最南端

Southern States, the *informal* the states of the southeastern US, especially the states that fought against the North in the US Civil War【非正式】南方诸州〔美国东南部诸州，尤指内战期间与北方作战的南方各州〕

Sou·they, Rob·ert /ˈsauðɪ, ˈrɑbət; ˈsaʊði, ˈrɒbət/ (1774-1843) a British writer and poet who became POET LAUREATE in 1813. His best-known works are his book *Life of Nelson* and short poems such as *The Battle of Blenheim*. 骚塞（1774-1843），英国作家、诗人。1813年成为桂冠诗人。代表作有《纳尔逊传》、短诗《布莱尼姆之战》等〕

South Geor·gia /ˌ· ˈ· ·/ an island in the South Atlantic, East of Cape Horn, which is under British control. Nobody lives there except British soldiers and a few scientists. Both the UK and Argentina think the island should belong to them. 南乔治亚岛〔南大西洋一岛屿。位于合恩角以东，目前属英国管辖。除英国军人和少数科学家外，岛上无其他居民。英国和阿根廷各自都认为对该岛享有主权〕

South Gla·mor·gan /ˌsauθ gləˈmɔrgən; ˌsaʊθ gləˈmɔːgən/ a former COUNTY in South Wales, now divided into the new county of Cardiff and the new county BOROUGH of Vale of Glamorgan 南格拉摩根〔曾为南威尔士一郡。重新划分后并入加的夫郡和郡级行政自治区格拉摩根谷〕

South Is·land /ˈ· ˌ· ·/ one of the two main islands of New Zealand, whose main towns are Christchurch and Dunedin. It is important for sheep farming and the growing of wheat. 南岛〔新西兰两大主岛之一。其主要城镇有克赖斯特彻奇和达尼丁。该岛是养羊业和种植小麦的重要地区〕

South Ken·sing·ton /ˌ· ˈ· · ·/ an area of southwest central London, informally called 'South Ken', where there are several large and important MUSEUMs, including the Science Museum, the Natural History Museum, and the Victoria and Albert Museum. It is also a fashionable and expensive place to live. 南肯辛顿〔伦敦市中心西南部一区域，俗称 South Ken。这里坐落着多家重要的大型博物馆，包括科学博物馆、自然历史博物馆、维多利亚和阿尔伯特博物馆等。南肯辛顿还是一个时尚豪华的住宅区〕

South Ko·re·a /ˌ· ˈ· ·/ a country in East Asia, officially called the Republic of Korea. Population: 47,904,000 (2001). Capital: Seoul. 韩国〔东亚一国家。正式名称：大韩民国，人口：47,904,000（2001），首都：首尔〕—see also 另见 KOREA, NORTH KOREA

South of France, the /ˌ· · ˈ·/ the part of France along the coast of the Mediterranean Sea, from Marseilles to the French border with Monaco. It is also called the 'Riviera' and it includes the Côte d'Azur. 南法，法国南部〔指法国地中海沿岸地区，自马赛延伸至法国－摩纳哥边境，包括蓝色海岸在内，又称"里维埃拉"〕

CULTURAL NOTE 文化注释

The South of France is a popular place for British people to go on holiday. In the past only very rich people went there, and many fashionable, rich, and famous people still go to places like Cannes, Nice, and St Tropez. 法国南部是受英国人欢迎的度假胜地。过去只有十分有钱的人才去那儿，现在仍有很多时尚人士、富人和名人去戛纳、尼斯和圣特罗佩度假。

South Pa·cif·ic /,· ·'· ·/ a very popular US musical play, written in 1949 by Richard Rodgers and Oscar Hammerstein, which was later made into a film《南太平洋》〔一部备受青睐的美国音乐剧。由理查德·罗杰斯和奥斯卡·哈默斯坦因于 1949 年共同创作，后来被搬上银幕〕

south·paw /ˈsauθ,pɔ; ˈsaʊθpɔː/ *n* [C] someone who uses their left hand more than their right hand, especially a PITCHER (3) in BASEBALL or a BOXER 左撇子；左撇子棒球投手[拳击手]

South Pole, the /,· ·'·/ *n* the most southern point on the Earth's surface, and the land around it 南极（地带） —see also 另见 MAGNETIC POLE, NORTH POLE —see picture at 参见 EARTH[1] 图

South Sea Bub·ble, the /,· · ·'· ·/ a serious financial problem in the UK in 1720, which led to many people losing all their money. The South Sea company made large profits by trading with South America, and this encouraged many people to invest their money in it (=lend the company money, in the hope of making more money). But the company was very dishonestly run, and in the end it failed and the money people had invested became worthless. 南海泡沫事件〔1720 年英国一场严重的金融风波，令许多人血本无归。南海公司曾与南美开展贸易，赚取了巨额利润，从而吸引大量股民投资。但该公司经营极度缺乏诚信，最终倒闭，使人们的投资变得一文不值〕

South Seas, the /,· '·/ *old use* or *literary* the southern Pacific Ocean, especially when people think of it as a place of white sand beaches, PALM trees, and beautiful girls who wear grass skirts【旧或文】南太平洋〔该词常让人联想起白色的沙滩、棕榈树和身穿草裙的美貌女郎〕 —**South Sea** /'· ·/ *adj* [only before noun 仅用于名词前]: *a beautiful South Sea island* 一座美丽的南太平洋岛屿

South Wales /,· '·/ the southern part of Wales, which formerly contained many coal mines, but now has a lot of modern industries. People from South Wales are sometimes called 'South Wallians'. 南威尔士〔威尔士南部。以前曾开办大批煤矿，如今已有了多处现代产业。南威尔士人有时叫做 South Wallians〕 —see also 另见 NEW SOUTH WALES

south·ward /ˈsauθwɚd; ˈsaʊθwəd/ *adj* going towards the south 往南行的: *the southward journey* 去南方的旅程

south·wards /ˈsauθwɚdz; ˈsaʊθwədz/ also 又作 **southward** *adv* towards the south 向南方: *The ship sailed southwards.* 这艘船向南航行。

South·wark /ˈsʌðɚk; ˈsʌðək/ a BOROUGH of London, south of the River Thames, which has a very old CATHEDRAL (=a large impressive church). The Globe Theatre, where Shakespeare's plays were first performed, is in Southwark. 萨瑟克〔伦敦一行政区，位于泰晤士河南岸。拥有一座非常古老的大教堂，也坐落着最早上演莎士比亚戏剧的环球剧院〕

south·west[1] /,sauθˈwɛst; ,saʊθˈwest◂/ *n* [U] **1** the direction that is exactly between south and west 西南，西南方 **2 the southwest** the southwestern part of a country 〔一国的〕西南部 —**southwest** *adv*: *We headed southwest.* 我们向西南进发。

CULTURAL NOTE 文化注释

The southwest of the US is known for its style of buildings, decorations, and cooking, which are all influenced by Native American and Mexican styles. Typical examples of these styles are ADOBE buildings, and patterns done in brown, dark orange, and TURQUOISE (=green mixed with blue), which are based on traditional Native American and Mexican designs. It is also known for the desert and for its large cacti (CACTUS). 美国西南部以其建筑、装饰和厨艺风格著称，而这些深受美国原住民和墨西哥风格的影响。最典型的是砖建筑，以及褐色、深橙色和青绿色的图案设计，这些都取材于传统的美国原住民和墨西哥的设计风格。美国西南部还以沙漠及高大的仙人掌而广为人知。

southwest[2] *adj* [only before noun 仅用于名词前] **1** a southwest wind comes from the southwest 〔风〕来自西南方的 **2** in the southwest of a place 〔一地的〕西南部: *down in the southwest corner of France* 在法国西南隅

south·west·er /,sauθˈwɛstɚ; ,saʊθˈwestə/ also 又作 **sou'wester** *n* [C] a strong wind or storm from the southwest 西南强风[风暴]

south·west·er·ly /,sauθˈwɛstɚlɪ; ,saʊθˈwestəli/ *adj* **1** towards or in the southwest 向西南的，在西南方向的 **2** a southwesterly wind comes from the southwest 〔风〕来自西南方的

south·west·ern /,sauθˈwɛstɚn; ,saʊθˈwestən/ *adj* in or from the southwest part of a country 住在[来自]〔一国〕西南部的

south·west·ward /,sauθˈwɛstwɚd; ,saʊθˈwestwəd/ *adj* going towards the southwest 往西南行进的: *in a southwestward direction* 朝西南方向 —**southwestwards, southwestward** *adv*

South York·shire /,· '· ·/ a COUNTY in the north of England, whose largest city is Sheffield 南约克郡〔英格兰北部一郡。最大城市为设菲尔德〕

sou·ve·nir /,suvəˈnɪr; ,suːvəˈnɪə/ *n* [C] an object that you keep to remind yourself of a special occasion or a place you have visited 纪念品，纪念物: [+of] *I bought a model of the Eiffel Tower as a souvenir of Paris.* 我买了一个埃菲尔铁塔模型作为去过巴黎的纪念品。| *a souvenir shop* 纪念品商店 | *a souvenir programme from the Gala Concert* 庆典音乐会的纪念节目单

sou'west·er /,sauˈwɛstɚ; saʊˈwestə/ *n* [C] **1** a hat made of shiny material that keeps the rain off, with a wide piece at the back that covers your neck 〔后沿宽至颈后的〕防水帽 **2** a SOUTHWESTER 西南强风[风暴]

sove·reign[1] /ˈsɑvrɪn; ˈsɒvrn̩/ *n* [C] **1** *formal* a king or queen【正式】国王；女王；君主 **2** a former British gold coin worth £1 〔从前英国的〕一英镑金币

sovereign[2] *adj* **1** having the highest power in a country 〔国家内〕权力至高无上的: *Most European monarchs no longer have sovereign control.* 大多数欧洲君主不再拥有至高无上的控制权了。**2** a sovereign country or state is independent and governs itself 〔国家〕独立自主的，具有独立主权的: *The UN was designed as an association of sovereign states.* 联合国是作为主权国家的联盟而成立的。**3 sovereign remedy** *old-fashioned* an excellent way of curing all kinds of illnesses and problems【过时】万能药，灵丹妙药

sove·reign·ty /ˈsɑvrɪntɪ; ˈsɒvrn̩ti/ *n* [U] **1** complete freedom and power to govern 至高无上的权威: *the sovereignty of Parliament* 议会至高无上的权威 **2** the power that an independent country has to govern itself 国家的主权，国家的独立自主

So·vi·et /ˈsovɪət; ˈsəʊviət/ *adj* from or connected with the former USSR (Soviet Union) or its people （前）苏联的；（前）苏联人民的

soviet *n* [C] an elected council in a Communist country 苏维埃〔共产党领导的国家中通过选举产生的委员会〕

Soviet bloc, the /,· · · '·/ a name for the former Soviet Union, together with the countries of Eastern Europe which it partly controlled, and other Communist countries that supported it, such as North Korea, Vietnam, and Cuba 苏联阵营〔指前苏联和部分受其控制的东欧国家以及朝鲜、越南、古巴等其他一些支持它的共产党执政国家〕

Soviet U·nion, the /,· · · '· ·/ a country in Europe and Asia between 1917 and 1991, whose full name was the Union of Soviet Socialist Republics (the USSR). The Soviet Union was the largest country in the world and was made up of 15 REPUBLICS (=separate nations), the most important of which was Russia. It was formed after the Russian Revolution in 1917 as a Communist state, led by Lenin. It was one of the most powerful countries in the world, and many people regarded it as the enemy of the US and western Europe during the Cold War. In the 1990s the Soviet Union began to break up as many of the republics made themselves independent. 苏联〔全称为"苏维埃社会主义共和国联盟"（简称 USSR），1917 年成立，1991 年解体。地跨欧亚两洲，是当时世界上面积最大的国家，由以俄罗斯为主的 15 个加盟共和国组成。1917 年俄国革命后成立，为列宁领导的共产党执政国家。苏联是当时世界上最强大的国家之一，冷战期间被视为美国和西欧各国的敌国。20 世纪 90 年代，许多加盟共和国纷纷宣布独立，苏联解体〕

sow[1] /so; səʊ/ *past tense* **sowed** *past participle* **sown** /son; səʊn/ *or* **sowed** *v* **1** [I,T] to plant or scatter seeds on a piece of ground 播（种）: *Sow the seeds in late March.* 三月底播这些种子。| **sow sth with sth** *We're sowing the field with grass.* 我们正在这块地里种草。**2 sow the seeds of** to do something that will cause a bad situation in the future 播下〔导致坏情况的〕种子，造成〔问题〕的根源: *repressive policies that are sowing the seeds of future conflicts* 正在播下未来冲突的种子的高压政策 —**sower** *n* [C]

sow² /saʊ; saʊ/ *n* [C] a fully grown female pig〔已成熟的〕母猪 —opposite 反义词 BOAR

So·wet·o /sə`wɛto; sə'wetəʊ/ a large TOWNSHIP that was established near Johannesburg in South Africa for black people to live in, because they were not allowed to live in Johannesburg under the old system of APARTHEID, although they were allowed to work there. In 1976 a student protest against the use of the Afrikaans language instead of English in schools became a riot and almost 200 people, including many children, were killed by the South African police and army. As a result, Soweto became an important centre for opposition to the white government. 索韦托〔南非约翰内斯堡附近一座大型城镇，原种族隔离制度下的黑人居住区。当时，黑人可获准在约翰内斯堡工作，但不得居住。1976 年，一名学生抗议学校用南非荷兰语替代英语，后来演变成为一场暴乱，包括许多儿童在内的近 200 人被南非军警打死。此后，索韦托成为反对白人政府的重要中心〕

sown /son; səʊn/ the past participle of sow

sox /sɑks; sɒks/ *n* [plural] an American spelling of socks, used especially in advertising 袜子〔socks的美式拼法，尤用于广告中〕

soy /sɔɪ; sɔɪ/ also 又作 **soy·a** /`sɔɪə; 'sɔɪə/ *n* [U] soy beans 大豆

soy bean /'· ·/ also 又作 **soya bean** /'·· ·/ *n* [C] the bean of an Asian plant from which oil and food containing a lot of PROTEIN is produced 大豆

So·yin·ka /sɔr`jɪŋkə; sɔɪ'jɪŋkə/, **Wo·le** /`wole; 'wəʊleɪ/ (1934-) a Nigerian writer of plays, poems, and NOVELs who won the Nobel Prize for Literature in 1986. 索因卡〔(1934-)，尼日利亚剧作家、诗人、小说家。1986 年获诺贝尔文学奖〕

soy sauce /,· '·/ *n* [U] a dark brown liquid that is used especially in Japanese and Chinese cooking〔尤指日本和中国烹饪用的〕酱油

soz·zled /`sɑzəld; 'sɒzəld/ *adj BrE humorous* drunk【英，幽默】喝醉酒的

S

spa /spɑ; spɑː/ *n* [C] **1** a place that has a spring of mineral water that people believe makes you healthy 矿泉疗养地: *the spas of Germany* 德国的矿泉疗养地 **2** *AmE* a bath or pool that sends currents of hot water around you; JACUZZI【美】热水漩水式浴缸[浴池]，按摩式浴缸[浴池]

CULTURAL NOTE 文化注释

Spas became very fashionable places in the UK and Europe in the 18th and 19th centuries. People still visit some spas, but to look at the old buildings rather than to go in the water. The most famous English spa is in Bath, in the west of England. 矿泉疗养地在18、19世纪的英国和欧洲风行一时。现在人们仍然会去这些地方，但目的是去看古建筑而不是泡矿泉疗养。英国最著名的矿泉疗养地在英格兰西部的巴斯。

space¹ /spes; speɪs/ *n*

1 ►AMOUNT OF SPACE 空间大小◄ [U] the amount of an area, room, container etc that is empty or available to be used 空间，空地方: *There's space for a table and two chairs.* 有空间放得下一张桌子和两把椅子。| *How much space is there on each disk?* 每张磁盘有多大容量？| **make space** *I'm trying to make space for all Tom's canoeing gear.* 我正在设法给汤姆的划船工具腾出地方。| **leave space** *Leave enough space for the suitcases.* 留出足够的地方放衣箱。| **closet/cupboard/office space** *There's plenty of closet space in our new apartment.* 我们的新公寓有足够的壁橱空间。| **sense/feeling of space** (=the feeling that a room has plenty of space) 空间宽大的感觉 *Mirrors give a sense of space.* 镜子给人空间宽大的感觉。 see 见 PLACE¹ (USAGE)

2 ►PIECE OF SPACE 空间范围◄ [C,U] an area, especially one used for a particular purpose〔有特定目的的〕空位，处所: *a parking space* 停车处 | *There was just an empty space where the book had been.* 原来放书的地方正好有个空位。| **clear a space** *Lucy cleared a space on her desk for her new computer.* 露西在她的书桌上清理出一块空地方放新电脑。

3 ►BETWEEN EARTH AND STARS 地球与各个星体之间◄ [U] the area outside the Earth's air where the stars and PLANETs are 太空: *space travel* 太空旅行，宇宙飞行 | **outer space** (=far away in space) 外太空 *creatures from outer space* 来自外太空的生物

4 ►ALL AROUND EVERYTHING 万物周围◄ [U] all of the space in which everything exists, and in which everything has a position or direction 空间，空中: *the exact point in space where two lines meet* 两线在空间中的确切交点 | *beyond the dimensions of space and time* 在空间与时间两维之外

5 ►BETWEEN THINGS 在物体之间◄ [C] an empty space between two things, or between two parts of something; GAP (1)〔两物或某物两部分之间的〕空间，距离；空隙: *The children hid in the space between the wall and the shed.* 孩子们躲在墙和棚屋之间的空隙里。

6 ►TIME 时间◄ **a) in/during the space of** within a particular period of time 在一段…的时间里，在…期间: *Mandy had four children in the space of four years.* 曼迪在四年里生了四个孩子。**b) a short space of time** a short period of time during which a lot of things happen 短短的一段时间〔指期间有许多事情发生〕: *It's amazing how well we knew each other after such a short space of time.* 令人惊奇的是我们在短短的一段时间里彼此就这么了解。

7 ►EMPTY LAND 空地◄ [C,U] land, or an area of land that has not been built on〔尚无建筑物的〕空地: **open space** *a pleasant town centre with plenty of open space* 开阔宜人的城市中心区 | **wide open spaces** *the wide open spaces of the prairies* 辽阔的大草原

8 ►IN WRITING 在书写方面◄ [C] **a)** an empty space between written or printed words, lines etc〔字或行之间的〕间隔，距离 **b)** the width of a typed letter of the alphabet 打出一个字母所占的宽度: *The word 'the' takes up three spaces.* the 这个词占三格。**c)** a place provided for you to write your name or other information on a document, piece of paper etc〔纸上预留的〕空白处: *Please write any comments in the space provided.* 请把意见写在预留的空白处。

9 ►IN A NEWSPAPER 在报纸上◄ [U] the amount of space in a newspaper, magazine or book that is used for a particular subject〔报纸、书刊对某题目的〕篇幅: *Endless space has been devoted to Princess Di.* 对戴妃的报道已经用去无数篇幅了。

10 ►FREEDOM 自由◄ [U] the freedom to do what you want or do things on your own, especially in a relationship with someone else〔个人的〕生活空间，〔不受别人牵制的〕个人自由: *I've split up with Phil because I need more space.* 我和菲尔分手了，因为我需要更多个人空间。

11 look/stare into space to look straight in front of you without looking at anything in particular, usually because you are thinking〔常因为思考〕凝视前方，茫然直视: *What's wrong with Jenny? She's just been staring into space all day.* 珍妮怎么了？她整天只是瞪着眼睛发呆。—see also 另见 BREATHING SPACE

space² *v* also 又作 **space out 1** [T always+adv/prep] to arrange objects or events so that they have equal spaces or periods of time between them 将…均匀地隔开: **space sth ↔ out/along etc** *Try to space out your classes and study in between.* 设法将上课时间分开，当中进行温习。| *Space the desks one metre apart.* 把这些书桌隔开一米排列。| **be evenly spaced** (=with equal spaces) 均匀相隔 **2** also 又作 **space out** [I] *AmE informal* to stop paying attention and just look in front of you without thinking, especially because you are bored or because you have taken drugs【美，非正式】〔尤指因无聊或吸毒后〕变得昏昏沉沉，瞪着眼发呆: *I was so tired I just spaced out, completely unable to concentrate.* 我累得很，只知道愣着发呆，根本不能集中思想。—see also 另见 SPACED OUT

space-age /'· ·/ *adj informal* very modern【非正式】太空时代的，非常现代化的: *This space-age device can remember up to 100 phone numbers.* 这个非常现代化的装置能存储多达一百个电话号码。

space bar /'· ·/ *n* [C] the part at the bottom of a TYPEWRITER that you press to make a space〔打字机的〕间隔档，空格杆[键]

space ca·det /'· ·,·/ *n* [C] *informal* someone who forgets things, does not pay attention, and often behaves strangely【非正式】健忘散漫的人，马大哈式的人: *I like her, but she's kind of a space cadet.* 我喜欢她，不过她这个人有点"马大哈"。

space cap·sule /'· ,··/ *n* [C] the part of a space vehicle that carries people into space to obtain information and then comes back to Earth 太空舱，航天舱

space·craft /`spes,kræft; 'speɪs-krɑːft/ *n* [C] a vehicle that is able to travel in space 航天器，太空船，宇宙飞船

spaced out /,· '·◄/ *adj informal* not fully conscious of what is happening around you, for example because you are extremely tired or because you have taken drugs【非正式】〔因极度疲倦或吸毒后〕头脑不清醒的，迷迷糊糊的: *JD looked spaced out, face flushed, hair in disarray.* JD 看上去头脑不清，脸色发红，头发蓬乱。—see also 另见 **space** (SPACE² (2))

space heat·er /'· ,··/ *n* [C] a small machine for heating a room 小型供暖器

space·man /`spes,mæn; 'speɪsmæn/ *n plural* **spacemen** /-,mɛn; -men/ [C] **1** *informal* a man who travels into space; ASTRONAUT【非正式】宇航员，航天员，太空人 **2** someone in stories who visits the Earth from another world〔小说中的〕外星人: *little green spacemen from Mars* 来自火星的小个绿色外星人

Space Nee·dle, the /ˈ· ,·/ a tall tower (185 metres) which is the most famous building in Seattle, Washington State, US, and which is sometimes used in pictures to represent Seattle 太空针塔〔一座高达185米的塔楼。美国华盛顿州西雅图市最著名的建筑，有时用在图片中代表西雅图市〕

space probe /ˈ· ·/ *n* [C] a SPACECRAFT without people in it, that is sent into space to collect information about the conditions there and send it back to Earth 宇宙探测器，太空探测船：*a space probe investigating Jupiter* 探测木星的宇宙探测器

space·ship /ˈspes,ʃɪp; ˈspeɪs,ʃɪp/ *n* [C] a vehicle for carrying people through space, especially in stories〔尤指小说中的〕宇宙飞船，太空船

space shut·tle /ˈ· ,··/ *n* [C] a vehicle that is designed to go into space and back to Earth several times to do experiments and carry people 航天飞机，太空穿梭机

space sta·tion /ˈ· ,··/ *n* [C] a large SPACECRAFT that stays above the Earth and is a base for people travelling in space or for scientific tests 航天站，宇航站，太空站：*Mir, the Soviet space station orbiting earth* 围绕地球运行的前苏联太空站"和平号"

space·suit /ˈspes,sut; ˈspeɪs-suːt/ *n* [C] a special suit for wearing in space, that covers and protects your whole body and provides an air supply 航天服，太空服

space-time con·tin·u·um /,· ·ˈ··,···/ *n* [U] *technical* the universe considered as having four measurements: length, width, depth, and time【术语】时空一体，时空体〔指有长度、宽度、深度与时间四种量度的宇宙〕

space·walk /ˈspes,wɔk; ˈspeɪswɔːk/ *n* [C] the act of moving around outside a spacecraft while in space, or the time spent outside it 太空行走〔指离开航天器外出活动〕；太空行走的时间

space·wom·an /ˈspes,wumən; ˈspeɪs,wʊmən/ *n plural* **spacewomen** /-,wɪmɪn; -,wɪmɪn/ [C] *informal* a woman who travels into space; ASTRONAUT【非正式】女宇航员，女航天员，女太空人

spac·y /ˈspesɪ; ˈspeɪsi/ *adj informal* behaving as though you are not fully conscious of what is happening around you【非正式】头脑不清醒的，迷迷糊糊的：*June is pretty spacey; I'd never let her take care of the kids.* 琼相当糊涂，我绝不会让她带孩子。—**spacey** *adv*: *Dan acts kind of spacey.* 丹的举动有点儿糊里糊涂。

spac·ing /ˈspesɪŋ; ˈspeɪsɪŋ/ *n* [U] the amount of space between each printed letter, word, or line on a page〔印刷的字母与字母、单词与单词或行与行之间的〕间隔，空白：**single spacing** (=lines with no empty lines between them) 单行行距〔行与行之间不留空行〕| **double spacing** (=lines with one empty line between each one) 双行行距〔行与行之间留一行间隔〕

spa·cious /ˈspeʃəs; ˈspeɪʃəs/ *adj* a spacious house, room etc is large and has plenty of space to move around in 宽敞的，广阔的；广大的：*a spacious, comfortably furnished living room* 一间宽敞的、陈设舒适的起居室 —**spaciously** *adv* —**spaciousness** *n* [U]

spack·le /ˈspækl; ˈspækl/ *n* [U] *AmE* a substance used to fill holes in walls, that becomes very hard when it dries【美】〔填墙洞用的〕填泥料

spade /sped; speɪd/ *n* [C] **1** a tool for digging that has a long handle and a broad metal blade you push into the ground 铲，铁锹 **2** [C] a PLAYING CARD belonging to the set of cards that have one or more black shapes that look like pointed leaves printed on them 印有黑桃的纸牌：*the queen of spades* 黑桃王后 **3 call a spade a spade** to say exactly what you think is true, without trying to be polite 有一说一，照直说，直言不讳 **4 in spades** *informal especially AmE* to a much greater degree, or in a much greater amount, than you expected【非正式，尤美】非常，极其：*It may have been tough, but Ginny's effort was repaid in spades.* 这事也许艰苦，但金尼的努力得到了非常丰厚的回报。**5** [C] *old-fashioned* a very offensive word for a black person【过时】黑鬼〔极具冒犯性的用语〕

spade·work /ˈsped,wɝk; ˈspeɪd-wɜːk/ *n* [U] hard work that has to be done in preparation before something can happen 艰苦的准备工作：*Credit must go to the researchers, who did a lot of the spadework.* 功劳应当归于研究人员，他们做了大量艰苦的准备工作。

spa·ghet·ti /spəˈgɛtɪ; spəˈgeti/ *n* [U] a type of PASTA in very long thin pieces, that is cooked in boiling water 意大利粉，意大利面条 —compare 比较 MACARONI, TAGLIATELLE, VERMICELLI —see picture at 参见 PASTA 图

Spaghetti Junc·tion /·,··ˈ··/ *n* **1** *AmE* a place where a lot of roads cross over each other【美】复式公路枢纽 **2** a place in Birmingham in central England where a lot of roads meet and cross over each other 复式公路枢纽〔位于英格兰中部的伯明翰〕

spaghetti west·ern /·,··ˈ··/ *n* [C] a film about American COWBOYS in the Wild West, especially one made in Europe by an Italian director〔尤指意大利导演在欧洲摄制的〕美国西部牛仔影片

Spain /spen; speɪn/ a country in southwest Europe, between France and Portugal, which includes the Balearic and Canary Islands. It is a member of the EU. Population: 40,038,000 (2001). Capital: Madrid. For many British people, Spain is a popular place to go for a holiday because of its hot, dry summers. People from Spain are called Spaniards. 西班牙〔欧洲西南部一国家。位于法国和葡萄牙之间，包括巴厘阿里群岛和加那利群岛。为欧盟成员国。人口：40,038,000 (2001)，首都：马德里。西班牙夏季炎热干爽，是颇受英国欢迎的度假之地。西班牙人称作 Spaniard〕—see also 另见 SPANISH

spake /spek; speɪk/ *biblical or poetic*【圣经或诗】a past tense of SPEAK

Spam /spæm; spæm/ *n* [U] *trademark* a type of inexpensive CANNED meat made mainly of PORK【商标】好味宝午餐肉

spam *v* [I,T] *technical* to send copies of the same information to many different groups on the INTERNET【术语】在网上广发垃圾邮件：*spamming the newsgroups* 向各新闻组发送垃圾邮件

span[1] /spæn; spæn/ a past tense of SPIN

span[2] *n* [C] **1** the length of time over which someone's attention, life etc continues〔注意力、生命等持续的〕时间：*A four-year-old's concentration span is usually about 10 minutes.* 一个四岁孩子的注意力持续时间通常为10分钟左右。**2** a period of time between two dates or events〔两个日期或两件事之间的〕时距，期间：*Over a span of ten years, the company has made great strides.* 10年间，这家公司有了很大的发展。**3** the part of a bridge, ARCH[1] (1) etc that goes across from one support to another〔桥梁、拱门等的〕跨距；墩距 **4** the distance from one side of something to the other〔从一端到另一端的〕全长：*a bird with a large wing span* 一只翼展宽大的鸟

span[3] *v* **spanned, spanning** [T] **1** to include all of a period of time〔时间〕持续，延伸：*a career spanning four decades* 长达40年的职业生涯 **2** to include all of a particular space or area〔空间、地域〕跨越，包括：*The Mongol Empire spanned much of Central Asia.* 蒙古帝国包括了中亚的许多地区。**3** if a bridge spans an area of water it goes from one side to the other〔桥梁〕跨越〔水面〕，横跨

span·gle[1] /ˈspæŋgl; ˈspæŋgəl/ *v* [T] to cover something with shiny spots 用闪亮的斑点覆盖，使闪闪发亮：**be spangled with** *His mackintosh was spangled with drops of rain.* 他的雨衣上布满了闪闪发亮的雨珠。—**spangled** also 又作 **spangly** *adj*: *acrobats in spangled tights* 穿着闪亮紧身衣的杂技演员

spangle[2] *n* [C] a small piece of shiny metal or plastic sewn on to clothes to give them a shining effect; SEQUIN〔衣服上用作装饰的〕闪亮的金属[塑料]片，闪光饰片

Spang·lish /ˈspæŋglɪʃ; ˈspæŋglɪʃ/ *n* [U] *especially AmE* a mixture of the Spanish and English languages【尤美】西英混合语〔西班牙语和英语的混合语〕

Span·iard /ˈspænjəd; ˈspænjəd/ *n* [C] a Spanish person 西班牙人

Span·iel /ˈspænjəl; ˈspænjəl/ *n* [C] a type of dog with long ears that hang down 西班牙猎犬〔一种长毛垂耳狗〕—see picture at 参见 DOG[1] 图

Span·ish[1] /ˈspænɪʃ; ˈspænɪʃ/ *adj* from or connected with Spain 西班牙的

Spanish[2] *n* [U] the language of Spain and parts of South America 西班牙语

Spanish-A·mer·i·can War, the /,· ··,···ˈ·/ a war in 1898 between the US and Spain, which the US started because it wanted Cuba to be independent from Spain and because the US battleship Maine was mysteriously destroyed by an explosion near Havana, Cuba. After Spain was defeated, Cuba became independent, and the US took control of the islands of the Philippines, Guam, and Puerto Rico. Theodore Roosevelt, who later became president, first became famous through his military success in this war, when he led a group of men called the Rough Riders. 西美战争〔1898年美国和西班牙之间的一场战争。战争由美国发动，以支持古巴摆脱西班牙统治争取独立，并对美国战舰"缅因"号在古巴哈瓦那附近神秘被毁作出反应。西班牙战败后，古巴获得独立，美国则赢得对菲律宾群岛、关岛和波多黎各的控制权。西奥多·罗斯福在这场战争中率领一支号称"莽骑兵"的部队，因战功卓著脱颖而出，他后来成为美国总统〕

Spanish Civ·il War, the /,··,··ˈ·/ a war fought in Spain, from 1936 to 1939, between the RIGHT-WING Nationalists, led by General Franco, and the LEFT-WING Republicans. Many people from other countries joined the International Brigade to help

the Republicans, including well-known writers and poets such as George Orwell, and the US writer Ernest Hemingway wrote about the war as a news reporter. The Nationalists won the war, and from 1939 to 1975 Spain was ruled by Franco. 西班牙内战〔1936 年至 1939 年间西班牙发生的一场内战。交战一方是以佛朗哥将军为首的右翼民族主义分子，另一方是左翼共和派。许多外国人组成国际纵队支持共和派，其中包括著名作家、诗人乔治·奥威尔等。美国作家欧内斯特·海明威当时曾以新闻记者的身份对这场内战进行报道。民族主义分子最终获胜，佛朗哥于 1939 年至 1975 年间统治西班牙〕

Spanish fly /,·· '·/ *n* [U] a substance made from dried insects, that is supposed to be an APHRODISIAC (=drug causing sexual excitement) 斑蝥剂〔一种用风干昆虫制成的药，据说可以引起性欲〕

Spanish Main, the /,·· '·/ the area around the coast of northern South America, from which Spanish ships carried gold and treasure back to Spain during the 16th and 17th centuries. Many of these ships were attacked by PIRATE*s*, and there are many stories and films about the exciting adventures of the people who sailed the Spanish Main. 南美洲北岸地区，加勒比海地区〔南美大陆北岸沿海一带。16、17 世纪，西班牙船只沿此线路将黄金和财宝运回西班牙，很多船只遭到海盗袭击。不少小说和电影描写了人们沿西班牙大陆航行时惊险刺激的冒险经历〕

Spanish ome·lette /,·· '··/ *n* [C] a thick OMELETTE made with cooked vegetables〔拌以蔬菜的〕西班牙煎蛋卷

Spanish Steps /,·· '·/ some famous steps built in the 18th century, that climb to the main French church in Rome, the Trinita dei Monti. 西班牙阶梯〔建于 18 世纪的著名阶梯，通往罗马市内主要的法国教堂圣三一教堂〕

spank /spæŋk; spæŋk/ *v* [T] to hit a child, on their bottom with your open hand〔用手掌〕打〔小孩的〕屁股 —compare 比较 SMACK[1] —**spanking, spank** *n* [C,U]: *If you don't stop that noise, you'll get a spanking.* 如果你继续吵闹的话，那就要打屁股了。

spank·ing[1] /ˈspæŋkɪŋ; ˈspæŋkɪŋ/ *adj old-fashioned*【过时】**at a spanking pace/rate** very fast 快速地: *They started walking at a spanking rate.* 他们开始以很快的速度走。

spanking[2] *adv old-fashioned*【过时】**spanking new/clean etc** very new, clean etc 非常新/干净等: *a spanking new car* 崭新的汽车

span·ner /ˈspænə; ˈspænə/ *n* [C] **1** *BrE* a metal tool that fits over a nut (NUT[1] (2)) and is used for turning it to make it tight or to undo it【英】扳手，扳子; WRENCH[2] (3) *AmE*【美】—see also 另见 RING SPANNER —see picture at 参见 TOOL[1] 图 **2 put/throw a spanner in the works** *BrE informal* to unexpectedly do something that prevents a plan or process from continuing or succeeding【英，非正式】打乱〔计划〕，破坏〔过程〕: *He won't lend us the money? Well, that really puts a spanner in the works.* 他不肯借钱给我们？哦，那可真要坏事了。

spar[1] /spɑr; spɑː/ *v* **sparred, sparring** [I] **1** to practise BOXING with someone〔与某人〕练拳: *He once sparred with Mike Tyson.* 他曾与迈克·泰森练拳。**2** to argue with someone but not in an unpleasant way〔友好地〕争论，争辩: *gentle sparring between the generations* 两代人之间并不激烈的争论

spar[2] *n* [C] a thick pole, especially one used on a ship to support sails or ropes 圆材〔尤用作船舶的桅杆、帆桁等〕—compare 比较 MAST (1)

[S2] **spare[1]** /spɛr; speə/ *adj*

1 ▶ADDITIONAL 附加的◀ **spare key/bulb/battery etc** a key etc that you have in addition to the ones you normally use, so that it is available if another is needed 备用钥匙/灯泡/电池等

2 ▶AVAILABLE 可用的◀ not being used by anyone and available to be used 多余的，现成的: *Have you got any spare boxes?* 你有没有多余的盒子？

3 spare time time when you are not working 空闲时间: *What do you do in your spare time?* 你闲下来时干什么？

4 spare change coins of little value that you do not need and can give to other people 多余的零钱: *Do you have any spare change for the phone?* 你有打电话用的零钱吗？

5 be going spare *spoken* if something is going spare it is available for you to have or use【口】可以使用; 可以拥有: *I'll have some of that cake if it's going spare.* 如果那蛋糕没有人要，我就吃一点。

6 ▶THIN 瘦的◀ *literary* tall and thin【文】瘦削的，又高又瘦的: *an old man with a spare wiry frame* 一位精瘦结实的老人

7 go spare *BrE informal* to become very angry or worried【英，非正式】非常生气，气急败坏: *Dad would go spare if he knew I'd stayed out all night.* 爸爸如果知道我整夜不归，他会气坏的。

[S3] **spare[2]** *v* [T]

1 ▶GIVE 给予◀ if you can spare something, you can give it to someone because you are not using it or do not need it〔把不用的或多余的东西〕拨出，抽出，腾出，让给: *I can't spare the time.* 我抽不出时间。| *We're too busy to spare anyone to help you right now.* 我们目前太忙，腾不出人来帮助你。| **spare sb sth** *Could you spare me £5?* 你能给我五英镑吗？

2 money/time to spare if you have time, money etc to spare, there is some left in addition to what you have used or need 余钱/余暇: *We had an hour to spare so we looked round the shops.* 我们有一小时的空余时间，于是就去逛商店。| *They got there with seconds to spare.* 他们到那里时只剩几秒钟了。

3 spare sb trouble/difficulty/pain etc to prevent someone from having to experience something difficult or unpleasant 免除某人的麻烦/困难/痛苦等: *They did what they could to spare him any pain.* 他们尽了一切努力使他免受任何痛苦。

4 spare a thought for to think about another person who is in a worse situation than they are 想一想〔某人〕: *Spare a thought for Nick, who's doing his exams while we lie in the sun.* 想一想尼克吧，他正在考试，而我们在躺着晒太阳。

5 spare no expense to spend as much money as necessary to make something really good and not worry about the cost 不惜工本: *Janet's parents spared no expense on her wedding.* 珍妮特的父母不惜工本，给她办婚礼。

6 spare sb the details to not tell someone all the details about something, because it is unpleasant or boring 不对某人谈…的细节〔以免使人不快或厌烦〕

7 ▶NOT DAMAGE OR HARM 不损坏或伤害◀ to not damage or harm someone or something even though other people or things are being damaged, killed or destroyed 使免受〔损坏、伤亡〕，幸免: *Only the children were spared.* 只有孩子们得以幸免。

8 spare sb's feelings to avoid doing something that would upset someone 免使某人难过: *We carefully avoided mentioning Cathy's break-up to spare her feelings.* 我们小心地避免提起凯茜离婚的事，以免让她难过。

9 spare sb's blushes *BrE* to avoid doing something that would embarrass someone【英】不使某人难为情

spare[3] *n* **1** [C] an additional thing of a particular kind that you keep so that it is available 备用品: *If the fuse has gone, the spares are kept in the garage.* 保险丝如果断了，车库里有备用的。**2** [C] a SPARE TYRE (1) 备用轮胎 **3 spares** [plural] *BrE* new parts for vehicles or machines【英】〔车辆或机器的〕零件，备件，配件

spare part /,· '·/ *n* [C] a new part for a vehicle or machine, that is used to replace a part that is damaged or broken〔车辆或机器的〕备用零件，备件

spare-part sur·ge·ry /,· · '···/ *n* [U] *informal* an operation to put an artificial organ, or an organ from a dead person, into the body of a living person【非正式】器官移植手术

Spare Rib /,· '·/ *trademark* a magazine produced in Britain by a group of women working together. It has articles on political subjects as well as stories by women and information on subjects of interest to women, especially RACISM and FEMINISM, and is read mainly by feminists.【商标】《多出的肋骨》〔由一批英国女性编印的杂志。文章内容不仅涉及政治话题，还包括女性创作的故事、女性感兴趣的话题，尤其是种族主义和女权主义等。读者多为女权主义者〕

spare·ribs /ˈspɛr,rɪbz; ˈspeə,rɪbz/ *n* [plural] the ribs (RIB[1] (2)) of a pig and the meat on them served as a food〔食用的〕带肉猪排骨

spare room /,· '·/ *n* [C] a bedroom in your house, that is kept for guests to use when they come to stay〔家中的〕备用卧室，客房

spare tyre *BrE*【英】, **spare tire** *AmE*【美】/,· '·/ *n* [C] **1** an additional wheel with a tyre on it, that you keep in a car for use if another tyre gets damaged 备用轮胎 **2** *humorous* a large ring of fat around someone's waist【幽默】肥胖的腰腹部

spar·ing /ˈspɛrɪŋ; ˈspeərɪŋ/ *adj* using or giving only a little of something; FRUGAL 省着用的，节约的，节俭的: **[+with]** *There's not much shampoo left, so be sparing with it.* 剩下的洗发剂不多了，所以要省着点用。| **[+in]** *The critics were sparing in their praise.* 那些批评家很少赞扬别人。—**sparingly** *adv*: *Apply the glue sparingly.* 少涂点胶水。

spark[1] /spɑrk; spɑːk/ *n*

1 ▶FIRE 火◀ [C] a very small bit of brightly burning material produced by a fire or by hitting or rubbing together two hard objects 火花，火星: *In a gas leak, any small spark will cause an explosion.* 煤气泄漏时，任何一个小火花都会引起爆炸。| *a shower of sparks from the fire* 从火中飞出的一阵火花

2 ▶ELECTRICITY 电◀ [C] a flash of light caused by electricity passing across a space 电火花

3 **spark of interest/excitement/anger etc** a small amount of a feeling or quality, that can be noticed in someone's expression or behaviour 一点点兴趣/激动/怒气等: *Meg's eyes lacked their usual spark of humour.* 梅格的眼睛里缺少了常有的幽默的火花。

4 ►**INTELLIGENCE/ENERGY** 智慧/精力◄ [U] a quality of intelligence or energy that makes someone successful or fun to be with 生气, 活力, 〔才智的〕焕发: *Ali has plenty of spark and wit.* 阿里充满了活力和智慧。

5 ►**CAUSE** 原因◄ [C] a small action or event that quickly causes trouble or violence 〔麻烦、暴力等的〕起因, 祸根: *Hani's murder was the spark that started the riot.* 哈尼被杀是引起这次暴乱的根源。

6 **sparks fly** if sparks fly between two people, they argue angrily 激烈争吵: *Sparks were flying at the Conroy's last night!* 昨晚在康罗伊家发生了激烈的争吵!

spark² *v* **1** also 又作 **spark off** [T] to be the cause of trouble or violence 引起, 导致〔麻烦、暴力等〕: *a minor incident that sparked off the conflict* 引发了这场冲突的一件小事 **2** [T] to start someone's interest in something 激发〔兴趣〕, 激励, 鼓舞: *Going to an exhibition sparked Chris's interest in photography.* 参观一次展览会激发了克里斯对摄影的兴趣。**3** [I] to produce sparks of fire or electricity 发出火花[电火花] **4** [I] *AmE old-fashioned* to pay special attention to someone you are sexually attracted to【美, 过时】受到某人吸引, 为某人倾倒

sparking plug /ˈ‥ ˌ/ *n* [C] *BrE* a SPARK PLUG【英】火花塞

spar·kle¹ /ˋsparkl; ˈspɑːkəl/ *v* [I] **1** to shine in small bright flashes 闪闪发光, 闪耀, 闪烁: *The diamond ring sparkled in the sunlight.* 钻石戒指在阳光下闪闪发光。**2** if someone's eyes sparkle, they shine brightly, especially because the person is happy or excited 〔眼睛〕发亮, 闪耀〔尤因快乐或兴奋〕: [+with] *Ron's eyes sparkled with excitement.* 罗恩的眼睛闪烁着兴奋的神情。—see also 另见 SPARKLING

sparkle² *n* [C,U] **1** a bright shiny appearance, with tiny points of flashing light 闪耀, 闪光 **2** a quality that makes something seem interesting and full of life 生气, 活力: *The dialogue doesn't have much sparkle.* 这对话不是很生动。

spar·kler /ˋsparklɚ; ˈspɑːklə/ *n* [C] **1** a FIREWORK in the shape of a thin stick, that gives off sparks of fire as you hold it in your hand 〔燃烧时发出火花的手持〕烟花棒 **2 sparklers** [plural] *informal* diamonds【非正式】钻石

spark·ling /ˋsparklɪŋ; ˈspɑːklɪŋ/ *adj* **1** shining brightly with points of flashing light 闪亮的, 闪光的: *a sparkling lake* 湖光潋滟 **2** a sparkling drink has bubbles (BUBBLE¹ (1)) of gas in it 〔饮料〕起泡沫的: *a sparkling wine* 气泡葡萄酒 **3** full of life and intelligence 充满生气的, 才智焕发的: *sparkling wit* 才华横溢

spark plug /ˈ· ˌ/ *n* [C] *technical* a part in a car engine that produces an electric SPARK¹ (2) to make the petrol mixture start burning【术语】〔汽车引擎的〕火花塞

spark·y /ˋsparkɪ; ˈspɑːki/ *adj* full of life and energy 活泼的, 充满活力的: *a sparky debating partner* 一位充满活力的辩论伙伴

sparring match /ˈ‥ ˌ/ *n* [C] a friendly argument that is not serious 友好的争论

sparring part·ner /ˈ‥ ˌ‥/ *n* [C] **1** someone you practise BOXING with 练拳的对手 **2** someone you regularly have friendly arguments with 〔经常地〕友好争论的对手

spar·row /ˋspæro; ˈspærəʊ/ *n* [C] a small brown bird, very common in many parts of the world 麻雀

sparse /spars; spɑːs/ *adj* existing only in small amounts 稀少的, 稀疏的: *sparse vegetation* 稀疏的植被 | *Data on fatal accidents are sparse and difficult to obtain.* 关于死亡事故的资料很少, 也很难获得。—**sparsely** *adv*: *a sparsely populated area* 人烟稀少的地区 —**sparseness** *n* [U]

Spar·ta /ˋspartə; ˈspɑːtə/ a city of ancient Greece which was famous for the bravery and skill of its soldiers, and for the simple way in which its people lived without any comforts 斯巴达〔古希腊城邦。以其士兵骁勇善战、人民生活极其俭朴而著称〕—**Spartan** *n, adj*

Spar·ta·cus /ˋspartəkəs; ˈspɑːtəkəs/ (died 71 BC) a Roman GLADIATOR (=a man who fought against other men or wild animals to entertain people), who led a large army of SLAVEs in a REVOLT against their Roman owners. Eventually they were defeated by Roman armies, and many of them were killed by being crucified (CRUCIFY). 斯巴达克〔卒于公元前71年〕, 古罗马角斗士。他率领一支庞大的奴隶起义军反抗罗马奴隶主, 但最终被罗马军队击败, 大部分起义者被钉死在十字架上〕

spar·tan /ˋspartn̩; ˈspɑːtn/ *adj* spartan conditions or ways of living are simple and without any comfort 〔生活条件或方式〕简朴而艰苦的: *spartan accommodation* 简朴的住处 | *adjusting to the spartan life of boarding school* 适应寄宿学校的清苦生活

spas·m /ˋspæzəm; ˈspæzəm/ *n* [C] **1** a sharp pain when your muscles suddenly become tighter in an uncontrolled way 痉挛, 抽搐 **2 a spasm of grief/laughter/coughing** a sudden strong feeling or reaction that lasts for a short period 一阵悲伤/欢笑/咳嗽

spas·mod·ic /spæzˋmadɪk; spæzˈmɒdɪk/ *adj* **1** happening for short irregular periods, not continuously 间歇的, 不规则的, 断断续续的: *spasmodic bursts of energy* 一阵阵的精力迸发 **2** like or connected with a muscle spasm 痉挛性的, 抽搐的 —**spasmodically** /-klɪ; -kli/ *adv*

spas·tic /ˋspæstɪk; ˈspæstɪk/ *adj* **1** *slang* an offensive word meaning stupid or lacking in skill, used especially by children【俚】愚笨的, 拙劣的〔冒犯语, 尤用于儿语〕**2** *old-fashioned* having CEREBRAL PALSY, a disease that prevents control of the muscles【过时】患大脑性麻痹的 —**spastic** *n* [C]

spat¹ /spæt; spæt/ the past tense and past participle of SPIT

spat² *n* **1** [C] *informal* a short unimportant quarrel【非正式】口角, 小争吵: *It's just your normal, average sibling spat.* 那只是你们兄弟间正常的小争吵而已。**2** [plural] special pieces of cloth worn in former times by men above their shoes and fastened with buttons 〔旧时男子穿的〕鞋罩, 鞋套

spate /spet; speɪt/ *n* **1 a spate of** a large number of similar unpleasant things that happen in a short period of time 大量, 大批, 许多〔短时间内发生类似的不愉快事件〕: *a spate of burglaries* 接连发生的多宗入室盗窃案 **2 in spate** a river, stream etc that is in spate, is very full and flowing very fast 〔河水等〕猛涨, 泛滥

spa·tial /ˋspeʃəl; ˈspeɪʃəl/ *adj technical* concerning the position, size, shape etc of things【术语】空间的; 关于空间的 —**spatially** *adv*

spat·ter /ˋspætɚ; ˈspætə/ *v* **1** [T] to scatter or throw small amounts of mud, dirt etc all over a surface 溅, 洒: **spatter sb/sth with** *a passing car spattered with mud* 一辆驶过的车身溅满污泥的汽车 | **spatter sth on/over etc** *Grey flicked his brush spattering paint over my shirt.* 格雷甩了甩刷子, 把油漆溅到了我的衬衣上。**2** [I] if liquid spatters on a surface, drops of it fall or are thrown on it 〔液体〕洒落, 滴下: [+on] *The first drops of rain spattered on the stones.* 开始落下的雨滴洒落在石头上。—**spatter** *n* [C]

spat·u·la /ˋspætʃələ; ˈspætjʊlə/ *n* [C] **1** a kitchen tool with a wide flat blade used for spreading, mixing, or lifting soft substances 〔厨房里煎炒东西用的〕铲 **2** *BrE* a small instrument with a flat surface, used by doctors to hold your tongue down so that they can examine your throat【英】〔医生用的〕压舌板

spawn¹ /spɔn; spɔːn/ *v* **1** [I,T] if a fish or FROG spawns it produces eggs in large quantities together 〔鱼、蛙等〕大量产〔卵〕**2** [T] to make a series of things happen or start to exist 使大量出现, 使大量产生; 酿成: *the massive bureaucracy spawned by these programs* 这些计划所引起的官僚主义泛滥

spawn² *n* [U] the eggs of a fish, FROG etc laid together in a soft mass 〔鱼、蛙等产的〕成团的卵, 卵块

spay /spe; speɪ/ *v* [T] to remove part of the sex organs of a female animal so that it is not able to have babies 切除〔雌性动物的〕卵巢, 阉割〔雌性动物〕

SPCK /ˌɛs pi si ˋke; ˌes piː siː ˈkeɪ/ Society for Promoting Christian Knowledge; a British organization which produces and sells Christian books in order to teach people more about Christianity 基督教知识普及协会〔英国一组织。编著并出售基督教书籍, 以便向民众传播更多基督教知识〕

speak /spik; spiːk/ *v past* **spoke** /spok; spəʊk/ *past participle* **spoken** /ˋspokən; ˈspəʊkən/ S1 W1

1 ►**IN CONVERSATION** 在会话中◄ [I always+adv/prep] to talk to someone about something or have a conversation 谈话, 交谈: **speak to sb about sth** *I intend to speak to the manager about the way I have been treated.* 我想对经理谈谈我所受到的那种待遇。| *I know her by sight but not to speak to* (=not well enough to talk to her). 我只认得她的模样, 但没跟她说过话。| **speak with** *especially AmE*【尤美】*Sally would like to speak with you for a minute.* 萨莉想和你谈一会儿。| **speak of** *formal*【正式】*It was the first time she had ever spoken of marriage.* 那是她头一次谈及婚姻问题。—see 见 SAY¹ (USAGE)

2 ►**SAY WORDS** 说话◄ [I] to use your voice to produce words 说话, 讲话: *I was so shocked I couldn't speak.* 我震惊得说不出话来。| [+to] *John! Speak to me! Are you alright?* 约翰! 跟我说话呀! 你没事吧?

3 ►**A LANGUAGE** 一种语言◄ [T not in progressive 不用进行时] to be able to speak a particular language 会说, 会讲〔某种语

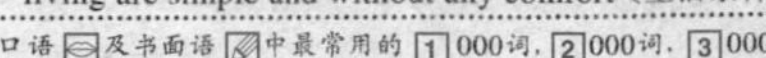

言〕: *Do you speak English?* 你会说英语吗? | **not speak a word of** (=not speak it at all) 一个字也不会说/完全不会说 *He doesn't speak a word of French.* 他一句法语也不会说。| **French-speaking/Italian-speaking etc** *a German-speaking secretary* 会说德语的秘书

4 ▶FORMAL SPEECH 正式演讲◀ [I] to make a formal speech 演说, 演讲; 发言: *Diana's been invited to speak at the annual conference.* 戴安娜被邀请在年会上作演讲。| **speak in favour of/against** (=support or oppose) 发言支持/反对 *Only one MP spoke against the bill.* 只有一位议会议员发言反对那项提案。— see also 另见 SPEAKER

5 be not speaking/not be on speaking terms if two people are not speaking they will not be polite or talk to each other, especially because they have quarrelled 彼此不说话/互不理睬〔尤因为吵架了〕

6 ▶EXPRESS IDEAS/OPINIONS 表达想法/意见◀ [T] to say something that expresses your ideas or opinions 表达, 表明〔观点、意见〕: *Not a word was spoken about the whole affair.* 对于整个事件没有人表达过半点意见。| **speaking as a parent/teacher/democrat etc** *Speaking as a parent, I would like to see more discipline in schools.* 作为一位家长来说, 我希望看到学校能加强纪律。| **speak well/badly/ill of** (=say good or bad things about someone) 说某人的好话/坏话 *It's wrong to speak ill of the dead.* 说死者的坏话是不对的。| **speak highly of** (=praise someone) 赞扬〔某人〕 *I'm so pleased to meet you – my wife has always spoken very highly of you.* 见到你真高兴 —— 我太太经常称赞你。| **speak your mind** (=tell people exactly what you think, even if it offends them) 坦率地说出自己的想法, 直言不讳 *She's very direct, the kind of person who believes in speaking their mind.* 她这个人非常坦率, 是那种认为说话应当直言不讳的人。

7 generally/personally/technically speaking used when you are expressing a general, personal etc opinion 一般来说/就个人来说/从技术上说〔用于表示从某个角度发表意见〕: *Generally speaking, rural schools provide a better environment for the students.* 一般来说, 乡村学校能给学生提供更好的环境。

8 speak out of turn to say something when you do not have the right or authority to say it 说话鲁莽, 讲话不合身份: *I hope I haven't spoken out of turn – I didn't know it was supposed to be a secret.* 真希望我没有说那些冒失的话 —— 我不知道这是应当保密的。

9 none/nothing to speak of not large or important enough to mention 不值一提: *There's been no rain to speak of – only a few drops.* 没有下过像样的雨, 只是下过几滴。

10 so to speak used when you are saying something in words that do not have their usual meaning 可以说〔在使用不平常表达方法时说的话〕: *We all learned this theory, so to speak, at our mother's knee.* 可以说, 还在妈妈膝头的时候, 我们大家就都知道了这种说法。

11 speak volumes to express something very clearly, without using words 〔不用说话〕有力地说明, 充分地证明: *Mary could not express the high hopes she had for her daughter, but her actions spoke volumes.* 玛丽不能表达她对女儿的深厚期望, 但她的行动充分说明了这一点。

speak for sb/sth *phr v* [T] **1** to express the feelings, thoughts, or beliefs of a person or group of people 代表…讲话, 充当…的代言人: *I think I speak for everyone here when I say we wish you all the best.* 祝你一切顺利, 我想我的话代表了大家的心意。**2 speak for yourself** *spoken* used to tell someone that you do not have the same opinion as they do【口】你只代表你自己说话〔用于表示不同意对方的意见〕: *"We were all bored in that lecture." "Speak for yourself! I liked it."* "那次讲座我们都听得很厌烦。" "你只是说你自己吧! 我是喜欢那次讲座的。" **3 be spoken for** if something or someone is spoken for, it has already been promised to someone else 已被预订, 已被订购: *The first 300 cars off the production line have already been spoken for.* 第一批300辆汽车刚刚离开生产线便已被订购一空。**4 speak for itself/themselves** to show something so clearly that no explanation is necessary 不言而喻, 不辩自明: *1994 has been a very good year for us – the figures speak for themselves.* 1994年对我们是很好的一年 —— 一看数字便知道。—see also 另见 **actions speak louder than words** (ACTION (15)), **in a manner of speaking** (MANNER (4))

speak of sth *phr v* [T] *literary* to show clearly that something happened or that it exists【文】表明…: *The lush vegetation spoke of a richer, damper climate.* 茂盛的草木表明气候湿润, 适宜植物生长。

speak out *phr v* [I] to publicly speak in protest about something, especially when protesting could be dangerous 公开地说出来〔尤指冒险表示抗议〕: **[+about/against]** *Five students who had spoken out against the regime were arrested.* 五名公开地抗议政府的学生均遭逮捕。

speak to sb *phr v* [T] *informal* to talk to someone who has done something wrong, to tell them not to do it again【非正式】当面提醒, 责备, 告诫: *Joe was late again today, you'll have to speak to him.* 乔今天又迟到了, 你得说说他。

speak up *phr v* [I] **1** used to ask someone to speak louder 大声地说, 提高嗓门说〔用于要求别人〕: *Speak up, please, I can't hear you.* 请说大声一点, 我听不见你说的话。**2** to express your opinion freely and clearly 自由地、清楚地表达意见: *"Is that wise?" Isidore spoke up, gathering courage.* "那样明智吗?" 伊西多尔鼓起勇气, 直截了当地问道。**3 speak up for** to speak in support of someone 替…说话, 支持: *It's about time someone spoke up for single mothers.* 该是有人替单身母亲说话的时候了。

USAGE NOTE 用法说明: SPEAK

WORD CHOICE 词语辨析: **speak, talk, discuss, describe, say**

Speak is a little formal and often gives the idea that one person is saying more than any others in a conversation. speak这个词略为正式, 并常表示在谈话中一个人说得比其他人多: *He won't listen to me – will you speak to him?* 他不肯听我的 —— 你去跟他说说好吗? | *Could you speak a little louder please?* 请你讲大声一点好吗?

Talk is over twice as frequent in spoken English and usually suggests that two or more people are having a conversation. talk在口语中的使用频率要高一倍多, 并通常表示两人或更多的人在进行谈话: *We stayed up all night talking.* 我们整个晚上都在谈话, 没有睡觉。| *Are you two talking about me?* 你们两个是不是在谈论我?

If you **talk about** something with someone, for example, in order to reach a decision, you **discuss** it. talk about 表示讨论某事以便作出决定时, 也就是说在 discuss: *The boss wants to discuss next year's budget at the meeting.* 老板想在会议上讨论明年的预算问题。You can **discuss** or **describe** something either in speech or in writing. discuss 或describe既可以表示口头上的讨论或描述, 也可以表示书面的讨论或描述。

In British English **speak with** and **talk with** often mean a longer more formal talk than **speak to** or **talk to**, but in American English they are used more generally. 在英国英语中, speak with 和 talk with 常用于比 speak to 和 talk to 更长、更为正式的谈话, 但在美国英语中一般无此区别。

Compare **speak** a language and **speak in** a language. 比较 speak 和 speak in 在表示说某种语言时的用法: *Catherine may speak Greek* means either 'she may know Greek' or 'she knows Greek and may use it on this occasion'; *'Catherine may speak in Greek'* means only the second of these. Catherine may speak Greek 这个句子可以表示"她可能会说希腊语"或"她懂希腊语, 而且她这次可能用希腊语发言"这两种意思。但Catherine may speak in Greek 只表示上述第二种意思。

GRAMMAR 语法

When **speak** is transitive, its object is usually a language. 当speak用作及物动词时, 其宾语通常为某种语言: *What's she speaking* (=what language)? 她讲的是什么语言? | *I don't speak a word of Thai* (NOT 不用 *talk*). 我一句泰语也不会讲。You **say** other things 说其他事情则用 say: *What's she saying?* (=what words?) 她在说些什么? Note that you say 注意, 我们可以说: *I didn't say it/anything/those things* (NOT 不用 *speak it* etc). 我没说过这件事/任何事/那些事。| *I gave my opinion* (NOT 不用 *spoke* my opinion). 我提出我的意见。But you would sometimes say 但我们有时候会说: *She spoke the truth* (=told the truth). 她说了真话。

In writing **talk** is rarely transitive and can take only a few objects. 在书面语中, talk很少用作及物动词, 只有一些单词可用作它的宾语: *He's talking nonsense/business.* 他在胡说八道/谈正经事。Otherwise you need to say **talk about** 一般则必须说talk about: *She talked about her childhood for a long time.* 她谈自己的童年谈了很久。In informal spoken English, however, you will hear things like 不过, 在非正式口语中, 有时也可以听到这些用法: *We're talking big bucks!* (=there is a lot of money involved in this situation) 我们在谈大笔钱的事! or 或 *They're talking cars again* (=they are talking about cars). 他们又在谈汽车了。

When it is transitive neither **talk** nor **speak** can have a person as its object. 在用作及物动词时, talk 和 speak 都不能用人作宾语: *I spoke to him yesterday* (NOT 不用 *spoke him*). 我昨天跟他说过了。| *They should talk to each other more* (NOT 不用 *talk each other*). 他们应当多互相交谈。See also 另见 SAY[1] (WORD CHOICE).

-speak /spik; spiːk/ *suffix* [in nouns 构成名词] the special language, especially slang words or words that are difficult to understand, used in a particular business or activity 行话, 术语, 语言: *computerspeak* 电脑语言

speak·eas·y /ˈspikˌizɪ; ˈspiːkˌiːzi/ *n* [C] a place in the US in the 1920's and 1930's where you could buy alcohol illegally〔20 世纪 20、30年代美国的〕非法经营的售酒处

2 2 **speak·er** /ˈspikɚ; ˈspiːkə/ *n* [C] **1** someone who makes a speech, usually at a meeting 演讲者: *Our speaker tonight is Mr Pearson.* 我们今晚的演讲者是皮尔逊先生。| **after-dinner speaker** (=someone who makes a speech after a formal meal) 宴会后的演讲者 **2 French speaker/English speaker etc** someone who speaks French etc 讲法语/讲英语等的人 **3** the part of a radio or record player where the sound comes out〔收音机或唱机的〕扬声器 **4 the Speaker** an official who controls discussions in a parliament〔议会的〕议长

Speaker's Cor·ner /ˌ‥ ˈ‥/ an area in the northeast corner of Hyde Park in London, where ordinary people can go, especially on Sunday mornings, to make a speech about any subject, and other people listen to them and sometimes argue with them. People often stand on a box to make their speeches. 演讲角〔伦敦海德公园东北角一区域。星期天早晨, 普通百姓可以到那里就任何话题发表演讲, 其他人可以聆听, 并可与演讲者辩论。演讲者通常站在箱子上发表演说〕

speaking tube /ˈ‥ ˌ/ *n* [C] a pipe through which people in different rooms can talk to each other〔各个房间之间的〕通话管

spear[1] /spɪr; spɪə/ *n* [C] **1** a pole with a sharp pointed blade at one end, used as a weapon in the past 矛, 标枪 **2** a thin pointed stem of a plant, shaped like a spear 嫩芽, 嫩枝, 嫩茎: *asparagus spears* 芦笋嫩茎

spear[2] *v* [T] **1** to push or throw a spear into something, especially in order to kill it 用矛刺: *The huntsmen were spearing fish from the river.* 猎人正从河中叉鱼。**2** to push a pointed object, usually a fork, into something, so that you can pick it up 用叉叉起, 用尖物叉起

spear·head[1] /ˈspɪrˌhɛd; ˈspɪəhed/ *v* [T] to lead an attack or organized action 当…的先锋, 带头〔做某事〕: *Ross spearheaded a campaign to improve sales.* 罗斯带头发起一场促销活动。

spearhead[2] *n* [C usually singular 一般用单数] a person or group of people who lead an attack or organized action 先锋, 前导, 先头部队: *The group became the spearhead of the labor union movement.* 这个团体成了工会运动的先锋。

spear·mint /ˈspɪrˌmɪnt; ˈspɪəˌmɪnt/ *n* [U] **1** a fresh MINT[1] (1) taste, often used in sweets 留兰香〔味〕: *spearmint chewing gum* 留兰香味口香糖 **2** the MINT[1] (2) plant that this taste comes from 留兰香〔植物〕

spec /spɛk; spek/ *n BrE informal*【英, 非正式】**1 on spec** if you do something on spec, you do it without being sure that you will get what you are hoping for 碰运气: *I sent in an application on spec.* 我寄去一份申请书碰碰运气。**2 specs** [plural] glasses (GLASS[1] (3)) to help you see 眼镜

1 1 **spe·cial[1]** /ˈspɛʃəl; ˈspeˌʃəl/ *adj* **1** not ordinary or usual but different in some way and often better or more important 特殊的, 特别的: *a special case, deserving special treatment* 一种应加以特殊处理的特殊情况 | *diabetics on a special diet* 实行特殊饮食的糖尿病患者 | **special occasion** (=an important social event) 特殊场合 *I keep this suit for special occasions.* 我把这套西服留在特殊场合穿。| **anything special** *spoken*【口】*Are you doing anything special for Christmas?* 你过圣诞节有什么特别活动吗? | **special edition** (=a special type of car, watch etc produced only for a short time)〔只在一段短时间内生产的汽车、手表等的〕特别版本 **2 special offer** a low price charged for a product for a short time 特价出售: *There's a special offer on this shampoo – two for the price of one.* 这种洗发剂特价出售 —— 买一瓶送一瓶。**3** particularly important to someone and deserving attention, love etc 特别亲密的, 特别受喜爱的: *Rob's a special friend of mine.* 罗布是我一位特别亲密的朋友。| *a wonderful teacher who made every child feel special* 能使每个孩子都感到自己受重视的优秀教师 **4** unusually good 特别好的: *I'd like you to try some of this whisky. It's rather special.* 我想请你尝一尝这种威士忌酒。这是一种不同寻常的好酒。| **nothing special** (=not particularly good) 并非特别好的, 一般的 *"What was the food like?" "Nothing special."* "饭菜怎么样?" "只是一般。" **5** more than usual 格外的, 特别的: *Take special care on the roads tonight – it's icy.* 今晚在路上要格外小心 —— 结冰了。—see 见 ESPECIALLY (USAGE)

special[2] *n* [C usually singular 一般用单数] **1** something that is not usual or ordinary, and is made or done for a special purpose 特别的东西, 特殊的事物: *a two-hour television special on famine in Africa* 长达两小时的关于非洲饥荒的电视特别节目 **2** *informal, especially AmE* a lower price than usual for a particular product for a short period of time【非正式, 尤美】特价: *The supermarket has a special on chicken.* 超级市场有特价鸡出售。| **on special** *Breyer's ice cream is on special this week.* 布雷耶店的冰淇淋本周特价。**3** *ScotE* a type of beer【苏格兰】一种啤酒

special a·gent /ˌ‥ ˈ‥/ *n* [C] *AmE* someone who works for the FBI【美】〔联邦调查局的〕特工, 特别调查员

Special Branch /ˈ‥ ˌ/ *n* [U] a department of the British police force that deals with political crimes or crimes affecting the safety of the government, for example TERRORISM〔英国警察部门的〕政治保安处

special con·sta·ble /ˌ‥ ˈ‥‥/ *n* [C] someone in Britain who has an ordinary job, but is sometimes employed as a police officer when the police need more help〔英国在警力不足时协助维持社会治安的〕特种警察

special de·liv·e·ry /ˌ‥ ˈ‥‥/ *n* [C,U] a service that delivers a letter or package very quickly〔邮件〕快递, 限时专送

special ed·u·ca·tion /ˌ‥ ‥ˈ‥/ *n* [U] the education of children who have particular physical problems or learning problems〔向身体或智力有缺陷的学生提供的〕特殊教育

special ef·fect /ˌ‥ ‥ˈ/ *n* [C] an unusual image or sound in a film or television programme that has been produced artificially〔电影、电视等的〕特技效果: *the amazing special effects in 'Jurassic Park'*《侏罗纪公园》中惊人的特技效果

special forc·es /ˌ‥ ˈ‥/ *n* [plural] soldiers who have been specially trained to fight against GUERRILLA or TERRORIST groups〔从事反游击战和反恐怖主义的〕特种部队

special in·terest group /ˌ‥ ˈ‥ ˌ/ *n* [C] a group of people who all share the same aims 特殊利益集团

spe·ci·al·is·m /ˈspɛʃəlˌɪzəm; ˈspeʃəlɪzəm/ *n* **1** [U] the practice of limiting your interests or activities to particular subjects 专门研究, 专修 **2** [C] an activity or subject that you know a lot about 特长, 专长, 专门学科

spe·cial·ist /ˈspɛʃəlɪst; ˈspeʃəlɨst/ *n* [C] **1** someone who knows a lot about a particular subject, or is very skilled at it 专家: [+in] *a specialist in African history* 非洲史专家 **2** a doctor who knows more about one particular type of illness or treatment than other doctors 专科医生: *a heart specialist* 心脏专科医生 3 3

spe·ci·al·i·ty /ˌspɛʃɪˈælətɪ; ˌspeʃiˈælɨti/ *n plural* **specialities** [C] *BrE*【英】**1** a kind of food that is always very good in a particular restaurant or area〔一家饭馆或某地方的〕特色菜, 名菜; SPECIALTY (1) *AmE*【美】: *Try the mushroom paté – it's our speciality.* 试试肉酱蘑菇吧 —— 这是我们的特色菜。**2** a subject or skill that you know a lot about or have a lot of experience of 专业, 专门研究; 专长; SPECIALTY (2) *AmE*【美】: *Preston's speciality was night photography.* 普雷斯顿的专长是夜间摄影。

spe·cial·ize also 又作 **-ise** *BrE*【英】/ˈspɛʃəlˌaɪz; ˈspeʃəlaɪz/ *v* [I] to limit all or most of your study, business etc to a particular subject or activity 专门研究, 专门从事, 专攻: [+in] *After qualifying, Zelda decided to specialize in contract law.* 取得资格后, 泽尔达决定专门从事合同法业务。—**specialization** /ˌspɛʃələˈzeʃən; ˌspeʃəlaɪˈzeɪʃən/ *n* [C,U] 3

spe·cial·ized also 又作 **-ised** *BrE*【英】/ˈspɛʃəlˌaɪzd; ˈspeʃəlaɪzd/ *adj* trained, designed, or developed for a particular purpose or type of work 专门的; 专用的: *Don't try repairing it yourself – it requires specialized knowledge.* 不要试着自己去修理 —— 这需要具有专业知识。| **highly specialized** (=very specialized) 高度专业化的 *a highly specialized field of study* 高度专门化的研究领域

special li·cence /ˌ‥ ˈ‥/ *n* [C,U] special permission given by the Church of England for a marriage to take place at a time or place not usually allowed 结婚特许证〔英国教会发出的, 允许在通常不准结婚的时间或地点结婚〕

spe·cial·ly /ˈspɛʃəlɪ; ˈspeʃəli/ *adv* **1** for one particular purpose, and only for that purpose 为了特殊目的, 特意地, 专门地: *I had this dress made specially for the wedding.* 我特地为那次婚礼做了这件连衣裙。**2** *especially spoken* much more than usual, or much more than other people or things; ESPECIALLY【尤口】特

S

别, 尤其: *We specially wanted to visit Disneyland.* 我们特别想去参观迪斯尼乐园。—see 见 ESPECIALLY (USAGE)

special needs /ˌ··ˈ·/ *n* [plural] needs that someone has because they have mental or physical problems〔智力或身体有缺陷的人的〕特殊需要: *children with special needs* 有特殊需要的儿童

Special O·lym·pics, the /ˌ·· ·ˈ··/ an international programme of sports events and sports training for adults and children who have mental or physical problems 特殊奥林匹克运动会, 特奥会〔专门为智力障碍或生理缺陷的成人和儿童安排的国际性体育训练计划和比赛〕

special school /ˈ··ˌ·/ *n* [C] a school for children with physical problems or problems with learning〔专为智力或身体有缺陷的孩子开办的〕特殊学校

spe·cial·ty /ˈspɛʃəltɪ; ˈspeʃəlti/ *n* [C] *especially AmE*【尤美】**1** a kind of food that is always very good in a particular area or restaurant〔一地或一家饭馆的〕特色菜, 拿手菜; SPECIALITY (1) *BrE*【英】: *Our specialty is clam chowder.* 我们的特色菜是蛤肉汤。**2** a subject or job that you know a lot about or have a lot of experience of 专业, 专门研究; 专长; SPECIALITY (2) *BrE*【英】*Johnson's specialty is Medieval European history.* 约翰逊的专业是中世纪欧洲史。

W3 **spe·cies** /ˈspiʃiz; ˈspiːʃiːz/ *n plural* **species** [C] a group of animals or plants which are all similar and can breed together to produce young animals or plants of the same kind as them〔动植物的〕物种, 种: **endangered species** (=one that may soon no longer exist) 濒危物种 *This type of rattlesnake has been declared an endangered species.* 这类响尾蛇已被宣布为濒危物种了。

S1 W1 **spe·cif·ic¹** /spɪˈsɪfɪk; spəˈsɪfɪk/ *adj* **1** [only before noun 仅用于名词前] a specific thing, person, or group is one particular thing etc 具体的, 特定的, 特有的: *Is this game meant for a specific age-group?* 这种游戏是专为特定年龄组的人安排的吗? **2** detailed and exact 详细的, 明确的, 确切的: *Una gave us very specific instructions.* 尤娜给了我们非常详尽的指示。| *You said you live in the West Country, could you be a bit more specific?* 你说你住在英格兰西南部, 你能说得更确切一点吗? **3 specific to** *formal* limited to, or affecting only one particular thing【正式】仅限于…的, 只对…有影响的: *a disease specific to horses* 只有马才会得的病

specific² *n* **1 specifics** [plural] particular details that must be decided exactly 细节, 详情: **get down to/go into specifics** *I can't go into specifics at this time, but I can tell you that we have an agreement.* 我现在不能详谈具体情况, 但我可以告诉你我们已经有一项协议。**2** [C] *technical* a drug that has an effect only on one particular DISEASE【术语】特效药

S2 W3 **spe·cif·ic·ally** /spɪˈsɪfɪklɪ; spəˈsɪfɪkli/ *adv* **1** concerning or intended for one particular type of person or thing only 特定地, 具体地, 专门地: *a video specifically aimed at teenagers* 专门以青少年为对象的录像片 **2** in a detailed or exact way 明确地: *I specifically asked you not to do that!* 我明确地要求你不要那样做! **3** [sentence adverb 句子副词] used when you are adding more exact information 说明确些, (说具体些) 就是: *Tom's hoping to move to Spain, or more specifically, Barcelona.* 汤姆希望迁往西班牙, 说具体些就是巴塞罗那。

spe·ci·fi·ca·tion /ˌspɛsəfəˈkeʃən; ˌspesəfəˈkeɪʃən/ *n* **1** [C usually plural 一般用复数] a detailed instruction about how something should be designed or made 规格说明, 明细规范: *a car manufactured according to exact specifications* 按照严格的规格制造的汽车 | **job specification** (=detailed description of what a job involves) 工作职责说明 **2** [C] a clear statement of what is needed or wanted 具体[明确]说明: *Any student can apply for a loan, the only specification being that you must be in full-time education.* 任何学生均可申请贷款, 唯一要求是申请人必须是全日制学生。

specific grav·i·ty /ˌ·ˌ·· ˈ···/ *n* [U] *technical* the weight of a substance divided by the weight of the amount of water that would fill the same space【术语】比重

W3 **spe·ci·fy** /ˈspɛsəˌfaɪ; ˈspesəfaɪ/ *v* **specified, specifying** [T] to state something in an exact and detailed way 具体指明, 明确规定, 详述: *Names and numbers were not specified.* 名字和号码都没有具体指明。| **specify who/what/how etc** *Did you specify where the new work station has to go?* 你有没有指明新的工作站必须设在什么地方? | **specify that** *The rules clearly specify that competitors must not accept payment.* 规则清楚地说明参赛者不得接受报酬。

spe·ci·men /ˈspɛsəmən; ˈspesəmən/ *n* [C] **1** a small amount or piece of something that is taken from a plant or animal, so that it can be tested or examined 样品, 样本, 标本: *a zoological specimen* 动物标本 | [+of] *The doctor will need a specimen of your blood.* 医生需要你的血样。**2** a single example of something 实例, 范例: *a very fine specimen of 12th century glass* 12世纪玻璃的极好的样品 **3** *humorous* a person you are describing in a particular way, usually in an unpleasant way【幽默】某种类型的人, 家伙: *Who's that revolting specimen your daughter's going out with?* 那个和你女儿出双入对的讨厌家伙是谁?

spe·cious /ˈspiʃəs; ˈspiːʃəs/ *adj formal* seeming to be true or correct, but actually false【正式】似是而非的, 貌似正确的: *a specious argument* 貌似有理的论据 —**speciously** *adv* —**speciousness** *n* [U]

speck /spɛk; spek/ *n* [C] a very small mark, spot, or piece of something 小斑点; 小片: *The boat was soon just a speck on the horizon.* 那艘船很快就变成了地平线上的一个小点。—see picture on page A7 参见 A7 页图

speck·le /ˈspɛkl; ˈspekəl/ *n* [plural] small marks or spots covering a background of a different colour〔许多〕小斑点

speck·led /ˈspɛkld; ˈspekəld/ *adj* covered with many small marks or spots 带有许多小斑点的, 布满小斑点的: *speckled eggs* 蛋壳上布满小斑点的鸡蛋 —see picture on page A16 参见 A16 页图

spec·ta·cle /ˈspɛktəkl; ˈspektəkəl/ *n* [C] **1** a very impressive show or scene 奇观, 壮观的场面[景象]: *The military parade was a magnificent spectacle.* 这次军事检阅场面非常壮观。**2** [usually singular 一般用单数] an unusual thing or situation to be seen or noticed 不同寻常的事[现象]: [+of] *the curious spectacle of a cat actually chasing a dog* 一只猫竟然在追逐一只狗的稀奇事 **3 make a spectacle of yourself** to behave in a way that is likely to make other people notice you and laugh at you 出洋相 **4 spectacles** [plural] *formal* two pieces of round glass in a frame, worn in front of your eyes to help you to see clearly; glasses (GLASS¹ (3))【正式】眼镜 —see also 另见 **see sth through rose-coloured spectacles** (ROSE-COLOURED (2))

spec·tac·u·lar¹ /spɛkˈtækjələ; spekˈtækjələ/ *adj* **1** very impressive and exciting 壮观的, 精彩的, 引人注目的: *a spectacular fireworks display* 壮观的烟火表演 **2** unusually great or large 巨大的, 辉煌的: *His new show is a spectacular success.* 他的新演出取得巨大的成功。—**spectacularly** *adv*

spectacular² *n* [C] an event or performance that is very large and impressive 壮观的场面; 盛大的演出: *a television spectacular* 场面浩大的电视节目

spec·tate /ˈspɛktet; spekˈteɪt/ *v* [I] to watch a sports event 观看体育比赛

spec·ta·tor /ˈspɛktetə; spekˈteɪtə/ *n* [C] someone who is watching an event or game〔体育运动或比赛的〕观看者, 观众: *The match attracted over 40,000 spectators.* 这场比赛吸引了四万多名观众。

Spectator, The a magazine which contains articles about politics, important events, and the arts. There are separate British and US magazines called *The Spectator*. The magazine was started in the UK in 1711, by Joseph Addison and Sir Richard Steele.《旁观者》〔一杂志名称, 刊载政治、重大时事以及艺术类文章, 有英国版和美国版两种。约瑟夫·艾迪生和理查德·斯蒂尔爵士于 1711 年在英国创刊〕

spectator sport /ˈ··· ˌ·/ *n* [C] a sport that people go and watch 观众众多的体育运动

spec·ter /ˈspɛktə; ˈspektə/ *n* [C] the American spelling of SPECTRE spectre 的美式拼法

Spec·tor /ˈspɛktə; ˈspektə/, **Phil** /fɪl; fɪl/ (1940-) a US record producer and songwriter, who had an important influence on pop music in the 1960s. He developed a style called the 'wall of sound', which was used as a background for groups such as The Crystals and The Ronettes. 斯佩克特〔(1940-), 美国唱片制作人、词作家。曾对20世纪60年代的流行音乐产生过重大影响。首创"音墙"风格, "水晶"和"罗内特"等演唱组合均以此为音乐背景〕

spec·tra /ˈspɛktrə; ˈspektrə/ the plural of SPECTRUM

spec·tral /ˈspɛktrəl; ˈspektrəl/ *adj* **1** *literary* connected with or like a spectre【文】鬼魂的; 幽灵般的: *a spectral apparition* 幽灵 **2** *technical* connected with or made by a SPECTRUM【术语】光谱的, 由光谱所作的

spec·tre *BrE*【英】, **specter** *AmE*【美】/ˈspɛktə; ˈspektə/ *n* **1 the spectre of** something that people are afraid of because it may affect them soon 引起恐惧的事物: *the spectre of unemployment* 失业的恐惧 **2** [C] *literary* a GHOST【文】鬼魂, 幽灵

spec·tro·scope /ˈspɛktrəˌskop; ˈspektrəskəʊp/ *n* [C] an instrument used for forming and looking at spectra (SPECTRUM (2)) 分光镜 —**spectroscopy** /spɛkˈtrɑskəpɪ; spekˈtrɒskəpi/ *n* [U] —**spectroscopic** /ˌspɛktrəˈskɑpɪk; ˌspektrəˈskɒpɪk◂/ *adj*

spec·trum /ˋspɛktrəm; ˈspektrəm/ *n plural* **spectra** /-trə; -trə/ [C] **1** a complete range of opinions, ideas, situations etc, going from one extreme to its opposite〔观点、思想、情况等的〕范围，幅度: *Our speakers tonight come from both ends of the political spectrum.* 我们今晚的演讲人来自政坛的两个极端。| [+of] *a wide spectrum of opinion* 众说纷纭 **2** the set of bands of coloured light into which a beam of light may be separated by passing it through a PRISM 光谱 **3** a complete range of radio, sound etc waves 频谱: *the electromagnetic spectrum* 电磁（波）谱

spec·u·late /ˋspɛkjəˌlet; ˈspekjʊleɪt/ *v* **1** [I,T] to think or talk about the possible causes or effects of something without knowing all the facts or details 猜测，推测: **[+on/about]** *We can only speculate about why he did it.* 我们只能猜测他为什么那样做。| **speculate that** *George began to speculate that the two events might be linked.* 约翰开始猜测那两件事可能有联系。**2** [I] to buy goods, property, shares (SHARE[2] (5)) in a company etc hoping that you will make a large profit when you sell them 投机，做投机买卖: **[+in]** *Ned had speculated in gold and lost heavily.* 内德曾作黄金投机买卖，损失惨重。—**speculator** *n* [C]: *property speculators* 房地产投机者[炒家]

spec·u·la·tion /ˌspɛkjəˋleʃən; ˌspekjʊˈleɪʃən/ *n* [C,U] **1** the act of guessing without knowing all the facts about something, or the guesses that you make 猜测，推测: **[+about]** *increased speculation about the possibility of tax cuts* 关于减税可能性的诸多猜测 | **speculation that** *There is some speculation that the president was aware of the situation.* 有人猜测总统是了解情况的。| **pure speculation** (=speculation that is not based on any facts) 纯属猜测 *The jury should disregard the witness's last statement as pure speculation.* 陪审团应当认为证人的最后陈述毫无事实根据而不予考虑。| **wild/idle speculation** (=speculation that is unlikely to be true) 胡乱猜测 **2** the act of trying to make a profit by speculating (SPECULATE (2)) 投机买卖，投机生意: *property speculation* 房地产投机买卖

spec·u·la·tive /ˋspɛkjəˌletɪv; ˈspekjʊlətɪv/ *adj* **1** based on guessing, not on information or facts 猜测的，猜想的: *These figures are, at best, speculative.* 这些数字顶多也是个猜测。**2** bought or done in the hope of making a profit later 投机的: *speculative investments* 投机性的投资 —**speculatively** *adv*

sped /spɛd; sped/ the past tense and past participle of SPEED

2 2 **speech** /spitʃ; spiːtʃ/ *n* **1** [C] a talk, especially a formal one about a particular subject, given to a group of people 演说，演讲: *an election speech* 竞选演说 | **give/make/deliver a speech** *Dr Ozu made a brilliant speech about the need for change.* 奥祖博士发表了关于必须进行改革的精彩演说。**2** [U] the ability to speak 说话的能力: *Only humans are capable of speech.* 只有人类才具备说话能力。| **power of speech** (=the ability to speak) 说话能力 *brain damage resulting in the loss of the power of speech* 导致说话能力丧失的脑部损伤 | **speech impediment** (=a physical or nervous problem that affects your speech) 言语障碍 **3** [U] spoken language rather than written language 口语: *In speech we use a smaller vocabulary than in writing.* 在口语中我们用的词汇比在书面语中用的少。| **freedom of speech** (=the right to say whatever you want) 言论自由 **4** [U] the particular way in which someone speaks〔某人的〕说话方式: *Bob's speech was slurred, and he sounded drunk.* 鲍勃说话含糊不清，听起来像是喝醉了酒。**5** [C] a set of lines that an actor must say in a play〔演员的〕台词: *Hamlet's longest speech* 哈姆雷特最长的那段台词 —see also 另见 DIRECT SPEECH, FIGURE OF SPEECH, INDIRECT SPEECH, PART OF SPEECH, REPORTED SPEECH, **speech bubble** (BUBBLE[1] (3))

speech day /ˈ· ·/ *n* [C] an occasion held once a year in some British schools, when prizes are given to children〔英国的一些学校一年一度的〕授奖演讲日

spee·chi·fy /ˋspitʃəˌfaɪ; ˈspiːtʃɪfaɪ/ *v* [I] *informal* to make speeches in order to seem important【非正式】〔高谈阔论地〕发表演说: *speechifying about the dishonesty of politicians* 高谈阔论地大谈政客的不诚实问题

speech·less /ˋspitʃlɪs; ˈspiːtʃləs/ *adj* unable to speak because you feel very angry, upset etc〔因愤怒、难过等而〕说不出话的，哑口无言的: **[+with]** *speechless with rage* 气得说不出话来 —**speechlessly** *adv* —**speechlessness** *n* [U]

speech marks /ˈ· ·/ *n* [plural] the marks (" ") or (' ') that show when someone starts speaking and when they stop 引号〔表示说话开始和结束的符号" "或' '〕

speech syn·the·siz·er /ˈ· ,···/ *n* [C] a computer system that produces sounds like human speech 言语合成器〔能产生类似人声的电脑系统〕

speech ther·a·py /ˌ· ˈ···/ *n* [U] treatment that helps people who have difficulty in speaking properly 言语障碍矫治（法），言语治疗 —**speech therapist** *n* [C]

speed[1] /spid; spiːd/ *n* 1 2

1 ►OF MOVEMENT 运动的◄ [C,U] how fast something moves or travels 速度，速率: *What speed are we doing?* 我们的速度如何？| *Police are advising motorists to reduce speed.* 警方劝告驾车者减速。| **pick up/gather speed** (=gradually start to travel faster) 逐渐加快速度 *Once outside the station, the train began to pick up speed.* 一出车站，火车就开始加速。| **a speed of 60 mph/80 kph etc** *a truck traveling at a speed of 50 mph* 以每小时50英里的速度行驶的卡车 | **at top/full speed** (=as fast as possible) 以最高速度，全速 *Forster was bundled into a waiting car and driven away at top speed.* 福斯特被匆匆塞进一辆正在等候的汽车，然后车子全速开走了。| **at high/low speed** (=very fast or very slow) 以高速/慢速 *a metal disc revolving at high speed* 高速转动着的金属盘 | **at breakneck speed** (=dangerously fast) 以极危险的高速 | **at speed** *formal* (=fast)【正式】快速 *The bus was already travelling at speed.* 这辆公共汽车已经在疾驰了。

2 ►OF ACTION 行动的◄ [U] the rate at which something happens or is done〔事物发生或进行的〕速度，快速: *Everyone was surprised by the speed of events.* 每个人都为这些事件发生得如此之快而感到吃惊。| **with speed** *formal* (=quickly)【正式】迅速地 *The government acted with speed and efficiency.* 政府的行动迅速而有效。| **reading/operating speed** (=the speed at which a person reads or a machine operates) 阅读速度/〔机器〕运行速度

3 ►PHOTOGRAPHY 摄影◄ [C] **a)** the degree to which photographic film is sensitive to light〔摄影胶片的〕感光速度 **b)** the time it takes for a camera SHUTTER (2) to open and close 快门速度: *a shutter speed of 1/250 second* 1/250秒的快门速度

4 ►DRUG 毒品◄ [U] *slang* an illegal drug that makes you very active; AMPHETAMINE【俚】安非他明，苯丙胺〔一种兴奋剂〕

5 five-speed/ten-speed etc having five etc gears (GEAR[1] (1)) 五挡的/十挡的等: *a five-speed gearbox* 有五挡的变速箱

speed[2] *v past* **sped** /spɛd; sped/ *also* 又作 **speeded** **1** [I always+adv/prep] to go quickly 快行，急走: **[+along/by/off etc]** *The robbers sped off in their getaway car.* 劫匪们开着逃跑用的汽车疾驰而去。**2** [T always+adv/prep] take someone or something somewhere very quickly 挟[带]着…快走: **speed sb to/away/back etc** *Security guards sped her to a waiting helicopter.* 保安员把她迅速带往一架正在等候的直升机。**3 be speeding** to be driving faster than the legal limit 超速驾驶: *I got caught speeding on Route 40 yesterday.* 我昨天在40号公路上超速驾驶被抓住了。 3

speed by *phr v* [I] if time speeds by, it seems to pass very quickly〔时间〕很快地过去，飞逝: *The weeks sped by and soon it was time to go back to school.* 几个星期转眼就过去了，很快又到了开学的时候。

speed up *phr v* [I,T] to move or happen faster or make something move or happen faster（使）加快速度: *We'd better speed up if we want to be on time.* 我们如果想要准时赶到，最好还是加快速度。| **speed sth ↔ up** *The new system will speed up the registration process.* 这个新制度将加快注册过程。

speed·boat /ˋspidˌbot; ˈspiːdbəʊt/ *n* [C] a small boat with a powerful engine designed to go fast 快艇

speed bump /ˈ· ·/ *n* [C] a narrow raised part across a road that forces traffic to go slowly〔横在路面上的〕交通减速板

speed·ing /ˋspidɪŋ; ˈspiːdɪŋ/ *n* [U] the offence of driving faster than the legal limit 超速驾驶: *Liz was found guilty of speeding and fined £50.* 莉兹被判犯有超速驾驶罪，罚款50英镑。

speed lim·it /ˈ· ,··/ *n* [C] the fastest speed allowed by law on a particular piece of road〔为特定路段设定的〕限速，速度限制: *a 30 mph speed limit* 每小时30英里的限速

speed·om·e·ter /spiˋdɑmətɚ; spɪˈdɒmɪtə/ *n* [C] an instrument in a vehicle that shows how fast it is going〔车辆上的〕速度计 —see picture on page A2 参见A2页图

speed read·ing /ˈ· ,··/ *n* [U] the skill of reading very quickly 快速阅读

speed skat·ing /ˈ· ,··/ *n* [U] the sport of racing on ice wearing ICE SKATES 速度滑冰

speed trap /ˈ· ·/ *n* [C] a place on a road where police wait to catch drivers who are going too fast 车速监视区[路段]

speed·way /ˋspidˌwe; ˈspiːdweɪ/ *n* [U] **1** the sport of racing MOTORCYCLES or cars on a special track 摩托车赛；汽车比赛 **2** [C] a special track for this sport 赛车跑道

speed·well /ˋspidwɛl; ˈspiːdwel/ *n* [U] a small European wild plant with light blue or white flowers 婆婆纳〔一种小型欧洲野生植物，开浅蓝色或白色花〕

speed·y /ˋspidɪ; ˈspiːdi/ *adj* **1** happening or done quickly or without delay 迅速的，很快的；及时的: *We hope you make a*

speedy recovery. 我们希望你迅速康复。| *The accusations brought a speedy denial.* 那些指责迅即遭到否认。**2** a speedy car goes fast〔汽车〕快速的 —**speedily** *adv* —**speediness** *n* [U]

spe·le·ol·o·gy /ˌspiliˋɑlədʒɪ; ˌspiːliˈɒlədʒi/ *n* [U] *technical*【术语】**1** the sport of walking and climbing in CAVES 洞穴攀行运动 **2** the scientific study of CAVES 洞穴学 —**speleologist** *n* [C] —**speleological** /ˌspiliəˋlɑdʒɪkl; ˌspiːliəˈlɒdʒɪkəl◂/ *adj*

spell[1] /spɛl; spel/ *v past tense and past participle* **spelt** /spɛlt; spelt/ *especially BrE*【尤英】, **spelled** *especially AmE*【尤美】**1** [I,T] to form a word by writing or naming the letters in the correct order〔用字母〕拼写, 拼出: *"How do you spell your name?" "S-M-Y-T-H."* "你的名字怎样拼写?" "是S-M-Y-T-H。" | **can spell** (=be good at spelling words correctly) 拼写能力强 *I used to fail exams because I couldn't spell.* 我过去考试总是不及格, 因为我的拼写能力很差。| **spell sth wrong/wrongly** *You've spelled my name wrong.* 你把我的名字拼错了。**2** [T not in passive 不用被动态] if letters spell a word, they form it〔字母〕拼成〔某词〕: *B-O-O-K spells 'book'.* B-O-O-K 拼成 book(书)。**3 spell trouble/disaster/danger etc** if a situation or action spells trouble etc, it makes you expect trouble etc 招致[带来]麻烦/灾难/危险等: *Such a scandal could spell disaster for the government.* 这样的丑闻可能给政府带来灾难。**4** [T] *AmE & AustrE* to do someone else's work for them for a short period so that they can rest【美和澳】暂时代替〔某人的工作〕: *Can I spell you at the wheel?* 我替你开会儿车好吗?

spell sth ↔ **out** *phr v* [T] **1** to show how a word is spelled by writing or saying the letters separately in the right order 逐个字母写[读]出〔某个单词〕: *"Could you spell that out for me?" "F-A-H-E-R-T-Y."* "你能给我逐个字母拼出那个词吗?" "F-A-H-E-R-T-Y。" **2** to explain something clearly and in detail 清楚地说明; 详细地解释: **spell out how/what etc** *Will the Minister spell out exactly how he intends to finance these tax cuts?* 部长会具体地详细解释他打算怎样填补减税所造成的财政缺口吗? **3** to write a word in its complete form instead of using an ABBREVIATION 写出〔某词的〕全部字母〔而不是其缩略式〕: *If you are using initials for the title of a group, be sure to spell them out at least once in your article.* 如果你要用首字母代表一个团体的名称, 在文章中至少要有一次把它的全名拼写出来。

spell[2] *n* [C] **1** a piece of magic that someone does or the special words or ceremonies used in doing it 魔法; 符咒, 咒语: **put a spell on/cast a spell over** (=do a piece of magic to change something) 用符咒镇住 *The wizard had put a spell on the city to send all its people to sleep.* 巫师对那个城市施了咒语, 让所有人都进入梦乡。| **break the spell** (=stop the spell from working) 破除符咒 | **under a spell** *The frog was really a handsome young prince under a spell.* 那只青蛙其实是一位中了魔咒的年轻英俊的王子。**2** a period of a particular kind of activity, weather etc, usually a short period〔某种活动, 天气等的〕一段时间, 一阵子: *After a brief spell in the army I returned to teaching.* 我在军队干了很短一段时间之后, 又回到了教学岗位。| [+of] *a spell of bad luck* 倒霉的日子 | **a cold/wet/dry spell** *Do you remember that foggy spell we had in April?* 你还记得我们四月份那段大雾时期吗? **3** a power that attracts and influences you so strongly that it completely controls your feelings 吸引力, 魅力; 迷惑力: **be/fall under sb's spell** *Maya fell under his spell within minutes of meeting him.* 梅亚认识他几分钟后就被他的魅力迷住了。**4** a very short period of feeling ill〔疾病的〕一阵发作: *a dizzy spell* 一阵头晕

spell·bind·ing /ˋspɛlˌbaɪndɪŋ; ˈspelbaɪndɪŋ/ *adj* extremely interesting and holding your attention completely 极有趣的, 使人入迷的: *a spellbinding tale* 引人入胜的故事 —**spellbinder** *n* [C]

spell·bound /ˋspɛlˌbaund; ˈspelbaʊnd/ *adj* extremely interested in something you are listening to 听得入迷的: **hold sb spellbound** *The storyteller held his audience spellbound.* 那个讲故事的人使听众听得入迷。

spell-check·er /ˈ·ˌ··/ *n* [C] a computer PROGRAM that checks what you have written and makes your spelling correct〔电脑的〕拼写检查程序 —**spell-check** *v* [I,T]

spel·ler /ˋspɛlɚ; ˈspelə/ *n* [C] **1 good/bad/poor speller** someone who is good or bad at spelling words correctly 拼写能力好/不好的人 **2** *AmE* a book for teaching spelling【美】单词拼写课本

spell·ing /ˋspɛlɪŋ; ˈspelɪŋ/ *n* **1** [U] the act of spelling words correctly or the ability to do this 拼写能力; 拼字: *Her spelling has improved.* 她的拼写能力有进步。**2** [C] the way in which a word is spelled〔单词的〕拼(写)法: *What's the American spelling of 'colour'?* colour 这个词的美式拼法是什么?

spelling bee /ˈ·· ˌ·/ *n* [C] *AmE* a competition in which the winner is the one who spells the most words correctly【美】单词拼写比赛

spelt /spɛlt; spelt/ *especially BrE*【尤英】the past tense and past participle of SPELL

spe·lunk·ing /spɪˋlʌŋkɪŋ; spɪˈlʌŋkɪŋ/ *n* [U] *AmE* the sport of walking and climbing in CAVES【美】洞穴攀行运动 —**spelunker** *n* [C]

Spence /spɛns; spens/, **Sir Basil** (1907-76) a British ARCHITECT, who designed Coventry Cathedral 斯彭斯爵士〔(1907-1976), 英国建筑师, 考文垂大教堂的设计者〕

spend /spɛnd; spend/ *past tense and past participle* **spent** /spɛnt; spent/ *v*

1 ▶MONEY 钱◀ [I,T] to use your money to buy or pay for things 用(钱), 花费: **spend money/£5/$10/a lot** *I spent so much money this weekend!* 我这个周末花钱太多! | **spend money etc on sth** *More money should be spent on health and education.* 应该把更多的钱花在医疗保健和教育上。| **spend money etc on sb** (=buy things for someone) 花钱买东西给某人 *Cecilia spends far too much money on those spoilt kids of hers.* 塞西莉亚在她那些惯坏了的孩子身上花的钱太多了。| **money well spent** (=a sensible way of spending money) 值得花的钱 *The repairs cost a lot, but it's money well spent.* 维修费用很高, 但这些钱是值得花的。

2 ▶TIME 时间◀ [T] to pass or use time 度过, 消磨: **spend time in/with etc** *We'll have to spend the night in a hotel.* 我们将不得不住旅馆过夜。| *I want to spend more time with my family.* 我想花更多的时间和家人在一起。| **spend time doing sth** *Much of my time is spent studying financial reports.* 研究财政报告花去我很多时间。

3 spend the night with to stay for the night and have sex with someone 同…一起过夜并发生性关系

4 ▶FORCE/EFFORT 力量/努力◀ [T] *literary* to use all of something【文】用尽, 耗尽: *The storm had spent its force.* 暴风雨已经停了下来。

5 spend a penny *BrE spoken* an expression meaning to URINATE, used when you want to avoid saying this directly【英口】小便〔委婉说法〕: *I need to spend a penny – where are the loos?* 我要方便一下——请问洗手间在哪儿?

spend·er /ˋspɛndɚ; ˈspendə/ *n* [C] someone who spends money 花钱者, 用钱的人: **big spender** (=someone who regularly spends very large amounts of money) 花钱大手大脚的人

Spender, Sir Ste·phen /ˋstivən; ˈstiːvən/ (1909-95) a British poet and critic whose books of poetry include *The Still Centre* and *The Generous Days* 斯彭德爵士〔(1909-1995), 英国诗人、评论家。著有诗集《静止的中心》和《慷慨的日子》等〕

spend·ing /ˋspɛndɪŋ; ˈspendɪŋ/ *n* [U] the amount of money spent, especially by a government or organization〔尤指政府或组织的〕开销, 花费: **government/public/defence spending** *a reduction in government spending on defense* 政府国防开支的下降

spending mon·ey /ˈ·· ˌ··/ *n* [U] money that you have available to spend on your own personal pleasures 零用钱, 零花钱: *$25 a week in spending money* 每星期25美元的零花钱

spend·thrift /ˋspɛndˌθrɪft; ˈspendˌθrɪft/ *n* [C] someone who spends money carelessly, even when they do not have a lot of it 挥霍者, 浪费金钱的人

Spen·ser /ˋspɛnsɚ; ˈspensə/, **Ed·mund** /ˌɛdmənd; ˈedmənd/ (?1552-99) an English poet famous especially for his EPIC poem *The Faerie Queene* which he never finished 斯宾塞〔(?1552-1599), 英国诗人。其史诗《仙后》虽未完成, 但尤为著名〕

spent[1] /spɛnt; spent/ the past tense and past participle of SPEND

spent[2] *adj* **1** already used, and now empty or useless 用过的; 失效的: *spent cartridges* 空弹壳 **2 be a spent force** if a political idea or organization is a spent force, it no longer has any power or influence〔政治思想〕已丧失影响; 〔政治组织〕已经失去权力: *They had written Wilson off as a spent force in British politics.* 他们已经认定威尔逊在英国政治中不再具有影响力了。**3** *literary* extremely tired【文】精疲力竭的

sperm /spɝm; spɜːm/ *n* **1** *plural* **sperm** *or* **sperms** [C] a cell produced by the sex organs of a male animal, which is able to join with the female egg to produce a new life 精子 **2** [U] the liquid from the male sex organs that these cells swim in; SEMEN 精液

sper·ma·cet·i /ˌspɝməˋsɛtɪ; ˌspɜːməˈseti/ *n* [U] a solid oily substance found in the head of the SPERM WHALE and used in making skin creams, CANDLES etc 鲸蜡, 鲸脑油

sper·ma·to·zo·on /ˌspɝmətəˋzoən; ˌspɜːmətəˈzəʊɒn/ *n plural* **spermatozoa** /-ˋzoə; -ˈzəʊə/ [C] *technical* a sperm【术语】精子

sperm bank /ˈ· ·/ *n* [C] a place where SEMEN is kept to be used in medical operations to help women to become PREGNANT〔供人工授精用的〕精子库

sper·mi·cide /ˋspɝməˌsaɪd; ˈspɜːmɪ̣saɪd/ *n* [C,U] a cream or liquid that kills SPERM*s*, used while having sex to prevent the woman from becoming PREGNANT〔用于避孕的〕杀精子剂 —**spermicidal** /ˌspɝməˋsaɪdəl; ˌspɜːmɪ̣ˈsaɪdl◂/ *adj*: *spermicidal jelly* 杀精膏

sperm whale /ˈ· ·/ *n* [C] a large WHALE, hunted for its oil, fat and SPERMACETI 抹香鲸

Sper·ry /ˋspɛrɪ; ˈsperi/, **El·mer Am·brose** /ˋɛlməˋæmbroz; ˈelmə ˈæmbrəʊz/ (1860-1930) a US engineer and inventor, who invented equipment that helps ships to sail in the right direction 斯佩里〔(1860-1930)，美国工程师、发明家，发明了帮助船只控制航向的仪器〕

spew /spju; spjuː/ *v* **1** also 又作 **spew out/forth** [I always+adv/prep,T] to flow out of something in large quantities, or to make something flow out in this way (使)喷出，(使)涌出：[**+from/into/over**] *Lava spewed from the volcano.* 熔岩从火山口喷出。| **spew sth (out)** *The burst pipe was spewing out dirty water.* 污水正从破裂的管子中涌出来。**2** also 又作 **spew up** [I,T] *BrE informal* to VOMIT【英，非正式】呕吐

SPF /ˌɛs pi ˋɛf; ˌes piː ˈef/ Sun Protection Factor; a number on a bottle of SUNTAN cream that tells you how much protection it gives you from the sun〔防晒霜的〕防晒系数：*SPF 25* 防晒系数 25

sphag·num /ˋsfægnəm; ˈsfægnəm/ *n* [C,U] *technical* a type of MOSS【术语】泥炭藓〔一种苔藓〕

sphere /sfɪr; sfɪə/ *n* [C] **1** a ball shape 球，球形，球体：*The Earth is not a perfect sphere.* 地球并不是一个标准的球体。—see picture at 参见 SHAPE[1] 图 **2** a particular area of activity, work, knowledge etc〔活动、工作、知识等的〕范围，领域：*His reputation lies in the scientific sphere.* 他在科学领域中颇有声誉。**3 sphere of influence** a person or country's sphere of influence is the area where they have power to change things 势力范围，影响所及的范围

-sphere /sfɪr; sfɪə/ *suffix technical* [in nouns 构成名词] the air surrounding the Earth at a particular height【术语】距离地球表面某一高度的气体外层：*the stratosphere* 平流层

spher·i·cal /ˋsfɛrəkḷ; ˈsferɪkəl/ *adj* having the shape of a sphere 球形的，球状的

sphe·roid /ˋsfɪrɔɪd; ˈsfɪərɔɪd/ *n* [C] *technical* a shape that is similar to a ball, but not a perfect sphere【术语】扁球体，椭球体

sphinc·ter /ˋsfɪŋktə; ˈsfɪŋktə/ *n* [C] *technical* a muscle that surrounds a passage in your body, and can tighten in order to close it【术语】括约肌：*the anal sphincter* 肛门括约肌

sphinx /sfɪŋks; sfɪŋks/ *n* [C] an ancient Egyptian image of a lion with a human head lying down〔古埃及的〕狮身人面像，斯芬克斯(像)

Sphinx, the 1 also 又作 **the great sphinx** a large, very ancient sphinx which is close to the Pyramids of El Giza in Egypt and is visited by many tourists 狮身人面像〔极为古老的巨型斯芬克斯雕像，位于埃及吉萨金字塔附近，前去观赏者众多〕**2** in Greek MYTHOLOGY, a creature with the head of a woman and the body of a lion. She lay outside Thebes and killed people who could not answer her RIDDLE (=very difficult question). Oedipus answered the riddle, and the Sphinx killed herself. 斯芬克斯〔希腊神话中的一个怪物，头为美女，身为狮子。她卧于底比斯城外，凡猜不中其谜语者均被杀死。俄狄浦斯猜中谜底后，她便自杀身亡〕

spic, spik /spɪk; spɪk/ *n* [C] *AmE* a very offensive word meaning a Spanish-speaking American【美】讲西班牙语的美国佬〔极具冒犯性的用语〕

spice[1] /spaɪs; spaɪs/ *n* **1** [C,U] one of the various types of powder or seed, taken from plants, that you put into food you are cooking to give it a special taste〔从植物中提取，烹调用的〕香料；调味品：*Indian spices such as cumin and saffron* 小茴香、番红花之类的印度香料 **2** [singular,U] interest or excitement that is added to something〔为某事增添〕趣味，情趣，风味：*They need gossip to add a bit of spice to their dull lives.* 他们需要流言飞语来给枯燥乏味的生活增添一点趣味。—see also 另见 **variety is the spice of life** (VARIETY (5))

spice[2] *v* [T] **1** also 又作 **spice up** to add interest or excitement to something 使增添趣味：*an essay that needs spicing up* 需要增添趣味的小品文 **2** to add spice to food 给〔食物〕加香料：[**+with**] *baked apples spiced with cinnamon and nutmeg* 加进肉桂和肉豆蔻的烤苹果

spick-and-span /ˌspɪk ən ˋspæn; ˌspɪk ən ˈspæn/ *adj* a room, house etc that is spick-and-span is completely clean and tidy〔房间、房子等〕干干净净的，整洁的

spic·y /ˋspaɪsɪ; ˈspaɪsi/ *adj* **1** food that is spicy has a pleasantly strong taste, and gives you a pleasant burning feeling in your mouth〔食物〕加有香料的，辛辣的：*pasta with a spicy tomato sauce* 加上辣番茄酱的面条 **2** a story that is spicy is slightly shocking or rude〔故事〕下流的，粗俗的：*a spicy rumour* 猥亵的传闻 —**spicily** *adv* —**spiciness** *n* [U]

spi·der /ˋspaɪdə; ˈspaɪdə/ *n* [C] a small creature with eight legs which makes networks of thread for catching insects 蜘蛛

Spi·der·man /ˋspaɪdəˌmæn; ˈspaɪdəmæn/ *trademark* an imaginary hero of CARTOON STRIPS and films who is able to climb very high walls like a SPIDER and catch criminals in a web which he throws over them【商标】蜘蛛侠〔连环漫画和电影中一个虚构的英雄。能像蜘蛛一样攀爬高墙，并将一张网撒向罪犯，将他们一举捕获〕

spi·der·web /ˋspaɪdəˌwɛb; ˈspaɪdəweb/ *n* [C] *AmE* a very fine network of sticky threads made by a spider to catch insects【美】蜘蛛网；COBWEB *BrE*【英】

spi·der·y /ˋspaɪdərɪ; ˈspaɪdəri/ *adj* writing that is spidery is untidy with long thin lines〔字迹〕细长而不整齐的

spiel /spil; ʃpiːl/ *n* [C,U] *informal* fast talk that the speaker has used many times before and that is intended to persuade people to buy something【非正式】喋喋不休的游说；〔为了推销商品的〕长串流利言辞：*the salesman's spiel* 推销员一番流畅油滑的话

Spiel·berg /ˋspilbɝg; ˈspiːlbɜːg/, **Ste·ven** /ˋstivən; ˈstiːvən/ (1946-) one of the most successful film DIRECTOR*s* in the history of the US cinema, famous for making films that are full of exciting events and special effects. His many popular films include *Jaws* (1975), *Raiders of the Lost Ark* (1981), *E.T.* (1982), *Jurassic Park* (1993), and *SCHINDLER'S LIST* (1994). 斯皮尔伯格〔(1946-)，美国电影史上最成功的导演之一。其影片以惊心动魄的情节和特技效果著称。执导了许多深受欢迎的影片，如《大白鲨》(1975)、《夺宝奇兵》(1981)、《外星人》(1982)、《侏罗纪公园》(1993) 和《辛德勒的名单》(1994) 等〕

spif·fing /ˋspɪfɪŋ; ˈspɪfɪŋ/ *adj BrE old-fashioned* excellent【英，过时】极好的，出色的，一流的

spif·fy /ˋspɪfɪ; ˈspɪfi/ *adj informal especially AmE* very neat and fashionable【非正式，尤美】非常整洁而时髦的：*a spiffy little red car* 一辆漂亮时髦的红色小汽车

spig·ot /ˋspɪgət; ˈspɪgət/ *n* [C] **1** a TAP[1] (1,2) in a large container that controls the flow of liquid from it〔大容器的〕塞子，栓 **2** *especially AmE* an outdoor TAP[1] (1)【尤美】室外水龙头

spik /spɪk; spɪk/ *n* [C] another spelling of SPIC spic 的另一种拼法

spike[1] /spaɪk; spaɪk/ *n* [C] **1** something long and thin with a sharp point, especially a pointed piece of metal 尖状物；金属钉状物：*spikes along the top of a fence* 栅栏的尖头 **2 spikes** [plural] metal points on the bottom of a shoe used for running, or the shoe itself〔跑鞋鞋底上的〕鞋钉；钉鞋 —see picture at 参见 STUD[1] 图 **3** *technical* a sharp point on a GRAPH【术语】〔图表〕曲线上的陡升线 **4** *technical* the head of a plant that produces grain such as corn or wheat【术语】〔玉米、麦子等的〕穗

spike[2] *v* [T] **1** to push a sharp point into something〔把尖物〕刺进，刺穿：*a guy spiking litter and putting it in a garbage bag* 用尖头棍子戳起废纸放进垃圾袋的人 **2** to add a strong alcoholic drink to a weak or non-alcoholic one 加烈酒于〔淡酒或不含酒精的饮料中〕：[**+with**] *Bill's drink had been spiked with vodka.* 比尔的饮料掺了伏特加酒。**3** to prevent someone from saying something or printing something in a newspaper 阻止〔某人〕在报纸上发表〔言论〕：*a clumsy attempt to spike rumours of a cabinet split* 企图阻止在报刊上发表内阁分裂传闻的笨拙做法 **4 spike sb's guns** *BrE* to spoil an opponent's plans【英】打乱〔破坏〕对手的计划

spik·y /ˋspaɪkɪ; ˈspaɪki/ *adj* **1** having long sharp points 带〔尖〕刺的，有刺的：*a spiky cactus* 带刺的仙人掌 **2** hair that is spiky is stiff and stands up on top of your head〔头发〕挺直的，竖起的 —see picture on page A6 参见 A6 页图 **3** *BrE informal* easily offended or annoyed【英，非正式】暴躁的，易怒的 —**spikiness** *n* [U]

3 **spill¹** /spɪl; spɪl/ *past tense and past participle* **spilt** /spɪlt; spɪlt/ *especially BrE*【尤英】, **spilled** *especially AmE*【尤美】*v* **1** [I, T] if you spill a liquid or if it spills, it accidentally flows over the edge of a container（使）溢出，（使）泼出，（使）洒落: **spill sth down/on/over** *Oh no! I've spilt coffee all down my shirt!* 糟糕，我把咖啡洒在衬衫上了！| [+on/over] *He slipped and the wine spilled all over the carpet.* 他滑倒，酒洒了一地毯。**2** [I always+ adv/prep] if people spill out of somewhere, they move out in large groups〔人群〕涌出: [+out/into/onto etc] *Crowds from the theatre were spilling onto the street.* 人群从戏院涌到了街上。**3 spill the beans** *informal* to tell something that someone else wanted you to keep a secret【非正式】泄露秘密，走漏风声 **4 spill your guts** *AmE* to tell someone everything you know about something, especially because you are upset【美】〔尤指因心情不好〕把自己知道的一切和盘托出: *some drunk spilling his guts to me at the bar* 在酒吧里把心事向我和盘托出的一个醉汉 **5 spill blood** *literary* to kill or wound people【文】杀人；伤人 —see also 另见 **cry over spilt milk** (CRY¹ (5))

spill 洒落

spill over *phr v* [I] if a problem or bad situation spills over, it spreads and begins to affect other places, people etc〔问题或坏情况〕蔓延，扩散: [+into] *There is a danger that the conflict will spill over into neighbouring towns.* 这场冲突有蔓延到邻近城镇的危险。

spill² *n* **1** [C,U] an act of spilling something or an amount of something that is spilled 洒出，溢出；洒出量，溢出量: **oil spill** *The oil spill in Alaska threatens ecological catastrophe.* 阿拉斯加的溢油将给生态环境带来灾难。**2** [C] a piece of wood or twisted paper for lighting lamps, fires etc〔用于点灯、生火等的〕木片；纸捻 **3** [C] *old-fashioned* a fall from a horse, bicycle etc【过时】〔从马、自行车等上的〕摔下

spil·lage /ˈspɪlɪdʒ; ˈspɪlɪdʒ/ *n* [C,U] a SPILL² (1) 洒出（量），溢出（量）

spill·way /ˈspɪl,we; ˈspɪlweɪ/ *n* [C] a passage for water to flow over or around a DAM (=wall for holding back water)〔水坝的〕溢洪道

spilt /spɪlt; spɪlt/ *especially BrE*【尤英】the past tense and past participle of SPILL

3 **spin¹** /spɪn; spɪn/ *past tense and past participle* **spun** /spʌn; spʌn/ *v*

1 ►TURN AROUND 旋转◄ [I,T] to turn around and around very quickly, or to make something do this（使）快速旋转: *The ice skater was spinning faster and faster.* 滑冰者转得越来越快。| *spin the roulette wheel* 转动轮盘赌的转轮 | **spin (sth/sb) around** *Liz spun around on her heel to face me.* 莉兹猛地转过身来面对着我。

spin 快速旋转

2 ►WOOL/COTTON 羊毛/棉花◄ [I,T] to make cotton, wool etc into thread by twisting it 将〔棉花、羊毛等〕纺成〔纱、线〕，纺〔纱、线〕: *The wool is spun into thread and then woven.* 先将羊毛纺成线，然后再织。

3 ►WET CLOTHES 湿衣服◄ [T] to get water out of clothes using a machine after you have washed them〔用机器〕使〔洗过的衣物〕脱水，旋干

4 ►INSECT 昆虫◄ [T] if a SPIDER or insect spins a WEB (1) or COCOON, it produces thread to make it〔蜘蛛〕吐丝结网；〔昆虫〕吐丝作茧

5 sb's head spins if your head spins, you feel as if you might FAINT because you are shocked, excited, or drunk〔因震惊、兴奋、醉酒等〕某人头都晕了: *My head was spinning with all this new information.* 所有这些新资料把我头都弄晕了。

6 spin a story/yarn/line [T] to tell someone a story that is not true in order to deceive them〔为了骗人〕编造故事: *beggars spinning hard-luck stories* 编造倒霉故事骗人的乞丐

7 ►DRIVE 驾驶◄ [I always+adv/prep] to drive or travel quickly 开车疾驰: [+past/along etc] *Barbara waved as she spun past in her new sportscar.* 芭芭拉一边招手一边开着她那辆新跑车飞驰而过。

spin sth ↔ **off** *phr v* [T] **1** to produce a new television programme using characters from another programme〔根据另一个电视节目〕编出〔新的节目〕: *'The Rifleman' spun off another new series, 'Wanted Dead or Alive.'*《步枪手》又派生出一部新的电视系列剧《亡命天涯》。**2** to form a separate and partly independent company from parts of an existing company〔从现存公司中〕组成〔一个部分独立的子公司〕: *The company spun off its financial services division in 1988.* 这家公司于1988年组成了它的金融服务子公司。

spin sth ↔ **out** *phr v* [T] **1** to make something continue for longer than is necessary 拖长，拖延: *I'm paid by the hour, so I spin the work out as long as I can.* 我拿计时工资，所以我尽量把工作拖长。**2** to use money, food etc as carefully and slowly as possible because you do not have very much of it 尽可能延长使用〔钱、食物等〕: [+over] *I've only got £10 left, so we'll have to spin it out over the whole week.* 我只剩10英镑，所以我们必须省着用，使它能维持整个星期。

spin² *n*

1 ►TURNING 旋转◄ [C] an act of turning around quickly 快速旋转: *the spin of a top* 陀螺的快速旋转 | *The dance ended with a dramatic spin.* 这场舞蹈以一阵激动人心的快速旋转结束。

2 ►CAR 汽车◄ [C] *informal* a short trip in a car for pleasure【非正式】〔乘车〕兜风: *Let's go for a spin in the country.* 我们开车到乡下去兜兜风吧。

3 ►BALL 球◄ [U] if you put spin on a ball in a game such as tennis or CRICKET (2), you deliberately make the ball turn very quickly so that it is difficult for your opponent to hit〔网球、板球等的〕旋转（球）

4 fall/go into a (flat) spin a) to become very confused and anxious 陷入恐慌，变得惊慌失措: *The sudden fall on the stockmarket sent brokers into a spin.* 股市暴跌使经纪人惊慌失措。**b)** if an aircraft goes into a spin it falls suddenly, turning around and around〔飞机的〕螺旋下降，旋冲

5 ►WET CLOTHES 湿衣服◄ **give sth a spin** *BrE* to turn clothes around very fast in a machine to remove water from them【英】〔用机器〕给〔湿衣服〕脱水

6 ►INFORMATION 消息◄ [singular] *informal especially AmE* a way of providing information that makes it seem to be favourable for a particular person or political party【非正式，尤美】〔对某人或政党有利的〕倾向性的报道[看法]: *trying to put a positive spin on the economic figures* 试图对经济数字作倾向性的乐观报道 —see also 另见 SPIN DOCTOR

7 ►SCIENCE 科学◄ [singular] a quality of an ELEMENTARY PARTICLE that influences its behaviour with other particles〔基本粒子的〕自旋

spi·na bif·i·da /ˌspaɪnə ˈbɪfɪdə; ˌspaɪnə ˈbɪfɪdə/ *n* [U] a serious condition in which a person's SPINE is split down the middle from birth, leaving their SPINAL CORD unprotected 脊柱裂

spin·ach /ˈspɪnɪtʃ; ˈspɪnɪdʒ/ *n* [U] a vegetable with large dark green leaves 菠菜 —see picture on page A9 参见A9页图

spin·al /ˈspaɪnl; ˈspaɪnl/ *adj* belonging to or affecting your SPINE (1) 脊柱的；脊椎的: *spinal injuries* 脊柱受伤

spinal col·umn /ˈ·· ˌ··/ *n* [C] *technical* your SPINE (1)【术语】脊柱

spinal cord /ˌ·· ˈ·/ *n* [C] the thick string of nerves enclosed in your SPINE (1) by which messages are sent to and from your brain 脊髓

spin·dle /ˈspɪndl; ˈspɪndl/ *n* [C] **1** a part of a machine shaped like a stick, around which something turns〔机器的〕轴；心轴 **2** a round pointed stick used for twisting the thread when you are spinning wool 纺锤；纱锭

spin·dly /ˈspɪndlɪ; ˈspɪndli/ *adj* long and thin in a way that looks weak 细长的，纤弱的: *spindly legs* 细长的双腿

spin doc·tor /ˈ· ˌ··/ *n* [C] *informal* someone whose job is to give information to the public in a way that gives the best possible advantage to a politician or organization【非正式】舆论导向专家: *The White House spin doctors are hard at work explaining the President's about-face on taxes.* 白宫的舆论导向专家正在努力为总统在税收问题上的彻底改变作出解释。

spin-dry·er /ˌ· ˈ··/ *n* [C] *especially BrE* a machine that removes most of the water from washed clothes by spinning them around and around very fast【尤英】旋转式脱水机 —**spin-dry** *v* [T]

spine /spaɪn; spaɪn/ *n* [C] **1** the row of bones down the centre of your back that supports your body and protects your SPINAL CORD 脊柱，脊椎 —see picture at 参见 SKELETON 图 **2** a stiff sharp point on an animal or plant〔动植物的〕刺，刺毛: *cactus spines* 仙人掌的刺 **3** the part of a book that the pages are fastened onto 书脊

spine-chil·ling /ˈ· ,· ·/ *adj* a spine-chilling story or film is very frightening in a way that people enjoy〔故事、电影〕令人毛骨悚然的 —**spine-chiller** /ˈspaɪn ˌtʃɪlɚ; ˈspaɪn ˌtʃɪlə/ *n* [C]

spine·less /ˈspaɪnlɪs; ˈspaɪnləs/ *adj* **1** lacking courage and determination 没有骨气的, 懦弱的: *a bunch of spineless do-gooders* 一群懦弱的空想的社会改良家 **2** without a spine 无脊柱的: *spineless creatures such as jellyfish* 水母一类的无脊椎动物 —**spinelessly** *adv* —**spinelessness** *n* [U]

spi·net /ˈspɪnɪt; spɪˈnet/ *n* [C] a musical instrument of the 16th and 17th centuries, which is played like a piano 斯皮耐琴〔16、17世纪类似钢琴的一种键琴〕

spin·na·ker /ˈspɪnəkɚ; ˈspɪnəkə/ *n* [C] a sail with three points at the front of a boat, used when the wind is directly behind〔赛艇的〕大三角帆 —see picture at 参见 YACHT 图

spin·ner /ˈspɪnɚ; ˈspɪnə/ *n* [C] **1** someone whose job is to make thread by twisting cotton, wool etc 纺纱工 **2** a BOWLER in a game of CRICKET (2) who throws the ball with a spinning action〔板球的〕旋转球投手 **3** a thing used for catching fish that moves around and around when pulled through the water〔钓鱼用的〕旋式诱饵 —see also 另见 MONEY-SPINNER

spin·ney /ˈspɪnɪ; ˈspɪni/ *n* [C] *BrE* a small area of trees and bushes【英】小树林, 灌木丛

spinning jen·ny /ˈspɪnɪŋ ˌdʒɛnɪ; ˈspɪnɪŋ ˌdʒeni/ *n* [C] an industrial machine used in the past for making cotton, wool etc into thread〔旧时的〕珍妮纺纱机

spinning wheel /ˈ· · ,·/ *n* [C] a simple machine consisting of a wheel on a frame that people used in their homes in the past for making cotton, wool etc into thread〔从前家用的〕纺车

spin-off /ˈ· ·/ *n* [C] **1** an unexpected but useful result of something, that happens in addition to the intended result 副产品, 派生产品; 附带的结果: *Laser research has had important spin-offs for eye surgery.* 激光研究产生了一些适用于眼科手术的重要附带成果。—see also 另见 **spin off** (SPIN¹) **2** a television programme involving characters that were previously in another programme or film〔利用其他节目或电影中人物编成的〕派生电视节目: *'Maude' was a spin-off from 'All in the Family'.*《莫德》是《一家人》的派生电视剧。

spin·ster /ˈspɪnstɚ; ˈspɪnstə/ *n* [C] *old-fashioned* an unmarried woman, usually one who is no longer young and seems unlikely to marry【过时】〔年龄不小的〕未婚女人, 老处女 —**spinsterhood** *n* [U]

CULTURAL NOTE 文化注释

There is an old STEREOTYPE of a spinster as a MIDDLE-AGED woman who lives alone, is not very attractive, and has never been asked by any man if she will marry him. Spinster is, however, an old-fashioned word which is not used much now. 人们旧观念中的老处女是一个独自生活的中年女性, 相貌平平, 从没有男人向其求过婚。不过, spinster 是一个过时的词, 现在已经很少使用。

spin the bot·tle /,· · ˈ· ·/ *n* [U] a game in which people sitting in a circle spin a bottle in the middle and when the bottle stops spinning and points to someone, that person must do something, such as kissing another person 转瓶游戏〔玩时大家围成一圈, 转动放在中间的瓶子, 瓶子停下来时瓶口所指的人得做一事, 如亲吻某人〕

spin·y /ˈspaɪnɪ; ˈspaɪni/ *adj* having a lot of spines (SPINE (2)) 多刺的: *a spiny gorse bush* 多刺的荆豆丛

spi·ral¹ /ˈspaɪrəl; ˈspaɪərəl/ *adj* in the form of a continuous line or curve that winds around a central point, moving further away from it all the time 螺旋形的, 螺线形的: *a spiral watch spring* 螺旋形的手表发条 —**spirally** *adv*

spiral² *n* [C] **1** a spiral curve 螺线 **2** a process, usually a harmful one, in which something gradually but continuously rises, falls, gets worse etc 螺旋式过程〔持续上升或下降、恶化等, 通常指有害的变化〕: *Shipbuilding entered a spiral of decline.* 造船业陷入了持续衰退之中。| **upward/downward spiral** *a vicious downward spiral of debt* 债务的恶性持续增加 **3 inflationary spiral** a situation where wages and prices rise continuously because the level of INFLATION (1) is high 恶性通货膨胀

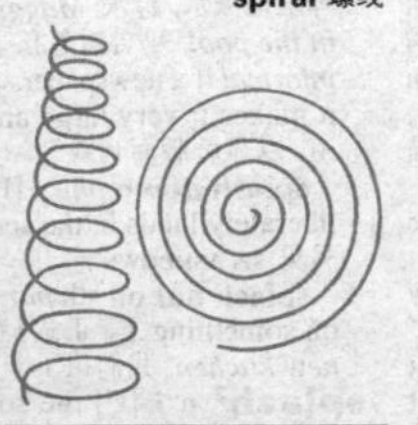
spiral 螺线

spiral³ *v* **spiralled, spiralling** *BrE*【英】, **spiraled, spiraling** *AmE*【美】[I] **1** [always+adv/prep] to move in a continuous curve that gets nearer to or further from its central point as it goes round 螺旋形地上升[下降]: [+to/around etc] *The damaged plane spiralled to the ground.* 损坏了的飞机盘旋堕地。**2** if debt or the cost of something spirals, it increases quickly and uncontrollably〔债务、物价〕急剧而失控地上升: *the spiraling cost of legal services* 法律服务费的急剧上涨

spiral stair·case /,· · ˈ· ·/ *n* [C] a set of stairs arranged in a circular pattern so that they go around a central point as they get higher 螺旋状楼梯

spire /spaɪr; spaɪə/ *n* [C] a roof that rises steeply to a point on top of a tower, especially on a church〔教堂等的〕塔尖, 尖顶

spir·it¹ /ˈspɪrɪt; ˈspɪrɨt/ *n* S3 W2

1 ▶INNER PART 内部◀ [singular,U] an inner part of someone that includes their thoughts and feelings, and is thought of as making them what they are 精神, 心灵〔指人的内部世界, 包括思想、感情〕: *His spirit was untameable.* 他的精神不可驯服。| *strong in spirit* 内心坚强的 | **independent/proud/free etc spirit** (=a person with a particular type of character) 独立/骄傲/自由等的人 *a toddler already showing an independent spirit* 已经表现出独立性格的学步的小孩

2 ▶SOUL 灵魂◀ [C] the part of someone that is believed to continue to live after they have died 灵魂: *Although Laurie is dead, I can feel his spirit with me.* 劳里虽然已经死了, 但我还能感觉到他的灵魂和我在一起。—compare 比较 SOUL (1)

3 ▶DEAD PERSON 死人◀ [C] a dead person who is believed to have returned to this world and has strange or magical powers; GHOST¹ (1) 鬼, 鬼魂: *Some people believe that evil spirits can be removed by exorcism.* 有些人相信驱邪术可驱除恶鬼。

4 ▶HAPPY/SAD 快乐的/悲伤的◀ spirits [plural] the way someone feels at a particular time, for example if they are cheerful or sad 心境, 情绪, 兴致: **be in good/low spirits** (=be happy or sad) 心情好/不好 | **be in high spirits** (=be excited) 情绪高涨 *We started our journey in high spirits.* 我们兴高采烈地踏上旅途。| **keep sb's spirits up** (=make sure someone does not become less cheerful) 使某人保持心情开朗 | **raise/lift sb's spirits** (=make someone feel happier and more hopeful) 鼓舞/振奋某人的情绪 *long, hot summer days that lift the spirits* 令人精神焕发的炎热长夏 | **sb's spirits lift/sink** (=become more or less cheerful) 某人高兴起来/不起来 *My spirits sank when I saw the mess they'd left.* 我看见他们弄得那样乱七八糟就高兴不起来。

5 in spirit you say you will be somewhere in spirit or with someone in spirit, when you cannot be with them but are thinking about them 在内心里, 在精神上: *I can't come to your wedding but I'll be there in spirit.* 我不能参加你们的婚礼, 但到时候我的心会和你们在一起的。

6 ▶DRINK 酒◀ [C usually plural 一般用复数] **a)** *especially BrE* a strong alcoholic drink such as WHISKY or BRANDY【尤英】烈(性)酒〈如威士忌或白兰地〉 **b)** *BrE* liquid such as alcohol, used for cleaning【英】〔用于清洁的〕酒精

7 get into the spirit/enter into the spirit *BrE* to start to feel as happy, excited etc as the people around you【英】融入欢乐的气氛中: *Judith couldn't really enter into the spirit of the occasion.* 朱迪思不能真正投入那场合的欢乐气氛中。

8 ▶ATTITUDE 态度◀ [singular] the attitude that you have towards something 心态, 态度: *You've got to approach this meeting in the right spirit.* 你一定要以正确的心态来对待这个会议。| *a true spirit of friendship* 友谊的真正态度

9 ▶DETERMINATION 决心◀ [U] *approving* courage, energy, and determination【褒】勇气; 活力; 决心: *Our team played with great spirit.* 我们队打[踢]得劲头十足。| **fighting spirit** (=brave determination) 斗志 | **break sb's spirit** (=make someone lose their courage and determination) 挫某人的锐气 *slaves whose spirits had been broken* 锐气已经受挫的奴隶

10 that's the spirit *spoken* used to express approval of someone's behaviour or attitude【口】这就对了, 这种精神才对〔用于认可某人的行为或态度〕

11 team/community/public etc spirit a strong feeling of belonging to a particular group and wanting to help them 团队/团体/公益等精神

12 the spirit of the age/times the set of ideas, beliefs, and aims that are typical of a particular period in history 时代精神

13 when/as the spirit moves you when you feel that you want to do something 当你有心要做的时候

spirit² *v* [T] **spirit sb/sth away/off** to remove someone or something in a secret or mysterious way 秘密[神秘地]把某人/某物带[弄]走: *At the end of the press conference Jackson was*

spirited away through a back door. 记者招待会结束时，杰克逊被偷偷地从后门送走了。

spir·it·ed /ˈspɪrɪtɪd; ˈspɪrɨtɨd/ *adj approving* having energy and determination【褒】精神饱满的，生气勃勃的；有决心的：*Raphael is so young and spirited.* 拉斐尔非常年轻，生气勃勃。| **a spirited defence/debate** *a spirited defence of her decisions* 对她的决定所作的有力辩护 —see also 另见 HIGH-SPIRITED, LOW-SPIRITED, MEAN-SPIRITED, PUBLIC-SPIRITED

spirit lamp /ˈ‥ ·/ *n* [C] *BrE* a small lamp that burns METHYLATED SPIRITS【英】酒精灯

spir·it·less /ˈspɪrɪtlɪs; ˈspɪrɨtləs/ *adj* **1** having no energy or determination 没精打采的，无朝气的；没有决心的 **2** not cheerful 情绪低落的，垂头丧气的 —**spiritlessness** *n* [U]

spirit lev·el /ˈ‥ ˌ‥/ *n* [C] a tool for testing whether a surface is level 水准仪，气泡式水准仪，水泡水平仪；LEVEL[1] (11) *AmE*【美】

Spirit of St. Lou·is, The /ˌspɪrɪt əv sənt ˈluɪ; ˌspɪrɨt əv sənt ˈluːi/ the aircraft in which Charles Lindbergh made the first flight by one person across the Atlantic Ocean "圣路易斯精神"号〔查尔斯·林白首次单独驾机飞越大西洋时使用的飞机〕

spir·i·tu·al[1] /ˈspɪrɪtʃuəl; ˈspɪrɨtʃuəl/ *adj* **1** connected with your spirit rather than with your body or mind 精神（上）的，心灵的：*As a priest I'm responsible for your spiritual welfare.* 作为一个神父，我对你精神上的幸福负责。| *spiritual values* 精神价值 **2** connected with religion 宗教（上）的：*the spiritual authority of the church* 教会的宗教权威 **3 spiritual home** a place where you feel you belong because you share the ideas and attitudes of that society 精神家园，精神归宿〔指一个自己能认同其思想和态度的地方〕—**spiritually** *adv*

spiritual[2] *n* [C] a religious song of the type sung originally by the black people of the US 灵歌〔一种原为美国黑人唱的宗教歌曲〕

spir·i·tual·is·m /ˈspɪrɪtʃuəlˌɪzəm; ˈspɪrɨtʃʊlɪzəm/ *n* [U] the belief that dead people may send messages to living people, usually through a MEDIUM (=someone with special powers) 招魂说，降灵说〔认为死人可以通过灵媒把信息传给活人〕—**spiritualist** *n* [C] —**spiritualistic** /ˌspɪrɪtʃuəˈlɪstɪk; ˌspɪrɨtʃʊˈlɪstɪk◂/ *adj*

spir·i·tu·al·i·ty /ˌspɪrɪtʃuˈæləti; ˌspɪrɨtʃuˈælɨti/ *n* [U] the quality of being interested in religion or religious matters 灵性，对宗教[宗教事物]的热衷

spir·i·tu·ous /ˈspɪrɪtʃuəs; ˈspɪrɨtʃuəs/ *adj* [only before noun 仅用于名词前] *technical* containing alcohol【术语】含酒精的

spit[1] /spɪt; spɪt/ *past tense and past participle* **spat** /spæt; spæt/ also 又作 **spit** *AmE*【美】; *present participle* **spitting** *v*

1 ▶LIQUID FROM YOUR MOUTH 口水◀ [I] to blow a small amount of SALIVA (=the liquid in your mouth) out of your mouth 吐口水，吐唾沫：**[+at/on]** *Mom, Judy spit at me!* 妈妈，朱迪向我吐口水！| *Kevin cleared his throat and spat on the path.* 凯文清了清喉咙，往路上啐了一口。| *Don't get too close to the camels – they spit!* 不要太靠近那些骆驼 —— 它们会喷唾沫的！

2 ▶FOOD ETC 食物等◀ [T] to force something out of your mouth 吐：*spit blood* 吐血 | **spit sth out** *Ian was chewing on some gristle but was too polite to spit it out.* 伊恩嚼到一些软骨头，但他很讲礼貌，没有把它吐出来。

3 ▶RAIN 雨◀ **be spitting** to rain very lightly 下小雨：*You don't need an umbrella, it's only spitting.* 你不用带雨伞，只飘着一点小雨。

4 ▶SAY STH 说话◀ [T] also 又作 **spit out** to say something quickly in a very angry way 急促愤怒地说：*"Don't even think of taking it!" she spat.* "你甚至连想也别想拿它！"她愤怒地说。

5 spit it out *spoken* used to ask someone to tell you something that they seem too frightened or embarrassed to say【口】爽快地说出来〔用于让人说其不敢或不愿说的话〕：*Come on Jean, spit it out!* 说吧，琼，爽爽快快地说出来吧！

6 ▶SMALL PIECES 小片片◀ [I] to send out small bits of something, for example fire or hot oil, into the air〔火花、滚烫的油花等〕进溅，发出噼啪[毕剥]声：*sausages spitting in a pan* 在锅里噼啪作响的香肠 | *The van drove off, gravel spitting from under the wheels.* 小货车开走了，碎石从轮子下噼噼啪啪地弹出。

7 ▶CAT 猫◀ [I] if a cat spits it makes short, angry sounds〔猫在愤怒时〕发出咕噜咕噜声

8 be within spitting distance *spoken* to be very close to where you are【口】在很近处

9 I could just spit *spoken* used to say that you are very angry or annoyed【口】我简直气坏了

spit[2] *n* **1** [U] the watery liquid that is produced in your mouth; SALIVA 唾液，唾沫，口水 **2** [C] a long thin stick that you put through meat to turn it and cook it over a fire 烤肉扦子，炙扦子 **3** [C] a long narrow piece of land that sticks out into the sea, a river etc 沙嘴〔伸入水域中的狭长条陆地〕—see picture on page A12 参见 A12 页图 **4 be the (dead) spit of** *BrE spoken* to look exactly like someone else【英口】一模一样：*Sam is the dead spit of his dad.* 萨姆长得和他爸爸一模一样。**5 spit and polish** *informal* thorough cleaning and polishing【非正式】彻底的打扫擦洗 **6 spit and sawdust** *BrE spoken* a spit and sawdust PUB is rough, dirty and simple in style【英口】〔酒馆〕破旧的，肮脏的，简陋的

Spit·al·fields /ˈspɪtl̩fildz; ˈspɪtlfiːldz/ a place in East London where there used to be a market selling fruit, vegetables, and flowers. There is now a new market which sells organic vegetables. 斯皮塔尔费尔茨〔东伦敦过去的果蔬、鲜花市场。该地现有一处新市场，专营有机蔬菜〕

spit·ball /ˈspɪtˌbɔl; ˈspɪtbɔːl/ *n* [C] *AmE* a small piece of paper that children put in their mouth and then throw at each other【美】小孩放进嘴里弄湿后投向别人的小纸团

spite[1] /spaɪt; spaɪt/ *n* **1 in spite of** without being prevented by something; DESPITE 虽然；不顾；尽管…（仍…）：*We went out in spite of the rain.* 尽管下着雨，我们还是出去了。| **in spite of the fact that** *Kelly loved her husband in spite of the fact that he drank too much.* 虽然她丈夫喝酒很凶，凯莉仍然爱着他。**2** [U] a feeling of wanting to hurt or upset people, for example because you are JEALOUS or think you have been unfairly treated 恶意，怨恨，坏心眼：**out of spite** (=because of spite) 出于恶意 *She broke it just out of spite.* 她就是出于恶意把它打破的。| **pure/sheer spite** (=spite and nothing else) 纯属恶意 **3 in spite of yourself** if you do something in spite of yourself, you do it although you did not expect or intend to do it 不由自主地，身不由己地

spite[2] *v* [T only in infinitive 仅用于不定式] to deliberately annoy or upset someone 故意与〔某人〕作对，恶意对待：*The neighbours throw things over the garden wall just to spite us.* 邻居把东西扔过花园围墙，故意和我们作对。—see also 另见 **cut off your nose to spite your face** (CUT OFF (9))

spite·ful /ˈspaɪtfʊl; ˈspaɪtfəl/ *adj* deliberately nasty to someone in order to hurt or upset them 有恶意的，怀恨在心的：*What I can't forgive is that it was such a spiteful thing to do.* 我不能原谅的是，竟然干出那样可恶的事。—**spitefully** *adv* —**spitefulness** *n* [U]

Spit·fire /ˈspɪtˌfaɪr; ˈspɪtfaɪə/ a type of small fighter aircraft used by the British air force during World War II. It was especially important in the Battle of Britain. "喷火式"战斗机〔二战时期英国空军使用的一种小型战斗机。在"不列颠之战"中发挥了至关重要的作用〕

spitfire *n* [C] someone, especially a woman, who becomes angry very easily 烈性子的人〔尤指女人〕

spitting im·age /ˌ‥ ˈ‥/ *n* **be the spitting image of sb** to look exactly like someone else 长相与某人一模一样

spit·tle /ˈspɪtl̩; ˈspɪtl/ *n* [U] *old-fashioned* the liquid in your mouth; SPIT[2] (1)【过时】唾沫，口水

spit·toon /spɪˈtun; spɪˈtuːn/ *n* [C] a container used to SPIT[1] (1) into 痰盂

spiv /spɪv; spɪv/ *n* [C] *BrE old-fashioned* a man who gets money from small dishonest business deals【英，过时】不务正业、专靠欺诈谋生的人

splash[1] /splæʃ; splæʃ/ *v* **1** [I] if a liquid splashes, it hits or falls on something noisily or it moves noisily〔液体〕溅泼，飞溅，溅落：**[+against/on/over]** *Great drops of rain splashed on the window.* 大滴大滴的雨点噼里啪啦地打在窗户上。**2** [T always+adv/prep] to make someone or something wet with a lot of small drops of water or other liquid 泼溅〔液体〕于：**splash sth on/over/with etc sth** *Shivering, he splashed cold water on his face and washed his hands.* 他一边发抖，一边用冷水泼脸、洗手。**3** also 又作 **splash about/around** [I] to make water fly up in the air with a loud noise by hitting it or by moving around in it 哗啦哗啦地溅水，蹚水：*Maggie watched the children splashing about in the pool.* 玛吉看着孩子们在游泳池里哗啦哗啦地玩水。**4** [T] *informal* if a newspaper splashes a story or picture over its pages, it makes it very large and easy to notice【非正式】以大篇幅报道，以显著版面刊载

splash down *phr v* [I] if a SPACECRAFT splashes down it deliberately lands in the sea〔宇宙飞船在海面上〕溅落 —see also 另见 SPLASHDOWN

splash out on sth *phr v* [T] *informal* to spend a lot of money on something【非正式】在…上花很多钱：*We splashed out on a new kitchen.* 我们花了一大笔钱重新装备厨房。

splash[2] *n* **1** [C] the sound of a liquid hitting something or being moved around quickly〔液体〕溅泼声，飞溅声：*Rachel fell into the river with a loud splash.* 雷切尔扑通一声掉进河里。—

see picture on page A19 参见 A19 页图 **2** [C] a mark made by a liquid splashing onto something else 洒溅的斑点: *There were splashes of paint all over my clothes.* 我衣服上溅满了油漆斑点。**3 a splash of colour** small area of bright colour 一片鲜艳的颜色 **4 make a splash** *informal* to do something that gets a lot of public attention【非正式】惹人注目, 引起轰动: *Russell's new show made a big splash in New York.* 拉塞尔的新演出在纽约引起很大的轰动。**5** [singular] *especially BrE* a small amount of liquid added to a drink【尤英】〔加入饮料中的〕少量液体: *Just a splash of milk in my coffee, please.* 请给我的咖啡加点牛奶。

splash³ *adv informal* with a splash【非正式】扑通一声地: *You should have seen Rex – he jumped splash into the lake!* 可惜你没有亲眼看见雷克斯——他扑通一声跳进湖里!

splash·back /ˈsplæʃˌbæk; ˈsplæʃbæk/ *BrE*【英】, **splashboard** /ˈsplæʃˌbɔrd; ˈsplæʃbɔːd/ *AmE*【美】*n* [C] the area of a bathroom or kitchen wall that is behind TAPS and covered in tiles (TILE¹ (1))〔浴室或厨房水龙头后面贴有瓷砖的〕挡溅板

splash·down /ˈsplæʃˌdaʊn; ˈsplæʃdaʊn/ *n* [C,U] a landing by a SPACECRAFT in the sea〔宇宙飞船在海上的〕溅落

splash guard /ˈ· ·/ *n* [C] *AmE* a flat piece of rubber hanging behind the wheel of a vehicle to prevent mud being thrown up【美】〔汽车车轮后的〕挡泥板; MUDFLAP *BrE*【英】

splash·y /ˈsplæʃɪ; ˈsplæʃi/ *adj AmE* big, bright and very easy to notice; FLASHY【美】显眼的, 惹人注意的

splat¹ /splæt; splæt/ *n* [singular] *informal* a noise like something wet hitting a surface hard【非正式】〔湿物击打表面时发出的〕啪哒声

splat² *v* **splatted, splatting** [I,T] to make a noise like something wet hitting a surface, or to make something make this noise (使)发啪哒声: **[+against]** *Big raindrops splatted against the windscreen.* 很大的雨点啪哒啪哒地打在挡风玻璃上。

splat·ter /ˈsplætɚ; ˈsplætə/ *v* [I,T] to cover something with small drops of liquid 飞溅(在), 溅泼(于): *Mud splattered the hem of her kimono.* 污泥溅在她的和服下摆上。

splay /sple; spleɪ/ also 又作 **splay out** *v* [I,T] if fingers or legs splay or are splayed, they spread further apart, often in a way that looks strange (使)〔手指、双腿〕张开: *He sat sturdily on the floor, legs splayed apart.* 他张开双腿, 扎扎实实地坐在地板上。

splay foot·ed /ˌ· ˈ··◂/ *adj* having very flat wide feet 八字脚的, 外翻足的

spleen /splin; spliːn/ *n* **1** [C] an organ near your stomach that controls the quality of your blood 脾脏 —see picture at 参见 DIGESTIVE 图 **2** [U] *formal* anger【正式】怒气: **vent your spleen on sb** (=get angry with someone) 向某人大发脾气, 拿某人出气

splen·did /ˈsplɛndɪd; ˈsplendɪd/ *adj formal*【正式】**1** excellent or very fine 极好的, 优秀的, 杰出的: *a splendid person* 杰出的人物 | *a splendid suggestion* 极好的建议 **2** beautiful and impressive 壮丽的, 华丽的, 辉煌的, 灿烂的: *There are some splendid villas near Rome.* 罗马附近有一些豪华别墅。| *a splendid view of the port* 港口的壮丽景象 —**splendidly** *adv*: *Joe and my father are getting along splendidly.* 乔和我父亲相处得极好。

splen·dif·e·rous /splɛnˈdɪfərəs; splenˈdɪfərəs/ *adj BrE informal humorous* splendid【英, 非正式, 幽默】极好的, 华丽的, 壮丽的

splen·dour *BrE*【英】, **splendor** *AmE*【美】/ˈsplɛndɚ; ˈsplendə/ *n* **1** [U] impressive beauty and richness, usually in a large building or large place 壮丽, 华丽, 壮观: *the gothic splendor of the cathedral* 大教堂哥特式风格的壮丽 **2 splendours** [plural] impressive, beautiful, rich features, especially of a large building or place〔尤指大建筑物或地方的〕雄伟[华丽]的特质: *the splendours of Versailles* 凡尔赛宫的雄伟之处

sple·net·ic /splɪˈnɛtɪk; splɪˈnetɪk/ *adj literary* bad-tempered and often angry【文】脾气坏的, 易怒的

splice¹ /splaɪs; splaɪs/ *v* [T] **1** to join the ends of two pieces of rope, film etc so that they form one continuous piece 将〔两条绳子、胶片等的头〕连接[捻接, 黏接] **2 get spliced** *BrE informal* to get married【英, 非正式】结婚

splice² *n* [C] the act of joining the ends of two things together, or the place where this join has been made 连接, 接合; 连接处, 接合点

splic·er /ˈsplaɪsɚ; ˈsplaɪsə/ *n* [C] a machine for joining pieces of film or recording TAPE¹ (1a) neatly together〔胶片或磁带的〕连接器

splint /splɪnt; splɪnt/ *n* [C] a flat piece of wood, metal etc, used for keeping a broken bone in position while it mends〔用以固定断骨的〕夹板

splin·ter¹ /ˈsplɪntɚ; ˈsplɪntə/ *n* [C] a small sharp piece of wood, glass, or metal, that has broken off a larger piece〔木头、玻璃或金属的〕碎片, 尖片: *I've got a splinter in my finger.* 我的手指扎了一根刺。| **[+of]** *splinters of glass* 玻璃碎屑 —**splintery** *adj*: *splintery plywood* 容易碎裂的胶合板 —see picture on page A7 参见 A7 页图

splinter² *v* [I,T] if something such as wood splinters, or you splinter it, it breaks into thin sharp pieces (使)裂成碎片: *Soft wood splinters easily.* 软木容易碎裂。

splinter group /ˈ· · ˌ·/ also 又作 **splinter or·ga·niz·a·tion** /ˈ· · · · ·, · ·/ *n* [C] a group of people that has separated from a political or religious organization because they have different ideas etc〔因意见分歧而从政治、宗教等团体〕分裂出来的小团体[小派别]: *Green Realignment, a splinter group of the British Green Party* 绿色新联盟——从英国绿党分裂出来的小派别

split¹ /splɪt; splɪt/ *v past tense and past participle* **split** *present participle* **splitting** [S2] [W3]

1 ▶INTO GROUPS 成为几个团体◀ also 又作 **split up** [I,T] if a group of people splits or is split, it divides into two or more groups, because one group strongly disagrees with the other〔由于意见严重分歧而〕分裂: *The issue of women's ordination is splitting the church.* 关于给妇女授神职的问题正使教会陷于分裂。| **[+over/on]** *The party split over segregation.* 这个党在种族隔离问题上分歧严重。| **be split on/over** *The National Defense Committee is split over the use of military force.* 国防委员会在如何使用军事力量的问题上意见有分歧。

2 ▶INTO PARTS 成为几部分◀ also 又作 **split up** [I,T] to divide or separate something into different parts, or to be divided into different parts 分割, 把…分开〔成几部分〕: **[+into]** *Each district was split up into a number of sub-divisions.* 每个区被分成若干个分区。| *At the end of the bridge the expressway split into two roads.* 这条高速公路在桥的尽头分成两条路。

3 ▶BREAK OR TEAR 裂开或撕开◀ [I,T] if something splits or if you split it, it tears or breaks along a straight line (使)裂开, 撕开: *Harry split his trousers climbing over the fence.* 哈里在爬过围栏时撕破了裤子。| **[+open]** *One of the pumpkins had split open.* 有一个南瓜裂开了。| **split (sth) in two/half** *The board had split in two.* 这块板裂成了两块。| **split (sth) down/across/along etc** *He split the stone down the middle.* 他把石头从中间破成两半。

4 ▶SHARE 分摊◀ [T] to divide something into separate parts so that two or more people each get a part 均分, 分配: **split sth between** *Profits will be split between three major charities.* 利润将在三个主要慈善机构之间分配。| **split sth three/four etc ways** (=into three, four, or more equal parts) 将某物平均分成三份/四份等 *I think we should split what's left three ways.* 我认为我们应当把剩下的均分成三份。| **split the bill/cost** *It's only fair to split the cost of the bills.* 分摊这些账单的费用才是公平的。

5 ▶INJURE 损伤◀ also 又作 **split open** [T] to cut someone's head or lip, by hitting them 碰破〔头或嘴唇〕, 把…碰得裂开: *The poor guy had his head split right open.* 那个可怜的家伙把头撞破了。

6 ▶LEAVE 离开◀ [I] *slang* to leave quickly【俚】迅速离去: *They grabbed her purse and split.* 他们抢了她的钱包后逃之夭夭。

7 split hairs to argue that there is a difference between two things, when the difference is really too small to be important 在琐碎的问题上争辩: *Let's stop splitting hairs and get back to the main issue.* 我们别再在琐碎问题上争辩了, 还是回到主要的问题上来吧。

8 split the difference to agree on an amount that is exactly between two amounts that have been mentioned〔在数额上〕互相让步, 折中, 妥协: *You want $20, I'm offering $10. Why don't we split the difference?* 你要 20 美元, 我出 10 美元, 我们为什么不各让一步, 折中一下呢?

9 split your sides to laugh very hard 捧腹大笑

split off *phr v* **1** [I] to completely separate from a group〔从群体中〕分离出来: **[+from]** *The ancestors of this animal split off from the rest and established themselves as an independent species.* 这种动物的祖先从原种分离出来后自己成为一个独立的物种。**2** [I,T] to break something away from something so that it is completely separate, or to break off in this way (使)分离(出来): *Huge boulders had split off and rolled down the mountainside.* 巨石崩裂开来, 滚下山坡。

split on sb *phr v* [T] *informal especially BrE* to tell someone in authority about something wrong that someone else has done【非正式, 尤英】告发: *You wouldn't split on a pal would you?* 你不会告发老朋友吧?

S

split up *phr v* **1** [I] to end a marriage or relationship 离婚；决裂，绝交：*Steve's parents split up when he was four.* 史蒂夫四岁时父母离了婚。| [+with] *Jackie's splitting up with her boyfriend.* 杰姬要和男友分手。**2** [I,T] to divide into groups 分组：*Please don't split up when we get to the museum.* 到达博物馆后请大家不要散开。| **split sth ↔ up** *The teacher split up the class into three groups.* 老师把全班分成三组。**3** [T **split** sth ↔ **up**] to divide or separate something into different parts 把…分成若干部分：*The article is easier to read if you split it up into sections.* 这篇文章如果分成几部分就更容易读了。

split² *n* [C] **1** a long straight hole caused when something breaks or tears 裂口，裂缝：*a split in the seat of his trousers* 他裤子臀部上的裂缝 **2** a serious disagreement that divides an organization or group of people into smaller groups〔团体内部的〕分裂，分离：*Arguments over admitting women to the club may lead to a split.* 接受妇女参加俱乐部的争论可能导致俱乐部分裂。**3** the part of something you receive when something, especially money, is shared〔尤指钱的〕一份，份额：**a three-way/four-way etc split** (=a share of something that is divided equally between three, four etc people) 三人/四人等均分的一份 **4** *informal* a difference between two things, ideas etc【非正式】〔两者之间的〕差别，差异：*the split between ideals and reality* 理想和现实之间的差别 **5 do the splits** to spread your legs wide apart so that your legs touch the floor along their whole length 劈叉，劈一字腿 —see also 另见 BANANA SPLIT

split ends /ˌ·ˈ·/ *n* [plural] a condition of someone's hair in which the ends have split into several parts 开叉的发梢

split in·fin·i·tive /ˌ·····/ *n* [C] a phrase in which you put an adverb or other word between 'to' and an INFINITIVE, as in 'to easily win'. Some people think this is incorrect English. 分裂不定式〔副词或其他词插在to和动词原形之间，如to easily win。有些人认为这是不正确的英语〕

split-lev·el /ˌ·ˈ··◂/ *adj* a split-level house, room or building has floors at different heights in different parts〔房子、房间或建筑物〕错层式的

split pea /ˌ·ˈ·◂/ *n* [C] a dried PEA split into its two halves 干豌豆瓣

split per·son·al·i·ty /ˌ·····/ *n* [C] *not technical* a condition in which someone has two very different ways of behaving; SCHIZOPHRENIA【非术语】分裂人格，双重人格

split ring /ˌ·ˈ·/ *n* [U] a metal ring, used for keeping keys on, that can be opened to allow the keys to be put on or taken off 开口[叠口]钥匙圈

split screen /ˌ·ˈ·◂/ *n* [C] a method used in films and on television screen (SCREEN¹ (1,2)) to show different scenes or pieces of information at the same time〔电影或电视的〕分画面：*a split-screen movie* 分画面电影

split sec·ond /ˌ·ˈ··◂/ *n* **a split second** an extremely short period of time 一刹那，顷刻：*I just turned round for a split second and she vanished!* 我转过身去就那么一转眼的时间，她就没了人影儿！—**split-second** *adj*: *a split-second decision* 刹那间作出的决定

split shift /ˌ·ˈ·/ *n* [C] a period of work that is divided into two or more parts on the same day 间隔班〔一天的上班时间分成两段或几段的轮班〕：*Chefs work a split shift.* 厨师上间隔班。

split tick·et /ˌ·ˈ··/ *n* [C] a vote in US elections in which the voter has voted for some CANDIDATES of one party and some of the other party〔美国选举的〕分裂票〔一个选民同时选两党候选人的选票〕—**split-ticket** *adj*: *split-ticket voting* 分裂票选举

split·ting /ˈsplɪtɪŋ; ˈsplɪtɪŋ/ *adj* a splitting HEADACHE is very bad〔头痛〕剧烈的

splodge /splɑdʒ; splɒdʒ/ *n* [C] *informal* a large mark of mud, paint etc with an irregular shape【非正式】〔污泥、油漆等的〕斑块，污渍：*a splodge of ketchup on his shirt* 他衬衣上的大片番茄酱污渍 —**splodgy** *adj*

splosh /splɑʃ; splɒʃ/ *v* [I always+adv/prep] *BrE informal* to make a noise by falling into or moving through water; SPLASH¹【英，非正式】啪啦啪啦地溅水，泼水 —**splosh** *n* [C]: *a discreet splosh as the eel-fisherman cast off* 捕鳗者在解缆开船时尽量小的声音

splotch /splɑtʃ; splɒtʃ/ *n* [C] a SPLODGE 斑块，污迹

splurge /splɝdʒ; splɜːdʒ/ *v* [I] *informal* to spend more money than you can usually afford【非正式】乱花钱，挥霍金钱：*Let's splurge and take a cab.* 我们奢侈一回，叫出租车吧。—**splurge** *n* [C]

splut·ter /ˈsplʌtɚ; ˈsplʌtə/ *v* [I] **1** to talk quickly in short confused phrases, especially because you are angry or surprised 急促而慌乱地说话〔尤因生气或吃惊〕：*"But...But...I can't believe...how could you?" she spluttered.* "可…可是…我不能相信…你怎么能?" 她语无伦次地说。| [+with] *Katie was spluttering with rage.* 凯蒂气得说话结结巴巴。**2** to make short sharp noises, like someone spitting (SPIT¹ (6)) 发出噼啪[毕剥]声：*Bill was coughing and spluttering.* 比尔在咳嗽，唾沫星子四溅。| *The boat's engine spluttered and stopped.* 小船的发动机噼噼啪啪响了几下就停了。—**splutter** *n* [C]

Spock /spɑk; spɒk/, **Dr Ben·ja·min** /ˈbɛndʒəmɪn; ˈbendʒəmɪ̩n/ (1903-1998) a US doctor who wrote books giving advice on how parents should take care of their children, including *The Common Sense Book of Baby and Childcare* (1946), which suggested that parents should allow their children more freedom than was fashionable at the time, and which had a great influence on parents in the US and UK. Some people later criticized him for encouraging parents to be too PERMISSIVE (=not strict enough) with their children. Dr Spock was also known for his opposition to the Vietnam War. 斯波克医生〔(1903-1998)，美国医生。著有育婴养子类书籍，如《婴幼儿保健常识》(1946) 等。该书建议父母给孩子更多自由，这超越了当时流行的做法，对英美两国的家长产生了很大影响。有人后来批评他鼓动家长放纵孩子。斯波克医生还以反对越战而闻名〕

Spock, Mr a character from the US television programme *Star Trek*. Mr Spock is a man from an imaginary PLANET called Vulcan, who has pointed ears and green blood, and is always completely LOGICAL, so that his ideas and decisions are based only on facts, not on emotions. He is also known for saying to his commander, Captain James Kirk, "It's life, Jim, but not as we know it". 斯波克先生〔美国电视剧《星际旅行》中的一个角色。斯波克先生来自一个虚构的星球"瓦肯星"。他长着一对尖耳朵，流着绿色的血液，做事始终极有逻辑，作决定时仅以事实为依据，决不为感情所左右。他给指挥官詹姆斯·柯克船长的报告非常著名："是生物，吉姆，但不是我们了解的那种"〕

Spode /spod; spəʊd/ *trademark* a type of fine CHINA, such as plates and TEAPOTS, made in the UK【商标】斯波德陶瓷〔一种产于英国的细瓷制品，有盘子、茶壶等〕

spoil /spɔɪl; spɔɪl/ *past tense and past participle* **spoiled** *or* **spoilt** /spɔɪlt; spɔɪlt/ *BrE*【英】*v*

1 ▶RUIN STH 毁掉某物◀ [T] to have a bad effect on something so that it is no longer attractive, enjoyable, useful etc 损坏，糟蹋，破坏：*The countryside has been spoiled by the new freeway.* 乡村被新修的高速公路破坏了。| *Don't spoil your sister's birthday by crying at her party.* 不要在你妹妹的聚会上哭，使她的生日扫兴。| **spoil everything** (=completely ruin someone's plan) 完全打乱某人的计划 *Mom arrived home just then, which spoiled everything.* 妈妈就在这时回家了，完全打乱了我们的计划。—see also 另见 **spoil/ruin your appetite** (APPETITE (1)) —see 见 DESTROY (USAGE)

2 ▶FOOD 食物◀ [I] to start to decay〔开始〕变坏，变质；腐败：*Food will spoil if the temperature in your freezer rises above 8°C.* 冷藏箱里的温度如果高于8摄氏度，食物就会变坏。

3 ▶CHILD 小孩◀ [T] to give a child whatever they want, or let them do what they want, with the result that they behave badly 宠坏，惯坏，溺爱〔小孩〕：**spoil sb with sth** *Jimmy's grandmother spoils him with toys and candy.* 吉米的祖母用玩具和糖果把他惯坏了。

4 ▶TREAT KINDLY 体贴地对待◀ [T] to look after someone in a way that is kind or too kind 无微不至地关心；过分地照顾，纵容：*You know you're spoiling me with all this good cooking.* 你用这么多美味佳肴招待我，太让我受宠若惊了。| **spoil yourself** *Go on, spoil yourself. Have another piece of cake.* 来吧，纵容自己一下，再来一块蛋糕。

5 ▶VOTING PAPER 选票◀ [T] to mark a BALLOT PAPER wrongly so that your vote is not included〔因划票不符规定〕使〔选票〕成废票

6 be spoiling for a fight/argument to be very eager to fight or argue with someone 一心想打架/吵架 —see also 另见 SPOILS, SPOILER

spoil·age /ˈspɔɪlɪdʒ; ˈspɔɪlɪdʒ/ *n* [U] *technical* waste resulting from something being spoiled【术语】变坏，变质，腐败；〔因变坏造成的〕浪费

spoiled /spɔɪld; spɔɪld/ *usually* 一般作 **spoilt** *BrE*【英】*adj* **1** someone, especially a child, who is spoiled is rude and behaves badly because their parents have always given them what they want and allowed them to do what they want〔小孩〕惯坏的，宠坏的：**spoiled brat** (=spoiled, annoying child) 宠坏的孩子 | **spoiled rotten** (=very spoiled) 极度惯坏的 **2 be spoilt for choice** *BrE* to have so many good things to choose from that

you cannot decide which one to choose【英】可供选择的好东西太多［以至无从下手］

spoil·er /ˋspɔɪlɚ; ˈspɔɪlə/ *n* [C] **1** a piece of an aircraft wing that can be lifted up to slow the plane down〔机翼上用以降低飞行速度的〕扰流器 **2** a raised part on a racing car that stops the car lifting off the road at high speeds〔赛车上〕气流偏导器 **3** a book, article etc that is produced to take attention away from another similar book and spoil its success 捣乱作品〔指为分散读者对某作品的注意并破坏其成功而同时出版的类似的书或文章等〕**4** *AmE* a person or team that spoils another's winning record【美】〔个人或团队〕妨碍他人取胜者，拆台者

spoils /spɔɪlz; spɔɪlz/ *n* [plural] *formal or literary*【正式或文】**a)** things taken by an army from a defeated enemy, or things taken by thieves 战利品，掠夺物；赃物：*the spoils of war* 战利品｜*dividing up the spoils* 分赃 **b)** profits gained through political power 通过政治权力获得的利益

spoil·sport /ˋspɔɪlˌspɔrt; ˈspɔɪlspɔːt/ *n* [C] *informal* someone who spoils other people's fun【非正式】扫兴者，破坏别人兴致的人：*Don't be a spoilsport, Richard. We can't play without you.* 不要扫兴，理查德，你不参加我们就玩不成了。

spoilt /spɔɪlt; spɔɪlt/ *adj* another form of the word SPOILED spoiled的另一种形式

spoke[1] /spok; spəʊk/ the past tense of SPEAK

spoke[2] *n* [C] **1** one of the thin metal bars which connect the outer ring of a wheel to the centre, especially on a bicycle〔尤指自行车轮子上的〕轮辐，辐条 —see picture at 参见 BICYCLE[1] 图 **2 put a spoke in sb's wheel** to prevent someone from doing something they have planned 破坏某人的计划：*I feel like telling the press everything. That'd put spoke in their wheel.* 我很想向报界公开一切。那样他们的计划就行不通了。

-spoken /spokən; spəʊkən/ *suffix* [in adjectives 构成形容词] speaking in a particular way 以…方式说话的：*a softly-spoken girl* (=who speaks quietly) 说话柔声细气的姑娘

spok·en[1] /ˋspokən; ˈspəʊkən/ the past participle of SPEAK

spoken[2] *adj* **1 spoken English/language** the form of language that you speak rather than write 英语口语／口语 **2 quietly/softly/well-spoken** speaking in a quiet, educated etc way 说话轻轻的／柔柔的／有教养的 **3 be spoken for** *informal*【非正式】**a)** if something is spoken for, you cannot buy it because it is being kept for someone else〔东西〕为某人保留 **b)** if someone is spoken for, they are married or already have a serious relationship with someone 已结婚；已与别人有正式关系

2 **spokes·man** /ˋspoksmən; ˈspəʊksmən/ *n plural* **spokesmen** /-mən; -mən/ [C] someone who has been chosen to speak officially for a group, organization or government 发言人，代言人：*a White House spokesman* 白宫发言人｜[+for] *a spokesman for victims' families* 受害者家属代言人

spokes·per·son /ˋspoksˌpɝsn̩; ˈspəʊksˌpɜːsən/ *n plural* **spokespeople** /-ˌpipl̩; -ˌpiːpəl/ [C] a word meaning spokesman or spokeswoman which some people use because they think that 'spokesman' should not be used for both sexes 发言人，代言人

spokes·wom·an /ˋspoksˌwʊmən; ˈspəʊksˌwʊmən/ *n plural* **spokeswomen** /-ˌwɪmɪn; -ˌwɪmɪn/ [C] a woman who has been chosen to speak officially for a group, organization, or government 女发言人，女代言人

spo·li·a·tion /ˌspolɪˋeʃən; ˌspəʊliˈeɪʃən/ *n* [U] *formal* the violent or deliberate destruction or spoiling of something【正式】〔粗暴或故意的〕破坏，毁坏：*the spoliation of the environment* 自然环境的破坏

sponge[1] /spʌndʒ; spʌndʒ/ *n* **1** [C,U] a piece of a soft natural or artificial substance full of small holes, which can suck up liquid and is used for washing (一块)海绵；海绵状物：*The physio ran onto the field with a wet sponge.* 物理治疗师拿着一块湿海绵跑到赛场上去。**2** [C] a simple sea creature from which natural sponge is produced 海绵〔一种可以产生天然海绵的海洋生物〕**3** [singular] *especially BrE* an act of washing something with a sponge【尤英】用海绵擦拭：*Give my back a quick sponge, would you?* 你用海绵替我擦几下背，好吗？**4** [C] a SPONGER 寄生者 **5** [C,U] *BrE* SPONGE CAKE【英】海绵蛋糕

sponge[2] *v* **1** also 又作 **sponge down** [T] to wash something with a wet cloth or sponge 用湿布[海绵]擦洗：*Sponge down the walls before you paint them.* 先用海绵洗墙，再上涂料。**2** [T always+adv/prep] to remove liquid or a mark with a wet cloth or sponge 用湿布[海绵]吸掉〔液体〕，揩掉〔斑点〕：**sponge sth off/out/up** *Wendy tried to sponge the wine off her dress.* 温迪试图用海绵吸干洒在她连衣裙上的酒。**3** [I] to get money, free meals etc from other people, without doing anything for them 依赖他人生活，寄生：*Right-wing politicians accuse the poor of sponging.* 右翼政客指责穷人过着寄生生活。｜**sponge off sb** *Carl's been sponging off his family ever since he left college.* 卡尔大学毕业后，一直依赖家庭生活。

sponge bag /ˈ· ·/ *n* [C] *BrE* a small bag for carrying the things that you need to wash with【英】盥洗用具袋

sponge bath /ˈ· ·/ *n* [C] an act of washing your whole body with a wet cloth when you cannot use a BATHTUB or SHOWER[1] (1)〔不入水的〕海绵擦身浴

sponge cake /ˈ· ·/ *n* [C,U] a light cake made from eggs, sugar, and flour but usually no fat 海绵蛋糕

sponge pud·ding /ˌ· ˈ··/ *n* [C] *BrE* a food made of eggs, butter, flour and sugar which is eaten hot【英】海绵布丁

spon·ger /ˋspʌndʒɚ; ˈspʌndʒə/ *n* [C] someone who gets money, free meals etc, from other people and does nothing for them 依赖他人生活者，寄生者

spong·y /ˋspʌndʒɪ; ˈspʌndʒi/ *adj* soft and full of holes that contain air or liquid like a SPONGE[1] (1) 松软多孔的，海绵似的：*The earth was soft and spongy underfoot.* 脚下的地像海绵一样松软。—**sponginess** *n* [U]

spon·sor[1] /ˋspɑnsɚ; ˈspɒnsə/ *n* [C] **1** a person or company that pays for a show, broadcast, sports event etc in exchange for the right to advertise at that event〔出资举办表演、广播、体育比赛等以在其中做广告的〕赞助者，赞助商：*the Championship's sponsor, Martell Cognac* 锦标赛的赞助商马爹利白兰地公司 **2** someone who agrees to give someone else money for a CHARITY (2) if they walk, run, swim etc a particular distance 慈善募捐活动的赞助者 **3** someone who officially agrees to help someone else, or to be responsible for what they do 担保人，保证人：*You need a sponsor to get a working visa.* 你必须有担保人才能获得工作签证。**4** someone who officially introduces or supports a proposal for a new law 提案人；发起者，倡议者 **5** a GODPARENT 教父；教母

sponsor[2] *v* [T] **1** to give money to a sports event, theatre etc 赞助，资助〔体育比赛、演出等〕：*The bank is sponsoring a sports day for children in the area.* 银行在赞助为本区儿童举办的运动日。**2** to agree to give someone money for CHARITY if they walk, run etc a particular distance 赞助〔某人的慈善募捐活动〕：*I've sponsored Alison $1 for every mile in the walkathon.* 艾莉森在步行马拉松中每走一英里我赞助一美元。**3** to officially support a proposal for a new law 倡议〔法案〕；支持〔法案〕

spon·sored /ˋspɑnsɚd; ˈspɒnsəd/ *adj* **sponsored walk/swim etc** *BrE* an event in which many people walk, swim etc a particular distance in order to collect money for a CHARITY (2)【英】慈善步行／游泳等〔一种募捐活动〕

spon·sor·ship /ˋspɑnsɚˌʃɪp; ˈspɒnsəʃɪp/ *n* [U] support, usually financial support for an activity or event 赞助，资助：*The expedition is looking for sponsorship from one of the major banks.* 探险队正在向其中一家大银行寻求赞助。

spon·ta·ne·ous /spɑnˋtenɪəs; spɒnˈteɪniəs/ *adj* happening or done without being planned or organized, but because you suddenly feel you would like to do it 自发的，自动的；一时冲动的：*The crowd gave a spontaneous cheer when the result was announced.* 宣布结果时人群即时爆发出一阵欢呼声。—**spontaneously** *adv* —**spontaneousness, spontaneity** /ˌspɑntəˋniətɪ; ˌspɒntəˈniːɪti/ *n* [U]

spontaneous com·bus·tion /·ˌ··· ·ˈ··/ *n* [U] burning caused by chemical changes inside something rather than by heat from outside 自发燃烧，自燃

spoof /spuf; spuːf/ *n* [C] a funny book, play, film etc that copies a serious or important one and makes it seem silly 嘲讽性的模仿作品：[+of/on] *'A Five Minute Hamlet' is an amusing spoof of Shakespeare's most famous play.*《五分钟哈姆雷特》是一出模仿莎士比亚最著名戏剧的滑稽剧。—**spoof** *v* [T]

spook[1] /spuk; spuːk/ *n* [C] *informal*【非正式】**1** a GHOST[1] (1) 鬼 **2** *slang* a SPY[1]【俚】密探，间谍：*Yup. He was a real live CIA spook.* 是的。他是个真正的中央情报局间谍。

spook[2] *v* [T] *informal especially AmE* to frighten someone【非正式，尤美】使惊慌，惊吓：*You've really spooked me with that story about plane crashes.* 你讲的那个飞机坠毁故事让我听了很害怕。

spook·y /ˋspukɪ; ˈspuːki/ *adj informal* strange or frightening in a way that makes you think of ghosts (GHOST[1] (1))【非正式】阴森恐怖的，使人毛骨悚然的：*a spooky old house with creaking stairs* 楼梯嘎吱作响的阴森恐怖的老房子

spool /spul; spuːl/ *n* [C] **1** an object shaped like a wheel that you wind electric wire, recording TAPE[1] (1a), photographic film etc around〔电线、录音带、胶卷等的〕卷轴；线轴 **2** *AmE* a REEL[1] (1a)【美】〔电线、棉纱等的〕一卷；〔胶片、磁带等的〕一盘；〔电影的〕一本：*Don't forget to rewind the spool.* 别忘记倒带子。

S

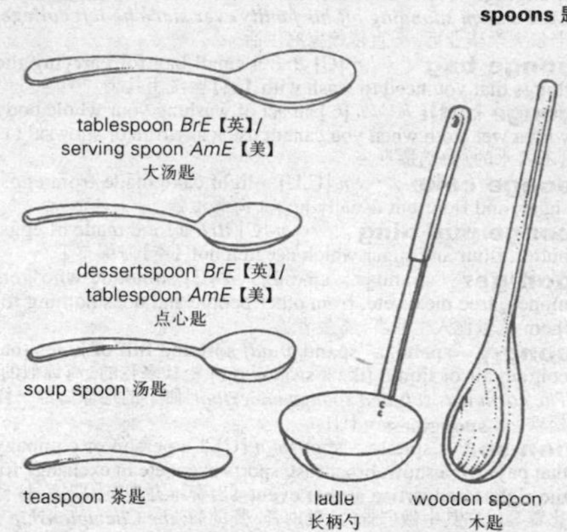

spoon¹ /spun; spuːn/ *n* [C] **1** a thing used for eating, cooking, or serving food, consisting of a small bowl-shaped part and a long handle 匙子, 勺 **2** a SPOONFUL 一匙之量, 一满匙 —see also 另见 **be born with a silver spoon in your mouth** (BORN² (11)), DESSERTSPOON, GREASY SPOON, SOUP SPOON, WOODEN SPOON

spoon² *v* [T] to pick up or move food with a spoon 用匙舀: [+into/on] *Spoon the mixture into glasses.* 用匙把混合物舀进玻璃杯里。

spoo·ner·is·m /ˈspunəˌrɪzəm; ˈspuːnərɪzəm/ *n* [C] a phrase in which the speaker makes the mistake of exchanging the first sounds of two words, with a funny result, for example 'sew you to a sheet' for 'show you to a seat'〔两个词的〕首音误置〔如把 show you to a seat 说成 sew you to a sheet, 因而产生可笑的效果〕

spoon-feed /ˈ· ·/ *v past tense and past participle* **spoon-fed** [T] **1** to give too much information and help to someone 填鸭式地给…灌输〔信息等〕: *Spoon-feeding students does not help them remember things.* 对学生进行填鸭式灌输并不能帮助他们记住东西。**2** to feed someone, especially a baby, with a spoon 用匙喂〔尤指婴儿〕

spoon·ful /ˈspunˌful; ˈspuːnfʊl/ *n* [C] the amount that a SPOON will hold 一匙之量, 一满匙: **[+of]** *Two spoonfuls of sugar, please.* 请放两匙糖。

spoor /spʊr; spɔː/ *n* [C] the track of foot marks or FAECES (=solid waste) left by a wild animal〔野生动物留下的〕脚印, 足迹; 臭迹

spo·rad·ic /spəˈrædɪk; spəˈrædɪk/ *adj* happening often but not regularly; INTERMITTENT 偶尔发生的, 零星的, 分散的: *sporadic fighting in the west of the city* 城西的零星战斗 —**sporadically** /-klɪ; -kli/ *adv*

spore /spɔr; spɔː/ *n* [C] a cell like a seed, produced by some plants such as MUSHROOMS, and by some very simple animals, which is able to develop into a new plant or animal 孢子; 芽孢

spor·ran /ˈspɑrən; ˈspɒrən/ *n* [C] a special bag made of leather or fur, worn in front of a KILT by a Scotsman〔苏格兰男子佩于短裙前面的〕毛皮袋

sport¹ /sport; spɔːt/ *n*

1 ►GAMES 运动◄ **a)** [C] a physical activity in which people compete against each other 运动, 体育运动; 体育比赛: *My favourite sports are tennis and swimming.* 我最喜爱的运动是网球和游泳。| *I was never any good at sports when I was young.* 我年轻时一点也不擅长运动。| **spectator sport** (=one which is watched by large groups of people) 人们喜欢观看的运动 *Football is one of the most popular spectator sports.* 足球是最受观众喜爱的体育运动之一。**b)** [U] *BrE* sports in general【英】体育运动〔总称〕: *Here's news about today's sport.* 现在是今天的体育新闻。| *Why is there so much sport on TV?* 为什么电视上的体育节目这么多?

2 ►HUNTING 打猎◄ [C] a country outdoor activity such as hunting or fishing 野外运动〈如打猎、钓鱼等〉: **blood sports** (=sports that involve killing animals) 以猎杀〔鸟兽〕为乐的运动

3 sports [plural] *BrE* an occasion when people compete in running, jumping, throwing etc【英】运动会: **school/county sports** *The school sports are usually held in July* 学校运动会通常在7月份举行。

4 ►HELPFUL PERSON 热心人◄ also 又作 **good sport** *old-fashioned* a helpful cheerful person who lets you enjoy yourself and never complains when there is trouble【过时】热情开朗的人; 大度的人: *His Mum will let us have a party. She's a good sport.* 他妈妈会让我们开聚会的。她是个慷慨大度的人。| **be a sport** (=used when asking someone to help you) 大方一点〔用于向人求助时〕*Be a sport and lend me your bike.* 慷慨一点, 把自行车借我用一下。

5 ►MAN/BOY 男子/男孩◄ *spoken*【口】**a)** *AustrE* a friendly way of addressing someone, especially a man【澳】老兄, 朋友〔用作友好的称呼, 尤用于男子〕**b)** *AmE old-fashioned* a friendly way of addressing a young boy【美, 过时】小伙子, 小朋友, 哥儿〔用作对小男孩的友好称呼〕

6 ►FUN 玩笑◄ [U] *old use* fun or amusement【旧】玩笑, 戏谑

7 make sport of *old use* to joke about someone in a way that makes them seem stupid【旧】开…的玩笑, 嘲笑〔某人〕

8 ►PLANT/ANIMAL 植物/动物◄ [C] *technical* a plant or animal that is different in an important way from its usual type【术语】变态的动[植]物, 变种

9 the sport of kings horse racing 赛马 —see also 另见 FIELD SPORTS, WINTER SPORTS, WATER SPORTS

sport² *v* **1 be sporting sth** to be wearing or showing something publicly, especially in a proud way 炫耀某物, 卖弄某物: *Eric was sporting a new camel-hair coat.* 埃里克炫耀地穿着一件骆驼毛外衣。**2** [I] *literary* to play together happily【文】嬉戏, 玩耍: *dolphins sporting amidst the waves* 在波浪中嬉戏的海豚

sport car /ˈ· ·/ *n* [C] *AmE* a SPORTS CAR【美】跑车

sport coat /ˈ· ·/ *n* [C] *AmE* a SPORTS JACKET【美】〔男子作便服穿的〕外套

sport·ing /ˈsportɪŋ; ˈspɔːtɪŋ/ *adj* **1 a)** [only before noun 仅用于名词前] related to or taking part in sports (有关或参加)体育运动的: **sporting goods** *especially AmE* (=sports equipment)【尤美】体育用品 | **sporting event** (=occasion on which a sport is played) 体育比赛项目 **b)** related to or joining in country sports like hunting or horse racing 有关[从事]野外运动〈如打猎或赛马〉的: *the sporting gentry* 喜欢野外运动的绅士们 **2** *BrE* fair and generous, especially in sports【英】有运动家风度的, 公正大度的: **it is sporting of sb** *It was sporting of him to admit that his last shot was out.* 他有运动家风度, 承认最后一枪打飞了。**3 a sporting chance** a fairly good chance of succeeding or winning 相当大的成功[取胜]机会: *Neil has a sporting chance of getting in the football team.* 尼尔有相当大的机会入选足球队。—**sportingly** *adv*

Sporting Life /ˌ·· ˈ·/ a British daily newspaper which dealt mainly with horse racing. It stopped being published in 1998.【商标】《体育生活》〔英国一日报。主要报道赛马情况, 1998 年起停刊〕

spor·tive /ˈsportɪv; ˈspɔːtɪv/ *adj literary* enjoying fun and making jokes in a friendly way; PLAYFUL【文】嬉戏的, 欢闹的 —**sportively** *adv* —**sportiveness** *n* [U]

sport jack·et /ˈ· ˌ··/ *n* [C] *AmE* a SPORTS JACKET【美】〔男子作便服穿的〕外套

sports /sports; spɔːts/ *adj* [only before noun 仅用于名词前] **1** connected with sport or used for sport 有关体育活动的; 体育运动用的: *a sports field* 运动场 | *sports equipment* 运动装备 | *sports clubs* (体育)运动俱乐部 **2** on the subject of sport〔内容〕关于体育的: *When I buy a newspaper, I always read the sports page first.* 我买到报纸总是先看体育版。| *a sports commentator on television* 电视体育评论员

sports car /ˈ· ·/ *n* [C] a low fast car, often with a roof that can be folded back or removed 跑车〔车身低、车速快、通常车顶可以折叠或拆卸的汽车〕

sports·cast /ˈsportsˌkæst; ˈspɔːtskɑːst/ *n* [C] *AmE* a television broadcast of a sports match【美】电视的体育比赛播放 —**sportscaster** *n* [C]

sports cen·tre /ˈ· ˌ··/ *n* [C] *BrE* a building where many different types of indoor sports are played【英】体育运动中心, 体育馆

sports coat /ˈ· ·/ *n* [C] a SPORTS JACKET〔男子作便服穿的〕外套

sports day /ˈ· ·/ *n* [C] *especially BrE* a day on which the children at a school have sports competitions【尤英】〔中小学生进行比赛的〕运动日; FIELD DAY (2) *AmE*【美】

sport shirt /ˈ· ·/ *n* [C] *AmE* a SPORTS SHIRT【美】〔男子作便服穿的〕运动衫

Sports Il·lus·trat·ed /ˌ· ˈ····/ *trademark* a weekly US magazine with articles about different sports, teams, professional players etc【商标】《运动画刊》〔美国一周刊, 刊登关于各类体育运动、球队以及职业球员的文章〕

sports jack·et /ˈ· ,··/ *n* [C] a man's comfortable JACKET (1), usually made of TWEED, worn on informal occasions〔男子作便服穿的〕外套, 粗花呢夹克

sports·man /ˈspɔrtsmən; ˈspɔːtsmən/ *n plural* **sportsmen** /-mən; -mən/ [C] a man who plays several different sports, especially outdoor sports〔尤指户外运动的〕运动员; 参加运动者 —see also 另见 SPORTSWOMAN

sports·man·like /ˈspɔrtsmən,laɪk; ˈspɔːtsmənlaɪk/ *adj* behaving in a fair, honest, and polite way when competing in sports〔在体育比赛中〕公平、诚实、有礼貌的; 有运动家风度[品格]的: *gentlemanly and sportsmanlike behaviour* 绅士般的、有运动家风度的行为

sports·man·ship /ˈspɔrtsmən,ʃɪp; ˈspɔːtsmənʃɪp/ *n* [U] behaviour that is fair, honest and polite in a game or sports competition 运动家风度[品格], 体育精神: **good/bad sportsmanship** *We try to teach the kids good sportsmanship.* 我们力求教育孩子们要有良好的体育精神。

sports schol·ar·ship /ˈ· ,···/ *n* [C] money given to some college students in America to pay for all or part of their education because they are good enough to play for one of the college's sports teams〔美国大学颁给运动成绩优秀的学生的〕体育奖学金

sports shirt /ˈ· ·/ *n* [C] a shirt for men that is worn on informal occasions〔男子作便服穿的〕运动衫

sports·wear /ˈspɔrts,wɛr; ˈspɔːtsweə/ *n* [U] **1** clothes that are worn to play sports or when you are relaxing 运动服装; 休闲服装 **2** *AmE* clothes that are suitable for informal occasions【美】便服, 便装

sports·wom·an /ˈspɔrts,wʊmən; ˈspɔːts,wʊmən/ *n plural* **sportswomen** /-,wɪmɪn; -,wɪmɪn/ [C] a woman who plays many different sports, especially outdoor sports〔尤指户外运动的〕女运动员; 参加运动的女子

sport·y /ˈspɔrtɪ; ˈspɔːti/ *adj informal*【非正式】**1** designed to look attractive in a bright informal way 漂亮的, 花哨的, 潇洒的: *a sporty jacket and skirt* 一套花哨的外套和裙子 **2** *especially BrE* good at and fond of sport【尤英】擅长[喜欢]运动的: *I'm not a very sporty person.* 我不是一个擅长运动的人。—**sportiness** *n* [U]

S2 W2 **spot¹** /spɑt; spɒt/ *n* [C]

1 ►PLACE 地方◄ a particular place or area, especially a pleasant place where you spend time〔尤指休闲的〕地点, 场所: *an ideal spot for a picnic* 野餐的理想地点 | *We walked along the beach looking for a spot to sit.* 我们沿着海滩往前走, 想找个地方坐下。| **camping/swimming/holiday spot** (=a place that is suitable for a particular activity) 适合野营/游泳/度假的地方 *We found several good camping spots by the river.* 我们在河边找到几处很好的露营地点。| **the exact/very/same spot** (=the exact place where something happens)〔某事发生的〕准确地点 | **a sunny/shady spot** *These plants grow best in a sunny spot.* 这些植物在阳光充足的地方长得最好。—see 见 POSITION (USAGE) —see graph at 参见 LOCATION 图表

2 ►AREA 面积◄ a usually round area on a surface, that is a different colour or is rougher, smoother etc than the rest（圆）点, 斑点: *Dalmatian dogs have white coats with black or brown spots.* 斑点狗毛皮白色, 带有黑色或棕色斑点。| **[+of]** *Her pink suit made a bright spot of colour against the white steps.* 她的粉红色衣服在白色台阶的衬托下形成一片亮丽的色彩。

3 ►MARK 痕迹◄ a small mark on something, especially one that is made by a liquid 污渍, 斑点: *There are a lot of grease spots on the shirt.* 衬衣上沾了许多油渍。| *spots of paint on the carpet* 地毯上的油漆斑点

4 on the spot if you do something on the spot, you do it immediately, often without thinking about it very carefully 立即, 马上; 当场: *He bought the car on the spot.* 他立即买下了那辆汽车。| *The police could give you an on the spot fine.* 警察可以对你当场罚款。

5 be on the spot to be in the place where something is happening 在现场: *As the man on the spot, Coen was in a position to take vital decisions.* 作为在场唯一能作主的人, 库恩能够作重大的决定。

6 ►MARK ON SKIN 皮肤上的斑点◄ **a)** a small round red area on someone's skin that shows that they are ill〔皮肤上的〕红斑: *I was covered in spots when I had measles.* 我患麻疹时全身长满了红斑。**b)** *BrE* a small raised red mark on someone's skin, especially on their face; PIMPLE【英】〔尤指脸上红色的〕丘疹; 粉刺: *This cream clears up teenage spots in days.* 这种乳膏用上几天就能消除青少年脸上的粉刺。

7 ►POSITION 地位◄ a position in a competition, event, television programme etc〔在比赛、电视节目等中的〕地位, 位置: *The Bulldogs earned a spot in the semifinals.* 斗牛犬队赢得了半决赛资格。| *A bluegrass band has the second spot on the program.* 一支蓝草乡村乐队表演第二个节目。| **guest spot** (=part of a television or radio programme showing someone who does not usually appear on the programme)〔电视或电台节目中的〕特邀嘉宾栏目: *a guest spot on the Johnny Carson show* 约翰尼·卡森节目中的客串表演

8 run/dance/hop etc on the spot to run etc in one place, without moving forwards or around the area 原地跑步/跳舞/跳跃等

9 weak spot a) a point at which someone or something is not very good 弱点, 不足（之处）: *He'd look at my work and immediately find every weak spot.* 他会检查我的工作, 并立即会发现每一点毛病。**b)** *AmE* if someone has a weak spot for something, they like it very much【美】〔对某物的〕特别喜爱, 偏爱

10 put sb on the spot to deliberately ask someone a question that is difficult or embarrassing to answer〔故意〕使某人处于难堪地位: *Reporters put the governor on the spot with questions about his involvement in the bribery scandal.* 记者们向州长提出一些关于他卷入贿赂丑闻的问题, 使他狼狈不堪。

11 in a spot *informal* in a difficult situation【非正式】处于困难境地: **put sb in a spot** *You've put us in one hell of a spot by telling them that, you know.* 你知道吗, 你把那件事告诉他们, 使我们的处境非常糟糕。

12 bright spot something that is good in a bad situation 亮点, 困境中使人高兴的事: **the one/only bright spot** *Being able to visit my folks was the one bright spot of the vacation.* 能够看望亲人, 是这个假期中唯一一件令人高兴的事。

13 a spot of *BrE informal* a small amount of something【英, 非正式】一点点: *I could do with a spot of whisky.* 我可以喝一点点威士忌。| **a spot of bother** (=a small amount of trouble) 一点麻烦

14 ►ON CLOTH 在布上面◄ **spots** *BrE* small round areas that form a pattern on a piece of cloth; POLKA DOTS【英】〔指布上的〕圆点图案, 斑点: *a dark blue dress with white spots* 带白点的深蓝色连衣裙

15 spots of rain *BrE* a few drops of rain【英】几滴雨

16 ►LIGHT 灯◄ a SPOTLIGHT[1] (1) 聚光灯

17 five-spot/ten-spot etc *AmE spoken* a piece of paper money worth five dollars, ten dollars etc【美口】一张五美元/十美元等钞票

18 ►ADVERTISEMENT 广告◄ a short radio or television advertisement, especially one for a politician 广告插播〔尤指为政客作的广播或电视短广告〕: *a 30-second spot on the local radio station* 在地方广播电台插播的30秒短讯 —see also 另见 BEAUTY SPOT, BLACK SPOT, BLIND SPOT, **not change your spots** (CHANGE[1] (1)), G-SPOT, **high point/spot** (HIGH[1] (13)), **hit the spot** (HIT[1] (27)), **hot spot** (HOT[1] (30)), **knock spots off** (KNOCK[1] (13)), **be rooted to the spot** (ROOT[2] (4)), **have a soft spot for** (SOFT (10)), TROUBLE SPOT

spot² *v* [T]

1 ►NOTICE 注意到◄ to notice something, especially something that is difficult to see, or that you are looking for 看出, 认出; 找出: *Luckily, the enemy planes were spotted early.* 幸亏及早发现了敌机。| *I spotted a break in the fence and headed towards it.* 我看到篱笆上有个缺口, 便朝那里走去。| **spot sb doing sth** *Meg spotted someone coming out of the building.* 梅格发现有人走出大楼。| **difficult/easy to spot** *Dick's very tall, so he's easy to spot in a crowd.* 迪克个子很高, 所以在人群中容易被认出来。

2 ►RECOGNIZE 辨认出◄ to recognize the good or bad qualities in someone or something 发现, 辨认出〔某人或某事的特性〕: *You must learn to spot trouble ahead and prevent it.* 你一定要学会预先发现问题并加以防范。| **spot sb's potential** *Island Records were the first to spot his potential.* 海岛唱片公司最早发现了他的潜质。

3 be spotted to have small round marks on the surface〔表面〕有斑点, 有污渍: **[+with]** *The floor was spotted with paint.* 地板上有很多油漆的污渍。

4 ►GAME 比赛◄ *AmE* to give the other player in a game an advantage【美】〔在比赛中〕让〔对手〕: **spot sb sth** *He spotted me six points and he still won.* 他让了我六分, 但还是赢了。

spot³ *adj technical* for buying or paying immediately, not at some future time【术语】现货的; 现付（款）的: **spot cash/price** *They won't take credit; they want spot cash.* 他们不赊账, 他们要现钱。| *What's the spot price for oil?* 石油的现货价是多少?

spot check /ˌ· ˈ·/ *n* [C] a quick examination of a few things or people from a group, to check whether everything is correct or satisfactory 抽样检查, 抽查: *spot checks by customs officers* 海关官员进行的抽查

spot·less /ˈspɑtlɪs; ˈspɒtləs/ *adj* **1** completely clean 一尘不染的，干干净净的: *Joe's house is spotless.* 乔的房子收拾得很干净。**2 spotless reputation/record/character** a completely honest and good character 毫无瑕疵的名誉/记录/品格: *Before his arrest, the suspect's record was spotless.* 嫌疑犯在被逮捕之前的记录是完全清白的。—**spotlessly** *adv* —**spotlessness** *n* [U]

spot·light¹ /ˈspɑtˌlaɪt; ˈspɒtlaɪt/ *n* **1 a)** [C] a light with a very bright beam which can be directed at someone or something 聚光灯 —see picture at 参见 LIGHT¹ 图 **b)** [singular] the round area of light made by this beam on the ground, stage etc 聚光灯照出的光圈: *Step into the spotlight so we can see you!* 走进光圈，让我们看得见你！**2 be in the spotlight** to receive a lot of attention in the newspapers, on television etc 受到报纸[电视等]经常注意: *Now that he's entered politics he is constantly in the spotlight.* 他既然进了政界，就经常为公众所瞩目了。

spotlight² *v past tense and past participle* **spotlighted** *or* **spotlit** [T] **1** to direct attention to someone or something 使显眼，使突出，使受注意: *The article spotlights the problems of the homeless.* 这篇文章突出报道了无家可归者的种种问题。**2** to shine a strong beam of light on something 将聚光灯射向〔某物〕，聚光照明 —**spotlit** /ˈspɑtˌlɪt; ˈspɒtlɪt/ *adj*

spot-on /ˌ·ˈ·◂/ *adj, adv BrE informal* exactly right【英，非正式】完全正确的[地]: *Judith is always spot-on with her advice.* 朱迪丝的劝告总是完全正确的。

spot·ted /ˈspɑtɪd; ˈspɒtɪ̣d/ *adj* [usually before noun 一般用于名词前] having small round marks or DOTS on the surface〔表面上〕有圆点的，有斑点的: *red and white spotted pyjamas* 有红白色圆点的睡衣 —see picture on page A16 参见 A16 页图

spotted dick /ˌ··ˈ·/ *n* [U] a boiled PUDDING (1) with CURRANTS which is eaten in Britain〔英国的〕葡萄干布丁

spot·ter /ˈspɑtə; ˈspɒtə/ *n* [C] **bird/train etc spotter** *especially BrE* someone who spends time watching birds, trains etc【尤英】鸟类/火车等观察者

spot·ty /ˈspɑtɪ; ˈspɒti/ *adj* **1** *BrE informal* having spots on your face【英，非正式】〔脸上〕有粉刺的: *a spotty youth* 长粉刺的青年 **2** *AmE* good only in some parts, but not in other parts; PATCHY【美】〔质量〕有好有坏的，参差不齐的

spouse /spaus; spaʊs/ *n* [C] *formal* a husband or wife【正式】配偶〔指丈夫或妻子〕

spout¹ /spaut; spaʊt/ *n* [C] **1** a small tube or pipe on a container that you pour liquid out through 容器嘴，壶嘴 **2 a spout of water/blood etc** a sudden strong stream of liquid which comes out of somewhere very fast 水柱/血柱等: *The whale blew a spout of water into the air.* 鲸向空中喷出一条水柱。—see also 另见 **water-spout 3 up the spout** *BrE informal*【英，非正式】**a)** if someone's plans have gone up the spout, they cannot succeed〔计划等〕不成功的: *Her chances of studying medicine have gone up the spout.* 她学医的机会已经告吹了。**b)** completely wrong 完全错的: *His calculations are completely up the spout.* 他的计算完全错误。**c)** *old-fashioned* going to have a baby; PREGNANT【过时】怀孕的

spout² *v* **1 a)** [I always+adv/prep] if liquid or fire spouts from somewhere, it comes out very quickly in a powerful stream〔液体或火〕涌出；喷出: [+from] *Blood was spouting from the wound in her arm.* 血从她手臂的伤口涌出来。**b)** [T] to send out liquid or flames very quickly in a powerful stream 喷出，喷射〔液体或火焰〕: *a volcano spouting lava* 喷射着熔岩的火山 **2** also 又作 **spout off** [I,T] *informal* to talk a lot about something in a boring way, especially without thinking about what you are saying【非正式】喋喋不休[滔滔不绝]地说: [+about] *I'm tired of listening to Jim spouting about politics.* 吉姆滔滔不绝地谈政治，我都听腻了。| **spout (off) sth** *It's no use spouting theories about education if you've never actually taught anyone.* 你如果从来没有实际教过任何学生，大谈教育理论是不顶用的。**3** [I] if a WHALE spouts it sends out a stream of water from a hole in its head〔鲸〕喷水柱

sprain /spren; spreɪn/ *v* [T] to damage a joint in your body by suddenly twisting it 扭伤〔关节〕: *I fell down the steps and sprained my ankle.* 我摔下台阶，扭伤了脚踝。—**sprain** *n* [C]

sprang /spræŋ; spræŋ/ the past tense of SPRING

sprat /spræt; spræt/ *n* [C] a small European HERRING〔欧洲产的〕小西鲱

Sprat, Jack —see 见 JACK SPRAT

sprawl¹ /sprɔl; sprɔːl/ *v* **1** also 又作 **sprawl out** [I always+adv/prep] to lie or sit with your arms or legs stretched out in a lazy or careless way〔懒洋洋地〕伸开手脚躺[坐]着: [+in/on etc] *He just sprawls out in his chair and expects me to bring his dinner.* 他就这样摊开四肢坐在椅子上，等我来给他端上晚餐。| **be sprawled out** *The students were sprawled out on the grass.* 学生们伸开手脚躺在草地上。| **send sb sprawling** (=hit someone with such force that they fall over) 把某人打趴在地上 **2** [I always+adv/prep] if buildings or a town sprawl, they spread out over a wide area in an untidy and unattractive way〔建筑群或城镇〕杂乱地延伸[扩展]: *An industrial estate sprawled across the valley.* 一个工业区杂乱无章地在山谷中延伸。

sprawl² *n* [singular] **1** a large area of buildings that are spread out in an untidy and unattractive way 杂乱无章地扩展的大面积建筑群: *a vast sprawl of industrial development* 一大片肆意扩展的工业开发区 | **urban sprawl** *Los Angeles' huge urban sprawl* 洛杉矶市区无计划的大规模扩张 **2** [singular] a position in which you have your arms or legs stretched out in a lazy or careless way 懒洋洋地伸开四肢躺卧的姿势

spraw·ling /ˈsprɔlɪŋ; ˈsprɔːlɪŋ/ *adj* spreading over a wide area in an untidy or unattractive way 杂乱地延伸的，无计划地扩展的: *a sprawling metropolis* 一座杂乱无章地扩展的大城市

spray¹ /spre; spreɪ/ *v* **1** [T] to make a stream of small drops of liquid come out of a small tube or several small holes 喷: **spray sb with sth** *She sprayed herself with perfume.* 她往自己身上喷香水。| **spray sth on/over sth** *Vandals had sprayed graffiti on the walls.* 破坏公物者在墙上胡乱喷涂。| **spray crops/plants** (=cover them with liquid to protect them from insects or disease) 给农作物/植物喷杀虫药 **2** [I always+adv/prep] if liquids or small bits spray somewhere they are quickly scattered through the air〔液体或碎屑〕飞溅出来: [+over/around/from etc] *Grass started spraying from the blades of the lawn mower.* 碎草开始从剪草机的刀片上飞溅出来。**3 spray (sb/sth with) bullets** to shoot many bullets from a gun quickly（向某人/某物）开枪扫射: *Gunmen sprayed the crowd with bullets.* 持枪歹徒向人群开枪扫射。

spray 喷 3

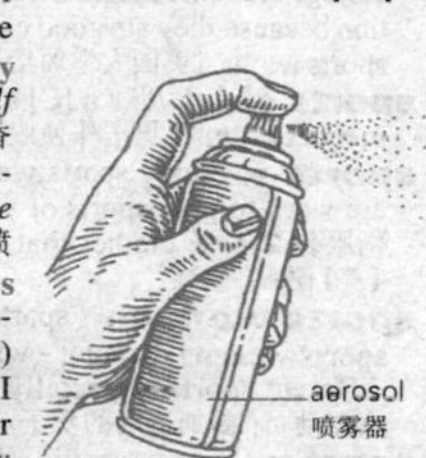

spray² *n*

1 ▶**LIQUID** 液体◀ [C,U] liquid which is forced out of a special container in a stream of very small drops 喷雾液体: **hair spray** (=spray which you put on your hair to keep it tidy) 喷发定型剂 | **insect spray** (=spray used for killing insects) 杀虫喷剂

2 ▶**A CAN** 一罐◀ [C] a can or other container with a special tube which forces liquid out in a stream of small drops 喷雾罐，喷雾器: *Avoid sprays that contain harmful CFCs.* 避免使用装着有害的含氯氟烃的喷雾器。

3 ▶**FROM THE SEA** 海上来的◀ [U] water in very small drops blown from the sea or a wet surface 浪花，水花: *A thunderous plume of spray leapt half-way up the cliff.* 一大片浪花扑向悬崖的半腰，发出雷鸣般的轰响。

4 ▶**BRANCH** 树枝◀ [C] a small branch from a tree or plant used for decoration〔装饰用的〕小树枝: [+of] *sprays of holly* 冬青树枝

5 ▶**FLOWERS/JEWELS** 花朵/珠宝◀ [C] an attractive arrangement of flowers or jewels 带花[镶有珠宝]的枝状饰物

6 a spray of bullets/dust etc a lot of very small objects or bits moving quickly through the air 一阵枪弹/灰尘等

spray can /ˈ··/ *n* [C] a can from which paint is sprayed 喷漆罐

spray·er /ˈspreə; ˈspreɪə/ *n* [C] a piece of equipment used for spraying liquid, especially to protect crops from insects or disease〔尤指施杀虫药用的〕喷雾器

spray gun /ˈ··/ *n* [C] a piece of equipment held like a gun, which sprays liquid in very small drops 喷枪

spray paint /ˈ··/ *n* [U] paint that is sprayed from a can 喷漆 —**spray-paint** *v* [I,T]

spread¹ /sprɛd; spred/ *v past tense and past participle* **spread** 2 2

1 ▶**OPEN OR ARRANGE** 打开或安排◀ also 又作 **spread sth ↔ out** [T] to open something so that it covers a bigger area, or arrange a group of things, so that they cover a flat surface 伸开，展开，张开，铺开: **spread sth on** *Let's spread the map out on the floor.* 我们把地图摊开在地板上吧。| **spread sth over/across etc** *She spread the towel over the radiator to dry.* 她把毛巾铺在暖气上烘干。| *The market women had spread out their goods on the pavement.* 女商贩在人行道上把货物摆开。

2 ▶**DISEASE/FEELING/PROBLEM/FIRE** 疾病/感情/问题/火◀ [I,T] to increase, or be increased, and affect more and more

people or affect a larger area（使）传播，（使）蔓延：*The fire spread very quickly.* 大火迅速蔓延开来。| [+through/to/across etc] *Cholera is spreading through the refugee camps at an alarming rate.* 霍乱正以惊人的速度在难民营中传播开来。| **spread sth** *She's the sort of woman who enjoys spreading bad feeling.* 她是那种喜欢散布敌意的女人。

3 ►INFORMATION/IDEAS 消息/思想◄ **a)** [I] to become known about or used by people more and more 变得广为人知，散布：*News of the explosion spread swiftly.* 发生爆炸的消息迅速传播开来。| [+to/through/over etc] *Buddhism spread to China from India.* 佛教从印度传到中国。| **the word spread** (=the news became known by more and more people) 消息传开 *The word spread that Louise had resigned.* 有传闻说路易丝已经辞职了。| **spread like wildfire** (=become known very quickly) 不胫而走 **b)** [T] to tell a lot of people about something 散播，散布；通知：**spread lies/rumours/gossip** *Andy loves spreading rumours about his colleagues.* 安迪很喜欢散播关于同事的谣言。| **spread the word** *Can you spread the word that the meeting is at 10.30?* 请你通知大家会议在10点半开始，好吗？

4 ►PEOPLE/PLANTS/ANIMALS 人/植物/动物◄ [I always+adv/prep] to begin to live or grow in other areas or countries 分布，散布：**throughout/over etc** *The Moors spread all over Southern Spain.* 摩尔人遍布西班牙南部。

5 ►SOFT SUBSTANCE 软的物质◄ **a)** [T] to put a soft substance onto a surface in order to cover it 涂，敷：**spread sth on/over** *He spread plaster on the walls.* 他往墙上涂灰泥。| **spread sth with sth** *Spread the toast thinly with butter.* 给烤面包涂上薄薄的黄油。—see picture on page A11 参见A11页图 **b)** [I] to be soft enough to be put onto a surface in order to cover it〔够软〕容易涂敷：*If you warm up the butter it'll spread more easily.* 如果你把黄油加热一下，就更容易涂开。

6 ►COVER A LARGE AREA 覆盖大的面积◄ **a)** also 又作 **spread out** [I always+adv/prep] to cover or stretch over a large area 绵延；扩展：[+across/over etc] *Leafy branches spread above her forming a canopy.* 叶子茂密的树枝在她头顶散开形成一个罩篷。**b) be spread across/over etc** to exist or be present over a large area 遍布，散布：*The population is fairly evenly spread across the country.* 这个国家的人口分布相当均匀。

7 spread (out) your legs/arms/fingers etc to push your legs, fingers, arms etc as far apart as possible 张开双腿/双臂/手指等

8 ►DO STH GRADUALLY 逐步进行某事◄ also 又作 **spread sth ↔ out** [T] to do something gradually over a period of time 将…分散于一段时间内：**spread sth over sth** *Could I spread the repayments over a longer period?* 我可以把分期还款的期限延长一些吗？

9 ►WORK/RESPONSIBILITY/MONEY 工作/责任/钱◄ [T] to share work, responsibility, or money among several people 分配，分摊：*The work will be spread across the departments.* 这项工作将由各部门分担。| **spread the load/burden** *If we type five pages each that should help spread the load.* 如果我们每人打五页字，那样工作量就会分摊开了。

10 ►EXPRESSION 表情◄ [I always+adv/prep] to gradually cover all of someone's face 满脸流露：[+across/over] *A mischievous grin spread over her face.* 她满脸调皮的微笑。

11 spread seeds/manure/fertilizer to scatter seeds, MANURE etc on the ground 撒种/施粪肥/施肥料

12 spread your wings to start to have an independent life 开始独立生活：*A year spent studying abroad should allow him to spread his wings a bit.* 在外国留学一年，他应当可以独立一些了。

13 spread its wings if a bird or insect spreads its wings it stretches them wide〔鸟或昆虫〕张开翅膀

14 spread a/the table (with) *old-fashioned* to put food and drink on a table【过时】〔在桌上〕摆上饭菜饮料

spread out *phr v* **1** [I] if a group of people spread out, they move apart from each other so that they cover a wider area〔人群〕散开：*The detective ordered the officers to spread out and search the surrounding fields.* 探长命令警员散开，搜查周围的田野。**2** [T **spread** sth ↔ **out**] to open something out or arrange a group of things on a flat surface 打开，摊开，排开：*Sue spread out her notes on the kitchen table and began to write.* 休把笔记本打开放在厨房桌子上，然后开始写字。**3** [I] to cover or stretch over a large area 伸展，延伸：*A lush green valley spread out below us.* 一片茂密翠绿的山谷在我们下面延伸。**4** [T **spread** sth ↔ **out**] to do something gradually over a period of time 将…分散在一段时间内：*You can spread out the cost over a year.* 你可以把费用分散在一年内支付。

spread² *n*

1 ►INCREASE 增长◄ [singular] the increase in the area, or number of people, affected by something, or in the number of people who do something 传播；扩展；蔓延：**the spread of** *the spread of liberal ideas in the 19th century* 19世纪自由思想的传播

2 ►SOFT FOOD 软质食物◄ [C,U] a soft food which you spread on bread 涂面包的酱：**cheese/chocolate etc spread** (=cheese, chocolate etc in a soft form) 干酪酱/巧克力酱等

3 ►LARGE MEAL 丰盛的饭菜◄ [singular] *informal* a large meal for several guests on a special occasion【非正式】丰盛的饭菜，宴会：*She organized a marvellous spread for the soiree afterwards.* 她后来为那次社交晚会举行了盛大的筵席。

4 ►RANGE 范围◄ [singular] a range of people or things 范围；广度；幅度：*We have a good spread of ages in the department.* 我们部门人员的年龄分布很好。

5 double-page spread/centre spread a special article or advertisement in a newspaper or magazine, which covers two pages or covers the centre pages〔报刊中〕横跨两版的/中心页跨页的文章[广告]

6 ►HAND/WINGS 手/两翼◄ [U] the area covered when the fingers of a hand, or a bird's wings, are fully stretched 手指伸直时手的全长；〔鸟的〕两翼全长，翼展

7 a spread of land/water an area of land or water 一片土地/水域

8 ►FARM 农场◄ [C] *AmE* a large farm or RANCH【美】大农场；大牧场

9 ►MONEY 钱◄ *technical* the difference between the buying price and the selling price of shares (SHARE² (5)) on the STOCK EXCHANGE【术语】〔股票的买入价和卖出价之间的〕差价，差额 —see also 另见 MIDDLE-AGED SPREAD

spread-ea·gled /ˈsprɛdˌiɡld; spredˈiːɡəld/ *adj* lying with arms and legs stretched out 伸开四肢躺着的：*He lay spreadeagled on the bed.* 他伸开四肢躺在床上。

spread·sheet /ˈsprɛdˌʃit; ˈspredʃiːt/ *n* [C] *technical* a kind of computer PROGRAM that can show and calculate information about sales, taxes, profits etc【术语】电子数据表，试算表〔能显示和计算销售、交税、利润等数据资料的电脑程序〕

spree /spri; spriː/ *n* [C] a short period of time doing something that you enjoy, especially spending money or drinking 作乐，狂欢〔尤指花钱、喝酒等〕：**go (off) on a spree** *He's gone off on a drinking spree with his friends.* 他外出和朋友喝酒狂欢。| **a shopping/spending etc spree** *I'm going on a shopping spree to cheer myself up.* 我要去大买特买一番让自己高兴高兴。

sprig /sprɪɡ; sprɪɡ/ *n* [C] a small stem or part of a branch with leaves or flowers on it 带叶[花]的小枝：[+of] *a sprig of parsley* 一小枝带叶的欧芹

spright·ly /ˈspraɪtlɪ; ˈspraɪtli/ *adj* an old person who is sprightly is still active and full of energy〔老人〕活跃的，有活力的 —**sprightliness** *n* [U]

spring¹ /sprɪŋ; sprɪŋ/ *n* S2 W2

1 ►SEASON 季节◄ [C,U] the season between winter and summer when leaves and flowers appear 春天，春季：*It was a cold, sunny day in early spring.* 那是早春里寒冷而阳光灿烂的一天。| *the spring of 1933* 1933年春季 | *spring flowers* 春花

2 ►BED/CARS ETC 床/汽车等◄ **a)** [C usually plural 一般用复数] something, usually a twisted piece of metal, that will return to its previous shape after it has been pressed down 弹簧；发条 **b)** [U] the ability of a chair, bed etc to return to its normal shape after being pressed down 弹性，弹力：*There's not much spring in this old sofa.* 这张旧沙发已经没有多少弹性了。

3 ►WATER 水◄ [C] a place where water comes up naturally from the ground 泉，泉源：*The islands are renowned for their thermal springs and sulphur baths.* 这些海岛以其温泉及硫磺浴而享有盛名。

4 with a spring in your step if you walk with a spring in your step, you move quickly and cheerfully 步伐轻快

5 ►SUDDEN JUMP 突然一跳◄ [singular] a sudden quick movement or jump in a particular direction 跳，跳跃

spring² *v past tense* **sprang** /spræŋ; spræŋ/ also 又作 **sprung** /sprʌŋ; sprʌŋ/ *AmE*【美】, *past participle* **sprung**

1 ►MOVE SUDDENLY 突然移动◄ [I always+adv/prep] to move suddenly and quickly in a particular direction, especially by jumping 跳，跳跃，跳起：[+out of/from/towards etc] *Tom sprung out of bed and rushed to the window.* 汤姆从床上跳起来冲到窗前。| *A kitten sprang from under the bush.* 一只小猫从矮树丛下蹿了出来。| **spring to your feet** (=stand up suddenly) 突然站起

S

2 ▶EXPRESSION/TEARS 表情/眼泪◀ [I always+adv/prep] to appear suddenly on someone's face or in their eyes〔在脸上或眼中〕突然出现，冒出：**[+into/to]** *Tears sprang into her eyes as she started telling them what had happened.* 她开始向他们诉说发生了什么事时，突然泪如泉涌。
3 ▶MOVE BACK 复原◀ [I always+adv/prep] to move quickly back again after being pushed downwards or sideways 弹回原处，反弹：**[+back/up]** *The branch sprang back and hit him in the face.* 树枝弹回来打在他脸上。
4 spring to mind if someone or something springs to mind you immediately think of them 马上想到：*Nobody's name actually springs to mind as an ideal candidate.* 的确一时想不出什么理想的人选。
5 spring into action also 又作 **spring to life** to suddenly become active 突然活跃起来：*The whole town would spring into action at carnival time.* 狂欢节时，全镇的人都会突然活跃起来。
6 spring into existence to suddenly begin to exist 突然出现：*A lot of small businesses sprang into existence during the 1980s.* 20世纪80年代突然冒出了许多小公司。
7 spring open/shut to open or close suddenly and quickly 突然打开/合上：*The lid of the box sprang open.* 盒盖突然弹开。
8 spring a trap a) if an animal springs a trap, it makes the trap move and catch it〔动物〕触发捕捉器〔而被捉〕 **b)** to make someone say or do something by tricking them 诱使某人说出[干]某事
9 spring a leak if a boat or a container springs a leak, it begins to let liquid in or out through a crack or hole〔船或容器〕出现裂缝〔开始漏水〕
10 spring to sb's defence to quickly defend someone who is being criticized 迅速为某人辩护：*Charlene sprang immediately to her son's defence.* 查伦马上挺身而出为她儿子辩护。
11 spring to attention if soldiers spring to attention they stand suddenly upright〔士兵〕霍然立正
12 spring a surprise to make something unexpected or unusual happen 使突然发生，使大吃一惊
13 ▶PRISON 监狱◀ [T] *informal* to help someone escape from prison【非正式】帮助〔某人〕越狱：*A gangland boss was recently sprung from Dartmoor prison.* 一个黑社会头目最近在别人帮助下从达特穆尔监狱逃跑。

spring from *phr v* [T] *spoken*【口】**1** to be caused by something 由…引起：*Her rudeness to other people springs from a basic insecurity.* 她对别人的不礼貌是由于她缺乏基本的安全感所致。**2 where did you/she etc spring from?** used to express surprise when you suddenly see someone who you thought was somewhere else 你/她等是从哪儿冒出来的？〔用于表示惊讶〕

spring sth **on** sb *phr v* [T] to tell someone some news that surprises or shocks them 向〔某人〕突然说〔某事，令人惊讶或震惊〕

spring up *phr v* [I] to suddenly appear or start to exist 突然出现：*Fast-food restaurants are springing up all over town.* 突然市区到处都出现了快餐店。| *A strong wind seemed to have sprung up from nowhere.* 不知从哪儿突然刮来一阵强风。

Spring Bank Hol·i·day /ˌ· ˈ· ˈ···/ a public holiday in the UK, on the last Monday in May 春季银行假日〔英国一公众假日，五月的最后一个星期一〕

spring·board /ˈsprɪŋˌbɔrd; ˈsprɪŋbɔːd/ *n* [C] **1** something that helps you to start doing something, especially by giving you ideas about how to do it〔工作的〕起点，起步方法：**[+for]** *Teachers can use these ideas as a springboard for planning their own lessons.* 教师在备课时可以利用这些想法作为起点。**2** a strong board for jumping on or off, used when diving (DIVE[1] (1)) or doing GYMNASTICS〔跳水运动的〕跳板，〔体操运动的〕踏跳板

spring·bok /ˈsprɪŋˌbɑk; ˈsprɪŋbɒk/ *n* [C] a small DEER that can run fast and lives in South Africa 跳羚〔南非的一种小羚羊〕

spring break /ˌ· ˈ·/ *n* [C] *AmE* a holiday from college or university in the spring, that is usually two weeks long【美】春假〔大学里在春天放的假，通常为两周〕

spring chick·en /ˌ· ˈ··/ *n* [C] **she's/you're no spring chicken** *humorous* used to say that someone is no longer young【幽默】她/你已经不再年轻了

spring-clean /ˌ· ˈ·◂/ *v* [I,T] to clean a house thoroughly, usually once a year〔通常一年一度对房屋的〕彻底打扫，大扫除：**do the spring-cleaning** *Judith's busy doing the spring-cleaning.* 朱迪思在忙于大扫除。—**spring-clean** *n* [singular] *BrE*【英】

spring fe·ver /ˌ· ˈ··/ *n* [U] a sudden feeling of energy and wanting to do something new and exciting that you have in the spring 春躁症〔指在春季突然觉得精力充沛、想尝试新鲜刺激事物的心理状态〕

spring on·ion /ˌ· ˈ··/ *n* [C] *BrE* a strong-tasting onion with a small white round part and a long green stem, usually eaten raw【英】大葱；SCALLION, GREEN ONION *AmE*【美】

spring roll /ˌ· ˈ·/ *n* [C] a type of Chinese food consisting of a piece of rolled PASTRY filled with vegetables and sometimes meat and cooked in oil 春卷；EGG ROLL *AmE*【美】

Spring·steen /ˈsprɪŋstin; ˈsprɪŋstiːn/, **Bruce** /brus; bruːs/ (1949-) a US ROCK singer and songwriter whose songs often deal with the problems faced by young WORKING CLASS people in the US. He is sometimes called 'the Boss'. His ALBUMs include *Born to Run* and *Born in the USA*. 斯普林斯廷〔(1949-)，美国摇滚歌手、词作家，有时被称为"老板"。歌曲内容多涉及美国蓝领阶层年轻人面临的种种问题。专辑有《生就奔忙》和《生在美国》〕

spring tide /ˌ· ˈ·/ *n* [C] a large rise and fall in the level of the sea at the time of the NEW MOON and the FULL MOON〔新月和满月时的〕大潮，满潮，朔望大潮

spring·time /ˈsprɪŋˌtaɪm; ˈsprɪŋtaɪm/ *n* [U] the time of the year when it is spring 春天，春季：*Paris in the springtime* 春天的巴黎

spring train·ing /ˌ· ˈ··/ *n* [U] *AmE* the period during which a BASEBALL team gets ready for competition【美】〔棒球队的〕赛前训练

spring·y /ˈsprɪŋɪ; ˈsprɪŋi/ *adj* **1** something that is springy comes back to its former shape after being pressed or walked on 有弹性的，有弹力的：*The turf felt springy underfoot.* 脚下的草皮踩起来有弹性。**2 springy step/walk** a way of walking which is quick and full of energy 轻快有力的步伐 —**springily** *adv* —**springiness** *n* [U]

sprin·kle[1] /ˈsprɪŋkl; ˈsprɪŋkəl/ *v* **1** [T] to scatter small drops of liquid or small pieces of something 洒〔小水滴〕；撒〔小片固体〕：**sprinkle sth on/over sth** *She sprinkled perfume on the pillow.* 她往枕头上洒香水。| **sprinkle sth with sth** *Sprinkle the pasta with cheese.* 给面条撒些干酪。—see picture on page A11 参见A11页图 **2 be sprinkled with jokes/quotations etc** to be full of jokes etc 插进了许多笑话/引语等：*Dr Krowik's conversation was liberally sprinkled with literary allusions.* 克罗威克博士在交谈中用了大量的文学典故。**3 it is sprinkling** *AmE* if it is sprinkling, it is raining lightly【美】下着小雨

sprinkle[2] *n* [singular] **1** a sprinkling 少量，一点：*Add a sprinkle of salt.* 放少量的盐。**2** *AmE* a light rain【美】小雨

sprin·kler /ˈsprɪŋklɚ; ˈsprɪŋklə/ *n* [C] **1** a piece of equipment with holes, used for scattering water on grass or soil〔浇草地的〕洒水器 **2** a piece of equipment with holes that is on a ceiling and scatters water if there is a fire〔天花板上的〕自动喷水火火装置

sprin·kling /ˈsprɪŋklɪŋ; ˈsprɪŋklɪŋ/ *n* **a sprinkling of** a small quantity or amount of something 少量，一点：*The hilltops were covered with a sprinkling of snow.* 山顶上覆盖着薄薄的一层雪。

sprint[1] /sprɪnt; sprɪnt/ *v* [I] to run very fast for a short distance〔短距离〕快速奔跑，冲刺：**[+along/across/up etc]** *Bill sprinted up the steps.* 比尔快速跑上台阶。

sprint[2] *n* **1** [singular] a short period of running very fast 短距离的快速奔跑：**put on a sprint/make a sprint** (=run very quickly for a short distance) 全速短跑 **2** [C] a short race in which the runners run very fast over a very short distance 短距离赛跑，短跑比赛：*the 100 metre sprint* 100米短跑

Sprint·er /ˈsprɪntɚ; ˈsprɪntə/ *n* a type of fast train used for fairly short rail journeys in the UK 斯普林特火车〔英国一种用于短途旅行的快速列车〕

sprinter *n* [C] someone who runs in fast races over short distances 短跑运动员：*sprinter Linford Christie* 短跑运动员林福德·克里斯蒂

Sprite /spraɪt; spraɪt/ *trademark* a type of sweet, clear, not alcoholic drink with BUBBLEs that has a LEMON and LIME taste【商标】雪碧〔一种甜味软饮料。无色，有气泡，带柠檬和酸橙口味〕

sprite *n* [C] **1** a FAIRY (1), especially one who is graceful or who likes playing tricks on people 小精灵 **2** an image produced by a special type of computer, that is drawn in layers to look real〔电脑屏幕上的多层次、有立体感的〕子图形，子画面

spritz /sprɪts; sprɪts/ *v* [T] *AmE* to SPRAY a liquid in short bursts【美】喷〔液体〕：*Spritz a little water on the fern every day.* 每天给这棵蕨类植物喷一点水。—**spritz** *n* [C] *a spritz of hair spray* 喷洒喷发定型剂

spritz·er /ˈsprɪtsɚ; ˈsprɪtsə/ *n* [C,U] a drink made with SODA WATER and white wine〔用汽水和白葡萄酒调制的〕汽酒

sprock·et /ˈsprɑkɪt; ˈsprɒkɪ̣t/ *n* [C] **1** also 又作 **sprocket wheel** a wheel with a row of teeth (TOOTH (2)) for fitting into and turning a bicycle chain or a photographic film with holes〔自行车的〕链轮;〔电影放映机的〕输片齿轮, 带齿卷盘 **2** one of the teeth on a wheel of this kind 链轮[输片齿轮]的齿

sprog /sprɑg; sprɒg/ *n* [C] *BrE humorous* a child or baby【英, 幽默】小孩; 婴儿

sprout¹ /spraut; spraʊt/ *v* **1** [I] if leaves or BUDs sprout they appear and begin to grow〔树叶或新芽〕开始长出来 **2** [I,T] if vegetables, seeds, or plants sprout they start to produce SHOOTs, or BUDs〔种子等〕发芽, 抽芽: *Keep the tray away from direct sunlight until the seeds begin to sprout.* 种子开始发芽之前, 花盆要放在没有阳光直射的地方。| **sprout sth** *The plant had sprouted a few flower stalks.* 那棵植物长出了几根花柄。**3** also 又作 **sprout up** [I always+adv/prep] to appear suddenly in large numbers 突然大量出现, 大量冒出: [+in/throughout] *Office blocks seem to be sprouting up everywhere.* 好像到处都有办公大楼冒出来。**4** [T] to grow suddenly, or grow something suddenly, especially hair, horns, or wings〔尤指头发、角、翅膀等〕突然长出, 突然产生: *Jim seemed to have sprouted a beard overnight.* 吉姆好像一夜之间便长出了胡子。

sprout² *n* [C] **1** a small green vegetable like a very small CABBAGE; BRUSSELS SPROUT 球芽甘蓝 **2** a new growth on a plant; SHOOT² (1)〔植物的〕苗; 芽, 嫩枝 **3** [usually plural 一般用复数] *AmE* an ALFALFA seed which has grown a stem and is eaten【美】〔可食的〕苜蓿芽 **4** *AmE* a BEANSPROUT【美】豆芽

spruce¹ /sprus; spruːs/ *n* [C,U] a tree that grows in northern countries and has short leaves shaped like needles 云杉

spruce² *v*

spruce up *phr v* [I,T] *informal* to make yourself or something look neater and tidier【非正式】把〔自己或某物〕打扮得整齐干净: *I'll just go upstairs and spruce up a bit before dinner.* 宴会之前我得上楼去打扮一下。| **spruce sb/sth ↔ up** *We need to spruce the house up a bit before we sell it.* 我们需要把房子稍微收拾一下再卖。

spruce³ *adj* neat and clean 整齐干净的: *Mr Bailey was looking very spruce in a white linen suit.* 贝利先生穿着一身白色亚麻布衣服, 看起来真帅。—**sprucely** *adv*

sprung¹ /sprʌŋ; sprʌŋ/ a past tense and the past participle of SPRING

sprung² *adj* supported or kept in shape by SPRINGs 装有弹簧的, 用弹簧支撑的: *a sprung mattress* 弹簧床垫

spry /spraɪ; spraɪ/ *adj* a spry old person is active and cheerful〔老人〕充满活力的, 开朗的: *a spry ninety-year old* 一位矫健的 90 岁老人 —**spryly** *adv*

spud /spʌd; spʌd/ *n* [C] *informal* a POTATO【非正式】马铃薯, 土豆

spume /spjum; spjuːm/ *n* [U] *literary* FOAM¹ (1) that forms on the top of waves when the sea is rough【文】〔海浪的〕泡沫, 浮沫

spun /spʌn; spʌn/ the past tense and past participle of SPIN

spunk /spʌŋk; spʌŋk/ *n* [U] **1** *informal* courage【非正式】胆量, 勇气 **2** *BrE slang* SEMEN【英俚】精液 —**spunky** *adj*: *Clare's a spunky team captain.* 克莱尔是个有胆量的球队队长。

spur¹ /spɝ; spɜː/ *n* [C] **1** a sharp pointed object on the heel of a rider's boot which is used to encourage a horse to go faster 马刺 **2** a fact or event that makes you try harder to do something 激励因素; 鼓舞; 鞭策: *Did your father's success act as a spur when you started in business?* 你开始从商时, 你父亲的成功对你是一种鞭策吗? **3 do sth on the spur of the moment** to do something suddenly, without thinking about it before you do it 一时冲动之下做某事: *On the spur of the moment she picked up the phone and called Mike.* 她一时冲动, 拿起话筒给迈克打电话。—see also 另见 SPUR-OF-THE-MOMENT **4** a piece of high ground which sticks out from the side of a hill or mountain 山嘴, 尖坡 **5** a railway track or road that goes away from a main line or road〔铁路或公路的〕支线 **6** the stiff sharp part that sticks out from the back of a male chicken's leg〔公鸡腿上的〕距

spur² *v* **spurred, spurring 1** also 又作 **spur on** [T] to encourage someone to try harder in order to succeed 激励, 鼓励: **spur sb (on) to** *It's unlikely that harsh criticism will spur a child on to greater efforts.* 严厉的批评不大可能激励孩子作出更大的努力。| **spur sb into action** (=to make someone start doing something) 促使某人行动起来 **2** [T] to make an improvement or change happen faster 促进: *Lower taxes would spur investment and help economic growth.* 降低税率将刺激投资, 有助于经济增长。**3** [I,T] to encourage a horse to go faster, especially by pushing it with special points on the heels of your boots〔尤指用马刺〕策马前进; 使〔马〕快跑

spu·ri·ous /ˈspjurɪəs; ˈspjʊəriəs/ *adj* **1** a spurious statement, argument etc, is not based on facts or good reasoning and is likely to be incorrect〔声明、论据等〕站不住脚的, 谬误的: *a cosy and entirely spurious view of family life* 对家庭生活的美妙而虚幻的看法 **2** insincere 虚假的, 不诚实的: *spurious sympathy* 虚假的同情 —**spuriously** *adv* —**spuriousness** *n* [U]

spurn /spɝn; spɜːn/ *v* [T] *especially literary* to refuse to accept something or to have a relationship with someone, especially because you are too proud【尤文】轻蔑地拒绝, 对…不屑一顾: *She spurned all offers of help.* 她轻蔑地拒绝一切帮助。| *a spurned lover* 遭到轻蔑拒绝的爱慕者

spur-of-the-mo·ment /ˌ· · · ˈ··◂/ *adj* [only before noun 仅用于名词前] a spur-of-the-moment decision or action is made or done suddenly without planning 出于一时冲动的

Spurs /spɝz; spɜːz/ a famous English football team, whose full name is 'Tottenham Hotspur'. Their football ground is at White Hart Lane in north London. 热刺队〔英国一支著名足球队。全称为"托特纳姆热刺队", 主场设在伦敦北部的白鹿巷体育场〕

spurt¹ /spɝt; spɜːt/ *v* **1** [I] if liquid or flames spurt from something they pour out of it quickly and suddenly〔液体或火焰〕喷出; 迸出: [+from/out of] *Water began spurting from a hole in the pipe.* 水开始从水管的裂口涌出来。**2** [T] to send out liquid or flames 喷出〔液体或火焰〕 **3** [I always+adv/prep] to move somewhere very quickly 迅速行进; 冲刺: [+towards/across] *He spurted towards the finishing line.* 他向终点线冲刺。

spurt² *n* [C] **1** a sudden pouring out of liquid or flames〔液体或火焰的〕喷出; 涌出: [+of] *The fire sent up spurts of flame.* 火中蹿出一股股火焰。| **in spurts** (=quickly for short periods) 突然一阵阵地 *The water came out of the tap in short spurts.* 水一阵阵地从水龙头里喷出。**2** a short sudden increase of activity, effort, or speed〔活动、努力或速度的〕突然增加; 迸发: [+of] *a sudden spurt of academic progress* 学业的突然进步 | **put on a spurt** (=to suddenly move more quickly for a short period) 冲刺 *Eric put on a spurt to try and catch up with the others.* 埃里克突然加速, 试图赶上其他人。| **in spurts** (=in sudden short periods of effort) 短期的突然努力 *I tend to work in spurts.* 我经常会拼命地工作一阵子。

Sput·nik /ˈspʌtnɪk; ˈspʌtnɪk/ a SATELLITE put into space by the former Soviet Union. There were several Sputniks, but the first of these (Sputnik I in 1957) was the first satellite ever to go around the Earth. "史泼尼克"号〔前苏联发射的人造卫星。名为史泼尼克号的卫星有好几颗, 其中最早的一颗是 1957 年发射的"史泼尼克一号", 为首颗绕地球飞行的人造卫星〕

sput·ter /ˈspʌtɚ; ˈspʌtə/ *v* **1** [I] to make several sudden soft sounds like someone spitting (SPIT¹ (1)) 发出噼噼啪啪声, 毕剥作响: *The engine began sputtering as the car climbed the hill.* 汽车上坡时, 引擎开始噼噼啪啪作响。**2** [I,T] to talk quickly in short confused phrases, especially because you are angry or shocked; SPLUTTER (1)〔因气愤或震惊而〕语无伦次地说

spu·tum /ˈspjutəm; ˈspjuːtəm/ *n* [U] *technical* liquid in your mouth which you have coughed up from your lungs【术语】痰

spy¹ /spaɪ; spaɪ/ *n* [C] someone whose job it is to find out secret information about another country, organization, or group 间谍: *a British spy in World War II* 第二次世界大战中的一名英国间谍 | *a spy film* 间谍片

CULTURAL NOTE 文化注释

In CARTOONs a spy is usually drawn as a man wearing a RAINCOAT. The collar of his coat sticks up so that it hides the lower part of his face, and he typically wears a hat that helps to hide his eyes. A spy in a cartoon usually walks on his toes so that he does not make any noise, and he often hides behind trees or around the corner of a building when he is spying on someone. 漫画里的间谍通常被刻画成穿着雨衣。他上衣的领子竖起来遮住下半边脸, 而且他通常还戴着帽子, 这样可以遮住他的双眼。漫画里的间谍走起路来蹑手蹑脚, 不弄出任何声响, 而且经常躲在树后或者墙角处秘密监视目标。

spy² *v* **1** [I] to secretly collect information about an enemy country or an organization you are competing against 从事间谍活动; 秘密收集情报: [+on] *He was charged with spying on top-secret naval bases.* 他被指控刺探绝密的海军基地情报。**2 spy on sb** to watch someone secretly 秘密监视某人: *Jean's always spying*

on the neighbours. 琼总是窥探她的邻居。**3** [T] *especially literary* to suddenly see someone or something, especially after searching for them【尤文】〔尤指通过搜索后〕突然看见, 突然发现: *Ellen suddenly spied her friend in the crowd.* 埃伦突然在人群中看到了她的朋友。

spy sth ↔ **out** *phr v* [T] **1** to secretly find out information about something 暗中查明 **2 spy out the land** to secretly find out more information about a situation before deciding what to do〔作决定前〕暗中摸清情况

spy·glass /ˈspaɪˌglæs; ˈspaɪglɑːs/ *n* [C] a small TELESCOPE used by sailors in the past〔旧时水手用的〕小型望远镜

Spy Who Came in from the Cold, The /ˌ· · ·ˌ· · ˈ·/ (1963) a NOVEL by John Le Carré about a British SPY (=someone whose job it is to find out secret information about another country) in East Germany who wants to go back to the West《寒国谍影》〔(1963), 约翰·勒·卡雷的小说。描写一名在前东德活动的英国间谍设法返回西方的故事〕

sq the written abbreviation of 缩写= SQUARE

squab·ble /ˈskwabl̩; ˈskwɒbəl/ *v* [I] to quarrel continuously about something unimportant〔为琐事〕争吵, 发生口角: *[+about/over] The kids are still squabbling about whose turn it is to wash the dishes.* 孩子们仍然在为该轮到谁洗碗而争吵。—**squabble** *n* [C]

3 **squad** /skwad; skwɒd/ *n* [C] **1** a group of players from which a team will be chosen for a particular sports event〔为参加某体育比赛而组成的〕运动队; 球队: *the Italian World Cup squad* 代表意大利参加世界杯赛的球队 **2** the police department responsible for dealing with a particular kind of crime〔警察的〕特别行动小组: **drugs/fraud/vice squad** *Officers of the narcotics squad raided the club.* 缉毒小组的警员突击搜查这个俱乐部。**3** a small group of soldiers working together as a unit〔士兵组成的〕班, 小队: *a drill squad* 操练(示范)班 **4** *AmE* a group of CHEERLEADERS【美】拉拉队 —see also 另见 DEATH SQUAD, FIRING SQUAD, FLYING SQUAD

squad car /ˈ· ·/ *n* [C] a car used by police on duty; PATROL CAR 巡逻警车: *He was bundled into the back of a squad car.* 他被塞进巡逻警车的后座。

squad·dy, squaddie /ˈskwadɪ; ˈskwɒdi/ *n* [C] *BrE informal* a soldier who is not an officer【英, 非正式】士兵

squad·ron /ˈskwadrən; ˈskwɒdrən/ *n* [C] a military force consisting of a group of aircraft or ships 飞行中队; 海军分遣舰队: *a squadron of bombers* 轰炸机中队

squadron lead·er /ˈ· · ˌ· ·/ *n* [C] an officer in the British AIRFORCE below a WING COMMANDER〔英国〕空军少校[中队长]

squal·id /ˈskwalɪd; ˈskwɒlɪ̈d/ *adj* **1** dirty and unpleasant because of a lack of care or money〔因无人料理或缺钱而〕污秽的, 肮脏的: *How can anyone live in such squalid conditions?* 人怎么能住在如此污秽的环境中? | *a tiny squalid apartment* 肮脏的小套房 **2** involving low moral standards or dishonesty; SORDID (1) 道德败坏的; 卑鄙的; 低贱的: *a squalid tale of sex and corruption* 涉及色情和腐败的下流故事 —see also 另见 SQUALOR —**squalidly** *adv* —**squalidness** *n* [U]

squall[1] /skwɔl; skwɔːl/ *n* [C] a sudden strong wind, especially one that brings rain or snow 飑〔突起的狂风, 常夹有雨或雪〕: *A violent squall sank both ships.* 一阵强烈的飑把两艘船都刮沉了。

squall[2] *v* [I] if a baby or child squalls, it cries noisily〔婴儿或小孩〕大声哭喊; 尖叫

squal·ly /ˈskwɔlɪ; ˈskwɔːli/ *adj* squally rain or snow comes with sudden strong winds 风狂雨暴的, 多飑的: *squally showers* 狂风暴雨

squal·or /ˈskwalɚ; ˈskwɒlə/ *n* [U] the condition of being SQUALID 污秽, 肮脏: *The refugees are forced to live in squalor.* 难民们被迫生活在肮脏的环境里。

squan·der /ˈskwandɚ; ˈskwɒndə/ *v* [T] to spend money or use your time carelessly on things that are not useful 浪费, 挥霍: **squander sth on** *They squandered millions on that film.* 他们在那部电影上浪费了几百万。—**squanderer** *n* [C]

Squan·to /ˈskwanto; ˈskwɒntəʊ/ (?1585-1622) a Native American who helped the Pilgrim Fathers, the first English people to come to America, by showing them where to hunt and fish and how to plant corn 斯夸托〔(?1585-1622), 美洲印第安人。曾帮助最早抵达美洲的清教徒前辈移民, 教他们到何处捕鱼、打猎以及如何种植谷物〕

2 3 **square**[1] /skwɛr; skweə/ *adj*

1 ►**SHAPE** 形状◄ having four straight equal sides and 90° angles at the corners 正方形的, 四方形的: *a square flower bed* 正方形的花坛

2 ►**ANGLE** 角◄ forming a 90° angle 成直角的: *a square corner* 成直角的拐角 | *a square jaw* 方下巴 | *square shoulders* 宽肩膀

3 square metre/mile etc an area of measurement equal to a square with sides a metre long, a mile long etc 平方米/平方英里等: *about four square meters of ground* 大约四平方米的土地 | *There isn't a café within a square mile of here.* 这地方一平方英里内没有咖啡馆。

4 5 feet/2 metres etc square having the shape of a square with sides that are 5 feet, 2 metres etc long 五英尺/两米见方等: *The room is six metres square.* 这个房间为六米见方。

5 ►**LEVEL** 水平的◄ parallel with a straight line 平行的, 水平的: *[+with] I don't think the shelf is square with the floor.* 我觉得这块搁板与地板不平。

6 a square deal honest and fair treatment from someone, especially in business 公平对待; 公平交易: *I try to give my workers a square deal, decent wages, and a clean room.* 我尽量对我的工人公平合理, 给他们像样的工资和清洁的住房。—see also 另见 **hit sth fair and square** (FAIR[2] (2)), **tell sb fair and square** (FAIR[2] (3))

7 a square meal a good satisfying meal 丰盛的一顿饭

8 be all square to have the same number of points as your opponent in a competition 比分相同, 平局: *The teams were all square at the end of the first half.* 上半场结束时两队打成平局。

9 (all) square *informal* if two people are square they do not owe each other any money【非正式】〔彼此〕两不欠账的: *Here's your £10 back, that makes us square.* 还你 10 英镑, 这样我们谁也不欠谁的了。

10 ►**UNFASHIONABLE** 不合时尚的◄ *old-fashioned* boring and unfashionable【过时】古板的; 守旧的

11 a square peg in a round hole *informal* someone who is in a job or situation that is not suitable for them【非正式】不适宜做某工作的人; 与周围环境格格不入的人 —**squareness** *n* [U]

square[2] *n* [C] 2

1 ►**SHAPE** 形状◄ **a)** a shape with four straight equal sides with 90° angles at the corners 正方形, 四方形: *First of all, draw a square.* 首先, 画一个正方形。—see picture at 参见 SHAPE[1] 图 **b)** a piece of something in this shape (正)方形物: *[+of] a square of cloth* 一块方布 —see picture on page A7 参见 A7 页图

2 ►**IN A TOWN** 在城镇里◄ **a)** a broad open area in the middle of a town usually in the shape of a square, or the buildings surrounding it 广场; 广场周围的建筑物: *There's a market in the square every Tuesday.* 每星期二广场上有集市。**b) Square** used in addresses 广场〔用于地址中〕: *She lives in Hanover Square.* 她住在汉诺威广场。

3 be back to square one to be back in exactly the same situation that you started from, so that you have made no progress 退回起点〔毫无进展〕; 从头开始: *Police have released the suspect and are now back to square one.* 警方释放了那个嫌疑人, 现在又得从头开始。

4 ►**NUMBER** 数字◄ the result of multiplying a number by itself 平方, 二次幂: *The square of 4 is 16.* 4 的平方是 16。—see also 另见 SQUARE ROOT

5 ►**IN A GAME** 在游戏中◄ a space on a board used for playing a game such as CHESS〔棋盘等上的〕方格

6 ►**PERSON** 人◄ *old-fashioned* someone who is boring because they are not interested in the newest styles of music, clothes etc【过时】古板守旧的人; 老古板

7 ►**TOOL** 工具◄ a flat tool with a straight edge, often shaped like an L, used for drawing or measuring 90° angles 直角尺, 丁字尺, 曲尺 —see also 另见 SETSQUARE

8 be on the square *old-fashioned* to behave or speak honestly【过时】行为正直; 说话诚实: *Are you really on the square?* 你是真心的吗?

square[3] *v* [T]

1 ►**MULTIPLY** 乘◄ to multiply a number by itself 使〔某数〕自乘一次; 使〔某数〕成平方

2 ►**IN A COMPETITION** 在竞赛中◄ to win the same number of points or games as your opponent 把〔比分〕拉平, 使〔比赛〕打成平局: *India won the second match to square the series at one each.* 印度队赢了第二场, 使循环赛积分为一平。

3 ►**PAY SB MONEY** 付钱给某人◄ to pay money to someone in an official position, so that they do what you want 收买, 贿赂: *We'll have to square a few government officials, if we're going to get this scheme approved.* 我们要想使这个计划得到批准, 就得买通几位政府官员。

4 square your shoulders to push back your shoulders with your back straight, usually to show your determination 挺直肩膀〔以显示决心〕

5 ►MAKE STH STRAIGHT 使某物变直◄ to make something straight or parallel 使…变直[变平行]

6 square the circle to attempt something impossible 尝试做不可能的事

square sth ↔ **away** *phr v* [T usually passive 一般用被动态] *AmE* to finish something, especially by putting the last details in order【美】完成〔尤指做完最后细节〕: *Get your work squared away before you leave.* 把工作完成后再走。

square off *phr v* [T] **1** [T **square** sth ↔ **off**] to make something square with straight edges 把…弄成方形 **2** [I] *AmE* to get ready to fight someone【美】摆好打斗的架势

square up *phr v* **1** [I] to pay money that you owe 清账; 结账: *I'll pay for the drinks and you can square up later.* 我来付饮料的钱, 你可以过后再结算。**2** [I] *BrE* to get ready to fight someone【英】摆好打斗的架势 **3** [T **square up to** sb/sth] to deal with a difficult situation or person in a determined way 果敢地面对〔某人或困难的处境〕: *I admire the way she squared up to the problem.* 我钦佩她正视问题的勇气。

square with *phr v* **1** [I,T not in progressive 不用进行时] if you square two ideas, statements etc with each other or if they square with each other they can be accepted together even though they seem different (使)〔两种观点、说法等〕一致: *Ben's story doesn't square with Jane's version.* 本的说法跟简的不一致。| **square sth with sth** *How do you square fighting in a war, with being a Christian?* 你作为一名基督徒还去打仗, 这怎么说得通呢? | **square sth with your conscience** (=make yourself believe that what you are doing is morally right) 使自己对某事感到心安理得 **2** [T **square** sth **with** sb] to arrange something with someone by persuading them to agree to it or allow it 取得〔某人的〕同意[认可]: *I'll take the day off if I can square it with my boss.* 我要是能征得老板的同意, 就休一天假。

square[4] *adv* [only after verb 仅用于动词后] **1** directly and firmly; SQUARELY 直接地; 果断地: **square in the eye** *Look him square in the eye and say no.* 直视着他的眼睛说不。**2** [+to] at 90° to a line; SQUARELY (4) 成直角; 垂直地

square-bash·ing /ˈ· ˌ··/ *n* [U] *BrE informal* practice in marching as part of military training【英, 非正式】〔军队的〕操练步伐

square brack·ets /ˌ· ˈ··/ *n* [plural] *BrE* a pair of BRACKETS [ ], used for enclosing information【英】方括号

squared /skwɛrd; skweəd/ *adj* **1** divided into squares or marked with squares 方格的: *squared paper* 方格纸; 座标纸 **2 3/9/10 etc squared** the number 3, 9, 10 etc multiplied by itself 数字3/9/10等的自乘: *3 squared equals 9.* 3的平方是9。

square dance /ˈ· ·/ *n* [C] a type of COUNTRY DANCE in which four pairs of dancers face each other in a square〔四对男女跳的〕方形舞

square knot /ˈ· ·/ *n* [C] *AmE* a double knot that will not come undone easily; REEF KNOT【美】方结, 平结〔一种不易松脱的双结〕

square·ly /ˈskwɛrlɪ; ˈskweəli/ *adv* [only after verb 仅用于动词后] **1** directly and firmly; SQUARE[4] (1) 直接地, 坚定地: *He turned and faced her squarely.* 他转过身来径直地面对着她。**2** completely and with no doubt 完全地, 毫无疑问地: *The report puts the blame squarely on the government.* 这份报告毫不含糊地把责任归在政府头上。**3** straight on something and centrally 端端正正地: *Dr Soames jammed his hat squarely on his head.* 索姆斯博士把帽子端端正正地扣在头上。**4** at 90° to a line; SQUARE[4] (2) 成直角; 垂直地

Square Mile, the /ˌ· ˈ·/ another name for the City of London (=the financial and banking centre of London), used especially in news reports. It is called this because the area of the City is about one square mile. 平方英里城〔伦敦老城区金融中心的别称, 多见于新闻报道。因面积约为一平方英里, 故名〕

square-rigged /ˌ· ˈ·◄/ *adj* a ship that is square-rigged has its sails set across it and not along its length〔船〕有横帆装置的

square root /ˌ· ˈ·/ *n* [C] the square root of a number is the number which, when multiplied by itself, equals that number 平方根: *The square root of nine is three.* 9的平方根是3。

squar·ish /ˈskwɛrɪʃ; ˈskweərɪʃ/ *adj* shaped almost like a square 近似方形的, 呈方形的

squash[1] /skwɑʃ; skwɒʃ/ *v* **1** [T] to press something into a flat shape, often breaking or damaging it 挤扁; 压碎; 压坏: *I don't want my hat getting squashed in your bag.* 我不想我的帽子在你的包里给压扁。| *Hey! You're squashing me!* 嗨, 你挤着我啦! **2** [I always+adv/prep, T always+adv/prep] to push yourself or something else into a space that is too small 挤进; 塞进: [+into] *Seven of us squashed into the car.* 我们中有七个人挤进了汽车。**3** [T] *informal* to use your power or authority to stop something that is causing trouble; QUASH【非正式】镇压, 压制

squash[2] *n* **1** [U] a game played by two people who use rackets (RACKET[1] (3)) to hit a small rubber ball against the four walls of a square court 壁球 **2 it's a squash** *spoken* used to say that there is not enough space for everyone to fit comfortably in【口】太挤了: *Sorry it's a squash with six in the car.* 对不起, 这辆车坐六个人太挤了。**3** [C,U] one of a group of large vegetables with solid flesh and hard skins, such as PUMPKINS and ZUCCHINI 南瓜属植物〈如南瓜、西葫芦〉—see picture on page A9 参见A9页图 **4** [U] *BrE* a drink made from fruit juice, sugar, and water【英】果汁饮料

squashed /skwɑʃt; skwɒʃt/ *adj* broken or made flat by being pressed hard 压碎的; 压扁的: *a bag of squashed tomatoes* 一袋压烂了的番茄

squash rack·ets /ˈ· ˌ··/ *n* [U] SQUASH[2] (1) 壁球

squash·y /ˈskwɑʃɪ; ˈskwɒʃi/ *adj* soft and full of liquid 软而多汁的: *squashy overripe tomatoes* 过熟发软的番茄 —**squashiness** *n* [U]

squat[1] /skwɑt; skwɒt/ *v* **squatted, squatting** [I] **1** also 又作 **squat down** to sit with your knees bent under you, your bottom off the ground, and balancing on your feet 蹲, 蹲坐: [+on/behind/in etc] *Parsons squatted down beside the footprints to get a better look.* 帕森斯蹲在脚印旁, 以便看得更清楚。—see picture at 参见 CROUCH 图 **2** to live in a building or on a piece of land without permission and without paying rent 擅自占用建筑物[空地]: *There are people squatting in the house next door.* 有人擅自居住在隔壁的房子里。

squat[2] *adj* unattractively short and thick or low and wide 矮胖的; 粗矮的: *squat stone cottages roofed in slate* 矮宽的石板瓦屋顶的小石屋

squat[3] *n* **1** [C] a squatting position 蹲坐; 蹲姿 **2** [singular] *BrE* a house that people are living in without permission and without paying rent【英】被擅自占用的房子: *She lives in a draughty squat in Camden.* 她居住在卡姆登一间私占的四周透风的房子里。

squat·ter /ˈskwɑtə; ˈskwɒtə/ *n* [C] someone who lives in an empty building or on a piece of land without permission and without paying rent 擅自占用建筑物[空地]的人: *crudely built squatters' shacks* 私占空地者搭建的简陋的棚屋

CULTURAL NOTE 文化注释

A small number of people in the UK and the US, usually younger people in big cities, live in a squat instead of renting or buying a home. Local councils and local governments sometimes ignore the fact that squatters are in their property, especially if they plan to pull the building

squash 壁球

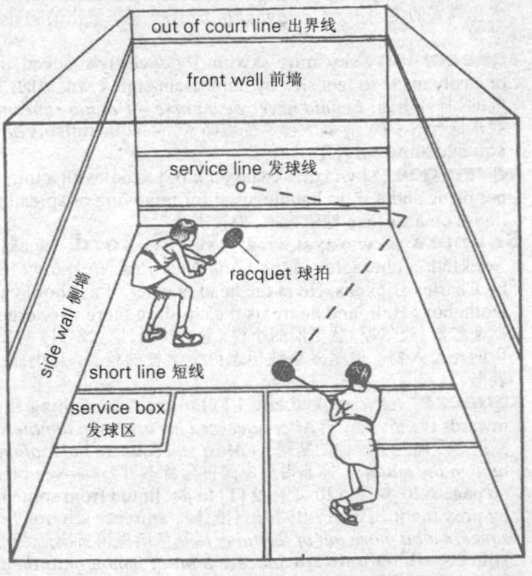

out of court line 出界线
front wall 前墙
service line 发球线
racquet 球拍
side wall 侧墙
short line 短线
service box 发球区

a squash court 壁球场

down in the near future. If the property is privately owned, however, the owners may take legal action against the squatters in order to force them to move out. 在英国和美国有少数一些人，通常是大城市中的年轻人，擅自搬到空房中住而不是住在租来或买来的房子里。地方政务委员会和地方政府有时对这些擅自占用他们房产的人放任不管，尤其是在他们计划不久将拆除这些建筑时更是如此。但是，如果房产为私人所有，房主可以通过法律手段强迫擅自占用房屋者搬出去。

Many squatters believe that they have a moral right to live in empty buildings when these buildings are not being used for any purpose by the owner. Other people, however, disapprove of squatters and believe that they should pay rent for their homes. 很多擅自占用空房者认为他们有道义上的权利搬到空房中去住，不管房主因何种目的不用这些房子。可是另外一些人对此持反对意见，认为擅自占用空房者应该支付房租。

squaw /skwɔ; skwɔː/ *n* [C] *old use* a word for a Native American woman, which many people think is offensive【旧】美洲印第安女子〔许多人认为该词具有冒犯性〕

squawk /skwɔk; skwɔːk/ *v* [I] **1** if a bird squawks, it makes a loud sharp angry sound〔鸟〕发出响亮的尖叫声: *Behind her a peacock squawked.* 在她身后，一只孔雀大声尖叫起来。**2** *informal* to complain loudly and angrily【非正式】大声气愤地抱怨 —**squawk** *n* [C]

squeak¹ /skwik; skwiːk/ *v* [I] **1** to make a very short high noise or cry that is not loud 发出吱吱声[短促的尖叫声]: *I can hear mice squeaking in the walls.* 我能听到墙内老鼠在吱吱叫。| *a squeaking hinge* 吱吱作响的铰链 **2** [always+adv/prep] *informal* to succeed, win, or pass a test by a very small amount so that you only just avoid failure【非正式】侥幸成功；险胜；勉强通过：[+**through/by**] *She only just squeaked through her maths test.* 她数学考试只是勉强及格。

squeak² *n* [C] a very short high noise or cry 吱吱声，短促的尖叫声: *a squeak of alarm* 闹钟短促的响声

squeak·y /ˈskwikɪ; ˈskwiːki/ *adj* **1** making very high noises that are not loud 发出短促而尖利声音的；吱吱叫的: *a squeaky voice* 尖利的嗓音 | *a squeaky door* 吱吱作响的门 **2 squeaky clean** *informal*【非正式】**a)** never having done anything morally wrong 品行端正的；行为正直的: *You're not exactly squeaky clean either.* 你的品行也并不是无懈可击的。**b)** completely clean 极其干净的: *squeaky clean hair* 非常干净的头发 —**squeakily** *adv* —**squeakiness** *n* [U]

squeal¹ /skwil; skwiːl/ *v* [I] **1** to make a long loud high sound or cry 发出长而尖锐的声音[叫声]: *squealing tires* 嘎吱作响的轮胎 | [+**with/in**] *The children squealed with delight.* 孩子们高兴得尖叫了起来。**2 squeal (on sb)** *informal* to tell the police or someone in authority about someone you know who has done something wrong【非正式】举报〔某人〕，告密

squeal² *n* [C] a long loud high sound or cry 长而尖锐的声音[叫声]: [+**of**] *Squeals of delight came from the children.* 孩子们发出高兴的尖叫声。| *a squeal of brakes* 刹车发出的刺耳的嘎吱声

squeam·ish /ˈskwimɪʃ; ˈskwiːmɪʃ/ *adj* easily shocked, upset or easily made to feel sick by unpleasant sights 易受惊的；易呕吐的；神经质的: *I could never be a nurse – I'm too squeamish.* 我永远当不了护士，我太容易受惊吓了。—**squeamishly** *adv* —**squeamishness** *n* [U]

squee·gee /ˈskwidʒi; ˈskwiːdʒiː/ *n* [C] a tool with a thin rubber blade and a short handle, used for removing or spreading a liquid on a surface 橡胶拖把，橡胶刷帚

Squeers /skwɪrz; skwɪəz/, **Wack·ford** /ˈwækfərd; ˈwækfəd/ a character in the book *Nicholas Nickelby* (1838) by Charles Dickens. He is the head teacher of a school called Dotheboys Hall, and he treats the children there very cruelly. 斯奎尔斯〔查尔斯·狄更斯的小说《尼古拉斯·尼克尔贝》(1838)中的一个人物。他是多斯波伊思男童学校的校长，对小孩十分残酷〕

squeeze¹ /skwiz; skwiːz/ *v* **1** [T] to press something firmly inwards 压；挤；捏；榨: *Alice squeezed his arm affectionately.* 艾丽斯疼爱地捏了捏他的胳膊。| *Must you squeeze the toothpaste tube in the middle?* 你非得从中间挤牙膏不可吗？—see picture on page A20 参见 A20 页图 **2** [T] to get liquid from something by pressing it 压出；挤出；榨出〔液体〕: **squeeze sth out** *Try to squeeze a bit more out of the tube.* 尽量从筒里再挤出一点儿。| **squeeze sth on/onto sth** *Squeeze a bit of lemon onto the fish.* 往鱼上挤点柠檬。—see picture on page A11 参见 A11 页图 **3** [I always+adv/prep, T always+adv/prep] to try to make something fit into a space that is too small, or to try to get into such a space (使)挤进；塞入: [+**into/through/past/between**] *Five of us squeezed into the back seat of the car.* 我们五个人挤进了汽车的后座。| *Move your chair and I'll try to squeeze past.* 挪一下你的椅子，我尽量挤过去。| **squeeze sth into** *You'll never squeeze yourself into that dress.* 那件连衣裙你根本套不进去。**4 squeeze sth out of sb** to force someone to tell you something 强迫某人说出某事: *See if you can squeeze more information out of them.* 看看你能否逼他们说出更多的东西。**5 squeeze sb out (of sth)** to make it difficult for someone to continue in business, by attracting their customers〔通过吸引某人的顾客〕将某人挤出〔某行业〕: *It's the big operators squeezing the independents out of the market.* 那些大企业正在把独立经营者挤出市场。**6** [T] to manage to do something although you are very busy〔在很忙的时候〕设法安排〔做某事〕: **squeeze sth in/into** *How do you manage to squeeze so much into one day?* 你一天里怎么能有时间做那么多事情？| **squeeze sb in** (=have time to see them) 挤出时间见某人 *I can squeeze you in at four o'clock.* 我能挤出时间在 4 点钟见你。**7 squeeze in/into/through** to succeed, win, or pass a test by a very small amount so that you only just avoid failure 侥幸成功；险胜；勉强通过〔考试〕**8** [T] to strictly limit the amount of money that is available to a company or organization 紧缩〔公司或机构的〕资金；使…经济拮据: *The failure of the levy has squeezed the school district's budget.* 税款征收不利使学区预算拨款变得拮据。

squeeze² *n* **1 a (tight) squeeze** a situation in which there is only just enough room for things or people to fit somewhere 拥挤；密集: *It'll be a squeeze with six people in the car.* 这辆汽车坐六个人会很拥挤。**2** [C] an act of pressing something firmly, usually with your hands 紧捏；紧握；挤压: **give sb/sth a squeeze** *Marty gave her hand a little squeeze.* 马蒂轻轻地捏了一下她的手。**3 a squeeze of lemon/lime etc** a small amount of juice obtained by squeezing a piece of fruit 挤出微量的柠檬汁/酸橙汁等 —see picture on page A7 参见 A7 页图 **4 a squeeze** a situation in which wages, prices, borrowing money etc are strictly controlled 拮据；紧缩: *a credit squeeze* 信贷紧缩 **5 put the squeeze on sb** *informal* to try to persuade someone to do something【非正式】试图说服某人 **6 your/her/his main squeeze** *AmE informal* someone's BOYFRIEND or GIRLFRIEND【美，非正式】你/她/他的男[女]朋友

squeeze·box /ˈskwizˌbɑks; ˈskwiːzbɒks/ *n* [C] *informal* an ACCORDION【非正式】手风琴

squeez·er /ˈskwizə; ˈskwiːzə/ *n* [C] a small tool for squeezing juice from fruit such as LEMONS 榨汁器

squelch /skwɛltʃ; skweltʃ/ *v* [I] **1** to make a sucking sound by walking in soft wet mud〔在泥沼中走时〕发出咯吱咯吱声: [+**through/along/up**] *We squelched up the sodden path.* 我们咯吱咯吱地走过浸透水的小路。—see picture on page A19 参见 A19 页图 **2** [T] *AmE* to stop something such as an idea from continuing to develop or spread【美】扼杀，消除〔念头等〕: *Such rigid teaching methods only serve to squelch kids' creativity.* 如此僵化的教学方法只会扼杀孩子的创造力。—**squelch** *n* [C]

squelch·y /ˈskwɛltʃɪ; ˈskweltʃi/ *adj* squelchy mud or ground is soft and wet and makes a sucking noise when you walk on it〔泥泞或地面〕软湿的，踩上去发出咯吱咯吱声的

squib /skwɪb; skwɪb/ *n* [C] **1** a small exploding FIREWORK 小爆竹，甩炮 **2** *literary* a short amusing piece of writing that attacks someone【文】讽刺短文 —see also 另见 **damp squib** (DAMP¹ (2))

squid /skwɪd; skwɪd/ *plural* **squid** *or* **squids** *n* [C] a sea creature with a long body and ten arms around its mouth 枪乌贼，鱿鱼

squidg·y /ˈskwɪdʒɪ; ˈskwɪdʒi/ *adj BrE* soft and wet, like thick mud【英】〔像泥一样〕软而湿的

squif·fy /ˈskwɪfɪ; ˈskwɪfi/ *adj BrE old-fashioned* slightly drunk【英，过时】微醉的

squig·gle /ˈskwɪgl; ˈskwɪgəl/ *n* [C] a short irregular line in writing or drawing that curls and twists 扭曲、不规则的短线: *I can't read the signature, it's just a squiggle.* 我看不懂这个签名，它只是一条歪歪扭扭的线。—**squiggly** *adj*: *squiggly lines* 弯曲的短线

squint¹ /skwɪnt; skwɪnt/ *v* [I] **1** to look at something with your eyes partly closed in order to see better 眯着眼睛看: *Anna squinted in the sudden bright sunlight.* 太阳光突然变强，安娜眯起眼睛看。| [+**at**] *Squinting at the target, Mark took careful aim.* 马克眯着眼睛，认真瞄准靶子。**2** [not in progressive 不用进行时] to have a squint 患斜视(症)

squint² *n* [singular] **1** a condition of your eye muscles that makes each eye look in a different direction 斜视，斜视症 **2**

have/take a squint at sth *informal* to look at something【非正式】看一眼某物；瞟一眼某物

squire /skwaɪr; skwaɪə/ *n* [C] **1** the man who in the past owned most of the land around a country village in England〔从前英国乡村的〕大地主，乡绅 **2** a young man in the Middle Ages who learned how to be a KNIGHT[1] (1) by serving one〔中世纪〕骑士的随从 **3** *BrE spoken* used by some men to address a man when they do not know his name【英口】先生〔某些男人对其不知道姓名的男性的称呼〕

squirm /skwɝm; skwɜːm/ *v* [I] **1** to twist your body from side to side because you are uncomfortable or nervous〔因不舒服或紧张而〕扭动身体: *Stop squirming so I can finish doing your hair!* 别扭来扭去，让我把你的头发梳好！ **2** to feel very embarrassed or ashamed 感到尴尬[惭愧]: **[+with]** *Greg turned red, squirming with guilt.* 格雷格的脸变红了，因内疚而局促不安。—**squirm** *n* [singular]

squir·rel[1] /ˈskwɝəl; ˈskwɪrəl/ *n* [C] a small animal with a long furry tail that climbs trees and eats nuts 松鼠

squirrel[2] *v* [T+away] *especially AmE* to keep something in a safe place to use later【尤美】储存，贮藏〔供以后使用〕

squir·rel·y /ˈskwɝəlɪ; ˈskwɪrəli/ *adj AmE informal* unable to stay still; RESTLESS【美，非正式】静不下来的；焦躁不安的

squirt[1] /skwɝt; skwɜːt/ *v* **1** [I,T] if you squirt liquid or if it squirts, it is forced out of a narrow hole in a thin fast stream 使喷出；射出；喷射: *Water's squirting from about five different leaks.* 水正从五个不同的裂缝中喷出。| **squirt sth** *Squirt some oil in the lock.* 往锁里面喷些油。**2** [T] to hit or cover someone or something with a thin fast stream of liquid 向…喷射〔液体〕: **squirt sb/sth with sth** *Mom! Chad's squirting me with the hose!* 妈！查德用水管喷我！

squirt[2] *n* [C] **1** a fast thin stream of liquid 喷射的液体，细的喷流 —see picture on page A7 参见 A7 页图 **2 little squirt** *spoken* an insulting word for a short person, especially someone who is annoying you【口】小矮子，小东西〔侮辱性用语〕: *You're just an ignorant little squirt.* 你只不过是个无知的小矮子！

squirt gun /ˈ· ·/ *n* [C] *AmE* a WATER PISTOL【美】玩具水枪

squish /skwɪʃ; skwɪʃ/ *v* **1** [I always+adv/prep] to make a soft sucking sound by moving in or through something soft and wet like mud 发出咯吱声 —see picture on page A19 参见 A19 页图 **2** [I,T] *AmE informal* to SQUASH[1] something, or to become squashed【美，非正式】(被) 挤扁；(被) 压碎

squish·y /ˈskwɪʃɪ; ˈskwɪʃi/ *adj* soft and wet or full of liquid 湿软的: *squishy mud* 湿软的烂泥 —**squishiness** *n* [U]

Sr *BrE*【英】, **Sr.** *AmE*【美】**1** [only after noun 仅用于名词后] the written abbreviation of 缩写= SENIOR 老，大: *Douglas Fairbanks, Sr.* 老道格拉斯·费尔班克斯 **2** [only before noun 仅用于名词前] the written abbreviation of 缩写= SEÑOR 先生: *Sr Lopez* 洛佩斯先生 **3** the written abbreviation of 缩写= Sister, used in front of the name of a NUN 修女〔用于名字前〕: *Sr Bernadette* 贝尔纳黛特修女 **4** *BrE* the written abbreviation of 缩写= Sister, used in front of the name of a nurse【英】护士长〔用于名字前〕

Sri Lan·ka /sri ˈlæŋkə; sriː ˈlæŋkə/ a country in southern Asia, which is an island in the Indian Ocean, southeast of India. Population: 19,409,000 (2001). Capital: Colombo. Sri Lanka was formerly called Ceylon, and it was ruled by Britain from 1798 to 1948. About 70% of the population are Sinhalese, who are mostly Buddhists. The other main group are the Tamils, who are mostly Hindus, and many of them want to become independent from Sri Lanka. 斯里兰卡〔南亚印度洋一岛国。位于印度东南。人口：19,409,000 (2001)，首都：科伦坡。1789 至 1948 年由英国统治，旧称锡兰。人口的 70% 为僧伽罗人，其中大多为佛教徒。另一主要群体为泰米尔人，多为印度教徒，其中有不少人希望从斯里兰卡独立出去〕—**Sri Lankan** *n, adj*

SS /ˌɛs ˈɛs; ˌes ˈes/ [only before noun 仅用于名词前] the abbreviation of 缩写= STEAMSHIP

[S3] **ssh** /ʃ; ʃ/ *interjection* used to ask for silence or less noise 嘘〔用于要求别人保持安静〕: *Ssh! You'll wake everybody up.* 嘘！你会把大家都吵醒的。

SSI /ˌɛs ɛs ˈaɪ; ˌes es ˈaɪ/ Supplemental Security Income; for the Aged, Blind, and Disabled a system of monthly payments made by the US government to adults over 65 who do not have much money, or to people of any age who are blind or disabled 补充保障收入〔美国政府一项月津贴补助计划。资助对象为 65 岁以上的低收入老人、任何年龄的盲人或残疾人〕

St *BrE*【英】also 又作 **St. 1** [only after noun or adjective 仅用于名词或形容词后] the written abbreviation of 缩写= street 大街: *Wall St.* 华尔街 | *Church St* 教堂街 **2** the written abbreviation of 缩写= SAINT 圣…: *St Luke's Gospel* (圣) 路加福音 **3 st** the written abbreviation of 缩写= STONE[1] (6) 英石

-st /st; st/ *suffix* **1** forms written ORDINAL numbers with 1〔加在数字 1 后构成序数词〕: *the 1st* (=first) *prize* 一等奖 | *my 21st birthday* 我的 21 岁生日 **2** *old use or biblical* another form of the suffix -EST (2)【旧或圣经】〔后缀 -est (2) 的另一种形式〕: *thou dost* (=you do) 你做

stab[1] /stæb; stæb/ *v* **stabbed, stabbing 1** [T] to push a knife into someone or something〔用刀〕刺，戳，捅: **stab sb to death** *Smith was found stabbed to death in a burning car.* 在一辆燃烧着的汽车中发现史密斯被人刺死了。| **stab sb in the heart/arm etc** *Luca stabbed her in the thigh with a breadknife.* 卢卡用一把面包刀刺她的大腿。**2** [I,T] to make quick pushing movements with your finger or something pointed; JAB[1]〔用手指或尖的东西〕戳 **3 stab sb in the back** to do something that harms someone who likes and trusts you; BETRAY 背后中伤某人；背叛某人 —see also 另见 STABBING

stab[2] *n* [C] **1** an act of stabbing or trying to stab someone 刺，戳，捅: *severe stab wounds* 严重的刺伤 | **[+at]** *He made a vicious stab at me with a broken bottle.* 他拿破瓶子狠狠地朝我刺过来。**2 a stab of fear/disappointment/pain etc** a sudden sharp feeling of fear etc 一阵恐惧/失望/痛苦等: *A quick stab of excitement ran through him.* 他突然感到一阵兴奋。**3 have/make a stab at (doing) sth** *informal* to try to do something【非正式】试图[尝试]做某事 **4 a stab in the back** an attack from someone you thought was a friend 背后中伤；背叛: *One of them smiles in your face while the other one stabs you in the back.* 他们两个中一人当面对你友好，另一个人则在背后向你施放暗箭。

stab·bing[1] /ˈstæbɪŋ; ˈstæbɪŋ/ *adj* a stabbing pain is sharp and sudden, as if it had been made by a knife〔疼痛〕突然而剧烈的，如刀刺的: *stabbing headaches* 刀刺般的头痛

stabbing[2] *n* [C] a crime in which someone is stabbed 持利器伤人罪

sta·bil·i·ty /stəˈbɪlətɪ; stəˈbɪlɪti/ *n* [U] **1** the condition of being strong, steady and not changing 稳固，稳定: **[+of]** *the stability of the dollar* 美元的稳固 | *a long period of political stability* 长期的政治稳定 **2** *technical* the ability of a substance to stay in the same state【术语】〔物质的〕稳定性 —opposite 反义词 INSTABILITY

sta·bil·ize also 又作 **-ise** *BrE*【英】/ˈstebl̩ˌaɪz; ˈsteɪbɪlaɪz/ *v* [I,T] to become firm, steady or unchanging, or to make something firm or steady (使) 稳固；(使) 稳定: *The patient's condition has now stabilized.* 病人的情况已经稳定下来了。—**stabilization** /ˌstebələˈzeʃən; ˌsteɪbɪlaɪˈzeɪʃən/ *n* [U]

sta·bil·iz·er also 又作 **-iser** *BrE*【英】/ˈstebəˌlaɪzɚ; ˈsteɪbɪlaɪzə/ *n* [C] **1** a chemical that helps something such as a food to stay in the same state〔食物等的〕稳定剂 **2** a piece of equipment that helps make something such as an aircraft, ship, or bicycle steady〔飞机、轮船或自行车的〕稳定器，平衡器

sta·ble[1] /ˈstebl̩; ˈsteɪbəl/ *adj* **1** steady and not likely to move or change 稳定的；安定的；不变的: *Be careful, that ladder isn't stable.* 小心，那把梯子不稳。| *a stable marriage* 稳定的婚姻 | *a politically stable country* 政局稳定的国家 **2** calm, reasonable, and not easy to upset 平静的；稳重的: *Norman's a bit neurotic, but his wife's a very stable person.* 诺曼有点神经质，但他的妻子是很稳重的人。**3** *technical* a stable substance tends to stay in the same chemical or ATOMIC state【术语】〔物质〕稳定的，不易分解[变化]的 —opposite 反义词 UNSTABLE —see also 另见 STABILITY —**stably** *adv* [W3]

stable[2] *n* [C] **1** *BrE* a building where horses are kept【英】马厩，马房 **2** *AmE* a building where horses, cattle etc are kept【美】牲口棚 **3 a)** a group of racing horses that has one owner or trainer〔一位马主或驯马师所拥有的〕一群赛马 **b)** a group of people working for the same company or with the same trainer〔在同一家公司工作或受同一教练训练的〕一群人: *actors from the same Hollywood stable* 同在一家好莱坞公司旗下的演员 **4 shut/close the stable door after the horse has bolted** to try to prevent something when it is too late, and harm has already been done 亡羊补牢，贼去关门

stable[3] *v* [T] to put or keep a horse in a stable 置〔马〕于马房

sta·ble·boy /ˈstebl̩ˌbɔɪ; ˈsteɪbəlbɔɪ/ also 又作 **stable lad** /ˈ· · ·/ *BrE*【英】, **stableman** /ˈstebl̩ˌmæn; ˈsteɪbəlmæn/ *AmE*【美】*n* [C] a man or boy who works in a stable and looks after horses〔在马房照顾马匹的〕马夫；马童

sta·ble·mate /ˈstebl̩ˌmet; ˈsteɪbəlmeɪt/ *n* [C] something or someone that is like other things or people 类似的事物: *ambient music and its stablemate techno* 氛围音乐及与它相似的高技术音乐

sta·bles /ˈstebḷz; ˈsteɪbəlz/ *n* [plural] a stable or a group of stables 马厩; 马房

sta·bling /ˈstebliŋ; ˈsteɪbliŋ/ *n* [U] space for horses to be stabled 拴马处, 拴马位; 马厩

stac·cat·o /stəˋkɑto; stəˈkɑːtəʊ/ *adv* when music is played staccato the notes are cut short and do not flow smoothly〔音乐〕断断续续地; 不连贯地 —compare 比较 LEGATO —**staccato** *adj*

stack¹ /stæk; stæk/ *n* [C] **1** a neat pile of things one on top of the other〔叠放整齐的〕一叠, 一堆, 一摞: **[+of]** *a stack of papers* 一叠文件 | *stacks of dishes waiting to be washed* 一摞摞待洗的盘碟 **2** a large pile of grain, grass etc that is stored outside〔储放于户外的〕粮垛; 草堆 —see also 另见 HAYSTACK **3 a stack of/stacks of** *informal especially BrE* a large amount【非正式, 尤英】大量, 大批, 许多: *Mr. Truman has stacks of money.* 杜鲁门先生有很多很多的钱。**4** a tall chimney 高大的烟囱 **5 the stacks** a part of a library where books are stored close together〔图书馆的〕书库; 藏书书架 **6** a temporary store of information on a computer〔电脑临时储存资料的〕存储栈; 栈式存储 —see also 另见 **blow your top/stack** (BLOW¹ (20))

stack² *v* **1** also 又作 **stack up** [I,T] to form a neat pile or make things into a neat pile 整齐地堆起; (使)成堆; 摞起: *These chairs are designed to stack easily.* 这些椅子设计得易于叠放在一起。| **stack sth** *Stack the books up against the wall.* 把图书靠墙堆起来。| *a stacking hi-fi system* 组合式高保真音响系统 **2** [T usually passive 一般用被动态] to put piles of things on a place or in a place 把…堆放在〔某处〕; 堆满: **[+with]** *The floor was stacked with boxes.* 地板上堆满了箱子。**3 have the odds stacked against you** *informal* to be at a great disadvantage【非正式】处于非常不利的地位, 处于困境: *The home team can't win; the odds are stacked against them.* 主队赢不了啦, 形势对他们极为不利。**4 stack the cards** *BrE*【英】, **stack the deck** *AmE*【美】*informal* to arrange cards dishonestly in a game【非正式】洗牌作弊 **5** also 又作 **stack up** [I,T] if aircraft stack or are stacked around an airport, they are made to fly around it until they can land (使)飞机在机场上空作定高分层盘旋〔等待着陆〕

stack up *phr v* [I] *informal* to have a particular appearance when compared with something else【非正式】比较, 比高低: **[+against]** *How does their product stack up against our own?* 他们的产品跟我们的产品相比怎么样?

stacked /stækt; stækt/ *adj informal* an offensive word meaning having large breasts【非正式】胸部丰满的〔冒犯语〕

stack sys·tem /ˈ· ˌ··/ *n* [C] an arrangement of equipment for playing music, in which one piece stands on top of another 组合音响

stack-up /ˈ· ·/ *n* [C] a situation in which several aircraft are flying around an airport waiting to land〔数架飞机在机场上空等候着陆时的〕定高分层盘旋

sta·di·um /ˈstedɪəm; ˈsteɪdiəm/ *n plural* **stadiums** or **stadia** /-dɪə; -diə/ [C] a building for sports, consisting of a field surrounded by rows of seats〔有多层看台的〕体育场, 运动场: *a baseball stadium* 棒球场

2 2 **staff¹** /stæf; stɑːf/ *n*

1 ►WORKERS 工作人员◄ a) [C, also+plural verb *BrE* 英] the people who work for an organization, especially a school or business〔尤指学校或公司的〕全体职员, 员工: *The school's staff is excellent.* 这所学校的教职员工是优秀的。| *We now employ a staff of 25.* 我们现在雇了25名员工。| **member of staff** *complaints by members of staff about sick pay* 雇员关于病假工资的投诉 | **on the staff** (=being a member of staff) 成为一名职员 *It's good to have you on the staff.* 很高兴你成为我们的职员。**b)** [plural] the members of such a group 职员, 人员: *Andrea's in charge of about 20 staff.* 安德烈娅负责管理约20名员工。| *a special car park for senior staff* 高级雇员专用的停车场

2 ►STICK 棍, 棒◄ [C] *plural* **staves** /stevz; steɪvz/ **a)** *old use* a long thick stick to help you walk【旧】手杖, 拐杖 **b)** a long thick stick that an official holds in some ceremonies 权杖

3 ►FLAG 旗◄ [C] a pole for flying a flag on; FLAGPOLE 旗杆

4 ►MUSIC 音乐◄ [C] the set of five lines that music is written on; STAVE¹ (1) 五线谱

5 the staff of life *literary* a basic food, especially bread【文】主食〔尤指面包〕—see also 另见 GENERAL STAFF, GROUND STAFF

staff² *v* [T usually passive 一般用被动态] to provide the workers for an organization 为…配备职员: *The refuge is staffed mainly by volunteers.* 在避难所工作的主要是志愿人员。—see also 另见 OVERSTAFFED, UNDERSTAFFED —**staffing** *n* [U]: *staffing levels* 人员配备水平

staff nurse /ˈ· ˌ·/ *n* [C] a British hospital nurse whose rank is just below a sister's (SISTER (2))〔英国〕医院护士〔地位仅次于护士长〕

staff of·fi·cer /ˈ· ˌ···/ *n* [C] an officer who helps a military commander of a higher rank 参谋

Staf·ford·shire /ˈstæfɚdʃɚ; ˈstæfədʃə/ a COUNTY in central England famous for its factories making CHINA (=plates, cups etc) 斯塔福德郡〔英格兰中部一郡, 以瓷器工厂闻名〕

staff ser·geant /ˈ· ˌ··/ *n* [C,U] a lower rank in the army or the US Air Force or Marines, or someone who has this rank〔美国空军的〕中士;〔海军陆战队的〕上士 —see table on page C6 参见C6页附录

stag /stæg; stæg/ *n* [C] **1** a fully grown male DEER 成年雄鹿, 牡鹿 **2** *BrE* someone who buys shares (SHARE² (5)) in a new company, hoping to sell them quickly and make a profit【英】认购新股并迅速抛出获利者, 炒新股者 **3 go stag** *AmE informal* if a man goes stag he goes to a party without a woman【美, 非正式】〔指男子〕不带女伴参加社交聚会 —see also 另见 STAG NIGHT, STAG PARTY

stage¹ /stedʒ; steɪdʒ/ *n* 1 1

1 ►TIME/STATE 时间/状态◄ [C] a particular time or state that something reaches as it grows or develops 时期; 阶段: *The plan is still in its early stages.* 这项计划仍处于初期阶段。| *the different stages of a child's development* 孩子成长的不同阶段 | **at this stage** *It would be unwise to comment at this stage of the negotiations.* 在谈判的这个阶段发表评论是不明智的。| **stage by stage** (=gradually) 逐步地, 逐渐地 | **at a later stage** *The design may well be modified at a later stage.* 这个设计以后很可能要修改。—compare 比较 PHASE¹ (1), STEP¹ (4)

2 ►THEATRE 戏院◄ [C] the raised floor in a theatre on which plays are performed 舞台: **on stage** *She is on stage for most of the play.* 在这部戏里, 大部分时间她都出场。| **stage left/right** (=from the left or right side of the stage) 从舞台的左侧/右侧 —see picture at 参见 THEATRE 图

3 ►ACTING 表演◄ the stage acting as a profession 舞台生涯; 戏剧表演: **go on the stage** (=become an actor) 当演员

4 take centre stage/be at the centre of the stage to have everyone's attention, or to be very important 成为大家注意的中心; 非常重要: *Sally just loves to take center stage.* 萨莉就是喜欢吸引大家的注意。| *The hostage question has returned to the centre of the stage.* 人质问题再次成为人们关注的焦点。

5 ►PLACE 地方◄ [singular] a place where something important happens〔重大事件发生的〕地点, 场所: *Geneva has been the stage for many such conferences.* 日内瓦已成为众多此类会议的举办地点。| *the European political stage* 欧洲政治舞台

6 set the stage for to prepare for something or make something possible 为…做准备; 使…成为可能: *Will this agreement merely set the stage for another war?* 这个协议是否只会酿成另一场战争?

7 he's/she's going through a stage *informal* used to say that someone young will soon stop behaving badly or strangely【非正式】他/她正在经历成长阶段〔指年轻人度过此阶段后, 不良或奇怪的行为就会很快消失〕—see also 另见 LANDING STAGE

stage² *v* [T] to organize an event that people will come to see, or that you hope many people will notice 举办; 举行: *We hope to stage four plays this season.* 我们希望在本季上演四部话剧。| *They'll be staging a Hockney exhibition.* 他们将举办一场霍克尼画展。| **stage a strike/demonstration/sit-in etc** *School teachers are staging a protest against the cuts.* 教师正在为反对减薪而举行抗议活动。

stage·coach /ˈstedʒˌkotʃ; ˈsteɪdʒkəʊtʃ/ *n* [C] a closed vehicle pulled by horses that in former times carried passengers who paid to go to a particular place〔旧时的〕驿站马车

stage di·rec·tion /ˈ· ·ˌ··/ *n* [C] a written instruction to an actor to do something in a play 舞台指示

stage door /ˌ· ˈ·◄/ *n* [C] the side or back door in a theatre, used by actors and theatre workers〔供演员及舞台工作人员使用的〕剧院侧门[后门]

stage fright /ˈ· ·/ *n* [U] nervousness felt by someone who is going to perform in front of a lot of people 怯场

stage·hand /ˈstedʒˌhænd; ˈsteɪdʒhænd/ *n* [C] someone who works on a theatre stage, getting it ready for a play or for the next part of a play 舞台工作人员

stage-man·age /ˈ· ˌ··/ *v* [T] *informal* to organize a public event, such as a meeting, in a way that will give you the result that you want【非正式】对…进行幕后策划[安排]: *The press conference was cleverly stage-managed.* 记者招待会安排得很巧妙。

stage man·ag·er /ˈ· ˌ···/ *n* [C] someone in charge of a theatre stage during a performance 舞台监督

stage name /ˈ· ·/ *n* [C] a name used by an actor instead of his or her real name〔演员的〕艺名

stage·struck /ˈstedʒˌstrʌk; ˈsteɪdʒstrʌk/ *adj* loving to see plays, or wanting very much to become an actor 爱看戏剧的; 渴望当演员的

stage whis·per /ˌ· ˈ··/ *n* [C] **1** an actor's loud WHISPER that other actors on the stage seem not to hear 舞台上的低声旁白 **2** a loud WHISPER that is intended to be heard by everyone 有意使大家都能听见的耳语: *"What's going on?" I demanded in a stage whisper.* "发生了什么事?" 我用大家都能听见的低声问道。

stage·y /ˈstedʒɪ; ˈsteɪdʒi/ *adj* another spelling of STAGY stagy 的另一种拼法

stag·fla·tion /ˌstægˈfleʃən; stægˈfleɪʃən/ *n* [U] an economic condition in which there is INFLATION (=a continuing rise in prices) but many people do not have jobs and businesses are not doing well 停滞性通货膨胀, 滞胀〔指出现通货膨胀、许多人失业和商业萧条的一种经济状况〕

stag·ger[1] /ˈstægɚ; ˈstægə/ *v* **1** [I always+adv/prep] to walk or move unsteadily, almost falling over 蹒跚; 摇摇晃晃地走: **[+away/into/down etc]** *The old man staggered drunkenly to his feet.* 老汉醉醺醺地摇晃着站了起来。| *Marcus came staggering through the door with his groceries.* 马库斯拿着食品杂货摇摇晃晃地走进门。—see picture on page A24 参见 A24 页图 **2** [T usually passive 一般用被动态] to make someone feel very surprised or shocked 使〔某人〕惊愕[震惊]: *What staggered us was the sheer size of her salary.* 令我们感到惊愕的是她的巨额工资。**3** [T] to arrange people's working hours, holidays etc so that they do not all begin and end at the same time 错开〔工作时间、假期等〕 **4** [T] to start a race with each runner at a different place on a curved track 梯形起跑〔指环形跑道上运动员在不同的位置起跑〕

stagger[2] *n* [C usually singular 一般用单数] an unsteady movement of someone who is having difficulty in walking 蹒跚; 摇晃不稳的脚步

stag·gered /ˈstægɚd; ˈstægəd/ *adj* [not before noun 不用于名词前] very surprised at something that has happened to you, or some news that you have heard that is hard to believe 非常吃惊的; 难以置信的: **[+by/at]** *I was staggered by the size of the phone bill.* 电话账单上的金额使我感到非常吃惊。| **staggered to hear/see/find etc** *We were staggered to find that we were not entitled to any money.* 我们非常吃惊地发现我们无权得到一分钱。

stag·ger·ing /ˈstægərɪŋ; ˈstægərɪŋ/ *adj* very surprising, shocking, and almost unbelievable 令人吃惊[震惊]的; 令人难以置信的: *The cost was a staggering $10 million.* 费用竟高达1000万美元。—**staggeringly** *adv*: *a staggeringly high phone bill* 费用高得惊人的电话账单

stag·ing /ˈstedʒɪŋ; ˈsteɪdʒɪŋ/ *n* **1** [C,U] the activity or art of performing a play〔戏剧的〕上演, 演出; 演技: *a modern-dress staging of 'Hamlet'* 穿现代服装演出的《哈姆雷特》 **2** [U] movable boards and frames for standing on 脚手架; 台架, 棚架

staging a·re·a /ˈ·· ˌ···/ *n* [C] a place where soldiers meet and where military equipment is gathered before it is moved to another place〔军队的〕集结待命地区

staging post /ˈ·· ·/ *n* [C] a place where a stop is regularly made on a long journey〔长途旅行中的〕中途站: *Bahrain is a staging post on the flight from Britain to Australia.* 巴林是从英国飞往澳大利亚的中途站。—compare 比较 STOPOVER

stag·nant /ˈstægnənt; ˈstægnənt/ *adj* **1** stagnant water or air does not move or flow and often smells bad〔水或空气〕不流动的, 静止的; 有臭味的: *a stagnant pond* 一潭死水 **2** not changing, developing, or making progress; inactive 不发展的, 停滞(不前)的; 不活跃的: *Industrial output has remained stagnant.* 工业生产一直停滞不前。—**stagnancy** *n* [U] —**stagnantly** *adv*

stag·nate /ˈstægnet; stægˈneɪt/ *v* [I] to stop developing or making progress 停滞; 不发展: *a stagnating economy* 停滞不前的经济 | *I don't want to spend the rest of my life stagnating in that office.* 我不想一辈子在那间办公室里毫无前途地干下去。—**stagnation** /stægˈneʃən; stægˈneɪʃən/ *n* [U]: *economic stagnation* 经济停滞

stag night /ˈ· ·/ *n* [C] *BrE* the night before a man's wedding, which he spends with his male friends, drinking or having a party【英】单身汉之夜〔指男子结婚前一个晚上, 和男性朋友共同度过这个夜晚, 一起喝酒或举行聚会〕

stag par·ty /ˈ· ˌ··/ *n* [C] a party for men only, especially on the night before a man's wedding〔尤指男子结婚前一晚举办的〕只限男人参加的社交聚会

stag·y, stagey /ˈstedʒɪ; ˈsteɪdʒi/ *adj* behaviour that is stagy is not natural and is like the way an actor behaves on a stage〔行为等〕不自然的; 演戏似的; 做作的: *a very stagy manner* 非常做作的举止 —**stagily** *adv*

staid /sted; steɪd/ *adj* serious, old-fashioned, and boring in the way you live, dress, or work 严肃呆板的; 古板的; 枯燥的: *a staid old bachelor* 一个严肃呆板的老单身汉 | *staid attitudes* 古板的态度 —**staidly** *adv* —**staidness** *n* [U]

stain[1] /sten; steɪn/ *v* **1** [I,T] to accidentally make a mark on something, especially one that cannot be removed, or to be marked in this way 染污, 沾污; 留下难以清除的污迹: **[+with]** *teeth stained with nicotine from years of smoking* 因多年抽烟而被尼古丁熏黄的牙齿 | *Pale carpets stain too easily.* 浅色的地毯太容易沾污。—see picture on page A18 参见 A18 页图 **2** [T] to change the colour of something, especially something made of wood, by using a special chemical or DYE 给〔某物, 尤指木制品〕染色[着色] **3 stain sb's name/honour/reputation etc** *literary* to damage the good opinion that people have about someone【文】玷污某人的名誉

stain[2] *n* **1** [C] a mark that is difficult to remove, especially one made by a liquid such as blood, coffee, or ink〔尤指液体做成的〕污迹, 污点: *There's a big stain on your tie.* 你的领带上有一大块污迹。| **blood/ink/wine etc stain** *How do you get wine stains out of a tablecloth?* 怎样把桌布上的葡萄酒污迹洗掉? **2** [C,U] a chemical for darkening something, especially wood〔尤指木材的〕着色剂, 染色剂 **3 a stain on sb's character/reputation etc** something that makes people think that someone has done something wrong or illegal 某人性格/名声等上的污点

stained glass /ˌ· ˈ·/ *n* [U] glass of different colours used for making pictures and patterns in windows, especially in a church〔尤指教堂窗户上的〕彩色玻璃

stain·less /ˈstenlɪs; ˈsteɪnləs/ *adj literary* without any sign of illegal or immoral behaviour【文】〔行为〕无污点的; 清白的; 无瑕疵的: *a lady of beauty, rank and stainless reputation* 一位有地位的名誉清白的美丽女士

stainless steel /ˌ·· ˈ·/ *n* [U] a type of steel that does not RUST 不锈钢: *stainless steel cutlery* 不锈钢餐具

stair /stɛr; steə/ *n* **1 stairs** [plural] a set of steps built for going from one level of a building to another〔楼层之间的〕楼梯: **up/down the stairs** *Jerry ran up the stairs.* 杰里跑上楼梯。| **the top/head of the stairs** *Kate was standing at the top of the stairs.* 凯特站在楼梯的最上面。| **the foot of the stairs** (=the bottom) 楼梯下端 | **a flight of stairs** (=between two floors of a building)〔建筑物两层之间的〕一段楼梯 *The attic's up five flights of stairs.* 阁楼在第五层。—see also 另见 DOWNSTAIRS, UPSTAIRS[2] —see picture on page A4 参见 A4 页图 **2** [C] one of the steps in a set of stairs 楼梯的一级: *Lucy sat down on the bottom stair.* 露西坐在楼梯最下面的一阶上。**3** [C] *especially literary* a set of stairs【尤文】阶梯: *a steep winding stair to the tower* 通向塔楼陡峭而回旋的阶梯 **4 below stairs** *old-fashioned BrE* in the servants' part of a large house, in the past【过时, 英】〔旧时〕在佣人的住处 S2 W3

stair·case /ˈstɛrˌkes; ˈsteəkeɪs/ *n* [C] a set of stairs inside a building with its supports and the side parts that you hold on to〔包括扶手、栏杆的〕楼梯

stair·way /ˈstɛrˌwe; ˈsteəweɪ/ *n* [C] a staircase, especially a large or impressive one〔尤指大的或气派的〕楼梯

stair·well /ˈstɛrˌwɛl; ˈsteəwel/ *n* [C] the space going up through all the floors of a building, where the stairs go up 楼梯井

stake[1] /stek; steɪk/ *n* W3

1 ▶SHARP POST 尖桩◀ [C] a pointed piece of wood, metal etc that is pushed into the ground to hold a rope, mark a particular place etc〔尖状木头或金属等的〕桩; 柱

2 the stake a post to which a person was tied in former times to be killed by being burnt〔旧时捆绑并处死犯人的〕火刑柱: **burn sb at the stake** *Witches were often burnt at the stake.* 巫婆经常被绑在火刑柱上烧死。

3 have a stake in to have an important part or share in a business, plan etc so that you will gain if it succeeds 在〔公司、计划等中〕有股份; 与…有利害关系: *a 33% stake in the business* 该公司33%的股份 | *I just don't feel I have a stake in the country's future.* 我就是感觉不到我与国家的未来休戚相关。

4 be at stake if something that you value very much is at stake, you will lose it if a plan or action is not successful 濒于险境; 处于成败关头: *If we lose the contract, hundreds of jobs are at stake.* 我们如果失去这项合同, 几百人将濒于失业的境地。

5 (be prepared to) go to the stake for/over sth to take great risks to protect or defend an idea, belief etc (准备)为保护[捍卫]某事物冒巨大风险: *That's my opinion, but I wouldn't go to the stake for it.* 那是我的观点, 但我不会冒大险去捍卫它。

6 ▶RISK 风险◀ [C usually singular 一般用单数] money risked on the result of something, especially a horse race; BET[2] (1)〔尤指赛马的〕赌注; 赌金

7 stakes [plural] money that people risk on the result of a game, race etc, all of which is taken by the winner〔游戏、比赛等的〕赌金; 赌注: *We're playing for very high stakes here.* 我们这里下的赌注都很大。

8 play for high stakes a) to risk a lot of money in a game〔在比赛中〕下大赌注 **b)** to be in a situation where you gain or lose a lot 处于利害攸关的境地

9 the popularity/fashion etc stakes a situation that can be considered as if it were a competition 声望/时尚大赛: *Ben wouldn't score very highly in the popularity stakes.* 本的声望不会很高。

10 pull up stakes *AmE*【美】, **up stakes** *BrE*【英】*informal* to leave your job or home【非正式】辞职; 离家; 搬家: *We're going to pull up stakes and move to Montana.* 我们打算把家搬到蒙大拿州去。

stake² *v* [T] **1** to risk money on a race or competition 把〔钱〕押下打赌: *Hargreave staked his whole fortune on one card game.* 哈格雷夫把他的全部财产都押在一场纸牌戏上。**2** to risk losing something that is valuable or important to you, if a plan or action is not successful 拿…去冒险: **stake sth on sb/sth** *The President is staking his reputation on these trade talks.* 总统把自己的声誉都押在这些贸易谈判上。| *I've staked all my hopes on you.* 我把我所有的希望都寄托在你身上了。**3** also 又作 **stake up** to fasten or strengthen something with stakes 用桩支撑; 把…系在柱上: *Those young trees will have to be staked.* 那些小树得用桩子支撑起来。**4** also 又作 **stake off** to mark or enclose an area of ground with stakes 用标桩标出[围起]〔某一地区〕: *The muddiest corner of the field has been staked off.* 这块地最泥泞的一角已用标桩围了起来。**5 stake (out) a claim** to say publicly that you think you have a right to have or own something 公开声明对…拥有所有权: *Joe staked his claim to the land where he found the gold.* 乔声明拥有他发现黄金的那块土地的所有权。

stake sth ↔ **out** *phr v* [T] *informal* to watch a place secretly and continuously【非正式】持续监视〔某处〕: *The vice squad have been staking out the club for weeks.* 警察缉捕队已经对这个俱乐部监视了几个星期。—**stakeout** *n* [C]

stake·hold·er /ˈstek,holdɚ; ˈsteɪk,həʊldə/ *n* [C] **1** someone chosen to hold the money that is risked by people on a race, competition etc and to give all of it to the winner 赌金保管人 **2** someone, usually a lawyer, who takes charge of a property during a quarrel or a sale〔争执或销售时的〕财产保管人〔常指律师〕

stal·ac·tite /stəˈlæktaɪt; ˈstæləktaɪt/ *n* [C] a sharp pointed object hanging down from the roof of a CAVE, which is formed gradually by water that contains minerals as it drops slowly from the roof〔钟乳洞中的〕钟乳石, 石钟乳

stal·ag·mite /stəˈlægmaɪt; ˈstæləgmaɪt/ *n* [C] a sharp pointed object coming up from the floor of a CAVE, formed by drops from a stalactite〔钟乳洞中的〕石笋

stale¹ /stel; steɪl/ *adj* **1** bread or cake that is stale is no longer fresh or good to eat〔面包、蛋糕〕不新鲜的; 变味的: **go stale** *This loaf has gone stale.* 这条面包变味了。**2** air that is stale is not fresh or pleasant〔空气〕不新鲜的; 污浊的 **3** news or jokes that are stale are no longer interesting or exciting〔新闻、笑话〕不再有趣的, 没有新意的, 乏味的: *the same stale old jokes we've all heard before* 我们以前都曾听过的那些老掉牙的笑话 **4** someone who is stale has no new ideas, interest, or energy, because they have been doing the same thing for too long〔因长期从事同一工作而〕疲沓的, 没有生气的: **feel/get/go stale** *I'm getting stale in this job – I need a change.* 这个工作我已经干腻了, 需要换一换工作。—**staleness** *n* [U]

stale² *v* [I] *formal* to become less interesting or exciting【正式】变得疲沓[不再有趣]

stale·mate /ˈstel,met; ˈsteɪlmeɪt/ *n* [C,U] **1** a situation in which it seems impossible to settle an argument or disagreement, and neither side can get an advantage; DEADLOCK 僵局; 僵持: *The discussions with the miners' union ended in stalemate.* 同矿工工会的谈判以陷入僵局告终。**2** a position in CHESS in which neither player can win〔国际象棋的〕和棋 —**stalemate** *v* [T]

Sta·lin /ˈstalɪn; ˈstɑːlɪn/, **Joseph** (1879-1953) a Russian politician, born in Georgia, who was leader of the former Soviet Union from the death of Lenin (1924) until his own death. Stalin was responsible for developing farming and industry in his country, and for successfully leading it in the war against Germany (1941-45), but most people now remember his great cruelty. Thousands of political opponents were killed or sent to prisons in Siberia. 斯大林〔(1879-1953), 前苏联政治家, 生于格鲁吉亚。列宁逝世 (1924) 后任苏联领导人, 直至去世。斯大林推动了苏联工农业的发展, 并成功带领苏联对德作战 (1941-1945)。然而, 他做事极为残酷, 人们对此记忆犹新。成千上万名持不同政见者惨遭杀害, 或被送进西伯利亚的监狱〕

Sta·lin·grad /ˈstalɪŋgræd; ˈstɑːlɪngræd/ the old name for the city of Volgograd in the former Soviet Union, on the River Volga. The city was almost destroyed in the Battle of Stalingrad in 1942-43 and many Russians were killed, when the German army tried unsuccessfully to take control of it. 斯大林格勒〔伏尔加格勒在前苏联时期的旧称。该城在 1942-1943 年的斯大林格勒保卫战中几乎毁于一旦, 当时, 德军企图占领该城, 苏联方面伤亡惨重, 但最终取得胜利〕

Sta·lin·is·m /ˈstalɪn,ɪzəm; ˈstɑːlɪnɪzəm/ *n* [U] the political system and methods used by Joseph Stalin when he was the leader of the former Soviet Union. The main features of Stalinism were that all plans and policies were made by Stalin himself and a small group of followers, and violence and fear were used to prevent any opposition. 斯大林主义〔主要特征为: 所有计划和政策均由斯大林本人及其幕僚制定; 采用暴力或恫吓手段防止任何反对声音的出现〕—**Stalinist** *adj*

stalk¹ /stɔk; stɔːk/ *n* [C] **1** a long narrow part of a plant that supports leaves, fruits, or flowers; stem〔植物的〕茎; 柄; 梗: *celery stalks* 芹菜梗 **2** a thin upright object 柄状物: *a microphone on a short stalk* 短柄麦克风 **3 eyes out on stalks** *BrE informal* if your eyes are out on stalks you are surprised or shocked【英, 非正式】吃惊的, 震惊的

stalk² *v* **1** [T] to follow a person or animal quietly in order to catch or kill them〔为捉拿或杀死某人或某动物而〕悄悄地跟踪; 潜近: *a tiger stalking its prey* 悄悄跟踪猎物的老虎 | *We know the rapist stalks his victims at night.* 我们知道那个强奸犯在夜间偷偷地跟踪受害人。**2** [I always+adv/prep] to walk in a proud or angry way, with long steps〔高傲或气愤地〕大步地走: **[+out/off/away]** *Yvonne turned and stalked out of the room in disgust.* 伊冯娜转身气愤地大踏步走出了房间。

stalk·er /ˈstɔkɚ; ˈstɔːkə/ *n* [C] a criminal who follows a woman over a period of time in order to force her to have sex, or kill her〔伺机强奸或杀害妇女的〕暗中尾随的罪犯

stalk·ing /ˈstɔkɪŋ; ˈstɔːkɪŋ/ *n* [U] the crime of following someone over a period of time in order to force them to have sex or kill them〔伺机强奸或杀害妇女的〕暗中尾随犯罪

stalking horse /ˈ‥ ,‥/ *n* [C] someone or something that hides someone's true purpose, especially a politician who says he wants his leader's job when the real plan is that another, more important politician should get it 掩护者; 障眼物;〔尤指竞选中的〕掩护性候选人

stall¹ /stɔl; stɔːl/ *n* **1** [C] a table or a small shop with an open front, especially outdoors, where goods are sold〔尤指户外的〕货摊, 摊位: *a market stall* 市场摊位 **2** [C] an enclosed area in a building for an animal 畜栏, 畜棚, 厩 **3** [C usually singular 一般用单数] an occasion when an engine stops working〔引擎〕停止运转, 熄火: *The plane went into a stall.* 这架飞机进入了失速状态。**4** [C usually plural 一般用复数] a seat in a row of fixed seats for priests and singers in some larger churches〔一些大教堂中的〕牧师[唱诗班]座位: *choir stalls* 唱诗班席位 **5 shower/toilet stall** a small enclosed private area for washing or using the toilet 淋浴间/厕所的小隔间 **6 the stalls** *BrE* the seats on the main level of a theatre or cinema【英】〔戏院、剧院的〕正厅座位: *a good seat in the front row of the stalls* 正厅前排的好座位 —see picture at 参见 THEATRE 图

stall² *v* **1** [I,T] if an engine stalls or you stall it, it stops because there is not enough power or speed to keep it going〔引擎因动力或速度不足而〕停止运转; 熄火; 使〔引擎〕停止运转: *Stupid car! It always stalls on hills.* 破车! 总是在山坡上抛锚。| **stall sth** *An inexperienced pilot may easily stall a plane.* 没有经验的飞行员很容易会使飞机失速。**2** [I] *informal* to deliberately delay because you are not ready to do something, answer questions etc【非正式】故意拖延: *Quit stalling and answer my question!* 别拖延时间了! 快回答我的问题! **3** [T] *informal* to make someone wait or stop something from happening until you are ready【非正式】搪塞; 拖延: *Maybe we can stall the sale until the prices go up.* 也许我们可以拖到价格上涨时再出售。| *Dad's coming! Stall him for a minute while I hide this.* 爸爸来了! 把他拖住一会儿, 等我把这个藏起来。

stall·hold·er /ˈstɔl,holdɚ; ˈstɔːl,həʊldə/ *n* [C] *BrE* someone who rents and keeps a market stall【英】摊主, 摊贩

stal·lion /ˈstæljən; ˈstæljən/ *n* [C] a male horse kept for breeding 种马 —compare 比较 MARE

Stal·lone /stəˈlon; stəˈləʊn/, **Syl·ves·ter** /sɪlˈvɛstɚ; sɪlˈvestə/ (1946-) a US film actor, famous for appearing as strong men who are good at fighting, such as the characters of Rocky, a boxer, and Rambo, a US soldier 史泰龙〔(1946-), 美国电影

演员。以饰演精通打斗的硬汉形象著称，如拳击手洛奇、美军士兵兰博〕

stal·wart¹ /ˈstɔlwɚt; ˈstɔːlwət/ *n* [C] someone who works hard and is loyal to a particular organization or set of ideas〔某组织或思想的〕忠实拥护者: *Conservative party stalwarts* 保守党的忠实拥护者

stalwart² *adj* **1 stalwart supporter/ally etc** a very loyal and strong supporter etc 忠实的拥护者/盟友等 **2** *formal* strong in appearance【正式】强壮的; 雄健的 —**stalwartly** *adv*

sta·men /ˈstemən; ˈsteɪmən/ *n* [C] *technical* the male part of a flower that produces POLLEN【术语】〔花的〕雄蕊

Stam·ford Bridge /ˌstæmfɚd ˈbrɪdʒ; ˌstæmfəd ˈbrɪdʒ/ **1** a village in northern England where the English King Harold won a battle against the King of Norway, a short time before he was killed at the Battle of Hastings in 1066 斯坦福布里奇, 斯坦福桥〔英格兰北部一村庄。英国国王哈罗德曾在此战胜挪威国王, 但不久即在1066年的黑斯廷斯战役中阵亡〕 **2** the football ground of Chelsea Football Club in West London 斯坦福桥足球场〔伦敦西区切尔西足球俱乐部的主场〕

stam·i·na /ˈstæmənə; ˈstæmɪ̣nə/ *n* [U] physical or mental strength that lets you continue doing something for a long time without getting tired 持久力, 耐力, 毅力: *You need stamina to be a long-distance runner.* 当长跑运动员需要有耐力。

stam·mer¹ /ˈstæmɚ; ˈstæmə/ *v* [I,T] to speak or say something with a lot of pauses and repeated sounds, either because you have a speech problem, or because you are nervous, excited etc 口吃地说, 结结巴巴地说: *Whenever he was angry he would begin to stammer slightly.* 他一生气, 说话就开始有点结巴。—compare 比较 STUTTER¹ (1) —**stammerer** *n* [C] —**stammeringly** *adv*

stammer² *n* [C usually singular 一般用单数] a speech problem which makes someone speak with a lot of pauses and repeated sounds 结巴, 口吃: *He's got a bad stammer.* 他口吃非常严重。

2 **stamp¹** /stæmp; stæmp/ *n* [C]

1 ▶MAIL 邮件◀ also 又作 **postage stamp** *formal*【正式】a small piece of paper that you buy and stick onto an envelope or package before posting it 邮票: *a 29-cent stamp* 29美分的邮票 | **a sheet/book of stamps** (=set of stamps that you buy) 一版/一本邮票

2 ▶TOOL 工具◀ a tool for pressing or printing a mark or pattern onto a surface, or the mark made by this tool 印章, 图章; 印记, 戳记: *a date stamp* 日期戳 | *a passport stamp* 护照印

3 the stamp of sth if something has the stamp of a particular quality, it clearly has that quality 具有…的特点[特征]: **bear the stamp of sth** *The speech bore the stamp of authority.* 这个讲话有权威性。

4 ▶PAYMENT 支付, 付款◀ *BrE* a small piece of paper that is worth a particular amount of money and is bought and collected for something over a period of time【英】代币券; 购物券: *television licence stamps* 电视机许可证代金券

5 ▶TAX 税◀ a piece of paper for sticking to some official papers to show that British tax has been paid 印花税票〔在英国贴在官方文件上证明税已交讫的票据〕

6 a man/woman of his/her stamp *formal* someone with a particular kind of character【正式】他/她这类人〔指具有某种特征的人〕: *I wouldn't trust a man of his stamp.* 我不会相信他这种人。

7 an act of stamping, especially with your foot 跺; 跺脚, 顿足: *an angry stamp* 气愤的跺脚

1 1 **stamp²** *v*

1 ▶FOOT 脚◀ [I] to lift your foot off the ground and put it down hard on something 跺脚; 用力踩: **[+on]** *Marta shrieked and started stamping on the cockroach.* 玛尔塔尖声大叫, 并开始用力踩那只蟑螂。| **stamp around** (=walk this way) 跺着脚到处走 *Just because you're mad you don't have to stamp around like that.* 你就算生气也不必那样来回跺脚。

2 stamp your foot to lift your foot off the ground and bring it down again very hard because you are angry〔气愤地〕跺脚; 顿足: *"I will not!" yelled Bert, and stamped his foot.* "我不会的!"伯特大喊道, 并气愤地跺着脚。

3 stamp your feet to keep lifting each foot and bringing it down again very hard, to make a noise or because you are cold〔为发出声响或因寒冷而〕跺脚: *She stood at the bus stop stamping her feet to keep warm.* 她站在公共汽车站那里, 跺着脚以保持暖和。

4 ▶MAKE A MARK 留下印记◀ [T] to put a pattern, sign or letters on something using a special tool 在…上面印盖〔图案、记号、字等〕: **stamp sth on sth** *Stamp the date on all the letters.* 在所有的信上加盖日期〔戳〕。| **stamp sth with sth** *Your passport must be stamped with your entry date.* 你的护照上必须盖上入境日期。

5 stamp on sb/sth *informal* to use force or your authority to stop someone from doing something, or stop something from happening【非正式】镇压[压制]某人/某事: *Roberts stamped on every suggestion we made and then decided to end the project.* 罗伯茨压制我们提出的每一项建议, 然后决定终止那个计划。

6 ▶AFFECT SB/STH 影响某人/某物◀ [T] to have an important or permanent effect on someone or something 对…有重要[永久性]的影响: **be stamped on sb's memory** *That awful experience is indelibly stamped on my memory.* 那个可怕的经历给我留下了不可磨灭的记忆。| **stamp sb with sth** *His army years had stamped him with an air of brisk authority.* 多年的军旅生涯使他养成了一种雷厉风行的作风。

7 stamp sb as sth to show that someone has a particular type of character 表明某人有某种特征: *The latest scandal clearly stamped her as a liar.* 最近的丑闻清楚地说明她是个说谎者。

8 ▶MAIL 邮政◀ [T] to stick a stamp onto a letter, parcel etc 在…上贴上邮票

stamp sth ↔ **out** *phr v* [T] **1** to prevent something bad from continuing 消除; 杜绝: *We aim to stamp out poverty in our lifetimes.* 我们的目标是在有生之年消除贫困。**2** to put out a fire by stepping hard on the flames 踏灭〔火〕 **3** to make a shape or object by pressing hard on something using a machine or tool〔用机器或工具〕冲压制成

Stamp Act, the /ˈ· ·/ a British law made in 1765 which put a tax on Britain's colonies (COLONY) in North America. According to this law, various documents had to carry a stamp, which had to be paid for. This caused a lot of anger in the colonies, and opponents of the law used the phrase "No taxation without representation", meaning that it was unfair to make them pay taxes to Britain when they did not have any representatives in the British parliament. Although the tax was removed in 1766, the Stamp Act and the anger that it caused was one of the events that led to the American Revolutionary War.《印花税条例》〔1765年英国向北美殖民地征税的一项法案, 规定各类文件均需贴上买来的印花税票。这在殖民地引起强烈不满, 反对者提出口号: "没有代表权, 就不纳税", 意即他们在英国议会中没有代表, 要他们向英国纳税有失公平。虽然《印花税条例》于1766年取消, 但该法案及其引发的不满情绪却成为美国独立战争的诱因之一〕

stamp du·ty /ˈ· ,· ·/ *n* [U] a tax that must be paid in Britain on particular legal documents that have to be officially checked〔英国的〕印花税

stamped ad·dressed en·ve·lope /,· ·,· ˈ· · ·/ *n* [C] *BrE* an SAE; an envelope with your name, address and a stamp on it, which you send to a person or organization so that they can send you information【英】贴有邮票的回邮信封; SELF-ADDRESSED *AmE*【美】

stam·pede¹ /stæmˈpid; stæmˈpiːd/ *n* [C] **1** a sudden rush of frightened animals〔受惊动物的〕奔逃, 逃窜 **2** a sudden rush by a lot of people, all wanting to do the same thing or go to the same place〔人群的〕蜂拥; 争先恐后的行动: *stampede of producers offering her roles in their films* 争先恐后请她拍影片的制片商 **3** *AmE* an entertainment event at which COWBOYS show their skills, and there are competitions, dancing etc【美】牛仔竞技表演 —compare 比较 RODEO

stampede² *v* [I,T] **1** if animals stampede, they suddenly start running together, because they are frightened〔动物因受惊而〕奔逃, 逃窜: *a herd of stampeding buffalo* 一群惊逃的水牛 **2 be/get stampeded** to be made frightened or worried so that you do something too quickly 因受惊吓而蜂拥去做某事: **[+into]** *Don't get stampeded into any rash decisions.* 不要因惊慌失措而作出草率的决定。

stamp·ing ground /ˈ· · ·/ *n* [C] **sb's stamping ground** a favourite place where someone often goes 某人常去的地方

stance /stæns; stɑːns/ *n* [C usually singular 一般用单数] **1** an opinion that is stated publicly〔公开表明的〕观点; 立场; 看法: **[+on]** *an uncompromising stance on nuclear disarmament* 在核裁军问题上的坚定立场 | **take/adopt a stance** *The President has adopted a tough stance on terrorism.* 总统对恐怖主义采取强硬的立场。**2** a position in which you stand, especially when doing a particular activity〔尤指在做某活动时的〕站姿: *A good relaxed stance is essential when skiing.* 滑雪时良好、放松的站姿是非常重要的。—compare 比较 POSTURE¹ (1)

stanch /stæntʃ; stɑːntʃ/ *v* [T] an American spelling of STAUNCH² staunch²的美式拼法

stan·chion /ˈstæntʃən; ˈstɑːntʃən/ *n* [C] a strong upright bar used to support something 立柱, 支柱

stand¹ /stænd; stænd/ *v past tense and past participle* **stood** /stud; stud/

① BE UPRIGHT 直立, 站立
② CAN'T STAND 无法忍受
③ ACCEPT/BEAR 接受/忍受
④ IN A PARTICULAR STATE/SITUATION 处于某种状态/境地
⑤ CONTINUE/NOT CHANGE 继续/不改变
⑥ NOT MOVED OR USED 没有移动或使用过
⑦ FEELINGS/OPINIONS 感觉/看法
⑧ LEVEL/AMOUNT/VALUE/HEIGHT 水平/数量/价值/高度
⑨ BE RESPONSIBLE 负责
⑩ LAW 法律
⑪ BE PROUD/INDEPENDENT 自豪/独立
⑫ COULD STAND 需要; 应该
⑬ OTHER MEANINGS 其他意思

① BE UPRIGHT 直立, 站立

1 [I] to support yourself on your feet in an upright position 站立: *It looks like we'll have to stand – there are no seats left.* 看来我们只能站着, 没有座位了。| *Can you see any better from where you're standing?* 在你站的地方是不是看得更清楚? | **stand and do sth** *Diane stood and waved until his car was gone.* 黛安娜站在那儿挥手, 直到他的汽车远去。| **stand still** (=not move) 站着不动 *Stand still and let me wipe your face.* 站着别动, 让我给你擦擦脸。| **stand there** (=stand and not do anything) 闲站着 *Don't just stand there – help me!* 不要光站在那里, 帮帮我! | **stand on your toes/stand on tiptoe** (=support yourself on your toes) 踮着脚站着 *If you stand on tiptoe you can just about reach it.* 如果你踮起脚就差不多能够着了。—see also 另见 STANDSTILL, **stand up**

2 ►STAND SOMEWHERE TO DO STH 站在某处做某事◄ [I always+adv/prep] to take a particular position or do something in particular while standing 站在某个位置; 站着做某事: *Everybody stand in a circle.* 大家站成一圈。| *You don't need to stand closer to the microphone.* 你不必站得离麦克风很近。| [+at/beside/by etc] *Ouida, you stand at the door and greet people.* 奥维达, 你站在门口迎接大家。| **stand on sth** *We used to get in trouble for standing on the seats.* 我们以前常因站在座位上而惹麻烦。| **stand somewhere doing sth** *They just stood there laughing.* 他们只是站在那儿笑。| **stand back/aside** (=step backwards or sideways) 向后站/靠边站 *Stand back and give her some air!* 向后站, 让她透透气! | **stand clear (of)** (=move away) 移开; 不靠近 *Stand clear of the doors, please.* 请勿靠近门口。

3 ►RISE 起立◄ also 又作 **stand up** [I,T] to rise to an upright position, or to make someone do this (使)起立[站立]: *Suddenly, everyone stood up and cheered.* 突然, 大家都站了起来大声欢呼。| *Please stand and face the judge.* 请起立面对法官。| *Come on, stand up and say something.* 快, 站起来, 说点什么。| **stand sb (up) on sth** *Stand Molly up on a chair so she can see.* 让莫莉站在椅子上, 她就看得见了。

4 ►ON A BASE 在基础上◄ [I,T always+adv/prep] to stay upright on a base or on an object, or to put something there (使)竖立[屹立]: *Few houses were left standing after the tornado.* 龙卷风过后, 剩下没倒的房子寥寥无几。| *A green lamp stood on the leather-topped desk.* 皮面的桌子上摆着一盏绿色的台灯。| *There's a parking lot where the theater once stood.* 以前剧院的位置现在是一个停车场。| **stand sth on/in/over etc** *Can you stand that pole in the corner for now?* 你能不能暂时把那根竿子立在角落里?

5 stand to attention if soldiers stand to attention, they stand very straight and stiff to show respect〔士兵〕立正

6 stand on your head/hands to support yourself on your head or hands, with your feet in the air 用头/手支撑倒立

7 stand in line *AmE* to wait to be able to do something until the people ahead of you have done it【美】排队; queue up (QUEUE²) *BrE*【英】: *Gail has men standing in line wanting to go out with her.* 想跟盖尔约会的男人都排成队了。

8 stand fast/stand firm/stand your ground to refuse to be forced to move backwards 拒不后退; 拒不让步

② CAN'T STAND 无法忍受

9 [T] *usually spoken* to not like someone or something at all, or think that something is extremely unpleasant【一般口】不能忍受〔某人或某物〕: *I can't stand whiskey.* 威士忌我喝不了。| **can't stand the sight of** *I'm so mad, I can hardly stand the sight of him.* 我非常恼火, 几乎一看见他就讨厌。| **can't stand to see/hear/do etc** *I can't stand to see good food going to waste.* 我不能忍受看到好好的食物被浪费。| **can't stand seeing/hearing/doing etc** *Lily can't stand working in an office.* 在办公室工作, 莉莉受不了。| **can't stand sb/sth doing** *I can't stand people dropping litter.* 我讨厌人们乱扔垃圾。—see also 另见 **stand for** (STAND¹), **can't bear sb doing sth** (BEAR¹ (1))

③ ACCEPT/BEAR 接受/忍受

10 [I,T] to be able to accept or deal well with a difficult situation; TOLERATE 接受, 对付; 忍受: *I've had about as much as I can stand of your arguing!* 你们的争吵我快要听腻了! | *I don't know if I can stand the waiting any longer.* 再等下去, 我不知道我是否受得了。| **stand sb doing sth** *How can you stand Marty coming home late all the time?* 你怎么能容忍马蒂总是晚回家? | **not stand any nonsense** *Get up to bed, and I won't stand any nonsense.* 上床睡觉去吧, 不许跟我胡闹。—see graph at 参见 BEAR 图表

11 ►BE GOOD ENOUGH 够好的◄ [T] to be done or made well enough to be successful, strong, or useful for a long time 经得起, 经受: **stand close examination** (=be proved to be correct, well made etc) 经得起仔细检验 *I suspect Murray's theory won't stand close examination.* 我怀疑默里的理论经受不住仔细检验。| **stand the test of time** (=stay strong) 经受时间的考验 *It's nice to see their marriage has stood the test of time.* 很高兴看到他们的婚姻经得起时间的考验。

12 if you can't stand the heat, get out of the kitchen used to say that you should leave a job or situation if you cannot deal with its difficulties 受不了热就别在厨房待着〔指如果对付不了困难, 就应该离开〕

④ IN A PARTICULAR STATE/SITUATION 处于某种状态/境地

13 [I always+adv/prep, linking verb 连系动词] to be in, stay in, or get into a particular state 处于[保持; 进入]某种状态: *Court stands adjourned until 2 p.m.* 法庭休庭至下午2点。| **as sth stands** *The law, as it stood, favoured the developers.* 从法律本身来看对开发商有利。| **the way things stand/as things stand** (=used when talking about the state that a situation has reached) 目前的状况/就目前的情况看 *I'm not too thrilled with the way things stand at the moment.* 我对目前的情况并不感到很高兴。| **where/how do things stand?** (=used to ask what is happening in a situation) 目前情况如何? *Where do things stand in terms of the budget?* 现在预算的情况怎么样? | **stand united/divided** (=agree or disagree completely) 意见统一/有分歧 *The committee stands divided on this issue.* 委员会在这个问题上有分歧。| **stand prepared/ready to do sth** (=be prepared to do something whenever it is necessary) 准备好做某事 | **stand together** (=stay united) 团结一致 *If we all stand together, they can't beat us.* 如果我们团结一致, 他们就无法击败我们。| **stand in awe of sb** (=admire them, be afraid of them, or both) 敬畏某人

⑤ CONTINUE/NOT CHANGE 继续/不改变

14 stand alone to continue to do something alone, without help from anyone else 继续独自做某事: *Harper stood alone in his refusal to sell to the railroad.* 哈珀独自坚持着拒不卖给铁路。

15 ▶STILL EXIST 依然存在◀ [I not in progressive 不用进行时] to continue to exist, be correct, or be VALID 继续存在; 保持正确; 保持有效: *My offer of a place to stay still stands.* 我愿提供住处的意愿仍没有变。| *The court of appeal has ruled that the conviction should stand.* 上诉法庭的判决是维持原判。

16 stand still to not change or progress at all although time has passed 毫无变化; 停滞不前: *Nothing stands still in the computer industry.* 在计算机行业, 一切都在不停地变化。| **time stands still** *Going back home, it's as if time has stood still and I'm ten years old.* 回到家里, 时光好像停顿了下来, 而我彷佛才10岁。

17 stand your ground/stand firm/stand fast also 又作 **stand your guns** *AmE*【美】to refuse to change your opinions, intentions, or behaviour 坚持立场; 拒不让步: *Stand your ground, don't let them talk you into anything you don't want.* 要坚定, 不要听他们的劝说而做你自己不愿做的事情。| [+on/against] *I call on you as citizens to stand firm against racism!* 我呼吁你们作为公民要坚决反对种族主义!

18 stand pat *AmE informal* to refuse to change a decision, plan etc【美, 非正式】坚持不变: [+on] *Harry's standing pat on his decision to fire Janice.* 哈里坚持决定要解雇贾尼丝。

⑥ NOT MOVED OR USED 没有移动或使用过

19 [I, linking verb 连系动词] to stay in a particular position, place, or state without being moved or used 停放在某位置, 处于某状态; 没有移动[使用]过: *The car's been standing in the garage for weeks.* 这辆汽车停放在车库里好几个星期了。| **stand empty/idle** (=not being used) 空置/闲置 *scores of derelict houses standing empty* 几十幢无人居住的废弃房屋

20 ▶LIQUID 液体◀ [I] a liquid that stands does not flow or is not made to move〔液体〕不流动; 处于静止状态: *standing pools of marsh water* 一潭潭沼泽的积水

⑦ FEELINGS/OPINIONS 感觉/看法

21 know how/where you stand (with sb) to know how someone feels about you 知道某人对自己的看法: *Yvonne may be blunt, but you always know where you stand with her.* 伊冯娜也许有点迟钝, 但你总能了解她对你有什么看法。

22 where sb stands someone's opinion about something, or the official rule about something 某人对某事的看法; 对某事的正式规定: [+on] *The voters want to know where you stand on abortion.* 选民们想知道你对堕胎的看法。

23 from where I stand according to what you know or feel 据我所知; 在我看来: *Well from where I'm standing, it seems like she's being unreasonable.* 我觉得她好像是不讲道理的。

24 I stand corrected *spoken formal* used to admit that your opinion or something that you just said was wrong【口, 正式】我承认错误〔用于承认自己的观点或刚才说过的话是错误的〕

⑧ LEVEL/AMOUNT/VALUE/HEIGHT 水平/数量/价值/高度

25 [I always+adv/prep] to be at a particular level or amount 处于某水平[数量]: [+at] *Inflation currently stands at four percent.* 目前的通货膨胀为百分之四。| *Your bank balance stands at $720.92.* 你的银行存款余额为720.92美元。

26 [I always+adv/prep] to have a particular rank or position when compared to similar things or people〔与类似事物或人相比〕处于某等级[地位]: *I know your son stands high on the list of suitable candidates.* 我知道你儿子在合适的候选人名单中排在前面。| **stand in relation to** *How do their sales stand in relation to those of similar firms?* 他们的销售额与类似的公司相比如何?

27 [I always+adv/prep, linking verb 连系动词] *usually written* to be a particular height【一般书面】高度为…: **stand four feet etc (high)/stand 20 metres etc (tall)** *The Eiffel Tower stands 300m high.* 埃菲尔铁塔的高度为300米。

⑨ BE RESPONSIBLE 负责

28 [linking verb 连系动词] to take a particular responsibility 承担某种职责: **stand guard (over)** *If you stand guard over our stuff, I'll run get the tickets.* 要是你来看管我们的东西, 我就跑过去买票。| **stand bail** (=pay money as a promise that someone will return to a court to be judged)〔为某人〕提供保释金, 做保释人 | **stand surety** (=be responsible for the results if someone else does not do what they promise to) 作担保

⑩ LAW 法律

29 stand trial to be brought to a court of law to have your case examined and judged〔在法庭上〕受审: [+for] *Gresham will stand trial for murder.* 格雷沙姆将因谋杀罪而受审。

30 stand accused to be the person in a court of law who is being judged for a crime 被指控, 被控告: *Vincent Amis, you stand accused of murder.* 文森特·埃米斯, 你被指控犯有谋杀罪。

⑪ BE PROUD/INDEPENDENT 自豪/独立

31 stand on your own (two) feet to be able to earn what you need without help from others 自立: *I'll think of him as equal when he's learnt to stand on his own two feet.* 当他学会了自立后, 我就对他平等看待。

32 stand tall *AmE* to be proud and feel ready to deal with anything【美】自豪; 自信

33 stand on your dignity to demand to be treated with respect 要求受到应有的礼遇; 保持自己的尊严[身份]: *Never one to stand on her dignity, Eva joined in with the fun.* 伊娃从来不爱摆架子, 她和大家一起玩了起来。

⑫ COULD STAND 需要; 应该

34 used to say very directly that it would be a good idea for someone to do something or for something to happen〔用于直言〕〔某人〕最好做〔某事〕;〔某事〕应该发生: **sb could stand to do sth** *You could stand to lose a few pounds.* 你最好能减肥几磅。| **sth could stand another look/more attention etc** (=it ought to be looked at more closely) 某事物需要再仔细查看 *Your report could stand another read-through for typos.* 你的报告得再通读一次, 看看是否有打字错误。

35 I could stand sth *AmE spoken humorous* used to say that you would like something【美口, 幽默】我想要某物: *I could stand another piece of pie!* 我想再吃一块馅饼!

⑬ OTHER MEANINGS 其他意思

36 stand a chance/hope (of doing sth) to be likely to be able to do something or to succeed 有机会/有希望(做某事): *You'll stand a better chance of getting a job with a degree.* 你有了学位找到工作的机会就更大。| **not stand a chance** *I'm afraid she doesn't stand a chance.* 恐怕她没有什么机会。| **stand little chance** (=not be likely to succeed) 成功的可能性不大 *The bill stands little chance of becoming law.* 这项议案几乎没有可能成为法律。

37 stand to gain/lose/win etc to be likely to do or have something 很可能获得/失去/赢得等: *We stand to make a lot of money from the merger.* 通过这次合并, 我们很可能赚到一大笔钱。

38 do sth standing on your head to do something easily 轻而易举地做某事: *Get Anne to help – she can fix things like that standing on her head.* 请安妮来帮忙, 她能轻而易举地修理好那样的东西。

39 stand on your head to do sth to make a great effort to do something 努力[竭力]去做某事: *You won't find me standing on my head to help him any more.* 你再也不会看到我尽力去帮助他了。

40 it stands to reason used to say that something should be completely clear to anyone who is sensible 显然; 合乎情理: *If the thefts are all in the same area, it stands to reason it's the same kids doing it.* 如果盗窃都发生在同一地区, 那显然是同一伙年轻人干的。

41 ▶ELECTION 选举◀ [I] to try to become elected to a council, parliament etc 竞选; 当候选人: *Who's standing for the Democrats in the 44th district?* 谁是第44区的民主党候选人? —see also 另见 **stand against**

42 stand in sb's way/path to prevent someone from doing something 妨碍某人; 阻碍某人: *If you really want to marry Liam, I'm not going to stand in your way.* 你如果真的想跟利亚姆结婚, 我不会阻止你的。

43 stand sb in good stead to be very useful to someone when needed 需要时对某人很有用: *Now that I'm emigrating to the United States, my being able to speak English should stand me in good stead.* 我要移民去美国了, 而我能讲英语对我应该是有益处的。

44 stand sb a drink/meal etc to pay for something as a gift to someone; TREAT[1] (5) 请某人喝酒/吃饭等: *Come on, Jack, I'll stand you a drink if you like.* 来吧, 杰克, 我请你喝一杯。赏光吗?

45 not stand on ceremony to not worry about the formal rules of polite behaviour 随便; 不拘礼节: *Don't stand on ceremony – if you want a drink, have one.* 别客气, 想喝就来一杯吧。

46 stand or fall by/on to depend on something for success 成败取决于: *The whole project must stand or fall on the quality of its research.* 整个项目的成败取决于研究的质量。
47 stand sth on its head to show that a belief, idea etc is completely untrue 证明〔信念、观点等〕完全不真实, 把某事彻底推翻: *Galileo's discovery stood medieval thought on its head.* 伽利略的发现彻底推翻了中世纪的思想。
48 [I+on/in] *BrE* to accidentally step on or in something【英】意外地踩到: *Mind you don't stand on Fluffy's tail.* 小心别踩到弗拉菲的尾巴。—see also 另见 **make sb's hair stand on end** (HAIR (6)), **leave sb/sth standing** (LEAVE[1] (31)), **not have a leg to stand on** (LEG[1] (8))

stand against sb/sth *phr v* [T] to oppose a person, organization, plan, decision etc 反对: *If we don't stand against the cutbacks, they'll cut even more next year.* 我们如果不反对这次削减, 明年他们就会减得更多。

stand around *phr v* [I] to stand somewhere and not do anything〔无所事事地〕闲站着: *It's too cold to stand around out here – I'm going back inside.* 在外面闲站着太冷了, 我要进屋里去了。

stand by *phr v* **1** [T] to not do anything to help someone or prevent something from happening 袖手旁观: *We are not prepared to stand by and let them close our schools.* 我们不会袖手旁观, 听任他们关闭我们的学校。**2** [T **stand by** sth] to keep a promise, agreement etc, or to declare that something is still true 信守〔诺言〕; 遵守〔协定〕; 坚持: *I stand by what I said earlier.* 我坚持原先说的话。**3** [T **stand by** sb] to stay loyal to someone and support them, especially in a difficult situation〔尤指在困难情况下〕继续忠于; 支持: *Wes needs to know we'll always stand by him.* 韦斯需要确定我们总是会支持他。**4** [I] to be ready to do something if necessary 准备行动: **be standing by** *A rescue boat is always standing by in case of trouble.* 一艘营救船随时待命, 以防发生事故。| [+for] *Stand by for the countdown.* 请作好倒数准备。| **stand by to do sth** *Stand by to cue the commercial.* 请准备好播广告。—see also 另见 BYSTANDER, STANDBY

stand down *phr v* **1** [I] to agree to leave your position or to stop trying to be elected, so that someone else can have a chance 辞职; 退出竞选: *I'm prepared to stand down in favor of a younger candidate.* 我准备退出竞选, 让位给一个年轻点的候选人。—see also 另见 **step down** (STEP[2]) **2** [I] to leave the WITNESS BOX in court 离开证人席 **3** [I,T **stand** sb ↔ **down**] *BrE* to send a soldier away from work after they have done their work for the day, or to stop working for the day; **go off duty** (DUTY (3))【英】撤走〔值过班的士兵〕;〔士兵〕下班[不值勤]

stand for sth *phr v* [T] **1** if a letter, number or sign stands for something, it represents it as a short form of a word, name, or idea 代表; 象征; 意味着: *"My name is Dean E. Beller." "What does the E stand for?"* "我的名字是迪安·E.贝勒。" "E代表的是什么?" **2** [usually in questions and negatives 一般用于疑问句和否定句] to allow something to continue to happen without complaining about it or trying to stop it 忍受; 容忍: *We will not stand for this sort of behavior, young man!* 小伙子, 我们不会容忍这种行为! | **stand for being** *I won't stand for being treated like a child.* 我不会容忍被当做孩子对待。**3** to support a particular set of ideas, values, or principles 主张; 支持; 拥护: *I want to know what she stands for before I'll vote for her.* 在我投她的票之前, 我想知道她主张什么。

stand in *phr v* [I] to temporarily do someone else's job 暂时代替〔某人〕: [+for] *Can you stand in for Meg while she's on vacation?* 梅格休假期间, 你能暂时代替她吗? —see also 另见 STAND-IN

stand out *phr v* [I] **1** to be very easy to see or notice by looking or sounding different from other things or people 显眼; 突出: *I think black lettering will stand out best on a yellow sign.* 我认为黄色标志上用黑色字体最醒目。| **stand out in a crowd** *Well, that dress will make you stand out in a crowd!* 好, 那件连衣裙会使你在人群中很显眼! **2 stand out a mile** to be very clear or noticeable 显而易见; 极醒目: *They thought no one knew but it stood out a mile they were interested in each other.* 他们以为没有人知道, 但他们互相有好感是明摆着的事。**3** to be clearly better or the best 显然比…好; 最杰出: **stand out as** *Among mystery writers, P D James stands out as a superior storyteller.* 在侦探小说作家中, P.D.詹姆斯最突出, 是最好的小说家。| [+from/among/above] *Nathan stands out from the rest of the singers.* 内森从其他歌手中脱颖而出。—see also 另见 STANDOUT

stand out against sth *phr v* [T] to be strongly opposed to an idea, plan etc 坚决[强烈]反对: *We must stand out against bigotry.* 我们必须坚决反对偏见。

stand over sb *phr v* [T] to stand very close behind someone and watch as they work to make sure they do nothing wrong〔站在某人身后〕严密监督[监视]: *I can't concentrate with him standing over me like that.* 他那样监视着我, 我无法专心工作。

stand to *phr v* [I,T **stand** sb ↔ **to**] *BrE* to order a soldier to move into a position so that they are ready for action, or to move into this position【英】命令〔士兵〕进入战备状态;〔士兵〕进入战备状态

stand up *phr v* **1** [I usually in progressive 一般用进行时] to stand 站立, 站: *Boy am I tired, I've been standing up all day.* 哎呀, 我真的累坏了, 我已经站了一整天。| **stand up straight** *Stand up straight, boy, don't slouch!* 站直, 孩子, 别没精打采的! **2** [I always+ adv/prep] to stay healthy in a difficult environment or in good condition after a lot of hard use 耐久; 耐用; 经得起: [+to] *The trees stood up pretty well to the frosts this winter.* 这些树经得起今年冬天的霜冻。**3** [I] to be proved to be true, correct, useful etc when tested 站得住脚; 证明真实[正确, 有用等]: **stand up under/to** *stand up under close scrutiny* 经得起仔细推敲 | **stand up in court** (=be successfully proved in a court of law) 在法庭上站得住脚 *Without a witness, the charges will never stand up in court.* 如果没有证人, 这些指控在法庭上是绝对站不住脚的。**4** [T **stand** sb **up**] *informal* to not meet someone after you have promised to do something with them【非正式】未如约与…见面, 爽约: *I was supposed to go to a concert with Kyle on Friday, but he stood me up.* 我星期五本来要跟凯尔一起去听音乐会的, 但他失约了。**5 stand up and be counted** to make it very clear what you think about something when this is dangerous or might cause trouble for you〔尤指对危险或可能引起麻烦的事物〕公开表明立场[态度] —see also 另见 STAND-UP

stand up for sb/sth *phr v* [T] to support or defend a person or idea when they are being attacked 支持; 保卫; 维护: *It's time we stood up for our rights.* 我们该维护自己的权利了。| *Didn't anyone stand up for James and say it wasn't his fault?* 难道没有人支持詹姆斯, 说那不是他的过错?

stand up to sb/sth *phr v* [T] to refuse to accept unfair treatment from a person or organization 拒绝接受〔某人或组织〕的不公平对待: *He'll respect you more if you stand up to him.* 如果你向他提出抗议, 他会更尊重你。

stand² *n*

1 ▶FOR SUPPORT 作支撑用◀ [C] a piece of furniture or equipment for supporting something 架; 台; 座: *a music stand* 乐谱架 | *an umbrella stand* 伞架 | *Can we put another microphone stand here?* 我们可以在这里再放一个话筒架吗? | **coat-stand/hat-stand** (=for hanging coats or hats on) 衣架/帽架

2 ▶FOR SELLING 作销售用◀ [C] a small structure used for selling or showing things; STALL[1] (1) 售货台[亭]; 货摊, 摊位: *a hotdog stand* 热狗摊 | *Come by our stand at the exhibition and see the new products.* 到我们在展览会上设的摊位来看看新产品。—see also 另见 NEWSSTAND

3 ▶OPINION/ATTITUDE 观点/态度◀ [C usually singular 一般用单数] a position or opinion that you state firmly and publicly〔公开表明的〕坚定主张[立场]: **take a stand (on)** *The Labour Party has not taken a stand on the political position of the monarchy.* 工党还没有就君主的政治地位表明立场。

4 ▶SPORTS GROUND 运动场◀ [C] also 又作 **stands** *plural* a building where people stand or sit to watch the game at a sports ground〔运动场里的〕看台 —see also 另见 GRANDSTAND

5 ▶OPPOSE/DEFEND 反对/防御◀ [C] a strong effort to defend yourself or to oppose something 防御; 反抗, 抵抗: **make a stand** *In February 1916 the French army made a stand at Verdun.* 1916年2月, 法国军队在凡尔登进行了奋力抵抗。| **make/mount a stand against** *Somebody's got to make a stand against the parish council.* 得有人站出来反对行政区议会。

6 ▶SPORTS GAME 体育比赛◀ [C] the period of time in which two batsmen (BATSMAN) are playing together in a game of CRICKET (2), or the points that they get〔在一局板球赛中两个击球员的〕持续坚守; 得分

7 the stand *AmE* a WITNESS BOX【美】证人席: **take the stand** *Will the next witness please take the stand?* 请下一位证人到证人席来。—see also 另见 ONE-NIGHT STAND

stand·a·lone /ˈstændəˌlon; ˈstændələʊn/ *adj technical* a standalone computer works on its own without being part of a NETWORK[1] (4)【术语】〔计算机〕独立的

[S3] [W2] **stan·dard**[1] /ˈstændəd; ˈstændɚd/ *n*
1 ▶LEVEL OF QUALITY 质量水平◀ [C often plural 常用复数, U] a level of quality, skill, ability or achievement by which someone or something is judged, that is considered to be necessary or acceptable in a particular situation 水平; 水准; 标准: *The airline has rigorous safety standards.* 这家航空公司有严格的安全标准。| [+of] *Inspections are meant to ensure the standard of teaching is acceptable.* 视察是为了确保教学水准合格。| **(of a) high/low standard** *Our students achieve very high standards of musical ability.* 我们的学生达到了很高的音乐水平。| *Articles of a low standard will not be accepted.* 质量差的论文不会被接受。| **set a standard** (=decide what people are expected to do) 制定标准 *The International Atomic Energy Agency sets standards for the industry.* 国际原子能机构为该行业制定标准。| **meet/reach/attain a standard** *They have to reach a certain standard or they won't pass.* 他们必须达到一定水准, 不然就无法通过。| **to standard** (=well enough) 合乎标准; 足够好 *completing work to standard and on time* 合乎标准并准时完成工作 | **maintain standards** (=keep them the way they are) 保持水平; 保持水准 *After his early success, Cameron was unable to maintain such high standards.* 卡梅伦起初获得了成功, 但他没能把如此高的水平保持下去。| **above/below standard** (=better than usual, or not good enough) 超过/低于标准 *The accommodation here is really below standard.* 这里的住宿条件实在低于标准。| **up to standard** (=good enough) 合乎[达到]标准 *Your recent work just hasn't been up to standard.* 你最近的工作就是没有达到标准。| **raise/lower a standard** *We're not about to lower our standards just to make a cheaper product.* 我们不会为了制造更廉价的产品而降低我们的标准。| **let standards fall/drop/slip** (=allow them to get worse) 允许标准下降/下滑 *On no account must we let standards slip.* 我们无论如何也不能允许水准下滑。
2 ▶COMPARING 比较◀ [C usually plural 一般用复数] the ideas of what is good or normal that someone uses to compare one thing with another 标准; 规范; 规格: **by sb's standards** *They were all pretty excitable by our quiet English standards.* 按我们英国人性情平和的标准来看, 他们都相当容易激动。| **by any standard(s)** (=by anyone's opinion or values) 无论在谁看来; 不论以什么标准 *It's a deprived area by any standard.* 不论以什么标准来看, 那都是个贫困地区。
3 ▶MORAL RULE 道德准则◀ [C usually plural 一般用复数] rules for behaviour based on an idea of what is morally good and right 道德标准; 道德准则: *Nobody could live up to his standards.* 没有人能够达到他的道德标准。
4 ▶MEASUREMENT 计量, 测量◀ [C] a fixed official rule for measuring weight, purity, value etc〔重量、纯度、价值等的〕标准, 基准: *an official government standard for the purity of silver* 白银纯度的政府法定标准
5 ▶SONG 歌曲◀ [C] a popular song that has been sung by many different singers〔很多歌星演唱过的〕流行歌曲
6 ▶FLAG 旗◀ [C] a flag used in ceremonies 仪式用旗帜: *the royal standard* 王室的旗帜
7 ▶MILITARY POLE 军队旗杆◀ [C] a pole with a picture or shape at the top carried in the past at the front of an army〔旧时军队的〕军旗旗杆 —see also 另见 DOUBLE STANDARD, LIVING STANDARD

This graph shows some of the words most commonly used with the noun **standard**. 本图表所示为含有名词 standard 的一些最常用的词组。

high standard
set a standard
meet a standard
to standard
low standard
maintain standards
reach/attain a standard
2 4 6 8 10 per million 每百万

Based on the British National Corpus and the Longman Lancaster Corpus
据英国国家语料库和朗文兰开斯特语料库

[S3] [W2] **standard**[2] *adj* **1** accepted as normal or usual 正常的; 普通的; 普遍接受的: *We paid them the standard rate for the job.* 这工作我们付给他们标准的工钱。| **standard practice/procedure** (=the usual way of doing things) 例行的做法/程序 *Searching luggage at airports is now standard practice.* 在机场检查行李现在已成为例行的做法。**2** regular and usual in shape, size, quality etc〔形状、大小、质量等〕规则的; 标准的: *We make shoes in standard and wide sizes.* 我们做标准码和加宽码的鞋子。| *All these vans are made to a standard design.* 这些客货两用车都是按标准设计制造的。**3** a standard book, work, author etc is read by everyone studying a particular subject〔某一学科的书、作品、作者等〕公认为标准的; 有权威的 **4 standard English/spelling/pronunciation etc** *BrE* the form of English, spelling, pronunciation etc that most people in Britain use, and that is not limited to one area or group of people【英】标准英语/拼法/发音等 —see also 另见 NON-STANDARD, SUBSTANDARD

Standard, The —see 见 The EVENING STANDARD

standard-bear·er /ˈ· ·, ·ˌ·/ *n* [C] **1** an important leader in a moral argument or political group 领导者; 倡导者; 领袖; 旗手 **2** a soldier who carried the STANDARD (=flag) at the front of an army〔军队的〕旗手

standard de·duc·tion /ˌ·· ·ˈ··/ *n* [C usually singular 一般用单数] *AmE* a fixed amount of the money you earn that you do not have to pay tax on【美】标准扣减额, 工资免税额〔指收入中无需纳税的一笔固定金额〕

standard de·vi·a·tion /ˌ·· ··ˈ··/ *n* [C] *technical* a number in statistics (STATISTIC (1)) that shows how widely members of a mathematical set vary from the average set【术语】〔统计学上的〕标准差

standard-is·sue /ˌ·· ˈ··◂/ *adj* included in ordinary military equipment〔军队装备〕标准配给的, 统一分发的

stan·dard·ize also 又作 **-ise** *BrE*【英】/ˈstændədˌaɪz; ˈstændɚdaɪz/ *v* [T] to make all the things of one particular type the same as each other 使…标准化[统一规格]: *Attempts to standardize English spelling have never been successful.* 统一英语拼写的尝试从未成功过。—**standardization** /ˌstændədaɪˈzeɪʃən; ˌstændɚdəˈzeɪʃən/ *n* [U]

standard lamp /ˈ·· ·/ *n* [C] *BrE* a tall lamp that stands on the floor【英】落地灯; FLOOR LAMP *AmE*【美】—see picture at 参见 LIGHT[1] 图

standard of liv·ing /ˌ·· · ˈ··/ *n* [C usually singular 一般用单数] the amount of wealth, comfort, and things that can be bought that a particular person, group, country etc has 生活水平, 生活水准: *a nation with a high standard of living* 生活水准高的国家

standard time /ˈ·· ·/ *n* [singular] the time to which all clocks in a particular area of the world are set 标准时间

stand·by, stand-by /ˈstændˌbaɪ; ˈstændbaɪ/ *n* **1** [C] something that is kept ready so that it can be used when needed 备用物: *Powdered milk is a good standby in an emergency.* 奶粉是紧急情况下很好的备用品。| *The hospital has a standby generator.* 这家医院有备用发电机。**2 on standby** ready to help immediately if you are needed 随时待命: *A special team of police were kept on standby.* 一支警察特遣队随时待命。**3** [U] the condition of being ready to travel on a plane if there are any seats left when it is ready to leave〔飞机乘客〕等候剩余机票的, 候补的: *a cheap standby ticket* 便宜的剩余机票 | **on standby** *All the seats are taken, but we can put you on standby.* 机位已满, 但我们可以让你做候补乘客。**4** [C] someone or something that you can always depend on or that will always be suitable 可依靠的人[事物]; 总是合适的人[事物]: *It's useful to have a little black dress as a standby.* 备一件黑色小礼服很有用。—see also 另见 **stand by** (STAND[1])

stand-in /ˈ· ·/ *n* [C] **1** someone who does the job or takes the place of someone else for a short time〔职位或工作的〕临时替代者: *Gilbert failed to find a stand-in and so could not go to their dinner party.* 吉尔伯特找不到人临时替代他, 因此无法参加他们的晚宴。**2** someone who takes the place of an actor for some scenes in a film〔电影中的〕替身 —see also 另见 **stand in** (STAND[1])

stand·ing[1] /ˈstændɪŋ; ˈstændɪŋ/ *adj* [only before noun 仅用于名词前] **1** permanently agreed or arranged 永久的; 长期有效的; 常置的: *You have to pay standing charges whether or not you use the service.* 无论你是否使用这项服务, 你都必须交纳固定费用。| **standing invitation** (=permission to visit someone whenever you like) 长期有效的邀请 **2 standing order(s)** **a)** an agreement to pay for something regularly from your bank account〔要求银行定期付款的〕长期自动转账委托 **b)** a permanent rule that a committee, council etc follows when it meets〔委员会、议会等的〕议事规则 **3** done from a standing position 直立着做的; 站着做的: *The runners set off from a standing start.* 赛跑者站着起跑。| **standing ovation** (=when people stand up

to CLAP[1] (1) after a performance) 起立鼓掌 **4 standing joke** something that happens often and that people make jokes about 经常引人发笑的笑话: *My spelling mistakes had become a standing joke in the office.* 我的拼写错误已经成为办公室里讲不厌的笑话。

standing² *n* [U] **1** someone's rank or position in a system, organization, society etc, based on what other people think of them 地位; 身份; 声望: *The scandal will certainly damage the Governor's standing in the polls.* 丑闻肯定会损害州长在选举中的声望。| **high/low standing** *a lawyer of high standing* 名望高的律师 **2 of five/many etc years' standing** used to show the time during which something such as an agreement has existed〔协议等〕已经存在五年的/多年的等: *an arrangement of several years' standing* 执行了好几年的安排

standing ar·my /,·· '··/ *n* [C] a professional, permanent army, rather than one that has been formed for a war 常备军; 正规军

Standing Com·mit·tee /'·· ,··/ *n* [C] a committee of members in the British Parliament or in the US House of Representatives, whose purpose is to examine a BILL (=new law that has been suggested) and to consider whether it needs any changes 常务委员会〔英国议会或美国众议院审查议案并决定是否需要作出修改的一个委员会〕—see 见 SELECT COMMITTEE

standing or·der /,·· '··/ *n* [C,U] an arrangement by which a bank pays a fixed amount of money from your account every month, year etc〔要求银行定期付款的〕长期自动转账委托 —compare 比较 DIRECT DEBIT

standing room /'·· ·/ *n* [U] space for standing in a theatre, sports ground etc〔戏院、运动场等的〕站位: **standing room only** (=no seats are left) 只有站位

stand·off /ˋstænd,ɔf; 'stændɒf/ *n* [C] a situation in which neither side in a fight or battle can gain an advantage〔战斗的〕僵持(状态)

stand-of·fish /,stænd ˋɔfɪʃ; ,stænd 'ɒfɪʃ/ *adj informal* rather unfriendly and formal【非正式】不友好的; 冷淡的; 疏远的: *She was cold and stand-offish.* 她态度冷漠, 不甚友好。—**stand-offishly** *adv* —**stand-offishness** *n* [U]

stand·out /ˋstænd,aut; 'stændaʊt/ *n* [C] *AmE* someone who is better at doing something or more attractive than other people in a group【美】突出的人; 引起注意的人: *In that class, Mary's a standout.* 玛丽在那个班里很是突出。—**standout** *adj*: *a standout performance* 一场出色的演出

stand·pipe /ˋstænd,paɪp; 'stændpaɪp/ *n* [C] a pipe that provides water in a public place in the street〔在街上给公共场所供水的〕竖管

stand·point /ˋstænd,pɔɪnt; 'stændpɔɪnt/ *n* [C usually singular 一般用单数] a way of thinking about people, situations, ideas etc; POINT OF VIEW 立场; 观点; 立足点: *the feminist standpoint* 女权主义立场 | [+of] *Let's look at this from the standpoint of the voters.* 让我们从选民的角度来看待这个问题。

St An·drews /sent ˋændruz; sənt 'ændruːz/ a city in eastern Scotland known especially for its old university and its GOLF courses 圣安德鲁斯〔苏格兰东部一城市, 尤以当地历史悠久的大学和高尔夫球场闻名〕

stand·still /ˋstænd,stɪl; 'stænd,stɪl/ *n* [singular] a situation in which there is no movement or activity at all 静止(状态); 停顿, 停滞: **come to a standstill/bring sth to a standstill** *Strikers brought production to a standstill.* 罢工者使生产陷于停顿。| **at a standstill** *Traffic was at a standstill on the freeway.* 高速公路上的交通完全瘫痪了。

stand-up¹, standup /ˋstænd,ʌp; 'stændʌp/ *adj* [only before noun 仅用于名词前] **1** stand-up COMEDY involves one person telling jokes as a performance〔喜剧〕单人说笑表演的: *a stand-up comedian* 从事单人说笑表演的喜剧演员 **2** done or intended to be used by people who are standing up 站着做的; 站着使用的: *We had a stand-up buffet.* 我们站着吃了一顿自助餐。**3** a stand-up fight, argument etc is loud and violent〔打斗、争论等〕喧闹而激烈的: *If it came to a stand-up fight, I wouldn't have a chance.* 要是硬碰起来, 我根本不是对手。**4** able to stay upright 能够直立的: *a photo in a stand-up frame* 竖立相架中的照片 | *a stand-up collar* 直立的衣领 —see also 另见 **stand up**

stand-up² also 又作 **standup** *n* [U] stand-up COMEDY 单人说笑喜剧, 独角喜剧: **do stand-up** *Mark used to do stand-up at Roxy's bar.* 马克曾在罗克西的酒吧里表演独角喜剧。

Stan·ford /ˋstænfɚd; 'stænfəd/ a famous American university in California, south of San Francisco 斯坦福大学〔美国一知名大学, 位于加利福利亚州旧金山市以南〕

Stan·i·slav·sky Con·stan·tin /,stænɪˋslɑvskɪ; ,stænɪ'slævski/ /ˋkɑnstəntin; 'kɒnstəntiːn/ (1863-1938) a Russian actor and theatre DIRECTOR who developed a new way of acting, called method acting. This involves actors using their own emotions and remembering their own experiences so that they feel as if they really become the character they are playing. 斯坦尼斯拉夫斯基〔(1863-1938), 俄罗斯演员、戏剧导演。首创"体验派表演法", 要求演员发掘内心感情、回忆自己的亲身经历, 从而完全融入所扮演的角色〕

stank /stæŋk; stæŋk/ the past tense of STINK

Stan·ley /ˋstænlɪ; 'stænli/, **Henry Morton** (1841-1904) a British EXPLORER. In 1871 he was sent by a US newspaper to find David Livingstone in Africa, and is famous for saying "Dr Livingstone, I presume" when he found him. People sometimes say this as a joke when they meet someone. 斯坦利〔(1841-1904), 英国探险家。1871 年, 他受美国一家报社派遣前往非洲寻找戴维·利文斯通。找到后, 他说了一句话, 非常有名: "我想您就是利文斯通博士吧。"今天人们见面时偶尔也会用这句话来开玩笑〕

Stanley, Port —see 见 PORT STANLEY

Stanley Cup, the /,·· '·/ a prize given to the winner of the National Hockey League, which is made up of ice hockey teams from Canada and the US 斯坦利杯〔奖给国家冰球联盟冠军队的奖杯。国家冰球联盟由美国和加拿大两国的冰球队组成〕

stan·za /ˋstænzə; 'stænzə/ *n* [C] a group of lines in a repeated pattern forming part of a poem〔诗的〕节, 段

sta·ple¹ /ˋstepl; 'steɪpəl/ *n* [C] **1** a small piece of thin wire that is pushed into sheets of paper and bent over to hold them together 订书钉 **2** a small U-shaped piece of metal with pointed ends, used to hold something in place U形钉 **3** a food that is needed and used all the time 常用食物; 主食: *staples like flour and rice* 面粉和大米等主食 **4** *technical* the main product that is produced in a country【术语】〔一国的〕主要产品: *Bananas and sugar are the staples of Jamaica.* 香蕉和糖是牙买加的主要产品。

staple² *v* [T] to fasten two or more things together with a staple 用订书钉把…订住

staple³ *adj* [only before noun 仅用于名词前] **1** forming the greatest or most important part of something 主要的; 最重要的: *Oil is Nigeria's staple export.* 石油是尼日利亚的主要出口产品。| *a staple ingredient of comedy* 喜剧最重要的成分 **2 staple diet** **a)** the food that you normally eat 主食: *They live on a staple diet of rice and vegetables.* 他们以大米和蔬菜为主食。**b)** something that is always being produced, seen, bought etc 经常制作[看到, 购买等]的东西: *television's staple diet of soap operas and quiz shows* 以肥皂剧和问答比赛为主的电视节目 **3** used all the time 常用的, 惯用的: *Marty's staple excuses* 马蒂惯用的借口

staple gun /'·· ·/ *n* [C] a tool used for putting strong staples into walls U形钉枪

sta·pler /ˋsteplɚ; 'steɪplə/ *n* [C] a tool used for putting staples into paper 订书机

star¹ /stɑr; stɑː/ *n* [C]

1 ►IN THE SKY 在空中◄ a burning mass of gases in space that can be seen at night as a point of light in the sky 星; 恒星: *I lay on my back and looked up at the stars.* 我仰面躺着看天上的星星。—see also 另见 FALLING STAR, SHOOTING STAR

2 ►PERFORMER 表演者◄ **a)** a famous and successful performer in entertainment or sport〔娱乐或体育的〕明星, 名角: **film/movie star** *There were pictures of film stars all over the walls.* 墙上挂满了电影明星的照片。| **pop star** (=famous popular music singer) 流行歌星 | **big star** (=very famous performer) 大明星 *By the age of twenty she was already a big star.* 她20岁时就已经是大明星了。| **star quality** (=something that makes you seem special, and likely to be a star) 明星气质 | **rising star** (=someone who is becoming successful and famous) 崭露头角的明星, 新秀 *a rising star in the music world* 音乐界的后起之秀 **b)** someone who acts the part of the main character in a film or play〔电影或戏剧中的〕主角: *The star of his next movie was an unknown young actress.* 他下一部电影中的主角是一位名不见经传的年轻女演员。| **the star part** (=the most important part in a film or play)〔电影或戏剧中〕最主要的角色 | **child star** (=a child who has an important part in a film) 童星 | **the star of the show** (=the person who gives the best performance in a play, film etc)〔电影、戏剧等中〕表演最精彩的演员 —see also 另见 STAR²

3 ►SHAPE 形状◄ **a)** a shape with four or more points which is supposed to look like a star in the sky 星状, 星形: *A five-pointed star is called a pentagram.* 五个角的星称为五角星。—see picture at 参见 SHAPE[1] 图 **b)** a mark in this shape, used to draw attention to something written; ASTERISK 星号 **c)** a piece of cloth or metal in this shape, worn to show someone's rank or position〔表示级别或地位的〕星章

4 ▶**HOTELS/RESTAURANTS** 酒店/餐馆◀ a mark used in a system for judging the quality of hotels and restaurants〔评判酒店和餐馆质量等级的〕星（级）: **three-star/four-star/five-star** *a two-star bed and breakfast* 提供住宿和次日早餐的二星级旅馆

5 **the stars a)** *informal* a HOROSCOPE (=description of what will happen to you in the future) that is printed in newspapers or magazines【非正式】〔报纸或杂志上刊登的〕星象: **read your stars** *I never read my stars – I don't believe any of it anyway.* 我从来不看星象，反正我一点儿也不信这个。**b)** *literary* a force that controls what will happen in the future; FATE (2)【文】命运，运气: **written in the stars** (=decided by this) 命中注定的 —see also 另见 STAR-CROSSED

6 ▶**SUCCESSFUL PERSON** 成功的人◀ *informal* someone who is particularly successful at a job, course of study etc【非正式】〔在某工作、课程等中〕特别成功的人: *I was the star of my village because I won a place at the school in Nayoumi.* 我是我们村里的明星，因为我考上了在拿犹米的那所学校。| **a star player/performer/salesman etc** *the Academy's star pupil* 学院最优秀的学生 | **shining star** (=very successful person) 非常成功的人

7 **you're/she's a star!** *informal* used to say that someone is very good at something or thank someone for helping you【非正式】你/她（真是）太棒[太好]了！〔称赞某人或感谢某人帮助时使用〕

8 **star turn** the main or best performer or event in a performance 主角；最佳演员；主要[最精彩]节目: *Our star turn was a fire-eating act.* 我们最精彩的节目是吞火表演。

9 **star attraction** the most interesting person or thing, that most people want to see 最有吸引力的人[事物]

10 **see stars** to see flashes of light, especially because you have been hit on the head 眼冒金星〔尤指因头部被击所致〕: *I felt a little dizzy and could see stars.* 我觉得有点头晕，眼冒金星。

11 **have stars in your eyes** to imagine that something you want to do is much more exciting or attractive than it really is 充满不切实际的幻想 —see also 另见 STARRY-EYED

12 **four star (petrol)** *BrE* high quality petrol that has lead (LEAD[3] (1)) in it【英】高质量含铅汽油 —see also 另见 EVENING STAR, FIVE-STAR GENERAL, FOUR-STAR GENERAL, MORNING STAR, **guiding star** (GUIDING), **be born under a lucky/unlucky star** (BORN (10)), **reach for the stars** (REACH[1] (8)), **thank your lucky stars** (THANK (6))

star[2] **starred, starring** *v* **1** [I] to act the part of the main character in a film or play〔在电影或戏剧中〕担任主角；主演: [**+in**] *She will star in the Los Angeles production of 'Phantom' this year.* 今年她将担任在洛杉矶上演的《歌剧的幽灵》的主角。**2** [T] if a film or play stars someone, that person acts the part of the main character 由…担任主角；由…主演: *a film starring Meryl Streep* 由梅丽尔·斯特里普主演的电影 **3** **starring role** the most important acting part in a film, play etc〔电影、戏剧等中的〕主角 **4** to put an ASTERISK (=a star-shaped mark) next to something written 给…加上星号: *The starred items will be available from July.* 加星号的货品将于七月份起有售。

star·board /ˈstɑrˌbɔrd; ˈstɑːbəd/ *n* [U] the side of a ship or aircraft that is on your right when you are facing forwards〔船舶或飞机的〕右舷，右侧 —**starboard** *adj* —opposite 反义词 PORT (4)

starch[1] /stɑrtʃ; stɑːtʃ/ *n* **1** [U] a white substance that has no taste and forms an important part of foods such as grain, rice, and potatoes 淀粉 **2** [C,U] a food that contains this substance 含淀粉的食物: *Avoid fatty foods and starches.* 不要吃高脂肪和含淀粉的食物。**3** [U] a substance that is mixed with water and is used to make cloth stiff〔用于浆布的〕浆粉

starch[2] *v* [T] to make cloth stiff, using starch 给…上浆: *a starched white tablecloth* 浆洗过的白桌布

star cham·ber /ˌ· ˈ··/ *n* [C] a group of people that meets secretly and makes decisions that are important or judgements that are severe 星室法庭〔秘密地开会，并作出重要决定或重判的团体〕；专横暴虐的团体

starch·y /ˈstɑrtʃɪ; ˈstɑːtʃi/ *adj* **1** containing a lot of STARCH[1] (1) 含大量淀粉的: *starchy foods* 含大量淀粉的食物 **2** very formal and correct in your behaviour 古板的；拘谨的；生硬的: *Not knowing what to say or do he became stiff and starchy.* 他不知道说什么和做什么，显得古板而又拘谨。—**starchily** *adv* —**starchiness** *n* [U]

star-crossed /ˈ· ·/ *adj literary* star-crossed lovers can never be happy because their situation prevents them from being together【文】〔恋人〕命运不佳的，不幸的

star·dom /ˈstɑrdəm; ˈstɑːdəm/ *n* [U] the situation of being a famous performer 明星的地位: *Her triumphs were clouded by the loneliness of stardom.* 她成功的喜悦被做明星的孤独冲淡。| **shoot/rise to stardom** (=become famous very quickly) 迅速登上明星宝座

star·dust /ˈstɑrˌdʌst; ˈstɑːdʌst/ *n* [U] *literary* an imaginary magic substance like shiny powder【文】虚无缥缈之物〔想象中具有魔力的粉状闪光物〕

stare[1] /stɛr; steə/ *v* [I] **1** to look at something or someone for a long time without moving your eyes 凝视；盯着看: [**+out**] *Stop staring out of the window and do some work!* 别盯着窗外看了，快做点事吧！| [**+at**] *What are you staring at?* 你在盯着看什么呢？| **stare into space** (=look for a long time at nothing) 瞪着眼睛发愣，出神 —see 见 GAZE[1] (USAGE) **2** **be staring sb in the face a)** *informal* to be very clear and easy to see; be OBVIOUS【非正式】非常清楚而容易看见；明显的: *The solution is staring you in the face.* 解决办法就明摆在你面前。**b)** to seem impossible to avoid 看来无法避免: *Defeat was staring us in the face.* 看来我们输定了。—see also 另见 **stark staring mad** (STARK[2] (2))

stare sb **out** *BrE*【英】, **stare** sb **down** *AmE*【美】*phr v* [T] to look at someone for so long that they start to feel uncomfortable and look away 盯得〔某人〕不敢再对视

stare[2] *n* [C] a long steady look or a way of staring 盯视；凝视: *a disapproving stare* 不赞成的目光 | *She ignored the stares of everyone around her.* 她不理会周围所有人凝视的目光。| **hold sb's stare** (=not look away when someone is staring at you) 与某人对视

star·fish /ˈstɑrˌfɪʃ; ˈstɑːˌfɪʃ/ *n* [C] a flat sea animal that has five arms forming the shape of a star 海星

star·fruit /ˈstɑrˌfrut; ˈstɑːˌfruːt/ *n* [C] a pale green fruit that has a shape similar to a star 杨桃，五敛子

star·gaz·er /ˈstɑrˌgezɚ; ˈstɑːˌgeɪzə/ *n* [C] **1** someone who studies ASTRONOMY or ASTROLOGY 天文学家；占星家 **2** someone with ideas or plans that are impossible or not practical 空想家；不切实际的人 —**stargazing** *n* [U]

star jump /ˈ· ·/ *n* [C usually plural 一般用复数] *BrE* one of a series of exercise jumps that you do from a standing position with your arms and legs pointing out at each side; JUMPING JACK【英】星状跳跃，跳跃运动〔健身动作，从站立姿势起跳，四肢叉开〕

stark[1] /stɑrk; stɑːk/ *adj* **1** very simple and severe in appearance〔外表上〕简陋的；荒凉的: *In the cold dawn light the castle looked stark and forbidding.* 在黎明冰冷的光线下，城堡看上去荒凉而令人生畏。| *the stark beauty of the New Mexico desert* 新墨西哥沙漠的荒凉之美 **2** unpleasantly clear and impossible to avoid; HARSH 明摆着的；严峻的: **stark reality** *The film shows the stark realities of life in the slums.* 这部电影反映贫民窟里严酷的生活现实。| **stark choice** *The Tories are facing a stark choice between cutting the deficit and maintaining benefits.* 保守党面临着减少赤字或保留救济金的困难选择。**3** [only before noun 仅用于名词前] complete; total 完全的；全然的；十足的: *Jerry's eyes were wide open with a look of stark terror.* 杰里的眼睛睁得很大，神色极度恐惧。| **in stark contrast to** (=completely opposite) 与…形成鲜明对照 *Their poverty was in stark contrast to the luxury all around them.* 他们的贫穷与周围的奢华形成了鲜明的对照。—**starkly** *adv* —**starkness** *n* [U]

stark[2] *adv* **1** **stark naked** *informal* not wearing any clothes at all; completely NAKED【非正式】一丝不挂，赤裸裸 **2** **stark raving mad** also 又作 **stark staring mad** *BrE* completely crazy【英】完全疯了的

stark·ers /ˈstɑrkɚz; ˈstɑːkəz/ *adj* [not before noun 不用于名词前] *BrE informal* not wearing any clothes; NAKED【英，非正式】一丝不挂的，赤裸裸的

star·less /ˈstɑrlɪs; ˈstɑːləs/ *adj* with no stars showing in the sky 无星的；没有星光的

star·let /ˈstɑrlɪt; ˈstɑːlɪ̵t/ *n* [C] a young actress who plays small parts in films and is hoping to become famous 常演配角而渴望成名的年轻女演员

star·light /ˈstɑrˌlaɪt; ˈstɑːlaɪt/ *n* [U] the light that comes from the stars, often considered to be romantic 星光〔常被认为有浪漫气息〕

star·ling /ˈstɑrlɪŋ; ˈstɑːlɪŋ/ *n* [C] a greenish black bird that is very common in Europe（紫翅）椋鸟〔常见于欧洲〕

star·lit /ˈstɑrˌlɪt; ˈstɑːˌlɪt/ *adj literary* made brighter by stars【文】星光照耀的: *a starlit night* 星光照耀的夜晚

Star of Beth·le·hem, the /ˌ· · ˈ···/ the star which, in the Bible, appeared in the sky when Jesus was born, to show the way to the place of his birth 伯利恒之星，圣诞星〔据《圣经》记载，这颗星在耶稣降生时出现在天空，是前往其出生地的引路之星〕

Star of Da·vid /ˌstɑr əv ˈdevɪd; ˌstɑːr əv ˈdeɪvɪ̵d/ *n* [C usually singular 一般用单数] a star with six points that is strongly

connected with Judaism or the state of Israel 大卫之星〔为犹太教和以色列国标志的六角星〕

Starr /stɑr; stɑː/, **Rin·go** /ˈrɪŋgo; ˈrɪŋgəʊ/ (1940-) a British musician who played the drums in the pop band The Beatles 斯塔尔〔(1940-), 英国音乐人。曾任流行乐队甲壳虫乐队的鼓手〕

Starr Re·port, the /ˌ· ˈ··/ a very long report written in 1998 by Kenneth Starr, the lawyer responsible for finding out about the relationship between President Bill Clinton and Monica Lewinsky and whether the President had lied in order to hide the relationship. The report was made available on the Internet for anyone to read.《斯塔尔报告》〔肯尼斯·斯塔尔 1998 年起草的一份长篇报告。斯塔尔是一名律师, 负责调查克林顿总统与莫尼卡·莱温斯基的两性关系, 并调查克林顿是否说谎隐瞒了真相。这份报告被上传至互联网, 供大众阅览〕

star·ry /ˈstɑrɪ; ˈstɑːri/ *adj* having many stars 布满星星的: *a starry winter sky* 满天星斗的冬夜

starry-eyed /ˌ·· ˈ·◂/ *adj informal* happy and hopeful about things in a way that is silly or UNREALISTIC【非正式】过分乐观的; 不切实际的: *a starry-eyed optimist* 不切实际的乐天派

Stars and Bars, the /ˌ·· ˈ·/ the Confederate flag 星杠旗, 邦联旗〔美国南北战争时期南部邦联政府的旗帜〕

Stars and Stripes /ˌ·· ˈ·/ *n* [singular] *AmE* the flag of the US【美】星条旗, 美国国旗

CULTURAL NOTE 文化注释

There are 50 stars on the US flag to represent the 50 states in the US, and there are 13 STRIPEs to represent the 13 original colonies (COLONY) that became the first states of the US. In the past, when there were fewer states, there were fewer stars. 美国国旗上有50颗星, 分别代表美国的50个州。此外国旗上还有13个条分别代表原先的13个殖民地, 这些殖民地成为美国最早的13个州。过去因为州的数目较少, 国旗上星的数目也相应较少。—see Cultural Note at FLAG 见 FLAG 文化注释

Star·ship En·ter·prise /ˌstɑrʃɪp ˈɛntəpraɪz; ˌstɑːʃɪp ˈentəpraɪz/ the name of the spaceship in the television show *Star Trek* "进取"号飞船〔电视剧《星际旅行》中太空船的名称〕

star sign /ˈ· ·/ *n* [C] one of the twelve signs of the ZODIAC (=the system that uses people's birth dates to say what will happen to them in the future)〔黄道十二宫之一的〕宫; 星座

Star-Span·gled Ban·ner /ˌ· ·· ˈ··/ *n* [singular] **1** the NATIONAL ANTHEM (=national song) of the US《星条旗永不落》,《星条旗之歌》〔美国国歌〕 **2** *AmE literary* the flag of the US【美, 文】星条旗, 美国国旗

CULTURAL NOTE 文化注释

The Star-Spangled Banner is typically sung at the beginning of a professional sports event in the US, such as a baseball or an American football game. People are expected to stand up, remove their hats, and put their right hand over their hearts while the song is being sung in order to show respect and support for the US. Some people dislike this song, because it is about war and is difficult to sing. These people think a song such as *America the Beautiful* would be a better national anthem. 在美国, 每逢棒球和美式橄榄球等职业比赛开始, 就要演唱《星条旗永不落》这首歌。歌声唱起时, 人们要起立、脱帽、将右手放在胸前, 以此表示对美国的崇敬和支持。有人不喜欢这首歌, 认为它与战争有关并且很难唱。他们认为像《美丽的亚美利加》这样的歌用作国歌更好。

star-stud·ded /ˈ· ˌ··/ *adj* including many famous performers 明星云集的: *a star-studded cast* 明星云集的演员阵容

START /stɑrt; stɑːt/ Strategic Arms Reduction Talks; talks between the US and the former Soviet Union, which aimed to reach agreement about reducing the number of NUCLEAR weapons that each country kept. Two START Treaties (=official agreements) were signed, START I (1991) and START II (1993), in which each country promised to destroy several types of nuclear weapons. 削减战略武器会谈〔美国和前苏联之间举行的会谈, 旨在就削减核武器数量问题达成一致。双方先后签署过两个条约, 即《削减战略武器条约 I》(1991) 和《削减战略武器条约 II》(1993)。双方在条约中均承诺销毁若干种核武器〕

S2 W2 **start¹** /stɑrt; stɑːt/ *v*

1 ▶BEGIN DOING STH 开始做某事◀ [I,T] to begin doing something 开始〔做某事〕: **start doing sth** *I've just started learning German.* 我刚开始学德语。| *We'd better start getting dressed soon.* 我们最好赶快穿好衣服。| **start to do sth** *When Tom heard this he started to laugh uncontrollably.* 汤姆在听到这事时, 忍不住笑了起来。| *Things started to go wrong after we reached Cairo.* 我们到达开罗后, 情况开始不对劲了。| *Damn! It's just started to rain.* 该死! 开始下雨了。| **start sth** *Haven't you started that book yet?* 你开始读那本书了没有? | *There was so much to do we didn't know where to start.* 要做的事情太多了, 我们不知道从哪里开始。| *Do start,* (=begin to eat a meal) *or it'll go cold.* 开始吃吧, 不然要凉了。| **[+from]** *Starting from point A draw a straight line down to point B.* 从A点画一条直线至B点。| **start (off) with** (=deal with something as the first part of an activity) 从…开始做起 *Decorating the place was going to be a major job, and we decided to start with the kitchen.* 装修这个地方是项大工程, 我们决定先从厨房开始做起。| **start (off) by doing** *Start by melting the butter in the frying pan.* 先在平底煎锅里把黄油融化。| **start again** (=begin doing something again) 又开始做某事 *Billy was afraid to say anything in case she started crying again.* 比利怕她又哭起来, 所以什么也不敢说。| **get started** (=start doing something, especially when you have not been able to do anything yet, or have been lazy) 开始干; 着手做 *We'd better get started if we want to finish this job by midday.* 我们要想在中午前完成这项工作, 最好现在就开始干。| **start from scratch** (=start a job or activity from the beginning) 从头开始〔做某事〕 *They had to start from scratch redecorating the house.* 他们不得不从头开始, 重新装修房子。| **start afresh/anew** (=start doing something again better or differently) 重新开始 *Lisa saw the new job as a chance to start afresh.* 莉莎把这个新工作当做一次重新开始的机会。—see graph at 参见 COMMENCE 图表

2 ▶BEGIN HAPPENING 开始发生◀ also 又作 **start off** [I,T] to begin happening or make something begin happening (使) 开始发生: *Do you know what time the match starts?* 你知道比赛几点钟开始吗? | **[+in]** *The marathon race starts in the city centre.* 马拉松赛跑从市中心出发。| **start sth** *The avalanche was started by a rock fall on the higher slopes.* 雪崩是由高坡上一块石头滚落引起的。| **start sb doing sth** *The conversation he overheard had started him thinking.* 他无意中听到的那段对话令他沉思起来。| **start with** *The festivities started with a huge fireworks display.* 庆祝活动一开始是大型烟花表演。| **starting from now/tomorrow/next week etc** *You have two minutes to answer the following questions starting from now.* 从现在开始, 你有两分钟时间回答下列问题。| **get started** (=start happening, especially after a delay)〔尤指在延误后〕开始 *The match finally got started at 2.30 p.m.* 比赛最终于下午2时30分开始。

3 to start with a) used when talking about the beginning of a situation, especially when it changes later 起初, 开始时〔尤指情况后来发生变化〕: *I felt nervous to start with, but soon began to relax.* 我起初觉得有点紧张, 但很快就开始放松了。**b)** used to emphasize the first of a list of facts or opinions you are stating 首先, 第一〔用于强调所叙述的一系列事实、观点等中的第一条〕: *We're not going on holiday this year; to start with we haven't got the money and then there's still a lot we need to do on the house.* 我们今年不去度假了, 首先我们没有钱, 其次这房子还有很多活要干。—see 见 FIRSTLY (USAGE)

4 ▶PERIOD OF TIME 一段时间◀ [I always+adv/prep, T always+adv/prep] if a fixed period of time starts in a certain way, or you start it in a certain way, it begins in that way 以某种方式开始: **[+badly/well]** *The season started badly for United when they lost their first three matches.* 赛季一开始联队就出师不利, 前三场比赛都输掉了。| **start sth with/on etc** *Jerome always starts the day with a cup of coffee and a cigarette.* 杰尔姆每天起来总要来一杯咖啡和一根香烟。

5 be back where you started to have failed to do what you have been trying to do 试图做某事失败; 白费劲: *Liz hasn't got his address, so we're back where we started.* 利兹没有他的地址, 所以我们是在白费工夫。

6 ▶JOB/SCHOOL 工作/学校◀ [I,T] to begin a new job, or to begin going to school, college etc 开始 (新的工作); 开始 (上学): *The sales manager phoned this morning to ask if I could start next week.* 销售经理今天上午来电话, 问我能否下周上班。| **start school/college/work** *Simon's starting school in September.* 西蒙9月份就要开始上学了。

7 ▶JOURNEY 旅程, 旅行◀ also 又作 **start off/out** [I] to begin a journey 启程, 动身, 出发: *We'll have to start early to get to Edinburgh by midday.* 我们必须早早出发, 才能在中午之前到达爱丁堡。| **[+from]** *We start out from Harlow at seven.* 我们7点钟从哈洛起程。

8 ▶LIFE/PROFESSION 生活/职业◀ also 又作 **start off/out** [I always+adv/prep, T always+adv/prep] to begin your life or profession in a certain way 开始生活; 开始立业: **[+as/in]** *Rob*

started off as a salesman and now he's managing director. 罗布从一名推销员开始做起，现在成了总经理。| **start sth** *We started married life living in a caravan.* 我们刚结婚时住在一辆旅行拖车里。

9 ▶ROAD/RIVER 道路/河流◀ [I always+adv/prep] if a river, road etc starts somewhere it begins in that place 起源，起始：**[+in/at]** *The Mississippi starts in Minnesota.* 密西西比河发源于明尼苏达州。

10 ▶CAR 汽车◀ also 又作 **start up** [I,T] if you start a car or engine or if it starts, it begins to work（使）发动，（使）开始运作，启动：*The car wouldn't start this morning.* 今天早上这辆车发动不起来。| **get the car/engine started** *He couldn't get his motorbike started.* 他的摩托车发动不起来。

11 ▶PRICES 价格◀ [I always+adv/prep] if prices start at or from a particular figure, that is the lowest figure at which you can get or buy something〔价格等〕自…起：**[+at/from]** *Prices for bed and breakfast start at £15 a night.* 宿夜加次日早餐的价钱由15英镑起。

12 ▶BUSINESS/CLUB 公司/俱乐部◀ also 又作 **start up** [T] to make something begin to exist 创办；建立：*Sally decided to start up a club for single mums in the neighbourhood.* 萨莉决定在街区成立一个单亲妈妈俱乐部。| **start a business/company/firm** *Bruno started his own plumbing business when he was only 24.* 布鲁诺年仅24岁时就创办了自己的管道设备公司。

13 start a family to have your first baby 生第一个孩子：*At 34 she thought it was about time they started a family.* 34岁那年，她觉得他们应该生个孩子了。

14 start a fire to deliberately cause a fire 点火，生火

15 start a fight/argument etc to deliberately cause a fight, argument etc 挑起打斗/争吵等：*Don't let him drink too much – he'll only start a fight with someone.* 别让他喝太多的酒，不然他只会找人寻衅打架。

16 start a rumour to tell other people something, usually something unpleasant or untrue 造谣，散布流言：*She wondered who could have started such a vicious rumour.* 她想知道是谁在散布如此恶毒的谣言。

17 Don't (you) start! *BrE spoken* used to tell someone to stop complaining, arguing or annoying you【英口】别招人烦！〔用于叫某人停止抱怨、争吵或骚扰〕：*"Mum, I don't like this ice-cream." "Oh, don't you start!"* "妈妈，我不喜欢这冰淇淋。" "哦，你别招我厌烦了！"

18 you started it! *spoken* used to tell someone that they caused an argument or problem【口】是你挑起来的！〔用于表示争论或问题是某人引起的〕：*"Stop arguing with me Dave!" "It was you who started it."* "戴夫，别再跟我争论了！" "这是你先挑起的。"

19 start something/anything to begin causing trouble 惹麻烦，闯祸：*I was worried in case my mate Ronnie started anything.* 我担心万一我的朋友龙尼惹出麻烦。

20 ▶MOVE SUDDENLY 突然移动◀ [I] to move your body suddenly, especially because you are surprised or afraid〔尤指因吃惊或害怕〕突然移动；惊起，吓一跳：*A loud knock at the door made her start.* 巨大的敲门声把她吓了一跳。| **[+from]** *Emma started from her chair and rushed to the window.* 埃玛从椅子上惊跳起来，向窗口冲去。

21 ▶LIQUID 液体◀ [I always+adv/prep] if a liquid or substance starts from somewhere, it comes out quickly〔液体等〕涌出；突然出现：*Blood started from the wound.* 血从伤口涌出。

22 start young to begin doing something when you are young 很年轻就开始（做某事）：*"Marcia's only ten and she's already got a boyfriend." "Yes, they start young nowadays!"* "马西娅才10岁就已经有男朋友了。" "是啊，现在的孩子早恋！"

start off *phr v* **1** [I,T] to begin happening or make something begin happening（使）开始：**start sth ↔ off** *Richard started the discussion off by telling us about his experiences in Africa.* 理查德向我们讲述了他在非洲的经历，作为讨论的开场白。| *The match started off at a fast and furious pace.* 比赛一开始节奏急速，战况激烈。**2** [I] to begin a journey 起程，动身：*What time will we have to start off in the morning?* 我们必须早上几点钟动身？**3** [I] to move in a particular direction 朝〔某方向〕移动：*The bus started off slowly up the road.* 公共汽车慢慢地上路了。**4** [T **start** sb ↔ **off**] to help someone begin an activity 帮助〔某人〕开始：*I tried to start the children off by giving them ideas for things to write about.* 我给孩子们提供一些题材，帮助他们动笔。**5** [T **start** sb ↔ **off**] *informal* to make someone get angry, or start laughing, by saying something【非正式】〔说某事〕使〔某人〕生气[发笑]：*Don't mention Steve's name to Jenny; it'll only start her off!* 别跟珍妮提起史蒂夫的名字，那只会惹她生气！| **start sb off doing sth** *David's remarks started the girls off giggling.* 戴维的话令女孩们咯咯地笑了起来。

start sb **on** sth *phr v* [T] to make someone start doing something regularly, especially because it will be good for them 使开始有规则地做〔尤指做对某人有益的事〕：*We started Gemma on solid foods when she was four months old.* 杰玛四个月大的时候，我们开始喂她吃固体食物。

start on sth *phr v* [T] to begin doing something or using something 开始做；开始使用：*Let's start on the wine shall we?* 我们开始喝酒好吗？| *I guess it's time we started on the packing.* 我想我们该开始收拾行李了。

start on at sb *phr v* [T] to begin criticizing someone or complaining to them about something 开始批评，开始抱怨：*Ray's wife started on at him about how he spent too much time in the pub.* 雷的太太开始抱怨他怎么花那么多的时间泡酒吧。

start over *phr v* [I] *AmE* to start doing something again from the beginning, especially because you want to do it better【美】重新开始，从头做起：*If you make a mistake when you're keying, just press delete and start over.* 如果键盘输入出错，就按删除键重新开始。

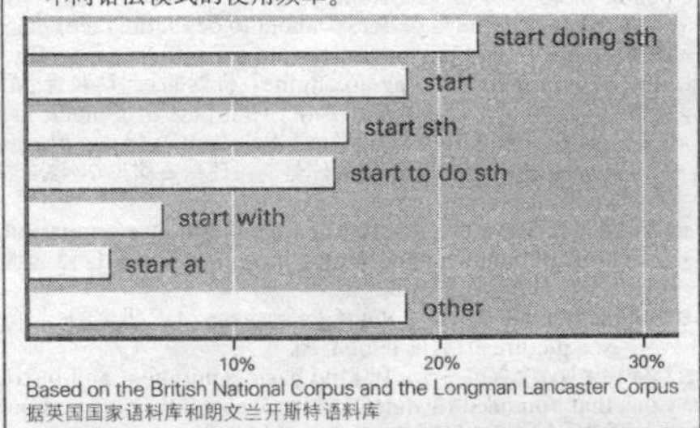

start² *n*

S2 W3

1 ▶OF AN ACTIVITY/EVENT 用于活动/事件◀ [C usually singular 一般用单数] the beginning of an activity or event or the point at which it starts to develop〔活动或事件的〕开始，开端；起始点：**[+of]** *This fighting marked the start of more widespread civil unrest.* 这场战斗标志着更广泛的国内动荡的开始。| *We arrived late and missed the start of the film.* 我们迟到了，错过了电影的开头。| **(right) from the start** *We've had problems with this project right from the start.* 这个项目从刚一开始起我们就遇到许多难题。| **from start to finish** *The concert was a fiasco from start to finish.* 这场音乐会从头到尾都很失败。| **get off to a good/bad start** (=begin well or badly) 开始时很好/不好 *Chelsea got off to a good start, beating their opponents 5-0.* 切尔西队开局顺利，以5:0击败对手。

2 ▶OF A PERIOD OF TIME 一段时间的◀ [C usually singular 一般用单数] the beginning of a fixed period of time 一段时间的开始：**the start of the year/day/season** *The start of the season was marred by the awful weather.* 这个季节一开始就给糟糕的天气破坏了。| **get off to a good/bad start** *The day got off to a bad start when I missed the train.* 我那天误了火车，从一开始就不顺利。

3 make a start (on sth) to begin doing something 着手〔做某事〕：*I guess it's time I made a start on the housework.* 我想我该着手做家务了。

4 ▶SPORT 体育运动◀ the start the place where a race begins〔比赛的〕起点；起跑线：*The horses were all lined up at the start.* 马匹在起跑线上各就各位。

5 ▶ADVANTAGE 优势◀ [C usually singular 一般用单数] a situation in which you have an advantage over other people 优势地位；有利条件：*George was grateful to his parents for the start they'd given him.* 乔治感谢父母为他提供有利条件。| **a start in life** (=things that will help you to succeed in life) 人生中有利于成功的优势 *Naturally we want to give our kids the best possible start in life.* 当然，我们想给孩子们尽可能好的人生起步条件。

6 ▶IN A RACE/COMPETITION 在赛跑/比赛中◀ [C usually singular 一般用单数] the amount of time or space by which one person is ahead of another, especially in a race or competition〔尤指在赛跑或比赛中的〕抢先之时间[距离]：*They decided to give the younger boys a sixty metre start.* 他们决定让那些年龄小的男孩先跑60米。| **[+on]** *The prisoners had a three hour start on their pursuers.* 囚犯们逃跑了三个小时后，追捕的人才开始追。

7 ►SUDDEN MOVEMENT 突然移动◄ [singular] a sudden movement of the body, usually caused by fear or surprise〔因恐惧或吃惊〕突然移动; 惊起: **with a start** *Ted woke up with a start and felt for the light switch.* 特德猛然惊醒过来, 摸索着找电灯开关。| **give you a start** (=frighten or surprise you) 令某人吃了一惊 *The sound of footsteps gave me quite a start.* 脚步声吓了我一大跳。

8 for a start used to emphasize the first of a list of facts or opinions you are stating 首先, 第一〔用于强调一系列事实或观点的第一条〕: *Vincent should never have been picked for the team; for a start he has not had enough experience.* 文森特根本就不该入选球队, 首先他经验不足。—see also 另见 FALSE START, **in/by fits and starts** (FIT[3] (6))

start·er /ˈstɑrtɚ; ˈstɑːtə/ *n* [C] **1** a person, horse, car etc that is in a race when it starts〔赛跑、赛马、赛车等的〕参赛者[马、汽车等]: *Of the eight starters, only three finished the race.* 参赛的八名选手中, 只有三名赛完全程。**2 for starters** *informal* a phrase meaning to begin with, used to tell someone what should be done or said first【非正式】首先, 第一, 作为开头: *Well, for starters, you'd better get an application form.* 哦, 首先, 你最好拿一张申请表。**3** someone who gives the signal for a race to begin〔赛跑的〕发令员: *The starter fired his gun.* 发令员鸣枪发令。| **under starter's orders** (=about to begin the race) 准备起跑 **4** a piece of equipment for starting a machine, especially an electric motor for starting an engine〔机器的〕起动装置〔尤指使发动机起动的电动机〕 **5** *BrE* the first part of a meal; APPETIZER【英】〔一顿饭的〕第一道菜, 开胃小吃: *Would you like soup or melon as a starter?* 第一道菜你是要汤还是要甜瓜? —see also 另见 NONSTARTER, SELF-STARTER

starter home /ˈ· · ·/ *n* [C] *BrE* a small house or apartment bought by people who are buying their first home【英】起步房〔第一次置业者购买的小房子或小公寓〕

starter mo·tor /ˈ· ·, · ·/ *n* [C] a STARTER (4)〔机器的〕起动装置 —see picture at 参见 ENGINE 图

starter pack /ˈ· · ·/ *n* [C] the basic equipment and instructions that you need to start working, especially on a computer〔尤指电脑操作的〕启动包, 基础设备和指令

start·ing block /ˈ· · ·/ *n* [C] one of a pair of blocks fixed to the ground that a runner pushes their feet against at the start of a race 起跑器

starting gate /ˈ· · ·/ *n* [C] a gate or pair of gates that open to allow a horse or dog through at the start of a race〔赛马或赛狗比赛的〕起跑闸

starting price /ˈ· · ·/ *n* [C] the last PRICE (=amount of money that is returned for money risked) that is offered just before a horse or dog race begins〔赛马或赛狗的〕临赛赔率, 赌率

start·le /ˈstɑrtl; ˈstɑːtl/ *v* [T] to make someone suddenly surprised or slightly shocked 使[某人]吃惊; 吓[某人]一跳: *You startled me! I didn't hear you come in.* 你吓了我一跳! 我没有听见你进来。| **startled to see/hear/learn etc** *I was startled to see Amanda there.* 我看到阿曼达在那里, 吃了一惊。

start·ling /ˈstɑrtlɪŋ; ˈstɑːtlɪŋ/ *adj* very unusual or surprising 惊人的; 令人震惊的: *Paddy's words had a startling effect on the children.* 帕迪的话在孩子们身上产生了惊人的效果。—**startlingly** *adv*: *startlingly pale* 苍白得惊人

Star Trek /ˈ· ,·/ a very popular US science fiction television programme of the 1960s about the adventures of a group of people travelling through space in the Starship Enterprise. The characters include Captain Kirk, Scotty, and Mr Spock. There are several well-known phrases from the programme, such as "Space – the final frontier", "to boldly go where no man has gone before", and "Beam me up, Scotty". There have been several new programmes based on the original idea, including *Star Trek – The Next Generation, Star Trek – Deep Space Nine, Star Trek – Voyager*, and *Enterprise*. There have also been several successful films based on the *Star Trek* stories.《星际旅行》〔一部 20 世纪 60 年代备受欢迎的美国系列科幻电视剧。讲述柯克船长、斯科蒂、斯波克先生等人乘坐"进取"号星际飞船遨游太空的历险故事。片中不少台词为人们所熟知, 如"太空 —— 最后的边疆"、"勇敢驶向人迹未至的领域"、"斯科蒂, 快把我送走"。根据原创意还制作了几部新剧, 其中包括《星际旅行: 银河飞龙》、《星际旅行: 银河前哨》、《星际旅行: 航海家号》、《星际旅行: 进取号》等。此外, 还有数部优秀影片也是以《星际旅行》故事为蓝本拍摄的〕—see 另见 KLINGON

start-up /ˈ· ·/ *adj* start-up costs are connected with beginning and developing a new business 创业时的〔成本〕; 起始(阶段)的: *a start-up budget of $90,000* 九万美元的创业预算

starv·a·tion /stɑrˈveʃən; stɑːˈveɪʃən/ *n* **1** [U] suffering or death caused by lack of food 挨饿, 饥饿; 饿死: *people dying of starvation in the famine* 在饥荒中饿得濒临死亡的人 **2 starvation diet** *informal* very little food【非正式】极少量的食物 **3 starvation wages** extremely low wages 挨饿工资, 极低的工资

starve /stɑrv; stɑːv/ *v* [I,T] **1** to suffer or die because you do not have enough to eat, or to make someone else do this (使)挨饿; (使)饿死: *Thousands of people will starve if food doesn't reach the stricken city.* 如果食物不能运到那座受灾的城市, 数以千计的人就要饿死。| **starve sth** *The dog looked like it had been starved.* 这只狗看上去像是被饿坏了。| **starve to death** (=die from lack of food) 饿死 *They'll either die from the cold or starve to death.* 他们要么将被冻死, 要么将被饿死。**2** to not give or not be given something very important, for example love or money, with harmful results〔使某人〕得不到某物〈如爱或钱〉而受苦; 缺乏: [+of] *The schools are understaffed and starved of funds.* 学校师资不足, 资金匮乏。| **be starved for sth** *AmE* (=not get any at all)【美】得不到某物 *That poor kid's just starved for attention.* 那个可怜的孩子极需关注。**3 be starving** also 又作 **be starved** *especially AmE spoken*【尤美, 口】to be very hungry 感觉很饿, 饿极了: *You must be starving! Come and eat lunch.* 你肯定饿坏了! 快来吃午饭吧。

starve sb **into** *phr v* [T] to force someone to do something, by preventing them from getting food or money 以饥饿迫使…, 使〔某人〕饿得只好做〔某事〕: *The miners were starved into submission.* 矿工们被饿得只好屈服。

starve sb **out** *phr v* [T] to force someone to leave a place by preventing them from getting food 使〔某人〕挨饿而被迫离开〔某处〕: *If we can't blast them out, we'll starve them out.* 如果不能把他们炸出来, 我们就把他们饿出来。

starve·ling /ˈstɑrvlɪŋ; ˈstɑːvlɪŋ/ *n* [C] *literary* a person or animal that is thin and unhealthy from lack of food【文】〔因饥饿而〕瘦弱不堪的人[动物]

starving /ˈstɑrvɪŋ; ˈstɑːvɪŋ/ *adj* **1** so hungry that you will die soon if you do not eat 饥饿的, 挨饿的: *pictures of starving children* 饥饿儿童的照片 | **the starving** (=people who are starving) 饥民 **2** [not before noun 不用于名词前] *spoken* very hungry【口】很饿的: *Can we get something to eat – I'm absolutely starving.* 我们弄点吃的吧, 我饿极了。

Star Wars[1] /,· ˈ·/ an informal name for SDI 星球大战计划〔战略防御计划的俗称〕

Star Wars[2] (1977) a very popular US film made by George Lucas, about people in the future who live in a distant part of the universe. The film describes the battles between the forces led by Luke Skywalker and those led by the evil Darth Vader. The good characters in the film are helped and protected by a magic power called 'the Force'. Other films show what happened both before and after the action of this story.《星球大战》〔(1977), 一部备受欢迎的美国影片。由乔治·卢卡斯执导。影片描写居住在宇宙深处的未来人的故事, 讲述分别由天行者路克和邪恶的达斯·维达统领的两支力量之间的较量。正面人物得到一种名为"原力"的神奇力量的帮助和保护。《星球大战》系列的其他电影多为此故事的前传或续集〕

stash[1] /stæʃ; stæʃ/ *v* [T always+adv/prep] *informal* to store something in a safe, often secret, place【非正式】储藏, 存放; 藏匿: **stash sth away** *He has money stashed away in the Bahamas.* 他把钱藏在巴哈马。| [+in/under] *You can stash your gear in here.* 你可以把你的工具存放在这里。

stash[2] *n* [C] *informal* an amount of something that is kept in a secret place【非正式】隐藏的东西: [+of] *a stash of drugs* 藏匿的一批毒品

Sta·si /ˈstɑzɪ; ˈstɑːzi/ the secret government police of the former East Germany. The Stasi secretly watched ordinary citizens and collected information about them for the government. 国家安全部〔前东德政府的秘密警察组织。负责秘密监视普通百姓, 收集他们的情况并向政府汇报〕

state[1] /stet; steɪt/ *n* 

1 ►CONDITION 状况◄ [C] the mental, emotional, or physical condition that someone or something is in at a particular time 状况, 状态; 情况, 情形: *Frankly I wouldn't trust his emotional state right now.* 坦白地说, 我不相信他目前的情绪状态。| *Water exists in three states: liquid, gaseous, and solid.* 水有三种状态: 液态、气态和固态。| **in a bad/good etc state** *The roads are in a terrible state after the severe winter weather.* 严冬过后, 公路的路面情况极差。| [+of] *The driver was in a state of shock.* 司机处于休克状态。| **not in a fit state to do sth** (=not healthy enough or in a good enough condition) 因健康状况不佳而不适宜做某事 *David's in no fit state to go out yet.* 戴维健康状况不佳, 仍不适宜外出。| **state of mind** (=the way you feel) 思想状态; 心情 *Ames' dismissal had left him in a distressed state of mind.* 埃姆斯因被解雇而心烦意乱。| **be in a good/bad state of**

repair (=not need repairing, or need repairing) 维修良好/亟待修葺 *The house we're buying is in a good state of repair.* 我们要买的房子维修得很好。| **a state of war** (=officially fighting another country) 战争[交战]状态 —see also 另见 STATE OF EMERGENCY

2 ▶GOVERNMENT 政府◀ also 又作 **State** [singular,U] the government or political organization of a country 国家, 政府: *If elected, they want to cut back the powers of the state.* 如果当选, 他们要削减政府的权力。| *The State has allocated special funds for the emergency.* 国家已拨出专款应付紧急状况。| **state employees/property/regulations etc** *limits on salary increases for state workers* 对政府职员加薪的限制 | **state-owned/state-funded/state-subsidized etc** (=owned, paid for etc by the government) 国有的/政府投资的/政府补贴的 *a state-funded community housing project* 政府资助的社区住房项目 | **matters of state** (=the business of the government) 国家大事 —see also 另见 POLICE STATE, WELFARE STATE —see 见 RACE[1] (USAGE)

3 ▶A COUNTRY 国家◀ [C] a country considered as a political organization〔作为政治组织的〕国家: **democratic/totalitarian/one-party state** (=with that type of government) 民主/极权主义/一党制的国家 | **member state** (=a country belonging to an international organization) 成员国, 会员国 *NATO's member states* 北约成员国 —see 见 RACE[1] (USAGE)

4 ▶PART OF A COUNTRY 国家的一部分◀ also 又作 **State** [C] one of the areas with limited law-making powers that together make up a country controlled by a central government 州; 邦: *Queensland is one of the states of Australia.* 昆士兰是澳大利亚的一个州。

5 ▶CEREMONY 仪式◀ [U] the grand, official ceremonies and events connected with governments and rulers〔与政府和统治者有关的〕盛礼; 隆重仪式: **state visit** (=official visit to another country) 国事访问 *the President's state visit to Moscow* 总统对莫斯科的国事访问 | **state occasions** (=special public events) 隆重的盛典 *Their band often plays at the White House on state occasions.* 他们的乐队经常在白宫的隆重盛典上演奏。| **in state** (=with a lot of comfort and public attention) 豪华地; 隆重地 *The empress travelled in state with all her ladies.* 女皇带着她所有的贵族夫人、小姐隆重出行。—see also 另见 **lie in state** (LIE[1] (12))

6 the States *spoken* a word meaning the US, used especially by someone when they are outside the US【口】美国〔尤在美国境外时使用〕: *Which part of the States would you suggest I should visit?* 你会建议我去美国的哪个地方?

7 be in a state/get into a state *spoken* to be or become very nervous, anxious, or excited【口】处于/陷入紧张[焦虑、兴奋]之中: *Mom and Dad were in a state when I didn't come home until very late.* 我很晚才回到家, 爸爸妈妈非常着急。

8 state of affairs a situation 情况, 局势, 事态: *I must say this is a very unsatisfactory state of affairs.* 必须承认, 目前的局势令人很不满意。

9 the state of play a) the position reached in an activity or process that has not finished yet〔某一活动或过程的〕当前进展情况: *What is the state of play in the current negotiations?* 目前谈判的最新情况怎么样? **b)** the score points that have been gained at one time in a sports game〔体育比赛在某一时刻的〕得分

state[2] *v* [T] **1** to formally give a piece of information or your opinion, especially by saying it clearly 陈述, 说明, 阐明: *Please state your name and address.* 请说出你的姓名和地址。| *The Government needs to clearly state its policy on UN intervention.* 政府需要就联合国干预问题清楚地阐明其政策。| [+(that)] *The witness stated that he had not seen the woman before.* 证人说他以前从未见过那个女人。| **state the obvious** (=say something that is completely unnecessary because it is already clear) 陈述明显的事实 **2** if a document, newspaper, ticket etc states information, it contains the information written clearly〔文件、报纸、票据等〕写明: *The price of the tickets is stated on them.* 票价清楚地印在票上。

state at·tor·ney /ˌ. ˈ.../ *n* [C] *AmE* a lawyer who represents the state in court cases【美】州检察官

state ben·e·fit /ˌ. ˈ.../ *n* [C,U] money given by the government in Britain to people who are poor, without a job, ill etc〔英国的〕政府救济金

state court /ˈ. ./ *n* [C] a court in the US which deals with legal cases that are concerned with state laws or a state's CONSTITUTION (1)〔美国的〕州法院

State De·part·ment /ˈ. .,../ *n* the American government department that deals with anything connected with foreign countries 美国国务院

state·hood /ˈstethud; ˈsteɪthʊd/ *n* [U] **1** the condition of being an independent nation 独立国家的地位 **2** the condition of being one of the states making up a nation, such as the US〔美国等国的〕州 [邦] 的地位

State·house /ˈstetˌhaus; ˈsteɪthaʊs/ *n* [C usually singular 一般用单数] the building where the lawyers in a US state do their work〔美国的〕州议会大厦

state·less /ˈstetlɪs; ˈsteɪtləs/ *adj* not officially being a citizen of any country 无国籍的: *All stateless individuals were presumed to be lawless vagabonds.* 所有无国籍的人均被推定是没有法律控制的流浪者。—**statelessness** *n* [U]

state line /ˌ. ˈ./ *n* [C] the line between two states in the US〔美国的〕州界线: *At the end of the trip we crossed the state line into California.* 行程最后, 我们跨过州界线进入加利福尼亚州。

state·ly /ˈstetlɪ; ˈsteɪtli/ *adj* **1** done slowly and with a lot of ceremony; formal 缓慢而庄严的; 正式的: *the stately progress of the procession* 队伍缓慢而庄严的行进 **2** impressive in style and size; NOBLE[1] (2) 雄伟的; 高贵的; 堂皇的: *the stately trees of the pine forest* 松树林里的参天大树

stately home /ˌ.. ˈ./ *n* [C] a large house in the countryside in Britain which has historical interest 豪华宅第〔英国有历史价值的乡村大宅〕

state·ment[1] /ˈstetmənt; ˈsteɪtmənt/ *n* **1** [C] something you say or write publicly or officially to let people know your intentions or opinions, or to record facts〔正式的〕陈述; 声明: *False statements on your tax form could land you in jail.* 在报税表上作不实申报会把你送进监狱的。| **make a statement (about)** *Before we begin, I'd like to make a statement about my involvement.* 在我们开始之前, 我想就我和此事的关系作一声明。| **issue a statement** (=write something that can be read in public or given to newspapers) 发表声明 *The Congressman issued a statement to the press.* 这位国会议员向新闻界发表了一份声明。| **get/take a statement** (=officially write down what someone says) 正式记录〔某人的〕陈述 | **sworn statement** (=that you officially declare to be true) 经宣誓的证词 **2** [C] a list showing amounts of money paid, received, owing etc and their total 结算表, 财务报表: *the company's annual financial statement to shareholders* 公司给股东的年度财务报表 | **bank statement** (=sent regularly from your bank about your account) 银行账户结算单 **3** [U] *formal* the act of expressing something in words【正式】措词; 表达: *The details of the agreement need more exact statement.* 这项协议中细节的措词需要更加准确。

S

statement[2] *v* [T] *BrE* if an education authority statements a child who has special educational needs, they give a school additional money to help teach that child【英】〔教育部门为有特殊教育需要的学生的所在学校〕提供额外教育经费 —**statemented** *adj*

Stat·en Is·land /ˈstætn̩ ˌaɪlənd; ˈstætn ˌaɪlənd/ an island in the US which is the smallest of the five BOROUGHS of New York City. A boat called the Staten Island FERRY takes passengers between Manhattan and Staten Island. Many people whose family origins are Italian or Irish live there. 斯塔滕岛〔美国一岛屿, 纽约市下属五个行政区中最小的一个。"斯塔滕岛"号渡轮往返于曼哈顿和斯塔滕岛之间运送乘客。岛上居民多为意大利或爱尔兰后裔〕

state of e·mer·gen·cy /ˌ. . .ˈ.../ *n* [C] a situation that a government officially declares to be very dangerous, and in which it uses special laws so that it can react very quickly 紧急状态: *There has been a call for the lifting of the state of emergency.* 有人呼吁解除紧急状态。

state-of-the-art /ˌ. . . ˈ.◀/ *adj* using the most modern and recently developed methods, materials, or knowledge 使用最先进技术的, 达到最新水平的: *state-of-the-art technology* 最先进的技术

State of the U·nion ad·dress, the /ˌ. . . ˈ.. . .ˈ./ a speech given in January each year by the President of the US to Congress and the nation, in which he gives his opinion of the condition of the country and explains his plans for the future 国情咨文〔美国总统每年1月向国会及全国发表的讲话。总统就美国国情提出见解, 并阐述未来的施政纲领〕

State O·pen·ing of Par·lia·ment, the /ˌ. ˌ.. . . ˈ.../ the occasion each year when the British queen or king officially opens the Parliament after its summer RECESS (=the period when Parliament is closed), and makes a speech saying what the government plans to do during the next year 议会开幕式〔英国议会每年夏季休会结束后举行的典礼, 由英国女王或国王正式宣布议会开幕, 并就政府来年的工作计划发表演说〕

state park /ˌ. ˈ./ *n* [C] a large park owned and managed by a US state, often in an area of natural beauty〔美国的〕州立公园

state·room /ˈstetˌrum; ˈsteɪtrʊm/ *n* [C] one of the large rooms in a palace〔宫殿里的〕豪华房间

States, the /stets; steɪts/ an informal name for the United States of America 美国〔美利坚合众国的非正式名称〕

State's at·tor·ney /ˌ· ˈ··/ *n* [C] *AmE* STATE ATTORNEY【美】州检察官

state school /ˈ· ,·/ *n* [C] a British school which receives money from the government and provides free education〔英国的〕公立学校

State's ev·i·dence /ˌ· ˈ···/ *n AmE*【美】**turn State's evidence** if a criminal turns State's evidence, they give information in a court of law about other criminals〔罪犯向法庭〕提供对同案犯不利的证据;〔罪犯〕作为污点证人指控同党; QUEEN'S EVIDENCE *BrE*【英】

State·side /ˈstetˌsaɪd; ˈsteɪtsaɪd/ *adj, adv AmE informal* a word meaning in the US or connected with the US, used by people when they are not in the US【美, 非正式】美国的; 在美国〔谈话者不在美国时使用〕: *When were you last Stateside?* 你最近什么时候在美国?

states·man /ˈstetsmən; ˈsteɪtsmən/ *n* [C] a political or government leader, especially one who is respected as being wise, honourable, and fair〔尤指贤明公正的〕政治家 —**statesmanlike** *adj*: *a statesmanlike performance in dealing with the crisis* 在处理危机中表现出的政治家风范 —**statesmanship** *n* [U]

state tax /ˈ· ·/ *n* [C,U] *AmE* a tax in the US that is paid to the state rather than to the central government【美】州税 —compare 比较 FEDERAL TAX

state troop·er /ˌ· ˈ··/ *n* [C] *AmE* a member of a police force that is controlled by one of the US state governments who works anywhere in that state【美】州警察

state u·ni·ver·si·ty /ˌ· ··ˈ····/ *n* [C] *AmE* a university in the US which receives money from a state to help pay its costs【美】州立大学

state·wide /ˈstetˈwaɪd; ˈsteɪtwaɪd/ *adj AmE* affecting an entire US state【美】影响全州的; 全州范围的: *Regulations will be local rather than statewide.* 规章将适用于当地, 而不是整个州。

stat·ic¹ /ˈstætɪk; ˈstætɪk/ *adj* not moving, changing, or developing, especially when movement or change would be good 不动的; 不变化的; 不发展的; 静（止）的: *Economists predict that house prices will stay static for a long period.* 经济学家预测, 房价将长期保持稳定。—compare 比较 DYNAMIC¹ (2,3)

static² *n* [U] **1** noise caused by electricity in the air that blocks or spoils the sound from radio or TV 静电干扰 **2** static electricity 静电 **3** *AmE informal* complaints or opposition to a plan, situation, or action【美, 非正式】〔对计划、状况或行动的〕抱怨, 指责, 反对: *His promotion has caused a lot of static.* 他的晋升招致很多人不满。—**statically** /-klɪ; -kli/ *adv*

static e·lec·tri·ci·ty /ˌ·· ··ˈ····/ *n* [U] electricity that is not flowing in a current, but collects on the surface of an object and gives you a small ELECTRIC SHOCK 静电

stat·ics /ˈstætɪks; ˈstætɪks/ *n* [U] the science dealing with the forces that produce balance in objects that are not moving 静力学 —compare 比较 **dynamics** (DYNAMIC² (1b))

sta·tion¹ /ˈsteʃən; ˈsteɪʃən/ *n*

1 ►TRAVEL 旅行◄ [C] **a)** a place where public vehicles regularly stop so that passengers can get on and off, goods can be loaded etc 车站: *the city bus station* 城市公共汽车站 | **train station** *especially AmE*【尤美】, **railway station** *especially BrE*【尤英】*It's time to meet Daddy at the train station.* 该去火车站接爸爸了。| **subway station** *AmE*【美】, **underground station** *BrE*【英】(=for trains that run under the ground) 地铁站 **b)** the building or buildings at such a place 车站建筑: *Is there a waiting room in the station?* 车站里有候车室吗? | *Grand Central Station* 中央火车站

2 ►ACTIVITY OR SERVICE 活动或服务◄ [C] a building or place that is a centre for a particular kind of service or activity 所; 站; 台; 局: **(police/fire) station** *You'll have to go with the officer to the station.* 你必须跟警察到警察局去。| **petrol station** *BrE*【英】, **gas station** *AmE*【美】(=where petrol is sold) 汽车加油站 | **polling station** (=where you vote in an election) 投票站 | **research station** *Frank spent six months at an arctic research station.* 弗兰克在一个北极研究所度过了六个月。—compare 比较 ACTION STATIONS

3 ►BROADCASTING 广播◄ [C] **a)** one of the many different signals you can receive on your radio or television, that a company broadcasts on〔电台或电视台的〕频率, 台: *Tom tuned the radio to a country music station.* 汤姆把收音机调到一个乡村音乐台。| **get/pick up a station** *I can't get many stations on this thing.* 这玩意能收到的频道不是很多。**b)** an organization which makes television or radio broadcasts, or the building where this is done 电视台; 广播电台: *That woman from the local TV station is here for your interview.* 当地电视台的那位女士来这里采访你。—compare 比较 CHANNEL¹ (1,2)

4 ►POSITION 位置◄ [C] a place where someone stands or sits in order to be ready to do something quickly if needed 岗位; 位置: *You're not to leave your station unless told.* 没有命令, 你不得离开岗位。

5 ►FARMING 畜牧业◄ [C] a large sheep or cattle farm in Australia or New Zealand〔澳大利亚或新西兰的〕大牧羊场; 大牧牛场

6 ►SOCIAL RANK 社会地位◄ [C] *old-fashioned* your position in society【过时】社会地位; 身份: **above your station** (=higher than your social rank) 高于自己的地位 *Don't get ideas above your station.* 不要有超越自己地位的想法。

7 ►MILITARY 军事◄ [C] a small military establishment 军队小型的驻地; 基地

8 ►SHIPS 船◄ [U] *technical* a ship's position in relation to others in a group, especially a military ship【术语】〔船只的, 尤指军舰的〕编队位置, 战位

station² *v* [T usually passive 一般用被动态] to put someone in a particular place in order to do a particular job or military duty 部署〔某人〕于; 安置; 使驻扎: *He's still in the Army, stationed in Washington.* 他仍在部队, 驻扎在华盛顿。| *Two guards were stationed at the back of the room.* 在房间的后面布置了两名卫兵。

sta·tion·a·ry /ˈsteʃənˌɛrɪ; ˈsteɪʃənəri/ *adj* standing still instead of moving 不（移）动的; 静止的: *How did you manage to drive into a stationary vehicle?* 你是怎么开车的, 竟会撞上一辆停着不动的车子?

station break /ˈ·· ·/ *n* [C] *AmE* a pause during a radio or television broadcast in the US, so that local stations can give their names【美】〔美国电台、电视台的〕广播间歇〔在节目中途的间歇用以插播台名〕

sta·tion·er /ˈsteʃənə; ˈsteɪʃənə/ *n* [C] *BrE*【英】**1 stationer's** a shop that sells stationery 文具店 **2** someone in charge of a shop that sells stationery 文具商, 文具店店主

sta·tion·e·ry /ˈsteʃənˌɛrɪ; ˈsteɪʃənəri/ *n* [U] **1** materials that you use for writing, such as paper, pens, pencils etc 文具 **2** paper for writing letters on, usually with matching envelopes〔一般指有信封配套的〕信纸: *a letter on hotel stationery* 用酒店信纸写的信

sta·tion-house /ˈ·· ,·/ *n* [C] *AmE old-fashioned* the local office of the police in a town, part of a city etc; POLICE STATION【美, 过时】〔城镇等的〕警察（分）局

station mas·ter /ˈ·· ,··/ *n* [C] someone who is in charge of a train station 火车站站长

station wag·on /ˈ·· ,··/ *n* [C] *AmE* a large car with extra space at the back, with a door there for loading and unloading【美】客货两用车; ESTATE CAR *BrE*【英】

sta·tis·tic /stəˈtɪstɪk; stəˈtɪstɪk/ *n* **1 statistics a)** [plural] a collection of numbers which represent facts or measurements 统计数字[资料]: *Statistics on illness are used in planning health care.* 疾病统计数字被用于制定保健计划。| *Statistics show that 35% of new businesses fail in their first year.* 统计资料显示, 35% 的新企业在第一年即倒闭。**b)** [U] the science of dealing with and explaining such numbers 统计学: *Statistics is a branch of mathematics.* 统计学是数学的一个分支。**2** [singular] a single number which represents a fact or measurement 数据; 统计数字中的一项: *Is he aware of the statistic that women make up 40% of the workforce?* 女性占劳动力的40%, 他知道这个数据吗? —see also 另见 VITAL STATISTICS —**statistical** *adj*: *statistical evidence* 以统计数字表明的证据 —**statistically** /-klɪ; -kli/ *adv*: *The variation is not statistically significant.* 这一变化在统计学上是没有显著意义的。

CULTURAL NOTE 文化注释

Many people believe that you can use statistics to prove anything that you want to prove, and that politicians and companies sometimes use them in dishonest ways. People also sometimes mention a famous remark made by the US writer Mark Twain: "There are three kinds of lies: lies, damned lies, and statistics." 很多人相信可以用数字来证明自己想证明的一切, 而政治家和公司常以不诚实的手段耍数字把戏。人们有时也会提起美国作家马克·吐温说的一句著名的话, "有三种谎言: 谎言, 该死的谎言和数字。"

stat·is·ti·cian /ˌstætəˈstɪʃən; ˌstætɪˈstɪʃən/ *n* [C] someone who works with statistics 统计学家; 统计员

sta·tive /ˋstetɪv; ˈsteɪtɪv/ *adj technical* a stative verb describes a state rather than an action or event, and is not usually used in PROGRESSIVE[1] (3) forms, for example 'belong' in the sentence 'this book belongs to me'【术语】【动词】表示状态的〔一般不用进行时, 如 this book belongs to me 中的 belong〕

stats /stæts; stæts/ *n* [plural] *informal* statistics【非正式】统计学

stat·u·a·ry /ˋstætʃʊˌɛrɪ; ˈstætʃuəri/ *n* [U] *technical* statues【术语】雕像; 塑像; 雕塑作品: *a fine collection of Greek statuary* 一批精美的希腊雕塑收藏品

stat·ue /ˋstætʃu; ˈstætʃuː/ *n* [C] an image of a person or animal that is made in solid material such as stone or metal and is usually large 雕像; 塑像: *a bronze statue of a horse* 一座马的铜像 | *People say Rome is a city with many statues.* 人们说罗马是一座有很多雕像的城市。—compare 比较 SCULPTURE

Statue of Lib·er·ty, the /ˌ‥ ˈ‥‥/ a statue of a woman on Liberty Island, in New York Harbour, given to the US by France in 1884 to celebrate the American and French revolutions. The woman is holding up a TORCH in her right hand and represents freedom. 自由女神像〔纽约港自由女神岛上的一尊女神塑像。1884 年由法国赠送给美国, 以庆祝美国革命和法国革命的胜利。女神右手高擎火炬, 象征自由〕

stat·u·esque /ˌstætʃʊˋɛsk; ˌstætʃuˈesk/ *adj* large and beautiful in a formal way, like a statue 雕像般端庄优美的: *a tall statuesque woman* 一个身材高大、端庄优美的女人

stat·u·ette /ˌstætʃʊˋɛt; ˌstætʃuˈet/ *n* [C] a very small statue for putting on a table or shelf〔放在桌子或架子上的〕小雕像; 小塑像 —compare 比较 BUST[2] (1)

stat·ure /ˋstætʃɚ; ˈstætʃə/ *n* [C,U] *formal*【正式】**1** the degree to which someone is admired or regarded as important 名声, 声望: *Louis Armstrong was a musician of world stature.* 路易斯·阿姆斯特朗是一位享誉世界的音乐家。**2** someone's height or size 身高; 身材: *short in stature* 身材矮小

2 **sta·tus** /ˋstetəs; ˈsteɪtəs/ *n* **1** [C,U] the legal position or condition of a person, group, country etc〔人、组织、国家等的〕法律地位; 身份, 状况: *What is her immigration status?* 她的移民状况如何? | *Don't accept any money if it will affect your amateur status.* 如果会影响你的业余选手身份的话, 就不要接受任何金钱。| **marital status** (=whether you are married or not) 婚姻状况 *Please state your name, age and marital status.* 请说明你的姓名、年龄和婚姻状况。**2** [U] **a)** your social or professional rank or position, considered in relation to other people 社会地位; 专业资格; 职位: **high/low status** *high status businessmen* 地位高的商人 **b)** high social position that makes people recognize and respect you 重要地位; 重要身份: *Barnes has a great status in the community.* 巴恩斯在这个社区有很高的地位。| **status symbol** (=something that you have or own that you think shows high social status) 社会地位的象征 *A secretary is a boss's status symbol.* 秘书是老板的身份象征。**3** [C] a situation at a particular time, especially in an argument, discussion etc〔尤指争论、讨论等的〕状态; 状况: *What's the status of the trade talks?* 贸易谈判进行到何种程度了?

status quo /ˌstetəs ˋkwo; ˌsteɪtəs ˈkwəʊ/ *n* **the status quo** the state of a situation as it is 现状: **maintain the status quo** (=not make any changes) 维持现状 *Managers want to maintain the status quo because they're afraid to take risks.* 经理们想维持现状, 因为他们害怕冒险。

stat·ute /ˋstætʃʊt; ˈstætʃuːt/ *n* [C] **1** a law passed by a parliament, council etc and formally written down 法令, 法规; 成文法: **by statute** *Protection for the consumer is laid down by statute.* 保障消费者权益已在法令里作了规定。**2** a formal rule of an institution or organization〔某机构、组织的〕条例; 章程: *College statutes forbid drinking on campus.* 大学校规禁止在校园内喝酒。

statute book, the /ˈ‥ ‥/ *n not technical*【非术语】a real or imaginary written collection of the laws in existence 成文法典, 法令全书: **on the statute book** (=in operation) 在实施中 *The government would like to see this new law on the statute book as soon as possible.* 政府希望看到这项新法令尽快付诸实施。

statute law /ˈ‥ ‥/ *n* [U] the whole group of written laws established by a parliament, council etc 成文法 —compare 比较 COMMON LAW[2]

statute of lim·i·ta·tions /ˌ‥‥ ˈ‥/ *n* [C] *AmE technical* a law which gives the period of time within which action may be taken on a legal question or crime【美, 术语】诉讼时效法规; 〔法律上的〕时效

stat·u·to·ry /ˋstætʃʊˌtorɪ; ˈstætʃətəri/ *adj* fixed or controlled by law 依照法令的; 法定的: *statutory employment rights* 法定就业权利 | *She's below the statutory age for school attendance.* 她还不到法定的入学年龄。—**statutorily** *adv*

statutory of·fence /ˌ‥‥ ‥ˈ‥/ *n* [C] *AmE technical* a crime that is described by a law and can be punished by a court【美, 术语】法定罪行

statutory rape /ˌ‥‥ ˈ‥/ *n* [C] *law* the act of having sex with someone who is not allowed by law to have sex【法律】法定强奸罪〔指与未成年人发生性关系〕

staunch¹ /stɔntʃ; stɔːntʃ/ *adj* giving strong, loyal support to another person, organization, belief etc; STEADFAST 坚定的; 忠实可靠的: *They are staunch trade unionists.* 他们是坚定的工会主义者。| *a staunch friend and ally* 坚定可靠的朋友和盟友 —**staunchly** *adv* —**staunchness** *n* [U]

staunch² also 又作 **stanch** *AmE*【美】—*v* [T] to stop the flow of liquid, especially of blood from a wound 止住〔液体的〕流出; 使〔伤口〕止血: *The blood seemed to pour from the wound and I thought I would never staunch the flow.* 血好像从伤口里不停地往外涌, 我以为再也止不住了。

stave¹ /stev; steɪv/ *n* [C] **1** the set of five lines on which music is written 五线谱 **2** one of the thin curved pieces of wood fitted close together to form the sides of a BARREL[1] (1)〔桶边上弧形的〕桶板, 侧板

stave² *v*

stave in *phr v past tense and past participle* **staved** *or* **stove** [I,T] to break something inwards or be broken inwards by something〔从外向里〕打破, 砸破: **stave sth ↔ in** *The ship's side was stove in when it went onto the rocks.* 船撞到了岩石上, 船舷被撞穿了。

stave sth **↔ off** *phr v past tense and past participle* **staved** [T] to keep someone or something from reaching you or affecting you for a period of time 挡开; 避开: *She'd brought some fruit on the journey to stave off hunger.* 她旅途上带了些水果充饥。| *Amazingly, the protestors have staved off the army for three nights running.* 令人惊奇的是, 抗议者们已经连续三个晚上把军队挡住。

staves /stevz; steɪvz/ the plural of STAFF

stay¹ /ste; steɪ/ *v* 1 1

1 ▶IN A PLACE 在某处◀ [I] to stop and remain in a place rather than go or leave 停留, 逗留, 留下: **stay (for) an hour/a while etc** *Can't you stay a little longer?* 你能再多待一会儿吗? | **stay late** *I had to stay later than planned at work.* 我不得不比原计划晚些下班。| **stay here/there** *Stay right there! I'll be back in a minute.* 待在那儿别动! 我一会儿就回来。| **stay to dinner/stay for lunch** *Can you stay for supper?* 你能留下来吃晚饭吗? | **stay behind** (=remain after others have gone)〔在别人走后〕留下来 *I stayed behind to help clean up after the party.* 聚会结束后, 我留下来帮助收拾东西。—see graph at 参见 REMAIN 图表

2 ▶IN A POSITION 处于某位置◀ [I, linking verb 连系动词] to continue to be in a particular position, place, or state, without changing 保持原状; 维持: **stay calm/quiet/warm etc** *It's going to stay cold for the next few days.* 在接下来的几天里天气仍然寒冷。| *You'd think he could stay sober for once.* 你可能会认为这一次他能保持清醒。| [+away/back/on etc] *Stay away from my daughter!* 不要缠着我女儿! | *Get out of this house and stay out!* 滚出这幢房子, 别再回来! | *You stay on this road for one mile before turning off.* 顺着这条路走一英里, 然后拐弯。| **stay in/out** (=not leave your home, or remain away from home) 待在家里/不在家中 *I won't have you staying out on a school night.* 第二天要上学, 我不许你晚上不回家。| **stay up** (=not go to bed) 熬夜, 不睡觉 *I stayed up late to watch the film.* 我为看那部电影很晚才睡觉。| **stay in a job** (=keep doing it) 继续做某工作 *I don't know whether to stay in teaching or not.* 我不知道是否该继续当教师。| **stay around** *informal* (=not leave someone)【非正式】不离开某人 *How do you know he'll stay around?* 你怎么知道他会待在你身边? | **stay up/down/the same etc** (=remain at the same level) 保持不跌/不涨/不变等 *House prices have stayed down for a whole year.* 房价一整年都没有上涨。| **stay out of** *spoken* (=not get involved)【口】不要卷入 *Stay out of this, Ben, it's none of your business.* 本, 别卷入这件事, 这跟你无关。

3 ▶LIVE SOMEWHERE 住在某处◀ [I] to live in a place for a while as a visitor or guest〔过访或做客时〕留宿, 暂住: [+at/with] *We stayed at the hotel for four nights.* 我们在那家旅店住了四晚。| *My mother is staying with us this week.* 我母亲这星期来我们家住。| **stay the night/stay overnight/stay over** (=stay from one evening to the next day) 过夜 *You can stay overnight if you don't want to drive home.* 你要是不想开车回家, 可以在这儿过夜。

4 stay put *spoken* to remain in one place and not move【口】待在原处, 不动: *You stay put in the car while I run into the store!* 我跑去商店, 你待在汽车里别动!

5 be here to stay to become accepted and used by most people 被普遍接受[使用]; 成为风尚: *Do you think computers are here to stay?* 你认为电脑会得到广泛使用吗?

6 stay after school to remain at school after the day's classes are finished, often as a punishment 课后留在学校〔常作为惩罚〕

7 stay the course *informal* to finish something in spite of difficulties【非正式】坚持到底: *Working in sales is very demanding and not many of our people stay the course.* 做销售非常费力, 我们的很多销售员都不能坚持到最后。

8 ►STOP 停止◄ [I,T] *literary* to stop doing something, or stop someone from doing something【文】停止; 制止

9 stay! used to tell a dog not to move 别动!〔作为对狗的命令〕

stay on *phr v* [I] to continue to do a job or to study after the usual or expected time for leaving〔在通常或预定的时间后〕继续留下工作[学习]: *"I thought your contract was done." "It is, but I'm staying on."* "我以为你的合同期满了。" "是的, 但我继续留下来。"

stay² *n* **1** [C usually singular 一般用单数] a limited time of living in a place 停留, 逗留, 暂住: *I met her towards the end of my stay in Los Angeles.* 我在洛杉矶暂住快要结束时结识了她。| *a short stay in the hospital* 短期住院 **2** [C,U] *law* the stopping or delay of an action because a judge has ordered it【法律】延缓, 延期, 推迟: **stay of execution** (=a delay of the punishment) 刑罚的缓期执行 **3** [C] a strong wire or rope used for supporting a ship's MAST (1) 支索〔支撑船桅的绳索、钢索〕 **4** [C] a short piece of plastic, bone, or wire used to keep a shirt COLLAR[1] (1) or a CORSET stiff〔衬衫衣领、紧身胸衣等的〕撑条 **5 stays** [plural] a CORSET〔妇女穿的〕紧身胸衣, 紧身褡

stay-at-home /ˈ· · ,·/ *n* [C] *informal* someone who always stays at home and never does exciting things【非正式】不爱出门的人, 深居简出的人

S

stay·er /ˈsteɚ; ˈsteɪə/ *n* [C] *BrE* a horse or person who can keep going to the end of a long race, job etc【英】有耐力的马[人]

stay·ing pow·er /ˈ·· ,··/ *n* [U] the ability or energy to keep doing something difficult until it is finished 耐力, 持久力: *They showed their staying power in the long-distance races.* 他们在长跑比赛中显示了耐力。

St Ber·nard /ˌsent bɚˈnɑrd; sənt ˈbɜːnəd/ *n* [C] a large strong Swiss dog that was trained in the past to help find people who were lost in the snow 圣伯纳狗〔一种瑞士大狗, 过去被训练用来寻找在雪中迷路的人〕

STD /ˌɛs ti ˈdi; ˌes tiː ˈdiː/ *n* [U] **1** subscriber trunk dialling; the telephone system in Britain that allows people to connect their own LONG-DISTANCE calls〔英国的〕用户直拨长途电话 **2** sexually transmitted disease; a disease that is passed on through having sex, such as AIDS, HERPES etc 性传播疾病〈如艾滋病、疱疹等〉

std the written abbreviation of 缩写= STANDARD

stead /stɛd; sted/ *n* **do sth in sb's stead** *formal* to do something that someone else usually does or was going to do【正式】代替某人做某事 —see also 另见 **stand sb in good stead** (STAND[1] (43))

stead·fast /ˈstɛdˌfæst; ˈstedfɑːst/ *adj literary* faithful and very loyal【文】忠实的, 忠诚的: [+in] *Harold remained steadfast in his Christian faith throughout his life.* 哈罗德一辈子虔诚地信奉基督教。—**steadfastly** *adv* —**steadfastness** *n* [U]

3 **stead·y¹** /ˈstɛdɪ; ˈstedi/ *adj*

1 ►NOT MOVING 不移动的◄ firmly held in a particular position and not moving or shaking 稳定的, 牢固的, 不摇晃的: *Keep the camera steady while you take a picture.* 照相时把照相机拿稳。| **a steady hand** *You need a steady hand for such a delicate job.* 做这样精细的工作手要稳。

2 ►CONTINUOUS 持续的◄ moving, happening, or developing in a continuous gradual way 平稳进行的; 持续的; 逐渐的: *a steady decline in manufacturing output* 制造业产量的持续下降 | *Paul has made steady progress this year.* 保罗今年有持续的进步。| **a steady stream of visitors/enquiries etc** *a steady stream of East Germans making their way through the new gap in the wall* 源源不断地穿越柏林墙的新缺口过来的东德人

3 ►NOT CHANGING 不变的◄ a steady level, speed etc stays about the same〔水平、速度等〕平稳的, 固定不变的: *We were driving at a steady 60 mph.* 我们一直以60英里的时速行驶。

4 ►PERSON 人◄ someone who is steady is sensible and you can depend on them 稳健的; 靠得住的: *a steady worker* 可靠的工人

5 steady job/work/income a job or work that will definitely continue over a long period of time 稳定的职位/工作/收入

6 steady boyfriend/girlfriend someone that you have been having a romantic relationship with 关系固定的男朋友/女朋友

7 steady relationship a serious and strong relationship that continues for a long time 稳定的关系 —**steadily** *adv* —**steadiness** *n* [U]

steady² *v* **1** [T] to hold something steady or make it steady 拿稳, 扶稳; 使稳定[稳固]: **steady yourself** (=get back your balance in order to prevent yourself from falling) 使自己站稳 *He tried to steady himself by grabbing the tree.* 他抓住那棵树, 试图使自己站稳。**2** [I] to stop increasing or decreasing and remain about the same 停止升降, 稳定下来: *The dollar has steadied after early losses on the money markets.* 美元在货币市场经历了早些时候的下跌之后, 现在已经稳定下来。**3 steady your nerves** to make yourself calm 使自己镇定: *She had a brandy to steady her nerves.* 她喝了一杯白兰地酒, 使自己镇定下来。

steady³ *adv* **go steady (with sb)** to have a long regular romantic relationship with a BOYFRIEND or GIRLFRIEND (与某人)有固定的恋爱关系

steady⁴ *n* [C] *AmE informal* a BOYFRIEND or GIRLFRIEND that someone has been having a romantic relationship with【美, 非正式】关系确定的男朋友[女朋友]: *Jill is Ray's steady.* 吉尔是雷的对象。

steady⁵ *interjection BrE informal*【英, 非正式】**1** used when you want to tell someone to be careful or not to cause an accident 当心; 稳一点: *Steady! You nearly knocked me over.* 小心点! 你差点儿把我撞倒了。**2 Steady on!** used when you think that what someone is saying is too strong or extreme 说话当心点〔当某人说话太重或太极端时用作提醒〕: *Steady on! Derek's not that bad.* 说话小心点! 德里克没有那么坏!

steady state the·o·ry /ˌ·· ˈ· ˌ···/ *n technical* the idea that things in space have always existed and have always been moving away from each other as new atoms begin to exist【术语】(宇宙学中的)稳恒状态理论 —**compare** 比较 BIG BANG THEORY

steak /stek; steɪk/ *n* **1** [C,U] good quality BEEF (=meat from a cow), or a large thick piece of any good quality red meat 牛排; 〔红色肉类的〕肉排: *I like my steak rare.* 我喜欢牛排烧得生一点。**2** [U] *BrE* beef that is not of such good quality and is used in making CASSEROLES etc【英】用来做炖锅菜的质量一般的牛肉 **3 cod/salmon/tuna etc steak** [C] a large thick piece of fish 鳕鱼/三文鱼/金枪鱼排

steak·house /ˈstekˌhaus; ˈsteɪkhaʊs/ *plural* **steakhouses** /-ˌhauzɪz; -haʊzɪz/ *n* [C] a restaurant that serves steak 牛排餐厅

steak tar·tare /ˌ· ·ˈ·/ *n* [U] steak that is cut into very small pieces and eaten raw, usually with a raw egg〔通常配生鸡蛋供生吃的〕鞑靼牛肉末

steal 偷

He stole her purse *BrE*【英】/wallet *AmE*【美】.
He robbed the woman (of her purse *BrE*【英】/ wallet *AmE*【美】). 他偷了那位女士的钱包。

steal¹ /stil; stiːl/ *v past tense* **stole** /stol; stəʊl/ *past participle* **stolen** /ˈstolən; ˈstəʊlən/ 3 3

1 ►TAKE STH 拿走某物◄ [I,T] to take something that belongs to someone else 偷, 窃取: [+from] *Some drug users steal from their own families to finance their habit.* 有些吸毒者偷自己家里的钱来购买毒品。| **steal sth** *Sean has a long history of stealing cars.* 肖恩偷汽车有很长时间了。| **steal sth from sb** *He was accused of stealing ideas from a rival studio.* 他被指控盗用敌对设计室的概念。

2 ▶MOVE SOMEWHERE 向某处移动◀ [I always+adv/prep] to move quietly without anyone noticing you 悄悄地移动: [+into/across etc] *I tried to steal out of the room without waking Stefan.* 我尽量悄悄地溜出房间，免得吵醒斯蒂芬。

3 **steal the show/limelight/scene** to do something, especially when you are acting in a play, that makes people pay more attention to you than to other people〔尤指演戏时〕抢出风头

4 **steal a look/glance etc** to look at someone or something quickly and secretly 偷偷地看一眼/瞥一眼等

5 ▶SPORT 体育运动◀ [I,T] to run to the next BASE[2] (8) in the game of BASEBALL before someone hits the ball〔在棒球比赛中〕偷(垒)

6 **steal a kiss** to kiss someone quickly when they are not expecting it 偷吻(一下)

7 **steal sb's thunder** to get the success and praise someone else should have got, by doing what they had intended to do 抢在别人前面做某事而获得成功和赞赏; 抢别人的功劳

8 **steal a march on sb** to secretly or unexpectedly start something that someone else had planned to do, so that you gain an advantage over them 偷偷地[出其不意地]抢在某人前头; 抢占先机

9 **steal sb's heart** *literary* to make someone fall in love with you【文】使某人爱上自己; 获得某人的欢心

USAGE NOTE 用法说明: STEAL

WORD CHOICE 词语辨析: **steal, take, rob, burgle, burglarize, pick sb's pocket**

People **steal** things (from people, cars, houses, shops, banks etc). steal 用于从某人那里，或从汽车、房屋、商店、银行等中偷窃: *He's stolen my Walkman!* (NOT 不用 *stolen me* or 或 *robbed my Walkman*) 他偷了我的随身听。| *Someone stole his passport while he was asleep.* 他睡着时，有人偷了他的护照。

Take is also often used in this sense. take 也常常用来表达这个意思: *Someone's taken my wallet.* 有人把我的钱包偷走了。

People **rob** other people (of things) especially in a public place. rob 用于抢劫某人(身上的东西)，尤指在公共场所: *A man was robbed by three youths as he walked home from work yesterday.* 一名男子昨天下班回家时被三名青年抢劫。

People **rob** banks, or gas stations, but usually **burgle** (*BrE*) or **burglarize** (*AmE*) a house or office. 抢劫银行或汽车加油站用 rob，但闯入别人房子或办公室行窃，一般用 burgle【英】或 burglarize【美】: *At least 10 houses in the area had been burgled during the night.* 这个地区起码有10户住宅在夜间被盗。

If someone **picks your pocket**, they steal things from your pocket, usually when you are in a crowd of people. pick your pocket 指"扒窃，掏某人的腰包"，一般是在人多拥挤的地方。

steal[2] *n* [C] *informal*【非正式】**1 be a steal** to be very cheap 便宜极了: *At 20 bucks the camera was a steal.* 这台照相机只要20美元，实在太便宜了。—see 见 CHEAP[1] (USAGE) **2** the act of running to the next BASE[2] (8) in the game of BASEBALL before someone hits the ball〔棒球比赛中的〕偷垒

stealth /stɛlθ; stelθ/ *n* [U] the action of doing something very quietly, slowly, or secretly so that no one notices you 悄悄的行动，秘密行动: *Cats rely on stealth to catch their prey.* 猫悄无声息地行动以捕捉猎物。| **by stealth** *They are trying to carry out their aims by stealth, after failing to impose them by law.* 他们的目标未能通过法律手段来达到，现正试图秘密地实施。

stealth bomb·er /ˈ· ˌ·· / *n* [C] an American military aircraft that cannot be discovered by RADAR instruments〔美国的〕隐形轰炸机

stealth·y /ˈstɛlθɪ; ˈstelθi/ *adj* moving or doing something quietly and secretly 悄悄的，鬼鬼祟祟的，偷偷摸摸的: *His eye caught a stealthy movement at the edge of the wood.* 他看到树林边有人悄悄地在移动。—**stealthily** *adv*

[3] **steam**[1] /stim; stiːm/ *n* [U]

1 ▶GAS 气体◀ the hot mist that water produces when it is boiled 蒸汽，水蒸气: *Be careful of the steam from the kettle.* 小心水壶冒出来的蒸汽。

2 ▶MIST ON A SURFACE 表面的雾气◀ the mist that forms on windows, mirrors etc when warm wet air suddenly becomes cold 水汽; 雾气

3 ▶POWER 动力◀ power that is produced by boiling water to make steam, in order to make things work or move 蒸汽动力[压力]: *The engines are driven by steam.* 发动机是由蒸汽驱动的。| **steam engine/train etc** (=an engine etc that works by the power produced by steam) 蒸汽机车/火车等

4 **let off steam** to get rid of your anger or excitement in a way that does not harm anyone by doing something active 发泄怒火; 宣泄激情: *PE is a good time for the kids to let off steam!* 体育课是孩子们宣泄过剩精力的好时机!

5 **run out of steam** to no longer have the energy or the desire to continue doing something, especially because you are tired〔尤指因疲劳而〕泄气; 失去动力: *The home team began to run out of steam in the last quarter.* 主队在最后一节开始泄气了。

6 **get/pick up steam a)** if an engine gets up steam, it gradually starts to go faster〔指发动机〕逐渐加速 **b)** if plans, beliefs etc get up steam, they gradually become more important and more people become interested in them〔计划、观念等〕逐渐变得重要，逐渐得到关注

7 **under your own steam** if you go somewhere under your own steam, you get there without help from anyone else 靠自己的力量: *I'll get to the restaurant under my own steam.* 我会自己设法赶到那家餐馆。

8 **go full steam ahead with** to do something with as much energy and eagerness as possible 全力以赴地做(某事)

9 ▶RAILWAY 铁路◀ a railway system in which the trains use steam for power 使用蒸汽机车的铁路系统: *the age of steam* 蒸汽机车时代

steam[2] *v* **1** [I] if something steams, steam rises from it, especially because it is hot 散发蒸汽，冒热气: *a mug of steaming coffee* 一杯冒着热气的咖啡 **2** [T] to cook something in steam〔用蒸汽〕蒸: *Steam the vegetables lightly.* 把蔬菜稍蒸一下。**3** [I always+adv/prep] to travel somewhere in a boat or train that uses steam to produce power 乘汽船[蒸汽火车]旅行: [+into/from etc] *During the next two weeks, we steamed from port to port.* 在接下来的两周里，我们乘汽船到了一个又一个港口。**4 be steamed** *AmE spoken* to be very angry【美口】非常生气

steam sth ↔ **open/off** *phr v* [T] to use steam to open an envelope or to remove a stamp from an envelope 用蒸汽把〔信封〕打开/把〔邮票〕揭下来

steam up *phr v* [I,T] to cover or become covered with steam (使)蒙上水汽: **steam sth ↔ up** *The warm room steamed up my glasses.* 温暖的房间使我的眼镜结了一层水汽。—see also 另见 STEAMED-UP

steam·boat /ˈstimˌbot; ˈstiːmbəʊt/ *n* [C] a boat that uses steam to produce power and is used for sailing along rivers and coasts 汽船，汽艇

steam clean /ˈ· ·/ *v* [T] to clean something made of cloth by using a machine that produces steam 蒸汽洗涤

steam·ed-up /ˌ· ˈ·/ *adj* [not before noun 不用于名词前] *informal* excited and angry or worried【非正式】激动的; 生气的; 焦虑的: *Don't get so steamed-up about it – it's not really important.* 别为这事生那么大的气，其实这无关紧要的。

steam·er /ˈstimɚ; ˈstiːmə/ *n* [C] **1** a STEAMSHIP 汽船，大轮船 **2** a container used to cook food in steam 汽锅，蒸锅

steam·ing /ˈstimɪŋ; ˈstiːmɪŋ/ *adv* **1 steaming hot** very hot 十分炎热的; 滚烫的: *It was a steaming hot day.* 那天天气很热。**2** *ScotE* very drunk【苏格兰】大醉的，烂醉的

steam i·ron /ˈ· ˌ··/ *n* [C] an electric iron that produces steam in order to make clothes easier to iron 蒸汽熨斗

steam·roll /ˈstimˌrol; ˈstiːmrəʊl/ *v* [T] *AmE* to steamroller【美】〔以权力、影响力〕强迫，迫使; 强行

steam·roll·er[1] /ˈstimˌrolɚ; ˈstiːmˌrəʊlə/ *n* [C] a heavy vehicle with very wide wheels that you drive over road surfaces to make them flat 蒸汽压路机

steamroller[2] *v* [T] *informal* to force someone to do what you want them to do, or to make sure something happens by using all your power and influence【非正式】〔以权力、影响力〕强迫，迫使; 强行; STEAMROLL *AmE*【美】: *He steamrollered his bill through Parliament against fierce opposition.* 他不顾别人的强烈反对，以高压手段强行使议会通过这项法案。

steam·ship /ˈstimˌʃɪp; ˈstiːmˌʃɪp/ *n* [C] a large ship that uses steam to produce power 汽船，大轮船

steam shov·el /ˈ· ˌ··/ *n* [C] *AmE* a large machine that digs and moves earth in a large bucket【美】挖土机，电铲

steam·y /ˈstimɪ; ˈstiːmi/ *adj* **1** full of steam or covered in steam 充满蒸汽的; 水汽覆盖的: *steamy windows* 被水汽覆盖的窗户 **2** sexually exciting and slightly shocking 色情而狂放的: *a steamy love affair* 狂放的性关系

steed /stid; stiːd/ *n* [C] *poetic* a strong fast horse【诗】骏马

steel[1] /stil; stiːl/ *n* **1** [U] strong metal that can be shaped easily, consisting of iron and CARBON 钢，钢铁: *a bridge made of steel* [2] [3]

钢铁大桥 | **stainless steel** *stainless steel cutlery* 不锈钢餐具 **2** [U] the industry that makes steel 钢铁工业: *Sheffield is a major steel town.* 设菲尔德是主要的钢铁城市。**3 nerves of steel** the ability to be brave and calm in a dangerous or difficult situation 超人的胆量, 巨大的勇气: *You need nerves of steel to be a racing driver.* 要做赛车手, 你必须具有超人的胆量和勇气。**4** [C] a thin bar of steel used to sharpen knives〔磨刀用的〕钢棒

steel[2] *v* [T] **steel yourself** to prepare yourself to do something that you know will be unpleasant or upsetting 使自己坚强起来〔去应付不愉快的事〕: **steel yourself to do sth** *Bob steeled himself to tell her about her father's death.* 鲍勃硬起心肠把她父亲的死讯告诉了她。

steel band /,ˈ·/ *n* [C] a group of people who play a type of music from the West Indies, in which you hit different areas on drums made from metal oil BARRELs to produce different musical sounds 钢鼓乐队〔以金属油桶制成的鼓为乐器, 演奏一种西印度群岛音乐的乐队〕

Steele /stil; stiːl/, **Sir Richard** (1672-1729) an Irish writer who started the magazine *The Tatler*. His friend Joseph Addison also wrote articles for it. 斯蒂尔爵士〔(1672-1729), 爱尔兰作家。曾创办《闲谈者》杂志。他的朋友约瑟夫·艾迪生也为该杂志撰稿〕

steel gui·tar /,· ·ˈ·/ *n* [C] a musical instrument with ten strings that is played using a steel bar and a PEDAL (=a bar you press with your foot) 钢吉他〔一种有10根弦、用钢棒和踏板演奏的乐器〕

steel wool /,· ˈ·/ *n* [U] a rough material made of fine steel threads, that is used to make surfaces smooth, remove paint etc 钢丝绒, 钢棉〔用于磨光表面、擦除油漆等〕—compare 比较 WIRE WOOL

steel·works /ˈstil,wɝks; ˈstiːlwɜːks/ *n* [C] *plural* **steelworks** a factory where steel is made 炼钢厂 —**steelworker** *n* [C]

steel·y /ˈstilɪ; ˈstiːli/ *adj* **1 steely determination/expression etc** an extremely strong and determined attitude, expression etc 坚定[钢铁般]的决心/表情等 **2** having a grey colour like steel 钢一样灰白的, 钢灰色的: *a steely sky* 钢灰色的天空

3 **steep**[1] /stip; stiːp/ *adj* **1** a road, hill etc that is steep slopes at a high angle〔路、山等〕陡的, 陡峭的: *The road's too steep to ride up on a bike.* 这路太陡了, 骑自行车上不去。**2 steep prices, charges etc** are unusually expensive〔价格、收费等〕过高的, 过分昂贵的: *landlords asking steep rents* 收租过高的房东 **3** a steep increase or rise in something is a very big increase〔增加、上升〕大幅度的; 急遽的: *a steep increase in the number of car thefts in the area* 该地区汽车盗窃案的急剧上升 **4 that's/it's a bit steep** *BrE spoken* used to say that a request or action is unreasonable【英口】那太不合理了〔指要求或行动〕: *They want us to work on New Year's Day? That's a bit steep!* 他们要我们在元旦上班? 这太过分了! —**steeply** *adv* —**steepness** *n* [U]

steep[2] *v* [I,T] **1 be steeped in history/tradition etc** to have a lot of a particular quality such as history etc 有丰富历史/传统等: *a town steeped in history* 历史悠久的小城 **2** to put food in a liquid and leave it there so that it becomes soft or has the same taste as the liquid 浸泡〔食物〕: *Steep the raisins in sherry.* 把葡萄干泡在雪利酒中。

steep·en /ˈstipən; ˈstiːpən/ *v* [I,T] if a slope, road etc steepens or something steepens it, it becomes steeper (使) 变得陡峭

stee·ple /ˈstipl̩; ˈstiːpəl/ *n* [C] a tall pointed tower on the roof of a church〔教堂的〕尖塔

stee·ple·chase /ˈstipl̩,tʃes; ˈstiːpəltʃeɪs/ *n* [C] **1** a long race in which horses jump over gates, water etc 越野障碍赛马 **2** a long race in which people run and jump over fences, water etc 障碍赛跑

stee·ple·jack /ˈstipl̩,dʒæk; ˈstiːpəldʒæk/ *n* [C] someone whose work is repairing towers, tall CHIMNEYs etc 尖塔、高烟囱等的修理工

steer[1] /stɪr; stɪə/ *v*

1 ►CAR/BOAT ETC 汽车/船等◄ [I,T] to control the direction a vehicle is going, for example by turning a wheel 操纵〔车、船的行驶方向〕; 驾驶〔车、船等〕: [+for/towards etc] *I tried to steer around the bollard.* 我试图驾车绕过安全柱。| *We turned about and steered for Port of Spain.* 我们转向朝西班牙港驶去。

2 ►CHANGE SB/STH 改变某人/某物◄ [T] to guide someone's behaviour or the way a situation develops without anyone noticing it 引导, 指导, 带领〔某人的行为〕: **steer sb towards/away from** *We steered Noel towards less expensive hobbies.* 我们引导诺埃尔培养花钱较少的业余爱好。| **steer the conversation** *Helen tried to steer the conversation away from school.* 海伦试图把谈话从学校这个话题上引开。

3 ►BE IN CHARGE OF 负责◄ [T always+adv/prep] to be in charge of an organization, team etc and make decisions that help it be successful, especially during a difficult time 掌管, 控制; 〔尤指在困难时期〕带领…渡过: **steer sth through/to etc** *McKinney steered the company through the hard years of recession.* 麦金尼带领公司渡过经济衰退的艰难岁月。

4 ►GUIDE SB TO A PLACE 引领某人到某处◄ to guide someone to a place, especially by putting your hand on their back, shoulder etc and gently pushing them 带领, 引导〔尤指用手轻推某人的背或肩等〕: **steer sb towards/to etc** *Joel steered the visitors towards the backyard.* 乔尔领着客人们向后院走去。

5 steer clear (of) *informal* to try to avoid someone or something unpleasant or difficult【非正式】避开; 从…脱身: *Paul's in a bad mood, so I'd steer well clear if I were you.* 保罗现在情绪不好, 所以我要是你的话, 我就远远地躲着他。

6 steer a middle course to choose a course of action that is not extreme 选择一条中间路线, 不走极端

steer[2] *n* [C] a young male cow that has had its sex organs removed〔阉过的〕小公牛 —compare 比较 BULLOCK, HEIFER

steer·age /ˈstɪrɪdʒ; ˈstɪərɪdʒ/ *n* [U] the part of a passenger ship where people who had the cheapest tickets used to travel in the past〔旧时的〕下等客舱, 统舱

steer·ing /ˈstɪrɪŋ; ˈstɪərɪŋ/ *n* [U] the parts of a car, boat etc that allow you to control its direction〔汽车、船等的〕转向装置, 操纵装置: *power steering* 动力转向装置 | *The steering on this car is lighter.* 这辆汽车的转向装置比较灵便。

steering com·mit·tee /ˈ·· ·,·ˈ·/ *n* a committee that guides or directs a particular activity〔某项活动的〕指导委员会, 督导委员会

steering wheel /ˈ·· ·/ *n* [C] a wheel that you turn to control the direction of a car 方向盘 —see picture on page A2 参见 A2 页图

Steer·pike /ˈstɪɚpaɪk; ˈstɪəpaɪk/ a character in the NOVEL *Gormenghast* by Mervyn Peake, who only wants power and will do anything to get what he wants 斯蒂派克〔默文·皮克的小说《戈尔曼加斯特》中的一个人物。他权欲熏心, 为达目的不择手段〕

steers·man /ˈstɪrzmən; ˈstɪəzmən/ *n* [C] someone who steers a ship 舵手

Stef·fens /ˈstɛfənz; ˈstefənz/, **Lincoln** (1866-1936) a US newspaper writer who had a special interest in CORRUPTION (=dishonest behaviour by people in official positions). He is famous especially for his magazine articles about crime and dishonesty in city governments, some of which also appear in his book *The Shame of the Cities*. 斯蒂芬斯〔(1866-1936), 美国报刊撰稿人, 特别关注腐败问题。尤以在杂志上撰文揭露市政府不法欺诈的黑幕而闻名, 其中部分文章收入其《城市的耻辱》一书〕

stein /staɪn; staɪn/ *n* [C] a tall cup for drinking beer, often decorated and with a lid〔常指有装饰、带盖的〕啤酒杯 —see picture at 参见 CUP 图

Stein·beck /ˈstaɪnbɛk; ˈstaɪnbek/, **John** (1902-68) a US writer whose NOVELs, including *The Grapes of Wrath*, *East of Eden*, and *Of Mice and Men* show great sympathy for poor people and their problems. He is one of the most popular and admired US writers of the 20th century, and he won the Nobel Prize for Literature in 1962. 斯坦贝克〔(1902-1968), 美国作家。其小说《愤怒的葡萄》、《伊甸园东》和《人鼠之间》反映了他对穷人及其困难的深切同情。他是20世纪最受欢迎和崇敬的美国作家之一, 1962年获诺贝尔文学奖〕

Stei·nem /ˈstaɪnəm; ˈstaɪnəm/, **Glo·ri·a** /ˈglorɪə; ˈglɔːriə/ (1934-) a US writer and FEMINIST who was a leading member of the women's movement in the 1960s, and started the magazine called *Ms.* 斯坦恩〔(1934-), 美国作家, 女权主义者。她是20世纪60年代女权运动的领袖人物, 曾创办《女士》杂志〕

Stei·ner /ˈstaɪnɚ; ˈstaɪnə/, **Ru·dolf** /ˈrudalf; ˈruːdɒlf/ (1861-1925) an Austrian PHILOSOPHER who believed that human beings can be trained to develop their spiritual powers. He developed his own system for educating children, and started schools, called Steiner schools or Waldorf schools, that use his educational methods. 斯坦纳〔(1861-1925), 奥地利哲学家。他认为人可以通过训练发掘其精神机能。他创立了自己的儿童教育理论体系, 并创办学校实施自己的教育方法。其学校称为"斯坦纳学校"或"华德福学校"〕

Stein·way /ˈstaɪnwe; ˈstaɪnweɪ/ *trademark* a type of piano of very good quality, made by a company that was established in New York by Henry Steinway in the 19th century【商标】施坦威钢琴〔一种优质钢琴, 由亨利·施坦威于19世纪在纽约创办的一家公司制造〕

Stel·la Ar·tois /,stɛlɚ arˈtwa; ,stelər ɑːˈtwɑː/ also 又作 **Stella** *trademark* a strong type of LAGER (=beer)【商标】斯泰拉啤酒, 时代啤酒〔一种口味浓郁的啤酒〕

stel·lar /ˈstɛlɚ; ˈstelə/ *adj* [only before noun 仅用于名词前] **1** *technical* connected with the stars【术语】星的, 星球的 —see also 另见 INTERSTELLAR **2** *AmE* done extremely well【美】非常出色的, 优秀的: **stellar performance** *Well, it wasn't exactly a stellar performance, was it Mike?* 哦, 那场演出并不算很出色, 对吗, 迈克?

stem¹ /stɛm; stem/ *n* [C] **1** the long thin central part of a plant above the ground or the smaller parts that grow from it, from which leaves grow; STALK¹ (1)〔植物的〕茎; 梗; 柄 **2** the long thin part of a wine glass, VASE etc, between the base and the wide top〔葡萄酒杯、花瓶等的〕颈, 柄, 脚 **3** the narrow tube of a pipe used to smoke tobacco 烟斗柄 **4** the part of a word that stays the same when different endings are added to it, for example 'driv-' in 'driving' and 'driven' 词干〈如driving和driven中的driv-〉 **5 from stem to stern** all the way from the front to the back, especially of a ship 从船头到船尾; 从头到尾; 到处

stem² *v* **stemmed, stemming** [T] **1 stem the tide/flow of** to stop something from spreading or developing 阻止…的扩散; 遏制…的发展: *The public apology was intended to stem the tide of complaints from viewers.* 公开道歉的目的是为了阻止观众大量的投诉。**2** *formal* to stop the flow of a liquid【正式】阻止〔液体的流动〕; 堵住; 止住: *stem the bleeding* 止住流血 **3 long-stemmed/short-stemmed etc** having a long stem, a short stem etc 长/短茎的; 高/矮脚的: *long-stemmed wine glasses* 高脚酒杯

stem from sth *phr v* [T not in progressive 不用进行时] to develop as a result of something else 源于…, 来自…; 由…发生: *Most of the difficulties stemmed from poor workmanship.* 麻烦大多是由于工艺差造成的。

stench /stɛntʃ; stentʃ/ *n* [C usually singular 一般用单数] **1** a very strong unpleasant smell 恶臭, 臭气: *the stench of urine* 尿臭味 **2** something unpleasant that makes you believe that something very bad and dishonest is happening 歪风邪气; 不诚实: **the stench of privilege/injustice etc** *The stench of corruption hangs over this whole affair.* 整件事笼罩着腐败的邪气。

sten·cil¹ /ˈstɛnsl; ˈstensəl/ *n* [C] a piece of plastic etc in which patterns or letters have been cut, or the decorative pattern or words made by putting paint or ink over this〔镂有图案或文字的〕模板, 型板; 刻字蜡纸; 用模板印制的文字[图案]

stencil² *v* [T] to make a pattern, letters etc using a stencil 用模板制作; 用蜡纸印

Sten·dhal /stɛnˋdɑl; ˈstɒndɑːl/ (1783-1842) a French writer whose best-known books are *Le Rouge et le Noir* and *La Chartreuse de Parme* 司汤达〔(1783-1842), 法国作家。最著名的小说有《红与黑》和《巴马修道院》〕

Sten gun /ˈstɛn ˌgʌn; ˈsten ˌgʌn/ *n* [C] a small British SUBMACHINE GUN 斯特恩式轻机枪, 史登冲锋枪〔英国一种小型冲锋枪〕

sten·o /ˈstɛno; ˈstenəʊ/ *n* [C] *informal*【非正式】**1** [C] a stenographer 速记(打字)员 **2** [U] stenography 速记(法)

ste·nog·ra·pher /stəˋnɑgrəfɚ; stəˈnɒgrəfə/ *n* [C] *AmE or BrE old-fashioned* someone whose job is to write down what someone else is saying, using stenography, and then type a copy of it【美或英, 过时】速记(打字)员; SHORTHAND TYPIST *BrE*【英】

ste·nog·ra·phy /stəˋnɑgrəfɪ; stəˈnɒgrəfi/ *n* [U] *AmE or BrE old-fashioned* a system of writing quickly by using signs or shorter forms for letters, words, and phrases; SHORTHAND【美或英, 过时】速记(法)

sten·to·ri·an /stɛnˋtorɪən; stenˈtɔːriən/ *adj literary* a stentorian voice is very loud and powerful【文】〔声音〕极其洪亮的

step¹ /stɛp; step/ *n* (S2 W2)

1 ▶MOVEMENT 移动◀ [C] the movement you make when you put one foot in front of the other when walking 脚步, 步: *With every step my bags seemed heavier.* 我每走一步都觉得行李越来越重。| **take a step** *Take two steps forward and one step back.* 向前走两步, 再往后退一步。| **retrace your steps** (=go back the way you came) 顺原路返回 | **direct/bend your steps** *literary* (=walk in a particular direction)【文】往某个方向走 *The sun was setting as he bent his steps towards home.* 他往家走时, 太阳开始落山了。

2 ▶ACTION 动作, 行动◀ [C] one of a series of things that you do in order to deal with a problem or to succeed〔一系列行动中的〕步骤; 措施: *Dole's first step will be to unite the party.* 多尔的第一步就是要把党团结起来。| **[+towards]** *The talks are an important step towards reconciliation.* 谈判是迈向和解的重要一步。| **take steps** (=take action) 采取措施 *We must take steps to make sure such an accident can never happen again.* 我们必须采取措施确保此类事故不会再次发生。| **a step forward** *The discovery of penicillin was a major step forward in the treatment of infections.* 青霉素的发现在治疗感染方面前进了一大步。| **a step in the right direction** (=an action that is not complete, but is good as a beginning) 朝正确方向迈出的一步 | **step backward** (=something you do that makes a situation worse) 退步, 倒退 *Many teachers see an emphasis on written tests as a step backwards in education.* 很多教师认为, 强调笔试是教育的一个倒退。

3 ▶STAIR 楼梯◀ [C] a flat narrow piece of wood or stone, especially one in a series, that you put your foot on when you are going up or down in a building 梯级, 台阶: *Jenny waited on the church steps.* 珍妮在教堂的台阶上等着。| **flight of steps** (=set of steps) 一段台阶 —see also 另见 DOORSTEP¹ (1)

4 ▶IN A PROCESS 在过程中◀ [C] a stage in a process or a position on a scale 阶段; 进程; 等级, 级别: *Every year you go up one step on the salary scale.* 你的工资每年增长一级。| **every step of the way** (=continuously during every stage of something) 在每一个阶段; 从头到尾 *Pam's husband has supported her every step of the way.* 帕姆的丈夫自始至终一直支持她。| **a step up** *Nina's promotion is quite a step up for one so young.* 尼娜的晋升对于一个这么年轻的人来说是相当大的一步。—compare 比较 STAGE¹ (1)

5 ▶DANCING 舞蹈◀ [C] a movement of your feet in dancing 舞步: *Wayne's learning the steps for the new routine.* 韦恩正在学习一套新的舞蹈动作。

6 mind *BrE*【英】**/watch your step a)** to be careful about what you say or how you behave 谨慎地说话[做事]: *You'll get into trouble if you don't watch your step.* 你要是不谨慎行事就会惹麻烦。**b)** to be careful when you are walking 小心行走: *Mind your step – the railing's loose.* 走路小心一点, 栏杆松动了。

7 be/keep in step a) if people or their ideas are in step, they agree with each other or with what is usual, acceptable etc〔与他人〕一致/保持一致: *Suzie tries to keep in step with fashion.* 苏西试图紧跟时尚。**b)** to march with a group of people so that your right feet all go forward at the same time〔与他人〕步伐一致/保持步伐一致

8 be out of step a) if people or their ideas are out of step, they are different from the other people in a group〔与他人或他人的观点〕不一致, 不合拍: *Joshua's out of step with modern life.* 乔舒亚与现代生活不合拍。**b)** if someone marching with a group is out of step, they are marching with their right foot going forward at a different time than everyone else〔与他人〕步伐不一致

9 ▶SOUND 声音◀ [C] the sound you make when you set your foot down while walking 脚步声: *I heard a step in the corridor.* 我听到走廊里有脚步声。—compare 比较 FOOTSTEP

10 ▶DISTANCE 距离◀ [C] the short distance you move when you take a step while walking 一步(的距离): *There's a pub just a few steps down the road.* 顺着这条路几步远就有一家酒吧。—compare 比较 PACE¹ (3)

11 fall into step to walk so that you are putting your right foot forward at the same time as the people you are walking with〔与他人〕步伐一致起来: *Mr. Jones soon fell into step beside her.* 琼斯先生很快就跟她的步伐一致起来。

12 step by step slowly and gradually from one stage to the next 逐渐地, 一步一步地: *Adam's learning the rules of chess step by step.* 亚当正在一步一步地学习国际象棋的规则。

13 be one step ahead to be better prepared for something or know more about something〔比某人〕准备充分; 了解更多: *A good teacher should always be one step ahead of his students.* 好教师应该总是比学生先一步。

14 ▶WAY SB WALKS 某人走路的方式◀ [C usually singular 一般用单数] the way someone walks, which often tells you how they are feeling 步态; 走路的姿势: *Gianni's usual bouncy step* 詹妮一贯的生气勃勃的步伐

15 steps [plural] *BrE* a STEPLADDER【英】活(动)梯(子), 折梯

16 ▶EXERCISE 锻炼◀ [C,U] a type of exercise you do by walking onto and off a flat piece of equipment several inches high, or that piece of equipment itself 踏板运动; 踏板: *Beginners' step class 7 pm.* 踏板运动初级班晚上7点上课。

17 ▶MUSIC 音乐◀ [C] *AmE* the difference in pitch (PITCH¹ (3)) between two musical notes that are separated by one key (KEY² (4)) on the piano【美】〔音乐中的〕音级; TONE¹ (8) *BrE*【英】

step² *v* **stepped, stepping** [I always+adv/prep] (W3)

1 ▶TAKE ONE STEP 走一步◀ to raise one foot and put it down in front of the other one 跨步, 迈步: **[+forward/back/down etc]** *Step aside, let the doctor through.* 站到一边去, 让医生过去。

2 ▶WALK 步行◀ to walk a short distance〔短距离〕行走: **[+inside/outside etc]** *I stepped into the hall to wait.* 我走进大厅里去等。| **step this way** (=come the way I am showing you) 往这边走

S

3 ►STAND ON STH 站在某物上◄ to bring your foot down on something 踏, 踩; TREAD[1] (1) *BrE*【英】: [+in/on etc] *I stepped in a puddle and got my shoes wet.* 我踩进一个水坑里把鞋弄湿了。

4 **step forward** to come and offer help 前来提供帮助: *Police are appealing for witnesses to step forward.* 警方呼吁目击者前来协助。

5 **step out of line** to behave badly by breaking rules or disobeying orders 行为出轨; 违反规矩[命令]

6 **step on it/step on the gas** *AmE spoken* to drive faster【美口】加速, 加快; 踩油门: *If you don't step on it we'll miss the plane.* 你要是不加快速度, 我们就赶不上飞机了。

7 **step lively!** *BrE spoken* used to tell someone to hurry【英口】快点〔用于催促某人〕 —see also 另见 **step into the breach** (BREACH[1] (5))

step down also 又作 **step aside** *phr v* [I] to leave your job or official position 辞职; 下台; 让位: **step down as sth** *Eve has stepped down as chairperson.* 伊芙已经辞去主席一职。| **step down in favour of sb/sth** *Lister is stepping down in favor of a younger man.* 利斯特准备退下来, 让位给一个更年轻的人。

step in *phr v* [I] to become involved in a discussion or disagreement, especially in order to stop the trouble; INTERVENE 介入, 干涉, 插手: *If the dispute continues, the government will have to step in.* 如果争端继续下去, 政府将不得不进行干涉。

step out *phr v* [I] **1** *AmE* to go out for a short time【美】出去一会儿, 暂时离开: *Molly just stepped out but she'll be back soon.* 莫莉刚出去一会儿, 不过她很快就会回来。—see also 另见 POP[1] (1) **2** *old-fashioned* to start walking fast【过时】加快步伐, 快走

step sth ↔ **up** *phr v* [T] to increase the amount of an activity or the speed of a process in order to improve a situation 使增加; 使上升; 使加快: *We will be stepping up production to meet the increased demand.* 为满足需求的增长, 我们将增加产量。

step- /stɛp; step/ *prefix* related not by birth but because a parent has remarried 继的〔无血缘关系, 但因父母一方再婚而构成亲缘关系的〕: *my stepfather* (=not my real father, but a man who has married my mother) 我的继父 | *her stepchildren* 她的继子女

step·broth·er /ˋstɛp,brʌðɚ; ˈstepbrʌðə/ *n* [C] a boy or man whose father or mother has married your father or mother 继父[继母]的儿子

step-by-step /ˌ· · ˈ·◄/ *adj* [only before noun 仅用于名词前] a step-by-step plan, method etc does things carefully and in a particular order 一步接着一步的; 循序渐进的

step·child /ˋstɛp,tʃaɪld; ˈsteptʃaɪld/ *n* [C] a stepdaughter or stepson 继女; 继子〔妻子与前夫或丈夫与前妻所生的孩子〕

step·daugh·ter /ˋstɛp,dɔtɚ; ˈstepdɔːtə/ *n* [C] a daughter that your husband or wife has from being married to someone else before 继女〔妻子与前夫或丈夫与前妻所生的女儿〕

step·fa·ther /ˋstɛp,fɑðɚ; ˈstepfɑːðə/ *n* [C] the man who is married to your mother but who is not your father 继父

Step·ford Wives, The /ˌstɛpfɚd ˋwaɪvz; ˌstepfəd ˈwaɪvz/ (1975) a horror film based on a book by Ira Levin, about a group of married women in a US village whose husbands secretly replace them with ROBOTS. The robots look exactly like the women, but they are designed to be interested only in cooking, cleaning their houses, and pleasing their husbands in every way. The phrase is sometimes used to describe women who behave in this way.《斯特福德郡的妻子们》, 又译《复制娇妻》〔(1975), 根据艾拉·莱文同名小说改编的恐怖电影, 讲述美国一个村庄有一群已婚妇女被丈夫用机器人秘密替代的故事。机器人看起来与她们完全一样, 但被设计成只关心烧菜做饭、打扫屋子、千方百计取悦丈夫的女性。这一短语有时用来指此类女性〕

Ste·phen·son /ˋstivənsn̩; ˈstiːvənsən/, **George** (1781-1848) a British engineer who developed the first steam-powered railway engine. He also built the first public railway to carry passengers in 1825 (the Stockton and Darlington Railway in northern England). His most famous steam train was called The Rocket. 斯蒂文森〔(1781-1848), 英国工程师, 蒸汽机车的发明者。1825 年, 他建成了世界上第一条客运铁路。其最著名的蒸汽机车名为"火箭号"〕

Stephenson, Rob·ert (1803-59) a British engineer, the son of George Stephenson. He continued his father's work on the development of the steam train, and also built bridges, including the railway bridge over the Menai Straits in North Wales. 斯蒂文森〔(1803-1859), 英国工程师。乔治·斯蒂文森之子。他不仅继承父业研究蒸汽机车, 而且设计建造桥梁, 其中包括北威尔士的梅奈海峡铁路大桥〕

step·lad·der /ˋstɛp,lædɚ; ˈstep,lædə/ *n* [C] a LADDER with two sloping parts that are joined at the top and that can be folded flat 活(动)梯(子), 梯凳

step·moth·er /ˋstɛp,mʌðɚ; ˈstepmʌðə/ *n* [C] a woman who is married to your father but who is not your mother 继母

CULTURAL NOTE 文化注释

In children's stories, especially FAIRY TALES, the stepmother is usually a very evil character who is cruel to her stepchildren (STEPCHILD). Sometimes she is called the 'wicked stepmother' as in the story *Cinderella*, and sometimes she is actually a WITCH as in the story of *Snow White and the Seven Dwarfs*. 在儿童故事, 特别是在童话中, 继母是个很坏的角色, 她对待继子继女们很不好。有时继母被叫做"邪恶的后妈", 像在《灰姑娘》中就是这样; 有时她实际上就是个巫婆, 像《白雪公主和七个小矮人》中的继母那样。

step·par·ent /ˋstɛp,pɛrənt; ˈstep,peərənt/ *n* [C] a stepfather or stepmother 继父, 后父; 继母, 后母

steppes, the /stɛps; steps/ *n* a large area of land without trees, especially an area in Russia, parts of Asia, and southeast Europe〔尤指俄罗斯、亚洲和欧洲东南部分地区的〕无树木的大草原, 干草原

step·ping-stone /ˈ· · ·/ *n* [C] **1** something that helps you to progress towards achieving something especially in your work〔尤指工作上〕达到成功的手段, 进身之阶: *Think of this job as a stepping-stone to something better.* 把这个工作看做是通往更好工作的阶梯。**2** one of a row of large flat stones that you walk on to get across a stream〔过河用的〕踏脚石

step·sis·ter /ˋstɛp,sɪstɚ; ˈstepsɪstə/ *n* [C] a girl or woman whose father or mother has married your mother or father 继父[继母]的女儿

step·son /ˋstɛp,sʌn; ˈstepsʌn/ *n* [C] a son that your husband or wife has from being married to someone else before 继子〔妻子与前夫或丈夫与前妻所生的儿子〕

-ster /stɚ; stə/ *suffix* [in nouns 构成名词] **1** someone who has a particular quality 有…特征[品性]的人: *a youngster* (=a young person) 年轻人 **2** someone who is connected with, deals with, or uses a particular thing 与…有关的人; 参与…的人: *a trickster* (=someone who plays deceiving tricks) 骗子 | *a gangster* (=a member of a GANG)〔结成团伙的〕歹徒 | *a pollster* (=someone who carries out POLLS) 民意调查者

ster·e·o[1] /ˋstɛrɪo; ˈsteriəʊ/ *n* **1** [C] a machine for playing records, CDs etc that produces sound from two speakers (SPEAKER (3)) 立体声音响器材 **2** **in stereo** if music, a radio programme etc is in stereo, it is being played or broadcast using a system in which sound is directed through two speakers 用立体声播放的: *This programme is being broadcast in stereo.* 本节目是用立体声播放的。 3

stereo[2] also 又作 **ster·e·o·phon·ic** /ˌstɛrɪəˋfɑnɪk; ˌsteriəˈfɒnɪk◄/ *adj* using a system of sound recording or broadcasting in which the sound is directed through two speakers (SPEAKER (3)) to make it seem more real 立体声的: *stereo recording* 立体声录音 —compare 比较 MONO[2], QUADRAPHONIC

ster·e·o·gram /ˋstɛrɪə,græm; ˈsteriəgræm/ *n* [C] a picture that looks like a repeating pattern, but in which some people can see THREE-DIMENSIONAL objects 立体相片[图片]

ster·e·o·scop·ic /ˌstɛrɪəˋskɑpɪk; ˌsteriəˈskɒpɪk◄/ *adj* a stereoscopic photograph, picture etc is made so that when you look at it through a special machine it looks solid 立体的, 有立体感的

stereo sys·tem /ˈ· · · , · ·/ *n* [C] a set of equipment for playing music on, usually including a record player, CASSETTE PLAYER, and radio 立体声音响设备

ster·e·o·type[1] /ˋstɛrɪə,taɪp; ˈsteriətaɪp/ *n* [C] a fixed idea or image of what a particular type of person or thing is like 模式化的思想[形象]; 老一套; 旧框框: *racial stereotypes* 种族陈规 | [+of] *the stereotype of a woman who stays at home with the children* 待在家里照看小孩的妇女的典型形象 —**stereotypical** /ˌstɛrɪəˋtɪpɪkl̩; ˌsteriəˈtɪpɪkəl◄/ *adj*

stereotype[2] *v* [T usually passive 一般用被动态] to decide, usually unfairly, that certain people have particular qualities or abilities because they belong to a particular race, sex, or social class 对…有老一套看法; 把…模式化: [+as] *Homeless people are often stereotyped as a bunch of alcoholics.* 无家可归者经常被看成是一群酗酒者。—**stereotyping** *n* [U]: *sexual stereotyping* 性的公式化 —**stereotyped** *adj*

ster·ile /ˋstɛrəl; ˈsteraɪl/ *adj* **1** not able to have babies 不能生育的: *She became sterile because of exposure to radiation.* 她因接触辐射而失去了生育能力。—compare 比较 FERTILE (2) **2** completely clean and not containing any BACTERIA 无菌的, 消过毒的: *Operations must be carried out in a sterile environ-*

ment. 手术必须在无菌的环境下进行。**3** land that is sterile cannot be used for growing crops〔土地〕贫瘠的，不毛的，不长植物的 **4** lacking new ideas or imagination 缺乏新意念[想象力]的: *sterile thought* 缺乏新意的想法 —**sterility** /stɛˋrɪlətɪ; stəˈrɪlɪ̈ti/ *n* [U]

ster·il·ize also 又作 **-ise** *BrE*【英】/ˈstɛrə͵laɪz; ˈsterɪ̈laɪz/ *v* [T usually passive 一般用被动态] **1** to make something completely clean and kill any BACTERIA in it 给…消毒[杀菌]: *sterilized milk* 消毒牛奶 | *Sterilize the bottles with boiling water.* 用沸水把这些瓶子消毒。**2** to perform an operation that makes a person or animal unable to have babies 为…做绝育手术，使…失去生殖能力 —**sterilizer** *n* [C] —**sterilization** /͵stɛrələˋzeʃən; ͵sterɪ̈laɪˈzeɪʃən/ *n* [C,U]

ster·ling¹ /ˈstɝlɪŋ; ˈstɜːlɪŋ/ *n* [U] the standard unit of money in the United Kingdom, based on the pound 英国货币

sterling² *adj* **1 sterling silver/gold** silver or gold of a particular standard or pureness 标准纯银/纯金 **2 sterling qualities/effort/character etc** *especially BrE* qualities etc that are excellent and dependable【尤英】优秀的品质/出色的努力/高尚的品德等

stern¹ /stɝn; stɜːn/ *adj* **1** strict in a very serious and often unpleasant way 严格的，苛刻的: *a stern teacher* 严格的教师 | *groups calling for sterner penalties for drug offences* 呼吁对毒品犯罪施以更严厉惩处的团体 **2 stern look/expression/rebuke** something that someone says or does that expresses disapproval 严厉的神色/表情/指责 —**sternly** *adv* —**sternness** *n* [U]

stern² *n* [C usually singular 一般用单数] the back part of a ship 船尾，艉部 —compare 比较 BOW² (2) —see picture at 参见 YACHT 图

Sterne /stɝn; stɜːn/, **Laur·ence** /ˈlɔrəns; ˈlɒrəns/ (1713-68) an Irish writer whose best-known work is his humorous NOVEL *Tristram Shandy*, one of the earliest novels in English. His style influenced later writers who used the stream of consciousness method. 斯特恩〔(1713-1768)，爱尔兰作家。其幽默小说《项迪传》最为出名，这是最早用英语撰写的小说之一。斯特恩的创作风格对其后的意识流小说家具有一定影响〕

ster·num /ˈstɝnəm; ˈstɜːnəm/ *n* [C] *plural* **sternums** or **sterna** /-nə; -nə/ *technical* a BREASTBONE【术语】胸骨 —see picture at 参见 SKELETON 图

ste·roid /ˈstɪrɔɪd; ˈstɪərɔɪd/ *n* [C] a chemical compound produced in the body, but also given as a drug by doctors for injuries and used illegally by people doing sports to improve their performance 类固醇，甾族化合物

ster·to·rous /ˈstɝtərəs; ˈstɜːtərəs/ *adj* stertorous breathing makes a noisy sound〔呼吸〕打鼾的，发出呼噜声的: *His breathing was stertorous but regular.* 他呼吸声粗重但很均匀。

steth·o·scope /ˈstɛθə͵skop; ˈsteθəskəʊp/ *n* [C] an instrument used by doctors to listen to someone's heart or breathing 听诊器

stet·son /ˈstɛtsn̩; ˈstetsən/ *n* [C] *trademark* a tall hat with a wide BRIM (=edge), worn especially in the American West【商标】〔尤指在美国西部戴的〕斯特森高顶宽边帽 —see picture at 参见 HAT 图

ste·ve·dore /ˈstivə͵dɔr; ˈstiːvɪ̈dɔː/ *n* [C] *AmE* someone whose job is loading and unloading ships【美】码头装卸工，搬运工; DOCKER *BrE*【英】

Stevens /ˈstivənz; ˈstiːvənz/, **Thad·de·us** /ˈθædɪəs; ˈθædiəs/ (1792-1868) a US politician in the Republican Party who was strongly opposed to SLAVERY and was an important supporter of the programme of Reconstruction after the American Civil War 史蒂文斯〔(1792-1868)，美国共和党政治家。他极力反对奴隶制，是美国内战后南方重建计划的重要支持者〕

Stevens, Wallace /ˈwɑlɪs; ˈwɒlɪ̈z/ (1879-1955) a US poet whose collections of poems include *Harmonium* and *The Man with the Blue Guitar* 史蒂文斯〔(1879-1955)，美国诗人。创作有诗集《簧风琴》和《携蓝色吉他的男人》〕

Ste·ven·son /ˈstivənsn̩; ˈstiːvənsən/, **Ad·lai** /ˈædlaɪ; ˈædlaɪ/ (1900-65) a US politician in the Democratic Party who competed in the elections for President in 1952 and 1956, but was beaten by Eisenhower both times. He helped to establish the UN (=United Nations) in 1946, and was the US DELEGATE (=elected representative) to the UN from 1961 to 1965. 史蒂文森〔(1900-1965)，美国民主党政治家。1952、1965 年两度参加总统竞选，但均输给艾森豪威尔。1946 年参加了联合国的组建工作，1961 至 1965 年任美国驻联合国代表〕

Stevenson, Rob·ert Lou·is /ˈrɑbɚt ˈluɪ; ˈrɒbət ˈluːiː/ (1850-94) a Scottish writer whose books *Treasure Island* and *Kidnapped* are among the best-known adventure stories in English. He also wrote *The Strange Case of Dr Jekyll and Mr Hyde* 史蒂文森〔(1850-1894)，苏格兰作家。创作的《金银岛》和《绑架》属于最著名的英语冒险故事。另著有《化身博士》〕

stew¹ /stu; stjuː/ *n* **1** [C] a cooked dish, made of meat and vegetables that are cooked slowly together in liquid 炖煮的菜肴: *beef stew* 炖牛肉 **2 in a stew** *informal* to be confused or anxious, especially because you are in a difficult situation【非正式】〔尤指因处于困境而〕困惑的; 焦虑的: *You're in a real stew about this interview, aren't you?* 你很担心这次面试，对吗？

stew² *v* **1** [T] to cook something slowly in liquid 炖，煨，焖: *stewed apples* 炖苹果 **2 stew (in your own juice)** *informal* to worry because of something bad that has happened or a mistake you have made【非正式】自作自受

stew·ard /ˈstuɚd; ˈstjuːəd/ *n* [C] **1** a man who serves food and drinks to the passengers on a plane or ship〔飞机、轮船上的〕男乘务员，男服务员 **2** a man whose job is to look after a house and its lands, such as a farm〔房屋、田地的〕看管人 **3** a man who arranges the supply and serving of food in a club, college etc〔俱乐部、学校等的〕伙食管理员 **4** *BrE* someone who is in charge of a horse race, meeting, or other public event【英】〔赛马、聚会或其他公共活动的〕负责人，管事，干事 —see also 另见 SHOP STEWARD

Stewart /ˈstjuɚt; ˈstjuːət/, **James** (1908-97) a very popular US film actor, who had a soft, slow way of speaking and was known for often playing very ordinary, honest characters. His many films include *Mr Smith Goes to Washington* (1939) and *It's a Wonderful Life* (1946), and he also acted in several films by the DIRECTOR Alfred Hitchcock, including *Rear Window*. 斯图尔特〔(1908-1997)，深受欢迎的美国演员。其说话方式柔缓，以经常饰演普通的老实人而著名。主演过《史密斯先生到华盛顿》(1939) 和《美妙人生》(1946) 等多部影片。还曾出演希区柯克执导的《后窗》等影片〕

stew·ard·ess /ˈstuɚdɪs; ˈstjuːədɪ̈s/ *n* [C] a woman who serves food and drinks to the passengers on a plane or ship〔飞机、轮船上的〕女乘务员，女服务员

stew·ard·ship /ˈstuɚd͵ʃɪp; ˈstjuːədʃɪp/ *n* [U] the way in which someone controls and looks after an event or organization〔某活动或组织的〕管理方式

stewed /stud; stjuːd/ *adj* **1** [not before noun 不用于名词前] *informal* drunk【非正式】喝醉酒的 **2** *BrE* tea that is stewed tastes too strong and bitter because it has been left too long before being drunk【英】〔茶因为时间久而〕泡得太浓的

St Hel·ens /sent ˋhɛlənz; sənt ˈhelənz/, **Mount** a VOLCANO in Washington State in the northwestern US, which ERUPT*ed* in 1980 after a quiet period of over a hundred years, sending out ASH (=powder produced when something has been burnt) and LAVA (=hot liquid rock) over a wide area. The large amount of ash in the air affected the weather in many northern parts of the world for some time. 圣海伦斯火山〔美国西北部华盛顿州一火山。在休眠一百多年后于 1980 年爆发，喷射出的火山灰和熔岩覆盖了大片地区。大量火山灰飘浮在空气中，曾一度影响了北半球许多地区的天气状况〕

stick¹ /stɪk; stɪk/ *v past tense and past participle* **stuck** /stʌk; stʌk/ S2 W3

1 ►PUSH 推◄ [T always+adv/prep, I always+adv/prep] if a pointed object sticks into something or you stick it into something, it is pushed into it 刺，戳，插: **stick sth in/into/through etc** *They stuck pins in the map to mark enemy positions.* 他们把针插在地图上，标出敌人的位置。| **stick in/through etc** *Joe had cactus spines sticking in his finger.* 仙人掌的刺扎进了乔的手指。

2 ►FIX 固定◄ [I,T] to fix something to something else with a sticky substance, or to become fixed to a surface 粘，粘住，贴上: *I can't get this stamp to stick.* 这张邮票我贴不上。| **stick sth to/in/on etc** *It took hours to stick all these photos in my album.* 把这些照片都贴进我的相册花了好几个小时。| **[+to]** *It was so hot his shirt was sticking to his back.* 天气太热，他的衬衫都粘在背上了。

3 ►PUT 放置◄ [T always+adv/prep] *informal* to put something somewhere quickly and without thinking carefully; SHOVE¹ (2)【非正式】随便摆放: **stick sth in/on/there etc** *Just stick your coat on that chair.* 把你的外衣放在那张椅子上就行了。

4 ►DIFFICULT TO MOVE 难以移动◄ [I] if something sticks it becomes fixed in one position so that it is difficult to move 卡住; 钉住: *This cupboard door keeps sticking.* 这扇柜门老是卡住。

5 stick in sb's mind if something sticks in your mind, you remember it very well, especially because it is unusual or interesting〔尤因不同寻常或有意思而〕留在某人的脑海里，令某人记

忆犹新: *What really sticks in my mind is how sad the woman looked.* 真正令我难忘的是那个女人悲伤的神情。

6 stick it [T usually in negatives 一般用于否定句] to continue to deal with a difficult or unpleasant situation 继续应付困境; 坚持下去: *College is harder than I thought, I don't think I can stick it much longer.* 上大学比我想象的更难, 我想我是坚持不了多久了。

7 make sth stick *informal* to prove that someone is guilty【非正式】证明…有罪: *The police won't bring the case to court because they don't think they can make the charges stick.* 警方不会把这案件提交法院, 因为他们认为他们无法使指控成立。

8 you/they can stick sth *spoken* used to say angrily that you do not want what someone is offering you【口】留给你(们)/他们自己吧〔用于生气地表示自己不要所给的东西〕: *You can stick your job if you won't pay me more than that!* 你如果不愿意出更多的钱, 那就把这工作留给你自己干吧!

9 be stuck fast to be fixed in one position and unable to move 牢牢粘住; 卡住不能移动: *His arm was stuck fast in the drainpipe.* 他的胳膊卡在排水管里不能动了。

10 stick fast to a belief/idea etc to continue to believe something although it may be difficult 坚守某一信仰/观点等: *Through it all Stella has stuck fast to her belief in the Communist system.* 经过了所有这一切, 斯特拉坚持对共产主义制度的信仰。

11 be stuck for *spoken* to be unable to think or to find something that you need to have【口】无法想出; 找不到〔需要的东西〕: *If you're stuck for a babysitter, Alison's always free.* 如果你找不到人照顾孩子, 艾莉森总是有空的。

12 stick in your throat *BrE*【英】**/stick in your craw** *AmE*【美】**a)** if a situation or someone's behaviour sticks in your throat, it is so annoying that you cannot accept it〔指某种处境或某人的行为〕使人难以接受 **b)** if words stick in your throat, you are unable to say what you want〔指言词〕难以启齿, 说不出口

13 ►NAME 名字◄ [I] if a name that someone has invented sticks, people continue to use it〔指绰号〕被继续使用: *One newspaper dubbed him 'Eddie the Eagle' and the name stuck.* 一家报纸戏称他为"老鹰埃迪", 这个绰号就叫开了。

14 ►CARD GAME 纸牌戏◄ [I] to decide not to take any more cards in some card games 决定不再要牌: *I'm sticking.* 我不再要牌了。

15 can't stick *BrE spoken* to dislike someone or something very much【英口】极不喜欢; 无法忍受: *I can't stick her husband, he's always so rude.* 我无法忍受她的丈夫, 他总是那么粗鲁。| **can't stick sb doing sth** *Lena can't stick anybody reading over her shoulder.* 莉娜不喜欢别人在她背后一起阅读。—see also 另见 **stick/poke your nose into** (NOSE¹ (4))

stick around *phr v* [I] *informal* to stay in the same place for a little longer, especially in order to wait for something that you expect to happen【非正式】〔在某处〕逗留, 待在…附近〔尤指等待某事发生〕: *Stick around, there'll be dancing later.* 不要走开, 一会儿有舞蹈。

stick at sth *phr v* [T] *BrE*【英】**1** to continue to study or work hard at something in a very determined way 坚持…, 继续不懈地做…: **stick at it** *Just stick at it and you'll pass your exams easily.* 坚持下去, 你会轻松通过考试的。**2 stick at nothing** *informal* to be willing to do anything, even if it is illegal, in order to achieve something【非正式】无所顾忌, 不择手段: *Des'll stick at nothing to make money.* 德斯为了赚钱什么都做得出来。

stick by sb/sth *phr v* [T] **1** to continue to give your support to a friend who has problems 继续支持〔有困难的朋友〕: *Samuel promised to stick by her, whatever happened.* 塞缪尔答应无论发生什么事都会支持她。**2** to do what you said you would do or what you think you should do 坚持〔承诺等〕: **stick by a decision/promise etc** 坚持决定/坚守诺言等

stick sth **on** sb *phr v* [T] *informal* to prove or make it seem that someone is guilty of a crime【非正式】证明〔某人〕有罪; 诬告, 陷害: *They can't stick it on me – I wasn't even in the country at the time.* 他们无法诬告我, 我当时根本不在国内。

stick out *phr v*

1 ►COME UP OR FORWARD 向上或向前突出◄ [I] if a part of something sticks out, it comes out further than the rest of a surface or comes out through a hole 突出; 突出来: *Francis wore glasses and his front teeth stuck out.* 弗朗西斯戴眼镜, 门牙外突。| **stick out of/from/through** *Careful – there's a nail sticking out of that board.* 小心, 那块板上有颗钉子突了出来。

2 ►PUT STH OUT 伸出某物◄ [T **stick** sth ↔ **out**] to deliberately make part of your body come forward or out from the rest of your body〔有意〕伸出〔身体的一部分〕, 探出: *Carl stuck his leg out and tripped the man up.* 卡尔伸出一条腿, 将那个男人绊倒。| **stick your tongue out** (=show your tongue in order to be rude to someone) 伸舌头〔对某人无礼〕

3 stick it out to continue to the end of an activity that is difficult, painful, or boring〔把困难、棘手或枯燥的活动〕坚持到底: *The movie was really boring but we stuck it out.* 那部影片的确枯燥, 但我们还是坚持把它看完。

4 stick out like a sore thumb *informal* to look very unsuitable and different from everyone or everything around【非正式】碍眼, 惹人注目: *I'm not going to the party dressed like this, I'd stick out like a sore thumb.* 我不会穿成这个样子去参加聚会, 那会显得很碍眼。

5 it sticks out a mile *informal* used to say that a fact about someone's character or feelings is very clear and easily noticed【非正式】〔某人的性格或情绪〕很明显, 显而易见, 一目了然: *It always sticks out a mile when Jenny doesn't like someone, she just can't hide her feelings.* 珍妮不喜欢谁总是很明显, 她就是不会掩饰自己的感情。

6 stick your neck out *informal* to give your opinion about something when you know there is a risk that you may be wrong or that people may disagree with you【非正式】说冒风险[惹祸]的话

stick out for sth *phr v* [T] *informal* to refuse to accept less than what you asked for【非正式】坚持索取[要求]: *The unions are sticking out for a higher pay offer.* 工会坚持要求提高工资。

stick to sth *phr v* [T]

1 ►PROMISE/BELIEF 承诺/信仰◄ to do or keep doing what you said you would do or what you believe in 遵守, 信守; 坚持: *Just make a decision and stick to it.* 作个决定, 然后照着去做吧。| **stick to your decision/principles etc** *We have stuck to our election promises.* 我们遵守了我们竞选时的承诺。

2 ►CONTINUE WITH SAME THING 继续使用同一东西; 继续做同一件事◄ to keep using or doing one particular thing and not change to anything else 继续使用; 继续做: *If you're driving, stick to soft drinks.* 你如果要开车, 那还是坚持喝软饮料。| *Reporters should stick to investigating the facts.* 记者应该继续调查事实。

3 stick to it to continue to work or study in a very determined way in order to achieve something 坚持下去; 继续做下去: *I hated practicing, but I stuck to it and now I can play pretty well.* 我讨厌练习, 但还是坚持了下来, 现在我弹得很好了。

4 stick to the point/subject/facts to talk only about what you are supposed to be talking about or what is certain 紧扣主题/题目/事实: *We'll never finish this meeting if people don't stick to the point.* 如果大家不能紧扣主题, 我们这个会就永远开不完。

5 stick to the path/road etc to stay on a marked path or road so that you do not get lost 沿着小径/大路等走〔以免迷路〕

6 stick to the rules *informal* to do something exactly according to the rules【非正式】遵守规则

7 stick to your guns *informal* to refuse to change your mind about something even though other people are trying to persuade you that you are wrong【非正式】〔虽然受攻击仍〕坚持自己的立场[观点]

8 That's my story and I'm sticking to it. *spoken* used to say that you are not going to change any part of what you have already said【口】这就是我说的情况, 我坚持这一说法〔用于表示自己不会对已经说过的话作出任何改变〕

stick together *phr v* [I] *informal* if people stick together, they continue to support one another even when they have problems【非正式】互相支持; 团结一致: *If we stick together we've got a better chance.* 我们如果同心协力, 希望就更大。

stick out 突出; 伸出

Peter's ears stick out. 彼得长着一副招风耳。

Lucy stuck her tongue out. 露西伸出舌头。

stick up *phr v* **1** [I] if a part of something sticks up, it is raised up or points upward above a surface 向上突起; 竖起: *His hair stuck up as though he hadn't had time to comb it.* 他的头发都竖了起来，好像他没有时间梳理似的。| [**+from/out of/through etc**] *We could just see part of the boat sticking up out of the water.* 我们只能看见船的一部分露出水面。**2 stick 'em up** *slang* used to tell someone to raise their hands when threatening them with a gun【俚】〔被枪指着时〕举起手来〔威胁语〕

stick up 竖起

Dad's hair sticks up.
爸爸的头发直竖着。

stick up for sb *phr v* [T] *informal* to defend someone who is being criticized, especially when no one else will defend them【非正式】为…辩护; 支持; 维护: *At least my friends stuck up for me.* 起码我的朋友支持我。| **stick up for yourself** *She's always known how to stick up for herself.* 她总是知道如何保护自己。

stick with sb/sth *phr v* [T] *informal*【非正式】**1** to stay close to someone 紧跟; 跟…在一起，不离开…: *If you don't want to get lost, you'd better stick with me.* 你如果不想迷路的话，最好跟紧我。**2** to continue doing or using something the way you did or planned to do before 继续做[使用]，不放弃: *Let's stick with the original arrangements.* 我们按原先的安排去做吧。**3** to continue doing something, especially something difficult 坚持〔做某事，尤指困难的事情〕: **stick with it** *Stick with it and you'll win through in the end.* 坚持下去，你最终会成功的。**4** *informal* to remain in someone's memory【非正式】留在…的记忆里: *One thing he said then has stuck with me ever since.* 他当时说的一件事我一直记忆犹新。

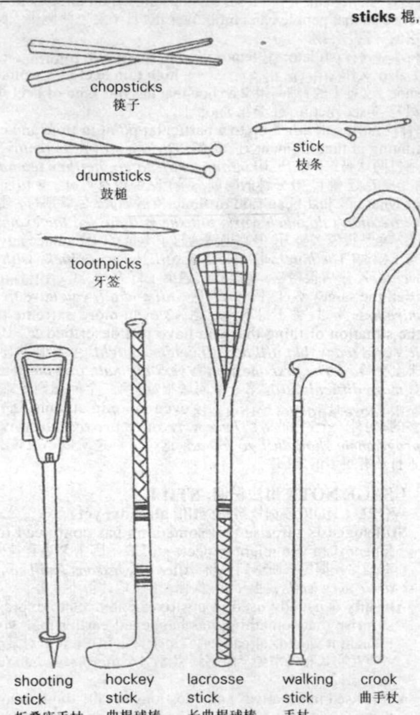

3 3 **stick²** *n*

1 ▶FROM A TREE 来自树上◀ [C] a long thin piece of wood that has fallen or been cut from a tree 柴枝, 枝条

2 ▶FOR WALKING 供走路用◀ a long thin piece of wood or metal that you use to help you walk 手杖, 拐杖 —see also 另见 CANE¹ (1)

3 ▶SPORT 体育运动◀ a long thin piece of wood that you use for hitting the ball in sports such as HOCKEY〔曲棍球等体育运动中使用的〕棍, 棒

4 ▶FOR HITTING SB 用于打人◀ a long thin piece of wood that you use to hit someone or something〔打击用的〕棍, 棒

5 stick of celery/dynamite etc a long thin piece of CELERY etc 一根芹菜/一条棍状炸药等

6 get (hold of) the wrong end of the stick *spoken* to misunderstand one small thing that makes you misunderstand everything about a particular situation【口】完全误解

7 give sb stick *BrE spoken* to criticize someone for something they have done, sometimes in a humorous way【英口】批评某人; 嘲讽某人

8 (out) in the sticks very far from a town or city 远离城镇: *They live somewhere out in the sticks.* 他们住在远离城市的某个地方。

9 ▶CAR 汽车◀ *AmE informal* a STICK SHIFT【美, 非正式】〔汽车的〕变速杆, 换挡杆

10 up sticks *BrE spoken* if you up sticks, you move to a different area or house【英口】搬家, 迁居: *He'd upped sticks and moved to London.* 他搬家去了伦敦。

11 old stick *BrE old-fashioned* used to describe someone in a friendly way【英, 过时】某种类型的人〔用于友善地描述某人〕: *Ned's a good old stick.* 内德是个蛮不错的家伙。

stick·ball /ˈstɪkˌbɔl; ˈstɪkbɔːl/ *n* [U] a game like BASEBALL that is played in the street by children in the US, using a small ball and a stick 棍球〔美国儿童在街头玩的类似棒球的游戏〕

stick·er /ˈstɪkɚ; ˈstɪkə/ *n* [C] **1** a small piece of paper or plastic with a picture or writing on it that you can stick on to something〔有图或文字的〕粘贴标签, 贴纸 —compare 比较 LABEL¹ (1) —see picture at 参见 SIGN¹ 图 **2** *BrE informal* someone who keeps trying to do something even when it becomes very difficult【英, 非正式】坚持不懈的人, 锲而不舍的人 3

stick·ing point /ˈ· · , ·/ *n* [singular] the thing that prevents an agreement being made in a discussion〔谈判中的〕症结, 障碍: *The question of equal pay is likely to be the sticking point.* 同等报酬的问题可能成为症结之所在。

stick in·sect /ˈ· , · ·/ *n* [C] an insect with a long thin body that looks very like a small stick 竹节虫

stick-in-the-mud /ˈ· · · , ·/ *n* [C] someone with old-fashioned attitudes who is not willing to try anything new 守旧的人, 墨守成规的人

stick·ler /ˈstɪklɚ; ˈstɪklə/ *n* **be a stickler for rules/punctuality etc** to think that rules etc are very important and that other people should behave according to them as well 坚持遵守规则/时间

stick-on /ˈ· ·/ *adj* [only before noun 仅用于名词前] stick-on material has a sticky substance on its back so that you can stick it on to something 可粘贴的, 背后带胶的: *stick-on sequins* 可粘贴的闪光装饰片

stick·pin /ˈstɪkˌpɪn; ˈstɪkˌpɪn/ *n* [C] *AmE* a decorated pin worn as jewellery【美】装饰别针

stick shift /ˈ· ·/ *n* [C] *AmE*【美】**1** a movable metal bar in a car that you use to control its gears〔汽车的〕变速杆, 换挡杆; GEAR LEVER *BrE*【英】**2** a car that uses a stick shift system to control its gears 使用变速杆系统的汽车 —compare 比较 AUTOMATIC² (2)

stick-to-it·ive·ness /ˌstɪk ˈtu ɪtɪvnɪs; stɪk ˈtuː ɪtɪvnɪs/ *n* [U] *AmE informal* the ability to continue doing something that is difficult or tiring to do【美, 非正式】坚韧不拔, 不屈不挠

stick-up /ˈ· ·/ *n* [C] *informal* a situation in which someone steals money from people in a bank, shop etc by threatening them with a gun【非正式】持枪抢劫

stick·y /ˈstɪkɪ; ˈstɪki/ *adj*

1 ▶SWEETS/HONEY ETC 糖果/蜂蜜等◀ made of or covered with a substance that sticks to surfaces 黏性的, 黏的: *Jeremy's hands were sticky with jam.* 杰里米的手上都是黏糊糊的果酱。| *tea and sticky buns* 茶和黏牙的圆面包

2 sticky label/tape etc *BrE* a LABEL¹ (1) etc that has glue on one side so that it sticks to surfaces【英】粘贴标签/黏胶带

3 ▶WEATHER 天气◀ making you feel uncomfortable and very hot, wet, and dirty 湿热得令人难受的: *a hot sticky day in August* 8月里一个湿热得令人难受的日子

4 ▶EMBARRASSING 令人尴尬的◀ *informal* a sticky situation, conversation, or event is embarrassing and makes you feel worried or nervous【非正式】〔情况、对话或事件〕令人尴尬的; 令人

焦虑的: *We were in for a long, sticky evening.* 我们注定要经历一个令人不安的漫漫长夜。

5 ▶DIFFICULT 困难的◀ a sticky situation, question, or problem is difficult or dangerous to deal with〔处境、问题等〕困难的, 棘手的: *The band now have a minder to get them out of sticky situations.* 乐队现在有个保镖帮助他们应付麻烦的情况。

6 ▶NOT HELPFUL 不肯帮忙的◀ *BrE* not willing to help you or do what you want【英】不肯帮忙的; 不大方的: *I asked him to lend me some money, but he was rather sticky about it.* 我要他借一点钱给我, 可是他不大乐意。

7 have sticky fingers *informal* to be likely to steal something【非正式】好偷窃的, 有偷窃习惯的

8 come to/meet a sticky end *BrE informal* to die violently especially because you have been doing something bad【英, 非正式】〔尤因做了坏事〕横死; 不好的下场, 悲惨的结局: *The gangsters in his novels always come to a sticky end.* 他小说中的歹徒都没有好下场。

9 be on a sticky wicket *BrE informal* to be in a situation that is difficult or that may become difficult【英, 非正式】处于困难的境遇, 处于不利的形势 —**stickiness** *n* [U]

stiff¹ /stɪf; stɪf/ *adj*
1 ▶BODY 身体◀ if a part of your body is stiff or you are stiff, your muscles hurt and it is difficult to move 僵直的, 不灵活的; 疼痛的: *Arthritis makes your joints stiff and sore.* 关节炎令关节发僵疼痛。| **stiff neck/back/joint** *Alastair woke up with a stiff neck.* 阿拉斯泰尔一觉醒来感到颈部僵直。| **feel stiff** *I felt really stiff after playing basketball last week.* 我上星期打完篮球后感到身体发僵。

2 ▶DOOR/DRAWER ETC 门/抽屉等◀ difficult to move, bend or turn 难移动的; 难弯曲的; 难转动的: *Pull hard – that drawer's very stiff.* 使劲拉, 那个抽屉很紧。

3 ▶PAPER/MATERIAL 纸/材料◀ hard and difficult to bend 硬的, 难折叠的: *a sheet of stiff cardboard* 一张硬纸板

4 ▶MIXTURE 混合物◀ thick and almost solid, so that it is not easy to stir 稠的, 难搅拌的: *Beat the egg whites until stiff.* 把蛋白打到发稠。| *stiff dough* 硬面团

5 ▶UNFRIENDLY 不友好的◀ unfriendly or very formal, so that other people feel uncomfortable 不友好的; 拘谨的: *He replied in a stiff, ironic voice.* 他用生硬、讽刺的口气回答。

6 ▶VERY HARD 非常严厉的◀ more difficult, strict, or severe than usual 艰难的; 严格的; 严厉的: **stiff sentence/penalty/fine** *There's a stiff fine for speeding.* 超速驾驶要受重罚。| **stiff competition** *He'll be facing stiff competition for that job.* 要得到那份工作, 他将面临激烈的竞争。

7 a stiff wind/breeze a fairly strong wind etc 强劲的风

8 a stiff drink/whisky etc a very strong alcoholic drink 烈性酒/威士忌等

9 keep a stiff upper lip to try to keep calm and not show your feelings in a situation when most people would become upset 保持沉着坚强; 咬紧牙关 —**stiffly** *adv* —**stiffness** *n* [U]

stiff² *adv* **1 bored/scared/worried stiff** *informal* extremely bored etc【非正式】极其腻烦/害怕/担心: *As a child I was scared stiff of going down to the cellar.* 小时候, 我非常害怕到地下室去。**2 frozen stiff a)** extremely cold 非常寒冷的, 冻僵的: *Joey was frozen stiff after walking through the snow.* 乔伊在雪中步行后快冻僵了。**b)** cloth that has frozen stiff is hard because the water in it has become ice〔布〕冻得坚硬的

stiff³ *n* [C] *slang*【俚】**1** the body of a dead person 死尸, 尸体 **2 working stiff** *AmE informal* an ordinary person who works to earn enough money to live【美, 非正式】〔挣钱谋生的〕普通人, 劳动者

stiff⁴ *v* [T] *AmE informal* to not pay someone money that you owe them or that they expect to be given, especially by not leaving a tip (TIP¹ (2)) in a restaurant【美, 非正式】不给〔某人〕付钱; 不给〔侍者〕小费

stiff·en /ˈstɪfən; ˈstɪfən/ *v* **1** [I] to suddenly become unfriendly, angry, or anxious〔突然〕变得冷淡; 顿时强硬起来: *Francesca stiffened at his suggestion that it was her fault.* 他暗示那是她的过错, 弗朗西斯卡一下子就变得强硬起来。**2** [I,T] to become stronger and more determined (使) 变得更坚强[坚定]: *The advancing army met stiffening resistance.* 推进中的部队遇到更加顽强的抵抗。| **stiffen sb's resolve** *His emotional speech was sure to stiffen their resolve.* 他那感人的演说一定会增强他们的决心。**3** [T] to make material stiff so that it will not bend easily 使〔材料〕变硬[坚挺]: *a spray to stiffen shirt collars* 能使衣领坚挺的喷剂 **4** [I] to become painful and difficult to move 变得酸痛[僵硬]: *His joints had stiffened.* 他的关节变得僵硬。

stiff-necked /ˌ· ˈ·◂/ *adj* proud and refusing to change or obey; OBSTINATE (1) 顽固而傲慢的, 倔强的

sti·fle /ˈstaɪfl; ˈstaɪfəl/ *v* **1** [I,T] to stop someone from breathing or be unable to breathe comfortably, especially because the air is too hot or not fresh (使) 感到窒息, (使) 透不过气来: *He was almost stifled by the fumes.* 他差点被烟熏得喘不过气来。**2** [T] to stop something from happening or developing 抑制, 阻止, 压制: *rules and regulations that stifle initiative* 压制积极性的规章制度 **3** [T] to stop a feeling from being expressed 强忍住, 压抑〔感情〕: *He stifled an urge to hit her.* 他强忍住冲动, 没有打她。| **stifle a yawn/smile/laughter etc** *Nancy stifled a yawn as the teacher's voice droned on.* 南希忍住呵欠, 听老师不停地唠叨。

sti·fling /ˈstaɪflɪŋ; ˈstaɪflɪŋ/ *adj* **1** a room or weather that is stifling is very hot and difficult to breathe in〔房间、天气〕闷热的, 令人窒息的: *a stifling, crowded carriage* 闷热拥挤的车厢 **2** a situation that is stifling stops you from developing your own ideas and character〔境况〕令人窒息的; 压制个性发挥的: *the stifling atmosphere of the court* 法庭上令人窒息的气氛

stig·ma /ˈstɪgmə; ˈstɪgmə/ *n* **1** [singular,U] a strong feeling in society that a type of behaviour is shameful 耻辱, 羞辱, 见不得人的感觉: *There is a strong stigma attached to suicide.* 自杀被认为是非常见不得人的事情。| **the stigma of alcoholism/abortion etc** *The stigma of alcoholism makes it a more difficult problem to treat.* 酗酒的羞耻感使之变得更加难以治疗。**2** [C] *technical* the top of the centre part of a flower that receives the POLLEN that allows it to form new seeds【术语】〔植物的〕柱头

stig·ma·ta /ˈstɪgmətə; ˈstɪgmətə/ *n* [plural] the marks on Christ's body caused by nails, or similar marks on the bodies of some holy people 圣痕〔耶稣(受难时)身上的钉痕或其他一些圣人身上相似的伤痕〕

stig·ma·tize also 又作 **-ise** *BrE*【英】/ˈstɪgməˌtaɪz; ˈstɪgmətaɪz/ *v* [T] **be stigmatized** to be treated by society as if you should be ashamed of your situation or actions 被视为可耻: *People with handicaps shouldn't be stigmatized.* 有生理缺陷的人不应该被人看不起。—**stigmatization** /ˌstɪgmətəˈzeɪʃən; ˌstɪgmətaɪˈzeɪʃən/ *n* [U]

stile /staɪl; staɪl/ *n* [C] a set of steps placed on either side of a fence so that people can climb over it〔设于篱笆两侧供人跨越用的〕梯磴, 台阶

sti·let·to /stɪˈleto, stɪ̮ˈletəʊ/ *plural* **stilettos** or **stilettoes** *n* [C] **1** also 又作 **stiletto heel** /·, ·· ˈ·/ a high thin heel of a woman's shoe〔女鞋上的〕细高跟 **2** a shoe that has this kind of heel 细高跟鞋 —see picture at 参见 SHOE¹ 图

still¹ /stɪl; stɪl/ *adv* **1** up to a particular point in time and continuing at that moment 还, 仍然: *Do you still play tennis?* 你还打网球吗? | *With 30 minutes still to go, neither team had scored.* 还剩下 30 分钟的时间, 两个队都没有得分。**2** in spite of what has just been said or done 虽然如此, 尽管那样, 然而: *Clare didn't do much work, but she still passed the exam.* 克莱尔虽然没怎么努力, 但她仍然通过了考试。| [sentence adverb 句子副词] *The hotel was terrible. Still, we were lucky with the weather.* 旅店很糟糕, 幸而我们遇上了好天气。| **still and all** (=all the same) 不过; 依然; 毕竟 *Still and all, you have to admire her.* 不过, 你不得不佩服她。**3** even more extreme than the situation or thing that you have just described 更, 还要: *It's cold today, but it'll be still colder tonight.* 今天很冷, 但晚上会更冷。| *The first question is very difficult, and the second is more difficult still.* 第一个问题很难, 第二个问题则更难。**4 still more/another/other etc** even more in amount 还有更多的/另外一个/别的等: *There were still more reasons why the programme shouldn't go ahead.* 这个节目之所以不应该继续进行还有更多的原因。

USAGE NOTE 用法说明: STILL
WORD CHOICE 词语辨析: **still, already, yet**

Still suggests surprise that something has continued for longer than you might expect. still 表示因为某事物持续时间比预期更久而感到惊讶: *After fifty lessons I still can't drive very well.* 我上了 50 次课, 车还是开得不太好。

Already is usually used in positive sentences to express surprise that something has happened earlier than you thought it would. already 通常用于肯定句中, 表示对某事物发生得比预料中更早而感到惊讶: *Are they here already?* 他们已经到了?

Yet is used in negatives and questions to talk about things that you expect to happen, but have not happened or might not have happened. yet 用于否定句和疑问句中, 表示某事物预期应该发生但还未发生或可能还未发生: *I haven't had breakfast yet.* 我还没有吃早餐。| *Has Bill arrived yet?* 比尔到了吗?

Compare **yet** with **already** in a question. 比较疑问句中 yet 和 already 的区别: *Have you had lunch yet?* asks for information, while *Have you had your lunch already?* expresses surprise that lunch has already been eaten. Have you had lunch yet?（你吃过午饭了吗?）这句话是询问信息, Have you had your lunch already?（你已经吃过午饭了?）则表示感到惊讶。

Yet used instead of **still** in a positive sentence is rare and a little formal. 肯定句中用 yet 替代 still 的情况很少见, 而且较正式: *We have yet to hear the truth.* 我们还没有听到实情。| *The Council may yet surprise us.* 地方议会也许仍会令我们吃惊。In conversation, however, you are more likely to say something like 但在对话中, 更常用类似下面例句的说法: *We don't know the truth yet.* 我们仍然不知道实情。

GRAMMAR 语法

Still usually comes immediately before any negative word. still 通常直接出现在否定词前: *She still isn't ready.* 她还没有准备好。| *They still don't know.* 他们仍然不知道。| *A solution has still not been found* (or 或 *...still hasn't,* NOT 不用 *...has not still*). 目前还没有找到解决的办法。

Still usually comes immediately after a positive modal verb. still 通常紧跟在肯定的情态动词后: *I can still remember* (NOT 不用 *still can remember*). 我仍然记得。| *He may still be there* (or 或 *...be still there...*). 他可能还在那里。

Otherwise **still** comes after the verb **to be** and immediately before any main verb. still 还出现在动词 to be 之后或直接用于其他主要动词之前: *He's still eating* (NOT 不用 *still is eating*). 他还在吃。| *It's still wet outside.* 外面还是湿的。| *We still have time* (NOT 不用 *have still time*). 我们还有时间。| *I still love her.* 我依然爱她。

still² *adj* **1** not moving 静止的, 不动的: *a still pool* 不流动的池塘 | **keep/stand/lie etc still** *Keep still while I tie your shoe.* 别动, 我给你系鞋带。**2** not windy 无风的: *a hot, still, airless day* 无风、闷热的一天 **3** quiet, calm, and without any activity 寂静的; 安宁的; 宁静的: *It was so still you could have heard a pin drop.* 真静啊, 静得连掉下一根针都听得见。**4** *BrE* a still drink does not contain gas【英】〔饮料〕不含气体的 **5 still waters run deep** used to say that someone who is quiet may have very strong feelings or a lot of knowledge 静水流深〔指沉默寡言者可能有强烈的情感或丰富的知识〕—**stillness** *n* [U]

still³ *n* [C] **1** a photograph of a scene from a cinema film〔电影的〕剧照; 定格画面 **2** a piece of equipment for making alcoholic drinks out of grain or potatoes〔酿酒用的〕蒸馏器 **3 the still of the night/evening etc** *literary* the calm and quiet of the night etc【文】夜间/傍晚等的寂静

still⁴ *v* [T] *literary*【文】**1** to make someone or something become quiet or calm 使安静, 使静止: *The food stilled the baby's cries.* 婴儿有了吃的便不哭了。**2** if a doubt or fear is stilled, it becomes weaker or goes away 使〔疑虑或恐惧〕减轻[消除]; 使平静

still·birth /ˈstɪlˌbɜθ; ˈstɪlbɜːθ/ *n* [C,U] a birth in which the baby is born dead 死产, 死胎 —compare 比较 ABORTION, MISCARRIAGE

still·born /ˈstɪlˌbɔrn; ˈstɪlbɔːn/ *adj* **1** born dead 死产的: *a stillborn baby* 死产儿 **2** ending before having had a chance to start 未开始便结束的; 夭折的: *a stillborn romance* 夭折的罗曼史

still life /ˌ· ˈ·◂/ *plural* **still lifes** *n* [C,U] a picture of an arrangement of objects, especially flowers and fruit 静物画

stilt /stɪlt; stɪlt/ *n* [C usually plural 一般用复数] **1** one of two poles on which you can stand and walk high above the ground 高跷: *A clown crossed the ring on stilts.* 一个小丑踩着高跷走过圆形表演场。**2** one of a set of poles that support a building so it is raised above ground or water level〔将建筑物撑离地面或水面的〕支撑物, 支材

stilt·ed /ˈstɪltɪd; ˈstɪltʲd/ *adj* a stilted style of writing or speaking is formal, and unnatural〔文体、言谈〕呆板的, 生硬的, 不自然的: *a stilted conversation* 生硬的对话 —**stiltedly** *adv*

Stil·ton /ˈstɪltn̩; ˈstɪltən/ *n* [U] a kind of English cheese that is white with grey-blue marks and has a strong taste〔英国的〕斯提尔顿干酪, 蓝芝士

stim·u·lant /ˈstɪmjələnt; ˈstɪmjʊ̈lənt/ *n* [C] **1** a drug or substance that makes you feel more active and full of energy 兴奋剂[药]; 引起兴奋的物质: *Caffeine is a stimulant.* 咖啡因是一种兴奋剂。| [+to] *a stimulant to appetite* 刺激食欲的兴奋剂 | **stimulant effects/properties etc** *a drug with stimulant properties* 具有兴奋剂性能的药品 **2** something that encourages more of a particular activity; STIMULUS 刺激(物): *economic stimulants* 刺激经济增长的措施 | [+to] *Travel can be a stimulant to learning.* 旅游能够成为刺激学习的因素。

stim·u·late /ˈstɪmjəˌlet; ˈstɪmjʊ̈leɪt/ *v* [T] **1** to encourage an activity to begin or develop further 刺激, 促使, 促进: *The discussions stimulated a free exchange of ideas.* 讨论促进了思想的自由交流。| **stimulate growth/demand/the economy etc** (=make economic growth etc start or become stronger) 刺激增长/需求/经济等 **2** to encourage someone by making them excited about and interested in something 激发; 鼓励, 激励: **stimulate sb to do sth** *An inspiring teacher can stimulate students to succeed.* 一个富有启发性的教师可以激励学生取得成功。**3** to make a plant or part of the body become active or stronger 使活跃; 使强壮: *Light stimulates plant growth.* 光会促进植物的生长。—**stimulative** /-ˌletɪv; -lətɪv/ *adj* —**stimulation** /ˌstɪmjəˈleʃən; ˌstɪmjʊ̈ˈleɪʃən/ *n* [U]

stim·u·lat·ing /ˈstɪmjəˌletɪŋ; ˈstɪmjʊ̈leɪtɪŋ/ *adj* **1** exciting or full of new ideas 使人兴奋的; 充满新思想的: *We had a most stimulating conversation.* 我们进行了一次很有启发性的谈话。**2** making you feel more active and healthy 使人振奋的: *I find mountain air much more stimulating.* 我觉得山上的空气非常使人振奋。

stim·u·lus /ˈstɪmjələs; ˈstɪmjʊ̈ləs/ *plural* **stimuli** /-laɪ; -laɪ/ *n* **1** [singular,U] something that helps a process to develop more quickly or more strongly 刺激(物), 促进因素: [+to] *The discovery of oil acted as a stimulus to the local economy.* 石油的发现促进了当地的经济。**2** [C] something that causes a reaction in a plant or part of the body 使植物[人体]产生反应之物, 刺激物: *A reflex action is a response to a stimulus.* 反射行为是对刺激的一种反应。

Sting /stɪŋ; stɪŋ/ (1951-) a British songwriter, singer, and actor who sang with the group The Police until they separated, and has worked successfully on his own since then. He is also well known for his work to protect the environment. 斯汀〔(1951-), 英国词作家、歌手、演员。他曾是"警察"乐队的一名歌手, 乐队解散后, 他独立发展, 并大获成功。他还以参与环保工作而闻名〕

sting¹ *v past tense and past participle* **stung** /stʌŋ; stʌŋ/ **1** [I,T] if an insect or a plant stings you, it causes a sharp pain and that part of your body swells 刺, 蜇, 叮: *Henry was stung by a bee at the picnic.* 亨利在野餐时被蜜蜂蜇了一下。**2** [I,T] to hurt or to make something hurt with a sudden sharp pain for a short time (使)刺痛, (使)产生〔短时间的〕剧痛: *The antiseptic might sting a little.* 这消毒剂可能会引起轻微刺痛。| *Chopping onions makes my eyes sting.* 切洋葱把我的眼睛辣得很痛。**3** [T usually passive 一般用被动态] if a remark or criticism stings, it makes you feel upset and embarrassed 使感到气愤[尴尬]: *Days later she was still stung by the accusations.* 好多天后, 她仍因受到指控而感到气愤。| **sting sb into (doing) sth** *Her harsh words stung him into action.* 她严厉的批评刺激他采取了行动。| **stinging rebuke/sarcasm etc** (=severe and strongly expressed criticism etc) 尖刻的指责/挖苦等

sting sb **for** sth *informal*【非正式】**1** *especially BrE* to charge someone too much for something【尤英】向〔某人〕索取过高的价钱, 在…上敲〔某人的〕竹杠: *The garage stung him for £300.* 汽车修理站敲了他300英镑。**2** *BrE* to borrow money from someone【英】向〔某人〕借钱: *Can I sting you for a fiver?* 我能跟你借五英镑吗?

sting² *n*

1 ▶**INSECT/ANIMAL** 昆虫/动物◀ [C] *BrE* a sharp needle-like part of an animal or insect's body that can be pushed through the skin of a person or animal, often leaving poison【英】刺, 螯刺, 螯针; STINGER *AmE*【美】

2 ▶**WOUND** 伤(口)◀ [C] a wound or mark made when an insect or plant stings you 刺伤处, 蜇伤处: *Rub ointment on to the wasp sting.* 把药膏涂在黄蜂蜇伤的地方。

3 ▶**PAIN** 疼痛◀ [singular] a sharp pain in your eyes or skin, caused by being hit, smoke etc 刺痛, 剧痛: *the sting of salt in a wound* 盐入伤口的剧痛

4 a sting in the tail an unexpected end to a story, suggestion etc, that makes the whole thing less pleasant for the person listening〔指故事或建议等的〕使人不快的结尾

5 take the sting out of to make something unpleasant easier to deal with 使不引起刺痛; 使不快的事较易应付: *She smiled to take the sting out of her words.* 她微笑着, 使自己的话不至于刺痛别人。

6 ▶**CRIME** 犯罪◀ [C] *AmE*【美】**a)** a situation in which criminals obtain a large amount of money by cheating someone; SWINDLE²〔巨额〕诈骗 **b)** a situation in which the police catch criminals by pretending to be involved in criminal activity themselves〔警方假装参与犯罪以抓获罪犯的〕圈套

sting·er /ˈstɪŋɚ; ˈstɪŋə/ *n* [C] *AmE* the sharp needle-like part of an animal or insect's body that can be pushed through the

skin of a person or animal, often leaving poison【美】刺，螯刺，螯针；STING² (1) *BrE*【英】

stinging net·tle /ˈ‥,‥/ *n* [C] a wild plant with leaves that sting and leave red marks on the skin 带刺荨麻

sting·ray /ˈstɪŋ,re; ˈstɪŋreɪ/ *n* [C] a large fish with a flat body and several sharp points on its back near its tail 刺魟

stin·gy /ˈstɪndʒɪ; ˈstɪndʒi/ *adj* **1** *informal* not generous, especially with money, when you can easily afford to be【非正式】吝啬的，小气的：*Jim's too stingy to give money to charity.* 吉姆太小气，不愿捐钱行善。**2** a stingy amount of something, especially food, is too small to be enough 极少量的，不足的：*The helpings here are pretty stingy.* 这里的一份食物量很少。—**stingily** *adv* —**stinginess** *n* [U]

3 **stink¹** /stɪŋk; stɪŋk/ *past tense* **stank** /stæŋk; stæŋk/ *past participle* **stunk** /stʌŋk; stʌŋk/ *v* [I] **1** to have a strong and very unpleasant smell 散发恶臭，发臭味：*That paint stinks!* 那种油漆味道难闻极了！| **[+of]** *The place stank of old fish.* 那地方有陈鱼的臭味。| **it stinks** *It stinks of smoke in here.* 这里有难闻的烟味。| **stink to high heaven** (=stink very much) 臭气熏天 **2 it stinks!** *spoken* used to say that you do not like something【口】糟透了〔用于表示不喜欢某事物〕：*"What did you think of the show?" "It stank!"* "你觉得那演出怎么样?" "糟透了!" **3** to make you think that something dishonest has been done secretly 让人感觉不对劲：*The whole business really stinks.* 这整件事让人感觉很不对头。

stink sth **out** *BrE*【英】, **stink** sth **up** *AmE*【美】*phr v* [T] to fill a place with a very unpleasant smell 使…充满难闻的味道：*Those onions are stinking the whole house out.* 那些洋葱弄得满屋子都是难闻的气味。

stink² *n* [C] **1** a terrible smell 恶臭，难闻的气味：*What a stink!* 这味道真臭！| **[+of]** *a stink of rotten eggs* 变质鸡蛋的臭味 **2 make/raise/cause etc a stink** to complain very strongly because you are annoyed about something 强烈抱怨；大吵大闹：*I'm going to kick up a stink if they don't get us onto a flight soon.* 如果他们不尽快安排我们上飞机，我就要大闹一场。**3 work/run/go like stink** *BrE* to work etc as fast and as well as you can【英】卖力地工作/奔跑/行走：*We had to work like stink to meet the deadline.* 为了能在最后期限之前完成，我们不得不卖命工作。

S

stink bomb /ˈ‥ ,/ *n* [C] a small container that produces an extremely bad smell when it is broken〔爆炸时发出恶臭的〕臭弹

stink·er /ˈstɪŋkɚ; ˈstɪŋkə/ *n* [C] *informal*【非正式】**1** something that is very difficult or unpleasant 非常困难[令人不快]的事：*This cold I've got is a real stinker.* 这次我得的感冒真是令人难受。**2** someone who behaves badly 行为恶劣的人，非常无礼的人：*That son of theirs is a little stinker!* 他们那个儿子是个讨厌的小家伙！

stink·ing /ˈstɪŋkɪŋ; ˈstɪŋkɪŋ/ *adj* **1** having a very strong unpleasant smell 臭的，发(恶)臭味的：*an alley full of stinking garbage cans* 满是发出恶臭的垃圾桶的巷子 **2** *spoken* used to emphasize what you are saying when you are angry【口】令人讨厌的〔生气时用以加强语气〕：*Just keep your stinking money then.* 那你就留着你的臭钱吧。**3** [only before noun 仅用于名词前] *informal, especially BrE* very unpleasant【非正式，尤英】讨厌的，糟糕的：*Stinking weather we've had lately!* 最近的天气真糟糕！| **a stinking cold** *I've got an absolutely stinking cold.* 我得了讨厌的重感冒。**4 stinking rich** *informal* an expression meaning extremely rich, used especially when you think this is unfair【非正式】十分富有的，非常有钱的〔尤用于表示这是不公平的〕 **5 a stinking letter** *BrE* an angry letter in which you complain very strongly about something【英】言辞激烈的投诉信

stink·y /ˈstɪŋkɪ; ˈstɪŋki/ *adj informal* smelling unpleasant; SMELLY【非正式】难闻的，有臭味的：*stinky socks* 臭袜子

stint¹ /stɪnt; stɪnt/ *n* [C usually singular 一般用单数] **1** a limited or fixed period of work or effort 固定的工作期限；固定的工作量：**[+as]** *the beginning of her stint as waitress* 她做服务员的初期 | **do a stint** *Mark did a two-year stint in the army.* 马克服过两年的兵役。| **do your stint** (=do some work that other people also have to do and that you do not expect to enjoy much) 做自己的那份工作 *Has he done his stint at the bar yet?* 他在酒吧的那份工作做完了吗？**2 without stint** *formal* very generously【正式】不吝惜地，非常慷慨地：*Sarah gave of her time and money without stint.* 萨拉毫不吝惜地出了时间出了钱。

stint² *v* [I usually in negatives 一般用于否定句] to give or use too little of something 节制，吝惜；限量：**stint on sth** *You can't stint on the butter with that recipe.* 按那个食谱烹饪时，可不能吝惜黄油。

sti·pend /ˈstaɪpɛnd; ˈstaɪpend/ *n* [C] an amount of money paid regularly to someone such as a priest or student as wages or money to live on〔尤指给牧师、学生等的〕薪俸，薪金；助学金

sti·pen·di·a·ry¹ /staɪˈpɛndɪ,ɛrɪ; staɪˈpendiəri/ *adj* receiving a stipend 有薪俸的，领薪金的

stipendiary² also 又作 **stipendiary ma·gis·trate** /‚ˈ‥‥ˈ‥/ *n* [C] a MAGISTRATE in Britain who is paid by the state〔英国的〕领薪治安官，领薪地方法官

stip·ple /ˈstɪpl̩; ˈstɪpəl/ *v* [T] to draw or paint a picture or pattern using short STROKEs or spots instead of lines 点画；点刻 —**stippled** *adj* —**stippling** *n* [U]

stip·u·late /ˈstɪpjə,let; ˈstɪpjʊleɪt/ *v* [T] to say that something must be done, when you are making an agreement or offer〔在协议或提议中〕规定，约定：*Vanessa clearly stipulated payment in advance.* 瓦妮莎清楚地说明要预先付款。| **stipulate that sth be done** *Tony stipulated that all expenses be refunded.* 托尼讲明所有的开支都必须报销。

stip·u·la·tion /,stɪpjəˈleʃən; ,stɪpjʊˈleɪʃən/ *n* [C,U] a specific condition that is stated as part of an agreement 条款，约定[规定]的条件：**[+that]** *Kay signed, with the stipulation that she would take 10% of the profits.* 凯签字了，附加的条件是她要得到利润的10%。

stir¹ /stɝ; stɜː/ *v* 3 3

stir 搅动

1 ►MIX 混合◄ [T] to move a liquid or substance around with a spoon or stick in order to mix it together 搅，搅拌，搅动：*Stir the paint to make sure it is smooth.* 将油漆搅拌至均匀。| **stir sth in/into** *When the sauce has cooled, add the grated cheese and stir it in.* 调味汁冷却后，拌入磨碎的乳酪。

2 ►FEELINGS 感情◄ a) [T] to make someone have a strong feeling or reaction 激发，激起〔强烈的感情〕；引起〔强烈的反应〕：*He was stirred by the man's enthusiasm.* 他被那个人的热情所打动。| **stir sb's memory/imagination etc** *Her imagination was stirred by the scene.* 那场景激发了她的想象。| **stir memories/emotions etc** *The news stirred memories of their own persecution.* 该新闻唤起他们对自己受迫害的回忆。**b)** [I] a feeling stirs in you, you begin to feel it〔感情〕激起，唤起，挑起：*Excitement stirred inside her.* 她内心开始兴奋起来。

3 ►MOVE SLIGHTLY 微动◄ [I] **a)** to move slightly or change your position because you are uncomfortable or just before you wake up〔睡觉时〕轻轻地移动[挪动]：*I never stirred all night long.* 我睡觉整夜都一动也不动。**b)** to move slightly 微微地动：*Something stirred in the long grass.* 深深的草丛中有东西轻轻地动了一下。

4 ►DO STH 做某事◄ [T] to make someone feel they must do something 激发，激励〔某人做某事〕：*The incident stirred them to action.* 该事件激励他们行动起来。| **stir yourself** *especially BrE*【尤英】*He stirred himself to answer the door.* 他赶快去开门。

5 ►CAUSE TROUBLE 导致麻烦◄ [I] *BrE informal* to cause trouble between people by spreading false or secret information【英，非正式】〔通过散布谣言〕搬弄是非，挑拨：*Ben's always stirring!* 本总是搬弄是非！

6 ►MAKE STH MOVE 使某物移动◄ [T] to make something move slightly 使轻轻地移动：*The wind stirred the fallen leaves.* 风吹动落叶。

stir sth ↔ **up** *phr v* [T] **1** to deliberately try to cause arguments or problems between people 惹起[麻烦]，挑起[争吵]：*The new leader was accused of stirring up trouble.* 新领导人被指责挑起事端。| **stir things up** *Dave's just trying to stir things up because he's jealous.* 戴夫只不过因为嫉妒而试图搬弄是非。**2** to make something move around in the air or in water 搅起，搅动，使扬起：*The horse's hooves stirred up a lot of dust.* 马蹄扬起很多尘土。

stir² *n* **1** [C usually singular 一般用单数] an act of stirring something 搅拌，搅动：**give sth a stir** *Give that pan a stir, will you?* 把锅搅一下，行吗？**2** [C usually singular 一般用单数] a feeling of excitement or annoyance 激动[烦恼]的感觉：**[+of]** *a stir of disapproval* 一阵不满的骚动 | **create/cause a stir** *Plans for the motorway caused quite a stir among local residents.* 修建高速公路的计划在当地居民中引起了相当大的轰动。

stir-cra·zy /,ˈ ‥◂/ *adj informal* extremely nervous and upset, especially because you feel trapped in a place【非正式】〔尤指因感觉被困在某处而〕极度紧张的，神经失常的

stir-fry /ˈ‥ ,/ *v* [T] to cook something by mixing it in hot oil for a short time 炒〔菜〕，爆炒：*stir-fried vegetables* 爆炒的蔬菜 —**stir-fry** *n* [C]

Stirling /ˈstɝlɪŋ; ˈstɜːlɪŋ/ a COUNTY in central Scotland 斯特灵郡〔苏格兰中部一郡〕

stir·rer /ˈstɝə; ˈstɜːrə/ *n* [C] *BrE informal* someone who likes to cause trouble between people by spreading false or secret information【英, 非正式】煽动者; 搬弄是非者; 捣乱分子

stir·ring /ˈstɝɪŋ; ˈstɜːrɪŋ/ *adj* producing strong feelings or excitement in someone; ROUSING 激动人心的, 令人振奋的: *stirring music* 激动人心的音乐 | *a stirring speech* 令人振奋的演讲 — **stirringly** *adv*

stir·rings /ˈstɝɪŋz; ˈstɜːrɪŋz/ *n* **stirrings of love/doubt/rebellion etc** early signs that love etc is starting 爱情/疑虑/反叛等的先兆

stir·rup /ˈstɪrəp; ˈstɪrəp/ *n* [C] a ring of metal that hangs from each side of a horse's SADDLE¹ (1) for someone to put their foot in 马镫 —see picture at 参见 HORSE¹ 图

stitch¹ /stɪtʃ; stɪtʃ/ *n*

1 ▶**SEWING** 缝纫◀ [C] one of the short pieces of thread that you can see in a piece of cloth where it has been sewn〔缝纫中的〕一针: *Some of the stitches have come out of this shirt sleeve.* 这件衬衫的袖子有几针开线了。

2 ▶**WITH WOOL** 用毛线◀ [C] one of the small circles that join together to make a SWEATER etc, formed when you are knitting (KNIT (2)) with wool〔编织中的〕一针: **drop a stitch** (=lose a stitch because the wool has come off the needle) 漏掉一针

3 ▶**STYLE** 风格◀ [C,U] a particular way of sewing or knitting (KNIT¹ (2)) that makes a particular pattern 缝法, 针法; 编结法: *Purl and plain are the two main stitches in knitting.* 反针和平针是编织中的两种主要织法。

4 ▶**FOR WOUND** 缝合伤口◀ [C] a piece of thread that fastens the edges of a wound together〔缝合伤口的〕缝线: *The cut needed 15 stitches.* 这伤口需要缝15针。| *He had three stitches in it.* 他在该处缝了三针。

5 ▶**PAIN** 疼痛◀ [singular] a sharp pain in the side of your body, that you can get by running or laughing very hard〔跑步或大笑引起的〕胁部的突然剧痛: *I can't go any faster – I have a stitch.* 我无法跑得更快了, 我觉得胁部剧痛。

6 **in stitches** laughing uncontrollably 忍不住大笑, 忍俊不禁: **have sb in stitches** (=make sb laugh) 使某人忍不住大笑 *Her jokes had us all in stitches.* 她的笑话使我们大家都忍俊不禁。

7 **not have a stitch on** *informal* to be wearing no clothes【非正式】一丝不挂, 赤身露体

8 **not have a stitch to wear** to not have any clothing that is suitable for a particular occasion〔在某一场合〕没有什么衣服可穿

9 **a stitch in time (saves nine)** *spoken* used to say that it is better to deal with problems early than to wait until they get worse【口】一针及时, 可省九针; 及时处理, 事半功倍

stitch² *v* [T] to SEW two pieces of cloth together, or to sew a decoration onto a piece of cloth 缝, 缝合, 缝补; 缝缀: *She stitches the pieces together to make a quilt.* 她把小布块缝在一起做成被子。| **stitch sth onto** *Nina stitched a flower onto the skirt.* 尼娜把一朵花缝在裙子上。

stitch up *phr v* [T] **1** [**stitch** sth ↔ **up**] to put stitches in cloth or a wound in order to fasten parts of it together 缝合, 缝拢: *She stitched up the cut and left it to heal.* 她把伤口缝好让它愈合。**2** [**stitch** sth ↔ **up**] to get a deal or agreement completed satisfactorily so that it cannot be changed 圆满地完成: *The deal was stitched up in minutes.* 那交易几分钟就完成了。**3** [**stitch** sb ↔ **up**] *BrE informal* to make someone seem guilty of a crime by providing false information; FRAME² (3)【英, 非正式】陷害, 诬陷: *George said he'd been stitched up.* 乔治说他是被人陷害的。

stitch·ing /ˈstɪtʃɪŋ; ˈstɪtʃɪŋ/ *n* [U] a line of stitches in a piece of material 针脚

St Ives /sent ˈaɪvz; sənt ˈaɪvz/ a small town on the coast of Cornwall in southwest England, popular with tourists and also a centre for water sports and painters 圣艾夫斯〔英格兰西南部康沃尔郡沿岸一小镇。该镇为旅游胜地、水上运动中心、画家云集之地〕

St James's Pal·ace /ˌ· ˌ·· ˈ··/ a royal palace in central London 圣詹姆斯宫〔伦敦市中心的一座皇家宫殿〕

St James's Park /ˌ· ˌ·· ˈ·/ a small royal park near Buckingham Palace in London 圣詹姆斯公园〔伦敦白金汉宫附近一小型皇家公园〕

St John Am·bu·lance /ˌ· ˌ· ˈ···/ also 又作 **St John's Ambulance** a British organization whose unpaid members are trained to give first aid to anyone who is hurt or becomes ill. They often attend sports and other public events. 圣约翰救护机构, 圣约翰救伤队〔英国一组织。其会员不领取报酬, 接受训练后为各类伤病员提供急救服务, 经常出现在体育比赛等公共场合〕

St Kath·a·rine's Dock /sent ˌkæθərɪnz ˈdɑk; sənt ˌkæθərɪnz ˈdɒk/ a DOCK on the River Thames near the Tower of London, where ships used to be loaded and unloaded. It is now a centre for sailing boats. 圣凯瑟琳码头〔泰晤士河畔一码头。位于伦敦塔附近, 曾用于货物装卸, 现为帆船集中地〕

St Kil·da /sent ˈkɪldə; sənt ˈkɪldə/ a rocky island in the Atlantic Ocean, west of Scotland. People used to live there, but the last people left in 1930. It is now a nature reserve, with many interesting birds. 圣基尔达岛〔苏格兰以西大西洋一岩石岛。过去曾有人居住, 但1930年最后一批居民迁出该岛。现为自然保护区, 栖息着大量有趣的鸟类〕

St Kitts-Ne·vis /sent ˌkɪts ˈnivɪs; sənt ˌkɪts ˈniːvɪs/ a country in the east Caribbean Sea, officially called St Christopher Nevis, and consisting of three islands: St Kitts, Nevis, and Anguilla. Population: 38,756 (2001). Capital: Basseterre. 圣基茨—尼维斯〔东加勒比海一国家。正式名称为圣里克斯托弗—尼维斯。由圣基茨、尼维斯、安圭拉三座岛屿组成。人口: 38,756 (2001), 首都: 巴斯特尔〕

St Law·rence Riv·er, the /ˌ· ˌ·· ˈ··/ a North American river which flows from Lake Ontario to the Gulf of St Lawrence and forms part of the border between the US and Canada 圣劳伦斯河〔北美洲一河流。源于安大略湖, 注入圣劳伦斯湾。该河是美国和加拿大分界线的一部分〕

St Lawrence Sea·way, the /ˌ· ˌ·· ˈ··/ a waterway in North America through the St Lawrence River and all the Great Lakes, which can be used by large ships. It was built by the US and Canada by digging passages out of the ground to connect the river and the lakes, and was opened in 1959. 圣劳伦斯海道〔北美地区连接圣劳伦斯河与五大湖的一条航道, 可供大型船只航行。美国和加拿大共同挖掘了一条人工河道才将圣劳伦斯河与五大湖贯通。圣劳伦斯海道1959年投入使用〕

St Le·ger, the /sent ˈlɛdʒɚ; sənt ˈledʒə/ a well-known British horse race run in September at Doncaster. It is for three-year-old horses and was established in 1776. 圣莱杰赛马〔每年9月在唐克斯特镇举行的英国著名赛马比赛。该比赛只限3龄马参加, 初创于1776年〕

St Lou·is /sent ˈluɪs; sənt ˈluːi/ a city in the state of Missouri in the eastern central US, which is a port and an industrial centre. It is also famous for its JAZZ and BLUES music, and for the Gateway Arch, a very large ARCH built in the 1960s. 圣路易斯〔美国中东部密苏里州一城市, 为港口城市和工业中心。以爵士乐、布鲁斯音乐和20世纪60年代修建的大拱门著称〕

St Lu·cia /sent ˈluʃə; sənt ˈluːʃə/ a country in the east Caribbean Sea, one of the Windward Islands, south of Martinique. Population: 158,178 (2001). Capital: Castries. 圣卢西亚〔加勒比海东部一国家。位于马提尼克岛以南, 为向风群岛一岛屿。人口: 158,178 (2001), 首都: 卡斯特里〕—**St Lucian** *n, adj*

St Mar·tin-in-the-Fields /ˌ· ˌ···· ˈ·/ a church in London which has a small ORCHESTRA that performs concerts there. It is also an important centre for helping people who do not have homes. 圣马丁教堂〔伦敦一座教堂。拥有一支小型管弦乐队, 经常举办音乐会。亦是一处重要的无家可归者救助中心〕

St Mo·ritz /ˌsæn moˈrɪts; ˌsæn məˈrɪts/ a town in southeast Switzerland which is a fashionable and expensive centre for winter sports 圣莫里茨〔瑞士东南部一城镇, 时尚豪华冬季体育中心〕

stoat /stot; stəʊt/ *n* [C] a small thin animal with brown fur that is similar to a WEASEL, and kills other animals 白鼬, 短尾鼬, 扫雪

the stocks 足枷

stock¹ /stɑk; stɒk/ *n* [S3] [W3]

1 ▶**SUPPLIES** 供应◀ [C] also 又作 **stocks** *plural* a supply of something that you keep and can use when you need to 储备物, 备用物; 供应物: *stocks of flour and sugar* 储备的面粉和糖 |

build up a stock *The country has been building up its stock of weapons.* 该国一直在加强其武器储备。

2 ▶IN A SHOP 在商店◀ [C,U] a supply of a particular type of thing that a shop has to sell〔商店的〕存货, 现货: *Buy now while stocks last!* 欲购从速, 余货售完即止! | **out of/in stock** (=unavailable or available in a particular shop) 没有货/有现货 *I'm sorry, that swimsuit is completely out of stock in your size.* 对不起, 你要的尺寸的游泳衣全卖光了。| **take stock** (=check and count the goods in a shop) 盘点存货

3 ▶FINANCE 金融◀ **a)** [C] *technical* a SHARE[2] (5) in a company【术语】股份 **b)** [U] the total value of a company's shares (SHARE[2] (5))〔某公司的〕总股值

4 ▶COOKING 烹饪◀ [C,U] a liquid made by boiling meat or bones and vegetables, which is used to make soups etc 汤汁, 原汤〈如肉汤、骨头汤等〉: *chicken stock* 原汁鸡汤

5 ▶AMOUNT AVAILABLE 可利用的量◀ [singular] also 又作 **stocks** *plural* the total amount of something that is available to be used in a particular area 可供利用的数量, 总储备量: *Cod stocks in the North Atlantic have dropped radically.* 北大西洋鳕鱼的总量已大幅下降。

6 ▶ANIMALS 动物◀ [U] farm animals, especially cattle; LIVESTOCK 家畜, 牲畜〔尤指牛〕

7 take stock (of sth) to think carefully about the things that have happened in a situation in order to decide what to do next〔对形势〕作出估计[判断], 估量: *Turning 40 is a time to take stock of your life.* 到40岁了, 该检讨一下自己的人生了。

8 be of peasant/Protestant/Scottish stock etc to be related to a particular type of family in the past 出身于农民/新教徒/苏格兰家庭等

9 sb's stock is high/low if someone's stock is high or low, they are very popular or very unpopular 某人很受人/不受人喜爱; 某人的声望高/低: *The government's stock was high just before the election.* 政府在选举前夕声望很高。

10 ▶FLOWER 花◀ [C] a plant with pink, white, or light purple flowers and a sweet smell 紫罗兰

11 ▶PLANT 植物◀ **a)** a plant that you can cut stems off to make new plants grow〔从其上获取接穗的〕苗木 **b)** a thick part of a stem onto which another plant can be added so that the two plants grow together 砧木

12 ▶DOCUMENT 文件◀ [C] an official document promising that a government will pay back the money it has borrowed with a fixed amount of INTEREST[1] (4) 公债

13 a stock of jokes/knowledge/courage etc the jokes, knowledge etc that someone knows or has 一堆笑话/一套知识/一股勇气等: *John seems to have an inexhaustible stock of funny stories.* 约翰似乎有讲不完的滑稽故事。

14 the stocks a) a wooden structure in a public place to which criminals were fastened by their feet or hands in former times 足枷; 手枷〔旧时一种木制的刑具〕 **b)** a wooden structure in which a ship is held while it is being built〔造船用的〕船台

15 ▶ACTORS 演员◀ [C] *AmE* a STOCK COMPANY (2)【美】〔演出几种不同保留剧目的〕专业剧团 | **summer stock** (=a group of actors who work together on several plays during the summer) 夏季剧团〔夏季在一起演出几种不同剧目的一群演员〕| **do stock** (=work as an actor in this group) 做专业剧团的演员 *Jim's doing stock in Northern California.* 吉姆正在北加州做专业剧团的演员。

16 ▶CLOTHING 衣服◀ [C] a wide band of cloth worn around the neck so that the ends hang in front of your chest, especially by some priests 领圈;〔尤指牧师衣领下的〕阔领带 —see also 另见 **laughing stock** (LAUGH[1] (9)), **lock, stock, and barrel** (LOCK[2] (3)), ROLLING STOCK

stock[2] *v* [T] **1** if a shop stocks a particular product, it keeps a supply of it to be sold〔商店为销售而〕储备: *Do you stock English wines?* 你们备有英国葡萄酒出售吗? **2** to provide a supply of something so that it is ready to use 供应, 提供: *The fridge was stocked with all the butter and eggs needed for the Christmas baking.* 冰箱里存足了做圣诞糕饼所需的黄油和鸡蛋。**3** to put fish in a lake or river〔在湖或河里〕放养〔鱼〕: **[+with]** *rivers stocked with trout* 放养鳟鱼的河 —see also 另见 WELL-STOCKED

stock up *phr v* [I] to buy a lot of something to use when you need to 囤积, 贮存: **[+on]** *We stocked up on wine when we went to Paris.* 我们去巴黎时买了很多葡萄酒。

stock[3] *adj* **1 stock excuse/question/remark etc** an excuse etc that people often say or use, especially when they cannot think of anything more interesting or original 老一套的借口/问题/评论等 **2** [only before noun 仅用于名词前] kept in a shop as goods to be sold〔商店〕库存的, 常备的: *shoes in all the stock sizes* 所有常备尺码的鞋子

stock·ade[1] /stɑkˋed; stɒˈkeɪd/ *n* [C usually singular 一般用单数] a wall or fence made of large upright pieces of wood, built to defend a place〔防御用的〕栅栏, 围桩

stockade[2] *v* [T] to put a stockade around a place in order to defend it 用栅栏防卫, 用围桩围住

stock·breed·er /ˈstɑkˌbridɚ; ˈstɒkˌbriːdə/ *n* [C] a farmer who breeds cattle 牲畜饲养人

stock·brok·er /ˈstɑkˌbrokɚ; ˈstɒkˌbrəʊkə/ *n* [C] someone whose job is to buy and sell stocks (STOCK[1] (3)), bonds (BOND[1] (1)), and shares (SHARE[2] (5)) for other people 证券[股票]经纪人 —**stockbroking** *n* [U]

stock car /ˈ· ·/ *n* [C] **1** a car that has been made stronger so that it can compete in a race where cars often crash into each other〔用普通车改装的〕赛车 **2** *AmE* a railway carriage for cattle【美】〔火车的〕牲畜运载车厢

stock cer·tif·i·cate /ˈ· ·,··/ *n* [C] *AmE* an official document that shows that you own shares (SHARE[2] (5)) in a company【美】股份证书, 股票, 股权证

stock com·pa·ny /ˈ· ,···/ *n* [C] *AmE*【美】**1** a company whose money is divided into shares (SHARE[2] (5)) so that many people own a small part of it; JOINT-STOCK COMPANY 股份公司 **2** a group of actors who work together doing several different plays〔演出几种不同保留剧目的〕一群演员, 专业剧团

stock cube /ˈ· ·/ *n* [C] a small piece of solid substance made of dried juices from meat and vegetables, that is mixed with water to make STOCK[1] (4)〔经脱水的〕粒状汤料, 固体汤料

stock ex·change /ˈ· ·,·/ *n* [C usually singular 一般用单数] **1** the business of buying stocks (STOCK[1] (3)) and shares (SHARE[2] (5)) 证券交易, 股票交易: *She made a fortune on the stock exchange.* 她买卖股票赚了一大笔钱。**2** a place where stocks and shares are bought and sold 证券[股票]交易所

stock·hold·er /ˈstɑkˌholdɚ; ˈstɒkˌhəʊldə/ *n* [C] *especially AmE* someone who owns stocks (STOCK[1] (3)) in a business【尤美】股票[证券]持有人, 股东; SHAREHOLDER *BrE*【英】

Stock·holm /ˈstɑkhom; ˈstɒkhəʊm/ the capital city of Sweden. It is a port and also an important centre of business, art, and education 斯德哥尔摩〔瑞典首都, 港口城市, 重要的商业、艺术、教育中心〕

stock·i·nette /ˌstɑkɪnˋɛt; ˌstɒkɪˈnet/ *n* [U] *especially BrE* a soft cotton material that stretches, used especially for BANDAGES【尤英】松紧棉织物, 弹力棉织物〔尤用作绷带〕

stock·ing /ˈstɑkɪŋ; ˈstɒkɪŋ/ *n* [C usually plural 一般用复数] **1** a thin close-fitting piece of clothing that covers a woman's leg and foot (女式) 长筒袜 —compare 比较 PANTYHOSE, TIGHTS **2** *old-fashioned* a man's sock【过时】男袜 **3 in your stockinged feet** not wearing any shoes 只穿袜而不穿鞋的 —see also 另见 BODY STOCKING, CHRISTMAS STOCKING

stock-in-trade /,· · ˈ·/ *n* [U] **1** words or behaviour that a particular type of person often uses 惯用言辞; 惯有行为; 惯用手段[伎俩]: *A pleasant manner is part of a politician's stock-in-trade.* 待人亲切热情是政治家惯用的策略之一。**2** *old-fashioned* the things you need to do your job【过时】经营某行业所需的一切

stock·ist /ˈstɑkɪst; ˈstɒkɪst/ *n* [C] *BrE* a person, shop, or company that keeps a particular product or particular goods to sell【英】备有某种产品[货物]供出售的商人[商店、公司], 零售商 (店)

stock·man /ˈstɑkmən; ˈstɒkmən/ *n* [C] a man whose job is to look after farm animals 畜牧工人, 饲养员

stock mar·ket /ˈ· ,··/ *n* [C usually singular 一般用单数] the STOCK EXCHANGE 证券[股票]交易所, 证券市场

stock·pile[1] /ˈstɑk,paɪl; ˈstɒkpaɪl/ *n* [C+of] a large supply of goods, weapons etc that are kept ready to be used in the future, especially when they may become difficult to obtain〔尤指为有可能短缺而准备的物资、武器等的〕贮存, 储备

stockpile[2] *v* [T] to keep adding to a supply of goods, weapons etc that you are keeping ready to use if you need them in the future 贮存, 积聚〔物资、武器等〕: *The Superpowers are stockpiling nuclear arms.* 超级大国在加强他们的核武器贮备。

stock·pot /ˈstɑk,pɑt; ˈstɒkpɒt/ *n* [C] a pot in which you make STOCK[1] (4) 汤锅

stock·room /ˈstɑk,rum; ˈstɒkrʊm/ *n* [C] a room for storing things in a shop or office〔商店或办公室的〕仓库, 储藏室

stock-still /,· ˈ·/ *adv* not moving at all 静止地, 一动不动 (地): *Oscar stood stock-still and listened.* 奥斯卡站在那儿一动不动地听着。

stock·tak·ing /ˈstɑk,tekɪŋ; ˈstɒk,teɪkɪŋ/ *n* [U] *BrE* an occasion when you make a list of all the goods that you have a supply of at a particular time, especially in a shop【英】〔存货的〕盘点, 清点存货; INVENTORY (2) *AmE*【美】

Stockton-on-Tees /ˌ··ˈ·/ also 又作 **Stockton** a town in Cleveland, northeast England, near the point where the River Tees joins the sea. The first passenger railway in the world, running from Stockton to Darlington, was established in 1825. 蒂斯河畔的斯托克顿〔英格兰东北部克利夫兰郡一城镇，位于蒂斯河入海口附近。斯托克顿至达灵顿铁路为世界上第一条客运铁路，于1825年建成〕

stock·y /ˈstɑkɪ; ˈstɒki/ *adj* a stocky person is short and heavy and looks strong〔人〕矮而结实的，粗壮的 —**stockily** *adv* —**stockiness** *n* [U]

stock·yard /ˈstɑkˌjɑrd; ˈstɒkjɑːd/ *n* [C] a place where cattle, sheep etc are kept before being taken to a market and sold〔在运往市场出售之前临时的〕牲畜围栏

stodge /stɑdʒ; stɒdʒ/ *n* [U] **1** heavy food that makes you feel full very quickly 油腻易使人饱的食物 **2** *BrE informal* something written that is very dull and difficult to read【英，非正式】乏味难懂的作品

stodg·y /ˈstɑdʒɪ; ˈstɒdʒi/ *adj* **1** stodgy food is heavy and makes you feel full very quickly〔食物〕油腻易使人饱的 **2** *BrE informal* stodgy writing is dull and difficult to read【英，非正式】〔作品〕乏味难懂的 **3** a stodgy person is dull and behaves rather formally〔人〕墨守成规的，古板而乏味的 —**stodginess** *n* [U]

sto·gie /ˈstogɪ; ˈstəʊgi/ *n* [C] *AmE informal* a CIGAR, especially a thick cheap one【美，非正式】雪茄〔尤指廉价的粗雪茄〕

sto·ic /ˈsto·ɪk; ˈstəʊɪk/ *n* [C] someone who does not show their emotions and does not complain when something unpleasant happens to them 坚忍克己的人；不以苦乐为意的人；恬淡寡欲的人；禁欲（主义）者

sto·ic·al /ˈsto·ɪkl̩; ˈstəʊɪkəl/ *adj* also 又作 **stoic** not complaining or feeling unhappy when bad things happen to you 坚忍的；不以苦乐为意的；恬淡寡欲的；禁欲的 —**stoically** /-klɪ; -kli/ *adv*

sto·i·cis·m /ˈsto·ɪˌsɪzəm; ˈstəʊɪ̣sɪzəm/ *n* [U] patience and calmness when bad things happen to you 坚忍（精神）；不以苦乐为意；恬淡寡欲；禁欲

stoke /stok; stəʊk/ also 又作 **stoke up** *v* [I,T] to add more coal or wood to a fire used for cooking or heating 添加〔煤、柴火等燃料〕；给…添加〔燃料〕：**stoke sth with sth** *Stoke the furnace with wood.* 给炉子添加柴火。

stoke up *phr v* [T] **1** to add more coal or wood to a fire 添〔火〕：**stoke sth ↔ up** *Get the fire stoked up.* 把火添旺。**2 to stoke up fear/anger etc** to make a lot of people feel frightened etc about something 引发恐惧/愤怒等：*The leaflets stoked up a lot of fears of an invasion.* 传单引起很多人对侵略的恐惧。**3 stoke up on/with a)** to eat a lot of food, for example because you will not eat again for a long time 饱餐一顿，大吃一顿：*We stoked up on hot soup before going out in the snow.* 我们冒雪出门之前喝了很多热汤。**b)** to buy a lot of something that you need 大量购置，大量添置：*stoking up on warm clothing* 大量购置保暖的衣服

stoked /stokt; stəʊkt/ *adj AmE spoken* very excited about something good that is happening and that you did not expect【美口】〔因意外的惊喜而〕振奋的，非常兴奋的

Stoke Man·de·ville /ˌstok ˈmændəvɪl; ˌstəʊk ˈmændəvɪl/ a hospital in Buckinghamshire, southern England, which treats people who have severe injuries to the SPINE 史托克·曼德维尔医院〔英格兰南部白金汉郡一所医院，专门治疗脊椎严重损伤〕

Stoke-on-Trent /ˌ··ˈ·/ a city in Staffordshire, central England, on the River Trent. It is the centre of the area known as the Potteries, famous for making CHINA and POTTERY since the end of 18th century. 特伦特河畔的斯托克〔英格兰中部斯塔夫德郡一城市，濒临特伦特河。18世纪末以来，以制作瓷器和陶器而闻名，为"陶瓷区"的中心〕

stok·er /ˈstokɚ; ˈstəʊkə/ *n* [C] someone whose job is to put coal or other FUEL[1] (1) into a FURNACE 烧火工，司炉，火夫

Stoker, Bram /bræm; bræm/ (1847-1912) an Irish writer whose most famous work is his book *Dracula*. 斯托克〔(1847-1912)，爱尔兰作家。其最著名的作品为小说《吸血鬼德拉库拉》〕

Sto·kow·ski /stəˈkɑfskɪ; stəˈkɒfski/, **Le·o·pold** /ˈliəpold; ˈliːəpəʊld/ (1887-1977) a US CONDUCTOR who helped to make CLASSICAL music more popular in the US. As conductor of the Philadelphia Symphony Orchestra, he directed the music for, and appeared in, the Walt Disney film *Fantasia* (1940). 斯托科夫斯基〔(1887-1977)，美国指挥家，推动了古典音乐在美国的普及。曾以费城交响乐团指挥的身份为迪斯尼音乐片《幻想曲》(1940)担任指挥，并在该片中出现〕

stole[1] /stol; stəʊl/ the past tense of STEAL

stole[2] *n* [C] a long straight piece of cloth or fur that a woman wears across her shoulders 女用披肩，长围巾

sto·len /ˈstolən; ˈstəʊlən/ the past participle of STEAL: *stolen cars* 被盗的汽车 | *books stolen from libraries* 从图书馆偷出来的书

stol·id /ˈstɑlɪd; ˈstɒlɪ̣d/ *adj* someone who is stolid does not react to situations or seem excited by them when most people would react; IMPASSIVE 不易激动的；麻木不仁的；无动于衷的 —**stolidly** *adv* —**stolidness** also 又作 **stolidity** /stəˈlɪdətɪ; stəˈlɪdɪ̣ti/ *n* [U]

stom·ach[1] /ˈstʌmək; ˈstʌmək/ *n* [C] **1** the organ inside your body where food begins to be digested (DIGEST[1] (1)) 胃 —see picture at 参见 DIGESTIVE SYSTEM 图 **2** the front part of your body, below your chest 腹部：*Andrew was lying on his stomach.* 安德鲁俯卧着。**3 do sth on an empty stomach** to do something when you have not eaten 空着肚子做某事：*Don't go to work on an empty stomach.* 别空着肚子去工作。**4 have a strong stomach** to be able to see or do things that are unpleasant without feeling sick or upset 有很强的承受能力：*Don't watch that film unless you have a strong stomach.* 除非你忍受得了，否则不要去看那部电影。**5 turn your stomach** to make you feel sick or upset 使某人感到恶心，令某人反胃：*The sight of the slaughtered cow turned my stomach.* 看到被宰杀的牛令我感到恶心。**6 have no stomach for a fight/task etc** to have no desire to do something because you do not like doing it etc 不想打架/没兴趣做某工作等 3 3

stomach[2] *v* [T usually in questions and negatives 一般用于疑问句和否定句] **1** to be able to accept something, especially something unpleasant; ENDURE 承受，容忍，忍耐 | **can't stomach** *Tracy couldn't stomach the idea of moving to Glasgow.* 特雷西不能接受移居到格拉斯哥的主意。| **hard/difficult to stomach** *Rob found Cathy's attitude hard to stomach.* 罗布觉得凯茜的态度令人难以忍受。**2** to eat something without becoming ill 吃…而不感到难受[不适]：*I can't stomach fried food.* 我不能吃油炸的食物。

S

stom·ach·ache /ˈstʌməkˌek; ˈstʌmək-eɪk/ *n* [C,U] pain in your stomach or near your stomach 胃痛；肚子痛

stomach pump /ˈ·· ·/ *n* [C] a machine with a tube that doctors use to suck out the food etc inside someone's stomach, especially after they have swallowed poison 胃唧筒〔抽吸胃中食物等的医疗器具，尤用于给服毒者洗胃〕

stomp /stɑmp; stɒmp/ *v* [I always+adv/prep] **1** to walk with heavy steps, especially because you are angry〔尤指因生气〕跺脚，重踩：*Alex stomped angrily up the stairs.* 亚历克斯怒气冲冲地重步走上楼梯。**2 sb's stomping ground** a favourite place where someone often goes 某人喜欢常去的地方

stone[1] /ston; stəʊn/ *n* 2 1

1 ►ON THE GROUND 在地上◄ [C] a small piece of rock of any shape, found on the ground 石子，石块，石头：*Round, flat stones are the best for skimming across water.* 圆圆扁扁的石子打水漂最好。

2 ►ROCK 石，石料◄ [U] a hard mineral substance or rock 矿石；石料：*honey colored stone* 蜜黄色的矿石 | *stone statues* 石像

3 ►JEWELLERY 珠宝◄ [C] a jewel 宝石：*gem stones* 宝石

4 ►FRUIT 水果◄ [C] *BrE* a large hard single seed at the centre of some fruits【英】〔某些果实中的〕核；PIT[1] (9) *AmE*【美】—compare 比较 PIP[1] (1)

5 ►MEDICAL 医学的◄ [C] a ball of hard material that can form in organs such as your BLADDER or KIDNEYs〔膀胱或肾脏等器官中的〕结石

6 ►WEIGHT 重量◄ [C] *plural* **stone** or **stones** a measurement of weight used in Britain that is equal to 6.35kg 英石，听〔英国的重量单位，等于6.35公斤〕—see table on page C4 参见C4页附录

7 a stone's throw (away) very close to something 投石可及的距离，非常靠近，附近：*The villa was only a stone's throw from the beach.* 该度假别墅离海滩很近。

8 be made of stone also 又作 **have a heart of stone** to not show any emotions or pity for someone 冷酷无情，有一副铁石心肠 —see also 另见 FOUNDATION STONE, PAVING STONE, STEPPING-STONE

stone[2] *v* [T] **1** to throw stones at someone or something 向…扔石头，用石头掷击：**stone sb to death** (=kill someone with stones, especially as a punishment in the past) 投掷石头砸死某人〔旧时作为惩罚手段〕**2** *BrE* to take the stone out of fruit【英】去掉〔水果的〕核；PIT[2] (2) *AmE*【美】：*stoned dates* 去核的枣 **3 stone the crows!** also 又作 **stone me!** *BrE old-fashioned* used to express surprise or shock【英，过时】哎呀，啊〔表示惊讶或震惊〕

Stone, Ol·i·ver /ˈɑlɪvɚ; ˈɒlɪ̣və/ (1946-) a US film DIRECTOR and film writer whose films deal with recent US history

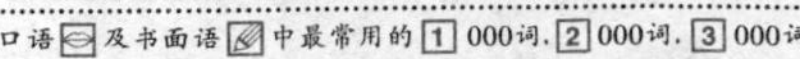

and modern US society, often in a critical way that some people disagree with. His films include *Platoon* (1986), *Born on the Fourth of July* (1989), *JFK* (1991), about the murder of the President John F. Kennedy, and *Natural Born Killers* (1994). 斯通〔(1946-), 美国电影导演、电影剧本作家。他的影片关涉美国近代历史和现代美国社会, 其批判风格经常招致非议。作品包括《野战排》(1986)、《生于七月四日》(1989)、讲述约翰·F.肯尼迪总统遇刺案的《惊天大刺杀》(1991)以及《天生杀人狂》(1994)等〕

Stone Age /ˈ· ·/ *n* the earliest known time in human history, when only stone was used for making tools, weapons etc 石器时代 —compare 比较 BRONZE AGE, IRON AGE

stone-cold /ˌ· ˈ·◂/ *adj* **1** completely and unpleasantly cold 冰冷的, 完全凉的: *The body's stone-cold.* 尸体已经冰凉。**2 stone-cold sober** having drunk no alcohol at all 完全清醒的, 一点酒也没有喝

stoned /stond; stəʊnd/ *adj* [not before noun 不用于名词前] **1** *informal* feeling very excited or extremely relaxed because you have taken an illegal drug【非正式】〔吸食毒品后〕极度兴奋[松弛]的 **2** very drunk 烂醉如泥的

stone dead /ˌ· ˈ·◂/ *adj* completely dead 完全死了的

stone deaf /ˌ· ˈ·◂/ *adj* completely unable to hear 完全聋的

stone-ground /ˈ· ·/ *adj* stone-ground flour is made by crushing grain between two MILLSTONES〔面粉〕用石磨研磨的

Stone·henge /ˈstonhɛndʒ; ˌstəʊnˈhendʒ◂/ a group of very large, tall stones that are arranged into a large circle with a smaller circle inside it, which stand on Salisbury Plain in Wiltshire, southern England. People think that they were put there about 4000 years ago and were used for studying the movements of the Sun, Moon, and stars. Some people also believe that they were used by the Druids (=ancient priests before the Christian period) in religious ceremonies. 巨石阵〔英格兰南部威尔特郡索尔兹伯里平原上一组巨石。石块排列成一个大圈, 中间还有一小圈。据认为, 这一石柱群大约4000年前就安置在那里, 用以研究太阳、月亮、星星的运行情况。也有人认为巨石阵是德鲁伊特教祭师举行宗教仪式的场所〕

stone·ma·son /ˈstonˌmesn̩; ˈstəʊnˌmeɪsən/ *n* [C] someone whose job is cutting stone into pieces to be used in buildings 石匠, 石工

Stone of Scone, the /ˌston əv ˈskun; ˌstəʊn əv ˈskuːn/ a stone seat that was traditionally used in the Scottish ceremony for officially making someone King or Queen of Scotland. It is also called the Stone of Destiny. The stone was taken from Scotland in 1296 and kept in Westminster Abbey in London, but Scottish Nationalists, who believed that the stone belonged in Scotland, tried to steal it. In 1996 it was officially returned to Scotland. 斯库恩石座〔曾在苏格兰君主加冕庆典中使用的石制宝座, 又称"命运之石"。1296年从苏格兰运至伦敦, 保存在威斯敏斯特教堂, 但苏格兰民族主义者认为它属于苏格兰, 甚至企图将其盗走。1996年, 斯库恩石座正式归还苏格兰〕

Stone·wall /ˌstonˈwɔl; ˌstəʊnˈwɔːl/ a British organization that works to improve the legal rights of HOMOSEXUAL men and women, and to persuade politicians to change any laws that treat homosexuals unfairly "石墙"组织〔英国一机构。其职责是为同性恋者争取合法权利, 说服政治家修改对同性恋者不公的所有法规〕

stonewall *v* [I] to delay a discussion, decision etc by talking a lot and refusing to answer questions〔用冗长的发言或拒绝回答问题的办法〕拖延[阻碍]〔议事、作出决定等〕

stone·ware /ˈstonˌwɛr; ˈstəʊnweə/ *n* [U] pots etc that are made from a special hard clay 粗陶器

stone-washed /ˌ· ˈ·◂/ *adj* stonewashed JEANS etc have been made softer by a washing process in which they are beaten with stones〔牛仔裤等〕石洗的, 石磨的

stone·work /ˈstonˌwɝk; ˈstəʊnwɜːk/ *n* [U] the parts of a building that are made of stone, especially when they are decorative 建筑物的石制部分〔尤指带有装饰的〕

stonk·ered /ˈstɑŋkɚd; ˈstɒŋkəd/ *adj AustrE informal* very tired【澳, 非正式】筋疲力竭的, 非常疲劳的

stonk·ing /ˈstɑŋkɪŋ; ˈstɒŋkɪŋ/ *adj BrE informal* surprisingly good【英, 非正式】好得出奇的, 非常好的: *He scored a stonking goal.* 他进了很漂亮的一球。

ston·y /ˈstonɪ; ˈstəʊni/ *adj* **1** covered by stones or containing stones 铺着石头的; 多石的; 石质的: *stony soil* 多石的土壤 **2** without emotion or pity 冷酷的, 无情的; 无同情心的: *stony faces* 冷酷的面孔 | *a stony silence* 事不关己的沉默 **3 fall on stony ground** if a request, suggestion, joke etc falls on stony ground, it is ignored or people do not like it 被忽视; 不受喜欢; 没有引起反响 —**stonily** *adv*

stony-faced /ˌ· · ˈ·◂/ *adj* showing no emotion or friendliness 面无表情的, 冷漠的

stood /stud; stʊd/ the past tense and past participle of STAND[1]

stooge /studʒ; stuːdʒ/ *n* [C] **1** one of two performers who is the subject of the jokes made by the other performer〔作为另一演员引逗或打趣对象的〕配角 **2** *informal* someone who always does what someone else wants them to【非正式】唯命是从的人, 傀儡

stook·ie /ˈstukɪ; ˈstʊki/ *n* [C] *ScotE* a PLASTER CAST【苏格兰】石膏模型

stool /stul; stuːl/ *n* [C] **1** a seat without any supporting part for your back or arms 凳子: *a bar stool* 酒吧凳子 —see picture at 参见 CHAIR[1] 图 **2** *technical* a piece of solid waste from your body【术语】大便, 粪便

stool·pi·geon /ˈstulˌpɪdʒən; ˈstuːlˌpɪdʒɪn/ *n* [C] *AmE informal* someone, especially a criminal, who helps the police to catch another criminal; INFORMER【美, 非正式】〔警察的〕眼线; 用来诱捕罪犯的人; 告密者

stoop[1] /stup; stuːp/ *v* [I] **1** also 又作 **stoop down** to bend your body forwards and down 俯身, 弯腰: *The doorway was so low that Martin had to stoop to go in.* 门口很低, 马丁不得不弯腰进去。**2** to stand with your back and shoulders bent forwards 弓背, 弯腰曲背站立

stoop to sth *phr v* [T] to do something, even though you know it is morally wrong, because you think it will help you achieve something 降低道德标准去做…: *Ray would stoop to anything to get what he wants.* 雷为了得到自己想要的东西什么事都做得出来。| **stoop to doing sth** *I didn't expect you to stoop to lying.* 我没料到你竟然会下贱到去撒谎。

stoop[2] *n* **1** [singular] if you have a stoop, your shoulders slope forward or seem too round 曲背; 弯腰: *Jeff's developed a stoop.* 杰夫有些驼背。**2** [C] *AmE* a raised area at the door of a house, usually big enough to sit on【美】门廊, 门阶

stooped /stupt; stuːpt/ *adj* having a stoop 弯腰的; 驼背的: *a stooped old man* 驼背的老人

stoop·ing /ˈstupɪŋ; ˈstuːpɪŋ/ *adj* stooping shoulders are bent forwards or have become too round〔肩膀〕弯曲的

stop[1] /stɑp; stɒp/ *v* **stopped, stopping**

1 ►NOT MOVE OR CONTINUE 不再移动或继续◄ [I,T] to no longer move or continue to do something, or to make someone or something do this (使)停止, (使)停下来: *Stop, thief!* 站住, 小偷! | **stop sth** *Apply pressure to stop the bleeding.* 压住伤口止血。| *You'll have to stop the generator, it's overheating.* 你得把发电机停下来, 机器过热了。| **stop doing sth** *Lena's trying to stop smoking.* 莉娜正试图戒烟。| **stop that/it** *spoken*【口】*Stop it! You're hurting me.* 住手! 你弄痛我了。| **stop short** (=stop walking suddenly) 突然止步, 突然停住脚步 | **stop and do sth** *People stopped and stared as she screamed at him.* 她对他尖叫时, 人们停下来盯着他们看。| **stop (dead)/stop in your tracks** (=stop walking or running very suddenly) 突然停止走[跑], 猛然止步 | **stop (sth) at/outside/in etc** *Jill stopped the car outside the post office.* 吉尔在邮局外面把汽车停下。| **stop on a dime** *AmE* (=stop very quickly)【美】迅速停止

2 ►PREVENT 防止, 阻止◄ [T] to prevent someone from doing something or something from happening 防止, 阻止, 阻挡: *I'm leaving home and you can't stop me.* 我要离开这个家, 你无法阻止我。| **stop sb (from) doing sth** *Lynn's parents tried to stop her seeing him.* 琳恩的父母企图阻止她和他见面。| **there's nothing to stop sb** *There's nothing to stop you calling her to say you're sorry.* 你完全可以给她打电话向她道歉。

3 ►END 结束◄ [I,T] to end or make something end (使)结束, (使)终止: *We'll go out when the rain stops.* 雨停了我们就出去。| **stop sth** *The referee stopped the fight.* 裁判终止了这场拳击赛。| **[+at]** *The road stops at the farm.* 这条路通到农场就没了。

4 ►PAUSE 暂停◄ [I] to pause in an activity, journey etc in order to do something before continuing 中止, 暂时停下来: **stop for sth** *We stopped for a drink on the way home.* 我们在回家的路上停下来喝点东西。| **stop to do sth** *Maya stopped to tie her shoelace.* 马娅停下来系鞋带。| **stop to think/consider etc** *It's time we stopped to think about our next move.* 我们该停下来想一想下一步的行动了。

5 stop at nothing (to do sth) to be ready to do anything, even if it is cruel, dishonest, or illegal, to get what you want (做某事)不择手段, (做某事)无所顾忌: *Franca will stop at nothing to get a part in the film.* 为了能在那部电影中扮演一个角色, 弗兰卡会不择手段。

6 stop short of (doing) sth to decide that you are not willing to do something wrong or dangerous, though you will do some-

thing similar that is less dangerous 决定不去做〔错误或危险的事情〕; 不愿逾矩: *The US government supported sanctions but stopped short of military action.* 美国政府支持制裁, 但不愿采取军事行动。

7 ►STAY 停留◄[I] *BrE informal* to stay somewhere for a short time, especially at someone's house【英, 非正式】〔尤指在某人家里〕逗留, 短时间停留: *I won't sit down – I'm not stopping.* 我不坐了, 我不打算逗留。| **[+for]** *Can you stop for a chat?* 你能停下来聊聊天吗?

8 ►WALKING/TRAVELLING 步行/旅行◄[T] to go to someone and speak to them or make them stop when they are walking or travelling somewhere 使〔某人〕停下, 拦住, 截住: *Someone stopped me in the street and asked the way.* 有人在街上拦住我问路。| *If they try to get away, they'll be stopped at the border.* 他们要是企图逃跑, 在边境上将会被截住。

9 ►MONEY 钱◄to prevent money from being paid after you agreed to pay it 停付; 扣留: **stop sth from sth** *Money for breakages will be stopped from your wages.* 损耗费将从你的工资中扣除。| **stop a cheque** (=tell your bank not to pay the money) 停止兑付支票

10 ►BLOCK 堵塞◄[T] also 又作 **stop up** to block something such as a pipe so that water, smoke etc cannot go through it 堵塞, 塞住, 堵住

stop back *phr v* [I] *AmE* to go back to a place you have been to earlier【美】返回: *Can you stop back later? I'm real busy right now.* 你能过一会再来吗? 我现在实在很忙。

stop by *phr v* [I,T] to make a short visit to a place or person, especially when you are on your way to somewhere else 顺便拜访, 顺路探望: *Daniel stopped by the newsagent's on his way home.* 丹尼尔在回家的路上顺便去了一趟报摊。

stop sth ↔ **down** *phr v* [T] to make the hole in a camera LENS (2) smaller so that less light gets in when you take a photograph〔摄影时〕缩小〔镜头的〕光圈

stop in *phr v* [I] *informal*【非正式】**1** to make a short visit to a place or person, especially when you are on your way to somewhere else 顺便拜访, 顺路探望: **[+at]** *Let's stop in at Vera's on our way.* 我们顺路去薇拉家坐坐吧。**2** *BrE* to stay at home【英】待在家里: *I'm stopping in to wash my hair tonight.* 我今晚待在家里洗头。

stop off *phr v* [I] to make a short visit to a place during a journey, especially to rest or to see someone〔在旅途中〕中途停留: *Shall we stop off somewhere on the way to Cornwall?* 我们去康沃尔的路上要在哪里逗留吗? | **[+in/at etc]** *We stopped off in Santa Rosa for a day.* 我们在圣罗莎停留了一天。

stop out *phr v* [I] *BrE informal* to stay out later than usual【英, 非正式】待在外面, 晚归: *Lizzie stopped out all night on Saturday.* 莉齐星期六整夜外出未归。

stop over *phr v* [I] to make a short stay somewhere before continuing a long journey 中途作短暂停留: *The plane stops over in Dubai on the way to India.* 飞机飞往印度的途中在迪拜作短暂停留。

stop up *phr v* [I] *BrE informal* to stay up late【英, 非正式】熬夜, 迟睡: *Joe stopped up till 3 o'clock to watch the boxing.* 乔为看那场拳击赛一直熬到3点钟才睡觉。

This graph shows how common the different grammar patterns of the verb **stop** are. 本图表所示为动词 stop 构成的不同语法结构的使用频率。

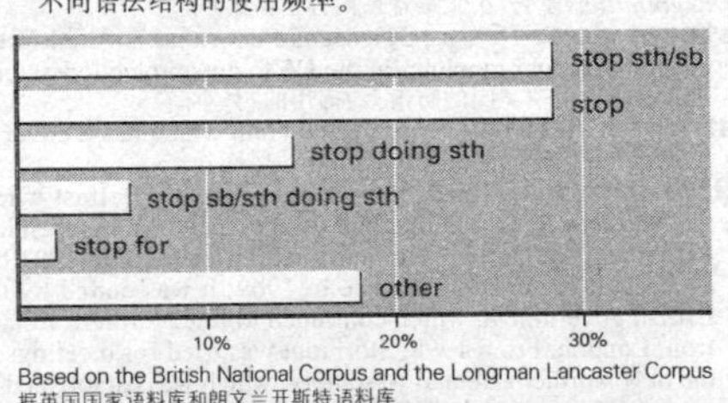

Based on the British National Corpus and the Longman Lancaster Corpus
据英国国家语料库和朗文兰开斯特语料库

3 3 **stop[2]** *n* [C]

1 bring sth to a stop to stop something moving or happening 使…停下来; 使…停止: *David brought the truck to a shuddering stop.* 戴维使卡车摇摇晃晃地停了下来。

2 come/roll to a stop if a vehicle, an activity etc comes to a stop, it stops moving or happening〔车辆、活动等〕停下来, 停止: *Work on the project has come to a stop because of lack of funding.* 因缺乏资金, 该项目已经停下来了。

3 ►DURING JOURNEY 旅途中◄a time or place when you stop during a journey for a short time 中途停留(处): *Our first stop was Paris, and then we traveled on to Marseilles.* 我们旅行的第一站是巴黎, 接着我们又到了马赛。| **make a stop** (=stop somewhere while travelling) 途中停留 *We only made two stops on the long drive down through France.* 我们开车穿越法国的漫长旅途中只作了两次停留。

4 ►BUS/TRAIN 公共汽车/火车◄a place where a bus or train regularly stops for people to get on and off 车站: *This is your stop, isn't it?* 你到站该下车了, 对吗?

5 put a stop to sth to prevent something from continuing or happening 制止; 使…停下来: *The new law should put a stop to this tax evasion.* 新法规应该制止这种偷税漏税的行为。

6 pull out all the stops to do everything you possibly can to make something happen and succeed 竭尽全力; 全力以赴: *The Bianchis had pulled out all the stops for their daughter's wedding.* 比安基夫妇为女儿的婚礼全力以赴。

7 ►MUSIC 音乐◄**a)** a set of pipes on an ORGAN (2) that produce sound〔风琴的〕(一排) 音管 **b)** a set of handles that you push in or out in an organ to control the amount of sound it produces〔风琴的〕音栓

8 ►CONSONANT 子音◄a consonant sound, like /p/ or /k/, made by stopping the flow of air completely and then suddenly letting it out of your mouth; PLOSIVE (闭) 塞音 —see also 另见 FULLSTOP

stop·cock /ˈstɑp,kɑk; ˈstɒpkɒk/ *n* [C] a VALVE (1) that can be opened or closed with a TAP (=object you turn) to control the flow of a liquid in a pipe〔调节管道中液体流量的〕管闩, 活栓, 阀门; TURNCOCK *BrE*【英】

Stopes /stops; stəʊps/, **Ma·rie** /məˈri; ˈmɑːri/ (1880-1958) a British scientist who in 1921 started the first CLINIC (=a place where people can go for medical treatment and advice) offering practical help with BIRTH CONTROL (=methods for controlling the number of children you have). She also wrote two popular books about sex education. At the time, her work was strongly criticized and opposed by the Roman Catholic Church and by many doctors with traditional opinions. 斯托普斯〔(1880-1958), 英国科学家。1921 年开设了世界首家节育诊所。她还撰写了两本有关性教育的大众读本, 但遭到当时的罗马天主教会和传统派医生的强烈批评和抵制〕

stop·gap /ˈstɑp,gæp; ˈstɒpgæp/ *n* [C] something or someone that you use for a short time until you can replace it with something better 临时替代的物[人]; 补缺者: *a stopgap measure* 临时措施

stop-go /,· ˈ·◂/ *adj* **stop-go approach/policies etc** *BrE* a way of controlling the economy by restricting government spending for a period of time and then not restricting it so severely for a time【英】〔用作调控经济的〕紧缩与膨胀交替的应变方法/政策等

stop·light /ˈstɑp,laɪt; ˈstɒplaɪt/ *n* [C] also 又作 **stoplights** *plural AmE* a set of coloured lights used to control and direct traffic; TRAFFIC LIGHTS【美】交通信号灯, 红绿灯

stop·o·ver /ˈstɑp,ovɚ; ˈstɒp,əʊvə/ *n* [C] a short stay somewhere between parts of a journey, especially on a long plane journey〔尤指长途飞行中的〕中途停留: *a two-day stopover in Hong Kong* 在香港逗留两天

stop·page /ˈstɑpɪdʒ; ˈstɒpɪdʒ/ *n* **1** [C] a situation in which workers stop working for a short time as a protest 停工, 罢工: *time lost in disputes and stoppages* 因纠纷和停工损失的时间 **2** [C] something that blocks a tube or container 堵塞(物), 阻塞(物): *an intestinal stoppage* 肠堵塞 **3** [C,U] *BrE* the act of stopping something from moving or happening【英】停止, 中止; 阻止: *complete stoppages of production* 生产的完全停顿 | *stoppages due to injury* 因伤暂停 **4 stoppages** [plural] *BrE* money kept back from your wages by your employer in order to pay your tax, for your PENSION etc【英】〔从工资中的〕扣除部分, 扣除额

Stoppard /ˈstɑpard; ˈstɒpɑːd/, **Sir Tom** (1937-) a British writer of plays, born in the Czech Republic. He first became well-known for his play *Rosencrantz and Guildenstern Are Dead* and has since written many other plays. 斯托帕特爵士〔(1937-), 英国剧作家, 生于捷克共和国。成名作为戏剧《罗森克兰茨与吉尔登斯特恩之死》, 之后又创作了不少剧本〕

stop·per /ˈstɑpɚ; ˈstɒpə/ *n* [C] the thing that you put in the top part of a bottle to close it 瓶塞, 栓 —**stopper** *v* [T] —see picture at 参见 LABORATORY 图

stopping dis·tance /ˈ·· ,··/ *n* [C,U] the distance that a driver is supposed to leave between their car and the one in front in order to be able to stop safely 安全车距

stop press /ˌ· ˈ·◂/ *n* [singular] late news added to a newspaper after the main part has been printed〔报纸开印后临时插入的〕最新消息

stop·watch /ˈstɑpˌwɑtʃ; ˈstɒpwɒtʃ/ *n* [C] a watch used for measuring the exact time it takes to do something, especially to finish a race〔尤用于赛跑的〕秒表, 跑表

stor·age /ˈstɔrɪdʒ; ˈstɔːrɪdʒ/ *n* [U] **1** the act of keeping or putting something in a special place while it is not being used 储存, 贮藏, 保管: *the storage of radioactive material* 放射性材料的存放 | **storage space/capacity** (=space etc for storing things) 贮存空间/容量 **2 in storage** if furniture or other goods are in storage, they are being kept in a special place until you need to use them〔家具等〕被存放着 **3** the price you pay for having goods or furniture stored 贮存费, 仓租

storage heat·er /ˈ·· ˌ··/ *n* [C] *BrE* a HEATER that stores heat at times when electricity is cheaper【英】电蓄热器

store¹ /stɔr; stɔː/ *n* [C]

1 ►LARGE SHOP 大商店◄ a large place that sells many different kinds of goods 大商店: *At Christmas the stores stay open late.* 圣诞节期间, 大商店营业到很晚。—see also 另见 CHAIN STORE, DEPARTMENT STORE, GENERAL STORE

2 ►SHOP 商店◄ *AmE* a place where goods are sold to the public; SHOP¹ (1)【美】商店, 店铺: *There are about 60 different stores in the Fallbrook Mall.* 福尔布鲁克购物中心有大约60家不同的商店。| **a shoe/clothing/grocery etc store** (=one that sells one type of goods) 鞋店/服装店/(食品)杂货店等 *She worked in a book store during college.* 她读大学时在一家书店打工。| **go to the store** *I need to go to the store for some milk.* 我需要去商店买些牛奶。—see graph at 参见 SHOP¹ 图表

3 ►SUPPLY 供应◄ a supply of something that you keep to use later 储备, 贮存物: [+of] *Granny always had a special store of chocolate for us.* 奶奶总是特地为我们储备一些巧克力。

4 ►PLACE TO KEEP THINGS 储存物品的地方◄ a large building in which goods are stored so they can be used or sold later; WAREHOUSE 仓库: *a grain store* 粮仓

5 be in store if something unexpected such as a surprise or problem is in store for someone, it is about to happen to them 将要发生, 就要出现: *He's got a few surprises in store if he thinks he can order us around.* 如果他认为他可以把我们差来遣去, 他将会感到有点吃惊。

6 stores [plural] **a)** supplies of food and equipment that are used by an army, navy etc 军需品, 补给品 **b)** the building or room in an army camp, ship etc where these are kept〔军营或船上等的〕补给品仓库

7 set great store by sth to consider something to be very important 认为某事非常重要: *Anne sets great store by that training course.* 安妮非常重视那个培训课程。

store² *v* [T] **1** also 又作 **store away** to put things away and keep them until you need them 贮藏, 储存, 积蓄: *Squirrels are storing up nuts for the winter.* 松鼠正在为冬天储存坚果。**2** to keep facts or information in your brain or a computer〔在头脑或电脑中〕储存〔事实或信息〕: *A mass of data is stored in the computer.* 大量数据存入了电脑。**3 store up trouble/problems etc** to behave in a way that will cause trouble for you later 制造麻烦/难题等: *Sarah is storing up problems for herself by lying to him.* 萨拉对他说谎是在为自己制造麻烦。

store brand /ˈ· ·/ *n* [C] *especially AmE* a type of goods that are produced for a particular shop and have the shop's name on them【尤美】商店品牌〔专为某商店生产并标有该商店店名的商品〕

store de·tec·tive /ˈ· ·ˌ··/ *n* [C] someone who is employed in a large shop to watch the customers and to stop them stealing 店铺侦探, 专抓在商店里行窃者的人

store·front /ˈstɔrˌfrʌnt; ˈstɔːfrʌnt/ *n* [C] *AmE*【美】**1** the part of a store that faces the street〔临街的〕店面, 铺面 **2 storefront law office/church/school** a small law office etc in a shopping area〔购物区内〕临街的小型律师事务所/教堂/学校

store·house /ˈstɔrˌhaus; ˈstɔːhaʊs/ *n* [C] **1 a storehouse of information/memories etc** something that contains a lot of information etc 信息/记忆等的宝库 **2** *old-fashioned* a building where things are stored; WAREHOUSE【过时】仓库, 栈房

store·keep·er /ˈstɔrˌkipə; ˈstɔːˌkiːpə/ *n* [C] *AmE* someone who owns or manages a shop【美】店主; SHOPKEEPER *BrE*【英】

store·room /ˈstɔrˌrum; ˈstɔːrʊm/ *n* [C] a room where goods are stored 贮藏室

sto·rey *BrE*【英】, **story** *AmE*【美】/ˈstɔrɪ; ˈstɔːri/ *n* [C] **1** a floor or level of a building〔建筑物的〕层 **2 two-storey/five-storey etc** having two etc storeys 两/五层楼等的

stor·ied /ˈstɔrɪd; ˈstɔːrid/ *adj* **1 two-storied/five storied etc** *AmE* having two etc storeys【美】有两/五层楼等的 **2** [only before noun 仅用于名词前] *literary* being the subject of many stories; FAMOUS【文】传说[故事]中有名的

stork /stɔrk; stɔːk/ *n* [C] a tall white bird with long legs and a long beak (白)鹳

> **CULTURAL NOTE 文化注释**
>
> In the past, when parents had to explain to young children where new babies come from, they often used to say that the stork brought them. Cards, birth announcements, and CARTOONS often show a stork holding a big cloth bag in its beak, with a new baby sitting inside the bag. 过去, 父母不得不向小孩子回答小婴孩是从哪儿来的时候, 他们常说是鹳衔来的。贺卡、新生儿告示和漫画上通常画着鹳用嘴叼着大布袋, 布袋里有个小婴孩。

storm¹ /stɔrm; stɔːm/ *n* **1** [C] a period of very bad weather when there is a lot of rain, strong winds, and often lightning 暴风雨: *crops damaged by recent heavy storms* 最近被暴风雨毁坏的庄稼 | **the storm broke** (=suddenly started) 暴风雨突然来临 —see picture on page A13 参见 A13 页图 **2** [C usually singular 一般用单数] a situation in which people suddenly express very strong feelings about something that someone has said or done 感情的突然爆发, 迸发: *The governor found himself at the centre of a political storm.* 州长发现自己处于一场政治风暴的中心。| **a storm of protest/abuse/laughter etc** *Government plans for hospital closures provoked a storm of protest.* 政府关闭医院的计划激起了强烈的抗议。**3 take somewhere by storm a)** to be very successful in a particular place 在某地大获成功: *The new show took London by storm.* 新剧轰动了伦敦。**b)** to attack a place using large numbers of soldiers and succeed in getting possession of it 大举进攻并占领某地, 直捣某地 **4 a storm in a teacup** an unnecessary expression of strong feelings about something that is very unimportant 茶杯里的风波; 小题大做; 大惊小怪 **5 dance/sing/party up a storm** *AmE* to do something with all your energy【美】尽情地跳舞/唱歌/狂欢: *They're dancing up a storm in there.* 他们正在那里尽情地跳舞。

storm² *v* **1** [T] to suddenly attack and enter a place using a lot of force 猛烈攻击, 突然袭击: *An angry crowd stormed the embassy.* 愤怒的人群突然袭击大使馆。**2** [I always+adv/prep] to go somewhere in a noisy fast way that shows you are extremely angry 气冲冲地走: [+out of/into/off etc] *Alan stormed out of the room.* 艾伦气冲冲地走出房间。**3** [I,T] *literary* to shout something because you feel extremely angry【文】怒吼, 愤怒地喊叫: *"What difference does it make?" she stormed.* "那又怎么样?"她嚷道。

storm cel·lar /ˈ· ˌ··/ *n* [C] *AmE* a place under a house where you can go to be safe during violent storms【美】暴风雨避难窖, 防风地窖

storm cloud /ˈ· ·/ *n* [C] **1** a dark cloud which you see before a storm 暴风雨前的乌云, 暴风云 **2** [usually plural 一般用复数] a sign that something very bad is going to happen 不祥的预兆, 凶兆: *Storm clouds are gathering over the East-West trade negotiations.* 乌云正笼罩着东西方贸易谈判。

storm door /ˈ· ·/ *n* [C] a second door that is fitted to the outside of a door in winter in the US to give protection against rain, snow etc〔美国的防雨、雪等用的〕外重门

storm lan·tern /ˈ· ˌ··/ *n* [C] a lamp which has a cover to protect the flame against the wind 防风灯

Stor·mont /ˈstɔrmənt; ˈstɔːmənt/ a castle in Belfast where the Northern Ireland Parliament used to meet. An independent Parliament for Northern Ireland was started there in 1921 but as a result of serious violence in 1969, it was ended by the British government, which continued to rule Northern Ireland from London. From 1998, Stormont was used for meetings of the new Northern Ireland Assembly, which was established as a result of peace talks. 斯托蒙特〔贝尔法斯特一城堡, 曾为北爱尔兰议会所在地。1921年, 在此成立了一个独立的北爱尔兰地方议会, 但因1969年发生严重暴力事件, 遭英国政府取缔, 北爱尔兰继续接受英国政府的管辖。经过一系列和平谈判, 新的北爱尔兰议会得以成立, 1998年起, 斯托蒙特成为其会址〕

storm·troop·er /ˈstɔrmˌtrupə; ˈstɔːmˌtruːpə/ *n* [C] a member of a special group of German soldiers in the Second World War who were trained to be particularly violent〔第二次世界大战中德国的〕冲锋队员, 突击队员

storm win·dow /ˈ· ,··/ *n* [C] a second window fitted to the outside of a window in winter in the US to give more protection against rain, snow etc〔美国的防雨、雪等用的〕外重窗

storm·y /ˈstɔrmɪ; ˈstɔːmi/ *adj* **1** stormy weather, sky etc is full of strong winds, heavy rain, and dark clouds 暴风雨的: *The sky was starting to look rather stormy.* 天空乌云密布，暴风雨即将来临。**2** a stormy relationship, meeting etc is full of strong and often angry feelings 激烈的，冲动的；多风波的：*a stormy meeting* 争论激烈的会议 | *a stormy affair* 一波三折的事情

S2 W2 **sto·ry** /ˈstɔrɪ; ˈstɔːri/ *n* [C]

1 ▶FOR ENTERTAINMENT 供娱乐◀ a description of how something happened, that is intended to entertain people, and may be true or imaginary〔真实或虚构的〕故事；叙述；描述：*the story of Cinderella* 灰姑娘的故事 | *Don't be frightened, Connie – it's only a story.* (=it is imaginary) 康妮，别害怕，这只是一个虚构的故事。| [+about] *a story about gangsters* 一个关于匪徒的故事 | **fairy/ghost/love story** *a true-life love story* 一个真实的爱情故事 | **tell/read sb a story** *Mommy, will you read me a story?* 妈妈，你能给我讲一个故事吗？

2 ▶EVENTS 事件◀ a description of the most important events in someone's life or in the development of something 事迹；记事；史话：*the story of the railways* 铁路史话 | *the Tina Turner Story*《蒂娜·特纳传记》| **sb's life story** *Nobody wants to hear your life story the first time you meet them.* 谁也不想第一次见面就听你的生活经历。

3 ▶NEWS 新闻◀ a report in a newspaper or news broadcast about a recent event〔报刊或广播中的〕(新闻) 报道：*a front-page story in 'The Times'*《泰晤士报》的头版新闻报道 | **run a story** (=report an event) 刊登对某事件的报道 *'The Observer' ran a big story about the scandal.*《观察家报》刊登了有关该丑闻的长篇报道。| **cover story** (=the main story in a magazine that is about the picture on the cover)〔杂志的〕封面故事[专题报道] | **success story** *Calvin's life was a success story – from farm boy to business tycoon.* 卡尔文的一生是一个从农村孩子成为商业巨头的成功故事。—see graph at 参见 NEWS 图表

4 ▶OF A FILM/PLAY ETC 电影/戏剧等的◀ what happens in a film, play, or book; PLOT[1] (1)〔电影、戏剧、书的〕(故事) 情节：*Tom Hanks was brilliant, but the story was boring.* 汤姆·汉克斯演技很出色，但电影情节十分枯燥。

5 ▶EXCUSE 借口◀ an excuse or explanation, especially one that you have invented〔尤指编造的〕借口，遁词：*Where were you? And don't give me any story about working late!* 你去了哪里？不要给我找借口，说晚上加班什么的！| *Well that's my story* (=that is what I say happened), *and I'm sticking to it.* 哦，这就是我要说的情况，而且我坚持这一说法。

6 my/your side of the story the way that a particular person describes what happened 我/你对事情的描述：*Before we decide who is to blame, we want to hear your side of the story.* 在决定是谁的错之前，我们想听一听你对这件事情的解释。

7 ▶WHAT PEOPLE SAY 人们的说法◀ information which people tell each other, but which may be untrue; RUMOUR 传闻，传说，谣传：*There are a lot of wild stories going around.* 有很多荒诞的谣言在流传。| **so the story goes** (=people are saying this) 据说如此，传说是这样 *He was having an affair with Julie, or so the story goes.* 他跟朱莉有暧昧关系，至少大家是这么传的。

8 it's a long story *spoken* used to tell someone that you do not want to give them all the details that a full answer to their question would need【口】说来话长〔表示不想讲细节〕

9 it's the same story in/here/there etc used to say the same thing is happening in another place 这里/那里等也是同样的情况：*Unemployment is falling in the US and it's the same story in Europe.* 美国的失业人数正在减少，欧洲也是如此。

10 it's the same old story *spoken* used to say that the present bad situation has often happened before【口】又是那老一套〔表示目前糟糕的情况以前经常发生〕：*It's the same old story – too much work and not enough time.* 情况还是跟过去一样 —— 工作太多，但时间不够。

11 to cut a long story short *BrE spoken*【英口】, **to make a long story short** *AmE spoken*【美口】used when you want to finish a story quickly 长话短说；简而言之；总之

12 but that's another story *spoken* used when you have mentioned something that you are not going to talk about on this occasion【口】那是另一回事了〔表示不打算谈论所提及的某事〕

13 that's not the whole story *spoken* used to say that there are more details which people need to know in order to understand the situation【口】情况还不止这样，那还不是事情的全部

14 that's the story of my life *spoken* used after a disappointing experience to mean that similar disappointing things always seem to happen to you【口】我总是这样倒霉〔在经历失望的事情之后表示自己经常遭遇类似的不幸〕

15 end of story *BrE spoken* used to mean that there is nothing more to say about a particular subject【英口】就这样〔表示对某话题再没有什么好谈论的了〕：*As far as I'm concerned Terry is still a friend, end of story.* 在我看来，特里仍然是我的朋友，就这么简单。

16 ▶A LIE 谎言◀ a word used by or to children meaning a lie 谎言，假话〔儿语〕：**tell stories** *Have you been telling stories again?* 你又在说谎了吗？

17 the American spelling of STOREY storey 的美式拼法 —see also 另见 SHORT STORY, **cock and bull story** (COCK[1] (3)), **hard-luck story** (HARD[1] (23)), SOB STORY

sto·ry·book[1] /ˈstɔrɪ,buk; ˈstɔːribʊk/ *n* [C] a book of stories for children〔为儿童编写的〕故事书：*a creature standing in front of us like something out of a storybook* 一个像是从故事书里走出来的生物，站在我们的面前

storybook[2] *adj* **a storybook ending/romance etc** an ending etc that is so happy or perfect that it is like one in a children's story 传奇故事式的结局/爱情等：*I walked up the path in front of a lopsided storybook cottage.* 我走在一座村舍前的一条小路上，那村舍歪歪斜斜，像童话故事里讲的那样。

story line /ˈ·· ·/ *n* [C] the main set of connected events in a story; PLOT[1] (1) (故事) 情节

sto·ry·tell·er /ˈstɔrɪ,tɛlɚ; ˈstɔːri,telə/ *n* [C] someone who tells stories, especially to children〔尤指给儿童〕讲故事的人；说书人

stoup /stup; stuːp/ *n* [C] **1** a container for holy water near the entrance to a church〔教堂入口附近的〕圣水钵 **2** a glass or MUG[1] (1,2) used for drinking in former times〔旧时用的〕玻璃杯；大酒杯，圆筒形有柄大杯

stout[1] /staut; staʊt/ *adj* **1** fairly fat and heavy or having a thick body 胖的，粗壮的：*a short, stout man* 体格粗壮的矮个子男人 | *She's gotten pretty stout since you last saw her.* 自从你上次见到她以来，她变得富态了。—see 见 FAT[1] (USAGE) **2** *literary* strong and thick【文】粗壮的，结实的：*a stout stick* 粗大的棍子 | *a stout pair of shoes* 一双结实的鞋子 **3** *literary* brave and determined【文】勇敢的；坚定的；坚决的：**stout defence/support/resistance** *Michael offered his usual stout support.* 迈克尔一如既往地给予坚定的支持。—**stoutly** *adv*: *He stoutly maintained his innocence.* 他坚称自己是无辜的。—**stoutness** *n* [U]

stout[2] *n* [U] a strong dark beer (烈性) 黑啤酒

stout·heart·ed /,stautˈhartɪd; ,staʊtˈhɑːtɪd◀/ *adj literary* brave and determined【文】勇敢的；坚定的

stove[1] /stov; stəʊv/ *n* [C] **1** a thing used for heating a room or for cooking, which works by burning wood, coal, oil or gas〔炊事或取暖用的〕炉子，火炉：*a wood-burning stove* 烧木柴的火炉 | *a camp stove* 野营火炉 —compare 比较 COOKER (1) **2** *AmE* the top of a COOKER【美】厨灶，炉头

stove[2] *v* the past tense and past participle of STAVE[2]

stove·pipe hat /,stovpaɪp ˈhæt; ,stəʊvpaɪp ˈhæt/ *n* [C] *AmE* a tall black silk hat worn by men in the past【美】〔旧时的〕高筒窄边男用丝绒大礼帽

stow /sto; stəʊ/ also 又作 **stow away** *v* [T always+adv/prep] to put or pack something tidily away in a space until you need it again 将…装好收起：*You can stow your gear under the bed.* 你可以把你的工具装好放在床底下。

stow away *phr v* **1** [I] to hide on a ship or plane in order to travel secretly or without paying 偷乘〔船或飞机〕：*The boy was caught trying to stow away on a plane bound for India.* 那男孩在企图偷乘一架开往印度的飞机时被捉住了。**2** [T **stow** sth ↔ **away**] to stow something 将…装好收起 —see also 另见 STOWAWAY

stow·age /ˈstoɪdʒ; ˈstəʊɪdʒ/ *n* [C] space available on a boat for storing things〔船舶的〕装载空间

stow·a·way /ˈstoə,we; ˈstəʊəweɪ/ *n* [C] someone who hides on a ship or plane in order to avoid paying or to travel secretly 无票偷乘船[飞机]者；偷渡者

Stowe /sto; stəʊ/, **Har·ri·et Beech·er** /ˈhærɪət ˈbitʃɚ; ˈhæriət ˈbiːtʃə/ (1811-96) a US writer whose NOVEL *Uncle Tom's Cabin* influenced many people in the US, especially in the North, to oppose SLAVERY (=the system where black people were owned by white people and made to work for them). In the 20th century, the book was criticized for the way it shows the relationship between SLAVES and their owners, and the expression 'Uncle Tom' is used in a disapproving way to describe a black person who is too eager to please white people. 斯托夫人〔(1811-1896)，美国作家。其小说《汤姆叔叔的小屋》对不少美国人，尤其是北方人产生了巨大影响，促使他们加入到

反对奴隶制的行列中。而在20世纪，书中所描写的黑奴与奴隶主之间的关系遭到批评，"汤姆叔叔"一词成为贬义词，用以形容那些竭力讨好白人的黑人〕

St Pan·cras /sent `pæŋkrəs; sənt 'pæŋkrəs/ a railway station in London, next to King's Cross, famous for the impressive Gothic style of its buildings 圣潘克拉斯站〔伦敦一火车站。与国王十字站相邻，以其壮观的哥特式建筑风格著称于世〕

St Paul /·ˈ·/ the capital city of the US state of Minnesota and an important industrial and business centre. It is a port on one side of the Mississippi River, with Minneapolis on the other side. Together, they are known as the Twin Cities. 圣保罗〔美国明尼苏达州首府、重要工商业中心和港口城市。位于密西西比河畔，与明尼阿波利斯市隔河相望，合称"双子城"〕

St Pe·ters·burg /sent `pitɚzbɝg; sənt 'pi:təzbɜ:g/ a city on the Baltic Sea which was the capital of Russia from 1712 to 1918. It was called Petrograd from 1914 to 1924, then Leningrad until 1991, and then after the end of the Soviet Union, it was given back its original name. Russia's most famous MUSEUM, the Hermitage, is there. 圣彼得堡〔波罗的海沿岸一城市。1712至1918年为俄国首都，1914至1924年称为彼得格勒，后改称列宁格勒并一直沿用至1991年，苏联解体后恢复其旧称。俄罗斯最著名的博物馆艾尔米塔什博物馆位于该市〕

Stra·chey /ˈstretʃɪ; 'streɪtʃi/, **Lyt·ton** /ˈlɪtn; 'lɪtn/ (1880-1932) a British writer who was a member of the Bloomsbury Group. His best-known book, *Eminent Victorians*, describes the lives of four famous 19th century country people in a humorous and not very respectful way 斯特雷奇〔(1880-1932)，英国作家，布卢姆斯伯里派成员。其代表作是《维多利亚女王时代名人传》，以调侃的语气描述19世纪英国四位著名人物的生平〕

strad·dle /ˈstrædl; 'strædl/ *v* [T] **1** to sit or stand with your legs on either side of someone or something 跨坐；跨立：*Joe sat straddling the beam.* 乔跨坐在横梁上。**2** if something straddles a line, road, or river, part of it is on one side and part on the other side 横跨…的两边，跨越…的两边：*a little town straddling the frontier between France and Germany* 横跨法德两国边境线的一座小城镇 **3** to include different areas of activity 包括〔不同的活动领域〕：*Her job straddled marketing and public relations.* 她的工作包括市场营销和公共关系两个领域。

Strad·i·va·ri·us /ˌstrædɪˈvɛrɪəs; ˌstrædɪ'veəriəs/ also 又作 **Strad** /ˈstræd; 'stræd/ *informal* a VIOLIN made by the Italian maker Antonio Stradivari (1644-1737). Violin players today consider his violins to be the best ever made, and they are extremely valuable.【非正式】斯特拉迪瓦里小提琴〔意大利小提琴制作大师安东尼奥·斯特拉迪瓦里(1644-1737)制作的一种小提琴。是当今的小提琴演奏者们公认的最好的小提琴，非常名贵〕

strafe /stref; streɪf/ *v* [T] to attack a place by flying low and firing many bullets 低空〔飞行〕扫射[袭击]

strag·gle /ˈstrægl; 'strægəl/ *v* [I] **1** to move at a slower speed than the group you are with so that you remain at a distance behind them 掉队，落伍，落后：[+**in**] *runners straggling in two hours after the leaders* 比领先者落后两小时到达的赛跑者 **2** to move, grow, or spread out untidily in different directions 蔓延，蔓生；零乱地散布：*thin, black, straggling hair* 稀疏、散乱的黑发 | *Her handwriting straggled over the page.* 她的字迹毫无规则地散布在那一页纸上。

strag·gler /ˈstræglɚ; 'strægla/ *n* [C] someone who is too slow to stay with the others in a group so that they move along some distance behind 掉队的人，落伍者：*Wait for the stragglers to catch up.* 等那些掉队的人赶上来。

strag·gly /ˈstræglɪ; 'strægəli/ *adj* growing untidily and spreading out in different directions 蔓延的；散落的；零乱的：*a straggly moustache* 蓬乱的小胡子 —see picture on page A6 参见A6页图

straight¹ /stret; streɪt/ *adv*

1 ►IN A STRAIGHT LINE 成直线地◄ moving in a straight line 笔直地，成直线地：**straight ahead/at/down/in front of etc** *The book is on the table straight in front of you.* 那本书就在你面前的桌子上。| *She was looking straight at me.* 她直盯着我看。| *We're stuck in the middle of the road with this truck heading straight towards us.* 我们陷在路中间无法动弹，这辆卡车朝我们直冲过来。| *She walked straight past me.* 她就从我身边一直走了过去。| *Terry was so tired he couldn't walk straight.* 特里累得路都走不稳了。| *The cat sat in front of him, its tail stretched out straight.* 那只猫坐在他的前面，尾巴伸得直直的。

2 ►IMMEDIATELY 立即◄ [+adj/adv] immediately or without delay 立即；径直，不延误地：**straight to/after/down/back etc** *Let's get straight down to business.* 我们直接谈正题吧。| *Go straight home and tell your mother.* 马上回家告诉你妈妈。| *We can meet straight after lunch.* 我们午饭后马上就可以见面。

3 ►ONE AFTER THE OTHER 一个接一个◄ happening one after the other in a series, especially an unusually long series 连续地：*He's been without sleep now for three days straight.* 他已经连续三天没有睡觉了。

4 ►SEE/THINK 看见/思考◄ if you cannot think or see straight, you cannot think or see clearly 清楚地：*Turn the radio down, I can't think straight.* 把收音机的音量调低点，我思绪很乱。

5 tell sb straight/straight out *spoken* to tell someone something clearly without trying to hide your meaning【口】坦率地告诉某人：*She told him straight out that she wouldn't work on Saturday.* 她直率地对他说她不愿意星期六上班。| **straight to his/her face** *I'll tell him straight to his face what I think of him.* 我会当着他的面坦白地告诉他我对他的看法。

6 go straight *informal* to stop being a criminal and live an honest life【非正式】改邪归正，重新做人：*Tony's been trying to go straight for about six months.* 托尼努力改邪归正大约有六个月了。

7 straight off also 又作 **straight away** *BrE spoken* immediately or at once【英口】立即，立刻，马上：*I guessed it was you straight off.* 我一下子就猜出是你。

8 straight up *BrE spoken*【英口】**a)** used to ask someone if they are telling the truth 真的吗〔用于询问某人是否在说实话〕：*"The shoes cost £250." "Straight up?"* "这双鞋要250英镑。" "真的吗？" **b)** used to emphasize that what you are saying is true 的确，真的〔用于强调自己所说的是实话〕：*I don't know where she is, straight up.* 我不知道她在哪里，真的。

9 straight from the shoulder *AmE informal* expressed plainly and directly, without trying to avoid unpleasantness【美，非正式】直截了当地，坦诚地

10 damn straight *AmE spoken* used to explain that something is completely true or right【美口】绝对真实，绝对正确：*Damn straight that's good.* 那绝对好。

straight² *adj*

1 ►NOT BENDING OR CURVING 不弯曲的◄ something such as a line or road that is straight goes in one direction and does not bend or curve (笔)直的：*Anne loved Rome with its open spaces and long straight avenues.* 安妮喜欢罗马开阔的空地和笔直的大街。| **in a straight line** *After five beers I was incapable of walking in a straight line.* 五杯啤酒下肚，我路都走不直了。| **straight hair** (=hair without curls) 直发 —see picture on page A6 参见A6页图

2 ►LEVEL/UPRIGHT 平正的/竖直的◄ level, upright, or flat in position or shape 平正的，端正的；竖直的：*Stand up straight.* 站直。| *Is my tie straight?* 我的领带系得正吗？

3 ►ONE AFTER ANOTHER 一个接一个的◄ immediately one after another in a series, especially in an unusually long series 一个接一个的，连续的：*an amazing record of 43 straight wins* 连赢43场的惊人记录

4 ►TIDY 整齐的◄ [not before noun 不用于名词前] a room that is straight is clean and tidy and everything is in its proper place 整洁的，整齐的，有条理的：*I'm trying to get the room straight before your parents get here.* 我正设法在你父母到达前把房间收拾好。

5 ►TRUTHFUL 真诚的◄ honest and truthful 诚实的；真实的：**be straight with sb** *Are you going to be straight with me or not?* 你是打算对我说老实话，还是不？| **a straight answer** *It's difficult to get a straight answer out of him.* 很难得到他的坦率答复。| **straight talk/honesty** *No more of this fancy playing with words – I want some straight talk here.* 不要再玩这种文字游戏了，我要听实话。

6 get this/it straight *spoken* to understand the true facts about a situation【口】清楚无误地了解情况；弄清楚事实：*Let me get this straight – Tom sold the car and gave you the money?* 让我先把这件事弄清楚 —— 汤姆卖掉了汽车，把钱给了你，对吗？

7 set/put sb/sth straight (about) to make someone understand the true facts about a situation 使某人正确了解事实，使某人弄清楚情况：*Tell him to ask Ruth – she'll put him straight.* 叫他去问露丝 —— 她会帮他把情况弄清楚的。| **set/put the record straight** *I'd like to put the record straight about Bill's resignation.* 我想弄清楚比尔辞职的事。

8 get/put/set things straight (between) *spoken* to deal with the small problems you have in your relationship with someone【口】说明情况；理顺〔与某人的〕关系：*I think it's best to get things straight from the start. This job is not easy.* 我认为最好一开始就把事情说清楚，这份工作并不容易。

9 ►CHOICE/FIGHT 选择/打斗◄ a straight choice or contest involves only two possible choices or opponents 〔选择〕只有两

个可能的;〔竞赛〕只涉及两个对手的: *The election is seen as a straight fight between the Socialists and the ruling coalition.* 这次选举被认为是社会党人和执政联盟之间的直接交锋。| *How about a straight swap, my U2 album for this one?* 作个简单直接的交换如何? 我的U2唱片换你这个。—see also 另见 STRAIGHTFORWARD (2)

10 ▶NOT LIMITED 无限制的◀ simple and not limited by any conditions; STRAIGHTFORWARD (3) 简单的; 无(条件)限制的: *Did you do it? Just give me a straight yes or no.* 这是不是你干的? 明确地回答我是或不是。

11 a straight face someone who has a straight face looks serious although they really want to smile or laugh 严肃的表情: **keep a straight face** *She looked so ridiculous it was hard to keep a straight face.* 她看上去很滑稽, 让人忍俊不禁。

12 ▶ALCOHOLIC DRINKS 酒精饮料◀ alcoholic drinks that are straight have no water or ice or any other liquid added; NEAT (4) 纯的, 不加水[冰、其他饮料]的: *I like my vodka straight.* 我喜欢喝纯的伏特加酒。

13 ▶NORMAL 正常的◀ *slang* someone who is straight behaves in a way that is accepted as normal by many people but which you think is dull and boring【俚】正经的; 枯燥的: *Dave's OK, but his wife is really straight.* 戴夫还不错, 但他的妻子太一本正经了。

14 ▶NOT OWING SB MONEY 不欠债的◀ [not before noun 不用于名词前] no longer owing money to someone or being owed money by someone 不欠债的; 不被别人欠钱的: *If you give me £10 then we're straight.* 如果你给我10英镑, 我们就谁也不欠谁了。

15 ▶SEX 性行为◀ *slang* HETEROSEXUAL【俚】异性恋的

16 ▶DRUGS 毒品◀ *slang* not using drugs【俚】不吸毒的

straight³ *n* **1** [C] *slang* someone who is attracted to people of the opposite sex【俚】异性恋者 **2** [C] *slang* someone who is not a drug user【俚】不吸毒的人 **3** [singular] *especially BrE* the straight part of a RACETRACK【尤英】跑道的直道(部分); STRAIGHTAWAY² *AmE*【美】**4 keep to/stray from the straight and narrow** *humorous* to live in an honest and moral way, or to fail to do this【幽默】循规蹈矩地/不循规蹈矩地生活; 安分守己/不安分守己

straight ar·row /,·ˈ··/ *n* [C] *AmE informal* someone who never does anything illegal or unusual and exciting【美, 非正式】循规蹈矩的人, 安分守己的人

straight·a·way¹ /ˈstretəˌwe; ˌstreɪtəˈweɪ/ *adv* at once; immediately 立即, 立刻; 马上: *Let's start work straightaway.* 我们立即开始工作吧。

straight·a·way² /ˈstretəˌwe; ˈstreɪtəweɪ/ *n* [singular] *AmE* the straight part of a RACETRACK【美】跑道的直道(部分); STRAIGHT³ (3) *BrE*【英】

straight·en /ˈstretn̩; ˈstreɪtn/ *v* **1** also 又作 **straighten out** [I, T] to become straight or make something straight (使)变直; 把…弄直: *Straighten your tie.* 把你的领带弄直。| *The road twisted and turned and then straightened out.* 那条路先是弯弯曲曲的, 后来就变得笔直了。**2** also 又作 **straighten up** [I] to make your back straight, or to stand up straight after bending down 挺直身子, 直起身来 **3** also 又作 **straighten up** to make something tidy 把…弄整齐: *You can't go out till you straighten your room.* 你把房间整理好才能出去。

straighten sb/sth ↔ **out** *phr v* [T] **1** to settle a difficult situation by dealing with the things that are causing problems or confusion 解决〔问题〕; 清理, 整顿〔混乱情况〕: *There are a few things that need straightening out between us.* 我们之间有几件事情需要弄清楚。**2** to deal with someone's bad behaviour or personal problems 使改好, 使变好: *We try to help these kids straighten themselves out and get back into school.* 我们试图帮助这些孩子改邪归正, 重新回去上学。

straighten up *phr v* [I] *AmE* to begin to behave well after behaving badly【美】改邪归正, 重新做人: *You'd better straighten up, young lady!* 小姑娘, 你最好循规蹈矩一点!

straight-faced /ˌstretˋfest; ˌstreɪtˈfeɪst◂/ *adj* not showing by the expression on your face that you are really joking or doing something funny〔在开玩笑或做好玩的事时〕表情严肃的: *"I've never been so serious in all my life," Bart said straightfaced.* "我这辈子从来没有如此认真过。"巴特一本正经地说。—**straightfacedly** /-ˋfesədlɪ; -ˈfeɪsɨ̣dli◂/ *adv*

S3 **straight·for·ward** /ˌstretˋfɔrwəd; ˌstreɪtˈfɔːwəd◂/ *adj* **1** honest about your feelings or opinions and not hiding anything 诚实的, 坦率的, 老实的: *Jack is tough, but always straightforward and fair.* 杰克很强硬, 但总是坦诚公正的。**2** simple and easy to understand 简单的, 易懂的: *The system itself is perfectly straightforward.* 该系统本身非常简单。**3** [only before noun 仅用于名词前] not limited by any conditions 无条件限制的, 明确的: *a straightforward cash settlement* 直接的现金结算 —**straightforwardly** *adv* —**straightforwardness** *n* [U]

straight·jack·et /ˋstretˌdʒækɪt; ˈstreɪtˌdʒækɨ̣t/ *n* [C] another spelling of STRAITJACKET straitjacket 的另一种拼法

straight man /ˈ· ·/ *n* [C] a male entertainer who works with a COMEDIAN, providing him or her with opportunities to make jokes〔喜剧演员的〕男搭档, 男配角

straight shoot·er /ˈ· ˌ·· / *n* [C] *AmE informal* an honest person who you can trust【美, 非正式】〔可以信赖的〕正派人, 老实人

straight tick·et /ˌ·ˈ··/ *n* [C] a vote in which someone chooses all the candidates of a particular political party in the US〔美国〕只投同一政党所有候选人票的选票

straight·way /ˋstretˌwe; ˈstreɪtweɪ/ *adv old use* STRAIGHTAWAY【旧】立即, 立刻, 马上

strain¹ /stren; streɪn/ *n*

1 ▶WORRY 焦虑◀ [C,U] worry caused by having to deal with a problem or work too hard over a long period of time 焦虑; 紧张: *The trial has been a terrible strain for both of us.* 法庭审判令我们两人都非常焦虑。| **put a strain on sb/sth** *Nick's frequent trips were putting a strain on their marriage.* 尼克经常出行使他们的婚姻关系趋于紧张。| **be under (a) strain** *I know you've been under a lot of strain lately.* 我知道你最近压力很大。| **stresses and strains** (=problems and worries) 紧张和压力 *the stresses and strains of everyday working life* 日常工作中的紧张和压力

2 ▶DIFFICULTY 困难◀ [C] a problem or difficulty that is caused when something is used more than is normal or acceptable 问题, 困难; 负担; 紧张: *The drought has put a heavy strain on our water resources.* 干旱给我们的水资源带来了很重的负担。

3 ▶FORCE 力, 力量◀ [U] a force that pulls, stretches or pushes something 拉力, 张力, 推力: **[+on]** *The strain on the cables supporting the bridge is enormous.* 支撑桥梁的这些钢缆拉力极强。| **under the strain** (=because of the force) 因受拉力 *The rope snapped under the strain.* 绳子因拉得太紧而断了。

4 ▶INJURY 损伤◀ [C,U] an injury to a muscle or part of your body caused by using it too much〔肌肉〕拉伤, 扭伤, 损伤: *a back strain* 背部扭伤 —compare 比较 SPRAIN

5 ▶DISTRUST 不信任◀ [C,U] a situation in which two people, groups etc have stopped being friendly or trusting each other; TENSION (2)〔人或团体之间的〕不友好[不信任]状态; 紧张: *the current strain in relations between the two countries* 目前两国之间的紧张关系

6 ▶PLANT/ANIMAL 植物/动物◀ [C] a breed or type of animal, plant etc 系, 品系, 品种, 类型: **[+of]** *trying to develop a new strain of wheat* 试图开发小麦的新品种

7 the strains of sth *literary* the sound of music being played【文】曲调, 旋律: **[+of]** *the strains of the Blue Danube Waltz*《蓝色多瑙河圆舞曲》的旋律

8 ▶QUALITY 特点◀ [singular] a particular quality which people have, especially one that is passed from parents to children〔尤指遗传的〕性格倾向, 气质, 性情: **[+of]** *There's a strain of madness in his family.* 他一家都有疯癫的倾向。

9 take the strain to pull on something such as a rope until it is tight, then keep it in that position 拉紧〔绳子等〕

10 ▶WAY OF SAYING STH 说话的方式◀ [singular] *formal* the meaning of what you are saying or writing, or the way it is expressed【正式】表达方式; 口吻, 语气; 笔调: *a strain of bitterness in Young's later work* 扬后期作品中伤感的笔调

strain² *v*

1 ▶PART OF BODY 身体的一部分◀ [T] to injure a muscle or part of your body by making it work too hard〔因过分用力而〕拉伤, 扭伤, 损伤: *strain a muscle in your leg* 拉伤你的腿部肌肉 | *You'll strain your eyes trying to read in this light.* 在这样的光线下看书会伤害眼睛。

2 ▶EFFORT 努力◀ [I,T] to try very hard to do something using all your physical or mental strength 使劲, 竭力, 用尽全力: **strain to do sth** *The singer had to strain to reach the high notes.* 那位歌手费了很大的劲才唱到那高音。| **strain for sth** *Bill choked and gasped, straining for air.* 比尔噎住了, 使劲喘息着吸气。| **strain your ears/eyes** (=try very hard to hear or see) 费劲地听/看 *I strained my ears, listening for any sound in the silence of the cave.* 我竖起耳朵, 试图在寂静的山洞里听到些声音。| **strain yourself** (=try too hard) 努力过度 *Don't strain yourself! You need to rest more.* 别累坏了自己! 你需要多休息。

3 ▶LIQUID 液体◀ [T] to separate solid things from a liquid by pouring the mixture through something with very small holes in it 滤, 过滤 —see picture on page A11 参见 A11 页图

4 ▶BEYOND A LIMIT 超过限度◀ [T] to force something to be used to a degree that is beyond a normal or acceptable limit 使用…到超过正常限度, 使用…到极限: *The influx of refugees is straining our limited facilities.* 难民的涌入使我们有限的设施不堪重负。| **strain sth to the limit** *I tell you, my patience has been strained to the limit!* 我告诉你, 我的忍耐已经到了极限!
5 **strain a friendship/relationship etc** to behave in a way that causes problems in a friendship etc 损害友谊/关系等, 使友情/关系等出现问题: *Too many arguments about money can strain a relationship.* 因钱而发生过多的争吵会使关系变得紧张。
6 ▶PULL/PUSH 拉/推◀ [I] to pull hard at something or push hard against something 使劲拉[推], 绷紧: [+against] *Buddy's huge gut strained against the buttons on his shirt.* 巴迪的大肚子把他衬衫的纽扣绷得紧紧的。| [+at] *a ship straining at its moorings* 把缆索拉得很紧的船
7 **strain every nerve** to try as hard as possible to do something 全力以赴: *a comedian straining every nerve to get a laugh* 竭力逗乐的喜剧演员
8 **straining at the leash** eager to be allowed to do what you want 急欲获准做某事, 跃跃欲试: *30,000 troops straining at the leash and the generals locked in indecision* 三万大军跃跃欲试, 将军却在犹豫不决中

strained /strend; streɪnd/ *adj* **1** a situation or behaviour that is strained makes people feel nervous and uncomfortable, and unable to behave naturally; TENSE[1] (1) 紧张的; 不自在的: *I couldn't stand the strained atmosphere at dinner anymore.* 我再也忍受不了饭桌上的那种紧张气氛了。**2** showing the effects of worry or too much work 心力交瘁的; 焦虑的; 疲惫的: *Dinah's face looked white and strained.* 黛娜脸色苍白, 疲惫不堪。

S

strain·er /ˋstrenɚ; ˈstreɪnə/ *n* [C] a kitchen tool for separating solids from liquids 滤器, 滤网: *a tea strainer* 茶叶过滤网

strait[1] /stret; streɪt/ *n* [C] **1** also 又作 **straits** [plural] a narrow passage of water between two areas of land, usually connecting two seas 海峡; 狭窄的水道: *the Strait of Gibraltar* 直布罗陀海峡 **2 be in dire straits** to be in a difficult situation, especially a financial one, that could have very bad or dangerous results 陷于恶劣的困境中〔尤指财务困境〕: *If one of the family is in dire straits, we try to help each other out.* 家中如果有人陷入困境, 我们尽量互相帮助, 使其摆脱困难。

strait[2] *adj biblical* narrow and therefore usually difficult to pass through【圣经】狭窄的, 由于狭窄而难以通过的

strait·ened /ˋstretn̩d; ˈstreɪtnd/ *adj formal*【正式】**in straitened circumstances** in a difficult situation because of a lack of money 因经济拮据而陷入困境: *an elderly spinster living in straitened circumstances* 穷困潦倒的老姑娘

strait·jack·et, straightjacket /ˋstret,dʒækɪt; ˈstreɪt,dʒækɪ̣t/ *n* [C] **1** a special piece of clothing that is used to control the movements of someone who is mentally ill and violent〔用于约束精神病人的〕约束衣, 紧身衣 **2** something such as a law or set of ideas that puts unfair limits on someone 约束, 不公平的限制〈如法律、思想等〉: *the straitjacket of censorship* 审查制度的约束

strait-laced /ˋstretˋlest; ˌstreɪtˈleɪst◂/ *adj* having strict, old-fashioned ideas about moral behaviour〔道德方面〕一本正经的; 守旧的, 古板的: *So then Sally and her straitlaced friend showed up and we all had to shut up.* 后来, 萨莉和她那个古板的朋友来了, 我们大家都不得不停止谈话。

Strait of Ma·gel·lan, the /ˌstret əv məˋdʒɛlən; ˌstreɪt əv məˈgelən/ a narrow area of sea between Tierra del Fuego and the mainland of South America. It connects the Atlantic Ocean with the Pacific Ocean and was discovered by Ferdinand Magellan in 1520. 麦哲伦海峡〔火地岛与南美洲大陆之间的一片狭窄海域, 连接大西洋和太平洋。1520 年由斐迪南·麦哲伦发现〕

strand〔线、绳的〕股; 缕

strand /strænd; strænd/ *n* [C] **1** a single thin piece of thread, wire, hair etc〔线、绳、毛发等的〕股; 缕: *a strand of yarn* 一股线 **2** one of the parts of a story, problem etc 故事的情节; 问题的一部分: *Plato draws all the strands of the argument together at the end.* 柏拉图最后把各个论点归结起来。

Strand, the a famous street in central London where the Savoy Hotel and many theatres are 斯特兰德大街〔伦敦市中心一著名街道。沿街有萨伏伊酒店和许多剧院〕

strand·ed /ˋstrændɪd; ˈstrændɪ̣d/ *adj* a person or vehicle that is stranded is unable to move from the place where they are〔人或交通工具〕被滞留的;〔船〕搁浅的: **leave sb/sth stranded** *The tide had gone out, leaving the boat stranded on the rocks.* 潮水退了, 小船搁浅在礁石上。| [+in/on/at] *There I was, stranded in Rome with no passport and no money.* 我当时就这样被困在罗马, 没有护照, 也没有钱。

strange[1] /strendʒ; streɪndʒ/ *adj* **1** unusual or surprising, especially in a way that is difficult to explain or understand 奇怪的, 不寻常的; 不可思议的: *a strange noise* 奇怪的噪声 | *Does Geoff's behaviour seem strange to you?* 你觉得杰夫的行为奇怪吗? | **that's strange** *spoken*【口】*That's strange. I was sure Jude was right here a second ago.* 真奇怪, 我敢肯定刚才祖德就在这里。| **it's strange that/how** *It's strange that you've never met him.* 很奇怪, 你居然从来没有见过他。| **there's something strange about** *There's something strange about that house.* 那所房子有点奇怪。| **strange to say** *BrE* (=strangely)【英】说来奇怪 *Strange to say, I was just thinking that myself.* 说来奇怪, 我自己刚才也是那么想的。**2** someone or something that is strange is not familiar because you have not seen or met them before 陌生的, 不熟悉的: *all alone in a strange city* 独自一人在一个陌生的城市里 **3 feel strange** to feel unpleasant physically or emotionally 觉得不舒服: *Can you get me a glass of water? I feel a bit strange.* 你能帮我拿杯水吗? 我觉得有点不舒服。—**strangeness** *n* [U] S2 W2

strange[2] *adv* [only after verb 仅用于动词后] *AmE* in a way that is different from what is normal【美】古怪地: *The cat's been acting really strange – I wonder if it's sick.* 这只猫的行为怪怪的, 不知道是不是病了。

strange·ly /ˋstrendʒlɪ; ˈstreɪndʒli/ *adv* **1** in an unusual way 奇怪地, 不寻常地: *Mick's been acting very strangely lately.* 米克最近的行为很怪。| *a strangely shaped shell* 形状奇特的贝壳 **2 strangely enough** [sentence adverb 句子副词] used to say that although something seems unlikely, it is true 真奇怪〔表示某事虽然似乎不可能, 但却是真的〕: *Strangely enough, I wasn't really that disappointed.* 真奇怪, 我并不是那么失望。**3** in a way that is surprising or unexpected 令人吃惊地, 出乎意料地: *Her voice was strangely familiar.* 她的声音出乎意料地熟悉。

strang·er /ˋstrendʒɚ; ˈstreɪndʒə/ *n* [C] **1** someone whom you do not know 陌生人: *Children must not talk to strangers.* 小孩子千万不要同陌生人说话。| **perfect/complete/total stranger** (=used to emphasize that you do not know them) 根本不相识的人, 完全陌生的人 *A perfect stranger waved to me in the street this morning.* 今天上午, 一个我根本不认识的人在街上向我招手。**2 be no stranger to sth** to have had a lot of a particular kind of experience 有过很多某事的经历, 对某事并不陌生: *My sister is no stranger to hard times.* 我的姐姐饱经磨难。**3** someone in a new and unfamiliar place 异乡人; 外地人; 新来者: *"Where's the station?" "Sorry, I'm a stranger here myself."* "车站在哪里?" "对不起, 我也不是本地人。" **4 Hello, stranger!** *spoken humorous* used to greet someone you have not seen for a long time【口, 幽默】你好, 陌生人! 嗨, 久违了!〔用于跟好久不见的人打招呼〕

Strangers' Gal·le·ry, the /ˋ· ·, ··/ *n* the part of the British House of Commons or of the House of Lords where members of the public can sit and watch what happens in Parliament 旁听席〔英国下议院或上议院的一部分。公众可坐在这里观看议会活动〕

Strange·ways /ˋstrendʒwez; ˈstreɪndʒweɪz/ a prison in Manchester in northwest England, where prisoners took control and did a lot of damage in 1990, as a protest against bad conditions in British prisons 斯特兰奇威监狱〔英格兰西北部曼彻斯特市的一座监狱。1990 年, 囚犯们控制了该监狱, 并进行大肆破坏, 以抗议英国监狱恶劣的生活条件〕

stran·gle /ˋstræŋgl̩; ˈstræŋgəl/ *v* [T] **1** to kill someone by pressing on their throat with your hands, a rope etc 扼死, 勒死, 绞死: *The victim had been strangled with a nylon stocking.* 受害者是被人用尼龙长袜勒死的。**2** to limit or prevent the growth or development of something 限制[阻止]…的成长[发展]; 扼杀: *UN sanctions are slowly strangling the economy.* 联合国的制裁正在逐渐扼杀该国的经济。—**strangler** *n* [C]

stran·gled /ˋstræŋgl̩d; ˈstræŋgəld/ *adj* **strangled cry/gasp/sound etc** a cry etc that is suddenly stopped before it is finished 突然止住的哭泣/喘息/声音等

stran·gle·hold /ˋstræŋgl̩hold; ˈstræŋgəlhəʊld/ *n* **1** [C usually singular 一般用单数] complete control over a situation,

organization etc〔对局势、组织等的〕完全控制: **have a stranglehold on** *firms have a stranglehold on the production of CDs* 完全控制了激光唱片生产的公司 | **break the stranglehold of sb** (=stop someone having complete control) 打破某人的完全控制 **2** [C] a strong hold around someone's neck that is meant to stop them from breathing 勒颈, 卡脖子

stran·gu·late /ˈstræŋgjəˌlet; ˈstræŋgjʊ̈leɪt/ *v* [I,T] if a part of your body strangulates or is strangulated, it becomes tightly pressed so that the flow of blood stops 绞扼, 绞窄, 扼住, 压紧〔以阻止血流〕

stran·gu·la·tion /ˌstræŋgjəˈleʃən; ˌstræŋgjʊ̈ˈleɪʃən/ *n* [U] the act of killing someone by strangling them STRANGLE (1), or the fact of being killed in this way 扼死, 勒死, 绞死; 窒息而死

strap[1] /stræp; stræp/ *n* [C] a narrow band of strong material that is used to fasten, hang, or hold onto something 带子: *a leather watch strap* 皮表带 | *a backpack with adjustable straps* 背带长度可调整的背包 —see also 另见 CHINSTRAP, SHOULDER STRAP

strap[2] *v* **strapped, strapping** [T] **1** [always+adv/prep] to fasten something or somebody in place with one or more straps 用带子束住, 捆绑: **strap sb/sth in/on/down etc** *Strap that saddle on good and tight.* 把那副马鞍系好绑紧。| **be strapped in** (=have a belt fastened around you in a car) 系好安全带 *Are the kids strapped in?* 孩子们系好安全带了吗? **2** *BrE*【英】also 又作 **strap up** [often passive 常用被动态] to tie BANDAGEs firmly round a part of your body that has been hurt〔用绷带〕包扎〔伤口〕; TAPE[2] (4) *AmE*【美】

strap·hang·ing /ˈstræpˌhæŋɪŋ; ˈstræpˌhæŋɪŋ/ *n* [U] *BrE informal* supporting yourself while standing in a moving bus, train etc by holding onto a strap that hangs from the roof【英, 非正式】〔乘车时〕拉着吊带站着 —**straphanger** *n* [C]

strap·less /ˈstræplɪs; ˈstræpləs/ *adj* **strapless dress/gown** a dress that leaves your shoulders completely bare 露肩[无带]连衣裙/晚装

strapped /stræpt; stræpt/ *adj* **strapped (for cash)** *informal* having little or no money at the moment【非正式】钱不多的; 身无分文的: *Can you lend me ten dollars? I'm a little strapped for cash.* 你能借给我10美元吗? 我身上现金不多了。

strap·ping /ˈstræpɪŋ; ˈstræpɪŋ/ *adj* [only before noun 仅用于名词前] a strapping young man or woman is strong, tall, and looks healthy and active 身材高大的, 魁梧的; 强健的: *a strapping young man of 15 or so* 15岁上下的壮小子

Stras·berg /ˈstræzbɝg; ˈstræzbɜːg/, **Lee** (1901-82) a US teacher of acting and theatre DIRECTOR who was the first person in the US to use and develop the ideas about acting, called method acting, that were invented by Constantin Stanislavsky. From 1948 to 1982 he was in charge of the Actor's Studio in New York City. 斯特拉斯伯格〔(1901-1982), 美国表演艺术指导教师、戏剧导演。他是最早继承并发展康斯坦丁·斯坦尼斯拉夫斯基首创的体验派表演理论的美国人。1948至1982年曾主管纽约市演员工作室〕

Stras·bourg /ˈstrɑsbɝg; ˈstræzbɜːg/ a city in northeast France where the European Parliament and the Council of Europe are based 斯特拉斯堡〔法国东北部一城市。欧洲议会和欧洲理事会所在地〕

stra·ta /ˈstretə; ˈstrɑːtə/ *n* **1** the plural of STRATUM stratum的复数形式 **2** a plural form often used instead of STRATUM 常用来代替stratum的复数形式

strat·a·gem /ˈstrætədʒəm; ˈstrætədʒəm/ *n* [C] *formal* a trick or plan to deceive an enemy or gain an advantage【正式】〔蒙蔽敌人或谋取利益的〕计谋, 策略; 花招

W3 **stra·te·gic** /strəˈtidʒɪk; strəˈtiːdʒɪk/ also 又作 **stra·te·gic·al** /-dʒɪkḷ; -dʒɪkəl/ *adj* **1** done as part of a plan, especially in a military, business, or political situation 战略(性)的; 策略(上)的: *UN forces have made a strategic withdrawal to regroup.* 联合国部队进行了战略性撤退, 以便重新部署。| *strategic bombing* 战略轰炸 **2** useful or right for a particular purpose〔对某特定目的〕有用的; 合适的: *Marksmen were placed at strategic points along the president's route.* 在总统经过路线的重要位置上安排了神枪手。**3** used in fighting wars 用于战争的: *secret purchases of strategic materials* 秘密购买战略物资 | **strategic arms/weapons** (=weapons designed to reach an enemy country from your own) 战略性武器 —**strategically** /-kḷɪ; -kli/ *adv*

Strategic De·fense I·ni·tia·tive, the /·,··· ·'··,···/ the full name of SDI〔美国〕战略防御计划〔SDI的全称〕

strat·e·gist /ˈstrætədʒɪst; ˈstrætɪ̈dʒɪ̈st/ *n* [C] someone who is good at planning, especially military movements 善于策划的人; 〔尤指〕战略家

strat·e·gy /ˈstrætədʒɪ; ˈstrætɪ̈dʒi/ *n* **1** [U] the skill of planning in advance the movements of armies or equipment in a war〔战争中的〕战略; 战略学 **2** [C] a well-planned series of actions for achieving an aim, especially success against an opponent〔为实现某目标, 尤指为战胜对手而制定的〕行动计划; 计谋, 策略: *Our strategy was to defend and then counterattack.* 我们的策略是先防御后反攻。| [+for] *a strategy for dealing with unemployment* 对付失业问题的行动计划 **3** [U] skilful planning in general 战略, 策略: *the need to focus on strategy for the entire company* 把注意力集中到公司整体策略的必要性 W2

Strat·ford-upon-A·von /ˌstrætfəd əpɑn ˋevən; ˌstrætfəd əpɒn ˈeɪvən/ a town in Warwickshire, central England, on the River Avon. It is famous as the place where William Shakespeare was born, and is very popular with tourists. 埃文河畔的斯特拉特福〔英格兰中部沃里克郡一城镇, 位于埃文河畔。因威廉·莎士比亚诞生于此而著名, 是颇受欢迎的旅游胜地〕

Strath·clyde /stræθˋklaɪd; stræθˈklaɪd/ a former local government region in central Scotland, that included the city of Glasgow 斯特拉斯克莱德〔曾为苏格兰中部一地方政府辖区, 包括格拉斯哥市〕

strat·i·fi·ca·tion /ˌstrætəfəˋkeʃən; ˌstrætɪ̈fɪ̈ˈkeɪʃən/ *n* **1** [C, U+ of] the way that a society develops into different social classes〔社会的〕分层, 阶层形成 **2** [C,U] the way that different layers of earth, rock etc develop over time 层理; 地层 **3** [C,U] the position that different layers of something have in relation to each other 层叠(现象)

strat·i·fied /ˈstrætəˌfaɪd; ˈstrætɪ̈faɪd/ *adj* **1** having different social classes 有不同社会等级的, 分层的: *a stratified society* 等级社会 **2** having several layers of earth, rock etc〔土壤、岩石等〕成层的: *stratified rock* 成层岩

strat·os·phere /ˈstrætəˌsfɪr; ˈstrætəsfɪə/ *n* **1 the stratosphere** the outer part of the air surrounding the Earth, starting at about ten kilometres above the Earth 平流层, 同温层 **2 the fashion/pop music etc stratosphere** a very high position in fashion etc that makes you famous 最高档次的时装/流行音乐等

stra·tum /ˈstretəm; ˈstrɑːtəm/ *n plural* **strata** /-tə; -tə/ [C] **1** a layer of rock of a particular kind, especially one with different layers above and below it 岩层 **2** a layer of earth, such as one where tools, bones etc from an ancient civilization are found by digging 地层〈如考古层〉 **3** a social class in a society 社会阶层

Strauss /straus; straʊs/, **Jo·hann** /ˈjohɑn; ˈjəʊhæn/ (1825-99) an Austrian COMPOSER who wrote more than 400 WALTZes including the very popular *Blue Danube* and *Tales from the Vienna Woods* 施特劳斯〔(1825-1899), 奥地利作曲家。创作了四百多首圆舞曲, 其中包括深受欢迎的《蓝色多瑙河》和《维也纳森林的故事》〕

Strauss, Richard (1864-1949) a German COMPOSER whose best-known works are his SYMPHONIC poems, his OPERAs, especially *Der Rosenkavalier* (1911), and his *Four Last Songs* (1948). One of his symphonic poems, *Also sprach Zarathustra* (1895) was used in the film *2001: A Space Odyssey* (1968). 斯特劳斯〔(1864-1949), 德国作曲家, 以交响诗和歌剧著称。代表作有《玫瑰骑士》(1911)和《最后四首歌》(1948)等。其交响诗《查拉图斯特拉如是说》(1895)被电影《2001太空漫游》(1968)所采用〕

Stra·vin·sky /strəˋvɪnskɪ; strəˈvɪnski/, **I·gor** /ˈigɔr; ˈiːgɔː/ (1882-1971) a Russian musician, famous especially for his BALLET music, including *The Firebird* and *The Rite of Spring*, which he wrote for the ballet producer Diaghilev. His work was very different from anything done before. 斯特拉文斯基〔(1882-1971), 俄国音乐家, 尤以芭蕾音乐闻名。代表作有《火鸟》和《春之祭》, 是应芭蕾舞编导达吉烈夫之约创作的曲目, 风格独树一帜〕

straw /strɔ; strɔː/ *n* **1 a)** [U] the dried stems of wheat or similar plants that are used for animals to sleep on, and for making things such as baskets, mats etc〔干的〕麦秆, 稻草, 禾秆: *a straw hat* 草帽 **b)** [C] a single dried stem of wheat etc〔单根的〕麦秆, 稻草秆: *Some straws were sticking to his jacket.* 他的夹克衫上粘着几根稻草。**2** [C] a thin tube of paper or plastic for sucking up liquid〔喝饮料用的〕吸管: *a boy happily drinking a chocolate milkshake through a straw* 高兴地用吸管喝着巧克力奶昔的男孩 **3 the last straw/the straw that breaks the camel's back** the last problem in a series of problems that finally makes you give up, get angry etc 压垮骆驼的最后一根稻草; 〔一系列问题中〕最终使人无法承受的事; 终于使人不堪重负的因素 **4 a straw in the wind** *BrE* a sign of what might happen in the future【英】〔未来事态的〕迹象, 征兆; 苗头: *These* S3

stories of food riots may well be straws in the wind. 这些因食物引起暴乱的传闻很可能就是要出事的苗头。**5 straw man** *AmE* a weak opponent or imaginary argument that can easily be defeated【美】稻草人; 不堪一击的假想对手; 不值一驳的虚构论点 —see also 另见 **you can't make bricks without straw** (BRICK[1] (4)), **clutch at straws** (CLUTCH[1]), **draw the short straw** (DRAW[1] (26))

straw·ber·ry /ˈstrɔˌbɛri; ˈstrɔːbəri/ *n* **1** [C] a soft red juicy fruit with small pale seeds on its surface, or the plant that grows this fruit 草莓〔指植物或其果实〕: *strawberries and cream* 奶油草莓 | *strawberry jam* 草莓果酱 —see picture on page A8 参见 A8 页图 **2** [U] a dark pink colour 紫红色, 草莓色

strawberry blonde /ˌ··· ˈ·/ *n* [C] a woman with light reddish yellow hair 头发略带红色的金发女子 —**strawberry blonde** *adj*

strawberry mark /ˈ··· ·/ *n* [C] a reddish mark on your skin at birth that never goes away; BIRTHMARK 莓状痣; 红色胎记

straw boat·er /ˌ· ˈ··/ *n* [C] *BrE* a stiff hat made of straw that is usually worn in summer【英】〔夏天戴的〕硬草帽

straw-col·oured /ˈ· ˌ··/ *adj* light yellow 浅黄色的, 麦秆色的

straw poll /ˌ· ˈ·/ also 又作 **straw vote** *n* [C] an unofficial test of people's opinions before an election, to see what the result is likely to be〔大选前为测验民意进行的〕非正式投票

stray[1] /stre; streɪ/ *v* [I] **1** to leave the place where you should be without intending to 走离; 走失, 迷路: *a warship that had strayed into enemy waters* 误入敌方水域的战舰 **2** to begin to deal with a different subject than the main one, without intending to 偏离〔主题〕: **stray into/onto sth** *We're straying into ethnic issues here.* 我们现在偏离主题, 讨论起种族问题来。| **stray from the subject/point/question** *Try not to stray from the point in your answers.* 你在回答中尽量不要离题。

S

stray[2] *adj* [only before noun 仅用于名词前] **1** a stray animal walks around because it is lost or has no home〔动物〕走失的, 迷路的, 流浪的 **2** accidentally separated from other things of the same kind 离散的; 零落的: *A stray spark must have started the blaze.* 一定是一颗散落的火花引起了这场大火。| *a few stray wisps of hair* 几缕散发

stray[3] *n* [C] **1** an animal that is lost and cannot find its home or has no home 走失[流浪]的动物 **2** *informal* someone or something that has become separated from others of the same kind【非正式】离开同类的人; 离开原位的东西 —see also 另见 **waifs and strays** (WAIF (2))

streak[1] /strik; striːk/ *n* [C] **1** a coloured line, especially one that is not straight or has been made accidentally 色条; 条痕; 斑纹: *Sue has blonde streaks in her hair.* 休的头发里夹杂着几缕金发。**2** a part of someone's character that is different from the rest of their character 个性特征, 特点: *Mel has a romantic streak in him.* 梅尔个性有点浪漫。| *a sadistic streak* 有点儿虐待狂 **3** a period of time during which you continue to be successful or to fail〔不断成功或失败的〕一段时期: *a streak of good luck* 一阵子好运气 | **be on a winning/losing streak** (=have a period of time when you continue to win or lose) 一段时期连赢/连输 *After a month-long losing streak we finally won a game.* 我们一连输了一个月后, 终于赢了一场。**4 a streak of lightning** a long straight burst of LIGHTNING 一道闪电: **like a streak of lightning** (=very fast) 迅速地; 风驰电掣地 *The cat shot out the door like a streak of lightning.* 那只猫闪电般地跑出门去。

streak[2] *v* **1** [I always+adv/prep] to run or fly somewhere so fast you can hardly be seen 飞速地跑[飞]: **[+across/along/down etc]** *Two jets streaked across the sky.* 两架喷气式飞机从空中迅速地飞过。**2** [T usually passive 一般用被动态] to cover something with streaks 使布满条纹: **[+with]** *Colin's face was streaked with tears.* 科林的脸上挂着条条泪痕。**3** [I] to run across a public place with no clothes on to shock people 裸跑

streak·er /ˈstrikɚ; ˈstriːkə/ *n* [C] someone who runs across a public place with no clothes on to shock people 裸跑的人

streak·y /ˈstrikɪ; ˈstriːki/ *adj* marked with streaks 有条纹的; 有纹理的: *When I washed the shirt it went all streaky.* 我洗了这件衬衫后, 它变得尽是条痕。

streaky ba·con /ˌ·· ˈ··/ *n* [U] *BrE* smoked or salted pig meat that has lines of fat between the meat【英】五花熏咸肉; BACON *AmE*【美】

stream[1] /strim; striːm/ *n* [C]

1 ►SMALL RIVER 小河◄ a natural flow of water that moves across the land and is narrower than a river 小河, 小溪: *a mountain stream* 山涧 —see also 另见 DOWNSTREAM, UPSTREAM

2 ►CONTINUOUS SERIES 连续的系列◄ a long and almost continuous series of events, people, objects, etc〔事件、人、物等的〕一连串, 一系列, 流: **[+of]** *a stream of traffic* 川流不息的车辆 | *A steady stream of visitors came to the house.* 参观这所房子的人络绎不绝。| *a stream of abuse* 一连串的辱骂

3 ►AIR/WATER 空气/水◄ a current of water or air, or the direction in which it is flowing 水流(方向); 气流(方向): *A stream of cold air rushed through the open door.* 一股冷风穿门而过。—see also 另见 GULF STREAM, JET STREAM

4 come on stream *technical* to start producing something such as oil, electricity, goods etc【术语】投入生产〔石油、电、货品等〕: *The new plant will come on stream at the end of the year.* 新工厂将于年底投产。

5 go/swim against the stream to do or think something differently from what people in general do or think 反潮流; 不随大流

6 ►SCHOOL 学校◄ *especially BrE* a level of ability within a group of students of the same age【尤英】同龄学生按能力水平划分的班[组]: *Caroline's in the top stream.* 卡罗琳在智力最高组。—see also 另见 BLOODSTREAM, STREAM OF CONSCIOUSNESS

stream[2] *v*

1 ►POUR 倾注◄ [I always+adv/prep,T] to flow quickly and in great amounts, or to make something flow in this way; pour (使)奔流; (使)倾注; (使)涌流: **[+out/in/onto etc]** *Water came streaming out of the burst pipe.* 水从爆裂的水管中涌出来。| *Tears streamed down her cheeks.* 泪水顺着她的脸颊流下来。

2 ►FLOW 流动◄ [I always+adv/prep] to move in a continuous flow in the same direction 不断地流动; 〔朝同一方向〕涌: **[+out/across/past etc]** *The crowd streamed out of the football ground.* 人群从足球场蜂拥而出。

3 ►MOVE FREELY 自由移动◄ [I always+adv/prep, usually in progressive 一般用进行时] to move freely in a current of wind or water〔在风或水中〕自由飘动, 自由流动: **[+in/out/behind etc]** *Elise ran, her hair streaming out behind her.* 埃莉斯跑着, 头发向后飘。

4 ►GIVE OUT LIQUID 流出液体◄ [I,T] to produce a continuous flow of liquid 流淌; 不断地流出: **[+with]** *The onions made my eyes stream with tears.* 洋葱辣得我眼睛直流泪。

5 ►SCHOOL 学校◄ [T] *especially BrE* to put school children in groups according to their ability【尤英】将〔学生〕按能力水平分组[分班]; TRACK[2] (5) *AmE*【美】

6 a streaming cold *BrE* a very bad cold, with liquid flowing from your nose【英】会流鼻涕的重感冒

stream·er /ˈstrimɚ; ˈstriːmə/ *n* [C] **1** a long narrow piece of coloured paper, used for decoration at special occasions〔装饰用的〕彩色纸带, 饰带 **2** a long narrow flag 长条旗

stream·line /ˈstrimˌlaɪn; ˈstriːmlaɪn/ *v* [T] **1** to form something into a smooth shape so that it moves easily through the air or water 使…成为流线型: *All these new cars have been aerodynamically streamlined.* 所有这些新汽车都被做成了流线型。**2** to make something such as a business, organization etc work more simply and effectively 精简〔企业、组织等〕; 简化使效率更高: *efforts to streamline the production process* 简化生产过程以提高效率的努力 —**streamlined** *adj*

stream of con·scious·ness /ˌ· · ˈ··· ·/ *n* [U] the expression of thoughts and feelings in writing exactly as they pass through your mind, without the usual ordered structure they have in formal writing 意识流〔一种创作方式〕

street /strit; striːt/ *n* [C] **1** a public road in a city or town that has houses, shops etc on one or both sides 大街, 街道: *101 Oxford Street, London* 伦敦牛津街 101 号 | **street map** (=showing the names and positions of all the roads) 街道图 | **street musicians** (=performing outdoors in towns) 街头演奏音乐家 —see also 另见 HIGH STREET **2 the streets** a phrase meaning the roads of a city, used to mean a place where people live who have no home and where it is difficult to survive〔无家可归的穷人居住的〕街头: **on the streets** *young people living on the streets* 流落街头的年轻人 **3 the man/woman in the street** the average person, who represents the general opinion about things 普通人, 一般人: *The man in the street wouldn't have a clue what a dongle is.* 一般人根本不知道加密狗为何物。**4 (right) up your street** a job or course that is up your street is exactly right for you because you have the right skills and are interested in it〔指工作或课程因在某人的技能和兴趣范围内〕刚好适合某人 **5 one-way/two-way street** a process that fully involves the opinions and feelings of only one person or group, or of both people or groups 单方面/双方参与的过程: *Trust is not a one-way street.* 信任不是单向的。**6 walk the streets** *old-fashioned* an expression meaning to be a PROSTITUTE【过时】当妓女, 卖淫

7 streets ahead (of) *BrE informal* much better than someone or something else【英, 非正式】比…好得多: *James is streets ahead of the rest of the class at reading.* 詹姆斯在阅读方面远远超过班里的其他同学。—see also 另见 BACKSTREET, **be on easy street** (EASY[1] (11)), STREET SMARTS

USAGE NOTE 用法说明: STREET
WORD CHOICE 词语辨析: **street, road**
A **street** is in the middle of a town, and usually has shops and other buildings and pavements (*BrE* 英)/sidewalks (*AmE* 美). street 是指城镇的街道, 两旁通常有商店等建筑物和人行道: *a street corner* (NOT 不用 *road corner*) 街角
A **road** can be in the town or in the country, and usually leads to another town, or to another part of a town. road 是指城镇或乡间的公路, 通常连接一个城镇与另一城镇或城镇的一个地区与另一个地区: *the road to Birmingham* (NOT 不用 *street*) 往伯明翰的公路
BRE-AME DIFFERENCES 英国英语和美国英语的区别
British speakers often say **in a street or road** where American speakers say **on a street or road**. 英国人常在 street 或 road 前用介词 in, 美国人则常用 on: *the shops in the High Street* 大街上的商店 (*BrE* 英) | *the stores on Main Street* 大街上的商店 (*AmE* 美) | *a house in Bristol Road* (*BrE* 英)在布里斯托尔路的一栋房子 | *a house on Boston Road* (*AmE* 美)在波士顿路的一栋房子
In spoken American English words like **street** are often left out especially when giving directions to numbered streets. 在美国口语中, 尤其在告诉别人如何去某条有编号的大街时, street 等词常被省去: *Where's the Empire State Building? At 34th and 5th.* 到帝国大厦怎么走? 在 34 街和第 5 大街的交汇处。In British English this would be 英国英语则说: *At the junction of 34th Street and 5th Avenue.* 在 34 街和第 5 大街的交汇处。

street·car /ˈstritˌkɑr; ˈstriːtkɑː/ *n* [C] *AmE* a type of bus that runs on electricity along metal tracks in the road【美】有轨电车; TRAM *BrE*【英】

Streetcar Named Desire, A /,.. , . ˈ. ./ (1947) a play by Tennessee Williams, made into a film with Marlon Brando and Vivien Leigh in 1951, about a beautiful woman who is becoming old and her violent younger brother-in-law《欲望号街车》〔(1947), 田纳西·威廉斯的名剧。1951 年拍成电影, 由马龙·白兰度和费雯丽主演。影片讲述一个青春渐去的美丽女子和她粗暴的妹夫之间的故事〕

street-cred /ˈstrit ˌkrɛd; ˈstriːt kred/ also 又作 **street cred·i·bil·i·ty** /,. .ˈ. ../ *n* [U] popular acceptance and approval among young people, especially because you know how to survive in a city〔在年轻人中认同的〕街头信誉: *It'll wreck your street cred if you're seen helping the police.* 如果有人看到你帮助警察, 会损害你的街头信誉。—**street-credible** /ˈ. , ..ˈ/ *adj*

street·lamp /ˈstritˌlæmp; ˈstriːtlæmp/ *n* [C] a streetlight 街灯, 路灯

street·light /ˈstritˌlaɪt; ˈstriːtlaɪt/ *n* [C] a light at the top of a tall post in the street 街灯, 路灯 —see picture on page A4 参见 A4 页图

street peo·ple /ˈ. ,../ *n* [plural] people who have no home and live on the streets 无家可归的人, 漂泊街头的人

street smarts /ˈ. ./ *n* [U] *AmE* the ability to deal with difficult situations on the streets of a big city【美】在城市街头应付困境的能力: *unsuspecting tourists with no street smarts whatsoever* 根本没有城市街头适应能力的、毫无提防的游客

street style /ˈ. ./ *n* [U] style connected with the clothes, music etc of ordinary young people〔衣服、音乐等的〕普通年轻人的风格, 大众风格

street val·ue /ˈ. ,../ *n* [C,U] the price for which a drug can be sold illegally to people〔毒品的〕街头黑市行情[价格]: *The drugs haul had a street value of £100,000.* 这批毒品的黑市价格为 10 万英镑。

street·walk·er /ˈstritˌwɔkɚ; ˈstriːtˌwɔːkə/ *n* [C] *old-fashioned* a PROSTITUTE who stands on the street to attract customers【过时】〔街头拉客的〕妓女

street·wise /ˈstritwaɪz; ˈstriːtwaɪz/ *adj informal* clever and experienced enough to deal with difficult situations on the streets of a big city【非正式】善于在街头营生的; 圆滑世故能在城市街头混得开的: *streetwise drug dealers overtaking the neighborhood* 称霸街坊、常在街头混的毒品贩子

S2 W2 **strength** /strɛŋθ; streŋθ/ *n*

1 ►**PHYSICAL STRENGTH** 体力◄ [U] the physical power and energy that makes someone strong 体力, 力气, 力量: *It took Susan weeks to regain her strength after the illness.* 苏珊病愈后过了好几个星期才恢复体力。| **the strength to do sth** *I don't have the strength to climb any further.* 我没有力气再往上爬了。| **with all your strength** *Diana pulled on the rope with all her strength.* 黛安娜用尽全身的力气拉绳子。| **not know your own strength** (=not realize how strong you are) 没有意识到自己的力量 —see also 另见 **outgrow your strength** (OUTGROW (4))

2 ►**OF AN OBJECT** 某物体的◄ [U] how strong an object or structure is, especially its ability to last for a long time without breaking 强度: [**+of**] *I have doubts about the strength of that beam in the ceiling.* 我怀疑天花板上那条横梁的强度。

3 ►**OF CHARACTER** 性格上的◄ [U] the ability to deal with difficult or unpleasant situations in a brave or determined way〔处理困境等的〕意志力: *moral strength* 道德力量 | **strength to do sth** *Where did you find the strength to keep trying?* 你不断进行尝试的意志力是从哪儿来的? | **strength of character** (=strong ability to deal with difficult situations) 性格的坚强 *the underlying strength of character behind Roosevelt's easy charm* 罗斯福平易近人的外表下潜在的坚强性格 | **inner strength** (=strength of spirit) 精神力量 *His troubles have bred in him an inner strength he'll never lose.* 他所经受的磨难使他产生一种永不磨灭的精神力量。—see also 另见 **tower of strength** (TOWER[1] (3))

4 ►**OF FEELING/BELIEF/RELATIONSHIP** 感情/信仰/关系的◄ [U] how strong a feeling, belief, or relationship is 坚强; 坚定; 强度: [**+of**] *We can't ignore the strength of public opinion.* 我们不能忽视公众舆论的力量。| *the strength of family bonds* 家庭纽带的力量 | **strength of feeling** *Don't underestimate the strength of feeling that the abortion issue will generate.* 不要低估堕胎问题将会引发的强烈情绪。| **strength of purpose** (=determination) 决心 *I began to feel my strength of purpose failing me.* 我开始觉得自己的决心在动摇。

5 ►**POLITICAL/MILITARY/ECONOMIC** 政治/军事/经济(上)的◄ [U] political, military or economic power〔政治、军事或经济上的〕实力: [**+of**] *the strength of the US economy* 美国的经济实力 | **a show of strength** (=an occasion when a country shows how powerful its army etc is)〔军事等的〕实力显示, 显示力量

6 ►**OF A SUBSTANCE/MIXTURE** 物质/混合物的◄ [C,U] how strong a substance or mixture is 强度; 浓度; 烈度: *The drug is available in two strengths.* 这种毒品有两种不同的烈度。| **full-strength/half-strength/double-strength etc** *acid diluted to half-strength* 浓度被稀释了一半的酸

7 ►**USEFUL QUALITY OR ABILITY** 有用的特征或能力◄ [C] a particular quality or ability that gives someone or something an advantage 强点, 长处, 优势: *The great strength of our plan lies in its simplicity.* 我们这个计划的最大长处在于它的简单明了。

8 position of strength a position where you have an advantage over someone, especially in discussions〔尤指在讨论中的〕优势地位: *If we keep our nuclear weapons, we can negotiate from a position of strength.* 我们如果保存自己的核武器, 就能在谈判中处于强势地位。

9 ►**OF A TEAM/ARMY ETC** 团队/军队等的◄ [U] the number of people in a team, army etc 人力, 人数; 兵力: **below strength** *The police force is below strength at the moment.* 目前警力不足。| **in strength** (=in large numbers) 大批地, 大量地

10 ►**OF MONEY** 金钱的◄ [U] the value of a country's money〔某国家货币的〕价值; 价格坚挺程度: [**+of**] *the strength of the dollar on the international money markets* 美元在国际货币市场上的强势

11 ►**COLOUR/LIGHT** 颜色/光线◄ [U] how strong a light or colour is〔光线或颜色的〕强度: *the strength of the beam of light* 光束的强度

12 ►**OF A WIND/CURRENT** 风/水流的◄ [U] how strong a wind or current of water is〔风或水流的〕强度

13 go from strength to strength to have one success after another 不断取得成功; 日益壮大: *Since the advent of the personal computer, the software industry has gone from strength to strength.* 自从有了个人电脑, 软件业不断壮大。

14 on the strength of sth because of something that persuaded you 基于…; 受…的鼓励: *I bought the book on the strength of your recommendation.* 我是因为你的推荐才买这本书的。

15 give me strength *spoken* used when you are annoyed or angry about something【口】给我力量吧! 真叫人受不了!〔用于表示烦恼或生气〕

S

strength·en /ˋstrɛŋθən; ˈstreŋθən/ *v*
1 ▶FEELING/BELIEF/RELATIONSHIP 感情/信仰/关系◀ [I,T] to become stronger or make something stronger (使) 变强, 加强; 使更坚固: *Our friendship has steadily strengthened over the years.* 我们的友谊逐年加深。| **strengthen sth** *Steve's opposition only strengthened her resolve to go ahead.* 史蒂夫的反对只有加强了她继续下去的决心。
2 ▶TEAM/ARMY ETC 团队/军队等◀ [T] to make an organization, army etc more powerful, especially by increasing the number or quality of the people in it 增强〔某组织或军队等的〕实力: *The team has been strengthened by the arrival of two Brazilian players.* 两位巴西球员的到来增强了该球队的实力。
3 ▶MONEY 钱◀ [I,T] to increase in value or to increase the value of money〔货币〕增值; 增加〔货币的〕价值: *The pound has strengthened against other currencies.* 英镑对其他货币的比值上升了。
4 ▶FINANCIAL SITUATION 财政状况◀ [T] to improve the financial situation of a country or company 增强, 改善〔某国或公司的财政状况〕: *measures to strengthen the economy* 增强经济的措施
5 ▶STRUCTURE 结构◀ [T] to make something physically or structurally stronger 加固: *Metal supports were added to strengthen the outer walls.* 增加了金属支架以加固外墙。
6 ▶PROOF/REASON 证据/理由◀ [T] to give support to a reason or an attempt to prove something 为…提供更有力的理由[证据]: *Evidence from independent witnesses would greatly strengthen your case.* 独立证人的证词更有利于你的案子。
7 ▶WIND/CURRENT 风/水流◀ [I] to increase in force 加强, 增大: *The wind had strengthened during the night.* 风在夜里刮得更大了。

stren·u·ous /ˋstrɛnjuəs; ˈstrenjuəs/ *adj* **1** needing great effort or strength 艰苦的, 须作出努力的, 要花工夫的: *a strenuous climb* 艰难的攀登 | *The doctor advised Ken to avoid strenuous exercise.* 医生建议肯不要做剧烈运动。**2** active and determined 积极的; 坚决的: **make strenuous efforts** *the strenuous efforts the council is making to improve security* 地方议会为改进安全所作出的积极努力 —**strenuously** *adv*: *She strenuously denied the accusations.* 她极力否认那些指控。

strep throat /ˌstrɛp ˋθrot; ˌstrep ˈθrəʊt/ *n* [C,U] *informal* an illness in which your throat is very painful【非正式】链球菌性咽喉炎, 脓毒性咽喉炎

strep·to·coc·cus /ˌstrɛptəˋkɑkəs; ˌstreptəˈkɒkəs/ *n plural* **streptococci** /-kaɪ; -kaɪ/ [C] a BACTERIA that causes infections, especially in your throat 链球菌 —**streptococcal** *adj*

strep·to·my·cin /ˌstrɛptəˋmaɪsɪn; ˌstreptəʊˈmaɪsɪn/ *n* [U] a strong drug used in medicines to kill BACTERIA 链霉素

stress[1] /strɛs; stres/ *n* **1** [C,U] continuous feelings of worry about your work or personal life, that prevent you from relaxing 压力; 忧虑; 紧张: *Your headaches are due to stress.* 你的头痛是紧张造成的。| **under stress** *Janet's been under a lot of stress since her mother's illness.* 珍妮特自从母亲生病以来承受了很大的压力。| **stresses and strains** (=problems and worries) 紧张和压力 | **stress-related** (=caused by stress) 与紧张有关的 *a stress-related illness* 与紧张有关的疾病 **2** [C,U] the physical force or pressure on an object 应力: *the stress exerted on an aircraft's wing* 施加于飞机机翼的应力 **3** [U] the special attention or importance given to a particular idea, fact, or activity; EMPHASIS 强调; 重要性: **put/lay stress on** *Pugh laid particular stress on the need for discipline.* 皮尤特别强调纪律的必要性。**4** [C,U] the degree of force or loudness with which a part of a word is pronounced or a note in music is played, which makes it sound stronger than other parts or notes 重音, 重读; 〔音乐中的〕加强

stress[2] *v* [T] **1** to emphasize a statement, fact, or idea 强调, 着重: *I can't stress enough the need for cooperation.* 无论我如何强调合作的必要性都不过分。**2** to pronounce a word or part of a word more forcefully or loudly 重读: *The word 'machine' is stressed on the second syllable.* machine 这个词的第二个音节要重读。

stressed /strɛst; strest/ *adj* **1** [not before noun 不用于名词前] so worried and tired that you cannot relax 焦虑的, 紧张的, 无法放松的 **2** *technical* an object, especially a metal object, that is stressed has had a lot of pressure or force put on it【术语】〔尤指金属物体〕受力的

stressed out /ˌ· ˈ·◂/ *adj informal* so worried and tired that you cannot relax【非正式】极度焦虑的; 非常紧张的, 压力大的: *Rob looks so stressed out since he started this new job.* 罗布自从开始做这份新工作以来, 看上去一直非常紧张。

stress·ful /ˋstrɛsfəl; ˈstresfəl/ *adj* a job, experience, or situation that is stressful makes you worry a lot 充满压力的, 紧张的: *Moving to a new house is a very stressful experience.* 搬新家是件很劳心的事。

stress mark /ˈ· ·/ *n* [C] a mark that shows which part of a word is pronounced more forcefully 重音符号

stretch[1] /strɛtʃ; stretʃ/ *v*
1 ▶MAKE STH BIGGER/LOOSER 使某物更大/更松◀ **a)** [I,T] to make something bigger or looser by pulling it, or to become bigger or looser as a result of being pulled (使) 变大; (使) 变松; 拉长: *My big, blue sweater has stretched completely out of shape.* 我那件蓝色大毛线衫已经松得完全变了形。**b)** [I not in progressive 不用进行时] if material stretches, it can become bigger or longer when you pull it and then return to its original shape when you stop 可伸展, 可延伸, 有弹性: *Lycra shorts will stretch to fit you perfectly.* 莱卡短裤有弹性, 穿着很贴身。
2 ▶ARM/BODY 手臂/身体◀ [I,T] to straighten your arms, legs, or body to full length 伸开, 张开, 伸展〔肢体〕: *Carl sat up in bed, yawned and stretched.* 卡尔从床上坐了起来, 边打呵欠边伸懒腰。
3 ▶MAKE STH TIGHT 使某物变紧◀ [T] to pull something so that it is tight 拉紧, 拽紧: *a rope stretched between two poles* 在两根柱子间扯着的绳子 | **stretch sth tight** *Stretch the canvas tight over the frame.* 把油画布紧绷在画框上。
4 ▶IN SPACE 在空间上◀ [I always+adv/prep] to spread out or cover a large area of land 延伸, 绵延: [+to/into/away] *The desert stretched away as far as the eye could see.* 沙漠绵延, 一望无际。| *a line stretching around the block* 围绕着街区的一条线
5 ▶IN TIME 在时间上◀ [I always+adv/prep] to continue over a period of time 延续, 延伸: [+into/on/over] *a research program stretching over several years* 一个历时数年的研究项目
6 ▶RULE/LIMIT 规则/限制◀ [T] to allow something that would not normally be allowed by a rule or limit 放宽规则[限制]: *This once I'll stretch the rules and let you leave work early.* 这一次我就放宽规定让你早下班。| **stretch a point** (=allow a rule to be broken) 破例; 放宽规定 *We'll stretch a point and let the baby travel free this time.* 我们这次破例让婴儿免费旅行。
7 stretch sb's patience/credulity etc to be almost beyond the limits of what someone can accept, believe etc 使某人难以忍受/相信等: **stretch sth to the limit** *Barry's behaviour has stretched my patience to the limit.* 巴里的行为已经使我忍无可忍。
8 ▶ABILITIES 能力◀ [T] to make someone use all of their skill, abilities or intelligence 使〔某人〕施展才华: *The work's too easy. The students aren't being stretched enough.* 作业太容易, 没有让学生充分发挥出来。
9 be stretched (to the limit) to have hardly enough money or supplies for your needs 手头拮据, 没有足够的钱[日用品]: *We're stretched at the moment, otherwise I'd offer to lend you some money.* 我们目前手头拮据, 不然我会主动提出借一些钱给你。
10 stretch the truth to make something seem more important, bigger etc than it really is 夸大事实, 言过其实: **be stretching it** *He's a good player, but 'world class' is stretching it.* 他是一位优秀的选手, 但要说是"世界级的", 那就有点夸张了。
11 not stretch to sth if someone's money will not stretch to something, they cannot afford it 买不起某物, 支付不起某物的费用: *Our savings don't stretch to a vacation this year.* 今年我们的存款不够去度假。
12 stretch your legs *informal* to go for a walk, especially after sitting for a long time【非正式】〔尤指久坐后〕伸伸腿; 散散步 —**stretchable** *adj*

stretch out *phr v* **1** [I always+adv/prep] *informal* to lie down, usually in order to sleep or rest【非正式】躺下〔睡觉或休息〕: *I'm just going to stretch out on the couch for ten minutes.* 我打算在沙发上躺10分钟。**2** [T **stretch** sth ↔ **out**] to put out your hand, foot etc in order to reach something 伸出, 伸开〔手、脚等〕: *Jimmy stretched out his hand to take the candy.* 吉米伸出手去拿糖果。

stretch[2] *n*
1 ▶LENGTH OF LAND/WATER 一片地域/水域◀ [C] an area of land or water, especially one that is long and narrow〔尤指长而窄的〕一片地域; 一片水域: [+of] *The boat rocked as it entered the stretch of rough water.* 船进入那段风浪大的水域后摇晃起来。| *a beautiful stretch of countryside* 一片乡村美景 |

home/final/finishing stretch (=the last part of a track before the end of a race) 临近终点的一段跑道
2 ▶TIME 时间◀[C] a continuous period of time 连续的一段时间: [+of] *a stretch of three weeks without sunshine* 一连三个星期没有阳光 | **at a stretch** (=without stopping) 不停地, 连续地 *I couldn't stand for hours at a stretch.* 我无法连续站立几个小时。
3 ▶BODY 身体◀[C] the action of stretching a part of your body out to its full length, or a particular way of doing this 伸展动作;〔肢体的〕伸展, 伸开, 张开: *The ski instructor showed us some special stretches.* 滑雪教练给我们示范了几个特别的伸展动作。
4 ▶MATERIAL 材料◀[U] the ability a material has to increase in length or width without tearing 伸展性, 弹性: *This elastic has lost its stretch.* 这条松紧带已经失去了弹性。—compare 比较 STRETCHY
5 not by any stretch of the imagination used to say that something cannot be true, even if you try very hard to imagine or believe it 无论怎样想象都不〔表示某事怎么想象或推想也不可能是真实的〕: *You wouldn't call him smart by any stretch of the imagination, but he did ok for himself.* 无论你如何想象, 也不能说他是聪明人, 但他自己生活得还可以。
6 ▶JAIL 监狱◀[C usually singular 一般用单数] *informal* a period of time spent in prison【非正式】服刑期, 徒刑
7 at full stretch *BrE*【英】**a)** using everything that is available 全力以赴, 竭尽所能: *The emergency services were at full stretch after the motorway pile-up.* 高速公路发生连环撞车事故之后, 紧急救护部门正全力以赴 (进行处理)。**b)** with your body or part of your body stretched as far as possible 身体[肢体]伸直: *He dived and caught the ball at full stretch.* 他一个鱼跃伸手把球接住。

stretch·er[1] /ˈstrɛtʃɚ; ˈstretʃə/ *n* [C] a covered frame for carrying someone who is too injured or ill to walk 担架

stretcher[2] *v* [T always+adv/prep] to carry someone on a stretcher 用担架抬送〔某人〕: **stretcher sb off/into etc** *Ward was stretchered off early in the game after a tackle by Townley.* 沃德在比赛初段遭汤利的一次阻截之后被担架抬下了场。

stretcher-bear·er /ˈ·· ˌ··/ *n* [C] someone, usually a soldier, who carries one end of a stretcher 抬担架的人〔通常为士兵〕

stretch lim·o /ˈstrɛtʃ ˌlɪmo; ˈstretʃ ˌlɪməʊ/ also 又作 **stretch lim·ou·sine** /ˈ· ˌ···/ *n* [C] a very large comfortable car that has been made longer than usual 加长豪华轿车, 特大豪华轿车

stretch·mark /ˈstrɛtʃmɑrk; ˈstretʃmɑːk/ *n* [C usually plural 一般用复数] a mark left on your skin as a result of it stretching too much, especially during PREGNANCY〔尤指怀孕时留下的〕萎缩纹, 妊娠纹

stretch·y /ˈstrɛtʃɪ; ˈstretʃi/ *adj* material that is stretchy can stretch when you pull it and then return to its original shape 有弹性的, 可伸张的: *stretchy cotton leggings* 弹性棉护腿

strew /stru; struː/ *v past participle* **strewn** /strun; struːn/ or **strewed** [T usually passive 一般用被动态] **1** to scatter things around a large area 撒, 散播: [+around/about/over] *I found papers strewn all over the room.* 我发现整个房间散满了文件。| **be strewn with** *The yard was strewn with garbage.* 院子里到处散落着垃圾。**2** *literary* to lie scattered over something【文】散布于, 点缀于: *Flowers strewed the path.* 花散落在小径上。**3 strewn with** containing a lot of something 充满: *conversation liberally strewn with swear words* 充斥着脏话的谈话

strewth /struθ; struːθ/ *interjection BrE and AustrE* used to express surprise, annoyance etc【英和澳】哎呀, 天哪〔表示惊讶、烦恼等〕

stri·at·ed /ˈstraɪetɪd; straɪˈeɪtɪ̈d/ *adj technical* having narrow lines or bands of colour; STRIPED【术语】有线条的, 有条纹的

stri·a·tion /straɪˈeʃən; straɪˈeɪʃən/ *n* [C usually plural 一般用复数] *technical* one of a number of narrow lines or bands of colour; STRIPE (1)【术语】线条, 条纹

strick·en /ˈstrɪkən; ˈstrɪkən/ *adj formal* very badly affected by trouble, illness, unhappiness etc【正式】受灾的; 患病的; 受困扰的; 受苦的: *Supplies of medicine were rushed to the stricken city.* 药品被迅速送往受灾城市。| [+by/with] *stricken with a fatal disease* 患致命的疾病 | **poverty stricken** (=very poor) 非常贫穷的, 极度贫困的 *poverty stricken areas riddled with disease* 受疾病侵扰的极度贫困地区 | **panic stricken** (=filled with sudden terror) 惊慌失措的, 惊恐至极的 *Panic stricken crowds swarmed into the square.* 惊慌失措的人群纷纷涌进广场。| **grief stricken** *A grief stricken mother from Kansas wrote in to tell me of her tragedy.* 堪萨斯的一位悲痛欲绝的母亲写信来向我诉说她的悲剧。

strict /strɪkt; strɪkt/ *adj* **1** someone who is strict demands that rules should always be obeyed 严格的, 严厉的: *a strict teacher* 严格的老师 | [+with] *The Stuarts are very strict with their children.* 斯图尔特夫妇管子女很严。| [+about] *This company is very strict about punctuality.* 这公司严格要求准时。**2** a strict order or rule is one that must be obeyed〔命令、规则〕必须严格遵守的: *You had strict instructions not to tell anybody.* 你得到严格指示不得告诉任何人。| **in the strictest confidence** (=it must be kept completely secret) 极其秘密地 *I'm telling you this in the strictest confidence.* 我告诉你这事, 你要严加保密。**3** [usually before noun 一般用于名词前] exact and correct, but often unreasonably exact 严谨的; 精确的, 确凿的: *He's using 'trust' in the strict legal sense.* 他是在严格的法律意义上使用 trust (信任) 这个词。**4 strict Muslim/vegetarian etc** someone who obeys all the rules of a particular religion, belief etc 不折不扣的穆斯林/素食者等 —**strictness** *n* [U] 3

strict·ly /ˈstrɪktlɪ; ˈstrɪktli/ *adv* **1** exactly and completely 完全地; 确切地: *That isn't strictly true.* 那并不全是真的。**2 strictly speaking** used when you are using words or explaining rules in an exact and correct way 严格地说: *Strictly speaking, spiders are not insects, although most people think they are.* 严格地说, 蜘蛛不是昆虫, 虽然大多数人都认为它们是昆虫。**3** only for a particular person or thing and no one else 严格限定地; 只限于某人[某物]: *This is strictly between us. Nobody else must know.* 此事仅限于我们知道, 不可告诉其他任何人。**4** in a way that must be obeyed 严格地, 严明地: *Discipline will be strictly enforced.* 我们将严格执行纪律。

stric·ture /ˈstrɪktʃɚ; ˈstrɪktʃə/ *n* [C often plural 常用复数] *formal*【正式】**1** a severe criticism 严厉批评 **2** [+on/against] a rule that strictly limits you morally or physically 约束; 限制; 束缚

S

stride[1] /straɪd; straɪd/ *v past tense* **strode** /strod; strəʊd/ *past participle* **stridden** /ˈstrɪdn̩; ˈstrɪdn/ [I always+adv/prep] to walk quickly with long steps 迈大步走, 大踏步走: [+across/into/down] *Clarice jumped off the porch and strode across the lawn.* 克拉丽斯从门廊上跳下, 大步走过草坪。

stride[2] *n*
1 ▶WALKING 走, 步行◀[C] a long step 大步, 阔步: *Paco reached the door in only three strides.* 帕科三大步就走到了门口。
2 ▶PATTERN OF STEPS 步态◀[U] the pattern of your steps or the way you walk or run; GAIT 步法, 步态: *the runner's long, loping stride* 跑步者大步轻快的步法
3 ▶IMPROVEMENT 改进◀[C] an improvement in a situation or in the development of something 进步, 进展, 发展: **make great/big/giant strides** *We've made great strides in medical technology this century.* 本世纪我们在医疗技术方面有了很大的进展。
4 get into your stride *BrE*【英】, **hit your stride** *AmE*【美】to become comfortable with a job so you can do it continuously and well〔做某工作〕开始上轨道, 驾轻就熟: *Once I get into my stride I can finish the essay in a few hours.* 我一旦写顺手, 几个小时就能写完那篇论文。
5 take sth in your stride to not allow something to annoy, embarrass, or upset you in any way 从容地对付: *Eva took all the setbacks in her stride.* 伊娃从容地应对所有的挫折。
6 put sb off their stride to make someone stop giving all their attention to what they are doing 使某人分心: *Knowing that Bob was watching the game really put me off my stride.* 知道鲍勃正在观看比赛, 这使得我实在无法集中注意力。
7 (match sb) stride for stride to manage to be just as fast, strong, skilled etc as someone else even if they keep making it harder for you (设法与某人) 并驾齐驱
8 without breaking stride *especially AmE* without allowing something to interrupt or annoy you【尤美】不加停顿地; 心平气和地: *Zeke dealt with the reporters' questions without breaking stride.* 齐克从容地应付了记者的提问。
9 strides [plural] *AustrE informal* trousers【澳, 非正式】裤子

stri·dent /ˈstraɪdn̩t; ˈstraɪdənt/ *adj* **1** a sound or voice that is strident is too loud and high and sounds unpleasant 刺耳的, 尖声的: *the strident blaring of a military band* 军乐队刺耳的演奏声 **2** forceful and determined 强烈的; 坚定的: *the strident demands of the American media* 美国媒体的强烈要求 —**stridently** *adv* —**stridency** *n* [U]

strife /straɪf; straɪf/ *n* [U] *formal* trouble between two people or groups; CONFLICT[1]【正式】〔两个人或团体之间的〕冲突, 纠纷, 争斗: *a time of political strife* 政治斗争的时代

strike¹ /straɪk; straɪk/ *v past tense and past participle* **struck** /strʌk; strʌk/

① THINK/NOTICE 想/注意
② STOP WORK 停止工作
③ HIT 击，打
④ LIGHTNING 闪电
⑤ ATTACK/HARM 攻击/伤害
⑥ EXPRESS AN OPINION/FEELING 表达观点/感情
⑦ CLOCKS 时钟
⑧ STRONG FEELINGS 强烈的感情
⑨ FIND 发现
⑩ DO STH 做某事
⑪ OTHER MEANINGS 其他意思

① THINK/NOTICE 想/注意

1 [T not in progressive 不用进行时] if a thought or idea strikes you, you suddenly realize that it is important, interesting, surprising, bad etc 突然意识到，突然想到: *The funny side of the affair suddenly struck her.* 她突然意识到事情可笑的一面。| **it strikes sb that** *It struck Carol that what he'd said about Helen applied to her too.* 卡罗尔突然意识到他说海伦的那些话也适用于自己。| **be struck by** *We were struck by the generosity of even the poorest citizens.* 使我们深受感动的是，甚至最贫穷的市民也慷慨大方。—see 见 OCCUR (USAGE)

2 strike sb as sth to seem to have a particular quality or feature 给某人…的印象: *His jokes didn't strike Jack as being very funny.* 杰克不觉得他的笑话好笑。| *How did he strike you?* (=how did he seem to you?) 他给你的印象如何？| **it strikes sb as** *It strikes me as a great idea.* 我觉得这个主意好极了。| **strike sb as strange/odd/funny etc** *It struck me as odd at the time.* 我当时觉得这很古怪。

3 strike the eye to be particularly noticeable 显眼，醒目: *What strikes your eye at once is her gorgeous red hair.* 一下子吸引你注意力的是她那一头美丽的红发。

② STOP WORK 停止工作

4 [I] to deliberately stop working for a time because of a disagreement about pay, working conditions etc 罢工: *The police are forbidden to strike.* 警察被禁止罢工。| **strike for** *We're striking for another two dollars an hour.* 我们为争取每小时多发两美元而罢工。

③ HIT 击，打

5 [I always+adv/prep,T] *formal* to hit or knock hard against something【正式】打，击，撞: **strike (sth) against** *Then my shovel struck against something metallic.* 然后我的铲子碰到一件像金属的东西。| **strike sb/sth on** *A snowball struck him on the back of the head.* 一团雪球打中他的后脑勺。| **strike sth** *My foot struck a rock.* 我的脚碰到一块石头。| **be struck by sth** *The car had been struck by a falling tree.* 汽车被一棵倒下的树砸中了。

6 ▶WITH YOUR HAND 用手◀ [T] *formal* to deliberately hit someone or something hard, especially with your hand【正式】〔尤指用手〕打，击: *I wouldn't dream of striking a woman.* 我做梦也不会打女人。| *strike the buss drum* 打低音鼓 | **strike sth with** *He struck the table with his fist.* 他用拳头砸桌子。| **strike a blow** *The blow was almost certainly struck with the left hand.* 那一拳几乎可以肯定是用左手打的。| **strike home** (=hit something exactly where you were aiming to hit it) 击中目标，击中要害 *His sword struck home deep into the bull's neck.* 他的剑正中目标，深深地扎在公牛的脖子上。

7 strike a match/light to light a match by hitting it against a hard surface 划火柴

④ LIGHTNING 闪电

8 [I,T] when LIGHTNING strikes something, it hits and damages it〔闪电〕击中，击毁: *That old forked tree was once struck by lightning.* 那棵分杈的老树曾经被闪电击中过。

⑤ ATTACK/HARM 攻击/伤害

9 [I] to attack quickly and suddenly 猛然攻击，突然袭击: *When the snake strikes, its mouth opens wide.* 蛇发起攻击时嘴张得很大。| *Police fear that the killer will strike again.* 警方担心凶手会再次作案。| **strike at** *This law strikes at the most vulnerable groups in our society.* 这项法律打击的是我们社会中最弱势的群体。| **strike at the heart of** *spending cuts that strike at the heart of socialized medicine* 给公费医疗以沉重打击的削减开支

10 [I] if something unpleasant strikes, it suddenly happens〔不愉快的事〕突然发生: *Tragedy struck two days later when Tammy was in a serious car accident.* 两天后悲剧突然发生，塔米遭遇严重车祸。

11 [I] to do something that gives you an advantage or harms your opponent in a fight, competition etc 主动出击，抢占优势: *Brazil struck first with a goal in the third minute.* 巴西队先发制人，在第三分钟时就进了一球。| **strike the first blow** (=gain the first advantage) 先发制人，抢占最初的优势

12 strike a blow for to do something to help an idea, belief, or organization 以实际行动拥护〔某主意、信念或团体〕: *It's time we struck a blow for women's rights.* 我们以实际行动维护妇女权益的时候到了。

13 strike a blow at to have a harmful effect on people's behaviour or beliefs 危害，伤害: *This latest research strikes a blow at the foundations of psychiatry.* 这项最新研究动摇了精神病学的基础。

⑥ EXPRESS AN OPINION/FEELING 表达观点/感情

14 strike a chord to express an opinion or idea that other people agree with or have sympathy with 引起共鸣，打动: *Powell's angry speech struck a deep chord with his audience.* 鲍威尔愤怒的演说深深地打动了听众。

15 strike a happy/cheerful/cautious etc note to express a particular feeling or attitude 表达出高兴/振奋/谨慎等的感情[态度]: *The article struck a conciliatory note.* 那篇文章表达了和解的姿态。| **strike the right note/a discordant note** (=express or fail to express what people are feeling) 说出大家的心声/发出不和谐的声音 *Her speech appeared to strike exactly the right note.* 她的演说似乎正好表达了大家的心声。

16 strike home if something that you say strikes home, it has exactly the effect on someone that you intended 产生预期的效果: *Anna's criticism of his laziness really struck home.* 安娜批评他懒惰，的确击中了他的要害。

⑦ CLOCKS 时钟

17 [I,T] when a clock strikes or strikes one, six etc, its bell sounds a certain number of times to show what the time is 敲钟，报时: *The church clock began to strike twelve.* 教堂的钟开始敲12下。| **strike the hour** (=strike when it is exactly one o'clock, two o'clock etc) 整点报时

⑧ STRONG FEELINGS 强烈的感情

18 strike terror/fear/a chill into sb's heart to make someone feel afraid 使某人感到恐惧/害怕/毛骨悚然: *The word 'cancer' still strikes terror into many hearts.* "癌症"这个词仍然使很多人感到恐惧。

19 be struck dumb to be unable to speak, usually because you are very surprised〔常指吃惊得〕说不出话来: *When the Queen shook my hand, I was struck dumb.* 女王跟我握手，我惊得一时说不出话来。

⑨ FIND 发现

20 strike gold/oil etc to suddenly find gold, oil etc, especially after you have been looking for it〔尤指经过挖掘〕找到黄金/石油等: *They finally struck gold in 1886.* 他们终于在1886年发现了金矿。

21 strike it rich/lucky to suddenly make a lot of money or

have good luck 发横财/交好运: *With her last book she's really struck it rich.* 她靠最近的那本书发了大财。

⑩ **DO STH** 做某事

22 strike a balance to give the correct amount of importance or attention to two opposing things 使达到平衡, 两者兼顾: **strike the right balance** *The speech strikes the right balance between humour and seriousness.* 演说幽默而不失严肃, 恰到好处。

23 strike a bargain/deal to agree to do something if someone else does something for you 达成协议/交易: *The US and China have recently struck a deal over trade.* 美国和中国最近就贸易问题达成一项协议。

24 strike while the iron is hot [usually imperative 一般用祈使句] to do something immediately rather than waiting until a later time when you are less likely to succeed 趁热打铁, 趁机行事

⑪ **OTHER MEANINGS** 其他意思

25 ►LIGHT 光线◄[T] to fall on a surface 射在〔某表面〕: *What happens when light strikes a glass lens?* 光射在玻璃镜片上会怎么样?

26 be within striking distance to be very close to something or very near to achieving something 非常靠近〔某物〕; 即将实现〔某目标〕

27 strike a pose/an attitude to stand or sit with your body in a particular position 以某种姿势站[坐]; 摆姿势: *Eva walked to the middle of the room, turned, and struck a pose with her head to one side.* 伊娃走到房间中央, 转过身来, 头一歪摆了个姿势。

28 strike sb/sth off/from to remove a name or a thing from a written list 从〔名单〕上删去某人/某物, 涂掉某人/某物: *We had to strike him off the short list.* 我们不得不从决选名单上删去他的名字。

29 ►TENT/SAIL 帐篷/帆◄[T] to take down a tent or sail 拆除〔帐篷或船帆〕: **strike camp** (=take down tents when leaving a camping place) 〔离开野营地时〕拆除帐篷

strike back *phr v* [I] to attack someone who has attacked you first 回击, 反击: *The rebels struck back within hours.* 叛军在几小时内进行了反击。

strike sb ↔ down *phr v* [T] **1** to hit someone so hard that they fall down 将〔某人〕击倒 **2** [usually passive 一般用被动态] to make someone die or become seriously ill 使丧命; 使病倒: *Hundreds died that winter, struck down by pneumonia.* 那年冬天数百人因患肺炎而死去。

strike off *phr v* **be struck off** *BrE* if a doctor, lawyer etc is struck off, their name is removed from the official list of people who are allowed to work as doctors etc【英】将〔医生、律师等〕除名

strike on/upon sth *phr v* [T] **1** to discover something or have a good idea about something 发现; 想出: *At last I've struck on a plan that might work.* 最后, 我想出了一个可能行得通的计划。**2 be struck on** *BrE informal* to think that something is good or well-made【英, 非正式】喜欢, 认为…好: *I'm not very struck on these chocolates.* 我不是很喜欢这些巧克力。

strike out *phr v*

1 ►NAME 名字◄[T **strike** sth ↔ **out**] to draw a line through something written on a piece of paper 划掉, 删去, 涂掉

2 ►WALK/SWIM 步行/游泳◄[I always+adv/prep] to start walking or swimming in a particular direction, especially in a determined way 〔朝某方向〕坚定地行进[游去]: *He decided to follow her, striking out in the same direction.* 他决定跟着她, 朝同一个方向坚定地走下去。

3 strike out on your/his/their own to start doing something new or living by yourself, without other people's help 开始独立做新的事情; 开始独立的生活: *Eric left the family business and struck out on his own.* 埃里克离开了家族企业, 自行创业。

4 ►NOT SUCCEED 不成功◄[I] *informal especially AmE* to be unsuccessful at something【非正式, 尤美】不成功, 失败: *"Did she say she'd go out with you?" "No, I struck out."* "她说愿意跟你外出约会吗?" "没有, 我碰了钉子。"

5 ►BASEBALL 棒球◄**a)** [I] to be unable to continue trying to hit the ball in BASEBALL, because you have already missed it three times 三击不中出局 **b)** [T **strike** sb ↔ **out**] to put a player out in BASEBALL by making them fail to hit the ball three times 使〔某球员〕三击不中出局

strike up *phr v* **1** [I,T] to begin playing a piece of music 开始演奏〔乐曲〕: **strike up the band** (=tell it to begin playing) 叫乐队开始演奏 **2 strike up a friendship/relationship/conversation** to start to become friendly with someone 建立友谊/建立关系/交谈起来

3 3 **strike²** *n* [C]

1 ►STOP WORK 停止工作◄ a period of time when a group of workers deliberately stop working because of a disagreement about pay, working conditions etc 罢工; 罢课: **miners'/train/electricity etc strike** *During the teachers' strike, all the schools were closed.* 教师罢课期间, 所有的学校都关闭了。| **go on strike/on strike** *The Boston police went on strike in 1919.* 1919年波士顿警察罢工。| **be (out) on strike** *Within half an hour, all the drivers were out on strike.* 半个小时内, 所有的司机都罢工了。| **come out/go out on strike** (=start one) 开始罢工 | **call a strike** (=ask people to stop working) 号召举行罢工 | **call off a strike** (=decide not to continue it) 停止罢工 | **strike action** *The mine-workers were solidly in favour of strike action.* 矿工们坚决支持罢工行动。| **general strike** (=involving most workers in the country) 总罢工, 全国大罢工

2 hunger/rent strike a time when someone refuses to eat or pay rent as a protest about something 绝食抗议/拒交房租: *a hunger strike by political prisoners* 政治犯的绝食抗议

3 ►ATTACK 打击, 攻击◄ a military attack, especially by aircraft dropping bombs 军事打击〔尤指空袭〕: **[+against/on]** *nuclear strikes on several targets* 对几个目标进行的核打击 | **launch a strike** *American aircraft carriers have launched several strikes.* 美国的航空母舰发动了数次袭击。—see also 另见 FIRST STRIKE

4 oil strike the discovery of oil under the ground 石油的意外发现

5 ►SPORT 体育运动◄**a)** a situation in BOWLING (1) in which you knock down all the PINS (=bottle shaped objects) with one of two balls 〔保龄球〕一击全倒 **b)** an attempt to hit the ball in BASEBALL in which you miss hitting the ball 〔棒球〕好球

strike·bound /ˈstraɪkˌbaund; ˈstraɪkbaʊnd/ *adj* unable to move, travel, or happen because of a STRIKE² (1) 由于罢工而停顿的: *a strikebound port* 由于罢工而陷入停顿的港口

strike·break·er /ˈstraɪkˌbrekɚ; ˈstraɪkˌbreɪkə/ *n* [C] someone who takes the job of someone who is striking (STRIKE¹ (4)) 代替罢工者工作的人, 破坏罢工者 —compare 比较 BLACKLEG, SCAB (2) —**strikebreaking** *n* [U]

strike-out /ˈstraɪkˌaut; ˈstraɪkaʊt/ *n* [C] if the PITCHER (3) in BASEBALL throws a strikeout, he puts the player out by throwing three strikes (STRIKE² (5)) 〔棒球〕三击不中(击球员)出局 —see also 另见 **strike out** (STRIKE¹)

strike pay /ˈ· ·/ *n* [U] money paid to workers who are striking (STRIKE¹ (4)) by their union 〔工会在罢工期间给工人的〕罢工津贴

strik·er /ˈstraɪkɚ; ˈstraɪkə/ *n* [C] **1** someone who is striking (STRIKE¹ (4)) 罢工者; 罢课者 **2** a player in football whose main job is to kick a GOAL (2) 〔足球队的〕前锋(队员)

strik·ing /ˈstraɪkɪŋ; ˈstraɪkɪŋ/ *adj* **1** unusual or interesting enough to be noticed 惊人的; 显著的: **a striking contrast** *a striking contrast between the luxury hotels and the ghettos just a block away* 豪华旅店和一个街区之隔的贫民窟之间的天壤之别 **2** someone who is striking is very attractive, often in an unusual way 吸引人的, 惹人注目的: *a dark man with striking features* 相貌动人的黝黑男子 —see also 另见 **be within striking distance** (STRIKE¹ (26)) —**strikingly** *adv*

string¹ /strɪŋ; strɪŋ/ *n* 3 2

1 ►THREAD 线◄[C,U] a strong thread made of several threads twisted together, used for tying or fastening things 〔由几股合成的〕线; 细绳; 带子: *Can you find me some string to tie up this package?* 你能帮我找些绳子来捆这个包裹吗? | *Puppets are worked by strings.* 木偶是用线来操纵的。| *a piece of string* 一根绳子

2 ►GROUP/SERIES 组/系列◄[C] **a)** a number of similar things or events coming one after another 一连串, 一系列〔事件等〕: **[+of]** *a string of hit albums* 一系列非常成功的唱片 **b)** a group of similar things 一系列〔类似的事物〕: **[+of]** *She owns a string of health clubs.* 她拥有多家类似的健身俱乐部。**c)** *technical* a group of letters, words, or numbers, especially in a computer PROGRAM【术语】〔尤指电脑程序中字符的〕串

3 a string of pearls/beads/onions several objects of the same kind connected with a thread 一串珠/珠子/洋葱

4 ►MUSIC 音乐◄**a)** [C] one of the long thin pieces of wire, NYLON etc that is stretched across a musical instrument and produces sound 〔乐器上的〕弦 **b) strings** [plural] the people in an

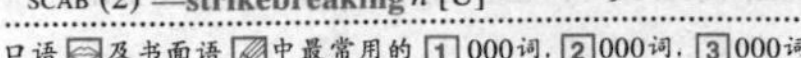

ORCHESTRA who play the instruments that have strings, such as VIOLINS 乐队的弦乐器演奏者〈如小提琴手〉

5 have sb on a string *informal* to be able to make someone do whatever you want【非正式】操纵[支配]某人: *Susie has her mother on a string.* 苏茜竟能任意支配她的母亲。

6 no strings (attached) if an agreement or relationship has no strings, there are no special conditions or limits〔协议或关系〕无附带条件, 无任何限制: *The policy offers 15% interest with no strings attached.* 该保险单支付15%的利息, 不附带任何条件。

7 pull strings to secretly use your influence with important people in order to get what you want or help someone else 暗中施加影响; 走后门: *Phil had to pull a few strings to get them to give me the job.* 菲尔只得动用一些私人关系, 让他们把那份工作给我。| **pull sb's strings** (=control them) 控制某人, 操纵某人

8 have more than one string to your bow to have more than one skill, idea, plan etc that you can use if you need to 有后备技能[想法、计划等]; 有两手准备 —see also 另见 G-STRING, **hold/control the purse strings** (PURSE¹ (6))

string² *v past tense and past participle* **strung** /strʌŋ; strʌŋ/ [T] **1** to put things together onto a thread, chain etc 用〔线、链等〕穿起来: *beads strung on a silver chain* 穿在银链上的珠子 **2** [always+adv/prep] to hang things in a line, high up, especially for decoration 悬挂〔尤指作为装饰〕: [+**string sth up/along/across etc**] *Dad had strung brightly-colored lights up in the backyard.* 爸爸在后院里挂起了鲜艳的彩灯。**3** to put a string or a set of strings onto a musical instrument 给〔乐器〕装弦

string along *phr v informal*【非正式】**1** [T] to deceive someone for a long time by making them believe that you will help them, that you love them etc 哄骗; 吊〔某人〕胃口: *Timms will never pay you back; he's just stringing you along.* 蒂姆斯根本不会还钱给你, 他只是在骗你而已。**2** [I] *BrE* to go somewhere with someone for a short time, especially because you do not have anything else to do【英】〔尤因找不到别的事情干而〕跟随, 暂与〔某人〕结伴: [+**with**] *If you're going into town, I'll string along with you.* 你如果进城, 我就和你结伴同行。

string sth ↔ **out** *phr v* [T] **1** [usually passive 一般用被动态] to spread something out in a long line 把…排成一条线, 使摆成一行: *The islands were strung out along the coastline.* 那些岛屿沿海岸线排成一行。—see also 另见 STRUNG-OUT **2** *informal* to make something last longer【非正式】使拖长, 拉长: *The whole deal was strung out for a lot longer than necessary.* 整个交易被拖了很长时间。

string sth ↔ **together** *phr v* [T] **string two words/sentences together** to say something that makes sense to other people 说出令人听懂的话: *He was so drunk he could hardly string two words together.* 他醉得几乎连话都说不成句了。

string sth/sb ↔ **up** *phr v* [T] *informal* to kill someone by hanging them【非正式】绞死, 吊死: *He should be strung up for what he did to that girl.* 就他对那个女孩的所作所为, 他应该被绞死。—see also 另见 STRUNG-UP

string bean /ˌ· ˈ·/ *n* [C] *especially AmE* a green bean with long thin pods (POD¹ (1)) that are eaten as food【尤美】红花菜豆; RUNNER BEAN *BrE*【英】—see picture on page A9 参见 A9 页图

stringed in·stru·ment /ˌ· ˈ···/ *n* [C] a musical instrument that produces sound from a set of strings (STRING¹ (4)), such as a VIOLIN 弦乐器〈如小提琴〉

strin·gent /ˈstrɪndʒənt; ˈstrɪndʒənt/ *adj* **1 stringent rule/test/condition** very strict and must be obeyed 严格的规则/测验/条件: *stringent anti noise regulations* 严格的防噪音条例 **2** stringent economic conditions exist when there is a severe lack of money and strict controls on the supply of money〔经济状况〕银根紧的, 紧缩的 —**stringently** *adv* —**stringency** *n* [U]

string·er /ˈstrɪŋə; ˈstrɪŋə/ *n* [C] someone who regularly sends in news stories to a newspaper, but who is not employed by that newspaper 特约记者[通讯员]

string tie /ˌ· ˈ·/ *n* [C] a thick string worn around your neck and held in place by a decorative object, worn by men in the western US〔美国西部男士戴的〕厚狭领结[带], 绳领带

string·y /ˈstrɪŋɪ; ˈstrɪŋi/ *adj* **1** meat, fruit, or vegetables that are stringy are full of thin pieces that are difficult to eat 纤维多的; 有筋的: *Scoop out the pumpkin's stringy fibres.* 用勺子把南瓜中的筋挖出来。**2** hair that is stringy is very thin and looks like string, especially because it is dirty〔尤指毛发因脏而〕呈线状的: *old men with stringy beards leaning on walking sticks* 拄着拐杖、胡须打绺的老人 **3** someone or a part of their body that is stringy is very thin so that their muscles show through their skin; WIRY 瘦的, 青筋毕露的: *I'd like to wring his stringy little neck!* 我要把他的细脖子拧断!

strip¹ /strɪp; strɪp/ *v* **stripped, stripping**

1 ▶TAKE OFF CLOTHES 脱衣服◀ also 又作 **strip off** [I,T] to take off your clothes or take off someone else's clothes 脱去(…的)衣服: *Jack stripped off and jumped into the shower.* 杰克脱掉衣服, 跳进淋浴间。| **strip sb** *The police stripped us all, looking for drugs.* 警察剥光我们大家的衣服搜查毒品。| **stripped to the waist** (=not wearing any clothes on the top half of your body) 上身脱得精光的 | **strip down to your pants/socks etc** (=take off all your clothes except your pants etc) 脱得只剩内裤/袜子等 | **strip naked** (=remove all your clothes) 脱光所有的衣服

2 ▶REMOVE A LAYER 除去一层◀ [T] to remove something that is covering the surface of something else 剥去, 除去: **strip sth off/from** *We need to strip the wallpaper off the walls first.* 我们得先把墙纸刮掉。| **strip sth of** *a branch stripped of its bark* 剥去树皮的树枝

3 strip sb of sth to take away something important from someone as a punishment, for example their title, property, or power〔作为惩罚〕剥夺某人的头衔、财产或权力: *Captain Evans was found guilty and stripped of his rank.* 埃文斯上尉被判有罪, 免去了军衔。

4 ▶ENGINES/EQUIPMENT 发动机/设备◀ also 又作 **strip down** [T] to separate an engine or piece of equipment into pieces in order to clean or repair it; DISMANTLE 拆卸〔发动机或设备以进行清理或检修〕

5 ▶BUILDING/SHIP 建筑物/轮船◀ [T] to remove everything that is inside a building, ship, car etc so that it is completely empty 搬走〔建筑物、轮船、汽车等中的〕所有东西, 搬空: *The house was stripped by thieves.* 那所房子被盗贼洗劫一空。—see also 另见 ASSET STRIPPING

strip sth ↔ **away** *phr v* [T] to gradually get rid of habits, customs etc 逐渐摆脱〔习惯、风俗等〕: *Changes in society have stripped away men's role as protector and breadwinner.* 社会的变迁已使男人不再充当保护者和挣钱养家者的角色。

strip² *n* [C] **1** a long narrow piece of paper, cloth etc 条, 狭条状物〔纸、布料等〕: *a strip of paper* 一张纸条 **2** a long narrow area of land 狭长的一块土地: *a strip of sand between the cliffs and the sea* 悬崖和大海之间的一块沙地 **3 do a strip** to take your clothes off, especially in a sexually exciting way as a form of entertainment 表演脱衣舞 **4** *AmE* a road with a lot of shops, restaurants etc along it【美】〔沿途有许多商店、餐馆等的〕公路: *I could see the outline of the neon lights of the strip through the haze.* 从薄雾中我可以看到商业街上霓虹灯的轮廓。**5** *BrE* the clothes of a particular colour worn by a team【英】〔运动队穿的某种颜色的〕运动服, 队服: *Liverpool's famous red strip* 利物浦队著名的红色运动服 **6** a STRIP CARTOON 连环漫画 —see also 另见 COMIC STRIP, LANDING STRIP, **tear sb off a strip** (TEAR² (9)) 3

strip car·toon /ˌ· ·ˈ·/ *n* [C] *BrE* a series of drawings inside a row of small boxes that tells a short story【英】连环漫画; COMIC STRIP *AmE*【美】—compare 比较 CARTOON (1)

strip club /ˈ· ·/ *n* [C] a place where people go to see performers who take off their clothes to music 表演脱衣舞的夜总会

stripe /straɪp; straɪp/ *n* [C] **1** a line of colour, especially one of several lines of colour all close together 条纹, 线条: *a shirt with black and white stripes* 黑白条纹相间的衬衣 **2** a narrow piece of material worn on the arm of a uniform as a sign of rank〔军服袖子上〕表示军衔的条纹: *A sergeant has three stripes.* 军士军服上有三条杠。**3 earn your stripes** *informal* to do something to deserve a particular rank or position【非正式】〔为对得起某官职或地位而〕须作出努力

striped /straɪpt; straɪpt/ *adj* having lines or bands of colour 有不同颜色条纹的: *a blue and white striped T-shirt* 蓝白条纹相间的T恤 —see picture on page A16 参见 A16 页图

strip joint /ˈ· ·/ *n* [C] *informal* a strip club【非正式】表演脱衣舞的夜总会

strip light·ing /ˈ· ˌ··/ *n* [U] lighting provided by long, white FLUORESCENT tubes, usually in public buildings rather than in houses〔通常在公共建筑中的〕荧光灯管照明 —see picture at 参见 LIGHT¹ 图

strip·ling /ˈstrɪplɪŋ; ˈstrɪplɪŋ/ *n* [C] *literary* a boy who is almost a young man【文】青年男子, 小伙子

strip mall /ˈ· ·/ *n* [C] *AmE* a small shopping centre that consists of a single row of shops with parking spaces in front of them【美】小型购物中心

strip min·ing /ˈ· ˌ··/ *n* [U] *especially AmE* a method of getting metal, coal etc by removing the earth from the surface of

the ground, rather than by digging a passage under the ground 【尤美】露天采矿 —compare 比较 OPENCAST

strip·per /ˈstrɪpɚ; ˈstrɪpə/ *n* [C] **1** someone, especially a woman, who takes off their clothes in a sexually exciting way in order to entertain people 表演脱衣舞者; 〔尤指〕脱衣舞舞女 **2** a tool or liquid used to remove something from a surface 剥离表面物的器具; 清除表层物的液体: *paint stripper* 除漆剂

strip pok·er /ˌ· ˈ·· / *n* [C] a game of POKER (=card game) in which players that lose take off pieces of their clothing "剥猪猡"扑克牌戏〔输者被罚剥去衣服〕

strip search /ˈ· · / *n* [C] a process in which you have to remove your clothes so that your body can be checked, usually for hidden drugs 〔通常指为寻找隐藏的毒品而作的〕裸体搜查

strip show /ˈ· · / *n* [C] a form of entertainment where people, especially women, take off their clothes in a sexually exciting way 脱衣舞表演

strip·tease /ˈstrɪpˌtiz; ˈstrɪptiːz/ *n* [C,U] a performance in which someone, especially a woman, takes off their clothes in a sexually exciting way 脱衣舞(表演) —**striptease** *v* [I]

strip·y /ˈstraɪpɪ; ˈstraɪpi/ *adj BrE* STRIPED 【英】有不同颜色条纹的

strive /straɪv; straɪv/ *v past tense* **strove** /strov; strəʊv/ *past participle* **striven** /ˈstrɪvən; ˈstrɪvən/ [I] *formal* to make a great effort to achieve something 【正式】〔为获得某物而〕努力, 奋斗: [**+for/after**] *We must continue to strive for greater efficiency.* 我们必须继续争取提高效率。| **strive to do sth** *The film studio is striving to improve its public image.* 该电影制片厂正在努力改善其公众形象。

strobe light /ˈstrob ˌlaɪt; ˈstrəʊb ˌlaɪt/ also 又作 **strobe** *n* [C] a light that flashes on and off very quickly, often used in places where you can dance 〔常用于跳舞场所的〕频闪闪光灯

strode /strod; strəʊd/ the past tense of STRIDE

S3 **stroke¹** /strok; strəʊk/ *n* [C]

1 ▶ILLNESS 疾病◀ an occasion when a blood tube in your brain suddenly bursts or is blocked 中风: *He was paralyzed by a severe stroke.* 他因严重中风而瘫痪。| **have/suffer a stroke** *I'm afraid your aunt has had a slight stroke.* 你姑姑怕是患了轻度中风。

2 ▶SWIMMING/ROWING 游泳/划船◀ a) one of a set of movements in swimming or rowing in which you move your arms or the OAR forward and then back repeatedly 〔游泳或划船的〕一次划水: *She swam with strong steady strokes.* 她平稳地用力划水游泳。**b)** a style of swimming or rowing 〔游泳的〕游法; 〔划船的〕划法: *the backstroke* 仰泳 **c)** the person who sets the speed at which everyone in the boat rows 〔指挥划桨速度的〕尾桨手, 领桨手

3 a) at a/one stroke with a single sudden action 一举, 一下子: *Brian saw a chance of solving all his problems at one stroke.* 布莱恩找到一个可以一下子解决所有问题的机会。**b) a bold stroke** something that someone does to achieve something that seems very brave 勇敢的行动

4 ▶A HIT 击, 打◀ an action in which you hit someone with something such as a whip or thin stick 一击, 一抽: *He cried out at each stroke of the whip.* 鞭子每抽一下, 他都叫出声来。

5 on the stroke of seven/nine etc at exactly seven o'clock etc 在7点整/9点整等: *She arrived punctually on the stroke of five.* 她在5点整准时到达。

6 ▶CLOCK/BELL 时钟/铃◀ a single sound made by a clock giving the hours, or by a bell, GONG etc 〔时钟、铃等报时的〕一次鸣响, 敲击声: *Maria appeared on the final stroke of the dinner gong.* 玛丽亚在晚饭铃敲最后一响时出现了。

7 a stroke of luck/fortune something lucky that happens to you unexpectedly 一桩意外的幸事/运气: *By an amazing stroke of luck, I ran into her that very evening.* 非常幸运的是, 我就在那天晚上碰到了她。

8 a stroke of lightning a bright flash of lightning, especially one that hits something 〔尤指击中某物的〕闪电的一击

9 a stroke of genius/inspiration etc a very good idea about what to do to solve a problem 聪明之举/绝妙的主意等: *It was a stroke of genius to make her the party chairman.* 让她做党的主席实在是个聪明之举。

10 ▶SPORT 体育运动◀ a hitting of the ball in games such as tennis, golf and cricket 〔网球、高尔夫球、板球等的〕击球; 一击, 一抽: *learn to play the basic backhand strokes* 学打基本的反手击球

11 ▶A MOVEMENT OF YOUR HAND 手的动作◀ a gentle movement of your hand over something 轻抚, 抚摸: **give sth a stroke** *She gave the dog a stroke.* 她抚摸了一下那只狗。

12 ▶PEN/BRUSH 钢笔/毛笔◀ a) a single movement of a pen or brush when you are writing or painting 〔钢笔或毛笔的〕一挥, 挥笔动作: *Max made a few quick decisive strokes with his brush.* 马克斯用画笔迅速、果断地画了几笔。**b)** a line made by doing this 一笔, 一画; 笔画: *the thick downward strokes of the characters* 字体中那些向下的粗笔画

13 with/at a stroke of the pen if you do something with a stroke of the pen, you do it by signing a piece of paper 大笔一挥〔签字〕: *You cannot wipe out a thousand years of history at the stroke of a pen.* 你不能把一千年的历史一笔勾掉。

14 not do a stroke (of work) *informal* to not do any work at all 【非正式】什么〔工作〕也不做

15 put sb off their stroke *informal* to make someone stop giving all their attention to what they are doing 【非正式】使某人分心: *Seeing Frank watching me put me off my stroke.* 发现弗兰克在看我, 我无法专心。

16 ▶IN NUMBERS 在数字中◀ *BrE* used when you are saying a number written with the mark (/) in it 【英】斜线(号): *The serial number is seventeen stroke one.* (=17/1) 编号是17/1。

stroke² *v* [T] **1** to move your hand gently over something 轻抚, 抚摸: *He reached out and stroked her cheek tenderly.* 他伸手轻柔地抚摸她的脸颊。—see picture on page A21 参见A21页图 **2** [always+adv/prep] to move something somewhere with gentle movements of your hand 用手轻轻地移动〔某物〕

stroll /strol; strəʊl/ *v* [I] to walk somewhere in a slow relaxed way 散步, 漫步, 闲逛, 溜达: [**+along/across/around**] *We strolled around the park for an hour or so.* 我们在公园里闲逛了一个小时左右。—**stroll** *n* [C] —see picture on page A24 参见A24页图

stroll·er /ˈstrolɚ; ˈstrəʊlə/ *n* [C] *AmE* a small chair on wheels in which a small child sits and is pushed along 【美】(手推)轻便婴儿车; PUSHCHAIR *BrE* 【英】—see picture at 参见 PRAM 图

stroll·ing /ˈstrolɪŋ; ˈstrəʊlɪŋ/ *adj* [only before noun 仅用于名词前] a strolling entertainer travels around the country giving informal performances on the way 〔艺人〕巡回的, 流浪的

S1 W1 **strong** /strɔŋ; strɒŋ/ *adj*

1 ▶PHYSICAL STRENGTH 体力◀ having a lot of physical power so that, for example, you can lift heavy things 强健的, 健壮的, 力气大的: *He was a very strong man.* 他是个很强壮的人。| *her strong hands* 她那强有力的双手

2 ▶THINGS 事物◀ not easily broken or destroyed 坚固的, 结实的, 不易损坏的: *a tall, strong tree* 一棵高而茁壮的树 | *a pair of strong scissors* 一把结实的剪刀

3 ▶ABLE TO DEAL WITH DIFFICULTY 能够对付困难◀ determined and able to deal with a difficult or upsetting situation 〔处理困境时〕坚强的, 坚定的: *I wasn't sure whether I was strong enough to go to the funeral.* 我不知道我是否坚强得能去参加那个葬礼。| *My grandmother was a strong woman.* 我祖母是位坚强的女性。

4 ▶POWER 权力◀ having a lot of power or influence 强大的, 强有力的; 影响力大的: *Margaret Thatcher was certainly a strong leader.* 玛格丽特·撒切尔无疑是位强有力的领袖。| *a strong navy* 强大的海军

5 ▶HEALTHY 健康的◀ healthy, especially after you have been ill 〔尤指病后〕健康的, 强健的: *I don't think her heart is very strong.* 我认为她的心脏不太健康。| **have a strong constitution** (=be healthy and not easily become ill) 体质强壮; 健壮

6 ▶FEELINGS/OPINIONS 感情/观点◀ strong emotions, opinions, beliefs etc are ones that you feel or believe a lot and are very serious about 〔感情、观点、信仰等〕强烈的, 坚定的, 不会动摇的: *The subject of abortion always arouses strong emotions.* 堕胎问题总会激起强烈的情绪。| *Harris has received strong support from her colleagues.* 哈里斯得到了同事们坚定的支持。| **strong sense of sth** *He has always had a strong sense of duty.* 他总是有强烈的责任感。

7 ▶AFFECT/INFLUENCE 影响◀ a strong desire, influence etc affects you very much 〔欲望、影响等〕强烈的, 深刻的: *I was overcome by a strong desire to speak to her.* 我很想跟她讲话, 不能自持。| *The temptation is very strong.* 那种诱惑力很强。

8 ▶RELATIONSHIP 关系◀ a strong relationship, friendship etc is very loyal and likely to last a long time 〔关系、友情等〕忠诚的; 牢固的; 持久的: *There is a very strong bond between the two of us.* 我们两人的关系非常牢固。| *He has strong links with the drugs trade.* 他与毒品贸易关系密切。

9 ▶ARGUMENT/REASON ETC 论据/理由等◀ a set of reasons that are likely to persuade other people that something is true or the correct thing to do 强有力的, 有说服力的: *There is strong evidence to support Evan's discrimination claim.* 埃文说有歧视, 是有确凿证据的。

10 ▶LIKELY 可能的◀ likely to succeed or happen 〔成功或发生〕可能性大的: *She's a strong candidate for the party leader-*

ship. 她是该党领袖的有力候选人。| **strong possibility/probability/chance** *I think there's a strong possibility that the Cowboys will win.* 我认为牛仔队获胜的可能性极大。

11 ►**GROUP OF PEOPLE** 小组, 团队◄ a strong team or other group of people is very good at doing something 强有力的; 善于…的: *A strong cast was led by Leo McKern.* 强大的演员阵容由利奥·麦克恩率领。| *Germany has one of the strongest teams in the tournament.* 德国队是锦标赛中最强的队伍之一。

12 ►**GOOD AT** 擅长…的◄ something that someone is strong on is the thing that they do well 擅长的: *Offence is where she's strong – her defensive play isn't good.* 她擅长进攻, 不善于防守。| **be sb's strong point/suit** *Tact never was my strong point.* 我一向不够老练。| **be strong on** (=be good at doing something) 擅长做… *My family has always been strong on science.* 我们家的人一向在理科方面比较强。| **strong subject** (=something you are studying that you are good at) 擅长的学科 *French was always my strong subject.* 法语一直是我擅长的学科。

13 **be in a strong position** to be in a situation where you have power over other people or are likely to get what you want 处于优势地位: *The party has never been more popular and is in a strong position to win the election.* 该党从来没有如此受欢迎, 很可能在大选中取胜。

14 ►**FOOD/DRINK** 食物/饮料◄ having a lot of taste or a lot of the substance that gives something its effect 强烈的; 味道浓的; 烈性的: *strong coffee* 浓咖啡 | *a strong curry* 很辣的咖喱 | **strong drink** (=alcoholic drinks) 烈性酒 *He hasn't touched strong drink for years.* 他很多年没喝过烈性酒了。

15 ►**TASTE/SMELL** 味道/气味◄ having a taste etc that you notice easily 〔气味〕强烈的; 味道重的: *This cheese has a very strong flavour.* 这乳酪味道很重。| *a strong smell of bonfires* 浓浓的篝火味

16 ►**LIGHT/COLOUR** 光/颜色◄ bright and easy to see 强烈的; 深的; 鲜明的: *The light was not very strong.* 光线不是很强。

17 **strong wind/current/tide** a wind etc that moves with great force 强风/急流/汹涌的潮水: *strong spring tides* 汹涌的春潮

18 **strong language** speech or writing that contains a lot of swearing 激烈的语言, 骂人的话: *This film is not suitable for children under 12 as it contains strong language.* 这部电影里有脏话, 不适合12岁以下的儿童观看。

19 **strong accent** the way that someone pronounces words that shows clearly that they come from a particular area or country 浓重的口音: *a strong German accent* 浓重的德国口音

20 **strong nose/chin/features** a nose etc that is large and noticeable, especially in an attractive way 好看的高鼻梁/好看的突下巴/轮廓分明的容貌: *She has the same strong features as her mother.* 她有跟她妈妈一样轮廓分明的动人容貌。

21 **a strong pound/dollar/mark etc** a CURRENCY (=the type of money used in a country) that does not easily lose its value compared with other currencies 坚挺的英镑/美元/马克等

22 **600/10,000 etc strong** [only after number 仅用于数字后] used to give the number of people in a crowd or organization 人数达600/10,000等: *the 70,000 strong South African Domestic Workers Union* 有70,000名会员的南非家庭帮佣协会

23 **strong verb** *technical* a verb that does not add a regular ending in the past tense, but may change a vowel【术语】不规则变化的动词

24 **have a strong stomach** to be able to watch something unpleasant without feeling sick or upset 〔看到讨厌的事情〕不感到恶心[烦恼]; 耐力强: *It's a very violent film. You'll need a strong stomach to sit through it.* 这部电影暴力镜头很多, 要把它看完你得耐得住才行。

25 **be still going strong** to continue to be active or successful, even after a long time 〔长时间后〕仍然强壮; 继续保持成功: *I'm glad to see that the printing classes are still going strong.* 我很高兴地看到, 印刷课依旧很受欢迎。

26 **be a bit strong** *especially BrE informal* to be too severe or extreme【尤英, 非正式】太严厉; 过分: *Describing him as 'evil' was a bit strong, I thought.* 我觉得, 说他"邪恶"有点过分。—see also 另见 **come on strong** (COME[1]) —**strongly** *adv*

strong-arm /'· ·/ *adj* [only before noun 仅用于名词前] *informal*【非正式】**strong-arm methods/tactics etc** methods etc that use force or violence, especially when this is not necessary 〔尤指不必要的〕强制手段/策略等 —**strong-arm** *v* [T]

strong·box /'strɔŋˌbɑks; 'strɒŋbɒks/ *n* [C] a box, usually made of metal, that can be locked and is used for keeping valuable things in 保险箱[柜]

strong·hold /'strɔŋˌhold; 'strɒŋhəʊld/ *n* [C] **1** an area where there is a lot of support for a particular way of life, political party etc 〔某生活方式、政党等〕备受支持的地方; 据点, 大本营: *The area is a Republican stronghold.* 该地区是共和党的大本营。**2** *old-fashioned* a FORTRESS【过时】要塞, 堡垒

strong-mind·ed /ˌ· '··◄/ *adj* not easily influenced by other people to change what you believe or want 意志坚强的, 果断的, 坚定的: *You have to be pretty strong-minded to say "no" to him.* 你得很坚定才能对他说"不"。—**strong-mindedly** *adv* —**strong-mindedness** *n* [U]

strong room /'· ·/ *n* [C] a special room in a bank, shop etc where valuable objects can be kept safely 〔银行、商店等贮藏贵重物品的〕保险库

strong-willed /ˌ· '·◄/ *adj* knowing exactly what you want to do and being determined to achieve it, even if other people advise you against it 意志坚强的, 坚决的

stron·ti·um /'strɑnʃɪəm; 'strɒntiəm/ *n* [U] a soft metal that is one of the chemical elements (ELEMENT (1)) 锶〔一种金属元素〕

strop /strɑp; strɒp/ *n* [C] **1** a narrow piece of leather used for sharpening a RAZOR 磨剃刀用的皮带, 革砥 **2 be in a strop** *BrE informal* to be annoyed about something【英, 非正式】因某事而烦恼

strop·py /'strɑpɪ; 'strɒpi/ *adj BrE informal* bad-tempered and easily offended or annoyed【英, 非正式】脾气坏的, 易生气的: *Aaron, we won't go anywhere if you're going to be stroppy!* 阿伦, 如果你要发脾气的话, 我们就哪儿也不去了! —**stroppily** *adv* —**stroppiness** *n* [U]

strove /strov; strəʊv/ the past tense of STRIVE

struck /strʌk; strʌk/ the past tense of STRIKE

struc·tur·al /'strʌktʃərəl; 'strʌktʃərəl/ *adj* connected with the structure of something 结构(上)的, 构造(上)的: *structural damage* 建筑结构方面的破坏 | *structural changes in the economy* 经济的结构性变化 —**structurally** *adv*

structural en·gi·neer /ˌ··· ··'·/ *n* [C] an engineer skilled in planning the building of large structures such as bridges 〔设计桥梁等大型建筑的〕结构工程师 —**structural engineering** *n* [U]

struc·tur·al·is·m /'strʌktʃərəlɪzm; 'strʌktʃərəlɪzəm/ *n* [U] a method of studying language, literature, society etc in which you examine the different parts or ideas in a subject to find a common pattern 结构主义〔语言学、文学、社会学等学科采用的研究方法, 注重通过分析不同的部分或观点以寻找共同的模式〕—**structuralist** *adj, n*

struc·ture[1] /'strʌktʃə; 'strʌktʃə/ *n*

1 ►**PARTS FORMING A WHOLE** 构成整体的部分◄ [U] the way in which the parts of something are connected with each other and form a whole 结构, 构造; 组织: *the structure of the brain* 大脑的结构 | *sentence structure* 句子结构

2 ►**BUILDING/BRIDGE ETC** 建筑物/桥梁等◄ [C] a large building, bridge etc, especially one that has many parts 〔尤指拥有多个部分的〕建筑物, 结构物: *a six-storey concrete structure* 一座六层的混凝土建筑物

3 ►**PEOPLE/ORGANIZATIONS ETC** 人/组织等◄ [C] the way in which relationships between people or groups are organized in a society or in an organization 〔社会或组织中的〕关系结构, 体系: *the power structure of world politics* 世界政治的权力结构

4 ►**ORGANIZED ACTIVITY** 有组织的活动◄ [C,U] an activity that is carefully organized and planned 条理性的活动, 组织性的活动: *Children need some sort of structure to their day.* 儿童一天的生活需要有点条理性。—see also 另见 **career structure** (CAREER[1] (1))

structure[2] *v* [T] to arrange the different parts of something into a pattern or system in which each part is connected to the others 组织; 安排: *You need to structure your arguments more carefully.* 你需要更为仔细地组织好自己的论点。

stru·del /'strudəl; 'struːdl/ *n* [C,U] a type of Austrian or German cake, made of PASTRY with fruit inside 果馅卷〔一种奥地利或德国糕点〕: *apple strudel* 苹果馅卷

strug·gle[1] /'strʌgl; 'strʌgəl/ *v* [I] **1** to try extremely hard to achieve something, even though it is very difficult and you have a lot of problems 奋斗, 拼搏, 作出极大的努力: **struggle to do sth** *She's struggling to bring up a family on a very low income.* 她靠着微薄的收入艰难地供养一群孩子。| [+for] *a young artist struggling for recognition* 一位为获得承认而奋斗的青年艺术家 **2** to fight someone who is attacking you or holding you, especially so that you can escape 〔尤指为逃脱而与他人〕搏斗; 挣扎: [+with] *Liz struggled fiercely with her attacker.* 莉兹同攻击她的人进行激烈的搏斗。**3** if two people struggle, they fight each other for something, especially something one of them is holding 争斗, 争抢: *They struggled briefly, then Ray grabbed the bag and ran.* 他们争抢了一会, 后来雷抓住那个袋子跑了。

4 to move somewhere with great difficulty 艰难地〔向某处〕行进: [+towards/into etc] *Kim struggled out of the wreckage, her head bleeding badly.* 金艰难地从残骸中爬了出来，头上血流不止。

struggle on *phr v* [I] to continue doing something that you find difficult, tiring etc 挣扎着坚持下去: *We've lost two of our best players, but we're struggling on.* 我们失去了两名最好的运动员，但我们仍努力坚持下去。

3 **struggle²** *n* [C] **1** a long hard fight to get freedom, political rights etc〔为争取自由、政治权利等而进行的〕斗争，奋斗: *the nation's struggle for independence* 该国争取独立的斗争 | **power struggle** (=a fight to get power in a country or organization) 权力斗争 **2** a fight between two people for something, especially something one of them is holding 争斗，争抢: *After a short struggle I got the knife off him.* 经过短暂的搏斗，我从他手里夺过了刀子。**3** an attempt to fight or escape from someone who is attacking you or holding on to you 搏斗; 挣扎: *Police examined the body but found no signs of a struggle.* 警察检查了尸体，但没有发现搏斗的痕迹。**4 be a struggle** if an activity, job etc is a struggle for someone, they find it very difficult to do 是困难[费劲]的事: [+for] *Reading is a struggle for Tim.* 阅读对蒂姆来说是件费劲的事。

strum /strʌm; strʌm/ *v* **strummed, strumming** [I,T] to play an instrument such as a GUITAR by moving your fingers up and down across its strings 弹奏，拨弄〔吉他等弦乐器〕

strum·pet /ˈstrʌmpɪt; ˈstrʌmpə̩t/ *n* [C] *old use* an insulting word meaning a woman who has sex for money【旧】妓女，婊子

strung /strʌŋ; strʌŋ/ the past tense and past participle of STRING²

strung-out /ˌ· ˈ·◂/ *adj* [not before noun 不用于名词前] *informal*【非正式】**1** if you are strung-out on a drug, that drug is affecting you a lot, so that you cannot react normally 有毒瘾的: [+on] *strung-out on heroin* 吸海洛因成瘾的 **2** extremely tired and worried 极其疲惫焦虑的

strung-up /ˌ· ˈ·◂/ *adj BrE informal* very nervous, worried, or excited【英，非正式】极其紧张[焦虑; 兴奋]的

strut¹ /strʌt; strʌt/ *v* **strutted, strutting** [I] **1** to walk proudly with your head high and your chest pushed forwards, showing that you think you are important 趾高气扬地走，架子十足地走: [+about/across etc] *Ryan was strutting around the office, issuing orders.* 瑞安在办公室里趾高气扬地走来走去，发号施令。**2 strut your stuff** *informal* to show your skill at doing something【非正式】炫耀自己的本领: *Look at Dave strutting his stuff on the dance floor.* 看，戴夫正在舞池里大显身手。

strut² *n* **1** [C] a long thin piece of metal or wood used to support a part of a building, the wing of an aircraft etc 支柱，撑杆，支杆 **2** [singular] a proud way of walking, with your head high and your chest pushed forwards 趾高气扬的步态，昂首阔步的样子

strych·nine /ˈstrɪknin; ˈstrɪkniːn/ *n* [U] a very poisonous substance sometimes used in small amounts as a medicine 士的宁，马钱子碱〔有毒，微量可作药用〕

St Thom·as /· ˈ··/ an island in the US Virgin Islands in the Caribbean Sea 圣托马斯岛〔加勒比海美属维尔京群岛一岛屿〕

St Trin·i·an's /sent ˋtrɪnɪənz; sənt ˈtrɪniənz/ an imaginary British private school for girls in humorous CARTOON stories of the 1950s and later in a number of humorous films. The girls are very badly behaved and the teachers cannot control them, and they have many amusing and exciting adventures, often involving illegal activities. 圣特里尼恩女校〔20 世纪 50 年代的幽默连环漫画及之后的许多喜剧片中虚构的一所英国私立女校。该校女生行为不端，教师无法管束。她们有许多滑稽而刺激的冒险之举，常有违法之嫌〕

St Tro·pez /ˌsæn trəˋpe; ˌsæn trəˈpeɪ/ a fashionable holiday town on the south coast of France, which used to be very popular with rich and famous people. It became famous in the 1960s for being one of the first holiday towns to allow women on the beach to wear nothing on their breasts. 圣特罗佩〔法国南部海岸一时尚度假小镇，曾经颇受富豪名流青睐。20 世纪 60 年代，该地是最早允许女性在海滩上裸露乳房的度假城镇之一，并因此而出名〕

Stu·art /ˈstuɚt; ˈstjuːət/ the name of the royal family that ruled Scotland from 1371 to 1603 and Britain from 1603 to 1649 and from 1660 to 1714 斯图亚特〔王室家族的名称。该家族 1371 至 1603 年统治苏格兰，1603 至 1649 年、1660 年至 1714 年统治不列颠〕

Stuart, Charles Edward —see 见 BONNIE PRINCE CHARLIE

Stuart, Gil·bert /ˈgɪlbɚt; ˈgɪlbət/ (1755-1828) a US painter who painted many PORTRAITS of famous people. His best-known work is his picture of George Washington. 斯图亚特〔(1755-1828)，美国画家。创作有大量名人肖像画，以乔治·华盛顿的肖像画最为著名〕

Stuart, James Edward (1688-1766) the son of the British king James II, sometimes also called the Old Pretender, and the father of Bonnie Prince Charlie (Charles Edward Stuart). He believed he had the right to be the British king instead of King George I, but his attempt to become king, during the first Jacobite Rising of 1715-16, was a failure. 斯图亚特〔(1688-1766)，又称老僭王，英国国王詹姆斯二世之子，英俊王子查理之父。他认为当国王的应该是自己，而不是乔治一世，并企图夺取王位，1715 至 1716 年发动了第一次詹姆斯党人起义，但以失败告终〕

Stuart, Mary —see 见 MARY QUEEN OF SCOTS

stub¹ /stʌb; stʌb/ *n* [C] **1** the short part that is left when the rest of something long and thin, such as a cigarette or pencil, has been used 残头，残根; 烟蒂; 铅笔头 **2** the part of a ticket that is returned to you after it has been torn, as proof that you have paid 票根，存根 **3** a piece of a cheque left in a cheque book as a record after the main part has been torn out 支票的存根

stub² *v* [T] **stub your toe** to hurt your toe by hitting it against something 使脚趾碰到〔某物〕

stub sth ↔ **out** *phr v* [T] to stop a cigarette burning by pressing the end of it against something 把〔香烟〕捻灭 —see picture at 参见 PUT 图

stub·ble /ˈstʌbl; ˈstʌbəl/ *n* [U] **1** short stiff hairs that grow on a man's face if he does not SHAVE¹ (1) 胡子茬，须茬，短须: **designer stubble** (=stubble that a man has to look fashionable) 时髦的短须 **2** short stiff pieces left in the fields after wheat, corn etc has been cut〔作物收割后遗留在地里的〕残茎，茬(子) —**stubbly** *adj*

stub·born /ˈstʌbɚn; ˈstʌbən/ *adj* **1** determined not to change your mind, even when people think you are being unreasonable 固执的，顽固的，执拗的; 倔强的: **a stubborn streak** (=a stubborn part of your character) 个性中固执的倾向 *I knew you'd be too stubborn to listen!* 我早就知道你太固执，不会听的! | **stubborn as a mule** (=very stubborn) 非常执拗[固执] **2 stubborn opposition/persistence etc** very strong and determined opposition etc 顽强的抵抗/坚持不懈等: *The Broncos provided stubborn opposition throughout the whole game.* 在整场比赛中野马队进行了顽强的抵抗。**3** difficult to remove, deal with, or use 难以去除[对付; 使用]的: *stubborn stains* 很难洗掉的污渍 —**stubbornly** *adv* —**stubbornness** *n* [U]

Stubbs, George /stʌbs; stʌbs/ (1724-1806) a British artist whose best-known works are his paintings of horses and other animals 斯塔布斯〔(1724-1806)，英国艺术家，以画马和其他动物著称〕

stub·by /ˈstʌbɪ; ˈstʌbi/ *adj* short and thick or fat 短粗的，矮胖的: *stubby little fingers* 短粗的小手指

stuc·co /ˈstʌko; ˈstʌkəʊ/ *n* [U] a type of PLASTER¹ (1) surface on the outside walls of buildings〔涂外墙用的〕灰泥

stuck¹ /stʌk; stʌk/ the past tense and past participle of STICK¹

stuck² *adj* [not before noun 不用于名词前]

1 ▶**FIXED** 固定的◀ fixed in a particular position and impossible to move 卡住的，无法移动的，动不了的: *Sheila tried to open the window but it was stuck.* 希拉试图打开窗户，可窗户卡住了。| **get stuck** *The bus got stuck in the snow and we had to walk the rest of the way.* 公共汽车陷在雪中开不动了，剩下的路我们只好步行了。| **get sth stuck** *Tommy got his head stuck between the railings.* 汤米的头卡在栏杆之间动不了。

2 ▶**DIFFICULTY** 困难◀ unable to do any more of something that you are working on because it is too difficult 被难倒的，困住的; 没法进行下去的: *Can you help me with my homework Dad? I'm stuck.* 爸爸，你能帮我做作业吗? 我给难倒了。

3 ▶**SITUATION** 处境◀ unable to escape from an unpleasant or boring situation 无法摆脱困境的: [+in/at] *I wouldn't be able to stand being stuck in an office all day.* 我无法忍受整天被困在办公室里。| [+with] *I was stuck with my aunt all afternoon.* 我整个下午都被我姑姑缠住了。

4 be stuck with sth to have something you do not want because you cannot get rid of it 不得不接受某事物; 无法摆脱某事物: *We're renting the house, so we're stuck with this ugly wallpaper.* 我们将租用这房子，不得不接受这难看的墙纸。

5 be stuck on sb *informal* to be attracted to someone【非正式】非常喜欢某人，被某人吸引: *Jane's really stuck on the new boy in her class.* 简真的很喜欢班里新来的那个男孩。

6 get stuck in *BrE spoken* to start doing something eagerly and with a lot of energy【英口】积极地开始做某事，急切地做…: *Let's get stuck in and see if we can finish this by lunchtime.* 我们快开始干吧，看午饭前能否把这事做完。

stuck³ *n* [U] **be in stuck** *BrE informal* to be in trouble【英，非正式】陷入麻烦

stuck-up /ˌ· ˈ·◂/ *adj informal* proud and unfriendly because you think you are better and more important than other people【非正式】傲慢的，自以为了不起的：*a stuck-up officious little man* 一个自命不凡、爱管闲事的小男人

stud 鞋底防滑凸起物

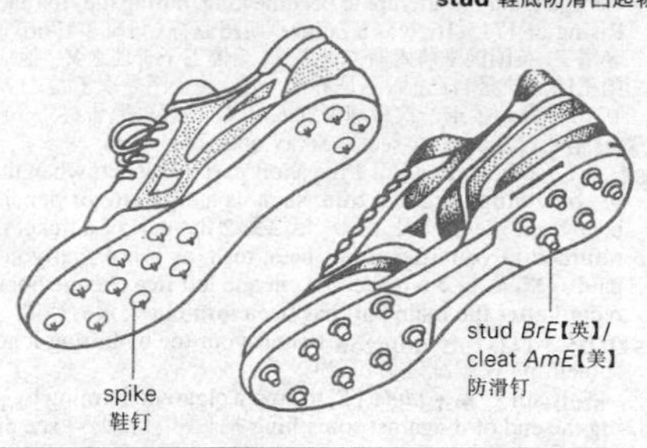

stud¹ /stʌd; stʌd/ *n*

1 ►**ON SHOES** 在鞋上◄[C] one of a set of small pointed pieces of metal or plastic that are fixed onto the bottom of a running shoe, football boot etc to stop you from slipping〔跑鞋、足球鞋等的〕鞋底防滑凸起物；〔鞋底的〕防滑钉

2 ►**IN YOUR EAR** 在耳朵上◄[C] a small, round EARRING 圆形小耳环，螺栓式耳环，耳钉 —see picture at 参见 JEWELLERY 图

3 ►**DECORATION** 装饰◄[C] a round piece of metal that is stuck into a surface for decoration 饰钉，大头钉：*a leather jacket with studs around the collar and cuffs* 领子和袖口有饰钉的皮夹克

4 ►**FOR A SHIRT** 供衬衫用◄[C] a small thing for fastening a shirt or collar that consists of two round, flat pieces of metal joined together by a bar 领扣，饰纽 —see also 另见 PRESS-STUD

5 ►**ANIMAL** 动物◄[C,U] animals such as horses that are kept for breeding 种畜；种马：*a stud farm* 种马饲养场 | **put an animal out to stud** (=use the animal for breeding) 为配种而饲养某动物

6 ►**MAN** 男人◄[C] *informal* an insulting word for a man who has a lot of sexual partners and who is very proud of his sexual ability【非正式】为自己的性能力骄傲的男子，乱搞性关系的男人〔侮辱性用语〕

7 ►**BOARD** 木板◄[C] *AmE* the kind of board that is used to make the frame of a house【美】板墙筋，壁骨；立柱

stud² *v* [T usually passive 一般用被动态] *literary* to cover a surface or area with many small things【文】覆盖，散布于：*field studded with daisies* 雏菊遍地的田野

stud·book /ˈstʌdˌbʊk; ˈstʌdbʊk/ *n* [C] a list of names of race horses from which other race horses have been bred 赛马血统记录簿；马种系谱

stud·ded /ˈstʌdɪd; ˈstʌdʒd/ *adj* decorated with a lot of studs or small jewels etc 镶满饰纽[宝石]的：*a studded leather belt* 镶满饰钉的皮带

stu·dent /ˈstudn̩t; ˈstjuːdənt/ *n* [C] **1** someone who is studying at a school, university etc 学生，学员：*a first year student at the University of Oslo* 奥斯陆大学一名一年级学生 | **law/medical/engineering etc student** *A lot of art students live in this dorm.* 许多学艺术的学生住在这个宿舍。| **student teacher/nurse** (=someone who is learning to be a teacher or nurse) 实习教师／护士 | **A/B/C etc student** *AmE* (=someone who always earns A's etc for their work)【美】学业成绩总是得 A/B/C 等的学生 —see also 另见 MATURE STUDENT **2** **be a student of sth** to be very interested in a particular subject 对某学科非常感兴趣：*Myles was a profound student of human nature.* 迈尔斯对研究人性非常感兴趣。

CULTURAL NOTE 文化注释

In the UK, when people think about students, they often think of someone who doesn't study very much, enjoys drinking a lot of alcohol, misses classes because they always wake up late, and complains about not having enough money. Although this stereotype still exists, there have been many changes in student life in recent years. Far more people study at university than in the past and they come from a wider range of social classes. In the past, students were given money by the government to help pay for their living costs and courses were free, but now most students must get LOANS to help pay for both living costs and university FEES. Almost all students have a lot of debts by the time they get their degrees. Many of them have to do PART-TIME jobs in order to earn money while they are at university. 在英国，人们印象中的学生形象是学习不用功、酗酒，因总是睡懒觉而缺课，还有抱怨钱不够花。尽管这样的学生仍然存在，最近一些年学生的生活还是有了不少变化。上大学的人比过去多了，而且来自更加广泛的社会阶层。过去政府公费为学生解决生活费，而且课程也是免费的；但是现在大多数学生必须自己贷款解决生活费和学费。几乎所有学生在拿到学位的时候都要欠下不少的债，很多在校大学生不得不靠做些兼职来挣钱。

In the US, people do not really have a stereotype of what students are like. Universities have always cost a lot of money, and most students work while they are in university. Students are given special loans to help pay for university, which they must pay back over a period of many years after they finish. 在美国，人们对学生实际上没有一个固定的印象。上大学总会花很多钱，因此多数学生边学习边打工。学生能申请到特别的贷款来缴付上大学的费用，这些贷款需要毕业后多年才能还清。— see also 另见 **town and gown** (TOWN (9)); compare Cultural Note at SORORITY 比较 SORORITY 文化注释

student bod·y /ˌ·· ˈ··/ *n* [C] *AmE* all of the students in a HIGH SCHOOL, college, or university, considered as a group【美】〔一所中学或大学的〕全体学生

student gov·ern·ment /ˌ·· ˈ···/ also 又作 **student council** /ˌ·· ˈ··/ *n* [C] *AmE* an elected group of students in a HIGH SCHOOL, college, or university who represent the students in meetings and who organize school activities【美】学生自治会〔指中学或大学里推选出来代表学生参加会议并组织学校活动的学生团体〕

student loan /ˌ·· ˈ·/ *n* [C] a method of paying for your education in which students at a college or university borrow money from a bank or the government and repay it when they start working 学生贷款

students' u·nion /ˌ·· ˈ··/ also 又作 **student union** *n* [C] **1** a building where students go to meet socially 学生活动大楼 **2** *BrE* an association of students in a particular college or university【英】〔大专院校的〕学生会

student teach·ing /ˌ·· ˈ··/ *n* [U] *AmE* the period of time during which students who are learning to be teachers practise teaching in a school【美】教学实习；TEACHING PRACTICE *BrE*【英】

stud·ied /ˈstʌdɪd; ˈstʌdid/ *adj* a studied way of behaving is deliberate and often insincere because you have planned your behaviour carefully 经过深思熟虑的；有意的；装模作样的：*She spoke with studied politeness.* 她故作有礼地说话。

stu·di·o /ˈstudɪˌo; ˈstjuːdiəʊ/ *n* [C]

1 ►**FOR TELEVISION/RECORDS** 供电视/录音用◄ a room where television and radio programmes are made and broadcast or where music is recorded 录音室，播音室，演播室：*a TV studio* 电视录制室

2 ►**FILMS** 电影◄ also 又作 **studios** a film company or the buildings it owns and uses to make its films 电影制片公司，电影制片厂：*Depardieu is making a film with one of the big Hollywood studios.* 德帕尔迪厄正与好莱坞的一家大制片公司合作拍摄一部电影。

3 ►**FOR PAINTING/PHOTOGRAPHY** 供绘画/摄影用◄ **a)** a room where a painter or photographer regularly works〔画家、摄影师的〕工作室 **b)** a company that produces pictures or photographs 画室；照相馆，摄影室

4 ►**FOR DANCING** 供舞蹈用◄ a room where dancing lessons are given or that dancers use to practise in 舞蹈练习厅

5 ►**APARTMENT** 公寓◄ also 又作 **studio apartment** *AmE*【美】，**studio flat** *BrE*【英】a small apartment with one main room 一室的公寓房

studio au·di·ence /ˌ··· ˈ···/ *n* [C] a group of people who watch and are sometimes involved in a radio or television programme while it is being made〔广播或电视节目的〕现场观众

stu·di·ous /ˈstudɪəs; ˈstjuːdiəs/ *adj* **1** spending a lot of time studying and reading 好学的，勤奋的，用功的：*a quiet studious young man* 文静好学的年轻人 **2** careful in your work〔工作〕认真的，仔细的，小心的：*studious attention to detail* 认真注意细节 —**studiously** *adv* —**studiousness** *n* [U]

stud·y¹ /ˈstʌdɪ; ˈstʌdi/ *n*

1 ►**PIECE OF WORK** 一项工作◄[C] a piece of work that is done to find out more about a particular subject or problem,

and usually includes a written report〔对某一课题或问题的〕研究: [+of/into] *We're doing a study into how much time people spend watching television.* 我们正在进行一项研究，调查人们看电视所花的时间。| *a study of Australian wild birds* 一项对澳大利亚野生鸟类的研究 | **make/carry out/conduct a study** *a study of children's eating habits carried out in 1976* 1976年对儿童饮食习惯进行的研究

2 ▶ROOM 房间◀[C] a room in a house that is used for work or study 书房，书斋

3 ▶SCHOOL WORK 功课◀[U] the activity of studying 学习；读书: *Set aside a period of time specifically for study.* 专门留出一段时间来学习。

4 studies [plural] subjects that people study, especially several related subjects〔尤指几个相关专业的〕学科；学业: *the Department of Russian Studies* 俄语系

5 ▶ART 艺术◀[C] a small detailed drawing, especially one that is done to prepare for a large painting〔绘画的〕试画，习作: *Renoir's studies of small plants and flowers* 雷诺阿的小植物和花卉试画

6 ▶MUSIC 音乐◀[C] a piece of music, usually for piano, that is often intended for practice〔尤指钢琴的〕练习曲

7 be a study in sth to be a perfect example of something 是…的最佳例子，是…的典型: *His face was a study in incredulity.* 他的脸上完全是难以置信的神色。

8 be in a brown study *old-fashioned* to be thinking deeply about something【过时】在沉思中，正在默想

S3 W3 **study²** *v* **studied, studying** **1** [I,T] to spend time reading, going to classes etc in order to learn about a subject 学习，攻读: *I've been studying English for 6 years.* 我学英语已有6年了。| *I can't study with that music playing all the time.* 那音乐一直播放，我无法学习。| **study to be a doctor/lawyer etc** *My brother's studying to be an accountant.* 我弟弟在读会计。| **study for an exam/diploma etc** *I've only got three weeks left to study for my exams.* 我只剩下三个星期的学习时间为考试作准备。| **study under sb** (=be trained by a famous teacher) 师从某人，跟某名师学习 *a psychologist who studied under Jung in Zurich* 曾在苏黎世师从荣格的心理学家 —see 见 KNOW[1] (USAGE) **2** [T] to watch and examine something carefully over a period of time in order to find out more about it 仔细端详，仔细察看；研究: *Goodall was studying the behavior of gorillas in the wild.* 古多尔在仔细观察野生状态的大猩猩的行为。| **study how/why/when etc** *studying how stress affects body chemistry* 研究压力如何影响人体的化学反应 **3** [T] to spend a lot of time carefully examining a plan, document, problem etc 仔细研究〔计划、文件、问题等〕: *I haven't had time to study the proposals yet.* 我还没有时间去仔细研究那些提议。

study hall /'‥ ‚/ *n* [U] *AmE* a period of time during a school day in which a student does not have a class and usually goes somewhere to study【美】〔学校的〕自习时间，自修（课）

S1 W3 **stuff¹** /stʌf; stʌf/ *n* [U]

1 ▶SUBSTANCE 物质◀*informal* a kind of substance or material【非正式】材料，东西: *What's that stuff you're drinking?* 你喝的那是什么东西？| *The dress was made of silky stuff.* 那件衣服是用丝绸料子做的。

2 ▶THINGS 事物◀*informal* a number of different things【非正式】几种不同的物品，东西: *How do you think you're going to fit all that stuff into a car?* 你认为怎样才能把那些东西都装进汽车里呢？

3 ▶SUBJECT 话题◀*informal* the subject of something such as a book, television programme, lesson etc【非正式】〔书、电视节目、课程等的〕题材，话题: *What kind of stuff do you like to read?* 你喜欢读哪一类的题材？

4 ▶ACTIVITIES 活动◀all the activities that someone does〔某人从事的〕活动，事情: *I've got so much stuff to do this weekend.* 我这个周末有很多事情要做。

5 sb's stuff *informal* things that belong to someone【非正式】某人的物品，某人的所有物: *I'm leaving in an hour and I still haven't packed my stuff.* 我一小时后就要出发，可我还没有收拾东西呢。

6 ▶EQUIPMENT 设备◀*informal* the equipment you need for a particular activity【非正式】做某事所需的东西: *Where's the camping stuff?* 野营用的东西在哪儿？

7 the stuff of dreams/life/politics exactly the kind of thing that dreams etc consist of 梦/生活/政治的内容: *an enchanting place – the very stuff of dreams* 一个迷人的地方——正如梦中所见的那样

8 ▶CHARACTER 性格◀the qualities of someone's character〔某人的〕本质，品质: **the right stuff** (=qualities that make you able to deal with difficulties) 对付困难的能力 | **be made of sterner stuff** (=be more determined) 性格更加坚强 *I thought you were made of sterner stuff – don't just give up.* 我原以为你是个性格比较坚强的人——别这样就放弃了。

9 do/show your stuff to do what you are good at when everyone wants you to do it 拿出自己的本领，显身手: *Come on Gina, get on the dance floor and do your stuff!* 来吧，吉娜，到舞池里一显身手！

10 that's the stuff! *spoken* used to express approval of what someone is doing or saying【口】这就对啦！好呀！〔用于对某人所做或所说的事情表示赞同〕

11 stuff and nonsense *spoken* used to say that you think something is stupid or untrue【口】胡说八道，废话 —see also 另见 **a bit of stuff** (BIT[1] (19)), **be hot stuff** (HOT[1] (18)), **kid's stuff** (KID[1] (4)), **know your stuff** (KNOW[1] (13)), **strut your stuff** (STRUT[1] (2))

stuff² *v* [T]

1 ▶PUSH 推◀[always+adv/prep] to push something soft into a small space in a careless hurried way 填，塞: **stuff sth into/in/up** *She stuffed two more sweaters into her bag.* 她又往袋子里塞了两件毛线衫。| **be stuffed with** *a huge picnic basket stuffed with delicacies* 塞满美食的野餐大篮子 | **stuffed full of** *a briefcase stuffed full of papers* 装满文件的公文包

2 ▶FILL 装满◀to fill something tightly with soft material, so that it becomes firm 填满，装满: *a pillow stuffed with feathers* 塞满羽毛的枕头

3 ▶FOOD 食物◀to fill a chicken or another type of food, such as a TOMATO, with a mixture of bread, rice etc 给〔鸡、番茄等〕填馅，填料于〔食物〕

4 ▶DEAD ANIMAL 死的动物◀to fill the skin of a dead animal in order to make the animal look real 填塞〔死动物〕的皮以做标本: *a stuffed parrot* 制成标本的鹦鹉

5 stuff yourself also 又作 **stuff your face** *informal* to eat so much food that you cannot eat anything else【非正式】吃饱，吃足: [+with] *The kids have been stuffing themselves with candy.* 孩子们一直在吃糖果，都吃饱了。

6 get stuffed *spoken* used to tell someone very rudely and angrily that you do not want to talk to them or accept their offer【口】走开，不要烦了，去你的吧〔以非常粗鲁和生气的语气表示不想与某人交谈或拒绝接受某人的提议〕: *He only offered me £10 for it, so I told him to get stuffed.* 他只出10英镑想买下它，所以我就叫他滚开。

7 you/they can stuff sth *spoken* used to say very angrily or rudely that you do not want what someone is offering【口】见你的鬼去吧〔非常气愤或粗鲁地表示不接受某人的提议〕: *Yeah? Well you can stuff your damn contract!* 是吗？那你就和你那该死的合同一起见鬼去吧！

8 ▶GAME 比赛◀to defeat an opposing team easily 轻易击败〔对手〕: *We stuffed them, 15-2, 15-4, 15-3.* 我们以15:2, 15:4, 15:3轻取对手。

stuffed /stʌft; stʌft/ *adj* completely full, so that you cannot eat any more 吃饱了的: *No, no dessert, I'm stuffed.* 不，不要甜点了，我吃饱了。

stuffed an·i·mal /‚ ˈ‥‥/ *n* [C] *AmE* a toy animal covered and filled with soft material【美】〔填充松软材料的〕动物玩具；SOFT TOY *BrE*【英】

stuffed shirt /‚ ˈ ‚/ *n* [C] someone who behaves in a very formal way and thinks that they are important 神气十足的人，妄自尊大的人

stuffed-up /‚ ˈ ◂/ *adj* unable to breathe properly through your nose because you have a cold 鼻塞的，〔因感冒鼻塞而〕无法正常呼吸的

stuff·ing /ˈstʌfɪŋ; ˈstʌfɪŋ/ *n* [U] **1** a mixture of bread, onion, egg and HERBS that you put inside meat before cooking it 填在肉食中的馅；〔肉食中的〕填料；DRESSING (2) *AmE*【美】: *sage and onion stuffing* 洋苏叶和洋葱填料 **2** soft material that is used to fill something such as a CUSHION〔垫子等中的〕填料，填充物 —see also 另见 **knock the stuffing out of** (KNOCK[1] (10))

stuff·y /ˈstʌfɪ; ˈstʌfi/ *adj* **1** a room or building that is stuffy does not have enough fresh air in it〔房间或建筑物〕通风不好的，空气不新鲜的，闷的: *It's getting stuffy in here – do you mind if I open the window?* 这里有点儿闷热，我打开窗户行吗？**2** someone who is stuffy is too formal and has old-fashioned ideas〔指人〕一本正经的，古板的，拘谨的 —**stuffily** *adv* —**stuffiness** *n* [U]

stul·ti·fy·ing /ˈstʌltəˌfaɪ-ɪŋ; ˈstʌltɨfaɪ-ɪŋ/ *adj* so boring that you feel as though you are losing your ability to think 使人呆滞的；使人厌倦[迟钝]的: *a stultifying exercise* 枯燥刻板的练习 —**stultify** *v* [T] —**stultification** /ˌstʌltəfəˈkeʃən; ˌstʌltɨfɨˈkeɪʃən/ *n* [U]

stum·ble /ˈstʌmbḷ; ˈstʌmbəl/ *v* [I] **1** to hit your foot against something or put your foot down awkwardly while you are walking or running, so that you almost fall 绊脚, 绊跌, 绊了一下: *In her hurry she stumbled and spilled the milk all over the floor.* 匆忙中她绊了一下, 把牛奶全洒到地上。| [+over/on] *Vic stumbled over the step as he came in.* 维克进来时在台阶上绊了一下。**2** to walk unsteadily and often almost fall 蹒跚而行, 踉跄: [+in/out/across etc] *I finished the whisky and then stumbled upstairs and into bed.* 我喝完威士忌, 然后踉跄地爬上楼倒在床上。**3** to stop or make a mistake when you are reading to people or speaking〔朗读或说话时〕打结巴; 说错: [+over/at/through] *I hope I don't stumble over any of the long words.* 但愿我说那些长字眼时不结巴。**4 stumbling block** a problem or difficulty that prevents you from achieving something 阻碍成功的困难[难题], 障碍物, 绊脚石: [+to] *a territorial dispute which is the main stumbling block to a peace settlement* 成为达成和平协议主要障碍的领土纠纷 —**stumble** *n* [C]

stumble on/across sth *phr v* [T] to discover something or meet someone by chance and unexpectedly 偶然发现[碰见]: *Boyce was killed because he stumbled across something he shouldn't have seen.* 博伊斯因偶然看到自己不应看到的事而被杀害了。

stump¹ /stʌmp; stʌmp/ *n* [C]

1 ▶TREE 树◀ the bottom part of a tree that is left in the ground after the rest of it has been cut down; TREE STUMP〔树被砍下后留下的〕树桩, 树墩

2 ▶SOMETHING BROKEN 打破的东西◀ the small useless part of something that remains after most of it has broken off or worn away 残余部分; 残段; 残根: *the stump of a broken tooth* 坏牙的残根

3 ▶ARM/LEG 胳膊/腿◀ the short part of someone's leg, arm etc that remains after the rest of it has been cut off 残肢

4 ▶IN SPORT 在体育运动中◀ one of the three upright sticks in CRICKET (2) that you throw the ball at〔板球〕三柱门的任何一柱

5 stump speech *AmE* a speech made while travelling around to get political support【美】巡回政治演说

stump² *v* **1** [T] to ask someone such a difficult question that they are completely unable to think of an answer 把〔某人〕难住, 难倒: *trying to stump the teacher* 企图把老师难倒 | **be stumped** *Nobody knows – even the experts are stumped.* 谁也不知道, 连专家都被难住了。| **get/have sb stumped** *This question'll have them all stumped.* 这个问题会把他们都难住的。**2** [I+up/along/across] to walk with heavy steps; STOMP 迈着沉重的步子走; 跺着脚走 **3** [T] to put a BATSMAN out of the game in CRICKET (2) by touching the stumps with the ball when he is out of the hitting area〔板球〕以球触三门柱而使〔跑分的击球员〕出局 **4** [I,T] *AmE* to travel around an area, meeting people and making speeches in order to gain political support【美】作巡回政治演说: *I'm too old to keep stumping around the state.* 我太老了, 不能继续在州内到处作巡回演说了。

stump up *phr v* [I,T] *BrE informal* to pay money, even if it is difficult【英, 非正式】〔勉强地〕支付(钱): *That's ten quid you owe me. Come on, stump up.* 你欠我10英镑, 快掏钱吧。

stump·y /ˈstʌmpɪ; ˈstʌmpi/ *adj BrE* stumpy legs, fingers etc are short and thick in an unattractive way; STUBBY【英】〔腿、手指等〕短粗的, 敦实的

stun /stʌn; stʌn/ *v* **stunned, stunning** [T not in progressive 不用进行时] **1** to surprise or upset someone so much that they do not react immediately 使大吃一惊, 使震惊: *Sacha was too stunned by what had happened to say anything.* 萨夏对发生的事情感到十分震惊, 一时说不出话来。| **stunned silence** (=silence because everyone is too surprised to speak) 瞠目结舌 **2** to make someone unconscious for a short time 使〔某人〕短暂失去知觉, 使晕过去: *Thank God that punch only stunned you!* 感谢上帝, 那一拳只是把你打昏了而已!

stung /stʌŋ; stʌŋ/ the past tense and past participle of STING¹

stun gun /ˈ· ·/ *n* [C] a weapon that produces a very strong electric current and can be used to make animals or people unconscious〔使被击中者晕眩的〕电击枪

stunk /stʌŋk; stʌŋk/ a past tense and the past participle of STINK¹

stun·ner /ˈstʌnɚ; ˈstʌnə/ *n* [C] *old-fashioned* someone or something that is very attractive, especially a woman【过时】极具吸引力的人[物]; 〔尤指〕极漂亮的女人

stun·ning /ˈstʌnɪŋ; ˈstʌnɪŋ/ *adj* **1** extremely attractive or beautiful 极具吸引力的, 极漂亮的: *You look absolutely stunning in that dress.* 你穿上那件衣服, 看上去非常迷人。| *a stunning view* 非常美丽的景色 **2** very surprising or shocking 令人惊奇的, 令人震惊的: *stunning news* 令人震惊的新闻 —**stunningly** *adv*

stunt¹ /stʌnt; stʌnt/ *n* [C] **1** a dangerous action that is done to entertain people, especially in a film〔尤指电影中的〕特技表演, 绝技: *Not many actors do their own stunts.* 很多演员并不亲自表演特技动作。**2** something that is done to attract people's attention, especially in advertising or politics〔尤指广告或政治中的〕噱头, 引人注目的花招: **publicity stunt** *Todd flew over the city in a hot air balloon as a publicity stunt.* 托德乘坐热气球从城市上空飞过, 作为一种宣传花招。**3 pull a stunt** to do something that is silly or that is slightly dangerous 做愚蠢[惊险]的事: *Next time you pull a stunt like that don't expect me to get you out of trouble.* 下次你要再做那样的蠢事, 别指望我帮你解围。

stunt² *v* [T] to stop something or someone from growing to their full size or developing properly 抑制, 阻碍…的成长[发育]: *Lack of sunlight will stunt the plant's growth.* 缺乏阳光会阻碍植物的生长。

stunt man /ˈ· ·/ *n* [C] a man who is employed to take the place of an actor when something dangerous has to be done in a film〔电影中受雇替代男演员做惊险动作的〕男替身演员

stunt wom·an /ˈ· ˌ··/ *n* [C] a woman who is employed to take the place of an actress when something dangerous has to be done in a film〔电影中受雇替代女演员做惊险动作的〕女替身演员

stu·pe·fied /ˈstupəˌfaɪd; ˈstjuːpḷfaɪd/ *adj* so surprised, tired, or bored that you cannot think clearly〔因吃惊、疲劳或厌倦而〕目瞪口呆的: *a stupefied expression* 目瞪口呆的表情 —**stupefaction** /ˌstupəˈfækʃən; ˌstjuːpḷˈfækʃən/ *n* [U]

stu·pe·fy·ing /ˈstupəˌfaɪ·ɪŋ; ˈstjuːpḷfaɪ-ɪŋ/ *adj* making you feel extremely surprised, tired, or bored 令人非常吃惊[疲劳; 厌倦]的: *stupefying inefficiency* 令人惊讶的低效率 —**stupefy** *v* [T]

stu·pen·dous /stuˈpɛndəs; stjuːˈpendəs/ *adj* surprisingly large or impressive 巨大的; 惊人的; 了不起的: *a stupendous achievement* 了不起的成就 —**stupendously** *adv*

stu·pid /ˈstupɪd; ˈstjuːpḷd/ *adj* **1** showing a lack of good sense or good judgment; silly 愚蠢的, 傻的: *stupid mistakes* 愚蠢的错误 | *I was very drunk last night – I hope I didn't do anything stupid.* 我昨晚喝得烂醉, 希望我没干什么蠢事。| **it is stupid (of sb) to do sth** *It was stupid of me to lose my temper.* 我大发脾气, 真是太愚蠢了。**2** having a low level of intelligence, so that you have difficulty learning or understanding things 笨的, 头脑迟钝的: *Charlie understands perfectly well what you mean. He's not stupid.* 查利完全理解你的意思, 他并不笨。**3** *informal* used when you are talking about something that makes you annoyed or impatient【非正式】恼人的, 讨厌的〔用以表示气恼或不耐烦〕: *I can't get this stupid radio to work.* 我无法弄响这台讨厌的收音机。**4** [singular] an insulting way of talking to someone who you think is being stupid 笨蛋, 蠢货〔侮辱性的说法〕: *No, stupid, don't do it like that!* 不, 笨蛋, 不要那样做! **5 stupid with cold/sleep/shock etc** unable to think clearly because you are extremely tired, cold etc 冻得/睡得/惊得等头昏脑胀 —**stupidly** *adv*: *Stupidly I forgot my umbrella and ended up getting soaked.* 我糊涂得忘记带雨伞了, 结果淋得浑身都湿透了。

stu·pid·i·ty /stuˈpɪdətɪ; stjuːˈpɪdḷti/ *n* **1** [C usually plural 一般用复数, U] behaviour or actions that show a lack of good sense or good judgment 愚蠢的行为: *all the horrors and stupidities of war* 战争中的所有恐怖事和愚蠢行为 **2** [U] the quality of being stupid or unintelligent 愚蠢, 愚笨; 糊涂

stu·por /ˈstupɚ; ˈstjuːpə/ *n* [C,U] a state in which you cannot think, speak, see or hear clearly, usually because you have drunk too much alcohol or taken drugs〔因过量喝酒或吸毒引起的〕昏迷, 恍惚, 不省人事: **drunken stupor** *We found him lying at the bottom of the stairs in a drunken stupor.* 我们发现他躺在楼梯口, 醉得不省人事。

stur·dy /ˈstɝdɪ; ˈstɜːdi/ *adj* **1** someone who is sturdy is strong, short, and healthy looking〔指人〕健壮的, 强健的, 壮实的: *a sturdy young man* 健壮的小伙子 | *sturdy legs* 结实的双腿 **2** an object that is sturdy is strong, well-made, and not easily broken〔指物〕结实的, 坚实的, 坚固的: *a sturdy wall* 坚固的墙 **3** determined and not easily persuaded to change your opinions 坚定的, 坚决的, 不易改变主意的: *They kept up a sturdy opposition to the plan.* 他们一直坚决反对那项计划。—**sturdily** *adv* —**sturdiness** *n* [U]

stur·geon /ˈstɝdʒən; ˈstɜːdʒən/ *n* [C,U] a large fish, from which CAVIAR is obtained, or the flesh of this fish which can be eaten 鲟(鱼)〔其卵可制鱼子酱〕; 鲟鱼肉

stut·ter¹ /ˈstʌtɚ; ˈstʌtə/ *v* **1** [I,T] to speak with difficulty because you cannot stop yourself from repeating the first CONSONANT of some words; STAMMER¹ 结结巴巴地说: *"I'm D-d-david," he stuttered.* "我叫戴…戴…戴维。"他结结巴巴地说。**2** [I] if a

machine stutters, it keeps making little exploding noises and does not work smoothly〔机器〕发出突突的噪声，不顺畅地运转

stutter² *n* [singular] an inability to speak normally because you stutter 结巴，口吃: *a nervous stutter* 紧张性的口吃

St Vin·cent /sent ˈvɪnsn̩t; sənt ˈvɪnsənt/ a country in the east Caribbean Sea consisting of a main island called St Vincent, and some smaller islands called the Grenadines. Population: 115,942 (2001). Capital: Kingstown. 圣文森特〔圣文森特和格林纳丁斯为东加勒比海沿岸一国家。由主岛圣文森特和较小的格林纳丁斯群岛组成。人口: 115,942 (2001)，首都: 金斯敦〕

sty /staɪ; staɪ/ *n* [C] **1** a place where pigs are kept; PIGSTY (2) 猪圈，猪栏 **2** also 又作 **stye** an infected place on the edge of your EYELID, which becomes red and swollen 睑腺炎，麦粒肿

Sty·gi·an /ˈstɪdʒɪən; ˈstɪdʒiən/ *adj literary* unpleasantly dark【文】阴暗的；阴森森的: *the Stygian gloom* 阴森森的昏暗地区

style¹ /staɪl; staɪl/ *n*
1 ►WAY OF DOING/MAKING 做事/制作方式◄ [C] a particular way of doing something, designing something, or producing something, especially one that is typical of a particular period of time or of a particular group of people〔某个时期或某个团体的〕风格，作风: *styles of architecture* 建筑风格 | *The Dutch created a completely new style of football.* 荷兰人创造出一种全新的足球风格。| **Swedish/new/country etc style** (=done or made in a way that is typical of Sweden etc) 瑞典/新/乡村等风格的 *a gangland-style killing* 黑社会式的谋杀 | *The cathedral is one of the earliest examples of the gothic style.* 这座大教堂是最早的哥特式建筑之一。
2 ►WAY OF BEHAVING/WORKING 行为/工作方式◄ [C] the particular way that someone does something or deals with other people〔某人做事或待人的〕方式，特点: **[+of]** *an authoritarian style of leadership* 专断的领导作风 | **management/teaching etc style** *an attempt to use Japanese management style in a European business* 在欧洲企业中使用日本管理方式的尝试 | **it's not his/her style** (=it is not the way someone usually behaves) 那不是他/她的做事风格 *I can't ask a man out – it's just not my style.* 我不会请一个男士出去玩，那不是我的作风。| **like sb's style** (=approve of the way someone does things, used especially by someone in authority) 赞赏某人的作风〔尤作权威人士用语〕*I like your style, Simpson. I think you'll do well here.* 辛普森，我喜欢你做事的风格。我认为你在这儿会很有前途的。| **be more sb's style** *spoken* (=used as a joking way of saying that you prefer something that does not need as much skill or bravery as something that has been mentioned)【口】那才是我做的事〔玩笑用语，表示跟刚提及的事相比，自己更喜欢做不需要那么多技巧或勇气的事情〕*I don't think the parachuting weekend is for me – the art class is more my style.* 我认为周末去跳伞不适合我，上绘画课才是我做的事。| **in true British/student etc style** (=in a way that is very typical of the behaviour of a particular type of person) 典型的英国人/学生等风格 *Then the sailors, in true navy style, drank a bottle of rum each.* 然后，那些水手们每人喝了一瓶朗姆酒——典型的水手风格。
3 ►DESIGN 设计◄ [C] the design of something, which decides what shape or appearance it will have〔某物的〕设计，款式: *Car styles have changed radically in the past 20 years.* 在过去20年里，汽车的款式彻底地改变了。
4 ►FASHION 时装◄ [C,U] a fashion in clothes or hair〔衣服或头发的〕流行式样，款式: *70's styles look very odd today.* 70年代的时装式样今天看来很古怪。
5 ►WRITING/LITERATURE 写作/文学◄ [C,U] the particular way someone uses words to express ideas, tell stories etc 文体，文风: *The stories are typical of Kelman's robust prose style.* 这些故事是凯尔曼典型的、尖锐有力的散文文体。—see also 另见 STYLISTIC
6 ►ART/MUSIC/FILM 绘画/音乐/电影◄ [C,U] the typical way that someone paints, writes music etc, or a typical way of painting etc from a particular period of time〔某人或某时期的〕风格: *a modern musician who composes in the style of Bach* 用巴赫风格作曲的现代音乐家
7 ►SPECIAL QUALITY 特征◄ [U] a confident and attractive quality that makes people admire you, and that is shown in your appearance, or the way you do things 风度，气派，格调: **have style** *You may not like her, but she certainly has style!* 你也许不喜欢她，但她确实有风度！—see also 另见 STYLISH
8 in style done in a way that people admire, especially because it is unusual, shows great determination, or involves spending a lot of money 有气派；有风度；摆排场: **in great/grand/fine etc style** *Sampras won the title in fine style, not losing a single game.* 桑普拉斯没输过一局比赛，非常潇洒地赢得了冠军。—see also 另见 **cramp sb's style** (CRAMP² (2))

style² *v* [T] **1** to design clothing, furniture, or the shape of someone's hair in a particular way 设计；把…制作成某种式样: *These shoes have been styled for maximum comfort.* 这双鞋精心设计，力求达到最大限度的舒适。| **have sth styled** *She has her hair styled by Giorgio.* 她请乔治为她做头发。**2 style yourself Lord/Dr etc** *formal* to give yourself a particular title or name【正式】称自己为勋爵/博士等: *They style themselves 'the terrible twins'.* 他们称自己为"可怕的双胞胎"。—see also 另见 SELF-STYLED

styling brush /ˈ···ˌ·/ *n* [C] a heated brush used, especially by women, to make their hair a particular shape〔尤指女性用于做发型的〕定型刷子

styl·ish /ˈstaɪlɪʃ; ˈstaɪlɪʃ/ *adj* attractive in a fashionable way 有风度[气派]的；时髦的: *a stylish dresser* 穿着很时髦的人 —**stylishly** *adv* —**stylishness** *n* [U]

styl·ist /ˈstaɪlɪst; ˈstaɪlɪ̵st/ *n* [C] **1** someone who cuts or arranges people's hair as their job 发型师 **2** someone who has carefully developed a good style of writing 文体家，追求优美写作风格的人

styl·is·tic /staɪˈlɪstɪk; staɪˈlɪstɪk/ *adj* related to the style of a piece of writing or art 写作文体上的；艺术风格上的 —**stylistically** /-klɪ; -kli/ *adv*

styl·is·tics /staɪˈlɪstɪks; staɪˈlɪstɪks/ *n* [U] the study of style in written or spoken language 文体学，风格学

sty·lized also 又作 **-ised** *BrE*【英】/ˈstaɪˌlaɪzd; ˈstaɪlaɪzd/ *adj* drawn or written in an artificial style, that does not include natural detail〔绘画或写作〕程式化的: *a stylised picture of a car* 程式化的汽车图形 —**stylize** *v* [T]

sty·lus /ˈstaɪləs; ˈstaɪləs/ *n* [C] **1** the small pointed part of a RECORD PLAYER, that touches the record〔唱机的〕唱针 **2** a pointed instrument used in the past for writing on WAX¹ (1)〔旧时在蜡板上写字的〕尖笔，铁笔

sty·mie /ˈstaɪmɪ; ˈstaɪmi/ *v* [T] *informal* to prevent someone from doing what they have planned or want to do; THWART【非正式】阻碍，妨碍，使不能实施: *He desperately wanted to save his marriage, but felt stymied and doomed to fail.* 他极力想挽救自己的婚姻，但感觉阻力很大，注定要失败。

Sty·ro·foam /ˈstaɪrəˌfom; ˈstaɪərəˌfəʊm/ *n* [U] *AmE trademark* a soft light plastic material that prevents heat or cold from passing through it, used especially to make containers【美，商标】聚苯乙烯泡沫塑料; POLYSTYRENE *especially BrE*【尤英】: *a Styrofoam cup* 聚苯乙烯泡沫塑料杯

Styx, the /stɪks; stɪks/ in Greek MYTHOLOGY, a river in Hades. The souls of dead people were carried across it in a boat by Charon. 冥河，斯提克斯河，守誓河〔希腊神话中冥府的一条河。卡隆用船将亡灵运到河的彼岸〕

suave /swɑv; swɑːv/ *adj* someone who is suave is polite, confident, and relaxed, especially in an insincere way 温文尔雅的；自信而老于世故的: *a suave and sophisticated gentleman* 温文尔雅的绅士 —**suavely** *adv* —**suavity, suaveness** *n* [U]

sub- /sʌb; sʌb/ *prefix* **1** under; below 在…下面的: *subzero temperatures* 零度以下的温度 | *subsoil* (=beneath the surface)〔土壤的〕底土层 **2** less important or powerful than someone or something, or of lower rank than someone〔重要性或级别〕次于…，低于…: *a subcommittee*〔委员会下设的〕专门小组 | *a sublieutenant* 陆军少尉 **3** part of a bigger whole 分支: *a subsection* 分部 **4** used to say that something is like something else, but not as good or not real 仿，近似的: *dreary rows of sub-Victorian villas* 几排单调的仿维多利亚时代的花园别墅 **5** *technical* almost【术语】近于，亚: *subtropical heat* 亚热带的高温

sub¹ /sʌb; sʌb/ *n* [C] *informal*【非正式】**1** a SUBMARINE 潜水艇 **2** a SUBSTITUTE in sports such as football〔足球等体育运动的〕替补队员 **3** a SUBSCRIPTION 捐赠款；会费 **4** *BrE* part of your wages that you receive earlier than usual because you need money【英】〔工资中的〕预支款; ADVANCE¹ (4) *AmE*【美】**5** *AmE* a long bread roll split open and filled with meat, cheese etc【美】潜艇[大型]三明治〔长面包纵向切开，中间夹肉、干酪等〕**6** *AmE* a SUBSTITUTE TEACHER【美】代课教师 **7** *BrE* a SUBEDITOR【英】助理编辑，文字编辑

sub² *v* **subbed, subbing** *informal*【非正式】**1** [I **+for**] to act as a SUBSTITUTE for someone 代替；作替补队员 **2** [T] *BrE* to give someone part of their wages earlier than usual or lend them money【英】预支工资给…，预付；借钱给…: *I subbed Fenella a tenner to get a decent bunch of flowers.* 我预付给费内拉10英镑，去买一束像样的鲜花。**3** [T] *BrE* to SUBEDIT something【英】审校〔文稿〕，对〔稿件〕作文字加工

sub·al·tern /səbˈɔltən; ˈsʌbəltən/ *n* [C] a middle rank in the British army, or someone who has this rank〔英国〕陆军中尉(军衔)

sub·aq·ua /sʌb ˋækwə; sʌb ˈækwə/ *adj* [only before noun 仅用于名词前] *BrE* related to sports that take place under water 【英】水下运动的: *sub-aqua diving* 潜泳

sub·arc·tic /sʌbˋɑrktɪk; sʌbˈɑːktɪk◂/ *adj* near or typical of the Arctic Circle 近北极圈的; 亚北极区的

sub·a·tom·ic /ˌsʌbəˋtɑmɪk; ˌsʌbəˈtɒmɪk◂/ *adj* smaller than an atom or existing within an atom 亚原子的, 次原子的; 原子内的

sub·com·mit·tee /ˋsʌbkəˌmɪtɪ; ˈsʌbkəˌmɪti/ *n* [C] a small group formed from a committee to deal with a particular subject in more detail〔委员会下设的〕专门小组

sub·con·scious¹ /sʌbˋkɑnʃəs; sʌbˈkɒnʃəs/ *adj* subconscious feelings, desires etc are hidden in your mind and you do not know that you have them〔感觉、欲望等〕下意识的, 潜意识的: *a subconscious fear of failure* 对失败的潜意识恐惧 —**subconsciously** *adv*

subconscious² *n* [singular] the part of your mind that has thoughts and feelings you do not know about; UNCONSCIOUS² 下意识, 潜意识

sub·con·ti·nent /sʌbˋkɑntənənt; ˌsʌbˈkɒntɪ̣nənt/ *n* [C] **1** a very large area of land that is part of a CONTINENT 次大陆 **2 the subcontinent** *especially BrE* the area of land that includes India, Pakistan, and Bangladesh【尤英】印度次大陆〔包括印度、巴基斯坦和孟加拉国〕

sub·con·ti·nen·tal /ˌsʌbkɑntəˋnɛntḷ; ˌsʌbkɒntɪ̣ˈnentl◂/ *adj* *AmE* related to a subcontinent【美】次大陆的

sub·con·tract /sʌbˋkɑntrækt; ˌsʌbkənˈtrækt/ *v* [T] if a company subcontracts work, they pay other people to do part of their work for them 将〔已签合约的工作〕分包[转包]给〔他人〕: *We will be subcontracting most of the electrical work.* 我们将把大部分的电工活转包出去。—**subcontract** /sʌbˋkɑntrækt; sʌbˈkɒntrækt/ *n* [C]

sub·con·trac·tor /ˌsʌbˋkɑntræktɚ; ˌsʌbkənˈtræktə/ *n* [C] someone who does part of the work of another person or firm 分包者

sub·cul·ture /ˋsʌbˌkʌltʃɚ; ˈsʌbˌkʌltʃə/ *n* [C] a particular group of people within a society and their behaviour, beliefs, and activities, which many people disapprove of 亚文化群; 亚文化: *the drug subculture of the inner city* 旧城区的吸毒亚文化群

sub·cu·ta·ne·ous /ˌsʌbkjuˋtenɪəs; ˌsʌbkjuːˈteɪniəs◂/ *adj* *technical* beneath your skin【术语】皮下的: *subcutaneous fat* 皮下脂肪 —**subcutaneously** *adv*

sub·di·vide /ˌsʌbdəˋvaɪd; ˌsʌbdɪ̣ˈvaɪd/ *v* [T] to divide into smaller parts something that is already divided 把〔分过的东西〕再分, 重分, 细分: *The house was subdivided into apartments about ten years ago.* 这房子大约 10 年前被细分成一间间的公寓房。

sub·di·vi·sion /ˌsʌbdəˋvɪʒən; ˌsʌbdɪ̣ˈvɪʒən/ *n* **1** [C,U] the act of dividing something that has already been divided, or the parts that result from doing this 再分, 进一步细分; 进一步分成的部分 **2** [C] *AmE* an area of land that has been subdivided for building houses on【美】〔为建房而划分的〕一块土地

sub·due /səbˋdu; səbˈdjuː/ *v* [T] **1** to stop a person or group from behaving violently, especially by using force 镇压, 制伏: *Police managed to subdue the angry crowd.* 警察设法控制了愤怒的人群。**2** *formal* to prevent your emotions from showing【正式】克制, 抑制〔情绪〕: *Frank subdued his grief in order to comfort Cathy.* 为安慰凯茜, 弗兰克抑压住自己的悲痛。**3** *formal* to take control of a place by defeating the people who live there【正式】征服, 控制〔某地〕: *Napoleon subdued much of Europe.* 拿破仑征服了大半个欧洲。

sub·dued /səbˋdud; səbˈdjuːd/ *adj* **1** subdued lighting, colours etc are less bright than usual〔照明、颜色等〕柔和的, 不强烈的 **2** a person or sound that is subdued is unusually quiet〔人〕抑郁的, 沉默寡言的, 闷闷不乐的;〔声音〕压低的: *Richard seems very subdued tonight.* 理查德今晚似乎很消沉。**3** an event or business activity that is subdued does not have as much excitement or interest as you would expect〔事件、生意〕冷清的, 沉闷的: *The housing market is fairly subdued.* 住房市场相当萧条。

sub·ed·it /sʌbˋɛdɪt; ˌsʌbˈedɪ̣t/ *v* [T] *BrE* to examine other people's writing for mistakes and make them correct【英】审校〔文稿〕, 对…作文字加工; COPYEDIT *AmE*【美】

sub·ed·i·tor /sʌbˋɛdɪtɚ; ˌsʌbˈedɪ̣tə/ *n* [C] *BrE* someone whose job is to examine other people's writing, such as a newspaper article, and to change mistakes【英】助理编辑, 文字编辑

sub·group /ˋsʌbˌgrup; ˈsʌbgruːp/ *n* [C] a separate, smaller, and sometimes less important part of a group 小团体, 小集团, 小分组

sub·head·ing /ˋsʌbˌhɛdɪŋ; ˈsʌbˌhedɪŋ/ *n* [C] a short phrase used as a title for a small part within a longer piece of writing 副标题, 小标题

sub·hu·man /sʌbˋhjumən; sʌbˈhjuːmən/ *adj* behaving or thinking in a way that you do not expect from people, especially when this is very bad〔行为、思维〕低于人类的: *subhuman intelligence* 低于人的智能

Su·bic Bay /ˌsubɪk ˋbe; ˌsuːbɪk ˈbeɪ/ a large US military base in the Philippines 苏比克湾〔美国在菲律宾的一个大型军事基地〕

sub·ject¹ /ˋsʌbdʒɪkt; ˈsʌbdʒɪkt/ *n* [C] S2 W2

1 ▶THING TALKED ABOUT 谈论的东西◀ the thing you are talking about or considering in a conversation, discussion, book, film etc〔对话、讨论、书、电影等的〕主题, 题目; 话题: *Subjects covered in this chapter are exercise and nutrition.* 本章讨论的问题是运动和营养。| *Paul has strong opinions on most subjects.* 保罗在大多数话题上观点激烈。| **change the subject** (=start talking about something different) 改变话题 *Stop trying to change the subject!* 别想改变话题! | **get onto the subject (of)** (=start talking about it) 开始谈论…话题 *How did we get onto the subject of drugs?* 我们是怎样谈起毒品这个话题的? | **get off the subject (of)** (=start talking about something else instead of what you were supposed to be talking about) 离开…话题〔而谈论别的事情〕 *Somehow we got off the subject of homework altogether.* 不知怎的, 我们完全偏离了家庭作业的话题。| **be on the subject (of)** (=be talking about) 正在谈论…话题 *While we're on the subject of money, have you got the £10 you owe me?* 既然我们谈到了钱的问题, 你欠我的那 10 英镑现在能还我吗? | **be the subject of** (=be what is dealt with) 是…的主题 *Truffaut's childhood memories were the subject of his first film.* 特吕弗的童年记忆是他第一部电影的主题。| **be a subject of/for debate/discussion etc** *Genetic engineering is very much a subject for debate.* 基因工程是个很有争议的话题。

2 ▶ART 艺术◀ the thing you are dealing with when you paint a picture, take a photograph etc〔绘画、摄影等的〕主题: *Monet loved to use gardens as his subjects.* 莫奈喜欢以花园作为绘画的主题。

3 ▶SCHOOL 学校◀ an area of knowledge that you study at a school or university 学科, 科目; 课程: *My favourite subject at school was English.* 我上学时最喜欢的学科是英语。

4 ▶TEST 实验◀ a person or animal that is used in a test 实验对象, 接受实验的人[动物]: *The subjects of this experiment were all men aged 18-35.* 本实验的对象均为年龄在 18 至 35 岁的男性。

5 ▶GRAMMAR 语法◀ a noun, noun phrase, or PRONOUN that usually comes before a main verb and represents the person or thing that performs the action of the verb, or about which something is stated, such as 'She' in 'She hit John' or 'elephants' in 'Elephants are big'〔文法中的〕主语, 主词〈如 She hit John 中的 she, 或 Elephants are big 中的 elephants〉—compare 比较 OBJECT¹ (6)

6 ▶COUNTRY 国家◀ someone who was born in a country that has a king or queen, or someone who has a right to live there〔君主国的〕臣民, 国民: *a British subject* 英国国民 —compare 比较 CITIZEN (2), NATIONAL²

subject² *adj* **1** [not before noun 不用于名词前] likely to be affected by something, especially something unpleasant 易受…影响的; 易患…的: **[+to]** *areas subject to strong winds* 易受强风袭击的地区 | *Kieran is subject to fits of depression.* 基兰常患忧郁症。**2 subject to** dependent on something else 取决于…; 有待于…: *Your planning application is subject to review by the local council.* 你的建房申请有待当地议会的审查。**3** [only before noun 仅用于名词前] *formal* a subject country, state, people etc are strictly governed by another country【正式】〔国家、人民等〕被他人统治的, 受人管辖的

subject³ /səbˋdʒɛkt; səbˈdʒekt/ *v* [T] *formal* to force a country or group of people to be ruled by you and control them very strictly【正式】使隶属, 使顺从; 征服

subject sb/sth **to** sth *phr v* [T often passive 常用被动态] to force someone or something to experience something very unpleasant or difficult, especially over a long time 使遭受, 使经历, 使蒙受: *Barker subjected his victim to a terrifying ordeal.* 巴克使其受害者遭受痛苦的折磨。| **be subjected to** *All our products are subjected to rigorous testing.* 我们所有的产品都经过严格的检验。

sub·jec·tion /səbˋdʒɛkʃən; səbˈdʒekʃən/ *n* [U] *formal*【正式】**1** the act of forcing a country or group of people to be ruled by you 征服, 镇压; 强行统治: *Rome was intent on the subjection of the world.* 罗马曾试图征服全世界。**2 in subjection (to)** strictly controlled by someone 被(某人)严格控制, 受(某人)支配: *Grandfather kept the whole household in subjection to his wishes.* 爷爷让全家人都对他言听计从。

sub·jec·tive /səb`dʒɛktɪv; səb'dʒektɪv/ *adj* **1** a statement, report, attitude etc that is subjective is influenced by personal opinion and can therefore be unfair 主观的: *As a critic, his writing is far too subjective.* 作为评论家，他的文章太主观了。—opposite 反义词 OBJECTIVE² (1) **2** [no comparative 无比较级] existing only in your mind or imagination 主观想象的，只存在于想象之中的: *our subjective perception of colours* 我们对颜色的主观感知 **3** *technical* related to the subject in grammar【术语】主语的，〔文法中〕主词的 —**subjectively** *adv* —**subjectivity** /ˌsʌbdʒɛk`tɪvətɪ; ˌsʌbdʒek'tɪvəti/ *n* [U]

subject mat·ter /'·· ,··/ *n* [U] what is being talked about in speech or writing, or represented in art〔讲话、著作或艺术作品的〕题材；内容: *The movie has been rated 'R' due to adult subject matter.* 这部电影因其成人题材而被列为"限制级"。

sub·join /ˌsʌb`dʒɔɪn; ˌsʌb'dʒɔɪn/ *v* [T+to] *technical* to add a sentence or phrase at the end of a statement【术语】〔在末尾〕增补，补述，添加〔一句话等〕

sub ju·di·ce /sʌb `dʒudɪsɪ; ˌsʌb 'dʒuːdɪsi/ *adv* [only after verb 仅用于动词后] *law* a legal case being considered sub judice is now being dealt with by a court, and therefore is not allowed to be publicly discussed, for example in a newspaper【法律】〔司法案件〕在审理中的，尚未裁决的；〔因尚未裁决〕不准公诸于众的

sub·ju·gate /`sʌbdʒəˌget; 'sʌbdʒəgeɪt/ *v* [T] to defeat a person or group and make them obey you 使屈服，征服，降伏: *a subjugated people* 被征服的民族 —**subjugation** /ˌsʌbdʒə`geʃən; ˌsʌbdʒə'geɪʃən/ *n* [U]

sub·junc·tive /səb`dʒʌŋktɪv; səb'dʒʌŋktɪv/ *n* [C] a verb form or a set of verb forms in grammar, used in some languages to express doubt, wishes〔文法中〕假设语气，虚拟语气: *In 'if I were you' the verb 'to be' is in the subjunctive.* 在 if I were you 中动词 to be 是虚拟语气。—compare 比较 IMPERATIVE¹ (3), INDICATIVE² —**subjunctive** *adj*

sub·lease /`sʌbˌlis; 'sʌb-liːs/ *n* [C] an agreement in which someone who rents property from its owner then rents that property to someone else 转租，分租 —**sublease** /sʌb`lis; sʌb'liːs/ *v* [I,T]

sub·let /sʌb`lɛt; sʌb'let/ *v* **subletted, subletting** [I,T] to rent to someone else a property that you rent from its owner 将〔租来的物业〕转租，分租 —**sublet** /`sʌblɛt; 'sʌblet/ *n* [C]

sub·lieu·ten·ant /ˌsʌblu`tɛnənt; ˌsʌb-lə'tenənt/ *n* [C] a middle rank in the Royal Navy, or someone who has this rank 海军中尉 —see table on page C6 参见 C6 页附录

sub·li·mate /`sʌbləˌmet; 'sʌblɪmeɪt/ *v* [I,T] *technical* to use the energy that comes from sexual feelings to do something, such as work or art, that is more acceptable to your society【术语】(使)〔性欲〕转化为社会接受的行为；(使)升华，(使)高尚化

sub·li·ma·tion /ˌsʌblə`meʃən; ˌsʌblɪ'meɪʃən/ *n* [U] **1** the process of sublimating (SUBLIMATE) 净化，高尚化 **2** *technical* the process of changing a solid substance to a gas by heating it and then changing it back to a solid in order to make it pure【术语】升华，纯化

sub·lime¹ /sə`blaɪm; sə'blaɪm/ *adj* **1** excellent in a way that makes you feel extremely happy 卓越的，超群的；令人赞叹的: *We had a sublime view over the Mediterranean.* 我们在地中海上空看到令人叹为观止的景色。**2** not caring or thinking at all about the result of your actions 不顾后果的: *sublime insensitivity to other people's feelings* 完全不顾他人感受 —**sublimely** *adv* —**sublimeness** *n* [U] —**sublimity** /sə`blɪmətɪ; sə'blɪmɪti/ *n* [U]

sublime² *n* **1 the sublime** something that is excellent and makes you feel extremely happy 高尚，崇高；壮观，宏伟；庄严: *The sublime, unlike beauty, can inspire awe.* 与美不同的是，庄严使人敬畏。**2 from the sublime to the ridiculous** used to say that a serious and important thing or event is being followed by a silly thing or event〔指事物或事件〕从高超到荒谬，从一个极端到另一个极端: *First Hamlet, now pantomime? That's going from the sublime to the ridiculous.* 演完《哈姆雷特》后演童话剧？这太煞风景了。

sub·lim·i·nal /sʌb`lɪmənl; sʌb'lɪmɪnəl/ *adj* at a level of your mind that you are not conscious of 潜意识的，下意识的；潜在的: **subliminal messages** *Reverend Jones claims there are subliminal Satanic messages on that album.* 琼斯牧师声称，那张唱片中有潜在的邪恶信息。| **subliminal advertising** (=with hidden messages and pictures in it) 潜意识广告

sub·ma·chine gun /ˌsʌbmə`ʃin ˌgʌn; ˌsʌbmə'ʃiːn gʌn/ *n* [C] a type of MACHINE GUN that is light and easily moved 冲锋枪，轻机枪

submarine 潜(水)艇

sub·ma·rine¹ /`sʌbməˌrin; 'sʌbməriːn/ *n* [C] a ship, especially a military one, that can stay under water 潜(水)艇: *a nuclear submarine* 核潜艇

submarine² *adj technical* growing or used under the sea【术语】海底的，海中的；生于海底[海中]的；海底使用的: *submarine plant life* 海生植物

sub·mar·i·ner /ˌsʌbmə`rinɚ; sʌb'mærɪnə/ *n* [C] a sailor living and working in a submarine 潜水艇水手

submarine sand·wich /,··· '··/ *n* [C] *AmE* a SUB¹ (5)【美】潜艇[大型]三明治〔长面包纵向切开，中间夹肉、干酪等〕

sub·merge /səb`mɝdʒ; səb'mɜːdʒ/ *v* **1** [I,T] to go under the surface of water, or to put something under water or another liquid (使)潜入水中，(使)没入水中；(使)浸没；淹没: *The tunnel entrance was submerged by rising sea water.* 隧道入口被涨起的海水淹没。**2** [T] to cover or completely hide something 完全掩盖，遮掩；使完全消失: *Feelings she thought she'd submerged were surfacing again.* 她以为她已经掩饰的感情又显露了出来。**3 submerge yourself in sth** to make yourself very busy doing something 埋头于某事: *Alice submerged herself in work to try and forget about Tom.* 艾丽斯埋头工作，试图忘记汤姆。—**submergence** *n* [U]

sub·merged /səb`mɝdʒd; səb'mɜːdʒd/ *adj* just under the surface of water or another liquid 在水下的，没入液体中的: *submerged rocks* 没入水中的礁石

sub·mersed /səb`mɝst; səb'mɜːst/ *adj* submersed plants etc live under the water〔植物〕生长于水下的

sub·mer·si·ble /səb`mɝsəbl; səb'mɜːsɪbəl/ *n* [C] a vehicle that can travel under water 可潜入水中的交通工具

sub·mer·sion /səb`mɝʃən; səb'mɜːʃən/ *n* [U] the act of going under water, or the state of being completely covered in liquid 没入水中，浸没，淹没

sub·mis·sion /səb`mɪʃən; səb'mɪʃən/ *n* **1** [U] the state of being completely controlled by a person or group, and accepting that you have to obey them 屈服，屈从；顺从: **force/frighten etc sb into submission** *The prisoners were eventually starved into submission.* 囚犯们最终因饥饿被迫屈服了。| **in submission to** (=in obedience to) 顺从…，服从…，听从… *I offer my resignation in submission to your request.* 我按你的要求提交辞呈。**2** [C,U] the act of giving a plan, piece of writing etc to someone in authority for them to consider or approve, or the plan, piece of writing etc itself 提交(物)，呈递(书): *The deadline for the submission of proposals is May 1st.* 提交建议的最后期限是5月1日。**3** [U] *formal* an opinion or thought that you state【正式】意见，建议，看法: **in my submission** *It is important, in my submission, that a wider view be taken.* 我认为持更开明的见解是很重要的。**4** [C] *law* a request or suggestion that is given to a judge for them to consider【法律】提交仲裁的要求；提请考虑的建议 S2

sub·mis·sive /səb`mɪsɪv; səb'mɪsɪv/ *adj* always willing to obey someone even if they are unkind to you 服从的，顺从的；恭顺的: *Martin expects his wife to be meek and submissive.* 马丁期望妻子温顺，对他言听计从。—**submissively** *adv* —**submissiveness** *n* [U]

sub·mit /səb`mɪt; səb'mɪt/ *v* **submitted, submitting** **1** [I,T] to obey someone when you have no choice about it because they have power over you 顺从，服从；屈从: [+to] *I will not submit to your bullying.* 我不会屈服于你的欺侮。| **submit yourself to sb/sth** *Derek agreed to submit himself to questioning.* 德里克同意接受审问。**2** [T] to give a plan, piece of writing etc to someone in authority for them to consider or approve 呈送，提交，呈递〔计划等〕: *All applications must be submitted by Monday.* 所有申请必须在星期一前递交。**3** [T] *formal* to agree to obey a S2 W3

S

person, group, or set of rules【正式】同意服从[遵守]: **submit sth to** *We are willing to submit to arbitration.* 我们愿意接受仲裁。**4** [T] *formal* to suggest or say something【正式】建议, 主张: **submit that** *I submit that the jury has been influenced by the publicity in this case.* 我认为, 在本案的审理过程中, 陪审团受到了外界宣传的影响。

sub·nor·mal /sʌb`nɔrml; ˌsʌb'nɔːməl◂/ *adj* less or lower than normal 比正常少的, 低于正常的: *subnormal temperatures* 低于正常的温度

sub·or·bit·al /sʌb`ɔrbɪtl; sʌb'ɔːbɨtl/ *adj technical* making less than one complete ORBIT (=journey around the Earth)【术语】〔轨道〕不满一整圈的, 亚轨道的: *a suborbital space flight* 亚轨道太空飞行

sub·or·di·nate¹ /sə`bɔrdn̩ɪt; sə'bɔːdɨnət/ *adj* less important than something else, or in a lower position with less authority 次要的; 下级的; 从属的: *a subordinate role on the committee* 委员会中次要的角色 | [+to] *a commission that is subordinate to the Security Council* 隶属于安理会的委员会 —compare 比较 SUBSERVIENT

subordinate² *n* [C] someone who has a lower position and less authority than someone else in an organization 部下, 下级, 部属

sub·or·di·nate³ /sə`bɔrdəˌnet; sə'bɔːdɨneɪt/ *v* [T] to put someone or something in a less important position 使处于次要地位, 使从属于…: **subordinate sth to sb/sth** *Joe subordinated his wishes to those of the group.* 乔使自己的愿望服从于全组的愿望。—**subordination** /səˌbɔrdə`neʃən; səˌbɔːdɨ'neɪʃən/ *n* [U]

subordinate clause /·ˌ···'·/ *n* [C] a DEPENDENT CLAUSE 从句, 从属子句

sub·orn /sə`bɔrn; sə'bɔːn/ *v* [T] *law* to persuade someone to tell lies in a court of law or to do something else that is illegal, especially for money【法律】唆使; 收买〔某人〕作伪证[做其他非法的事] —**subornation** /ˌsʌbɔr`neʃən; ˌsʌbɔː'neɪʃən/ *n* [U]

sub·plot /`sʌbˌplɑt; 'sʌbplɒt/ *n* [C] a PLOT (=set of events) that is less important than and separate from the main plot in a story, play etc〔小说、剧本等的〕次要情节, 从属情节

sub·poe·na¹ /sə`pinə; sə'piːnə/ *n* [C] *law* a written order that you must come to a court of law and be a witness【法律】〔传唤出庭的〕传票

subpoena² *v past tense* **subpoenaed** [T] *law* to order someone to come to a court of law and be a witness【法律】用传票传唤〔某人〕出庭

sub-post of·fice /ˌ·'··,··/ *n* [C] a small British post office that has fewer services than a main post office〔英国的〕小邮局, 邮政所

sub·rou·tine /ˌsʌbru`tin; ˌsʌbruː'tiːn/ *n* [C] a part of a computer PROGRAM containing a set of instructions for doing a small job that is part of a larger job〔电脑的〕子程序

sub·scribe /səb`skraɪb; səb'skraɪb/ *v* **1** [I] to pay money regularly to have copies of a newspaper or magazine sent to you 订阅〔报纸或杂志〕: [+to] *What newspaper do you subscribe to?* 你订阅哪种报纸? **2** [I] *BrE* to pay money regularly to be a member of an organization or to help its work【英】定期缴纳会员费; 定期捐款赞助: [+to] *Chris subscribes to an environmental action group.* 克里斯定期捐款给一个环保行动组织。**3** [T] *BrE* to give money regularly for a service【英】〔为某项服务〕定期交费: *People in the office subscribe £1 a week for coffee.* 办公室的人每周出一英镑支付咖啡的费用。**4** [T] *formal* to sign your name【正式】签〔名〕: *Please subscribe your name to the document.* 请在文件上签名。

subscribe for sth *phr v* [T] to agree to buy or pay for shares (SHARE² (5)) 认购〔股票〕: *Each employee may subscribe for up to £2000 worth of shares.* 每个雇员可以认购价值不超过2000英镑的股票。

subscribe to sth *phr v* [T usually in questions and negatives 一般用于疑问句和否定句] if you subscribe to an idea, view etc, you agree with it or support it 同意, 赞同; 支持: *I have never subscribed to the view that schooldays are the happiest days of your life.* 我从来没有同意过校园生活是人生最快乐的日子的看法。

sub·scrib·er /səb`skraɪbɚ; səb'skraɪbə/ *n* [C] **1** someone who pays money regularly to receive copies of a newspaper or magazine〔报纸或杂志的〕订阅者, 订户 **2** *BrE* someone who pays money to be part of an organization or to help its work【英】〔某组织的〕会员;〔某项活动的〕赞助者 **3** *BrE* someone who gives money regularly for a service【英】〔某项服务的〕用户 **4** someone who signs their name on a document〔文件的〕签名者

sub·scrip·tion /səb`skrɪpʃən; səb'skrɪpʃən/ *n* [C] **1** an amount of money you pay regularly, especially once a year, to receive copies of a newspaper or magazine 订阅费 **2** *BrE* an amount of money you pay regularly to be a member of an organization or to help its work【英】会(员)费; 捐赠款

sub·sec·tion /sʌb`sɛkʃən; 'sʌbsekʃən/ *n* [C] a part of a SECTION 分部; 小节, 小段

sub·se·quent /`sʌbsɪˌkwɛnt; 'sʌbsɨkwənt/ *adj formal* coming after or following something else【正式】随后的, 继…之后的: *These skills were then passed on to subsequent generations.* 然后, 这些技术被传给了后代。| **subsequent to** (=after) 在…之后 *events that happened subsequent to the accident* 在那场事故之后发生的事情 —compare 比较 CONSEQUENT 2

sub·se·quent·ly /`sʌbsəkwəntlɪ; 'sʌbsɨkwəntli/ *adv formal* after an event in the past【正式】后来, 随后, 接着: *The book was subsequently translated into 15 languages.* 那本书后来被翻译成15种语言。 3

sub·ser·vi·ent /səb`sɝvɪənt; səb'sɜːviənt/ *adj* **1** someone who is subservient is too willing to do what other people want them to do 恭顺的, 屈从的, 卑躬屈膝的 **2** *formal* less important than something else; SUBORDINATE【正式】次要的, 从属的: [+to] *Your own needs must be subservient to those of the group.* 你个人的需要必须服从于团队的需要。—**subserviently** *adv* —**subservience** *n* [U]

sub·set /`sʌbˌsɛt; 'sʌbset/ *n* [C] a set that is part of a larger set 子集;〔大套中的〕一小套

sub·side /səb`saɪd; səb'saɪd/ *v* [I] **1** if a feeling or noise subsides, it gradually decreases〔情绪、噪声〕逐渐减弱; 平静下来, 平息: *Simon waited until the laughter subsided.* 西蒙一直等到笑声平息下来。**2** if a building subsides, it gradually sinks further into the ground〔建筑物〕沉降, 下陷 **3** if land subsides, its surface sinks to a lower level〔土地〕塌陷, 下陷: *After the heavy rains, part of the road subsided.* 大雨过后, 部分路段塌陷了。**4** if bad weather conditions subside, they gradually return to a normal state〔恶劣天气〕平息, 平静下来: *Then the wind subsided, and all was quiet.* 后来风渐渐停了, 一切又恢复了平静。

sub·si·dence /səb`saɪdn̩s; səb'saɪdəns/ *n* [C,U] the process by which land sinks to a lower level, or the state of land or buildings that have sunk〔建筑物的〕沉降;〔土地的〕塌陷, 下陷: *Is your house insured against subsidence?* 你给房子投保了沉降险吗?

sub·sid·i·ar·i·ty /səbˌsɪdɪ`ærɪtɪ; səbˌsɪdi'ærɨti/ *n* [U] a word meaning a political POLICY (1) in which more power, for example to make decisions, is given to a smaller group of people, used especially about the European Community giving power to its member countries 权力下放政策, 权力自主(原则)〔尤指给予欧盟各成员国更多自主权的政策〕

sub·sid·i·a·ry¹ /səb`sɪdɪˌɛrɪ; səb'sɪdiəri/ *n* [C] a company that is owned or controlled by another company 子公司, 附属公司: *a subsidiary of a US parent company* 美国总公司的一家子公司

subsidiary² *adj* connected with, but less important than, the main plan, subject, event etc 附带的, 附属的; 次要的: [+to] *The smaller workshops are subsidiary to the main conference.* 这些小规模的研讨会是这次主要会议的附带活动。

sub·si·dize also 又作 **-ise** *BrE*【英】/`sʌbsəˌdaɪz; 'sʌbsɨdaɪz/ *v* [T] to pay part of the cost of something so that the buyer can pay less for it 给…津贴[补贴]: *Farming is partly subsidized by the government.* 农业得到政府的部分补贴。—**subsidizer** *n* [C] —**subsidization** /ˌsʌbsədə`zeʃən; ˌsʌbsɨdaɪ'zeɪʃən/ *n* [U]

sub·si·dy /`sʌbsədɪ; 'sʌbsɨdi/ *n* [C] money that is paid by a government or organization to make prices lower, reduce the cost of producing goods etc〔政府或组织为平抑物价、降低生产成本等而发放的〕津贴, 补贴, 补助金: *international disagreement over trade subsidies* 有关贸易津贴的国际纠纷

sub·sist /səb`sɪst; səb'sɪst/ *v* [I] to stay alive on only small amounts of food or money〔以很少的食物或钱〕维持生活, 生存下去: [+on] *We had to subsist on bread and water.* 我们不得不靠面包和水维持生存。

sub·sis·tence /səb`sɪstəns; səb'sɪstəns/ *n* [U] **1** the ability to live with very little money or food〔以很少的食物或钱〕维持生活; 生存, 生计: *Not even subsistence is possible in such conditions.* 在这种条件下连维持生存都不可能。**2** a small amount of money or food that is just enough to survive 仅够维持生存的钱[食物]: **subsistence allowance** (=money given to you to live on) 仅够维持最低限度生活的补贴[津贴] | **subsistence diet** (=only enough food to keep living) 仅够维持生存的饮食 | **subsistence farmers** (=who produce just enough food to live on) 生产的粮食只够自己食用的农民

subsistence crop /·'···ˌ·/ *n* [C] a crop that is grown to be used by the farmer rather than to be sold〔农民生产只供自己食用的〕自给作物 —compare 比较 CASH CROP

sub·sis·tence lev·el /ˈ‥ ˌ‥/ *n* [singular] a very poor standard of living, which only provides the things that are completely necessary and nothing more 勉强糊口的生活水平: *Many of the poorer farmers live at subsistence level.* 许多穷苦的农民只能勉强糊口。

sub·soil /ˋsʌbˌsɔɪl; ˈsʌbsɔɪl/ *n* [U] the layer of soil between the surface and the lower layer of hard rock 下层土, 底土层, 心土

sub·son·ic /sʌbˋsɑnɪk; ˌsʌbˈsɒnɪk◂/ *adj* slower than the speed of sound 亚音速的: *subsonic flight* 亚音速飞行

sub·spe·cies /ˋsʌbˌspiʃiz; ˈsʌbˌspiːʃiːz/ *n* [C] a group of similar plants or animals that is smaller than a SPECIES〔动植物的〕亚种

sub·stance /ˋsʌbstəns; ˈsʌbstəns/ *n*
1 ▶MATERIAL 物质◀ [C] a type of solid or liquid that has particular characteristics 物质: *a sticky substance* 黏性物质, 胶黏物 | *radioactive substances* 放射性物质 | *Heroin is an illegal substance.* 海洛因是一种违禁品。
2 ▶IDEAS 思想◀ [singular,U] *formal* the most important ideas contained in an argument or piece of writing; ESSENCE (1)【正式】〔论点、著作的〕主旨, 主要内容; 真谛: **the substance of** *The substance of his argument was that too many people live below the poverty line.* 他的主要论点就是太多的人生活在贫困线之下。| **in substance** *What she said in substance was that the mayor must resign.* 她所说的中心意思就是市长必须辞职。
3 ▶IMPORTANCE 重要性◀ [U] *formal* importance, especially because of dealing with things that are necessary; SIGNIFICANCE【正式】重要性: *It was an entertaining speech, but without much substance.* (=without many important or serious ideas) 那是一篇吸引人的演讲, 但是没有多少实质内容。| **matters/issues of substance** *Instead of debating points of procedure, we should be discussing matters of substance.* 我们与其争辩程序问题, 还不如讨论一些实质性的东西。
4 ▶TRUTH 事实◀ [U usually in questions and negatives 一般用于疑问句和否定句] *formal* basic facts that are true【正式】事实: [+to] *There is no substance to the rumour that the princess is pregnant.* 公主怀孕的传言不是真的。| **without substance** (=untrue) 失实(的)
5 **substance abuse** *technical* the habit of taking too many drugs so that you are harmed by them【术语】药物滥用
6 **a man/woman of substance** *literary* a rich man or woman【文】富人, 有财产的人
7 ▶REAL 真实的◀ [U] something that really exists that you can feel 真实存在的事物: *phantoms without substance* 不真实的幻影

sub·stan·dard /sʌbˋstændɚd; ˌsʌbˈstændəd◂/ *adj* not as good as the average, and not acceptable 低于标准的, 次等的: *substandard housing* 不够标准的住房 —compare 比较 NON-STANDARD, STANDARD[2]

sub·stan·tial /səbˋstænʃəl; səbˈstænʃəl/ *adj* 1 large enough in amount or number to be noticeable or to have an important effect 大量的; 重要的; 有重要影响的: *The document requires substantial changes.* 该文件需要作重大修改。| *We have the support of a substantial number of parents.* 我们有许多家长的支持。2 large enough to be satisfactory 多的; 可观的: *a substantial salary* 可观的薪水 | *a substantial breakfast* 丰盛的早餐 3 large and strongly made 坚固的, 结实的: *a substantial mahogany desk* 坚固的红木书桌 4 *formal* having a lot of influence or power, usually because of wealth【正式】〔常指因富有而〕有影响力[权势]的: *a very substantial family in the wool trade* 羊毛业中一个举足轻重的家族

sub·stan·tial·ly /səbˋstænʃəlɪ; səbˈstænʃəli/ *adv* 1 when considering the most important parts 主要地; 大体上, 基本上: *There are one or two minor differences, but they're substantially the same text.* 这些文本有一两处小的差异, 但他们大体上是一样的。2 very much 大量地; 可观地: *substantially higher prices* 高出许多的价格

sub·stan·ti·ate /səbˋstænʃɪˌet; səbˈstænʃieɪt/ *v* [T] *formal* to prove the truth of something that someone has said, claimed etc【正式】证明, 证实: *Can you substantiate your claim in a court of law?* 你能在法庭上证明你声称的事是有根据的吗? —**substantiation** /səbˌstænʃɪˋeʃən; səbˌstænʃiˈeɪʃən/ *n* [U]

sub·stan·tive[1] /səbˋstæntɪv; səbˈstæntɪv/ *adj* 1 *formal* dealing with things that are important or real【正式】实质的; 真实的, 实际的: **substantive discussions** (=in which important matters are discussed) 实质性的讨论 2 *technical* expressing existence, in grammar【术语】〔语法中〕表示存在的: *The substantive verb is 'to be'.* to be 是表示存在的动词。3 [only before noun 仅用于名词前] *formal* real and continuing, rather than being only for a limited time【正式】永久的, 终身的: *the substantive rank of colonel* 终身的上校军衔 —**substantively** *adv*

sub·stan·tive[2] /ˋsʌbstəntɪv; ˈsʌbstəntɪv/ *n* [C] *technical* a noun【术语】名词 —**substantival** /ˌsʌbstənˋtaɪvḷ; ˌsʌbstənˈtaɪvəl◂/ *adj*

sub·sta·tion /ˋsʌbˌsteʃən; ˈsʌbˌsteɪʃən/ *n* [C] a place where electricity is passed on from the place that produces it into the main system 变电站, 变电所, 配电室

sub·sti·tute[1] /ˋsʌbstəˌtut; ˈsʌbstɨtjuːt/ *n* [C] 1 someone who does someone else's job for a limited period of time especially in a sports team or performance 代替者; 替补队员[演员]: *The lead singer was ill and her substitute wasn't nearly as good.* 主唱歌手病了, 替代她的演员远远比不上她。2 something new or different that you use instead of something else that you used previously 代替物, 替代品: *a sugar substitute* 糖的代用品 3 **be no substitute for sth** to not have the same good or desirable qualities as something or someone else 没有…那样好, 不如…称心: *Vitamin pills are no substitute for healthy eating.* 维生素片不能替代健康饮食。

substitute[2] *v* 1 [T] to use something new or different instead of something else 用〔新的或不同的事物〕代替: **substitute sth for/with sth** *You can substitute yogurt for the sour cream.* 你可以用酸奶代替酸味奶油。2 [I,T] to do someone's job until the person who usually does it is able to do it again 替代, 顶替; 替换: [+for] *Bill substituted for Larry who was off sick.* 拉里因病没有上班, 比尔替了他。

substitute teach·er /ˌ‥ ˈ‥ ‥/ *n* [C] *AmE* a teacher who teaches a class when the usual teacher is ill【美】代课教师; SUPPLY TEACHER *BrE*【英】

sub·sti·tu·tion /ˌsʌbstəˋtuʃən; ˌsʌbstɨˈtjuːʃən/ *n* [C,U] someone or something that you use instead of the person or thing you would usually use, or the act of using them 代替的人[物]; 代替, 替换: *Coach Packard made two substitutions in the second half.* 帕卡德教练在下半场两次换人。

sub·stra·tum /sʌbˋstretəm; ˌsʌbˈstrɑːtəm/ *n plural* **substrata** /-tə; -tə/ [C] 1 a layer that lies beneath another layer, especially in the earth〔尤指土壤的〕下层, 底(土)层: *a substratum of rock* 底层岩石 2 *formal* a quality that is hidden【正式】隐藏的特点: *a substratum of truth in the argument* 该论据中隐含的真实性

sub·struc·ture /ˋsʌbˌstrʌktʃɚ; ˈsʌbˌstrʌktʃə/ *n* [C] 1 one of the structures (STRUCTURE[1] (3)) within a society or organization that combines with others to form a whole〔组成社会或机构的〕基础, 下层结构 2 a solid base under the ground that supports a building above the ground〔支持地面建筑的〕基础, 下层结构, 地下建筑, 根基

sub·sume /səbˋsum; səbˈsjuːm/ *v* [T] *formal* to include someone or something as a member of a group or type, rather than considering it separately【正式】把…归入[纳入]某一类: **subsume sb/sth under sth** *For the purpose of the survey, typists are subsumed under office workers.* 为了便于调查, 打字员被算作办公室工作人员。

sub·ten·ant /sʌbˋtɛnənt; ˌsʌbˈtenənt/ *n* [C] someone who pays rent for an apartment, office etc to the person who is renting it from the owner〔公寓、办公室等的〕转租承租人, 次承租人 —**subtenancy** *n* [C,U]

sub·tend /səbˋtɛnd; səbˈtend/ *v* [T] *technical* to be opposite to a particular angle or ARC, and form the limits of it in GEOMETRY【术语】〔几何中〕对向〔某角或某弧度〕

sub·ter·fuge /ˋsʌbtɚˌfjudʒ; ˈsʌbtəfjuːdʒ/ *n* [C,U] *formal* a secret trick or slightly dishonest way of doing something, or the use of this【正式】花招, 诡计, 手段: *Sereni was lured to Moscow by subterfuge.* 塞雷尼被人施诡计引诱到了莫斯科。

sub·ter·ra·ne·an /ˌsʌbtəˋrenɪən; ˌsʌbtəˈreɪniən◂/ *adj* beneath the surface of the Earth 地下的, 地表下的: *subterranean passages* 地下通道

sub·text /ˋsʌbˌtɛkst; ˈsʌbtekst/ *n* [C] a hidden or second meaning in something that someone says or writes 潜在含义, 字面下的意思, 潜台词: *Whatever their text, the subtext is always this: political repression.* 不论他们的原文是什么, 潜台词总是这四个字: 政治镇压。

sub·ti·tle /ˋsʌbˌtaɪtḷ; ˈsʌbˌtaɪtl/ *n* [C] 1 **subtitles** [plural] the words printed over a film in a foreign language to translate what is being said by the actors〔外国电影的〕字幕, 对白译文: *a French film with English subtitles* 有英语字幕的法国电影 2 a less important title below the main title in a book 副标题, 小标题 —**subtitle** *v* [I,T]

sub·ti·tled /ˋsʌbˌtaɪtḷd; ˈsʌbˌtaɪtld/ *adj* having subtitles or a particular subtitle 有副标题的; 以…为副标题的

sub·tle /ˋsʌtl; ˈsʌtl/ *adj* **1** not easy to notice or understand unless you pay careful attention 难以捉摸[理解]的; 微妙的, 细微的: *a subtle flavor of oranges* 少许的橙子味 | *The pictures are similar, but there are subtle differences between them.* 这些图画很相似, 但它们之间有细微的差别。**2** someone who is subtle uses indirect methods to hide what they really want or intend to do 含蓄的, 隐晦的: *Hugo didn't even try to be subtle about it – he stared right at her.* 雨果毫不含蓄, 直直地看着她。**3** clever, especially in order to deceive people 狡猾的, 狡诈的: *a subtle plan* 巧妙狡猾的计划 **4** very clever in noticing and understanding things; SENSITIVE (1) 敏感的, 敏锐的; 有辨别力的: *a subtle mind* 敏锐的头脑 —**subtly** *adv*

sub·tle·ty /ˋsʌtḷtɪ; ˈsʌtlti/ *n* **1** [U] the quality of being subtle 敏锐, 机敏; 微妙, 巧妙; 狡猾: *She argued her case with considerable subtlety.* 她相当机敏地为自己的论点辩护。**2** [C usually plural 一般用复数] a thought, idea, or detail that is important but difficult to notice or understand 微妙的思想; 〔想法等中的〕细微之处: [+of] *Some of the subtleties of the language are lost in translation.* 语言中的一些微妙之处在译文中丢失了。

sub·to·tal /ˋsʌbˏtotḷ; ˈsʌbˌtəʊtl/ *n* [C] the total of a set of numbers, especially on a bill, that is added to other numbers to form a complete total 〔尤指账单上的〕小计, 部分累计数

sub·tract /səbˋtrækt; səbˈtrækt/ *v* [T] to take a number or an amount from something larger 减去, 减掉: **subtract sth from sth** *If you subtract 10 from 30 you get 20.* 30 减去 10 等于 20。—compare 比较 ADD (2), DEDUCT, MINUS[1] (1)

sub·trac·tion /səbˋtrækʃən; səbˈtrækʃən/ *n* [C] the act of subtracting 减; 减法 —compare 比较 ADDITION (4)

sub·trop·i·cal /sʌbˋtrɑpɪkḷ; ˌsʌbˈtrɒpɪkəl◂/ *adj* related to an area near to a tropical area, or typical of that area 副热带的, 亚热带的: *subtropical vegetation* 亚热带植被

S

sub·urb /ˋsʌbɝb; ˈsʌbɜːb/ *n* [C] an area away from the centre of a town or city, where a lot of people live 〔城镇的〕郊区, 近郊, 城郊住宅区: [+of] *Blackheath is a suburb of London.* 布莱克希斯是伦敦的一个郊区。| **the suburbs** (=this type of area) 市郊, 市郊住宅区 *a naive kid from the suburbs* 一个来自市郊的天真孩子

CULTURAL NOTE 文化注释

The STEREOTYPE of people who live in the suburbs is a married couple who go to the nearest city to work, and have two children, and a fairly new car. Most of the families own their home rather than rent it. Suburbia is generally considered to be a boring but safe place to live. 住在郊区的人给人的典型印象是去最近的城市上班的已婚夫妇, 有两个孩子和一辆比较新的汽车。多数家庭有自己的房子而不是租房子住。一般认为郊区是个乏味但安全的居住之地。

sub·ur·ban /səˋbɝbən; səˈbɜːbən/ *adj* **1** related to a suburb, or in a suburb 郊区的, 市郊的: *suburban life* 郊区的生活 | *suburban streets with houses that all look the same* 房屋一模一样的郊区街道 **2** boring and having very traditional beliefs and interests 乏味的; 古板的; 传统的: *suburban attitudes* 狭隘的态度

sub·ur·ban·ite /səˋbɝbənˏaɪt; səˈbɜːbənaɪt/ *n* [C] someone who lives in a suburb 郊区居民, 住在郊区的人

sub·ur·bi·a /səˋbɝbɪə; səˈbɜːbiə/ *n* [U] **1** the behaviour, opinions, and ways of living that are typical of people who live in a suburb 郊区人的行为、观念和生活方式; 郊区习俗: *middle-class suburbia* 郊区中产阶级的生活方式 **2** suburban areas in general 郊区

sub·ven·tion /səbˋvɛnʃən; səbˈvenʃən/ *n* [C] *formal* a gift of money for a special use 【正式】〔特殊用途的〕资助金; 补贴费; 津贴

sub·ver·sion /səbˋvɝʒən; səbˈvɜːʃən/ *n* [U] secret activities that are intended to encourage people to oppose the government 〔对政府的〕颠覆, 暗中破坏

sub·ver·sive[1] /səbˋvɝsɪv; səbˈvɜːsɪv/ *adj* ideas, activities etc that are subversive are often secret and intended to encourage people to oppose a government, religion etc 〔对政府、宗教等〕颠覆性的: *subversive political activities* 颠覆性政治活动 —**subversively** *adv* —**subversiveness** *n* [U]

subversive[2] *n* [C] someone who is subversive 颠覆分子, 破坏分子

sub·vert /səbˋvɝt; səbˈvɜːt/ *v* [T] *formal* 【正式】**1** to try to destroy the power and influence of a government or established system etc 颠覆; 暗中破坏〔现政府、现有制度等〕: *attempts to subvert the democratic process* 破坏民主进程的企图 **2** to destroy someone's beliefs or loyalty 腐蚀; 败坏; 使放弃〔信念、忠诚等〕

sub·way /ˋsʌbˏwe; ˈsʌbweɪ/ *n* [C] **1** *BrE* a path for people to walk under a road or railway 【英】〔公路或铁路下的〕地下通道, 地下人行道; UNDERPASS *AmE* 【美】 **2** *AmE* a railway that runs under the ground 【美】地下铁道, 地铁; UNDERGROUND[3] *BrE* 【英】

sub-ze·ro /ˌ·ˈ··◂/ *adj* below zero in temperature 〔温度〕零度以下的

suc·ceed /səkˋsid; səkˈsiːd/ *v*

1 ►**NOT FAIL** 没有失败◄[I] to do what you have tried or wanted to do 成功, 达成: *I'm sure you'll succeed if you work hard.* 你只要努力, 我肯定你会成功的。| **succeed in doing sth** *Negotiators have not yet succeeded in establishing a ceasefire.* 谈判者仍未达成停火协定。| **succeed only in doing sth** (=fail and do the opposite of what you had wanted) 取得相反的效果; 弄巧反拙 *You've only succeeded in upsetting your mother.* 你这样反而弄得你妈妈不高兴了。

2 ►**HAVE A GOOD RESULT** 取得好结果◄[I] to have the result or effect something was intended to have 达到目的, 取得预期效果: *The anti-smoking campaign has only partly succeeded.* 反吸烟运动只是部分地获得成功。

3 ►**REACH A HIGH POSITION** 升到高位◄[I] to do well in your job, especially because you have worked hard at it for a long time 〔在事业上〕取得成功, 功成名就: [+as] *I'm not sure he has the determination to succeed as an actor.* 我不敢肯定他有当一名出色演员的决心。| [+in] *Women need to be tough to succeed in the male-dominated world of business.* 在男性主宰的商界里, 妇女必须坚强才能取得成功。

4 ►**FOLLOW IN A POSITION** 继位◄[I,T] to be the next person to take a position or rank after someone else 接替; 继任; 继承: **succeed sb as sth** *Gingrich will succeed Foley as speaker of the house.* 金里奇将接替福利担任议院议长。

5 ►**REPLACE** 替代◄[T] *formal* to come after and replace something else 【正式】替代, 替换: *a new generation of computers designed to succeed their existing range* 为替代现有的电脑系列而设计的新一代电脑

6 nothing succeeds like success used to say that success often leads to even greater success 一事成, 事事成; 一顺百顺

suc·ceed·ing /səkˋsidɪŋ; səkˈsiːdɪŋ/ *adj* coming after something else 随后的, 接着的: *Over the succeeding weeks things went from bad to worse.* 在接下来的几个星期里, 情况越来越坏。

suc·cess /səkˋsɛs; səkˈses/ *n* **1** [U] the achieving of something you have been trying to do, with a good result 成功, 胜利, 成就: *success in a highly competitive market* 在竞争激烈的市场中取胜 | *She puts her success down to hard work and good luck.* 她认为自己的成功是由于努力和幸运。| **have success in doing sth** *Did you have any success in persuading Adam to come?* 你劝说亚当来成功了吗? **2** [C] something that has a good result or effect 成功的事, 达到目的的事: *The play was an overnight success.* 这部剧作一夜走红。| **a great/huge/big success** *Kathy's wedding shower was a great success.* 凯茜的结婚送礼会搞得极为成功。| **make a success of sth** *Dick's taken over a pub, I bet he makes a success of it.* 迪克接手开了一家酒吧, 我肯定他会取得成功。| **prove a success** (=become successful) 表明是成功的; 取得成功 **3** [C] someone who does very well in their job 成功者; 取得成就的人: [+in] *Janet is determined to be a success in whatever field she chooses.* 珍妮特下了决心, 不管自己选择什么行业都要做个成功者。| [+as] *Tony's been a great success as our new coach.* 作为我们的新教练, 托尼一直干得极为出色。**4 success story** someone or something that becomes successful in spite of difficulties 大获成功的人[事物]; 成功的范例: *Ewing has turned the business into a success story.* 尤因把公司经营得很成功。

suc·cess·ful /səkˋsɛsfəl; səkˈsesfəl/ *adj* **1** having the effect or result you intended 成功的; 如愿以偿的, 达到目的的: *Well, it wasn't a very successful meeting.* 哎, 那次会议不大成功。| **successful in doing sth** *Were you successful in persuading him to change his mind?* 你劝他改变主意, 他听了吗? **2** a successful business, film etc makes a lot of money 〔公司、影片等〕利润丰厚的, 非常赚钱的: *The show's had a pretty successful run.* 这戏相当成功, 已连演多场。**3** a successful person earns a lot of money or is very well known and respected 〔人〕有成就的; 赚钱多的; 出人头地的: *luxury apartments for the successful young executive* 供飞黄腾达的年轻高管居住的豪华公寓 | [+in] *successful in politics* 在政坛上飞黄腾达 —opposite 反义词 UNSUCCESSFUL —**successfully** *adv*

suc·ces·sion /səkˋsɛʃən; səkˈseʃən/ *n* **1 in succession** happening one after the other without anything different happening in between 连续不断; 一个接一个: *She won the championship four times in succession.* 她连续四次夺得冠军。| **in close/quick succession** (=quickly one after the other) 一个紧接一个

2 a succession of a number of people or things of the same kind following, coming or happening one after the other 连续不断的〔人或物〕: *A succession of visitors came to the door.* 登门造访者接踵而来。**3** [U] the act of taking over an office or position, or the right to be the next to take it 接替, 继承, 继任; 继承权: *If Prince Charles dies, the succession passes to his son.* 查尔斯王子如果去世, 继承权就传给他的儿子。| **succession to sth** *the queen's succession to the throne* 女王对王位的继承 —compare 比较 ACCESSION (1)

suc·ces·sive /sək`sɛsɪv; sək'sesɪv/ *adj* coming or following one after the other 连续的, 接连的, 相继的: *The hockey team has had five successive victories.* 这支曲棍球队已经连续五次获胜了。—**successively** *adv*

suc·ces·sor /sək`sɛsɚ; sək'sesə/ *n* [C] **1** someone who takes a position previously held by someone else 继承人; 继任者, 接班人: [+as] *His successor as chairman takes over next week.* 接替他担任主席的人下周上任。**2** *formal* a machine, system etc that exists after another one in a process of development【正式】〔机器、操作系统等的〕换代产品, 接替的事物: *the transistor's successor, the microchip* 晶体管的换代产品, 微晶片 —opposite 反义词 PREDECESSOR

suc·cinct /sək`sɪŋkt; sək'sɪŋkt/ *adj approving* clearly expressed in a few words【褒】言简意赅的, 简明扼要的, 简练的: *a very succinct explanation* 非常简明的解释 —**succinctly** *adv* —**succinctness** *n* [U]

suc·cor /`sʌkɚ; 'sʌkə/ *n* [U] the American spelling of SUCCOUR succour 的美式拼法 —**succor** *v* [T]

suc·co·tash /`sʌkə,tæʃ; 'sʌkətæʃ/ *n* [U] *AmE* a dish made from corn, beans, and TOMATOes cooked together【美】豆煮玉米〔用玉米、豆子和番茄一起煮成的食品〕

suc·cour¹ *BrE*【英】, **succor** *AmE*【美】/`sʌkɚ; 'sʌkə/ *n* [U] *literary* help that is given to someone who is having problems【文】救济, 援助, 救助

succour² *BrE*【英】, **succor** *AmE*【美】—*v* [T] *literary* to help someone who has problems【文】救济, 援助, 救助: *succouring the needy* 救济贫困的人们

suc·cu·bus /`sʌkjəbəs; 'sʌkjʊbəs/ *n plural* **succubi** /-baɪ; -baɪ/ [C] *literary* a female devil that has sex with a sleeping man【文】〔传说中与睡眠中的男子性交的〕女梦淫妖 —compare 比较 INCUBUS (2)

suc·cu·lent¹ /`sʌkjələnt; 'sʌkjʊlənt/ *adj* **1** juicy and delicious 多汁美味的: *a succulent steak* 美味多汁的牛排 **2** *technical* a succulent plant has thick soft leaves or stems that can hold a lot of liquid【术语】〔植物〕茎叶肥厚多水分的, 肉质的—**succulence** *n* [U]

succulent² *n* [C] *technical* a succulent plant such as a CACTUS【术语】肉质植物〈如仙人掌〉

suc·cumb /sə`kʌm; sə'kʌm/ *v* [I] *formal*【正式】**1** to stop opposing someone or something that is stronger than you, and allow them to take control 屈服, 屈从; 不再抵抗: *After an intense artillery bombardment the town finally succumbed.* 经过一番猛烈炮轰后, 该镇终于投降了。| **succumb to temptation** *Gina finally succumbed to temptation and had some ice cream.* 吉娜终于抵不住诱惑, 吃了一些冰激凌。**2** if you succumb to an illness you become very ill or die of it 病情加重; 〔因病而〕死

such¹ /sʌtʃ; sʌtʃ/ *predeterminer, determiner* **1** used to talk about a person, thing etc which is of the same kind as that which has already been mentioned 上述一类的, 诸如此类的, 这样的, 这类的〔用于指已提到的人或事物〕: *Such behavior is just not acceptable in this school.* 此类行为在本校是绝对不能接受的。| *The rules make it quite clear what should be done in such a situation.* 条例中明确规定在这种情况下应当如何处理。| [+as] *It was against such a background as this that the President made his speech.* 总统正是在这种背景下发表演说的。**2 such as** used when giving an example of something 像, 诸如, 例如〔用于举例〕: *The local community is still reliant on traditional industries such as farming and mining.* 当地仍然依赖务农和采矿之类的传统产业。| *"There are lots of ways to increase productivity." "Such as?"* "提高生产力的途径多得很。" "例如?" | **people/things etc such as** *professional people such as bank managers and solicitors* 诸如银行经理和事务律师一类的专业人士 **3 such a kind man/such tall women etc** used to emphasize how kind a man is, how tall particular women are etc 如此和善的男人/如此高大的女士等〔用于表示强调〕: *Did you have to buy such an expensive coat?* 你非得买这样昂贵的外套吗? | *You haven't invited Ron have you? He's such a bore.* 你没有邀请罗恩吧? 他可是够讨厌的。| *I've seen an eagle before, but never at such close quarters.* 我以前见过老鹰, 但从来没有离这么近看到过。| [+(that)] *It's such a tiny kitchen that I don't have to do much to keep it clean.* 这个厨房很小, 我不必太费事就可以把它保持清洁了。| *He's such an idiot, I don't even ask him to help any more.* 他这个人蠢得很, 我根本不会再找他帮忙了。**4 or some such person/thing etc** a person, thing etc like the one just mentioned 或诸如此类的人/东西等: *He said she looked scruffy, or made some such helpful comment.* 他说她看上去邋里邋遢, 并作了一些诸如此类的有益的点评。**5 such as it is/such as they are etc** *especially spoken* used when you do not think that something is good enough or impressive enough【尤口】虽然它不过如此/虽然它们不怎么样等: *You're welcome to borrow my car such as it is.* 欢迎你借用我的汽车, 虽然它不怎么样。**6 there's no such person/thing etc as** used to say that a particular person or thing does not exist 没有…这样的人/物等〔用于表示某一类人或物并不存在〕: *These days there's no such thing as a job for life.* 如今已经没有终身职位这种事儿了。**7 such...as** *formal or literary* used to emphasize that there is a small amount of something or that it is of poor quality【正式或文】…的那些; …的那种〔用于强调某物数量不多或质量不好〕: *Such food as they gave us was warm and nutritious.* 他们给我们的那些食物是热的, 而且有营养。

such² *pron* **1** used to talk about a person, thing, etc that is of the same kind as that which has already been mentioned 这样的人[事物], 上述的人[事物]〔用于指已提到的人或事物〕: *A Welsh victory had been predicted and such indeed was the result.* 有人预言威尔士队会获胜, 果然不出所料。**2 such...as/that** *formal or literary* used to give a reason or explanation for something【正式或文】到如此程度; 如此…以致〔用于给出理由或作解释〕: *The nature of the job was such that he felt obliged to tell no one about it.* 那种工作的性质就如此, 他觉得只好秘而不宣了。| *His manner was such as to offend everyone who he met.* 他态度如此恶劣, 以致到处得罪人。**3 and such** *spoken* and people or things like that【口】以及诸如此类的人[物]: *It won't be anything special, just a few cakes and sandwiches and such.* 不会有什么特别的东西, 只是几块蛋糕和三明治以及诸如此类的点心罢了。**4 not...as such** *spoken* used to say that something is not really what you are calling it【口】并不是真正的…, 并非名副其实的…〔用于表示某物名不副实〕: *There isn't a garden as such, just a little vegetable patch.* 那里并不是一个真正的菜园, 只是一小块菜地罢了。**5 such...as** *formal* those people or things of a particular group or kind【正式】凡是…; 那些…: *Such of you as wish to leave may do so now.* 你们想走的现在都可以走了。

such and such /`· · ,·/ *predeterminer spoken* a certain time, amount etc that is not named【口】某某; 这样那样的〔表示未具体指明的时间、数量等〕: *If they tell you to come on such and such a day, don't agree unless it's convenient.* 如果他们叫你在某一天来, 你若不方便就不要答应。

such·like¹ /`sʌtʃ,laɪk; 'sʌtʃlaɪk/ *pron spoken* things of that kind【口】这一类的事物, 诸如此类的东西: *Do you enjoy plays, films and suchlike?* 你喜欢看戏剧、电影这类东西吗?

suchlike² *adj* [only before noun 仅用于名词前] *spoken* of that kind; SIMILAR【口】这一类的, 诸如此类的, 类似的: *tennis and baseball and suchlike summer sports* 网球、棒球以及类似的夏季运动

suck¹ /sʌk; sʌk/ *v* [I,T]

1 ▶DRINK 喝◀ to take liquid into your mouth by tightening your lips into a small hole and using the muscles of your mouth to pull the liquid in 吸, 吮, 啜: **suck at sth** *a baby sucking at its mother's breast* 在妈妈怀里吃奶的婴儿 | **suck sth up** *Jennie sucked up the last bit of milkshake with her straw.* 珍妮用吸管喝完最后一点奶昔。

2 ▶PUT IN MOUTH 放在嘴里◀ to hold something in your mouth and pull on it with your tongue and lips 含在嘴里吮食: *Don't suck your thumb, dear!* 不要吮大拇指, 宝贝! | **suck on sth** *Lara's been sucking on that jawbreaker for half an hour.* 那块圆硬糖劳拉已经吮了半个钟头了。

3 ▶PULL 拉◀ to pull someone or something with great power and force to a particular place 抽, 吸; 以强大的吸力吞没, 把…卷入: [+down/into] *Something got sucked down into the boiler and clogged it.* 有个东西给吸进了锅炉里, 把它塞住了。| **suck sb under/along** *Be careful of rip tides! They'll suck you right under.* 当心急流! 它会把你直卷进海底的。

4 suck sb into sth to make someone become involved in a particular situation, event etc, especially a bad one 使某人卷入某事〔尤指坏事〕: *Gullible people can easily get sucked into religious cults.* 轻信的人很容易被引入邪教。

5 sth sucks *informal especially AmE* an impolite expression meaning that something is very bad in quality or that a situation is very bad【非正式, 尤美】某事物真差劲, 某事物糟透了: *Her acting sucks.* 她的演技糟透了。

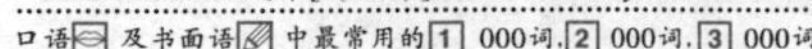

suck up *phr v* [I] *informal* to say or do a lot of nice things in order to make someone like you or to get what you want【非正式】奉承, 巴结, 拍马屁: **suck up to sb** *He's always sucking up to the boss.* 他总是拍老板的马屁。

suck² *n* [C] an act of sucking 吸, 吮, 啜

suck·er¹ /ˈsʌkɚ; ˈsʌkə/ *n* [C]

1 ▶**PERSON** 人◀ *informal* someone who is easily deceived, tricked, or persuaded to do something they do not want to do【非正式】容易上当受骗的人; 傻瓜: *You fell for that old line? Sucker!* 你居然相信了那一套骗人的老话? 真是大傻瓜!

2 **be a sucker for sth** to like something so much that you cannot refuse it 对某物入迷, 非常喜欢某物: *She's a real sucker for old movies.* 她非常爱看老电影。

3 ▶**PART OF AN ANIMAL** 动物身体的部位◀ *not technical* a part of an insect or of an animal's body that it uses to hold on to a surface【非术语】〔动物的〕吸盘: *Tree frogs have suckers on their feet.* 树蛙脚上有吸盘。

4 ▶**SWEET** 甜的◀ *AmE* a LOLLIPOP (2)【美】棒棒糖

5 ▶**PLANT** 植物◀ a part of a plant that grows from the root or lower stem of the plant to become a new plant 根出条〔从植物的根部或底部长出的新枝〕

6 ▶**RUBBER** 橡胶◀ a flat piece of rubber that sticks to a surface by SUCTION 橡皮吸盘

sucker² *v*

sucker sb **into** sth *phr v* [T] *AmE* to persuade someone to do something they do not want to do, especially by tricking them or lying to them【美】骗〔某人〕去做〔某事〕: **sucker sb into doing sth** *Laurie got suckered into babysitting her little sister.* 劳丽被哄去照看她的小妹妹。

suck·le /ˈsʌkḷ; ˈsʌkəl/ *v* **1** [T] to feed a baby or young animal with milk from the breast 给〔婴儿或小动物〕喂奶, 哺乳: *a sheep suckling her lamb* 给羊羔哺乳的绵羊 **2** [I] if a baby or young animal suckles, it sucks milk from a breast〔婴儿或小动物〕吮吸〔母乳〕, 吸奶 —compare 比较 BREASTFEED, NURSE² (6)

suck·ling /ˈsʌklɪŋ; ˈsʌklɪŋ/ *n* [C] *literary* a young human or animal still taking milk from its mother【文】乳儿; 乳兽

suckling pig /ˈ··· ·/ *n* [C] a young pig still taking milk from its mother, which is often cooked and eaten on special occasions 乳猪

su·crose /ˈsukros; ˈsuːkrəʊz/ *n* [U] *technical* the common form of sugar【术语】蔗糖 —compare 比较 FRUCTOSE, LACTOSE

suc·tion /ˈsʌkʃən; ˈsʌkʃən/ *n* [U] the process of removing air or liquid from an enclosed space so that another substance is sucked in, or so that two surfaces stick together〔对水或空气的〕吸, 抽吸, 吸出

suction cap /ˈ·· ·/ *BrE*【英】, **suction cup** *AmE*【美】*n* [C] a small round piece of rubber or plastic that sticks to a surface by suction 吸盘, 吸杯

suction pump /ˈ·· ·/ *n* [C] a pump that works by removing air from an enclosed space, so that the substance to be pumped is sucked in 抽吸泵, 真空泵

Su·dan /suˈdæn; suˈdæn/ also 又作 **the Sudan** a country in northeast Africa, south of Egypt and west of Ethiopia, which is the largest country in Africa. Population: 36,080,000 (2001). Capital: Khartoum. Sudan suffered from FAMINE (=serious lack of food) during the 1990s. 苏丹〔非洲东北部一国家。位于埃及以南、埃塞俄比亚以西, 是非洲最大的国家。人口: 36,080,000 (2001), 首都: 喀土穆。20 世纪 90 年代曾遭受严重饥荒〕—**Sudanese** *n, adj*

sud·den /ˈsʌdṇ; ˈsʌdn/ *adj* **1** happening, coming, or done quickly and unexpectedly 突然的, 忽然的, 迅速而意外的: *I keep having sudden bouts of dizziness.* 我总是突然觉得一阵阵的眩晕。| *a sudden change in temperature* 温度的突然变化 | *Marry you? Why, George, this is all so sudden!* 嫁给你? 啊哟, 乔治, 这太突然了! **2** **(all) of a sudden** suddenly 突然地, 突如其来地, 猛然地: *We were driving along, when all of a sudden a car pulled straight out in front of us.* 我们正开着车子往前走, 冷不防一辆汽车径直冲到我们前面。—**suddenness** *n* [U]

sudden death /ˌ·· ˈ·/ *n* [U] if a game goes into sudden death, it continues after its usual ending time until one player or team gains the lead and wins 突然死亡法〔指加时赛以先得分者为胜方的决胜方法〕

sud·den·ly /ˈsʌdṇlɪ; ˈsʌdnli/ *adv* quickly and unexpectedly 迅速而意外地, 突然地, 突如其来地: *Suddenly there was a huge bang.* 突然传来一声巨响。| *George died very suddenly.* 乔治死得非常突然。

Su·de·ten·land /suˈdetṇlænd; suːˈdeɪtənlænd/ an area in the northwest of the Czech Republic which Hitler attacked and took control of in 1938, just before World War II 苏台德区〔捷克共和国西北部一地区。1938 年二战爆发前夕被希特勒军队袭击和控制〕

suds /sʌdz; sʌdz/ *n* [plural] **1** the mass of BUBBLES (BUBBLE¹ (1)) formed on the top of water with soap in it 一团肥皂泡, 肥皂泡沫 **2** *AmE informal* beer【美, 非正式】啤酒 —**sudsy** *adj*

sue /su; sjuː/ *v* [I,T] to make a legal claim against someone, especially for an amount of money, because you have been harmed in some way〔尤指为要求赔偿损失而〕控告, 起诉, 告…的状: *If the builders don't fulfil their side of the contract, we'll sue.* 如果建筑商一方不履行合同, 我们就要提出诉讼。| **sue sb for libel/negligence/malpractice etc** (=because of something they have done wrong) 控告某人诽谤/玩忽职守/渎职等 *Elton John sued a newspaper for libel.* 埃尔顿·约翰控告一家报社诽谤。| **sue sb for £100,000/damages** (=in order to get money) 对某人提起诉讼, 索赔 10 万英镑/索要赔偿金 *I'll sue them for every penny they've got.* 被他们弄去的每一分钱我都要打官司拿回来。| **sue sb for divorce** (=in order to end a marriage) 对某人提出诉讼要求离婚

sue for sth *phr v* [T] *formal* to BEG or ask for something【正式】乞求; 要求: **sue for peace** *The rebels were forced to sue for peace.* 叛乱分子被迫要求和解。

> **CULTURAL NOTE 文化注释**
>
> The practice of suing people and organizations is called LITIGATION and is especially common in the US. Typical examples include drivers who have been sued for causing road accidents, and doctors who have been sued by PATIENTS who believe that they have not received good medical treatment. Sometimes people have sued and won large amounts of money for reasons that seem silly to many people, such as suing a restaurant because its coffee was too hot. Suing is rarer in the UK, but it is becoming more common. 起诉个人或团体的行为被称为诉讼, 尤其常见于美国。典型的诉讼有: 司机导致了交通事故被起诉, 医生被病人起诉没有给予他们良好的治疗。有时人们通过起诉赢得一大笔钱, 而他们起诉的理由看起来有些荒诞可笑, 例如起诉饭店说咖啡太烫。英国的起诉要少很多, 但现在正逐渐变得普遍起来。

suede /swed; sweɪd/ *n* [U] soft leather with a slightly rough surface〔外表略粗糙而料子柔软的〕绒面革, 软皮革: *suede shoes* 绒面革皮鞋 —see picture on page A16 参见 A16 页图

su·et /ˈsuɪt; ˈsuːɪt/ *n* [U] hard fat from around an animal's KIDNEYS, used in cooking〔动物腰部的〕板油, 硬脂肪油〔用于烹调〕—**suety** *adj*

Suez Ca·nal, the /suˌɛz kəˈnæl; ˌsuːɪz kəˈnæl/ a CANAL (=artificial river) in northeast Egypt which was opened in 1869 and which joins the Mediterranean Sea with the Gulf of Suez and the Red Sea. It is used by ships going between Europe and the Indian Ocean. 苏伊士运河〔埃及东北部一运河。连接地中海与苏伊士湾和红海, 1869 年贯通, 供来往于欧洲和印度洋之间的船只通行〕

Suez Cri·sis, the /ˈ·· , ·ˈ·/ the events in 1956 that followed the decision by the government of Egypt to take control of the Suez Canal. Before this, the canal was owned and operated by a foreign company. When Egypt took control, the UK and France sent ships and soldiers to the area to try to get the canal back. This attempt failed, and it was criticized by most other countries, including the US and the former Soviet Union. The British and French forces left Egypt after a few months, and the British Prime Minister, Anthony Eden, gave up his position as a result of this. For many people in the UK, the Suez Crisis was a serious defeat and a sign that the UK was no longer an important international power. In the UK, the Suez Crisis is often simply called Suez. 苏伊士运河危机〔1956 年埃及政府决定控制苏伊士运河而引发的一系列事件。在此之前, 苏伊士运河为一家外国公司所有和经营。埃及政府接管运河时, 英、法两国向该地派遣军舰和部队, 试图夺回运河控制权, 但以失败告终, 并遭到包括美国和前苏联在内的大多数国家的抨击。数月之后, 英、法军队撤离埃及, 英国首相安东尼·艾登因此而辞职。对许多英国人来说, 苏伊士运河危机是一次惨败, 是英国从此丧失世界大国地位的标志。在英国, 苏伊士运河危机一般简称 Suez (苏伊士)〕

suf·fer /ˈsʌfɚ; ˈsʌfə/ *v* 

1 ▶**PAIN** 疼痛◀ [I,T] to experience physical or mental pain 感到疼痛; 遭受痛苦; 蒙受, 遭受: *At least he died suddenly and didn't suffer.* 起码他死得很突然, 没有遭受痛苦。| [**+from**] *Simon suffers from migraines.* 西蒙患有偏头痛。| **I/you/she will suffer for it** (=will feel very ill or sore) 我/你/她会因此而吃苦头 *I know I'll suffer for it in the morning, but give me another*

gin. 我知道我明天早上会因此而难受，不过，还是再给我来一杯杜松子酒吧。

2 ▶BAD SITUATION 不好的形势◀ [I,T] to be in a very bad situation that makes things very difficult for you 遭受困难，吃苦头，受损害：*Small businesses have suffered financially during the recession.* 小公司在经济不景气期间遭受了经济损失。| **suffer the consequences** (=be punished) 承担后果，受到惩罚 *If you break the law, you must be prepared to suffer the consequences.* 如果你犯法，你就要准备为此承担后果。

3 ▶EXPERIENCE 经历◀ [T] if someone suffers an unpleasant or difficult experience, it happens to them 经受，经历〔不愉快或困难的事〕：**suffer a defeat** *The Democrats have just suffered a huge defeat in the polls.* 民主党刚在选举中遭到了惨败。| **suffer damage/injury/loss** *The car suffered severe damage in the accident.* 汽车在事故中受到严重损坏。

4 ▶WORSE 更坏◀ [I] to become worse in quality because a bad situation is affecting something or because nobody is taking care of it 变差，变坏，变糟：*The ferry operators denied that safety would suffer if costs were cut.* 渡轮经营者否认降低成本就会影响安全的说法。

5 not suffer fools gladly to not be patient with people you think are stupid 对愚蠢的人没有耐心，不能耐着性子与蠢人相处 **6 suffer sb to do sth** *old use* to allow someone to do something【旧】容许某人做某事

suf·fer·ance /ˋsʌfrəns; ˈsʌfərəns/ *n* **on sufferance** *formal* if you live or work somewhere on sufferance, you are allowed to do it by someone who would rather you did not do it【正式】勉强〔被容许〕地：*Martha made it clear I was only staying with them on sufferance.* 玛尔塔说得很清楚，我只是勉强被容许和他们住在一起。

suf·fer·er /ˋsʌfərə; ˈsʌfərə/ *n* [C] someone who suffers, especially from a particular illness 受害者，受苦者；〔尤指某种疾病的〕患者：*a huge increase in the number of asthma sufferers* 哮喘患者的剧增

suf·fer·ing /ˋsʌfrɪŋ; ˈsʌfərɪŋ/ *n* [C,U] physical or mental pain and difficulty, or an experience of this〔肉体或精神上的〕痛苦；痛苦经历：*the suffering of innocent people during a war* 无辜人民在战争期间遭受的痛苦

suf·fice /səˋfaɪs; səˈfaɪs/ *v* [not in progressive 不用进行时] **1** [I] *formal* to be enough【正式】足够，满足…的需要：*A light lunch will suffice.* 少量的午餐就够了。| **suffice to do sth** *Two examples should suffice to illustrate my point.* 举两个例子就足以说明我的观点了。**2 suffice (it) to say (that)** used to say that the statement that follows is enough to explain what you mean, even though you could say more 只要说…就够了：*Suffice to say it was a local person who called the police.* 就说是一个当地人给警方打的电话，其他的就不必多说了。**3** [T] *formal* to be enough to satisfy someone【正式】足够〔某人〕之用，使满足：*Just some bread and soup will suffice me.* 我只要点面包和汤就够了。

suf·fi·cien·cy /səˋfɪʃənsɪ; səˈfɪʃənsi/ *n formal*【正式】**1** [U] the state of being or having enough 足够，充足 **2 a sufficiency of** a supply that is enough 足够的供应；足够的量：*Eating fruit should ensure a sufficiency of Vitamin C.* 吃水果应能保证维生素C的足量补充。

suf·fi·cient /səˋfɪʃənt; səˈfɪʃənt/ *adj formal* as much as is needed for a particular purpose; enough【正式】足够的，充足的：*We can only prosecute if there is sufficient evidence.* 我们只有在证据充足时才能提出起诉。| **sufficient to do sth** *His income is sufficient to keep him comfortable.* 他的收入足够供他舒适地生活。| [+for] *There is sufficient food for everyone.* 有足够的食物供所有人吃。—opposite 反义词 INSUFFICIENT —see 见 ADEQUATE (USAGE)

suf·fix /ˋsʌfɪks; ˈsʌfɪks/ *n* [C] a letter or letters added to the end of a word to form a new word 后缀，词尾：*You can add the suffix 'ness' to the word 'kind' to form 'kindness'.* 在kind后加后缀ness可以构成kindness。—see also 另见 AFFIX —compare 比较 PREFIX[1] (1)

suf·fo·cate /ˋsʌfəˌket; ˈsʌfəkeɪt/ *v* **1** [I,T] to die or make someone die by preventing them from breathing (使)窒息而死，(使)闷死：*She rolled onto her baby and actually suffocated it!* 她翻身压在婴儿身上，竟把宝宝闷死了！**2 be suffocating** to feel uncomfortable because there is not enough fresh air 感到窒息，感到呼吸困难：*Can you open a window? I'm suffocating.* 请你打开窗户好吗？我觉得很闷。**3** [T] to prevent a relationship, plan, business etc from developing well or being successful 压制，扼杀，阻碍：*Jealousy can suffocate any relationship.* 妒忌可以扼杀任何人际关系。—**suffocation** /ˌsʌfəˋkeʃən; ˌsʌfəˈkeɪʃən/ *n* [U]

Suf·folk /ˋsʌfək; ˈsʌfək/ a COUNTY on the east coast of southeast England. It has no big cities, and its countryside can be seen in the paintings of the 19th century artist John Constable. 萨福克〔英格兰东南部东海岸一郡。境内无大城市，秀丽的乡村景色在19世纪英国画家约翰·康斯坦布尔的作品中可见一斑〕

suf·fra·gan /ˋsʌfrəgən; ˈsʌfrəgən/ *adj* [only before noun 仅用于名词前] a suffragan BISHOP (1) helps another bishop of higher rank in their work〔指主教〕协助上级主教的，副的 —**suffragan** *n* [C]

suf·frage /ˋsʌfrɪdʒ; ˈsʌfrɪdʒ/ *n* [U] the right to vote in national elections 选举权，投票权

> **CULTURAL NOTE 文化注释**
>
> In the UK, women were first allowed to vote in 1918, but only if they were over 30 years old. Women over 21 were finally allowed to vote in 1928. In the US, women were allowed to vote from 1920. 英国1918年首次给予女性选举权，但规定年龄必须在30岁以上。1928年终于授予年龄21岁以上的女性选举权。美国从1920年开始女性就拥有选举权。

suf·fra·gette /ˌsʌfrəˋdʒɛt; ˌsʌfrəˈdʒet/ *n* [C] a woman who tried to gain the right to vote for women especially as a member of a group in Britain or the US in the early 20th century 为妇女争取选举权的女子〔尤指20世纪初英国或美国某团体的成员〕

suffragette为妇女争取选举权的女子

suf·fuse /səˋfjuz; səˈfjuːz/ *v* [T] *especially literary* if warmth, colour, liquid etc suffuses something or someone, it covers or spreads through them【尤文】〔温暖、颜色、液体等〕充满，布满，弥漫于：*The light of the setting sun suffused the clouds.* 夕阳映红了浮云。—**suffusion** /səˋfjuʒən; səˈfjuːʒən/ *n* [U]

sug·ar[1] /ˋʃʊgə; ˈʃʊgə/ *n* **1** [U] a sweet white or brown substance that is obtained from plants and used to sweeten food and drinks 食糖〈如白糖、红糖〉：*Do you take sugar in your coffee?* 你喝咖啡加糖吗？**2** [C] the amount of sugar that a small spoon can hold 一茶匙的糖：*How many sugars do you want in your tea?* 你的茶里要放几茶匙糖？**3** *technical* one of several sweet substances formed in plants【术语】糖〔植物中形成的甜味物质〕—compare 比较 GLUCOSE **4** *BrE spoken* used to address someone you like very much【英口】亲爱的，心肝，宝贝〔用于称呼自己非常喜爱的人〕**5 (oh) sugar!** *spoken especially BrE* used when you are very annoyed about something stupid that you have just done, or when something goes wrong【口，尤英】(噢)糟了！(哦)真糟糕！〔用于因做了蠢事感到恼火或某事出了麻烦之时〕

sugar[2] *v* [T] **1** to add sugar or cover something with sugar; SWEETEN (1) 加糖于，裹糖于…上：*Did you sugar my coffee?* 你给我的咖啡加糖了吗？**2 sugar the pill** *especially BrE* to do something that makes an order, activity etc less unpleasant【尤英】把苦药包上糖衣；降低〔某项命令、活动等〕令人讨厌的程度 —**sugared** *adj*: *sugared almonds* 糖杏仁

sugar beet /ˋ‥ ˏ/ *n* [U] a vegetable that grows under the ground from which sugar is obtained; BEET (1)〔制糖用的〕甜菜，糖萝卜

Sugar Bowl, the /ˋ‥ ˏ/ an important college football game held every year in New Orleans, Louisiana 蔗糖杯赛〔每年在美国路易斯安那州新奥尔良进行的高校橄榄球大赛〕

sug·ar·cane /ˋʃʊgəˌken; ˈʃʊgəkeɪn/ *n* [U] a tall tropical plant from whose stems sugar is obtained 甘蔗

sugar-coat·ed /ˌ‥ˈ‥◂/ *adj* **1** covered with sugar 裹糖的，包有糖衣的 **2** made to seem better than something really is 粉饰过的：*I'm tired of hearing Fred's sugar-coated promises.* 我已经听腻了弗雷德那些甜言蜜语的许诺。

sugar cube /ˋ‥ ˏ/ *n* [C] a sugar lump 方糖

sugar dad·dy /ˋ‥ ˌ‥/ *n* [C] *informal* an older man who gives a young woman presents and money in return for her company and often for sex【非正式】〔以礼物和金钱换取年轻女人陪伴或性好处的〕老色迷，阔干爹，甜爹

Sug·ar·loaf Moun·tain /ˌʃʊgəlof ˋmaʊntn; ʃʊgələʊf ˈmaʊntɪn/ a mountain in Rio de Janeiro in southeast Brazil 塔糖峰，面包山〔巴西东南部里约热内卢的一座山〕

sugar lump /ˈ· · ˌ·/ *n* [C] *especially BrE* a square piece of solid sugar【尤英】方糖

sugar ma·ple /ˈ· · ,· ·/ *n* [C] a kind of MAPLE tree that grows in North America whose SAP (=liquid from the tree) is used to make MAPLE SYRUP 糖槭〔产于北美，其树液可制成槭糖浆〕

sug·ar·y /ˈʃʊgəri; ˈʃʊgəri/ *adj* **1** containing sugar or tasting like sugar 含糖的，甜的：*sugary snacks* 甜点心 **2** language, emotions etc that are sugary are too nice and seem insincere〔语言、情感等〕过于甜蜜的，媚人的，甜言蜜语的：*songs full of sugary sentiments about love* 充满柔情蜜意的歌曲

sug·gest /səgˈdʒɛst; səˈdʒest/ *v* [T] **1** to tell someone your ideas about what they should do, where they should go etc 建议，提议：*If this is not convenient, please suggest another date.* 要是这个日期不方便，那就请另选一个日子吧。| **suggest doing sth** *John suggested going together in one car.* 约翰建议大家坐同一辆汽车去。| **suggest (that)** *She suggested that we write that into the contract.* 她建议我们把那一点写进合同。| **can/may I suggest** (=used to politely suggest a different idea) 我可以提个建议…吗？〔用于客气地表示不同的想法〕*May I suggest that you see a financial advisor?* 我可否建议你去找个理财顾问咨询一下？| **suggest how/where etc** *Can you suggest where to stay in Rio?* 你能建议在里约热内卢住什么地方吗？—see 见 PROPOSE (USAGE) **2** to tell someone about a suitable person for a job 推荐〔某职务的合适人选〕：**suggest sb for** *Mr Roberts Guarino has been suggested for the post of director.* 罗伯茨·瓜里诺先生已被推荐担任主任一职。**3** to make someone think that a particular thing is true; INDICATE (1) 显示，间接表明；暗示：*The actual number of rapes may be higher than the statistics suggest.* 实际的强奸数字可能要比统计资料所显示的更高。| [+(that)] *There was nothing to suggest that she intended to kill herself.* 没有任何迹象显示她有意自杀。**4** to make someone have a new idea 使产生〔新想法〕；启发：**suggest sth to sb** *It was a magazine article that suggested the idea to me.* 是杂志上的一篇文章使我产生这个想法的。**5 I'm not suggesting** *spoken* used to say that what you are going to say is not meant to criticize someone as much as it may seem【口】我并不是说〔用于表示自己并非要强烈批评某人〕：*I'm not suggesting that you are lying, but it is very misleading.* 我并不是说你在撒谎，但你的话误导性很强。**6** to remind someone of something or help them to imagine it 使人想起；使人联想到：*The stage was bare, with only the lighting to suggest a prison.* 舞台上空无一物，只有灯光使人联想到监狱。

sug·ges·ti·ble /səgˈdʒɛstəbl; səˈdʒestɨbəl/ *adj* easily influenced by other people or by things you see and hear 易受影响的：**highly/very suggestible** *At that age, kids are highly suggestible.* 小孩在那种年龄非常容易受影响。

sug·ges·tion /səgˈdʒɛstʃən; səˈdʒestʃən/ *n* **1** [C] an idea, plan, or possibility that someone mentions 建议，提议，意见：**have a suggestion** *We've had several suggestions on a name for the baby.* 我们已经得到好几个关于给宝宝取个什么名字的建议了。| **make a suggestion** *Can I just make one suggestion about how we might do this?* 关于如何做此事，我能否提一个建议？| [+that] *He rejected my suggestion that we appoint Roger.* 他拒绝了我提出的我们应任命罗杰的建议。—see 见 PROPOSE (USAGE) **2 a suggestion of** a slight amount of something 微量的…；…的迹象：*There was just a suggestion of a smile on her face.* 她脸上微微露出一丝笑意。**3** [U] the act of telling someone your idea about what they should do 提议，建议：**at sb's suggestion** (=because someone suggested something) 由于某人的提议，根据某人的建议 *At her father's suggestion, she left Paris and returned home.* 根据父亲的建议，她离开巴黎回到了家中。| **open to suggestions** (=willing to listen to ideas) 愿意听取意见；欢迎提建议 **4 suggestion that/of** [usually in questions and negatives 一般用于疑问句及否定句] a slight possibility 些微的可能；细微的迹象：*There was never any suggestion of criminal involvement.* 没有发现涉及犯罪的任何迹象。**5** [U] an indirect way of making you accept an idea, for example by HYPNOTISM 通过间接方式〈如催眠术〉作出的暗示，示意

sug·ges·tive /səgˈdʒɛstɪv; səˈdʒestɪv/ *adj* **1** a remark, behaviour etc that is suggestive makes you think of sex〔话语、行为等〕挑动色情的，性挑逗[暗示]的 **2** reminding you of something 暗示的；示意的；启发的；引起联想的：**suggestive of sth** *an abstract painting suggestive of a desert landscape* 一幅使人联想起荒漠景色的抽象画 —**suggestively** *adv* —**suggestiveness** *n* [U]

Su·har·to /suˈharto; suːˈhɑːtəʊ/, **T. N. J.** (1921-2008) the President of Indonesia from 1967 to 1998. In the late 1990s, when Indonesia experienced serious economic problems, there were many public protests against his government, and he agreed to give up his position as President. 苏哈托〔(1921-2008)，1967 至 1998 年任印度尼西亚总统。20 世纪 90 年代晚期，印尼经济出现严重问题，反政府抗议活动此起彼伏，苏哈托被迫同意辞职〕

su·i·cid·al /ˌsuəˈsaɪdl; ˌsuːɨˈsaɪdl◂/ *adj* **1** wanting to kill yourself 想自杀的，有自杀倾向的：*After his wife left him he was suicidal.* 在妻子离他而去之后，他很想自杀。| **suicidal tendencies** *For many years before treatment, Clare had suicidal tendencies.* 在治疗前许多年，克莱尔曾有自杀倾向。**2** likely to lead to death 自杀性的；可能导致死亡的：*the suicidal challenge of jumping over 50 cars on a motorcycle* 骑摩托车跃过 50 辆汽车的玩命逞强之举 **3** likely to lead to a lot of damage or trouble 可能造成大破坏[麻烦]的：*It would be suicidal for the senator to oppose this policy.* 如果反对这项政策，这位参议员将会自毁前程。

su·i·cide /ˈsuəˌsaɪd; ˈsuːɨsaɪd/ *n* [C,U] **1** the act of killing yourself 自杀：**attempt suicide** (=try to kill yourself) 企图自杀 | **commit suicide** (=kill yourself) 自杀 *Gill committed suicide last year after losing her job.* 吉尔去年失业之后自杀了。—see 见 KILL[1] (USAGE) **2 political/social suicide** something you do that ruins your good position in politics or society 断送自己政治前程/社会地位之举

suicide pact /ˈ· · · ˌ·/ *n* [C] an arrangement between two or more people to kill themselves at the same time 自杀合约〔指两人以上约定一起自杀〕

suit[1] /sut; suːt/ *n* [C]

1 ▶CLOTHES 衣服◀ a set of clothes made of the same material, usually including a JACKET (=short coat) with trousers or a skirt 一套衣服〔通常包括用相同衣料做的短上衣和裤子或裙子〕：*a cream linen suit* 一套米色亚麻衣服 | *a grey winter suit* 一套灰色冬装 —see also 另见 MORNING SUIT

2 jogging/swim suit a piece or pieces of clothing used for a special purpose 慢跑运动服/游泳衣 —see also 另见 BOILER SUIT, SHELL SUIT, WET SUIT

3 ▶CARDS 纸牌◀ one of the four types of cards in a set of playing cards〔一副纸牌中的〕四种花色的牌中的任何一种

4 ▶LAW 法律◀ an argument brought to a court of law by a private person or company, not by the police or government; LAWSUIT〔个人或公司而非警方或政府提出的〕诉讼；讼案：**file suit** (=bring an argument to a court of law) 提出诉讼

5 sb's strong suit *especially AmE* something that you are good at【尤美】某人擅长的事，某人的专长，某人的特长：*Politeness is not his strong suit.* 他不擅长客套。

6 plead/press your suit *old use* to ask a woman to marry you【旧】〔向女子〕求婚 —see also 另见 **in your birthday suit** (BIRTHDAY (2)), **follow suit** (FOLLOW (15))

suit[2] *v* [T] **1** to be acceptable or CONVENIENT for a particular person or in a particular situation 适合；中…的意；对…方便：*Finding a date that suits us all is very difficult.* 很难找到一个对我们大家都合适的日期。| *Buy a database program to suit your needs.* 买个数据库程序来满足你的需要吧。| **suit sb (fine)** *spoken* (=be completely acceptable)【口】(很) 合某人的意；对某人(很) 合适 *"Eight o'clock?" "That suits me fine."* "8点钟行吗？" "行，这对我很合适。" | **suit sb down to the ground** (=be exactly right for someone) 对某人非常合适 *Yup, this little car suits me down to the ground.* 好，这辆小汽车对我再合适不过了。**2** [not in passive 不用被动态] to make someone look attractive 使显得漂亮：*That coat really suits Paul.* 保罗穿那件外套真好看。| *Red suits you.* 你穿红色很漂亮。—see 见 FIT[1] (USAGE)

3 well/best/ideally suited to have the right qualities to do something 非常适合〔做某事〕；具备做某事的特质：*Dirk would be ideally suited to the job.* 德克做这工作再合适不过了。

4 suit yourself *spoken* used to tell someone they can do whatever they want to, even though it annoys you【口】随你的便吧；你想怎样就怎样吧：*"I don't really feel like going out after all." "Suit yourself."* "我还是不是特别想出去。" "随你的便。"

5 suit sb's book *BrE informal* to fit well into someone's plans【英，非正式】适合某人的计划，合某人的心意

suit sth **to** sth *phr v* [T] *formal* to make something exactly right for something else【正式】使〔某物〕适合于〔另一物〕：*Suit the punishment to the crime, I say.* 我说呀，要按罪量刑。

suit·a·bil·i·ty /ˌsutəˈbɪlətɪ; ˌsuːtəˈbɪlɨti/ *n* [U] the degree to which something or someone has the right qualities for a particular purpose 合适，适合，适宜：[+for] *There's no doubt about Christine's suitability for the job.* 克里斯蒂娜适合做这份工作，这是毫无疑问的。

suit·a·ble /ˈsutəbl; ˈsuːtəbəl/ *adj* having the right qualities for a particular person, purpose, or situation 合适的，适合的，适宜的：*We are hoping to find a suitable school.* 我们希望能找到

一所合适的学校。| [+for] *The house is not really suitable for a large family.* 这所房子不是很适合大家庭居住。| **suitable to do sth** *Would this be suitable to wear to Deb's wedding?* 穿这套衣服参加德布的婚礼合适吗? —opposite 反义词 UNSUITABLE —**suitableness** *n* [U]

suit·a·bly /ˋsutəblɪ; ˈsuːtəbli/ *adv* **1 suitably dressed/prepared/equipped etc** wearing the right clothes, having the right information, equipment etc for a particular situation 衣着得体/准备停当/装备完善等: *We were relieved that Gordon had arrived at the wedding suitably dressed.* 看见戈登衣着得体地来参加婚礼,我们都松了一口气。**2 suitably impressed/amazed** showing the amount of feeling you would expect in a particular situation 合乎情理地佩服/吃惊: *The others were suitably impressed by the huge trout I caught.* 大家对我抓到的特大鳟鱼表示钦佩,也是合情合理的。

suitcases 手提箱

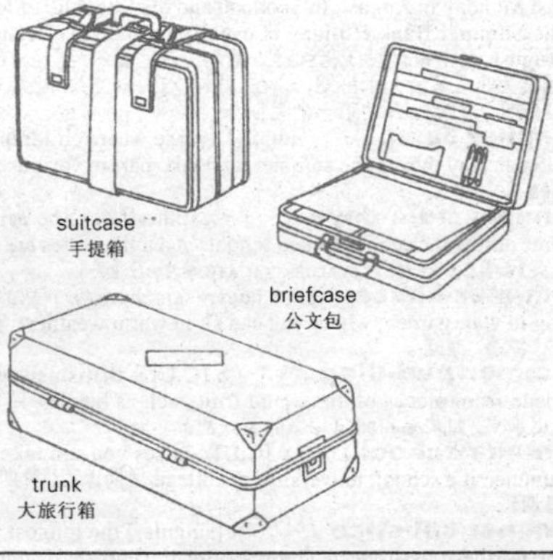

suitcase
手提箱

briefcase
公文包

trunk
大旅行箱

suit·case /ˋsutˏkes; ˈsuːtkeɪs/ *n* [C] a large case with a handle, used for carrying clothes and possessions when you travel〔旅行用的〕手提箱

suite /swit; swiːt/ *n* [C]

1 ▶ROOMS 房间◀ a set of rooms, especially expensive ones in a hotel〔旅馆的〕套房〔尤指豪华套房〕: *a honeymoon suite* 蜜月套房 | **suite of rooms** *a suite of rooms for palace guests* 王室宾客套房

2 ▶FURNITURE 家具◀ *especially BrE* a set of matching furniture for a room【尤英】一套家具: *a pink bathroom suite* 一套粉红色浴室家具 | **three-piece suite** (=a large seat and two chairs) 三件套家具〔一张长沙发加两张单座沙发〕

3 ▶MUSIC 音乐◀ a piece of music made up of several short parts〔音乐的〕组曲: *the Nutcracker Suite*《胡桃夹子组曲》

4 ▶POLITICS 政治◀ the people who work for, advise, or help an important person; RETINUE〔要人的〕〔一批〕随员,随从

5 ▶COMPUTERS 电脑◀ *technical* a group of related computer PROGRAMS that make a set【术语】〔电脑的〕程式组

suit·ing /ˋsutɪŋ; ˈsuːtɪŋ/ *n* [U] *technical* material used for making suits, especially woven wool【术语】西服衣料,羊毛衣料

sui·tor /ˋsutɚ; ˈsuːtə/ *n* [C] *old use* a man who wants to marry a particular woman【旧】〔女子的〕追求者,求婚者

Su·kar·no /suˋkarno; suːˈkɑːnəʊ/, **Ach·mad** /ˋakmad; ˈɑːkmɑːd/ (1902-70) the first President of Indonesia (1945-67) 苏加诺〔(1902-1970),印度尼西亚第一任总统(1945-1967)〕

Suk·koth /ˋsukoθ; ˈsʊkəʊθ/ also 又作 **Feast of Tabernacles** a Jewish festival which celebrates the gathering of the crops, and remembers the time in Jewish history when small shelters (sukkahs) were made by the Jews when they were in the wilderness 住棚节,收获节〔犹太节日。庆祝丰收和纪念历史上犹太人在旷野搭建棚舍的日子〕

Sul·ei·man I /sulɪˏman ðə ˋfɝst; sʊlɪˌmɑːn ðə ˈfɜːst/ (?1494-1566) a Turkish ruler, also known as Suleiman the Magnificent, who greatly improved the Ottoman Empire in its government and culture 苏莱曼一世(?1494-1566)〔土耳其统治者,也有"伟人苏莱曼"之称。他曾极大地促进了奥斯曼帝国的管理和文化〕

sul·fate /ˋsʌlfet; ˈsʌlfeɪt/ *n* [C,U] the American spelling of SULPHATE sulphate 的美式拼法

sul·fide /ˋsʌlfaɪd; ˈsʌlfaɪd/ *n* [C,U] the American spelling of SULPHIDE sulphide 的美式拼法

sul·fur /ˋsʌlfɚ; ˈsʌlfə/ *n* [U] the American spelling of SULPHUR sulphur 的美式拼法

sulfur di·ox·ide /ˌ‥ ·ˋ··/ *n* [U] the American spelling of SULPHUR DIOXIDE sulphur dioxide 的美式拼法

sul·fu·ric a·cid /sʌlˏfjurɪk ˋæsɪd; sʌlˌfjʊərɪk ˈæsɪ̇d/ *n* [U] the American spelling of SULPHURIC ACID sulphuric acid 的美式拼法

sul·fu·rous /ˋsʌlfərəs; ˈsʌlfərəs/ *adj* the American spelling of SULPHUROUS sulphurous 的美式拼法

sulk[1] /sʌlk; sʌlk/ *v* [I] to show that you are annoyed about something by being silent and having an unhappy expression on your face 生闷气,愠怒: *Stuart's sulking because I told him he couldn't go out and play.* 斯图尔特在生闷气,因为我不许他到外面去玩。

sulk[2] *n BrE*【英】**in a sulk** angry and silent 愠怒(的),生着闷气(的): *Neil's in a sulk because Paul won't play football with him.* 尼尔在生闷气,因为保罗不肯跟他踢足球。

sulk·y /ˋsʌlkɪ; ˈsʌlki/ *adj* **1** showing that you are sulking 生闷气的,绷着脸的: *a sulky frown* 郁郁不乐的皱眉 **2** tending to sulk 爱生闷气的,动辄不高兴的: *a sulky child* 爱生闷气的孩子 —**sulkily** *adv* —**sulkiness** *n* [U]

sul·len /ˋsʌlən; ˈsʌlən/ *adj* **1** silently showing anger or bad temper 闷闷不乐的,愠怒的: *a look of sullen resentment* 满脸的愠怒怨恨 **2** *literary* sky or weather that is sullen is dark and unpleasant【文】〔天空或天气〕阴沉的 —**sullenly** *adv* —**sullenness** *n* [U]

Sul·li·van /ˋsʌlɪvən; ˈsʌlɪ̇vən/, **John L.** (1858-1918), a US BOXER who was the last world HEAVYWEIGHT CHAMPION to have fought without wearing gloves. However, he wore special GLOVES when he lost his title to James J. Corbett in 1892. He was called the Boston Strong Boy. 沙利文〔(1858-1918),美国拳击手。他是最后一位徒手搏击的世界重量级拳王。然而,他戴上特制的手套后,却于 1892 年输给詹姆斯·J.科比特,卫冕失利。有"波士顿硬汉"之称〕

Sullivan, Louis Henry (1856-1924) a US ARCHITECT who worked in Chicago and built some of the first SKYSCRAPERS (=very tall buildings), such as the Wainwright Building in St Louis 沙利文〔(1856-1924),美国建筑师。他曾在芝加哥工作,设计了美国最早的一批摩天大楼,如圣路易斯市的温赖特大厦〕

Sullivan, Sir Arthur (1842-1900) a British COMPOSER who worked with W.S. Gilbert to write humorous OPERETTAS (=plays with songs) 沙利文爵士〔(1824-1900),英国作曲家。曾与 W.S. 吉尔伯特共同创作幽默轻歌剧〕—see also 另见 GILBERT AND SULLIVAN

sul·ly /ˋsʌlɪ; ˈsʌli/ *v* [T] *formal or literary* to spoil or reduce the value of something that was perfect【正式或文】弄脏,玷污;破坏: *a scandal that sullied his reputation* 玷污了他名誉的丑闻

sul·phate *BrE*【英】, **sulfate** *AmE*【美】/ˋsʌlfet; ˈsʌlfeɪt/ *n* [C,U] a SALT[1] (4) formed from SULPHURIC ACID 硫酸盐: *copper sulphate* 硫酸铜

sul·phide *BrE*【英】, **sulfide** *AmE*【美】/ˋsʌlfaɪd; ˈsʌlfaɪd/ *n* [C,U] a mixture of sulphur with another substance 硫化物

sul·phur *BrE*【英】, **sulfur** *AmE*【美】/ˋsʌlfɚ; ˈsʌlfə/ *n* [U] an ELEMENT (=simple substance) especially in the form of a light yellow powder, used in drugs, explosives, and industry 硫,硫黄

sulphur di·ox·ide *BrE*【英】, **sulfur dioxide** *AmE*【美】/ˌ‥ ·ˋ··/ *n* [U] a poisonous gas that is a cause of air POLLUTION in industrial areas 二氧化硫〔污染空气的有毒气体〕

sul·phu·ric ac·id *BrE*【英】, **sulfuric acid** *AmE*【美】/sʌlˏfjurɪk ˋæsɪd; sʌlˌfjʊərɪk ˈæsɪ̇d/ *n* [U] a powerful acid 硫酸

sul·phu·rous *BrE*【英】, **sulfurous** *AmE*【美】/ˋsʌlfərəs; ˈsʌlfərəs/ *adj* related to, full of, or used with sulphur 硫的,含硫的

sul·tan /ˋsʌltn̩; ˈsʌltən/ *n* [C] a ruler in some Muslim countries 苏丹〔某些伊斯兰教国家统治者的称号〕

sul·ta·na /sʌlˋtænə; sʌlˈtɑːnə/ *n* [C] **1** a small pale RAISIN (=dried fruit) without seeds, used in baking〔做糕饼用的〕无籽小葡萄干; GOLDEN RAISIN *AmE*【美】**2** also 又作 **Sultana** the wife, mother, or daughter of a sultan 苏丹的女眷〔指其妻子、母亲或女儿〕

sul·tan·ate /ˋsʌltn̩ɪt; ˈsʌltəneɪt/ *n* [C] **1** a country ruled by a sultan 苏丹统治的国家,苏丹国: *the sultanate of Oman* 阿曼苏丹国 **2** the position of a sultan, or the period of time during which he rules 苏丹的职位;苏丹的统治期

sul·try /ˋsʌltrɪ; ˈsʌltri/ *adj* **1** weather that is sultry is unpleasantly hot with no wind〔天气〕闷热的 **2** a woman who is sultry makes other people feel strong sexual attraction to her〔女子〕风骚的,性感迷人的: *a sultry look* 撩人的一瞥 —**sultriness** *n* [U]

sum¹ /sʌm; sʌm/ *n*
1 ►MONEY 钱◄ [C] an amount of money 金额, 款项: **a large/small sum (of)** *Sid was left a large sum of money by his aunt.* 锡德的姑母给他遗留下一大笔钱。| **for the sum of** *It was mine for the sum of £20.* 我是花了20英镑把它买来的。—see also 另见 LUMP SUM, **princely sum** (PRINCELY (1))
2 the sum of the total produced when you add two or more numbers together 和; 总和, 总数: *The sum of 6 and 4 is 10.* 6加4之和为10。
3 greater/more than the sum of its parts a group of things or people that is greater than the sum of its parts has a quality or effectiveness as a group that you would not expect from looking at each member〔总体的作用〕大于各部分的总和
4 ►CALCULATION 计算◄ [C] *BrE* a simple calculation by adding, multiplying, dividing etc, especially one done by children at school【英】简单的计算, 算术〔尤指小学生的加减乘除运算〕
5 do your sums *informal BrE* to calculate whether you have enough money to do something【非正式, 英】算一算是否有足够的钱做某事: *Well I've done my sums, and I think I can afford a holiday.* 我已经算过了, 我想我有足够的钱去度假。
6 in sum *old-fashioned* used before a statement that gives the main information about something in a few simple words【过时】总之, 简而言之: *It was, in sum, a complete failure.* 总之, 这是一次彻底的失败。—see also 另见 SUM TOTAL

sum² *v* **summed, summing**
sum up *phr v* **1** [I,T] to give the main information about a report, speech, TRIAL¹ (1) etc in a short statement at the end; SUMMARIZE 概括, 总结, 概述: **to sum up** *So, to sum up, we need to concentrate on staff training.* 因此, 概括地说, 我们需要集中精力对员工进行培训。| **sum** sth ↔ **up** *The last chapter sums up the arguments.* 最后一章概括了全部论点。**2** [T **sum** sb/sth ↔ **up**] to form a judgment or opinion about someone or something 对…作出判断; 对…形成意见: *Pat summed up the situation at a glance.* 帕特一眼就看清了当时的情势。**3 that (about) sums it up** *spoken* used to say that you have said everything that is important about a subject【口】主要情况就是这样 —see also 另见 SUMMING-UP

Su·ma·tra /sʊˋmɑtrə; sʊˈmɑːtrə/ the second largest of the islands that form the country of Indonesia. Its largest city is Padang. 苏门答腊岛〔印度尼西亚第二大岛。岛上最大城市为巴东〕—**Sumatran** *n, adj*

Su·mer /ˋsumɚ; ˈsuːmə/ the southern part of ancient Mesopotamia (modern Iraq), where people called the Sumerians lived from about 3500 BC, in one of the world's earliest societies. One of the cities of Sumer was the city of Ur. The Sumerians developed a type of writing known as cuneiform, and many scientists think that they invented the wheel. 苏美尔〔古代美索不达米亚(今伊拉克)南部地区。其居民称为苏美尔人, 约公元前3500年开始在这里生活, 并建立了世界上最早的社会之一。乌尔城为苏美尔人建立的城邦之一。苏美尔人发明了"楔形文字", 不少科学家认为轮子也是苏美尔人发明的〕

sum·ma cum lau·de /ˋsʌmə ˌkʌm ˋlɔdı; ˌsʌmə kʌm ˈlɔːdi/ *adj, adv AmE* the highest level of HONOURS given to American university or college students【美】〔给予美国大学生的〕最高荣誉 —compare 比较 CUM LAUDE

sum·mar·ize also 又作 **-ise** *BrE*【英】/ˋsʌməˌraɪz; ˈsʌməraɪz/ *v* [I,T] to make a short statement giving only the main information and not the details of a plan, event, report etc 总结, 概括, 概述: *Jack quickly summarized the main points of his plan.* 杰克很快地概述了他计划中的要点。

sum·ma·ry¹ /ˋsʌmərı; ˈsʌməri/ *n* [C] a short statement that gives the main information about something, without giving all the details 总结, 摘要, 概要: *Please write a one-page summary of this report.* 请给这份报告写一个一页纸的摘要。| *a news summary* 新闻提要 | **in summary** *So, in summary, we've got to try to get further funding.* 因此, 概括地说, 我们必须努力争取更多的资金。

summary² *adj* [only before noun 仅用于名词前] *formal* done immediately, without paying attention to the usual processes, rules etc【正式】立即的; 速决的〔未顾及惯常的程序、规定等〕: *a summary execution* 立即处决—**summarily** *adv*: *Franklin was summarily dismissed.* 富兰克林被立即开除了。

sum·mat /ˋsʌmət; ˈsʌmət/ *pron dialect* a spoken form of SOMETHING【方言】某事, 某物, 某种东西〔something的口语形式〕

sum·ma·tion /sʌmˋeʃən; səˈmeɪʃən/ *n* [C] *formal*【正式】**1** a summary; SUMMING-UP 总结, 概括, 概述 **2** the total amount or number you get when two or more things are added together 总和, 总数, 合计

sum·mer¹ /ˋsʌmɚ; ˈsʌmə/ *n* **1** [C,U] the time of the year when the sun is hottest and the days are longest, between spring and autumn 夏天, 夏季: *Are you going on vacation this summer?* 今年夏天你去度假吗? | *the summer of 1940* 1940年夏季 | **be summer** *I'm so glad it's summer!* 夏天到了, 我很高兴! | **summer clothes/sports etc** (=used or done in summer) 夏季衣服/运动等 *a summer dress* 一件夏装 | **high summer** (=the hottest part of summer) 盛夏 **2 summer rental** [C] *AmE* a house or apartment that you rent only during the summer【美】夏季出租房〔只在夏天租用的房子或公寓〕**3 your 50/70 etc summers** *literary* a way of saying how old someone is【文】50岁/70岁等, 50个/70个等春秋: *looking younger than his 70 summers* 他看起来要比70高龄显得年轻 —see also 另见 INDIAN SUMMER

summer² *v* [I] to spend the summer in a particular place〔在某地〕过夏天, 度夏

Summer Bank Hol·i·day, the /ˌ‥ ˈ ‥ˈ/ a public holiday in England, Wales, and Northern Ireland, usually on the last Monday in August. In Scotland and the Republic of Ireland, the Summer Bank Holiday is usually on the first Monday in August. 夏季银行假日〔英格兰、威尔士及北爱尔兰一公众假日, 通常为8月最后一个星期一。在苏格兰与爱尔兰共和国, 夏季银行假日一般是8月的第一个星期一〕

summer camp /ˈ‥ ˌ·/ *n* [C,U] a place where children in the US can stay during the summer, and take part in various activities 夏令营

summer hol·i·days /ˌ‥ ˈ‥·/ *n* [plural] *BrE* the period of time during the summer when schools and universities are closed【英】〔学校的〕暑假; SUMMER VACATION *AmE*【美】

sum·mer·house /ˋsʌmɚˌhaʊs; ˈsʌməhaʊs/ *n* [C] a building in your garden, where you can sit in warm weather〔花园中的〕凉亭, 凉棚

summer pud·ding /ˌ‥ ˈ‥/ *n* [C,U] a British sweet dish made from pieces of bread and fruit such as berries 夏令布丁〔用水果, 如浆果和面包片做的英式甜品〕

summer school /ˈ‥ ·/ *n* [C,U] courses you can take in the summer at a school, university, or college 暑期课程, 暑期学校, 暑期班

summer sol·stice /ˌ‥ ˈ‥/ *n* [singular] the longest day in the northern HEMISPHERE (=top half of the earth), around June 22nd 夏至〔北半球白天最长的一天, 在6月22日前后〕

CULTURAL NOTE 文化注释

Summer solstice is not usually celebrated in Britain or the US, but in Britain a few people, especially Druids, do celebrate it by watching the sun rise on that day at STONEHENGE. 在夏至这天英美两国通常没有庆祝活动, 但是英国会有一些人, 特别是德鲁伊特教的祭司, 通过在巨石阵观日出的方式来庆祝夏至。

sum·mer·time /ˋsʌmɚˌtaım; ˈsʌmətaım/ *n* [U] the season when it is summer 夏天, 夏季 —see also 另见 BRITISH SUMMER TIME

summer va·ca·tion /ˌ‥ ·ˈ‥/ *n* [U] *AmE* the period of time during the summer when schools and universities are closed【美】〔学校的〕暑假; SUMMER HOLIDAYS *BrE*【英】

sum·mer·y /ˋsʌmərı; ˈsʌməri/ *adj* suitable for, or reminding you of the summer 适合夏季的; 夏季的: *a light summery dress* 一件轻薄的夏装

summing-up /ˌ‥ ˈ·/ *n plural* **summings-up** [C] a statement giving the main facts but not the details of something, especially made by a judge at the end of a TRIAL¹ (1)〔尤指法官在审判结束时所作的〕总结, 总括性概述: *In his summing-up, the judge said it was dangerous to convict on this evidence alone.* 法官在总结中说, 单凭这点证据就宣判有罪是危险的。—see also 另见 **sum up** (SUM²)

sum·mit /ˋsʌmıt; ˈsʌmɪt/ *n* [C] **1** the top of a mountain 山顶: *The climbers reached the summit of Mount Everest yesterday.* 登山者昨天登上珠穆朗玛峰的峰顶。—see picture on page A12 参见A12页图 **2** a set of meetings between the leaders of several governments 首脑会议, 最高级会议, 峰会: *the recent Geneva summit* 最近召开的日内瓦首脑会议 | **summit meeting** (=for a particular purpose) 首脑会议, 最高级会议; 高峰会 **3 the summit of** *formal* the greatest amount or highest level of something【正式】…的顶峰, …的极点: *the summit of scientific achievement* 科学成就的顶峰

sum·mon /ˋsʌmən; ˈsʌmən/ *v* [T] *formal*【正式】**1** to officially order someone to come to a meeting, a court of law etc 召集〔开会〕; 传唤〔出庭〕: **summon sb to sth** *We were all summoned to a meeting with the principal.* 我们都被叫去和校长开

会。| **summon sb to do sth** *They'll probably be summoning you to appear in court.* 他们也许要传唤你出庭。**2** also 又作 **summon** sth ↔ **up** to make a great effort to use your strength, courage, energy etc 鼓起〔勇气〕; 振作〔精神〕; 使出〔力气〕: *Summoning all her strength, Julia gave one last pull.* 朱莉娅使尽全身力气最后再拉了一次。| *I couldn't summon up the courage to ask you out until now.* 我直到现在才鼓起勇气约你出来。**3 summon a meeting/conference etc** to arrange for a meeting to take place and order people to come to it; CONVENE 召开会议等

sum·mons¹ /ˈsʌmənz; ˈsʌmənz/ *n plural* **summonses** [C] an official order to appear in a court of law〔法庭的〕传票: **serve a summons on sb** (=order someone to appear in court) 发出传票传唤某人出庭

summons² *v* [T usually passive 一般用被动态] to order someone to appear in a court of law 发传票给〔某人〕, 传唤, 传讯: *I was summonsed to appear as a witness.* 我被传唤出庭作证。

su·mo /ˈsumo; ˈsuːməʊ/ also 又作 **sumo wrest·ling** /ˌ.. ˈ../ *n* [U] a Japanese form of wrestling (WRESTLE (1)), done by men who are very large 相扑〔日本的一种摔跤运动〕 —**sumo wrestler** *n* [C]

sump /sʌmp; sʌmp/ *n* [C] **1** the lowest part of a DRAINAGE system where liquids or wastes remain〔排水系统的〕集液池, 污水坑 **2** *BrE* the part of an engine that contains the supply of oil【英】〔发动机的〕油盘, 润滑油箱; OIL PAN *AmE*【美】

sump·tu·ous /ˈsʌmptʃuəs; ˈsʌmptʃuəs/ *adj* very impressive and expensive; LUXURIOUS 豪华的, 奢华的, 奢侈的: *a sumptuous banquet* 盛宴 —**sumptuously** *adv*: *sumptuously dressed in velvet* 身穿华贵天鹅绒衣服 —**sumptuousness** *n* [U]

sum to·tal /ˌ. ˈ../ *n* **the sum total of** the whole amount of something, especially when this is less than expected or needed 全部〔东西〕; 总数, 总量, 总额〔尤用于表示比预料或所需的少〕: *Is that the sum total of what they've taught you?* 这就是他们教给你的全部东西了吗?

Sun the written abbreviation of 缩写= SUNDAY

S2 W1 **sun¹** /sʌn; sʌn/ *n* **1** [singular] the large bright thing in the sky that gives us light and heat, and around which the Earth moves 太阳 —see picture at 参见 SOLAR SYSTEM 图 **2** [U] the heat and light that come from the sun 阳光, 日光: *Too much sun is bad for you.* 过多的太阳光对你没有好处。| **in the sun** *Tanya sat in the sun, reading a book.* 塔尼娅坐在阳光下看书。**3** [C] any star around which PLANETs move〔有行星的〕恒星 **4 catch the sun** *BrE*【英】, **get the sun** *AmE*【美】**a)** if someone catches or gets the sun, they become slightly red or brown because they have been outside in the sun〔人〕被晒黑 **b)** if a place or room catches or gets the sun, it is very bright and warm when the sun shines〔地方或房间〕阳光充足 **5 under the sun** used to emphasize that you are talking about something that includes very large numbers of ideas or things etc 世界上, 天(底)下〔用于表示强调〕: *Santos could talk about any subject under the sun.* 桑托斯可以谈论世界上的任何话题。—see also 另见 **make hay while the sun shines** (HAY (3))

sun² *v* **sunned, sunning** [T] **sun yourself** to sit or lie outside when the sun is shining 晒太阳: *a cat sunning itself on the patio* 在露台上晒太阳的猫

Sun, the a British TABLOID daily newspaper which generally supports RIGHT-WING and nationalist political ideas. It has some articles about events in the news and politics, but many of its stories are about the private lives of well-known people, such as the royal family, television actors, and sports players.《太阳报》〔英国一每天刊行的通俗小报。通常支持右翼和民族主义政治观点。除刊登新闻和政治类文章外, 主要报道王室成员、电视演员、体育明星等名人的私生活〕

sun-baked /ˈ. ./ *adj* made very hard and dry by the sun〔太阳〕晒干的, 晒硬的: *the sun-baked earth of the western desert* 被太阳晒硬了的西部沙漠土地

sun-bathe /ˈsʌnˌbeð; ˈsʌnbeɪð/ *v* [I] to sit or lie outside in the sun, especially in order to become brown 沐日光浴, 晒太阳: *a good beach for sunbathing* 日光浴的理想海滩 —see 见 BATH² (USAGE)

CULTURAL NOTE 文化注释

Sunbathing is very popular with people in the US and the UK, and many people think it is attractive to have a SUNTAN (=brown skin that white people get from spending time in bright sunlight). However, it is now known that sunbathing can cause skin CANCER and people are worried about this, especially since the hole in the OZONE LAYER was discovered. As a result, people are more careful than in the past about using SUNBLOCK and wearing hats to protect themselves from the sun. 日光浴在英美两国非常流行, 很多人认为褐色的皮肤更有魅力。然而, 自从知道了日光曝晒会导致皮肤癌, 特别是臭氧层的空洞被发现之后, 人们开始担心起来。因此现在人们比过去更加小心, 注意涂抹防晒霜和戴遮阳帽等来躲避日晒。

sun·beam /ˈsʌnˌbim; ˈsʌnbiːm/ *n* [C] a beam of light from the sun that you can see because it is shining through a cloud〔一道〕日光, 阳光光束

sun·bed /ˈsʌnbɛd; ˈsʌnbed/ *n* [C] **1** a metal structure the size of a bed that you lie on to make your skin brown using light from special lamps 太阳灯浴浴床 **2** a SUN LOUNGER〔室外用的〕轻便折椅 —see also 另见 SUNLAMP

Sun·belt, the /ˈsʌnbɛlt; ˈsʌnbelt/ *n* [singular] the southern and southwestern parts of the US, from Virginia to South California, called this because of the hot, sunny climate in this area 阳光地带〔美国南部和西南部从弗吉尼亚到加利福尼亚州南部的一个区域。这里气候温和, 日照充足, 故得此名〕

sun blind /ˈ. ./ *n* [C] *BrE* the thing you pull down over a window to keep the sun out of a room【英】〔阻挡阳光照进室内的〕百叶窗, 遮阳帘

sun·block /ˈsʌnblɑk; ˈsʌnblɒk/ *n* [C,U] cream or oil that you rub into your skin, in order to completely stop the sun's light from burning you 防晒霜, 防晒油 —compare 比较 SUNSCREEN

sun·bon·net /ˈsʌnˌbɑnɪt; ˈsʌnbɒnɪ̣t/ *n* [C] a hat worn in the past by women as protection from the sun〔旧时的〕阔边遮阳女帽

sun·burn /ˈsʌnˌbɝn; ˈsʌnbɜːn/ *n* [U] the condition of having skin that is red and painful, as a result of spending too much time in the sun 晒伤, 〔晒太阳过量而引起的〕皮肤灼痛 —**sunburned** also 又作 **sunburnt** *adj* —compare 比较 SUNTAN

sun cream /ˈ. ./ *n* [C,U] *BrE* a cream or oil that you rub into your skin to stop the sun from burning you too much; SUNTAN LOTION【英】防晒霜, 防晒油

sun·dae /ˈsʌndɪ; ˈsʌndeɪ/ *n* [C] a dish made from ICE CREAM, fruit, sweet SAUCE, nuts etc 圣代冰激凌, 新地〔一种加水果、糖浆、果仁等的冰激凌〕: *a chocolate sundae* 巧克力圣代冰激凌

Sun·day /ˈsʌndɪ; ˈsʌndi/ written abbreviation 缩写为 **Sun** *n* [C,U] **1** the day between Saturday and Monday. In Britain, Sunday is considered the last day of the week, and in the US it is considered the first day of the week 星期日, 星期天〔在英国被看作是一周的最后一天, 在美国则被看作是一周的第一天〕: *I went to a concert last Sunday.* 上星期天我去听了一场音乐会。| *We're going to a match on Sunday.* 我们星期天要去看比赛。| *Sunday nights are usually pretty quiet.* 星期天晚上一般都相当安静。| **on Sundays** (=each Sunday) 每逢星期天, 在星期天 *Do you go to church on Sundays?* 你每个星期天都上教堂做礼拜吗? | **a Sunday** (=one of the Sundays in the year)〔一年中的〕某个星期日 *My birthday is on a Sunday this year.* 我今年的生日是在一个星期天。| **the Sunday** *BrE* (=the Sunday of the week being mentioned)【英】所提及的一周的星期日 *Nan came on the Monday and left on the Sunday.* 南星期一来的, 星期天就走了。**2 Sunday best** your best clothes, worn only for special occasions or for church〔某人衣服中〕最好的衣服, 节日盛装 **3 Sunday driver** an insulting word meaning someone who annoys other people by driving too slowly 星期日司机〔侮辱性用语, 指开车慢得令人厌烦的人〕—see also 另见 **never in a month of Sundays** (MONTH (7))

Sunday Ex·press, The /ˌ.. ˈ../ a British TABLOID newspaper sold every Sunday, which generally supports the ideas of the Conservative Party《星期日快报》〔英国一星期日发行的通俗小报。通常支持保守党的观点〕—see also 另见 The EXPRESS

Sunday Mir·ror, The /ˌ.. ˈ../ a British tabloid newspaper sold every Sunday, which generally supports the ideas of the Labour Party《星期日镜报》〔英国一星期日发行的通俗小报。通常支持工党观点〕—see also 另见 The MIRROR

Sunday Post, the /ˌ.. ˈ./ also 又作 **the Post** a scottish sunday newspaper which supports traditional values and has many stories also about ordinary people. It is very popular in Scotland and is also read by Scottish people in many other parts of the world.《星期日邮报》〔苏格兰一星期日报纸。该报支持传统价值观念, 多刊载百姓故事。在苏格兰颇受读者青睐, 旅居世界其他许多地区的苏格兰人也阅读此报〕

Sunday school /ˈ.. ./ *n* [C,U] a place where children are taught about Christianity on Sundays 主日学校〔星期日对儿童进行基督教教育的场所〕

Sunday Sport, The /ˌ.. ˈ./ a British TABLOID newspaper sold every Sunday which has almost no serious news stories but has many stories about sex and SCANDAL (=immoral or shock-

ing events involving famous people)《星期日体育报》〔英国一星期日发行的通俗小报。几乎没有严肃类的新闻报道,而登载不少的名人性丑闻〕

Sunday Tel·e·graph, The /,‥'‥/ a serious British newspaper with generally RIGHT-WING political opinions《星期日电讯报》〔英国一严肃类星期日报纸。其政治观点通常偏右〕

Sunday Times, The /,‥'·/ a serious British Sunday newspaper whose political opinions are fairly RIGHT-WING. The Sunday Times was one of the first papers to be divided into SECTIONS (=separate parts), such as a Sports Section and a Business Section, and it has a very large number of these.《星期日泰晤士报》〔英国一严肃类星期日报纸。其政治观点较为右翼。该报是最早划分版面的报纸之一,辟有体育、商业等诸多版面〕

sun·deck /'sʌn,dɛk; 'sʌndek/ *n* [C] a part of a ship where people can sit in the sun〔大船上供乘客坐在阳光下的〕日光甲板

sun·der /'sʌndɚ; 'sʌndə/ *v* [T] *literary* to break something into parts, especially violently【文】〔尤指猛烈地〕将〔某物〕分开; 使碎开; 割开; 切开 —see also 另见 ASUNDER

sun·dial /'sʌn,daɪəl; 'sʌndaɪəl/ *n* [C] an object used in the past for telling the time, by looking at the position of a shadow made on a stone circle by a pointed piece of metal〔旧时用以测量时间的〕日规, 日晷

sun·down /'sʌn,daun; 'sʌndaʊn/ *n* [U] *old-fashioned* SUNSET (1)【过时】日落

sun·down·er /'sʌn,daunɚ; 'sʌn,daʊnə/ *n* [C] *informal especially BrE* an alcoholic drink drunk in the evening【非正式, 尤英】〔黄昏时喝的〕日落酒

sun-drenched /'· ·/ *adj* a sun-drenched place is one where the sun shines most of the time〔地方〕阳光充足的, 充满阳光的: *sun-drenched tropical islands* 阳光充足的热带海岛

sun·dress /'sʌn,drɛs; 'sʌndres/ *n* [C] a dress that you wear in hot weather, that does not cover your arms, neck, or shoulders 太阳裙〔一种天热时穿的无袖连衣裙〕

sun-dried /'· ·/ *adj* [only before noun 仅用于名词前] sun-dried food has been left in the sun to dry in order to give it a particular taste〔食物〕晒干的: *sun-dried tomatoes*〔晒成的〕番茄干

sun·dries /'sʌn,drɪz; 'sʌndriz/ *n* [plural] *formal* small objects that are not important enough to be named separately【正式】杂物; 杂项 —see also 另见 SUNDRY

sun·dry /'sʌndrɪ; 'sʌndri/ *adj* [only before noun 仅用于名词前] *formal*【正式】**1 all and sundry** everyone, not just a few carefully chosen people 每个人〔而不是精心挑选的某些人〕: *In the 80s the economy was booming and banks dished out loans to all and sundry.* 在 80 年代, 经济繁荣, 银行贷款人人可得。**2** not similar enough to form a group; various 各种各样的, 杂七杂八的: *pens, books, and other sundry articles* 钢笔、书本及各种其他物品

sun·fish /'sʌn,fɪʃ; 'sʌnfɪʃ/ *n* [C,U] a fish that lives in the sea and has a large round body 太阳鱼, 棘臀鱼〔一种海鱼〕

sun·flow·er /'sʌn,flauɚ; 'sʌn,flaʊə/ *n* [C] a very tall plant with a large yellow flower and seeds that can be eaten 向日葵

sung /sʌŋ; sʌŋ/ the past participle of SING

sun·glass·es /'sʌn,glæsɪz; 'sʌn,glɑːsɪz/ *n* [plural] dark glasses that you wear to protect your eyes when the sun is very bright 太阳镜, 墨镜

sun god /'· ·/ *n* [C] a god in some ancient religions who represents the sun or has power over it〔古代某些宗教信仰中的〕太阳神

sun hat /'· ·/ *n* [C] a hat that you wear to protect your head from the sun〔阔边〕遮阳帽 —see picture at 参见 HAT 图

sunk /sʌŋk; sʌŋk/ the past tense and past participle of SINK[1]

sunk·en /'sʌŋkən; 'sʌŋkən/ *adj* **1** [only before noun 仅用于名词前] having fallen to the bottom of the sea 沉没的, 沉在海底的: *a sunken ship* 一艘沉船 | *sunken treasure* 沉在海底的宝物 **2** [only before noun 仅用于名词前] built or placed at a lower level than the surrounding floor, ground etc 低于周围地面的, 沉降式的, 下沉式的: *a sunken bath* 低于地面的浴缸 | *a sunken garden* 沉降式花园 **3 sunken cheeks/eyes etc** cheeks or eyes that have fallen inwards, especially because you are old, or ill 凹陷的双颊/两眼等〔尤指因年老或患病所致〕

sun·lamp /'sʌn,læmp; 'sʌnlæmp/ *n* [C] a lamp that produces a special light used for making your skin brown 太阳灯, 紫外线灯

sun·less /'sʌnlɪs; 'sʌnləs/ *adj* having no light from the sun 无阳[日]光的: *the sunless depths of the ocean* 没有阳光的海洋深处

sun·light /'sʌn,laɪt; 'sʌnlaɪt/ *n* [U] natural light that comes from the sun 阳光, 日光: *bright sunlight* 灿烂的阳光 | *plants that need a lot of sunlight* 需要大量日光的植物

sun·lit /'sʌn,lɪt; 'sʌnlɪt/ *adj* made brighter by light from the sun 阳光照耀的: *a sunlit garden* 阳光灿烂的花园

sun lounge /'· ·/ *n* [C] *BrE* a room with large windows and often a glass roof, designed to let in lots of light【英】日光浴室〔窗户很大, 房顶常用玻璃建造以吸收阳光〕; SUN PORCH *AmE*【美】

sun loun·ger /'·, ‥/ *n* [C] a light chair like a folding bed, that you can sit or lie on outside〔室外用的〕轻便折椅

Sun·na, Sun·nah /'sunə; 'sʊnə/ *n* **the Sunna** a set of Muslim customs and rules based on the words and acts of Muhammad 逊奈〔伊斯兰教根据穆罕默德言行建立的穆斯林言行规范〕

Sun·ni /'sunɪ; 'sʊni/ *n* [C] a Muslim who follows one of the two main branches of the Muslim religion 逊尼派教徒〔逊尼派是伊斯兰教的两支主要教派之一〕—compare 比较 SHIITE

sun·ny /'sʌnɪ; 'sʌni/ *adj* **1** full of light from the sun 阳光充足的: *a sunny day* 阳光明媚的日子 | *a sunny room* 阳光充足的房间 **2** *informal* cheerful and happy【非正式】兴高采烈的, 快乐的: *a sunny smile* 快活的微笑

sunny-side up /,‥ '· '·/ *adj* [not before noun 不用于名词前] *AmE* an egg that is cooked sunny-side up is cooked in hot fat on one side only, and not turned over in the pan【美】〔煎蛋〕单面煎的, 只煎一面的

sun porch /'· ·/ *n* [C] *AmE* a room with large windows and often a glass roof, designed to let in lots of light【美】日光浴室〔窗户很大, 房顶常用玻璃建造以吸收阳光〕; SUN LOUNGE *BrE*【英】

sun·rise /'sʌn,raɪz; 'sʌnraɪz/ *n* [U] **1** the time when the sun first appears in the morning 日出(时分); 黎明; 拂晓: *We got up at sunrise.* 我们黎明时起床。**2** the part of the sky where the sun first appears in the morning 晨曦, 朝霞: *sunrise over Mount Fuji* 富士山山顶的晨曦

sunrise in·dus·try /'‥, ‥'/ *n* [C] an industry, such as ELECTRONICS or making computers, that uses modern processes and takes the place of older industries 朝阳工业, 新兴工业〈如电子工业、电脑制造业等〉—compare 比较 HEAVY INDUSTRY

sun·roof /'sʌn,ruf; 'sʌnruːf/ *n* [C] **1** a part of the roof of a car that you can open to let in air and light〔汽车的〕活动车顶, 滑动顶板 —see picture on page A2 参见 A2 页图 **2** a flat roof of a building where you can sit when the sun is shining〔可晒太阳的〕平屋顶, 楼顶平台

sun·screen /'sʌn,skrin; 'sʌnskriːn/ *n* [C,U] a cream or oil that you rub into your skin to stop the sun from burning you 防晒霜, 防晒油 —see also 另见 SUNBLOCK

sun·set /'sʌn,sɛt; 'sʌnset/ *n* **1** [U] the time of day when the sun disappears and night begins 日落(时分), 薄暮, 黄昏: **at sunset** *The builders stop work at sunset.* 建筑工人傍晚时分收工。**2** [C,U] the part of the sky where the sun gradually disappears at the end of the day 晚霞, 落日余晖: *We sat on the beach and watched the sunset.* 我们坐在海滩上观看落日余晖。

Sunset Boule·vard /,‥ '‥/ a long road in Hollywood, California, the eastern part of which is called the Sunset Strip. 日落大道〔加利福尼亚州好莱坞的一条长道。大道的东段称作"日落带"〕

sun·shade /'sʌn,ʃed; 'sʌnʃeɪd/ *n* [C] an object shaped like an UMBRELLA, used especially in the past as protection from the sun; PARASOL 太阳伞; 遮阳篷

sun·shine /'sʌn,ʃaɪn; 'sʌnʃaɪn/ *n* [U] **1** a word meaning the light and heat that come from the sun, used when you want to say that this is pleasant 阳光, 日照: *Northern Ireland will start dry with some sunshine.* 北爱尔兰一早天气干燥, 有些阳光。**2** *informal* happiness【非正式】快乐, 幸福: **ray of sunshine** *Zoe was the only ray of sunshine during those depressing months.* 在令人忧愁的那几个月里, 佐伊是唯一能带来快乐的人。

sun·spot /'sʌn,spɑt; 'sʌnspɒt/ *n* [C] **1** *technical* a small dark area on the sun's surface【术语】〔太阳表面的〕黑子, 日斑 **2** *informal* a place where the sun shines a lot, that many people go to on holiday【非正式】阳光充沛的度假地

sun·stroke /'sʌn,strok; 'sʌnstrəʊk/ *n* [U] fever, weakness etc caused by being outside in the sun for too long 日射病, 中暑

sun·tan /'sʌntæn; 'sʌntæn/ *n* [C] attractively brown skin which you get when you spend a lot of time in bright sunlight; TAN[2] (2)〔皮肤的〕晒黑 —**suntanned** *adj* —compare 比较 SUNBURN

suntan lo·tion /'‥, ‥/ also 又作 **suntan oil** /'‥, ·/ *n* [C,U] a cream or oil that you rub into your skin to stop the sun from burning you too much 防晒霜, 防晒油

sun·trap /'sʌn,træp; 'sʌntræp/ *n* [C] a place that is sheltered and gets a lot of heat and light from the sun 避风向阳处: *Our terrace is a real suntrap.* 我们的露台真是个向阳避风的地方。

sun-up /ˈ·ˌ·/ *n* [U] *old-fashioned* SUNRISE【过时】日出

sun-wor·ship·per /ˈ·ˌ·ˌ··/ *n* [C] *informal* someone who likes to lie in the sun to get a SUNTAN【非正式】极爱日光浴的人

Sun Yat Sen /ˌsʊn ˌjæt ˈsɛn; ˌsʊn jæt ˈsen/ (1866-1925) a Chinese political leader who established the National Party in China, and helped to remove the last Manchu emperor from power. He became the first President of the new Republic of China in 1911. 孙中山，又叫孙逸仙〔(1866-1925)，中国政治领袖。他创立了中国国民党，推翻了满清末代皇帝，1911年成为中华民国第一任总统〕

sup /sʌp; sʌp/ *v* **1** [T] to drink something, especially slowly in small amounts 一点点地喝，呷: *Mrs Holliday was supping porridge in the back kitchen.* 霍利迪太太在后边厨房里慢慢地喝粥。 **2** *old use* to eat supper【旧】吃晚饭 —**sup** *n* [C]

super- /ˈsupɚ; ˈsuːpə/ *prefix* more, larger, greater, or more powerful than usual 超，特别，过于: *a supertanker* (=a ship that can carry extremely large loads) 超级货轮[油轮] | *superglue* 超强力胶水 | *super-rich film stars* 特别阔气的电影明星 | *superheated steam* 过热蒸气

S2 **su·per**[1] /ˈsupɚ; ˈsuːpə/ *adj informal* extremely good; WONDERFUL【非正式】极好的，了不起的: *It's a super place for a holiday.* 这是个度假的绝佳去处。| *That sounds super.* 那听起来棒极了。| *What a super idea!* 这个主意好极了!

super[2] *n* [C] *informal* a SUPERINTENDENT (3)【非正式】看门人

super[3] *adv AmE spoken* extremely【美口】十分，非常，极: *Sorry, I'm super tired, I have to turn in.* 对不起，我累得很，得上床睡觉了。

su·per·a·bun·dance /ˌsupərəˈbʌndəns; ˌsuːpərəˈbʌndəns/ *n formal*【正式】**a superabundance of** more than enough of something 过多，过剩 —**superabundant** *adj*

su·per·an·nu·at·ed /ˌsupɚˈænjuˌetɪd; ˌsuːpərˈænjueɪtɪ̈d/ *adj formal* old and no longer useful or no longer able【正式】陈旧的；过时无用的；老弱无能的: *a load of superannuated computer equipment* 一大堆过时的电脑设备 | *superannuated Tory politicians* 老朽无能的保守党政客

su·per·an·nu·a·tion /ˌsupɚˌænjuˈeʃən; ˌsuːpərænjuˈeɪʃən/ *n* [U] *technical especially BrE* money paid as a PENSION[1], especially from your former employer【术语，尤英】〔尤指由前雇主支付的〕退休金

superannuation scheme /ˌ····ˈ·· ·/ *n* [C] *BrE* a type of PENSION PLAN that is paid for by your employer【英】〔由雇主支付的〕退休金方案

su·perb /suˈpɝb; sjuːˈpɜːb/ *adj* [no comparative 无比较级] extremely good; excellent 极好的，超级的；杰出的，卓越的: *The food was superb.* 食物好极了。| *a superb performance* 极其精彩的演出 —**superbly** *adv*

Super Bowl, the /ˈ·· ·/ a football game played in the US each year in late January on a Sunday, known as Super Bowl Sunday, that decides which team is the winning team of the year in the NFL. It was first held in 1967, and is watched on television by millions of people. 超级杯〔美国一年一度的橄榄球比赛，为美国全国橄榄球联盟的年度冠军赛。一月下旬的某个星期天举行，这一天称为“超级杯星期天”。超级杯始于1967年，每年收看电视直播的观众有数百万〕

su·per·bug /ˈsupɚˌbʌg; ˈsuːpəbʌg/ *n* [C] *not technical* a type of BACTERIA that cannot be killed by traditional drugs【非术语】〔不能用传统药物消灭的〕超级病菌

su·per·charg·er /ˈsupɚˌtʃɑrdʒɚ; ˈsuːpəˌtʃɑːdʒə/ *n* [C] *technical* a piece of equipment that increases the power of an engine by supplying air or FUEL[1] (1) at a pressure that is higher than normal【术语】〔发动机的〕增压(助燃)器 —**supercharged** *adj*

su·per·cil·i·ous /ˌsupɚˈsɪlɪəs; ˌsuːpəˈsɪliəs◂/ *adj* behaving as if you think that other people are less important than you; HAUGHTY 高傲的，傲慢的，目中无人的: *She's got a supercilious way of speaking that makes me want to scream!* 她那种目中无人的讲话态度让我真想大叫! | *a supercilious smile* 傲慢的微笑 —**superciliously** *adv* —**superciliousness** *n* [U]

su·per·con·duc·tiv·i·ty /ˌsupɚˌkɑndʌkˈtɪvətɪ; ˌsuːpəkɒndʌkˈtɪvɪ̈ti/ *n* [U] the ability of some substances to allow electricity to flow through them very easily, especially at very low temperatures 超导(电)性

su·per·con·duc·tor /ˌsupɚkənˈdʌktɚ; ˌsuːpəkənˈdʌktə/ *n* [C] a substance that allows electricity to flow through it very easily, especially at very low temperatures 超导体

su·per·du·per /supɚˈdupɚ; ˌsuːpəˈduːpə◂/ *adj old-fashioned* extremely good; SUPER[1]【过时】极好的，极棒的，了不起的

su·per·e·go /ˌsupɚˈigo; ˌsuːpərˈiːgəʊ/ *n* [C] *technical* a word meaning your conscience, used in Freudian PSYCHOLOGY【术语】〔弗洛伊德精神分析学中的〕超我 —compare 比较 EGO (3), ID

su·per·fi·cial /ˌsupɚˈfɪʃəl; ˌsuːpəˈfɪʃəl◂/ *adj*

1 ▶APPEARANCE 外表◀ seeming to have a particular appearance at first, although this is not true or real 表面(上)的: *Despite their superficial similarities, the two novels are in fact very different.* 这两本小说尽管表面上有相似之处，但实际上很不相同。| *a superficial air of tranquility* 表面上平静的气氛

2 ▶NOT LOOKING/STUDYING CAREFULLY 不仔细察看/研究的◀ not studying or looking at something carefully and only noticing the most obvious things 肤浅的，浅薄的，不深入的: *theories based on a superficial knowledge of Japanese business methods* 以对日本经营方法肤浅了解为基础的理论

3 ▶WOUND/DAMAGE 伤口/损伤◀ affecting only the surface of your skin or the outside part of something, and therefore not serious 表皮的；外部的；不严重的: *She escaped with only superficial cuts and bruises.* 她逃了出来，只是皮肤有几处刮破和青肿。| **superficial examination/study etc** *Even a superficial inspection revealed grave flaws.* 即使从表面查看也看出了严重的缺点。

4 ▶PERSON 人◀ someone who is superficial does not think about things that are serious or important; SHALLOW[1] (2) 浅薄的，肤浅的: *a weak-minded and superficial husband who seemed only interested in football* 意志薄弱、头脑简单、只对足球感兴趣的丈夫

5 ▶NOT IMPORTANT 不重要的◀ superficial changes, difficulties etc are not important and do not have a big effect〔变化、困难等〕不重要的，影响不大的: *superficial changes in government policies on the environment* 政府在环境政策方面微不足道的改变

6 ▶TOP LAYER 表层◀ existing in or connected with the top layer of something, especially soil, rock etc〔尤指土壤、岩石等〕表层的 —**superficially** *adv* —**superficiality** /ˌsupɚˌfɪʃɪˈælətɪ; ˌsuːpəfɪʃiˈælɪ̈ti/ *n* [U]

su·per·flu·i·ty /ˌsupɚˈfluətɪ; ˌsuːpəˈfluːɪ̈ti/ *n formal*【正式】**a superfluity of** a larger amount of something than is necessary 多余；过多；过剩

su·per·flu·ous /suˈpɝfluəs; suːˈpɜːfluəs/ *adj formal* more than is needed or wanted; unnecessary【正式】多余的；过剩的；不必要的: *We could all see what was going on, so the commentary was superfluous.* 我们都能看出正在发生的一切，所以那些解说是多余的。—**superfluously** *adv* —**superfluousness** *n* [U]

su·per·glue /ˈsupɚglu; ˈsuːpəgluː/ *n* [U] *trademark* a very strong glue that sticks very quickly and is difficult to remove【商标】超强力胶水 —**superglue** *v* [T]

su·per·grass /ˈsupɚˌgræs; ˈsuːpəgrɑːs/ *n* [C] *BrE* a criminal who gives the police information about many other criminals, in order to get a less severe punishment【英】〔为获得减刑而〕向警方告密的罪犯

su·per·he·ro /ˈsupɚˌhɪro; ˈsuːpəˌhɪərəʊ/ *n* [C] a character in stories who uses special powers, such as great strength or the ability to fly, to help people〔故事中以特异本领助人的〕超级英雄

su·per·high·way /ˈsupɚˌhaɪwe; ˈsuːpəˌhaɪweɪ/ *n* [C] *AmE* a very large road on which you can drive distances quickly【美】高速公路 —see also 另见 INFORMATION SUPERHIGHWAY

su·per·hu·man /ˌsupɚˈhjumən; ˌsuːpəˈhjuːmən◂/ *adj* much greater than ordinary human powers or abilities 超人的，超出常人能力的；非凡的: **superhuman effort/strength** *It will require a superhuman effort to get the job done on time.* 要按时完成这件工作需要付出非凡的努力。

su·per·im·pose /ˌsupərɪmˈpoz; ˌsuːpərɪmˈpəʊz/ *v* [T] **1** to put one picture, image, or photograph on top of another so that both can be partly seen 使〔图画、图像、照片〕重叠，使叠加: **superimpose sth on/onto sth** *His face had been superimposed onto a different background.* 他的脸部被叠加到一个不同的背景上。**2** to combine two systems, ideas, opinions etc so that one influences the other 使〔两种制度、思想、意见等〕相结合，使融合: *Eastern themes superimposed onto Western architecture* 与西方建筑学融合的东方主题 —**superimposition** /ˌsupərɪmpəˈzɪʃən; ˌsuːpərɪmpəˈzɪʃən/ *n* [U]

su·per·in·tend /ˌsuprɪnˈtɛnd; ˌsuːpərɪnˈtend/ *v* [T] *formal* to be in charge of something, and control how it is done【正式】主管；监督；控制 —**superintendence** *n* [U]

su·per·in·tend·ent /ˌsuprɪnˈtɛndənt; ˌsuːpərɪnˈtendənt/ *n* [C] **1** someone who is officially in charge of a place, job, activity etc 主管人；负责人 **2** a middle rank in the British police, or someone who has this rank〔英国的〕警察长，警司 **3** *AmE* someone who is in charge of an apartment building【美】〔公寓楼的〕管房人，看门人 CARETAKER (1) *BrE*【英】**4** also 又作 **superintendent of schools** someone who is in charge of all the schools in a particular area in the US〔美国的〕地区教育主管

su·pe·ri·or[1] /sʊˋpɪrɪɚ; suːˈpɪəriə/ *adj* **1** having a higher position or rank than someone else 职位[级别]更高的; 上级的: *I'll report you to your superior officer.* 我要向你的上司投诉你。| *a superior court* 上级法院 **2** better, more powerful, more effective etc than a similar person or thing, especially one that you are competing against 更好的; 更强的; 更有效的: *Fletcher's fitness and superior technique brought him victory.* 弗莱彻的体能和出色的技术使他取得了胜利。| [+to] *The new mark IV engine is superior to its rivals.* 新的IV型发动机强于其竞争产品。| **vastly superior** (=very much better than others) 比其他的好得多 **3** a word meaning of very good quality, used especially in advertising 质量上乘的, 优质的〔尤用于广告〕: *a superior wine* 优质[上等]葡萄酒 | *superior craftsmanship* 高超的手艺 **4** thinking that you are better than other people 有优越感的, 高傲的, 傲慢的: *He has such a superior attitude, I feel like spitting at him.* 他的态度如此傲慢, 我真想往他的脸上吐唾沫。**5** *technical* higher in position; upper【术语】上面的, 上部的: *the superior limbs* (=arms) 上肢 **6 Mother Superior** a title for the woman in charge of a group of NUNs 女修道院院长 —compare 比较 INFERIOR[1]

superior[2] *n* [C] someone who has a higher rank or position than you, especially in a job 上级, 上司, 长官: **sb's immediate superior** (=the person in a position directly above you) 某人的顶头上司 —compare 比较 INFERIOR[2]

Superior, Lake the largest of the Great Lakes on the border between Canada and the US, which is also the largest FRESHWATER lake (=whose water does not contain salt) in the world 苏必利尔湖〔五大湖最大的一个湖。位于加拿大与美国边境, 是世界上最大的淡水湖〕

su·per·i·or·i·ty /sʊ,pɪrɪˋɔrətɪ; suː,pɪəriˈɒrɪ̣ti/ *n* [U] **1** the quality of being better, more skilful, more powerful etc than other things 优秀; 优势; 优越: [+over] *the intellectual superiority of humans over other animals* 人类与其他动物相比所具有的智力优势 | [+in] *US superiority in air power* 美国空军的优势 **2** an attitude that shows you think you are better than other people 优越感; 骄傲自大: *Janet always spoke with an air of superiority.* 珍妮特说话时总带着一种优越感。

su·per·la·tive[1] /sʊˋpɝlətɪv; suːˈpɜːlətɪv/ *adj* **1** excellent 最好的, 最优秀的: *a superlative performance* 精彩绝伦的表演 **2** a superlative adjective or adverb expresses the highest degree of a particular quality〔形容词或副词〕最高级的: *The superlative form of 'good' is 'best'.* good的最高级形式是best。—compare 比较 COMPARATIVE[1] (4)

superlative[2] *n* **1 the superlative** the superlative form of an adjective or adverb〔形容词或副词的〕最高级(形式): *'Biggest' is the superlative of 'big'.* biggest是big的最高级形式。**2** [C] a word in this form, used especially when expressing great praise or admiration〔尤指表示赞赏的〕最高级形式的形容词[副词]: **a string of superlatives** (=several superlative adjectives praising someone or something) 一连串的盛赞之词

su·per·la·tive·ly /sʊˋpɝlətɪvlɪ; suːˈpɜːlətɪvli/ *adv* extremely 极其, 非常: *superlatively happy* 极为高兴

Su·per·man /ˋsupɚ,mæn; ˈsuːpəmæn/ *trademark* a character in US COMICS (=magazines with stories told in pictures), films, and television programmes. He came to Earth as a baby from an imaginary PLANET called Krypton, and he has great strength and special powers, including the ability to fly and to see through objects using X-ray vision. He uses his powers to save the world from being destroyed by evil characters. Most of the time he lives a normal life as Clark Kent, a reporter for the newspaper *The Daily Planet*, and no one knows that he is Superman, not even his girlfriend, Lois Lane, who also works for the same newspaper. When his help is needed, he quickly changes from his ordinary clothes into a special uniform and becomes Superman.【商标】超人〔美国漫画杂志、电影和电视剧中的人物。他还是婴儿的时候就从虚构的克莱普顿星球来到地球。他力大无比, 具有特异功能, 如飞行能力和能透视物体的X光视力。他利用自己的特殊本领使地球免遭坏人的破坏。他大部分时间以《每日星球报》记者克拉克·肯特的身份过着普通人的生活, 没有人知道他是超人, 甚至和他在同一报社工作的女友洛伊丝·莱恩也不例外。一旦有需要, 他就会迅速脱去便装, 换上一套特制的服装, 变为超人〕

superman *plural* **supermen** /-mɛn; -men/ *n* [C] a man of unusually great ability or strength 超人〔具有超常能力或力量的人〕

3 **su·per·mar·ket** /ˋsupɚ,markɪt; ˈsuːpə,mɑːkɪ̣t/ *n* [C] a very large shop where customers can choose from a large number of different kinds of food and other regularly needed goods 超级市场, 超市

su·per·nal /sʊˋpɝnl; suːˈpɜːnl/ *adj formal* connected with the sky or heaven【正式】〔来自〕天上的; 天国的

su·per·nat·u·ral[1] /,supɚˋnætʃrəl; ,suːpəˈnætʃərəl◂/ *adj* impossible to explain by natural causes, and therefore seeming to involve the powers of gods or magic 超自然的; 奇异的; 神奇的: *supernatural forces* 超自然力量 —**supernaturally** *adv*

supernatural[2] *n* **the supernatural** supernatural events, powers, and creatures 超自然事件; 超自然力; 超自然生命: *belief in the supernatural* 相信超自然力量

su·per·no·va /,supɚˋnovə; ,suːpəˈnəʊvə/ *n* [C] a very large exploding star〔天文中的〕超新星 —compare 比较 NOVA

su·per·nu·me·ra·ry /,supɚˋnjumə,rɛrɪ; ,suːpəˈnjuːmərəri/ *n* [C] *formal* someone or something that is additional to the number of people or things that are needed【正式】多余的人[物]; 额外的人[物] —**supernumerary** *adj*

su·per·pow·er /,supɚˋpauɚ; ˈsuːpə,paʊə/ *n* [C] a nation that has very great military and political power 超级大国

su·per·script /ˋsupɚ,skrɪpt; ˈsuːpəskrɪpt/ *adj* written or printed above a number, letter etc 上标的〔写或印在数字、字母等上方或上角的〕—**superscript** *n* [C,U]

su·per·sede /,supɚˋsid; ,suːpəˈsiːd/ *v* [T often passive 常用被动态] if a new idea, product, or method supersedes another one, it becomes used instead because it is more modern or effective 替代, 取代: *Television superseded radio in the fifties.* 电视在50年代取代了无线电广播。

su·per·ser·ver /ˋsupɚ,sɝvɚ; ˈsuːpə,sɜːvə/ *n* [C] a very powerful computer that controls other computers〔电脑的〕超级服务器

su·per·son·ic /,supɚˋsanɪk; ,suːpəˈsɒnɪk◂/ *adj* faster than the speed of sound 超声速的: *supersonic aircraft* 超音速飞机 —compare 比较 SUBSONIC

su·per·star /ˋsupɚ,star; ˈsuːpəstɑː/ *n* [C] an extremely famous performer, especially a musician or film actor〔尤指音乐或电影中的〕超级巨星

su·per·sti·tion /,supɚˋstɪʃən; ,suːpəˈstɪʃən/ *n* [C,U] a belief that some objects or actions are lucky and some are unlucky, based on old ideas of magic 迷信: *the old superstition that walking under a ladder is unlucky* 认为在梯子下走不吉利的那种古老的迷信思想

CULTURAL NOTE 文化注释

Although most American and British people do not consider themselves to be superstitious, people do still mention a lot of superstitions. If someone spills salt, they sometimes pick up a small amount of it and throw it over their left shoulder to avoid bad luck. When people talk about something good that they hope will happen, they often say "knock on wood" or "touch wood" while touching a piece of wood to make sure that it does happen: *"The car will be fixed on Monday, touch wood."* To be funny, people sometimes touch their own head when they say "touch wood". People also say "fingers crossed" and put their middle finger over their INDEX FINGER when they hope that something will happen. *"Fingers crossed, we should arrive in Paris before 10 pm."* 尽管大多数英美人认为自己并不迷信, 人们仍然会提到很多迷信的事。如果有人不小心将盐撒出, 他们有时会捡起一小撮并从左肩膀上扔过去, 以此来消灾。当人们希望谈及的好事发生时, 经常说knock wood或touch wood("敲木头"或"摸木头", 意为但愿如此或希望好运), 同时用手摸一块木头来确保好事发生: "星期一汽车就能修好了, 但愿如此。" 为了搞笑, 人们有时摸着自己的脑袋口里照样说着touch wood。也有说fingers crossed("手指交叉", 意为上帝保佑)并把中指与食指交叉, 人们以此希望某事出现, 如"上帝保佑, 让我们晚上10点之前到达巴黎。" — see also Cultural Note at LUCKY, UNLUCKY 另见 LUCKY, UNLUCKY 文化注释

su·per·sti·tious /,supɚˋstɪʃəs; ,suːpəˈstɪʃəs◂/ *adj* influenced by old-fashioned beliefs about luck and magic 迷信的 —**superstitiously** *adv*

su·per·store /ˋsupɚ,stor; ˈsuːpəstɔː/ *n* [C] *BrE* a very large shop that sells many different types of goods, usually just outside a town【英】超级商场, 大型商场〔通常在市外, 出售各类商品的大型商店〕

su·per·struc·ture /ˋsupɚ,strʌktʃɚ; ˈsuːpə,strʌktʃə/ *n* [singular,U] **1** a structure that is built on top of the main part of something such as a ship or building〔船、建筑物等的〕上部结构, 上部建筑, 上层建筑物 **2** *formal* political and social systems that are based on a simpler system【正式】〔政治和社会制度等

的〕上层建筑: *a superstructure of religion based on nature worship* 以自然崇拜为基础的宗教上层建筑

su·per·tank·er /ˈsupɚˌtæŋkɚ; ˈsuːpəˌtæŋkə/ *n* [C] an extremely large ship that can carry large quantities of oil or other liquids 超级油轮, 巨型油轮

Super Tues·day /ˌ‥ ˈ‥/ in the US, the second Tuesday in March during a year when there is an election for the position of President. Before the main election in November, there is a series of PRIMARY elections, in which the people in each state choose the person that they want as their party's candidate for President. On Super Tuesday there are several important primaries in different states all on the same day. 超级星期二〔美国总统大选年3月份的第二个星期二。美国大选在11月份举行, 但此前要进行一系列初选, 各州公民选出自己所支持政党的总统候选人。在超级星期二这天, 数场重要初选在各州同期举行〕

su·per·vene /ˌsupɚˈvin; ˌsuːpəˈviːn/ *v* [I] *formal* to happen unexpectedly, especially in a way that stops or interrupts an event or situation【正式】意外发生〔尤指因而终止或干扰某事〕

su·per·vise /ˈsupɚˌvaɪz; ˈsuːpəvaɪz/ *v* [I,T] to be in charge of a group of workers or students and be responsible for making sure that they do their work properly 监督; 管理; 指导 —**supervisor** *n* [C] —**supervisory** /ˌsupɚˈvaɪzərɪ; ˌsuːpəˈvaɪzəri◂/ *adj*: *She works there in a supervisory capacity.* 她在那里担任监督指导的工作。

su·per·vi·sion /ˌsupɚˈvɪʒən; ˌsuːpəˈvɪʒən/ *n* [U] the act of supervising someone or something 监督; 管理; 指导; 主管: *The patient is improving, but still needs constant supervision.* 病人已在好转, 但还需要不间断地进行监护。| **under sb's supervision** *We work under the Chief Engineer's supervision.* 我们在总工程师的指导下进行工作。

su·pine /suˈpaɪn; ˈsuːpaɪn/ *adj formal*【正式】**1** lying on your back 仰卧的 —opposite 反义词 PRONE (2) **2** allowing other people to make decisions instead of you in a way that seems very weak-minded 无所作为的; 消极的; 优柔寡断的: *a supine and cowardly press, scared by government threats of censorship* 消极软弱、被政府的审查威胁吓破了胆的新闻界 —**supinely** *adv*

sup·per /ˈsʌpɚ; ˈsʌpə/ *n* [C,U] the last meal of the evening 晚饭, 晚餐

sup·plant /səˈplænt; səˈplɑːnt/ *v* [T] to take the place of a person or thing so that they are no longer used, no longer in a position of power etc 取代, 代替; 将…排挤掉: *Barker was soon supplanted as party leader.* 巴克在该党中的领导地位很快就被人取代了。

sup·ple /ˈsʌpl̩; ˈsʌpəl/ *adj* **1** someone who is supple bends and moves easily and gracefully 〔身体〕柔软的, 灵活的: *She exercises every day to keep herself supple.* 她每天锻炼以保持身体灵活。**2** leather, skin, wood etc that is supple is soft and bends easily 〔皮革、皮肤、木料等〕柔软易弯的; 柔韧的 —**suppleness** *n* [U]

sup·ple·ment¹ /ˈsʌpləmənt; ˈsʌpl̩mənt/ *n* [C] **1** something that you add to something else to improve it or make it complete 增补物, 补充物, 补给品: *a dietary supplement* 饮食的补充物 **2** an additional part at the end of a book, or a separate part of a newspaper, magazine etc 〔书的〕补编, 补遗; 〔报纸、杂志的〕增刊: *the Sunday supplements* 星期天的增刊 **3** an amount of money that is added to the price of a service, hotel room etc 〔服务、旅馆房费等的〕附加费: *There is a £5 supplement for extra sheets and towels.* 额外的床单和毛巾收附加费5英镑。

sup·ple·ment² /ˈsʌpləˌmɛnt; ˈsʌpl̩ment/ *v* [T always+ adv/prep] to add something, especially to what you earn or eat, in order to increase it to an acceptable level 补充, 增补, 增加: **supplement sth by/with** *Kia supplements her regular salary by tutoring in the evenings.* 基娅靠在晚上当家庭教师来补贴她固定的薪水。—**supplementation** /ˌsʌpləmɛnˈteʃən; ˌsʌpl̩menˈteɪʃən/ *n* [U]

sup·ple·men·ta·ry /ˌsʌpləˈmɛntərɪ; ˌsʌpl̩ˈmentəri◂/ *adj* provided in addition to what already exists 补充的, 增补的, 附加的: *There is a supplementary water supply in case the main supply fails.* 万一主要供水系统出现故障, 还有补充供水。

sup·pli·ant /ˈsʌplɪənt; ˈsʌpliənt/ *n* [C] *literary* a supplicant【文】恳求者, 哀求者 —**suppliant** *adj*

sup·pli·cant /ˈsʌplɪkənt; ˈsʌplɪkənt/ *n* [C] *literary* someone who asks for something, especially from someone in a position of power or from God【文】恳求者, 哀求者, 祈求者〔尤指向有权者或上帝请求〕

sup·pli·cate /ˈsʌplɪˌket; ˈsʌpl̩keɪt/ *v* [I,T] *literary* to ask or pray for help from someone in power or from God【文】恳求, 祈求; 哀求〔有权势者或上帝〕—**supplication** /ˌsʌplɪˈkeʃən; ˌsʌpl̩ˈkeɪʃən/ *n* [U]: *Paolo knelt and bowed his head in supplication.* 保罗跪着在低头祈祷。

sup·pli·er /səˈplaɪɚ; səˈplaɪə/ *n* [C] also 又作 **suppliers** a company that provides a particular product 供应商: *Continental is one of the world's biggest suppliers of grain.* 大陆公司是世界最大的谷物供应商之一。

sup·ply¹ /səˈplaɪ; səˈplaɪ/ *n*

1 ▶AMOUNT AVAILABLE 可用量◀ [C] an amount of something that is available to be used 供应量, 供给量: **[+of]** *a regular supply of fresh vegetables* 新鲜蔬菜的经常供应 | *More donors are needed as blood supplies are running low.* 由于血液供应不足, 需要更多的捐血者。

2 be in short supply if something is in short supply, there is very little of it available and it is difficult to get 供应不足, 不充裕: *Chocolate was in short supply during the war.* 战争期间巧克力供应不足。

3 gas/electricity/water supply a system that is used to supply gas etc 煤气/电力/自来水供应(系统): **cut off a supply** (=stop the supply) 停止[中断]供应 *During the drought some households had their water supply cut off.* 在干旱期间有些住户的自来水供应被中断。

4 ▶NECESSARY THINGS 必需品◀ supplies [plural] food, clothes and things necessary for daily life, especially for a group of people over a period of time 日用(必需)品〔尤指供一些人在一段时间内用的东西〕: *A convoy of trucks packed with vital medical supplies succeeded in reaching the town.* 一个满载重要医药用品的卡车车队成功抵达那个城镇。

5 supply and demand [U] the relationship between the amount of goods for sale and the amount that people want to buy, especially the way it influences prices 供求关系

6 ▶ACT OF SUPPLYING 供应◀ [U] the act or process of supplying something 供应, 供给, 补给: *The military government is trying to stop the supply of guns to the rebels.* 军政府在试图切断叛军的枪支补给。| *supply of oxygen to the brain* 对大脑的氧气供应

7 supply ship/convoy/route etc a ship etc used for bringing or storing supplies 补给船/车[船]队/路线等 —see also 另见 MONEY SUPPLY

supply² *v* [T] to provide people with something that they need or want, especially regularly over a long period of time 供应, 供给, 提供〔所需物品〕: **supply sb with sth** *US forces mounted a massive air operation to keep the city supplied with food.* 美军进行大规模空运以保持那个城市的食品供应。| *An informer supplied the police with the names of those involved in the crime.* 一位告密者向警方告发了与罪案有牵连的人。| **supply sth to sb** *They were arrested for supplying drugs to street dealers.* 他们因给街头毒品贩子提供毒品而被逮捕。

supply-side e·co·nom·ics /ˌ‥ ‥ˈ‥/ *n* [U] *technical* the idea that if the government reduces taxes, producers will be able to make more goods and this will improve a country's economic situation【术语】供应经济学〔主张通过减税以刺激生产和投资从而有利于国家经济形势的理论〕

supply teach·er /ˈ‥ ˌ‥/ *n* [C] *BrE* a teacher who does the work of another teacher who is ill, on a course etc【英】代课教师; SUBSTITUTE TEACHER *AmE*【美】

sup·port¹ /səˈpɔrt; səˈpɔːt/ *v* [T]

1 ▶AGREE WITH SB/STH 赞同某人/某事◀ to say that you agree with an idea, group, person etc and want them to succeed 支持; 赞成; 拥护: *The bill was supported by a large majority in the Senate.* 这项法案得到参议院里大多数人的支持。| **support sb in sth** *We support the police wholeheartedly in their work against crime.* 我们全力支持警方打击犯罪活动的工作。| **strongly support** (=support something very much) 大力支持

2 ▶HOLD STH UP 撑起某物◀ to hold the weight of something, keep it in place, or prevent it from falling 支撑, 承受〔某物的重量〕: *The middle part of the bridge is supported by two huge towers.* 桥的中部由两个巨型桥塔支撑着。| *I grabbed the rail to support myself.* 我抓住栏杆来支撑自己。

3 ▶PROVIDE MONEY TO LIVE 提供生活费◀ to provide enough money for someone to pay for all the things they need 供养, 抚养, 资助: *She needs a high income to support such a large family.* 她需要一份高收入来养活这么一大家子。| *It's difficult to support yourself on this salary.* 靠这份薪水来养活你自己是困难的。

4 ▶GIVE MONEY TO STH 给某事物出钱◀ to encourage a group, organization or event etc by giving it money 出钱帮助, 为…提供资金, 资助: *Please support your local theatre, buy some tickets today!* 请资助本地的剧院, 今天就买几张票吧!

5 ▶HELP SB 帮助某人◀ to help someone by being sympathetic and kind to them during a difficult time in their life〔在困难时期〕帮助，支持：*My wife supported me enormously when my mother died.* 我母亲去世时，我妻子给了我极大的安慰。
6 ▶LAND 土地◀ if land can support people or animals, it is of good enough quality to grow enough food for them to live〔指土地提供足够的食物〕养活，维持〔人和动物的生命〕：*This land isn't fertile enough to support many cattle.* 这片土地不够肥沃，养不活许多牛。
7 ▶A BAD HABIT 不良习惯◀ to get money in order to pay for a bad habit such as taking drugs 支付…的花费，用钱维持〔不良习惯〕：*He stole from his mother's savings to support his drug habit.* 他偷母亲的积蓄来维持自己的吸毒恶习。
8 ▶PROVE STH 证明某事物◀ to show or prove that something is true or correct 证明，证实：*The results support our original theory.* 这些结果证明了我们最初的理论。
9 ▶SPORTS TEAM 运动队◀ *especially BrE* to like a particular sports team and go to watch the games they play【尤英】为〔某运动队〕捧场，支持：*Trev supports Arsenal, but I like Spurs.* 特雷夫是阿森纳队的球迷，而我喜欢热刺队。
10 ▶BEAR STH 忍受某事◀ [usually in negatives 一般用于否定句] *formal* to be able to bear something; ENDURE【正式】忍受：*She could not support the heat any longer.* 她再也不能忍受这种酷热了。—see also 另见 INSUPPORTABLE

2 2 **support²** *n*
1 ▶APPROVAL 赞同◀ [U] approval and encouragement for an idea, plan etc 支持，拥护，赞同：*Local people have given us a lot of support in our campaign.* 当地人民对我们的活动给予了很多支持。| **in support of** *They signed a petition in support of the pay claim.* 他们在请愿书上签名支持这次的加薪要求。| **drum up support** (=get many people's approval) 争取人们的支持 *The Americans used the story to drum up support for the stronger measures against Libya.* 美国人利用这个借口争取人们支持对利比亚采取更加强硬的措施。
2 ▶SYMPATHY/HELP 同情/帮助◀ [U] sympathetic encouragement and help that you give to someone 同情；鼓励；帮助：*Thanks for all your support at this difficult time.* 谢谢你们在这困难时刻所给予的一切帮助。—see also 另见 **moral support** (MORAL¹ (3))
3 ▶HOLD STH UP 撑起某物◀ [C,U] something such as a piece of wood that presses up on something else to hold it up or in position 支撑物；支柱；支架；支座：*The roof may need extra support.* 这个房顶需要额外的支撑物。| *the supports of a bridge* 桥梁的支座
4 ▶INJURED PART OF BODY 身体的受伤部位◀ [C] something that you wear to hold a weak or damaged part of your body in the right place〔用以支撑身体虚弱或受伤部位等的〕支持(器)，托
5 ▶PEOPLE WHO SUPPORT STH 支持某事的人◀ [U] the people who support a political party, an idea, a team etc〔某政党、思想、球队等的〕支持者，拥护者：*There isn't much local support for the new candidate.* 新候选人得不到多少当地人的支持。

sup·por·ta·ble /səˋpɔrtəbl; səˈpɔːtəbəl/ *adj* [usually in negatives 一般用于否定句] *formal* possible to bear; TOLERABLE【正式】可忍受的

2 2 **sup·port·er** /səˋpɔrtɚ; səˈpɔːtə/ *n* [C] **1** someone who supports a particular person, group, or plan 支持者，拥护者：**strong/firm/staunch supporter** *one of Clinton's staunchest supporters* 克林顿最坚定的支持者之一 | *supporters of animal rights legislation* 支持为动物权利立法的人们 **2** *especially BrE* someone who supports a sports team, especially by regularly going to watch them play; FAN¹ (1)【尤英】〔球队的〕支持者，球迷：*Manchester United supporters* 曼彻斯特联队的支持者

support group /ˈ· · ·/ *n* [C] a group of people who meet to help each other with a particular problem, for example ALCOHOLISM〔为解决酗酒等问题而成立的〕互助组

sup·port·ing /səˋpɔrtɪŋ; səˈpɔːtɪŋ/ *adj* **1 supporting part/role/actor etc** a small part in a play or film, or the actor who plays such a part〔戏剧或电影中的〕配角/演配角的男演员等 **2 supporting wall/beam etc** a wall etc that supports the weight of something 支撑墙/梁等

sup·por·tive /səˋpɔrtɪv; səˈpɔːtɪv/ *adj approving* giving help or encouragement, especially to someone who is in a difficult situation【褒】支持的；给予帮助和鼓励的：*I can always count on Gail to be supportive when things go wrong.* 出问题时我总能依靠盖尔的帮助。

1 1 **sup·pose¹** /səˋpoz; səˈpəʊz/ *v* [T] **1 be supposed to do sth a)** used when saying what someone should or should not do, especially because of rules or what someone in authority has said 被期望做某事；应该做某事：*You're supposed to ask the teacher if you want to leave the classroom.* 你如果要离开教室，应该先问问老师。| *We're not supposed to smoke here.* 我们不应该在这里抽烟。**b)** used when saying what people intended should happen, especially when it failed to happen 本应，本该〔用于表示某事本应发生而没有发生〕：*The new laws are supposed to prevent crime.* 这些新法令本应起到防止犯罪的作用。| *The meeting was supposed to take place on Tuesday, but we've had to postpone it.* 这会本应该星期二举行，但我们不得不把它推迟了。**2 be supposed to be sth** to be believed to be something by many people 被相信是…，被认为…：*The castle is supposed to be haunted.* 这座城堡据说在闹鬼。| *'Dirty Harry' is supposed to be one of Eastwood's best films.*《辣手神探夺命枪》被认为是伊斯特伍德的最佳影片之一。**3** to think that something is probably true, based on what you know 认为，料想，猜想，假定：*There were many more deaths than was first supposed.* 死亡人数要比早先预想的多得多。| **suppose (that)** *What makes you suppose we're going to sell the house?* 你凭什么认为我们准备把这房子卖掉？| **be generally supposed** (=most people think that something was probably true) 被多数人认为，一般认为 *Mr Tyke was generally supposed to have left the country.* 一般认为泰克先生已经离开这个国家了。| **There is no reason to suppose (that)** (=used to say that you think something is unlikely) 没有理由推测〔表示某事不大可能〕*There's no reason to suppose her new book will be any better than her last one.* 没有理由推测她的新书会比上一本好。**4** *formal* to expect that something will happen and base your plans on it【正式】假定，预期；以…为条件：*The company's plan supposes a steady increase in orders.* 公司的计划是假定订单将持续稳定地增加。

Frequencies of the verb **suppose** in spoken and written English 动词 suppose 在英语口语和书面语中的使用频率

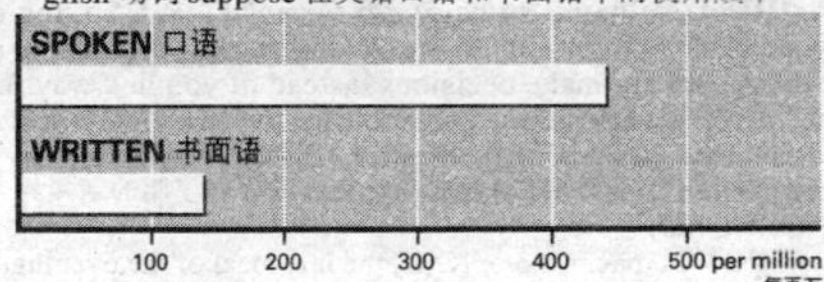

Based on the British National Corpus and the Longman Lancaster Corpus
据英国国家语料库和朗文兰开斯特语料库

This graph shows that the verb **suppose** is much more common in spoken English than in written English. This is because it is used in some common spoken phrases. 本图表显示，动词 suppose 在英语口语中的使用频率远远高于书面语，因为口语中一些常用的短语是由 suppose 构成的。

suppose (*adv*) **SPOKEN PHRASES**
含 suppose 的口语短语

5 I suppose *especially BrE*【尤英】**a)** used to say you think something is true, although you are uncertain about it 我想，我认为〔用于认为某事真实，但不敢肯定〕：**I suppose (that)** *I suppose he could have shot himself, but where would he have got the gun?* 我想他可能是开枪自杀的，但他从哪里弄到枪的？| *I suppose Philip will be late, as usual.* 我想菲利普照例又会迟到的。**b)** used when agreeing to let someone do something, especially unwillingly 我想〔尤用于表示勉强同意某人做某事〕：**I suppose so** *"Can we come with you?" "Oh, I suppose so."* "我们可以跟你一起去吗？" "噢，我看可以吧。" **c)** used when guessing that something is true 我猜想〔用于表示猜测〕：*She looked about 50, I suppose.* 我看她大约50岁。**d)** used when saying in an angry way that you expect something is true 我看〔用于生气地表示预料某事真实〕：**I suppose (that)** *I suppose you thought you were being smart!* 我看你是自作聪明！**e)** used to say that you think that something is probably true, although you wish it was not and hope someone will tell you it is not 恐怕〔用于表示某事很可能真实，虽然自己希望并非如此〕：**I suppose (that)** *I suppose it's too late to apply for that job now.* 恐怕现在申请那份工作已经太迟了。**6 suppose/supposing** used to ask someone to imagine what would happen if a particular situation existed 假设，假定〔用于要某人设想如果某情况存在会发生什么事〕：*Look, suppose you lost your job tomorrow, what would you do?* 哎，假设你明天丢掉了工作，你会怎么办呢？**7 I don't suppose (that)** *especially BrE*【尤英】**a)** used to ask for something in a very polite way〔用于很礼貌地提出要求〕：*I don't suppose you'd give me a lift to the station?* 我能否顺便搭你的车子去车站？**b)** used to say that you think it is unlikely something will happen 我

以为不会〔用于表示某事不大可能发生〕: *I don't suppose I'll ever see her again.* 我想我再也不会见到她了。**8 who/what etc do you suppose** used to ask someone who, what etc they think did something, is something etc 你认为是谁/什么等…: *Who on earth do you suppose could have done this?* 你认为到底是谁能干出这种事来? **9 what's that supposed to mean?** used when you are annoyed by what someone has just said 这是什么意思?〔用于表示对某人刚说的话感到恼火〕: *"I'll bear your offer in mind." "Bear it in mind! What's that supposed to mean?"* "你的提议我会记在心上。" "记在心上! 那是什么意思?"

suppose[2] *conjunction especially spoken* 【尤口】**1** used when imagining what the result would be if something happened; SUPPOSING 假设, 假定〔用于假设某事发生后带来的后果〕: **suppose (that)** *It's not worth the risk, suppose your mother found out?* 不值得冒这个险, 万一你妈妈发现了怎么办? **2** *informal* used to suggest something; SUPPOSING 【非正式】〔用于提出建议〕: *Suppose we try to sort this out before we go.* 咱们尽量在走之前把这事解决了吧。

sup·posed /sə`pozd; sə'pəʊzd/ *adj* [only before noun 仅用于名词前] claimed by other people to be true or real, although you do not think they are right 据说的, 假定的: *the supposed benefits and advantages of privatizing state industries* 所谓的国家工业私有化带来的利益和优越性

sup·pos·ed·ly /sə`pozɪdlɪ; sə'pəʊzɨdli/ *adv* used when saying what many people say or believe is true, especially when you disagree with them 据说, 据称; 一般相信, 一般看来: *In April 1912 this supposedly unsinkable ship hit an iceberg.* 1912年4月, 这艘据称不会沉没的海轮撞上了冰山。| [sentence adverb 句子副词] *Supposedly, she's a rich woman.* 据推测, 她是个很有钱的女人。

sup·pos·ing /sə`pozɪŋ; sə'pəʊzɪŋ/ *conjunction* SUPPOSE[2] 假设, 假定

sup·po·si·tion /ˌsʌpə`zɪʃən; ˌsʌpə'zɪʃən/ *n* [C,U] something that you think is true even though you are not certain and cannot prove it 假定; 推测; 猜测: *His version of events is pure supposition.* 他对事件的说法纯属推测。| **supposition (that)** *The police are acting on the supposition that she took the money.* 警方正按照她偷了钱的推测采取行动。

sup·pos·i·to·ry /sə`pɑzəˌtorɪ; sə'pɒzɨtəri/ *n* [C] a small piece of solid medicine that is placed in someone's RECTUM or VAGINA 〔放入直肠或阴道的〕栓剂, 坐药 —compare 比较 PESSARY (1)

sup·press /sə`prɛs; sə'pres/ *v* [T] **1** to stop people from opposing the government, especially by using force 〔尤指用武力〕镇压, 制止, 压制: *The revolt was ruthlessly suppressed by the military.* 叛乱受到军方的残酷镇压。**2** to prevent important information or opinions from becoming known, especially from people who have a right to know 禁止发表〔消息、言论等〕; 查禁, 封锁: *attempts by the Pentagon to suppress documents connected with the case* 五角大楼想封锁与该案件有关文件的企图 **3** to stop yourself from showing your feelings 抑制〔感情〕, 忍住: *Susan could hardly suppress a giggle.* 苏珊差点忍不住要咯咯地笑出声来。| *suppressed anger* 强忍的怒火 **4** to prevent something from growing or developing, or from working effectively 抑制〔生长、发展、起作用等〕: *The virus suppresses the body's immune system.* 这种病毒破坏人体的免疫系统。—**suppressible** *adj* —**suppression** /-`prɛʃən; -'preʃən/ *n* [U]: *the suppression of free speech* 压制言论自由

sup·pu·rate /`sʌpjəˌret; 'sʌpjʊ̈reɪt/ *v* [I] *technical* if a wound suppurates it produces or gives out PUS (=infected liquid) 【术语】〔伤口〕化脓 —**suppuration** /ˌsʌpjə`reʃən; ˌsʌpjʊ̈'reɪʃən/ *n* [U]

su·pra·na·tion·al /ˌsuprə`næʃənl; ˌsuːprə'næʃənəl/ *adj* involving more than one country 超国家的, 多国的: *a supranational organization* 超国家组织

su·prem·a·cist /sə`prɛməsɪst; sə'preməsɨst/ *n* [C] someone who believes that their own particular group or race is better than any other 〔某团体或种族〕至上主义者: *a white supremacist group* 白人至上主义者团体

su·prem·a·cy /sə`prɛməsɪ; sə'preməsi/ *n* [U] the position in which you are more powerful or advanced than anyone else 至高无上; 最高地位: *Japan's unchallenged supremacy in the field of electronics* 日本在电子领域未受到挑战的最高地位

su·preme /su`prim; suː'priːm/ *adj* **1** having the highest position of power, importance, or influence 〔权力、地位、重要性或影响力〕最高的, 至高无上的: *the Supreme Allied Commander in Europe* 欧洲盟军最高司令 | **reign supreme** *where justice reigns supreme* 在正义主宰一切的地方 **2** [only before noun 仅用于名词前] the greatest possible 〔程度〕最大的, 极度的: *supreme courage in the face of terrible danger* 在极大危险面前表现出的高度勇气 | **supreme effort** *It required a supreme effort to stop myself from giving up.* 我尽了最大努力才使自己没有半途而废。| **of supreme importance** *a matter of supreme importance* 极为重要的事情 **3 make the supreme sacrifice** to die for your country, for a principle etc 为国捐躯; 〔为原则等〕牺牲

Supreme Be·ing /·ˌ· '··/ *n* [singular] *literary* God 【文】上帝

Supreme Court /·ˌ· '·/ *n* [singular] the most important court of law in some countries or some states of the US 〔一些国家或美国一些州的〕最高法院

CULTURAL NOTE 文化注释

The Supreme Court deals with cases that are concerned with people's CONSTITUTIONAL rights (=rights that are written down in the US CONSTITUTION), such as the right to speak freely and the right to fair and equal treatment. Cases that are dealt with in the Supreme Court are often related to things that people have very strong opinions about, such as ABORTION. 美国联邦最高法院处理涉及到人们宪法权利的案件, 例如言论自由的权利以及获得公正和平等对待的权利。联邦最高法院处理的案件通常涉及一些人们强烈支持或反对的事物。

Supreme Court Jus·tice /·ˌ· · '··/ one of the nine judges of the US Supreme Court. Each Supreme Court Justice is chosen by the President of the US and must then be accepted by Congress, and they usually have this position for the rest of their lives. The most important judge is called the Chief Justice. 最高法院大法官〔美国联邦最高法院九名大法官之一。每位大法官均由美国总统提名并须经国会批准。该职务通常为终身制。最重要的大法官称作"首席大法官"〕

su·preme·ly /su`primlɪ; suː'priːmli/ *adv* [+adj/adv] extremely or to the greatest possible degree 极度地; 极其: *a supremely talented player* 极有才能的选手

su·prem·o /su`primo; suː'priːməʊ/ *n* [C] *BrE informal* someone who controls a particular activity, organization, or industry, and has unlimited powers 【英, 非正式】〔具有无限权力的〕最高权威; 最高领导人

Supt. the written abbreviation of 缩写= SUPERINTENDENT

sur·charge[1] /`sɝˌtʃɑrdʒ; 'sɜːtʃɑːdʒ/ *n* [C] money that you have to pay in addition to the basic price of something 附加费, 额外费用: **[+on]** *a 10% surcharge on airline tickets* 飞机票10%的附加费

surcharge[2] *v* [T] to make someone pay an additional amount of money 向〔某人〕收取附加费

sur·coat /`sɝˌkot; 'sɜːkəʊt/ *n* [C] a piece of clothing with no arms which was worn over ARMOUR (1) in the past 〔古代穿在铠甲外面的〕无袖罩袍

sure[1] /ʃur; ʃɔː/ *adj*

1 ►CERTAIN YOU KNOW STH 肯定知道某事◄ [not before noun 不用于名词前] confident that you know something or that something is true or correct 确信的, 有把握的: *"What time does the show start?" "I'm not sure."* "表演什么时候开始?" "我拿不准。" | **sure (that)** *I'm sure there's a logical explanation for all this.* 我确信所有这些问题都是有合理解释的。| *Are you sure you know how to get there?* 你肯定知道怎样到那里去吗? | **[+of]** *You need to be sure of your facts before making any accusations.* 你在提出任何指控之前必须对自己所掌握的事实很有把握才行。| **[+about]** *"That's the man I saw in the building last night." "Are you quite sure about that ?"* "那就是我昨晚在大楼里看见的那个男人。" "你能完全肯定吗?" | **not sure how/where/whether etc** *I'm not sure where Michael is, to be honest.* 老实说, 我拿不准迈克尔现在在哪儿。| **not sure if** *Mr Watkins isn't sure if he'll be able to come.* 沃特金斯先生不敢肯定他是不是能来。| **pretty sure** (=almost certain) 几乎可以肯定 *I'm pretty sure Barbara still works there.* 我几乎可以肯定芭芭拉还在那儿工作。

2 ►CERTAIN ABOUT YOUR FEELINGS 清楚自己的感觉◄ [not before noun 不用于名词前] certain about what you feel, want, like etc 〔对自己的感觉、要求、喜爱等〕肯定的, 确实的, 无疑的: *"Are you sure you really want a divorce?"* "你肯定你确实想要离婚吗?"

3 make sure a) to find out if something is true or to check that something has been done 〔把某事〕弄清楚, 查明: *"Did you lock the front door?" "I think so, but I'd better make sure."* "你锁前门了吗?" "我想是的, 但我最好还是去查看一下。" | **make sure (that)** *Emma peered into the room to make sure that Ruth was asleep.* 埃玛往房间里仔细查看, 要搞清楚露斯确实是睡着了。**b)**

to do something so that you can be certain of the result 设法确保: **make sure (that)** *I made sure that the rope was firmly fastened around his waist.* 我检查了绳子，确保其牢牢系在他的腰部。| **make sure of sth** *Ben made sure of winning by betting on all the horses.* 本对所有的马都下了注，确保能赢。

4 ▶CERTAIN TO BE TRUE 肯定（真实）的◀ certain to be true 肯定真实的，肯定的，确切的: **one thing is (for) sure** *One thing's for sure, we'll never be able to move this furniture on our own.* 有一点是肯定的，我们自己绝对搬不动这些家具。| **sure sign/indication** (=a sign that something is certainly going to happen) 某事肯定会发生的征兆/标志 *Those black clouds are a sure sign of rain.* 那些黑云是肯定要下雨的征兆。

5 ▶CERTAIN TO SUCCEED 肯定要成功◀ certain to succeed 肯定会成功的: **sure way/means** (=a way of doing something that will certainly achieve a particular result) 万无一失的方法 *Arriving at work in pyjamas is a sure way of attracting attention to yourself!* 穿睡衣去上班肯定是惹人注目的一种做法！| **a sure bet** *AmE* (=something that is certain to succeed)【美】一定成功的事，十拿九稳的事 | **a sure thing** *AmE* (=something that will definitely happen, win, succeed etc)【美】一定会发生的事；肯定会赢[成功]的事

6 be sure of to be certain to get something or be certain that something will happen 一定会，肯定会: *United must beat Liverpool to be sure of winning the championship.* 联队要稳拿冠军就必须打败利物浦队。| *You can be sure of one thing – there'll be a lot of laughs.* 有一点可以肯定 —— 将会笑声不断。

7 sure of yourself confident in your own abilities and opinions, sometimes in a way that annoys other people 有自信心；〔过分〕自信: *Kids nowadays seem very sure of themselves.* 如今的小孩显得非常自信。

8 be sure to do sth *spoken* used to tell someone to remember to do something【口】一定要做某事，务必要做某事〔用于告诉某人记住做某事〕: *Be sure to ring and let us know you've got back safely.* 一定要来个电话，让我们知道你已经平安返回。

9 sure to do sth certain to happen or to do something〔某事〕一定会发生；肯定会做某事: *He's sure to get nervous and say something stupid.* 他肯定会精神紧张，说些蠢话。

10 (as) sure as hell *spoken especially AmE* used to emphasize a statement【口，尤美】绝对肯定〔用于强调〕: *I'm sure as hell not gonna do it.* 我绝对肯定不去做那件事。

11 to be sure *BrE spoken* used to admit that something is true, before saying something that is the opposite【英口】不能否认；诚然，固然〔用于要说相反意见之前〕: *Jamie's had his problems to be sure, but he's got potential.* 无可否认，杰米固然有他自己的问题，但他是有潜力的。

12 sure thing *AmE spoken* used to agree to something【美口】当然；没问题: *"See you next week?" "Sure thing."* "下星期再见?" "当然。"

13 have/get a sure hold/footing if you have a sure hold or footing your hands or feet are placed firmly so they cannot slip 抓紧/站稳 —see also 另见 SURELY

14 sure as eggs are eggs *BrE old-fashioned* used to say that something is definitely true【英，过时】的的确确，千真万确，毫无疑问 —**sureness** *n* [U]

Frequencies of the word **sure** in spoken and written English 单词sure在英语口语和书面语中的使用频率

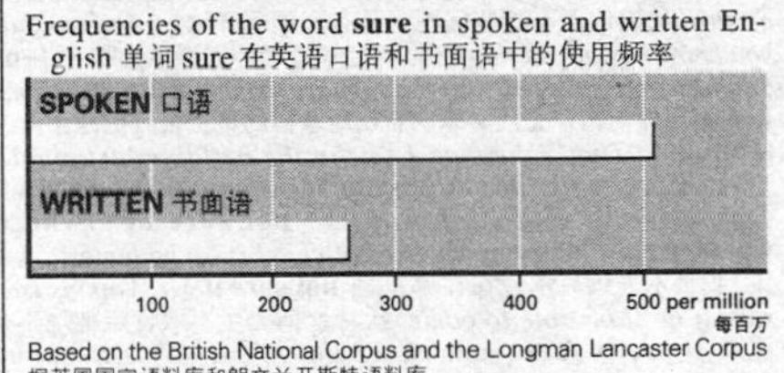

Based on the British National Corpus and the Longman Lancaster Corpus
据英国国家语料库和朗文兰开斯特语料库

This graph shows that the word **sure** is much more common in spoken English than in written English. This is because it has special uses in spoken English and is used in some common spoken phrases. 本图表显示，单词sure在英语口语中的使用频率远远高于书面语，因为它在口语中有特殊的用法，而且口语中一些常用短语是由sure构成的。

sure² *adv*

1 for sure *spoken*【口】**a)** certainly 肯定地，确切地: *No one knows for sure what really happened.* 没有人确切地知道到底发生了什么事。**b)** used to emphasize that something is true 毫无疑问〔用于强调某事真实〕: *I know one person who won't be happy with the decision, that's for sure.* 我知道有一个人会对这个决定感到不高兴，这一点毫无疑问。**c)** *AmE* used to agree with someone【美】当然；肯定〔用于表示同意〕

2 sure enough used to say that something did actually happen in the way that you said it would 果真，果然（如此）〔表示发生的事与预料的相符〕: *Sure enough Mike managed to get lost.* 迈克果然迷路了。

3 ▶USED TO SAY 'YES' 用于表示"是"◀ *spoken especially AmE* used to say 'yes' to someone【口，尤美】当然，好的: *"Can you give me a ride to work tomorrow?" "Sure."* "明天我可以顺路搭你的车子上班去吗?" "当然可以。"

4 ▶USED AS A REPLY 用作回答◀ *AmE spoken* used as a way of replying to someone when they thank you【美口】不（用）谢，不（用）客气: *"Thanks for your help Karen." "Sure."* "谢谢你的帮助，卡伦。" "不用谢。"

5 ▶USED TO EMPHASIZE STH 用于强调某事◀ *AmE informal* used to emphasize a statement【美，非正式】必定，无疑: *Mom's sure gonna be mad when she gets home.* 妈妈回到家时一定会大为恼火。

6 ▶USED BEFORE STATEMENT 用于陈述的内容之前◀ *AmE spoken* used at the beginning of a statement admitting that something is true, especially before adding something very different【美口】的确，无可否认〔用于陈述的开始，承认某事真实，但往往接着补充不同看法〕: *Sure Joey's happy now, but will it last?* 乔伊现在的确是快乐的，但这能持久吗?

sure·fire /ˈʃʊrˌfaɪr; ˈʃɔːfaɪə/ *adj* [only before noun 仅用于名词前] *informal* certain to succeed【非正式】一定能成功的: *There's no surefire way to get rid of cockroaches.* 没有什么方法一定能把蟑螂灭掉。| **surefire success** *I think the new show will be a surefire success with kids.* 我认为这个新节目一定会大受孩子们的欢迎。

sure·foot·ed /ʃʊrˋfʊtɪd; ˌʃɔːˈfʊtɪd◂/ *adj* able to walk without sliding or falling in a place where it is not easy to do this 脚步稳的；不会摔倒的

sure·ly /ˈʃʊrlɪ; ˈʃɔːli/ *adv* **1** [sentence adverb 句子副词] used to show that you think something must be true, especially when people seem to be disagreeing with you 想必，谅必〔尤用于当别人似乎不同意时〕: *You must have heard about the riots surely?* 想必你已经听到发生骚乱的事了吧? | *There must surely be some explanation.* 肯定是有某种解释吧。| *Surely we can't just stand back and let this happen?* 我们总不能袖手旁观任由此事发生吧? **2 surely not** *spoken* used to show you cannot believe that something is true【口】绝不可能，绝对不会〔用于表示不相信〕: *"The chairman's just handed in his resignation." "Surely not."* "主席刚递交了辞呈。" "绝不可能。" **3** *old-fashioned* certainly【过时】必定，无疑: *Such sinners will surely be punished.* 这样的罪人必定会受到惩罚。**4** *AmE old-fashioned* used to say 'yes' to someone or to express agreement with them【美，过时】当然；可以〔用于表示同意〕

USAGE NOTE 用法说明: SURELY

WORD CHOICE 词语辨析: **surely, certainly, sure, definitely, of course, naturally, obviously**

Surely is usually used to show that you believe something, and would be surprised if others did not agree. surely通常用于表示相信某事，并会对其他人不同意感到惊讶: *Surely they must realize that* (=I think they should realize that, and don't you agree?). 想必他们已认识到这一点了〔=我想他们应已认识到这一点，你说是吧?〕。| *They've gone home, surely* (=you seem to be still expecting to see them, but I'm sure they have gone). 他们谅必已经回家了〔=你似乎还在期待见到他们，但我敢肯定他们已经走了〕。| *He surely doesn't expect me to pay him immediately* (=I hope he doesn't expect this and I don't think he ought to). 他想必不会以为我会马上付钱给他吧〔=我希望他不会这样想，而且我认为他不应该这样〕。

A sentence with **surely**, especially near the beginning, usually sounds like a question, even if nobody actually answers, and could easily be followed by a question tag. 句子里〔尤其在接近句首的地方〕用surely时，通常听起来像个问句，但并不要求真的给予回答。这种句子往往带有一个附加疑问句: *Surely they know, don't they?* 他们想必知道，不是吗?

Certainly is four times as frequent as **surely** in spoken English and shows that you strongly believe something, in spite of what others think. 在英语口语中，certainly的使用频率是surely的四倍，表示你坚决相信某事，而不管别人怎样想: *He certainly doesn't expect me to pay him immediately* (=I know he doesn't expect the money now).

他肯定不认为我会马上付钱给他的〔=我知道他并不认为现在就会拿到那笔钱〕。| *She was amazed and I was certainly surprised too* (NOT *surely* because it would be strange to expect others to know how you feel). 她大为惊讶，我也着实吃了一惊〔不用 surely，因为不能期待别人知道你的感觉如何〕。

Certainly often suggests that there may also be a slight doubt or condition, even if it is not actually followed by **but**. certainly 常暗示可能同时包含轻微的疑问或条件，即使句子后面不一定跟用 but: *It's certainly very beautiful, but it's far too expensive.* 它无疑是很漂亮的，但实在太贵了。| *"He's a brilliant student, isn't he?" "Well, he certainly works very hard."* (=but I do not agree that he is brilliant) "他是个很聪明的学生，不是吗？""噢，他确实很勤奋。"〔=但我不认为他很聪明〕

In informal spoken American English **sure** is often used, especially just before the verb, with a similar meaning to **certainly**, but is often stronger and may show annoyance or impatience. 在非正式美国口语中，sure 常用在动词前面，意义和 certainly 相似，但一般语气较强，且可能表示恼火或不耐烦: *They sure are late* (=they're late and isn't that surprising/annoying?)! 他们确实迟到了〔=他们竟然迟到，这真让人惊讶/恼火〕!

Definitely shows that you believe something so strongly that there is no doubt or question about it at all. definitely 表示对某事坚决相信，毫无疑问: *He's definitely the best player in the team.* 他无疑是队里最佳的选手。

Of course, **naturally**, and **obviously** show that you not only think something is true but also that it is not surprising. of course, naturally 和 obviously 表示认为某事不但真实，而且不足为奇: *They broke down on the way so of course they were late.* 他们的车子在路上坏了，所以他们自然迟到了。| *Naturally my mother loved me.* 我妈妈自然是爱我的。| *A vacation in Switzerland would obviously be expensive.* 在瑞士度假不用说会是很费钱的。

For information about using these words in answer to questions see **of course** (WORD CHOICE). 关于这些词用于回答问题时的用法，请参阅 of course（词语辨析）。

sur·e·ty /ˈʃʊrtɪ; ˈʃɔːrɪ̣ti/ *n* [C,U] *law*【法律】**1** someone who will pay a debt, appear in court etc if someone else fails to do so 保证人，担保人 **2 stand surety (for sb)** be responsible for paying a debt, appearing in court etc if someone else fails to do so 做（某人的）担保人 **3** money someone gives to make sure that someone will appear in court〔交给法院保证出庭的〕保证金

surf¹ /sɜf; sɜːf/ *v* [I] **1** to ride on waves standing on a special board 冲浪: **go surfing** *When we were in Hawaii we went surfing every day.* 我们在夏威夷时每天都去冲浪。**2 surf the net** to look quickly through information on the computer INTERNET for anything that interests you 在互联网上冲浪，上网浏览信息: *surfing the net with a high-speed modem* 用高速调制解调器在互联网上浏览信息 —**surfer** *n* [C]

CULTURAL NOTE 文化注释

Surfing is considered to be an activity for young and fashionable people. It is associated especially with California, Hawaii, and Australia, and it usually makes people think of a sunny CLIMATE and the lifestyle that goes with it. Many people also think of the Beach Boys, who recorded popular songs about surfing. 冲浪被认为是年轻人和时尚人士的运动。人们常把冲浪同加利福尼亚、夏威夷和澳大利亚联系起来。冲浪也会让人们想起晴朗的天气和与之有关的生活方式。很多人还会联想到"沙滩男孩"组合，他们录制了很多有关冲浪的流行歌曲。

surf² *n* [U] the white substance that forms on top of waves as they move towards the shore 浪头的白色泡沫

sur·face¹ /ˈsɜfɪs; ˈsɜːfɪ̣s/ *adj* [only before noun 仅用于名词前] appearing to be true or real, but not representing what someone really feels or what something is really like; SUPERFICIAL 表面（上）的；外表的: *The surface calm of the city was shattered by a massive explosion.* 这个城市表面的宁静被巨大的爆炸声打破了。| *surface resemblance* 外表相似

surface² *n* [C]

1 ►WATER/LAND 水/陆◄ the top layer of an area of water or land〔水或陆地的〕表面，面: *the Earth's surface* 地球表面 | *Pieces of trash were floating on the surface of the river.* 一片片的垃圾漂浮在河面上。| *the surface of the road* 路面

2 ►TOP LAYER 表层◄ the outside or top layer of an object〔物体的〕外层，表层，面: *a frying pan with a non-stick surface* 不粘（的煎）锅

3 on the surface if someone or something is calm, nice etc on the surface, they seem that way until you know them better 表面上；外表上: *On the surface Mrs Lewis seemed nice enough but she had a nasty temper at times.* 刘易斯太太表面上显得非常和蔼可亲，但有时脾气很坏。

4 below/beneath/under the surface if an emotion or quality is below, beneath, under the surface, it is not easy to notice at first〔情感等〕隐藏的: *I sensed a lot of tension and jealousy beneath the surface.* 我感觉到表面之下隐藏着非常紧张和嫉妒的情绪。

5 come/rise to the surface if unpleasant feelings or attitudes come or rise to the surface they become noticeable after being hidden〔不愉快的情绪或态度〕显露，显现；表现出来: *Violence and prejudice have risen to the surface in a lot of inner-city areas.* 暴力和偏见在很多市中心贫民区已经显露出来。

6 ►FOR WORKING ON 供工作用的◄ an area on a desk, table etc used for working 桌面，台面；〔某物的〕面: *Make sure all kitchen surfaces are clean and tidy.* 一定要把厨房所有表面都搞得清洁整齐。

7 ►SIDE OF AN OBJECT 物体的面◄ *technical* one of the sides of an object【术语】〔物体的一个〕面: *How many surfaces does a cube have?* 立方体有几个面？—see also 另见 **scratch the surface** (SCRATCH¹ (7))

surface³ *v* **1** [I] to rise to the surface of water 浮出水面: *The bird dived and didn't surface for at least a minute.* 鸟潜入水里，至少有一分钟没有浮出水面。**2** [I] if information or feelings surface, they become known after being hidden〔信息或情感〕显露，暴露，公开: *A few personality clashes have surfaced within the department.* 这个部门里的一些个人冲突已经公开化了。**3** [I] *humorous* to get up, especially after being in bed for a long time【幽默】〔尤指久睡后〕起床: *Joe never surfaces before midday on Sunday.* 乔在星期天不睡到中午是不会起床露面的。**4** [T] to put a surface on a road 给…铺路面

surface a·re·a /ˈ‥ ˌ‥‥/ *n* [C] the area of the outside of an object that can be measured〔物体可量度的〕表面面积

surface mail /ˈ‥ ˌ‥/ *n* [U] the system of sending letters or packages by land or sea 陆路[水路]邮件，平（寄）邮（件）

surface ten·sion /ˌ‥ ˈ‥‥/ *n* [U] the way the MOLECULEs in the surface of a liquid stick together so that the surface is held together 表面张力

surface-to-air /ˌ‥‥ ˈ‥◂/ *adj* **surface-to-air missile** a MISSILE (1) that is fired at planes from the land or from a ship 地[舰]对空导弹

surface-to-surface /ˌ‥‥ ˈ‥‥◂/ *adj* **surface-to-surface missile** a MISSILE (1) that is fired from land or a ship at another point on land or at another ship 地对地[舰]导弹；舰对舰[地]导弹

surf·board /ˈsɜfˌbɔrd; ˈsɜːfbɔːd/ *n* [C] a long piece of plastic, wood etc that you stand on to ride the waves 冲浪板 —see picture at 参见 SURF 图

sur·feit /ˈsɜfɪt; ˈsɜːfɪ̣t/ *n formal*【正式】**a surfeit of sth** an amount of something that is too large or that is more than you need 过量的某物；过度的某事物: *a surfeit of food and drink* 过量的食物和饮料

surf·ing /ˈsɜfɪŋ; ˈsɜːfɪŋ/ *n* [U] **1** the activity or sport of riding over the waves on a special board 冲浪（运动）**2 channel/cyber surfing** looking quickly from one television programme to

another, or looking through the computer INTERNET for something that interests you〔为寻找有趣的内容〕频繁更换电视频道/网上冲浪

surge¹ /sɝdʒ; sɜːdʒ/ *v* **1** [I always+adv/prep] if a crowd of people surges, they suddenly move forward together very quickly〔人群〕迅速涌动; 蜂拥向前: [**+forward/through etc**] *The crowd surged through the gates.* 人群蜂拥通过各个进出口。 **2** also 又作 **surge up** [I] if a feeling surges or surges up you begin to feel it very strongly〔情感〕涌起, 涌现: *Helpless rage surged up within me.* 无法抑制的怒火在我胸中涌起。 **3** [I always+adv/prep] if a large amount of water surges, it moves very quickly and suddenly〔大水〕汹涌, 奔腾

surge² *n* [C usually singular 一般用单数] **1 a surge of** a sudden, large increase in a feeling〔情感〕激增; 涌现: *a surge of excitement* 一阵兴奋 **2** a sudden increase in something such as demand, profit, interest etc〔需求、利润、兴趣等的〕急剧增加: [**+in**] *stores expecting the usual surge in demand as Christmas approaches* 期望着圣诞来临时需求照例陡增的商店 **3** a sudden movement of a lot of people〔人群的〕蜂拥: [**+of**] *a surge of refugees into the country* 涌入这个国家的难民潮

sur·geon /ˈsɝdʒən; ˈsɜːdʒən/ *n* [C] a doctor who does operations in hospital 外科医生 —see also 另见 DENTAL SURGEON

Surgeon Gen·e·ral /ˌ‥ ˈ‥‥/ **1** the chief medical officer of the US Public Health Service. The Surgeon General is responsible for giving advice about health and finding out whether particular chemicals, foods etc are safe. For example, bottles of alcohol and packages of cigarettes that are sold in the US must have labels with the Surgeon General's warning. 卫生局局长〔美国公共卫生署医务主管。其职责是就公共卫生问题建言献策, 核实某些化学品、食品的安全性。比如, 在美国出售的酒类和香烟, 包装上都必须印有公共卫生署卫生局局长的警示标志〕 **2** the chief medical officer of the US army, navy, or air force〔美国海、陆、空三军〕军医处处长

S2 W3 **sur·ge·ry** /ˈsɝdʒəri; ˈsɜːdʒəri/ *n* **1** [U] medical treatment in which a surgeon cuts open your body to repair or remove something inside 外科手术: *major heart surgery* 心脏大手术 —see also 另见 COSMETIC SURGERY, PLASTIC SURGERY **2** [C,U] *especially AmE* the place where operations are done in a hospital【尤美】手术室; THEATRE (3) *BrE*【英】**3** [C] *BrE* a place where a doctor or DENTIST gives treatment【英】〔医生或牙医的〕诊所; OFFICE *AmE*【美】**4** [U] *BrE* a regular period each day when people can see a doctor or DENTIST【英】门诊时间; **office hours** (OFFICE (3)) *AmE*【美】: *Surgery is from 9am – 1pm on weekdays.* 周一至周五的门诊时间为上午9时至下午1时。 **5** [C] *BrE* a special period of time when people can see a MEMBER OF PARLIAMENT to discuss problems【英】〔议员的〕接待时间

sur·gi·cal /ˈsɝdʒɪkl; ˈsɜːdʒɪkəl/ *adj* [only before noun 仅用于名词前] **1** connected with or used for medical operations 外科的; 外科手术的: *surgical techniques* 外科技术 **2 surgical stocking/collar etc** a STOCKING etc that someone wears to support a part of their body that is injured or weak 外科治疗袜/领圈[护颈]等 —**surgically** /-klɪ; -kli/ *adv*: *The growth was surgically removed.* 用外科手术把肿瘤给切除了。

surgical spir·it /ˌ‥ ˈ‥/ *n* [U] *BrE* a type of alcohol used for cleaning wounds or skin【英】〔用以清洗伤口等的〕消毒用酒精; RUBBING ALCOHOL *AmE*【美】

surgical strike /ˌ‥ ˈ·/ *n* [C] a carefully planned quick military attack intended to destroy something in a particular place without damaging the surrounding area 外科手术式打击, 精确的军事攻击

Su·ri·nam, Suriname /ˌsʊrɪˈnɑm; ˌsʊərɪˈnæm/ a country on the northern coast of South America between Guyana and French Guiana, which used to be called Dutch Guiana when it was a COLONY of the Netherlands. Population: 434,000 (2001). Capital: Paramaribo. 苏里南〔南美洲北部沿海一国家。位于圭亚那与法属圭亚那之间。曾为荷兰殖民地, 当时称荷属圭亚那。人口: 434,000 (2001), 首都: 帕拉马里博〕—**Surinamese** /ˌsʊrɪnəˈmiz; ˌsʊərɪnəˈmiːz◂/ *n, adj*

sur·ly /ˈsɝlɪ; ˈsɜːli/ *adj* **surlier, surliest** bad-tempered, unfriendly, and often rude 脾气暴躁的, 粗暴的: *Passengers complain of frequent delays and surly staff.* 乘客投诉航班经常延误和工作人员粗暴无礼。—**surliness** *n* [U]

sur·mise /sɚˈmaɪz; səˈmaɪz/ *v* [T] *formal* to guess that something is true using the information you know already【正式】推测, 猜测, 臆测 —**surmise** *n* [C,U]

sur·mount /sɚˈmaunt; səˈmaʊnt/ *v* [T] *formal*【正式】**1** to succeed in dealing with a problem or difficulty; OVERCOME 克服〔困难〕: *a program designed to help couples surmount marital difficulties* 为帮助夫妻克服婚姻问题而设计的项目 **2** [usually passive 一般用被动态] to be above or on top of something 耸立于…之上; 在…顶上: *a stone tower surmounted by a tall spire* 有高耸塔尖的石塔 —**surmountable** *adj*

sur·name /ˈsɝˌnem; ˈsɜːneɪm/ *n* [C] the name that you share with your parents, or often with your husband if you are a married woman, and which in English comes at the end of your full name; LAST NAME 姓

sur·pass /sɚˈpæs; səˈpɑːs/ *v* [T] **1** to be even better or greater than someone or something else 超过; 胜过: *Gower became England's highest run scorer, surpassing Geoff Boycott's old record.* 高尔超过了杰夫·博伊科特的旧纪录, 成为英格兰得分最高的板球选手。| **surpass expectations/hopes/dreams** (=be better than you had expected, hoped etc) 比期望/希望/梦想的更好 **2 surpass yourself** an expression meaning to do something even better than you have ever done before, often used jokingly when someone has done something badly 超越自己〔表示比自己过去做得更好, 但常用于开玩笑, 表示做得很差〕: *You've really surpassed yourself this time!* 你这回真的超越自己了!

sur·pass·ing /sɚˈpæsɪŋ; səˈpɑːsɪŋ/ *adj* [only before noun 仅用于名词前] *literary* much better than that of other people or things【文】出色的, 卓越的: *a picture of surpassing beauty* 一幅优美绝伦的画作

sur·plice /ˈsɝplɪs; ˈsɜːplɪs/ *n* [C] a piece of clothing made of white material worn over other clothes by priests or singers in church〔教士或唱诗班成员穿的〕白色罩袍, 白色法衣

sur·plus¹ /ˈsɝpləs; ˈsɜːpləs/ *n* [C,U] **1** an amount of something that is more than what is needed or used 剩余, 过剩; 剩余额, 多余的量: *Apply paste thinly to the back of the wallpaper taking care to remove any surplus.* 把糨糊薄薄地涂在墙纸背面, 注意抹去多余的。| [**+of**] *an enormous surplus of crude oil* 大量过剩的原油 **2** the amount of money that a country or company has left after it has paid for all the things it needs 盈余; 顺差 —see also 另见 TRADE SURPLUS

surplus² *adj* **1** more than what is needed or used 过剩的, 剩余的, 多余的: *Companies are likely to continue laying off surplus staff well into the recovery.* 各公司很可能继续解雇冗员, 直至经济明显复苏。 **2 be surplus to requirements** *formal* be no longer necessary【正式】不再需要: *Most of this furniture is now surplus to requirements.* 这些家具现在大多都用不着了。

sur·prise¹ /sɚˈpraɪz; səˈpraɪz/ *n* S3 W2

1 ►**EVENT** 事件◄ [C] an unexpected or unusual event 意想不到的事; 不同寻常的事: *Joan! What a lovely surprise to see you again!* 琼! 再次见到你真是惊喜万分! | **surprise visit/announcement/attack etc** *Let's pay grandma a surprise visit.* 咱们去看望奶奶给她一个惊喜。| *US forces launched a surprise attack on the Panamanian capital.* 美军对巴拿马首都发动突袭。| **come as a surprise (to sb)** (=happen unexpectedly) 出乎(某人)意料, 使(某人)感到来得突然 *The news that George was leaving came as a surprise to everyone.* 乔治要离开的消息使大家都感到意外。| **it came as no surprise** (=you expected it would happen) 来得并不突然 *It came as no surprise when Sarah announced she was pregnant.* 萨拉宣布她怀孕时, 人们并不感到意外。| **there is a surprise in store for sb** (=something unexpected is going to happen to them) 将有意想不到的事发生在某人身上

2 ►**FEELING** 感觉◄ [U] the feeling you have when something unexpected or unusual happens 惊奇, 惊讶, 诧异: *Imagine my surprise when she told me she'd been married twice already.* 当她告诉我她已结过两次婚时, 想象一下我有多么吃惊吧。| **get/have a surprise** *Harwich police got a nasty surprise yesterday when someone left a suspected unexploded bomb inside the police station.* 昨晚有人将一枚可疑的未爆的炸弹放在哈威治警察局内, 这使警方吃了一惊。| **in/with surprise** *She noticed with surprise the change in his appearance.* 她吃惊地注意到他外表的变化。| **much to my surprise** (=in a way that surprises you) 使我十分惊讶的是 *Much to my surprise they offered me the job.* 使我非常惊奇的是, 他们把那份工作给了我。

3 take sb by surprise to happen unexpectedly 出乎某人意料: *The heavy snowfall had taken us all by surprise.* 这场大雪使我们大家猝不及防。

4 take sb/sth by surprise to suddenly attack a place or an opponent when they are not ready 出其不意地袭击某人/某地: *Rebel forces took the town by surprise.* 叛军突袭了该镇。

5 ►**GIFT/PARTY ETC** 礼物/聚会等◄ [C usually singular 一般用单数] an unexpected present, trip etc which you give to someone or organize for them, often on a special occasion 令某人意外惊喜的事物〈如礼物、旅行等〉: *I've got a little surprise waiting for you at home.* 我有一件让你意想不到的礼物在家等着你。| *Jim's organized a trip to the opera as a surprise for his mum.* 吉姆安排去看歌剧, 要给妈妈一个惊喜。

6 surprise guest/visitor etc someone who arrives somewhere unexpectedly 不速之客

7 surprise! *spoken* used when you are just about to show someone something that you know will surprise them【口】有个你想不到的东西!〔用于即将给某人看令其惊奇的东西时〕

8 a) surprise, surprise used when saying in a joking way that you expected something to happen or be true 啊, 真出乎意料〔玩笑语, 用于表示自己预料某事属实或将会发生〕: *The American TV networks are – surprise, surprise, full of stories about the royal divorce.* 真想不到! 美国各个电视网竟大肆报道王室离婚的新闻。**b)** *spoken* used when you suddenly appear in front of someone who you know is not expecting to see you【口】没想到吧〔出其不意地突然出现在某人面前时说的话〕

9 ►METHOD 方法◄ [U] the use of methods which are intended to cause surprise 令人惊奇[感到意外]的方法: **an element of surprise** *An element of surprise is important to any attack.* 出其不意在任何进攻中都是非常重要的。

surprise[2] *v* [T] **1** to make someone feel surprised 使惊奇, 使诧异, 使感到意外: *Paul's news surprised her.* 保罗的消息使她感到意外。| **it surprises sb to see/find/know etc** *It surprised them to see Jane up so early.* 他们看到简那么早起床感到惊奇。| **it doesn't surprise me** *"Howard and Shari have split up." "I have to say it doesn't surprise me."* "霍华德和夏丽已经分手了。""我得说这不足为奇。" | **what surprises sb is** *What surprised me most was that she didn't seem to care.* 最令我感到意外的是, 她好像毫不在乎。—see 见 SHOCK[1] (USAGE) **2** to find, catch, or attack someone when they are not expecting it, especially when they are doing something they should not be doing 出其不意地发现; 当场抓获; 突然袭击: **surprise sb doing sth** *A security guard surprised the burglars in the store room.* 一名保安员出其不意地在储藏室当场抓住了小偷。

[S2] [W2] **sur·prised** /sə`praɪzd; sə'praɪzd/ *adj* having a feeling of surprise 吃惊的, 惊奇的, 惊讶的, 诧异的: *Mr Benson looked surprised when I told him I was leaving.* 当我告诉他我要离去时, 本森先生显得非常惊讶。| **[+at/by]** *We were all surprised at Sue's outburst.* 苏突然情绪激动起来, 我们大家都很惊讶。| **surprised (that)** *Harry was surprised that Carl didn't say anything to defend himself.* 卡尔没为自己作任何辩护, 这使哈里感到很惊奇。| **surprised to see/hear/learn etc** *I was pleasantly surprised to learn that I had passed.* 我知道自己已经通过, 感到非常惊喜。| **surprised look/expression** *She just sat there with a surprised expression on her face.* 她只是坐在那里, 脸上带着惊愕的表情。| **don't be surprised if...** *spoken* (=used when saying that something is likely to happen)【口】要是…不必感到惊奇〔用于表示很可能发生某事〕*Don't be surprised if they ask a lot of difficult questions.* 他们如果提出很多难以解答的问题, 你不要感到奇怪。| **I wouldn't be surprised** *spoken* (=used when saying that you expect something will happen)【口】我不会觉得意外, 我认为那是意料中的事 *"Do you think they'll get married?" "I wouldn't be at all surprised."* "你认为他们会结婚吗?" "如果他们结婚, 我一点也不会感到吃惊。"

[S3] [W3] **sur·pris·ing** /sə`praɪzɪŋ; sə'praɪzɪŋ/ *adj* unusual or unexpected 令人惊奇的, 使人吃惊的, 出人意料的: *a surprising lack of communication between management and staff* 管理部门和职工之间令人吃惊地缺少沟通 | **it is surprising (that)** *It's not really surprising that only a few people came tonight.* 今晚只来了几个人, 这实际上并不出人意料。| **it is surprising how/what etc** *It's surprising how quickly those in the public eye fade.* 那些公众人物转眼就淡出了人们的视线, 快得令人吃惊。| **it is hardly/scarcely surprising** *It's hardly surprising that she won't talk to you after what you said to her.* 在你对她说了那些话以后, 她不愿跟你说话就不足为奇了。

[W3] **sur·pris·ing·ly** /sə`praɪzɪŋlɪ; sə'praɪzɪŋli/ *adv* unusually or unexpectedly 惊人地, 使人吃惊地, 出人意料地: **[+adj/adv]** *The exam was surprisingly easy.* 这次考试简单得出人意料。| **not surprisingly** [sentence adverb 句子副词] *Not surprisingly, the UK has the highest divorce rate in the Community.* 毫不奇怪, 英国的离婚率在欧洲共同体中是最高的。

sur·real /sə`riəl; sə'rɪəl/ *adj* a situation or experience that is surreal is very strange, like something from a dream〔情况或经历〕超现实的; 离奇的, 荒诞的: *American politics has always been more surreal than any satire.* 美国政治向来比任何讽刺作品都更加荒诞离奇。

sur·real·is·m /sə`riəl,ɪzəm; sə'rɪəlɪzəm/ *n* [U] 20th century art or literature in which the artist or writer connects unrelated images and objects in a strange way〔20 世纪文学、艺术上的〕超现实主义 —**surrealist** *adj*: *a surrealist painting* 一幅超现实主义绘画 —**surrealist** *n* [C]

sur·real·is·tic /sə,riəl`ɪstɪk; sə,rɪə'lɪstɪk◂/ *adj* **1** seeming very strange because of a combination of many unusual, unrelated events, images etc 梦幻般的; 离奇的; 超现实的 **2** connected with surrealism 超现实主义的 —**surrealistically** /-klɪ; -kli/ *adv*

sur·ren·der[1] /sə`rɛndə; sə'rendə/ *v* **1** [I] to say officially that you want to stop fighting because you realize that you cannot win 投降: *The terrorists were given ten minutes to surrender.* 恐怖分子被限定在10分钟之内投降。| **surrender to sb** *The unit was forced to surrender to the enemy.* 这支部队被迫向敌人投降。**2 surrender to sth** to allow yourself to be controlled or influenced by something 听任…摆布; 屈服于…: *Colette surrendered to temptation and took out a cigarette.* 科利特经不起诱惑, 拿出了一支香烟。**3** [T] to give your soldiers or land to an enemy after they have beaten you in a battle〔向敌人〕交出〔部队〕; 放弃〔土地〕: *The General had to surrender his troops.* 将军不得不交出他的部队。**4** [T] to give up something that is important or necessary, often because you feel forced to〔被迫〕放弃: *Critics feel that Boyer has surrendered his artistic identity in his later films.* 评论家们感到博耶在他后期的电影里放弃了自己的艺术风格。**5** [T] *formal* to give something such as a ticket or a PASSPORT to an official【正式】〔向官员〕交出〔票证、护照等〕: **surrender sth to sb** *The court ordered Bond to surrender his passport to the authorities.* 法院命令邦德把护照交给当局。

surrender[2] *n* [singular,U] **1** the act of saying officially that you want to stop fighting because you realize that you cannot win 投降: **unconditional surrender** (=act of accepting total defeat) 无条件投降 **2** the act of allowing yourself to be controlled or influenced by something 屈服; 让步: *a surrender to the forces of evil* 向恶势力屈服

sur·rep·ti·tious /,sɝəp`tɪʃəs; ,sʌrəp'tɪʃəs◂/ *adj* done secretly or quickly because you do not want other people to notice 秘密的, 偷偷摸摸的, 鬼鬼祟祟的: *Robert stole a surreptitious glance at Myrna to see her reaction.* 罗伯特偷偷扫了默纳一眼, 看看她的反应。—**surreptitiously** *adv* —**surreptitiousness** *n* [U]

Sur·rey /`sɝɪ; 'sʌri/ a COUNTY in southeast England which is one of the Home Counties. Many of the people who live there travel to London every day to work, and most people think of Surrey as a wealthy, mainly MIDDLE-CLASS area. 萨里郡〔英格兰东南部一郡, 伦敦周围诸郡之一。该郡的许多居民每天去伦敦上班。多数人认为萨里郡为富庶之地, 居民以中产阶级为主〕

surrey *n* [C] *AmE* a light carriage with two seats, which was pulled by a horse and was used in the past【美】〔旧时的〕双座轻便马车

sur·ro·gate /`sɝəget; 'sʌrəgeɪt/ *adj* [only before noun 仅用于名词前] a surrogate person or thing is one that takes the place of someone or something else 替代的, 代理的: *Uncle Giles became a sort of surrogate father to them after the accident.* 在那次事故以后贾尔斯叔叔便成了他们的代理父亲。—**surrogate** *n* [C]

surrogate moth·er /,... '../ *n* [C] a woman who has a baby for another woman who cannot have one 代孕妇, 代母〔替不育妇女生育的妇女〕

CULTURAL NOTE 文化注释

There is some disagreement about the ETHICS of this practice, especially when the surrogate mother decides that she wants to keep the baby after it is born. In Britain and the US, it is now against the law to pay a surrogate mother, but she can agree to become one as a favour for a friend or relative. 关于为人代孕的道德问题, 特别是代孕母亲在孩子出生后决定自己留养时, 人们有不同的观点。在英国和美国, 现在花钱请人代孕是违法的, 但是女性帮助朋友或亲属代孕是可以的。

sur·round[1] /sə`raund; sə'raʊnd/ *v* [T] **1** [usually passive 一般用被动态] to be all around someone or something on every side 环绕, 围绕: *The city is surrounded on all sides by hills.* 这个城市四面环山。| **be surrounded by sth** *Jill was sitting on the floor surrounded by boxes.* 吉尔坐在地板上, 周围摆满了箱子。**2 be surrounded by sb/sth** to have a lot of a particular kind of people or things near you 周围有很多…; 被…围住: *How can I work when I'm surrounded by idiots.* 周围都是白痴, 叫我怎么工作? **3** if police or soldiers surround a place they arrange themselves in positions all the way around it 包围, 围困〔某处〕: *We've got the place surrounded. Come out with your hands up.* 这个地方已被我们包围了, 举起手出来吧。**4** to be closely connected with a situation or event 与〔某情况或事件〕密切相关: *the controversy surrounding the group's 'Cop Killer' track* 围绕着该演唱组《警察杀手》这首歌曲的争论 **5 surround yourself** [W2]

with to choose to have certain people or things near you all the time 和…在一起，与…为伍: *David loved to surround himself with young people.* 戴维很喜欢和年轻人在一起。

surround² *n* [C] an area around the edge of something, especially one that is decorated or made of a different material 围饰，缘饰

sur·round·ing /səˋraʊndɪŋ; səˈraʊndɪŋ/ *adj* [only before noun 仅用于名词前] near or around a particular place 附近的，四周的: *the surrounding towns* 附近的城镇 | *After the explosion the army sealed off the surrounding area.* 爆炸发生后，军队封锁了周围地区。

sur·round·ings /səˋraʊndɪŋz; səˈraʊndɪŋz/ *n* [plural] the objects, buildings, natural things etc that are around a person or thing at a particular time 环境；周围的事物: *It took me a few weeks to get used to my new surroundings.* 我花了好几个星期才适应这个新环境。

sur·tax /ˈsɝˌtæks; ˈsɜːtæks/ *n* [U] an additional tax on money you earn if it is higher than a particular amount〔对超过一定额的收入征收的〕附加税

sur·veil·lance /səˋveləns; səˈveɪləns/ *n* [U] the act of carefully watching a person or place because they may be connected with criminal activities〔对可疑的人或地方的〕监视；盯梢: **keep sb/sth under surveillance** *Police are keeping the area under constant surveillance.* 警察在不间断地监视这个地区。

sur·vey¹ /sɝˋve; ˈsɜːveɪ/ *n* [C] **1** a set of questions that you ask a large number of people in order to find out about their opinions or behaviour 调查: **to carry out/conduct a survey** (=do a survey) 进行调查 *a recent survey conducted by Manchester University into children's attitudes to violence on television* 曼彻斯特大学最近进行的关于儿童对电视暴力所持态度的调查 **2** an examination of a house or other building done especially for someone who wants to buy it〔尤指为购房者所做的〕房屋鉴定［查勘］ **3** an examination of an area of land in order to make a map of it〔绘制地图前对某地的〕勘测，测量，测绘 **4** a general description or report about a particular subject or situation〔对某一专题或形势的〕概论，概述: *a survey of modern English literature* 现代英语文学概论

sur·vey² /sɚˋve; səˈveɪ/ *v* [T] **1** [often passive 常用被动态] to ask a large number of people questions in order to find out their attitudes or opinions 调查: *Almost 60% of those surveyed said they supported the President's action.* 在被调查人中有将近60%的人支持总统的行动。**2** to look at or consider someone or something carefully, especially in order to form an opinion about them〔尤指为形成某种意见而〕审视，仔细考虑: *He leaned back in his chair and surveyed her critically for a moment.* 他靠在椅子上，挑剔地审视了她一番。**3** to examine the condition of a house or other building and make a report on it, especially for people who want to buy it〔尤指为购房者〕鉴定〔房屋〕 **4** to examine and measure an area of land and record the details on a map 测量，勘测，勘定: *a surveying expedition* 一次勘测之行

survey course /ˈ‥ ˌ‥/ *n* [C] *AmE* a university course that gives an introduction to a subject for people who have not studied it before【美】〔大学里介绍一门学科的〕概论课

sur·vey·or /sɚˋveɚ; səˈveɪə/ *n* [C] someone whose job is to examine the condition of a building, or to measure and record the details of an area of land〔建筑物的〕鉴定人，房产检视员；〔土地〕测量员，勘测员 —see also 另见 QUANTITY SURVEYOR

sur·viv·al /sɚˋvaɪvl̩; səˈvaɪvəl/ *n* [U] **1** the state of continuing to live or exist 继续生存；幸存: *His doctors said he had a 50-50 chance of survival.* 医生说他有50%的生存机会。| *Our disregard for the environment threatens the long-term survival of the planet.* 我们对环境的漠视威胁着地球的长久存在。| **fight for survival** (=struggle or work hard in order to continue to exist) 为生存而奋斗 *A lot of small companies are having to fight for survival.* 很多小公司正不得不为生存而奋斗。**2 survival of the fittest** a situation in which only the strongest and most successful people or things continue to exist 适者生存 **3 a survival from** *especially BrE* something that has continued to exist from a much earlier period, especially when similar things have disappeared; RELIC【尤英】…时代的残存物；遗风；遗迹

survival kit /ˈ‥ ˌ/ *n* [C] a collection of things that you need to help you stay alive if you get hurt or lost 救生包，救生箱〔装有受伤或迷路时维持生命所必需的救生用品〕

sur·vive /sɚˋvaɪv; səˈvaɪv/ *v* **1** [I,T] to not die in an accident or war or from an illness〔经历事故、战争或疾病后〕活下来，幸存；幸免于难: *Only 12 of the 140 passengers survived.* 在140名乘客中只有12人幸免于难。| **survive sth** *There are concerns that the refugees may not survive the winter.* 人们担心那些难民可能熬不过冬天。**2** [I,T] to continue to exist in spite of many difficulties and dangers〔经历困难和危险后〕仍然存在，保存下来: *A few pages of the original manuscript still survive.* 有几页原始手稿保存了下来。**3** [I,T] *often spoken* to continue to live normally and not be too upset by your problems【常口】从〔困难中〕挺过来；挣扎着过下去: *I don't think I could survive another year as a teacher; it's just too stressful.* 再当一年教师我想我是挺不过去了，压力实在太大。| *"How are you?" "Oh, surviving!"* "你过得怎么样？" "噢，凑合着过呗！" **4 survive on** to continue to live a normal life even though you have very little money〔靠很少钱〕继续维持生活: *I don't know how you all manage to survive on Jeremy's salary.* 我真不知道你们只靠杰里米的薪金是怎样生活的。**5** [T] to live longer than someone else, usually someone closely related to you 比〔尤指亲人〕活得更长，比〔某人〕长寿: *Harry survived his wife by three months.* 哈里比他妻子多活了三个月。

sur·vi·vor /sɚˋvaɪvɚ; səˈvaɪvə/ *n* [C] **1** someone or something that still exists in spite of having been nearly destroyed or almost dead 生还者，幸存者；残存物: **sole/lone survivor** (=only person who survives) 唯一生还者 *Major Hawkins was the lone survivor of the crash.* 霍金斯少校是这次坠机事件中的唯一生还者。**2** someone who manages to live their life without being too upset by problems 善于在困境中生存的人，善于求存者: *Don't worry about Kurt; he's a survivor.* 不用为库尔特担心，他善于在困境中生存。

sus·cep·ti·bil·i·ty /səˌsɛptəˋbɪlətɪ; səˌseptɪ̈ˈbɪlɪ̈ti/ *n* **1** [U] the condition of being easily affected or influenced by something 敏感；易受影响（的状况）；过敏性: *susceptibility to disease* 易于得病（的体质） **2 sb's susceptibilities** someone's feelings, especially when they are easily offended or upset 某人易受伤害的感情，某人的敏感心理: *The policy has no regard for the susceptibilities of minority groups.* 这项政策忽视了少数民族的敏感心理。

sus·cep·ti·ble /səˋsɛptəbl̩; səˈseptɪ̈bəl/ *adj* **1 susceptible to sth a)** likely to suffer from a particular illness or be affected by a particular problem 易得病的；易受某事影响的: *Certain people are more susceptible to stress than others.* 有些人比其他人更受不了压力。**b)** easily influenced or affected by something 易受…影响的: *Men are supposedly easily susceptible to feminine charms.* 男人据称容易受女性魅力的诱惑。**2** *literary* tending to experience strong feelings easily and be easily influenced by other people; IMPRESSIONABLE【文】多情的；易动情的: *a susceptible young boy* 容易动感情的少年 **3 susceptible of change/interpretation/analysis etc** *formal* able to be changed etc【正式】可以改变/解释/分析等的

su·shi /ˈsuʃɪ; ˈsuːʃi/ *n* [U] a Japanese dish consisting of pieces of raw fish on top of cooked rice 寿司〔一种在米饭上加生鱼片的日本主食〕

sus·pect¹ /səˋspɛkt; səˈspekt/ *v* [T not in progressive 不用进行时] **1** to think that something is probably true or likely, especially something bad 猜想，怀疑，觉得〔尤指坏事〕可能是事实: 
suspect (that) *She strongly suspected her husband had been lying.* 她觉得她丈夫很可能一直在说谎。| **suspect murder/foul play** (=suspect that someone has been murdered) 疑为谋杀 | **I suspect** *spoken*【口】: *It was a decision, I suspect, that he will later regret.* 这个决定我认为他以后会后悔的。**2** to think that someone is probably guilty 怀疑〔某人〕有罪，认为〔某人〕有嫌疑: *Who do you suspect?* 你怀疑是谁？| **suspect sb of sth** *He's suspected of murder.* 他有杀人嫌疑。| **suspect sb of doing sth** *Pilcher was suspected of being a spy.* 皮尔彻被怀疑是间谍。**3** to distrust someone or doubt the truth of something 不信任，不相信；怀疑…的真实性: *I began to suspect his motives when he asked to borrow more.* 当他提出要借更多的钱时，我开始怀疑起他的动机来了。

sus·pect² /ˈsʌspɛkt; ˈsʌspekt/ *n* [C] someone who is thought to be guilty of a crime〔犯罪〕嫌疑人，可疑分子: *Two suspects were arrested today in connection with the robbery.* 两个与抢劫案有关的嫌疑人今天被捕了。

suspect³ *adj* **1** something that is suspect seems likely to have something wrong with it and should not be trusted, believed, or depended on 可疑的；不可信任的；不可靠的: *The evidence against the four Irishmen was highly suspect.* 指控那四个爱尔兰人的证据很不可靠。| **highly suspect** 非常值得怀疑的 **2** [only before noun 仅用于名词前] suspect packages, goods etc look as if they contain something illegal or dangerous〔包裹、货物等〕可疑的: *Customs officers impounded the suspect crates.* 海关人员扣押了那些可疑的货箱。

sus·pect·ed /səˋspɛktɪd; səˈspektɪ̈d/ *adj* **1 suspected terrorist/spy etc** someone the police believe is a TERRORIST etc〔被警方〕疑为恐怖分子/间谍等的人 **2 a suspected broken**

knee/heart attack etc if you have a suspected broken knee etc, doctors think that you may have a broken knee etc 疑似膝部骨折/心脏病发作等

sus·pend /sə`spɛnd; sə'spend/ *v* [T] **1** to officially stop something from continuing, especially for a short time 暂停, 中止: *Sales of the drug will be suspended until more tests are completed.* 这种药品在完成进一步检验之前暂停销售。**2** to make someone leave school, a job, or an organization temporarily, especially because they have broken the rules〔尤指因违反纪律〕使…暂时停学[停职]: **suspend sb from sth** *Dave was suspended from school for a week.* 戴夫被停学一个星期。**3** *formal* to hang something from something else【正式】悬, 挂, 吊: **suspend sth from sth** *The long fluorescent tubes were suspended from the ceiling.* 一支支长长的荧光管悬在天花板上。| **suspend sth by sth** *a ball suspended by a rope from a branch* 用绳子悬挂在树枝上的球 **4 suspend judgment** to decide not to make a firm judgment about something until you know more about it 暂不作出判断 **5 be suspended in** *technical* if something is suspended in a liquid or in air, it floats in it without moving【术语】悬浮在: *an insect suspended in a piece of amber* 悬浮在琥珀中的昆虫

suspended an·i·ma·tion /·,·· ··'··/ *n* [U] **1** a state in which someone's body processes are slowed down to a state almost like death 假死 **2** a feeling that you cannot do anything because you have to wait for what happens next 焦灼

suspended sen·tence /·,·· '··/ *n* [C] a punishment given by a court in which the criminal will only go to prison if they do something else illegal within a particular period of time 缓刑: *a two-year suspended sentence* 缓刑两年

sus·pend·er /sə`spɛndɚ; sə'spendə/ *n* [C] **1** *BrE* something that hangs down from a woman's underwear to hold STOCKINGS up【英】吊袜带; GARTER (2) *AmE*【美】**2 suspenders** *AmE* two bands of cloth that go over your shoulders and fasten to your trousers to hold them up【美】〔男裤的〕吊带, 背带; braces (BRACE[2] (5)) *BrE*【英】

suspender belt /·'·· ·/ *n* [C] *BrE* a piece of women's underwear with suspenders joined to it【英】〔女用的〕吊袜束腰带; GARTER BELT *AmE*【美】

sus·pense /sə`spɛns; sə'spens/ *n* [U] a feeling of excitement or anxiety when you do not know what will happen next 悬念; 焦虑; 紧张感: **in suspense** *The children waited in suspense to hear the end of the story.* 孩子们紧张地等着听故事的结局。| **keep sb in suspense** *We were kept in suspense waiting for the results of the contest.* 我们焦急地等待比赛的结果。| **the suspense is killing me!** (=used when you are excited or anxious because you do not know what will happen) 我等得急死了!〔表示因不知接下来会发生什么事而感到紧张〕

sus·pen·sion /sə`spɛnʃən; sə'spenʃən/ *n* **1** [U] the act of officially stopping something from continuing for a period of time 暂停, 中止: **[+of]** *EC sanctions included suspension of the 1980 trade agreement and import limits on textiles.* 欧共体的制裁包括中止1980年的贸易协定和限制纺织品进口。**2** [C] the removal of someone from a team, job, school etc for a period of time, especially to punish them〔尤指作为处分〕暂时停职[停学]; 暂时〔从球队等〕除名: *Sean McCarthy is set to return to football after a three match suspension.* 肖恩·麦卡锡在被罚停赛三场之后将再出场比赛。**3** [U] equipment fixed to the wheels of a vehicle to make it more comfortable on roads that are not smooth〔装在车轮上以减少震动的〕悬架, 减震装置 **4** [C] *technical* a liquid mixture consisting of very small pieces of solid material that are contained in the liquid but have not combined with it【术语】悬浮液; 悬浮体 —compare 比较 COLLOID **5** [U] the act of hanging something from something else 悬, 挂, 吊: *suspension cables* 悬缆

suspension bridge /·'·· ·/ *n* [C] a bridge that is hung from strong steel ropes fixed to towers 悬索桥, 吊桥

sus·pi·cion /sə`spɪʃən; sə'spɪʃən/ *n* **1** [C,U] a feeling that someone is probably guilty of doing something wrong or dishonest 怀疑, 嫌疑: **have your suspicions** (=think you probably know who did something wrong) 心中有怀疑对象 *I'm not sure who took it, but I have my suspicions.* 我不能肯定是谁拿走了它, 但我心中有怀疑对象。| **have a sneaking suspicion** (=have a slight feeling that someone has done something wrong without having any definite information) 有点怀疑 | **arouse sb's suspicions** *Neighbours' suspicions were aroused by the bruises on the child's arms.* 孩子手臂上的伤痕引起了邻居们的怀疑。**2 on suspicion of** because someone is thought to be guilty of a crime 因受到怀疑, 涉嫌: *She was arrested on suspicion of killing her boyfriend.* 她因涉嫌谋杀男友而被捕。**3 under suspicion** someone who is under suspicion of a crime is thought to be guilty of it 被怀疑犯了罪的, 有作案嫌疑的: **come/fall under suspicion** *Yet another politician came under suspicion of being in the pay of big business.* 又有一名政客涉嫌被大企业收买。**4 above/beyond suspicion** if someone is above or beyond suspicion, they definitely could not be guilty of a crime or have done something wrong 无可怀疑的, 没有嫌疑的: *Just because she knew and liked Dysart did not mean that the man was necessarily above suspicion.* 仅仅因为她认识并喜欢戴萨特并不等于他就肯定没有嫌疑。**5** [C,U] a feeling that you do not trust someone 不信任, 猜疑: *She always treated us with suspicion.* 她总是对我们疑神疑鬼的。| **look upon/regard sb with suspicion** *Anyone who expressed any kind of liberal opinion was regarded with deep suspicion.* 凡是表达过开明思想的人都受到极大的怀疑。**6** [C] a feeling that something has happened is true 疑心; 怀疑: *There is always a suspicion that the legal system is designed to suit lawyers rather than to protect the public.* 人们总是觉得, 法律制度的制定是为了迎合律师而不是为了保护公众。| **suspicion (that)** *I had a suspicion she might be hurt.* 我隐约觉得她可能受到了伤害。**7 a suspicion of sth** a very small amount of something seen, heard, tasted etc 一点儿, 些微: *I could see the faintest suspicion of a tear in her eyes.* 我能看到她眼睛里有一丁点儿泪水。

sus·pi·cious /sə`spɪʃəs; sə'spɪʃəs/ *adj* **1** thinking that someone might be guilty of doing something wrong or dishonest, without being sure 怀疑的, 猜疑的: *His behaviour that day made the police suspicious.* 他那天的行为使警方产生了怀疑。| **[+of/about]** *I'm suspicious of Jen's intentions.* 我怀疑珍的动机。**2** making you think that something bad or illegal is happening 可疑的, 引起怀疑的: *Anyone who saw anything suspicious is asked to contact the police immediately.* 任何人看到可疑的事请立即与警方联系。| *They found a suspicious package under the seat.* 他们在座位底下发现了一个可疑的包裹。| *a suspicious-looking character* 一个形迹可疑的人物 | **in suspicious circumstances** *Her mother had died in suspicious circumstances.* 她母亲的死亡情况可疑。—see also 另见 SUSPECT[3] **3** feeling that you do not trust someone or that there is something wrong 感到怀疑的, 认为有问题的: **[+of]** *Both parents and pupils are deeply suspicious of the new exams.* 家长和学生都对这种新的考试深感怀疑。 S3

sus·pi·cious·ly /sə`spɪʃəslɪ; sə'spɪʃəsli/ *adv* **1** in a way that shows you think someone has done something wrong or dishonest 怀疑地, 猜疑地: *Meg looked at me very suspiciously.* 梅格疑心重重地看着我。**2** in a way that makes people think that something bad or illegal is happening 可疑地, 值得怀疑地: *He saw two youths acting suspiciously outside the pub.* 他看到酒馆外面两个年轻人行动鬼祟, 形迹可疑。**3** in a way that shows you think there is probably something wrong with something 怀疑地: *They sat in silence, eyeing the food suspiciously.* 他们沉默地坐着, 怀疑地看着那些食物。**4 looks/sounds etc suspiciously like** *often humorous* used when saying that something is very like something else【常幽默】看起来/听起来等十分像…: *That pen looks suspiciously like the one I lost last week!* 那支笔看起来十分像我上星期丢失的那一支!

suss /sʌs; sʌs/ *v* [T] *BrE informal* to realize something【英, 非正式】认识到, 明白; 发现: **suss (that)** *We soon sussed she wasn't telling the truth.* 我们很快就发现她没有讲真话。

suss sb/sth ↔ **out** *phr v* [T] *BrE informal* to understand the important things about someone or something, especially things they are trying to hide【英, 非正式】发现…的真相, 探明…的隐情: *She's bound to suss out the truth sooner or later.* 她迟早一定会了解真相的。

sussed /sʌst; sʌst/ *adj BrE informal* knowing all about someone or something【英, 非正式】对…完全了解的: *These boys are too sussed to believe their own hype.* 这些男孩什么都知道, 所以根本不相信他们自己天花乱坠的宣传。| **get sth sussed** *It's so annoying, you get something sussed and then they change the rules.* 真烦人, 你刚把事情弄明白, 他们又改变规则了。

Sus·sex /`sʌsɪks; 'sʌsɪks/ an area and former COUNTY on the south coast of England, divided since 1974 into East Sussex and West Sussex. It has many attractive small villages, and people think of it as a wealthy, mainly MIDDLE-CLASS area. 萨塞克斯〔英格兰南部沿海一地区。曾是一个郡, 1974年起分为东萨塞克斯和西萨塞克斯。境内有许多漂亮的小村庄, 人们心目中的萨塞克斯为富庶之地, 居民以中产阶级为主〕

sus·tain /sə`sten; sə'steɪn/ *v* [T] W3

1 ►MAKE STH CONTINUE 使某事继续◄ to make something continue to exist over a period of time; MAINTAIN (1) 保持, 维持, 使持续: *The teacher tried hard to sustain the children's interest.* 老师努力保持孩子们的兴趣。—see also 另见 SUSTAINED

2 ▶GIVE STRENGTH 给予力量◀ to make it possible for someone to stay strong or hopeful 使保持强壮; 使保持信心[希望]: *A good breakfast will sustain you all morning.* 丰富的早餐会使你整个上午保持精力充沛。| *They were sustained by the knowledge that help would come soon.* 他们知道援助很快就会到来, 因此得以支撑下去。

3 sustain damage/an injury/defeat/heavy losses etc *formal* to be damaged, hurt or defeated or lose a lot of soldiers, money etc【正式】遭受破坏/伤害/失败/严重损失等: *Allied forces sustained heavy losses in the first few weeks of the campaign.* 盟军在战役的最初几个星期中遭受惨重的损失。

4 ▶WEIGHT 重量◀ *formal* to hold up the weight of something【正式】支撑, 承受〔重量〕: *The floor wouldn't sustain the weight of a piano.* 这地板承受不了一架钢琴的重量。

5 ▶IDEA 意见◀ *formal* to support an idea, argument etc【正式】支持〔某意见、论点等〕: *There was no proof to sustain his views.* 没有证据支持他的观点。

6 ▶LAW 法律◀ objection sustained *spoken* used by a judge when saying that someone was right to object to another person's statement【口】反对有效〔法官说的话, 表示某人提出的异议正当〕

sus·tain·a·ble /sə`stenəbḷ; səˈsteɪnəbəl/ *adj* an action or process that is sustainable can continue or last for a long time 能长期保持的; 能长期维持的; 能持续的: *sustainable economic growth* 可持续的经济增长

sus·tained /sə`stend; səˈsteɪnd/ *adj* something that is sustained continues for a long time 持续的, 持久的: *Paula owes her success to sustained hard work.* 葆拉把她的成就归功于坚持不懈的努力。| *sustained economic development* 持续的经济发展

sus·te·nance /`sʌstənəns; ˈsʌstənəns/ *n* [U] **1** *formal* food that keeps people strong and healthy; NOURISHMENT【正式】〔使人健康强壮的〕食物; 营养: *The children were thin and badly in need of sustenance.* 孩子们身体瘦弱, 极需营养。**2** *informal* food you feel you need because you are tired and hungry【非正式】〔因疲劳或饥饿而需要的〕食物: *I need sustenance! Let's go get some food!* 我需要补充一下! 咱们去弄点吃的来! | *There's not much sustenance in a bag of crisps.* 一包油炸马铃薯片没有什么营养。**3** the act of sustaining something 保持; 维持; 支持

Suth·er·land /`sʌðələnd; ˈsʌðələnd/, **Dame Joan** /dʒon; dʒəʊn/ (1926-) an Australian OPERA singer, who is one of the most important SOPRANOS (=women with high singing voices) of the 20th century. She is known as La Stupenda because of the great beauty of her singing, and she sang in opera houses all over the world from the 1950s to the 1980s. 萨瑟兰〔(1926-), 澳大利亚歌剧演唱家, 20 世纪最重要的女高音歌唱家之一。演唱十分优美, 被誉为"神奇女高音", 20 世纪 50 至 80 年代在世界各大歌剧院巡回演出〕

Sutherland, Gra·ham /`greəm; ˈgreɪəm/ (1903-80) a British artist, famous especially for his picture of Winston Churchill, which Lady Churchill (Churchill's wife) later burned because she did not like it 萨瑟兰〔(1903-1980), 英国画家。尤以创作的温斯顿·丘吉尔肖像画闻名, 但丘吉尔夫人并不喜欢, 后来就把它烧了〕

su·tra /`sutrə; ˈsuːtrə/ *n* [C] a piece of Hindu or Buddhist holy writing〔印度教或佛教中的〕经

sut·tee /sʌ`ti; ˈsʌtiː/ *n* [U] the ancient custom in the Hindu religion of burning a wife with her dead husband 殉夫自焚〔古时印度教中寡妇在亡夫火葬时与其俱焚的习俗〕

Sut·ton Hoo /ˌsʌtṇ `hu; ˌsʌtn ˈhuː/ a place in Suffolk, eastern England, where people digging in 1939 found a 7th century Saxon ship with weapons, jewellery, and other things believed to have been buried with a king 萨顿胡〔英格兰东部萨福克郡一地区。1939 年, 该地区挖掘出 7 世纪撒克逊时期的一艘船, 船上有武器、珠宝等物品, 被认为是某位国王的陪葬品〕

su·ture /`sutʃə; ˈsuːtʃə/ *n* [C,U] the act of sewing a wound together, or a stitch used in this〔伤口的〕缝合; 〔伤口缝合的〕一针, 缝针 —**suture** *v* [T]

Suva /`suvə; ˈsuːvə/ the capital city of Fiji. The University of the South Pacific is in Suva. 苏瓦〔斐济首都, 也是南太平洋大学所在地〕

Su·wan·nee, the /sə`wɑnɪ; səˈwɒni/ also 又作 **the Swanee** a river in the south of the US, flowing through Georgia and Florida to the Gulf of Mexico, and made famous by the old song '*Swanee River*' by Stephen Foster 萨旺尼河〔美国南部一河流。流经佐治亚州和佛罗里达州, 最后注入墨西哥湾。因斯蒂芬·福斯特的老歌《萨旺尼河》而闻名〕

su·ze·rain·ty /`suzərɪntɪ; ˈsuːzəreɪnti/ *n* [U] the right of a country or leader to rule over another country 宗主权, 宗主国的地位 —**suzerain** /-rɪn; -reɪn/ *n* [singular]

Su·zu·ki meth·od, the /·`··, ·ˈ·/ *trademark* a system of teaching young children to play the VIOLIN, by making them copy the music teacher, often taught in very large classes【商标】铃木教学法〔一种教幼儿拉小提琴的音乐教育体系。通常为大班教学, 幼儿在课堂上模仿音乐老师的动作〕

svelte /svɛlt; svelt/ *adj* someone, especially a woman, who is svelte is thin and graceful〔尤指女子〕身材苗条的, 修长的: *a svelte young lady* 身材苗条的年轻女子

Sven·ga·li /svɛn`gɑlɪ; svenˈgɑːli/ *n* [C] a man who has the power to control people's minds and make them behave in a bad way 斯文加利式人物〔指能控制别人思想并令其作恶的人〕

SW the written abbreviation of 缩写= SOUTHWEST and SOUTHWESTERN

swab[1] /swɑb; swɒb/ *n* [C] **1** a small piece of material used by a doctor or nurse to clean a wound or take liquid from someone's body〔医生或护士用以清洁伤口等的〕拭子, 药棉棒: *a cotton swab* 棉签 **2** a test using such a piece of material 用棉签取样所作的检验: *Take a swab of his throat, nurse.* 护士, 用棉签从他的咽喉取样做检查。

swab[2] *v* **swabbed, swabbing** [T] **1** also 又作 **swab down** to clean something, especially the floors of a ship 擦洗〔尤指船上的地板〕 **2** also 又作 **swab out** to clean a wound with a piece of material〔用拭子等〕拭抹〔伤口〕

swad·dle /`swɑdḷ; ˈswɒdl/ *v* [T] *old-fashioned* to wrap a baby tightly to protect it【过时】用襁褓包裹〔婴孩〕

swaddling clothes /`·· ·/ *n* [plural] *old use* the pieces of cloth wrapped around babies to protect them【旧】襁褓

swag /swæg; swæg/ *n* **1** [U] *slang* the goods stolen when someone is robbed【俚】〔偷或抢来的〕赃物; 掠夺物 —compare 比较 LOOT[1] (1) **2** [C] a deep fold of material, especially in or above a curtain〔帐子、窗帘等的〕深褶子 **3** [U] *AustrE* a set of clothes and possessions wrapped in a cloth and carried by someone who is travelling on foot【澳】〔徒步旅行者的〕行囊, 包袱

swag·ger[1] /`swægə; ˈswægə/ *v* [I] **1** [always+adv/prep] to walk proudly, swinging your shoulders in a way that shows too much confidence 昂首阔步, 大摇大摆地走, 趾高气扬地走: **[+down/in/out etc]** *He swaggered down the street with a foolish grin on his face.* 他大摇大摆地走在街道上, 脸上带着傻笑。**2** *old-fashioned* to talk or behave in a very proud way; BOAST[1] (1)【过时】自我吹嘘; 狂妄自大; 自鸣得意 —**swaggerer** *n* [C] —**swaggeringly** *adv*

swagger[2] *n* [singular,U] a way of behaving or walking that is too confident or unusually confident 趾高气扬; 狂妄自大; 自鸣得意: *He combines the cocky swagger of Johnny Rotten with the animal sexuality of Prince.* 他身上兼有约翰尼·罗顿的狂妄与歌手普林斯的原始性感。

swain /swen; sweɪn/ *n* [C] *poetic* a young man from the country who loves a girl【诗】乡下情郎

swal·low[1] /`swɑlo; ˈswɒləʊ/ *v*

1 ▶FOOD 食物◀ [T] to make food or drink go down your throat and towards your stomach 吞下, 咽下〔食物或饮料〕: *He swallowed the last of his coffee and asked for the bill.* 他喝下最后一口咖啡, 要求结账。

2 ▶NERVOUSLY 紧张地◀ [I] to make this kind of movement with your throat, especially because you are nervous〔尤指因为心情紧张〕做吞咽动作, 咽口水: *Leo swallowed hard and walked into the interview.* 利奥使劲咽了一下口水, 然后走进去面试。

3 ▶BELIEVE/ACCEPT 相信/接受◀ [T] *informal* to immediately believe a story, explanation etc that is not actually true【非正式】轻信, 轻易接受〔不真实的解释等〕: **swallow sth whole** (=believe something without asking questions) 对某事深信不疑; 全盘相信某事 *Her excuse was obviously a lie, but Eric swallowed it whole.* 她的辩解明显是在撒谎, 但埃里克竟然全盘相信了。| **hard to swallow** (=difficult to believe) 难以置信 *I find those old superstitions hard to swallow.* 我觉得那些古老的迷信思想难以置信。

4 ▶FEELINGS 感情◀ [T] to stop yourself from showing your feelings 使〔感情、想法等〕不流露: *Daisy tried hard to swallow her doubts.* 戴西尽力不露出自己的疑心。

5 swallow your pride to ignore your feelings and do something that is very embarrassing for you because you have no choice 忍辱含垢; 抑制羞耻感: *When Ken lost his job he had to swallow his pride and borrow money.* 肯失业的时候, 他不得不抛开面子去借钱。—see also 另见 **a bitter pill (to swallow)** (BITTER[1] (7))

swallow sb/sth **up** *phr v* [T usually passive 一般用被动态] **1** if something such as a company or a country is swallowed up by a large company, organization etc it becomes part of it and

no longer exists on its own 吞并: *Their company was swallowed up by a multinational.* 他们的公司为一家跨国公司所吞并。**2** if something such as an amount of money is swallowed up by something else, it is made to disappear completely 耗尽〔金钱〕, 用尽: *I got a pay rise, but it was swallowed up by the increase in train fares.* 我加了工资, 但让火车票涨价给完全抵消了。

swallow² *n* [C] **1** a small bird with a tail that comes to northern countries in the summer 燕子 **2** an act of making food go down your throat 吞, 咽: *He downed his whisky in one swallow.* 他一口把威士忌喝完。

swallow dive /'·· ·/ *n* [C] *BrE* a DIVE² (1) into water, that starts with your arms stretched out from the sides of your body 【英】燕式跳水; SWAN DIVE *AmE*【美】

Swallows and Am·a·zons /,····'···/ (1930) the first book in a series of popular NOVELs for children by the British writer Arthur Ransome, about the adventures of a group of children sailing, camping, and looking after themselves in the Lake District in northern England《燕子与亚马孙人》〔(1930), 英国作家阿瑟·兰塞姆儿童系列流行小说的第一部。讲述一群孩子在英格兰北部湖区驾船航行、野营、独立生活的冒险故事〕

swam /swæm; swæm/ the past tense of SWIM¹

swa·mi /ˈswɑmɪ; ˈswɑːmi/ *n* [C] a Hindu religious teacher〔印度教的〕宗教教师

swamp¹ /swɑmp; swɒmp/ *n* [C,U] land that is always very wet or slightly covered with water 沼泽(地) —compare 比较 MARSH —**swampy** *adj*: *swampy ground* 湿地

swamp² *v* [T] **1** [usually passive 一般用被动态] to suddenly give someone a lot of work, problems etc to deal with 使陷入〔大量工作〕; 使面临〔大量问题〕: **swamp sb with sth** *We've been swamped with calls since we put the ad in the paper.* 我们自从在报纸上登出广告之后, 电话就多得应接不暇。**2** to suddenly cover something with a lot of water, especially in a way that causes damage〔骤然〕淹没, 浸没: *The shoreline was swamped by the high tides.* 海岸线被高涨的潮水淹没了。

swan¹ /swɑn; swɒn/ *n* [C] a large white bird with a long graceful neck that lives on rivers and lakes 天鹅

swan² *v* **swanned, swanning** [I always+adv/prep] *BrE informal* to do things in a relaxed way that is not very responsible 【英, 非正式】悠闲地工作; 马马虎虎地做事: **[+off/around]** *You can't just swan off to the cinema when you're supposed to be working!* 你可不能在上班时间溜出去看电影啊!

swan dive /'· ·/ *n* [C] *AmE* a DIVE² (l) into water, that starts with your arms stretched out from the sides of your body【美】燕式跳水; SWALLOW DIVE *BrE*【英】

Swa·nee /ˈswɑnɪ; ˈswɒni/ **1 the Swanee** another name for Suwannee 萨旺尼河〔别称〕 **2 go down the Swanee** *BrE informal* if a plan goes down the Swanee, it fails or does not happen in the way you intended【英, 非正式】〔计划〕失败, 未按预想进行

swank¹ /swæŋk; swæŋk/ *v* [I] *informal especially BrE* to behave or speak too confidently, especially to try and make other people admire you【非正式, 尤英】炫耀, 吹嘘, 摆阔: *Stop swanking; you're not the only person who's got a flash car.* 别炫耀了, 又不是只有你一个人才有花哨的汽车。

swank² *n informal especially BrE*【非正式, 尤英】**1** [U] proud, confident behaviour that is intended to make people admire you, but is annoying 炫耀; 摆架子; 卖弄 **2** [C] someone who talks and behaves confidently in order to make people admire them 爱吹嘘的人, 爱出风头的人

swank³ *adj especially AmE* swanky【尤美】非常时髦的; 奢华的

swank·y /ˈswæŋkɪ; ˈswæŋki/ *adj informal*【非正式】**1** very fashionable or expensive; POSH 非常时髦的; 奢华的: *a really swanky reception* 很有排场的招待会 **2** *especially BrE* tending to act too confidently to get attention【尤英】爱出风头的; 爱吹嘘的; 爱摆阔的

Swan Lake /,· '·/ (1877) a BALLET with music by Tchaikovsky. It tells the story of Prince Siegfried who falls in love with a SWAN (=a large white bird) which changes into the beautiful Princess Odette. At the end of the ballet, Odette dies of unhappiness and disappears under the water of the lake, and the music from this scene, called 'The Dying Swan', is very well-known.《天鹅湖》〔(1877), 由柴可夫斯基配乐的一部芭蕾舞剧。讲述的是齐格弗里德王子爱上了一只天鹅, 天鹅后来变成漂亮的奥迪塔公主。舞剧结束时奥迪塔郁郁而死, 消失在湖水中。这一幕的音乐非常有名, 称为《天鹅之死》〕

Swan·sea /ˈswɑnsɪ; ˈswɒnzi/ a city in Wales that was once an industrial port used for coal, and is now attractive to tourists for the nearby mountains of the Brecon Beacons 斯旺西〔威尔士一城市。曾为工业港口, 用于煤炭转运。现在, 附近的布雷肯山的风光吸引游人纷至沓来〕

swan·song /ˈswɑn,sɔŋ; ˈswɒnsɒŋ/ *n* [C] the last piece of work or performance of a poet, painter etc〔诗人、画家等的〕最后一个作品; 最后一次表演: *The 1992 tour was a swansong for the two Irish players.* 1992 年的巡回比赛是这两位爱尔兰球员的告别演出。

swap¹, **swop** /swɑp; swɒp/ *v* **swapped, swapping** [I,T] **1** to exchange something with someone, especially so that each of you get what you want; TRADE² (1) 交换〔尤指双方各得所需之物〕: *I liked her coat and she liked mine, so we swapped.* 我喜欢她的外套, 她也喜欢我的, 所以我们就交换了。| **swap sth for sth** *Adam swapped three of his stickers for three of Alex's.* 亚当用自己的三张贴纸跟亚历克斯换了三张。| **swap sth with sb** *I swapped hats with Mandy.* 我和曼迪交换了帽子。| **swap sb sth for sth** *I'll swap you two of mine for one of yours.* 我可以用我的两张换你的一张。**2 swap places** also 又作 **swap round** *BrE* to let someone sit or stand in your place, so that you can have their place【英】互换位置[座位]: *I want to sit by Val; can we swap places?* 我想坐在瓦尔旁边, 我们可以互换座位吗? 3

swap², **swop** *n* [C] *informal*【非正式】**1** [usually singular 一般用单数] an exchange of one thing for another 交换, 交易: *a swap of arms for hostages* 以武器交换人质 | **do a swap** *I like your doll better; let's do a swap.* 我更喜欢你的玩具娃娃, 咱们交换吧。**2** something that has been or may be exchanged 交换物; 可交换之物

swap meet /'· ,·/ *n* [C] *AmE* an occasion when people meet to buy and sell used goods, or to exchange them【美】〔买卖或交换旧货的〕二手货集市

SWAPO /ˈswɑpo; ˈswɑːpəʊ/ the South West Africa People's Organization; a political party which began when Namibia was called South West Africa, and which sometimes used violence to achieve its aim. When Namibia finally gained its independence from South Africa, SWAPO won the first free elections there in 1989, and won power again in the 1994 elections. 西南非洲人民组织〔纳米比亚(旧称西南非洲)一政党。有时采用暴力手段达到目的。纳米比亚最终摆脱南非统治获得独立之后, 该组织在 1989 年首次自由选举中胜出, 并于 1994 年再次赢得选举成为执政党〕

sward /swɔrd; swɔːd/ *n* [C] *literary* a piece of grassy land【文】一片草地[草皮]

swarf /swɔrf; swɔːf/ *n* [U] small bits of metal, plastic etc that are produced when you use a cutting tool〔金属或塑料等的〕细屑, 切屑

swarm¹ /swɔrm; swɔːm/ *n* [C] **1** a large group of insects, especially BEEs, or animals moving together 移动中的一群昆虫〔或动物, 尤指蜂群〕 **2** a crowd of people who are moving quickly〔迅速移动的〕人群: **[+of]** *Swarms of tourists jostled through the square.* 一群群游客熙熙攘攘地穿过广场。

swarm 蜂群

a swarm of bees
一群蜜蜂

swarm² *v* [I] **1** [always+adv/prep] if people swarm somewhere, they go there as a large, uncontrolled crowd 成群结队地移动; 蜂拥; 涌往: **[+through/over/out etc]** *photographers swarming around the princess* 一窝蜂地拥到公主周围的摄影记者们 **2** if BEEs swarm they leave a HIVE (=place where they live) in a large group to look for another home〔蜜蜂〕成群飞离蜂巢寻觅新巢

swarm with sb/sth *phr v* **be swarming with** to be full of a moving crowd of people or animals 挤满〔移动的人群或动物〕: *The museum was swarming with tourists.* 博物馆里挤满了观光客。

swar·thy /ˈswɔrðɪ; ˈswɔːði/ *adj* someone who is swarthy has dark skin that is considered unattractive〔人〕肤色黝黑的

swash·buck·ling /ˈswɑʃ,bʌklɪŋ; ˈswɒʃ,bʌkəlɪŋ/ *adj* enjoying adventures, sword fighting etc 喜欢冒险[斗剑]的: *swashbuckling pirates* 冒险成性的海盗 —**swashbuckler** *n* [C]

swas·ti·ka /ˈswɑstɪkə; ˈswɒstɪkə/ *n* [C] an ancient sign consisting of a cross with each end bent at 90°, used in the twentieth century as a sign for the Nazi Party 卐字〔20 世纪时用作纳粹党的党徽〕

swat /swɑt; swɒt/ *v* **swatted, swatting** [T] to hit an insect to try to kill it 重拍, 猛击〔昆虫〕 —**swat** *n* [C]

Swatch /swɑtʃ; swɒtʃ/ *trademark* a type of watch made by a Swiss company, often made of brightly coloured plastic【商标】斯沃琪〔一款瑞士手表，通常用色泽鲜亮的塑料制成〕

swatch *n* [C] a piece of cloth that is used as an example of a type of material or its quality〔小块〕布样，样品

swathe[1] /sweð; sweɪð/ also 又作 **swath** /swɑθ; swɒθ/ *n* [C] **1** a long band of cloth 长布条: *swathes of cotton* 长条的棉布 **2** a line or area of grass or crops that has been cut by a machine or a cutting tool〔用机器、镰刀等割出的〕一行草[作物] **3** any large area of land that is different from the land on either side of it〔与两旁土地不同的〕大片土地: *Acid rain is now affecting great swathes of Western Europe.* 酸雨现正影响着西欧的广大地区。 **4 cut a swath through** if a fire, severe storm etc cuts a swath through a place, it destroys almost everything around it〔大火、暴风雨等〕把…夷为平地; 严重摧毁

swathe[2] *v* [T usually passive 一般用被动态] *literary*【文】**be swathed in sth** to be wrapped or covered in something, especially cloth 用某物包裹; 用某物覆盖: *women swathed in expensive furs* 身穿名贵毛皮衣服的女士们

sway[1] /swe; sweɪ/ *v* **1** [I,T] to move slowly from one side to another (使) 摇摆, (使) 摆动, (使) 摇晃: *trees swaying gently in the breeze* 在微风中轻轻摇动的树木 | **sway sth** *Melanie swayed her hips in time with the music.* 梅拉妮随着音乐节拍扭动着臀部。 **2** [T often passive 常用被动态] to influence someone who has not yet decided about something so that they change their opinion 影响〔某人〕; 使改变看法: *Don't allow yourself to be swayed by his promises.* 你可不要听了他的许诺就改变主意呀。

sway[2] *n* [U] **1** swinging movement from side to side 摇摆, 摆动, 摇晃: *the sway of the ship* 船的摇晃 **2** *literary* power to rule or influence people; control【文】影响力, 支配, 统治: **hold sway** (=have great power or influence) 拥有大权; 有巨大影响力 *In medieval times the Church held great sway politically.* 在中世纪, 教会在政治上处于支配地位。

S

sway·back /ˈswe͵bæk; ˈsweɪbæk/ *n* [C usually singular 一般用单数] *AmE* a condition in which your back curves inward too much【美】脊椎前凸

Swa·zi·land /ˈswɑzɪ͵lænd; ˈswɑːzilænd/ a country in southeast Africa between South Africa and Mozambique. Population: 1,104,000 (2001). Capital: Mbabane. 斯威士兰〔非洲东南部一国家, 位于南非与莫桑比克之间。人口: 1,104,000 (2001), 首都: 姆巴巴内〕

2 **swear** /swɛr; sweə/ *v past tense* **swore** /swɔr; swɔː/ *past participle* **sworn** /swɔrn; swɔːn/

1 ▶OFFENSIVE LANGUAGE 无礼的语言◀ [I] to use offensive language, especially because you are angry〔尤指因生气〕咒骂; 用粗话骂人; 说脏话: *Don't swear in front of the children.* 不要在孩子们面前骂人。| [+at] *Rich tripped over the dog and swore at it.* 里奇被狗绊了一跤, 就咒骂起它来。| **swear like a trooper** (=use very offensive language) 满口脏话

2 ▶SERIOUS PROMISE 严肃的许诺◀ [T] to make a very serious promise 起誓保证: **swear to do sth** *Mona swore never to return home.* 莫娜发誓不再回家。| **swear (that)** *Victor swore he would get his revenge.* 维克托发誓要报仇。| [+on/by] *Do you swear on your honour never to tell anyone?* 你能以你的名誉发誓永远不会告诉任何人吗?

3 ▶PUBLIC PROMISE 公开承诺◀ [I,T] to make a public official promise, especially in a court of law〔尤指在法庭上〕宣誓, 起誓: [+on] *Witnesses have to swear on the Bible.* 证人必须用手按着《圣经》宣誓。| **swear an oath** *Before giving evidence you have to swear an oath to tell the truth.* 在提供证词前, 你必须宣誓保证说实话。| **swear allegiance** *Presidents must swear allegiance to the US Constitution.* 总统必须宣誓效忠美国宪法。

4 ▶STATE THE TRUTH 说真话或实话◀ [T not in progressive 不用进行时] *informal* to say that what you have said is the truth【非正式】保证〔自己说的是真话〕; 郑重说明: **swear (that)** *He says he was there all the time, but I swear I never saw him.* 他说他自始至终都在那里, 但我保证我根本没有见到他。| **swear blind (that)** *informal* (=used to empasize you are telling the truth)【非正式】一口咬定〔自己说的是实话〕*She swore blind that she had never met the man.* 她一口咬定她从未见过那个男子。| **I could have sworn (that)** *informal* (=I was almost certain)【非正式】我几乎可以肯定 *I could have sworn I left the keys on that table.* 我几乎可以肯定是把钥匙放在那张桌子上的。| **swear to God** *I never touched her I swear to God.* 我对上帝发誓我从未碰过她。

5 swear sb to secrecy/silence to make someone promise not to tell anyone what you have told them 使某人发誓保守秘密

swear by sth *phr v* [T not in progressive 不用进行时] *informal* to have great confidence in the effectiveness of something【非正式】极其信赖: *He swears by vitamin C pills, and says he never gets ill.* 他非常相信维生素C片, 说他因此从不生病。

swear sb ↔ **in** *phr v* [T usually passive 一般用被动态] **1** to make someone promise publicly to be loyal to a country, official job etc 使〔某人〕宣誓就职: *The new governor was sworn in.* 新州长宣誓就职。| *the swearing-in ceremony* 宣誓就职仪式 **2** to make someone give an official promise in a court of law 使〔某人〕在法庭宣誓: *The jury had to be sworn in first.* 陪审团必须首先宣誓。

swear off sth *phr v* [T] to promise to stop doing something that is bad for you 承诺终止〔某种不良行为〕: *I'm swearing off alcohol after last night!* 昨晚之后, 我保证戒酒了!

swear to *phr v* [T] **not swear to (doing) sth** to be unwilling to say that something is true because you are not sure about it 不能保证某事属实: *I think it was Sue I saw, but I wouldn't swear to it.* 我觉得我看到的人是休, 但我不敢保证是她。

swear word /ˈ· ·/ *n* [C] a word that is considered to be offensive or shocking by most people 脏话, 粗话

CULTURAL NOTE 文化注释

Although swearing is common, many people believe that it is rude or offensive to swear a lot. Words that are marked taboo in this dictionary, such as SHIT, FUCK, and BOLLOCKS, are considered extremely offensive by most people. In the UK, if these words are used in television programmes, they are sometimes covered with a BLEEP (=high electronic sound). In the US, these words are not used in ordinary programmes, and they are always covered by a bleep sound in talk shows or other live programmes. In the UK and US, if a play or film on television contains a lot of swearing, there is usually a warning before the programme starts, which typically says that the programme includes 'strong language'. 尽管脏话随处可以听到, 很多人还是认为说太多脏话是粗鲁或冒犯人的行为。本词典中标记为【讳】的词, 如shit, fuck和bollocks等, 被大多数人认为极具冒犯性。在英国, 如果电视节目中说出这些词, 有时就播出"哔哔"声来盖过。在美国, 这些词不用在普通的节目中, 而一旦在访谈节目或现场直播节目中说出时, 总会被"哔哔"声干扰。在英国和美国, 如果电视上的演出和电影中含有不少脏话, 那么在节目开始之前就会有警示提醒, 一般会说本节目包含一些"猛话"。

Many people use swear words when they are with their friends, but would not use them in front of their parents or strangers. Most people believe that you should not swear in front of children, and most people think that it is totally unacceptable for children to swear. Some men believe that it is also impolite to swear in front of women, although many people consider this to be an old-fashioned belief. 很多人在朋友面前说脏话, 可从来不会在父母和陌生人面前说。大多数人都相信在孩子面前说脏话是不对的, 而小孩说脏话是完全不能接受的。有些男性认为在女性面前说脏话也是不礼貌的, 尽管很多人认为这个看法已经过时。

Other swear words, such as DAMN, HELL, or BLOODY, are less strong and more acceptable, especially if you have hurt yourself or something has gone wrong, but even these words are considered offensive by some people, especially older people or very religious people. 其他脏话如damn, hell, bloody等, 给人的感觉不是那么强烈, 也更易接受, 特别是在弄伤自己或某事出错时脱口而出地说出这些词。但在有些人, 特别是老年人或笃信宗教的人看来, 这些词也具有冒犯性。— see 见 FOUR-LETTER WORD

sweat[1] /swɛt; swet/ *v*

1 ▶LIQUID FROM SKIN 皮肤冒出的液体◀ [I] to have liquid coming out through your skin, especially because you are hot or frightened 出汗, 流汗, 冒汗: *I was sweating after the long climb.* 我长时间攀爬后出汗不止。| **sweat heavily/profusely** (=sweat a lot) 出大汗; 流很多汗 | **sweat like a pig** *informal* (=sweat a lot)【非正式】汗流浃背, 浑身是汗 | **sweat buckets** *informal* (=sweat a lot)【非正式】汗如雨下, 大汗淋漓

2 ▶WORK 工作◀ [I] *informal* to work hard【非正式】辛苦工作, 拼命干活: *For years she had struggled and sweated to keep the family fed.* 多少年来, 她为了养家糊口在拼命干活。| [+over] *Tim really sweated over that thesis.* 蒂姆写那篇论文真是费了劲。| **sweat blood** (=work very hard) 拼命地干

3 ▶WORRY 担心◀ [I] *informal* to be anxious, nervous, or worried about something【非正式】焦虑; 精神紧张; 担心: *We were all really sweating as we waited for the results.* 我们在等待结

果时心情真是紧张得很。| *Don't tell them yet – let them sweat a bit first!* 暂时不要告诉他们——先让他们着急一下!

4 don't sweat it *AmE spoken* used to tell someone not to worry about something【美口】别担心, 别着急: *Don't sweat it, I'll lend you the money.* 不用担心, 我会借钱给你的。

5 don't sweat the small stuff *AmE spoken* used to tell someone not to worry about unimportant things【美口】不要为小事担心

6 sweat bullets *AmE informal* to be very worried, anxious, or frightened【美, 非正式】非常担心; 十分着急; 非常害怕

7 ►PRODUCE LIQUID 产生液体◄ [I] if something such as cheese sweats, liquid from inside appears on its surface〔乳酪等〕表面渗出水分

8 ►COOK 烹调◄ [T] *BrE* to heat food gently in a little water or fat【英】用文火熬: *Sweat the vegetables until the juices run out.* 用文火煮这些蔬菜, 直至熬出菜汁。

sweat sth ↔ **out** *phr v* [T] **1 sweat it out a)** to continue doing something until it is finished, even though it is difficult 坚持做完〔困难的工作〕: *You can't leave the course now. Just sweat it out until the summer.* 你现在不能放弃这门课程, 坚持到夏季把它修完吧。**b)** to do hard physical exercise 吃力地锻炼身体: *They were sweating it out in the gym.* 他们正拼命地在健身房里进行训练。**2** to get rid of an illness by making yourself sweat a lot 通过发汗把〔疾病〕治好 **3 sweat your guts out** *informal* to work very hard, especially using physical effort【非正式】拼命工作〔尤指体力劳动〕: *I've sweated my guts out trying to get this shed built on time.* 为了争取按时建好这间棚屋, 我一直在拼命苦干。**4 sweat sth out of sb** *AmE informal* to find out information from someone by asking lots of questions in a threatening way【美, 非正式】反复威逼某人说出某情况: *Finally they sweated the other names out of him.* 他们终于逼他说出了其他人的名字。

sweat sth ↔ **off** *phr v* [T] to lose weight by sweating a lot 通过大量流汗减轻〔体重〕: *He sweated off two pounds in the sauna.* 他通过洗桑拿浴大量出汗, 体重减轻了两磅。

sweat[2] *n*

1 ►LIQUID ON SKIN 皮肤上的液体◄ [U] liquid that comes out through your skin when you are hot, frightened, or doing exercise 汗, 汗水, 汗液: *Ian came off the squash court dripping with sweat.* 伊恩大汗淋漓地走出壁球场。| **work up a sweat** (=to do physical exercise or hard work that makes you sweat) 因锻炼[辛苦工作]而流汗 | **break out in a sweat** (=start to sweat, especially because you are frightened)〔尤指因惧怕〕冒汗 *I was ready to kill the guy, and he didn't even break out in a sweat!* 我恨不得杀死那个人, 而他竟然连汗也没有冒!

2 get into a sweat about sth *informal* to become nervous or frightened about something【非正式】因某事而紧张[害怕]: *Don't get into such a sweat about it! It's only a test.* 不要为这事那么紧张! 这只不过是一次测验。

3 a cold sweat a state of nervousness or fear, in which you start to sweat, even though you are not hot〔由于精神紧张或害怕出的〕一身冷汗: *I woke up from the nightmare in a cold sweat.* 我从噩梦中惊醒, 出了一身冷汗。

4 no sweat *spoken* used to say that you can do something easily【口】一点也不难, 毫不费力: *"Are you sure you can do it on time?" "Yeah, no sweat!"* "你有把握按时完成吗?" "是的, 没问题!"

5 sweats [plural] *AmE informal*【美, 非正式】**a)** clothes made of thick, soft cotton, worn especially for sport; SWEAT SUIT 运动服 **b)** trousers of this type; SWEAT PANTS 运动裤

6 the sweat of sb's brow *literary* the hard effort that someone has made in their work【文】〔某人所付出的〕艰苦努力

7 ►WORK 工作◄ [singular] *old-fashioned* hard work, especially when it is boring or unpleasant【过时】〔尤指枯燥或不愉快的〕艰苦的工作

8 (old) sweat *old-fashioned* someone who has a lot of experience, especially a soldier【过时】经验丰富的人〔尤指老兵〕

sweat·band /ˈswɛt͵bænd; ˈswetbænd/ *n* [C] **1** a narrow band of cloth that you wear around your head or wrist to stop sweat running down when you are doing sport〔运动时缠在头部或手腕的〕吸汗带 **2** a narrow piece of cloth that you wear sewn or stuck in the inside of a hat〔帽子内侧的〕防汗带

sweated la·bour *BrE*【英】, **sweated labor** *AmE*【美】/ˌ· ˈ··/ *n* [U] **1** hard work done for very low wages, especially in a factory 血汗劳动〔尤指工厂的艰苦而工资低微的工作〕**2** the people who do this work 血汗劳工

sweat·er /ˈswɛtɚ; ˈswetə/ *n* [C] a piece of warm WOOLLEN or cotton clothing for the top half of your body that has long SLEEVES and no buttons〔长袖〕毛线衣, 羊毛衫, 针织(套)衫, 运动衫; JUMPER (1) *BrE*【英】

sweat gland /ˈ· ·/ *n* [C] a small organ under your skin that produces sweat 汗腺

sweat pants /ˈ· ·/ *n* [plural] *AmE* thick cotton trousers, worn especially for sport【美】棉织厚长裤, 运动裤

sweat·shirt /ˈswɛt͵ʃɝt; ˈswet-ʃɜːt/ *n* [C] a piece of thick cotton clothing with long SLEEVES, worn on the top half of your body, especially for sport 棉织长袖衫, 长袖运动衫

sweat·shop /ˈswɛt͵ʃɑp; ˈswet-ʃɒp/ *n* [C] a small business, factory etc where people work hard in bad conditions for very little money 血汗工厂〔工作条件恶劣而工资低微的小厂等〕: *Sweatshops often employ female or immigrant workers.* 血汗工厂经常雇用妇女和移民劳工。

sweat suit /ˈ· ·/ *n* [C] *AmE* a set of clothes made of thick soft cotton, worn especially for sport【美】〔棉织〕运动套装, 运动衣裤

sweat·y /ˈswɛtɪ; ˈsweti/ *adj* **1** covered with SWEAT[2] (1) 有汗的; 满是汗的, 被汗水湿透的: *We came home hot and sweaty after the day's work.* 干完一天工作之后, 我们热得满身是汗地回家。| *sweaty palms* 有汗的掌心 **2** smelling unpleasantly of SWEAT[2] 发汗臭味的: *sweaty socks* 有汗臭味的袜子 **3** unpleasantly hot or difficult so that you SWEAT[1] 闷热的; 劳累的, 使人出汗的: *a sweaty August day* 8月里闷热的一天 | *a sweaty job* 吃力的工作 **4** cheese that is sweaty has drops of liquid on its surface〔乳酪〕表面渗出水分的

Swede /swid; swiːd/ *n* [C] someone who comes from Sweden 瑞典人

swede *n* [C,U] *BrE* a round yellow vegetable that grows under the ground【英】芜菁甘蓝; RUTABAGA *AmE*【美】

Swe·den /ˈswidn̩; ˈswiːdn/ a country in Scandinavia, northern Europe. Population: 8,875,000 (2001). Capital: Stockholm. It is a member of the EU, and has a generally high standard of living and a generous system of WELFARE. People from Sweden are called Swedes. 瑞典〔北欧一国家, 位于斯堪的纳维亚半岛。人口: 8,875,000 (2001), 首都: 斯德哥尔摩。为欧盟成员国, 生活水准较高, 实行高福利制度。瑞典人称作 Swede〕—see 见 SWEDISH

Swe·dish[1] /ˈswidɪʃ; ˈswiːdiʃ/ *n* [U] **1** the language spoken in Sweden 瑞典语 **2 the Swedish** the people of Sweden 瑞典人〔总称〕

Swedish[2] *adj* from or connected with Sweden 瑞典的; 来自瑞典的; 与瑞典有关的

sweep[1] /swip; swiːp/ *v past tense and past participle* **swept** /swɛpt; swept/ S3 W3

1 ►CLEAN STH 把…弄干净◄ [T] to clean the dust, dirt etc from the floor or ground using a special brush 扫, 打扫, 清扫: *Bert swept the path in front of the house.* 伯特清扫了门前的小路。| *Sweep the floor clean for me please.* 请帮我把地板打扫干净。—see picture at 参见 CLEAN[2] 图

2 ►PUSH STH SOMEWHERE 把某物推到某处◄ [T always+adv/prep] **a)** to clean a surface by pushing something to a particular place or in a particular direction with a special brush 扫去, 拂去, 清除: *Could you sweep the snow off the patio for me?* 你能帮我把露台上的雪清除掉吗? **b)** to move something to a particular place or in a particular direction with a brushing or swinging movement 卷走; 冲走; 移去; 刮走: *The wind swept the dead leaves away.* 风把枯叶刮走了。| *I swept the papers quickly into the drawer.* 我迅速地把那些文件塞进抽屉里。

3 ►CROWD 人群◄ [I always+adv/prep] if a group of people sweep somewhere, they quickly move there together 迅速地移动; 冲过: **[+through/along etc]** *The crowd swept through the gates of the stadium.* 人群冲过体育场的大门。

4 ►PERSON 人◄ [I always+adv/prep] if someone sweeps somewhere, they move quickly and confidently, especially because they are impatient or like to seem important 昂首阔步地走: **[+into/through etc]** *Eva swept into the meeting and demanded to know what was going on.* 伊娃大步冲进会场, 要求知道正在发生什么事情。

5 ►WIND/WAVES ETC 风/浪等◄ [I always+adv/prep,T] if winds, waves, storms etc sweep a place or sweep through, across etc a place, they move quickly and with a lot of force〔风、浪、风暴等迅速猛烈地〕扫过, 掠过(某地): **[+across/through etc]** *90 mile per hour winds swept across the plains.* 时速 90 英里的强风横扫平原。| **sweep sth** *Thunderstorms swept the country.* 雷暴横扫全国。

6 ►IDEA/FEELING 思想/感情◄ [I always+adv/prep,T] if an idea or feeling sweeps a group of people or sweeps across, over etc a group, it quickly becomes very popular with them 风行; (在…)迅速传播: **[+across/through etc]** *The new dance craze swept through the teenage population.* 这种新舞在青少年中风

靡一时。| **sweep sth** *a wave of nationalism sweeping the country* 席卷全国的民族主义浪潮

7 sweep sb along/away a) if a crowd sweeps someone along or away it forces them to move in the same direction it is moving in〔人群〕拥着某人向前: *I was swept away by the crowd and lost sight of Alyssa completely.* 我被人群拥着往前走, 完全看不到阿莉莎了。**b)** if a feeling or idea sweeps you along or away, you are so involved or interested in it that you forget about other things〔感情、思想〕令某人着迷; 使某人深受影响: *19th century scientists swept along on the tide of Darwin's theories* 19世纪深受达尔文理论思潮影响的科学家

8 sweep to victory/power to win something easily and in an impressive way 大获全胜/一举掌权: *Nixon and Agnew swept to victory with 47 million votes.* 尼克松和阿格纽赢得4700万张选票, 大获全胜。

9 sweep the board to win everything that can be won, especially very easily〔尤指轻易地〕大获全胜, 囊括全部奖项

10 ▶FORM A CURVE 形成曲线◀ [I always+adv/prep] to form a long curved shape 蜿蜒; 延伸: **[+down/along etc]** *The hills swept down to the sea.* 山丘延绵, 伸到了海边。

11 ▶LOOK 看◀ [I always+adv/prep,T] to look quickly at all of something〔目光等〕扫视: *The General's eyes swept the horizon.* 将军双目扫视着地平线。| **[+over/across/around etc]** *Her eyes swept over Marcia appraisingly.* 她用评价的目光迅速打量着马西娅。

12 sweep sb off their feet to make someone feel suddenly and strongly attracted to you in a romantic way 把某人一下子迷住, 使某人神魂颠倒: *Jill's been swept off her feet by an older man.* 吉尔被一位年长男子迷住了。

13 sweep sth under the carpet also 又作 **sweep sth under the rug** *AmE*【美】to try to keep something a secret, especially something you have done wrong 掩盖某事〔尤指错事〕

sweep sth ↔ **aside** *phr v* [T] to refuse to pay attention to something someone says 拒不理会, 无视

sweep sth ↔ **away** *phr v* [T] **1** to completely destroy something or make something disappear 扫除; 消灭; 摧毁: *houses swept away by the floods* 被洪水摧毁的房屋 | *A sudden feeling of nostalgia swept all my anger away.* 突然的一阵怀旧情绪使我怒气全消。**2 be swept away by** to be so interested or involved in something that you forget about other things 深受…感染, 被…打动: *We couldn't help being swept away by Bette's enthusiasm.* 我们都不禁被贝特的热情打动了。

sweep sth ↔ **back** *phr v* [T] if you sweep your hair back, you pull it back from your face, especially so that it stays in that style 把〔头发〕梳向后面, 向后掠〔头发〕: **[+in/into]** *Kerry swept her hair back into a bun.* 克丽把头发梳到后面盘成一个髻。

sweep up *phr v* **1** [I,T] to clean a place using a special brush, or to pick up dirt, dust etc in this way 打扫, 清扫: *The janitor was just sweeping up as I left the building.* 我离开大楼时, 看门人正在进行打扫。**sweep sth ↔ up** *Jan was left to sweep up the bits of paper and broken glass.* 简被留下来清扫那些纸屑和碎玻璃。**2** [T **sweep** sb ↔ **up**] to pick someone up in one quick movement 一下抱起〔某人〕: *Harriet swept the child up in her arms and stormed out.* 哈丽雅特一把抱起孩子, 怒气冲冲地跑了出去。**3 sweep sb's hair up** to pull someone's hair back away from their face, especially so that it stays in that style 把某人的头发梳到后面

sweep² *n* **1** [C] a long swinging movement of your arm, a weapon etc 挥动: *With one sweep of his sword, he cut through the rope.* 他剑一挥, 把绳索砍断了。**2** [C usually singular 一般用单数] *BrE* the act of sweeping something【英】打扫, 清扫: *The kitchen needs a good sweep.* 厨房需要好好打扫一下了。**3 the sweep of a)** a long curved line or area of land 长而弯曲的一段〔土地〕; 连绵弯曲的地带: **[+of]** *the sweep of the hills in the distance* 远处延绵的山丘 **b)** the quality that an idea, plan, piece of writing etc has of considering many different and important things〔思想、作品等的〕广度, 范围: *the grand sweep of Whitman's poetic vision* 惠特曼丰富的诗歌想象力 **4** [C usually singular 一般用单数] a search or attack that moves over a large area〔大面积的〕搜索, 搜查; 扫荡 **5 sweeps** [singular] *AmE informal* a SWEEPSTAKE【美, 非正式】赌金全赢制 **6** [C] a CHIMNEYSWEEP 烟囱清洁工 —see also 另见 **clean sweep** (CLEAN¹ (12))

sweep·er /ˈswipɚ; ˈswiːpə/ *n* [C] **1** someone or something that sweeps 清扫者, 清洁工; 清扫机: *a road sweeper* 马路清洁工; 马路清扫机 **2** *BrE* a football player who plays in a position behind other defending players【英】〔足球运动的〕自由中卫

sweep·ing /ˈswipɪŋ; ˈswiːpɪŋ/ *adj* **1** affecting many things, or making a big difference to things 影响大的; 范围广的; 广泛的: **sweeping changes/cuts etc** *sweeping changes that mean job cuts in every department* 意味着每个部门都要裁员的全面变革 | *sweeping proposals* 内容广泛的建议 **2** lacking knowledge of or consideration for facts or details 笼统的; 总括性的: *sweeping statements* 总括性的说法 | **sweeping generalization** *You shouldn't make sweeping generalizations about women drivers.* 你不该对女性驾驶员一概而论。

sweep·ings /ˈswipɪŋz; ˈswiːpɪŋz/ *n* [plural] dirt, dust etc that is left to be swept up 扫拢的垃圾[尘土等]: *a pile of sweepings* 一堆扫拢的垃圾

sweep·stake /ˈswipˌstek; ˈswiːpsteɪk/ *n* [C] a type of betting (BET¹), in which the winner gets all the money risked by everyone else〔胜者可获全部赌金的〕赌金全赢制: *a sweepstake on the horses* 赛马中的赌金全赢制

sweet¹ /swit; swiːt/ *adj* 2 3

1 ▶TASTE 味道◀ having a taste like sugar 甜的, 味甜的: *This tea is too sweet.* 这茶太甜了。| *a sweet apple* 甜苹果 | *sweet wine* 甜酒 —compare 比较 BITTER¹ (4), DRY¹ (9), SOUR¹ (1)

2 ▶CHARACTER 性格◀ kind, gentle, and friendly 和蔼的; 温柔的; 友好的: *a sweet smile* 和蔼的微笑 | *How sweet of you to remember my birthday!* 你真好, 还记得我的生日! —see also 另见 SWEET-TEMPERED

3 ▶CHILDREN/SMALL THINGS 小孩/小物品◀ *especially BrE* looking pretty and attractive; CUTE【尤英】漂亮的, 可爱的: *Your little boy looks very sweet in his new coat.* 你的小儿子穿着新外套真好看。

4 ▶THOUGHTS/EMOTIONS 思想/感情◀ making you feel pleased, happy, and satisfied 令人愉悦的, 惬意的; 使人满足的: *Revenge is sweet.* 报仇给人带来快感。

5 ▶SMELLS 气味◀ having a pleasant smell; FRAGRANT 芳香的, 芬芳的: *sweet-smelling flowers* 气味芳香的花朵

6 ▶SOUNDS 声音◀ pleasant to listen to 悦耳的, 动听的: *She had a very sweet singing voice.* 她唱歌的声音悦耳动听。

7 have a sweet tooth to like things that taste of sugar 爱吃甜食

8 keep sb sweet *informal* to behave in a pleasant, friendly way towards someone, because you want them to help you later【非正式】讨好某人, 巴结某人: *I'm trying to keep Angela sweet so that she'll lend me her notes.* 我在尽力向安杰拉献殷勤, 好让她把笔记借给我。

9 in your own sweet way if you do something in your own sweet way, you do it in exactly the way that you want to, without considering what other people say or think 只凭自己的意愿; 不考虑别人; 自私地: *I'd rather carry on in my own sweet way, if you don't mind.* 如果你不介意, 我就按我的想法做下去了。

10 sweet deal *AmE* a really good deal【美】赚钱的交易; 十分合算的买卖

11 sweet FA also 又作 **sweet Fanny Adams** *BrE informal* used to say FUCK ALL (=nothing at all) when you want to avoid using the word 'fuck'【英, 非正式】一点儿也没有〔fuck all 的委婉说法, 以避免使用 fuck 这个脏词〕: *"How much did they pay you for that job?" "Sweet FA!"* "干那件工作他们给了你多少报酬?" "一分钱也没有!"

12 sweet nothings things that lovers say to each other〔情侣之间的〕卿卿我我的话, 情话: *a couple whispering sweet nothings to each other* 悄悄地互相说着情话的一对情侣

13 be sweet on sb *old-fashioned* to be very attracted to or in love with someone【过时】钟情于某人, 爱上某人 —see also 另见 **home sweet home** (HOME¹ (16)), **short and sweet** (SHORT¹ (9)), SWEETNESS —**sweetly** *adv*

This graph shows how common the nouns **sweet** and **candy** are in British and American English. 本图表显示名词 sweet 和 candy 在英国英语和美国英语中的使用频率。

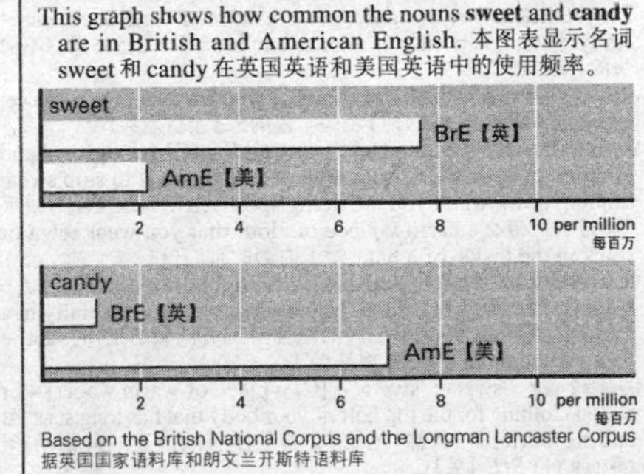

Based on the British National Corpus and the Longman Lancaster Corpus 据英国国家语料库和朗文兰开斯特语料库

In British English **sweet** is used to mean a small piece of sweet food made of sugar or chocolate. Americans use **candy** for this meaning. In British English **sweet** also means sweet food that is served at tne end of a meal. Americans use **dessert** for this meaning. 在英国英语中, sweet 指用糖或巧克力做的糖果, 而美国英语则用 candy 表示此意。英国英语中 sweet 也可指餐后的甜食, 而美国英语则用 dessert。

sweet² *n* **1** [C] *BrE* a small piece of sweet food made of sugar or chocolate【英】糖果; CANDY *AmE*【美】: *Eating sweets is bad for your teeth.* 吃糖果对牙齿不好。**2** [C,U] *BrE* sweet food served at the end of a meal; DESSERT【英】〔餐后的〕甜食, 甜点: *Would you like a sweet, or some cheese and biscuits?* 你是喜欢来点甜食, 还是干酪和饼干? **3 (my) sweet** *old-fashioned* used when speaking to someone you love【过时】亲爱的, 甜心〔用作爱称〕: *Don't cry, my sweet.* 亲爱的, 不要哭。

sweet-and-sour /ˌ· · ˈ·◂/ *adj* [only before noun 仅用于名词前] a sweet-and-sour dish in Chinese cooking has both sweet and sour tastes together〔中国菜〕甜酸的, 糖醋的: *sweet-and-sour pork* 咕咾肉

sweet·bread /ˈswitˌbrɛd; ˈswiːtbred/ *n* [C] *old-fashioned* a small organ from a sheep or young cow, used as food【过时】〔从羊或小牛身上取下供食用的〕胰脏, 杂碎

sweet·corn /ˈswitkɔrn; ˈswiːtkɔːn/ *n* [U] *BrE* the soft yellow seeds from MAIZE that are cooked and eaten【英】甜玉米〔可煮食〕; CORN (2b) *AmE*【美】

sweet·en /ˈswitn; ˈswiːtn/ *v* **1** [I,T] to make something sweeter, or become sweeter (使) 变甜; 加糖于: *Sweeten the mixture with a little honey.* 加点蜂蜜使混合料变甜。**2** also 又作 **sweeten sb ↔ up** [T] *informal* to try to persuade someone to do what you want, by giving them presents or money【非正式】〔通过送礼物或金钱〕笼络, 讨好: *We're going to have to sweeten them up if we want that contract.* 如果想签上那份合同, 我们就得花钱笼络他们一下。—see also 另见 SWEETENER (2) **3** [T] *literary* to make someone kinder, gentler etc【文】使和蔼; 使温和; 使温柔: *Old age had not sweetened her.* 年老并没有使她变得和蔼可亲。

sweetened con·densed milk /ˌ·· ˌ·· ˈ·/ *n* [U] *especially AmE* milk that has been made thicker and sweeter, and is usually sold in cans【尤美】甜炼乳; CONDENSED MILK *BrE*【英】

sweet·ener /ˈswitnə; ˈswiːtnə/ *n* **1** [C,U] a substance used to make something taste sweeter 甜味剂, 甜化剂: *No artificial sweeteners are used in this product.* 本产品没有使用人造甜味剂。**2** [C] *informal* something that you give to someone to persuade them to do something【非正式】贿赂物, 笼络物: *These tax cuts are just a preelection sweetener.* 这些减税措施只不过是选举前用来笼络人心的东西。

sweet gum /ˌ· ˈ·/ *n* [C] a tree with hard wood and groups of seeds like PRICKLY balls, common in North America〔产于北美的〕枫香树

sweet·heart /ˈswitˌhɑrt; ˈswiːthɑːt/ *n* [C] **1** a way of addressing someone you love 亲爱的, 宝贝, 甜心〔用作爱称〕: *Come here, sweetheart.* 到这儿来, 亲爱的。**2** an informal way of addressing a woman you do not know, which some women find offensive 甜心, 可爱的人〔对陌生女子的非正式称呼, 有些女子认为这种称呼带有冒犯性〕 **3** *old-fashioned* the person that you love【过时】情人, 恋人 —see also 另见 DARLING¹ (1), LOVE² (9)

sweet·ie /ˈswiti; ˈswiːti/ *n* [C] **1** *BrE informal* a word for a SWEET² (1), used by or to children【英, 非正式】糖果〔儿语〕 **2** *BrE informal* something or someone that is small, pretty, and easy to love【英, 非正式】小巧[漂亮, 可爱]的人[物]: *Look at that little dog – isn't he a sweetie!* 瞧那只小狗 — 它多逗人喜爱! **3** *informal* a way of addressing someone you love【非正式】亲爱的〔用作爱称〕

sweetie pie /ˈ·· ˌ·/ *n* [C] *AmE informal* a way of addressing someone you love【美, 非正式】亲爱的, 宝贝〔用作爱称〕

sweet·meat /ˈswitˌmit; ˈswiːtmiːt/ *n* [C] *BrE old-fashioned* a SWEET¹ (1), or any food made of or preserved in sugar【英, 过时】糖果; 甜食; 蜜饯

sweet·ness /ˈswitnɪs; ˈswiːtnɪ̈s/ *n* [U] **1** how sweet something is 甜度 **2 be all sweetness and light** to behave in a way that is very pleasant and friendly, especially when you do not normally behave like this〔尤指一反常态地〕和蔼可亲, 亲切友善: *She's all sweetness and light when Paul's around.* 每当保罗在场时, 她就异常地和蔼可亲。

sweet pea /ˌ· ˈ·/ *n* [C] a climbing plant with sweet-smelling flowers in pale colours 香豌豆

sweet pep·per /ˌ· ˈ··/ *n* [C] a green, red, or yellow vegetable that is hollow with many seeds 甜椒; BELL PEPPER *AmE*【美】

sweet po·ta·to /ˌ· ·ˈ··/ *n* [C] a vegetable that looks like a red potato, is yellow inside and tastes sweet 番薯, 红薯, 白薯 —compare 比较 YAM (1) —see picture on page A9 参见 A9 页图

sweet roll /ˈ· ·/ *n* [C] *AmE* a small sweet PASTRY【美】小甜油酥点心

sweet-talk /ˈ· ·/ *v* [T] *informal* to try to persuade someone to do something by talking to them in a pleasant way【非正式】用甜言蜜语劝诱: **sweet-talk sb into doing sth** *I managed to sweet-talk her into driving me home.* 我终于用花言巧语哄得她开车送我回家。—**sweet talk** *n* [U]

sweet-temp·ered /ˌ· ˈ··◂/ *adj* having a character that is kind and gentle 性情温和的, 脾气好的

sweet wil·liam /ˌswit ˈwɪljəm; ˌswiːt ˈwɪljəm/ *n* [C,U] a plant with sweet-smelling flowers 美国石竹

swell¹ /swɛl; swel/ *v past tense* **swelled** *past participle* **swollen** /ˈswolən; ˈswəʊlən/

1 ►PART OF YOUR BODY 身体部位◄ [I] also 又作 **swell up** to gradually increase in size 肿, 肿胀: *Her ankle was already starting to swell.* 她的脚踝已经开始肿了。

2 ►PEOPLE 人◄ [T] to gradually increase in amount or number〔数量〕逐渐增加, 增多, 增大: *We asked them to come to the meeting to swell the numbers.* 我们叫他们来开会以增加出席的人数。| *The crowd swelled.* 人群逐渐扩大。| **swell the ranks of sth** (=increase the number of people in a particular situation) 扩大…的队伍; 增加…的人数 *School leavers are swelling the ranks of the unemployed.* 离校生正在不断扩大失业者的队伍。

3 ►SOUND 声音◄ [I] *literary* to become louder【文】〔声音〕增强, 变响亮: *Music swelled around us.* 音乐声在我们四周逐渐增强。

4 ►SHAPE 形状◄ [I,T] also 又作 **swell (sth ↔) out** to get or give something a full round shape (使) 鼓起, (使) 隆起: *The wind swelled the sails.* 风吹得船帆鼓了起来。

5 swell with pride/anger etc to feel very proud, angry etc 扬扬得意/怒气冲冲等: *His heart swelled with pride as he watched his daughter collect her prize.* 他看着女儿领奖时心中充满了自豪。

6 ►SEA 海◄ [I] to move suddenly and powerfully upwards 波涛汹涌 —see also 另见 GROUNDSWELL, SWOLLEN

swell² *n* **1** [singular] the way the sea moves up and down 海面的起伏, 浪涌: **heavy swell** (=very strong swell) 大浪涛, 猛烈的浪涌 *We didn't go sailing that day, as there was a heavy swell.* 那天我们没有驾船出海, 因为海上浪涛很大。**2** [singular] an increase in sound level, especially in music; CRESCENDO (1)〔尤指音乐〕音量逐渐增强 **3** [singular] the roundness and fullness of something 膨胀; 鼓起; 隆起: *the firm swell of her breasts* 她丰满坚挺的乳房 **4** [C] *old-fashioned* a fashionable or important person【过时】时髦人物; 头面人物, 要人

swell³ *adj AmE old-fashioned* very good【美, 过时】极好的, 第一流的: *You look swell!* 你看起来漂亮极了!

swell-head·ed /ˌ· ˈ··◂/ *adj AmE informal* thinking that you are more important or clever than you really are【美, 非正式】自负的, 自命不凡的

swell·ing /ˈswɛlɪŋ; ˈswelɪŋ/ *n* **1** [C] an area of your body that has become larger than normal, because of illness or injury〔身体因患病或受伤产生的〕肿块, 肿胀处: *a nasty swelling on my neck* 我颈部严重的肿块 **2** [U] the condition of having swelled 膨胀; 肿胀: *The spider's bite can cause pain and swelling.* 蜘蛛的叮咬可能引起肿疼。

swel·ter /ˈswɛltə; ˈsweltə/ *v* [I] to feel unpleasantly hot 感到热得难受, 热得发昏: *sitting and sweltering in the classroom* 坐在教室里热得难受

swel·ter·ing /ˈswɛltərɪŋ; ˈsweltərɪŋ/ *adj* unpleasantly hot 热得使人难受的: *Open a window; it's sweltering in here!* 打开一扇窗子吧; 这里面热得难受!

swept /swɛpt; swept/ the past tense and past participle of SWEEP

swept-back /ˌ· ˈ·◂/ *adj* **1** hair that is swept-back is brushed backward from your face〔头发〕向后梳的 **2** swept-back wings on an aircraft look like the letter v〔飞机机翼〕后掠的

swerve /swɝv; swɜːv/ *v* [I] **1** to make a sudden sideways movement while moving forwards, especially in order to avoid hitting something〔尤指为了避免碰撞〕突然地转向一边: *Jo swerved to avoid a dog.* 乔为了避免撞着狗而突然转向一边。| **[+across/off etc]** *The car swerved across the road and crashed into a wall.* 汽车突然转向冲过马路, 撞在一堵墙上。—see picture on page A3 参见 A3 页图 **2** [usually in negatives 一般用于否定句] *formal* to change from an idea, course of action, purpose etc【正式】改变主意[做法, 目的等]; 背离: **[+from]** *He vowed he would not swerve from his declared aims.* 他发誓不

会背离他公开宣布的目标。—**swerve** *n* [C]: *a swerve to the left* 向左急转

swift¹ /swɪft; swɪft/ *adj* **1** happening quickly and immediately 迅速的; 立刻的: *My letter received a swift reply.* 我的信得到迅速的答复。**2** [only before noun 仅用于名词前] moving, or able to move, very fast (能) 迅速移动的; 速度非常快的: *a swift runner* 跑得快的人 | **swift of foot** *literary* (=able to run fast)【文】跑得快的, 健步如飞的 **3 be swift to do sth** to do something as soon as you can, without any delay 迅速做某事, 立刻做某事: *They were swift to deny the accusations.* 他们立刻否认了那些指控。—**swiftly** *adv* —**swiftness** *n* [U]

swift² *n* [C] a small brown bird that has pointed wings, flies very fast, and is similar to a SWALLOW² (1) 雨燕

Swift, Jon·a·than /ˈdʒɑnəθən; ˈdʒɒnəθən/ (1667-1745) an Irish writer whose best-known book is *Gulliver's Travels* but who also wrote many other SATIRICAL stories and clever articles, in which he used humour to criticize institutions such as the universities, the legal profession, and the political parties. He was also a priest in the Church of England, and became Dean (=a high-ranking priest) of St Patrick's Cathedral in Dublin. Because of this, he is sometimes called 'Dean Swift'. 斯威夫特〔(1667-1745), 爱尔兰作家。最著名的小说是《格列佛游记》, 同时还创作了大量讽刺故事和睿智文章, 以幽默的笔触批评诸如大学、法律、政党等机构。他还是英国国教会教士, 后成为都柏林圣帕特里克大教堂教长, 因此有时人们称他"斯威夫特教长"〕

swig /swɪg; swɪg/ *v* **swigged, swigging** [T] *informal* to drink something in large mouthfuls, especially from a bottle【非正式】〔尤指直接从瓶子〕大口地喝, 痛饮: *They sat there, swigging beer.* 他们坐在那里大口大口地喝啤酒。—**swig** *n* [C]: *He took a large swig from the bottle.* 他从瓶子里喝了一大口。

swill¹ /swɪl; swɪl/ *v* [T] **1** to wash an area by pouring a lot of water over it or into it〔用水〕冲洗, 涮: **swill sth ↔ down/out** *Get a bucket to swill the yard down.* 去拿个桶来把院子冲洗冲洗。**2** *informal* to drink something in large amounts【非正式】大口地喝, 痛饮: *He does nothing but swill beer all day.* 他一天到晚啥事也不做, 只是拼命地喝啤酒。

swill² *n* **1** [U] food for pigs, mostly made of unwanted bits of human food 泔脚饲料, 猪食 —see also 另见 PIGSWILL **2** [C] the act of washing something by pouring a lot of water over it 冲洗, 涮

swim¹ /swɪm; swɪm/ *v past tense* **swam** /swæm; swæm/ *past participle* **swum** /swʌm; swʌm/ *present participle* **swimming**

1 ►MOVE THROUGH WATER 在水里移动◄ [I] to move yourself through water using your arms, legs etc 游水, 游泳: *My dad taught me to swim.* 我爸爸教我游泳。| *Exotic fish swam around in the tank.* 奇异的鱼儿在缸里游来游去。| **go swimming** (=swim for fun) 去游泳 —see 见 BATH² (USAGE)

2 ►IN A PARTICULAR AREA OF WATER 在某特定水域◄ [T] to get across a particular area of water by doing this 游过〔某水域〕, 泅渡: *She was the first woman to swim the Channel.* 她是第一位游过英吉利海峡的女子。

3 ►A PARTICULAR STYLE 某种姿势◄ [T] to use a particular style of swimming 游〔某 泳式〕: *She can swim breaststroke, backstroke, and crawl.* 她会游蛙泳、仰泳和自由泳。

4 ►NOT THINKING/SEEING PROPERLY 思维/视觉不清◄ [I] **a)** if your head swims, you start to feel confused or DIZZY (1) 发晕, 眩晕: *My head was swimming after looking at that screen all day.* 我看了一整天屏幕之后觉得头昏眼花。**b)** if something you are looking at swims, it seems to move because you feel DIZZY (1)〔因晕眩而觉得眼前物体〕旋转: *The numbers swam before my eyes.* 那些数字在我眼前旋转。

5 be swimming with sth also 又作 **be swimming in sth** to be very full of liquid or completely surrounded by liquid 浸[泡]在液体里: *potatoes swimming in thick gravy* 泡在浓肉汁里的马铃薯

6 swim with the tide to do or say the same things as most other people want because you do not want to seem different 顺应潮流, 随大溜, 随波逐流

7 swim against the tide to do or say different things from what most people do, because you do not mind being different 反潮流, 不随大溜 —see also 另见 **sink or swim** (SINK¹ (17))

swim² *n* [C] **1** a period of time that you spend swimming 游泳: *Let's go for a swim.* 咱们游泳去吧。**2 in the swim** *informal* knowing about and involved in what is happening in modern life【非正式】了解并融入现代生活的; 不脱离潮流的

swim·mer /ˈswɪmɚ; ˈswɪmə/ *n* [C] **a)** someone who swims well, often as a competitor 游泳者; 游泳运动员: **good/strong swimmer** (=someone who swims well) 善于游泳者/游泳能手 **b)** someone who is swimming 正在游泳的人: *We watched the swimmers heading out across the lake.* 我们看着游泳的人向湖对岸游去。

swim·ming /ˈswɪmɪŋ; ˈswɪmɪŋ/ *n* [U] the sport of swimming 游泳 (运动): *Swimming is great exercise.* 游泳是项很好的锻炼。| *a swimming club* 游泳俱乐部 2

swimming bath /ˈ· · ·/ *n* [C] *BrE old-fashioned* a public swimming pool, usually indoors【英, 过时】〔一般指室内的〕公共游泳池

swimming cos·tume /ˈ· · ˌ· ·/ *n* [C] *BrE* a piece of clothing worn for swimming, especially the kind worn by women【英】〔尤指女用〕游泳衣, 泳装

swim·ming·ly /ˈswɪmɪŋlɪ; ˈswɪmɪŋli/ *adv old-fashioned*【过时】**go swimmingly** if something you plan goes swimmingly, it happens without problems 顺利地进行, 一帆风顺

swimming pool /ˈ· · · ·/ *n* [C] a hole in the ground that has been built and filled with water for people to swim in; POOL¹ (1) 游泳池: *a house with a swimming pool* 有游泳池的房子

swimming suit /ˈ· · · ·/ *n* [C] *AmE* a SWIMSUIT【美】游泳衣

swimming trunks /ˈ· · · ·/ *n* [plural] *BrE* a piece of clothing like trousers with very short legs, worn by men for swimming【英】〔男用〕游泳裤

swim·suit /ˈswɪmˌsut; ˈswɪmsuːt/ *n* [C] a piece of clothing worn for swimming 游泳衣, 泳装

swim·wear /ˈswɪmˌwɛr; ˈswɪmweə/ *n* [U] clothing used for swimming 游泳衣

Swin·burne /ˈswɪnbɚn; ˈswɪnbɜːn/, **Al·ger·non** /ˈældʒɚnən; ˈældʒənən/ (1837-1909) a British poet whose best-known work is *Atalanta in Corydon*, a TRAGEDY in ancient Greek style 斯温伯恩〔(1837-1909), 英国诗人。最著名的作品是古希腊风格的悲剧《阿塔兰忒在卡吕冬》〕

swin·dle¹ /ˈswɪndl; ˈswɪndl/ *v* [T] to get money from someone by deceiving them 诈骗, 欺诈, 骗取〔钱财〕: **swindle sb out of sth** *He made a fortune swindling old ladies out of their life savings.* 他靠诈骗老年妇女的终生积蓄发了大财。

swindle² *n* [C] a situation where someone gets money by deceiving someone else 骗局; 诈骗, 骗取钱财: *a big tax swindle* 巨额税款诈骗

swine /swaɪn; swaɪn/ *n* [C] **1** *plural* **swine** *or* **swines** *informal* someone who behaves very unpleasantly【非正式】下流坯, 猪猡: *Leave her alone you filthy swine!* 不许再缠着她, 你这无耻的下流坯! **2** *old use* a pig【旧】猪

swine·herd /ˈswaɪnˌhɝd; ˈswaɪnhɜːd/ *n* [C] *old use* someone who looks after pigs【旧】养猪人, 猪倌

swing¹ /swɪŋ; swɪŋ/ *v past tense and past participle* **swung** /swʌŋ; swʌŋ/ 3

1 ►MOVE BACKWARDS/FORWARDS 向后/向前移动◄ [I,T] to move backwards and forwards hanging from a fixed point, or to make something do this〔前后〕摆动, 摇摆, 摇荡: *a sign swinging in the wind* 风中摇摆的招牌 | *The soldiers swung their arms as they marched.* 士兵们行进时摆动着双臂。

2 ►MOVE IN A CURVE 成弧线移动◄ [I always+adv/prep, T always+adv/prep] to move quickly in a smooth curve, or to make something move like this (使) 旋转, (使) 转动; (使) 转弯: *The heavy gates swung shut.* 沉重的大门旋转着关上了。| **swing sth through/into etc sth** *She swung the car into the drive.* 她把车子拐进了汽车道。| *Bradley swung himself up into the saddle.* 布拉德利跨上了马鞍。

3 ►CHANGE 改变◄ [I,T] if emotions or opinions swing or something swings them, they change quickly to the opposite of what they were (使)〔感情、意见等〕剧变, 扭转: *His mood could swing suddenly from great joy to complete despair.* 他的情绪可以从欢天喜地突然变成彻底绝望。

4 ►ARRANGE STH 安排某事◄ [T] *informal* to make special arrangements for something to happen, especially something that is not usually allowed【非正式】设法做成, 想法办妥〔尤指通常不允许做的事〕: *I'll see if I can swing it so my wife can come on that business trip with me.* 我看这次出差能否设法把我太太也带去。

5 ►PLAY 游戏◄ [I] to sit on a SWING² (1) and make it move backwards and forwards by bending and unbending your legs 荡秋千: *The girl swung higher and higher.* 那个女孩秋千荡得越来越高。

6 swing for sth *old-fashioned* to be killed by hanging (HANG¹ (3)) as a punishment for a crime【过时】〔因犯罪〕被绞死, 被处以绞刑

7 swing both ways *informal* to be BISEXUAL【非正式】对男女两性都有性欲, 既搞异性恋也搞同性恋

8 the swinging sixties the years 1960 to 1969, thought of as a time when there was an increase in social and sexual freedom

放纵不羁的60年代〔20世纪60年代被认为是社会自由和性自由高涨的年代〕

9 swing the lead *BrE old-fashioned* to avoid doing your work or duty, especially by pretending to be ill【英, 过时】〔尤指以装病〕逃避工作[责任] —see also 另见 **there's not enough room to swing a cat** (ROOM[1] (2))

swing around/round *phr v* **1** [I,T] to turn around quickly or make something turn around quickly, to face in the opposite direction (使)突然转向; (使)突然转身: *He swung around and yelled "that's a damn lie!"* 他猛地转过身来大声喊道:"那完全是谎言!" | **swing sth ↔ around/round** *In seconds they had swung the big gun around.* 他们在几秒钟内就调转了大炮炮口的方向。**2** [I] if a wind swings around it changed direction suddenly and quickly〔风〕突然转向,〔风向〕急变: *The wind swung round to the North-East.* 风突然转向变为东北风。

swing by *phr v* [I,T] *AmE informal* to visit a place or person for a short time, usually for a particular purpose【美, 非正式】〔常指为某目的〕短时探访; 顺便过访: **swing by sth** *I'll swing by the grocery store on my way home.* 我将在回家的路上顺便到食品杂货店去一趟。

swing[2] *n*

1 ►SEAT WITH ROPES 有绳子的座位◄ [C] a seat hanging from ropes or chains, for children to play on 秋千: *kids playing on the swings in the park* 在公园里荡秋千的小孩子

2 ►MOVEMENT 动作◄ [C] a swinging movement with your arm, leg etc especially made in order to hit something〔手臂、腿等的〕挥动, 挥舞, 挥击: **take a swing at sth** *He took a swing at my head and missed.* 他挥拳向我头部打来, 但没有打着。

3 ►GOLF 高尔夫球◄ [singular] the swinging movement of your arms and body when you hit the ball in GOLF 挥杆击球动作: *I spent months correcting my swing.* 我花了几个月时间纠正我的挥杆击球动作。

4 ►CHANGE 变化◄ [C] a noticeable change, especially in opinions or ideas〔尤指意见或主意的〕明显改变: *a big swing towards right-wing ideology* 向右翼思想的大转变

5 ►MUSIC 音乐◄ [U] JAZZ music of the 1930s and 1940s with a strong regular beat, usually played by a big band 摇摆乐〔流行于20世纪30和40年代的强节奏爵士乐, 通常由大型乐队演奏〕

6 get into the swing of sth *BrE* to become fully involved in an activity or situation【英】完全投入某事: *As soon as you get into the swing of it, you'll find it's quite easy.* 你一旦完全投入进去就会觉得相当容易。

7 be in full swing if an event or process is in full swing it has reached its highest level of activity 正在热烈进行中, 正起劲: *The party was in full swing when the police burst in.* 晚会正进行得如火如荼的时候, 警察闯了进来。

8 swings and roundabouts *BrE informal* used to say that every situation or decision has advantages and disadvantages【英, 非正式】〔某种情况或决定〕有得也有失

9 go with a swing *BrE*【英】**a)** if a party or activity goes with a swing it is lively, enjoyable and successful〔聚会、活动等〕搞得很活跃, 进行得很成功 **b)** if music goes with a swing it has a strong beat and a clear tune that is easy to dance to〔音乐〕节奏强劲, 曲调明快

swing-boat /ˈ· ·/ *n* [C] a large SWING[2] (1) shaped like a boat that two people can sit in〔可供两人坐的〕船形秋千

swing bridge /ˌ· ˈ·/ *n* [C] *BrE* a bridge that can be swung to the side when tall ships need to pass through【英】平转桥, 平旋桥

swing door /ˌ· ˈ·/ *n* [C] a door that can be pushed open from either side, and swings shut afterwards 双开式弹簧门 —see picture on page A15 参见 A15 页图

swinge·ing /ˈswɪndʒɪŋ; ˈswɪndʒɪŋ/ *adj BrE*【英】**swingeing cuts** very severe reductions in spending, especially by a government or organization; SWEEPING (1)〔尤指政府或机构的〕大量削减开支: *swingeing cuts in public spending* 公共开支的大幅度削减

swing·er /ˈswɪŋɚ; ˈswɪŋə/ *n* [C] *old-fashioned*【过时】**1** someone who is very active and fashionable, and goes to many parties, NIGHTCLUBs etc 活跃而时髦的人, 常参加社交聚会[去夜总会等]的人 **2** someone who has sexual relationships with many people 性滥交的人; 放荡的人

swing·ing /ˈswɪŋɪŋ; ˈswɪŋɪŋ/ *adj informal* exciting, fun, and enjoyable【非正式】令人兴奋的; 欢快的: *a swinging party* 热闹而有趣的聚会 —see also 另见 **the swinging sixties** (SWING[1] (8))

Swing Low, Sweet Char·i·ot /ˌ· · ˌ· ˈ· · ·/ a SPIRITUAL (=a religious song) from the southern states of the US, originally sung by black SLAVEs working in the fields. It is now often sung at RUGBY matches by English supporters.《马车从天上来》〔美国南方一首灵歌。最早为在农场干活的黑奴传唱。现在, 英格兰球迷在观看橄榄球比赛时常会唱起这支歌〕

swing·om·e·ter /swɪŋˈɑmɪtɚ; swɪŋˈɒmɪtə/ *n* [C] *BrE informal* a special machine, used on television programmes during elections to show how much support each political party is getting as results become known【英, 非正式】选票显示器〔选举时电视节目中用的一种特殊装置, 用以显示各政党所得的票数〕

swing set /ˈ· ·/ *n* [C] *AmE* a tall metal frame with swings (SWING[2] (1)) hanging from it, for children to play on【美】〔儿童玩耍的〕秋千

swing shift /ˈ· ·/ *n* [singular] *AmE informal* workers who work from 3 or 4 o'clock in the afternoon until 11 or 12 o'clock at night, or the system of working these times【美, 非正式】〔三班制的〕中班〔通常从下午3或4点至晚上11点或12点〕; 中班工人

swin·ish /ˈswaɪnɪʃ; ˈswaɪnɪʃ/ *adj BrE* extremely unpleasant or difficult to deal with【英】极讨厌的; 可鄙的; 难对付的: *a swinish problem* 非常棘手的问题 | *swinish behaviour* 可鄙的行为

swipe[1] /swaɪp; swaɪp/ *v* **1** [I,T] to hit or to try to hit someone or something by swinging your arm very quickly〔挥臂〕重击, 猛击: *Jim swiped Bob across the face.* 吉姆往鲍勃脸上猛掴了一巴掌。| **[+at]** *The woman swiped at the child.* 那个女人猛掴那个孩子。**2** [T] *informal* to steal something【非正式】偷窃: *Who's swiped my pen?* 谁偷了我的笔? **3** [T] to pull a special plastic card through a machine to record information on a computer 刷〔卡〕: *You need to swipe your card to get in the building.* 你必须刷过卡后才能进入这幢大楼。

swipe[2] *n* [C] **1** an act of hitting someone or something by swinging your arm very quickly〔挥臂〕重击, 猛击: **take a swipe at** *He took a wild swipe at the policeman.* 他疯狂地挥臂打那位警察。**2 take a swipe at** to publicly criticize someone in a speech or in writing〔口头或书面〕公开批评, 抨击: *In her latest article she takes a swipe at her detractors.* 在最新的一篇文章里, 她公开抨击诋毁她的人。

swirl[1] /swɝl; swɜːl/ *v* [I,T] to turn around quickly in a twisting circular movement, or make something do this (使)旋动, (使)打旋: *He swirled the brandy around in his glass.* 他旋动杯中的白兰地酒。| *The river had become a swirling torrent.* 河水已变成了翻滚的洪流。

swirl[2] *n* [C] **1** a swirling movement 旋动, 打旋: **[+of]** *a swirl of dust* 滚滚飞扬的尘土 **2** a twisting circular pattern 旋涡状; 螺旋形

swish[1] /swɪʃ; swɪʃ/ *v* [I,T] to move or make something move quickly through the air with a smooth quiet sound (使)发出刷刷[嗖嗖]声; (使)刷刷[嗖嗖]地移动: *Her skirt swished as she walked.* 她走动时裙子窸窣作响。| *The horse swished his tail.* 那匹马刷刷地摆动着尾巴。—**swish** *n* [singular]

swish[2] *adj BrE* fashionable and expensive-looking【英】时髦的; 豪华的: *a really swish apartment* 一套非常豪华的公寓

Swiss /swɪs; swɪs/ *adj* coming from or related to Switzerland 瑞士的; 与瑞士有关的

Swiss chard /ˌ· ˈ·/ *n* [U] CHARD 瑞士甜菜; 莙荙菜

Swiss Fam·i·ly Rob·in·son, the /ˌ· ˌ· · · ˈ· · ·/ (1813) a NOVEL for children by the Swiss writer Johann Wyss, about a family who live on a desert island after their ship sinks. It was made into a Walt Disney film in 1960.《瑞士家庭鲁宾逊》, 又译《海角一乐园》〔(1831), 瑞士作家约翰·维斯创作的一部儿童小说, 讲述一个家庭沉船之后在荒岛上生活的故事。1960年由沃尔特·迪斯尼公司搬上银幕〕

Swiss Guard, the /ˌ· ˈ·/ a group of Swiss soldiers in the Vatican in Rome, whose job is to guard the Pope. They wear a special colourful uniform. 瑞士侍卫队〔罗马梵蒂冈城保护教皇的瑞士军人, 身着色彩鲜艳的特制制服〕

swiss roll /ˌ· ˈ·/ *n* [C,U] *BrE* a long thin cake that is rolled up with JAM[1] (1) or cream inside【英】〔夹有果酱或奶油的〕卷筒夹心蛋糕, 瑞士卷

swiss steak /ˌ· ˈ·/ *n* [C,U] *AmE* a thick flat piece of BEEF covered in flour and cooked in a SAUCE【美】〔外蘸面粉加调味汁烹调而成的〕瑞士牛排

Switch *trademark* a type of system used for paying for goods and services in the UK, by which customers use a type of plastic card called a debit card, and money is immediately taken out of their bank account【商标】斯威奇系统, 转账卡〔英国一种商品和服务支付系统。客户使用一种称作借记卡的塑制卡, 消费一旦发生, 款项即从其银行账户划出〕: *Do you take Switch?* 你们这里可以用斯威奇借记卡吗? | *I'll pay by Switch.* 我用斯威奇借记卡支付。

switch off 关上开关

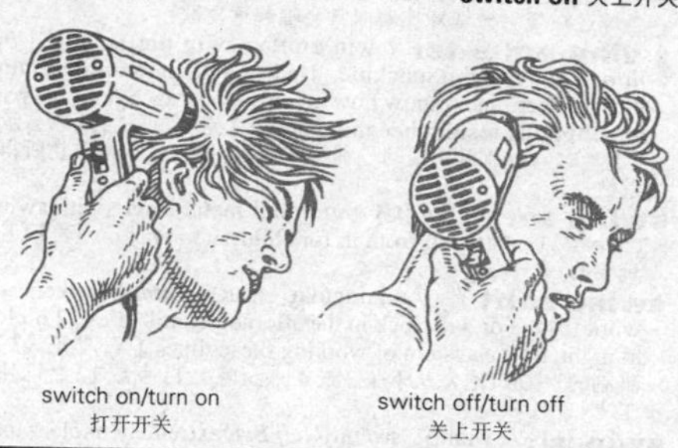

switch on/turn on
打开开关

switch off/turn off
关上开关

2 3 **switch¹** /swɪtʃ; swɪtʃ/ *v* **1** [I,T] to change from one thing to another, usually suddenly〔常指突然地〕转换, 转变, 改变: [+to] *He used to play tennis, but now he's switched to golf.* 他过去常打网球, 但现在改打高尔夫球了。| **switch sth to/from/away etc** *Duval switched easily and fluently from French to English.* 杜瓦尔流利自如地交替着讲法语和英语。| **switch jobs/positions etc** (=change from one job or position to another) 改变工作/职位等 **switch sth to/from/away etc** *We can switch the meeting to Tuesday if you like.* 如果你愿意的话, 我们可以把会议时间改到星期二。| **switch your attention** *Just switch your attention to the screen on your left.* 注意左边的屏幕。**2** [T] to secretly remove one object and put another similar object in its place〔秘密地〕换掉, 替换: *Someone must have switched suitcases at the airport.* 一定有人在飞机场把手提箱掉了包。**3** [I] to help someone you work with who needs time away from the job by agreeing to work certain hours for them if they do the same for you〔与同事〕调换上班时间, 调班: **switch with sb** *Can you switch with me on Monday night?* 你星期一晚上可以和我调班吗? **4** [T always+adv/prep] to change the way a machine operates by using a switch〔用开关〕改变〔机器的运转〕, 转换: *Switch the freezer to the 'extra cold' setting.* 把冰箱的冷冻室调到"特冷"挡。

switch off *phr v* **1** [I,T] to turn off a machine, electric light, radio etc by using a switch〔用开关〕关掉, 关上: *Don't forget to switch off when you've finished.* 用完后不要忘记关掉开关。| **switch sth ↔ off** *Can you switch the television off?* 请把电视机关掉好吗? —see 见 OPEN² (USAGE) **2** [I] *informal* to stop listening or paying attention【非正式】不听; 对…不加理睬[注意]: *He just switches off when you start talking to him.* 你要对他说话时, 他就不理不睬。

switch on *phr v* [I,T] to turn on a machine, electric light, radio etc by using a switch〔用开关〕开, 打开: **switch sth ↔ on** *Can you switch the light on?* 请你开灯好吗? —see 见 OPEN² (USAGE)

switch over *phr v* [I] **1** to change completely from one method, product etc to another〔方法、产品等〕完全改变, 完全转变: [+from/to] *A lot of banks are switching over to the new electronic system because it's more efficient.* 很多银行正在改用新的电子系统, 因为它效率更高。**2** [I,T] *BrE* to change from one radio or television station to another【英】转换〔电台或电视频道〕: *Switch over if you don't like the programme.* 如果你不喜欢这个节目, 就换个台吧。

3 **switch²** *n* [C] **1** the part on a light, radio, machine etc that starts or stops the flow of electricity when you press it up or down〔电灯、收音机、机器等的〕开关; 电闸: **light switch** *a light switch* 电灯开关 | *the on/off switch* 开关键 | **throw a switch** (=pull a large switch) 扳动电闸 *He threw a switch and all the lights in the theatre came on.* 他一扳电闸, 戏院里的灯全都亮了。**2** a complete, and usually sudden, change from one thing to another 骤变, 突变: *The switch to a free market economy will not be easy.* 向自由市场经济转变并不容易。| **that's a switch** *AmE* (=used to say that someone's behaviour is unusual for them)【美】那真不寻常〔用以指某人的行为一反往常〕*"Mark's doing the dishes tonight." "That's a switch!"* "马克今晚要洗盘子。" "那可真不寻常!" **3 make the switch** to secretly remove one object and put another similar object in its place〔偷偷地〕调换, 掉包: *The original painting has been replaced by a fake, and no one knows when the switch was made.* 这幅画的原件被一件赝品替换了, 但没有人知道是什么时候被掉包的。**4** a thin stick that bends easily 细软的枝条: *a willow switch* 柳枝

switch·back /ˈswɪtʃˌbæk; ˈswɪtʃbæk/ *n* [C] **1** a road or track that goes up and down steep slopes and around sharp bends〔陡坡上公路或铁路的〕之字形爬坡路段; 多急转弯的道路 **2** a ROLLER COASTER〔游乐场的〕环滑车, 过山车

switch·blade /ˈswɪtʃˌbled; ˈswɪtʃbleɪd/ *n* [C] *AmE* a knife with a blade inside the handle which springs out when you press a button【美】弹簧（小折）刀; FLICK KNIFE *BrE*【英】

switch·board /ˈswɪtʃˌbɔrd; ˈswɪtʃbɔːd/ *n* [C] a central system used to connect telephone calls in an office building, hotel etc, or the people who operate the system 电话交换台, 电话总机; 总机接线员: *Hello switchboard? Can I have an outside line?* 喂, 总机吗? 请接外线。| *switchboard operators* 交换台接线员 | **jam the switchboard** (=make too many calls for the switchboard to deal with) 电话太多使总机应接不暇

switch card /ˈ· ·/ also 又作 **switch** *n* [C] *BrE trademark* a plastic card from your bank that you use to pay for things and that allows the money to be taken straight from your account【英, 商标】〔银行〕代支卡〔由银行发放、供购物付款使用的一种塑料磁卡〕

switched-on /ˌ· ˈ·◂/ *adj old-fashioned* quick to notice new ideas and fashions【过时】紧跟时尚的, 对新观念[时尚]敏感的

Swith·in, Saint, Swithun /ˈswɪðɪn; ˈswɪðn̩/ —see 见 SAINT SWITHIN'S DAY

Swit·zer·land /ˈswɪtsələnd; ˈswɪtsələnd/ a country in western Europe with many mountains and lakes, surrounded by France, Germany, Austria, and Italy. Population: 7,283,000 (2001). Capital: Bern. Switzerland is a NEUTRAL country (=one that does not support any side in a war). It remained neutral in both World War I and World War II, and it does not belong either to the EU or to the UN. It is also a world centre for banking. People from Switzerland are called Swiss. 瑞士〔西欧一国家。境内有众多山脉和湖泊。毗邻法国、德国、奥地利、意大利等国家。人口: 7,283,000 (2001), 首都: 伯尔尼。瑞士为中立国, 在第一和第二次世界大战中均保持中立, 既非欧盟成员国, 也非联合国成员国。瑞士是世界银行业的中心。瑞士人称作 Swiss〕

swiv·el¹ /ˈswɪvl; ˈswɪvəl/ **swivelled, swivelling** *BrE*【英】, **swiveled, swiveling** *AmE*【美】also 又作 **swivel around/round** *v* **1** [I,T] to turn something around that is fixed to a moving central point (使) 旋转, (使) 转动: *He swivelled the camera on the tripod to follow the riders.* 他转动三脚架上的照相机追踪拍摄那些骑手。**2** [I] to turn around quickly in this way〔迅速地〕旋转, 转动

swivel² *n* [C] a thing that joins two parts of something in such a way that one or both parts can turn around freely 旋转接头; 旋轴

swivel chair /ˈ·· ·/ *n* [C] a chair that turns around on a swivel 转椅 —see picture at 参见 CHAIR¹ 图

swiz, swizz /swɪz; swɪz/ *n BrE spoken*【英口】**what a swizz!** used when something makes you feel cheated or disappointed 真是上当! 真令人扫兴!〔用于感到受骗或失望时〕

swiz·zle stick /ˈswɪzl ˌstɪk; ˈswɪzəl ˌstɪk/ *n* [C] a small stick for mixing drinks〔调饮料用的〕小棒; 搅酒棒

swol·len¹ /ˈswolən; ˈswəʊlən/ the past participle of SWELL¹

swollen² *adj* **1** a part of your body that is swollen is bigger than usual because of illness or injury〔身体某部位〕肿起的, 肿胀的; 膨胀的: *He bandaged his swollen ankle.* 他用绷带包扎肿起来的脚踝。**2** a river that is swollen has more water in it than usual〔河流〕涨满的, 涨水的 **3 have a swollen head/be swollen-headed** *BrE* to be too proud so that you think you are very clever or important【英】骄傲自满, 自负, 自高自大

swoon /swun; swuːn/ *v* [I] **1** to feel so much excitement, happiness, or admiration that you almost faint 欣喜若狂; 〔爱慕得〕神魂颠倒: *The audience was full of swooning girls.* 听众中有无数心醉神迷的女孩。**2** *old use* to become unconscious and fall down; FAINT² (1)【旧】失去知觉, 昏倒 —**swoon** *n* [singular]

swoop¹ /swup; swuːp/ *v* [I] **1** if a bird or aircraft swoops it moves suddenly and steeply down through the air, especially to attack something〔鸟或飞机〕突然下落; 向下猛冲, 猛扑: [+in/down etc] *The hawk swooped and seized a rabbit.* 老鹰猛冲下来, 抓住了一只兔子。**2** to make a sudden, surprise attack 突然袭击: [+in/on etc] *Police swooped in on gang hideouts in a series of raids.* 警方对歹徒藏身处进行了一系列的突击搜捕。

swoop² *n* [C] **1** a swooping movement or action 向下猛冲; 猛扑; 飞扑 **2** a sudden surprise attack 突然袭击: *Police hunting the killer arrested a man in a swoop on his flat last night.* 警方追捕杀人凶手, 昨晚突击搜查一公寓时逮捕了一名男子。—see also 另见 **at/in one fell swoop** (FELL⁴)

swoosh /swuʃ; swuːʃ/ *v* [I] to make a sound by moving quickly through the air〔在空气中移动时〕发出哗哗声, 嗖嗖作响 —**swoosh** *n* [C]

swop /swɑp; swɒp/ another spelling of SWAP swap 的另一种拼法

swords 剑，刀

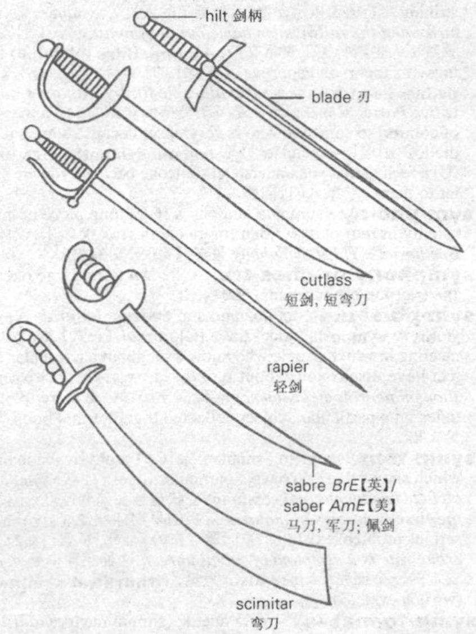

hilt 剑柄

blade 刃

cutlass 短剑，短弯刀

rapier 轻剑

sabre *BrE*【英】/ saber *AmE*【美】马刀，军刀；佩剑

scimitar 弯刀

sword /sɔrd; sɔːd/ *n* [C] **1** a weapon with a long pointed blade and a handle 剑；刀 **2 put sb to the sword** *old use* to kill someone with a sword【旧】用刀剑杀死某人 **3 sword of Damocles** *literary* the possibility of something bad or dangerous happening at any time【文】达摩克勒斯之剑〔喻指随时可能有祸事或危险临头〕: *The treaty hung like a sword of Damocles over French politics.* 这个条约好像一把达摩克勒斯之剑悬在法国政坛的头上。—see also 另见 **cross swords (with)** (CROSS[1] (15))

sword dance /ˈ· ·/ *n* [C] a Scottish dance in which people dance between and around swords that are laid on the ground 剑舞〔一种苏格兰舞，围着置于地上的刀剑或在其间起舞〕—**sword dancer** *n* [C] —**sword dancing** *n* [U]

sword·fish /ˈsɔrdˌfɪʃ; ˈsɔːdˌfɪʃ/ *n* [C] a large fish with a very long pointed upper jaw like a sword 剑鱼

swords·man /ˈsɔrdzmən; ˈsɔːdzmən/ *n* [C] someone who fights with a sword or someone who is skilled in this 剑客，刀剑手

swords·man·ship /ˈsɔrdzmənˌʃɪp; ˈsɔːdzmənʃɪp/ *n* [U] skill in fighting with a sword 剑术，刀术

swore /swɔr; swɔː/ the past tense of SWEAR

sworn[1] /swɔrn; swɔːn/ the past participle of SWEAR

sworn[2] *adj* **1 sworn enemies** two people or groups of people who will always hate each other 不共戴天的死敌 **2 sworn statement/evidence/declaration** a statement etc that someone makes after officially promising to tell the truth 宣誓后发表的陈述/证词/声明

swot[1] /swɑt; swɒt/ *n* [C] *BrE informal* someone who spends too much time studying and seems to have no other interests【英，非正式】只知道读书的人 —**swotty** *adj*

swot[2] *v* [I] *BrE informal* to study a lot in a short time, especially for an examination【英，非正式】〔尤指为准备考试临时〕刻苦学习，下死功夫读书; CRAM (3) *AmE*【美】: [+for] *I was busy swotting for my History exam.* 我正临阵磨枪，准备历史考试。

swot up *phr v* [I,T] *BrE* to study a subject a lot in a short time, especially to prepare for an examination【英】〔为准备考试〕刻苦学习〔某学科〕；临时抱佛脚地学: [+on] *Jill's busy swotting up on German.* 吉尔正忙于温习德语。| **swot sth ↔ up** *I've got to swot up French irregular verbs.* 我得用功学习法语的不规则动词。

SWP /ˌɛs dʌbl̩ju ˈpi; ˌes dʌbəljuː ˈpiː/ Socialist Workers' Party; a British political party that is very LEFT-WING. It produces a newspaper called *Socialist Worker*, which is sold by its members on the street, and its members are often involved in political DEMONSTRATIONS (=when a big crowd of people publicly protest about something). 社会主义工人党〔英国一极左翼政党。创办有《社会主义工人报》，由成员沿街出售。党员常参加政治游行〕

swum /swʌm; swʌm/ the past participle of SWIM[1]

swung /swʌŋ; swʌŋ/ the past tense and past participle of SWING[1]

syb·a·rit·ic /ˌsɪbəˈrɪtɪk; ˌsɪbəˈrɪtɪk◂/ *adj formal* wanting or enjoying expensive pleasures and comforts【正式】享受奢侈的，骄奢淫逸的 —**sybarite** /ˈsɪbəˌraɪt; ˈsɪbəraɪt/ *n* [C]

syc·a·more /ˈsɪkəˌmɔr; ˈsɪkəmɔː/ *n* [C] **1** a European tree that has leaves with five points and seeds with two parts like wings〔欧洲的〕西克摩槭树 **2** an American PLANE TREE 美国梧桐(树)，悬铃木

syc·o·phant /ˈsɪkəfənt; ˈsɪkəfənt/ *n* [C] *formal* someone who praises important or powerful people insincerely in order to get something from them【正式】阿谀奉承者，谄媚者，拍马屁者: *a dictator surrounded by sycophants* 被阿谀奉承者簇拥的独裁者 —**sycophantic** /ˌsɪkəˈfæntɪk; ˌsɪkəˈfæntɪk◂/ *adj*: *a sycophantic smile* 谄笑

Syd·ney /ˈsɪdnɪ; ˈsɪdni/ the largest city in Australia, which is the capital of the state of New South Wales and an important financial, industrial, and educational centre 悉尼〔澳大利亚最大城市，新南威尔士州首府，重要的金融、工业和教育中心〕

syl·la·ba·ry /ˈsɪləˌbɛrɪ; ˈsɪləbəri/ *n* [C] a list of syllables, sometimes represented as SYMBOLs 音节(符号)表

syl·lab·ic /sɪˈlæbɪk; sɪ̈ˈlæbɪk/ *adj* of or based on syllables 音节的；分音节的；由音节组成的: *syllabic stress* 音节重音 | *syllabic verse* 每行[每节]的音节数目固定的诗体

syl·la·ble /ˈsɪləbl̩; ˈsɪləbəl/ *n* [C] a word or part of a word which contains a single vowel sound 音节

syl·la·bub /ˈsɪləˌbʌb; ˈsɪləbʌb/ *n* [C,U] a sweet dish made with cream, wine or fruit juice, and usually eggs 乳酒冻〔一种用奶油、酒或果汁，经常还加鸡蛋混合而成的甜食〕

syl·la·bus /ˈsɪləbəs; ˈsɪləbəs/ *n* [C] *plural* **syllabuses** or **syllabi** /-baɪ; -baɪ/ a plan that states exactly what students at a school or college should learn in a particular subject〔某学科的〕教学大纲: *Dickens and Hardy are on this year's English syllabus.* 狄更斯和哈代的作品被列入今年的英语课程大纲。—compare 比较 CURRICULUM

S

syl·lo·gis·m /ˈsɪləˌdʒɪzəm; ˈsɪlədʒɪzəm/ *n* [C] a statement with three parts, the first two of which prove that the third part is true, for example 'all men will die; Socrates is a man; therefore Socrates will die' 三段论〔由大、小前提引出结论的推理，如"凡人必死，苏格拉底是人，因此苏格拉底必死。"〕—**syllogistic** /ˌsɪləˈdʒɪstɪk; ˌsɪləˈdʒɪstɪk◂/ *adj*

sylph /sɪlf; sɪlf/ *n* [C] **1** an attractively thin and graceful girl or woman 苗条高雅的女子 **2** an imaginary female spirit that, according to ancient stories lived in the air〔古代神话中空气里的〕女精灵

sylph·like /ˈsɪlfˌlaɪk; ˈsɪlflaɪk/ *adj literary* attractively thin and graceful【文】苗条而优雅的: *a sylphlike figure* 苗条的身材

syl·van /ˈsɪlvən; ˈsɪlvən/ *adj* in the forest or belonging to the forest; SILVAN 在森林中的；森林的

sym- /sɪm; sɪm/ *prefix* the form used for SYN- before b, m, or p 前缀 syn- 用于字母 b, m 或 p 前的形式

sym·bi·o·sis /ˌsɪmbaɪˈosɪs; ˌsɪmbaɪˈəʊsɪ̈s/ *n* [U] **1** *formal* a relationship between people or organizations that depend on each other equally【正式】〔人与人之间或机构之间平等的〕互相依赖(关系) **2** *technical* the relationship between two different living things that depend on each other for particular advantages【术语】〔生物的〕共生(关系) —**symbiotic** /ˌsɪmbaɪˈɑtɪk; sɪmbaɪˈɒtɪk◂/ *adj*: *a symbiotic relationship* 共生关系

sym·bol /ˈsɪmbl̩; ˈsɪmbəl/ *n* [C] **1** a picture or shape that has a particular meaning or represents an idea 象征，标志: [+of] *The dove is a symbol of peace.* 鸽子是和平的象征。**2** a letter, number, or sign that represents a sound, an amount, a chemical substance etc 符号，记号，标记: *'0' is the symbol for zero.* 0 是零的符号。—see picture at 参见 SIGN[1] 图 **3** someone or something that people think of as representing a particular quality or idea〔某一特性或思想的〕代表，代表性的人[物]: *Space exploration provides a symbol of national pride.* 宇宙探索是民族自豪感的象征。—see also 另见 SEX SYMBOL (W3)

sym·bol·ic /sɪmˈbɑlɪk; sɪmˈbɒlɪk/ also 又作 **sym·bol·i·cal** /-kl̩; -kəl/ *adj* used as a symbol, or containing symbols 象征的，象征性的: *a symbolic painting* 一幅有象征意义的画 | **be symbolic of sth** *The snake is symbolic of evil.* 蛇是邪恶的象征。—**symbolically** /-klɪ; -kli/ *adv*

sym·bol·is·m /ˈsɪmbl̩ˌɪzəm; ˈsɪmbəlɪzəm/ *n* [U] the use of symbols to represent something 象征主义(手法): *religious symbolism* 宗教象征主义

sym·bol·ize also 又作 **-ise** *BrE*【英】/ˈsɪmbḷˌaɪz; ˈsɪmbəlaɪz/ *v* [T] **1** to be a symbol of something 象征，是…的象征: *In Europe, the colour white symbolizes purity.* 在欧洲，白色象征纯洁。**2** to represent something with a symbol 用符号代表，用象征物表示: *Peace is symbolised by a dove.* 和平用鸽子作为象征。—**symbolization** /ˌsɪmbḷəˈzeʃən; ˌsɪmbəlaɪˈzeɪʃən/ *n* [U]

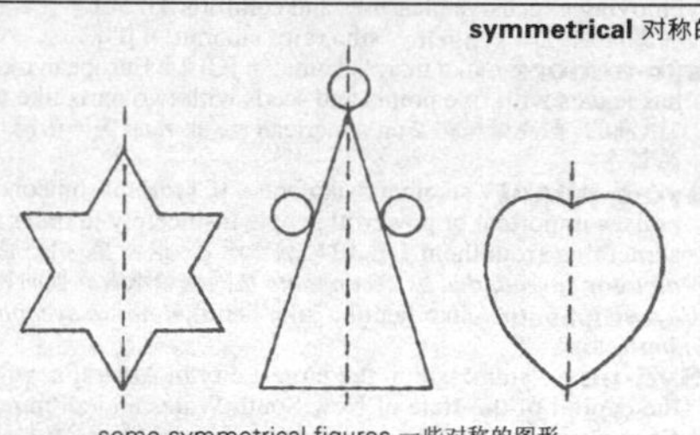

some symmetrical figures 一些对称的图形

sym·met·ri·cal /sɪˈmɛtrɪkḷ; sɪˈmetrɪkəl/ also 又作 **sym·met·ric** /sɪˈmɛtrɪk; sɪˈmetrɪk/ *adj* a thing or design that is symmetrical has two halves that are exactly the same shape and size 对称的: *The leaves of most trees are symmetrical.* 大多数树木的叶子是对称的。—opposite 反义词 ASYMMETRICAL —**symmetrically** /-klɪ; -kli/ *adv*

sym·me·try /ˈsɪmɪtrɪ; ˈsɪmḷtri/ *n* [U] exact likeness in size and shape between two sides of something 对称（性）: *the symmetry of the human body* 人体的对称（性）

sym·pa·thet·ic /ˌsɪmpəˈθɛtɪk; ˌsɪmpəˈθetɪk◂/ *adj* **1** willing to try to understand someone else's problems and give them any help they need 同情的；有同情心的: *You're not being very sympathetic, Joan.* 琼，你没有表现出很大的同情心。| **a sympathetic ear** (=willingness to listen to someone else's problems) 乐于倾听别人的困难 *Paul's great if you need a sympathetic ear or advice.* 假如你想倾诉衷肠或征求意见，保罗最合适不过了。**2** [not before noun 不用于名词前] willing to give approval and support to an aim or plan〔对某目的或计划〕赞成的，支持的: **[+to/towards]** *There is a group in the party sympathetic towards our aims.* 党内有一批人赞成我们的目标。**3** providing the right conditions to make the results you want to happen 合意的；合适的: *a sympathetic environment* 合适的环境 **4 sympathetic figure/character** *literary* someone in a book, play etc who the author intends you to like【文】〔书、戏剧等中〕令人喜爱的人物/角色 —**sympathetically** /-klɪ; -kli/ *adv*

sym·pa·thize also 又作 **-ise** *BrE*【英】/ˈsɪmpəˌθaɪz; ˈsɪmpəθaɪz/ *v* [I] **1** to feel sorry for someone because you understand their problems 同情，怜悯；体谅: *I sympathize; you need to know exactly what caused the accident.* 我非常同情，你需要了解导致事故发生的确切原因。| **[+with]** *I sympathize with the plight of the homeless.* 我很同情无家可归者的困境。**2** to support someone's ideas or actions 支持；赞同: **[+with]** *Many workers sympathized with the striking miners.* 很多工人都支持那些正在罢工的矿工。

sym·pa·thiz·er also 又作 **-iser** *BrE*【英】/ˈsɪmpəˌθaɪzɚ; ˈsɪmpəθaɪzə/ *n* [C] someone who supports the aims of an organization or political party but does not belong to it 同情者；支持者: *The anti-abortion rally attracted many sympathizers.* 反对人工流产的群众集会吸引了很多支持者。

sym·pa·thy /ˈsɪmpəθɪ; ˈsɪmpəθi/ *n* [U] **1** the feeling of being sorry for someone who is in a bad situation and understanding how they feel 同情；同情心: *He wants your sympathy so he's pretending to be sick.* 他想得到你的同情，所以在装病。| **have/feel sympathy for sb** *I've a lot of sympathy for her; she brought up the children on her own.* 我非常同情她，她是独自把孩子们抚养成人的。| **have no sympathy for sb** (=feel that someone deserves something bad that is happening to them) 不同情某人〔认为某人是自作自受〕| **play on sb's sympathy** (=make someone feel sorry for you in order to gain an advantage for yourself)〔为得到好处而〕利用某人的同情 | **you have my deepest sympathy** *formal* (=used in a letter to someone whose close relative has died)【正式】谨向你表示最深切的慰问〔用于慰唁信中〕| **offer your sympathy** *formal*【正式】*She wrote a letter offering her sympathy.* 她写了一封信去表示慰问。| **message/letter of sympathy** *The victim's parents have received thousands of messages of sympathy.* 罹难者的父母收到成千上万封的慰问信。**2 be in sympathy with** also 又作 **have sympathy for** to agree with and support someone's aims and actions 赞同，支持: *We have a lot of sympathy for your stand on lower taxes.* 我们非常支持你关于减税的立场。**3 come out in sympathy (with sb)** to STRIKE[1] (4) in order to give support to other people who are striking 举行罢工以示支持〔其他罢工的人〕: *The miners were on strike and the railwaymen came out in sympathy.* 矿工们罢工，铁路工人也举行罢工表示支持。**4 sympathies** [plural] **a)** feelings of support and approval〔感情上的〕支持，赞同: **sb's sympathies lie with** *Anne's sympathies lie firmly with the Conservative Party.* 安妮在感情上是坚决支持保守党的。**b)** a message of comfort to someone who is very upset because someone has died 唁函[电] —see also 另见 **tea and sympathy** (TEA (5)) **5** [U] a feeling that you understand someone because you are similar to them〔与某人的〕同感，共鸣

sym·pho·ny /ˈsɪmfənɪ; ˈsɪmfəni/ *n* [C] a long piece of music usually in four parts written for an ORCHESTRA 交响乐，交响曲: *Beethoven's Third Symphony* 贝多芬《第三交响曲》

symphony or·ches·tra /ˈ··· ˌ···/ *n* [C] a large ORCHESTRA (=group of musicians) 交响乐团

sym·po·si·um /sɪmˈpozɪəm; sɪmˈpəʊziəm/ *plural* **symposiums** *or* **symposia** /-zɪə; -ziə/ *n* [C] *formal*【正式】**1** a formal meeting in which people who know a lot about a particular subject have discussions about it 专题研讨会；讨论会: *a symposium on neurological science* 神经病学研讨会 **2** a group of articles on a particular subject collected together in a book 专题论文集

symp·tom /ˈsɪmptəm; ˈsɪmptəm/ *n* [C] **1** a physical condition 3
which shows that you have a particular illness 症状: *Symptoms include headaches and vomiting.* 症状包括头痛和呕吐。| **[+of]** *the first symptoms of malaria* 疟疾的早期症状 **2** a sign that a serious problem exists〔严重问题存在的〕征兆，征候: **[+of]** *The crime rate is a symptom of social unrest.* 这种犯罪率是社会不安定的一个征兆。—see also 另见 **withdrawal symptoms** (WITHDRAWAL (5))

symp·to·mat·ic /ˌsɪmptəˈmætɪk; ˌsɪmptəˈmætɪk◂/ *adj* **1 be symptomatic of sth** *formal* if a situation or kind of behaviour is symptomatic of something, it shows that a serious problem exists【正式】是…征兆；表明…: *Her irritation seems symptomatic of something deeper.* 她的烦躁可能是更深刻问题的征兆。**2** *technical* related to medical symptoms【术语】症状的 —**symptomatically** /-klɪ; -kli/ *adv*

syn- /sɪn; sɪn/ *prefix* together; sharing 共，同，合: *a synthesis* (=combining of separate things) 合成

syn·a·gogue /ˈsɪnəˌgɔg; ˈsɪnəgɒg/ *n* [C] a building where Jewish people meet for religious worship〔犹太〕会堂，犹太教堂

sync, synch /sɪŋk; sɪŋk/ *n informal*【非正式】**1 in sync** two or more parts of a machine, process etc that are in sync are working at the same rate 同步；协调 **2 out of sync** two or more parts of a machine, process etc that are out of sync are not working at the same rate 不同步；不协调

syn·chro·ni·city /ˌsɪŋkrəˈnɪsətɪ; ˌsɪŋkrəˈnɪsḷti/ *n* [U] the fact of two or more events happening at the same time or place, when these events are believed to be connected in some way〔有关联的事件的〕同时发生

syn·chro·nize also 又作 **-ise** *BrE*【英】/ˈsɪŋkrəˌnaɪz; ˈsɪŋkrənaɪz/ *v* **1** [T] to arrange for two or more actions to happen at exactly the same time 使同时发生，使同步: *If we synchronize our attacks they'll cause more disruption.* 假如我们同时发动攻击，造成的破坏就会更大。**2 synchronize your watches** to make two or more watches or clocks show exactly the same time 校准〔两个或多个〕钟表，使钟表显示同一时间 **3** [I,T] if the sound and action of a film synchronize or if you synchronize them, they go at exactly the same speed（使）〔电影〕声画同步，（使）〔影片的〕动作与声音同步 —**synchronization** /ˌsɪŋkrənəˈzeʃən; ˌsɪŋkrənaɪˈzeɪʃən/ *n* [U]

synchronized swim·ming /ˌ····ˈ··/ *n* [U] an activity in which swimmers move in patterns in the water to music 花样游泳

syn·chro·nous /ˈsɪŋkrənəs; ˈsɪŋkrənəs/ *adj* a synchronous signal on a computer is one in which the time between one BIT[1] (12) and the next is the same〔电脑信号〕同时的，同步的

syn·co·pa·tion /ˌsɪŋkəˈpeʃən; ˌsɪŋkəˈpeɪʃən/ *n* [U] a RHYTHM in a line of music in which the beats (BEAT[2] (3)) that are usually weak are emphasized〔音乐的〕切分音，切分节奏

syn·co·pe /ˈsɪŋkəpɪ; ˈsɪŋkəpi/ *n* [U] *technical*【术语】**1** the loss of consciousness when someone faints 晕厥 **2** a way of making a word shorter by leaving out of sounds or letters in the middle of it, for example changing 'cannot' to 'can't' 词中省略，中略〈如以 can't 代替 cannot〉

syn·di·cal·is·m /ˈsɪndɪkḷˌɪzəm; ˈsɪndɪkəlɪzəm/ *n* [U] a political system or belief whose aim is for workers to control industry 工团主义，工联主义〔以工人控制工业为目标的制度或主张〕—**syndicalist** *n* [C] —**syndicalist** *adj*

syn·di·cate¹ /ˈsɪndɪkɪt; ˈsɪndɪ̣kɪ̣t/ *n* [C] a group of people or companies who join together in order to achieve a particular aim 辛迪加，商业财团，企业联合组织: *a syndicate of local industrialists* 一个由本地工业家组成的集团

syn·di·cate² /ˈsɪndɪˌket; ˈsɪndɪ̣keɪt/ *v* **1** [T] to arrange for written work, photographs etc to be sold to a number of different newspapers, magazines etc 安排出售〔文章、照片等〕给多家报刊发表: **be syndicated** *His column is syndicated throughout America.* 他的专栏文章同时在美国全国各地的报刊发表。**2** [I,T] to form into a syndicate (把…) 组成辛迪加 —**syndication** /ˌsɪndɪˈkeʃən; ˌsɪndɪ̣ˈkeɪʃən/ *n* [U]

syn·drome /ˈsɪnˌdrom; ˈsɪndrəʊm/ *n* [C] **1** *technical* a set of physical or mental effects that show that someone has a particular disease【术语】综合征: *There is no satisfactory drug treatment for irritable bowel syndrome.* 肠易激综合征还没有令人满意的治疗药物。—see also 另见 DOWN'S SYNDROME **2** a set of qualities, events or behaviour that is typical of a particular kind of problem〔标明某类问题的〕一组典型特征[事件，行为]: *the syndrome of the bored middle-aged man* 感到厌烦的中年男性的种种典型表现

syn·er·gy /ˈsɪnɚdʒɪ; ˈsɪnədʒi/ *n* [U] *technical* additional energy that is produced by two people combining their energy and ideas【术语】〔两个人的精力和思想结合后产生的〕协同作用，增效作用

Synge /sɪŋ; sɪŋ/, **J. M.** (1871-1909) an Irish writer famous for his plays such as *The Playboy of the Western World* 辛格〔(1871-1909)，爱尔兰剧作家，以《西方世界的花花公子》等剧作闻名〕

syn·od /ˈsɪnəd; ˈsɪnəd/ *n* [C] an important meeting of church members to make decisions concerning the church〔对教会重大问题作决定的〕教会会议

syn·o·nym /ˈsɪnəˌnɪm; ˈsɪnənɪm/ *n* [C] a word with the same meaning or nearly the same meaning as another word in the same language, such as 'sad' and 'unhappy' 同义词，近义词〈如 sad 和 unhappy〉—compare 比较 ANTONYM

sy·non·y·mous /sɪˈnɑnəməs; sɪ̣ˈnɒnɪ̣məs/ *adj* **1** a situation, quality, idea etc that is synonymous with something else is the same or nearly the same as another 相同的；近似的: [+**with**] *She seems to think that being poor is synonymous with being lazy.* 她似乎认为，贫穷和懒惰是相同的。**2** two words that are synonymous have the same or nearly the same meaning〔单词〕同义的，近义的 —**synonymously** *adv*

sy·nop·sis /sɪˈnɑpsɪs; sɪ̣ˈnɒpsɪ̣s/ *n plural* **synopses** /-siz; -siːz/ [C+**of**] a short account of something longer, such as the story of a film, play, or book; SUMMARY¹〔电影故事、戏剧、书等的〕提要，概要，梗概

syn·tac·tic /sɪnˈtæktɪk; sɪnˈtæktɪk/ *adj technical* related to syntax【术语】句法的: *The two sentences have the same syntactic structure.* 这两个句子的句法结构相同。—**syntactically** /-klɪ; -kli/ *adv*

syn·tax /ˈsɪntæks; ˈsɪntæks/ *n* [U] *technical*【术语】**1** the rules of grammar that are used for ordering and connecting words to form phrases or sentences 句法；句法结构 **2** the rules that describe how words and phrases are used in a computer language〔电脑语言中使用的〕句法规则，语法 —compare 比较 MORPHOLOGY (1)

syn·the·sis /ˈsɪnθəsɪs; ˈsɪnθɪ̣sɪ̣s/ *n* **1** [C] something such as a substance or an idea, made by combining different things 综合物；综合体: [+**of**] *Their beliefs are a synthesis of Eastern and Western religions.* 他们的信仰是东西方宗教的综合体。**2** [U] the act of combining separate things, ideas etc into a complete whole 合成；综合: *the synthesis of rubber from petroleum* 用石油来合成橡胶 **3** [C] the production of the sounds of speech or music by electronic means〔用电子手段对语音或音乐的〕合成

syn·the·size also 又作 **-ise** *BrE*【英】/ˈsɪnθəˌsaɪz; ˈsɪnθɪ̣saɪz/ *v* [T] to produce something by combining different things, especially to make something similar to a natural product by combining chemicals 综合，合成〔尤指用化学物质合成人造产品〕: *Many minerals have been synthesized chemically.* 很多种矿物是通过化学方法合成的。

syn·the·siz·er also 又作 **synthesiser** *BrE*【英】/ˈsɪnθəˌsaɪzɚ; ˈsɪnθɪ̣saɪzə/ *n* [C] an electrical instrument that produces the sounds of various musical instruments〔电子〕音响合成器，电声合成器 —see also 另见 SPEECH SYNTHESIZER

syn·thet·ic /sɪnˈθɛtɪk; sɪnˈθetɪk/ *adj* produced by combining different artificial substances, rather than being naturally produced 合成的，人造的: *synthetic fabrics like nylon* 尼龙等人造纤维 —**synthetically** /-klɪ; -kli/ *adv*

syph·i·lis /ˈsɪflɪs; ˈsɪfɪ̣lɪ̣s/ *n* [U] a very serious disease, passed on during sexual activity or from parent to child 梅毒

sy·phon /ˈsaɪfən; ˈsaɪfən/ *n* [C] another spelling of SIPHON siphon 的另一种拼法

Syr·a·cuse /ˈsaɪrəkjuz; ˈsaɪrəkjuːz/ **1** a port and town on the east coast of the Italian island of Sicily, built by Greeks in the 8th century BC 锡拉丘萨〔意大利西西里岛东岸一港口城镇。公元前8世纪由古希腊人建立〕**2** a city in the northern part of New York State in the US 锡拉库萨〔美国纽约州北部一城市〕

Syr·i·a /ˈsɪrɪə; ˈsiriə/ a country in west Asia, south of Turkey and west of Iraq. Population 16,729,000 (2001). Capital: Damascus. 叙利亚〔西亚一国家，位于土耳其以南、伊拉克以西。人口: 16,729,000 (2001)，首都: 大马士革〕—**Syrian** *n, adj*

sy·ringe¹ /ˈsɪrɪndʒ; sɪ̣ˈrɪndʒ/ *n* [C] an instrument for taking blood from someone's body or putting liquid, drugs etc into it, consisting of a hollow plastic tube and a needle 注射器，注射筒

syringe² *v* [T] to clean something with a syringe〔用注射器〕灌洗；冲洗: *Get the doctor to syringe your ears.* 去找医生把你的耳朵冲洗一下。

syr·up /ˈsɪrəp; ˈsɪrəp/ *n* [U] **1** sweet liquid, especially sugar and water 糖水: *canned fruit in syrup* 糖水水果罐头 **2** thick sticky pale liquid made from sugar 糖浆: *golden syrup* 金黄色的糖浆 | *maple syrup* 槭糖浆 **3** medicine in the form of a thick sweet liquid 药用糖浆，含药糖浆: *cough syrup* 止咳糖浆

syr·up·y /ˈsɪrəpɪ; ˈsɪrəpi/ *adj* **1** thick and sticky like syrup or containing syrup 糖浆状的；含有糖浆的: *syrupy drinks* 糖浆似的饮料 **2** too sweet, nice or kind 太甜蜜的；过于多情的: *Her voice was syrupy.* 她说话嗲声嗲气的。

sys·tem /ˈsɪstəm; ˈsɪstɪ̣m/ *n* S1 W1

1 ►RELATED PARTS 相关部分◄ [C] a group of related parts that work together as a whole for a particular purpose 系统: *They have an alarm system in the house.* 他们房子里装有报警系统。| *the body's immune system* 身体的免疫系统 | *the banking system in the US* 美国的银行系统 | *the railway system* 铁路系统

2 ►METHOD 方法◄ [C] an organized set of ideas, methods, or ways of working 体制，制度；一套办法，一套工作方法: [+**of/for**] *What is the system for marking pronunciation in the dictionary?* 这本词典用什么系统注音？

3 ►THE BODY 身体◄ [C] your body considered as a set of working parts〔由各器官组成的〕整个身体: *All this overeating is bad for my system.* 这暴饮暴食对我身体有害。

4 ►COMPUTERS 电脑◄ [C] the way in which a computer or set of computers works〔电脑的〕工作系统[方式]: *a fault in the system* 系统中出的毛病 | *What software does the system use?* 这个系统用的是什么软件？—see also 另见 OPERATING SYSTEM

5 the system *informal* the combination of official rules and powerful groups or organizations that seem to govern your life and limit your freedom【非正式】〔操纵个人生活、限制个人自由的〕既成秩序；现行体制；制度: *You can't beat the system in this company!* 本公司的制度违反不得！

6 get sth out of your system *informal* to do something that helps you get rid of unpleasant strong feelings【非正式】消除强烈的不快情绪: *I was furious, so I went for a run to get it out of my system.* 我气坏了，便去跑步发泄怒火。

7 ►ORDER 秩序◄ [U] the use of sensible and organized methods 条理；秩序: *We need a bit more system in the way we organize our files.* 我们的档案管理需要安排得更有条理些。

sys·te·mat·ic /ˌsɪstəˈmætɪk; ˌsɪstɪ̣ˈmætɪk◄/ *adj* based on carefully organized methods; THOROUGH 有系统的，有条理的；仔细周到的: *The way they've collected their data is not very systematic.* 他们收集资料的方法条理性不够。| *a systematic search of the building* 对大楼的彻底搜查 —**systematically** /-klɪ; -kli/ *adv*

sys·te·ma·tize also 又作 **-ise** *BrE*【英】/ˈsɪstəməˌtaɪz; ˈsɪstɪ̣mətaɪz/ *v* [T] to put facts, numbers, ideas etc into a particular order 使条理化，使系统化 —**systematization** /ˌsɪstəmətəˈzeʃən; ˌsɪstɪ̣mətaɪˈzeɪʃən/ *n* [U]

sys·te·mic /sɪsˈtɛmɪk; sɪsˈtemɪk/ *adj technical* having an effect on the whole of something, especially a living thing【术语】影响全局的；〔尤指〕影响〔生物〕全身的: *systemic injection* 影响全身的注射 —**systemically** /-klɪ; -kli/ *adv*

systems an·a·lyst /ˈ‥ ˌ‥‧/ *n* [C] someone who studies business or industrial operations, and uses computers to plan them, improve them etc 系统分析员，系统分析专家 —**systems analysis** /ˌ‥ ˈ‥‧/ *n* [U]

T,t

T, t /ti; tiː/ *plural* **T's** or **t's 1** the 20th letter of the English alphabet 英语字母表的第二十个字母 **2 to a T** *informal* if something suits you to a T, it is exactly right for you【非正式】恰好, 精确地: *That dress suits you to a T.* 那件连衣裙你穿正合身。

T&G /ˌti ənd ˋdʒi; ˌtiː ənd ˈdʒiː/ a common name for the TGWU (英国) 运输与普通工人工会〔TGWU 常用名〕

TA /ˌti ˋe; ˌtiː ˈeɪ/ *n* [singular] the abbreviation of 缩写= TERRITORIAL ARMY

3 **ta** /tɑ; tɑː/ *interjection BrE informal* thank you【英, 非正式】谢谢

tab /tæb; tæb/ *n* [C]

1 ▶SMALL PIECE OF PAPER/CLOTH 小片纸/布◀ a small piece of paper, cloth etc that is fixed to the edge of something, especially giving information about it〔固定在某物边缘, 尤指列出其有关信息的〕小纸条; 小布条; 小标签

2 ▶ON A CAN 罐头上◀ *AmE* a small piece of metal that you pull to open a can of drink【美】〔开罐的金属〕小拉环

3 ▶IN A BAR/RESTAURANT 在酒吧/饭馆◀ a system used in some bars, restaurants etc in which they keep a record of what you have bought and you pay for it later〔某些酒吧或饭馆的〕赊账制; 账单: **put sth on a tab** *Don't worry about the meal. Put it on my tab.* 别担心吃饭的事, 记在我的账上。

4 keep tabs on sb *informal* to watch someone carefully to check what they are doing【非正式】密切注意某人, 监视某人的一举一动: *The police have been keeping tabs on Rogers since he got out of prison.* 自从罗杰斯出狱以来, 警察一直在严密监视他。

5 pick up the tab to pay for something, especially when it is not your responsibility to pay〔尤指代他人〕付账; 承担费用: *Taxpayers pick up the tab for government mismanagement of the economy.* 纳税人为政府经济管理不善而承担损失。

6 ▶CIGARETTE 香烟◀ *slang* a cigarette【俚】香烟

7 ▶IN TYPING 打字机上◀ a TAB STOP 跳格键, 制表键

8 *slang* a solid form of the illegal drug LSD【俚】迷幻药毒丸: *a tab of acid* 一粒迷幻药毒丸

Ta·bas·co /təˋbæsko; təˈbæskəʊ/ also 又作 **tabasco sauce** /ˌ·ˌ·· ˈ·/ *n* [U] *trademark* a very hot-tasting red liquid made from CHILLI (2) peppers, used in cooking【商标】〔烹调用的〕塔巴斯科辣酱汁

tab·by /ˋtæbɪ; ˈtæbi/ *n* [C] a cat with grey, brown, or orange marks on its fur〔毛皮上有灰色、褐色或橙色斑点的〕(虎) 斑猫 —**tabby** *adj*

tab·er·nac·le /ˋtæbɚˌnækl̩; ˈtæbənækəl/ *n* [C] **1 the tabernacle** the small tent in which the ancient Jews kept their most holy objects〔古代犹太人存放圣物的〕帐幕; 会幕 **2** a church or other building used by some Christian groups〔某些基督教派的〕教堂, 礼拜堂 **3** a box used for keeping holy bread and wine in Roman Catholic churches〔罗马天主教堂里存放圣餐用面包和葡萄酒的〕圣体柜

1 1 **ta·ble¹** /ˋtebl̩; ˈteɪbəl/ *n*

1 ▶FURNITURE 家具◀ a piece of furniture with a flat top supported by legs 桌子, 台子: *a kitchen table* 厨房用桌 | **table lamp** (=made to be put on a small table) 台灯 | **book a table** (=ask a restaurant to keep a table available for you)〔向饭馆〕预订餐桌 *I've booked a table for two for 8:00.* 我已经订好 8 点钟两个人的餐桌。| **lay the table** *BrE*【英】**set the table** *especially AmE*【尤美】(=put knives, forks etc on a table before a meal) 布置桌子〔指开饭前放餐具等〕| **clear the table** (=take all the empty plates, dishes etc off a table after eating)〔指饭后〕收拾桌子 | **at table** *BrE formal* (=sitting around a table having a meal)【英, 正式】就餐, 用餐 —see also 另见 COFFEE TABLE, HIGH TABLE

2 ▶LIST 表格◀ [C] a list of numbers, facts, or information arranged in rows across and down a page (一览) 表, 表格; 单子: **table of contents** *The table of contents at the front will tell you which page it's on.* 前面的目录会告诉你具体在哪页。

3 ▶MATHS 数学◀ a list that young children learn, in which all the numbers between 1 and 12 are multiplied by each other 乘法表: **three/four etc times table** *He's 12 years old and still doesn't know his three times table.* 他 12 岁了, 却还不会背三的乘法口诀。

4 on the table a) an offer, idea etc that is on the table has been officially suggested and you are considering it〔某事或某主意〕正式提交考虑, 被摆到桌面上: *The offer on the table at the moment is a 10% wage increase.* 此刻摆到桌面上的是增加 10% 工资的方案。**b)** *AmE* an offer, idea etc that is on the table is no longer being considered at the moment but will be dealt with in the future【美】〔某事或某主意〕暂时被搁置〔留待以后考虑〕

5 turn the tables (on sb) to suddenly become stronger than the opponent who used to be stronger than you〔突然〕转弱为强, 转败为胜: *Suddenly Harry felt that the tables had somehow been turned and that he was now the victim.* 突然间, 哈里觉得局势莫名其妙地对他变得不利起来, 他现在成了被动挨打的。

6 under the table *informal* money that is paid under the table is paid secretly and illegally to get what you want【非正式】〔指金钱〕非法支付, 秘密交易: *payments made under the table to local officials* 对当地官员的贿赂

7 ▶GROUP 一群人◀ the group of people sitting around a table〔饭桌上的〕一桌人, 同席的人: *His stories kept the whole table amused.* 他讲的故事让全桌人很开心。—see also 另见 **drink sb under the table** (DRINK² (2))

table² *v* [T] **1** *BrE* **table a proposal/question/demand etc** to suggest a proposal etc for other people to consider【英】提交议案/问题/要求等〔供讨论〕**2** *AmE* **table a bill/measure/proposal etc** to leave an offer, idea etc to be dealt with in the future【美】搁置法案/措施/议案等; 把…留到以后处理

tab·leau /ˋtæblo; ˈtæbləʊ/ *n* [C] a group of people who do not speak or move arranged on stage to show a famous event 舞台造型〔由一群人在舞台上塑造静态画面, 以表现著名事件〕

ta·ble·cloth /ˋtebl̩ˌklɔθ; ˈteɪbəlklɒθ/ *n* [C] a cloth used for covering a table 桌布 —see picture on page A15 参见 A15 页图

table d'hôte /ˋtɑbl̩ dot; ˌtɑːbəl ˈdəʊt/ *n* [singular] a complete meal served at a fixed price in a hotel or restaurant〔价格固定的〕套餐

ta·ble·land /ˋtebl̩ˌlænd; ˈteɪbəl-lænd/ also 又作 **tablelands** *n* [C] *technical* a large area of high flat land; PLATEAU (1)【术语】台地, 高地

table lin·en /ˋ·· ˌ··/ *n* [U] all the cloths used during the meal〔席间所有的〕餐桌用布〈如台布、餐巾、盆盘布垫等〉

table man·ners /ˋ·· ˌ··/ *n* [plural] the way in which someone eats their food, considered according to the usual rules of social behaviour about eating 进餐礼仪, 用餐时的礼节: *Piotr's got terrible table manners.* 皮埃特的餐桌礼仪糟透了。

table mat /ˋ·· ˌ·/ *n* [C] a small mat that you put under a hot dish or plate〔放在热食盘碟下的〕碗垫, 盘垫 —see picture on page A15 参见 A15 页图

Table Moun·tain /ˋ·· ˌ··/ a high mountain in South Africa with steep sides and a flat top like a table. It stands behind the city of Cape Town. 桌山〔南非一高山, 山坡陡峭, 山顶平坦, 形似桌子, 俯瞰开普敦市〕

ta·ble·spoon /ˋtebl̩ˌspun; ˈteɪbəlspuːn/ *n* [C] **1** *BrE* a large spoon used for serving food, or the amount held in it【英】大汤匙, 大调羹; 一大匙容量: *three tablespoons of sugar* 三大调羹白糖 **2** *AmE* a medium-sized spoon which you use for eating【美】〔进餐用的〕中号调羹 **3** *AmE* a spoon that holds exactly 1/128 of a US pint of liquid【美】〔刚好能盛放 1/128 美国品脱液体的〕茶匙 —see picture at 参见 SPOON¹ 图

ta·ble·spoon·ful /ˋtebl̩spunˌfʊl; ˈteɪbəlspuːnfʊl/ *n plural* **tablespoonfuls, tablespoonsful** [C] the amount that a tablespoon holds 一大调羹容量: **[+of]** *two tablespoonsful of flour* 两调羹面粉

tab·let /ˋtæblɪt; ˈtæbl̩ɪt/ *n* [C] **1** *especially BrE* a small round hard piece of medicine; PILL (1)【尤英】药片: *three tablets a day before meals* 一日三片药, 饭前服用 **2** a flat piece of soap 一块肥皂 **3** a flat piece of stone or metal with words cut into it〔铭刻有文字的〕石匾, 金属匾

table ten·nis /ˋ·· ˌ··/ *n* [U] an indoor game played on a table by two or four players who hit a small plastic ball to each other across a net; PING-PONG 乒乓球运动

ta·ble·ware /ˋtebl̩ˌwɛr; ˈteɪbəlweə/ *n* [U] the plates, glasses, knives etc used when eating a meal 餐具〔总称〕

table wine /ˋ·· ˌ·/ *n* [C,U] a fairly cheap wine intended for drinking with meals 佐餐酒

tab·loid /ˋtæblɔɪd; ˈtæblɔɪd/ *n* [C] **1** *BrE* a newspaper that has a lot of stories about sex, famous people etc, and not much serious news【英】〔刊载大量有关性、名人逸事等报道的〕通俗小报: *The tabloids had the story splashed all over their front pages.* 各通俗小报都在头版醒目位置刊载了这一报道。**2** a newspaper with a small page 小报〔开本小的报纸〕—compare 比较 BROADSHEET —**tabloid** *adj*: *the tabloid press* 小报新闻界

ta·boo¹ /tæˋbu; təˈbuː/ *adj* **1 taboo subject/area/word** a subject etc that people avoid because they think it is offensive or embarrassing 禁忌题材/禁区/禁忌语: *Death is still a taboo subject to some people.* 对某些人来说, 死亡仍然是一个忌讳的话题。**2** *technical* too holy or evil to be touched, or used【术语】〔因太神圣或太邪恶而〕禁止接触的, 禁止使用的

taboo² *n plural* **taboos** [C,U] **1** a social custom which means a particular activity or subject must be avoided 禁忌, 忌讳: **[+about/on/against]** *a strong taboo against fighting in public* 严格禁止在公共场所打架 **2** a religious custom that FORBIDS a particular activity because it may offend God〔宗教方面的〕清规戒律

ta·bor /ˋtebɚ; ˈteɪbə/ *n* [C] a small DRUM¹ (1) 小鼓

tab stop /ˋ· ·/ *n* [C] a button on a computer or TYPEWRITER that you push, in order to move forward to a particular place on a line of text〔电脑或打字机上的〕跳格键, 制表键

tab·u·lar /ˋtæbjəlɚ; ˈtæbjʊ̈lə/ *adj* arranged in the form of a TABLE (=set of numbers arranged in rows across and down a page)〔列成〕表格的, 表格式的

tab·u·la ra·sa /ˌtæbjələ ˋrɑzə; ˌtæbjʊ̈lə ˈrɑːzə/ *n* [C usually singular 一般用单数] *Latin literary* your mind in its original state, before you have learned anything【拉丁, 文】心灵白板〔出生后未曾学习任何外界东西之前的心灵原始状态〕

tab·u·late /ˋtæbjəˌlet; ˈtæbjʊ̈leɪt/ *v* [T] to arrange figures or information together in a set or a list so that they can be easily compared 把…制成表格; 以表格形式排列〔数字、资料等〕—**tabulation** /ˌtæbjuˋleʃən; ˌtæbjʊ̈ˈleɪʃən/ *n* [U]

tach·o·graph /ˋtækəˌgræf; ˈtækəgrɑːf/ *n* [C] a piece of equipment for recording the speed of a vehicle, the distance it has travelled etc 速度里程计

ta·chom·e·ter /təˋkɑmətɚ; tæˈkɒmɪ̈tə/ *n* [C] a piece of equipment used to measure the speed, at which the engine of a vehicle turns 转速表, 速度表

ta·cit /ˋtæsɪt; ˈtæsɪ̈t/ *adj* tacit agreement, support etc is accepted or understood without actually being officially agreed 心照不宣的, 默认的: *a tacit agreement that no company would cut their prices* 各公司之间不削价的默契 —**tacitly** *adv* —**tacitness** *n* [U]

ta·ci·turn /ˋtæsəˌtɝn; ˈtæsɪ̈tɜːn/ *adj* speaking very little, so that you seem unfriendly 沉默寡言的, 不苟言笑的 —**taciturnly** *adv* —**taciturnity** /ˌtæsəˋtɝnətɪ; ˌtæsɪ̈ˈtɜːnɪ̈ti/ *n* [U]

tack¹ /tæk; tæk/ *n*

1 ▶NAIL 针◀ [C] a small nail with a sharp point and flat top 平头针, 大头针

2 ▶PIN 钉◀ [C] *AmE* a short pin with a large round flat top, for fixing notices to boards, walls etc【美】图钉, 按钉; DRAWING PIN *BrE*【英】, THUMBTACK *AmE*【美】

3 change tack/try a different tack etc to do something completely different from what you were doing before, especially in order to achieve something 改变策略; 采取另一做法: *Rudy changed tack, his tone suddenly becoming friendly.* 鲁迪改变了方式, 他的语气突然变得友好起来。

4 ▶SHIP 船◀ [C,U] the direction of a sailing ship, based on the direction of the wind and the position of its sails〔帆船的〕航行方向〔由风向和帆的位置决定〕: *Ships on the starboard tack have right of way.* 右舷抢风行驶的船有先行权。

5 ▶SEWING 缝纫◀ [C] a long loose stitch used for fastening pieces of cloth together before SEWING them properly〔大针脚〕暂缝, 粗缝

6 ▶UGLY OBJECTS 丑陋的杂物◀ [U] small objects that are very ugly and cheap, but are sold as decorations〔难看而廉价的〕小装饰品; 劣质杂物: *souvenir shops full of tack* 廉价纪念品充斥的商店

7 ▶HORSES 马◀ [U] all the equipment you need for horse riding 马具, 鞍辔

tack² *v* **1** [T always+adv/prep] to fasten something with a tack〔用图钉〕把…钉上: **[+up]** *tacking notices up on the board* 把告示钉在板上 **2** [T] to fasten pieces of cloth together with long loose stitches, before SEWING them properly〔大针脚〕暂缝, 粗缝 **3** [I] to change the course of a sailing ship so that the wind blows against its sails from the opposite direction〔船〕抢风航行

tack sth ↔ **on** *phr v* [T] *informal* to add something to something that already exists or is complete, especially in a way that looks badly planned【非正式】〔尤指笨拙、多余地〕增补; 附加: *The environmental section of the bill was obviously tacked on afterwards.* 那个法案关于环境方面的内容显然是后来粗糙地增补上去的。| *a little porch tacked on to the front of the house* 屋前加的小门廊

tack·le¹ /ˋtækḷ; ˈtækəl/ *v* S3 W3

1 [T] to make a determined effort to deal with a difficult problem 处理, 对付〔难题〕: *It took twelve fire engines to tackle the blaze.* 用了12辆消防车来对付那场烈火。

2 [T] to talk to someone in order to deal with a difficult problem〔为了解决难题〕与…交涉: **tackle sb about sth** *When I tackled Didi about it, she admitted he'd tried to do too much.* 当我与迪迪交涉此事时, 她承认他过于卖力了。

3 [I,T] **▶SPORT 体育运动◀ a)** to try to take the ball away from an opponent in a game such as football or HOCKEY (1)〔足球或曲棍球〕把球抢走, 抢断; 铲球 —see picture on page A23 参见A23页图 **b)** to force someone to the ground so that they stop running, in a game such as American football or RUGBY〔橄榄球比赛中〕擒抱〔对方球员〕

4 [T] to fight against another person, organization etc 对付: *I certainly couldn't tackle both of them on my own.* 光我一个人当然对付不了他们两个。

tackle² *n* **1** [C] **a)** the act of trying to take the ball from an opponent in a game of football or HOCKEY (1)〔足球或曲棍球〕阻截得球, 抢断; 铲球 **b)** [C] the act of stopping an opponent by forcing them to the ground, especially in American football or RUGBY〔尤指橄榄球〕擒抱, 抱截〔通过拉倒对手来阻挡进攻〕**2** [C] a player in American football who stops other players by tackling them 阻截队员〔美式橄榄球的前线球员之一〕**3** [U] the equipment used in some sports, especially fishing〔体育〕器具〔尤指钓具〕**4** [U] *slang* a man's sexual organs【俚】男性性器官 **5** [C,U] ropes and PULLEYS (=wheels) used for moving a ship's sails, lifting heavy things etc 滑车, 滑轮组

tack·y /ˋtækɪ; ˈtæki/ *adj* **1** cheap looking and of very bad quality 模样寒碜的; 劣质的: *tacky ornaments* 劣质廉价的饰品 **2** slightly sticky 发黏的: *The paint's still slightly tacky.* 油漆还有些黏。—**tackily** *adv* —**tackiness** *n* [U]

ta·co /ˋtɑko; ˈtɑːkəʊ/ *n* [C] a type of Mexican food consisting of a flat circle made of CORN (2) flour folded and filled with BEEF¹ (1), beans etc〔牛肉、豆子等作馅的〕墨西哥玉米薄饼卷

tact /tækt; tækt/ *n* [U] the ability to be polite and careful about what you say or do so that you do not upset or embarrass other people 得体; 乖巧; 机敏: *With great tact, Aunt Jo persuaded Theo to apologize.* 乔姨妈十分巧妙地说服了西奥去道歉。

tact·ful /ˋtæktfəl; ˈtæktfəl/ *adj* careful not to say or do anything that will upset or embarrass other people 乖巧的; 机敏的; 圆通的: *Sam maintained a tactful silence as she ranted on.* 她大叫大嚷个不停时, 山姆很老练, 一声不吭。—**tactfully** *adv*: *Everyone tactfully refrained from mentioning his argument with the boss.* 大家都很乖巧, 避免提及他与老板的争论。

tac·tic /ˋtæktɪk; ˈtæktɪk/ *n* **1** [C] a method that you use to achieve something 手法; 策略: *Salesmen employ all sorts of clever tactics to try and persuade you.* 推销员用尽各种聪明的手法来努力说服你。| **delaying tactic(s)** (=something you do in order to give yourself more time) 拖延战术[策略] | **strong arm tactics** (=the use of violence to achieve your aim) 武力手段[策略] **2** [C usually plural 一般用复数] the way in which military forces are arranged in order to win a battle 战术

tac·tic·al /ˋtæktɪkḷ; ˈtæktɪkəl/ *adj* **1** done in order to achieve what you want at a later time, especially in a game or large plan 策略性的; 谋略性的: *a tactical move to avoid the threat of legal action* 为躲避可能的法律行动而采取的策略 **2 tactical error/mistake** a mistake that will harm your plans later 战术失误/错误: *Telling him your age was a tactical error.* 你把年龄告诉了他是一个策略性的错误。**3 tactical weapon/missile etc** a weapon etc that is only used over short distances〔只用于短距离的〕战术性武器/导弹等: *tactical nuclear missiles* 战术核导弹 **4** connected with the organizing of military forces in order to win battles 战术上的 —**tactically** /-kḷɪ; -kli/ *adv*

tactical vot·ing /ˌ··· ˋ··/ *n* [U] the practice of voting for a political party that you do not support in order to prevent another party from winning an election 策略性投票〔为防止另一政党赢得选举而把票投给自己并不支持的一个政党〕

tac·ti·cian /tækˋtɪʃən; tækˈtɪʃən/ *n* [C] someone who is very good at TACTICS 战术家; 谋略家

tac·tile /ˋtæktḷ; ˈtæktaɪl/ *adj* connected with your sense of touch 触觉的: *a tactile sensation* 触觉

tact·less /ˈtæktlɪs; ˈtæktləs/ *adj* likely to upset or embarrass someone without intending to 不乖巧的, 不圆通的; 不明智的: *I wanted to know about the divorce, but thought it would be tactless to ask.* 我想知道离婚的事, 但又觉得这样问欠妥当。| *a tactless remark* 不明智的话 —**tactlessly** *adv* —**tactlessness** *n* [U]

tad /tæd; tæd/ *n informal*【非正式】**a tad** *BrE dialect* a small amount, or to a small degree【英, 方言】少量; 轻微: *"Would you like some milk?" "Just a tad."* "你想要点牛奶吗?" "就一点点。"

tad·pole /ˈtæd,pol; ˈtædpəʊl/ *n* [C] a small creature that has a long tail, lives in water, and grows into a FROG (1) or TOAD 蝌蚪

Ta·dzhi·ki·stan /tɑ,dʒikɪˋstɑn; tɑː,dʒiːkɪˈstɑːn/ another spelling of TAJIKISTAN 塔吉克斯坦〔Tajikistan 的另一种拼法〕

taf·fe·ta /ˈtæfɪtə; ˈtæfɪ̣tə/ *n* [U] a shiny stiff cloth made from silk or NYLON 塔夫绸

Taf·fy /ˈtæfɪ; ˈtæfi/ *n* [C usually singular 一般用单数] *BrE slang* a word for someone who is Welsh, often considered to be offensive【英俚】威尔士佬〔常被认为不礼貌的称呼〕

taffy *n* [U] *especially AmE* a soft sweet usually made from sugar boiled brown【尤美】太妃糖, 乳脂糖

Taft /tæft; tæft/, **William Howard** (1857-1930) the twenty-seventh president of the US, from 1909 to 1913. He was also Chief Justice of the Supreme Court from 1921 to 1930. 塔夫脱〔(1857-1930), 美国第27任总统, 1909至1913年在任, 1921至1930年任美国最高法院首席大法官〕

tag¹ /tæg; tæg/ *n* **1** [C] a small piece of paper, plastic etc, fixed to something to show what it is, who owns it, what it costs etc 标签, 标牌: **name/identification/price tag** *Where's the price tag on this dress?* 这件衣服上的价格标签在哪里? **2** [U] a children's game in which one player chases and tries to touch the others〔儿童玩的〕捉人游戏 **3** [C] a phrase such as 'isn't it?', 'won't it?', or 'does she?', added to the end of a sentence to make it a question or to ask you to agree with it 附加疑问句 **4** [C] a metal or plastic point at the end of a piece of string or SHOELACE that prevents it from splitting〔绳子、鞋带末端的〕金属[塑料]包头

tag² **tagged, tagging** *v* [T] **1** to fasten a tag onto something 给…加上标签, 给…挂上标牌: *Tag the bottles now or we'll forget which one is which.* 现在给那些瓶子贴上标签, 否则我们会忘了哪个是哪个。**2 be tagged as stupid/a failure etc** to be thought of in a particular way that is difficult for you to change〔难以改变地〕被看作是笨蛋/没有出息的人等: *He quit after 4½ years because he didn't want to be tagged forever as a game show host.* 他干了四年半后辞职了, 因为他不想让人永远把他看作是一个游戏节目主持人。**3 Tag!** *spoken* used in a children's game when a player manages to touch someone they are chasing【口】捉到啦!〔儿童在玩捉人游戏时的用语〕**4** *slang* to illegally paint your name or sign on a wall, vehicle etc【俚】〔在墙壁、汽车等上面违法〕涂写〔名字或标记〕

tag along *phr v* [I] *informal* go somewhere with someone, especially when they do not want you to【非正式】〔尤指在对方并不情愿的情况下〕跟着〔某人〕去: *Mom, I can't do anything with her tagging along all the time.* 妈妈, 她老是跟着我, 我什么也干不了。

tag sth ↔ **on** *phr v* [T] to add something to something that already exists or is complete, especially in a way that looks badly planned 把…附加于…〔尤指安排不妥地多余添加〕: *Why don't you just tag on a paragraph about the latest research?* 你何不在后面加上一段, 把最新的研究情况包括进去?

ta·glia·tel·le /tæɡljəˋtɛlɪ; ,tæɡljəˈteli/ *n* [U] a kind of PASTA that is cut in very long, thin, flat pieces〔又长又薄的、扁平的〕意大利扁面条 —see picture at 参见 PASTA 图

Ta·gore /təˋgɔr; təˈgɔː/, **Ra·bin·dra·nath** /rəˋbɪndrənɑθ; rəˈbɪndrənɑːθ/ (1861-1941) a Bengali Indian writer, one of the most important Indian writers of the 20th century. His works include *Gitanjali*, and *Chitra*, a play which he translated into English 泰戈尔〔(1861-1941), 印度孟加拉语作家, 20世纪最重要的印度作家之一。作品包括《吉檀迦利》和《齐德拉》。他曾把《齐德拉》这一剧本译成英文〕

Ta·hi·ti /tɑˋhitɪ; təˈhiːti/ an island in French Polynesia, in the Pacific Ocean, which is governed by France. It is well known for being a very beautiful place. 塔希提岛, 又译大溪地〔法属波利尼西亚一岛屿。位于太平洋, 由法国管辖, 以景色优美著称〕

tai chi /,taɪ ˋtʃi; ,taɪ ˈtʃiː/ *n* [U] a Chinese form of physical exercise that trains your mind and body in balance and control 太极(拳)

S2 W3 **tail¹** /tel; teɪl/ *n*

1 ►ANIMAL 动物◄ [C] the movable part at the back of an animal's body 尾巴: *The dog wagged its tail.* 狗摇摆尾巴。| *a fish's tail* 鱼尾 —see picture at 参见 HORSE 图

2 ►AIRCRAFT 飞机◄ [C] the back part of an aircraft〔飞机的〕尾部 —see picture at 参见 AIRCRAFT 图

3 ►SHIRT 衬衫◄ [C] the bottom part of your shirt at the back, that you put inside your trousers〔衬衫的〕后下摆

4 ►BACK PART 末尾部分◄ [C usually singular 一般用单数] the back part of something, especially something that is moving away from you 末尾部分; 后部〔尤指某种从你面前移开的东西〕: *We saw the tail of the procession disappearing round the corner.* 我们看到游行队伍的队尾渐渐消失在拐角处。

5 tails a) [U] the side of a coin that does not have the head of the president, queen etc on it〔硬币的〕反面: *Which side do you want, heads or tails?* 你要哪一面, 正面还是反面? —opposite 反义词 **heads** (HEAD¹ (36)) **b)** [plural] a man's formal JACKET (1) with two long parts that hang down at the back〔男子的〕晚礼服, 燕尾服

6 ► FOLLOW 跟踪◄ [C] *informal* someone who is employed to watch and follow someone, especially a criminal【非正式】盯梢者: **put a tail on sb** (=order someone to follow another person) 派人跟踪某人

7 sit/be on sb's tail *BrE informal* to follow another car too closely【英, 非正式】〔开车时〕与前面车辆距离太小; TAILGATE² *AmE*【美】

8 turn tail to run away because you are too frightened to fight or attack〔因不敢抵抗或攻击而〕逃跑, 转身逃走

9 the tail end of a queue/meeting etc the very last part of a QUEUE etc 队列/会议等的末尾; 尾声

10 with your tail between your legs embarrassed or unhappy because you have failed or been defeated〔因失败或被打败而〕夹着尾巴; 垂头丧气

11 the tail is wagging the dog *informal* used to say that an unimportant thing is wrongly controlling a situation【非正式】尾巴摇狗〔用来比喻本末倒置或主次颠倒〕—see also 另见 **nose to tail** (NOSE¹ (19)), **a sting in the tail** (STING² (4))

tail² *v* [T] *informal* to follow someone and watch what they do, where they go etc【非正式】跟踪〔某人〕, 盯〔某人〕的梢

tail away *phr v* [I] to become quieter, thinner etc and then disappear 变得越来越静[稀少]; 逐渐消失: *The beach tailed away to nothing.* 沙滩逐渐消失得无影无踪了。

tail back *phr v* [I] *especially BrE* to form a tailback【尤英】形成塞车

tail off *phr v* [I] to become gradually smaller or weaker, sometimes stopping completely 逐渐变小[弱]; 完全消失: *Our profits tailed off towards the end of the year.* 我们的利润到年底几乎减至零了。

tail·back /ˈtel,bæk; ˈteɪlbæk/ *n* [C] *BrE* a line of traffic that is moving very slowly or not moving at all【英】〔因交通堵塞而形成的〕车辆长龙: *a five mile tailback on the M25* M25号公路上长达5英里的塞车长龙

tail·board /ˈtel,bɔrd; ˈteɪlbɔːd/ *n* [C] a TAILGATE¹〔汽车后部向外向下开的〕后门, 尾门

tail·bone /ˈtelbon; ˈteɪlbəʊn/ *n* [C] the bone at the very bottom of your back; COCCYX 尾骨

tail·coat /ˈtel,kot; teɪlˈkəʊt/ *n* [C] a coat worn by men to formal events such as weddings, that is short at the front and divides into two long pieces at the back〔男子在正式场合穿的〕燕尾服

tail·gate¹ /ˈtel,get; ˈteɪlgeɪt/ n [C] *AmE* a door at the back of a vehicle that opens outwards and downwards【美】〔汽车后部向外向下开的〕后门, 尾门

tailgate² *v* [I,T] *especially AmE* to drive too closely behind another vehicle【尤美】〔开车时〕与前面车辆距离太小

tailgate par·ty /ˈ· ·, · ·/ also 又作 **tailgate** *n* [C] a party before an American football game where people eat and drink in the CARPARK of the place where the game is played 车尾大聚餐〔指美式橄榄球开赛前人们在停车场就地吃喝的场面〕

tail-light /ˈ· ·/ *n* [C] one of the two red lights at the back of a vehicle〔车辆的红色〕尾灯 —see picture on page A2 参见 A2 页图

tai·lor¹ /ˈtelə; ˈteɪlə/ *n* [C] someone who makes men's clothes specially measured to fit each customer〔为男顾客量体裁衣的〕裁缝

tailor² *v* [T] **tailor sth to your needs/requirements** to make something so that it is exactly right for your particular needs 根据特定需要制作…: *We can tailor the insurance policy according to your family's needs.* 我们可以根据你家庭的需要制定保险单。

tai·lored /ˈteləd; ˈteɪləd/ *adj* **1** a piece of clothing that is tailored is made to fit very well〔衣服〕定做的 **2** made to fit a particular need or situation 适合〔特定需要或情况〕的: *tailored financial advice* 配合个别需要的财务咨询

tai·lor·ing /ˋteləɪŋ; ˈteɪlərɪŋ/ *n* [U] the work of making men's clothes or the style in which they are made〔制作男装的〕裁缝业; 裁缝手艺

tailor-made /ˌ‥ ˈ‥◂/ *adj* exactly right or suitable for someone or something 正好适合〔某人或某物〕的: [+for] *The job's tailor-made for John.* 这份工作正好适合约翰去做。

tail·piece /ˋtelˏpis; ˈteɪlpiːs/ *n* [C] a part added at the end of a book, story etc〔附加于书末或故事结尾处的〕附属部分; 补白

tail pipe /ˋ· ·/ *n* [C] *AmE* the pipe that takes unwanted gases out of a vehicle's engine【美】〔车辆发动机的〕尾部排气管, 尾喷管; EXHAUST² (1) *BrE*【英】

tail·spin /ˋtelˏspɪn; ˈteɪlˌspɪn/ *n* [C] an uncontrolled fall of a plane through the air, in which the back of the plane spins in a wider circle than the front〔飞机失控下坠时的〕尾旋

tail·wind /ˋtelˏwɪnd; ˈteɪlˌwɪnd/ *n* [C] a wind blowing in the same direction that a vehicle is travelling〔车辆等行驶时从后面吹来的〕顺风

taint¹ /tent; teɪnt/ *v* [T usually passive 一般用被动态] to make someone or something seem less pure and desirable by relating it to something unpleasant 玷污, 败坏〔某人的名誉〕; 弄脏〔某物〕: **be tainted by/with** *a political reputation tainted by association with the Mafia* 由于与黑手党来往而被玷污的政治声誉

taint² *n* [singular] the appearance of being related to something shameful or terrible 污点, 瑕疵; 腐坏: [+of] *court officials free from the taint of corruption* 一身清廉的法庭官员

taint·ed /ˋtentɪd; ˈteɪntɨd/ *adj especially AmE* food or drink that is tainted is no longer safe because it has decayed or contains poison【尤美】〔食物或饮料〕腐坏的, 变质的, 有毒的: *tainted milk* 变质牛奶

Taipei /ˋtaɪˋpe; ˈtaɪpeɪ/ the largest city of Taiwan, China. It is surrounded by mountains, and its most important industries are making TEXTILES, clothing, machinery, and ships. 台北〔中国台湾最大城市, 四面环山。其最重要的产业为纺织、服装、机械和造船〕

Tai·wan /ˌtaɪˋwɑn; ˌtaɪˈwɑːn/ a Chinese island off the southeast coast of China. Population: 22,370,000 (2001). Largest city: Taipei. Taiwan has experienced rapid economic development since the 1950s and has many factories. 台湾〔中国一岛屿, 位于东南沿海。人口: 22,370,000 (2001), 最大的城市: 台北。台湾自20世纪50年代起经济快速发展, 岛上建有许多工厂〕—**Taiwanese** /ˌtaɪwəˋniz; ˌtaɪwəˈniːz/ *n, adj*

Ta·ji·ki·stan /tɑˏdʒikɪˋstɑn; tɑːˌdʒiːkɪˈstɑːn/ a country in central Asia, between Uzbekistan and China, formerly part of the Soviet Union. Population: 6,579,000 (2001). Capital: Dushanbe. 塔吉克斯坦〔中亚一国家, 在乌兹别克斯坦和中国之间, 曾是苏联的一部分。人口: 6,579,000 (2001), 首都: 杜尚别〕—**Tajik** /tɑˋdʒik; tɑːˈdʒiːk/, **Tajikistani** /tɑˏdʒikɪˋstɑnɪ; tɑːˌdʒiːkɪˈstɑːni/ *n, adj*

Taj Ma·hal, the /ˌtɑdʒ məˋhɑl; ˌtɑːdʒ məˈhɑːl/ a beautiful building made of white MARBLE (=a type of smooth, hard rock) in Agra, northern India, built as a MAUSOLEUM (=a building containing a grave) for his wife by the emperor Shah Jahan in the 17th century. It is one of the world's most famous buildings, and is visited by many tourists. 泰姬陵〔印度北部阿格拉一幢漂亮的白色大理石建筑。该建筑是17世纪皇帝沙贾汗为亡妻建造的陵墓, 是世界上最著名的建筑物之一, 吸引许多游客前去观看〕

take¹ /tek; teɪk/ *v past tense* **took** /tʊk; tʊk/ *past participle* **taken** /ˋtekən; ˈteɪkən/

① MOVE STH 移动某物
② DO SOMETHING 做某事
③ NEED STH 需要某物
④ SCHOOL/EXAMS 学校/考试
⑤ GET SOMETHING IN YOUR POSSESSION 取得某物
⑥ TAKE PART 参加
⑦ TAKE PLACE 发生
⑧ ACCEPT SOMETHING 接受某物
⑨ SPOKEN PHRASES 口语短语
⑩ OTHER MEANINGS 其他意思
⑪ PHRASAL VERBS 短语动词

① MOVE STH 移动某物

1 [T] to move someone or something from one place to another 把〔某人或某物〕带(走); 拿(走); 取(走); 搬(走): *Don't forget to take your bag when you go.* 你走的时候别忘了拿自己的包。| *Paul doesn't know the way – can you take him?* 保罗不认识路, 你能带他去吗? | **take sb/sth to** *We take the kids to school in the car.* 我们用车送孩子们上学。| *Our neighbor was taken away in a police car.* 我们的邻居被一辆警车带走了。| *Take the car to the garage to be repaired.* 把车送到修理厂去修理一下。| **take sb sth** *Take your mother a cup of tea.* 给你妈拿杯茶去。| **take sb/sth with you** *I'll take the dogs with me when I go to the lake.* 我去湖边时会把狗都带上。—see 见 BRING (USAGE)

② DO SOMETHING 做某事

2 [T] a word meaning to do something, used with many different nouns to form a phrase that means 'do the actions connected with the nouns'〔与许多不同的名词连用, 构成短语, 意义相当于"做与该名词相关的动作"〕: *take a walk* 散步 | *take a bath* 洗澡 | *take a breath* 吸一口气 | *take a vacation* 度假

③ NEED STH 需要某物

3 take (sb) 2 hours/6 months etc to need a particular amount of time to do something or for something to happen 花〔某人〕两个小时/六个月等: *The journey takes three hours.* 这段路程要花三个小时。| **take 2 hours/6 months etc to do sth** *It took three hours to fix the washing machine.* 修理那台洗衣机花了三个小时。| *It took us half an hour to get there.* 我们花了半个小时到那儿。

4 ▶NEED MONEY/EFFORT/A QUALITY 需要钱/努力/某种品质◀ [T] to need a particular quality, amount of money, or effort, in order for you to do something or for something to happen〔为了做成某事或使某事发生〕需要〔某种特殊的品质、一定数量的钱或努力〕: *It takes strength and stamina to be a long-distance runner.* 要想成为一名长跑运动员, 需要体力和耐力。| **it takes sth to do sth** *It took a lot of courage to admit you were wrong.* 要承认自己错了, 需要很大的勇气。

5 ▶STH NEEDS STH〔某物〕需要〔某物〕◀ [T] if a machine, vehicle etc takes a particular kind of petrol, BATTERY (1) etc, you have to use that in it〔机器、车辆等〕需要使用〔某种特定的汽油、电池等〕: *The car only takes unleaded.* 这辆车只用无铅汽油。

6 have what it takes *informal* to have the qualities needed to be successful【非正式】具有成功的天资[品质]: *Neil's got what it takes to be a great footballer.* 内尔具有成为一名伟大足球运动员的天赋。

④ SCHOOL/EXAMS 学校/考试

7 ▶STUDY STH IN SCHOOL 在学校学习◀ [T] to study a particular subject in a school or college, in order to do an examination〔在学校〕攻读〔某一课程〕: *I only had to take 6 credits my senior year.* 我大四时只需修六个学分。

8 ▶TEACH 教书◀ [T] *BrE* to teach a particular group of students in a school or college【英】〔在学校〕教授〔某个班级〕: **take sb for sth** *Who takes you for French?* 谁教你们法语?

9 take an exam/test to do an examination or test 参加考试/测验: *I had to take my driving test three times before I passed.* 我参加了三次驾驶考试才通过。

⑤ GET SOMETHING IN YOUR POSSESSION 取得某物

10 ▶STEAL 偷窃◀ [T] to steal something, or borrow something without someone's permission 偷窃〔某物〕;〔未经某人允许〕拿走〔某物〕: *The burglars took most of our jewellery.* 入室窃贼偷走了我们的大多数珠宝。| *She's taken my pen.* 她拿走了我的笔。—see 见 STEAL (USAGE)

11 ▶GET CONTROL 得到控制◀ [T] to get possession or control of something 拥有; 控制〔某物〕: *Enemy forces have taken the airport.* 敌军已经控制了机场。| **take control/charge** Ann

took control of the division last month. 安上个月接管了该部门。

12 ►GET STH 得到某物◄ [T] to get something for yourself 把…据为己有: *Jim took all the credit, even though he hadn't done much of the work.* 吉姆把一切荣誉据为己有，尽管他并未干多少活。

13 take a seat to sit down 坐下

14 take the lead to take the leading position in a race, competition etc〔在比赛、竞赛等中〕领先

15 ►HOLD STH 拿着某物◄ [T] to get hold of something in your hands〔手里〕拿着〔某物〕: *Let me take your jacket.* 把你的夹克给我。| *She took my arm as we walked down the street.* 我们沿街走着时，她挽着我的手臂。

⑥ TAKE PART 参加

16 take part to do an activity, sport etc with other people 参加〔活动、体育运动等〕: *Greg was too sick to take part.* 格雷格病得太重，没法参加。| **take part in sth** *She was invited to take part in a TV debate.* 她被邀请参加一场电视辩论。

⑦ TAKE PLACE 发生

17 take place if an event takes place, it happens〔某一事件〕发生; 举行: *The contest takes place every four years.* 该赛事每四年举行一次。| *We don't know exactly what took place, but they both looked furious afterward.* 我们不知道到底出了什么事，但他们俩事后都是一脸愠怒。—see 见 OCCUR (USAGE)

⑧ ACCEPT SOMETHING 接受某物

18 a) [T] to accept something that someone offers you 接受〔某人给的东西〕: *If I were you I'd take the job.* 我要是你的话，我会接受聘请的。| **take it or leave it** *spoken* (=used to say that your offer will not change)【口】要不要随你的便: *I'll give you £50 – take it or leave it.* 我给你 50 英镑 —— 要不要随你的便。| **take sb's advice** *I took your advice and went to the doctor's.* 我听从了你的建议，去看过医生。**b)** [T not in progressive 不用进行时] to be willing to accept that something is true and correct 乐意接受; 相信…是真的/正确的: *I refuse to take the blame.* 我拒绝接受对我的指责。| *Do they take credit cards in this shop?* 这家商店接受信用卡吗? | **take sb's word for it** (=accept that what someone says is true) 相信某人说的是真的 *Don't take my word for it if you don't want – go back and see for yourself!* 如果你不乐意，就别信我的话 —— 回去自己看看去吧!

19 take sth as read to accept that something is correct because you have no other choice〔因别无选择而〕相信…是不会错的: *We can take it as read that Judith will want to come.* 朱迪思会希望来，我们可以肯定这是不会错的。

20 ►ACCEPT STH UNPLEASANT 接受令人不快的事◄ [T] *informal* to accept an unpleasant situation or someone's unpleasant behaviour without becoming upset【非正式】容忍，忍受: *I can't take any more of his lies and deceit.* 我再也无法忍受他的谎言和欺骗了。| *Steve's tough – He can take it.* 史蒂夫很坚强 —— 他能承受此事。| **hard to take** *All this uncertainty is really very hard to take.* 这种种患得患失的心情实在难以忍受。

Frequencies of the verb **take** in spoken and written English
动词 take 在英语口语和书面语中的使用频率

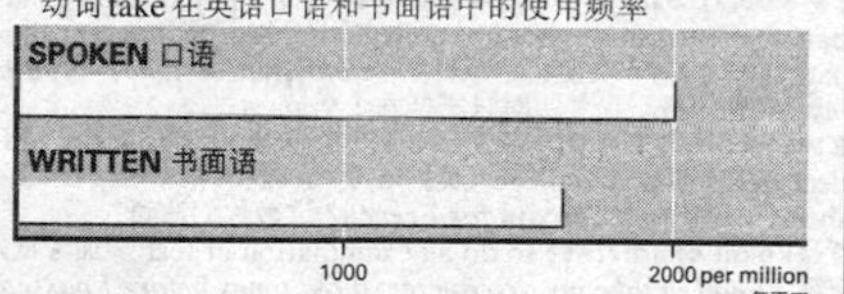

Based on the British National Corpus and the Longman Lancaster Corpus
据英国国家语料库和朗文兰开斯特语料库

This graph shows that the verb **take** is more common in spoken English than in written English. This is because it is used in some common spoken phrases. These are shown in the section marked SPOKEN PHRASES. 本图表显示，动词 take 在英语口语中的使用频率高于书面语，因为该词用于一些常用口语短语中。这些短语出现在标有"SPOKEN PHRASES 口语短语"的部分。

21 ►SUFFER STH 忍受某事◄ [T] to experience something unpleasant because you cannot avoid it 不得已而接受; 忍受: *Staff have agreed to take a 2% pay cut.* 员工已经同意接受削减 2% 的薪水。

⑨ SPOKEN PHRASES 口语短语

22 take sb/sth (for example) used when you want to give an example of something you have just been talking about 以某人/某事为例; 举例说明: *You don't need loads of qualifications – take me for example, I failed my exams, but still found a job.* 你不需要具备许多资格证书 —— 以我为例，我考试没有过关，但还是找到了一份工作。

23 I take it (that) used to say that you expect someone will do something, know something etc 我想; 我认为: *I take it you've heard that Rick's resigned.* 我想你已听说里克辞职了。

24 I take your point used when you are accepting that what someone has said is true 我同意你的观点; 我相信〔你的话是正确的〕: *Mr Chairman, I take your point, but I also support Mr Baxter's view.* 主席先生，我同意你的说法，但我也支持巴克斯特先生的观点。

25 take it from me used to persuade someone that what you are saying is true 请相信我的话，我敢担保: *Ken won't last long in this job, take it from me.* 这项工作，肯不会干长的，相信我的话吧。

26 take a hike *especially AmE* used to tell someone to go away【尤美】叫〔某人〕离开: *Look, Buddy, I'm tired of your mouth. Why don't you take a hike.* 瞧! 老兄，我对你的话已经厌烦了。你还是走人吧。

27 it takes all sorts (to make a world) used to show that you think what someone is doing, likes etc is very strange 世上什么人都有; 大千世界无奇不有

28 what do you take me for? used when someone has suggested you would do something and you want to say you would not do anything like that 你把我当什么人看了?: *I won't tell her the secret – what do you take me for?* 我不会把这秘密告诉她的 —— 你把我当什么人看了?

⑩ OTHER MEANINGS 其他意思

29 ►NUMBERS 数字◄ [T] to subtract one number from another number 从…中减去: **take something from** *Take four from nine and what do you get?* 九减去四，结果是多少?

30 ►HAVE SPACE FOR 给…留有空地◄ [T not in progressive or passive 不用进行时或被动态] to have only enough space to contain a particular amount of something, or a particular number of things 能装下，能盛下，能容纳: *The car takes five people.* 这辆车能装五个人。| *The shelf won't take any more books.* 书架上再也摆不下书了。

31 ►MEDICINE/DRUG 药，药品/毒品◄ [T] to take a drug into your body 服〔药〕，吃〔药〕: *Do you want to take an aspirin for your headache?* 你头痛，要吃一片阿斯匹林吗? | **take drugs** (=take illegal drugs) 吸毒

32 take sides to support one person more than another person in an argument〔在辩论中〕支持，偏袒〔某一方〕: *You always take sides with Maggie without even listening to me!* 你总是偏袒玛吉，根本不听我的!

33 be taken with/by to be attracted by a particular idea, plan or person 被吸引住，被迷住: *I'm quite taken by the idea of Christmas in Berlin.* 我完全被这个在柏林过圣诞节的想法所吸引。

34 be taken ill/sick etc to suddenly become ill 突然病倒

35 ►SEX 性◄ [T] *literary* if a man takes a woman, he has sex with her【文】和〔妇女〕发生性行为

36 ►EAT/DRINK 吃/喝◄ [T] used in some phrases meaning to eat or drink something 吃; 喝〔用于某些短语中〕: **do you take sugar** (=do you take sugar in your tea or coffee) 你〔喝茶或喝咖啡时〕加糖吗?

37 ►TAXI/BUS/TRAIN ETC 出租车/公共汽车/火车等◄ [T] to go somewhere by taxi, bus, or train 乘坐〔出租车、公共汽车或火车〕: *We were too exhausted to walk so we took the bus.* 我们累得实在走不动了，所以改乘公共汽车。

38 ►FEELINGS 感觉◄ [T] to have or experience a particular feeling, used in some phrases〔用于某些短语中，表示一种特定的感觉〕: *Lin takes no interest in her work.* 林对自己的工作毫无兴趣。| **take pity on** (=help someone that you feel pity for) 同情，可怜 *that nice young man who took pity on me and helped me with my bags* 那个同情我、帮我拿包的好小伙子 | **take offence** (=feel offended by something) 觉得被冒犯了 *Don't take offence. Roger says things like that to everybody.* 不要见怪，罗杰跟谁说话都是那样的。

39 take a picture/photograph to photograph someone or

something 给…拍照: [+of] *I took several pictures of the cottage we stayed in.* 我给我们住宿过的那间小农舍拍摄了好些照片。

40 ▶WRITE 写◀ [T] to write down information that you have just been given 把〔刚刚得知的情况〕写下, 记下: *Don't let me forget to take your address before you leave.* 你离开前别忘了给我留下地址。| *It might be a good idea to take notes during the lecture.* 听讲座时记笔记, 或许是个好办法。

41 take sth seriously/lightly to consider someone or something in a particular way 认真地/不当回事地对待某人或某事: *It's not the kind of comment you take lightly, is it?* 不是能掉以轻心的那一类评论, 是吗? | *I always take you seriously, don't I?* 我总是很认真地对待你, 不是吗?

42 take sth well/badly to react well or badly when you find something out 对某事作出好/不好的反应: *"How did she take it when you told her?" "Er, not too well."* "你告诉她时, 她有什么反应?" "呃, 反应不是很好。"

43 ▶TEST/MEASURE STH 测试/测量某物◀ [T] to test or measure something 测试; 测量〔某物〕: *He took my temperature and blood pressure.* 他测量了我的体温和血压。

44 take sth to bits/pieces to divide something into its separate parts 拆开; 分解: *We had to take the radio to pieces to find out what was wrong with it.* 我们只好把收音机拆开, 以搞清楚里面究竟出了什么故障。

45 take a bend/fence/corner etc [T] to try to get over or around something in a particular way 转过弯道/栅栏/角落等: *We took the bend at over 60 and lost control.* 我们以六十多英里的时速转弯, 结果失去了控制。

46 ▶SIZE 尺寸, 型号◀ [T] to wear a particular size of clothes or shoes 穿…尺寸[号码]的衣服[鞋子]: *I take size 6 shoes.* 我穿6码的鞋。

47 ▶STH WORKS 某物起作用◀ [I] if a DYE (=colouring substance) or INJECTION (=medicine) takes, it is successful〔染料或注射的药物等〕起了作用, 有了效果

⑪ PHRASAL VERBS 短语动词

take aback *phr v* [T] **be taken aback** to be very surprised about something 对…吃惊: *He seemed quite taken aback by the news.* 他好像对这一消息十分惊讶。

take after sb *phr v* [T not in progressive 不用进行时] to look or behave like an older relative〔在外貌、行为等方面〕与〔某个长辈〕相像: *Jenni really takes after her mother.* 珍妮真的长得很像自己的母亲。

take sb/sth **apart** *phr v* [T] **1** to separate something into pieces; DISMANTLE 拆开, 拆卸 **2 a)** to beat someone very easily in a game or sport〔比赛中〕把…打得一败涂地 **b)** to criticize someone very strongly 严厉批评; 把…驳得体无完肤

take away from sth *phr v* [T] to harm the good effect or success of something; DETRACT 减损; 贬低: *We won't allow a few troublemakers to take away from our enjoyment of the occasion.* 我们不会允许几个制造麻烦的人影响我们在这次活动中获得的乐趣。

take back *phr v* [T] **1** [**take** sth ↔ **back**] to admit that you were wrong to say something 收回〔说错的话〕: *I'm sorry I was rude, I take it all back.* 对不起, 我太粗鲁了, 我收回我说过的所有话。**2** [**take** sth ↔ **back**] to take something you have bought back to a shop because it is not suitable 退回〔从商店里购买的货物〕: *If the shirt doesn't fit, take it back.* 如果这件衬衣不合身, 就拿回来退货吧。**3** [**take** sb **back**] to make you remember a time in the past 使回忆起: *Seeing those old pictures really took me back.* 看到那些老照片, 真的使我想起了过去。

take sth ↔ **down** *phr v* [T] **1** to separate a large structure or machine into pieces 把〔大件物品或机器〕拆开, 拆卸: *They're taking the scaffolding down next week.* 他们下周要把脚手架拆除。**2** to write something down 写下, 记下: *Let me take down your name and number.* 让我记下你的名字和号码。**3** to lower your trousers, shorts (SHORT³ (2)) etc without actually removing them 褪下〔裤子等, 但不脱掉〕

take in *phr v* [T]

1 ▶PERSON 人◀ [**take** sb ↔ **in**] to let someone stay in your house, especially because they have nowhere else to stay 收留, 收容, 收养: *Brett's always taking in stray animals.* 布雷特总是收养那些走失的动物。

2 ▶INCLUDE 包括◀ [**take** sth ↔ **in**] if a price or cost takes in something it includes it〔价格或成本里〕包括: *This price takes in the cost of all the accommodation and food.* 这个价格包括了食宿等一切费用。

3 take in a movie/show etc *AmE* to go to see a film, play etc【美】观看电影/戏剧等

4 ▶CLOTHES 衣服◀ [**take** sth ↔ **in**] to make a piece of clothing narrower so that it fits you 改小〔衣服〕—opposite 反义词 **let out** (4) (LET¹)

5 ▶UNDERSTAND/REMEMBER STH 理解/记住某事◀ [**take** sth ↔ **in**] to understand and remember new facts and information 领会, 理解; 记住: *I told Grandpa we were going away, but I don't think he took it in.* 我告诉爷爷我们要走了, 但我认为他并没把话听进去。

6 be taken in to be completely deceived by someone so that you believe a lie 被骗: *Don't be taken in by products claiming to help you lose weight in a week.* 不要被那些声称在一周内会帮你减肥的产品给骗了。

take off 脱去〔衣服〕; 〔飞机〕起飞

He took his coat off. 他脱去了外衣。

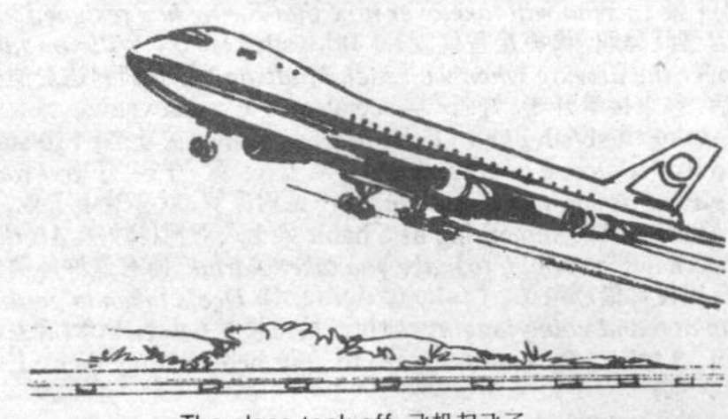

The plane took off. 飞机起飞了。

take off *phr v*

1 ▶REMOVE STH 除掉某物◀ [T **take** sth ↔ **off**] to remove something, especially a piece of clothing 脱下, 脱去〔尤指衣服〕: *Take your coat off.* 脱掉你的外衣。| *I forgot to take off my make-up last night.* 我昨天晚上忘了卸妆。—opposite 反义词 **put on**

2 ▶AIRCRAFT/SPACECRAFT 飞机/航天器◀ [I] to rise into the air at the beginning of a flight 起飞: *As the plane was taking off, I remembered I hadn't turned the iron off.* 飞机起飞时, 我才想起我没有给熨斗断电。

3 ▶COPY SB 模仿某人◀ [T **take** sb ↔ **off**] *informal* to copy the way someone speaks or behaves, in order to entertain people【非正式】〔为了逗笑而〕模仿〔某人的谈吐举止〕

4 ▶HOLIDAY 假日◀ [T **take** sth **off**] to have a holiday from work on a particular day, or for a particular length of time〔在某日或某段时间〕休假: *I'm taking Thursday off to do some Christmas shopping.* 我星期四要休假, 去买一些圣诞礼物。

5 ▶SUCCESS 成功◀ [I] to suddenly start being successful 突然开始成功; 开始走红: *I hear the business is really taking off.* 我听说生意真的开始兴隆了。

6 ▶LEAVE A PLACE 离开一个地方◀ [I] *informal* to leave somewhere suddenly, especially without telling anyone【非正式】〔尤指不打招呼就〕匆匆离开: *Clare just took off without saying goodbye.* 克莱尔没有道别就离开了。

take on *phr v* [T] **1** [**take** sb **on**] to start to employ someone 开始雇用〔某人〕: *We're taking on 50 new staff this year.* 我们今年要雇用50名新员工。—see 见 HIRE¹ (USAGE) **2** [**take on** sth] to begin to have a particular quality or appearance 开始具有〔某种特征、面貌等〕; 呈现; 露出: *His face took on a worried look.* 他的脸上开始露出焦虑的神情。| *These insects can take on the colour of their surroundings.* 这些昆虫能够呈现出与其

T

周围环境相同的颜色。**3** [**take** sb ↔ **on**] to start an argument or fight with someone 开始和…争吵[斗殴、较量等] **4** [**take** sth ↔ **on**] to agree to do some work or be responsible for something 接受〔工作等〕; 承担〔责任等〕: *I'm worried about Doug, he's taking on too much work. He looks awful.* 我担心道格, 他承担的工作太多了。他的气色很不好。

take out *phr v* [T]

1 ▶**PERSON** 人◀ [T **take** sb **out**] to take someone to a restaurant, cinema, club etc 带〔某人〕出去〔到饭馆、电影院、俱乐部等地〕: *We're taking my folks out for a meal next week.* 下周我们带父母出去吃饭。

2 ▶**GET STH** 获得某物◀ [**take** sth ↔ **out**] to arrange to get something officially, especially from an insurance company or a court of law 正式地获得…; 〔尤指从保险公司或法庭〕领到: *I'm thinking of taking out a life insurance policy.* 我正在考虑买一份人寿保险。| *They've taken out an ad in the local paper.* 他们在当地的报纸上登了一则广告。

3 take it out of sb to make someone feel very tired 使某人筋疲力尽: *Having the flu really takes it out of you!* 患了流感会让你真的觉得浑身没有劲!

4 ▶ **KILL/DESTROY** 杀害/摧毁◀ [**take** sb/sth ↔ **out**] *informal* to kill someone, or destroy something【非正式】杀害〔某人〕; 摧毁〔某物〕: *The building was completely taken out by a bomb.* 那幢大楼被一颗炸弹完全摧毁了。

5 take sb out of themselves to make someone feel less worried about their problems 使某人减少烦恼

take sth **out on** sb *phr v* [T] **take it out on sb** to make someone suffer because you are feeling angry, tired etc 向〔某人〕发泄〔不满等〕; 拿〔某人〕出气: *Don't take it out on me, it's not my fault you've had a bad day.* 别把火发泄到我身上, 你今天不顺心, 又不是我的错。

take over *phr v* [I,T] to take control of something 接管; 接任; 接手: *Who will take over now that Ewing has resigned?* 尤因已经辞职, 谁将接替他呢? | **take** sth ↔ **over** *Will you take over the driving when we reach Madison?* 等我们到达麦迪逊后, 你来接着开车, 好吗? —see also 另见 TAKEOVER

take to sb/sth *phr v* [T not in passive 不用被动态] **1** to start to like someone or something 喜欢上…; 对…产生好感: *I took to Paul as soon as I met him.* 我一见到保罗, 就喜欢上了他。**2** to start doing something as a habit 染上…习惯[嗜好]: *All this bad news is enough to make you take to drink.* 所有这种坏消息足以使你借酒消愁。| **take to doing sth** *Dee's taken to getting up at 6 and going jogging.* 迪伊开始习惯在6点起床, 然后去慢跑。**3 take to your bed** to go to your bed and stay there 上床〔休息〕

take up sth *phr v* [T]

1 ▶**ACTIVITY/SUBJECT** 活动/主题◀ [T **take up** sth] to become interested in a particular activity or subject and spend time doing it 对〔某项活动或主题〕产生兴趣; 开始花时间从事…: *Glenn has taken up pottery.* 格伦已开始喜欢上陶瓷制作。

2 ▶**JOB/RESPONSIBILITY** 工作/责任◀ [**take up** sth] to start a new job or have a new responsibility 开始从事〔一项新的工作〕/开始担当〔一项新的责任〕: *She took up her first teaching post in 1950.* 1950年, 她走上第一个教学岗位。

3 ▶**POSITION** 位置◀ [**take up** sth] to put yourself in a particular position ready for something to happen, or so that you can see better 占好位置以备…: *The runners took up their positions on the starting line.* 赛跑运动员已在起跑线上各就各位。

4 ▶**IDEA/SUGGESTION/SUBJECT** 想法/建议/主题◀ [**take** sth ↔ **up**] to do something about an idea or suggestion that you have been considering 着手处理, 着手进行: *I'm going to take this matter up with my lawyer.* 我将找我的律师着手处理此事。

5 ▶**OFFER** 建议◀ [**take** sth ↔ **up**] to accept an offer or CHALLENGE[1] (1) that someone has made 接受〔建议或挑战〕: *Are you going to take up the challenge of lasting a whole week without arguing?* 坚持一周内不争吵, 你打算接受这一挑战吗?

6 ▶**SPACE/TIME** 空间/时间◀ [**take up** sth] if something takes up a particular amount of time or space it fills it 占去〔时间或空间〕: *Writing the paper took up most of the weekend.* 写那篇论文占去了周末的大半时间。| *Your clutter takes up far too much space.* 你那些乱七八糟的东西占去了太多地方。

7 take up arms to fight a battle using weapons 拿起武器〔去战斗〕

8 take up residence to start living somewhere 开始在〔某地〕安顿下来; 在…定居

9 ▶**CLOTHES** 衣服◀ [**take** sth ↔ **up**] to reduce the length of a skirt or pair of trousers 收短〔裙子或裤子〕

10 ▶**CONTINUE AN ACTIVITY** 继续某项活动◀ [**take** sth ↔ **up**] to continue a story or activity that someone else started, or that you have started but had to stop 继续讲/做; 把…接着进行下去: *I'll take up the story where you left off.* 我将从你停下的地方把这个故事继续讲下去。

take sb **up on** sth *phr v* [T] to accept an invitation that someone has made 接受…邀请: *I'll take you up on that offer of a drink, if it still stands!* 我会接受你的邀请去喝一杯, 如果你说的话还算数!

take up with sb/sth *phr v* [T] **1** to become friendly with someone, especially someone who may influence you badly 开始与…亲密交往〔尤指会有不良影响〕: *Sean's taken up with a bunch of lazy hoods.* 肖恩开始与一群游手好闲的恶棍交往。**2 be taken up with** to be very busy dealing with someone or something 忙于: *Jo's completely taken up with work at the moment.* 乔此刻正全神贯注地工作。

take upon *phr v* [T] **take it upon yourself to do sth** to decide to do something without permission or approval 擅自决定做〔某事〕: *Stefan took it upon himself to sell the car while I was away.* 我不在时斯蒂芬自作主张地把那辆车卖了。

take² *n* [C] **1** the act of a scene for a film or television programme 〔电影或电视节目〕一次拍摄的镜头: *We had to do six takes for this particular scene.* 为了这个场景, 我们不得不拍了六个镜头。**2** [usually singular 一般用单数] the amount of fish or animals caught at one particular time 一次获得的捕鱼量; 捕获量 **3** [usually singular 一般用单数] *informal especially AmE* the amount of money earned by a shop or business in a particular period of time【非正式, 尤美】营业额 **4 be on the take** *informal* to be willing to do something wrong in return for money【非正式】〔愿意〕受贿, 贪赃枉法 **5 sb's take on sth** *AmE informal* someone's opinion about a situation or idea【美, 非正式】某人对某事的观点[立场]: *What's your take on the Middle East issue?* 你对中东问题的立场是什么?

take·a·way /ˈtekəˌwe; ˈteɪkəweɪ/ *n* [C] *BrE*【英】**1** a meal that you buy at a shop or restaurant to eat at home 〔商店或餐馆的〕外卖食品; TAKE-OUT (1) *AmE*【美】: *Let's have a takeaway tonight.* 我们今晚买点东西带回去吃吧。**2** a shop or restaurant that sells meals to be eaten somewhere else 外卖商店; 外卖餐馆; TAKE-OUT (2) *AmE*【美】

take-home pay /ˈ· · ˌ·/ *n* [U] the amount of money that you receive after you have paid tax etc 〔扣除税款等后的〕实得工资

tak·en /ˈtekən; ˈteɪkən/ the past participle of TAKE[1]

take-off /ˈ· ·/ *n* **1** [C,U] the time when a plane or ROCKET rises into the air 〔飞机或火箭的〕起飞, 升空 **2** [C] the act of leaving the ground as you make a jump 起跳 **3** [C] an amusing performance that copies the way someone behaves 〔对某人动作的〕滑稽模仿: *Suzie did a brilliant take-off of the principal.* 苏兹模仿校长的动作, 学得惟妙惟肖。—see also 另见 **take off** (TAKE[1])

take-out /ˈ· ·/ *n* [C] *AmE*【美】**1** a meal that you buy at a shop or restaurant to eat at home 〔商店或餐馆的〕外卖食品; TAKEAWAY (1) *BrE*【英】**2** a shop or restaurant that sells cooked meals to be eaten somewhere else 外卖商店; 外卖餐馆; TAKEAWAY (2) *BrE*【英】

take·o·ver /ˈtekˌovɚ; ˈteɪkˌəʊvə/ *n* [C] **1** the act of getting control of a company by buying most of its shares (SHARE[2] (5)) 购股兼并, 〔通过购买其大部分股票而实现对某企业的〕接管, 接收 | **takeover bid** (=an attempt to get control) 兼并要约, 盘进出价 **2** an act of getting control of a country or political organization, especially by using force 〔尤指通过武力对某国或某政治组织的〕接管, 接收: *the communist takeover in Laos* 共产党接管老挝政权

ta·ker /ˈtekɚ; ˈteɪkə/ *n* [C] **be no/few/not many takers** used to say that no one accepted or wanted something that was offered 〔对某种提供的东西〕没有/很少/不多的接受者: *There have been a few takers so far, but the price is a big obstacle.* 目前已有几个顾客, 但价格是个大的障碍。

take-up /ˈ· ·/ *n* [U] the rate at which people buy or accept something offered by a company, government etc 〔对公司、政策等推出东西的〕认购率; 接受率: *Despite all the advertisements, the take-up has been slow.* 尽管做了那么多广告, 认购率还是很低。

tak·ings /ˈtekɪŋz; ˈteɪkɪŋz/ *n* [plural] the money that a shop gets from selling its goods 〔商店〕收入, 营业额: *Someone broke*

in and stole the day's takings from the safe. 有人入室行窃，把当天的收入从保险柜里偷走了。

Talbot /ˈtɔlbət; ˈtɔːlbət/, **William Henry Fox** (1800-77) a British photographer who was the first to invent a way of making more than one photograph from the same NEGATIVE (=image on a piece of film that shows dark areas as light and light areas as dark) 塔尔博特〔(1800-1877)，英国摄影师。他最早发明了底片，同一底片可冲印多张照片〕

talc /tælk; tælk/ *n* [U] **1** talcum powder 滑石粉，爽身粉 **2** a soft smooth mineral that feels like soap and is used for making paints, plastics, etc〔用来制造颜料、塑料等的〕滑石

tal·cum pow·der /ˈtælkəm ˌpaudɚ; ˈtælkəm ˌpaʊdə/ *n* [U] a fine powder which you put on your skin after washing to make it dry or smell pleasant 滑石粉，爽身粉

[3] **tale** /tel; teɪl/ *n* [C] **1** a story of imaginary events, especially of an exciting kind 故事：*tales of far-off lands* 异国他乡的故事 **2** a spoken description of an event or situation that is often not completely true〔未必完全真实的〕陈述；传说，传闻：*tales of his life in post-war Berlin* 有关他在战后柏林的生活传闻 **3 tell tales** *especially BrE* to tell someone in authority something untrue, unfair, or unpleasant, often because you want to harm someone else【尤英】向上级诬告；搬弄是非；TATTLE *AmE*【美】：*Samantha's been telling tales to the teacher again.* 萨曼莎又在对老师说别人的坏话了。**4 tale of misery/woe** a description of events that made you very unhappy 痛苦的/悲惨的故事 **5 live/survive etc to tell the tale** *humorous* to still be alive after a dangerous or unpleasant event【幽默】〔经历危难后〕活下来/幸存等：*Yes, it's true. I've been to stay at my mother-in-law's and lived to tell the tale.* 是的，是真的。我暂住在我岳母家，总算度过来了。

[3] [3] **tal·ent** /ˈtælənt; ˈtælənt/ *n* **1** [C,U] a special natural ability or skill 天资，天赋；才能：*musical talent* 音乐天赋 | **[+for]** *She showed a talent for acting at an early age.* 她在很小的时候就显示出演戏的天赋。| **a man/woman of many talents** (=someone who has the ability to do several things very well) 一个多才多艺的男人/女人 | **talent contest/show/competition** (=a competition in which people show how well they can sing, dance, tell jokes etc) 新秀选拔赛〔指通过唱歌、跳舞、讲笑话等活动选拔出有演出才能的人〕**2** [U] people who have a special natural ability or skill 有才能的人，天才，才子：**footballing/golfing etc talent** (=people who are good at football, GOLF etc) 足球天才/高尔夫球天才等 *Britain has lost a lot of its footballing talent to clubs abroad.* 英国有许多足球天才流失到了国外的球队。**3** [U] *BrE slang* sexually attractive people【英俚】性感的人，尤物：*There's not much talent round here tonight.* 今晚这里没有多少尤物。

tal·ent·ed /ˈtæləntɪd; ˈtæləntɪ̣d/ *adj* very good at something such as singing, acting, or playing sports 有天资的，有才能的：*a talented actor* 一名很有天赋的演员

talent scout /ˈ· · ·/ *n* [C] someone whose job is to find young people who are good at a sport or activity〔擅长于发掘体育或其他活动人才的〕人才发掘者，新秀物色者〈如球探、星探〉

Tale of a Tub, A a SATIRE by Jonathan Swift about religious EXTREMISM. It tells of three brothers, Peter, who represents the Roman Catholic church; Jack, who represents the extreme Protestants, and Martin, who represents the Anglican church.《一只桶的故事》〔乔纳森·斯威夫特创作的一部讽刺宗教极端主义的作品。故事中有三个兄弟，彼得代表罗马天主教，杰克代表极端的新教徒，马丁代表英国圣公会〕

Tale of Two Cit·ies, A /ˌ· · · ˈ· ·/ (1859) a NOVEL by Charles Dickens, set in London and Paris at the time of the French Revolution. The start of the book is very well known: "It was the best of times, it was the worst of times ...". Another famous part is the thoughts of one of the main characters, Sydney Carton, when he is about to be killed by the GUILLOTINE instead of another man that he is pretending to be, so that the other man can live: "It is a far, far better thing that I do, than I have ever done".《双城记》〔(1859)，查尔斯·狄更斯创作的一部小说。故事发生在法国大革命时期的伦敦和巴黎。小说的开场白很有名："这是最好的年代，这是最糟的年代…"。小说中还有一个著名片段，作为主人公之一的西德尼·卡顿为了保全别人而冒名顶替上了断头台。当时他有一段内心独白："这么做好极了，我平生从未做过这么好的事情"〕

Tal·i·ban, the /ˈtɑlɛˌbɑn; ˈtɑːleˌbɑːn/ *n* [plural] a Muslim group which controlled most of Afghanistan from 1996 to 2001. The Taliban followed the laws of Islam very strictly. 塔利班〔一穆斯林组织。1996至2001年曾控制阿富汗大部分地区，成员严格遵守伊斯兰教规〕

tal·is·man /ˈtɛlɪzmən; ˈtælɪ̣zmən/ *n plural* **talismans** [C] an object that is believed to have magic powers of protection 辟邪物，护身符

[1] [1] **talk[1]** /tɔk; tɔːk/ *v*

1 ▶CONVERSATION 交谈◀ [I] to say things to someone, especially in a conversation 谈话，交谈：**talk to** *Who was that you were talking to at the party?* 晚会上与你说话的那一位是谁？| **talk with** *Bob was talking with a pretty woman from the fire department.* 鲍勃正在与消防部门的一位漂亮女士谈话。| **talk about/of** *We were talking about our childhoods and realized we both went to the same school.* 我们谈起了各自的童年，发现我俩上的是同一所学校。—see 见 SAY[1] (USAGE) | **get talking** (=start having a conversation) 开始交谈 *Once they got talking nothing could stop them.* 他们一开始谈起来，便会没完没了。| **talk sport/politics etc** (=have a conversation about sport etc) 谈论体育/政治等 *I can't stand it when you talk politics.* 你一谈政治，我就受不了。—see 见 SPEAK (USAGE)

2 ▶SERIOUS SUBJECT 严肃话题◀ [I] to discuss something with someone, especially an important or serious subject 讨论；商谈：*We need to talk before things get any worse.* 在事情变得更糟之前，我们需要好好谈一谈。| **talk about/of** *Jenny and I have talked about getting married some day.* 我和珍妮已经谈过了将来结婚的事。| **talk to** *I think I'm going to have to talk to a solicitor.* 我想我必须去跟律师讨论一下。—see also 另见 **talk shop** (SHOP[1] (6))

3 ▶SAY WORDS 说话◀ [I] to produce words in a language 说话：*Most babies start to talk by 18 months.* 大多数婴儿最晚18个月大时开始说话。| *Who would ever believe that computers would be able to talk?* 谁会相信电脑居然会说话？

4 people will talk/people are talking *informal* used to emphasize that people will think you are doing something bad【非正式】人们会说闲话的/人们正在传言：*Don't leave your car outside my house; people will talk.* 别把你的车停在我家外边。人们会说闲话的。

5 ▶SECRET INFORMATION 秘密情报◀ [I] to give someone important secret information because they force you to〔被迫〕说出内情，吐露秘密；招供：*Even after three days of interrogation, Maskell refused to talk.* 即使经过三天的审问，马斯克尔仍然拒不开口。

6 not be talking *informal* if two people are not talking they refuse to talk to each other because they have argued【非正式】〔两人因争吵过而〕互不理睬：*It's been 3 weeks and they're still not talking.* 已经三周了，他俩仍然互不理睬。

7 ▶A SPEECH 演讲◀ [I] to give a speech 演讲；谈论：**talk on/about** *This morning Mrs Elliott will be talking about the best way to cultivate roses.* 今天上午，埃利奥特夫人将介绍种植玫瑰花的最佳方法。

8 talk sense to give sensible opinions about things 说得有理：*He's a little old-fashioned but he talks a lot of sense.* 他的观点有些陈旧，但话都说得很有道理。

9 talk sense into to persuade someone to behave in a sensible way 以道理说服某人，以理服人：*Will you see if you can talk some sense into him – he says he wants to join the army.* 你是否愿意跟他谈一谈，晓以利害 — 他说他要参军。

10 talk your way out of *informal* to escape from an unpleasant or embarrassing situation by giving explanations, excuses etc【非正式】依靠口才使〔自己〕摆脱困境：*I'd like to see you talk your way out of this one!* 我倒想看看你如何凭借自己的口才摆脱这一困境！

11 talk the hind legs off a donkey *informal* to talk a lot, especially about unimportant things【非正式】唠叨个没完没了

12 talk nineteen to the dozen *informal*【非正式】**talk a blue streak** *AmE*【美】to talk very quickly and without stopping 说话滔滔不绝，口若悬河

13 talk turkey *informal AmE* to talk seriously about important things, especially in order to agree on something【非正式，美】〔尤指为了达成某事〕严肃地商谈：*"I'm ready to make a deal." "OK. Let's talk turkey."* "我是有意达成交易的。""好的，我们认真谈谈。"

14 talking point a subject, problem, piece of news etc that many people are interested in〔很多人感兴趣的〕话题，论题

15 talk dirty *informal* to talk in a sexual way to someone in order to make them feel sexually excited【非正式】说下流话〔以使某人性兴奋〕

16 talk tough *informal* to tell people very strongly what you want from them【非正式】说话口气强硬

17 be talking through your hat *informal* to say silly or stupid things about something that you think you know a lot about【非正式】信口开河，胡说八道

Frequencies of the verb **talk** in spoken and written English
动词 talk 在英语口语和书面语中的使用频率

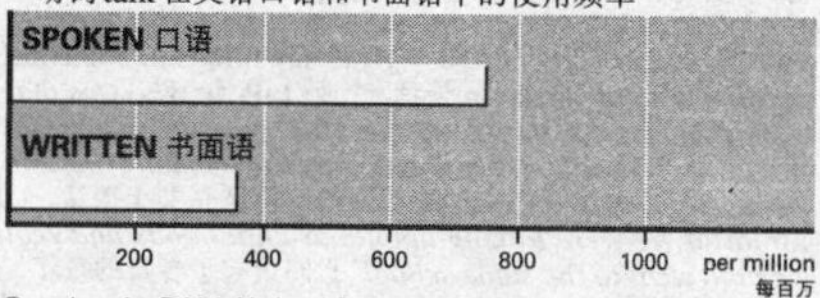

Based on the British National Corpus and the Longman Lancaster Corpus
据英国国家语料库和朗文兰开斯特语料库

This graph shows that the verb **talk** is much more common in spoken English than in written English. This is because it is used in a lot of common spoken phrases. 本图表显示，动词 talk 在英语口语中的使用频率远远高于书面语，因为口语中很多常用短语是由 talk 构成的。

talk (*v*) SPOKEN PHRASES
含 talk 的口语短语

18 what are you talking about? a) used when the person you are talking to has just said something stupid or annoying 你(们)在说些什么?〔用来指对方说的话显得愚蠢或令人恼怒〕: *"I'm sorry – I didn't do the report because my cat hurt his paw." "What on earth are you talking about?"* "对不起，我没有准备好那份报告，因为我的猫伤了爪子。""你到底在说些什么?" **b)** used to ask someone what their conversation is about 你(们)在说些什么?〔用来问对方谈论的话题〕
19 know what you are talking about to know a lot about a particular subject 对某一方面很了解，是行家: *I worked in hotels for years, so I know what I'm talking about.* 我在酒店工作过多年，所以我对这一行很了解。
20 talk about rich/funny/stupid etc used to emphasize that the person or thing you are talking about is very rich, funny, stupid etc 说到富有/可笑/愚蠢等〔用来强调所谈论的人或物很富有、可笑、愚蠢等〕: *Talk about luck! That's the second competition he's won in a week!* 说到运气！这可是一周内他赢的第二次比赛！
21 talking of/about used to say more about a subject that someone has just mentioned 谈到，论及〔用来承接刚才的话题〕: *Talking of Venice, have you seen the masks I bought there last year?* 谈到威尼斯，你见过我去年在那儿买的那些面具吗?
22 now you're talking used when you think someone's suggestion is a very good idea 你这话说得对了，太对了，正合我意: *"We could go for a pizza instead." "Now you're talking."* "我们可以改吃比萨饼。""正合我意!"
23 look who's talking/you're a fine one to talk/ you can talk used to tell someone they should not criticize someone else because they are just as bad 亏你有脸说别人〔意即你没资格批评别人，你同别人一样糟糕〕: *"Peggy shouldn't smoke so much." "Look who's talking!"* "佩姬不应该抽那么多烟。""你还有资格说别人!"
24 we're/you're talking (about) a) used to tell someone what will be necessary in order to do or get what they are asking you about 我们/你们需要〔用来告知对方为了满足要求需要付出…〕: *If you want the job done properly you're talking £10,000 at least.* 如果你想妥善处理此事，你至少需要付出 10,000 英镑。 **b)** used to explain something about a person or thing that is being discussed 我们/你们正在谈论的是…〔用来解释正在讨论中的某人或某事〕: *Don't forget, we're talking about a country where millions are starving.* 别忘了，我们正在谈论的是一个有几百万人在挨饿的国家。
25 don't talk rubbish/nonsense/crap etc *especially BrE* used to tell someone that what they are saying is silly and completely wrong【尤英】别说傻话，别胡说八道了: *The best goalkeeper in England! Him? Oh, don't talk rubbish!* 英格兰最优秀的守门员！就他？噢，别胡说八道了!
26 I'm talking to you! used when you are angry because the person you are talking to is not paying attention to you 我在跟你说话!〔用来表示你因对方未注意你说话而生气〕: *Hey! I'm talking to you! Look at me!* 嘿！我在跟你说话呢！看着我!

talk around *phr v* [T] **1** [**talk** sb ↔ **around**] to persuade someone to change their opinion and agree with you 说服〔某人〕改变主意: *Leave Betty to me. I'll soon talk her around.* 把贝蒂交给我吧。我会很快让她改变主意的。**2 talk around sth** to discuss a problem without really dealing with the important parts of it 不着边际地谈某事; 不得要领地谈某事

talk back *phr v* [I] to answer someone rudely after they have criticized you or told you to do something 回嘴，顶嘴: *I'd never let a child of mine talk back to me like that!* 我绝不允许我的孩子这样跟我顶嘴!

talk sb/sth ↔ **down** *phr v* [T] **1** to give instructions on a radio to a PILOT[1] (1) so that they can bring an aircraft safely to the ground〔通过无线电跟飞行员通话以〕引导〔飞机〕安全着陆 **2** to make something that is successful or good seem worse than it really is 以言辞贬损; 贬低…: *It's just like the Labour Party to talk down the achievements of the health service reforms.* 工党就是这样，喜欢贬低公共医疗保健改革的成就。**3** to persuade someone to come down from a high place when they are threatening to jump and kill themselves 说服〔想从高处跳下自杀的人〕下来

talk down to sb *phr v* [T] to talk to someone as if they were stupid when in fact they are not; PATRONIZE 以高人一等的口气对〔某人〕说话: *You have to realize that kids aren't stupid; they know when they're being talked down to.* 你必须注意到孩子们并不傻; 他们知道什么时候你在用居高临下的口气跟他们讲话。

talk sb **into** sth *phr v* [T] to persuade someone to do something 说服〔某人〕做〔某事〕: *She didn't want to come, but I talked her into it.* 她并不想来，不过我把她说服了。| **talk sb into doing sth** *Try to talk Liz into buying a ticket.* 尽量说服莉兹买一张票吧。

talk sth ↔ **out** *phr v* [T] *informal* to talk about a problem in order to solve it【非正式】通过商谈解决〔问题〕: *We need to spend a little time talking it out.* 我们需要花点时间谈谈，以解决这件事。

talk sb **out of** sth *phr v* [T] *informal* to persuade someone not to do something【非正式】说服〔某人〕不去做〔某事〕: *Stuart was threatening legal action but I think his sister talked him out of it.* 斯图尔特威胁说要采取法律行动，不过我想他姐姐已说服他不这样做了。| **talk sb out of doing sth** *Can't you talk them out of selling the house?* 难道你不能说服他们不要卖掉那幢房子?

talk sth ↔ **over** *phr v* [T] to discuss a problem or situation with someone before you decide what to do〔在作出决定前与某人〕商量，讨论: *Don't worry, we have plenty of time to talk it over.* 别担心，我们有足够的时间好好商量一下。| [**+with**] *Well obviously I wanted to talk it over with you first.* 当然啦，我首先要与你就此事认真地谈一谈。

talk sth ↔ **through** *phr v* [T] to discuss all of something so that you are sure you understand it 把〔某事〕彻底说清楚: *I think we really need to talk this one through – there are so many things that could go wrong.* 我想我们真的有必要把这件事情说清楚 —— 可能出错的地方有许多。

talk² *n* S1 W1

1 ▶**CONVERSATION** 交谈◀ [C] a conversation 交谈: [**+with/about**] *After a long talk, we decided to stop seeing each other.* 经过一次长谈之后，我们决定不再见面。| **have a talk** *Listen John, you're going to have a talk with Marty.* 听着，约翰，你必须跟马蒂谈一谈。
2 ▶**A SPEECH** 讲话◀ [C+**about/on**] a speech or LECTURE[1] (1) 讲话，演讲; 讲座，报告: *a series of talks about literary theory* 关于文学理论的系列讲座 | **give a talk** *Dr. Howard is giving a talk on homeopathy today.* 霍华德博士今天要作一次关于顺势疗法的报告。
3 ▶**DISCUSSION** 讨论◀ **talks** [plural] formally organized discussions between governments, organizations etc〔政府、机构等之间的〕正式会谈; 谈判: *Peace talks* 和平谈判 | *Talks with the rebels have failed yet again.* 与叛军的谈判再次破裂了。
4 ▶**TYPE OF CONVERSATION** 说话的方式◀ [U] type of conversation 说话的方式: *Some people would say that kind of talk was treason!* 有些人会说，那种讲话的口吻简直就是叛国! | **girls' talk/football talk/fighting talk etc** *All this football talk bores me stiff!* 全是足球行话，烦死我啦!
5 be all talk *spoken* to always be talking about what you have done or what you are going to do without ever actually doing anything【口】说空话，空谈: *Don't be scared of Jake. He's all talk!* 别害怕杰克，他全是放空炮!
6 be the talk of the town/company etc to be the person or thing that everyone is talking about because they are very interested, excited, shocked etc 街谈巷议的话题; 众人的谈资: *Tim's been the talk of the department since his affair with Janice.* 蒂姆自从和贾尼丝有了暧昧关系之后，成了整个部门的谈资。
7 just talk/only talk *informal* a story, claim etc that is just talk or only talk is very likely to be untrue【非正式】闲话; 流言飞语:

Everyone says he was a spy but if you ask me it's just talk. 人人都说他曾当过间谍，但如果要我说的话，那不过是流言飞语。 **8 there's talk of** used to say that a lot of people are talking about something that might happen in the future 有…的传闻[传言]:*There's talk of more factory closures in the area.* 有传言说本地区有更多的工厂将关闭。—see also 另见 SMALL TALK, SWEET-TALK

talk·a·tive /ˈtɔkətɪv; ˈtɔːkətɪv/ *adj* liking to talk a lot 爱说话的，健谈的，多嘴的 —**talkativeness** *n* [U]

talk·er /ˈtɔkɚ; ˈtɔːkə/ *n* [C] *informal* someone who talks a lot or talks in a particular way【非正式】健谈的人；以某种方式说话的人：*What a talker that man is!* 那家伙真是一个会讲话的人！| *We need a persuasive talker and a good organizer.* 我们需要一个会做说服工作的人和一个优秀的组织者。

talk·ie /ˈtɔkɪ; ˈtɔːki/ *n* [C] *old-fashioned* a cinema film with sounds and words【过时】有声电影 —see 见 SILENT (4)

talking book /ˌ.. ˈ./ *n* [C] a book that has been recorded for blind people to listen to〔供盲人使用的〕有声读物

talking head /ˌ.. ˈ./ *n* [C] *informal* someone on television who talks directly to the camera, for example when reading the news【非正式】〔出现在电视屏幕上面对摄像机〕说话的人〈例如新闻播音员〉

talking-to /ˈ.. ./ *n* **give sb a talking-to** *informal* to talk to someone angrily because you are annoyed about something they have done【非正式】申斥，责骂；给〔某人〕一顿教训：*If you ask me, what that girl needs is a good talking-to.* 要是问我的话，那姑娘需要狠狠地训一顿。

talk show /ˈ. ./ *n* [C] *AmE* a radio or television show on which famous people talk to each other and are asked questions【美】〔广播或电视上的〕名人访谈节目，脱口秀；CHAT SHOW *BrE*【英】

2 2 **tall** /tɔl; tɔːl/ *adj* **1** a person, building, tree etc that is tall has a greater than average height〔人、楼、树等〕高于一般的；高大的：**6 ft/2 metres etc tall** *I'm only five feet tall.* 我只有5英尺高。—see 见 HIGH[1] (USAGE) —see picture at 参见 HIGH[1] 图 **2** *AmE* a tall drink has a small amount of alcohol mixed with a large amount of a non-alcoholic drink and is served in a tall glass【美】〔含少量酒精的饮料〕一大杯的 **3 be a tall order** *informal* if a request or piece of work is a tall order, it will be almost impossible for you to do【非正式】极难办成的；很难做到的：*Fixed by Monday? That's a tall order.* 星期一之前修好？那可很难办到。**4 tall story** *BrE*【英】, **tall tale** *AmE*【美】a story that is difficult to believe, because it makes events seem more exciting, dangerous etc than they really were 荒诞的故事；难以置信的事：*Jim was full of tall stories about his travels.* 吉姆爱说旅行中碰见的荒诞不经的事。—see also 另见 **stand tall** (STAND[1] (32)), **walk tall** (WALK[1] (9)) —**tallness** *n* [U]

Tallahassee /ˌtæləˈhæsɪ; ˌtæləˈhæsi/ the capital city of the US state of Florida 塔拉哈西〔美国佛罗里达州首府〕

tall·boy /ˈtɔlˌbɔɪ; ˈtɔːlbɔɪ/ *n* [C] *BrE* a tall piece of wooden furniture containing several drawers【英】〔带有好几层抽屉的〕高脚橱柜；HIGHBOY *AmE*【美】

Tallinn /ˈtælɪn; ˈtælɪn/ the capital and largest city of Estonia. It is a port and its most important industries are fishing and making electrical goods. 塔林〔爱沙尼亚共和国首都，该国最大城市，为一港口。最重要的产业为捕鱼业和电气制造业〕

tal·low /ˈtælo; ˈtæləʊ/ *n* [U] hard animal fat used for making CANDLES〔用于制造蜡烛的〕硬动物脂肪

tal·ly[1] /ˈtælɪ; ˈtæli/ *n plural* **tallies** [C] **1** a record of how much you have spent, won, obtained etc so far〔花费的〕账目；〔比赛等活动中赢得的〕积分，得分：*England's tally at the moment is 15 points.* 英格兰队目前的积分是15分。| **keep a tally** (=write down or remember) 记录〔账单等〕**2** a special stick that was used in the past to show an amount of money owed, a quantity of goods delivered etc〔旧时用来记录欠款、交货数量等的〕记事木签，符木

tally[2] *v* **tallied, tallying 1** [I] if numbers or statements tally, they match each other exactly 符合；〔完全〕吻合：*If the figures don't quite tally you might be missing an invoice.* 如果数目不完全吻合，可能是你遗漏了一张发票。| **tally with** *Your account of the accident doesn't tally with the facts.* 你对这次事故的描述与事实不完全一致。**2** also 又作 **tally up** [T] to calculate the total number of points won, things done etc 计算〔得分、总数等〕

Tal·mud /ˈtælmʊd; ˈtælmʊd/ *n* **the Talmud** the collection of writings that make up Jewish law about religious and non-religious life《塔木德经》〔规范犹太人宗教及世俗生活的法典〕

tal·on /ˈtælən; ˈtælən/ *n* [C] a sharp powerful curved nail on the feet of some birds that catch animals for food〔某些鸟强有力的〕利爪

tam·a·rind /ˈtæmərɪnd; ˈtæmərənd/ *n* [C] a tropical tree, or the fruit of this tree 罗望子〔一种热带树木〕；罗望子的果实

Tam·bo /ˈtæmbo; ˈtæmbəʊ/, **Ol·i·ver** /ˈɑləvɚ; ˈɒləvə/ (1917-93) a South African NATIONALIST politician, president of the ANC from 1977-90 坦博〔(1917-1993)，南非民族主义政治家，1977至1990年任非洲人国民大会主席〕

tam·bour /ˈtæmbʊr; ˈtæmbʊə/ *n* [C] a circular wooden frame used to hold cloth firmly in place while patterns are being sewn (SEW) on to it; EMBROIDERY HOOP〔刺绣用的〕绷圈，圆形绷架

tam·bou·rine /ˌtæmbəˈrin; ˌtæmbəˈriːn/ *n* [C] a circular musical instrument with small pieces of metal around the edge that makes a sound when you shake it〔鼓边四周装有小金属片，一摇便发出声响的〕铃鼓

tame[1] /tem; teɪm/ *adj* **1** *informal* boring or unexciting and disappointing【非正式】平淡的；枯燥乏味的；令人失望的：*After all that hype, the film was a bit tame.* 经过铺天盖地的一阵宣传，那部电影还是怪没劲的。**2** an animal that is tame has been trained to live with people〔动物〕驯服的；由人驯养的 —**tamely** *adv* —**tameness** *n* [U]

tame[2] *v* [T] **1** to reduce the power or strength of something and prevent it from causing trouble 制服，控制；驾驭：*Over the years, a series of dams has tamed the might of the Colorado river.* 多年来通过一系列大坝的修建，把科罗拉多河的凶猛给制服了。**2** to train a wild animal to obey you and not to attack people 驯服〔野生动物〕，使驯化 —compare 比较 DOMESTICATE

Tamil Na·du /ˌtæmɪl nɑˈdu; ˌtæmɪl nɑːˈduː/ a state in southeast India, formerly called **Madras State**, whose capital and largest city is Chennai, formerly called Madras 泰米尔纳德邦〔印度东南部一邦，旧称马德拉斯邦。首府和最大城市是清奈，旧称马德拉斯〕

Tamil Ti·gers, the /ˌ.. ˈ../ a group of fighters who support a separate state for the Tamil Hindu people of Sri Lanka 泰米尔猛虎组织〔斯里兰卡一反政府武装组织，主张建立一个信奉印度教的泰米尔人独立国家〕

Taming of the Shrew, The /ˌ.. . . ˈ./ a humorous play by William Shakespeare about a woman called Kate. Kate is very honest and always tells people exactly what she thinks, and because of this some people think she is rude and unpleasant. But she eventually begins to behave like a quiet and OBEDIENT wife when Petruchio marries her.《驯悍记》〔威廉·莎士比亚的一部喜剧。剧中有一个名叫凯特的女人，为人十分诚实，总是想到什么就说什么。有些人因此认为她这个女人粗鲁而讨人嫌。后来，彼德鲁乔娶了她，她成了文静温顺的好妻子〕

tam-o'-shan·ter /ˌtæm ə ˈʃæntɚ; ˌtæm ə ˈʃæntə/ also 又作 **tam·my** /ˈtæmɪ; ˈtæmi/ *n* [C] a Scottish cap, usually made of wool, with a POMPOM (=small wool ball) in the centre 苏格兰式便帽〔一般用羊毛制成，帽顶中央有一小绒球〕

Tam O'Shanter /ˌtæm əˈʃæntɚ; ˌtæm əˈʃæntə/ (1791) a long, humorous poem by Robert Burns, which tells the frightening story of a farmer called Tam O'Shanter who is chased by WITCHes (=women with magic powers)《汤姆·奥桑特》〔(1791)，罗伯特·彭斯的一首幽默长诗，讲述农夫汤姆·奥桑特被一群女巫追赶的恐怖故事〕

tamp /tæmp; tæmp/ *v* [T always+adv/prep] also 又作 **tamp down** to press or push something down by lightly hitting it several times 压实；拍打…使坚实：*"Ah well," sighed Papa, absently tamping the tobacco down in his pipe.* "噢，是的。"爸爸一边叹气，一边心不在焉地把烟斗里的烟叶装实。

Tam·pa /ˈtæmpə; ˈtæmpə/ a city, port, and holiday RESORT in western Florida in the US 坦帕〔美国佛罗里达州西部一港口城市和度假胜地〕

Tam·pax /ˈtæmpæks; ˈtæmpæks/ *n plural* **Tampax** [C] *trademark* the name of a very common type of TAMPON【商标】丹碧丝〔一种常用的月经棉塞〕

tam·per /ˈtæmpɚ; ˈtæmpə/ *v*

tamper with sth *phr v* [T] to touch something or make changes to it without permission, especially in order to deliberately damage it 胡乱摆弄；擅自篡改；故意损坏：*How likely is it that the drugs could have been tampered with?* 药品的成分被人擅自改变，有多大可能呢？| *They just don't see the point in tampering with a system that's worked fine so far.* 他们不理解为什么要去破坏一套迄今一直运行不错的系统。

tamper-ev·i·dent /ˈ.. ˌ.../ *adj BrE* a package or container that is tamper-evident is made so that you can see if someone has opened it before it is sold in the shops【英】商品包装拆封后易于被识别的；TAMPER-RESISTANT *AmE*【美】

tamper-proof /ˈ.. ./ *adj* a package or container that is tamper-proof is made in a way that prevents someone opening it before it is sold〔商品包装〕防拆封的，防撕扯封条的

tamper-re·sist·ant /ˈ· · ˌ· ˈ·/ *adj AmE* TAMPER-EVIDENT【美】商品包装拆封后易于被识别的

tam·pon /ˈtæmpɑn; ˈtæmpɒn/ *n* [C] a tube-shaped mass of cotton or similar material that a woman puts inside her VAGINA during her PERIOD〔妇女用的〕月经棉塞

tan[1] /tæn; tæn/ *v* **tanned, tanning 1** [I] if you tan, your skin becomes darker because you spend time in the sun〔皮肤〕晒黑: *People with fair skin usually don't tan very easily.* 皮肤白皙的人通常不容易晒得很黑。**2** [T] if the sun tans you, it makes your skin become darker 使〔皮肤〕晒黑 **3** [T] to make animal skin into leather by treating it with TANNIN (=a kind of acid) 用鞣酸将〔兽皮〕制成皮革 **4 tan sb's hide** *old-fashioned* to hit someone a lot, as a punishment【过时】把某人狠揍一顿 —**tan** *adj AmE*【美】: *Did you see Lizzie? She's so tan!* 你看到莉齐了吗？她晒得真黑！

tan[2] *n* **1** [U] a light yellowish brown colour 棕黄色，黄褐色: *tan shoes* 棕黄色的鞋 —see picture on page A5 参见 A5 页图 **2** [C] the brown colour that someone with pale skin gets after they have been in the sun; SUNTAN〔被太阳晒成的〕棕褐色肤色: *I wish I could get a tan like that.* 但愿我能晒成那样的棕褐色肤色。**3** [C] an abbreviation of 缩写= TANGENT (3)

tan·dem /ˈtændəm; ˈtændəm/ *n* [C] **1** a bicycle built for two riders sitting one behind the other〔两人一前一后同骑的〕双人自行车 **2 in tandem with** happening at the same time 同时发生: *Hastings' appointment in tandem with McDougan's should improve our sales expertise.* 黑斯廷斯和麦克道根的同时就任应该使我们的销售水平得到提高。**3 work in tandem with** to work together with someone to get the best results 与〔某人〕协同工作，联合工作

tan·doo·ri /tɑnˋdʊrɪ; tænˈdʊəri/ *n* [U] a northern Indian method of cooking in a large closed clay pot 唐杜里烹饪法〔印度北部用密封大陶罐烹调的一种方法〕

Tandy /ˈtændɪ; ˈtændi/, **Jessica** /ˈdʒɛsɪkə; ˈdʒesɪkə/ (1909-94) a British actress who at the age of 80 became the oldest winner of an Oscar in 1989 for her part in the film *Driving Miss Daisy*. She moved to America in 1940. She acted mainly on stage, but her films include *Forever Amber* (1947) and *Fried Green Tomatoes at the Whistle Stop Cafe* (1991). 坦迪〔(1909-1994)，英国女演员。1989年80高龄的她因主演《为戴茜小姐开车》，成为奥斯卡历史上年龄最大的影后。1940年定居美国，主要演出舞台剧。她出演的电影有《除却巫山不是云》(1947)和《油炸绿番茄》(1991)〕

tang /tæŋ; tæŋ/ *n* [singular] a strong sharp taste or smell 强烈刺鼻的味道: *the salty tang of the sea air* 带强烈咸味的海上空气 —**tangy** *adj*: *tangy oranges* 味道浓烈的橙子

Tan·gan·yi·ka /ˌtæŋgənˈjikə; ˌtæŋgənˈjiːkə/, **Lake** a large lake between the Democratic Republic of Congo and Tanzania 坦噶尼喀湖〔位于刚果民主共和国与坦桑尼亚之间的一个大湖〕

tan·gent /ˈtændʒənt; ˈtændʒənt/ *n* [C] **1 go/fly off at a tangent** *informal* to suddenly start thinking or talking about a completely new and different subject【非正式】突然离开原来的思路；突然离题: *It's impossible to have a logical discussion with Rob because he keeps going off at a tangent.* 不可能跟罗布进行一次合乎逻辑的讨论，因为他老是不断地突然离题。**2** *technical* a straight line that touches the outside of a curve but does not cut across it【术语】切线 **3** *technical* the FRACTION (2) calculated for an angle by dividing the length of the side that would be opposite it in a TRIANGLE with a RIGHT-ANGLE by the length of the side that would be next to it【术语】〔三角学中的〕正切 —compare 比较 COSINE, SINE

tan·gen·tial /tænˋdʒɛnʃəl; tænˈdʒenʃəl/ *adj* **1** *formal* tangential information, comments etc are only indirectly related to a particular subject【正式】〔情况、评论等〕不直接相干的；略为触及〔主题〕的 **2** *formal* tangential lines, roads etc move or go out in different directions; DIVERGENT【正式】〔线条、道路等〕漫射开来的，朝不同方向的，分岔的 **3** *technical* like a tangent【术语】(像)切线的 —**tangentially** *adv*

tan·ge·rine /ˈtændʒəˌrin; ˌtændʒəˈriːn/ *n* [C] a small sweet fruit like an orange with a skin that comes off easily 橘子

tan·gi·ble /ˈtændʒəbl; ˈtændʒəbəl/ *adj* **1 tangible proof/results/benefits etc** proof, results, advantages etc that are easy to see so that there is no doubt 确凿的证据/明显的结果/实在的利益等: *Welfare reform has not yet brought any tangible benefits.* 福利改革还没有带来任何实在的好处。—opposite 反义词 INTANGIBLE **2** *formal* able to be felt by touch【正式】可触摸的，可触知的；有形的 —**tangibly** *adv* —**tangibility** /ˌtændʒəˋbɪlətɪ; ˌtændʒəˈbɪləti/ *n* [U]

tan·gle[1] /ˈtæŋgl; ˈtæŋgəl/ *v* [I,T] to become twisted together or make something become twisted together in an untidy mass (使)缠结在一起；(使)乱成一团: *My hair tangles easily.* 我的头发很容易缠在一起。| **tangle sth** *Somebody's tangled all these cables under my computer.* 有人把我电脑下面的电线搞得乱成一团。

tangle with sb *phr v* [T] *informal* to argue or fight with someone【非正式】和…争吵[打架]: *I wouldn't tangle with him if I were you.* 如果我是你的话，是不会跟他争吵的。

tangle[2] *n* [C] **1** a twisted mass of something such as hair or thread〔头发、线等的〕缠结，纠结，乱成一团: *Her hair was full of tangles after being out in the wind.* 在外面吹了风之后，她的头发变得乱糟糟的。| **tangle of branches/weeds/threads etc** *We had to cut our way through a tangle of branches.* 我们不得不砍掉缠在一起的树枝来开路前进。**2** a confused state 乱成一团，纷乱，混乱: *My emotions were in a complete tangle.* 我的情绪完全乱成一团了。**3** *informal* [+**with**] a quarrel or fight【非正式】争吵；打架

tan·gled /ˈtæŋgld; ˈtæŋgəld/ also 又作 **tangled up** *adj* **1** twisted together in an untidy mass 纠结的；缠绕在一起的: *The telephone cord is all tangled up.* 电话线全缠在一起了。**2** complicated or made up of many confusing parts 复杂的；混乱的；乱糟糟的: *What she needed was time to sort out her tangled feelings.* 她需要时间来整理一下纷乱的心情。

Tan·gle·wood /ˈtæŋgəlwʊd; ˈtæŋgəlwʊd/ a place in Massachusetts, US, where the Boston Symphony Orchestra performs concerts outdoors during the summer. It is also a school for training musicians, and many famous musicians and COMPOSERS have studied and taught at Tanglewood. 坦格尔伍德〔美国马萨诸塞州一地名。夏日时节，波士顿交响乐团常在此举办露天音乐会。该地还有一所专门培养音乐人才的学校，培养了许多著名音乐家和作曲家〕

tan·go[1] /ˈtæŋgo; ˈtæŋgəʊ/ *n plural* **tangos** [C] a lively dance from South America, or a piece of music for this dance 探戈舞；探戈舞曲

tango[2] *v* [I] **1** to dance the tango 跳探戈舞 **2 it takes two to tango** *spoken* used to say that if a problem involves two people then both people are equally responsible【口】探戈舞得两个人跳；一个巴掌拍不响

tank[1] /tæŋk; tæŋk/ *n* [C] **1** a large container for storing liquid or gas〔盛放液体或气体的〕大容器: *The hot water tank is leaking.* 热水箱在漏水。| **fish tank** (=for keeping fish in) 鱼缸 | **petrol tank** *BrE*【英】/**gas tank** *AmE*【美】(=part of a vehicle for holding petrol)〔汽车的〕油箱 **2** also 又作 **tankful** the amount of liquid or gas held in a tank〔液体或气体〕满满一箱的容量: *I'll do over 400 miles on a full tank.* 有满满一箱的油，我可以跑四百多英里。**3** a heavy military vehicle that has a large gun and runs on two metal belts fitted over its wheels 坦克(车) **4** a large artificial pool for storing water 人工大蓄水池 —see also 另见 THINK-TANK, SEPTIC TANK

tank[2] *v*

tank up *phr v* [I] *especially AmE* to put petrol in your car so that the tank is full【尤美】(给汽车)加满汽油

tan·kard /ˈtæŋkəd; ˈtæŋkəd/ *n* [C] a large metal cup, usually with a handle and lid, used for drinking beer〔通常有把手和杯盖的〕大金属啤酒杯 —see picture at 参见 CUP 图

tanked up /ˌ· ˈ·/ also 又作 **tanked** /tæŋkt; tæŋkt/ *AmE*【美】*adj* [not before noun 不用于名词前] *slang* drunk【俚】喝醉的: *Jim gets really funny when he's tanked.* 吉姆喝醉的时候真是滑稽可笑。

tank·er /ˈtæŋkɚ; ˈtæŋkə/ *n* [C] a vehicle or ship specially built to carry large quantities of gas or liquid, especially oil 油船，油轮；油罐车 —see also 另见 OIL TANKER

tank top /ˈ· ·/ *n* [C] **1** *BrE* a piece of clothing like a SWEATER but with no sleeves (SLEEVE (1))【英】〔像无袖套头毛衣的〕紧身短背心 **2** *AmE* a piece of clothing like a shirt but with no sleeves (SLEEVE (1))【美】〔无袖〕运动背心

tanned /tænd; tænd/ *adj* having a darker skin colour because you have been in the sun〔皮肤〕被晒黑的 —see picture on page A6 参见 A6 页图

tan·ner /ˈtænɚ; ˈtænə/ *n* [C] **1** someone whose job is to make animal skin into leather by tanning (TAN[1] (3)) 鞣皮工，制革工 **2** *BrE old use* SIXPENCE (=a coin)【英旧】六便士硬币

tan·ne·ry /ˈtænərɪ; ˈtænəri/ *n* [C] a place where animal skin is made into leather by tanning (TAN[1] (3)) 鞣皮厂，制革厂

tan·nin /ˈtænɪn; ˈtænɪn/ also 又作 **tan·nic acid** /ˌtænɪk ˋæsɪd; ˌtænɪk ˈæsɪd/ *n* [U] a reddish acid used in preparing leather, making ink etc 丹宁(酸)，鞣酸〔用于制革、制造墨水等〕

tan·noy /ˈtænɔɪ; ˈtænɔɪ/ *n* [C] *BrE trademark* a system for giving out information in public places by means of LOUDSPEAKERS【英，商标】天朗播音设备〔一种以扩音器向公众发布消

息的播音设备〕: **over the tannoy** *What were they saying about flight delays over the tannoy?* 他们在广播里就航班延误的事说了些什么?

tan·ta·lize also 又作 **-ise** *BrE*【英】/ˈtæntḷ͵aɪz; ˈtæntəl͵aɪz/ *v* [T usually passive 一般用被动态] to show or promise something that someone really wants, but then not allow them to have it 使〔某人〕因想要却得不到而干着急; 逗引; 撩拨

tan·ta·liz·ing also 又作 **tantalising** *BrE*【英】/ˈtæntḷ͵aɪzɪŋ; ˈtæntəl-aɪzɪŋ/ *adj* making you feel a strong desire to have something that you cannot have 逗引人的; 撩拨人的: *The tantalizing smell of warm bread wafted out of the shop.* 热面包诱人的味道从店里飘出。—**tantalizingly** *adv*

tan·ta·lus /ˈtæntḷəs; ˈtæntələs/ *n* [C] a case in which bottles of alcoholic drink can be locked up in such a way that they can be seen 上锁透明酒柜

tan·ta·mount /ˈtæntə͵maunt; ˈtæntəmaʊnt/ *adj* **be tantamount to sth** if an action, suggestion, plan etc is tantamount to something, it is almost the same thing as it 〔行动、建议、计划几乎〕等于某事, 相当于某事: *But that's tantamount to saying poor people are criminals!* 不过, 那等于是说穷人就是罪犯!

tan·trum /ˈtæntrəm; ˈtæntrəm/ *n* [C] a sudden moment of unreasonable bad temper and anger 〔突然无理的〕脾气发作: **have/throw a tantrum** *Some kid threw a tantrum in the middle of the store.* 有个孩子在商店里大发脾气。

Tan·za·ni·a /͵tænzəˈniə; ͵tænzəˈniːə/ a country in East Africa between Kenya and Mozambique, formed in 1964 when Tanganyika and Zanzibar joined together to make one country. Population: 36,232,000 (2001). Capital: Dodoma. 坦桑尼亚〔东非一国家, 位于肯尼亚和莫桑比克之间, 1964年由坦噶尼喀与桑给巴尔合并而成。人口: 36,232,000 (2001)。首都: 多多马〕—**Tanzanian** *n, adj*

Tao /tau; taʊ/ *n* [U] the natural force that unites all things in the universe, according to Taoism 〔道家学说中的〕道

Taoi·seach, the /ˈtiʃək; ˈtiːʃək/ *n* the title of the PRIME MINISTER of the Republic of Ireland 〔爱尔兰共和国的〕总理

Tao·is·m /ˈtauɪzəm; ˈtaʊɪzəm/ *n* [U] a way of thought developed in ancient China, based on the writings of Lao Tzu, emphasizing a natural and simple way of life 道家学说, 道教

S3 **tap¹** /tæp; tæp/ *n*

1 ►WATER/GAS 水/煤气◄ [C] a piece of equipment for controlling the flow of water, gas etc from a pipe or container 〔水、煤气等管道或容器的〕龙头, 阀门; FAUCET *AmE*【美】: **turn on the tap** (=so that water comes out of it) 打开(水)龙头 *Carla, don't leave the taps running!* 卡拉, 别让水龙头开着空流! | **tap water** *In some countries, the tap water isn't safe enough to drink.* 在某些国家自来水不够清洁, 不能直接饮用。| **cold/hot tap** (=the tap that cold or hot water comes from) 冷水龙头/热水龙头 —see picture on page A10 参见A10页图

2 ►BARREL 桶◄ [C] a specially shaped object used for letting liquid out of a BARREL¹ (1) 〔桶的〕塞子

3 ►A LIGHT HIT 轻轻的敲击◄ [C] an act of hitting something lightly, especially to get someone's attention 〔尤指为了引起某人注意而对某物的〕轻轻敲击, 轻叩, 轻拍: **[+at/on]** *There was a tap at the door.* 有人轻轻地敲了一下门。| *Suddenly, I felt a tap on my shoulder and turned round to see Sheila there.* 突然, 我感觉到有人在我肩膀上轻轻拍了一下, 我转过身一看是希拉。

4 on tap a) *informal* something that is on tap is ready to use when you need it【非正式】可随时取用[使用]的: *We've got a lot of experts on tap to advise us.* 我们有很多专家可以随时向我们提供咨询。**b)** beer that is on tap comes from a BARREL¹ (1) 〔桶装啤酒〕可随时旋开旋塞供饮用的

5 ►DANCING 跳舞◄ also 又作 **tap dancing** [U] dancing in which you wear special shoes with pieces of metal on the bottom which make a loud sharp sound on the floor 踢踏舞

6 ►TELEPHONE 电话◄ [C] an act of secretly listening to someone's telephone, using electronic equipment 电话窃听

7 ►TUNE 乐调◄ taps a song or tune played on the BUGLE at night in an army camp, and at military funerals 〔军营里的〕熄灯号; 〔军队的〕葬礼号

S3 **tap²** *v* **tapped, tapping**

1 ►HAND OR FOOT 手或脚◄ [I,T] to hit your hand or foot lightly against something, especially to get someone's attention or without thinking about it 〔用手或脚〕轻敲, 轻叩, 轻拍: *She tapped her feet in time to the music.* 她和着音乐用脚轻敲着节拍。| **tap sth on/against etc** *He sat tapping his fingers on the arm of the chair.* 他坐着, 手指轻轻敲着椅子的扶手。| **[+on]** *I went up and tapped on the window.* 我走上前去, 轻轻叩了一下窗户。| **tap sb on the arm/ shoulder etc** *"Hey Paul," she said, tapping him on the shoulder.* "嘿, 保罗。"她一边说着, 一边拍了拍他的肩膀。—compare 比较 KNOCK¹ —see picture on page A20 参见A20页图

2 ►ENERGY 能源◄ also 又作 **tap into** [T] to use or take what is needed from an energy supply or power supply 发掘, 开发〔能源或电力〕: *We have enormous reserves of oil still waiting to be tapped.* 我们有储量巨大的石油有待开发。

3 ►IDEAS 思想◄ [T] also 又作 **tap into** to make as much use as possible of the ideas, experience, knowledge etc that a group of people has 利用, 采用〔思想、经验、知识等〕: *Honestly, we have a vast pool of practical experience, just waiting to be tapped.* 老实说, 我们有大量的实际经验有待利用。

4 ►TELEPHONE 电话◄ [T] to listen secretly to someone's telephone by using a special piece of electronic equipment 电话窃听

5 ►TREE 树木◄ [T] to get liquid from the TRUNK of a tree by making a hole in it 在〔树干〕上凿孔以取其液汁: *tapping rubber trees* 割开橡胶树皮取胶乳

6 tap sb for sth *BrE informal* to get money from someone【英, 非正式】从某人处弄到钱: *Joey tapped me for a fiver.* 乔伊从我这儿弄走5英镑。

tap sth ↔ **in** *phr v* [T] to put information, numbers etc into a computer, telephone etc by pressing buttons or keys 把〔信息、数据等〕敲入[键入, 输入]〔电脑、电话等〕: *Tap in your password before you log on.* 登录前请先输入密码。

tap·as /ˈtɑpəs; ˈtæpəs/ *n* [plural] small dishes of food eaten as part of the first course of a Spanish meal 〔一种西班牙饭菜的〕餐前小吃

tap dan·cing /ˈ· ͵··/ *n* [U] dancing in which you wear shoes with pieces of metal on the bottom, which make a sharp sound 踢踏舞 —**tap dance** *n* [C] —**tap dancer** *n* [C]

tape¹ /tep; teɪp/ *n* S3 W3

1 ►FOR RECORDING 用于录制◄ a) [U] narrow plastic material covered with a special MAGNETIC substance, on which sounds, pictures, or computer information can be recorded and played 〔可以录音、录像或录制电脑信息的〕磁带, 带子: **on tape** (=recorded on tape) 录在磁带上 *We've got the film on tape.* 我们已把这部片子录在带子上了。| *I don't like the sound of my own voice on tape.* 我不喜欢录下来的我自己的声音。**b)** [C] a special plastic box containing a length of tape that you can record sound on; CASSETTE (盒式)磁带: *Turn the tape over when it's finished.* 磁带放完时要翻一面。| *William lent me some of his Beatles tapes.* 威廉把他的一些"甲壳虫"音乐磁带借给了我。| **blank tape** (=with nothing recorded on it) 空白磁带 **c)** [C] a special plastic box containing a length of tape that you can record sound and pictures on; VIDEOTAPE (盒式)录像带: *Police have seized a number of magazines and tapes.* 警察缴获了一些杂志和录像带。

2 ►PIECE OF MUSIC/FILM 音乐带子/影片带子◄ [C] a recording of a performance, piece of music, speech etc on tape 〔录有演出、音乐、演讲等的〕录音带: **[+of]** *I'd like a tape of the concert.* 我想要一盘音乐会的录音带。

3 ►STICKY MATERIAL 胶黏材料◄ [U] narrow length of sticky material used to stick things together 胶带, 胶布; SELLOTAPE *BrE*【英】; SCOTCH TAPE *AmE*【美】: *a parcel fastened with tape* 用胶带缠住的包裹

4 ►THIN PIECE OF MATERIAL 细长材料◄ [C,U] a long thin piece of material used for various purposes such as marking out an area of ground or to tie things together 〔划分地界或拴捆东西用的〕带子, 线带

5 the tape a string stretched out across the finishing line in a race and broken by the winner 〔比赛终点冲刺的〕终点线

6 ►FOR MEASURING 用于测量◄ a TAPE MEASURE 卷尺 —see also 另见 RED TAPE

tape² *v* S3

1 ►RECORD STH 录制某物◄ also 又作 **tape record** [I,T] to record sound or pictures onto a TAPE¹ (1) 〔用磁带〕录音[录像]

2 ►FASTEN STH 拴紧某物◄ also 又作 **tape up** [T] to fasten a package, box etc with TAPE¹ (3) 〔用胶带〕拴住, 捆扎

3 ►STICK STH 粘连某物◄ [T] to stick something onto something else using TAPE¹ (3) 用〔胶布〕粘贴: *He had a picture of his girlfriend taped to the inside of his locker door.* 他把一张女朋友的相片贴在寄存柜门的内侧。

4 ►INJURY 伤口◄ also 又作 **tape up** [T usually passive 一般用被动态] *especially AmE* to tie a BANDAGE¹ firmly around an injured part of someone's body【尤美】用〔绷带〕包扎〔受伤部位〕; STRAP² (2) *BrE*【英】: *We've got a nurse to tape that up for you.* 我们找了一名护士来为你包扎伤口。

5 have sth/sb taped *BrE informal* to understand someone or something completely and have learned how to deal with them

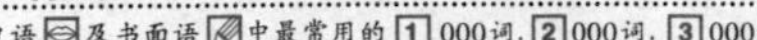

【英, 非正式】摸清某事 / 某人的底细: *You can't fool Liz – she's got you taped.* 你骗不了莉兹 —— 她摸清了你的老底。

tape deck /ˈ· ·/ *n* [C] the part of a TAPE RECORDER that winds the tape, and records and plays back sound〔录音机的〕磁带驱动器, 走带装置

tape drive /ˈ· ·/ *n* [C] a small machine attached to a computer that passes information from a computer to a tape or from a tape to a computer〔电脑上的〕磁带驱动器

tape mea·sure /ˈ· ,· ·/ *n* [C] a long narrow band of cloth or steel, marked with centimetres, metres etc, used for measuring something〔测量用的〕卷尺, 钢卷尺

ta·per[1] /ˋtepɚ; ˈteɪpə/ *v* [I,T] also 又作 **taper off** to become gradually narrower towards one end (使) 一端逐渐变得细小: *The jeans taper towards the ankle.* 牛仔裤的裤管到脚踝处逐渐变窄。

taper off *phr v* [I] to decrease gradually 逐渐变少; 逐渐减弱: *Interest in the scandal seems to be tapering off.* 人们对那件丑闻的兴趣似乎越来越小了。—**tapering** *adj*: *long tapering fingers* 细长的手指

taper[2] *n* [C] **1** [usually singular 一般用单数] a gradual decrease in the width of a long object〔长形物体的〕逐渐变细[变窄] **2** a very thin CANDLE 细蜡烛 **3** a piece of string covered in WAX[1] (1), used for lighting lamps and CANDLES〔点灯火和点蜡烛用的〕火媒

tape re·cord /ˈ· ·,·/ *v* [T] to record sound using a tape recorder〔用录音机〕录〔音〕

tape re·cord·er /ˈ· ·,· ·/ *n* [C] a piece of electrical equipment that can record sound on tape and play it back 盒式磁带录音机

tape re·cord·ing /ˈ· ·,· ·/ *n* [C] something that has been recorded with a tape recorder 磁带录音: *The court heard secretly obtained tape recordings of the meeting.* 法庭听取了偷录下的会议录音。

ta·pered /ˋtepɚd; ˈteɪpəd/ *adj* having a shape that gets narrower towards one end 一端逐渐变得尖细的; 锥形的: *tapered sleeves* 锥形袖

tap·es·try /ˋtæpɪstrɪ; ˈtæpɪstri/ *n* [C,U] heavy cloth or a large piece of cloth on which coloured threads are woven to produce a picture, pattern etc 挂毯, 壁毯: *the Bayeux Tapestry*〔法国〕巴约挂毯

tape·worm /ˋtep,wɝm; ˈteɪpwɜːm/ *n* [C] a long flat PARASITE that lives in the bowels (BOWEL (1)) of humans and other animals 绦虫〔肠内的一种寄生虫〕

tap·i·o·ca /,tæpɪˋokə; ,tæpiˈəʊkə/ *n* [U] small hard white grains made from the crushed dried roots of CASSAVA , used especially for making sweet dishes〔制作甜点心用的〕木薯淀粉 (颗粒)

ta·pir /ˋtepɚ; ˈteɪpə/ *n* [C] an animal like a pig with thick legs, a short tail, and long nose, that lives in tropical America and Southeast Asia 貘〔一种像猪的动物, 腿粗, 尾短, 鼻长, 生活于热带美洲和东南亚〕

tap·pet /ˋtæpɪt; ˈtæpɪt/ *n* [C] *technical* an engine part that moves up and down and makes another part of the engine move, open, close etc【术语】〔发动机内的〕挺杆, 推杆

tap·root /ˋtæp,rut; ˈtæpruːt/ *n* [C] the main root of a plant, that grows straight down and produces smaller side roots〔植物的〕主根

tar[1] /tɑr; tɑː/ *n* [U] **1** a black substance, thick and sticky when hot but hard when cold, used especially for making road surfaces〔尤指用于铺路的〕柏油; 沥青 —see also 另见 COAL TAR **2** a sticky substance that is formed by burning tobacco〔烟草的〕烟碱, 焦油: **high/low/medium tar** *high tar cigarettes* 焦油含量高的香烟

tar[2] *v* **tarred, tarring** [T] **1** to cover a surface with tar 用沥青覆盖〔路面〕 **2 be/get tarred with the same brush** to be blamed for someone else's faults or crimes 被认为有同样缺点, 被看作一路货色 **3 tar and feather** to cover someone in tar and feathers as a cruel unofficial punishment 把〔某人〕浑身涂上柏油再粘上羽毛以作为一种非官方的残酷惩罚

ta·ra·ma·sa·la·ta /,tærəməsəˋlɑtə; ,tærəməsəˈlɑːtə/ *n* [U] a Greek food consisting of a pink mixture made from fish eggs 希腊红鱼子酱

tar·an·tel·la /,tærənˋtɛlə; ,tærənˈtelə/ *n* [C] a fast Italian dance, or the music for this dance 塔兰台拉舞〔一种意大利快步舞〕; 塔兰台拉舞曲

Ta·ran·ti·no /,tærənˋtino; ,tærənˈtiːnəʊ/, **Quen·tin** /ˋkwɛntən; ˈkwentɪn/ (1963-) a US film DIRECTOR whose films include *Reservoir Dogs* (1992), *Pulp Fiction* (1994), and *Jackie Brown* (1997). His films are often very violent, and some people criticize him for this. But other people admire him for the clever way in which his stories are put together. 塔伦蒂诺〔(1963-), 美国电影导演。执导的作品有《落水狗》(1992)、《低俗小说》(1994) 和《危险关系》(1997)。他的电影常常充斥着暴力, 因此遭到一些人的批评, 而有些人则欣赏他对故事情节的巧妙安排〕

ta·ran·tu·la /təˋræntʃələ; təˈræntjʊlə/ *n* [C] a large poisonous SPIDER from Southern Europe and tropical America 塔兰托大蜘蛛〔南欧及热带美洲的一种有毒的大蜘蛛〕

Tar·dis, the /ˋtɑrdɪs; ˈtɑːdɪs/ the machine used by Dr Who and his friends for travelling through time in the British television programme *Dr Who*. On the outside, the Tardis is small and looks like a type of telephone box that was formerly used by the British police, but it is much larger inside. 塔迪斯〔英国电视剧《无名博士》中无名博士及其朋友使用的一台时空穿梭机。从外观上来看, 塔迪斯就像以前英国警察专用的电话间, 但里面空间却很大〕

tar·dy /ˋtɑrdɪ; ˈtɑːdi/ *adj formal*【正式】**1** done later than it should have been done 迟的, 晚了的: *We apologize for our tardy response to your letter.* 来函迟迟未复, 谨表歉意。**2** acting or moving slowly; SLUGGISH 行动缓慢的; 拖沓的 —**tardily** *adv* —**tardiness** *n* [U]

tare /tɛr; teə/ *n* **1** [usually singular 一般用单数] *technical* the weight of wrapping material in which goods are packed【术语】〔货物的〕包装材料的重量, 皮重 **2** [usually singular 一般用单数] *technical* the weight of an unloaded goods vehicle, used to calculate the actual weight of its goods【术语】空重, 车身重量 **3** [usually plural 一般用复数] *biblical* an unwanted plant growing in fields of grain; WEED[1] (1)【圣经】稗子, 莠草

tar·get[1] /ˋtɑrgɪt; ˈtɑːgɪt/ *n* [C]

1 ►OBJECT OF ATTACK 攻击对象◄ an object, person, or place that is deliberately chosen to be attacked〔有意攻击的〕目标; 攻击对象: [+for/of] *The docks are the main target for the bombing raids.* 码头区是空袭的主要目标。| **soft/easy target** *Cars without security devices are an easy target for the thief.* 没有安全装置的汽车很容易成为盗贼的目标。| **prime target** (=a very likely target) 首要攻击目标

2 ►AN AIM 目标◄ a result, such as a total, an amount, or a time, which you aim to achieve; GOAL (1) 想要达到的结果〈如总数、时限等〉; 目标; 指标: *I've set myself a target of saving £20 a month.* 我给自己定了一个目标: 每月存上 20 英镑。| **meet targets** (=achieve targets) 达到指标; 实现目标 *Dealers are under pressure to meet sales targets.* 经销商们受到要完成销售指标的压力。| **on target** (=likely to achieve a target) 有可能实现目标 *We're on target for 3% inflation by 1996.* 我们有可能在 1996 年前把通货膨胀率控制到 3%。

3 ►SHOOTING 射击◄ something that you practise shooting at, especially a round board with circles on it〔射击的〕靶子: *A target 300 yards away* 300 码以外的一个靶子 | **target practice** *The area is used by the army for target practice.* 这一地区被军队用来练习打靶。

4 target group/area/audience etc a limited group, area etc that a plan, idea etc is aimed at 特别针对的群体 / 领域 / 听众等: *We need to clearly identify our target market.* 我们需要明确我们的目标市场。

5 be the target of criticism/complaints etc to be criticized, blamed, etc for something 成为批评 / 抱怨等的对象: *She's become the target of much criticism since the affair became public.* 自从那一暧昧关系公开之后, 她便成了众矢之的。

target[2] *v* [T] **1** to aim something at a target 对…瞄准, 把…当作靶子: **target sth on/at** *missiles targeted on American and European cities* 瞄向美国和欧洲城市的导弹 **2** to make something have an effect on a particular limited group or area 以…为目标[对象]: [+on/at] *We want to target more welfare on the poorest groups in society.* 我们想给社会上最贫困的群体提供较多的福利。**3** to choose someone or something as your target 把…选作目标: *It's clear that smaller, more vulnerable banks have been targeted.* 很明显, 规模较小、力量较脆弱的银行已被确定为目标。

tar·iff /ˋtærɪf; ˈtærɪf/ *n* [C] **1** a tax on goods coming into a country or going out of a country〔对进口或出口商品征收的〕关税 **2** *especially BrE* a list of fixed prices, such as the cost of meals or rooms, charged by a hotel or restaurant【尤英】〔旅馆或餐厅对房间或餐饮等固定收费项目的〕收费表, 价目表

tar·mac[1] /ˋtɑr,mæk; ˈtɑːmæk/ *n* **1** also 又作 **tar·ma·cadam** /,tɑrməˋkædəm; ,tɑːməˈkædəm/ [U] a mixture of TAR and very small stones, used for making the surface of roads; ASPHALT〔铺路用的〕柏油碎石 (沥青和碎石的混合物) **2 the tarmac** an area covered with tarmac, especially where planes take off or land〔尤指飞机跑道用的〕铺有柏油碎石的地面

tarmac[2] *v* [T] to cover a road's surface with tarmac 在〔路面上〕铺柏油碎石

tar·nish¹ /ˋtɑrnɪʃ; ˈtɑːnɪʃ/ *v* **1** [T] if an event or fact tarnishes someone's REPUTATION, record, image etc, it makes it worse 玷污〔名誉〕; 损害〔形象〕: *a record tarnished by recent scandals* 被最近丑闻玷污的记录 **2** [I,T] if metals such as silver, COPPER (1), or BRASS (1) tarnish, or if something tarnishes them, they become dull and lose their colour (使)〔银器、铜器、黄铜器等金属〕失去光泽, 变暗淡: *tarnished silver spoons* 失去光泽的银匙

tarnish² *n* [singular, U] dullness of colour, or loss of brightness 颜色晦暗; 光泽变暗

ta·ro /ˋtɑro; ˈtɑːrəʊ/ *n* [C,U] a tropical plant grown for its thick root which is boiled and eaten 芋, 芋头

tar·ot /ˋtæro; ˈtærəʊ/ *n* [singular,U] a set of 78 cards, used for telling what will happen to someone in the future 塔罗牌〔一套用于占卜的纸牌, 共78张〕

tar·pau·lin /tɑrˋpɔlɪn; tɑːˈpɔːlɪ̵n/ *n* [C,U] a heavy cloth prepared so that water will not pass through it, used to keep rain off things 防水帆布, 油布

tar·ra·gon /ˋtærə͵gɑn; ˈtærəgən/ *n* [U] the leaves of a small European plant used as a HERB 龙蒿〔一种欧洲植物, 其叶是用于烹调的香草〕: *chicken with tarragon* 龙蒿叶煮鸡肉

tar·ry¹ /ˋtærɪ; ˈtæri/ *v* [I] *literary*【文】**1** to stay in a place, especially when you should leave; LINGER〔尤指应离开时〕逗留, 停留; 徘徊 **2** to delay or be slow in going somewhere 耽搁, 拖延

tar·ry² /ˋtɑrɪ; ˈtɑːri/ *adj* covered with TAR (=a thick black liquid) 涂了柏油的

tar·sus /ˋtɑrsəs; ˈtɑːsəs/ *n* [C] *technical* your ANKLE or one of the seven small bones in your ankle【术语】脚踝; 跗骨〔踝部的七块小骨头之一〕—**tarsal** *adj*

tart¹ /tɑrt; tɑːt/ *n* **1** [C,U] a PIE (1) without a top on it, containing something sweet〔顶部不用面皮密封的〕甜馅饼 **2** [C] *informal* a woman whose appearance or behaviour makes you think that she is too willing to have sex【非正式】荡妇 **3** [C] *slang* a PROSTITUTE【俚】妓女

tart² *adj* **1** food that is tart has a slightly sour taste that stings your tongue〔味道〕酸的: *a tart apple* 酸苹果 **2 tart reply/remark etc** a reply, remark etc that is sharp and unkind 尖刻的回答/话等: *Her tart reply upset me.* 她那尖刻的回答令我很难受。—**tartly** *adv*: *Colin replied tartly that he hadn't invited me.* 科林尖酸刻薄地说, 他并没有邀请我。—**tartness** *n* [U]

tart³ *v*

tart sth ↔ up *phr v* [T] *BrE informal*【英, 非正式】**1** to try to make something more attractive by decorating it, often in a way that other people think is cheap or ugly 把…装饰得刺眼而又俗气: *All they've done for the party is to tart up the old church hall.* 他们为那次晚会所做的就是把那座旧教堂的大厅装饰得俗不可耐。**2 tart yourself up** *often humorous* if a woman tarts herself up she tries to make herself look attractive, by putting on jewellery, MAKE-UP (1) etc【常幽默】把自己打扮得花枝招展

tar·tan /ˋtɑrtn̩; ˈtɑːtn/ *n* **1 a)** [U] woollen cloth, originally from Scotland woven with bands of different colours and widths that cross each other at right angles〔苏格兰〕格子花呢 —see picture on page A16 参见A16页图 **b)** [C] this pattern on other cloth 格子织物, 花格图案: *Her skirt is a red and green tartan.* 她的裙子是红绿相间花格图案的。**2** [C] a special pattern of this type worn by a particular Scottish CLAN (=large family group)〔作为苏格兰某大家族标志的〕格子花呢图案: *the MacGregor tartan* 麦格雷戈家族的格子花呢图案 —**tartan** *adj*: *a bright tartan shirt* 色彩鲜艳的格子衬衣

tar·tar /ˋtɑrtɚ; ˈtɑːtə/ *n* **1** [U] a hard substance that forms on your teeth 牙石, 牙垢 **2** [U] a reddish-brown substance that forms on the inside of wine barrels 酒石〔酒桶内壁上形成的一种赤褐色物质〕**3** [U] a white powder used in baking and in medicine 酒石英, 酒石酸氢钾〔一种用于烘烤面包糕点和医药的白色粉末〕**4** [C] *informal* someone who has a violent temper or is difficult to deal with【非正式】凶悍的人; 很难对付的人: *She's a real tartar.* 她真是一个悍妇。

tar·tare sauce /͵tɑrtɚ ˋsɔrs; ͵tɑːtə ˈsɔːs/ *n* [U] a cold white SAUCE often eaten with fish, made from egg, oil, GHERKINs and capers (CAPER² (1)) 塔塔酱, 蛋黄沙司〔吃鱼时常用的一种调味酱〕

tar·tar·ic ac·id /tɑrˋtærɪk ˋæsɪd; tɑː͵tærɪk ˈæsɪ̵d/ *n* [U] a strong acid that comes from a plant and is used in preparing some foods and medicines 酒石酸〔用于制作某些食品和医药〕

tart·y /ˋtɑrtɪ; ˈtɑːti/ *adj especially BrE* wearing the kind of clothes that people think a PROSTITUTE would wear【尤英】穿着打扮很妖冶的

Tar·zan /ˋtɑzn̩; ˈtɑːzən/ the main character in books by Edgar Rice Burroughs, which were later made into many films, about a baby who is left in the African forest and cared for by APEs until he becomes a man. He wears only a LOINCLOTH (=a piece of cloth worn around the waist), moves through the forest by swinging from tree to tree on ropes made of plants, and is very brave and strong, with big muscles. He meets a woman called Jane who becomes his girlfriend, and he is famous for saying 'Me Tarzan. You Jane' and also for making a loud cry as a warning. 人猿泰山〔埃德加·赖斯·巴勒斯系列小说中的主人公。该小说后来被改编成多部影片。故事中有一个婴儿被遗弃在非洲丛林中, 由几只猿抚养成人。他身上仅系一条缠腰布, 手握藤条荡来荡去, 在林间穿行。他十分勇敢强壮, 肌肉发达。他遇到了一个名叫简的姑娘, 简成了他的女朋友。"我, 泰山, 你, 简", 泰山说的这句话, 还有他大声呼叫的预警信号, 都十分有名〕

Tash·kent /tæʃˋkɛnt; tæʃˈkent/ a city in central Asia which is the capital city of Uzbekistan 塔什干〔中亚一城市, 乌兹别克斯坦首都〕

task /tæsk; tɑːsk/ *n* [C] **1** a piece of work that must be done, especially one that is difficult or unpleasant or that must be done regularly〔尤指困难或必须定期做的〕工作; 任务: **[+of]** *He was given the task of stacking the chairs in the auditorium.* 给他分派的任务是要把大礼堂的椅子堆放好。| *the grim task of identifying the dead* 辨认死者的令人生畏的工作 | *daily tasks* 日常工作任务 | **thankless task** (=a boring task that no one wants to do) 费力不讨好的事, 苦差事 *Volunteers had the thankless task of distributing campaign leaflets.* 志愿者们承担了散发宣传页这件苦差事。**2** a piece of work that is difficult but very important〔困难但又很重要的〕工作: *Our main task is to improve the economy.* 我们的主要工作是改善经济。**3 take someone to task** to tell someone that you strongly disapprove of something they have done〔为某人所做之事〕责备[严厉批评]某人

task force /ˋ· ·/ *n* [C] **1** a group formed for a short time to deal with a particular problem〔为处理某一特定问题而暂时组成的〕工作组: *a citizens' task force formed to rejuvenate the area* 为使该地区重振活力而由居民组成的一支工作小组 **2** a military force sent to a place for a special purpose〔军队的〕特别行动小组, 特遣部队

task·mas·ter /ˋtæsk͵mæstɚ; ˈtɑːsk͵mɑːstə/ *n* **be a hard/stern/tough taskmaster** to force people to work very hard or use a lot of effort 是一个严厉的监督人[监工, 工头]

Tas·ma·ni·a /tæzˋmenɪə; tæzˈmeɪniə/ a large island off the south east coast of Australia, which is one of the states of Australia 塔斯马尼亚〔与澳大利亚东南海滨隔海相望的一座大岛, 是澳大利亚诸州之一〕—**Tasmanian** *n, adj*

Tass, TASS /tæs; tæs/ the official national news organization of the former Soviet Union 塔斯社〔前苏联官方通讯社〕

tas·sel /ˋtæsl̩; ˈtæsəl/ *n* [C] a mass of threads tied together into a round ball at one end and hung as a decoration on clothes, curtains etc 流苏, 穗, 缨〔用作衣服、窗帘等的装饰〕—**tasselled** *BrE*【英】also 又作 **tasseled** *AmE*【美】*adj*

taste¹ /test; teɪst/ *n*

1 ►FOOD 食物◄ [singular,U] the special feeling that is produced by a particular food or drink when you put it in your mouth 味道, 滋味: *Sugar has a sweet taste.* 糖有甜味。| *Has the milk gone sour? It's got a funny taste.* 牛奶变酸了吗? 有一种怪味。| *the strong taste of the coffee* 浓郁的咖啡味道

2 ►JUDGEMENT 鉴赏力◄ [U] someone's judgement about what is good or suitable when they choose clothes, music etc〔对衣服、音乐等的〕鉴赏力; 品味; 趣味: **have (good) taste** (=make good judgements) 有(很好的)鉴赏力 *She has instinctive good taste.* 她天生就有不错的鉴赏力。| **have bad/no taste** *Mick has really bad taste in clothes.* 米克穿衣服很不得体。

3 ►STH YOU LIKE 你喜欢的东西◄ [C,U] the type of thing that you tend to like 喜爱, 爱好; 口味: **[+for/in]** *His tastes in films and books were very different from her own.* 他在电影和书籍方面的志趣与她大不相同。| **have a taste for** *I've always had a taste for jazz and blues music.* 我一向喜爱爵士乐和布鲁斯音乐。| **to sb's taste** (=in a way that someone likes) 合某人的口味; 称某人的心 *She had the whole house redecorated to her taste.* 她按照自己的品味把整座房子重新装修。| **have no taste for** (=not like something at all) 一点都不喜欢…

4 ►SMALL AMOUNT 少量◄ [usually singular 一般用单数] a small amount of food or drink that you put in your mouth to try it〔食物、饮料的〕少量, 一小口: *Have a taste of this soup and see if it needs more salt.* 尝一尝这汤, 看看是否还需要加盐。

5 ►WITH TONGUE 用舌头◄ [U] the sense by which you know one food from another 味觉: *You need a good sense of taste to be a chef.* 要想成为一名厨师, 你需要具备良好的味觉。

6 be in bad/poor taste jokes, remarks etc that are in bad taste are unacceptable, especially because they upset someone〔笑

话、讲话等〕格调低的，庸俗的: *I thought your terrorist joke was in pretty bad taste.* 我当时就认为你那个关于恐怖分子的笑话格调很庸俗。

7 a taste of fame/success etc a short experience of something that you want more of 对名望/成功等的〔短暂〕体验

8 leave a bad/nasty taste in your mouth to feel angry or upset as a result of seeing or hearing something unpleasant 留下难受的滋味: *The way he spoke to those children left a nasty taste in my mouth.* 他对那些孩子说话的方式让我觉得很不是滋味。

9 to taste a phrase meaning as much as is needed to make something taste the way you like, used in instructions for cooking 按照个人的口味，适量地〔用于烹调的说明语〕: *Add salt and pepper to taste.* 随个人口味适量加盐和胡椒。

10 an acquired taste something that you like only after you have tried it several times 多尝才会喜欢的东西: *Olives are something of an acquired taste.* 橄榄是一种需要多吃才会让人喜欢的食物。

11 there is no accounting for taste used to say that you do not understand why someone has chosen something 人各有所好: *He's so nice – I don't see why you don't like him. But there's no accounting for taste.* 他这么好，我不明白你为什么不喜欢他。人可是各有所好呢。

taste² *v* **1** [I not in progressive 不用进行时] to have a particular kind of taste 有…的味道: **taste delicious/sweet/fresh etc** *The mangoes tasted delicious.* 那些芒果味美可口。| *This wine tastes too acidic.* 这葡萄酒味道太酸了。| **taste like** *This chicken tastes more like turkey.* 这鸡肉的味道吃起来更像火鸡肉。| *What does pumpkin taste like?* 南瓜吃起来是什么味道？| **taste of** *overripe cheese tasting of ammonia* 有氨水味的熟过了头的干酪 | **sweet-tasting/strong-tasting etc** (=having a sweet, strong etc taste) 味道甜的/味道浓烈的等 *strong-tasting coffee* 味道浓郁的咖啡 **2** [T] to put a small amount of food or drink into your mouth to see what it is like 尝，品尝: *You'd better taste the soup to see if I put enough salt in it.* 你最好尝一下那汤，看看我是否放够了盐。| *Come on, just taste it!* 来，尝一尝吧！ **3** [T not in progressive 不用进行时] to experience the taste of food or drink 尝出…的味道: *I can hardly taste what I'm eating because of my cold.* 因为感冒了，我几乎尝不出食物的味道。 **4 taste fame/freedom etc** to have a short experience of something that you want more of 〔短暂地〕体验到出名/自由等的滋味: *We had tasted success and wanted more.* 我们已经体验到成功的滋味，还想取得更大的成功。

USAGE NOTE 用法说明: TASTE

WORD CHOICE 词语辨析: **taste, try, sample, savour** (*BrE* 英) **/savor** (*AmE* 美)

If you eat or drink a little of something just in order to find out its taste or flavour, you **taste** it. 尝食物或饮料的滋味用 taste: *Have you tasted this wine yet?* 你品尝过这种酒吗？ However, **taste** is much more often used in other meanings, where you receive the taste of something but do not actively search for it 然而，taste 有一种常见得多的用法，指不主动寻找而察觉出味道: *Can you taste the spices in this dish?* 你能尝出这道菜里的香料吗？| *This wine tastes great* (NOT 不用 *This wine is very good taste*). 这种酒十分香醇。

In fact most often people use the word **try** when they eat or drink something deliberately to see if they like it – not just what it tastes like, but also what it looks like, its smell etc. 其实，品尝食物或饮料，不仅尝它的味道，还看它的样子、闻它的气味等，最常用的词是 try: *You must try this wine/our local dishes/the salmon.* 你得尝一尝这种酒/我们本地的菜/鲑鱼。

You may also **sample** food or drink, that is try just a little, perhaps not a full dish or meal. 也可以浅尝 (sample) 食物或饮料，即不吃一整盘或一整餐: *You'll have a chance to sample all the cheeses of the region.* 你将有机会品尝本地区的各种干酪。

If you spend time enjoying the taste of something you **savour** it. savour 指专门花时间去享受美味: *Here you can relax, chat and savour a variety of local dishes.* 在这里，您可以休息、闲谈、品尝种种当地风味菜肴。

taste bud /ˈ· ·/ *n* [C usually plural 一般用复数] one of the small parts of the surface of your tongue which can tell the difference between foods according to their taste 味蕾

taste·ful /ˈtestfəl; ˈteɪstfəl/ *adj* made, decorated, or chosen with good TASTE¹ (2) 有鉴赏力的，趣味高雅的: *a simple but tasteful arrangement of flowers* 简单而显得趣味高雅的插花 —compare 比较 TASTY —**tastefully** *adv*: *tastefully decorated* 装饰得很大方 —**tastefulness** *n* [U]

taste·less /ˈtestlɪs; ˈteɪstləs/ *adj* **1** food or drink that is tasteless is unpleasant because it has no particular taste 〔食品或饮料〕无味道的: *The vegetables were tasteless and soggy.* 这些蔬菜淡而无味，湿乎乎的。 **2 tasteless joke/remark/comment etc** a joke etc that is unacceptable in a particular situation 格调不高的笑话/话语/评论等 **3** made, decorated or chosen with bad TASTE¹ (2) 格调很低的，庸俗的: *a tasteless outfit* 一套趣味庸俗的服装 —**tastelessly** *adv* —**tastelessness** *n* [U]

tast·er /ˈtestɚ; ˈteɪstə/ *n* [C] **1** someone whose job is to test the quality of foods, teas, wines etc by tasting them 品尝家，试味专家: *a wine taster* 品酒师 **2** *informal* a small example of something that is provided so that you can see if you like it【非正式】〔检验某物的一份〕小样: [**+of**] *Here's just a taster of what will be in print next month.* 这儿就有一份小样，从中可以看出下月将刊载些什么。

tast·ing /ˈtestɪŋ; ˈteɪstɪŋ/ *n* [C] an event that is organized so that you can try different foods or drinks to see if you like them 〔食品或饮料的〕品尝集会: *a wine and cheese tasting* 一次品尝酒和干酪的集会

tast·y /ˈtestɪ; ˈteɪsti/ *adj* **tastier, tastiest 1** food that is tasty has a good taste 味道好的，味美可口的: *a wide selection of tasty cold meats* 多种味美可口的冷荤 —compare 比较 TASTEFUL **2** *informal* tasty news, GOSSIP etc is especially interesting and often connected with sex or surprising behaviour【非正式】〔新闻、传闻等〕特别有趣的；与桃色事件相关的 **3** *informal* a word meaning attractive, used especially by men about women【非正式】有吸引力的，够味儿的〔尤指男子形容女性〕: *She's well tasty.* 她真够味儿。—**tastiness** *n* [U]

tat /tæt; tæt/ *n* [U] *BrE* things that are cheap and badly made【英】不值钱的东西；质量低劣的东西 —see also 另见 TIT FOR TAT

ta-ta /ˈtɑˌtɑ; tæˈtɑː/ *interjection BrE informal* goodbye【英，非正式】再见

Tate Bri·tain /ˌtet ˈbrɪtn; ˌteɪt ˈbrɪtn/ also 又作 **the Tate** an ART GALLERY in south central London which shows British art from the 16th century to the present day. There is a special part of the Tate that contains a large collection of work by J.M.W. Turner. 塔特英国美术馆〔位于伦敦中南部，藏品主要是16世纪至今的英国艺术品。该馆设有一特别展室，藏有J.M.W. 特纳的许多作品〕

Tate Gal·lery, the /ˌ· ˈ···/ also 又作 **the Tate** the former name for Tate Britain. There are also two smaller Tate Galleries outside London, one in Liverpool, and one in St Ives in south-west England. 塔特美术馆〔Tate Britain (塔特英国美术馆) 的旧称。伦敦以外另有两座规模较小的塔特美术馆，一座在利物浦，另一座在英格兰西南部的圣艾夫斯〕

Tate Modern /ˌ· ˈ··/ Britain's national MUSEUM of modern art in London, which was first opened to the public in May 2000. The building was formerly a power station, and it was changed into an ART GALLERY by two Swiss ARCHITECTS. The museum contains works by famous artists such as Pablo Picasso, Salvador Dali, and Francis Bacon. 塔特现代美术馆〔位于伦敦的英国国家现代艺术博物馆，2000年5月开馆。此处以前是一座发电站，由两位瑞士建筑师改建成美术馆，馆藏有巴伯罗·毕加索、萨尔瓦多·达利和弗朗西斯·培根等著名艺术家的作品〕

ta·ter /ˈtetɚ; ˈteɪtə/ *n* [C] *informal* a potato【非正式】马铃薯

Ta·ti /tæˈti; tæˈtiː/, **Jacques** /ʒɑk; ʒæk/ (1908-82) a French film actor and DIRECTOR who appeared in humorous films such as *Monsieur Hulot's Holiday* (1953) 塔蒂〔(1908-1982)，法国男电影演员、导演，曾主演过《胡洛先生的假期》(1953) 等喜剧片〕

Tat·ler /ˈtætlɚ; ˈtætlə/ **1** a famous magazine published in London in the early eighteenth century, started by Sir Richard Steele, containing poetry, stories, news etc. 《闲谈者》〔英国一著名杂志。18世纪早期由理查德·斯梯尔爵士在伦敦创办，刊载诗歌、小说、新闻报道等〕 **2** a British monthly magazine which reports on the social events and lives of rich and fashionable people 《闲谈者》〔英国一月刊，刊登有关社交盛会以及富豪名流的生活的文章〕

tat·tered /ˈtætɚd; ˈtætəd/ *adj* **1** clothes, books etc that are tattered are old and torn 〔衣服、书等〕破旧的，破烂的: *an old man in a tattered brown coat* 一个穿着一件棕色破旧外衣的老人 —see picture on page A18 参见 A18 页图 **2** dressed in old torn clothes 衣衫褴褛的

tat·ters /ˈtætɚz; ˈtætəz/ *n* [plural] **1** clothing or pieces of cloth that are old and torn 破旧衣服；破布 **2 in tatters a)** a plan, policy etc that is in tatters is ruined or badly damaged〔计划、政策等〕千疮百孔的: *The government's income policy was in*

tatters. 政府的收入政策彻底破产了。**b)** clothes that are in tatters are old and torn〔衣服〕破旧不堪的

tat·tie /ˈtætɪ; ˈtæti/ *n* [C] *ScotE* a potato【苏格兰】马铃薯

tat·ting /ˈtætɪŋ; ˈtætɪŋ/ *n* [U] a kind of LACE that you make by hand, or the process of making it〔手工〕梭织花边; 梭织花边工艺

tat·tle /ˈtætḷ; ˈtætl/ *v* [I] **1** *old-fashioned* to talk about small unimportant things, or about other people's private affairs; GOSSIP【过时】闲聊; 谈论他人隐私 **2** if a child tattles, they tell a parent or teacher that another child has done something bad〔小孩〕打小报告 —**tattler** *n* [C]

tat·tle·tale /ˈtætḷˌtel; ˈtætlteɪl/ *n* [C] *AmE informal* a word meaning someone who tattles, used by or to children【美, 非正式】〔小孩中的〕打小报告者; 搬弄是非者〔儿语〕; TELLTALE² *BrE*【英】

tat·too¹ /tæˈtu; təˈtuː/ *n plural* **tattoos 1** [C] a picture or message that is permanently marked on your skin with a needle and ink〔皮肤上的〕文身: *a tattoo of a snake* 一条蛇的文身 **2** [C] an outdoor military show with music, usually at night〔常在夜间举行的、有音乐伴奏的〕军队表演操 **3** [singular] a rapid continuous beating of drums, especially played as a military signal, or a sound like this〔尤指作为军事信号的〕连续快速的击鼓声

tattoo² *v* [T] **1** to make a permanent picture or message on someone's skin with a needle and ink DYES〔用针和墨水〕在〔皮肤上〕刺花纹, 文身 **2** to mark someone in this way 给〔某人〕刺花纹, 文身 —**tattooed** *adj*: *The Maori's face was heavily tattooed.* 那个毛利人的脸上刺有很多花纹。

tat·too·ist /tæˈtuɪst; təˈtuːɨst/ *n* [C] someone whose job is tattooing 专门替人文身的人, 文身师

tat·ty /ˈtætɪ; ˈtæti/ *adj* **tattier, tattiest** *informal especially BrE* untidy or in a bad condition; SHABBY【非正式, 尤英】不整洁的, 邋遢的; 破旧的: *tatty jeans* 破旧的牛仔裤 | *a few tatty old chairs* 几把破旧的椅子 —**tattily** *adv* —**tattiness** *n* [C]

Ta·tum /ˈtetəm; ˈteɪtəm/, **Art** (1910-56) a US JAZZ piano player, who was born almost blind, and was one of the greatest ever 塔特姆〔(1910-1956), 美国爵士钢琴演奏家。他一出生双目便几近失明, 是有史以来最伟大的爵士钢琴演奏家之一〕

taught /tɔt; tɔːt/ the past tense and past participle of TEACH: *She taught English in Prague.* 她曾在布拉格教英语。

taunt¹ /tɔnt; tɔːnt/ *v* [T] to try to make someone angry or upset by saying unkind things or laughing at their faults or failures etc 激怒; 嘲弄; 奚落: [+about/over] *The other children taunted him about his weight.* 别的孩子嘲笑他体胖。—**tauntingly** *adv*

taunt² *n* [C often plural 常用复数] a remark or joke intended to make someone angry or upset〔引人发怒或伤人感情的〕嘲弄, 讥笑: *The boy's taunts rang after her. 'Cry baby! Cry baby!'* 男孩的嘲笑还在她耳边回响: "哭鼻子大王! 哭鼻子大王!"

taupe /top; təʊp/ *n* [U] a brownish grey colour 褐灰色 —**taupe** *adj*

Tau·rus /ˈtɔrəs; ˈtɔːrəs/ *n* **1** [singular] the second sign of the ZODIAC, represented by a BULL, and believed to affect the character and life of people born between April 21 and May 22 金牛宫〔黄道十二宫的第二宫〕 **2** [C] someone who was born between April 21 and May 22 出生于金牛宫时段〔即4月21日至5月22日之间〕的人: *My husband's a Taurus.* 我的丈夫出生于金牛宫时段。

taut /tɔt; tɔːt/ *adj* **1** stretched tight 拉紧的, 绷紧的: *the taut strings of the guitar* 吉他绷紧的弦 | *The runners were crouching, muscles taut.* 赛跑运动员正蹲在地上, 肌肉绷得紧紧的。—opposite 反义词 SLACK¹ (3) **2** showing signs of worry or anxiety; TENSE¹ (1) 忧虑的; 紧张不安的: *Catherine looked upset, her face taut.* 凯瑟琳显得心绪不宁, 脸色紧张。

taut·en /ˈtɔtn; ˈtɔːtn/ *v* [I,T] to make something stretch tight, or to become stretched tight (使…) 拉紧, (使…) 绷紧

tau·tol·o·gy /tɔˈtɑlədʒɪ; tɔːˈtɒlədʒi/ *n* [C,U] a statement in which you unnecessarily say the same thing twice using different words, for example, 'He sat alone by himself.' 同义反复, 赘述〈如: "他自己独自坐着。"〉—**tautological** /ˌtɔtəˈlɑdʒɪkl; ˌtɔːtəˈlɒdʒɪkəl◂/ *adj* —**tautologically** /-klɪ; -kli/ *adv*

tav·ern /ˈtævən; ˈtævən/ *n* [C] **1** *BrE old use* a PUB where you can also stay the night【英旧】小旅店, 客栈 **2** word for a bar, often used in the name of a bar 酒馆; 酒吧: *Murphy's Tavern* 墨菲酒馆

taw·dry /ˈtɔdrɪ; ˈtɔːdri/ *adj* cheaply and badly made 廉价的, 不值钱的; 制作粗糙的: *tawdry jewellery and fake furs* 廉价珠宝和假毛皮 —**tawdriness** *n* [U]

taw·ny /ˈtɔnɪ; ˈtɔːni/ *adj* brownish yellow in colour 黄褐色的: *a lion's tawny fur* 狮子的黄褐色毛皮

[S1] [W1] **tax¹** /tæks; tæks/ *n* **1** [C,U] an amount of money that you must pay to the government according to your income, property, goods etc that is used to pay for public services 税, 税款: *The government claimed it would lower taxes.* 政府宣称将降低税收。| [+on] *If you cash in the investment early, then you have to pay tax on that.* 如果你提早把投资兑现, 那么你必须为此缴税。| **before/after tax** (=before or after paying tax on something) 税前/税后 *What are you earning before tax?* 你纳税之前挣多少? | **tax burden** (=the total amount of tax paid by an average person)〔平常人的〕纳税负担 **2** [singular] *formal* something that uses a lot of your strength, PATIENCE etc【正式】沉重的压力[负担] —see also 另见 CAPITAL GAINS TAX, **corporation tax** (CORPORATION (3)), INCOME TAX, PROPERTY TAX, SALES TAX, VAT

tax² *v* [T] **1** to charge a tax on something 对…征税, 向…课税: **heavily/lightly taxed** *Cigarettes are heavily taxed in Britain.* 在英国, 香烟要课以重税。**2 tax a car/motorbike etc** *BrE* to pay the sum of money charged each year for using a vehicle on British roads【英】缴纳汽车/摩托车等的牌照税 **3 tax sb's patience/strength etc** to use almost all of someone's patience, strength etc 使某人不耐烦/费尽力气等: *The kids are really taxing my patience today.* 这些孩子今天真让我够受的。—see also 另见 TAXING —**taxable** *adj*: *taxable income* 应予课税的收入

tax sb **with** sth *phr v* [T] *formal* to tell someone they have done something wrong, or blame them for it【正式】因…而责备〔某人〕; 为…而谴责〔某人〕

tax·a·tion /tækˈseʃən; tækˈseɪʃən/ *n* [U] **1** the system of charging taxes 征税, 课税, 税收(制度): *the reform of taxation* 税收改革 | **direct taxation** (=the taxing of income) 直接税〔即所得税〕| **indirect taxation** (=the taxing of the things people buy) 间接税〔即商品或货物税〕 **2** money collected from taxes 税额, 税款: *We'll have to consider even higher taxation in the next year or two.* 我们必须考虑在今后一两年再提高税额。 [W3]

tax a·void·ance /ˈ· ·,··/ *n* [U] legal ways of paying less tax 避税〔以合法的方式少缴税〕—compare 比较 TAX EVASION

tax brack·et /ˈ· ,··/ *n* [C] a particular range of income levels on which the same rate of tax is paid 征税范围〔按同一税率缴纳的收入范围〕

tax break /ˈ· ·/ *n* [C] *AmE* a special reduction in taxes that the government allows for a particular purpose【美】减税优惠: *a tax break for insulating your home* 为将你住所隔热保温而给予的减税优惠

tax-de·duc·ti·ble /ˌ· ·ˈ···◂/ *adj* tax-deductible costs can be taken off your total income before it is taxed〔在课税前〕可从个人总收入中扣除的: *If you're self-employed, your travel expenses are tax-deductible.* 如果你是个体经营, 你的旅行开支可在计税前从总收入中扣除。

tax-de·ferred /ˌ· ·ˈ·◂/ *adj AmE* not taxed until a later time【美】推迟扣税的: *tax-deferred savings* 推迟扣税的存款

tax disc /ˈ· ·/ *n* [C] a small round piece of paper on a car WINDSCREEN in Britain that shows the driver has paid ROAD TAX 圆形纳税证〔贴在汽车的挡风玻璃上, 表示路税已付〕

tax dodge /ˈ· ·/ *n* [C] a legal way of paying less tax 避税〔合法地少缴税的方式〕

tax e·va·sion /ˈ· ·,··/ *n* [U] illegal ways of paying less tax 逃税〔以非法的方式少缴税〕

tax ex·empt /ˌ· ·ˈ·◂/ *adj* tax exempt savings, income etc are not taxed 免税的, 不征税的

tax ex·ile /ˈ· ˌ··/ *n* [C] someone who lives abroad in order to avoid paying high taxes in their own country〔为躲避在国内缴纳高额税款而移居国外的〕避税者, 逃税者

tax ha·ven /ˈ· ˌ··/ *n* [C] a place where people go to live to avoid paying high taxes in their own country 逃税者乐园, 避税天堂〔指税率低的地方, 许多人为躲避在国内缴纳高额税款而移居此地〕

tax·i¹ /ˈtæksɪ; ˈtæksi/ *n* [C] a car and driver that you pay to take you somewhere; CAB (1) 出租车, 计程车 | **flag (down)/hail a taxi** (=wave or shout at a taxi to make it stop) 挥手拦下/叫住一辆出租车

taxi² *v* [I] if a plane taxis, it moves slowly along the ground before taking off or after landing〔飞机起飞前或着陆后在地面〕缓慢滑行

taxi·cab /ˈtæksɪˌkæb; ˈtæksikæb/ *n* [C] a taxi 出租车

tax·i·der·mist /ˈtæksəˌdɝmɪst; ˈtæksɨdɜːmɨst/ *n* [C] someone whose job is taxidermy 动物标本剥制师

tax·i·der·my /ˈtæksəˌdɝmɪ; ˈtæksɨdɜːmi/ *n* [U] the art of specially preparing the skins of dead animals, birds or fish then filling them with a special material so that they look as though they are alive 动物标本剥制术

tax·ing /ˈtæksɪŋ; ˈtæksɪŋ/ *adj* needing a lot of effort; DEMANDING 烦重的, 累人的; 费劲的: *The job is taxing but enjoyable.* 这项工作很累人, 但也很有乐趣。

tax in·spect·or /ˈ· ·,·ˌ·/ *n* [C] someone who works for the government, deciding how much tax a person or company should pay〔政府的〕税务稽查员

taxi rank /ˈ· · ·/ also 又作 **taxi stand** *n* [C] *BrE* a place where taxis wait to be HIRED【英】出租车候客点; CABSTAND *AmE*【美】

tax·man /ˈtæksmæn; ˈtæksmæn/ *n* [C] **1** a tax collector or tax inspector 税务员; 税务稽查员 **2 the taxman** the government department that collects taxes〔政府的〕税务部门

tax·on·o·my /tæksˋɑnəmɪ; tækˈsɒnəmi/ *n* [C,U] the process of organizing things such as plants or animals into different groups or sets that show their natural relationships〔动、植物等的〕分类学

tax·pay·er /ˈtæksˌpeɚ; ˈtæks-peɪə/ *n* [C] a person or organization that pays tax 纳税人; 纳税单位

tax re·lief /ˈ· ·,·ˌ/ *n* [U] *BrE* the right to not have to pay tax on part of what you earn【英】部分收入免税权

tax re·turn /ˈ· ·,·ˌ/ *n* [C] the form on which you have to give information so that your tax can be calculated 纳税申报单

tax shel·ter /ˈ· ·,·ˌ/ *n* [C] a plan or method that allows you to legally avoid paying tax 合法避税手段

tax year /ˈ· ·/ *n* [C] the period of 12 months in which your income is calculated for paying taxes. The tax year begins on April 6th in Britain, and January 1st in the US. 税务年度〔计数所得税的时段，为期12个月，在英国始于4月6日，在美国始于1月1日〕

Taylor /ˈtelɚ; ˈteɪlə/, **A J P** (1906-90) an English historian, writer, and television speaker. His books include *English History 1914-1945* (1965) and *The Origins of the Second World War* (1961). 泰勒〔(1906-1990)，英格兰历史学家、作家、电视播音员。著作包括《英国史1914-1945》(1965)和《第二次世界大战的起源》(1961)〕

Tay·lor, Elizabeth (1932-2011) a US film actress, often known as Liz Taylor, who was born in the UK and is famous for her beauty. Her films include *National Velvet* (1944), *Cat on a Hot Tin Roof* (1958), *Cleopatra* (1962), and *Who's Afraid of Virginia Woolf?* (1966). 泰勒〔(1932-2011)，美国女电影演员，亦名利兹·泰勒。她生于英国，以美貌著称。主演过的影片包括《玉女神驹》(1944)、《朱门巧妇》(1958)、《埃及艳后》(1962)、《谁害怕弗吉尼亚·沃尔夫》(又译《灵欲春宵》)(1966)等〕

Taylor /ˈtelɚ; ˈteɪlə/, **Zachary** /ˈzækərɪ; ˈzækəri/ (1784-1850) the twelfth president of the US, from 1849 to 1850 泰勒〔(1784-1850)，1849至1850年任美国第十二任总统〕

Tay·side /ˈtesaɪd; ˈteɪsaɪd/ a region in eastern Scotland in the area of the River Tay. Its main city is Dundee. 泰赛德〔苏格兰东部一行政区，位于泰河流域，主要城市为邓迪〕

TB *BrE*【英】, **Tb** *AmE*【美】/ˌti ˋbi; ˌtiː ˈbiː/ *n* [U] tuberculosis; a serious infectious disease that affects your lungs and other parts of your body 结核(病)

T-ball /ˈti ˌbɔl; ˈtiː bɔːl/ *n* [U] *trademark* an easy form of BASEBALL for young children; TEE-BALL【商标】〔一种供小孩玩的〕简易棒球

Tbilisi /ˌtəbəˈlisɪ; ˌtəbɪˈliːsi/ the capital city of the Republic of Georgia 第比利斯〔格鲁吉亚共和国首都〕

T-bill /ˈti bɪl; ˈtiː bɪl/ *informal* a US Treasury bill【非正式】短期国库券〔美国财政部发行的一种短期债券〕

T-bird /ˈti bɝd; ˈtiː bɜːd/ an informal name for a Thunderbird (=a type of car) 雷鸟汽车〔Thunderbird的俗称〕

T-bone steak /ˌti bon ˋstek; ˌtiː bəʊn ˈsteɪk/ *n* [C] a thinly cut piece of BEEF[1] (1) that has a T shaped bone in it T字骨牛排

TBS /ˌti bi ˋɛs; ˌtiː biː ˈes/ the abbreviation of 缩写= the TURNER BROADCASTING SYSTEM

tbs, tbsp *n* [C] the written abbreviation of 缩写= TABLESPOON: *1 tbs sugar* 一汤匙糖

TCCB, the /ˌti si si ˋbi; ˌtiː siː siː ˈbiː/ the abbreviation of 缩写 = TEST AND COUNTY CRICKET BOARD

Tchai·kov·sky /tʃaɪˋkɔfskɪ; tʃaɪˈkɒfski/, **Pe·ter Il·yich** /ˈpitɚ ˋɪlɪtʃ; ˈpiːtə ˈɪlɪtʃ/ (1840-93) a Russian COMPOSER who wrote symphonies (SYMPHONY) and BALLETs, such as *Swan Lake* and *The Sleeping Beauty*. Other well-known works are *The 1812 Overture* and his first piano CONCERTO. His music is romantic, emotional, and often rather sad. 柴可夫斯基〔(1840-1893)，俄国作曲家。他创作有交响曲和《天鹅湖》、《睡美人》等芭蕾舞剧。其他著名作品有《1812序曲》和首创的钢琴协奏曲。他的音乐浪漫、感人，通常颇为凄婉〕

TCP /ˌti si ˋpi; ˌtiː siː ˈpiː/ *trademark* a type of liquid ANTISEPTIC【商标】磷酸三甲苯酯〔一种防腐杀菌剂〕

tea /ti; tiː/ *n*

1 ►DRINK 饮料◄ [U] **a)** a hot brown drink made by pouring boiling water onto the dried leaves from a particular bush 茶: *Do you take milk and sugar in your tea?* 你的茶里面放牛奶和糖吗? **b)** [C] *especially BrE* a cup of tea【尤英】一杯茶: *Three teas and a coffee, please.* 请来三杯茶，一杯咖啡。

2 mint/camomile etc tea a hot drink made by pouring boiling water onto the leaves or flowers of a particular plant, sometimes used as a medicine 薄荷茶/甘菊茶等〔用某些叶子或花泡的饮料〕

3 ►LEAVES 叶子◄ [U] the dried, finely cut leaves of a particular Asian bush, that is used for making tea 茶叶: *China tea* 中国茶叶 | *Ceylon tea* 锡兰茶叶 | *tea plantations* 茶叶种植园

4 ►MEAL 饭餐◄ [U] *BrE*【英】**a)** a very small meal of cake or BISCUITs, eaten in the afternoon with a cup of tea 下午茶, 午后茶点 **b)** a large meal that is eaten early in the evening in some parts of Britain〔英国某些地方分量很大的〕傍晚茶 —compare 比较 DINNER, SUPPER —see also 另见 HIGH TEA

5 tea and sympathy *BrE* kindness and attention that you give someone when they are upset【英】〔对不幸者的〕安慰和同情

6 (not) for all the tea in China *informal* used to say that you would refuse to do something, whatever happened【非正式】绝对不, 无论如何都不: *I wouldn't do his job, not for all the tea in China.* 我无论如何都不会去干他那份工作。—see also 另见 **not be your cup of tea** (CUP[1] (8))

CULTURAL NOTE 文化注释

Tea has traditionally been a very popular drink in the UK. It is still popular even though a lot of people now prefer to drink coffee instead. If you visit a British person's home, they will often 'put the KETTLE on' and ask you if you would like a cup of tea, sometimes informally called a CUPPA or a BREW. It is considered polite to offer someone who is doing work for you in your home, such as someone who is fixing something, a cup of tea. Tea is usually served with milk and sometimes sugar. If you feel worried or have just experienced something bad or shocking, a British person will typically tell you to sit down while they make you 'a nice cup of tea' because it is believed that tea helps to make you feel calm. 茶是英国人十分青睐的传统饮品。尽管现在有不少人都跑去喝咖啡了，但饮茶仍然流行。去英国人家中做客，他们就会"把水壶坐在炉子上"并问你要不要来杯茶。茶有时也被非正式地称作cuppa或brew。家里来人帮忙，例如来修东西，那么给他们奉上一杯茶是礼貌之举。人们通常会在茶里面加牛奶，有时也加糖。如果你感觉忧虑，或刚经历了不好的事情或受了打击，英国人一般会让你坐下来，然后为你沏"一杯好茶"，因为在他们看来茶能让人镇定。— compare Cultural Note at COFFEE比较 COFFEE 文化注释

tea·bag /ˈtibæg; ˈtiːbæg/ *n* [C] a small paper bag with tea leaves inside, used for making tea 袋泡茶, 茶包

tea break /ˈ· ·/ *n* [C] *especially BrE* a short pause from work in the middle of the morning or afternoon for a drink, a rest etc; COFFEE BREAK【尤英】喝茶休息时间, 茶歇〔上午或下午工作中途的短暂休息〕

tea cad·dy /ˈ· ,· ·/ *n* [C] a small metal box that you keep tea in 茶叶罐, 茶叶盒

tea·cake /ˈtiˌkek; ˈtiːkeɪk/ *n* [C] *BrE* a small flat round cake made of a bread-like mixture with RAISINs or CURRANTs in it【英】茶点心〔一种带葡萄干的小圆饼〕

teach /titʃ; tiːtʃ/ *past tense and past participle* **taught** /tɔt; tɔːt/ *v* 

1 ►SCHOOL/COLLEGE ETC 学校/大学等◄ [I,T] to give lessons in a school, college, or university 教书; 讲授: *Guy's been teaching in France for 3 years now.* 盖伊已经在法国教了三年书。| **teach English/mathematics/history etc** *Janet teaches science at a local school.* 珍妮特在当地一所学校教自然科学。| **teach sth to sb** *I'm teaching English to Italian students.* 我给一些意大利学生讲授英语。| **teach school/college etc** *AmE* (=teach in a school etc)【美】教中、小学/大学等 *My Dad taught school in New York.* 我爸在纽约一所学校教书。

2 ►SHOW SB HOW 教某人如何做◄ [T] to show someone how to do something 教〔某人〕做〔某事〕: **teach sb (how) to do sth** *My father taught me to swim.* 父亲教我游泳。| *Hamad is teaching me how to play the guitar.* 哈马德教我如何弹吉他。| **teach sb sth** *Can you teach me one of your card tricks?* 你那些牌技能传授给我一点吗?

3 ►CHANGE SB'S IDEAS 改变某人的想法◄ [T] to show or tell someone how they should behave or what they should think 教导; 教育: **teach sb to do sth** *When I was young, children were taught to treat older people with respect.* 我小的时候, 人们教育孩子要尊重老人。| **teach sb sth** *The trouble is that parents don't teach their kids the difference between right and wrong.* 问题在于父母们不教自己的孩子分清是非。

4 ▶**EXPERIENCE SHOWS STH 经验说明了某事**◀ [T] if an experience or situation teaches you something, it helps you to understand something about life〔经验〕使〔某人〕明白: **teach sb to do sth** *Poverty taught us to appreciate the little things in life.* 贫穷教会了我们要珍惜生活中的一点一滴。

5 **that'll teach you!** *spoken* used when something unpleasant has just happened to someone because they ignored your warning【口】这下你知道了吧!: **that'll teach you to do sth** *That'll teach you to park your car in a restricted area!* 这下你知道不应该把车停放在禁止停车区域了吧!

6 **teach sb a lesson** *informal* to punish someone to make sure that they will not behave badly again【非正式】教训某人: *Next time he comes home drunk lock him out, that'll teach him a lesson.* 下次他再醉醺醺地回家, 就把他关在门外, 那样会给他一个教训。

7 **you can't teach an old dog new tricks** used to say that older people often do not want to change the way they do things 老家伙不会接受新东西; 积习难改

8 **teach your grandmother (to suck eggs)** *BrE* to give someone advice about something that they already know【英】班门弄斧

USAGE NOTE 用法说明: TEACH

WORD CHOICE 词语辨析: **teach, instruct, coach, tutor, train, educate**

Teach is the general word for helping a person or group of people to learn something. teach 泛指"教": *He teaches German at a local school.* 他在当地一所学校教德语。| *Mom taught me to drive.* 妈妈教我开车。

If you **instruct** someone you usually teach them, especially in a practical way and about a practical skill. instruct 指教导、指导, 尤指教授实用的技巧: *First of all you'll be instructed in the use of the safety equipment.* 首先, 将教你们如何使用安全设备。

In British English you can **coach** a person, often outside the ordinary educational system, and often in a particular subject that they need additional help with. 在英国英语中, coach 指针对某一特定学科的额外指导、辅导, 这种指导通常在普通教育系统之外进行: *She coaches kids in advanced mathematics, usually in their homes.* 她通常是到孩子们的家里给他们辅导高等数学。In American English, you **tutor** someone when they need help learning a particular subject. 在美国英语中, 针对某一特定学科的个别辅导的用词是 tutor: *tutoring in reading and arithmetic* 辅导阅读和算术。People also may **coach** a person or team to become better in a sport. coach 也指在体育运动方面的执教、担任教练: *Greg's coaching the football team this year.* 格雷格今年执教这支足球队。

You can **train** a person or group of people, especially in particular skills and knowledge, up to a necessary level for a job. train 是训练、培训人的意思, 尤其是训练特定的技能和知识, 以满足一定层次的工作需要: *It takes several years to train a doctor.* 培养一名医生需要花费好几年时间。| *Soldiers are trained to kill.* 士兵受训杀敌。You can also **train** an animal. train 也指训练动物: *The dogs are trained to attack any stranger that comes near.* 狗受训攻击任何靠近的陌生人。

Educate means to teach people over a long period of time, in all kinds of knowledge (not just school subjects). **Educating** someone is sometimes compared with **training** them in skills for jobs. educate 指长期地、全面地教育, 不仅指学科的教育, 有时与工作技能的培训 (training) 对比: *He was educated at Eton.* 他在伊顿公学受过教育。| *Parents should educate their children in how to behave.* 父母们应该教育自己的孩子注意行为举止。| *The government's campaign aims to educate everyone about AIDS.* 政府的宣传活动旨在教育大家对艾滋病有所了解。

GRAMMAR 语法

Teach is not usually used with **about** except when it is transitive. 除了在作及物动词时, teach 通常不与about 连用: *Children need to be taught about drugs.* 有必要给孩子们讲解毒品方面的知识。| *She taught us about the new computer system* (but NOT 但不用 *She taught about the new computer system*). 她给我们讲解有关这套新的电脑系统的情况。

Remember the past tense and past participle forms are **taught**, never *teached*. 记住其过去式和过去分词是 taught, 从不用 teached。

teach·er /ˈtitʃɚ; ˈtiːtʃə/ *n* [C] someone whose job is to teach 教师, 老师, 教员: *Miss Tindale's my favourite teacher.* 廷德尔小姐是我最喜欢的老师。

teacher's pet /ˌ··ˈ·/ *n* [singular] *informal* a child who everyone thinks is the teacher's favourite student and is therefore disliked by the other students【非正式】〔为其他学生所反感的〕老师的宠儿, 老师宠爱的学生

tea chest /ˈ··/ *n* [C] a large wooden box that used to have tea in it, often used afterwards for moving and storing things 茶叶箱〔装运茶叶的大木箱, 常用来搬运或储存其他东西〕

teach·ing /ˈtitʃɪŋ; ˈtiːtʃɪŋ/ *n* [U] **1** the work or profession of a teacher 教学工作; 教学事业: *She's thinking of going into teaching.* (=becoming a teacher) 她在考虑从事教学工作。| *a teaching career* 教学生涯 | **teaching practice** *BrE*【英】, **student teaching** *AmE*【美】(=a period of teaching done by someone who is training to be a teacher) 教学实习 **2** also 又作 **teachings** [plural] the moral, religious, or political ideas spread by a particular person or group〔道德、宗教、政治等方面的〕教义; 学说: *the teachings of Gandhi* 甘地的学说

teaching hos·pi·tal /ˈ··, ˌ···/ *n* [C] a hospital where medical students receive practical training from experienced doctors 教学医院

tea cloth /ˈ··/ *n* [C] *BrE*【英】**1** a TEA TOWEL 茶巾 **2** a small piece of material used to cover a tea-table〔铺在茶几上的〕小桌布

tea co·sy /ˈ·, ··/ *n* [C] a thick cover that you put over a TEAPOT to keep the tea hot〔用以保温的〕茶壶套

tea·cup /ˈtiˌkʌp; ˈtiːkʌp/ *n* [C] a cup that you serve tea in 茶杯 —see also 另见 **storm in a teacup** (STORM¹ (4))

tea gar·den /ˈ· ··/ *n* [C] a large area of land used for growing tea; tea PLANTATION (1) 茶叶种植园

tea·house /ˈtiˌhaus; ˈtiːhaʊs/ *n* [C] a special house in China or Japan where tea is served, often as part of a ceremony〔中国及日本的〕茶馆, 茶楼, 茶室

teak /tik; tiːk/ *n* **1** [U] a very hard, yellowish brown wood that is used for making ships and good quality furniture 柚木木材〔用于造船或做上等的家具〕**2** [C] the South Asian tree that this wood comes from 柚木(树)〔产于亚洲南部〕

teal /til; tiːl/ *n* **1** [C] a small wild duck 小野鸭 **2** [U] a greenish blue colour 绿光暗蓝色

tea·leaf /ˈtiˌlif; ˈtiːliːf/ *n* [C] **1 tealeaves** [plural] the small, finely cut pieces of leaf used for making tea 茶叶 **2** *BrE slang* a thief【英俚】贼, 小偷

team¹ /tim; tiːm/ *n* [C] **1** a group of people who play a game or sport together against another group〔游戏或体育运动的〕队; 小组: *There are nine players on a baseball team.* 一支棒球队有九名队员。| [also+plural verb *BrE* 英]: *Our team are winning.* 我们的球队目前领先。| **play for a team** *Tim plays for the national volleyball team.* 蒂姆为国家排球队效力。| **in a team** *BrE*【英】, **on a team** *AmE*【美】: *Is Mario going to be on the team this year?* 马里奥今年会在该队打球吗? | **make the team** *AmE* (=be chosen for a team)【美】入选球队 **2** a group of people who have been chosen to work together to do a particular job 工作队, 工作组: [+of] *a team of twelve scientists* 由12名科学家组成的工作组 **3** two or more animals that are used to pull a vehicle〔同拉一辆车的〕一组动物

team² *v*

team up *phr v* [I] to join with someone in order to work on something 结成一队; 合作: [+with] *You can team up with one other class member if you want.* 如果你愿意的话, 你可以与班里一个同学组成一队。

team·mate also 又作 **teammate** *especially AmE*【尤美】/ˈ··/ *n* [C] someone who plays in the same team as you 队友

team spir·it /ˌ·ˈ··/ *n* [U] willingness to work with other people as part of a team 团队精神

team·ster /ˈtimstɚ; ˈtiːmstə/ *n* [C] *AmE* someone whose job is to drive a TRUCK¹ (1)【美】卡车司机

Team·sters, the /ˈtimstɚz; ˈtiːmstəz/ the largest TRADE UNION in the US 国际卡车司机协会〔美国最大的工会组织〕

team·work /ˈtimˌwɝk; ˈtiːmwɜːk/ *n* [U] the ability of a group of people to work well together 团队合作, 协作, 配合

tea par·ty /ˈ·, ··/ *n* [C] **1** a small party in the afternoon at which tea, cake etc is served (午后)茶会 **2 be no tea party** *AmE informal* to be very difficult or unpleasant to do【美, 非正式】很难做; 令人很不愉快

tea·pot /ˈtiˌpɑt; ˈtiːpɒt/ *n* [C] a container for making and serving tea, which has a handle and a SPOUT¹ (1) 茶壶

tear¹ /tɪr; tɪə/ *n* **1** [C] a drop of salty liquid that flows from your eye when you are crying 眼泪, 泪水: *Tears just rolled down his*

face. 他简直是泪流满面。| *tear-stained cheeks* 泪水沾湿的双颊 | **(be) in tears** (=crying) 哭泣, 流泪 *My wife actually broke down in tears telling me.* 我妻子实际上是流着眼泪告诉我的。| **burst into tears** (=suddenly start crying) 突然大哭起来 *Bridget burst into tears and ran out.* 布丽奇特突然大声哭着跑了出去。| **be close to tears/be on the verge of tears** (=be almost crying) 眼泪快要夺眶而出 | **fight back tears** (=try very hard not to cry) 努力克制着不哭出来 | **bring tears to sb's eyes** (=make someone almost cry) 使某人禁不住流泪 *It's music that'll bring tears to the eyes of grown men.* 这种音乐使男子汉也禁不住流起泪来。| **reduce sb to tears** (=make someone cry, especially by being unkind to them) 逼得某人流泪 | **shed tears** (=cry because you are sad) 洒泪, 挥泪 *Few of us shed any tears when Miss Crabbe left.* 克拉布小姐走的时候, 我们当中没有几个人流泪的。| **tears of joy/laughter etc** *Tears of gratitude shone in his eyes.* 他的眼里闪动着感激的泪水。**2 it'll (all) end in tears** *BrE spoken* used to warn someone that what they are doing will have an unpleasant result and cause unhappiness【英口】〔警告某人〕不会有好结果的, 不会有好下场的 —see also 另见 **bore sb to tears** (BORE² (1)), **shed crocodile tears** (CROCODILE (4))

tear² /tɛr; teə/ *v past tense* **tore** /tɔr; tɔː/ *past participle* **torn** /tɔrn; tɔːn/

tear out 撕下

1 a) ►PAPER/CLOTH 纸/布◄ [T] to damage something such as paper or cloth by pulling it too hard or letting it touch something sharp 撕破; 扯破; 划破; 戳破: *Oh no! I've torn my T-shirt.* 哦, 不! 我把 T 恤衫扯破了。| **tear sth on sth** *Be careful you don't tear your sleeve on that nail.* 小心, 别让你的袖子被那钉子划了。| **tear sth out/off/away etc** (=remove something by tearing it away from something else) 把某物撕开/撕掉/扯掉等 *Someone's torn the last page out.* 有人把最后一页给撕掉了。| **tear a hole in sth** *"Oh Rick, you've torn a hole in your best pants."* "哎, 里克, 你这条最好的裤子给划了一道口子。" | **tear sth to shreds/pieces** (=tear something so much that it is in small pieces) 把…撕成碎片 *The contract lay on the ground, torn to shreds.* 合同被撕成碎片, 扔在地上。| **tear sth open** (=to open something very quickly by tearing it) 撕开; 拆开 *Lister grabbed the envelope and tore it open to see if he'd got the job.* 利斯特抢过信封后撕开, 看他是不是获得了那份工作。**b)** [I] if paper or cloth tears, a hole appears in it, or it splits, because it has been pulled too hard or has touched something sharp 〔纸或布〕破裂, 被撕裂; 被扯破: *Careful, the paper is very old and tears easily.* 小心点, 那纸很旧了, 很容易撕破。

2 ►MOVE QUICKLY 快速移动◄ [I always+adv/prep] to move somewhere very quickly, especially in a dangerous or careless way 〔尤指以危险的、粗心大意的方式〕疾驰; 飞跑; 狂奔: **[+away/up/past etc]** *The way the big kids tear around the garden on their bikes, it's dangerous for the little ones.* 大一些的孩子在花园里骑着自行车到处乱闯, 这对小一点的孩子是很危险的。

3 ►REMOVE STH 除掉某物◄ [T always+adv/prep] to pull something violently from the place where it is fixed or held 〔猛烈地〕撕扯; 拔掉; 掀掉: **tear sth from/away etc** *The wind tore the door from its hinges.* 风把门从铰链上给刮掉了。

4 tear loose to escape from something that is holding you by moving violently 挣脱束缚: *The dog tore loose and ran off.* 那条狗挣脱束缚跑掉了。

5 be torn between to be unable to decide between two people or things, because you want both 左右为难, 难以取舍: *I'm torn between getting a new car and going on vacation.* 我既想买一辆新车, 又想去度假, 这真让我左右为难。

6 be torn by sth a) to feel very worried, guilty, anxious etc because you are affected by a strong emotion or feeling 〔心理或情感上〕被折磨; 对…感到忧虑: *I was torn by conflicting impulses.* 相互冲突的欲望折磨着我。**b)** if a country or family is torn by an argument, war etc, it is very badly affected by it 〔国家或家庭〕饱受〔战争、争吵等的〕折磨: *a nation torn by war and riots* 一个饱受战争和动乱之苦的民族

7 tear sb/sth to shreds/pieces to criticize someone or something very severely 对某人严厉批评[驳斥]; 对某事大肆挑剔: *In the end the prosecutor's case was torn to shreds by Russell's lawyer.* 最后, 原告的辩词被拉塞尔的律师驳得体无完肤。

8 ►MUSCLE 肌肉◄ [T] to damage a muscle or LIGAMENT (=a strong band connected to your muscles) 使〔肌肉或韧带〕撕裂, 受伤

9 tear sb off a strip/tear a strip off sb *BrE informal* to criticize someone angrily because they have done something wrong【英, 非正式】怒斥某人, 严厉谴责某人

10 tear sb limb from limb *humorous* to attack someone in a very violent way【幽默】痛打某人; 猛烈攻击某人: *When I get hold of the person responsible, I'll tear them limb from limb.* 等我抓到肇事者, 我会把他打得骨头散架。

11 tear your hair out *informal* to be very anxious or angry about something【非正式】对〔某事〕极其担忧[愤怒]: *I've been tearing my hair out sorting out these wedding arrangements.* 我一直在急着要把婚礼的安排整理出一个头绪来。

12 be in a tearing hurry *BrE* to be doing something very quickly, especially because you are late【英】〔尤指迟于规定时刻〕非常匆忙〔地做某事〕

13 tear sb's heart out to make someone feel extremely upset 使心碎; 使极其难受: *She's so lonely – it's tearing my heart out.* 她是如此孤独, 这让我心里难受极了。

14 that's torn it! *BrE spoken* used when something bad has happened that stops you from doing what you intended to do【英口】这下完了; 这下倒霉了: *That's torn it! I've left my keys in the car!* 这下完了! 我把钥匙忘在车上了!

tear sb/sth **apart** *phr v* [T] **1** to make someone feel extremely unhappy or upset 使心里不快; 使极其难受: *It tears me apart to see them argue.* 看到他们争吵, 我难受极了。**2** to cause serious arguments in an organization, group etc 使〔机构、团体等〕严重内讧, 分裂: *Scandal is tearing the government apart.* 丑闻使政府面临分裂。**3** to break something into many small pieces, especially in a violent way 〔尤指粗暴地〕把…撕成碎片: *a carcass torn apart by wolves* 被狼群撕碎的动物尸体

tear at sb/sth *phr v* [T] to pull violently at someone or something 撕扯: *The children were screaming and tearing at each other's hair.* 孩子们尖叫着, 互相抓扯着对方的头发。

tear away *phr v* **1** [I] to suddenly start moving very quickly 〔突然迅速地〕离开: *The car tore away into the distance.* 汽车突然加速, 迅速消失在远方。**2 tear yourself away (from)** to leave a place or person very unwillingly because you have to 依依不舍地离开: *Could you please tear yourself away from the TV and help me for a minute.* 劳驾你先别看电视了, 来帮我一下。

tear sth ↔ **down** *phr v* [T] to knock down a large building or part of a building 推倒, 拆毁〔建筑物〕: *It's time some of these old apartment blocks were torn down.* 这里有些旧的住宅楼该拆了。

tear into sb/sth *phr v* [T not in passive 不用被动态] **1** to attack someone by hitting them very hard 猛攻; 向…猛扑: *boxers tearing into each other* 相互猛攻的拳击手 **2** to criticize someone very strongly, especially unfairly 〔尤指不公正地〕猛烈抨击〔某人〕: *All I said was that she could maybe try harder and she really tore into me.* 我只不过说她也许得更努力一些, 她倒真的向我开起火来了。

tear off *phr v* **1** [T **tear** sth ↔ **off**] to remove your clothes as quickly as you can 迅速脱掉〔衣服〕: *Ben tore off his coat and dived in to rescue the child.* 本迅速脱掉外衣, 跳下水去救那个孩子。**2** [I] to suddenly start moving very quickly 突然迅速走开[离开]: *I must tear off to the store before it closes.* 我必须在关门前赶到商店。**3** [T **tear** sth ↔ **off**] *BrE informal* to write something in a short time【英, 非正式】匆匆写成: *I tore off a letter.* 我匆匆写就了一封信。

tear sth ↔ **up** *phr v* [T] **1** to destroy a piece of paper or cloth by breaking it into small pieces 把〔纸或布〕撕碎: *Crying, she tore up his letter.* 她边哭边把他的信给撕碎了。**2** to damage or ruin a place, especially by behaving violently 〔尤指举止粗暴地〕捣毁, 破坏〔某个地方〕: *football fans tearing up the grounds* 足球迷们捣毁场地 **3 tear up an agreement/contract etc** to suddenly decide to stop being restricted by a contract etc 撕毁协议/合同等

tear up 撕碎

tear³ /tɛr; teə/ *n* [C] a hole in a piece of cloth, paper etc where it has been torn 〔布、纸等〕撕破的地方; 裂口 —see also 另见 **wear and tear** (WEAR² (4))

tear·a·way /ˈtɛrəˌwe; ˈteərəweɪ/ *n* [C] *informal* a young person who behaves badly and often gets into trouble【非正式】小流氓，暴徒；爱惹祸的小伙子：*One night some young tearaways set fire to the De Corizo house.* 一天夜里，几个小流氓放火烧了德·科里佐家的房子。

tear·drop /ˈtɪrˌdrɑp; ˈtɪədrɒp/ *n* [C] *especially literary* a single drop of salty liquid from your eye【尤文】泪滴，泪珠

tear·ful /ˈtɪrfʊl; ˈtɪəfəl/ *adj* crying a little or almost crying 噙满泪水的；欲哭出声的；垂泪的：*a tearful reunion at the airport* 机场上一次满含泪水的团聚 —**tearfully** *adv*

tear gas /ˈtɪr gæs; ˈtɪə gæs/ *n* [U] a gas that stings your eyes, used by the police to control crowds 催泪瓦斯，催泪弹 —**tear-gas** *v* [T]

tear·jerk·er /ˈtɪrˌdʒɝkɚ; ˈtɪəˌdʒɜːkə/ *n* [C] *informal* a film, book, story etc that makes you feel very sad【非正式】使人悲伤流泪的电影[图书，故事等]

tea·room /ˈtiˌrum; ˈtiːruːm/ *n* [C] a restaurant where tea and light meals are served〔供应茶和点心的〕茶馆，茶室

tease[1] /tiz; tiːz/ *v* **1** [I,T] to make jokes and laugh at someone in order to have fun by embarrassing them, either in a friendly way or in an unkind way 戏弄，逗弄；拿…取笑[开玩笑]：*Don't get upset, I was only teasing.* 别介意，我只是在开玩笑。| **tease sb** *Kids often tease each other.* 孩子们经常互相开玩笑。| **tease sb about** *I was teased about my weight as a child.* 我小的时候别人老取笑我长得胖。**2** [T] to deliberately annoy an animal〔故意地〕逗弄；激怒〔动物〕：*Stop teasing the cat!* 别再招惹那只猫了！**3** [I,T] to deliberately make someone sexually excited without intending to have sex with them 挑逗，撩拨〔使某人性兴奋而又不打算满足对方〕 **4** [T] *AmE* to comb your hair in the opposite direction to which it grows, so that it looks thicker【美】回梳，逆梳〔以使头发显得浓密〕；BACKCOMB *BrE*【英】

tease out *phr v* [T] **1 tease sth out of sb** to persuade someone to tell you something that they do not want to tell you 哄骗某人说出某事 **2** [**tease** sth ↔ **out**] to gently loosen or straighten hairs or threads that are stuck together 把〔缠绕在一起的毛发或线绳〕轻轻弄松[弄直]：*She teased out the knots in her hair.* 她把头发里的结弄开了。

tease[2] *n* [C] *informal*【非正式】**1** someone who enjoys making jokes at people, and embarrassing them, especially in a friendly way 爱开玩笑的人，爱戏弄别人的人〔尤指以无恶意的方式〕：*Don't take any notice of Joe – he's a big tease.* 千万不要搭理乔——他可特别爱戏弄人。**2** someone who deliberately makes you sexually excited, but has no intention of having sex with you 性挑逗者

tea·sel /ˈtizl̩; ˈtiːzəl/ *n* [C] **1** a plant with PRICKLY leaves and flowers 起绒草，川续断〔一种叶子和花都带刺的植物〕 **2** a dried flower from this plant, used for brushing cloth to give it a soft surface 晒干的起绒草花

teas·er /ˈtizɚ; ˈtiːzə/ *n* [C] *informal*【非正式】**1** a very difficult question, especially in a competition〔尤指竞赛中的〕难题 **2** a TEASE[2] 爱戏弄别人的人；性挑逗者

tea ser·vice /ˈ· ˌ··/ *n* [C] a matching set of cups, plates, teapot etc, used for serving tea〔包括茶杯、茶碟和茶壶等在内的〕一套茶具

tea shop /ˈ· ·/ *n* [C] a TEAROOM 茶馆

tea·spoon /ˈtiˌspun; ˈtiːspuːn/ *n* [C] **1** a small spoon used for mixing sugar into tea, coffee etc〔搅拌茶、咖啡等用的〕茶匙 —see picture at 参见 SPOON[1] 图 **2** also 又作 **tea·spoon·ful** /ˈtispunfʊl; ˈtiːspuːnfʊl/ the amount a teaspoon can hold 一茶匙容量

teat /tit; tiːt/ *n* [C] **1** *BrE* the rubber part on a baby's bottle that the baby sucks milk from【英】〔婴儿奶瓶上的〕橡皮奶头；NIPPLE (3) *AmE*【美】**2** one of the small parts on a female animal's body that her babies suck milk from〔雌性动物的〕奶头，乳头

tea tow·el /ˈ· ˌ··/ *n* [C] *BrE* a cloth for drying cups, plates etc, after you have washed them【英】〔用来擦干洗过的杯盘等的〕拭布；茶巾；DISH TOWEL *AmE*【美】—see picture on page A10 参见 A10 页图

tea trol·ley /ˈ· ˌ··/ *n* [C] *BrE* a small table on wheels, that you serve food and drinks from【英】〔用来端送食品和饮料的〕小餐车

tea urn /ˈ· ·/ *n* [C] a large metal container with a TAP[1] (1) used for heating the water to make tea〔烧水泡茶用的〕大茶壶，茶炊

tea·zel, teazle /ˈtizl̩; ˈtiːzəl/ *n* [C] another spelling of TEASEL teasel 的另一种拼法

TEC /tɛk; tek/ Training and Enterprise Council; a British organization paid for by the government which helps to train people for new jobs, especially people who are unemployed. It also helps people start their own business or learn how to manage it effectively. 培训与企业委员会〔英国政府资助的一个机构，专门为求职者、尤其是失业者提供培训，同时还为人们创业和有效管理企业提供帮助〕

tech /tɛk; tek/ *n* [C] *BrE informal* a TECHNICAL COLLEGE【英，非正式】技术学院

tech·ie /ˈtɛkɪ; ˈteki/ *n* [C] *AmE informal* a TECHNICIAN (1)【美，非正式】技术人员

tech·ni·cal /ˈtɛknɪkl̩; ˈteknɪkəl/ *adj* [S2] [W2]
1 ▶**INDUSTRY/SCIENCE** 工业/科学◀ connected with practical knowledge, skills, or methods, especially in industrial or scientific work 技术的，技能的；工艺的：*technical experts* 技术专家 | *technical training* 技术训练 —see 见 TECHNIQUE (USAGE)
2 ▶**LANGUAGE** 语言◀ using words in a special way that is difficult for most people to understand because it is connected with one particular subject 技术性的；与技术或专业相关的：*technical terms* 术语
3 technical problem/hitch a problem involving the way an engine or system works 技术故障，机件故障
4 ▶**ACCORDING TO RULES** 根据规则◀ according to the exact details in a set of rules 严格根据规则的；严格遵循某些规章的：*a technical infringement of the rules* 严格说来，是一次违规
5 ▶**IN MUSIC/ART** 在音乐/艺术方面◀ concerning the special skill of doing something difficult, especially in music, art, sport etc〔尤指在音乐、艺术、体育运动等方面〕技巧卓越的：*Navratilova's technical mastery of the game* 纳夫拉蒂洛娃对网球运动技巧的出色掌握

technical col·lege /ˈ··· ˌ··/ *n* [C] a college in Britain where students who have finished school study for further qualifications especially in practical subjects〔英国实用科目方面的〕专科学院，技术学院

tech·ni·cal·i·ty /ˌtɛknɪˈkælətɪ; ˌteknɪˈkæləti/ *n* [C] **1 technicalities** [plural] details of a system or process that you need a special knowledge to understand 技术细节：*Can you explain the technicalities of laser printing?* 你能不能解释一下激光打印的技术细节？**2** a small detail in a law or a set of rules, especially one that forces you to make a decision that seems unfair〔法律或规则上的〕细则〔尤指迫使人作出看似不公平决定的细则〕：*A legal technicality meant Tollitt had to be released, although the evidence was against him.* 根据法律上的一项细则，必须释放托利特，尽管证据对他不利。| **on a technicality** (=only because of a technicality) 因法律[规则]的细节 *Wild lost the competition on a technicality.* 怀尔德因规则的一项细节而输掉了那场比赛。

tech·ni·cally /ˈtɛknɪklɪ; ˈteknɪkli/ *adv* [S3] **1** [sentence adverb 句子副词] according to the exact details of rules, laws etc; STRICTLY (1) 严格根据法律地；严格遵循规则地：*Technically, I'm not supposed to do this, but we're short-staffed.* 按说，我不应该这样做，但我们实在是缺少人手。**2** [+adj/adv] showing the special skills connected with a particular activity 技巧上；与技巧有关地：*a technically brilliant pianist* 一位技巧卓越的钢琴家 **3 technically possible/impossible/difficult etc** possible etc using the scientific knowledge that is available now 技术上是可能的/不可能的/困难的等

tech·ni·cian /tɛkˈnɪʃən; tekˈnɪʃən/ *n* [C] **1** a skilled scientific or industrial worker 技师，技术人员：*a laboratory technician* 一名实验室技术人员 —see 见 TECHNIQUE (USAGE) **2** someone who is very good at the skills of a particular sport, art etc〔运动、艺术等〕精于技巧者；巧匠：*Whether he was a great artist or not, Dali was a superb technician.* 无论达利是不是一名伟大的艺术家，他确是一名卓越的技巧大师。

Tech·ni·col·or /ˈtɛknɪˌkʌlɚ; ˈteknɪkʌlə/ *n* [U] *trademark* a type of colour film process used for the cinema【商标】〔电影的〕彩色印片法

tech·ni·col·our *BrE*【英】, **technicolor** *AmE*【美】/ˈtɛknɪˌkʌlɚ; ˈteknɪkʌlə/ *adj* [only before noun 仅用于名词前] *humorous* having many very bright colours, usually too bright【幽默】色彩（过分）鲜艳的，艳丽多彩的

tech·nique /tɛkˈnik; tekˈniːk/ *n* [C] [S3] [W1] **1** a special skill or way of doing something, especially one that has to be learned 技巧；手法：*new techniques for producing special effects in movies* 制作电影特技效果的一些新技法 **2** [U] the level of skill or the set of skills that someone has 技术水平；技能：*a footballer with brilliant technique* 一名球技高超的足球运动员

USAGE NOTE 用法说明：TECHNIQUE
WORD CHOICE 词语辨析：**technique, technology, technical, technician, expert, high tech**
A **technique** [C] is a specific way of doing something, usually involving some skill. It may or may not be scientific or involve machines. 可数名词 technique 指技巧、技术，

它不一定与科学或机器有关: *a teaching/management/propaganda technique* 教学/管理/宣传技巧 | *a new technique that allows us to see inside the human body* 一种使我们得以看到人体内部的新技术

Technique [U] is the way you do something practical or skilful. 不可数名词technique 指做某实用或要求专门技巧的事情的水平、技能: *She's a wonderful skater, her technique is superb.* 她是一名了不起的滑冰高手, 她的水平是一流的。

Technology (usually [U]) is the general use of scientific knowledge for practical purposes, usually seen in actual machines or in industry. technology 一般用作不可数名词, 泛指针对实用目的的科学知识, 通常体现于具体的机器或工业方面: *high technology* (NOT 不用 *high techniques*) 高科技 | *Computer/medical technology is changing the world* (NOT 不用 *the technology is changing the world*). 电脑/医学技术正在改变着世界。| *An examination of the wrecked ship will tell us something about the technology of the past* (NOT 不用 *technique*). 通过对遇难船只的检查, 我们将会明白有关前人科技的一些东西。

Something that is **technical** often relates to detailed practical knowledge of something involving science, technology, or machines. technical 往往与科学技术或机械的具体实用知识相关: *a technical report on the plane crash* (=describing exactly what went wrong with the plane) 关于飞机坠毁的技术性报告〔详细描述失事飞机的问题所在〕| *The train is delayed due to a technical fault.* 火车因为技术故障而误点。| *technical progress/subjects/information/help/expertise* 技术进步/题材/情报/帮助/知识

More generally **technical** matters may involve knowledge about any job or subject that only someone specially trained would usually have. 较广义的technical 指与必须经过专门训练才能掌握的任何工作或学科有关的知识: *a technical point of law* 一个专业性的法律点 | *a technical grammatical term* 一个语法专业术语 | *a highly technical question* 一个高度专业性的问题

Someone who works with and mends scientific equipment or machines is a **technician**. Someone who knows all about a particular subject of any sort is an **expert** (NOT 不用 *a technical*). technician 是指在工作中使用科学设备或机器并会对其进行修理的技术人员。expert〔专家〕是指通晓某一学科的人。

A machine, process or industry may be **high tech** (=using the latest scientific ideas, especially electronic) (but NOT 但不用 *high technical*). high tech 形容机器、工序、行业等, 指使用最新科学思想尤其是电子学的高科技: *Surgeons now use the latest in high tech medical equipment.* 外科医生们现在使用最新的高科技医疗设备。| *high tech computer companies* 高科技电脑公司

SPELLING 拼写

Technique is never spelt *technic* or *tecnique*. technique 不能拼写成 technic 或 tecnique。

tech·no /ˈtɛkno; ˈteknəʊ/ *n* [U] a type of popular electronic dance music with a fast, strong beat 高技术音乐〔一种节奏快而强劲的电子舞蹈音乐〕

techno- /ˈtɛknə; ˈteknə/ *prefix* **1** concerning TECHNOLOGY 表示与技术相关的: *technocracy* (=rule by skilled specialists) 技术专家统治 | *technophobia* (=dislike of computers, machines etc) 技术恐惧〔指不喜欢电脑、机器等〕 **2** **techno-literacy/techno-babble/techno-theorist etc** connected with electronic equipment such as computers 对电脑的通晓/技术套语[行话]/电脑理论家等: *techno-literacy* (=skill in using computers) 会用[通晓]电脑

tech·noc·racy /tɛkˈnɑkrəsɪ; tekˈnɒkrəsi/ *n* [C,U] a social system in which people with a lot of scientific or technical knowledge have a lot of power 技术专家统治〔一种科学技术人才掌握大量权力的社会制度〕

tech·no·crat /ˈtɛknəˌkræt; ˈteknəkræt/ *n* [C] a highly skilled scientist who has a lot of power in industry or government 技术专家型官员; 〔在工业或政府内有很大权力的〕技术专家

tech·no·lo·gi·cal /ˌtɛknəˈlɑdʒɪkḷ; ˌteknəˈlɒdʒɪkəl◂/ *adj* related to technology 技术的; 科技的; 工艺的: *The steam engine was the greatest technological advance of the 19th century.* 蒸汽机是19世纪最伟大的科技进步。—**technologically** /-klɪ; -kli/ *adv*: *technologically developed countries* 科技发达国家

tech·nol·o·gist /tɛkˈnɑlədʒɪst; tekˈnɒlədʒɪst/ *n* [C] someone who has special knowledge of technology 技术专家; 工艺学专家

tech·nol·o·gy /tɛkˈnɑlədʒɪ; tekˈnɒlədʒi/ *n* **1** [C,U] knowledge about scientific or industrial methods or the use of these methods 技术; 科技; 工艺: *nuclear technology* 核工业技术 | *the application of modern technologies to agriculture* 现代科技在农业上的应用 —see 见 TECHNIQUE (USAGE) **2** [U] machinery and equipment used or developed as a result of this knowledge 技术设备; 技术应用: *The factory uses the very latest technology.* 工厂使用了最新的技术设备。

tech·no·phobe /ˈtɛknəˌfob; ˈteknəfəʊb/ *n* [C] someone who does not like modern machines, such as computers〔指不喜欢电脑等现代机器的〕技术恐惧者 —**technophobia** /ˌtɛknəˈfobɪə; ˌteknəˈfəʊbiə/ *n* [U]

Te·cum·seh /tɪˈkʌmsə; tɪˈkʌmsə/ (?1765-1813) a chief of the Shawnee tribe who tried to unite the Native American groups in North America so that together they could prevent the US from taking any more of their land. They were beaten at the battle of Tippecanoe in 1811, and Tecumseh was killed in a battle against the US army in 1813. 特库姆赛〔(?1765-1813), 印第安肖尼族酋长。他试图将北美的印第安各部族联合起来, 共同抵制美国政府进一步侵占他们的土地。1811年, 他们在蒂珀卡努河一役中战败。1813年, 特库姆赛在与美国军队作战中阵亡〕

ted·dy bear /ˈtɛdɪ bɛr; ˈtedi beə/ also 又作 **teddy** *BrE*【英】 *n* [C] a soft toy in the shape of a bear 玩具熊

teddy bear 玩具熊

Teddy Bears' Pic·nic, the /ˌ·· ˈ· ˈ··/ a children's song which was first popular in Britain the 1950s and which starts 《泰迪熊的野餐》〔20世纪50年代在英国最早流行的一首儿歌〕, 开头是这样的:

If you go down to the woods today,
You're sure of a big surprise.
If you go down to the woods today,
You'd better go in disguise...
如果你今天要去森林,
保准你会大吃一惊。
如果你今天要去森林,
化了装去才不打紧…

teddy boy /ˈ·· ·/ *n* [C] a member of a group of young men in Britain in the 1950's who had their own special style of clothes and music〔指英国20世纪50年代在衣着打扮和音乐爱好方面都很独特的〕男阿飞

te·di·ous /ˈtidɪəs; ˈtiːdiəs/ *adj* boring, tiring, and continuing for a long time 枯燥乏味的; 冗长的: *a tedious lecture* 一次很枯燥的讲座 —**tediously** *adv* —**tediousness** *n* [U]

te·di·um /ˈtidɪəm; ˈtiːdiəm/ *n* [U] the quality of being tedious 枯燥乏味; 冗长: *She hated the tedium of life in a small country village.* 她很厌烦小乡村里枯燥乏味的生活。

tee[1] /ti; tiː/ *n* [C] **1** a small object, used in GOLF to hold the ball above the ground before you hit it〔高尔夫球运动中用来放置球的〕球座 —see picture on page A23 参见A23页图 **2** a flat, raised area from which you hit the ball in a game of GOLF〔高尔夫球运动中的〕开球区, 发球区

tee[2]

tee off *phr v* **1** [I] to hit the ball off the tee in a game of GOLF〔从高尔夫球球座上〕开球, 发球 **2** [T **tee sb off**] *AmE informal* to make someone angry【美, 非正式】使〔某人〕生气, 激怒: *His attitude really tees me off.* 他的态度真的惹恼了我。**3** [T **tee off on** sb] *AmE informal* to be angry with someone or criticize them【美, 非正式】责骂; 严厉地批评〔某人〕

Tee-ball /ˈ· ·/ *n* [U] another spelling of T-BALL t-ball 的另一种拼法

teed off /ˌ· ˈ·/ *adj AmE slang* annoyed or angry; FED UP【美俚】恼怒的, 发怒的

teem /tim; tiːm/ also 又作 **teem down** *v* [I] *BrE* to rain very heavily【英】下大雨: *It's been teeming down all day.* 一整天都在下着大雨。

teem with sth *phr v* [T not in passive 不用被动态] to be full of people, animals etc 充满〔人或动物等〕: **be teeming with** *Times Square was teeming with theatergoers.* 时代广场上挤满了看戏的人。

teem·ing /ˈtimɪŋ; ˈtiːmɪŋ/ *adj* full of people, animals, etc that are all moving around 充满〔人或动物等〕的; 拥挤的; 万头攒动的: **teeming city/streets/market etc** *the teeming streets of Cairo* 万头攒动的开罗街道

teen¹ /tin; tiːn/ *adj informal*【非正式】[only before noun 仅用于名词前] teenage 青少年的, 十几岁的: *a teen magazine* 一本少年杂志

teen² *n* [C] *AmE informal* a teenager【美, 非正式】青少年, 十几岁的孩子

teen·age /ˈtinˌedʒ; ˈtiːneɪdʒ/ also 又作 **teen·aged** /ˈtinˌedʒd; ˈtiːneɪdʒd/ *adj* [only before noun 仅用于名词前] aged between 13 and 19, or concerning someone of that age 青少年的, 十几岁的〔13 到 19 岁之间的〕: *my teenage daughter* 我那十多岁的女儿

teen·ag·er /ˈtinˌedʒɚ; ˈtiːneɪdʒə/ *n* [C] also 又作 **teen** *AmE informal*【美, 非正式】someone who is between 13 and 19 years old 青少年, 十几岁的孩子〔13 到 19 岁之间的孩子〕: *a TV sex education series aimed at teenagers* 一部针对青少年的性教育电视系列片 —see 见 CHILD (USAGE)

teens /tinz; tiːnz/ *n* [plural] the period of your life when you are between 13 and 19 years old 青少年时期〔13 到 19 岁之间〕: **be in your teens** *They were in their teens when they first met.* 他们初次见面时都才十多岁。

tee·ny /ˈtinɪ; ˈtiːni/ *adj informal* very small; TINY【非正式】很小的, 小小的

tee·ny·bop·per /ˈtinɪˌbɑpɚ; ˈtiːniˌbɒpə/ *n* [C] *old-fashioned* a girl between the ages of about 9 and 14, who is very interested in popular music, teenage fashions etc【过时】〔年龄在大约 9 至 14 岁之间、热衷于流行音乐、青少年时尚等的〕时髦少女

tee·ny wee·ny /ˈtinɪ ˈwinɪ; ˌtiːni ˈwiːni◂/ also 又作 **teen·sy ween·sy** /ˌtinzɪ ˈwinzɪ; ˌtiːnzi ˈwiːnzi◂/ *adj informal* a word meaning very small, used especially by or to children【非正式】小小的; 一点点的〔尤指儿语〕

tee·pee /ˈtipi; ˈtiːpiː/ *n* [C] another spelling of TEPEE tepee 的另一种拼法

tee shirt /ˈ· ˌ·/ *n* [C] another spelling of T-SHIRT t-shirt 的另一种拼法

Tee·side, Teesside /ˈtizsaɪd; ˈtiːzsaɪd/ an area in northeast England around the place where the River Tees enters the North Sea. It is north of Yorkshire and south of Tyneside, and is an important industrial centre, especially for the oil and chemical industries. 蒂赛德〔英格兰东北部一地区, 蒂斯河在此流入北海。蒂赛德位于约克郡以北、泰尼赛德以南, 是一个以石油、化工为主导的重要工业中心〕

tee·ter /ˈtitɚ; ˈtiːtə/ *v* [I] **1** to stand or move unsteadily as if you are going to fall 站立不稳; 摇摇欲坠; 蹒跚行走: [+on/along/across etc] *She teetered along in her high-heeled shoes.* 她穿着高跟鞋踉踉跄跄地走着。**2 be teetering on the brink/edge of** to be very close to an extreme and dangerous situation 濒临〔危险形势〕: *teetering on the brink of revolution* 处于革命前夕

teeter-tot·ter /ˈ·· ˌ··/ *n* [C] *AmE* a large toy like a board on which two children sit, one at each end; SEESAW¹【美】跷跷板

teeth /tiθ; tiːθ/ *n* the plural of TOOTH

teethe /tið; tiːð/ *v* [I] **be teething** if a baby is teething, its first teeth are growing〔婴儿〕长乳牙 —**teething** *n* [U]

teething troub·les /ˈ·· ˌ··/ *n* [plural] small problems that a company, product, system etc has at the beginning〔公司、产品、系统等〕开始阶段的困难: *a few teething troubles with the new computer system* 这套新的电脑系统在启用阶段遇到的几个问题

tee·to·tal /tiˈtotl; ˌtiːˈtəʊtl◂/ *adj* never drinking alcohol 滴酒不沾的 —**teetotalism** *n* [U]

tee·to·tal·ler *BrE*【英】, **teetotaler** *AmE*【美】/tiˈtotlɚ; tiːˈtəʊtələ/ *n* [C] someone who never drinks alcohol 滴酒不沾的人: *There was a time when no self-respecting pop star would admit to being a non-smoking teetotaller.* 曾经有一段时间, 所有自尊自重的明星都不愿承认自己是烟酒不沾的人。

TEFL /ˈtɛfəl; ˈtefəl/ *n* [U] the teaching of English as a foreign language 作为外语的英语教学 —compare 比较 TESOL

Tef·lon /ˈtɛflɑn; ˈteflɒn/ *n* [U] *trademark* a plastic that stops things from sticking to it, often used in making pans【商标】特氟隆, 聚四氟乙烯〔一种不易粘的塑料, 常用于平底锅制造中〕

Tegucigalpa /təˌgusəˈgælpə; təˌguːsɪˈgælpə/ the capital city of Honduras 特古西加尔巴〔洪都拉斯首都〕

Teh·ran /tɛˈrɑn; ˌteəˈrɑːn/ also 又作 **Teheran** the capital and largest city of Iran, and the industrial centre of the country 德黑兰〔伊朗首都和最大城市, 也是该国的工业中心〕

Te Ka·na·wa /te ˈkɑnəwə; teɪ ˈkɑːnəwə/, **Dame Ki·ri** (1944-) an OPERA singer from New Zealand. Many people admire her SOPRANO voice. 卡纳瓦〔(1944-), 新西兰歌剧演唱家。她的女高音颇受青睐〕

tel the written abbreviation of 缩写= TELEPHONE NUMBER

Tel A·viv /ˌtɛl əˈviv; ˌtel əˈviːv/ the second largest city of Israel, which is on the coast of the Mediterranean Sea 特拉维夫〔以色列第二大城市, 位于地中海沿岸〕

tele- /ˈtɛlɪ; ˈteli/ *prefix* **1** at or over a long distance 远〔距离〕: *a telescope* (=for seeing a long way) 望远镜 | *telecommunications* 电信, 远程通信 | *telepathy* (=sending of thought messages) 通灵术 | *teleshopping*(=using a computer in your home to order goods) 网上购物 **2** by or for television 由电视; 为电视: *a teleplay* 电视剧 | *a telerecording* 电视屏幕录像

tel·e·cast /ˈtɛləˌkæst; ˈtelikɑːst/ *n* [C] a broadcast on television 电视广播

tel·e·com·mu·ni·ca·tions /ˌtɛləkəˌmjunəˈkeʃənz; ˌtelikəmjuːnɪ̈ˈkeɪʃənz/ *n* [plural] the process or business of sending and receiving messages by telephone, radio, television etc 电信, 远程通信〔指用电话、无线电、电视等发送和接收信息〕: *a telecommunications satellite* 通信卫星

tele·com·mut·er /ˈtɛləkəˌmjutɚ; ˈtelikəˌmjuːtə/ *n* [C] someone who works for a company at home using a computer connected to the main office 远距离工作者〔指在家里通过使用与公司办公室相连接的电脑而工作的人〕—**telecommuting** *n* [U]

Tel·e·com Tow·er, the /ˌtɛlɪkɑm ˈtauɚ; ˌtelɪkɒm ˈtaʊə/ a very tall, narrow, circular building in central London which was built in the 1960s and used to be called the **Post Office Tower**. It is used for sending and receiving electronic signals for radio, telephones, and television. 电信塔〔伦敦市中心一座又高又细的圆柱形建筑, 建于 20 世纪 60 年代, 旧称邮政塔, 用于发送和接收广播、电话与电视信号〕

tel·e·gram /ˈtɛləˌgræm; ˈtelɪ̈græm/ *n* [C] a message sent by telegraph 电报, 电文; WIRE¹ (6) *AmE*【美】: *telegrams of congratulations* 贺电

CULTURAL NOTE 文化注释

In the UK, the Queen traditionally sends a telegram to anyone who is celebrating their 100th birthday. The telegram service was stopped in 1982, and instead of a telegram, people receive a card, but they still call it a telegram. 在英国, 女王传统上会给每个百岁寿星发一封贺电。1982 年电报服务取消, 之后百岁老人收到的不是一封电报, 而是一张贺卡, 但他们仍习惯称之为"贺电"。

tel·e·graph¹ /ˈtɛləˌgræf; ˈtelɪ̈grɑːf/ *n* **1** [U] an old-fashioned method of sending messages using radio or electrical signals〔旧时用无线电或电信号发送信息的〕电报 **2** [C] a piece of equipment that receives or sends messages in this way 电报机 —see

teeth 牙齿

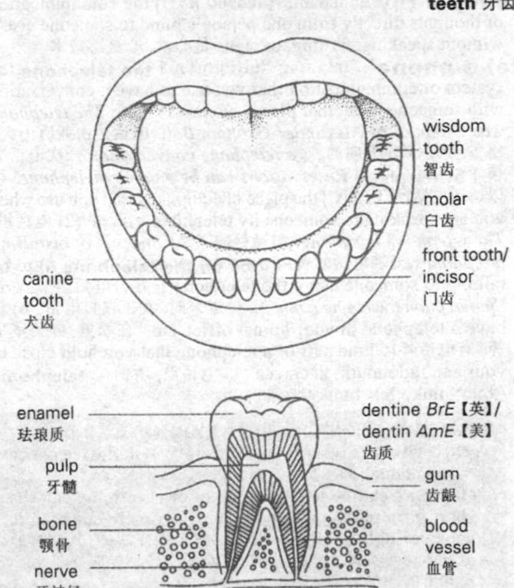

a cross-section of a tooth
牙齿的断面图

also 另见 BUSH TELEGRAPH —**telegraphic** /ˌtɛlə`græfɪk; ˌtelɨˈgræfɪk◂/ *adj* — **telegraphically** /-klɪ; -kli/ *adv*

telegraph² *v* **1** [I,T] to send a message by telegraph（给…）发电报，发电文：*Once he knew where we were, Lewis telegraphed every few hours.* 一知道了我们所在的地方，刘易斯每隔几小时便发来一份电报。**2** [T] *informal* to let people clearly see what you intend to do without saying anything【非正式】流露；暴露〔意图〕：*Sampras rather telegraphed that shot.* 桑普拉斯这球要怎么打，毫不含糊。

Telegraph, the —see 见 The DAILY TELEGRAPH

te·leg·ra·pher /tə`lɛgrəfɚ; tɨˈlegrəfə/ *n* [C] someone whose job is to send and receive messages by telegraph 电报员，报务员

tel·e·graph·ese /ˌtɛləgræ`fiz; ˌtelɨgrəˈfiːz/ *n* [U] the style of language used in TELEGRAMS in which you only include the really necessary words 电报文体

te·leg·ra·phist /tə`lɛgrəfɪst; tɨˈlegrəfɨst/ *n* [C] a telegrapher 电报员，报务员

telegraph line /ˈ··· ,·/ *n* [C] a telegraph wire 电报线（路）

telegraph pole /ˈ··· ,·/ *n* [C] *BrE* a tall wooden pole for supporting telephone wires【英】电话线杆；TELEPHONE POLE *AmE*【美】

telegraph post /ˈ··· ,·/ *n* [C] *BrE* a telegraph pole【英】电话线杆

telegraph wire /ˈ··· ,·/ *n* [C] a wire for sending messages by TELEGRAPH¹ 电报线

te·leg·ra·phy /tə`lɛgrəfɪ; tɨˈlegrəfi/ *n* [U] *technical* the process of sending messages by TELEGRAPH¹【术语】电报通讯（术）

tel·e·ki·nes·is /ˌtɛləkɪ`nisɪs; ˌtelikɪˈniːsɪs/ *n* [U] the ability to move physical objects using only the power of your mind 心灵致动〔仅凭心灵的力量可移动物体的能力〕

tel·e·mar·ket·ing /ˌtɛlə`mɑrkɪtɪŋ; ˌteliˈmɑːkɨtɪŋ/ *n* [U] a method of selling things in which you telephone people to see if they want to buy something 电话推销（术）—compare 比较 TELESALES —**telemarketer** *n* [C]

te·lem·e·try /tə`lɛmətrɪ; tɨˈlemɨtri/ *n* [U] *technical* the use of special scientific equipment to measure something and send the results somewhere by radio【术语】遥测

tel·e·ol·o·gy /ˌtɛlɪ`ɑlədʒɪ; ˌteliˈɒlədʒi/ *n* [U] the belief that all natural things and events were specially planned for a particular purpose 目的论〔认为自然界一切事物均被有意安排以达到某种目的〕—**teleological** /ˌtɛlɪə`lɑdʒɪkəl; ˌteliəˈlɒdʒɪkəl◂/ *adj*

tel·e·path·ic /ˌtɛlɪ`pæθɪk; ˌtelɨˈpæθɪk◂/ *adj* **1** having a mysterious ability to know what other people are thinking 有心灵感应能力的：*How did he know that? He must be telepathic.* 他怎么知道那件事的？他一定有心灵感应。**2** connected with or sent by telepathy 与心灵感应相关的；以心灵感应术传送的：*telepathic messages* 以心灵感应术传递的信息

te·lep·a·thy /tə`lɛpəθɪ; tɨˈlepəθi/ *n* [U] the communication of thoughts directly from one person's mind to someone else's without speaking, writing, or signs 传心术，心灵感应术

tel·e·phone¹ /`tɛlə,fon; ˈtelɨfəʊn/ *n* **1 the telephone** the system of communication that you use to have a conversation with someone in another place; PHONE¹ (1) 电话：*The telephone was invented by Alexander Graham Bell.* 电话是由亚历山大·格雷厄姆·贝尔发明的。| *a telephone conversation* 一次电话交谈 | **by telephone** *Reservations can be made by telephone.* 可以通过电话预订。**2** [C] the piece of equipment that you use when you are speaking to someone by telephone; PHONE¹ (2) 电话机：*The telephone is ringing.* 电话铃响了。| *the cost of installing telephones* 安装电话的费用 **3 be on the telephone a)** to be talking to someone using the telephone 正在打电话：*I was on the telephone when he came in.* 他进来时，我正在打电话。**b)** to have a telephone in your home, office etc〔在家里、办公室里等〕有电话 **4** [C] the part of a telephone that you hold close to your ear and mouth; RECEIVER (1) 电话筒；听筒 —**telephonic** /ˌtɛlə`fɑnɪk; ˌtelɨˈfɒnɪk◂/ *adj*

USAGE NOTE 用法说明：TELEPHONE

WORD CHOICE 词语辨析：words related to the telephone 与 telephone 有关的词

Telephone can be used as a noun or a verb, as can the short form **phone**, which is four times more common in spoken English. telephone可用作名词或动词，其缩写形式phone亦如此。phone 在口头英语中使用的频率是telephone的四倍。

If someone phones you, you **have or receive a call** (NOT 不用 *a telephone*) from them. have a call 或 receive a call 指接到一个电话。

If you want to **phone** a friend or **call** them (or **ring** them **(up)** (*BrE*), **give** them **a ring** (*BrE*)/**call**), you **dial** their **(phone) number**. 给朋友打电话（phone, call, ring … up【英】，或 give … a ring【英】/call），须拨（dial）他的电话号码（phone number）。

If you are phoning **long distance**, you will need to dial the **code** (*BrE*)/**area code** (*AmE*) (=number) for the region or country where they live, as well as their **local** number. 打长途电话（long distance），须拨区号（code【英】/area code【美】）和本地的号码（local number）。

All these numbers are found in the **phone book** or **directory** (*BrE*), or by phoning **directory enquiries** (*BrE*)/**information** (*AmE*). 电话号码可以在电话号码簿（phone book/directory【英】）中找到，也可以在查号台（directory enquiries【英】/information【美】）找到。

If you have a problem **getting through** to the person you are phoning, you may ring the **operator** for help. 电话接通是get through。接不通电话时可以找接线员（operator）帮忙。

When you phone someone, their phone will **ring**, and if they are at home they will answer by **picking up the phone** (or technically the **receiver**, or on cordless phones the **handset**). 你给人打电话时，他的电话铃声会响（ring）起来。如果他在家，他会拿起电话（pick up the phone）来听；严格地说是拿起听筒（receiver 或无绳电话的 handset）。

If they are busy they may ask you to **phone/call/ring back** later or to **hold on**, or more officially and in American English **hold** (=wait). 如果他正忙着，他会让你待会再打（phone/call/ring back）或等一下（hold on，正式用语或美式英语是 hold）。

If they do not want to speak to you, or have finished speaking to you, they may **hang up** (=replace the receiver or switch off the handset). 如果听电话的人不想跟你谈，或者已经谈完了，他会挂断电话（hang up）。

If someone is already **on the phone** when you call them, their number is **engaged** (*BrE*)/**busy** (*AmE*). 如果打电话时对方正在通话（on the phone），电话会占线（engaged【英】/busy【美】）。

If someone does not want to receive any calls, they may **leave their phone off the hook** (=the receiver is not in its proper place) so that no calls will get through. 不想接电话的人会把电话摘下来（leave the phone off the hook），那么什么电话都接不通。

A telephone in a public place is a **public phone** or **payphone**, often placed in a **phone/call box** (*BrE*) or **phone booth** (*AmE*). 在公共场所的电话是公用电话（public phone）或投币电话（payphone），它常设置在电话亭（phone/call box【英】，也叫 phone booth【美】）里。

GRAMMAR 语法

You **(tele)phone** a place or a person, NOT *to* them. telephone 的宾语是一个地方或人，不加 to：*Please phone Mary/the hospital.* 请给玛丽/医院打电话。But you often speak of being **on the phone to** someone. 但可以说 on the phone to …。

telephone² *v* [I,T] *BrE formal* to speak to someone by telephone; PHONE²【英，正式】（给…）打电话：*Mr Dodd telephoned to say he was ill.* 多德先生打电话说他病了。

Frequencies of the verbs **telephone, phone** and **call** in spoken and written English 动词telephone, phone 和 call 在英语口语和书面语中的使用频率

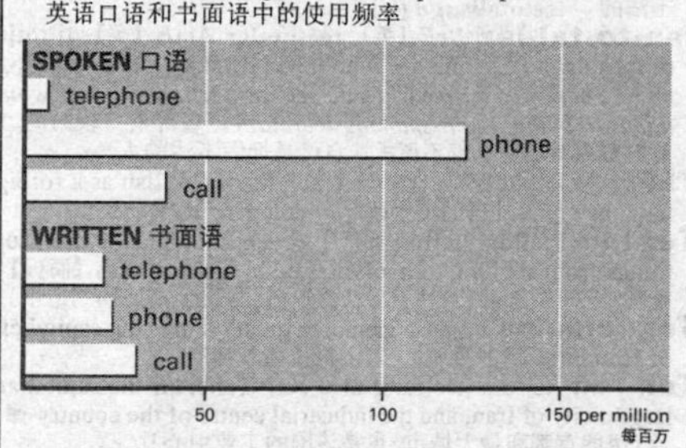

Based on the British National Corpus and the Longman Lancaster Corpus
据英国国家语料库和朗文兰开斯特语料库

This graph shows that it is much more usual in spoken English to use the verbs **phone** or **call** rather than **telephone**, which is formal and is therefore much more common in written English than in spoken English. 本图表显示，在英语口语中，动词phone和call的使用频率远远高于telephone，后者属正式用语，故而在英语书面语中常用得多。

telephone book /'···, ·/ *n* [C] a TELEPHONE DIRECTORY 电话号码簿

telephone box /'···, ·/ *BrE*【英】, **telephone booth** *AmE*【美】*n* [C] an enclosed structure containing a telephone that can be used by the public 公用电话亭[间]

telephone call /'···, ·/ *n* [C] an attempt to speak to someone by telephone 电话: *There's a telephone call for you, Mr Baron.* 巴伦先生，有电话找你。

telephone di·rec·to·ry /'···, ···/ *n* [C] a book containing an alphabetical list of the names, addresses, and telephone numbers of all the people in a particular area 电话号码簿

telephone ex·change /'··· ·, ·/ *n* [C] a central building or office where telephone calls are connected to other telephones 电话交换台; 电话局

telephone num·ber /'···, ··/ *n* [C] the number that you DIAL[2] to telephone a particular person or place 电话号码

telephone pole /'···, ·/ *n* [C] *AmE* a tall wooden pole for supporting telephone wires【美】电话线杆; TELEGRAPH POLE *BrE*【英】

te·leph·o·nist /tə'lɛfənɪst; tɪ̢'lefənɪ̢st/ *n* [C] *BrE* someone whose job is to connect telephone calls at a SWITCHBOARD or telephone exchange【英】接线员，话务员 —compare 比较 OPERATOR (1)

te·le·pho·to lens /ˌtɛləfoto 'lɛnz; ˌtelɪ̢fəʊtəʊ 'lenz/ *n* [C] a special camera LENS (2) used for taking clear photographs of things that are far away〔拍摄远处物体用的〕长焦距镜头，摄远镜头: *a time before the advent of chequebook journalism and telephoto lenses* 在媒体出高价征集名人隐私和摄远镜头问世之前的时代

tel·e·print·er /'tɛlɪˌprɪntə; 'telɪ̢ˌprɪntə/ *n* [C] a machine for writing TELEX messages that you are sending, and for printing messages received 电传打字机; TELETYPEWRITER *AmE*【美】

Tel·e·prompt·er /'tɛlɪˌprɑmptə; 'telɪ̢ˌprɒmptə/ *n* [C] *trademark* a machine that helps someone speaking on television by showing them the words of their speech on a screen【商标】〔在屏幕上为电视讲话人显示出讲稿的〕电子提词机

tel·e·sales /'tɛlɪselz; 'teliseɪlz/ *n* [U] the practice of telephoning people in order to try to sell them things 电话销售，电话售货 —compare 比较 TELEMARKETING

tel·e·scope[1] /'tɛləˌskop; 'telɪ̢skəʊp/ *n* [C] a piece of scientific equipment shaped like a tube, used for making distant objects look larger and closer 望远镜: *the 250-ft Lovell telescope at Jodrell Bank* 乔德雷尔班克天文台的250英尺直径的洛弗尔望远镜 —see also 另见 RADIO TELESCOPE

telescope[2] *v* [T] to make a process or set of events seem to happen in a shorter time 使〔某一过程或某事件〕缩短: *In the story the whole rebellion is telescoped into a few days.* 在这个故事里，整场叛乱的过程被缩短为几天。

tel·e·scop·ic /ˌtɛlə'skɑpɪk; ˌtelɪ̢'skɒpɪk◂/ *adj* **1** made of parts that slide over each other so that the whole thing can be made longer or shorter 可伸缩的; 套叠式的: *a tripod with telescopic legs* 支架可以伸缩的一个三脚架 **2** connected with a telescope 望远镜的; 关于望远镜的: *a telescopic lens* 一个望远镜镜头 | *a telescopic picture of Mars* 一张用望远镜拍摄的火星图片

tel·e·text, Teletext /'tɛləˌtɛkst; 'telitekst/ *n* [U] a system of broadcasting written information on television 电视文字播送

Tel·e·type /'tɛlɪˌtaɪp; 'telitaɪp/ *n* [C] *trademark* a TELEPRINTER【商标】电传打字机

tel·e·type·writ·er /ˌtɛlɪ'taɪpraɪtə; ˌteli'taɪpraɪtə/ *n* [C] *AmE* a TELEPRINTER【美】电传打字机

tel·e·vise /'tɛləˌvaɪz; 'telɪ̢vaɪz/ *v* [T] to broadcast something on television 用电视播放: *The game will be televised live on ABC tonight.* 这场比赛今晚将由美国广播公司现场直播。

S1 W1 **tel·e·vi·sion** /'tɛləˌvɪʒən; 'telɪ̢ˌvɪʒən/ *n* **1** [C] also 又作 **television set** *formal* a thing shaped like a box with a screen, on which you can watch programmes; TV【正式】电视(机): *a 16 inch colour television* 一台16英寸的彩色电视机 **2** [U] a way of broadcasting pictures and sounds in the form of programmes that people can watch 电视播放(技术): *Who invented television?* 电视播放技术是谁发明的? | *television and radio journalism* 电视广播新闻事业 **3** [U] the programmes broadcast in this way; TV 电视节目: **watch television** *In the evenings I like to relax and watch television.* 晚上，我喜欢放松下来，看看电视节目。| **television programme/show/commercial etc** *the television news* 电视新闻 **4 on (the) television** broadcast or being broadcast on television 在电视上播放: *What's on television tonight?* 今晚有什么电视节目? **5** [U] the business of making and broadcasting programmes on television 电视广播业: *Jean works in television.* 琼从事电视广播工作。| **television producer/reporter/newsreader etc** *a television film-crew* 一支电视影片工作组

television li·cence /'····, ··/ *n* [C] an official piece of paper that you need to buy in Britain in order to legally use a television in your home〔英国的〕电视机使用许可证

CULTURAL NOTE 文化注释

In the UK, it is a crime to own a television if you do not have a television licence. You have to buy a licence every year unless you are over 75 years old. DETECTOR VANS go around the streets and use special equipment to find out if anybody is using a television without a licence. The BBC does not receive any money from advertisements. Instead, the money collected from the television licence is used to pay for all of its programmes. Television companies which compete with the BBC think that this is unfair and would like the television licence to be ABOLISH*ed* (=officially ended). 在英国，不申领电视机使用许可证而使用电视是违法的。除非年龄达到75岁以上，人们每年都要花钱购买一张许可证。探测车走街串巷通过特殊的设备来找出那些没有许可证就看电视的人。英国广播公司的收入不是靠广告，相反，播出节目所需的费用来自发售电视许可证的钱。与英国广播公司竞争的电视公司认为这不公平，希望取缔电视许可证。

tel·e·work·er /'tɛlɪˌwɜkə; 'teliwɜːkə/ *n* [C] someone who works from home using a computer, FAX etc 家庭办公者〔指在家里使用电脑、传真机等办公的人〕

tel·ex[1] /'tɛlɛks; 'teleks/ *n* **1** [U] the system of sending messages from one business to another on the telephone network, by SATELLITE (1) etc 电传，电传打字: **by telex** *We'll send you the reply by telex.* 我们将通过电传给您回复。**2** [C] a message sent in this way 通过电传收发的信息

telex[2] *v* [I,T] to send a message, piece of information etc to someone using a telex 用电传将〔信息〕传给〔某人〕

Tel·ford /'tɛlfəd; 'telfəd/, **Thomas** (1757-1834) a Scottish ARCHITECT and engineer who built many bridges, roads, and canals. Some of his bridges are still used today, including the road bridge across the Menai Straits in North Wales. A new town called Telford, named after him, was built in central England in the 1960s. 特尔福特〔(1757-1834)，苏格兰建筑师、工程师，建造了许多桥梁、公路和运河。他建造的一些桥梁至今仍在使用，其中包括北威尔士的梅奈海峡路桥。20世纪60年代，英格兰中部兴建的一座新城镇以他的名字命名，即特尔福特〕

tell /tɛl; tel/ *v past tense and past participle* **told** /told; təʊld/ S1 W1
1 ▶SAY/INFORMATION 说/信息◀ [T] to give someone facts or information about something 把〔某事〕告诉〔某人〕; 说，讲: **tell sb (that)** *She wrote to tell me she couldn't come.* 她写信告诉我她不能来了。| *Don't tell me you've forgotten my birthday again.* 不要对我说你又忘了我的生日。| *Police will not name the body until the relatives have been told.* 在告知亲属之前，警察是不会公布死者的身份的。| **tell sb who/why/what etc** *There is a sign telling you where the emergency exits are.* 有标志告诉你紧急出口在哪里。| **tell sb about sth** *Harry's been telling me all about his last vacation.* 哈里一直在给我讲有关他上次度假的事。| **tell sb sth** *Tell me your name and address.* 告诉我你的名字和住址。| *Can you tell me the quickest way to Manchester?* 你能告诉我去曼彻斯特最快的方式吗? | **tell a story/joke/secret/lie** *When I was young my father told me stories about the war.* 我小的时候，我父亲给我讲过那次战争中的故事。| **tell the truth** *If Dan is telling the truth, the others are in danger.* 如果丹讲的是真话，那其余的人就有危险。| **tell sb straight** (=tell someone the true facts or your true feelings) 直截了当地告诉某人 *I told her straight I wasn't coming.* 我直截了当地告诉她，我不来了。—see 见 SAY[1] (USAGE)

2 ▶ORDER 命令◀ [T] to say that someone must do something; order 命令; 给…下命令: **tell sb to do sth** *The teacher told all the children to sit down quietly.* 老师要所有孩子都安安静静地坐下。| **tell sb what/how etc** *Don't tell me how to behave in public!* 不用你告诉我在公共场合该怎样怎样! | *Stop trying to*

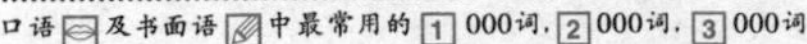

tell me what to do all the time. 别老是想命令我该做什么。| **tell sb (that)** *All the hostages were told that they had to lie on the floor.* 所有的人质被告知必须躺在地板上。| **do as you are told** (=obey) 按照告诉你的去做 *These kids will never do as they're told.* 这些孩子从来不按照要求去做。

3 tell yourself to remind yourself of the facts of a situation because it is difficult to accept or because it worries you 提醒自己；叮嘱自己：*I keep telling myself there is nothing I could have done to save him.* 我不断告诉自己，我实在是无力去救他。

4 ►RECOGNIZE THE SIGNS 辨别迹象◄ [I,T not in progressive 不用进行时] to know something or be able to recognize something because of certain signs that show this 知道；看出；认出：*Yes, I do dye my hair. How can you tell?* 是的，我的确经常染发。你怎么看出来的？| **tell (that)** *Even though it was so dark I could still tell it was you.* 尽管光线这么暗，我还是能认出这就是你。| **tell when/how etc** *It's hard to tell how long the job will take.* 很难说这工作要花多长时间。| **tell by/from** *You can tell by the way it walks that the dog has been injured.* 从这只狗走路的样子可以判断出它受伤了。| **tell a mile off** (=know very easily) 很容易看出 *You could tell a mile off that he was lying.* 很容易看出，他是在撒谎。

5 ►RECOGNIZE DIFFERENCE 识别◄ [T not in progressive 不用进行时] to be able to see how one person or thing is different from another 识别，辨别，分辨：**tell sth from sth** *Amateurs may be unable to tell the fake from the original painting.* 业余爱好者也许识别不了真迹与赝品。| **tell sb and sb apart** *It's almost impossible to tell Jackie and Moira apart since they had their hair cut.* 由于杰姬和莫伊拉都把头发剪了，所以几乎不可能把她俩区别开来。| **tell the difference** *Margarine and butter? I can't tell the difference.* 人造黄油和普通黄油？我说不出它们有什么区别。

6 ►WARN 警告◄ [T usually in past tense 一般用过去时] to warn someone that something bad might happen 警告；告诫：**tell sb (that)** *I told you it was a waste of time talking to him.* 我早就告诉过你，跟他谈话是在浪费时间。| **tell sb to do sth** *My mother told me not to trust Robert.* 我妈妈告诫我不要相信罗伯特。

T

7 ►BE A SIGN OF STH 显示某种情况◄ [T not in progressive or passive 不用进行时或被动态] to give information in ways other than talking which helps you know or understand more about a situation 显示；提示；说明：**tell sb (that)** *The bleeper tells you you've left your lights on.* 嘟嘟声提示你忘了关灯。| **tell sb what/why etc** *The red light tells you when the machine is ready to use.* 红灯提示你，机器已可以使用。| **tell sb about sth** *What do these fossils tell us about our ancestors?* 这些化石说明了我们祖先的什么情况？

8 tell the time *BrE*【英】, **tell time** *AmE*【美】to be able to know what time it is by looking at a clock 从钟表上读出时间

9 ►AFFECT 影响◄ [I not in progressive 不用进行时] to have an effect on someone, especially a harmful one 产生影响〔尤指有害的影响〕：*His years in the army certainly tell in his attitude to his work.* 他的多年军旅生涯当然会影响他对自己工作的态度。| **tell on sb** *These late nights are really beginning to tell on her.* 这些天的熬夜真的开始在影响她了。| *The stress of work told on their marriage.* 工作的紧张影响了他俩的婚姻生活。—see also 另见 TELLING

10 ►BAD BEHAVIOUR 不良行为◄ [I] *informal* to tell someone in authority about something wrong that someone has done【非正式】告发，举报：*I'm going to tell, if you don't stop messing around.* 如果你还是到处瞎混，我就要告发你。| **tell on sb** *If you promise not to tell on me I'll put the money back where I found it.* 如果你答应不去告发我，我就把这些钱放回到原处。

11 tell tales *BrE* to say something that is not true about someone else, especially to cause them trouble【英】造谣；搬弄是非：*Have you been telling tales again?* 你是不是又搬弄是非了？| **tell tales on sb** *an unpopular child, always telling tales on the other children* 一个不招人喜欢的、总爱给其他孩子打小报告的孩子 —see also 另见 TELLTALE[2]

12 tell sb where to get off *informal* to tell someone angrily that you are not interested in them, what they want etc【非正式】严厉斥责某人；使某人碰一鼻子灰：*"Did you give him the money?" "No, I told him where to get off."* "你把那钱给他了吗？""没有。我让他碰了一鼻子灰。"

13 all told altogether, when everyone or everything has been counted 总共，合计，总括起来：*There must have been eight cars in the accident, all told.* 这次大概总共有八辆车出了事故。

14 ►VOTES 票数◄ [T] *technical* to count the votes in an election【术语】数，计算〔选票〕—see also 另见 SAY[2] (1)

Frequencies of the verb **tell** in spoken and written English
动词tell在英语口语和书面语中的使用频率

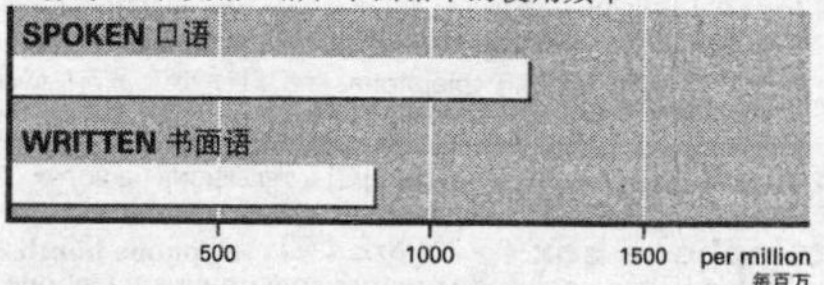

Based on the British National Corpus and the Longman Lancaster Corpus
据英国国家语料库和朗文兰开斯特语料库

This graph shows that the verb **tell** is more common in spoken English than in written English. This is because it is used in a lot of common spoken phrases. 本图表显示，动词tell在英语口语中的使用频率高于书面语，因为口语中很多常用短语是由tell构成的。

tell (*v*) **SPOKEN PHRASES**
含 tell 的口语短语

15 I'll tell you what used when you are suggesting or offering something 我的建议是，我的主张是：*I tell you what, we'll get you something to eat on the way.* 我的建议是，我们给你准备一点在路上吃的东西。

16 I told you so used when you have warned someone about a possible danger that has now happened and they have ignored your warning 我告诫过你吧；我原来说对了吧

17 to tell (you) the truth used to emphasize that you are being very honest 老实说，实话对你讲：*I don't really want to go out, to tell the truth.* 老实说，我并不是真的想出去。

18 I can tell you/I'm telling you used to emphasize that what you are saying is true even though it may be difficult to believe 我可以肯定地说/我说的没错；听我说：*I'm telling you Sheila, I've never seen anything like it in my life.* 听我说，希拉，我这辈子从来没见过这样的事。

19 tell me used before asking a question 告诉我〔用于提问之前〕：*Tell me, what do you think of the new boss?* 告诉我，你对这位新老板有什么看法？

20 I'll tell you something/one thing/another thing used when giving your opinion about something, especially to someone you disagree with 我来讲一点，我来发表一下我的观点〔尤用于表示反对〕：*I'll tell you one thing – you'll never get me to vote for him.* 我告诉你，你休想让我投他的票。

21 I couldn't tell you used to tell someone that you do not know the answer to their question 我不清楚，我没法说：*"How much would a rail ticket cost?" "I couldn't tell you, I always drive."* "一张火车票要花多少钱？""不清楚。我总是自己开车。"

22 I can't tell you a) used to say that you cannot tell someone something because it is a secret 不能告诉你〔因为保密〕：*"Where are you taking me?" "I can't tell you, it would spoil the surprise."* "你要把我带到哪儿去？""不能告诉你，不然那一份惊奇就没了。" **b)** used to say that you cannot express your feelings or describe something properly 无法表达；无法形容：**I can't tell you how/what etc** *I just can't tell you how worried I've been.* 我简直无法形容我一直是多么担心。

23 don't tell me used to interrupt someone because you know what they are going to say or because you want to guess 别告诉我〔用于打断对方的话，表示已经知道他要说什么或猜出他要说什么〕：*"I'm sorry I'm late but..." "Don't tell me – the car broke down again?"* "对不起，我迟到了，不过…""不会又是车子坏了吧？"

24 John/she etc tells me (that) used to say what someone has told you 约翰/她等告诉我：*Mike tells me you found a job.* 迈克告诉我，你找到了一份工作。

25 I'm not telling(you) used to say that you refuse to tell someone something 我不会告诉你的

26 that would be telling used to say that you cannot tell someone something because it is a secret 那可不能讲〔因为是秘密〕

27 you're telling me used to emphasize that you already know and agree with something that someone has just said 那还用说，你说得完全对：*"It's hot in here." "You're telling me!"* "这里面很热。""那还用说！"

28 tell me about it used to say that you already know how bad something is, especially because you have experienced it yourself 我早就知道了，我也有同感：*"I've been so tired*

lately." "Yeah, tell me about it!" "我近来一直感到很累。""是呀,我也是这样!"

29 you never can tell/you can never tell used to say that you cannot be certain about what will happen in the future 说不准; 对〔某事〕没有把握

30 there's no telling what/how etc used to say that it is impossible to know what has happened or what will happen next 不可能知道是什么/将发生什么事等: *She's desperate. There's no telling what she'll try next.* 她不顾一切了, 不知道她下一步会做什么。

31 tell me another used when you do not believe what someone has told you 我不信, 哪有这种事

tell against sb *phr v* [T no passive 无被动态] *BrE formal* if a bad quality or feature tells against you, it makes you unsuccessful in what you are trying to achieve【英, 正式】对…有不利影响, 不利于…: *She has the figure of a model but her height really tells against her.* 她具有模特儿的身材, 但她的身高真的对她不利。

tell sb/sth **apart** *phr v* [T not in progressive 不用进行时] to be able to see which person or thing is which, even though they are very similar 区分, 辨别: *I've never been able to tell the twins apart.* 我从来都不能区别出那对双胞胎。| **[+from]** *It's difficult to tell the forged stamp apart from the real one.* 很难把假的邮票与真的邮票区别开来。

tell of sb/sth *phr v* [T] *especially literary* to describe the details of an event or person【尤文】描述, 叙述: *The poem tells of the deeds of a famous warrior.* 这首诗描述了一位著名武士的壮举。

tell off 斥责

tell sb ↔ **off** *phr v* [T] **1** to talk angrily to someone because they have done something wrong 斥责; 训诫: **be/get told off** *Do your homework or you'll get told off again.* 做你的家庭作业吧, 不然你又要挨骂了。| **tell sb off for doing sth** *My dad told me off for swearing.* 我爸因为我骂人而训斥我。**2** *formal* to separate a group of people from a larger group, in order to do special work or tasks【正式】〔为担当特殊工作或任务而〕抽调出〔一部分人〕; 派出: *Ten soldiers were told off to dig ditches.* 10名士兵被抽调去挖壕沟。

William Tell 威廉·退尔

Tell, William a Swiss FOLK HERO of the 14th century, who opposed the Austrians who ruled Switzerland. According to a famous story, Tell was ordered by the Austrian governor to use his CROSSBOW to shoot an apple placed on his own son's head. He succeeded in doing this because of his great skill, and later killed the governor. This encouraged the Swiss people to fight and gain their independence. Tell's story is told in a well-known OPERA by Rossini. 退尔〔14世纪瑞士民间英雄。他反抗统治瑞士的奥地利人。据一著名传说所述, 奥地利总督令退尔用弩弓把他儿子头上的一只苹果射下来。凭着高超的射技, 他成功地将苹果射落, 后来还杀了总督。这一壮举鼓舞了瑞士人为争取独立而斗争。罗西尼创作的一部著名歌剧也讲述退尔的事迹〕

tell·er /ˈtɛlɚ; ˈtelə/ *n* [C] **1** someone whose job is to receive and pay out money in a bank 银行出纳员 **2** someone who counts votes 清点选票的人, 点[计]票员

tell·ing /ˈtɛlɪŋ; ˈtelɪŋ/ *adj* **1** having a great or important effect; SIGNIFICANT (1) 有力的; 有效的; 有重大影响的: a *telling argument* 有说服力的论点 —see also 另见 TELL (9) **2** a remark that is telling shows what you really think although you may not intend it to 显露内心活动的, 流露真实思想的 **—tellingly** *adv*

telling-off /ˌ‥ˈ‥/ *n* **give sb a telling-off** to talk angrily to someone because they have done something wrong 责备某人, 斥责某人: *They gave the children a good telling-off.* 他们给了那群孩子一顿痛骂。—see also 另见 **tell off** (TELL)

tell·tale¹ /ˈtɛltel; ˈtelteɪl/ *adj* **telltale signs/marks etc** signs that clearly show something that is unpleasant or is supposed to be secret 泄露秘密的, 暴露内情的: *the telltale scars of injecting heroin* 注射过海洛因的明显痕迹

telltale² *n* [C] *BrE* a word used by children, meaning a child who tells adults about other children's secrets or bad behaviour【英】爱搬弄是非的小孩; 打小报告者〔儿语〕; TATTLETALE *AmE*【美】

tel·ly /ˈtɛlɪ; ˈteli/ *n* [C,U] *BrE informal* television【英, 非正式】电视; 电视机: **on telly** *Is there anything good on telly tonight?* 今晚电视上有什么好节目吗? S3

te·me·ri·ty /təˈmɛrətɪ; təˈmerəti/ *n* [U] *formal* unreasonable confidence that is likely to offend someone【正式】鲁莽; 冒失; 不自量力: **have the temerity to do sth** *I was amazed that you had the temerity to ask the question.* 我感到很惊讶, 你竟冒失地提出那个问题。

temp¹ /tɛmp; temp/ *n* [C] an office worker who is only employed temporarily〔办公室的〕临时雇员

temp² *v* [I] to work as a temp 做临时雇员: *Carol's temping until she can find another job.* 卡罗尔在能找到另一份工作之前一直在做临时雇员。

tem·per¹ /ˈtɛmpɚ; ˈtempə/ *n*

1 ▶TENDENCY TO BE ANGRY 容易发怒◀ [C,U] a tendency to become angry suddenly 坏脾气: *That temper of hers will get her into trouble one of these days.* 她的那种脾气早晚会让她碰到麻烦的。| *If he can't control his temper, he should give up teaching.* 如果他控制不住自己的脾气, 他就应该放弃教书工作。| **quick/fiery/violent temper** *Be careful, he's got a pretty violent temper.* 小心点, 他的脾气非常暴躁。| **tempers become frayed** (=people become angry) 人们变得暴躁 *Tempers were becoming frayed as the day went on.* 随着这天时间过去, 大家的火气变得越来越大。

2 ▶SHORT ANGRY FEELING 短时间的怒气◀ [singular,U] an uncontrolled feeling of anger that lasts for a short time〔烦躁的〕情绪;〔难以控制的〕怒气: **be in a temper** *It's no use talking to him when he's in a temper.* 他心情烦躁时跟他谈是没有用的。| **be in a foul/awful temper** (=be angry) 发怒 | **a fit of temper** (=a quick expression of anger) 突发的一顿脾气 *Pete hit his brother in a fit of temper.* 皮特一气之下打了他的弟弟。| **fly into a temper** (=suddenly become very angry) 突然大发脾气 | **temper tantrum** (=sudden angry behaviour like that of a small child) 耍小孩子脾气

3 lose your temper to suddenly become so angry that you cannot control yourself 发脾气, 生气: *"Stop it," Helen shouted at the children, trying not to lose her temper.* "住手。"海伦朝孩子们大声嚷道, 尽量不让自己发脾气。

4 keep your temper to stay calm when it would be easy to get angry 捺住性子, 不让脾气发作: *I was finding it increasingly difficult to keep my temper.* 我发现越来越难控制住自己的脾气了。

5 good-tempered/foul-tempered etc having a good, bad temper etc 脾气好的/脾气坏的等

6 temper! temper! *spoken* used humorously to tell someone not to get angry【口】别生气啦! 别生气啦!〔幽默用法〕

7 ▶ATTITUDE 态度◀ [singular] *formal* the general attitude that people have in a particular place at one time【正式】〔某时某地人们普遍的〕态度, 看法: **[+of]** *the temper of life in Renaissance Italy* 文艺复兴时期意大利人的生活态度 —see also 另见 BAD-TEMPERED, EVEN-TEMPERED, ILL-TEMPERED

temper² *v* [T] **1** to make metal as hard as is needed by heating it and then putting it in cold water 使〔金属〕变坚韧, 锻炼, 使回火: *tempered steel* 回火钢 **2** *formal* to make something difficult or unpleasant more acceptable or pleasant【正式】使缓和; 使容易接受

tem·pe·ra /ˈtɛmpərə; ˈtempərə/ *n* [U] a method of painting in which the colour is mixed with a thick liquid such as egg 蛋彩画法

tem·pe·ra·ment /ˈtɛmprəmənt; ˈtempərəmənt/ *n* [C,U] the emotional part of someone's character, especially how likely they are to be happy, angry etc; DISPOSITION (1) 气质, 性情, 性格, 禀性: *a sunny temperament* 快活的性格

tem·pe·ra·men·tal /ˌtɛmprəˈmɛntḷ; ˌtempərəˈmentl◂/ *adj* **1** likely to suddenly become upset, excited, or angry 喜怒无常的; 易兴奋的; 易怒的: *It's difficult to work for someone who's so temperamental.* 为一个如此喜怒无常的人工作, 真是难啊。**2** a machine, system etc that is temperamental does not always work properly〔机器、系统等〕性能不稳定的 **3** related to the emotional part of someone's character 气质的, 性情的, 性格的: *serious temperamental differences between the couple* 那对夫妇之间严重的性格不合 **—temperamentally** *adv*

tem·pe·rance /ˈtɛmprəns; ˈtempərəns/ *n* [U] **1** the practice of never drinking alcohol for moral or religious reasons 戒酒; 禁酒〔因道德或宗教原因〕: *the Victorian virtues of thrift, temperance, and hard work* 节俭、戒酒、勤奋等这些维多利亚时代的美德 **2** *formal* sensible control of the things you say and do, especially the amount of alcohol you drink【正式】〔对言行, 尤指饮酒的〕自我克制, 节制

tem·pe·rate /ˈtɛmprɪt; ˈtempərət/ *adj* **1 temperate climate/region** a type of weather or a part of the world that is never very hot or very cold 温和的气候; 温带地区: *the temperate zone, north and south of the tropics* 热带以北和以南的温带地区 **2** *formal* behaviour that is temperate is calm and sensible【正式】〔行为〕温和的, 心平气和的; 自我节制的 —see also 另见 INTEMPERATE (1)

tem·pe·ra·ture /ˈtɛmprətʃɚ; ˈtempərətʃə/ *n* **1** [singular] a measure of how hot or cold a place or thing is 温度, 气温: *The temperature of the water was just right for swimming.* 这水温刚好适合游泳。| **a temperature of 20°/100° etc** *Water boils at a temperature of 100°C.* 水在100摄氏度达到沸点。| **the temperature rises/goes up** (=it gets hotter) 温度上升 | **high/low temperatures** *a material that can withstand high temperatures* 一种耐高温的材料 | **rise/fall etc in temperature** *a gradual rise in ocean temperatures* 海洋温度的逐步上升 | **room temperature** (=normal, comfortable temperature of a room) 室温, 常温 *Let the mixture cool to room temperature.* 让混合物的温度降到室温。| **air/water/body temperature** *You mustn't let the body temperature drop too low.* 你千万不要让体温降得太低。| **the temperature falls/drops etc** (=it gets colder) 温度下降等 *The temperature in New York dropped to minus 10° last night.* 纽约的温度昨晚降到了零下10度。| **temperature change** *a great temperature change from last week* 上周以来气温的大幅度变化 | **constant temperature** (=a temperature that does not change) 恒温 *The refrigerator keeps your food at a constant temperature.* 电冰箱以恒温状态保存食物。**2 sb's temperature** the temperature of your blood 某人血液的温度: **take sb's temperature** (=measure their temperature) 量某人的体温 *The nurse took my temperature.* 护士给我量过体温。| **have/run a temperature** (=have a temperature that is higher than normal) 发烧 *Susie has a temperature and has gone to bed.* 苏茜发烧, 已经上床歇着去了。**3** [C] the temperature of a situation is the way people are reacting, for example whether they are behaving angrily or calmly〔人们反应的〕情绪; 气氛: *Be careful what you say, the temperature's a bit hot in there.* 小心你的说话, 那儿的气氛有些紧张。

This graph shows some of the words most commonly used with the noun **temperature**. 本图表所示为含有名词temperature的一些最常用词组。

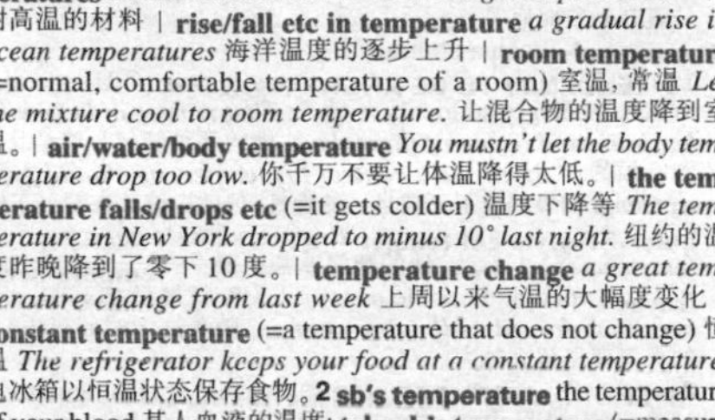

the temperature rises
high temperature
low temperature
rise/fall etc in temperature
room temperature
air/water/body temperature
the temperature falls/drops
temperature change

2 4 6 8 10 per million 每百万

Based on the British National Corpus and the Longman Lancaster Corpus 据英国国家语料库和朗文兰开斯特语料库

tem·pest /ˈtɛmpɪst; ˈtempəst/ *n* [C] *literary* a violent storm【文】暴风雨; 暴风雪

Tempest, The a play by William Shakespeare about Prospero, the Duke of Milan, who has been forced by his brother to live alone on a distant island with his daughter Miranda. The other main characters are Prospero's magical helper, Ariel, and his slave Caliban.《暴风雨》〔威廉·莎士比亚创作的一戏剧。故事中米兰公爵普洛斯彼罗被兄弟逐至一座荒岛, 与女儿米兰达过着与世隔绝的生活。剧中的其他主要人物还有精灵阿里尔及其奴仆卡利班〕

tem·pes·tu·ous /tɛmˈpɛstʃuəs; temˈpestʃuəs/ *adj* **1** a tempestuous relationship or period of time includes many strong emotions〔关系〕强烈情感错杂的;〔时代〕风云变幻的: *a tempestuous marriage* 爱恨交加的婚姻关系 **2** *literary* a tempestuous sea or wind is very rough and violent; STORMY【文】〔大海〕波涛汹涌的;〔天气〕狂风暴雨的: *lost in the dark tempestuous night* 迷失在狂风暴雨的黑夜里 **—tempestuously** *adv* **—tempestuousness** *n* [U]

tem·plate /ˈtɛmplɪt; ˈtempleɪt/ *n* [C] **1** a thin sheet of plastic or metal in a special shape or pattern used to help cut other materials in a similar shape〔切割材料时用的塑料或金属〕模板, 型板, 样板 **2** *technical* a system for arranging information on a computer screen【术语】〔在电脑上整理信息用的〕模板

Tem·ple /ˈtɛmpḷ; ˈtempəl/ an area in central London which contains the Inner Temple and the Middle Temple, two parts of the Inns of Court. Many lawyers and BARRISTERS work there. 圣殿〔伦敦市中心一地区。该区有内殿律师学院和中殿律师学院, 许多律师在此工作〕

temple *n* [C] **1** a building where people go to WORSHIP[1] (1), in the Hindu, Buddhist, Sikh, Mormon, or modern Jewish religions 庙宇, 寺院; 圣殿 **2** [usually plural 一般用复数] one of the two fairly flat areas on each side of your forehead 太阳穴 —see picture at 参见 HEAD[1] 图

Temple, Shir·ley /ˈʃɝlɪ; ˈʃɜːli/ (1928-) a US child actress who was very popular during the 1930s. She sang and danced and had BLONDE curly hair. Her films include *Little Miss Marker* (1934) and *Heidi* (1937). As an adult she became **Shirley Temple Black**, and worked as an ambassador for the US government. 邓波儿〔(1928-), 20世纪30年代走红的美国电影女童星。她能歌善舞, 留着一头鬈曲的金发。出演过的影片有《可爱的马克小姐》(1934) 和《海蒂》(1937) 。成年之后, 她更名为秀兰·邓波儿·布莱克, 曾任美国政府大使〕

tem·po /ˈtɛmpo; ˈtempəʊ/ *n* [C] **1** the speed at which music is played or should be played〔音乐演奏的〕速度 **2** the speed at which something happens; PACE〔事情进展的〕节奏; 步调: *the easy tempo of island life* 岛上生活的轻松节奏

tem·po·ral /ˈtɛmpərəl; ˈtempərəl/ *adj formal*【正式】**1** related to or limited by time 关于时间的; 受时间限制的; 短暂的: *the temporal character of human existence* 人生的短暂性 **2** related to practical instead of religious affairs〔与宗教相对应的〕尘世的, 世俗的: *The Church has no temporal power in the modern state.* 在现代国家里, 教会没有世俗权力。

tem·po·ra·ry /ˈtɛmpəˌrɛrɪ; ˈtempərəri/ *adj* **1** lasting for only a limited period of time 暂时的, 临时的: *A lot of work now is temporary or part-time.* 现在有很多工作都是临时的或非全日的。| *The accident caused a temporary disability.* 事故造成了暂时的残疾。**2** intended to be used for only a limited period of time 短期的, 短暂的: *The council have placed us in temporary accommodation.* 委员会给我们安排了临时住处。—compare 比较 PERMANENT[1], PROVISIONAL (1) **—temporariness** *n* [U] **—temporarily** /ˈtɛmpəˌrɛrəlɪ; ˈtempərərəli/ *adv*: *The library is temporarily closed for repairs.* 图书馆暂时关闭, 以便维修。

tem·po·rize also 又作 **-ise** *BrE*【英】/ˈtɛmpəˌraɪz; ˈtempəraɪz/ *v* [I] *formal* to delay or avoid making a decision in order to gain time【正式】〔为争取时间而〕拖延

tempt /tɛmpt; tempt/ *v* [T] **1** to make someone want to have or do something, even though they know they really should not 引诱, 诱使: *If you leave valuables in your car it will tempt thieves.* 如果你把贵重物品留在车上, 那是在招贼。| **be tempted** *I'm tempted to buy that dress even though it's expensive.* 尽管那件套裙很贵, 我还是动了心想买。**2** to try to persuade someone to do something by making it seem attractive 怂恿; 引诱〔某人去做〕: **tempt sb into doing sth** *The ads hope to tempt people into buying their brand of coffee.* 那些广告希望吸引人们去买他们那个品牌的咖啡。| **tempt sb to do sth** *free gifts to tempt people to join* 吸引人们参加的免费赠品 **3 tempt fate/providence a)** to do something that involves unnecessary risk and may cause serious problems 冒〔不必要的〕危险; 玩命 **b)** to say too confidently that something will have a good result,

that there will be no problems etc 言之过甚，说事情会有好结果、会很顺利等

temp·ta·tion /tɛmpˈteʃən; tempˈteɪʃən/ *n* **1** [C,U] a strong desire to have or do something even though you know you should not 引诱，诱惑: **temptation to do sth** *There might be a temptation to cheat if students sit too close together.* 如果同学们坐得太近，那有可能诱使他们去作弊。| **resist/overcome (the) temptation** (=not do something, even though you want to) 抵挡/战胜诱惑 | **give in to (the) temptation** (=do something although you know you should not) 经不住诱惑 *I finally gave in to the temptation and had a cigarette.* 我终于经不住诱惑，抽了一支烟。**2** [C,U] something that makes you want to have or do something, even though you know you should not 有诱惑力的东西: *Having candy in the house is a great temptation!* 在屋里放糖果，那多有诱惑力！

Temptations, The a US male popular music group which made many successful records from the mid-1960s to the 1990s, including *I'm Gonna Make You Love Me* (1969) and *Just My Imagination* (1971). 诱惑乐队〔美国一支男子流行乐队。20世纪60年代中至20世纪90年代发行过许多优秀唱片，其中包括《我要你爱我》(1969)和《我的想象》(1971)〕

temp·ting /ˈtɛmptɪŋ; ˈtemptɪŋ/ *adj* something that is tempting seems very good and you would like to have it or do it 诱人的，吸引人的: *a tempting job offer* 一次很诱人的工作机会 | *That pie looks tempting!* 那馅饼看上去太诱人了！| **it is tempting to do sth** *It's tempting to just ignore her when she's this upset.* 看她这么心烦意乱，真想不去理她。—**temptingly** *adv*

temp·tress /ˈtɛmptrɪs; ˈtemptrɪ̈s/ *n* [C] *old-fashioned* a woman who makes a man want to have sex with her【过时】引诱男人的女子，妖妇

tem·pus fu·git /ˌtɛmpəs ˈfjudʒɪt; ˈtempəs ˈfjuːdʒɪ̈t/ *Latin* a phrase meaning 'time flies'; used to say that time passes very quickly【拉丁】光阴似箭，时光易逝

ten /tɛn; ten/ *number* **1** 10 十 —see table on page C1 参见C1页附录 **2 ten to one** *informal* used to say that something is very likely【非正式】十之八九，极有可能，多半会: *Ten to one he'll have forgotten all about it tomorrow.* 他明天多半会把这事忘得一干二净。**3 be ten a penny** *BrE informal* to be very common and therefore not special or unusual【英，非正式】很普通，很平常，不稀罕 —see also 另见 **a dime a dozen** (DIME (2)) **4 ten out of ten** *BrE* used in schools to give a perfect mark, or humorously to praise someone【英】〔学校〕给打了满分；得了满分〔称赞人的幽默说法〕: *You get ten out of ten for effort, Simon.* 西蒙，你因为努力得了满分。—**tenth** *number*

ten·a·ble /ˈtɛnəbl; ˈtenəbəl/ *adj* **1** a belief, argument etc that is tenable is reasonable and can be defended successfully〔信仰、论点等〕有道理的，站得住脚的 —opposite 反义词 UNTENABLE **2 be tenable for** a job or position that is tenable for a particular length of time will continue for that length of time〔工作或职位〕可保持一段时间的；可担任一段时间的

te·na·cious /tɪˈneʃəs; tɪ̈ˈneɪʃəs/ *adj* determined to do something and unwilling to stop trying even when the situation becomes difficult 坚持的；坚韧不拔的；顽强的 —**tenaciously** *adv* —**tenaciousness** or **tenacity** /tɪˈnæsətɪ; tɪ̈ˈnæsɪ̈ti/ *n* [U]

ten·an·cy /ˈtɛnənsɪ; ˈtenənsi/ *n* **1** [C] the period of time that someone rents a house, land etc 租赁〔对住房、土地等的〕使用期，租用期: *a six-month tenancy* 六个月的租赁期限 **2** [C,U] the right to use a house, land etc that is rented〔住房、土地等的〕租赁权，租用权

S3 W2 **ten·ant** /ˈtɛnənt; ˈtenənt/ *n* [C] someone who lives in a house, room etc and pays rent to the person who owns it 房客；租户

tenant farm·er /ˌ.. ˈ../ *n* [C] someone who farms land that is rented from someone else 佃农，佃户

ten·ant·ry /ˈtɛnəntrɪ; ˈtenəntri/ *n* **the tenantry** *old use* all the farmers who rent land from the same person in one place【旧】〔在同一地区向同一地主租地耕种的〕佃户，承租人

Ten Com·mand·ments, the /ˌ. .ˈ..ˌ/ according to the Old Testament of the Bible, the set of rules that God gave to Moses on Mount Sinai, in order to tell people how they should behave. They are supposed to have been written on two stone TABLETS (=flat pieces of stone) and they appear in the Christian, Jewish, and Islamic religions. The ten rules include 'Thou shalt not kill' and 'Thou shalt not steal'. 十诫〔据《圣经·旧约》记载，十诫是上帝为了告诫人们如何规范行为而在西奈山上授予摩西的一套戒律。据说戒律刻写在两块石板上，其内容在基督教、犹太教和伊斯兰教中均有所反映。十诫包括"不可杀人"及"不可偷盗"等〕

S1 W1 **tend** /tɛnd; tend/ *v*
1 tend to do sth to often do a particular thing, especially something that is bad or annoying, and to be likely to do it again 易于；往往会做某事〔尤指不好的事〕: *Sally tends to interfere in other people's business.* 萨莉经常会干涉别人的事情。| *The car does tend to overheat.* 这车确实很容易过热。
2 tend towards sth to have a particular quality or feature more than others 有…的趋势；倾向于…: *Charles tends towards obesity.* 查尔斯有肥胖的趋势。
3 tend bar *especially AmE* to serve customers in a store, bar etc【尤美】〔在商店、酒吧等处〕接待顾客: *Theresa tends bar at the Irish Lion.* 特雷莎在"爱尔兰狮"酒吧做招待。
4 ►LOOK AFTER 照料◄ also 又作 **tend to** [T] *old-fashioned* to look after someone or something【过时】照顾，照料: *a shepherd tending sheep on the hillside* 在山坡上照料羊群的牧羊人
5 ►MOVE/DEVELOP 移动/发展◄ [I always+adv/prep] *formal* to move or develop in a particular direction【正式】朝〔某一特定方向〕移动；发展: **[+upwards/downwards]** *Interest rates are tending upwards.* 利率有提高的趋势。

Ten Days that Shook the World /ˌ. ˌ. ˌ. ˌ. ˌ. ˈ./ (1919) a book by the US journalist John Reed about the Russian Revolution of 1917. Reed was himself in St Petersburg during the Revolution, and actively supported it.《震撼世界的十日》〔(1919)，美国记者约翰·里德撰写的一本书，讲述1917年的俄国革命。当时，里德本人就在圣彼德堡，积极支持俄国革命〕

ten·den·cy /ˈtɛndənsɪ; ˈtendənsi/ *n* [C] **1** a PROBABILITY that you will develop, think or behave in a certain way〔发育、思想、行为等的〕倾向: **[+to/towards]** *Some people may inherit a tendency to alcoholism.* 有些人可能天生有酗酒的倾向。| **have a tendency to do sth** (=often do something and be more likely to do it than other people) 倾向于做某事，往往会做某事 *Jean's nice but she has a tendency to talk too much.* 琼人倒不错，就是往往太唠叨了。**2 artistic/alcoholic etc tendencies** particular skills, weaknesses or desires that make someone behave in a particular way 艺术的气质/酗酒的危险等: *kids with criminal tendencies* 有犯罪倾向的孩子 **3** a general change or development in a particular direction 趋势，趋向: **[+for]** *We've noticed a growing tendency for people to work at home instead of in offices.* 我们注意到一种趋势，越来越多的人在家里工作而不是在办公室里上班。| **[+to/towards]** *There has been a general tendency towards conservation and recycling.* 总的趋势一直是着眼于保护和回收。**4** [also+plural verb *BrE* 英] a group within a political party that supports ideas that are usually more extreme than those of the main party〔政党内部观点往往较为极端的〕激进派: *the growing fascist tendency* 日益增长的法西斯极端势力 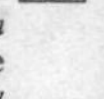 S3 W3

ten·den·tious /tɛnˈdɛnʃəs; tenˈdenʃəs/ *adj* a tendentious speech, remark, book etc expresses a strong opinion that is intended to influence people〔演讲、评论、书籍等的观点〕有强烈倾向性的，鼓动色彩浓厚的

ten·der¹ /ˈtɛndɚ; ˈtendə/ *adj*
1 ►MEAT/VEGETABLES 肉食/蔬菜◄ easy to cut and eat, especially because they have been well cooked 嫩的；软的；易炖烂的〔尤指烹饪恰到好处〕: *tender beef* 嫩牛肉 —opposite 反义词 TOUGH¹ (5)
2 ►PART OF YOUR BODY 身体的某一部分◄ a tender part of your body is painful if someone touches it 疼痛的，一触即痛的: *My arm is still tender where I bruised it.* 我手臂碰伤的地方仍然很痛。
3 ►GENTLE 温柔的◄ gentle and careful in a way that shows love 温柔的；体贴入微的；慈爱的: *Sam's voice was full of tender concern.* 萨姆的话语里充满了体贴入微的关怀。| *a tender look* 含情脉脉的一瞥
4 tender loving care *usually spoken* sympathetic treatment and a lot of attention【一般口】体贴入微的关怀
5 tender blossoms/plants etc plants etc that are easily damaged 娇弱的花朵/幼嫩的植株等
6 tender age *humorous or literary* the time when you are young or inexperienced【幽默或文】年幼时期；未成熟时期: *I don't know that your jokes are suitable for someone of my tender age!* 我不知道你那些笑话对于我这样年幼的人来说是不是合适！| **at the tender age of** *Nicholas was sent to boarding school at the tender age of seven.* 尼古拉斯在年仅七岁时就被送往寄宿学校。—**tenderly** *adv* —**tenderness** *n* [U]

tender² *n* [C] **1** a formal statement of the price you would charge for doing a job or providing goods or services 投标（书）: **put sth out to tender** (=ask for statements of the price for doing a particular job) 招标承办某事 **2** a small boat that takes people or supplies between the shore and a larger boat〔来往于岸边和大船之间运送人员或补给品的〕驳运船；补给船；交通艇 **3** part of a steam train used for carrying coal and water

for the train〔蒸汽火车的〕煤水车 —see also 另见 BARTENDER, LEGAL TENDER

tender³ *v* **1** [I] to make a formal offer to do a job or provide goods and services at a particular price 投标〔承办某事〕: **[+for]** *tendering for a road building contract* 投标承接一项公路修建合同 **2** [T] *formal* to give or show something to someone【正式】递呈, 呈交; 提出: *tender a proposal* 提出一项方案 | **tender your resignation** (=officially say that you are going to leave your job) 正式递交辞呈 **3** [T] *old-fashioned* to give money as a payment【过时】付款, 偿还

ten·der·foot /ˈtɛndɚˌfʊt; ˈtendəfʊt/ *n* [C] *AmE informal*【美, 非正式】**1** someone who has just arrived at a place where life is much harder than they are used to 新到艰苦地区的人; 还没吃过苦的新来者 **2** an inexperienced beginner 没有经验的新手, 初学者: *a political tenderfoot* 政界的新手

tender-heart·ed /ˌ‥ˈ‥◂/ *adj* very kind and gentle 心肠软的, 温柔慈善的: *She was too tender-hearted to refuse.* 她心肠太软, 拒绝不了。—**tender-heartedly** *adv* —**tenderheartedness** *n* [U]

ten·der·ize also 又作 **-ise** *BrE*【英】/ˈtɛndəˌraɪz; ˈtendəraɪz/ *v* [T] to make meat softer and easier to eat by preparing it in a special way〔通过特殊处理〕把〔肉〕烹制得嫩嫩的

ten·der·loin /ˈtɛndɚˌlɔɪn; ˈtendəlɔɪn/ *n* [U] meat that is soft and easy to eat, cut from each side of the backbone of cows or pigs〔牛或猪背腰处的〕嫩肉, 里脊肉: *pork tenderloin* 猪里脊肉

ten·don /ˈtɛndən; ˈtendən/ *n* [C] a thick strong string-like part of your body that connects a muscle to a bone〔连接肌肉和骨头的〕腱

ten·dril /ˈtɛndrɪl; ˈtendrɪl/ *n* [C] **1** a thin leafless curling stem by which a climbing plant fastens itself to a support〔攀缘植物的〕卷须 **2** a thin curling piece of hair 鬈发: *Ralph pushed the damp tendrils of hair out of his eyes.* 拉尔夫把几绺湿鬈发从眼前拨开。

ten·e·ment /ˈtɛnəmənt; ˈtenɪmənt/ *n* [C] a large building divided into apartments, especially in the poorer areas of a city〔尤指城市贫民区的〕公寓大楼

Ten·e·rife /ˌtɛnəˈrif; ˌtenəˈriːf/ one of the Canary Islands off the northwest coast of Africa, which is very popular with tourists 特内里费岛〔加那利群岛一岛屿, 与非洲西北海岸隔海相望, 著名度假胜地〕

ten·et /ˈtɛnɪt; ˈtenɪt/ *n* [C] a principle or belief, especially one that is part of a larger system of beliefs 教义; 信念, 信条: *the tenets of Buddhism* 佛教的教义

ten·fold /ˈtɛnfold; ˈtenfəʊld/ *adj, adv* ten times as much or as many of something 十倍的[地]: *Company turnover has risen tenfold to $550 million.* 公司营业额上升了九倍, 达到5.5亿美元。

ten-gal·lon hat /ˌ‥ˈ‥ˈ/ *n* [C] a tall hat made of soft material with a wide BRIM, worn especially by COWBOYS〔尤指美国牛仔戴的〕宽边高顶软帽

Ten Green Bot·tles /ˌ‥ˈ‥/ a song about ten green bottles hanging on a wall and becoming fewer and fewer as they fall off the wall《十只绿瓶子》〔歌名。歌词大意是, 墙上挂着十只绿颜色的瓶子, 一只一只往下掉, 墙上的瓶子越来越少〕

ten·ner /ˈtɛnɚ; ˈtenə/ *n* [C] *BrE informal* £10 or a ten-pound note【英, 非正式】十英镑; 十英镑钞票: *Can you lend me a tenner?* 你能借给我10英镑吗?

Ten·nes·see /ˌtɛnəˈsi; ˌtenəˈsiː/ abbreviation 缩写为 **TN** a state in the southeast of the US, whose cities include Memphis, Nashville, Chattanooga, and Knoxville. Tennessee is both an industrial and farming centre, with coal mines, chemical industries, and crops such as cotton and tobacco. 田纳西州〔美国东南部一州。境内的城市包括孟菲斯、纳什维尔、查塔努加和诺克斯维尔。田纳西既是一个工业中心, 又是一个农业中心, 有煤矿、化学工业以及棉花、烟草等农作物〕

Ten·ni·el /ˈtɛnɪəl; ˈteniəl/, **Sir John** (1820-1914) a British artist who drew the original pictures for the books *Alice's Adventures in Wonderland* and *Through the Looking-Glass.* He also drew CARTOONS (=funny drawings) for the magazine *Punch* for many years. 坦尼尔〔(1820-1914), 英国画家, 曾为《艾丽丝漫游奇境记》和《镜中世界》画过原始插图。多年来, 他还一直为《笨拙》杂志创作漫画〕

3 3 **ten·nis** /ˈtɛnɪs; ˈtenɪs/ *n* [U] a game for two people or two pairs of people who use rackets (RACKET¹ (3)) to hit a small soft ball backwards and forwards over a net 网球(运动)

tennis court /ˈ‥ ˌ/ *n* [C] the four-sided area that you play tennis on 网球场

tennis el·bow /ˌ‥ˈ‥/ *n* [U] a medical problem in which your elbow is very painful 网球肘〈病〉〔一种肘部十分疼痛的疾病〕

tennis shoe /ˈ‥ ˌ/ *n* [C] a strong shoe used for sports 网球(运动)鞋

Ten·ny·son /ˈtɛnɪsn; ˈtenɪsən/, **Al·fred** /ˈælfrɪd; ˈælfrɪd/ (1809-92) often called by his title, **Alfred, Lord Tennyson**; an English poet who was made POET LAUREATE (=the queen's official poet). His works include *In Memoriam,* a poem written for a friend of his who died, but he is best known for his narrative poems (=poems that tell a story), such as *Charge of the Light Brigade* and *The Lady of Shalott.* 丁尼生〔(1809-1892), 正式称谓为阿尔弗雷德·丁尼生勋爵。他是英格兰诗人, 曾获"桂冠诗人"称号。他的诗作《悼念》为纪念他的一位亡友而作。创作的叙事诗, 如《轻骑旅的冲锋》和《夏洛蒂小姐》, 最为有名〕

ten·on /ˈtɛnən; ˈtenən/ *n* [C] an end of a piece of wood, that has been cut to fit exactly into a MORTISE in order to form a strong joint 榫头, 榫舌

ten·or /ˈtɛnɚ; ˈtenə/ *n* **1** [C] a man with a singing voice that can reach the range of notes just below the lowest woman's voice 男高音(歌手): *the famous tenor, Luciano Pavarotti* 著名男高音卢西亚诺·帕瓦罗蒂 **2** [singular] the part of a piece of music this person sings 高音声部: *Can you sing the tenor?* 你能唱出高音声部吗? **3** [C] a musical instrument with the same range of notes as the singer 次中音乐器 **4 the tenor of a)** *formal* the general way in which an event or process takes place【正式】一般趋向; 一般(发展)进程: *The general tenor of the debate was stressful.* 那场辩论的总体过程充满了紧张气氛。**b)** the general meaning of something written or spoken〔文章或讲话的〕大意, 要旨: *the theological tenor of his speech* 他讲话中的神学要旨

ten·pin /ˈtɛnˌpɪn; ˈtenˌpɪn/ *n* [C] one of the ten bottle-shaped wooden objects that you try to knock down in BOWLING (1)〔保龄球运动中作为滚击目标的〕瓶形木柱, 木瓶

tenpin bowl·ing /ˌ‥ˈ‥/ *n* [U] *BrE* an indoor sport in which you roll a heavy ball along a floor to knock down bottle-shaped wooden objects【英】保龄球, 十柱滚木球运动; BOWLING *AmE*【美】

tense¹ /tɛns; tens/ *adj* **1** feeling very nervous and worried because of something bad that might happen 紧张的; 焦虑的: *The robbers were tense as they waited the long minutes for the van to arrive.* 劫匪们在运钞车到来之前的漫长等待中一直十分紧张。| **tense moment/atmosphere etc** *Marion spoke, eager to break the tense silence.* 玛丽昂说话了, 一心想要缓和紧张沉默的气氛。**2** unable to relax your body or part of your body because your muscles feel tight〔肌肉〕紧张的; 绷紧的: *Massage is great if your neck and back are tense.* 如果你的颈部和背部肌肉紧张的话, 按摩一下是很管用的。—see also 另见 TENSION —**tensely** *adv* —**tenseness** *n* [U]

tense² *v* [I,T] also 又作 **tense up** to make your muscles tight and stiff, or to become tight and stiff 使〔肌肉〕绷紧; 僵直: *Relax, and try not to tense up so much.* 放松, 试着不要绷得这么紧。| *She felt how his body tensed with anger.* 她感觉到他的身体因愤怒而绷得紧紧的。

tennis 网球

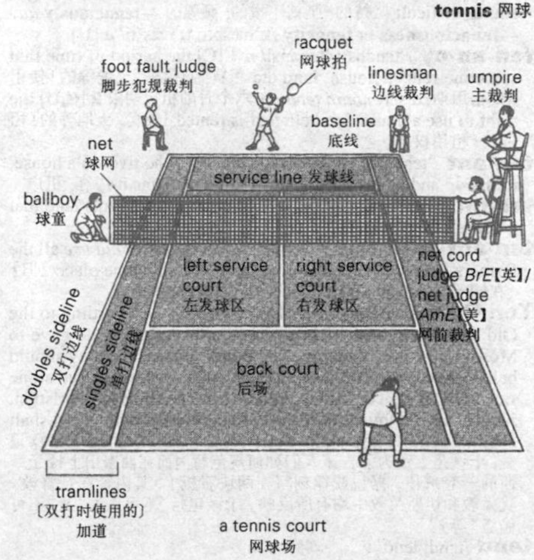

a tennis court
网球场

tense³ *n* [C,U] any of the forms of a verb that show the time, continuance or completion of an action or state that is expressed by the verb. 'I am' is in the present tense, 'I was' is past tense, and 'I will be' is future tense.〔动词的〕时态〔"I am"是现在时态,"I was"是过去时态,而"I will be"是将来时态〕

tensed up /,· ˈ·/ *adj* [not before noun 不用于名词前] *informal* feeling so nervous or worried that you cannot relax【非正式】紧张不安的: *Why are you so tensed up?* 你为什么这样紧张不安?

ten·sile /ˈtɛnsl; ˈtensaɪl/ *adj* able to be stretched 可伸展[拉长]的: *tensile rubber* 有伸缩性的橡胶

tensile strength /,·· ˈ·/ *n* [U] *technical* the ability of a particular kind of steel, CONCRETE² etc to bear pressure or weight【术语】抗拉强度

[3][2] **ten·sion** /ˈtɛnʃən; ˈtenʃən/ *n*

1 ▶NERVOUS FEELING 紧张感觉◀ [U] a nervous worried feeling that makes it impossible for you to relax 紧张; 焦虑; 焦急: *The tension was becoming unbearable, and I wanted to scream.* 这种紧张再也忍受不了,我真想尖声大叫。

2 ▶NO TRUST 不信任◀ [C usually plural 一般用复数, U] the feeling that exists when people or countries do not trust each other and may suddenly attack each other〔人与人、国家与国家之间的〕紧张关系, 紧张局势: *attempts to ease racial tensions in inner cities* 缓和市中心贫民区种族之间紧张关系的努力

3 ▶DIFFERENT INFLUENCES 不同的影响力◀ [singular] a situation in which different needs, forces or influences pull in different directions and make the situation difficult〔需求、势力或影响力之间的〕冲突; 紧张状况: **[+between]** *In business there's always a tension between the needs of customers and shareholders.* 在商业活动中,顾客和股东的需求之间始终存在着矛盾。

4 ▶TIGHTNESS 绷紧◀ [U] tightness or stiffness in a wire, rope, muscle etc〔电线、绳子、肌肉等的〕拉紧, 绷紧: *Tension in the neck muscles can cause headaches.* 颈部肌肉的紧张会导致头痛。

5 ▶FORCE 力量◀ [U] the amount of force that stretches something 张力, 拉力: *This wire will take 50 pounds tension.* 这根金属线能承受50磅的拉力。

1066 the year 1066, the year of the Battle of Hastings and the Norman Conquest of Britain 1066年〔是年发生了黑斯廷斯战役和诺曼人征服不列颠两个事件〕

1066 And All That (1930) a humorous book about British history written by R. I. Yeatman and W. C. Sellar. The writers claim that there are only two dates in British history which all British people remember: the arrival of Julius Caesar in Britain in 55BC, and the Battle of Hastings in 1066.《一〇六六大事记》〔(1930), 耶特曼与塞勒合写的一部英国历史著作, 风格诙谐幽默。作者声称, 英国历史上仅有两个日子为英国人所铭记, 即公元前55年尤利乌斯·凯撒征服不列颠和1066年的黑斯廷斯战役〕

tent /tɛnt; tent/ *n* [C] a shelter consisting of a sheet of cloth supported by poles and ropes, used especially for camping 帐篷: **pitch a tent** (=put up a tent) 搭帐篷 —see also 另见 OXYGEN TENT

ten·ta·cle /ˈtɛntəkl; ˈtentɨkəl/ *n* [C] one of the long thin parts of a sea creature such as an OCTOPUS, which it uses for holding things〔海洋动物如章鱼等的〕触手, 触角, 触须 —see picture at 参见 OCTOPUS 图

ten·ta·tive /ˈtɛntətɪv; ˈtentətɪv/ *adj* **1** not definite or certain, because you may want to change your mind 不确定的; 暂定的; 试探性的: *We've fixed a tentative date for the meeting.* 我们暂定了一个开会的日期。**2** done without confidence 踌躇不决的, 犹豫的: *a tentative smile* 勉强的笑容 —**tentatively** *adv*: *Albi knocked tentatively and entered.* 阿尔比犹犹豫豫地敲了一下门, 然后走了进去。—**tentativeness** *n* [U]

ten·ter·hooks /ˈtɛntɚ,hʊks; ˈtentəhʊks/ *n* **be on tenterhooks** to feel nervous and excited because you are waiting for something〔因等待而〕紧张不安: *She had been on tenterhooks all night, expecting Joe to return at any moment.* 她一晚上都焦虑不安, 期待着乔随时回来。

tenth¹ /tɛnθ; tenθ/ *n* 10th 第十

tenth² *n* [C] one of ten equal parts of something 十分之一

ten·u·ous /ˈtɛnjuəs; ˈtenjuəs/ *adj* **1 tenuous link/relationship/evidence** a link etc that seems weak or doubtful 薄弱的环节/暧昧的关系/无力的证据: *a tenuous link with my past* 与我过去的微弱的联系 **2** *literary* very thin and easily broken【文】纤细的; 易碎的 —**tenuously** *adv* —**tenuousness** *n* [C]

ten·ure /ˈtɛnjɚ; ˈtenjə/ *n* [U] **1** the right to stay permanently in a teaching job at university〔大学教师的〕终身职位 **2** *formal* the period of time when someone has an important job【正式】〔重要职位的〕任期: *throughout his tenure in office* 在他的整个任期内 **3** *law* the legal right to live in a house or use a piece of land for a period of time【法律】〔房屋的〕居住权;〔土地的〕使用期

Ten·zing /ˈtɛnsɪŋ; ˈtensɪŋ/, **Nor·gay** /ˈnɔrge; ˈnɔːgeɪ/ (1914-86) a Nepalese SHERPA (=a mountain climber employed to guide other climbers) who is often called **Sherpa Tenzing**. He and Sir Edmund Hillary were the first people to reach the top of Mount Everest, in 1953. 丹增〔(1914-1986), 尼泊尔登山向导, 常被称为夏尔巴人丹增。1953年, 他与埃德蒙·希拉里爵士一起成为最先登上珠穆朗玛峰的人〕

te·pee /ˈtipi; ˈtiːpiː/ *n* [C] a round tent used by Native Americans〔美洲土著人使用的〕圆锥形帐篷

tep·id /ˈtɛpɪd; ˈtepɨd/ *adj* **1** tepid liquid is slightly warm, especially in a way that seems unpleasant〔液体〕微温的, 微热的〔尤指温度不合适的〕: *I politely sipped my tepid coffee.* 我斯文地啜饮着微热的咖啡。—see picture at 参见 HOT¹ 图 **2** a feeling, reaction etc that is tepid shows a lack of excitement or interest〔感觉〕不够热情的;〔反应〕冷淡的: *The critics' reaction to the play was tepid.* 评论家对该剧的反应冷淡。—see also 另见 LUKEWARM —**tepidly** *adv* —**tepidness** or **tepidity** /tɪˈpɪdətɪ; teˈpɪdɨti/ *n* [U]

te·qui·la /təˈkilə; tɨˈkiːlə/ *n* [C,U] a strong alcoholic drink made in Mexico from the CACTUS plant 特奎拉酒〔一种墨西哥产用植物龙舌兰制成的烈酒〕

ter·cen·te·na·ry /,tɝˈsɛntə,nɛrɪ; ,tɜːsenˈtiːnəri/ *n* [C] the day or year exactly 300 years after a particular event 300周年〔纪念日〕

Teresa, Mother —see 见 MOTHER TERESA

Ter·kel /ˈtɝkl; ˈtɜːkəl/, **Studs** /stʌdz; stʌdz/ (1912-2008) a US writer and radio broadcaster whose books, including *Working* and *The Good War*, are based on the experiences and memories of ordinary American people 特克尔〔(1912-2008), 美国作家、电台播音员。作品包括《工作》和《美好的战争》等, 根据美国普通老百姓的经历和回忆写成〕

[1][1] **term¹** /tɝm; tɜːm/ *n* [C]

① ONE WAY OF REGARDING SOMETHING 看待某事的一种方式
② WORDS/LANGUAGE 字词/语言
③ PERIOD OF TIME 时段
④ CONDITIONS/AGREEMENT 条件/协议
⑤ RELATIONSHIP 关系
⑥ OTHER SENSES 其他意思

① ONE WAY OF REGARDING SOMETHING 看待某事的一种方式

1 in financial/artistic/psychological etc terms if you describe or consider something in financial etc terms, you are mainly interested in the financial etc side of it 就金融/艺术/心理学等而言: *In artistic terms, the film was revolutionary.* 从艺术角度来看, 这部电影具有革命性。| *the enormous cost of war, in human terms* 就人的生命而言战争的高昂代价

2 in terms of if you explain or judge something in terms of a particular fact or event, you are only interested in its connection with that fact or event 在…方面, 从…方面来说; 根据…来解释: *US foreign policy tended to see everything in terms of the Vietnam war.* 美国的外交政策往往根据越南战争的角度来看待一切。| *In terms of customer satisfaction, the policy cannot be criticized.* 说到顾客的满意情况, 这个政策无可挑剔。

3 in sb's terms according to one person's set of opinions 在某人看来, 根据某人的观点: *In their terms, cutting government spending is the most important thing.* 根据他们的观点, 削减政

府开支是最重要的事情。

4 in real terms a change of a price or cost in real terms has been calculated to include the effects of other changes such as price rises〔价格或费用的〕实际变化情况: *Our wages have gone down in real terms over the past year.* 我们的工资实际上比去年降低了。

② **WORDS/LANGUAGE** 字词/语言

5 ▶WORD/EXPRESSION 字词/词组◀ [C] a word or expression that has a particular meaning, especially in a technical or scientific subject 专门名词; 术语: **medical/legal/scientific term** *Contusion is the medical term for a bruise.* "挫伤"一词是磕碰受伤的医学名称。

6 a term of abuse/endearment etc a word or expression used to insult someone, say you love them etc 骂人的词/表示爱意的词等: *To an islander, tourist was just about the worst term of abuse.* 对一个岛上居民来说, 游客差不多是被用得最滥的词。

7 in glowing terms/in strong terms if you describe something in glowing terms or say something in strong terms, you show that you admire something very much or that you are very angry 以十分赞许的口吻/以强烈的措辞: *I complained to the manager in the strongest possible terms.* 我以最强烈的措辞向经理投诉。

8 in no uncertain terms in a clear and usually angry way〔通常带着怒气〕直截了当地: *He told me in no uncertain terms not to park near his house.* 他直截了当地告诉我, 别把车停在他家附近。—see also 另见 **a contradiction in terms** (CONTRADICTION (3))

③ **PERIOD OF TIME** 时段

9 ▶SCHOOL/UNIVERSITY 中小学/大学◀ [C] *BrE* one of the three periods that the school or university year is divided into【英】学期〔一学年分为三学期〕: **summer/autumn/spring term** *The main exams are at the end of the summer term.* 主要的考试都安排在夏季学期的期末。| **term time** (=during the term) 在学期内 *Teachers often feel overworked in term time.* 教师们在学期内经常觉得工作担子过重。—see also 另见 HALF-TERM —compare 比较 SEMESTER

10 in the long/short/medium term considered over a period from now until a long etc time in the future 就长期/短期/中期而言: *The company's prospects look good in the long term.* 这家公司的远景看好。

11 ▶TIME IN A JOB 工作的时间◀ [C] a period of time for which someone is elected to an important government job, or that a government has power〔一届政府或当选重要政府职务的〕任期, 期限: **term of office/term in office** *The president hopes to be elected to a second term of office.* 总统希望当选连任一届。

12 prison/jail term etc a period of time that someone must spend in prison 服刑期限: *The terrorists each received a 30 year prison term.* 每一名恐怖分子被判30年监禁。

13 ▶BUSINESS 商务◀ [singular] the period of time that a contract, LOAN[1] (1) etc continues for〔合同等的〕有效期限: *We're trying to extend the term on our mortgage.* 我们正在设法延长抵押的期限。

14 ▶END OF BUSINESS AGREEMENT 商务协议的终止◀ [singular] *technical* the end of the period of a business agreement【术语】〔商务协议的〕终止期: *The policy reaches its term next year.* 这份保险单在明年终止。

15 ▶HAVING A BABY 生孩子◀ [U] *technical* the end of the period of time when a woman is PREGNANT【术语】分娩期, 足月(分娩) —see also 另见 LONG-TERM, SHORT-TERM

④ **CONDITIONS/AGREEMENT** 条件/协议

16 ▶CONDITIONS 条件◀ **terms** [plural] **a)** the conditions of an agreement, contract, or legal document〔协议、合同或法律文件的〕条款: *Under the terms of the agreement, Hong Kong goes back to China in 1997.* 根据协议条款, 香港于1997年回归中国。**b)** the conditions under which you agree to buy or sell something 付款条件; 购买[出售]条件: *I bought this car on very reasonable terms.* 我以非常合理的价格买了这辆车。| **on easy terms** (=a way of paying for something gradually in small amounts) 以分期付款的方式

17 on your (own) terms according to the conditions that you ask for 按照自己的条件: *If I agree to do this it will be on my own terms.* 如果我同意做这事, 就要按我的条件来办。

18 terms of reference the agreed limits of what an official committee or report has been asked to study〔对某一官方委员会或报告的〕授权范围; 研究事项

⑤ **RELATIONSHIP** 关系

19 be on good/bad terms to have a friendly relationship or bad relationship with someone 关系好/关系不好: [+with] *We're on good terms with all our neighbours.* 我们与所有的邻居关系都好。| *He had been on bad terms with his father for years.* 他多年来一直与父亲关系不好。

20 be on speaking terms to be able to talk to someone and have a friendly relationship with them, especially after a quarrel〔尤指吵架后〕关系好, 友好地相互说话: *They were barely on speaking terms.* 他们关系不好, 相互之间几乎不说话。

⑥ **OTHER SENSES** 其他意思

21 come to terms with sth to accept an unpleasant situation or event and no longer feel upset or angry about it 与…妥协, 对…让步; 接受〔不愉快的事〕: *It's hard to come to terms with being unemployed.* 很难接受失业这个现实啊。

22 on equal terms/on the same terms having the same advantages, rights, or abilities as anyone else 在平等的条件下/在相同的条件下: *US companies want to be able to compete on equal terms with their overseas rivals.* 美国的公司想要在平等的条件下与他们的海外对手展开竞争。

23 be thinking/talking in terms of to be considering doing something, buying something, arranging something etc 正考虑做某事; 正打算做某事: *She's talking in terms of resigning.* 她正打算辞职。| *I was just thinking in terms of a small party.* 我只打算搞一次小型聚会。

24 ▶NUMBER/SIGN 数字/符号◀ [C] *technical* one of the numbers or signs used in a mathematical calculation【术语】〔数学运算中的〕项

term² *v* [T usually passive 一般用被动态] to use a particular word or expression to name or describe something 把…称为, 把…叫做: **be termed sth** *This condition is sometimes termed RSI, or repetitive strain injury.* 这种疾病有时称为RSI, 即重复性劳损。| *The meeting could hardly be termed a success.* 这次会议很难说是一次成功的会议。

ter·ma·gant /ˈtɝməgənt; ˈtɜːməgənt/ *n* [C] *literary* a noisy woman who often quarrels with people【文】悍妇, 泼妇 —**termagant** *adj*

ter·mi·nal¹ /ˈtɝmənl; ˈtɜːmɪ̣nəl/ *adj* **1** a terminal illness cannot be cured, and causes death〔疾病〕不治的, 致死的, 晚期的: *terminal cancer* 晚期癌症 **2 terminal decline/decay** the state of becoming worse and worse and never getting better 越来越糟; 一蹶不振: *Britain's industrial base seems in a terminal decline.* 英国的工业基础仿佛日薄西山。**3 terminal boredom** *humorous* the feeling of being extremely bored【幽默】极度的烦闷 **4** [only before noun 仅用于名词前] *technical* existing at the end of something【术语】终端的, 末端的, 末尾的: *terminal buds* 顶芽 —**terminally** *adv*: *terminally ill* 患不治之症的; 病入膏肓的

terminal² *n* [C] **1** a big building where people wait to get onto planes, buses, or ships, or where goods are loaded on〔飞机、公共汽车、轮船或货物运输的〕集散站; 终点站: *Terminal 4 at Heathrow airport* 希思罗机场的4号航站楼 **2** a piece of computer equipment consisting of at least a keyboard and a screen, that you use for putting in or taking out information from a large computer〔电脑的〕终端; 终端设备 **3** one of the points at which you can connect wires in an electrical CIRCUIT〔电路的〕端子

ter·mi·nate /ˈtɝməˌnet; ˈtɜːmɪ̣neɪt/ *v* [I,T] *formal* if something terminates, or if you terminate it, it ends【正式】(使) 结束, (使) 终止: *His contract was terminated immediately they found out who he was.* 他们发现他的身份后便立即终止了与他订的合同。

ter·mi·na·tion /ˌtɝməˈneʃən; ˌtɜːmɪ̣ˈneɪʃən/ *n* [C,U] **1** [C] *technical* a medical operation to end the life of a developing child before it is born; ABORTION【术语】终止妊娠 **2** *formal* the act of ending something, or the end of something【正式】结束, 终止, 停止: *You may face a reduction or termination of benefits.* 你可能会面临津贴的减少或停发。

Ter·min·a·tor, The /ˈtɝməˌnetɚ; ˈtɜːmɪ̣neɪtə/ (1984) a violent US film, in which Arnold Schwarzenegger appears as an ANDROID (=a machine that looks exactly like a person) who is sent back from the future to kill a woman before she can give birth to a child who will become a great leader in the future. In a second film, *Terminator II* (1991), Schwarzenegger appears

as another android, but this time he is a good character who wants to help the humans.《终结者》〔(1984),美国一暴力影片。阿诺德·施瓦辛格在剧中扮演机器人,他被未来世界派回来杀害一名女子,因为她腹中的胎儿将成为未来的伟大领袖。在续集《终结者II》(1991)中,阿诺德·施瓦辛格饰演另一个机器人,但这次是一个帮助人类的正面角色〕

ter·mi·nol·o·gy /ˌtɝməˋnɑlədʒi; ˌtɜːmɪ̵ˈnɒlədʒi/ *n* [C,U] the technical words or expressions that are used in a particular subject 术语,专门用语: *scientific terminology* 科学术语 —**terminological** /ˌtɝmɪnəˋlɑdʒɪkl; ˌtɜːmɪ̵nəˈlɒdʒɪkəl◂/ *adj*

ter·mi·nus /ˋtɝmənəs; ˈtɜːmɪ̵nəs/ *n* [C] the station or stop at the end of a railway line or bus service〔铁路、公共汽车线路的〕终点站

ter·mite /ˋtɝmaɪt; ˈtɜːmaɪt/ *n* [C] an insect that eats and destroys wood from trees and buildings 白蚁

term·ly /ˋtɝmli; ˈtɜːmli/ *adj BrE* happening each TERM (=one of the three periods in the school or university year)【英】每学期发生[举行]的

term pa·per /ˈ· ˌ··/ *n* [C] *AmE* a long piece of written work by a US school or college student, that is the most important piece of work in their course【美】学期论文

tern /tɝn; tɜːn/ *n* [C] a black and white sea-bird that has long wings and a tail with two points 燕鸥〔一种海鸟〕

ter·race /ˋtɛrɪs; ˈterɪ̵s/ *n* [C]

1 ▶HOUSES 房屋◀ *especially BrE* a row of houses that are joined to each other, or a street with one of these rows in it【尤英】〔互相连接的〕一排房屋,排屋;〔排屋面对的〕街道: *21 Chestnut Terrace* 栗树街21号

2 ▶PLACE YOU CAN SIT 可以坐的地方◀ an area, especially next to a hotel or restaurant, where people can sit outside to eat or drink〔尤指旅馆或餐馆人们可以坐在室外吃喝的〕露天平台

3 ▶FOOTBALL 足球◀ the terraces [plural] *BrE* the wide steps that the people watching a football match can stand on【英】〔足球赛观众站立的〕看台

4 ▶FLAT ROOF 平的屋顶◀ a flat roof used as an outdoor living area〔用作室外起居的〕屋顶平台

5 ▶FLAT LAND 平地◀ a flat area cut out of a slope, usually one in a series that rise up the slope, that is often used to grow crops〔修在坡地上的〕梯田;阶地

terraced house /ˌ·· ˈ·/ *n* [C] *BrE* a house which is part of a row of houses that are joined together【英】排屋中的一栋房屋; ROW HOUSE *AmE*【美】—see picture on page A4 参见A4页图

ter·ra·cot·ta /ˌtɛrəˋkɑtə; ˌterəˈkɒtə◂/ *n* [U] hard reddish-brown baked CLAY 赤陶土: *a terracotta pot* 赤陶罐子

ter·ra fir·ma /ˌtɛrə ˋfɝmə; ˌterə ˈfɜːmə/ *n* [U] *Latin, usually humorous* land rather than sea or air【拉丁,一般幽默】大地,陆地: *We were glad to be back on terra firma again.* 我们很高兴又踏上了陆地。

ter·rain /tɛˋren; teˈreɪn/ *n* [C,U] a word meaning a particular type of land, for example, hilly, rough etc 地形,地势;地面: *rocky terrain* 多石的地形

ter·ra·pin /ˋtɛrəpɪn; ˈterəpɪ̵n/ *n* [C] a small TURTLE (=animal with four legs and a hard shell) that lives in warm water areas 水龟〔生活在温暖水域中的一种小龟〕

ter·rar·ium /təˋrɛrɪəm; təˈreəriəm/ *n* [C] a large glass container that you grow plants in as a decoration〔栽培装饰性植物所用的〕大玻璃盆,陆栖植物培育箱

Ter·rence Hig·gins Trust, the /ˌtɛrəns ˋhɪgɪnz ˌtrʌst; ˌterəns ˈhɪgɪnz ˌtrʌst/ a British CHARITY organization which was started in 1983 and gives help and advice to people suffering from or worried about AIDS and HIV infection 泰伦斯·希金斯信托基金〔英国一慈善机构,成立于1983年,专为患有艾滋病和感染艾滋病毒的人或担心患上艾滋病的人提供帮助和咨询服务〕

ter·res·tri·al /təˋrɛstrɪəl; tɪ̵ˈrestriəl/ *adj technical*【术语】**1** connected with the Earth rather than with the moon or other planets 地球的 —see also 另见 EXTRATERRESTRIAL[2] **2** living on or connected with land rather than water 陆地的;陆生的,陆栖的 **3 terrestrial TV/broadcasting/channels etc** TV etc that is broadcast from the earth rather than from SATELLITES (=special equipment in outer space) 地面的〔而不是卫星的〕电视/广播/频道等 —**terrestrially** *adv*

1 3 **ter·ri·ble** /ˋtɛrəbl̩; ˈterɪ̵bəl/ *adj* **1** extremely severe in a way that causes harm or damage 剧烈的;厉害的;非常严重的: *a terrible accident* 一次严重事故 | *The poor lad took a terrible beating.* 那可怜的少年遭到一顿毒打。**2** making you feel afraid or shocked 可怕的,骇人的;令人震惊的: *There was a terrible noise and the roof caved in.* 随着一阵可怕的声音,房顶坍塌了。**3** *informal* extremely bad; AWFUL[1] (1)【非正式】很糟的,极差的: *The hotel was absolutely terrible.* 这家旅馆糟糕透了。| *I'm a terrible cook.* 我做的饭菜差极了。

ter·ri·bly /ˋtɛrəblɪ; ˈterɪ̵bli/ *adv* **1** [+adj/adv] *especially BrE* very; extremely【尤英】很,非常,极度: *We were terribly worried.* 我们非常担心。| *I'm terribly sorry to have kept you waiting.* 非常抱歉,让您久等了。**2** very badly; severely 非常糟地;严重地: *The little boy missed his mother terribly.* 那小男孩太想念妈妈了。 2

ter·ri·er /ˋtɛrɪɚ; ˈteriə/ *n* [C] a small active type of dog that was originally used for hunting 㹴〔一种原来用于狩猎的小型犬〕

ter·rif·ic /təˋrɪfɪk; təˈrɪfɪk/ *adj* **1** *informal* very good, especially in a way that makes you feel happy and excited【非正式】极好的,极棒的;非常愉快的: *We had a terrific time on holiday.* 我们度假时玩得特别愉快。| *I feel terrific!* 我感到特别开心!**2** very large in size or degree〔尺寸或程度〕极其巨大的,大得惊人的: *Suddenly, there was a terrific bang!* 突然"砰"的一声巨响!

ter·rif·i·cally /təˋrɪfɪklɪ; təˈrɪfɪkli/ *adv* [+adj/adv] *informal* very; extremely【非正式】非常;极度: *It's terrifically difficult for working parents to find adequate child care.* 双职工父母要找到妥善的托儿服务,真是非常的困难。

ter·ri·fied /ˋtɛrəˌfaɪd; ˈterɪ̵faɪd/ *adj* very frightened 非常害怕的,极度惊恐的: *a terrified animal* 一头受惊的动物 | **[+of]** *I'm terrified of heights.* 我有恐高的毛病。| **[+at]** *Mark was terrified at the thought of parachuting.* 马克一想到跳伞就害怕得要命。| **terrified (that)** *We were both terrified that the bridge would collapse.* 我们两人都很害怕桥会坍塌。

ter·ri·fy /ˋtɛrəˌfaɪ; ˈterɪ̵faɪ/ *v* [T] to make someone extremely afraid 使害怕,使恐惧: *Her husband's violence terrified her.* 她丈夫的暴力行为让她感到害怕。

ter·ri·fy·ing /ˋtɛrəˌfaɪɪŋ; ˈterɪ̵faɪ-ɪŋ/ *adj* extremely frightening 极其可怕的,骇人听闻的: *The hostages suffered a terrifying ordeal.* 人质们遭受了极其可怕的折磨。—**terrifyingly** *adv*

ter·rine /tɛˋrin; teˈriːn/ *n* [C,U] a dish made of cooked meat, fish etc, formed into a LOAF shape and served cold; PÂTÉ〔用肉类、鱼类等做成块状,用作冷盘的〕肉酱

ter·ri·to·ri·al[1] /ˌtɛrəˋtorɪəl; ˌterɪ̵ˈtɔːriəl◂/ *adj* **1** [no comparative 无比较级] related to land that is owned or controlled by a particular country〔某国家的〕领土的;属地的 **2** *technical* territorial animals, birds etc guard the area of land that they consider to be their own【术语】〔兽类、鸟类等〕守卫自身活动地域的;领域性的 —**territoriality** /ˌtɛrəˌtorɪˋælətɪ; ˌterɪ̵tɔːriˈælɪ̵ti/ *n* [U]

territorial[2] often 常作 **Territorial** *n* [C] a member of the British Territorial Army 英国国防义勇军成员

Territorial Ar·my, the /ˌ····· ˈ··/ *n* a military force of people in Britain who train as soldiers in their free time; TA〔业余时间接受军训的〕英国国防义勇军 —compare 比较 NATIONAL GUARD

territorial wa·ters /ˌ····· ˈ··/ *n* [plural] the sea near a country's coast, which that country has legal control over〔某一国的〕领海

ter·ri·to·ry /ˋtɛrəˌtorɪ; ˈterɪ̵təri/ *n* 2

1 ▶GOVERNMENT LAND 政府土地◀ [C,U] land that is owned or controlled by a particular government, ruler, or military force 领土,版图,领地: *We crossed the river into enemy territory.* 我们渡河进入敌军的领地。

2 ▶TYPE OF LAND 某一类土地◀ [U] land of a particular type〔某种特定的〕地区,地方: *an expedition through previously unexplored territory* 一次穿越未经勘探的地区的探险

3 US Territory land that belongs to the United States, but is not a state 美国属地

4 ▶EXPERIENCE 经验◀ [U] a particular area of experience or knowledge〔经验或知识的〕领域: *The company is moving into unfamiliar territory with this new software.* 该公司正通过这种新开发的软件进入一个陌生的领域。

5 ▶ANIMAL 动物◀ [C,U] the area that an animal, bird etc regards as its own and will defend against other animals〔兽类、鸟类等的〕地盘,领域

6 ▶BUSINESS 商务◀ [C,U] an area of business, especially in selling, for which someone is responsible〔商务活动、尤指商业销售的〕地区: *I'm in charge of the metropolitan Chicago territory.* 我负责芝加哥大都市地区的销售活动。

7 come/go with the territory to be a natural and accepted part of a particular job, situation, place etc〔在某种工作、情况等中〕难免碰到: *I'm a cop – so I could get shot – it goes with the territory.* 我是警察,所以我有可能挨枪弹——那恐怕是工作中难免碰到的事情。

T

ter·ror /ˈtɛrɚ; ˈterə/ *n*

1 ▶**FEAR** 恐惧◀ [U] a feeling of extreme fear 恐惧, 惊恐: *Paul screamed, the terror bursting out of him.* 保罗尖声大叫, 恐惧表露无遗。| **in terror** (=very frightened) 惊恐地 *The people fled in terror.* 人们惊恐而逃。| **live in terror of** (=be very frightened of someone or something) 非常害怕〔某人或某事〕 *After being bullied, Steven lived in terror of going to school.* 被人欺负后, 史蒂文非常害怕去上学。| **sheer terror** *There was a look of sheer terror on his face.* 他的脸上有一种非常恐怖的表情。| **in terror of your life** (=very frightened that you will be killed) 害怕丢命

2 ▶**VIOLENT ACTION** 暴力行动◀ [U] violent action for political purposes; TERRORISM 恐怖活动; 恐怖主义: *The resistance movement started a campaign of terror.* 抵抗运动开始搞恐怖活动。

3 ▶**FRIGHTENING SITUATION** 可怕的情况◀ [C] an event or situation that makes people feel extremely frightened, especially because they think they may die〔尤指令人担忧生命安危的〕可怕的事[情况]: *The hostages suffered untold terror.* 人质们遭受无法言喻的惊恐。

4 ▶**PERSON** 人◀ [C] *informal* a very annoying person, especially a child【非正式】讨厌的人〔尤指孩子〕: *That Johnson kid's a real terror!* 约翰逊家的那个孩子真是混世魔王!

5 **hold no terrors for sb** *formal* to not frighten or worry someone【正式】不让人害怕; 不让人焦虑: *Death held no terrors for me.* 死亡并不让我感到恐惧。—see also 另见 **reign of terror** (REIGN[1] (2)), **a holy terror** (HOLY (4)), **strike terror into sb's heart** (STRIKE[1] (18))

ter·ror·is·m /ˈtɛrəˌrɪzəm; ˈterərɪzəm/ *n* [U] the use of violence such as bombing, shooting or KIDNAPPING to obtain political demands 恐怖主义: *The government is determined to combat international terrorism.* 政府决心同国际恐怖主义作斗争。

ter·ror·ist /ˈtɛrəˌrɪst; ˈterərɪst/ *n* [C] someone who uses violence such as bombing, shooting etc to obtain political demands 恐怖分子: *Two of the terrorists were shot dead.* 恐怖分子中有两名被击毙。| **terrorist attack/activity** *Twenty people were killed in the latest terrorist attack.* 有20人死于最近的那次恐怖主义袭击。—compare 比较 GUERRILLA, PARTISAN[2] (2)

T

ter·ror·ize also 又作 **-ise** *BrE*【英】/ˈtɛrəˌraɪz; ˈterəraɪz/ *v* [T] to deliberately frighten people by threatening to harm them, especially so they will do what you want 恐吓…: *Many people have been terrorized into leaving their homes.* 许多人遭到恐吓, 离开了家园。

ter·ry·cloth /ˈtɛrɪˌklɔθ; ˈteriklɒθ/ also 又作 **ter·ry** /ˈtɛrɪ; ˈteri/ *n* [U] a type of thick cotton cloth with uncut threads on both sides, used to make TOWELS, bath mats etc 毛圈织物; 毛巾布 —see picture on page A16 参见A16页图

terse /tɝs; tɜːs/ *adj* a terse reply, message etc uses very few words and often shows that you are annoyed〔回答、信息等〕简短的〔常表示厌烦等〕: *Derek's terse reply ended the conversation.* 德里克的简短回答使谈话终止了。—**tersely** *adv*: *"Continue!" he said tersely.* "继续!"他简短地说道。—**terseness** *n* [U]

ter·tia·ry /ˈtɝʃɪˌɛrɪ; ˈtɜːʃəri/ *adj technical* third in place, degree, or order【术语】第三位的; 第三级的; 第三的

tertiary ed·u·ca·tion /ˌ····ˈ··/ *n* [U] *formal* education at a college, university etc; HIGHER EDUCATION【正式】高等教育, 大学教育

Te·ry·lene /ˈtɛrəlin; ˈterəliːn/ *n* [U] *BrE trademark* a light strong artificial cloth【英, 商标】涤纶〔一种人造纤维织物〕

TES /ˌti i ˈɛs; ˌtiː iː ˈes/ the abbreviation of 缩写= The TIMES EDUCATION SUPPLEMENT

TESL /ˈtɛsl; ˈtesəl/ *n* [U] the Teaching of English as a Second Language 作为第二语言的英语教学

TESOL /ˈtɛsɑl; ˈtesɒl/ *n* [U] *especially AmE* the teaching of English to speakers of other languages【尤美】向说其他语言的人讲授英语, 作为外语的英语教学

TESSA /ˈtɛsə; ˈtesə/ Tax-Exempt Special Savings Account; a special type of account with a bank or building society in the UK, in which you can save money and you do not have to pay tax on the interest you earn if you leave the money there for at least 5 years 免税特殊储蓄账户〔英国银行或购房互助协会设立的一种特殊存款项目, 存满五年即可免去利息税〕

tes·sel·la·ted /ˈtɛslˌetɪd; ˈtesəleɪtɪd/ *adj technical* made of small flat pieces in various shapes and colours that fit together to form a pattern【术语】用小块东西镶嵌成花纹的

Tess of the D'Ur·ber·villes /ˌtɛs əv ðə ˈdɝbəvɪlz; ˌtes əv ðə ˈdɜːbəvɪlz/ (1891) a NOVEL by Thomas Hardy about a young woman who is persuaded by a man from a higher social class to have sex with him. He treats her very badly and she finally kills him and is hanged for his murder.《德伯家的苔丝》〔(1891), 托马斯·哈代创作的一部小说。故事中有一位年轻姑娘, 被上层社会的一个男人诱奸, 并遭到虐待。最后, 她杀了那个男人, 自己也因谋杀罪而被处以绞刑〕

test¹ /tɛst; test/ *n* [C] 1 1

1 ▶**EXAM** 考试◀ a set of questions, exercises or practical activities to measure someone's skill, ability, or knowledge 测验, 测试; 考查, 考试: **spelling/driving/biology etc test** *How did you do on your maths test?* 你数学测验考得怎么样? | **pass/fail a test** *She passed her driving test when she was 17.* 她17岁时通过了驾驶考试。| **do/take/sit a test** (=take part in it) 参加考试 *The thought of taking the test terrifies me.* 一想到参加考试, 我就害怕。| **[+on]** *We have a test on irregular verbs tomorrow.* 我们明天测验不规则动词。| **test result** *When do you get your test results back?* 你什么时候拿回你的考试成绩?

2 ▶**MEDICAL** 医学的◀ **a)** a short medical examination on a part of your body, or to find out what is wrong with you〔医学〕检查; 化验: *an eye test* 眼睛检查 | **run a test** (=do one quickly) 对…作出快速的检查 *We'll just run some tests on your blood sample.* 我们将对你的血液样本很快作出检查。| **test results** *I'm still waiting for my test results from the hospital.* 我还在等待医院的化验结果。**b)** equipment for carrying out a medical test 医疗检查设备: *a pregnancy test* 怀孕检查设备

3 ▶**FOR CHECKING STH** 检验某物◀ a process used to find out whether equipment works correctly, or whether something contains a particular substance 检验; 试验: *nuclear weapons tests* 核武器试验 | **a test for sth** (=a test to find sth) 对某物的检验 *a test for chemicals in the water* 对水中化学物质的检验 | **test site/equipment/procedure** *We went to the test site in Nevada.* 我们前往内华达州的试验场地。

4 ▶**DIFFICULT SITUATION** 艰难处境◀ a situation in which the qualities of someone or something are clearly shown 考验: **a test of character/strength etc** *The problems she faced were a real test of character.* 她面临的那些问题是对她的品格的一次真正考验。| **put sb/sth to the test** (=find out how good someone or something is) 使某人/某事得到考验 *Living together will soon put their relationship to the test.* 一起生活会很快使他们的关系得到考验。

5 **stand the test of time** to be good enough, strong enough etc to last for a long time 经受时间的考验: *Our friendship has stood the test of time.* 我们的友谊经受住了时间的考验。

6 ▶**STANDARD** 标准◀ something that is used as a standard to judge or examine something else〔判断或检验某事的〕标准, 试金石: *It's difficult to know what's a good test of love.* 很难说什么是检验爱情的试金石。—see also 另见 TEST CASE

7 ▶**SPORT** 体育运动◀ *BrE*【英】the short form of 缩略式= TEST MATCH —see also 另见 BREATH TEST, MEANS TEST, SMEAR TEST

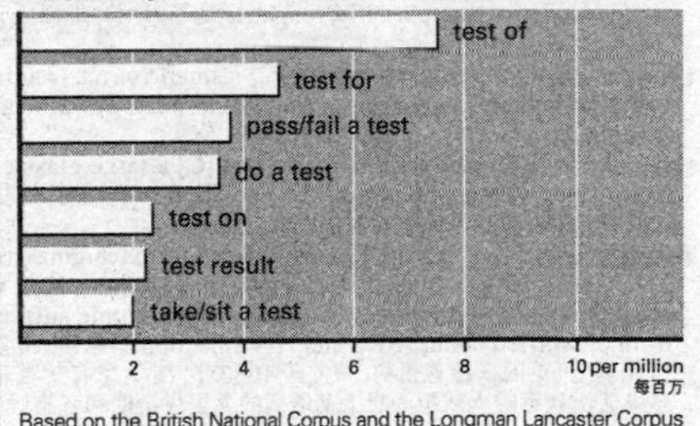

test² *v* 3 2

1 ▶**EXAM** 考试◀ [T] to ask someone spoken or written questions, or make them do a practical activity, to find out what they know about a subject 测验, 测试; 考查: **test sb on** *We're being tested on grammar tomorrow.* 我们明天要测验语法。| **test sth** *We'll have to test his knowledge of computers.* 我们得测试一下他的电脑知识。

2 ▶**MEDICAL** 医学的◀ **a)** [T] to give someone a short medical examination on a part of their body, or to find out what is wrong with them 检查〔身体的某个部分〕, 给…体检: *I must have my eyes tested.* 我必须检查一下我的眼睛。| **test sb for sth** *I'm going to test you for diabetes.* 我给你检查一下, 看有没有糖尿病。

b) to get a particular result when a medical test is done on you 化验结果为…: *He tested positive for HIV.* 他的艾滋病病毒化验结果呈阳性。

3 ►MACHINE/PRODUCT 机器/产品◄ [T] to use something for a short time to see if it works properly 试验; 检验: *testing nuclear weapons* 试验核武器 | **test sth on sb/sth** (=use something on someone or something to test it) 在某人/某物身上做试验 *None of this range of cosmetics has been tested on animals.* 这一化妆品系列从未在动物身上试验过。

4 ►FIND OUT 查出◄ [T] to examine something in order to find out something about it 检查, 查看: *Test the cake to see if it's done.* 查看一下糕点, 看看是否做好了。| **test sth for sth** *testing ore samples for quality* 检查矿石样品的质量

5 ►BE DIFFICULT 困难的◄ [T] to be so difficult that all of someone or something's good qualities will be needed to do it 考验, 考查: *The next six months will test your powers of leadership.* 接下来的六个月将考验你的领导能力。—see also 另见 TESTING

6 ►OIL/GAS 石油/天然气◄ [I,T] to search for oil, gas etc by carrying out tests 勘探, 探测: **[+for]** *testing for oil* 探测石油

7 test the water to check people's reaction to a plan before you decide to do anything 试探〔人们对某项计划的〕反应: *We'll have to test the water before we ban smoking in the staffroom.* 我们禁止在职工休息室吸烟之前, 得先看看大伙的反应。—see also 另见 **tried and tested** (TRIED[2])

Test Act, the /ˈ· ·/ a law made in 1673 in the UK which prevented Catholics from becoming members of Parliament or having jobs in the government. This law was ended in 1828. 《宗教考查法》〔英国于1673年颁布的一项法律。该法禁止天主教徒入选议会和担任公职, 1828年被废止〕

tes·ta·ment /ˈtɛstəmənt; ˈtestəmənt/ *n* [C] *formal*【正式】**1 a testament to sth** something that shows or proves something else very clearly 对某物的证明[证据]: *The aircraft's safety record is an impressive testament to its designers' skill.* 飞机的安全记录是对其设计师技能的一个有力证明。**2** a WILL[2] (2) 遗嘱 —see also 另见 NEW TESTAMENT, OLD TESTAMENT —**testamentary** /ˌtɛstəˈmɛntərɪ; ˌtestəˈmentəri◂/ *adj*

Test and Coun·ty Crick·et Board /ˌ· · ·, ·· ˈ· · ·, ·/ abbreviation 缩写为 **TCCB** an organization in the UK that governs the way professional CRICKET is played 英国职业板球管理委员会

test ban /ˈ· ·/ *n* [C] an agreement between countries to stop testing NUCLEAR WEAPONS 禁止核武器试验协定

test card /ˈ· ·/ *n* [C] a pattern or picture that is shown on television when there are no programmes〔检测电视上图案或画面效果的〕测试卡

test case /ˈ· ·/ *n* [C] a legal case that establishes a particular principle and is then used as a standard which other similar cases can be judged against 判例案件〔确定某种判决准则、供其他类似案件作判决依据的案件〕

test cer·tif·i·cate /ˈ· ·,·· ·/ *n* [C] *BrE* the official paper that proves that a car is legally safe enough to drive【英】〔汽车的〕安全证明书

test drive /ˈ· ·/ *n* [C] an occasion when you drive a car to see if it works correctly or if you like it so that you can decide if you want to buy it〔汽车的〕试验驾驶, 试车 —**test-drive** *v* [T]

test·er /ˈtɛstɚ; ˈtestə/ *n* [C] a small bottle of PERFUME[1] (1) etc, in a shop, for customers to try〔商店里供顾客试用的〕试用品〈如香水等〉

tes·ti·cle /ˈtɛstɪk]; ˈtestɪkəl/ *n* [C] one of the two round organs that produce SPERM in a male, that are enclosed in a bag of skin behind and below the PENIS 睾丸

tes·ti·fy /ˈtɛstəˌfaɪ; ˈtestɪ̣faɪ/ *v* **1** [I,T] to make a formal statement of what is true, especially in a court of law〔尤指在法庭上〕作证: **[+that]** *Can you testify that you saw the defendant at the scene of the crime?* 你能作证你看见被告在犯罪现场吗? | **[+against]** *It would not be easy to testify against people you know.* 要作证指控你相识的人, 真是不容易啊。| **[+for]** *Vicky agreed to testify for the accused.* 维基同意为被告作证。**2** [I,T] *formal* to be a clear sign that something is true【正式】证明, 证实: **[+to]** *Mrs Parson's nervous behaviour testified to the strain she was under.* 帕森夫人的紧张行为证明了她承受的压力有多大。**3** [I] *AmE* to stand up and tell people about how God has helped you in your life【美】作见证〔指基督徒向人诉说上帝的恩典〕

tes·ti·mo·ni·al /ˌtɛstəˈmonɪəl; ˌtestɪ̣ˈməʊniəl/ *n* [C] **1** a formal written statement describing someone's character and abilities〔对某人品格和能力的〕证明书, 推荐信 —see also 另见 REFERENCE (4) **2** something that is given or done to someone to show thanks, praise, or admiration 感谢信; 表扬信; 奖状; 奖励: *a testimonial dinner* 一次表示谢意的宴会

tes·ti·mo·ny /ˈtɛstəˌmonɪ; ˈtestɪ̣məni/ *n* [C,U] **1** a formal statement that something is true, such as the one a WITNESS makes in a court of law〔法庭上的〕证词: *Barker's testimony is crucial to the prosecution's case.* 巴克的证词对控告方的证据起到关键的作用。**2** a fact or situation that shows or proves something very clearly 证据; 证明: **[+to/of]** *These results are a testimony to your hard work.* 这些成果证明了你的辛勤劳动。

test·ing /ˈtɛstɪŋ; ˈtestɪŋ/ *adj* a testing situation, experience etc is difficult to deal with 很难对付的, 棘手的: *a testing time in their relationship* 他们的关系经受考验的时刻

testing ground /ˈ· · ·/ *n* [C] **1** a place where machines, cars etc are tried to see if they work properly〔机器、汽车等的〕测试场; 试验地 **2** a situation or problem in which you can try new ideas and methods to see if they work〔新思想、新方法的〕试验机会: *Eastern Europe has become a testing ground for high speed privatization.* 东欧已经成为高速私有化的试验场。

tes·tis /ˈtɛstɪs; ˈtestɪ̣s/ *n plural* **testes** /-tiz; -tiːz/ [C] *technical* a TESTICLE【术语】睾丸

test match /ˈ· ·/ *n* [C] a CRICKET (2) or RUGBY match that is played between the teams of different countries 板球[橄榄球]的国际比赛

tes·tos·ter·one /tɛsˈtɑstəˌron; teˈstɒstərəʊn/ *n* [U] the chemical in males that gives them their male qualities 睾丸素, 睾丸甾酮

test pi·lot /ˈ· ,· ·/ *n* [C] a pilot who flies new aircraft in order to test them〔新飞机的〕试飞员

test tube /ˈ· ·/ *n* [C] a small glass container that is shaped like a tube and is used in chemistry 试管 —see picture at 参见 LABORATORY 图

test-tube ba·by /ˈ· · ,· ·/ *n* [C] *not technical*【非术语】**1** a baby born as a result of ARTIFICIAL INSEMINATION〔人工授精产下的〕试管婴儿 **2** a baby that started to develop from an egg removed from a woman's body and was then put back inside the woman to continue developing〔体外受精后再移植入母体而产下的〕试管婴儿

tes·ty /ˈtɛstɪ; ˈtesti/ *adj* impatient and easily annoyed; IRRITABLE 不耐烦的; 急躁的: *a testy old man* 一位脾气暴躁的老头 | *testy remarks* 不耐烦的话 —**testily** *adv*: *"You can't!" Ralph interrupted him testily.* "你不可以!"拉尔夫不耐烦地打断了他的话。—**testiness** *n* [U]

tet·a·nus /ˈtɛtənəs; ˈtetənəs/ *n* [U] a serious illness caused by BACTERIA that enter your body through cuts and wounds and make your muscles, especially your jaw, go stiff; LOCKJAW 破伤风

tetched /tɛtʃt; tetʃt/ *adj AmE spoken* slightly crazy【美口】神经有点不正常的, 疯疯癫癫的

tetch·y /ˈtɛtʃɪ; ˈtetʃi/ *adj* likely to get angry or upset easily 急躁的; 容易生气的: *Jane's a bit tetchy this morning, watch what you say to her.* 简今天上午有点犯急, 你跟她说话得小心点。—**tetchily** *adv* —**tetchiness** *n* [U]

tête-à-tête[1] /ˈtet ə ˈtet; ˌteɪt ɑː ˈteɪt/ *n* [C] *French* a private conversation between two people【法】〔两人之间的〕私下交谈: *have a cosy tête-à-tête* 进行一次温馨的促膝交谈

tête-à-tête[2] *adv* [only after verb 仅用于动词后] *French* if two people meet, speak, or eat tête-à-tête they are together in private【法】〔两人之间〕私下地

teth·er[1] /ˈtɛðɚ; ˈteðə/ *n* [C] **1** a rope or chain that an animal is tied to so that it can only move around within a limited area〔拴牲畜用的〕系绳, 拴链 **2 be at the end of your tether** to be so worried, tired etc, that you feel you can no longer deal with a difficult or upsetting situation 忍无可忍; 走投无路; 一筹莫展: *Morel was at the end of his tether, too exasperated to answer.* 莫雷尔忍无可忍, 气得无言以对。

tether[2] *v* [T] to tie an animal to a post so that it can only move around within a limited area 拴住, 系住〔牲畜〕

tetra- /tɛtrə; tetrə/ *prefix* having four of something〔表示"四"〕: *a tetrahedron* (=solid shape with four sides) 一个四面体

Teu·ton·ic /tjuˈtɑnɪk; tjuːˈtɒnɪk/ *adj* **1** *humorous* having qualities that are thought to be typical of German people【幽默】〔品质等〕日耳曼人所独具的; 典型德国人风格的: *Teutonic efficiency* 日耳曼人的效率 **2** connected with the ancient German peoples of northwestern Europe〔古代西北欧的〕条顿民族的

Tex·as /ˈtɛksəs; ˈteksəs/ abbreviation 缩写为 **TX** a large state in the south of the US, which has a long border with Mexico. It is an important centre of the oil and gas industries, and also of cattle and crop farming. Its cities include Houston, Dallas, San Antonio, Austin, and El Paso. Before it became part of the US in 1845, Texas was briefly an independent country. 得克萨斯州〔美国南部一州, 与墨西哥之间有很长的边界。该州是重要的石油和天然气工业中心, 也是养牛和种植业中心。其城市包括休斯顿、

达拉斯、圣安东尼奥、奥斯汀和埃尔帕索。1845 年成为美国的一个州之前，得克萨斯曾一度为独立国家〕 **—Texan** *n, adj*

Texas Rang·ers, the /,·· ˈ··/ a group of police officers that was originally established in the 19th century to fight against criminals in the US state of Texas. They still exist today. 得克萨斯巡逻队〔一支警察部队，成立于 19 世纪。这支部队专门打击美国得克萨斯州的犯罪分子，至今仍然存在〕

Tex-mex /ˈtɛks mɛks; ˈteks meks/ *adj AmE informal* connected with the music, cooking etc of Mexican-American people【美，非正式】〔音乐、烹饪等〕墨西哥裔美国人的：*a Tex-Mex restaurant* 一家墨西哥裔美国人餐馆

2 1 **text** /tɛkst; tekst/ *n* **1** [U] the writing that forms the main part of a book, magazine etc rather than the pictures or notes〔书、杂志等的〕正文〔区别于图片、注释等〕；文字：*There ought not to be too much text in children's books.* 儿童书籍里不应该有太多的文字。**2** [U] any written material 文字材料：*One disk can store the equivalent of 500 pages of text.* 一张磁盘能够储存相当于 500 页的文字材料。**3 the text of sth** the exact words of a speech, article etc〔演说、文章等的〕原文：*Only 'The Times' printed the full text of the President's speech.* 只有《泰晤士报》刊载了总统演说的全文。**4** [C] a book or other piece of writing that is connected with learning or intended for study 课本，教科书；教材：**a set text** (=a book that must be studied for an examination)〔考试指定的〕必读课本 *'Hamlet' is a set text for this year's English exam.*《哈姆雷特》是今年英语考试的必读课文。**5** [C] a short piece from the Bible that someone reads and talks about〔某人诵读并讲述的一小段〕圣经经文

text·book¹ /ˈtɛkst,bʊk; ˈtekstbʊk/ *n* [C] a book that contains information about a subject that people study 教科书，教材，课本：*a biology textbook* 一本生物学教材 —see also 另见 COURSEBOOK

textbook² *adj* [only before noun 仅用于名词前] done or happening exactly as something should be done or as it should happen 合乎规范的；完善的：*That shot of Becker's was superb – textbook stuff.* 贝克尔那一球打得真棒，无懈可击！| **textbook case/example** *The advertising campaign was a textbook example of how to sell a product.* 这项广告宣传活动是如何销售产品的一个范例。

tex·tile /ˈtɛkstl; ˈtekstaɪl/ *n* [C] **1** a word used mainly in business for woven material that is made in large quantities 纺织品：*Their main exports are textiles, especially silk and cotton.* 他们的主要出口商品是纺织品，尤其是丝绸和棉布。| **textile industry/market etc** *a textile factory* 一家纺织厂 **2 textiles** *plural* the industry involved in making cloth 纺织业

tex·tu·al /ˈtɛkstʃuəl; ˈtekstʃuəl/ *adj* concerning the way that a book, magazine etc is written〔书、杂志等〕正文的，原文的：*a detailed textual analysis* 详细的文本分析

tex·ture /ˈtɛkstʃɚ; ˈtekstʃə/ *n* [C,U] **1** the way a surface, substance, or material feels when you touch it, especially how smooth or rough it is〔尤指光滑或粗糙的〕手感，质感，质地：*the smooth texture of silk* 丝绸的光滑质感 | *a soil with a loose sandy texture* 松散的沙质土壤 **2** *literary* the way the different parts are combined in a piece of writing, music, art etc in order to make a particular impression on you; CHARACTER (2)【文】〔写作、音乐、艺术等作品的〕神韵：*the rich texture of Shakespeare's English* 莎士比亚笔下的英语之丰富神韵 **—textural** *adj* **—texturally** *adv*

tex·tured /ˈtɛkstʃɚd; ˈtekstʃəd/ *adj* **1** having a surface that is not smooth 质地粗糙的：*textured wallpaper* 质地粗糙的墙纸 **2 coarse-textured/smooth-textured/fine-textured etc** having a texture that is smooth etc 质地粗糙的/质地光滑的/质感致密的等：*heart-shaped, rough-textured leaves* 质地粗糙的心形树叶

textured vege·ta·ble pro·tein /,·· ,··· ˈ··/ *n* [U] a substance made from beans, used instead of meat; TVP 结构性植物蛋白，植物组织蛋白

TGWU, the /ˌti dʒi dʌbljʊ ˈju; ˌtiː dʒiː dʌbəljuː ˈjuː/ also 又作 **T&G** the Transport and General Workers' Union; one of the largest TRADE UNIONs in the UK 运输与普通工人工会〔英国规模最大的工会之一〕

-th /θ; θ/ *suffix* **1** forms ORDINAL numbers, except with 1,2, or 3 第〔几〕〔构成除一、二、三之外的序数词〕：*the 17th of June* 6 月 17 日 | *a fifth of the total* 总数的五分之一 —see also 另见 -ND, -RD, -ST **2** *old use or biblical*【旧或圣经】another form of the suffix -ETH 后缀 -eth 的另一种拼法：*he doth* (=does) 他做

Thack·e·ray /ˈθækərɪ; ˈθækəreɪ/, **Wil·liam Make·peace** /ˈmek,pis; ˈmeɪkpiːs/ (1811-63) a British writer, born in India, whose best-known work is his NOVEL *Vanity Fair* 萨克雷〔(1811-1863)，英国作家。生于印度，以小说《名利场》最为著名〕

Thai·land /ˈtaɪlənd; ˈtaɪlænd/ a country in southeast Asia, between Malaysia and Myanmar. Population: 61,798,000 (2001). Capital: Bangkok. It is a popular place for tourists to visit. Before 1949, Thailand was called Siam. 泰国〔东南亚一国家，位于马来西亚和缅甸之间。人口：61,798,000 (2001)，首都：曼谷。该国为著名旅游胜地。1949 年前称暹罗〕

Tha·lid·o·mide /θəˈlɪdə,maɪd; θəˈlɪdəmaɪd/ *n* [U] *trademark* a drug given to people to make them calm, until it was discovered that it harmed the development of the arms and legs of unborn babies【商标】反应停，酞胺哌啶酮〔原用作镇静剂，发现影响胎儿四肢的发育后停用〕

Thames /tɛmz; temz/ **1 the Thames** the longest river in England, which flows from the west into the North Sea. In London, many well-known bridges across the Thames connect the north and south of the city, and many important buildings, including the Houses of Parliament and the Tower of London, are built next to the river. 泰晤士河〔英格兰最长的河流，源自西部，注入北海。伦敦有许多著名桥梁，横跨泰晤士河，连接市区南北。泰晤士河沿岸有许多著名建筑，其中包括议会大厦和伦敦塔〕：*She lives south of the Thames.* 她住在泰晤士河之南。**2 set the Thames on fire** [usually in negatives 一般用于否定句] *BrE old-fashioned* to achieve something unusually good or interesting, which makes people notice you【英，过时】做出惊人之举而声名大噪：*Phil was making a living as a writer, but he hadn't yet done anything to set the Thames on fire.* 菲尔以写作为生，但尚未写出什么惊人之作。

Thames Val·ley, the /,· ˈ··/ the area of land next to the River Thames, between London and Oxford 泰晤士河谷〔与泰晤士河毗邻的一个区域，位于伦敦和牛津之间〕

than¹ /ðən; ðən; *strong* 强读 ðæn; ðæn/ *conjunction* **1 higher than/cheaper than etc** used when comparing two things that are different to introduce the second thing 比…更高/更廉价等〔用于两个事物的比较，引入第二个事物〕：*The cost of the repairs was a lot cheaper than I thought.* 维修费用比我所想的要便宜许多。**2 would rather/would sooner...than...** used to say that you prefer one thing to another 宁愿…而不愿…：*If it's alright by you I'd rather walk than go by car.* 如果你没有问题的话，我宁愿走路，而不愿乘车。**3 hardly/scarcely/no sooner etc... than...** used to say that something had only just happened when something else happened 一…就…：*No sooner had I mailed the letter than I realized she'd changed address.* 我刚寄出那封信，就意识到她已更改了地址。**4** *informal* except【非正式】除…之外：*They left me with no option than to resign.* 除了辞职，他们没有给我任何选择。 1 1

than² *prep* **1 higher/more expensive than** used when comparing two things that are different to introduce the second thing 比…更高/更昂贵〔用于两个事物的比较，引入第二个事物〕：*Miranda has always been more intelligent than her two brothers.* 米兰达一直比她的两个兄弟更聪明。| *Richard's marrying a woman who's older than his own mother.* 理查德要跟一个比自己母亲还年长的女人结婚。| *The new tax system will definitely affect some people more than others.* 新的税收体制将对一些人产生比较明显的影响。**2 more/less/fewer etc than** used when comparing two different amounts, numbers etc to introduce the second amount or number 比…多/少等：*The programme doesn't last any longer than an hour.* 该节目长度不超过一个小时。| *He's been unemployed for more than 18 months now.* 他到现在已经失业 18 个多月了。| *It's a beautiful dress but it's much more than I can afford.* 这件连衣裙很漂亮，不过太贵了。 1 1

thane /θen; θeɪn/ *n* [C] a man who fought for the King but was below the rank of a KNIGHT¹ (1) in early English history〔英格兰早期历史上为国王服兵役、地位低于骑士的〕大乡绅

thank /θæŋk; θæŋk/ *v* [T] **1** to tell someone that you are pleased and grateful for something they have done, or to be polite about it 感谢，向…表示谢意：*Remember to thank Uncle Robin when you see him.* 你见到罗宾大叔别忘了向他致谢。| **thank sb for** *Meg and Jo ran to thank their aunt for the presents.* 梅格和乔跑过去感谢姨妈给他们送礼物。| **thank sb for doing sth** *I must write and thank him for sending the cheque.* 我必须写信感谢他送来了支票。**2 thank God/goodness/heavens** used to show that you are very glad about something 感谢上帝，谢天谢地：*Thank God that's over! I've never been so nervous in my life!* 感谢上帝，终于结束了！我一生中从来没有这么紧张过！| [+for] *"Your son is safe!" "Thank heavens for that!"* "你的儿子安全了！""那真要谢天谢地了！" —see 见 GOD (USAGE) **3 have sb to thank (for sth)** used when saying who is responsible for something helpful or, humorously, who is responsible for something unhelpful 因某事感谢某人；因某事责怪某人〔幽默用法〕：*I have Phil to thank for getting me my first job.* 我得感谢菲尔帮 1 2

我找到了我的第一份工作。| *And who do I have to thank for that mess on my desk?* 我的桌上那么乱，是谁干的好事？ **4 only have yourself to thank (for sth)** *spoken* used to say that you are responsible for something bad that has happened to you【口】只能怪自己，咎由自取：*She has only herself to thank if she doesn't have any friends.* 如果说她没有任何朋友，那只能怪她自己。**5 sb won't thank you (for doing something)** used to tell someone that another person will be annoyed because of what they have done 某人不会（因你做了某事而）感谢你的：*I know you're just trying to help, but he won't thank you for telling him how to do it.* 我知道你只不过是想帮帮他的忙，但他不会因为你告诉他如何做而感谢你的。**6 thank your lucky stars** *spoken* used to tell someone that they are very lucky, especially because they have avoided an unpleasant or dangerous situation【口】多亏自己的运气好：*You should thank your lucky stars I got here when I did!* 多亏你运气好，当时我刚巧来到这儿。**7 you'll thank me** *spoken* used to tell someone not to be annoyed with you for doing or saying something, because it will be helpful to them later【口】你将来会感谢我的：*You'll thank me for this one day, Laura.* 劳拉，你将来会晓得我是一片好心的。**8 I'll thank you to do sth** *spoken formal* used to tell someone in an angry way not to do something because it is annoying you【口，正式】请〔不要做某事〕好不好〔语气含有怒意〕：*I'll thank you to mind your own business.* 我请你别管闲事好不好？—see also 另见 THANK YOU

thank·ful /ˈθæŋkfəl; ˈθæŋkfəl/ *adj* [not before noun 不用于名词前] grateful and glad about something that has happened, especially because without it the situation would be much worse 感谢的，感激的；为…感到高兴的：**[+for]** *I'll be thankful for a good night's sleep after the week I've had.* 在经历了这样的一周之后，我能好好地睡上一个晚上就感激不尽了。| **thankful (that)** *You should be thankful that you have me to look after you.* 有我来照料你，你应该高兴才是。| **thankful to do sth** *I was thankful to make any sort of progress at all.* 能取得一点进步，我感到欣慰。—see also 另见 **be thankful for small mercies** (MERCY (5)) —**thankfulness** *n* [U]

thank·ful·ly /ˈθæŋkfəli; ˈθæŋkfəli/ *adv* **1** [sentence adverb 句子副词] used to say that you are glad that something has happened, especially because a difficult situation has ended or been avoided 高兴地，欣慰地：*Thankfully, I managed to pay off all my debts before we got married.* 感到欣慰的是，在我们结婚前，我已设法还清了所有债务。**2** feeling grateful and glad about something, especially because a difficult situation has ended or been avoided 满怀感激地〔尤指困境已过去或避免〕：*We came in and collapsed thankfully onto our beds.* 我们进到屋里，谢天谢地，终于可以瘫倒在床上了。

thank·less /ˈθæŋklɪs; ˈθæŋkləs/ *adj* **1** a thankless job is difficult and you do not get any praise for doing it 吃力不讨好的，为人作嫁的：**a thankless task** *Cooking for the family every day is a thankless task.* 每天给家里人做饭是一件费力不讨好的事。**2** *literary* a thankless person is not grateful【文】〔指人〕不知感激的，忘恩负义的：*a thankless child* 一个忘恩负义的孩子 —**thanklessly** *adv*

S1 W2 **thanks¹** /θæŋks; θæŋks/ *interjection* **1** used to tell someone that you are grateful for something they have given you or done for you; THANK YOU 感谢，谢谢：*"Pass the salt, please ... thanks."* "请把盐递过来…谢谢"。| **thanks for (doing) sth** *I'd love to go to the party. Thanks for asking me.* 我非常愿意去参加晚会。谢谢邀请了我。| *Thanks for the ride home – see you tomorrow!* 谢谢开车送我回家。明儿见！| **thanks a lot** *informal*【非正式】*Thanks a lot for the drink.* 多谢你请我喝酒。| **many thanks** (=often used in a formal business letter) 非常感谢〔常用于正式商务信函〕*Dear Mr Williams, Many thanks for the articles you sent me last week.* 亲爱的威廉斯先生，非常感谢您上周给我寄来的文章。**2** used as a polite way of accepting something that someone has offered you 谢谢〔表示礼貌地接受〕：*"Do you want another cup of coffee?" "Oh, thanks."* "你还想要一杯咖啡吗？" "呃，谢谢！" **3 fine thanks** *spoken* used when politely answering someone's question【口】很好，谢谢〔礼貌地回答某人的问候〕：*"Hi, Bill, how are you?" "Fine, thanks."* "嘿，比尔，你可好吗？" "很好，谢谢。" **4 no thanks** used to say politely that you do not want something 不用，谢谢〔礼貌地谢绝〕：*"How about some cake?" "Oh, no thanks, I'm on a diet."* "来点蛋糕怎么样？" "哦，不用，谢谢，我在节食。"

thanks² *n* [plural] **1** the things you say or do to show that you are grateful to someone 道谢的话；道谢的举动：*Joe got up and left without a word of thanks.* 乔起身离开了，一句感谢的话也没有说。**2 thanks to a)** used to say that someone has done something very helpful or useful 归功于：*Thanks to Germaine's tireless efforts, the concert was a huge success.* 多亏杰曼努力不懈，音乐会获得了巨大成功。—see 见 OWING (USAGE) **b)** used to say, angrily or humorously that someone has caused a problem 归咎于〔愤怒的或幽默的语气〕：*It was supposed to be a surprise, but thanks to your big mouth she knows all about it now.* 本来打算来一次惊喜的，但是，拜你多嘴，她现在什么都知道了。**c)** used to say that something good is caused by something else 由于，因为：*Thanks to the warm Autumn, our fuel bills have been very low.* 由于今年秋季温暖，我们的燃料费一直很低。**3 no thanks to** *spoken* an expression meaning 'in spite of', used when someone should have helped you but did not【口】不是因为〔某人〕才…〔表示尽管某人本该帮忙却没有〕：*It was no thanks to you that we managed to win the game.* 我们不是因为你才最终赢得了那场比赛。—see also 另见 VOTE OF THANKS

Thanks·giv·ing /ˌθæŋksˈgɪvɪŋ; ˌθæŋksˈgɪvɪŋ◂/ *n* [U] a public holiday in the US in November, when families have a large meal together and celebrate the origins of their country 感恩节〔美国11月份的一个公共假日〕

CULTURAL NOTE 文化注释

Celebrating Thanksgiving 庆祝感恩节

Thanksgiving is a very important event in the US. It is a holiday when all the members of a family eat a traditional meal of TURKEY, STUFFING, CRANBERRY SAUCE, YAMS, CORN BREAD, other types of cooked vegetables, and PUMPKIN PIE. Although Thanksgiving Day is on a Thursday, most schools and offices are also closed on the following day, so that people have a LONG WEEKEND. Many people watch television on Thanksgiving Day, and there is the Macy's Thanksgiving Day PARADE in New York City, which is shown on television across the country. The most popular thing to watch on Thanksgiving Day, however, is American football. Most large DEPARTMENT STORES are open on the Friday after Thanksgiving and have a big SALE (=a time when goods are sold at lower prices than usual). It is also the day when most stores start decorating their buildings for Christmas. Most people in the US consider the day after Thanksgiving to be the beginning of the Christmas holiday season. 感恩节是美国一个十分重要的节日。在节日里，全家人要聚餐吃一顿传统的饭菜，包括火鸡、填馅食品、越橘汁、山药、玉米面包和其他种类的炖蔬菜以及南瓜饼。尽管感恩节是在星期四，但大多数单位和学校还是会在接下来的星期五关门放假，这样人们就有了一个长周末。在感恩节这天很多人看电视，而电视向全国转播纽约梅西百货公司的感恩节大游行。然而最受欢迎的感恩节电视节目还是美式橄榄球比赛。很多大型百货商店会在感恩节第二天的星期五开门迎客，来个大甩卖。很多商店也是从这天开始为圣诞节装点店堂。美国的大多数人都把感恩节看成是圣诞假期的序幕。

The story of Thanksgiving 感恩节的由来

Thanksgiving celebrates the time when SETTLERS who came to North America from England were saved by Native Americans. Many of the settlers died of HUNGER during their first winter in the new land. The Native Americans showed them how to grow corn and other crops, so that they had enough food to eat during the next winter. The settlers and Native Americans celebrated together with a special meal, and gave their thanks to God for the food and help. Children at school sometimes perform this story as a play, wear special clothes to look like settlers, and have a parade or draw pictures of things related to Thanksgiving such as turkeys, pumpkins, corn, Pilgrims, and Native Americans. 感恩节是纪念从英格兰来到北美洲的定居者被美洲原住民搭救的事。来到新大陆的第一个冬天，很多定居者被饥饿夺走了生命。美洲原住民教会他们如何种植玉米和其他作物，这样他们在来年的冬天就有足够的食物可吃。定居者和美洲原住民特别设宴一起庆祝，感谢苍天赐予的食物和给予的帮助。在学校里，孩子们将此事改编成剧目上演，他们穿戴特殊的服装打扮成定居者的样子，并举行游行活动，或者画一些与感恩节有关的事物，例如火鸡、南瓜、玉米、清教徒前辈移民和美洲原住民等等。

thanksgiving *n* [C,U] an expression of thanks to God〔对上帝的〕感恩

thank you /ˈ· ·/ *interjection* **1** used to tell someone that you are grateful for something they have given you or done for you; THANKS 谢谢你，多谢：*Margaret handed him the butter. "Thank you," said Samuel.* 玛格丽特把黄油递给了他。"谢谢你。"塞缪尔说。| *Thank you very much, Brian.* 非常感谢你，布赖恩。| **thank**

you for (doing) sth *It's good to see you, Mr. Mathias. Thank you for coming.* 很高兴见到您，马赛厄斯先生。谢谢您的光临。| *Dear Grandma, thank you for the lovely shirt you sent me for Christmas.* 亲爱的外婆，谢谢您在圣诞节给我寄来的那件漂亮的衬衫。**2** used as a polite way of saying that you would like something that someone has offered 谢谢你〔礼貌地表示接受某事〕: *"Can I give you a lift into town?" "Oh, thank you."* "搭我的车进城好吗?" "噢，谢谢你。" **3** used when politely answering someone's question 谢谢你〔礼貌地回答某人的问候〕: *"How was your trip to Paris?" "Very pleasant, thank you."* "你的巴黎之行怎么样?" "非常愉快，谢谢。" **4 no thank you** used to say politely that you do not want something 不用，谢谢〔礼貌地表示谢绝〕: *"Would you like some more coffee?" "No, thank you, I'm fine."* "再来点咖啡吗?" "不用了，谢谢，我够了。" **5** used at the end of a sentence when telling someone firmly that you do not want their help or advice and are slightly annoyed by it 多谢啦〔略带气愤地谢绝提供的帮助或建议〕: *I can manage quite well on my own, thank you!* 我自己完全能做好，多谢你啦!

thank-you¹ *adj* **thank-you letter/note/card etc** a short letter etc in which you thank someone 感谢信/便条/卡片等

thank-you² *n* [C] something you say or do in order to thank someone 道谢的话；道谢的举动: *This present's a thank-you for helping me last week.* 这份礼物是为了感谢你上周帮了我的忙。

S1 W1 **that¹** /ðæt; ðæt/ *determiner plural* **those** /ðoz; ðəʊz/ **1** used to talk about a person, thing, idea etc that has already been mentioned or that the person you are talking to knows about already 那，那个；那些〔指已经提到或已经知道的人、事物、想法等〕: *Who was that man I saw you with last night?* 我看到昨天晚上跟你在一起的那个人是谁? | *Those flowers that you gave me lasted over a week.* 你给我的那些花搁了一个多星期都没有枯萎。| *Later that day the news was being broadcast all over the world.* 那天晚些时候，世界各地的广播都报道了这一消息。| *How much is that hat in the window?* 橱窗里的那顶帽子多少钱? | *The lawyer was expensive, but at that stage we wanted to make sure everything went smoothly.* 请律师是很贵的，但已经到了那一步，我们想要保证一切事情都进展顺利。**2** used to talk about the person or thing that is farthest from you, or the situation that is not happening at the moment 那，那个；那些〔指离你最远的人或物或尚未发生的情况〕: *That party of hers was great but this one will be even better.* 她那次聚会办得不错，但这一次会更好。| *So many cakes to choose from – I'll take that one over there.* 有这么多糕点可供选择，我要那边的那一块。| *Look at those men in that car. What on earth are they doing?* 瞧那辆车上的那些人。他们究竟在干什么?

S1 W1 **that²** *pron plural* **those 1** used to talk about a person, thing, idea etc that has already been mentioned or that the person you are talking to already knows about 那，那个；那些〔指已经提到或已经知道的人、事物或想法等〕: *Pregnant! Who told you that?* 怀孕啦! 谁告诉你的? | *Where did you get those? I've been looking for some shoes just like that.* 你是在哪儿买那双鞋的? 我一直就在找那样的鞋。| *So that's why you don't like him.* 所以，那就是你为什么不喜欢他的原因。| *I wish you wouldn't say things like that.* 我希望你不要说那样的话。| **with that** (=after doing that) 随后，随即 *She slammed the book on the table and with that ran out of the room.* 她把书摔在桌子上，随后跑出了房间。**2** used to talk about the person or thing that is farthest from you, the situation that is not happening at the moment etc 那个人；那事物〔指离你最远的人或物或尚未发生的情况〕: *No, that's your desk, this one's mine.* 不，那才是你的课桌，这个是我的。| *Those were great years at college, but I think that I'm even happier now.* 那些是大学时代的美好时光，不过我觉得我现在还要快乐一些。**3** *formal* used when talking about a particular person or thing, especially one which is a particular type or kind 【正式】〔特定的〕那一个；那一类: *In my opinion the finest wines are those from France.* 我认为，最好的葡萄酒要数法国产的那些。| **that of** *Rupert's manner was that of someone accustomed to mixing with aristocracy.* 鲁珀特的举止属于那种习惯与贵族打交道的人。**4 that's life/men/politics etc** *spoken* used to say that someone's actions are typical of a particular group of people, situation etc 【口】那便是生活/男人/政治等: *"I washed all my clothes only to find I'd left a £20 note in the pocket." "That's life I suppose."* "我把所有的衣服都洗了，结果发现口袋里留了一张20英镑的钞票。" "我想，人生就是这样!" | *We go out for a romantic meal and all he wants to do is talk about football. That's men for you.* 我俩出去是为了享受浪漫的一顿饭，但他只想谈论足球。男人就是这样! **5 at that** *especially spoken* used to give more information, about something mentioned before 【尤口】此外，而且: *He'll have to buy a new car and a big one at that. There are 8 children in his family.* 他不得不买一辆新车，而且要买一辆大的。他家里有八个孩子。**6 and (all) that** *BrE spoken* and similar people or things 【英口】等等，诸如此类: *There were lots of sandwiches and pies and that but I wasn't really hungry.* 有很多的三明治、馅饼等东西，不过我不很饿。**7 that is (to say)** *spoken* used to correct something that you have just said or written 【口】也就是说，即〔用于更正〕: *I know how to operate a computer. That is, I thought I did until I saw this one.* 我知道如何操作电脑。也就是说，在看到这台电脑之前，我想我是知道的。**8 that's a clever dog/that's a good girl** *spoken* used to praise children or animals 【口】这才是好乖乖/这才是好姑娘: *You've eaten all your supper – that's a good boy!* 你把晚饭全吃完了——这才是乖孩子! **9 that's it** *spoken* used when you are angry about a situation and you do not want it to continue 【口】完了，就这样〔表示愤怒〕: *That's it. I'm not taking any more. You can keep your rotten job.* 就这样。我不干了。你可以继续干那没有劲的活。**10 that's that** *spoken* used to say you will not change a decision 【口】就这么定了，就这样吧〔表示决心坚定〕: *I refuse to go and that's that!* 我不会去的。就是这样!

Frequencies of the pronoun **that** in spoken and written English 代词that在英语口语和书面语中的使用频率

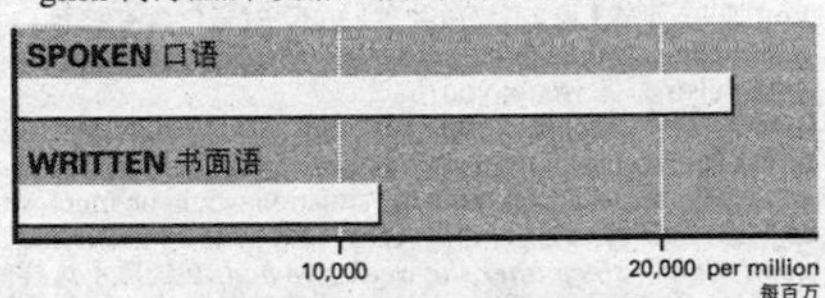

Based on the British National Corpus and the Longman Lancaster Corpus
据英国国家语料库和朗文兰开斯特语料库

This graph shows that the pronoun **that** is more common in spoken than in written English. This is because it is used a lot in conversation to refer to something that has already been mentioned, or when talking about the person or thing that is farthest from you, or a situation in the past. It is also used in some common spoken phrases. 本图表显示，代词that在英语口语中的使用频率高于书面语，因为该词经常用于会话中，指代前面已经提及过的事物，离自己很远的人或物，或者是过去的事情。它还用于一些常用的口语短语中。

that³ /ðət; ðət; *strong* 强读 ðæt; ðæt/ *conjunction* **1** used after verbs, nouns and adjectives to introduce a CLAUSE (2) which gives more information, a reason, an explanation etc 〔用在动词、名词或形容词后引入包含信息、理由、解释等的从句〕: *If she said that she'd come, she'll come.* 如果她说过她要来，她就会来的。| *The rules state that only the goal keeper can handle the ball.* 规则规定，只有守门员才能用手触球。| *Is it true that the Robinsons are emigrating?* 罗宾逊一家要移居国外，这是真的吗? | *The fact that he is your brother-in-law should not affect your decision.* 他是你的姐夫，但这一事实不应该影响你的决定。**2 a) so big/tall etc that...** very big, very tall etc with the result that something happens or someone does something 如此大/高等…〔用在so之后，表示结果〕: *She's so tall that she has to have her clothes made for her.* 她长得这么高，所以不得不定做衣服。**b) such a big man/such a tall house etc that** a very big man, a very tall house etc with the result that something happens or someone does something 如此一个大个子男人/如此一幢高房子等〔用在such之后，表示结果〕: *He's such a miserable so-and-so that none of the nurses like helping him.* 他是一个让人非常讨厌的家伙，没有哪个护士愿意帮助他。**3** used as a RELATIVE PRONOUN like 'who', and 'which' 〔用作关系代词，相当于 who 或 which〕: *Did you know the man that bought the sportscar?* 你认识那个买了跑车的男子吗? | *There are lots of things that I need to buy before the trip.* 我在旅行前有许多东西需要去买。**4** used with objects of a PREPOSITION in a CLAUSE (2) 〔在从句中用作介词的宾语〕: *The police have found the gun that she was shot with.* 警察已经找到打死她的那支枪。| *There's Betty, my sister that I've been telling you about.* 那就是贝蒂，我多次对你说过的我的妹妹。**5 the year/time etc that** the year, the time etc when something happened 〔某事发生的〕那一年/那一时刻等: *The day that my father died, I was on holiday in Greece.* 我父亲去世的那一天，我正在希腊度假。**6** used to introduce a clause after a SUPERLATIVE¹ (2) 〔用来引入最高级形容词或副词后的从句〕: *Veronica is the most boring person that I've ever met.* 韦罗尼卡是我遇见过的最讨厌的人。| *He was the greatest boxer that ever lived.* 他是历史上最伟大的拳击手。**7** *formal* in order S1 W1

that, or so that something may happen or someone may do something【正式】为了, 以便〔表示目的或可能的结果〕: *We pray that he may recover soon.* 我们祈愿他早日康复。**8** *literary* used when you wish that something would happen, that you could do something etc【文】〔用来引导对某种事情的愿望〕: *Oh, that I could fly.* 唉, 我要是能飞就好了! —see also 另见 **so (that)** (so² (2))

USAGE NOTE 用法说明: THAT
SPOKEN-WRITTEN 口语－书面语
In conversation it is not usual for **that** to actually be used in a *that* clause after a verb or adjective. This is especially true after the commonest verbs taking such clauses in spoken English – **think, say, know, see,** and after common adjectives like **sure, confident, afraid, sorry, aware, glad**. 在对话中, 实际上 that 往往并不用于动词或形容词后的 that 从句中。在口头英语中, 在诸如 think, say, know, see 等最常用的动词和 sure, confident, afraid, sorry, aware, glad 等形容词后, 用到此类的从句尤为常见: *I think Stuart's gone crazy.* 我想斯图尔特已经发疯了。| *I'm afraid it could be there for six months.* 我想可能这会持续六个月。
In written English there are differences between different styles of writing. **That** is hardly ever left out in academic writing, where in any case the commonest verbs are not the same as in spoken English, but are words like **show, ensure**. 在书面英语中, 不同的文体之间是有差异的。在学术性写作中, that 很少被省略掉, 此外, 学术性文字中最常用的动词不是口头英语中的那些, 而是 show, ensure 等词: *Empirical data show that similar processes can be guided quite differently.* 实际观察得来的数据表明, 类似的过程可以用完全不同的方法来引导。| *It is important that both groups are used in the experiment.* 重要的是, 两组都必须用于实验。
In newspapers **that** is used at least twice as much as it is left out. 在报刊中, 使用that的时候比被省略的时候至少要多出一倍: *The police say that they don't have the time to worry about marijuana.* 警察说, 他们没有时间去操心大麻的事。But in fiction it is left out more than it is kept in. 但是在小说中, 被省掉的时候多于被保留的时候: *I'm sorry I hit you just now!* 对不起, 我刚才打了你。
GRAMMAR 语法
That is more often left out when the subject of the *that* clause is the same as the subject of the main clause, or where it is a pronoun. 当 that 从句的主语与主句的主语一样时, 或者从句开头是代词时, that 更多是被省略掉: *I think I'll make a shopping list.* 我想我要开一张购物清单。| *They were glad she'd gone out.* 他们很高兴她已经出去了。But 但是, *I suspect that John was a bit drunk.* 我怀疑约翰有点儿醉了。
That is usually put in if the main verb is passive, or where the *that* clause does not immediately follow the verb. 如果主句动词是被动语态, 或者 that 从句不是紧跟在主句动词后, 通常要使用 that: *I was told that he had arrived.* 我被告知, 他已经到了。| *They warned him that it was dangerous.* 他们警告他, 这很危险。
PUNCTUATION 标点符号
That does not usually immediately follow a comma. *Who* and *which* may follow a comma in relative clauses that add information but do not restrict the meaning, but *that* is not used in these clauses. 一般来说, that 不直接跟在逗号之后。who 和 which 在关系从句中可以跟在逗号之后, 补充说明情况, 但并不限制性意义, 而 that 不用在这类从句中。Look at this restrictive clause 试看下面的限制性从句: *She visited her brother who/that lives in Detroit* (=she has more than one brother, and the relative clause with *who/that* tells us which one). 她探访了她那位住在底特律的兄弟〔她有不止一个兄弟, 而关系从句告诉了我们是哪一个〕。Compare this non-restrictive clause 试比较下面的非限制性从句: *She visited her brother, who lives in Detroit* (=she has only one brother, and the relative clause, which cannot begin with *that*, just adds further information about him). 她探访了她的兄弟, 他住在底特律〔她只有一个兄弟, 这里的关系从句不能以 that 开始, 它只是补充了有关他的情况〕。

S1 W2 **that⁴** /ðæt; ðæt/ *adv* [+adj/adv] **1 that long/many etc** *spoken* used to say how long or how many, especially because you are showing the size, number etc with your hands【口】那么长/那么多等〔尤指通过手势比划来表示大小、数目等〕: *The fish was that long, give or take an inch or two.* 那条鱼有那么长, 相差不超过一两英寸。| *He missed hitting the car in front by that much.* 他险些撞到前面那辆车, 就差那么一点点。**2 not that long/many** *spoken* used when you mean fairly short, only a few etc【口】没有那么长/那么多〔用来表示较短、较少等〕: *Will's not that tall, considering he's 16 already.* 威尔不很高, 他已经 16 岁了。| **not all that** *The film wasn't all that good really.* 那部电影实际上不怎么好看。**3 that long/many etc (that)** *BrE spoken* so long, so many etc that something happens, someone does something etc【英口】那么长/那么多等…〔表示程度、结果等〕: *She was that tired that she had to go upstairs and rest.* 她疲倦极了, 只好上楼去休息。| *I've eaten that much, I think I'm going to be sick.* 我已吃了那么多, 我想我会反胃的。

thatch¹ /θætʃ; θætʃ/ *v* [I,T] to make the roof of a building with dried STRAW (=strong stems), REEDs etc 用茅草[芦苇等]覆盖〔屋顶〕—**thatched** *adj*: *a thatched cottage* 茅屋, 茅舍 —**thatcher** *n* [C]

thatch² *n* **1** [C] a roof made of dried STRAW, REEDs etc 茅草屋顶 **2** [U] STRAW or REEDs used to make a roof〔用以盖屋顶的〕茅草; 芦苇 **3** [singular] *humorous* a thick untidy pile of hair on someone's head【幽默】浓密的乱发

Thatch·er /ˈθætʃə; ˈθætʃə/, **Margaret** (1925-) a British politician in the Conservative Party, now officially called **Baroness Thatcher**, and sometimes called **Maggie** in the newspapers. She became leader of her party in 1975, and in 1979 became the UK's first woman Prime Minister, a position she held until 1990. She won three General Elections one after the other, and she had a great influence on British politics and on British life. Her ideas, which have become known as **Thatcherism**, have also influenced politicians in other countries. She reduced taxes, took away power from TRADE UNIONs, and started a programme of PRIVATIZATION (=selling state-owned services such as electricity, gas, and the telephone service, so that they became private companies). She was a strong and determined leader who would not change her mind easily and would not accept disagreement among her ministers. For this reason, she was sometimes called 'the Iron Lady'. 撒切尔〔(1925-), 英国保守党政治家, 正式称撒切尔女男爵。报纸上有时称她为"玛姬"。1975 年, 她成为保守党的领导人, 1979 年成为英国历史上第一位女首相, 直到 1990 年离任。她连续三次在大选中获胜, 对英国的政治及国民生活产生了重大影响。她的思想被称为撒切尔主义, 对其他国家的政治家也有所影响。她降低税赋, 剥夺工会的权利, 启动私有化计划。她是个强硬领导人, 不会轻易改变主意, 也不能接受大臣有异议。因此, 她有时也被称作"铁娘子"〕

Thatch·er·is·m /ˈθætʃərɪzəm; ˈθætʃərɪzəm/ *n* [U] the general principles on which Margaret Thatcher's government was based when she was Prime Minister of the UK, especially her ideas about economic management 撒切尔主义〔撒切尔夫人执政期间英国政府遵循的基本原则, 尤指撒切尔的经济管理观念〕

thaw¹ /θɔ; θɔː/ *v* **1** [I,T] also 又作 **thaw out** if ice or snow thaws or is thawed, it becomes warmer and turns into water (使)〔冰雪〕融化: *The lake thawed in March.* 三月里, 湖水解冻了。| **it thaws** (=ice and snow melt) (冰、雪) 融化 *It thawed overnight.* 一夜之间冰雪就融化了。**2** also 又作 **thaw out** [T] to let frozen food unfreeze until it is ready to cook 解冻〔冷冻食品〕: *Thaw frozen meat in its packet and then cook as soon as possible.* 先让冻肉在包装盒里解冻, 然后尽快烹煮。**3** [I] to become friendlier and less formal〔态度〕变得温和, 随和: *After a few glasses of wine Robert began to thaw a little.* 几杯酒过后, 罗伯特开始变得比较温和了。

thaw² *n* **1** [singular] a period of warm weather during which snow and ice melt 融雪期; 化冰期; 解冻期: *The thaw begins in March.* 解冻期在三月份开始。**2** [C] an improvement in relations between two countries after a period of unfriendliness〔两国之间经历一段不和时期之后的关系〕缓和, 改善

the- /θɪ; θi/ *prefix* another form of the prefix THEO- 前缀 theo- 的另一种拼写

the¹ /ðə; ðə; *before vowels* 元音前作 ðɪ; ði; *strong* 强读 ði; ðiː/ *definite article, determiner* **1** used to refer to a particular thing or person when everyone knows which thing or person you are talking about, or because only one such person or thing exists〔用来指大家知道正在谈论的或唯一存在的某一特定的事物或人〕: *I've got two cats now; the black and white one's called Rosie and the ginger one's called Joseph.* 我现在有两只猫了, 黑白相间的那一只名叫罗西, 姜黄色的那只名叫约瑟夫。| *The audience clapped and cheered.* 观众鼓掌欢呼。| *Take these letters to the post office, will you.* 把这些信件拿到邮局去, 好吗? | *The sky was gray and overcast.* 天空灰蒙蒙、阴沉沉的。| *They're holding an election later in the year.* 他们要在下半年举行选 S1 W1

举。| *the tallest building in the world* 世界上最高的建筑 | **the United States/the Aegean Sea etc** (=used before the names of certain countries, seas etc) 美国/爱琴海等〔用于某些国家、海洋等名称之前〕| **His Holiness the Pope/the Defense Minister etc** (=used as part of someone's title) 教皇(陛下)/国防部长(阁下)等〔用于某些人的头衔中〕| **the Smiths/the Kings/the Mitchells etc** *especially spoken* (=used before the name of a family to refer to all the members of that family)【尤口】史密斯一家/金一家/米切尔一家等〔用于某个家庭的姓氏之前, 指全家的所有成员〕**2** used to refer to something that everyone knows because it happens in nature or is a part of daily life〔用来指自然界或日常生活中大家都知道的某事〕: *We drove through the night to get to New Orleans in time.* 我们彻夜驱车, 及时地赶到了新奥尔良。| *Ella's been complaining about the traffic keeping her awake at night.* 埃拉一直在抱怨来往车辆让她晚上睡不着觉。| *We would ask tenants to switch off the water supply before vacating the property.* 我们要求房客在搬出房屋前先把自来水关掉。**3** used to refer to a part of the body or to someone or something that belongs to someone〔用来指某人身体的某一部位或属于某人的某一东西或某人〕: *She hit him on the* (=his) *ear.* 她打了他一记耳光。| *How's the* (=your) *arm?* 手臂怎么样了? |*The* (=my) *car broke down again today.* 今天车又抛锚了。| **the wife** *spoken* (=used especially by men to refer to their own wife or to another man's wife and considered to be offensive by some women)【口】那婆娘〔尤为男人用来指自己的或别人的妻子, 一些妇女认为这是冒犯用语〕**4** used before an adjective to make it into a noun when you are referring to all the people who that adjective describes〔用在形容词前, 指某一类人〕: *We need more sheltered accommodation for the elderly.* 我们需要为老年人提供更多的安身之所。| **the rich/the poor** *She devoted her life to helping the poor.* 她毕生都在帮助穷人。| **the wounded/the disabled/the physically handicapped etc** *parking facilities for the disabled* 残疾人专用停车设施 | **the Germans/the Japanese/the British** (=used to refer to all the people from a particular country) 德国人/日本人/英国人〔用来指某一国的全体人民〕**5** *especially spoken* used before an adjective to make it into a noun when you are referring to a situation that that adjective describes【尤口】〔用在形容词前, 指某一类情况〕: *Her behaviour is verging on the manic.* 她的行为近于疯狂。| **the impossible/the ridiculous/the insane** *Come on now, that's asking for the impossible.* 得了吧, 那是强人所难。**6** used before a singular noun to make it general〔用于单数名词前, 表示泛指〕: *The condor is in danger of extinction.* 兀鹫有濒于灭绝的危险。| *The computer has revolutionized office work.* 电脑使办公室工作发生了革命性变化。**7** used before a plural noun to refer generally to a particular kind of thing〔用于复数名词前, 表示泛指〕: *I find it easier to get up when the mornings are lighter.* 晨光更明亮的时候, 我觉得更容易起床。| *The shops are always packed just before Christmas.* 圣诞节前几天, 商店里总是挤满了人。**8** used before activities that people do, especially musical activities, but usually not including sports〔用于人的活动前, 尤用于音乐活动前, 但一般不包括体育运动〕: *Fiona's learning the flute.* 菲奥纳正在学吹长笛。| *He plays the violin.* 他会拉小提琴。**9 the flu/the measles/the mumps** *spoken* used before the names of certain not very serious illnesses【口】流感/麻疹/流行性腮腺炎〔用于某些不太严重的疾病名称前〕: *Amy's off school with the measles.* 埃米因患麻疹而告假了。**10** *spoken* used before referring to a particular day, date, or month【口】〔用于某一特定的日期或月份前〕: *Tuesday the thirteenth of April* 4月13日星期二 | *We moved house in the first week of July.* 我们是在七月份的第一个星期里搬家的。| *The meeting was scheduled for the Thursday.* 会议定在星期四。**11** used to refer to a period of time that lasts ten or a hundred years〔用来指十年或一百年的一个时期〕: **the twenties/the thirties/the forties etc** *There was a severe recession in the mid-twenties.* 20年代中期曾有过一次严重的经济衰退。| **the sixteen-hundreds/the seventeen-hundreds/the eighteen-hundreds** *the great novelists of the nineteen-hundreds* 20世纪的伟大小说家 **12 by the metre/by the dozen/by the handful etc** used before the names of measurements when describing how something is calculated, sold, or used 论米/论打/论把等〔来计算、销售或使用, 用于量度名称之前〕: *This cloth is sold by the metre.* (=it is measured in metres in order to calculate its price) 这布匹论米卖〔按米尺度量来计算价格〕。| *We get paid by the hour.* 我们按小时计报酬。**13** used before a noun, especially in negative sentences to show an amount or degree needed for a particular purpose〔用于名词前、尤用于否定句中, 表示所需要的量或程度〕: *I haven't the time to talk just now.* 我现在没有时间谈话。| *Eric didn't even have the common sense to send for a doctor.* 埃里克甚至连去请医生的常识都没有。**14** used before the name of a thing that represents a particular activity〔用于某一物体名词前, 表示某一特定的活动〕: *Rupert took to the bottle* (=began to drink a lot of alcohol) *after his wife died.* 鲁珀特在妻子死后开始贪杯。| *He's already been under the knife* (=had a medical operation) *twice this year.* 他今年已经是两次开刀做手术了。**15** *spoken* used with strong pronunciation before a noun to show that it is the best, most famous etc person or thing of its kind【口】〔用于名词之前, 表示某一类人或事物中最好的、最有名的, 发音要重读〕: *"Apparently Paul McCartney's singing at the club tonight." "Not the Paul McCartney surely!"* "据我所知保罗·麦卡特尼今晚上要在俱乐部演唱了。" "当然不是那个保罗·麦卡特尼!" **16** *spoken* used when describing someone or something when you are angry, jealous, surprised etc【口】〔用于形容某人或某事, 表示愤怒、嫉妒、吃惊等〕: *He's stolen my parking space, the bastard!* 他偷占了我的停车位, 这个臭小子! | *I can't get this drawing pin out, the stupid thing.* 我没法取出这颗图钉, 这破烂玩意儿! | *"Jamie's won a holiday in Hawaii." "The lucky devil!"* "杰米赢得了去夏威夷度假的机会。" "这家伙真走运!" **17** *spoken* used in certain phrases that express anger, surprise etc【口】〔用于某些短语中, 表示愤怒、吃惊等〕: *What the hell are you doing here?* 你究竟在这里搞什么? | *For the love of God what will the boy do next!* 上帝知道那孩子下一步还会干些什么!

USAGE NOTE 用法说明: THE

GRAMMAR 语法

The is not used with uncountable or plural nouns when you mean 'all' of something in general, or when what you are talking about is not already specifically known about by the reader or listener. 当泛指某事物的"总体"时, 或者当谈论的事还没有为读者或听者具体知晓时, the不与不可数名词或复数名词一起使用: *I love life/rock music/wine/ice cold beer/silk shirts/bananas.* 我喜爱生活/摇滚乐/葡萄酒/冰镇啤酒/绸衬衫/香蕉。| *We sat around eating cheese and crackers and listening to rock music.* 我们随意地坐着, 一边吃着干酪和饼干, 一边听着摇滚乐。

The is used if you are mentioning specific things that are already known to the reader or listener. 如果你提到的具体事物是读者或听者已经知晓的, 要用 the: *We drank the beer and the wine and watched the video* (=the beer etc that I just told you about or that you know about). 我们一边喝着啤酒和葡萄酒, 一边看着录像〔指啤酒或葡萄酒是我刚告诉过你的或者你本来就知道的〕。

The is also used whenever you use an *of* phrase, relative clause, superlative etc, to say more specifically what kind of thing you mean. 在使用 of 短语、关系从句、最高级等以更具体地说出你所意指的某种事物时, 也要用 the: *I love the life of a writer/the food that you cook/the best things in life.* 我喜爱作家的生活/你做的那些食品/生活中最美好的东西。

The is not usually used at all in the following situations (though in a few specific cases it may be if the noun is restricted as just described). 在下列情况下, 通常不用 the〔然而在少数具体情况下, 如果名词像上述那样受到限制的话, 也可以用 the〕:

1. With many times of day and night and days, months etc, especially after **at, by,** and **on**. 表示白天、晚上、星期、月份等时, 尤其在 at, by 和 on 之后: *at sunset/noon/by night/on Monday* 在夕阳西下时/在中午时分/在晚上前/在星期一 (Compare 比较 *during the night/on the Monday after Christmas* 在那天晚上/在圣诞节后的那个星期一) Compare also 再比较以下两句: *Last week was awful* (=the one just before now) and 和 *The last week was awful* (=the last week of my vacation etc some time ago). 上周糟糕透了〔指现在之前的那一周〕/最后一周糟糕透了〔指先前度假中等的最后一周〕。

2. When you give dates in speech you say 讲话中提到日期时要说: *June the third* (*BrE* 英)/*June third* (*AmE* 美) or 或 *the third of June* 6月3日, but you would write 但写作时则用: *June 3rd*

3. When you are talking about meals, especially after **at, before, during, after, for,** and the verb **have**. 在谈论饭餐时, 尤其在 at, before, during, after, for 之后和动词 have 之后: *after/at/before/during breakfast* 早餐之后/吃早餐时/早餐之前/早餐期间 | *coffee for breakfast* 咖啡当早餐 | *When do you have breakfast?* 你什么时候吃早饭? | *Lunch is at one.* 午饭在一点吃。(Compare 比较 *The breakfast she gave us was good.* 她给我们准备的早餐很不错。)

4. In many fixed expressions such as 在许多固定表达方式里，诸如: *by car/bus etc* 坐汽车/公共汽车等 | *at/to school/university etc* 在学校/在大学/去上学/去上大学等 | *in/to bed/prison/church* 在床上/在监狱里/在教堂里/上床/进监狱/上教堂 | *arm in arm* 手臂挽着手臂 | *face to face* 面对着面 | *husband and wife* 夫妻 | *from beginning to end* 自始至终

5. With names of languages and most diseases 指语言和大多数疾病的名称时: *She speaks Greek.* 她说希腊语。| *He's got cancer/flu/mumps/a cold.* 他患了癌症/流感/流行性腮腺炎/感冒。In informal spoken English, however, people often use **the** before the names of several common diseases. 然而，在非正式的口头英语中，人们经常在一些常见疾病名称前使用the: *He has got the flu/the mumps.* 他患了流感/流行性腮腺炎。

6. With names of airports and railway stations 指机场、火车站的名称时: *I'm arriving at Heathrow airport/Grand Central Station.* 我将到达希思罗机场/中央大火车站。

7. With many names of streets, places, countries, mountains etc 指街道、地点、国家、山脉等名称时: *Madison Avenue/Oxford Street/New York/Texas/Holland/Mount Fuji.* 麦迪逊大街/牛津街/纽约/得克萨斯州/荷兰/富士山 (compare 比较 *This isn't the New York I remember.* 这不是我记忆中的纽约。)

8. However, some such names always contain **the**. 然而，有些这类名称总是含有the: *The Strand, The Bronx, The Hague, The Sudan* 斯特兰德大街，布朗克斯区，海牙，苏丹 This includes especially the names of countries that are plural or contain the word *state, republic* etc. 这尤其包括名称是复数或含有state, republic等词的国家: *The Netherlands, the USA, the UK, the Irish Republic.* 荷兰，美国，英国，爱尔兰共和国

9. **The** is usually needed with names of hotels and restaurants if they do not end in *'s*. 如果旅馆或餐馆的名称不是以's结尾，通常需要用the: *The Hilton/The Grand Hotel/The Mandarin.* 希尔顿酒店/贵宾酒店/文华酒店 Also with names of rivers, seas, and groups of mountains. 另外，用于河流、海洋和山脉的名称: *The Ganges/The Atlantic/The Rockies* 恒河/大西洋/落基山脉

the² *adv* **1** used in comparisons to show that two things happen together〔用于比较，表示两件事同时发生〕: *The more he eats the fatter he gets.* 他吃得越多就越胖。| *"When do you want this done?" "The sooner the better."* "你想要这事什么时候办成?" "越早越好。" **2** used in comparisons to show that someone or something has more or less of a particular quality than before〔用于比较，表示某人或某物与过去相比的某一品质〕: **the better/the worse** *You'll feel all the better for having some time away from work.* 你如能离开工作一段时间，就会感觉好一些。| **none the wiser** (=not knowing more about something than before) 仍然弄不明白 *Her lengthy explanation left me none the wiser.* 她冗长的解释还是让我弄不明白。**3** used in front of adjectives and adverbs to emphasize that something is as big, good etc as it is possible to be〔用于形容词或副词前，强调某事尽可能的程度〕: *He likes you the best.* 他最喜欢你。| *I had the greatest difficulty understanding her.* 我费了好大的劲才明白她的意思。

S2 W2 **the·a·tre** *BrE*【英】, **theater** *AmE*【美】/ˈθɪətə; ˈθɪətə/ *n*
1 ▶BUILDING 建筑物◀ [C] a building or place with a stage where plays are performed 剧场，戏院: *an open-air theatre* 露天剧场 | *the Mercury Theater* 墨丘利剧院
2 ▶PLAYS 戏剧◀ [U] **a)** plays as a form of entertainment 戏剧: *I enjoy theater and swimming.* 我喜欢看戏和游泳。| **the theatre** *He's really interested in literature and the theatre.* 他对文学和戏剧真的很感兴趣。| **good theatre** (=effective entertainment) 具有娱乐性 *Yeats' plays are great poetry but they are not good theatre.* 叶芝的剧作都是伟大的诗篇，但不能用来消闲解闷。**b)** the work of acting in, writing, or organizing plays 戏剧事业；剧作，剧本: *classes in theater and music* 戏剧音乐班 | *She's been working in the theatre for over thirty years.* 她从事戏剧工作已有三十余载。
3 ▶IN A HOSPITAL 在医院◀ [C,U] a special room in a hospital where medical operations are done〔医院里的〕手术室；OPERATING THEATRE *BrE*【英】
4 ▶AREA 区域◀ [C] a large area where a war is being fought 战区；战场: *the Pacific theater during World War II* 第二次世界大战期间的太平洋战区
5 ▶PLACE TO SEE A FILM 看电影的地方◀ [C] *AmE AustrE* a building where films are shown【美，澳】电影院；CINEMA (1) *BrE*【英】, MOVIE THEATER *AmE*【美】

the·a·tre·go·er *BrE*【英】, **theatergoer** *AmE*【美】/ˈθɪətə-ˌgəʊə; ˈθɪətəˌgəʊə/ *n* [C] someone who regularly watches plays at the theatre 戏院常客，戏迷: *Ken's a keen theatregoer.* 肯是一个狂热的戏迷。

theatre-in-the-round /ˌ‥ · · ˈ·/ *n* [U] the performance of a play on a central stage with the people watching sitting in a circle around it〔舞台在正中央、观众坐在四周的〕圆形剧场；圆形剧场戏剧技法

theatre weap·ons /ˈ‥ ˌ‥/ *n* [plural] *technical* weapons, especially MISSILEs that can only be fired a few hundred kilometres【术语】战术武器〔尤指射程只有几百公里的导弹〕

the·at·ri·cal /θɪˈætrɪkl; θiˈætrɪkəl/ *adj* **1** connected with the performing of plays 剧场的，剧院的；戏剧的；演剧的: *comic and theatrical skills* 喜剧演艺技能 **2** behaving in a loud or very noticeable way that is intended to get people's attention 戏剧性的；夸张的: *He took her hand and kissed it in a theatrical gesture.* 他捧起她的手，用一种夸张的姿势吻了一下。—**theatrically** /-klɪ; -kli/ *adv*

the·at·ri·cals /θɪˈætrɪklz; θiˈætrɪkəlz/ *n* [plural] **1** *BrE informal* deliberately emotional behaviour so that people will notice you【英，非正式】戏剧性行为；夸张行为: *We can do without all these theatricals, Andrew!* 安德鲁，我们不需要这些装模作样！**2** performances of plays 戏剧表演: *amateur theatricals* 业余戏剧表演

Thebes /θibz; θiːbz/ **1** an ancient city in southern Egypt, where there are ancient TEMPLEs (=religious buildings) and TOMBs (=places where dead people are buried) 底比斯〔埃及南部一古城，有古代庙宇和陵墓〕**2** an ancient city in eastern Greece, northwest of Athens, where Oedipus was king according to old Greek stories. It was destroyed by Alexander the Great. 第比斯〔希腊东部一古城，位于雅典西北。据古希腊传说，俄狄浦斯曾任第比斯国王。该城被亚历山大大帝摧毁〕—**Theban** *n, adj*

thee /ði; ðiː/ *pron old use* the object[1] (6) form of THOU; you【旧】汝，尔〔thou 的宾格〕

theft /θɛft; θeft/ *n* **1** [U] the crime of stealing 盗窃罪: *Car theft is on the increase.* 汽车盗窃犯罪越来越多。**2** [C] an act of stealing something 偷窃，偷盗: *There have been a number of thefts in the area.* 该地区已有几宗偷窃案发生。| [+of] *the theft of £150 from the office* 从办公室偷走的150英镑

S1 W1 **their** /ðə; ðə; *strong* 强读 ðɛr; ðeə/ *determiner* [possessive form of *they* they 的所有格形式] **1** of or belonging to them 他们的；她们的；它们的: *They washed their faces and went to bed.* 他们洗过脸，就上床睡觉了。| *The twins spend all their time together.* 那对双胞胎总是待在一起。**2** used to avoid saying 'his' or 'her' after words like 'anyone', 'no one', 'everyone' etc〔用在anyone, no one, everyone 等词后，泛指〕人人，大家: *Everyone is entitled to their own opinion.* 人人都可以有自己的意见。—compare 比较 HIS[1] —see 见 EACH[1] (USAGE)

theatre 剧场

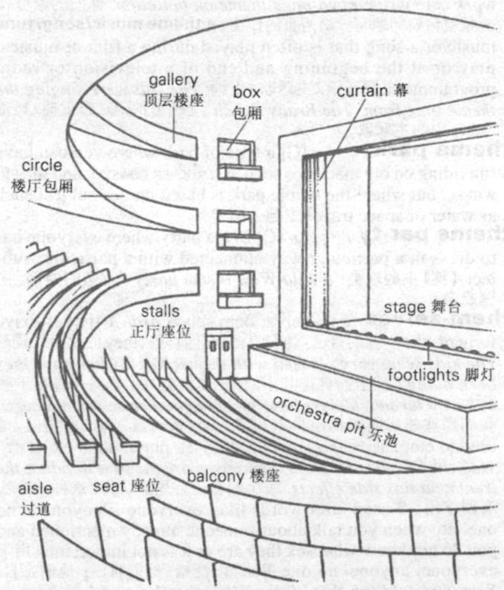

theirs /ðɛrz; ðeəz/ *pron* [possessive form of *they* they 的所有格形式] **1** of or belonging to the people or things that have already been mentioned〔对已经提到过的人或事物〕他们的; 她们的; 它们的〔东西〕: *When our washing machine broke, our neighbours let us use theirs.* 我们的洗衣机坏了的时候, 邻居让我们用他们的。| *They shared the prize money with a friend of theirs.* 他们与他们的一位朋友分享那笔奖金。**2** used to avoid saying 'his' or 'hers' after words like 'anyone', 'no one', 'everyone' etc〔用在 anyone, no one, everyone 等词后, 泛指〕人人, 大家: *Everyone wants what is theirs by right.* 人人都想得到权利赋予自己的东西。—compare 比较 HIS²

the·is·m /ˋθiɪzəm; ˈθiːɪzəm/ *n* [U] *technical* the belief that a personal God exists and that He has made His existence known to people through the Bible, church, dreams etc【术语】〔基督教的〕一神论 —**theistic** /θiˋɪstɪk; θiːˈɪstɪk/ *adj* —**theistically** /-klɪ; -kli/ *adv*

Thel·ma and Lou·ise /ˌθɛlmə ənd luˋiz; ˌθelmə ənd luˈiːz/ (1991) a US road movie about two women who kill a man because he tries to force one of them to have sex with him. They then drive across the US having exciting adventures, and they discover that they enjoy the freedom of not having any relationships with men, and they enjoy living as criminals.《末路狂花》〔(1991), 美国一公路电影。故事中, 两个女子因一男子强迫与她们中的一位发生性关系而将他杀死。然后, 她俩驾车横穿美国, 途中经历一连串刺激的冒险经历, 终于发现自己非常喜欢没有男人的自由生活, 而且还觉得当逃犯的日子很开心〕

them¹ /ðəm; ðəm; *strong* 强读 ðɛm; ðem/ *pron* **1** the object form of 'they' 他们; 她们; 它们〔they 的宾格〕: *Has anyone seen my keys? I can't find them anywhere.* 有人见到我的钥匙吗? 我到处都找不到。| *The police were very helpful when I spoke to them.* 当我向警察说明情况后, 他们很愿意帮忙。—see 见 ME (USAGE) **2** used to avoid saying 'him' or 'her' after words like 'anyone', 'no one', 'everyone' etc〔用在 anyone, no one, everyone 等词后, 泛指〕那人, 那些人: *If anyone phones, tell them I'll be back later.* 如果有人打电话来, 就说我要过一会儿才回来。

them² / ðɛm; ðem/ *determiner spoken* sometimes used to mean those, although most people think this is incorrect【口】那些〔多数人认为这是不正确的用法〕: *Can I have some of them biscuits, Mum?* 妈妈, 我可以吃一点那些饼干吗?

the·mat·ic /θɪˋmætɪk; θɪˈmætɪk/ *adj* concerned with a particular THEME 主题的; 专题的; 题目的: *thematic consistency* 主题的连贯性

theme /θim; θiːm/ *n* [C] **1** the main subject or idea in a piece of writing, speech, film etc〔文章、讲话、电影等的〕主题: *The book's theme is the conflict between love and duty.* 本书的主题是爱情与职责之间的冲突。**2** a short simple tune that is repeated and developed in a piece of music〔音乐的〕主调; 主旋律: *Freia's theme in Wagner's opera* 瓦格纳歌剧中的弗莱雅主旋律 **3** *AmE* a short piece of writing on a particular subject that you do for school【美】〔为某一特定学科写作的〕作文, 短论文: *Your homework is to write a two-page theme on pollution.* 你们的家庭作业是就污染问题写一篇两页的作文。**4 theme music/song/tune** music or a song that is often played during a film or musical play or at the beginning and end of a television or radio programme 主题音乐/主题歌/主调: *The kids were singing the theme song from 'The Brady Bunch'.* 孩子们唱着《布雷迪·邦奇一家》中的主题歌。

theme park /ˈ· ·/ *n* [C] a type of park where you can have fun riding on big machines such as a ROLLER COASTER and the BIG WHEEL, but where the whole park is based on one subject such as water or space travel 主题公园

theme par·ty /ˈ· ˌ· ·/ *n* [C] *BrE* a party where everyone has to dress in a particular way connected with a particular subject【英】主题晚会: *a wild West theme party* "荒蛮的西部"主题晚会

them·selves /ðəmˋsɛlvz; ðəmˈselvz/ *pron* **1** the reflexive form of 'they' 他们自己; 她们自己; 它们自己〔they 的反身代词〕: *The kids seem very pleased with themselves – what have they been doing?* 孩子们自得其乐, 似乎非常高兴。他们一直在干些什么? | *Our neighbours have just bought themselves a jacuzzi.* 我们那些邻居刚刚都给自家买了一个"极可意"牌按摩浴缸。**2** used to emphasize the pronoun 'they', a plural noun etc 自己, 自身〔用于强调〕: *Doctors themselves are the first to admit the treatment has side effects.* 医生们自己首先承认说, 这种治疗法有副作用。**3** used after words like 'everyone', 'anyone', 'no one' etc when you talk about someone already mentioned and you do not know what sex they are or it is not important〔用于 everyone, anyone, no one 等词后, 泛指〕他们自己; 他们亲自: *Someone told me they'd actually seen the accident happen themselves.* 有人告诉我说他们的确目击了那场事故的发生。**4 in themselves** used to say that ideas or situations only become important, serious etc when you consider other related ideas or situations 本身, 自身; 就本身而言: *None of the witnesses' statements prove anything in themselves, but together they are quite conclusive.* 没有哪一个证人的证词本身能证明什么, 但把它总括起来, 结论却相当明显。**5 (all) by themselves a)** alone 单独地, 独自地: *It is a sad fact that many pensioners now live by themselves.* 许多领取养老金的人现在都是独自生活, 这是一个令人悲哀的事实。**b)** without help 全靠自己地: *Did the children make the model all by themselves?* 孩子们是全靠自己做那个模型的吗? **6 (all) to themselves** if people have something to themselves, they do not have to share it with anyone 完全属于自己的: *In the new house the children will have a room to themselves.* 在新房子里, 孩子们将有一间属于自己的房间。**7 not be/feel themselves** if people are not themselves, they do not feel or behave in the way they usually do because they are nervous, upset or ill〔因神经紧张、烦恼、生病等而〕表现反常/心神不定

then¹ /ðɛn; ðen/ *adv* **1** at a particular time in the past or future 当时, 那时; 到时候, 届时: *It was then that I realised she'd tricked me.* 直到那个时候我才意识到她骗了我。| *I used to go to school with Mavis Butterwick, or Mavis O'Brien as she then was.* 我曾经同梅维丝·巴特韦克一道上学, 她当时名叫梅维丝·奥布赖恩。| *The furniture is being delivered next week so until then we'll have to sit on the floor.* 家具下周才送来, 所以在此之前, 我们只好坐在地板上。| **from then on** (=starting at that time) 从那时开始 *They met in 1942 and from then on they were firm friends.* 他们1942年相识, 从那时开始, 他们一直是好朋友。| **just then** *Silently she closed the door. Just then she heard a noise.* 她默不作声地关上了门, 就在那时, 她听到一阵嘈杂声。| **back then** (=a long time ago in the past, when things were different) 回首往事, 当年 *Back then we spent holidays in Blackpool.* 当年我们曾在布莱克浦度假。| **then and only then** *Tidy your room, then and only then can you go out with Mike.* 先整理好了你的屋子, 这样, 也只有这样, 你才可以跟迈克一块儿出去。**2** next; after something has happened 接下来, 然后: *You're doing it all wrong. Mix the flour and butter and then add the eggs.* 你弄错了。是先把面粉和黄油搅拌好, 然后加入鸡蛋。| *First the passengers and then the stewards jumped from the wreckage.* 先是乘客, 然后是乘务人员从失事的船上跳了下来。**3** used to say that because of what you know about the situation, something else is probably true 那么: *Still in your pyjamas? Have you just got out of bed then?* 你还穿着睡衣? 那么你是刚起床了? | **if...then...** *If x = 3 and y = 5 then xy = 15.* 假定x=3, y=5, 那么 xy=15。**4 but then (again)** *especially spoken* used to say that although something is true something else is also true which makes the first thing seem less important【尤口】不过话又说回来: *I don't spend much but then I don't really go out much.* 我花费不大, 不过话又说回来, 我实际上并不怎么出去。**5** *spoken* used at the end of questions, statements etc, especially to agree with someone or to make people aware that you are speaking【口】那么好吧〔用在句末, 尤表示赞同或引人注意〕: *So, what do you do then?* 这么说来, 你是干什么的? | *Right then, shall we start?* 那好吧, 我们开始吧? | *"Mom, will you play tennis with me?" "Get the balls out then."* "妈妈, 你跟我一块儿打网球好吗?" "那好吧, 把球拿出来吧。" **6** *especially spoken* used when giving your opinion or advice about something【尤口】那, 那就: *If you're going to go then go.* 如果你打算去, 那就去吧。| *"He's boring, rude and arrogant." "Then divorce him."* "他令人厌烦, 而且粗鲁傲慢。" "那就跟他离婚吧。" **7** so that something happens or so that someone does something 这样, 这样一来: *Wear a big hat and dark glasses then no one will recognize you.* 戴上一顶大帽子和一副墨镜, 这样, 就没有人会认出你来了。**8** used in a list of things when you have remembered something else you want to add 另外, 还有: *I do all the washing and cleaning and then there's the ironing too.* 所有的洗涤清理工作都是我在做, 另外还有熨烫的活。**9 then and there** also 又作 **there and then** immediately 立即, 当场: *I expected to have to wait a few days, but they issued the passport then and there.* 我原以为得等上几天时间, 但他们当场就办好了护照。—see also 另见 **now and then** (NOW¹ (6))

then² *adj* **the then President, Director etc** the President, Director etc at a particular time in the past 当时的总统/主任等: *secretary to the then Head of Light Entertainment* 当时的娱乐节目负责人的秘书

thence /ðɛns; ðens/ *adv formal*【正式】**1** from there 从那儿, 从那里: *We went by boat to Trieste, and thence by train to Prague.* 我们先坐船去的里雅斯特, 然后从那儿坐火车去布拉格。**2** for that reason 因为那个缘故; 因而

thence·forth /ˌðɛns`fɔrθ; ðens'fɔːθ/ also 又作 **thence·for·ward** /ˌðɛns`fɔrwəd; ðens'fɔːwəd/ *adv formal* starting from that time【正式】从那时起: *Thenceforth he made his life in England.* 从那时起，他开始在英格兰谋生。

theo- /θɪə; θɪə/ also 又作 **the-** *prefix* concerning God or gods 神的: *theology* (=study of religion) 神学

the·oc·ra·cy /θɪ`ɑkrəsɪ; θi'ɒkrəsi/ *n* [C] a social system or state controlled by religious leaders 神权政治; 神权政体 —**theo·cratic** /ˌθɪə`krætɪk; ˌθiːə'krætɪk◂/ *adj*: *the imposition of a theocratic State* 强迫实行神权政体

the·od·o·lite /θɪ`ɑdḷˌaɪt; θi'ɒdəlaɪt/ *n* [C] a piece of equipment used by a land SURVEYOR for measuring angles 经纬仪〔勘测人员用来测量角度的一种仪器〕

the·o·lo·gian /ˌθɪə`lodʒən; ˌθiːə'ləʊdʒən/ *n* [C] someone who has studied theology 神学家, 神学研究者

theological col·lege /·.··.., ·.·/ *BrE*【英】, **theological seminary** /ˌ·····'····/ *AmE*【美】*n* [C] a college for training people to become priests or church ministers 神学院〔训练人们成为牧师或教会神职人员的学院〕

the·ol·o·gy /θɪ`ɑlədʒɪ; θi'ɒlədʒi/ *n* **1** [U] the study of religion and religious ideas and beliefs 神学: *He studied theology at college.* 他在大学读神学。**2** [C,U] a particular system of religious beliefs and ideas 宗教信仰体系: *According to Muslim theology there is only one God.* 根据穆斯林的宗教信仰, 神只有一个。—**theological** /ˌθɪə`lɑdʒɪkḷ; ˌθiːə'lɒdʒɪkəl◂/ *adj*: *theological debate* 神学辩论 —**theologically** /-kḷɪ; -kli/ *adv*

theo·rem /`θɪərəm; 'θɪərəm/ *n* [C] *technical* a statement, especially in mathematics, that you can prove by reasoning【术语】〔尤指数学中依据推理可以证明的〕定理

theo·ret·i·cal /ˌθɪə`rɛtɪkḷ; θɪə'retɪkəl/ also 又作 **theo·ret·ic** /ˌθɪə`rɛtɪk; θɪə'retɪk/ *adj* **1** concerned with the study of scientific ideas rather than with practical uses of science or practical experience〔科学〕理论的: *theoretical physics* 理论物理 —compare 比较 PRACTICAL¹ (1) **2** a theoretical situation or condition is supposed to exist but does not really exist 理论上的; 推想的, 臆测的: *Equality between men and women in our society is still only theoretical.* 在我们这个社会里, 男女之间的平等仍然停留在理论上。| *a theoretical risk of an explosion* 臆测的爆炸的风险

theo·ret·i·cally /ˌθɪə`rɛtəkəlɪ; θɪə'retɪkli/ *adv* [sentence adverb 句子副词] **1** used to say what is supposed to happen in a particular situation when the opposite is true 根据推测来看, 按道理讲: *Theoretically, Damian's the boss, but I coordinate the team on a day-to-day basis.* 按理说, 达米安是老板, 但全队日常的协调工作是由我来做的。**2** according to a scientific idea that has not been proved to be true in a practical way 在理论上; 从理论上说: *It is theoretically possible for computers to be programmed to think like humans.* 对电脑进行编程, 使它像人一样思考, 这在理论上是可能的。

theo·rist /`θɪərɪst; 'θɪərɪ̵st/ also 又作 **theo·re·ti·cian** /ˌθɪərə`tɪʃən; ˌθɪərə'tɪʃən/ *n* [C] someone who develops ideas within a particular subject that explain why particular things happen or are true 理论家: *a leading economic theorist* 杰出的经济学理论家

theo·rize also 又作 **-ise** *BrE*【英】/`θɪəˌraɪz; 'θɪəraɪz/ *v* [I+**about/on**, T+**that**] to think of a possible explanation for an event or fact 建立学说; 阐释

theo·ry /`θɪərɪ; 'θɪəri/ *n* **1** [C] an idea or set of ideas that is intended to explain something about life or the world, especially one that has not yet been proved to be true 学说: *Darwin's theory of evolution* 达尔文的进化论 | **theory that** *the theory that light is made up of waves* 光是由波组成的这一学说 **2** [U] the general principles or ideas of a subject, especially a scientific subject 理论: *Freudian theory has had a great influence on psychology.* 弗洛伊德理论对心理学有着巨大的影响。**3 in theory** something that is true in theory is not actually true although it is supposed to be 理论上, 从理论上来说: *In theory, a child could live on breast milk for ever, but this is hardly practical.* 理论上, 一个孩子可以永远靠母乳养活, 但这实际上行不通。**4** [C] an idea that someone thinks is true but for which they have no proof 猜想; 假设: **theory that** *Detectives are working on a theory that his murderer was someone he knew.* 侦探的调查基于一个假设, 即谋杀他的人是他认识的。**5** [U] the set of rules on which a practical subject or skill is based 原理; 学理: *musical theory* 音乐理论

ther·a·peu·tic /ˌθɛrə`pjutɪk; ˌθerə'pjuːtɪk◂/ *adj* **1** intended to help treat or cure an illness 有助于治疗的: *Nettles contain vitamins that have a therapeutic value.* 荨麻含有几种具治疗价值的维生素。**2** making you feel calm and relaxed 使人镇静的; 使人放松的: *I find swimming very therapeutic.* 我觉得游泳能松弛神经。—**therapeutically** /-kḷɪ; -kli/ *adv*

ther·a·peu·tics /ˌθɛrə`pjutɪks; ˌθerə'pjuːtɪks/ *n* [U] *technical* the part of medical science concerned with the treatment and cure of illness【术语】治疗学

ther·a·pist /`θɛrəpɪst; 'θerəpɪ̵st/ *n* [C] someone who has been trained to give a particular form of treatment for physical or mental illness 治疗专家, 理疗师: *a speech therapist* 语言官能治疗专家

ther·a·py /`θɛrəpɪ; 'θerəpi/ *n* [C,U] **1** the treatment of an illness or injury over a fairly long period of time, especially without using drugs or operations〔尤指不使用药物或不施行手术的〕疗法, 治病术 **2** the treatment or examination of someone's mental problems by talking to them for a long time about their feelings; PSYCHOANALYSIS〔通过长时间言谈来治疗或了解病人的心理问题的〕心理疗法; 精神分析: **be in therapy** (=be having therapy) 接受心理疗法 *Rob was in therapy for several years.* 罗布接受心理治疗好几年。—see also 另见 OCCUPATIONAL THERAPY, SPEECH THERAPY

Ther·a·va·da /ˌθɛrə`vɑdə; ˌθerə'vɑːdə/ *adj* relating to the form of Buddhism practised in Cambodia, Laos, Myanmar, Sri Lanka, and Thailand. It is based on the teachings of the Buddha as recorded in the Pali Canon 上座部的〔上座部是柬埔寨、老挝、缅甸、斯里兰卡和泰国一带的佛教流派, 以《巴利大藏经》中记录的佛陀教义为正典〕—compare 比较 MAHAYANA

there¹ /ðɛr; ðeə/ *pron* **1 there is/there are/there must be** used to say that something exists 有〔表示存在〕: *Is there life after death?* 死后有生命存在吗? | *There's no special way of doing it – you just have to mix the dough slowly.* 做这没有什么特别的方法, 你只需要把面团慢慢地和好。| *There must be some explanation for such outlandish behaviour.* 如此怪异的行为, 一定事出有因。| **there seems/appears to be** *There seems to be some mistake. I've never met you before in my life.* 大概弄错了吧, 我以前从来没有见过你。| **there exists/there remains etc** *formal*【正式】*There remains the possibility that mistakes have been made.* 仍然有这个可能: 有人出了差错。**2 there was/there were etc** used to say that something happened〔表示过去某事发生的〕有过: *Suddenly there was a loud crash as the clock fell to the floor.* 突然传来一声巨响, 钟掉到了地板上。| *There were several fights outside the stadium but no one was hurt.* 在体育场外面发生了好几宗打斗事件, 但无人受伤。

T

there² /ðɛr; ðeə/ *adv* **1** in or to a particular place 在那里; 往那里: *Sit there and wait until the teacher's finished.* 坐在那儿, 等到老师完了事。| *Scotland? I've always wanted to go there.* 苏格兰? 我一直想去那儿。| *Don't just stand there – do something!* 别光站在那儿, 做点事吧! | **out/in/under etc there** *I know there's a mouse under there somewhere.* 我知道在那下面的什么地方有一只老鼠。| **over there** *How are you getting on over there in Paris?* 你在巴黎那边过得怎么样? —compare 比较 HERE¹ (1) **2** if something is there, it exists 那里, 那儿: *The chance was there, but I didn't take it.* 机会来临了, 不过我没有抓住。| *All the food is there to be eaten so please enjoy it.* 所有的食品放在那儿就是让人吃的, 所以请享用吧。| *When asked why he climbed Everest, Mallory just said "Because it was there."* 当问到他为什么要攀登珠穆朗玛峰时, 马洛里只是说"因为它就在那儿。" **3** *spoken* used to say which statement, idea or reason you agree with, you want to say something about etc【口】在那一点上, 有关那一点: *"I believe we are all products of our environment." "I'm sorry but I disagree with you there."* "我认为我们全是环境的产物。""对不起, 在这一点上我并不同意你的看法。" **4** *spoken* used to get someone's attention when you are speaking to them or to make them notice someone or something【口】〔用来引起某人注意〕: *Hey, you there! Watch out!* 喂! 说你呢! 小心! | *Hi there, I haven't seen you in ages.* 嗨! 好久都没看到你了。| *There goes the phone again. It's not stopped ringing all morning.* 电话铃又响了。整个上午都在响个不停。**5 get there a)** to arrive in a particular place 到达那儿: *Most of the food had been eaten by the time I got there.* 等我到那儿时, 已经没剩下多少吃的了。**b)** *spoken* to succeed in doing something【口】成功地做某事, 得以: *It took me a lot of time and effort to qualify as a doctor but I got there in the end.* 为了取得医生资格, 我花费了大量的时间和精力, 不过最终我还是成功了。**6 be there (for sb)** *spoken* to be ready to help someone or be kind to them when they have problems【口】随时乐于帮助(某人): *That's what I loved about my father – he was always there for me.* 这便是我那么爱我的父亲的原因, 因为他总是愿意帮我一把。**7 he's/she's not all there** *spoken* a phrase used to describe someone who is not very intelligent and seems slightly crazy, used when you want to avoid saying this directly【口】他/她有点不对劲〔以比

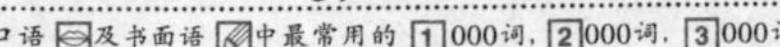

较含蓄的方式说某人不是很聪明，有一点疯癫〕 **8 there and back** the distance, cost etc there and back is the total distance or cost of the journey to a place, added to the distance or cost of the return〔旅程、旅费等的〕往返，来回: *The journey's not too bad – only four hours there and back.* 旅途上不算太糟——来回只花了四个小时。 **9 there and then** also 又作 **then and there** immediately 在彼时彼地，当场，立即: *I thought I'd have to wait but they offered me the job there and then.* 我原以为我得等着，但他们当场就把那份工作给了我。 **10 there's a good boy/there's a clever dog etc** *spoken* used to praise a child or animal【口】这才是乖孩子/这才是小乖乖等 **11 there you are/go** *spoken*【口】**a)** used to be polite when giving something to someone 行啊; 给你〔给某人某物时的礼貌用语〕: *"Can I have two bottles of beer please?" "There you are, that'll be £3.20 please."* "请来两瓶啤酒。" "给，请付3.20英镑。" **b)** used when someone is upset, complains etc, to tell them that what has happened is typical or they should have expected it 根本不足为奇; 原本就是这么回事〔对某人难受、抱怨时用的回答〕 **12 that book there/those shoes there etc** *spoken* used when showing or pointing to where something is【口】那边那本书/那边那双鞋等〔用来表示某物所在的地方〕: *Can you pass me that wine glass there?* 你能把那边那个酒杯递给我吗? | **that there book/those there shoes etc** (=a form of this expression that is sometimes used although most people think it is incorrect) 那本书/那双鞋等〔这种表达形式有时候有人使用，但大多数人认为是不正确的用法〕 *It was those there holes in the road which made me fall down.* 是路上的那些坑使我摔倒了。

there³ /ðɛr; ðeə/ *interjection* used to express success, satisfaction, sympathy etc 瞧好啦〔用来表示成功、满意、同情等〕: *There! I've done it! I've resigned.* 瞧! 我已经做了! 我已经辞职了。| *It only lasted a week but there! What can you expect for £2 an hour.* 只干了一周时间就打住了! 一小时两英镑，你能有什么指望? | **there, there!** (=used to comfort someone who is crying) 好啦! 好啦!〔用来安慰哭泣的人〕 *There, there, don't get so upset!* 好啦，好啦，别这么难过啦!

there·a·bouts /ˌðɛrəˋbauts; ˌðeərəˈbaʊts/ also 又作 **there·a·bout** /-ˋbaut; -ˈbaʊt/ *adv AmE* near a particular time, place, number etc, but not exactly【美】接近〔某一时间、地点、数目等〕; 近乎; 大约; 左右: **or thereabouts** *These houses were built in 1930 or thereabouts.* 这些房子是在1930年左右修建的。

there·af·ter /ðɛrˋæftɚ; ðeərˈɑːftə/ *adv formal* after a particular event or time; afterwards【正式】其后，此后: *10,000 men had volunteered by the end of September; thereafter, approximately 1,000 men enlisted each month.* 到9月底时已有10,000人志愿加入，此后，每个月差不多有1000人报名参加。

3 **there·by** /ðɛrˋbaɪ; ðeəˈbaɪ/ *adv formal* with the result that something else happens【正式】借此，由此: *He became a citizen in 1978, thereby gaining the right to vote.* 他在1978年成为公民，由此获得了投票权。

2 1 **there·fore** /ˋðɛrˌfɔr; ˈðeəfɔː/ *adv formal* as a result of something that has just been mentioned【正式】因此，为此，所以: *The dollar has gone down against the yen, therefore Japanese goods are more expensive for Americans.* 美元兑日元的汇率下跌了，因此日本商品对美国人来说涨价了。—see 见 THUS (USAGE)

there·in /ðɛrˋɪn; ðeərˈɪn/ *adv formal*【正式】**1** in that place, or in that piece of writing 在那里; 在那篇文章[那本书]里: *See Thompson, 1983, and the references cited therein.* 见汤普森(1983)以及该书里引用的参考资料。 **2 therein lies** used to say that something is caused by or comes from a particular situation 此即，缘此〔用以说明某事是由某种情况引起〕: *The treaty was imposed by force, and therein lay the cause of its ineffectiveness.* 该条约是通过武力强加于人的，它执行不力的原因就在于此。

there·in·af·ter /ˌðɛrɪnˋæftɚ; ˌðeərɪnˈɑːftə/ *adv law* later in the same official paper, statement etc【法律】在〔同一正式文件、声明等中的〕下文; 以下

there·of /ðɛrˋɑv; ðeərˈɒv/ *adv formal* concerning something that has just been mentioned【正式】其; 其中: *States differ in standards for products and the labelling thereof.* 各州产品的标准不同，其标签也不同。

there·on /ðɛrˋɑn; ðeərˈɒn/ *adv formal*【正式】**1** on the thing that has just been mentioned 在那件事情上 **2** THEREUPON 随即; 就此，在其上

there·to /ðɛrˋtu; ðeəˈtuː/ *adv formal* concerning an agreement or piece of writing that has just been mentioned【正式】关于〔已提及的协议、文字资料等〕: *the treaty and any conditions attaching thereto* 该条约及其所附的任何条件

there·un·der /ðɛrˋʌndɚ; ðeərˈʌndə/ *adv formal*【正式】**1** under something that has just been mentioned 在其下，在那一点下面 **2** according to a document, law, or part of an agreement that has just been mentioned 根据〔文件、法律或协议中的〕那一点

there·up·on /ˌðɛrəˋpɑn; ˌðeərəˈpɒn/ *adv formal*【正式】**1** immediately after something else has happened, and usually as a result of it; then 随即，随后; 于是: *Thereupon the whole audience stood up and began cheering.* 于是，全体观众起立，开始欢呼。 **2** concerning a subject that has just been mentioned 就此，在其上: *I have read your article, and wish to comment thereupon.* 我读过你的文章，并且想就此作一番评论。

therm /θɝm; θɜːm/ *n* [C] a measurement of heat equal to 100,000 British Thermal Units, used in Britain for measuring how much gas someone has used 撒姆〔一种测量热量的单位，相当于10万英制热单位，在英国用于测算某人所使用的煤气量〕

therm- /θɝm; θɜːm/ *prefix* another form of the prefix THERMO- 前缀 thermo- 的另一种拼法

ther·mal¹ /ˋθɝml; ˈθɜːməl/ *adj* [only before noun 仅用于名词前] **1** concerned with or caused by heat 热的; 热量的; 由热引起的: *thermal energy* 热能 | *thermal conductivity* 热导率 **2** thermal water is heated naturally under the earth〔水〕天然温热的: *thermal springs* 温泉 **3** thermal clothing is made from special material to keep you warm in very cold weather〔衣服〕保温的，保暖的: *thermal underwear* 保暖内衣

thermal² *n* [C] **1** a rising current of warm air used by birds〔鸟在飞翔过程中常借用的〕上升的热气流 **2 thermals** [plural] *informal* special warm clothing, especially underwear【非正式】保暖型衣服〔尤指保暖内衣〕

ther·mi·on·ics /ˌθɝmɪˋɑnɪks; ˌθɜːmiˈɒnɪks/ *n* [U] *technical* the part of science that deals with the flow of ELECTRONS from heated metal【术语】热离子学

thermo- /θɝmo; θɜːməʊ/ also 又作 **therm-** *technical prefix* concerning heat【术语】热的; 与温度有关的: a *thermostat* (=for controlling temperature) 恒温器 | *thermostable* (=not changing when heated) 热稳定的

ther·mo·dy·nam·ics /ˌθɝmodaɪˋnæmɪks; ˌθɜːməʊdaɪˈnæmɪks/ *n* [U] the science that deals with the relationship between heat and other forms of energy 热力学

ther·mom·e·ter /θəˋmɑmətɚ; θəˈmɒmɪtə/ *n* [C] a piece of equipment that measures the temperature of the air, of your body etc 温度计，寒暑表; 体温计: *The thermometer was reading over 100°C.* 温度计上的读数超过了摄氏100度。

ther·mo·nu·cle·ar /ˌθɝmoˋnuklɪɚ; ˌθɜːməʊˈnjuːkliə◂/ *adj* thermonuclear weapons use a NUCLEAR reaction, involving the splitting of atoms, to produce very high temperatures and a very powerful explosion 热核的: *a thermonuclear device* 热核装置

ther·mo·plas·tic /ˌθɝmoˋplæstɪk; ˌθɜːməʊˈplæstɪk◂/ *n* [C, U] *technical* a plastic that is soft and bendable when heated but hard when cold【术语】热塑性塑料〔加热时柔软可弯曲但在低温时坚硬的塑料〕

ther·mos /ˋθɝməs; ˈθɜːməs/ also 又作 **thermos flask** /ˈ· · ·/ *n* [C] *trademark* a special container like a bottle, that keeps drinks hot or cold【商标】保温瓶 —see picture at 参见 FLASK 图

ther·mo·set·ting /ˋθɝmoˌsɛtɪŋ; ˈθɜːməʊˌsetɪŋ/ *adj technical* thermosetting plastic becomes hard and unbendable after it has been heated【术语】〔指塑料〕加热后即硬化的，热固的

ther·mo·stat /ˋθɝməˌstæt; ˈθɜːməstæt/ *n* [C] an instrument used for keeping a room or a machine at a particular temperature〔使房间或机器保持一定温度的〕恒温器 —see picture at 参见 ENGINE 图

THES, The /ˌti etʃ i ˋɛs; ˌtiː eɪtʃ iː ˈes/ the abbreviation of 缩写= The TIMES HIGHER EDUCATION SUPPLEMENT

the·sau·rus /θɪˋsɔrəs; θɪˈsɔːrəs/ *n plural* **thesauruses** or **thesauri** /-raɪ; -raɪ/ [C] a book in which words are put into groups with other words that have similar meanings 同义词词典; 类义词汇编

these /ðiz; ðiːz/ the plural of THIS

The·se·us /ˋθisɪəs; ˈθiːsiəs/ in ancient Greek stories, a hero from Athens who killed the Minotaur and married the queen of the Amazons 忒修斯〔古希腊神话中的雅典英雄。他杀死怪物弥诺陶洛斯，并娶亚马孙人的女王为妻〕

the·sis /ˋθisɪs; ˈθiːsɪs/ *n plural* **theses** /-siz; -siːz/ [C] **1** a long piece of writing about a particular subject that you do as part of an advanced university degree such as an MA or a PhD 论文〔指大学的高级学位论文，如文学硕士论文或哲学博士论文〕: *Writing a thesis on dance clubs is not as strange as it seems.* 写一篇研究舞蹈俱乐部的论文似乎很奇怪，其实不然。 **2** *formal* an idea or theory that tries to explain why something happens【正式】〔设法解释某事的〕论点: *Their main thesis is that inflation*

is caused by increases in the money supply. 他们的主要论点是，通货膨胀是因为货币供应增加而引起的。

thes·pi·an /ˈθɛspɪən; ˈθespiən/ *n* [C] *formal or humorous* an actor【正式或幽默】演员 —**thespian** *adj: Aidan turns all his thespian charm on the beautiful Tara.* 艾丹竭尽他的演技才能来追求漂亮的塔拉。

they /ðe; ðeɪ/ *pron* [used as the subject of a verb 用作动词主语] **1** used to talk about two or more people or things that have been mentioned already or that the person you are talking to already knows about 他们；她们；它们：*Bob and Sue sold everything they owned and they now run a bar in Spain.* 鲍勃和休把他们拥有的一切东西都变卖了，他俩现在在西班牙开了一家酒吧。**2 they say/think etc** *especially spoken* used to say what people in general think or believe【尤口】据说/据信等：*They say his wife ran off with a younger man.* 他的妻子据说跟一个小伙子跑了。**3** *especially spoken*【尤口】**a)** the government, the police, the people who control an organization etc 他们〔泛指政府、警察或控制某一机构的人等〕：*I see they're threatening to put up taxes again.* 我明白他们又在威胁要提高税收。**b)** all the people in a group, such as all doctors, all scientists, all teachers etc 他们〔泛指医生、教师等某一团体中的所有人〕：*Apparently she has something they call 'glue ear'.* 看来她患了医生们称为"分泌性中耳炎"的耳疾。**4** used to avoid saying 'he' or 'she' after words like 'anyone', 'no one', 'everyone' etc〔用在 anyone, no one, everyone 等词后，泛指那些人〕：*If anyone has any information related to the crime will they please contact the police.* 任何人如果掌握有关这一案件的情况，请与警方联系。—see 见 HE (USAGE)

they'd /ðed; ðeɪd/ **1** the short form of 缩略式= 'they had'：*If only they'd been there.* 他们当时要在那儿就好了。**2** the short form of 缩略式= 'they would'：*It's a pity my parents didn't come, they'd have enjoyed it.* 很遗憾，我的父母没有来，要不然他们会很开心的。

they'll /ðel; ðeɪl/ the short form of 缩略式= 'they will'：*They'll be tired after the long journey.* 他们在这次长途旅行后会很疲劳的。

they're /ðer; ðə; *strong* 强读 ðɛə; ðeə/ the short form of 缩略式= 'they are'：*They're going to Crete next week.* 他们下周要去克里特。

they've /ðev; ðeɪv/ *especially BrE*【尤英】the short form of 缩略式= 'they have', used especially in verb compounds〔尤用在动词复合结构中〕：*They've had a lot of trouble with their car.* 他们的车子经常出毛病。| *They really need the money, because they've a new baby to think of now.* 他们确实需要那笔钱，因为他们现在得顾及刚出生的孩子。

thi·am·in /ˈθaɪəˌmin; ˈθaɪəmiːn/ also 又作 **thi·a·mine** /-min; -miːn/ *n* [U] a natural chemical in some foods, that you need in order to prevent particular illnesses 硫胺素，维生素 B_1

thick 厚的

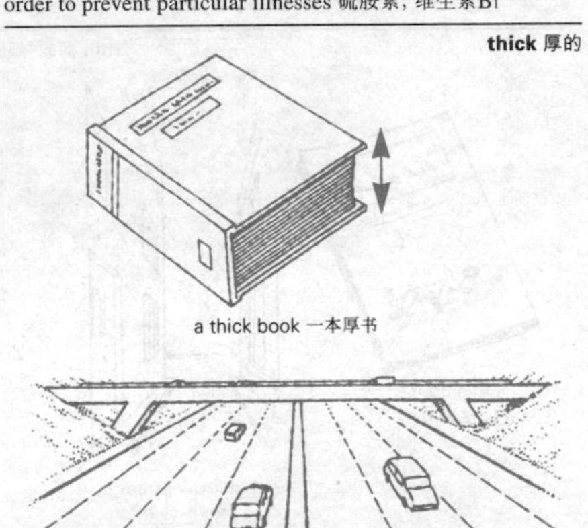

a thick book 一本厚书

a wide road 一条宽阔的路

thick¹ /θɪk; θɪk/ *adj*
1 ►THINGS 物体◄ **a)** measuring a particular amount, especially more than usual, between two surfaces or sides 厚的：*a thick oak door* 一扇厚重的橡木门 | *Wrap your baby in a thick towel or blanket.* 把你的婴儿裹在厚的毛巾或毛毯里面。| **3 feet/1 cm/two inches etc thick** *In some places, the walls are over two meters thick.* 在某些地方，墙壁有两米多厚。| [+with] (=forming a thick layer) 形成厚厚的一层 *The staircase was crumbling, and thick with dust.* 楼梯摇摇欲坠，积着厚厚的灰尘。**b)** measuring more around the middle than usual 粗的；粗大的：*Connect the battery using a thick cable.* 用一根粗电缆线把电池组连接起来。—opposite 反义词 THIN
2 ►PERSON 人◄ *BrE informal* stupid【英，非正式】愚笨的：*Don't think I can't see what's going on – I'm not that thick.* 别以为我不明白正在发生的事，我没那么蠢。| *He's a nice guy, but he's a bit thick.* 他是个不错的家伙，只是有点儿笨。| **(as) thick as two short planks** (=very stupid) 愚笨之极
3 ►LIQUID 液体◄ not solid, but moving or flowing slowly 稠的；浓的：*For a thicker gravy, add more flour.* 要想肉汁浓一点，就再加些面粉。| *thick porridge* 稠粥
4 ►SMOKE/CLOUD ETC 烟/云等◄ filling the air, and difficult to see through or breathe in 浓密的；不清明的：*At the scene of the riot, thick black smoke is still pouring from burning tires.* 在暴乱的现场，熊熊燃烧的轮胎仍然冒着浓密的黑烟。| *thick fog* 浓雾 | [+with] *The air was thick with exhaust fumes.* 空气中废气弥漫。
5 be thick on the ground to be present or available in large amounts or numbers 大量随处可见：*Cheap houses aren't as thick on the ground as they used to be.* 廉价房不再像从前那样随处可见了。—opposite 反义词 **be thin on the ground** (THIN¹ (12))
6 ►VOICE 口音◄ **a)** clearly belonging to a particular place or part of the country〔某地的口音〕浓重的；重浊的：**a thick German/Yorkshire/Brazilian etc accent** *TV viewers will get just one more chance to hear his thick Scottish accent.* 电视观众将还有一次机会听到他那浓重的苏格兰口音。**b)** not as clear or high as usual, for example because someone has been crying〔声音〕沙哑的；低沉的：*Bill's voice was thick and gruff.* 比尔说话粗声粗气。
7 ►TREES/BUSHES ETC 树木/灌木等◄ growing very close together, or having a lot of leaves, so there is not much space in between 茂密的；繁茂的：*The little animal tried to hide in the thick undergrowth.* 那头小动物试图躲藏在茂密的矮灌木丛中。| *a thick forest* 密林
8 ►HAIR/FUR ETC 头发/毛皮等◄ forming a deep, soft covering 浓密的：*She ran her fingers through her thick brown hair.* 她用手指揉搓她那浓密的褐色头发。
9 be (as) thick as thieves if two people are as thick as thieves, they are very friendly with each other and seem to share a lot of secrets 非常亲密：*I don't trust those two. Lately they've been as thick as thieves.* 我不信任那两个家伙，他俩近来一直很亲密。
10 give sb a thick ear/get a thick ear *BrE spoken* to hit someone or be hit on the head, as a punishment【英口】打某人的头部/头部被打：*Any more cheek from you and you'll get a thick ear.* 你再这样放肆，会挨耳光的。
11 have a thick skin to not care if people criticize you or do not like you 脸皮厚；抱着无所谓的态度 —see also 另见 THICK-SKINNED
12 be thick with sb to be very friendly with someone 与某人非常友好
13 (it's) a bit thick *BrE old-fashioned* used to say something is a little unfair or annoying【英，过时】不怎么公平；有点让人气愤 —**thickly** *adv*

thick² *adv* **1** if you spread, cut etc something thick, you spread or cut it in a way that produces a thick layer or piece〔某物被抹或被切得〕厚：*peanut butter spread thick* 抹得很厚的花生酱 **2 thick and fast** arriving or happening very frequently, in large amounts or numbers 大量而急速地；频繁且迅猛地：*Competition entries have been coming in thick and fast.* 参加比赛的作品纷至沓来。—see also 另见 **lay it on (a bit thick)** (LAY²)

thick³ *n* **1 be in the thick of sth** to be involved in the busiest, most active, most dangerous etc part of a situation 在〔最繁忙、最活跃、最危险的情况〕之中：*Following his recent operation, Governor Brown hopes to be back in the thick of the action as soon as possible.* 在经过最近的手术之后，布朗州长希望尽可能快地重新投入工作。**2 through thick and thin** in spite of any difficulties or problems 患难与共；同甘共苦：**stick together through thick and thin** *As kids we promised to stick together through thick and thin.* 小时候我们曾许下诺言，患难与共，团结一致。

thick·en /ˈθɪkən; ˈθɪkən/ *v* [I,T] to become thick, or make something thick 加厚；变厚；使浓；使密集：*The fog was beginning to thicken.* 雾开始变浓了。| **thicken sth** *You can thicken a sauce by adding cornstarch.* 你可以添加玉米粉使调味汁变浓。—see also 另见 **the plot thickens** (PLOT¹ (3))

T

thick·en·er /ˈθɪkənə; ˈθɪkənə/ also 又作 **thick·en·ing** /ˈθɪkənɪŋ; ˈθɪkənɪŋ/ *n* [C,U] a substance used to thicken a liquid〔使液体变稠的〕增稠剂

thick·et /ˈθɪkɪt; ˈθɪkɪt/ *n* [C] a group of bushes and small trees 灌木丛

thick-head·ed /ˌ·ˈ··◂/ *adj informal* extremely stupid【非正式】愚笨之极的: *He's so thick-headed he can't understand the simplest instructions.* 他愚笨极了，连最简单的用法说明都理解不了。

thick·ness /ˈθɪknɪs; ˈθɪknɪs/ *n* **1** [C,U] how thick something is 厚度: *The length of nails you need depends on the thickness of the plank.* 你所需要的钉子长度取决于木板的厚度。**2** [C] a layer of something〔某东西的〕层: [+of] *Wrap the cake in two thicknesses of greaseproof paper.* 用两层防油纸包蛋糕。

thick·o /ˈθɪko; ˈθɪkəʊ/ *n* [C] *informal* someone who is very stupid【非正式】笨蛋，傻瓜

thick·set, thick-set /ˌθɪkˈsɛt; ˌθɪkˈset◂/ *adj* having a wide strong body; STOCKY〔身体〕粗壮的; 粗实的: *a short thickset man* 一名矮而粗壮的男子

thick-skinned /ˌ·ˈ·◂/ *adj* not easily offended by other people's criticism or insults 厚脸皮的; 不易伤害的: *a thick-skinned insurance salesman* 一位厚脸皮的保险推销员

thief /θif; θiːf/ *n plural* **thieves** /θivz; θiːvz/ [C] someone who steals things, especially without using violence 小偷, 贼: *a car thief* 盗车贼 | *Leaving ground floor windows open will encourage thieves.* 让底楼的窗户敞开着，那是在招引小偷。—compare 比较 BURGLAR, ROBBER —see also 另见 **be (as) thick as thieves** (THICK[1] (9))

thiev·e·ry /ˈθivərɪ; ˈθiːvəri/ *n* [U] *formal* thieving【正式】偷窃行为

thiev·ing /ˈθivɪŋ; ˈθiːvɪŋ/ *n* [U] *informal especially BrE* the practice of stealing things【非正式，尤英】偷窃行为 —**thieving** *adj*: *He's a nasty thieving good-for-nothing.* 他是一个卑鄙龌龊、惯爱偷摸、一无是处的家伙。

thiev·ish /ˈθivɪʃ; ˈθiːvɪʃ/ *adj literary* like a thief【文】贼头贼脑的, 贼眉鼠眼的

T

thigh /θaɪ; θaɪ/ *n* [C] the top part of your leg, between your knee and your HIP[1] (1) 大腿, 股 —see picture at 参见 BODY 图

thim·ble /ˈθɪmbḷ; ˈθɪmbəl/ *n* [C] a small metal or plastic cap used to protect your finger when you are sewing〔缝纫时用来保护手指的〕顶针, 针箍

thim·ble·ful /ˈθɪmbḷˌful; ˈθɪmbəlfʊl/ *n* [C+of] *informal* a very small quantity of liquid【非正式】〔液体的〕少量, 些微

Thim·phu /ˈtɪmˌpu; tɪmpuː/ the capital city of Bhutan 廷布〔不丹首都〕

S2 W2 **thin**[1] /θɪn; θɪn/ *comparative* 比较级 **thinner** *superlative* 最高级 **thinnest** *adj*

1 ▶NOT THICK 不厚的◀ having a very small distance or a smaller distance than usual between two sides or two flat surfaces 薄的; 细的: *a thin nylon rope* 一条细的尼龙绳 | *She's only wearing a thin summer jacket.* 她只穿了一件很薄的夏季短上衣。| *two thin slices of bread* 两薄片面包 | *The road was covered with a thin layer of ice.* 路面上覆盖着一层薄薄的冰。| **paper thin** (=very thin) 薄如纸的; 非常薄的 *Keep your voice down, the walls are paper thin.* 小点儿声，这些墙像纸一样薄。—opposite 反义词 THICK[1] (1)

2 ▶NOT FAT 不肥胖的◀ having little fat on your body〔身体〕瘦的: *Larry was tall and thin with dark brown hair.* 拉里又高又瘦，长着一头深褐色的头发。| *I wish my legs were thinner.* 但愿我的腿再瘦一点。—opposite 反义词 FAT[1] (1)

3 ▶LIQUID 液体◀ a liquid that is thin flows very easily because it has a lot of water in it〔液体〕稀的; 淡的: *thin paint* 稀的油漆

4 ▶SMOKE/MIST 烟/雾霭◀ smoke or mist that is thin is easy to see through〔烟或雾霭〕稀薄的, 淡薄的: *The fog is quite thin in places.* 在某些地方，雾很稀薄。—opposite 反义词 THICK[1] (4)

5 ▶AIR 空气◀ air that is thin is more difficult to breathe than usual because it has less OXYGEN in it〔空气〕稀薄的: *the thinner air high in the mountains* 高山上较为稀薄的空气

6 ▶VOICE 话音◀ a thin voice is high and unpleasant to listen to 尖声细气的; 刺耳难听的: *a thin cracked singing voice* 尖细刺耳的歌声

7 ▶SOUND 声音◀ a thin sound is unpleasantly weak〔声音〕微弱而听着难受的: *the thin mewing of a bedraggled kitten* 一只浑身湿漉漉的小猫刺耳的喵喵声 —opposite 反义词 FULL[1] (15)

8 ▶HAIR/PLANTS 毛发/植物◀ hairs or plants that are thin have spaces between them〔毛发或植物〕稀疏的: *a thin straggly beard* 稀稀拉拉的胡子 | *thin vegetation* 稀疏的植被

9 ▶EXCUSE/ARGUMENT/EXPLANATION 借口/论据/解释◀ a thin excuse, argument, or explanation is not good or detailed enough to persuade you that it is true〔借口、论据或解释〕贫乏的; 空泛的; 不能令人信服的

10 ▶INFORMATION/DESCRIPTION 信息/描述◀ a piece of information or a description that is thin is not detailed enough to be useful or effective〔信息或描述〕不够充分的; 不够有效的: *The evidence for Viking settlements in America is pretty thin.* 有关北欧海盗在美洲开拓殖民地的证据很不充分。

11 the thin end of the wedge *especially BrE spoken* an expression meaning something that you think is the beginning of a harmful development【尤英，口】糟糕事情的开始: *These job cuts are just the thin end of the wedge.* 这次裁员只是开始，麻烦事还在后头。

12 be thin on the ground if a particular type of person or thing is thin on the ground, there are very few available 不是随处可见的, 少有的: *Taxis seem to be thin on the ground.* 出租车好像为数不多。

13 be having a thin time (of it) *spoken* to be in a difficult situation, especially one in which you do not have enough money【口】过窘迫日子〔尤指钱不够用〕

14 be (skating) on thin ice to be in a situation in which you are likely to upset someone or cause trouble 容易使人反感; 容易招惹麻烦: *I think the people who argue that discoveries in genetics should be commercially protected are on thin ice.* 有些人主张遗传学上的种种发现应该得到商业上的保护，我认为这些人是在招惹麻烦。

15 disappear/vanish into thin air to disappear or vanish completely in a mysterious way 神秘地消失不见

16 thin on top *informal* an expression meaning having little hair on your head used when you want to avoid saying this【非正式】头上稀疏〔一种表示某人头发稀少的含蓄说法〕—see also 另见 THINLY —**thinness** *n* [U]

USAGE NOTE 用法说明: THIN

WORD CHOICE 词语辨析: **thin, slim, slender, lean, skinny, underweight, emaciated, narrow**

Thin is a general word to describe people who have little or no fat on their bodies (opposite *fat*), but it often sounds a little negative. thin 泛指身体瘦, 瘦削 (其反义词是 fat), 但往往含一点贬义。

If you want to make clear that someone is **thin** in a pleasant way, you say they are **slim** or (less common) **slender**. 如果要说某人瘦得很好看, 用 slim 或〔不太常用的〕slender: *I wish I were as slim as you.* 但愿我有你那么苗条。| *with a slim build and long slender legs* 有着苗条的身段和修长的腿

You can also say **lean** (=thin in a strong and healthy way).

thin 薄的, 细的

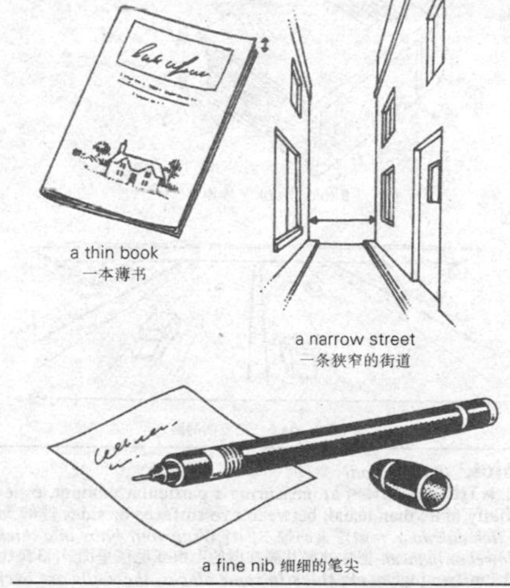

a thin book 一本薄书

a narrow street 一条狭窄的街道

a fine nib 细细的笔尖

形容瘦而健康的, 可以说 lean: *a lean, muscular body* 没多余脂肪、肌肉发达的身体

If someone is a bit too thin they are **skinny** (informal), **underweight** (the technical word), or (worst of all) **emaciated**. 形容太瘦的人可以用 skinny〔非正式用法〕、underweight〔术语〕, 最严重是 emaciated〔骨瘦如柴〕: *He looks skinny as a rake.* 他瘦得像一把耙子。| *skinny fashion models* 纤瘦的时装模特儿。| *The doctor says I'm a little underweight since my illness.* 医生说我自从生病以来体重有点过轻了。| *the emaciated bodies of the famine victims* 饥民皮包骨的身体

Thin (opposite **thick**) can also be used for things if the distance through them is not very big. thin 也指物体细、薄 (其反义词是 thick) : *a thin post/wire/dress/slice of cheese* 一根细柱子/一条细电线/一件薄连衣裙/薄薄的一片干酪

Narrow is usually used to describe something that is not very wide from side to side. narrow 一般用来形容物体狭窄: *a narrow road/bed/gap* 窄路/窄床/窄缝 However, in a few contexts, especially where something is both long and narrow, **thin** can be used in this sense too. 然而在少数情况下, thin 也可表示狭长: *a thin stripe/strip of tape/a dress with very thin straps* 细长的条纹/细长的录音磁带/吊带非常细长的连衣裙

thin² *adv* so as to be thin 薄地; 细地: *Don't cut the bread so thin.* 别把面包切得这么薄。

thin³ *v* **thinned, thinning** [T] **1** also 又作 **thin out** to make more room for plants to grow by removing the weaker ones 使〔植物〕稀疏, 给…间苗: *thinning out the carrots* 给胡萝卜间苗 **2 thin the ranks** if something thins the ranks of a group of people, there are less of them as a result of it 减少人员: *Illness had thinned our ranks.* 疾病使我们人员减少了。**3** to make a liquid weaker by adding water or another liquid 使〔液体〕稀释; 使变淡: *This paint needs thinning.* 这种油漆需要稀释。

thin out *phr v* [I] if a crowd thins out the people gradually separate and leave so there are fewer of them〔拥挤的人群〕变稀少; 散去: *By midnight the crowd outside the theatre was starting to thin out.* 到半夜时分, 剧院外面的人群开始散去了。

thine¹ /ðaɪn; ðaɪn/ *pron old use* yours【旧】你的; 你们的

thine² *determiner old use* a word meaning your, used before a word beginning with a vowel or 'h'; THY【旧】你的; 你们的〔用在元音或 h 开头的单词前〕

1 1 **thing** /θɪŋ; θɪŋ/ *n*

1 ▶IDEA/ACTION/FEELING/FACT 思想/行动/感觉/事实◀ [C] anything that you can think of as a single item, for example an idea, an action, a feeling, or a fact〔任何单一的〕事情: *The important thing is for us to tell the truth.* 重要的事情是我们要讲出真相。| *What a stupid thing to do.* 做的是一件多么蠢的事。| *A horrible thing happened yesterday.* 昨天发生了一件可怕的事。| **do the right/decent/honourable etc thing** *I kept wondering if I was doing the right thing.* 我一直在想我是不是在做正确的事情。

2 ▶OBJECT 物体◀ [C] an object 物体; 东西: *On top of the box there was a thing like a long handle.* 在盒子顶端有一个像长柄的东西。| *I need to pop into the supermarket to get a few things.* 我需要马上赶到超市去买几样东西。—see 见 MACHINE¹ (USAGE)

3 ▶SITUATION 情况◀ **things** [plural] life in general and the way it is affecting people 情况; 形势: *How are things with you?* 你们的情况怎么样? | *Things could be worse.* 情况有可能更糟。| *Things are going really well at the moment.* 此刻的形势真的很好。

4 there is no such thing used to emphasize that something does not really exist or happen 根本不存在这样的事情: *"There's no such thing as love," that's what she said.* "根本不存在爱这种东西。"她是这么说的。

5 not know a thing/not feel a thing/not see a thing etc to know, feel etc nothing 什么都不知道/什么都感觉不到/什么都看不见等: *I can't feel a thing – my mouth is completely numb.* 我什么都感觉不到——我的嘴完全麻木了。| *She doesn't do a thing to help around the house.* 她在家里什么事都不动手帮忙。

6 make a (big) thing out of sth to make something seem more important than it really is, by getting angry, excited etc〔由于气愤、激动等〕把事情闹大了: *OK, so we disagree, but let's not make a big thing out of it.* 好吧, 就算咱们意见不一致, 也别把事情闹大了。

7 the last thing sb wants/expects etc something that someone does not want, expect etc at all 根本不想要/不敢指望的事等: *The last thing I felt like doing was dancing.* 我最不想做的事便是跳舞。

8 ▶EQUIPMENT 设备◀ [C] *especially BrE* the tools, equipment, clothes etc that you need for a particular job, sport etc【尤英】〔某一工作或体育活动所需的〕用品; 设备; 物件: *I left my swimming things at home.* 我把游泳的那些用品忘在家里了。

9 ▶AT THE END 在最终◀ **last thing** at the end of a day, afternoon, evening etc〔某一天、某一下午或晚上等的〕最后事情: *He always polished his shoes last thing at night.* 他在晚上的最后一件事总是擦鞋子。

10 ▶AT THE BEGINNING 在开始◀ **first thing** at the beginning of a day, morning, afternoon etc〔某一天、某一上午或下午等的〕开头第一件事情: *I'll phone you first thing Monday morning.* 星期一上午第一件事, 我就给你打电话。

11 ▶CLOTHES/POSSESSIONS 衣服/所属物品◀ **things** [plural] *especially BrE* clothes and possessions【尤英】衣服等所属物品: *Pack your things. We're leaving.* 把你的衣物等装好。我们马上出发。

12 all things considered having considered all the facts about something 所有情况考虑进来; 综合考虑起来: *All things considered, the team didn't do too badly.* 总的来说, 该队的表现不算太差。

13 among other things used when you are giving one fact, reason, effect etc but want to suggest that there are many others 除了其他很多事情外(还…): *This led, among other things, to the resignation of the Director.* 这导致了局长的辞职, 以及其他许多事情。

14 make things easy/difficult to deliberately make it easy, difficult etc for someone to do something 故意使事情变得容易/困难: [+for] *He could make things difficult for you if he chooses.* 他可以给你制造麻烦, 如果他想那样做的话。

15 be onto a good thing *informal* to be in a situation that is very helpful, comfortable, or profitable for you【非正式】处于非常有利的形势: *When they offered to pay for her travel as well she realized she was onto a good thing.* 当他们提出还要为她支付旅费时, 她意识到自己有好事了。

16 the done thing *informal* the way of behaving or doing something that is socially acceptable【非正式】符合社会习俗的事情: *You can't serve beer with the meal. It's not the done thing.* 吃饭时是不能供应啤酒的, 这不符合习俗。

17 poor thing/lovely little thing/funny little thing etc a person or animal that is unlucky, attractive, funny etc 可怜的家伙/可爱的小家伙/可笑的小家伙等: *You poor thing.* 你这个可怜的家伙。

18 the (latest) thing *informal* the thing that is popular or fashionable at the moment【非正式】时下流行的东西: *Platform heels are the thing at the moment.* 厚底高跟鞋是时下流行的东西。

19 be a thing of the past to no longer exist or happen 明日黄花: *Good manners seem to be a thing of the past.* 良好的礼貌似乎已是明日黄花了。

20 do your own thing *informal* to do something in the way that you like instead of copying other people or following strict rules【非正式】按照自己的方式做事, 走自己的路: *Do you prefer a structured exercise class, or do you like to do your own thing?* 你是较喜欢一种有组织的练习课, 还是喜欢按自己的方式去做?

21 have a thing about *informal* to have very strong and often unreasonable feelings about someone or something【非正式】对〔某人或某事〕非常反感〔常指抱有成见〕: *He's got a real thing about people smoking.* 他对人们吸烟真的很反感。

22 breakfast things/dinner things etc *BrE* the plates, dishes etc used for a particular meal【英】早餐后的那一摊子〔碗筷碟盘等〕/晚餐后的那一摊子等: *I'll just wash up the breakfast things.* 我得把早餐后的那一摊子全部洗干净。

23 taking one thing with another *BrE* considering all the facts【英】综合考虑起来: *Taking one thing with another, I think it's a good scheme.* 综合考虑起来, 我认为这是一个不错的计划。

24 be all things to all men to behave in a way that makes everyone like you 八面玲珑, 面面俱到: *You must stop trying to be all things to all men.* 你千万不要再试图让每个人都喜欢你了。

25 the shape of things to come the way in which things will probably happen or develop in the future 未来事情的形态; 未来的发展趋势: *Perhaps shopping by computer is the shape of things to come.* 也许, 通过电脑购物是未来的发展趋势。

26 in all things in every situation 在一切事情上; 在各种情况下: *She believes in being honest in all things.* 她认为在一切事情上都应该诚实。

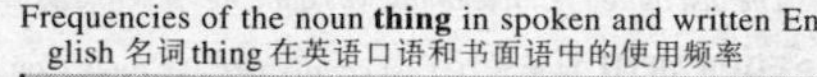
Frequencies of the noun **thing** in spoken and written English 名词thing在英语口语和书面语中的使用频率

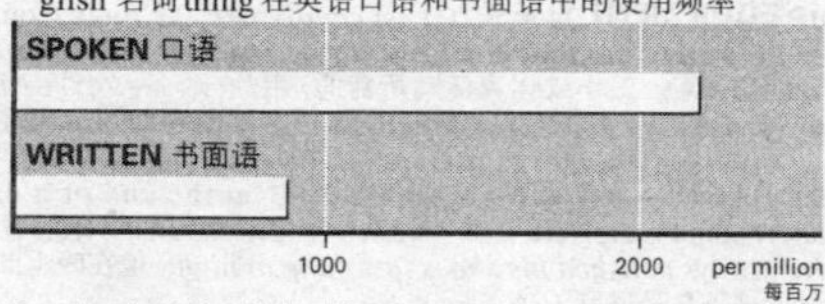

Based on the British National Corpus and the Longman Lancaster Corpus
据英国国家语料库和朗文兰开斯特语料库

This graph shows that the noun **thing** is much more common in spoken English than in written English. This is because it is used in a lot of common spoken phrases. 本图表显示, 名词thing在英语口语中的使用频率远远高于书面语, 因为口语中有很多常用短语是由thing 构成的。

thing (*n*) **SPOKEN PHRASES**
含thing的口语短语

27 the thing is used when explaining a problem or the reason for something 目前的问题是, 事情的原委是: *The thing is, I can't afford to buy a car.* 问题是, 我买不起一辆车。

28 thing to do something that someone does 所做的事: *That was a really stupid thing to do.* 那真是做了一件蠢事。

29 thing to say a remark 所说的话: *What a strange thing to say!* 多么奇怪的话!

30 light bulb thing/handle thing/switch thing etc used when you do not know the correct name for something 叫灯泡什么的东西/叫把手什么的东西/叫开关什么的东西等〔用于不知道某物正确名称之时〕: *Is that it – that handle thing under the shelf?* 是那个吗 —— 架子下面那个叫把手什么的东西?

31 for one thing used to give one reason for something 其中一个原因是: *I wouldn't work abroad. I don't like travelling for one thing.* 我不愿在国外工作。一个原因是, 我不喜欢旅行。

32 it is a good thing (that) used to say that it is lucky or good that something has happened 这是一件幸运的事[好事]: *It's a good thing we brought some food with us.* 我们随身带了一些食品, 真不错。

33 that sort/kind of thing used to mean 'other things of the same type', without giving more examples 那一类的事情: *Oh, we spent the time reading, listening to the radio, that kind of thing.* 噢, 那段时间我们所做的就是读书、听收音机之类的事情。

34 and things used to mean 'and other things', without giving more examples 等(其他)东西: *They sell jewellery and things, but it's all cheap stuff.* 他们卖珠宝首饰等东西, 不过全是些便宜货。

35 the thing with used to say what the problem with someone or something is〔某人或某事的〕问题所在: *That's the thing with him, isn't it? You can't trust him.* 那便是他的问题所在, 不是吗? 你不能信任他。

36 just one of those things used to say that something unpleasant or unlucky cannot be prevented 没办法的一件倒霉事: *It wasn't really the driver's fault, it was just one of those things.* 那实际上不是驾驶员的错, 那只是没办法的一件倒霉事。

37 it's (just) one thing after another used to say that a lot of unpleasant or unlucky things keep happening to you (简直)是接二连三的倒霉事, 祸不单行: *Train strikes, computer problems, illness – it's just one thing after another!* 铁路工人罢工, 电脑出问题, 生病 —— 真是祸不单行!

38 just the thing/the very thing exactly the thing that you want or that is necessary 正是想要的东西; 正是需要的东西: *"Would this help?" "That's just the thing I was looking for."* "这个有用吗?" "这正是我在找的东西。"

39 what with one thing and another used to explain that you have not done something because you have been too busy 忙了这个又要忙那个; 忙这忙那地: *Well, what with one thing and another, we never got round to getting it fixed.* 唉, 忙了这个又要忙那个, 我们根本没有时间来修理这个东西。

40 the way things are/stand used to say that because of the present situation you must do or cannot do something 目前的情况是: *The way things are we can't possibly afford a vacation this year.* 从目前的情况看来, 我们今年不可能有钱去度假。

41 it's no bad thing used to say that even though an event seems to be unlucky it does actually help 这算不上什么坏事: *We had to sell the car, although it was no bad thing really because it was too expensive to run.* 我们不得不把那辆车卖掉, 因为开车太花钱了, 所以这实际算不上是什么坏事。

42 of all things used to show that you are surprised or shocked by something that someone has done or said 偏偏, 真没想到: *And for breakfast he had curry, of all things!* 真没想到, 他早餐竟然吃咖喱!

43 it's one thing to..., it's another thing to..., used to say that doing one thing is very different from doing another thing 做…是一回事, 做…则是另一回事: *It's one thing to play a computer game; it's quite another thing to write your own programs.* 玩电脑游戏是一回事, 自己编写程序则完全是另一回事。

44 sb did/said etc no such thing used to say angrily that someone did not do or say something 某人根本没做这样的事/没说这样的话等: *"Jane says that you took the money out of the cash box." "I did no such thing!"* "简说你从钱柜里拿了钱。" "我绝没有做过这种事!"

45 (do) the...thing *AmE* used to talk about an activity and everything that is involved with it【美】(做) …方面的事: *Jody tried the college thing but finally dropped out.* 乔迪尝试了一下大学生活, 但最终还是辍学了。

thing·a·ma·jig /ˈθɪŋəməˌdʒɪɡ; ˈθɪŋəmɪdʒɪɡ/ also 又作 **thing·a·ma·bob** /ˈθɪŋəməˌbɑb; ˈθɪŋəmɪbɒb/ **thing·y** /ˈθɪŋɪ; ˈθɪŋi/ *n* [C] *spoken* used when you cannot remember or do not know the name of the person or thing you want to mention【口】某人; 某物〔用来指记不清或不知道你要提及的某人的名字或某东西的名称〕: *Have you got the thingamajig for opening the wine?* 你有开酒瓶的那个玩意儿吗?

Things Fall A·part /ˌ· · ˈ·/ (1958) a NOVEL by the Nigerian writer Chinua Achebe about the problems experienced by traditional African societies as their way of life changes in the 20th century. It was one of the first African novels to become well known in Europe and the US. 《瓦解》〔(1958), 尼日利亚作家希诺阿·阿契贝创作的一部小说。该小说反映传统的非洲社会随着20世纪生活方式的转变而遇到的诸多问题, 是最早为欧美读者熟知的非洲人创作的小说之一〕

think[1] /θɪŋk; θɪŋk/ *past tense and past participle* **thought** /θɔt; θɔːt/ *v*

1 ►OPINION/BELIEF 观点/信念◄ [T] to have an opinion or belief about something 认为; 以为: **think (that)** *I think that she should have paid the money back.* 我认为她应该偿还那笔钱。| *Harry thought it was a lousy idea.* 哈里认为那是一个很糟的主意。| *I didn't think anyone would believe me.* 我以为没有人会相信我。| *I remember thinking their behaviour was strange.* 我记得曾经认为他们的行为很奇怪。| *Well, Tom, what do you think?* 呃, 汤姆, 你怎么认为? | **think of sb/sth as sth** (=think that someone or something is something) 认为某人/某物是… *We now think of the car as being essential rather than a luxury.* 我们现在认为汽车是很重要的, 而不是什么奢侈品。| **think sb/sth (to be) sth** *We all thought her very intelligent.* 我们当时都认为她很聪明。| **think it right/important etc** *formal*【正式】*Do you think it right for the government to cut funding in this way?* 你认为政府以这种方式削减经费是正确的吗? | **be thought to be (doing sth)** *formal*【正式】*They are thought to be receiving arms from the Republic.* 有人认为他们正从该共和国那儿得到武器。

2 ►USE YOUR MIND 动脑◄ [I] to use your mind to solve something, decide something etc 思考; 思虑; 考虑: *We must think very carefully before we decide what to do.* 在决定做什么之前, 我们必须十分慎重地考虑。| *Wait a minute, I'm thinking.* 等一下, 我正在思考。| **[+about/of]** *She lay awake thinking about the money.* 她醒着躺在那儿, 心里想着那笔钱。| *I tried not to think of Richard or what he was doing.* 我尽量不去想理查德或者他在干什么。| **think deeply** (=think carefully, for a long time) 沉思, 深思 *They clearly haven't thought very deeply about the possible consequences.* 很明显, 他们对可能的后果并未作过深入的思考。

3 ►HAVE AN IDEA 有一个想法◄ [T] to have an idea or thought in your mind, especially one that appears suddenly 想, 想到: *And then I thought: "Why the hell shouldn't I?"* 然后我想: "我究竟为什么不应该呢?" | *"I certainly am in luck!" Katy thought.* "我当然是幸运的喽!" 凯蒂想道。

4 think of/about doing sth to consider the possibility of doing something 考虑做某事的可能性: *I had never thought of be-*

coming an actor. 我从未考虑过要当一名演员。| We did think about buying a flat in London. 我们确实考虑过要在伦敦买一套房子。

5 think better of it to not do something that you had planned to do, because you realize that it is not a good idea 认为还是不做的好: *He started to say something, then thought better of it.* 他开口想说点什么, 继而觉得还是不说为好。

6 think nothing of (doing sth) to do something easily or without complaining, even though other people would find it difficult 认为(做某事)没有什么困难: *The people here think nothing of walking ten miles to collect firewood.* 这里的人认为走10英里路去打柴算不上什么困难事。

7 think for yourself to have ideas and thoughts of your own rather than believing what other people say 独立思考: *Parents have to teach their children to think for themselves.* 父母们必须教育孩子自己动脑筋。

8 think sth to yourself to have a thought in your mind, but not tell it to anyone 自己心里想着某事: *I thought to myself, when I'm 60, Patrick will still only be in high school.* 我暗自思忖, 当我60岁时, 帕特里克还只在中学读书。

9 think twice (before doing sth) to think very carefully before deciding to do something, because you know about the dangers or problems (在做某事之前)再三考虑, 慎重思考: *I'll think twice before taking out such a large loan again.* 在再一次借出这么一大笔贷款之前, 我会慎重考虑的。

10 think again to think of a new idea or plan because you realize that you cannot use the first one that you thought of 重新考虑: *If we can't have the car we'll have to think again about how to get there.* 如果没有车, 我们得重新考虑如何去那儿。

11 think aloud/think out loud to say what you are thinking, without talking to anyone in particular 自言自语: *Oh, sorry; I guess I was thinking out loud.* 噢, 对不起, 我想我是在自言自语。

12 think a lot of sb/think highly of sb to admire or respect someone 佩服某人/看重某人: *I can assure you, the management thinks very highly of you.* 我可以肯定地告诉你, 管理层非常看重你。

13 think the world of sb to like or love someone very much 非常喜爱某人: *He thinks the world of those children.* 他非常喜爱那些孩子。

14 think badly of sb to disapprove of someone or what they have done 不赞同某人; 看不惯某人的所为: *Please don't think badly of me. I had no choice.* 请不要看不起我。我当时没有选择。

15 not think much of to think that someone or something is bad, useless etc 认为〔某人或某事〕不好[无用]: *I don't think much of that new restaurant.* 我对那家新饭馆评价不高。

16 think the best/worst of sb to consider someone's actions in a way that makes them seem as good as possible or as bad as possible 对某人的行为往最好处想/最坏处想: *Ellie's the type of person that always thinks the best of people.* 埃利属于那种总是认为人心尽善的人。

17 think big *informal* to plan to do things that are difficult, but will be very impressive, make a lot of profit etc【非正式】打算大干一番, 立大志: *We had money, materials, and the opportunity to think big. It was up to us to do something with it.* 我们有资金, 有原料, 也有大干一番的机会。得失成败全取决于我们自己。

18 think on your feet to answer questions or think of ideas quickly, without preparing in advance 思路敏捷: *A good teacher can think on her feet.* 一名优秀的教师头脑灵活, 能随机应变。

19 think to do sth *literary* to try to do something【文】设法做某事: *They had thought to deceive me.* 他们想骗我。

Frequencies of the verb **think** in spoken and written English 动词think在英语口语和书面语中的使用频率

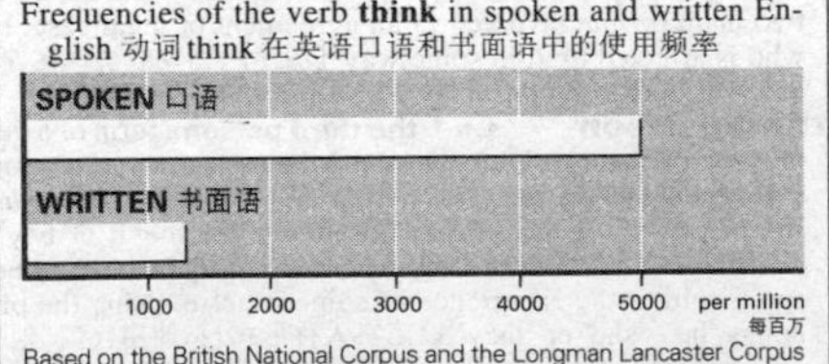

Based on the British National Corpus and the Longman Lancaster Corpus
据英国国家语料库和朗文兰开斯特语料库

This graph shows that the verb **think** is much more common in spoken English than in written English. This is because it is used in a lot of common spoken phrases. 本图表显示, 动词think在英语口语中的使用频率远远高于书面语, 因为口语中很多常用短语是由think构成的。

think (*v*) SPOKEN PHRASES
含 think 的口语短语

20 I think used when you are saying that you believe something is true, although you are not sure 我认为; 我想: *Mary is in the garden, I think.* 我想玛丽在花园里。| *I don't think Ray will mind.* 我认为雷不会介意的。

21 I think I'll used when saying what you will probably do 我想我将会: *I think I'll go into town today.* 我想我今天要进城去。

22 I think so/I don't think so/I think not used when answering a question, to say that you believe something is true or not true 我认为如此/我不认为如此/我认为不是: *"Is Jenny still living in Manchester?" "I think so."* "珍妮还住在曼彻斯特吗?" "我想是吧。"

23 I thought (that) a) used when you are politely suggesting something to do 我想〔用于礼貌地建议做某事〕: *I thought we could meet for lunch.* 我想我们可以一起吃顿午饭。| *I thought we'd go swimming tomorrow.* 我想我们明天可以去游泳。**b)** used to say what you thought or believed was true, although you were not sure 我原以为: *I thought he was honest, but I was wrong.* 我原以为他诚实, 但我错了。

24 I should/would think used when you are saying that you believe something is probably true 依我说; 依我认为: *We'll need about six yards of material, I should think.* 依我认为, 我们需要大约6码的材料。

25 I can't think who/where/what used to say that you cannot remember or understand something 我想不起[想不明白]是谁/是在哪里/是什么: *I can't think where I left my keys.* 我想不起我把钥匙忘在哪里了。| *I can't think why she ever married him.* 我想不明白她为什么居然嫁给了他。

26 do you think (that)...? a) used when you are asking someone politely to do something for you 〔用于礼貌地请某人为你做某事〕: *Do you think you could help me move these boxes?* 您能不能帮我搬一下这些箱子? **b)** used to ask someone's opinion 〔用来征求某人的意见〕: *Do you think I need to bring a jacket?* 你认为我有必要带一件夹克吗?

27 who/what etc do you think? a) used to ask someone's opinion 你认为谁/什么等?〔用来征求某人的意见〕: *Who do you think will win?* 你认为谁会赢? **b)** used when asking someone angrily about something 〔用于气愤地责问某人〕: *What do you think you're doing with that computer?* 你以为你在用那台电脑干些什么? | *Where do you think you're going?* 你以为你要去哪里呢?

28 (now I) come to think of it used when you are adding something more to what you have said, because you have just remembered it, or realized it (现在我)回想起来: *My father looked worried and, now I come to think of it, so did my brother.* 我父亲当时很焦虑, 现在我回想起来, 我哥哥当时也是那样。

29 who would have thought? used to say that something is very surprising 谁会想到呢?〔表示非常吃惊〕: *Who would have thought she'd end up dancing for a living?* 谁会想得到呢, 她最终竟靠跳舞谋生?

30 I thought as much used to say that you are not surprised by what you have just found out 我已经意料到, 我已看出个大概〔表示并不吃惊〕: *"Andy failed his driving test." "I thought as much when I saw his face."* "安迪没有通过驾驶考试。" "我看到他的表情时便已猜出个大概。"

31 just think! used to ask someone to imagine or consider something 试着想一想!: *Just think – we could be millionaires!* 试着想一想 —— 我们竟有可能成为百万富翁! | [+of] *It would be lovely, but just think of the expense!* 是很不错, 但想一想那费用!

32 you would have thought (that)/you would think (that) used to say that you expect something to be true, although it is not 你本来会以为…/你会以为…〔表示预期的事没发生〕: *You would have thought the school would do more to help a child like Craig.* 你本来会以为学校会做更多的事去帮助像克雷格这样的孩子。

33 anyone would think (that) used to say that someone behaves as if a particular thing were true, although it is not 谁都会以为…: *Anyone would think he owns the place, the way he talks!* 谁都会以为那个地方是他的, 瞧他说话的那副样子!

34 I wasn't thinking/I didn't think used as a way of saying you are sorry because you have upset someone 我没想清楚〔用于道歉〕: *Sorry, I shouldn't have said that. I wasn't*

thinking. 对不起，我不该说那样的话。那些话是脱口而出的。
35 to think (that)...! used to show that you are very surprised about something 真没想到…!: *To think that we lived next door to him and never realised what he was up to!* 真没想到我们住在他的隔壁，竟从不知道他在干什么勾当！
36 think nothing of it used when someone has thanked you for doing something, to say politely that you did not mind doing it 算不上什么事；不用谢
37 if you think..., you've got another think coming! used to tell someone that if they think someone is going to do something, they are wrong 如果你认为…，那你就大错特错了！: *If you think I'm going to wait around for you, you've got another think coming!* 如果你认为我会百般无聊地等你，那你就大错特错了！
38 when you think about it used to say that you realize something when you consider a fact or subject 你〔思考某一事实或主题时〕会意识到…；其实: *When you think about it, most of the things you worry about in life aren't that important.* 其实你生活中担心的大多数事情都不那么重要。
39 that's what you/they etc think! used to say that you strongly disagree with someone 那是你的/他们等的看法！〔表示你强烈反对某人的看法〕

think back *phr v* [I] to think about things that happened in the past 回想起；追忆: [+on/to] *When I think back to those nights, it is the crunch of snow and the warm lights from the windows that I remember.* 当我回想起那些夜晚时，我记得的是踩在雪地上的咯吱声和从窗户里映照出来的温暖灯光。

think of sb/sth *phr v* [T] **1** to produce a new idea, name, suggestion etc by thinking 想出〔新主意、名字、建议等〕: *They're still trying to think of a name for the baby.* 他们还在想方设法给那个婴儿取个名字。| *Can you think of anyone else who could do it?* 你能不能想出还有谁可以做这事？ **2** to remember a name or fact 想起，回忆起: *No, I can't think of the name of the hotel either.* 不，我也想不起那家酒店叫什么。 **3** to behave in a way that shows that you want to treat other people well 对〔某人〕关怀: *It was very good of you to think of me.* 感谢你的关怀。| *He never thinks of others, only of himself.* 他从来不关心别人，只关心他自己。 **4 what do you think of...?** used to ask what someone's opinion is about something 你怎么认为…?〔用来问询某人对某事的看法〕: *So what do you think of this new manager then?* 那么，你对这位新来的经理持什么看法？

think sth ↔ **out** *phr v* [T] to think about something carefully, considering all the possible problems, results etc 把〔某事〕考虑好: *He had spoken on the spur of the moment, without thinking things out first.* 他当场说了那番话，根本没有把事情首先考虑好。

think sth ↔ **over** *phr v* [T] to think about something carefully 认真考虑〔某事〕: *Why don't you think it over for a while, and give me a call in a couple of days.* 你何不认真地考虑一下，过一两天再给我打电话来。

think sth ↔ **through** *phr v* [T] to think carefully about the possible results of doing something 认真地考虑〔做某事可能产生的结果〕: *Having thought it through, I listed the pros and cons and made my decision.* 我把此事通盘想了一番，把赞同的和反对的意见都列了出来，然后作出了自己的决定。

think sth ↔ **up** *phr v* [T] to produce a new idea, name etc by thinking hard about something 想出，构思出〔主意、名字等〕: *We laugh at the absurdity of these laws and wonder how anyone ever thought them up.* 我们对这些法律的荒谬感到可笑，搞不懂怎么会有人想出这些东西来。

think² *n* **have a think** to think about a difficulty or question 想一想，想一下: *I don't know whether I'll go to the party, I'll have a think and let you know.* 我不知道我是否去参加那个聚会，我得想一想，然后再告诉你。

think·er /ˈθɪŋkɚ; ˈθɪŋkə/ *n* [C] someone who is famous for their important work in a subject such as science or PHILOSOPHY 思想家: *Einstein was one of the world's great thinkers.* 爱因斯坦是世界上伟大的思想家之一。

Think·er, The a SCULPTURE by Auguste Rodin of a man sitting and thinking, with his elbow on his knee and his chin on his hand《思想者》〔奥古斯特·罗丹创作的一尊雕塑。该雕塑为一男子的坐像，其肘部置于膝盖，手托下巴，作思索状〕

think·ing¹ /ˈθɪŋkɪŋ; ˈθɪŋkɪŋ/ *n* [U] your opinion about something or your attitude towards it 想法；看法；态度: *The Administration's thinking changed as the war progressed.* 随着战争的进展，本届政府的态度改变了。| **to my way of thinking** (=in my opinion) 依我所想，依我看来 *Well, to my way of thinking, they should have done that years ago.* 唉，依我看来，他们在几年前就应该做那件事了。| **put on your thinking cap** *informal* (=think seriously about a problem, in order to try and solve it)【非正式】开动你的脑筋；认真地想一想

thinking² *adj* [only before noun 仅用于名词前] a thinking person is intelligent and tries to think carefully about important subjects 有思想的；认真思考的: *No thinking person would seriously disagree with this point of view.* 没有哪一个有思想的人会强烈反对这一观点。

think-tank /ˈ· ·/ *n* [C also+plural verb] a committee of people with experience in a particular subject that an organization or government establishes to produce ideas and give advice 智囊团〔为某个机构或政府就某方面问题出谋划策的委员会〕: *a right-wing political think-tank* 一个右翼的政治智囊团

thinly /ˈθɪnlɪ; ˈθɪnli/ *adv* **1** in a way that has a very small distance between two sides or two flat surfaces 很薄地: *thinly sliced bread* 切得很薄的面包片 **2** scattered or spread over a large area, with a lot of space in between 稀疏地: *Sow the radish seeds thinly.* 把萝卜籽撒播得稀一些。| **thinly populated/settled etc** *The mountain regions are more thinly populated than the lowlands.* 高山地区比低地地区人烟稀少。 **3 thinly disguised/concealed etc** if something or someone is thinly disguised etc, you can easily see what it really is 伪装/隐瞒等不够巧妙的；很容易识破的: *moralism thinly disguised as fiction* 明显地以小说形式出现的说教

thin·ner /ˈθɪnɚ; ˈθɪnə/ *n* [U] a liquid such as TURPENTINE that you add to paint to make it less thick〔松节油等添加到油漆中的〕稀释液

thin-skinned /ˌ· ˈ·◂/ *adj* too easily offended or upset by criticism 脸皮薄的；一批评就脸红的

third¹ /θɝd; θɜːd/ *number* 3rd 第三: **third time lucky** *spoken* used when you have failed to do something twice and hope to be successful the third time【口】第三次会交好运〔指前两次均已失败而希望第三次取得成功〕

third² *n* [C] **1** one of three equal parts of something 三分之一 **2** the lowest type of degree that is given by a British university〔英国大学里颁发的〕第三等学位，三级荣誉学位

third class /ˌ· ˈ·◂/ *n* [U] **1** a cheap class of mail in the US, usually used for sending advertisements 三等邮件〔美国的一种廉价邮件，通常用来寄送广告〕 **2** a THIRD² (2) 第三等学位，三级荣誉学位 **3** *old use* the cheapest and least comfortable part of a train or ship【旧】〔火车最廉价的〕三等车厢；〔轮船的〕三等舱 —**third-class** *adj, adv*: *We travelled third-class to Marseilles.* 我们坐三等舱去马赛。

third de·gree /ˌ· ·ˈ·◂/ *n* **give sb the third degree** *informal* to ask someone a lot of questions in order to get information from them【非正式】〔为获得信息而〕严厉盘问某人: *I got home after midnight and Dad gave me the third degree.* 我半夜以后才回家，爸爸严厉盘问我一番。

third-degree burn /ˌ· · · ˈ·/ *n* [C] the most serious kind of burn, that goes right through your skin 三度烧伤〔最为严重的一种烧伤，伤及皮下深层〕

Third Man, The /ˌ· ˈ·/ (1949) a film directed by Carol Reed and written by Graham Greene, which is set in Vienna at the end of World War II. It tells the story of a writer who is trying to find his friend Harry Lime (played by Orson Welles), who has become a criminal. The music from the film, which is played on a ZITHER, is very well-known.《第三者》〔(1949)，卡罗尔·里德导演的一部电影，剧本为格雷厄姆·格林所写。故事发生在二战即将结束时的维也纳，有一位作家设法要找到自己的朋友哈里·莱姆(由奥森·威尔斯饰演)，而此时的哈里已成了一名罪犯。影片中有一段齐特琴演奏的音乐非常有名〕

third par·ty /ˌ· ˈ··◂/ *n* [C] *law* someone who is not one of the two main people involved in an agreement or legal case, but who is affected by it in some way【法律】〔协议或法律案件中的〕第三方，第三者: *third party insurance* 第三方责任险

third per·son /ˌ· ˈ··◂/ *n* **1 the third person** a form of a verb or PRONOUN that is used for showing the person, thing or group that is being mentioned〔动词或代词的〕第三人称: *'He', 'she', 'it' and 'they' are third person pronouns.* he, she, it 和 they 都是第三人称代词。 **2 in the third person** a story in the third person is told as the experience of someone else, using the pronouns 'he', 'she' or 'they' 以第三人称形式〔指使用代词"他"、"她"或"他们"来讲述故事〕 —see also 另见 FIRST PERSON, SECOND PERSON

third-rate /ˌ· ˈ·◂/ *adj* of very bad quality 三流的；劣质的: *a third-rate hotel* 一家三流酒店

Third Read·ing /ˌθɝd ˈridɪŋ; ˌθɜːd ˈriːdɪŋ/ *n* the third and final occasion when a BILL (=a suggested new law) is read out loud in the British Parliament or the US Congress 第三读〔指在

英国议会或美国国会中将一项提案第三次也是最后一次大声宣读出来〕

Third Reich, the /ˌθɜ·d ˈraɪk; ˌθɜːd ˈraɪk/ the period of Nazi government in Germany, led by Adolf HITLER, from 1933 to 45 第三帝国〔指 1933 至 1945 年阿道夫·希特勒领导下的德国纳粹政府统治时期〕

Third Way /ˌ· ˈ·/ *n* the idea of a system of government that does not have the state control and high taxes of SOCIALISM, but unlike CAPITALISM tries to give people equal opportunities and a good quality of life 第三条道路〔指有关国家政府制度的一种思潮。基于此理念建立的政府没有社会主义的国家控制和高额税赋，也有别于资本主义，它试图给人民带来平等的机会和高品质的生活〕

Third World, the /ˌ· ˈ·◂/ *n* the poorer countries of the world that are not industrially developed 第三世界〔指世界上工业不发达的贫穷国家〕—**Third World** *adj*: *Third World problems* 第三世界问题

thirst[1] /θɜ·st; θɜːst/ *n* **1** [singular] the feeling of wanting or needing a drink 渴，口渴: **quench your thirst** (=get rid of your thirst by drinking something) 止渴；解渴 *a thirst-quenching drink* 一种止渴的饮料 | **work up a thirst** (=do work or exercise that makes you thirsty) 干得/锻炼得口渴 *I really worked up a thirst during that game.* 我在那场比赛中真的累得十分口渴。| **raging thirst** (=an extremely strong thirst) 火烧火燎的口渴，口干舌燥 **2** [U] the state of not having enough to drink 饮水不足，缺水: *Half of the animals had died of thirst.* 有一半的动物死于饮水不足。**3 a thirst for knowledge/excitement/power etc** *literary* a strong desire for knowledge etc【文】对知识/刺激/权力等的渴望: *These new immigrants had a thirst for education.* 这些新来的移民渴望获得教育。

thirst[2] *v* [I] *old use* to be thirsty【旧】感到口渴；渴望，渴求
thirst for/after sth *phr v* [T] *literary* to want something very much【文】渴望，渴求〔某物〕: *young men thirsting for adventure* 渴望冒险的年轻人

thirst·y /ˈθɜ·stɪ; ˈθɜːsti/ *adj* **1** needing to drink or feeling that you want a drink 渴的，口渴的: *Can I have a glass of water, I'm really thirsty.* 我能喝一杯水吗？我真的很口渴。| **thirsty work** (=work that makes you want a drink) 使人口渴的工作 *All this digging is thirsty work.* 这种不断的挖掘是使人口渴的活儿。**2 thirsty for knowledge/power** *literary* having a strong desire for knowledge etc【文】渴望知识/权力 **3** *literary* fields or plants that are thirsty need water【文】〔田地或植物〕干旱的；缺水的 —**thirstily** *adv*

thir·teen /θɜ·ˈtin; ˌθɜːˈtiːn◂/ *number* 13 十三

thir·teenth[1] /θɜ·ˈtinθ; ˌθɜːˈtiːnθ/ *n* 13th 第十三

thirteenth[2] *n* [C] one of thirteen equal parts of something 十三分之一

thir·ty /ˈθɜ·tɪ; ˈθɜːti/ *number* **1** 30 三十 **2 the thirties** the years from 1930 to 1939 三十年代〔1930 年至 1939 年〕

CULTURAL NOTE 文化注释

When people in the US and UK think of the thirties, they think of the Great Depression, when the economies of Europe, the US, and other countries failed. Millions of people lost their jobs and many became extremely poor. 在美国和英国，人们提起 20 世纪 30 年代就会想到大萧条，这一时期欧洲和美国等国家的经济崩溃了，成千上万的人失去工作，很多人变得极度贫困。

Dust storms and a lack of rain caused severe problems for farmers in an area of the south central US. Much of the TOPSOIL blew away in the wind, nothing would grow, and the area became known as the Dustbowl. Many people left this area hoping to find jobs somewhere else. When they think of the thirties, Americans often think of the long lines that people waited in to get bread or soup, because they had nothing else to eat. 美国中南部一部分地区的沙尘暴和缺乏降雨给农民带来严重的问题。表层土壤被风吹走，庄稼不能成活，这个地区变成了黄尘地带。很多人离开此地希望能在其他地方找到工作。当美国人想到 30 年代的时候，他们就会想起领取面包或汤的人排起的长长队伍，因为这些人已经没有可以果腹的其他食物了。

3 in your thirties aged between 30 and 39 在三十多岁年纪: **in your early/late thirties** (=below or above 35) 在 30 到 35 岁之间/在 35 到 39 岁之间 **4 in the thirties** if the temperature is in the thirties, it is between 30° and 39° 在三十多度〔指温度在 30° 至 39° 之间〕: **in the high/low thirties** *a hot day, with temperatures in the low thirties* 气温 30 度出头的热天 —**thirtieth** *adj*

Thirty-nine Ar·ti·cles, the /ˌ· · ˈ· · ·/ a set of 39 statements which form the main beliefs of the Church of England. They were written in 1571 and people who become priests in the church must first formally accept these beliefs.《三十九条信纲》〔英国国教会的信仰纲要，拟定于 1571 年。任教会牧师者必须首先接受这些信条〕

thir·ty·some·thing /ˈθɜ·tɪˌsʌmθɪŋ; ˈθɜːtiˌsʌmθɪŋ/ *n* [C] *informal* someone in their thirties who is well educated with a good job, plenty of money etc【非正式】三十多岁的成功人士: *a glossy new magazine aimed at thirtysomethings* 一份针对三十多岁成功人士、用有光纸印刷的新杂志 —**thirtysomething** *adj*: *a thirtysomething lawyer* 一名三十多岁事业有成的律师

Thirty Years' War, the /ˌ· · · ˈ·/ a European war fought mainly in Germany between 1618 and 1648. It led to the Hapsburg and the Holy Roman Empire losing power in Europe. 三十年战争〔指 1618 至 1648 年的欧洲战争，主战区在德国。该战争使哈布斯堡王朝和神圣罗马帝国在欧洲的势力逐步削弱〕

this[1] /ðɪs; ðɪs/ *determiner plural* **these** /ðiz; ðiːz/ **1** used to talk about a person, thing, idea etc that has already been mentioned or that the person you are talking to already knows about 这，这个〔指已经提到的或已知的人、物、主意等〕: *Wait till you hear this joke.* 等着，你来听听这个笑话。| *What is the purpose of your visit to this country?* 你访问这个国家的目的是什么？| *There will be another meeting later this week.* 本周晚些时候还将有一个会议。| *How can we help these poor children?* 我们怎样才能帮助这些穷孩子？| *If we carry on at this rate we'll be bankrupt by the end of the week.* 如果我们以这种进度继续下去的话，我们到不了周末就会破产。**2** used to talk about the person or thing nearest to you or the time that is soonest etc 这，这个〔指人或事物最靠近的一个或时间最近的一个〕: *I'm going to visit my Mum this Wednesday.* 这个周三我要去看我妈。| *I'll look in these rooms if you look in all the rest.* 我来看看这些房间，你去看其余的所有房间。| *I'm surprised you like that photo – I prefer this one.* 真想不到你喜欢那张照片 — 我更喜欢这张。**3** *spoken* used in stories, jokes etc when you mean a person or thing, especially when you do not know their name【口】〔用于故事或笑话等中〕某一个〔人或事物〕: *When am I going to meet this boyfriend of yours?* 我什么时候能看到你的这一位男朋友？| *I met this really weird guy tonight.* 我今晚遇到一个真的很怪异的家伙。**4 this minute/second** immediately 立刻，马上: *I want to see you in my office this minute!* 我要你立即到办公室里来见我！

this[2] *pron plural* **these** **1** used to talk about a person, thing, idea etc that has already been mentioned or that the person you are talking to knows about already 这，这个〔指已提到的或已知的人、物、主意等〕: *Where did you find these?* 你在哪里找到这些的？| *This is terrible. What on earth are we going to do?* 真糟糕。我们究竟该怎么办呢？| *If you think that's funny wait till you hear this.* 如果你认为那很可笑，那就等着听听这件事吧。**2** used to talk about the person or thing nearest to you, the time that is soonest etc 这，这个〔指人或事物最靠近的一个或时间最近的一个〕: *These are your coats, aren't they?* 这些是你的外衣，是吗？| *That might be a much prettier dress but I feel more comfortable in this.* 那一件可能要漂亮得多，但我觉得穿着这一件要舒服些。**3 a)** *informal* used to introduce someone to someone else【非正式】这一位〔用于介绍某人〕: *Sam, this is my sister, Liz.* 萨姆，这位是我的妹妹莉兹。**b)** used when you have answered the telephone and you want to give your name〔用于接电话说出自己的名字时〕: *"Can I speak to Joan please?" "This is Joan speaking."* "请问琼在吗？""我就是琼。" **4** a particular time 某一时刻: *I thought he would have been back before this.* 我以为他会在这之前回来的。| *Well young lady, what time do you call this?* 唉，年轻的女士，你说这是什么时候了？**5 this, that and the other** also 又作 **this and that** *especially spoken* various different things, subjects etc【尤口】形形色色的东西；各种不同的话题: *"What have you two been gossiping about all evening?" "Oh this, that and the other."* "你们俩整个晚上一直在唠叨些什么？""哦，各种各样的杂事。" **6 what's (all) this?** *spoken* used to ask what is happening, what someone's problem is etc【口】出什么事了？怎么了？: *What's this? Crying again?* 怎么了？又哭了？

this[3] *adv* [+adj/adv] **this big/many etc** *spoken* used to say how big or how many, especially because you are showing the size, number etc with your hand【口】这么大/多等〔表示有多大或有多少的程度，尤其在用手势表示大小、数目等时〕: **this big/tall etc** *The table's about this high and this wide.* 那桌子大约有这么高，这么宽。| **this much/many** *Do you know he cut this much off my fringe without even asking me!* 你可知道，他连问都不问我一下就把我的刘海剪去这么多！

This·be /ˈθɪzbɪ; ˈθɪzbi/ the female lover of Pyramus 西斯贝〔皮拉姆斯的情人〕—see 见 PYRAMUS AND THISBE

This Is Your Life /ˌ· · · ˈ·/ a British and US television programme in which a famous person's life story is told. It begins when the presenter surprises someone and says "This Is Your Life", before taking him or her to a television STUDIO. The famous person's friends and relations have been secretly brought to the studio to meet them there and say something about them 《这就是你的人生》〔英美一电视节目。每期介绍一位名人的故事。节目一开始，主持人常会让请来的名人大吃一惊，总是以"这就是你的人生"为开场白，然后才把他或她请进演播室。名人的亲朋好友早已秘而不宣地被请到了演播室与名人见面，讲述这位名人的故事〕

this·tle /ˈθɪsl; ˈθɪsəl/ *n* [C,U] a wild plant with prickly leaves and purple or white furry flowers 蓟〔一种叶片带刺、开紫色或白色毛茸状花朵的野生植物〕

thistle 蓟

this·tle·down /ˈθɪsl̩ˌdaun; ˈθɪsəldaʊn/ *n* [U] the soft light feathery substance fastened to thistle seeds that helps them to float in the air 蓟种子冠毛〔蓟种子上的软翅，可帮助种子飘浮空中〕

thith·er /ˈðɪðɚ; ˈðɪðə/ *adv old use* in that direction【旧】向那边，到那边

tho' /ðo; ðəʊ/ *adv* a short form of 缩略式= 'though'

Thomas /ˈtɑməs; ˈtɒməs/**, Dy·lan** /ˈdɪlən; ˈdɪlən/ (1914-53) a Welsh poet and writer famous especially for his radio play *Under Milk Wood*. 托马斯〔(1914-1953)，威尔士诗人、作家。他创作的广播剧《奶树林下》尤为著名〕

Thomas, R S (1913-2000) a Welsh poet who wrote about Welsh people and their culture in poems such as *Song at the Year's Turning* 托马斯〔(1913-2000)，威尔士诗人。他以诗展现威尔士民族与文化，如《辞旧迎新歌》〕

Thomas à Kempis —see 见 Thomas à KEMPIS

Thomas Cook /ˌ· · ˈ·/ *trademark* a British company that sells holidays and also arranges flights, sells foreign money etc. It is one of the oldest companies providing services for travellers and was started in 1841 by Thomas Cook.【商标】通济隆〔英国一公司，提供假日旅游、订购机票、兑换外币等服务，是历史最悠久的旅游公司之一，由托马斯·库克于1841年创立〕

Thomas the Tank En·gine /ˌ· · · ˈ· ˌ·/ a little blue steam railway engine with a smiling face, which is the main character in a series of books, television programmes, and films for young children, which first became popular with British children in the 1950s 火车头托马斯〔一台小型蓝色蒸汽火车机车，面部设计形似一张笑脸。它是儿童系列读物、电视剧和电影中的主角，20世纪50年代开始为英国儿童所喜爱〕

thong /θɔŋ; θɒŋ/ *n* [C] **1** a long thin piece of leather used to fasten something or as part of a whip 皮带子；〔皮鞭的〕梢 **2 thongs** [plural] *AmE* a type of shoe that you hold on with your toes【美】平底人字拖鞋；FLIPFLOPS *BrE*【英】—see picture at 参见 SHOE[1] 图 **3** a pair of KNICKERS or the bottom half of a BIKINI that has a single string instead of the back part 短衬裤；〔后面狭窄如带子的〕比基尼泳装裤

Thor /θɔr; θɔː/ in Norse MYTHOLOGY, the god of THUNDER and the strongest of the gods. The word 'Thursday' is based on his name. 托尔〔北欧神话中的雷神，威力居众神之首。Thursday（星期四）一词即源于他的名字〕

tho·rax /ˈθɔræks; ˈθɔːræks/ *n plural* **thoraxes** *or* **thoraces** /-rəsiz; -rəsiːz/ [C] **1** *technical* the part of your body between your neck and your waist【术语】〔人的〕胸（部），胸廓 **2** the part of an insect's body between its head and its ABDOMEN (2)〔昆虫的〕胸（节） —**thoracic** /θɔˈræsɪk; θɔːˈræsɪk/ *adj*

Tho·reau /θəˈro; ˈθɔːrəʊ/**, Henry David** (1817-62) a US writer and PHILOSOPHER whose best-known works are *Walden, or Life in the Woods*, in which he describes his simple life in the countryside, and *Civil Disobedience*, an essay on refusing to obey unfair laws, which influenced Gandhi and Martin Luther King 梭罗〔(1817-1862)，美国作家、哲学家。代表作是《沃尔登，或林中生活》和《论公民的不服从》。前者描写他在乡村的简朴生活，后者是一篇政论文，主张拒绝遵守不公正的法律，对甘地和马丁·路德·金产生过影响〕

thorn /θɔrn; θɔːn/ *n* **1** [C] a sharp point that grows on the stem of a plant such as a rose〔植物茎上的〕刺 **2** [C,U] a bush or tree that has thorns 带刺的灌木，荆棘 **3 a thorn in your side** someone or something that annoys you or causes problems for a long period of time 长时间使人苦恼或招来麻烦的人[事]，肉中刺：*He's been a thorn in the side of the party leadership for years.* 他多年来一直是该党领导层的肉中刺。

thorn·y /ˈθɔrnɪ; ˈθɔːni/ *adj* **1 thorny question/problem/point/issue** a question etc that is complicated and difficult 棘手的问题/难题/难事：*The thorny question of redundancies will have to be tackled sooner or later.* 裁减冗员这一棘手问题迟早必须给以解决。**2** a thorny bush, plant etc has thorns〔灌木、植物等〕有刺的，多刺的 —**thorniness** *n* [U]

thor·ough /ˈθɝo; ˈθʌrə/ *adj* **1** including every possible detail 彻底的；全面的；详尽的：*My doctor gave me a thorough check-up.* 我的医生给我做了一次全面的检查。| *I made very thorough notes of the meeting.* 我对那次会议作了非常详尽的笔记。**2** careful to do things properly so that you avoid mistakes 仔细的；缜密的：*Our mechanics will check everything, they're very thorough.* 我们的机械师要对一切东西进行检查，他们的工作是非常仔细的。**3 a thorough pest/nuisance/mess** used to emphasize the bad qualities of someone or something 彻头彻尾的讨厌鬼/十足的麻烦/混乱不堪 —see also 另见 THOROUGHLY —**thoroughness** *n* [U]

thor·ough·bred /ˈθɝoˌbrɛd; ˈθʌrəbred/ *n* [C] **1** a horse that has parents of the same very good breed 纯种马 **2** someone who seems to do something naturally to a very high standard 天才：*If we are talking about batsmen, Gower is a thoroughbred.* 要讲击球手，高尔是一流的。

thor·ough·fare /ˈθɝoˌfɛr; ˈθʌrəfeə/ *n* **1** [C] the main road through a place such as a city or village〔穿城而过或穿过村镇的〕大街，大道：*The motel was off the main thoroughfare.* 那家汽车旅馆不靠大马路。**2 no thoroughfare** a written sign used to tell people that they cannot go on a particular road or path 此路不通；禁止通行〔标牌用语〕

thor·ough·go·ing /ˈθɝoˈgo·ɪŋ; ˌθʌrəˈgəʊɪŋ◂/ *adj* **1** very thorough and careful 彻底的；仔细的：*a thoroughgoing inspection of the site* 对现场的彻底检查 **2** [only before noun 仅用于名词前] a thoroughgoing action or quality is complete 完全的，十足的：*the thoroughgoing materialism of this generation* 这一代人十足的物质主义

thor·ough·ly /ˈθɝolɪ; ˈθʌrəli/ *adv* **1** completely 完全地；极度地：*She sat in her room feeling thoroughly miserable.* 她坐在房间里，感到痛苦极了。| *I thoroughly enjoyed the play this evening.* 我非常喜欢今天晚上演出的这部剧。**2** carefully, so that nothing is forgotten 彻底地；仔细地；详尽地：*to clean a room thoroughly* 彻底地打扫房间

those /ðoz; ðəʊz/ the plural of THAT

thou[1] /θau; θaʊ/ *n* [C] *spoken* a thousand or a thousandth【口】一千；一千分之一：*They paid about sixty nine thou for it.* 他们买它花了大约六万九千块。

thou[2] /ðau; ðaʊ/ *pron old use* a word meaning you, used as the subject of a sentence【旧】汝，尔〔用作主语〕—see also 另见 HOLIER-THAN-THOU

though[1] /ðo; ðəʊ/ *conjunction* **1** used to introduce a statement that makes the other main statement seem surprising or unlikely 虽然，尽管：*Though he was only twelve he could run faster than any kid in the school.* 尽管他只有12岁，他却比学校里的任何孩子都跑得快。| **though old/tired etc** *His childhood, though poverty stricken, had been a happy one.* 他的童年生活虽然贫困，却也很幸福。| **old though it is/tired though he was etc** *Odd though it may seem, I actually like housework.* 尽管可能说来奇怪，我实际上喜欢做家务活儿。**2** used to add a fact or opinion which makes what you have just said seem less serious, less important etc 可是，不过，然而：*These samosas are great, though there's not much meat in them.* 这些油炸三角肉饺味道真不错，虽然里面肉没有多少。| *The offenders were dealt with firmly though fairly.* 违规者受到了严厉的，不过也是很公平的处理。**3 as though** as if 好像，仿佛：*The lights were on as though everyone had left in a hurry.* 灯还亮着，好像大家是匆匆离去的。—see also 另见 ALTHOUGH, **even though** (EVEN[1] (6))

though[2] *adv* [sentence adverb 句子副词] *especially spoken* used at the end of a CLAUSE (2) to add a fact or opinion which makes what you have just said seem less important, or to add a very different fact or opinion etc【尤口】可是，不过，然而〔用在从句末〕：*Yeah, a Rolex for £150 is a great bargain. Is it real though?* 是呀，150英镑买一只劳力士表是很划算。不过那是真的吗？| *Two heart attacks in a year. It hasn't stopped him smoking though.* 一年两次心脏病发作，可是那也没让他把烟戒掉。

thought[1] /θɔt; θɔːt/ past tense and past participle of THINK[1]

thought[2] *n*

1 ▶**STH YOU THINK ABOUT** 你想到的某事◀ [C] something that you think of, remember, or realize; idea 思想，想法；观念：*I was just going to pick up the phone when a sudden thought*

made me hesitate. 我正要去拿电话，这时，一个突然出现的想法使我犹豫起来。| [+of] *a traveller's thoughts of home* 游子对家的思念 | **the thought (that)** *I'm bothered by the thought that I might not have a job next year.* 一想到明年可能没有工作，我就烦着呢。| **have a thought** (=suddenly think of something) 突然想起某事 *I've just had a thought – why don't we invite Judith?* 我刚刚有了一个想法 —— 我们何不把朱迪思请来呢？| **the thought crossed my mind** (=I considered it) 我心里有这个想法 *"Do you think we should cancel the holiday?" "The thought had crossed my mind."* "你认为我们应该取消这次度假吗？""我也这样想过。" | **a/the thought occurs to sb** (=someone thinks of something) 某人想起了某事 *The thought has just occurred to me, that we should get some insurance.* 我是刚刚才有这个想法的，我们应该买些保险。| **the very thought (of)** (=used when a thought produces strong feelings) 一想到… *The very thought of moving to New York filled him with dread.* 一想到迁居纽约，他心里便充满了恐惧。| **sobering thought** (=a serious and worrying thought) 发人深省的想法，令人忧虑的想法 *It's a sobering thought that this country spends more on weapons than on education.* 这个国家花在武器上的钱比花在教育上的钱多，这真让人忧虑。| **dark thoughts** (=evil or sad thoughts) 邪恶的想法；悲哀的想法 *You must put such dark thoughts out of your mind.* 你必须把这种邪恶的想法从心里弄掉。| **cannot bear the thought of** (=be unable to accept an idea) 无法接受…的想法 *Louis could not bear the thought of being parted from her.* 路易斯无法接受要与她分手的想法。

2 ▶ACT OF THINKING 思考行为◀ [U] the act of thinking 想，思考；思维: **lost/deep in thought** (=thinking so much that you do not notice what is happening around you) 陷入思索中/在沉思中 *Derek was staring out of the window, lost in thought.* 德里克凝视着窗外，陷入了沉思。| **thought process** (=the way people's minds work) 思维方式 *Piaget helped teachers to understand children's thought processes.* 皮亚杰帮助教师们了解孩子的思维方式。

3 ▶CAREFUL CONSIDERATION 认真考虑◀ [U] careful and serious consideration 考虑，思索: *With more thought and care this would have been a first class essay.* 如果再认真琢磨一下，这本来应该是一篇一流的散文。| **give sth thought** (=think carefully about sth) 认真考虑某事 *I've been giving your proposal a lot of thought.* 我一直在认真地考虑你的提议。

4 that's a thought! *spoken* used to say that someone has made a good suggestion【口】那是一个好主意!: *"Why don't you ask Walter's advice?" "That's a thought! – I'll phone him right away."* "你为什么不征求一下沃尔特的意见?" "那是个好主意！我这就给他打电话。"

5 it's just a thought *spoken* used to say that what you have just said is only a suggestion and you have not thought about it very much【口】仅仅是一个想法而已: *I was wondering if your brother could help us – it was just a thought.* 你哥哥是否能帮咱们的忙呢？那只是一个想法而已。

6 ▶SUGGESTION 建议◀ [C] a suggestion or opinion about something 建议；意见: [+on] *Do you have any thoughts on how we should spend the money?* 你有没有什么建议，我们应该怎样花这笔钱?

7 ▶INTENTION 意图◀ [C,U] intention or hope of doing something 意图，打算；希望: [+of] *I had no thought of gaining any personal advantage.* 我当时未曾想到要获得任何个人的好处。

8 ▶CARING ABOUT STH 关心某事◀ [C,U] a feeling of worrying or caring about something 对…的担心；关心: [+for] *Louis went back into the blazing building with no thought for his own safety.* 路易斯又回到熊熊燃烧的大楼里，根本没有考虑到自身的安全。| **you are always in my thoughts** (=used to tell someone that you think about them and care about them a lot) 我一直在想着你；我一直在关心着你

9 sb's thoughts turn to sth if your thoughts turn to something, you start to think about it 转而开始想到某事: *Debbie's thoughts had turned to more serious matters.* 黛比转而思考一些更重大的问题。

10 spare a thought for used to tell someone that they should think about someone who is in a worse situation than they are〔用于要求别人〕给〔某人〕一点关心: *Spare a thought for the homeless.* 给无家可归的人一点关心。

11 don't give it another thought *spoken* used to tell someone politely not to worry after they have told you they are sorry【口】别把它放在心上，不要再往心里去〔礼貌地告诉某人不要因为歉意而心里过不去〕

12 it's the thought that counts *spoken* used to say that someone's actions are very kind even if they have only done something small or unimportant【口】〔也许实效微小但〕情意胜过一切

13 ▶WAY OF THINKING 思想方法◀ [U] a way of thinking that is typical of a particular group, period of history etc〔某一团体的〕思想（方法）；〔某一历史时期的〕思潮: *ancient Greek thought* 古希腊思想 —see also 另见 **perish the thought** (PERISH (3)), SECOND THOUGHT, **school of thought** (SCHOOL[1] (8))

thought·ful /ˈθɔtfəl; ˈθɔːtfəl/ *adj* **1** serious and quiet because you are thinking a lot 认真思考的，沉思的；若有所思的: *a thoughtful expression* 若有所思的表情 **2** always thinking of the things you can do to make people happy or comfortable 想得周到的；体贴的，关心的: *You'll like Paul, he's very thoughtful.* 你会喜欢保罗的，他非常体贴人。| [+of] *It was really thoughtful of you to remember my birthday.* 你真是体贴人，还记得我的生日。—**thoughtfully** *adv* —**thoughtfulness** *n* [U]

thought·less /ˈθɔtlɪs; ˈθɔːtləs/ *adj* forgetting about the needs and feelings of other people because you are thinking about what you want 欠考虑的；不为他人着想的，自私的: *rash and thoughtless actions* 轻率的自私行动 | **it is thoughtless of sb to do sth** *It's so thoughtless of John to smoke when there's a baby around.* 约翰真是不为别人着想，旁边有一个婴儿，他竟然还抽烟。—**thoughtlessly** *adv* —**thoughtlessness** *n*

thought-out /ˌ· ˈ·◂/ *adj* **carefully/well/badly thought-out** planned and organized carefully, well etc 考虑仔细的/周密的/不周的: *a carefully thought-out speech* 字斟句酌的演讲

Thought Po·lice, the /ˈ· ·,·/ the police organization in George Orwell's story *1984*, whose job is to control what people think and the way that they think. The expression 'thought police' is sometimes used for describing any group that tries to tell other people what opinions they should have or what words they should use. 思想警察〔乔治·奥威尔的小说《一九八四》述及的警察组织，其职责是控制人的思想和思维方式。该词有时用于指设法左右人的思想和言语的团体或组织〕

thou·sand /ˈθauzn̩d; ˈθaʊzənd/ *number* **1** 1000 一千 —see 见 HUNDRED (USAGE) **2 thousands** a lot 许许多多；数以千计: [+of] *There were thousands of people at the concert.* 有数以千计的人出席这次音乐会。—**thousandth** *adj*

Thousand and One Nights, the /,· · · ˈ·/ —see 见 the ARABIAN NIGHTS

thral·dom *BrE*【英】, **thralldom** *AmE*【美】/ ˈθrɔldəm; ˈθrɔːldəm/ *n* [U] *literary* the state of being a slave; SLAVERY【文】奴役；奴隶制度

thrall /θrɔl; θrɔːl/ *n* **in sb's thrall** *literary* controlled or strongly influenced by someone or something【文】在某人的奴役[束缚，控制]之下: *The magic of the evening held them in thrall.* 那个晚会的魅力征服了他们。

thrash[1] /θræʃ; θræʃ/ *n* **1** [singular] a violent movement from side to side 剧烈的摆动；不断的挥动 **2** [C] *old-fashioned* a loud noisy party【过时】闹哄哄的聚会 **3** [U] *informal* a type of ROCK[1] (2) music with very loud fast electric guitar playing【非正式】刺耳摇滚乐

thrash[2] *v* **1** [T] to beat someone violently in order to punish them 毒打；痛打: *My poor brother used to get thrashed for all kinds of minor offences.* 我那可怜的哥哥曾经因为各种鸡毛蒜皮的违规行为而常常挨打。**2** [I always+adv/prep] to move or make something move from side to side in a violent or uncontrolled way 猛烈摆动；翻腾: [+about/around] *The fish were thrashing about in the bottom of the boat.* 鱼在船的底舱里乱蹦乱跳。**3** [T] *informal* to defeat someone very easily in a game【非正式】〔比赛中〕轻易地把…击败: *Brazil thrashed Italy 5-0.* 巴西队以五比零轻取意大利队。

thrash sth ↔ **out** *phr v* [T] to discuss a problem thoroughly with someone until you find an answer 彻底讨论〔直到找出解决办法〕；商讨: *We spent the whole day trying to thrash out a solution.* 我们花了一整天时间反复研究，尽力找出一个解决办法。

thrash·ing /ˈθræʃɪŋ; ˈθræʃɪŋ/ *n* [C] **give/get a thrashing a)** to beat someone or be beaten violently as a punishment 痛打/被痛打: *If you speak to your mother like that again, you'll get a thrashing.* 如果你再那样跟你的母亲说话，你会挨一顿痛打的。**b)** to defeat someone or be defeated easily in a game〔比赛中〕轻易地击败…；被…轻易地击败

thread[1] /θrɛd; θred/ *n*

1 ▶COTTON/SILK ETC 棉/丝绸等◀ [C,U] a long thin string of cotton, silk etc used to SEW or weave cloth〔缝衣服的〕线，细线: *Have you got a needle and thread?* 你有针线吗？

2 ▶IDEAS 思想◀ [singular] the connection between the different parts of an explanation, story etc 思路，头绪；贯穿的主线: *a common thread running through all the poems* 把所有诗歌贯穿起来的一条共同主线 | **lose the thread** (=stop understanding how

T

ideas or events are connected) 失去头绪；中断思路 *I'm sorry, I've lost the thread of your argument.* 对不起，我失去了头绪，不能理解你的论证。

3 pick up the threads to begin something again after a long period, especially a relationship or way of life〔尤指某种关系或生活方式中断很长时间后〕再继续下去: *It's difficult to pick up the threads when you've been travelling for so long.* 你已经旅行了这么长的时间，要恢复原来的生活方式是很困难的。

4 ►LIGHT/SMOKE ETC 光/烟等◄ [C] *literary* a long thin line of something【文】线一样细长的东西: [+of] *The Colorado River is just a thread of silver, 4,000 feet below.* 在下面4000英尺处的科罗拉多河就像一条银色的细线。

5 ►ON A SCREW 在螺钉上◄ [C] a continuous raised line of metal that winds around the curved surface of a screw 螺纹 —see picture at 参见 SCREW¹ 图

6 threads [plural] *old fashioned, especially AmE* clothes【过时，尤美】衣服 —see also 另见 **hang by a thread** (HANG¹ (5))

thread² *v* [T] **1** to put a thread or string through a hole 穿线于: *Williams threaded the rope through the karabiner and attached it to the safety point.* 威廉斯把绳索穿在登山铁环里，然后固定在桩子上。| **thread a needle** (=push a thread through the hole in a needle) 穿针（引线）**2** to put a film, tape etc correctly through parts of a camera, PROJECTOR or TAPE RECORDER 把〔胶卷、磁带等〕装放〔在照相机、录音机等里面〕**3** to connect objects by pushing a string through a hole in them 用线把…串连起来: *Thread the beads on a string and make a necklace.* 用线把珠子串连起来，做成一根项链。**4 thread your way through/into etc** to move through a place by carefully going around things that are blocking your way 小心〔避开障碍物〕穿过/进入〔某地〕等: *She came towards me, threading her way through the traffic.* 她小心地避过车辆行人，朝我走过来。

thread·bare /ˈθrɛd͵bɛr; ˈθredbeə/ *adj* **1** clothes, carpets etc that are threadbare are very thin and in bad condition because they have been used a lot〔衣服、地毯等〕破旧的；磨得很薄的: *a threadbare old sofa* 一张用得很旧的沙发 —see picture on page A18 参见A18页图 **2 threadbare excuse/argument/joke etc** an excuse etc that is no longer effective because it has been used too much 陈旧的托辞/论点/笑话等

Threadneedle Street —see 见 OLD LADY OF THREADNEEDLE STREET

threat /θrɛt; θret/ *n* **1** [C,U] a statement that you will cause someone pain, unhappiness, or trouble 威胁，恐吓: *Your threats don't scare me!* 你的那些威胁吓不倒我！| [+of] *the threat of strike action* 采取罢工行动的威胁 | **make/issue a threat against** *Threats have been made against the book's author.* 有人对那本书的作者发出恐吓。| **give in to threats** (=do what someone wants because they threaten you) 屈服于威胁 *The government will not give in to terrorist threats.* 政府不会屈服于恐怖分子的威胁。| **carry out a threat** (=do what you threatened to do) 把威胁付诸行动 | **empty threat** (=a threat to do something that you cannot really do) 虚张声势的威胁 *Take no notice – they're empty threats.* 不要在意，那些是虚张声势的威胁。| **death/bomb etc threat** *Police are investigating death threats made against the singer.* 警察正在调查针对那名歌手的死亡威胁。| **under threat of** *Mancini claims he was forced to carry out their orders under threat of death.* 曼西尼声称自己是在死亡的威胁下才被迫执行他们的命令的。**2** [C usually singular 一般用单数] the possibility that something very bad will happen〔灾难等〕坏事发生的可能: [+of] *There's a serious threat of famine.* 饥荒爆发的可能性极大。| **be under threat of closure/attack etc** (=be likely to be closed, attacked etc) 有可能遭到关闭/攻击等 *The factory is still under threat of closure.* 这家工厂仍然有关闭的可能。**3** [C usually singular 一般用单数] someone or something that is regarded as a possible danger 可能会带来危险的人[事]: [+to] *Automation presents the biggest threat to the workforce.* 自动化给劳动大军带来最大的威胁。| **pose a threat** *Nuclear weapons continue to pose a threat.* 核武器继续构成威胁。

threat·en /ˈθrɛtn; ˈθretn/ *v* **1** [T] to say that you will cause someone pain, unhappiness, or trouble if they do not do what you want 威胁，恐吓〔某人〕: **threaten to do sth** *Every time they quarrel, Jan threatens to leave.* 他俩每次吵架时，简都威胁说要离开。| **threaten sb with sth** *We were threatened with the sack if we didn't cooperate.* 我们受到威胁，不合作就会被解雇。| **threaten sb** *It's no use threatening me – I won't do it.* 威胁我是没有用的，我不会干这个的。| **threaten sth** *The unions are threatening a one-day strike.* 工会威胁说要举行一天的罢工。| **threaten that** *He's threatening that if he doesn't get his way, he'll resign.* 他威胁说，如果他不能如愿以偿的话，他就辞职。**2** [T] to be likely to harm or destroy something 威胁到；危害到: *Poaching threatens the survival of the rhino.* 偷猎危及犀牛的生存。**3** [I,T] if something threatens to cause an unpleasant situation, it seems likely that it will cause it〔不利的事〕将要发生；〔某事〕可能引起〔不利的后果〕: **threaten sb/sth with** *Large areas of the jungle are now threatened with destruction.* 大片的热带丛林现在面临被毁灭的危险。| **threaten to do sth** *The incident threatens to ruin his chances in the election.* 这一事件会毁了他在这次选举中当选的机会。

threat·en·ing /ˈθrɛtnɪŋ; ˈθretn-ɪŋ/ *adj* **1** talking or behaving in a way that is intended to threaten someone〔言行〕带有威胁口气的: *His voice sounded threatening.* 他的话音里带有威胁的口气。**2** making threats 威胁（性）的，恐吓（性）的: *a threatening letter* 一封恐吓信 **—threateningly** *adv*

three /θri; θriː/ *number* **1** 3 三 **2 the three R's** *old-fashioned* used when talking about children's education to mean reading, writing and ARITHMETIC【过时】〔儿童教育的〕三R技能〔指读、写、算三项基本技能〕

Three Blind Mice /͵· ·ˈ·/ a NURSERY RHYME (=an old song or poem for young children).《三只盲鼠》〔一首童谣〕The rhyme goes 该童谣如下:

Three blind mice, three blind mice,
See how they run, see how they run!
They all ran after the farmer's wife,
who cut off their tails with a carving knife.
Did you ever see such a thing in your life
As three blind mice?
三只盲鼠，三只盲鼠，
跑得快，跑得快。
一齐追赶农夫他老婆，
她挥刀割下鼠尾巴。
三只这样的盲鼠，
你可见过吗？

three-cor·nered /͵· ˈ··◄/ *adj* **1** having three corners 三角的，有三个角的 **2 three-cornered contest/fight** a competition which involves three people or groups 涉及三方的竞争/角逐

three-D, 3-D /͵θri ˈdi; ͵θriː ˈdiː◄/ *adj* a three-D film or picture is made so that it appears to be three-dimensional 三维的，立体的 **—three-D** *n* [U]: *a film in 3-D* 一部立体电影

three-day e·vent /͵· · ·ˈ·/ *n* [C] *BrE* a horse-riding competition that takes place for three days【英】三日马术赛

three-di·men·sion·al /͵· ·ˈ···◄/ *adj* **1** having or seeming to have length, depth, and height（似）有三维的，立体的: *a three-dimensional structure* 三维结构 **2** a three-dimensional character in a book, film etc, seems like a real person〔书、电影等中的人物〕有立体感的；逼真的

three·fold /ˈθri͵fold; ˈθriːfəʊld/ *adj* three times as much or as many 三倍的 **—threefold** *adv*

three-half·pence /͵·ˈ··/ *n* [U] *BrE old use* one and a half old pence【英旧】一个半便士

Three Kings, the /͵· ˈ·/ —see 见 the THREE WISE MEN

three-leg·ged race /͵· ͵·· ˈ·/ *n* [C] a race in which two people run together, and one person has their right leg tied to the other person's left leg 绑腿赛跑，二人三足赛跑〔一种两人为一组的赛跑，其中一人的右腿与另一人的左腿绑在一起〕

three-line whip /͵· · ˈ·/ *n* [C] an order from a leader of a British political party telling MPs in that party that they must vote in a particular way 紧急指令〔指英国政党领袖要求本党议员必须按照指示投票〕

Three Lit·tle Pigs, The /͵· ˈ·· ·/ an old children's story about three little pigs, each of whom builds a house of a different material, which the BIG BAD WOLF tries to blow down, saying "I'll huff and I'll puff and I'll blow your house down"《三只小猪》〔一个流传很久的童话故事。三只小猪各自用不同材料造好一间屋子，有只大坏狼想用嘴把屋子吹倒，它叫道："我要呼——呼——呼吹倒你的屋子"〕

Three Men in a Boat /͵· · · ˈ·/ (1889) a humorous book by Jerome K. Jerome about three men and a dog who go on holiday and row a boat up the River Thames《三人同舟》〔(1889)，杰罗姆·K.杰罗姆的一部幽默小说。故事中有三个男人带着一条狗一起去度假，他们划着一条船沿泰晤士河逆流而上〕

Three Mile Is·land /͵· · ˈ··/ a place in Pennsylvania in the US, where there was a serious accident of a NUCLEAR power station in 1979. The people in charge managed to prevent a MELTDOWN (=when the nuclear material melts and burns through its containers), but the accident increased opposition to nuclear power in the US and prevented new power stations from being built. 三英里岛〔美国宾夕法尼亚州一地名，1979年那里曾发生一起严重的核电站事故。有关人员经过努力消除了堆芯熔毁的危

险，但这次事故使美国人反对核能源的呼声日益高涨，并且阻止了新核电站的建设〕—compare 比较 CHERNOBYL

Three Mus·ket·eers, The /ˌθri mʌskəˋtɪr; ˌθriː mʌskɪˈtɪə/ (1844) a NOVEL by Alexandre Dumas, set in France in the 17th century, about three men called Porthos, Athos, and Aramis, who are members of a group of soldiers guarding Louis XIII, the king of France. They are very skilled at fighting with swords, and they have many exciting adventures with their friend D'Artagnan, who comes to Paris from the country and joins the Musketeers when he shows them what a good fighter he is.《三剑客》，又译《三个火枪手》〔(1844)，大仲马创作的一部小说，以17世纪的法国为背景。书中讲述三个男子波尔托斯、阿索斯和阿拉米斯的故事。他们是法国国王路易十三的护卫，个个剑术高超，与他们的朋友达达尼昂一起经历了许多冒险奇遇。达达尼昂从乡下来到巴黎，向三剑客展示了自己的高超武艺，随之加入到他们的行列〕

three·pence /ˈθrɪpəns; ˈθrepəns/ *n* [U] *BrE old use* three old pence【英旧】三便士

three·pen·ny bit /ˌθripɛni ˋbɪt; ˌθrepəni ˈbɪt/ *n* [C] a small coin used in Britain before 1971 that was worth three old pence〔1971年之前在英国使用的〕三便士小硬币

Threepenny Op·e·ra, The /ˌ···ˈ···/ (1928) an OPERA with music by Kurt Weill and words by Bertolt Brecht, based on *The Beggar's Opera* (1728) by John Gay《三便士歌剧》〔(1928)，库尔特·韦尔作曲、贝托尔德·布莱希特作词的一部歌剧，根据约翰·盖伊的《乞丐的歌剧》改编而成〕

three-piece suit /ˌ··ˈ·/ *n* [C] a suit that consists of a JACKET (1), WAISTCOAT, and trousers made from the same material 三件套的西装〔包括上衣、背心和裤子〕

three-piece suite /ˌ··ˈ·/ *n* [C] *especially BrE* two chairs and a SOFA covered in the same material【尤英】三件套的沙发

three-ply /ˈ··/ *adj* three-ply wood, wool, TISSUE (1) etc consists of three layers or threads〔木板等〕三层的；〔线等〕三股的

three-point turn /ˌ·ˈ·ˈ·/ *n* [C] a way of turning your car so that it faces the opposite way, by driving forwards, backwards, and then forwards again 三点转向〔指把汽车前驶、后退再前驶以转为相反方向的方法〕

three-quar·ter /ˌ·ˈ··/ *adj* [only before noun 仅用于名词前] three quarters of the full size, length etc of something〔大小、长度等〕四分之三的：*a three-quarter violin* 一把四分之三大小的小提琴 | **a three-quarter length coat** (=one that ends a little above your knees) 长及膝盖以上的外套

three-quar·ters /ˌ·ˈ··/ *n* [plural] an amount equal to three of the four equal parts that make up a whole 四分之三：[+of] *three-quarters of an hour* 45分钟

three-ring cir·cus /ˌ··ˈ··/ *n* [singular] *AmE informal* a place or situation that is confusing because there is too much activity【美，非正式】乱哄哄的地方[场面]：*I don't know how you can work in that office – it's like a three-ring circus.* 我不知道你怎么能够在那样的办公室里工作——那里就像一个闹哄哄的大马戏团。

three R's, the /ˌθri ˋɑrz; ˌθriː ˈɑːz/ *n old-fashioned* reading, writing, and ARITHMETIC (=working with numbers), considered as the basic things that children must learn【过时】〔儿童必须学会的〕三R技能〔指读、写、算〕

three·score /ˈθriskɔr; ˈθriːskɔː/ *number old use* 60【旧】六十 —see also 另见 SCORE[3] (1)

three·some /ˈθrisəm; ˈθriːsəm/ *n* [C usually singular 一般用单数] *informal* a group of three people or things【非正式】三人一组；三件一套

three-star /ˈ··/ *adj* a three-star hotel, restaurant etc is officially judged to be of a good standard〔宾馆、饭店等〕三星级的

Three Ten·ors, the /ˌ·ˈ··/ three OPERA singers, José Carreras, Placido Domingo, and Luciano Pavarotti, who are very popular TENORS (=men with high singing voices), and who have often appeared in concerts together and made records together 三大男高音〔指三位声望颇高的歌剧演唱家，即何塞·卡雷拉斯、普拉西多·多明戈和卢恰诺·帕瓦罗蒂。他们常在音乐会上一同演出，并一起录制唱片〕

three-wheel·er /ˌ·ˈ··/ *n* [C] a car that has three wheels 三轮汽车

Three Wise Men, the /ˌ··ˈ·/ also 又作 **the Three Kings**, **the Magi** in the New Testament of the Bible, three kings or wise men who came from the East, guided by a star, and brought gifts of gold, FRANKINCENSE, and MYRRH for the baby Jesus. 东方三博士，东方三贤士〔《圣经·新约》中来自东方的三位国王或贤哲。他们在一颗星星的指引下为新生的耶稣送去黄金、乳香和没药〕

Three Wise Mon·keys, the /ˌ··ˈ··/ three monkeys who are shown in pictures sitting in a row. The first has its hands covering its eyes, the second has its hands covering its ears, and the third has its hands covering its mouth. Together they represent the phrase "see no evil, hear no evil, speak no evil". 三只聪明的猴子〔图画中并排而坐的三只猴子，第一只用手遮住双目，第二只用手掩住双耳，第三只用手捂住嘴巴。合起来就代表了这句格言"非礼勿视，非礼勿听，非礼勿言"〕

thren·o·dy /ˈθrɛnədi; ˈθrenədi/ *n* [C] *literary* a funeral song for someone who has died【文】挽歌，哀歌

thresh /θrɛʃ; θreʃ/ *v* [I,T] to separate the grain from the rest of corn, wheat etc, by beating it with a special tool or machine (给)〔玉米、小麦等〕脱粒；打谷 —**thresher** *n* [C] —compare 比较 THRASH[2]

threshing ma·chine /ˈ·· ·ˌ·/ *n* [C] a machine used for separating the grain from the rest of corn, wheat etc〔给玉米、小麦等脱粒的〕打谷机，脱粒机

thresh·old /ˈθrɛʃold; ˈθreʃhəʊld/ *n* [C] **1** the entrance to a room or building, or the area of floor at the entrance 门槛 **2** the level at which something starts to happen or have an effect〔某事开始发生或产生效果的〕阈，限度：*my boredom threshold* 我忍受烦闷的限度 | **pain threshold** (=the amount of pain you can suffer before you react to it) 痛觉阈〔指能忍受疼痛的限度〕 | **have a high pain threshold** (=be able to suffer a lot of pain before you react) 痛觉阈高〔指忍受疼痛的能力高〕 | **have a low pain threshold** (=not be able to suffer much pain before you react) 痛觉阈低〔指忍受疼痛的能力低〕 **3 on the threshold of** at the beginning of a new and important event or development 在〔重要事件等〕的开端：*All Europe stands on the threshold of an era of prosperity.* 整个欧洲都处在一个繁荣时期的开端。

threw /θru; θruː/ the past tense of THROW[1]

thrice /θraɪs; θraɪs/ *adv old use* three times【旧】三倍；三次

thrift /θrɪft; θrɪft/ *n* [U] *old-fashioned* wise and careful use of money, so that none is wasted【过时】节省，节俭 —see also 另见 SPENDTHRIFT

thrift shop /ˈ· ·/ *n* [C] *AmE* a shop that sells used goods, especially clothes, often in order to get money for a CHARITY (2)【美】〔常为慈善机构筹募经费，尤其出售旧衣服的〕廉价旧货店

thrift·y /ˈθrɪftɪ; ˈθrɪfti/ *adj* using money carefully and wisely 节省的，节俭的：*hard-working, thrifty folk* 勤劳节俭的人们 —**thriftily** *adv* —**thriftiness** *n* [U]

thrill[1] /θrɪl; θrɪl/ *n* **1** [C] a sudden strong feeling of excitement and pleasure, or the thing that makes you feel this〔突然强烈的〕激动；狂喜：**get a thrill out of** *Even though I've been acting for years, I still get a thrill out of going on stage.* 尽管我多年来一直在演出，但一上舞台我仍然感到十分激动。| **give sb a thrill** *Pete reckons that using guns gives him a thrill.* 皮特认为使用枪会给他一种刺激感。| **the thrill of (doing sth)** (=the excitement you get from something)〔做某事获得的〕兴奋感 *the thrill of travelling at speed* 驾车飞驰的兴奋感 | **do sth for the thrill of it** (=do something for excitement and not for any serious reason) 为了寻求刺激而做某事 **2 thrills and spills** the excitement and danger involved in an activity, especially a sport〔尤指体育运动中的〕惊险刺激 —see also 另见 **cheap thrill** (CHEAP[1] (5))

thrill[2] *v* **1** [T] to make someone feel excited and happy 使兴奋，使冲动：*The magic of his music continues to thrill audiences.* 他那魔法般的音乐继续使听众感动。**2** [I] to feel excited 感到激动：[+to] *Thrill to the magic of the world's greatest guitarist.* 感受世界上最伟大的吉他手的魅力。

thrilled /θrɪld; θrɪld/ *adj* [not before noun 不用于名词前] very excited, happy, and pleased 非常激动的，兴奋的，高兴的：*We were so thrilled to hear about the baby.* 听到那个婴儿的消息，我们非常高兴。| **thrilled to bits** (=very thrilled) 兴奋得不得了

thrill·er /ˈθrɪlɚ; ˈθrɪlə/ *n* [C] a book or film that tells an exciting story about murder or crime〔关于谋杀或犯罪的〕惊险小说；惊险电影

thril·ling /ˈθrɪlɪŋ; ˈθrɪlɪŋ/ *adj* interesting and exciting 引人入胜的；令人激动的：*a thrilling climax to the championship* 争夺冠军的紧张高潮 —**thrillingly** *adv*

thrive /θraɪv; θraɪv/ *v past tense* **thrived** or **throve** /θrov; θrəʊv/ [I] *formal* if something such as a company or plant thrives, it becomes very successful or very strong and healthy【正式】兴旺，欣欣向荣；茁壮成长：*tree ferns that still thrive in tropical rainforests* 在热带雨林里仍然长势旺盛的桫椤 | *a free-market economy in which businesses can thrive* 使企业得以蓬勃发展的自由市场经济

thrive on sth *phr v* [T] to enjoy or be successful in conditions that other people, businesses etc find difficult or unpleasant 乐意做〔别人觉得难做或不乐意做的事〕；〔在其他人、企业等认为困难或不利的环境中〕成功：*I wouldn't want that much pressure,*

but she seems to thrive on it. 我不愿承担那么多的压力，但她好像乐在其中。

thri·ving /ˈθraɪvɪŋ; ˈθraɪvɪŋ/ *adj* a thriving company, business etc is very successful 欣欣向荣的，兴旺发达的：*a thriving tourist industry* 欣欣向荣的旅游业

throat /θrot; θrəʊt/ *n* [C] **1** the passage from the back of your mouth to the top of the tubes that go down to your lungs and stomach 喉咙，咽喉 —see picture at 参见 HEAD[1] 图 **2** the front of your neck 喉部，颈前部：*She fingered the pearls at her throat.* 她用手指拨弄着脖子上的珍珠。**3 clear your throat** to make a noise in your throat, especially before you speak, or in order to get someone's attention〔说话前或引人注意时〕清一下嗓子 **4 force/ram sth down sb's throat** *informal* to force someone to accept or listen to your ideas and opinions【非正式】强迫某人接受[听从]自己的意见 **5 be at each other's throats** if two people are at each other's throats, they are fighting or arguing 互相打斗；激烈争吵 **6 cut your own throat** to behave in a way that is certain to harm you, especially because you are proud or angry〔尤指因骄傲或发怒而〕自己害自己；自寻死路 —see also 另见 **bring a lump to sb's throat** (LUMP[1] (4)), **have a frog in your throat** (FROG (2)), **jump down sb's throat** (JUMP[1] (9)), **stick in your throat** (STICK[1] (12))

throat·y /ˈθrotɪ; ˈθrəʊti/ *adj* making a low rough sound when you speak or sing〔说话或唱歌时〕声音低沉的，声音沙哑的 —**throatily** *adv* —**throatiness** *n* [C,U]

throb[1] /θrɑb; θrɒb/ *v* [I] **throbbed, throbbing 1** if a part of your body throbs, you get a regular feeling of pain in it〔身体的某一部分〕抽痛：*Her foot was throbbing with pain.* 她的脚在阵阵抽痛。**2** if music or a machine throbs it makes a sound with a strong regular beat〔音乐或机器〕有规律地颤动发声 **3** if your heart throbs, it beats faster or more strongly than usual〔心脏急速强烈地〕跳动，搏动

throb[2] *n* [C] a low, strong, regular beat or sensation 颤动；震动；跳动：*the throb of distant drums* 远处鼓声的震动 —see also 另见 HEARTTHROB

throes /θroz; θrəʊz/ *n* [plural] **in the throes of** in the middle of a very difficult situation 处于…的困境之中：*a country in the throes of a profound economic crisis* 一个深陷于经济危机之中的国家 —see also 另见 DEATH THROES

throm·bo·sis /θrɑmˈbosɪs; θrɒmˈbəʊsɪs/ *n* [C,U] *technical* a serious medical problem caused by a CLOT[2] (1) forming in your blood, especially in your heart【术语】血栓形成

throne /θron; θrəʊn/ *n* **1** [C] a special chair used by a king or queen at important ceremonies〔君王的〕宝座，御座 **2 the throne** the position and power of being a king or queen 王位，帝位；王权，君权：**be on the throne** (=be ruling)〔君主〕在位 *in 1913 when George V was on the throne* 1913年乔治五世在位的时候 | **come to the throne** (=become king or queen)〔君主〕继位，登基 | **be next in line to the throne** (=be the person who will become king or queen when the present one dies) 身为储君

throng[1] /θrɔŋ; θrɒŋ/ *n* [C] *literary* a large group of people in one place; crowd【文】一大群人；人群：*a milling throng of excited spectators* 一群到处乱转、激动不已的观众 | **the throng** *She got lost in the throng.* 她在人群中迷路了。

throng[2] *v* **1** [I always+adv/prep,T] if people throng a place, they go there in large numbers〔人群〕蜂拥；群集；挤满〔某地〕：*tourists still thronging the bars and restaurants* 仍然挤满在酒吧和餐馆里的游客 **2 be thronged with** if a place is thronged with people, it is very crowded with them〔某地〕被…挤满：*streets thronged with Christmas shoppers* 挤满了圣诞购物者的街道

throt·tle[1] /ˈθrɑtl̩; ˈθrɒtl/ *v* [T] **1** to hold someone's throat very tightly so that they cannot breathe; STRANGLE (1) 掐〔某人的〕脖子，把〔某人〕勒得透不过气来；使窒息（而死）**2** to make it difficult or impossible for something to succeed 阻挡；压制；扼杀：*These policies are throttling individual initiative and effort.* 这些政策是在扼杀个人的进取和努力。

throttle back *phr v* [I,T] to reduce the amount of petrol or oil flowing into an engine, in order to reduce speed 减少〔流进发动机的〕汽油以减速

throttle[2] *n* [C] *technical*【术语】**1** a piece of equipment that controls the amount of petrol, oil etc going into a vehicle's engine〔控制汽车发动机油量的〕节流阀，油门（杆）**2 at full throttle** as fast as possible in your car, boat etc〔汽车、船只等〕油门大开地；全速地

through[1] /θru; θruː/ *prep* **1** entering something such as a door, passage, tube, or hole at one end or side and leaving it at the other 穿过，贯穿；从一端到另一端：*They were suddenly plunged into darkness as the train went through the tunnel.* 当火车通过隧道时，他们一下子陷入了黑暗之中。| *The ball went flying through the window.* 球从窗户飞穿了过去。| *As the water passes through the filter a lot of dirt is taken out.* 水在流过过滤器时，过滤掉大量的污物。**2** going into an area, group etc and moving across it or within it 穿过，通过〔某一地区、人群等〕：*He had to push his way through the crowd to get to her.* 他得挤过人群才能到达她跟前。| *The new ring road stops all the traffic driving through the centre of town.* 新的环城路使穿越城市中心的所有交通都受到了限制。| *gliding noiselessly through the air* 无声地滑过空中 —see picture on page A1 参见A1页图 **3** if you see something through glass, a window etc, you are on one side of the glass etc and it is on the other 透过〔玻璃、窗户等〕：*I could see her through the window.* 我能透过窗户看到她。| *Through the mist she could just make out his silhouette.* 透过雾霭，她只能看到他身体的轮廓。**4** passing a place where you are supposed to stop〔在应该停下的地方〕闯过：*The driver had gone straight through the traffic lights and hit an oncoming car.* 那名司机径直闯过交通灯，撞上了一辆迎面驶来的汽车。| *Once through passport control your luggage will be searched.* 过了护照检查站，你的行李就要接受检查。**5** cutting, breaking or making a hole from one side of something to the other 切断，断开；凿穿：*Not only did the drill pierce the wood but it went straight through the table underneath too!* 那钻头不仅钻穿了木头，还径直钻进了木头下面的桌子！| *The goat had eaten right through the rope.* 那只山羊径直啃断了绳子。**6** during and to the end of a period of time 在整个期间；自始至终：*Sometimes I go to bed at 5 a.m. and sleep right through the day.* 有时候我早上5点上床，然后睡一个白天。| *I wouldn't worry about Joe, he's just going through a difficult period.* 我不担心乔，他正在经历一个困难时期。**7** if you get through a difficult situation or experience you deal with it successfully 战胜〔困境〕；成功地渡过：*I've no idea how I managed to get through my exams last year.* 我不知道我去年是如何通过考试的。| *He has lots of friends which really helped him through the divorce.* 他有很多的朋友，这真的帮他渡过了离婚这一关。**8 look through/search through/go through etc** to do something from beginning to end and include all parts of it 彻底地查看/搜寻/检查等：*In the dress rehearsal he'll go through the play one final time.* 在最后彩排时，他要对全剧最后再审查一遍。| *I've searched through all my documents and I still can't find my passport.* 我找遍了我的所有文件，但仍然找不到我的护照。**9** because of someone or something 由于，因为：*How many working days were lost through sickness last year?* 去年因为员工生病损失了多少个工作日？| *Through your incompetence many of the hotel's regular guests have taken their business elsewhere.* 由于你的无能，酒店的许多常客去了别家。**10 get through/go through** to use a lot of something 大量用[消费]〔某物〕：*You wouldn't believe how many packets of cigarettes she gets through.* 你不会相信她抽多少盒烟。**11** using a particular person, organization etc to help you achieve something 通过，经由：*I got my first job through an employment agency.* 我通过一家职业介绍所获得了我的第一份工作。**12 May through June/Wednesday through Friday etc** *AmE* from May until June, from Wednesday until Friday etc【美】从5月到6月/从星期三到星期五等：*The store is open Monday through Saturday.* 商店从星期一到星期六都开门。—see 见 INCLUSIVE (USAGE) **13** if you go through a country, you travel across it 在…旅行；游遍：*It was while we were travelling through Africa that we decided to settle over there.* 正是在游历非洲期间，我们决定在那边定居。**14** if a law passes through a parliament, it is agreed and accepted as a law〔法律在议会的〕通过：*The bill's passage through Congress was not a smooth one.* 该议案在国会的通过不是很顺利。—see also 另见 THRU

through[2] *adv* **1** from one end or side of something to the other 穿过；通过：*Let me through – I'm a doctor!* 让我过去吧——我是医生！**2 read/think/talk etc sth through** to read, think etc about something very carefully from beginning to end 认真彻底地阅读/想想/谈谈等：*If you think it through – we have no choice but to agree to his demands.* 如果你认真彻底地想一想——我们没有选择，只有同意他的要求。**3 get through/come through/pull through etc** to deal with a difficult situation or experience successfully 渡过（难关）/战胜（困难）/坚持下来等：*I don't know why you worry about exams – you'll sail through as usual.* 我不知道你为什么担心考试——你会像平常一样顺利通过的。| *Doctors are unsure about whether she'll pull through.* 她是否会挺得过来，医生们没有把握。**4 get through/make it through etc** to reach a person, place etc after a difficult journey〔艰难地〕到达，抵达：*It's snowing too heavily, you'll never get through.* 雪下得太大了，你根本去不了的。| [+to] *After days of effort, rescue teams have finally made it through to the*

survivors. 经过几天的努力, 营救队终于到了幸存者那儿。**5 wet through/cooked through etc** *informal* very wet, cooked completely etc【非正式】湿透了/熟透了等: *You're wet through. What on earth have you been doing?* 你湿透了。你到底干什么去了? **6 get through/be through** *BrE* to be connected to someone by telephone【英】〔打电话〕接通了: [+to] *I managed to get through to her after several attempts.* 我试了好几次, 终于接通了她的电话。| **put sb through** (=connect someone by telephone to someone else) 给某人接通〔电话〕 *"Can I speak to Mr Henry please?" "I'm putting you through sir."* "请问亨利先生在吗?" "我这就给你接过去, 先生。" **7 go through to London/Paris etc** if something such as a train goes through to London it continues as far as London 通往伦敦/巴黎等 **8 through and through** if someone is a particular type of person through and through, they are completely that type of person 完完全全地, 彻底地: *I'll say one thing for Sandra – she's a professional through and through.* 我要为桑德拉说一句 —— 她完完全全是专家。

through³ *adj* **1 be through (with sb/sth)** *informal*【非正式】**a)** to have finished doing something, using something etc 完成〔某事〕; 用完〔某东西〕: *I'm not through just yet – I should be finished in an hour.* 我还没有做完 —— 一个小时后该做完了吧。**b)** to no longer be having a relationship with someone 与〔某人〕关系完结: *That's it! Simon and I are through.* 就这样! 我和西蒙一刀两断了。**c)** to have stopped doing something or using something that is bad or that you do not like 戒除, 戒掉〔恶习〕: *He says he's through with drugs but it's just not that easy.* 他说他已戒掉了毒品, 但事情没有那么容易。**2 through train/road** a train or road by which you can reach a place, without having to use other trains or roads 直达火车/直通路

S3 W1 **through·out¹** /θru`aut; θruː'aʊt/ *prep* **1** in every part of a particular area, place etc 遍及; 在…各处: *a large international organization with offices throughout the world* 在世界各地设有办事处的一家大型国际机构 **2** during all of a particular period, from the beginning to the end 在整个期间; 自始至终: *He had misled the court throughout the trial.* 在整个审判过程中, 他一直在误导法庭里所有的人。

throughout² *adv* [usually at the end of a sentence 一般用于句尾] **1** in every part of a particular area, place etc 到处, 各个地方: *The house is in excellent condition with fitted carpets throughout.* 这幢房子条件极好, 到处都铺了地毯。**2** during all of a particular period, from the beginning to the end 在整个期间; 自始至终: *He managed to remain calm throughout.* 他自始至终勉力保持镇静。

through·put /'θru,put; 'θruːpʊt/ *n* [U] the amount of work, materials etc that can be dealt with in a particular period of time 〔在一定时间内的〕工作量; 吞吐量; 处理能力: *an airport with a weekly throughput of 100,000 passengers* 一周旅客吞吐量达10万人的机场

Through the Look·ing-Glass /,··'···/ (1872) a book for children by Lewis Carroll in which the main character, Alice, a little girl, visits a strange world by stepping through a mirror. Many of the people she meets are chess pieces or characters from NURSERY RHYMES (=old songs or poems for young children) such as Humpty Dumpty. 《镜中世界》, 又译《镜中奇缘》〔(1872), 刘易斯·卡罗尔的一部儿童小说。书中的主人公是一个名叫艾丽丝的小女孩。她走进一面镜子来到一个奇幻世界, 见到的许多人物要么是一个个的棋子, 要么像童谣中的"矮胖子"〕— see also另见 ALICE IN WONDERLAND

through·way /'θru,we; 'θruːweɪ/ *n* [C] *AmE* a THRUWAY【美】高速公路

throve /θrov; θrəʊv/ *old-fashioned*【过时】the past tense of THRIVE

S1 W1 **throw¹** /θro; θrəʊ/ *v past* **threw** /θru; θruː/ *past participle* **thrown** /θron; θrəʊn/

1 ▶THROW A BALL/STONE ETC 扔球/石头等◀ [I,T] to make an object such as a ball move quickly through the air by moving your hand quickly 投, 扔, 抛, 掷: **throw sth at/to/towards etc** *Someone threw a stone at the car.* 有人朝那辆汽车扔了一块石头。| *Cromartie throws the ball back to the pitcher.* 克罗马蒂把球又扔回给投手。| **throw sb sth** *Throw me that towel, would you.* 请把那块毛巾扔给我。

2 ▶PUT STH CARELESSLY 随意放置某物◀ [T always+adv/prep] to put something somewhere quickly and carelessly 随手扔下〔某物〕: **throw sth on/onto/down etc** *Don't just throw your clothes on the floor – pick them up!* 不要随手把衣服扔在地板上 —— 把它们捡起来!

3 ▶PUSH ROUGHLY/VIOLENTLY 粗鲁地/猛烈地推◀ [T always+adv/prep] to push someone or something roughly and violently in a particular direction or into a particular position 〔粗鲁和猛烈地〕把…推向, 抛向: **throw sth ↔ open** *Smelling smoke, she threw open all the windows.* 她闻到烟的味道, 便用力推开所有的窗户。| **throw sb into the air** *Patrick was thrown into the air by the force of the explosion.* 爆炸的威力把帕特里克抛到了空中。| **throw sb to the ground** *The guards threw Biko to the ground and started kicking him.* 卫兵们猛力地把比科推倒在地, 开始用脚踢他。

4 ▶MAKE SB FALL 使某人倒下◀ [T] **a)** to make your opponent fall to the ground in WRESTLING or JUDO 〔摔跤或柔道比赛中〕把〔对手〕摔倒在地 **b)** if a horse throws its rider it makes them fall onto the ground 〔马〕把〔骑手〕抛落在地

5 throw yourself at/on/into/down etc to move or jump somewhere suddenly and with a lot of force 突然猛力地扑向/跳到/冲进/扑倒等: *I managed to open the door by throwing myself at it.* 我设法用身体撞开了门。

6 ▶MOVE HANDS/HEAD ETC 移动手/头等◀ [T always+ adv/prep] to suddenly and quickly move your hands, arms, head etc into a new position 急伸, 将〔手、臂、头等〕猛动: **throw sth back/up/around etc** *I threw my arms around her and kissed her.* 我猛地把她搂住并亲吻她。

7 throw sb into prison/jail to suddenly put someone in prison 把某人投进监狱: *Anyone who opposes the regime is liable to be thrown in jail.* 任何反对该政权的人都有可能被投进监狱。

8 throw sb out of work/office etc to suddenly take away someone's job or position in authority 突然把某人解雇/解职等: *Nixon was thrown out of office, following the Watergate scandal.* 在水门丑闻后, 尼克松被迫辞去职务。

9 throw sb into confusion/chaos/disarray etc to suddenly make a group of people very confused and uncertain about what they should do 突然使〔人们〕陷入困惑/混乱等中: *Everyone was thrown into confusion by this news.* 这一消息突然使大家茫然不解。

10 ▶CONFUSE SB 使某人困惑◀ [T] to confuse or shock someone, especially by suddenly saying something 〔尤指突然说出的话〕使人困惑; 使人震惊: **throw sb completely** *This handsome young stranger said "Hello, Maria," – it threw me completely.* 这位年轻英俊的陌生人说: "你好, 玛丽亚。" —— 这话让我完全怔住了。

11 be thrown back on to be forced to have to depend on your own skills, knowledge etc 被迫依靠〔自己的技能、知识等〕: *Once again we were thrown back on our own resources.* 我们再一次被迫依靠自己的力量解决困难。

12 throw suspicion/doubt on to make people think that someone is probably guilty or that something may not be true 使人们对…产生怀疑: *new discoveries that throw doubt on some basic scientific assumptions* 使人们对一些基本科学假设产生怀疑的新发现

13 throw sb a look/glance/smile etc to quickly look at someone with a particular expression that shows how you are feeling 朝某人看了一下/扫了一眼/笑了一下等

14 throw a fit/scene/tantrum etc to react in a very angry way 大发一通脾气: *I can't tell my parents – they'd throw a fit!* 我不能告诉我爸妈 —— 他们会大发脾气的!

15 throw questions/a remark to ask a lot of questions or suddenly say something 不断地提问题/突然说出一句话: *They kept throwing awkward questions at me.* 他们不断地向我提出一些尴尬的问题。

16 throw a switch/handle/lever to make a large machine or piece of electrical equipment start or stop working by moving a SWITCH² (1) 推一下开关/把手/控制杆〔使大型机器或电器设备启动或停止〕

17 throw a party to organize a party and invite people 举办一次聚会

18 throw yourself into sth to start doing an activity eagerly and using a lot of time and effort 积极投入到某项事中去: *Since her husband died, she's thrown herself into her work.* 自从丈夫去世后, 她积极投身到工作之中。

19 throw dice/a six/a four etc to roll DICE or to get a particular number by rolling dice 掷骰子/掷了个六点/掷出四点等: *You have to throw a six to start.* 你必须掷一个六点才能开始。

20 throw money at *informal* to try to solve a problem by spending a lot of money but without really thinking about the problem【非正式】靠大量花钱〔以解决某个问题, 但没经过深思熟虑〕

21 throw good money after bad/throw money down the drain to waste money by spending it on something that has already failed 花冤枉钱/花的钱打水漂了

22 throw your weight around to use your position of authority to tell people what to do in an unreasonable way 耀武扬威,

作威作福: *He's the sort of insensitive bully who enjoys throwing his weight around.* 他是那种毫无同情心的恶霸，喜欢到处耀武扬威。

23 throw your weight behind to publicly support a plan, person etc and use your power to make sure they succeed 公开支持…; 作为…的后盾: *The party leadership is throwing its weight behind the campaign.* 党的领导层公开支持这项活动。

24 throw cold water on to say that a plan, suggestion etc is unlikely to succeed 给〔计划、建议等〕泼冷水

25 throw light on to make something easier to understand by providing new information〔提供新资料〕使…更易理解: *startling revelations that throw new light on Elvis, the man* 有助于重新认识埃尔维斯其人的惊人发现

26 throw a light/shadows/rays [T] to make light, shadows etc fall on a particular place 发出光亮/投射影子/发射光束: *The trees threw long, dark shadows across the cornfield.* 树林在玉米地里投下长长的黑影。

27 throw the book at *informal* to punish someone as severely as possible or charge them with as many offences as possible【非正式】尽量从严惩罚〔某人〕; 尽量从严指控〔某人〕所犯的罪行

28 throw caution to the wind(s) to ignore the risks and deliberately behave in a way that may cause trouble or problems 不顾一切风险; 故意冒险行事

29 ▶DELIBERATELY LOSE 故意输掉◀ [T] to deliberately lose a fight or sports game that you could have won 故意输掉〔搏斗或体育比赛〕

30 throw sth (back) in sb's face to be unkind to someone after they have been kind to you or helped you 以怨报德; 忘恩负义

31 throw a punch/a left/a right etc to try to hit someone with your hand in a fight 打〔某人〕一拳/一记左拳/一记右拳等

32 throw yourself at sb *informal* to try very hard to attract someone's attention because you want to have a sexual relationship with them【非正式】努力引起某人的注意〔因为想与其发生性关系〕

33 throw your hat into the ring to officially announce that you will compete or take part in something〔正式宣布〕参加角逐[参与某事]

34 throw the baby out with the bath water to get rid of good useful parts of a system, organization etc when you are changing it in order to try and make it better〔在改革某系统、机构等时〕把好东西连同糟粕一起扔弃

35 ▶POT 陶罐◀ [T] to make a clay object such as a bowl, using a POTTER'S WHEEL〔在陶轮上〕制作〔陶器〕, 把…拉成坯

36 throw your voice to use a special trick to make your voice seem to be coming from a different place from the place you are standing〔利用口技〕使嗓音让人听来似乎来自他处 —see also 另见 **be thrown in at the deep end** (DEEP[1] (16))

throw sth ↔ **away** *phr v* [T] **1** to get rid of something that you do not want or need 扔掉, 抛弃〔某物〕: *I shouldn't have thrown away the receipt.* 我不应该扔掉那张收据的。**2** to lose or waste something good that you have, for example a skill or an opportunity 浪费掉〔本领〕; 错过〔机会〕: *This could be the best chance you'll ever have. Don't throw it away!* 这或许是你能得到的最好机会。别白白地错过了!

throw in sth *phr v* [T] **1** [**throw** sth ↔ **in**] to add something to what you are selling, without increasing the price 免费添加, 额外奉送: *We paid $2,000 for the boat, with the trailer and spares thrown in.* 我们花了2000美元买那只船, 拖车和备用件是额外赠送的。**2** [**throw** sth ↔ **in**] if you throw in a remark, you say it suddenly without thinking carefully 随口说〔话〕 **3 throw in the sponge/towel** *informal* to admit that you have been defeated【非正式】认输, 承认失败

throw sb/sth ↔ **off** *phr v* [T] **1** [**throw** sth ↔ **off**] to take off a piece of clothing in a quick, careless way 匆匆脱下〔衣服〕: *He threw off his sweater.* 他匆匆脱掉毛衣。**2** [**throw** sth ↔ **off**] to get free from something that has been limiting your freedom 摆脱〔束缚〕: *In 1845 they finally threw off the yoke of foreign rule.* 1845年, 他们最终摆脱了外国统治的枷锁。**3** [**throw** sth ↔ **off**] if you throw off a slight illness such as a COLD[2] (2), you succeed in getting better 摆脱〔感冒等小病〕 **4** [**throw** sb/sth ↔ **off**] to escape from someone or something that is chasing you 甩掉, 摆脱掉〔追赶者〕: **throw sb off the scent** (=make someone who is following you unable to find where you have gone) 甩掉跟踪的尾巴; 摆脱跟踪者 *If we cross the stream it might throw them off the scent.* 我们如果跨过小溪, 有可能甩掉他们的追踪。**5** [**throw** sth ↔ **off**] to produce large amounts of heat, light, RADIATION etc 散发出, 放射出〔热、光、辐射等〕: *The engine was throwing off so much heat that the air above it shimmered with haze.* 发动机散发出太多的热量, 使它上面因雾蒙蒙而发亮。

throw sth ↔ **on** *phr v* [T] to put on a piece of clothing quickly and carelessly 匆匆穿上〔衣服〕

throw sth ↔ **open** *phr v* [T] **1** to allow people to go into a place that is usually kept private 对公众开放〔某地〕: *plans to throw the Palace open to the public* 把这座宫殿对公众开放的计划 **2** to allow anyone to take part in a competition or a discussion 使〔竞赛或讨论〕对公众开放

throw sb/sth ↔ **out** *phr v* [T] **1** [**throw** sth ↔ **out**] to get rid of something that you do not want or need, especially when you are tidying〔尤指打扫时〕扔掉, 抛弃〔不想要的东西〕: *We usually throw out all our old magazines.* 我们通常把所有的旧杂志全部扔掉。**2** [**throw** sb ↔ **out**] to make someone leave a place, school, or organization etc quickly, especially because they have been behaving badly or made you angry 撵走; 解雇〔某人〕: *Nick got thrown out of college in the second year for taking drugs.* 因为吸毒, 尼克在大学二年级时被开除了。| **throw sb out on the street** (=make someone leave their house immediately, even if they have nowhere else to live) 把某人赶出家门 **3** [**throw** sth ↔ **out**] if parliament or another official or political organization throws out a plan or suggestion, they refuse to accept it and make it legal, especially after voting〔议会或某个政治机构〕拒绝接受〔计划或提议〕: *The bill was thrown out by the Senate.* 该议案遭到参议院的拒绝。**4** [**throw** sth ↔ **out**] if something throws out smoke, heat, dust etc, it produces a lot of it and fills the air with it 散发出〔大量烟雾、热量、灰尘等〕: *huge trucks throwing out noxious fumes from their exhausts* 排气管中散发出大量有毒烟雾的大型卡车

throw sb **over** *phr v* [T] *old-fashioned* to end a romantic relationship with someone【过时】断绝与〔某人〕的恋爱关系

throw sb/sth **together** *phr v* [T] **1** [**throw** sth ↔ **together**] to make something such as a meal quickly and not very carefully 匆匆张罗出〔饭菜等〕: *There's lots of food in the fridge – I'm sure I can throw something together.* 冰箱里有许多食物——我有把握能很快地做出一点吃的东西来。**2** [**throw** sb ↔ **together**] if a situation throws people together, it makes them meet and know each other 使〔人们〕相遇相识; 使偶然相聚在一起

throw up *phr v* **1** [I,T] to bring food or drink up from your stomach out through your mouth because you are ill or drunk etc; VOMIT[1]〔因生病或醉酒等〕呕吐, 呕出: *Georgia was bent over the basin, throwing up.* 乔治娅趴在洗脸盆边呕吐。—see 见 SICK[1] (USAGE) **2** [T **throw** sth ↔ **up**] to produce new ideas, problems, or new people 产生〔新思想、新问题〕; 带来〔新人〕: *It wasn't a long meeting, but it did throw up some interesting suggestions.* 会议时间并不长, 却提出了一些有意思的建议。**3** [T **throw** sth ↔ **up**] if a vehicle, runner etc throws up dust, water etc, they make it rise into the air as they move along〔汽车、跑步者等经过时〕扬起〔灰尘等〕; 溅起〔水等〕 **4** [T **throw** sth ↔ **up**] *informal* to suddenly leave your job, your home etc【非正式】突然辞去〔工作〕; 抛弃〔家庭〕: *I can't just throw up everything and come and live with you.* 我不可能抛弃一切, 过来与你一同生活。

throw² *n* [C] **1** an act of throwing something such as a ball 投, 扔, 抛, 掷: *The throw went straight to Marinelli on first base.* 那一投径直朝第一垒的马里内利飞去。**2** the distance which something is thrown 投掷的距离: *a throw of over eighty metres* 投出八十多米的距离 **3** the result of throwing something in a game such as darts (DART[2] (1)) or DICE[1] (1) 投掷飞标/骰子等的结果 **4 £5/ £10/50p etc a throw** *BrE informal* £5, £10 etc each【英, 非正式】每个的价格是5英镑/10英镑/50便士等

throw·a·way /ˈθroə,we; ˈθrəʊəweɪ/ *adj* **1 throwaway remark/line/comment etc** a short remark etc that is said quickly and without careful thought 脱口而出的话/即兴的台词/信口开河的评论等: *a comedy act full of short throwaway lines* 充满简短即兴台词的喜剧节目 **2 throwaway cup/plate/razor etc** a cup, plate etc that has been produced cheaply so that it can be thrown away after it has been used; DISPOSABLE (1) 用后即扔的; 一次性使用的杯子/盘子/剃须刀等 **3 the throwaway society** used to show disapproval when talking about modern societies in which products are not made to last a long time 一次性物品充斥的社会〔表达对现代社会的不满〕

throw·back /ˈθro,bæk; ˈθrəʊbæk/ *n* [C usually singular 一般用单数] something that is similar to or is a result of something that happened in the past 复旧; 返祖现象: **be a throwback to** *This year's fashions are a throwback to the 1950s.* 今年的时装是20世纪50年代流行的款式东山再起。

throw-in /ˈ· ·/ *n* [C] the act of throwing the ball back onto the field in football, after it has gone over the line at the side of the

field〔足球踢出边线后的〕掷边线球 —see picture on page A23 参见 A23 页图

thru /θru; θruː/ *adj, adv AmE informal*【美，非正式】a short form of 缩略式= THROUGH—**thru** *prep*

thrum /θrʌm; θrʌm/ *v* **thrummed, thrumming** [I,T] to make a low sound like something beating or shaking 低沉地嗡嗡作响: *the deep thrumming of the engine* 发动机低沉的隆隆声

thrush /θrʌʃ; θrʌʃ/ *n* **1** [C] a brown bird with spots on its front 鸫 **2** [U] an infectious disease that affects the VAGINA or mouth 鹅口疮，真菌性口炎；真菌性阴道炎

thrust¹ /θrʌst; θrʌst/ *v past tense and past participle* **thrust** [T] **1** to push something somewhere with a sudden or violent movement 猛推，猛塞：**thrust sth into/back** *The man thrust a package into Jake's hand and ran away.* 那名男子把一包东西塞进杰克的手里，然后跑开了。**2 have sth thrust upon you** to be forced to accept something that you did not expect or want〔被迫〕接受不指望得到或不想要的东西；身不由己 **3** [I+at] to make a sudden movement forward with a sword or knife〔用剑或刀〕刺，戳

thrust sth ↔ **aside** *phr v* [T] to refuse to think about something 把〔某事〕抛在一边；拒绝考虑〔某事〕：*Our complaints were thrust aside and ignored.* 我们的投诉被抛在一边，无人理睬。

thrust² *n* **1** [C] a sudden strong movement that pushes forward 猛冲，猛刺；推进：*the quick thrust of his sword* 他那一剑的猛刺 **2 the thrust** the main meaning or most important part of what someone says or does〔说话或做事的〕要旨，中心点：*the main thrust of Clinton's healthcare reforms* 克林顿的医疗保健改革的要旨 **3** [U] *technical* the force of an engine that pushes something such as a plane forward【术语】〔发动机推进飞机等的〕推力，推进力

thru·way, throughway /ˈθruˌwe; ˈθruːweɪ/ *n* [C] *AmE* a wide road for fast traffic that you pay to use【美】〔路面宽阔的〕付费高速公路

thud¹ /θʌd; θʌd/ *n* [C] the low sound made by a heavy object hitting something else〔重物碰击其他东西时发出的〕砰然声，低沉声：*His head hit the wall with a dull thud.* 他的头碰在墙上，发出低沉的一声。

thud² *v* **thudded, thudding** [I] to hit or fall onto something with a low sound〔砰地一声〕碰击；掉落〔在某物上〕

thug /θʌg; θʌg/ *n* [C] a violent man 恶棍，暴徒：a *bunch of thugs* 一群暴徒—**thuggery** *n* [U]

thumb¹ /θʌm; θʌm/ *n* [C] **1** the part of your hand that is shaped like a thick short finger and helps you to hold things〔手的〕拇指：*a baby sucking its thumb* 吮吸拇指的婴儿 **2** the part of a GLOVE that fits over your thumb〔手套的〕拇指部分 **3 be all (fingers and) thumbs** *informal* to be unable to do things neatly and carefully with your hands【非正式】笨手笨脚：*Would you do up these buttons for me? I seem to be all thumbs today.* 帮我扣上这些纽扣好吗？今天我感觉笨手笨脚的。**4 give sth the thumbs up/down** *informal* to officially accept or reject a plan, suggestion etc【非正式】正式接受/拒绝〔计划、建议等〕：*The project had been given the thumbs up and we could now get started.* 这项工程已经获得批准，我们现在可以开始了。**5 be under sb's thumb** to be so strongly influenced by someone that they control you completely 完全在某人的控制下；在某人的巨大影响之下 —see also 另见 **stick out like a sore thumb** (STICK¹), **rule of thumb** (RULE¹ (9))

thumb² *v* **1 thumb a lift** *BrE informal*【英，非正式】**thumb a ride** *AmE informal*【美，非正式】to persuade a driver of a passing car to stop and take you somewhere, by putting your hand out with your thumb raised〔伸出手并竖起拇指向过路的车〕请求搭车 **2 thumb your nose at** to show that you do not respect rules, laws etc or you do not care what someone thinks of you 蔑视〔规则、法律等〕；不在乎〔别人对自己的看法〕：*a chance to thumb his nose at authority* 一次让他可以表现蔑视权威的机会

thumb through sth *phr v* [I,T] to look through a book, magazine etc quickly 匆匆翻阅，浏览〔图书、杂志等〕：*thumbing through the pages of a gardening catalogue* 浏览园艺用品目录

thumb in·dex /ˈ·ˌ··/ *n* [C] a series of U-shaped cuts in the edge of a large book, usually showing the letters of the alphabet, that help you find the part you want〔在一本厚书的边缘上通常标有字母的〕拇指索引，书边挖月索引

thumb·nail¹ /ˈθʌmˋnel; ˈθʌmneɪl/ *adj* **thumbnail sketch/description** a short description giving only the main facts about something 简略的描述

thumbnail² *n* [C] the nail on your thumb 拇指甲

thumb·screw /ˈθʌmˌskru; ˈθʌmskruː/ *n* [C] an instrument used in the past to punish or TORTURE² (1) people by crushing their thumbs 拇指夹〔旧时的一种刑具〕

thumb·tack /ˈθʌmˌtæk; ˈθʌmtæk/ *n* [C] *AmE* a short pin with a broad flat top used especially for fixing notices on walls【美】图钉，按钉；DRAWING PIN *BrE*【英】—see picture at 参见 PIN¹ 图

thump¹ /θʌmp; θʌmp/ *v* **1** [T] *informal* to hit someone very hard with your hand closed【非正式】捶打，重击：*If you don't shut up, I'm going to thump you!* 如果你不住嘴的话，我就要狠狠揍你！—see picture on page A20 参见 A20 页图 **2** [I always+adv/prep,T] to make a dull loud sound by beating or falling against a surface 发出重击声；嘭地作响：[+against/on/into] *the dog's tail thumping against the floor* 狗尾巴击打着地板的声音 **3** [I] if your heart thumps, it beats very quickly because you are frightened or excited〔心脏因恐惧或激动〕怦怦地跳

thump² *n* **1** [C] the dull sound that is made when something hits a surface 重击声；嘭的一声：*We heard a loud thump and then a scream from upstairs.* 我们听到楼上传来嘭的一声，然后是一声尖叫。**2 give sb a thump on the back/head etc** *especially BrE* to hit someone on the back, head etc【尤英】给某人的背上/头上等一记重击

thump·ing /ˈθʌmpɪŋ; ˈθʌmpɪŋ/ also 又作 **thumping great/big** *adj* [only before noun 仅用于名词前] *BrE informal* very big【英，非正式】非常大的，极大的：*Mulroney swept to power with a thumping majority.* 穆罗尼以压倒性的多数票当选执政。

thun·der¹ /ˈθʌndɚ; ˈθʌndə/ *n* **1** [U] the loud noise that you hear during a storm, usually after a flash of lightning 雷声：**clap of thunder** (=one sudden noise of thunder) 一声霹雳 **2** [singular] a loud, deep noise like thunder 雷鸣般的响声，轰隆声：*the thunder of gunfire* 炮火的轰鸣声 **3 a face like thunder** looking very angry 满面怒容 —see also 另见 BLOOD-AND-THUNDER, **steal sb's thunder** (STEAL¹ (7))

thunder² *v* **1 it thunders** if it thunders, there is a loud noise in the sky, usually after a flash of lightning 打雷 **2** [I always+adv/prep] to move in a way that makes a very loud noise 轰隆隆地移动：*The children came thundering downstairs.* 孩子们轰隆隆地走下楼梯。| [+against/onto] *The sea thundered against the rocks.* 海水轰然地撞击着礁石。**3** [T] to shout loudly and angrily 愤怒地大声叫嚷，怒吼

Thun·der·bird /ˈθʌndɚˌbɝd; ˈθʌndəbɜːd/ *trademark*【商标】**1** also 又作 **T-bird** *informal*【非正式】a type of car made by Ford and sold in the US. Thunderbirds became very popular with young people in the late 1950s because they were fast and fashionable cars with tail FINS. 雷鸟〔福特公司生产的一种汽车，在美国销售。20 世纪 50 年代末，雷鸟属高速、时髦的尾鳍车型，深受青年人喜爱〕**2** a type of strong pale wine 雷鸟〔一种淡色烈性酒〕

thun·der·bolt /ˈθʌndɚˌbolt; ˈθʌndəbəʊlt/ *n* [C] **1** a flash of LIGHTNING and a noise of thunder together, which hits something〔击中某东西的〕雷电 **2** a sudden event or piece of news that shocks you 晴天霹雳般的事件；令人震惊的消息 **3** an imaginary weapon of thunder and lightning, used by gods to punish people 霹雷〔神惩罚人所用的一种雷电武器〕

thun·der·clap /ˈθʌndɚˌklæp; ˈθʌndəklæp/ *n* [C] a single loud noise of thunder 雷声，雷鸣

thun·der·cloud /ˈθʌndɚˌklaud; ˈθʌndəklaʊd/ *n* [C] a large dark cloud that you see before or during a storm〔暴风雨来临之前或暴风雨期间所看到的〕雷雨云

Thun·der·er, The /ˈθʌndrɚ; ˈθʌndərə/ an informal name for the British newspaper *The Times*, used in the past 大雷神〔英国《泰晤士报》旧时的俗称〕

thun·der·ing /ˈθʌndərɪŋ; ˈθʌndərɪŋ/ *adj, adv BrE old-fashioned* very bad, severe etc【英，过时】非常坏的，严重的：*That's a thundering great lie!* 那是一个极大的谎言！

thun·der·ous /ˈθʌndərəs; ˈθʌndərəs/ *adj* extremely loud 响声极大的，雷鸣般的：*thunderous applause* 雷鸣般的掌声 —**thunderously** *adv*

thun·der·storm /ˈθʌndɚˌstɔrm; ˈθʌndəstɔːm/ *n* [C] a storm with thunder and lightning 雷暴

thun·der·struck /ˈθʌndɚˌstrʌk; ˈθʌndəstrʌk/ *adj* [not before noun 不用于名词前] extremely surprised or shocked 极其震惊的，吓得目瞪口呆的：*Jeff was staring at me thunderstruck. "You mean it's been stolen?" he gasped.* 杰夫目瞪口呆地看着我。"你的意思是说它被偷走了？"他喘息着说。

thun·der·y /ˈθʌndərɪ; ˈθʌndəri/ *adj* thundery weather is the type of weather that comes before a thunderstorm〔天气〕雷暴前的

Thur·ber /ˈθɝbɚ; ˈθɜːbə/, **James** (1894-1961) a US humorous writer and CARTOONIST (=someone who does humorous drawings), whose work often appeared in the magazine *The New*

Yorker 瑟伯〔(1894-1961)，美国幽默作家，漫画家。他的作品常被《纽约人》杂志刊载〕

Thurs·day /ˋθɝzdɪ; ˈθɜːzdi/ written abbreviation 缩写为 **Thur.** or **Thurs.** *n* [C,U] the day between Wednesday and Friday. In Britain, Thursday is considered the fourth day of the week, and in the US it is considered the fifth day of the week 星期四，周四: *We went to the theatre last Thursday.* 我们上周四去看戏了。| *I'll phone you on Thursday.* 我星期四给你打电话。| *Christmas Day is on a Thursday this year.* 今年的圣诞节是个星期四。| **Thursday morning/evening etc** *Shall we go to a film Thursday night?* 星期四晚上我们去看电影好吗？| **on Thursdays** (=each Thursday) 每个星期四，每周四 *I go to night school on Thursdays.* 我每个周四去上夜校。| **the Thursday** *BrE* (=the Thursday of the week being mentioned)【英】所提及的那个星期的周四 *Angela's arriving on the Thursday and leaving on the Sunday.* 安吉拉周四到达，周日离开。

1 **thus** /ðʌs; ðʌs/ *adv formal*【正式】**1** [sentence adverb 句子副词] as a result of something that you have just mentioned; HENCE 因此，因而，从而: *Most of the evidence was destroyed in the fire. Thus it would be almost impossible to prove him guilty.* 多数证据已毁于火灾，因而要证明他有罪，几乎是不可能的。**2** in this manner or way 以此种方式；如此，这样: *He sold his car and used the money thus obtained to fly to Rio.* 他卖掉自己的汽车，用所得的钱坐飞机去了里约热内卢。**3 thus far** until now 到此为止，迄今: *Her political career thus far had remained unblemished.* 她的政治生涯至今还没有一丝污点。

USAGE NOTE 用法说明: THUS

WORD CHOICE 词语辨析: **thus, so, therefore, consequently, for this reason, as a result**

Thus is a little old-fashioned and only used in very formal English. thus 有点过时，仅用于非常正式的文体。In court you might hear 在法庭里可能听见: *They had no offer of finance, and thus were unable to achieve completion* (=they did not get the money so they could not buy the house). 他们无法提供资金，因而未能完成交易。

In spoken English you usually use **so**. 口语中一般用 so: *I don't use the language much, so I tend to forget it* (NOT 不用 *thus*). 那门语言我用得不多，所以往往会遗忘。

In formal speech and writing **therefore** will usually be used or, especially at the beginning of a sentence, **consequently**, **for this reason**, or **as a result**. 在正式的口头语和书面语中，一般用 therefore, consequently, for that reason 或 as a result, 后三者在句子的开头尤其常用: *The country was beautiful. Consequently I decided to return the next year./ I therefore decided to return the next year.* 那个国家很美丽，因此我决定第二年再回到那儿。

thwack[1] /θwæk; θwæk/ *n* [C] a short loud sound like something hitting a hard surface 拍打(声)；重击(声)

thwack[2] *v* [T] to hit someone or something making a short loud sound 拍打；重击

thwart[1] /θwɔrt; θwɔːt/ *v* [T] *formal* to prevent someone from doing what they are trying to do【正式】阻挠，阻碍: *My plans were thwarted by the intervention of the police.* 我的计划因警察的干预而受到阻挠。| *thwarted ambition* 受挫的雄心

thwart[2] *n* [C] *technical* a seat fixed across a ROWING BOAT【术语】〔划艇的〕座板

thy /ðaɪ; ðaɪ/ *determiner old use* your【旧】你的: *We praise thy name, O Lord.* 主啊，我们赞美你的圣名。

thyme /taɪm; taɪm/ *n* [U] a plant used for giving food a special taste 百里香〔用作食物的调味品〕

thy·roid /ˋθaɪrɔɪd; ˈθaɪrɔɪd/ also 又作 **thyroid gland** /ˈ‥, ‥ˈ/ *n* [C] an organ in your neck that produces substances that affect the way you develop and behave 甲状腺

thy·self /ðaɪˋsɛlf; ðaɪˈself/ *pron old use* yourself【旧】你自己

ti /ti; tiː/ *n* [singular] the seventh note in a musical SCALE[1] (8) according to the SOL-FA system 全音阶的第七音

Ti·a Ma·ri·a /ˌtiə məˋriə; ˌtiːə məˈriːə/ *trademark* a type of LIQUEUR (=strong alcoholic drink) made in the Caribbean, which tastes of coffee and is usually drunk from a small glass after a meal【商标】添万利，蒂玛丽亚〔加勒比海地区出品的一种甜露酒，咖啡味儿，通常在餐后用小杯酌饮〕

Tianjin /tjɛnˋdʒɪn; tjenˈdʒɪn/ a large industrial city in China 天津〔中国一大型工业城市〕

ti·a·ra /taɪˋɛrə; tiˈɑːrə/ *n* [C] a piece of jewellery like a small CROWN[1] (1a), that a woman wears on her head on formal occasions〔妇女在正式场合佩戴的〕冕状宝石头饰: *a diamond tiara* 冕状钻石头饰

Tiber, the /ˋtaɪbɚ; ˈtaɪbə/ the third longest river in Italy, which flows from the Apennines south to Rome and the sea 台伯河〔意大利第三大河流，流经亚平宁山脉南侧，最终流向罗马和大海〕

Ti·bet /tɪˋbɛt; tɪˈbet/ an Autonomous Region in southwest China. Population: 2,616,300 (2000). Capital: Lhasa. Most of Tibet consists of high plains surrounded by very high mountains. 西藏〔中国西南地区一自治区。人口: 2,616,300 (2000)，首府: 拉萨。西藏大部分地区为高原，四周高山环绕〕 —**Tibetan** *n, adj*

tib·i·a /ˋtɪbɪə; ˈtɪbiə/ *n plural* **tibiae** /-bɪˌi; -bi-iː/ *or* **tibias** [C] *technical* a bone in the front of your leg【术语】胫骨 —see picture at 参见 SKELETON 图

tic /tɪk; tɪk/ *n* [C] a sudden, uncontrolled movement of a muscle in your face, usually because of a nervous illness〔一般因神经疾病造成面部肌肉的〕抽搐

tick[1] /tɪk; tɪk/ *n* **1** [C] a mark (✓) written next to an answer, something on a list etc, to show that it is correct or has been dealt with〔在答案旁边或名单上标明正确或已经处理的〕勾号〔✓〕; CHECK[2] (9) *AmE*【美】: *Put a tick in the box if you agree with this statement.* 如果你同意这种说法，就在方格内打一个勾号。**2** [C] a very small animal like an insect that lives under the skin of other animals and sucks their blood〔动物身上的〕蜱，壁虱 **3** [singular] the short repeated sound that a clock or watch makes every second〔钟表发出的〕滴答声 —see picture on page A19 参见 A19 页图 **4** [singular] *spoken especially BrE* a very short time【口，尤英】一瞬间，一刹那: **in a tick** (=soon) 立刻，马上 *I'll be with you in a tick.* 我马上就过来。**5 on tick** *informal old-fashioned* if you get something on tick, you arrange to take it now and pay later【非正式，过时】赊购，赊账

tick[2] *v* **1** [I] if a clock or watch ticks, it makes a short sound every second〔钟表〕发出滴答声 **2** [T] *BrE* to mark a test, list of questions etc with a tick, usually to show that something is correct【英】给〔试卷、问题等〕打勾号; CHECK[1] (5) *AmE*【美】: *Tick the box next to the statement that best describes you.* 在最符合你的那种说法旁边的方格内打上勾号。**3 what makes sb tick** *informal* the thoughts, desires, opinions etc that give someone their character or make them behave in a particular way【非正式】形成某人的性格或影响他的行为的思想[欲望、见解等]

tick away/by *phr v* **1** [I] if time ticks away or by, it passes, especially when you are waiting for something to happen〔尤指等待某事发生时〕时光在流逝，时间一点一点地过去: *We're going to have to make a decision – time's ticking away.* 我们必须马上作出决定——时间正在一分一秒地过去。**2** [T **tick** sth ↔ **away**] if a clock or watch ticks away the hours, minutes etc, it shows them as they pass〔钟表〕以滴答声表示〔小时、分钟等的〕流逝

tick sb/sth ↔ **off** *phr v* [T] **1** *BrE informal* to tell someone angrily that you are annoyed with them or disapprove of them【英，非正式】责备，怒斥〔某人〕: *The teacher ticked us off for talking in class.* 因为在课堂上说话，老师责备了我们。**2** *BrE* to mark the things on a list with a tick to show that they are finished or have been dealt with【英】给…打勾号〔表明…已经完成或已作处理〕: *She should have ticked off Miss Vine's name on her list.* 她本应把瓦因小姐的名字从名单上勾掉。**3** *AmE informal* to annoy someone【美，非正式】使生气，激怒

tick over *phr v* [I] *BrE*【英】**1** if a vehicle's engine ticks over, it works slowly without moving the vehicle〔汽车发动机〕空转，慢转 **2** if a system, business etc ticks over, it continues working but without producing very much or without much happening〔某一系统、公司等〕在慢吞吞地延续；进展缓慢；停滞: *The business is just about ticking over.* 公司的业务无大进展。

tick·er /ˋtɪkɚ; ˈtɪkə/ *n* [C] *informal* your heart【非正式】心脏

ticker tape /ˈ‥ ‥/ *n* **1** [U] long narrow paper on which information is printed by a special machine〔一种特别的机器打印信息时用的窄长条〕纸带 **2 ticker tape parade** *AmE* an occasion when someone important or famous arrives in an American city and pieces of paper are thrown from high buildings to welcome them【美】抛扔纸带的迎宾式〔当某要人或名人抵达某城市时人们从高楼上扔出纸片的欢迎仪式〕

tick·et[1] /ˋtɪkɪt; ˈtɪkɪt/ *n* [C] 1 2

1 ▶CINEMA/BUS/TRAIN ETC 电影院/公共汽车/火车等◀ a printed piece of paper which shows that you have paid to enter a cinema, travel on a bus, plane etc〔进电影院或乘坐公共汽车、飞机等的〕票；入场券: **theatre/train/airline ticket** *The plane ticket only cost $170.* 飞机票只花了 170 美元。—see also 另见 SEASON TICKET

2 ▶DRIVING OFFENCE 驾驶违章◀ a printed note ordering you to pay money because you have done something illegal while driving or parking your car〔驾车或停车时因违章而收到的〕罚款通知: *a parking ticket* 停车罚款通知

3 ▶IN SHOPS 在商店◀ a piece of paper fastened to something in a shop that shows its price, size etc〔商店里货物的〕标签; 价格标签

4 ▶ELECTION 选举◀ [singular] *especially AmE*【尤美】**a)** a list of the people supported by a particular political party in an election〔政党的〕候选人名单: *He withdrew his name from the Democratic ticket.* 他从民主党候选人名单中撤了出来。**b)** the ideas that a political party supports in an election〔政党在选举中支持的〕政见; 纲领: *He fought the election on an openly racist ticket.* 他以公开的种族主义观点参加选举。

5 **ticket to success/fame etc** *especially AmE* a way of getting success etc【尤美】成功/出名等的手段: *The part in the movie was his ticket to stardom.* 他在这部电影里扮演一个角色, 因而成为明星。

6 **be just the ticket** *old-fashioned* to be exactly what is needed【过时】正是所需要的东西 —see also 另见 MEAL TICKET, DREAM TICKET

ticket² *v* [T] **1** to fasten a small piece of paper onto something to show its price, size etc 加标签于; 标明〔价格、尺码等〕**2** *AmE* to give someone a ticket for parking their car in the wrong place【美】对〔某人〕发出停车违章通知单 **3 be ticketed for** to be intended for a particular use, purpose, job etc 被指定, 被指派〔为某种用途、目的、工作等〕: *These cars have been ticketed for sale abroad.* 这些汽车被指定销往国外。

ticket tout /ˈ· · ,·/ *n* [C] *BrE* someone who sells tickets outside a theatre or sports ground at a high price because there are not many available【英】倒票的人, 黄牛; SCALPER *AmE*【美】

tick·ing /ˋtɪkɪŋ; ˈtɪkɪŋ/ *n* [U] a thick strong cotton cloth used for making MATTRESS and PILLOW¹ (1) covers〔用于制作床垫套或枕套的〕结实型厚棉布

ticking off /, · · ˈ·/ *n* **give sb a ticking off** *BrE informal* to tell someone that you disapprove of something they have done【英, 非正式】斥责, 责备 —see also 另见 **tick off** (TICK²)

tick·le¹ /ˋtɪkl; ˈtɪkəl/ *v* **1** [T] to rub someone's body gently with your fingers in order to make them laugh〔用手指轻触某人的身体〕使觉得痒; 搔〔某人的〕痒痒 —see picture on page A20 参见 A20 页图 **2** [I,T] if something touching your body tickles you, it makes you want to rub your body because it is uncomfortable (使)发痒; (使)感到痒: *Mommy, this blanket tickles.* 妈妈, 这毛毯让人痒痒。**3** [T] if a situation, remark etc tickles you, it amuses or pleases you〔情况、讲话等〕使开心; 使高兴: *I was tickled by her description of the wedding.* 我听了她对婚礼的描述感到很开心。| **be tickled pink** (=be very pleased or amused) 非常开心, 觉得非常有趣 *She was tickled pink to see you in the paper!* 她非常高兴在报纸上看到你的大名! **4 tickle sb's fancy** *old-fashioned* if something tickles your fancy, it seems interesting and makes you want to do it【过时】勾起了某人的兴趣: *The idea of appearing in a film rather tickled his fancy.* 想到要在电影里出头露面, 这让他跃跃欲试。**5 tickle the ivories** *old-fashioned* to play the piano【过时】弹钢琴

tickle² *n* [singular] **1** a slight sore feeling which makes you want to cough or rub yourself; ITCH² (1) 痒, 发痒: *I've got a tickle in my throat that won't go away.* 我的嗓子发痒, 总好不了。**2 give sb a tickle** to rub someone lightly with your fingers in order to make them laugh 搔某人痒痒

tick·lish /ˋtɪklɪʃ; ˈtɪklɪʃ/ *adj* **1** someone who is ticklish is sensitive to tickling 对痒敏感的, 怕痒的 **2** *informal* a ticklish situation or problem must be dealt with very carefully, especially because you may offend or upset people【非正式】〔情况或问题〕需小心对付的, 棘手的: *You'll have the ticklish task of explaining to Rita why she hasn't been promoted.* 你得来处理这个棘手的问题, 向丽塔解释她为什么没有得到晋升。—**ticklishly** *adv* —**ticklishness** *n* [U]

tick-tack-toe /, · · ˈ·/ *n* [U] *AmE* a children's game in which two players draw X's or O's in a pattern of nine squares【美】画"连城"游戏〔一种由两人在九个方格内填写"×"或"○"的儿童游戏〕; NOUGHTS AND CROSSES *BrE*【英】

tick-tock /,tɪk ˋtɑk; ,tɪk ˈtɒk/ *n* [singular] the noise that a large clock makes when it ticks〔大钟发出的〕滴答声

ticky-tacky /,tɪkɪ ˋtækɪ; ,tɪki ˈtæki◂/ also 又作 **ticky-tack** /-ˋtæk; -ˈtæk/ *n* [U] *AmE informal* a material, especially for building, that is cheap and of low quality【美, 非正式】廉价劣质的材料〔尤指建筑材料〕—**ticky-tacky** *adj*

tid·al /ˋtaɪdl; ˈtaɪdl/ *adj* connected with the regular rising and falling of the sea 潮汐的, 潮水的: *a tidal pool* 潮潭

tidal wave /ˈ· · ,·/ *n* [C] **1** a very large ocean wave that flows over the land and destroys things 海啸 **2** a very large amount of a particular kind of feeling or activity happening at one time〔感情或活动的〕浪潮: *a tidal wave of public condemnation* 公众谴责的浪潮

tid·bit /ˋtɪd,bɪt; ˈtɪd,bɪt/ *n* [C] *AmE*【美】**1** a small piece of food that tastes good 少量的精美食品, 珍馐; TITBIT *BrE*【英】**2** a small piece of interesting information, news etc 花絮, 趣闻; TITBIT *BrE*【英】: *tidbits of gossip* 闲话趣闻

tid·dler /ˋtɪdlɚ; ˈtɪdlə/ *n* [C] *BrE informal* a very small fish【英, 非正式】很小的鱼

tid·dly, tiddley /ˋtɪdlɪ; ˈtɪdli/ *adj BrE informal*【英, 非正式】**1** slightly drunk 微醉的 **2** very small 很小的: *a tiddly little insect* 一只很小的昆虫

tid·dly·winks /ˋtɪdlɪ,wɪŋks; ˈtɪdliwɪŋks/ *n* [U] a children's game in which you try to make small round pieces of plastic jump into a cup by pressing one edge with a larger piece 弹塑料片游戏〔一种以大塑料圆片压小塑料圆片, 使其弹跳落入杯中的儿童游戏〕

tide¹ /taɪd; taɪd/ *n* **1** [C usually singular 一般用单数] the regular rising and lowering of the level of the sea 海潮, 潮汐: *driftwood on the beach, brought in by the tide* 被潮水带到沙滩上的漂木 | **the tide is in/out** (=the sea is at a high or low level) 潮涨/潮落 —see also 另见 HIGH TIDE, LOW TIDE **2** [C] a current of water caused by the tide 潮水: *Strong tides make swimming dangerous.* 大的潮水使游泳很危险。**3** [C usually singular 一般用单数] the way in which events, opinions etc are developing 潮流, 趋势: **the tide turns against** (=people's opinions change so that they no longer approve of someone or something)〔舆论〕趋势朝不利于…的方向转变 *The tide of public opinion seems to be turning against the President.* 公众舆论的趋势看来在朝不利于总统的方向转变。| **swim with/against the tide** (=support or oppose what most people think) 随大溜/反潮流 | **stem the tide** (=prevent something from developing and getting worse) 阻止…的进一步恶化 *efforts to stem the tide of hysteria caused by the shootings* 努力阻止枪杀引起的歇斯底里恶化 **4** [singular] a large number of people or things moving along together 潮水般的人流; 洪流: *the tide of refugees crossing the border* 跨越边界的难民潮 | **stem the tide** (=stop this movement) 阻止人流; 阻止潮流 **5 Christmastide/eveningtide/morningtide etc** *old use* a particular time of the year or day【旧】圣诞节期间/晚上时间/早晨时光等

tide²

tide sb **over** *phr v* [T] to help someone through a difficult period 帮助〔某人〕渡过难关: *I can give you enough money to tide you over until next month.* 我可以给你足够的钱让你坚持到下个月。

tide·mark /ˈ· ,·/ *n* [C] **1** a mark left on the shore by the sea, that shows how high the water was〔潮水在海岸上留下的最高〕潮痕 **2** *BrE informal* a dirty mark left around the inside of a bath that shows how high the water was【英, 非正式】〔浴缸里水位留下的〕垢痕

tide pool /ˈ· ,·/ *n* [C] *AmE* a small area of water left among rocks by the sea when the tide goes out【美】〔潮水退走后在礁石间留下的〕潮水潭; ROCK POOL *BrE*【英】

tide·wa·ter /ˋtaɪd,wɔtɚ; ˈtaɪd,wɔːtə/ *n* **1** [U] water that flows onto the land when the tide rises to a very high level〔大潮时涌上陆地的〕潮水 **2** [U] water in the parts of rivers that are affected by tides〔江河里的〕潮水 **3** [C] *AmE* an area of land at or near the sea coast【美】沿海陆地, 滨海地区

tide·way /ˋtaɪd,we; ˈtaɪdweɪ/ *n* [C] *AmE*【美】**1** a narrow area of water through which the tide flows〔潮水流经的〕潮路 **2** a strong current flowing through a tideway〔经潮路流过的〕强潮流

tid·ings /ˋtaɪdɪnz; ˈtaɪdɪŋz/ *n* [plural] *old use* news【旧】消息: **good/glad tidings** (=good news) 佳音, 喜讯

ti·dy¹ /ˋtaɪdɪ; ˈtaɪdi/ *adj especially BrE*【尤英】**1** a room, house, desk etc that is tidy is neatly arranged with everything in the right place〔房间、房子、书桌等〕整洁的, 整齐的: **neat and tidy** *Ellen's room always looks neat and tidy.* 埃伦的房间看上去总是干净整洁。**2** someone who is tidy keeps their house, clothes etc neat and clean〔人〕整洁的, 爱整齐的: *I've always been a naturally tidy person.* 我天生爱干净, 始终如此。**3 a tidy sum/profit** *informal* a large amount of money【非正式】一大笔钱/利润: *We sold the house for a tidy sum and moved south.* 我们把那座房子卖了一大笔钱, 然后移居到了南方。—**tidily** *adv* —**tidiness** *n* [U]

tidy² also 又作 **tidy up** *v* [I,T] *especially BrE* to make a place look tidy【尤英】使整洁, 整理, 收拾: *You're not allowed to go out until you tidy up your room.* 你在整理好房间之前, 不准出去。| **tidy up after** (=tidy a place after someone has made it untidy) 收拾被人弄得很脏乱的地方 *I'm tired of tidying up*

after you boys. 你们这些男孩子常常把这里弄得又脏又乱，我真懒得去收拾。

tidy sth **away** *phr v* [T] *BrE* to put something back in the place where it should be【英】收拾好放回原处: *Let's tidy these papers away.* 我们把这些文件收拾起来吧。

tidy³ *n* [C] **desk/car/sink tidy** *BrE* a container for putting small objects in, used to keep your desk, car etc tidy【英】桌子上/汽车里/洗涤槽旁边用来放零星杂物的容器

tie¹ /taɪ; taɪ/ *v*

1 ▶STRING/ROPE 线/绳索◀ a) [T] to fasten one thing to another with a piece of string, rope etc〔用线、绳索等〕系，扎，拴，捆: **tie sth to/behind/onto etc** *Tie this label onto your suitcase.* 把这个标签拴在衣箱上。| **tie sb to sth** *They tied him to a lamp-post and beat him up.* 他们把他捆在一根灯杆上，然后狠狠地揍他。| **tie sb's hands/feet** (=tie them together) 捆住某人的手/脚 **b)** also 又作 **tie up** [T] to fasten a piece of string, rope etc around something to keep it closed or keep all its parts together 把…捆起来[缚在一起]: **tie sth with sth** *The package had been tied with strong green string.* 那包东西是用结实的绿色绳子捆起来的。| [+around/over/under etc] *I'll just tie my hair back out of my eyes.* 我只需把头发系在后边，不挡住眼睛就行。| **tie sth in bunches/bundles etc** *tie the sticks up in bundles* 把那些棍子一束一束捆起来 | **tie your hair back** (=fasten your hair to the back of your head so that it does not reach your face) 把头发系在脑后 **c)** [T] to make a knot in a piece of string, rope etc, for example to fasten shoes or other clothes 把〔线、绳索等〕打结；系上: **tie sb's shoelaces** *Can you tie your shoelaces by yourself?* 你自己会系鞋带吗？| **tie a knot/bow** *She pulled the ribbon tightly and tied a bow.* 她把丝带拉紧，打了一个蝴蝶结。**d)** [I] to be fastened using pieces of string, RIBBON (1) etc 用带子、丝带等系牢: *The dress ties at the back.* 这件连衣裙是在背后系带的。

2 ▶GAME/COMPETITION 比赛/竞赛◀ also 又作 **be tied** [I] if two players, teams etc tie or are tied in a game or competition, they finish it with an equal number of points〔在比赛或竞赛中双方〕得分相同，打成平局: [+with] *At the end of the season, we were tied with the Tigers.* 在本赛季结束时，我们与老虎队得分相同。| **tie for first/second place** *Woosnam and Lyle tied for fourth place on 264.* 伍斯纳姆和莱尔并列第四，总杆数都是 264。

3 be tied to a) to be connected with something or dependent on it 联系在一起；依附于: *The flat is tied to the job.* 住房是与工作联系在一起的。**b)** to be unable to leave the situation, place, job etc that you are in 束缚，约束，限制: *a housewife tied to the kitchen all day* 整天被束缚在厨房里的家庭主妇

4 tie the knot *informal* to get married【非正式】结婚

5 tie yourself (up) in knots *BrE informal* to become very confused when you are trying to explain something【英，非正式】〔解释某事时〕自己给自己搞糊涂了，自己把自己难住了

6 sb's hands are tied if someone's hands are tied, they cannot do what they want because of particular conditions, rules etc〔因某种条件、规则等〕某人无法做想做的事: *Team manager, Ron Jones, would like to buy some new players, but his hands are tied at the moment.* 球队主教练罗恩·琼斯想买几名新球员，但眼下还不能随心所欲。

7 tie one on *AmE slang* to get drunk【美俚】喝醉

tie sb **down** *phr v* [T] **1** to stop someone from being free to do the things they want to do 束缚，牵制〔某人〕: *He wouldn't marry her because he didn't want to feel tied down.* 他不愿意娶她，因为他不想有被拴住的感觉。**2 tie yourself down (to sth)** to make a promise or agreement that restricts what you do 使自己受到〔许诺或协议的〕约束: *I'm happy to do the job, but I don't want to tie myself down to a particular date.* 我很乐意做这份工作，不过我不想给自己定下一个具体的日期。

tie in *phr v* [I +with] **1** if one idea or statement ties in with another one, it helps to prove the same thing 同…一致，与…相符: *Marsden's conclusions tie in with our theory perfectly.* 马斯登的结论与我们的理论完全相符。**2** to happen at the same time as something else 与…同时发生: *We've planned the broadcast to tie in with the bicentenary celebrations.* 我们已计划使这次广播与二百周年纪念活动同时进行。

tie up *phr v*

1 ▶PERSON 人◀ [T **tie** sb ↔ **up**] to tie someone's arms, legs etc so that they cannot move 把〔某人〕捆绑起来: *The intruders tied Kurt up and put him in the closet.* 非法入室者把库尔特捆绑起来，然后关进壁橱里。

2 ▶OBJECT 物体◀ [T **tie** sth ↔ **up**] to fasten something together by using string or rope 把〔某物〕捆绑起来

3 ▶BUSY 忙◀ be tied up to be so busy that you cannot do anything else 忙得脱不开身: *I can't see you tomorrow – I'm going to be tied up all day.* 我明天没法见你 — 我会一整天忙得脱不开身的。

4 ▶TRAFFIC 交通◀ be tied up *especially AmE* if traffic is tied up, it is blocked and cannot move freely【尤美】〔交通〕阻塞，动弹不得

5 ▶MONEY 钱◀ be tied up if your money is tied up in something, it is all being used for that thing and you cannot use it for anything else〔钱用于某项事情上而〕不能动用: [+in] *My money's all tied up in the house.* 我的钱全投在房子上而不能动用。

6 ▶ARRANGEMENTS 安排◀ [T **tie** sth ↔ **up**] to finish arranging all the details of something such as an agreement or a plan 订妥〔协议或计划〕；安排好〔细节〕: *We'd better tie up the details with a solicitor.* 我们最好让律师把这些细节安排好。

7 be tied up with to be very closely connected with something 与…有密切联系: *Christianity in Africa is tied up with its colonial past.* 非洲的基督教与非洲的殖民历史有密切的关系。

8 tie up loose ends to do the things that are necessary in order to finish a piece of work 做收尾的工作: *I just have to tie up a few loose ends before I go on vacation.* 我只要处理完几件收尾的工作就去度假。

9 ▶BOAT 船◀ [I] to tie a boat to something〔船〕系泊: *We tied up alongside a barge.* 我们把船系泊在一艘驳船旁边。

tie² *n* [C] 

1 ▶MEN'S CLOTHES 男式服装◀ a long narrow piece of cloth that you wear around your neck, tied in a special knot in front 领结，领带; —see also 另见 BLACK-TIE, BOW TIE

2 ▶CONNECTION/RELATIONSHIP 联系/关系◀ a relationship between two people, groups, or countries that connects them〔人与人、团体与团体、国家与国家之间的〕关系，联系: *close economic ties between the two countries* 那两个国家之间密切的经济联系

3 ▶FOR CLOSING STH 用来捆扎某物◀ a piece of string, wire etc used to fasten or close something such as a bag〔用来捆扎某物的〕绳子，带子

4 ▶RESULT 结果◀ [usually singular 一般用单数] the result of a game, competition, or election in which two or more people get the same number of points, votes etc〔比赛、竞赛或选举中〕分数相同；票数相同；平局，平手: **end in a tie** *The match ended in a tie.* 这场比赛以平局告终。

5 ▶GAME 体育比赛◀ *BrE* one game, especially of football, that is part of a larger competition【英】〔尤指足球赛中的〕较大型比赛中的一场: *the fourth round tie of the FA cup* 足总杯第四轮的比赛

6 ▶PREVENT YOU FROM DOING STH 阻止做某事◀ something that forces you to stay in one place, job etc or prevents you from being free to do what you want 束缚，羁绊；牵累，累赘: *If you're the sort of person who enjoys travelling, young children can be a tie.* 如果你是那种喜好旅游的人，小孩子可能是个累赘。

7 ▶RAILWAY 铁路◀ *AmE* a heavy piece of wood or metal supporting a railway track【美】轨枕，枕木; SLEEPER (4) *BrE*【英】

tie·break·er /ˈtaɪˌbrekɚ; ˈtaɪˌbreɪkə/ also 又作 **tie·break** /ˈtaɪbrek; ˈtaɪbreɪk/ *n* [C] **1** an additional question in a game or QUIZ, used to decide who will win when two people have the same number of points〔游戏或抢答赛的〕决胜题 **2** the final game of a set (SET² (5)) in tennis when each player has won six games〔网球比赛中各胜六局后的〕决胜局

tied cot·tage /ˌ. ˈ../ *n* [C] *BrE* a house that a farm worker rents from a farmer while he is working in that farm【英】〔农场工人受雇于农场期间从农场主那儿租住的〕契约屋，雇工农舍

tied house /ˌ. ˈ./ *n* [C] *BrE* a PUB that can only sell the beer made by a particular company【英】〔只出售某公司所产啤酒的〕特约经销酒馆

tie-dye /ˈ. ./ *v* [T] to tie string around parts of a piece of material and colour it with DYE (=coloured liquid) in order to make a special pattern 扎染〔把布料捆扎后再用染料染色以形成特别的图案〕—see picture on page A16 参见 A16 页图

tie-in /ˈ. ./ *n* [C] a product such as a record, book, or toy that is connected with a new film, TV show etc 关联性产品〔指与一部新电影、电视剧等有关的唱片、图书或玩具〕

tie-pin /ˈ. ./ *n* [C] a thing used for keeping a man's TIE² (1) fastened to his shirt or as a decoration 领带别针

Tiepolo /tiˈɛpəlo; tɪˈepələʊ/, **Giovanni Battista** /dʒɔˈvɑnni bɑtˈtistɑ; dʒɔːˈvɑːnniː bɑːtˈtiːstɑː/ (1696-1770) an Italian artist in the Rococo period who is famous for his FRESCOes 提埃坡罗〔(1696-1770)，意大利洛可可时期的艺术家，以湿壁画著名〕

tier /tɪr; tɪə/ *n* [C] **1** one of several rows of seats that rise one behind another〔阶梯式座位的〕一排，一列 **2** one of several levels in an organization or system〔机构或系统的〕层次；等级：*The company has three tiers of management.* 该公司有三个管理层次。**3 two-tiered/three-tiered etc** having two, three etc layers 有两层的/有三层的等：*a three-tiered wedding cake* 三层的婚礼蛋糕

Ti·er·ra del Fue·go /tɪˌɛrə dɛl ˈfwego; tiˌerə del ˈfweɪgəʊ/ a group of islands off the south coast of South America, owned by Chile and Argentina 火地岛区〔与南美洲南海岸隔海相望的一群岛，分属智利和阿根廷〕

tie-up /ˈ· ·/ *n* [C] *informal*【非正式】**1** an agreement to become business partners〔公司的〕联营；联合：[**+with**] *IBM's tie-up with Auspex System Inc* IBM与Auspex系统合伙公司的联营 **2** *BrE* a close connection between two or more things, especially when one causes the other【英】〔因果〕关系，联系：[**+between**] *the tie-up between class interests and politics* 阶级利益与政治之间的关系 **3** *AmE* a situation in which traffic is prevented from moving or there is a problem which prevents a system or plan from working【美】〔交通的〕阻塞；〔系统或计划的〕停顿，停滞不前 —see also 另见 **tie up** (TIE[1])

tiff /tɪf; tɪf/ *n* [C] a slight argument between two people who are in love〔情侣之间的〕口角，吵嘴：*Dave's had a tiff with his girlfriend.* 戴夫同女友吵了嘴。

Tif·fa·ny glass /ˈtɪfənɪ glæs; ˈtɪfəni glɑːs/ a type of coloured glass which was originally produced in the early 1900s, and used for making LAMPSHADES, VASES, and other decorations 蒂芬尼玻璃〔一种彩色玻璃，20世纪初开始生产，用于制作灯罩、花瓶等饰品〕

tif·fin /ˈtɪfɪn; ˈtɪfɪn/ *n* [U] *BrE old use or IndE* a light meal eaten in the morning or the middle of the day【英旧或印】上午的茶点小吃；午餐

ti·ger /ˈtaɪgɚ; ˈtaɪgə/ *n* [C] a large strong animal that has yellow and black lines on its body and is a member of the cat family 虎，老虎 —see also 另见 **paper tiger** (PAPER[2] (4))

tiger lil·y /ˈ·· ,·ˈ·/ *n* [C] a LILY (=flower) that has large orange flowers with black spots 卷丹(花)

tiger moth /ˈ·· ·/ *n* [C] a type of MOTH (=flying insect) with black stripes on its wings 灯蛾

S2 W3 **tight**[1] /taɪt; taɪt/ *adj*

1 ▶CLOTHES 衣服◀ fitting a part of your body very closely, especially in a way that is uncomfortable 紧身的，贴身的：*tight trousers* 紧身裤 | *My shoes were far too tight and I was in agony by the time I got home.* 我的鞋太夹脚，等我走回家时，已痛苦不堪了。| **be a tight fit** (=only just fits someone) 刚好合身 *The top is rather a tight fit.* 上面刚刚合身。—see also 另见 SKIN-TIGHT, TIGHT-FITTING

2 ▶PULLED/STRETCHED 拉/绷◀ string, wire, cloth etc that is tight has been pulled or stretched firmly so that it is straight or cannot move 拉紧的，绷紧的：**pull sth tight** *Pull the thread tight.* 把线拉紧。| *The bandage must be tight enough to stop the bleeding.* 绷带必须拉紧，才能止住流血。

3 ▶FIRMLY FIXED/FASTENED 固定/拴或系得很牢◀ something such as a screw or lid that is tight is firmly fixed and is difficult to move 紧的，牢的：*Check that the screws are tight.* 查看一下螺丝钉是否拧紧了。

4 a tight hold/grip a firm hold on something 紧紧抓住：*His mother kept a tight hold on his hand.* 他的母亲一直紧紧地抓住他的手。

5 ▶STRICT CONTROL 严格控制◀ controlled very strictly and firmly〔控制〕严格的，严密的：*Spending is kept within very tight limits.* 开销受到非常严格的限制。| *Security was very tight for the president's visit.* 为了总统的来访，保安工作做得非常严密。| **keep a tight rein on** (=control someone or something very strictly) 严格控制住〔某人或某物〕| **run a tight ship** (=manage a company, organization etc very effectively by having strict rules) 对〔公司、组织机构等〕严格管理

6 ▶MONEY 钱◀ *informal*【非正式】**a)** if money is tight, you do not have enough of it 手头紧的，手头拮据的：**money is tight/things are tight** *Money was tight and he needed a job badly.* 他手头很拮据，急需找到工作。**b)** someone who is tight is not generous and tries very hard to avoid spending money; MEAN[2] (2) 花钱小气的，吝啬的 —see also 另见 TIGHT-FISTED

7 ▶LITTLE TIME 少量时间◀ if time is tight, it is difficult for you to do everything you need to do in the time available〔时间〕紧的：**tight schedule/deadline** (=one that gives you very little time to do or finish something) 排得满满的日程表/紧张的期限 *a tight deadline* 紧张的期限 | *It'll be a bit tight, but we should just get there and back in time.* 时间是有点紧，但我们应该可以赶到那儿并及时地赶回来。

8 ▶LITTLE SPACE 少量空间◀ if space is tight, there is only just enough space to fit something into a place 填满的，塞满的，挤满的：**a tight squeeze/fit** (=a situation where there is only just enough space for things or people to fit) 挤得满满的/贴得紧紧的状况 *It was a tight squeeze, but somehow we all got into the car.* 已经挤得满满的，但无论怎样我们还是全都挤进车里了。

9 ▶CLOSE TOGETHER 紧密地在一起◀ placed or standing very close together 紧密的，紧紧的：*She wore her hair in a tight bun.* 她把头发紧紧地盘成一个髻。

10 ▶CLOSE RELATIONSHIP 亲密关系◀ a tight group of people, countries etc have a close relationship with each other and are closely connected with each other〔人与人、国家与国家等之间〕关系密切的

11 ▶CHEST/STOMACH ETC 胸/胃等◀ feeling painful or uncomfortable, because you are ill or worried 憋闷的；不适的：*He had been complaining of a tight chest and sore throat.* 他当时一直在抱怨胸口闷、嗓子疼。

12 ▶SMILE/EXPRESSION/VOICE ETC 笑容/表情/声音等◀ showing that you are annoyed, or upset 显得生气的；不高兴的：*Her mother gave a tight, forced smile.* 她的母亲很不自然地勉强笑了一下。—see also 另见 TIGHT-LIPPED

13 ▶BEND/TURN 转弯/转向◀ very curved so that it turns very quickly to another direction 转得很急的：*Careful now, there's a tight bend coming up.* 现在小心点，马上有个急转弯。

14 in a tight corner/spot *informal* in a difficult situation【非正式】处境困难的：*I'm always willing to help a friend in a tight spot.* 我总是愿意帮助处境困难的朋友。

15 ▶PLAY/PERFORMANCE 表演/演出◀ performed very exactly, with no unnecessary pauses 准确的；紧凑的，一气呵成的：*a tight, well-rehearsed production* 经过充分排练、一气呵成的演出

16 ▶GAME/COMPETITION 比赛/竞赛◀ a tight game, competition etc is one in which the teams, competitors etc all play well and it is not easy to win 紧张激烈的；不相上下的，势均力敌的：*It was a tight match, with the winning goal scored in the final minute.* 那是一场难分难解的比赛，在最后一分钟才打进决定胜负的一球。

17 ▶DRUNK 醉的◀ [never before noun 从不用于名词前] *old-fashioned informal* drunk【过时，非正式】喝醉的 —see also 另见 AIRTIGHT, WATERTIGHT —**tightly** *adv*: *Marie held the baby tightly in her arms.* 玛丽把婴儿紧紧地抱在怀中。—**tightness** *n* [U]

tight[2] *adv* very firmly or closely; tightly 紧紧地，牢牢地：**hold tight** *Hold tight to the safety rail.* 把安全杆抓紧。| **keep sth tight shut** *I kept my eyes tight shut and hoped they would go away.* 我紧闭双眼，希望他们会走开。—see also 另见 **sit tight** (SIT (5)), **sleep tight** (SLEEP[1] (4))

tight·en /ˈtaɪtn; ˈtaɪtn/ also 又作 **tighten up** *v* **1** [T] to close or fasten something firmly by turning it 使变紧；使更牢固：*Tighten up the screws.* 把螺丝拧紧。| *You'll need to tighten the lid on the jar.* 你得把罐子上的盖拧紧。**2** [I,T] if you tighten a rope, wire etc, or if it tightens, it is stretched or pulled so that it becomes tight 绷紧，拉紧(绳子、线等)：*When you tighten guitar strings the note gets higher.* 你把吉他的弦绷紧一点，音就会变高。**3** [I,T] to become stiff or make a part of your body become stiff (使)〔身体的某一部分〕变得僵硬，变得僵直：*I can feel my neck tightening up.* 我能感觉到自己的脖子正变得僵硬起来。**4** [T] to make a rule, law, or system more strict 使〔规则、法律或制度〕更严格；加紧，加强：**tighten up on** *measures aimed at tightening up on security* 旨在加强保安的措施 **5 tighten your hold/grip on** to hold someone or something more firmly 更紧地抓住〔某人或某物〕：*Sarah tightened her grip on my arm.* 萨拉更紧地抓住我的手臂。**6 tighten your belt** *informal* to try to spend less money than you used to【非正式】勒紧裤带；设法更节俭地过日子：*When Maureen lost her job, we had to tighten our belts.* 莫琳失业之后，我们不得不勒紧裤带过日子。

tight-fist·ed /ˌtaɪt ˈfɪstɪd; ˌtaɪt ˈfɪstɪd◂/ *adj informal* not generous with money; STINGY【非正式】〔花钱〕非常小气的，吝啬的 —**tight-fistedness** *n* [U]

tight-fit·ting /ˌ· ˈ··◂/ *adj* fitting very closely or tightly〔衣服〕紧身的；贴身的；〔盖子〕严密的，严实的：*a tight-fitting skirt* 一条紧身的女裙 | *saucepan with a tight-fitting lid* 盖子严实的深平底锅

tight-knit /ˌ· ˈ·◂/ *adj* [only before noun 仅用于名词前] **1** a tight-knit group of people are closely connected with each other 紧密团结的：*a tight-knit island community* 一个紧密团结的岛上社区 **2** *AmE* a tight-knit plan is very carefully arranged so that nothing can go wrong【美】〔计划〕周密的

tight-lipped /ˌtaɪt ˋlɪpt; ˌtaɪt ˈlɪpt◂/ *adj* **1** unwilling to talk about something 不愿说话的, 缄默的: *Diplomats are remaining tight-lipped about the negotiations.* 外交官们对谈判的情况仍然闭口不谈。**2** with your lips tightly pressed together because you are angry 〔因为生气〕紧闭双唇的

tightly-knit /ˌ· · ˈ·◂/ *adj* TIGHT-KNIT 紧密团结的; 计划周密的

tight·rope /ˈtaɪtˌrop; ˈtaɪt-rəʊp/ *n* [C] **1** a rope or wire high above the ground that someone walks along in a CIRCUS (1) 〔马戏团表演用的〕钢丝, 绷索 **2 walk a tightrope** to be in a difficult situation in which you must be careful about what you say or do 走钢丝〔比喻处境困难, 言行必须谨慎〕

3 **tights** /taɪts; taɪts/ *n* [plural] **1** *BrE* a piece of women's clothing that fits closely around your feet and legs and up to your waist, made of very thin material【英】女用连裤袜; PANTYHOSE *AmE*【美】—see picture on page A17 参见 A17 页图 **2** a similar piece of clothing that is coloured and cannot be seen through, worn especially by dancers 〔尤指舞蹈演员穿的〕紧身衣

tight·wad /ˈtaɪtˌwɑd; ˈtaɪtwɒd/ *n* [C] *informal especially AmE* someone who hates to spend or give money【非正式, 尤美】吝啬鬼, 守财奴: *My allowance is very small – Dad's a real tightwad.* 我的零用钱很少 — 爸爸真是个吝啬鬼。

ti·gress /ˈtaɪgrɪs; ˈtaɪgrɪ̈s/ *n* [C] a female tiger 母虎, 雌老虎

Ti·gris, the /ˈtaɪgrɪs; ˈtaɪgrɪ̈s/ a river in southwest Asia, flowing through Turkey and Iraq. The area between the Tigris and another river, the Euphrates, is called Mesopotamia, and several of the world's most ancient cities were built in this area. 底格里斯河〔亚洲西南部一河流, 流经土耳其和伊拉克。底格里斯河与幼发拉底河之间的地区称作美索不达米亚, 世界上最古老的几座城市曾建于该地区〕

tike /taɪk; taɪk/ *n* [C] another spelling of TYKE tyke 的另一种拼法

til, 'til /tɪl; tɪl/ a short form of 缩略式 = TILL¹

til·de /ˈtɪldə; ˈtɪldə/ *n* [C] a mark (˜) placed over the letter 'n' in Spanish to show that it is pronounced /nj/ 〔西班牙语中置于字母 n 之上的〕腭化音符号

3 **tile¹** /taɪl; taɪl/ *n* **1** [C] a flat square piece of baked clay or other material, used for covering roofs, floors etc 〔屋顶、地板等上面用的〕瓷砖, 地砖: *bathroom tiles* 浴室瓷砖 **2** [C] a thin curved piece of baked clay used for covering roofs 〔盖屋顶用的〕瓦, 瓦片 **3 go out on the tiles** *BrE informal* to go out drinking, dancing etc for enjoyment【英, 非正式】纵情玩乐, 花天酒地

tile² *v* [T] to cover a roof, floor etc with tiles 铺瓦于〔屋顶〕; 贴地砖于〔地面等〕—**tiled** *adj*: *a tiled floor* 铺了地砖的地面 —**tiler** *n* [C]

til·ing /ˈtaɪlɪŋ; ˈtaɪlɪŋ/ *n* [U] a set of tiles used to cover a roof, floor etc 〔一套〕瓦; 瓷砖; 地砖

 **till¹** /tɪl; tɪl/ *prep, conjunction especially spoken* until【尤口】直到: *I didn't learn to drive till I was thirty three.* 我直到 33 岁才学开车。| *The shop's open till nine o'clock most evenings.* 这家商店大多数晚上要营业到 9 点。

till² /tɪl; tɪl/ *n* [C] *BrE* a machine used in shops, restaurants etc for calculating the amount of you have to pay, and storing the money【英】〔商店、饭馆等的〕现金出纳机; REGISTER¹ (5) *AmE*【美】—see also 另见 **be caught with your fingers in the till** (FINGER¹ (8))

till³ *v* [T] *old use* to prepare land for growing crops【旧】耕〔地〕, 犁〔地〕

till·age /ˈtɪlɪdʒ; ˈtɪlɪdʒ/ *n* [U] *old use* the activity of preparing land for growing crops【旧】耕作, 耕地

til·ler /ˈtɪlɚ; ˈtɪlə/ *n* [C] a long handle fastened to the RUDDER (=part that controls the direction) of a boat 〔控制船舶方向的〕舵柄 —see picture at 参见 YACHT 图

tilt¹ /tɪlt; tɪlt/ *v* **1** [I,T] to move or make something move into a position where one side is higher than the other (使)倾斜, (使)翘起: *The table tilted suddenly, spilling all the drinks.* 桌子突然倾斜, 饮料全都洒了出来。**2** [T] to move your head or chin upwards or to the side 仰起〔头, 下巴〕; 使〔头, 下巴〕侧偏, 偏向: *Jodi tilted her head and looked thoughtful.* 乔迪仰起头, 一副若有所思的样子。**3** [T] to influence an opinion or situation so that people prefer one person, belief etc 使倾向于, 使偏向于: *This new evidence may tilt the balance of opinion in his favour.* 这一新的证据可能使舆论有利于他。

tilt at sb *phr v* [T] **1** to attack someone by what you say or write 抨击〔某人〕**2** *old use* to move quickly on a horse towards someone, in order to attack them with a LANCE【旧】骑马持矛冲向〔某人〕

tilt² *n* **1 at full tilt** as fast as possible 全速地: *We rode down the hill at full tilt.* 我们骑着马全速冲下山去。**2** [C,U] a movement or position in which one side of something is higher than the other 倾斜, 倾侧 **3** [C] a spoken or written attack on someone or something 〔口头或文字的〕抨击, 攻击

tim·ber /ˈtɪmbɚ; ˈtɪmbə/ *n* **1** [U] *especially BrE* wood used for building or making things, or the trees that produce this wood【尤英】木材, 原木; 〔可作木材的〕树木; LUMBER² (2) *AmE*【美】**2** [C] a wooden beam, especially one that forms part of the main structure of a house 〔尤指构成房屋主要结构的〕栋木, 大梁 **3 timber!** *spoken* used to warn people that a tree being cut down is about to fall【口】倒啦! 避开! 〔用来警告人们所伐树木快要倒下〕—see also 另见 HALF-TIMBERED 3

tim·ber·line /ˈtɪmbɚˌlaɪn; ˈtɪmbəlaɪn/ *n* [singular] *technical*【术语】**1** the height above the level of the sea beyond which trees will not grow 林木线〔指树木生长的海拔高度上限〕**2** the northern or southern limit in the world beyond which trees will not grow 树木生长线〔指南半球或北半球树木生长的纬度上限〕

tim·bre /ˈtɪmbɚ; ˈtæmbə/ *n* [C,U] the quality of the sound made by a particular instrument or voice 〔乐器或嗓音的〕音质, 音品, 音色

tim·brel /ˈtɪmbrəl; ˈtɪmbrəl/ *n* [C] *old use* a TAMBOURINE【旧】铃鼓

Tim·buk·tu /ˌtɪmbʌkˋtu; ˌtɪmbʌkˈtuː/ a city on the edge of the Sahara Desert in Mali, West Africa, whose correct name is **Tombouctou**. People sometimes mention Timbuktu as an example of a place that is very far away 廷巴克图〔非洲西部马里境内撒哈拉沙漠边缘一城市, 正确名称为 Tombouctou (通布图)。人们有时借用廷巴克图指称一个遥远的地方〕: *enough cars to stretch from here to Timbuktu* 汽车多得足以从这里排到廷巴克图

Time /· · ·, ·/ also 又作 **Time magazine** a US weekly news magazine which is sold in the US and is also available in many countries around the world《时代周刊》〔美国一新闻周刊, 在世界许多国家都可买到〕

1
1
time¹ /taɪm; taɪm/ *n*

① TIME 时间	⑨ GOOD TIME/BAD TIME ETC 好时光/坏时光等
② TIME SHOWN ON A CLOCK 时刻	⑩ PERIOD IN HISTORY 历史阶段
③ OCCASION 场合	⑪ TIME NEEDED TO DO STH 做某事所需的时间
④ HOW OFTEN 频度	⑫ AVAILABLE TIME 可利用的时间
⑤ TIME WHEN STH HAPPENS 某事发生的时间	⑬ SLOWLY/QUICKLY 慢/快
⑥ TIME WHEN STH SHOULD HAPPEN 某事应发生的时间	⑭ MODERN 现代
⑦ SUITABLE TIME 合适的时机	⑮ IN TIME 及时
⑧ PERIOD OF TIME 一段时间	⑯ HOW MANY 多少

⑰ COMPARISONS 比较
⑱ GRADUALLY/EVENTUALLY 逐渐/最终
⑲ MUSIC 音乐
⑳ LIKE/DISLIKE 喜欢/不喜欢
㉑ OTHER MEANINGS 其他意思

① TIME 时间

1 [U] something that is measured in minutes, hours, years etc using clocks 时间: *a machine that can travel through time* 可以穿越时间的机器 | *The basic unit of time, the second, was redefined in 1967.* 1967年，时间的基本单位——秒——被重新定义。| **time passes/goes by** *Time goes by so quickly these days.* 这些天时间过得真快。

② TIME SHOWN ON A CLOCK 时刻

2 [singular] a particular point in time shown on a clock in hours and minutes 时间，时刻〔指钟表上显示的具体时间〕: *What time is it?* 几点了？| **what time do you make it?** *BrE*【英】**/what time do you have?** *AmE*【美】(=used to ask someone with a watch what time it is) 你的表几点了？| **have you got the time?** *BrE*【英】**/do you have the time?** *AmE*【美】(=used to ask someone if they know what time it is) 你知道几点钟了吗？| **tell the time** *BrE*【英】**/tell time** *AmE*【美】(=be able to know what time it is by looking at a clock) 讲出钟表上的时间，识钟表: *He's ten years old and he still can't tell the time.* 他已经10岁了，但还不会看表。| **look at the time** *spoken* (=used when it is later than you thought it was)【口】看看已经几点了〔表示已经很晚了〕*Oh look at the time – we'd better get moving.* 哦，瞧已经几点了——我们最好动身吧。

3 keep good/perfect etc time if a clock or watch keeps good or perfect time, it works very well〔钟表〕走得很准

4 ►IN PART OF THE WORLD 世界某地◄ [U] the time in one particular part of the world, or the time used in one particular area〔某一特定地区的〕时间: *Eastern Standard Time* 东部标准时间 | *British Summer Time* 英国夏令时间 | **local time** *We will be arriving in New York at 3 am local time.* 我们将在当地时间凌晨3点抵达纽约。

③ OCCASION 场合

5 [C] an occasion when something happens or someone does something 次，回: **every/each time** *It was the only time I ever saw her lose her temper.* 那是唯一一次我看见她发脾气。| *Every time I meet her I always forget her name.* 每次见到她时，我总忘了她的名字。| **next time** *Give us a call next time you're in town.* 下次你进城时，给我们来个电话。| **this time** *I won't report you this time but don't do it again.* 我这次不告发你，但别再做这事了。| **the last time** *When was the last time you were ill?* 你最近一次生病是在什么时候？| **one time** (=once) 有一次 *I came home one time and found that someone had smashed all the windows.* 我有一次回家，发现有人把所有窗户都给砸碎了。

④ HOW OFTEN 频度

6 three/four/ten etc times used to say how often something happens 三次/四次/十次等: *I must have called you about five times.* 我差不多给你打过五次电话。| *How many times have you visited the US?* 你去过美国多少次？| *We visit him two or three times a month.* 我们每个月去看他两三次。

7 nine times out of ten/99 times out of 100 used to say that something is almost always true or almost always happens 十之八九: *Nine times out of ten she's right.* 她十之八九是对的。

8 all the time continuously or very often 一直，始终；十分经常: *It's a really useful book – I use it all the time.* 这真是一本很有用的书，我总在用它。

9 most of the time very often or almost always 大多数时候: *Most of the time they seem to just sit around watching TV.* 大多数时候他们似乎只是闲坐着看电视。

10 the whole time if something happens the whole time, especially something annoying, it happens continuously 老是，总是〔尤指恼人的事〕: *The baby was crying the whole time.* 那婴儿老是哭个不停。

11 time after time/time and time again happening often over a long period, especially in a way that is annoying 反复多次；一而再，再而三: *I've told her time after time not to bring that dog in here.* 我已反复多次告诉她不要把那条狗带到这里来。

12 at times sometimes but not usually 有时，偶尔: *At times I wonder if it's worth all the effort.* 有时候我会想，这一切努力是否值得。

13 from time to time sometimes, but not regularly or very often 偶尔，有时: *I still see her from time to time.* 我偶尔还是会去见她。

14 half the time *especially spoken* if something happens half the time, especially something annoying, it happens quite often【尤口】经常〔尤指恼人的事〕: *Half the time they don't even bother to answer my letters.* 他们经常甚至不愿给我回信。

15 at no time used to say strongly that something never happened or should never happen 在任何时候都不(应该)，从来没有: **at no time do/did etc** *At no time did I tell you that you could use my car.* 我从没告诉过你，说你可以用我的车。

16 at all times used especially in official notices or announcements to say what always happens or should always happen (应该)随时，总是〔尤用于正式告示或通知〕: *Identification badges must be worn at all times.* 表示身份的徽章必须随时佩戴。

⑤ TIME WHEN STH HAPPENS 某事发生的时间

17 [C,U] the particular minute, hour, day etc when something happens or someone does something〔某事发生或某人做某事的〕具体时刻: *What time did you get to bed?* 你是几点上床的？| *Her note didn't give the time of the meeting.* 她的通知没有给出会议的具体时间。| *We both left college at around the same time.* 我们两人是差不多同时离开大学的。| **by the time** *By the time you get this letter I'll be in Canada.* 等你拿到这封信的时候，我已经在加拿大了。| **opening/closing time** (=the time when a shop, bar etc opens)〔商店、酒吧等的〕开门/关门时间 | **arrival/departure time** (=the time when a train, plane etc leaves)〔火车、飞机等的〕到达/出发时间: *Departure times for all flights to Spain are subject to delay.* 所有飞往西班牙的航班离港时间都可能推迟。| **lunch/dinner/break etc time** (=the time when you usually have lunch etc) 午饭/晚餐/中间休息等时间 | **at any one time** (=at any particular time) 在任何时候，随时 *There are always at least two nurses on duty at any one time.* 任何时候至少有两名护士在值班。| **this time tomorrow/last week etc** *This time tomorrow I'll be getting on a plane to Dallas.* 明天这个时候我将登上飞往达拉斯的飞机。

⑥ TIME WHEN STH SHOULD HAPPEN 某事应发生的时间

18 [singular] the time when you should do something, when something should happen, or when something is expected to happen〔应该做某事或某事应该发生的〕时间，时候: **it's time to do sth** *Come on kids, it's time to go home.* 来吧，孩子们，该回家了。| **it's time sb did sth/was doing sth** (=used when saying that someone should do something soon) 某人不久该做某事: *It's time we had a party.* 我们该举行一次聚会了。| **it's time for** *The voters felt it was time for a change.* 选民们认为到了该有改变的时候了。

19 it's about time *especially spoken* used to say strongly that you think something should happen soon or should already have happened【尤口】到了该做某事的时候: *It's about time he got himself a proper job.* 他该给自己找一份合适的工作。

20 and about time too/not before time *spoken* used when you are annoyed because someone arrives late or something happens later than you expected or than was arranged【口】早就到时间了/已经晚了: *"Here's Helen!" "And about time too – where has she been?"* "海伦来了！""她早该到了——她上哪儿去了？"

21 on time arriving or happening at the correct time or the time that was arranged 准时，按时: *These buses are never on time.* 这些公共汽车从来就不准时。| **right/bang/dead on time** (=at exactly the right time) 准时，一分不差地: *Our train arrived bang on time.* 我们的火车一分不差地准时到达。

22 ahead of/behind time earlier or later than the time when a piece of work should be finished, someone should arrive somewhere etc〔某项工作完成或某人到达的〕时间提前/晚了: *The dam was completed two years ahead of time.* 水坝提前两年竣工。

23 call time *BrE* to tell the customers in a PUB that it is time to stop drinking【英】到点了〔酒馆告诉顾客到打烊的时间了〕

⑦ **SUITABLE TIME** 合适的时机

24 [C,U] a suitable or convenient time for something to happen or someone to do something〔合适的或方便的〕时间: **good/bad time** (=a convenient or inconvenient time) 合适的/不合适的时间: *I'm afraid you've caught me at a bad time – Can you call back later?* 你在这个时候找我恐怕不合适, 能不能稍后再打来? | **not be the time/be hardly the time** *This is hardly the time to ask him for a loan.* 这不是向他借贷的时机。| **come at the right/wrong time** *The pay rise came at just the right time.* 加薪来得正是时候。

25 there's no time like the present *especially spoken* used to say that now is a good time to do something【尤口】再没有比现在更好的时机: *If you're thinking of buying a house, there's no time like the present.* 你如果想买房子, 再没有比现在更好的时机了。

26 the time is ripe (for) used to say that the conditions are suitable now for something to happen〔某事发生的〕时机[条件]已经成熟: *The time is ripe for a peace settlement.* 达成和平协议的时机已经成熟。

27 when the time comes when something that you expect to happen actually happens, or when something becomes necessary 当预期发生的事确实发生了; 必要时: *I'm sure she'll make the right choice when the time comes.* 我敢肯定, 必要时她会作出正确的选择。

⑧ **PERIOD OF TIME** 一段时间

28 [singular] a period of time during which something happens or someone does something 一段时间; 某段日子: *I enjoyed my time as a student.* (=the period when I was a student) 我在学生时代日子过得挺快活的。| **for a long time/for some time etc** *The cheering went on for quite some time.* 欢呼声持续了好一阵子。| **a long time ago/some time ago** *All this happened a very long time ago, before you were born.* 这一切都发生在很久以前, 你那时还没有出生。| **time of year/day etc** *It should be pretty out there at this time of the year.* 在一年中的这个时候, 那里的景色应该是不错的。

29 at the time at a particular moment or period in the past, especially when the situation is very different now 当时: *It seemed like a good idea at the time.* 在当时, 这似乎是一个好主意。| *I was living in Phoenix at the time.* 我当时住在菲尼克斯。

30 at one time at some time in the past but not now 曾经有一个时期, 一度: *This used to be a very pretty valley at one time.* 这里曾经是一处非常美丽的山谷。

31 at this time *AmE* at this particular moment【美】此时此刻: *I don't really want to start up any new relationships at this time.* 我真的不想在这个时候开始有什么新的恋爱关系。

32 for the time being for a short period of time from now, but not permanently 眼下, 暂时: *You can stay in the spare room for the time being.* 你可以暂时住在那间空房间里。

33 for a time for a fairly short time, until something happens to change the situation 有一段较短的时间: *For a time we all lived together peacefully. Then the trouble started.* 曾经有一段时间, 我们大家和睦地住在一起。然后, 麻烦开始来了。| *Peter lived in Italy for a time.* 彼得曾在意大利住过一段时间。

34 for some time for a fairly long time 好长一段时间, 较长时间: *I hadn't seen my family for some time.* 我已有好长一段时间没见到家人了。

35 for hours/months etc at a time for a period that continues for several hours, months etc 连续几个小时/几个月等: *Alex is happy to read for hours at a time.* 亚历克斯连续读几个小时的书, 乐在其中。

36 for any length of time for more than just a short time 稍长一段时间: *He seemed unable to keep the same job for any length of time.* 他好像不能将同一份工作干得稍微长久一点。

37 from time out of mind *literary* for a very long time【文】很长时间, 很久

⑨ **GOOD TIME/BAD TIME ETC** 好时光/坏时光等

38 [C] a good time, bad time, difficult time, etc is a period or part of your life when you have good, bad, difficult etc experiences〔好的、倒霉的、艰难的〕时光, 时日, 岁月: *This was the happiest time of her life.* 这是她一生中最幸福的时光。| **have a good/great/fantastic time** (=enjoy yourself a lot) 玩得很高兴/高兴极了/特别高兴: *Thanks for the meal – we both had a really good time.* 谢谢这顿美餐——我俩真的玩得很开心。| **good/bad/hard etc times** *It's best to forget the bad times and just remember the good ones.* 最好忘掉不愉快的岁月, 只记住美好的日子。

⑩ **PERIOD IN HISTORY** 历史阶段

39 [C] also 又作 **times** [plural] — a particular period in history〔历史上的〕时代, 时期: **Roman/Greek/ancient etc times** *a tradition that goes back to Medieval times* 可以追溯到中世纪的一种传统 | *The film takes us back to the time of the American War of Independence.* 这部电影把我们带回到了美国独立战争时期。| **our time(s)** (=the present period in history) 我们的时代 *peace in our time* 我们这个时代的和平

⑪ **TIME NEEDED TO DO STH** 做某事所需的时间

40 [C,U] the amount of time that it takes you to do something〔做某事需要花费的〕时间: *How much time will it take you to finish your essay?* 你完成这篇文章需要花多少时间? | **journey time/travel time** *The Channel Tunnel has cut the journey time from London to Paris by as much as 3 hours.* 英吉利海峡隧道使伦敦到巴黎的旅行时间减少了三个小时。

41 take time if doing something takes time, it needs a long period of time 需要时间, 花费时间: *Learning a language isn't easy – it takes time.* 学一门语言不容易——这需要时间。

42 ►IN A RACE 比赛中◄ [C] the amount of time taken by a runner, swimmer etc in a race〔赛跑、游泳等比赛中花费的〕时间: *the fastest time in the world this year over 400 metres* 今年世界上400米跑的最快时间

43 have (the) time to have enough time to do something 有足够时间〔做某事〕: [+for] *Do you have time for a coffee?* 你有时间喝杯咖啡吗? | **have time to do sth** *I don't have time to talk to you right now.* 我现在没有时间同你谈话。| *She hung up before I had time to say sorry.* 我还没来得及道歉, 她就挂断了电话。

44 make/find time to arrange your plans so that you have enough time to do something 抽出/找出时间: *You should try and make time to see a doctor.* 你应该尽量抽出时间去看医生。

45 there is time there is enough time for someone to do something 有足够时间〔做某事〕: *We thought we'd do some shopping after lunch, if there's time.* 我们想, 如果有时间的话, 午饭后去买点东西。| **there is time (for sb) to do sth** *We had to leave at once – there wasn't even time to pack.* 我们当时必须马上动身, 甚至连打点行李的时间都没有。

⑫ **AVAILABLE TIME** 可利用的时间

46 [U] the amount of time that is available for you to do something〔可以利用的〕时间: *You'd better hurry up – we don't have much time.* 你最好快点儿, 我们没有多少时间了。| *Time is running out in the hostage crisis.* 解决这次人质危机的时间不多了。| **sb's time** (=the time they have available) 某人可以利用的时间 *I seem to spend most of my time on the phone.* 我好像把大多数时间都花在打电话上了。| **precious time** (=time that is valuable because there is not much available) 宝贵的时间 *Hurry up – we're wasting precious time.* 快一点儿, 我们在浪费宝贵的时间。

47 have all the time in the world used to say that you have as much time as you want in which to do something 要多少时间就有多少时间, 有的是时间

48 time's up *spoken* used in competitions and examinations to tell people that there is no more time left【口】时间到, 没有时间了〔用于竞赛和考试中〕

49 be out of time an expression used on television and radio programmes when saying that there is no more time left〔电视和电台节目中说的〕时间到了, 〔节目〕要结束了: *Sorry, we're out of time – I'll have to stop you there.* 对不起, 时间到了, 我们不得不就此打住。

⑬ **SLOWLY/QUICKLY** 慢/快

50 take your time a) to do something slowly or carefully without hurrying 不用急; 慢慢来: *There's no need to rush back – just take your time.* 不用急着赶回来, 慢慢来吧。**b)** to do something more slowly than seems reasonable 慢吞吞, 拖拉: *The builders are certainly taking their time with our roof!* 这些建筑工人在建屋顶时肯定在磨洋工!

51 in no time at all/in next to no time very quickly or soon, especially in a way that is surprising 立刻, 马上〔尤指快得令人吃惊〕: *Jed got the car fixed in no time at all.* 杰德马上就把那辆车修理好了。

52 make good time if you make good time on a journey, you travel quickly, especially more quickly than you expected〔旅途中〕快速行进〔尤指比预期的要快〕: *There wasn't much traffic, so we made good time.* 交通流量不大, 所以我们一路快速行进。

53 there's no time to lose used to say that you must do something quickly because there is very little time 没有可以损失的时间; 必须抓紧时间

54 with time to spare sooner than expected or necessary 还有剩余的时间〔指比预期的要快〕: *There was very little traffic, and we got to the airport with time to spare.* 路上没有多少车辆, 因此我们去到机场后还有富余时间。

55 time is of the essence *formal* used to say that it is important that something is done quickly【正式】时间是关键; 时间上得赶快

56 time is money used to say that wasting time or delaying something costs money 时间就是金钱, 一寸光阴一寸金

⑭ MODERN 现代

57 ahead of your time someone who is ahead of their time uses the newest ideas and methods, which are later used by many other people 走在时代的前面; 〔思想或方法〕超前, 创新: *Matisse was well ahead of his time in his use of colour.* 马蒂斯在运用色彩方面大大超前于他那个时代。

58 ahead of its time a machine, system etc that is ahead of its time has a very modern and advanced design〔机器、制度等〕很现代化, 很先进; 超前: **way ahead of its time** (=a long way ahead of its time) 大大领先于同时代 *The car, which featured a turbo-charged engine and disc-brakes, was way ahead of its time.* 这种车配备了涡轮增压发动机和盘式制动器, 在当时遥遥领先于它那个时代。

⑮ IN TIME 及时

59 in 10 days/five years/a few minutes' etc time ten days, five years etc from now 十天/五年/几分钟等后: *Don't worry, we'll be at the hospital in a couple of minutes' time.* 不要担心, 我们几分钟后就赶到医院。

60 in time a) early or soon enough to do something 及时〔做某事〕: **in time to do sth** *Brian usually gets home in time to bath the children.* 布赖恩通常会及时赶回家里给孩子们洗澡。| **just in time** *"Did you catch your plane?" "Yes – we got there just in time."* "你赶上飞机了吗?" "是的, 我们刚刚赶上。" | **in good time/in plenty of time** (=early, so that you do not have to rush or you have enough time to get ready) 及早, 尽早; 及时 *Let me know in good time if you need any help.* 你如果需要帮助, 请尽早告诉我。**b)** after a certain period of time, especially after a gradual process of change and development 过一段时间, 迟早: *Don't worry – I'm sure things will get better in time.* 不要担心, 情况肯定迟早会有好转的。

⑯ HOW MANY 多少

61 one/three/a few etc at a time separately, or in groups of three, a few etc together at the same time 一次一个/三个/几个等: *We had to see the nurse one at a time.* 我们必须一个一个地去见护士。| *He dragged himself along a few steps at a time.* 他几步一停地拖着脚往前走。

⑰ COMPARISONS 比较

62 five/ten/many etc times used to say how much bigger, better etc one thing is than another 五倍/十倍/很多倍等: *Their garden is three times bigger than ours.* 他们的花园比我们的要大三倍。| *Sue earns five times as much as I do.* 休挣的钱是我的五倍。

63 the best/biggest etc...of all time the best, biggest etc of a particular kind of person or thing that has ever existed 有史以来最好的/最大的等…: *the most successful movie of all time* 有史以来最成功的一部电影

⑱ GRADUALLY/EVENTUALLY 逐渐/最终

64 all in good time used to tell someone to be patient because something they are waiting for will certainly happen eventually, and probably quite soon 完全来得及; 快了; 别急〔告诉某人他期待的事肯定最终会发生, 而且也许很快会发生〕

65 it's (only) a matter/question of time used to say that something will definitely happen at some time in the future, but you do not know when 这(只不过)是时间问题〔指某事肯定会发生〕: *That road's dangerous – it's only a matter of time before someone gets killed.* 那条路很危险, 早晚会有人在那里丧命。

66 (only) time will tell used to say that it will eventually become clear whether or not something is true, right etc, at some time in the future (只有)时间会说明一切: *I don't know if she's the best choice for the job – only time will tell.* 我不知道她是不是担任这项职务的最佳人选 —— 时间会说明一切。

67 over time if something happens over time, it happens gradually during a long period 渐渐地, 慢慢地: *Over time her husband's mood seemed to change.* 渐渐地, 她丈夫的情绪似乎有所改变。

68 with time/given time after a certain period of time, especially after a gradual process of change and development 随着时间的推移; 逐渐地: *I guess things will improve with time.* 我想情况会逐渐改善的。

69 time heals all wounds used to say that things you are worried or upset about will gradually disappear as time passes 时间会医治一切创伤

⑲ MUSIC 音乐

70 ►MUSIC 音乐◄ [U] the number of beats (BEAT[2] (4)) in each bar (BAR[1] (6)) in a piece of music〔音乐的〕拍子, 节拍: *Waltzes are usually in three-four time.* 华尔兹舞通常是四分之三拍。

71 in time to if you do something in time to a piece of music, you do it using the same RHYTHM and speed as the music 合着〔音乐的〕节拍: *She began moving her body in time to the music.* 她开始合着音乐的节拍晃动身体。

72 keep time to play a piece of music using the right RHYTHM and speed 按节拍〔演奏音乐〕

73 keep/beat time to show the RHYTHM and speed that a piece of music should be played at to a group of musicians, using your hands〔用手〕打着节拍

74 in/out of time (with) if you are in or out of time with someone who is playing a piece of music, you are or are not following the same RHYTHM and speed as them 合着/不合〔别人演奏的节拍〕

⑳ LIKE/DISLIKE 喜欢/不喜欢

75 have a lot of time for *informal* to like or admire someone or something【非正式】喜欢; 钦佩; 对…非常感兴趣

76 not have much time for/have no time for *informal* to dislike and not want to waste your time on someone or something【非正式】不喜欢, 讨厌〔某人或某事〕; 不想在…上浪费时间: *She's always complaining – I've got no time for people like that.* 她总爱发牢骚, 我可不喜欢那样的人。

㉑ OTHER MEANINGS 其他意思

77 before your time a) something that is before your time happened before you were born, before you started working or living somewhere etc 在…出生[开始工作, 到某地生活]之前; 早于…的时代: *The Beatles were a bit before my time.* 甲壳虫乐队略早于我的时代。**b)** if you do something before your time, you do it before the time when most people usually do it in their lives 过早: *She's growing old before her time.* 她过早地开始衰老了。

78 in my/your etc time during the period of time when you were living in a particular place or working in a particular company etc 我/你等〔在某地〕生活[工作]的那个年代: *Of course in my time we didn't have all these computers.* 当然啦, 在我那个年代, 我们可没有这些电脑。

79 in your own time if you do work or studying in your own time, you do it outside normal school or work hours 在自己的时间里, 在业余时间里

80 in your own good time *informal* when you are ready【非正式】在自己做好准备之时, 在自己认为方便之时: *I'll speak to him about it in my own good time.* 我在方便的时候会跟他说这事的。

81 (sb's) time is up *spoken* used to say that someone has to stop doing something, because they have done it for long enough【口】〔某人做某事〕该结束了: *OK kids! Time's up – get out of the pool.* 好啦, 孩子们! 游够了, 从池子里出来吧。

82 sb's time is up/sb's time is drawing near someone is going to die soon 某人快要死了/某人活不长了

83 be near her time *old-fashioned* if a woman is near her time, she is going to have a baby soon【过时】〔女人〕即将分娩

84 time is on your side used to say that someone is young enough to be able to wait before doing something or until something happens 你还年轻, 有的是时间

85 against time if you work against time to do something, you try to do it even though you have very little time 争分夺秒, 尽快

86 time was (when) used to say that there was a time when you used to be able to do something, when something used to happen etc 曾经有一个时候…: *Time was when you could buy a new car for less than $500.* 曾经有一段时间, 不到 500 美元就可以买一辆新车。

87 pass the time of day (with sb) to say hello to someone and have a short talk with them（与某人）打招呼，（与某人）寒暄
88 ▶PRISON 牢房◀ do time to spend a period of time in prison 坐牢服刑
89 time and a half one and a half times the normal rate of pay 相当于平时一倍半的工资 —see also 另见 BIG TIME, FULL TIME, HALF TIME, PART-TIME, **at the best of times** (BEST³ (12)), **it is high time** (HIGH¹ (20)), **bide your time** (BIDE (1)), **in the fullness of time** (FULLNESS (1)), **kill time** (KILL¹ (9)), **lose time** (LOSE¹ (14)), **mark time** (MARK¹ (11)), **move with the times** (MOVE¹ (19)), **in the nick of time** (NICK¹ (1)), **for old times' sake** (OLD (18)), **once upon a time** (ONCE¹ (14)), **play for time** (PLAY¹ (16)), **at the same time** (SAME¹ (3)), **sign of the times** (SIGN¹ (9)), **a stitch in time (saves nine)** (STITCH¹ (9)), **have a whale of a time** (WHALE¹ (2))

time² *v* [T] **1** [usually passive 一般用被动态] to arrange or choose that something should happen at a particular time 安排…的时间，选好…的时间: *You timed your arrival well; we're just going to eat.* 你来得正好；我们刚要吃饭。| **be timed to do sth** *The bomb was timed to go off in the rush-hour.* 炸弹设定在人流高峰时刻爆炸。| **be timed for sth** *The next show is timed for 8 o'clock.* 下一场演出定在 8 点。**2** to measure how fast someone or something is going, how long it takes to do something etc 测定…的速度；记录…所需的时间: *We timed our journey: it took two and a half hours.* 我们算了一下旅程的时间：一共花了两个半小时。| **time sb/sth at** *Christie was timed at 10.02 seconds.* 克里斯蒂用了 10.02 秒的时间。| **time how long** *Time how long it takes me to swim 4 lengths.* 测试一下我游两个来回要花多长时间。**3** to hit a ball or make a shot at a particular moment 看准〔击球、射门或投篮〕的时间: *a perfectly timed smash* 时间卡得很准的扣球 | **time sth well/badly etc** *Baggio timed that pass beautifully.* 巴乔那个球传得正是时候。—see also 另见 ILL-TIMED, MISTIME, WELL-TIMED

time and mo·tion stud·y /ˌ· · ˈ· · ˌ· ·/ *n* [C] a study of working methods to find out how effective they are 时间和动作研究〔指对工作方法的有效程度进行的一种研究〕

time bomb /ˈ· ·/ *n* [C] **1** a bomb that is set to explode at a particular time 定时炸弹 **2** a situation that is likely to become a very serious problem 潜在的严重问题: *the time bomb of youth unemployment* 年轻人失业的潜在问题

time cap·sule /ˈ· ˌ· ·/ *n* [C] a container that is filled with objects from a particular time, so that people in the future will know what life was like then 时代文物锦囊，当代史料储存器〔用来存放某个时代的物件，以供后人了解当时的生活情况〕

time card /ˈ· ·/ *n* [C] a piece of card on which the hours you have worked are recorded by a special machine 工作时间记录卡，考勤卡

time clock /ˈ· ·/ *n* [C] a special clock that records the exact time when someone arrives at and leaves work 上下班记时钟，考勤钟

time-con·sum·ing /ˈ· ·ˌ· ·/ *adj* taking a long time to do 耗费时间的；旷日持久的: *an expensive, complex, and time-consuming process* 一个昂贵、复杂、费时的过程

time-hon·oured /ˈ· ˌ· ·/ *adj* a time-honoured method, custom etc is one that has existed for a long time〔方法、习俗等〕古老的，历史悠久的: *the time-honoured patterns of sheep-grazing and cultivation* 历史悠久的牧羊和耕种方式

time·keep·er /ˈtaɪmˌkipɚ; ˈtaɪmˌkiːpə/ *n* [C] **1** someone who officially records the times taken to do something, especially at a sports event〔尤指体育赛事中的〕计时员 **2 good/bad timekeeper a)** someone who is good or bad at arriving at work at the right time 上班准时/不准时的人 **b)** a watch or clock that is good or bad at showing the right time 时间准/不准的钟[表] —**timekeeping** *n* [U]

time lag /ˈ· ·/ also 又作 **time lapse** *n* [C] the period of time between two connected events〔两个相关联事件之间的〕时间间隔，时间差: *There is a considerable time lag between the planning stage and the final product.* 在规划阶段和最终成品之间有相当大的时间间隔。

time-lapse /ˈ· ·/ *adj* time-lapse photography makes a very slow process seem to happen much faster〔摄影〕延时的，定时的〔以高速显示非常缓慢的过程的摄影技术〕

time·less /ˈtaɪmlɪs; ˈtaɪmləs/ *adj* **1** remaining beautiful, attractive etc and not becoming old-fashioned 万古长新的；永不过时的: *the timeless beauty of Venice* 威尼斯万古不变的美 **2** *literary* continuing for ever【文】永恒的，恒久的: *the timeless universe* 永恒的宇宙 —**timelessly** *adv* —**timelessness** *n* [U]

time lim·it /ˈ· ˌ· ·/ *n* [C] the longest time that you are allowed in which to do something 时限，期限: *the legal time limit for abortions* 堕胎的法定期限

time·ly /ˈtaɪmlɪ; ˈtaɪmli/ *adj* done or happening at exactly the right time 适时的，及时的: *a timely intervention* 及时的干预 | **timely reminder** (=one that makes you remember something at the right time) 让人及时想起某事的东西

time ma·chine /ˈ· ·ˌ·/ *n* [C] an imaginary machine in which people can travel backwards or forwards in time 时间机器〔一种想象中的机器，人们可以乘坐它到过去或未来〕

time off /ˌ· ˈ·/ *n* [U] time when you are officially allowed not to be at work or studying〔正式规定的〕休假，放假: **take/have etc time off** *If you're feeling tired you should take some time off.* 你如果觉得累，就应休一段时间的假。

Time Out /ˌ· ˈ·/ *trademark* a weekly London magazine which gives details of all the films, plays, sports games, and other events and activities taking place in the city【商标】《消闲》〔伦敦一周刊，详尽介绍伦敦市电影、戏剧、体育比赛等活动信息〕

time out /ˌ· ˈ·/ *n* [C] **1 take time out** *informal* to rest or do something different from your usual job or activities【非正式】〔日常工作或活动中〕暂停休息 **2** *technical* a short break during a sports match when the teams can rest, get instructions from their manager etc【术语】〔体育比赛过程中的〕暂停

time·piece /ˈtaɪmˌpis; ˈtaɪmpiːs/ *n* [C] *old use* a clock or watch【旧】钟；表

tim·er /ˈtaɪmɚ; ˈtaɪmə/ *n* [C] **1** an instrument that you use to measure time, when you are doing something such as cooking 定时器: *Set the timer on the cooker for three minutes.* 把饭锅上的定时器定为 3 分钟。—see also 另见 EGG-TIMER **2 part-timer/full-timer** someone who works part or all of a normal working week 兼职人员/全职人员

times /taɪmz; taɪmz/ *prep* multiplied by 乘，乘以: *Two times two equals four.* (2×2=4) 二乘（以）二等于四。

Times, The 1 an old and famous British daily newspaper. *The Times* is a serious paper, and generally supports fairly RIGHT-WING political ideas. At one time, especially before television and radio, *The Times* had great influence on British political life, and many important people used to give their opinions by writing letters to *The Times*. In the US it is sometimes called *The London Times* so that it is not confused with US newspapers such as *The Los Angeles Times* or *The New York Times*.《泰晤士报》〔英国一历史悠久且享有盛名的日报。该报内容严肃，总体上支持比较右翼的政治观点，曾一度对英国人的政治生活产生过重大影响，在电视、广播出现之前尤为如此。许多重要人物过去曾给《泰晤士报》写信表达自己的观点。在美国有时称之为《伦敦时报》以免与美国的《洛杉矶时报》或《纽约时报》相混淆〕**2** the New York Times《纽约时报》**3** the Los Angeles Times《洛杉矶时报》

time-sav·ing /ˈ· ˌ· ·/ *adj* designed to reduce the time usually needed to do something 节省时间的，省时的: *a time-saving device* 一种可以节省时间的装置 —**time-saver** *n* [C]

time·scale /ˈtaɪmˌskel; ˈtaɪmskeɪl/ *n* [C] the period of time it takes for something to happen or be completed 时标，时段〔某事发生或完成所需要的时间段〕

Times Ed·u·ca·tion Sup·ple·ment, The /ˌ· ˌ· ·ˈ· · ˌ· · ·/ abbreviation 缩写为 **TES** a weekly British newspaper with articles on education in schools and advertisements for teaching jobs, produced by *The Times*《泰晤士报教育增刊》〔英国一周报，刊登有关学校教育的文章与教师征聘广告，由《泰晤士报》编印〕

time·serv·er /ˈtaɪmˌsɝvɚ; ˈtaɪmˌsɜːvə/ *n* [C] *informal* someone who does the least amount of work possible【非正式】工作上混时间的人，得过且过的人 —**timeserving** *adj, n* [U]

time·share /ˈtaɪmʃɛr; ˈtaɪmʃeə/ *n* [C] a holiday home that you buy with other people so that you can each spend a period of time there every year〔每年分时段与别人共享的〕分时享用的度假住房 —**timeshare** *adj*

CULTURAL NOTE 文化注释

Companies that sell timeshares have a bad REPUTATION in Britain because some people have been tricked by dishonest businessmen into paying for properties that are much too expensive or which do not even exist. Some timeshare companies now call themselves 'holiday clubs' because of this bad reputation. Timeshare properties are especially common in countries such as Spain where many

British people enjoy spending their holidays. People who sell timeshares often arrange meetings at popular holiday RESORTs where they try to persuade people to buy timeshares in a very clever and AGGRESSIVE way. Britain and the EU have introduced laws to make it more difficult for timeshare companies to deceive people. 在英国，那些出售分时享用的度假住房的公司名声很差，因为很多人都被不诚实的销售人员敲了竹杠，他们付款买了些要么特别昂贵要么根本就不存在的房产。因为想避开这种坏名声，现在很多经营分时度假住房的公司易名为"假日俱乐部"。分时度假的房产在西班牙等国尤其普遍，因为很多英国人都爱去那里度假。销售分时度假房屋的人常在热点度假胜地举行推销会，他们以十分巧妙和强势的手段游说人们购买。英国和欧盟均通过立法来限制经营分时享用度假房屋的公司去坑害人们。

time-shar·ing /'·,··/ *n* [U] **1** *technical* the art of dealing with more than one computer PROGRAM at the same time【术语】〔电脑同时有不止一个程序在运转的〕分时操作，时间共享 **2** the practice of owning a timeshare 分时享用度假住房

time sheet /'· ·/ *n* [C] a piece of paper on which the hours you have worked are written or printed 工作时间记录单，考勤单

Times High·er Ed·u·ca·tion Sup·ple·ment, The /,·,··'··,··/ abbreviation 缩写为 **The THES** a weekly British newspaper with articles on education in universities and other institutions of higher education, as well as advertisements for jobs in these places, produced by *The Times*《泰晤士报高等教育增刊》〔英国一周报，刊登有关高等教育的文章与招聘广告，由《泰晤士报》编印〕

time sig·nal /'·,··/ *n* [C] a sound on the radio that shows the exact time〔收音机发出的〕报时信号

time sig·na·ture /'·,···/ *n* [C] two numbers at the beginning of a line of music that tell you how many beats (BEAT[2] (4)) there are in a BAR[1] (6)〔乐谱开头用以表示节拍数的〕拍号

Times Lit·e·ra·ry Sup·ple·ment, the /,·'····,···/ abbreviation 缩写为 **TLS** a British weekly newspaper which contains articles and information about literature, especially about new books, produced by *The Times*《泰晤士报文学增刊》〔英国一周报，刊登文学方面的文章和信息，尤其是新书介绍，由《泰晤士报》编印〕

Times Square /,·'·/ a large SQUARE (=a broad, open area with buildings on all sides) in New York City, close to many theatres. A New Year's Eve celebration is held there every year. 时代广场〔纽约市一宽阔广场，附近有许多剧场，每年都要在此举行新年除夕庆祝活动〕

time switch /'· ·/ *n* [C] an electronic control that can be set to start or stop a machine at a particular time 计时开关，定时开关

time·ta·ble[1] /ˈtaɪm,tebḷ; ˈtaɪm,teɪbəl/ *n* [C] *BrE*【英】**1** a list of the times at which buses, trains, planes, etc arrive and leave〔公共汽车、火车、飞机等的〕运行时间表，时刻表；SCHEDULE *AmE*【美】**2** a list of the times of classes in a school, college etc〔学校里的〕课程表；SCHEDULE *AmE*【美】**3** a plan of events and activities, with their dates and times; SCHEDULE〔活动计划的〕时间表，日程表

timetable[2] *v BrE*【英】**1** [T usually passive 一般用被动态] to plan that something will happen at a particular time in the future; SCHEDULE 为…安排[确定]时间: **timetable sth for** *The meeting has been timetabled for 2 o'clock.* 会议已经定在2点开。**2** [I,T] to arrange the times at which classes will take place in a school or college〔学校里〕安排课程时间表: *Timetabling is the responsibility of the deputy head.* 安排课程时间表是副校长的职责。

time warp /'· ·/ *n* [C] **1 be (caught/stuck) in a time warp** to have not changed even though everyone or everything else has 固步自封，僵化不变: *The whole college seems stuck in some 1960s time warp!* 整个大学似乎还停滞在20世纪60年代！**2** an imaginary situation in which the past or future becomes the present〔幻想中的〕时间异常，时空错乱

time·worn /ˈtaɪm,worn; ˈtaɪmwɔːn/ *adj* something timeworn is old and has been used a lot 陈旧的；年久而残破的: *timeworn phrases* 用滥了的语句

time zone /'· ·/ *n* [C] one of the 24 areas that the world is divided into, each of which has its own time 时区

tim·id /ˈtɪmɪd; ˈtɪmᵻd/ *adj* not having courage or confidence 胆小的，胆怯的；羞怯的: *a timid smile* 羞涩的一笑 | *a policy that is both timid and inadequate* 一项既无胆识又不完善的政策 —**timidly** *adv* —**timidity** /tɪˈmɪdətɪ; tᵻˈmɪdᵻti/ *n* [U]

tim·ing /ˈtaɪmɪŋ; ˈtaɪmɪŋ/ *n* [U] **1** a word meaning the time, day etc when someone does something or when something happens, especially when you are considering how suitable this is 时间的选择，时机的掌握: **good/bad/perfect etc timing** *Ah good timing! I was just thinking I needed a coffee.* 啊，真是好时候！我刚巧在想要一杯咖啡呢。| *What perfect timing! I was just finishing my work as you arrived to pick me up.* 时间真是恰到好处！你来接我的时候，我刚把工作做完。**2** the way in which electricity is sent to the SPARK PLUGs in a car engine〔汽车发动机内电传送到火花塞的〕时间配合，时间同步

Timor /ˈtimɔr; ˈtiːmɔː/ an island between the South China Sea and the Indian Ocean. Population: 1,382,207 (1980). Capital: Kupang 帝汶岛〔南中国海与印度洋之间一岛屿。人口: 1,382,207 (1980)，首府: 古邦〕

tim·o·rous /ˈtɪmərəs; ˈtɪmərəs/ *adj formal* lacking confidence and easily frightened【正式】胆怯的；缺乏自信的；易受惊吓的: *She was no helpless, timorous female.* 她决不是柔弱胆怯的女性。—**timorously** *adv* —**timorousness** *n* [U]

tim·pa·ni /ˈtɪmpənɪ; ˈtɪmpəni/ *n* [U] a set of KETTLEDRUMS〔一组〕定音鼓

tim·pa·nist /ˈtɪmpənɪst; ˈtɪmpənᵻst/ *n* [C] someone who plays the timpani 定音鼓手

tin[1] /tɪn; tɪn/ *n* **1** [U] a soft white metal that is often used to cover and protect iron and steel 锡: *a tin box* 锡盒 **2** [C] *BrE* a small metal container in which food or drink is sold【英】罐头；CAN *especially AmE*【尤美】: *a sardine tin* 沙丁鱼罐头 | *a tin of beans* 一罐豆子 —see picture at 参见 CONTAINER 图 **3** [C] a metal container with a lid in which food can be stored〔存放食物的〕金属盒: *a biscuit tin* 饼干盒 **4** [C] *BrE* a metal container in which food is cooked【英】〔烹饪食物的〕器皿；PAN[1] (2) *AmE*【美】: *a bread tin* 烤面包模子 3

tin[2] *adj* **1** made of TIN 锡制的，镀锡的: *a tin mug* 锡杯 | *a tin soldier* 锡兵 **2 have a tin ear** *AmE informal* to be unable to hear the difference between musical notes【美，非正式】不能辨别乐音，五音不辨 **3 tin god** *informal* someone gets much more admiration and respect than they really deserve【非正式】被盲目崇拜的人，浪得虚名的人

tinc·ture /ˈtɪŋktʃɚ; ˈtɪŋktʃə/ *n* [C,U] [+of] *technical* a medical substance mixed with alcohol【术语】酊剂〔药物与酒精的混合物〕

tin·der /ˈtɪndɚ; ˈtɪndə/ *n* [U] dry material that burns easily and can be used for lighting fires 引火物，火绒，火种

tin·der·box /ˈtɪndɚ,bɑks; ˈtɪndəbɒks/ *n* **1** [C usually singular 一般用单数] a place or situation that is dangerous and where there could suddenly be a lot of fighting or problems 危机四伏的地区[形势]: *Racial tension was high, and the southern states were a real tinderbox.* 种族关系紧张，南方各州真是一个火药桶。**2** [C] a box containing things needed to make a flame, used in former times〔旧时取火用的〕火绒盒

tinder-dry /,··'·◂/ *adj* extremely dry and likely to burn very easily 极干燥易燃的: *The whole forest is tinder-dry.* 整座森林如火绒般干燥。

tin·foil /ˈtɪn,fɔɪl; ˈtɪnfɔɪl/ *n* [U] thin shiny metal that bends like paper and is used for covering food etc〔用于包裹食物等的〕锡箔，锡纸

ting /tɪŋ; tɪŋ/ *n* [C] a high clear ringing sound 叮当声: *the ting of a bell* 钟发出的叮当声 —**ting** *v* [I,T]

ting-a-ling /,··'·◂/ *n* [C] *informal* the high clear ringing sound that is made by a small bell【非正式】〔小铃发出的〕叮当声

tinge[1] /tɪndʒ; tɪndʒ/ *n* [C] a very small amount of a colour, emotion, or quality 淡淡的色调；些许，一点，一丝〔情绪、特质等〕: [+of] *a tinge of sadness in her voice* 她声音里的一丝悲伤

tinge[2] *v* [T+with] to give something a small amount of a particular colour, emotion, or quality 着淡色于…；使带有一点…〔情绪、特质等〕

tinged /tɪndʒd; tɪndʒd/ *adj* **tinged with** showing a small amount of a colour, emotion or quality 略带一点〔颜色、情绪、特质等〕的: *black hair tinged with grey* 略带灰色的黑发

tin·gle /ˈtɪŋgḷ; ˈtɪŋgəl/ *v* [I] **1** if a part of your body tingles, you feel a slight uncomfortable feeling, especially on your skin〔尤指皮肤〕感到刺痛，刺痒: [+with] *My cheeks were tingling with the cold.* 我的脸颊冻得刺痛。**2 tingle with excitement** to feel very excited 感到很激动 —**tingle** *n* [C]: *A nervous tingle ran down her spine.* 一阵令人不安的刺痒沿着她脊背往下扩散。

tin hat /,·'·/ *n* [C] a metal hat worn by soldiers〔士兵的〕钢盔

tin·ker[1] /ˈtɪŋkɚ; ˈtɪŋkə/ *n* [C] **1** someone who travels from place to place selling things or repairing metal pots, pans etc〔游走四方的〕小贩；补锅匠 **2** *BrE old-fashioned* a disobedient or annoying young child【英，过时】顽童，小淘气 **3 not give a**

tinker's curse/cuss *BrE spoken*【英口】**not give a tinker's damn** *AmE spoken*【美口】to not care about something at all〔对…〕毫不在乎

tinker² *v* [+with] to make small changes to something in order to repair it or make it work better〔随便马虎地〕修理, 修补; 摆弄: *It's no use just tinkering with the legislation.* 对立法只是小修小补, 那是没用的。

Tin·ker·bell /ˈtɪŋkəˌbɛl; ˈtɪŋkəbel/ a FAIRY (=an imaginary creature who looks like a small person but has wings and can do magic) who helps Peter Pan in the play and book *Peter Pan* by J. M. Barrie. She talks to Peter Pan by making bell-like sounds. 小铃铛, 银铃仙子〔J.M.巴里的剧本和小说《彼得·潘》中帮助小飞侠的仙子。她与小飞侠说话的声音就像铃铛的声响〕

Tin·ker·toys /ˈtɪŋkəˌtɔɪz; ˈtɪŋkətɔɪz/ *trademark* a type of US toy consisting of different-sized coloured sticks and pieces shaped like wheels, which can be joined together to make models of buildings, cars etc【商标】廷克玩具〔一种美国玩具, 包括各种尺寸的彩色木杆和形似轮子的木块, 可拼装成房屋、小汽车模型等〕

tin·kle¹ /ˈtɪŋkl; ˈtɪŋkəl/ *n* [C usually singular 一般用单数] **1** a light ringing sound 叮当声: *She could hear the tinkle of coffee cups.* 她可以听到咖啡杯发出的叮当声。—see picture on page A19 参见 A19 页图 **2 give sb a tinkle** *BrE informal* to call someone on the telephone【英, 非正式】给某人打电话: *I'll give you a tinkle tomorrow.* 我明天给你打电话。**3 have a tinkle** an expression meaning to URINATE (=pass water from your body), used especially by or to children 撒尿, 尿尿〔尤为儿语〕

tinkle² *v* [I,T] to make light ringing sounds or to make something do this (使) 发出叮当声: *a tinkling bell* 叮叮当当的铃声

Tin Man, the /ˌ· ˈ·/ a character from the book and film *The Wizard of Oz*. He is made of metal and does not have a heart, but in the story goes to see the Wizard of Oz to ask him to give him a heart. 铁皮人〔小说和电影《绿野仙踪》中的人物。他是用金属做成的, 没有心脏。故事中, 他去拜望巫师, 想求得一颗心脏〕

tinned /tɪnd; tɪnd/ *adj BrE* tinned food is sold in a TIN¹ (2) and can be kept for a long time before it is opened【英】〔食品〕罐装的: *tinned tomatoes* 罐头番茄

tin·ni·tus /tɪˈnaɪtəs; ˈtɪnɪtəs/ *n* [U] *technical* an illness in which you hear noises, especially ringing, in your ears【术语】耳鸣 (症)

tin·ny /ˈtɪnɪ; ˈtɪni/ *adj* **1** a tinny sound is unpleasant to listen to, like small pieces of metal hitting each other〔声音〕尖细的, 像薄金属碰撞声的 **2** a tinny metal object is badly or cheaply made〔金属制品〕廉价的, 粗制的, 质量差的

tin o·pen·er /ˈ· ˌ···/ *n* [C] *BrE* a tool for opening tins【英】开罐器, 罐头刀; CAN OPENER *especially AmE*【尤美】—see picture on page A10 参见 A10 页图

Tin Pan Al·ley /ˌ· · ˈ··/ *informal old-fashioned* the people who produce popular music and their way of life, especially in the US【非正式, 过时】锡盘巷〔指美国流行音乐人及其生活方式〕

tin·plate /ˈtɪnˌplet, ˈtɪnpleɪt/ *n* [U] very thin sheets of iron or steel covered with tin 镀锡铁皮, 马口铁

tin-pot /ˈ· ·/ *adj* [only before noun 仅用于名词前] a tin-pot person, organization, etc is not very important, although they think that they are〔人、组织机构等〕卑微而又自负的: *a tin-pot dictator* 无足轻重却自我陶醉的独裁者

tin·sel /ˈtɪnsl; ˈtɪnsəl/ *n* [U] **1** thin strings of shiny paper used as decorations, especially at Christmas〔尤指圣诞节期间装饰用的〕锡箔纸, 闪光纸 **2** something that seems attractive but is not valuable or important 花哨而无用的东西, 华而不实的东西: *the tinsel and glamour of Hollywood* 好莱坞的浮华和魅力

Tin·sel·town /ˈtɪnsḷtaun; ˈtɪnsəltaun/ a humorous informal name for Hollywood, which is used to give the idea that people in Hollywood care only about GLAMOUR and the way things look, and not about anything serious 丝箔城, 浮华城〔好莱坞谑称。意指好莱坞的人关心的仅仅是浮华和外在, 而不注重有深度的东西〕

tin shears /ˈ· ·/ *n* [plural] *AmE* heavy scissors for cutting metal【美】〔切割金属的〕大剪刀; snips (SNIP¹ (1)) *BrE*【英】

tint¹ /tɪnt; tɪnt/ *n* [C] **1** a small amount of a particular colour 淡淡的色泽; 色调: *autumn tints* 淡淡的秋色 **2** artificial colour, used to slightly change the colour of your hair 染发剂: *She had put red tints in her hair.* 她把自己的头发染成了淡红色。

tint² *v* [T] **1** to slightly change the colour of someone's hair using artificial colour〔用染发剂〕稍微改变〔头发〕的颜色 **2** to give hair an artificial colour 给〔头发〕染成人工的颜色

tin·tack /ˈtɪnˌtæk; ˈtɪntæk/ *n* [C] a short nail made of iron and covered with tin 镀锡小铁钉

Tin·ta·gel /tɪnˈtædʒəl; tɪnˈtædʒəl/ an ancient castle on the north coast of Cornwall, where, according to old stories, King Arthur lived 廷塔杰尔〔康沃尔北部沿岸一古城堡。相传是亚瑟王居住的地方〕

tint·ed /ˈtɪntɪd; ˈtɪntḭd/ *adj* [only before noun 仅用于名词前] tinted glass is coloured, rather than completely transparent〔玻璃〕有色的

Tin·tin /ˈtɪntɪn; ˈtɪntɪn/ the main character in the CARTOON books by the Belgian writer Hergé, which were later made into cartoon films. Tintin is a young man whose hair has a long TUFT that sticks up at the front. He has many exciting adventures with his dog **Snowy**, trying to solve crimes and catch criminals. 丁丁〔比利时作家埃尔热的漫画故事中的主人公。其故事后来被改编成动画片。丁丁是个年轻人, 头发留成长长的一簇, 竖在脑门上。他和自己的小狗斯诺伊经历了不少刺激的冒险奇遇, 想方设法地破案并抓获罪犯〕

tin·tin·nab·u·la·tion /ˌtɪntɪˌnæbjəˈleʃən; ˌtɪntḭnæbjʊˈleɪʃən/ *n* [C,U] *literary* the sound of bells【文】铃声; 叮当声

Tin·to·ret·to /ˌtɪntəˈrɛto; ˌtɪntəˈretəʊ/ (1518-94) an Italian artist born in Venice, famous especially for his religious paintings and his PORTRAITS (=pictures of people) 丁托莱托〔(1518-1594), 意大利画家。生于威尼斯, 尤以宗教题材的作品与肖像画闻名〕

ti·ny /ˈtaɪnɪ; ˈtaɪni/ *adj* extremely small 极小的, 微小的: *a tiny baby* 很小的婴儿 | *The opium farmers receive only a tiny fraction of this sum.* 种植鸦片的农民们从这笔钱中只拿到极小的一部分。 S2 W2

Tiny Tim /ˌtaɪnɪ ˈtɪm; ˌtaɪni ˈtɪm/ a character in the story *A Christmas Carol* (1843) by Charles Dickens. He is the young son of Bob Cratchit, who works for Scrooge, and is very ill and cannot walk. At the end of the book, he says "God bless us, every one!" 小蒂姆〔查尔斯·狄更斯的小说《圣诞颂歌》(1843) 中的人物。他是斯克鲁奇的雇员鲍勃·克拉基伊特的小儿子, 病得很重, 连路也走不动了。在书的结尾部分, 他说道:"愿上帝保佑我们, 保佑每一个人!"〕

-tion /ʃən; ʃən/ *suffix* (in nouns 构成名词) another form of the suffix -ION 后缀 -ion 的另一种形式

tip¹ /tɪp; tɪp/ *n* S2 W3

1 ▶END 末端◀ [C] the end of something, especially something pointed 末端, 末梢; 尖端; 顶点: *Use the tip of the brush to paint fine lines.* 用画笔的尖端来绘细线。| *The tip of her nose was red.* 她的鼻尖是红的。—see also 另见 FINGERTIP

2 ▶MONEY 钱◀ [C] a small amount of additional money that you give to someone, such as a WAITER or a taxi driver 小费, 赏钱: *Did you leave a tip?* 你留下小费了吗? | *a 10% tip* 10% 的小费

CULTURAL NOTE 文化注释

In the US and the UK, people tend to give tips for particular services, although tipping is much more common and important in the US. In restaurants in the US, people usually give the waiter between 15% and 20% of the bill, but in the UK they give about 10%. If the service is bad, however, people in both countries give a smaller tip or do not leave any tip. It is also normal to give a tip to PORTERS who carry your bags at the airport or in a hotel, and to give a 10% tip to taxi drivers and to people who cut your hair. 在美国和英国, 人们会为特别服务提供小费, 尽管给予小费在美国更为普遍和被人重视。在美国的餐馆里, 人们通常按照账单的 15% 到 20% 给服务员小费, 而在英国只会给大约 10% 的小费。当然如果服务差, 人们可以少给或不给小费。在机场和酒店给予行李搬运工小费也是正常的事, 此外人们还会给出租车司机和理发师 10% 的小费。

3 ▶ADVICE 忠告◀ [C] a helpful piece of advice 有用的劝告, 忠告, 建议: [+on] *Steve gave me some useful tips on how to take good pictures.* 就如何拍好照片, 史蒂夫给了我一些很有用的建议。

4 ▶WASTE 垃圾◀ [C] *BrE* an area where unwanted waste is taken and left; DUMP² (1)【英】垃圾场: *a rubbish tip* 垃圾弃置场

5 ▶UNTIDY 不整洁◀ [singular] *BrE informal* an extremely dirty or untidy place【英, 非正式】极不干净[极不整洁]的地方: *Your room's a real tip! When are you going to clean it?* 你的房间简直成垃圾堆了! 你打算什么时候打扫打扫?

6 on the tip of your tongue if a word, name etc is on the tip of your tongue, you know it but cannot remember it 就在嘴边〔但记不起来了〕

7 the tip of the iceberg a small sign of a problem that is much larger 冰山的一角; 重大问题显露出表面的一小部分: *The offi-*

cial statistics are probably only the tip of the iceberg. 官方的统计数字可能只反映了冰山一角。
8▶HORSE RACE 赛马◀ [C] *informal* special information about which horse will win a race【非正式】〔关于赛马中哪匹马会赢的〕特别情报，内部情报

tip² *v* **tipped, tipping**
1▶FALL 倒下◀ [I,T] also 又作 **tip over/up** to fall or turn over, or make something do this（使）倒下；（使）倾翻：*Careful you don't tip the milk jug over!* 你小心点，别把牛奶罐弄翻了！| *If you lean on the table, it'll tip up.* 如果你斜靠在桌子上，它会翻的。
2▶POUR 倾倒◀ [T] to pour something from one place or container into another 把…从一个容器倒入另一容器；倾倒；倾卸：**tip sth out/into/onto etc** *She weighed out the flour and tipped it out into a bowl.* 她称了面粉，然后把它倒进一个碗里。
3▶LEAN 倾斜◀ [I,T] to lean at an angle instead of being level or straight, or to make something do this（使）倾斜，（使）倾侧：*Sit still and don't tip the chair back.* 坐定了，别把椅子往后倾斜。
4▶MONEY 钱◀ [I,T] to give an additional amount of money to someone such as a WAITER or taxi driver 给〔服务员或出租车司机等〕小费，给赏钱：*Did you remember to tip the waiter?* 你记得给服务员小费了吗？—see picture on page A15 参见 A15 页图
5▶LIKELY TO SUCCEED 可能成功的◀ [T usually passive 一般用被动态] *especially BrE* to say who you think is most likely to be successful at something【尤英】认为…最有可能成功：**tip sb as/for** *She's been tipped for promotion.* 有人认为她可能得到提升。| **tip sb/sth to do sth** *a horse that was tipped to win* 被认为有可能赢的赛马
6▶COVER 覆盖◀ be tipped with to have one end covered in something 顶端覆盖着…：*arrows tipped with poison* 箭头上涂有毒药的箭
7 it's tipping down *BrE spoken* it is raining【英口】天正下着雨
8 tip the balance/scales to give a slight advantage to someone or something 使平衡局面发生倾侧；使稍微有利于…：*Your support tipped the balance in our favour.* 你们的支持使整个局面对我们有利。
9 tip the scales at to weigh a particular amount before a BOXING or WRESTLING match〔参加拳击或摔跤比赛前〕称得重量为…：*He tips the scales at 180 pounds.* 他称得重量为 180 磅。
10 tip sb the wink *BrE informal* to give someone secret information【英，非正式】给某人秘密消息
11 tip your hat to *AmE* to show that you think someone is very good, helpful, successful etc【美】向…致敬
tip sb ↔ **off** *phr v* [T] to give someone a secret warning or piece of information, especially to the police about illegal activities 向…提出秘密警告；〔尤指给警察〕通风报信：*The police must have been tipped off.* 警察一定事先得知了风声。

tip-off /ˈ· ·/ *n* [C] *informal* a warning that something is going to happen, especially to the police about illegal activities【非正式】秘密的警告；〔尤指给警察的〕通风报信，密报：*Acting on an anonymous tip-off, police raided the house.* 警察根据匿名提供的情报采取行动，搜查了那所房子。

Tip·pe·ca·noe /ˌtɪpɪkəˈnu; ˌtɪpɪkəˈnuː/ a river in Indiana in the US, where US soldiers led by William Henry Harrison won a battle against the Shawnee, a Native American people, in 1811. Harrison himself, who later became President of the US, was given the NICKNAME 'Tippecanoe' after the battle. 蒂珀卡努河〔美国印第安纳州一河流。1811 年，威廉·亨利·哈里森领导美军在此打败了印第安人的肖尼族，他本人并据此被冠以"蒂珀卡努"的绰号。后来，哈里森成了美国总统〕

Tip·pe·ra·ry /ˌtɪpəˈrɛrɪ; ˌtɪpəˈreəri/ a town and COUNTY in the south of the Republic of Ireland. There is a well-known song from World War I called *It's a Long Way to Tipperary.* 蒂珀雷里〔爱尔兰共和国南部一城镇和郡名。一战期间有一首著名歌曲，名为《蒂珀雷里路迢迢》〕

Tip·pett /ˈtɪpɪt; ˈtɪpɪt/, **Sir Mi·chael** (1905-98) an English COMPOSER who wrote CLASSICAL music for both voices and instruments. He also wrote several OPERAs and his works include *A Child of Our Time.* 蒂皮特〔(1905-1998)，英国古典音乐作曲家。他创作有声乐和乐器作品以及数部歌剧，代表作是《我们这个时代的一个孩子》〕

Tipp-Ex /ˈtɪp ɛks; ˈtɪp eks/ *n* [U] *BrE trademark* white liquid that is used to cover over mistakes in writing, typing etc【英，商标】"迪美斯"牌修正液[涂改液]；WHITEOUT *AmE*【美】

tipp-ex /ˈtɪpɛks; ˈtɪpeks/ *v* [T+**out**] *BrE* to cover over a mistake in writing, typing etc, using white liquid【英】用修正液[涂改液]涂改

tip·ple /ˈtɪpl; ˈtɪpəl/ *n informal especially BrE*【非正式，尤英】**favourite tipple** someone's favourite alcoholic drink〔某人〕最喜爱喝的酒

tip·pler /ˈtɪplɚ; ˈtɪplə/ *n* [C] *informal especially BrE* someone who drinks alcohol【非正式，尤英】饮烈酒者，酒徒

tip·ster /ˈtɪpstɚ; ˈtɪpstə/ *n* [C] someone who gives information about which horse is likely to win a race〔提供赛马信息的〕情报贩子

tip·sy /ˈtɪpsɪ; ˈtɪpsi/ *adj informal* slightly drunk【非正式】微醉的 —**tipsily** *adv* —**tipsiness** *n* [U]

tip·toe¹ /ˈtɪpˌto; ˈtɪptəʊ/ *n* **on tiptoe(s)** if you stand on tiptoe you stand on your toes, in order to make yourself taller 踮着脚：*Anita stood on tiptoe and tried to see over the wall.* 安妮塔踮着脚尖，想看到墙那边。

tiptoe² *v* [I] to walk quietly and carefully on your toes 踮着脚走，蹑手蹑脚地走：[+**across/down etc**] *He tiptoed across the hall and followed her into the kitchen.* 他蹑手蹑脚地穿过走廊，跟着她进了厨房。—see picture on page A24 参见 A24 页图

tip-top /ˌ· ˈ·◂/ *adj informal* excellent【非正式】非常好的，顶呱呱的：**in tip-top condition/shape etc** *The car's in tip-top condition.* 这辆车的状况非常好。

ti·rade /ˈtaɪred; taɪˈreɪd/ *n* [C] a long angry speech criticizing someone or something 抨击性的长篇演说：*He launched into a tirade against the church.* 他发表了长篇抨击教会的演说。

Tirana /tɪˈrɑnə; tɪˈrɑːnə/ the capital city of Albania. Its main industries include metal, cotton TEXTILEs, and soap. 地拉那〔阿尔巴尼亚首都，主要产业是金属业、棉纺织业和肥皂业〕

tire¹ /taɪr; taɪə/ *v* **1** [I,T] to start to feel tired or make someone feel tired（使）感到累，（使）感到疲劳：*As we neared the summit, we were tiring fast.* 当接近山顶时，我们越来越累，快不行了。**2 tire of sth** to become bored with something 对某事感到厌烦：*Sooner or later he'll tire of politics.* 迟早他会厌烦政治的。**3 never tire of doing sth** to do something so much that it annoys other people 不厌其烦地做某事〔因此令人厌烦〕：*She never tires of telling everyone how wonderful her new house is.* 她不厌其烦地告诉每个人，说她的新房子是如何如何的好。
tire sb ↔ **out** *phr v* [T] to make someone very tired 使精疲力尽，使疲劳不堪

tire² *n* [C] the American spelling of TYRE tyre 的美式拼法

tired /taɪrd; taɪəd/ *adj* **1** feeling that you want to sleep or rest 困倦的；疲倦的，累的：*I'm so tired I could sleep for a week.* 我累极了，简直能睡上一个星期。| *She can't come tonight – she says she's too tired.* 她今晚不能来了，她说她太累。**2** bored with something because it is no longer interesting, or has become annoying 厌烦的，厌倦的：**tired of doing sth** *I'm tired of watching television, let's go for a walk.* 我看电视都看腻了，我们出去走走吧。| [+**of**] *I was getting tired of all her negative remarks.* 我对她那一整套消极言论感到越来越厌烦了。**3 tired out** very tired, especially after a lot of hard work, travelling etc〔尤指在干了大量繁重工作、旅行等之后〕精疲力竭的 **4 tired (old) subject/joke etc** a subject, joke etc that is boring because it is too familiar 枯燥乏味[老一套]的话题/笑话等 —see also 另见 DOG-TIRED, **be sick (and tired) of sth** (SICK¹ (4)) —**tiredness** *n* [U] —**tiredly** *adv* S1 W2

tire·less /ˈtaɪrlɪs; ˈtaɪələs/ *adj* working very hard in a determined way without stopping 不知疲倦的，孜孜不倦的：*the tireless efforts of the rescue workers* 营救人员坚持不懈的努力 —**tirelessly** *adv*

Ti·re·si·as /taɪˈrisiæs; taɪˈriːsiæs/ in ancient Greek stories, a blind man who had the ability to know what was going to happen in the future, and who told people about the crimes of Oedipus 提瑞西阿斯〔古希腊传说中一盲人。他有预见未来的能力，揭露过俄狄浦斯的罪行〕

tire·some /ˈtaɪrsəm; ˈtaɪəsəm/ *adj* making you feel annoyed or impatient 烦人的，令人厌烦的：*the whole tiresome business of filling out the forms* 填写表格这一整套烦人的事

tir·ing /ˈtaɪrɪŋ; ˈtaɪərɪŋ/ *adj* making you feel that you want to sleep or rest 令人困倦的；令人疲劳的，令人感到累的：*We've all had a very tiring day – let's go to bed.* 大家今天都很累，我们上床睡觉吧。

ti·ro /ˈtaɪro; ˈtaɪərəʊ/ *n* [C] someone who is only beginning to learn something 新手，生手，初学者

Ti·rol /tɪˈrol; tɪˈrəʊl/ —see 见 the TYROL

'tis /tɪz; tɪz/ *poetical*【诗】the short form of 缩略式= 'it is'

tis·sue /ˈtɪʃu; ˈtɪʃuː/ *n* **1** [C] a piece of soft thin paper, used especially for blowing your nose on 纸巾，面巾纸：*a box of tissues* 一盒面巾纸 **2** also 又作 **tissue paper** [U] light thin paper used for wrapping, packing etc〔包装等用的〕薄纸，绵纸 **3** [U] the material forming animal or plant cells〔动植物细胞的〕组 W3

织: **plant/lung/brain etc tissue** 植物/肺/脑等组织 **4 a tissue of lies** a story or account that is completely untrue 一派谎言

tit /'tɪt; tɪt/ *n* [C] **1** *informal* an offensive word for a woman's breast【非正式】(女人的)乳房, 奶子(冒犯用语) **2** *BrE slang* a stupid person【英俚】傻瓜, 笨蛋 **3 get on sb's tits** *BrE slang* to annoy someone a lot【英俚】让某人非常厌烦 **4** a small European bird 山雀(欧洲的一种小鸟)

ti·tan, Titan /'taɪtn̩; 'taɪtn/ *n* [C] a very strong or important person; GIANT[2] (4) 巨人, 大力士; 泰斗, 大师; 巨子

Ti·ta·ni·a /taɪ'tenɪə; taɪ'tɑːniə/ the queen of the fairies and the wife of Oberon in the play *A Midsummer Night's Dream* by William Shakespeare 泰坦尼娅(威廉·莎士比亚的剧本《仲夏夜之梦》中的仙后, 为奥伯朗之妻)

ti·tan·ic /taɪ'tænɪk; taɪ'tænɪk/ *adj* very big, strong, impressive etc 巨大的; 力大无比的; 重大的: *a titanic struggle* 大搏斗

Titanic, the a large British passenger ship which was people considered impossible to sink, but which hit an ICEBERG in the Atlantic Ocean on its first journey in 1912, and as a result sank, killing more than 1500 of its passengers. There have been many books and films about this event. People sometimes use the phrase 'like rearranging the deck chairs on the Titanic' to describe the actions of a person or organization which makes small and useless changes to a situation, when the situation is already hopeless and certain to fail. "泰坦尼克"号(英国一艘被认为是永不沉没的大型客轮。1912 年首航时在大西洋上撞上了一座冰山而最终沉没, 1500 余名乘客遇难, 许多书和电影中都有这一事件的描述。人们有时借用 like rearranging the deck chairs on the Titanic (像重新排列"泰坦尼克"号甲板上的座椅一样) 这一短语来形容某个人或组织面对一种毫无希望或注定失败的局面而做出的小而无用的举动)

ti·ta·ni·um /taɪ'tenɪəm; taɪ'teɪniəm/ *n* [U] a strong, light, and very expensive metal 钛(一种金属元素)

Ti·tans, the /'taɪtnz; 'taɪtnz/ in Greek MYTHOLOGY, the first gods who ruled the universe, before Zeus became the most powerful god. They were thought of as GIANT*s* (=like humans, but extremely large and tall). 泰坦诸神(希腊神话中在宙斯成为最强大的神之前统治宇宙的最早诸神。这些神灵被人们视为巨人)

tit·bit /'tɪt,bɪt; 'tɪt,bɪt/ *n* [C] *especially BrE*【尤英】**1** a small piece of food 少量的精美食品, 珍馐; TIDBIT *AmE*【美】**2 titbit of information/gossip/news etc** *plural* a small but interesting piece of information etc 趣闻/花絮/花边消息等

titch /tɪtʃ; tɪtʃ/ *n* [singular] *BrE* a humorous or insulting way of addressing a small person【英】矮个子, 小不点儿(对身材矮小的人的幽默或侮辱性的称呼语)

titch·y /'tɪtʃɪ; 'tɪtʃi/ *adj BrE informal* extremely small【英, 非正式】极小的

tit·fer /'tɪtfɚ; 'tɪtfə/ *n* [C] *BrE old-fashioned slang* a hat【英, 过时, 俚】帽子

tit for tat /,‥'‥/ *n* [U] *informal* something bad that you do to someone because they have done something bad to you【非正式】一报还一报, 以眼还眼

tithe /taɪð; taɪð/ *n* [C usually plural 一般用复数] a tax paid to the church, in former times 什一税(旧时支付给基督教会的一种税)

Ti·tian /'tɪʃən; 'tɪʃən/ (1490-1576) an Italian painter from Venice, whose work includes religious paintings and scenes from ancient Greek and Roman stories. Many people admire his use of colours, and his name is sometimes used to describe a brownish-orange colour that is typical of his paintings. 提香((1490-1576), 意大利威尼斯画家。作品包括宗教画和取材于古希腊和古罗马神话故事的画作。他对色彩的运用颇受人推崇, 他的名字有时用以指代多见于其作品的一种棕黄色)

Tit·i·ca·ca /,tɪtɪ'kɑkə; ,tɪtɪ'kɑːkə/, **Lake** the largest lake in South America, and the highest in the world, in the Andes mountains between Bolivia and Peru 的的喀喀湖(南美洲最大的湖泊, 也是世界上海拔最高的湖泊, 位于玻利维亚与秘鲁之间的安第斯山区)

tit·il·late /'tɪtl̩,et; 'tɪtɪleɪt/ *v* [T] if a picture or a story titillates someone, it makes them feel sexually excited or interested 使感到性兴奋; 使感到有趣: *the usual pin-ups to titillate the readers* 让读者感到性刺激的常见女人图片 **—titillating** *adj* **—titillation** /,tɪtl̩'eʃən; ,tɪtɪ'leɪʃən/ *n* [U]

tit·i·vate, tittivate /'tɪtə,vet; 'tɪtɪveɪt/ *v* [I,T] *informal* to make yourself pretty or tidy【非正式】打扮, 装饰, 梳整 **—titivation** /,tɪtə'veʃən; ,tɪtɪ'veɪʃən/ *n* [U]

ti·tle /'taɪtl̩; 'taɪtl/ *n* **1** [C] the name given to a particular book, painting, play etc (书籍、图画、戏剧等的)题目, 标题: *The title of this play is 'Othello'.* 这部剧作的标题是《奥赛罗》。**2** [C] a book (某一本)书: *His novel was one of last year's best-selling titles.* 他的小说是去年的畅销书之一。**3** [C] **a)** a name such as 'Sir' or 'Professor', or letters such as 'Mrs' or 'Dr', that are used before someone's name to show their rank or profession, whether they are married etc (表明某人地位或职业的)头衔, 称谓 **b)** a name that describes someone's job or position (表示某人工作的)职位, 职称: *Her official title is editorial manager.* 她的正式职位是编辑部经理。**4** [singular,U] *technical* the legal right to own something【术语】所有权: [+to] *He has title to the land.* 他拥有那块土地的所有权。**5** [C] the position of being the winner of an important sports competition (重大体育比赛中的)冠军: *Navratilova won a record number of Wimbledon titles.* 纳夫拉蒂洛娃创纪录地赢得了很多次温布尔登网球赛冠军。

ti·tled /'taɪtl̩d; 'taɪtld/ *adj* having a title such as 'lord', DUKE, EARL etc 有贵族头衔的, 有爵位的

title deed /'‥ ·/ *n* [C] a piece of paper giving legal proof that someone owns a particular property 房地产契据, 产权证

title hold·er /'‥ ,‥/ *n* [C] **1** a person or team that is the winner of an important sports competition (体育比赛的)冠军; 冠军队 **2** someone who owns a title deed 房地产契据持有人, 产权人

title page /'‥ ·/ *n* [C] the page at the front of a book which shows the book's name, writer etc (图书的)书名页, 扉页

title role /'‥ ·/ *n* [C] the main acting part in a play, which is the same as the name of the play (主角与剧作名称一样的)剧名角色

tit·mouse /'tɪt,maʊs; 'tɪtmaʊs/ *n* [C] a small European bird 山雀(欧洲的一种小鸟)

Ti·to /'tito; 'tiːtəʊ/, **Marshal Josip Broz** /,jɑsəp 'brɑs; jɒsɪp 'brɒs/ (1892-1980) a Yugoslav Communist politician, who was president of Yugoslavia from 1953 until his death. Although Yugoslavia was a Communist state at this time, it was not influenced or controlled by the Soviet Union. Some people now say that Tito's strong leadership kept Yugoslavia together as one country, and since his death it has separated into smaller parts. 铁托((1892-1980), 南斯拉夫共产党领导人, 1953 年起任南斯拉夫总统直至去世。当时, 南斯拉夫虽是一个共产党执政的国家, 但却没有受苏联的影响或控制。如今有些人说铁托的铁腕领导维系了南斯拉夫的团结和统一, 自他去世后, 南斯拉夫不断分崩离析)

tit·ter /'tɪtɚ; 'tɪtə/ *v* [I] to laugh quietly in a high voice, especially because you are nervous (尤指紧张时)窃笑; 傻笑: *At the word 'breast' some of the class tittered.* 听到"乳房"这个词, 班上的一些同学窃笑起来。**—titter** *n* [C]

tittle-tat·tle /'tɪtl̩ ,tætl̩; 'tɪtl ,tætl/ *n* [U] unimportant conversation about other people and what they are doing; GOSSIP[1] (1) (关于别人的)闲聊; 闲言碎语

tit·ty /'tɪtɪ; 'tɪti/ *n* [C] *slang* a woman's breast; TIT【俚】(女人的)乳房, 奶子

tit·u·lar /'tɪtʃəlɚ; 'tɪtʃʊlə/ *adj* [only before noun 仅用于名词前] **titular head/leader/monarch etc** someone who is the official leader or ruler of a country but who does not have real power or authority 挂名的头目/没有实权的领导/有名无实的君主等

Ti·tus An·dron·i·cus /,taɪtəs æn'drɑnɪkəs; ,taɪtəs æn'drɒnɪkəs/ a play by William Shakespeare, which people think is his first TRAGEDY. It is set in ancient Rome and is full of shocking violence and murder. 《泰特斯·安德洛尼克斯》(威廉·莎士比亚创作的一部戏剧。据认为, 这是他的第一部悲剧作品。该剧以古罗马为背景, 全剧充满了令人震惊的暴力和谋杀)

Ti·tus Groan /,taɪtəs 'gron; ,taɪtəs 'grəʊn/ (1946) a NOVEL by the British writer Mervyn Peake. It tells the story of Titus, the 77th Earl of Groan, in his castle called Gormenghast, and it is full of strange and frightening characters 《泰特斯·格罗恩》((1946), 英国作家默文·匹克的一部小说, 讲述第 77 代格罗恩伯爵泰特斯在自己的城堡歌门鬼城中生活的故事, 小说中有许多怪异恐怖的人物)

tiz·zy /'tɪzɪ; 'tɪzi/ also 又作 **tizz** /tɪz; tɪz/ *n* [singular] *informal*【非正式】**in a tizzy** feeling worried, nervous, and confused 焦虑不安, 心慌意乱

T-junc·tion /'ti ,dʒʌŋkʃən; 'tiː ,dʒʌŋkʃən/ *n* [C] *BrE* a place where two roads meet and form the shape of the letter T【英】(道路的)T 形交叉, 丁字路口

TLC /,ti ɛl 'si; ,tiː el 'siː/ *n* [U] *informal* tender loving care; kindness and love that you show someone to make them feel better and happier【非正式】亲切的关爱

TLS, the /,ti ɛl 'ɛs; ,tiː el 'es/ the abbreviation of 缩写= the TIMES LITERARY SUPPLEMENT

TM[1] a written abbreviation of 缩写= TRADEMARK

TM[2] /,ti 'ɛm; ,tiː 'em/ an abbreviation of 缩写= TRANSCENDENTAL MEDITATION

TN the written abbreviation of 缩写= TENNESSEE

TNT /ˌti ɛn ˋti; ˌtiː en ˈtiː/ *n* [U] a powerful explosive 梯恩梯〔一种烈性炸药〕

[1][1] **to¹** /tə; tə, *before vowels* 元音前作 tʊ; tʊ; *strong* 强读 tu; tuː/ **1** [used before a verb to show that it is the infinitive 用于动词前表示是不定式, but not before 但不用于 **can, could, may, might, will, would, shall, should, must,** or 或 **ought** 之前。The following senses show the patterns in which **to** is used. 下列义项表明了 to 的各种用法。] **2** used after verbs〔用于动词后〕: *He lived to be 90.* 他活到了90岁。| *I used to live in New York.* 我曾经住在纽约。| *He wants to leave.* 他想离开。| *Let her leave if she wants to.* 她如果想走, 就让她走吧。| *They allowed the hostages to go.* 他们允许人质离开。| *He told his men to shoot.* 他叫他的手下人射击。| *He told them not to.* 他告诉他们不要这样。**3** [used after 用于 **how, where, who, whom, whose, which, when, what,** or 或 **whether** 之后]: *I know where to go but I don't know how to get there.* 我知道去什么地方, 但我不知道怎样去那儿。| *She wondered whether or not to go.* 她不知道是不是该去。| *She wondered whether to go or not.* 她不知道是该去呢, 还是不该去。| *Would you tell me when to leave?* 你能告诉我什么时候动身吗? **4** used after nouns〔用于名词后〕: *an attempt to make a joke* 试图开一个玩笑 | *I haven't got the qualifications to apply.* 我没有资格申请。| *There seemed to be no reason to stay.* 似乎没有留下的理由。**5** after adjectives〔用于形容词后〕: *That's very easy to say.* 那是很容易说的。| *I'm glad to say she's making a good recovery.* 我很高兴地说, 她正恢复得很不错。| *We are sorry to announce the cancellation of the flight to Geneva.* 我们很抱歉地通知大家, 飞往日内瓦的航班被取消。**6** used to refer to, or to emphasize a particular verb〔用于指称或强调某一动词〕: *'To find' takes a direct object.* to find 加直接宾语。| *It would be best to wear waterproof clothing.* 最好是穿上防水服。| *What I really should have done was to say "no" straightaway.* 我当时真正应该做的是直截了当地说"不"。**7** used to show that someone intends to do something〔用于表示某人想做某事〕: *They left early to catch the train.* 为了赶火车他们很早就动身了。| *She wore a large hat to keep the sun off her head.* 她戴了一顶很大的帽子, 不让自己的头晒到太阳。| *I've taken some money out of the bank to buy Christmas presents.* 我从银行里取了一些钱好买圣诞礼物。**8** used after **too**+adjective〔用于 too+形容词后〕: *It's too cold to go out.* 天太冷了, 没法出去。| *Jim's too honest to play a trick like that.* 吉姆太老实了, 他不会那样搞恶作剧的。**9** used after an adjective and **enough**〔用于形容词和 enough之后〕: *I reckon it's warm enough to wear a T-shirt.* 我想天气够暖和了, 穿一件 T 恤衫就行。| *It's cold enough to snow.* 天够冷的, 会下雪的。**10** used to introduce a statement〔用于引导陈述句〕: *To be quite honest, I've never even heard of him.* 老实说, 我压根儿就没有听说过他。| *To put it another way, how are you going to get the cash to pay for it?* 换一种问法, 你打算如何搞到现金来买这东西? | *To begin with, let's look at Chapter 3.* 首先, 让我们来看第三章。**11** used after the pattern **There is**+noun〔用于 There is+名词这一句型之后〕: *There were plenty of things to eat.* 可以吃的东西很多。| *There's also the cost to consider.* 还有成本也要考虑到。

to² /tu; tuː/ *adv* **1** if you push a door to, or something moves a door to, it closes〔门〕在关上的位置: *The wind blew the door to.* 风把门吹得关上了。**2 come to** if someone comes to, they become awake or conscious after being asleep or unconscious 苏醒过来: *John didn't come to for half-an-hour after falling and hitting his head.* 约翰摔了一跤把头给撞了, 过了半个小时才苏醒过来。

[1][1] **to³** /tə; tə, *before vowels* 元音前作 tʊ; tʊ; *strong* 强读 tu; tuː/ *prep* **1** in a direction towards 向, 朝, 到, 往: *the road to London* 通往伦敦的路 | *a journey to China* 中国之行 | *She stood up and walked to the window.* 她站起来走到窗口。| *Sam threw the ball to his little sister.* 萨姆把球扔向他的小妹妹。**2** in a direction from a particular person or thing 在…方, 位于…方向: *Chongqing is about 150 miles to the south of Chengdu.* 重庆位于成都以南大约150英里处。| *I was sitting to the left of the President.* 我当时坐在总统的左边。**3** in order to be in a particular place or area 到…去: *We're hoping to go to Istanbul for our holidays this year.* 我们希望今年去伊斯坦布尔度假。| *Don't forget; we're going to Eve's for supper tomorrow night.* 别忘了, 我们明晚要去伊夫家里吃晚饭。| *I usually go to bed at 11p.m.* 我通常晚上11点上床睡觉。| *"Where's Emily?" "She's gone to the loo."* "埃米莉在哪儿?" "她去洗手间了。" **4** in order to be in a particular situation, or in a particular physical or mental state 为了到…情况; 为了达到…身体[精神]状态: *After two difficult years the company is now on the road to recovery.* 在渡过两年困难期之后, 该公司目前正在复苏中。| *She sang the baby to sleep.* 她唱歌哄婴儿入睡。| *The mob stoned her to death.* 这群暴徒用石头砸死了她。| *Wait until the lights change to green.* 等到变成绿灯为止。**5** reaching as far as a particular thing 达到〔某事物〕: *The water came right up to our knees.* 水一直涨到了我们的膝部。**6** in a position in which two things are touching〔相互之间〕贴着, 紧挨着: *The paper stuck firmly to the wall.* 那纸紧紧地贴在墙上。| **cheek to cheek** *They danced cheek to cheek.* 他俩脸贴着脸跳舞。**7** facing something or in front of it 对着, 面对着: *I sat with my back to the engine.* 我背对发动机坐着。| **face to face** *We stood face to face.* 我们面对面站着。| **back to back** *The two houses were back to back.* 那两座房子背向而立。**8** until and including 直到〔并包括在内〕: *She can already count from one to twenty.* 她已经能从1数到20了。| *They stayed from Friday night to Sunday morning.* 他们从星期五晚上一直待到星期天早上。| *It's ten kilometres from here to Angers.* 从这里到昂热有10公里。| **from beginning to end** *She read the novel from beginning to end.* 她从头到尾地读了这部小说。| **a nine-to-five job** (=a typical job in which you begin work at nine o'clock and finish at five o'clock) 朝九晚五的工作 **9** used to show the person or thing to which actions or words are directed or to whom things belong〔用于指出行动或语言的对象; 用于指出东西的拥有者〕: *This is a letter to Mildred from George.* 这是乔治写给米尔德丽德的一封信。| *Have you told all your news to John?* 你把全部消息都告诉约翰了吗? | *You have no right to this land.* 你对这块土地没有所有权。| *Will they give you an office to yourself?* 他们会给你一间属于自己的办公室吗? **10** used to show the person or thing that is affected by an action 对, 对于〔用来指出受行动影响的人或事物〕: *a danger to your health* 对你健康的威胁 | *She's very kind to animals.* 她对动物很仁慈。| *What have you done to the radio? It's not working.* 你是怎么摆弄这台收音机的? 它现在不响了。| *There's always an element of risk to starting up a new business.* 创业总会有风险的。**11** working for someone, or being a part of something that is necessary to make it work 为…〔工作〕; 是…的〔一部分〕: *Have you seen the key to the back door?* 你见过开后门的那把钥匙吗? | *Rona's secretary to the managing director.* 罗娜是总经理的秘书。**12** used when comparing two things, numbers etc 与…相比, 相对于…而言: *I know he's successful but he's nothing to what he could have been.* 我知道他有成就, 但与他本来可取得的成就相比, 这一点算不了什么。| *England beat Scotland by two goals to one.* 英格兰队以二比一击败了苏格兰队。**13** used especially after verbs such as 'seem', 'feel', 'sound' to show how things affect, concern, or influence someone 至于, 对于〔尤用于 seem, feel, sound 等动词后, 表示影响到或涉及某人〕: *The whole thing sounds very suspicious to me.* 整个事情在我听来都非常可疑。| *Tickets cost £10 each and to some people that's a lot of money.* 每张票10英镑, 对于某些人来说, 这是个大数目。**14** according to a particular feeling or attitude 合乎〔某一看法或态度〕: **to your liking/taste etc** *The decor wasn't really to our liking.* 这种装饰实在不合我们的口味。| **to your advantage** (=in a way that will help you or be good for you) 对你有利的 *You could use this information to your advantage.* 你可以利用这条信息。| **to your knowledge** (=according to what you know) 就你所知道的 *Brookner has not to my knowledge written any books since this one.* 据我所知, 布鲁克纳自从写了这本书以后就再也没有写过别的书。**15 to your surprise/annoyance/delight** in a way that makes you feel a particular emotion 让你吃惊/气恼/高兴的是: *Much to her surprise she passed the exam with distinction.* 让她十分惊奇的是, 她以出众的成绩通过了考试。| *To our amazement she climbed on the desk and started removing her clothes.* 让我们大为吃惊的是, 她竟爬到桌子上, 开始脱衣服了。**16** *especially spoken* forming something or being one of the separate parts that makes something up【尤口】形成, 组成: *We're only getting eight francs to the pound at the moment.* 现在我们用1英镑只能兑换8法郎。| *There are sixteen ounces to every pound.* 1磅合16盎司。| **there's more to sb/sth than meets the eye** (=used to say that a person or situation is more complicated than they seem to be) 某人/某事比看上去复杂得多 **17** used when adding one number to another or when thinking about two facts at the same time 加〔数目〕; 还有, 以及: *Add fifty to seventy-five.* 75再加上50。| *In addition to all Ron's other problems his father died yesterday.* 除了其他所有那些问题, 罗恩还有一件事, 他父亲昨天去世了。**18** used to show that there is a certain amount of time before an event or before a particular time 在…之前还有〔时间〕: *Only two weeks to Christmas.* 离圣诞节只有两个星期。| *How long is it to dinner?* 到开晚饭还有多长时间? | **ten to five/twenty to one etc** (=ten minutes, twenty minutes etc before a particular hour) 差10分到5点/差20分到1点等 **19** used between two numbers when

you try to guess an exact number …至…之间〔用来估计数字〕: *There must have been between eighteen to twenty thousand people at the concert.* 那场音乐会上一定有1.8万到2万人。| *He drowned in 10 to 12 feet of water.* 他淹死在10到12英尺的水深处。**20** used when saying what the chances of something happening are or giving the ODDS in betting (BET[1] (1)) 比〔用于表示某事发生的可能或打赌中的输赢比率〕: *It's 100-1 he'll lose.* 他输定了。| *Seagram is running at 11-8.* 西格拉姆的赔率是11比8。

Toad /tod; təʊd/ one of the main characters in the children's story *The Wind in the Willows* by Kenneth Graham. Toad is a rich, proud character who lives in a big house called Toad Hall and thinks he is very important. 蟾蜍〔肯尼思·格雷厄姆的儿童故事书《杨柳风》中的主人公之一。蟾蜍是一个富有且傲慢的角色, 住在蟾蜍宫, 总以为自己是举足轻重的人物〕

toad *n* [C] a small animal that looks like a large FROG and lives mostly on land 蟾蜍, 癞蛤蟆

toad-in-the-hole /ˌ· · · ˈ·/ *n* [U] a British dish made of SAUSAGES cooked in a mixture of eggs, milk, and flour 裹面糊香肠〔一种英国菜〕

toad·stool /ˈtodˌstul; ˈtəʊdstuːl/ *n* [C] a wild plant like a MUSHROOM, that can be poisonous (毒)蕈

toad·y[1] /ˈtodɪ; ˈtəʊdi/ *n* [C] *informal* someone who pretends to like an important person so that they will help you【非正式】谄媚者, 马屁精

toady[2] *v* [I] to pretend to like an important person so that they will help you 谄媚, 奉承, 拍马屁: [+to] *toadying to the boss* 拍老板的马屁

to and fro[1] /ˌtu ənd ˈfro; ˌtuː ənd ˈfrəʊ/ *adv* if someone or something moves to and fro, they move in one direction and then back again 来来往往地, 往复地: *People were walking to and fro on the promenade.* 步行大道上人来人往。—**to-and-fro** *adj*

to and fro[2] *n* [U] *informal* continuous movement of people or things from place to place【非正式】〔人或东西的〕来来往往, 川流不息 —see also 另见 TOING AND FROING

3 **toast[1]** /tost; təʊst/ *n* **1** [U] bread that has been heated so that it is brown on both sides and no longer soft 烤面包〔片〕, 吐司: *We had toast for breakfast.* 我们早餐吃的是烤面包片。**2** [C] an occasion when you ask people to all drink something in order to thank someone, wish someone luck etc〔为答谢或祝福某人而进行的〕祝酒, 干杯: **propose a toast** (=ask people to drink a toast) 提议干一杯 **3 warm as toast** comfortably warm 温暖舒适: *They sat near the fire, warm as toast.* 他们坐在火边, 温暖又舒适。**4 be the toast of Broadway/Hollywood etc** to be very popular and praised by many people for something you have done in a particular field of work 百老汇/好莱坞等的大名人 —see also 另见 FRENCH TOAST

toast[2] *v* [T] **1** to drink a glass of wine, etc to thank someone, wish someone luck etc 为…举杯祝酒: *We toasted our success with champagne.* 我们用香槟酒庆祝自己的成功。**2** to make bread or other food brown by placing it close to heat 烘, 烤〔面包或其他食品〕: *toasted cheese sandwiches* 烘烤干酪三明治 **3** to sit yourself near a fire to make yourself warm〔坐在火边〕使暖和

toast·er /ˈtostɚ; ˈtəʊstə/ *n* [C] a machine you use for toasting bread 烤面包机 —see picture on page A10 参见A10页图

toasting fork /ˈ· · ·/ *n* [C] a long fork used to hold bread over a fire to toast it〔烤面包等用的〕烤叉

toast·mas·ter /ˈtostˌmæstɚ; ˈtəʊstˌmɑːstə/ *n* [C] someone who introduces the speakers at a formal occasion such as a BANQUET (=large formal meal)〔在宴会等正式场合中介绍演讲者的〕(宴会)主持人

toast·y /ˈtostɪ; ˈtəʊsti/ *adj AmE informal* warm and comfortable【美, 非正式】暖烘烘的, 温暖舒适的

to·bac·co /təˈbæko; təˈbækəʊ/ *n* [U] the dried brown leaves that are smoked in cigarettes, pipes etc 烟叶, 烟草

to·bac·co·nist /təˈbækənɪst; təˈbækənǀst/ *n* [C] *BrE*【英】**1** someone who has a shop that sells tobacco, cigarettes etc 烟草店老板, 烟草经销商 **2 tobacconist's** a shop that sells tobacco, cigarettes etc 烟草销售店, 烟店

to·bog·gan[1] /təˈbɑgən; təˈbɒgən/ *n* [C] a light wooden board with a curved front, used for sliding down hills covered in snow 平底木板雪橇

toboggan[2] *v* [I] to slide down a hill on a toboggan 乘坐平底木板雪橇滑行

to·by jug /ˈtobɪ ˌdʒʌg; ˈtəʊbi dʒʌg/ *n* [C] a container for drinking from, shaped like a fat man wearing a hat (人形)小酒杯〔形如头戴帽子的胖人〕

toc·ca·ta /təˈkatə; təˈkɑːtə/ *n* [C] a piece of music, usually for piano or organ, that is played very quickly 托卡塔〔一种用钢琴或管风琴快速演奏的乐曲〕

Tocque·ville /ˈtokvɪl; ˈtɒkvɪl/, **A·lex·is de** /əˈlɛksɪs də; əˈleksǀs də/ (1805-59) a French writer and politician who travelled in the US and then wrote a book called *Democracy in America* which examined the strengths and weaknesses of the American system of government 托克维尔〔(1805-1859), 法国作家、政治家。他游历过美国, 著有《美国的民主》, 分析了美国政府制度的优点和不足〕

toc·sin /ˈtaksɪn; ˈtɒksǀn/ *n* [C] *literary* a signal of danger that is made by ringing a bell【文】警铃, 警钟

tod /tad; tɒd/ *n* **on your tod** *BrE slang* by yourself【英俚】独自, 自个儿

To·day /təˈde; təˈdeɪ/ also 又作 **the Today Programme** a morning news programme on BBC Radio, which many people consider to be the most important British radio news programme. It includes interviews with politicians and other people in the news. 《今日播报》〔英国广播公司一早间新闻节目。许多人普遍认为它是英国电台最重要的新闻节目, 内容包括对政治家等人物的访谈〕

today[1] *adv* **1** on the day that is happening now 今天, 今日: *I couldn't go shopping yesterday so I'll have to go today.* 我昨天没能去买东西, 所以今天我必须去。| *Ed has his music lesson today.* 埃德今天有音乐课。| **today week/a week today** *BrE* (=one week from today)【英】距今天一周之后/下周的今天 *We're going on holiday today week.* 我们一周之后要去度假。—see picture at 参见 DAY 图 **2** at the present time 现今, 现在, 时下: *Students today seem to know very little about geography.* 如今的学生似乎对地理知识所知甚少。 1 1

today[2] *n* [U] **1** the day that is happening now 今天, 今日 —see picture at 参见 DAY 图: *Today is my birthday!* 今天是我的生日! | *Have you read today's paper yet?* 你看过今天的报纸了吗? **2** the present period of time 现今, 现在, 眼下: *Today's computers are becoming much smaller and lighter.* 现在的电脑正变得越来越小、越来越轻了。| *The children of today have more choices than their parents.* 现在的孩子比他们的父母有更多的选择。

Todd /tad; tɒd/, **Sweeney** /ˈswinɪ; ˈswiːni/ a character in a 19th-century British play whose job is to cut men's hair, but who murders his customers and has them made into meat pies. He is known as 'the demon barber of Fleet Street'. 托德〔19世纪一部英国戏剧中的人物。他专门为男人理发, 杀害自己的顾客并做成馅饼。人称"舰队街魔鬼理发师"〕

tod·dle /ˈtadl; ˈtɒdl/ *v* [I] if a small child toddles, it walks with short, unsteady steps〔学步小孩〕蹒跚行走

tod·dler /ˈtadlɚ; ˈtɒdlə/ *n* [C] a very young child who is just learning to walk 刚学走路的小孩 —see 见 CHILD (USAGE)

tod·dy /ˈtadɪ; ˈtɒdi/ *n* [C] a hot drink made with WHISKY, sugar, and hot water 香甜热酒〔由威士忌加糖和热水调制而成〕

to-do /tə ˈdu; tə ˈduː/ *n* [singular] *informal* unnecessary excitement or angry feelings about something, FUSS[1] (2)【非正式】骚动, 喧闹; 大惊小怪: *What a to-do there was when I said I didn't want to be married in a church!* 我说我不想在教堂里举行婚礼, 就引起了那么大的骚动!

toe[1] /to; təʊ/ *n* [C] **1** one of the five movable parts at the end of your foot 脚趾: *He stubbed his toe on a rock.* 他的脚趾碰在了一块石头上。| **big toe** (=the largest of your toes) 大脚趾 **2** the part of a shoe or sock that covers the front part of your foot〔鞋或袜的〕足尖部 —see picture at 参见 SHOE[1] 图 **3 step on sb's toes** *AmE*【美】**tread on sb's toes** *BrE*【英】to offend someone, especially by becoming involved in something that they are responsible for〔尤指因涉足别人负责的范围而〕得罪某人, 触犯某人: *He's new in the department and will have to be careful not to step on anyone's toes.* 他是这个部门新来的, 必须小心谨慎, 不要得罪任何人。**4 keep sb on their toes** to make sure that someone is ready for anything that might happen 使某人随时准备行动; 使某人保持警觉: *She certainly keeps the children on their toes!* 她的确让孩子们保持警觉! **5 make sb's toes curl** to make someone feel very embarrassed or uncomfortable about something 使某人感到尴尬; 使某人感到不舒服 **6 touch your toes** to bend downwards so that your hands touch your toes 躬身用手摸脚趾 —see also 另见 **from head to toe** (HEAD[1] (2)), **from top to toe** (TOP[1] (20)) 3

toe[2] *v* [T] **toe the line** to do what other people in a job or organization say you should do, whether you agree with them or not〔不管同意与否〕听从命令; 服从纪律; 按规定行事: *You toe the line or you don't stay on the team!* 你要听从命令, 否则你就别待在队里!

toe-cap /ˈtokæp; ˈtəʊkæp/ *n* [C] a piece of metal or leather that covers the front part of a shoe〔鞋前部的〕外包头, 鞋头

TOEFL /ˈtofəl; ˈtəʊfəl/ Test of English as a Foreign Language; a test that students can take if their first language is not English, that shows how good their English is 托福〔即以英语作为外语的测试，旨在检测母语为非英语的学生的英语水平〕

toe·hold /ˈtoˌhold; ˈtəʊhəʊld/ *n* **1** [singular] your first involvement in a particular activity, from which you can develop and become stronger〔事业发展、增强的〕初步的立脚点: *The company has gained a toehold in the competitive computer market.* 该公司在竞争激烈的电脑市场站稳了脚跟。**2** [C] a small hole in a rock where you can put your foot when you are climbing〔攀登时仅可容纳一只脚的〕立足点

toe·nail /ˈtoˌnel; ˈtəʊneɪl/ *n* [C] the hard part that covers the top of each of your toes 脚趾甲 —see picture at 参见 FOOT[1] 图

toe·rag /ˈtoræg; ˈtəʊræg/ *n* [C] *BrE spoken* an offensive word for someone you dislike【英口】臭小子; 臭娘们〔冒犯用语〕: *That toerag cheated me!* 那个臭小子骗了我!

toff /tɑf; tɒf/ *n* [C] *BrE old-fashioned* someone who is rich or has a high social position【英, 过时】有钱人; 上流社会的人

tof·fee /ˈtɑfɪ; ˈtɒfi/ *n* [C,U] **1** a sticky sweet brown substance that you can eat, made by boiling sugar, water, and butter together, or a piece of this substance 太妃糖 **2 can't do sth for toffee** *BrE informal* to be very bad at doing something【英, 非正式】根本干不了某事, 完全无法胜任某事: *He can't sing for toffee!* 他根本就不会唱歌!

toffee ap·ple /ˈ·· ˌ··/ *n* [C] an apple covered with toffee and put on a stick 太妃糖苹果〔苹果外裹有太妃糖, 插于棍上〕

toffee-nosed /ˈ·· ·/ *adj BrE informal* a toffee-nosed person thinks that they are better than other people because of their social position【英, 非正式】势利的, 好摆架子的, 自命不凡的: *He's a toffee-nosed little creep!* 他是个自命不凡的小人!

to·fu /ˈtofu; ˈtəʊfuː/ *n* [U] a soft white food like cheese, that is made from SOY BEANS 豆腐

tog¹ /tɑg; tɒg/ *n* [C] **1 togs** [plural] *informal* clothes【非正式】衣服 **2** *technical* a unit for measuring the warmth of QUILTs etc【术语】托格〔测量被子保暖性的单位〕

tog² *v* **tog** yourself **up/out** *phr v* [T] *informal* to put on clothes for a particular occasion or activity【非正式】〔为出席特殊场合或活动而〕给〔自己〕打扮, 使〔自己〕穿得漂亮

to·ga /ˈtogə; ˈtəʊgə/ *n* [C] a long loose piece of clothing worn by people in ancient Rome 托加袍〔古罗马人穿的宽松长袍〕

to·geth·er¹ /təˋgɛðɚ; təˈgeðə/ *adv*

1 ▶MAKE ONE THING 制作一种东西◀ if you want to put two or more things together, you join them so that they form a single subject or group 结合起来: *Mix the butter and sugar together.* 把黄油和糖搅拌在一起。| *He added all the numbers together.* 他把所有的数目加在一起。| *We stuck the pieces together again.* 我们把那些碎片又重新粘合在一起。| *The model was held together with string.* 那个模型用绳子拴在一起。

2 ▶IN ONE PLACE 在一个地方◀ if you keep, collect etc things together, you keep or collect them all in one place 到一起, 集拢着: *I gathered all my favourite paintings together.* 我把我喜爱的所有画都收集到了一起。

3 close/packed/crowded etc together if people or objects are close together, packed together etc, they are placed very near to each other 紧挨在一起/塞在一起/挤在一起等: *The climbers were sitting huddled together for warmth.* 登山者们挤成一团取暖。| *Her ornaments were all bunched together at one end of the shelf.* 她的那些装饰品全都束在一起, 放在书架的一端。

4 ▶AGAINST EACH OTHER 相互◀ if you rub, bang etc things together, you rub or bang them against each other 相互, 彼此: *Max was rubbing his hands together with glee.* 马克斯高兴地搓着双手。| *Knock the brushes together to clean them.* 把刷子互相拍拍弄干净。

5 ▶WITH EACH OTHER 共同◀ if two or more people are together or do something together, they are with each other or do something with each other 共同; 一齐, 一块儿: *We were at school together.* 我们曾经在同一所学校上学。| *Let's all stay together or someone might get lost.* 我们全都待在一块儿, 以防有人走失。| *They've decided to spend more time together.* 他们决定花更多的时间在一起。| *I hear George and his wife have got back together.* 我听说乔治和他妻子复婚了。| **all together (now)** *spoken* (=used when you are asking a group of people to say or do something together)【口】(现在)大家一起上 *Right, men. All together now...Push!* 好的, 伙计们。现在大家一起…推!

6 ▶IN AGREEMENT 一致地◀ if people are together, come together etc they are or become united and work with each other 团结一致地, 齐心协力地, 合作地: *Together we can win.* 团结一致, 我们就能取胜。| *We must work closely together on this one.* 这回我们必须密切合作。| *bring the two sides in the dispute together* 使纠纷双方达成和解

7 ▶AT THE SAME TIME 同时◀ at the same time 同时, 一齐: *Why do all the bills always come together?* 为什么账单总是一下子同时来呢? | *You should have used both the tools together.* 你应该同时使用这两种工具。

8 together with in addition to; at the same time as 和…一起, 连同: *Just bring it back to the store, together with your receipt.* 把它连同收据一起拿回店里来就行了。

9 ▶WITHOUT STOPPING 不停地◀ *old use* without interruption【旧】不间断地, 接连地: *It rained for four days together.* 雨接连下了四天。—see also 另见 **get your act together** (ACT[1] (5)), **hold together** (HOLD[1]), **piece sth together** (PIECE[2]), **pull together** (PULL[1])

together² *adj spoken* someone who is together always thinks clearly and does things in a very sensible, organized way【口】思路清晰的, 处事明智的, 条理井然的: *I admire Rosie – she's such a together person.* 我佩服罗茜, 她是一位如此镇静自若的人。

to·geth·er·ness /təˋgɛðɚnɪs; təˈgeðənɪ̵s/ *n* [U] the feeling you have when you are part of a group of people who have a close relationship with each other 和睦团结; 亲密无间: *I really miss the togetherness we felt at college.* 我真怀念我们在大学时那种亲密无间的感觉。

tog·gle /ˈtɑgl; ˈtɒgəl/ *n* [C] **1** a small piece of wood or plastic that is used as a button on coats, bags etc〔用作外衣、背包等纽扣的〕栓扣, 棒形纽扣 —see picture at 参见 FASTENER 图 **2** something on a computer that lets you change from one operation to another〔电脑上的〕双态元件〔使一种操作转换为另一种操作的键等元件〕

toggle switch /ˈ·· ·/ *n* [C] *technical* a small part on a machine that is used to turn electricity on and off by moving it up or down【术语】〔上下开闭电源的〕拨动开关

To·go /ˈtogo; ˈtəʊgəʊ/ a country in West Africa between Benin and Ghana. Population: 5,153,000 (2001). Capital: Lomé. 多哥〔西非一国家, 位于贝宁与加纳之间。人口: 5,153,000 (2001), 首都: 洛美〕 —**Togolese** /ˌtogəˋliz; ˌtəʊgəˈliːz/ *n, adj*

toil¹ /tɔɪl; tɔɪl/ *v* [I always+adv/prep] **1** also 又作 **toil away** to work very hard for a long period of time 长时间地苦干, 辛苦劳作: [**+at/over**] *I've been toiling away at this essay all weekend.* 我整个周末一直在辛苦地写这篇文章。**2** to move slowly and with great effort 吃力地慢行, 跋涉: [**+up/through/against etc**] *They toiled slowly up the hill.* 他们吃力地慢慢爬上了山。

toil² *n* [U] *formal*【正式】**1** hard unpleasant work done over a long period 长时间的辛苦劳作: *a life of toil* 一生辛劳 **2 the toils of** *literary* if you are caught in the toils of an unpleasant feeling or situation, you are trapped by it【文】困境; 困惑; 迷惑

toi·let /ˈtɔɪlɪt; ˈtɔɪlɪ̵t/ *n* **1** [C] a large bowl that you sit on to get rid of waste liquid or waste matter from your body 抽水马桶, 便池: *He flushed the toilet.* 他放水冲了马桶。**2** [C] *especially BrE* a room or building containing a toilet【尤英】厕所, 洗手间, 卫生间; BATHROOM (2) *AmE*【美】: *public toilets* 公共厕所 **3 go to the toilet** *BrE* to pass waste liquid or waste matter from your body【英】上厕所: *Mummy, I need to go to the toilet!* 妈妈! 我得去上厕所! **4** [U] *old-fashioned* the act of washing and dressing yourself【过时】梳洗, 打扮  2

toilet bag /ˈ·· ·/ *n* [C] a bag in which you keep things such as soap, TOOTHPASTE etc when travelling〔旅行时带着的〕梳洗用具袋; SPONGE BAG *BrE*【英】—see picture at 参见 BAG[1] 图

toilet pa·per /ˈ·· ˌ··/ *n* [U] soft thin paper used for cleaning yourself after you have used the toilet 卫生纸, 手纸

toi·let·ries /ˈtɔɪlɪtrɪz; ˈtɔɪlɪ̵triz/ *n* [plural] things such as soap and TOOTHPASTE that are used for washing yourself 梳洗用具; 梳妆用品

toilet roll /ˈ·· ·/ *n* [C] *BrE* toilet paper that is wound around a small tube【英】卫生卷纸

toilet-train·ing /ˈ·· ˌ··/ *n* [U] the act of teaching a child to use a toilet〔教孩子〕使用便盆的训练 —**toilet-train** *v* [T] —**toilet-trained** *adj*

toilet wa·ter /ˈ·· ˌ··/ *n* [U] a kind of PERFUME (=pleasant smelling liquid) that does not have a very strong smell 花露水

to·ing and fro·ing /ˌtuɪŋ ənd ˋfroɪŋ; ˌtuːɪŋ ənd ˈfrəʊɪŋ/ *n* [U] **1** movement backwards and forwards many times between two or more places 来来回回, 往复多次 **2** a lot of activity that does not help you to do something 瞎忙; 忙乱: *After much toing and froing they finally reached a decision.* 忙乱了一阵之后, 他们终于作出了决定。

to·ken¹ /ˈtokən; ˈtəʊkən/ *n* [C] **1** a round piece of metal that you use instead of money in some machines〔在某些机器上用

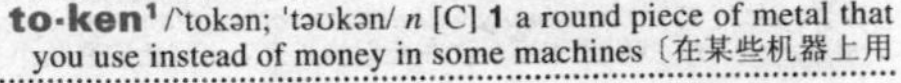

来代替钱的〕金属代币 **2** *formal* something that represents a feeling, fact, event etc【正式】象征，标志：**a token of your gratitude/respect/appreciation etc** *Please accept this gift as a small token of our appreciation.* 区区薄礼，略表谢意，请笑纳。—see also 另见 **by the same token** (SAME¹ (8)) **3 book/record/gift token** *BrE* a special piece of paper that you can exchange for a book, record etc in a shop【英】〔商店的〕购书礼券/唱片礼券/礼券；GIFT CERTIFICATE *AmE*【美】：*a £10 book token* 一张价值10英镑的购书券

token² *adj* [only before noun 仅用于名词前] **1** a token action, change etc is only done so that someone can pretend that they are dealing with a problem 装门面的；装模作样的：*The government thinks it can get away with token gestures on environmental issues.* 关于解决环保问题，政府以为做点表面文章就能掩人耳目。| **token black/woman etc** (=someone who is included in a group to make everyone think that it has all types of people in it, when this is not really true) 〔放进某些团体以示公正的〕装点门面的黑人/妇女等 **2** done as a first sign that an agreement, promise etc will be kept and that more will be done later 象征性的〔指为了表示守信而做，并将会做得更多〕：*A small token payment will keep the bank happy.* 一小笔象征性的付款会让银行感到满意。

to·ken·ism /ˈtokənˌɪzəm; ˈtəʊkənɪzəm/ *n* [U] actions that are intended to make people think that an organization deals fairly with people or problems when in fact it does not 装点门面，做表面文章

To Kill a Mock·ing·bird /ˈ·, · · ˈ· · ·/ (1960) a NOVEL by the US writer Harper Lee, which was later made into a film. The story is set in the southern US state of Alabama and is about a white lawyer, Atticus Finch, who defends a black man who has been charged with the RAPE of a white woman. The story deals with racial PREJUDICE, and especially with the effect it has on children. 《杀死一只知更鸟》〔(1960)，美国作家哈柏·李的一部小说，成书后被拍成电影。故事以美国南部的亚拉巴马州为背景，讲述白人律师阿蒂克斯·芬奇为一名被控强奸了白人女子的黑人男子辩护的故事。这部小说关涉种族歧视问题，尤其是种族歧视对儿童的影响〕

To·ky·o /ˈtokɪo; ˈtəʊkiəʊ/ the capital and largest city of Japan, and its main financial and business centre. Population: 11,549,100 (1995). 东京〔日本首都和最大城市，也是日本主要的金融和商业中心。人口：11,549,100 (1995)〕

told /told; təʊld/ the past tense and past participle of TELL

Toledo /təˈlido; təˈleɪdəʊ/ **1** a city in central Spain famous for the manufacture of swords. Its churches contain some of the greatest works of art in Spain. 托莱多〔西班牙中部一城市，以造剑闻名。该市的教堂收藏有许多优秀艺术品〕 **2** a city in northwest Ohio whose natural HARBOUR is an important port on the Great Lakes-St. Lawrence Seaway 托莱多〔俄亥俄州西北部一城市。该市的天然港口是五大湖－圣劳伦斯航道的一个重要港口〕

tol·e·ra·ble /ˈtɑlərəbl; ˈtɒlərəbəl/ *adj* **1** a situation that is tolerable is not very good, but you are able to accept it〔状况〕可接受的，过得去的，尚好的：*The apartment is really too small, but it's tolerable for the time being.* 这套公寓真的太小了，不过暂时还过得去。**2** unpleasant or painful and only just able to be accepted 令人不快[痛苦]的，仅仅可以忍受的：*The heat in this room is barely tolerable.* 这房间里热得简直无法忍受。

tol·e·ra·bly /ˈtɑlərəblɪ; ˈtɒlərəbli/ *adv* [+adj/adv] fairly, but not very much 相当；尚可：*We were tolerably happy for the first year.* 第一年，我们还算比较幸福。

tol·e·rance /ˈtɑlərəns; ˈtɒlərəns/ *n* **1** [U] willingness to allow people to do, say, or believe what they want without criticizing them 忍受，容忍；宽容：**[+of/towards]** *tolerance towards religious minorities* 对宗教上的少数派所持的宽容态度 **2** [C,U] the degree to which someone can suffer pain, difficulty etc without being harmed or damaged〔痛苦、困难等的〕忍受程度，忍耐力：**[+of/to]** *Many old people have a very limited tolerance to cold.* 许多老年人特别怕冷。**3** [C,U] *technical* the amount by which the size, weight etc of something can change without causing problems【术语】〔某物在大小、重量等方面的〕公差〔偏离公差则不能正常工作〕

tol·e·rant /ˈtɑlərənt; ˈtɒlərənt/ *adj* allowing people to do, say, or believe what they want without punishing or criticizing them 宽容的；容忍的：*Luckily, my parents were tolerant of my choice of music.* 幸运的是，我的父母对我选择音乐持宽容态度。

tol·e·rate /ˈtɑləˌret; ˈtɒləreɪt/ *v* [T] **1** to allow people to do, say, or believe something without criticizing or punishing them 容忍，容许；宽容：*We simply will not tolerate vigilante groups on our streets.* 我们根本不容许在我们的街道上出现治安联防小组。**2** to be able to accept something unpleasant or difficult, even though you do not like it 忍受；忍耐：*Many workers said they couldn't tolerate the long hours.* 许多工人都说他们无法忍受长时间的工作。

tol·e·ra·tion /ˌtɑləˈreʃən; ˌtɒləˈreɪʃən/ *n* [U] willingness to allow people to believe what they want without being punished 容忍(精神)；宽容(态度)：*a long history of religious toleration* 宗教宽容的漫长历史

Tol·kien /ˈtɑlkin; ˈtɒlkiːn/, **J.R.R.** (1892-1973) a British writer and university teacher, known for his NOVELS about imaginary characters who live in a strange, magical world, especially *The Hobbit*, and *The Lord of the Rings* 托尔金〔(1892-1973)，英国作家、大学教师，以《霍比特人》和《魔戒》等小说闻名。他在小说中虚构的人物生活在奇异的魔幻世界里〕

toll¹ /tol; təʊl/ *n* [C] **1** the money you have to pay to use a particular road, bridge etc〔道路、桥梁等的〕通行费 **2** [usually singular 一般用单数] the number of people killed or injured in a particular accident, by a particular illness etc〔事故、疾病等造成的〕伤亡人数：**death toll** *The death toll has risen to 83.* 死亡人数已上升到83人。**3 take its toll (on)** to have a very bad effect on something or someone over a long period of time 对…产生严重的不良影响：*Years of smoking have taken their toll on his health.* 多年的吸烟已严重损害了他的健康。**4** the sound of a large bell ringing slowly〔大钟的〕缓慢敲击声

toll² *v* [I,T] if a large bell tolls, or you toll it, it keeps ringing slowly, especially to show that someone has died〔尤表明某人已死而缓慢持续地〕敲(钟)，鸣(钟)

toll·booth /ˈtolˌbuθ; ˈtəʊlbuːθ/ *n* [C] a place where you pay to drive on a road, bridge etc〔道路、桥梁等征收通行费的〕收费亭[处]

toll·bridge /ˈ· ·/ *n* [C] a bridge that you pay to drive across 收费桥

toll-free /ˌ· ˈ·◂/ *adv AmE* if you telephone a particular number toll-free, you do not have to pay for the call【美】〔打某个电话号码时〕无须付费的，免费的 —**toll-free** *adj*: *Call this toll-free number for details!* 详情请拨打这个免费电话！

toll·gate /ˈtolˌget; ˈtəʊlgeɪt/ *n* [C] a gate across a road, at which you have to pay money before you can drive any further〔公路上收通行费的〕收费站，收费处

toll road /ˈ· ·/ *n* [C] a road that you pay to use 收费道路

toll·way /ˈtolwe; ˈtəʊlweɪ/ *n AmE* a large long road that you pay to use【美】收费公路

Tol·pud·dle Mar·tyrs /ˌtɑlpʌdl ˈmartəz; ˌtɒlpʌdl ˈmɑːtəz/ a group of six English farm workers who were put in jail for organizing a TRADE UNION (=organization that represents workers) in Tolpuddle, Dorset, in 1833-34. They were sent to Australia as criminals, but many people protested and in 1836 the men were brought home and set free. 托尔普德尔蒙难者〔指八名英国农场工人。他们因1833至1834年在英国多塞特郡的托尔普德尔组建工会而被判入狱，放逐澳大利亚，但遭众人抗议，遂于1836年被送回英国并获释〕

Tol·stoy /ˈtolstɔɪ; ˈtɒlstɔɪ/, **Count Leo** (1828-1910) a Russian writer famous for his long NOVELS *War and Peace* and *Anna Karenina* 托尔斯泰〔(1828-1910)，俄国作家，以长篇小说《战争与和平》与《安娜·卡列尼娜》闻名〕

tom /tɑm; tɒm/ *n* [C] *informal* a TOMCAT【非正式】雄猫，公猫

tom·a·hawk /ˈtɑməˌhɔk; ˈtɒməhɔːk/ *n* [C] a light AXE¹ (1) used by Native Americans〔北美印第安人用的〕轻斧，战斧

Tom and Jer·ry /ˌ· · ˈ· ·/ *trademark* two characters in humorous CARTOON films by Hanna and Barbera. Tom, who is a cat, is always chasing Jerry, who is a mouse, but Jerry is more clever than Tom and always finds ways of escaping.【商标】汤姆和杰里〔汉娜和巴伯拉导演的滑稽动画影片中的两个角色。汤姆是一只猫，总是追逐老鼠杰里，但杰里比汤姆聪明，总是能找到逃脱的办法〕

to·ma·to /təˈmeto; təˈmɑːtəʊ/ *n plural* **tomatoes** [C] a round soft red fruit eaten raw or cooked as a vegetable 番茄，西红柿 —see picture on page A9 参见A9页图 ⊖3

tomb /tum; tuːm/ *n* [C] a grave, especially a large one above ground〔尤指较大的〕坟，墓，冢：*the tomb of the Unknown Soldier* 无名战士墓

Tomb of the Un·knowns, the /ˌ· · · · ˈ·/ a national MONUMENT in Arlington National Cemetery in Virginia, US, where soldiers whose names were not known are buried from World Wars I and II, the Korean War, and the Vietnam War. It represents all the US people who died in those wars. 无名战士纪念碑〔美国弗吉尼亚州阿灵顿国家公墓的一处国家纪念碑，安葬着在一战、二战、朝鲜战争以及越南战争中阵亡的无名战士。该纪念碑代表在这些战争中阵亡的所有美国人〕

tom·bo·la/ˈtɑmbələ; tɒmˈbəʊlə/ *n* [U] *BrE* a game in which you buy a ticket with a number on it in order to try and win a prize【英】"担保乐"〔一种摸彩游戏〕

Tom·bouc·tou/ˌtɑmbukˋtu; ˌtɒmbuːkˈtuː/ the correct name of Timbuktu, a city in West Africa 通布图〔Timbuktu (廷巴克图)的正确拼法, 为西非一城市〕

tom·boy/ˈtɑmˌbɔɪ; ˈtɒmbɔɪ/ *n* [C] a girl who likes playing the same games as boys 野丫头, 假小子〔指喜欢像男孩子那样打闹的女孩子〕: *I was just coming out of my tomboy stage.* 我刚度过我的野丫头阶段。

Tom Brown's School·days /ˌ· ˈ· ˈ··/ (1857) a NOVEL by Thomas Hughes which describes life in a 19th century British PUBLIC SCHOOL (=a private school) for UPPER CLASS boys. The main character, Tom Brown, is shown as having high moral values. Another character, Flashman, who is a cruel BULLY, treats Tom Brown and his friends, who are younger than Flashman, very badly.《汤姆·布朗的求学时代》〔(1857), 托马斯·休斯的一部小说, 描写19世纪英国上层社会男孩读公学的生活。书中的主人公汤姆·布朗具有高尚的道德观。另一个人物名叫弗莱希曼, 恃强凌弱, 总是欺负年龄比他小的汤姆·布朗及其朋友〕

Tombstone a city in Arizona in the US, where the gunfight at the OK Corral took place 汤姆斯通〔美国亚利桑那州一城市。奥凯马厩大决战发生在此地〕

tomb·stone/ˈtumˌston; ˈtuːmstəʊn/ *n* [C] a stone that is put on a grave and shows the dead person's name, dates of birth and death etc; GRAVESTONE 墓石, 墓碑

tom·cat /ˈtɑmkæt; ˈtɒmkæt/ *n* [C] a male cat 雄猫, 公猫

tome/tom; təʊm/ *n* [C] *literary* a large heavy book【文】大部头书, 厚本书: *hefty leather-bound tomes of uncertain age* 沉重的、年代不详的皮装大部头书

tom·fool /ˌtɑmˋful; ˌtɒmˈfuːl◂/ *adj* very silly 极傻的, 笨透的: *That was a tomfool thing to do!* 那件事做得愚蠢透顶!

tom·fool·e·ry/ˌtɑmˋfulərɪ; tɒmˈfuːləri/ *n* [U] silly behaviour 愚蠢行为

Tom Jones /ˌ· ˈ·/ (1749) a humorous NOVEL by Henry Fielding about the travels, adventures, and sexual relationships of a young man, Tom Jones, whose behaviour is not always moral, but who is still likeable. It is one of the first modern English novels, and it influenced many later writers.《汤姆·琼斯》〔(1749), 亨利·菲尔丁创作的一部幽默小说。该书描写年轻人汤姆·琼斯的游历、奇遇以及风流韵事。尽管他的行为不总是合乎道德, 但他仍然讨人喜爱。这是最早的英国现代小说之一, 对菲尔丁之后的许多作家产生了一定影响〕

tom·my gun/ˈtɑmɪ ˌɡʌn; ˈtɒmi ɡʌn/ *n* [C] *informal* a small gun that can fire many bullets very quickly【非正式】汤姆式冲锋枪, 轻机枪

S1 W2 **to·mor·row¹** /təˋmɔro; təˈmɒrəʊ/ *adv* on or during the day after today (在)明天: *Our class is going to London tomorrow.* 我们全班明天要去伦敦。| **a week tomorrow** also 又作 **tomorrow week** *BrE*【英】(=a week from tomorrow) 从明天算起的一周 *James's new job starts a week tomorrow.* 詹姆斯的新工作从明天算起的一周之后开始。

tomorrow² *n* **1** [U] the day after today 明天: *I'll see you at tomorrow's meeting.* 在明天的会上再见吧。—see picture at 参见 DAY 图 **2** the future, especially the near future 来日, 未来〔尤指不久的将来〕: *The computers of tomorrow will be smaller and more powerful.* 未来的电脑将更小巧, 功能将更强大。**3** **do sth like there's no tomorrow** do something very quickly and carelessly, without worrying about the future 毫无节制地做某事, 不考虑将来地做某事: *Rita's spending money like there's no tomorrow.* 丽塔花起钱来根本不考虑将来。

Tom Sawyer —see 见 Tom SAWYER

Tom Thumb /ˌ· ˈ·/ a character in a FAIRY TALE (=a story for children in which magical things happen) who was only as big as a person's thumb 拇指汤姆〔童话故事中一人物, 身材如同人的拇指〕

tom-tom/ˈ· ·/ *n* [C] a long narrow drum you play with your hands〔一种狭长的〕手鼓, 长筒鼓

S3 **ton** /tʌn; tʌn/ *n* [C] **1** *plural* **tons** or **ton** a unit for measuring weight, equal to 2,240 pounds or 1,016 kilos in Britain, and 2,000 pounds or 907.2 kilos in the US 英吨〔2240磅或1016公斤〕; 美吨〔2000磅或907.2公斤〕—compare 比较 TONNE —see table on page C3 参见C3页附录 **2** **tons of** *informal* a lot of【非正式】大量的: *We've bought tons of beer for the party tonight.* 我们已经为今晚的聚会买了大量啤酒。**3** **weigh a ton** *informal* to be very heavy【非正式】非常重: *Your bag weighs a ton!* 你的包重得不得了! **4** **do a ton** *BrE informal* to drive at 100 miles an hour【英, 非正式】以每小时100英里的速度驾驶 **5** **come down on sb like a ton of bricks** *informal* to get very angry with someone about something they have done【非正式】对某人大发脾气

ton·al/ˈtonl; ˈtəʊnl/ *adj* **1** connected with tones of colour or sound 色调的; 音调的: *The tonal range she uses is wide and varied.* 她使用的音域宽广, 富于变化。**2** *technical* a piece of music that is tonal is based on a particular KEY² (4)【术语】〔音乐〕调性的 —opposite 反义词 ATONAL

to·nal·i·ty/toˋnælətɪ; təʊˈnælɪ̣ti/ *n* [C,U] *technical* the character of a piece of music that depends on the KEY² (4) of the music and the way in which the tunes and harmonies (HARMONY (1)) are combined【术语】〔音乐的〕调性

W2 **tone¹**/ton; təʊn/ *n*

1 ►VOICE SHOWING FEELING 表明情感的说话声◄ [C] [plural] the way your voice sounds that shows how you are feeling, or what you mean〔说话的〕语气, 口气; 腔调: *"Why would I lie?" Nora asked in an injured tone.* "我为什么要撒谎?"诺拉用委屈的口气问道。| *She spoke in warm tones about her family.* 她以亲切的语气谈论她的家庭。| **tone of voice** *spoken* (=used about someone's rude or angry way of speaking)【口】说话的腔调〔带有粗鲁或愠怒〕*I don't like your tone of voice.* 我不喜欢你说话的腔调。| **don't take that tone with me** *spoken* (=do not speak to me in that rude or unpleasant way)【口】别用那种口吻跟我说话

2 ►SOUND 声音◄ [C,U] the quality of a sound especially the sound of a musical instrument or someone's voice〔尤指乐器或某人说话的〕音调; 音色, 音质: *Your piano has a beautiful tone.* 你这架钢琴音色很美。| **in tone** (=having a particular tone) 在音质上 *Margaret's voice was shrill in tone.* 玛格丽特尖声尖气地说话。| **deep-toned/even-toned/shrill-toned etc** (=having a low, calm etc tone) 声音低沉/平和/很尖等的 *My father spoke in an even-toned voice.* 我父亲以平和的声音说话。

3 ►GENERAL FEELING/ATTITUDE 一般的感觉/态度◄ [singular,U] the general feeling or attitude expressed in a piece of writing, activity etc〔作品、活动等的〕基调, 格调; 气氛: *Sara had kept the tone of the meeting businesslike.* 萨拉一直使会议保持着务实的气氛。| **set the tone** (=establish the general attitude or feeling of an event, activity etc) 确定基调 *Unfortunately, their disagreement set the tone for the whole evening.* 不幸的是, 他们的不和笼罩着整个晚会。

4 ►SOCIALLY ACCEPTABLE 社会可以接受的◄ [U] the degree to which something is considered polite, interesting, socially acceptable etc 风气; 格调, 情调: *The formal setting gave a certain tone to the evening.* 正式而拘谨的环境使晚会带上了某种气氛。| **lower/raise the tone** *That horrible building lowers the whole tone of the neighborhood.* 那栋难看的建筑物降低了周围的格调。

5 ►COLOUR 颜色◄ [C] one of the many types of a particular colour, each slightly darker, lighter, brighter etc than the next 色调; 色彩的层次: *The entire painting was in tones of blue.* 整幅画都是蓝色调。—see also 另见 TWO-TONE

6 ►ELECTRONIC SOUND 电子声音◄ [C] a sound made by electronic equipment, such as a telephone〔电话等发出的〕电子声音: *Please leave a message after the tone.* 请在提示音后留言。| **dial/busy** *AmE*【美】**/engaged** *BrE*【英】**tone** (=the sound you hear on a telephone that means you can dial, it is busy etc)〔电话的〕拨号音/忙音 —see also 另见 DIALLING TONE

7 ►BODY 身体◄ [U] *technical* how firm and strong your muscles, skin etc are【术语】〔肌肉、皮肤等的〕强健, 健康状况: *Swimming improves your muscle tone.* 游泳会使你的肌肉更强健。

8 ►MUSIC 音乐◄ [C] *technical* the difference in PITCH² (3) between two musical notes that are separated by one KEY² (4) on the piano【术语】音程, 音级; STEP¹ (17) *especially AmE*【尤美】

9 ►VOICE LEVEL 语音调子◄ [C] *technical* the PITCH¹ (3) of someone's voice as they speak【术语】〔说话的〕声调; 语调: *The Chinese language has several tones.* 汉语有几种声调。

tone² *v* [T] to improve the strength and firmness of your skin, muscles etc 使〔皮肤、肌肉等〕更强健, 使更健康: *It cleanses and tones your skin.* 它清洁你的皮肤, 使之更加健康。

tone sth ↔ **down** *phr v* [T] **1** to reduce the effect of a speech or piece or writing, so that people will not be offended 缓和…语气: *His advisers told him to tone down his speech.* 他的顾问们告诉他要缓和讲话的语气。**2** to make a colour less bright 使〔颜色〕暗淡, 柔和

tone sth/sb ↔ **up** *phr v* [T] to make your body or part of your body feel healthier and stronger 使更健康, 使更强健: *Aerobics really tones up your muscles.* 有氧健身法的确会使你的肌肉更加强健。

tone-deaf /ˌ·ˈ·◂/ *adj* unable to tell the difference between different musical notes 不会辨别音调的: *the tone-deaf morons in today's pop groups* 在今天的流行音乐乐队里五音不辨的蠢才

tone lan·guage /ˈ·ˌ··/ *n* [C] *technical* a language such as Chinese in which the way a sound goes up or down affects the meaning of the word【术语】声调语言〔声调的高低会影响单词意思的语言，如汉语〕

tone·less /ˈtonlɪs; ˈtəʊnləs/ *adj* a toneless voice does not express any feelings〔声音〕单调的，平板的: *"I'm sorry," he said, in a flat toneless voice.* "对不起。"他以一种平淡的声调说道。—**tonelessly** *adv*

tone po·em /ˈ·ˌ··/ *n* [C] a piece of music written to represent an idea, scene, or story 交响诗，音诗〔表达思想、场面、故事的音乐作品〕

ton·er /ˈtonɚ; ˈtəʊnə/ *n* [U] **1** a type of ink used in computer PRINTERs, PHOTOCOPIERs etc〔电脑打印机、复印机等用的〕增色剂，色粉 **2** a liquid that you put on your face to make your skin feel good〔抹在脸上的〕润肤水

Tong·a /ˈtɑŋə; ˈtɒŋə/ a country consisting of about 170 small islands in the southwest Pacific Ocean. Population: 104,227 (2001). Capital: Nuku'alofa. It is ruled by a king and is a member of the British Commonwealth. 汤加〔太平洋西南部一国家，由大约170个小岛组成。人口: 104,227 (2001)，首都: 努库阿洛法。该国由国王统治，为英联邦成员国〕—**Tongan** *n, adj*

tongs /tɔŋz; tɒŋz/ *n* [plural] a tool that consists of two moveable bars joined at one end, used to pick up an object 夹子，钳子，镊子 —see picture at 参见 LABORATORY 图

tongue /tʌŋ; tʌŋ/ *n*

1 ▶MOUTH 嘴◀ [C] the soft, moveable part inside your mouth that you use for tasting, eating, and speaking 舌，舌头: *Joe ran his tongue over his dry lips.* 乔用舌头舔舔干燥的嘴唇。| *The dog panted, his tongue hanging out in the heat.* 那只狗在酷暑中把舌头伸在外面，喘着粗气。| **stick your tongue out** (=put your tongue outside your mouth as a rude gesture) 伸出舌头〔不礼貌的表示〕*Kim stuck her tongue out at the teacher.* 金不礼貌地朝老师伸出舌头。

2 sharp/eloquent/silver/acid etc tongue if you have a sharp, silver etc tongue, you speak in a way that shows your anger, use beautiful language etc 尖刻/流利/动听/尖酸等的话: *Gina's sharp tongue will get her into trouble one day.* 吉娜说话尖酸刻薄，总有一天会给自己惹上麻烦的。| **rough-tongued/sharp-tongued/silver-tongued etc** (=speaking in an angry, beautiful etc way) 说话愤怒/尖刻/动听等的 *He was clever and acid-tongued.* 他伶牙俐齿的，老爱挖苦人。

3 tongue in cheek if you say something with your tongue in your cheek, you say it as a joke〔说话〕不当真地; 开玩笑地 —see also 另见 TONGUE-IN-CHEEK

4 slip of the tongue a mistake in something you say 说漏了嘴，说错了话，口误: *Did I say $100? It must have been a slip of the tongue.* 我说过100美元吗? 那一定是口误。

5 bite your tongue to stop yourself saying something because it is better not to 停止说话，保持缄默: *I wanted to argue but I had to bite my tongue.* 我想辩驳，但又不得不保持缄默。| **bite your tongue!** (=used to tell someone angrily that they should not say the type of thing they have just said) 闭上你的嘴! 别再说了!

6 Cat got your tongue? also 又作 **Lost your tongue?** *spoken* used to ask someone why they are not talking【口】怎么不说话了?

7 get your tongue around *informal* to be able to say a difficult word or phrase【非正式】说出〔某个拗口的词或短语〕: *I can't get my tongue around the names of these Welsh towns.* 这些威尔士城镇的名字很拗口，我念不出来。

8 ▶LANGUAGE 语言◀ *literary* a language【文】语言; 方言: *Anton lapsed into his own tongue when he was excited.* 安东激动的时候就说自己的家乡话了。—see also 另见 MOTHER TONGUE, **native tongue** (NATIVE[1] (3))

9 watch your tongue! *spoken* used to tell someone that they should not have said something rude【口】注意你的话!

10 ▶FOOD 食物◀ [U] the tongue of a cow or sheep, cooked and eaten cold〔牛、羊等动物可供冷食的〕舌头

11 trip/roll off the tongue *humorous* if a name, phrase etc trips or rolls off your tongue, it is easy or pleasant to say【幽默】〔名字、短语等〕流畅地讲出: *Agatha Boglewood: it doesn't exactly trip off the tongue, does it?* 阿加莎·博格尔伍德: 说起来并不那么容易，是吧?

12 ▶SHAPE 形状◀ [C] something that has a long thin shape 舌状物: [+of] *tongues of fire* 火舌

13 ▶SHOE 鞋◀ the part of a shoe that lies on top of your foot, under the part where you tie it 鞋舌 —see picture at 参见 SHOE[1] 图

14 loosen sb's tongue if something, such as alcohol loosens your tongue, it makes you talk a lot〔喝酒等〕使某人话多，使某人管不住嘴: *Tongues loosened by drink, they told me what I needed to know.* 他们喝了酒话多，结果把我需要知道的都告诉了我。

15 find your tongue to speak after being silent because you were afraid or shy〔因害怕或害羞而沉默之后〕终于开口说话: *Dana finally found his tongue and told them how he'd hated his first day at school.* 达纳终于开口说话了，他告诉他们，他是多么讨厌上学的第一天。

16 hold your tongue! *old-fashioned spoken* used to angrily tell someone to stop speaking【过时，口】闭嘴! 不要讲话!

17 wagging tongues if you talk about tongues wagging, you mean that people are talking about someone in an unkind way 风言风语，说长道短: *Angela's divorce will certainly set tongues wagging.* 安杰拉的离婚肯定会让人们说三道四的。

18 keep a civil tongue in your head *spoken* used when you think someone should speak politely【口】说话要讲礼貌〔认为别人说话粗鲁时使用〕

19 speak with forked tongue *humorous* to tell lies【幽默】说谎

20 speak in tongues to speak using strange words as part of a religious experience 说别国的话，说其他民族的话〔一种宗教体验〕

21 tongue and groove joint *technical* a way of joining two pieces of wood【术语】〔两块木头的〕舌槽式接合 —see also 另见 **on the tip of your tongue** (TIP[1] (6)), **give sb the rough side of your tongue** (ROUGH[1] (18))

tongue de·press·or /ˈ·ˌ·ˌ··/ *n* [C] *AmE* a little flat piece of wood a doctor uses to hold down your tongue while examining your throat【美】〔医生检查病人喉咙时用的〕压舌板; SPATULA *BrE*【英】

tongue-in-cheek /ˌ·ˌ·ˈ·◂/ *adj* a tongue-in-cheek remark, comment etc is said as a joke〔讲话、评论等〕不可当真的，开玩笑的: *a splendidly tongue-in-cheek account of their first meeting* 对他们第一次见面的情景所作的天花乱坠的、不可当真的描述 —**tongue-in-cheek** *adv*: *I believe he said this tongue-in-cheek.* 我认为他说的这一点是开玩笑。

tongue-tied /ˈ··/ *adj* unable to speak easily to other people, especially because you feel embarrassed〔尤指因感到难堪而〕张口结舌的，说不出话的: *He sat tongue-tied, like a shy schoolboy.* 他笨嘴拙舌地坐在那里，活像个害羞的小学生。

tongue twist·er /ˈ·ˌ··/ *n* [C] a word or phrase that is difficult to say quickly and correctly 绕口的词语[句子]，绕口令

ton·ic[1] /ˈtɑnɪk; ˈtɒnɪk/ *n* **1** [C,U] also 又作 **tonic water** a clear bitter tasting drink that is mixed with alcoholic drinks such as GIN or VODKA 奎宁水: *a gin and tonic* 加奎宁水的杜松子酒 **2** [C usually singular 一般用单数] *BrE* something that improves your health, strength, or confidence【英】增进健康[增强信心]的东西: *The holiday was a real tonic.* 那次度假确实让人精神焕发。**3** [C] a medicine that is designed to give you more energy or strength when you feel tired 强身剂，补药: *a herbal tonic* 滋补性草药 **4** [C usually singular 一般用单数] *technical* the first note in a musical SCALE[1] (8)【术语】〔音阶中的〕主音

tonic[2] *adj formal* giving you energy and strength【正式】强身健体的，有利于健康的: *Sea air has a tonic quality.* 海洋空气有增进健康的作用。

to·night[1] /təˈnaɪt; təˈnaɪt/ *adv* on or during the night of today (在)今晚: *I've been really tired all day so I think I'll go to bed early tonight.* 我整天都觉得累极了，所以今晚想早点上床睡觉。| *at 9 o'clock tonight* 在今晚9点钟

tonight[2] *n* [U] the night of today 今晚: *Tonight is a very special occasion.* 今晚是个非同寻常的场合。| *tonight's news bulletin* 今晚的新闻发布

ton·nage /ˈtʌnɪdʒ; ˈtʌnɪdʒ/ *n* [C,U] **1** the size of a ship or the amount of goods it can carry, shown in TONs〔表示船舶大小的〕吨位; 载重吨位 **2** the total number of TONs that something weighs〔以吨计的〕总重量，总吨数

tonne /tʌn; tʌn/ *n plural* **tonnes** *or* **tonne** [C] a metric unit for measuring weight, equal to 1,000 kilograms 公吨〔等于1000公斤〕—see table on page C3 见C3页附录

tons /tʌnz; tʌnz/ *adv informal* very much【非正式】非常，极其: *I feel tons better after a rest.* 休息之后，我感觉好多了。

ton·sil /ˈtɑnsḷ; ˈtɒnsəl/ *n* [C] one of two small round pieces of flesh at the sides of the throat near the back of the tongue 扁桃体，扁桃腺: *She had to have her tonsils out.* 她得把扁桃体切除。—see picture at 参见 RESPIRATORY 图

ton·sil·li·tis /ˌtɑnsḷˈaɪtɪs; ˌtɒnsɪˈlaɪtɪs/ *n* [U] a serious infection of the tonsils 扁桃体炎，扁桃腺炎

tools 工具

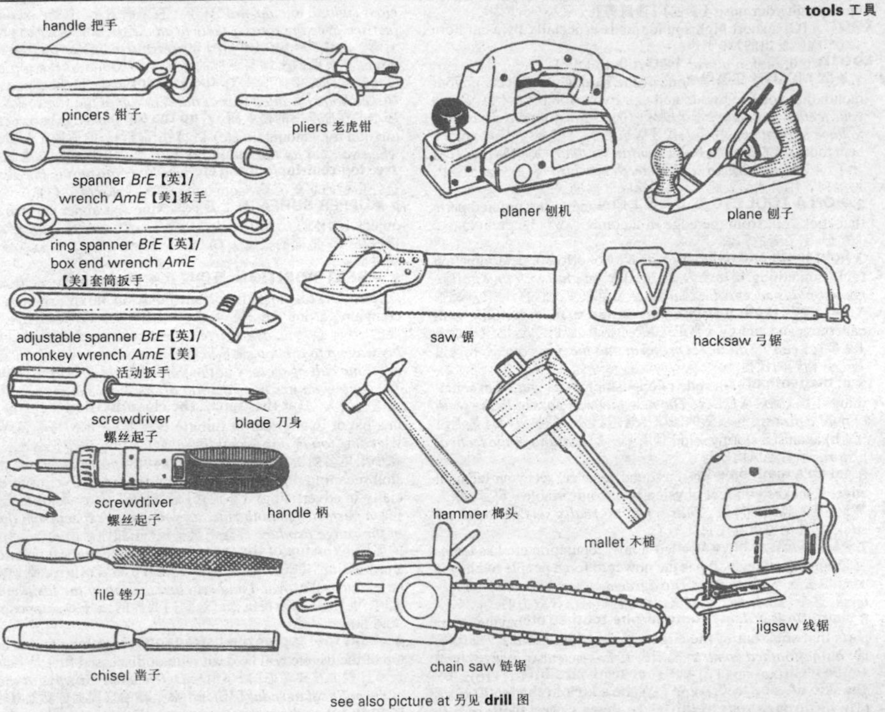

handle 把手
pincers 钳子
pliers 老虎钳
spanner *BrE*【英】/ wrench *AmE*【美】扳手
ring spanner *BrE*【英】/ box end wrench *AmE*【美】套筒扳手
adjustable spanner *BrE*【英】/ monkey wrench *AmE*【美】活动扳手
screwdriver 螺丝起子
blade 刀身
screwdriver 螺丝起子
handle 柄
file 锉刀
chisel 凿子
planer 刨机
plane 刨子
saw 锯
hacksaw 弓锯
hammer 榔头
mallet 木槌
jigsaw 线锯
chain saw 链锯

see also picture at 另见 **drill** 图

ton·so·ri·al /tɑn`sɔriəl; tɒn'sɔːriəl/ *adj humorous* connected with cutting hair【幽默】理发的; 理发师的: *a display of tonsorial perfection* 理发师精湛手艺的展示

ton·sure /'tɑnʃə; 'tɒnʃə/ *n* **1** [U] the act of removing all the hair from the top of your head to show that you are a MONK〔出家为僧的〕削发〔仪式〕**2** [C] the top part of your head that has had the hair removed for this reason〔出家僧人的〕头顶剃光部分,〔出家僧人的〕光顶 **—tonsured** *adj*

ton-up /'· ·/ *adj BrE old-fashioned*【英, 过时】**ton-up driver/biker etc** someone who likes to drive very fast 喜欢开快车的驾驶员/喜欢骑快车的自行车手等

Tony A·ward /'· · ·, ·/ also 又作 **Tony** *n* [C] a prize given to the best theatre actor, best actress, best play etc, shown in New York in a particular year 托尼奖〔美国一奖项。授予某年度在纽约上演的最佳剧目以及最佳男演员和最佳女演员〕

S1 W1 **too** /tu; tuː/ *adv* **1** [+adj/adv] more than is reasonable, possible, or necessary 太, 过分: *That music is too loud, turn the radio down.* 那音乐太闹了, 把收音机关小一点。| **too much/little/many etc sth** *There's too much talking! Open your books and get down to work.* 话太多了! 打开书本, 开始学习吧。| **much/far/a little etc too** *Amanda is much too young to get married.* 阿曼达太年轻了, 还不能结婚。| **too tall/old etc for** *That crossword is too difficult for me.* 那个拼字游戏对我来说太难了。| **too good/hot/big (a sth) to do sth** *My coffee is too hot to drink.* 我的咖啡太烫, 没法喝。| *A free cruise to Acapulco – that's too good an opportunity to miss.* 免费乘船游览阿卡普尔科——那个机会太好了, 不能错过。**2** [at the end of a sentence or clause 用于句子或从句的末尾] also 也, 亦, 还: *It's a nutritious meal and cheap too!* 这是富于营养的一餐饭, 而且还很便宜。| *Sheila wants to come too.* 希拉也想来。—compare 比较 EITHER **3** [+adj/adv] very 很, 非常: *Dinner shouldn't be too long. Would you like a drink first?* 晚餐应该不会等很久。你要不要先喝上一杯? | *You shouldn't have bought flowers. You're too kind.* 你本来不必买花, 你太客气了。**4 all too/only too** used to say that something is very easy to do, happens very often etc when it should not 很, 极, 非常: *Sadly this kind of attack is becoming all too common these days.* 现在这种袭击太常见了, 令人悲哀。**5** used to emphasize that you are angry, surprised, or agree with something〔用于强调愤怒、吃惊或赞同某事〕: *"They've just built another car park next to the supermarket." "About time too."* "他们刚在超市旁边修建了另外一个停车场。" "是该修了。" **6 I am/he is/you are etc too** *informal especially AmE* used to emphasize that you disagree with what someone has said about you【非正式, 尤美】我/他/你等其实[一定]…〔用于断然表示不同意〕: *"You're not smart enough to use a computer." "I am too!"* "你脑子不够机灵, 不会用电脑。" "我其实可以!"

took /tuk; tʊk/ the past tense of TAKE

S2 W2 **tool[1]** /tul; tuːl/ *n* [C] **1** something such as a hammer that you hold in your hand and use to do a particular job 工具: *Rob didn't have the right tool to repair the engine.* 罗布没有合适的工具来修理发动机。**2** something such as a piece of equipment or skill that is useful for doing your job 器具; 技能: *Television is an important tool for the modern teacher.* 对于现代教师来说, 电视是一种重要的工具。| **tools of the trade** *The poet is a craftsman and words are the tools of his trade.* 诗人是工匠, 文字是他这一行必不可少的工具。**3** someone who is used unfairly by someone else 被人利用的工具; 爪牙; 傀儡: **[+of]** *The king was merely a tool of the military government.* 这位国王只不过是军人政府的傀儡。**4** *taboo slang* a PENIS (=the male sex organ)【讳, 俚】阴茎, 鸡巴 —see also 另见 **down tools** (DOWN[4] (3))

tool[2] *v* **[I+along/down]** *AmE informal* to drive along a street, especially for fun【美, 非正式】〔尤指悠闲地〕驾驶车辆

tool up *phr v* [I,T **tool** sth ↔ **up**] to prepare a factory for production by providing the necessary tools and machinery〔以必要的工具和机器等〕装备〔工厂〕: *tooled up to produce light weapons* 装备工厂以生产轻型武器

tooled /tuld; tuːld/ *adj* tooled leather has been decorated using a special tool〔皮革〕手工压花的

tool kit /'· ·/ *n* [C] a set of various tools 工具包, 工具箱

tool shed /'· ·/ *n* [C] a small wooden building in a garden, where tools are kept〔园圃里的〕工具房

toot[1] /tut; tuːt/ *v* [I,T] **1** *especially BrE* if you toot your car horn, or if it toots, it makes a short, high sound【尤英】(使)〔汽车喇叭〕发嘟嘟声: *The taxi driver was angrily tooting his horn.*

那位出租车司机在愤怒地按着喇叭。**2** *AmE slang* to take COCAINE up through your nose【美俚】〔通过鼻孔〕吸入（可卡因）

toot² *n* [C] a short high sound, made especially by a car horn〔汽车喇叭发出的〕嘟嘟声

tooth /tuθ; tuːθ/ *n plural* **teeth** /tiθ; tiːθ/ [C]

1 ►IN MOUTH 在嘴里◄ one of the hard white objects in your mouth that you use to bite and CHEW your food 牙，牙齿: *Brush your teeth twice a day.* 每天刷牙两次。| *I'm going to the dentist to have a tooth out.* 我要去找牙医拔牙。| **cut a tooth** (=grow a new tooth) 长新牙 *The baby's cutting a tooth.* 那个婴儿在长新牙了。| *The Doberman sank its teeth into his leg.* 那只多伯曼氏短尾狗咬住了他的大腿，牙齿深深咬进肉里。

2 ►ON A TOOL ETC 在工具等上面◄ one of the pointed parts that sticks out from the edge of a comb, SAW² (1), COG (1), etc〔梳子、锯子等的〕齿

3 fight tooth and nail to try with a lot of effort or determination to do something 竭尽全力；坚决: *We fought tooth and nail to get our plans accepted.* 我们竭尽全力争取使我们的计划被采纳。

4 get your teeth into *informal* to start to do something with eagerness and energy【非正式】开始认真处理；急迫地想开始做〔某事〕: *I can't wait to get my teeth into the new course.* 我真想马上开始新的课程。

5 in the teeth of a) in spite of opposition or danger from something 不顾〔反对或危险〕: *The new law was passed in the teeth of public protest.* 这项新的法律尽管遭到公众的抗议可还是通过了。**b)** against a stormy wind 顶着〔暴风〕: *sailing in the teeth of a storm* 顶着暴风雨航行

6 set sb's teeth on edge if a sound, taste etc sets your teeth on edge, it makes you feel physically uncomfortable〔声音、味道等〕使某人感到不舒服: *That scraping really sets my teeth on edge.* 那种刮擦声真让我受不了。

7 ►LAW 法律◄ have teeth if a law, regulation etc has teeth, or if you give it teeth, it has the power to force people to obey it〔法律、法规等〕具有效力: *The agreement works because it has teeth.* 这个协议并非一纸空文，因为它是有法律效力的。

8 sharp-toothed/saw-toothed/fine-toothed etc having sharp parts that stick out of the edge, etc 尖牙利齿/锯齿般/细齿等的: *a fine-toothed comb* 一把细齿梳子 —see also 另见 **armed to the teeth** (ARMED (1)), **cut your teeth on sth** (CUT¹ (16)), **by the skin of your teeth** (SKIN¹ (5)), **be a kick in the teeth** (KICK² (4)), **lie through your teeth** (LIE² (1)), **have a sweet tooth** (SWEET¹ (7)), **take the bit between your teeth** (BIT¹ (17))

tooth·ache /ˈtuθˌek; ˈtuːθ-eɪk/ *n* [C,U] a pain in a tooth 牙痛

tooth·brush /ˈtuθˌbrʌʃ; ˈtuːθbrʌʃ/ *n* [C] a small brush for cleaning your teeth 牙刷 —see picture at 参见 BRUSH¹ 图

tooth·less /ˈtuθləs; ˈtuːθləs/ *adj* **1** having no teeth 没有牙齿的: *a toothless smile* 不露齿的笑 **2** a law that is toothless has no power to make someone obey it〔法律〕无效的，无约束力的，不起作用的: *Without legal sanctions it is toothless.* 没有法律上的认可，这是无约束力的。

tooth·paste /ˈtuθˌpest; ˈtuːθpeɪst/ *n* [U] a substance used to clean your teeth 牙膏

tooth·pick /ˈtuθˌpɪk; ˈtuːθˌpɪk/ *n* [C] a very small pointed stick for removing bits of food that are stuck between your teeth 牙签

tooth pow·der /ˈ· ˌ··/ *n* [U] a special powder used to clean your teeth 牙粉

tooth·some /ˈtuθsəm; ˈtuːθsəm/ *adj humorous* tasting good; DELICIOUS【幽默】味道好的，美味可口的: *the less toothsome corners of English cuisine* 英国烹调中不太可口的方面

tooth·y /ˈtuθɪ; ˈtuːθi/ *adj* **toothy smile/grin** a smile in which you show a lot of teeth 露齿的笑

toot·le /ˈtutl̩; ˈtuːtl/ *v* [I] *BrE*【英】**1** *old-fashioned* to move slowly in a car【过时】〔汽车〕缓慢地行驶 **2** to play an instrument such as a FLUTE without producing any particular tune〔长笛等乐器〕连续发出不成音调的声音

toots /tuts; tʊts/ *n* [C] *AmE old-fashioned* a way of addressing a woman, sometimes considered offensive【美，过时】宝贝儿〔该称呼有时被认为具有冒犯性〕: *Hey toots! How're you doing?* 嘿，宝贝儿！过得怎么样？

toot·sie /ˈtutsɪ; ˈtʊtsi/ *n* [C] **1** *AmE spoken* a way of addressing a woman, sometimes considered offensive【美口】宝贝儿〔该称呼有时被认为具有冒犯性〕**2 tootsies** [plural] *informal* a word meaning toes, used especially by or to children【非正式】脚趾〔尤为儿语〕

top¹ /tɑp; tɒp/ *n* [C]

1 ►THE HIGHEST PART 最高部分◄ the highest part of something 顶部，顶端，上端: **the top of** *Place the mixture in the top of the oven.* 把混合物放在烤箱的上半部分。| *The top of the mountain is covered with snow.* 山顶覆盖着白雪。| *I filled the glass right to the top.* 我把杯子一直斟满为止。| *She could only just see over the tops of their heads.* 她仅仅能越过他们的头顶看看。| **at the top (of sth)** *Write your name at the top of the page.* 在页面的上端写下你的名字。| *I stood at the top of the stairs.* 我站在楼梯顶端。| **the very top** (=the highest part) 最上端 *The book I wanted was at the very top of the stack.* 我想要的那本书在那堆书的最上面。| **up the top** *spoken* (=at or near the top of a tree, mountain etc)【口】在[靠近]…的顶端 *You'll see it when you get up the top of the hill.* 你到山顶时就会看到的。| **tree top/roof-top/hill-top etc** *the white cliff-tops in the distance* 远处白色的峭壁顶端 —opposite 反义词 BOTTOM¹ (1)

2 ►UPPER SURFACE 上方表面◄ the flat upper surface of an object〔物体的〕上面: *papers spread all over the top of piano* 摊放在钢琴上面的报纸 | *The table has a glass top.* 这桌子是玻璃桌面。

3 ►BEST POSITION 最佳位置◄ the top the best, most successful, or most important position in an organization, company, group etc〔机构、公司、团体等中的〕最好位置；最重要的职位；最高位: *He started life at the bottom and worked his way up to the top.* 他从最低层干起，然后一步步升到了最高层。| *the cult of secrecy at the top* 上层对保密的热衷 | **the top of** *people who are near the top of the wages league* 差不多最高工资的人 | **(at the) top of the class/division etc** (=the best in a list or in an order of things) 在班上/在部门里等名列前茅 *We came top of our group three years running.* 我们连续三年在小组里名列榜首。| **top of the range** *informal* (=an expression meaning one of the best or most expensive, used especially in advertising)【非正式】最佳[最贵]的产品〔尤广告上使用〕*a perfectly smooth ride, as you would expect from the top of the range product* 行驶绝对平稳，正如你对顶尖产品所期望的那样 | **the top of the tree** *informal* (=the highest position in a profession)【非正式】〔在某一行业中〕高居首位；达到顶峰 *By now Vivien Westwood had reached the top of the fashion tree.* 此时，维维恩·韦斯特伍德已达到时装界的顶峰。—opposite 反义词 BOTTOM¹ (5)

4 be (at the) top of the list/agenda something that is at the top of the list etc will be dealt with or discussed first 是名单上/议事日程上首要考虑的〔事情〕: *Defence isn't always at the top of the political agenda!* 国防并不总是政治议程上首要考虑的事！

5 on top a) on the highest point or surface of something 在最上面，在顶部: *Sprinkle some Parmesan on top and grill.* 在面上撒一些帕尔梅森干酪，然后加以烧烤。| *a hat with a red pompom on top* 顶部有一个红色小绒球的帽子 | **on top of** *There's $10 on top of the refrigerator.* 冰箱上面有10美元。| **one on top of the other** also 又作 **on top of one another** (=in a pile) 一个一个地码成一堆 *The workmen were stacking the crates on top of one another.* 工人们把那些板条箱一个挨一个地码起来。—opposite 反义词 UNDERNEATH **b)** in the most successful or important position in business, a game etc〔在商务、体育比赛等中〕处于领先地位，占上风: *The All Blacks stayed on top throughout the match.* "全黑"队整场比赛一直领先。**c)** on the highest part of your head 在头顶部: *Cut it short on top, please.* 请把头顶上的头发剪短。

6 on top of if something dangerous or threatening is on top of you, it is very near you〔危险或威胁〕非常接近，逼近: *The truck was almost on top of us.* 那辆卡车几乎把我们撞倒。**a)** if something bad happens to you on top of something else, it happens when you have other problems 除…之外〔还有其他烦恼〕: *On top of everything else, I now owe my parents $10,000 for the fines!* 除了其他一切之外，我现在还因为那些罚金欠了父母10,000美元。**b)** in complete control of a job, situation etc 完全控制着…；对…摸得一清二楚: *Don't worry; I'm back on top of things now.* 不要担心，我现在又完全控制了局面。

7 come out on top to win a difficult struggle or argument, especially one that has lasted for a long time〔尤指经过长期努力后〕获得成功: *It's very difficult to predict who will come out on top.* 很难预测谁将最后胜出。

8 get on top of if work, a problem etc gets on top of you, it begins to make you feel unhappy and upset〔工作、问题等〕压得人受不了: *Things are starting to get on top of him.* 事情开始压得他受不住了。

9 on top of the world *informal* extremely happy【非正式】极其高兴的: *When I heard she'd been released I felt on top of the world!* 听说她已被释放，我感到高兴极了！

10 ►COVER 盖子◄ something that you put on a pen, bottle etc to close it, especially something that you push or turn〔笔〕帽；〔瓶〕盖: *You've left the top off the toothpaste again!* 你又没有拧上牙膏盖！| *Where's the top of this pen?* 这支笔的笔帽到哪

去了?| **bottle/pen etc** *milk bottle tops* 牛奶瓶盖子 —see also 另见 SCREW TOP

11 ▶CLOTHES 衣服◀ a piece of clothing that you wear on the upper part of your body 上衣,上装: *her stripy top* 她那件条纹上衣 | *a skirt with a matching top* 一条配有上装的裙子 | *slip your pyjama top off* 脱掉你的睡衣上装

12 ▶PLANT 植物◀ the part of a fruit or vegetable where it was attached to the plant, or the leaves of a plant whose root you can eat〔植物的〕顶梢部分;〔根部可食用的植物的〕叶子: *Cut the tops off the tomatoes.* 把番茄的蒂削掉。| *carrot tops* 胡萝卜茎叶

13 the top of the milk *BrE* the creamy part that rises to the top of a bottle of milk【英】〔瓶装牛奶最上面的〕顶层乳

14 ▶STREET/FIELD ETC 街道/田地等◀ the part of the street or of a piece of land that is the furthest away either from you or from the most important entrance to it〔街道或田地的〕最远处;末端,尽头: *I waited at the top of East Street.* 我在东街的尽头等着。

15 the top of the table the part of a long dinner table where the most important people sit〔长条形餐桌上地位最高的人坐的〕餐桌首席,上席,上座 —see also 另见 TOP TABLE

16 off the top of your head *informal* if you answer a question or provide information off the top of your head, you do it immediately without checking the facts【非正式】立即,马上;不加思索地〔回答问题、提供信息〕: *Just off the top of my head I'd say there were about 50.* 只是信口说一说的话,我会说大约有50个。

17 sing/shout at the top of your voice to sing etc as loudly as you possibly can 放开嗓子唱歌/叫喊: *We yelled at the tops of our voices.* 我们敞开嗓门叫喊着。

18 from the top *spoken* an expression meaning from the beginning, used especially in the theatre【口】从头,从最开始〔尤用于戏剧〕: *Alright. Once more from the top. Action!* 好的,从头再来一遍。开始!

19 from top to bottom if you clean or search somewhere from top to bottom, you do it very thoroughly 彻底地〔清理、寻找等〕

20 from top to toe if a person is dressed or covered in something from top to toe, they are completely dressed or covered in it 从头到脚,完完全全〔指穿衣服或被覆盖〕: *expensive Parisian couture from top to toe* 从头到脚一身昂贵的巴黎时装

21 the top and bottom of *BrE spoken* the general result or meaning of a situation, expressed in a few words【英口】〔用三言两语概括的某情况的〕结果;实质: *He's trying to embarrass you, that's the top and bottom of it.* 他想让你难堪,那便是他所作所为的本意。

22 not have much up top *BrE spoken* to be not very intelligent【英口】不怎么精明,没什么头脑

23 tops *BrE spoken* used after a number to say that it is the highest possible amount of money you will get【英口】〔用于一笔钱的数目后表示可能得到的〕最高数目: *You'll make £200 from it, £250 tops.* 你会从中赚到200英镑,最高还可赚到250英镑。

24 be (the) tops *old-fashioned informal* to be the best【过时,非正式】是最好,为最佳

25 ▶TOY 玩具◀ a child's toy that spins around on its point when the child twists it 陀螺

26 spin like a top to spin or turn round very quickly 很快地转动: *The impact sent me spinning like a top.* 这一撞使我晕头转向。

27 sleep like a top *BrE* to sleep very deeply and well【英】睡得很香,熟睡

S1 W1 **top²** *adj* [only before noun 仅用于名词前]

1 ▶HIGHEST 最高◀ at the top; highest 顶端的;最高的: *the top button of his shirt* 他衬衫最上面的那颗纽扣 | *I can dive off the top board.* 我能从最高那层跳板跳水。| *Sprinkle cheese over the top layer of tomatoes.* 在最上面一层的番茄上撒些干酪。| **top floor** *Andrew lives on the top floor.* 安德鲁住在顶层。| **top priority** *We are giving the matter top priority.* 我们优先处理这件事情。| **the top 50/third/20% etc** *She is among the top 5% of earners in this country.* 她在这个国家属于收入最高的5%这一行列。| *We weren't even in the top 100 companies.* 我们甚至还没有进入前100家大公司的行列。—opposite 反义词 BOTTOM² (1)

2 top left/right/centre expressions meaning the picture at or nearest the top of the pages on the left or right or in the centre, used in magazines and newspapers 左上/右上/中间顶端〔指报刊杂志等图片在页面上的位置〕: *Top right: Silk Blouse £95 from Harrods.* 右上图:哈罗德的女式丝绸衬衫,价格95英镑。

3 ▶BEST 最佳◀ best or most successful 最佳的,最好的;最成功的: *one of our top tennis players* 我们最优秀的网球运动员之一 | *a top New York salon* 纽约的一家顶级美容院 | *people in top jobs* 工作职位最高的人 | *top quality ingredients* 优质配料 | *She got top marks.* 她获得了最高分。| **be on top form** (=to be doing something that you are good at especially well) 处于最佳状态 *Our team's on top form at the moment.* 我们队此时处于最佳状态。

4 top speed the fastest speed a vehicle can move at〔交通工具的〕最高速,全速: *We chased after them at top speed.* 我们以最快速度追赶他们。

5 top copy a piece of written material that is produced first and from which copies have been or can be made〔书面材料的〕正本

6 the top brass *informal* people in positions of high rank, especially in the army, navy etc【非正式】达官贵人;〔尤指〕高级军官

7 top dog *informal* the person in the highest or most important position especially after a struggle or effort【非正式】〔尤指经过竞争和努力而〕夺魁者;居高位的人

8 ▶HIGH SOCIAL CLASS 上层社会◀ *old-fashioned informal* from the highest social class【过时,非正式】上层社会的: *a top people's magazine* 上层社会人士的一份杂志

top³ *v* **topped, topping** [T]

1 ▶BE HIGHER 更高◀ to be higher or more than something 高于;超过: *Their profits have reportedly topped £1,000,000 this year.* 据报道,他们的利润今年已超过1,000,000英镑。

2 top an offer/bid etc to offer more money than someone else 超过某一开价/标价等: *A rival company has topped our offer by $5 million.* 同我们竞争的一家公司以500万美元超过了我们的开价。

3 ▶BE BETTER 更好◀ if you top someone else's remarks or actions you say or do something better, funnier or more exciting 优于,胜过: **top that** *And we also met Michael Jackson. Bet you can't top that!* 况且我们还见过迈克尔·杰克逊。我敢说没有比这更带劲的事情了!

4 top the bill/charts etc to come first in a list or in an order of things 在名单/列表等上面成为第一名: *Their party topped the poll in only 12 seats.* 他们的政党在仅有的12个选举席位中位列第一。—see also 另见 CHART-TOPPING

5 be topped by sth if something, especially an article of clothing, a mountain, or a building, is topped by something else, it has that thing on its top 某物在…的顶部: *roofs topped by fat chimneys* 矗立着粗大烟囱的房顶 | *trellis-topped brick walls* 墙头搭了棚的砖墙

6 topped with cream/onions etc with cream etc on the top …上面盖了一层奶油/洋葱等: *spicy new pizzas topped with curry sauce* 浇了一层咖喱酱的新式香辣比萨饼 —see also 另见 TOPPING

7 to top it all *spoken* in addition to other bad things that have happened to you【口】更有甚者,更糟糕的是: *To top it all I lost my job.* 更糟糕的是,我还丢了工作。

8 top and tail *BrE* to cut the top and bottom off a piece of fruit or a vegetable【英】削掉〔水果或蔬菜〕的根和叶;去掉…的两端

9 ▶REACH THE TOP 达到顶点◀ *literary* if you top a rising piece of ground, you reach the top of it【文】到达…的顶部;上升到…的顶点: *Our wagon topped the crest of the hill and we gasped at the view before us.* 马车到达了山顶,我们对眼前的景色惊叹不已。

10 top yourself *BrE slang* to kill yourself deliberately【英俚】自杀

top sth ↔ **off** *phr v* [T] to complete something successfully by doing a last action or adding a last detail〔完成一个行动或增加最后一点细节从而〕圆满地完成〔某事〕: *Let's top off the evening with a drink.* 咱们喝上一杯来圆满地结束今晚的活动。| *A cherry on each cake would top them off nicely.* 每块蛋糕上加一颗樱桃就大功告成了。

top out *phr v* [I] if something such as a price that is increasing tops out, it reaches its highest point and stops rising〔价格等达到最高点后〕不再上升: *Do you think interest rates have topped out now?* 你认为利率现在已经上升到最高点了吗?

top sth/sb ↔ **up** *phr v* [T] *especially BrE*【尤英】**1** to fill a partly empty container with liquid 注满〔半空的容器〕: *I'll just top up the coffee pot.* 我把咖啡壶装满就行。**2** to put more drink in someone's glass or cup 给〔某人的杯子〕加满: *Can I top you up?* 我给你的杯子加满好吗? **3** to increase the level of something slightly so as to bring it back to the level you want 稍微增加〔某物〕以回复到想要达到的水平: *Top up your tan this winter!* 今冬把你的皮肤晒得更漂亮! —see also 另见 TOP-UP

to·paz /ˈtopæz; ˈtəʊpæz/ *n* [C,U] a transparent yellow jewel or the mineral that it is cut from 黄玉;黄玉矿

top-class /ˌ·ˈ·◂/ *adj* being the best, most skilful etc 最优秀的, 第一流的: *top-class athletes such as Linford Christie* 像林福德·克里斯蒂那样的顶尖运动员 | *a top-class restaurant* 一流的餐馆

top·coat /ˈtɑpˌkot; ˈtɒpkəʊt/ *n* **1** [C,U] the last layer of paint that is put on a surface〔油漆的〕外涂层 **2** [C] *old-fashioned* a warm long coat【过时】长大衣, 宽大衣

top-down /ˌ·ˈ·◂/ *adj BrE* a top-down plan etc is one in which you start with a general idea of what you want and then add the details later【英】〔规划等〕从总体构思到具体细节的; 自上而下的: *adopting a top-down managerial philosophy* 采纳一套自上而下的管理理念

top-drawer /ˌ·ˈ·◂/ *adj informal* of the highest quality or social class【非正式】最优质的; 社会最上层的, 上流社会的: *top-drawer entertainment* 上流社会的娱乐

top-dress·ing /ˈtɑpˌdrɛsɪŋ; ˌtɒpˈdresɪŋ/ *n* [C,U] *technical* a layer of FERTILIZER that is spread over land【术语】〔撒在土地上的〕表层肥料, 顶肥

to·pee, topi /toˈpi; ˈtəʊpiː/ *n* [C] a hard hat for protecting your head in tropical sunshine〔热带地区的〕太阳帽

To·pe·ka /təˈpikə; təˈpiːkə/ the capital city of the US state of Kansas 托皮卡〔美国堪萨斯州首府〕

top-flight /ˌ·ˈ·◂/ *adj* most successful, skilful, or important 最成功的; 第一流的; 最重要的. *They've hired a really top-flight sales team.* 他们雇用了一支真正称得上第一流的销售队伍。

top gear /ˌ·ˈ·/ *n* [U] **1** the highest GEAR of a car, bus etc〔汽车等的〕高速挡: **in top gear** *The car will cruise at 80 mph in top gear.* 这辆车在高速挡能以每小时80英里的速度平稳地行驶。**2** **be in top gear** to be at the highest level of activity 处于最活跃的状态: *The party's election campaign is now in top gear.* 该党的选举活动现在进行得如火如荼。

top-gross·ing /ˈ·ˌ··/ *adj* a top-grossing film earns more money than any other film at a particular time〔电影〕票房收入高的

top hat /ˌ·ˈ·/ *n* [C] a man's tall black or grey hat, now worn only on formal occasions〔仅在正式场合戴的〕男子高顶大礼帽 —see picture at 参见 HAT 图

top-heav·y /ˌ·ˈ··◂/ *adj* **1** too heavy at the top and therefore likely to fall over 上重下轻的, 头重脚轻的 **2** an organization that is top heavy has too many managers compared to the number of ordinary workers〔机构等〕高层管理人员过多的: *burdened by a top-heavy bureaucracy* 在高层管理人员过多的官僚机构的重负下

to·pi /toˈpi; ˈtəʊpiː/ *n* [C] another spelling of TOPEE topee 的另一种拼法

to·pi·a·ry /ˈtopɪˌɛrɪ; ˈtəʊpiəri/ *n* [U] trees and bushes cut into the shapes of birds, animals etc, or the art of cutting them in this way 树木整形(术)〔把乔木或灌木修剪成鸟、兽等的形状〕

2 **top·ic** /ˈtɑpɪk; ˈtɒpɪk/ *n* [C] a subject that people talk or write about〔讲话或写作的〕话题, 论题, 题目: *The environment is a popular topic these days.* 近来环境是一个很流行的话题。| **topic of conversation** *The wedding has been the only topic of conversation for weeks!* 那次婚礼是几周以来唯一的话题!

top·ic·al /ˈtɑpɪkl̩; ˈtɒpɪkəl/ *adj* a story, subject, problem etc that is topical is interesting because it deals with something that is important at the present time 热门话题的; 当前受到关注的: *a new TV comedy dealing with topical issues* 一部反映热门问题的新电视喜剧 —**topically** /-klɪ; -kli/ *adv* —**topicality** /ˌtɑpɪˈkælətɪ; ˌtɒpɪˈkæləti/ *n* [U]

top·knot /ˈtɑpˌnɑt; ˈtɒpnɒt/ *n* [C] a way of arranging your hair, often tied with RIBBONS, on top of your head 顶髻

top·less /ˈtɑplɪs; ˈtɒpləs/ *adj* a woman who is topless is not wearing any clothes on the upper part of her body, so that her breasts are bare〔妇女〕无上装的, 上身裸露的: *topless sunbathing* 上身裸露的日光浴 | **topless bar/show** (=one in which the women serving or performing are topless) 雇用袒胸女招待的酒吧/女子袒胸表演

top-lev·el /ˌ·ˈ··◂/ *adj* [only before noun 仅用于名词前] involving the most powerful people in a country, organization etc 最高阶层的, 最高级的: *Top-level talks are to be held between the heads of state.* 最高级会谈将在两国元首之间举行。

top·most /ˈtɑpˌmost; ˈtɒpməʊst/ *adj* [only before noun 仅用于名词前] the topmost part of something is its highest part 最高的; 最上面的; 绝顶的: *The topmost branches were still bathed in sunlight.* 顶端的枝丫仍然沐浴在阳光下。

top-notch /ˌ·ˈ·◂/ *adj informal* having the highest quality or standard【非正式】最高级的; 顶呱呱的; 第一流的: *I was lucky and got myself a job with a top-notch company.* 我当时很幸运, 在一家顶尖的公司找到了一份工作。

Top of the Pops /ˌ···ˈ·/ a British television programme on which singers and bands appear and music videos are shown, especially when the singers or bands have records in the current CHARTS. The programme always ends with the record that has sold the most copies in that week.《流行音乐榜中榜》〔英国一电视节目。该节目播出歌手和乐队的现场表演, 播放音乐录像, 尤其播出近期上榜的歌手或乐队的节目。节目结束时总是播放本周销量最高的一张唱片〕

to·pog·ra·phy /toˈpɑgrəfɪ; təˈpɒgrəfi/ *n* [U] **1** the science of describing an area of land, or making maps of it 地形学; 地形测绘学 **2** [+of] the shape of an area of land, including its hills, valleys etc 地形, 地貌 —**topographer** *n* [C] —**topographical** /ˌtɑpəˈgræfɪkl̩; ˌtɒpəˈgræfɪkəl◂/ *adj*

top·per /ˈtɑpə; ˈtɒpə/ *n* [C] *informal* a TOP HAT【非正式】男子高顶大礼帽

top·ping[1] /ˈtɑpɪŋ; ˈtɒpɪŋ/ *n* [C,U] something you put on top of food to make it look nicer or taste better〔加在食品上面使之更好看或更好吃的〕配料, 浇头: *a pizza with extra cheese topping* 额外加了干酪配料的比萨饼

topping[2] *adj BrE old-fashioned* excellent【英, 过时】极好的, 顶呱呱的

top·ple /ˈtɑpl̩; ˈtɒpəl/ *v* **1** [I,T] to become unsteady and then fall over, or to make something do this (使)不稳而倒下, (使)倒塌: [+over] *A stack of plates swayed, and began to topple over.* 一大堆盘子摇晃着, 然后开始倒塌了。**2** [T] to take power away from a leader or government, especially by force; OVERTHROW[1] (1)〔尤指通过暴力〕从…夺取政权; 推翻: *This scandal could topple the government.* 这一丑闻有可能使政府倒台。

top-rank·ing /ˌ·ˈ··◂/ *adj* most powerful and important within an organization 最高级别的: *top-ranking diplomats* 最高级别的外交官

top-rat·ed /ˌ·ˈ··◂/ *adj informal* very popular with the public【非正式】受欢迎的: *a top-rated TV show* 大受欢迎的电视节目

top round /ˈ··/ *n* [U] *AmE*【美】〔牛肉的〕内大腿肉; TOPSIDE[1] *BrE*【英】

top-se·cret /ˌ·ˈ··◂/ *adj* top-secret documents or information must be kept completely secret〔文件或情报〕绝密的: *a top-secret military code* 绝密军事代码

top·side[1] /ˈtɑpˌsaɪd; ˈtɒpsaɪd/ *n* [U] *BrE* high quality BEEF cut from the upper leg of the animal【英】〔牛的〕大腿肉; TOP ROUND *AmE*【美】

topside[2] also 又作 **top·sides** /-ˌsaɪdz; -saɪdz/ *adv AmE* towards or onto the DECK (=upper surface) of a boat or ship【美】朝向甲板; 在甲板上

top·soil /ˈtɑpˌsɔɪl; ˈtɒpsɔɪl/ *n* [U] the upper level of soil in which most plants have their roots 表土层; 耕作层

top·spin /ˈtɑpˌspɪn; ˈtɒpˌspɪn/ *n* [U] the turning movement of a ball that has been hit or thrown in such a way that it spins forward〔球的〕上旋

Top·sy /ˈtɑpsɪ; ˈtɒpsi/ a small black girl character in the NOVEL *Uncle Tom's Cabin* (1851-52) by Harriet Beecher Stowe. When somebody asks her whether she knows who made her (that is, whether she has heard of God), she replies "I expect I grow'd (=grew)". 托普茜〔哈丽特·比彻·斯托的小说《汤姆叔叔的小屋》(1851-1852) 中的一个黑人小女孩。有人问她是否知道是谁创造了她时, 她总是回答说"我想我是长出来的"。〕

CULTURAL NOTE 文化注释

People in the US say something "just grew, like Topsy" when they are talking about something whose real origin is not known or about something that has gradually become very large. 在美国当人们聊到某些真实来源不详或者逐渐变大的事物时, 他们就会说: "像托普茜一样是长出来的。"

top·sy-tur·vy /ˈtɑpsɪ ˈtɝvɪ; ˌtɒpsi ˈtɜːvi◂/ *adj informal* in a state of complete disorder or confusion【非正式】乱七八糟的, 一团糟的: *He left his room all topsy-turvy.* 他的房间完全是一团糟。

top tab·le /ˌ·ˈ··/ *n* [C] *BrE* a table at a formal meal, for example at a wedding, where the most important people sit【英】〔正式宴会上重要人物坐的〕首席餐桌; HEAD TABLE *AmE*【美】

top-up /ˈ··/ *n* [C] *BrE* an amount of liquid that you add to a glass, cup etc in order to make it full again【英】加至满杯的量: *Would you like a top-up?* 您来一个满杯好吗?

tor /tɔr; tɔː/ *n* [C] *BrE* a rocky hill【英】多岩石的小山

Tor·ah /ˈtɔrə; ˈtɔːrə/ *n* [singular] all the writings and teachings concerned with Judaism, especially the first five books of the Jewish Bible 托拉〔指犹太教的全部律法教条, 尤指《犹太圣经》的首五卷书〕

torch¹ /tɔrtʃ; tɔːtʃ/ *n* [C] **1** *BrE* a small electric lamp that you carry in your hand【英】手电筒; FLASHLIGHT *AmE*【美】: *We shone our torches around the walls of the cavern.* 我们用手电筒照山洞的四壁。**2** a long stick with burning material at one end that produces light 火把; 火炬: *the Olympic torch* 奥林匹克火炬 | *a torch-light procession* 火炬游行 **3 carry a torch for** *old-fashioned* to secretly love and admire someone【过时】暗恋〔某人〕

torch 手电筒

torch² *v* [T] *informal* to deliberately make a building start to burn【非正式】故意点燃: *Rioters torched several abandoned cars.* 暴徒放火烧毁了几辆被遗弃的汽车。

torch·light /ˈtɔrtʃˌlaɪt; ˈtɔːtʃlaɪt/ *n* [U] **1** *BrE* the light produced by a torch【英】手电筒光 **2** the light produced by burning torches 火炬光

tore /tɔr; tɔː/ the past tense of TEAR²

to·re·a·dor /ˈtɔrɪəˌdɔr; ˈtɒriədɔː/ *n* [U] the person who fights bulls (BULL¹ (1)) in a Spanish BULLFIGHT〔西班牙斗牛的〕斗牛士

tor·ment¹ /ˈtɔrmɛnt; ˈtɔːment/ *n* **1** [U] severe mental or physical suffering, often lasting a long time〔精神或肉体上的〕折磨, 痛苦: **in torment** *She lay awake all night in torment.* 她一晚都没有睡着, 在痛苦中煎熬。**2** [C] someone or something that makes you suffer 使人痛苦的人[物]

tor·ment² /tɔrˈmɛnt; tɔːˈment/ *v* [T] **1** to make someone suffer a lot, especially so that they feel guilty or very unhappy 折磨, 使痛苦; 使苦恼: *Seth was tormented by feelings of guilt.* 塞思备受负罪感的折磨。| *tormented by hunger* 饱受饥饿的折磨 **2** to deliberately treat someone cruelly by annoying them or hurting them 骚扰; 烦扰: *The older boys would torment him whenever they had the chance.* 那些年岁较大的男孩子一有机会就骚扰他。—**tormentor** *n* [C]

torn /tɔrn; tɔːn/ the past participle of TEAR² —see picture on page A18 参见 A18 页图

tor·na·do /tɔrˈnedo; tɔːˈneɪdəʊ/ *n plural* **tornadoes** *or* **tornados** [C] an extremely violent storm consisting of air that spins very quickly and causes a lot of damage 龙卷风 —compare 比较 HURRICANE, CYCLONE

To·ron·to /təˈrɑnto; təˈrɒntəʊ/ a city and port on Lake Ontario, Canada. Toronto is the capital of the PROVINCE of Ontario and the largest city in Canada. 多伦多〔加拿大安大略湖沿岸一港口城市, 为安大略省首府和加拿大最大城市〕

tor·pe·do¹ /tɔrˈpido; tɔːˈpiːdəʊ/ *n plural* **torpedoes** [C] a long narrow weapon that is fired under the surface of the sea and explodes when it hits something 鱼雷

torpedo² *v* [T] **1** to attack or destroy a ship with a torpedo 用鱼雷攻击[摧毁] **2** to stop something such as a plan from succeeding 破坏〔计划等〕; 使失败: *New threats of violence have effectively torpedoed the peace talks.* 新的暴力威胁实际上破坏了和平谈判。

tor·pid /ˈtɔrpɪd; ˈtɔːpɪ̈d/ *adj formal* not active because you are lazy or sleepy, or making you feel like this【正式】(使人) 迟钝的, (使人) 懒散的; (使人) 昏昏欲睡的, 有气无力的: *a torpid mind* 迟钝的头脑 | *the heavy torpid warmth of the evening air* 夜晚闷热、使人昏昏欲睡的空气—**torpidly** *adv*

tor·por /ˈtɔrpɚ; ˈtɔːpə/ *n* [singular,U] *formal* a state of being not active because you are lazy or sleepy【正式】〔因懒散或困倦而〕不活跃: *stirring the wasps from their winter torpor* 把黄蜂从冬天的慵懒中惊醒 —**torpidity** /tɔrˈpɪdətɪ; tɔːˈpɪdɪ̈ti/ *n* [U]

torque /tɔrk; tɔːk/ *n* [U] *technical* the force or power that makes something turn around a central point, especially in an engine【术语】〔尤指发动机的〕转矩, 力矩

Tor·que·ma·da /ˌtɔrkəˈmɑdə; ˌtɔːkwɪˈmɑːdə/, **Tom·ás de** /ˈtɑmɑs də; ˈtɒməs də/ (1420-98) a Spanish Christian leader who started the Spanish Inquisition, the Roman Catholic organization that persecuted and punished HERETICS (=people whose religious beliefs are considered unacceptable). He was responsible for hurting and killing thousands of people in very cruel ways. 托尔克马达〔(1420-1498), 西班牙基督教领袖。他设立了西班牙异端裁判所, 即罗马天主教迫害和惩罚异教徒的机构。他以极为残忍的手段折磨并杀害过成千上万的异教徒〕

Tor·re·mo·li·nos /ˌtɔrəməˈlinos; ˌtɒrɪ̈məˈliːnɒs/ a town on the Mediterranean coast of Spain which is popular with tourists. 托雷莫利诺斯〔西班牙地中海沿岸一城镇, 为旅游胜地〕

tor·rent /ˈtɔrənt; ˈtɒrənt/ *n* [C] **1** a large amount of water moving very rapidly and strongly in a particular direction〔水的〕湍流, 急流: **a raging torrent** (=a very violent torrent) 汹涌的急流 *After five days of heavy rain the Telle river was a raging torrent.* 经过五天的大雨之后, 泰勒河成了汹涌的急流。**2 torrent of abuse/criticism/protest etc** a lot of insults, criticism etc that someone suddenly receives 连珠炮似的痛骂/批评/抗议等: *a torrent of protest over the proposed tax* 针对拟议税收的抗议浪潮

tor·ren·tial /tɔˈrɛnʃəl; tɒˈrenʃəl/ *adj* **torrential rain** very heavy rain 倾盆大雨

tor·rid /ˈtɔrɪd; ˈtɒrɪ̈d/ *adj* **1** involving strong emotions, especially of sexual love〔尤指性爱〕热烈的; 〔情欲〕炽烈的: *a torrid love affair* 狂热的风流韵事 **2** *literary* torrid weather is very hot【文】〔天气〕灼热的, 炎热的: *the torrid desert sun* 沙漠中灼热的太阳

tor·sion /ˈtɔrʃən; ˈtɔːʃən/ *n* [U] *technical* the twisting of a piece of metal【术语】〔金属的〕扭转, 扭曲

tor·so /ˈtɔrso; ˈtɔːsəʊ/ *n* [C] **1** your body, not including your head, arms, or legs〔头和四肢除外的〕人体躯干: *Police have found the headless torso of a woman.* 警察发现了一名妇女的无头躯体。**2** a STATUE of a torso 人体躯干雕像

tort /tɔrt; tɔːt/ *n* [C] *law* an action that is wrong but not criminal and can be dealt with in a CIVIL (3) court of law【法律】〔不构成刑事罪的〕民事侵权行为

tor·til·la /tɔrˈtijə; tɔːˈtiːjə/ *n* [C] a piece of thin flat bread made from corn or wheat flour from Mexico〔墨西哥的一种〕薄玉米[小麦面]饼, 玉米粉[小麦面]圆饼

tor·toise /ˈtɔrtəs; ˈtɔːtəs/ *n* [C] a slow-moving land animal that can pull its head and legs into the hard round shell that covers its body 陆龟 —compare 比较 TURTLE (1)

Tortoise and the Hare, the /ˌ· · · · ˈ·/ a FABLE (=a traditional story that teaches a moral lesson) by Aesop in which a TORTOISE and a HARE have a race. The tortoise unexpectedly wins by moving slowly but steadily, while the hare, because he knows he can run much faster than the tortoise, stops halfway and falls asleep. The lesson of the story is 'Slow and steady wins the race.'《龟兔赛跑》〔伊索寓言故事。故事中一只乌龟和一只兔子赛跑。乌龟跑得慢, 但始终不松懈, 于是出人意料地赢了这场比赛。兔子自以为跑起来比乌龟快得多, 就在途中停下来睡着了。这则故事的寓意是"慢而不懈, 赢得比赛"〕

tor·toise·shell /ˈtɔrtəsˌʃɛl; ˈtɔːtəsʃel/ *n* **1** [U] a hard, shiny brown and white material made from the shell of a tortoise 龟甲; 玳瑁壳 **2** [C] a cat that has yellow, brown, and black marks on its fur 花斑家猫 **3** [C] a BUTTERFLY that has brown and orange wings〔翅膀呈褐色和橙色的〕蛱蝶

tor·tu·ous /ˈtɔrtʃuəs; ˈtɔːtʃuəs/ *adj* **1** a tortuous path, stream, road etc has a lot of bends in it and is therefore difficult to travel along 弯弯曲曲的; 曲折的: *a tortuous path over the mountains to Kandahar* 翻山越岭通往坎大哈的一条蜿蜒小径 **2** complicated and long and therefore confusing 转弯抹角的, 绕圈子的; 复杂的; 令人费解的: *The book begins with a long, tortuous introduction.* 这本书的开头是一篇冗长的、令人费解的前言。—**tortuously** *adv* —**tortuousness** *n* [U]

tor·ture¹ /ˈtɔrtʃɚ; ˈtɔːtʃə/ *n* [C,U] **1** an act of deliberately hurting someone in order to force them to tell you something, to punish them, or to be cruel 拷打, 拷问; 酷刑: *He died after five days of excruciating torture.* 在经历五天的严刑拷打后, 他死了。**2** severe physical or mental suffering〔身心所受的〕折磨, 煎熬: *Hearing her practice the violin is torture!* 听她练小提琴, 简直是受罪!

torture² *v* [T] **1** to deliberately hurt someone to force them to give you information, to punish them, or to be cruel 拷打, 拷问; 对…施以酷刑: *Political opponents of the regime may be tortured.* 反对该政权的政治犯可能要受酷刑。**2** if a feeling or knowledge tortures you, it makes you suffer mentally 使〔精神上〕受到折磨; 使痛苦; 使苦恼: *tortured by guilt* 因内疚而感到痛苦 —**torturer** *n* [C]

To·ry /ˈtɔrɪ; ˈtɔːri/ *n* [C] a member of the British Conservative Party〔英国的〕保守党成员, 托利党人: *a lifelong Tory* 一名终身的保守党党员 | *Tory principles* 保守党的各项原则

Tory Par·ty /ˈ· ·ˌ·ˈ/ *n* [singular] another name for the British Conservative Party 托利党〔英国保守党的别称〕

Tos·ca·ni·ni /ˌtɑskəˈninɪ; ˌtɒskəˈniːni/, **Ar·tu·ro** /ɑrˈturo; ɑːˈtʊərəʊ/ (1867-1957) an Italian CONDUCTOR (=someone who directs a group of musicians) who worked at La Scala in Milan, Italy, at the Metropolitan Opera Company in New York City, and with the NBC Symphony Orchestra in New York City 托斯卡尼尼〔(1867- 1957), 意大利指挥家。他先后在意大利米兰的

斯卡拉歌剧院、纽约市大都会歌剧院以及纽约市国家广播公司交响乐团担任指挥〕

toss[1] /tɔs; tɒs/ *v*

1 ►THROW 扔◄[T] to throw something, especially something light, with a quick gentle movement of your hand 扔，掷，抛〔尤指轻快地抛较轻的东西〕: **toss sth into/down/out of etc** *Toss that book over here, will you?* 把那本书扔过来，好吗？| **toss sth to sb** *"Catch!" said Sandra, tossing her bag to him.* "接着！"桑德拉一边说着，一边把包扔给他。| **toss sb sth** *Frank tossed her the newspaper.* 弗兰克把报纸扔给了她。

2 ►MOVE 移动◄[I,T] to move and turn around continuously in a violent or uncontrolled way, or make something do this （使）动来动去；（使）翻转不停: **toss sth about/around** *Our small boat was tossed about like a cork.* 我们的小船像软木塞一样颠簸不停。| **toss and turn** (=keep changing your position in bed because you cannot sleep) 辗转反侧 *I've been tossing and turning all night.* 我整个晚上翻来覆去睡不着。

3 ►THROW A FLAT OBJECT 抛扔扁平的物体◄[T] *BrE* to throw a flat object upwards so that it turns over in the air before it falls again【英】把〔扁平的物体〕抛向空中使其翻转落下；FLIP[1] (2) *AmE*【美】: *tossing pancakes on Pancake Day* 薄烤饼日那天抛薄饼

4 ►A COIN 硬币◄also 又作 **toss up** [I,T] *especially BrE* to make a coin go upwards and spin in the air, as a way of deciding something【尤英】把〔硬币〕抛向空中〔决定某事〕；FLIP[1] (2) *especially AmE*【尤美】: *They tossed a coin to decide who would go first.* 他们抛硬币决定谁先走。| **toss (up) for it** *Well we can't make up our minds; we'll just have to toss for it.* 既然我们无法下定决心，那就只好抛硬币来决定了。

5 ►IN COOKING 烹调过程中◄[T] to cover food in a liquid by shaking it around in the liquid〔在液体中〕摇晃，搅拌〔食物〕: *Toss the carrots in some butter before serving.* 用一些黄油把胡萝卜搅拌一下，然后端上桌子。

6 toss your head to move your head back suddenly, often with a shaking movement showing anger 把头往后一仰〔表示气愤〕: *He tossed his head angrily and left the room.* 他气愤地把头往后一仰，离开了房间。

7 toss your cookies *AmE spoken* to VOMIT[1]【美口】呕吐

toss off *phr v* **1** [T **toss** sth ↔ **off**] to produce something quickly and without much effort 轻而易举地完成〔某事〕: *one of those painters who can toss off a couple of pictures before breakfast* 那种能够在早餐之前轻松地完成两三幅绘画的画家 **2** [T **toss** sth ↔ **off**] *old-fashioned* to drink something quickly【过时】将…一饮而尽: *He tossed off a few whiskies.* 他一口气喝下几杯威士忌酒。**3** [I,T **toss** sb ↔ **off**] *BrE taboo* to MASTURBATE【英讳】手淫

toss[2] *n* [C] **1** the act of throwing a coin in the air to decide something 抛硬币〔决定某事〕: *The toss of a coin decided who would serve first.* 通过抛硬币决定谁首先发球。**2** a sudden backwards movement of your head, so that your hair moves 猛一仰头: *"I'll see," the nurse said, with an officious toss of her head.* 这名护士猛一仰头，以发号施令的口吻说："我来看看。" **3 win/lose the toss** *especially BrE* to win or lose the right to make a choice at the beginning of a game or race, according to the result of tossing a coin【尤英】〔在比赛或游戏开始时〕抛硬币赢了/输了 **4** the act of gently throwing something〔轻轻的〕抛，扔，投: *Will distracted me and I missed the toss.* 威尔分散了我的注意力，所以我没有投中。**5 not give a toss** *BrE spoken* to not care about something at all【英口】根本不在乎: *I really couldn't give a toss what Dermot thinks.* 我真的根本就不在乎德莫特是怎么想的。—see also 另见 **argue the toss** (ARGUE (5))

toss-up /ˈ· ·/ *n* **1 it's a toss-up** *spoken* used when you do not know which of two things will happen, or which of two things to choose【口】这件事尚未分晓[难以定夺]: *"I don't know who'll get the job – it's a toss-up between Carl and Steve."* "我不知道谁会得到这份工作——卡尔和史蒂夫两人的机会不相上下。" **2** [C usually singular 一般用单数] *BrE* an act of tossing a coin in order to decide something【英】抛硬币〔决定某事〕

tot[1] /tɑt; tɒt/ *n* [C] **1** *informal* a very small child【非正式】小娃娃 **2** *especially BrE* a small amount of an alcoholic drink【尤英】少量酒

tot[2] *v* **totted, totting**

tot sth ↔ **up** *phr v* [T] *informal* to add together numbers or amounts of money in order to find the total【非正式】把〔数字或钱〕加起来: *The waiter quickly totted up the bill.* 服务生很快便把账单算好了。

to·tal[1] /ˈtotl̩; ˈtəʊtl/ *adj* **1** [only before noun 仅用于名词前] complete, and affecting or including everything 完全的，彻底的: *The sales campaign was a total disaster.* 那次促销活动完全是一场灾难。| *a total ban on cigarette advertising* 彻底禁止香烟广告 **2 total number/amount/cost etc** the number, amount etc that is the total 总数/总量/总成本等: *total sales of 200,000 per year* 每年20万的销售总额

total[2] *n* [C] **1** the final number or amount of things, people etc when everything has been counted 总数，总量，总额: *If you add 30 and 45 the total is 75.* 30加45，总数是75。| **a total of** *They were jailed for a total of thirty years.* 他们在监牢里总共被关了30年。| **in total** *There were probably about 40 people there in total.* 那里总共可能有40人左右。| **the sum total** (=the whole of an amount when everything is considered together) 全部，总数 **2 grand total a)** the final total, including all the totals added together 总计 **b)** *humorous* used when you think the final total is small【幽默】〔自认为很小的〕总数: *I earned a grand total of $4.15.* 我总共才挣了四块一毛五。

total[3] *v* **totalled, totalling** *BrE*【英】, **totaled, totaling** *AmE*【美】**1** [T, linking verb 连系动词] to reach a particular total 总数为，总共达: *losses totalling $3 million* 总计达300万美元的损失 **2** [T] *AmE informal* to damage a car so badly that it cannot be repaired【美，非正式】使〔汽车〕彻底毁坏: *Chuck ran into a telephone pole and totaled his dad's new Toyota.* 查克撞到一根电线杆上，使他爸爸那辆新丰田车完全报废了。

total sth ↔ **up** *phr v* [T] to find the total number or total amount of something by adding 求得…的总数，把…相加起来: *At the end of the game total up everyone's score to see who has won.* 在游戏结束时，把每个人的总分加起来，看看是谁赢了。

to·tal·i·tar·i·an /toˌtæləˈtɛrɪən; təʊˌtæl̩ˈteəriən/ *adj* based on a political system in which ordinary people have no power and are completely controlled by the government 极权主义的: *a totalitarian régime* 极权主义政权 —**totalitarianism** *n* [U]

to·tal·i·ty /toˈtælətɪ; təʊˈtæl̩ti/ *n* [U] *formal*【正式】**1** the whole of something 整体，全部: **in its totality** (=as a complete thing) 作为一个整体，从整体上 *It's essential that we look at the problem in its totality.* 重要的是，我们应从整体上看待这个问题。**2** a total amount 总数，总额

to·tal·i·za·tor also 又作 **-isator** /ˈtotl̩əˌzetɚ; ˈtəʊtəlaɪˌzeɪtə/ *n* [C] *BrE formal* a TOTE[2]【英，正式】〔赛马的〕赌金计算器

tot·al·ly /ˈtotlɪ; ˈtəʊtli/ *adv* completely 完全地，彻底地: *That's a totally different matter.* 那是一件完全不同的事情。| *It's like learning a totally new language.* 这就好像在学一门全新的语言。| *a totally unexpected situation* 完全没有预料到的情况

tote[1] /tot; təʊt/ also 又作 **tote around** *v* [T] *informal especially AmE* to carry something, especially regularly【非正式，尤美】〔尤指经常性地〕随身携带: *having to tote around heavy textbooks* 不得不随身携带着厚重的课本

tote[2] *n* [C] a machine that adds together the amounts of money BET on a race and divides it among the winners〔赛马的〕赌金计算器

tote bag /ˈ· ,· / *n* [C] *AmE* a large bag for carrying things【美】〔装东西的〕大手提带，购物袋 —see picture at 参见 BAG[1] 图

to·tem /ˈtotəm; ˈtəʊtəm/ *n* [C] an animal, plant etc that is thought to have a special spiritual connection with a particular tribe, especially in North America, or a figure made to look like the animal etc 图腾；图腾形象 —**totemic** /toˈtɛmɪk; təʊˈtemɪk/ *adj*

totem pole /ˈ· · ·/ *n* [C] **1** a tall wooden pole with one or more totems cut or painted on it, made by the Native Americans of northwest North America〔北美土著的〕图腾柱 **2 low man on the totem pole** *AmE* someone of low rank in an organization or business【美】〔在机构或公司中〕级别较低的人

To·to /ˈtoto; ˈtəʊtəʊ/ the dog belonging to Dorothy in *The Wizard of Oz* 托托〔《绿野仙踪》中多萝西的小狗的名字〕

toto —see 见 IN TOTO

Tot·ten·ham Court Road /ˌtɑtnəm kɔrt ˈrod; ˌtɒtnəm kɔːt ˈrəʊd/ a street in central London with many shops selling electronic goods such as STEREO systems, televisions, and computer equipment 托特纳姆考特路〔伦敦市中心的一条街。街上的许多商店出售电子产品，如立体声系统、电视及电脑设备〕

Tottenham Hot·spur /ˌtɑtnəm ˈhɑtspɚ; ˌtɒtnəm ˈhɒtspɜː/ the full name of Spurs, a football team from North London 托特纳姆热刺队〔热刺队全称，为北伦敦一支足球队〕

tot·ter /ˈtɑtɚ; ˈtɒtə/ *v* [I] **1** to walk or move unsteadily from side to side as if you are going to fall over 摇摇晃晃，跌跌撞撞: *Lorrimer swayed a little, tottered, and fell.* 洛里默歪了一下，然后摇摇晃晃地倒了下去。—see picture on page A24 参见 A24 页图 **2** if a political system or organization totters, it becomes less strong and is likely to stop working〔政治制度或机构〕摇摇欲坠

tou·can /ˈtukæn; ˈtuːkən/ *n* [C] a tropical American bird with bright feathers and a very large beak 巨嘴鸟〔美洲热带的一种鸟〕

2 2

tou·ch¹ /tʌtʃ; tʌtʃ/ *v*

① FEEL SB/STH PHYSICALLY 触到某人/某物
② AFFECT SB'S FEELINGS 影响某人的感情
③ USE/HANDLE 使用/触摸
④ DEAL/ATTEND TO 处理
⑤ HAVE AN EFFECT ON 产生影响
⑥ OTHER MEANINGS 其他意思

① FEEL SB/STH PHYSICALLY 触到某人/某物

1 [T] to put your hand or another part of your body on something or someone so that you can feel them〔手或身体其他部位〕触到, 摸到, 碰到: *Small children are constantly moving and wanting to touch everything.* 小孩子总是不断地活动, 什么都想摸一摸。| *She couldn't bear the thought of touching a dead body.* 要去触摸一具死尸, 她连想都不敢想。

2 to put your hand or any part of your body on someone in a sexual way〔因性欲而〕接触〔别人的身体〕: *Ben hadn't touched her yet. Hadn't even kissed her.* 本没有碰过她, 甚至还没有吻过她。| *She bent over me, touching me with her lips.* 她朝我俯过身来, 吻了我一下。

3 [T] to put your hand on someone in order to show them kindness or affection 抚摸〔表示亲切、怜爱等〕: *He put his hand out to touch the young man's shoulder.* 他伸出手, 摸了一下那位小伙子的肩膀。| *He was a remote man who hardly ever played with or even touched his children.* 他是个孤僻的人, 难得跟自己的孩子一起玩, 也不去爱抚他们。

4 [I,T] if two things are touching, they reach each other so that there is no space between them 触碰; 触及; 接触: *I sat facing him, our knees touching.* 我面向他坐, 我俩的膝盖相互靠着。| **touch sth** *The little boy's legs were too short to touch the ground.* 那个小男孩的两条腿太短了, 够不着地面。

5 not touch sb to not hit someone or hurt them physically 不伤害某人〔身体〕: *The older boys swore they hadn't touched the child.* 那些年长的男孩子发誓说没有打过那个小孩。

② AFFECT SB'S FEELINGS 影响某人的感情

6 [T] to make someone feel upset, sympathetic, interested etc 使感到难受[同情, 有趣等]: *His harsh words had obviously touched her although she tried not to show it.* 她尽管竭力不表现出来, 但对他那些苛刻的言辞明显地感到难受。| *Politics didn't touch me an awful lot those days.* 在那些日子里, 政治对我的影响并不很大。

7 touch a nerve to mention a subject that makes someone feel upset, or angry 触到某人的痛处: *I think you touched a nerve when you brought up the subject of divorce.* 我认为, 你提及离婚这个话题是触到了痛处。

8 be touched by sth to feel grateful for or pleased about something nice that someone does 被某事感动, 打动: *I was very touched by his kind letter.* 我被他那封亲切的信深深打动了。— see also 另见 TOUCHING

③ USE/HANDLE 使用/触摸

9 not touch sth a) ▶OBJECT/POSSESSION 物体/财产◀ to not use or handle something 不使用[不接触]某物: *I've never touched a penny of that money.* 那笔钱我从来没有用过一分。| *He has a car but I'm sure he wouldn't let you touch it.* 他有一辆车, 但我敢说他是不会让你用的。| **Don't touch (sth)** *spoken* (=used when you are warning someone not to handle or touch something because it is dangerous or not allowed)【口】不准碰〔警告语〕*"Don't touch that switch!" his father shouted.* "不要碰那个开关!"他父亲嚷道。**b)** ▶FOOD/DRINK 食品/饮料◀ to not eat or drink the thing mentioned 不吃; 不喝: *She went to school without touching her breakfast.* 她没吃早饭就上学去了。| *He rarely ever touches alcohol, except at Christmas.* 除了在圣诞节, 他平常几乎不喝酒。| **not/never touch the stuff** (=not drink alcohol) 不喝/从不喝酒 *My grandfather was an alcoholic and as a result my father never touched the stuff.* 我祖父酗酒成性, 因此我父亲滴酒不沾。

④ DEAL/ATTEND TO 处理

10 ▶PRACTICAL MATTER/SITUATION 实际的问题/情况◀ [T] to deal with or become involved with a particular matter, situation or problem 处理; 参与: *He was the only lawyer who would touch the case.* 他是唯一愿意处理此案的律师。| *He's a walking disaster! Everything he touches goes wrong.* 他真是一个灾星! 他涉及的每一件事都会出错。

11 not touch sth to not do any work on or give any time to something which needs work or attention 没有做某事; 没有关注某事: *The garden looks awful – I'm afraid I haven't touched it for weeks.* 花园看上去乱糟糟的 —— 我恐怕有好几个礼拜没有清理它了。

12 wouldn't touch sth/sb (with a bargepole) *BrE*【英】**ten-foot pole** *AmE*【美】used as a way of saying that you think something or someone is bad in some way and you do not want to get or advise getting involved with them〔因趋利避害而〕不想与某事/某人有瓜葛; 不建议别人与其有瓜葛: *I wouldn't touch that house with a bargepole – it's almost falling down.* 我才不想跟那座房子扯上任何关系呢 —— 它都快要倒塌了。

⑤ HAVE AN EFFECT ON 产生影响

13 [T] to have an effect on someone or something so that it changes or influences them 对…有影响: *They had lived in such isolation that the outside world had barely touched them.* 他们生活在这么与世隔绝的环境里, 外界对他们几乎没有影响。

14 be touched by sth to be affected by a particular quality 受…的影响; 带有…的特性: *All the family were touched by a common genius.* 全家人都带有一种共同的天赋。| *There was no denying that his motivation was touched by self interest.* 不可否认的是, 他的动机里带有自私的成分。

15 [T] if an expression such as a smile touches your face, your face has that expression for a short time〔脸上〕露出, 闪现〔笑容等〕: *A rare frown touched his normally placid face.* 他那通常平静的脸上出现了难得一见的皱眉。

⑥ OTHER MEANINGS 其他意思

16 [T] to concern a particular subject, situation, or problem 涉及, 关系到: *Though the question touched a new vein, Nelson answered promptly.* 尽管这个问题涉及一个新的方面, 纳尔逊还是迅速地作了回答。

17 nothing/no one to touch sth/sb, nothing/no one that can touch sth/sb nothing or no one that is as good as something or someone 没有什么/没有人能比得上某事物/某人: *She's a brilliant tennis player – there's no one else here to touch her.* 她是一名杰出的网球选手, 这里没有谁能比得上她。| *You can listen to a recording of a concert but nothing can touch actually being there.* 你可以听音乐会的录音, 不过这根本无法与在现场听相比。

18 touch bottom a) to reach the ground at the bottom of a sea, river etc 下降到[碰到]〔海、河等的〕底部: *He swam down and down but could not touch bottom.* 他往下面游啊游, 但还是碰不到底。**b)** to reach the lowest level or worst condition 达到最低点; 落到最坏的地步: *After weeks of uncertainty, morale in the company has touched bottom.* 经过几周的动荡, 公司的士气已经跌落到最低点。

19 touch wood *especially BrE* used when you have just said that you have been lucky in some way in the past, because this expression is traditionally supposed to help your good luck to continue【尤英】摸摸木头以求福〔英国民俗认为说这话能使好运气延续下去〕: *I haven't been ill yet this winter – touch wood.* 我今年冬天还没有生过病, 但愿一直好福气。

touch down *phr v* [I] if an aircraft touches down, it lands on the ground〔飞机等〕降落, 着陆: *We all sighed with relief when the plane finally touched down safely.* 当飞机最终安全着陆时, 我们全都松了一口气。

touch sb **for** sth *phr v* [T] *informal* to persuade someone to give or lend you something, especially money【非正式】求某人给[借]某物〔尤指钱〕: *Can I touch you for a fiver until next week?* 我能向你借五块钱, 等下周再还吗?

touch sth ↔ **off** *phr v* [T] to cause a difficult situation or violent events to begin 使产生〔困境〕; 引发〔暴力事件〕: *The government's actions touched off a storm of protest.* 政府的行动激发了抗议风暴。

touch on/upon sth *phr v* [T] to mention or deal with a particular subject briefly when talking or writing〔说话或写作时〕简略地提到, 提及: *There is one factor we have not touched on, so far, in talking about personality.* 在讨论个性方面, 有一个因素我们迄今还未谈到。

touch sth **up** *phr v* [T] to improve something by changing it or adding to it slightly 修改, 改进, 润色: *The speech he finally gave had been touched up by his staff.* 他最后所作的发言是经他的工作班子润色过的。| *She quickly touched up her lipstick.* 她很快地添补了一点唇膏。

touch sb **up** *phr v* [T] to touch someone in a sexual way when you should not 对〔异性〕动手动脚: *He had a reputation for touching up his secretaries.* 他因为对自己的秘书动手动脚而名声不好。

touch² *n*

1 ▶SENSE 感觉◀[U] the sense that you use to discover what something feels like, by putting your hand or another part of your body on it 触觉: *Visually impaired people orient themselves by touch.* 视力有障碍的人通过触觉确定自己的方位。| **to the touch** *Natural fabrics feel much nicer to the touch.* 天然纤维摸起来感觉要好得多。

2 ▶ACT OF TOUCHING 触摸行为◀[C usually singular 一般用单数] what you do when you put your hand or another part of your body on or against something or someone either deliberately or not 触, 碰, 摸: *A smile, a friendly gesture, a touch – any of these can be of an enormous help.* 一个微笑, 一个友好的姿态, 一下触摸——任何这些行为都可能有巨大的帮助。| *I couldn't move. The slightest touch hurt.* 我不能动, 轻轻碰一下都疼。| **at the touch of a button** (=used to emphasize how easily something practical can be done) 只需按一下按钮〔用以强调某事很容易做成〕*We can contact people on the other side of the world at the touch of a button nowadays.* 今天, 我们只需按一下按钮就能与远在天涯海角的人联系上。

3 ▶FEEL SB/STH 感觉某人/某物◀[C usually singular 一般用单数] the way that someone or something feels and the effect they have on your body〔触摸的〕感觉: *She longed to see him again and feel his touch.* 她渴望着能再次见到他, 感受他的抚摸。| *The child recoiled from the thought of the cold slimy touch of the snake's body.* 一想到蛇身那种冷冰冰、黏糊糊的感觉, 这孩子退缩了。

4 be in touch to speak especially on the telephone, or write to someone about something〔尤指通过电话或写信〕联系: *I'll be in touch when I get back from Paris.* 我从巴黎回来后就可以联系上了。| **[+with]** *My officials have been in touch with the department concerning their comments.* 我手下的官员已经与提出意见的那个部门联系上了。

5 get in touch to write or speak to someone on the telephone in order to tell them something〔写信或打电话〕取得联系: *We'll get in touch as soon as we know the results of the test.* 我们一知道测试的结果就尽快进行联系。| **[+with]** *You can get in touch with me at the office if necessary.* 如果必要的话, 你可以在办公室与我取得联系。

6 keep/stay in touch to speak or write to someone when you can no longer see them as often as you used to 保持联系: **[+with]** *Our neighbours are moving away but I hope that we'll still keep in touch with each other.* 我们的邻居要搬走了, 不过我希望我们仍然会保持联系。

7 lose touch to no longer speak or write to someone because they do not live near you, work with you etc 失去联系: **[+with]** *I've lost touch with most of my friends from college.* 我与大学时代的大多数朋友已经失去了联系。

8 put sb in touch with sb to give someone the name, address, or telephone number of a person or organization they need 安排某人与某人联系: *Your doctor should be able to put you in touch with a specialist.* 你的医生应该能够安排你与一位专科医生取得联系。

9 be/keep/stay in touch with sth to have the latest information, knowledge, and understanding about a subject 获得某方面的最新情况[知识, 了解等]: *Through the media we are able to keep in touch with events on the other side of the world almost as they happen.* 通过媒体, 我们几乎立即就能够了解到在世界另一端发生的事件。

10 be out of touch with sth/lose touch with sth to no longer have the correct information or a good understanding about a subject 不再了解某事, 与某事已很生疏: *Government ministers are often being accused of being out of touch with real life.* 政府部长们经常被指责与实际生活脱节。

11 ▶DETAIL/ADDITION 细节/补充◀[C] a small detail that improves or completes something〔细节上的〕润色, 修饰, 点缀: *The flowers on every table were a very nice touch.* 每张桌子上摆放的花是非常美丽的点缀。| *She was just adding the final touches to her speech.* 她正在给她的演讲作最后的润色。| **finishing touch/touches** *The necklace was the finishing touch to her wedding outfit.* 那串项链是她结婚礼服的点睛之笔。

12 ▶WAY OF DOING STH 做某事的方式◀[C] a particular way of doing something 手法, 风格, 技巧: *A more sensitive touch is needed in our approach to this problem.* 我们解决这一问题需要一种更加细腻的技巧。| *The room was decorated with a very artistic touch.* 这个房间的装饰很有艺术风格。

13 a touch of sth a very small amount of something 少量, 一点儿: *"I'm afraid I don't agree," said Hazel, with a touch of irritation.* 黑兹尔略带气愤地说:"我恐怕不同意。" | *She had a touch of fever in the night.* 她夜里稍微有点发烧。

14 a touch cold/strange/unfair etc slightly cold, strange etc 有点冷/奇怪/不公平等的: *He sounded a touch upset when I spoke to him on the phone.* 我在电话里跟他说话时, 他似乎有点不高兴。

15 lose your touch to lose your ability to do something 失去〔做某事的〕能力: *He's been playing so badly recently that it seems he's losing his touch.* 他最近的表演一直很差劲, 他似乎失去了表演能力。—see also 另见 **the common touch** (COMMON[1] (8)), **a soft touch** (SOFT (11))

touch-and-go /ˌ· · ˈ·/ *adj informal* in a touch-and-go situation, there is a serious risk that something bad could happen【非正式】一触即发的, 危险的; 没有把握的: *It was touch-and-go whether the doctor would get there on time.* 医生能否会按时赶到那儿是没有把握的。

touch·down /ˈtʌtʃˌdaʊn; ˈtʌtʃdaʊn/ *n* [C] **1** the moment at which a plane or SPACECRAFT lands〔飞机、航天器等的〕降落, 着陆 **2** an act of touching the ball down on the ground behind your opponent's GOAL (3) in RUGBY〔橄榄球赛中越过对方底线的〕触地得分 **3** an act of moving the ball across the opposing team's GOAL LINE in American football〔美式橄榄球赛中的〕达阵, 持球过底线得分 —see picture on page A22 参见 A22 页图

tou·ché /tuˋʃe ˈtuːʃeɪ/ *interjection* used when you want to emphasize in a humorous way that someone has made a very good point during an argument 说得好, 说到点子上了〔用于强调某人在辩论中论点有力的一种幽默说法〕: *"You should be ashamed." "So should you." "Touché," he replied, not at all put out.* "你应该感到羞耻。""你也应该如此。""说得好!"他回答说, 一点也不恼怒。

touched /tʌtʃt; tʌtʃt/ *adj* [not before noun 不用于名词前] **1** feeling happy and grateful because of someone's actions 高兴的; 感激的; 受感动的: *We were deeply touched by their present.* 他们送来礼物, 我们非常感激。| **touched that** *Cathryn was touched that Sarah had come to see her off.* 令凯瑟琳感动的是, 萨拉来为她送行了。—see also 另见 TOUCH[1] (8) **2** *informal* slightly strange in your behaviour【非正式】行为有点古怪的: *He seems a bit touched to me!* 我觉得他的行为显得有点古怪!

touch foot·ball /ˈ· ˌ··/ *n* [U] *AmE* a type of American football in which you touch the person with the ball instead of tackling (TACKLE[1] (3)) them【美】触身式橄榄球〔美式橄榄球的变种, 持球球员被对方接触到就不得再跑, 但不允许擒抱持球球员〕

touch·ing¹ /ˈtʌtʃɪŋ; ˈtʌtʃɪŋ/ *adj* making you feel pity, sympathy, sadness etc 令人同情的; 感人的; 伤感的: *a touching reunion of father and son* 感人的父子团聚情景 —see also 另见 TOUCH[1] (6) **—touchingly** *adv*

touching² *prep formal* concerning【正式】关于, 有关: *matters touching the conduct of diplomacy* 有关外交事务的问题

touch·line /ˈtʌtʃˌlaɪn; ˈtʌtʃlaɪn/ *n* [C] a line along each of the two longer sides of a sports field, especially in football〔尤指足球场的〕边线

touch·pa·per /ˈtʌtʃˌpepɚ; ˈtʌtʃˌpeɪpə/ *n* [C] a piece of slow-burning paper, that you light in order to start a FIREWORK burning〔引发烟花爆竹用的〕导火线, 火绒线: *Light the blue touchpaper, then retire to a safe distance.* 点燃蓝色的火绒线, 然后退到安全距离之外。

touch·stone /ˈtʌtʃˌston; ˈtʌtʃstəʊn/ *n* [C] something used as a test or standard 试金石; 检验标准: **[+of]** *Pupil behaviour was*

seen as 'the touchstone of quality' of the school system. 学生的行为表现被认为是学校系统的"质量检验标准"。

touch-tone phone /'· · , -/ *n* [C] a telephone that produces different sounds when different numbers are pushed 按钮式电话机

touch-type /'· -/ *v* [I] to be able to use a TYPEWRITER without having to look at the letters while you are using it〔不用看键盘上的字母而〕盲打

touch·y /ˈtʌtʃɪ; ˈtʌtʃi/ *adj* **1** easily becoming offended or annoyed 过分敏感的; 易动怒的: *Since his girlfriend left him, he's been very touchy.* 自从女朋友离开他后, 他一直动不动就发脾气。 **2 touchy subject/question etc** a subject etc that needs to be dealt with very carefully 需小心对待的话题/问题等: *Asking about a reporter's sources can be a touchy business.* 要使一名记者透露他的消息来源, 需要非常谨慎。 **—touchily** *adv* **—touchiness** *n* [U]

tough¹ /tʌf; tʌf/ *adj*
1 ▶DIFFICULT 困难的◀ difficult to do or deal with, and needing a lot of effort and determination 难办的, 棘手的; 费力的: *Life as a single mother can be tough and depressing.* 单身母亲的生活可能会艰难而令人沮丧。| *a tough decision* 艰难的决定 | *The reporters were asking a lot of tough questions.* 记者们问了许多难以回答的问题。
2 ▶STRONG PEOPLE 坚强的人◀ able to live through difficult or severe conditions 坚强的, 顽强的; 能吃苦耐劳的: *The men who work on the oil rigs are a tough bunch.* 在石油钻塔上工作的那些人是一群能吃苦耐劳的人。| **as tough as nails/as tough as old boots** (=very tough) 非常坚强的; 能吃大苦的 *He's as tough as nails – a good man to have on the mountain rescue team.* 他非常坚强——是山区营救队的得力成员。
3 ▶STRONG THING 坚固的东西◀ not easily broken or made weaker 结实的, 不易破损的; 坚固的: *a very tough, hard-wearing cloth* 非常结实而耐磨损的布料
4 ▶DETERMINED 坚定的◀ very determined or strict 坚定的; 强硬的; 严格的: *Congress is taking a tough anti-inflation line.* 国会正在采取一条强硬的反通货膨胀的路线。| **get tough with** (=punish or deal with someone in a determined and strict way) 以强硬的方式惩罚[对付] *It's time to get tough with drunk drivers.* 该对酒后驾车采取强硬手段了。| **be tough on** (=treat someone very strictly) 严格对待; 严格对付 *My mother was tougher on my older sister than she was on me.* 我母亲对我姐姐比对我要严厉一些。| *It's time to get tough on crime.* 到了该严厉打击犯罪的时候了。| **tough nut/cookie/customer** *informal* (=someone who is very determined to do what they want and not what other people want)【非正式】〔态度坚决〕很难对付的人/家伙/顾客
5 ▶FOOD 食物◀ difficult to cut or eat 切不下的; 咬不动的; 不嫩的, 老的: *The meat was tough and hard to chew.* 这肉太硬, 很难嚼动。| *the tough outer leaves of the cabbage* 洋白菜外面那几层老菜叶 —opposite 反义词 TENDER¹ (1)
6 ▶ANGRY/NOT SORRY 生气的/不同情的◀ *spoken* used when you do not have any sympathy with someone【口】气愤的/不怜悯的: **tough!** *"I'm getting wet." "Tough! You should've brought your umbrella."* "我淋湿了。" "活该! 你本该带把雨伞的。" | *She didn't tell us she was coming, so if this screws up her plans that's just tough.* 她没有告诉我们她要来, 所以, 如果这打乱了她的计划, 也是活该。
7 tough luck *spoken*【口】**a)** also 又作 **tough shit** *taboo*【讳】used when you do not have any sympathy for someone's problems 活该倒霉: *Well, that's just their tough luck. It was their mistake.* 唉, 活该他们倒霉。那是他们自己的错。**b)** *BrE* used when you feel sympathy about something bad that has happened to someone【英】倒霉的, 可怜的〔表示同情〕: *You didn't get the job? Oh, tough luck.* 你没有得到那份工作? 噢, 真不走运。
8 ▶VIOLENT PERSON 粗暴的人◀ likely to behave violently and having no gentle qualities 粗暴的, 凶恶的; 灭绝人性的: *tough young thugs looking for trouble* 像凶神恶煞、到处滋事的年轻暴徒
9 ▶VIOLENT AREA 暴力地区◀ a tough part of a town has a lot of crime or violence〔城区〕暴力犯罪多发的, 治安很差的: *tough areas of Chicago* 芝加哥治安很差的地区
10 ▶UNFORTUNATE 不幸的◀ unfortunate in a way that seems unfair 不幸的; 不公平的: [**+on**] *It's really tough on him – his wife divorces him, then he has all these problems at work.* 他真是不幸——妻子与他离了婚, 接着工作上又出现了这么多问题。
11 tough love *AmE* love and strictness at the same time【美】严厉的爱 **—toughly** *adv* **—toughness** *n* [U]

tough² *n* [C] *old-fashioned* someone who often behaves in a violent way【过时】暴徒, 恶棍

tough³ *v* **tough it out** to manage to stay in a difficult situation by being determined 渡过难关, (从困境中)挺过来: *We toughed it out, knowing the boss would soon be leaving.* 我们坚定地挺了过来, 因为知道老板快要离任了。

tough·en /ˈtʌfn̩; ˈtʌfən/ also 又作 **toughen up** *v* [I,T] to become tougher or make someone or something tougher (使)变坚韧; (使)变坚强: *toughened glass* 强化玻璃 | *Three years in the army toughened him up.* 三年的军队生活使他变得坚强起来。

Tou·louse-Lau·trec /tuˌluz loˈtrɛk; tuːˌluːz ləʊˈtrek/, **Hen·ri de** /ɑnˈri də; ˈɒnri də/ (1864-1901) a French artist who lived in Montmartre in Paris and painted many pictures of PROSTITUTES, dancers, actors etc. He also painted POSTERS advertising performances by famous entertainers of his time, in theatres such as the Moulin Rouge. 图卢兹-洛特雷克〔(1864-1901), 法国画家。他居住在巴黎蒙马特, 创作有许多人物肖像画, 其中包括妓女、舞蹈演员和戏剧演员, 还为当时的著名艺人在红磨坊等剧场的演出活动画宣传海报〕

tou·pée /tuˈpe; ˈtuːpeɪ/ *n* [C] a small artificial piece of hair that some men wear over a place on their heads where the hair no longer grows〔男子用来遮盖秃发处的〕假发

tour¹ /tʊr; tʊə/ *n* [C] **1** a journey for pleasure, during which you visit several different towns, areas etc〔观光〕旅游, 旅行: *a bicycle tour* 骑自行车旅游 | [**+round/around/of**] *a 10-day tour of China* 中国10日游 —see also 另见 PACKAGE TOUR **2** a short trip through a place to see it〔对某地的〕参观, 游览: [**+of/round/around**] *a guided tour around the Kennedy Space Center* 有向导陪同的肯尼迪太空中心游览 **3** a planned journey made by musicians, a sports team etc in order to perform or play in several places 巡回演出; 巡回比赛: [**+of**] *the England cricket team's tour of India* 英格兰板球队在印度的巡回比赛 | **on tour** *The Moscow Symphony Orchestra is here on tour.* 莫斯科交响乐团巡回演出, 来到此地。| **a leg of a tour** (=one part of it) 巡回演出的一站 *the first leg of U2's European tour* U2演唱组欧洲巡回演出的第一站 **4** a period during which you go to live somewhere, usually abroad, to do your job, especially military work 外地工作期〔尤指在海外的军方工作〕: *a two-year tour in Vietnam* 在越南的两年派驻期 **5 tour of inspection** an official visit to a place, institution, group etc in order to check its quality or performance〔官员的〕视察访问, 巡察

tour² *v* [I,T] to visit somewhere on a tour 游览, 观光: *We're touring the Greek islands this summer.* 我们今年夏天要去游览希腊诸岛。

tour de force /ˌtʊr də ˈfɔrs; ˌtʊə də ˈfɔːs/ *n* [singular] something that is done very skilfully and successfully, in a way that impresses people 绝技, 绝活, 拿手好戏: *His speech to the Democratic Convention was a tour de force.* 他在民主党大会上的演说精彩极了。

Tour de France, the /ˌ· · ˈ·/ a famous bicycle race that takes place in France each year. The race goes all over France and continues for about three weeks. On each day the rider who is leading the race wears a special yellow shirt. 环法自行车赛〔每年在法国举行的一项著名自行车赛事。比赛路线环绕法国全境, 历时约为三周。每天在比赛中领先的运动员身着一件特制的黄色运动衫〕

tour·is·m /ˈtʊrɪzm̩; ˈtʊərɪzəm/ *n* [U] the business of providing things for people to do, places for them to stay etc while they are on holiday 旅游业, 观光业: *The country depends on tourism for most of its income.* 该国的大部分收入依靠旅游业。

tour·ist /ˈtʊrɪst; ˈtʊərɪst/ *n* [C] someone who is travelling or visiting a place for pleasure 游客, 游人, 观光客: *Cambridge is always full of tourists in the summer.* 剑桥在夏季总是挤满了游客。

tourist at·trac·tion /ˈ· · ·, · -/ *n* [C] a place or event that a lot of tourists go to 旅游胜地; 旅游盛事: *The Statue of Liberty is a major tourist attraction.* 自由女神像是一处重要的旅游景点。

tourist class /ˈ· · ·/ *n* [U] the cheapest standard of travelling conditions on a plane, ship etc〔飞机、轮船等上面最廉价的〕旅游舱, 经济舱

tourist of·fice /ˈ· · , · -/ also 又作 **tourist in·for·ma·tion of·fice** /ˌ· · · ˈ· · , · -/ *n* [C] an office that gives information to tourists in an area 旅游信息咨询处

tourist trap /ˈ· · , -/ *n* [C] a place that many tourists visit, but where drinks, hotels etc are more expensive 敲游客竹杠的地方〈如餐饮店、旅店等〉

tour·ist·y /ˈtʊrɪstɪ; ˈtʊərɪsti/ *adj informal*【非正式】**1** a place that is touristy is unpleasantly full of tourists and the things that attract tourists 挤满游客的, 充满吸引游客的东西的: *Benidorm is too touristy for me.* 贝尼多姆对我来说游客太多了一点。**2** a touristy activity is unpleasantly typical of the things that tour-

ists do〔活动〕像旅游似的; 走马观花似的: *The boat trip was kind of touristy, but we did get to see a lot.* 那次乘船旅行有点走马观花似的, 不过我们还是看到了不少风景。

tour·na·ment /ˈtɜnəmənt; ˈtʊənəmənt/ *n* [C] **1 tennis/chess/badminton etc tournament** a competition in which players compete against each other in a series of games until there is one winner 网球/国际象棋/羽毛球等锦标赛 **2** a competition to show courage and fighting skill between soldiers in the Middle Ages〔中世纪的〕骑士比武大会

tour·ni·quet /ˈtɜnɪˌkɛt; ˈtʊənɪkeɪ/ *n* [C] a band of cloth that is twisted tightly around an injured arm or leg to stop it bleeding 止血带

tour of du·ty /ˌ· · ˈ· ·/ *n* [C] a period of time when you are working in a particular place or job, especially abroad while you are in the army etc 工作期;〔尤指军队中派驻海外的〕服役期

tour op·e·rat·or /ˈ· ˌ· · · ·/ *n* [C] *BrE* a company that arranges travel tours【英】旅游公司, 旅行社

tou·sle /ˈtauzl; ˈtaʊzəl/ *v* [T] to make someone's hair look untidy 弄乱〔头发〕

tou·sled /ˈtauzld; ˈtaʊzəld/ *adj* tousled hair or a tousled appearance looks untidy〔头发〕蓬乱的; 蓬头垢面的: *She had just awakened, her eyes sleepy and her hair tousled.* 她刚睡醒, 一副睡眼惺忪、头发蓬乱的样子。

Tous·saint l'Ou·ver·ture /tuˌsæn luvɛrˈtjʊɚ; ˌtuːsæn luːveəˈtjʊə/ (1746-1803) a former SLAVE who became a leader of the people in Haiti, in opposition to French rule there. He died in a French prison. 图森-路维杜尔〔(1746-1803), 海地人民领袖, 奴隶出身。他反对法国在海地的统治, 死于法国的一座监狱中〕

tout¹ /taut; taʊt/ *v* **1** [T] to praise something or someone in order to persuade people that they are important or worth a lot 赞扬; 吹捧: *the much touted delights of England in the spring* 众口交誉的英格兰春天的乐趣 | **be touted as sth** *Bates was widely touted as the next Olympic star.* 贝茨被大家预测为下一届奥林匹克之星。**2** [I,T] *especially BrE* to try to persuade people to buy goods or services you are offering【尤英】兜售, 推销〔商品或服务〕: **tout for business/custom** (=look for customers) 拉生意/招徕顾客 **3** [I,T] *AmE* to give someone information about a horse in a race【美】(向…) 提供赛马情报

tout² *n* [C] *BrE*【英】**1** someone who buys tickets for a concert, sports match etc and sells them at a very high price 票贩子, 黄牛党; SCALPER *AmE*【美】**2** someone who tries to sell goods or services to people passing on the street 沿街兜售者, 拉生意者

tow¹ /to; təʊ/ *v* [T] to pull a vehicle or ship along behind another vehicle using a rope or chain 牵引, 拖, 拉〔车或船〕: *The ship had to be towed into the harbor.* 那艘轮船不得已被拖进了港口。

tow² *n* **1** [C] an act of pulling a vehicle behind another vehicle using a rope or chain 牵引, 拖, 拉〔车船等〕: *Can you give us a tow?* 你能帮我们拖一下吗? **2 in tow** *informal* following closely behind someone or something【非正式】紧跟在后: *Hannah arrived with her four kids in tow.* 汉娜来了, 她的四个孩子紧跟在后面。**3 take sth in tow** to connect a rope or a chain to a vehicle or ship so that it can be towed〔用绳索或链条〕拖着〔车或船〕**4 on tow** *BrE* a vehicle that is on tow is being pulled along by another vehicle【英】〔车〕被拖着走

to·wards /tɔrdz; təˈwɔːdz/ *especially BrE*【尤英】, **to·ward** /tɔrd; təˈwɔːd/ *especially AmE*【尤美】*prep* **1** moving, looking, or pointing in a particular direction 向(着), 朝(着): *He noticed two policemen coming towards him.* 他觉察到两名警察正朝他走来。| *All the windows face toward the river.* 所有的窗户都朝向河。| *He was standing with his back towards me.* 他背对我站着。—see picture on page A1 参见 A1 页图 **2** if you do something towards something, you do it in order to achieve it 为了(…目的): *These negotiations are the first step toward reaching an agreement.* 这些谈判是为了达成一项协议而迈出的第一步。| *The council is constantly working towards racial and sexual equality.* 该委员会正不断努力争取种族和性别上的平等。**3** a feeling, attitude etc towards something is how you feel or what you think about it 对于; 关于〔指感觉、态度等〕: *Brian's attitude towards his work has always been very positive.* 布赖恩对工作的态度总是非常积极主动的。**4** money put, saved, or given towards something is used to pay for it〔钱〕用于支付…: *A lot of the donations will be put towards repairing the church roof.* 捐款中的很大部分将用于维修教堂的屋顶。**5 a)** just before a particular time 快要到〔某个时刻〕: *Toward the end of the afternoon it began to rain.* 快到傍晚时, 天下起雨来了。**b)** near a particular place 接近〔某一地方〕: *As you get towards the coast you notice more and more hotels and restaurants.* 快接近海边时, 你会注意到有许许多多的旅馆和饭店。

tow-a·way zone /ˈtoəwe ˌzon; ˈtəʊəweɪ ˌzəʊn/ *n* [C] *AmE* an area where cars are not allowed to park, and from which they can be taken away by the police【美】禁止停车区〔违章车有可能被警察拖走〕

tow·bar /ˈtobɑr; ˈtəʊbɑː/ *n* [C] a metal bar on the back of a car for towing (TOW¹) a CARAVAN (1) or boat〔用以牵引车、船等的〕牵引杠

tow·el¹ /ˈtauəl; ˈtaʊəl/ *n* [C] a piece of cloth that you use for drying your skin or for drying things such as dishes 毛巾, 纸巾; 抹布: *a bath towel* 浴巾 —see also 另见 PAPER TOWEL, TEA TOWEL, **throw in the towel** (THROW¹)

towel² *v* [T] *AmE* also 又作 **towel down** to dry yourself using a towel【美】用毛巾擦干 —see also 另见 TOWELLING

tow·el·ette /ˌtauəˈlɛt; ˌtaʊəˈlet/ *n* [C] a small piece of soft wet paper that you use to clean your hands or face 小毛巾; 湿餐巾纸

tow·el·ling *BrE*【英】, **toweling** *AmE*【美】/ˈtauəlɪŋ; ˈtaʊəlɪŋ/ *n* [U] thick soft cloth, used especially for making towels or BATHROBES 毛巾布 —see picture on page A16 参见 A16 页图

towel rail /ˈ· · ·/ also 又作 **towel rack** *n* [C] a bar or frame on which towels can be hung, especially in a bathroom〔尤指浴室里的〕毛巾架

tow·er¹ /ˈtauɚ; ˈtaʊə/ *n* [C] **1** a tall narrow building either built on its own or forming part of a castle, church etc 塔; 塔楼: *They rebuilt the church tower in the 1870s.* 他们在19世纪70年代重修了那座教堂的钟楼。**2** a tall structure, often made of metal, used for signalling, broadcasting etc〔发送信号或广播等用的〕铁塔, 塔状建筑物: *an air traffic control tower* 空中交通管制塔 **3 tower of strength** someone who gives you a lot of help, sympathy, and support when you are in trouble〔在遇到麻烦时〕可依靠的人; 支柱: *Her father was a tower of strength to her when her marriage broke up.* 她的婚姻破裂时, 父亲成了她可以依靠的支柱。—see also 另见 COOLING TOWER, **ivory tower** (IVORY (6)), WATER TOWER

tower² *v* [I] **1** to be much taller than the people or things around you〔比周围的人或物体〕高出许多; 高耸, 屹立: [+about/over] *Graham was 6 ft 5, and towered over the rest of us.* 格雷厄姆身高6英尺5英寸, 比我们其余的人都要高出许多。**2** to be much better than any other person or organization that does the same thing as you〔比…〕优秀许多; 高踞〔于…之上〕: [+about/over] *Mozart towers over all other composers.* 莫扎特高踞于其他所有作曲家之上。

Tower, the —see 见 the TOWER OF LONDON

tower block /ˈ· · ·/ *n* [C] *BrE* a tall building containing apartments or offices【英】〔作公寓或办公用的〕高层建筑

Tower Bridge /ˌ· · ˈ·/ a bridge which crosses the River Thames in London, just to the east of the Tower of London. The part of the bridge which carries the road divides in the middle into two separate parts, which can be pulled up so that tall ships can pass under it. Tower Bridge is one of London's best-known buildings, and is often used as a symbol representing London. 塔桥〔伦敦市区横跨泰晤士河的一座桥, 位于伦敦塔东面。路桥部分可从中间一分为二, 并可吊起以便让桥下的大船通过。塔桥是伦敦最著名的建筑物之一, 常作为伦敦的标志〕

tower computer /ˌ· · ˈ· ·/ *n* [C] a computer in the shape of a tall box 塔式计算机 —see picture on page A14 参见 A14 页图

tow·er·ing /ˈtauərɪŋ; ˈtaʊərɪŋ/ *adj* [only before noun 仅用于名词前] **1** very tall 高大的, 高耸的: *great towering cliffs* 宏伟高耸的峭壁 **2** much better than other people of the same kind; OUTSTANDING (1) 出众的, 杰出的: *a towering genius of his time* 他那个时代一名杰出的天才 **3 in a towering rage** very angry 怒气冲天

Tower of Ba·bel, the /ˌ· · · ˈ· ·/ a tower in a story in the Old Testament of the Bible. According to the story, everyone originally spoke the same language, but when the people of Babel tried to build a tower that would reach to Heaven, God prevented them by making them all speak different languages. The people could not understand each other, and were unable to finish building the tower. People sometimes use the word 'babel' to talk about a situation in which many people are talking at the same time and it is impossible to understand anyone. 巴别塔, 通天塔〔《圣经·旧约》故事中的一座塔。据称, 太初人们讲同一种语言, 只是当巴别人想建一座通往天堂的宝塔时, 上帝才让他们讲了不同的语言, 这样就可以阻止他们造塔。巴别人相互听不懂彼此的话, 因而无法将塔建成。人们有时借用 babel 一词指许多人同时开口说话但谁也听不懂谁的情形〕

Tower of Lon·don, the /ˌ·· ·ˈ·/ also 又作 **the Tower** a FORTRESS (=protected group of buildings including a castle) in London next to the River Thames, built in the 11th century but originally built in Roman times. The kings and queens of England lived there in the past, and many important people were kept as prisoners there. It is now a MUSEUM. 伦敦塔〔伦敦市一堡垒，位于泰晤士河畔，始建于罗马时代，目前的塔楼建于11世纪。过去，伦敦塔曾住过英格兰国王或女王，也曾囚禁过许多要人。伦敦塔现为博物馆〕

tow·head /ˈtoˌhɛd; ˈtəʊhed/ *n* [C] someone with very light-coloured hair 亚麻色头发的人 —**towheaded** *adj*

tow·line /ˈtolaɪn; ˈtəʊlaɪn/ *n* [C] a TOWROPE 拖索，纤绳

town /taʊn; taʊn/ *n*

1 ▶PLACE 地方◀ [C] a large area with houses, shops, offices etc where people live and work, that is smaller than a city and larger than a village〔大于村庄、小于城市的〕镇，城镇，市镇：*an industrial town in the Midlands* 英格兰中部地区的一座工业城镇 | *the town of Norwalk, Connecticut* 康涅狄格州诺沃克镇

2 ▶MAIN CENTRE 主要中心◀ [U] the business or shopping centre of a town〔市镇的〕商业中心区，闹市区：*We're going into town tonight to see a film.* 我们今晚要去市中心看电影。| *They have a small apartment in town.* 他们在市中心有一套不大的公寓。

3 ▶PEOPLE 人们◀ [singular] all the people who live in a particular town 镇民，市镇居民：*The whole town turned out to watch the procession.* 全镇的人都出来观看游行队伍。

4 ▶WHERE YOU LIVE 居住地◀ [U] *AmE* the town or city where you live【美】〔居住的〕城镇；城市：*Cam left town about an hour ago, he should be out at the farm by now.* 卡姆大约一个小时前离开城里，他现在应该在城外的农场上了。| **out of town** *I'll be out of town for about a week.* 我将离开城里大约一个星期。| **in town** *Guess who's in town? Jodie's sister!* 猜猜谁到城里来了？乔迪的妹妹！| **be from out of town** (=live in a different town than the one you are in) 来自另一个城镇 *Do you know of a good place to eat? I'm from out of town.* 你能介绍个吃饭的好地方吗？我是外地人。

5 ▶VILLAGE 村庄◀ [C] *AmE* several houses forming a small group around a church, shops etc【美】乡镇，集镇；VILLAGE *BrE*【英】：*Rowayton is a small town of around 4,000 people.* 罗威顿是一个大约有4000人的小乡镇。

6 ▶NOT COUNTRY 不是乡下◀ the town life in towns and cities in general 城镇生活，城市生活〔统称〕：*Which do you prefer, the town or the country?* 城市生活与乡村生活，你较喜欢哪一种？

7 go to town (on) *informal* to do something in a very eager or thorough way, often spending a lot of money【非正式】拼命地干〔某事〕；花大钱〔做某事〕：*Angela really went to town on buying things for her new house.* 安杰拉在为自己的新房子买东西时真是舍得花钱。

8 go/be out on the town *informal* to go to restaurants, bars, theatres etc for entertainment in the evening【非正式】〔晚间去娱乐场所〕寻欢作乐

9 town and gown *BrE* used to describe the situation in which the people living in a town and the students in a town seem to be separate and opposing groups【英】〔分成两派、相互对立的〕城镇居民和学生 —see also 另见 GHOST TOWN, **blow town** (BLOW¹ (11)), MARKET TOWN, NEW TOWN, **paint the town red** (PAINT² (6))

town cen·tre /ˌ·ˈ··/ *n* [C] *BrE* the main business area in the centre of a town【英】市中心，城里商业区；DOWNTOWN *AmE*【美】

town clerk /ˌ·ˈ·/ *n* [C] an official who keeps records, advises on legal matters etc〔主管档案、提供法律事务咨询等工作的〕镇执事

town coun·cil /ˌ·ˈ··/ *n* [C] *BrE* a group of people who are responsible for public areas and services, such as roads, parks etc, in a particular town【英】〔负责管理某一城镇公共事务的〕镇议会，市议会 —**town councillor** *n* [C]

town cri·er /ˌ·ˈ··/ *n* [C] someone employed in former times to walk around the streets of a town, shouting news, warnings etc〔昔日受雇沿街〕大声宣读公告的人

town hall /ˌ·ˈ·/ *n* [C] a public building used for a town's local government 市政厅，镇公所，镇政府办公楼

town house /ˈ· ·/ *n* [C] **1** a house in a town or city, especially a fashionable one in a central area 市镇住宅〔尤指市镇中心区的新式住宅〕**2** a house in a town that belongs to someone who also owns a house in the countryside〔在乡间拥有住所者的〕市内住宅：*the Duke's town house in Mayfair* 公爵在梅费尔的市内住宅 **3** *AmE* a house in a group of houses that share one or more walls【美】〔边墙共用的〕排屋，连栋房屋

town·ie /ˈtaʊnɪ; ˈtaʊni/ *n* [C] *informal* someone who lives in a town or city and does not know anything about life in the countryside【非正式】〔对乡村生活一无所知的〕城里人

town meet·ing /ˌ·ˈ··/ *n* [C] *AmE* a meeting at which the people who live in a town discuss subjects or problems that affect their town【美】镇民大会

Town Mouse and the Coun·try Mouse, the /ˌ·ˌ·ˈ··ˌ·/ an old story about a mouse who lives in a town and who invites a poor mouse who lives in the country to come and stay with him. The country mouse does not like the town, and when he invites the town mouse to come and stay with him in the country, the town mouse does not like the country. The lesson of the story is that a way of life that is suitable for one person may not be suitable for another.《城里老鼠和乡下老鼠》〔一则古老的故事。故事中一只城里老鼠邀请一只乡下穷老鼠与它同住，可乡下老鼠并不喜欢城里。接着，乡下老鼠请城里老鼠去乡下与它一起住，可城里老鼠也不喜欢乡下。这个故事的寓意是，适合一个人的生活方式未必适合另一个人〕

town plan·ning /ˌ·ˈ··/ *n* [U] the study of the way towns work, so that roads, houses, services etc can be provided as effectively as possible 城镇规划

town·ship /ˈtaʊnʃɪp; ˈtaʊnʃɪp/ *n* [C] **1** a town in Canada or the US that has some local government〔加拿大或美国享有一定地方行政权的〕乡，镇区 **2** a town in South Africa where black citizens live〔过去南非的〕黑人居住的城市，镇：*the black township of Soweto* 黑人城镇索韦托

towns·peo·ple /ˈtaunzˌpipḷ; ˈtaʊnzˌpiːpəl/ also 又作 **towns·folk** /-fok; -fəʊk/ *n* [plural] **1** all the people who live in a particular town 城镇居民：*the proud townspeople of Semer Water* 塞默沃特城自豪的居民们 **2** people who live in towns and not in the country 镇民，城里人

tow·path /ˈtoˌpæθ; ˈtəʊpɑːθ/ *n* [C] a path along the side of a CANAL or river used especially in former times by horses pulling boats〔运河或河流两岸昔日供马拉船的〕曳船道，纤路

tow·rope /ˈtoˌrop; ˈtəʊrəʊp/ also 又作 **towline** *n* [C] a rope or chain used for pulling vehicles along 拖索，拖缆，纤绳

tow·truck /ˈtoˌtrʌk; ˈtəʊtrʌk/ *n* [C] *AmE* a strong vehicle that can pull cars behind it【美】拖运车，牵引车；BREAKDOWN TRUCK *BrE*【英】

tox·ae·mi·a *BrE*【英】, **toxemia** *AmE*【美】/tɑksˈimɪə; tɒkˈsiːmiə/ *n* [U] a medical condition in which your blood contains poisons 毒血症

tox·ic /ˈtɑksɪk; ˈtɒksɪk/ *adj* containing poison, or caused by poisonous substances 有毒的；由有毒物质引起的：*toxic fumes* 有毒烟气 | *a toxic waste dump* 有毒废物弃置场 —**toxicity** /tɑksˈɪsətɪ; tɒkˈsɪsəti/ *n* [U]

tox·i·col·o·gy /ˌtɑksɪˈkɑlədʒɪ; ˌtɒksɪˈkɒlədʒi/ *n* [U] the science and medical study of poisons and their effects 毒物学，毒理学

toxic shock syn·drome /ˌ··ˈ·ˌ··/ *n* [U] a serious illness that causes a high temperature and is thought to be connected with the use of TAMPONS 中毒性休克综合征〔严重疾病，患者发高烧，被认为与使用月经棉塞有关〕

toxic waste /ˌ··ˈ·/ *n* [C,U] waste products from industry that are harmful to people, animals, or the environment 有毒〔工业〕垃圾

tox·in /ˈtɑksɪn; ˈtɒksɪn/ *n* [C] a poisonous substance, especially one that is produced by BACTERIA and causes a particular disease 毒素〔尤指细菌产生的致病物质〕

toy¹ /tɔɪ; tɔɪ/ *n* [C] **1** an object for children to play with 玩具：*some toys for the baby* 给婴儿的一些玩具 | **toy boat/car/truck etc** *Davey wanted some toy soldiers for Christmas.* 戴维想要一些玩具兵作为圣诞礼物。| **soft/cuddly toy** *BrE* (=a toy that looks like an animal and is covered in fur)【英】毛绒/让人想搂抱的动物玩具 **2** an object that you buy because it gives you pleasure and enjoyment 小玩艺儿，小摆设：*The food mixer is her latest toy.* 食品搅拌器是她最近买来的小玩艺儿。

toy² *v*

toy with sth *phr v* [T] **1** to think about an idea or possibility, usually for a short time and not very seriously〔通常指短暂而不认真地〕考虑：**toy with the idea of doing sth** *I've been toying with the idea of going to Japan to visit them.* 我一直打算去日本探访他们，只是从来没有认真地想过。**2** to play with an object, often while you are thinking about something else 摆弄，戏耍〔常指一边想其他事情一边摆弄〕：*Elsa toyed with her coffee cup.* 埃尔莎摆弄着自己的咖啡杯。

toy³ *adj* [only before noun 仅用于名词前] a toy animal or dog is a type of dog that is specially bred to be very small〔动物〕体形非常小的：*a toy poodle* 小小的长鬈毛狗

toy boy /ˈ· ·/ *n* [C] *informal* a young man who is having a sexual relationship with an older woman【非正式】〔与年龄较大的妇女有性关系的〕小男人, 小情夫

trace¹ /tres; treɪs/ *v* [T]

1 ▶FIND SB/STH 发现某人/某物◀ to find someone or something that has disappeared by searching for them carefully 仔细找寻: *She had given up all hope of tracing her missing daughter.* 她已经放弃了寻找到失踪女儿的一切希望。

2 ▶ORIGINS 来源◀ to find the origins of something, or where something came from 追溯; 追查: **trace sth (back) to** *The style of these paintings can be traced back to early medieval influences.* 这些绘画的风格可以追溯到中世纪早期的影响。

3 ▶HISTORY/DEVELOPMENT 历史/发展◀ to study or describe the history, development, or progress of something 研究…的历史; 探索…的发展; 追寻…的轨迹: *Sondheim's book traces the changing nature of the relationship between men and women.* 桑德海姆的这本书探索了男人与女人之间关系不断变化的本质。

4 ▶COPY 誊写◀ to copy a drawing, map etc by putting a piece of transparent paper over it and then drawing the lines you can see through the paper〔用透明纸在图上〕描摹, 描绘

5 ▶DRAW 勾画◀ to draw real or imaginary lines on the surface of something, usually with your finger or toe〔用手指或脚趾在物体表面〕画〔线〕; 留下〔印迹〕: **trace sth on/in/across** *Rosie's fingers traced a delicate pattern in the sand.* 罗西用手指在沙地上留下了精美的图案。

6 trace a call to use special electronic equipment to find out who made a telephone call〔利用特殊的电子设备〕追查打电话的人 —**traceable** *adj*

trace² *n*

1 ▶SIGN OF STH 某物的迹象◀ [C,U] a small sign that shows that someone or something was present or existed 踪迹, 痕迹, 迹象: **no trace** *There was no trace of anyone having entered the room since then.* 没有任何迹象表明有人在那以后进过这间屋子。| **all trace** *Petra's lost all trace of her German accent.* 佩特拉已完全没有德国口音了。| **any trace** *Officers were unable to find any trace of drugs.* 警察未能找到毒品存在的任何迹象。| **disappear/vanish/sink without trace** (=disappear completely, without leaving any sign of what happened) 消失/隐没/沉没得无影无踪 *The Roanoke colony vanished without trace.* 罗阿诺克殖民地消失得无影无踪了。

2 ▶SMALL AMOUNT 小量◀ [C] a very small amount of a quality, emotion, substance etc that is difficult to see or notice 微量; 痕量: **[+of]** *I saw the faintest trace of a smile cross Sandra's face.* 我看到在桑德拉的脸上闪过一丝微笑。| *traces of poison* 微量毒素

3 ▶TELEPHONE 电话◀ [C] *technical* a search to find out where a telephone call came from, using special electronic equipment【术语】〔利用特殊电子设备对电话的〕追查, 追踪: *The police were able to put a trace on the call.* 警察能够追查到电话是从什么地方打过来的。

4 ▶INFORMATION RECORDED 记录的信息◀ [C] the mark or pattern made on a SCREEN or on paper by a machine that is recording an electrical signal〔记录电信号的机器在屏幕或纸上作的〕描记线: *This trace shows the heartbeat.* 这条描记线显示了心脏跳动的情况。

5 kick over the traces to stop following the rules of a social group and do what you want 挣脱羁绊, 摆脱约束

6 ▶CART/CARRIAGE 大车/马车◀ [C] one of the two pieces of leather, rope etc by which a cart or carriage is fastened to the animal that is pulling it〔大车或马车上的〕挽绳

trac·er /ˈtresɚ; ˈtreɪsə/ *n* [C] a bullet that leaves a line of smoke or flame behind it 曳光弹

trac·e·ry /ˈtresərɪ; ˈtreɪsəri/ *n* [C,U] **1** *technical* the curving and crossing lines of stone in the upper parts of some church windows【术语】〔教堂窗户上部的〕窗花格 **2** *literary* an attractive pattern of lines that cross each other【文】线条交错的美丽图案: *the delicate tracery of the bare branches against the sky* 在天空衬托下光秃秃的枝丫交错成的细致图案

tra·che·a /ˈtrekɪə; trəˈkiːə/ *n* [C] *technical* the tube that takes air from your throat to your lungs【术语】气管 —see picture at 参见 RESPIRATORY 图

trach·e·ot·o·my /ˌtrekɪˈɑtəmɪ; ˌtrækiˈɒtəmi/ *n* [C] *technical* an operation to cut a hole in someone's throat so that they can breathe【术语】气管切开术

tra·cho·ma /trəˈkomə; trəˈkəʊmə/ *n* [U] *technical* a painful illness that affects the transparent covering over your eyes【术语】沙眼〔一种眼病〕

trac·ing /ˈtresɪŋ; ˈtreɪsɪŋ/ *n* [C] a copy of a map, drawing etc made by tracing (TRACE¹ (4)) it 描摹

tracing pa·per /ˈ· ·, ·ˈ/ *n* [U] strong transparent paper used for tracing (TRACE¹ (4)) 描图纸

track¹ /træk; træk/ *n*

1 ▶ROAD 道路◀ [C] a narrow road with a rough uneven surface that cars can travel on〔路面粗糙不平的、可行车的〕小道, 窄路: *The road leading to the farm was little more than a rough track.* 通往农场的道路基本上只是一条凹凸不平的小路。| *a deeply-rutted cart track* 车辙很深的小道

2 ▶PATH 小径◀ [C] a narrow path, especially one made by people or animals frequently walking in the same place〔尤指经常行走踩出来的〕小路, 小径: *a mountain track* 山间小路 | *The track led through dense forest.* 小径穿过茂密的森林。

3 ▶FOR RACING 用于比赛◀ [C] a circular course around which runners, cars etc race, often with a specially prepared surface 跑道: *To run a mile, you have to run four circuits of the track.* 要跑一英里, 你必须沿着跑道跑四圈。—see also 另见 DIRT TRACK

4 ▶RAILWAY 铁路◀ [C] the two metal lines along which trains travel or the narrow strip of land to which they are fixed; RAILWAY LINE〔铁路的〕轨道, 铁路线: *The track was damaged in several places.* 这条铁路线有好几处地方都毁坏了。—see picture at 参见 TUNNEL¹ 图

5 tracks [plural] a line of marks left on the ground by a moving person, animal, or vehicle〔人、兽等的〕足迹, 痕迹; 〔车辆的〕轨迹, 车辙: *We followed the tyre tracks across a muddy field.* 我们顺着车胎的辙印穿过一片泥泞的田野。| *The tracks, which looked like a fox's, led into the woods.* 这些看上去像狐狸足迹的痕迹延伸到树林里。

6 be on the right/wrong track to think in a way that is likely to lead to a correct or incorrect result 思路正确/错误: *He's not interested in her at all – you're on the wrong track there.* 他对她根本不感兴趣—你在这一点上想错了。

7 ▶MUSIC/SONG 音乐/歌曲◀ [C] one of the songs or pieces of music on a record, CASSETTE, or CD〔唱片、录音带或CD上的〕一首歌; 一支曲子: *There's a great Miles Davis track on side two.* 在第二面有迈尔斯·戴维斯的一首名曲。

8 keep/lose track of to pay attention to someone or something so that you know where they are or what is happening to them, or to fail to do this 掌握/失去…的线索; 了解/不了解…的动态: *It's difficult to keep track of all the new discoveries in genetics.* 要全面掌握遗传学的新发现是困难的。

9 stop (dead) in your tracks to suddenly stop, especially because something has frightened or surprised you〔尤指因惊吓而〕突然停下: *Fay stopped in her tracks and pointed at the house.* 费伊突然停了下来, 指着那座房子。

10 cover/hide your tracks to be careful not to leave any signs that could let people know where you have been or what you have done because you want to keep it a secret 掩盖/隐匿自己的行踪[活动]: *We don't know where Ford is, he's been very clever in covering his tracks.* 我们不知道福特在哪儿, 他非常狡猾, 来无影去无踪的。

11 be on the track of to hunt or search for someone or something 追踪, 追寻: *Police are on the track of a gang that has robbed five post offices in the last month.* 警察正在追踪过去一个月里抢劫了五家邮局的一帮匪徒。

12 ▶SPORT 体育运动◀ [U] *AmE*【美】**a)** sport that involves running on a track 径赛运动: *The next year he didn't run track or play football.* 第二年他没有参加径赛运动, 也没有踢足球。**b)** all the sports in an ATHLETICS competition such as running, jumping, or throwing the JAVELIN 田径运动: *a famous track star* 田径运动名星 | *She went out for track in the spring.* (=she joined the school's track team) 她在春季加入了学校的田径队。

13 I'd better make tracks *spoken* used to say you must leave a place, especially when you do not want to leave【口】我得马上离开〔尤指自己并不想离开〕: *I'd love to stay, but it's time we started making tracks.* 我倒很想留下, 不过我们该离开了。

14 ▶DIRECTION 方向◀ [C] the direction or line taken by something as it moves〔物体移动的〕方向; 行动路线: **[+of]** *islands that lie in the track of North Atlantic storms* 位于北大西洋风暴运行路线上的岛屿

15 ▶ON A VEHICLE 交通工具上◀ [C] an endless metal band driven by the wheels of a vehicle such as a BULLDOZER that allows it to move over uneven ground〔车辆的〕履带

16 ▶FOR RECORDING 录音用的◀ [C] a band on a TAPE¹ (1) on which music or information can be recorded〔录音带的〕音轨, 磁迹: *Sergeant Pepper was recorded on eight tracks.*《佩珀中士》是用八轨磁带录音的。

17 be on track *spoken* to be likely to achieve the result you want【口】有可能获得〔想要的结果〕: *We're still on track for 10% growth.* 我们仍然有可能达到 10% 的增长率。

18 get off the track *spoken* to begin to deal with a new subject rather than the main one which was being discussed【口】偏离正题，离题：*Don't get off the track, we're looking at this year's figures not last year's.* 别偏离正题了，我们关注的是今年的数字，而不是去年的。—see also 另见 **off the beaten track** (BEATEN (3)), ONE-TRACK MIND, **be from the wrong side of the tracks** (WRONG[1] (14))

track² *v*

1 ▶SEARCH 搜寻◀ [T] to search for a person or animal by following the marks they leave behind them on the ground, their smell etc 追踪，跟踪：**track sb to sth** *The dogs tracked the wolf to its lair.* 一群狗追踪那只狼一直到它的巢穴。

2 ▶AIRCRAFT/SHIP 飞行器/轮船◀ [T] to follow the movements of an aircraft or ship by using RADAR〔用雷达〕跟踪〔飞机或轮船〕：*a tracking station* 跟踪站

3 ▶CAMERA 摄像机◀ [I+in/out] to move a film or television camera away from or towards a scene in order to follow the action that you are recording〔电影或电视摄像机〕跟踪摄影，移动摄影

4 ▶RECORD 唱片◀ [I] if a PICK-UP (4) tracks, it moves in the grooves (GROOVE[1] (1)) on a record〔唱针在唱片纹道中〕移动

5 ▶SCHOOL 学校◀ [T] *AmE* to put school children in groups according to their ability【美】把〔学生〕按能力分组；STREAM[2] (5) *BrE*【英】

6 ▶MARK 印迹◀ [T] *AmE* to leave behind a track of something such as mud or dirt when you walk【美】留下…的足印：*Which of you boys tracked mud all over the kitchen floor?* 是你们中哪个男孩子在厨房地板上到处留下带泥的脚印？—**tracker** *n* [C]: *a police tracker dog* 警方的追捕者

track sb/sth ↔ **down** *phr v* [T] to find someone or something that is difficult to find by searching or making inquiries in several different places 追踪到；追查到：*I finally managed to track down the book you wanted in a shop near the station.* 我在车站附近的一家书店里终于找到了你想要的那本书。

track and field /ˌ· · ˈ·/ *n* [U] *AmE* sports such as running and jumping【美】田径运动；ATHLETICS *BrE*【英】

track·ball /ˈtrækˌbɔl; ˈtrækbɔːl/ *n* [C] a small ball connected to a computer, that you turn in order to move the CURSOR 轨迹球〔一种与电脑连接的用来控制光标移动的小球〕

tracker dog /ˈ· · ˌ·/ *n* [C] a dog that has been specially trained to follow and find people 搜索用警犬

track e·vent /ˈ· ·ˌ·/ *n* [C] *AmE* a running race【美】径赛项目

tracking sta·tion /ˈ· · ˌ· ·/ *n* [C] a place from which objects moving in space, such as SATELLITES and ROCKETS, can be recognized and followed〔对在太空中运行的人造卫星、火箭等进行识别、追踪的〕跟踪站

track·lay·er /ˈtrækˌleɚ; ˈtrækˌleɪə/ *n* [C] *AmE* a workman who builds or repairs railway tracks【美】〔铁路的〕铺轨工人；养路工；PLATE-LAYER *BrE*【英】

track meet /ˈ· ·/ *n* [C] *AmE* a sports event consisting of competitions in running, jumping etc【美】田径运动会

track rec·ord /ˌ· ˈ· ·/ *n* [singular] all the things that a person or organization has done in the past, which show how good they are at doing their job, dealing with problems etc〔个人或机构在工作、解决问题等方面的〕成绩记录，业绩记录：*We're looking for someone with a proven track record in selling advertising.* 我们正在寻找一位在广告销售业绩方面有良好记录的人。

track·suit /ˈtrækˌsut; ˈtræksuːt/ *n* [C] *BrE* loose clothes consisting of trousers and a JACKET (1), worn especially for sport【英】宽松式运动衣裤，田径服

tract /trækt; trækt/ *n* [C] **1 digestive/reproductive/urinary etc tract** a system of connected organs that have one main purpose in a part of your body〔身体器官系统中的〕消化道/生殖道/泌尿道等 **2** a large area of land〔土地的〕一大片：*vast tracts of woodland* 大片林地 **3** *formal* a short piece of writing, especially about a moral or religious subject【正式】〔尤指道德或宗教题材的〕短文，小册子：*a tract on the dangers of drink* 一本关于饮酒之种种危险的小册子

trac·ta·ble /ˈtræktəbl; ˈtræktəbəl/ *adj formal* easy to control or deal with【正式】易控制的；易对付的：*Separating a problem into separate chunks often makes it more tractable.* 把一个问题分成不同的几大部分往往会使它更容易处理。—opposite 反义词 INTRACTABLE —**tractability** /ˌtræktəˈbɪlətɪ; ˌtræktəˈbɪlɪ̣ti/ *n* [U]

trac·tion /ˈtrækʃən; ˈtrækʃən/ *n* [U] **1** the process of treating a broken bone with special medical equipment that pulls it〔治疗骨折用的〕牵引术：**be in traction** (=be receiving this kind of treatment) 接受牵引治疗 *He was in traction for weeks after the accident.* 事故后他接受了几个星期的牵引治疗。**2** the force that prevents something such as a wheel sliding on a surface〔防止车轮在路面滑动的〕附着摩擦力：*The tires were bald and lost traction on the wet road.* 那些轮胎都磨光了，在湿的路面上失去了附着摩擦力。**3** the type of power needed to make a vehicle move, or to pull a heavy load〔使汽车或重物等移动的〕牵引力

trac·tor /ˈtræktɚ; ˈtræktə/ *n* [C] a strong vehicle with large wheels, used for pulling farm machinery 拖拉机；牵引车

Tra·cy, Spen·cer /ˈspɛnsɚ; ˈspensə/ (1900-67) a US film actor known especially for appearing as characters who were honest and had high moral principles. He often worked with Katharine Hepburn, with whom he had a romantic relationship with for many years. His films include *Captains Courageous* (1937), *Adam's Rib* (1949), and *Guess Who's Coming to Dinner* (1967). 屈赛〔(1900-1967)，美国电影演员。他在影片中尤以饰演为人诚实、道德高尚的形象而著称，常与凯瑟琳·赫本合作，并与其保持多年恋人关系。他出演的电影包括《怒海余生》(1937)、《亚当的肋骨》(1949) 和《猜猜谁来吃晚餐》(1967)〕

trade¹ /tred; treɪd/ *n*

1 ▶BUYING/SELLING 买/卖◀ [U] the activity of buying, selling, or exchanging goods within a country or between countries 买卖，交易，贸易：*There has been a marked increase in trade between East and West.* 东西方之间的贸易已经有了明显的增长。| **the arms trade** (=the buying and selling of weapons) 武器买卖，军火生意 —see also 另见 BALANCE OF TRADE, FREE TRADE, SLAVE TRADE

2 the hotel/banking/tourist etc trade the business done by banks, hotels etc 酒店业/银行业/旅游业等：*My husband worked in the jewellery trade all his life.* 我丈夫一辈子都在珠宝行业工作。

3 ▶AMOUNT OF BUSINESS 营业额◀ [U] business activity, especially the amount of goods or products that are sold 营业额，交易量：*A lot of pubs nowadays do most of their trade at lunch-times.* 现在的许多小酒馆主要是午饭时有生意。—see also 另见 **do a roaring trade** (ROARING (3))

4 ▶JOB/WORK 职业/工作◀ [C] a particular job, especially one needing special skill with your hands〔尤指需要特殊手工技巧的〕职业；手艺：*In those days people would leave school at fourteen to learn a trade.* 在那个年代，人们14岁时便辍学去学一门手艺。| **be sth by trade** (=be trained to do a particular job) 职业是〔干某种工作〕*My grandfather was a plumber by trade.* 我祖父的职业是管道工。| **tools of your trade** (=the things that you need to do your job) 干某项工作所需的工具 —see 见 JOB (USAGE)

5 the trade a particular kind of business, and the people who are involved in it 某一行业和从事该行业的人：*I could get Ron to look at your car for you; he works in the trade.* 我可以让罗恩为你看看车子，他是干这行的。

6 passing trade people who go into a shop, restaurant etc because they see it, but are not regular customers 过路客生意：*Souvenir shops rely mainly on passing trade.* 纪念品商店主要做的是过路客生意。—see also 另见 STOCK-IN-TRADE, JACK-OF-ALL-TRADES, **tricks of the trade** (TRICK[1] (5))

trade² *v* **1** [I,T] to buy and sell goods, services etc 做买卖，进行贸易，从事交易：**[+with]** *Britain built up her wealth by trading with other countries.* 英国通过与其他国家进行贸易而积累起财富。| **[+in]** *These companies trade mainly in furs and animal skins.* 这些公司主要从事动物毛皮的交易。| **trade sth** *Salesmen traded the new products all over the country.* 推销员们在全国各地推销这些新产品。| **trading partner** (=a country that buys your goods and sells their goods to you) 贸易伙伴(国) **2** [I] to exist and operate as a business 做生意，开展业务：*The firm now trades under the name Lanski and Weber.* 这家公司现在使用兰斯基和韦伯的名称开展业务。| **cease trading** (=stop being a business) 结束业务 **3** [T usually passive 一般用被动态] *technical* to buy or sell something on the STOCK EXCHANGE【术语】从事〔股票〕交易：*Over a million shares were traded during the day.* 那天成交了一百多万股。**4 trade insults/blows etc** *informal* to insult or hit each other during an argument or fight【非正式】对骂/对打等 **5** [I,T] *especially AmE* to exchange something you have for something someone else has【尤美】用…交换…，互相交换：**trade sth for** *I'll trade my Roberto Clemente card for your Hank Aaron one.* 我用我的罗伯托·克莱门特棒球卡换取你的汉克·阿伦棒球卡。| *We traded necklaces.* 我们互相交换了项链。| **I'll trade you** *spoken* (=used to say you want to exchange something)【口】我要与你交换东西 *"I have peanut butter and jelly today." "Trade you. I have cream cheese."* "我今天有花生酱和果酱。""与你交换吧，我有奶油干酪。"

trade sth ↔ **down** *phr v* [T] *especially AmE* to sell something such as a car in order to buy one that costs less【尤美】卖出〔某物〕以买进较廉价的同类物

trade sth ↔ **in** *phr v* [T] to give something such as a car to the person you are buying a new one from, so that you pay less 以〔某物〕折价换购同类的新货物: *He traded his old car in for a new model.* 他把旧车折价换购了一辆新的款式。—see also 另见 TRADE-IN

trade sth ↔ **off** *phr v* [T] to balance one situation or quality against another, in order to produce an acceptable result 在…和…之间取得平衡: *We have to trade off the cost of research against the danger that our competitors will overtake us.* 我们必须在研究成本和保持竞争力之间取得平衡。—see also 另见 TRADE-OFF

trade on/upon sth *phr v* [T] to use a situation or someone's kindness in order to get an advantage for yourself 利用〔某一形势或某人的善良〕: *If you ask me they're just trading on Sam's good nature.* 如果你问我的话, 他们只不过是在利用萨姆的善良本性。

trade up *phr v* [I,T] to give a used item, such as a car, for a similar item which is more expensive or valuable 以〔旧物〕折价换购〔同类中更贵或更有价值的货物〕: **trade up sth** *Diego's traded up his old car for a more expensive model.* 迪戈把他那辆旧车折价换购了一款更贵的车。

trade def·i·cit /ˈ· ˌ···/ also 又作 **trade gap** *n* [C] the amount by which the value of what a country buys from abroad is more than the value of what it sells 贸易赤字, 贸易逆差

Trade De·scrip·tions Act /ˌ· ·ˈ·· ˌ·/ a British law that is intended to prevent companies from lying about the quality or effectiveness of their goods and services in their advertisements and LABELS《商品说明法》〔英国的一条法律, 旨在防止公司在广告和标签中对其产品和服务的品质或效果进行欺骗性宣传〕

trade dis·count /ˈ· ˌ··/ *n* [C] a special reduction in the price of goods sold to people who are going to sell the goods in their own shop or business 同行折扣, 批发折扣

trade fair /ˈ· ·/ *n* [C] a large event when several companies show their goods or services in one place, to try to sell them 交易会

trade gap /ˈ· ·/ *n* [C] TRADE DEFICIT 贸易逆差

trade-in /ˈ· ·/ *n* [C] *AmE* a used item, often a car, given to reduce the price of the new one that you are buying【美】〔以旧物折价抵销新物部分价格的〕折价贴换交易; PART-EXCHANGE *BrE*【英】: *Are you going to give your Ford as a trade-in?* 你打算以折价贴换的形式卖掉你的福特车吗? | **trade-in price/value/figure** *The trade-in value of the car is roughly $3,000.* 这辆汽车的折价贴换价值大约是3000美元。

trade·mark /ˈtredˌmark; ˈtreɪdmɑːk/ *n* [C] **1** a special name, sign, or word that is marked on a product to show that it is made by a particular company〔公司生产某一产品的〕商标, 注册商标 **2** a particular way of behaving, dressing etc by which someone or something can be easily recognized〔某人或某物在行为、穿着等方面很容易被识别出来的〕标记, 特征: *The striped T-shirt became the comedian's trademark.* 那件带条纹的T恤衫成了这位喜剧演员的标志。

trade name /ˈ· ·/ *n* [C] a name given to a particular product, that helps you recognize it from other similar products; BRAND NAME〔某种产品的〕商标名, 商品名

trade-off /ˈ· ·/ *n* [C] an acceptable balance between two opposing things that you want〔两种对立因素之间的〕平衡; 妥协; 协调: *There has to be a trade-off between quality and quantity if we want to keep prices low.* 如果我们想要保持低价格的话, 必须在质量和数量之间取得平衡。

trade price /ˈ· ·/ *n* [C] the price at which goods are sold to shops by the companies that produce them 批发价格, 同行价格

trad·er /ˈtredɚ; ˈtreɪdə/ *n* [C] someone who buys and sells goods 商人, 买卖人, 经商者

trade route /ˈ· ·/ *n* [C] a way across land or sea often used by traders' vehicles, ships etc 商队路线; 商船航线; 贸易路线; 贸易航线

trade school /ˈ· ˌ·/ *n* [C] *especially AmE* a school where people go in order to learn a particular trade (TRADE[1] (4))【尤美】中等职业学校

trade se·cret /ˌ· ˈ··/ *n* [C] **1** a piece of secret information about a particular business, that is only known by the people who work there〔只有商家内部人知道的〕行业秘密: *The Coca-Cola formula is a well kept trade secret.* 可口可乐的配方是一个保守很严的行业秘密。**2** *informal* a piece of information about how to do or make something, that you do not want other people to know【非正式】秘密: *Could you give me the recipe for that 'coq au vin' or is it a trade secret?* 你能把那道"红酒烩鸡"的食谱给我吗? 难道那是一个秘密不成?

trades·man /ˈtredzmən; ˈtreɪdzmən/ *n* [C] **1** *especially BrE* someone who buys and sells goods, especially in a shop【尤英】商人, 买卖人; 〔尤指商店里的〕零售商, 店主 **2** *especially BrE* someone who goes to people's houses to sell or deliver goods【尤英】上门推销员; 送货员 **3** *especially AmE* someone who works at a job or trade (TRADE[1] (4)) that involves skill with your hands【尤美】手艺人; 技工

Trades U·nion Con·gress /ˌ· ·ˈ·· ˌ··/ *n* the TUC〔英国的〕工会代表大会; 工会联合会

trade sur·plus /ˌ· ˈ··/ *n* [C] *technical* the amount by which the value of the goods that a country sells to other countries is more than the value of what it buys from them【术语】贸易盈余〔指一个国家的出口商品总值超过进口总值〕

trade u·nion /ˌ· ˈ··/ also 又作 **trades union** *BrE*【英】*n* [C] an organization, usually in a particular trade or profession, that represents workers, especially in meetings with employers〔某一行业的〕工会; LABOR UNION *AmE*【美】—**trade unionist** *n* [C]

trade wind /ˈ· ·/ *n* [C] a tropical wind that blows continually towards the EQUATOR from either the northeast or the southeast 信风, 贸易风〔指从东北或东南方向不停地吹向赤道的热带风〕

trading es·tate /ˈ·· ·ˌ·/ *n* [C] *BrE* an area of land, often at the edge of a city, where there are small factories and businesses【英】工商业区, 工业园区〔通常位于市郊〕

trading post /ˈ·· ·/ *n* [C] a place where people can buy and exchange goods in a country area, especially in the US or Canada in the past〔尤指昔日美国或加拿大的〕贸易站: *a remote trading post in the Yukon* 育空地区一处偏远的贸易站

tra·di·tion /trəˈdɪʃən; trəˈdɪʃən/ *n* **1 a)** [C] a belief, custom, or way of doing something that has existed for a long time 传统: *Christmas traditions* 圣诞传统 | [+of] *a long tradition of wine-making* 悠久的酿酒传统 | **tradition that** *the tradition that the eldest son inherits the property* 长子继承财产的传统 —see 见 HABIT (USAGE) **b)** [U] beliefs or customs like this in general 传统信仰; 传统习俗: *The British are lovers of tradition.* 英国人很看重传统。| **by tradition** *By tradition, it is the bride's parents who pay for the wedding.* 根据传统习俗, 由新娘的父母支付婚礼的费用。**2** [C,U] the way in which things are done in a particular country, group of people etc 传统方式, 惯例, 老规矩: *the Western tradition in art* 西方的艺术传统方式 | *It had become a tradition in our house to stay up all night at New Year.* 在新年时守夜已成了我们家的惯例。| **break with tradition** (=stop doing something in the way it has always been done) 打破了传统, 打破老规矩 *Breaking with family tradition, they decided not to send Laura to boarding school.* 他们打破家庭的老规矩, 决定不送劳拉上寄宿学校。**3 be in the tradition of** to have the same features as something that has been made or done in the past 沿袭…的传统: *His paintings are very much in the tradition of Picasso and Matisse.* 他的绘画在很大程度上沿袭了毕加索和马蒂斯的传统。

tra·di·tion·al /trəˈdɪʃənḷ; trəˈdɪʃənəl/ *adj* **1** being part of the traditions of a country or group of people 传统的; 习俗的; 惯例的: *Kumar gave the traditional Hindu greeting.* 库玛按照印度习俗打招呼。| *traditional music* 传统音乐 | **it is traditional (for sb) to do sth** *It is traditional for the bridegroom to make a speech.* 按照惯例, 新郎要致辞。**2** following ideas and methods that have existed for a long time, without being interested in anything new or different; CONVENTIONAL 因袭的; 守旧的; 传统的: *I went to a very traditional school.* 我上的是一所非常传统的学校。—**traditionally** *adv*

tra·di·tion·al·is·m /trəˈdɪʃənḷˌɪzəm; trəˈdɪʃənəlɪzəm/ *n* [U] belief in the importance of TRADITIONS and customs 传统主义, 崇尚传统

tra·di·tion·al·ist /trəˈdɪʃənḷɪst; trəˈdɪʃənəlɪst/ *n* [C] someone who respects TRADITION and does not like change 传统主义者, 崇尚传统者; 墨守成规者 —**traditionalist** *adj*

tra·duce /trəˈdjus; trəˈdjuːs/ *v* [T] *formal* to deliberately say things that are untrue or unpleasant【正式】诽谤, 中伤, 诋毁

Tra·fal·gar /trəˈfælgɚ; trəˈfælgə/**, Cape** the most southwesterly point of Spain. In the sea near the cape, British ships under Nelson won an important sea battle against the French and Spanish in 1805. 特拉法尔加角〔西班牙的最西南端。1805年, 纳尔逊指挥的英国舰队在特拉法尔加角附近海域的一次重要海战中击败了法国和西班牙联合舰队〕

Trafalgar, the Battle of an important sea battle fought off Cape Trafalgar in southwest Spain in 1805, when British

ships led by Admiral Nelson beat the French and Spanish forces. Nelson was killed in the battle, and Trafalgar Square was built in his honour. 特拉法尔加海战〔1805年在西班牙西南部的特拉法尔加角附近海域发生的一场重要海战。海军上将纳尔逊率领的英国战舰打败了法国和西班牙联合舰队，纳尔逊在此次战役中阵亡。特拉法尔加广场就是为了纪念纳尔逊而修建的〕

Trafalgar Square /, ·· ˈ·/ a SQUARE (=a broad, open area with buildings on all sides) in central London, where Nelson's Column stands 特拉法尔加广场〔伦敦市中心一广场，矗立着纳尔逊纪念柱〕

S1 W2 **traf·fic¹** /ˈtræfɪk; ˈtræfɪk/ *n* [U] **1** the vehicles moving along a road or street〔道路或街道上的〕车辆交通: *The noise of the traffic kept me awake.* 道路上车辆的噪音使我无法入睡。| **heavy traffic** (=a large amount of traffic) 拥挤的交通 *We were stuck in heavy traffic for more than an hour.* 我们在拥挤的交通中被堵了一个多小时。**2** the movement of aircraft, ships, trains etc from one place to another〔飞机、轮船、火车等的〕往来，交通: *air traffic control* 空中交通管制 **3** *formal* the movement of people or goods by aircraft, ships, or trains【正式】〔飞机、轮船或火车等运送人或货物的〕交通运输: [+of] *Most long-distance traffic of heavy goods is done by ships.* 大多数重型货物的长途运输都使用轮船。**4** the secret buying and selling of illegal goods〔秘密进行的〕非法买卖，非法交易: *drugs traffic* 毒品买卖 | [+in] *traffic in firearms* 非法军火交易

traffic² *v past tense and past participle* **trafficked**

traffic in sth *phr v* [T] to buy and sell illegal goods〔非法地〕贩卖，交易: *Lewis was found guilty of trafficking in drugs.* 刘易斯贩卖毒品，被判有罪。

traffic calm·ing /ˈ·· ,··/ *n* [U] *BrE* changes made to a road to stop people driving too fast along it【英】〔路面上设置的阻止驾车速度过快的〕交通减速措施

traffic cir·cle /ˈ·· ,··/ *n* [C] *AmE* a raised circular area that cars must drive around, where three or more roads join【美】环形交叉路口，环岛; ROUNDABOUT¹ (1) *BrE*【英】

traffic cone /ˈ·· ,·/ *n* [C] a plastic marker in the shape of a CONE that is put on the road to show where repairs are being done 锥形交通路标〔放在路面上表示该段道路正在维修〕

traffic cop /ˈ·· ,·/ *n* [C] *AmE informal*【美，非正式】**1** a police officer who stands in the road and directs traffic〔站在马路上指挥交通的〕交通警察 **2** a police officer who stops drivers who drive in an illegal way〔阻截违章驾车司机的〕交通巡警

traffic court /ˈ·· ,·/ *n* [C] *AmE* a court in a town or city in the US that deals with people who have done something illegal while driving【美】交通法庭

traffic is·land /ˈ·· ,··/ *n* [C] a raised area in the middle of the road where people can wait for traffic to pass〔马路中间的〕交通安全岛

traffic jam /ˈ·· ,·/ *n* [C] a long line of vehicles on a road that cannot move, or that can only move very slowly 交通阻塞，塞车: *We were stuck in a traffic jam on the freeway for two hours.* 我们在高速公路上碰上了交通阻塞，被堵了两个小时。

traf·fick·er /ˈtræfɪkə; ˈtræfɪkə/ *n* [C] someone who buys and sells illegal goods, especially drugs 做非法买卖的人〔尤指毒品贩子〕

traf·fick·ing /ˈtræfɪkɪŋ; ˈtræfɪkɪŋ/ *n* [U] the buying and selling of illegal goods, especially drugs〔尤指毒品的〕非法买卖，非法交易: *drug trafficking* 毒品贩卖

traffic lights /ˈ·· ,·/ *n* [C] special lights at a place where roads meet, that control the traffic by means of red, yellow, and green lights 交通信号灯，红绿灯

traffic school /ˈ·· ,·/ *n* [C] *AmE* a class that teaches you about driving laws, that you can go to instead of paying money for something you have done wrong while driving【美】交通法规学校〔违章司机可以上这种学校而免交罚金〕

traffic war·den /ˈ·· ,··/ *n* [C] *BrE* someone whose job is to check that vehicles have not parked illegally on the streets【英】〔市区负责监控车辆停放的〕交通督导员

tra·ge·di·an /trəˈdʒidɪən; trəˈdʒiːdiən/ *n* [C] *formal* an actor or writer of tragedy【正式】悲剧演员；悲剧作家

tra·ge·dy /ˈtrædʒədɪ; ˈtrædʒədi/ *n* **1** [C,U] a very sad event, that shocks people because it involves death 悲剧性事件，惨剧，惨案: *Tragedy struck the family when their two-year old son died of leukemia.* 悲剧降临到这个家庭，他们两岁的儿子因白血病死了。**2** [C] *informal* something that seems very sad and unnecessary because something will be wasted, lost, or harmed【非正式】〔因浪费、失去或伤害而造成的〕不幸；遗憾: *It's a tragedy to see so much talent going to waste.* 看到这么多的人才浪费掉，真是可惜啊。**3 a)** [C] a serious play or book that ends sadly, especially with the death of the main character 悲剧作品: *'Hamlet' is one of Shakespeare's best known tragedies.*《哈姆雷特》是莎士比亚最有名的悲剧作品之一。**b)** [U] this type of plays or books 悲剧〔文学类别之一〕: *an actor specializing in tragedy* 一名擅长演悲剧的演员

tra·gic /ˈtrædʒɪk; ˈtrædʒɪk/ *adj* **1** a tragic event or situation makes you feel very sad 悲惨的，不幸的: *Lillian Board's death at 22 was a tragic loss for the world of British athletics.* 莉莲·博德22岁时就去世了，这对英国田径界来说是一个不幸的损失。**2** [only before noun 仅用于名词前] connected with tragedy in books or plays 悲剧的: *a great tragic actor* 一名伟大的悲剧演员 | **tragic hero** (=the main character in a tragedy) 悲剧主角 **3 tragic flaw** a weakness in the character of the main person in a tragedy that causes their own problems and usually death 悲剧性缺陷〔指悲剧主人公性格上的弱点，这些弱点引发诸多问题，通常会导致自身毁灭〕: *Jealousy is Othello's tragic flaw.* 妒忌是奥赛罗的悲剧性缺陷。

tra·gic·ally /ˈtrædʒɪklɪ; ˈtrædʒɪkli/ *adv* in a very sad or unfortunate way 悲惨地，不幸地: [sentence adverb 句子副词] *Tragically, her dancing career ended only six months later.* 很不幸的是，她的舞蹈生涯仅在六个月后就结束了。| [+adj/adv] *Alan died tragically young.* 很不幸，艾伦年纪轻轻就去世了。

tra·gi·com·e·dy /ˌtrædʒɪˈkɑmədɪ; ˌtrædʒɪˈkɒmɪdi/ *n* [C,U] a play or a story that is both sad and funny 悲喜剧 —**tragicomic** /ˌtrædʒɪˈkɑmɪk; ˌtrædʒɪˈkɒmɪk◂/ *adj*

trail¹ /trel; treɪl/ *v* **1** [I,T always+adv/prep] if something trails behind you, or if you trail it behind you, it gets pulled behind you as you move along 拖，拉；拖在后面: [+across/in/through] *She walked slowly along the path, her skirt trailing in the mud.* 她慢慢地沿着小径走着，裙子拖在泥地上。| **trail sth in/on/through** *Rees was leaning out of the boat trailing his hand through the water.* 里斯把身体倾斜在船外边，让手在水里荡着。**2** also 又作 **trail along** [I always+adv/prep] to walk slowly, especially because you are tired or bored, and often following other people〔尤指因疲倦或厌烦〕慢吞吞地走〔在后面〕: [+behind/around] *Susie trailed along behind her parents.* 苏茜慢吞吞地走在她父母的身后。**3** [I,T usually in progressive 一般用进行时] to be losing in a game, competition, or election〔体育比赛、竞赛或选举中〕落后于: *The Democrats are still trailing in the latest poll.* 在最近的民意调查中，民主党仍然落后。| **trail (sb) by** *At the end of the first half Bolton were trailing by two goals to nil.* 在上半场结束时，博顿队以0:2落后。**4** [T] to follow a person or animal by looking for signs that they have gone in a particular direction 跟踪，追踪: *Police trailed the gang for several days.* 警察花了好几天的时间跟踪那帮家伙。—see also 另见 TRAILER

trail away/off *phr v* [I] if someone's voice trails away or off, it becomes gradually quieter and then stops〔说话的声音〕逐渐变小，减弱: *She trailed off, silenced by the look Kris gave her.* 她看到克里斯给她的眼色，说话的声音越来越小，终于默不作声了。

trail² *n* [C] **1 be on sb's trail** to be finding out where someone has gone in order to find or catch them 跟踪，追踪某人: *Police believe they are on the trail of a dangerous killer.* 警方相信他们追踪的是一名危险的杀手。| **be hard/hot on sb's trail** (=be close to finding someone you are trying to catch) 紧追不舍〔并即将发现某人〕**2 while the trail is still hot** if you chase someone while the trail is still hot, you follow them soon after they have left〔某人〕刚离开〔就随后追赶〕**3** the track or smell of a person or animal by which it can be hunted or followed〔人或动物的〕足迹，踪迹；嗅迹: *The hunters lost the tiger's trail in the middle of the jungle.* 猎人们在丛林中找不到那只老虎的踪迹了。**4** a rough path across open country or through a forest 小路，小径: *The trail led over Boulder Pass before descending to a lake.* 那条小路穿过博尔德山口，然后向下通向一个湖。**5 trail of blood/dust etc** a line or series of marks left by someone or something that is moving 血迹/尘土等的痕迹: *They left a trail of muddy footprints on the living room carpet.* 他们在客厅的地毯上留下了一长串泥脚印。| **trail of destruction** (=damage left by a moving storm or army)〔暴风雨或军队过后留下的〕毁坏痕迹，断壁残垣 **6 a trail of broken hearts/unpaid bills etc** *humorous* a series of unhappy people or bad situations all caused by the same person【幽默】〔某人留下的〕一串破碎的心/一大摞未支付的账单等: *He left a trail of broken hearts, of deserted women behind him.* 他留下一长串破碎的心 —— 一个个被遗弃的妇人。—see also 另见 **blaze a trail** (BLAZE¹ (4))

trail·blaz·er /ˈtrelˌblezə; ˈtreɪlˌbleɪzə/ *n* [C] someone who is the first to discover or develop new methods of doing something 开路人；先驱，创始人: *a trailblazer in the field of medical research* 医学研究领域的先驱

trail·er /ˈtrelə; ˈtreɪlə/ *n* [C] **1** *AmE* a vehicle that can be pulled behind a car, used for living and sleeping in during a holiday【美】〔度假期间拖在汽车后面用作起居和睡觉的〕活动房屋; CARAVAN (1) *BrE*【英】**2** a vehicle that can be pulled behind a vehicle, used for carrying something such as a boat or large piece of equipment 拖车, 挂车 **3** *especially BrE* an advertisement for a new film or television show, usually consisting of small scenes taken from it【尤英】〔电影、电视节目的〕新片预告, 预告片

trailer park /ˈ· · ·/ also 又作 **trailer court** *n* [C] *AmE* an area where TRAILERs are parked and used as people's homes【美】拖车式活动房屋停车场

trail·ing /ˈtrelɪŋ; ˈtreɪlɪŋ/ *adj* a trailing plant grows along the ground or hangs down〔植物〕蔓生的: *ivy and other trailing plants* 常春藤及其他蔓生植物

Trail of Tears, the /ˌ· · ˈ·/ the path that the Cherokees were forced to travel by the US government to RESERVATIONs west of the Mississippi River. The journey was extremely long, cold, and difficult, and about 4000 Cherokees died. 血泪之路〔切罗基人在美国政府的强迫之下迁往位于密西西比河西面的保留地时走过的一条路。这条路格外漫长, 一路寒风凛冽, 十分艰难, 约有4000切罗基人死于途中〕

train[1] /tren; treɪn/ *n* [C]

1 ▶RAILWAY 铁路◀ a number of connected carriages pulled by an engine along a railway line 火车, 列车: *Jeff just missed the six o'clock train.* 杰夫刚好错过了6点钟的那班火车。| [**+to**] *I caught the early train to Bruges.* 我赶早班火车去了布鲁日。| **by train** *It's more relaxing to travel by train.* 坐火车旅行让人更为放松。| **train driver/journey/service** *There's no train service between here and Wales.* 这里与威尔士之间没有通火车。—see also 另见 BOAT TRAIN

2 ▶SERIES 系列◀ train of a series of connected events, actions etc 一系列, 一连串〔相关事件、行动等〕: *That one incident sparked off a whole train of events.* 那一次事件引发了一连串事件。

3 train of thought a connected series of thoughts developing in your mind 一连串想法; 思路: *The phone rang and interrupted my train of thought.* 电话铃响了, 打断了我的思路。

4 set sth in train *formal* to make something start happening【正式】使…开始启动: *Plans to modernize have been set in train.* 现代化的计划已经开始启动。

5 bring sth in its train *formal* if an action or event brings something in its train, that thing happens as a result of it【正式】引发某事: *a decision that brought disaster in its train* 带来灾难的一项决定

6 ▶PEOPLE/ANIMALS 人/动物◀ a long line of moving people, animals, or vehicles〔行进中的〕行列, 队列: *a camel train* 一支驼队

7 ▶DRESS 裙子◀ a part of a long dress that spreads out over the ground behind the person who is wearing it 长裙拖在地上的下摆, 拖裾: *a wedding dress with a long train* 下摆很长的结婚礼服

8 ▶SERVANTS 仆从◀ a group of servants or officers following an important person, especially in former times〔尤指旧时重要人物的〕随行人员, 随从

train[2] *v* **1** [I,T] to teach someone or be taught the skills of a particular job or activity (接受) 训练; (被) 培训: [**+as**] *Nadia trained as a singer under a famous professor of music.* 纳迪亚曾在一著名音乐教授的指导下接受歌手的训练。| **train sb in** *Soldiers trained in hand-to-hand combat.* 接受过徒手格斗训练的士兵。| **train to do sth** *Hugh's training to be a doctor.* 休正在接受培训, 准备当医生。—see 见 TEACH (USAGE) **2** [T] to teach an animal to do something or to behave correctly 训练〔动物〕: **train sth to do sth** *These dogs are trained to detect explosives.* 这些狗受过训练, 能搜寻爆炸物。| *a well-trained puppy* 训练有素的小狗 **3** [I,T] to prepare for a sporting event or tell someone how to prepare for it, especially by exercising〔为准备体育赛事而〕训练, 操练: [**+for**] *Brenda spends two hours a day training for the marathon.* 布伦达为了马拉松比赛每天训练两个小时。**4** [T] to aim a gun, camera etc at someone or something 把〔枪、照相机等〕对准, 瞄准: **train sth on/at** *The firemen trained their hoses on the burning building.* 消防人员把水管对准那幢燃烧着的建筑物。**5** [T] to make a plant grow in a particular direction by bending, cutting, or tying it 使〔植物〕按照特定方向生长 —**trained** *adj*: *a highly trained technician* 技巧娴熟的技术人员 —**trainable** *adj* —see also 另见 TRAINING

train·bear·er /ˈtrenˌberə; ˈtreɪnˌbeərə/ *n* [C] someone who holds the train (TRAIN[1] (7)) of a dress, especially at a wedding〔尤指婚礼中牵新娘婚纱的〕牵纱者, 挽裙裾者

train·ee /trenˈi; ˌtreɪˈniː◂/ *n* [C] someone who is being trained for a job 接受工作培训的人; 实习生: *The new trainees will start next week.* 新一批实习生下周开始上班。| **trainee reporter/engineer/salesman etc** *a trainee hairdresser* 实习美发师

train·er /ˈtrenə; ˈtreɪnə/ *n* [C] **1** someone who trains people or animals for sport, work etc 教练(员); 驯兽师: *a teacher trainer* 培训教师的人 **2** *BrE* a type of strong shoe that you wear for sport【英】运动鞋, 跑鞋; SNEAKER *AmE*【美】—see picture at 参见 SHOE[1] 图

train·ing /ˈtrenɪŋ; ˈtreɪnɪŋ/ *n* **1** [singular,U] the process of training or being trained 训练, 培训; 受训: [**+in**] *On the course we received training in every aspect of the job.* 在培训课上, 我们接受了有关工作的全面训练。| *a training manual* 培训手册 **2** [U] special physical exercises that are part of a plan for keeping someone fit and healthy〔保持体形的〕训练, 锻炼: *Lesley does weight training twice a week.* 莱斯利一周进行两次器械训练。| **be in/out of training** (=be fit or not fit for a sport) 正处于良好/不佳的竞技状态 *The champion is in training for his next fight.* 这位冠军正在为下一场比赛进行训练。—see also 另见 SPRING TRAINING

Training and En·ter·prise Coun·cil, the /ˌ· · ˈ· · · ˌ· ·/ the TEC

training col·lege /ˈ· · ˌ· ·/ *n* [C,U] *BrE* a college for adults that gives training for a particular profession【英】〔为成人开设的〕职业培训学院, 进修学院: *a teacher training college* 教师进修学院 | *a training college for pilots* 飞行员培训学院

train set /ˈ· ·/ *n* [C] a toy train with railway tracks〔包括车轨在内的〕玩具火车

train spot·ter /ˈ· ˌ· ·/ *n* [C] *BrE*【英】**1** someone who collects the numbers of railway engines and other information about them for fun〔作为娱乐爱好〕收集火车机车号码及其他相关信息的人 **2** someone who you think is boring and only interested in unimportant details 无聊的人; 只关心芝麻小事的人 —**trainspotting** *n* [U]

> **CULTURAL NOTE 文化注释**
>
> People often make jokes about train spotters because they are considered to be boring people who are only interested in small details and boring facts and always wear unfashionable clothing such as ANORAKs. 爱好收集火车机车号码及其他相关信息的人常常成为人们开玩笑的对象, 因为他们被认为是一群乏味的家伙, 只关心一些细枝末节和无聊的事实, 并且总是穿着带兜帽的短风雨衣之类的过时衣服。

traipse /treps; treɪps/ *v* [I always+adv/prep] *informal* to walk somewhere slowly and unwillingly when you are tired【非正式】闲荡: [**+up/down/around etc**] *I've been traipsing round the shops all morning.* 我整个上午一直在逛商店。

trait /tret; treɪt/ *n* [C] *formal* a particular quality in someone's character【正式】〔人性格中的〕特性, 品质: *Anne's generosity is one of her most pleasing traits.* 安妮的慷慨是她最受人喜爱的品性之一。

trai·tor /ˈtretə; ˈtreɪtə/ *n* [C] someone who is not loyal to their country or friends 卖国者; 叛徒, 背叛者: *He was hanged as a traitor.* 他因叛国罪被绞死。| *a traitor to the cause of women's rights* 女权运动的背叛者

trai·tor·ous /ˈtretərəs; ˈtreɪtərəs/ *adj especially literary* not loyal to your country or friends【尤文】卖国的; 叛变的, 背叛的 —**traitorously** *adv*

tra·jec·to·ry /trəˈdʒɛktərɪ; trəˈdʒektəri/ *n* [C] *technical* the curved path of an object that is fired or thrown through the air【术语】〔物体射向或抛向空中形成的〕轨道, 轨迹; 弹道

tram /træm; træm/ also 又作 **tram·car** /ˈtræmˌkɑr; ˈtræmkɑː/ *n* [C] *especially BrE* an electric vehicle for carrying passengers, which moves along the streets on metal tracks【尤英】有轨电车; STREETCAR *AmE*【美】

tram·lines /ˈtræmˌlaɪnz; ˈtræmlaɪnz/ *n* [plural] *BrE*【英】**1** the metal tracks in the road that trams run along 有轨电车的轨道 **2** *BrE informal* a pair of parallel lines at the edge of a tennis court【英, 非正式】〔网球场两侧供双打时用的〕加道 —see picture at 参见 TENNIS 图

tram·mels /ˈtræmḷz; ˈtræməlz/ *n* [plural] *formal* something that limits or prevents free movement, activity, or development【正式】限制, 拘束, 束缚, 妨碍: *an urge to shake off the trammels of respectability* 一种想摆脱礼俗束缚的愿望 —see also 另见 UNTRAMMELLED

tramp[1] /træmp; træmp/ *n* [C] **1** someone who has no home or job and moves from place to place, often asking for food or

money 流浪者，游民：*a group of tramps huddled around a fire* 围坐在火边的一群流浪汉 **2** a long or difficult walk（长途）跋涉：*It was a long tramp home through the snow.* 那天冒雪走回家，是一次长途跋涉。**3** *old-fashioned especially AmE* a woman who has too many sexual partners【过时，尤美】荡妇 **4 the tramp of** the sound of heavy walking …沉重的脚步声：*the steady tramp of soldiers' feet on the road* 士兵们走在路上发出的重重脚步声

tramp² *v* [I always+adv/prep,T] to walk around or through somewhere with firm or heavy steps 用重重的脚步走（过）；踩，踏（遍）：**tramp sth** *I've tramped the streets all day looking for work.* 我一整天走遍大街小巷，寻找工作。| [**+across/over/up etc**] *Who's been tramping all over the floor in muddy shoes?* 谁穿着沾满泥的鞋子在地板上到处乱踩？

tram·ple /ˋtræmpḷ; ˈtræmpəl/ *v* [I always+adv/prep, T] **1** to step heavily on something so that you crush it with your feet 踩，践踏：[**+on/over/through etc**] *You trampled on my beautiful flowerbeds!* 你踩坏了我那些美丽的花坛！| **trample sb/sth underfoot** *She dropped her jacket and it was trampled underfoot.* 她的外衣掉在地上，被踩在脚下。| **trample sb to death** (=kill someone by stepping heavily on them) 踩死某人 *Several people were nearly trampled to death in the rush to get out.* 大家往外冲的时候，好几个人差点被踩死。**2 trample on sth/trample sth underfoot** to behave in a way that shows that you do not care about someone's rights, hopes, ideas etc 侵犯；无视〔某人的权利、愿望、想法等〕：*The colonial government had trampled on the rights of the native people.* 殖民政府侵犯了本土人民的权利。

tram·po·line /ˌtræmpəˋlin; ˈtræmpəliːn/ *n* [C] a piece of equipment that you jump up and down on as a sport, made of a sheet of material tightly stretched across a metal frame 蹦床，弹床〔一种体育用具〕 **—trampoline** *v* [I] **—trampolining** *n* [U]

trance /træns; trɑːns/ *n* [C] **1** a state in which you behave as if you were asleep but are still able to hear and understand what is said to you 恍惚状态：*a hypnotic trance* 催眠后的恍惚状态 **2** a situation in which you are thinking about something so much that you do not notice what is happening around you 恍惚；出神，发呆：**be in a trance** *What's the matter with you? You've been in a trance all day!* 你怎么啦？一整天都恍恍惚惚的！

tran·quil /ˋtræŋkwɪl; ˈtræŋkwḷl/ *adj* pleasantly calm, quiet, and peaceful 平静的，宁静的，安谧的：*a tranquil village scene* 宁静的乡村景色 **—tranquilly** *adv* **—tranquillity** *BrE*【英】, **tranquility** *AmE*【美】/træŋˋkwɪlətɪ; træŋˈkwɪlḷti/ *n* [U]: *the tranquillity of the Tuscan countryside* 托斯卡乡下的宁静

tran·quil·lize also 又作 **-ise** *BrE*【英】, **tranquilize** *AmE*【美】/ˋtræŋkwɪˌlaɪz; ˈtræŋkwḷlaɪz/ *v* [T] to make a person or animal calm or unconscious by using a drug〔用药物〕使〔人或动物〕镇静[昏迷]

tran·quil·lizer also 又作 **-iser** *BrE*【英】, **tranquilizer** *AmE*【美】/ˋtræŋkwɪˌlaɪzɚ; ˈtræŋkwḷlaɪzə/ *n* [C] a drug used to reduce nervous anxiety and make you calm 镇静剂，安定药

trans- /træns; træns/ *prefix* **1** on or to the far side of something; across 在[到]…的另一边；横穿，横贯：*trans-atlantic flights* 横跨大西洋的航班 | *the trans-Siberian railway* 西伯利亚横贯铁路 **2** between two things or groups; INTER- 在…之间的：*transracial fostering* 异族间的收养 **3** shows a change 表示变化：*He's been transformed by the experience.* 那次经历改变了他。| *the transmutation of base metal into gold* 贱金属变为黄金

trans·act /trænzˋækt; trænˈzækt/ *v* [I,T] *formal* to do business【正式】办理（业务），做（交易）：*Most deals are transacted over the phone.* 大多数交易是在电话上做成的。

S3 W3 **trans·ac·tion** /trænzˋækʃən; trænˈzækʃən/ *n formal*【正式】**1** [C] a business deal（一笔）交易；（一件）事务：*The bank charges a fixed rate for each transaction.* 银行对办理的每一笔交易收取固定比例的费用。| *financial transactions* 金融业务 **2** [U] the process of doing business〔业务等的〕办理；执行：*the transaction of his public duties* 执行他的公共职责 **3 transactions** [plural] discussions that take place at the meetings of a society, or a written record of these〔学会等的〕讨论，议事；议事录，公报

Trans-Am Cham·pi·on·ship, the /ˌtrænz ˋæm ˌtʃæmpɪənʃɪp; ˌtrænz ˈæm ˌtʃæmpiənʃɪp/ a number of sports car races held in the US and Canada 环美赛车锦标赛〔在美国和加拿大举行的多场次赛车比赛〕

Trans·a·mer·i·ca Build·ing, the /ˌtrænzəˋmɛrɪkə ˌbɪldɪŋ; ˌtrænzəˈmerḷkə ˌbɪldɪŋ/ a famous building in San Francisco which is shaped like a PYRAMID, and which is sometimes used in pictures to represent San Francisco 泛美大厦〔旧金山一座著名建筑。该大厦形似金字塔，有时用于图片，代表旧金山市〕

trans·at·lan·tic /ˌtrænzətˋlæntɪk; ˌtrænzətˈlæntɪk◂/ *adj* [only before noun 仅用于名词前] **1** crossing the Atlantic Ocean 横跨大西洋的：*transatlantic flights* 横跨大西洋的航班 **2** involving countries on both sides of the Atlantic Ocean 大西洋两岸国家的：*a transatlantic agreement* 大西洋两岸国家的一项协定 **3** on the other side of the Atlantic Ocean 大西洋彼岸的：*one of America's transatlantic military bases* 美国在大西洋彼岸的军事基地之一

trans·cei·ver /trænsˋsivɚ; trænˈsiːvə/ *n* [C] a radio that can both send and receive messages 无线电收发两用机

tran·scend /trænˋsɛnd; trænˈsend/ *v* [T] *formal* to go above or beyond the limits of something【正式】超越；超过，超出：*The desire for peace transcended political differences.* 对和平的渴望超越了政治上的分歧。

tran·scen·dent /trænˋsɛndənt; trænˈsendənt/ *adj formal* going far beyond ordinary limits【正式】超常的，卓越的，出类拔萃的：*the transcendent genius of Mozart* 莫扎特的卓越天才 **—transcendently** *adv*

tran·scen·den·tal /ˌtrænsɛnˋdɛntḷ; ˌtrænsenˈdentl◂/ *adj* experiences or ideas going beyond human knowledge, understanding, and experience 超出人类知识范围的；超出一般经验的 **—transcendentally** *adv*

tran·scen·den·tal·is·m /ˌtrænsɛnˋdɛntḷˌɪzəm; ˌtrænsenˈdentəl-ɪzəm/ *n* [U] the belief that knowledge can be obtained by studying thought and not necessarily by practical experience 先验论〔认为无需通过实践经验，只凭研究思想即可获得知识的哲学观点〕 **—transcendentalist** *n* [C]

transcendental med·i·ta·tion /ˌ····· ··ˋ··/ *n* [U] a method of becoming calm by repeating special religious words in your mind 超脱禅定（法）

trans·con·ti·nen·tal /ˌtrænzkɑntəˋnɛntḷ; ˌtrænzkɒntḷˈnentl/ *adj* crossing a CONTINENT 横贯大陆的：*a transcontinental railway* 一条横贯大陆的铁路

tran·scribe /trænˋskraɪb; trænˈskraɪb/ *v* [T] *formal*【正式】**1** to write an exact copy of something 誊写，抄写：*transcribing an ancient manuscript* 抄写一本古代手稿 **2** to write down something exactly as it was said 逐字逐句记录，记下〔所说的话〕：*A secretary transcribed the witnesses' statements.* 秘书记下了证人的口供。**3** *technical* to represent speech sounds with special PHONETIC letters【术语】用音标记下〔语音〕，标注〔音标〕 **4** [**+into**] *formal* to change a piece of writing into the alphabet of another language【正式】把〔一篇文字〕用另一种语言的字母写出[记下] **5** to arrange a piece of music for a different instrument or voice 改编〔一段音乐使适于其他乐器演奏或用其他声调演唱〕：**transcribe sth for sth** *a piece transcribed for piano* 改编成钢琴曲的一首乐曲 **6** to copy recorded music, speech etc from one system to another, for example from TAPE¹ (1) to CD 复制，转录〔音乐、话语等，如从录音带转换成光碟〕

tran·script /ˋtrænˌskrɪpt; ˈtrænskrɪpt/ *n* [C] **1** an exact written or printed copy of something 抄本，副本；转录本：[**+of**] *A transcript of the tapes was presented in court as evidence.* 那些录音带的文本被呈交法庭作为证据。**2** *AmE* an official document of a college or university that has a list of a student's classes and the results they received【美】〔大学的〕学生成绩单

tran·scrip·tion /trænˋskrɪpʃən; trænˈskrɪpʃən/ *n* **1** [U] the act or process of transcribing something 抄写；记录；转录；标音：*Pronunciation is shown by a system of phonetic transcription.* 发音用音标系统表示。**2** [C] an exact written or printed copy of something; transcript 抄本，副本，文字记录

tran·sept /ˋtrænsɛpt; ˈtrænsept/ *n* [C] one of the two parts of a church that are built out from the main area of the church to form a cross shape〔建在教堂主体两边、呈十字形的〕耳堂

trans·fer¹ /trænsˋfɝ; trænsˈfɜː/ *v* **transferred, transferring** W2

1 ▶PERSON 人◀ [I,T] to move or arrange for someone to move from one place or job to another, especially within the same organization 转移（地方）；调动（工作）〔尤指在同一机构中〕：**transfer sb to** *They're transferring me to the Edinburgh office.* 他们要把我调往爱丁堡办事处。

2 ▶THING/ACTIVITY 东西/活动◀ [T] *formal* to move something from one place or position to another【正式】搬运；迁移：**transfer sth (from sth) to** *Transfer the cookies to a wire rack to cool.* 把小甜饼放到金属丝制的架子上冷却。| *We're transferring production to Detroit.* 我们正在把生产移到底特律。

3 ▶MONEY 钱◀ [T] to move money from the control of one account or institution to another 把〔钱〕转到另一账户上：*I'd like to transfer £500 into my current account.* 我想把500英镑转到我的活期账户上。| *Will I be able to transfer my pension rights?* 我能把我的退休金转账吗？

4 transfer your affection/loyalty etc to change from loving or supporting one person to loving or supporting a different one 移情于别人/转而支持别人等: [+to] *I immediately transferred my support to the other candidate.* 我立即转而支持另一位候选人。

5 ▶PROPERTY 财产◀ [T] *law* to officially give property or money to someone else【法律】把〔财产〕转让给另一人: *The assets were transferred into his wife's name.* 那些资产转让到了他妻子的名下。

6 transfer power/responsibility/control (to) to officially give power etc to another person or organization 转让权力/责任/控制权（给…）: *transferring control of public land to the states* 把公共土地控制权转让给各州

7 ▶PLANE 飞机◀ [I,T] to change from one plane to another during a journey, or arrange for someone to do this 转机; 转乘, 改乘: *You'll have to transfer at Los Angeles.* 你必须在洛杉矶转机。

8 ▶RECORDING 录音◀ [T] to copy recorded information, music etc from one system to another, for example from TAPE[1] (1) to CD 录制, 转录〔信息、音乐等, 如从录音带转换成光碟〕: *I decided to transfer the files onto floppy disk.* 我决定把这些文件转录到软盘上去。—**transferable** *adj*: *Airline tickets are not transferable.* 飞机票不得转让。

2 **trans·fer²** /ˋtrænsfɚ; ˈtrænsfɜː/ *n* **1 a)** [C,U] the process by which someone or something moves or is moved from one place, job etc to another〔地点的〕转移;〔工作的〕调动: *Penny's applied for a transfer to another part of the company.* 彭尼已申请调到公司的其他部门工作。| *data transfer* 资料传送 **b)** [C] someone or something that has been moved in this way 已调动的人; 已转移的东西 **2 transfer of power** a process by which the control of a country is taken from one person or group and given to another 权力的转让[过渡]: *the peaceful transfer of power in South Africa* 南非权力的和平过渡 **3** [C] *especially BrE* a drawing, pattern etc that can be stuck or printed onto a surface【尤英】〔可粘贴或印制的〕图画, 图案; DECAL *especially AmE*【尤美】**4** [C] *especially AmE* a ticket that allows a passenger to change from one bus, train etc to another without paying more money【尤美】〔公共汽车、火车等的〕转乘票证

trans·fer·ence /trænsˋfɝəns; ˈtrænsfərəns/ *n* [U] *formal* a process by which someone or something is moved from one place, position, job etc to another【正式】调任, 调职; 转移; 转让

transfer fee /ˈ‥ ˌ/ *n* [C] *BrE* the money that is paid to one football club by another for the transfer of a player【英】〔足球运动员的〕转会费

transfer list /ˈ‥ ˌ/ *n* [C] a list of the football players at one club who can transfer to other clubs〔足球运动员的〕转会名单

trans·fig·ure /trænsˋfɪgjɚ; trænsˈfɪgə/ *v* [T] *literary* to change the way someone or something looks, especially so that they become more beautiful【文】使变形, 使改观; 美化: *a face transfigured with joy* 因喜悦而容光焕发的脸 —**transfiguration** /ˌtrænsfɪgjəˋreʃən; trænsˌfɪgəˈreɪʃən/ *n* [C,U]

trans·fix /trænsˋfɪks; trænsˈfɪks/ *v* [T] *literary* to make a hole through something or someone with a sharp pointed weapon【文】刺穿, 戳破, 钉住

trans·fixed /trænsˋfɪkst; trænsˈfɪkst/ *adj* [not before noun 不用于名词前] unable to move because you are very shocked, frightened etc〔因震惊、害怕等〕不能动弹的; 惊呆的: *Joe stood transfixed when I told him the terrible news.* 当我把这可怕的消息告诉乔时, 他惊呆了。

3 **trans·form** /trænsˋfɔrm; trænsˈfɔːm/ *v* [T] to completely change the appearance, form, or character of something or someone, especially in a way that improves it 使改观, 使变形; 使转化: **transform sth into** *In the last 20 years Korea has been transformed into an advanced industrial power.* 在最近的20年里, 韩国已变成一个先进的工业强国。| **transform sb/sth** *Put yourself in the hands of our experts, who will transform your hair and makeup.* 你把自己交给我们的专家吧, 他们会使你的发型和化妆彻底改观。—**transformable** *adj*

trans·for·ma·tion /ˌtrænsfɚˋmeʃən; ˌtrænsfəˈmeɪʃən/ *n* [U] a complete change in someone or something〔彻底的〕改变, 改观: *In recent years the film industry has undergone a complete transformation.* 近年来, 电影业发生了彻底的改变。

trans·form·er /trænsˋfɔrmɚ; trænsˈfɔːmə/ *n* [C] a piece of equipment for changing electricity from one VOLTAGE to another 变压器

trans·fu·sion /trænsˋfjuʒən; trænsˈfjuːʒən/ *n* [C,U] *formal* the process of putting blood from one person into another person's body【正式】输血: *A blood transfusion saved his life.* 输血挽救了他的性命。

trans·gress /trænsˋgrɛs; trænzˈgres/ *v* [I,T] *formal* to do something that is against the rules of social behaviour or against a moral principle【正式】违背, 违反〔社会规范或道德准则〕: *Those who have transgressed against custom must be punished.* 那些违背了习俗的人必须受到惩罚。—**transgressor** *n* [C] —**transgression** /-ˋgrɛʃən; -ˈgreʃən/ *n* [C,U]

tran·si·ent¹ /ˋtrænʃənt; ˈtrænziənt/ *adj formal*【正式】**1** continuing only for a short time; TRANSITORY 短暂的, 转瞬即逝的, 一时的: *transient fashions* 短暂的时尚 **2** passing quickly through a place or staying there for only a short time 逗留时间很短的; 流动性的: *a transient population of gold prospectors* 探寻黄金的流动人口 —**transience, transiency** *n* [U]

transient² *n* [C] *AmE* someone who has no home and moves around from place to place; TRAMP[1] (1)【美】流浪者; 游民

tran·sis·tor /trænˋzɪstɚ; trænˈzɪstə/ *n* [C] **1** a small piece of electronic equipment in radios, televisions etc that controls the flow of electricity 晶体管, 电晶体 **2** a transistor radio 晶体管收音机, 电晶体收音机

tran·sis·tor·ize also 又作 **-ise** *BrE*【英】/trænˋzɪstəˌraɪz; trænˈzɪstəraɪz/ *v* [T] *technical* to put transistors into something so that it can be made smaller【术语】装晶体管于; 使电晶体化

transistor ra·di·o /ˌ‥ ˈ‥‥/ *n* [C] a small radio that has transistors in it instead of valves (VALVE (3)) 晶体管收音机, 电晶体收音机

Tran·sit /ˋtrænsɪt; ˈtrænsɪt/ *trademark* a type of large VAN (=a vehicle that is used for carrying goods) made by the Ford Motor Company in the UK【商标】全顺〔福特汽车公司在英国制造的一种小型货车〕

transit *n* **1** [U] the process of moving goods or people from one place to another〔人或货物的〕运输: **in transit** (=in the process of being moved) 在运输过程中 *goods damaged in transit* 在运输中受损的货物 **2** [C,U] *technical* the movement of a PLANET or moon in front of a larger object in space, such as the sun【术语】凌（日）〔行星或月球在太阳等较大天体前面经过〕

transit camp /ˈ‥ ˌ/ *n* [C] a place where REFUGEES stay before moving to somewhere more permanent〔难民暂居的〕过境营地, 临时难民营

tran·si·tion /trænˋzɪʃən; trænˈzɪʃən/ *n* [C,U] *formal* the act or process of changing from one form or state to another【正式】过渡; 转变, 变迁: *the band's gradual transition from hard rock hipsters to kings of pop* 乐队从赶时髦的硬摇滚乐手向流行音乐之王的逐渐转变 | **in transition** (=in the process of changing) 在演变之中 *The book takes an interesting look at a marriage in transition.* 这本书描写了一段婚姻的演变, 引人入胜。 3

tran·si·tion·al /trænˋzɪʃənḷ; trænˈzɪʃənəl/ *adj* **1 transitional stage/period etc** a period during which something is changing from one state or form into another 过渡阶段/时期等: *maintaining law and order in the transitional period between governments* 在两届政府过渡时期维持法治和秩序 **2 transitional government** a government that is temporary during a period of change 过渡政府 —**transitionally** *adv*

tran·si·tive /ˋtrænsətɪv; ˈtrænsətɪv/ *adj technical* a transitive verb must have an object, for example the verb 'break' in the sentence 'I broke the cup'. Transitive verbs are marked [T] in this dictionary.【术语】〔动词〕及物的〔如在句子 I broke the cup 中的 break。本辞典的及物动词均标以 [T]〕—compare 比较 DITRANSITIVE, INTRANSITIVE —**transitive** *n* [C] —**transitively** *adv*

transit lounge /ˈ‥ ˌ/ *n* [C] an area in an airport where passengers can wait〔机场的〕中转候机厅

tran·si·to·ry /ˋtrænsəˌtɔrɪ; ˈtrænzətəri/ *adj* continuing or existing for only a short time; TRANSIENT 短暂的, 一时的

transit vi·sa /ˈ‥ ˌ‥/ *n* [C] a VISA (=special document) that allows someone to pass through one country on their way to another 过境签证

Trans·kei /trænsˋkaɪ; trænsˈkaɪ/, **the Transkei** an area of South Africa that is part of the Eastern Cape Province. It was formerly a HOMELAND (a partly independent area set aside for the black population during the APARTHEID period). 特兰斯凯〔南非东角省一地区。种族隔离时期曾为"黑人家园", 即黑人保留地〕

trans·late /trænsˋlet; trænsˈleɪt/ *v* **1** [I,T] to change speech or writing into another language 翻译, 把〔话语或文字〕译成〔另一种语言〕: *Robin doesn't speak German so I'll have to translate.* 罗宾不会讲德语, 所以我得翻译。| **translate sth (from sth) into** *We translated the text from Italian into English.* 我们把文本从意大利语译成了英语。—compare 比较 INTERPRET (2) **2** [I] to be changed from one language into another（被）翻译: *Most poetry doesn't translate easily.* 大多数诗歌都是不容易翻译的。**3** [T] to change something from one form into another 把…变成另一种形状, 转化为…: **translate sth into** *We're hoping to trans-*

late our ideas into action. 我们希望把自己的思想转化为行动。—**translatable** *adj*

trans·la·tion /træns`leʃən; træns'leɪʃən/ *n* **1** [C,U] the act of translating something or something that has been translated 翻译；翻译作品：*a translation of Aristotle's 'Ethics'* 亚里士多德的《伦理学》译本 | **translation (from sth) into** *translation from Latin into English* 由拉丁语到英语的翻译 | **in translation** *I've only read "Madame Bovary" in translation.* 我只读过《包法利夫人》的翻译本。| **be lost in translation** (=be no longer effective when translated) 在翻译中丢失了 *Much of the book's humour has been lost in translation.* 这本书的很多幽默之处在翻译中丢失了。**2** [U] *formal* the process of changing something into a different form【正式】转化：*the translation of ideas into deeds* 思想转化为行动

trans·la·tor /træns`letɚ; træns'leɪtə/ *n* [C] someone who changes speech or writing into a different language 翻译（者），译员 —compare 比较 INTERPRETER

trans·lit·e·rate /træns`lɪtə͵ret; trænz'lɪtəreɪt/ *v* [T] to write a word, sentence etc in the alphabet of a different language or writing system 把〔词、句子等〕用另一种语言的字母[另一种书写系统]写出 —**transliteration** /͵trænslɪtə`reʃən; trænz͵lɪtə'reɪʃən/ *n* [C,U]

trans·lu·cent /træns`lusn̩t; trænz'luːsənt/ *adj* not transparent, but clear enough to allow light to pass through 半透明的：*translucent paper* 半透明纸 —**translucence** *n* [U]

trans·mi·gra·tion /͵trænsmaɪ`greʃən; ͵trænzmaɪ'greɪʃən/ *n* [U] *technical* the time when the soul passes into another body after death, according to some religions【术语】〔死后灵魂的〕轮回，转世

trans·mis·sion /træns`mɪʃən; trænz'mɪʃən/ *n* **1** [U] the process of sending out of electrical signals, messages etc, by radio or similar equipment〔电子信号、信息等的〕发送，播送：*We apologize for the break in transmission earlier in the programme.* 我们为节目初期出现的播放中断表示歉意。**2** [C] *formal* something that is broadcast on television, radio etc【正式】〔电视、广播等的〕播送节目 **3** [C] the parts of a vehicle that take power from the engine to the wheels〔汽车的〕传动装置，变速器：*My car has automatic transmission.* 我的汽车具有自动传动装置。**4** [U] *formal* the process of sending or passing of something from one person, place, or thing to another【正式】传递，传播：*the transmission of disease* 疾病的传播

trans·mit /træns`mɪt; trænz'mɪt/ *v* **transmitted, transmitting** **1** [I,T] to send out electric signals, messages etc by radio or other similar equipment; broadcast 发送，播送，播放（电子信号、信息等）：*The US Open will be transmitted live via satellite.* 美国公开赛将通过卫星现场直播。**2** [T] to send or pass something from one person, place or thing to another 传送，传递，传播：*an infection transmitted by mosquitoes* 由蚊子传播的一种传染病 —see also 另见 SEXUALLY TRANSMITTED DISEASE **3** [T] *technical* if an object or substance transmits sound or light, it allows sound or light to travel through or along it【术语】传播〔声音或光〕

trans·mit·ter /træns`mɪtɚ; trænz'mɪtə/ *n* [C] equipment that sends out radio or television signals〔发送无线电或电视信号的〕发射机，发报机

trans·mog·ri·fy /træns`mɑgrə͵faɪ; trænz'mɒgrɪ̣faɪ/ *v* [T] *humorous* to change the shape of something completely, as if by magic【幽默】〔变魔术般〕完全改变

trans·mute /træns`mjut; trænz'mjuːt/ *v* [T] *formal* to change one substance or type of thing into another【正式】使变化；把…变成…：*Alchemists tried to transmute lead into gold.* 炼金术士试图把铅变成金。—**transmutable** *adj* —**transmutation** /͵trænsmju`teʃən; ͵trænzmjuː'teɪʃən/ *n* [C,U]

tran·som /`trænsəm; 'trænsəm/ *n* [C] **1** a bar of wood above a door, separating the door from a window above it〔门的〕横档，横楣 **2** a bar of wood or stone across a window, dividing the window into two parts〔把窗户分隔为二的〕过梁 **3** *AmE* a small window over a door or over a larger window【美】门顶窗；楣窗；气窗；FANLIGHT *BrE*【英】

trans·par·en·cy /træn`spɛrənsɪ; træn'spærənsi/ *n* **1** [C] a piece of photographic film through which light can be shone to show a picture on a large screen; SLIDE² (4) 幻灯片 **2** [U] the quality of glass, plastic etc that makes it possible for you to see through it〔玻璃、塑料等的〕透明（性）

trans·par·ent /træn`spɛrənt; træn'spærənt/ *adj* **1** something that is transparent allows light to pass through it, so that you can see the things through it 透明的：*Plain glass is transparent.* 普通玻璃是透明的。| *a transparent silk blouse* 透明的丝绸女衬衫 —compare 比较 OPAQUE, TRANSLUCENT **2** a lie, excuse etc that is transparent does not deceive people〔谎言、借口等〕骗不了人的；显而易见的 **3** *formal* speech or writing that is transparent is clear and easy to understand【正式】〔讲话或文字〕含意清楚的 —**transparently** *adv*

tran·spi·ra·tion /͵trænspə`reʃən; ͵trænspɪ̣'reɪʃən/ *n* [U] *technical* the process of transpiring (TRANSPIRE (3))【术语】蒸腾（作用）

tran·spire /træn`spaɪr; træn'spaɪə/ *v* **1** **it transpires that** *formal* if it transpires that something is true, people find out that it is true【正式】泄露，被人所知：*It now transpires that he kept all the money for himself.* 他把所有的钱都据为己有，这点现在已大白于天下了。**2** [T] to happen 发生：*Let's wait and see what transpires.* 让我们等着瞧会发生什么事吧。**3** [I,T] *technical* when a plant transpires, it gives off water from its surface【术语】〔植物〕蒸腾

trans·plant¹ /træns`plænt; træns'plɑːnt/ *v* [T] **1** to move a plant from one place and plant it in another 移植，移栽〔植物〕**2** to move an organ, piece of skin etc from one person's body to another 移植〔器官、皮肤等〕**3** *formal* to move something or someone from one place to another【正式】搬运，搬迁，迁移 —**transplantation** /͵trænsplæn`teʃən; ͵trænsplɑːn'teɪʃən/ *n* [U]

trans·plant² /`trænsplænt; 'trænsplɑːnt/ *n* [C,U] **1** the operation of transplanting an organ, piece of skin etc〔器官、皮肤等〕移植（手术）：*heart transplant surgery* 心脏移植外科 **2** the organ etc that is transplanted in this type of operation 移植的器官，移植物 —compare 比较 IMPLANT²

trans·po·lar /træns`polɚ; ͵trænz'pəʊlə◂/ *adj* across the area around the North or South Pole 穿越北极[南极]的；穿越极地的

trans·pond·er /træn`spɑndɚ; træn'spɒndə/ *n* [C] *technical* a piece of radio or RADAR equipment that sends out a particular signal when it receives a signal telling it to do this【术语】发射机应答器

trans·port¹ /`trænsport; 'trænspɔːt/ *n* **1** [U] a system for carrying passengers or goods from one place to another〔旅客或货物的〕运输，运送；TRANSPORTATION (2) *AmE*【美】：**public transport** (=buses, trains etc) 公共交通 *Public transport in Prague was excellent.* 布拉格的公共交通很好。**2** [U] a method of travelling from one place to another 交通工具，运输途径：*It's easier to get to the college if you have your own transport* (=car, bicycle etc). 如果你有自己的交通工具，要去这所学院就容易了。| **means of transport** *Horses provided the only means of transport.* 马匹曾是唯一的交通工具。**3** [U] the process or business of taking goods from one place to another 运输（过程）；运输（业务）；TRANSPORTATION (1) *AmE*【美】：[+of] *The transport of freight by air is very expensive.* 航空货运是非常昂贵的。**4** [C] a ship or aircraft for carrying soldiers or supplies〔运送士兵或供给品的〕运输船；运输机 **5** **be in a transport of delight/joy etc** *literary* to be feeling very strong emotions of pleasure, happiness etc【文】感到非常高兴/快乐等

trans·port² /træns`port; træn'spɔːt/ *v* [T] **1** to take goods, people etc from one place to another in a vehicle 运输，运送〔货物、人等〕：*Transporting goods by rail reduces pollution.* 通过铁路运输货物可以减少污染。| **transport sb/sth to** *You will be transported to the resort by coach.* 将用游览车把你们运送到度假胜地。**2** **be transported back/into etc** to imagine that you are in another place or time because of something that you see or hear〔想象中〕被带回到/被带入〔另一地点或时间等〕：*Walking around the town, I was transported back to my youth.* 我在城里到处走着，好像回到了青少年时代。**3** to send a criminal to a distant country as a punishment in former times〔旧时〕流放，放逐〔犯人〕**4** **be transported with delight/joy etc** *literary* to feel very strong emotions of pleasure, happiness etc【文】欣喜若狂，喜不自胜 —**transportable** *adj*

Transport and Gen·e·ral Work·ers' U·nion, the /͵‥‥‥`‥‥/ the full name of the TGWU（英国）运输与普通工人工会〔TGWU 全称〕

trans·por·ta·tion /͵trænspɚ`teʃən; ͵trænspɔː'teɪʃən/ *n* [U] **1** the process or business of taking goods from one place to another 运输（过程）；运输（业务）：*the transportation of dangerous chemicals by road* 通过公路运输危险的化学品 **2** *AmE* a system for carrying passengers or goods from one place to another【美】〔旅客或货物的〕运输，运送；TRANSPORT¹ (1) *BrE*【英】**3** *old use* the punishment of sending a criminal to a distant country【旧】〔犯人的〕流放，放逐

transport caf·e /`‥ ‥͵‥/ *n* [C] *BrE* a cheap restaurant beside a main road, used mainly by drivers of heavy vehicles【英】〔主要为重型货车司机服务的〕路边廉价餐馆；TRUCK STOP *AmE*【美】

trans·port·er /træns`portɚ; træn'spɔːtə/ *n* [C] a long vehicle that can carry one or more other vehicles〔运载其他车辆的〕长型货车

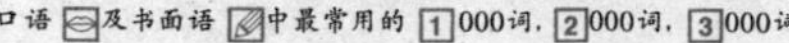

transport plane /ˈ‥, ˌ/ *n* [C] a plane that is used especially for carrying military equipment or soldiers〔尤指运送军事设备或士兵的〕运输机

transport ship /ˈ‥, ˌ/ *n* [C] a ship used especially for carrying soldiers〔尤指运送士兵的〕运输船

trans·pose /trænsˋpoz; trænˈspəʊz/ *v* [T] *technical*【术语】**1** *formal* to change the order or position of two or more things【正式】变换，调换〔顺序或位置〕**2** to write or perform a piece of music in a musical KEY[2] (4) that is different from the one that it was first written in 使〔乐曲〕变调，移调 —**transposition** /ˌtrænspəˋzɪʃən; ˌtrænspəˈzɪʃən/ *n* [C,U]

trans·put·er /trænsˋpjutɚ; trænzˈpjuːtə/ *n* [C] *technical* a powerful computer MICROCHIP that can deal with very large amounts of information very fast【术语】〔能迅速处理大量信息、功率强大的〕电脑微晶片

trans·sex·u·al /ˌtrænsˋsɛkʃuəl; trænˈsekʃuəl/ *n* [C] someone who wants to be or look like a member of the opposite sex, especially by having a medical operation〔尤指通过医学手术〕欲改变性别者，易性癖者 —**transsexual** *adj* —**transsexualism** *n* [U]

Trans-Si·be·ri·an Rail·way, the /ˌ‥ˌ‥, ‥ˈ‥/ a railway that connects the Russian cities of St Petersburg and Vladivostok, the longest railway line in the world 西伯利亚大铁路〔连接俄罗斯的圣彼德堡与符拉迪沃斯托克(海参崴)的一条铁路，是世界上最长的铁路〕

tran·sub·stan·ti·a·tion /ˌtrænsəbˌstænʃɪˋeʃən; ˌtrænsəbstænʃiˈeɪʃən/ *n* [U] *technical* the belief of some Christians that the bread and wine in the MASS (=a religious ceremony) become the actual body and blood of Christ【术语】圣餐变体〔认为弥撒仪式上的面包和葡萄酒实际上变成耶稣基督的肉和血的一种论点〕

Trans·vaal, the /ˌtrænsˋvɑl; ˈtrænzvɑːl/ an area in the north-east of South Africa. Boer farmers first went to live there in the 1830s, and it became a centre of the Afrikaner people and their culture, and of the opposition to British rule in South Africa, which led to the Boer War. 德兰士瓦省〔南非东北部一省。19世纪30年代，布尔人最早前往该地定居，该地后来成为阿非利加人(荷兰人后裔)的文化中心和反对英国殖民统治的中心，最终导致了布尔战争〕

T

trans·verse /trænsˋvɝs; trænzˈvɜːs/ *adj* [no comparative 无比较级] *technical* lying or placed across something【术语】横向的，横断的: *a transverse beam* 横梁

trans·ves·tite /trænsˋvɛstaɪt; trænzˈvestaɪt/ *n* [C] someone who enjoys dressing like a person of the opposite sex 异性装癖者，爱穿异性服装的人 —**transvestite** *adj* —**transvestism** *n* [U]

Tran·syl·va·ni·a /ˌtrænsɪlˋvenɪə; ˌtrænsɪ̣lˈveɪniə/ an area of central Romania with many mountains and forests, now a centre for the steel and chemical industries, but famous for being the place where Count Dracula is supposed to have lived 特兰西瓦尼亚〔罗马尼亚中部一地区。那里群山连绵，从林密布，现为钢铁和化工中心。该地据说是吸血鬼德拉库拉伯爵住过的地方，并因此而出名〕—**Transylvanian** *adj*

trap[1] /træp; træp/ *n* [C]

1 ▶FOR ANIMALS 用于动物的◀ a piece of equipment for catching animals〔捕捉动物的〕夹子，罗网，陷阱: *a mouse caught in a trap* 被夹子夹住的老鼠 | **set a trap** (=prepare it) 设置陷阱，布下圈套 —see also 另见 MOUSETRAP

2 ▶BAD SITUATION 恶劣的处境◀ an unpleasant or difficult situation that is difficult to escape from 圈套；困境: *Amanda felt that marriage was a trap.* 阿曼达觉得婚姻是一个陷阱。

3 ▶CLEVER TRICK 聪明的计策◀ a clever trick that is used to catch someone or to make them do or say something that they did not intend to 计谋，策略；陷阱: **fall/walk into a trap** *Hopefully, the thief will fall right into our trap.* 如果顺利的话，那个贼会恰好落入我们设置的圈套。| **lay a trap (for)** (=arrange a trap for someone) 为…设下圈套

4 fall into the trap of doing sth to do something that seems good at the time but is not sensible or wise 做某事不明智: *Don't fall into the trap of investing all your money in one place.* 不要把你所有的钱都投资到一个地方，那样做并不明智。

5 keep your trap shut *spoken* to not say anything about things that are secret【口】不把…说出去，不泄密: *Just keep your trap shut, and we won't get into trouble.* 你只要不说出去，我们就不会有麻烦。

6 shut your trap! *spoken* a rude way of telling someone to stop talking【口】闭上你的嘴!

7 ▶VEHICLE 车辆◀ a light vehicle with two wheels, pulled by a horse 双轮轻便马车: *a pony and trap* 小马拉的双轮轻便马车

8 ▶SPORT 体育运动◀ *AmE* a place on a GOLF COURSE where there is sand, and from which it is difficult to hit the ball【美】〔高尔夫球场的〕沙坑; BUNKER (3) *BrE*【英】

9 ▶DOG RACE 赛狗◀ a special gate from which a dog is set free at the beginning of a GREYHOUND race〔赛狗开始时放狗出笼的〕围栏 —see also 另见 BOOBY TRAP, DEATH TRAP, POVERTY TRAP, SPEED TRAP

trap[2] *v* [T]

1 ▶IN A DANGEROUS PLACE 在危险的地点◀ [usually passive 一般用被动态] to prevent someone from escaping from a dangerous place 困住，关住；使陷于危险中: *Twenty miners were trapped underground.* 20名矿工被困在地下。

2 ▶IN A BAD SITUATION 在恶劣的处境中◀ **be trapped** to be in a bad situation from which you cannot escape 使陷于困境: *Julia felt trapped in a dead end job.* 朱莉娅觉得工作没有出路，陷于困境。

3 ▶ANIMAL 动物◀ to catch an animal or bird using a trap 用陷阱捕猎〔兽或鸟〕

4 ▶CATCH SB 抓住某人◀ to catch someone by forcing them into a place from which they cannot escape 把〔某人〕困住〔以便捕捉〕；使陷入罗网: *The police trapped the terrorists at a roadblock.* 警察在设有路障的地方围困恐怖分子。

5 ▶TRICK SB 欺骗某人◀ to trick someone so that you make them do or say something that they did not intend to 诱骗，诱使: **trap sb into (doing) sth** *I was trapped into signing a confession.* 我被诱骗在供词上签了字。

6 ▶CRUSH 压扁◀ to get a part of your body crushed between two objects 被夹住；被压扁: *a four-year-old who had trapped his fingers in the door* 手指被夹在门里的一个四岁小孩 | *pain from a trapped nerve in the back* 因背上一根神经被压迫而引起的疼痛

7 ▶GAS/WATER ETC 气/水等◀ to hold and keep gas, water etc so that it can be used later 把〔气、水等〕储存；留存: *solar panels that trap the sun's heat* 把太阳热量储存起来的太阳能电池板

trap·door /ˋtræpdɔr; ˈtræpdɔː/ *n* [C] a small door that covers an opening in a roof or floor〔房顶的〕活动天窗；〔地板的〕活板门

tra·peze /træˋpiz; trəˈpiːz/ *n* [C] a short bar hanging from two ropes high above the ground, used by ACROBATS〔杂技演员用的〕空中吊杠，空中秋千

tra·pe·zi·um /trəˋpizɪəm; trəˈpiːziəm/ *n* [C] *technical*【术语】**1** *BrE* a shape with four sides, of which only two are parallel【英】梯形 **2** *AmE* a shape with four sides of which none are parallel【美】不规则四边形 —see picture at 参见 SHAPE 图

trap·e·zoid /ˋtræpəˌzɔɪd; ˈtræpɪ̣zɔɪd/ *n* [C] *technical*【术语】**1** a shape with four sides, of which none are parallel 不规则四边形 **2** *AmE* a shape with four sides of which only two are parallel【美】梯形 —see picture at 参见 SHAPE 图

trap·per /ˋtræpɚ; ˈtræpə/ *n* [C] someone who traps wild animals, especially for their fur〔尤指为获取毛皮的〕设陷阱捕兽者

trap·pings /ˋtræpɪŋz; ˈtræpɪŋz/ *n* [plural] things such as clothes, possessions etc that show someone's rank, success, or position〔表明某人官职或地位的〕服饰；标志: [+of] *all the trappings of fame* 名望的各种标志

Trap·pist /ˋtræpɪst; ˈtræpɪ̣st/ *n* [C] a member of a Roman Catholic religious society whose members never speak〔罗马天主教中缄默无言的〕特拉普派修士

trap·shoot·ing /ˋtræpˌʃutɪŋ; ˈtræpˌʃuːtɪŋ/ *n* [U] the sport of shooting at special clay objects fired into the air 飞靶射击

trash[1] /træʃ; træʃ/ *n* [U] **1** *AmE* waste material that will be thrown away【美】废物，垃圾; RUBBISH *BrE*【英】—see graph at 参见 RUBBISH[1] 图表 **2** *informal* something that is of very poor quality【非正式】质量粗劣的东西: *There's a lot of trash on TV these days.* 近来电视上有大量粗制滥造的东西。**3** *informal especially AmE* a very insulting word for people who you think do not deserve your respect【非正式，尤美】废物〔极具侮辱性的用语，指不值得尊敬的人〕

trash[2] *v* [T] *informal* to destroy something completely, either deliberately or by using it too much【非正式】〔因故意或过分使用而〕捣毁，破坏: *The place got trashed last time we had a party!* 我们上一次举行聚会的时候把这个地方搞得乱七八糟的!

trash·can /ˋtræʃˌkæn; ˈtræʃkæn/ *n* [C] *AmE*【美】**1** a large container with a lid for holding waste material from people's homes 垃圾桶; DUSTBIN *BrE*【英】**2** a container for waste paper etc in a public place 废纸篓；公用垃圾箱; LITTER BIN *BrE*【英】

trash com·pac·tor /ˈ‥, ˌ‥/ *n* [C] *AmE* a machine that presses waste material together into a very small mass【美】垃圾压实机

trashed /træʃt; træʃt/ *adj AmE spoken*【美口】**1** very drunk 烂醉的: *We went out and got trashed last night.* 我们昨晚外出喝酒，喝得烂醉。**2** completely destroyed 完全毁坏的: *We need a new map – this one's trashed.* 我们需要一张新地图 —— 这张已完全毁坏了。

trash·y /ˈtræʃɪ; ˈtræʃi/ *adj* of extremely bad quality 质量极其粗劣的; 毫无价值的: *trashy novels* 垃圾小说 —**trashiness** *n* [U]

trau·ma /ˈtrɔmə; ˈtrɔːmə/ *n* **1** [C] a very unpleasant and upsetting experience 痛苦的经历: *the trauma of an attack or rape* 遭到袭击或强奸的痛苦经历 **2** [U] a mental state of extreme shock caused by a very frightening or unpleasant experience 心理创伤: *compensation for the emotional trauma he had suffered since childhood* 对他童年以来所受感情创伤的补偿 **3** [C,U] *technical* injury【术语】损伤, 外伤: *the hospital's trauma unit* 医院的外伤科

trau·mat·ic /trɔˋmætɪk; trɔːˈmætɪk/ *adj* a traumatic experience is so shocking and upsetting that it affects you for a long time〔某种经历〕痛苦难忘的, 造成精神创伤的: *The death of his son was the most traumatic event in Stan's life.* 儿子的死是斯坦一生中最痛苦难忘的事。—**traumatically** /-klɪ; -kli/ *adv*

trau·ma·tized also 又作 **-ised** *BrE*【英】/ˈtrɔməˌtaɪzd; ˈtrɔːmətaɪzd/ *adj* so shocked by something that you are unable to forget it or to continue your life as normal 精神上受到创伤的, 痛苦难忘的: *totally traumatized by his war experiences* 因其战争经历而精神上倍受打击

trav·ail /ˈtrævel; ˈtræveɪl/ *n* [U] *old use*【旧】**1** also 又作 **travails** [plural] very tiring work 很累人的工作, 苦活 **2 in travail** a woman who is in travail is feeling the pain of giving birth〔妇女〕分娩的阵痛

2 2 **trav·el**[1] /ˈtrævl; ˈtrævəl/ *v* **travelled, travelling** *BrE*【英】**traveled, traveling** *AmE*【美】

1 ▶JOURNEY 旅途◀ **a)** [I] to go from one place to another, or to several places, especially to distant places〔尤指长途〕旅行: *If I had a lot of money I'd travel.* 我如果有很多的钱, 就外出去旅行。| *They're travelling down from Edinburgh on Monday.* 他们星期一要从爱丁堡来。| **travel by train/car etc** *We travelled by train across Eastern Europe.* 我们乘火车游历了东欧。| **travel widely** (=go to many different places) 到过很多地方 | **travel around** (=go to different places over a period of time)〔在某段时间里〕四处漫游 *I met Tim while I was travelling around.* 在我四处漫游期间, 遇见了蒂姆。| **travel light** (=without taking many bags) 轻装旅行 **b) travel the world/country** to go to most parts of the world or most parts of a particular country 周游世界/周游全国

2 well-travelled/widely travelled having travelled to many different countries 到过很多地方的, 游历很广的

3 ▶DISTANCE 距离◀ [I,T] to go a particular distance or at a particular speed 走过〔某距离〕;〔以某速度〕行进: *The train was travelling at 100 mph.* 火车前进的速度是每小时100英里。| *They travelled 200 miles on the first day.* 他们第一天走了200英里。

4 ▶FOOD/WINE 食品/酒◀ **travel well** to remain in good condition when taken long distances 经得起长途运输而保持优良品质

5 ▶LIGHT/SOUND 光/声音◀ [I] to move at a particular speed or in a particular direction〔以某一速度或朝某一方向〕前进: *Light travels faster than sound.* 光速比音速快。

6 ▶FOR BUSINESS 用于商务◀ [I] to go from place to place to sell and take orders for your company's products 做旅行推销; 四处兜售商品: [+for] *My wife travels for a London firm.* 我妻子为伦敦一家公司做旅行推销。

7 ▶MOVE QUICKLY 快速移动◀ [I] *informal* to go very fast【非正式】快速行进, 飞驰: *That motorbike was really travelling.* 那辆摩托车开得真快。

8 ▶NEWS 消息◀ [I] to be passed quickly from one place to another 很快地传播开来: *News travels fast.* 消息传得很快。

9 ▶SPORT 体育运动◀ [I] *technical* to run while you are holding the ball in BASKETBALL【术语】〔篮球比赛中〕持球走, (带球)走步

USAGE NOTE 用法说明: TRAVEL

WORD CHOICE 词语辨析: **travel** (*n,v*), **sb's travels, journey, trip, voyage, flight**

Travel [U] is only used for the general activity of moving from place to place. travel〔不可数〕只用于泛指从某地去另一地: *He came home after years of foreign travel.* 他在国外旅行多年后回到了家。The *-ing* form of the verb **travel** is also used widely with a similar meaning. travel的 -ing 形式也用得广泛, 表达类似的意义: *I do a bit of travelling abroad* (NOT 不用 *travel(s)*). 我经常去国外走走。| *travel/travelling expenses* 旅行花费 | *air travel/travelling by air* 航空旅行

If someone moves from place to place over a period of time, you talk about **their travels**. 如果某人在某段时间里到处走, 可用 travels: *Did you go to Rome during your travels?* 你在旅行期间去罗马了吗? | *He's on his travels again.* 他又旅行去了。

A particular time spent and distance covered when you go somewhere is a **journey**, especially if it is long or travelled regularly. journey 表示去某地所花的时间和旅行的距离, 尤指较长距离的或定期的旅行: *I get tired of the journey to work every day.* 我厌烦了每天去上班的那段路程。| *The journey to Darjeeling was awful – I was sick all the way* (NOT 不用 *travel*). 前往大吉岭的那段路太糟糕了, 我一直想吐。

A journey to a place and back that is not made regularly, and is perhaps short, is a **trip**. 表示非定期的, 也许较短的往返旅行, 则用 trip: *This is my first trip abroad.* 这是我第一次出国旅行。| *The kids are going on a trip to the castle.* 孩子们要去那座城堡走一趟。| *How long does the trip take?* 来回要花多长时间? (*travel* would not be used in any of these).〔travel 不用于这些句子中〕。

A journey by sea or in space is a **voyage**, and by plane a **flight**. You **take** a **flight** or **trip** and **make** or **go** on a **voyage** or **journey** (but NOT 但不用 *a travel*). 海上旅行或太空旅行的用词是 voyage, 乘飞机旅行是 flight。与 flight 或 trip 搭配的动词是 take, 与 voyage 或 journey 搭配的动词是 make 或 go。

GRAMMAR 语法

Travel (*v*) is not often used transitively travel 通常不用作及物动词 except when you are talking about 下列说法除外: *travelling the country/the world* 走遍全国/世界。Otherwise it is usually intransitive and a preposition is used with the place involved. 其他情况通常用作不及物动词, 要用介词连接所指地点: *He travels a lot/all over the world.* 他游历甚广/游遍世界。| *We travelled to Paris/in India/through many foreign countries* (NOT 不用 *travelled many countries*). 我们去了巴黎/在印度旅行/游历了许多国家。

2 2 **travel**[2] *n* [U] **1** the act or activity of travelling 旅行; 移动; 运动: *Snow has disrupted travel in many parts of the country.* 该国很多地方都下雪, 影响了交通。**2 travels** [plural] journeys, especially to places that are a long way away〔尤指长途的〕旅行, 游历: *Tell us more about your travels.* 给我们多讲讲你的旅行经历。| **be off on your travels** *informal* (=be travelling for pleasure)【非正式】外出旅游 *Are you off on your travels again this summer?* 你今年夏天又要外出旅游吗?

travel a·gen·cy /ˈ‥ ˌ‥/ *n* [C] an office or company that arranges travel and holidays for people 旅行社

travel a·gent /ˈ‥ ˌ‥/ *n* [C] someone who owns or works in a travel agency 旅行代理人; 开办旅行社的人

trav·el·a·tor /ˈtrævletə; ˈtrævəleɪtə/ *n* [C] another spelling of TRAVOLATOR travolator 的另一种拼法

travel bu·reau /ˈ‥ ˌ‥/ *n* [C] a TRAVEL AGENCY 旅行社

trav·el·ler *BrE*【英】, **traveler** *AmE*【美】/ˈtrævlə; ˈtrævələ/ *n* [C] **1** someone who is on a journey or someone who travels often 旅客, 旅行者; 经常旅行的人: *Rail travellers will suffer as a result of fare increases.* 铁路旅客将会因票价上涨而吃苦头。**2** *BrE* someone who travels around from place to place in a CARAVAN as a way of life【英】驾驶旅行拖车过漂泊生活的人 — compare 比较 GYPSY

traveller's cheque *BrE*【英】, **traveler's check** *AmE*【美】/ˈ‥ ˌ‥/ *n* [C] a special cheque that can be exchanged for the money of a foreign country 旅行支票

trav·el·ling *BrE*【英】, **traveling** *AmE*【美】/ˈtrævlɪŋ; ˈtrævəlɪŋ/ *adj* **1 travelling musician/circus etc** a musician etc that goes from place to place in order to work or perform 巡回演出的音乐家/马戏团等 **2 travelling rug/clock etc** a clock etc designed to be used when you are travelling 旅行用毛毯/时钟等 **3 travelling people/folk** travellers (TRAVELLER (2)) 过漂泊生活的人

travelling sales·man *BrE*【英】, **traveling salesman** *AmE*【美】/ˌ‥ ˈ‥/ *n* [C] someone who goes from place to place, selling their company's products 旅行推销员

trav·el·ogue also 又作 **travelog** *AmE*【美】/ˈtrævəˌlɔg; ˈtrævəlɒg/ *n* [C] a film or talk that describes travel in a particular country, or a particular person's travels 旅行纪录片; 旅行见闻讲座

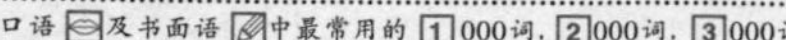

travel-sick /ˈ· · ·/ *adj* feeling ill because you are travelling in a vehicle 晕车的; 晕船的; 晕飞机的: *Many children get travel-sick on long journeys.* 许多孩子在长途旅行时都会头晕。—**travel sickness** *n* [U]

tra·verse[1] /trəˋvɝs; ˈtrævɜːs/ *v* [T] *formal* to move across, over, or through something【正式】跨过, 穿过, 横越, 横穿: *They traversed the desert slowly.* 他们缓慢地穿过沙漠。

trav·erse[2] /ˋtrævɝs; ˈtrævɜːs/ *n* [C] *technical* a sideways movement across a very steep slope in mountain-climbing【术语】〔爬山时的〕斜向[横向]攀上〔陡坡〕: *the traverse of the mountain's north face* 斜向攀登山的北坡

trav·es·ty /ˋtrævɪstɪ; ˈtrævəsti/ *n* [C] an extremely bad example of something; especially one that is very unfair or morally wrong and has the opposite result to the one it should have 歪曲模仿, 曲解; 嘲弄: *O'Brien described his trial as a travesty of justice.* 奥布赖恩把对他的审讯描述成是对司法的嘲弄。

trav·o·la·tor, travelator /ˋtrævəletɚ; ˈtrævəleɪtə/ *n* [C] *BrE formal* a flat moving band of material on the floor, that people can step onto so that they do not have to walk, especially in airports【英, 正式】〔尤指机场的〕自动人行道

trawl[1] /trɔl; trɔːl/ *v* [I,T] **1** to search through a lot of documents, lists, etc in order to find out information〔在大量文件、名单等中〕搜寻〔资料〕: [**+through**] *I'll have to trawl through all my lecture notes again.* 我不得不把所有讲座笔记再翻一遍。**2** to fish by dragging a special wide net behind a boat 以拖网捕鱼: *trawling the bay for herring* 在海湾里用拖网捕鲱鱼

trawl[2] *n* [C] **1** an act of searching through a lot of documents, lists etc in order to find something〔在大量文件、名单等中的〕搜寻 **2** a wide net that is pulled along the bottom of the sea to catch fish 拖网 **3** a TRAWL LINE 排钩绳

trawl·er /ˋtrɔlɚ; ˈtrɔːlə/ *n* [C] a fishing boat that trawls 拖网渔船

traw·ler·man /ˋtrɔlɚˏmæn; ˈtrɔːləmən/ *n* [C] someone who works on a trawler 拖网渔民; 拖网渔船工人

trawl line /ˈ· ·/ *n* [C] *AmE* a long fishing line to which many smaller lines are fastened【美】排钩绳〔挂有许多小钓线的长的钓线〕

trays 浅盘

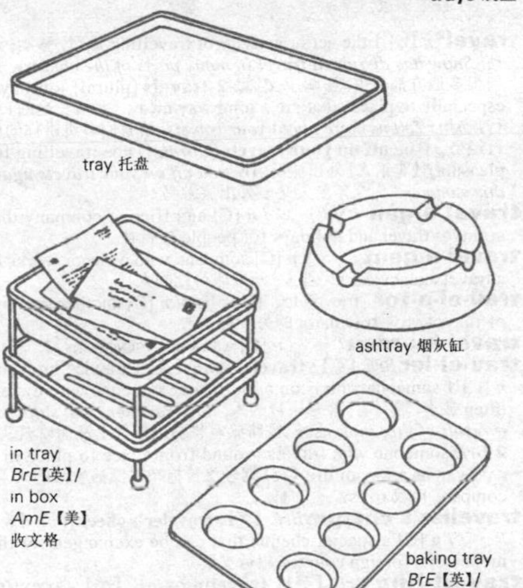

tray 托盘

in tray *BrE*【英】/ in box *AmE*【美】 收文格

ashtray 烟灰缸

baking tray *BrE*【英】/ cupcake tin *AmE*【美】 杯形糕饼烤盘

tray /tre; treɪ/ *n* [C] **1** a flat piece of plastic, metal, or wood, with raised edges, used for carrying things such as plates, food etc〔浅〕盘, 托盘: *The waiter brought drinks on a tray.* 服务员用托盘端来饮料。**2** *especially BrE* a flat open container with three sides used for holding papers, documents etc on a desk【尤英】〔办公桌上存放文件等的〕格子: **in tray** (=for holding documents you still have to deal with)〔放置待处理文件的〕收文格 | **out tray** (=for holding documents you have dealt with)〔放置已处理文件的〕发文格 —see also 另见 BAKING TRAY

treach·e·rous /ˋtrɛtʃərəs; ˈtretʃərəs/ *adj* **1** someone who is treacherous cannot be trusted because they are disloyal and secretly intend to harm you 背信弃义的, 不忠的, 阴险的: *a treacherous plot to overthrow the leader* 一项推翻领导人的阴谋 **2** ground or conditions that are treacherous are particularly dangerous because you cannot see the dangers 暗藏危险的: *There are treacherous currents in the bay.* 海湾中有暗流。—**treacherously** *adv*

treach·e·ry /ˋtrɛtʃərɪ; ˈtretʃəri/ *n* **1** [U] behaviour that is not loyal to someone who trusts you, especially when this helps their enemies 背信弃义, 不忠, 背叛: *the treachery of those who plotted against the king* 那些阴谋叛乱的人对国王的不忠 **2** [C usually plural 一般用复数] a disloyal action against someone who trusts you 背叛行为; 欺骗行为

trea·cle /ˋtrikḷ; ˈtriːkəl/ *n* [U] *BrE*【英】**1** a thick sweet black sticky liquid that is obtained from the sugar plant and used in cooking 糖蜜; MOLASSES *AmE*【美】**2** GOLDEN SYRUP 糖浆: *a treacle tart* 糖浆馅饼

trea·cly /ˋtriklɪ; ˈtriːkli/ *adj BrE*【英】**1** thick and sticky, like treacle 稠的, 黏的; 糖蜜似的: *treacly black mud* 又稠又黑的泥泞 **2** expressing feelings of love or fondness in a way that seems insincere 过分多情的; 讨好的

tread[1] /trɛd; tred/ *v past tense* **trod** /trɑd; trɒd/ *past participle* **trodden** /ˋtrɑdṇ; ˈtrɒdn/

1 ►STEP IN/ON 踩到里面/上面◄ [I always+adv/prep] *BrE* to put your foot on or in something while you are walking; STEP【英】踩, 踏: [**+in/on**] *Sorry – did I tread on your foot?* 对不起, 我踩到你的脚了吗? | *Be careful not to tread on that broken glass.* 小心别踩到那块碎玻璃上。

2 ►CRUSH 压扁◄ a) [T] *BrE* to press or crush something into the floor or ground with your feet【英】用力踩; 踩烂; TRACK[2] (6) *AmE*【美】: **tread sth into/onto/over** *Stop treading mud all over my clean kitchen floor!* 不要把我干净的厨房地板到处都踩上泥! | *Bits of the broken vase got trodden into the carpet.* 破花瓶的一些碎片被踩进了地毯里面。**b) tread grapes** to crush GRAPES with your feet in order to produce the juice from which wine is made 用脚踩烂葡萄〔以酿酒〕

3 tread carefully/warily/cautiously etc to be very careful about what you say or do in a difficult situation 步步为营, 言行谨慎: *We can't risk the talks breaking down – we'll have to tread carefully.* 我们不能冒谈判破裂的风险, 必须步步为营。

4 tread a path *formal* to take a particular action or series of actions【正式】采取某种[系列]行动: *Anyone who makes such serious allegations is treading a very dangerous path.* 任何人提出如此严重的指控, 都要冒极大的风险。

5 tread water a) to stay floating upright in deep water by moving your legs as if you were riding a bicycle〔游泳时〕踩水 **b)** to make no progress in a particular situation, especially because you are waiting for something to happen〔尤指因等待某事发生而〕裹足不前

6 tread the boards *humorous* to work as an actor【幽默】当演员, 演戏

7 ►WALK 走路◄ [I always+adv/prep,T] *literary especially BrE* to walk【文, 尤英】行走, 步行: *David trod wearily along behind the others.* 戴维疲惫地走在别人的后面。—see also 另见 **step/tread on sb's toes** (TOE[1] (3))

tread[2] *n* **1** [C,U] the pattern of lines on the part of a tyre that touches the road 轮胎胎面花纹 **2** [C] the part of a stair that you put your foot on〔楼梯的〕梯面, 踏步板 **3** [singular] the particular sound that someone makes when they walk 脚步声, 走路声: *I could hear our father's heavy tread outside the door.* 我能听到门外父亲重重的脚步声。

trea·dle /ˋtrɛdḷ; ˈtredl/ *n* [C] a flat piece of metal or wood that you move with your foot to turn a wheel in a machine〔机器上踩踏使轮子转动的〕踏板

tread·mill /ˋtrɛdˏmɪl; ˈtredˌmɪl/ *n* **1** [singular] work or a way of life that seems very boring because you always have to do the same things 单调而枯燥的工作[生活] **2** [C] a MILL[1] (1) worked in the past by prisoners treading on steps fixed to a very large wheel〔过去用以惩罚犯人的〕踏车

trea·son /ˋtrizṇ; ˈtriːzən/ *n* [U] the crime of being disloyal to your country or its government, especially by helping its enemies or trying to remove the government using violence 叛国(罪), 通敌(罪): [**+against**] *an act of treason against the state* 叛国行为 | **commit treason** (=do something that is treason) 犯叛国罪 | **high treason** (=treason of the worst kind) 严重叛国罪

trea·son·a·ble /ˋtrizṇəbḷ; ˈtriːzənəbəl/ also 又作 **trea·son·ous** /-zṇəs; -zənəs/ *adj* a treasonable offence can be punished as trea-

son 叛逆的，叛国的：*a treasonable act against the head of state* 针对国家元首的一次叛逆行动

trea·sure[1] /ˈtrɛʒɚ; ˈtreʒə/ *n* **1** [U] a store of gold, silver, jewels etc 金银财宝，宝藏：*buried treasure* 埋在地下的财宝 | **treasure chest** (=box containing treasure) 珠宝箱 **2** [C] a very valuable and important object such as a painting or ancient document 珍宝，珍品：*the art treasures of the Louvre* 卢浮宫的艺术珍品 **3** *informal old-fashioned* [singular] someone who is very useful or important to you【非正式，过时】很有用的人，得力帮手：*Our housekeeper is a real treasure.* 我们的管家真是个难得的好帮手。

treasure[2] *v* [T] to treat something as being very special, important, or valuable 珍藏，珍惜，珍视：*Thank you; I shall treasure this gift always.* 谢谢您！我会永远珍惜这件礼物的。| *treasured memories of happier days* 对幸福时光的珍贵回忆

treasure hunt /ˈ.. ,./ *n* [C] a game in which you have to find something that has been hidden by answering questions that are left in different places 寻宝游戏〔通过解答留在不同地点的问题来找到隐藏的东西〕

Treasure Is·land /,.. ˈ../ (1883) an adventure story for children by Robert Louis Stevenson about a young man called Jim Hawkins who is trying to find some TREASURE (=gold, jewels, coins etc) that has been buried on an island. He discovers that some of the sailors on his ship are PIRATES (=sailors who violently rob other ships) led by Long John Silver.《金银岛》〔(1883)，罗伯特·路易斯·史蒂文森的一部儿童历险小说，讲述一个名叫吉姆·霍金斯的年轻人努力寻找藏在一座海岛上的财宝的故事。他发现自己船上的有些水手是海盗，他们的头子是朗·约翰·西尔弗〕

trea·sur·er /ˈtrɛʒərɚ; ˈtreʒərə/ *n* [C] someone who is in charge of the money for an organization, club, political party etc〔团体、机构等的〕司库，财务主管

treasure trove /ˈtræʒɚ ,trov; ˈtreʒə trəʊv/ *n* [U] *BrE law* valuable objects, coins etc that are found where they have been hidden or buried, which are not claimed by anyone【英，法律】〔被发现埋藏的〕无主财宝

> **CULTURAL NOTE 文化注释**
>
> In Britain, these valuable objects legally belong to the king or queen, but the finder may be allowed to keep them. In the US, the finder is usually allowed to keep them. 在英国，法律规定这些宝物属于国王或女王所有，但是允许发现者自己保存。在美国，人们发现宝物后通常都可以据为己有。

trea·su·ry /ˈtrɛʒərɪ; ˈtreʒəri/ *n* **1 the Treasury** a government department that controls the money that the country collects and spends〔政府的〕财政部：*a senior civil servant at the Treasury* 财政部的一位高级公务员 **2** [C] a place where money or valuable objects are kept in a castle, church, PALACE etc〔城堡、教堂、宫殿等的〕金库，宝库

Treasury Bench, the /ˈ... ,./ the first row of seats to the right of the Speaker in the British House of Commons, where all the most important government ministers sit 国务大臣席〔英国下议院议长右侧的首排座位，所有政府重臣在此就座〕

Treasury bill /ˈ... ,./ also 又作 **T-bill** *informal*【非正式】an American government bond. Treasury bills are sold to raise money for the government and usually bought by large financial institutions around the world. 短期国库券〔美国政府发行的一种债券。发售短期国库券旨在为政府筹集资金，购买者通常为世界各国的大型金融机构〕

treat[1] /trit; triːt/ *v* [T]

1 ▶**BEHAVE TOWARDS SB** 对待某人◀ [always+adv/prep] to behave towards someone in a particular way 对待，看待：**treat sb like/as** *She treats me like one of the family.* 她把我当作家人来看待。| *Even though they were much younger, we treated them as equals.* 他们即便年轻得多，我们还是平等地对待他们。| **badly treated/well treated** *The prisoners were well treated by their guards.* 囚犯受到卫兵很好的对待。| **treat sb with respect/contempt/kindness etc** *Despite her seniority, Margot was never treated with much respect.* 玛戈特尽管是长辈，但从未受到多少尊重。| **treat sb like dirt/a dog** (=treat someone unkindly and without respect) 把某人不当人看待/当狗看待

2 ▶**DEAL WITH STH** 处理某事◀ [always+adv/prep] to deal with or discuss something in a particular way 处理；讨论：**treat sth as** *Please treat this information as completely confidential.* 这项资料请绝对保密。| **treat sth favourably/seriously/carefully etc** *Any complaint about safety standards must be treated very seriously.* 任何有关安全标准的投诉意见必须十分认真地对待。

3 ▶**MEDICAL** 医学的◀ to try to cure an illness or injury by using drugs, hospital care, operations etc 治疗，医治：*Nowadays malaria can be treated with drugs.* 如今，疟疾可以用药物医治。

4 ▶**REGARD** 看待◀ [always+adv/prep] to regard an idea, subject, statement etc in a particular way 把…看作；看待：**treat sth as** *She treats everything I say as some kind of joke.* 她把我说的每一件事都当成是玩笑。

5 ▶**BUY STH FOR SB** 为某人买某物◀ to buy something special for someone that you know they will enjoy 请客，款待，招待：**treat sb to sth** *We treated Mom to lunch at the Savoy.* 我们在萨沃伊酒店请妈妈吃午饭。| **treat yourself to sth** (=buy yourself something special) 自己花钱享受某物 *I treated myself to a new dress.* 我给自己买了一条新连衣裙。

6 ▶**PROTECT/CLEAN** 保护/清理◀ to put a special substance on something or use a chemical process in order to protect, clean, or preserve it 为…涂上保护层；〔用化学方式〕处理；清理：*It is possible to treat sewage so that it can be used as fertilizer.* 可以对污水进行处理，使之可以用作肥料。—see also 另见 TRICK OR TREAT

treat with sth *phr v* [T] *formal* to try to reach an official agreement with someone【正式】与…协商[谈判、交涉]

treat of sth *phr v* [T] *formal* if a book, article etc treats of something, it is about that subject【正式】〔著作、文章等就某主题〕探讨，论述

treat[2] *n* **1** [C] something special that you give someone or do for them because you know they will enjoy it〔给某人的〕特别待遇，款待，招待：*Steven took his son to the zoo as a birthday treat.* 史蒂文带儿子去动物园作为生日的特别招待。**2** [singular] an unexpected event that gives you a lot of pleasure 意外的乐事，幸事：*I really miss everyone, and getting a letter from home is a big treat.* 我真的很想念大家，收到家里的来信成了我的一大乐事。**3 my treat** *spoken* used to tell someone that you will pay for something such as a meal for them【口】我来付钱，我请客：*Let's go out for dinner – my treat this time.* 咱们出去吃饭吧——这次由我来请客。**4 go down a treat** *BrE informal* if something goes down a treat, people like it very much【英，非正式】深受喜爱：*Brightly coloured building blocks always go down a treat with toddlers.* 色彩鲜艳的积木总是深得幼童的喜爱。**5 look/work a treat** *BrE informal* to look very good or work very well【英，非正式】看上去很好/工作得很出色：*The sports ground looked a treat, with all the flags flying.* 运动场看上去很漂亮，到处都是彩旗飘扬。

treat·a·ble /ˈtritəbl; ˈtriːtəbəl/ *adj* a treatable illness or injury can be helped with drugs or an operation〔病或伤〕可医治的

trea·tise /ˈtritɪs; ˈtriːtɪ̱s/ *n* [C **+on**] a serious book or article about a particular subject 专著；专题论文：*a treatise on medical ethics* 论述医学伦理的专著

treat·ment /ˈtritmənt; ˈtriːtmənt/ *n*

1 ▶**MEDICAL** 医学的◀ [C,U] a method that is intended to cure an injury or illness 治疗；疗法：[**+for**] *The best treatment for a cold is to rest and drink lots of fluids.* 治疗感冒的最佳方法是休息和多喝流质。| **give sb treatment** *She was given emergency treatment by paramedics.* 她接受了护理人员的紧急治疗。| **receive treatment** *receiving treatment for skin cancer* 接受皮肤癌治疗 | **respond to treatment** (=get better when you are treated) 有疗效

2 ▶**BEHAVIOUR TOWARDS SB** 对待某人的行为◀ [U] a particular way of behaving towards someone or of dealing with them 对待(方式)；待遇：[**+of**] *Henchard's cruel treatment of his wife* 亨查德对妻子的虐待 | **special/preferential treatment** (=when one person is treated better than another) 特殊的待遇/优待 *The two young princes were not singled out for special treatment at school.* 两位年轻的王子在学校里并没有享受特殊待遇。| **give sb the full treatment** *informal especially BrE* (=treat someone in a very special way and give them a lot of attention)【非正式，尤英】给某人特殊的礼遇

3 ▶**OF A SUBJECT** 有关某一主题◀ [C,U] a particular way of dealing with or talking about a subject〔针对某一主题的〕讨论，论述：*I didn't think the film gave the issue serious enough treatment.* 我认为这部电影对那个问题并没有给予足够严肃的阐述。

4 ▶**CLEAN/PROTECT** 清理/保护◀ [U] a process by which something is cleaned, protected etc 处理〔指清理、保护等的过程〕：*the treatment of waste oils and solvents* 对废弃油料及溶剂的处理

treat·y /ˈtritɪ; ˈtriːti/ *n* **1** [C] a formal agreement between two or more countries or governments〔国家或政府间的〕条约：*the Treaty of Versailles* 凡尔赛条约 | **peace treaty** *A peace treaty was signed between the US and Vietnam.* 美国和越南签订了一 

项和平条约。**2** [U] *technical* formal agreement between two people, especially to buy a house【术语】〔尤指为了购房，两人之间签订的〕协议，协定

Treaty of Brest-Li·tovsk, the /ˌtritɪ əv ˌbrɛst lɪˋtɒfsk; ˌtriːti əv ˌbrest lɪˈtɒfsk/ a peace agreement made on March 3rd, 1918, between Germany and its allies (ALLY) and Soviet Russia《布列斯特－立陶夫斯克和约》〔1918年3月3日德国及其盟国与苏维埃俄国签订的和平条约〕

Treaty of Rome, the /ˌ‥ˈ/ the formal agreement made in 1958 between France, West Germany, Italy, Belgium, the Netherlands, and Luxembourg, which established the European Economic Community, which later became the EU (European Union)《罗马条约》〔1958年法国、西德、意大利、比利时、荷兰及卢森堡共同签署的正式协议。据此建立了欧洲经济共同体，后来成为欧洲联盟〕

Treaty of Ver·sailles, the /ˌ‥‥ˈ/ a peace agreement made in 1919 at Versailles in France, following the defeat of Germany in World War I, between Germany and the Allies (=the countries that fought against Germany in the war, including France, Russia, the UK, and the US). According to the treaty, Germany lost some of its land and had to agree to pay large amounts of money to the Allies for damage caused by the war. The treaty also established the League of Nations.《凡尔赛条约》〔一战德国战败后，1919年德国与协约国（包括法国、俄国、英国和美国）在法国凡尔赛宫签订的一项和约。该条约规定德国割让部分土地，并给协约国支付大笔钱款以赔偿战争造成的破坏。该条约还促成了国际联盟的创立〕

treb·le¹ /ˋtrɛbl; ˈtrebəl/ *predeterminer* three times as big, as much, or as many as something else 三倍的，三重的：*They sold the house for treble the amount they paid for it.* 他们以购进价的三倍出售了这所房子。

treble² *v* [I,T] to become three times as big in amount, size, or number, or to make something increase in this way（使）成三倍：*Their profits have trebled in the last two years.* 他们的利润在最近两年里增加了两倍。

treble³ *n* **1** [U] the upper half of the whole range of musical notes〔音乐的〕最高音部 —compare 比较 BASS¹ (3) **2** [C] a boy with a high singing voice 能唱最高音部的男孩子 —**treble** *adj, adv*: *a clear treble voice* 嘹亮的高音

T

treble clef /ˌ‥ˈ/ *n* [C] *technical* a sign (𝄞) at the beginning of a line of written music which shows that the note written on the bottom line of the STAVE¹ (1) is an E above MIDDLE C【术语】高音谱号 —see picture at 参见 MUSIC 图

1 1 **tree** /tri; triː/ *n* [C] **1** a very tall plant that has a wooden trunk, branches, and leaves, and lives for many years 树（木），乔木：*We planted an orange tree in the backyard.* 我们在后院种了一棵柑橘树。| *Children love to climb trees.* 小孩喜爱爬树。**2** a drawing with many branching lines that shows how several things are related to each other 树形图；家谱图 —see also 另见 FAMILY TREE **3 be out of your tree** *informal* to not be thinking in a sensible or practical way【非正式】不理智的，傻里傻气的 —see also 另见 CHRISTMAS TREE, **the top of the tree** (TOP¹ (3)), **it doesn't grow on trees** (GROW (9)), **be up a gum tree** (GUM TREE (2))

tree fern /ˈ‥ ˌ/ *n* [C] a large tropical FERN 桫椤〔一种高大的热带木本蕨类植物〕

tree·house /ˋtrihaus; ˈtriːhaʊs/ *n* [C] a wooden structure built in the branches of a tree for children to play in〔供孩童玩的〕树上小屋

tree·less /ˋtriləs; ˈtriːləs/ *adj* a treeless area has no trees in it 无树木的

tree line /ˈ‥ ˌ/ *n* [singular] the TIMBERLINE 林木线

tree-lined /ˈ‥ ˌ/ *adj* a tree-lined road has trees on both sides〔道路两旁〕植有树木的

Tree of Know·ledge, the /ˌ‥ˈ‥/ according to a story in the Old Testament of the Bible, a tree in the Garden of Eden whose fruit Adam and Eve were forbidden by God to eat. When they disobeyed God and ate the fruit God forced them to leave the Garden of Eden. 智慧之树〔据《圣经·旧约》所述，上帝禁止亚当和夏娃食用伊甸园中智慧之树上的果实，但他们违背上帝的旨意，偷吃了树上的果实，于是上帝把他们赶出了伊甸园〕

tree sur·ge·ry /ˈ‥ˌ‥‥/ *n* [U] the treatment of damaged trees, especially by cutting off branches 树木整形（术），树木修补（术）

tree·top /ˋtritɑp; ˈtriːtɒp/ *n* [C usually plural 一般用复数] the branches at the top of a tree 树梢：*looking out over the treetops* 从树梢上方望出去

tree-trunk /ˈ‥ ˌ/ *n* [C] the thick central part of a tree 树干

tre·foil /ˋtrifɔɪl; ˈtriːfɔɪl/ *n* [C] **1** a type of small plant that has leaves which divide into three parts 三叶植物 **2** a pattern in the shape of these leaves 三叶形

trek¹ /trɛk; trek/ *v* **trekked, trekking** [I always+adv/prep] to make a long and difficult journey, especially on foot 艰苦跋涉〔尤指徒步长途旅行〕: [**+in/across etc**] *trekking in the Himalayas* 在喜马拉雅山地区的艰苦跋涉

trek² *n* [C] **1** a long and difficult journey especially on foot〔尤指徒步的〕长途艰苦旅行：*the long trek to the Pole* 前往极地的长途跋涉 **2** *informal* a distance that seems long when you walk it【非正式】〔显得很漫长的〕一段路程：*I'm afraid it's a bit of a trek to the station.* 到车站恐怕有一大段路程吧。

trel·lis /ˋtrɛlɪs; ˈtrelɪs/ *n* [C] a frame made of long narrow pieces of wood that cross each other, used to support climbing plants〔用以支撑攀缘植物的〕棚，架

trem·ble /ˋtrɛmbl; ˈtrembəl/ *v* [I] **1** to shake slightly in a way that you cannot control, especially because you are upset or frightened〔尤指因难受或受到惊吓而〕颤抖，发抖，战栗：*His lip started to tremble and then he started to cry.* 他的嘴唇开始颤抖，然后就哭了起来。| **tremble with anger/fear etc** *I stood there trembling with humiliation and rage.* 我站在那儿，因屈辱和愤怒而发抖。**2** to shake slightly〔轻微地〕摇晃，震颤：*The whole house trembled as the train went by.* 火车经过时，整座屋子都在震颤。**3** if your voice trembles, it sounds nervous and unsteady〔说话声〕紧张，发抖 **4** to be worried or frightened about something 焦虑，担忧；担惊受怕：**I tremble to think what/how** *I tremble to think what will happen when she finds out.* 一想到她发现真相后会发生的事，我就不寒而栗。—**tremble** *n* [C] —**trembly** *adj*

tre·men·dous /trɪˋmɛndəs; trɪˈmendəs/ *adj* **1** very big, fast, powerful etc 巨大的；极快的；强有力的：*a tremendous explosion* 猛烈的爆炸 | *I learned a tremendous amount in a short time.* 我在短时间内学到了大量东西。**2** excellent 极好的，特棒的：*She's got a tremendous voice, hasn't she?* 她有一副绝好的嗓子，不是吗？ 2

trem·o·lo /ˋtrɛməˌlo; ˈtreməlәʊ/ *n* [C] rapidly repeated musical notes〔音乐中的〕颤音，震音

trem·or /ˋtrɛmə; ˈtremə/ *n* [C] **1** a small EARTHQUAKE in which the ground shakes slightly〔大地的〕轻微震动：*an earth tremor* 小地震 **2** a slight shaking movement that you cannot control, especially because you are ill, weak, or upset〔尤指因生病、虚弱或激动而不能控制的〕颤抖，发抖：*He was left with a slight tremor in his hand after his stroke.* 中风之后，他的手有点轻微的颤抖。

trem·u·lous /ˋtrɛmjələs; ˈtremjʊləs/ *adj literary* shaking slightly, especially because you are nervous【文】〔尤指因紧张而〕颤抖的，微微发抖的：*a tremulous voice* 颤抖的嗓音 —**tremulously** *adv*

trench /trɛntʃ; trentʃ/ *n* [C] **1** a long narrow hole dug into the surface of the ground 壕沟，沟渠：*Plant your roses in a trench filled with manure.* 把玫瑰种植在填满肥料的沟里。**2** a deep trench dug in the ground as a protection for soldiers 战壕，堑壕：*the trenches of World War I* 第一次世界大战时的堑壕 **3** *technical* a long narrow valley in the ground beneath the sea【术语】海沟：*the Mariana Trench in the Pacific Ocean* 太平洋中的马里亚纳海沟

tren·chant /ˋtrɛntʃənt; ˈtrentʃənt/ *adj* expressed very strongly, effectively, and directly without worrying about offending people 尖锐的，尖刻的，直言不讳的：*a trenchant attack on the principle of 'political correctness'* 对"政治正确性"原则的尖锐抨击 —**trenchantly** *adv* —**trenchancy** *n* [U]

trench coat /ˈ‥ ˌ/ *n* [C] a military style raincoat with a belt〔有腰带的〕军用雨衣

CULTURAL NOTE 文化注释

Trench coats are often thought of in connection with PRIVATE DETECTIVES because many of them wear coats like this in books and films. 人们常把军用雨衣同私家侦探联系起来，因为在图书和影视中很多私家侦探穿着此类外衣。

trench·er /ˋtrɛntʃɚ; ˈtrentʃə/ *n* [C] a wooden plate used in former times for serving food〔旧时用来盛食物的〕木盘

trench war·fare /ˌ‥ˈ‥/ *n* [U] a method of fighting in which soldiers from opposing armies are in TRENCHes facing each other 堑壕战

trend /trɛnd; trend/ *n* [C] **1** a general tendency in the way a situation is changing or developing 趋势，趋向，倾向，动向：[**+in**] *recent trends in education* 教育的最新动向 | [**+towards**] *The current trend is towards more part-time employment.* 现行的趋 2 2

势是更多的人在兼职。| **reverse a trend** (=make a trend go in the opposite direction) 使趋势逆转，扭转趋势 *These figures reverse the trend of spending increases.* 这些数字表示开支增加的趋势得到了扭转。| **underlying trend** (=the trend over a long period of time) 基本趋势，长期趋势 **2 set the trend** to start doing something that other people copy 开创潮流: *'Rambo' set the trend for a whole wave of violent action movies.*《第一滴血》开创了暴力动作影片的新潮流。

trend·set·ter /ˈtrɛnd͵sɛtɚ; ˈtrend͵setə/ *n* [C] someone who starts a new fashion or makes it popular 开创新潮流的人；开创新风的人 —**trendsetting** *adj*

trend·y¹ /ˈtrɛndɪ; ˈtrendi/ *adj* influenced by the most fashionable styles and ideas 时尚的；受新潮思想影响的: *He's a trendy photographer in Santa Monica.* 他在圣莫尼卡工作，是个时尚的摄影师。—**trendily** *adv* —**trendiness** *n* [U]

trendy² *n* [C] *BrE informal* someone who is trendy because they want other people to think they are very modern【英，非正式】时尚人物；思想新潮的人: *young trendies with left-wing ideas* 有左翼思想的新潮年轻人

Trent, the /trɛnt; trent/ a river in the Midlands of England, flowing northeast into the Humber 特伦特河〔位于英格兰中部，流向东北注入亨伯河〕

Trenton /ˈtrɛntən; ˈtrentən/ the capital city of the US state of New Jersey 特伦顿〔美国新泽西州首府〕

tre·pan /trɪˈpæn; trɪˈpæn/ *v* [T] to cut a round piece of bone out of your SKULL (=head) as part of a medical operation 在〔颅骨〕施行环钻术〔即在颅骨上开圆形的洞，是一种外科手术〕

trep·i·da·tion /͵trɛpəˈdeʃən; ͵trepɪˈdeɪʃən/ *n* [U] a feeling of anxiety or fear about something that is going to happen 恐惧不安，惴惴不安: *With some trepidation, I opened the door.* 我有些惴惴不安地打开了门。

tres·pass¹ /ˈtrɛspəs; ˈtrespəs/ *v* [I+on] **1** to go onto someone's private land without their permission 未经许可进入私人宅地，擅自进入 **2** *old use* to do something wrong; SIN² 【旧】做坏事 —**trespasser** *n* [C]

trespass on sth *phr v* [T] to unfairly use more than you should of someone else's time, help etc, for your own advantage 过多占用〔别人的时间〕；过多利用〔别人的帮助〕: *It would be trespassing on their hospitality to accept any more from them.* 要是再接受他们的款待，就太过意不去了。

trespass² *n* **1** [C,U] the offence of going onto someone's land without their permission 擅自进入私人宅地，非法进入: *prosecute him for trespass* 起诉他擅入禁地 **2** [C] *biblical* something you have done that is morally wrong; SIN【圣经】过错，罪过

tress·es /ˈtrɛsɪz; ˈtresɪz/ *n* [plural] *literary* a woman's beautiful long hair【文】〔女人的〕漂亮长发

tres·tle /ˈtrɛsl; ˈtresəl/ *n* [C] *especially BrE* an A-shaped frame used as one of the two supports for a temporary table【尤英】〔用来支撑临时性桌面的〕支架，搁凳

trestle ta·ble /ˈ·· ͵··/ *n* [C] *especially BrE* a temporary table made of a long board supported on trestles【尤英】〔临时性的〕搁板桌

Trevi Fountain /ˈtrevi ͵faʊntn; ˈtreɪvi ͵faʊntɪn/ an 18th century FOUNTAIN in Rome, Italy. There is a saying that if you throw a coin over your shoulder into the fountain, you will be sure to return. 特雷维喷泉，许愿泉〔18世纪意大利罗马市内一喷泉。罗马人有一个传说，如果你掷过肩膀向水池里投一枚硬币，你准会有机会再次造访罗马〕

Tre·vith·ick /trɪˈvɪθɪk; trɪˈvɪθɪk/, **Richard** (1771-1833) a British engineer who invented a new type of steam engine, which was used in 1804 in the first train ever built 特里维西克〔(1771-1833)，英国工程师。他发明了一种新型蒸汽机车，1804年用于世界首列火车〕

trews /truz; truːz/ *n* [plural] a pair of trousers, especially with a TARTAN pattern 裤子〔尤指有苏格兰格子花呢图案的裤子〕

trey /tre; treɪ/ *n* [C] *AmE* a playing card or the side of a DICE with three marks on it【美】三点的纸牌；〔骰子〕刻有三点的一面: *I have two pairs, treys and sevens.* 我有两对牌，一对三点和一对七点。

tri- /traɪ; traɪ/ *prefix* three; three times〔表示"三"，"三次"，"三倍"〕: *trilingual* (=speaking three languages) 说三门语言的 | *triangle* (=a shape with three sides) 三角形

tri·ad /ˈtraɪæd; ˈtraɪæd/ *n* [C] **1** [singular] a Chinese secret criminal group 三合会〔华人黑社会组织〕 **2** a group of three people or things that are related or similar to each other 三人组合；三种事物的组合

S3 W2 **tri·al¹** /ˈtraɪəl; ˈtraɪəl/ *n*

1 ►COURT 法庭◄ [C,U] a legal process in which a court of law examines a case to decide whether someone is guilty of a crime 审判，审理: *a murder trial* 一宗谋杀案的审判 | *The defendant has a right to a fair trial.* 被告有权利得到公正的审判。| **stand trial/be on trial (for)** (=be judged in a court of law) 接受审判/因…受到审判 *Brady was on trial for assault.* 布雷迪因袭击他人而受到审判。| *a bank employee who is due to stand trial on embezzlement charges* 因被控侵吞公款而将受到审判的一名银行职员 | **come to trial** *formal* (=when a case is brought to a court of law)【正式】提交法庭审判 *By the time the case comes to trial he will have spent a year behind bars.* 到这个案子提交法庭审判时，他将已经在监狱里待上一年了。—see also 另见 SHOW TRIAL

2 ►TEST 试验◄ [C,U] **a)** a process of testing to find out whether something works effectively and is safe 试验，试用: *a new drug that is undergoing clinical trials* 正在接受临床试验的一种新药 **b)** a short period during which you use something or employ someone to find out whether they are satisfactory for a particular purpose or job 试验期，试用期: **take/have sth on trial** (=test something without having to buy it first) 把某物拿来试用 *Take the vacuum cleaner on trial for a week; if you don't like it you pay nothing.* 把那个真空吸尘器拿去试用一周；你如果不满意的话，不必付钱。| **trial period** *The security system will be reviewed after a three-month trial period.* 这套安全系统在经过三个月试用期后将进行复查。

3 by trial and error if you do something by trial and error, you test many different methods of doing something in order to find the best 反复试验〔以得出最佳效果〕: *You'll find out by trial and error which flowers grow best.* 你通过反复试验就会发现哪些花长得最好。

4 ►WORRY/ANNOY 焦虑/厌烦◄ be a trial (to) to be very worrying or annoying to someone〔令某人〕焦虑[厌烦]: *My brothers and I were always a real trial to my parents.* 我们几兄弟总是让父母心烦。

5 trials and tribulations difficulties and troubles 艰难困苦: *After many trials and tribulations we reached our destination.* 历经艰难困苦后我们终于到达了目的地。

6 ►SPORTS 体育运动◄ trials [plural] *BrE* a sports competition that tests a player's ability【英】预赛，选拔赛

trial² *v* [T] to thoroughly test something to see if it works correctly or is effective〔全面彻底地〕测试，试验，试用: *These techniques were trialled by teachers in 300 schools.* 教师们在300所学校里试用过这些技巧。

trial run /͵·· ˈ·/ *n* [C] an occasion when you test a new method or system to see if it works well 试行；试验；试车；试航: *This year is something of a trial run for the new service.* 今年可以说是新的服务项目的试行年。

trials bike /ˈ·· ·/ *n* [C] *BrE* a type of MOTORCYCLE that you can ride on very rough ground【英】〔可以在非常崎岖不平的路面上行驶的〕越野摩托车

tri·an·gle /ˈtraɪ͵æŋgl; ˈtraɪæŋgəl/ *n* [C] **1** a flat shape with three straight sides and three angles 三角形 —see picture at 参见 SHAPE¹ 图 **2** something that is shaped like a triangle 三角形物体: *a triangle of land* 一块三角地 **3** a musical instrument made of metal bent in the shape of a triangle, that you hit to make a ringing sound 三角铁〔一种打击乐器〕 **4** *AmE* a flat plastic object with three sides that has one angle of 90° and is used for drawing angles【美】〔直角〕三角板，三角尺; SET-SQUARE *BrE*【英】

tri·an·gu·lar /traɪˈæŋgjəlɚ; traɪˈæŋgjʊlə/ *adj* **1** shaped like a triangle 三角形的 **2** involving three people or teams 三者之间的: *a triangular sporting competition* 一次由三方参加的体育比赛

tri·an·gu·la·tion /͵traɪæŋgjəˈleʃən; traɪ͵æŋgjʊˈleɪʃən/ *n* [U] a method of finding your position by measuring the lines and angles of a triangle on a map 三角测量法

triangulation sta·tion /···ˈ·· ͵··/ *n* [C] *formal* a TRIG POINT【正式】三角测量点〔在山顶上通常用石块标志的一个点，用以测定你在地图上所处的位置〕

tri·ath·lon /traɪˈæθlən; traɪˈæθlən/ *n* [C] a sports competition in which competitors run, swim, and cycle long distances 三项全能运动〔赛跑、游泳、自行车〕

trib·al /ˈtraɪbl; ˈtraɪbəl/ *adj* connected with a tribe or tribes 部落的: *a tribal dance* 部落舞蹈 | *tribal warfare* 部落战争

trib·al·is·m /ˈtraɪbl͵ɪzm; ˈtraɪbəl-ɪzəm/ *n* [U] **1** the state of being organized into tribes 部落制度 **2** behaviour and attitudes that are based on strong loyalty to your tribe 部落意识[习性]

tribe /traɪb; traɪb/ *n* [C] **1** a social group consisting of people of the same race who have the same beliefs, customs, language etc, and usually live in one particular area ruled by a chief 部落，部落社会: *the tribes living in the Amazonian jungle* 生活在

亚马孙热带丛林里的部落 —see 见 RACE[1] (USAGE) **2** a group of related animals or plants 族, 群〔动植物的一类〕: *the cat tribe* 猫族 **3** *humorous* a large family【幽默】大家庭: *We were only expecting Jack and his wife, but the whole tribe turned up.* 我们只想着杰克和他的妻子会来，但结果是全家大小都来了。

tribes·man /ˈtraɪbzmən; ˈtraɪbzmən/ *n* [C] a man who is a member of a tribe 部落男性成员

tribes·wom·an /ˈtraɪbzˌwumən; ˈtraɪbzˌwumən/ *n* [C] a woman who is a member of a tribe 部落女性成员

trib·u·la·tion /ˌtrɪbjəˈleʃən; ˌtrɪbjʊˈleɪʃən/ *n* [C,U] *formal* serious trouble or a serious problem【正式】苦难, 艰难: *the tribulations of his personal life* 他个人生活中的种种艰辛 —see also 另见 **trials and tribulations** (TRIAL[1] (5))

tri·bu·nal /trɪˈbjunl; traɪˈbjuːnl/ *n* [C] a type of court that is given official authority to deal with a particular situation or problem 特别法庭; 审理委员会: *The case of your redundancy will be heard by an independent tribunal.* 一个独立的审理委员会将审理有关你们裁员的案子。

trib·une /ˈtrɪbjun; ˈtrɪbjuːn/ *n* [C] an official in ancient Rome who was elected by the ordinary people to protect their rights〔古罗马由普通人民选出的〕护民官, 保民官

trib·u·ta·ry[1] /ˈtrɪbjəˌtɛrɪ; ˈtrɪbjʊtəri/ *n* [C] a stream or river that flows into a larger river〔河流的〕支流

tributary[2] *adj formal* having a duty to pay TRIBUTE (3)【正式】需交纳贡赋的

trib·ute /ˈtrɪbjut; ˈtrɪbjuːt/ *n* **1** something that you say, do, or give in order to express your respect or admiration for someone〔向某人表示敬慕而献出的〕礼品, 赠品; 颂词: **pay tribute to** (=praise and thank someone publicly) 公开赞扬和感谢 *I'd like to pay tribute to the party workers for all their hard work.* 我谨对党内工作人员的辛苦工作表示赞扬和感谢。**2 be a tribute to** to be a clear sign of the good qualities that someone or something has〔某种优良品质的〕标示, 证明: *It was a tribute to her teaching methods that so many children passed the test.* 这么多孩子通过了考试, 这就是对她的教学方法的一种证明。**3** [C,U] a payment of goods or money by one ruler or country to another more powerful one〔一国向强国交付的〕贡品, 贡赋, 贡金 **4 floral tribute** flowers sent to a funeral 敬献给葬礼的鲜花

trice /traɪs; traɪs/ *n* **in a trice** *BrE literary* very quickly【英, 文】一刹那, 瞬间

tri·ceps /ˈtraɪsɛps; ˈtraɪseps/ *n* [C] the large muscle at the back of your upper arm〔手臂上的〕三头肌

3 **trick[1]** /trɪk; trɪk/ *n* [C]

1 ▶DECEIVING SB 欺骗某人◀ something you do in order to deceive someone 骗局, 花招, 诡计: *He pretended to be ill, but it was just a trick.* 他假装生病了, 不过那只是一个花招。| *a clever trick to cheat the authorities* 欺骗当局的诡计

2 dirty/rotten/mean trick an unkind or unfair thing to do 下流的/无耻的/卑鄙的诡计: *He didn't turn up? What a rotten trick!* 他没有露面? 多么无耻的诡计!

3 ▶JOKE 玩笑◀ something you do to surprise someone and to make other people laugh 恶作剧: *I'm getting tired of your silly tricks.* 我对你那些愚蠢的恶作剧感到厌烦了。| **play a trick on sb** *The girls were always playing tricks on their teacher.* 这些女孩子总是捉弄她们的老师。

4 do the trick *spoken* if something does the trick it solves a problem or provides what is needed to get a good result【口】奏效, 达到预期效果: *A bit more flour should do the trick.* 再来一点面粉应该就可以了。

5 ▶CLEVER METHOD 巧妙办法◀ a clever way of doing something that works very well 诀窍; 技巧, 技法: *The trick is to bend your knees as you catch the ball.* 诀窍是接球时要屈膝。| **tricks of the trade** (=clever methods used in a particular job) 某一行工作的诀窍 *a salesman who knew all the tricks of the trade* 一个对本行业诀窍全都通晓的推销员

6 use every trick in the book to use every clever or dishonest method that you know to achieve what you want 使出各种绝招, 使出浑身解数: *Ed used every trick in the book to get that contract.* 埃德使出浑身解数想要得到那份合同。

7 sb can teach/show you a trick or two *informal* used to say that someone knows a lot more than you【非正式】某人可以教你一两招, 某人比你懂得多

8 be up to your (old) tricks *informal* to be doing the same dishonest things that you have often done before【非正式】耍(老)花招: *Watch out for Joe, he's up to his old tricks again.* 小心乔, 他又要耍老花招了。

9 ▶MAGIC 魔术◀ a skilful set of actions that seem like magic, done to entertain people 戏法, 把戏: *We spent the next hour performing card tricks.* 我们在接下来的一个小时里表演纸牌戏法。

10 a trick of the light a strange effect of the light that changes the way things look or makes you see something that is not really there 灯光引起的错觉: *For a moment I thought you were Duncan, but it was just a trick of the light.* 有那么一会儿, 我以为你就是邓肯, 不过那只是灯光在捉弄人罢了。

11 ▶CARDS 纸牌◀ the cards played or won in one part of a game of cards〔纸牌游戏中出的或赢的〕一圈牌, 一墩牌: *He won the first three tricks easily.* 他轻松地赢了头三圈牌。

12 ▶HABIT 习惯◀ have a trick of doing sth to have a habit of using a particular expression or of moving your face or body in a particular way 有〔使用某句口头禅或以特别的方式活动脸部或身体〕的习惯: *She had this trick of raising her eyebrows at the end of a question.* 她有一个习惯, 在提问结束时总要扬起眉头。

13 never miss a trick *informal* to always know exactly what is happening even if it does not concern you【非正式】对所发生的事无所不晓; 了如指掌: *Dave's found out. He never misses a trick, does he?* 戴夫已经知道了。他从不漏过一点东西, 是吗?

14 how's tricks? *spoken* used to greet someone in a friendly way【口】近来如何?〔寒暄语〕: *Hello Bill! How's tricks?* 你好, 比尔! 近来怎么样?

15 turn a trick *AmE slang* to have sex with someone for money【美俚】卖淫 —see also 另见 CONFIDENCE TRICK, HAT-TRICK

trick[2] *v* **1** [T] to deceive someone in order to get something from them or to make them do something 欺骗, 诱骗, 哄骗: *He knew he'd been tricked, but it was too late.* 他知道自己被骗了, 但为时已晚。| **trick sb into doing sth** *Clients were tricked into believing their money was being invested.* 客户们被骗了, 以为他们的钱正用于投资。| **trick sb out of** *The corporation was tricked out of $20 million.* 那家公司被骗走了2000万美元。**2 be tricked out with/in** *literary* to be decorated with something【文】装饰, 打扮: *a hat tricked out with ribbons* 一顶用缎带作装饰的帽子

trick[3] *adj* **1 trick photography** photography that cleverly changes the way things look 特技摄影 **2 trick question** a question which seems easy to answer but has a hidden difficulty 看似容易其实困难的问题 **3 trick knee/ankle etc** *AmE* a joint that is weak and can suddenly cause you problems【美】软弱无力而突然撑不住的膝关节/脚踝骨等

trick·e·ry /ˈtrɪkərɪ; ˈtrɪkəri/ *n* [U] the use of tricks to deceive or cheat people 耍花招, 欺骗, 哄骗

trick·le[1] /ˈtrɪkl; ˈtrɪkəl/ *v* [I always+adv/prep] **1** if liquid trickles somewhere, it flows slowly in drops or in a thin stream 滴, 淌; 涓涓地慢流: [**+down/into/out**] *The tears trickled down her cheeks.* 泪水一滴一滴地从她面颊上流下。**2** if people, vehicles, goods etc trickle somewhere, they move there slowly in small groups or amounts〔人、车辆、货物等〕缓慢而零星地移动: [**+in/into/away**] *The first few fans started to trickle into the stadium.* 最早到达的几位球迷开始三三两两地走进体育场。

trickle[2] *n* [singular] **1** a thin slow flow of liquid 涓涓细流: *The water in the stream had been reduced to a trickle.* 溪流中的水已减少成涓涓细流了。**2** a movement of people, vehicles, goods etc into a place in very small numbers or amounts 小批的移动, 少量的流动: *Recent legislation has reduced immigration to a trickle.* 最近的立法已使移民减少到很小数量。

trickle charg·er /ˈ· · ˌ· ·/ *n* [C] a piece of equipment used to put electricity into a car BATTERY (1)〔汽车蓄电池的〕点滴式充电器, 连续补允充电器

trickle-down ef·fect /ˌ· · ˈ· · ˌ·/ *n* [singular] a belief that additional wealth gained by the richest people in society will have a good economic effect on the lives of everyone 滴入效应〔一种认为社会中最富有的一批人获得的额外财富会对每一个人的生活产生良好经济效应的理论〕

trick or treat /ˌ· · ˈ·/ *v* **go trick or treating** if children go trick or treating, they go from house to house on HALLOWE'EN saying 'trick or treat' in order to get small presents "不请吃就捣蛋"〔万圣节前夕孩子们挨家逐户索要小礼物时说的话〕

trick·ster /ˈtrɪkstə; ˈtrɪkstə/ *n* [C] someone who deceives or cheats people 骗子: **confidence trickster** *a slick, fast-talking confidence trickster* 一个花言巧语、口若悬河、欺诈钱财的骗子

trick·y /ˈtrɪkɪ; ˈtrɪki/ *adj* **1** a tricky job is difficult to do because it is complicated and needs great care 困难的; 复杂的; 需慎重对待的: *Finding the electrical fault was really tricky.* 查找电路故障真是复杂, 需要谨慎。**2** a tricky situation is difficult to deal with and is full of problems 难对付的, 棘手的; 问题很多的: *I find myself in a very tricky situation.* 我发觉自己处境十分难堪。**3** a tricky person is likely to deceive you; CRAFTY 狡猾的; 会耍花招的, 诡计多端的 —**trickiness** *n* [U] —**trickily** *adv* 3

tri·col·our *BrE*【英】, **tricolor** *AmE*【美】/ˈtraɪˌkʌlə; ˈtrɪkələ/ *n* [C] a flag with three equal bands of different colours, especially the national flags of France or Ireland 三色旗〔有三条宽度相等的色带的旗, 尤指法国或爱尔兰的国旗〕

tri·cy·cle /ˈtraɪsɪkl; ˈtraɪsɪkəl/ *n* [C] a bicycle with three wheels, especially for young children〔尤指幼儿骑的〕三轮自行车[脚踏车]

Trident[1] *trademark* a powerful type of NUCLEAR MISSILE developed in the US. It is fired from SUBMARINES, and can attack several different places at the same time.【商标】三叉戟导弹〔美国一种威力强大的核导弹。该导弹从潜艇上发射, 可同时攻击若干不同目标〕

Trident[2] *trademark* a type of CHEWING GUM without any sugar in it, sold in the US【商标】三圣果口香糖〔美国销售的一种无糖口香糖〕

tri·dent /ˈtraɪdn̩t; ˈtraɪdənt/ *n* [C] a weapon with three points that looks like a large fork 三叉戟〔一种武器〕

tried[1] /traɪd; traɪd/ the past tense and past participle of TRY[1]

tried[2] *adj* **tried and tested/trusted** a tried and tested method has been used successfully many times 经实践反复证明的, 屡试不爽的: *tried and tested safety procedures* 经实践反复证明的安全守则 | *a tried and trusted formula* 一个屡试不爽的公式

tri·en·ni·al /traɪˋɛnɪəl; traɪˈeniəl/ *adj* happening every three years 三年一次的

tri·er /ˈtraɪə; ˈtraɪə/ *n* [C] *informal* someone who always makes a great effort, even if they do not often succeed【非正式】〔不计成败〕尽心竭力[埋头苦干]的人

trif·fid /ˈtrɪfɪd; ˈtrɪfɪ̣d/ *n* [C] an imaginary plant that grows very large, moves about, and attacks people 巨型三裂植物〔想象中的一种植物, 能到处行走, 攻击人类〕

tri·fle[1] /ˈtraɪfl; ˈtraɪfəl/ *n* **1 a trifle** *formal* slightly; rather【正式】有点儿, 稍稍: *You seem a trifle nervous.* 你似乎有点儿紧张。**2** [C] *old-fashioned* something unimportant or not valuable【过时】琐碎事; 无价值的东西: *I don't know why you waste your money on such trifles.* 我不明白你为什么把钱浪费在这种无价值的东西上。**3** [C,U] a cold sweet dish that consists of layers of cake, fruit, JELLY (1), CUSTARD (1), and cream 蛋糕甜食〔一种由蛋糕、水果、果冻、牛奶蛋糊、奶油等层层制成的冷甜食〕

trifle[2] *v*

trifle with sb/sth *phr v* [T] to treat someone or something without proper respect or seriousness 轻视, 小看; 随便对待: *The boss is not a man to be trifled with.* 这位老板不是一个可以小看的人。

tri·fling /ˈtraɪflɪŋ; ˈtraɪflɪŋ/ *adj* unimportant or of little value 不重要的, 微不足道的: *a trifling matter* 小事 | *a trifling sum* 一小笔钱

trig·ger[1] /ˈtrɪgə; ˈtrɪgə/ *n* [C] **1** the part of a gun that you press with your finger to fire it〔枪的〕扳机 | **pull/squeeze the trigger** *He aimed carefully and squeezed the trigger.* 他仔细地瞄准, 然后扣动了扳机。—see picture at 参见 GUN[1] 图 **2 be the trigger (for)** to be the thing that quickly causes a serious problem 成为引发〔严重问题〕的因素: *Even a minor incident could be the trigger for renewed fighting.* 即便是一件小事, 也有可能成为重新开战的导火线。

trigger[2] also 又作 **trigger off** *v* [T] to make something happen very quickly, especially a series of violent events 引发, 激发〔尤指一系列暴力事件〕: *The assassination triggered off a wave of rioting.* 这次暗杀事件引发了一轮暴乱。| **trigger a feeling/memory** (=make you suddenly feel or remember something) 使人突然觉得/突然记起 *The song triggered many happy memories.* 那首歌勾起许多幸福的回忆。

trigger-hap·py /ˈ‥ ˌ‥/ *adj informal* much too willing to shoot at people【非正式】随便就开枪的: *He nearly got shot by some trigger-happy cop.* 他差点被某个乱开枪的警察射中。

trig·o·nom·e·try /ˌtrɪgəˋnɑmətrɪ; ˌtrɪgəˈnɒmɪ̣tri/ *n* [U] the part of mathematics that is concerned with the relationship between the angles and sides of TRIANGLES〔数学中的〕三角学 —**trigonometrical** /ˌtrɪgənəˋmɛtrɪkl; ˌtrɪgənəˈmetrɪkəl/ *adj*

trig point /ˈtrɪg ˌpɔɪnt; ˈtrɪg pɔɪnt/ *n* [C] *BrE* a point often marked by a stone block on top of a hill, used for measuring your position on a map【英】三角点〔在山顶上通常用石块标志的一个点, 用以测定你在地图上所处的位置〕

trike /traɪk; traɪk/ *n* [C] *informal* a TRICYCLE【非正式】三轮自行车

tril·by /ˈtrɪlbɪ; ˈtrɪlbi/ *n* [C] *especially BrE* a man's soft FELT[2] hat【尤英】〔一种男人戴的〕软毡帽

tri·lin·gual /traɪˋlɪŋgwəl; ˌtraɪˈlɪŋgwəl◂/ *adj* able to speak or use three languages 会三种语言的

trill[1] /trɪl; trɪl/ *v* [I,T] **1** to sing with repeated short high notes 用颤音唱; 发出颤音: *birds trilling in the trees* 在树上啭鸣的鸟 **2** to say something in a pleasant high cheerful voice 以悦耳欢乐的高嗓音说话: *"Have a nice time, darling," she trilled.* "玩得开心点, 亲爱的。"她欢快地高声叫道。

trill[2] *n* [C] **1** *technical* a musical sound made by quickly going up and down several times between two notes a SEMITONE apart【术语】〔音乐的〕颤音 **2** a sound like this, especially one made by a bird〔尤指鸟的〕啭鸣声, 啼啭声 **3** *technical* a speech sound produced by quickly moving the end of your tongue against the top part of your mouth when you say 'r'【术语】〔发 r 音时发出的〕颤音

tril·lion /ˈtrɪljən; ˈtrɪljən/ *number, quantifier* **1** one million million; 1,000,000,000,000 一万亿 **2** also 又作 **trillions** *informal* a very large number of something【非正式】大量, 巨额

tri·lo·bite /ˈtraɪləˌbaɪt; ˈtraɪləbaɪt/ *n* [C] a small simple sea creature that lived millions of years ago and is now a FOSSIL (1) 三叶虫〔一种生活于海洋的古生物〕

tril·o·gy /ˈtrɪlədʒɪ; ˈtrɪlədʒi/ *n* [C] a group of three connected plays, books, films etc about the same characters〔戏剧、图书、电影等的〕三部曲: *the second part of a trilogy* 三部曲中的第二部

trim[1] /trɪm; trɪm/ **trimmed, trimming** *v* [T]

1 ▶CUT 剪◀ to make something look neater by cutting small pieces off it 修剪: *Your hair needs trimming.* 你的头发需要修剪了。| *Can you trim the hedge?* 你能修剪一下树篱吗?

2 ▶REDUCE 减少◀ to remove parts of a plan to reduce its cost 削减: *We need to trim the Defence budget by a further £500m.* 我们有必要把国防预算再削减 5 亿英镑。

3 ▶DECORATE 装饰◀ [usually passive 一般用被动态] to decorate the edges of clothes by adding a piece of different material 装饰, 点缀〔衣服的边缘部分〕: **trim sth with** *a dress trimmed with lace* 饰有花边的连衣裙

4 ▶SAIL 航行◀ to move the sails of a boat into a position that makes the boat go faster 调整船帆使航行加快

5 trim your sails *informal* to spend less money【非正式】减少开支

trim sth **↔ off** *phr v* [T] to cut small pieces off something so that it looks neater 去掉〔细碎部分, 使之更整齐〕: *Trim off the ragged edges.* 剪去不整齐的边缘。

trim[2] *adj* **1** thin, attractive, and healthy looking 修长的, 健康好看的: *I play tennis regularly to keep trim.* 我定期打网球, 以保持体形。| *a trim figure* 匀称的身材 **2** neat and well looked after 整齐的, 整洁的: *a trim suburban garden* 整洁的郊区花园

trim[3] *n* **1** [singular] an act of cutting something to make it look neater 修剪: *My beard needs a trim.* 我的胡子需要修剪了。**2 be in (good) trim** *informal* to be in good physical condition【非正式】处于良好状态: *The team is in good trim for the match.* 球队为这场比赛已做好了准备。**3** [singular, U] additional decoration on a car, piece of clothing etc〔汽车等的〕额外装饰: *1983 Ford Escort, metallic black with white trim* 一辆配以白色饰边的 1983 年产黑色福特"护卫"车 **4** [U] the degree to which an aircraft is level in relation to the horizon 配平〔飞机相对于地平线的倾斜度〕

tri·ma·ran /ˌtraɪməˋræn; ˈtraɪməræn/ *n* [C] a sailing boat that has three separate but connected parts that float on the water 三体帆船

Trim·ble /ˈtrɪmbl̩; ˈtrɪmbəl/, **David** (1944-) a British politician who is leader of the Ulster Unionist Party, a political party in Northern Ireland which is supported mostly by Protestants and believes strongly that Northern Ireland should remain part of the UK. He had an important part in attempts to bring peace to Northern Ireland. In 1998 he became First Minister in the new Northern Ireland assembly (parliament) and shared the Nobel Prize for peace with John Hume. 特林布尔〔(1944-), 英国政治家、北爱尔兰统一党领袖。该党的主要支持者是新教徒, 他们坚信北爱尔兰应继续留在英国。特林布尔在北爱尔兰和平进程中具有重要作用。1998 年, 他成为新建的北爱尔兰议会的首席大臣, 并与约翰·休姆一起荣获诺贝尔和平奖〕

tri·mes·ter /traɪˋmɛstə; trɪˈmestə/ *n* [C] **1** *AmE* one of three periods of equal length that the year is divided into in some schools【美】〔有些学校实行的一年三学期制的〕一学期; TERM[1] (9) *BrE*【英】**2** one of the three-month periods of a PREGNANCY 三月期〔怀孕的三个为期三个月的阶段之一〕

trim·mer /ˈtrɪmə; ˈtrɪmə/ *n* [C] a machine for cutting the edges of HEDGES, LAWNS etc 修剪器; 剪草机

trim·mings /ˈtrɪmɪŋz; ˈtrɪmɪŋz/ *n* [plural] **1** pieces of material used to decorate clothes〔衣服的〕装饰品, 花饰: *the fur trimmings on a hat* 帽子上的毛皮装饰品 **2** the small pieces that are

T

left after you have cut something larger 剪下来的细小碎片: *hedge trimmings* 从树篱上修剪下来的细枝碎叶 **3 all the trimmings** *BrE informal* all the other types of food that are traditionally served with the main dish of a meal【英, 非正式】〔主菜的〕全部配菜: *Christmas dinner with all the trimmings* 有各种配菜的圣诞晚餐

Trin·i·dad and To·ba·go /ˈtrɪnəˌdæd ənd təˈbego; ˌtrɪnɪdæd ənd təˈbeɪgəʊ/ a country consisting of the islands of Trinidad and Tobago in the south Caribbean Sea, close to the coast of Venezuela. Population: 1,170,000 (2001). Capital: Port of Spain. 特立尼达和多巴哥〔南加勒比海一国家, 靠近委内瑞拉海岸, 由特立尼达岛和多巴哥岛组成。人口: 1,170,000 (2001), 首都: 西班牙港〕

trin·i·ty /ˈtrɪnətɪ; ˈtrɪnɪti/ *n* **1 the Trinity** the union of Father, Son, and Holy Spirit in one God according to the Christian religion〔基督教关于圣父、圣子、圣灵合一的〕三位一体 **2** [C] *literary* a group of three people or things【文】三人一组; 三件东西一组; 三合一

Trinity House /ˌ··· ˈ·/ a British organization that provides LIGHTHOUSEs and LIGHTSHIPs around the coast of the UK 三一领港服务公司〔英国一机构, 为沿海地区提供灯塔及灯塔船〕

Trinity term /ˈ··· ˌ·/ the name given to the SUMMER TERM (=one of the three periods that the school year is divided into) in some British schools and universities〔英国某些中小学和大学的〕夏季学期

trin·ket /ˈtrɪŋkɪt; ˈtrɪŋkɪt/ *n* [C] a piece of jewellery or a small pretty object that is not worth much money 廉价珠宝; 小件饰物: *a shop selling little trinkets and souvenirs* 一家销售小件饰物和纪念品的商店

tri·o /ˈtrio; ˈtriːəʊ/ *n plural* **trios** [C] **1** a group of three people or three connected things 三人一组; 三件一套: **[+of]** *He was met by a trio of smiling executives.* 迎接他的是三位面带笑容的主管。**2** a group of three singers or musicians who perform together 三重唱[奏]团 **3** a piece of music for three performers 三重唱(曲); 三重奏(曲) —compare 比较 DUET, QUARTET

2 2 **trip**[1] /trɪp; trɪp/ *n* **1** [C] a journey to a place and back again〔往返〕旅行, 外出: *Did you have a good trip?* 你外出一趟还好吗? | **make a trip** *I couldn't carry everything at once, so I had to make several trips.* 我不能一次就扛走所有的东西, 所以不得不来回跑几趟。| **go on/take a trip** *We're thinking of taking a trip to the mountains.* 我们正在考虑去山里旅行一趟。| **coach/boat trip** *a boat trip up the Thames* 沿泰晤士河而上的一次乘船旅行 | **business/school/skiing etc trip** *a business trip to Japan* 去日本出差 | **day trip** (=a pleasure trip done in one day) 一日游 —see 见 TRAVEL (USAGE) **2** [C] *slang* the experiences someone has while their mind is affected by a drug such as LSD【俚】〔吸毒时经历的〕幻觉: *a bad trip* 不舒服的一阵迷幻感觉 **3** [C] an act of falling as a result of hitting something with your foot 绊倒 **4** [singular] *AmE slang* a person or experience that is amusing and very different from normal【美俚】让人开心的奇人; 奇妙有趣的体验: *She's a real trip.* 她真是个开心果。—see also 另见 **ego trip** (EGO (2)), ROUND TRIP

trip[2] *v*

1 ►FALL 倒下◄ also 又作 **trip up** [I] to hit something with your foot while you are walking or running so that you fall or almost fall 绊倒: *I didn't push him, he tripped.* 我没有推他, 他自己绊倒的。| **[+over]** *Pick up that box or someone will trip over it.* 把那个箱子捡起来, 不然会把人绊倒的。

2 ►MAKE SB FALL 使某人倒下◄ also 又作 **trip sb up** [T] to make someone fall by putting your foot in front of them when they are moving 把〔某人〕绊倒: *Baggio was clearly tripped inside the penalty area.* 巴乔在禁区里很明显是被人绊倒的。

3 ►WALK/DANCE 走路/跳舞◄ [I always+adv/prep] *literary* to walk or run with quick light steps as if you are dancing【文】轻快地走; 小跑: **trip along/over/down etc** *a little girl tripping along the lane* 轻快地沿着小巷走的小姑娘

4 trip off the tongue to be easy to say or pronounce 很容易说出[发音]: *Monofluorophosphate! It doesn't exactly trip off the tongue, does it?* 单氟磷酸盐! 不容易上口, 是吗?

5 trip a switch/wire to accidentally make an electrical system operate by moving part of it〔偶然地〕触动开关/电线: *Alarm bells were ringing so I must have tripped a switch on my way in.* 警铃都响起来了, 所以一定是我在进来的时候不小心触动了开关。

6 ►DRUG 毒品◄ also 又作 **trip out** [I] *slang* to experience the effects of an illegal drug such as LSD【俚】〔服用迷幻药等后〕产生幻觉

7 trip the light fantastic *humorous* to dance【幽默】跳舞

trip up *phr v* **1** [T **trip** sb **up**] to trick someone into making a mistake 使〔某人〕犯错误: *The questions look simple, but they're designed to trip you up.* 这些问题看上去很简单, 但其用意就是为了迷惑人。**2** [T **trip** sb **up**] to make someone fall by putting your foot in front of them when they are walking 使〔某人〕绊倒 **3** [I] to hit something with your foot while you are walking so that you fall 绊倒 **4** [I] to make a mistake 犯错误, 出差错: **[+over]** *It's easy to trip up over some of the regulations.* 很容易在一些规定上出差错。

tri·par·tite /traɪˈpɑrtaɪt; traɪˈpɑːtaɪt/ *adj formal*【正式】**1 tripartite agreement/alliance etc** involving three groups or nations 三方之间的协定/联盟等 **2** having three parts 由三部分组成的: *a tripartite structure* 由三部分组成的结构

tripe /traɪp; traɪp/ *n* [U] **1** the stomach of a cow or pig used for food〔供食用的〕牛肚; 猪肚 **2** *informal* something that has been said or written which is stupid or untrue【非正式】瞎说[瞎写]的东西; 废话, 蠢话: *Why do you read such tripe?* 你为什么看这种蹩脚的东西?

trip·le[1] /ˈtrɪpl; ˈtrɪpəl/ *adj* [only before noun 仅用于名词前] **1** having three parts or involving three members 有三部分的, 有三个成员的: *a triple alliance* 三方同盟 **2 triple circle/line/coil etc** a set of three circles etc 三重圆/线/圈等 **3 triple murder/killing etc** the murder etc of three people 三重谋杀/杀害等

triple[2] *v* [I,T] to become three times as much or as many, or to make something do this (使)成为三倍, 增加两倍: *The company has tripled in size in the last twenty years.* 在最近20年里, 该公司在规模上已扩大了两倍。| **triple sth** *We should triple our profits next year.* 我们明年应该使利润增长两倍。

triple[3] *n* [C] a hit of the ball in BASEBALL that allows the BATTER[2] (3) to get to the third BASE[2] (8)〔棒球中的〕三垒打

Triple Crown, the /ˌ··· ˈ·/ a title for winning all three of a set of important events in various sports. In British horse racing, it is especially for winning the St Leger, the Derby, and the Two Thousand Guineas. In US horse racing, it is especially for winning the Preakness, the Belmont Stakes, and the Kentucky Derby. In Rugby Union, the Triple Crown is for beating all three of the other home countries 三冠王〔授予各种体育项目的三项系列重要赛事冠军得主的称号。在英国, 尤指圣莱格赛、德比赛和二千几尼赛三次赛马冠军的得主。在美国, 尤指普利克内斯赛马、贝尔蒙特赛马大奖赛、肯塔吉德比赛马三项比赛冠军的得主。英式橄榄球的三冠王指在英格兰、苏格兰、威尔士和爱尔兰之间的比赛中击败其他三支球队的冠军队〕

triple jump /ˈ·· ·/ *n* [singular] an ATHLETICS event in which you try to jump as far as you can by jumping with one foot, then onto the other foot, and finally with both feet 三级跳远

trip·let /ˈtrɪplɪt; ˈtrɪplɪt/ *n* [C] one of three children born at the same time to the same mother 三胞胎中的一个 —compare 比较 COUPLET

trip·lex /ˈtrɪplɛks; ˈtrɪpleks/ *n* [C] *AmE* an apartment which has rooms on three floors of a building【美】三层一套式公寓

Triplex *n* [U] *BrE trademark* a special type of safety glass used in car windows【英, 商标】〔汽车窗户上的〕三层安全玻璃, 夹层玻璃

trip·li·cate /ˈtrɪpləˌket; ˈtrɪplɪkɪt/ *n* **in triplicate** if a document is written in triplicate, there are three copies of it〔文件的〕一式三份

tri·pod /ˈtraɪpɑd; ˈtraɪpɒd/ *n* [C] a support with three legs, used for a camera, TELESCOPE[1] etc〔照相机、望远镜等的〕三脚架 —see picture at 参见 LABORATORY 图

Trip·ol·i /ˈtrɪpəlɪ; ˈtrɪpəli/ a city and port in northwest Libya, the capital of Libya and its largest industrial centre 的黎波里〔利比亚西北部一港口城市, 为利比亚首都和最大工业中心〕

trip·per /ˈtrɪpɚ; ˈtrɪpə/ *n* [C] *BrE old-fashioned* someone visiting a place on a short pleasure trip for one day【英, 过时】〔一日游的〕游客: **day tripper** *The beach was crowded with day trippers.* 沙滩上挤满了一日游的游客。

trip·tych /ˈtrɪptɪk; ˈtrɪptɪk/ *n* [C] *technical* a picture, especially a religious one, painted on three pieces of wood that are joined together【术语】三联画〔在三块相连的木板上的绘画, 尤指宗教题材绘画〕

trip·wire /ˈtrɪpˌwaɪr; ˈtrɪpˌwaɪə/ *n* [C] a wire stretched across the ground as part of a trap〔陷阱在地面上绷紧的〕绊脚线, 触发线

tri·reme /ˈtraɪrim; ˈtraɪriːm/ *n* [C] an ancient warship with three rows of OARs on each side〔古代的〕三列划桨战船

tri·sect /traɪˈsɛkt; traɪˈsekt/ *v* [T] *technical* to divide a line, angle etc into three equal parts【术语】把〔线、角等〕分成三等份

Tris·tan and I·sol·de /ˌtrɪstn̩ ənd ɪˋsold; ˌtrɪstən ənd ɪˈzɒldə/ two characters in an old love story. Tristan falls in love with Isolde, who is the wife of his uncle, when they drink a magic love POTION without realizing what they are drinking. Their story is told in an OPERA by Richard Wagner. 特里斯坦与伊索尔德〔一则古老爱情故事中的两个人物，即特里斯坦和他的舅母伊索尔德。他俩在不知情的状况下喝了迷药，顿然热恋在一起。其爱情故事可见于理查德·瓦格纳的同名歌剧〕

Tris·tan da Cun·ha /ˋtrɪstn̩ də ˋkunjə; ˌtrɪstən də ˈkuːnə/ a group of islands in the South Atlantic Ocean, between South Africa and South America. The people living there had to be taken away when a VOLCANO ERUPT*ed* in 1961, but they were able to return two years later. 特里斯坦－达库尼亚群岛〔南大西洋一群岛，位于南非与南美洲之间。1961 年，当地居民因火山爆发而被迫迁移，两年后才重返家园〕

tri-state /ˋtraɪstet; ˈtraɪsteɪt/ *adj AmE* related to a group of three states in the US【美】三个州的，三州之间的

Tris·tram Shan·dy /ˌtrɪstrəm ˋʃændɪ; ˌtrɪstrəm ˈʃændi/ the main character and NARRATOR (=person who tells the story) in the book *The Life and Opinions of Tristram Shandy* (1759-67) by Laurence Sterne. The NOVEL does not have a clear story, and its style greatly influenced 20th century stream of consciousness writers . 特里斯特拉姆〔劳伦斯·斯特恩的《项狄传》(1759-1767) 的主人公和叙事人。该小说没有清晰的情节，其创作风格对 20 世纪的意识流作家产生了很大影响〕

trite /traɪt; traɪt/ *adj* a trite remark, idea etc has been used so often that it seems boring and not sincere〔话〕老一套的；〔思想〕陈腐的: *a dull speech full of trite clichés* 充满陈词滥调的枯燥演讲 —**triteness** *n* [U]

tri·umph[1] /ˋtraɪəmf; ˈtraɪəmf/ *n* **1** [C] an important victory or success, especially after a difficult struggle〔尤指艰苦战斗后获得的〕胜利，成功: *Winning the championship represents a personal triumph for the team's manager.* 赢得冠军标志着该队主教练个人的成功。| [+over] *a brave man's triumph over adversity* 一位勇者战胜逆境 **2** a feeling of pleasure and satisfaction that you get from victory or success 胜利[成功]的喜悦: *yells of triumph* 胜利的欢呼 **3** [C] a very successful example of something 杰出的模范，榜样: *The gallery is a triumph of design.* 这个画廊是卓越设计的典范。

triumph[2] *v* [I] to gain a victory or success, especially after a difficult struggle 战胜，获胜: [+over] *We know that in the end we shall triumph over evil.* 我们知道，我们最终将战胜邪恶。

tri·um·phal /traɪˋʌmfl; traɪˈʌmfəl/ *adj* [only before noun 仅用于名词前] done or made in order to celebrate a triumph 为庆祝胜利而进行的[制作的]: *a triumphal procession* 庆祝胜利的游行 | *a triumphal arch* 一座凯旋门

tri·um·phal·is·m /traɪˋʌmflɪzəm; traɪˈʌmfəlɪzəm/ *n* [U] the expression of being too proud about a victory and too pleased about your opponent's defeat〔因胜利而〕耀武扬威；趾高气扬

tri·um·phant /traɪˋʌmfənt; traɪˈʌmfənt/ *adj* **1** having gained a victory or success 胜利的，成功的: *the triumphant army* 得胜的军队 **2** expressing pleasure and pride because of your victory or success〔因胜利或成功而〕扬扬得意的；耀武扬威的 —**triumphantly** *adv*: *"I've done it!" he shouted triumphantly.* "我成功了！"他得意扬扬地喊道。

tri·um·vir·ate /traɪˋʌmvərɪt; traɪˈʌmvɪ̈rɪ̈t/ *n* [C] *formal* a group of three very powerful people who share control over something【正式】三头政治，三雄执政

triv·et /ˋtrɪvɪt; ˈtrɪvɪ̈t/ *n* [C] **1** a metal support, placed under a hot pot or dish to protect the surface of a table〔桌面上放置滚烫菜锅或菜盘的〕金属台架 **2** a support for holding a pot over a fire〔放在火上支撑炊具的〕三脚架

triv·i·a /ˋtrɪvɪə; ˈtrɪviə/ *n* [plural] **1** unimportant or useless details 琐事；微不足道的细节: *I'm not going to waste my time on such trivia.* 我不打算把时间浪费在这一类琐事上。**2** detailed facts about past events, famous people, sport etc used in QUIZ games〔问答游戏中有关历史事件、名人或体育运动等的〕详细知识，细节

triv·i·al /ˋtrɪvɪəl; ˈtrɪviəl/ *adj* **1** unimportant or of little value 微不足道的，没有什么价值的: *I'm sorry to bother you with what must seem a trivial problem.* 用一个似乎微不足道的问题打扰您，我感到抱歉。| *a trivial sum* 很小的一笔钱 **2** ordinary 普通的，平常的: *trivial everyday duties* 普通的日常事务 —**trivially** *adv*

triv·i·al·i·ty /ˌtrɪvɪˋælətɪ; ˌtrɪviˈælɪ̈ti/ *n* **1** [U] the fact of being not at all important or serious 琐碎；平凡 **2** [C] something that is very unimportant 琐事: *Don't waste your time on trivialities.* 别把时间浪费在鸡毛蒜皮的小事上。

triv·i·al·ize also 又作 -ise *BrE*【英】/ˋtrɪvɪəlˌaɪz; ˈtriviəlaɪz/ *v* [T] to make an important subject seem less important than it really is 使显得琐碎[平凡]: *The article trivializes the whole issue of equal rights.* 这篇文章使整个有关平等权利的问题显得琐碎无聊。—**trivialization** /ˌtrɪvɪəlaɪˋzeʃən; ˌtrɪviəlaɪˈzeɪʃən/ *n* [U]

Trivial Pur·suit /ˌ···ˈ·/ *n* [U] *trademark* a game in which people have to answer questions about many different subjects【商标】难题答问棋赛〔一种参与者必须回答许多不同题材问题的游戏〕

Troc·a·de·ro, the /ˌtrakəˋdero; ˌtrɒkəˈdɪərəʊ/ a large building near Piccadilly Circus in central London, with many shops and EXHIBITION*s*, and a place where you can play virtual reality computer games 特罗卡德罗大厦〔伦敦市中心皮卡迪利广场附近一大型建筑。内有许多商店和展室，还有一个仿真电子游戏娱乐场〕

tro·chee /ˋtrokɪ; ˈtrəʊkiː/ *n* [C] *technical* a unit in poetry consisting of one strong or long beat followed by one weak or short beat, as in 'father'【术语】〔英语诗歌的〕扬抑格，长短格

trod /trad; trɒd/ the past tense of TREAD[1]

trod·den /ˋtradn̩; ˈtrɒdn/ the past participle of TREAD[1]

trog·lo·dyte /ˋtragləˌdaɪt; ˈtrɒglədaɪt/ *n* [C] someone living in a CAVE[1], especially in very ancient times〔尤指远古时代的〕穴居人

troi·ka /ˋtrɔɪkə; ˈtrɔɪkə/ *n* [C] **1** a Russian carriage pulled by three horses side by side〔俄罗斯的〕三驾马车 **2** a group of three people working together, especially in government〔尤指政府中的〕三人组，三头政治

Troi·lus and Cres·si·da /ˌtrɔɪləs ənd ˋkrɛsɪdə; ˌtrɔɪləs ənd ˈkresɪ̈də/ a play by William Shakespeare, set at the time of the Trojan War, about the unhappy love affair between two lovers, Troilus and Cressida《特洛伊罗斯与克瑞西达》〔威廉·莎士比亚创作的一部戏剧。该剧以特洛伊战争时期为背景，讲述特洛伊罗斯与克瑞西达的悲剧爱情故事〕

Tro·jan /ˋtrodʒən; ˈtrəʊdʒən/ **1** *trademark* a type of condom sold in the US【商标】特洛伊〔在美国出售的一种安全套〕**2** *old-fashioned* **work like a Trojan** to work very hard【过时】像特洛伊人一样埋头苦干，非常勤奋地工作

Trojan Horse, the /ˌ·· ˈ·/ *n* a wooden horse used by Greek soldiers to trick their enemies the Trojans during the Trojan War. The Greeks hid inside a large wooden model of a horse and were taken into Troy by Trojan soldiers, who thought that it was a gift. 特洛伊木马〔特洛伊战争期间希腊士兵蒙骗特洛伊人的一匹木马。希腊士兵藏身于木马之中，特洛伊士兵以为是件礼物，就将木马拉进特洛伊城〕

Trojan War, the /ˌ·· ˈ·/ according to ancient Greek stories, a war which was fought between the Greeks and the Trojans because the Trojan prince Paris had carried off Helen, wife of Menelaus, a Greek king. The war was won by a trick in which Greek soldiers, hidden inside a wooden model of a horse, were taken into Troy by the Trojans, who thought that the horse was a gift. Homer describes the Trojan War in his book *The Iliad*. 特洛伊战争〔据古希腊传说，这是特洛伊王子帕里斯诱拐希腊国王墨涅拉俄斯之妻海伦而引发的一场战争。希腊士兵施巧计，藏身于木马之中。特洛伊人误以为是件礼物，就把木马拉进特洛伊城。希腊人最后赢了这场战争。特洛伊战争在荷马的《伊利亚特》中有所描述〕

troll /trol; trəʊl/ *n* [C] an imaginary creature in ancient Scandinavian stories, like a very large or very small ugly person〔古代斯堪的纳维亚传说中的〕山精，巨人，侏儒

trol·ley /ˋtralɪ; ˈtrɒli/ *n* [C] **1** *especially BrE* a large metal basket or frame on wheels that you push along, used for carrying bags, shopping etc【尤英】购物手推车; CART[1] (2) *AmE*【美】: *a supermarket trolley* 超市的购物手推车 **2** *BrE* a small table on very small wheels from which food and drinks are served【英】〔送食品饮料的〕手推车; CART[1] (3) *AmE*【美】: *a tea trolley* 茶具车 **3** *AmE* an electric vehicle for carrying passengers which moves along the street on metal tracks【美】有轨电车; TRAM *BrE*【英】**4** a TROLLEYBUS 无轨电车 **5** the part of an electric vehicle that connects it to the electric wires above〔电车与其上方电线相连接的〕触轮 **6 be off your trolley** *BrE humorous* to be crazy【英，幽默】疯疯癫癫，失去理智

trol·ley·bus /ˋtralɪˌbʌs; ˈtrɒlibʌs/ *n* [C] a bus that gets its power from electric wires above the street 电车，无轨电车

trol·lop /ˋtraləp; ˈtrɒləp/ *n* [C] **1** *old-fashioned* an offensive word for a very untidy woman【过时】邋遢女人〔冒犯用语〕**2** an offensive word for a sexually immoral woman 行为不检的女人，荡妇

Trol·lope /ˋtraləp; ˈtrɒləp/, **Anthony** (1815-82) a British writer whose NOVEL*s*, such as *Barchester Towers*, are famous

T

for their description of Victorian England. 特罗洛普〔(1815-1882),英国作家。他创作的《巴切斯特塔》等小说以描写维多利亚时代的英格兰而出名〕

trom·bone /trɑm`bon; trɒm'bəʊn/ *n* [C] a large musical instrument made of metal which you blow into and which has a long tube that you slide in and out to change the notes 长号, 伸缩喇叭〔一种乐器〕

trom·bon·ist /trɑm`bonɪst; trɒm'bəʊnɪst/ *n* [C] a musician who plays a trombone 长号手, 长号演奏者

troop[1] /trup; tru:p/ *n* **1 troops** [plural] soldiers, especially in organized groups 部队; 军人: *Troops were sent in to stop the riots.* 派部队进来制止暴乱。**2 troop movements/concentrations** movements or gatherings of troops 部队调动/集结 **3** [C] a group of soldiers, especially on horses or in tanks (TANK[1] (3)) 〔一支部队, 尤指〕骑兵连; 装甲连 **4** [C] a group of people or wild animals, especially when they are moving 〔尤指行进中的〕一群人; 一群动物 **5** [C] a group of about 32 SCOUTS led by an adult〔由成人带领 32 人一队的〕童子军中队 —compare 比较 TROUPE

troop[2] *v* [I always+adv/prep] to move together in a group 成群结队地移动: [+**into/along/out etc**] *We all trooped into the meeting.* 我们全都一起走进会场。

troop car·ri·er /'·,··/ *n* [C] a ship, aircraft, or vehicle used for carrying soldiers 运兵船;〔运送军人的〕运输机; 运兵车

troop·er /`trupɚ; 'tru:pə/ *n* **1** [C] the lowest ranking soldier in the part of the army that uses tanks (TANK[1] (3)) or horses〔军阶最低的〕装甲兵; 骑兵 **2 swear like a trooper** to swear a lot 满口粗话 **3** [C] a member of a state police force in the US〔美国的〕州警察

Trooping the Col·our, the /,·· ·'··/ a traditional British ceremony held every year in London on the official birthday of the Queen or King. Many soldiers on horses or on foot, march across Horse Guards Parade carrying their 'colours' (=flags), and they SALUTE the queen or king as they march past. It is a very colourful ceremony and is popular especially with tourists. 军旗敬礼分列式〔英国每年逢女王或国王的法定诞辰日在伦敦举行的一项传统仪式。许多骑兵或步兵高举彩旗, 列队通过皇家骑兵卫队阅兵场, 向女王或国王致敬。这项仪式色彩夺目, 颇受游人欢迎〕

troop·ship /`trup,ʃɪp; 'tru:p,ʃɪp/ *n* [C] a ship used for carrying a large number of soldiers 部队运输船, 运兵船

trope /trop; trəʊp/ *n* [C] *technical* a FIGURE OF SPEECH【术语】比喻

tro·phy /`trofɪ; 'trəʊfi/ *n* [C] **1** a prize for winning a race or other competition, especially a silver cup or a PLAQUE (2)〔比赛等赢得的〕奖杯, 奖牌: *the Football League Trophy* 足球联赛奖杯 **2** something that you keep to show something successful that you have done, especially in war or hunting〔尤指战争或狩猎中的〕战利品, 猎获物, 胜利纪念品: *A lion's head was among the trophies of his African trip,* 在他的非洲之行的战利品中有一个狮子头。

trop·ic /`trɑpɪk; 'trɒpɪk/ *n* **1** [C] one of the two imaginary lines around the world, either the Tropic of Cancer which is 23 ½° north of the EQUATOR, or the Tropic of Capricorn which is 23 ½° south of the EQUATOR〔赤道以北或以南的〕回归线 —see picture at 参见 EARTH[1] 图 **2 the tropics** the hottest part of the world, which is between the two tropics 热带

trop·i·cal /`trɑpɪkḷ; 'trɒpɪkəl/ *adj* **1** coming from or existing in the hottest parts of the world 热带的: *the tropical rain forests* 热带雨林 | **tropical medicine** (=study of diseases that are common in hot countries) 热带医学 **2** weather that is tropical is very hot and wet〔天气〕湿热的: *a steamy tropical night* 一个闷热潮湿的夜晚

Tros·sachs, the /`trɑsəks; 'trɒsəks/ an area in central Scotland famous for its beauty, and especially the valley between Loch Achray and Loch Katrine 特罗萨克斯〔苏格兰中部一地区。风景秀美, 颇为有名, 尤其是阿克雷湖和卡特琳湖之间的谷地风光〕

trot[1] /trɑt; trɒt/ *v* **trotted, trotting 1** [I] if a horse trots, it moves fairly quickly with each front leg moving at the same time as the opposite back leg〔马〕小跑 **2** [I always+adv/prep] **a)** to run fairly slowly, taking short steps 小跑, 慢跑: *William trotted along happily beside his parents.* 威廉在父母旁边高兴地一路小跑。**b)** *spoken* to walk or go somewhere【口】走, 去〔某地〕: *I'm just trotting down to the shops.* 我正要去商店。

trot sth ↔ **out** *phr v* [T] *informal* to give opinions, excuses, reasons etc that you have used too often to seem sincere【非正式】重复说〔老一套的东西〕: *Steve trotted out the same old excuses.* 史蒂夫重复的又是老一套借口。

trot[2] *n* **1** [singular] the movement of a horse at trotting (TROT[1]) speed〔马的〕小跑: *We set off at a brisk trot.* 我们以轻快的步伐出发了。**2** [C] a ride on a horse at trotting (TROT[1]) speed 骑马小跑: *I'm going for a trot down the lane.* 我要沿着小路骑马慢跑。**3** [singular] a fairly slow way of running in which you take short steps 慢跑, 快步: **break into a trot** (=increase your speed to a trot) 开始小跑 **4 on the trot** *BrE informal*【英, 非正式】**a)** one after the other 一个接一个地: *Sally's won three races on the trot.* 萨莉连续赢了三项比赛。**b)** busy doing something 马不停蹄地忙于某事: *I've been on the trot all day.* 我整天都在马不停蹄地忙着。**5** [C] *AmE* a book of translations or answers used by students; a CRIB[1] (4b)【美】〔学生用来作弊的〕译本; 答案 **6 the trots** *humorous* DIARRHOEA【幽默】腹泻, 跑肚

troth /trɔθ; trəʊθ/ *n old use*【旧】**1 by my troth** used when expressing an opinion strongly 请相信我; 我保证; 我发誓〔用以表示强烈的意见〕**2 in troth** truly; INDEED 真的, 的确 —see also 另见 **plight your troth** (PLIGHT[2])

Trot·sky /`trɑtskɪ; 'trɒtski/, **Le·on** /`liɑn; 'li:ɒn/ (1879-1940) a Russian political leader, born in the Ukraine, who had an important part in the Russian Revolution of 1917. He was also a writer on Communism and he believed in revolution by workers all over the world. He lost power when his enemy Stalin took control of Russia after the death of Lenin (1924), and he was later forced to leave the country. He was eventually murdered in Mexico on the orders of Stalin. 托洛茨基〔(1879-1940), 俄国政治领袖, 生于乌克兰, 在 1917 年俄国革命中起过重要作用。他也是一位共产主义理论家, 主张世界性的工人革命。列宁去世后 (1924), 托洛茨基因政敌斯大林控制了苏联而丧失权力, 后被迫离开苏联, 最终经斯大林指示在墨西哥遇害〕

Trot·sky·ite /`trɑtskɪ,aɪt; 'trɒtskiaɪt/ also 又作 **Trot·sky·ist** /-skɪɪst; -skiɪst/ *n* [C] someone who believes in the political ideas of Leon Trotsky, especially that the working class should take control of the state 托洛茨基主义者, 托派分子 —**Trotskyite** *adj*

trot·ter /`trɑtɚ; 'trɒtə/ *n* [C] a pig's foot, cooked and used as food〔煮熟供食用的〕猪蹄

trou·ba·dour /`trubə,dur; 'tru:bədɔ:/ *n* [C] a type of singer and poet who travelled around the PALACES and castles of Southern Europe in the 12th and 13th centuries〔12、13 世纪周游于南欧一带宫殿和城堡的〕行吟诗人

troub·le[1] /`trʌbḷ; 'trʌbəl/ *n* 

1 ▶PROBLEMS 问题◀ [C,U] problems that make something difficult, spoil your plans, make you worry etc 麻烦; 烦扰; 忧虑: *Every time there's trouble, I have to go along and sort it out.* 每次有麻烦时, 我都得坚持下去, 把问题化解掉。| [+**with**] *They're having a lot of trouble with the new baby.* 新生的婴儿给他们添了许多麻烦。| **trouble doing sth** *I never have any trouble getting to sleep.* 我从来不会失眠。| **what's the trouble?** *spoken* (=used to ask someone what is causing a particular problem)【口】出什么麻烦了? 怎么了? | **the trouble is** *spoken* (=used when explaining why something is impossible or difficult)【口】麻烦是, 问题是 *I'd like to give you the money now – the trouble is, I don't get paid till Friday.* 我倒想现在就把钱给你, 但麻烦的是, 我要到星期五才发薪。| **sb's troubles** (=all the problems that you have in your life) 生活中的种种问题 *Because I'm a good listener people often come to me with their troubles.* 人们有麻烦就往往来找我, 因为我善于倾听。| **teething troubles** (=small problems at the beginning) 初始阶段遇到的小问题 *After a few teething troubles, the new system worked perfectly.* 这套新系统在开始阶段出了几个小问题, 后来就运转得非常好。

2 ▶FAULT 过错◀ the trouble with *spoken* used when explaining what is unsatisfactory about something or someone【口】过错, 不足, 缺点: *The trouble with you is that you don't listen.* 你的缺点是不好好听讲。| *That's the trouble with lasagne – it takes so long to make.* 那便是做宽面条的麻烦之处 —— 需要花太长的时间来做。

3 ▶HEALTH 健康◀ [U] a problem that you have with your health 毛病: [+**with**] *He sometimes has trouble with his breathing.* 他有时候呼吸系统有毛病。| **heart/stomach/skin etc trouble** *Irene's at home today with stomach trouble.* 艾琳今天因犯胃病待在家里了。

4 ▶MACHINE/SYSTEM 机器/系统◀ [U] something that is wrong with a machine, vehicle, or system〔机器、车辆等的〕故障, 毛病: *engine trouble* 发动机故障 | [+**with**] *trouble with the central heating system* 中央供暖系统的毛病

5 ▶BAD SITUATION 恶劣处境◀ [U] a difficult or dangerous situation 困境, 险境: **be in trouble** *an SOS from a ship in trouble*

一艘遇险轮船发出的求救信号 | **get/run into trouble** *The company ran into trouble when it tried to expand too quickly.* 这家公司扩展业务的步伐太快，陷入了困境。| **in serious/deep/big trouble** *If you connect the wrong wires to the power supply, you'll be in deep trouble.* 如果接电源时接错了线，你会惹出大麻烦的。

6 be asking for trouble *informal* to take risks or do something stupid that is likely to cause problems【非正式】自寻麻烦，自讨苦吃：*You're just asking for trouble if you don't get those brakes fixed.* 你如果不把那些刹车修好，简直就是在自讨苦吃。

7 ►EFFORT 努力◄ [U] an amount of effort and time that is needed to do something, especially when it is inconvenient for you to do it 麻烦，费事；不方便：**put sb to a lot of trouble** (=make someone use a lot of time and effort) 给某人添了很多麻烦 *I'm sorry, I didn't mean to put you to so much trouble.* 对不起，我并不是有意要给你添这么多的麻烦。| **take the trouble to do sth** (=make a special effort to do something) 费[尽]力地做某事 *The teacher took the trouble to learn all our names on the first day.* 第一天老师就努力地记住我们所有人的名字。| **go to/take a lot of trouble** (=use a lot of time and effort doing something carefully) 不厌其烦地〔做某事〕| **save sb the trouble (of doing sth)** (=make it unnecessary for sb to do sth) 为某人省去了〔做某事〕的麻烦 *I thought if I phoned you, it would save you the trouble of writing a letter.* 我当时想，如果我给你打电话，就不用麻烦你写信了。| **be more trouble than it's worth** *spoken* (=when something takes too much time and effort to do)【口】太花时间，太费事 *I find that making my own clothes is more trouble than it's worth.* 我觉得自己做衣服太费事，不值得。

8 no trouble/it's no trouble *spoken* used to say that you are very willing to do something because it is not inconvenient for you【口】一点也不麻烦

9 be no trouble *informal* if someone is no trouble, they do not annoy or worry you【非正式】〔某人〕不会添麻烦：*You can leave the children with me. They're no trouble.* 你可以把孩子们留给我照管。他们不会给我添麻烦的。

10 ►ARGUMENT/VIOLENCE 争论/暴力◄ also 又作 **troubles** [plural] a situation in which people quarrel or fight with each other 纠纷；骚乱，动乱：*The trouble started when the police tried to break up the demonstration.* 警察试图驱散这次游行示威，结果爆发了骚乱。| *the recent troubles in Northern Ireland* 最近发生在北爱尔兰的骚乱 | **cause/make trouble** (=deliberately cause trouble) 惹麻烦/闯祸 *Don't give him another drink or he'll start causing trouble.* 别让他再喝了，不然他会开始惹出麻烦来的。

11 ►BLAME 责怪◄ [U] a situation in which someone in authority is angry with you or is likely to punish you 惹出麻烦的处境：*There'll be trouble when your father finds out what you've done.* 要让你父亲发现你干了什么，麻烦就来了。| **be in trouble (with)** *My brother's in trouble with the police again.* 我弟弟又同警察扯上麻烦了。| **get into trouble** *Don't copy my work or we'll both get into trouble.* 不要抄我的作业，不然我们两人都会有麻烦的。

12 get sb into trouble a) to put someone into a situation in which they are likely to be punished 给某人惹来麻烦：*Diane told a lie rather than get her friend into trouble.* 为了不给朋友惹麻烦，黛安娜说了谎话。**b)** *old-fashioned* to make a woman PREGNANT【过时】使女人怀孕

Frequencies of the noun **trouble** in spoken and written English 名词 trouble 在英语口语和书面语中的使用频率

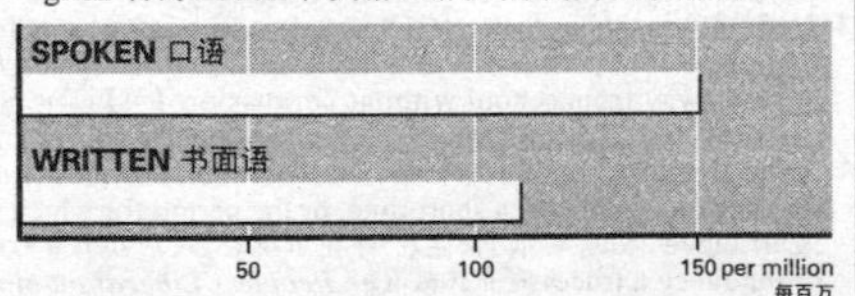

Based on the British National Corpus and the Longman Lancaster Corpus
据英国国家语料库和朗文兰开斯特语料库

This graph shows that the noun **trouble** is more common in spoken English than in written English. This is because it is used in some common spoken phrases. These are marked '*spoken*' in the entry. 本图表显示，名词 trouble 在英语口语中的使用频率远远高于书面语，这是因为该词用于一些常用的口语短语中。在词条里，这些短语用"【口】"标示。

USAGE NOTE 用法说明: TROUBLE

WORD CHOICE 词语辨析: **trouble** (*n,v*), **problem**, **troubles**, **troubled**, **worried**, **bother**

Trouble [usually U] is usually used to talk about the worry etc that people have in some situations (especially when there is some specific difficulty). trouble〔一般作不可数名词〕通常用来指人们在某些情况下〔尤指在有某种具体困难时〕产生的忧虑、担心等：*Her back is giving her a lot of trouble* (=pain). 她的背给她带来不少痛苦。| *Do you have much trouble with the kids?* (=do they behave badly?) 孩子们给你惹了很多麻烦吗？| *Thanks for your trouble* (=effort). 你辛苦了。

When you speak of a **problem** [C], you are thinking more of a person, thing, or situation that is difficult (either for things or people). problem〔可数名词〕指造成困难的人、事或情况：*Acid rain is an increasing environmental problem.* 酸雨是一个日趋严重的环境问题。| *my biggest problem* (NOT 不用 *my best trouble*) 我最大的问题

In many situations a **problem** is a source of **trouble**, so there are some contexts where both words may be used. 在许多情况下 problem（问题）就是 trouble（麻烦）的根源。所以这两个词有时可以互换：*What's the trouble/problem?* 怎么了？| *I had a bit of trouble/a bit of a problem.* 我有了一点麻烦。| *the trouble/problem with my car* 我车子的麻烦 However sometimes there is a clear difference in meaning. 然而，有时候两者在意思上有着明显的差别：*There's trouble in the bar* (perhaps means people are fighting). 酒吧里有麻烦了〔也许意味着有人在殴斗〕。But *There's a problem in the bar* (perhaps means there is no beer left). 酒吧里出了点问题〔也许意味着没有啤酒了〕。

In some contexts only **problem** can be used. You can *solve* problems but not trouble(s). Something may *pose* a problem but not trouble. In spoken English **trouble** is frequent only in certain phrases. 有时只能用 problem。可以用 solve problems（解决问题），但不能用 solve trouble(s)；某事可能 pose a problem（引起问题），但不能 pose trouble(s)。在英语口语中 trouble 仅仅常用于某些短语中：*The (only) trouble is/was...*（唯一的）麻烦是… | *This/that is/was the trouble.* 这/那正是麻烦所在。| *...Just don't cause any trouble...* 只要不惹任何麻烦… | *...have (no) trouble with...* 有[没有]…的麻烦 | *be in (real/a lot of) trouble* 陷入（真正的/大量的）麻烦中 | *...get into trouble...* …陷入麻烦…

Problem is more common in technical or formal contexts, **trouble** in informal or conversational ones. problem 在术语或正式语境中用得较为普遍，而 trouble 则较多地用于非正式或对话语境中：*the nuclear problem* 核问题 | *the problem with BCCI is more common* 国际商业信贷银行的问题更为普遍。But you are more likely to say 不过更有可能说：*tummy trouble* 肚子痛 | *The trouble with Paul is that he has no sense of humour.* 保罗的问题在于他没有幽默感。

Troubles (plural) is used with a much more specific meaning either for all the things that worry a person,or all the difficulties of an organization or country. troubles〔复数〕可用来更具体地指某人所焦虑的一切事情或某一组织或国家的所有困难：*money troubles* 经济困难 | *the troubles besetting the government* 困扰政府的麻烦 | *the troubles in Northern Ireland* 北爱尔兰的麻烦。But you would say 但人们会说：*world/traffic problems* (NOT 不用 *troubles*) 世界/交通问题

Trouble (*v*) and **troubled** (*adj*) are not very common in ordinary spoken English. trouble〔动词〕和 troubled〔形容词〕在普通的口头英语中用得并不很普遍：*I was worried about my work* (in writing you might perhaps use *troubled*). 我很担心我的工作〔写作时也许会用 troubled 代替 worried〕。| *Don't bother me while I'm watching TV.* 我看电视时不要烦我。| *My car had a problem* (NOT 不用 *was troubled*). 我的车子出了点问题。

GRAMMAR 语法

Usually someone *has trouble* (NOT *troubles*) doing something (NOT *has trouble to do it*). 一般用 has trouble〔不用 troubles〕doing something〔不用 has trouble to do it〕。

You may be *in trouble* (NOT *in a trouble/troubles*). 可以用 in trouble〔不用 in a trouble/troubles〕。

trouble² *v* **1** [T] if a problem troubles you, it makes you feel worried 使忧虑，使苦恼：*You must talk to your daughter and find out what's troubling her.* 你必须跟女儿谈谈，弄清楚什么

事在让她苦恼。**2** [T] *formal* to ask someone to do something for you when it is inconvenient for them【正式】麻烦〔某人〕，给〔某人〕添麻烦: *I promise not to trouble you again.* 我保证不再给你添麻烦了。**3 may I trouble you?/sorry to trouble you** *spoken formal* used when politely asking someone to do something for you or give you something【口, 正式】我可以麻烦您一下吗?/对不起, 麻烦您一下: *Sorry to trouble you, but could you tell me the way to the station, please.* 对不起, 麻烦您一下, 请问到车站怎么走? | *May I trouble you for the salt?* 麻烦你递一下盐好吗? | *Can I trouble you to close the door.* 麻烦你把门关上。**4 not trouble to do sth** to not do something because it needs too much effort 不用费神[操心]做某事: *They never troubled to ask me what I would like.* 他们从来不费神问我喜欢什么。**5** [T] if a medical problem troubles you, it causes you pain or makes you suffer 使疼痛, 使不舒服: *Roy has been troubled by a stomach ulcer for months.* 罗伊已被胃溃疡折磨好几个月了。

troub·led /ˈtrʌbl̩d; ˈtrʌbəld/ *adj* **1** feeling worried or anxious 忧虑的; 烦恼的, 苦恼的: *Benson looked troubled when he heard the news.* 本森听到这消息时面露忧色。—see 见 TROUBLE (USAGE) **2** having many problems 问题丛生的, 混乱的: *These are troubled times for the coal industry.* 对于煤炭工业来说, 现在是多事之秋。

trouble-free /ˌ·· ˈ·◂/ *adj* causing no difficulty or worry 没有困难的; 没有问题的; 没有忧虑的: *Since we changed our car we've had two years of trouble-free motoring.* 自从换了这辆车后, 我们开了两年都没出过故障。

troub·le·mak·er /ˈtrʌbl̩ˌmekɚ; ˈtrʌbəlˌmeɪkə/ *n* [C] someone who deliberately causes problems, especially by complaining or making people argue with each other 惹事生非者, 捣蛋鬼: *a handful of troublemakers who are damaging the club's reputation* 毁坏俱乐部名声的一群惹是生非者

Troub·les, the /ˈtrʌbl̩z; ˈtrʌbəlz/ *n* [plural] a name used, especially in Ireland, for the political problems connected with Ireland's relationship with the UK. The events in the early 1920s, when Ireland was fighting to become an independent country, were called the Troubles, and the name is also used for the problems and violence in Northern Ireland since the late 1960s. 北爱问题〔在爱尔兰专门使用的一个名词, 指关涉北爱尔兰和英国关系的政治问题。20世纪20年代初北爱尔兰为争取独立而组织的一系列事件被称为"北爱问题"。该词也指20世纪60年代末以来在北爱尔兰发生的一系列问题及暴力事件〕

T

troub·le·shoot·er /ˈtrʌbl̩ˌʃutɚ; ˈtrʌbəlˌʃuːtə/ *n* [C] someone who is employed by a company to deal with serious problems〔公司雇用的〕处理难题的人

troub·le·some /ˈtrʌbl̩səm; ˈtrʌbəlsəm/ *adj* causing you trouble or anxiety, over a long period of time 引起麻烦的; 令人烦恼[讨厌]的: *a troublesome child* 烦人的孩子

trouble spot /ˈ·· ˌ·/ *n* [C] a place where trouble often happens, especially war or violence〔尤指经常发生战争或暴力的〕麻烦地区, 不安定地区: *Extra police were drafted in to patrol late-night trouble spots.* 又增加了一些警察在后半夜经常出事的地区巡逻。

trough /trɔf; trɒf/ *n* [C] **1** a long narrow open container that holds water or food for animals〔喂动物的〕食槽, 饮水槽 **2** the hollow area between two waves in the sea or between two hills〔海中的〕浪谷, 波谷;〔山间的〕槽谷 **3** a short period of low activity, low prices etc in something that is continuously measured over a longer period〔商业活动、价格等的〕低谷期, 萧条期: *the peaks and troughs of economic cycles* 经济周期中的高峰和低潮 **4** *technical* a long area of fairly low pressure on a weather map between two areas of high pressure【术语】〔气象图上标示的〕低压槽

trounce /trauns; traʊns/ *v* [T] to defeat someone completely 彻底打败, 击溃: *We were trounced 13-0.* 我们以0:13的比分被打得一败涂地。

troupe /trup; truːp/ *n* [C] a group of singers, actors, dancers etc who work together 演出团, 剧团, 歌舞团

troup·er /ˈtrupɚ; ˈtruːpə/ *n* [C] *informal* someone who has a lot of experience of work in the entertainment business【非正式】从事娱乐业多年的人, 老演员, 老艺人

trouser press /ˈ·· ·/ *n* [C] a piece of equipment that you can keep your trousers in to keep them flat and smooth〔使裤子保持平整不皱的〕压裤器

2 **trou·sers** /ˈtrauzɚz; ˈtraʊzəz/ *n* [plural] a piece of clothing that covers the lower half of your body, with a separate part fitting over each leg 裤子: *I need a new pair of trousers for work.* 我需要一条新的工作裤。| *short trousers* 短裤 —**trouser** *adj* [only before noun 仅用于名词前]: *The tickets are in my trouser-pocket.* 票在我的裤子口袋里。—see also 另见 **wear the trousers** (WEAR[1] (8)), **catch sb with their trousers down** (CATCH[1] (3)) —see picture on page A17 参见 A17 页图

This graph shows how common the nouns **trousers** and **pants** are in British and American English. 本图表所示为名词 trousers 和 pants 在英国英语和美国英语中的使用频率。

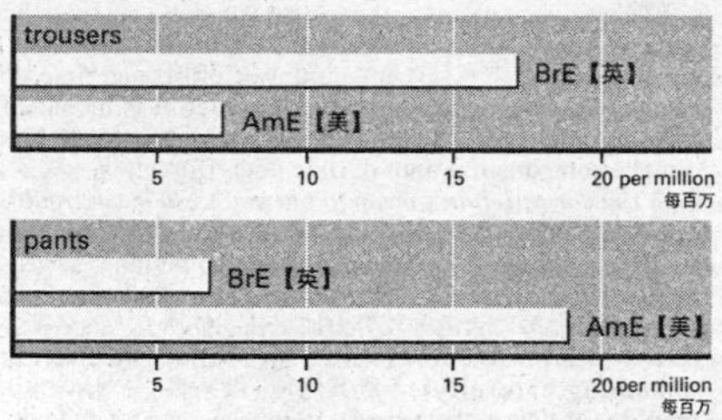

Based on the British National Corpus and the Longman Lancaster Corpus
据英国国家语料库和朗文兰开斯特语料库

In British English **trousers** is used to mean a piece of clothing that covers the lower half of your body, with a separate part fitting over each leg. In American English **pants** is used for this meaning. **Pants** is commonly used in British English to mean underwear, but Americans use the word **underwear**. 在英国英语中, trousers 用来指裤子。在美国英语中, 裤子是 pants。pants 在英国英语中普遍用来指内裤, 而美国人则用 underwear 指内裤。

trouser suit /ˈ·· ·/ *n* [C] *BrE* a woman's suit consisting of a JACKET and matching trousers【英】〔女子的上衣与配套的裤子组成的〕长裤套装; PANTSUIT *AmE*【美】

trous·seau /truˋso; ˈtruːsəʊ/ *n* [C] *old-fashioned* the personal possessions that a woman brings with her when she marries【过时】嫁妆

trout /traut; traʊt/ *n* **1** *plural* **trout** [C,U] a common river-fish, often used for food, or the flesh of this fish 鳟鱼〔一种河鱼〕; 鳟鱼肉 **2 old trout** *BrE spoken* an unpleasant or annoying old person, especially a woman【英口】老家伙; 老厌物〔尤指老妇人〕

trove /trov; trəʊv/ *n* —see 见 TREASURE TROVE

trow·el /ˈtrauəl; ˈtraʊəl/ *n* [C] **1** a garden tool like a very small SPADE 小泥铲, 小铲子〔一种园艺工具〕 **2** a small tool with a flat blade, used for spreading CEMENT on bricks etc〔泥瓦匠使用的〕瓦刀, 镘刀, 抹子

Troy /trɔɪ; trɔɪ/ according to ancient Greek stories, a city in Asia Minor (=modern Turkey) which the Greeks eventually gained control of in the Trojan War. In the 19th century, Heinrich Schliemann, a German ARCHAEOLOGIST discovered the ruins of an ancient city in northwest Turkey, which he claimed was Troy. 特洛伊〔古希腊传说中小亚细亚一城市。特洛伊战争期间, 希腊人最后占领了该城。19世纪, 德国考古学家海因里希·谢里曼在土耳其西北部发现了一处古城遗址, 声称为特洛伊〕

troy weight /ˈtrɔɪ ˌwet; ˈtrɔɪ weɪt/ *n* [U] a British weights system, used in former times for weighing gold, silver etc〔英国旧时称量金银等用的〕金衡制

tru·an·cy /ˈtruənsɪ; ˈtruːənsi/ *n* [U] the practice of deliberately staying away from school without permission 逃学, 旷课

tru·ant /ˈtruənt; ˈtruːənt/ *n* [C] **1** a student who stays away from school without permission 逃学者, 旷课生 **2 play truant** *BrE* to stay away from school without permission【英】逃学, 旷课 —**truant** *v* [I]

truce /trus; truːs/ *n* [C] an agreement between enemies to stop fighting or arguing for a short time, or the period for which this is arranged 休战, 停战(协定); 停止争辩(协议): **call a truce** (=announce a truce) 宣布休战 *The People's Liberation Movement called a truce for the elections.* 人民解放运动组织宣布在选举期间休战。

Tru·cial States, the /ˌtruʃəl ˋstets; ˌtruːʃəl ˈsteɪts/ a former name for the United Arab Emirates 特鲁西尔诸国〔阿拉伯联合酋长国旧称〕

truck[1] /trʌk; trʌk/ *n* **1** [C] a large road vehicle used to carry goods 货车, 卡车; LORRY *BrE*【英】: *The trucks were loaded at the docks.* 这些卡车在码头上装货。**2** [C] *BrE* a railway vehicle that is part of a train and carries goods【英】〔铁路的〕货车; CAR (3) *AmE*【美】: *coal trucks* 运煤车 **3** [C] a simple piece of equip- 

ment on wheels used to move heavy objects 手推车，手拉车 4 **have no truck with sb** to avoid speaking or doing business with someone 不与…打交道，不同…来往

truck[2] *v especially AmE*【尤美】1 [T] to take something somewhere by truck 用货车装运 2 [I always+adv/prep] *informal* to go, move, or travel【非正式】去往，移动，行进：**truck along/down etc** *We were trucking on down to Jack's place.* 我们在去杰克家的路上。3 **get trucking** *informal* to leave【非正式】离开，上路

truck·er /ˈtrʌkɚ; ˈtrʌkə/ *n* [C] *AmE* a truck driver【美】货车司机

truck farm /ˈ· ·/ *n* [C] *AmE* an area for growing vegetables and fruit for sale【美】商品果蔬农场；MARKET GARDEN *BrE*【英】

truck·ing /ˈtrʌkɪŋ; ˈtrʌkɪŋ/ *n AmE*【美】1 [U] the business of taking goods from place to place by road 货车运输业 2 **keep on trucking** *spoken* used to encourage someone to continue what they are doing【口】继续干下去〔鼓励人的话〕

truck·le /ˈtrʌkl; ˈtrʌkəl/ *v*

truckle to sb/sth *phr v* [T] *old-fashioned* to do what someone tells you in a way that seems weak【过时】屈从，对…唯命是从

truckle bed /ˈ· · ,/ *n* [C] *BrE* a low bed on small wheels, that you can slide under a larger bed【英】〔不用时可推入大床下的〕装有脚轮的矮床；TRUNDLE BED *AmE*【美】

truck·load /ˈtrʌk,lod; ˈtrʌkləʊd/ *n* [C] the amount that fills a truck 货车装载量

truck stop /ˈ· ·/ *n* [C] *AmE* a cheap place to eat on a main road, used mainly by TRUCK[1] (1) drivers【美】〔主要为货车司机服务的〕路边廉价餐馆；TRANSPORT CAFE *BrE*【英】

truc·u·lent /ˈtrʌkjələnt; ˈtrʌkjʊlənt/ *adj* bad-tempered and always willing to argue with people 脾气暴躁的；好斗的，寻衅的：*Most people resented his truculent manner.* 大多数人都不满他那寻衅好斗的作派。—**truculently** *adv* —**truculence** *n* [U]

trudge[1] /trʌdʒ; trʌdʒ/ *v* [I always + adv/prep] to walk with slow, heavy steps, especially because you are tired〔尤指因疲倦而〕艰难地走，步履沉重地走：**trudge home/along/through etc** *The old man trudged home through the snow.* 老人步履艰难地穿过雪地走回了家。—see picture on page A24 参见 A24 页图

trudge[2] *n* [singular] a long tiring walk 长途疲惫的步行，长途跋涉

S1 W1 **true**[1] /tru; truː/ *adj*

1 ▶**NOT FALSE** 不假的◀ based on facts and not imagined or invented 符合事实的，真的，真实的：*No, honestly, it's a true story.* 不，老实说，这是一个真实的故事。| **it is true (that)** *Is it true that you're leaving?* 你是真的要走了吗？| **be true of sb** *Babies need a lot of sleep and this is particularly true of newborns.* 婴儿需要大量的睡眠，新生儿尤其如此。—opposite 反义词 FALSE

2 **the true value/seriousness/nature etc** the real value etc of something rather than what seems at first to be correct 真正的价值/严重性/本性等：*I didn't realize the true seriousness of the problem until I checked the fuel gauge.* 我直到检查了燃料表后才意识到这个问题的真正严重性。| *The house was sold for only a fraction of its true value.* 这房子卖出去了，价格比它真正的价值低得多。

3 ▶**REAL FEELINGS** 真实的感情◀ your true emotions, beliefs, opinions etc are the ones that you really have and not the ones that you pretend to have〔情感、信仰、意见等〕真实的，实际的：*Her true motives only emerged later.* 她真实的动机是后来才显露出来的。

4 ▶**ADMITTING STH** 承认某事◀ *spoken* used when you are admitting that something is true, but saying that in spite of this something else is also true【口】诚然，固然，的确〔用来承认某事的真实性，但同时指出另一事情也真实〕：*"He's very hard-working." "True, but I still don't think he's the right man for the job."* "他工作非常勤奋。""的确如此，不过我还是认为他不是这项工作的合适人选。"

5 **true love/courage/freedom etc** the type of love etc that is strong and has all the qualities that it should have 真正的爱情/勇气/自由等：*True courage includes the recognition of your own fear.* 真正的勇气包括承认自己的恐惧。

6 **come true** if wishes, dreams etc come true, they happen in the way that someone has said or hoped that they would〔愿望、梦想等〕实现，成真：*By 1975 the worst economic predictions had come true.* 到 1975 年，对经济最糟糕的预测已经成为现实。—see also 另见 **a dream come true** (DREAM[1] (5))

7 ▶**LOYAL** 忠心的◀ faithful and loyal to someone, whatever happens 忠实的，忠贞的：[+to] *Throughout the whole ordeal, she remained true to her husband.* 在整个磨难时期，她对丈夫忠贞不渝。

8 **true friend/believer/sportsman etc** someone who behaves in the way that a good friend etc should behave 真正的朋友/信仰者/体育爱好者等：*You find out who your true friends are at times like this.* 在这种时候，你会发现哪些人才是你真正的朋友。

9 **true to form/type** used to say that someone is behaving in the bad way that you expect them to〔不良行为〕一如既往：*True to form, Henry turned up late.* 像往常一样，亨利很晚才露面。

10 **true to life** a book, play, description etc that is true to life seems very real and natural; REALISTIC〔图书、戏剧、描述等〕逼真的，活灵活现的

11 **true to your word** doing exactly what you have promised to do 说话算数，履行诺言：*True to his word, John arrived promptly at 2 o'clock.* 约翰说话算数，在两点钟时就准时来了。

12 **be true to your principles/beliefs etc** to behave according to the principles that you claim to believe in 忠实于原则/信仰等：*He remains true to the traditions of his profession.* 他一直忠实于他这一行业的传统。

13 **only (too true)** used to say that you know something is true, especially when you do not like it 千真万确的〔用来表示知道某事是真的，尤指不喜欢的事〕：*It is only too true that people are judged by their accents.* 人们总以口音来判断人，真没办法。

14 **true mammal/fish/plant etc** having all the qualities of a particular class of object, animal, plant etc according to an exact description of it 真正的哺乳动物/鱼类/植物等〔表示合乎严格的定义，有某类的全部特征〕：*Despite its appearance, the whale is a true mammal.* 尽管有那样的外表，鲸是真正的哺乳动物。

15 ▶**STRAIGHT/LEVEL** 直的/平的◀ [not before noun 不用于名词前] *technical* fitted, placed, or formed in a way that is perfectly flat, straight, correct etc【术语】〔安装、放置等〕端正的；正确的：*If the door's not true, it won't close properly.* 这门如果安得不正，就关不严。

16 **sb's aim is true** if your aim is true, you hit the thing that you were throwing or shooting at〔投掷、射击等〕命中目标

17 **(there's) many a true word spoken in jest** used to say that when people are joking they sometimes say things that are true and important 玩笑中也有不少实话 —see also 另见 **be too good to be true** (GOOD[1] (23)), **show yourself in your true colours** (COLOUR[1] (11)), **not ring true** (RING[2] (5)), TRULY, TRUTH

true[2] *adv* 1 in an exact straight line 端正地；笔直地：*The arrow flew straight and true to its target.* 箭不偏不斜地朝靶子飞去。2 *old use* truthfully【旧】真实地，确实地 3 *technical* if a type of animal breeds true, the young animals are exactly like their parents【术语】〔动物〕子代与亲代完全相同地，与原种相同地，纯种地

true[3] *n* **out of true** not completely straight, level, or balanced 不直；不平；不正：*The walls are slightly out of true.* 这墙壁稍微有点不直。

true-blue /, · ˈ·/ *adj* 1 *BrE informal* believing completely in the ideas of the British CONSERVATIVE PARTY【英，非正式】忠于保守党思想的：*a true-blue Tory* 忠诚的保守党党员 2 *AmE* completely loyal to a person or idea【美】非常忠诚的，忠心耿耿的：*a true-blue friend* 忠心耿耿的朋友

True Con·fes·sions /, · ˈ· ·/ *trademark* a magazine which contains stories about people's problems in love, marriage, and relationships. The stories, which are supposed to be true, are told in a way that is intended to make them as strange, exciting, or shocking as possible【商标】《真实忏悔》〔一杂志名。该杂志刊载真实的故事，关涉爱情、婚姻或人际关系问题。这些故事在叙述时被有意写得十分离奇、刺激或令人震惊〕：*Her private life is right out of 'True Confessions'.* 她的私生活与《真实忏悔》中的故事别无二致。

true-heart·ed /, · ˈ· ·/ *adj literary* faithful; loyal【文】忠实的；忠心的

true-life /, · ˈ·/ *adj* [only before noun 仅用于名词前] based on real facts and not invented 以事实为依据的〔而不是虚构的〕：*a true-life adventure* 一次真实的冒险活动

true·love /ˈtru,lʌv; ˈtruːlʌv/ *n* [C] *poetic* the person that you love【诗】爱人，恋人，心上人

true north /, · ˈ·/ *n* [U] north as it appears on maps, calculated as a line through the centre of the earth rather than by using the MAGNETIC POLE 真北〔地图上的北方，即根据地球中轴线而不是用磁极计算的正北方〕

Truf·faut /truˈfo; ˈtrʊfəʊ/, **Fran·çois** /franˈswa; ˈfrɒnswaː/ (1932-84) a French film DIRECTOR who was part of the New Wave, and whose films include *Les Quatre Cents Coups* (1959), *Jules et Jim* (1961) and *Day for Night* (1973). 特吕弗，又译杜鲁福〔(1932-1984)，法国电影导演，新浪潮运动的发起人之一。执导的影片有《四百击》(1959)、《朱尔与吉姆》(1961) 和《白昼之夜》(1973) 等〕

truf·fle /ˈtrʌfl; ˈtrʌfəl/ *n* [C] **1** a black or light brown FUNGUS that grows underground, and is a very expensive food 块菌〔生长于地下的一种很昂贵的食用真菌〕 **2** a soft creamy sweet made with chocolate 巧克力软糖: *a rum truffle* 朗姆酒心巧克力软糖

tru·is·m /ˈtruɪzəm; ˈtruːɪzəm/ *n* [C] a statement that is clearly true, so that there is no need to say it 自明之理, 不言而喻的话: *His speech was just a collection of clichés and truisms.* 他说的只不过是一堆陈词滥调和不言而喻的话。

tru·ly /ˈtrulɪ; ˈtruːli/ *adv* [+adj/adv] **1** used to emphasize that the way you are describing something is really true 真实地, 确实地: *There was a truly beautiful view from the bedroom.* 从卧室望出去的风景确实很美。| *a truly amazing story* 确实令人惊异的故事 | *Truly, this is an honour.* 的确, 这是一项荣誉。**2** *formal* sincerely【正式】诚挚地, 真诚地: *I am truly sorry.* 我真的感到抱歉。**3** in an exact or correct way 准确地; 正确地: *A spider cannot truly be described as an insect.* 准确地说, 蜘蛛不能算是昆虫。**4 well and truly** *especially spoken* completely; totally【尤口】彻底地, 完全地: *We were well and truly trapped.* 我们完全被困住了。**5 really and truly** *spoken* used to emphasize that something is definitely true【口】的的确确地, 千真万确地〔用于强调〕: *I couldn't believe we were really and truly going at last.* 我无法相信我们终于真的可以走了。**6 yours truly a)** used at the end of a business letter, before the signature 你忠实的〔用于公文书信结尾, 签名前〕—see also 另见 **yours faithfully/truly** (YOURS (3)) **b)** *informal humorous* used to mean yourself【非正式, 幽默】本人, 我自己: *So, yours truly was left to clean up.* 于是, 留下我自己来收拾残局。

Tru·man /ˈtrumən; ˈtruːmən/**, Harry S** (1884-1972) a US politician in the Democratic Party who was President of the US from 1945 to 1953. He took the decision to drop NUCLEAR bombs on Japan in 1945, and helped to establish NATO. He also organized the Marshall Plan, and began US involvement in the Korean War in 1950. 杜鲁门〔(1884-1972), 美国民主党政治家, 1945至1953年任美国总统。1945年, 他决定向日本投掷原子弹, 参与创立北大西洋公约组织。他还组织过马歇尔计划, 1950年使美国开始卷入朝鲜战争〕

trump¹ /trʌmp; trʌmp/ *n* [C] **1** a card from the SUIT (=one of the four types of cards in a set) that has been chosen to have a higher value than the other suits in a particular game〔牌戏中的〕王牌, 将牌 **2 trumps** [plural] also 又作 **trump** *AmE*【美】the SUIT¹ (3) chosen to have a higher value than the other suits in a particular game 王牌的花色: *Hearts are trumps.* 红桃是王牌。**3 come up trumps/turn up trumps** to provide what is needed, especially unexpectedly and at the last moment〔在最后时刻意外地〕提供需要之物: *Paul came up trumps and managed to borrow a car for us.* 保罗送来及时雨, 为我们借到了一辆汽车。

trump² *v* [T] to play a trump that beats someone else's card in a game〔牌戏中〕打出王牌赢〔别人的牌〕

trump sth ↔ **up** *phr v* [T] to use false information to make someone seem guilty of a crime 捏造〔罪名〕, 假造〔罪证〕: *They had trumped the whole thing up to get rid of him.* 为了除掉他, 他们捏造了所有罪证。—see also 另见 TRUMPED-UP

trumped-up /ˌ. ˈ.◂/ *adj* **trumped-up charges/evidence etc** false information that has been used to make someone seem guilty of a crime 捏造的罪名/证据等: *Dissidents were routinely arrested on trumped-up charges.* 异己经常因捏造的罪名被逮捕。

trump·e·ry /ˈtrʌmpərɪ; ˈtrʌmpəri/ *adj old use* not valuable【旧】毫无价值的

trum·pet¹ /ˈtrʌmpɪt; ˈtrʌmpɨt/ *n* **1** [C] a musical instrument that you blow into, which consists of a curved metal tube that is wide at the end with three buttons to change the note 小号, 喇叭〔一种铜管乐器〕 **2** [singular] the loud noise that an ELEPHANT makes 大象的吼声 —see also 另见 **blow your own trumpet** (BLOW¹ (21))

trumpet² *v* **1** [T] to tell everyone about something that you are proud of, in an annoying way 吹嘘, 大肆宣扬: *She's always trumpeting her son's achievements.* 她总是到处吹嘘儿子的成就。**2** [I] if an ELEPHANT trumpets, it makes a loud noise〔大象〕吼叫

trun·cate /ˈtrʌŋket; trʌŋˈkeɪt/ *v* [T] *formal* to make something shorter【正式】把…截短 —**truncation** /trʌŋˈkeʃən; trʌŋˈkeɪʃən/ *n* [U]

trun·cat·ed /trʌŋˈketɪd; trʌŋˈkeɪtɨd/ *adj* made shorter than before, or shorter than usual 缩短了的

trun·cheon /ˈtrʌntʃən; ˈtrʌnʃən/ *n* [C] *especially BrE* a short thick stick that police officers carry as a weapon【尤英】警棍 —compare 比较 NIGHTSTICK *AmE*【美】

trun·dle /ˈtrʌndl; ˈtrʌndl/ *v* [I always+adv/prep,T] to move slowly along on wheels, or to make something do this by pushing or pulling it (使)慢慢地移动[滚动]: *Two large wagons trundled by.* 两辆大马车缓慢地驶过。

trundle bed /ˈ.. ˌ./ *n* [C] *AmE* a low bed on wheels that you can slide under a larger bed【美】〔不用时可推入大床下的〕装有脚轮的矮床; TRUCKLE BED *BrE*【英】

trunk /trʌŋk; trʌŋk/ *n* [C] **1** the thick central wooden stem of a tree 树干 **2** *AmE* the part at the back of a car where you can put bags, tools etc【美】〔汽车后部的〕行李厢; BOOT¹ (3) *BrE*【英】**3** the very long nose of an ELEPHANT 象鼻 **4 trunks** [plural] a piece of clothing like very short trousers, worn by men for swimming 男式游泳裤 **5** *technical* the main part of your body, not including your head, arms, or legs【术语】〔人体的〕躯干 **6** a very large box made of wood or metal, in which clothes, books etc are stored or packed for travel 大箱子; 大旅行箱 —see picture at 参见 SUITCASE 图

trunk call /ˈ. ./ *n* [C] *BrE old-fashioned* a telephone call between places that are a long distance apart【英, 过时】长途电话

trunk road /ˈ. ./ *n* [C] *BrE* a main road used for travelling long distances【英】干道, 干线公路

truss¹ /trʌs; trʌs/ *v* [T] **1** also 又作 **truss up** to tie someone's arms, legs etc very firmly with rope so that they cannot move 捆, 扎, 绑〔人的手脚, 使人动弹不得〕: *They trussed up their victim and left him for dead.* 他们把受害人捆绑起来, 把他当作死尸一样。**2** to prepare a chicken, duck etc for cooking by tying its legs and wings into position 捆扎〔鸡、鸭等的腿、翅以便烹煮〕

truss² *n* [C] **1** a special belt worn to support a HERNIA (=medical problem that affects the muscles below your stomach)〔患疝病者用的〕疝带 **2** a frame supporting a roof or bridge〔支撑屋顶或桥梁的〕桁架, 构架

trust¹ /trʌst; trʌst/ *n*

1 ►BELIEF 相信◄ [U] a strong belief in the honesty, goodness etc of someone or something 信任, 信赖, 相信: *an agreement made on the basis of mutual trust* 在相互信任基础上达成的一项协议 | **put your trust in** *You shouldn't put your trust in a man like that.* 你不应该相信那样的一个男人。| **betray sb's trust** (=do something that shows someone should not have trusted you) 辜负某人的信任

2 take sth on trust to believe that something is true without having any proof 凭空相信: *I just had to take it on trust that he would deliver the money.* 我只好指望他守信用, 会把那笔钱送来。

3 ►FINANCIAL ARRANGEMENT 金融安排◄ [U] an arrangement by which someone has legal control of your money or property, especially until you are old enough to use it〔金钱或财产的〕信托, 托管〔尤指为少年儿童代管〕: **hold sth in trust** *The money your father left you will be held in trust until you are 21.* 你父亲给你留下的这笔钱将委托他人代管, 直至你满21岁。

4 ►ORGANIZATION 机构◄ [C usually singular 一般用单数] an organization or group that has control over money that will be used to help someone else 信托机构: *a charitable trust* 慈善信托机构 —see also 另见 TRUST FUND

5 a position of trust a job or position in which you have been given the responsibility of making important decisions 重任, 要职

6 ►COMPANIES 公司◄ [C] *especially AmE* a group of companies that illegally work together to reduce competition and control prices【尤美】托拉斯〔企业为减少竞争和操纵价格而非法形成的组合〕: *anti-trust laws* 反托拉斯法 —see also 另见 **breach of trust** (BREACH¹ (2)), UNIT TRUST

trust² *v*

1 ►HONEST PEOPLE 诚实的人◄ [T] to believe that someone is honest and will not harm you, cheat you etc 信任, 相信: *I trusted Max, so I lent him the money.* 我相信马克斯, 所以我把钱借给了他。| **trust sb to do sth** *Can they be trusted to look after the house?* 能信任他们会把房子照管好吗? | **trust sb completely/implicitly** *You must trust her implicitly and do everything she says.* 你必须绝对地信任她, 一切按照她所说的去做。| **not trust sb an inch** *BrE informal* (=not trust someone at all)【英, 非正式】一点都不信任某人 —opposite 反义词 DISTRUST

2 ►DEPEND ON FACTS 取决于事实◄ [T] to be sure that something is true or will happen 对…有把握, 信得过: *I wouldn't trust any information I get from them.* 从他们那儿获得的任何信息我都信不过。| **trust sth to do sth** *You can't trust the trains to run on time.* 你不能指望火车会准时。

3 trust sb's judgement to think that someone is likely to make the right decisions 相信某人的判断

4 trust you/him/them etc (to do sth)! *spoken* used to say that someone has behaved in a bad way that is typical of them【口】你/他/他们等肯定(要做某事)!〔指做不好的事〕: *Trust you to be late!* 知道你肯定要迟到!

5 I trust (that) *spoken formal* used to say politely that you hope something is true【口, 正式】我希望…: *I trust that your family is well.* 我希望你的家人都好。

6 trust sb with sth to believe that someone would be careful with something valuable or dangerous if you gave it to them 放心地把某物交给某人: *Would you trust that kid with a hammer?* 把锤交给那个孩子, 你放心得下吗? —see also 另见 TRUSTING, **tried and tested/trusted** (TRIED)

trust in sth/sb *phr v* [T] *formal* to believe in someone or something【正式】相信; 信仰: *We trust in God.* 我们信仰上帝。

trust to sth *phr v* [T] **trust to luck/chance/fate etc** to hope that luck etc will help you, usually because there is nothing else you can do 依靠运气/机会/命运等; 听其自然, 听天由命

2 **trust·ee** /trʌsˈtiː; ˌtrʌsˈtiː◂/ *n* [C] **1** someone who has control of money or property that is in a TRUST[1] (3) for someone else〔金钱或财产的〕受托人 **2** a member of a group that controls the money of a company, college, or other organization〔公司、学院或机构的〕理事, 董事会成员

trust·ee·ship /trʌsˈtiʃɪp; trʌsˈtiːʃɪp/ *n* **1** [C,U] the job of being a trustee 受托人的职位; 理事[董事]职位 **2** [U] government of an area by a country or countries that are given authority by the United Nations 托管〔联合国委托某国或某几国管理某地区〕

trust·ful /ˈtrʌstfəl; ˈtrʌstfəl/ *adj* ready to trust other people 容易相信他人的 —**trustfully** *adv* —**trustfulness** *n* [U]

trust fund /ˈ· ·/ *n* [C] money belonging to someone that is controlled for them by a trustee 信托基金

trust·ing /ˈtrʌstɪŋ; ˈtrʌstɪŋ/ *adj* willing to believe that other people are good and honest 容易相信他人的, 轻信的: *Sara's trusting nature led her to believe Tony's lies.* 萨拉轻信的性格使她相信了托尼的谎言。

trust·wor·thy /ˈtrʌstˌwɝðɪ; ˈtrʌstˌwɜːði/ *adj* someone who is trustworthy can be trusted and depended upon; DEPENDABLE 值得信赖的, 可靠的 —**trustworthiness** *n* [U]

trust·y /ˈtrʌstɪ; ˈtrʌsti/ *adj* [only before noun 仅用于名词前] *old use or humorous* a trusty weapon, vehicle, animal etc is one that you have had for a long time and can depend on【旧或幽默】〔武器、车辆、动物等〕久经考验的, 可靠的: *his trusty sword* 他那把历久弥坚的剑 | *My trusty old car will get us home.* 我那辆经久耐用的旧车将载我们回家。

1 2 **truth** /truθ; truːθ/ *n*

1 ►TRUE FACTS 事实◄ the truth the true facts about something, as opposed to what is untrue, imagined, or guessed 真实, 真相, 实情: **[+about]** *We never found out the truth about Mike's past.* 我们从未搞清楚迈克的来历。| **tell the truth** *How can we be sure that she's telling the truth?* 我们怎么能确信她说的是实情? | **be the truth** *It's the truth. She really did it.* 这是真的, 的确是她干的。| **get to the truth** (=find out what really happened) 弄清真相 *Only after several days of questioning did the police finally get to the truth.* 经过好几天的审问以后, 警方才最终弄清了真相。| **the truth of the matter** *Reforms were promised, but the truth of the matter is that nothing has changed.* 改革的许诺已经作出, 但事情的真实情况是, 什么都没有改变。

2 ►BEING TRUE 真实性◄ [U] the state or quality of being true 真实性: *Do you think there's any truth in these rumours?* 你认为这些谣传有什么真实性吗? | **a grain of truth** (=a small amount of truth) 些许真实性 *There wasn't a grain of truth in what he said.* 他的话一点真实性都没有。

3 ►IMPORTANT IDEAS 重要思想◄ [C usually plural 一般用复数] *formal* an important fact or idea that is accepted as being true【正式】真理: *the fundamental truths about mankind* 关于人类的基本真理

4 to tell (you) the truth *spoken* used when giving your personal opinion or admitting something【口】老实说, 实话对你说: *Well, to tell you the truth, I've never really liked her.* 唉, 实话对你说吧, 我从来就没有真正喜欢过她。

5 if (the) truth be known used when telling someone the real facts about a situation, or your real opinion 如果要把事实说出来的话: *If the truth be known, that was the main reason why we left.* 如果要实话实说, 那便是我们离开的主要原因。

6 nothing could be further from the truth used to say that something is definitely not true 那绝对不是事实

7 the gospel truth if you think something is the gospel truth, you believe completely that it is true 绝对的真理: *I thought everything my teachers told me was the gospel truth.* 我曾认为老师们告诉我的一切都是绝对真理。

8 in (all) truth *old-fashioned* in fact; really【过时】事实上; 的确: *In truth, I did not mind whether we went or not.* 事实上, 当时我们去不去我都无所谓。

9 the truth will out *old-fashioned* used to say that even if you try to stop people from knowing something, they will find out in the end【过时】真相终会大白的 —see also 另见 HALF-TRUTH, **home truths** (HOME[3] (6)), **the moment of truth** (MOMENT (11))

Truth, Soj·our·ner /ˈsodʒɝnɚ; ˈsɒdʒənə/ (1797-1883) a female US SLAVE (=a black person who was owned by a white person) with strong Christian beliefs, who was allowed to become a free person and who then travelled around the US teaching people about God and speaking publicly against SLAVERY (=the practice of owning slaves). 特鲁斯〔(1797-1883), 美国一女黑奴, 笃信基督教。她获准成为自由人之后, 走遍全美向人们传道, 并公开反对奴隶制度〕

Truth and Rec·on·cil·i·a·tion Com·mis·sion, the /, · · · · ·ˈ· · ·, · ·/ abbreviation 缩写为 **the TRC** in South Africa, a group of people chosen by the government to find out the truth about crimes committed during the time of APARTHEID, in order to help the people of South Africa to live together in peace 真相与和解委员会〔南非一组织, 成员由政府选任。其职责是调查种族隔离时期各种罪行的真相, 帮助南非人民和平共处〕

truth drug /ˈ· ·/ *BrE*【英】, **truth serum** /ˈ· ,· ·/ *AmE*【美】*n* [C,U] a drug that is supposed to make people tell the truth 吐真药〔一种据说能使人吐露真言的药〕

truth·ful /ˈtruθfəl; ˈtruːθfəl/ *adj* **1** someone who is truthful does not usually tell lies 诚实的, 一向说实话的: *a truthful child* 一个从不说谎的孩子 **2** a truthful statement gives the true facts about something 真实的, 如实的 —**truthfully** *adv* —**truthfulness** *n* [U]

try[1] /traɪ; traɪ/ *v* 1 1

1 ►ATTEMPT 试图◄ [I,T] to attempt to do or get something 试, 尝试; 试图; 努力: **try to do sth** *Don't shout at him; he's only trying to help.* 别对他大叫大嚷的; 他只是想帮忙。| **try sth** *Roberts tried a shot at goal.* 罗伯茨试着射门。| **try and do sth** *You must try and control your temper.* 你必须尽量控制自己的脾气。| **try** *Tim may not be good at math but at least he tries.* 蒂姆的数学也许不是很好, 但至少他很努力。| **try doing sth** (=try to do something) 试着做某事 *I'm going to try cooking a paella this evening.* 我打算今晚上试着做一道西班牙肉菜饭。| **try hard/desperately** (=make a lot of effort to do something) 极力/拼命地努力 *Sharon tried hard to keep a straight face.* 莎伦竭力忍住不笑。| **try your best/hardest** (=make as much effort as possible to do something) 尽最大努力 *I'll try my best to finish the work for this evening.* 我会尽最大努力完成今晚的工作。| **try and try** (=keep making an effort to do something) 试了又试; 一再努力 *He tried and tried to make her stay but she refused.* 他一再努力挽留她, 但遭到了她的拒绝。| **try as you might** (=used to say that someone is making a lot of effort to do something) 尽管努力了 *Try as I might, I could not overcome my fear of heights.* 我尽管努力了, 但还是无法克服恐高症。| **it wasn't for lack/want of trying** (=used to say that if someone does not achieve something it is not because they have not tried) 并不是因为没有努力 *If Simon doesn't get through his accountancy exams it won't be for lack of trying.* 如果西蒙通不过会计考试, 那并不是因为他没有努力。| **you couldn't do sth if you tried** *spoken* (=used to say that someone does not have the skill or ability to do something)【口】再努力也做不了某事 *My Dad couldn't fix a car if he tried.* 我爸爸再努力也修不了车。

2 ►TEST/USE 试验/使用◄ [T] to do or use something for a short while to discover if it is suitable, enjoyable etc 试一下; 试验; 试用: *It works really well – you should try it.* 这东西真的很好使, 你应该试试。| **try doing sth** *Try taking deep, slow breaths.* 试着慢慢地做深呼吸。| **try sth on sb/sth** *Scientists are trying the new drugs on rats.* 科学家们在老鼠身上试验这些新药。| **try sb on sth** *Petra's trying the baby on solid foods.* 彼德拉试着让婴儿吃些固体食品。| **try something new/different** (=do or use something that is different from what you usually do or use) 尝试新的/不同的东西 *a different kind of holiday for those who are willing to try something new* 为那些愿意尝试新玩法的人设计的一种另类假日 | **try sth for size** (=put on a piece of clothing to find out whether it fits you) 试穿〔衣服〕看是否合身

3 ►FOOD/DRINK 食品/饮料◄ [T] to taste food or drink to find out if you like it 尝一尝, 品尝: *You must try that home-made apple pie.* 你一定要尝一尝那自制的苹果馅饼。—see 见 TASTE[2] (USAGE)

4 ►TRY TO FIND SB/STH 试图找到某人/某物◄ [I,T] to go to a place or person, or call them, in order to find something or someone 问〔某人〕; 去〔某地〕找; 试一试; 找一找: *"Where's the*

glue?" "Try Charles; maybe he knows." "胶水在哪儿?""去问问查尔斯, 他也许知道。" | *We tried several hotels before finding one with two single rooms.* 我们试着找了好几家旅馆之后才找到一家有两个单人房间的。| *I'm sorry, but Ms Bouvier is out of the office. Could you try again later.* 对不起, 布维尔女士不在办公室, 请稍后再打来。

5 ▶DOOR/WINDOW 门/窗户◀ [T] to try to open a door, window etc in order to see if it is locked 试着打开〔门、窗等〕: *I tried the top drawer but it was locked.* 我试着打开最上面那格抽屉, 但它上了锁。| **try the lock/latch/handle** (=try to open a door, window etc by moving or pushing a lock etc) 转动锁/闩/把手〔来开门、窗等〕

6 ▶LAW 法律◀ [T usually passive 一般用被动态] to examine and judge a legal case, or someone who is thought to be guilty of a crime in a court 审判, 审理: *Lansman was tried for murder.* 兰斯曼因谋杀罪受到审判。

7 try sb's patience/temper/nerves etc to make someone feel impatient, angry, nervous etc 考验某人的耐心/脾气/神经等: *The constant noise from next door was trying my nerves to the utmost.* 隔壁那没完没了的噪声使我的神经都要崩溃了。| **it's enough to try the patience of a saint** *spoken* (=used to say that something or someone is very annoying)【口】〔令人烦扰的事或人〕连圣人也受不了 *These computer crashes are enough to try the patience of a saint.* 这些电脑故障让圣人也受不了。

8 try your hand at sth to try a new activity in order to see whether it interests you or whether you are good at it 对某事作新的尝试: *You ought to try your hand at portrait painting.* 你应该尝试一下肖像画。

9 try your luck to try to achieve something or get something you want, usually by taking a risk 试一试运气: *After his singing career failed so miserably in England, he decided to try his luck abroad.* 他在英国的演唱事业惨败之后, 决定去国外碰碰运气。

This graph shows how common the different grammar patterns of the verb **try** are. 本图表所示为动词try构成的不同语法模式的使用频率。

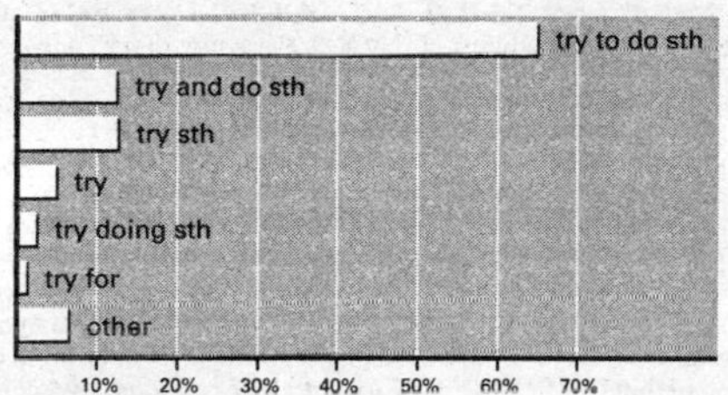

Based on the British National Corpus and the Longman Lancaster Corpus
据英国国家语料库和朗文兰开斯特语料库

try for sth *phr v* [T] *BrE* to try to get something you really want such as a job, prize, or a chance to study somewhere【英】试图获得; 争取, 谋求: *Alison's trying for a job as a research assistant.* 艾莉森正在争取一份研究助理的工作。

try sth ↔ **on** *phr v* [T] **1** to put on a piece of clothing to see if it fits you or if it suits you 试穿; 试戴: *She tried the shoes on but they were too small.* 她试穿了那些鞋, 但都太小了。**2 try it on** *BrE spoken* to behave badly in order to find out how bad you can be before people become angry【英口】〔故意表现恶劣以〕试探, 刺探: *During your first few days' teaching the kids will probably try it on just to see how you react.* 在你刚开始教学的几天里, 孩子们可能会故意捣蛋, 试探你的反应。

try sth ↔ **out** *phr v* [T] **1** to test something such as a method or a piece of equipment to see if it is effective or works properly 试用; 试验; 检验: *Jamie could hardly wait to try out his new bike.* 杰米迫不及待地想试一下他那辆新自行车。**2** to practise a skill in order to improve it 练习〔技巧〕: **try sth out on sb/sth** *She enjoyed trying her French out on Jean-Pierre.* 她喜欢找让-皮埃尔练习法语。

try out for sth *phr v* [T] *AmE* to try to be chosen as a member of a team, for a part in a play etc【美】参加选拔; 争取成为〔团队的一员等〕: *Joan tried out for the school basketball team.* 琼参加了校篮球队的选拔。

S3 **try²** *n* [C] **1** [usually singular 一般用单数] an attempt to do something 尝试, 试: *She didn't manage to break the record, but it was a good try.* 她没有能够打破纪录, 但这不失为一次很好的尝试。| **have a try** *Let me have a try; I might be able to open it.* 让我试一试; 我或许能打开。| **give it a try** *I'm not sure I can make him change his mind, but I'll give it a try.* 我不敢保证我能使他改变主意, 不过我会试一下。| **worth a try** *My idea may not work, but it's worth a try.* 我的主意也许行不通, 但值得一试。**2 give sth/sb a try** to try using or doing something to see if it is suitable or successful, or to ask if someone can help you 试一下某事/试一下向某人求助: *Shall we give that Tibetan restaurant a try?* 我们要不要尝一下那家藏族饭馆? **3** four points won by putting the ball on the ground behind the opponents' GOAL LINE in RUGBY〔橄榄球赛中〕在对方球门线后带球触地得四分

try·ing /ˈtraɪ-ɪŋ; ˈtraɪ-ɪŋ/ *adj* annoying or difficult in a way that makes you feel worried, tired etc 令人难受的; 恼人的; 困难的: *That child is very trying.* 那个孩子非常磨人。—see also 另见 TRY[7]

try·out /ˈtraɪaʊt; ˈtraɪaʊt/ *n* [singular] *AmE* a time when people who want to be in a sports team, activity etc are tested, so that the best can be chosen【美】〔体育运动队成员等的〕挑选, 选拔; TRIAL[1] (6) *BrE*【英】: *Cheerleading tryouts will be held on Friday afternoon.* 星期五下午将进行啦啦队选拔。

try-out /ˈ· ·/ *n* [C] *BrE* a period of time spent trying a new method, tool, machine etc to see if it is useful【英】〔新方法、工具、机器等的〕试用期; 试验期

tryst /trɪst; trɪst/ *n* [C] *old use or humorous*【旧或幽默】**1** an arrangement between lovers to meet in a secret place or at a secret time〔情人的〕幽会 **2** a place where lovers meet secretly 幽会处

tsar, tzar, czar /tsɑr; zɑː/ *n* [C] a male ruler of Russia before 1917〔1917年以前统治俄国的〕沙皇

tsa·ri·na, tzarina, czarina /tsɑˋrinə; zɑːˈriːnə/ *n* [C] a female ruler of Russia before 1917, or the wife of a tsar〔1917年以前统治俄国的〕女沙皇; 沙皇皇后

tsar·ism, tzarism, czarism /ˋtsɑrɪzm̩; ˈzɑːrɪzəm/ *n* [U] a system of government controlled by a tsar, especially the system in Russia before 1917〔尤指1917年以前俄国的〕沙皇制度; 沙皇统治 —**tsarist** *n* [C] —**tsarist** *adj*

tset·se fly, tzetze fly /ˋtsɛtsɪ flaɪ; ˈtetsi flaɪ/ *n* [C] an African fly that sucks the blood of people and animals and spreads serious diseases 舌蝇, 采采蝇〔非洲一种吸吮人和动物血液并传播严重疾病的苍蝇〕

T-shirt, tee-shirt /ˋti ˌʃɜt; ˈtiː ʃɜːt/ *n* [C] a soft, usually cotton shirt that stretches easily, has short SLEEVES and no collar T恤(衫); 短袖运动衫: *She was wearing jeans and a T-shirt.* 她穿着牛仔裤和T恤衫。

tsp the written abbreviation of 缩写= TEASPOON: *1 tsp of salt* 一茶匙盐

T-square /ˋti ˌskwɛr; ˈtiː skweə/ *n* [C] a large T-shaped piece of wood or plastic used to draw exact plans or pictures〔画图用的〕丁字尺

tsu·na·mi /tsuˋnɑmɪ; tsʊˈnɑːmi/ *n* [C] *technical* a TIDAL WAVE【术语】海啸

TT, the /ˌti ˋti; ˌtiː ˈtiː/ Tourist Trophy; a set of British MOTORCYCLE races, held every year on the Isle of Man 旅游杯摩托车赛〔英国每年在马恩岛举行的系列摩托车赛〕

tub /tʌb; tʌb/ *n* [C]

1 ▶CONTAINER 容器◀ **a)** a small container made of paper or plastic with a lid, in which food is bought or stored〔盛食物的〕小钵: *a tub of margarine* 一小钵人造黄油 **b)** a large round container without a lid, used for washing, storing things in etc 盆, 缸: *There were roses in tubs on the balcony.* 在阳台上的大盆里种有玫瑰花。

2 ▶BATH 洗澡◀ *AmE* a large container in which you sit to wash yourself; BATHTUB【美】浴缸

3 ▶AMOUNT 数量◀ also 又作 **tubful** the amount of liquid, food etc that a tub can contain 一钵/一盆的容量: *We ate a whole tub of ice-cream.* 我们吃了整整一盒冰淇淋。

4 ▶BOAT 船◀ *humorous* an old boat that travels slowly【幽默】行驶缓慢的旧船, 老爷船

5 ▶PERSON 人◀ *AmE informal* someone who is short and fat【美, 非正式】矮胖子: *Their children are all tubs.* 他们的孩子全都是矮胖子。

tu·ba /ˋtjubə; ˈtjuːbə/ *n* [C] a very large musical instrument, consisting of a curved metal tube, larger than a TRUMPET[1] (1) which you blow into and which produces a very deep sound 大号〔一种铜管乐器〕

tub·by /ˋtʌbɪ; ˈtʌbi/ *adj informal* short and slightly fat, with a round stomach; PLUMP[1] (1)【非正式】矮胖的, 大腹便便的 —see 见 FAT[1] (USAGE)

tube /tub; tjuːb/ *n*

1 ▶PIPE FOR LIQUID 液体输送管◀ [C] a round pipe made of metal, glass, rubber etc, especially for liquids or gases to go through〔输送液体或气体的〕圆管, 管子, 筒 —see also 另见 INNER TUBE, TEST TUBE

2 ▶CONTAINER 容器◀ [C] a narrow container made of plastic or soft metal and closed at one end, that you press between your fingers in order to push out the soft substance that is inside〔装有柔软物质的〕软管: *a tube of toothpaste* 一管牙膏

3 ▶IN YOUR BODY 在人体内◀ [C] a tube-shaped part inside your body〔身体内的〕管, 道: *the bronchial tubes* 支气管

4 ▶TRAINS 列车◀ **the tube** *BrE* the system of trains that run under the ground in London【英】地下铁道, 地铁: *Smoking is forbidden on the Tube.* 地铁里禁止吸烟。| *a tube station* 地铁站 | **by tube** *It's quicker by tube.* 坐地铁要快一些。—compare 比较 SUBWAY (2) —see also 另见 UNDERGROUND[3]

5 go down the tubes *informal* if a situation goes down the tubes, it quickly becomes ruined or spoiled【非正式】被毁灭; 被破坏: *I wasn't going to sit and watch my career go down the tubes.* 我不会坐视我的事业被毁掉。

6 ▶TELEVISION 电视◀ **the tube** *AmE informal* the television【美, 非正式】电视机

7 ▶ELECTRICAL EQUIPMENT 电子设备◀ [C] *technical* the part of a television that creates the picture; CATHODE RAY TUBE【术语】电视机显像管; 阴极射线管

tubes 管子, 筒

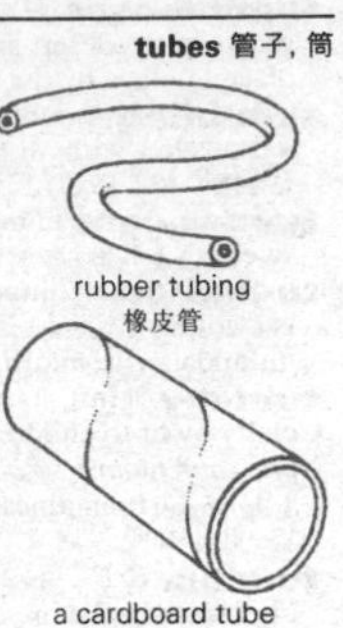

tu·ber /ˈtubɚ; ˈtjuːbə/ *n* [C] a round swollen part that grows below the ground on the stem of certain plants such as the potato, from which new plants grow〔马铃薯等植物的〕块茎 —**tuberous** *adj*

tu·ber·cu·lar /tuˋbɝkjəlɚ; tjuːˈbɜːkjʊlə/ also 又作 **tuberculous** /-kjələs; -kjʊləs/ *adj* connected with tuberculosis 结核病的

tu·ber·cu·lo·sis /tuˏbɝkjəˋlosɪs; tjuːˌbɜːkjʊˈləʊsʒs/ *n* [U] a serious infectious disease that affects many parts of your body, especially your lungs; TB 结核病〔尤指肺结核〕

tube top /ˈ· ·/ *n* [C] *AmE informal* a piece of women's clothing that goes around your chest and back to cover your breasts but does not cover your shoulders or stomach【美, 非正式】〔妇女的〕管状胸褡; 抹胸; BOOB TUBE *BrE*【英】

tub·ing /ˈtubɪŋ; ˈtjuːbɪŋ/ *n* [U] tubes in general, especially when connected together into a system〔尤指连成一个系统的〕管道, 管子: *rubber tubing* 橡皮管

Tub·man /ˈtʌbmən; ˈtʌbmən/, **Har·riet** /ˈhærɪət; ˈhæriət/ (?1820-1913) a US SLAVE who escaped to the northern US (where slavery was not allowed) and became an important member of the Underground Railroad, a system for helping slaves who were trying to escape. She also worked for the army of the North in the Civil War. 塔布曼〔(?1820-1913), 美国一黑奴。她逃到美国北方后成为"地下铁路"的重要联络员, 帮助奴隶设法出逃。美国内战期间, 她还替北方军队做事〕

tub-thump·ing /ˈ· ˌ··/ *adj* [only before noun 仅用于名词前] *BrE informal* trying to persuade people about your opinions in a loud and forceful way【英, 非正式】〔设法说服人时〕大喊大叫的, 气焰逼人的: *a tub-thumping speech* 慷慨激昂的演讲 —**tub-thumping** *n* [U] —**tub-thumper** *n* [C]

tu·bu·lar /ˈtubjəlɚ; ˈtjuːbjʊlə/ *adj* **1** made of tubes or in the form of a tube 用管子做成的; 管状的: *tubular metal furniture* 用金属管制作的家具 **2** *AmE* a word meaning very good or excellent, used especially by young people【美】非常出色的, 挺好的〔尤为年轻人使用〕

TUC /ˌti ju ˈsi; ˌtiː juː ˈsiː/ *n* the abbreviation of 缩写= Trades Union Congress; the association of British trade unions〔英国的〕职工大会; 工会联合会

tuck¹ /tʌk; tʌk/ *v* **1** [T always+adv/prep] to push the edge of a piece of cloth or paper into something so that it looks tidier or stays in place 把〔衣服或纸张〕塞进〔某处〕: **tuck sth into/under** *Nick was tucking his shirt into his trousers when she walked in.* 她走进去的时候, 尼克正把衬衫下摆塞进裤子里。**2** [T always+adv/prep] to put something into a small space, especially in order to protect or hide it 把…收藏起来: **tuck sth behind/under/into sth** *I tucked the letter into my bag.* 我把那封信塞进包里。**3** [T] to put a TUCK (=a special fold) in a piece of clothing 在〔衣服里〕缝褶子

tuck sth ↔ away *phr v* [T] **1 be tucked (away) somewhere a)** if a place is tucked away it is in a quiet area〔某处所〕隐藏在〔寂静的地方〕: *The inn was tucked away in a remote mountain village.* 那家客栈隐藏在一个偏远的山村里。**b)** if someone or something is tucked away they are hidden or difficult to find 躲藏, 隐藏; 被收藏: *The key to the cellar was tucked away at the back of the shelf.* 地窖的钥匙被藏在架子的背后。**2** *informal* to store something, especially money, in a safe place【非正式】把某物〔尤指钱〕收藏在安全处: *Over the years, she had tucked away over £2,000.* 这些年来, 她一共攒了两千多英镑。**3** *informal* to eat a lot of food, usually quickly and with enjoyment【非正式】大吃〔尤指狼吞虎咽地美美地吃〕: *I watched as he tucked away a huge plate of pie.* 我看着他狼吞虎咽地吃完了一大盘馅饼。

tuck in *phr v* **1** [I] *informal especially BrE* to eat eagerly【非正式, 尤英】大吃: *Come on everyone, tuck in!* 来吧, 各位, 大吃一顿吧! **2** [T **tuck** sb ↔ **in**] to make a child comfortable in bed by arranging the sheets around them 帮助〔孩子〕盖好被子安睡: *I'll come up and tuck you in in a minute.* 我一会儿上来帮你盖好被子。**3** [T **tuck** sth ↔ **in**] to put the edge of a piece of clothing, paper etc inside something so that it looks tidier or stays in place 把〔衣服、纸张等〕塞进〔某处〕: *The blanket was too short to tuck in at the bottom.* 毯子太短了, 底端塞不进去。**4** [T **tuck** sth ↔ **in**] to move a part of your body inwards so that it does not stick out so much 使〔身体的某一部分〕紧贴身体: *When you dive, keep your elbows tucked in.* 你在跳水的时候要夹紧肘部。

tuck into sth *phr v* [T] *informal* to eat something eagerly【非正式】大吃, 狼吞虎咽地吃: *They were tucking into the Christmas turkey.* 他们狼吞虎咽地吃着圣诞火鸡。

tuck sb ↔ **up** *phr v* [T] **1** to make a child comfortable in bed by arranging the sheets around them 帮助〔孩子〕盖好被子安睡 **2 be tucked up** *informal* to be lying or sitting in bed【非正式】卧〔坐〕在床上: *He was tucked up in bed doing a crossword.* 他坐在床上玩纵横填字谜游戏。

tuck² *n* **1** [C] a narrow flat fold of cloth sewn into a piece of clothing for decoration or to give it a special shape〔衣服的〕褶, 缝褶 **2** [U] *BrE old-fashioned* a word for cakes, sweets etc used especially by schoolchildren【英, 过时】糖果糕点〔此词多为小学生使用〕 **3** [C] a small medical operation done to make your face or stomach look flatter and younger〔脸部或腹部的〕整容小手术: *tiny tucks behind her ears* 她耳朵背后的细微整容

Tuck, Friar —see 见 FRIAR TUCK

tuck·er¹ /ˈtʌkɚ; ˈtʌkə/ *v*

tucker sb **out** *phr v* [T] *AmE informal* to make someone very tired【美, 非正式】使非常疲乏: *The kids were tuckered out after the walk.* 孩子们在步行之后疲倦极了。

tucker² *n* [U] *AustrE, NZE informal* food【澳, 新西兰, 非正式】食物 —see also 另见 **your best bib and tucker** (BIB (3))

Tucson /ˈtusɑn; ˈtuːsɒn/ a city in South Arizona in the US, surrounded by mountains. It is a popular retirement and health centre. 吐桑〔美国亚利桑那州南部一城市。四面环山, 是大众喜爱的退休疗养和保健中心〕

-tude /tud; tjuːd/ *suffix* [in nouns 构成名词] another form of the suffix -ITUDE 后缀 -itude 的另一种形式: *disquietude* (=anxiety) 忧虑不安 | *desuetude* 废弃不用

Tu·dor /ˈtudɚ; ˈtjuːdə/ *adj* connected with the period in British history between 1485 and 1603〔英国历史从1485-1603年〕都铎王朝的; 都铎王室的: **Tudor house/ buildings/architecture etc** (=built in the style used in the Tudor period) 都铎式房子/大楼/建筑等 *a rambling Tudor house overlooking the river* 一幢俯瞰河面的大而无当的都铎式房屋

Tudor, Henry —see 见 King HENRY VII

Tu·dors, the /ˈtudɚ; ˈtjuːdə/ the members of the Tudor family 都铎王朝: *After the Tudors, James I came to the throne.* 继都铎王朝之后, 詹姆斯一世登上王位。

Tues·day /ˈtuzdɪ; ˈtjuːzdi/ written abbreviation 缩写为 **Tue.** or **Tues.** *n* [C,U] the day between Monday and Wednesday. In Britain, Tuesday is considered the second day of the week, and in the US it is considered the third day of the week 星期二: *We moved in last Tuesday.* 我们上星期二搬进来的。| *The results come out on Tuesday.* 结果在星期二出来。| *His birthday is on a Tuesday this year.* 今年他的生日是在一个星期二。| **Tuesday morning/evening etc** *Let's go out for a meal Tuesday night.* 星期二晚上我们出去吃饭吧。| **on Tuesdays** (=each Tuesday) 每周二 *I usually stay in on Tuesdays.* 周二我通常在家。| **the Tuesday** *BrE* (=the Tuesday of the particular week being mentioned)【英】〔指提及的某周的〕星期二 *We went out on the Tuesday.* 那个星期二我们出去了。

tuft /tʌft; tʌft/ *n* [C] a bunch of hair, feathers, grass etc growing or held closely together at their base〔头发、羽毛、草等的〕一束，一簇: *a few scrawny goats chewing at tufts of grass* 几只正在咀嚼簇簇青草的骨瘦如柴的山羊

tuft·ed /ˈtʌftɪd; ˈtʌftɨ̣d/ *adj* with a tuft or tufts 有簇饰的; 有羽冠的: *a tufted duck* 一只长着羽冠的鸭子

tug¹ /tʌg; tʌg/ *v* **tugged, tugging** [I,T] also 又作 **tug at** to pull with one or more short, quick pulls〔迅猛地〕拉，拖，拽: *She kept tugging insistently at Alan's sleeve.* 她执意不停地拽艾伦的袖子。

tug² *n* [C] **1** also 又作 **tug boat** /ˈ· ·/ a small strong boat used for pulling or guiding ships into a port, up a river etc 拖船 **2** [usually singular 一般用单数] a sudden strong pull 猛拉，拖，拽: *He gave the rope a sharp tug and I fell sprawled on the deck.* 他猛地拉了一下绳子，我四脚朝天地倒在甲板上。

tug-of-war /ˌ· · ˈ·/ *n* [singular] **1** a test of strength in which two teams pull against each other on a rope 拔河赛 **2** a situation in which two people or groups try very hard to get or keep the same thing 激烈的争夺: *The children are trapped in an emotional tug-of-war when their parents quarrel.* 当父母吵架时，孩子们陷入了情感上的激烈斗争。

Tuil·e·ries, the /ˈtwiləri; ˈtwiːləri/ a large public garden in central Paris, near the Louvre 土伊勒里公园〔巴黎市中心一大型公园，位于卢浮宫附近〕

tu·i·tion /tuˈɪʃən; tjuˈɪʃən/ *n* [U] **1** teaching, especially in small groups〔尤指学生人数不多的〕教学，讲课: *I had to have extra tuition in maths.* 我不得不上数学的补习课。| **tuition fees** (=the money you pay for being taught) 学费 **2** *AmE* the money you pay for being taught【美】学费: *When I started college, tuition was $350 a quarter.* 我开始念大学的时候，学费是一个学期350美元。

tu·lip /ˈtuləp; ˈtjuːlɨ̣p/ *n* [C] a brightly coloured flower that is shaped like a cup and grows from a BULB (2) in spring 郁金香(花)

Tull /tʌl; tʌl/, **Jeth·ro** /ˈdʒɛθro; ˈdʒeθrəʊ/ (1674-1741) a British farmer and inventor, who developed new methods of farming and invented a machine for putting seeds in the ground 塔尔〔(1674-1741)，英国农场主、发明家。他发明了新的播种方法和播种机〕

tulle /tul; tjuːl/ *n* [U] a thin soft silk or NYLON material like a net〔丝绸或尼龙的〕薄纱，绢网

Tul·sa /ˈtʌlsə; ˈtʌlsə/ a city in northeast Oklahoma in the US. It is an important centre of the US oil industry. 塔尔萨〔美国俄克拉何马州东北部一城市，为美国重要的石油工业中心〕

tum·ble¹ /ˈtʌmbl̩; ˈtʌmbəl/ *v* [I] **1** [always+adv/prep] to fall quickly and suddenly downwards, especially with a rolling movement 倒下，跌倒，摔倒; 滚下; 翻滚: [**+over/backwards/down**] *She lost her balance and tumbled backwards.* 她失去了平衡，朝后倒去。**2** [always+adv/ prep] to move in an uncontrolled way 莽莽撞撞地行动; 胡乱地走: [**+into/through**] *The kids tumbled out of the car.* 孩子们一窝蜂地下了车。**3** if prices or figures tumble, they go down suddenly and by a large amount〔价格或数字〕猛跌，暴跌: *Stock market prices have tumbled over the past week.* 股市价格在过去的一周里猛跌。**4** [always+adv/ prep] if someone's hair tumbles down, it is long and thick and has curls〔长而鬈曲的浓发〕垂下，垂落: *Long blonde hair tumbled about her face.* 金色的长发垂落在她的脸上。**5** *AmE* to do TUMBLING【美】翻跟斗，空翻

tumble to sth *phr v* [T] *informal* to suddenly understand or realize something【非正式】忽然明白: *It was a long time before she tumbled to what I meant.* 过了很久她才忽然明白我的意思。

tumble² *n* [C] a fall, especially from a high place〔尤指从高处〕倒下，跌倒，摔倒 —see also 另见 ROUGH-AND-TUMBLE

tum·ble·down /ˈtʌmbl̩ˌdaun; ˈtʌmbəldaʊn/ *adj* [only before noun 仅用于名词前] **tumbledown building/house/cottage etc** old and beginning to fall down, often in a way that seems attractive 摇摇欲坠的大楼/房子/小屋等: *a row of tumbledown labourer's cottages* 一排摇摇欲坠的劳工小屋

tumble dry·er /ˌ·· ˈ··/ *n* [C] *BrE* a machine that uses hot air to dry clothes after they have been washed; DRYER【英】衣服烘干机

tum·bler /ˈtʌmblɚ; ˈtʌmblə/ *n* [C] **1** a glass with a flat bottom and no handle 无柄的平底玻璃杯 —see picture at 参见 GLASS¹ 图 **2** also 又作 **tumblerful** /-ful; -fʊl/ the amount of liquid that this type of glass can contain 一平底玻璃杯的容量: *Jack must have had about six tumblers of whisky last night.* 杰克昨晚上一定喝了差不多六杯威士忌。**3** *old-fashioned* someone who performs special movements such as doing SOMERSAULTS (=a jump in which you turn over completely in the air); ACROBAT【过时】翻跟头杂技演员

tum·ble·weed /ˈtʌmbl̩ˌwid; ˈtʌmbəlwiːd/ *n* [U] a plant that grows in the desert areas of North America and is blown from place to place by the wind〔北美沙漠地区的〕风滚草

tum·bling /ˈtʌmblɪŋ; ˈtʌmblɪŋ/ *n* [U] a sport similar to GYMNASTICS but with all the exercises done on the floor 翻腾运动〔与体操相似的运动，但所有动作是在地上做的〕

tu·mes·cent /tuˈmɛsn̩t; tjuːˈmesənt/ *adj technical* swollen or swelling【术语】肿胀的，肿大的 —**tumescence** *n* [U]

tu·mid /ˈtumɪd; ˈtjuːmɨ̣d/ *adj technical* a tumid part of the body is swollen【术语】〔身体某一部分〕肿胀的，肿大的 —**tumidity** /tuˈmɪdətɪ; tjuːˈmɪdɨ̣ti/ *n* [U]

tum·my /ˈtʌmɪ; ˈtʌmi/ *n* [C] a word for STOMACH, used especially by or to children 肚子〔尤为儿语〕: *Touch your head and pat your tummy.* 摸摸自己的脑袋，拍拍自己的肚子。| **tummy bug/upset** (=an illness of the stomach that makes you feel sick) 胃/肚子难受

tu·mour *BrE*【英】, **tumor** *AmE*【美】/ˈtumɚ; ˈtjuːmə/ a mass of diseased cells in your body that have divided and increased too quickly 肿瘤: *a brain tumour* 脑瘤 | **malignant/benign tumour** (=dangerous/harmless tumour) 恶性/良性肿瘤 —**tumourous** *adj*

tu·mult /ˈtumʌlt; ˈtjuːmʌlt/ *n* [C,U] *formal*【正式】**1** a state of confusion, noise, and excitement, often caused by a large crowd〔通常由一大群人引起的〕混乱，骚乱; 吵闹，喧哗: *His announcement was drowned in the tumult.* 他的宣读被淹没在一片喧哗声中。| **in tumult** (=in a state of confusion or change) 混乱/动荡之中 *The whole country is in tumult.* 全国一片混乱。**2** a state of mental confusion caused by strong emotions such as anger, sadness etc〔思想上的〕波动，激动: **in tumult** (=anxious, confused, or unhappy) 焦急不安，心烦意乱 *His mind was in tumult.* 他心里烦躁不安。

tu·mul·tu·ous /tuˈmʌltʃuəs; tjuːˈmʌltʃuəs/ *adj* **1** full of activity, confusion, or violence 混乱的，骚乱的，乱哄哄的: *the tumultuous weeks leading up to the revolution* 革命爆发前混乱的几个星期 **2** very loud 嘈杂的，吵闹的，喧哗的: *Tumultuous applause rang through the hall.* 整个大厅里掌声雷动。—**tumultuously** *adv*

tu·mu·lus /ˈtumjələs; ˈtjuːmjɨ̣ləs/ *n* [C] a very large pile of earth put over a grave by people in former times〔古时的〕坟头

tu·na /ˈtunə; ˈtjuːnə/ *n* **1** [C] a large sea fish caught for food 金枪鱼〔一种食用海鱼〕**2** [U] the flesh of this fish, usually sold cooked in tins 金枪鱼肉〔通常以熟食罐装形式销售〕

Tun·bridge Wells /ˌtʌnbrɪdʒ ˈwɛlz; ˌtʌnbrɪdʒ ˈwelz/ a town in Kent, southeast England, which was an important SPA (=a place with a spring of mineral water) in the 17th and 18th centuries. Tunbridge Wells is a very wealthy and rather conservative place. 坦布里奇韦尔斯〔英格兰东南部肯特郡一城镇。17和18世纪，该镇为一重要温泉疗养地，是一个非常富裕但相当保守的地方〕

tun·dra /ˈtʌndrə; ˈtʌndrə/ *n* [U] the large flat areas of land in the north of Russia, Canada etc, where it is very cold and there are no trees 冻原，苔原

tune¹ /tun; tjuːn/ *n* [C] **1** a series of musical notes that are played or sung one after the other to make a pattern of sound that is usually pleasant to listen to 调子，曲调，旋律: *I recognize that tune but I can't remember the name of the song.* 我记得那个调子，但忘记了那首歌的名称。**2** **in tune** playing or singing the correct musical note 合调: *Sadle can't sing in tune.* 萨迪唱歌跑调。**3** **out of tune** playing or singing higher or lower than the correct musical note 走调: *That old piano's completely out of tune.* 那架旧钢琴完全走调了。**4** **be in tune with/out of tune with** to be able or unable to realize, understand, or agree with what someone else thinks or wants 与…协调(一致)/不协调: *Many politicians are totally out of tune with the needs of ordinary people.* 许多政客完全不考虑普通人的需求。**5** **to the tune of $1,000/£2 million etc** *informal* used to emphasize how large an amount or number is【非正式】达到1000美元/200万英镑等〔用来强调数量或数目大〕: *We're already in debt to the tune of £5,000.* 我们已经欠下高达5000英镑的债了。—see also 另见 **call the tune** (CALL¹ (25)), **change your tune** (CHANGE¹ (13)), **dance to sb's tune** (DANCE² (6))

tune² *v* [T] **1** to make a musical instrument play at the right PITCH¹ (3) 为〔乐器〕调音: *Someone's coming tomorrow to tune the piano.* 明天会有人来给钢琴调音。**2** to make an engine work as well as possible 把〔发动机〕调到最佳运转状态 **3** to make a radio or television receive broadcasts from a particular place 把〔收音机或电视机〕调到某一频道; 收听; 收看: *The radio was tuned to a classical station.* 收音机被调到了一个古典音乐台。| **stay tuned to (sth)** (=continue watching or listening to the same

radio station or television programme) 继续收听或收看〔同一个电台或电视节目〕 *Stay tuned for the latest news from Washington.* 请继续收听来自华盛顿的最新消息。**4 finely tuned sense/perception/ balance etc** a very careful and skilful way of judging something, understanding situations etc 细致的理解/深入的认识/微妙的平衡等: *She had a finely tuned sense of right and wrong.* 她对是非有细致入微的理解。

tune in *phr v* [I,T] **1** to watch or listen to a broadcast on radio or television 收听(广播); 收看(电视): *60 million people tuned in to watch the Royal Wedding.* 有6000万人收看了这次王室婚礼。| **tune sth ↔ in (to sth)** *Tune the radio in to KCRW.* 把收音机调到 KCRW 电台。**2 tuned in** able to realize or understand what is happening or what other people are thinking 了解, 熟悉〔情况或别人的想法等〕: *She doesn't seem very tuned in to these new developments.* 她对这些新的动态似乎不很了解。

tune out *phr v* [I,T] *informal especially AmE* to ignore or stop listening to someone【非正式, 尤美】不理睬, 置之不理: *She tuned out after I said no extra money was involved.* 我说了没有额外追加的钱款之后, 她便不加理睬了。| **tune sb/sth ↔ out** *I learned to tune out the background noise.* 我学会了对背景杂音听而不闻。

tune up *phr v* **1** [I] when musicians tune up, they prepare their instruments to play at the same PITCH[1] (3) as each other〔音乐家演奏前〕把乐器调好音 **2** [T **tune** sth ↔ **up**] to make a musical instrument play at the right PITCH[1] (3) 给〔乐器〕调好音

tune·ful /ˈtunfʊl; ˈtjuːnfəl/ *adj* pleasant to listen to 悦耳动听的, 曲调优美的: *tuneful melodies from light opera* 轻歌剧悦耳动听的旋律 —**tunefully** *adv* —**tunefulness** *n* [U]

tune·less /ˈtunlɪs; ˈtjuːnləs/ *adj* not having a pleasant tune 不合调的, 不悦耳的: *tuneless humming* 不成曲调的乱哼哼 —**tunelessly** *adv*

tun·er /ˈtunɚ; ˈtjuːnə/ *n* [C] the part of a radio or television that you can change to receive different TV stations and radio stations〔电视机或收音机上的〕调谐器

tune-up /ˈ· ·/ *n* [C] the process of making small changes to an engine so that it works as well as possible〔发动机的〕微调保养

tung·sten /ˈtʌŋstən; ˈtʌŋstən/ *n* [U] a hard metal that is one of the ELEMENTS (=simple substances) used in making steel 钨〔一种硬金属元素〕

tu·nic /ˈtunɪk; ˈtjuːnɪk/ *n* [C] **1** a long loose piece of clothing worn in former times, usually without sleeves (SLEEVE (1)) or a belt〔古人穿的一种〕(无袖) 长袍 **2** *BrE* a specially shaped short coat worn by soldiers, police officers etc as part of a uniform【英】〔士兵、警察等穿的〕紧身短上衣

tuning fork /ˈ·· ·/ *n* [C] a small U-shaped steel instrument that makes a particular musical note when you hit it〔为乐器调音用的〕音叉 —see picture at 参见 FORK[1] 图

tuning peg /ˈ·· ·/ *n* [C] a wooden screw used for tightening the strings on a VIOLIN, GUITAR etc〔小提琴、吉他等上面的〕调音弦轴, 琴栓 —see picture at 参见 PEG[1] 图

Tu·nis /ˈtunɪs; ˈtjuːnɪs/ the capital city of Tunisia, in the north-east of the country. The ruins of the ancient city of Carthage are close to Tunis. 突尼斯〔突尼斯首都, 位于该国东北部。迦太基古城遗址位于该市附近〕

Tu·nis·i·a /tjuˈnɪʃə; tjuːˈnɪziə/ a country in northwest Africa, between Libya and Algeria. Population: 9,705,000 (2001). Capital: Tunis. The south of the country forms part of the Sahara Desert. 突尼斯〔非洲西北部一国家, 位于利比亚和阿尔及利亚之间。人口: 9,705,000 (2001), 首都: 突尼斯。该国南部为撒哈拉大沙漠的一部分〕—**Tunisian** *n, adj*

tunnel 隧道

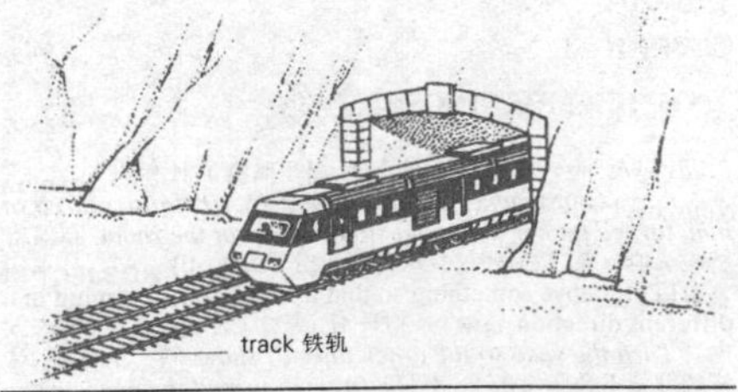

[3] **tun·nel**[1] /ˈtʌnl; ˈtʌnl/ *n* [C] **1** a passage that has been dug under the ground for cars, trains etc to go through〔汽车、火车等通行的〕隧道 **2** a passage under the ground that animals have dug to live in〔动物挖掘的〕地道, 坑道

tunnel[2] *v* **tunnelled, tunnelling** *BrE*【英】, **tunneled, tunneling** *AmE*【美】[I always+adv/prep,T] to dig a long passage under the ground 挖掘(隧道、地道): [**+under/through etc**] *tunneling through hard rock* 掘隧道穿过坚硬的岩石 | **tunnel your way into/through/under etc** (=move somewhere by digging a passage) 掘隧道进入/穿过; 在…下面掘隧道 *The prisoners tunneled their way under the fence.* 囚犯们在栅栏下面挖了一条地道。

tunnel vi·sion /ˌ·· ˈ··/ *n* [U] **1** the tendency to only think about one part of something such as a problem or plan, instead of considering all the parts of it 狭隘的眼光, 一孔之见, 井蛙之见: *He had the paranoia and tunnel vision of the knee-jerk patriot.* 他具有盲目的爱国者那种多疑和狭隘。**2** a condition in which someone's eyes are damaged so that they can only see things that are straight ahead 管状视〔视力受损而只能直视前方的物体〕

tun·ny /ˈtʌnɪ; ˈtʌni/ *n* [C,U] a British form of the word TUNA tuna 的英式拼写

tup·pence /ˈtʌpəns; ˈtʌpəns/ *n* [C,U] a British spelling of TWOPENCE twopence 的英式拼法

tup·penny /ˈtʌpənɪ; ˈtʌpni/ *adj* [only before noun 仅用于名词前] a British spelling of TWOPENNY twopenny 的英式拼法

Tup·per·ware /ˈtʌpɚˌwɛr; ˈtʌpəweə/ *n* [U] *trademark* a type of plastic container that closes very tightly and is used to store food【商标】"特百惠"塑料容器〔带有密闭盖子, 用来存放食物等〕

tur·ban /ˈtɝbən; ˈtɜːbən/ *n* [C] a long piece of cloth that you wind tightly round your head, worn by men in parts of North Africa and Southern Asia and sometimes by women as a fashion〔北非、南亚地区男性缠在头上的〕头巾; 女用头巾

tur·bid /ˈtɝbɪd; ˈtɜːbɪd/ *adj formal* turbid water or liquid is dirty and muddy【正式】〔水或液体〕混浊的, 不清的: *the silty, turbid waters of the Congo river* 淤泥阻塞、混浊不清的刚果河河水 —**turbidity** /tɝˈbɪdətɪ; tɜːˈbɪdɪti/ *n* [U]

tur·bine /ˈtɝbɪn; ˈtɜːbaɪn/ *n* [C] an engine or motor in which the pressure of a liquid or gas moves a special wheel around 涡轮机, 透平机 —see also 另见 GAS TURBINE, WIND TURBINE

tur·bo·charg·er /ˈtɝboˌtʃɑrdʒɚ; ˈtɜːbəʊˌtʃɑːdʒə/ also 又作 **turbo** *n* [C] a system that makes a vehicle more powerful by using a turbine to force air and petrol into the engine under increased pressure 涡轮增压器: *The 2.4 litre turbo charger diesel is the top-seller.* 2.4 升的涡轮增压器柴油车是最畅销的。—**turbocharged** *adj*

tur·bo·jet /ˈtɝboˌdʒɛt; ˈtɜːbəʊdʒet/ *n* [C] **1** a powerful engine that makes something, especially an aircraft, move forwards, by forcing out hot air and gases at the back 涡轮喷气发动机 **2** an aircraft that gets power from this type of engine 涡轮式喷气飞机

tur·bo·prop /ˈtɝboˌprɑp; ˈtɜːbəʊprɒp/ *n* [C] **1** a turbine engine that drives a PROPELLER 涡轮螺旋桨发动机 **2** an aircraft that gets power from this type of engine 涡轮式螺旋桨飞机

tur·bot /ˈtɝbət; ˈtɜːbɒt/ *n* [C,U] a large flat European fish 大菱鲆〔欧洲产的一种扁平的大鱼〕

tur·bu·lence /ˈtɝbjələns; ˈtɜːbjʊləns/ *n* [U] **1** irregular and violent movements of air or water that are caused by the wind〔由风造成的空气或水的〕湍流; 不稳定的强气流: *The flight was very uncomfortable because of turbulence.* 由于遇上不稳定的强气流, 这次飞行很不舒服。**2** a political or emotional situation that is very confused〔政治或情感上的〕骚乱, 骚动: *A period of political turbulence followed the civil war.* 内战之后是一段政治动荡的时期。

tur·bu·lent /ˈtɝbjələnt; ˈtɜːbjʊlənt/ *adj* **1** a turbulent situation or period of time is one in which there are a lot of sudden changes and often wars or violence 骚乱的, 动乱的: *The Reformation was one of the most turbulent periods in English history.* 宗教改革是英国历史上最为动荡的时期之一。**2** turbulent air or water moves around a lot because of the wind 风大浪高的; 狂风大作的: *turbulent weather conditions* 狂风大作的天气状况 **3** turbulent crowds or people are noisy and violent〔人群〕骚动的; 暴戾的: *the turbulent populace of the city's teeming ghettos* 该市拥挤的贫民窟里骚动不安的人们

turd /tɝd; tɜːd/ *n* [C] **1** *informal* a slightly rude word for a piece of the solid waste material you pass from your body【非正式】大便〔稍微粗俗的用语〕**2** *taboo* an insulting word for an unpleasant person【讳】混蛋, 臭小子: *You stupid little turd!* 你这个愚蠢的臭小子!

tu·reen /tuˈrin; tjʊˈriːn/ *n* [C] a large dish with a lid used for serving soup or vegetables〔盛汤用的〕大盖碗, 汤碗

turf¹ /tɝf; tɜːf/ *n* **1** [U] a surface that is made up of soil and a thick covering of grass 草皮: *the springy turf of the lawn* 草坪上有弹性的草皮 **2** *plural* **turfs** *or* **turves** /tɝvz; tɜːvz/ [C] *BrE* a square piece of turf cut out of the ground【英】一块草皮; SOD¹ (4) *AmE*【美】**3** **the turf** the sport of horse racing, or the track on which horses race 赛马（运动）; 赛马跑道: *devotees of the turf* 赛马爱好者 **4** [U] *AmE informal* an area that you think of as being your own【美，非正式】〔自己划定的〕地盘: *They resented these strangers invading their turf.* 他们对这些陌生人侵入他们的地盘感到愤怒。| **turf war** (=a fight or argument over the things you think belong to you) 地盘之争，地盘争夺战 **5** [C,U] *AmE, IrishE* a soft brown substance like earth that is used for burning instead of coal, especially in Ireland; PEAT【美，爱尔兰】〔尤指爱尔兰的〕泥炭，泥煤

turf² *v* [T] to cover an area of land with TURF¹ (1) 用草皮覆盖〔某块地〕

turf sb/sth ↔ **out** *phr v* [T] *BrE informal* to get rid of someone or something【英，非正式】赶走〔某人〕; 扔掉〔某物〕: *He's been turfed out of the golf club for bad behaviour.* 他因为行为不端而被逐出了这家高尔夫俱乐部。

turf ac·coun·tant /ˈ· ·,··/ *n* [C] *BrE* someone who has a business where people can BET¹ (1) on the results of horse races, football games etc; BOOKMAKER【英】〔经营赛马、足球比赛等赌博的〕赌注登记经纪人

Tur·ge·nev /tʊəˋgenjɛf; tʊəˈgeɪnjef/**, I·van** /ˈaɪvən; ˈaɪvən/ (1818-83) a Russian writer of books, short stories, and plays. His best-known works are his play *A Month in the Country* and his book *Fathers and Sons* 屠格涅夫〔(1818-1883)，俄国作家、短篇小说家和剧作家。最著名的作品有剧作《村居一月》和小说《父与子》〕

tur·gid /ˈtɝdʒɪd; ˈtɜːdʒɪd/ *adj* **1** turgid writing or speech is boring and difficult to understand〔写作或讲话〕枯燥乏味的; 很难理解的: *The whole play is turgid, amateurish drivel.* 整场戏枯燥乏味，全是业余水准的废话。**2** *formal* full and swollen with liquid or air【正式】〔因有液体或空气〕鼓得满满的; 肿胀的 —**turgidly** *adv* —**turgidity** /tɝˋdʒɪdətɪ; tɜːˈdʒɪdɪti/ *n* [U]

Tu·rin /tʊˋrɪn; tjʊəˈrɪn/ a city on the River Po in northwest Italy, which is the capital of the Piedmont region and is an important centre of the Italian car-making industry. Its Italian name is Torino. 都灵〔意大利西北部一城市。位于波河河畔，为皮埃蒙特区首府，也是意大利重要的汽车制造业中心。该市的意大利语名为 Torino〕

Tu·ring /ˈturɪŋ; ˈtjʊərɪŋ/**, A·lan** /ˈælən; ˈælən/ (1912-54) a British MATHEMATICIAN and computer scientist, who developed ideas which were later used to build the first electronic computer, and which also influenced the development of the study of ARTIFICIAL INTELLIGENCE. During World War II he helped to find out the meaning of the German military CODES (=secret writing system used for sending messages). 图灵〔(1912-1954)，英国数学家、电脑科学家。他提出的观点被应用于世界首台计算机的研发，也影响到人工智能研究的发展。二战期间，他参与了破译德军电码的工作〕

Turin Shroud, the /,· ·ˈ·/ a piece of cloth which is believed by some people to have covered the dead body of Jesus Christ after he had been crucified (CRUCIFY) and to be marked with an image of his face. But scientists who tested the cloth using CARBON DATING methods believe that it is not as old as that. 都灵裹尸布〔一些人认为耶稣基督钉死在十字架上之后裹盖其尸体使用的就是这块布，布上有耶稣的头像。科学家用碳-14年代测定法对这块布测定后认为，它的年代没有那样久远〕

Turk /tɝk; tɜːk/ *n* [C] someone from Turkey 土耳其人

Tur·key /ˈtɝkɪ; ˈtɜːki/ a country which is mainly in west Asia but partly in southeast Europe, between the Mediterranean and Black Seas. Population: 66,494,000 (2001). Capital: Ankara. Until the early 20th century, Turkey was the centre of the large Ottoman Empire, whose capital city was Istanbul, Turkey's largest city. 土耳其〔国名。国土大部分在西亚，一部分在东南欧，位于地中海与黑海之间。人口: 66,494,000 (2001)，首都: 安卡拉。20世纪初以前，土耳其是庞大的奥斯曼帝国的中心，帝国的都城伊斯坦布尔是土耳其的最大城市〕

turkey *n* **1** [C] a bird that looks like a large chicken and is often eaten at Christmas and at Thanksgiving 火鸡 **2** [U] the meat from a turkey eaten as food 火鸡肉: *roast turkey* 烤火鸡肉 **3** [C] *AmE informal* someone who is silly or stupid【美，非正式】傻瓜，笨蛋: *That guy's a real turkey.* 那家伙真是个笨蛋。**4** *AmE informal* an unsuccessful film or play【美，非正式】〔电影、戏剧等的〕失败之作 **5** **talk turkey** *informal especially AmE* to talk seriously about details, especially in business【非正式，尤美】认真地谈论〔细节，尤指商务谈判〕—see also 另见 COLD TURKEY

Turk·ish¹ /ˈtɝkɪʃ; ˈtɜːkɪʃ/ *n* [U] the language of Turkey 土耳其语

Turkish² *adj* from or connected with Turkey 土耳其的; 土耳其人的

Turkish bath /,·· ˈ·/ *n* [C] a health treatment that involves sitting in a very hot steamy room 土耳其浴，蒸汽浴: *I walked into the club and it was like a Turkish bath!* 我走进俱乐部，里面简直就像蒸汽浴一样!

Turkish cof·fee /,·· ˈ··/ *n* [C,U] very strong black coffee that you drink in small cups with sugar 土耳其咖啡〔一种不加奶的浓烈咖啡〕

Turkish de·light /,·· ·ˈ·/ *n* [U] a type of sweet made from firm JELLY (1) that is cut into pieces and covered in sugar or chocolate〔外包糖粉或巧克力的〕土耳其软糖

Turk·men·i·stan /,tɝkmɛnɪˋstæn; ,tɜːkmenɪˈstɑːn/ a country in central Asia between Iran and Uzbekistan, formerly part of the Soviet Union. Population: 4,603,000 (2001). Capital: Ashkhabad. 土库曼斯坦〔中亚一国家，位于伊朗和乌兹别克斯坦之间，以前是苏联的一部分。人口: 4,603,000 (2001)，首都: 阿什哈巴德〕—**Turkmen** /ˈtɝkmɛn; ˈtɜːkmen/ *adj*

Turks and Cai·cos Is·lands, the /,tɝks ənd ˋkekəs ,aɪləndz; ,tɜːks ənd ˈkeɪkəs ,aɪləndz/ a group of 30 islands in the British West Indies, southeast of the Bahamas. Population: 18,122 (2001). Capital: Grand Turk. 特克斯和凯科斯群岛〔英属西印度群岛地区由30个岛屿组成的一群岛，位于巴哈马群岛东南。人口: 18,122 (2001)，首府: 大特克岛〕

tur·me·ric /ˈtɝmərɪk; ˈtɜːmərɪk/ *n* [U] yellow powder used to give a special colour or taste to food, especially CURRY¹ 姜黄根粉〔用作食品调色或调味之用，尤用于咖喱〕

tur·moil /ˈtɝmɔɪl; ˈtɜːmɔɪl/ *n* [U, singular] a state of confusion, excitement, and trouble 混乱，骚乱，动乱: *The country is in complete turmoil.* 这个国家陷入一片混乱之中。

turn¹ /tɝn; tɜːn/ *v*

① CHANGE DIRECTION/POSITION 改变方向/位置	④ CHANGE 改变
② COLOUR 颜色	⑤ PAGE 书页
③ AGE/TIME 年龄/时间	⑥ VEHICLE 车辆
	⑦ OTHER MEANINGS 其他意思

① CHANGE DIRECTION/POSITION 改变方向/位置

1 a) ►**YOUR BODY** 人的身体◄ [I] to move your body so that you are looking in a different direction 转过身，翻身: *Ricky turned and walked away.* 里基转身走了。| [+**around/round/away etc**] *I turned around quickly to see if someone was following.* 我迅速转过身来，看看是否有人在后面跟着。| *Dan turned away so Brody couldn't see the fear in his eyes.* 丹转过身去，这样布罗迪就看不到他眼中的恐惧了。| **turn to do sth** *She turned to look back at him as she got on the plane.* 她登上飞机时转过身来看了他一眼。| *He turned to face Kim with tears in his eyes.* 他转过身来面对着金，眼里噙满了泪水。| **turn on your heel** (=turn away suddenly) 突然转身 *Brigitte glared at him, turned on her heel, and stomped out of the room.* 布丽吉特瞪了他一眼，然后转过身跺着脚走出了房间。**b)** ►**OBJECT** 物体◄ [T] to move something so that it is pointing or aiming in a different direction 转动〔某物〕; 使〔某物〕对准或瞄准〔某一方向〕: *Turn the vase so the crack doesn't show.* 转一下花瓶，这样裂缝就不会露出来了。| *The firemen turned the hose on the burning building.* 消防队员把水管对准正在燃烧的大楼。| **turn sth to face sth** *I turned the chair to face him and began to talk.*

我转过椅子，面朝着他开始说话。

2 ▶**ROAD/RIVER/PATH ETC** 路/河流/小径等◀ [I] to curve in a particular direction〔向某方向〕转弯: *The river turns east and flows down out of the mountains.* 河流折向东边，然后从山里流了出来。| *a small path twisting and turning through the woods* 曲折蜿蜒穿过树林的一条小径

3 ▶**MOVE AROUND CENTRAL POINT** 沿中心点转动◀ [I,T] to move around a central or fixed point, or make something move in this way (使)旋转，转圈: *The wheel creaked as it turned.* 轮子在旋转的时候嘎吱作响。| **turn sth** *Turn the handle as far as it will go to the right.* 向右转动手柄直到转不动为止。

② **COLOUR** 颜色

4 ▶**OBJECT** 物体◀ [linking verb 连系动词] to become a different colour 变色: *The clothes all turned pink in the wash.* 衣服在洗涤过程中全变成粉红色了。| *The leaves turned red, orange, and yellow in the autumn air.* 树叶在秋季变成了红、橙、黄几种颜色。—see 见 BECOME (USAGE)

5 ▶**PERSON** 人◀ [linking verb 连系动词] if a person turns a particular colour, their skin looks that colour because they feel ill, embarrassed etc〔某人因生病、尴尬等肤色〕改变: *Vy turned white when she saw all the blood on the floor.* 看到地板上全是血，维伊脸都变白了。| *Every time Inge speaks to Hans, he turns bright red.* 每次英奇跟汉斯说话时，他的脸都会变得通红。

6 ▶**HAIR** 头发◀ [linking verb 连系动词] if your hair turns grey or white, it becomes that colour because you are getting older〔因年老头发〕变色: *Her face was lined and her hair was already turning grey.* 她的脸上有了皱纹，头发已变成灰白色了。

③ **AGE/TIME** 年龄/时间

7 ▶**AGE** 年龄◀ [linking verb 连系动词] if someone turns a particular age, they become that age 到达〔某年龄〕: *"How old is Dennis?" "He's just turned 40."* "丹尼斯有多大了？" "他刚满40岁。"

8 ▶**TIME** 时间◀ [linking verb 连系动词] if it has turned a particular time, that time has just passed 到达〔某时间〕: *"What time is it?" "It's just turned 3:00."* "什么时间了？" "刚3点钟。"

④ **CHANGE** 改变

9 **turn nasty/mean/violent etc** to suddenly become angry, violent etc 突然变得愤怒/卑鄙/凶暴等: *One day the dog just turned nasty and bit me.* 一天，那只狗一怒之下咬了我。| *The police are worried that the situation could turn violent.* 警察担忧的是有可能会出现暴力行为。—see 见 BECOME (USAGE)

10 **turn cold/nasty** if the weather turns cold or nasty, it suddenly becomes cold, unpleasant etc〔天气〕变冷/变坏: *The forecast says it's going to turn nasty.* 预报说天气会变得很糟糕。

11 ▶**ACTIVITY** 活动◀ [I] to stop one activity and start something completely different 改变; 转向: [+to] *Our laughter turned to horror when we realized Jody really was hurt.* 当我们意识到乔迪真的受伤了，我们的笑声一下变成了恐惧。| *Many people here have turned to solar power as an alternative to electricity.* 这里的许多人改用太阳能替代电能。

12 **actor turned politician/football player turned author etc** someone who has done one job and then does something completely different 演员变成了政治家/足球运动员变成了作家等

13 **turn traitor** to be disloyal to a person, group, or idea that you have strongly supported before 成了叛徒: *Ramirez's lieutenant turned traitor and told the military where he was hiding.* 拉米雷斯的中尉叛变了，把他藏身的地方告诉了军方。

⑤ **PAGE** 书页

14 [T] if you turn a page in a book, you move it so that you can read the next page 翻动〔书页〕—see also 另见 **turn to** (TURN[1])

⑥ **VEHICLE** 车辆

15 [I,T] if you turn a vehicle or it turns, it changes direction (使)〔汽车〕转向，拐弯: [+into/off/left/right] *Turn left at the next light.* 在下一个红绿灯向左转。| *The car in front of me turned into a driveway.* 我前面的那辆车拐弯上了一条私用车道。| **turn sth around/into** *Jason turned the car around while I brought the suitcases.* 贾森在我去拿衣箱时把车子调了头。

⑦ **OTHER MEANINGS** 其他意思

16 ▶**INJURY** 受伤◀ [T] if you turn your ankle, you twist it in a way that injures it; SPRAIN 扭伤〔踝关节〕: *Is it bad? No, I just turned my ankle on the step.* 很严重吗？不，我只是在台阶上扭了脚踝。

17 ▶**MILK** 牛奶◀ [I] if milk turns, it becomes sour〔牛奶〕变酸

18 **turn your back (on)** **a)** to refuse to help or give sympathy to someone when they need it 对…置之不理; 对…撒手不管: *How can you turn your back on your own mother?* 你怎么能对自己的母亲撒手不管呢？**b)** to deliberately stop being involved in something that used to be very important for you 不再参与〔某事〕: *Isn't it hard to turn your back on tennis after so many years at the top?* 这么多年你一直处在最高峰，现在决定不再打网球了，难道不感到难受吗？**c)** to turn so that your back is pointing towards someone or something 转身背对着〔某人或某物〕: *He turned his back on her and spoke quietly into the phone.* 他转过身背对着她，对着话筒轻声说话。| *As soon as you turn your back on these kids, they're acting like maniacs again!* 你刚转过身不理这些孩子，他们就又发狂似地闹开了！

19 **turn sth inside out** **a)** to pull a piece of clothing, bag etc so that the inside is facing outwards 把〔衣服、口袋等〕里朝外翻: *Just turn the bag inside out to make sure there's nothing left in it.* 只需把口袋里朝外翻，确保里面没有留下任何东西。**b)** also 又作 **turn sth upside down** to search everywhere for something, in a way that makes a place very untidy 到处搜寻〔某物〕，翻了个底朝天: *The thieves had turned the house upside down looking for the papers.* 小偷把屋子翻了个底朝天，想寻找那些文件。

20 **turn (people's) heads** if something turns people's heads, they are surprised by it 让(人)吃惊: *Yes, it did turn a few heads when he moved back to the village.* 是的，他搬回村里居住，着实让一些人吃了一惊。

21 **turn sb's head** to be attractive in a romantic or sexual way to a particular person 使某人爱慕: *You mean that horrible old man actually managed to turn Jo's head?* 你指的是那个可怕的老头，竟然使乔爱上了他？

22 **have turned the corner** to have done the most difficult part of something, so that the rest looks fairly easy 已经渡过了最困难的阶段 —see also 另见 **turn a blind eye** (BLIND[1] (2)), **turn the other cheek** (CHEEK[1] (6)), **sb would turn in their grave** (GRAVE[1] (3)), **not turn a hair** (HAIR (8)), **turn your hand to** (HAND[1] (10)), **turn over a new leaf** (LEAF[1] (3)), **turn your nose up (at)** (NOSE[1] (6)), **turn the tables (on sb)** (TABLE[1] (5)), **turn tail** (TAIL[1] (8))

turn against sb/sth *phr v* [T] to decide that you do not like someone or agree with something any more 转而讨厌; 转而反对: *Public opinion in Panama turned against him.* 巴拿马的舆论转而反对他。

turn sb **against** sb/sth *phr v* [T] to make someone not to like someone any more or not to agree with something any more 使与…为敌; 离间…: *After the divorce, Dave accused Christina of turning the kids against him.* 离婚后，戴夫指责克里斯蒂娜挑唆孩子们与他作对。

turn around also 又作 **turn round** *BrE*【英】*phr v* **1** [T **turn** sth ↔ **round**] to complete the process of making a product or providing a service 完成; 提供; 生产出: *We can turn around a batch of 50 pressings in two hours.* 我们能够在两小时内压制出50张唱片。**2** [T **turn** sth ↔ **round**] to manage an unsuccessful business so well that it becomes successful again 使〔业务〕好转: *In under three years she had completely turned the company around.* 在不到三年的时间里，她已完全使公司的业务好转起来。**3** **turn around and say/tell** *spoken* to tell someone something that they think is unfair or unreasonable【口】反而说/讲〔不合理的话〕: *I complained about it but they just turned round and said it was my own fault.* 我投诉时，他们却说是我自己的过错。

turn away *phr v* **1** [T **turn** sb ↔ **away**] to refuse to let someone into a place such as a theatre, cinema etc, because there is no more space〔戏院等因满座〕不让…进入: *They turned about 1,000 people away at the Arena because all the tickets were gone.* 因为所有的票都已卖光了，他们把大约1000人拒在场馆外面。**2** [I,T] to refuse to give someone sympathy, help, or support 拒绝给…同情[援助，支持]: *Europe cannot in good conscience turn away from these refugees.* 欧洲不能心安理得地拒绝援助这些难民。| **turn sb ↔ away** *I can't turn her away. She's my brother's child.* 我不能拒绝她，她是我的侄女。

turn back *phr v* **1** [I] to go in the opposite direction 折回，掉转头: *It was late afternoon when we finally decided it was time to turn back.* 下午晚些时候，我们最终决定该往回走了。| *One of the boats had to turn back because it was taking in water.* 其中一只船因为进水不得不折回来。**2** [T **turn** sb ↔ **back**] to tell someone to go in the opposite direction, often because there is danger ahead〔常指因前方有危险〕使…折返: *We were turned back at the border because of the fighting.* 因为战火，我们在边

T

境处被迫折返。**3 turn back the clock a)** if you want to turn back the clock, you wish you had the chance to do something again so you could do it better 回复到从前; 重新有机会做〔某事〕: *"I'd like to be able to turn back the clock and make things right with Brett," said Gloria.* "我希望能够有机会回到从前, 与布雷特重归于好。" 格洛丽亚说道。**b)** to do something the way it was done at an earlier time, especially when that is worse than the way it is done now 回到过去的老一套, 倒退: *legislation that turns back the clock on human rights* 人权立法的倒退

turn down *phr v* [T] **1** [**turn** sth ↔ **down**] to make a machine such as an oven, radio etc produce less heat, sound etc 调低〔机器的热度、音量等〕: *Can you please turn the TV down? I can't hear myself think!* 请你把电视的声音关小一点行吗? 我没法静下心来思考! **2** [**turn** sb/sth ↔ **down**] to refuse an offer, request, or invitation 拒绝〔建议、要求、邀请等〕: *Pauline's turned down offers from several different law firms.* 保利娜拒绝了好几家律师事务所提供的工作机会。| *Jimmy offered to marry her again, but she'd already turned him down three times.* 杰米再向她求婚, 但她已经拒绝了他三次。—see 见 REFUSE¹ (USAGE)

turn in *phr v* **1** [T **turn** sth ↔ **in**] to give something back to the person that owns it, especially when it has been lost or borrowed 交回, 交还〔尤指失物或借来的东西〕: *Make sure to turn your security badge in before you leave the company.* 在离开公司之前一定要交回保安徽章。| [**+to**] *My wallet was turned in to the police two days after it was stolen.* 我的钱包在被盗两天后被交还给了警察。**2** [T **turn** sth ↔ **in**] *especially AmE* to give a piece of work to a teacher, your boss etc【尤美】交〔作业给老师〕; 交〔已完成的工作给老板〕: *Have you all turned in your homework from last night?* 你们全都交了昨晚的家庭作业没有? **3** [T **turn** sb ↔ **in**] to tell the police who or where a criminal is 〔向警方〕告发〔罪犯〕: *Margrove's wife finally turned him in after months of silence.* 在沉默了几个月后, 马格洛夫的妻子最终向警方告发了他。**4** [I] to go to bed 上床睡觉: *Well, I think I'll turn in. I've got to get up early.* 呃, 我想我要去睡觉了, 我得早起。

turn into sth *phr v* **1** [T] to become something different, or make someone or something do this 使…变成; 把…变成: **turn into sth** *In a few weeks, the caterpillar will turn into a butterfly.* 几周之后, 毛虫就会变成蝴蝶了。| *The sofa turns into a bed.* 沙发变成了床。| **turn sth into sth** *Lieutenant, do you have to turn everything into a question?* 中尉, 你什么样的事都得提问吗? | **turn sb into sth** *You'll never turn me into a salesman, Dad. I'm not made for it.* 爸爸, 你千万别指望我会成为推销员, 我天生不是那块料。**2** [T] to change by magic from one thing into another, or make something do this 〔通过魔法〕变成; 使…变成: **turn into sth** *In a flash of light, the prince turned into a frog.* 一阵闪光之后, 王子变成了一只青蛙。| **turn sb/sth into sth** *The fairy godmother turned the pumpkin into a coach.* 仙后把那只南瓜变成了一辆马车。**3** [T] if one season turns into another season, it changes gradually from one to the next 〔季节〕变化, 转换: *The snows melted, and winter turned into spring.* 积雪融化, 冬去春来。**4 days turned into weeks/months turned into years etc** used to say that time passed slowly while you waited for something to happen 几天之后又是几周/几个月之后又是几年等〔用于表示等待某事发生时日子过去〕: *Weeks turned into months, and still there was no letter from Renata.* 几周之后又是数月, 但仍然没有雷纳塔的来信。

turn off 关上

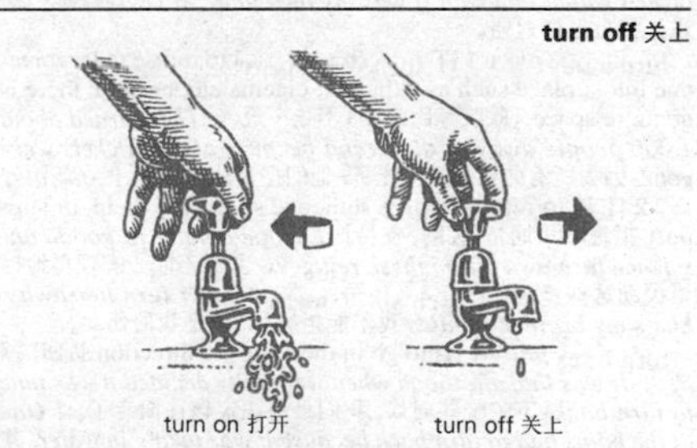

turn on 打开　　turn off 关上

turn off *phr v* **1** [T **turn** sth ↔ **off**] to stop the supply of water, gas etc from flowing by turning a handle or TAP as far as it will go 关掉〔自来水、煤气等的〕开关: *Turn off the hot water.* 把热水关掉。| *They've turned the gas off for a couple of hours.* 他们已把煤气关闭几个小时了。**2** [T **turn** sth ↔ **off**] to make a machine or piece of electrical equipment such as a television, car, light etc stop operating by pushing a button, turning a key etc 关闭〔电视机、汽车引擎、电灯等〕: *Don't forget to turn off the lights when you leave.* 离开时别忘了关灯。| *Turn the TV off now.* 现在把电视机关了。**3** [I,T] to leave one road, especially a large one, and drive along another one 离开〔某条路, 尤指大路〕而转上另一条路: **turn off at/near etc** *I'm sure we should have turned off at the last exit.* 我敢肯定, 我们本来应该在上一个出口驶出。| **turn off sth** *Gill turned off the A10 and started heading west.* 吉尔离开A10号公路, 开始奔西而去。—see also 另见 TURN-OFF **4** [T **turn** sb ↔ **off**] to do something that makes someone decide they do not like something 使〔人〕不喜欢: *Don't oversell the product. If your salespeople are pushy, they'll turn the customer off.* 推销产品不要没有分寸——你们的推销员如果咄咄逼人, 会让顾客不喜欢的。**5** [T **turn** sb ↔ **off**] to do something that makes someone feel that they are not attracted to you in a sexual way 使丧失性的吸引力: *It really turns me off when Richard wears his smelly socks to bed.* 理查德穿着他的臭袜子上床, 真让我倒胃口。

turn on *phr v* **1** [T **turn** sth ↔ **on**] to make the supply of water, gas etc start flowing from something by turning a handle or TAP¹ (1) 打开〔自来水、煤气等的〕开关: *I turned the water on in the shower.* 我打开了淋浴间的水龙头。| *We'll be turning on the gas in about an hour.* 我们在大约一小时后开启煤气。**2** [T **turn** sth ↔ **on**] to make a machine or piece of electrical equipment such as a car, television, light etc start operating by pushing a button, turning a key etc 启动〔汽车〕; 打开〔电视机、电灯等〕: *Could you turn on the light, please?* 请把灯打开好吗? | *When I turned the engine on it made a funny noise.* 当我启动发动机时, 它发出了异常的声音。—see 见 OPEN² (USAGE) **3** [T **turn on** sb] to suddenly attack someone or treat them badly, using physical violence or unpleasant words 突然袭击〔某人〕; 恶劣地对待〔某人〕: *Peter turned on Rae with eyes blazing and screamed, "Get out of my sight!"* 彼得眼冒怒火, 转向雷高声叫道: "从我面前滚开!" **4** [T **turn on** sth] if a situation, event, argument turns on a particular thing or idea, it depends on that thing in order to work 取决于, 依…而定: *The negotiations turned on getting the Italian delegation to agree.* 谈判取决于能否获得意大利代表团的同意。**5** [T **turn** sb **on**] to make someone feel sexually excited 使感到性刺激: *A lot of guys are turned on by the idea of women in uniform.* 许多家伙一想到穿着制服的女性就感到十分刺激。—see also 另见 TURN-ON **6** [T **turn** sb **on to** sth] to make someone become interested in a product, idea etc 使产生兴趣: *Mark's that friend of mine who turned me on to classical music.* 马克就是那位使我对古典音乐产生兴趣的朋友。

turn out *phr v* **1** [linking verb 连系动词] to happen in a particular way, or to have a particular result, especially one that you did not expect 最后结果是, 最终成为: *I hate the way my hair turned out. The colour's all wrong.* 我不喜欢我的头发最终做成的样子, 颜色完全不对劲。| *Don't worry, I'm sure it will all turn out fine.* 不要担心, 我敢肯定一切最终会好起来的。| **it turns out that** *It turned out that she didn't get the job in the end.* 结果是, 她没有得到那份工作。| **turn out to be** *That guy we met turned out to be Maria's second cousin.* 我们遇到的那个家伙原来是玛丽亚的堂弟。| *His statement turned out to be false.* 他说的那番话后来证明是一派谎言。**2** [T **turn** sth ↔ **out**] if you turn out a light, you stop the flow of electricity to it by pushing a button, pulling a string etc 关上, 关掉〔电灯〕: *Don't forget to turn out the lights when you go!* 你走的时候不要忘了关灯! **3** [T **turn** sb ↔ **out**] to force someone to leave a place 驱逐, 赶走: *Benjamin turned his son out of the house without any money.* 本杰明把儿子赶出了家门, 没给他一分钱。**4** [I] if people turn out for an event, they gather together to see it happen 〔为看热闹〕蜂拥而出: *Crowds of people turned out to watch the filming of the final scene of Rocky.* 人群蜂拥而至, 前来观看《洛奇》这部电影拍摄最后一场戏。—see also 另见 TURNOUT **5** [T **turn** sth ↔ **out**] to produce or make something 生产, 制造: *The factory turns out 300 units a day.* 这家工厂一天生产300台。**6 well/beautifully/badly turned out** to be dressed in good, beautiful etc clothes 衣着很好/很漂亮/很差劲: *elegantly turned-out young ladies* 衣着雅致的年轻女士

turn over *phr v* **1** [T **turn** sb ↔ **over to** sb] to bring a criminal to the police or other official organization 把〔犯人〕交给〔警方等〕: *The FBI caught Rostov and turned him over to the CIA.* 联邦调查局拘捕了罗斯托夫并把他移交给中央情报局。**2** [T

turn sth ↔ **over to** sb] to give someone the right to own or the responsibility for something such as a plan, business, piece of property etc 把〔所有权〕交给〔某人〕; 交托〔某人〕负责〔某事〕: *I'm turning the shop over to my son when I retire.* 我退休时就把商店托付给儿子去经营。| *When you leave, the project will be turned over to Mathias.* 你离开时, 这项工程就交给马赛厄斯来负责。**3** [T **turn over** sth] if a business turns over a particular amount of money, it makes that amount in a particular period of time 营业额达到: *We were turning over $1,500 a week when business was good.* 生意好的时候, 我们一周的营业额可达1500美元。**4** [I] *BrE* to turn a page in a book or a sheet of paper to the opposite side【英】〔书页或纸张〕翻过 **5** [I] *BrE* to change the CHANNEL[1] (1) on a television【英】变换电视频道: *I hate this programme. Can we please turn over?* 我讨厌这个节目, 请问能换个频道吗? **6 turn sth over in your mind** to think about something carefully, considering all the possibilities 认真考虑某事, 从多方面考虑某事: *I turned Zeke's comments over in my mind for a long time that night.* 我那天晚上很长时间都在反复思考齐克的评语。

turn to *phr v* **1** [T **turn to** sb/sth] to try to get help, advice, or sympathy from someone or by doing something 求助于, 求教于: *Nobody seems to understand. I don't know who to turn to.* 似乎没有人明白, 我不知道该向谁求教。| *Paul turned to drink* (=drinking alcohol) *to try to forget his problems at work.* 保罗借酒浇愁, 想忘掉工作中的烦恼。**2** [T **turn to** sth] to look at a particular page in a book 翻到〔书中的某页〕: *Turn to page 655 for more information on this subject.* 翻到655页就可以知道有关这一论题的更多情况。**3 turn your attention/thoughts/efforts etc to sth** to begin to think about or do something different from what you have been doing 开始注意到/想到/致力于某事 **4** [I] *old-fashioned* to begin to work hard【过时】开始努力工作: *We'll really have to turn to in order to finish this on time.* 为了按时完成工作, 我们真的必须开始努力了。

turn up *phr v* **1** [T **turn** sth ↔ **up**] to make a machine such as an oven, radio etc produce more heat, sound etc 调大, 开大〔热度、音量等〕: *Turn the oven up to 220°C.* 把烤箱调高到220°C。| *Turn up the radio!* 把收音机开大声一点! **2** [I] to suddenly appear after having been lost or searched for 突然露面, 重新出现: *I couldn't find my watch for ages, but then one day it turned up in a coat pocket.* 我有好长时间找不着手表了, 但有一天, 它在一件外衣的口袋里出现了。**3** [I always+adv/prep] to arrive at a place 到达, 来到: *Steven turned up late as usual.* 史蒂文像往常一样来迟了。**4** [I] if an opportunity or situation turns up, it happens, especially when you are not expecting it〔机会或情况〕突然发生, 不期而至: *Don't worry, I'm sure a job will turn up soon.* 不要着急, 我敢肯定工作不久就会有的。**5** [T **turn** sth ↔ **up**] to find something by thoroughly searching for it〔经过彻底搜寻〕发现, 发掘出: *The police investigation hasn't turned up any new evidence.* 警方还没有调查到任何新的证据。**6** [T **turn** sth ↔ **up**] *BrE* to shorten a skirt, trousers etc by folding up the bottom and SEWING it【英】〔把裙脚、裤脚卷起缝上〕改短… —see also 另见 **come up trumps/turn up trumps** (TRUMP[1] (3))

turn upon sb *phr v* [T] to suddenly attack someone or treat them badly, using physical violence or unpleasant words 突然袭击; 恶劣对待

turn² *n*

1 it is sb's turn if it is your turn to do something, it is the time when you can or should do it, because you are one of a number of people doing the same activity in a particular order 轮到某人〔做某事〕: *It's your turn. Roll the dice.* 轮到你了, 掷骰子吧。| **sb's turn to do sth** *I think it's our turn to drive the kids to school this week.* 我想这周该轮到我们开车送孩子们上学了。**2 take turns** also 又作 **take it in turns** *BrE* if many people take turns doing work or playing a game, they each do it one after the other in order to share work or play fairly【英】轮流, 依次: *You'll have to take turns being captain of the team.* 你们得轮流当球队的队长。| **take turns doing sth** *We took turns doing the driving on the way up to Canada.* 在去往加拿大的途中, 我们轮流开车。| **take turns to do sth** *brainstorming sessions where we all took turns to throw in ideas* 我们都轮流献计献策的攻关会议

3 in turn a) as a result of something 因此, 因而: *Interest rates were cut, and in turn, share prices rose.* 利率降了, 因而股票价格涨了。**b)** one after the other, especially in a particular order 轮流地, 依次地: *He asked each of us in turn to describe how alcohol had affected our lives.* 他要我们每个人依次描述一下酒是如何影响自己的生活的。

4 ▶VEHICLE 车辆◀ [C] the act of changing direction in a vehicle, or making it do this〔车辆的〕转向, 转弯: **make a left/right turn** *Make a left turn after the bank.* 过了银行后向左拐。

5 ▶ACT OF TURNING STH 转动某物的动作◀ [C] the act of turning something completely around a fixed point 转动, 旋转: *Tighten it another two or three turns.* 再给它拧紧两三圈。

6 ▶ROAD 道路◀ [C] the place where one road goes in a different direction from another〔道路的〕转弯处, 交叉处: *According to the map, we missed our turn back there at the light.* 从地图上来看, 我们错过了在交通灯那儿转弯。

7 the turn of the century the beginning of a century 世纪之交: *At the turn of the century, new technologies will already be in place.* 到世纪之交时, 新的技术将已经投入使用了。

8 take a turn for the worse/better to suddenly become worse or better 突然变得更糟/更好: *Paul's health took a turn for the worse on Tuesday.* 保罗的健康状况在星期二突然恶化起来。

9 turn of events a change in what is happening, especially an unusual one 事态的变化〔尤指不同寻常的变化〕: *The General's agreement to the peace talks is a welcome but unexpected turn of events.* 将军同意和谈, 这是值得欢迎的, 但也是未曾预料到的事态变化。

10 turn of phrase a) a particular way of saying something; expression 言谈方式; 说法; 措辞: *I've never liked that turn of phrase – when people say 'I won't detain you any longer'.* 我从来就不喜欢"我不再耽误你的时间了"这种说法。**b)** the ability to say things in a clever or funny way 巧妙风趣的口才: *Kate has a witty turn of phrase.* 凯特的言谈妙趣横生。

11 on the turn a) if the TIDE is on the turn, it is starting to come in or go out〔潮水〕在涨[落] **b)** starting to change, or in the process of changing 开始转变, 正在转变: *I began to think that maybe my luck was on the turn.* 我开始想我的运气也许正在变。**c)** *especially BrE* if milk, fish, or other food is on the turn, it is starting to become sour【尤英】〔牛奶、鱼等食品〕开始变馊

12 speak out of turn to say something you should not say in a particular situation, especially because you do not have enough authority to say it 说不该说的话〔尤指超越本分说话〕: *I hope I'm not speaking out of turn, sir, but I don't think this is the best way to proceed.* 我希望我没有冒昧无礼, 先生, 但我认为这并不是最好的做法。

13 do sb a good/bad turn to do something that is helpful or unhelpful for someone 做有利/有损于某人的行为: *You'll be doing me a good turn by driving Max home tonight.* 你今晚开车送马克斯回家, 就是帮了我一个大忙。

14 at every turn if something happens at every turn, it happens again and again 每一回; 总是; 处处: *We were frustrated at every turn in our efforts to get money for the project.* 我们努力想为这个项目筹钱, 但总是处处碰壁。

15 by turns if someone shows different feelings or qualities by turns, they change from one to another 轮流地, 依次〔表现某些情感或特质〕: *That evening he was silly, witty, and mournful by turns.* 那天晚上, 他先是傻乎乎的, 然后变得妙趣横生, 最后又悲从心来。

16 turn of mind *literary* the way that someone usually thinks or feels【文】性情; 习性, 天性: *He was of a melancholy turn of mind.* 他性情忧郁。

17 done/cooked to a turn to be perfectly cooked 烹调得恰到好处

18 one good turn deserves another used to say that if someone does something nice for you, you should do something nice for them to thank them 好心应该得到好报; 以德报德

19 take a turn in/on etc *old-fashioned* to walk somewhere just for pleasure【过时】悠闲地散步, 闲逛: *I think they're out taking a turn in the gardens.* 我想他们正在花园里悠闲地散步。

20 give sb a turn *old-fashioned* to frighten someone【过时】惊吓某人

21 have a turn *BrE old-fashioned* to feel slightly ill or faint【英, 过时】感觉有点不舒服; 有点头昏

turn·a·bout /ˈtɜːnəˌbaʊt; ˈtɜːnəbaʊt/ *n BrE*【英】[C usually singular 一般用单数] **1** a complete change in someone's opinions or ideas〔观点或思想的〕彻底改变, 变卦: *an extraordinary turnabout in public opinion* 舆论的异常转变 **2 turnabout is fair play** *AmE* used to say that because someone else has done something you can do it too【美】一人一遭, 天公地道; 以其人之道还治其人之身乃是公道

turn·a·round /ˈtɜːnəˌraʊnd; ˈtɜːnəraʊnd/ *n* [C usually singular 一般用单数] *especially AmE* a TURNROUND【尤美】收到某物、处理并送回所需的时间; 好转, 转机;〔观点或思想的〕彻底改变

turn·coat /ˈtɝnˌkot; ˈtɜːnkəʊt/ *n* [C] someone who stops supporting a political party or group and joins the opposing side 叛党者，变节者：*Casson was pilloried as a turncoat and a traitor.* 卡森因叛党变节而臭名昭彰。

turn·er /ˈtɝnɚ; ˈtɜːnə/ *n* [C] someone who uses a LATHE (=special tool) to make shapes out of wood or metal 车工，旋工

Turner, J.M.W. (1775-1851) one of the greatest British painters, who painted many pictures of the countryside, the sea, and the sky, in which he uses colour and light to show the force of the wind and sea 特纳，又译透纳〔(1775-1851)，英国最伟大的画家之一。他创作有许多绘画作品，表现乡村、大海和天空，以色彩和光线反映风与海的力量〕

Turner, Nat /næt; næt/ (1800-31) a US SLAVE who organized a successful REVOLT (=an attack against people in authority) against Southern slave owners in 1831. He was caught and later hanged for his actions. 特纳〔(1800-1831)，美国一奴隶。1831年，他成功组织了一次反对南方奴隶主的起义，被捕后处以绞刑〕

Turner, Ted (1938-) a US businessman and sportsman who started CNN (Cable News Network), a cable television company that was the first to broadcast news all day and night 特纳〔(1938-)，美国实业家、运动员。他创办了首家24小时连续播出新闻的有线电视新闻网〕

Turner Broad·cast·ing Sys·tem, the /ˌ·· ˈ··· ˌ ·ˈ/ abbreviation 缩写为 **TBS** a US television company, based in Atlanta, Georgia, whose programmes are shown mainly on cable and SATELLITE television. It is owned by Ted Turner. 特纳广播系统〔美国一电视公司。总部设在佐治亚州亚特兰大，节目主要在有线及卫星电视频道播出。公司为泰德·特纳所有〕

turn·ing /ˈtɝnɪŋ; ˈtɜːnɪŋ/ *n* [C] *BrE* a road that connects with the one you are on【英】从所在的路分出的路；〔道路的〕拐弯处；TURN² (6) *AmE*【美】：*Take the first turning on the left.* 到第一个拐弯处就向左拐。

turning cir·cle /ˈ·· ˌ··/ *n* [C] the smallest space in which a vehicle can drive around in a circle 回转圆〔汽车能转弯的最小行车圈〕

turning point /ˈ·· ·/ *n* [C] the time when an important change starts, especially one that improves the situation 转折点；关键时刻：*The Battle of El Alamein was a turning point in the war.* 阿拉曼战役是这次战争的一个转折点。

T

tur·nip /ˈtɝnɪp; ˈtɜːnə̩p/ *n* [C,U] a large round pale yellow vegetable that grows under the ground, or the plant that produces it 芜菁 —see picture on page A9 参见 A9 页图

turn·key¹ /ˈtɝnki; ˈtɜːnkiː/ *n* [C] *old use* a JAILER【旧】监狱看守

turnkey² *adj* [only before noun 仅用于名词前] ready to be used immediately 立即可以使用的：*low-cost turnkey systems for retail applications* 低成本的、马上可以交付使用的零售应用系统

turn-off /ˈ· ·/ *n* **1** [C] a smaller road that leads off a main road 岔路，支路 **2** [singular] *informal* something that makes you lose interest in something, especially sex【非正式】〔尤指在性方面〕使人失去兴趣的东西：*The music was a real turn-off so we left.* 那音乐真是让人倒胃口，所以我们就离开了。—see also 另见 **turn off** (TURN¹)

Turn of the Screw, The /ˌ· · ˈ ·/ (1898) a GHOST story by Henry James about a woman who believes that evil dead people are influencing two children she is caring for《螺丝在拧紧》，又译《碧庐冤孽》〔(1898)，亨利·詹姆斯的一部鬼怪小说。书中有一个妇人认为恶鬼在惊扰她照管的两个孩子〕

turn-on /ˈ· ·/ *n* [singular] *informal* something that makes you feel excited, especially sexually【非正式】〔尤指在性方面〕使人感到兴奋的东西：*I found the whole thing a real turn-on.* 我觉得这整件事真的让人感到兴奋。—see also 另见 **turn on** (TURN¹)

turn·out /ˈtɝnˌaut; ˈtɜːnaʊt/ *n* **1** [singular] the number of people who go to a party, meeting, or other organized event〔聚会、会议等〕出席人数，到场人数：*Despite the rain, there was a good turnout.* 尽管下雨，到场的人数还是不少。**2** [singular] the number of people who vote in an election〔选举中的〕投票人数：**high turnout** (=a lot of people voting) 高投票率 *Feelings about the election were strong, which ensured a high turnout.* 这次选举群情鼎沸，从而确保了高投票率。—see also 另见 **turn out** (TURN¹) **3** [C] *AmE* a place at the side of a narrow road where cars can wait to let others pass【美】〔窄路上的〕避车道

turn·o·ver /ˈtɝnˌovɚ; ˈtɜːnˌəʊvə/ *n* **1** [singular] the amount of business done in a particular period, measured by the amount of money earned 营业额：*an annual turnover of £5.6 million* 560万英镑的年营业额 **2** [singular] the rate at which people leave an organization and are replaced by others 人事变动率；人员流动率：*Low pay accounts for the high turnover of staff.* 低薪金是职员流动率高的原因。**3** [singular] the rate at which a particular type of goods is sold〔货物的〕销售量，成交量：*Supermarkets depend on a high turnover at low prices.* 超市依赖于低价格和高销售量。**4** [C] a small fruit PIE (1) 水果小馅饼：*an apple turnover* 苹果馅饼 **5** [C] *AmE* a situation in a game of American football or basketball in which something happens so that one team loses the ball and the other team gets it【美】〔美式橄榄球或篮球中的〕失球，〔球的〕易手

turn·pike /ˈtɝnˌpaɪk; ˈtɜːnpaɪk/ *n* [C] **1** *AmE* a large road for fast traffic, especially one that drivers have to pay to use【美】〔尤指需要付费的〕高速公路：*the New Jersey Turnpike* 新泽西收费高速公路 **2** *BrE* a road in Britain in the 18th century that travellers had to pay to use【英】〔18世纪英国的一种〕收费公路，收税路

turn·round /ˈtɝnˌraund; ˈtɜːnraʊnd/ *BrE*【英】，**turnaround** *especially AmE*【尤美】*n* [C] **1** the time it takes to receive something, deal with it and send it back, especially on a plane, ship etc〔尤指使用飞机、轮船等〕收到某物、处理并送回所需的时间：*Some drivers are on a bonus for fast turnround and deliveries.* 一些司机因周转快、送货快而获得奖金。—see also 另见 **turn around** (TURN¹) **2** [usually singular 一般用单数] a complete change from a bad situation to a good one 好转，转机：*This year's profits will confirm the company's remarkable turnaround.* 今年的利润将证实该公司的情况已有明显好转。**3** [usually singular 一般用单数] a complete change in someone's opinion or ideas〔观点或思想的〕彻底改变，转变；TURNABOUT (1) *BrE*【英】：*a turnround in government policy* 政府政策的彻底转变

turn sig·nal /ˈ· ˌ··/ *n* [C] *AmE* one of the lights on a car that flash to show which way the car is turning【美】〔汽车上的〕转向指示灯；INDICATOR (2) *BrE*【英】

turn·stile /ˈtɝnˌstaɪl; ˈtɜːnstaɪl/ *n* [C] a small gate that spins around and only lets one person at a time go through an entrance〔入口处的〕旋转式栅门：*We're getting far more spectators through the turnstiles than last year.* 我们吸引进场的观众大大超过去年。

turn·ta·ble /ˈtɝnˌtebḷ; ˈtɜːnˌteɪbəl/ *n* [C] **1** the round flat surface on a RECORD PLAYER that you put records on〔唱机的〕转盘，唱盘 **2** a large flat round surface on which railway engines are turned around〔铁路机车掉转方向的〕转车台

turn-up /ˈ· ·/ *n* **1** [C] *BrE* the bottom of a trouser leg that is folded up for decoration or to make it shorter【英】〔裤腿的〕卷起部分，卷边；CUFF *AmE*【美】—see picture on page A17 参见 A17 页图 **2 a turn up for the book(s)** *BrE informal* an unexpected and surprising event【英，非正式】意想不到的事，突发事件：*Keith's buying the drinks – that's a turn up for the books!* 基思请客买饮料呢——这可是没料到啊！

tur·pen·tine /ˈtɝpənˌtaɪn; ˈtɜːpəntaɪn/ *n* [U] a type of oil used for making paint more liquid or removing it from clothes, brushes etc 松节油

Tur·pin /ˈtɝpɪn; ˈtɜːpɪn/, **Dick** (1706-39) an English HIGHWAYMAN (=a criminal who stole from people travelling in carriages). He was hanged for his crimes, but there are many popular stories about his adventures. 特平〔(1706-1739)，英国一拦路劫匪。他罪行累累，被处以绞刑。他的冒险经历被写成了许多故事，颇为读者喜欢〕

tur·pi·tude /ˈtɝpəˌtud; ˈtɜːpə̩tjuːd/ *n* [U] *formal* evil【正式】邪恶，堕落：*gross moral turpitude* 道德沦丧

turps /tɝps; tɜːps/ *n* [U] *BrE informal* turpentine【英，非正式】松节油

tur·quoise /ˈtɝkwɔɪz; ˈtɜːkwɔɪz/ *n* **1** [C,U] a valuable greenish-blue stone or a jewel that is made from this 绿松石；绿松石首饰 **2** [U] a greenish-blue colour 绿松石色，青绿色 —**turquoise** *adj* —see picture on page A5 参见 A5 页图

tur·ret /ˈtɝɪt; ˈtʌrə̩t/ *n* [C] **1** a small tower on a large building, especially a CASTLE (1)〔尤指城堡的〕小塔楼 **2** the place on a TANK (=army vehicle) from which guns are fired〔坦克上的〕炮塔 —**turreted** *adj*

tur·tle /ˈtɝtḷ; ˈtɜːtl/ *n* [C] **1** an animal that lives mainly in water and has a soft body covered by a hard shell 海龟，龟 **2 turn turtle** a ship or boat that turns turtle turns upside down〔船〕倾覆

tur·tle·dove /ˈtɝtḷˌdʌv; ˈtɜːtldʌv/ *n* [C] a type of bird that makes a pleasant soft sound and is sometimes used to represent love 斑鸠

tur·tle·neck /ˈtɝtḷˌnɛk; ˈtɜːtlnek/ *n* [C] *AmE* a type of sweater with a high, close-fitting band that folds down as a collar【美】高领套头毛线衫；POLO NECK *BrE*【英】：*wearing a tweed skirt and a turtleneck sweater* 穿着一条粗花呢裙和一件高领毛衣 —**turtlenecked** *adj*

turves /tɜvz; tɜːvz/ *n* [plural] the plural of TURF[1] (2)

Tus·ca·ny /ˈtʌskənɪ; ˈtʌskəni/ an area of north central Italy which is famous for its wine and for its beautiful old cities such as Pisa, Siena, and its capital city, Florence. Tuscany is a popular place for MIDDLE CLASS British people to go on holiday. 托斯卡纳〔意大利中北部一地区。当地的葡萄酒和漂亮古城十分有名,如比萨、锡耶纳和首府佛罗伦萨等。托斯卡纳是英国中产阶级的度假胜地〕

tush[1] /tʌʃ; tʌʃ/ *interjection old use* used to say that something is not worth considering【旧】呸, 啐〔表示轻蔑等〕

tush[2] /tʊʃ; tʊʃ/ *n* [C] *AmE slang* the part of your body that you sit on; BOTTOM[1] (7)【美俚】屁股

tusk /tʌsk; tʌsk/ *n* [C] one of a pair of very long pointed teeth, that stick out of the mouth of animals such as ELEPHANTS〔大象等动物的〕长牙, 獠牙

Tus·ke·gee In·sti·tute, the /tʌsˋkigɪ ˌɪnstɪtjut; tʌsˈkiːgi ˌɪnstɨtjuːt/ one of the first colleges for black people in the US. It was started by Booker T. WASHINGTON in 1881 in Tuskegee, Alabama. 塔斯基吉学院〔美国最早的黑人学院之一。1881年由布克·T.华盛顿在亚拉巴马州的塔斯基吉创建〕

Tus·saud /tuˋso; təˈsɔːd/, **Madame** (1760-1850) a Swiss woman who made models of people in wax, including famous people who were killed by the GUILLOTINE in the French Revolution. In 1802 she established her WAXWORKS, called Madame Tussaud's, in London. 图索德夫人〔(1760-1850),瑞士女蜡像家。作品包括法国大革命时期被推上断头台那些名人的蜡像。1802年, 她在伦敦创办了图索德夫人蜡像馆〕

tus·sle[1] /ˋtʌsl; ˈtʌsəl/ *n* [C] *informal* a struggle or fight using a lot of energy, especially one in which you pull or push someone rather than hit them【非正式】搏斗〔尤指互相揪扯的打斗〕: *After quite a tussle I finally wrenched the letter from him.* 经过好一阵撕扯, 我终于从他手上夺走了那封信。

tussle[2] *v* [I+with] *informal* to fight or struggle without using any weapons, by pulling or pushing someone rather than hitting them【非正式】〔不持武器地〕揪扯, 搏斗: *tussling with the other boys in the queue* 与队列中其他男孩揪扯

tus·sock /ˋtʌsək; ˈtʌsək/ *n* [C] a small thick mass of grass 一簇草, 丛生草

tut[1] /tʌt; tʌt/ *interjection* a sound that you make by touching the top of your mouth with your tongue in order to show disapproval 咂嘴声, 啧啧声〔表示不赞同〕—**tut** *n* [C]

tut[2] *v* [I] to express disapproval by making a tut sound 啧啧〔表示不赞同〕: *The nurses rushed in, tutting with irritation.* 护士们冲了进去, 气得直咂嘴。

Tu·tan·kha·men, Tutankhamon /ˌtutŋˋkɑmən; ˌtuːtənˈkɑːmən/ (14th century BC) an Egyptian PHARAOH (=ruler) whose burial place and the valuable things in it were discovered in 1922. Many of these things can now been seen in Cairo. 图坦卡门, 又译图特安哈门〔(公元前14世纪), 埃及法老。其陵墓于1922年被发掘, 发现了大量有价值的文物, 其中许多在开罗展出〕

tu·te·lage /ˋtutlɪdʒ; ˈtjuːtɨlɪdʒ/ *n* [U] *formal*【正式】**1** the state or period of being taught or looked after by someone 受指导(期); 受监护(期): **under sb's tutelage** (=being taught by someone) 在某人的指导下 *Under Sir Edward's meticulous tutelage, I soon developed a discriminating taste.* 在爱德华爵士的悉心指导下, 我很快培养了鉴别能力。**2** regular teaching over many years or months 经年累月的定期教导[指导] **3** responsibility for someone's education, actions or property 监护, 保护

tu·tor[1] /ˋtutɚ; ˈtjuːtə/ *n* [C] **1** someone who teaches one pupil or a small group, and is paid directly by them 家庭教师, 私人教师: *a reading tutor* 指导阅读的家庭教师 **2** a teacher in a British university or college〔英国大学里的〕助教, 导师: *She was my tutor at Durham.* 她是我在达勒姆大学时的导师。

tutor[2] *v* [T+in] to teach someone as a tutor 给…当家庭教师; 指导 —see 见 TEACH (USAGE)

tu·to·ri·al[1] /tuˋtɔrɪəl; tjuːˈtɔːriəl/ *n* [C] a period of teaching and discussion with a tutor, especially in a British university〔尤指英国大学里的〕导师辅导(时间): *the tutorial system* 导师制

tutorial[2] *adj* connected with a tutor or their work 家庭教师的; 助教的; 大学导师的; 辅导的, 指导的

tut·ti frut·ti /ˌtutɪ ˋfrutɪ; ˌtuːti ˈfruːti/ *n* [U] a type of ICE CREAM that has very small pieces of fruit and nuts in it 什锦水果坚果冰淇淋

tut-tut[1] /ˋtʌt ˋtʌt; ˌtʌt ˈtʌt/ *interj* a sound made by touching the top of the mouth with the tongue twice, in order to show disapproval 咂嘴声, 啧啧声〔表示不赞同〕

tut-tut[2] *v* [I] to express disapproval by saying tut-tut 啧啧〔表示不赞同〕

tu·tu /ˋtutu; ˈtuːtuː/ *n* [C] a short skirt made of many folds of stiff material worn by BALLET dancers 芭蕾舞裙〔芭蕾舞演员穿的短裙〕

Tutu, Des·mond /ˋdɛzmənd; ˈdezmənd/ (1931-) a South African priest in the Anglican religion, who was Archbishop of Cape Town (1986-96). He had a leading part in the fight against APARTHEID, and he was given the Nobel Peace Prize in 1984. Nelson Mandela later made him head of the Truth and Reconciliation Commission. 图图〔(1931-), 南非圣公会牧师、开普敦大主教(1986-1996)。他在抵制种族隔离制度的斗争中起了主要作用, 1984年获诺贝尔和平奖。纳尔逊·曼德拉后来任命他为真相与和解委员会主席〕

Tu·va·lu /tuˋvɑlu; tuːˈvɑːluː/ a country in the South Pacific Ocean, east of the Solomon Islands, made up of nine CORAL islands, and formerly called the Ellice Islands. Population: 10,991 (2001). Capital: Fongafale. 图瓦卢〔南太平洋所罗门群岛以东一国家, 由九个珊瑚岛组成, 旧称埃利斯岛。人口: 10,991 (2001), 首都: 丰阿法莱〕

tu-whit tu-whoo /tu ˋhwɪt tu ˋhwu; tə ˌwɪt tə ˈwuː/ *n* [C] the sound made by an OWL 嘟噎嘟呜〔猫头鹰叫声〕

tux /tʌks; tʌks/ *n* [C] *informal* a tuxedo【非正式】男式无尾礼服

tux·e·do /tʌkˋsido; tʌkˈsiːdəʊ/ *n* [C] **1** a man's JACKET (1) that is usually black, worn on formal occasions〔在正式场合穿的〕男式无尾礼服上衣 **2** a man's suit that includes this type of jacket 一套男式无尾礼服

TV /ˌtiˋvi; ˌtiː ˈviː◂/ *n* [C,U] television 电视: **TV programme/series/drama/star etc** *a new TV series about exploration* 一部关于探险的新电视系列片 | *Jonathan Ross, the TV personality* 电视名人乔纳森·罗斯 | **on TV** *Did you see it on TV? What a game!* 你在电视上看到了吗? 多精彩的比赛! | *a TV in every room* 每个房间一台电视机 S2

CULTURAL NOTE 文化注释

Daytime TV 白天的电视

In the US, there are usually SOAP OPERAS, TALK SHOWS, old films, and old television programmes on during the day. In the UK, there are a variety of programmes, including children's programmes and shows about homes and cooking. People often think that the people who watch daytime television are at home because they do not have a job, because they are ill, or because they are women who are bored with doing their HOUSEWORK. 在美国, 电视上白天通常放些肥皂剧、访谈节目、旧电影和旧电视剧等。在英国, 电视上各式各样的节目比较多, 包括儿童节目和有关居家、烹饪的节目。人们常常认为是那些没有工作或者生病在家的人, 再就是那些干腻了家务活的妇女会大白天在家里看电视。

TV din·ner /ˌ‥ˈ‥/ *n* [C] a meal that is sold already prepared, so that you just need to heat it before eating〔只需加热即可食用的〕电视便餐

TV Guide /ˌ‥ˈ‥/ a US weekly magazine which gives the times and details of television programmes, as well as articles about programmes, actors etc《电视指南》〔美国一周刊。内有电视节目播出时间等具体信息及相关文章〕

TVP /ˌti vi ˋpi; ˌtiː viː ˈpiː/ *n* [U] the abbreviation of 缩写= TEXTURED VEGETABLE PROTEIN

TV Times /ˌ‥ˈ‥/ a British weekly magazine that gives the times and details of television programmes, as well as articles about programmes, actors etc《电视指南》〔英国一周刊。内有电视节目播出时间等具体信息及相关文章〕

twad·dle /ˋtwɑdl; ˈtwɒdl/ *n* [U] *informal* something that someone has said or written that you think is stupid; nonsense【非正式】〔说的或写的〕无聊话, 废话: *a load of self-indulgent twaddle* 大量自我陶醉的废话

twain /twen; tweɪn/ *prep old use*【旧】**1** two 二, 两, 双 **2 never the twain shall meet** used to say that two things are so different that they can never exist together 两者永远合不到一起

Twain, Mark (1835-1910) a US writer best known for his NOVELS *The Adventures of Tom Sawyer* and *The Adventures of Huckleberry Finn*, and for his descriptions of life on the Mississippi River. His real name was **Samuel Langhorne Clemens**. 马克·吐温〔(1835-1910), 美国著名作家。代表作有《汤姆·索耶历险记》和《哈克贝里·费恩历险记》, 其中描写有自己在密西西比河上的生活经历。真名为塞缪尔·兰霍恩·克莱门斯〕

twang[1] /twæŋ; twæŋ/ *n* [C usually singular 一般用单数] **1** a quality in the way someone speaks, produced when the air used to speak passes through your nose as well as your mouth 鼻音: *a rural twang* 乡下鼻音 **2** a quick ringing sound like the one

made by pulling a very tight wire and then suddenly letting it go 拨弦声

twang² *v* [I,T] if you twang something or if it twangs, it makes a quick ringing sound by being pulled and then suddenly let go (使) 发出拨弦声; (使) 发出"嘣"的一声: *She twanged the guitar strings.* 她拨弄吉他弦, 发出嘣嘣声。

twas /twɑz; twɒz/ *poetic*【诗】= it was

twat /twɑt; twɒt/ *n* [C] *BrE taboo*【英讳】**1** a stupid or unpleasant person 蠢人, 讨厌鬼 **2** the female sex organ 屄〔女性性器官〕

tweak /twik; twiːk/ *v* [T] **1** to suddenly pull or twist something 捏, 拧: *Matthew tweaked her nose.* 马修捏了她的鼻子。**2** to make small changes to a machine, vehicle, or system in order to improve the way it works 对〔机器、汽车或系统〕作小小的改进: *Of course the programme still needs tweaking to maximize efficiency.* 当然这套程序仍然需要作些小的改进才能发挥最高效率。—**tweak** *n* [C usually singular 一般用单数]

twee /twi; twiː/ *adj BrE* something that is twee looks too pretty or perfect【英】太花哨的; 过分艳丽的; 完美得过分的: *That picture of little cottages with lace curtains is rather twee.* 那张有蕾丝纱帘的小屋图画有点造作。

tweed /twid; twiːd/ *n* [U] **1** rough WOOLLEN cloth woven from threads of different colours, used mostly to make jackets (JACKET (1)), suits, and coats 粗花呢 —see picture on page A16 参见 A16 页图 **2 tweeds** [plural] a suit of clothes made from this type of cloth 粗花呢套装

Twee·dle·dum and Twee·dle·dee /twidlˌdʌm ənd twidlˈdi; twiːdlˌdʌm ənd ˈtwiːdlˈdiː/ two characters in the book *Through The Looking-Glass* by Lewis Carroll. They are fat little men, who are both dressed in school uniform and look exactly like each other. Their names are often used to describe two people or groups who are almost exactly the same as each other, especially when they both seem to be bad 特威德尔德姆和特威德尔迪〔刘易斯·卡罗尔的小说《镜中世界》中的两个人物。他俩是一对小胖子, 身穿校服, 看上去极为相像。两人的名字多用以指称外在相似、品行不端的两个人或组织〕: *Some voters felt there was little real difference between the two party leaders – a case of choosing between Tweedledum and Tweedledee.* 一些选民觉得这两个政党领袖没有实质性区别 —— 歪果子烂桃子, 选谁都一样。

tweed·y /ˈtwidɪ; ˈtwiːdi/ *adj* **1** *BrE* wearing tweed clothes in a way that is thought to be typical of the British upper class【英】爱穿粗花呢服装的; 典型英国上层阶级的: *the epitome of the tweedy country squire* 爱穿粗花呢服装的乡绅典型 **2** made of tweed or like tweed 粗花呢 (似) 的

tween /twin; twiːn/ *prep poetic* between【诗】在…之间

tweet /twit; twiːt/ *v* [I] to make the short high sound of a small bird〔小鸟〕啾啾地叫 —**tweet** *n* [C]

tweet·er /ˈtwitɚ; ˈtwiːtə/ *n* [C] a SPEAKER (=piece of equipment) through which the high sounds from a STEREO etc are made louder 高频扬声器 —compare 比较 WOOFER

twee·zers /ˈtwizɚz; ˈtwiːzəz/ *n* [plural] a small tool that has two narrow pieces of metal joined at one end, used to pull or move very small objects 镊子, 小钳子: *plucking her eyebrows with a pair of tweezers* 用一副镊子拔她的眉毛

tweezers 镊子

twelfth /twɛlfθ; twelfθ/ *n* [C] one of 12 equal parts of something 十二分之一

Twelfth Night /ˌ· ˈ·/ **1** the evening before the Epiphany (6 January), which represents the end of the Christmas period. Christmas cards and decorations are usually taken down on Twelfth Night 主显节前夕, 主显节之夜〔主显节 (1月6日) 前夕标志着圣诞节节庆的结束。此夜通常开始取下悬挂的圣诞贺卡及各种饰物〕**2** a humorous play by William Shakespeare , which tells a complicated story about a young woman called Viola, who dresses as a boy to work as a servant of the Duke Orsino. Eventually she marries the Duke and finds her brother, Sebastian, whom she believed to be dead.《第十二夜》〔威廉·莎士比亚的一部喜剧作品, 讲述一个错综复杂的故事。年轻姑娘维奥拉装扮成男孩去奥西诺公爵的府上做仆人, 最后她与公爵结了婚, 并找到了原以为已经死去的弟弟塞巴斯蒂安〕

twelve /twɛlv; twelv/ *number* 12 十二

twelve-month /ˈ· ·/ *n* [C] *old-fashioned* a year【过时】一年

Twelve Step /ˌ· ˈ·/ also **12-step a Twelve Step program** a method of helping people stop drinking alcohol, using drugs etc., developed by Alcoholics Anonymous 十二步戒酒[毒]法〔匿名嗜酒者互戒协会发明的一种方法, 采用药物等方法帮助人们戒酒或戒毒等〕—see 见 RECOVERY PROGRAM

20th Cen·tu·ry Fox /ˌtwɛntɪəθ sɛntʃərɪ ˈfɑks; ˌtwentiəθ sentʃəri ˈfɒks/ *trademark* a US film production company【商标】20世纪福克斯〔美国一家电影制片公司〕

twen·ty /ˈtwɛntɪ; ˈtwenti/ *number* **1** 20 二十 **2 the twenties** also 又作 **the 20's** the years from 1920 to 1929 二十年代〔指1920年–1929年〕: *a photo showing how the street looked in the early twenties* 一张展现这条街道20年代初期风貌的照片

CULTURAL NOTE 文化注释

The twenties are also known as the roaring twenties, and are thought of as a time when life in the US and UK was exciting and fun. When people think of the twenties in the US, they think of GANGSTERs (=members of criminal groups who carried guns and wore very good clothes), and fashionable young women known as FLAPPERs who went to 'speakeasies' (=illegal places where you could dance and drink alcohol) during Prohibition (=the time when alcohol was illegal in the US). 20世纪20年代亦被称为"兴旺的20年代", 这个时期英美的生活被认为既刺激又有趣。美国人由20年代想到的是匪徒和禁酒令期间年轻时髦女郎出入"地下酒吧"的情景。

3 be in your twenties to be aged between twenty and twenty nine〔年龄〕在二十多岁时: *She met him when she was in her twenties.* 她二十多岁时认识了他。

twenty-first /ˌ·· ˈ·◂/ *n* [C usually singular 一般用单数] your twenty-first BIRTHDAY or the celebration you have for it 21岁生日; 21岁生日庆祝会

24 hour clock /ˌtwɛntɪ fɔr aʊr ˈklɑk; ˌtwenti fɔːr aʊə ˈklɒk/ *n* a clock, or a system of telling the time, according to which, for example, one o'clock in the afternoon is called 1300 hours (pronounced '13 hundred hours'). 24小时制时钟; 24小时制〔如下午1点可叫做13点〕: *The trains run according to the 24 hour clock.* 火车按24小时计时系统运行。

twenty-one /ˌ·· ˈ·◂/ *n* [U] *AmE* a card game, usually played for money【美】21点牌戏〔一种赌博游戏〕; PONTOON (1) *BrE*【英】

20 Questions /ˌtwɛntɪ ˈkwɛstʃənz; ˌtwenti ˈkwestʃənz/ also 又作 **Animal, Vegetable or Mineral** *n AmE* a game in which one person thinks of an object and others have to guess what it is by asking questions about it which can only be answered with 'Yes' or 'No'. You sometimes mention the game when you think that someone is asking you too many questions or making you ask them too many questions instead of simply giving you the information you want.【美】20问答游戏〔又称动物、蔬菜、矿物竞猜游戏, 由一人想好一样东西, 其他人通过提问来猜出是什么, 被问者只能回答"是"或"不是"。当形容某人问题问得过多或者不肯直截了当说出你想要的信息而让你不得不反复探问时, 有时会提到这种游戏〕: *Just tell me straight – don't make me play '20 Questions'.* "直截了当说吧, 别让我玩20问答游戏啦。"

Twenty-Third Psalm, the /ˌ·· ·ˈ·/ the best-known Psalm in the Old Testament of the Bible, which is often sung at funerals. It starts with the words 'The Lord is my shepherd'. 诗篇第二十三篇〔《圣经·旧约》中最有名的诗篇, 常在葬礼上吟唱, 首句为"耶和华是我的牧者"〕

twenty-twenty vi·sion, 20/20 vision /ˌ·· ·· ˈ··/ *n* [U] the ability to see perfectly 极好的视力; 正常视力: *To be a pilot you must have twenty-twenty vision.* 要想当飞行员, 你必须具有极好的视力。

twenty-two, .22 /ˌtwɛntɪˈtu; ˌtwentiˈtuː/ *n* [C] a gun that fires small bullets, used for hunting small animals .22口径的猎枪

twerp /twɝp; twɜːp/ *n* [C] *informal* a stupid or annoying person【非正式】蠢人; 讨厌鬼

twice /twaɪs; twaɪs/ *predeterminer* two times 两次; 两倍 —see also 另见 **once bitten, twice shy** (ONCE¹ (17)), **once or twice** (ONCE¹ (7)), **think twice** (THINK¹ (9))

twid·dle¹ /ˈtwɪdl; ˈtwɪdl/ *v* [T] **1** also 又作 **twiddle with** to move or turn something around with your fingers many times, especially because you are bored〔尤指因为厌烦而反复地用手指〕捻弄, 摆弄 **2 twiddle your thumbs** *informal*【非正式】**a)** to do nothing while you are waiting for something to happen 闲着无事, 闲得无聊 **b)** to join your fingers together and move your thumbs in a circle around each other, because you are bored〔因无聊而把〕两手的手指互扣, 旋转大拇指 —**twiddle** *n* [C]

twiddle² *n* [C] a small twist or turn, especially in a decorative pattern〔尤指装饰图案中的〕修饰性小曲线, 小螺旋形线条

twiddly /ˈtwɪdlɪ; ˈtwɪdli/ *adj* **twiddly bit** *spoken* used to talk about a small part of an object without naming it【口】小东西〔用来代替正确名称, 指物体的一小部分〕: *Where's the twiddly bit for the top?* 放在上面的那个小东西到哪去了?

twig[1] /twɪg; twɪg/ *n* [C] a small very thin stem of wood that grows from a branch on a tree〔树枝上的〕细枝, 嫩枝 —**twiggy** *adj*

twig[2] *v* [I,T] *BrE informal* to suddenly realize something about a situation【英, 非正式】突然懂得: *Do you mean he still hasn't twigged?* 你的意思是指他仍旧没有明白?

twi·light /ˈtwaɪˌlaɪt; ˈtwaɪlaɪt/ *n* **1** [U] the small amount of light in the sky as the day ends 暮色, 黄昏的天色: *It appeared shadowy and insubstantial in the twilight.* 暮色中显得阴影模糊, 虚幻不清。**2** [U] the time when day is just starting to become night 黄昏时分, 薄暮时分 **3** [singular] the period just before the end of the most active part of someone's life〔人生的〕暮年时期: *the twilight of her acting career* 她演艺生涯的晚期 | **twilight years** (=the last ones of your life)〔人生的〕暮年, 晚年 **4 twilight world** *literary* a strange situation involving mystery, dishonesty etc【文】朦胧世界; 阴暗世界: *the twilight world of espionage* 间谍活动的阴暗世界

Twilight Zone, the /ˈ· · ·, ·/ a US television programme, originally made between 1959 and 1963, and then again in the 1980s, with a different story and characters each week. The stories usually deal with SUPERNATURAL events or science FICTION.《迷离境界》, 又译《阴阳魔界》〔美国一电视节目。初创于1959年至1963年期间, 20世纪80年代恢复播出, 每周讲述一个不同的故事和一些不同的人物, 通常讲述超自然事件或科幻故事〕

twi·lit /ˈtwaɪˌlɪt; ˈtwaɪlɪt/ *adj literary* lit by twilight【文】暮色下的: *the twilit gray of the sea* 暮色下灰暗的海面

twill /twɪl; twɪl/ *n* [U] strong cloth woven to produce parallel sloping lines across its surface 斜纹织物: *grey twill trousers* 灰色的斜纹裤子

twin[1] /twɪn; twɪn/ *n* [C] one of two children born at the same time to the same mother 双胞胎中的一个: *My brother and I look so alike that people often think we are twins.* 我和我的兄弟长得太像了, 人们经常认为我们是双胞胎。| **twin sister/brother/daughters etc** *Meet my twin sister.* 认识一下我的孪生妹妹。—see also 另见 IDENTICAL TWIN, SIAMESE TWIN

twin[2] *adj* [only before noun 仅用于名词前] **1 twin problems/goals etc** happening at the same time and related to each other 两个同时出现、密切相关的问题/目标等: *a policy to combat the twin problems of poverty and unemployment* 解决贫困和失业这两个密切相关问题的一项政策 **2 twin beds/engines etc** two similar things that are intended to be used as a pair 成对的(单人)床/双引擎等 —see also 另见 TWINSET, TWIN TOWN, TWIN TUB —see picture at 参见 BED 图

twin[3] *v* [T usually passive 一般用被动态] *BrE* to form a relationship between two similar towns in different countries in order to encourage visits between them【英】〔不同国家的两个类似城市〕结为姐妹城市: [+with] *Harlow in England is twinned with Stavanger in Norway.* 英国的哈洛与挪威的斯塔万格结成了姐妹城市。—see also 另见 TWIN TOWN

twin bed /ˌ· ˈ·/ *n* [C] **1** [usually plural 一般用复数] one of a pair of beds in a room for two people 双人房间中的对床之一 **2** *AmE* a bed for one person【美】单人床 —**twin-bedded** *adj*: *twin-bedded rooms* 有两张床的双人房间

Twin Cit·ies, the /ˌ· ˈ· ·/ the cities of Minneapolis and St Paul, in the US state of Minnesota 双子城〔指美国明尼苏达州的明尼阿波利斯和圣保罗两座城市〕

twine[1] /twaɪn; twaɪn/ *n* [U] strong string made by twisting together two or more threads or strings 两[多]股的线: *a bundle of papers tied up with twine* 用双股线捆扎起来的一摞文件

twine[2] *v* [I,T] to wind or twist around something else 缠绕, 盘绕; 捻: **twine sth around sth** *She twined her fingers round the empty cup.* 她手指交叉地捧着那个空杯子。| [+around] *Ivy twined around the balcony.* 常春藤缠绕着阳台。

twin-en·gined /ˌtwɪn ˈɛndʒɪnd; ˌtwɪn ˈendʒɪnd◂/ *adj* a twin-engined aircraft has two engines〔飞机〕双引擎的

twinge /twɪndʒ; twɪndʒ/ *n* [C] **1** a sudden feeling of slight pain 一阵刺痛: *I felt a twinge in my back.* 我感到背部一阵刺痛。**2 a twinge of guilt/jealousy/fear etc** a sudden slight feeling of guilt etc 感到一阵内疚/嫉妒/恐惧等: *John felt a twinge of regret as he walked away.* 约翰走开的时候感到一阵后悔。

Twin·kie /ˈtwɪŋkɪ; ˈtwɪŋki/ *trademark* a type of small, sweet, sticky yellow cake filled with a white cream, sold in the US【商标】特温奇〔美国销售的一种甜味奶油黄色小黏糕〕

twin·kle[1] /ˈtwɪŋkl; ˈtwɪŋkəl/ *v* [I] **1** if a star or light twinkles, it shines in the dark, quickly changing from bright to faint 闪烁, 闪耀: *The lights of the town twinkled below us.* 小镇的灯光在我们下方闪烁。**2** if someone's eyes twinkle, they have a cheerful expression〔眼睛〕闪闪发光: [+with] *Don's eyes twinkled with laughter.* 唐的双眼笑意盈盈。**3 in the twinkling of an eye** *old-fashioned* very quickly【过时】转眼间, 瞬间, 霎时

twinkle[2] *n* [C usually singular 一般用单数] **1 a twinkle in your eye** an expression in your eyes that shows you are happy or amused 眼睛里闪烁着愉悦的光芒: *"I can get that at home!" she said with a twinkle in her eye.* "我家里有!"她说道, 眼里闪烁着喜悦的光芒。**2 when you were just a twinkle in your father's eye** before you were born 在你还未出世的时候 **3** a small bright shining light that becomes brighter and then fainter 闪烁的光

Twinkle, twinkle, lit·tle star /ˌ· ·, · ·, · · ˈ·/ a NURSERY RHYME (=an old song or poem for children).《天上星星亮晶晶》〔一首童谣〕The rhyme goes 该童谣如下:

Twinkle, twinkle, little star,
How I wonder what you are.
Up above the world so high,
Like a diamond in the sky.
天上星星亮晶晶,
你是什么我说不清。
高高挂在夜空中,
宛如钻石放光明。

twin·set /ˈtwɪnˌsɛt; ˈtwɪnset/ *n* [C] *BrE* a woman's SWEATER and CARDIGAN that are meant to be worn together【英】女装两件套毛衣〔由套头毛衣和开襟衫组成〕: *twinset and pearls* 珍珠和女装两件套毛衣

twin town /ˌ· ˈ·/ *n* [C] *BrE* a town that has formed a relationship with a similar town in another country in order to encourage visits between them【英】〔与外国某个类似城市结成的〕姐妹城: *Oxford's twin town is Bonn.* 牛津的姐妹城是波恩。

twin tub /ˌ· ˈ·/ *n* [C] *BrE* a type of WASHING MACHINE with one part for washing and one for spin-drying (SPIN-DRYER)【英】双缸洗衣机

twirl[1] /twɜl; twɜːl/ *v* [I,T] to turn around and around or make something do this (使)旋转; (使)转动; (使)缠绕: [+around/round] *twirling around the dance floor* 围绕着舞池旋转 | **twirl sth around/round** *He twirled the gun round in his hand.* 他转动手上的枪。

twirl[2] *n* [C] a sudden quick spinning movement 快速的旋转, 转动 —**twirly** *adj*

twist[1] /twɪst; twɪst/ *v* S3

1 ▶BEND 弯曲◀ [T] to bend and turn something several times, especially in order to make something or to tie it to something 扭, 拧; 扭转成; 使弯曲: **twist sth into/around etc** *She twisted the wire into the shape of a star.* 她把金属丝扭成了星形。

2 ▶MOVE 移动◀ [I] to turn a part of your body around or change your position by turning 扭动身体: *He twisted to try and get free of the ropes.* 他扭动着身体, 设法挣脱掉绳子。

3 ▶TURN 转动◀ [T] to turn something using your hand〔用手〕转动, 旋动: **twist sth off** *Jack twisted the cap off the bottle.* 杰克拧开了瓶上的盖子。

4 ▶WIND 盘绕◀ [T always+adv/prep] to wind something in a particular way 盘绕, 缠绕; 捻, 搓: **twist sth round/around** *She twisted the streamers round the banisters.* 她把那些饰带缠绕在楼梯扶手上。| **twist sth together** *Twist the two ends of the wire together.* 把这根电线的两头绕在一起。

5 ▶ROAD/RIVER 道路/河流◀ [I] if a road, river etc twists, it changes direction in a series of curves 盘旋; 蜿蜒: *The track twisted into the hills.* 小道蜿蜒进入了山区。

6 ▶WORDS 词语◀ [T] to change the true or intended meaning of a statement, especially in order to get some advantage for yourself; DISTORT 歪曲, 曲解: *Every time I try to discuss the situation, he twists what I say.* 每次我想要讨论形势时, 他总歪曲我说的话。

7 twist your wrist/ankle/knee to hurt your wrist etc by pulling or turning it too suddenly while you are moving 扭伤手腕/踝关节/膝盖

8 twist and turn a) if a path, road, stream etc twists and turns, it has a lot of bends in it〔道路、溪流等〕弯弯曲曲, 蜿蜒 **b)** if a person or animal twists and turns, they make twisting movements〔人或动物〕曲折地行走; 扭动身体: *The snake twisted and turned through the mud.* 那条蛇蠕动身体穿过泥地。

9 twist sb's arm a) *informal* to persuade someone to do something they do not want to do【非正式】强迫某人做某事, 向某人施加压力: *I'm sure he'll come to the party if you twist his arm.* 如果你给他施加一点压力, 我敢说他会来参加聚会的。**b)** to bend someone's arm upwards behind their back in order to hurt them 把某人的手臂反扭到背后 **c) twist my arm!** *spoken* used hu-

morously to accept an invitation, a drink etc【口】敢强迫我！〔接受邀请、喝酒等；一种幽默用法〕: *Oh, go on, twist my arm! I'll have a red wine.* 好啊，继续来吧，敢强迫我喝酒！那我就喝杯红酒。—see also 另见 **twist/wrap sb around your little finger** (FINGER[1] (13)), **twist/turn the knife** (KNIFE[1] (4))

twist² *n* [C] **1** a twisting action or movement 扭，拧；捻；搓: *Give that lid a twist – it's coming loose.* 拧一下那个盖子，它快要松动了。**2** a bend in a river or road〔河流或道路的〕弯曲处 **3** an unexpected change in the meaning of a situation or in the progress of a series of events〔形势或事态的〕意外转折: *The story ends with a strange twist – the detective turns out to be the murderer.* 这个故事的结尾有一个奇特的转折——那侦探原来就是杀人凶犯。| **a twist of fate/fortune** *By an amazing twist of fate, we met again in Madrid five years later.* 命运巧合得令人惊奇，我们五年以后又在马德里相遇了。**4** a small piece of something that is twisted into a particular shape 搓捻成某一形状的东西: [+of] *a twist of tobacco* 烟叶卷 | *a twist of lemon* 柠檬卷片 **5 round the twist** *BrE* crazy【英】发疯的: **drive/send sb round the twist** (=make someone angry by continuously doing something) 不断做某事逼得某人发怒 **6 the twist** a popular fast dance in the 1960s in which you twist your body from side to side〔流行于20世纪60年代的〕扭摆舞 —**twisty** *adj*: *a twisty road* 一条弯弯曲曲的路 —see also 另见 **get your knickers in a twist** (KNICKERS (3))

Twist, Ol·i·ver /ˈɑlɪvɚ; ˈɒlɪvə/ the main character in the book *Oliver Twist* by Charles Dickens 特威斯特〔查尔斯·狄更斯的小说《雾都孤儿》的主人公〕

twist·ed /ˈtwɪstɪd; ˈtwɪstɪ̣d/ *adj* **1** bent in many directions, so that it has lost its original shape 扭曲的，变形的: *a mass of twisted wreckage* 一堆变形的残骸 **2** seeming to enjoy things that are cruel or shocking, in a way that is not normal〔兴趣〕反常的，变态的: *Whoever sent those letters has a twisted mind.* 寄那些信的人有变态心理。

twist·er /ˈtwɪstɚ; ˈtwɪstə/ *n* [C] **1** *BrE informal* someone who cheats other people【英，非正式】骗子；奸诈的人 **2** *AmE informal* a TORNADO【美，非正式】龙卷风

twit /twɪt; twɪt/ *n* [C] *informal* a stupid or silly person【非正式】笨蛋，傻瓜

twitch¹ /twɪtʃ; twɪtʃ/ *v* **1** [I,T] if a part of someone's body twitches, it makes a small, sudden, uncontrolled movement〔身体的某个部分〕颤动，抽动，抽搐: *My eye won't stop twitching.* 我的眼皮跳个不停。**2** [T] to move something quickly and suddenly 猛拉，急扯: *Sarah twitched the reins, and we moved off.* 萨拉猛地一拉缰绳，我们出发了。

twitch² *n* [C] **1** a quick movement of a muscle that you cannot control〔肌肉的〕抽搐，颤动: *a nervous twitch* 神经性抽搐 **2** a sudden, quick movement 猛的一拉，一动: *A twitch of the line means you've caught a fish.* 线猛地一动，意味着你钓着鱼了。

twitch·y /ˈtwɪtʃɪ; ˈtwɪtʃi/ *adj* **1** behaving in a nervous way because you are anxious about something 焦急的；紧张的: *Why are you so twitchy today?* 你今天为何如此焦躁不安？**2** repeatedly making sudden small movements 反复抽动的，抽搐的；痉挛性的: *a cat with a twitchy tail* 尾巴老是抽动的猫

twit·ter¹ /ˈtwɪtɚ; ˈtwɪtə/ *v* [I] **1** if a bird twitters, it makes a lot of short high sounds〔鸟〕鸣啭，啾啾叫，吱吱叫: *the twittering of larks overhead* 头上啾啾叫着的云雀 **2** if a woman twitters, she talks very quickly and nervously in a high voice〔妇女〕喊喊喳喳地说话

twitter² *n* **1** [singular] the short, high sounds that birds make〔鸟的〕鸣啭声，啾啾声，吱吱声 **2 be all of a twitter** also 又作 **be in a twitter** to be excited and nervous 很兴奋；很紧张: *She's been all of a twitter since her daughter's engagement.* 自从她女儿订婚以来，她一直兴奋得不得了。—**twittery** *adj*

twixt /twɪkst; twɪkst/ *prep old use* between【旧】在…之间

two /tu; tuː/ *number* **1** 2 二 **2 put two and two together** to guess the meaning of something you have heard or seen 根据现有情况推论，综合起来判断: *I didn't call to say I'd be late, but she put two and two together when she heard the weather reports.* 我没打电话说要迟到，但她听天气预报便知道了。**3 that makes two of us** *spoken* used to tell someone that you are in the same situation and feel the same way【口】我们两人的情况一样；我跟你有同感: *"Well, I don't want to be the one to tell him." "That makes two of us."* "唉，我不想充当去告诉他的那个人。""彼此彼此。" **4 two can play at that game** *spoken* used to tell someone that they will not have an advantage over you by doing something because you can do it too【口】这一套你会我也会 **5 two cents (worth)** [plural] *AmE informal* your opinion or what you want to say about a subject【美，非正式】〔对所讨论问题的〕意见，观点: *Everyone had to get in their two cents worth.* 每个人都得发表自己的意见。**6 for two cents** *AmE spoken* used when you are describing angrily what you would like to do to change a situation【美口】恨不得〔用于愤怒地表示要做某事〕: *For two cents I'd kick him out.* 我恨不得把他踢出去。**7 two bits** *AmE informal* twenty five CENTS, or a coin that is worth this amount of money【美，非正式】25美分（硬币），二毛五 **8 two's company, three's a crowd** used to say that it is better to leave two people alone to spend time with each other 两人成伴，三人不欢 —see also 另见 **don't care two hoots** (HOOT[1] (5)), **be in two minds about** (MIND[1] (6)), **two of a kind** (KIND[1] (8)), **be two a penny** (PENNY (11)), **it takes two to tango** (TANGO[2] (2))

two-bit /ˈ· ·/ *adj informal* not at all good or important【非正式】差劲的；微不足道的，不重要的: *She's just a two-bit movie star.* 她只是一名末流的电影明星。

two-di·men·sion·al /ˌ· ·ˈ···◂/ *adj* **1** a two-dimensional character in a book, play etc does not seem like a real person〔书本或剧中的人物〕描写没有深度的；没有真实感的 **2** flat 二维的，平面的: *a two-dimensional shape* 平面形状

two-edged /ˌ· ˈ·◂/ *adj* **1** having disadvantages or bad effects that are less easy to see than the good effects 优劣混杂的〔缺点不及优点明显的〕: *the two-edged triumphs of technology* 有利有弊的技术成就 | **a two-edged sword** (=with as many bad results as good ones) 双刃剑，双锋刀 *Strong leadership is a two-edged sword.* 强硬的领导是一把双刃剑。**2** having two edges that can cut 双刃的

two-faced /ˌ· ˈ·◂/ *adj informal* changing what you say according to who you are talking to, in a way that is insincere and unpleasant【非正式】两面派的，虚伪圆滑的: *He came out of the affair as a two-faced hypocrite.* 他在那件事上终于显出伪君子两面派的嘴脸。

two·fold /ˈtufold; ˈtuːfəʊld/ *adj* **1** two times as much or as many of something 两倍的: *a twofold increase in the incidence of TB* 结核病发病率呈两倍的增加 **2** having two important parts 有两部分的；双重的: *The reasons for the collapse are twofold.* 倒塌的原因是双重的。—**twofold** *adv*

two-hand·ed /ˌ· ˈ··◂/ *adj* **1** using both hands to do something 用双手操作的: *the tennis star's famous two-handed backhand* 那位网球名星著名的双手反手击球 **2** a two-handed tool is used by two people together〔工具〕两人操作的

two-line whip /ˌ· · ˈ·/ *n* [C] a written order given to members of the British Parliament about how they should vote on a particular subject〔发给英国议员就某一议题如何投票的〕书面通知

two-man /ˈ· ·/ *adj* designed to be used by two people 为二人设计的；限于二人使用的: *a two-man tent* 双人帐篷

two-one, 2-1 /ˌtu ˈwʌn; ˌtuː ˈwʌn/ *n* [C] the higher of two levels of a second-class university degree in Britain 二级一等〔英国大学学位第二类中较高的一级〕

two·pence, tuppence /ˈtʌpəns; ˈtʌpəns/ *n BrE*【英】**1** [U] an amount of money worth two pence 两便士 **2** [C] a British coin in former times that was worth two pence〔英国旧时的〕两便士硬币 **3 not care twopence** *old-fashioned* to not care at all about something or someone【过时】一点也不在乎

two·pen·ny /ˈtuˌpɛnɪ; ˈtʌpəni/ *adj BrE old-fashioned*【英，过时】**1** [only before noun 仅用于名词前] costing two pence; TUPPENNY 值两便士的 **2 twopenny-halfpenny** worth almost nothing 几乎没有价值的，一文不值的

two-per·cent milk /ˌ· ·ˈ· ˈ·/ *n* [U] *AmE* milk that has had about half the fat removed【美】半脱脂牛奶；SEMI-SKIMMED *BrE*【英】

two-piece /ˌ· ˈ·◂/ *adj* [only before noun 仅用于名词前] a two-piece suit consists of a matching JACKET (1) and trousers〔衣服〕两件套的〔指相配的短上衣和裤子〕

two-ply /ˈ· ˌ·/ *adj* consisting of two threads or layers 双股的；两层的: *two-ply wool* 双股毛线 | *two-ply tissues* 双层纸巾

two seat·er /ˌ· ˈ··◂/ *n* [C] a car, aircraft etc with seats for two people 双座汽车；双座飞机

two-sid·ed /ˌ· ˈ··◂/ *adj* having two different parts 两方面的，双重的: *a two-sided problem* 一个双重问题 —see also 另见 ONE-SIDED, MANY-SIDED

two·some /ˈtusəm; ˈtuːsəm/ *n* [C usually singular 一般用单数] two people who work together or spend a lot of time together〔两人组成的〕一对，一双；搭档: *the talented comedy twosome, French and Saunders* 才华横溢的喜剧搭档弗伦奇和桑德斯

two-star /ˈ· ·/ *adj* [only before noun 仅用于名词前] a level of quality used to judge hotels, restaurants etc, that shows they are of a medium standard〔旅馆、饭馆等〕二星级的，中档的

two-step /ˈ· ·/ *n* [singular] a dance with long sliding steps or the music for this type of dance 两步舞; 两步舞曲

two-stroke /ˈ· ·/ *adj* a two-stroke engine is one in which there is a single up-and-down movement of a PISTON〔发动机〕二冲程的

Two Thou·sand Guin·eas, the /ˌ· ·· ˈ··/ also 又作 **2000 Guineas** a famous British horse race run at Newmarket 二千几尼赛〔英国纽马基特举行的一项著名马赛〕

two-time /ˈ· ·/ *v* [T] *informal* to have a secret relationship with someone who is not your regular partner【非正式】背着…偷情; 对〔恋人〕不忠: *If you're two-timing me, I'll kill you I swear!* 如果你背着我偷情, 我发誓会杀了你! —**two-timer** *n* [C]

two-tone /ˈ· ·/ *adj* **1** two-tone furniture, clothes etc are made of material in two colours〔家具、衣服等〕两色的, 双色的: *two-tone shoes* 双色鞋 **2** making two different sounds 发双音的

two-two, 2-2 /ˌ· ˈ·/ *n* [C] the lower of two levels of a second-class university degree in Britain 二级二等〔英国大学学位第二类中较低的一级〕: *She got a 2-2 in French.* 她有个二级二等的法语学位。

two-way /ˌ· ˈ·◂/ *adj* **1** moving or allowing movement in both directions 双向的; 可双向通行的: *two-way traffic* 双向行驶的车辆交通 | *two-way trade* 双向贸易 **2** two-way radio both sends and receives messages〔无线电〕收发两用的

two-way mir·ror /ˌ· · ˈ··/ *n* [C] glass that looks like a mirror from one side, but that you can see through from the other〔从一面看是镜子, 从反面看是透明的〕双向镜

two-way street /ˌ· · ˈ·/ *n* [C usually singular 一般用单数] *AmE informal* a situation that depends on two people working well together【美, 非正式】依靠两人和睦相处的关系: *Marriage has to be a two-way street.* 婚姻之道在于相互沟通。

TX the written abbreviation of 缩写= TEXAS

-ty /tɪ; ti/ *suffix* [in nouns 构成名词] another form of the suffix -ITY 后缀 -ity 的另一种拼写: *certainty* (=being certain) 确定

ty·coon /taɪˋkun; taɪˈkuːn/ *n* [C] someone who is successful in business or industry and has a lot of money and power〔工商界的〕巨头, 大亨: *Millionaire computer tycoon, Alan Sugar* 计算机巨头百万富翁艾伦·休格

ty·ing /ˈtaɪ·ɪŋ; ˈtaɪ-ɪŋ/ the present participle of TIE

tyke /taɪk; taɪk/ *n* [C] **1** *spoken BrE* a child who is behaving badly【口, 英】淘气的孩子, 小淘气 **2** *AmE* a small child【美】小孩子 **3** *BrE informal* someone from Yorkshire【英, 非正式】约克郡人

Ty·le·nol /ˈtaɪlənɔl; ˈtaɪlənɒl/ *trademark* a type of medicine used for stopping pain such as headaches and for reducing fevers. Tylenol does not contain ASPIRIN.【商标】泰诺〔一种止痛解热药, 不含阿斯匹林〕

Ty·ler /ˈtaɪlɚ; ˈtaɪlə/, **John** (1790-1862) the tenth president of the US, from 1841 to 1845 泰勒〔(1790-1862), 1841 至 1845 年任美国第十任总统〕

Tyler, Wat /wɑt; wɒt/ (?-1381) an Englishman who was the leader of the Peasants' Revolt in 1381, a protest in which thousands of poor people marched to London to complain about their bad economic situation. He was murdered by the Lord Mayor of London. 泰勒〔(?-1381), 1381 年英国农民起义领袖。当时, 成千上万的穷人向伦敦进发, 以抗议自身所处的恶劣经济状况。最后, 泰勒遭到伦敦市长杀害〕

tym·pa·num /ˈtɪmpənəm; ˈtɪmpənəm/ *n* [C] *technical* an EARDRUM【术语】鼓膜

Tyn·dale /ˈtɪndl̩; ˈtɪndəl/, **William** (?1492-1536) an English priest who supported the Reformation (=the time when many Christians in Europe left the Catholic religion and started the Protestant religion). The Authorized Version of the Bible is partly based on his translations. He was killed by being burned to death because of his religious beliefs. 廷德尔〔(?1492-1536), 英国牧师, 支持宗教改革。《钦定本英文圣经》部分基于他的翻译。最后, 他因宗教信仰而被处以火刑〕

Tyne, the /taɪn; taɪn/ a river in northeast England, flowing through Newcastle-upon-Tyne to the North Sea 泰恩河〔英格兰东北部一河流, 流经泰恩河畔的纽卡斯尔, 最后注入北海〕

Tyne and Wear /ˌtaɪn ənd ˋwɪr; ˌtaɪn ənd ˈwɪə/ a METROPOLITAN COUNTY in northern England, made up of parts of Northumberland and Durham, and including Newcastle-upon-Tyne 泰恩－威尔郡〔英格兰北部一大都市郡, 由诺森伯兰郡和达勒姆郡部分地区组成, 包括泰恩河畔的纽卡斯尔〕

Tyne·side /ˈtaɪnsaɪd; ˈtaɪnsaɪd/ an area in northeast England on the banks of the River Tyne from Newcastle to the east coast. Tyneside formerly had a lot of industry, including shipbuilding and coal mining, and much of this closed down in the 1970s and 1980s, leaving many people without work. 泰恩赛德〔英格兰东北部一地区, 位于泰恩河沿岸, 从纽卡斯尔至东部海滨。过去, 泰恩赛德的工业十分繁荣, 包括造船业及采煤业等。20 世纪 70、80 年代, 多数工厂停产关闭, 造成许多人失业〕

Tyn·wald /ˈtɪnwəld; ˈtɪnwəld/ the parliament of the Isle of Man〔英国的〕马恩岛议会

type[1] /taɪp; taɪp/ *n* **1** [C] one member of a group of people or things that have similar features or qualities 类型, 种类: *There have been several incidents of this type in recent weeks.* 最近几周已经发生好几宗类似事件了。| *Buy the right shampoo for your hair type.* 买适合你发质的洗发剂。| [+of] *She's the type of person I admire.* 她是我欣赏的那一类人。**2** [U] printed letters 印刷字体: *italic type* 斜体字 **3** [C,U] a small block with a raised letter on it that is used to print with, or a set of these〔印刷用的〕活字 **4** [C] someone with particular qualities or interests 某种类型的人: *the sporty type* 爱好运动的人 **5 be sb's type** *especially spoken* to be the kind of person someone is sexually attracted to【尤口】在性方面对某人有吸引力的那类人: *He wasn't my type really.* 其实他不是对我有吸引力的那种人。 S1 W1

type[2] *v* **1** [T] to print a document on a piece of paper using a TYPEWRITER〔用打字机〕打字: *Does the report need to be typed?* 那份报告需要打出来吗? **2** [I] to write using a TYPEWRITER or a computer〔用打字机或电脑〕打字: *He types with two fingers.* 他用两个手指打字。**3** [T] *technical* to find out what type a plant, disease etc is【术语】找出〔植物、疾病等〕的类型; 把…分类

type·cast /ˈtaɪpˌkæst; ˈtaɪpkɑːst/ *v* [T] **1** to always give an actor the same type of character to play 总是给〔演员〕分配同一类型的角色: *He always gets typecast as the villain.* 他总是被分派去演坏蛋。**2** to give someone a particular type of job, activity etc to do, because you think it suits their character 给〔某人〕分派〔合乎其性格的工作、活动等〕

type·face /ˈtaɪpˌfes; ˈtaɪpfeɪs/ *n* [C] a group of letters, numbers etc of the same style and size, used in printing〔印刷用的〕字体

type·script /ˈtaɪpˌskrɪpt; ˈtaɪpˌskrɪpt/ *n* [C] a copy of a document, made using a TYPEWRITER〔用打字机打出的〕原稿, 打字稿

type·set·ter /ˈtaɪpˌsɛtɚ; ˈtaɪpˌsetə/ *n* [C] a person or machine that arranges the letters, words etc on a page or SCREEN[1] (1) for printing 排字工; 排字机

type·set·ting /ˈtaɪpˌsɛtɪŋ; ˈtaɪpˌsetɪŋ/ *n* [U] the job or activity of arranging TYPE[1] (3) for printing 排字 (工作) —**typeset** *v* [T]

type·writ·er /ˈtaɪpˌraɪtɚ; ˈtaɪpˌraɪtə/ *n* [C] a machine that prints letters of the alphabet onto paper 打字机

type·writ·ten /ˈtaɪpˌrɪtn; ˈtaɪpˌrɪtn/ *adj* written using a TYPEWRITER 用打字机打出的: *three sides of typewritten notes* 三页打字稿

ty·phoid /ˈtaɪfɔɪd; ˈtaɪfɔɪd/ also 又作 **typhoid fe·ver** /ˌ·· ˈ··/ *n* [U] a serious infectious disease that is caused by dirty food or drink 伤寒: *a sudden outbreak of typhoid* 伤寒的突然爆发

Typhoid Ma·ry /ˌ·· ˈ··/ (died 1938) an Irishwoman in the US who had the disease TYPHOID, and who was believed to have infected many people with it. The name is sometimes used to mean someone who is avoided because they are expected to cause a lot of trouble or problems. 伤寒玛丽〔(卒于1938年), 生活在美国的一名爱尔兰裔女子, 死于伤寒。据认为, 她的伤寒病当时传染了许多人。现在, 人们有时借用此名意指会给大家带来不少麻烦或问题因而应予以回避的一个人〕

ty·phoon /taɪˋfun; ˌtaɪˈfuːn◂/ *n* [C] a very violent storm in tropical areas in which the wind moves in circles 台风

ty·phus /ˈtaɪfəs; ˈtaɪfəs/ *n* [U] a serious infectious disease carried by insects that live on the bodies of people and animals 斑疹伤寒

typ·i·cal /ˈtɪpɪkl̩; ˈtɪpɪkəl/ *adj* **1** having the usual features or qualities of a particular group or thing 典型的, 有代表性的: *a typical British summer* 典型的英国夏季 | [+of] *This painting is fairly typical of his early work.* 这幅画在他早期作品中是相当典型的。**2** behaving or happening in the usual way 表现出个性的, 一向如此的: [+of] *It was typical of him to get angry about it.* 他因此发怒了, 这正是他的个性。**3 typical!** *spoken* used to show that you are annoyed when something bad happens again【口】老是这样!〔表示气愤〕 S2 W2

typ·i·cally /ˈtɪpɪklɪ; ˈtɪpɪkli/ *adv* **1** in a way that a person or group is generally believed to behave 典型地, 有代表性地: *It's a typically British bureaucratic response.* 这是典型的英国官僚式的回答。**2** in the way that a particular type of thing usually happens 一向, 向来, 通常: *The disease typically takes several weeks to appear.* 这种病通常要等几个星期才发作。

typ·i·fy /ˈtɪpəˌfaɪ; ˈtɪpɪ̈faɪ/ *v* [T not in progressive 不用进行时] **1** to be a typical example of something 是…的典型: *the arro-*

gance that typifies this government's approach 这届政府在处事上典型的傲慢态度 **2** to be a typical part or feature of something 是…的一部分; 是…的一向特征: *the long complicated sentences that typify legal documents* 法律文件一向具有的长而复杂的句子

typ·ing /ˈtaɪpɪŋ; ˈtaɪpɪŋ/ *n* [U] the activity of using a TYPEWRITER to write something 打字(工作): *I've got a lot of typing to do today.* 今天我有大量的打字工作要做。

typing pool /ˈ·· ·/ *n* [C] a group of typists in a large office who type letters for other people〔大办公室里的〕打字组

typ·ist /ˈtaɪpɪst; ˈtaɪpɪ̵st/ *n* [C] **1** a secretary whose main job is to TYPE letters 打字员 **2** someone who uses a TYPEWRITER 打字者: *I'm a slow typist.* 我打字很慢。

ty·po /ˈtaɪpo; ˈtaɪpəʊ/ *n* [C] *informal* a small mistake in the way something has been typed (TYPE² (2)) or printed【非正式】打字错误; 排印错误

ty·pog·ra·pher /taɪˋpɑgrəfɚ; taɪˈpɒgrəfə/ *n* [C] **1** someone who designs TYPEFACES 设计印刷字体的人 **2** a COMPOSITOR 排字工

ty·po·graph·ic /ˌtaɪpəˋgræfɪk; ˌtaɪpəˈgræfɪk◂/ also 又作 **ty·pograph·i·cal** /-fɪkl̩; -fɪkəl/ *adj* connected with typography 排印的; 印刷文字设计的 **—typographically** /-kl̩ɪ; -kli/ *adv*

ty·pog·ra·phy /taɪˋpɑgrəfi; taɪˈpɒgrəfi/ *n* [U] **1** the work of preparing written material for printing 排印 **2** the arrangement, style and appearance of printed words 印刷文字设计

ty·ran·ni·cal /tɪˋrænɪkl̩; tɪ̵ˈrænɪkəl/ *adj* **1** behaving in a cruel and unfair way towards someone you have power over 暴虐的, 专横的: *a tyrannical father* 专横的父亲 **2** tyrannical rules or laws etc are based on a system in which a single ruler uses their power unfairly 专制的: *the tyrannical laws relating to debtors* 针对债务人的苛刻法律

tyr·an·nize also 又作 **-ise** *BrE*【英】/ˋtɪrəˌnaɪz; ˈtɪrənaɪz/ *v* [T] to use power over someone cruelly or unfairly 对…施以暴政; 专横地对待: *a family tyrannized by their grandfather* 一个受到祖父专横管制的家庭

ty·ran·no·sau·rus /tɪˌrænəˋsɔrəs; tɪ̵ˌrænəˈsɔːrəs◂/ also 又作 **tyrannosaurus rex** /ˌ·,···ˈ·/ *n* [C] a very large, flesh-eating DINOSAUR 霸王龙〔一种大型食肉恐龙〕

tyr·an·nous /ˋtɪrənəs; ˈtɪrənəs/ *adj old-fashioned* TYRANNICAL【过时】暴虐的, 专制的

tyr·an·ny /ˋtɪrənɪ; ˈtɪrəni/ *n* **1** [U] unfair and strict control over someone 暴虐, 专横: *He longed to escape from the tyranny of his aunt.* 他渴望摆脱姨妈的专横管制。**2** [C,U] government by one person or a small group that has gained power unfairly and uses it cruelly 暴政, 苛政, 专制统治 **3 the tyranny of fashion/the clock etc** the way that fashion etc limits people's freedom to do things the way they want to do 潮流/时间等的残酷无情〔比喻潮流等限制人们的自由〕**4** [C often plural 常用复数] a cruel or unfair action that limits someone's freedom 暴行: *the tyrannies of Louis XVI's court* 路易十六宫廷的暴行

ty·rant /ˋtaɪrənt; ˈtaɪərənt/ *n* [C] **1** a ruler who has complete power and uses it in a cruel and unfair way 暴君, 专制君主: *Caligula and Nero, the two great tyrants* 卡利古拉和尼禄这两个大暴君 **2** someone who has power over other people, and uses it cruelly or unfairly 暴君似的人, 专横的人

tyre *BrE*【英】, **tire** *AmE*【美】/taɪr; taɪə/ *n* [C] **1** a thick, round band of rubber that fits around the wheel of a car, bicycle etc 轮胎: **a flat tyre** (=one that has lost all its air) 瘪轮胎 —see also 另见 SPARE TYRE —see picture on page A2 参见 A2 页图 **2** a round band of metal that fits around the outside of a wooden wheel〔木轮上的〕轮箍 3

Ty·rol, the /tɪˋrol; tɪˈrəʊl/ also 又作 **the Tirol** an area in Austria in the Alps that is popular with tourists who go there to SKI and climb mountains 蒂罗尔〔奥地利一地区, 位于阿尔卑斯山区, 是游人滑雪和登山的好去处〕**—Tyrolean** /ˌtɪroˋliən; ˌtɪrəˈliːən/ *n, adj*

Ty·son /ˋtaɪsn̩; ˈtaɪsən/, **Mike** (1966-) a US BOXER who was the youngest person to win the world HEAVYWEIGHT title in 1986. He was sent to prison for five years for RAPE and served three (1992-95). After this he won the heavyweight title again, but lost it to Evander Holyfield in 1996. In 1997, he was in the news for biting Holyfield's ear during a fight. 泰森〔(1966-), 美国拳击手, 1986 年获世界重量级冠军, 成为获此殊荣的最年轻拳手。他曾因强奸罪被判处五年监禁, 服刑三年(1992-1995)。出狱后, 他再次夺得重量级冠军, 1996年输给伊万德·霍利菲尔德。1997 年, 他因在比赛中咬伤霍利菲尔德的耳朵而成为新闻人物〕

tzar /tsɑr; zɑː/ *n* [C] another spelling of TSAR tsar 的另一种拼法 **—tzarist** *adj*

tza·ri·na /tsɑˋrinə; zɑːˈriːnə/ *n* [C] another spelling of TSARINA tsarina 的另一种拼法

tzar·is·m /ˋtsɑrɪzəm; ˈzɑːrɪzəm/ *n* [U] another spelling of TSARISM tsarism 的另一种拼法

tze·tze fly /ˋtsɛtsɪ ˌflaɪ; ˈtetsi flaɪ/ *n* [C] another spelling of TSETSE FLY tsetse fly 的另一种拼法

U,u

U, u /ju; juː/ *plural* **U's, u's** *n* [C] the 21st letter of the English alphabet 英语字母表的第二十一个字母

U /ju; juː/ *n* **1** [C] a letter used in Britain to officially show that a film is suitable for people of any age U级电影〔英国的一种电影标签，指适合各种年龄的观众观看〕 **2** [C] a mark used in schools and examinations to show that your work or behaviour is extremely bad〔表示在学校的表现或考试成绩〕"很差"的符号 **3** [C] *BrE* a GRADE[1] (5) given in an examination to show that the work is too bad to be marked at all【英】极差〔考试的评分〕 **4** [singular] *AmE old-fashioned*【美，过时】an abbreviation for 缩写= UNIVERSITY: *Indiana U* 印第安纳大学

UAE /ˌju e ˋi; ˌjuː eɪ ˈiː/ the written abbreviation of 缩写= the UNITED ARAB EMIRATES

UB40 /ˌju bi ˋfɔrtɪ; ˌjuː biː ˈfɔːti/ in the UK, an official card which shows that the person named on the card is receiving unemployment benefit (=money paid by the government to someone who does not have a job) UB40卡〔英国官方给失业者签发的失业救济卡〕

u·biq·ui·tous /juˋbɪkwətəs; juːˈbɪkwɪ̌təs/ *adj formal or humorous* seeming to be everywhere【正式或幽默】普遍存在的，无处不在的: *We were tormented in the outback by the ubiquitous Australian fly.* 在内陆腹地，我们被无处不在的澳大利亚苍蝇所折磨。 —**ubiquitously** *adv* —**ubiquity** *n* [U]

U-boat /ˋju ˌbot; ˈjuː bəʊt/ *n* [C] a German SUBMARINE, especially one that was used in the Second World War〔尤指第二次世界大战期间所用的〕德国潜艇，U型潜艇

UCAS /ˋjukæs; ˈjuːkæs/ the Universities and Colleges Admission Service; the official British organization which deals with APPLICATIONS (=official written requests) from students who want to study for a degree at a British university or college 高校招生服务局〔英国一官方组织，受理学生在英国高校攻读学位的正式书面申请〕

UC Berkeley /ˌju si ˋbɜːklɪ; ˌjuː siː ˈbɜːkli/ the University of California at Berkeley; one of the nine universities that are part of the University of California 加州大学伯克利分校〔加利福尼亚大学九所分校之一〕

UCLA /ˌju si ɛl ˋe; ˌjuː siː el ˈeɪ/ the University of California at Los Angeles; one of the nine universities that are part of the University of California 加州大学洛杉矶分校〔加利福尼亚大学九所分校之一〕

UDA /ˌju di ˋe; ˌjuː diː ˈeɪ/ Ulster Defence Association; an illegal Protestant PARAMILITARY organization in Northern Ireland, which has used violence against Catholic paramilitary groups such as the IRA and against ordinary Catholics 北爱尔兰防务协会〔北爱尔兰一非法新教徒准军事组织，以暴力手段对抗爱尔兰共和军等天主教准军事组织，并袭击普通天主教徒〕

ud·der /ˋʌdɚ; ˈʌdə/ *n* [C] the part of a female cow, goat etc that hangs down between its back legs and that produces milk〔母牛、母山羊等的〕乳房

UDR, the /ˌju di ˋar; ˌjuː diː ˈɑː/ Ulster Defence Regiment; a PARAMILITARY force in Northern Ireland from 1969 to 1999. 北爱尔兰防卫军〔北爱尔兰一支准军事力量，存在于1969至1999年间〕

UFO /ˋjuˌfo; ˈjuːfəʊ/ *n* [C] Unidentified Flying Object; a strange object in the sky, sometimes thought to be a SPACESHIP from another world 不明飞行物，幽浮〔空中的神秘飞行物体，有时被认为是来自另一个星球的宇宙飞船〕

UFW /ˌju ɛf ˋdʌbl̩ju; ˌjuː ef ˈdʌbəljuː/ the abbreviation of 缩写= UNITED FARM WORKERS

U·gan·da /juˋgændə; juːˈgændə/ a country in east central Africa, between the Democratic Republic of Congo and Kenya. Population: 23,986,000 (2001). Capital: Kampala. 乌干达〔中非东部一国家，位于刚果民主共和国与肯尼亚之间。人口：23,986,000 (2001)，首都：坎帕拉〕 —**Ugandan** *n, adj*

ugh /ux; ʊx/ *interjection* used to show strong dislike 哎，呀〔表示强烈厌恶〕: *Ugh! This medicine tastes awful!* 哎！这药味道真恶心！

ug·ly /ˋʌglɪ; ˈʌgli/ *adj* **1** extremely unattractive and unpleasant to look at 丑陋的；难看的: *He's just so ugly!* 他竟是这么丑！| *heavy, ugly furniture* 笨重丑陋的家具 | **ugly as sin** (=very ugly) 非常丑陋 **2** making you feel frightened, nervous, or threatened 可怕的，恐怖的: *There were ugly scenes as rival gangs started attacking each other.* 敌对团伙互相打起来，场面很可怕。 **3 rear its ugly head** to appear and start to cause problems〔不好的东西〕抬头，冒头: *Scandal has reared its ugly head yet again.* 流言飞语又抬头了。 **4 ugly duckling** [C] someone who is less attractive, skilful etc than other people when they are young, but who becomes beautiful and successful later 丑小鸭〔指小时候难看笨拙、但日后变得好看或有出息的人〕 —**ugliness** *n* [U]

Ugly Sis·ters, the /ˌ‥ ˈ‥/ two characters in the FAIRY TALE about Cinderella. They are Cinderella's sisters, and are ugly and treat her very badly. 丑恶姐姐〔童话故事《灰姑娘》中的两个人物。她们是灰姑娘的姐姐，相貌丑陋，经常虐待灰姑娘〕

UHF /ˌju etʃ ˋɛf; ˌjuː eɪtʃ ˈef/ *n* [U] ultra-high frequency; a range of radio waves (WAVE[1] (3)) that produces a very good quality of sound 超高频

uh huh /ʌ ˋhʌ; ʌ ˈhʌ/ *interjection informal* used to show that you understand or agree with what someone is saying to you【非正式】嗯〔表示理解或赞同〕: *"He's what, six years old?" "Uh huh."* "他什么，六岁了？" "嗯。"

UHT milk /ˌju etʃ ti ˋmɪlk; ˌjuː eɪtʃ tiː ˈmɪlk/ *n* [U] *BrE* milk that has been heated to a very high temperature to preserve it【英】超高温消毒牛奶

uh-uh /ˋʌ ʌ; ˈʌ ʌ/ *interjection informal* used to say no【非正式】啊，哦〔表示否定〕

UK /ˌju ˋke; ˌjuː ˈkeɪ◂/ *n* the abbreviation of 缩写= the United Kingdom 联合王国

u·ke·le·le /ˌjukəˋlelɪ; ˌjuːkəˈleɪli/ *n* [C] a musical instrument with four strings, like a small GUITAR 尤克莱利琴〔一种类似吉他的四弦琴〕

U·kraine /juˋkren; juːˈkreɪn/ a country in eastern Europe, between Poland and Russia. Population: 48,760,000 (2001). Capital: Kiev. It was formerly part of the Soviet Union. 乌克兰〔东欧一国家，位于波兰与俄罗斯之间，曾为前苏联的一部分。人口：48,760,000 (2001)，首都：基辅〕

UL /ˌju ˋɛl; ˌjuː ˈel/ Underwriters' Laboratories; a US organization which tests the safety of electrical equipment and makes rules for the companies that produce it. Electrical equipment that is approved by the UL has a special SEAL (=mark) on it 保险商实验室〔美国一机构，负责测试电器产品的安全性能，制订电器制造企业的规范。凡经其认证的电器产品均印有一个特殊标识〕

U·laan·baa·tar /ˌulan ˋbatar; ˌuːlɑːn ˈbɑːtɑː/ the capital city of Mongolia, formerly called Ulan Bator 乌兰巴托〔蒙古国首都，英文旧称 Ulan Bator〕

-ular /julɚ; jʊ̌lə/ *suffix* [in adjectives 构成形容词] of or concerning something …的；关于…的: *glandular fever* 腺热，传染性单核细胞增多症 | *tubular steel* 管形钢

ul·cer /ˋʌlsɚ; ˈʌlsə/ *n* [C] a sore area on your skin or inside your body that may BLEED or produce poisonous substances 溃疡: *stomach ulcers* 胃溃疡 —**ulcerous** *adj*

ul·cer·ate /ˋʌlsəˌret; ˈʌlsəreɪt/ *v* [I,T] to form an ulcer, or become covered with ulcers (使) 形成溃疡; (使) 溃烂 —**ulcerated** *adj* —**ulceration** /ˌʌlsəˋreʃən; ˌʌlsəˈreɪʃən/ *n* [U]

-ule /jul; juːl/ *suffix* [in nouns 构成名词] *technical* a small type of something【术语】小型物: *a granule* (=small grain) 小粒，细粒

Ulls·wa·ter /ˋʌlzwɔtɚ; ˈʌlzwɔːtə/ one of the lakes in the Lake District, northwest England 阿尔斯沃特湖〔英格兰西北部湖区的湖泊之一〕

ul·na /ˋʌlnə; ˈʌlnə/ *n* [C] *technical* the inner bone of your lower arm, on the side opposite to your thumb【术语】尺骨 —see picture at 参见 SKELETON 图

Ul·ster /ˋʌlstɚ; ˈʌlstə/ another name for Northern Ireland. The name Ulster is often used in news reports, and it is also the name preferred by the mainly Protestant political parties and groups who want Northern Ireland to remain part of the UK. 阿尔斯特〔北爱尔兰别称，常用于新闻报道。此名也倍受以新教徒为主要成员的政党和团体的青睐，他们主张北爱尔兰应继续留在英国〕

Ulster De·fence As·so·ci·a·tion /ˌ‥ ‥ˈ‥ ‥ˌ‥/ the full name of the UDA 北爱尔兰防务协会〔UDA的全称〕

Ulster Defence Re·gi·ment, the /ˌ‥ ‥ ˌ‥/ the full name of the UDR 北爱尔兰防卫军〔UDR的全称〕

U

Ul·ster Dem·o·crat·ic U·nion·ist Par·ty, the /ˌ···ˌ····ˈ···ˌ··/ a Protestant political party in Northern Ireland. Its members are LOYALISTs who believe very strongly that Northern Ireland should remain part of the UK, and are opposed to Roman Catholic parties having any political power. 北爱尔兰民主统一党〔北爱尔兰一新教政党, 其成员为效忠派, 坚决主张北爱尔兰应继续留在英国, 同时反对罗马天主教各政党拥有任何政治权力〕

Ulster U·nion·ists, the /ˌ··ˈ···/ the members of the Ulster Unionist Party, the political party in Northern Ireland that is supported mostly by Protestants. They believe that Northern Ireland should remain part of the UK. 北爱尔兰统一党人〔指北爱尔兰统一党党员。该党是北爱尔兰政党, 支持者多为新教徒。他们主张北爱尔兰应继续留在英国〕

Ulster Vol·un·teer Force /ˌ···ˈ·ˌ·/ the full name of the UVF 北爱尔兰志愿军〔UVF的全称〕

ul·te·ri·or /ʌlˋtɪrɪɚ; ʌlˈtɪəriə/ *adj* **ulterior motives/purpose etc** reasons for doing something that you deliberately hide in order to get an advantage for yourself 别有用心的动机/目的等: *In some countries, Peace Corps volunteers were suspected of having ulterior motives, such as spying for the CIA.* 在一些国家, 和平队志愿者被怀疑别有用心, 例如为中情局当间谍。

3 **ul·ti·mate**[1] /ˋʌltəmɪt; ˈʌltɪmɪt/ *adj* [only before noun 仅用于名词前] **1** better, bigger, worse etc than all other objects of the same kind〔同类中〕最出色的; 最糟糕的: *the ultimate sports car* 最棒的跑车 **2** an ultimate aim, purpose etc is the final and most important one〔目标等〕最终的; 首要的: *Complete disarmament was the ultimate goal of the conference.* 全面裁军是这次会议的最终目标。**3** an ultimate decision, responsibility etc is one that you cannot pass on to someone else〔决定、责任等〕最大的, 最高的: *Ultimate responsibility lies with the President.* 总统肩负着最大的责任。

ultimate[2] *n* **the ultimate in stupidity/luxury/technology etc** something that shows the highest possible level of stupidity etc 极端的愚蠢/极度的奢侈/尖端的技术等: *This video-sound system is the ultimate in home entertainment technology.* 这种音像系统是家庭娱乐技术的尖端。

3 **ul·ti·mate·ly** /ˋʌltəmɪtlɪ; ˈʌltɪmɪtli/ *adv* [sentence adverb 句子副词] after everything or everyone else has been done or considered 最后; 最终: *Ultimately the decision rests with the child's parents.* 最终要由孩子的父母作出决定。

ul·ti·ma·tum /ˌʌltəˋmetəm; ˌʌltɪˈmeɪtəm/ *n* [C] a threat saying that if someone does not do what you want by a particular time, you will do something to punish them 最后通牒, 哀的美敦书: **give sb an ultimatum** *Well, give him an ultimatum: either he pays by Friday or he finds somewhere else to live.* 好吧, 给他下个最后通牒: 要么在星期五之前付款, 要么另找住处。

ultra- /ʌltrə; ʌltrə/ *prefix* **1** *technical* above in a range; beyond【术语】外; 超: *ultrasound* (=too high to hear) 超声 —compare 比较 INFRA- **2** extremely 极(度): *an ultramodern building* 极现代的建筑 | *an ultracautious approach* 极其谨慎的办法

ul·tra-high fre·quen·cy /ˌ···ˈ···/ *n* [U] = UHF 超高频

ul·tra·ma·rine /ˌʌltrəməˋrin; ˌʌltrəməˈriːn◂/ *n* [C,U] a very bright blue colour 佛青色, 深蓝色 —**ultramarine** *adj*

ul·tra·son·ic /ˌʌltrəˋsɑnɪk; ˌʌltrəˈsɒnɪk◂/ *adj* ultrasonic sound waves are too high for humans to hear〔声波〕超声的

ultra·sound /ˋʌltrəˌsaund; ˈʌltrəsaʊnd/ *n* **1** [U] sound that is too high for humans to hear, and is often used in medical processes 超声(波) **2** [C] a medical process using this type of sound that produces an image of something inside your body, especially a baby〔医学中的〕超声波检查

ul·tra·vi·o·let /ˌʌltrəˋvaɪəlɪt; ˌʌltrəˈvaɪəlɪt◂/ *adj* **1** ultraviolet light is beyond the purple end of the range of colours that people can see 紫外(线)的 **2** [only before noun 仅用于名词前] an ultraviolet lamp, treatment etc uses this light to treat skin diseases or make your skin darker 利用紫外线的

u·lu·la·tion /ˌjuljəˋleʃən; juːljʊˈleɪʃən/ *n* [C] *literary* a long low sound made with your voice【文】呼喊(声); 嚎叫(声) —**ululate** /ˋjuljəˌlet; ˈjuːljʊleɪt/ *v* [I]

U·lu·ru /ˋuluru; ˈuːlʊruː/ a very large red rock in the Northern Territory, Australia, which is the world's largest MONOLITH (=block of stone). It was formerly known as Ayers Rock, but the original Australian Aboriginal name for it, Uluru, is now preferred. 乌卢鲁巨岩〔一巨型红岩。位于澳大利亚北方领地, 是世界上最大的独块巨石。旧称埃尔斯巨岩, 澳大利亚土著语称为乌卢鲁, 现多沿用此名〕

U·lys·ses /juˋlɪsiz; juːˈlɪsiːz/ the name for Odysseus in ancient Roman stories 尤利西斯〔古罗马神话中奥德修斯的名字〕

um /ʌm; ʌm/ *interjection* used when you cannot immediately decide what to say next 嗯〔说话时表示犹豫〕: *Um, yeah, I guess so.* 嗯, 是的, 我猜是这样。

um·ber /ˋʌmbɚ; ˈʌmbə/ *n* [C,U] a brown colour like earth 棕土色; 赭色 —**umber** *adj*

um·bil·i·cal cord /ʌmˋbɪlɪkl ˌkɔrd; ʌmˈbɪlɪkəl ˌkɔːd/ *n* [C] a long narrow tube of flesh that joins an unborn baby to its mother 脐带

um·bil·i·cus /ʌmˋbɪlɪkəs; ʌmˈbɪlɪkəs/ *n* [C] *technical* the small hollow place on your stomach; NAVEL【术语】脐, 肚脐

um·brage /ˋʌmbrɪdʒ; ˈʌmbrɪdʒ/ *n* **take umbrage (at)** to be offended by something that someone has done or said (为…)生气; (因…)见怪: *James took umbrage at Mrs Dubose's remarks.* 詹姆斯为杜博斯太太说的话而生气。

um·brel·la /ʌmˋbrɛlə; ʌmˈbrelə/ *n* [C] **1** a circular folding frame covered in cloth that you hold above you when it is raining 雨伞 —compare 比较 SUNSHADE, PARASOL **2 umbrella organization** an organization that includes many smaller groups〔有众多附属团体的〕伞状组织[机构] **3 umbrella term/word** a word whose meaning includes many different types of a particular object〔包括多种含义的〕综合术语/词 **4** the protection given by a powerful country, army, a weapons system etc 保护(伞): *the political umbrella of the United Nations* 联合国的政治庇护

umbrella 雨伞

UMIST /ˋjumɪst; ˈjuːmɪst/ the University of Manchester Institute of Science and Technology; a part of the University of Manchester which teaches science, engineering, electronics, and similar subjects 曼彻斯特大学理工学院〔曼彻斯特大学一分院, 开设理学、工程、电子等相近专业〕

um·laut /ˋumlaut; ˈʊmlaʊt/ *n* [C] a sign (¨) written over a German vowel to show how it is pronounced〔标在德语元音上方的〕变音符号(¨), 曲音符号

ump /ʌmp; ʌmp/ *n* [C] *AmE spoken* an umpire【美口】裁判员

um·pire[1] /ˋʌmpaɪr; ˈʌmpaɪə/ *n* [C] the person in some sports who makes sure that the players obey the rules 裁判员 —see picture at 参见 TENNIS 图

umpire[2] *v* [I,T] to be the umpire for a game or competition (给…)当裁判

ump·teen /ˋʌmpˋtin; ˌʌmpˈtiːn◂/ *determiner informal* a large number of【非正式】无数的; 许许多多的: *There seemed to be umpteen rules and regulations to learn.* 似乎有无数的规章制度要学习。—**umpteenth** *number*

'un /ən; ən/ *pron BrE spoken*【英口】**good 'un/bad 'un etc** a short form of 缩略式= one, used to say that someone or something is bad, good etc 一个好/坏人[东西]: *He's a bad 'un.* 他是个坏家伙。| *Those apples are little 'uns.* 那都是些小苹果。

UN /ˌju ˋɛn; juː ˈen/ *n* [singular] the United Nations; an international organization that tries to find peaceful solutions to world problems 联合国

un- /ʌn; ʌn/ *prefix* [especially in adjectives and adverbs 尤构成形容词和副词] **1** shows a negative, a lack, or an opposite; not 不〔表示"否定"、"缺乏"、"相反"之意〕: *unfair* 不公平的 | *unhappy* 不高兴的 | *unfortunately* 不幸地 **2** [especially in verbs 尤构成动词] shows an opposite〔表示做相反的动作〕: *to undress* (=take your clothes off) 脱去衣服

un·a·bashed /ˌʌnəˋbæʃt; ˌʌnəˈbæʃt◂/ *adj* not ashamed or embarrassed, especially when doing something unusual or rude 不害臊的, 不怕羞的; 满不在乎的: *She stared at him with unabashed curiosity.* 她好奇地盯着他看, 一点也不害臊。

un·a·bat·ed /ˌʌnəˋbetɪd; ˌʌnəˈbeɪtɪd◂/ *adj, adv* continuing without becoming any weaker or less violent 不减弱的[地]; 不衰退的[地]: *The storm continued unabated throughout the night.* 暴风雨持续了一夜, 丝毫没有减弱。| *his unabated ambition* 他那锐气不减的抱负

un·a·ble /ʌnˋebl; ʌnˈeɪbəl/ *adj* not able to do something 不能…的; 不会…的: **be unable to do sth** *Many passengers were unable to reach the lifeboats.* 许多乘客无法到达救生艇。 3 2

U·na·bomb·er /ˋjunəˌbɑmɚ; ˈjuːnəˌbɒmə/ the name given in newspapers to a man who, over a period of 18 years, sent 16 bombs through the mail to US universities and other

organizations, in order to protest against technology. In 1996 the FBI arrested Theodore Kaczynski, a former university professor, for these crimes. 大学炸弹客, 匿名投寄邮件炸弹者〔报界用语, 特指美国前大学教授西奥多·卡辛斯基。此人在18年共向美国高校等机构邮寄了16枚邮包炸弹, 目的是反对科技进步。1996年, 联邦调查局根据上述罪证将其逮捕〕

un·a·bridged /ˌʌnəˋbrɪdʒd; ˌʌnəˈbrɪdʒd◂/ *adj* a piece of writing, speech etc that is unabridged is in its full form without being made shorter〔文章、演讲等〕未删节的, 全文的: *the complete and unabridged works of Dickens* 未删节的狄更斯全集

un·ac·cept·a·ble /ˌʌnəkˋsɛptəbl̩; ˌʌnəkˈseptəbəl◂/ *adj* **1** something that is unacceptable is so wrong or bad that you think it should not be allowed 不能接受的: *unacceptable levels of unemployment* 不能接受的失业水平 **2 the unacceptable face of** the bad or unfair part of a system, activity etc …难以接受的一面: *property speculation, the unacceptable face of capitalism* 房地产投机, 资本主义不可接受的一面 —**unacceptably** *adv*

un·ac·com·pa·nied /ˌʌnəˋkʌmpənɪd; ˌʌnəˈkʌmpənid◂/ *adj* **1** someone who is unaccompanied has no one with them 无人陪伴的; 无随从的: *Unaccompanied children are not allowed on the premises.* 儿童无人陪伴不得入内。**2** an unaccompanied singer or musician sings or plays alone 无伴奏的: *a piece for unaccompanied voices* 一段适于清唱的曲子 **3 unaccompanied bags/luggage etc** bags, cases etc that are sent on a plane, train etc without their owner 托运的包裹/行李等

un·ac·count·a·ble /ˌʌnəˋkaʊntəbl̩; ˌʌnəˈkaʊntəbəl◂/ *adj formal*【正式】**1** very surprising and difficult to explain 莫名其妙的; 无法解释的; 不可理解的: *Patrick's disappearance was quite unaccountable.* 帕特里克的失踪相当令人费解。**2** not having to explain your actions or decisions to anyone else〔对本身的行为或决定〕不用解释的: *It is not acceptable that the governors of this institution should be largely unaccountable.* 令人不能接受的是这一机构的主管人员多数情况下竟然可以独断专行。—**unaccountably** *adv*

un·ac·count·ed /ˌʌnəˋkaʊntɪd; ˌʌnəˈkaʊntɪd◂/ *adj* something or someone that is unaccounted for cannot be found or their absence cannot be explained 失踪的; 不明去向的: *Two people are still unaccounted for after the floods.* 有两人在洪水过后仍下落不明。

un·ac·cus·tomed /ˌʌnəˋkʌstəmd; ˌʌnəˈkʌstəmd◂/ *adj formal*【正式】**1 unaccustomed to** not used to something 对…不习惯的: *a country boy, unaccustomed to city ways* 不习惯城市生活方式的乡下男孩 **2** [only before noun 仅用于名词前] not usual, typical, or familiar 不寻常的; 非惯例的; 不熟悉的: *unaccustomed physical exertion* 超常的体力付出 **3 unaccustomed as I am (to)** *spoken formal* used before saying something in front of a lot of people【口, 正式】尽管我不习惯于〔用于当众讲话时〕

un·ac·knowl·edged /ˌʌnəkˋnɑlɪdʒd; ˌʌnəkˈnɒlɪdʒd◂/ *adj* **1** not generally or publicly known for something that should be rewarded, thanked, or praised 未被公认的; 未被承认的; 未答谢的; 未受赞扬的: *Women's work in the home tends to be both unpaid and unacknowledged.* 妇女料理家务往往既得不到报酬, 也不被赞扬。**2 the unacknowledged leader/authority etc** a leader etc who is not officially or publicly recognised 自封的[未经正式认可的]领导/权威等: *Grandma was the unacknowledged boss of the family.* 祖母当时是非正式的一家之主。**3** ignored or not noticed 未受到注意[重视]的: *The tap on the door went unacknowledged for some time.* 轻轻的敲门声过了好一阵子才有人回应。

un·a·dopt·ed /ˌʌnəˋdɑptɪd; ˌʌnəˈdɒptɨd◂/ *adj BrE* an unadopted road must be repaired by the people who live along it and not by a town council【英】〔道路〕不由地方当局承担保养的

un·a·dul·te·rat·ed /ˌʌnəˋdʌltəˌretɪd; ˌʌnəˈdʌltəreɪtɨd◂/ *adj* **1** not mixed with other less pure substances 不掺杂的, 纯的 **2** [only before noun 仅用于名词前] complete or total 完全的; 十足的: *What unadulterated nonsense!* 真是一派胡言!

un·af·fect·ed /ˌʌnəˋfɛktɪd; ˌʌnəˈfektɨd◂/ *adj* **1** not changed or influenced by something 未改变的; 未受影响的: [+by] *The northwest was unaffected by the drought.* 西北部没有受到干旱影响。**2** *approving* natural in the way you behave【褒】〔举止〕不装腔作势的, 自然的: *her easy, unaffected manner* 她那从容、自然的举止 —**unaffectedly** *adv*

un·aid·ed /ʌnˋedɪd; ʌnˈeɪdɨd/ *adj, adv* without help 无助的[地]; 独立的[地]: *It was the first time she had walked unaided since her illness.* 这是她生病以来第一次独立行走。

un·al·loyed /ˌʌnəˋlɔɪd; ˌʌnəˈlɔɪd◂/ *adj literary* not mixed with anything else【文】不掺杂的; 纯的: *unalloyed happiness* 纯真的幸福

un·al·ter·a·ble /ʌnˋɔltərəbl̩; ʌnˈɔːltərəbəl/ *adj formal* not possible to change【正式】不可变更[改变]的: *an unalterable fact* 不可改变的事实 —**unalterably** *adv*

un·am·big·u·ous /ˌʌnæmˋbɪgjuəs; ˌʌnæmˈbɪgjuəs◂/ *adj* a statement, instruction etc that is unambiguous is clear and easy to understand because it can only mean one thing 清楚的, 明确的, 不含糊的: *a brief, unambiguous description of the problem* 对该问题简洁明确的表述 —**unambiguously** *adv*

un-A·mer·i·can /ˌ· ·ˋ···◂/ *adj* not loyal to generally accepted American customs and ways of thinking〔习俗、思维方式等〕不合美国的; 非美国的: **un-American activities** (=political activity believed to be harmful to the US) 非美活动〔被认为不利于美国的政治活动〕

u·na·nim·i·ty /ˌjunəˋnɪmɪtɪ; juːnəˈnɪmɨti/ *n* [U] *formal* a state or situation of complete agreement among a group of people【正式】一致同意

u·nan·i·mous /juˋnænəməs; juːˈnænɨməs/ *adj* **1** a unanimous decision, statement etc is one that everyone agrees with〔决定、声明等〕一致通过的, 无异议的 **2** agreeing completely about something 一致同意的: **unanimous that** *The jury was unanimous that the defendant was guilty.* 陪审团一致同意被告有罪。—**unanimously** *adv*

un·an·nounced /ˌʌnəˋnaʊnst; ˌʌnəˈnaʊnst◂/ *adj, adv* happening without anyone expecting or knowing about it 出人意料的[地]; 未经通报的[地]: *We arrived unannounced.* 我们未经通报就到了。

un·an·swer·a·ble /ʌnˋænsərəbl̩; ʌnˈɑːnsərəbəl/ *adj* **1** definitely true and therefore impossible to argue against 无可辩驳的: *an unanswerable case in law* 无法申辩的法律案件 **2** an unanswerable question is one that seems to have no possible answer or solution〔问题〕无法回答的, 没有答案的

un·ap·peal·ing /ˌʌnəˋpilɪŋ; ˌʌnəˈpiːlɪŋ◂/ *adj* not pleasant or attractive 无吸引力的: *an unappealing bowl of watery soup* 一碗淡而无味的稀汤

un·ap·proach·a·ble /ˌʌnəˋprotʃəbl̩; ˌʌnəˈprəʊtʃəbəl◂/ *adj* seeming unfriendly and therefore difficult to talk to 不可亲的, 冷淡的, 难以接近的: *Jo appeared, looking grim and unapproachable.* 乔出现了, 表情阴冷, 难以接近。

un·ar·gu·a·ble /ʌnˋɑrgjuəbl̩; ʌnˈɑːgjuəbəl/ *adj* something that is unarguable is definitely true or correct 不容置疑的; 无可争辩的 —**unarguably** *adv*

un·armed /ʌnˋɑrmd; ʌnˈɑːmd◂/ *adj* not carrying any weapons 未带武器的, 徒手的: **unarmed combat** (=fighting without weapons) 徒手格斗

un·a·shamed /ʌnəˋʃemd; ˌʌnəˈʃeɪmd◂/ *adj* not feeling embarrassed or ashamed about something that people might disapprove of 不害羞的; 恬不知耻的: *the unashamed luxury of our marble bath* 我们家里大理石浴缸的恣意奢华 —**unashamedly** *adv*

un·asked /ʌnˋæskt; ʌnˈɑːskt/ *adj, adv* **1** if a question is unasked, no one asks it, often because they are embarrassed〔常因不便过问而〕未被问及的[地] **2** if you do something unasked, you do it without anyone asking or inviting you to 未被要求的[地]; 未受邀请的[地]: *Jerry entered unasked, and stood by the fire.* 杰里主动走进来, 站在炉火旁边。| **unasked for** *hundreds of pounds in unasked for donations* 自发捐赠的数百英镑

un·as·sail·able /ˌʌnəˋseləbl̩; ˌʌnəˈseɪləbəl◂/ *adj formal* not able to be criticized, attacked, or made weaker【正式】不容置疑的; 攻不破的: *an unassailable argument* 无懈可击的论据

un·as·sum·ing /ˌʌnəˋsumɪŋ; ˌʌnəˈsjuːmɪŋ◂/ *adj* showing no desire to be noticed or given special treatment; MODEST 谦逊的, 不摆架子的: *an unassuming middle-class family* 谦逊的中产阶级家庭

un·at·tached /ˌʌnəˋtætʃt; ˌʌnəˈtætʃt◂/ *adj* **1** not involved in a romantic relationship; SINGLE[1] (3) 未恋爱的; 单身的: *Sure, he's handsome, but is he unattached?* 没错, 他挺帅, 可他是否单身呢? **2** not connected or fastened to anything 无关系的; 非附属的; 独立的

un·at·tain·a·ble /ˌʌnəˋtenəbl̩; ˌʌnəˈteɪnəbəl◂/ *adj* impossible to achieve 达不到的: *an unattainable goal* 达不到的目标

un·at·tend·ed /ˌʌnəˋtɛndɪd; ˌʌnəˈtendɨd◂/ *adj* left alone without anyone in charge 无人照看[负责]的: *unattended luggage* 无人照看的行李 | **leave sb/sth unattended** *Children should not be left unattended in the playground.* 孩子们在游乐场不应该没人照管。

un·at·trac·tive /ˌʌnəˋtræktɪv; ˌʌnəˈtræktɪv◂/ *adj* **1** not attractive, pretty, or pleasant to look at 无吸引[诱惑]力的; 不漂亮的: *an unattractive man* 没有魅力的男子 **2** not good or desirable 不好的; 讨厌的: *the unattractive aspects of nationalism* 民族主义令人生厌的方面 —**unattractively** *adv*

U

un·au·tho·rized /ʌnˋɔθə͵raɪzd; ʌnˈɔːθəraɪzd/ also 又作 **-ised** *BrE*【英】*adj* without official approval or permission 未经授权[批准]的: *laws to prevent unauthorized photocopying* 防止擅自影印的法规

un·a·vail·a·ble /͵ʌnəˋveləbḷ; ͵ʌnəˈveɪləbəl/ *adj* [not before noun 不用于名词前] **1** not able to be obtained 得不到的: *Funding for the new school is unavailable.* 新学校的资金无法到位。**2** not able or willing to meet someone 没空的: *I'm sorry, the principal is unavailable just now.* 对不起，校长这会儿没空。

un·a·vail·ing /͵ʌnəˋvelɪŋ; ͵ʌnəˈveɪlɪŋ/ *adj literary* not successful or effective【文】徒劳的; 无益的, 无用的: *unavailing efforts* 徒劳

un·a·void·a·ble /͵ʌnəˋvɔɪdəbḷ; ͵ʌnəˈvɔɪdəbəl/ *adj* impossible to prevent 不可避免的: *There are now fears that war is unavoidable.* 人们现在担心战争不可避免。—**unavoidably** *adv*: *Molly was unavoidably delayed.* 莫莉不得已被耽搁了。

un·a·ware /͵ʌnəˋwɛr; ͵ʌnəˈweə/ *adj* not noticing or realizing what is happening 未觉察到的; 未意识到的: [**+of**] *Mike seems unaware of the trouble he's causing.* 迈克看来还未意识到他所惹的麻烦。| **unaware that** *She remained unaware that she was being watched.* 她一直未察觉到自己在被监视。—**unawareness** *n* [U]

un·a·wares /͵ʌnəˋwɛrz; ͵ʌnəˈweəz/ *adv* **1 take/catch sb unawares** to happen or to do something in a way that someone was not expecting and so was not prepared for 让某人措手不及: *Caught unawares like that, I was unable to think of an excuse.* 冷不防被人这样抓住，我什么借口也想不出来了。**2** *formal* without noticing【正式】不知不觉地; 无意中: *We had walked unawares over the border.* 我们无意中越过了边界。

un·bal·anced /ʌnˋbælənst; ͵ʌnˈbælənst/ *adj* **1** someone who is unbalanced seems slightly crazy〔人〕精神失常[错乱]的 **2** a report, argument etc that is unbalanced is unfair because it emphasizes one opinion too much〔报告、论点等〕有失公允的, 片面的 **3** a relationship that is unbalanced is not equal because one person has more influence, power etc〔关系〕不平衡的, 不平等的

un·bear·a·ble /ʌnˋbɛrəbḷ; ʌnˈbeərəbəl/ *adj* too unpleasant, painful, or annoying to bear; INTOLERABLE 忍受不了的; 承受不住的; 无法容忍的: *Their constant arguments were unbearable.* 他们持续不断的争论让人无法忍受。—**unbearably** *adj*: *an unbearably hot day* 热得让人无法忍受的一天

un·beat·a·ble /ʌnˋbitəbḷ; ʌnˈbiːtəbəl/ *adj* **1** something that is unbeatable is the best of its kind〔同类中〕无与伦比的: *unbeatable prices* 无与伦比的价格 **2** a team, player etc that is unbeatable cannot be defeated 打不垮的, 无法击败的

un·be·com·ing /͵ʌnbɪˋkʌmɪŋ; ͵ʌnbɪˈkʌmɪŋ◂/ *adj old-fashioned*【过时】**1** clothes that are unbecoming do not make you look attractive〔衣服等〕不相配的; 不合身的; 难看的: *a blouse in an unbecoming green colour* 颜色难看的绿色衬衫 **2** behaviour that is unbecoming is shocking or unsuitable〔行为〕不合礼节的, 不得体的: [**+to**] *conduct unbecoming to a teacher* 与教师身份不相称的行为

un·be·known /͵ʌnbɪˋnon; ͵ʌnbɪˈnəʊn/ also 又作 **unbeknownst** [sentence adverb 句子副词] **unbeknown to sb** without that person knowing about it 不为某人所知的: *Unbeknown to him, his wife had been trying to phone him all morning.* 他不知道的是，他妻子一上午都在想方设法打电话给他。

un·be·lief /͵ʌnbɪˋlif; ͵ʌnbḷˈliːf/ *n* [U] *formal* a lack of belief or a refusal to believe in a religious faith【正式】无信仰;〔对宗教的〕不信 —compare 比较 DISBELIEF

3 **un·be·lie·va·ble** /͵ʌnbɪˋlivəbḷ; ͵ʌnbḷˈliːvəbəl◂/ *adj* **1** extremely surprising 极其惊人的: *Dealers were paying unbelievable prices for her paintings.* 商人开出惊人的高价来收购她的画。**2** very difficult to believe and therefore probably untrue 不可信的, 难以相信的: *Yvonne's excuse for being late was totally unbelievable.* 伊冯娜迟到的理由根本不可信。—**unbelievably** *adv*: *an unbelievably bad movie* 糟糕透顶的电影

un·be·liev·er /͵ʌnbəˋlivɚ; ͵ʌnbḷˈliːvə◂/ *n* [C] someone who does not believe in a particular religion 不信教者

un·bend /ʌnˋbɛnd; ʌnˈbend/ *v* **1** [I,T] to become straight or make something straight（把…）弄直 **2** [I] to relax and start behaving in a less formal way 放松; 变得随意: *She'd be a lot more likeable if she'd unbend a little.* 她如果放松一点，会变得更可爱。

un·bend·ing /ʌnˋbɛndɪŋ; ʌnˈbendɪŋ/ *adj* unwilling to change your opinions, decisions etc 不妥协的; 固执的: *a stern, unbending man* 严厉而又固执的男子

un·bi·ased /ʌnˋbaɪəst; ʌnˈbaɪəst/ *adj* able to make a fair judgment, especially because you are not influenced by your own or other people's opinions 不偏不倚的; 无偏见的; 公正的: *With all the publicity surrounding the case, it's going to be hard to find an unbiased jury.* 这个案件已闹得沸沸扬扬，要找一个不偏不倚的陪审团将很困难。

un·bid·den /ʌnˋbɪdṇ; ͵ʌnˈbɪdn/ *adv literary* without being asked for, expected, or invited【文】未被要求的; 意想不到的; 未受邀请的

un·blem·ished /ʌnˋblɛmɪʃt; ͵ʌnˈblemɪʃt/ *adj* not spoiled by any mistake or bad behaviour 无瑕疵的; 清白的: *an unblemished reputation* 清白的名声

un·born /ʌnˋbɔrn; ͵ʌnˈbɔːn◂/ *adj* not yet born 未出生的: *an unborn child* 未出生的孩子

un·bos·om /ʌnˋbuzəm; ͵ʌnˈbʊzəm/ *v* [T] *literary* **unbosom yourself to** to tell someone about the things that are worrying you【文】向〔某人〕吐露心事, 向〔某人〕倾诉心曲

un·bound·ed /ʌnˋbaundɪd; ʌnˈbaʊndḷd/ *adj formal* extreme or without any limit【正式】无边际的, 无限的: *unbounded energy* 无限的能量

un·bri·dled /ʌnˋbraɪdḷd; ʌnˈbraɪdld/ *adj literary* not controlled and too extreme or violent【文】放纵的, 不受控制的; 激烈的: *unbridled passion* 奔放的热情

un·bro·ken /ʌnˋbrokən; ʌnˈbrəʊkən/ *adj* continuing without being broken or interrupted 未破损的, 完整的; 未中断的: *an unbroken silence* 未打破的沉寂 | *the unbroken prosperity of the last 25 years* 过去25年的持续繁荣

un·buck·le /ʌnˋbʌkḷ; ͵ʌnˈbʌkəl/ *v* [T] to unfasten the BUCKLE on something 解开…的搭扣: *He unbuckled his belt.* 他解开了皮带的搭扣。

un·bur·den /ʌnˋbɝdṇ; ͵ʌnˈbɜːdn/ *v* [T] **1 unburden yourself/your heart** to tell someone your problems, secrets etc so that you feel better 吐露心事; 倾诉衷肠: *Jane unburdened herself of a terrible secret.* 简讲出了一个可怕的秘密。| [**+to**] *He felt an urge to unburden his heart to this stranger.* 他迫切地想向这个陌生人倾诉衷肠。**2** *literary* to take a heavy load away from someone【文】卸去…的负担

un·called-for /ʌnˋkɔld ͵fɔr; ʌnˈkɔːld fɔː/ *adj informal* behaviour or remarks that are uncalled-for are unfair or unsuitable【非正式】〔行为、评论等〕不公正的, 不合适的: *That comment was totally uncalled-for.* 那番评论毫无道理。

un·can·ny /ʌnˋkænɪ; ʌnˈkæni/ *adj* very strange and difficult to explain 离奇的; 不可思议的: *an uncanny coincidence* 不可思议的巧合 —**uncannily** *adv*

un·cared for /ʌnˋkɛrd ͵fɔr; ʌnˈkeəd ͵fɔː/ *adj* not looked after or not looked after properly 没人照顾的; 未得到适当照顾的: *The dogs looked hungry and uncared for.* 这几只狗看起来又饿又没人管。

un·ceas·ing /ʌnˋsisɪŋ; ʌnˈsiːsɪŋ/ *adj* never stopping 不停的; 不断的: *an unceasing barrage of questions* 没完没了的连珠炮似的问题 —**unceasingly** *adv*

un·ce·re·mo·ni·ous /͵ʌnsɛrəˋmonɪəs; ͵ʌnserḷˈməʊniəs◂/ *adj* without paying any attention to politeness or good manners 无礼的; 随便的: *Philippa finished her meal with unceremonious haste.* 菲莉帕狼吞虎咽地吃完了饭。—**unceremoniously** *adv* —**unceremoniousness** *n* [U]

un·cer·tain /ʌnˋsɝtṇ; ʌnˈsɜːtn/ *adj* **1** [not before noun 不用于名词前] not sure or feeling doubt 不确定的; 不能断定的: *Lee moved awkwardly and looked uncertain.* 李动作笨拙，看起来很迟疑。| [**+how/what/where etc**] *She hesitated, uncertain what to do next.* 她犹豫不决，拿不定主意下一步做什么。**2** likely to change, often in a way that is bad 无常的, 易变的: *My whole future now seemed uncertain.* 我的整个未来现在看起来变化无常。**3** [not before noun 不用于名词前] not definite or decided 未确定的: *Our holiday plans are still uncertain.* 我们的度假计划仍未确定。**4 in no uncertain terms** if you tell someone something in no uncertain terms, you tell them very clearly without trying to be polite 直截了当地: *I told Colin in no uncertain terms what I thought of him.* 我直截了当地告诉科林我对他的看法。—**uncertainly** *adv* —**uncertainty** *n* [C,U]

un·chal·lenged /ʌnˋtʃælɪndʒd; ʌnˈtʃælḷndʒd/ *adj* **1** accepted and believed by everyone and not doubted 未引起争论的; 无异议的, 未引起质疑的: *Roy's authority was unchallenged.* 罗伊的权威未受到挑战。**2** someone who goes somewhere unchallenged is not stopped and asked who they are or what they are doing〔人〕未受到阻碍的, 未受到盘查的: *How did the prisoners manage to get to the outer fence unchallenged?* 那些犯人是如何未受阻碍地顺利到达外层围栏的?

un·chang·ing /ʌnˋtʃendʒɪŋ; ʌnˈtʃeɪndʒɪŋ/ *adj* always staying the same 不变的, 恒定的

un·char·ac·ter·is·tic /ʌn͵kærəktəˋrɪstɪk; ʌn͵kærḷktəˈrɪstɪk◂/ *adj* not typical of someone or something and therefore

surprising 不典型的; 无任何特性的: [+of] *It's uncharacteristic of her to be late.* 迟到不是她的特点。—**uncharacteristically** /-kḷi; -kli/ *adv*

un·char·i·ta·ble /ʌnˈtʃærətəbḷ; ʌnˈtʃærɨtəbəl/ *adj* unkind or unfair in the way you judge people 苛刻的, 不宽厚的; 不公正的; 挑剔的: *It's very uncharitable to say Phillip's problems are all his own fault.* 说菲利普的问题都是他自己的错, 这未免太苛刻了。

un·chart·ed /ʌnˈtʃartɪd; ʌnˈtʃɑːtɨd/ *adj literary* 【文】 **1** not marked on any maps 地图上没有标明的: *The ship arrived at a previously uncharted island.* 这艘船到达了一个以前地图上没有标明的海岛。**2 uncharted waters/territory** a situation or activity that you have never experienced or tried before 未知的水域/领域: *This new operation was uncharted territory for the surgeons.* 这种新手术对外科医生来说是个未知的领域。

un·checked /ʌnˈtʃɛkt; ˌʌnˈtʃekt◂/ *adj* **1** an unchecked activity, illness etc develops and gets worse because it is not controlled or stopped 〔活动、疾病等〕未受抑制的, 未受制止的: *We cannot allow such behaviour to continue unchecked.* 我们不能允许这样的行为继续下去而不加制止。**2** not tested for quality, safety etc 未经检查[检验]的: *The goods should not have left the factory unchecked.* 产品不该在未经检验的情况下出了厂。—see also 另见 CHECK

un·civ·i·lized also 又作 **-ised** *BrE* 【英】 /ʌnˈsɪvḷˌaɪzd; ʌnˈsɪvɨlaɪzd/ *adj* **1** uncivilized behaviour is rude or socially unacceptable 野蛮的; 不文明的: *uncivilized incidents of racial violence* 野蛮的种族暴力事件 **2 an uncivilized hour** *informal* extremely early in the morning 【非正式】一大清早

un·cle /ˈʌŋkl; ˈʌŋkəl/ *n* [C] **1** the brother of your mother or father, or the husband of your aunt 伯[叔, 舅]父; 姑[姨]丈 —see picture at 参见 FAMILY 图 **2** a man whose brother or sister has a child 伯[叔, 舅]父: *Enrique was very excited about becoming an uncle.* 恩里克就要当伯伯[叔叔, 舅舅]了, 非常兴奋。**3** used as a name for a man who is a close friend of your parents 叔叔; 伯伯〔用于称呼父母的男性好朋友〕 **4 say uncle** *AmE spoken* used by children to tell someone to admit they have been defeated 【美口】讨饶, 认输〔儿童用语, 用于要求某人认输、承认失败〕 —see also 另见 **talk like a dutch uncle** (DUTCH[2] (3))

un·clean /ʌnˈklin; ˌʌnˈkliːn◂/ *adj* **1** *biblical* morally or spiritually bad 【圣经】不纯洁的; 肮脏的; 邪恶的: *an unclean spirit* 邪恶的精灵 **2** unclean food, animals etc are those that must not be eaten, touched etc in a particular religion 〔宗教上认为〕〔食物〕不宜食用的; 〔动物〕不可接触的 —**uncleanness** *n* [U]

un·clear /ʌnˈklɪr; ˌʌnˈklɪə◂/ *adj* **1** difficult to understand or be sure about, so that there is doubt or confusion 难懂的; 不清楚的; 不肯定的: *The terms of the contract are very unclear.* 合同的条款非常含糊不清。**2 be unclear about** to not understand something clearly 对…含糊不清: *I'm rather unclear about what I'm supposed to be doing here.* 我不太明白自己在这儿该做些什么。

Uncle Re·mus /ˌʌŋkḷ ˈriməs; ˌʌŋkəl ˈriːməs/ a character in the children's stories about Brer Rabbit by the US writer, Joel Chandler Harris. In the books, Uncle Remus is the narrator (=the character who tells the stories). 雷穆斯大叔〔美国作家乔尔·钱德勒·哈里斯所著兔子大哥系列儿童故事中的人物。书中的雷穆斯大叔是故事的讲述者〕

Uncle Sam /ˌʌŋkḷ ˈsæm; ˌʌŋkəl ˈsæm/ *n* [singular] *informal* the US, or the US government, sometimes represented by the figure of a man with a white BEARD and tall hat 【非正式】山姆大叔〔美国或美国政府的绰号, 有时用一个戴着高帽的白胡子老头的画像来表现〕

CULTURAL NOTE 文化注释

Uncle Sam first appeared in the 1800s, especially on POSTERS asking people to join the army. He is usually shown pointing his finger and saying "Uncle Sam needs you!" His TOP HAT and clothes are always decorated with the STARS AND STRIPES from the US flag. Political CARTOONS use his picture to represent the US, and newspapers often use the expression 'Uncle Sam' to mean the US government. 山姆大叔首次出现在19世纪, 特别是被画在劝导民众参军的海报上。他通常的形象是用手指着人并说"山姆大叔需要您!"他戴的高顶大礼帽和穿的衣服上总是饰有美国国旗的星条图案。政治漫画用他来代表美国, 而报纸经常用"山姆大叔"来指代美国政府。

Uncle Tom /ˌʌŋkḷ ˈtam; ˌʌŋkəl ˈtɒm/ *n* [C] *AmE* a black person who is too friendly or respectful to white people, used in a disapproving way by other black people 【美】汤姆叔叔〔指对白人毕恭毕敬的黑人, 黑人用此语常含不赞同的意味〕

un·clothed /ʌnˈkloðd; ʌnˈkləʊðd/ *adj formal* not wearing clothes or not covered by clothes; NAKED 【正式】未穿衣服的, 赤裸的

un·coil /ʌnˈkɔɪl; ˌʌnˈkɔɪl/ *v* [I,T] if you uncoil something, or if it uncoils, it stretches out straight, after being wound around in a circle 解开〔卷着的东西〕; (使)展开: *Slowly the snake uncoiled.* 蛇慢慢地伸展开盘着的身体。

un·com·fort·a·ble /ʌnˈkʌmfɚtəbḷ; ʌnˈkʌmftəbəl/ *adj* **1** not feeling physically comfortable, or not making you feel comfortable 不舒服的; 不舒适的: *This sofa is so uncomfortable.* 这张沙发太不舒服了。**2** unable to relax because you are embarrassed 不自在的; 不安的: *an uncomfortable silence* 令人不安的沉寂 —**uncomfortably** *adv*

un·com·mit·ted /ˌʌnkəˈmɪtɪd; ˌʌnkəˈmɪtɨd◂/ *adj* not having decided or promised to support a particular group, political belief etc 未作承诺的; 不受约束的; 未表态的; 中立的: *A large proportion of voters remain uncommitted.* 一大部分选民尚未表态。

un·com·mon /ʌnˈkamən; ʌnˈkɒmən/ *adj* rare or unusual 罕见的; 不平常的: *Violent crimes against the elderly are fortunately very uncommon.* 针对老年人的暴力犯罪幸好非常罕见。| **it is not uncommon for sb to do sth** *It is not uncommon nowadays for students to have bank loans.* 学生获银行贷款如今已不足为奇。—see 见 RARE (USAGE)

un·com·mon·ly /ʌnˈkamənlɪ; ʌnˈkɒmənli/ *adv* [+adj/adv] *old-fashioned* very 【过时】非常: *That's uncommonly kind of you.* 你真是太好了。

un·com·plain·ing /ˌʌnkəmˈplenɪŋ; ˌʌnkəmˈpleɪnɪŋ◂/ *adj* willing to accept a difficult or unpleasant situation without complaining 顺从的; 没有怨言的, 不诉苦的: *A dog can make a wonderful, uncomplaining walking companion.* 狗可以成为称心如意的散步伙伴。—**uncomplainingly** *adv*

un·com·pre·hen·ding /ˌʌnkamprɪˈhɛndɪŋ; ˌʌnkɒmprɪˈhendɪŋ/ *adj* not understanding what is happening 不理解的 —**uncomprehendingly** *adv*

un·com·pro·mis·ing /ʌnˈkamprəˌmaɪzɪŋ; ʌnˈkɒmprəmaɪzɪŋ/ *adj* unwilling to change your opinions or intentions 不妥协的, 不让步的; 坚定的: *an uncompromising opponent of democratic reform* 民主改革的坚决反对者 —**uncompromisingly** *adv*

un·con·cern /ˌʌnkənˈsɝn; ˌʌnkənˈsɜːn/ *n* [U] an attitude of not caring about something that other people worry about 漠不关心, 冷漠: *In view of the deepening crisis, we are surprised at the government's apparent unconcern.* 鉴于日益严重的危机, 我们对政府表现出来的漠不关心感到惊讶。

un·con·cerned /ˌʌnkənˈsɝnd; ˌʌnkənˈsɜːnd/ *adj* **1** not worried about something because you think it does not affect you 不关心的; 不忧虑的: [+about] *Many large companies seem totally unconcerned about the environment.* 许多大公司似乎丝毫不关心环境问题。**2** not interested in a particular aim or activity 不感兴趣的: [+with] *unconcerned with making a profit* 不注重赢利 —**unconcernedly** /-ndlɪ; -nɨdli/ *adv*

un·con·di·tion·al /ˌʌnkənˈdɪʃənəl; ˌʌnkənˈdɪʃənəl◂/ *adj* not limited by or depending on any conditions 不加限制的; 无条件的: *the unconditional release of all political prisoners* 所有政治犯的无条件释放 | **unconditional surrender** *The Allies declared they would accept nothing less than unconditional surrender.* 同盟国声明他们只接受无条件投降。—**unconditionally** *adv*

un·con·firmed /ˌʌnkənˈfɝmd; ˌʌnkənˈfɜːmd◂/ *adj* **unconfirmed report/story/rumour etc** a report etc that has not been proved or supported by official information 未经证实的报道/故事/传闻等: *We've received unconfirmed reports of an explosion in central London.* 我们收到一些未经证实的报道, 说伦敦市中心发生了爆炸。

un·con·scion·a·ble /ʌnˈkanʃənəbḷ; ʌnˈkɒnʃənəbəl/ *adj formal* much more than is reasonable or acceptable 【正式】不合理的; 过度的; 难以接受的: *an unconscionable amount of suffering* 极大的痛苦 —**unconscionably** *adv*

un·con·scious[1] /ʌnˈkanʃəs; ʌnˈkɒnʃəs/ *adj* **1** unable to see, move, feel etc in the normal way because you are not conscious 不省人事的, 失去知觉的: *She was found alive but unconscious.* 她被发现还活着, 但失去了知觉。| **knock/beat sb unconscious** *Murphy was attacked and beaten unconscious.* 默菲遭到袭击, 被打得不省人事。**2** a feeling or thought that is unconscious is one that you have without realizing it 〔感觉、想法〕无意识的; 不自觉的: *an unconscious need to be loved* 一种无意识的需要被人爱的想法 —compare 比较 SUBCONSCIOUS[1] **3 be unconscious of** to not realize the effect of something you have said or done

U

未意识到…，未觉察到…: *Doreen appeared to be unconscious of the amusement she had caused.* 多琳似乎并未意识到是她把大家逗乐了。**4** an action that is unconscious is not deliberate〔动作〕无意的 —**unconsciously** *adv* —**unconsciousness** *n* [U]

unconscious² *n* **the/sb's unconscious** the part of your mind in which there are thoughts and feelings that you do not realize you have; SUBCONSCIOUS² 无意识/某人的潜意识

un·con·sid·ered /ˌʌnkənˋsɪdɚd; ˌʌnkənˈsɪdəd◂/ *adj* **1** unconsidered remarks or actions are made without thinking about the possible results〔评论或行动〕未经思考的, 轻率的 **2** *formal* not important or not noticed【正式】不重要的; 未被注意的: *unconsidered trifles* 琐碎的小事

un·con·sti·tu·tion·al /ˌʌnkɑnstəˋtuʃənḷ; ˌʌnkɒnstɪ̣ˈtjuːʃənəl/ *adj* not allowed by the CONSTITUTION (=set of rules or principles by which a country or organization is governed) 违反宪法的: *the debate over whether flag-burning is an unconstitutional form of protest* 关于焚烧国旗是否属于违反宪法的抗议形式的争论 —**unconstitutionality** /ˌʌnkɑnstəˌtuʃənˋælətɪ; ˌʌnkɒnstɪ̣tjuːʃəˈnælɪ̣ti/ *n* [U]

un·con·trol·lable /ˌʌnkənˋtroləbḷ; ˌʌnkənˈtrəʊləbəl◂/ *adj* **1** uncontrollable emotions, desires or actions are ones that you cannot control or stop〔情感、欲望或动作〕控制不住的, 管束不了的: *I felt an uncontrollable urge to scream.* 我感到一种控制不住的要尖叫的冲动。**2** someone who is uncontrollable behaves badly and will not obey anyone〔人〕无法无天的 **3** situations or conditions that are uncontrollable cannot be changed〔情况〕失控的; 难以挽回的

un·con·trolled /ˌʌnkənˋtrold; ˌʌnkənˈtrəʊld◂/ *adj* uncontrolled emotions or behaviour continue because you are not trying to stop or control them 不加约束的; 无抑制的: *uncontrolled weeping* 放声大哭

un·con·ven·tion·al /ˌʌnkənˋvɛnʃənḷ; ˌʌnkənˈvenʃənəl◂/ *adj* very different from the way people usually behave, think, dress etc 非常规的, 不落俗套的: *unconventional political views* 异乎寻常的政治观点

un·co·op·er·a·tive /ˌʌnkoˋɑpəˌretɪv; ˌʌnkəʊˈɒpərətɪv◂/ *adj* not willing to work with or help someone 不愿合作的, 不配合的: *The immigration authorities were brusque and uncooperative.* 移民当局粗暴而又不合作。

un·co·ordi·nat·ed /ˌʌnkoˋɔrdṇˌetɪd; ˌʌnkəʊˈɔːdɪ̣neɪtɪ̣d◂/ *adj* **1** someone who is uncoordinated is not good at physical activities because they cannot control their movements effectively; CLUMSY〔动作〕不协调的; 笨拙的: *I was always too uncoordinated to be good at tennis.* 我总是太笨手笨脚了, 所以打不好网球。**2** a plan or operation that is uncoordinated is not well organized with the result that the different parts of it do not work together effectively〔计划、行动〕不协调的

un·cork /ʌnˋkɔrk; ʌnˈkɔːk/ *v* [T] to open a bottle by removing its CORK¹ (2) 拔去〔瓶子〕的塞子 —see picture on page A15 参见A15页图

un·count·a·ble /ʌnˋkauntəbḷ; ʌnˈkaʊntəbəl/ *adj* a noun that is uncountable has no plural form and means something which cannot be counted or regarded as either singular or plural, for example 'water', or 'beauty'. In this dictionary uncountable nouns are marked [U]; MASS NOUN〔名词〕不可数的〔如 water, beauty 等, 在本辞典中不可数名词以[U]标示〕

un·couth /ʌnˋkuθ; ʌnˈkuːθ/*adj* behaving and speaking in a way that is rude or socially unacceptable〔言语、行为〕粗鲁的, 不文明的: *rough, uncouth men* 粗暴无礼的男人 —**uncouthly** *adv* —**uncouthness** *n* [U]

un·cov·er /ʌnˋkʌvɚ; ʌnˈkʌvə/ *v* [T] **1** to find out about something that has been kept secret 发现, 破获, 揭露: *Customs officials uncovered a plot to smuggle weapons into the country.* 海关官员发现了一个走私武器入境的阴谋。**2** to remove the cover from something 揭开…的盖子; 移去…的覆盖物

un·crit·i·cal /ʌnˋkrɪtɪkḷ; ʌnˈkrɪtɪkəl/ *adj* unable or unwilling to see faults in something or someone 无鉴别力的; 不加批评的: [+of] *John's mother is totally uncritical of his behaviour.* 约翰的母亲对他的行为完全不加批评。—**uncritically** /-kḷɪ; -kli/ *adv*

un·crowned /ʌnˋkraund; ˌʌnˈkraʊnd◂/ *adj* **the uncrowned king/queen of** the person who is thought to be the best or most famous in a particular activity〔某活动〕的无冕之王/后; …最出色者: *Martina Navratilova, the uncrowned queen of women's tennis* 玛蒂娜·娜芙拉蒂洛娃女子网球的无冕之后

un·crush·a·ble /ʌnˋkrʌʃəbḷ; ʌnˈkrʌʃəbəl/ *adj* **1** material or cloth that is uncrushable is easy to keep smooth〔布料等〕揉不皱的 **2** very determined and not easily discouraged 坚强的, 压不垮的: *her uncrushable will to survive* 她那求生的坚强意志

unc·tu·ous /ˋʌŋktʃuəs; ˈʌŋktʃuəs/ *adj formal* too friendly and praising people too much in a way that seems very insincere【正式】甜言蜜语的, 假殷勤的, 谄媚的: *There is something smug and unctuous about him.* 他这人有点沾沾自喜, 虚情假意。—**unctuously** *adv* —**unctuousness** *n* [U]

un·curl /ʌnˋkɝl; ˌʌnˈkɜːl/ *v* [I,T] to stretch out straight from a curled position, or to make something do this (使) 伸直; (使) 变直

un·cut /ʌnˋkʌt; ˌʌnˈkʌt◂/ *adj* **1** a film, book etc that is uncut has not been made shorter, for example by having violent or sexual scenes removed〔影片、书籍等〕未删节[剪辑]的: *the uncut version of 'Lady Chatterley's Lover'*《查特莱夫人的情人》的未删节版本 **2** an uncut jewel that is still in its natural form has not been cut into a particular shape〔宝石〕未经雕琢的: *uncut gem stones* 未经琢磨的宝石

un·daunt·ed /ʌnˋdɔntɪd; ʌnˈdɔːntɪ̣d/ *adj* not afraid of continuing to try to do something in spite of difficulties or danger 无畏的, 大胆的; 不泄气的: [+by] *Undaunted by the enormity of the task, they began rebuilding the village.* 他们不畏任务艰巨, 开始重建村庄。

un·de·ceive /ˌʌndɪˋsiv; ˌʌndɪˈsiːv/ *v* [T] *formal* to tell someone what the real facts are when they have previously believed something that was untrue【正式】使不再受骗; 使明真相, 使醒悟

un·de·cid·ed /ˌʌndɪˋsaɪdɪd; ˌʌndɪˈsaɪdɪ̣d/ *adj* **1** [not before noun 不用于名词前] not having made a decision about something important 未决定的: [+about] *A third of the electorate remain undecided about how they will vote.* 三分之一的选民仍未决定投票意向。| [+what/which/whether etc] *Nadine was undecided whether or not to go to college.* 娜丁尚未决定是否去上大学。**2** a game or competition that is undecided has no definite winner〔比赛〕未定局的 —**undecidedly** *adv*

un·de·mon·stra·tive /ˌʌndɪˋmɑnstrətɪv; ˌʌndɪˈmɒnstrətɪv/ *adj* not showing your feelings of love or friendliness, especially by not touching or kissing people 含蓄的, 感情不外露的〔尤指不触摸或吻别人〕

un·de·ni·a·ble /ˌʌndɪˋnaɪəbḷ; ˌʌndɪˈnaɪəbəl◂/ *adj* definitely true or certain 不可否认的, 无可争辩的: *undeniable proof* 确证 —**undeniably** *adv*

under- /ʌndɚ; ʌndə/ *prefix* **1** too little 不足: *under-development* 欠发达 | *undercooked cabbage* 未煮熟的洋白菜 **2** going underneath something 在…下面: *an underpass* 地下通道 **3** inner; beneath others 内部的; 在…之下: *undergarments* 内衣 **4** less important or lower in rank〔重要性或等级〕次的, 低的: *a head gardener and three under-gardeners* 一个园艺主管和三个园艺助理

un·der¹ /ˋʌndɚ; ˈʌndə/ *prep*

1 ►**BELOW** 在…下面◄ directly below something, or covered by it 在…下面, 在…底下; 在…里面: *Write your name under your picture.* 在你的照片下面写上名字。| *She was carrying her handbag under her arm.* 她胳膊下夹着个手提包。| *I could see something glittering under the water.* 我能看见水里有东西在闪闪发光。

2 ►**LESS THAN** 少于◄ less than a particular number, amount, age, or price〔数字、数量、年龄或价格〕低于, 少于, 在…以下: *gifts for under ten dollars* 不到10美元的礼物 | *nursery education for children under five* 五岁以下儿童的幼儿教育 | *I spend just under four hours a day seeing customers.* 我一天接待顾客所花的时间将近四小时。| **be under age** (=not be old enough to drink, have sex etc legally) 未成年; 未及法定年龄 *You're not allowed in the bar if you're under age.* 未成年者不准进酒吧。

3 **be under construction/discussion/attack etc** to be in the process of being constructed, discussed etc 在建设/讨论/攻击等中: *The possibility of replacing the computers remains under consideration.* 更换电脑的可能性仍在考虑之中。| *The National Health Service is very much under attack from the Tory government.* (英国) 国民保健制度遭到保守党政府的猛烈抨击。

4 ►**CONTROLLED** 被控制的◄ being controlled by a particular leader, government, system etc 在…指挥[支配, 管理]下: *foreign policy under Kohl* 科尔指导下的外交政策 | *The Los Angeles Philharmonic is under the baton of Esa-Pekka Salonen.* 洛杉矶爱乐乐团由埃萨－佩卡·萨洛宁担任指挥。

5 ►**LAW/AGREEMENT** 法律/协议◄ according to a particular agreement, law etc 根据…, 依照…: *an exemption under Article 85* 根据第85条作出的豁免

6 ►**AFFECTED BY** 受…的影响◄ being affected by particular conditions or situations 在…影响下: *She's been under a lot of pressure at work.* 她工作中有很大压力。| *driving under the influence of alcohol* 酒后开车 | *The solicitor has said that*

under no circumstances must I pay it. 律师说我无论如何都不需要付款。

7 be under (sb's) control/influence/spell etc if someone or something is under someone's control etc, they control or influence it 在〔某人〕控制/影响/吸引等之下: *I'm glad to see that you have everything under control.* 我很高兴看到一切都在你控制之中。| *She seems to be coming under Gina's influence.* 她似乎在受吉娜的影响。

8 ▶CLASS/GROUP 类别/组◀ if an object, book, name etc is under a particular letter, list, system etc, that is where you can find it or that is the group it belongs to 在…类别下，属于…之类: *The baby's records are filed under the mother's last name.* 婴儿的档案记录归在母亲的姓下。

9 ▶POSITION AT WORK 工作职位◀ if people are under someone in authority, they work for that person and have a lower position 在…手下工作；在…的管辖下: *Guerrero works under him directly.* 格雷罗直接在他手下工作。

10 be under an impression/delusion to believe something is true, especially when you are wrong in believing it 留下印象/错觉: *I was under the impression that he was going on vacation that week.* 我的印象是他那周在休假。

11 be under anaesthesia/sedation/treatment etc to be treated by a doctor using a particular drug or method 在麻醉/镇静/治疗等中

12 ▶DIFFERENT NAME 别名◀ if you write something under another name, you write it using a name that is not your real name 用〔某个名字〕；假托…: *Eric Blair wrote under the name of George Orwell.* 埃里克·布莱尔用乔治·奥威尔的名字写作。

USAGE NOTE 用法说明: UNDER

WORD CHOICE 词义辨析: **under, underneath, below, beneath**

Under is the most common word used to talk about one thing being placed or moving directly under another, or being covered by it. 表示一物在另一物的正下方或在其中，under 是最常用的一个词: *I found it under the table/cushion.* 我发现它在桌子/垫子下面。| *The railway runs directly under the main street.* 铁路在主街的正下方穿过。| *Just push the note under the door.* 把便条直接塞在门下。| *The police all wear bullet-proof vests under their shirts.* 警察衬衣里面都穿上防弹背心。

Underneath is often used intead of **under** to slightly emphasize the idea of covering, touching, or hiding. 强调"遮盖"、"接触"、"藏匿"之意时，常用 underneath 而不用 under: *He keeps his money in a secret safe underneath the floor boards.* 他把钱保存在地板下面一个秘密的保险柜中。| *I wonder what's underneath that cover?* 我想知道那个盖子下面藏了什么? | *a creature that makes its nest underneath desert rocks* 把窝筑在沙漠岩石底下的动物

You use **under** to talk about something that is covered by something that is also all around it, but you would not use **underneath** so often in this way. under 用以表示处于某物之下并为之包围，underneath 则不常这么用: *Sea lions can travel much faster under water.* 海狮在水中行进的速度要快得多。

Beneath can also be used in all these ways, but is a little old-fashioned or literary. beneath 含以上三种用法，但有点过时或较常用于文学作品中。In a romantic story, for example, you might read 爱情故事中偶可遇见这种用法: *They strolled hand in hand beneath the summer moon.* 他们手拉着手，在夏日的月光下徜徉。

Below suggests that one thing is in a lower position than another, perhaps a little to one side or in front. below 表示一物处于另一物的下方，位置稍微靠边或靠前: *Jed and Jackie live in the apartment below us.* 杰德和杰姬住在我们楼下的公寓。| *There was a lake below the village, further down the valley.* 在村庄下面，山谷更低处有一个湖。

S2 W2 **under²** *adv* **1** in or to a place below something or covered by it 在下面；往下面；在底下: *He crawled under the blankets.* 他在毯子下面爬。**2** less in age, number, amount etc than the age etc mentioned 〔年龄、数量等〕低于，少于: *Children twelve and under must be accompanied by an adult.* 12岁及以下儿童必须有大人陪伴。

un·der·a·chiev·er /ˌʌndərəˋtʃivɚ; ˌʌndərəˈtʃiːvə/ *n* [C] someone who does not do as well as they could do, especially at school 未能充分发挥〔学习〕潜力者，学习成绩不理想者 —**underachieve** *v* [I] —**underachievement** *n* [U]

un·der·age /ˈʌndɚˋedʒ; ˌʌndərˈeɪdʒ◂/ *adj* too young to legally buy alcohol, drive a car, vote etc 未成年的，未及法定年龄的: *underage drinking* 未成年饮酒

un·der·arm¹ /ˈʌndɚˌɑrm; ˈʌndərɑːm◂/ *adv* if you throw a ball underarm, you throw it without moving your arm above your shoulder〔击球时〕低手地，手不过肩地; UNDERHAND² *AmE*【美】—see picture on page A23 参见 A23 页图

underarm² *adj* **underarm deodorant/antiperspirant** a substance which smells pleasant that you put under your arms 腋下除臭剂/止汗剂

un·der·bel·ly /ˈʌndɚˌbɛlɪ; ˈʌndəˌbeli/ *n literary*【文】**1** the weakest or most easily damaged part of a country, plan etc 易受攻击的区域；最薄弱部分: *regional warfare tearing at the country's underbelly* 攻击该国薄弱地区的局部战争 **2** the stomach of an animal such as a fish〔动物的〕下腹部〔如鱼肚〕

un·der·brush /ˈʌndɚˌbrʌʃ; ˈʌndəbrʌʃ/ *n* [U] *especially AmE* bushes, small trees etc growing under and around larger trees in a forest; UNDERGROWTH【尤美】〔长在树林中大树下的〕下层灌木丛，矮树丛

un·der·cap·i·tal·ize also 又作 -ise *BrE*【英】/ˌʌndɚˋkæpɪtḷˌaɪz; ˌʌndəˈkæpɪtl-aɪz/ *v* [T usually passive 一般用被动态] to not give a business enough money with the result that it cannot operate effectively 对〔企业〕投资不足

un·der·car·riage /ˈʌndɚˌkærɪdʒ; ˈʌndəˌkærɪdʒ/ *n* [C] the wheels of an aircraft and the structure that holds them〔飞机的〕起落架 —see picture at 参见 AIRCRAFT 图

un·der·charge /ˌʌndɚˋtʃɑrdʒ; ˌʌndəˈtʃɑːdʒ/ *v* [I,T] to charge too little or less than the correct amount of money for something〔对…〕少要价，少收…的价钱: **undercharge sb by £1/$2 etc** *They undercharged me by about two dollars.* 他们少要了我大约两美元。—opposite 反义词 OVERCHARGE (1)

un·der·class /ˈʌndɚˌklæs; ˈʌndəklɑːs/ *n* [singular] the lowest social class, consisting of people who are very poor 下层社会，最低阶层

un·der·class·man /ˌʌndɚˋklæsmən; ˌʌndəˈklɑːsmən/ *n* [C] *AmE* a student in the first two years of school or college【美】低年级学生〔指大学或中学的一、二年级学生〕

un·der·clothes /ˈʌndɚˌkloðz; ˈʌndəkləʊðz/ also 又作 **un·der·clo·thing** /-ˌkloðɪŋ; -ˌkləʊðɪŋ/ *n* [plural] clothes that you wear next to your body under your other clothes; UNDERWEAR 内衣

un·der·coat /ˈʌndɚˌkot; ˈʌndəkəʊt/ *n* [C] a layer of paint that you put onto a surface before you put the final layer on 内[底]涂层

un·der·cov·er /ˈʌndɚˋkʌvɚ; ˌʌndəˈkʌvə◂/ *adj* [only before noun 仅用于名词前] used or employed secretly, in order to catch criminals or find out information 暗中进行的；秘密干的: *an undercover operation* 秘密行动

un·der·cur·rent /ˈʌndɚˌkɝənt; ˈʌndəˌkʌrənt/ *n* [C] **1** a feeling, especially of anger or dissatisfaction, that people do not express openly 潜伏的情绪〔尤指愤怒、不满〕: [+of] *He sensed an undercurrent of resentment among the crowd.* 他觉察到人群中有潜在的怨恨。**2** a hidden and often dangerous current of water that flows under the surface of the sea or a river〔河或海中的〕暗流

un·der·cut /ˌʌndɚˋkʌt; ˌʌndəˈkʌt/ *v* [T] to sell goods or services more cheaply than another company 削价与…抢生意

un·der·de·vel·oped /ˌʌndɚdɪˋvɛləpt; ˌʌndədɪˈveləpt◂/ *adj* **1 underdeveloped country/region etc** a country, region etc that is poor and where there is not much modern industry 不发达的国家/地区等 —compare 比较 **developing country** (DEVELOPING) **2** not having grown or developed as much as is usual or necessary 发育不全的: *a skinny, underdeveloped child* 骨瘦如柴、发育不全的孩子

un·der·dog /ˈʌndɚˌdɔg; ˈʌndədɒg/ *n* [C] **1 the underdog** the person or team in a competition that is expected to lose 处于劣势的人[队]；〔竞赛中〕可能会输的人[队] **2** a person, country etc that is weak and is always treated badly 弱者；弱国

un·der·done /ˈʌndɚˋdʌn; ˌʌndəˈdʌn◂/ *adj* meat that is underdone is not completely cooked〔肉〕未煮透的；半生不熟的 —compare 比较 OVERDONE

un·der·dressed /ˌʌndɚˋdrɛst; ˌʌndəˈdrest◂/ *adj* wearing clothes that are too informal for a particular occasion 穿着过于随便的

un·der·em·ployed /ˌʌndərɪmˋplɔɪd; ˌʌndərɪmˈplɔɪd◂/ *adj* working in a job where you cannot use all your skills or where there is not enough work for you to do 大材小用的，未能人尽其才的；就业不足的

un·der·es·ti·mate¹ /ˈʌndɚˋɛstəˌmet; ˌʌndərˈestɪmeɪt/ *v* **1** [I,T] to think that something is smaller, cheaper, less important

U

etc than it really is (对…)估计不足, 低估; 看轻: *People often underestimate the importance of training.* 人们常常低估培训的重要性。**2** [T] to think that someone is not as good, clever, or skilful, as they really are 轻视, 小看〔某人〕: *Don't underestimate Manville – he's a skilful campaigner.* 不要小看曼维尔——他可是个出色的活动家。

un·der·es·ti·mate² /ʌndɚ`ɛstəmɪt; ˌʌndər'estɪ̣mɪt/ *n* [C] a guessed amount or number that is too low 估量过低; 低估: *14% may be an underestimate.* 14%也许是估计不足。

un·der·ex·pose /ʌndərɪk`spoz; ˌʌndərɪk'spəʊz/ *v* [T] to not let enough light reach the film when you are taking a photograph 使〔底片〕曝光不足

un·der·fed /ˌʌndɚ`fɛd; ˌʌndə'fed/ *adj* not given enough food to eat 未吃饱的; 喂食不足的

un·der·felt /`ʌndɚ`fɛlt; 'ʌndəfelt/ *n* [U] *BrE* soft material that you put between a CARPET¹ (1) and the floor【英】地毯垫毡〔置于地板与地毯之间的软材料〕

un·der·foot /ˌʌndɚ`fʊt; ˌʌndə'fʊt/ *adv* **1** under your feet where you are walking 在脚下: **wet/dry/firm etc underfoot** *The wet wood is very slippery underfoot.* 脚下的湿木头很滑。**2 trample sb/sth underfoot a)** to crush someone or something on the ground by stepping heavily on them 把某人/某物踩在脚下 **b)** to completely destroy someone or something 彻底毁灭某人/某物

un·der·fund /ˌʌndɚ`fʌnd; ˌʌndə'fʌnd/ *v* [T] **be underfunded** to not be provided with enough money 资金不足: *The childcare program is seriously underfunded.* 儿童保育计划的资金严重不足。—**underfunding** *n* [U]

un·der·gar·ment /`ʌndɚˌgɑrmənt; 'ʌndəˌgɑːmənt/ *n* [C] *old-fashioned* a piece of underwear【过时】内衣

un·der·go /ˌʌndɚ`go; ˌʌndə'gəʊ/ *v past tense* **underwent** /-`wɛnt; -'went/ *past participle* **undergone** /-`gɔn; -'gɒn/ [T not in passive 不用被动态] if you undergo a change, an unpleasant experience etc, it happens to you, or is done to you 经历, 经受; 遭受: *She's undergoing surgery.* 她正在接受手术。| *The company underwent several major changes.* 公司经历了几次重大变化。

un·der·grad·u·ate /ˌʌndɚ`grædʒuɪt; ˌʌndə'grædʒuɪ̣t◂/ *n* [C] *especially BrE* a student who is doing a university course for a first degree【尤英】〔尚未取得学位的〕大学(本科)生 —compare 比较 GRADUATE¹ (1)

un·der·ground¹ /`ʌndɚ`graund; 'ʌndəgraʊnd/ *adj* **1** below the surface of the earth 地下的: *an underground passage* 地下通道 **2** [only before noun 仅用于名词前] an underground group, organization etc is secret and illegal〔组织、机构等〕秘密的, 不合法的: *an underground terrorist organization* 地下恐怖主义组织

un·der·ground² /`ʌndɚ`graund; ˌʌndə'graʊnd/ *adv* **1** under the earth's surface 在地(面)下: *nuclear waste buried deep underground* 深埋在地下的核废料 | *The prairie dog burrows underground.* 草原犬鼠会打地洞。**2 go underground** to start doing something secretly, or hide in a secret place 转入地下; 隐匿: *The ANC was forced to go underground when the government arrested its leaders.* 在政府逮捕其领导人之后, 非洲人国民大会被迫转入地下。

un·der·ground³ /`ʌndɚ`graund; 'ʌndəgraʊnd/ *n* **the Underground a)** *BrE* a railway system under the ground【英】地下铁路, 地铁; SUBWAY (2) *AmE*【美】: *a map of the London Underground* 伦敦地铁图 **b)** an illegal group working in secret against the rulers of a country 反政府的非法地下组织; 秘密团体

Underground Rail·road, the /ˌ‥ˈ‥ /a group of people in the US who illegally helped SLAVES to become free by helping them to escape to the northern US and Canada, in the period before the Civil War. One of its best-known members was Harriet Tubman. 地下铁道, 地下交通网〔美国废奴主义组织。在美国内战之前的一段时期曾帮助奴隶逃往美国北部及加拿大, 使其获得自由, 此举在当时属违法行为。其成员以哈丽雅特·塔布曼最负盛名〕

un·der·growth /`ʌndɚˌgroθ; 'ʌndəgrəʊθ/ *n* [U] bushes, small trees, and other plants growing around and under bigger trees〔长在大树下的〕下层灌木丛, 矮树丛: *Something rustled in the undergrowth.* 有东西在灌木丛中沙沙作响。

un·der·hand¹ /`ʌndɚ`hænd; ˌʌndə'hænd◂/ also 又作 **un·der·hand·ed** /ˌʌndɚ`hændɪd; ˌʌndə'hændɪ̣d/ *adj* dishonest and done secretly 欺诈的; 秘密进行的: *underhand dealings* 秘密[私下]交易 —**underhandedly** *adv* —**underhandedness** *n* [U]

underhand² *adv AmE* if you throw a ball underhand, you throw it without moving your arm above your shoulder; UNDERARM¹【美】〔击球〕手不过肩地, 低手地

un·der·lay /`ʌndɚˌle; 'ʌndəleɪ/ *n* [C,U] a large piece of material put under a CARPET¹ (1)〔地毯下的〕垫料, 垫层

un·der·lie /ˌʌndɚ`laɪ; ˌʌndə'laɪ/ *v past tense* **underlay** /-`le; -'leɪ/ *past participle* **underlaid** /-`led; -'leɪd/ [T] *formal* to be the real cause of or reason for something【正式】构成…的真正起因: *Social problems and poverty underlie much of the crime in today's big cities.* 社会问题和贫困是当今大城市许多犯罪的根本原因。

un·der·line /ˌʌndɚ`laɪn; ˌʌndə'laɪn/ *v* [T] **1** to draw a line under a word to show that it is important 在…之下划线〔以示重要〕**2** to show that something is important 强调; 使突出: *This tragic incident underlines the need for immediate action.* 这一悲剧事件表明有必要立即采取行动。

un·der·ling /`ʌndɚlɪŋ; 'ʌndəlɪŋ/ *n* [C] an insulting word for someone who has a low rank 下属, 部下; 走卒〔侮辱性用词〕

un·der·ly·ing /ˌʌndɚ`laɪɪŋ; ˌʌndə'laɪ-ɪŋ/ *adj* **underlying reason/cause/aim etc** the reason, cause etc that is the most important, although it is not easily noticed 根本的理由/原因/目标等: *the underlying causes of her depression* 她意志消沉的根本原因 W3

un·der·manned /ˌʌndɚ`mænd; ˌʌndə'mænd◂/ *adj* not having enough workers 人员不足的

un·der·men·tioned /`ʌndɚ`mɛnʃənd; ˌʌndə'menʃənd◂/ *adj formal*【正式】**1** mentioned later in the same piece of writing 下述的: *Please supply me with the undermentioned goods.* 请给我供应下述货物。**2 the undermentioned** the people or things that are mentioned in the list that is written immediately below 下列的人员[物品]: *The undermentioned will report for duty.* 下列人员将前来报到。

Under Milk Wood /ˌ‥ ˌ ˈ ˈ/ (1954) a play by the Welsh poet Dylan Thomas, originally performed on the radio, which is set in an imaginary fishing village in Wales and describes, often in a humorous way, the people who live there and the things they do on a particular day《奶树林下》〔(1954), 威尔士诗人迪兰·托马斯的剧作, 最初为广播剧。该剧以威尔士一个虚构的渔村为背景, 采用幽默的笔触描写当地居民的日常生活琐事〕

un·der·mine /ˌʌndɚ`maɪn; ˌʌndə'maɪn/ *v* [T] **1** to gradually make someone or something less strong or effective 逐渐削弱[损害]: *She tried to undermine his authority at every opportunity.* 她试图利用一切机会来削弱他的权威。| *economic policies that threaten to undermine the health care system* 可能会损害卫生保健制度的经济政策 **2** to gradually take away the earth from under something 挖去…(底下)的土

un·der·neath¹ /ˌʌndɚ`niθ; ˌʌndə'niːθ/ *prep, adv* **1** directly under or below another object, used especially when one thing is covering or hiding another 在…下面; 在…底下〔尤指某物覆盖或藏着另一物〕: *It's near where the railway goes underneath the road.* 它在临近铁路从公路下通过的地方。| *A translation was written underneath.* 译文写在下面。—see 见 UNDER¹ (USAGE) —see picture on page A1 参见A1页图 **2** if someone is nice, shy etc underneath, they really are nice etc even though their behaviour shows a different character〔人〕本质上: *She seems aggressive, but underneath she's pretty shy.* 她看起来咄咄逼人, 实际上却相当腼腆。 S2

underneath² *n BrE*【英】**the underneath** the bottom surface of something, or the part of something that is below or under something else 下面; 下部; 底部, 底层: *We need to paint the underneath with a rust preventer.* 我们需要用防锈漆把底部刷一下。

un·der·nour·ished /ˌʌndɚ`nɝɪʃt; ˌʌndə'nʌrɪʃt◂/ *adj* unhealthy and weak because you have not had enough food 营养不足的 —**undernourishment** *n* [U]

un·der·paid /ˌʌndɚ`ped; ˌʌndə'peɪd◂/ *adj* earning less money than you deserve for your work 所得工资不足[过低]的: *Teachers are generally overworked and underpaid.* 教师一般都工作过度, 报酬过低。—**underpay** *v* [T]

un·der·pants /`ʌndɚˌpænts; 'ʌndəpænts/ *n* [plural] **1** *BrE* a short piece of underwear worn by men under their trousers【英】〔男用〕衬裤, 内裤 —see picture at 参见 UNDERWEAR 图 **2** *AmE* a short piece of underwear of this type, worn by men or women【美】〔男或女用的〕内裤, 衬裤

un·der·pass /`ʌndɚˌpæs; 'ʌndəpɑːs/ *n* [C] a road or path that goes under another road or a railway 地下通道; 下穿交叉道; 高架桥下的通道

un·der·pay /`ʌndɚ`pe; ˌʌndə'peɪ/ *v past tense and past participle* **underpaid** /-`ped; -'peɪd/ [T] to pay someone too little for their work 付给…过低的工资

un·der·pin /ˌʌndɚ`pɪn; ˌʌndə'pɪn/ *v* [T] **1** to give strength or support to an idea, belief etc 巩固, 支持〔想法、信念等〕: *A solid*

basis of evidence underpins their theory. 基础坚实的证据巩固了他们的理论。**2** to put a solid piece of metal under something such as a wall in order to make it stronger 加固〔墙等〕的基础 —**underpinning** *n* [C,U]

un·der·play /ˌʌndɚˈple; ˌʌndəˈpleɪ/ *v* [T] **1** to make something seem less important than it really is 淡化[贬低]…的重要性，使显得不如实际重要 **2 underplay your hand** to discuss something with someone without telling them everything about your plans, abilities etc 不动声色地小心行事，不露锋芒

un·der·priv·i·leged /ˈʌndɚˈprɪvəlɪdʒd; ˌʌndəˈprɪvəlɪdʒd◂/ *adj* very poor, with worse living conditions, educational opportunities etc than most people in society 贫困的；社会地位低下的；下层社会的

un·der·rate /ˈʌndɚˈret; ˌʌndəˈreɪt/ *v* [T] to think that someone or something is less good, effective, skilful etc than they really are 看轻；低估：*a much underrated novel* 评价过低的小说

un·der·re·sourced /ˌʌndərɪˈsorst; ˌʌndərɪˈzɔːst/ *adj* not provided with enough money, equipment etc〔资金、设备等〕供应不足的

un·der·score /ˌʌndɚˈskor; ˌʌndəˈskɔː/ *v* [T] *especially AmE*【尤美】**1** to emphasize something so that people pay attention to it 强调 **2** to draw a line under a word or phrase to show that it is important; UNDERLINE 在〔单词、短语〕底下划线〔以示强调〕

un·der·sea /ˈʌndɚˈsi; ˈʌndəsiː/ *adj* [only before noun 仅用于名词前] happening or existing below the surface of the sea 海底的；海面下的；在海面下进行的：*undersea exploration* 海底探险

un·der·sec·re·ta·ry /ˌʌndɚˈsɛkrəˌtɛrɪ; ˌʌndəˈsekrətəri/ *n* [C] **1** someone who is in charge of the daily work of a British government department〔英国的〕政务次官 **2** *AmE* a very important official in a government department who is one position in rank below the SECRETARY【美】副部长；副国务卿

un·der·sell /ˌʌndɚˈsɛl; ˌʌndəˈsel/ *v past tense and past participle* **undersold** /-ˈsold; -ˈsəʊld/ [T] **1** to sell goods at a lower price than someone else 以低于〔他人〕的价格出售；廉价出售 **2** to make other people think that someone or something is less good, effective, skilful etc than they really are 让人轻视；过于自谦；过低评价：*I think he undersold himself at the interview.* 我认为他在面试时过于自谦。

under·served /ˌ‥ˈ‥◂/ *adj AmE* not getting enough care and help from the government【美】〔政府〕关照不足的，服务不周到的：*the under-served communities of the inner city* 未获充分关照的旧城区贫民

un·der·sexed /ˌʌndɚˈsɛkst; ˌʌndəˈsekst◂/ *adj* having less desire to have sex than is normal 性欲不强的，性冷淡的

un·der·shirt /ˈʌndɚˌʃɝt; ˈʌndəʃɜːt/ *n* [C] *AmE* a piece of underwear with or without arms, worn under a shirt【美】内衣；汗衫，背心；VEST[1] (1) *BrE*【英】

un·der·side /ˈʌndɚˌsaɪd; ˈʌndəsaɪd/ *n* [singular] **the underside** the bottom side or surface of something 下侧；下面；底部

un·der·signed /ˌʌndɚˈsaɪnd; ˈʌndəsaɪnd/ *adj formal*【正式】**the undersigned** the person or people who have signed a piece of writing, used especially in formal letters〔尤指正式信件的〕签名者，署名人

un·der·sized /ˈʌndɚˈsaɪzd; ˌʌndəˈsaɪzd◂/ also 又作 **un·der·size** /-ˈsaɪz; -ˈsaɪz◂/ *adj* smaller than usual, or too small 小于一般尺寸的；太小的

un·der·staffed /ˌʌndɚˈstæft; ˌʌndəˈstɑːft◂/ *adj* not having enough workers, or fewer workers than usual 人员不足的，人手不够的

S1 W1 **un·der·stand** /ˌʌndɚˈstænd; ˌʌndəˈstænd/ *v past tense and past participle* **understood** /-ˈstʊd; -ˈstʊd/ [not in progressive 不用进行时]

1 ▶MEANING 意思◀ [I,T] to know the meaning of what someone is telling you, or the language that they speak 懂；理解；明白：*She doesn't understand English – try Spanish.* 她不懂英语——试试西班牙语吧。| *I'm sorry, I don't understand. Can you explain that again?* 对不起，我不明白，你能再解释一遍吗？| **understand perfectly** *I understand perfectly, the children must be in bed by 8 o'clock.* 我很清楚，孩子们8点前必须上床睡觉。

2 ▶FACT/IDEA 事实/想法◀ [I,T] to know or realize how a fact, process, situation etc works, especially through learning or experience〔尤指通过学习或经历〕了解；熟悉：*I don't really understand the political situation in Northern Ireland.* 我真的不了解北爱尔兰的政治形势。| **understand how/why/where etc** *You don't need to understand how computers work to be able to use them.* 你不必熟悉电脑的工作原理，会用就行。| **fully understand** *How the drug actually works isn't fully understood.* 这种药的实际作用尚未完全了解。

3 ▶PERSON 人◀ [I,T] to know and sympathize with how someone feels, and why they behave the way they do 理解，谅解；同情：*My parents just don't understand me.* 我父母就是不理解我。| *Don tried to understand.* 唐试图去谅解。| **understand how/what etc** *I understand how you feel, but I think you're overreacting.* 我理解你的感受，但我认为你的反应过头了。| **understand sb doing sth** *I can understand her wanting to live alone and be independent.* 我能理解她想独自生活，不再依赖别人。

4 I understand (that) *spoken formal* used to say that someone has told you that something is true【口，正式】获悉；听说：*I understand that you'll be coming to work here soon.* 我听说你很快要来这儿工作了。

5 make yourself understood to be able to express simple things in another language〔用外语〕表达自己的意思：*I'm not very good at German, but I can make myself understood.* 我的德语不太好，但我能表达自己的意思。

6 do you understand? *spoken* used when you are telling someone what they should or should not do, especially when you are angry with them【口】明白了吗？〔用于告诫〕：*Never speak to me like that again! Do you understand?* 别再那样对我说话！明白了吗？

7 be understood *formal* used to say that something has been agreed and there is no need to discuss it【正式】〔某事〕已商定：**be understood that** *I thought it was understood that if we worked late we'd get paid double.* 我原以为已经商定，我们加班就会得到双份报酬。

8 understand sth/sb to mean sth accept something as having a particular meaning 领会某事/某人的含义：*In this document, 'children' is understood to mean people under 14.* 本文件中，"儿童"是指14岁以下的人。

9 give sb to understand sth *formal* to make someone believe that something is true, something is going to happen etc, without telling them this directly【正式】〔不直接说明而〕使某人相信某事：*I was given to understand that the property was in good condition.* 我得到的感觉是，这房子维护得不错。

This graph shows how common the different grammar patterns of the verb **understand** are. 本图表所示为动词 understand 构成的不同语法模式的使用频率。

Pattern	Approx. frequency
understand sth	~50%
understand how/why/where etc	~17%
understand (that)	~15%
understand	~7%
understand sth/sb to mean sth	~1%
understand sb doing sth	~1%
other	~12%

10% 20% 30% 40% 50%

Based on the British National Corpus and the Longman Lancaster Corpus
据英国国家语料库和朗文兰开斯特语料库

un·der·stand·a·ble /ˌʌndɚˈstændəbl; ˌʌndəˈstændəbəl/ *adj* **1** able to be understood; COMPREHENSIBLE 可懂的；易于理解的：*The announcement was barely understandable.* 通告几乎看不懂。**2** understandable behaviour, reactions etc seem normal and reasonable because of the situation you are in〔行为、反应等〕可以理解的，合情理的：*Her anger was entirely understandable in the circumstances.* 她的愤怒在当时情况下是完全可以理解的。—**understandably** *adv*

un·der·stand·ing[1] /ˌʌndɚˈstændɪŋ; ˌʌndəˈstændɪŋ/ *n* **1** [C usually singular 一般用单数] a private, unofficial agreement〔私底下、非正式的〕协议，协定：**come to/reach an understanding** *I thought we had come to an understanding on this matter.* 我认为我们在这件事上已达成了协议。| **on the understanding that** (=on the condition that) 以…为条件 *I lent him the money on the strict understanding that he paid it back next month.* 我借钱给他，条件是他必须在下个月归还。**2** [singular,U] knowledge about something, based on learning or experience 了解；熟悉：**have an understanding of** *The present Industry Secretary has only a limited understanding of economics.* 现任工业部长对经济学所知有限。**3** [singular,U] sympathy towards someone's character and behaviour 谅解；同情：*Mutual understanding is important in all relationships.* 互相谅解在所有关系中都是重要的。**4** [U] the way in which you judge the meaning of something 领会；理解：[+of] *According to my understanding of the letter, it* W3

U

means something quite different. 根据我对该信的理解，它表示的意思完全不同。**5** [U] the ability to know and learn; INTELLIGENCE (1) 理解力；智力：*beyond a child's understanding* 超出了孩子的理解力

understanding² *adj* sympathetic and kind about other people's problems 能谅解的，宽容的：*Luckily, I have a very understanding boss.* 幸运的是，我有一个非常通情达理的上司。

un·der·state /ˈʌndɚˋstet; ˌʌndəˈsteɪt/ *v* [T] to describe something in a way that makes it seem less important than it really is 没有如实地陈述；淡化：*This report understates the seriousness of the situation.* 这个报告没有如实陈述形势的严峻。

un·der·state·ment /ˈʌndɚˌstetmənt; ˌʌndəˈsteɪtmənt/ *n* **1** [C] a statement that is not strong enough to express how good, bad, impressive etc something really is 不充分的陈述，轻描淡写的陈述：*To say the movie was bad is an understatement.* 说这电影不好是低调的说法。**2** [U] a way of describing things as being less good, bad, important etc than they really are 轻描淡写；少说，少报

un·der·stood /ˌʌndɚˋstʊd; ˌʌndəˈstʊd/ the past tense and past participle of UNDERSTAND

un·der·stud·y¹ /ˈʌndɚˌstʌdɪ; ˈʌndəˌstʌdi/ *n* [C] an actor who learns a part in a play so that they can act if the usual actor is ill 预备演员，替角

understudy² *v* [T] to be an understudy for a particular actor in a play 充当〔某演员〕的替角

un·der·sub·scribe /ˌʌndɚsəbˋskraɪb; ˌʌndəsəbˈskraɪb/ *v* [T] **be undersubscribed** if an activity, sale, service etc is undersubscribed, not many people want it 参加者[订户，用户]不足

3 **un·der·take** /ˌʌndɚˋtek; ˌʌndəˈteɪk/ *v past tense* **undertook** /-ˋtʊk; -ˈtʊk/ *past participle* **undertaken** /-ˋtekən; -ˈteɪkən/ [T] *formal*【正式】**1** to accept that you are responsible for a piece of work, and start to do it 着手做；承担，接受：*She undertook full responsibility for the new changes.* 她为新变化承担全部责任。**2 undertake to do sth** to promise or agree to do something 答应做某事；同意做某事：*He undertook to pay the money back in six months.* 他保证六个月内还款。

un·der·tak·er /ˌʌndɚˋtekɚ; ˈʌndəteɪkə/ *n* [C] *BrE* someone whose job is to arrange funerals; FUNERAL DIRECTOR【英】承办丧葬者，殡仪员

un·der·tak·ing /ˌʌndɚˋtekɪŋ; ˌʌndəˈteɪkɪŋ/ *n* **1** [C usually singular 一般用单数] an important job, piece of work, or activity that you are responsible for 任务；事业：*Starting a new business can be a risky undertaking.* 创办新企业是一项有风险的事情。**2** [C] *formal* a promise to do something【正式】许诺，保证：*an undertaking to respect people's privacy* 尊重人们隐私的承诺 **3** [U] the business of an undertaker 丧葬事宜；殡仪业

under-the-coun·ter /ˌ‥ ·ˈ‥◂/ *adj informal* under-the-counter goods are bought or sold secretly, especially because they are illegal【非正式】〔商品〕暗中[私下]成交的；违法交易的

un·der·tone /ˈʌndɚˌton; ˈʌndətəʊn/ *n* **1** a feeling or quality that is not directly expressed but can still be recognized 潜在的情感；〔隐约的〕含意：[+of] *There was an undertone of sadness in her letter.* 她的信中流露出伤感的情绪。**2** [C] a quiet voice or sound 低声，低音 —see also 另见 OVERTONE

un·der·tow /ˈʌndɚˌto; ˈʌndətəʊ/ *n* [singular] the water current under the surface that pulls back towards the sea when a wave comes onto the shore〔海浪冲上岸后退回去时形成的〕回流，退浪

un·der·used /ˌʌndɚˋjuzd; ˌʌndəˈjuːzd◂/ *adj* something that is underused is not used as much as it could be 未充分利用的

un·der·val·ue /ˌʌndɚˋvælju; ˌʌndəˈvæljuː/ *v* [T] to think that someone or something is less important or valuable than they really are 小看，轻视；低估：*She felt that the company undervalued her work.* 她觉得公司低估了她的工作。

underwater 水下的

swimming underwater 潜泳

un·der·wa·ter /ˈʌndɚˌwɔtɚ; ˌʌndəˈwɔːtə◂/ *adj* [only before noun 仅用于名词前] below the surface of an area of water, or able to be used there 水下的；水下(使)用的：*underwater cameras* 水下摄影机 —**underwater** *adv*

un·der·way /ˌʌndɚˋwe; ˌʌndəˈweɪ/ *adj* [not before noun 不用于名词前] **1** happening now 在进行中的：*Plans to merge the two companies are already underway.* 合并两家公司的计划已经在实施中。| **get underway** (=start happening) 开始进行；启动 **2** something such as a boat or train that is underway is moving〔船、火车等〕在行进中的 —see also 另见 **under way** (WAY¹ (67))

underwear 内衣

camisole 贴身胸衣

body *BrE*【英】/ body suit *AmE*【美】女紧身衣

vest *BrE*【英】/ undershirt *AmE*【美】背心

boxer shorts 平脚短裤

underpants/pants *BrE*【英】内裤

knickers *BrE*【英】/ panties *AmE*【美】女用短衬裤

bra 乳罩

un·der·wear /ˈʌndɚˌwɛr; ˈʌndəweə/ *n* [U] clothes that you wear next to your body under your other clothes 内衣；衬衣

un·der·weight /ˈʌndɚˋwet; ˌʌndəˈweɪt/ *adj* weighing less than is expected or usual 重量不足的；标准重量以下的 —opposite 反义词 OVERWEIGHT —see 见 THIN (USAGE)

un·der·went /ˌʌndɚˋwɛnt; ˌʌndəˈwent/ the past tense of UNDERGO

un·der·whelm /ˌʌndɚˋwɛlm; ˌʌndəˈwelm/ *v* [T] *humorous* to not be very impressive【幽默】未给…留下深刻印象

un·der·world /ˈʌndɚˌwɝld; ˈʌndəwɜːld/ *n* [singular] **1** the criminals in a particular place and the criminal activities they are involved in〔某地的〕罪犯；黑社会；犯罪活动 **2** the place where the spirits of the dead are believed to live, especially in Ancient Greek stories〔尤指古希腊神话中的〕地狱，阴间

un·der·write /ˌʌndɚˋraɪt; ˌʌndəˈraɪt/ *v past tense* **underwrote** /-ˋrot; -ˈrəʊt/ *past participle* **underwritten** /-ˋrɪtn̩; -ˈrɪtn/ [T] **1** *formal* to support an activity, business plan etc with money, so that you are financially responsible for it【正式】(同意)负担…的费用；以金钱支持：*The government has agreed to underwrite the project with a grant of £5 million.* 政府已同意拨款500万英镑资助该项目。**2** *technical* to be responsible for an insurance agreement【术语】为…保险

un·der·writ·er /ˈʌndɚˌraɪtɚ; ˈʌndəˌraɪtə/ *n* [C] someone who makes insurance contracts 保险商；保险业务受理人

Underwriters' La·bor·a·tories /ˈ‥‥ ‥ˈ‥/ the full name of the UL 保险商实验室〔UL的全称〕

un·de·served /ˌʌndɪˋzɝvd; ˌʌndɪˈzɜːvd◂/ *adj* undeserved criticism, praise etc is unfair because you do not deserve it 不该受的；冤枉的；不应得的：*She had an undeserved reputation for making trouble.* 她有个爱惹麻烦的名声，真是冤枉。

un·de·sir·a·ble /ˌʌndɪˋzaɪrəbl̩; ˌʌndɪˈzaɪərəbəl◂/ *adj formal* something or someone that is undesirable is not welcome or wanted because they may affect a situation or person in a bad way【正式】不受欢迎的；不合意的；讨厌的：*The incident could have undesirable consequences for the government.* 这事件会给政府带来不良的后果。

un·de·sir·a·bles /ˌʌndɪˋzaɪrəbl̩z; ˌʌndɪˈzaɪərəbəlz/ *n* [plural] people who are considered to be immoral, criminal, or socially unacceptable 不良分子；不受欢迎的人

un·de·vel·oped /ˌʌndɪˋvɛləpt; ˌʌndɪˈveləpt◂/ *adj* not yet developed 不发达的；未成熟的；未开发的 —compare 比较 UNDERDEVELOPED

un·did /ʌnˋdɪd; ʌnˈdɪd/ the past tense of UNDO

un·dies /ˋʌndɪz; ˈʌndiːz/ *n* [plural] *informal* underwear【非正式】内衣，衬衣

un·dig·ni·fied /ʌnˋdɪgnəˌfaɪd; ʌnˈdɪgnɪ̈faɪd/ *adj* behaving in a way that is embarrassing or makes you look silly 不庄重的；有损尊严的；不像样子的：*Sally made an undignified exit with her bathrobe clutched about her.* 萨莉裹着浴衣不雅观地退了出去。

un·di·lut·ed /ˌʌndaɪˋlutɪd; ˌʌndaɪˈluːtɪ̈d◂/ *adj literary* an undiluted feeling is very strong and not mixed with any other feelings【文】〔感情〕未淡化的；没有掺杂的；纯真的：*undiluted joy* 浓浓的乐趣

un·dis·charged /ˌʌndɪsˋtʃɑrdʒd; ˌʌndɪsˈtʃɑːdʒd◂/ *adj technical*【术语】**1** an undischarged debt is one that has not been paid〔债务〕未偿清的 **2 an undischarged bankrupt** someone who still owes money and is not legally allowed to stop repaying their debt 债务未偿付的破产者

un·dis·crim·i·nat·ing /ˌʌndɪˋskrɪməˌnetɪŋ; ˌʌndɪˈskrɪmɪ̈neɪtɪŋ/ *adj* not having the ability to see a difference in value between two people or things, and therefore unable to make judgments about them 无鉴别力的；区别不了的；不加区别的

un·dis·guised /ˌʌndɪsˋgaɪzd; ˌʌndɪsˈgaɪzd◂/ *adj* clearly shown and not hidden 公开的；坦率的；不加掩饰的：*undisguised contempt* 不加掩饰的蔑视

un·di·sput·ed /ˌʌndɪˋspjutɪd; ˌʌndɪˈspjuːtɪ̈d◂/ *adj* **1** known to be definitely true 无可争辩的，毫无疑问的：*They talk about an after-life as if it were an undisputed truth.* 他们谈论来世就好像这是无可置疑的事实。**2** accepted by everyone 公认的：*The brand has now become the undisputed market leader.* 这个牌子现已成为公认的市场主导品牌。

un·dis·turbed /ˌʌndɪˋstɝbd; ˌʌndɪˈstɜːbd◂/ *adj* not interrupted or moved 没受到干扰的；未被动过的：*At last I was able to work undisturbed.* 我终于可以不受干扰地工作了。| *The documents lay undisturbed for years.* 文件有数年未曾动过。

un·di·vid·ed /ˌʌndɪˋvaɪdɪd; ˌʌndɪˈvaɪdɪ̈d◂/ *adj* complete 完整的；全部的：**undivided attention** *Please give the matter your undivided attention.* 请专心处理这件事。

un·do /ʌnˋdu; ʌnˈduː/ *v past tense* **undid** /-ˋdɪd; -ˈdɪd/ *past participle* **undone** /-ˋdʌn; -ˈdʌn/ [T] **1** to unfasten something that is tied or wrapped 解开，打开，松开〔某物〕：*She carefully undid the parcel.* 她小心翼翼地打开了包裹。—see 见 OPEN[2] (USAGE) **2** to try to remove the bad effects of something you have done 消除…的坏影响：*Well, the mistake has been made now and can't be undone.* 唉，错已铸成，无可挽回。

un·do·ing /ʌnˋduɪŋ; ʌnˈduːɪŋ/ *n* **be sb's undoing** to cause someone's shame, failure etc 是某人蒙羞[失败]的原因[祸根]：*In the end gambling was his undoing.* 最后，赌博是他堕落的原因。

un·done /ʌnˋdʌn; ˌʌnˈdʌn◂/ *adj* [not before noun 不用于名词前] **1** not fastened 解开的，松开的：**come undone** (=become unfastened) 松开了 *One of your buttons is coming undone.* 你的一个纽扣要松开了。**2 leave sth undone** not finish something 未完成某事 **3** *old use* destroyed and without hope【旧】毁掉的；完蛋了的：*I am undone! My secret has been discovered!* 我完了！秘密已经被揭穿！

W3 **un·doubt·ed** /ʌnˋdaʊtɪd; ʌnˈdaʊtɪ̈d/ *adj* definitely true or known to exist 毋庸置疑的；肯定的：*her undoubted talent* 她那毋庸置疑的天才 —**undoubtedly** *adv*: *That is undoubtedly true.* 那是千真万确的。

un·dreamed-of /ʌnˋdrimd ɑv; ʌnˈdriːmd ɒv/ also 又作 **undreamt-of** /ʌnˋdrɛmt-; ʌnˈdremt-/ *adj* much more or much better than you could imagine 梦想不到的，想象不到的：*undreamed-of wealth* 意外的财富 | *These technological advances were undreamt-of even 20 years ago.* 这些技术进步甚至在20年前还是不可想象的。

un·dress[1] /ʌnˋdrɛs; ʌnˈdres/ *v* [I,T] to take your clothes off, or take someone else's clothes off 脱去（…的）衣服

undress[2] *n* [U] *formal* a state in which you are wearing few or no clothes【正式】穿衣很少；裸体：*The dancers walked around in various stages of undress.* 舞蹈演员身穿各式暴露的装束走来走去。

un·dressed /ʌnˋdrɛst; ˌʌnˈdrest◂/ *adj* **1** [not before noun 不用于名词前] not wearing any clothes 不穿衣服的，裸体的：**get undressed** (=take your clothes off) 脱去衣服 **2** an undressed wound has not been covered to protect it〔伤口〕未包扎的

un·due /ʌnˋdu; ˌʌnˈdjuː◂/ *adj* [only before noun 仅用于名词前] *formal* more than is reasonable, suitable, or necessary【正式】不适当的；过度的，过分的：*We managed to get through Customs without undue difficulty.* 我们没费多大周折便通过了海关。

un·du·late /ˋʌndʒəˌlet; ˈʌndjʊleɪt/ *v* [I] *formal* to move or be shaped like waves that are rising and falling【正式】起伏，波动：*undulating hills* 起伏的山峦 —**undulation** /ˌʌndʒəˋleʃən; ˌʌndjʊˈleɪʃən/ *n* [C,U]

un·du·ly /ʌnˋdulɪ; ʌnˈdjuːli/ *adv formal* too extreme or too much【正式】过度地，过分地：*Perhaps I have been unduly severe in my judgment of him.* 也许我对他的评价过于苛刻了。

un·dy·ing /ʌnˋdaɪɪŋ; ʌnˈdaɪ-ɪŋ/ *adj* [only before noun 仅用于名词前] continuing for ever 不朽的；永恒的：*They declared their undying love for each other.* 他们宣称永远爱对方。

un·earth /ʌnˋɝθ; ʌnˈɜːθ/ *v* [T] **1** to find out the truth about something 揭露；发现：*The reporter had unearthed some important secrets about her.* 记者发现了有关她的一些重要秘密。**2** to find something after searching for it, especially something that has been buried in the ground 发掘，掘出〔尤指埋藏于地下的东西〕

un·earth·ly /ʌnˋɝθlɪ; ʌnˈɜːθli/ *adj* **1** very strange and unnatural 奇异的；不自然的：*I felt an unearthly presence in the room.* 我感觉房间里怪怪的。**2 unearthly hour/time etc** *informal* very early or very late and therefore extremely inconvenient【非正式】早[晚]得不合适的时间等：*We had to set off at some unearthly hour of the morning.* 我们天没亮就得动身。—**unearthliness** *n* [U]

un·ease /ʌnˋiz; ʌnˈiːz/ *n* [U] a feeling of nervousness and anxiety that makes you unable to relax 不自在；心神不宁

un·eas·y /ʌnˋizɪ; ʌnˈiːzi/ *adj* **1** nervous, anxious, and unable to relax because you think something bad might happen 心神不安的，忧虑的，不自在的：*Katie felt uneasy about what she had done.* 凯蒂对自己所做的事感到忧心忡忡。—see 见 NERVOUS (USAGE) **2** an uneasy period of time is one when people have agreed to stop fighting or arguing, but which is not really calm 不稳定的；不安定的：*An uneasy peace descended on the area.* 一种不稳定的和平降临到这个地区。**3** not comfortable, peaceful, or relaxed 不舒服的；不踏实的；不安的：*She eventually fell into an uneasy sleep.* 她最后睡着了，但睡得并不踏实。| *an uneasy conscience* 不安的良心 —**uneasily** *adv* —**uneasiness** *n* [U]

un·eat·able /ʌnˋitəbḷ; ʌnˈiːtəbəl/ *adj* a word meaning unpleasant or unsuitable to eat, that some people think is incorrect; INEDIBLE 不可食的；不适合食用的〔有些人认为这词不正确〕

un·e·co·nom·ic /ˌʌnikəˋnɑmɪk; ˌʌniːkəˈnɒmɪk◂/ *adj* **1** not making enough money or profit 赚钱不多的；利润不大的；没有效益的：*Uneconomic mines will have to be closed.* 没有效益的矿井将不得不关闭。**2** uneconomical 不经济的；浪费的

un·e·co·nom·ic·al /ˌʌnikəˋnɑməkḷ; ˌʌniːkəˈnɒmɪkəl/ *adj* using too much effort, money or materials 不经济的；浪费的：*The project was considered uneconomical and shelved.* 这个项目被认为太浪费而搁置了。—**uneconomically** /-kḷɪ; -kli/ *adv*

un·ed·u·cat·ed /ʌnˋɛdʒəˌketɪd; ʌnˈedjʊkeɪtɪ̈d/ *adj* not educated to the usual level, or showing that someone is not well educated 没受过教育的；未受过良好教育的；没有教养的：*ignorant and uneducated opinions* 无知无识的观点

un·e·mo·tion·al /ˌʌnɪˋmoʃənḷ; ˌʌnɪˈməʊʃənəl◂/ *adj* not showing your feelings 不流露感情的；冷漠的：*He remained completely unemotional as the judge read out the sentence.* 法官宣读判决时，他仍然无动于衷。

un·em·ploy·able /ˌʌnɪmˋplɔɪəbḷ; ˌʌnɪmˈplɔɪəbəl◂/ *adj* not having the skills or qualities needed to get a job〔由于缺乏必要技能或素质而〕不能被雇用的

un·em·ployed[1] /ˌʌnɪmˋplɔɪd; ˌʌnɪmˈplɔɪd◂/ *adj* without a job 未被雇用的，失业的 S2 W3

unemployed[2] *n* **the unemployed** [plural] people who have no job 失业者：**the long-term unemployed** (=people who have not had a job for a long time) 长期失业者

un·em·ploy·ment /ˌʌnɪmˋplɔɪmənt; ˌʌnɪmˈplɔɪmənt/ *n* [U] **1** the number of people in a country who do not have a job 失业人数：*levels of unemployment* 失业率 | **high unemployment** (=lots of people without a job) 高失业率 **2** the fact of having no job 失业：*Closure of the plant will mean unemployment for 500 workers.* 这家工厂的倒闭意味着500个工人要失业。**3** *AmE informal* money paid regularly by the government to people who have no job【美，非正式】失业救济金 S2 W2

unemployment ben·e·fit /ˈ···· ˌ···/ *BrE*【英】, **unemployment com·pen·sa·tion** /ˈ···· ··ˌ··/ *AmE*【美】—*n* [U] money paid regularly by the government to people who do not have a job 失业津贴；失业救济金

un·end·ing /ʌn`ɛndɪŋ; ʌn'endɪŋ/ *adj* something unpleasant or tiring that is unending seems as if it will continue for ever 无休止的, 不停的, 不断的: *an unending struggle to survive* 无休止的挣扎求存

un·en·du·ra·ble /ˌʌnɪn`djʊrəbl̩; ˌʌnɪn'djʊərəbəl◂/ *adj formal* too unpleasant, painful etc to bear【正式】不可容忍的, 难以忍受的: *The pain was unendurable.* 疼痛无法忍受。

un·en·vi·a·ble /ʌn`ɛnvɪəbl̩; ʌn'enviəbəl/ *adj* difficult and unpleasant 艰难的; 令人不快的; 尴尬的: **unenviable task** *the unenviable task of informing the victim's relations* 通知受害人亲属的为难差事

un·e·qual /ʌn`ikwəl; ʌn'iːkwəl/ *adj* **1** not equal in number, amount, or level〔数目、数量或水平〕不相等的, 不相同的: **of unequal size/length etc** *two posts of unequal length* 不同长度的两根柱子 | **be unequal in size/weight etc** *The baskets were unequal in weight and looked likely to topple.* 篮子的重量不一, 看来要倒下。**2** unfairly treating different people or groups in different ways 不平等的, 不公正的; 不均匀的: *an unequal contest* 不公平的竞赛 | *the unequal distribution of wealth* 财富的分配不均 **3 be unequal to the task/job etc** to not have enough strength, ability etc to do something 不胜任任务/工作等 —**unequally** *adv*

un·e·qualled *BrE*【英】, **unequaled** *AmE*【美】/ʌn`ikwəld; ʌn'iːkwəld/ *adj* better than any other 无可比拟的, 无与伦比的: *The school's success rate is unequalled in the area.* 该校的成功率在本地区首屈一指。

un·e·quiv·o·cal /ˌʌnɪ`kwɪvəkl̩; ˌʌnɪ'kwɪvəkəl◂/ *adj formal* completely clear and without any possibility of doubt【正式】明确的; 毫不含糊的: *His answer was an unequivocal "No".* 他的回答是毫不含糊的"不"。—**unequivocally** /-klɪ; -kli/ *adv*

un·er·ring /ʌn`ɝɪŋ; ʌn'ɜːrɪŋ/ *adj* always exactly right 一贯准确的, 毫无偏差的: **unerring accuracy/judgement etc** *Max hit the target with unerring accuracy.* 马克斯准确无误地击中了目标。—**unerringly** *adv*

UNESCO /ju`nɛsko; juː'neskəʊ/ United Nations Educational, Scientific, and Cultural Organization; a part of the UN, based in Paris, which is concerned especially with providing help for poorer countries with education and science 联合国教科文组织〔联合国下属一机构, 总部设在巴黎, 主要负责向贫困国家提供教育及科技援助〕

un·eth·i·cal /ʌn`ɛθɪkl̩; ʌn'eθɪkəl/ *adj* not obeying rules of moral behaviour, especially those concerning a profession 不道德的〔尤指违反职业道德〕: *It is considered highly unethical for a psychiatrist to have a relationship with a patient.* 精神科医生与患者发生性关系被认为是极不道德的。—**unethically** /-klɪ; -kli/ *adv*

un·e·ven /ʌn`ivən; ʌn'iːvən/ *adj* **1** not smooth, flat, or level 不平坦的, 崎岖的: *The ground was very uneven in places.* 这地上有些地方非常不平坦。**2** not regular 不规则的; 不匀的: *His breathing had become uneven.* 他的呼吸变得不均匀。**3** not equal or equally balanced 不平等的; 不平衡的: *an uneven contest* 实力不对等的竞赛 **4** good in some parts and bad in others 不稳定的, 不一致的: *a rather uneven performance* 颇不稳定的演出 —**unevenly** *adv* —**unevenness** *n* [U]

un·e·vent·ful /ˌʌnɪ`vɛntfəl; ˌʌnɪ'ventfəl◂/ *adj* with nothing exciting or unusual happening 平淡的; 平静的; 平凡的: *a quiet, uneventful life in a small town* 小镇中宁静而平淡的生活 —**uneventfully** *adv* —**uneventfulness** *n* [U]

un·ex·am·pled /ˌʌnɪg`zæmpl̩d; ˌʌnɪg'zɑːmpəld◂/ *adj formal* better than anything else of the same type; EXCEPTIONAL (1)【正式】绝无仅有的; 无先例的, 空前的

un·ex·ci·ting /ˌʌnɪk`saɪtɪŋ; ˌʌnɪk'saɪtɪŋ◂/ *adj* ordinary and slightly boring 平淡的; 单调的: *a good quality but unexciting wine* 一种优质但味道淡的葡萄酒

un·ex·pect·ed /ˌʌnɪk`spɛktɪd; ˌʌnɪk'spektɪd◂/ *adj* an unexpected event, remark etc is one that is surprising because you were not expecting it 未曾意料到的, 意外的; 突然的: *Her angry outburst was totally unexpected.* 她的勃然大怒完全出人意料。—**unexpectedly** *adv* —**unexpectedness** *n* [U]

un·ex·plained /ˌʌnɪk`splend; ˌʌnɪk'spleɪnd◂/ *adj* something that is unexplained is something you cannot understand because you do not know the reason for it 无法解释的; 莫名其妙的; 原因不明的: *her unexplained death* 她莫名其妙的死亡

un·ex·pur·gat·ed /ʌn`ɛkspɚˌgetɪd; ʌn'ekspəgeɪtɪd/ *adj* an unexpurgated book, play etc is complete and has not had parts that might offend people removed〔书、剧本等〕完整的, 未删节的

un·fail·ing /ʌn`felɪŋ; ʌn'feɪlɪŋ/ *adj* always there, even in times of difficulty or trouble 经久不衰的, 永恒的; 始终可靠的: *His unfailing good humour made him popular with everyone.* 他那始终不变的好脾气使他受到大家的欢迎。—**unfailingly** *adv*

un·fair /ʌn`fɛr; ˌʌn'feə◂/ *adj* **1** not right or fair 不公平的, 不公正的: *It's so unfair – Mary gets more money for less work!* 太不公平了——玛丽做的事少, 拿的钱却多! **2** not giving a fair or equal opportunity to everyone〔机会〕不平等的, 不均等的: *an unfair advantage* 不平等的优势 | *American workers feel threatened by unfair competition from abroad.* 美国工人感受到来自国外的不平等竞争的威胁。**3 unfair dismissal** a situation in which someone is illegally dismissed from their job 非法解雇 —**unfairly** *adv* —**unfairness** *n* [U]

un·faith·ful /ʌn`feθfəl; ʌn'feɪθfəl/ *adj* **1** someone who is unfaithful has sex with someone who is not their wife, husband, or usual partner〔对妻子、丈夫或伴侣〕不忠的, 有外遇的: **[+to]** *Edward discovered that Leonie had been unfaithful to him.* 爱德华发现利奥妮对自己不忠。**2** not loyal to a principle, person etc〔对原则、人等〕不忠诚的, 不守信的 —**unfaithfully** *adv* —**unfaithfulness** *n* [U]

un·fal·ter·ing /ʌn`fɔltərɪŋ; ʌn'fɔːltərɪŋ/ *adj formal* strong, determined, and not becoming weaker【正式】坚决的; 坚定的: *His gaze was direct and unfaltering.* 他的凝视直接而又坚定。—**unfalteringly** *adv*

un·fa·mil·i·ar /ˌʌnfə`mɪljɚ; ˌʌnfə'mɪliə◂/ *adj* not known to you 不熟悉的, 不了解的: **[+to]** *The name was unfamiliar to me.* 我对这个名字不熟悉。| **[+with]** *Voters are unfamiliar with the real issues.* 投票者对真正的议题并不了解。—**unfamiliarity** /ˌʌnfəmɪlɪ`ærətɪ; ˌʌnfəmɪli'ærɪti/ *n*

un·fash·ion·a·ble /ʌn`fæʃənəbl̩; ʌn'fæʃənəbəl/ *adj* not popular or fashionable at the present time 不流行的; 不时髦的, 过时的: *an unfashionable old dress* 过时的旧连衣裙 | *His ideas have been unfashionable for some time.* 他的想法已经相当过时。

un·fas·ten /ʌn`fæsn̩; ʌn'fɑːsn/ *v* [T] to undo something such as a button, belt, rope etc 解开〔纽扣、带子、绳子等〕: *She unfastened her blouse.* 她解开了衬衫。

un·fath·om·a·ble /ʌn`fæðəməbl̩; ʌn'fæðəməbəl/ *adj literary* too strange or mysterious to be understood【文】莫测高深的, 难解的: *the unfathomable mysteries of human nature* 人性的不解之谜 —**unfathomably** *adv*

un·fa·vou·ra·ble *BrE*【英】, **unfavorable** *AmE*【美】/ʌn`fevrəbl̩; ʌn'feɪvərəbəl/ *adj* **1** unfavourable conditions, situations etc are not as good as they should be or usually are 不适宜的; 不利的: *unfavourable weather* 不适宜的天气 **2** expressing disapproval 反对的; 不同意的: *That new television series has had unfavourable reviews.* 那部新电视连续剧得到不好的评价。—**unfavourably** *adv*

un·feel·ing /ʌn`filɪŋ; ʌn'fiːlɪŋ/ *adj* not sympathetic towards other people's feelings 无情的, 冷酷的, 冷漠的: *an unfeeling college bureaucracy* 大学里冷漠的官僚主义 —**unfeelingly** *adv*

un·fet·tered /ʌn`fɛtɚd; ʌn'fetəd/ *adj formal* not restricted by laws or rules【正式】不受〔法规〕约束的; 自由的: *free and unfettered trade* 自由、不受约束的贸易

un·fin·ished /ʌn`fɪnɪʃt; ʌn'fɪnɪʃt/ *adj* not completed 未竟的, 未完成的: *She looked away, leaving her sentence unfinished.* 她眼望别处, 话在中途打住。| **unfinished business** (=something that has to be done or dealt with that you have not yet done) 未竟之事

un·fit /ʌn`fɪt; ʌn'fɪt/ *adj* **1** not in a good physical condition 身体不健康的, 体格不佳的: *She never gets any excercise – she must be really unfit.* 她从不锻炼, 身体一定不好。| **[+for]** *He was found to be medically unfit for overseas duty.* 他体检不合格, 不能到海外执行任务。**2** not good enough for a particular purpose 不合适的, 不适宜的; 不胜任的: **[+for]** *unfit for public office* 不适宜担任公职 | **unfit for human habitation/consumption** *dwellings unfit for human habitation* 不适宜人类居住的住处

un·flag·ging /ʌn`flægɪŋ; ʌn'flægɪŋ/ *adj* continuing strongly and never becoming tired or weak 持久的; 不倦的; (经久) 不衰的: **unflagging energy/interest etc** *We couldn't have done it without your unflagging enthusiasm.* 没有你持久不衰的热情, 我们不可能完成它。—**unflaggingly** *adv*

un·flap·pa·ble /ʌn`flæpəbl̩; ʌn'flæpəbəl/ *adj informal* having the ability to stay calm and not get upset, even in difficult situations【非正式】临危不乱的, 镇定自若的: *My unflappable assistant worked steadily on as the argument raged around her.* 尽管周围争论激烈, 我那处乱不惊的助手仍从容地继续工作。—**unflappably** *adv*

un·flinch·ing /ʌn`flɪntʃɪŋ; ʌn'flɪntʃɪŋ/ *adj* not changing or becoming weaker, even in a very difficult or dangerous situation 坚定的, 不畏缩的: *unflinching courage* 无畏的勇气 —**unflinchingly** *adv*

un·fo·cused, unfocussed /ʌnˋfokəst; ʌnˈfəʊkəst/ *adj* **1** not dealing with or paying attention to the important ideas, causes etc 无焦点的；不专心的：*The discussion was becoming unfocused.* 讨论变得漫无目的。**2** eyes that are unfocused are open, but are not looking at anything〔张大眼睛〕什么都不看的；〔目光〕茫然的

un·fold /ʌnˋfold; ʌnˈfəʊld/ *v* [I,T] **1** to open something that was folded 展开，打开，摊开〔卷着的东西〕：*Chiara unfolded the map and spread it on the table.* 基娅拉摊开地图，把它铺在桌子上。**2** if a story, plan etc unfolds, it becomes clearer as you hear or learn more about it〔故事、计划等〕逐渐明确；逐渐呈现；展示：*As the tale unfolds we learn more about Max's childhood.* 随着故事的展开，我们对马克斯的童年了解得更多。

un·fore·see·a·ble /ˌʌnforˋsiəbḷ; ˌʌnfɔːˈsiːəbəl/ *adj* an unforeseeable event, situation etc could not have been expected 不可预见的；预料不到的

un·fore·seen /ˌʌnforˋsin; ˌʌnfɔːˈsiːn◂/ *adj* an unforeseen situation is one that you did not expect to happen 预料不到的，意料之外的：*unforeseen delays* 出乎意料的延迟 | **unforeseen circumstances** *Due to unforeseen circumstances, the play has been cancelled.* 由于意料不到的一些情况，这部戏取消了。

un·for·get·ta·ble /ˌʌnfɚˋgɛtəbḷ; ˌʌnfəˈgetəbəl◂/ *adj* an unforgettable experience, sight etc affects you so strongly that you will never forget it, especially because it is particularly good or beautiful〔尤指因经历、景色等极其美好而〕难以忘怀的：*The colours of New England in the fall are unforgettable.* 新英格兰秋天的缤纷色彩令人难忘。—**unforgettably** *adv*

un·for·giv·a·ble /ˌʌnfɚˋgɪvəbḷ; ˌʌnfəˈgɪvəbəl◂/ *adj* an unforgivable action is so bad or cruel that you cannot forgive the person who did it 不可原谅的；不可饶恕的：*Her husband had deceived her, and this was unforgivable.* 她丈夫欺骗了她，这是不可原谅的。—**unforgivably** *adv*

un·for·giv·ing /ˌʌnfɚˋgɪvɪŋ; ˌʌnfəˈgɪvɪŋ◂/ *adj* someone who is unforgiving does not forgive people easily〔人〕不原谅人的；无情的

un·formed /ʌnˋfɔrmd; ˌʌnˈfɔːmd◂/ *adj* not yet completely developed 未成形的；未充分发展的：*The foetus's fingers and toes are as yet unformed.* 胎儿的手指和脚趾尚未成形。

S3 **un·for·tu·nate**[1] /ʌnˋfɔrtʃənɪt; ʌnˈfɔːtʃənɪt/ *adj* **1** happening because of bad luck and often having serious or dangerous results 不幸的；倒霉的：*an unfortunate accident* 不幸的事故 | *his unfortunate death at the height of his career* 他在事业巅峰时的不幸去世 **2** an unfortunate situation is one that you wish was different or had never happened 可叹的；令人遗憾的：*an unfortunate turn of events* 事态发生的让人遗憾的变化 | **most unfortunate** *formal* (=very unfortunate)【正式】非常不幸；真遗憾 *It's most unfortunate that your father can't come to the wedding.* 真遗憾，你父亲不能来参加婚礼。**3** *formal* unfortunate behaviour, remarks etc make people feel embarrassed or offended【正式】不适宜的，不得体的；粗野的：*I thought his choice of music was a little unfortunate.* 我认为他挑选的音乐有点不恰当。

unfortunate[2] *n* [C] *literary* someone who has no money, home, job etc【文】不幸的人

S1 W3 **un·for·tu·nate·ly** /ʌnˋfɔrtʃənɪtlɪ; ʌnˈfɔːtʃənɪ̥tli/ *adv* [sentence adverb 句子副词] used when you are mentioning a fact that you wish were not true 不幸地；令人遗憾地：*Unfortunately, you were out when we called.* 很遗憾，我们打电话时你出去了。

un·found·ed /ʌnˋfaʊndɪd; ʌnˈfaʊndɪ̥d/ *adj* statements, feelings, opinions etc that are unfounded are wrong because they are not based on true facts 没有事实根据的；无稽的；虚幻的：*Fears about the side-effects are largely unfounded.* 对副作用的担心大多没有事实根据。

un·fre·quent·ed /ˌʌnfrɪˋkwɛntɪd; ˌʌnfrɪˈkwentɪ̥d◂/ *adj formal* not often visited by many people【正式】人迹罕至的；冷落的：*an unfrequented spot* 人迹罕至的地方

un·frock /ʌnˋfrɑk; ʌnˈfrɒk/ *v* [T usually passive 一般用被动态] to remove someone from their position as a priest as a punishment for behaviour or beliefs that the church does not approve of 免去〔牧师或神父〕的圣职 —**unfrocked** *adj*

un·ful·filled /ˌʌnfʊlˋfɪld; ˌʌnfʊlˈfɪld◂/ *adj* **1** a wish, desire, hope etc that is unfulfilled has not been achieved 未实现的；未达到的：*All her own dreams and ambitions remained unfulfilled.* 她所有的梦想和抱负仍未实现。**2** someone who is unfulfilled feels they could be achieving more in their job, relationship etc〔人在工作、关系等上〕未得到满足的：*Her job left her feeling unfulfilled and unappreciated.* 她的工作使她感到壮志未酬，怀才不遇。

un·furl /ʌnˋfɝl; ʌnˈfɜːl/ *v* [T] to unroll and open a flag, sail etc 打开，展开〔旗、帆等〕

un·fur·nished /ʌnˋfɝnɪʃt; ʌnˈfɜːnɪʃt/ *adj* an unfurnished room, house etc has no furniture in it 无家具设备的

un·gain·ly /ʌnˋgenlɪ; ʌnˈgeɪnli/ *adj* moving in a way that does not look graceful〔动作〕笨拙的；难看的；不优雅的：*I had been a tall, ungainly teenager with a bad haircut and National Health glasses.* 我十几岁时个子高，动作笨拙，发型难看，还戴着国民保健制度免费提供的眼镜。—**ungainliness** *n* [U]

un·glued /ʌnˋglud; ʌnˈgluːd/ *adj* **come unglued** *AmE informal*【美，非正式】**a)** to become extremely upset or angry about something 烦恼不堪；异常愤怒：*Pat came unglued when I told him about the accident.* 当我把事故告诉帕特时，他不安极了。**b)** if your plans come unglued, they do not work well〔计划〕落空

un·god·ly /ʌnˋgɑdlɪ; ʌnˈgɒdli/ *adj* **1** [only before noun 仅用于名词前] *informal* an ungodly time or noise is unreasonable and annoying【非正式】〔时间或噪音〕不合情理的，恼人的，不适当的：*Why did you wake me up at such an ungodly hour?* 你怎么在这个时候把我叫醒？**2** *literary* showing a lack of respect for God【文】不敬神的，不虔诚的

un·gov·er·na·ble /ʌnˋgʌvɚnəbḷ; ʌnˈgʌvənəbəl/ *adj* **1** *formal* feelings that are ungovernable are impossible to control【正式】〔感情〕难控制的：**ungovernable temper** (=extreme anger that cannot be controlled) 难以控制的暴怒 **2** a country or area that is ungovernable is one in which the people cannot be controlled by the government, the police etc〔国家或地区〕难统治[控制]的

un·gra·cious /ʌnˋgreʃəs; ʌnˈgreɪʃəs/ *adj* not polite or friendly, especially towards someone who has said they are sorry to you or are being friendly to you〔尤指对已经道歉或表示友好的人〕无礼的，粗野的 —**ungraciously** *adv*

un·grate·ful /ʌnˋgretfəl; ʌnˈgreɪtfəl/ *adj* not expressing thanks for something that someone has given to you or done for you 忘恩负义的；不领情的：*Don't be so ungrateful!* 不要如此忘恩负义！—**ungratefully** *adv* —**ungratefulness** *n* [U]

un·guard·ed /ʌnˋgɑrdɪd; ʌnˈgɑːdɪ̥d/ *adj* **1** an unguarded remark, statement etc is one that you make carelessly without thinking of the possible effects〔说话、声明等〕粗心大意的；不慎重的，轻率的 **2 in an unguarded moment** at a time when you are not paying attention to what you are doing or saying 一不留神；一不小心：*In an unguarded moment, I told her I was leaving.* 我一不留神，告诉她我要走了。

un·guent /ˋʌŋgwənt; ˈʌŋgwənt/ *n* [C] *literary* an oily substance used on your skin; OINTMENT【文】油膏，软膏

un·hand /ʌnˋhænd; ʌnˈhænd/ *v* [T] *old use* to stop holding someone you have caught【旧】放开〔某人〕：*Unhand me, sir!* 放了我吧，先生！

un·hap·pi·ly /ʌnˋhæpɪlɪ; ʌnˈhæpḷi/ *adv* **1** in a way that shows you are not happy 不高兴地：*Zack looked at her unhappily.* 扎克不高兴地看着她。**2** [sentence adverb 句子副词] *old-fashioned* used when you are mentioning a fact that you wish were not true; UNFORTUNATELY【过时】不幸地，令人遗憾地：*Unhappily, she was not able to complete the course.* 很遗憾，她不能完成这门课程。

un·hap·py /ʌnˋhæpɪ; ʌnˈhæpi/ *adj* **unhappier, unhappiest** **1** not happy 不幸福的；不快乐的：*If you're so unhappy, why don't you change jobs?* 你要是这么不快乐，为什么不换换工作？**2** feeling worried or annoyed because you do not like what is happening in a situation 忧愁的；不满的：**[+about]** *We were unhappy about the press reports of the demonstration.* 我们对有关游行示威的新闻报道感到不满。| **[+with]** *If you're unhappy with your results, you can always take the exam again.* 你如果对成绩不满意，不论什么时候都可以重考。**3** *formal* an unhappy remark, situation etc is unsuitable or unlucky【正式】不适当的；不幸运的：*an unhappy turn of phrase* 不恰当的措辞 | *an unhappy coincidence* 不幸的巧合 —**unhappily** *adv* —**unhappiness** *n* [U] S3 W3

un·harmed /ʌnˋhɑrmd; ʌnˈhɑːmd/ *adj* [not before noun 不用于名词前] not hurt or harmed 未受伤（害）的；无恙的，平安的：*They managed to escape unharmed.* 他们得以平安脱险。

UNHCR /ˌju ɛn ˌetʃ si ˋɑr; juː en ˌeɪtʃ siː ˈɑː/ United Nations High Commission for Refugees; an international organization that is part of the UN and is responsible for giving help and support to REFUGEES (=people who have been forced to leave their country, because of wars, political problems etc) 联合国难民事务高级专员公署〔联合国下属一国际机构，负责向难民提供帮助和支援〕

un·health·y /ʌnˋhɛlθɪ; ʌnˈhelθi/ *adj* **1** likely to make you ill 对健康有害的；不卫生的：*unhealthy living conditions* 不利于健

康的生活条件 **2** not healthy 不健康的: *unhealthy children who don't get enough exercise* 缺乏锻炼的不健康的孩子 **3** unhealthy skin, hair etc shows that you are ill or not healthy〔皮肤、头发等〕显出病态的, 显得不健康的: *an unhealthy pale complexion* 苍白的病容 **4** behaviour that is unhealthy is not normal and may be harmful〔行为〕反常的; 病态的: **an unhealthy interest in** *Gareth had an unhealthy interest in death.* 加雷思对死亡有种病态的兴趣。—**unhealthily** *adv* —**unhealthiness** *n* [U]

un·heard /ʌnˋhɝd; ˌʌnˈhɜːd/ *adj* [not before noun 不用于名词前] not listened to 没听到的; 不予倾听的: **go unheard** *Her cries for help went unheard.* 没有人听到她的呼救声。

unheard-of /·ˈ··ˌ·/ *adj* something that is unheard-of is so unusual that it has not happened or been known before 前所未闻的; 空前的: *It's unheard-of for anyone to pass the exam so young.* 从未听说过有人这么年轻就通过了考试。

un·heed·ed /ʌnˈhidɪd; ʌnˈhiːdɨd/ *adj literary* noticed but not listened to, accepted, or believed【文】没有受到注意的, 被忽视的: **go unheeded** *Her prayers went unheeded.* 她的祈祷并无效验。

un·help·ful /ʌnˋhɛlpfəl; ʌnˈhelpfəl/ *adj* not willing or able to help in a situation and sometimes making it worse 不予帮助的; 不起帮助作用的, 无用的: *The authorities are being particularly unhelpful.* 当局尤其不予帮助。—**unhelpfully** *adv* —**unhelpfulness** *n* [U]

un·her·ald·ed /ʌnˋhɛrəldɪd; ʌnˈherəldɨd/ *adj formal* not previously announced or mentioned【正式】未事先宣布的; 未预告的

un·hinge /ʌnˋhɪndʒ; ʌnˈhɪndʒ/ *v* [T] to make someone become mentally ill 使〔某人〕精神失常, 使错乱: *The terrible experience seemed to have unhinged him slightly.* 这一可怕的经历似乎使他有点精神失常了。—**unhinged** *adj*

un·hip /ʌnˋhɪp; ʌnˈhɪp/ *adj slang* unfashionable【俚】不时髦的

un·hitch /ʌnˋhɪtʃ; ʌnˈhɪtʃ/ *v* [T] **1** to unfasten something that is joined to something else 解开; 放松 **2 get unhitched** *AmE informal* to get divorced (DIVORCE[1] (1))【美, 非正式】离婚, 离异

un·ho·ly /ʌnˋholɪ; ʌnˈhəʊli/ *adj* **1** [only before noun 仅用于名词前] *informal* unreasonable and annoying【非正式】不合理的; 惹人讨厌的: *The kids were making an unholy noise in the playroom.* 孩子们在游戏室发出讨厌的吵嚷声。**2** not holy or not respecting what is holy 不神圣的; 不虔敬的; 亵渎的 **3 unholy alliance** an unusual agreement between two people or organizations who would not normally work together, usually for a bad purpose 邪恶的同盟

U

un·hoped-for /ʌnˋhopt ˌfɔr; ʌnˈhəʊpt fɔː/ *adj* much better than had been expected 没有料到的, 出乎意料的: *unhoped-for success* 意外的成功

un·hur·ried /ʌnˋhɝɪd; ʌnˈhʌrid/ *adj* done slowly and calmly 不慌不忙的, 从容不迫的; 悠闲的: *He began to sketch with precise, unhurried strokes.* 他开始不慌不忙、一丝不苟地画起素描来。—**unhurriedly** *adv*

un·hurt /ʌnˋhɝt; ʌnˈhɜːt/ *adj* [not before noun 不用于名词前] not hurt 未受伤害的: *He was shaken and frightened, but unhurt.* 他受到惊吓, 但没有受伤。

u·ni /ˈjunɪ; ˈjuːni/ *n* [C] *BrE, AustrE spoken* university【英, 澳, 口】大学

uni- /junɪ; juːnɨ/ *prefix* one; single 单, 一: *unidirectional* 单向(性)的

UNICEF /ˈjunɪsef; ˈjuːnɨsef/ *n* United Nations International Children's Fund; an organization that helps children in the world suffering from disease, HUNGER etc 联合国儿童基金会

u·ni·corn /ˈjunɪˌkɔrn; ˈjuːnɨkɔːn/ *n* [C] an imaginary animal like a white horse with a long straight horn growing on its head〔传说中似白马的〕独角兽

u·ni·cy·cle /ˈjunɪˌsaɪkḷ; ˈjuːniˌsaɪkəl/ *n* [C] a vehicle that is like a bicycle but has only one wheel 独轮(自行)车

un·i·den·ti·fied /ˌʌnaɪˋdɛntɪˌfaɪd; ˌʌnaɪˈdentɨfaɪd◂/ *adj* an unidentified person or thing is one that you do not recognize, do not know the name of etc 未辨别出来的; 身份不明的: *An unidentified man was spotted near the scene of the crime.* 有人在犯罪现场附近发现了一个身份不明的男子。

u·ni·fi·ca·tion /ˌjunəfəˋkeʃən; ˌjuːnɨfɨˈkeɪʃən/ *n* [U] the act of combining separate countries to make a single country with one government〔国家的〕统一: *the unification of Germany* 德国的统一

Unification Church, the /ˌ····ˈ··, ·/ the official name for the Moonies 统一教团〔Moonies 的正式名称〕

3 **u·ni·form**[1] /ˈjunəˌfɔrm; ˈjuːnɨfɔːm/ *n* [C,U] **1** a particular type of clothing worn by all the members of a group or organization such as the police, the army etc〔警察、军人等穿的〕制服: *school uniform* 校服 **2 be in uniform a)** to be wearing a uniform 穿着制服 **b)** to be a member of the army, navy etc 做一名军人, 当兵

uniform[2] *adj* being the same in all its parts or among all its members 全部相同的, 一致的: *a plank of uniform width* 一块宽度均匀的木板 —**uniformly** *adv*

u·ni·formed /ˈjunəˌfɔrmd; ˈjuːnɨfɔːmd/ *adj* wearing a uniform 穿制服的: *uniformed police officers* 穿制服的警察

u·ni·form·i·ty /ˌjunəˋfɔrmətɪ; ˌjuːnɨˈfɔːmɨti/ *n* [U] the quality of being or looking the same as all other members of a group 相同(性); 统一(性); 一致(性): *the dull uniformity of the houses in the area* 该地区的房屋千篇一律

u·ni·fy /ˈjunəˌfaɪ; ˈjuːnɨfaɪ/ *v* [T] **1** to combine the parts of a country, organization etc to make a single unit 统一〔国家、组织等〕, 使成一体: *Spain was unified in the 16th century.* 西班牙是在16世纪统一的。**2** to change a group of things so that they are all the same 使相同, 使一致

u·ni·lat·e·ral /ˌjunɪˋlætərəl; ˌjuːnɨˈlætərəl◂/ *adj formal* a unilateral action or decision is done by only one of the groups involved in a situation【正式】〔行动或决定〕一方的, 单边的; 单方面的: *a unilateral declaration of independence* 单方面宣布独立 | **unilateral disarmament** (=the process of a country getting rid of its own NUCLEAR weapons without waiting for other countries to do the same) 单方面(核)裁军 —compare 比较 BILATERAL, MULTILATERAL —**unilateralism** *n* —**unilaterally** *adv*

un·i·ma·gin·a·ble /ˌʌnɪˋmædʒɪnəbḷ; ˌʌnɪˈmædʒɨnəbəl◂/ *adj* not possible to imagine 不能想象的, 想象不到的: *an unimaginable amount of money* 想象不到的款额

un·i·ma·gin·a·tive /ˌʌnɪˋmædʒɪnətɪv; ˌʌnɪˈmædʒɨnətɪv◂/ *adj* **1** lacking the ability to think of new or unusual ideas 缺乏想象力的 **2** too ordinary and boring 平淡的, 无趣的: *an unimaginative shop window display* 单调的橱窗陈设 **3** an unimaginative solution to a problem does not work very well because it does not involve any new or intelligent ideas 无新意的; 无创见的: *unimaginative housing policies* 无创意的住房政策

un·im·paired /ˌʌnɪmˋpɛrd; ˌʌnɪmˈpeəd◂/ *adj* not damaged by an unpleasant or unlucky experience 未受损的: *She survived the accident with her sight unimpaired.* 她从事故中幸存下来, 视力也未受损伤。

un·im·pea·cha·ble /ˌʌnɪmˋpitʃəbḷ; ˌʌnɪmˈpiːtʃəbəl◂/ *adj formal* so good or definite that criticism or doubt is impossible【正式】无可指摘的, 无懈可击的; 不容置疑的; 可靠的: *unimpeachable moral principles* 无可指摘的道德原则 —**unimpeachably** *adv*

un·im·por·tant /ˌʌnɪmˋpɔrtn̩t; ˌʌnɪmˈpɔːtənt◂/ *adj* not important 不重要的: *Women's issues were assumed to be unimportant, especially in the political arena.* 妇女问题总被认为无关紧要, 特别是在政治舞台上。

un·im·pressed /ˌʌnɪmˋprɛst; ˌʌnɪmˈprest/ *adj* not thinking that someone or something is good, interesting, unusual etc 没有印象的; 未受感动的: *Jay seemed unimpressed by the array of finery.* 杰伊似乎不为一系列的华丽服饰所动。

un·im·pres·sive /ˌʌnɪmˋprɛsɪv; ˌʌnɪmˈpresɪv◂/ *adj* someone or something that is unimpressive is not as good, large, important, skilful etc as you expected or as they are supposed to be 给人印象不深的; 不惹人注意的; 平淡的: *The new building is singularly unimpressive.* 新大楼非常不起眼。

un·in·formed /ˌʌnɪnˋfɔrmd; ˌʌnɪnˈfɔːmd◂/ *adj* not having enough knowledge or information 无知的; 不了解情况的: *uninformed criticism* 无根据的批评 —see also 另见 INFORMED

un·in·hab·it·a·ble /ˌʌnɪnˋhæbɪtəbḷ; ˌʌnɪnˈhæbɨtəbəl◂/ *adj* **1** an uninhabitable place is impossible to live in 不能居住的 **2** an uninhabitable house or apartment is too dirty, cold etc to live in〔房子或公寓〕不适于居住的〈如太肮脏、太冷等〉—opposite 反义词 HABITABLE

un·in·hab·it·ed /ˌʌnɪnˋhæbɪtɪd; ˌʌnɪnˈhæbɨtɨd◂/ *adj* an uninhabited place does not have anyone living there 无人居住的; 杳无人迹的: *an uninhabited island* 杳无人迹的荒岛

un·in·hib·it·ed /ˌʌnɪnˋhɪbɪtɪd; ˌʌnɪnˈhɪbɨtɨd◂/ *adj* expressing your feelings easily without feeling embarrassed 不受约束的; 无拘无束的; 随意的: *uninhibited laughter* 开怀大笑 —**uninhibitedly** *adv*

un·i·ni·ti·at·ed /ˌʌnɪˋnɪʃɪˌetɪd; ˌʌnɪˈnɪʃieɪtɨd◂/ *n* **the uninitiated** [plural] people who do not have special knowledge or experience of something 无某种专业知识[经验]者: *To the uninitiated, this will make little sense.* 对非专业人士来说, 这并无什么意义。—**uninitiated** *adj*

un·in·spired /ˌʌnɪnˋspaɪrd; ˌʌnɪnˈspaɪəd◂/ *adj* not showing any imagination 缺乏创见的, 没有想象力的; 平凡的: *an uninspired performance* 毫无创意的演出

un·in·spir·ing /ˌʌnɪnˋspaɪrɪŋ; ˌʌnɪnˈspaɪərɪŋ/ *adj* not at all interesting or exciting 引不起兴趣的；不令人振奋的：*an uninspiring piece of architecture* 一幢呆板的建筑

un·in·tel·li·gi·ble /ˌʌnɪnˋtɛlədʒəbl; ˌʌnɪnˈtelɪ̆dʒɪ̆bəl◂/ *adj* impossible to understand 难以理解的，晦涩难懂的：*Eva muttered something unintelligible.* 伊娃咕哝了些无人能懂的话。—**unintelligibly** *adv*

un·in·ten·tion·al /ˌʌnɪnˋtɛnʃənl; ˌʌnɪnˈtenʃənəl◂/ *adj* not said or done deliberately 不是故意的，无心的：*I know she upset you, but I'm sure it was unintentional.* 我知道她惹你心烦，但我肯定这不是故意的。—**unintentionally** *adv*

un·in·terest·ed /ʌnˋɪntərɪstɪd; ʌnˈɪntrɪ̆stɪ̆d/ *adj* not interested 不感兴趣的；不关心的：[+in] *Kevin seems uninterested in learning anything.* 凯文似乎对学任何东西都不感兴趣。—compare 比较 DISINTERESTED

un·in·ter·rupt·ed /ˌʌnɪntəˋrʌptɪd; ˌʌnɪntəˈrʌptɪ̆d◂/ *adj* continuous 不间断的，连续的：*a long, uninterrupted sleep* 长时间的连续睡眠 —**uninterruptedly** *adv*

un·in·vit·ed /ˌʌnɪnˋvaɪtɪd; ˌʌnɪnˈvaɪtɪ̆d◂/ *adj* not having been asked for 未被邀请的：*uninvited guests* 不速之客

un·in·vit·ing /ˌʌnɪnˋvaɪtɪŋ; ˌʌnɪnˈvaɪtɪŋ◂/ *adj* an uninviting place seems unattractive or unpleasant〔地方〕无吸引力的；令人讨厌的：*an uninviting, desolate landscape* 一派索然无味的荒凉景象

S1 W1 **u·nion** /ˋjunjən; ˈjuːnjən/ *n* **1** [C] an organization formed by workers to protect their rights; TRADE UNION 工会：*the air traffic controllers' union* 空中交通调度员工会 **2** a group of countries or states with the same central government 联邦；联盟：*the Soviet Union* 苏联 **3** [singular,U] *formal* the act of joining two or more things together or the state of being joined together【正式】联合，合并；结合：*The artist's work shows the perfect union of craftsmanship and imagination.* 这位艺术家的作品表现出技艺和想象力的完美结合。| [+with] *Scotland's union with England in 1603* 1603 年苏格兰与英格兰的合并 **4** [singular,U] *formal* marriage【正式】结婚，婚姻

U·nion·is·m /ˋjunjənɪzṃ; ˈjuːnjənɪzəm/ *n* [U] the principles of those people in Northern Ireland, mainly Protestants, who want Northern Ireland to remain as part of the UK. There are several political parties that support these principles, including the Ulster Unionists and the Democratic Unionist Party. 统一主义〔指以新教徒为主的部分北爱尔兰人的政治主张。他们要求北爱尔兰继续留在英国。这一主张得到北爱尔兰统一党、民主统一党等政党的支持〕—**Unionist** *n, adj*

unionism *n* [U] belief in the principles of TRADE UNIONS 工会主义；工联主义

U·nion·ist /ˋjunjənɪst; ˈjuːnjənɪ̆st/ *n* [C] a member of a political party that wants Northern Ireland to remain part of the United Kingdom〔主张北爱尔兰仍与英国保持统一的〕统一党党员 —**Unionism** *n* [U]

u·nion·ize also 又作 -ise *BrE*【英】/ˋjunjənˌaɪz; ˈjuːnjənaɪz/ *v* [I,T] if workers unionize or are unionized, they become members of a TRADE UNION (使) 成立工会；(使) 加入工会 —**unionization** /ˌjunjənəˋzeʃən; ˌjuːnjənaɪˈzeɪʃən/ *n* [U]

Union Jack /ˌ·· ˈ·/ *n* [C] the national flag of Great Britain and Northern Ireland 联合王国国旗，英国国旗

Union of So·vi·et So·cia·list Re·pub·lics, the /ˌ··· ,··· ,··· ·ˈ··/ the full name of the Soviet Union 苏维埃社会主义共和国联盟〔苏联的全称〕

Union Sta·tion /ˌ·· ˈ··/ the name of the main passenger train station in many US cities 联合火车站〔美国许多城市主要客运火车站的名称〕：*Chicago Union Station* 芝加哥联合火车站

u·nion suit /ˈ·· ˌ·/ *n* [C] *AmE* woollen underwear that covers the whole body【美】连衣裤；COMBINATIONS *BrE*【英】

S3 W2 **u·nique** /juˋnik; juːˈniːk/ *adj* **1** [no comparative 无比较级] being the only one of its kind 独一无二的；独特的：*Each person's fingerprints are unique.* 每个人的指纹都是不同的。**2** *informal* unusually good and special【非正式】极好的；难得的，不同寻常的；特别的：*a unique opportunity to travel* 难得的旅行机会 —**uniquely** *adv*: *an actor uniquely suited to the part* 唯一适合该角色的演员 —**uniqueness** *n* [U]

USAGE NOTE 用法说明: UNIQUE

WORD CHOICE 词语辨析: **unique, only**

If you want to say that something has features or qualities that make it different from anything else, especially when this makes it better, you say it is **unique**. unique表示某物具有独特之处，尤其是使之变得更为优秀：*His interpretation of the original screenplay is quite unique.* 他对这部原创电影剧本的解读确有独到之处。| *a style of folk art unique to these tribespeople* (=they are the only people who do it). 这些部落人独具的民间艺术风格。

If you want to say that there is just one of something available in a particular place at a particular time out of all the others that may exist, you say it is the **only** one. only 表示在某时某地独有的：*She was the only woman doctor in the district.* 她是该区唯一的女医生。| *After the attack, only one building was left standing.* 攻击过后，只有一栋楼还矗立着。

GRAMMAR 语法

Before a singular noun **unique** usually follows *a*, **only** often follows *the*. 用在单数名词前，unique 前面通常加 a；only 经常前面加 the：*This is a unique opportunity/the only opportunity I'll get.* 这是一次难得的机会/我能得到的唯一机会。

Many people think it is not correct to say something is *fairly* or *rather unique*, or *very unique*, as if **unique** can only be used in sense one. However, native speakers will often say this, because they are using **unique** in sense two to mean **unusual** or **special**. 许多人认为说某事 fairly 或 rather unique，或 very unique 不正确，似乎 unique 只能用于释义 1。然而母语为英语的人常这样说，他们用的是 unique 释义 2 的意思，即"难得的"或"特别的"。

u·ni·sex /ˋjunəsɛks; ˈjuːnɪseks/ *adj* intended for both men and women 不分男女的，男女皆适用的：*a unisex hairdressing salon* 男女通用的美发厅

u·ni·son /ˋjunəsn̩; ˈjuːnɪ̆sən/ *n* **1 in unison a)** if people speak in unison, they say the same words at the same time 一起〔说〕；齐声：*"No way!" the twins replied in unison.* "不行!"双胞胎异口同声地回答。**b)** if two groups, governments etc do something in unison they do it together because they agree with each other 共同〔做某事〕，一致：*Management and workers must act in unison to compete with foreign business.* 管理层和员工必须行动一致，与外国企业竞争。**2** [C] a way of singing or playing music in which everyone plays or sings the same tune〔音乐中的〕齐奏；齐唱

u·nit /ˋjunɪt; ˈjuːnɪ̆t/ *n* [C] W3

1 ▶PART 部分◀ a thing, person or group that is regarded as one single whole part of something larger 单位，单元〔指构成更大整体的人、物、群体〕：*The family is the smallest social unit.* 家庭是社会最小的基本单位。

2 ▶GROUP 团体◀ a group of people working together as part of the structure of a larger group, organization, company etc 科；室；部门：*She works in the emergency unit at the hospital.* 她在医院的急诊室工作。

3 ▶FOR MEASURING 用于计量◀ an amount or quantity of something used as a standard of measurement〔计量用的〕单位：[+of] *The dollar is the basic unit of currency in the US.* 美元是美国的基本货币单位。| *The patient was given 2 units of blood.* 给病人输了两个单位的血。

4 ▶FURNITURE 家具◀ a piece of furniture such as a cupboard, especially one that can be fitted to others of the same type〔家具的〕组合件，一套中的一件：**kitchen/office/storage unit** (=a unit designed for the kitchen etc) 厨房/办公室/贮藏设备组合件

5 ▶PART OF A MACHINE 机器的部分◀ a piece of machinery which is part of a larger machine〔机械的〕部件，元件：**control/filter/cooling unit** *The cooling unit must be replaced.* 冷却元件必须更换。

6 ▶PART OF A BOOK 书的部分◀ one of the numbered parts into which a TEXTBOOK (=a book used in schools) is divided〔教科书中的〕单元

7 ▶PRODUCT 产品◀ *technical* a single complete product made by a company【术语】一台[一套]成品：*The factory's output is now up to 150,000 units each month.* 这家工厂的产量现已上升到每月 15 万台。

8 ▶SCHOOL/UNIVERSITY 学校/大学◀ *AmE* an amount of work that a student needs to do in a particular course【美】〔课程的〕学习量

9 ▶APARTMENT 公寓◀ *AmE* a single apartment in a larger building【美】〔大楼中的〕一套住房

10 ▶NUMBER 数字◀ **a)** *technical* the smallest whole number; the number 1【术语】最小整数，〔数字〕1 **b)** any whole number less than ten 十以下的整数，个位数：*hundreds, tens, and units* 百位数、十位数和个位数

U·ni·ta·ri·an /ˌjunəˋtɛrɪən; ˌjuːnɪ̆ˈteəriən◂/ *adj* connected with a Christian group that believes its members should be free to believe what they want〔基督教中主张信仰自由的〕一位论教派的 —**unitarian** *n* [C]

U·ni·tas /juˈnaɪtəs; juːˈnaɪtəs/, **Johnny** (1933-2002) a US football player who was a famous QUARTERBACK for the Baltimore Colts team from 1956 to 1972. He was called 'the Golden Arm' because the passes he threw often became TOUCHDOWN*s* (=actions that win points). 尤尼塔斯〔(1933-2002)，美国橄榄球运动员，著名的四分卫。1956至1972年效力于巴尔的摩马驹队，因传出的球经常过对方球门线得分而被誉为"金臂"〕

u·nite /juˈnaɪt; juːˈnaɪt/ *v* [I,T] to join together with other people, organizations to achieve something 联合，团结: *two nations that are united by a bond of friendship* 以友谊的纽带联合起来的两个民族 | [+in/against/behind] *In a crisis, party members will always unite behind their leader.* 在危机中，党员总会团结起来支持他们的领导人。| **unite to do sth** *We must unite to fight against racism.* 我们必须联合起来反对种族主义。

U·nit·ed /juˈnaɪtɪd; juːˈnaɪtɪ̈d/ a word used in the names of many British football clubs 联队〔用于英国许多足球俱乐部的名称之中〕: *Manchester United* 曼彻斯特联队 | *We're going to the football on Saturday – United are playing Arsenal.* 我们周六要去看一场足球赛，联队对阿森纳队。

united *adj* **1** joined or closely connected by feelings, aims etc 团结的，联合的，统一的: *working for a united Europe* 致力于建设一个统一的欧洲 **2** involving or done by everyone 共同的，一致的: *a united effort to clean up the environment* 共同努力使环境清洁 —**unitedly** *adv*

United Ar·ab Em·ir·ates, the /·,·· ,·· '··/ abbreviation 缩写为 **UAE** a country in the Middle East, between Qatar and Oman, made up of seven small EMIRATE*s*, including Abu Dhabi and Dubai. Population: 2,407,000 (2001). Capital: Abu Dhabi. The land is mainly desert, but the country sells a lot of oil. 阿拉伯联合酋长国〔中东一国家。位于卡塔尔与阿曼之间，由七个小酋长国组成，其中包括阿布扎比和迪拜。人口: 2,407,000 (2001)，首都: 阿布扎比。该国大部分地区为沙漠，盛产石油〕

United Ar·tists /·,·· '··/ *trademark* a large US film company based in Hollywood, which has made many famous films【商标】联艺公司〔美国一大型电影公司。总部设在好莱坞，制作过不少著名影片〕

United Farm Work·ers /·,·· '· ,··/ abbreviation 缩写为 **UFW** a TRADE UNION in the US for people who work on farms, especially poor MIGRANT workers who pick fruit and vegetables at many different farms in order to earn enough to live 农场工人联合会〔美国一工会组织。成员为农场工人，尤其是贫穷的流动农场工人。他们辗转于各农场之间靠采摘蔬菜、水果维持生计〕

United King·dom, the /·,·· '··/ a country in northwest Europe, officially called the United Kingdom of Great Britain and Northern Ireland, made up of England, Wales, Scotland, and Northern Ireland. Population: 58,789,194 (2001). Capital: London. The name 'United Kingdom' was first used in 1707, when the parliaments of England and Scotland united to form one country. The country's government consists of a Queen or King, a Prime Minister, and two Houses of Parliament, the House of Commons and the House of Lords. The United Kingdom has been a member of the EU since 1972. 联合王国〔欧洲西北部一国家，正式名称为大不列颠及北爱尔兰联合王国，由英格兰、威尔士、苏格兰、北爱尔兰组成。人口: 58,789,194 (2001)，首都: 伦敦。"联合王国"一名最早见于1707年，当时英格兰和苏格兰议会合并，组成一个统一国家。其政府由女王(或国王)、首相、议会组成，议会分为上议院和下议院两院。1972年开始成为欧盟成员国〕—see also 另见 ENGLAND; NORTHERN IRELAND; SCOTLAND; WALES

United Na·tions /·,·· '··/ *n* [singular] an international organization that tries to find peaceful solutions to world problems 联合国

United Nations High Com·mis·sion for Ref·u·gees /·,··,·· ·· ·,·· ·,·· '·/ the full name of the UNHCR 联合国难民事务高级专员公署〔UNHCR 的全称〕

United Ne·gro Col·lege Fund /·,·· ,·· '·· ,·/ a CHARITY organization in the US which gives money and support to black students and black universities 黑人大学联合基金会〔美国一慈善机构，专为黑人学生及黑人大学提供资助〕

United Re·formed Church /·,·· ·,·· ,·/ a Christian religious group that formed in 1972 when the Presbyterian Church of England joined with the Congressional Church of England and Wales 联合归正教会〔1972年英格兰长老教会与英格兰及威尔士公理会合并而成的一个基督教会〕

United States of A·mer·i·ca, the /·,·· ,·· ·'···/ also 又作 **the United States, the US, the USA** a country in North America, made up of 50 states and the District of Columbia, where the capital is. Population: 278,059,000 (2001). Capital: Washington, D.C. The United States is the world's most important industrial nation, and one of its richest countries. With its powerful armed forces, it is the world's only real military 'superpower'. The US is often called 'America', but this is not really correct. 美利坚合众国〔简称美国。北美洲一国家，由50个州及首都所在地哥伦比亚特区组成。人口: 278,059,000 (2001)，首都: 华盛顿哥伦比亚特区。美国是世界上最重要的工业国家，也是最富裕的国家之一。该国军力强大，是当今世界上唯一真正意义上的军事"超级大国"。常被称作America，但这一称谓并不完全准确〕—see 见 AMERICA

CULTURAL NOTE 文化注释

People 人民

The Native American people, who lived in the US before Europeans came, now form only about 1% of the population. The rest is made up mainly of people whose families were IMMIGRANT*s* (=people who leave their own country to go and live somewhere else) and of African-Americans whose families were originally brought to the US from Africa to work as SLAVE*s*. European immigrants, from places such as Britain, Ireland, Poland, Italy, and Scandinavia, came to the US mainly in the 19th and early 20th centuries. More recently, many HISPANIC people have come to the US from places such as Puerto Rico and Mexico, and there have also been immigrants from Asian countries such as Korea, Japan, and China. 在欧洲人到来之前就一直居住在美洲的土著现在只占到美国总人口的1%左右。移民的后裔以及祖先从非洲被贩卖到美国做奴隶的非裔人构成了美国其余人口的绝大部分。欧洲移民主要是在19世纪和20世纪早期登陆美国的，他们来自英国、爱尔兰、波兰、意大利和斯堪的纳维亚等地。稍近一些时候，波多黎各和墨西哥等地的大量西班牙裔移民涌向美国。此外还有来自亚洲国家的移民，像来自韩国、日本和中国的移民。

History 历史

British people first went to live in the US in the 17th century and took control of the land and built towns and cities. Growing disagreement between Britain and the Americans led to the American Revolutionary War and the Declaration of Independence in 1776. More land was added to the nation over the following century. Disagreements between the North and the South led to the Civil War from 1861 to 1865. 英国人最早在17世纪进入美国定居，他们占领土地并修建城镇。英国和美国人逐渐失和，这导致了美国独立战争的爆发和1776《独立宣言》的发表。在接下来的一个世纪中，更多的土地被并入美国。而美国北方和南方的分歧导致1861年至1865年内战的爆发。

Government 政府

Government in the US is divided between the 'federal' government (=the national government), which is based in Washington D.C. and consists of the President and the Congress, and the 'state' governments, the local government of each separate state. The states have quite a lot of power to make their own laws and set their own taxes, and each state has its own state capital and law-making system. 在美国，政府分为"联邦"政府和"州"政府。前者设在华盛顿特区，包括总统和国会。后者是各州的地方政府。各州拥有制定自己的法律和确定赋税的诸多权力，而且每个州都有自己的首府和立法体系。

United Way /·,·· '·/ a CHARITY organization in the US which collects money from the public, and then divides this money to give to many different charities 联合之路〔美国一慈善组织，向公众募集资金，再将所得善款分配给众多不同的慈善机构〕

unit price /'·· ,·/ *n* [C] the price that is charged for each single thing or quantity that is sold 单价

unit trust /,·· '·/ *n* [C] *BrE* a company through which you can buy shares (SHARE² (5)) in many different businesses【英】单位投资信托公司，共同基金; MUTUAL FUND *AmE*【美】

u·ni·ty /ˈjunəti; ˈjuːnɪ̈ti/ *n* **1** [singular,U] a situation in which a group of people or countries work together for a particular purpose 团结; 联合; 一致: *European unity* 欧洲的统一 **2** [U] the quality of being complete 整体(性); 协调(性): *The design has a pleasing unity and appearance.* 该设计具有一种悦人的整体感和外观。**3** [U] *technical* the number 1【术语】〔数字〕1

Univ *n* a written abbreviation of 缩写= UNIVERSITY

U·ni·ver·sal /ˌjunəˈvɜsl; ˌjuːnɪ̈ˈvɜːsəl◂/ *trademark* a large US film company based in Hollywood, which has made many famous films【商标】环球影片公司〔美国一大型电影公司。总部设在好莱坞，制作过多部著名影片〕

3 **universal** *adj* **1** done by all the members of a group 全体（做）的，一致的：*There was universal agreement on the issue of sex education.* 关于性教育问题，大家的意见是一致的。**2** involving or understood by everyone in the world 普遍的，一般的：*a topic of universal interest* 人人都感兴趣的话题 **3** true or suitable in every situation 通用的；万能的：*a universal truth* 举世公认的真理 —**universally** *adv* —**universality** /ˌjunəvɝˈsæləti; juːnɪ̩vɜːˈsælɪ̩ti/ *n* [U]

Universal Dec·la·ra·tion of Hu·man Rights /ˌ······ˈ·/ an official statement made by the UN in 1948 which says all people in the world should have human rights, such as the right to express their beliefs without being punished and the right to be treated fairly according to the law《世界人权宣言》〔联合国1948年颁布的一份正式宣言，声明全世界人民都应享有人权，如自由表达信仰而不受惩罚的权利、依法受到公正待遇的权利等〕

universal joint /ˌ····ˈ·/ *n* [C] a part in a machine, at the point where two other parts join together, that can turn in all directions〔机器的〕万向接头

3 **u·ni·verse** /ˈjunəˌvɝs; ˈjuːnɪ̩vɜːs/ *n* [singular] **1 the universe** all space, including all the stars and PLANETS 宇宙；天地万物；万象 **2** the place where a particular person lives or works, including the people they know〔某人生活或工作的〕活动领域：**be the centre of sb's universe** (=be the most important thing to someone) 是某人生活的中心

2 1 **u·ni·ver·si·ty** /ˌjunəˈvɝsəti; juːnɪ̩ˈvɜːsɪ̩ti◂/ *n* [C,U] an educational institution at the highest level, where you study for a DEGREE 大学：**go to university** (=study at a university) 上大学

University of Lon·don, the /ˌ·,····ˈ··/ —see 见 LONDON UNIVERSITY

un·just /ʌnˈdʒʌst; ˌʌnˈdʒʌst◂/ *adj* not fair or reasonable 非正义的；不公平的；不公正的；不合理的：*unjust laws* 不公正的法律 —**unjustly** *adv*

un·just·i·fi·a·ble /ʌnˈdʒʌstəˌfaɪəbl; ʌnˈdʒʌstɪ̩faɪəbəl/ *adj* completely wrong and unacceptable 错误的；不能接受的：*Poisoning the earth's atmosphere is ecologically and morally unjustifiable.* 污染地球大气在生态上和道德上都是错误的。—**unjustifiably** *adv*

un·just·i·fied /ʌnˈdʒʌstəˌfaɪd; ʌnˈdʒʌstɪ̩faɪd/ *adj* criticism, bad treatment etc that is unjustified is unfair〔批评、处理等〕不合理的，不公正的：*I think your criticisms of Mr Ward are completely unjustified.* 我认为你对沃德先生的批评完全缺乏公正。

un·kempt /ʌnˈkɛmpt; ˌʌnˈkempt◂/ *adj* not neat or tidy 不整洁的，凌乱的：*an unkempt garden* 乱糟糟的花园

un·kind /ʌnˈkaɪnd; ˌʌnˈkaɪnd◂/ *adj* nasty, unpleasant, or cruel 不仁慈的；不和善的；刻薄的：*an unkind remark* 刻薄的说话 | [+to] *Her husband is very unkind to her.* 她丈夫对她非常刻薄。—**unkindly** *adv* —**unkindness** *n* [U]

un·know·ing /ʌnˈnoɪŋ; ʌnˈnəʊɪŋ/ *adj* [only before noun 仅用于名词前] *formal* not realizing what you are doing or what is happening; UNAWARE【正式】不知道的；没察觉的：*Buying the stolen property made her an unknowing accomplice to the crime.* 购买赃物使她无意中成了犯罪活动的共犯。—**unknowingly** *adv*

2 **un·known¹** /ʌnˈnon; ˌʌnˈnəʊn◂/ *adj* **1** not known about 不知道的，未知的：*a voyage through unknown territory* 穿越未知海域的航行 | *The murderer's identity remains unknown.* 谋杀者的身份仍然不明。**2** not famous 不知名的：*an unknown artist* 无名艺术家 **3 unknown to sb** without someone knowing 不为某人所知的：*Unknown to the general public, peace negotiations were already taking place.* 公众还不知道，和平谈判已在进行中。—see also 另见 UNBEKNOWN **4 be an unknown quantity** if someone or something is an unknown quantity, you do not know what their abilities are or how they are likely to behave 是未被人所了解的人[物]

unknown² *n* **1** [C] someone who is not famous 不出名的人：*At that point in her career she was still an unknown.* 她那时仍是个无名小卒。**2 the unknown a)** a place that is not known about or that has not been visited by humans 不为人知[人类尚未到达]的地方：*The astronauts began their journey into the unknown.* 宇航员开始了探索未知世界的旅行。**b)** things that you do not know or understand 未知事物：*a fear of the unknown* 对未知的恐惧

Unknown Sol·dier, the /ˌ··ˈ··/ a soldier, whose name is not known, and whose body is buried in a national MONUMENT, which is usually called the Tomb of the Unknown Soldier. He represents all the soldiers of the same nation who died in a war, especially in World War I or World War II. 无名战士〔身份无法确认的战士。安葬于常称作无名烈士墓的国家公墓里，代表各国在战争中，尤其是两次世界大战中牺牲的所有战士〕

un·law·ful /ʌnˈlɔfəl; ʌnˈlɔːfəl/ *adj law* not legal【法律】不合法的，非法的，违法的 —**unlawfully** *adv*

un·lead·ed /ʌnˈlɛdɪd; ʌnˈledɪ̩d/ *adj* unleaded petrol does not contain any LEAD³ (1) so is less harmful to the environment〔汽油〕不含铅的，无铅的

un·learn /ʌnˈlɝn; ˌʌnˈlɜːn/ *v* [T] *informal* to deliberately forget something you have learned【非正式】设法忘记〔已学会的东西〕；抛弃：*It's difficult to unlearn bad driving habits.* 很难改掉不好的驾驶习惯。

un·leash /ʌnˈliʃ; ʌnˈliːʃ/ *v* [T] **1** to suddenly let a strong force, feeling etc have its full effect 释放出，发泄〔力量、感情等〕：*forces of change unleashed by the war* 战争释放出来的变革力量 **2** to let a dog run free after it has been held on a LEASH¹ (1) 解开皮带以放开狗

un·leav·ened /ʌnˈlɛvənd; ʌnˈlevənd/ *adj* unleavened bread is flat because it is not made with YEAST〔面包〕未经发酵的

un·less /ʌnˈlɛs; ʌnˈles/ *conjunction* used when one thing will only happen or be true as long as another thing happens or is true 如果不…；除非…：*Milk quickly turns sour unless it's refrigerated.* 牛奶如果不冷藏，很快就会变酸。| *Unless some extra money is found, the theatre will close.* 要是不能额外弄一些钱，剧院将要关闭。 1 1

USAGE NOTE 用法说明: UNLESS

WORD CHOICE 词语辨析: **unless, if...not, if, provided/providing that**

You do not use **unless** about something that did not happen or you know is not true, but you can use **if...not** in this way. 某事没发生或明知某事不真实时，不用unless，但可用if...not。For example, you could not use **unless** in these sentences 例如下列句子中均不能用unless: *She would have died if the doctor hadn't operated immediately* (=but they did). 医生如果不是立即给她做了手术〔实际做了〕，她就死定了。| *If he wasn't such an idiot* (=but he is), *he would understand.* 他如果不是个大傻瓜〔他就是〕，他会明白的。

You use **unless** about something that *could* happen if something else does not happen or is not done, or if something *could* be true. unless表示如果另一事不发生，或没有做，或可能是真的，那么某事很可能会发生：*Unless the doctors operate immediately, she'll die./She'll die unless the doctors operate immediately* (=the doctors have not operated yet, and may or may not do). 医生如果不立即给她做手术〔医生还没有做，可能做，也可能不做〕，她会死去的。| *Unless he's a complete idiot, he'll understand* (=he may or may not be a complete idiot). 他如果不是个大傻瓜〔他可能是也可能不是个大傻瓜〕，他会明白的。

Unless and **if...not** can both be used to say that what you will do depends on something else happening.unless和if ... not均可表示要做的事情取决于另一事的发生：*Unless he comes soon, I'm going without him.* | *If he doesn't come soon, I'm going without him.* 他如果不马上来，我就自己走了。

You use **provided (that)** or **providing (that)** when the condition is that something definitely happens or is definitely true. provided (that)或providing (that)用于某事肯定会发生或一定是真实的时候：*Providing the weather's OK, we'll make the trip next Saturday.* 天气如果可以，我们下周六就去旅行。

You often use **unless** to add a condition that you think of after you have finished speaking. unless还常用于表示说话后又想起来的某个附加条件：*We'll go there next Saturday – unless it's raining of course.* 我们下周六会去那里——当然是如果不下雨的话。

un·let·tered /ʌnˈlɛtɚd; ʌnˈletəd/ *adj formal* unable to read or uneducated【正式】文盲的；未受教育的

un·li·censed /ʌnˈlaɪsənst; ʌnˈlaɪsənst/ *adj* without a LICENSE (=official document that gives you permission to do or have something) 没有执照的；未得到许可证的：*unlicensed firearms* 未取得许可证的火器 | *unlicensed traders* 没有营业执照的商人

un·like¹ /ʌnˈlaɪk; ˌʌnˈlaɪk◂/ *prep* **1** completely different from a particular person or thing 不像…；和…不同：*In his jeans and T-shirt, Charles looked most unlike a lawyer.* 查尔斯身穿牛仔裤和T恤衫，看上去一点儿也不像个律师。**2** not at all typical of something or someone 不是…的特点：*It's unlike Beth to drink so much, I wonder if she's all right.* 贝丝喝这么多可不像她，我不知道她有没有事。 3

unlike² *adj literary* not alike; different【文】不同的；不相似的

un·like·ly /ʌn`laɪklɪ; ʌn'laɪkli/ *adj* **1** not likely to happen 未必会发生的，不大可能的: *Donna might come, but it's very unlikely.* 唐娜也许会来，不过这不大可能。| **it is unlikely that** *It's unlikely that the thieves will be caught.* 这伙窃贼被抓住的可能性不大。| **in the unlikely event of** (=if something which is unlikely happens) 万一 *In the unlikely event of a fire, passengers should move to the top deck.* 万一发生火警，乘客应到顶层甲板上去。**2** not likely to be true 不大可能是真的，靠不住的: *an unlikely story* 不大真实的报道 **3 unlikely couple** two people who are having a relationship but do not seem suitable for each other 不般配的一对

un·lim·i·ted /ʌn`lɪmɪtɪd; ʌn'lɪmɨtɨd/ *adj* **1** without a fixed limit 无界限的; 无限制的: *unlimited credit* 无限的贷款 **2** very large amount 数量极大的，无数的: *an unlimited variety of cookies* 种类繁多的甜饼干

un·list·ed /ʌn`lɪstɪd; ʌn'lɪstɨd/ *adj* **1** not shown on an official STOCK EXCHANGE list〔证券〕未上市的 **2** *AmE* not in the list of numbers in the telephone DIRECTORY【美】电话号码不列入电话簿的; EX-DIRECTORY *BrE*【英】

un·lit /ʌn`lɪt; ˌʌn'lɪt◂/ *adj* dark because there are no lights 未被照明的，未点亮的: *an unlit stairway* 暗无灯光的楼梯

un·load /ʌn`lod; ʌn'ləʊd/ *v*

1 ▶VEHICLE/SHIP 车/船◀ a) to remove a load from a vehicle, ship etc 从〔车、船等〕卸下〔货物〕: **unload sth from sth** *The driver unloaded some boxes from the back of the truck.* 司机从卡车后部卸下了几只箱子。**b)** [I,T] if a vehicle, ship etc unloads, the goods that it carries are removed from it〔车、船等〕卸〔货〕: *The ship is unloading at the dock right now.* 船目前在码头卸货。

2 ▶GUN 枪、炮◀ [I,T] to remove the bullets or shells (SHELL[1] (2,3)) from a gun〔从枪、炮中〕退出子弹[弹壳]

3 ▶CAMERA 照相机◀ to remove the film from a camera〔从照相机中〕取出胶卷

4 ▶GET RID OF 除去◀ [T] *informal*【非正式】**a)** to get rid of something illegal or not very good by selling it quickly 把〔非法或不是很好的东西〕脱手，抛售; 倾销: **unload sth on/onto** *Hundreds of cheap videos were unloaded on the British market.* 数百种廉价录像带在英国市场上抛售。**b)** to get rid of work or responsibility by giving it to someone else 摆脱，推卸〔工作或责任〕: **unload sth on/onto sb** *Don't let him unload his problems onto you.* 别让他把他的问题都推到你身上。

un·lock /ʌn`lɑk; ʌn'lɒk/ *v* [T] **1** to unfasten the lock on a door, box etc 开…的锁 **2 unlock the secret of** to discover the most important facts about something 揭开…的秘密

un·looked-for /ʌn`lukt ˏfɔr; ʌn'lʊkt fɔː/ *adj informal* not expected【非正式】出乎意料的，意外的

un·loose /ʌn`lus; ʌn'luːs/ *v* [T] *formal* to untie or unfasten something【正式】解开，松开: *She unloosed her hair.* 她把头发松开。

un·loved /ʌn`lʌvd; ʌn'lʌvd/ *adj* not loved by anyone 无人喜爱的

un·love·ly /ʌn`lʌvlɪ; ʌn'lʌvli/ *adj literary* ugly【文】不可爱的，丑陋的

un·luck·y /ʌn`lʌkɪ; ʌn'lʌki/ *adj* **1** having bad luck 不幸的; 不走运的，不顺利的: *He gambled frequently, but was usually unlucky.* 他经常赌博，但往往运气不佳。| [+with] *We were unlucky with the weather this weekend. It rained constantly.* 我们真不走运，这个周末天公不作美，不停地下雨。**2** happening as a result of bad luck 倒霉的: **it is unlucky (for sb) that** *It was unlucky for Stephen that the boss happened to walk in just at that moment.* 史蒂文真倒霉，碰巧老板在那一刻走了进来。**3** causing bad luck 不吉的，不祥的 —**unluckily** *adv*

CULTURAL NOTE 文化注释

The most common things that people in the UK and US consider to be unlucky are Friday the 13th, walking under a ladder, and breaking a mirror. Every time a Friday is the thirteenth day of the month, people expect more accidents and problems to happen. Many people also avoid walking under a ladder that is leaning against a wall because they say it will bring them bad luck. People also say that you will have seven years of bad luck if you break a mirror. People in the US believe that it is unlucky if a black cat walks in front of you, but in the UK this is considered to be lucky. Although people say these things are unlucky, few people really believe that they are. 最为英美人所熟知的不吉利的事情是: 13号和星期五赶在同一天，走在梯子下和打碎镜子。如果某个月的13号碰巧是星期五，人们便认为要出更多的事故和麻烦。很多人对斜靠在墙上的梯子刻意回避，不在它下面走，说这样会让自己倒霉。人们还说，打碎了镜子将遭受七年的背运。美国人看到黑猫走在身前以为要遭殃，但是英国人视之为大吉。这些不走运的事人们也只是嘴上说说，没有谁会真的相信。— see also Cultural Notes at LUCKY, SUPERSTITION 另见 LUCKY, SUPERSTITION文化注释

un·made /ʌn`med; ˌʌn'meɪd◂/ *adj* an unmade bed is not tidy because the sheets, BLANKETS etc have not been arranged since someone slept in it〔床〕未铺好的

un·man·age·a·ble /ʌn`mænɪdʒəbḷ; ʌn'mænɪdʒəbəl/ *adj* difficult to control or deal with 难控制的; 难处理的; 难办的

un·man·ly /ʌn`mænlɪ; ˌʌn'mænli/ *adj* not thought to be suitable for or typical of a man 不适于男子的; 非男子汉的，柔弱的

un·manned /ʌn`mænd; ˌʌn'mænd◂/ *adj* a machine, vehicle etc that is unmanned does not have a person operating or controlling it〔机器、车辆等〕无人驾驶[操纵]的: *an unmanned spacecraft* 无人驾驶的宇宙飞船

un·man·ner·ly /ʌn`mænəlɪ; ʌn'mænəli/ *adj formal* not polite; rude【正式】没有礼貌的; 粗野的: *a rough, unmannerly security guard* 粗鲁无礼的保安员

un·marked /ʌn`mɑrkt; ˌʌn'mɑːkt◂/ *adj* something that is unmarked has no words or sign on it to show where or what it is 未做标记的; 没有标志的: *an unmarked grave* 未做标记的坟墓 | *an unmarked police car* 无标志的警车

un·mar·ried /ʌn`mærɪd; ˌʌn'mærid◂/ *adj* not married; SINGLE[1] (3) 未婚的; 独身的: *unmarried mothers* 未婚母亲

un·mask /ʌn`mæsk; ʌn'mɑːsk/ *v* [T] to make known the hidden truth about someone 揭露; 暴露〔真相〕: *Sherlock Holmes once again unmasked the murderer.* 歇洛克·福尔摩斯又一次揭露了杀人犯。

un·matched /ʌn`mætʃt; ˌʌn'mætʃt◂/ *adj literary* better than any other【文】无可比拟的，无与伦比的: *a woman of unmatched beauty* 美貌绝伦的女子

un·men·tion·a·ble /ʌn`mɛnʃənəbḷ; ʌn'menʃənəbəl/ *adj* too shocking or embarrassing to talk about〔因太震惊或尴尬而〕说不出口的

un·men·tion·a·bles /ʌn`mɛnʃənəbḷz; ʌn'menʃənəbəlz/ *n* [plural] *old-fashioned* underwear【过时】内衣，衬衣

un·mis·tak·a·ble, unmistakeable /ˌʌnmə`stekəbḷ; ˌʌnmɨ'steɪkəbəl◂/ *adj* familiar and easy to recognize 不会弄错的; 清楚明白的，显然的: *the unmistakable smell of rotting eggs* 明显的臭鸡蛋味 —**unmistakably** *adv*

un·mit·i·gat·ed /ʌn`mɪtəˏgetɪd; ʌn'mɪtɨgeɪtɨd/ *adj* [only before noun 仅用于名词前] **unmitigated disaster/failure etc** something that is completely bad 十足的灾难/失败等: *The tour was an unmitigated disaster.* 那次旅行完全是一场灾难。

un·moved /ʌn`muvd; ʌn'muːvd/ *adj* [not before noun 不用于名词前] feeling no pity, sympathy, or sadness, especially in a situation where most people would feel this 无动于衷的，冷漠的: *Richard remained unmoved throughout the funeral.* 理查德在整个葬礼期间，一直无动于衷。

un·named /ʌn`nemd; ˌʌn'neɪmd◂/ *adj* an unnamed person, place, or thing is one whose name is not known publicly 不知其名的: *The journalist cited an unnamed source in parliament.* 记者援引议会中一位不透露姓名的消息提供者。

un·nat·u·ral /ʌn`nætʃərəl; ʌn'nætʃərəl/ *adj* **1** different from what you would normally expect 不正常的，反常的: *It seems unnatural for a child to prefer the company of adults.* 小孩子宁愿与大人为伍，这似乎不大正常。**2** different from anything produced by nature 不自然的: *Her hair was an unnatural orange colour.* 她的头发是不自然的橘黄色。**3** different from normal human behaviour in a way that seems morally wrong〔行为〕违反常理的; 违背人道的: *unnatural sexual practices* 变态的性行为—**unnaturally** *adv*

un·ne·ces·sa·ry /ʌn`nɛsəˏsɛrɪ; ʌn'nesəsəri/ *adj* **1** not needed or more than is needed 不必要的; 多余的: *I'm trying to cut down on all my unnecessary spending.* 我正在尝试削减所有不必要的开支。**2** a remark or action that is unnecessary, is unkind or unreasonable〔说话或行动〕刻薄的; 无理的 —**unnecessarily** /ʌn`nɛsəˏsɛrəlɪ; ʌn'nesəsərəli/ *adv*: *I don't want to worry you unnecessarily.* 我不想给你徒添烦恼。

un·nerve /ʌn`nɝv; ˌʌn'nɜːv/ *v* [T] to upset or frighten someone so that they lose their confidence or their ability to think clearly 使气馁; 使不知所措: *Her first encounter with the boss unnerved her.* 她第一次与老板相遇时吓得不知所措。—**unnerving** *adj*

un·no·ticed /ʌn`notɪst; ʌn'nəʊtɨst/ *adj, adv* without being noticed 不被注意的[地]: *Elsa stood unnoticed at the edge of the*

crowd. 埃尔莎悄悄地站在人群的边沿。| **go/pass unnoticed** *His remark went unnoticed by everyone except me.* 他的话除了我别人都没注意到。

un·num·bered /ʌnˋnʌmbəd; ˌʌnˈnʌmbəd◂/ *adj* **1** not having a number 未编号的: *an unnumbered Swiss bank account* 未编号的瑞士银行账户 **2** *literary* too many to be counted【文】(多得)不可胜数的

un·ob·served /ˌʌnəbˋzɜvd; ˌʌnəbˈzɜːvd/ *adj, adv* not noticed 未受注意的[地]: *Ruth slipped out of the meeting unobserved.* 露丝溜出会议而未被察觉。

un·ob·tain·a·ble /ˌʌnəbˋtenəbl̩; ˌʌnəbˈteɪnəbəl◂/ *adj* impossible to get 不能得到的, 弄不到的: *Fresh fruit was unobtainable in the winter.* 新鲜水果在冬季弄不到的。

un·ob·tru·sive /ˌʌnəbˋtrusɪv; ˌʌnəbˈtruːsɪv◂/ *adj* not attracting attention and therefore not likely to be noticed 不引人注目的, 不显眼的: *a quiet unobtrusive student* 文静而不引人注目的学生 **—unobtrusively** *adv*

un·oc·cu·pied /ʌnˋɑkjəˌpaɪd; ʌnˈɒkjʊ̈paɪd/ *adj* **1** a seat, house, room etc that is unoccupied has no one in it〔座位、房屋等〕未被占用的, 空着的: *We moved in right away, as the flat was unoccupied.* 因为房子没人住, 我们立刻搬了进去。**2** an unoccupied country or area is not controlled by the enemy during a war〔国家、地区在战争中〕未被(敌人)占领的, 未沦陷的: *The family fled to unoccupied France.* 一家人逃到了未沦陷的法国。

un·of·fi·cial /ˌʌnəˋfɪʃəl; ˌʌnəˈfɪʃəl◂/ *adj* **1** without formal approval and permission from the organization or person in authority 非官方[非正式]批准的: *unofficial experiments carried out in secret laboratories* 在秘密实验室进行的未经正式批准的实验 **2** not made publicly known as part of an official plan 非正式公布的: *The President made an unofficial visit to the Senator's house on Cape Cod.* 总统去那位参议员在科德角的房子进行了一次非正式的拜访。**—unofficially** *adv*

un·or·ga·nized also 又作 **-ised** *BrE*【英】/ʌnˋɔrgənˌaɪzd; ʌnˈɔːgənaɪzd/ *adj* people who are unorganized do not have an organization, TRADE UNION, group etc to help or support them 未组织起来的; 没有组织的—compare 比较 DISORGANIZED

un·or·tho·dox /ʌnˋɔrθədɑks; ʌnˈɔːθədɒks/ *adj* unorthodox beliefs or methods are different from what is usual or accepted by most people〔信念或方法〕非常规的; 非正统的: *a tennis player with an unorthodox style* 风格独特的网球手

un·pack /ʌnˋpæk; ʌnˈpæk/ *v* **1** [I,T] to take everything out of a box or SUITCASE 打开(盒子或手提箱)取出(物品): *Let's go upstairs and unpack.* 我们上楼去打开箱子吧。**2** [T] *technical* to change information in a computer so that it is easier to understand but takes up more space【术语】解压〔压缩的电脑信息〕

un·paid /ʌnˋped; ˌʌnˈpeɪd◂/ *adj* **1** an unpaid bill or debt has not been paid 未支付的; 未偿还的 **2** done without receiving payment 不收报酬的; 无偿的: *unpaid voluntary work* 无报酬的志愿工作

un·pal·at·a·ble /ʌnˋpælətəbl̩; ʌnˈpælətəbəl/ *adj formal*【正式】**1** an unpalatable fact or idea is very unpleasant and difficult to accept〔事实或想法〕使人不快的; 令人讨厌的; 难以接受的: *We were trying to avoid the unpalatable truth – that the whole plan had failed.* 我们正设法回避这一使人不快的事实——整个计划失败了。**2** unpalatable food tastes unpleasant 难吃的, 不可口的 **—unpalatably** *adv*

un·par·al·leled /ʌnˋpærəˌlɛld; ʌnˈpærəleld/ *adj formal* greater or better than all others【正式】无比的, 无双的; 空前的: *a period of unparalleled economic prosperity* 一段经济空前繁荣的时期

un·par·don·a·ble /ʌnˋpɑrdnəbl̩; ʌnˈpɑːdnəbəl/ *adj formal* unpardonable behaviour is completely unacceptable【正式】不可宽恕的, 不可原谅的: *Your behaviour was unpardonable!* 你的行为不可饶恕! **—unpardonably** *adv*

UN peace·keep·ing force /ˌ· ˈ· ˌ··· ˌ·/ a group of soldiers from several different countries, who are sent by the UN to places where there has been a war, in order to prevent fighting from starting again. They wear light-blue BERETS (=a soft, flat hat). 联合国维和部队〔多国部队。由联合国派往战乱地区执行维和任务, 以防止战火再起。维和士兵头戴浅蓝色贝雷帽〕

un·pick /ʌnˋpɪk; ʌnˈpɪk/ *v* [T] to take out stitches from a piece of cloth or KNITTING 拆去〔衣料或编结物上〕的针脚[缝线]

un·placed /ʌnˋplest; ˌʌnˈpleɪst◂/ *adj BrE* not one of the first three to finish in a race or competition【英】〔在比赛中〕未获前三名的; 无名次的; 落选的

un·pleas·ant /ʌnˋplɛznt; ʌnˈplezənt/ *adj* **1** not pleasant or enjoyable 使人不愉快的, 不合意的, 讨厌的: *the unpleasant side-effects of the drug* 这种药讨厌的副作用 | *an unpleasant surprise* 令人不快的意外 **2** not kind and friendly 不友善的, 不客气的: *Our neighbours are extremely unpleasant.* 我们的邻居极不友善。**—unpleasantly** *adv*

un·pleas·ant·ness /ʌnˋplɛzntnɪs; ʌnˈplezəntnɪ̈s/ *n* [U] trouble or arguments 不愉快的事; 争执: *I hate all this unpleasantness.* 我讨厌所有这些争执。

un·plug /ʌnˋplʌg; ʌnˈplʌg/ *v* [T] to disconnect a piece of electrical equipment by taking its PLUG[1] (1a,c) out of a SOCKET (1) 拔去…的(电源)插头: *Unplug the TV before you go to bed.* 睡前拔下电视的插头。—see picture at 参见 PLUG[2] 图

un·plumbed /ʌnˋplʌmd; ˌʌnˈplʌmd◂/ *adj* **the unplumbed depths of** something that is not known about because it has never been examined or explored 未经探究的…深处: *the unplumbed depths of the ocean* 未经探究的海洋深处

un·pop·u·lar /ʌnˋpɑpjələ; ʌnˈpɒpjʊ̈lə/ *adj* not liked by most people 不受欢迎的, 不得人心的: *an unpopular decision* 不得人心的决定 | *He was very unpopular at school.* 他在学校里非常不受欢迎。**—unpopularity** /ʌnˌpɑpjəˋlærətɪ; ʌnˌpɒpjʊ̈ˈlærɪ̈ti/ *n* [U]

un·pre·ce·dent·ed /ʌnˋprɛsəˌdɛntɪd; ʌnˈpresɪ̈dentɪ̈d/ *adj* never having happened before, or never having happened so much 空前的, 前所未有的: *unprecedented price increases* 前所未有的价格上涨 **—unprecedentedly** *adv*

un·pre·dict·a·ble /ˌʌnprɪˋdɪktəbl̩; ˌʌnprɪˈdɪktəbəl◂/ *adj* **1** something that is unpredictable changes a lot so it is impossible to know what will happen〔因改变太多而〕无法预测的: *The weather in Britain is very unpredictable.* 英国的天气变幻莫测。**2** someone who is unpredictable tends to change their behaviour or ideas suddenly so that you never know what they are going to do or think〔人〕反复无常的, 捉摸不透的

un·pre·ju·diced /ʌnˋprɛdʒədɪst; ʌnˈpredʒʊ̈dɪ̈st/ *adj* willing to consider different ideas and opinions 无偏见的, 公正的

un·pre·pared /ˌʌnprɪˋpɛrd; ˌʌnprɪˈpeəd◂/ *adj* not ready to deal with something 无准备的: **[+for]** *Doug was unprepared for the boredom that followed his retirement.* 道格对退休以后的乏味无聊没有准备。

un·pre·pos·sess·ing /ˌʌnpripəˋzɛsɪŋ; ˌʌnpriːpəˈzesɪŋ/ *adj formal* not very attractive or noticeable【正式】不吸引人的; 不引人注意的

un·pre·ten·tious /ˌʌnprɪˋtɛnʃəs; ˌʌnprɪˈtenʃəs◂/ *adj approving* not trying to seem better, more important etc than you really are【褒】不炫耀的, 不招摇的; 不装模作样的: *an unpretentious restaurant* 简朴的餐馆 **—unpretentiously** *adv* **—unpretentiousness** *n* [U]

un·prin·ci·pled /ʌnˋprɪnsəpl̩d; ʌnˈprɪnsɪ̈pəld/ *adj formal* not caring about whether what you do is morally right; UNSCRUPULOUS【正式】不讲道德的, 不择手段的

un·print·a·ble /ʌnˋprɪntəbl̩; ʌnˈprɪntəbəl/ *adj* words that are unprintable are very rude or shocking〔词语因粗鲁或骇人听闻而〕不宜刊印的, 不能印刷的

un·pro·duct·ive /ˌʌnprəˋdʌktɪv; ˌʌnprəˈdʌktɪv◂/ *adj* not producing any good results 无结果的, 徒劳的: *I've had a very unproductive week.* 我度过了毫无收获的一周。

un·pro·fes·sion·al /ˌʌnprəˋfɛʃənl̩; ˌʌnprəˈfeʃənəl◂/ *adj* someone who is unprofessional does not behave according to the standard that is expected in a particular profession or activity 违反行业准则的: *Johnson was fired for unprofessional conduct.* 约翰逊因为有违反职业道德的行为而被开除了。**—unprofessionally** *adv*

un·prof·it·a·ble /ʌnˋprɑfɪtəbl̩; ʌnˈprɒfɪ̈təbəl/ *adj* **1** making no profit 无利润的: *unprofitable businesses* 无利可图的买卖 **2** *formal* bringing no advantage or gain【正式】无益的, 徒劳的: *It would be unprofitable to commit yourself to any firm plans at the moment.* 现在承诺做任何确切的计划都是无益的。

un·prompt·ed /ʌnˋprɑmptɪd; ʌnˈprɒmptɪ̈d/ *adj formal* unprompted actions are things that you do without anyone asking you to【正式】未经鼓动的; 未经提示的; 自发的

un·pro·nounce·a·ble /ˌʌnprəˋnaunsəbl̩; ˌʌnprəˈnaʊnsəbəl◂/ *adj* an unpronounceable word or name is very difficult to say〔单词或名字〕难发音的

un·pro·tect·ed /ˌʌnprəˋtɛktɪd; ˌʌnprəˈtektɪ̈d◂/ *adj* **1** something that is unprotected could hurt someone or be damaged 无保护的; 无掩护的, 没有防卫的: *Unprotected machinery can be dangerous.* 无保护的机器可能很危险。**2 unprotected sex** sex without a CONDOM 不用安全套的性交

un·pro·ven /ʌnˋpruvən; ˌʌnˈpruːvən, *ScotE*【苏格兰】-ˋprəvən; -ˈprəvən/ *adj* not tested, and not shown to be definitely true 未经检验的; 未经证实的: *unproven allegations* 未经证实的指控

un·pro·voked /ʌnprəˋvokt; ˌʌnprəˈvəʊkt◂/ *adj* unprovoked anger, attacks etc are directed at someone who has not done anything to deserve them〔愤怒、攻击等〕无端的, 无缘无故的: *The assault was completely unprovoked.* 这次攻击完全是无缘无故的。

un·qual·i·fied /ʌnˋkwɑləˌfaɪd; ʌnˈkwɒlɪ̵faɪd/ *adj* **1** not having the right knowledge, experience, or education to do something 无资格的; 不合格的: **unqualified to do sth** *I feel unqualified to advise you.* 我觉得自己没有资格向你提出忠告。**2 unqualified success/approval etc** success etc that is complete and without any criticism 极大的成功/无条件的同意等: *The play was an unqualified success.* 这部剧取得了全面的成功。

un·ques·tion·a·ble /ʌnˋkwɛstʃənəbl̩; ʌnˈkwestʃənəbəl/ *adj* impossible to doubt; certain 不成问题的, 无可置疑的; 确实的 —**unquestionably** *adv*

un·ques·tioned /ʌnˋkwɛstʃənd; ʌnˈkwestʃənd/ *adj* something that is unquestioned is accepted or believed by everyone 无争议的; 公认的: *the monarch's unquestioned right to rule* 公认的君主统治权

un·ques·tion·ing /ʌnˋkwɛstʃənɪŋ; ʌnˈkwestʃənɪŋ/ *adj* an unquestioning faith, attitude etc is very certain and without doubts〔信念、态度等〕无疑问[异议]的: *an unquestioning belief in God* 对上帝的深信不疑 | *unquestioning loyalty* 绝对的忠诚 —**unquestioningly** *adv*

un·qui·et /ʌnˋkwaɪət; ʌnˈkwaɪɪ̵t/ *adj literary* tending to make you feel nervous【文】焦虑的, 不安的: *His unquiet gaze moved away from her.* 他不安的凝视从她身上移开了。

un·quote /ʌnˋkwot; ʌnˈkwəʊt/ *adv* see 见 **quote...unquote** (QUOTE[1] (4))

un·rav·el /ʌnˋrævl̩; ʌnˈrævəl/ *v* **unravelled, unravelling** *BrE*【英】, **unraveled, unraveling** *AmE*【美】 **1** [I,T] if you unravel threads or if they unravel, they become separated 解开, 拆散〔线等〕; 散开 **2** [T] to understand or explain something that is very complicated 理解; 解释, 阐明: *It is difficult to unravel complex human emotions.* 很难阐明复杂的人类感情。

un·rea·da·ble /ʌnˋridəbl̩; ʌnˈriːdəbəl/ *adj* **1** an unreadable book or piece of writing is difficult to read because it is boring or complicated〔因平淡无味或复杂而〕难读懂的 **2** unreadable writing is so untidy that you cannot read it; ILLEGIBLE 字迹模糊的, 难以辨认的

un·real /ʌnˋrɪəl; ˌʌnˈrɪəl◂/ *adj* **1** [not before noun 不用于名词前] an experience, situation etc that is unreal seems so strange that you think you must be imagining or dreaming it 不真实的, 虚幻的: *The evening was so bizarre that it was beginning to seem unreal.* 那个晚上如此离奇, 似乎如梦幻一般。**2** not related to real things that happen 假的; 虚拟的: *Exam questions often deal with unreal situations.* 考试题常常讨论一些虚拟的情景。**3** *spoken* very exciting; excellent【口】很刺激的, 极棒的: *Our trip to Disneyland was unreal.* 我们的迪斯尼乐园之旅棒极了。 —**unreality** /ˌʌnrɪˋælətɪ; ˌʌnrɪˈælɪ̵ti/ *n* [U]

un·rea·lis·tic /ˌʌnrɪəˋlɪstɪk; ˌʌnrɪəˈlɪstɪk◂/ *adj* unrealistic ideas, hopes are not based on facts 不现实的, 不切实际的: *Predictions that Labour would win the election began to look unrealistic.* 关于工党会在大选中获胜的预言开始显得不切实际。| **it is unrealistic to do sth** *It is unrealistic to expect children to sit still for hours.* 指望孩子们安安静静地坐上几个小时, 那是不切实际的。| **be being unrealistic** *John, I think you're being totally unrealistic – we'll never be ready by then.* 约翰, 我认为你完全是在做白日梦 —— 我们到那时根本不可能准备好。—**unrealistically** /-klɪ; -kli/ *adv*

un·rea·son·a·ble /ʌnˋriznəbl̩; ʌnˈriːzənəbəl/ *adj* **1** behaving in an unfair, unpleasant, or stupid way 不讲理的; 超越情理的, 过分的: *Will thinks I'm being unreasonable in not lending him the car.* 威尔认为我不借车给他有点过分。**2** an unreasonable belief, request, action etc is wrong or unfair〔信念、要求、行动等〕不合理的; 荒谬的: **it is unreasonable to do sth** *I think it's unreasonable to expect you to work Sundays.* 我认为期望你星期天工作是没有道理的。| **make unreasonable demands** *Get assertive if your boss makes unreasonable demands.* 如果老板提出无理的要求, 你不要让步。**3** unreasonable prices, costs etc are too high〔价格、成本等〕过高的 —opposite 反义词 REASONABLE —**unreasonably** *adv* —**unreasonableness** *n* [U]

un·rea·son·ing /ʌnˋriznɪŋ; ʌnˈriːzənɪŋ/ *adj formal* an unreasoning feeling is one that is not based on fact or reason【正式】缺乏理智的; 不讲理的

un·rec·og·niz·a·ble also 又作 **-isable** *BrE*【英】/ʌnˋrɛkəgˌnaɪzəbl̩; ʌnˈrekəgnaɪzəbəl/ *adj* someone or something that is unrecognizable has changed or been damaged so much that you do not recognize them 不能识别的, 认不出来的: *They've built so many new buildings that the town centre was unrecognisable.* 他们盖了那么多新大楼, 镇中心都认不出来了。

un·rec·og·nized also 又作 **-ised** *BrE*【英】/ʌnˋrɛkəgˌnaɪzd; ʌnˈrekəgnaɪzd/ *adj* **1** someone who is unrecognized for something they have done has not received the admiration or respect they deserve 未被承认的: *one of the great unrecognized jazzmen of the 1930s* 未得到承认的20世纪30年代杰出爵士乐演奏者之一 **2** not noticed or not thought to be important 不被注意的; 遭到轻视的: **go unrecognized** *Domestic violence went unrecognized for years.* 家庭暴力问题已多年未引起人们的注意。

un·re·cord·ed /ˌʌnrɪˋkɔrdɪd; ˌʌnrɪˈkɔːdɪ̵d◂/ *adj* not written down or recorded 未写下来的; 未记录的; 未登记的: **go unrecorded** *Many of the complaints have gone unrecorded.* 许多投诉都未作记录。

un·re·fined /ˌʌnrɪˋfaɪnd; ˌʌnrɪˈfaɪnd◂/ *adj* **1** [no comparative 无比较级] an unrefined substance has not been separated from the other substances that it is combined with in its natural form 未精制的; 未提炼的: *unrefined oil* 未提炼的石油 | *unrefined sugar* 非精制的糖 **2** *formal* not polite or educated【正式】不优雅的; 无教养的 —opposite 反义词 REFINED

un·re·gen·e·rate /ˌʌnrɪˋdʒɛnərɪt; ˌʌnrɪˈdʒenərɪ̵t◂/ *adj formal* making no attempt to change your bad habits or bad behaviour【正式】不改悔的, 不思改过的; 顽固不化的: *an unregenerate liar* 不改悔的说谎者

un·re·lat·ed /ˌʌnrɪˋletɪd; ˌʌnrɪˈleɪtɪ̵d◂/ *adj* **1** not connected to each other in any way 无关的, 不相关的: *The police think that the two incidents are unrelated.* 警方认为这两个事件互不相关。**2** people who are unrelated are not members of the same family 无亲戚关系的; 非亲属的

un·re·lent·ing /ˌʌnrɪˋlɛntɪŋ; ˌʌnrɪˈlentɪŋ◂/ *adj formal* an unpleasant situation that is unrelenting continues for a long time without stopping【正式】〔令人不愉快的局面〕持续的, 不断的: *the unrelenting pressures of the job* 持续的工作压力 | *two days of unrelenting rain* 连续下了两天的雨 —see also 另见 RELENT, RELENTLESS —**unrelentingly** *adv*

un·re·li·a·ble /ˌʌnrɪˋlaɪəbl̩; ˌʌnrɪˈlaɪəbəl◂/ *adj* unable to be trusted or depended on 不可信赖的; 不可靠的: *The car's becoming very unreliable.* 这部汽车变得非常不可靠了。| **unreliable witness** (=someone who may not tell the truth in a court) 不可靠的证人 —opposite 反义词 RELIABLE

un·re·lieved /ˌʌnrɪˋlivd; ˌʌnrɪˈliːvd◂/ *adj* an unpleasant situation that is unrelieved continues for a long time because nothing happens to change it〔令人不愉快的情况〕未减轻的, 未解除的: *unrelieved pain* 未减轻的疼痛 —see also 另见 RELIEVE —**unrelievedly** /-ˋlivdlɪ; -ˈliːvɪ̵dli/ *adv*

un·re·mark·a·ble /ˌʌnrɪˋmɑrkəbl̩; ˌʌnrɪˈmɑːkəbəl◂/ *adj formal* not especially beautiful or interesting【正式】不引人注意的, 不显著的; 平凡的: *unremarkable buildings* 不起眼的建筑物

un·re·mit·ting /ˌʌnrɪˋmɪtɪŋ; ˌʌnrɪˈmɪtɪŋ◂/ *adj formal* an action or effort that is unremitting continues for a long time and probably will not stop【正式】〔行动或努力〕不间断的; 无休止的: *lives of unremitting drudgery* 无休止的苦工生活 —**unremittingly** *adv*

un·re·peat·a·ble /ˌʌnrɪˋpitəbl̩; ˌʌnrɪˈpiːtəbəl◂/ *adj* **1** something that someone says that is unrepeatable is too rude or offensive for you to want to say it again〔说话因粗俗或冒犯而〕不宜重复的: *Tim's comment was unrepeatable.* 蒂姆的评论不便重复。**2** unable to be done again 不能重做的

un·re·pent·ant /ˌʌnrɪˋpɛntənt; ˌʌnrɪˈpentənt◂/ *adj* not feeling ashamed of behaviour, or beliefs that other people may disapprove of 不改悔的, 不悔悟的; 顽固的: *an unrepentant right-winger* 顽固不化的右翼分子

un·rep·re·sen·ta·tive /ˌʌnrɛprɪˋzɛntətɪv; ˌʌnreprɪˈzentətɪv/ *adj* **1** not typical of a group or type, and therefore not giving you any information about the other members of the same group or type 不能代表的; 不典型的: **[+of]** *This painting is unrepresentative of the rest of her work.* 这幅画不代表她其余的作品。**2** an unrepresentative government only has a few members from a variety of social groups, so that the opinions of many people are ignored〔政府〕不代表全体民意的

un·re·quit·ed /ˌʌnrɪˋkwaɪtɪd; ˌʌnrɪˈkwaɪtɪ̵d◂/ *adj* **unrequited love** romantic love that you feel for someone, but that they do not feel for you 单恋, 单相思

un·re·served /ˌʌnrɪˋzɝvd; ˌʌnrɪˈzɜːvd◂/ *adj* complete and without any doubts 无保留的; 完全的, 充分的 —**unreservedly** /-ˋzɝvɪdlɪ; -ˈzɜːvɪ̵dli/ *adv*: *The company apologized unreservedly for its mistake.* 公司坦诚地就其错误道了歉。

UN res·o·lu·tion /ˌ· · · ˈ· ·/ an official decision made by the UN (=United Nations), which its members have voted for and are expected to obey 联合国决议〔联合国作出的正式决定。由成员国投票通过并遵守〕

un·re·solved /ˌʌnrɪˋzɑlvd; ˌʌnrɪˈzɒlvd◂/ *adj* an unresolved problem or question has not been answered or solved 未解答的；未解决的

un·res·pon·sive /ˌʌnrɪˋspɑnsɪv; ˌʌnrɪˈspɒnsɪv/ *adj* **1** not reacting to something or affected by it 无反应的；不受影响的：[+to] *The disease is unresponsive to conventional treatment.* 这种病常规疗法不起作用。**2** not reacting to what people say to you 不作出答复的；无反应的；冷淡的：*She remained still and unresponsive.* 她一动不动，没有任何反应。

un·rest /ʌnˋrɛst; ʌnˈrest/ *n* [U] a social or political situation in which people protest and tend to behave violently 不安宁；动乱；骚动：*The country was in a state of unrest.* 该国处于动乱之中。| **social/civil/political etc unrest** *These drastic measures were necessary to prevent further social unrest.* 这些严厉措施对防止进一步的社会动乱是必需的。

un·re·strained /ˌʌnrɪˋstrend; ˌʌnrɪˈstreɪnd◂/ *adj* not controlled or limited 无限制的；无拘束的；自由自在的：*unrestrained laughter* 放声大笑 —**unrestrainedly** *adv*

un·ripe /ʌnˋraɪp; ˌʌnˈraɪp/ *adj* unripe fruit, grain etc is not fully developed or ready to be eaten 未成熟的，生的：*green, unripe peaches* 青色的生桃子

un·ri·valled *BrE*【英】, **unrivaled** *AmE*【美】/ʌnˋraɪvl̩d; ʌnˈraɪvəld/ *adj formal* better than any other【正式】无敌的，无双的：*an unrivalled collection of Chinese art* 无与伦比的中国艺术珍品

un·ruf·fled /ʌnˋrʌfl̩d; ʌnˈrʌfəld/ *adj approving* calm and not upset by a difficult situation【褒】平静的；沉着的：*The Under-Secretary remained completely unruffled.* 那位副部长一直保持镇定自若。

un·ru·ly /ʌnˋrulɪ; ʌnˈruːli/ *adj* **1** behaving in an uncontrolled or violent way〔行为〕难驾驭的，难控制的；粗暴的：*unruly children* 难管教的孩子 **2** unruly hair is untidy〔头发〕乱蓬蓬的 —**unruliness** *n* [U]

un·sad·dle /ʌnˋsædl̩; ʌnˈsædl/ *v* [T] **1** to remove the SADDLE (=leather seat) from a horse 给〔马〕卸鞍 **2** if a horse unsaddles someone, it throws them off its back; UNSEAT〔马〕把〔某人〕摔下来，使坠马

un·said /ʌnˋsɛd; ʌnˈsed/ *adv* **be left unsaid** if something is left unsaid, you do not say it although you might be thinking it〔话〕未说出口：*Some things are better left unsaid.* 有些事不说出来更好。—**unsay** /ʌnˋse; ʌnˈseɪ/ *v* [T]

un·san·i·ta·ry /ˌʌnˋsænəˌtɛrɪ; ˌʌnˈsænɪ̵təri/ *adj especially AmE* conditions or places that are unsanitary are very dirty and likely to cause disease; INSANITARY【尤美】不卫生的；有碍健康的

un·sa·vour·y *BrE*【英】, **unsavory** *AmE*【美】/ʌnˋsevərɪ; ʌnˈseɪvəri/ *adj* unpleasant or morally unacceptable 令人不快的；〔道德上〕令人厌恶的：*I hope that ends the whole unsavoury business.* 我希望这会结束整桩令人讨厌的事。| **unsavoury light** *The latest revelations show the actor in a very unsavoury light.* 最近的新发现使那个演员的可恶之处暴露无遗。| **unsavoury character** (=an unpleasant and dishonest person) 缺德的小人

un·scathed /ʌnˋskeðd; ʌnˈskeɪðd/ *adj* [not before noun 不用于名词前] not hurt by a bad or dangerous situation 没有受伤的，未遭受伤害的：*Faye walked away from the accident completely unscathed.* 费伊在事故中脱险，安然无恙。

UNSCOM the United Nations Special Commission; an organization that was set up after the Gulf War to find and destroy Iraq's weapons that could kill many people at once 联合国特别委员会〔海湾战争后联合国设立的一个机构，旨在核查并销毁伊拉克的大规模杀伤性武器〕

un·scram·ble /ʌnˋskræmbl̩; ʌnˈskræmbəl/ *v* [T] to change a television SIGNAL or a message that has been sent in CODE (=a deliberately confusing way) so that it can be seen or read 使〔电视信号〕还原；译出〔密电码〕

un·screw /ʌnˋskru; ʌnˈskruː/ *v* [T] **1** to undo something by twisting it 拧开，旋开〔某物〕**2** to take the screws out of something 从〔某物〕旋出螺丝

un·script·ed /ˌʌnˋskrɪptɪd; ˌʌnˈskrɪptɪ̵d◂/ *adj* an unscripted broadcast, speech etc is not written or planned before it is actually made〔广播、演讲等〕不用稿子的；不事前准备的

un·scru·pu·lous /ʌnˋskrupjələs; ʌnˈskruːpjɪ̵ləs/ *adj* behaving in an unfair or dishonest way 不择手段的；不讲道德的；无耻的：*a cunning and unscrupulous politician* 狡猾而不择手段的政客 —**unscrupulously** *adv* —**unscrupulousness** *n* [U]

un·sea·son·a·ble /ʌnˋsiznəbl̩; ʌnˈsiːzənəbəl/ *adj* unseasonable weather is unusual for the time of year〔天气〕不合时令〔季节〕的

un·seat /ʌnˋsit; ʌnˈsiːt/ *v* [T] **1** to remove someone from a position of power or strength 使退位；使退职：*You'll see – we'll unseat the President at the next election.* 你瞧着吧，下次选举我们就会把总统赶下台。**2** if a horse unseats someone, it throws them off its back〔马〕把〔某人〕摔下来

UN Se·cu·ri·ty Coun·cil, the /ˌ· ·ˈ· · · ˌ· ·/ —see 见 the SECURITY COUNCIL

un·seed·ed /ʌnˋsidɪd; ˌʌnˈsiːdɪ̵d◂/ *adj* not chosen as a SEED (=someone with a numbered rank in a competition), especially in a tennis competition〔尤指网球比赛中〕未被挑选为种子选手的

un·see·ing /ʌnˋsiɪŋ; ˌʌnˈsiːɪŋ◂/ *adj especially literary* not noticing anything even though your eyes are open【尤文】视而不见的：*Jack gazed unseeing out of the window.* 杰克视而不见地盯着窗外。—**unseeingly** *adv*

un·seem·ly /ʌnˋsimlɪ; ʌnˈsiːmli/ *adj formal* unseemly behaviour is not polite or not suitable for a particular occasion【正式】〔行为〕不体面的；不合礼节的；不得体的：*Ann thought it unseemly to kiss her husband in public.* 安认为当众与丈夫接吻不太合适。—**unseemliness** *n* [U]

un·seen[1] /ʌnˋsin; ˌʌnˈsiːn◂/ *adj formal* not noticed or seen【正式】未被看见〔察觉〕的；未受注意的 —**unseen** *adv*: *She crept out of the building unseen.* 她蹑手蹑脚地从大楼里走出来，没让人看见。

unseen[2] *n* [C] *BrE* a piece of writing in a foreign language that you have not seen before and that you must translate into your own language in an examination【英】〔考试中〕需即席翻译成本国语的文章

un·set·tle /ʌnˋsɛtl̩; ʌnˈsetl/ *v* [T] to make someone feel upset or nervous 使心绪不宁；使担忧：*The sudden changes unsettled Judy.* 突如其来的变化使朱迪心神不宁。—**unsettling** *adj*

un·set·tled /ʌnˋsɛtl̩d; ʌnˈsetld/ *adj*

1 ▶SITUATION 形势◀ making people feel uncertain about what will happen 动荡不定的；不稳定的：*the unsettled times during the war* 战争期间的不稳定时期

2 ▶FEELING 感情◀ worried or excited about something so that you feel upset or nervous 心烦意乱的；不安的：*Children feel unsettled if their parents divorce.* 父母如果离婚，孩子们会感到心神不安。

3 ▶ARGUMENT OR DISAGREEMENT 争论或分歧◀ still continuing without reaching any agreement 未定的；未解决的：*The dispute between teachers and governors remains unsettled.* 教师与学校董事之间的争议仍然没有解决。

4 ▶WEATHER 天气◀ changing a lot in a short period of time 变幻莫测的；易变的

5 ▶STOMACH 胃◀ making you feel uncomfortable and a little sick 不舒服的，稍感不适的：*My stomach's a bit unsettled after all that rich food.* 吃了那么多油腻食物之后，我觉得胃有点不舒服。

un·sha·kea·ble, unshakable /ʌnˋʃekəbl̩; ʌnˈʃeɪkəbəl/ *adj* unshakable faith, beliefs etc are very strong and cannot be destroyed or changed〔信仰、信念等〕不可动摇的，坚定不移的

un·shav·en /ʌnˋʃevən; ʌnˈʃeɪvən/ *adj* a man who is unshaven has very short hairs growing on his face because he has not shaved (SHAVE[1] (1))〔男子〕未剃须的，未修面的

un·sight·ly /ʌnˋsaɪtlɪ; ʌnˈsaɪtli/ *adj* unpleasant to look at 不悦目的，难看的，不雅观的：*unsightly power stations ruining the landscape* 丑陋的毁坏风景的发电站 —**unsightliness** *n* [U]

unscrew 旋开

He tried to unscrew the lid. 他试图拧开盖子。

U

un·skilled /ʌn`skɪld; ˌʌn'skɪld◂/ *adj* **1** an unskilled worker has not been trained for a particular type of job〔工人〕无特殊技能的，未受专门训练的: **unskilled labour** (=people who have no special training) 非熟练工人 **2** unskilled work, jobs etc do not need people with special skills〔工作等〕无需特殊技能的 —compare 比较 SKILLED

un·so·cia·ble /ʌn`soʃəbl; ʌn'səʊʃəbəl/ *adj* not liking to be with people or to go to social events 不爱交际的，不合群的 —see also 另见 UNSOCIAL

un·so·cial /ʌn`soʃəl; ˌʌn'səʊʃəl◂/ *adj* **work unsocial hours** also 又作 **work unsociable hours** to work very early in the morning, during the night etc when most people do not work 非正常时间工作〔即在凌晨或夜间等时段工作〕

un·solved /ʌn`sɑlvd; ˌʌn'sɒlvd◂/ *adj* a problem, mystery, or crime that is unsolved has never been solved 未解决的

un·so·phis·ti·cat·ed /ˌʌnsə`fɪstɪˌketɪd; ˌʌnsə'fɪstɪkeɪtɪd◂/ *adj* **1** having little knowledge or experience of modern fashionable things, and showing this by the way you talk or behave 不谙世故的，天真无邪的: *an unsophisticated boy from the provinces* 来自外省的天真男孩 **2** unsophisticated tools, methods, or processes are simple, without many of the features of more modern ones〔工具、方法、过程〕不复杂的，简单的

un·sound /ʌn`saund; ˌʌn'saʊnd◂/ *adj* **1** unsound arguments, methods etc are not based on fact or reason〔论点、方法等〕谬误的；无根据的: *ideologically unsound* 观念上谬误的 **2** an unsound building or structure is in bad condition〔建筑物或结构〕不安全的，不稳固的 **3 of unsound mind** *formal* mentally ill and not responsible for your actions【正式】心智不健全的

un·speak·a·ble /ʌn`spikəbl; ʌn'spiːkəbəl/ *adj* **1** unspeakable actions or people are extremely bad 坏得无法形容的，坏透了的: *the unspeakable atrocities in Bosnia* 在波斯尼亚发生的难以形容的暴行 **2** *literary* unspeakable feelings are so extreme that it is impossible to describe them【文】〔感觉〕难以形容的: *unspeakable terror* 无法形容的恐怖 **—unspeakably** *adv*

un·spoiled /ʌn`spɔɪld; ˌʌn'spɔɪld◂/ also 又作 **un·spoilt** /-`spɔɪlt; -'spɔɪlt◂/ *especially BrE*【尤英】*adj* **1** *approving* an unspoiled place has not been changed for a long time, especially by new roads, buildings etc【褒】〔地方〕长时间未发生变化的；未丧失原有自然美的 **2** someone who is unspoiled has not changed in spite of the good or bad things that have happened to them〔人〕未受影响的；未被宠坏的: *She remained unspoilt by her success.* 她虽然事业有成，却依然保持本色。

un·sta·ble /ʌn`stebl; ʌn'steɪbəl/ *adj* **1** dangerous and likely to fall over because not balanced or properly supported 不稳固的；不牢靠的 **2** likely to change suddenly and perhaps become worse 易变的；动荡不定的: *an unstable economy* 不稳定的经济 **3** someone who is unstable changes very suddenly so that you do not know how they will react or behave〔人〕反复无常的，动摇不定的 **4** an unstable chemical is likely to separate into simpler compounds〔化合物〕不稳定的

un·stint·ing /ʌn`stɪntɪŋ; ʌn'stɪntɪŋ/ *adj* unstinting support, help, agreement etc is complete and given willingly〔支持、帮助、协议等〕慷慨的，大方的 **—unstintingly** *adv*

un·stop /ˌʌn`stɑp; ˌʌn'stɒp/ *v* [T] if you unstop a pipe, DRAIN[2] (1) etc, you remove something that is blocking it 除去〔管道、下水道等〕的堵塞物

un·stop·pa·ble /ʌn`stɑpəbl; ʌn'stɒpəbəl/ *adj* unable to be stopped 制止不住的，阻止不了的: *Once Janet gets an idea, she's unstoppable.* 珍妮特一旦拿定主意，谁也挡不住她。

un·stuck /ˌʌn`stʌk; ˌʌn'stʌk◂/ *adj* **come unstuck a)** if something comes unstuck, it becomes separated from something that it was stuck to 脱落；松开 **b)** *BrE informal* if someone comes unstuck, something that they are doing starts to go wrong【英，非正式】出毛病；失灵；失败

un·stud·ied /ʌn`stʌdɪd; ˌʌn'stʌdid/ *adj formal* an unstudied quality seems natural and is not a result of effort or practice【正式】非造作的，自然的: *unstudied grace* 自然的优雅

un·suit·able /ʌn`sjutəbl; ˌʌn'suːtəbəl/ *adj* not having the right qualities for a particular person, purpose, or situation 不合适的；不适宜的: **[+for]** *Those books are quite unsuitable for children.* 那些书对儿童颇不适宜。| *beaches judged unsuitable for swimming* 被断定为不适合游泳的海滩

un·sul·lied /ʌn`sʌlɪd; ʌn'sʌlid/ *adj literary* not spoiled【文】未受污染的，洁净的: *unsullied lush vegetation and wide open spaces* 一尘不染的茂盛草木和开阔的空地

un·sung /ʌn`sʌŋ; ˌʌn'sʌŋ◂/ *adj* not praised or famous for something you have done although you deserve to be〔该受赞而〕未被赞颂的；〔该出名而〕未出名的: **unsung hero** *Liam was an unsung hero during the crisis.* 利亚姆是这次危机期间默默无闻的英雄。

un·sure /ʌn`ʃur; ˌʌn'ʃʊə◂/ *adj* **1** not certain about something or about what you have to do 无把握的；不确知的: *If you are unsure about the operation, ask your doctor to explain it.* 你如果对手术无把握，请医生讲解一下。**2 unsure of yourself** to lack confidence 缺乏自信: *Chris seemed nervous and unsure of herself.* 克里斯显得紧张，缺乏自信。

un·sur·passed /ˌʌnsɚ`pæst; ˌʌnsə'pɑːst◂/ *adj* a skill, quality, or achievement that is unsurpassed is better than all the others〔技能、品质或成就〕无与伦比的，超群的: *Her knowledge of the subject is unsurpassed.* 她对这一学科的知识无人能比。

un·sus·pect·ing /ˌʌnsə`spɛktɪŋ; ˌʌnsə'spektɪŋ◂/ *adj* not knowing that something bad is about to happen 不怀疑的，无疑心的: *unsuspecting victims* 无提防之心的受害人

un·swerv·ing /ʌn`swɝvɪŋ; ʌn'swɜːvɪŋ/ *adj* an unswerving belief or attitude is one that is very strong and never changes〔信念、态度〕坚定不移的: **unswerving in sth** *Liz was unswerving in her determination to be a journalist.* 莉兹矢志不移地要成为一名记者。| **unswerving loyalty/admiration** *Nina has always shown unswerving loyalty to the family.* 尼娜总是对家庭表现出绝对的忠诚。

un·tan·gle /ʌn`tæŋgl; ˌʌn'tæŋgəl/ *v* [T] **1** to undo pieces of string etc that are twisted together 解开〔纠结〕: *fisherman untangling their nets* 正在解开缠结的渔网的渔民 **2** to make something less complicated 理顺，整理〔某物〕

un·tapped /ʌn`tæpt; ˌʌn'tæpt◂/ *adj* an untapped RESOURCE[1], market etc has not yet been used〔资源、市场等〕未开发的；未利用的

un·ten·a·ble /ʌn`tɛnəbl; ʌn'tenəbəl/ *adj* an untenable THEORY, argument etc is impossible to defend against criticism〔理论、论点等〕站不住脚的；不堪一击的: **untenable position** *The scandal left the President in an untenable position.* 丑闻使总统无可辩白。

un·thin·ka·ble /ʌn`θɪŋkəbl; ʌn'θɪŋkəbəl/ *adj* impossible to accept or imagine 不能接受的；难以置信的；难以想象的: *It would have been unthinkable ten years earlier to choose a woman as party leader.* 10年前选妇女作党的领袖是难以想象的。

un·think·ing /ʌn`θɪŋkɪŋ; ʌn'θɪŋkɪŋ/ *adj* not thinking about the effects of something you say or do 不考虑后果的 **—unthinkingly** *adv*

un·ti·dy /ʌn`taɪdɪ; ʌn'taɪdi/ *adj especially BrE*【尤英】**1** not neat; MESSY (1) 不整洁的，凌乱的: *an untidy room* 凌乱的房间 **2** someone who is untidy does not keep their house, possessions etc neat〔人〕不整齐的，无条理的 **—untidily** *adv* **—untidiness** *n* [U]

un·tie /ʌn`taɪ; ʌn'taɪ/ *v* [T] to undo the knots in something or undo something that has been tied 解开〔结或捆着之物〕**—untied** *adj*: *walking about with shoelaces untied* 鞋带不系四处走

un·til /ən`tɪl; ʌn'tɪl/ *prep, conjunction* **1** used to say that something stops happening or someone stops doing something at a particular time or when something else happens; TILL[1] 直到…为止: *Gary was working for IBM until 1969, when he got a job at Sperry.* 加里为国际商业机器公司一直工作到1969年，接着他在斯佩里公司找到了一份工作。| *Black people were denied the vote in the US until well into the 1950s.* 美国黑人直到20世纪50年代才获得选举权。| **up until** *This ticket is valid up until the 12th of March.* 这张票的有效期一直到3月12日。**2** used to say that you should stop travelling at a particular place 直到〔某地〕: *Stay on the train until Birmingham, and then change for Peterborough.* 坐火车一直到伯明翰，然后换乘到彼得伯勒的车。

un·time·ly /ʌn`taɪmlɪ; ʌn'taɪmli/ *adj* **1 untimely death/end etc** a death etc that is much earlier than usual or expected 过早死亡/结束等 **2** not suitable for a particular occasion or time 不适时的；不合时宜的 **—untimeliness** *n* [U]

un·tir·ing /ʌn`taɪrɪŋ; ʌn'taɪərɪŋ/ *adj approving* never stopping while working hard or trying to do something【褒】不倦的；坚持不懈的: *untiring efforts to help the homeless* 坚持不懈地致力于帮助无家可归的人 **—untiringly** *adv*

un·to /`ʌntu; 'ʌntuː/ *prep old use* to【旧】对，向: *Thanks be unto God.* 感谢上帝。

un·told /ʌn`told; ˌʌn'təʊld◂/ *adj* too much or too many to be measured (多得) 数不清的；不可计量的: **untold misery** *The floods have caused untold misery to hundreds of homeowners.* 洪水给数以百计的家庭造成了不可估量的痛苦。| **untold damage** *The scandal has done untold damage to his reputation.* 丑闻给他的名声造成了极大的损害。

un·touch·a·ble /ʌn`tʌtʃəbl; ʌn'tʌtʃəbəl/ *adj* **1** someone who is untouchable is in such a strong position that they cannot be affected by, or punished for, anything〔人因地位牢固而〕碰不得的；不受影响的: *He was the boss's husband and therefore*

untouchable. 他是老板的丈夫,因而碰不得。**2** belonging to the lowest social group, especially in the Hindu CASTE system 贱民的〔尤指印度种姓制度最低层者〕**—untouchable** *n* [C]

un·touched /ʌn`tʌtʃt; ˌʌn'tʌtʃt◂/ *adj* untouched food has not been eaten〔食物〕未动过的,未吃[喝]过的: *The food looked so awful that it was left untouched.* 食物看起来太糟糕了,结果没人动过。

un·to·ward /ʌn`tɔrd; ˌʌntə'wɔːd/ *adj* **anything/nothing untoward** *formal* something or nothing that is unexpected, unusual, or not wanted【正式】有/没有意外[异常,不幸]: *We walked past the house but didn't notice anything untoward.* 我们走过那栋房子,但没有注意到任何反常的情况。

un·tram·melled *BrE*【英】, **untrameled** *AmE*【美】/ʌn`træmḷd; ʌn'træməld/ *adj formal* without any limits【正式】不受限制的,不受妨碍的

un·treat·ed /ʌn`tritɪd; ʌn'triːtɪ̈d/ *adj* **1** an untreated illness or injury has not had medical attention〔疾病、伤处〕未予治疗的 **2** harmful substances that are untreated have not been made safe〔有害物质〕未经处理的: *untreated sewage* 未处理过的污水

un·tried /ʌn`traɪd; ˌʌn'traɪd◂/ *adj* **1** not having any experience of doing a particular job 无经验的,不熟练的: *a young and untried minister* 年轻而无经验的部长 **2** not yet tested to see whether it is successful 未经试验的: *a relatively new and untried method* 相当新颖但未经试验的方法

un·true /ʌn`tru; ʌn'truː/ *adj* **1** a statement that is untrue does not give the right facts; false 不真实的,假的 **2** *literary* someone who is untrue to their husband, wife etc is not faithful to them【文】不忠的

un·truth /ʌn`truθ; ʌn'truːθ/ *n* [C] *formal* a word meaning a lie, used because you want to avoid saying this directly【正式】谎言,假话〔委婉语〕

un·truth·ful /ʌn`truθfəl; ʌn'truːθfəl/ *adj* dishonest or not true 不诚实的;不真实的 **—untruthfully** *adv*

un·used[1] /ʌn`juzd; ˌʌn'juːzd◂/ *adj* not being used, or never used 不在使用的;未用过的: *unused office blocks* 空着的办公大楼

un·used[2] /ˌʌn`just; ʌn'juːst/ *adj* **unused to** not experienced in dealing with something 不习惯于…: *a sensitive man unused to publicity* 不习惯于抛头露面的敏感的人 | **unused to doing sth** *Maggie was unused to being told what to do.* 玛吉不习惯被人呼来唤去。

S2 W3 **un·u·su·al** /ʌn`juʒuəl; ʌn'juːʒuəl/ *adj* **1** different from what is usual or ordinary 异常的,不平常的: *The cake has a very unusual flavor.* 那块蛋糕有一种异乎寻常的味道。| **it is unusual to do sth** *It is unusual to find diamonds of this size.* 很难得发现这样大小的钻石。| **it is unusual for sb to do sth** *Earlier last century, it was unusual for women to have a career.* 上世纪初,妇女就业是很少见的。—see 见 RARE (USAGE) **2** interesting or attractive because of being different 独特的,与众不同的: *Alan's artwork is very unusual.* 艾伦的工艺品非常独特。

un·u·su·al·ly /ʌn`juʒuəlɪ; ʌn'juːʒuəli/ *adv* **1 unusually hot/difficult etc** more hot etc than is usual 异常地热/困难等 **2** in an unusual way 异乎寻常地: *The house was unusually quiet.* 那所房子异常地安静。

un·ut·ter·a·ble /ʌn`ʌtərəbḷ; ʌn'ʌtərəbəl/ *adj formal* an unutterable feeling is too extreme to be expressed in words【正式】〔感受〕无法用言语表达的: *unutterable sadness* 难以形容的忧伤 **—unutterably** *adv*

un·var·nished /ʌn`vɑrnɪʃt; ʌn'vɑːnɪʃt/ *adj* [only before noun 仅用于名词前] **1** plain and without additional decoration or description 未加修饰的,直率的: *the unvarnished truth* 不经修饰的真相 **2** without any VARNISH (=a transparent substance like paint, used to protect the surface of wood etc) 未上清漆的

un·veil /ʌn`vel; ˌʌn'veɪl/ *v* [T] **1** to show or tell people something that was previously kept secret 透露;揭露: *Reagan unveiled a series of budget cuts totaling $44 billion.* 里根透露了总计440亿美元的一系列预算削减。**2** to remove the cover from something, especially as part of a formal ceremony〔尤指举行仪式时〕揭去…上的覆盖物: *The Queen unveiled a statue of Prince Albert.* 女王为阿尔伯特亲王塑像揭幕。**—unveiling** *n* [C]

un·versed /ʌn`vɝst; ˌʌn'vɜːst/ *adj formal*【正式】**unversed in sth** without any knowledge or experience of something 对某事不了解[无经验]: *unversed in city ways* 不熟悉城市(生活)方式

un·voiced /ʌn`vɔɪst; ˌʌn'vɔɪst◂/ *adj* **1** not expressed in words 未用语言表达的,没说出来的: *unvoiced fears* 未说出来的恐惧 **2** *technical* unvoiced CONSONANTs are produced without moving the VOCAL CORDs【术语】清音的,无声的: */d/ and /g/ are voiced consonants, and /t/ and /k/ are unvoiced.* /d/和/g/是浊辅音,而/t/和/k/是清辅音。

un·waged /ʌn`wedʒd; ˌʌn'weɪdʒd◂/ *adj BrE* not having a paid job; UNEMPLOYED【英】没有工资收入的;失业的

un·want·ed /ʌn`wɑntɪd; ʌn'wɒntɪ̈d/ *adj* not wanted or needed 不需要的,多余的: *an unwanted pregnancy* 不希望有的怀孕

un·war·rant·ed /ʌn`wɔrəntɪd; ʌn'wɒrəntɪ̈d/ **unwarrantable** *adj* done without good reason, and therefore annoying 没有根据的;无正当理由的: *unwarranted interference in our affairs* 对我们事务的无理干涉

un·wa·ry /ʌn`wɛrɪ; ʌn'weəri/ *adj* not knowing about possible problems or dangers, and therefore easily harmed or deceived 不警惕的,粗心的〔因而容易受伤或受骗〕: **the unwary** (=people who are unwary) 粗心大意的人 **—unwarily** *adv* **—unwariness** *n* [U]

un·wel·come /ʌn`wɛlkəm; ʌn'welkəm/ *adj* **1** something that is unwelcome is not wanted, especially because it might cause embarrassment or problems 不想要的: *unwelcome publicity* 不受欢迎的宣传 **2** unwelcome guests, visitors etc are people that you do not want in your home〔客人等〕不受欢迎的,讨厌的

un·well /ʌn`wɛl; ʌn'wel/ *adj* [not before noun 不用于名词前] *formal* ill, especially for a short time【正式】〔尤指短时间的〕不舒服的,有病的 —see 见 SICK[1] (USAGE)

un·wield·y /ʌn`wildɪ; ʌn'wiːldi/ *adj* **1** an unwieldy object is big and heavy and difficult to carry〔物体〕庞大的,笨重的,难以搬运的 **2** an unwieldy system, argument, or plan is difficult to control or manage because it is too complicated〔因太复杂而〕难操纵的;难控制的: *unwieldy bureaucracy* 难以控制的官僚机构 **—unwieldiness** *n* [U]

un·will·ing /ʌn`wɪlɪŋ; ʌn'wɪlɪŋ/ *adj* **1** [not before noun 不用于名词前] not wanting to do something and refusing to do it 不愿意的,不乐意的: **unwilling to do sth** *They were unwilling to fund a project that had little chance of success.* 他们不愿意为一个不大可能成功的项目提供资金。**2** [only before noun 仅用于名词前] not wanting to do something but doing it 勉强(做)的,不情愿的: *an unwilling helper* 不情愿的助手 **—unwillingly** *adv*

un·wind /ʌn`waɪnd; ʌn'waɪnd/ *v past tense and past participle* **unwound** /-`waʊnd; -'waʊnd/ **1** [I] to relax and stop feeling anxious 放松,松弛: *I love cooking. It helps me unwind.* 我喜欢烹饪,它可以让我放松。**2** [I,T] to undo something that has been wrapped around something else 解开;展开(卷起的东西)

un·wit·ting·ly /ʌn`wɪtɪŋlɪ; ʌn'wɪtɪŋli/ *adv* in a way that shows you do not know or realize something 不知情地;未意识到地: *Friedmann had unwittingly stumbled upon a vital piece of evidence.* 弗里德曼无意中发现一个极重要的证据。**—unwitting** *adj* [only before noun 仅用于名词前]: *an unwitting accomplice* 不知情的同谋

un·wont·ed /ʌn`wontɪd; ʌn'wəʊntɪ̈d/ *adj* [only before noun 仅用于名词前] *formal* unusual and not what you expect to happen【正式】不寻常的,异常的: *"Good day" he cried with unwonted good humour.* "你好",他带着难得的好兴致大声说。

un·world·ly /ʌn`wɝldlɪ; ʌn'wɜːldli/ *adj* not interested in money or possessions 对钱财不感兴趣的;脱俗的,超凡的

un·wound /ʌn`waʊnd; ʌn'waʊnd/ the past tense and past participle of UNWIND

un·writ·ten /ʌn`rɪtṇ; ʌn'rɪtn/ *adj* known about and understood by everyone but not formally written down 非书面的;不成文的: **unwritten rule/law** *It was an unwritten law among my friends that we never told our mothers what we did.* 我们从不把所做的事告诉母亲,这在我的朋友中是一种不成文的规定。

un·zip /ʌn`zɪp; ˌʌn'zɪp/ *v* [T] to unfasten the ZIP on a piece of clothing, bag etc 拉开…的拉链

up- /ʌp; ʌp/ *prefix* **1** making something higher 使升级;使更高: *to upgrade a job* (=make it higher in importance) 提高工作的重要性 **2** [especially in adverbs and adjectives 尤构成副词和形容词] at or towards the top or beginning of something 在[向]…高处[源头]的: *uphill* 上坡的;往上坡 | *upriver* (=nearer to where the river starts) 在上游的;向上游 **3** [especially in verbs 尤构成动词] taking something from its place or turning it upside down 使起来〔离开原位〕;使颠倒过来: *an uprooted tree* 被连根拔起的树 | *She upended the bucket.* 她把水桶倒了过来。**4** [especially in adjectives and adverbs 尤构成形容词和副词] at or towards the higher or better part of something 在[向]更高处;在[向]更好处: *up-market* (=suitable for the higher social groups) 高档的;适合高消费阶层的 —compare 比较 DOWN-

up[1] /ʌp; ʌp/ *adv* **1** towards a higher position from the floor, ground, or bottom of something 从下往上地,向上地: *She picked her pen up off the floor.* 她从地板上捡起钢笔。| *Can you lift that box up onto the shelf for me?* 你能帮我把那个箱子提起来放到架子上去吗? | *After swimming for several seconds underwater he came up for air.* 他在水下游了几秒钟后,浮上来换

气。| **up you come** *spoken* (=used especially to children when lifting them)【口】你上来了〔尤抱起儿童时用语〕**2** at or in a high position 在高处: *John's up in his bedroom.* 约翰在楼上他的卧室里。| *The plane was flying 30,000 feet up.* 飞机在3万英尺高空飞行。**3** into an upright or raised position 处于[趋于]直立的位置; 起来: *Everyone stood up for the National Anthem.* 奏国歌时每个人都起立。| *Mick turned his collar up against the biting winds.* 米克翻起衣领抵挡刺骨的寒风。**4** in or towards the North 在[向]北方: *We're going to fly up to Scotland from London.* 我们将从伦敦向北飞往苏格兰。| *They live up North.* 他们住在北方。**5** towards someone so that you are near, or in the place where they are 向; 靠近: *He came right up and asked my name.* 他径直走过来问我的名字。| *A man sidled up to her and asked for money.* 一个男子悄悄地走过来向她讨钱。**6** increasing in loudness, strength, level of activity etc〔声音、力量、水平等〕由小变大, 由低变高: *Can you turn the telly up a bit?* 你能把电视机调大声点吗? | *Competition between these two companies is really hotting up.* 这两家公司的竞争真的愈来愈激烈了。**7** so as to be completely finished or used so that there is nothing left …完; …光: *Our savings are all used up.* 我们的积蓄都用光了。| *She won't eat up her vegetables.* 她吃不完自己的蔬菜。**8** so as to be in small pieces or divided into equal parts 成碎片; 平分: *They divided up the money.* 他们把钱分了。| *The plane hit the mountainside and broke up on impact.* 飞机撞在山坡上撞了个粉碎。**9** so as to be firmly fastened, covered, or joined〔拴、盖、连接〕紧地; 牢牢地: *Mr Cain was boarding up the windows.* 凯恩先生正用木板封紧窗户。**10** so as to be brought or gathered together 在一起, 合起来: *Let's just add up these figures quickly.* 让我们快把这些数字加起来吧。| *Could you collect up the pens?* 你能把那些钢笔收拢在一起吗? **11** if a surface or part of something is a particular way up, it is on top 朝上: **right side up/right way up** (=with the part that is going to be used, or that has words or pictures on it on top) 正面朝上 *Put the playing cards right side up on the table.* 把纸牌正面朝上放在桌上。**12** so as to receive attention 提出(以引起注意): *The question of a pay rise came up again during the meeting.* 增加工资的问题又在会议上提了出来。**13** above and including a certain amount or level 在…及以上: *Power was lost from the tenth floor up.* 10楼及以上没有电。| *Children of twelve up must pay full fare.* 12岁及以上儿童必须购全票。**14 up and down a)** higher and lower 一上一下; 起伏地: *The crowd were jumping up and down and screaming excitedly.* 人群跳上跳下, 激动得尖声喊叫。| **look sb up and down** (=look at someone in order to judge their appearance or character) 上下打量某人; 审视 *Maisie looked her rival critically up and down.* 梅茜挑剔地上下打量着对手。**b)** backwards and forwards 来来回回; 往返地: *Ralph paced up and down the room looking agitated.* 拉尔夫在屋里踱来踱去, 显得焦虑不安。**15 up to a)** up to and including a certain amount or level 多达, 至多…: *Up to six people* (=any number between one and six) *can sleep in the caravan.* 篷车最多可以睡六个人。**b)** also 又作 **up till** if something happens up to a certain time, date etc it happens until that time〔时间上〕一直到: *She continued to care for her father up to the time of his death.* 她一直照顾父亲, 直到他去世。**c)** clever, good, or well enough for a particular purpose or in order to do something 胜任〔工作等〕; 有资格做; 适于: *I'm afraid Tim just isn't up to the job* (=not good enough to do it properly). 我恐怕蒂姆干不了这份工作。| *Gemma isn't really up to long walks at the moment* (=too ill to do them). 杰玛眼下真的走不了这么长的路。| **up to doing** *My German isn't up to translating that letter.* 我的德语还不足以翻译那封信。**d)** if something is up to a particular standard it is good enough to reach that standard 达到〔标准〕: *The new CD is not up to the group's usual standard.* 新推出的激光唱片没有达到该演唱组通常的水准。**e)** doing something secret or something that you shouldn't be doing 干秘密或不应该干的事: *The children are very quiet; I wonder what they're up to.* 孩子们很安静, 我不知道他们在搞什么鬼。| **up to no good** (=doing something wrong or illegal) 做坏事 *I'll bet that Joe and his mates are up to no good as usual.* 我敢肯定乔和他的同伙跟往常一样在干坏事。**16 it's up to you** *spoken* used to tell someone that they must make a decision themselves【口】由你作主, 取决于你: *"Shall we have red wine or white?" "It's up to you."* "我们要红酒还是白酒?" "由你决定吧。" **17 up to your ears/eyes/neck in** *informal* deeply involved in a difficult or illegal situation【非正式】深陷于…; 埋头于…: *Rona and Colin are up to their ears in debt* (=they owe a lot of money). 罗娜和科林债台高筑。**18 up the workers!/up the reds! etc** *spoken* used to express support and encouragement for a particular group of people or for a sports team【口】工人加油!/红队加油!

up² *prep* **1** towards or in a higher place 向[在]…上: *We climbed slowly up the hill.* 我们缓缓地爬上山。| *The water was getting up my nose.* 水呛入我的鼻子里。**2** towards or at the top or far end of 向[在]…顶上; 向[在]…的远端: *Her office is up those stairs.* 她的办公室在楼上。| *They live just up the road* (=further along the road from here). 他们就住在路的那一头。**3** if you sail or go up a river you go towards its SOURCE¹ (4) 向…的上游: *a boat trip up the Bosphorus* 乘船沿博斯普鲁斯海峡而上 **4** *BrE spoken* used to mean to or at a particular place, although most people think this is incorrect【英口】到[在]…地方〔多数人认为此用法不正确〕: *Do you fancy going up the town?* 你想过到城里去吗? **5 up yours!** *spoken taboo* used to insult someone when they have done or said something that annoys you【口讳】去你的!〔用于被某人做的事或说的话激怒时〕: *"You'll never get promoted, you're not good enough." "Up yours!"* "你永远别想得到提升, 你不够资格。" "去你的!"

up³ *adj* **1** [not before noun 不用于名词前] not in bed 起床的, 没睡觉的: *Are the kids still up?* 孩子们还没睡吗? **2** [not before noun 不用于名词前] if a road is up, its surface is being repaired〔路面〕正在翻修的 **3** [not before noun 不用于名词前] if a computer system is up, it is working〔电脑系统〕正在工作的, 运行的 —opposite 反义词 DOWN³ (5) **4** [not before noun 不用于名词前] if a number, level, or amount is up, it is higher than before〔数目、水平、数量〕上涨的: *Inflation is up by 2 %.* 通货膨胀上涨2%。| [+on] *Profits are up on last year.* 利润与去年比较增加了。| **two goals up/three points up** (=having two goals, three points etc more than your opponents) 领先两球/三分 *United were a goal up at half time.* 联队在上半场结束时领先一球。**5** [not before noun 不用于名词前] if a ball is up in tennis or similar sports, it has only hit the ground once and therefore can be hit back by the opponent〔网球等在被击回前〕只落地一次的 **6 be up and about** *informal* to be well enough to walk about and have a normal life after you have been in bed because of an illness or accident【非正式】〔病后或事故后〕能起床走动 **7 be up to here (with)** *spoken* to be very upset and angry because of a particular situation or person【口】(对…)感到气愤: *I'm up to here with this job; I'm resigning!* 这份工作我干够了, 我要辞职! **8 be up and down** if someone is up and down, they sometimes feel well or happy and sometimes do not〔情绪〕波动不定: *Jason's been very up and down since his girlfriend left him.* 自从女朋友离开他以后, 贾森的情绪就很不稳定。**9 be up against** to have to deal with a difficult situation or fight an opponent 面临, 必须对付〔困境或对手〕: *He came up against a lot of problems with his previous boss.* 上一个老板给他不少麻烦。| **be up against it** *Murphy will be really up against it when he faces the reigning champion this afternoon.* 今天下午要面对本届冠军, 真够墨菲受的。**10 be up before** *informal* to appear in a court of law because you have been accused of a crime【非正式】出庭受审: *He was up before the Magistrates court charged with grievous bodily harm.* 他被控犯有严重人身伤害罪而在地方法庭受审。**11 be up for a)** to be intended for a particular purpose 用于…的: *The house is up for sale.* 这房现供出售。| *Even the most taboo subjects were up for discussion.* 连最禁忌的话题也供讨论了。**b)** to appear in a court of law because you have been accused of a crime〔因被控有罪而〕出庭受审: *Ron's up for drinking and driving next week.* 罗恩因酒后开车将于下周出庭受审。**12 be (well) up on/in/with** *informal* to know a lot about something【非正式】非常熟悉〔某事〕; 精通 **13** *spoken* if something is up, someone is feeling unhappy because they have problems, or there is something wrong in a situation【口】出事的; 发生不快的: *I could tell by the look on Joan's face that something was up.* 看琼的脸色, 我就知道出事了。| [+with] *Is something up with Julie? She looks really miserable.* 朱莉出了什么事? 她看起来真的很痛苦。| **what's up?** *What's up? Why are you crying?* 怎么啦? 你为什么哭? **14 not be up to much** *spoken* to not be of a very good quality or standard【口】不太好: *The food in that restaurant isn't up to much.* 那家餐馆的饭菜不怎么样。**15** [not before noun 不用于名词前] *informal* if a period of time is up, it is finished【非正式】到期的: *The President may be asked to resign before his four-year term is up.* 四年任期不到, 总统就可能被要求辞职。**16** [not before noun 不用于名词前] *informal* when food or drink is up it is ready to be eaten or drunk【非正式】〔饭菜〕准备好的: *Dinner's up!* 晚饭准备好了! **17 be up and running** if a new system or process is up and running, it is working properly〔新系统、新程序〕运行正常: *The New York office was up and running in about half the time it took us in Paris.* 只用了我们在巴黎所花时间的一半, 纽约办事处的工作就安排就绪了。**18 up to speed** knowing the necessary latest information or situation 跟上形势, 不落伍: *getting top-*

level managers up to speed on developments in on-line services 使高层管理人员掌握在线服务的最新发展

up⁴ *n* **1 be on an up** *spoken* to feel happy, especially after being upset and unhappy【口】开心〔尤指忧伤过后〕: *Kevin seems to be on an up at the moment; I hope it lasts.* 凯文眼下似乎很开心，我希望这种好心情能保持下去。**2 ups and downs** *informal* the mixture of good and bad experiences that happen in any situation or relationship【非正式】盛衰；浮沉；苦乐: *We have our ups and downs like all couples.* 我们有苦有乐，跟所有的夫妻一样。**3 on the up and up** *informal*【非正式】**a)** *BrE* improving and becoming more successful, especially financially【英】〔尤指经济上〕走上坡路，蒸蒸日上 **b)** *AmE* not hiding anything; HONEST【美】坦诚的；诚实的

up⁵ *v* **1** [T] to increase the amount or level of something 提高；增加: *They've upped their offer by a further 5%.* 他们把出价又提高了5%。**2 up and ...** if you up and do something, you suddenly start to do something different or surprising 突然开始〔做某事〕: **up and leave** *Without saying another word, he upped and left.* 他没再说一句话，突然站起来走了。

up-and-com·ing /ˌ· · ˈ·· ◂/ *adj* [only before noun 仅用于名词前] likely to be successful or popular 有希望的，有前途的: *an up-and-coming band from Manchester* 来自曼彻斯特的大有前途的乐队

up-and-un·der /ˌ· · ˈ· ·/ *n* [C] a situation in RUGBY when the ball is kicked forwards high into the air, and the players all rush towards the place where the ball lands〔橄榄球的〕过顶高球

U·pan·ish·ads, the /uˋpɑnɪʃɑd; uːˈpʌnɪʃəd/ *n* [plural] a collection of ancient holy books containing the main principles of Hindu religion and PHILOSOPHY《奥义书》〔记载印度教教义和哲学基本原理的古代圣书集〕

up·beat /ˋʌpˌbit; ˈʌpbiːt/ *adj* cheerful and making you feel that good things will happen 乐观的；欢笑的: *a comedy film with an upbeat ending* 以皆大欢喜为结局的喜剧电影

up·braid /ʌpˋbred; ˌʌpˈbreɪd/ *v* [T] *formal* to tell someone angrily that they have done something wrong【正式】责备，申斥〔某人〕

up·bring·ing /ˋʌpˌbrɪŋɪŋ; ˈʌpˌbrɪŋɪŋ/ *n* [singular] the care and training that parents give their children when they are growing up 抚育，养育；培养: *Mike had had a strict upbringing.* 迈克从小家教很严。

up·chuck /ˋʌpˌtʃʌk; ˈʌptʃʌk/ *v* [I] *AmE informal* to bring food or drink up from your stomach and out through your mouth because you are ill or drunk; VOMIT¹【美，非正式】呕吐

up·com·ing /ˋʌpˌkʌmɪŋ; ˈʌpˌkʌmɪŋ/ *adj* [only before noun 仅用于名词前] happening soon 即将来临的；即将发生的: *the upcoming elections* 即将来临的选举

up·coun·try /ˌʌpˋkʌntrɪ; ˌʌpˈkʌntri◂/ *adj* from an area of land without many people or towns, especially in the middle of a country 来自内地的〔尤指一国的中部，人或城镇不多的地区〕: *upcountry people* 内地人 —**upcountry** *adv*

up·date¹ /ʌpˋdet; ʌpˈdeɪt/ *v* [T] **1** to add the most recent information to something 为…提供最新信息；更新: *The files need updating.* 档案需要更新。**2** to make something more modern in the way it looks or operates 使现代化，使不过时

up·date² /ˋʌpdet; ˈʌpdeɪt/ *n* [C] the most recent news about something 最新消息: **[+on]** *the latest update on the Whitewater affair* 有关白水事件的最新消息

Up·dike /ˋʌpdaɪk; ˈʌpdaɪk/, **John** (1932-2009) a US writer who has written several NOVELs about the lives, relationships, and problems of MIDDLE CLASS people in the US, such as *Rabbit, Run* and *Rabbit is Rich*. His novel *The Witches of Eastwick* was made into a successful film. 厄普代克（1932-2009），美国作家。他创作的系列小说关乎美国中产阶级的生活、情感关系及面临的问题，如《兔子，快跑》和《兔子富了》等。小说《伊斯特威克的女巫们》被改编成一部优秀影片

up·end /ʌpˋɛnd; ʌpˈend/ *v* [T] to turn something over so that it is standing upside down 倒着放置〔某物〕

up·front /ˌʌpˋfrʌnt; ˌʌpˈfrʌnt/ *adj* [not before noun 不用于名词前] behaving or talking in a direct and honest way〔行为、谈话〕坦率的，诚实的: *Mo's very upfront with him about their relationship.* 莫在跟他的关系上很坦诚。—see also 另见 **up front** (FRONT¹ (15))

up·grade /ˌʌpˋgred; ˌʌpˈgreɪd/ *v* **1** [I,T] to make a computer or other machine better and able to do more things（使）〔电脑等〕升级 **2** [T] to give someone a more important job 提升〔某人〕，给〔某人〕升职 **3** [T] to be given a better seat on a plane than the one you paid for 飞机座位提级，升舱 —opposite 反义词 DOWNGRADE —**upgrade** /ˋʌpgred; ˈʌpgreɪd/ *n* [C]

up·heav·al /ʌpˋhivl̩; ʌpˈhiːvəl/ *n* [C,U] **1** a very big change that often causes problems 激变，剧变；动乱: *political upheaval* 政治动乱 **2** a very strong movement upwards, especially of the earth〔尤指地面的〕隆起

up·hill¹ /ˋʌpˋhɪl; ˌʌpˈhɪl◂/ *adj* **1** towards the top of a hill 上坡的，上山的: *an uphill climb* 向山上爬 **2** an uphill battle, struggle, job etc is very difficult and needs a lot of effort〔战斗、斗争、工作等〕艰难的，费力的

uphill² *adv* towards the top of a hill 往上坡；往山上

up·hold /ʌpˋhold; ʌpˈhəʊld/ *v* *past tense and past participle* **upheld** /-ˋhɛld; -ˈheld/ [T] **1** to defend or support a law, system, or principle so that it is not made weaker 支持，维护〔法规、制度或原则〕: *They want to uphold traditional family values.* 他们想坚持传统的家庭价值观念。**2** if a court upholds a decision made by another court, it states that the decision was correct〔法庭〕维持〔原判〕—**upholder** *n* [C]

up·hol·ster /ʌpˋholstɚ; ʌpˈhəʊlstə/ *v* [T] to cover a chair with material 为〔椅子〕装垫子[套子] —**upholstered** *adj* —**upholsterer** *n* [C]

up·hol·ster·y /ʌpˋholstərɪ; ʌpˈhəʊlstəri/ *n* [U] **1** material used to cover chairs 椅子套；垫衬料 **2** the process of covering chairs with material 座椅的加套装饰

up·keep /ˋʌpˌkip; ˈʌpkiːp/ *n* [U+of] the care needed to keep something in good condition 保养，维修

up·lands /ˋʌpləndz; ˈʌpləndz/ *n plural* the parts of a country that are away from the sea and are higher than other areas 高地；高原；山地 —**upland** *adj*: *upland forests* 山地森林

up·lift¹ /ˋʌpˌlɪft; ˈʌplɪft/ *n* [U] a sudden happy feeling 振奋

up·lift² /ʌpˋlɪft; ʌpˈlɪft/ *v* [T] *formal*【正式】**1** to make someone feel more cheerful 使〔某人〕振奋，鼓舞 **2** to make something higher 举起，抬起，抬高〔某物〕

up·lift·ed /ʌpˋlɪftɪd; ʌpˈlɪftɪ̣d/ *adj* **1** feeling happier 振奋的 **2** *literary* raised upwards【文】被提[抬]起的

up·lift·ing /ʌpˋlɪftɪŋ; ʌpˈlɪftɪŋ/ *adj* making you feel more cheerful 令人振奋的

up·mar·ket /ˌʌpˋmɑrkɪt; ˌʌpˈmɑːkɪ̣t◂/ *adj* connected with people who belong to a high social class or who have a lot of money 适合高消费阶层的；高档的；UPSCALE *AmE*【美】: *an upmarket fashion retailer* 高档时装零售商 —compare 比较 DOWNMARKET

up·on /əˋpɑn; əˈpɒn/ *prep formal*【正式】= on: *an honour bestowed upon the association* 授予该协会的荣誉 | *We are completely dependent upon your help.* 我们完全依赖你的帮助。—see also 另见 **once upon a time** (ONCE¹ (14)) —see picture on page A1 参见A1页图 3 1

up·per¹ /ˋʌpɚ; ˈʌpə/ *adj* [only before noun 仅用于名词前] **1** in a higher position than something else〔位置〕较上的，较高的，上面的: *the upper lip* 上唇 **2** near or at the top of something 靠近顶部的；在顶部的: *The monkeys live in the upper branches.* 猴子生活在靠近顶端的树枝上。**3 have/gain the upper hand** to have more power than someone else, so that you are able to control a situation 占上风；处于有利地位；控制: *Police have gained the upper hand over the drug dealers in the area.* 警察打击该地区的毒品贩子，处于上风。**4** more important than other parts or ranks in an organization, system etc 较高级的，上级的: **the upper echelons** (=the most important and most senior members of an organization) 最高层 **5 the upper limit** the highest limit 上限，最大限度: *sounds that are at the upper limit of our hearing capability* 处在我们听力极限的声音 **6** further from the sea or further north than other parts of an area 上游的；北部的: **the upper reaches** (=the parts of a river that are the furthest from the sea) 上游 *the upper reaches of the Nile* 尼罗河的上游 —see also 另见 **keep a stiff upper lip** (STIFF¹ (9)) 2

upper² *n* [C] **1** the top part of a shoe that covers your foot 鞋面，鞋帮: *leather uppers* 皮革鞋帮 —see picture at 参见 SHOE¹ 图 **2 uppers** [plural] *slang* illegal drugs that make you feel happy and give you a lot of energy; AMPHETAMINE【俚】兴奋剂；安非他明 **3 be on your uppers** *BrE old-fashioned* to have very little money【英，过时】一贫如洗

upper case /ˌ·· ˈ·◂/ *n* [U] *technical* letters written in capitals (A, B, C) rather than in small form (a, b, c)【术语】大写字母

upper class, the /ˌ·· ˈ·◂/ *n* [C] the group of people who belong to the highest social class 上流社会，上层社会: *upper class families* 上流阶层家庭 —**upper class** *adj*

up·per·class·man /ˌʌpɚˋklæsmən; ˌʌpəˈklɑːsmən/ *n* [C] *AmE* a student in the last two years at a school or university【美】〔中学或大学的〕高年级学生 —compare 比较 UNDERCLASSMAN

up·per·class·wom·an /ˌʌpɚˋklæswumən; ˌʌpəˈklɑːswʊmən/ *n* [C] *AmE* a female student in the last two years of school or university【美】高年级女生

up·per crust /ˌ‥ˈ◂/ *n* [singular] *informal* the group of people who belong to the highest social class【非正式】上流社会，上层社会 —**upper-crust** *adj*

up·per·cut /ˋʌpɚˌkʌt; ˈʌpəkʌt/ *n* [C] a way of hitting someone in which you swing your hand upwards into their chin 上钩拳

Up·per House /ˌ‥ˈ·/ *n* [singular] a group of elected representatives in a country, that is smaller and less powerful than the country's LOWER HOUSE 上议院

up·per·most /ˋʌpɚˌmost; ˈʌpəməʊst/ *adj* **1 uppermost in your mind** if something is uppermost in your mind, you think about it a lot because it is very important to you 心目中最主要的: *It is Tom's safety that is uppermost in our minds.* 汤姆的安全是我们心中最牵挂的事。**2** more important than other things 最重要的，压倒一切的: *As he looked at her, curiosity was his uppermost feeling.* 他望着她时，最主要的感觉是好奇。**3** higher than anything else 最高的: *the uppermost leaves on the tree* 树上最高处的叶子

upper school /ˈ‥ ·/ *n* [C] the classes of a school in Britain that are for older pupils, usually aged 14 to 18〔英国学校为 14 至 18 岁学生开设的〕大龄班

Upper Vol·ta /ˋʌpɚ ˋvɑltə; ˌʌpə ˈvɒltə/ the former name for Burkina Faso 上沃尔特〔布基纳法索的旧称〕

up·pi·ty /ˋʌpəti; ˈʌpɪ̇ti/ also 又作 **up·pish** /ˋʌpɪʃ; ˈʌpɪʃ/ *BrE*【英】*adj informal* behaving as if you are more important than you really are【非正式】傲慢的，盛气凌人的: *Now, don't start getting uppity with me, young man.* 好了，别对我这么傲慢，年轻人。

up·right[1] /ˋʌpˌraɪt; ˈʌp-raɪt/ *adj* **1** standing straight up 垂直的，笔直的 **2** always behaving in an honest way 正直的，诚实的: *decent, upright citizens* 正派诚实的公民 —**uprightness** *n* [U]

upright[2] *adv* **1** sitting or standing with your back straight 笔直地: **sit/stand bolt upright** *He sat bolt upright, startled by the scream.* 他挺直地坐着，被尖叫声吓呆了。**2** if something is pulled, held etc upright, it is put into a position in which it is standing straight up 竖直地

upright[3] *n* [C] a long piece of wood or metal that stands straight up and supports something〔木头或金属的〕直立支撑物

upright pi·an·o /ˌ‥ ·ˈ‥/ *n* [C] a piano with strings that are set in an up and down direction 竖[立]式钢琴

up·ris·ing /ˋʌpˌraɪzɪŋ; ˈʌpˌraɪzɪŋ/ *n* [C] an occasion when a group of people use violence to try to change the rules, laws etc in an institution or country 起义，暴动: *the 1956 Hungarian uprising* 1956 年的匈牙利起义

up·riv·er /ˌʌpˈrɪvɚ; ˌʌpˈrɪvə/ *adv* away from the sea towards the place where a river begins 向上游；从上游

up·roar /ˋʌpˌror; ˈʌp-rɔː/ *n* [singular, U] a lot of noise or angry protest about something 喧嚣；吵闹；骚动: **be in an uproar** *The house was in an uproar, with babies crying and people shouting.* 房子里婴儿在哭，人们在喊叫，一片喧闹。

up·roar·i·ous /ʌpˋrorɪəs; ʌpˈrɔːriəs/ *adj* very noisy, because a lot of people are laughing or shouting 喧闹的，人声鼎沸的 —**uproariously** *adv*

up·root /ʌpˋrut; ˌʌpˈruːt/ *v* [T] **1** to pull a plant and its roots out of the ground 把〔植物〕连根拔起 **2** to make someone leave their home for a new place, especially when this is difficult or upsetting 使〔某人〕迁移他处居住: *My father was in the army, so every two years we were uprooted and moved again.* 我父亲在军队中，所以每隔两年我们就要搬迁一次。

ups-a-dai·sy /ˋʌps ə ˋdezɪ; ˈʌps ə ˌdeɪzi/ *interjection* another spelling of OOPS-A-DAISY oops-a-daisy 的另一种拼法

up·scale /ˋʌpˌskel; ˈʌpskeɪl/ *adj AmE* connected with people from a high social class who have a lot of money; UPMARKET【美】适合高消费阶层的，高档的

up·set[1] /ʌpˋsɛt; ʌpˈset/ *v past tense and past participle* **upset** [T] **1** to make someone feel unhappy or worried 使〔某人〕心烦意乱，使生气: *I'm sorry, I didn't mean to upset you.* 对不起，我不是故意惹你不高兴的。**2** to change a plan or situation in a way that causes problems 打乱，搅乱〔计划、形势等〕: *The delicate ecological balance of the area was upset.* 该地区脆弱的生态平衡被打乱了。**3** to push something over without intending to〔无意地〕打翻，弄翻〔某物〕: *He upset a bottle of ink over the map.* 他无意中把一瓶墨水打翻在地图上。**4 upset sb's stomach** to make someone feel sick 使某人肠胃不适 **5 upset the apple cart** completely spoil someone's plans 搅乱某人的计划 —**upsetting** *adj*

up·set[2] /ˋʌpˌsɛt; ˈʌpset/ *n* **1** [C] an unexpected problem or difficulty 意外的挫折: *Despite this upset, the General decided to go ahead with the attack.* 尽管有此变故，将军还是决定发起攻击。**2** an occasion when a person or team surprisingly beats a stronger opponent in a competition, election etc〔比赛、竞选等〕意外的击败: *It was a major upset when the young skater took the gold medal.* 那个年轻的滑冰选手夺得金牌，这可真是个出乎意料的结果。**3 stomach/tummy upset** an illness that affects the stomach and makes you feel sick 肠胃/肚子不适 **4** [C,U] worry and unhappiness caused by an unexpected problem〔因意外问题引起的〕烦恼

up·set[3] /ʌpˋsɛt; ˌʌpˈset◂/ *adj* **1** [not before noun 不用于名词前] unhappy and worried because something unpleasant or disappointing has happened 不快的，心烦意乱的，烦恼的: **[+about/by/over etc]** *She was still upset about the argument she'd had with Harry.* 她依然为跟哈里发生的争论而感到烦恼。| **upset that** *Dad was very upset that you didn't phone.* 你没打电话来，爸爸很不高兴。**2 an upset stomach/tummy** an illness that affects the stomach and makes you feel sick 肠胃/肚子不适

up·shot /ˋʌpˌʃɑt; ˈʌpʃɒt/ *n* **the upshot (of)** the final result of a situation 结果，结局: *The upshot was that Jane decided to leave home.* 结局是简决定离家出走。

up·side[1] /ˋʌpˌsaɪd; ˈʌpsaɪd/ *n* [singular] *especially AmE* the positive part of a situation that is generally bad【尤美】〔不利局面中〕好的一面，积极面: *The upside of the whole thing is that we got a free trip to Jamaica.* 整个事情的好处是我们免费去了一趟牙买加。

upside[2] *prep* **upside the head/face etc** *AmE informal* on the side of someone's head etc【美，非正式】在头/脸等的侧面

up·side down /ˌ‥ˈ·/ *adv* **1** with the top at the bottom and the bottom at the top 倒置地，颠倒地: *You've hung that picture upside down!* 你把那幅画倒挂了！**2** disorganized or untidy 混乱地，乱七八糟地 —see also 另见 **turn sth upside down** (TURN[1] (19b))

up·stage[1] /ˋʌpˋstedʒ; ˌʌpˈsteɪdʒ◂/ *v* [T] to do something that takes people's attention away from someone else who is more important 将他人注意力从〔某人〕引向自己；抢〔更重要人物〕的镜头: *All the big name stars were upstaged by twelve-year-old Katy Rochford.* 所有的大明星都被 12 岁的凯蒂·罗奇福德抢去了风头。

upstage[2] *adv* towards the back of the stage in a theatre 朝着舞台后方 —**upstage** *adj*

up·stairs[1] /ʌpˋstɛrz; ˌʌpˈsteəz◂/ *adv* **1** towards a higher floor in a building, using the stairs 往楼上: *Lucy came rushing upstairs after her sister.* 露西追着妹妹跑上楼。—opposite 反义词 DOWNSTAIRS (1) **2** on an upper floor in a building, especially a house 在楼上: *My office is upstairs on the right.* 我的办公室在楼上右边。—compare 比较 DOWNSTAIRS (1) —see also 另见 **kick sb upstairs** (KICK[1] (10)) —**upstairs** *adj*: *an upstairs window* 楼上的窗户

upstairs[2] *n* [singular] **1 the upstairs** one or all of the upper floors in a building 楼层 **2 not have much upstairs** to not be very intelligent 不太有头脑 **3 the man upstairs** *informal* God【非正式】上帝

up·stand·ing /ʌpˋstændɪŋ; ˌʌpˈstændɪŋ/ *adj formal*【正式】**1** honest and responsible 诚实的，正直的: *an upstanding citizen* 正直的公民 **2** tall and strong 高大强壮的

up·start /ˋʌpˌstɑrt; ˈʌpstɑːt/ *n* [C] someone who is new in their job and behaves as if they are more important than they really are 暴发户；新贵；自命不凡的家伙: *an impudent young upstart* 粗鲁无礼的年轻新贵 —**upstart** *adj*

up·state /ˋʌpˌstet; ˈʌpsteɪt/ *adj* [only before noun 仅用于名词前] *AmE* in the northern part of a particular state【美】州的北部地区的: *upstate New York* 纽约州的北部地区 —**upstate** *adv*

up·stream /ˋʌpˋstrim; ˌʌpˈstriːm◂/ *adv* along a river, in the opposite direction from the way the water is flowing 向上游；逆流（地）—**upstream** *adj* —opposite 反义词 DOWNSTREAM

up·surge /ˋʌpsɝdʒ; ˈʌpsɜːdʒ/ *n* [C] **1** a sudden increase 猛增，急剧上升: **[+in]** *There's been an upsurge in complaints about the police.* 对警察的投诉猛然增多。**2** sudden strong feelings〔情绪的〕高涨，激发: **[+of]** *Adolescence is marked by an upsurge of sexual feeling.* 青春期的特点是性感觉骤增。

up·swing /ˋʌpˌswɪŋ; ˈʌpˌswɪŋ/ *n* [C] an improvement or increase in the level of something 进步；改进；改善；上升: *an upswing in the economy* 经济的回升

up·take /ˋʌpˌtek; ˈʌpteɪk/ *n* **1 be slow/quick on the uptake** *informal* to be slow or fast at learning or understanding things【非正式】领会[理解]慢/快 **2** [C,U] *technical* the rate at which a substance is taken into a system, machine etc【术语】吸收，摄

取(率): *the uptake of food and oxygen into an organism* 有机体对食物和氧气的吸收

up·tem·po /ˌ·ˈ··◂/ *adj* moving or happening at a fast rate 快速度的: *music with an up-tempo beat* 快节奏的音乐

up·tight /ˈʌpˌtaɪt; ˈʌptaɪt/ *adj informal* behaving in an angry way because you are feeling nervous and worried【非正式】〔行为因紧张不安而〕愤怒的

up-to-date /ˌ··ˈ·◂/ *adj* **1** modern or fashionable 现代的; 时髦的: *up-to-date ideas on education* 有关教育的现代理念 | **bring sth up-to-date** (=make something more modern) 使某事物更新潮 **2** including all the newest information 包含最新信息的: *up-to-date news* 最新消息 | *an up-to-date map* 包含最新资料的地图 | **keep/bring sb up-to-date** (=give someone all the newest information about something) 给某人提供〔有关某事物的〕全部最新信息

up-to-the-min·ute /ˌ····ˈ··◂/ *adj* **1** including all the newest information 包含最新信息的: *up-to-the-minute financial information* 最新金融信息 **2** very modern or fashionable 最新式的; 最时髦的

up·town /ˈʌpˌtaun; ˌʌpˈtaʊn◂/ *adv AmE* towards the northern areas of a city, especially the areas where people have more money【美】向城市的北部〔尤指有钱人的住宅区〕—**uptown** *adj*: *an uptown bar* 非商业区酒吧 —**uptown** *n* [U]

up·trend /ˈʌpˌtrɛnd; ˈʌptrend/ *n* [C] a period of time when business or economic activity increases〔经济方面〕向上[好转]的趋势

up·turn /ˈʌpˌtɝn; ˈʌptɜːn/ *n* [C] an increase in the level of something 好转; 上升, 提高: [+in] *an upturn in the housing market* 房产市场的好转

up·turned /ˌʌpˈtɝnd; ˈʌptɜːnd◂/ *adj* **1** turning upwards at the end 朝上翘的, 向上翻的: *an upturned nose* 翘鼻子 **2** turned upside down 翻转的, 倒置的: *upturned tables* 折起的桌子

up·ward /ˈʌpwɚd; ˈʌpwəd/ *adj* [only before noun 仅用于名词前] **1** moving or pointing towards a higher position 向上的: *an upward movement of the hand* 手的向上运动 **2** increasing to a higher level 升高的, 上升的: *the upward trend in house prices* 房价的上升趋势 —opposite 反义词 DOWNWARD

upwardly mo·bile /ˌ···ˈ··/ *adj* moving up through the social classes and becoming richer 向较高社会阶层流动的, 向上爬的 —**upward mobility** *n* [U]

up·wards /ˈʌpwɚdz; ˈʌpwədz/ also 又作 **upward** *adv AmE*【美】**1** moving or pointing towards a higher position 向上, 朝上: *Hold the gun so that it points upwards.* 握住枪, 使枪口朝上。—opposite 反义词 DOWNWARDS **2** increasing to a higher level 上升: *Salary scales have been moving steadily upwards.* 薪金级别一直在稳步上升。—opposite 反义词 DOWNWARDS **3** more than a particular amount, time etc〔数量、时间等〕…以上: *children of 14 and upwards* 14岁及14岁以上的儿童 | **upwards of** *informal*【非正式】*The waiting time for an operation can be upwards of two years.* 等待手术的时间可达两年以上。

Ur /ɝ; ɜː/ also 又作 **Ur of the Chaldees** /ˌɝ əv ðə kɒlˈdiz; ˌɜːr əv ðə kælˈdiːz/ an city in ancient Mesopotamia (modern Iraq), which existed from about 3500 BC to about the sixth century BC. According to the Old Testament of the Bible, Abraham was born there. 乌尔〔古代美索不达米亚(今伊拉克)一城市。乌尔存在于公元前3500至公元前6世纪前后, 据《圣经·旧约》记载, 为亚伯拉罕的出生地〕

U·rals, the /ˈjurəlz; ˈjʊərəlz/ also 又作 **the Ural Mountains** a group of mountains that stretch all the way down from the north to the south of Russia. Many people think of the Urals as the border between Europe and Asia 乌拉尔山脉〔俄罗斯境内贯通南北的山系。许多人视其为欧亚两洲的分界线〕

u·ra·ni·um /juˈrenɪəm; jʊˈreɪniəm/ *n* [U] a heavy white metal that is an ELEMENT (=simple substance), is RADIOACTIVE, and is used to produce NUCLEAR power and weapons 铀(元素)

U·ra·nus /ˈjurənəs; ˈjʊərənəs/ *n* [singular] **1** the PLANET seventh in order from the sun 天王星〔太阳系第七个行星〕—see picture at 参见 SOLAR SYSTEM 图 **2** the ruler of the universe, in ancient Greek stories 乌拉诺斯〔古希腊神话中的宇宙的统治者〕

W2 **ur·ban** /ˈɝbən; ˈɜːbən/ *adj* [only before noun 仅用于名词前] connected with a town or city 城市的, 都市的: *urban crime* 城市犯罪 | *the urban population* 城市人口

ur·bane /ɝˈben; ɜːˈbeɪn/ *adj* behaving in a relaxed and confident way in social situations 温文尔雅的, 彬彬有礼的: *Garroway's easy, urbane charm* 加罗韦从容而温文尔雅的魅力 —**urbanely** *adv* —**urbanity** *n* [U]

ur·ban·ize also 又作 **-ise** *BrE*【英】/ˈɝbənˌaɪz; ˈɜːbənaɪz/ *v* [T] to build houses, towns etc in the countryside 使城市化, 使都市化 —**urbanization** /ˌɝbənəˈzeʃən; ˌɜːbənaɪˈzeɪʃən/ *n* [U]

urban myth /ˌ··ˈ·/ *n* [C] a well-known story that many people believe, about an unusual or terrible event that has happened to an ordinary person 都市神话〔指发生在普通人身上的不寻常或恐怖的事〕

urban re·new·al /ˌ·· ·ˈ··/ *n* [U] the process of improving poor city areas by building new houses, shops etc 旧城区改建, 城市更新[美化]

urban sprawl /ˌ··ˈ·/ *n* [U] the spread of city buildings and houses into an area that was countryside 城区〔向乡村的〕扩展

ur·chin /ˈɝtʃɪn; ˈɜːtʃɪn/ *n* [C] *old-fashioned* a small dirty untidy child【过时】衣衫脏乱的小孩 —see also 另见 SEA URCHIN

Ur·du /ˈɝdu; ˈʊəduː/ *n* [U] the official language of Pakistan, also used in India 乌尔都语〔巴基斯坦的官方语言, 也通行于印度〕

-ure /jɚ; jə/ *suffix* [in nouns 构成名词] the action of doing something, or condition of being treated in a particular way〔表示"动作"或"动作之结果"〕: *the closure* (=closing) *of the factory* 工厂的关闭 | *exposure* 暴露; 曝光

u·re·thra /juˈriθrə; jʊˈriːθrə/ *n* [C] *technical* the tube through which waste liquid flows from your BLADDER and through which the SEMEN of males flows【术语】尿道

urge[1] /ɝdʒ; ɜːdʒ/ *v* [T] **1** to strongly advise someone to do something 催促, 力劝〔某人〕: **urge sb to do sth** *Brown urged her to reconsider her decision.* 布朗极力劝说她重新考虑她的决定。| **urge that** *I urge that you read this report carefully.* 我劝你仔细看看这份报告。**2** *formal* to strongly suggest that something should be done【正式】极力主张; 强调; 强烈要求: *The UN has urged restraint in the current crisis.* 联合国极力主张在当前危机中要保持克制。| **urge sth on/upon sb** *This course of action was urged upon us by all parties.* 这个行动是各方力促我们作出的。**3** [always+adv/prep] to make someone or something move by shouting, pushing them etc 推进; 驱策: **urge sb/sth into/forward** *Daniel urged the horses forward with a whip.* 丹尼尔用马鞭策马前进。 W3

urge sb ↔ **on** *phr v* [T] to encourage a person or animal to work harder, go faster etc 激励〔人〕; 驱策〔动物〕: *Urged on by the crowd, the Italian team scored two more goals.* 受到观众的激励, 意大利队又进了两球。

urge[2] *n* [C] a strong wish or need 强烈的欲望; 迫切的要求; 冲动: *sexual urges* 性冲动 | **urge to do sth** *I felt a sudden urge to scream.* 我突然很想大声喊叫。

ur·gent /ˈɝdʒənt; ˈɜːdʒənt/ *adj* **1** very important and needing to be dealt with immediately 紧急的, 急迫的, 需迅速处理的: *an urgent message* 紧急的消息 | **be in urgent need of** *in urgent need of medical attention* 急需医疗 **2** *formal* done or said in a way that shows that you want something to be dealt with immediately【正式】强求的; 急切的: *an urgent whisper* 急切的私语 —**urgency** *n* [U]: *a matter of great urgency* 极为迫切的问题 —**urgently** *adv* S3

U·ri·ah Heep —see 见 Uriah HEEP

u·ric /ˈjurɪk; ˈjʊərɪk/ *adj* related to URINE 尿的

u·ri·nal /ˈjurənḷ; ˈjʊərɪnəl/ *n* [C] **1** a type of toilet that men use that is fixed onto the wall〔固定在墙上的〕男用小便池 **2** a building or room containing urinals 小便处[所]

u·ri·na·ry /ˈjurəˌnɛrɪ; ˈjʊərɪnəri/ *adj technical* connected with urine or the parts of your body through which urine passes【术语】尿的; 泌尿器官的

u·ri·nate /ˈjurəˌnet; ˈjʊərɪneɪt/ *v* [I] *technical* to make urine flow out of your body【术语】排尿 —**urination** /ˌjurəˈneʃən; ˌjʊərɪˈneɪʃən/ *n* [U]

u·rine /ˈjurɪn; ˈjʊərɪn/ *n* [U] the liquid waste that comes out of your body when you go to the toilet 尿

urn /ɝn; ɜːn/ *n* [C] **1** a decorated container, especially one that is used for holding the ashes (ASH (3)) of a dead body 瓮; 〔尤指〕骨灰瓮 **2** a metal container that holds a large amount of tea or coffee〔金属的〕大茶壶; 大咖啡壶

Ur·sa Ma·jor /ˌɝsə ˈmedʒɚ; ˌɜːsə ˈmeɪdʒə/ also 又作 **the Great Bear** a large CONSTELLATION (=group of stars) near the North Pole, which can easily be seen from Earth. The seven brightest stars in Ursa Major are called the **Plough** (in the UK) or **the Big Dipper** (in the US). 大熊星座〔靠近北极的一大星座。从地球上很容易看到, 其中最亮的七颗星在英国称作 the Plough, 在美国称作 the Big Dipper, 即北斗七星〕

Ursa Mi·nor /ˌ··ˈ··/ a group of stars in the northern sky, close to Ursa Major, which can easily be seen from Earth, and which includes the Pole Star. It is also called **the Little Bear** or (in the US) **the Little Dipper** 小熊星座〔北方天空中的一星座。靠近大熊星座, 从地球上很容易看到, 其中包括北极星。该星座又称 the Little Bear, 在美国称 the Little Dipper〕

U·ru·guay /ˈjʊrəˌgwe; ˈjʊərəgwaɪ/ a country in South America, between Argentina and Brazil. Population 3,360,000 (2001). Capital: Montevideo. 乌拉圭〔南美洲一国家，位于阿根廷和巴西之间。人口：3,360,000（2001），首都：蒙得维的亚〕—**Uruguayan** *n, adj*

US /ˌju ˋɛs◂/ ju: ˈes◂/ *n* also 又作 **USA** /ˌju ɛs ˋe; ju: es ˈeɪ◂/ the United States of America 美国 —**US** *adj*: *the US Navy* 美国海军

1 1 **us** /əs; əs, *strong* 强读 ʌs; ʌs/ *pron* **1** the object form of 'we'〔we 的宾格〕: *Do you think Dave saw us?* 你认为戴夫看见我们了吗? | *The house is too small for us now.* 这房子现在对我们来说太小了。| *Emilio bought us a drink.* 埃米利奥请我们喝了一杯。**2** *BrE spoken* used instead of 'me', although most people think this incorrect【英口】我〔用于代替 me, 然而多数人认为这种用法不正确〕: *Give us a kiss.* 吻我一下。| *Lend us a pound, will you?* 借我一英镑好吗? —see 见 ME (USAGE)

U.S.A. also 又作 **USA** /ˌju ɛs ˋe; ju: es ˈeɪ/ the United States of America 美国

us·a·ble /ˈjuzəbḷ; ˈju:zəbl/ *adj* something that is usable is in a suitable state to be used 可用的

USAF /ˌju ɛs e ˋɛf; ju: es eɪ ˋef/ the abbreviation of 缩写= the United States Air Force 美国空军

us·age /ˈjusɪdʒ; ˈju:sɪdʒ/ *n* **1** [C,U] the way that words are used in a language〔语言的〕惯用法: *a book on modern English usage* 关于当代英语用法的书 **2** [U] the way in which something is used, or the amount of it that is used 使用方法; 使用量

USA To·day /ˌ· · · ˈ· ·/ *trademark* a newspaper that is sold in every state of the US and is also available in many countries around the world【商标】《今日美国》〔一份在美国各州发行的报纸，在世界许多国家也可以买到〕

USDA /ˌju ɛs di ˋe; ju: es di: ˈeɪ/ United States Department of Agriculture; the US government organization which helps farmers and makes sure they follow the laws concerning food production 美国农业部〔美国一政府机构，专为农场主提供支持，并确保他们遵守食品生产的有关法律〕

1 1 **use¹** /juz; ju:z/ *v* [T]

1 ►USE STH 使用某物◄ if you use a particular tool, method, service, ability etc, you do something with that tool, by means of that method etc, for a particular purpose 用; 使用; 应用: *Can I use your phone?* 我可以用一下你的电话吗? | *More people are using the library than ever before.* 使用图书馆的人比以往多。| *I can't tell you what to do – you must use your own discretion.* 我不能告诉你要做什么 —— 你必须运用你自己的判断力。| **use sth for doing sth** *We use this room for keeping all our junk in.* 我们用这房间存放所有的废旧杂物。| **use sth as** *My mother uses old socks as dusters.* 我母亲用旧袜子当抹布。| **use force** (=use violent methods) 使用武力

2 ►AMOUNT OF STH 某物的数额◄ to take something from a supply of food, gas, money etc with the result that there is less left 耗费, 消费〔某物〕: *We use about £40 worth of electricity a month.* 我们每月耗去大约价值40英镑的电。

3 ►USE A PERSON 利用人◄ to make someone do something for you in order to get something you want 利用〔某人〕: **use sb to do sth** *Smugglers use innocent people to carry drugs through customs.* 走私贩子利用无辜的人把毒品带过海关。| **use sb for your own ends** *Gerald had been using her for his own ends.* 杰拉尔德一直在利用她来达到自己的目的。

4 ►AN ADVANTAGE 优势◄ to take advantage of a situation 利用〔优势〕: **use sth for** *Gordon used his family's wealth for his own publicity.* 戈登利用家财使自己出名。| **use sth to do sth** *She used her position as manager to get jobs for her friends.* 她利用自己的经理职位为朋友谋职。

5 could use *spoken* if you say you could use something, you mean you would really like to have it【口】想要; 真想: *I could use a drink.* 我真想喝一杯。

6 ►PRODUCT 产品◄ to buy a particular product regularly 定期购买〔某商品〕: *I always use the same deodorant.* 我总是用同一种除臭剂。

7 ►WORD 言词◄ to say or write a particular word or phrase 使用〔词语〕: *an expression that would never be used in polite conversation* 在礼貌谈话中从来不使用的用语

8 ►DRUGS 毒品◄ to regularly take illegal drugs 吸食〔毒品〕

9 ►NAME 名字◄ to call yourself by a name that is not yours in order to keep your name secret 用〔假名〕: *Grant had checked into a Miami hotel using a false name.* 格兰特用假名入住迈阿密的一家旅馆。

use sth ↔ **up** *phr v* [T] to use all of something 用完, 用光: *Don't use up all the hot water.* 别把热水都用完。

3 2 **use²** /jus; ju:s/ *n* **1** [C] a way in which something can be used, or a purpose for which it can be used 用法; 用途: *Robots have many different uses in modern industry.* 机器人在现代工业中有许多不同的用途。**2** [singular, U] the act of using something or the amount that is used 使用; 用量: [+of] *the increasing use of computers in education* 教育领域电脑的使用日益增多 | *the poet's use of metaphor* 诗人对隐喻的运用 **3 make use of** to use something that is available in order to achieve something or get an advantage for yourself 利用, 使用: *Not enough people are making use of the children's play scheme.* 没有足够的人在利用儿童娱乐计划。| *The artist makes use of scrap iron in her sculpture.* 那位艺术家把废铁用于雕塑中。| **make good use of** (=get as much advantage as possible from something) 充分利用 *We must make the best possible use of the resources we have.* 我们必须充分利用我们现有的资源。**4 put sth to (good) use** to use knowledge, skills etc for a particular purpose (好好) 利用: *an opportunity to put her medical training to good use* 让她所受的医学培训能派上用场的机会 **5** [U] the ability or right to use something 运用能力; 使用权: *Joe's given me the use of his office till he gets back.* 乔让我使用他的办公室直到他回来。| *He lost the use of both legs as a result of the accident.* 他因事故而双腿残废了。**6 be no use** also 又作 **be of no use** *formal* to be completely useless【正式】没用处: *This map's no use – it doesn't show the minor roads.* 这张地图没用 —— 它没有标明小路。| **be (of) no use to sb** *Have this sweater – it's of no use to me any more.* 带上这件毛线衫吧 —— 我用不着了。**7 it's no use doing sth** *spoken* used to tell someone not to do something because it will have no effect【口】做某事没用: *It's no use arguing with her – she won't listen.* 跟她争论没有用 —— 她不会听的。**8 it's no use!** *spoken* used to say that you are going to stop doing something because you do not think it will be successful【口】白搭!〔用于表示停止做某事因认为不会成功〕: *Oh, it's no use! I can't fix it.* 唉, 算了吧! 我修不好它。**9 what's the use (of)?** *spoken* used to say that something seems to be a waste of time【口】(…) 有什么用?〔用于表示做某事是浪费时间〕: *What's the use of getting so angry?* 生这么大气有什么用? **10 be in use** a machine, place etc that is in use is being used〔机器、场所等〕在使用中: *All the machines are in use at the moment.* 眼下所有的机器都在使用中。**11 for the use of** provided for a particular person or group of people to use 供…用: *This parking lot is for the use of employees only.* 本停车场仅供员工使用。**12 come into use/go out of use** to start or stop being used 开始使用/停止使用: *New printing techniques have recently come into use.* 新的印刷技术最近开始投入使用。**13 out of use** a machine, place etc that is out of use is not being used〔机器、场所等〕废弃不用, 不再使用 **14 be of use** *formal* to be useful【正式】有用: *I wondered if this book might be of use to you.* 我不知道这本书对你是否有用。**15 have no use for** to have no respect for someone or something 厌恶, 不喜欢: *She has no use for people who are always complaining.* 她讨厌老是抱怨的人。**16 he/she/it has its uses** *spoken often humorous* used to say that something or someone can sometimes be useful【口, 常幽默】他/她/它自有其用处 **17** [C] one of the meanings of a word, or the way that a particular word is used〔某个词的〕(一项) 词义; 用法

use³ *v negative form* 否定式为 **usedn't, usen't** *old-fashioned BrE*【过时, 英】**used to do sth** if something used to happen, it happened regularly or all the time in the past, but does not happen now 过去常做某事: *I used to go to the cinema a lot, but I never get the time now.* 我过去常看电影, 但现在根本没有时间看了。| *Beth used to like rock 'n' roll when she was young.* 贝丝年轻时喜欢摇滚乐。| **used to** *"Do you play golf?" "No, but I used to."* "你打高尔夫球吗?" "不打, 但过去常打。" | **did not use to** also 又作 **used not to** *BrE old-fashioned*【英, 过时】*I'm surprised to see you smoking. You didn't use to.* 看见你抽烟我很惊讶, 你过去是不抽的。| *The shops usedn't to open on Sundays.* 这些商店过去在星期天是不营业的。| **used to be** (=something was true in the past but is not true now) 过去是 *She used to be such a happy lively girl.* 她过去可是个活泼快乐的姑娘。| **did there use to be?** also 又作 **used there to be?** *formal*【正式】*Did there use to be a hotel on that corner?* 过去那个拐角处有家旅馆吗? 1 2

used /just; ju:st/ *adj* **be used to** to have experienced something so that it no longer seems surprising, difficult, strange etc 习惯于〔某事物〕: *Lady Whitton wasn't used to people disagreeing with her.* 惠顿夫人不习惯别人跟她意见相左。| **get used to** *I'm sure I'll get used to the hard work.* 我肯定会习惯这项艰苦的工作。1 2

used /juzd; ju:zd/ *adj* **1 used cars/clothes etc** cars, clothes etc that have already had an owner; SECOND-HAND 旧汽车/衣服等: *a used car salesman* 二手车推销员 **2** dirty as a result of use 用脏了的: *a used tissue* 脏纸巾

[1] [1] **use·ful** /ˈjusfəl; ˈjuːsfəl/ *adj* **1** helping you to do or get what you want 有用的; 有益的: *useful information* 有用的信息 | *Dean's a really useful person to have around when things go wrong.* 遇上什么事时, 迪安确实是个好帮手。| **useful to sb** *information that may be useful to the enemy* 可能对敌人有用的情报 | **useful for sth** *These yellow stickers are useful for leaving messages.* 这些黄色粘贴标签可用于留言。| **prove useful** (=be useful in a particular situation) 派上用场 *Clive's experience in the building trade proved useful for re-roofing the garage.* 克莱夫在建筑业的经历在给车库换屋顶时派上了用场。| **make yourself useful** (=help someone) (给人) 帮忙 *Can I do anything to make myself useful?* 我能帮上什么忙吗? | **come in useful** (=be useful in a particular situation) 用得着 *Keep that, it might come in useful later.* 留着那东西, 也许以后用得上。**2** *BrE informal* satisfactory【英, 非正式】令人满意的: *The England cricket team scored quite a useful total.* 英格兰板球队的总得分很令人满意。—**usefully** *adv*

use·ful·ness /ˈjusfəlnɪs; ˈjuːsfəlnəs/ *n* [U] the state of being useful 有用; 实用性: **outlive its usefulness** (=not be useful any more) 不再有用

use·less /ˈjuslɪs; ˈjuːsləs/ *adj* **1** not useful or effective in any way 无用的; 无效的: *This bag is useless – it has a hole in it.* 这个袋子没用了, 上面有个洞。| *a useless piece of information* 一则无用的情报 | **completely/totally/utterly useless** *At that time, art was considered a completely useless activity.* 那时, 艺术被认为是一项全然无用的活动。| **useless for** *It's a nice watch, but it's useless for scuba diving.* 这手表挺好看, 但戴水肺潜水时不能用。| **it is useless to do sth** *It was useless to complain.* 抱怨是没有用的。**2** *informal* unable or unwilling to do anything properly【非正式】差劲的, 无能的: *Don't ask Tim to fix it. He's completely useless.* 别叫蒂姆来修理, 他根本不行。—**uselessly** *adv* —**uselessness** *n* [U]

Usenet /ˈjuznɛt; ˈjuːznet/ a very large organization of newsgroups and news SERVERs on the Internet Usenet 友思网〔巨型新闻组与新闻服务器网络系统〕

[3] **us·er** /ˈjuzɚ; ˈjuːzə/ *n* [C] someone or something that uses a product, service etc 使用者, 用户: *road users* 道路使用者 —see also 另见 END USER

user fee /ˈ‥ ˌ/ *n* [C] *AmE* a tax on a service provided for the public【美】使用费〔一种服务税〕

user friend·ly /ˌ‥ ˈ‥◂/ *adj* easy to use or operate 易使用[操作]的: *a user friendly guide to computing* 电脑操作便利指南 —**user-friendliness** *n* [U]

user in·ter·face /ˌ‥ ˈ‥ˌ/ *n* [C] the part of a computer PROGRAM or SOFTWARE package that contains the commands and operations for the person using the computer〔电脑〕用户接口, 用户界面

US Ge·o·lo·gi·cal Sur·vey /ˌ· ‥‥ ˈ‥/ a US government organization, part of the Department of the Interior, which makes detailed maps of the US and lists of minerals found in the US. In the UK there is a similar organization called the Ordnance Survey 美国地质勘探局〔美国一政府机构, 隶属内政部, 负责绘制精确的美国地图, 列出在美国发现的矿产清单。英国也有一类似机构, 称 Ordnance Survey (地形测量局)〕

ush·er¹ /ˈʌʃɚ; ˈʌʃə/ *n* [C] **1** someone who shows people to their seats at a theatre, cinema, wedding etc〔剧院、戏院、婚礼等的〕引座员, 迎宾员, 招待员 **2** *BrE* someone who works in a law court whose job is to make sure there is no trouble【英】〔法院的〕庭警

usher² *v* [T] to help someone to get from one place to another, especially by showing them the way 引, 领; 招待: **usher sb into/to** *The guard ushered him into the room.* 警卫领他进入房间。

usher in sth *phr v* [T] to be the start of something new 宣告, 开创: *The Stockholm Conference ushered in a new era of international cooperation.* 斯德哥尔摩会议开创了国际合作的新纪元。

ush·er·ette /ˌʌʃɚˈɛt; ˌʌʃəˈret/ *n* [C] *especially BrE* a woman who works in a cinema, showing people to their seats【尤英】〔电影院的〕女引座员, 女服务员

USIA, the /ˌju ɛs aɪ ˈe; ˌjuː es aɪ ˈeɪ/ United States Information Agency; a government department which sends representatives abroad to provide information about the United States 美国新闻署〔美国一政府部门, 向国外派驻代表, 负责美国对外宣传〕

USM, the /ˌju ɛs ˈɛm; ˌjuː es ˈem/ Unlisted Securities Market; a part of the London Stock Exchange for smaller companies which cannot be listed officially with the Stock Exchange 非上市证券市场; 非挂牌证券市场〔伦敦证券交易所为未能在交易所正式上市的小公司设立的交易场所〕

US Mas·ters Tour·na·ment, the /ˌ· ‥ ˈ‥, ‥/ also 又作 **the Masters Tournament** an important US GOLF competition 美国名人赛〔美国一项重要的高尔夫球赛事〕

USMC /ˌju ɛs ɛm ˈsi; ˌjuː es em ˈsiː/ the abbreviation of 缩写= the United States Marine Corps 美国海军陆战队

USN /ˌju ɛs ˈɛn; ˌjuː es ˈen/ the abbreviation of 缩写= the United States Navy 美国海军

USO /ˌju ɛs ˈo; ˌjuː es ˈəʊ/ United Service Organization; a US organization which arranges performances, builds libraries, and provides equipment such as telephones and televisions for people in the US armed forces 劳军联合组织〔美国一机构, 负责为美国军方人员安排演出活动, 兴建图书馆, 提供电话和电视等设备〕

U.S. of A. *spoken* the (good ol') U.S. of A. the United States of America【口】美国

US O·pen, the /ˌ· ˈ‥/ **1** an important GOLF competition that takes place in the US each year 美国公开赛〔每年在美国举行的一项重要的高尔夫球赛事〕**2** an important tennis competition that takes place in the US each year, in Forest Hills near New York City. The US Open is one of the Grand Slam events in tennis. 美国网球公开赛〔每年在美国举行的一项重要的网球赛事。比赛地点设在纽约市附近的森林山。美国公开赛是网球大满贯赛中的一项赛事〕

USS /ˌju ɛs ˈɛs; ˌjuː es ˈes◂/ United States Ship; letters which go before the name of a ship to show that it belongs to the American government 美国舰船〔写在舰名前面, 表示该舰属于美国政府〕: *USS Arizona* 美国"亚利桑那号"舰

USSR, the /ˌju ɛs ɛs ˈɑr; ˌjuː es es ˈɑː/ the official name of the Soviet Union 苏维埃社会主义共和国联盟〔苏联的正式名称〕

usu the written abbreviation of 缩写= USUALLY

u·su·al /ˈjuʒuəl; ˈjuːʒuəl/ *adj* **1** the same as what happens most of the time or in most situations 通常的; 惯常的; 平常的: [2] [2]
I'll meet you at the usual time. 我将在往常一样的时间见你。| *Gina was her usual cheerful self.* 吉娜跟平常一样快乐。| **it is usual for sb to do sth** *Is it usual for lectures to start so early?* 讲座通常这么早就开始吗? | **better/more etc than usual** *It seemed colder than usual in the house.* 房子里似乎比平时冷。**2 as usual** in the way that happens or exists most of the time 像往常一样, 照例: *As usual, they'd left the children at home with Susan.* 像往常一样, 他们把孩子留在家里跟苏珊在一起。**3 as per usual** *spoken* used to say that something bad that often happens has just happened again【口】〔坏事〕照常发生: *Matthew was drunk as per usual.* 马修像往常一样又喝醉了。**4 the usual** *spoken* the drink that you usually have【口】常喝的饮料

u·su·al·ly /ˈjuʒuəlɪ; ˈjuːʒuəli/ *adv* used when describing what happens on most occasions or in most situations 通常地; 惯常地, 平常地: *I'm usually in bed by 11.30.* 我通常11点半以前上床睡觉。| *Women usually live longer than men.* 女人通常比男人长寿。—see picture at 参见 FREQUENCY 图 [1] [1]

u·sur·er /ˈjuʒərɚ; ˈjuːʒərə/ *n* [C] *formal* someone who lends money to people and makes them pay too high a rate of INTEREST¹ (4)【正式】放高利贷者

u·su·ri·ous /juˈʒurɪəs; juːˈzjʊəriəs/ *adj formal* a usurious price or rate of INTEREST¹ (4) is unfairly high【正式】〔价格或利息〕过高的

u·surp /juˈzɝp; juːˈzɜːp/ *v* [T] *formal* to take someone else's power, position, job etc when you do not have the right to【正式】篡夺, 夺取〔权力、地位、工作等〕: *his deep jealousy at the thought of another man usurping his role as father* 想到另一个人夺走他身为父亲的角色时他那深深的嫉妒 —**usurper** *n* [C] —**usurpation** /ˌjuzɚˈpeʃən; ˌjuːzɜːˈpeɪʃən/ *n* [U]

u·su·ry /ˈjuʒərɪ; ˈjuːʒəri/ *n* [U] *formal* the practice of lending money to people and making them pay unfairly high rates of INTEREST¹ (4)【正式】放高利贷

UT the written abbreviation of 缩写= UTAH

U·tah /ˈjutɔ; ˈjuːtɑː/ abbreviation 缩写为 **UT** a state in the west of the US, whose capital, Salt Lake City, is a centre of the Mormon religion. Most of the people who live in Utah are Mormons. 犹他州〔美国西部一州。其首府盐湖城为摩门教中心, 该州大部分居民信奉摩门教〕

u·ten·sil /juˈtɛnsl; juːˈtensəl/ *n* [C] a tool or object with a particular use, especially in cooking 器皿, 用具〔尤指烹调用具〕: *kitchen utensils* 厨房用具

u·te·rus /ˈjutərəs; ˈjuːtərəs/ *n plural* **uteri** /-raɪ; -raɪ/ or **uteruses** [C] *technical* the organ in a woman or female MAMMAL where babies develop; WOMB【术语】子宫 —**uterine** /-raɪn; -raɪn/ *adj*

U·ther Pen·drag·on /ˌjuθɚ pɛnˈdrægən; ˌjuːθə penˈdrægən/ a king of the ancient Britons and the father of King

Arthur in old stories 犹瑟王, 大头龙犹瑟〔古时英国国王, 传说中的亚瑟王之父〕

u·til·i·tar·i·an /ˌjutɪləˋtɛrɪən; juːˌtɪlɪ̈ˈteəriən/ *adj* **1** *formal* useful and practical rather than being used for decoration【正式】有用的; 实用的: *ugly utilitarian buildings* 丑陋但实用的建筑物 **2** *technical* based on a belief in utilitarianism【术语】功利主义的; 实利主义的 —compare 比较 MATERIALISTIC

u·til·i·tar·i·an·is·m /ˌjutɪləˋtɛrɪənɪzṃ; juːˌtɪlɪ̈ˈteəriənɪzəm/ *n* [U] *technical* the belief that an action is good if it helps the greatest possible number of people【术语】功利主义; 实利主义

u·til·i·ty /juˋtɪlətɪ; juːˈtɪlɪ̈ti/ *n* **1** [usually plural 一般用复数] *especially AmE* a service such as gas or electricity provided for people to use【尤美】公用事业〈如燃气、电力等〉: *Does your rent include utilities?* 你的房租包括公用事业费吗? **2** [U] *formal* the amount of usefulness that something has【正式】效用, 实用

utility pole /ˈ·ˋ··· ˌ·/ *n* [C] *AmE* a tall wooden pole for supporting telephone and electric wires【美】〔木制〕电线杆

utility room /ˈ·ˋ··· ˌ·/ *n* [C] a room in a house where washing machines, FREEZERs etc are kept〔放置洗衣机、冰箱等的〕杂用室, 家用器具存放室

u·til·ize also 又作 **-ise** *BrE*【英】/ˋjutḷˌaɪz; ˈjuːtɪ̈laɪz/ *v* [T] *formal* to use something effectively【正式】利用, 使用: *a heating system that utilizes solar energy* 利用太阳能的供暖系统 **—utilizable** *adj* **—utilization** /ˌjutḷaɪˋzeʃən; ˌjuːtɪ̈laɪˈzeɪʃən/ *n* [U]

ut·most¹ /ˋʌtˌmost; ˈʌtməʊst/ *adj* **the utmost importance/respect/care etc** the greatest possible importance etc 极度的重要/尊敬/关心等: *a matter of the utmost importance* 极重要的事情

utmost² *n* [singular] **1** the most that can be done 极度, 极限, 最大可能: *Both runners had pushed themselves to the utmost.* 两个赛跑运动员都尽了最大努力。**2 do your utmost** to try as hard as you can to achieve something 竭尽全力: *We've done our utmost to make the process as simple as possible.* 为使工序尽可能简单, 我们已尽了全力。

u·to·pi·a /juˋtopɪə; juːˈtəʊpiə/ *n* [C,U] an imaginary perfect world where everyone is happy 乌托邦〔想象中的完美世界〕**—utopian** *adj*

ut·ter¹ /ˋʌtɚ; ˈʌtə/ *adj* [only before noun 仅用于名词前] **utter failure/rubbish/fool etc** a complete failure etc 彻头彻尾的失败/废物/傻瓜等: *What an utter waste of time!* 完全是浪费时间! | *We all watched in utter amazement.* 我们都万分惊奇地看着。

utter² *v* [T] *formal or literary*【正式或文】**1** to make a sound with your voice, especially with difficulty〔吃力地〕发出〔声音〕: *The wounded prisoner uttered a groan.* 受伤的囚犯发出一声呻吟。**2** to say things 讲; 说出: *Uttering a stream of filthy curses, Medlock stomped away.* 梅德洛克不干不净地咒骂了一通后, 跺着脚走了。

ut·ter·ance /ˋʌtərəns; ˈʌtərəns/ *n formal*【正式】**1** [C] something you say 言论, 言辞: *Politicians are judged by their public utterances.* 人们根据政治家公开的言论来评判他们。**2 give utterance to** to express something in words〔用言辞〕表达 **3** [U] the action of saying something 发声; 说话; 表达

ut·ter·ly /ˋʌtəlɪ; ˈʌtəli/ *adv* completely or totally 完全地, 十足地: *You look utterly miserable.* 你看起来难受极了。

ut·ter·most /ˋʌtɚˌmost; ˈʌtəməʊst/ *adj literary or formal* UTMOST¹【文或正式】极度的

U-turn /ˋjuˌtɜn; ˈjuː tɜːn/ *n* [C] **1** a turn that you make in a car, on a bicycle etc, so that you go back in the direction you came from〔汽车、自行车等的〕U 形转弯, 180 度调头 **2** *informal* a complete change of ideas, plans etc【非正式】〔观念、计划等的〕彻底改变, 180 度大转变: *a government U-turn on economic policy* 政府在经济政策上180度的大改变

UVF /ˌju vi ˋɛf; ˌjuː viː ˈef/ Ulster Volunteer Force; a PARAMILITARY organization in Northern Ireland which has used violence against people who want Northern Ireland to leave the UK and become part of the Irish Republic 北爱尔兰志愿军〔北爱尔兰一准军事组织, 曾以暴力手段袭击要求北爱尔兰脱离英国而加入爱尔兰共和国的人们〕

u·vu·la /ˋjuvjələ; ˈjuːvjɪ̈lə/ *n* [C] *technical* a small soft piece of flesh which hangs down from the top of your mouth at the back【术语】腭垂, 悬雍垂, 小舌

u·vu·lar /ˋjuvjələ; ˈjuːvjɪ̈lə/ *n* [C] a CONSONANT sound that you make with the back of your tongue touching, or nearly touching, your uvula〔辅音的〕小舌音 **—uvular** *adj*

Uz·bek·i·stan /ʊzˌbɛkɪˋstæn; ˌʊzbekɪˈstɑːn/ a country in central Asia between Turkmenistan and Kazakhstan. Population: 25,155,000 (2001). Capital: Tashkent. It was formerly part of the Soviet Union. 乌兹别克斯坦〔中亚一国家, 位于土库曼斯坦和哈萨克斯坦之间。人口: 25,155,000 (2001), 首都: 塔什干。该国曾是前苏联的一部分〕**—Uzbek** *n, adj*

U·zi /ˋuzɪ; ˈuːzi/ *trademark* a type of SUBMACHINE gun【商标】乌兹冲锋枪

V,v

V, v /vi; viː/ **1** *plural* **V's, v's** the 22nd letter of the English alphabet 英语字母表的第二十二个字母 **2** the number 5 in the system of ROMAN NUMERALS〔罗马数字的〕五

V *n* [C usually singular 一般用单数] something that has a shape like the letter V V字形物: *She cut the material into a V.* 她把材料裁成V字形。

v **1** the written abbreviation of 缩写= VERB **2** *informal*【非正式】the written abbreviation of 缩写= VERY

v. the British abbreviation of 英国英语缩写= VERSUS, used when talking about games in which two teams or players play against each other, or in the names of legal trials (TRIAL[1] (1))〔体育比赛或法庭审讯中〕〔一方〕对〔另一方〕; vs *AmE*【美】: *the England v. Australia cricket match* 英格兰对澳大利亚的板球比赛

V & A, the /ˌvi ənd ˈe; ˌviː ənd ˈeɪ/ *BrE informal* a short form of the Victoria and Albert Museum【英, 非正式】维阿博物馆〔维多利亚和阿尔伯特博物馆的缩写〕

V8 /ˌvi ˈet; ˌviː ˈeɪt/ *trademark* a type of drink made from tomato juice and other vegetable juices【商标】八珍果汁, V8饮料〔一种用番茄汁和其他蔬菜汁调制的饮料〕

VA[1] the written abbreviation of 缩写= VIRGINIA

VA[2] /ˌvi ˈe; ˌviː ˈeɪ/ the abbreviation of 缩写= the VETERANS AFFAIRS

vac /væk; væk/ *n* [C usually singular 一般用单数] *BrE informal* a university VACATION[1] (2)【英, 非正式】〔大学的〕假期

S3 **va·can·cy** /ˈvekənsɪ; ˈveɪkənsi/ *n* **1** [C] a room that is not being used in a hotel and is available for someone to stay in〔旅馆中的〕空房间: *'No vacancies', the sign read.* 告示牌上写着"客满"。**2** [C] a job that is available for someone to start doing〔职位〕空位, 空缺: *Judge Ginsburg is to fill the vacancy on the US supreme court.* 金斯伯格法官将填补美国最高法院的空缺。| [+for] *vacancies for drivers* 司机的空缺 **3** [U] lack of interest or thought 无聊; 心灵空虚; 失神: *His mouth fell open and the look of vacancy returned.* 他的嘴张着, 又显出了茫然若失的神情。

va·cant /ˈvekənt; ˈveɪkənt/ *adj* **1** a vacant seat, room etc is empty and available for someone to use〔座位、房屋等〕空的, 未被占用的: *Only a few apartments were still vacant.* 只有几套公寓仍然空着。**2** *formal* a vacant job or position in an organization is available for someone to start doing【正式】〔工作或职位〕空缺的: **fall vacant** (=become vacant) 出缺 **3** **vacant expression/smile/stare etc** an expression that shows that someone is not thinking about anything 茫然的表情/微笑/凝视等 **4** **situations vacant** the part of a newspaper where jobs are advertised〔报纸上的〕招聘栏 —**vacantly** *adv*: *Cindy was staring vacantly into space.* 辛迪茫然地凝视着天空。

vacant lot /ˌ·· ˈ·/ *n* [C] *especially AmE* an area of land that is not being used and on which nothing has been built, especially in a city【尤美】〔尤指城市中的〕空地

vacant pos·ses·sion /ˌ·· ·ˈ··/ *n* [U] *BrE technical*【英, 术语】**house/flat with vacant possession** a home or other building whose previous owner has left, so that the new owner can move into it immediately〔原房主搬离后, 新房主可立即迁入的〕闲置房屋/公寓

va·cate /ˈveket; vəˈkeɪt/ *v* [T] *formal*【正式】**1** to leave a job or position so that it is available for someone else to do 辞〔职〕, 腾出〔职位〕**2** to leave a seat, room etc so that someone else can use it 空出, 搬出: *Guests must vacate their rooms by 11 o'clock.* 客人必须于11点前腾出房间。

S2 W3 **va·ca·tion[1]** /veˈkeʃən; vəˈkeɪʃən/ *n* **1** [C] *especially AmE* a holiday, or time spent not working【尤美】假期, 休假: **on vacation** *They're on vacation for the next two weeks.* 未来两周他们要去度假。—see graph at 参见 HOLIDAY[1] 图表 **2** [C] one of the periods of time when universities are closed〔大学的〕假期 —see also 另见 LONG VACATION **3** [U] *formal* the act of leaving a place【正式】〔工作的〕辞去; 〔房屋等的〕腾出

vacation[2] *v* [I] *AmE* to go somewhere for a holiday【美】度假, 休假: [+in/at] *The Bernsteins are vacationing in Europe.* 伯恩斯坦一家正在欧洲度假。

va·ca·tion·er /veˈkeʃənə; vəˈkeɪʃənə/ *n* [C] *AmE* someone who has gone somewhere for a holiday【美】度假者; HOLIDAYMAKER *BrE*【英】

vac·cin·ate /ˈvæksn̩ˌet; ˈvæksɪ̈neɪt/ *v* [T] to protect someone from a disease by putting a small amount of a substance containing that disease into their body 给…接种疫苗, 给…打预防针: **vaccinate sb against sth** *All children should be vaccinated against measles.* 所有儿童都应接种疫苗以预防麻疹。—see also 另见 IMMUNIZE, INOCULATE —**vaccination** /ˌvæksn̩ˈeʃən; ˌvæksɪ̈ˈneɪʃən/ *n* [C,U]

vac·cine /vækˈsin; ˈvæksiːn/ *n* [C,U] a substance which contains the VIRUS that causes a disease and is used to protect people from that disease 疫苗: *a polio vaccine* 天花[小儿麻痹]疫苗 —compare 比较 SERUM (1)

vac·il·late /ˈvæsl̩ˌet; ˈvæsɪ̈leɪt/ *v* [I] to continue to change your opinions, ideas etc; WAVER (2) 犹豫, 踌躇, 拿不定主意: *The administration is still vacillating over the Health Care issue.* 行政部门在保健问题上仍然举棋不定。—**vacillation** /ˌvæsəˈleʃən; ˌvæsɪ̈ˈleɪʃən/ *n* [C,U]

va·cu·i·ty /væˈkjuətɪ; vəˈkjuːɪ̈ti/ *n* [U] *formal* a lack of intelligent, interesting, or serious thought【正式】空虚; 茫然; 愚蠢

vac·u·ous /ˈvækjuəs; ˈvækjuəs/ *adj formal*【正式】**1** a vacuous look or expression shows no sign of any feelings or intelligence〔神情或表情〕茫然的, 空洞的, 没有思想感情的 **2** a vacuous life or existence seems to have no useful purpose〔生活等〕空虚的, 无聊的, 漫无目的的 —**vacuously** *adv* —**vacuousness** *n* [U]

vac·u·um[1] /ˈvækjuəm; ˈvækjuəm/ *n* **1** [C] a space that is completely empty of all gas, especially one from which all the air has been taken away 真空 **2** [singular] a situation in which someone or something is missing or lacking, especially one that causes problems or makes you feel unhappy 失落感; 空虚(感): *Her husband's death left a vacuum in her life.* 丈夫的去世使她的生活变得空虚。| **power/political etc vacuum** *Nixon's departure from office created a political vacuum.* 尼克松的离任造成了一个政治真空状态。**3** **in a vacuum** existing completely separately from other people or things and having no connection with them 在真空状态中; 与外界隔绝 **4** [C] *old-fashioned* a vacuum cleaner【过时】真空吸尘器

vacuum[2] *v* [I,T] to clean a place using a vacuum cleaner 用真空吸尘器打扫 —see picture at 参见 CLEAN[2] 图

vacuum clean·er /ˈ··· ˌ··/ *n* [C] a machine that cleans floors by sucking up the dirt from them 真空吸尘器; HOOVER *BrE trademark*【英, 商标】

vacuum flask /ˈ··· ˌ·/ *n* [C] *BrE old-fashioned* a special container that keeps liquids hot or cold; THERMOS【英, 过时】保温瓶, 热水瓶

vacuum-packed /ˈ··· ˌ·/ *adj* vacuum-packed food is surrounded by plastic from which most of the air has been removed, so that the food will stay fresh for longer〔食物〕真空包装的

vacuum pump /ˈ··· ˌ·/ *n* [C] a pump for removing gas or air from an enclosed space 真空泵

vacuum tube /ˈ··· ˌ·/ *n* [C] *AmE* a VALVE (3)【美】真空管

Vaduz /vɑˈduts; vɑːˈduːts/ the capital city of Liechtenstein 瓦杜兹〔列支敦士登首都〕

vag·a·bond /ˈvægəˌbɑnd; ˈvægəbɒnd/ *n* [C] *especially literary* someone who has no home but travels from place to place【尤文】流浪者, 漂泊者 —compare 比较 VAGRANT

va·ga·ries /ˈvegərɪz; ˈveɪgəriz/ *n* [plural] *formal* unusual or unexpected events, changes, ideas etc, that have an effect on your life【正式】〔事件、想法等〕不可捉摸[异常]的变化: *the vagaries of the English weather* 英格兰天气的变幻无常

va·gi·na /vəˈdʒaɪnə; vəˈdʒaɪnə/ *n* [C] the passage from a woman's outer sexual organs to her WOMB 阴道 —**vaginal** *adj*

va·gran·cy /ˈvegrənsɪ; ˈveɪgrənsi/ *n* [U] the criminal offence of living on the street and BEGGING from people 流浪罪

va·grant /ˈvegrənt; ˈveɪgrənt/ *n* [C] *formal* someone who has no home or work, especially someone who begs【正式】流浪者, 乞丐

vague /veg; veɪg/ *adj* **1** unclear because someone does not give enough details or does not say exactly what they mean 含糊的, 不明确的, 不清楚的: *vague promises of support* 含糊其辞表示支持的承诺 | [+about] *Maria was very vague about her plans for the future.* 玛丽亚对自己未来的打算很不明确。**2** **have a** S3

vague idea/feeling/recollection etc that to think that something might be true or that you remember something, although you cannot be sure 隐约地想到/感到/忆起等 **3** not having a clear shape or form; INDISTINCT 模糊不清的: *The vague shape of a figure loomed through the mist.* 薄雾中隐隐出现一个模糊的人影。—**vagueness** *n* [U]

vague·ly /ˋveglɪ; ˈveɪgli/ *adv* **1** slightly 稍微: *There was something vaguely familiar about him.* 对他稍微有点熟悉。**2** in a way that shows you are not thinking about what you are doing 心不在焉地: *He smiled vaguely at the ceiling.* 他心不在焉地笑看着天花板。**3** not exactly 不精确地; 不确切地; 不完全地: *vaguely round* 略有点儿圆

Vail /vel; veɪl/ a city in Colorado in the western US, which is a popular place and fashionable for skiing 韦尔〔美国西部科罗拉多州一城市, 为深受欢迎的时尚滑雪胜地〕

vain /ven; veɪn/ *adj* **1** someone who is vain is very proud of their good looks, abilities, or position; CONCEITED 自负的, 自视过高的 **2 in vain** without success in spite of your efforts 徒劳, 无结果: *I tried in vain to get Sue to come with us.* 我想带休一起来, 结果白费心机。**3 vain attempt/hope/effort etc** an attempt, hope etc that fails to achieve the result you wanted 徒劳的尝试/希望/努力等 **4 vain threat/promise etc** *literary* a threat, promise etc that is not worrying because the person cannot do what they say they will【文】空洞的威胁/承诺等 **5 take sb's name in vain** *humorous* to talk about someone, while they are not there, especially in a way that shows a lack of respect for them【幽默】〔趁其不在场而〕轻慢地谈论某人 **6 take the Lord's name in vain** *old use* to swear using the words 'God', 'Jesus' etc【旧】亵渎上帝之名 —**vainly** *adv*: *The instructor struggled vainly to open his parachute.* 教官拼命想打开降落伞, 但没有成功。—see also 另见 VANITY

vain·glo·ri·ous /venˋglorɪəs; veɪnˈglɔːriəs/ *adj literary* too proud of your own abilities, importance etc【文】非常自负的; 极度虚荣的 —**vaingloriously** *adv* —**vainglory** *n* [U]

val·ance /ˋvæləns; ˈvæləns/, **valence** *n* [C] **1** a narrow piece of cloth that hangs from the edge of a shelf or from the frame of a bed to the floor〔装饰橱柜、床沿等的〕挂帘, 短帷幔, 挂布 **2** *especially AmE* a narrow piece of cloth above a window, covering the RAIL the curtains hang on【尤美】〔窗帘上端的〕布帷幔; PELMET *BrE*【英】

vale /vel; veɪl/ *n* [C] **1** *especially literary* a broad low valley【尤文】谷; 山谷 **2 the vale of tears/misery etc** *literary* used to mean the difficulties of life【文】尘世, 现世

val·e·dic·tion /ˌvæləˋdɪkʃən; ˌvælǝˈdɪkʃən/ *n* [C,U] *formal* the act of saying goodbye, especially in a formal speech【正式】〔尤指正式演讲中的〕告别

val·e·dic·to·ri·an /ˌvælədɪkˋtorɪən; ˌvælǝdɪkˈtɔːriən/ *n* [C] *AmE* the student who has received the best marks all the way through school, and usually makes a speech【美】致告别辞的毕业生代表〔通常为成绩最优者〕

val·e·dic·to·ry /ˌvæləˋdɪktərɪ; ˌvælǝˈdɪktəri◂/ *adj formal* connected with saying goodbye, especially on a formal occasion【正式】〔尤指在正式场合中〕告别的: *a valedictory speech* 告别辞

va·lence[1] /ˋveləns; ˈveɪləns/ *n* [C] *especially AmE* valency【尤美】原子价, 化合价

va·lence[2] /ˋvæləns; ˈvæləns/ *n* [C] another spelling of VALANCE valance 的另一种拼法

va·len·cy /ˋvelənsɪ; ˈveɪlənsi/ *n* [C] *technical especially BrE* a measure of the power of atoms to combine together to form compounds【术语, 尤英】原子价, 化合价

val·en·tine /ˋvæləntaɪn; ˈvæləntaɪn/ *n* [C] **1** someone you love or think is attractive, that you send a card to on St Valentine's Day (February 14th) (在圣瓦伦丁节〔2月14日〕向之赠送贺卡的)情人: *Be my valentine.* 做我的情人吧。**2** a card you send to someone on St Valentine's Day 在圣瓦伦丁节赠送给某人的贺卡, 情人卡

Valentine's Day /ˋ··· ,·/ —see 见 SAINT VALENTINE'S DAY

Val·en·ti·no /ˌvælənˋtino; ˌvælənˈtiːnəʊ/, **Ru·dolph** /ˋrudɑlf; ˈruːdɒlf/ (1895-1926) a US film actor, born in Italy, who appeared as romantic characters in SILENT FILMS (=films made with no sound). He was famous for being sexually attractive, and for being loved by millions of women who watched his films. These films include *The Four Horsemen of the Apocalypse* (1921) and *The Sheikh* (1921). 瓦伦蒂诺〔(1895-1926), 美国电影演员, 生于意大利, 曾在无声电影中饰演过许多浪漫角色。他性感迷人, 受到数百万女影迷的追捧, 主演过《启示录四骑士》(1921) 和《酋长》(1921) 等著名影片〕

valet[1] /ˋvælɪt; ˈvælǝt/ *n* [C] **1** a male servant who looks after a man's clothes, serves his meals etc〔男子的〕贴身男仆, 男仆从 **2** *BrE* someone who cleans the clothes of people staying in a hotel【英】〔为旅馆客人洗衣服的〕服务员 **3** *AmE* someone who parks your car for you at a hotel or restaurant【美】〔旅馆或餐厅中〕为客人泊车的人: *valet service* 停车服务

valet[2] *v* [T] *BrE* to clean someone's car【英】洗车: *a valeting service* 洗车服务

Val·hal·la /vælˋhælə; vælˈhælə/ in Norse MYTHOLOGY, a place in Asgard, the Norse heaven, to which the souls of those who died bravely in battle are taken by the Valkyries 瓦尔哈拉神殿, 英灵殿〔北欧神话中天宫内的一处宫殿。仙女瓦尔基里将阵亡勇士的英灵带到此地〕

valiant /ˋvæljənt; ˈvæliənt/ *adj* very brave, especially in a difficult situation〔尤指在困境中〕勇敢的, 英勇的: *a valiant attempt to break the world record* 破世界纪录的勇敢尝试

val·id /ˋvælɪd; ˈvælǝd/ *adj* **1** a valid ticket, document, or agreement can be used legally or is officially acceptable, especially for a fixed period of time or according to certain conditions 有效的: *a valid passport* 有效的护照 | *Your return ticket is valid for three months.* 你的回程票有效期为三个月。**2 valid reason/argument/criticism etc** a reason, argument etc that is based on what is true or sensible, and so should be accepted or treated in a serious way 正当的[有根据的]理由/论点/批评等: *His point about staff shortages was a valid one.* 他的关于员工短缺的观点是有根据的。—**validity** /vəˋlɪdətɪ; vəˈlɪdǝti/ *n* [U]: *I would question the validity of that statement.* 我要质疑那个声明的有效性。

val·i·date /ˋvæləˌdet; ˈvælǝdeɪt/ *v* [T] *formal* to prove that something is true or correct, or to make a document or agreement officially and legally acceptable【正式】证实; 使生效; 使合法化 —**validation** /ˌvæləˋdeʃən; ˌvælǝˈdeɪʃən/ *n* [C,U]

va·lise /vəˋlis; vəˈliːz/ *n* [C] *old-fashioned* a small SUITCASE【过时】小旅行袋

Val·i·um /ˋvælɪəm; ˈvæliəm/ *n* [U] a drug to make people feel calmer and less anxious 安定〔一种镇静剂〕

Valjean, Jean /ʒɑŋ; ʒɒŋ/ the main character in the book *Les Misérables* (1862) by the French writer Victor Hugo. Valjean is sent to prison for stealing bread to feed his sister's family, but he escapes. Later, he becomes a successful man, but he is hunted by a DETECTIVE, Javert, who wants to put him back in prison. 冉·阿让〔法国作家维克多·雨果所著小说《悲惨世界》(1862) 中的主人公。冉·阿让因偷面包给姐姐一家糊口而被捕, 后来越狱, 成为成功人士, 但却一直遭到想把他抓捕归案的侦探沙威的追踪〕

Val·ky·rie /vælˋkɪrɪ; ˈvælkǝriː/ in Norse MYTHOLOGY, one of Odin's female servants, who ride on their horses into battles and decide which brave soldiers will die. They then take the souls of the dead soldiers to Valhalla. 瓦尔基里, 女武神〔北欧神话中奥丁神的众侍女。她们骑着战马来到战场决定哪些勇士将战死, 然后将这些阵亡勇士的灵魂带至瓦尔哈拉神殿〕

val·ley /ˋvælɪ; ˈvæli/ *n* [C] an area of land between two lines of hills or mountains, usually with a river flowing through it 谷; 山谷〔常有河流流过〕: *the San Fernando valley* 圣费尔南多谷地 S3 W3

Valley Forge /ˌ·· ˋ·/ a place in Pennsylvania in the US where George Washington's soldiers stayed during the winter in 1777-78 in the American Revolutionary War. Many men died because of the cold and lack of food. 福奇谷〔美国宾夕法尼亚州一地。1777至1778年美国独立战争期间乔治·华盛顿的部队在此驻扎, 不少士兵因饥寒交迫而死〕

val·our *BrE*【英】, **valor** *AmE*【美】/ˋvælə; ˈvælə/ *n* [U] *literary* great courage, especially in war【文】〔尤指在战争中的〕勇猛, 勇武 —see also 另见 **discretion is the better part of valour** (DISCRETION (3))

val·u·a·ble /ˋvæljuəbl; ˈvæljuəbəl/ *adj* **1** worth a lot of money 值钱的, 贵重的: *a valuable painting* 一幅名贵的画 **2** valuable help, advice etc is very useful because it helps you to do something〔帮助、劝告等〕有价值的, 有用的 **3** important because there is only a limited amount available 宝贵的, 珍贵的: *I won't waste any more of your valuable time.* 我不再浪费你的宝贵时间了。 W3

val·u·a·bles /ˋvæljuəblz; ˈvæljuəbəlz/ *n* [plural] things that you own that are worth a lot of money, such as jewellery, cameras etc〔珠宝、照相机等〕贵重物品: *Guests should leave their valuables in the hotel safe.* 客人应把贵重物品存放在旅馆的保险柜中。

val·u·a·tion /ˌvæljuˋeʃən; ˌvæljuˈeɪʃən/ *n* [C,U] a judgment about how much something is worth, how effective or useful a particular idea or plan will be etc 估价; 评价: **put a valuation on** *The valuation they put on the house was far too high.* 他们对房子的估价太高。

val·ue¹ /vælju; ˈvælju:/ *n* [U]

1 ▶MONEY 钱◀ [C,U] the amount of money that something is worth 价值: *The alterations doubled the value of the house.* 改建使房子的价值翻了一番。| **increase/go down etc in value** *Shares can go down as well as go up in value.* 股票的价值会上升，也会下跌。| **market value** (=the amount of money that something can usually be sold for) 市场价值，市价，市值 *We paid a price that was well above the market value.* 我们付出的价钱远远高于市价。| **of value** (=worth a lot of money) 值钱的 *The thieves took nothing of value.* 小偷没偷走任何值钱的东西。| **street value** (=the value of drugs when they are sold illegally) 〔毒品的〕黑市价 | **hold its value** (=continue to be worth the same amount of money) 保值 *It's a beautiful carpet – it should hold its value.* 这地毯很漂亮，应该能保值。—see 见 WORTH (USAGE)

2 be good/excellent etc value *BrE*【英】also 又作 **be (good) value for money** used to say that you get a lot of something or that its quality is good, considering the price you pay for it 很划算 —see 见 CHEAP¹ (USAGE)

3 be bad/poor etc value *BrE* used to say that you do not get much of something or its quality is not very good, considering the price you pay for it【英】不划算: *I thought £10 for a record that only lasts 14 minutes was incredibly poor value.* 我认为花10英镑买一张只有14分钟的唱片太不值了。

4 ▶IMPORTANCE/USEFULNESS 重要性/有用性◀ [U] the importance or usefulness of something 重要性，用处，益处: **of great/little value** *His research has been of little practical value.* 他的研究没多大实用价值。| **sentimental value** (=importance that something has for you because someone you like gave it to you, because it reminds you of the past etc) 情感价值

5 ▶PRINCIPLES 准则◀ values [plural] your principles about what is right and wrong, or your ideas about what is important in life 准则；价值观（念）: *Western liberal values* 西方的自由价值观

6 ▶AMOUNT 数额◀ [C] *technical* a mathematical quantity shown by a letter of the alphabet or sign【术语】〔由字母或符号表示的〕（数）值: *Let x have the value 25.* 设 x 的值为 25。

7 ▶MUSIC 音乐◀ [C] the length of a musical note 音符长度，时值

8 curiosity/novelty/snob etc value a quality something has that makes it seem interesting or desirable because it is different, new, or typical of high class people 〔某物所呈现出的〕在趣味性/新奇性/虚荣性等方面的价值

9 family values an expression meaning the belief that the family is very important, used especially by politicians 家庭观念 —see also 另见 FACE VALUE

value² *v* [T] **1** to think that something is important to you 尊重，重视: *I value your advice.* 我很重视你的意见。| *a valued friend* 看重的朋友 **2** [usually passive 一般用被动态] to decide how much money something is worth, by comparing it with similar things 估价，计算…的价格: **value sth at** *We decided to get the house valued.* 我们决定给房子估估价。| *Paintings valued at over $200,000 were stolen from her home.* 几幅估价为二十多万美元的画从她家里被盗走了。

value-ad·ded tax /ˌ‥ ‥ ˈ‥/ *n* [U] VAT 增值税

value judg·ment /ˈ‥ ˌ‥/ *n* [C] a decision or judgment about how good something is, based on opinions not facts 价值判断〔根据见解而不是根据事实所作的判断〕

val·u·er /ˈvæljuə; ˈvæljuə/ *n* [C] someone whose job is to decide how much money things are worth 估价者；鉴定人

valve /vælv; vælv/ *n* [C] **1** a part of a tube or pipe that opens and shuts like a door to control the flow of liquid, gas, air etc passing through it 阀，活门；瓣（膜）: *the valves of the heart* 心脏瓣膜 —see picture at 参见 BICYCLE¹ 图 **2** the part on a TRUMPET¹ (1) or similar musical instrument that you press to change the sound of the note 〔乐器上的〕活塞，栓塞 **3** *BrE* a closed glass tube used to control the flow of electricity in old radios, televisions etc【英】电子管，真空管; VACUUM TUBE *AmE*【美】—see also 另见 BIVALVE, SAFETY VALVE

vamoose /væˈmus; væˈmu:s/ *interjection AmE old-fashioned* used to tell someone to go away【美，过时】〔用于叫某人〕走开

vamp¹ /væmp; væmp/ *n* [C] *old-fashioned* a woman who uses her sexual attractiveness to make men do things for her【过时】利用色相勾引男子为其效劳的女子；女骗子

vamp² *v*

vamp sth ↔ **up** *phr v* [T] *informal* to make a story, music etc seem more exciting by adding things to it【非正式】〔通过补充〕编造〔故事、音乐等〕；使…翻新

vam·pire /ˈvæmpaɪr; ˈvæmpaɪə/ *n* [C] an evil spirit that is believed to suck people's blood by biting their necks 吸血鬼〔传说中咬破人脖子吸血的恶鬼〕

CULTURAL NOTE 文化注释

In stories, vampires are only awake at night and will die if go into the sun's light. They do not have a REFLECTION if they stand in front of a mirror; they do not like GARLIC; they are afraid of the CROSS (=the sign of the Christian religion); they sleep in a COFFIN, and they can only be killed if someone pushes a wooden STAKE (=pointed stick) through their heart. A vampire can also change into a BAT. There are many books about vampires, and the most famous one is called *Dracula*, by Bram Stoker. There are also many films about vampires, especially Count Dracula. 故事中，吸血鬼只在夜间苏醒，一旦被阳光照到它们就会死去。站在镜子前面的吸血鬼是照不出影像的，它们不喜欢大蒜并惧怕十字架，它们睡在棺材里。人们只有用尖木棍刺中吸血鬼的心脏才能将其杀死。吸血鬼能够变成一只蝙蝠。写吸血鬼的书很多，而最有名的一本是布拉姆·斯托克写的《德拉库拉》。拍摄吸血鬼，特别是拍德拉库拉伯爵的电影也有很多。

vampire bat /ˈ‥ ‥/ *n* [C] a south American BAT that sucks the blood of other animals 〔南美的〕吸血蝙蝠

van /væn; væn/ *n* [C] **1** a vehicle used especially for carrying goods, which is smaller than a TRUCK and has a roof and usually no windows at the sides （厢式）小型货车: *a delivery van* 运货车 | *a van driver* 小型货车司机 **2** *especially BrE* a railway carriage with a roof and sides, used especially for carrying goods【尤英】带篷盖的铁路货车；行李车: *a luggage van* 行李车 —see also 另见 GUARD'S VAN

Van·brugh /vænˈbru; ˈvænbrə/, **Sir John** (1664-1726) an English ARCHITECT and Restoration COMEDY writer. He designed large houses for UPPER CLASS people, including **Blenheim Palace**, one of the best examples of the Baroque style in the UK, and **Castle Howard**. His plays include *The Relapse* and *The Provok'd Wife*. 范布勒爵士〔(1664-1726)，英国建筑师、王政复辟时期的喜剧作家。他为上流社会人士设计豪宅，其中包括英国巴洛克风格的典范之作布伦海姆宫以及霍华德城堡。其创作的剧作包括《故态复萌》和《恼怒的妻子》〕

Van Buren /væn ˈbjurən; væn ˈbjuərən/, **Martin** (1782-1862) the eighth president of the US, from 1837 to 1841 范布伦〔(1782-1862)，美国第八任总统，任期从 1837 至 1841 年〕

Van·cou·ver /vænˈkuvə; vænˈku:və/ **1** a city in British Columbia, Canada, on the Pacific Ocean. Vancouver is Canada's third largest city and is an important port and industrial and business centre. 温哥华〔加拿大不列颠哥伦比亚省一城市，濒临太平洋。加拿大第三大城市、重要港口及工商业中心〕 **2** also 又作 **Vancouver Island** an island off the southwest coast of British Columbia, Canada 温哥华岛〔加拿大不列颠哥伦比亚省西南近海的一座岛屿〕

van·dal /ˈvændl; ˈvændl/ *n* [C] someone who deliberately damages things, especially public property 故意破坏（公共）财物者

van·dal·is·m /ˈvændlˌɪzəm; ˈvændəl-ɪzəm/ *n* [U] the crime of deliberately damaging things, especially public property 故意破坏（公共）财物的行为

van·dal·ize also 又作 **-ise** *BrE*【英】/ˈvændlˌaɪz; ˈvændəl-aɪz/ *v* [T] to damage or destroy things deliberately, especially public property 故意破坏〔财物，尤指公物〕

Van·der·bilt /ˈvændəbɪlt; ˈvændəbɪlt/ a US family famous for being very rich. Cornelius Vanderbilt (1794-1877) became extremely rich by building STEAMSHIPs and railways in the 19th century. 范德比尔特家族〔美国一豪门世家。科尼利厄斯·范德比尔特 (1794-1877) 19 世纪通过制造汽船和修建铁路而成为巨富〕

Van Dyck /væn ˈdaɪk; væn ˈdaɪk/, **Sir Anthony** (1599-1641) a Flemish painter who lived for some time in England, and painted PORTRAITs of the British king Charles I and his family 凡·戴克爵士〔(1599-1641)，佛兰德斯画家。他曾一度旅居英格兰，为英王查理一世及其家族创作肖像画〕

vane /ven; veɪn/ *n* [C] a flat blade that is moved by wind or water to produce power to drive a machine 〔风车、螺旋桨等的〕翼，叶片: *the vanes of a propellor* 螺旋桨的叶片 —see also 另见 WEATHER VANE

Van Gogh /væn ˈgo; væn ˈgɒx/, **Vin·cent** /ˈvɪnsnt; ˈvɪnsənt/ (1853-90) a Dutch painter who went to live in southern France and who helped to develop the style of post-impressionism. His paintings typically use bright colours and have thick lines of paint in circular patterns, and the most fa-

mous ones include *Sunflowers* and *Irises*. He is also famous for being mentally ill and for cutting off one of his ears and later killing himself. 梵高〔(1853-1890), 荷兰画家, 旅居法国南部, 为后印象派风格的代表人物之一。明快的色彩和粗重的弧形线条构成其绘画的典型特征, 代表作为《向日葵》和《鸢尾花》。梵高同样为世人所熟知的是, 他因精神失常割掉了自己的一只耳朵, 后来自杀身亡〕

van·guard /ˈvænˌgɑrd; ˈvængɑːd/ *n* **1 in the vanguard** in the most advanced position of development 在前沿: *In the 19th century, Britain was in the vanguard of industrial progress.* 在19世纪, 英国是工业发展的前驱。**2 the vanguard** [singular] the leading position at the front of an army or group of ships moving into battle, or the soldiers who are in this position〔军队或舰队的〕前卫, 前锋

Van Helsing /væn ˋhɛlsɪŋ; væn ˈhelsɪŋ/, **Professor Abraham** a VAMPIRE hunter who hunts down Dracula in the NOVEL by Bram Stoker 范·海辛教授〔布拉姆·斯托克所著小说中的吸血鬼猎人, 猎杀了吸血鬼德拉库拉〕

va·nil·la¹ /vəˈnɪlə; vəˈnɪlə/ *n* [U] a substance used to give a special taste to ICE CREAM, cakes etc, made from the beans of a tropical plant 香草精, 香子兰精

vanilla² *adj* having the taste of vanilla 香草味的: *vanilla ice cream* 香草冰淇淋 | *vanilla essence* 香精

van·ish /ˈvænɪʃ; ˈvænɪʃ/ *v* [I] **1** to disappear suddenly, especially in a way that cannot easily be explained 突然不见, 消失〔尤指以一种不易解释的方式〕: *When I turned round again, the boy had vanished.* 当我再回头时, 那个男孩已经不见了。| **vanish into thin air** (=disappear completely in a very mysterious way) 化为乌有 | **vanish without trace/vanish off the face of the earth** (=disappear so that no sign remains) 消失得无影无踪 **2** to suddenly stop existing 灭绝: *Many species in South America have vanished completely.* 南美的许多物种已经灭绝。**3 do a vanishing act** *informal* to suddenly disappear, especially when someone is looking for you【非正式】突然消失〔尤指当有人在寻找你时〕

vanishing point /ˈ‥ ˌ‧/ *n* [singular] *technical* the point in the distance, especially on a picture, where parallel lines seem to meet【术语】消失点〔尤指透视画中平行线的会聚点〕

van·i·ty /ˈvænətɪ; ˈvænəti/ *n* [U] **1** too much PRIDE in yourself, so that you are always thinking about yourself and your appearance 虚荣(心); 自负 **2 the vanity of sth** *literary* the lack of importance of something compared to other things that are much more important【文】某事物的无用[无价值]: *The poem warns of the vanity of mental ambition.* 这首诗提醒世人, 不付诸实践的抱负毫无用处。

vanity case /ˈ‥ ˌ‧/ *n* [C] a small bag used by a woman for carrying MAKE-UP etc〔女性放置化妆品的〕小手袋, 小手提包[盒]

Vanity Fair /ˌ‥ ˈ‧/ **1** *trademark* a magazine sold in the US and UK that has articles on fashion, some news articles, and some articles or stories by well-known writers【商标】《名利场》〔在美国和英国出售的一种杂志, 刊登时尚、新闻类文章以及名家撰写的文章和故事〕**2** (1847-48) a NOVEL by William Thackeray about UPPER CLASS English society at the time of the war against Napoleon. The characters in the book, who include Becky Sharp, are often shown to be stupid or to have no moral principles.《名利场》〔(1847-1848), 威廉·萨克雷所著长篇小说, 描写与拿破仑交战期间英国上流社会的生活。书中描写的人物, 如贝基·夏普等, 往往不是愚蠢, 就是不讲道德〕**3** *literary* a place where people have no serious thoughts or beliefs, and where only money, fashion, and entertainment are considered to be important. The name comes from an imaginary place like this in *The Pilgrim's Progress* by John Bunyan.【文】浮华世界〔指一个缺乏深刻思想和信仰, 只追求金钱、时尚和享乐的场所。此名源自约翰·班扬所著《天路历程》一书中一个类似的虚构之地〕

vanity plate /ˈ‥ ˌ‧/ *n* [C] *AmE* a car NUMBERPLATE that has a special combination of numbers or letters, for example the first letters of the driver's names【美】特别车牌〈如由司机姓名首字母组合而成〉

vanity press /ˈ‥ ˌ‧/ also 又作 **vanity pub·lish·er** /ˈ‥ ˌ‥‧/ *n* [C usually singular 一般用单数] a company that writers pay to print their books 由作者自费出版书籍的出版社

vanity ta·ble /ˈ‥ ˌ‥/ *n* [C] *AmE*【美】梳妆台; a DRESSING TABLE *BrE*【英】

van·quish /ˈvæŋkwɪʃ; ˈvæŋkwɪʃ/ *v* [T] *literary* to defeat someone or something completely【文】彻底征服, 击败

van·tage point /ˈvæntɪdʒ ˌpɔɪnt; ˈvɑːntɪdʒ pɔɪnt/ *n* [C] **1** a good position from which you can see something〔能观察某物的〕有利位置: *From my vantage point on the hill, I could see the whole procession.* 从山上的有利位置, 我可以看到整个游行队伍。**2** a way of thinking about things that comes from your own particular situation; POINT OF VIEW 见解, 观点: *speaking from his vantage point as a major developer* 从他作为主要开发者的观点来说

Van·u·a·tu /ˌvænuˈɑtu; ˌvænuˈɑːtuː/ a country in the southwest Pacific Ocean, East of Australia, made up of a chain of VOLCANIC islands. Population: 192,190 (2001). Capital: Vila. Vanuatu was formerly called the New Hebrides, and it is an independent member of the British commonwealth. 瓦努阿图〔太平洋西南部一岛国, 位于澳大利亚以东, 由一系列火山岛组成。人口: 192,190 (2001), 首都: 维拉港。瓦努阿图旧称新赫布里底群岛, 现为英联邦的一个独立成员国〕

Van Winkle, Rip —see 见 RIP VAN WINKLE

vap·id /ˈvæpɪd; ˈvæpɪ̈d/ *adj formal* lacking intelligence, interest, or imagination【正式】缺少灵性的; 乏味的, 平庸的: *vapid piped music* 乏味的管乐 —**vapidly** *adv* —**vapidness** *n* [U] —**vapidity** /væˈpɪdətɪ; vəˈpɪdɪ̈ti/ *n* [U]

va·por /ˈvepɚ; ˈveɪpə/ *n* [C,U] the American spelling of VAPOUR vapour 的美式拼法

va·por·ize also 又作 **-ise** *BrE*【英】/ˈvepəˌraɪz; ˈveɪpəraɪz/ *v* [I,T] to change into a vapour, or to make something do this (使)蒸发, (使)变成蒸气: *Water vaporizes when it boils.* 水沸腾时就变成蒸气。—**vaporization** /ˌvepərəˋzeʃən; ˌveɪpəraɪˈzeɪʃən/ *n* [U]

va·pour *BrE*【英】, **vapor** *AmE*【美】/ˈvepɚ; ˈveɪpə/ *n* **1** [C, U] a mass of small drops of a liquid which float in the air, for example because the liquid has been heated 蒸气, 水汽,〔某种液体的〕蒸气: *water vapour* 水蒸气 **2 the vapours** [plural] *old use* a condition when you suddenly feel faint【旧】突然眩晕感 —**vaporous** *adj*

vapour trail *BrE*【英】, **vapor trail** *AmE*【美】/ˈ‥ ˌ‧/ *n* [C] the white line that is left in the sky by a plane〔飞机在高空飞行时产生的〕雾化尾流

var·i·a·ble¹ /ˈvɛrɪəbl; ˈveəriəbəl/ *n* [C] **1** something that may be different in different situations, so that you cannot be sure what will happen 易变的事, 可变因素: *There are too many variables in the experiment to predict the result accurately.* 实验中可变因素太多, 难以准确预测结果。**2** *technical* a mathematical quantity which can represent several different amounts【术语】〔数学中的〕变量, 变数 —compare 比较 CONSTANT²

variable² *adj* **1** likely to change often 易变的, 多变的: *the variable nature of the English climate* 英格兰气候的多变性 | *Consumer preferences are so variable that planning is almost impossible.* 消费者的爱好如此易变, 要计划几乎是不可能的。**2** sometimes good and sometimes bad; UNEVEN 时好时坏的: *The team's performance has been very variable lately.* 这个队近来的成绩时好时坏。**3** able to be changed 可变的: *The machine has variable temperature settings.* 这台机器设有调温装置。**variably** *adv* —**variability** /ˌvɛrɪəˋbɪlətɪ; ˌveərɪəˈbɪlɪ̈ti/ *n* [U]

var·i·ance /ˈvɛrɪəns; ˈveəriəns/ *n* [U] *formal*【正式】**1 be at variance with** if two people or things are at variance with each other, they do not agree or are very different 与…有分歧; 与…大相径庭: *Tradition and culture are often at variance with the needs of modern living.* 传统和文化常常与现代生活的需要不相符合。**2** the amount by which two or more things are different or by which they change 差异, 不一致

var·i·ant /ˈvɛrɪənt; ˈveəriənt/ *n* [C] **1** something that is slightly different from the usual form of something 变体: [+on] *a variant on the archetypal Hollywood hero* 好莱坞典型男主角的变体 **2** *technical* a slightly different form of a word or phrase【术语】〔同一词或短语的〕异体: *regional spelling variants in British and American English* 英国英语和美国英语中地域性的不同拼法 —**variant** *adj*: *a variant form of the word* 该词的异体

var·i·a·tion /ˌvɛrɪˋeʃən; ˌveəriˈeɪʃən/ *n* **1** [C,U] a difference or change from the usual amount or form of something〔数量或形式的〕变化, 变动: [+in] *There are wide regional variations in house prices.* 房价的地域性差异很大。**2** [C] something that is done in a way that is different from the way it is usually done〔做事方式的〕变更: [+on] *an interesting variation on the theme of betrayal and revenge* 对背叛与复仇这一主题的趣味性变更 **3** [C] one of a set of short pieces of music, each based on the same simple tune〔音乐中的〕变奏(曲): *Bach's Goldberg Variations* 巴赫的《哥德堡变奏曲》 2

var·i·cose veins /ˌværɪkos ˋvenz; ˌværɪ̈kəʊs ˈveɪnz/ *n* [plural] a medical condition in which the VEINs in your leg become swollen and painful〔腿部的〕静脉曲张

var·ied /ˈvɛrɪd; ˈveərid/ *adj* consisting of or including many different kinds of things or people, especially in a way that seems interesting 各种各样的, 形形色色的: *The work's very*

varied. 这项工作内容繁多。| *human nature, in all its many and varied forms* 形形色色的人性 | *products as varied as car bumpers and cigarette filters* 各式各样的产品，如汽车的保险杠和香烟的过滤嘴

var·ie·gat·ed /ˈvɛrɪˌgetɪd; ˈveərɪgeɪtɪ̣d/ *adj* **1** a variegated plant, leaf etc has different coloured marks on it〔植物〕杂色的；斑驳的：*variegated ivies* 杂色的常春藤 **2** *formal* consisting of a lot of different types of thing【正式】多样化的

var·ie·ga·tion /ˌvɛrɪˈgeʃən; ˌveərɪ̣ˈgeɪʃən/ *n* [U] marks of varied colours, especially in plants〔尤指植物的〕杂色；斑驳

[2][1] **va·ri·e·ty** /vəˈraɪətɪ; vəˈraɪəti/ *n*

1 a variety of a lot of a particular type of things that are different from each other 种种：*The girls come from a variety of different backgrounds.* 女孩们的出身背景各异。| **a wide variety of** *The T-shirts are available in a wide variety of colors.* 这些T恤有各种各样的颜色可供选择。

2 ▶DIFFERENCES 差异◀ [U] the differences within a group, set of actions etc that make it interesting 多样化，变化：**add variety to** (=make something more interesting) 给…增加趣味性 *There was little she could do to add variety to her daily routine.* 她无法给单调的日常生活增添些趣味。

3 ▶PLANT/ANIMAL 植物/动物◀ [C] a type of plant or animal that is different from others in the same group〔动、植物的〕种类，品种：[+of] *a new variety of apple* 新品种的苹果

4 ▶TYPE OF PERSON/THING 人/物的类型◀ [C usually singular 一般用单数] *often humorous* a particular type of person or thing【常幽默】〔人或物的〕类型：**of the...variety** *The men are mostly of the noble, long-suffering husband variety!* 男人大多属于高尚、刻苦耐劳的丈夫类型！

5 variety is the spice of life used to say that doing a lot of different things, meeting different people etc is what makes life interesting 变化让生活丰富多彩

6 ▶ENTERTAINMENT 娱乐◀ [U] a type of entertainment for theatre or television that includes a lot of different short performances〔剧院或电视的〕综艺节目

Variety Club of Great Brit·ain, the /·,···,·····/ a British CHARITY organization which gives money, holidays, vehicles etc to poor or sick children. Its members are people who work in television, films, and popular theatre. 大不列颠综艺俱乐部〔英国一慈善组织，资助贫困或残疾儿童，为其安排度假活动，提供交通工具等。其成员为影视、大众戏剧等演艺界人士〕

variety store /·ˈ···,·/ *n* [C] *AmE* a shop that sells many different kinds of goods, often at low prices【美】杂货店

[1][1] **var·i·ous** /ˈvɛrɪəs; ˈveəriəs/ *adj* [usually before noun 一般用于名词前] several different 各种各样的：*available in various colours* 各种颜色应有尽有

var·i·ous·ly /ˈvɛrɪəslɪ; ˈveəriəsli/ *adv* **variously described/estimated etc** used to introduce a number of different descriptions, amounts etc, that people have made or used about something 各种不同描述/估价等的：*His fortune has been variously estimated at between $1 and $2 billion.* 对他的财产有各种不同的估价，从10亿到20亿美元不等。

var·let /ˈvarlɪt; ˈvɑːlɪ̣t/ *n* [C] *old use* a bad man【旧】无赖，恶棍

var·mint /ˈvarmɪnt; ˈvɑːmɪ̣nt/ *n* [C] *old-fashioned* someone, especially a child, who causes a lot of trouble【过时】老闯祸的人〔尤指顽童〕

var·nish[1] /ˈvarnɪʃ; ˈvɑːnɪʃ/ *n* [C,U] **1** a clear liquid that is painted onto things, especially things made of wood, to protect them and give them a hard shiny surface〔尤指刷在木制品上的〕清漆，罩光漆 **2 the varnish** the clear shiny surface of something that has been covered in this liquid〔涂清漆后产生的〕光泽的表面 —compare 比较 LACQUER[1] (1)

varnish[2] *v* [T] to cover something with varnish 给…涂上清漆

var·si·ty /ˈvarsətɪ; ˈvɑːsɪ̣ti/ *n* [C,U] **1** *AmE* the main team that represents a university, college, or school in a sport【美】〔学校体育比赛中的〕代表队；校队：*the varsity football team* 大学足球代表队 —compare 比较 JUNIOR VARSITY **2** *BrE old-fashioned* a university, especially Oxford or Cambridge【英，过时】大学〔尤指牛津大学或剑桥大学〕

[2][2] **var·y** /ˈvɛrɪ; ˈveəri/ *v* **1** [I] if several things of the same type vary, they are all different from each other（彼此）相异，存在不同之处：**vary greatly/considerably/enormously** *Teaching methods vary greatly from school to school.* 每所学校的教学方法大不相同。| **vary in price/quality/size** *flowers that vary in color and size* 色彩各异大小不一的花朵 | **varying degrees of** *varying degrees of success* 不同程度的成功 **2** [I] to change often 多变，变化无常：*Quentin's mood seems to vary according to the weather.* 昆廷的情绪似乎随天气而变化。| **it varies** *"What do you normally have for lunch?" "Well, it varies from day to day."* "你午饭通常吃什么？" "噢，每天都不一样。" **3** [T] to regularly change what you do or the way that you do it 经常改变，使多样化：*My doctor said I should vary my diet more.* 医生说我的日常饮食应该更为多样化。—see also 另见 VARIED

vas·cu·lar /ˈvæskjələ; ˈvæskjɪ̣lə/ *adj technical* connected with the tubes through which liquids flow in the bodies of animals or in plants【术语】〔动物〕脉管的；〔植物〕维管的：*the vascular system* 维管系统

vase /ves; vɑːz/ *n* [C] a glass or baked clay container used to put flowers in or for decoration 花瓶，〔装饰用的〕瓶

va·sec·to·my /vəsˈɛktəmɪ; vəˈsektəmi/ *n* [C,U] a medical operation to cut the small tube that carries a man's SPERM so that he is unable to produce children 输精管切除术

Vas·e·line /ˈvæslˌin; ˈvæsɪ̣liːn/ *n* [U] *trademark* a soft clear substance used for various medical and other purposes【商标】凡士林

vas·sal /ˈvæsl; ˈvæsəl/ *n* [C] **1** a man in the MIDDLE AGES who was given land to live on by a lord in return for promising to work or fight for him〔中世纪的〕封臣，家臣〔对国君或领主效忠，作为回报获封土地者〕**2** *formal* a country that is controlled by another country【正式】（附）属国：*a vassal state* 附庸国

Vas·sar Col·lege /ˌvæsə ˈkalɪdʒ; ˌvæsə ˈkɒlɪdʒ/ also 又作 **Vassar** a college in the state of New York, US. It was established in 1861 as a college for women, but it has accepted male students since the late 1960s. 瓦瑟学院〔美国纽约州一学院。始建于1861年，最初为女子学院。自20世纪60年代末起开始招收男生〕

vast /væst; vɑːst/ *adj* **1** extremely large 巨大的，广大的，广阔的：*vast areas of rainforest* 广阔的雨林地区 | **vast expense** *A huge palace was constructed at vast public expense.* 用巨额公费建起了一座庞大的宫殿。| **in vast numbers** *The refugees came across the border in vast numbers.* 大量难民越过边界。**2 the vast majority/bulk of** used when you want to emphasize that something is true about almost all of a group of people or things …的绝大多数：*The vast majority of young people don't take drugs.* 绝大多数年轻人不吸毒。—**vastness** *n* [U] [2][2]

vast·ly /ˈvæstlɪ; ˈvɑːstli/ *adv* very much 非常：*This film is vastly superior to his last one.* 这部影片远比他上一部优秀。

VAT /ˌvi e ˈti; ˌviː eɪ ˈtiː/ *n* [U] value added tax; a tax added to the price of goods and services in Britain and the EU 增值税

vat /væt; væt/ *n* [C] a very large container for storing liquids such as WHISKY or DYE, when they are being made〔酿酒、盛染料用的〕大缸，大桶 [3]

Vat·i·can, the /ˈvætɪkən; ˈvætɪkən/ *n* **a)** the large PALACE in Rome where the Pope (=head of the Roman Catholic Church) lives and works 梵蒂冈〔罗马教廷所在地〕**b)** the government of the Pope 罗马教廷：*The Vatican is taking a hard line on birth control.* 罗马教廷在节育的问题上采取强硬路线。

Vatican City /,···ˈ··/ the independent state within Italy in the city of Rome which contains the Vatican and has its own PASSPORTS, money, etc. It has buildings which contain many of the greatest works of art in the world. Population: 1,000 (1995). 梵蒂冈城〔位于意大利罗马城内的独立国家，罗马教廷所在地，有自己的护照、货币等。城内建筑中藏有大量世界顶级艺术杰作。人口：1000（1995）〕

Vatican Coun·cil, the /,···ˈ··/ either of two important series of meetings in the Roman Catholic Church, in which leading members of the church discussed questions of belief and practice. **The First Vatican Council** (1869-70) developed the idea that the Pope was INFALLIBLE (=always right when talking about matters of belief). **The Second Vatican Council** (1962-65) discussed the relationship of the church with the modern world, and one of its results was that church services began to use modern languages instead of Latin. 梵蒂冈会议〔指罗马天主教会召开的两次重要系列会议中的任何一次。与会教会领袖讨论了有关信仰及宗教活动方面的问题。第一届梵蒂冈会议（1869-1870）确立了教皇绝无谬误的观点。第二次梵蒂冈会议（1962-1965）讨论了教会与现代世界的关系问题。会议的成果之一是，教堂礼拜仪式开始使用现代语言，而不再用拉丁文〕

vau·de·ville /ˈvodəˌvɪl; ˈvɔːdəvɪl/ *n* [U] *AmE* a type of theatre entertainment, popular from 1880 to 1950, in which there were many short performances of different kinds, including singing, dancing, jokes etc【美】歌舞杂耍表演，综艺节目〔盛行于1880年至1950年的一种剧院娱乐形式，有演唱、舞蹈、笑话等〕

Vaughan Wil·liams /ˌvɔn ˈwɪljəmz; ˌvɔːn ˈwɪljəmz/, **Ralph** /ref; reɪf/ (1872-1958) a British COMPOSER who collected English folk music and used it in his work. He is best known for his *Fantasia on a Theme by Thomas Tallis*, his VIO-

LIN music *The Lark Ascending*, and his symphonies (SYMPHONY). 沃恩·威廉斯〔(1872-1958)，英国作曲家。他曾收集英国民间音乐，并将其融入自己的作品，代表作有《托马斯·塔利斯主题幻想曲》、小提琴曲《云雀高飞》及数部交响曲〕

vault¹ /vɔlt; vɔːlt/ *n* [C] **1** also 又作 **vaults** [plural] a room with thick walls and a strong door where money, jewels etc are kept to prevent them from being stolen or damaged〔贵重财物的〕保管库，保险库 **2** also 又作 **vaults** [plural] a room where people from the same family are buried, often under the floor of a church〔常指教堂地下的〕墓穴，地下墓室 **3** a jump over something 撑竿跳 —see also 另见 POLE VAULT **4** a roof or CEILING (1) that consists of several ARCH*es* that are joined together, especially in a church〔尤指教堂的〕拱顶

vault² also 又作 **vault over** *v* [T] to jump over something in one movement, using your hands or a pole to help you〔尤指以手撑物或撑竿〕跳跃: *He vaulted over the fence and ran off into the night.* 他跃过篱笆，消失在夜色之中。—**vaulter** *n* [C]

vault·ed /ˈvɔltɪd; ˈvɔːltɪ̣d/ *adj* **vaulted roof/ceiling etc** a roof, ceiling etc that consists of several ARCH*es* which are joined together 拱状屋顶/顶篷等

vault·ing¹ /ˈvɔltɪŋ; ˈvɔːltɪŋ/ *n* [U] arches in a roof〔屋顶的〕拱；拱形圆顶

vaulting² *adj* **vaulting ambition** *literary* the desire to achieve as much as possible【文】极度的野心

vaulting horse /ˈ· ·· ·/ *n* [C] *BrE* a large wooden box used for jumping over in GYMNASTICS【英】跳马〔体育运动器械〕

vaunt /vɔnt; vɔːnt/ *v* **much-vaunted** a much-vaunted achievement is one that people often say is very good, important etc, especially with too much pride 大肆吹嘘的，过分夸耀的〔尤指因过于骄傲〕: *Reagan's much vaunted economic miracle* 里根时期被过分夸耀的经济奇迹

VC /ˌviˈsi; ˌviː ˈsiː/ *n* [C] **1** Victoria Cross; a special medal given to members of the British armed forces who have performed acts of very great bravery in war. The VC is the highest British military honour. 维多利亚十字勋章〔颁发给英国军人的特殊勋章，以表彰他们在战争中的英勇表现，是英国军队中的最高荣誉〕 **2** *AmE informal* the abbreviation of【美，非正式】缩写= the VIET CONG

VCR /ˌvi si ˈɑr; ˌviː siː ˈɑː/ *n* [C] *especially AmE* video cassette recorder; a machine which is used to record television programmes or to play VIDEOTAPES【尤美】录像机; VIDEO¹ (3) *BrE*【英】

VD /ˌvi ˈdi; ˌviː ˈdiː/ *n* [U] venereal disease; a disease that is passed from one person to another during sex 性病，花柳病

VDU /ˌvi di ˈju; ˌviː diː ˈjuː/ *n* [C] visual display unit; a machine like a television that shows the information from a computer or WORD PROCESSOR〔电脑或文字处理器的〕视频显示器

've /v; v, əv/ the short form of 缩略式= 'have': *We've finished.* 我们已经完成了。

veal /vil; viːl/ *n* [U] meat from a CALF (=a young cow) 小牛肉

vec·tor /ˈvɛktɚ; ˈvektə/ *n* [C] *technical*【术语】**1** a quantity that has a direction as well as a size, usually represented by an ARROW (2) 矢量，向量 **2** the course taken by a plane 飞机航线，航道

Ve·da /ˈvedə; ˈveɪdə/ *n* [plural] the oldest writings of the Hindu religion《吠陀》〔印度教最古老的文献〕

Ve·dan·ta /vɪˈdɑntə; vɪ̣ˈdɑːntə/ *n* the system of Hindu thought about religion 吠檀多〔印度的宗教思想体系〕

V-E Day /ˌvi ˈi ˌde; ˌviː ˈiː ˌdeɪ/ Victory in Europe Day; MAY 8th 1945, the day on which victory in Europe in World War II was celebrated 欧洲胜利日〔纪念1945年5月8日二战在欧洲战场取得胜利〕

vee·jay /ˌviˈdʒe; ˌviːˈdʒeɪ/ *n* [C] a VIDEO JOCKEY 电视音乐节目主持人

veep /vip; viːp/ *n* [C] *AmE informal* VICE PRESIDENT【美，非正式】副总统

veer /vɪr; vɪə/ *v* [I] **1** [always+adv/prep] to change direction suddenly 突然改变方向，转向: **[+off/away/across etc]** *The car veered sharply to the right and crashed.* 小轿车向右猛地一拐撞了车。**2** [always+adv/prep] to change suddenly to a very different belief, opinion, or subject〔信仰、观点或主题等〕突然改变: **[+towards/away from etc]** *The country's leaders seemed to veer towards nationalism.* 该国的领导人似乎突然转向了民族主义。**3** *technical* if the wind veers in a particular direction, it changes round to that direction【术语】〔风向〕顺转

veg¹ /vɛdʒ; vedʒ/ *n* [plural] *BrE informal* vegetables【英，非正式】蔬菜: *fruit and veg* 水果和蔬菜

veg² *v*

veg out *phr v* [I] *informal* to relax by doing something that needs very little effort, such as watching television【非正式】放松

ve·gan /ˈvɛgən; ˈviːgən/ *n* [C] someone who does not eat meat, fish, eggs, cheese, or milk 纯素食者，严格的素食主义者〔肉、鱼、蛋、乳酪、牛奶均不吃的人〕—**vegan** *adj*: *a vegan diet* 纯素食者的饮食

Ve·gas /ˈvegəs; ˈveɪgəs/ an informal name for Las Vegas 韦加斯〔拉斯韦加斯的俗称〕

ve·ge·bur·ger /ˈvɛdʒɪˌbɝgɚ; ˈvedʒiˌbɜːgə/ *n* [C] *BrE* a BURGER made with vegetables, beans etc, but no meat【英】素汉堡（包）

Ve·ge·mite /ˈvɛdʒɪmaɪt; ˈvedʒɪmaɪt/ *trademark* a type of soft, dark-brown salty food that can be spread, usually eaten on bread. Vegemite is similar to Marmite and is especially popular in Australia.【商标】维吉麦特〔一种深褐色涂酱。质感黏滑，味道略咸，涂在面包上吃，与玛迈特涂酱很相似，在澳大利亚尤其受欢迎〕

vege·ta·ble /ˈvɛdʒətəbl̩; ˈvedʒtəbəl/ *n* **1** [C,U] a plant such as a CABBAGE, CARROT, or potato which is eaten raw or cooked and is usually not sweet 蔬菜: *vegetable oil* 植物油 | **green vegetables** *citrus fruits and fresh green vegetables* 柑橘类水果与新鲜的绿色蔬菜 —see picture on page A9 参见A9页图 **2** [C] *informal* someone who cannot think or move because their brain has been damaged in an accident【非正式】植物人

vegetable mar·row /ˌ··· ˈ··/ *n* [C] a MARROW (2) 西葫芦〔葫芦科蔬菜〕

veg·e·tar·i·an /ˌvɛdʒəˈtɛrɪən; ˌvedʒɪ̣ˈteəriən◂/ *n* [C] someone who eats only vegetables, bread, fruit, eggs etc and does not eat meat or fish 素食主义者 —compare 比较 VEGAN —**vegetarian** *adj*: *a vegetarian restaurant* 素餐馆

veg·e·tar·i·an·is·m /ˌvɛdʒəˈtɛrɪənɪzəm; ˌvedʒɪ̣ˈteəriənɪzəm/ *n* [U] the practice of not eating meat or fish 素食主义

veg·e·tate /ˈvɛdʒəˌtet; ˈvedʒɪ̣teɪt/ *v* [I] not to do anything and feel bored because there is nothing interesting for you to do 无所事事地生活，过枯燥呆板的生活: *I got fed up with vegetating at home.* 在家里过懒散单调的生活，我腻烦极了。

veg·e·ta·tion /ˌvɛdʒəˈteʃən; ˌvedʒɪ̣ˈteɪʃən/ *n* [U] plants in general, especially in one particular area〔尤指某一地区的〕植被，植物，草木〔总称〕: *There was little vegetation on the island.* 岛上几乎没有什么植物。

veg·gie /ˈvɛdʒɪ; ˈvedʒi/ *n* [C] *informal*【非正式】**1** *BrE* a VEGETARIAN【英】素食主义者 **2** *AmE* a VEGETABLE (1)【美】蔬菜

vehe·ment /ˈviəmənt; ˈviːəmənt/ *adj* showing very strong feelings or opinions 感情强烈的；意见激烈的: *a vehement attack on the President's budget proposals* 对总统预算提案的激烈反对 —**vehemently** *adv*: *Dan vehemently denies the charges.* 丹断然否认指控。—**vehemence** *n* [U]

ve·hi·cle /ˈviɪkl; ˈviːɪkəl/ *n* [C] **1** *especially formal* a thing such as a car, bus etc that is used for carrying people or things from one place to another【尤正式】运载工具；车辆: *"Is this your vehicle, sir?" asked the policeman.* "这是你的车吗，先生？"警察问道。| *a heavy goods vehicle* 重型货车 **2 vehicle for (doing) sth** something that you use in order to achieve something or as a way of spreading your ideas, expressing your opinions etc 媒介（物）；用作…的工具: *The government used the press as a vehicle for its propaganda.* 政府把新闻媒体用作宣传的工具。

ve·hic·u·lar /viˈhɪkjələ; viːˈhɪkjɪ̣lə/ *adj formal* connected with road vehicles【正式】车辆的: *vehicular traffic* 车辆交通

veil¹ /vel; veɪl/ *n* [C] **1** a thin piece of material worn by women to cover their faces at formal occasions such as weddings, or for religious reasons 面纱 **2 the veil** the system in Islamic countries in which women must keep their faces covered in public places〔伊斯兰教国家的妇女在公共场所〕戴面纱的习俗 **3 draw a veil over** deliberately not to talk about something that happened in the past because it is unpleasant or embarrassing 把…掩盖起来；避而不谈〔不愉快或难堪的事〕: *I think it's better if we draw a veil over the whole sorry affair.* 我认为最好避而不谈这件不愉快的事。**4 veil of secrecy/deceit/silence etc** something that stops you knowing the full truth about a situation 蒙着神秘/虚假/静默等的色彩: *A veil of mystery surrounds Kelly's death.* 凯利的死笼罩着一层神秘的色彩。**5 veil of mist/cloud etc** a thin layer of mist, cloud etc that covers something so that you cannot see

veil 面纱

it clearly 一层薄雾/云等 **6 take the veil** *old-fashioned* to become a NUN【过时】当修女

veil² *v* [T] **1 be veiled in mystery/secrecy** if something is veiled in mystery etc, very little is known about it and it seems mysterious 隐在神秘/秘密之中 **2** to cover something with a veil 以面纱掩盖

veiled /veld; veɪld/ *adj* **veiled criticism/threats/hints etc** criticisms, threats etc that are hidden because you do not say directly what you think or mean 含蓄的批评/威胁/暗示等: **thinly veiled** (=only slightly hidden) 几乎不加遮掩的 *thinly veiled threats of retaliation* 几乎不加掩饰的报复恫吓

vein /ven; veɪn/ *n* **1** [C] one of the tubes through which blood flows to your heart from other parts of your body 静脉 —compare 比较 ARTERY (1) **2** [C] **a)** one of the thin lines on a leaf or on the wing of an insect〔植物的〕叶脉;〔昆虫的〕翅脉 **b)** one of the thin lines on a piece of wood, cheese, MARBLE (1) etc〔木头、干酪、大理石等的〕纹理, 纹路 **3** [C] a thin layer of a valuable metal or mineral which is contained in rock 矿脉; 岩脉; 矿层: *a rich vein of silver*〔蕴藏量〕丰富的银矿脉 **4** [singular] a particular style or way, especially when speaking or writing about something〔尤指说话、写作的〕风格; 方式: **in the same vein/in a similar vein** *His second novel is in very much the same vein as the first.* 他的第二部小说跟第一部风格几乎一模一样。| **in a serious/light-hearted vein** *The rest of the speech was in a more light-hearted vein.* 演讲的余下部分语调轻松多了。**5 a vein of humour/malice etc** a small amount of a particular quality 一丝幽默/恶意等: **a rich vein** *There's a rich vein of humour running through her stories.* 她的故事透出浓浓的幽默感。

veined /vend; veɪnd/ *adj* having a pattern of thin lines on its surface that looks like veins 有纹理的: *black-veined marble* 有黑色纹理的大理石

ve·lar /ˋvilɚ; ˈviːlə/ *adj* a velar CONSONANT such as /k/ or /g/ is pronounced with the back of your tongue close to the soft part at the top of your mouth 软腭音的〈例如 /k/ 或 /g/〉—**velar** *n* [C]

Ve·las·quez /vəˋlɑskes; vɪ̌ˈlæskwɪz/, **Di·e·go Ro·drig·uez de Sil·va y** /dɪˋego rɑˋdrigɛz də ˋsɪlvə i; diˈeɪgəʊ rɒˈdriːgez də ˈsɪlvə iː/ (1599-1660) a Spanish painter famous for his PORTRAITS of the Spanish royal family 委拉斯开兹〔(1599-1660), 西班牙画家, 以绘制的西班牙王室肖像闻名〕

Vel·cro /ˋvɛlkro; ˈvelkrəʊ/ *n* [U] *trademark* a material used for fastening clothes, which sticks together when you press a piece with a rough surface against a piece with a soft surface【商标】维克罗搭扣, 尼龙黏带 —see picture at 参见 FASTENER 图

veldt, veld /vɛlt; velt/ *n* **the veldt** the high flat area of land in South Africa that is covered in grass and has few trees〔南非高原上的〕草原

vel·lum /ˋvɛləm; ˈveləm/ *n* [U] a material used for making book covers, and in the past for writing on, made from the skins of young cows, sheep, or goats〔用小牛皮或小羊皮制的〕精制皮纸, 犊[羊]皮纸〔用作书皮或在过去用于书写〕

ve·lo·ci·pede /vəˋlɑsəˌpid; vɪ̌ˈlɒsɪ̌piːd/ *n* [C] a kind of bicycle, used in former times〔旧时用的〕自行车, 脚踏车

ve·lo·ci·ty /vəˋlɑsətɪ; vɪ̌ˈlɒsɪ̌ti/ *n* **1** [C,U] *technical* the speed at which something moves in a particular direction【术语】〔沿一定方向的〕速度: *the velocity of light* 光速 | *a high velocity bullet* 高速子弹 **2** [U] *formal* a high speed【正式】高速

vel·o·drome /ˋvɛləˌdrom; ˈveləʊdrəʊm/ *n* [C] a circular track for bicycle racing〔圆形赛道的〕自行车赛车场

ve·lour, velours /vəˋlʊr; vəˈlʊə/ *n* [U] heavy cloth which has a soft surface like velvet 棉绒; 丝绒

Vel·vee·ta /vɛlˋvitə; velˈviːtə/ *trademark* a type of soft processed orange cheese which is sold in a box. Velveeta melts easily, and people in the US use it especially for GRILL*ed* cheese SANDWICH*es* and on HAMBURGER*s*.【商标】韦尔维塔干酪〔一种橙黄色软质干酪, 盒装出售。这种干酪易融化, 美国人多用它做烤乳酪三明治, 或涂抹在汉堡上〕

vel·vet /ˋvɛlvɪt; ˈvelvɪ̌t/ *n* [U] cloth with a soft surface on one side which is used for making clothes, curtains etc 天鹅绒, 丝绒 —see picture on page A16 参见 A16 页图

vel·ve·teen /ˌvɛlvəˋtin; ˌvelvɪ̌ˈtiːn◂/ *n* [U] cheap material which looks like velvet 平绒, 棉天鹅绒

vel·vet·y /ˋvɛlvɪtɪ; ˈvelvɪ̌ti/ *adj* looking, feeling, tasting or sounding smooth and soft 柔软光滑的; 圆润轻柔的: *His voice had a wonderful velvety sound.* 他的嗓音轻柔圆润, 美妙极了。

ve·nal /ˋvinḷ; ˈviːnl/ *adj formal* using power in a dishonest or unfair way and accepting money as a reward for doing this【正式】〔利用职权〕贪污[受贿]的; 腐败的 —compare 比较 VENIAL —**venally** *adv* —**venality** /viˋnælətɪ; viːˈnælɪ̌ti/ *n* [U]

vend /vɛnd; vend/ *v* [T] *formal or law* to sell something【正式或法律】出售

ven·det·ta /vɛnˋdɛtə; venˈdetə/ *n* [C] **1** a quarrel which continues for a long time in which one group or person tries to harm another because they feel angry about something that happened in the past 世仇, 宿怨: *The two sides have been engaged in a bitter private vendetta against each other.* 双方积怨甚深, 彼此怀有深仇大恨。**2** a quarrel that has continued for a long time between two families who try to kill each other because of murders in the past; a FEUD 家族间的血仇, 族际仇杀

vending ma·chine /ˈ· · ˌ·/ *n* [C] a machine that you can get cigarettes, chocolate, drinks etc from by putting in a coin〔投币式〕自动售货机

vend·or /ˋvɛndɚ; ˈvendə/ *n* [C] **1** someone who sells things 小贩: **news-vendor/ice-cream vendor etc** (=someone who sells ice-creams, newspapers etc in the street) 报贩/售冰淇淋的小贩等 | **street vendor** *I could hear the shouts of the street vendors.* 我能听见街头小贩的叫卖声。**2** *law* someone who is selling something such as a house or an area of land【法律】〔房地产的〕卖主, 卖方

ve·neer¹ /vəˋnɪr; vɪ̌ˈnɪə/ *n* **1** [C,U] a thin layer of good quality wood that covers the outside of a piece of furniture which is made of a cheaper material 饰面薄板, 镶板〔镶嵌于用廉价材料制成的家具表面的优质薄木板〕: *walnut veneer* 胡桃木镶板 **2 a veneer of** *formal* behaviour that hides someone's real character or feelings【正式】〔掩饰真实性格或感情的〕举止; 虚饰: *a veneer of self-confidence* 貌似自信

veneer² *v* [T+with/in] to cover something with a veneer 贴镶板于〔某物的表面〕, 镶饰

ven·e·ra·ble /ˋvɛnərəbḷ; ˈvenərəbəl/ *adj* **1** *formal or humorous* a venerable person or thing is very old and respected because of their age, experience, historical importance etc【正式或幽默】〔由于年龄、经验〕令人尊敬的; 年高德劭的;〔因历史意义等〕神圣庄严的, 珍贵的: *venerable financial institutions such as the Bank of England* 像英格兰银行那样历史悠久的金融机构 **2 the Venerable... a)** the title given to a priest with the rank of ARCHDEACON in the Church of England 最尊敬的…〔英国国教中对副主教的尊称〕 **b)** the title given by the Roman Catholic Church to a dead person who is very holy but not yet a SAINT (1) 最圣洁的…〔天主教对非常圣洁但还不是圣徒的已故者的称号〕

ven·e·rate /ˋvɛnəˌret; ˈvenəreɪt/ *v* [T] *formal* to treat someone or something with great respect, especially because they are old or connected with the past【正式】尊敬, 崇拜, 敬重: *The Chinese venerate their ancestors.* 中国人尊敬自己的祖先。—**veneration** /ˌvɛnəˋreʃən; ˌvenəˈreɪʃən/ *n* [U]

ve·ne·re·al dis·ease /vəˋnɪrɪəl dɪˌziz; vɪ̌ˈnɪəriəl dɪˌziːz/ *n* [C,U] VD 性病, 花柳病

Ve·ne·tian blind /vəˌniʃən ˋblaɪnd; vəˌniːʃən ˈblaɪnd/ *n* [C] a set of long flat bars of plastic or metal which can be raised or lowered to cover a window 百叶窗帘 —see picture at 参见 BLIND³ 图

Ven·e·zue·la /ˌvɛnəˋzwilə; ˌvenɪ̌ˈzweɪlə/ a country in the north of South America between Colombia and Brazil. Population: 23,917,000 (2001). Capital: Caracas. It is an important producer of oil and COFFEE. 委内瑞拉〔南美洲北部一国家, 位于哥伦比亚和巴西之间。人口: 23,917,000 (2001), 首都: 加拉加斯。该国是重要的石油和咖啡生产国〕—**Venezuelan** *n, adj*

ven·geance /ˋvɛndʒəns; ˈvendʒəns/ *n* **1** [U] something violent or harmful that you do to someone in order to punish them for harming you, your family etc 报仇, 报复, 复仇: *Hamlet is driven by a desire for vengeance after his father is killed.* 父亲被杀之后, 哈姆雷特被复仇的欲望所驱使。**2 with a vengeance** if something is done with a vengeance, it is done much more than is expected or normal 过度地; 猛烈地: *The music started up again with a vengeance.* 音乐再度响起, 更加激昂。

venge·ful /ˋvɛndʒfəl; ˈvendʒfəl/ *adj literary* very eager to punish someone who has harmed you【文】有复仇心理的; 图谋报复的, 复仇的: *a vengeful God* 复仇之神 —**vengefully** *adv*

ve·ni·al /ˋvinɪəl; ˈviːniəl/ *adj formal* a venial fault, mistake etc is not very serious and can therefore be forgiven【正式】〔错误等〕轻微的; 可原谅的: *a venial sin* 可饶恕的罪孽 —compare 比较 VENAL

Ven·ice /ˋvɛnɪs; ˈvenɪ̌s/ a city in northeast Italy that is built on a system of CANAL*s* (=artificial rivers) and famous for its many beautiful buildings and works of art. In former times, Venice was a powerful independent state and an important trading nation. It is now a popular place for tourists to visit. 威尼斯〔意大利东北部一城市, 建在一运河系统之上, 以众多精美的建筑和艺术品著称。历史上曾经是强大的独立国家和重要的贸易国。今为旅游胜地〕—**Venetian** *n, adj*

ven·i·son /ˈvɛnəzn; ˈvenɪ̣zən/ *n* [U] the meat of a DEER 鹿肉

Venn di·a·gram /ˈvɛn ˌdaɪəgræm; ˈven ˌdaɪəgræm/ *n* [C] a picture that shows the relationship between a number of things by using circles that OVERLAP each other〔用圆表示集与集之间关系的〕维恩图

ven·om /ˈvɛnəm; ˈvenəm/ *n* [U] **1** a liquid poison that some snakes, insects etc produce and that they use when biting or stinging another animal or insect〔蛇、昆虫等的〕毒液 **2** extreme anger or hatred 痛恨, 怨恨, 憎恨: *There was real venom in her voice.* 她的声音中有着切齿怨恨。

ven·om·ous /ˈvɛnəməs; ˈvenəməs/ *adj* **1** full of extreme hatred or anger 充满怨恨的: *a venomous look* 充满怨恨的表情 **2** a venomous snake, insect etc produces poison to attack its enemies〔蛇、昆虫等〕有毒的, 分泌毒液的 —**venomously** *adv*

ve·nous /ˈvinəs; ˈviːnəs/ *adj* related to the VEINS (=tubes that carry the blood) in your body 静脉的

vent[1] /vɛnt; vent/ *n* [C] **1** a hole or pipe through which gases, smoke, liquid etc can enter or escape from an enclosed space or a container〔供气体或液体流通的〕孔口; 通风孔; 排气道: *an air vent* 通风孔 **2 give vent to** *formal* to do something to express a strong feeling, especially of anger【正式】抒发〔强烈感情〕, 发泄〔尤指怒火〕: *Joshua gave vent to his anger by kicking the chair.* 乔舒亚踢椅子以发泄怒气。**3** *technical* the small hole through which small animals, birds, fish, and snakes get rid of waste matter from their bodies【术语】〔小动物、鸟、鱼、蛇的〕肛门 **4** *technical* a narrow straight opening at the bottom of a jacket or coat, at the sides or back【术语】衣服底部的开衩

vent[2] *v* [T] to do something to express your feelings, especially anger, often in a way that is unfair〔指常用不公正的方式〕发泄〔感情, 尤指怒火〕: **vent sth on sb** *Paul had a bad day at work and vented his anger on his family.* 保罗整天工作不顺心, 就把怒气发泄到家人身上。

ven·ti·late /ˈvɛntḷˌet; ˈventɪ̣leɪt/ *v* [T] **1** to let fresh air into a room, building etc 使通风: **well-ventilated/poorly ventilated etc** *a well-ventilated kitchen* 通风良好的厨房 **2** *formal* to express your opinions or feelings about something【正式】发表〔意见或看法〕; 表达〔感情〕: *Doctrinal issues were never ventilated.* 教义的问题从未讨论过。—**ventilation** /ˌvɛntḷˈeʃən; ˌventɪ̣ˈleɪʃən/ *n* [U]: *Workers complained about the factory's lack of ventilation.* 工人抱怨工厂缺乏通风设施。| *a ventilation system* 通风系统

ven·ti·la·tor /ˈvɛntḷˌetɚ; ˈventɪ̣leɪtə/ *n* [C] **1** a thing designed to let fresh air into a room, building etc 通风装置; 排气风扇, 送风机 **2** a piece of equipment that pumps air into and out of someone's lungs when they cannot breathe without help 人工呼吸机

ven·tri·cle /ˈvɛntrɪkl; ˈventrɪkəl/ *n* [C] *technical*【术语】**1** one of the two spaces in the bottom of your heart that pump blood out into your body 心室 —compare 比较 ATRIUM (1) **2** a small hollow place in your body or in your brain〔人体内的〕腔室; 脑室

ven·tril·o·quis·m /vɛnˈtrɪləˌkwɪzəm; venˈtrɪləkwɪzəm/ *n* [U] the art of speaking without moving your lips, so that the sound seems to come from someone else 口技, 腹语术 —**ventriloquist** *n* [C]

ven·ture[1] /ˈvɛntʃɚ; ˈventʃə/ *n* [C] a new business activity that involves taking risks 风险项目, 风险投资; 冒险事业: *a commercial venture* 商业冒险 | **joint venture** (=an agreement between two companies to do something together) 合资企业

venture[2] *v formal*【正式】**1** [I always+adv/prep] to risk going somewhere when it could be dangerous 冒风险〔去某处〕, 冒险: **[+out/through/into etc]** *Today's the first time I've ventured out of doors since my illness.* 自生病以来, 今天是我第一次冒险走到室外。**2** [T] to say something although you are afraid of how someone may react to it 敢于说, 大胆表示: **venture to do sth** *Nobody ventured to say a word.* 没人敢说一句话。| **venture an opinion** (=say what you think) 大胆提出意见 *If I may venture an opinion, I'd say the plan needs more thought.* 我斗胆提一点意见, 我认为对这个计划需多加思量。**3** [T] to take the risk of losing something; GAMBLE[1] (1) 冒失去…的风险; 以…作为赌注: **venture sth on sth** *Jeff ventured his whole fortune on one throw of the dice.* 杰夫把全部财产都押在这次的掷色子上。**4 nothing ventured, nothing gained** used to say that you cannot achieve anything unless you take a risk 不入虎穴, 焉得虎子

venture on/upon sth *phr v* [T] to try to do something that involves risks 冒险做〔有风险或危险的事〕: *Now is not the time to venture on such an ambitious project.* 现在不是承担这种野心勃勃的项目的时候。

venture cap·i·tal /ˈ‥ ˌ‥ˈ/ *n* [U] money that is lent to someone so that they can start a new business 风险资本

Venture Scout /ˈ‥ ˌ‥/ a member of the Venture Scouts, part of the British Scout Association for boys and girls who are 16 to 20 years old 冒险童子军〔英国16至20岁的大龄童子军队员, 隶属于英国童子军总会〕

ven·ture·some /ˈvɛntʃɚsəm; ˈventʃəsəm/ *adj especially literary*【尤文】**1** a venturesome person is always ready to take risks〔人〕好冒险的; 大胆的 **2** a venturesome action involves taking risks〔行动〕有风险的 —**venturesomeness** *n* [U]

ven·ue /ˈvɛnju; ˈvenjuː/ *n* [C] a place where something such as a concert or a meeting is arranged to take place 举办地点, 举行场所, 会场: *the venue for the latest round of talks* 举行最新一轮谈判的地点

Ve·nus /ˈvinəs; ˈviːnəs/ *n* [singular] the PLANET second in order from the sun and nearest to the Earth 金星 —see picture at 参见 SOLAR SYSTEM 图

Venus de Mi·lo, the /ˌvinəs də ˈmilo; ˌviːnəs də ˈmiːləʊ/ a Greek STATUE of the GODDESS Venus that can be seen in the Louvre in Paris. It is badly damaged and is famous for having no arms. 米洛的维纳斯〔一尊维纳斯女神的古希腊塑像。现藏于巴黎卢浮宫, 塑像受损严重, 以断臂而闻名〕

Venus fly·trap /ˌvinəs ˈflaɪtræp; ˌviːnəs ˈflaɪtræp/ *n* [C] a plant that catches and eats insects 捕蝇草

ve·ra·ci·ty /vəˈræsətɪ; vəˈræsɪ̣ti/ *n* [U] *formal* the quality of being true or of telling the truth【正式】诚实; 真实; 讲实话 —**veracious** *adj*

ve·ran·da, verandah /vəˈrændə; vəˈrændə/ *n* [C] an open area with a floor and a roof that is built on the side of a house on the ground floor〔房屋侧面有屋顶和地板的〕走廊, 游廊: *Hannah sat sewing in the shade on the veranda.* 汉娜坐在游廊的阴凉处做针线活。

verb /vɝb; vɜːb/ *n* [C] a word or group of words that is used to describe an action, experience, or state, for example 'come', 'see', 'be', 'put on' 动词: *to conjugate a verb* 列举动词的词形变化 —see also 另见 AUXILIARY VERB, PHRASAL VERB

verb·al /ˈvɝbḷ; ˈvɜːbəl/ *adj* **1** spoken, not written 口头的, 非书面的: *a verbal agreement* 口头协议 —opposite 反义词 NONVERBAL **2** connected with words or using words 与言辞有关的, 用言辞的; 文字上的: *verbal skill* 使用言辞的技能 | *verbal abuse* 恶言, 谩骂 **3** related to a verb 动词的

verb·al·ize also 又作 **-ise** *BrE*【英】/ˈvɝbḷˌaɪz; ˈvɜːbəlaɪz/ *v* [I,T] *formal* to express something in words【正式】用言语表达: *He couldn't verbalize his fears.* 他无法用言语表达他的恐惧。

verb·al·ly /ˈvɝbḷɪ; ˈvɜːbəli/ *adv* in spoken words and not in writing 口头地, 口头上

verbal noun /ˌ‥ ˈ/ *n* [C] a noun that describes an action or experience and has the form of a PRESENT PARTICIPLE. For example 'building' is a verbal noun in 'The building of the bridge was slow work', but simply a noun in 'The bank was a tall building'; GERUND 动名词〔动词的现在分词形式作名词用〕—see also 另见 NOUN

ver·ba·tim /vɚˈbetɪm; vɜːˈbeɪtɪ̣m/ *adj, adv* repeating the actual words that were spoken or written 逐字的[地], 一字不差的[地]: *a verbatim account of our conversation* 对我们谈话内容的逐字报道

ver·bi·age /ˈvɝbɪɪdʒ; ˈvɜːbi-ɪdʒ/ *n* [U] *formal* too many unnecessary words in speech or writing【正式】〔说话或写作的〕冗词, 啰唆; 赘语: *eliminate irrelevant verbiage* 删去无关的冗词

ver·bose /vɚˈbos; vɜːˈbəʊs/ *adj formal* using or containing too many words【正式】啰唆的; 累赘的; 冗长的: *a verbose sermon* 喋喋不休的说教 —compare 比较 VERBAL —**verbosely** *adv* —**verboseness** or **verbosity** /vɚˈbɑsətɪ; vɜːˈbɒsɪ̣ti/ *n* [U]

ver·bo·ten /vəˈbotn; vəˈbəʊtən/ *adj German* not allowed; forbidden【德】不允许的; 被禁止的: *Being impolite to grown-ups was absolutely verboten in our household.* 我们家绝对不允许对大人无礼。

ver·dant /ˈvɝdn̩t; ˈvɜːdənt/ *adj literary* verdant land is covered with freshly growing green grass and plants【文】〔土地〕长满青翠草木的: *verdant fields* 青翠的田野

Ver·di /ˈvɛrdɪ; ˈveədi/, **Giu·sep·pe** /dʒuˈzɛpɪ; dʒʊˈzepi/ (1813-1901) an Italian COMPOSER whose best-known works are his *Requiem* and his OPERAS, including *La Traviata*, *Aida*, and *Rigoletto* 威尔第〔(1813-1901), 意大利作曲家。代表作有《安魂曲》、歌剧《茶花女》、《阿伊达》和《弄臣》等〕

ver·dict /ˈvɝdɪkt; ˈvɜːdɪkt/ *n* [C] **1** an official decision made by a JURY in a court of law about whether someone is guilty or not guilty of a crime〔法庭上陪审团作出的〕裁决, 裁定: *a ma-*

jority verdict of 10 to 2 一项10比2的多数裁决 | **return a verdict** *formal* (=give a verdict)【正式】作出裁决 | **reach a verdict** (=make a decision) 作出裁定 *After a week the jury had still not reached a verdict.* 一周过去了，陪审团仍未作出裁决。**2** an official decision or opinion made by a person or group that has authority〔由当权者作出的〕正式决定；正式意见：*The panel will be giving their verdict tomorrow.* 专责小组明天将提出正式意见。—see also 另见 OPEN VERDICT **3** *informal* an opinion or decision about something【非正式】意见；决定：[+on] *What's your verdict on the movie?* 你觉得那部电影怎么样？

ver·di·gris /ˈvɝdɪˌgris; ˈvɜːdɪ̣griː/ *n* [U] a greenish-blue substance that forms a thin layer on COPPER (1) or BRASS (1) that is kept in wet conditions〔铜器等的〕铜绿

ver·dure /ˈvɝdʒɚ; ˈvɜːdʒə/ *n* [U] *literary* the bright green colour of grass, plants, trees etc, or the plants themselves【文】草木的青翠；青翠的草木

verge[1] /vɝdʒ; vɜːdʒ/ *n* [C] **1** *especially BrE* the edge or border of a road or path etc【尤英】〔路等的〕边缘，边界：*the grass verge* 草地的边缘 **2 be on the verge of** to be about to do something 濒于，即将：*Jessica was on the verge of tears.* 杰茜卡几乎就要哭了。| *scientists on the verge of a major breakthrough* 即将取得重大突破的科学家

verge[2] *v*

verge on/upon sth *phr v* [T] to be very close to a harmful or extreme state 接近，濒于：**verge on madness/panic/chaos etc** *Daniela's strange behaviour sometimes verges on madness.* 丹妮拉的怪异行为有时近乎疯狂。| **verging on the impossible/ridiculous** (=almost impossible etc) 近乎不可能/荒谬

ver·ger /ˈvɝdʒɚ; ˈvɜːdʒə/ *n* [C] *especially BrE* someone whose job is to look after the contents of a church and perform small duties like showing people where to sit【尤英】教堂司事[堂守]

Ver·gil /ˈvɝdʒɪl; ˈvɜːdʒɪ̣l/ —see 见 VIRGIL

ver·i·fy /ˈvɛrəˌfaɪ; ˈverɪ̣faɪ/ *v* **verified, verifying** [T] **1** to find out if a fact, statement etc is correct or true; check 查证；核实：**verify sth with sb** *These details must be verified with the Home Office.* 这些细节必须向内政部核实。| **verify that** *The bank will have to verify that you are the owner of the property.* 银行必须核实你是该财产的所有者。**2** to state that something is true; CONFIRM 证实；确认：*The prisoner's statement was verified by several witnesses.* 犯人的供述得到几个证人的证实。—**verifiable** *adj* —**verification** /ˌvɛrɪfɪˈkeʃən; ˌverɪ̣fɪ̣ˈkeɪʃən/ *n* [C,U]: *the verification of scientific laws* 科学定律的验证

ver·i·ly /ˈvɛrəlɪ; ˈverɪ̣li/ *adv biblical* really【圣经】真实地，确实

ver·i·si·mil·i·tude /ˌvɛrəsəˈmɪləˌtud; ˌverɪ̣sɪ̣ˈmɪlɪ̣tjuːd/ *n* [U] *formal* the quality of a piece of art, a performance etc that makes it seem like something real【正式】貌似真实；逼真

ver·i·ta·ble /ˈvɛrətəbl̩; ˈverɪ̣təbəl/ *adj formal* a word used to emphasize a comparison that you think is correct【正式】名副其实的：*The male bird is a veritable rainbow of colors.* 雄鸟色彩斑斓，如彩虹一般。—**veritably** *adv*

ver·i·ty /ˈvɛrətɪ; ˈverɪ̣ti/ *n* [C usually plural 一般用复数] *formal* an important principle or fact about life, the world etc, that is true in all situations【正式】重要的真理[准则、事实]：*one of the eternal verities* 永恒的真理之一

Ver·laine /vɚˈlen; vəˈleɪn/, **Paul** (1844-96) a French poet whose works include *Romances sans Paroles* 魏尔兰〔(1844-1896)，法国诗人。代表作为《无题浪漫曲》〕

Ver·meer /vɚˈmɪɚ; vəˈmɪə/, **Jan** /jæn; jæn/ (1632-75) a Dutch painter who painted ordinary scenes from daily life, and is famous especially for his pictures of rooms, often with one woman in them 弗美尔〔(1632-1675)，荷兰画家。他常从日常生活的普通场景中发掘绘画题材，尤以室内画闻名，画中通常有一位女子〕

ver·mi·cel·li /ˌvɝməˈsɛlɪ; ˌvɜːmɪ̣ˈseli/ *n* [U] Italian PASTA (=food that is made from a mixture of flour, eggs, and water) that is shaped into very thin strings and cooked in boiling water〔意大利〕细面条 —see picture at 参见 PASTA 图

ver·mil·lion /vɚˈmɪljən; vəˈmɪljən/ *n* [U] a bright reddish-orange colour 朱红色，鲜红色 —**vermillion** *adj*

ver·min /ˈvɝmɪn; ˈvɜːmɪ̣n/ *n* [plural] **1** small animals or birds that destroy crops, spoil food etc, and are difficult to control 害兽；害鸟；害虫：*a barn infested with vermin* 遭害虫侵扰的谷仓 —compare 比较 PEST **2** insects that live on people's or animals' bodies, bite them, and drink their blood〔寄生在人或动物身上并吸血的〕寄生虫：*a bed alive with vermin* 满是寄生虫的床铺 **3** unpleasant people who cause problems for society 危害社会的人，害人虫，败类：*He thinks all beggars are vermin.* 他认为所有的乞丐都是寄生虫。

ver·min·ous /ˈvɝmɪnəs; ˈvɜːmɪ̣nəs/ *adj* **1** full of insects that bite you 长满寄生虫的：*the tramp's verminous old coat* 流浪乞丐满是虱子的旧外套 **2** very unpleasant or nasty 污秽的，讨厌的：*verminous blackmail letters* 言语污秽的敲诈信

Ver·mont /vɚˈmɑnt; vəˈmɒnt/ abbreviation 缩写为 VT a state in the northeastern US, which is part of New England. Vermont produces many minerals, and also MAPLE SYRUP, and attracts many visitors for SKIING, hunting, and fishing. 佛蒙特州〔美国东北部一州，为新英格兰地区一部分。该州矿产资源丰富，盛产槭糖浆，吸引众多游客前去滑雪、打猎、垂钓〕

ver·mouth /ˈvɝməθ; ˈvɜːməθ/ *n* [U] a drink made from wine that has strong-tasting substances added to it, usually drunk before a meal 味美思酒，苦艾酒

ver·nac·u·lar /vɚˈnækjəlɚ; vəˈnækjɪ̣lə/ *n* [C usually singular 一般用单数] the language spoken in a country or area, especially when it is not the official language〔尤指非官方语言的〕本国语；本地语，土话，方言 —**vernacular** *adj*

ver·nal /ˈvɝnl̩; ˈvɜːnl/ *adj* [only before noun 仅用于名词前] *literary or technical* connected with the spring season【文或术语】春季的，与春天有关的

Verne /vɝn; vɜːn/, **Jules** /dʒulz; dʒuːlz/ (1828-1905) a French writer who wrote science FICTION. His most famous books are *Journey to the Centre of the Earth*, *Twenty Thousand Leagues Under the Sea*, and *Around the World in Eighty Days* 凡尔纳〔(1828-1905)，法国科幻小说家。代表作有《地心游记》、《海底两万里》、《八十天环游地球》等〕

ver·ru·ca /vəˈrukə; vəˈruːkə/ *n* [C] a small hard infectious thing that can be painful and grows on the skin on the bottom of your foot〔脚底生的〕疣，肉赘；WART *AmE*【美】

versa —see 见 VICE VERSA

Ver·sailles /vɛrˈsaɪ; veəˈsaɪ/ a beautiful palace with gardens outside the city of Versailles near Paris, France. It was built for King Louis XIV and is now owned by the French state. Several peace agreements were signed there, including the one which formally ended World War I. 凡尔赛宫〔法国巴黎附近凡尔赛镇郊外的一处带有花园的精美宫殿。该宫殿为法王路易十四所建，现为法国政府所有。历史上若干重大和平协定均在此签署，其中包括一战的停战协定〕

ver·sa·tile /ˈvɝsətɪl; ˈvɜːsətaɪl/ *adj approving*【褒】**1** good at doing a lot of different things and able to learn new skills quickly and easily 多才多艺的：*a very versatile performer* 多才多艺的表演者 **2** having many different uses 有多种用途的，多功能的，万用的：*Nylon is a versatile material.* 尼龙是一种有多种用途的材料。—**versatility** /ˌvɝsəˈtɪlətɪ; ˌvɜːsəˈtɪlɪ̣ti/ *n* [U]

verse /vɝs; vɜːs/ *n* **1** [C] a set of lines that forms one part of a song 一节歌词：*Let's sing the last verse again.* 我们把最后一节再唱一遍吧。—compare 比较 CHORUS[1] (1) **2** [C] a set of lines of poetry that forms one part of a poem, and that usually has a pattern that is repeated in the other parts 诗节：*Learn the first two verses of the poem.* 把这首诗的头两节记住。**3** [U] words arranged in the form of poetry 诗；诗体；韵文：*a book of comic verse* 一本滑稽诗集 —compare 比较 PROSE —see also 另见 BLANK VERSE, FREE VERSE **4** [C] one of the numbered groups of sentences that make up each CHAPTER (=numbered part) of a book of the Bible〔《圣经》中标有数码的〕节 —see also 另见 **give/quote chapter and verse** (CHAPTER (5))

versed /vɝst; vɜːst/ *adj* **be (well) versed in** to know a lot about a subject or to be skilled in doing something 精通…，通晓…，对…造诣很深：*a woman well versed in the art of diplomacy* 熟谙外交艺术的女人

ver·si·fi·ca·tion /ˌvɝsəfəˈkeʃən; ˌvɜːsɪ̣fɪ̣ˈkeɪʃən/ *n* [U] *technical* the particular pattern that a poem is written in【术语】诗体；诗律

ver·sion /ˈvɝʒən; ˈvɜːʃən/ *n* [C] **1** a copy of something that has been changed slightly so that it is different from the thing being copied〔同一种物件稍有不同的〕样式，型号；复制件，变体：[+of] *The dress is a cheaper version of one seen at the Paris fashion shows.* 这套服装是巴黎时装展上看到的那一款的廉价复制品。| **old/first/later etc version of** *This is a sophisticated version of the old tripod camera.* 这是老式三角架相机中的精致款式。**2** a description of an event given by one person, especially when it is compared with someone else's description of the same thing〔某人对某一事件作出的〕描述；说法，讲法：[+of] *The two newspapers gave different versions of what happened.* 两家报纸对发生的事说法不一。**3** a play, film, piece of music etc that is slightly different from the book, piece of music etc on which it is based〔依据书、音乐等稍作改编的戏剧、电影、音乐等的〕版本；改编本：[+of] *an abridged version of the play* 该剧的节略本 **4 an English/Japanese/Spanish version** an En-

glish etc translation of a book, poem, or other piece of writing 英文/日文/西班牙文译本: [+of] *an English version of a German play* 德语剧本的英译本

ver·so /ˈvɝso; ˈvɜːsəʊ/ *n* [C] *technical* a page on the left-hand side of a book【术语】〔书的〕左页 —compare 比较 RECTO —**verso** *adj*

ver·sus /ˈvɝsəs; ˈvɜːsəs/ written abbreviation 缩写为 **v** *or* **vs** *prep* **1** used to show that two people or teams are against each other in a game or court case〔比赛或诉讼中〕…对…: *the New York Knicks versus the Los Angeles Lakers* 纽约尼克斯队对洛杉矶湖人队 | *the Supreme Court decision in Roe versus Wade* 最高法院关于罗对韦德诉讼案的裁决 **2** used when comparing the advantages of two different things, ideas etc 与…相对; 与…相比: *The Finance Minister must weigh up the benefits of a tax cut versus those of increased public spending.* 财政部长必须权衡是减税还是增加公共开支更有利。

ver·te·bra /ˈvɝtəbrə; ˈvɜːtɪ̥brə/ *n plural* **vertebrae** /-brɪ; -bri/ [C] one of the small hollow bones down the centre of your back 脊椎, 椎骨 —**vertebral** *adj*

ver·te·brate /ˈvɝtəˌbret; ˈvɜːtɪ̥brɪ̥t/ *n* [C] a living creature that has a BACKBONE (1) 脊椎动物 —compare 比较 INVERTEBRATE —**vertebrate** *adj*

ver·tex /ˈvɝtɛks; ˈvɜːteks/ *n plural* **vertices** /-təˌsiz; -tɪ̥siːz/ *or* **vertexes** [C+of] *technical*【术语】**1** the angle opposite the base of a shape such as a PYRAMID, CONE, TRIANGLE etc〔圆锥体、三角形等的〕顶角 **2** the point where the two lines of an angle meet〔一个角两线相交的〕顶点 **3** the highest point 最高点: *the vertex of an arch* 拱门的顶

ver·ti·cal¹ /ˈvɝtɪkl̩; ˈvɜːtɪkəl/ *adj* **1** pointing straight up and down in a line and forming an angle of 90 degrees with the ground or with another straight line 垂直的; 直立的: *a vertical line* 垂直线 | *blue and green vertical stripes* 蓝绿相间的竖条 | *a sheer, vertical cliff* 陡直的峭壁 **2** having a structure in which there are top, middle, and bottom levels 立体式的, 各种层次的, 从上到下的: *a vertical power relationship between top decision makers and the rest of the organization* 从高层决策者到机构其余人员的立体式权力关系 —compare 比较 HORIZONTAL —**vertically** /-kl̩ɪ; -kli/ *adv*

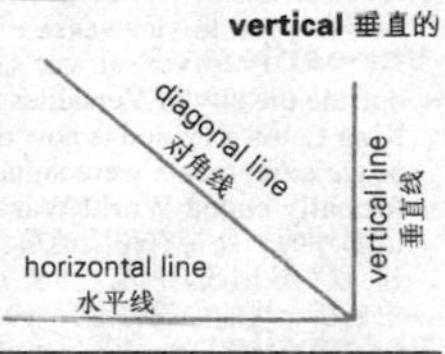

vertical² *n* **the vertical** the direction of something that is vertical 垂直方向; 垂直物, 垂直线: *an angle of about 30 degrees off the vertical* 与垂直线大约成30°角

ver·tig·i·nous /vɝˋtɪdʒənəs; vɜːˈtɪdʒɪ̥nəs/ *adj formal* a vertiginous place or position makes you feel ill because it is so high【正式】高得令人眩晕的; 感到眩晕的: *a vertiginous drop to the valley below* 直达谷底令人眩晕的垂直落差

ver·ti·go /ˈvɝtɪˌgo; ˈvɜːtɪgəʊ/ *n* [U] a sick DIZZY (1) feeling caused by looking down from a very high place〔因从高处俯视而产生的〕眩晕, 头晕

verve /vɝv; vɜːv/ *n* [U] the quality of being cheerful and exciting which is shown in the way someone does something 活力; 热情: *Cziffra played the Hungarian dances with great verve.* 奇夫拉热情洋溢地演奏匈牙利舞曲。

S1 W1 **ve·ry¹** /ˈvɛrɪ; ˈveri/ *adv* **1** [+adj/adv] used to emphasize an adjective or adverb or to add force to an expression 很, 非常〔用于强调所修饰的形容词或副词, 或加强语气〕: *"Can I help you with those bags?" "Thanks, that's very nice of you."* "我能帮你提那些包吗?" "谢谢, 你真是太好了。" | *It feels very cold up in the bedrooms.* 卧室里冷极了。| *I feel a lot better today thanks very much.* 我今天好多了, 非常感谢。| *We must be aware of the very real problems that these people face.* 我们必须清楚这些人所面临的非常现实的问题。| *The traffic's moving very slowly this morning.* 今天早上路上来往的车辆开得很慢。| *James was very much hoping you'd be able to come to the wedding.* 詹姆斯非常希望你能来参加婚礼。| **the very same** (=used to emphasize the fact that one thing is exactly the same as something else) 完全相同的, 一模一样的 *She was wearing the very same shoes as me.* 她穿的鞋跟我的一模一样。**2** [+adj] used to emphasize superlative adjectives〔用于形容词最高级前以加强语气〕: *We only use the very best ingredients.* 我们只用最好的配料。| *He might have told you he wasn't coming at the very least.* 他本来至少应该告诉你他不来了。| *This is the very last time I lend you money.* 这是我最后一次借钱给你。**3** **your very own** used to emphasize the fact that something belongs to one particular person and to no one else 完全属于某人自己的〔强调某物归某人所有〕: *She was thrilled at the idea of having her very own toys to play with.* 想到能玩完全属于自己的玩具, 她感到极为兴奋。**4** **not very a)** used before a quality to mean exactly the opposite of that quality 绝不, 根本不〔表示相反〕: *The teacher wasn't very pleased* (=was angry) *when she saw a dead mouse on the desk.* 看到桌子上有一只死老鼠时, 老师很是恼火。**b)** only slightly 不很, 不大, 稍微: *"Was the play interesting?" "Not very."* "这出戏好看吗?" "不怎么好看。"

S2 W1 **very²** *adj* [only before noun 仅用于名词前] used to emphasize a noun 正是那一个的, 正是的〔用以加强名词的语气〕: *He died in this very room.* 他就是在这个房间里去世的。| **this very minute** (=now) 就现在 *You'd better start doing some work this very minute.* 你最好现在就开始干点活。| **the very thought** (=just thinking about something) 一想到… *The very thought of food makes me feel ill.* 一想到食物, 我就觉得不舒服。| **the very idea!** (=used to express shock at what someone says or suggests) 亏你想得出来!〔对某人所说的表示震惊〕*Of course you shouldn't travel on your own at that time of night. The very idea!* 你当然不该在夜里那个时候独自外出。亏你想得出来! | **the very thing** (=used to describe an object or idea that is exactly right for a particular purpose) 正是它〔表示某物或意见正是所需要的〕*This gadget is the very thing for turning stiff taps.* 这个小玩意正好用来拧过紧的龙头。

very high fre·quen·cy /ˌ‥ ˈ‥ˈ‥/ *n* [U] VHF 甚高频

Very light /ˈvɛrɪ ˌlaɪt; ˈvɪəri laɪt/ *n* [C] *trademark* a bright light produced by a kind of burning bullet that is fired into the air as a signal that a ship needs help【商标】维利式(彩色)信号弹, 闪光信号弹〔船只求助时所发的信号弹〕

Very pis·tol /ˈ‥ ˌ‥/ *n* [C] the gun from which a Very light is shot 维利式(彩色)信号枪

ves·pers /ˈvɛspɚz; ˈvespəz/ *n* [U] the evening service in some types of Christian church 晚祷

Ves·puc·ci, **A·mer·i·go** /vɛˋsputʃɪ; veˈspuːtʃi/, /æˋmɛrigo; æˈmeriːgəʊ/ (1454-1512) an Italian sailor and EXPLORER who sailed to the Caribbean Sea and South America and discovered the place where the Amazon River flows into the sea. The name 'America' comes from his name. 韦斯普奇〔(1454-1512), 意大利航海家、探险家。他曾航行至加勒比海和南美洲, 发现了亚马孙河的入海口。America(亚美利加)一词即源于他的名字〕

ves·sel /ˈvɛsl̩; ˈvesəl/ *n* [C] **1** *formal* a ship or large boat【正式】船; 舰: *a fishing vessel* 渔船 **2** *old use or formal* a container for holding liquids【旧或正式】〔盛液体用的〕容器, 器皿 **3** *technical* a tube that carries blood through your body, such as a VEIN, or that carries liquid through a plant【术语】〔人体的〕血管; 脉管; 〔植物的〕导管

vest¹ /vɛst; vest/ *n* [C] **1** *BrE* a piece of underwear without SLEEVEs that you wear under a shirt【英】内衣背心, 汗衫; UNDERSHIRT *AmE*【美】—see picture at 参见 UNDERWEAR 图 **2** *AmE* a piece of clothing without arms that has buttons down the front and is usually worn under a JACKET, especially by men as part of a suit【美】马甲, 西装背心; WAISTCOAT *BrE*【英】**3** a piece of special clothing without SLEEVEs that is worn to protect your body 防护用背心: *a bullet-proof vest* 防弹背心

vest² *v*

vest in *phr v* [T] **1** [**vest** sth **in** sb] to give someone the official legal right to use power, property etc 授予, 赋予, 给予〔某人法律权力〕: **be vested in** *In most countries the right to make new laws is vested in the people's representatives.* 在大多数国家, 制订新法律的权力授予给人民的代表。**2** [**vest in** sb/sth not in passive 不用被动态] if property, power etc vests in someone, it belongs to them legally or officially〔财产、权力等〕归属于: *In former times this power vested in the Church.* 在过去, 这一权力属于教会。

vest sb **with** sth *phr v* [T] *formal* to give someone the official or legal right to use power, property etc【正式】授予〔某人〕使用〔某种权力或财产等〕的权利

ves·tal vir·gin /ˌvɛstl̩ ˋvɝdʒɪn; ˌvestl ˈvɜːdʒɪ̥n/ *n* [C] a young unmarried woman who had duties in one of the ancient Roman temples 维斯太贞女〔在古罗马庙宇中侍奉的年轻未婚女子〕

vested in·terest /ˌ‥ ˈ‥/ *n* [C] **1** if you have a vested interest in something happening, you have a strong reason for wanting it to happen because you will get an advantage from it 既得利益: *The tobacco companies have a vested interest in claiming that smoking isn't harmful.* 烟草公司声称抽烟无害, 因当中有其既得利益。**2** **vested interests** [plural] the groups of people who have a vested interest in something 既得利益集团: *The new reforms were opposed by both vested interests and welfare groups.* 新的改革既受到既得利益集团的反对, 也受到福利团体的反对。

ves·ti·bule /ˋvɛstə,bjul; ˈvestɪ̣bjuːl/ *n* [C] *formal*【正式】**1** a wide passage or small room inside the front door of a public building〔公共建筑物前门内的〕门厅，前厅 **2** *AmE* the enclosed passage at each end of a railway carriage that connects it with the next carriage【美】〔火车车厢与另一车厢之间的〕通廊，连廊

ves·tige /ˋvɛstɪdʒ; ˈvestɪdʒ/ *n* [C] *formal*【正式】**1** a small part or amount of something that still remains when most of it no longer exists 痕迹，遗迹；残余：**[+of]** *The new law removed the last vestiges of royal power.* 新法律扫除了王权的最后残余。**2** the smallest possible amount of a quality or feeling 一点儿，丝毫：**[+of]** *There's not a vestige of truth in the story.* 这个故事毫无真实性可言。

ves·ti·gi·al /vɛsˋtɪdʒɪəl; veˈstɪdʒiəl/ *adj* **1** *technical* a vestigial part of the body has never developed completely or has almost disappeared because it is no longer used【术语】〔器官等〕退化的：*Some snakes have vestigial legs.* 某些蛇有退化了的脚。**2** *formal* remaining as a sign that something existed after most of it has disappeared【正式】残余的，残留的，遗迹的：*vestigial traces of a past civilization* 昔日文明的遗迹 —**vestigially** *adv*

vest·ment /ˋvɛstmənt; ˈvestmənt/ *n* [C often plural 常用复数] a piece of clothing worn by priests during church services〔神职人员主持宗教仪式时穿的〕法衣，祭服；礼仪服

ves·try /ˋvɛstrɪ; ˈvestri/ *n* [C] a small room in a church where the priest and CHOIR change into their vestments and where holy plates, cups etc are stored〔教堂的〕法衣室，圣具室〔供放置各种圣器以及穿法衣用〕

Ve·su·vi·us /vɪˋsuvɪəs; vɪ̣ˈsuːviəs/ also 又作 **Mount Vesuvius** a VOLCANO (=a mountain with a large hole at the top) in southeast Italy. When Vesuvius ERUPT*ed* in AD 79, sending out ash and LAVA (=hot liquid rock), it buried the ancient Roman city of Pompeii. Vesuvius is still an 'active' volcano, which could erupt again at any time. 维苏威火山〔意大利东南部一火山。公元79年喷发时，大量火山灰和熔岩埋没了罗马古城庞贝。该火山仍是一座"活火山"，随时可能再次喷发〕

S3 **vet**[1] /vɛt; vet/ *n* [C] **1** someone who is trained to give medical care and treatment to sick animals 兽医；VETERINARIAN *AmE*【美】**2** *AmE informal* a VETERAN (1)【美，非正式】退伍军人：*a Vietnam vet* 越战退伍军人

vet[2] *v* [T] **1** *BrE* to check someone's past activities, relationships etc in order to make sure they are suitable for a particular job, especially one that involves dealing with secret information【英】审查〔某人过去的活动、亲属关系等〕：*The candidates are vetted by Central Office.* 候选人受到中央办公室的审查。**2** to check a report or speech carefully to make sure it is acceptable 检审〔报告或演讲等〕

vetch /vɛtʃ; vetʃ/ *n* [C] a plant with small flowers, often used to feed farm animals 巢菜，野豌豆

vet·e·ran /ˋvɛtərən; ˈvetərən/ *n* [C] **1** someone who has been a soldier, sailor etc in a war〔经历过战争的〕老军人，老水兵；退伍军人：*D Day veterans* 参加过二次大战中盟军诺曼底登陆的老兵 | *a veteran of the Second World War* 第二次世界大战时的老兵 **2** someone who has had a lot of experience of a particular activity 老手，〔在某方面〕经验丰富的人：*a veteran traveller* 富有经验的旅行家 | **[+of]** *a veteran of the anti-apartheid movement* 反对种族隔离的老战士 | **veteran politician/campaigner/statesman etc** (=someone who has been a politician etc for a long time) 老资格的政客/活动家/政治家等 *veteran Soviet politician Andrei Gromyko* 苏联资深政治家安德雷·葛罗米柯

veteran car /,‥ˋ·/ *n* [C] *BrE* a car built before 1905【英】〔1905年前制造的〕老爷车

Veterans Af·fairs, the /ˋ‥‥·/ also 又作 **the Veterans Administration** /ˋ‥ ‥,‥/ abbreviation 缩写为 **the VA** a US government organization which deals with things relating to former members of the armed forces, such as HEALTHCARE, education, and PENSION*s* (=money given to someone when they stop working) 退伍军人事务部，退伍军人管理局〔美国一政府机构，负责办理退伍军人的相关事宜，如医疗、教育和退休金等〕

Veterans As·so·ci·a·tion /ˋ‥‥,‥/ an organization whose members fought in a war in the past 退伍军人协会〔以有作战经历的军人为成员的一个组织〕：*the Vietnam Veterans Association* 越战退伍军人协会

Veterans of For·eign Wars /,‥‥,‥ˋ·/ abbreviation 缩写为 **VFW** a US organization for former soldiers who have fought in wars abroad. This organization sometimes works as a pressure group to influence the US government when it makes military decisions. 海外服役退伍军人协会〔美国为参加过海外战争的退伍军人服务的组织。该组织有时作为压力集团对美国政府的军事决定施加影响〕

vet·e·ri·na·ri·an /,vɛtərəˋnɛrɪən; ,vetərɪ̣ˈneəriən/ *n* [C] *AmE* someone who is trained to give medical care and treatment to sick animals; VET[1] (1)【美】兽医

vet·e·ri·na·ry /ˋvɛtərə,nɛrɪ; ˈvetərɪ̣nəri/ *adj* [only before noun 仅用于名词前] *technical* connected with the medical care and treatment of sick animals【术语】兽医的：*veterinary science* 兽医学

veterinary sur·geon /ˋ‥‥ ,‥/ *n* [C] *BrE formal* a VET[1] (1)【英，正式】兽医

ve·to[1] /ˋvito; ˈviːtəʊ/ *v* **vetoed, vetoing** [T] **1** to officially refuse to allow something to happen, especially something that other people or organizations have agreed 否决〔他人或其他组织已赞同之事〕：*The president vetoed a tax increase on gasoline last week.* 总统上周否决了增收汽油税的议案。**2** to refuse to accept a particular plan or suggestion 不同意，反对〔某个计划或建议〕：*Jenny wanted to invite all her friends, but I quickly vetoed that idea.* 珍妮想把她的朋友都请来，但我马上对此表示反对。

veto[2] *n plural* **vetos** [C,U] a refusal to give official permission for something, or the right to refuse to give such permission 否决（权）：**[+on]** *There is the threat of a presidential veto on this legislation.* 存在着总统否决这项立法的可能。| **power/right of veto** *They exercised their right of veto in the Security Council to prevent the resolution being passed.* 他们在安理会行使了否决权，阻止那项决议通过。

vex /vɛks; veks/ *v* [T] *old-fashioned* to make someone feel annoyed or worried【过时】使恼怒；使烦恼

vex·a·tion /vɛksˋeʃən; vekˈseɪʃən/ *n* **1** [U] *formal* the feeling of being worried or annoyed by something【正式】烦恼，苦恼；恼火 **2** [C] *old-fashioned* something that worries or annoys you【过时】令人烦恼[恼火]的事

vex·a·tious /vɛksˋeʃəs; vekˈseɪʃəs/ *adj old-fashioned* making you feel annoyed or worried【过时】令人恼火[烦恼]的 —**vexatiously** *adv*

vexed /vɛkst; vekst/ *adj* **1** **[+at/with]** *old-fashioned* annoyed or worried【过时】恼火的；烦恼的 **2** **vexed question/issue** a complicated problem that has caused a lot of arguments and is difficult to solve 引起争论的问题，棘手的问题：*the vexed question of how to deal with hunger-strikers* 如何对付绝食抗议者这一难题

V-for·ma·tion /ˋvi fɔr,meʃən; ˈviː fɔː,meɪʃən/ *n* [C] if birds or planes fly in a V-formation, they form the shape of the letter V as they fly〔鸟或飞机成群飞行时的〕V形队形；人字形队列

VFW /,vi ɛf ˋdʌblju; ,viː ef ˈdʌbəljuː/ the abbreviation of 缩写= VETERANS OF FOREIGN WARS

VGA /,vi dʒi ˋe; ,viː dʒiː ˈeɪ/ *n* [singular] Video Graphics Array; a standard of GRAPHICS (=pictures and letters) on a computer screen that has many different colours and is of a high quality 视频图形阵列

VHF /,vi ɛtʃ ˋɛf; ,viː eɪtʃ ˈef/ *n* [U] *technical* very high frequency; radio waves that move very quickly and produce good sound quality【术语】〔无线电的〕甚高频

VH1 /,vi ɛtʃ ˋwʌn; ,viː eɪtʃ ˈwʌn/ a cable television station in the US which shows especially music videos, talk shows, and some films. VH一台〔美国一家有线电视台。播出内容以音乐录像、访谈节目和电影为主〕

vi·a /ˋvaɪə; ˈvaɪə/ *prep* **1** travelling through a place on the way to another place 经过；取道：*We flew to Athens via Paris.* 我们经由巴黎飞往雅典。**2** using a particular person, machine etc to send something 通过〔某人或某机器等〕传送〔某物〕；借助于：*I sent a message to Kitty via her sister.* 我通过姬蒂的妹妹给她带去一封信。 W2

vi·a·ble /ˋvaɪəbl; ˈvaɪəbəl/ *adj* **1** a viable plan or system can work successfully〔计划或系统〕切实可行的：**a viable proposition/alternative/method etc** *Nuclear energy is only one viable alternative to coal or gas.* 核能只是煤或天然气的一种可行的替代物。| **economically/commercially viable** *The project is not economically viable.* 这个项目从经济效益来看是不可行的。**2** *technical* able to continue to live or to develop into a living thing【术语】能存活的；能生长发育的 —**viably** *adv* —**viability** /,vaɪəˋbɪlətɪ; ,vaɪəˈbɪlɪ̣ti/ *n* [U]: *the long term viability of the company* 该公司长期存在的可能性

vi·a·duct /ˋvaɪə,dʌkt; ˈvaɪədʌkt/ *n* [C] a long high bridge across a valley that has a road or railway on it〔架于山谷上的公路或铁路〕高架桥

vi·al /ˋvaɪəl; ˈvaɪəl/ *n* [C] a PHIAL 小瓶；小药瓶

vi·ands /ˋvaɪəndz; ˈvaɪəndz/ *n* [plural] *old use* food【旧】食物

vibes /vaɪbz; vaɪbz/ *n* [plural] *informal*【非正式】**1** the good or bad feelings that a particular person, group of people, or situation seems to produce and that you react to 感应，共鸣：**good/**

bad/strange vibes *I'm getting strange vibes from this guy, I think he's maybe lying to us.* 这家伙给我的感觉怪怪的，我想他可能在对我们说谎。**2** a VIBRAPHONE 电颤琴

vi·brant /ˋvaɪbrənt; ˈvaɪbrənt/ *adj* **1** exciting and full of activity and energy 令人兴奋的；充满活力的，精力充沛的，活跃的：*Hong Kong is a vibrant, fascinating city.* 香港是个富有活力的迷人城市。**2** a vibrant light or colour is bright and strong〔光或颜色〕明亮的；鲜艳的：*vibrant paintings of bullfights* 色彩鲜艳的斗牛画 —**vibrancy** *n* [U] —**vibrantly** *adv*

vi·bra·phone /ˋvaɪbrəˌfon; ˈvaɪbrəfəʊn/ *n* [C] an electronic musical instrument that consists of metal bars that you hit to produce a sound 颤音琴〔一种打击乐器〕

vi·brate /ˋvaɪbret; vaɪˈbreɪt/ *v* [I,T] to shake or make something shake continuously with small fast movements（使）颤动；（使）震动；（使）振动：*We could feel the floor vibrating to the beat of the music.* 我们能感觉到地板随着音乐的节拍而颤动。| *The vocal cords vibrate as air passes over them.* 声带在气流通过时产生振动。

vi·bra·tion /vaɪˋbreʃən; vaɪˈbreɪʃən/ *n* [C,U] **1** a continuous slight shaking movement 颤动，振颤；震动：*You can feel the vibrations of the ship's engine.* 你能感觉到船上发动机的震动。**2 vibrations** [plural] VIBES (1) 感应，共鸣

vi·bra·to /vɪˋbrɑto; vɪˈbrɑːtəʊ/ *n* [U] a way of singing or playing a musical note so that it goes up and down very slightly in PITCH[1] (3)〔演唱或演奏的〕颤动效果，颤音

vi·brat·or /ˋvaɪbretɚ; vaɪˈbreɪtə/ *n* [C] a piece of electrical equipment that produces a small shaking movement, used especially in MASSAGE or to get sexual pleasure 振动器；〔尤指按摩或获取性快感时用的〕振动按摩器，颤震器

vic·ar /ˋvɪkɚ; ˈvɪkə/ *n* [C] a priest in the Church of England who is in charge of a church in a particular area〔英国国教的〕教区牧师

vic·ar·age /ˋvɪkərɪdʒ; ˈvɪkərɪdʒ/ *n* [C] a house where a vicar lives 教区牧师的住宅

vi·car·i·ous /vaɪˋkɛrɪəs; vɪˈkeəriəs/ *adj* [only before noun 仅用于名词前] experienced by watching or reading about someone else doing something, rather than by doing it yourself 间接体验他人感受的；产生同感[共鸣]的：**vicarious pleasure/satisfaction/excitement etc** *the vicarious pleasure that parents get from their children's success* 父母因子女的成功而获得的同样的快乐 —**vicariously** *adv*

3 **vice** /vaɪs; vaɪs/ *n* **1** [U] evil or criminal activities that involve sex or drugs〔涉及性或毒品的〕罪恶，邪恶行径；不道德行为：**vice ring** (=a group of criminals involved in vice) 犯罪团伙 *The police have smashed a vice ring in Chicago.* 警察捣毁了芝加哥的一个犯罪团伙。**2** [C] a bad habit 恶习。*Smoking is my only vice.* 吸烟是我唯一的恶习。**3** [C] a bad or immoral quality in someone's character〔性格上的〕缺陷，弱点；劣根性：*the vice of greed* 贪婪的劣根性 —opposite 反义词 VIRTUE **4** usually 一般作 **vise** *AmE*【美】[C] a tool that holds an object firmly so that you can work on it using both your hands 老虎钳，台钳

vice- /vaɪs; vaɪs/ *prefix* the person next in official rank below someone, who can represent them or act instead of them〔官阶职位〕副；代（理）：*the Vice-President of the USA* 美国副总统 | *the vice-captain of the cricket team* 板球队的副队长

vice-ad·mi·ral /ˌ· ˈ ···/ *n* [C] a high rank in the British or US navy, or someone who has this rank〔英、美海军中的〕中将军衔；海军中将 —see table on page C6 参见 C6 页附录

vice-chan·cel·lor /ˌ· ˈ···/ *n* [C] **1** someone who is in charge of a British university〔英国主管大学事务的〕（副）校长 —compare 比较 CHANCELLOR (2) **2** someone who is next in rank to the CHANCELLOR (=person in charge) of a university in the US〔美国大学的〕副校长

vice·like /ˋvaɪsˌlaɪk; ˈvaɪslaɪk/ *adj* **a vicelike grip** a very firm hold 像老虎钳一般的紧握，抓牢

vice pres·i·dent /ˌ· ˈ···/ *n* [C] **1** the person who is next in rank to the president of a country and who is responsible for the president's duties if he or she is ill 副总统 **2** *AmE* someone who is responsible for a particular part of a company【美】〔公司等负责某个部门的〕副总裁：*our executive vice president for marketing* 主管营销的执行副总裁

vice·roy /ˋvaɪsrɔɪ; ˈvaɪsrɔɪ/ *n* [C] a man who was sent by the king or queen to rule another country, especially in the British Empire〔尤指在英帝国时期由国王或女王派去管理另一国家的〕总督：*the viceroy of India* 印度总督

vice squad /ˈ· ·/ *n* [C usually singular 一般用单数] the part of the police force that deals with crimes involving sex or drugs〔处理与性、吸毒等有关的案件的〕警察缉捕队

vice ver·sa /ˋvaɪsɪ ˋvɝsə; ˌvaɪs ˈvɜːsə/ *adv* used when the opposite of a situation you have just described is also true 反过来也是如此，反之亦然：*Anything the men wanted the women didn't, and vice versa.* 男人想要的东西女人不想要，反之亦然。

Vi·chy /ˋviʃɪ; ˈviːʃi/ a city in south central France where the government of France was based during World War II. The authority of the Vichy government was not accepted by many French people because it followed the rules and laws given to it by the Germans who had taken control of France. When people discuss this period of France's history they sometimes call the country **Vichy France**. 维希〔法国中南部一城市，二战期间法国政府所在地。维希当局执行德国占领军的法令和法规，大部分法国民众拒不接受其傀儡统治。人们有时以 Vichy France（维希法国）指称法国的这段历史〕

vi·cin·i·ty /vəˋsɪnətɪ; vəˈsɪnəti/ *n* **1 in the vicinity (of)** in the area around a particular place 在…附近：*The car was found abandoned in the vicinity of Waterloo Station.* 汽车被发现弃置在滑铁卢车站附近。**2 in the vicinity of** *formal* close to a particular amount or measurement【正式】在…左右，大约…：*a price somewhere in the vicinity of £25,000* 大约 25,000 英镑的价格

vi·cious /ˋvɪʃəs; ˈvɪʃəs/ *adj* **1** violent and dangerous, and likely to hurt someone 凶险的；会造成伤害的：*a vicious attack* 凶狠的攻击 | *a vicious criminal* 凶暴的罪犯 | *Keep away from that dog, he can be vicious.* 离那只狗远点，它很凶猛。**2** cruel and deliberately trying to hurt someone's feelings or make their character seem bad 狠毒的，恶意的：*Sarah can be quite vicious at times.* 萨拉有时相当狠毒。| **vicious attack/campaign/rumour etc** *Senator Logan launched a vicious attack on the president and his advisors.* 参议员洛根对总统及其顾问发动了一场恶毒的攻击。**3** unpleasantly strong or severe 剧烈的；恶劣的：*a vicious gust of wind* 一股很猛烈的风 | *a vicious headache* 剧烈的头痛 —**viciously** *adv*: *He twisted her arm viciously.* 他凶狠地拧她的胳膊。—**viciousness** *n* [U]

vicious cir·cle /ˌ·· ˈ··/ *n* [singular] a situation in which one problem causes another problem that then causes the first problem again, so that the whole process continues to be repeated 恶性循环

vi·cis·si·tudes /vəˋsɪsəˌtudz; vəˈsɪsətjuːdz/ *n* [plural] *formal* the continuous changes and problems that affect a situation or someone's life【正式】〔影响某种局面或个人生活的〕改变，变迁；兴衰：*the vicissitudes of married life* 婚后生活的变化

Vicks·burg /ˋvɪksbɝg; ˈvɪksbɜːg/ a city in Mississippi, US, where an important battle was fought during the American CIVIL WAR 维克斯堡〔美国密西西比州一城市。美国南北战争期间在此爆发了一场重要战役〕

vic·tim /ˋvɪktɪm; ˈvɪktəm/ *n* [C] **1** someone who has been attacked, robbed, or murdered 受害者；牺牲者：*In most sexual offences the attacker is known to the victim.* 在大多数性侵犯事件中，施暴者是受害者认识的人。| **rape/murder etc victim** *Most homicide victims are under 30.* 大多杀人案的受害者不足30岁。**2** someone who suffers because they are affected by a bad situation or by an illness〔恶劣情况的〕受灾者；〔疾病的〕患者：*a victim of circumstances* 环境的受害者 | **famine/earthquake/flood victims** *a massive aid program for the famine victims* 对遭受饥荒者的大规模援助计划 | **polio/cholera/AIDS victim** *Many cholera victims were being left to die.* 许多霍乱患者被置于等死的境地。**3** something that is badly affected or destroyed by a situation or action 牺牲品：**fall victim to** (=become a victim of something) 成为…的牺牲品 *Vital public services have fallen victim to budget cuts.* 一些重要的公共服务项目成了削减预算的牺牲品。**4 be a victim of its own success** to be badly affected by some unexpected results of being very successful 因成功而反受其害：*The once-peaceful village has attracted so many tourists that it has become a victim of its own success.* 那个曾经宁静的村子吸引了如此众多的游客，结果反受其害。**5 sacrificial victim** a person or animal that is killed and offered as a SACRIFICE[1] (3) (=gift) to a god 献祭用的人[牲畜]，牺牲品 **6 fashion/style victim** *informal* someone who always wears the newest fashions whether it suits them or not【非正式】盲目追求时尚者 2 2

vic·tim·ize also 又作 **-ise** *BrE*【英】/ˋvɪktɪmˌaɪz; ˈvɪktəmaɪz/ *v* [T] to treat someone unfairly, especially because you dislike their beliefs or the race they belong to〔尤指因厌恶某人的信仰或所属的人种而〕不公正地对待，使受害；迫害：*The sacked men claim they have been victimized because of their political activity.* 被解雇者声称他们是由于自己的政治活动而受到迫害。—**victimization** /ˌvɪktɪməˋzeʃən; ˌvɪktəmaɪˈzeɪʃən/ *n* [U]

vic·tor /ˋvɪktɚ; ˈvɪktə/ *n* [C] *formal* the winner of a battle, game, competition etc【正式】〔战斗、比赛等中的〕得胜者，胜利者：*After the game the victors returned in triumph.* 得胜者赛后凯旋。

vɪkˈtɔrɪə; vɪkˈtɔːriə/ **1** a large railway station in ...on, from which trains go to various parts of south-...d 维多利亚车站〔伦敦市中心一大型火车站。多趟列...往英格兰东南部各地〕 **2** the capital city of the Cana-...VINCE of British Columbia 维多利亚市〔加拿大不列颠...亚省首府〕 **3** a state in southeast Australia, which has a ...industry. Capital: Melbourne. 维多利亚州〔澳大利亚东南...州, 工业发达。首府: 墨尔本〕

...toria, Lake the largest lake in Africa, which is sur-...unded by Uganda, Tanzania, and Kenya 维多利亚湖〔非洲最大的湖泊。周边国家有乌干达、坦桑尼亚和肯尼亚〕

...ictoria, Queen (1819-1901) the British queen from 1837 until her death, who also had the title 'Empress of India'. She was queen for 64 years, longer than any other British king or queen, during a period of great change. While she was queen, the UK became one of the richest and most powerful countries in the world, as a result of the growth of industry and the development of the British Empire. People think now of the 'Victorian' period as a time of strict moral standards, when people were very serious, marriages were always permanent, and sex was never mentioned. Victoria was married to a German prince, Prince Albert. 维多利亚女王〔(1819-1901), 英国女王, 1837 年即位, 在位 64 年, 为英国历史上在位时间最长的君主。她还享有"印度女皇"的称号。在位期间, 英国经历了巨大变革, 工业迅猛发展, 帝国版图不断扩大, 成为当时世界上最富强的国家之一。"维多利亚"时代以严格的道德标准著称, 民风刻板拘谨, 婚姻关系稳定, 从不谈及与性有关的话题。维多利亚女王的丈夫为德国亲王阿尔伯特〕

Victoria and Al·bert Mu·se·um, the /ˌ·, ··· ˌ·, ·· ˈ· ·/ also 又作 **the V & A** a MUSEUM in central London that has valuable decorative objects of all styles and periods and from all over the world, such as paintings, glass, clothes, and jewellery 维多利亚和阿尔伯特博物馆〔伦敦市中心一博物馆。藏有来自不同国家、不同时代、风格各异的名贵饰品, 如绘画、玻璃制品、服装及珠宝等〕

Victoria Cross /ˌ·, ··· ˈ·/ *n* the full name of the VC 维多利亚十字勋章〔VC 的全称〕

Victoria Day /ˈ··· ˌ·/ a public holiday held in May in Canada 维多利亚日〔加拿大一公众假日, 定于每年 5 月〕

Victoria Falls /ˌ·, ··· ˈ·/ a WATERFALL on the Zambezi River between Zimbabwe and Zambia in southern Africa, which is about 1.5 kilometres/1 mile wide and about 120 metres/400 feet high. It is one of the most popular places in Africa for tourists to visit. 维多利亚瀑布〔赞比西河上的一大瀑布。位于非洲南部, 津巴布韦和赞比亚之间, 宽约 1.5 千米 (即约 1 英里), 落差约 120 米 (即 400 英尺), 是非洲境内最受游客喜爱的景点之一〕

Vic·to·ri·an¹ /vɪkˈtɔrɪən; vɪkˈtɔːriən/ *adj* **1** connected with the period from 1837-1901 when Victoria was Queen of England 维多利亚 (女王) 时代的 **2** having the strict moral attitudes typical of the society of this period 〔道德标准〕维多利亚 (女王) 时代特有的: *Victorian prudery* 维多利亚女王时代的那种故作正经

Victorian² *n* [C] an English person living in the period when ...ria ruled 维多利亚 (女王) 时代的人

vic·to·ri·ous /vɪkˈtɔrɪəs; vɪkˈtɔːriəs/ *adj* having won a victory ...胜利的, 战胜的: *The victorious team held the tro-...* 的球队把奖杯高高举起。| *We were confident that ... emerge victorious.* (=finally win) 我们确信盟军最... —**victoriously** *adv*

vic·to·ry ... /ˈvɪktəri/ *n* [C,U] **1** the success you achieve by wi... a game, race etc 胜利, 成功, 赢: *The streets ... celebrating an Italian victory.* 街上的人群... 的胜利。| [+over] *A great shot by ... over the Celtics.* 约翰逊一记 ... 队。| **win a victory** *The ... in a row.* 共和党... (=win easily and ... scored four ... as the ... 球, 使公羊队在比...中大 ... (=very great victory) 大胜, ... **a victory for common** ... 的裁决 ... ling a quarrel, which ... 常理获胜, 不偏不倚

Victory, ... 1805 when ... French and ... 战舰。海军 ... Nelson used in ... 法尔加角海... against the ... 战的胜利〕

口语 ... 及书面语 ...

vict·ual /ˈvɪtl; ˈvɪtl/ *v* [T] to supply a large number of people with food 为〔数量众多的人〕供应食物

vict·uals /ˈvɪtlz; ˈvɪtlz/ *n* [plural] *old use* food and drink 【旧】食物和饮料

vi·cu·ña /vɪˈkjunə; vɪˈkjuːnə/ *n* **1** [C] a large South American animal related to the LLAMA, from which soft wool is obtained 骆马〔产于南美, 与美洲驼近缘, 以其柔软的毛而著称〕 **2** [U] the cloth made from this wool 骆马毛织品

vi·de·li·cet /vɪˈdɛləsɪt; vɪˈdiːlɪset/ *adv Latin formal* VIZ 【拉丁, 正式】即, 也就是

vid·e·o¹ /ˈvɪdɪˌo; ˈvɪdiəʊ/ *n* **1** [C] a copy of a film or television programme recorded on VIDEOTAPE 〔电影或电视节目在录像带上的〕录影, 录像: *I've borrowed the video of 'Gone with the Wind'.* 我把《乱世佳人》的录像带借来了。| *a video shop* 出租录像带的商店 **2** [C, U] a VIDEOTAPE 录像带: *Have we got a blank video anywhere?* 我们哪里有空白的录像带吗? | **on video** *'Jurassic Park' is now available on video.* 《侏罗纪公园》的录像带现已有售。**3** [C] *BrE* a VIDEO CASSETTE RECORDER 【英】(盒式磁带) 录像机 —see picture on page A14 参见 A14 页图 **4** [U] the process of recording and showing television programmes, films, real events etc using video equipment 录影, 录像〔录制和播放电视节目、电影、真实事件等的过程〕: *Interactive learning has been greatly advanced by the introduction of video.* 录像的引进极大地促进了互动式教学。 S1 W2

video² *v* [T] to record a television programme, film, or a real event on a VIDEOTAPE; TAPE² (1) 把〔电视节目、电影或真实事件等〕录在录像带[录影带]上: *Could you video 'The Elvis Presley Story' for me at 8.00?* 你能帮我录下 8 点钟的《埃尔维斯·普雷斯利的故事》吗? | *They got a friend to video the wedding.* 他们找了一位朋友把婚礼场面录下来。

video³ *adj* **1** [only before noun 仅用于名词前] related to or used in the process of recording and showing pictures on television 电视的, 视频的, 影像的: **video equipment/recording/system etc** *The VHS and Beta video systems are not compatible.* VHS 和 Beta 录像系统互不兼容。—compare 比较 AUDIO **2** using VIDEOTAPE 用录像磁带[录影带]的: *a video recording* 录影, 录像

video ar·cade /ˈ··· ·ˌ·/ *n* [C] *AmE* a public place where there are a lot of VIDEO GAMES that you play by putting money in the machines 【美】电子游戏室

video cam·e·ra /ˈ··· ˌ···/ *n* [C] a special camera that can be used to film events using VIDEOTAPE 摄像机

video cas·sette /ˌ··· ·ˈ·/ *n* [C] a VIDEOTAPE 盒式录像带, 录像(磁)带

video cas·sette re·cord·er /ˌ··· ·ˈ· ·ˌ··/ *n* [C] a machine used to record television programmes or show videos (VIDEO¹ (1)) (盒式磁带) 录像机; VCR *especially AmE* 【尤美】, VIDEO¹ (3) *BrE* 【英】

video con·fe·ren·cing /ˈ··· ˌ···/ *n* [U] a system that allows people to communicate with each other by sending pictures and sounds electronically 电视会议, 视频会议 (系统)

vid·e·o·disc /ˈvɪdɪoˌdɪsk; ˈvɪdiəʊˌdɪsk/ *n* [C] a round flat piece of plastic from which films can be played in the same way as from a VIDEOTAPE 〔激光〕视盘, 录像盘, 影碟

video game /ˈ··· ˌ·/ *n* [C] a game in which you move images on a screen by pressing electronic controls 电视游戏

vid·e·og·ra·phy /ˌvɪdɪˈɑgrəfɪ; ˌvɪdiˈɒgrəfi/ *n* [U] *formal* the art of recording events with a VIDEO CAMERA 【正式】摄像 —**videographer** *n* [C]

video jock·ey /ˈ··· ˌ··/ *n* [C] someone who introduces short VIDEO films on television, especially those showing performances of popular music; VJ 〔尤指播放流行音乐的〕电视短片节目主持人

vid·e·o nas·ty /ˌ··· ˈ··/ *n* [C] *BrE informal* a VIDEO that includes very violent scenes 【英, 非正式】凶杀录像片, 暴力录影片

vid·e·o·phone /ˈvɪdɪoˌfon; ˈvɪdiəʊfəʊn/ *n* [C] a type of telephone that allows you to see the person you are talking to on a machine like a television 电视电话, 可视电话

video re·cord·er /ˈ··· ·ˌ··/ *n* [C] a VIDEO CASSETTE RECORDER (盒式磁带) 录像机

vid·e·o·tape¹ /ˈvɪdɪoˌtep; ˈvɪdiəʊteɪp/ *n* [C,U] a long narrow band of MAGNETIC material in a flat plastic container, on which films, television programmes etc can be recorded 盒式录像带, 录像(磁)带

videotape² *v* [...] to record a television programme, film etc on a videotape; VIDEO² 把〔电视节目、电影等〕录在录像带上

vid·e·o·tex /ˈvɪdɪoˌtɛks; ˈvɪdiəʊˌteks/ *n* [U] *trademark* a form ...ation that allows information to be exchanged us-... 【商标】〔通过...视传送的〕可视图文 (系...

vie /vaɪ; vaɪ/ *v* **vied, vying** [I] to compete very hard with someone in order to get something〔为获得某物与某人〕竞争: [+for] *Simon and Julian were vying for her attention all through dinner.* 西蒙和朱利安整个席间都在争着吸引她的注意力。| **vie with sb to do sth** *The major record companies are vying with each other to sign the group.* 两家主要唱片公司互相竞争，都想与这个乐队签约。

Vi·en·na /vɪˋɛnə; viˈenə/ the capital city of Austria, famous as a centre for music since the 18th century, and the home of many famous COMPOSERS, including Mozart and Beethoven. 维也纳〔奥地利首都，18世纪以来著名的音乐中心，莫扎特和贝多芬等众多著名作曲家的故乡〕—**Viennese** *n, adj*

Vientiane /ˌvjɛˋtjɑn; ˌvjeˈtjɑːn/ the capital city of Laos 万象〔老挝首都〕

Viet Cong, the /ˌvjɛt ˋkɑŋ; ˌvjet ˈkɒŋ/ also 又作 **the Vietcong** the group of GUERILLAS (=unofficial soldiers) who were supported by the Communist government of North Vietnam during the Vietnam War, and fought against US and South Vietnamese forces 越共〔越战期间在北越共产党政权支持下对美军和南越军队作战的游击队组织〕

Viet·nam /ˌviɛtˋnɑm; ˌvjetˈnæm/ a country in southeast Asia, next to Cambodia and China. Population: 79,939,000 (2001). Capital: Hanoi. Vietnam was ruled by France, as part of French Indochina, from the mid-19th century. It became independent in 1954 as two countries, the pro-western South Vietnam and the Communist North Vietnam. Attempts to unite the two countries led to the Vietnam War and eventually succeeded in 1975. The war caused great suffering and serious economic problems. Since the war, Vietnam has gradually improved its economic position and it is now a member of ASEAN. 越南〔东南亚一国家，毗邻柬埔寨和中国。人口: 79,939,000 (2001)，首都: 河内。19世纪中叶起，越南沦为法国殖民地，成为法属印度支那的一部分。1954年独立，但建立了两个国家，即亲西方的南越和共产党执政的北越。之后，实现南北统一的努力连续不断，最终引发了越南战争，直至1975年才宣告结束。这场战争带来了巨大的浩劫和严重的经济问题。战争结束后，越南逐渐提升自身的经济地位，现为东盟成员国〕

Vietnam Vet·e·rans Me·mo·ri·al, the /ˌ‥ˈ‥ ‥ˌ‥/ also 又作 **the Vietnam Memorial** two long walls made of polished black stone which are arranged in a V-shape on the Mall (=park area) in Washington, D.C. The walls have more than 58,000 names carved on them, which is to remind people of all the US soldiers who died in the Vietnam War or never returned from Vietnam. 越战纪念碑〔由光洁的黑石砌成的两道长墙。成V字形矗立在华盛顿特区的草地广场，上面刻有58,000多个名字，以纪念在越战期间阵亡或失踪的美军官兵〕

Vietnam War, the /ˌ‥ˈ·/ (1954-75) a long CIVIL WAR between the Communist forces of North Vietnam and the non-Communist forces of South Vietnam, which ended when South Vietnam was finally defeated in 1975, and Vietnam was united again as one country. Between 1965 and 1973, US soldiers fought in Vietnam to support the army of South Vietnam, and when people in the west talk about the Vietnam War, or simply about Vietnam they usually mean this period of US involvement. 越南战争〔(1954-1975)，北越的共产党军队与南越的非共产党军队之间进行的一场旷日持久的内战，1975年以南越战败、越南重获统一告终。1965至1973年，美军为支持南越军队开赴越南作战。西方人谈到越战或提及越南时，通常指美国介入越战的这段时期〕

CULTURAL NOTE 文化注释

The Vietnam War had a deep and lasting effect on US society and on the way that Americans thought about their own country. This is shown, for example, in the many films made about the war, such as *Apocalypse Now* (1979) and *Born on the Fourth of July* (1989). For a long time, people worried about the US becoming involved in any war, because they were afraid it would become 'another Vietnam', meaning that they were afraid many soldi… and foreign citizens would be killed without the U… ing able to achieve its aim. 越南战争对美国社会… 看待自己国家的观念有着深远的影响。例如… 很多题材取自越战的电影上看出来，这… 录》(1979) 和《生于七月四日》(1… 心美国会介入到任何战争中去… 一个越南"，意思是他们害… 而还造成大量美国士…

At first, most pe… war gradua… dents and other young people, as more US… killed and as the television news showed ter… of ordinary Vietnamese people being killed a… Many young men became 'draft dodgers' (=th… to accept the DRAFT, the system by which every … zen had to do military service), and many of them … country or went to jail in protest. There were large … **test marches**, many popular **protest songs**, and the … ing 'make love, not war' became popular. Military f… ures and loss of public support eventually forced the go… ernment to bring US forces back from Vietnam in 1973. 最初，大多数人支持这场战争。随着越来越多的美国兵战死和电视新闻中有关越南平民被杀害和致残的可怖画面的播出，尤其是在大学生和其他年轻人中反战逐步升级。很多年轻人成了"逃避兵役者"，其中许多人离开美国或因抗议而被投入监狱。有大型的反战游行和十分走红的反战歌曲，而且"做爱而不是作战"的说法很是流行。军事上的失败和缺少公众的支持最终迫使美国政府于1973年从越南撤回军队。

American people have very divided feelings about the war. Some people feel guilty about the terrible damage that it did to Vietnam, and most Americans now believe that the US should not have got involved in the war. Many 'Vietnam veterans' (=US soldiers who fought in the war) feel angry that they were made to fight. Many veterans are also angry because they were not praised like the soldiers from World War II when they came home, but were sometimes criticized by people who opposed the war. But some Americans still believe that the US was right to fight against Communism and should have remained in Vietnam until they won. 美国人对这场战争的感受差别极大。有人因为对越南造成的巨大破坏而心怀愧疚，而现在更多的美国人相信美国本不应该介入这场战争。很多越战老兵对自己被投入战争感到愤怒。因为没有像二战归来的军人那样受到褒扬，有时甚至会被反战人士批评，很多越战老兵对此气上加气。但是有些美国人仍然坚信美国去越南与共产主义作战的行为是对的，而且还应该一直待在越南直至胜利。

In the election for president in 2004, many people believed that John F. Kerry was a better candidate than George W. Bush because he had fought in the Vietnam War, and Bush had not. 在2004年的总统大选中，很多人认为约翰·F.克里作为候选人比乔治·W.布什更有优势，因为他参加过越南战争而布什没有。

view 视野，景色

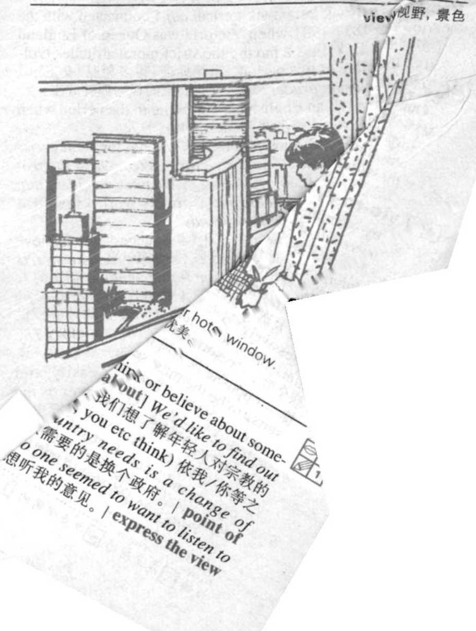

…r hotel window.

…ink or believe about some-… [about] We'd like to find out … 我们想了解年轻人对宗教的 … you etc think) 依我/你等之 … country needs is a change of … 需要的是换个政府。| **point of** … no one seemed to want to listen to … 想听我的意见。| **express the view** …

…ing a televisi… 电视观… (统)… of c…

that (=say you think that) 表达…的看法 *The chairman expressed the view that it would be better not to increase investments.* 董事长表达了自己的看法，认为最好不要增加投资。| **take the view that** (=have the opinion that) 持…的观点 *The judge took the view that a prison sentence would not be appropriate in this case.* 法官认为判决入狱对这一案件并不恰当。

2 ▶WAY OF CONSIDERING 思考方式◀ [C usually singular 一般用单数] a way of considering or understanding something 思考[理解]的方式[方法]，考虑: **[+of]** *Has your view of the role of women changed since you got married?* 自结婚以来，你对妇女所起作用的看法改变了吗？| *James always did have a rather romantic view of life.* 詹姆斯对生活一向有一种相当浪漫的想法。| **an inside view** (=based on actual experience in an organization, group etc) 局内人的看法 *Healey's autobiography gives the reader an inside view of the Labour party.* 希利的自传使读者得以了解工党的内幕。| **clear view** (=a definite and specific idea about something) 明确的想法 *Before doing anything you need to have a clear view of the kind of book you want to write.* 在开始之前，你需要对要写什么类型的书有明确的计划。| **take a dim/poor view of** (=disapprove) 不赞成 *She takes a pretty dim view of her son's recent behaviour.* 她对儿子近来的所作所为很不赞成。

3 ▶SIGHT 视觉◀ [C,U] what you are able to see or the possibility of seeing it 能[可能]看见的东西; 视力; 视野; 视线: **have a good/bad/wonderful etc view (of)** (=be able to see a lot, very little etc) 看得见/看不见/看得非常清楚等 *We had a really good view of the whole stage from where we were sitting.* 从我们坐的位置看，整个舞台尽收眼底。| **be in view** (=can be seen from where you are) 在视野中 *She waited until the whole island was in view and then took a photograph.* 她一直等到看得见整个岛后才拍了一张照片。| **come into view** (=begin to be seen) 出现在视野中 *As we rounded the bend in the river the castle came into view.* 我们绕过河湾时，城堡便映入了眼帘。| **in full view of** (=happening where people can see it clearly) …都清楚看见 *Francine screamed and slapped her husband in full view of all the guests.* 芙朗辛尖声大叫，当着所有客人的面给了丈夫一记耳光。| **block sb's view** (=stop someone from seeing something) 挡住某人的视线 *There was a tall guy sitting in front of me, blocking my view completely.* 有个高个子坐在我的前面，把我的视线全挡住了。| **bird's eye view** (=a view seen from above) 鸟瞰 *We've got a bird's eye view of the football stadium from our office window.* 从我们办公室的窗口可以鸟瞰足球场。

4 ▶SCENERY 景色◀ [C] the whole area, especially a beautiful place, that you can see from somewhere 风景，景色: *a spectacular view across the valley* 峡谷另一边的壮丽景色 | **spoil the view** (=make a view look less beautiful) 杀风景 *A huge nuclear reactor now spoils the view of the coastline.* 一个庞大的核反应堆使海岸的风景大打折扣。

5 ▶PICTURE 图片◀ [C] a photograph or picture showing a beautiful or interesting place 风景照; 风景画: *The book contains over fifty scenic views of Cambridge.* 该书有五十多幅剑桥的风景照。

6 be on view if paintings, photographs etc are on view, they are in a public place where people can go to look at them〔画作、照片等〕在展览[陈列]: *The Toulouse Lautrec posters are currently on view at the Hayward gallery.* 图卢斯·劳特雷克的招贴画正在海华德美术馆展出。

7 in view of used to introduce the reason for your decision or action 鉴于，考虑到，由于: *In view of Sutton's recent conduct the club has decided to suspend him until further notice.* 考虑到萨顿近来的表现，俱乐部决定暂停其会员资格，直至另行通知。

8 with a view to doing sth because you are planning to do something in the future 打算做某事: *We bought the cottage with a view to moving there when we retired.* 我们买了一间小屋，打算退休后搬去住。

9 have sth in view to have something in your mind as an aim 心里有做某事的打算: *He wants to find work, but he has nothing particular in view.* 他想找工作，但没有什么具体的打算。

10 take the long view (of) to think about the effect that something will have in the future rather than what happens now 对…作长远打算

view² *v* **1** [T] *formal* to look at something, especially because you are interested【正式】〔尤指出于兴趣〕看，查看，观察: **view sth from** *The buildings are much more impressive when viewed from the other side of the river.* 从河的另一边看，这些大楼要雄伟得多。| **view a house/apartment/property** (=go to see the inside of a house etc which you are interested in buying)〔因有兴趣购买而〕看房子/公寓/房产 | **view an exhibition/a garden etc** (=walk around it and look at it) 参观展览/花园等 *Thousands of tourists came to view the gardens every year.* 每年有成千上万的游客参观这些花园。 **2** [T always+ adv/ prep] to regard something in a particular way〔从某种方面〕考虑: *Viewed from a financial standpoint, the show was a failure.* 从经济的观点看，演出是不成功的。| **view sth as** *Conflict is viewed as an inevitable part of the child-parent relationship.* 冲突被视为子女与父母之间关系不可避免的一部分。| **view sth with caution/enthusiasm/horror etc** *Offers of rides from strangers should always be viewed with suspicion.* 如果有陌生人主动提出让你搭车，你一定要有戒备心理。**3** [I,T] *formal* to watch a television programme, film etc【正式】看（电视、电影等）: *an opportunity to view the film before it goes on general release* 观看尚未公映的影片的一次机会

view·er /ˈvjuə; ˈvjuːə/ *n* [C] **1** someone who watches television 电视观看者，电视观众: *The new series has gone down well with viewers.* 这个新系列片很受电视观众的欢迎。**2** a small box with a light in it used to look at SLIDES (=colour photographs on special film) 看片器〔用于看幻灯片的内置灯的小箱子〕

view·find·er /ˈvjuˌfaɪndə; ˈvjuːˌfaɪndə/ *n* [C] the small square of glass on a camera that you look through to see exactly what you are photographing〔照相机的〕取景器 —see picture at 参见 CAMERA 图

view·point /ˈvjuˌpɔɪnt; ˈvjuːpɔɪnt/ *n* [C] **1** a particular way of thinking about a problem or subject 观点，看法，见解: **from a different/practical/religious etc viewpoint** *From an ecological viewpoint, the new motorway has been a disaster.* 从生态学的角度看，这条新公路是个灾难。**2** a place from which you can see something 观察点

vig·il /ˈvɪdʒəl; ˈvɪdʒl/ *n* [C,U] **1** a period of time, especially during the night, when you stay awake in order to pray or remain with someone who is ill〔尤指为祷告或守护病人的〕守夜，值夜: **keep (a) vigil** *For three weeks Jeff kept a vigil while his son lay in a coma.* 儿子昏迷期间，杰夫一连三周日夜守护。**2** a silent political protest in which people wait outside a building, especially during the night〔尤指夜间〕静坐抗议: **hold a vigil** *Over 2,000 demonstrators held a candlelit peace vigil in front of the US embassy.* 二千多名示威者在美国大使馆前举行了一次烛光和平静坐抗议。

vig·i·lance /ˈvɪdʒələns; ˈvɪdʒlləns/ *n* [U] careful attention that you give to what is happening, so that you will notice any danger or illegal activity 警惕，警戒: *Constant vigilance is essential to combat drug-smuggling.* 始终保持警惕是打击毒品走私所必需的。

vig·i·lant /ˈvɪdʒələnt; ˈvɪdʒllənt/ *adj* giving careful attention to what is happening, so that you will notice any danger or illegal activity 警惕的，警觉的，警戒的: *Please remain vigilant at all times and report anything suspicious.* 请随时保持警惕，报告任何可疑情况。—**vigilantly** *adv*

vig·i·lan·te /ˌvɪdʒəˈlæntɪ; ˌvɪdʒlˈlænti/ *n* [C] a member of an unofficial group of people who join together to catch or punish criminals, usually because they think the police are ineffective〔非官方的〕治安维持会成员

vi·gnette /vɪnˈjɛt; vɪˈnjet/ *n* [C] **1** a short description in a book or play showing the typical features of a person or situation〔书本或剧本中对人物或场景的〕简介 **2** a small drawing or pattern placed at the beginning of a book or CHAPTER (1)〔书的扉页上或某章节前的〕小装饰图案

vig·or /ˈvɪgə; ˈvɪgə/ *n* [U] the American spelling of VIGOUR vigour 的美式拼法

vig·o·rous /ˈvɪgərəs; ˈvɪgərəs/ *adj* **1** using a lot of energy and strength or determination 强有力的; 积极的: *Vigorous efforts will be made to find alternative employment for those made redundant.* 将积极为失业人士另找一份职业。| *Your dog needs at least 20 minutes of vigorous exercise every day.* 你的狗每天需要进行至少20分钟的激烈运动。**2 a vigorous opponent/defender etc** someone who opposes or defends something strongly 顽强的反对者/捍卫者等: *a vigorous campaigner for human rights* 争取人权的顽强斗士 **3** strong and very healthy 强健的，精力旺盛的: *a vigorous man in the prime of life* 一个精力充沛的壮年男子 —**vigorously** *adv*: *Boil vigorously for five minutes.* 用猛火煮5分钟。

vig·our *BrE*【英】, **vigor** *AmE*【美】/ˈvɪgə; ˈvɪgə/ *n* [U] physical and mental energy and determination 活力，精力; 气势，魄力: *He set about his task with renewed vigour.* 他恢复了体力，开始了工作。

Viking 北欧海盗, 维京人

Vi·king /ˈvaɪkɪŋ; ˈvaɪkɪŋ/ *n* [C] one of a race of Scandinavian people in the 8th to 10th centuries who sailed in ships to attack areas along the coasts of northern and western Europe 北欧海盗, 维京人〔公元8到10世纪时乘船劫掠北欧和西欧海岸的斯堪的纳维亚人的一支〕

vile /vaɪl; vaɪl/ *adj* **1** *informal* very unpleasant or nasty【非正式】坏透的; 讨厌的: *This soup is vile.* 这汤太难喝了。| *She has a vile temper.* 她的脾气太糟了。**2** evil 可耻的; 邪恶的: *a vile slander* 卑鄙的诽谤 —**vilely** *adv* —**vileness** *n* [U]

vil·i·fy /ˈvɪləˌfaɪ; ˈvɪlɪfaɪ/ *v* [T] *formal* to say bad things about someone, especially things that are not true, in order to influence other people against them【正式】诬蔑, 中伤, 诽谤 —**vilification** /ˌvɪləfəˈkeʃən; ˌvɪlɪfɪˈkeɪʃən/ *n* [C]: *his vilification by the popular press* 通俗报刊对他的中伤

vil·la /ˈvɪlə; ˈvɪlə/ *n* [C] **1** a big country house with large gardens〔带有大花园的乡间〕别墅 **2** *BrE* a house in another country that you can rent for your holidays【英】〔国外可出租的〕度假别墅: *a holiday villa* 一幢度假别墅 **3** an ancient Roman house with its own farm〔古罗马带有农场的〕庄园, 邸宅

Vil·la /ˈviə; ˈviːə/, **Pan·cho** /ˈpɑntʃo; ˈpæntʃəʊ/ (about 1878-1923) a Mexican leader of a revolution against the Mexico government 维亚〔(约1878-1923), 墨西哥反政府革命运动的领袖〕

vil·lage /ˈvɪlɪdʒ; ˈvɪlɪdʒ/ *n* [C] **1** *BrE* a very small town in the countryside【英】乡村, 村庄: **village school/sports/life** *The village fête happens every year in May.* 乡村游乐会每年5月举行。**2 the village** the people who live in a village 全体村民: *The whole village came to the wedding.* 全村的人都来参加婚礼。

> **CULTURAL NOTE 文化注释**
> When American people use the word 'village' they usually mean an old, attractive, small town in Europe or a small area of simple houses in a less developed country, for example in Africa. 'Village' is not usually used to talk about places in the US. In British English, however, 'village' is used for small towns in general, whether they are new, busy, old, or quiet. 美国人用到village一词时, 通常指古老迷人的欧洲小镇或者非洲等地欠发达国家小片的简易住房; village通常不用来指代美国的某个地方。然而在英国英语中, village通指小城镇, 不管它们是新是旧, 是喧闹还是平静。

village green /ˌ·· ˈ·/ *n* [C] an area of grass in the middle of an English village〔英国〕村镇(公用)绿地

> **CULTURAL NOTE 文化注释**
> People often think of a game of CRICKET on the village green in the summer as being a very TRADITIONAL English scene. 人们通常把夏季在村镇公用绿地上举行一场板球比赛看成是非常传统的英国场景。

village id·i·ot /ˌ·· ˈ···/ *n* [C] someone living in a village who is very stupid and does not understand the modern world 乡巴佬, 乡下傻子

vil·lag·er /ˈvɪlɪdʒɚ; ˈvɪlɪdʒə/ *n* [C] someone who lives in a village 村民

Village Voice, The /ˈ··, ·/ a weekly newspaper produced in Greenwich Village, the artistic centre of New York City, which includes news and articles about politics, books, films etc, and alternative entertainment《村声周报》〔在纽约市艺术中心格林尼治村编印的一份周报, 刊登政治、新书、电影、另类娱乐等方面的报道与评论〕

vil·lain /ˈvɪlən; ˈvɪlən/ *n* [C] **1** the main bad character in a film, play, or story〔电影、戏剧或小说中的〕主要反面人物, 反派角色 **2** *BrE informal* a bad person or criminal【英, 非正式】坏人; 罪犯: *Watch him – he's a bit of a villain!* 提防他——他不是好人! **3 the villain of the piece** *often humorous* the person or thing that has caused all the trouble in a particular situation【常幽默】首犯, 主要肇事者; 为害的事物: *The CIA is commonly regarded as the villain of the piece.* 中央情报局被普遍视为惹祸者。

vil·lain·ous /ˈvɪlənəs; ˈvɪlənəs/ *adj* **1** *literary* evil【文】邪恶的: *He gave a villainous leer.* 他不怀好意地瞥了一眼。**2** *informal* unpleasant or nasty【非正式】坏透的; 讨厌的: *a villainous smell* 讨厌的气味

vil·lain·y /ˈvɪlənɪ; ˈvɪləni/ *n* [U] evil or criminal behaviour 恶行; 罪恶的行为

-ville /vɪl; vɪl/ *suffix old-fashioned slang, especially AmE*【过时, 俚, 尤美】**dullsville/squaresville etc** a place or thing that is dull etc 令人厌倦的地方[事物等]: *This party is really dullsville.* 这个聚会真是无聊极了。

vil·lein /ˈvɪlɪn; ˈvɪlɪn/ *n* [C] a poor farm worker in the Middle Ages who was given a small piece of land in return for working on the land of a rich lord〔中世纪的〕农奴, 佃农 —compare 比较 PEASANT (1)

Vilnius /ˈvɪlnɪəs; ˈvɪlniəs/ the capital city of Lithuania 维尔纽斯〔立陶宛首都〕

vim /vɪm; vɪm/ *n* [U] *old-fashioned* energy【过时】精力, 活力: *bursting with vim and vigour* 精神焕发

vin·ai·grette /ˌvɪnəˈgrɛt; ˌvɪnɪˈgret/ *n* [U] a mixture of oil, VINEGAR, salt, and pepper that you put on a SALAD〔油、醋、盐、胡椒混合成的〕沙拉调味汁

Vinci —see 见 LEONARDO DA VINCI

vin·di·cate /ˈvɪndəˌket; ˈvɪndɪkeɪt/ *v* [T] *formal*【正式】**1** to prove that someone or something is right or true; JUSTIFY 证明…正确[属实]: **vindicate an idea/method/decision** *Your decision not to resign has been fully vindicated.* 事实充分证明你不辞职的决定是正确的。**2** to prove that someone who was blamed for something is in fact not guilty 证明…清白; 为…辩护, 为…辩白: *The outcome of the trial vindicates Howells completely.* 庭审结果彻底证明了豪厄尔斯的清白。—**vindication** /ˌvɪndəˈkeʃən; ˌvɪndɪˈkeɪʃən/ *n* [singular,U]: *Improved economic growth is seen as a vindication of government policies.* 人们认为经济增长加快证明了政府决策的正确。

vin·dic·tive /vɪnˈdɪktɪv; vɪnˈdɪktɪv/ *adj* deliberately cruel and unfair, especially to someone who has harmed you 报复(性)的; 怀恨在心的; 恶意的: *After the divorce Joan's ex-husband became increasingly vindictive.* 离婚后, 琼的前夫报复心越来越重。—**vindictively** *adv*: *"That'll teach her," he thought vindictively.* "这对她倒是个教训。"他恶狠狠地想道。—**vindictiveness** *n* [U]

vine /vaɪn; vaɪn/ *n* [C] **1** a plant that produces GRAPES 葡萄属植物; 葡萄藤 **2** *technical* any plant that has thin twisting stems and grows up walls or posts or along the ground【术语】藤本植物, 攀缘植物

vin·e·gar /ˈvɪnɪgɚ; ˈvɪnɪgə/ *n* [U] an acid tasting liquid made from MALT or wine that is used to improve the taste of food or to preserve it 醋

vin·e·gar·y /ˈvɪnɪgərɪ; ˈvɪnɪgəri/ *adj* **1** tasting of vinegar 酸的 **2** bad-tempered and always ready to say unkind things 尖酸的; 刻薄的; 乖戾的

vine·yard /ˈvɪnjɚd; ˈvɪnjəd/ *n* [C] a piece of land where VINES are grown in order to produce wine 葡萄园

vi·no /ˈvino; ˈviːnəʊ/ *n* [U] *informal* wine【非正式】(葡萄)酒

vi·nous /ˈvaɪnəs; ˈvaɪnəs/ *adj formal*【正式】**1** connected with wine (似)酒的; 有酒味的; 由酒引起的 **2** having the colour of red wine 有红葡萄酒颜色的

vin·tage[1] /ˈvɪntɪdʒ; ˈvɪntɪdʒ/ *adj* **1** vintage wine is good quality wine made in a particular year〔某特定年份中酿制的酒〕佳酿的 **2** showing all the best or most typical qualities of something 最好的; 最典型的: *His latest film is vintage Spielberg.* 斯皮尔伯格最近的一部电影是他的代表作。**3** *often humorous* old【常幽默】旧式的, 老式的: *Our plane was a vintage Cessna.* 我们的飞机是一架老式的塞斯纳小型飞机。**4 vintage year a)** a year when a good quality wine was produced 美酒酿成的年份 **b)** a year when something of very good quality was produced 某高品质事物的出产年份: *1963 was not a vintage year for movies.* 1963年是电影业不景气的一年。

vintage[2] *n* [C] a particular year in which a wine is made 酒的酿造年份: *1961 was a very good vintage.* 1961年是酿酒的好年份。

vintage car /ˌ·· ˈ·/ *n* [C] *BrE* a car made between 1919 and 1930【英】〔1919-1930年间制造的〕老爷车

vint·ner /ˈvɪntnɚ; ˈvɪntnə/ *n* [C] someone who buys and sells wines 酒商

vi·nyl /ˈvaɪnɪl; ˈvaɪnḷl/ *n* [U] **1** a type of strong plastic 乙烯基（塑料）: *a vinyl chair* 乙烯基塑料椅子 | *vinyl flooring* 乙烯基地板材料 **2** a word for records that are played on a RECORD PLAYER, used when comparing them to CDs or TAPES 乙烯基唱片: *This album is no longer available on vinyl.* 这张专辑的乙烯基唱片版已买不到了。

vi·o·la /vɪˋolə; viˈəʊlə/ *n* [C] a musical instrument like a VIOLIN but larger and with a lower sound 中提琴

vi·o·late /ˋvaɪəˌlet; ˈvaɪəleɪt/ *v* [T] **1** to disobey or do something against an official agreement, law, principle etc 违背，违反；侵犯: *practices that violate health and safety regulations* 违反健康与安全条例的做法 | *The arrest and detention of the protestors violated their civil liberties.* 逮捕和拘留抗议者是侵犯了他们的公民自由。**2** *formal* to break open a grave, or force your way into a holy place without showing any respect【正式】（用暴力）打开〔坟墓〕；强行进入〔圣地〕；亵渎: *The thieves violated the graves searching for gold.* 盗贼们为寻找黄金而掘开了坟墓。**3 violate the peace/privacy of** *literary* to suddenly spoil a place or situation so that it is no longer peaceful or private【文】破坏…的和平/惊扰…的独处 **4** *literary* to force a woman to have sex; RAPE【文】强奸 —**violator** *n* [C]

vi·o·la·tion /ˌvaɪəˋleʃən; ˌvaɪəˈleɪʃən/ *n* [C,U] **1** an action that breaks a law, agreement, principle etc 违背，违反〔官方协议、法律、原则等〕: *human rights violations* 违反人权 | [+of] *violations of the ceasefire* 违反停火协议 | **in violation of** *The court's ruling is in violation of the UN Charter.* 法院的裁决违反了联合国宪章。| *a violation of the 3-second rule in basketball* 违反了篮球的三秒规则 **2** [C,U] *formal* an action that causes harm or damage by treating someone or their possessions without respect【正式】侵害；妨害；妨碍: [+of] *I felt her visits were a violation of my privacy.* 我认为她几次三番地来妨碍了我的私生活。| *He regarded the burglary as a violation of his home.* 他把这次偷盗视为对他住宅的侵害。

[S2] [W2] **vi·o·lence** /ˋvaɪələns; ˈvaɪələns/ *n* [U] **1** behaviour that is intended to hurt other people physically〔指伤害他人身体的〕暴力（行为）: *There is too much sex and violence shown on television.* 电视上性和暴力场面太多了。| *sporadic outbreaks of violence* 零星发生的暴力事件 | *robbery with violence* 暴力抢劫 | **domestic violence** (=violence between family members) 家庭暴力 | **act of violence** *acts of violence against the new immigrants* 针对新移民的暴力行为 | **resort to violence** (=use violence when nothing else is effective) 诉诸暴力 **2** an angry way of speaking or reacting〔言语或反应的〕愤怒；激烈: *She spoke with a violence that surprised them both.* 她言辞激烈，令他们俩都很惊讶。**3** extreme force 极大[强烈]的力量: *the violence of the wind* 猛烈的风 **4 do violence to** *formal* to spoil something【正式】破坏，对…损害

[S3] [W3] **vi·o·lent** /ˋvaɪələnt; ˈvaɪələnt/ *adj*

1 ▶ACTION 动作，行为◀ involving actions that are intended to injure or kill people, by hitting them, shooting them etc 暴力的；暴力引起的: *violent crimes such as murder or rape* 谋杀或强奸等暴力犯罪 | *violent clashes between the police and demonstrators* 警察和示威者之间发生的暴力冲突 | **violent death** (=murder) 惨死 *He met a violent death at the hands of the mob.* 他惨死在暴徒手中。

2 ▶PERSON 人◀ likely to attack, hurt, or kill other people 狂暴的，凶暴的: *My father was a violent and dangerous man.* 我父亲脾气暴躁，是个危险人物。| **turn/get violent** (=suddenly become violent)〔突然〕变得暴躁不安 *Keep the handcuffs on the prisoner in case he turns violent.* 别打开犯人的手铐，以防他发狂。

3 ▶ARGUMENT/WORDS 论据/言辞◀ showing very strong angry emotions or opinions〔情绪、意见等〕愤怒的；激烈的: *They had a violent quarrel over Dave's drinking.* 他们为戴夫喝酒的事而大吵了一架。| *His speech was full of violent denunciations of the government's promises.* 他的发言满篇都是对政府承诺的猛烈谴责。

4 ▶EMOTIONS 情绪◀ strong and very difficult to control 极端的；暴躁的: *She has a violent temper.* 她脾气暴躁。| *They took a violent dislike to each other.* 他们彼此极端厌恶。

5 violent film/play/drama a film etc that shows a lot of violent actions 暴力影片/戏/剧

6 violent storm/earthquake/explosion etc a storm etc that happens with a lot of force 强烈的风暴/地震/爆炸等

7 a violent headache/fit/coughing etc a physical feeling or reaction that is very painful or difficult to control 剧烈的头痛/痉挛/咳嗽等

8 ▶COLOUR 颜色◀ extremely bright〔色彩〕强烈的，非常明艳的: *Her cheeks turned a violent red colour.* 她的双颊腾地变得通红。—**violently** *adv*: *She became violently aggressive.* 她变得咄咄逼人，气势汹汹。| *Matthew trembled violently.* 马修颤抖得很厉害。

vi·o·let /ˋvaɪəlɪt; ˈvaɪəlḷt/ *n* [C] **1** a small plant with sweet-smelling dark purple flowers 紫罗兰 —see also 另见 SHRINKING VIOLET **2** [C,U] a colour between purple and blue 蓝紫色 —**violet** *adj* —see picture on page A5 参见 A5 页图

vi·o·lin /ˌvaɪəˋlɪn; ˌvaɪəˈlɪn/ *n* [C] the smallest instrument in the group of wooden musical instruments that are played by pulling a special stick across wire strings 小提琴 —**violinist** *n* [C]

vi·o·lin·cel·lo /viəlanˋtʃɛlo; ˌvaɪəlɪnˈtʃeləʊ/ *n* [C] a CELLO 大提琴

VIP /ˌvi aɪ ˋpi; ˌviː aɪ ˈpiː/ *n* [C] a very important person; someone who is very famous or powerful and is treated with special care and respect 要人；大人物: *the VIP lounge at the airport* 机场贵宾休息室

vi·per /ˋvaɪpɚ; ˈvaɪpə/ *n* [C] **1** a small poisonous snake 蝰蛇〔小毒蛇〕**2** *literary* someone who behaves in a nasty way and harms other people【文】阴险恶毒的人

vi·ra·go /vəˋrego; vḷˈrɑːgəʊ/ *n* [C] *formal* a BAD-TEMPERED woman with a loud voice【正式】泼妇，悍妇

vi·ral /ˋvaɪrəl; ˈvaɪərəl/ *adj* connected with or caused by a VIRUS 病毒（性）的，病毒引起的: *viral pneumonia* 病毒性肺炎

Vir·gil, Vergil /ˋvɝdʒɪl; ˈvɜːdʒḷl/ (70-19 BC) an ancient Roman poet whose best-known poem is *The Aeneid*, a long EPIC poem telling the story of how Aeneas left the city of Troy and eventually arrived in Italy 维吉尔〔（公元前70年-前19年），古罗马诗人。最著名的作品为长篇史诗《埃涅阿斯纪》，讲述埃涅阿斯离开特洛伊城并最终抵达意大利的故事〕

vir·gin[1] /ˋvɝdʒɪn; ˈvɜːdʒḷn/ *n* [C] **1** someone who has never had sex 处女 **2 the Virgin Mary** the mother of Jesus 圣母马利亚

virgin[2] *adj* **1 virgin land/forest/soil etc** land etc that is still in its natural state and has not been used or changed by people 处女地/原始森林/未开垦地等: **virgin snow** (=fresh and not spoiled) 初雪 **2** [only before noun 仅用于名词前] without sexual experience 贞洁的: *a virgin bride* 贞洁的新娘

vir·gin·al /ˋvɝdʒɪnḷ; ˈvɜːdʒḷnəl/ *adj* like a virgin 处女（般）的

vir·gin·als /ˋvɝdʒɪnḷz; ˈvɜːdʒḷnəlz/ *n* [plural] a small square musical instrument like a piano with no legs, popular in the 16th and 17th centuries 维金纳琴〔16 和 17 世纪流行的一种小方形钢琴状乐器，无支架〕

virgin birth /ˌ‥ ˋ‥/ *n* [singular] the birth of Jesus, which Christians believe was caused by God, not by sex between a man and a woman 圣灵感孕〔基督徒相信的耶稣基督的诞生方式〕

Vir·gin·i·a /vɚˋdʒɪnjə; vəˈdʒɪniə/ **1** abbreviation 缩写为 **VA** a state on the east coast of the US, south of Washington, D.C., which is one of the 13 original states of the US 弗吉尼亚州〔美国东海岸一州，位于华盛顿特区以南，为美国最早的13个州之一〕—see also 另见 WEST VIRGINIA **2** [U] a type of tobacco grown originally in the US state of Virginia 弗吉尼亚烟草〔一种最初在美国弗吉尼亚州种植的烟草〕

vir·gin·i·a creep·er /vɚˌdʒɪnjə ˋkripɚ; vɜːˌdʒɪniə ˈkriːpə/ *n* [C,U] a garden plant that grows up walls and has large leaves that turn deep red in autumn 五叶地锦〔一种攀爬于墙、秋天叶子会变红的大叶植物〕; WOODBINE *AmE*【美】

Virgin Is·lands, the /ˈ‥ ˌ‥/ a group of about 100 small islands in the east Caribbean Sea, some of which are ruled by the US as the US Virgin Islands, and some by the UK, as the British Virgin Islands 维尔京群岛〔位于加勒比海东部，包括约100个小岛，其中部分归美国所有，称美属维尔京群岛，部分归英国所有，称英属维尔京群岛〕

vir·gin·i·ty /vɚˋdʒɪnətɪ; vɜːˈdʒɪnḷti/ *n* [U] the condition of never having had sex 童贞，处女状态: **lose your virginity** (=have sex for the first time) 失去童贞 *She was 17 when she lost her virginity.* 她 17 岁时失去童贞。—compare 比较 CHASTITY

Virgin Ma·ry, the /ˌ‥ ˈ‥/ in the Christian religion, the mother of Jesus Christ. According to the New Testament of the Bible, when Mary was a young woman an ANGEL came to her from God and told her that she was going to have a baby, although she had never had sex, and that the baby would be the son of God. She is especially important to Roman Catholics, who have pictures and statues of her in their churches and homes, and who often pray to her for help. 圣母马利亚〔基督教中耶稣基督之母。据《圣经·新约》记载，马利亚还年轻时，上帝派使者降临到她身边，告诉她即将怀孕，尽管她从未与人有过性行为，并且

告诉她所生的婴孩将是上帝之子。马利亚在天主教徒中享有崇高的地位，他们在教堂及家中供奉马利亚的画像和塑像，向她祈求帮助〕

Virgin Queen, the /ˌ··ˈ·/ a name sometimes given to the English queen, Elizabeth I, because she never married 贞洁女王〔有时指英国女王伊丽莎白一世，因她终身未嫁，故名〕

Vir·go /ˈvɝgo; ˈvɜːgəʊ/ *n* **1** [singular] the sixth sign of the ZODIAC, represented by a young woman, and believed to affect the character and life of people born between August 23 and September 22 处女座，室女座；室女宫〔黄道十二宫的第六宫〕 **2** [C] someone who was born between August 23 and September 22 生于室女宫时段〔8月23日至9月22日〕的人

vir·ile /ˈvɪrəl; ˈvɪraɪl/ *adj* **1** looking or behaving in a way that is typical of a man by being strong, brave, full of energy etc and therefore sexually attractive 有男子气概的；充满阳刚活力的：*He had a muscular and virile body.* 他长得身强体壮，威武雄健。**2** virile qualities and actions show typically male strength and energy〔特质和行动〕强劲的，强健的，雄浑的：*virile sports such as rugby* 像橄榄球这样的典型男子运动项目

vi·ril·i·ty /vəˈrɪləti; vəˈrɪlɪti/ *n* [U] **1** the typically male quality of being strong, brave, and full of energy, in a way that is sexually attractive 雄壮；男子气概 **2** the ability of a man to have sex; POTENCY〔男性〕生殖能力

vi·rol·o·gy /vaɪˈrɑlədʒɪ; vaɪəˈrɒlədʒi/ *n* [U] the scientific study of VIRUS*es* or of the diseases caused by them 病毒学

vir·tu·al /ˈvɝtʃuəl; ˈvɜːtʃuəl/ *adj* **1 virtual peace/darkness/destruction etc** something that is so nearly complete peace etc that any difference is unimportant 实际上的和平/黑暗/毁灭等：*We have achieved virtual perfection in sound reproduction.* 我们在声音复制方面已经取得实际上的完美效果。| **be a virtual certainty/impossibility etc** (=be almost certain, impossible etc) 几乎是肯定/不可能的等 *Car ownership is a virtual necessity when you live in the country.* 住在乡下，拥有汽车几乎是必要的。**2 virtual leader/prisoner etc** someone who is in fact a leader, prisoner etc but not officially one 事实上的领袖/囚犯等：*The president was so much under his wife's influence that she was the virtual ruler of the country.* 总统受其妻子的影响很大，以至她成了国家实际上的统治者。

vir·tu·al·ly /ˈvɝtʃuəlɪ; ˈvɜːtʃuəli/ *adv* so nearly that any difference is not important; ALMOST 实际上，事实上；差不多：*Many species of wild animals have virtually disappeared from the face of the earth.* 许多野生动物物种实际上已经从地球上消失了。| *Virtually all the children come to school by bus.* 几乎所有儿童都是乘公共汽车来上学的。

virtual re·al·i·ty /ˌ··· ·ˈ···/ *n* [U] an image produced by a computer that surrounds the person looking at it and seems almost real 虚拟现实

vir·tue /ˈvɝtʃu; ˈvɜːtʃuː/ *n* **1** [U] *formal* moral goodness of character and behaviour【正式】善；德：*a man of the highest virtue* 品德极为高尚的人 —opposite 反义词 VICE **2** [C] a particular good quality in someone's character 美德；德行：*Among her many virtues are loyalty, courage and truthfulness.* 忠诚、勇敢和坦率是她诸多美德中的一部分。**3** [C,U] an advantage that makes something better or more useful than something else 优点，长处：*Free trade has a number of virtues.* 自由贸易有许多优点。| **the virtue of** *The Johnson plan has the virtue of flexibility.* 约翰逊的计划优点是灵活。**4 by/in virtue of** *formal* by means of or as a result of something【正式】凭借；由于，因为：*She became a British citizen by virtue of her marriage.* 她通过结婚成了英国公民。**5 make a virtue of necessity** to get an advantage out of doing something that you have to do 爽爽快快[心甘情愿]地做非做不可的事

vir·tu·os·i·ty /ˌvɝtʃuˈɑsəti; ˌvɜːtʃuˈɒsɪti/ *n* [U] *formal* a very high degree of skill in performing【正式】〔表演方面的〕精湛技巧，高超技艺：*the violinist's incredible virtuosity* 小提琴演奏家那不可思议的精湛技巧

vir·tu·o·so /ˌvɝtʃuˈoso; ˌvɜːtʃuˈəʊsəʊ/ *n* [C] someone who is a very skilful performer, especially in music〔尤指音乐上的〕大演奏家，艺术大师：*a virtuoso performance* 名家表演

vir·tu·ous /ˈvɝtʃuəs; ˈvɜːtʃuəs/ *adj* **1** *formal* behaving in a very honest and moral way【正式】有德行的；正直的：*Thomas Dunlop was a virtuous man and a leader in the community.* 托马斯·邓洛普为人正直，是社区的领导。**2** too satisfied with your own good behaviour and showing this in a way that annoys other people 自命清高的；自以为高尚的：*She threw up her hands in virtuous indignation.* 她双手挥过头顶，显出自以为是的愤慨。—**virtuously** *adv* —**virtuousness** *n* [U]

vir·u·lent /ˈvɪrulənt; ˈvɪrɪlənt/ *adj* **1** *formal* virulent emotions or speeches are full of hatred and very strongly expressed【正式】〔情感或言辞〕充满仇恨的，刻毒的，恶毒的：*virulent anti-Semitism* 恶毒的反犹太主义 **2** a poison, disease etc that is virulent is very dangerous and affects people very quickly〔毒药、疾病等〕剧毒的，迅速致命的：*a virulent form of malaria* 恶性疟疾 —**virulence** *n* [U]: *the virulence of an epidemic* 流行病的致命性 —**virulently** *adv*

vi·rus /ˈvaɪrəs; ˈvaɪərəs/ *n* **1** [C] a very small living thing, smaller than BACTERIA, that causes infectious illnesses 病毒：*the common cold virus* 普通感冒病毒 | *virus infections* 病毒感染 **2** [C] the illness caused by a virus 病毒性疾病：*She's got some virus.* 她患了病毒性疾病。**3** [C,U] a set of instructions secretly put into a computer, that can destroy information stored in the computer〔电脑〕病毒

vi·sa /ˈvizə; ˈviːzə/ *n* [C] an official mark put on your passport by the representative of a foreign country, that gives you permission to enter, pass through, or leave that country〔护照上的〕签证：**tourist/exit/entry visa** *She came here on a tourist visa, but it has expired.* 她是持旅游签证来这里的，但签证已经到期。—**visa** *v* [T]

Visa card /ˈ·· ·/ also 又作 **Visa** *trademark* a type of CREDIT CARD (=plastic card used to obtain goods and services, which the buyer pays for later) which can be used all over the world【商标】维萨卡，威世卡〔一种全球通用的信用卡〕

vis·age /ˈvɪzɪdʒ; ˈvɪzɪdʒ/ *n* [C] *literary* a face【文】脸；面容

vis-à-vis /ˌviz ə ˈvi; ˌviːz ɑː ˈviː/ *prep formal* in relation to or in comparison with something or someone【正式】关于，对于；同…相比：*the bargaining position of the worker vis-à-vis the employer* 和雇主相比雇员在谈判中所处的地位

vis·ce·ra /ˈvɪsərə; ˈvɪsərə/ *n* [plural] *technical* the large organs inside your body, such as your heart, lungs, stomach etc【术语】内脏，脏腑〈如心、肺、胃等〉

vis·ce·ral /ˈvɪsərəl; ˈvɪsərəl/ *adj* **1** *literary* visceral beliefs and attitudes are the result of strong feelings rather than careful thought【文】〔信仰、态度〕出自内心的，发自肺腑的：*Thatcher's visceral dislike of the European Monetary System* 撒切尔对欧洲货币体系发自肺腑的厌恶 **2** *technical* connected with the viscera【术语】内脏的

vis·cid /ˈvɪsɪd; ˈvɪsɪd/ *adj* VISCOUS 黏性的

vis·count /ˈvaɪkaunt; ˈvaɪkaʊnt/ *n* [C] a British NOBLEMAN with a rank between that of an EARL and a BARON〔英国的〕子爵

vis·count·cy /ˈvaɪkauntsɪ; ˈvaɪkaʊntsi/ *n* [C] the rank or title of a viscount 子爵的地位[头衔]

vis·count·ess /ˈvaɪkauntɪs; ˈvaɪkaʊntɪs/ *n* [C] the wife of a viscount, or a woman who has the rank of a viscount 子爵夫人；女子爵

vis·cous /ˈvɪskəs; ˈvɪskəs/ *adj technical* a viscous liquid is thick and sticky and does not flow easily【术语】〔液体〕黏滞的，黏性的 —**viscosity** /vɪsˈkɑsəti; vɪˈskɒsɪti/ *n* [U]

vise /vaɪs; vaɪs/ *n* [C] the usual American spelling of VICE (4) vice (4) 的一般美式拼法

Vish·nu /ˈvɪʃnu; ˈvɪʃnuː/ one of the three main gods in the Hindu religion. He is 'the Preserver' and has many Avatars (=different forms in which a god can actually be seen), the most important of which is Krishna. 毗湿奴〔印度教的三大主神之一。毗湿奴为守护神，有多种化身，其中最重要的化身为克利须那〕—see also 另见 BRAHMA; SIVA

vis·i·bil·i·ty /ˌvɪzəˈbɪləti; ˌvɪzɪˈbɪlɪti/ *n* [U] **1** how far it is possible to see, especially when this is affected by weather conditions〔尤指受天气状况影响时的〕能见度；视程：*Visibility is down to 20 metres due to heavy fog.* 由于有浓雾，能见度降至20米。| **good/poor visibility** *The search for survivors was abandoned because of poor visibility.* 由于能见度低，对幸存者的搜寻工作已经放弃。**2** the fact of something being easy to see 清晰度，明显度

vis·i·ble /ˈvɪzəbl̩; ˈvɪzɪbəl/ *adj* **1** something that is visible can be seen 看得见的；可见的：*The outline of the mountains was clearly visible.* 群山的轮廓清晰可见。**2** an effect that is visible is strong enough to be noticed〔影响〕明显的，显然的，可察觉的：*There is a visible change in attitudes to working women.* 人们在对待劳动妇女的态度上有了明显的变化。| *She showed visible signs of annoyance.* 她显然有些不高兴。**3** someone who is visible is always on television, in the newspapers etc〔经常在电视上、报纸上等〕露面的：*highly visible politicians* 高度曝光的政治家

vis·i·bly /ˈvɪzəblɪ; ˈvɪzɪbli/ *adv* in a way that is easy to see or notice 显然，明显地，显而易见地：*He was visibly shaken by her accusation.* 她的指控显然使他大为震惊。

vi·sion /ˈvɪʒən; ˈvɪʒən/ *n*

1 ►SIGHT 视力◄ [U] your ability to see 视力：*With my new glasses my vision is perfect!* 戴上新配的眼镜，我的视力好极

了！| *Tears blurred her vision.* 泪水模糊了她的视线。| **field of vision** (=the area in which you are able to see things) 视野 *As the cars overtake you, they are temporarily outside your field of vision.* 汽车超车时，会暂时处于你的视野之外。| **20-20 vision** (=perfect vision) 极好的视力

2 ▶IDEA 概念◀ [C] a picture in your mind of a possible situation or scene〔对一可能情况或场景的〕构想，设想；念头：[+of] *He conjured up a vision of a world without national divisions.* 他想象出一幅没有国别之差的世界景象。| **have visions of** (=think a situation is likely to happen) 有…的念头，认为…会发生 *The airport bus broke down and Tim had visions of missing his plane.* 机场班车坏了，蒂姆觉得这下赶不上飞机了。

3 ▶IN A DREAM 在梦中◀ [C] something that you seem to see, especially in a dream, as part of a powerful religious experience〔尤指梦中有关宗教的经历〕幻想，幻觉，梦幻：*She had a vision in which Jesus appeared before her.* 她在梦幻中看见耶稣出现在她面前。

4 ▶FUTURE PLANS 未来的计划◀ [U] the knowledge and imagination that are needed in planning for the future with a clear purpose 远见卓识：*At last we have a leader with vision and strong principles.* 我们终于有了一个有远见、原则性强的领导。

5 a vision of innocence/beauty etc *literary* something you see which shows a particular quality or attitude【文】天真/美丽等的形象

6 ▶TELEVISION 电视◀ [U] the quality of a picture that you can see on a television〔电视〕图像（质量）：*interference affecting sound and vision* 对声音和图像的干扰

vi·sion·a·ry[1] /ˈvɪʒənˌɛrɪ; ˈvɪʒənəri/ *adj* **1** having clear ideas of what the world should be like in the future 有远见的，有眼光的：*Le Corbusier was a great visionary architect.* 勒·科布西耶是一个有真知灼见的建筑师。**2** existing only in someone's mind and unlikely to ever exist in the real world 梦幻中的；空想的

visionary[2] *n* [C] **1** someone who has clear ideas and strong feelings about the way something should be in the future 有预见的人；有远见的人：*a visionary with a passionate belief in liberty* 一个崇尚自由、有远见卓识的人 **2** a holy person who has visions (VISION (3)) 看见神灵显现的人；有幻觉的人

S2 W1 **vis·it[1]** /ˈvɪzɪt; ˈvɪzɪ̈t/ *v* **1** [I,T] to go and spend time in a place or with someone, especially for pleasure or interest 参观，游览；拜访，访问：*"Do you live here?" "No, we're just visiting."* "你们住在这里吗？""不，我们只是来旅游的。" | **visit sth** *We hope to visit the Grand Canyon on our trip.* 我们希望旅途中能去游览大峡谷。| **visit sb** *Aunt Jane usually visits us for two or three weeks in the spring.* 简姑妈通常在春天到我们家住上两三周。| [+in/on/at/with] *AmE*【美】*When you are visiting in Washington, be sure to see the Air and Space Museum.* 到华盛顿时，一定要去航空航天博物馆看看。**2** [T] to go to see a doctor, lawyer etc in order to get treatment or advice 去〔医生、律师等〕处就诊[咨询] **3** [T] to go to a place in order to examine it officially 视察，巡视：*The building inspector is visiting the new housing project.* 建筑监察员正在视察这个新的住房项目。**4** [I] *AmE* to talk socially with someone【美】叙谈，闲谈：[+with] *While Mom visited with Phyllis we played in the yard.* 妈妈跟菲莉丝聊天时，我们在院子里玩耍。

visit sth **on** sb/sth *phr v* [T] *especially biblical* to do something to punish someone or show them that you are angry【尤圣经】惩罚某人〔表示愤怒〕：*God's wrath will be visited on sinners.* 上帝一定会惩罚罪人。

> **USAGE NOTE 用法说明: VISIT**
> WORD CHOICE 词语辨析: **visit, go to, go and see, have been to, come and see**
> **Visit** is slightly formal. More often you would say you **go to** a place or **go and see/go to see** a place or a person. visit 为略显正式的用语。表示去某地或到某处观光或探望某人时，更为常用的是 go to 或 go and see/go to see。You might write 可写作：*We visited the Grand Canyon*（我们游览了大峡谷）or 或 *I visited my mother*（我去探望了母亲）but in spoken English you are more likely to say 但在口语中更可能这样说：*We went to the Grand Canyon* or 或 *I went to see my mother.* Note that you would also say 注意，还可以说：*I've been to Hong Kong several times*（我已去过香港好几次了）and 和 *When you are in Tokyo you must come and see me*（你来东京时一定要来看我）。

W3 **visit[2]** *n* [C] **1** an occasion when someone visits a place or person 游览；参观；拜访：[+to] *a visit to New York* 游览纽约 | **on a visit** *We're just here on a short visit.* 我们来这儿只是短期逗留。| **pay sb a visit** *I must pay our new neighbors a visit.* 我必须拜访一下新邻居。| **have a visit from** *I've just had a visit from the police.* 警察刚到我这里来过。| **flying visit** (=a very short visit) 短暂访问 *We made a flying visit to my mother's to pick up the wedding presents.* 我们匆匆去了母亲那儿一趟，拿结婚礼物。**2** an occasion when you see a doctor, lawyer etc for treatment or advice 就诊；法律咨询：**pay a visit** *I must pay a visit to the dentist.* 我得去看牙医。| **home visit** (=when a doctor comes to your home)〔医生〕出诊，探视 **3** *AmE* an occasion when you talk socially with someone, or the time you spend doing this【美】叙谈；闲谈的时间：*Barbara and I had a nice long visit.* 芭芭拉和我作了一次愉快的长谈。

vis·i·ta·tion /ˌvɪzəˈteʃən; ˌvɪzɪ̈ˈteɪʃən/ *n* [C] **1** *formal* an official visit, usually made in order to examine something or someone【正式】视察，巡视：*a parental visitation of the school* 家长对学校的造访 **2** *literary* an event that is believed to be God's punishment for something【文】天谴，天祸：[+of] *visitations of plague, famine, and war* 瘟疫、饥荒及战争等天谴 **3** *humorous* a long visit from someone that you do not want to see【幽默】令人讨厌的过长的拜访

visiting card /ˈ··· ˌ·/ *n* [C] a small card with your name printed on it that people used to give to the people they visited 名片

visiting fire·man /ˌ··· ˈ··/ *n* [C] *especially AmE* an important visitor that you need to entertain in a special way【尤美】〔需给予特别招待的〕贵宾

visiting hours /ˈ··· ˌ·/ *n* [plural] the times during which you can visit people who are ill in hospital〔医院的〕探望时间

visiting pro·fes·sor /ˌ··· ·ˈ··/ *n* [C] a university teacher who has come from another university to teach for a period of time 客座教授

vis·it·or /ˈvɪzɪtɚ; ˈvɪzɪ̈tə/ *n* [C] someone who comes to visit a place or a person 观光者，参观者；访问者，探望者：*They were expecting visitors and had cleaned the house.* 他们把房子打扫得干干净净，等待着来客。| *travel tips for visitors to the USA* 给旅美游客的旅行提示 —see also 另见 HEALTH VISITOR S2 W2

visitors' book /ˈ··· ˌ·/ *n* [C] a book, especially in a church or other important building, in which visitors write their names and addresses〔尤指教堂或其他重要建筑的〕来客登记簿

vi·sor /ˈvaɪzɚ; ˈvaɪzə/ *n* [C] **1** the part of a HELMET (=protective hard hat) that can be lowered to protect your face〔头盔上可移下来保护脸部的〕面甲，脸盔 **2** *AmE* the curved part of a cap that sticks out in front above your eyes【美】帽舌；PEAK[1] (4) *BrE*【英】—see picture at 参见 CAP[1] 图 **3** a flat piece of material above the front window inside a car that can be pulled down to keep the sun out of your eyes; SUN VISOR〔汽车挡风玻璃内上方的〕遮阳板 **4** a curved piece of plastic that you wear on your head so that it sticks out above your eyes and protects them from the sun 护目镜；〔遮阳〕眼罩

vis·ta /ˈvɪstə; ˈvɪstə/ *n* [C] **1** *literary* a far view of beautiful scenery, especially looking between rows of trees, buildings etc【文】〔尤指从成排树木或建筑等中间看出去的〕长条形景色，远景：*The balcony commanded a vista of the harbour.* 从阳台上看海港的景色一览无遗。**2** the possibility of new experiences, ideas, events etc〔对新经历、想法、事件等的〕展望：*Exchange programs open up new vistas for students.* 交流项目为学生拓展了新的前景。

vi·su·al /ˈvɪʒuəl; ˈvɪʒuəl/ *adj* connected with seeing 视觉的，视力的：*visual identification of the subject by a witness* 证人对物件的视觉辨认 | *a powerful visual impact* 强大的视觉效果 W3

visual aid /ˌ··· ˈ·/ *n* [C] something such as a map, picture, film etc that helps people understand, learn, or remember information 直观教具〈如地图、图片、电影等〉

visual arts /ˌ··· ˈ·/ *n* [plural] art such as painting, SCULPTURE etc that you look at, as opposed to literature or music that you read or hear 视觉艺术〈如绘画、雕塑等〉

visual dis·play u·nit /ˌ··· ·ˈ· ˌ··/ *n* [C] VDU〔电脑或文字处理器的〕视频显示器

vi·su·al·ize also 又作 **-ise** *BrE*【英】/ˈvɪʒuəlˌaɪz; ˈvɪʒuəlaɪz/ *v* [T] to form a picture of someone or something in your mind; IMAGINE 设想，想象：*Try to visualize a successful future.* 试着设想一个成功的未来。| **visualize sb doing sth** *Somehow I can't visualize myself teaching adults.* 不知怎的，我想象不出自己教成年人的情景。| **visualize how/what etc** *It's hard to visualize how these tiles will look in our bathroom.* 很难想象这些瓷砖铺在我们浴室里会是什么样子。—**visualization** /ˌvɪʒuələˈzeʃən; ˌvɪʒuəlaɪˈzeɪʃən/ *n* [U]

vi·su·al·ly /ˈvɪʒuəlɪ; ˈvɪʒuəli/ *adv* **1** in appearance 表面上，外观上：*a visually stunning production* 看起来极好的生产情况 **2 visually impaired/handicapped** unable to see normally 视力受损的/有缺陷的：*She teaches visually impaired children.* 她

给有视力障碍的孩子讲课。**3** if you explain something visually, you let people see it by using pictures or films, or by showing real things〔用图画、电影或实物〕直观地〔解释某物〕: *The process is easy to understand when it is demonstrated visually.* 用直观演示，这个过程就容易理解了。

2 **vi·tal** /ˈvaɪtl̩; ˈvaɪtl/ *adj* **1** extremely important and necessary for something to succeed or exist 极其重要的，必不可少的: *Choosing the right equipment is vital.* 挑选合适的设备极其重要。| **[+to]** *Such measures are vital to national security.* 这些措施对国家安全是必不可少的。| **[+for]** *Regular exercise is vital for your health.* 经常锻炼对健康非常重要。| **it is vital that** *It is vital that you keep accurate records.* 保持准确的记录非常重要。| **vital importance** *The industry is of vital importance to the national economy.* 工业对国家经济极其重要。| **play a vital role** *Richardson played a vital role in the team's success.* 理查森对本队的成功起了极重要的作用。**2** full of energy in a way that is exciting and attractive 有生命力的；充满活力的，生机勃勃的: *The drawings were crude but wonderfully vital.* 这些绘画虽然粗糙，但充满惊人的活力。| *a strong, vital man* 一个身体强壮、朝气勃勃的男子 **3** [only before noun 仅用于名词前] necessary in order to keep you alive 维持生命所必需的: *the body's vital processes* 基本的生命活动 | *the vital organs* (=heart, brain etc) 要害器官〈如心、脑等〉

vi·tal·i·ty /vaɪˋtælətɪ; vaɪˈtæləti/ *n* [U] **1** great energy and cheerfulness 精力；活力: *Despite her eighty years Elsie was full of vitality.* 尽管已 80 岁了，埃尔茜依然充满活力。**2** the ability of an organization, country etc to continue working effectively〔组织、国家等的〕生命力: *The process of restructuring has injected some much-needed vitality into the company.* 重组为公司注入了一些急需的生命力。

vi·tal·ly /ˋvaɪtl̩ɪ; ˈvaɪtl-i/ *adv* in a very important or necessary way 极大地: *The way we treat our planet now will vitally affect the future of the human race.* 我们现在对待地球的方式将极大地影响人类的未来。| **vitally important** (=extremely important) 极其重要的 *It's vitally important that you all attend the meeting.* 你们都要参加会议，这极为重要。

vi·tals /ˋvaɪtl̩z; ˈvaɪtlz/ *n* [plural] *old use* the parts of your body that are necessary to keep you alive, such as your heart and lungs【旧】〔维持生命的〕重要器官〈如心、肺等〉

vital sta·tis·tics /ˌ‥ ·ˈ··/ *n* [plural] **1** *BrE humorous* a woman's chest, waist, and HIP measurements【英，幽默】妇女的三围（尺寸）〔指腰围、胸围和臀围〕**2** figures that show the number of births, deaths, marriages etc within a population 人口动态统计〔指对出生、死亡、婚姻等人口资料的统计〕

vit·a·min /ˋvaɪtəmɪn; ˈvɪtəmɪn/ *n* [C] a natural substance found in food that is necessary for good health 维生素，维他命: *Milk is rich in vitamins.* 牛奶富含维生素。| *vitamin pills* 维生素片 | **vitamin A/B/C etc** (=a particular type of vitamin) 维生素 A/B/C 等 *Lack of vitamin A can cause blindness.* 缺乏维生素A可导致失明。

vi·ti·ate /ˋvɪʃɪˌet; ˈvɪʃieɪt/ *v* [T usually passive 一般用被动态] *formal* to make something less effective or spoil it【正式】削弱〔某物〕的效能；破坏，损害: *The conclusions were vitiated by doubts concerning the scientific evidence.* 由于科学依据方面存疑，结论无效。—**vitiation** /ˌvɪʃɪˋeʃən; ˌvɪʃiˈeɪʃən/ *n* [U]

vit·i·cul·ture /ˋvɪtɪˌkʌltʃɚ; ˈvɪtɪkʌltʃə/ *n* [U] the study or practice of growing GRAPES for making wine〔为酿酒的〕葡萄栽培（学）；葡萄栽培术

vit·re·ous /ˋvɪtrɪəs; ˈvɪtriəs/ *adj* made of or looking like glass 玻璃做的；玻璃（状）的

vit·ri·fy /ˋvɪtrəˌfaɪ; ˈvɪtrɪfaɪ/ *v* [I,T] *technical* if a substance vitrifies or is vitrified, it changes into glass【术语】（使）成玻璃，（使）玻璃化 —**vitrification** /ˌvɪtrɪfəˋkeʃən; ˌvɪtrɪfɪˈkeɪʃən/ *n* [U]

vit·ri·ol /ˋvɪtrɪəl; ˈvɪtriəl/ *n* [U] **1** *literary* very cruel remarks that are intended to hurt someone's feelings【文】尖刻[刻薄]的话；讽刺 **2** *old-fashioned* SULPHURIC ACID【过时】硫酸

vit·ri·ol·ic /ˌvɪtrɪˋɑlɪk; ˌvɪtriˈɒlɪk◂/ *adj* vitriolic language is very cruel and intended to hurt someone's feelings〔言语〕尖刻的，辛辣的: *a vitriolic attack on homosexuals* 对同性恋者的刻薄攻击 —**vitriolically** /-klɪ; -kli/ *adv*

vitro *n* —see 见 IN VITRO FERTILIZATION

vi·tu·pe·ra·tion /vaɪˌtupəˋreʃən; vɪˌtjuːpəˈreɪʃən/ *n* [U] *formal* angry and cruel criticism【正式】谩骂，咒骂，辱骂: *the subject of daily vituperation and abuse* 每日辱骂的对象

vi·tu·pe·ra·tive /vaɪˋtupəˌretɪv; vɪˈtjuːpərətɪv/ *adj formal* full of angry and cruel criticism【正式】谩骂的，充满辱骂的

vi·va[1] /ˋvaɪvə; ˈvaɪvə/ *n* [C] *BrE informal* a spoken examination taken at the end of a university course; VIVA VOCE【英，非正式】〔大学某门课程结束时的〕口试，口头测验

viva[2] *interjection* used to show that you approve of someone and want them to continue to exist or be successful 万岁！〔表示赞许或祝愿的欢呼声〕: *Viva Eliot!* 艾略特万岁！

vi·va·ce /vɪˋvɑtʃɪ; vɪˈvɑːtʃi/ *adj, adv* music that is vivace is played quickly and with a lot of energy〔音乐〕活泼的[地]，轻快的[地]

vi·va·cious /vaɪˋveʃəs; vɪˈveɪʃəs/ *adj* a woman who is vivacious has a lot of energy and a happy attractive manner〔女性〕活泼的，快活的，生气勃勃的: *a vivacious and outgoing personality* 活泼外向的个性 —**vivaciously** *adv* —**vivaciousness** *n* [U] —**vivacity** /vaɪˋvæsətɪ; vɪˈvæsɪti/ *n* [U]

Vi·val·di, An·to·ni·o /ænˋtonɪo; ænˈtəʊniəʊ/ (1678-1741) an Italian COMPOSER who wrote many OPERAS and a lot of church music, but is most famous for *The Four Seasons*, one of the most popular pieces of CLASSICAL music 维瓦尔第〔(1678-1741)，意大利作曲家。他创作有大量歌剧和宗教音乐，其中以《四季》最为著名，为古典音乐中最受欢迎的曲目之一〕

vi·var·i·um /vaɪˋvɛrɪəm; vaɪˈveəriəm/ *n* [C] a place indoors where animals are kept in conditions that are as similar as possible to their natural environment〔模拟自然生态环境的〕动物饲养室

viv·a voc·e /ˌvaɪvə ˋvosɪ; ˌvaɪvə ˈvəʊsi/ *n* [C] *BrE formal* a VIVA[1]【英，正式】口试，口头测验

viv·id /ˋvɪvɪd; ˈvɪvɪd/ *adj* **1** vivid memories, dreams, descriptions etc are so clear that they seem real〔记忆、梦境、描述等〕生动的，逼真的，清晰的: *a vivid account of their journey across the desert* 对他们穿越沙漠旅行的生动记述 **2 vivid imagination** an ability to imagine unlikely situations very clearly 活跃的想象力 **3** vivid colours or patterns are very bright〔色彩、图案〕鲜艳的；鲜明的: *The lake was a vivid blue.* 湖水湛蓝。—**vividly** *adv*: *I can vividly remember the day we met.* 我能清楚地记得我们相遇的那一天。—**vividness** *n* [U]

viv·i·sec·tion /ˌvɪvəˋsɛkʃən; ˌvɪvɪˈsekʃən/ *n* [U] the practice of cutting open the bodies of living animals in order to do medical or scientific tests on them〔为做医学或科学实验而进行的〕动物活体解剖 —**vivisectionist** *n* [C]

vix·en /ˋvɪksn̩; ˈvɪksən/ *n* [C] **1** a female FOX[1] (1) 雌狐 **2** *old-fashioned* a BAD-TEMPERED woman【过时】悍妇，泼妇 —**vixenish** *adj*

Viz /vɪz; vɪz/ *trademark* a British COMIC (=magazine with stories told in pictures) for adults, which is full of rude jokes and is popular especially with students and other young adults. Most of its characters are STEREOTYPES (=people who are supposed to be very typical representatives of a certain type of person).【商标】《味滋》〔英国成人连环漫画，充斥着粗俗的笑话，尤为学生和青年人喜爱。画中多为脸谱型人物〕

viz *adv formal* used to introduce specific details that make your meaning clearer; NAMELY【正式】即，也就是，就是说

vi·zier /vɪˋzɪr; vɪˈzɪə/ *n* [C] an important politician in certain Muslim countries in the past 维齐尔〔旧时某些伊斯兰国家的高官、大臣〕

VJ /ˌvi ˋdʒe; ˌviː ˈdʒeɪ/ *n* [C] a VIDEO JOCKEY〔尤指播放流行音乐的〕电视音乐节目主持人

V-J Day /ˌvi ˋdʒe ˌde; ˌvɪ ˈdʒeɪ ˌdeɪ/ Victory over Japan Day; August 15th 1945, the day on which victory over Japan in World War II was celebrated 抗日战争胜利日，对日作战胜利日〔即 1945 年 8 月 15 日，纪念二战时期对日战争的胜利〕

Vlad·i·vos·tok /ˌvlædɪˋvɑstɑk; ˌvlædɪˈvɒstɒk/ a port and city on the east coast of Russia. The Trans-Siberian railway goes from Moscow to Vladivostok. 符拉迪沃斯托克，又名海参崴〔俄罗斯东部海岸一港口城市。西伯利亚大铁路自莫斯科延伸至此〕

V-neck /ˋvi nɛk; ˈviː nek/ *n* [C] an opening for the neck shaped like the letter V, in a piece of clothing V 形（衣）领，鸡心领 —**V-necked** *adj*: *a V-necked sweater* 鸡心领毛线衫 —see picture on page A17 参见 A17 页图

VOA, the /ˌvi o ˋe; ˌviː əʊ ˈeɪ/ the abbreviation of 缩写 = the VOICE OF AMERICA

vo·cab /ˋvokæb; ˈvəʊkæb/ *n* [U] *informal* VOCABULARY (5)【非正式】词汇表

vo·cab·u·la·ry /vəˋkæbjəˌlɛrɪ; vəˈkæbjʊləri/ *n* **1** [C,U] all the words that someone knows, learns, or uses〔一个人学会或使用的〕词汇量，语汇: *Considering he's only six, he has an excellent vocabulary.* 考虑到他只有六岁，他的词汇量已经相当大了。| **wide/limited vocabulary** (=a large or small vocabulary) 丰富/有限的词汇量 | **increase/extend/build up/enrich your vocabulary** *You should read more literature to enrich your vocabulary.* 你应该多看些文学作品，以丰富你的词汇量。**2** [C,U] the words that are typically used when talking about a particular subject

专业词汇，术语: *Most technical jobs use a specialized vocabulary.* 许多技术性工作都要用专业词汇。| [+of] *the vocabulary of politics* 政治学词汇 **3** [C] all the words in a particular language〔某种语言的〕词汇 **4 the word failure/compromise etc is not in sb's vocabulary** used to say that someone never thinks of accepting failure etc 某人的词汇中没有失败/妥协等词语〔指从不接受失败、妥协等〕 **5** [C] a list of words with explanations of their meanings, in a book for learning foreign languages〔外语教科书中有释义的〕词汇表 **6** [C,U] a list of the codes (CODE[1] (7)) or terms (TERM[1] (5)) used in a computer system〔电脑系统的〕词汇表，符号集

vo·cal[1] /ˈvokl; ˈvəʊkəl/ *adj* **1** protesting or complaining strongly and loudly about something 强烈反对的，大声抱怨的；直言不讳的，说话不客气的: *a vocal critic of the government* 对政府直言不讳的批评者 **2** [only before noun 仅用于名词前] connected with the voice 声音的；使用嗓音的: *The song suited the singer's vocal range.* 这首歌适合这位歌手的音域。—**vocally** *adv*

vocal[2] *n* [C usually plural 一般用复数] the part of a piece of music that is sung rather than played on an instrument〔音乐的〕歌唱部分〔相对于乐器演奏部分〕: *vocals by John Lennon and Paul McCartney* 约翰·列侬和保罗·麦卡特尼的演唱

vocal cords, vocal chords /ˈ· · ·/ *n* [plural] thin pieces of muscle in your throat that produce sounds when you are speaking 声带

vo·cal·ist /ˈvoklɪst; ˈvəʊkəl̩ɪst/ *n* [C] someone who sings popular songs, especially with a band〔尤指与乐队配合演唱流行歌曲的〕歌手 —compare 比较 INSTRUMENTALIST

vo·ca·tion /voˈkeʃən; vəʊˈkeɪʃən/ *n* **1** [C] a job that you do because you have a very strong feeling that doing this job is the purpose of your life, and especially because you want to help other people〔指自己非常热爱的〕工作，职业，使命: *Teaching isn't just a job – it's a vocation.* 教书并不单单是一份工作——它是一种使命。| **find your vocation** *She felt that she had found her vocation when she began writing children's books.* 她开始创作儿童文学后，才感到自己找到了所热爱的工作。—see 见 JOB (USAGE) **2** [C,U] a special ability to do a particular job or activity, especially one that gives service to other people〔尤指从事某种服务性行业的〕素质，才能: [+for] *He has a vocation for teaching.* 他有教书的禀赋。**3** [C,U] a strong belief that you have been chosen by God to be a priest or a NUN; CALLING 神召；天职，〔宗教上的〕使命感: *a vocation for the priesthood* 当牧师的使命感

vo·ca·tion·al /voˈkeʃənl; vəʊˈkeɪʃənəl/ *adj* **vocational training/guidance/course etc** training etc that teaches you the skills you need to do a particular job 职业培训/指导/课程等

voc·a·tive /ˈvɑkətɪv; ˈvɒkətɪv/ *n* [C] *technical* a particular form of a noun in certain languages, used when speaking or writing to someone【术语】〔某些语言中的〕呼格；呼格词 —**vocative** *adj*

vo·cif·er·ate /voˈsɪfəˌret; vəˈsɪfəreɪt/ *v* [I] *formal* to shout loudly, especially when complaining【正式】〔尤指抱怨地〕大叫大嚷 —**vociferation** /voˌsɪfəˈreʃən; vəˌsɪfəˈreɪʃən/ *n* [C, U]

vo·cif·er·ous /voˈsɪfərəs; vəˈsɪfərəs/ *adj formal*【正式】**1** expressing your opinions loudly and strongly〔表述自己观点时〕大声的，激昂的: *vociferous protesters* 吵吵嚷嚷的抗议者 **2** vociferous opinions are loudly and strongly expressed〔意见〕大声疾呼地提出的: *a vociferous debate* 大叫大嚷的辩论 —**vociferously** *adv* —**vociferousness** *n* [U]

vod·ka /ˈvɑdkə; ˈvɒdkə/ *n* [U] a strong clear alcoholic drink from Russia 伏特加〔俄罗斯出产的烈酒〕

Vogue /vog; vəʊg/ *trademark* a fashion magazine for women, which includes photographs of expensive clothes and articles about new fashions, health, and beauty.【商标】《时尚》〔一女性时尚杂志，刊登各类高档服装的图片及时装、健康、美容方面的文章〕

vogue *n* [singular, U] if something is the vogue, it is popular or fashionable for a period of time 时尚；流行: [+for] *the vogue for childbirth at home* 在家中分娩的时尚 | **be in vogue/be the vogue** *Short skirts are very much in vogue just now.* 短裙目前非常流行。

vogue word /ˌ· ˈ·/ *n* [C] a word that is fashionable for a short period of time 时髦词，时兴词

S2 W1 **voice**[1] /vɔɪs; vɔɪs/ *n*

1 ▶SPEAKING 说话◀ [C,U] the sounds that you make when you speak 说话声，嗓音: *He recognized her voice instantly.* 他立刻听出了她的声音。| *I could hear voices in the next room.* 我能听见隔壁房间里的说话声。| **a loud/deep/soft/husky etc voice** *a child with a squeaky voice* 说话尖声尖气的小孩 | **angry/excited/worried etc voice** *the angry voices of disgruntled passengers* 不满意的乘客发出的愤怒声 | **in a deep/angry etc voice** *He spoke in a pleasantly deep voice.* 他说话声音深沉，非常悦耳。| **a small voice** (=a quiet and shy voice) 小而羞怯的声音 | **sb's tone of voice** (=the quality of someone's voice which expresses their attitude) 某人的语气[声调] *I could tell from his tone of voice that he was not impressed.* 我能从他的语气中听出他不感兴趣。| **raise your voice** (=speak more loudly, especially in an angry way)〔尤指生气地〕提高嗓门 *I know what you're saying – there's no need to raise your voice.* 我明白你的意思，你没必要提高嗓门。| **lower/drop your voice** (=speak more quietly) 放低声音 *She moved closer and lowered her voice so Alex wouldn't hear.* 她往前凑了凑，放低了声音，这样亚历克斯就听不见了。| **keep your voice down** *spoken* (=used to tell someone to speak more quietly)【口】小声点 | **at the top of your voice** (=shouting as loudly as you can) 扯着喉咙，放开嗓子〔喊叫〕 *I could hear him screaming and yelling at the top of his voice.* 我能听到他扯着嗓子又喊又叫。| **sb's voice breaks** (=when a boy's voice becomes deeper like a man's) 某人的嗓子变声 *He was 13 and his voice was already starting to break.* 他13岁，嗓子已经开始变声了。—see 见 NOISE[1] (USAGE)

2 deep-voiced/husky-voiced etc having a voice that is deep etc 嗓音低沉的/沙哑的等

3 ▶ABILITY TO SPEAK 说话能力◀ [U] the ability to use your voice 嗓子；发声能力: *You won't have any voice left if you keep shouting like that.* 这么大喊大叫下去，你会喊坏嗓子的。| **close your voice** (=be unable to speak because you have a sore throat) 无法发声〔因嗓子疼而无法讲话〕

4 ▶SINGING 歌唱◀ a) [C,U] the quality of sound you produce when you sing〔唱歌的〕声音，音质: *a young man with a fine singing voice* 音色优美的青年 | **be in good voice** (=be singing well) 唱得好 **b)** [C] a person singing 演唱者: *a piece written for six voices and piano* 为六声部和钢琴谱的曲子

5 ▶OPINION 意见◀ a) [singular,U] the right or ability to express an opinion, to vote, or to influence decisions 表达意见权；发言权；投票权；影响力: **have a voice (in)** *It is important that parents should have a voice in deciding how their children are educated.* 重要的是父母应有权决定其子女受什么样的教育。| **give voice to** (=express opinions or feelings openly) 公开表达〔意见、感情〕 *Only Hartman dared to give voice to their discontent.* 只有哈特曼敢于公开表达他们的不满情绪。**b)** [C] an opinion or wish that is expressed〔表达出的〕意见，愿望: *The government should listen to the voice of the black community.* 政府应该听取黑人社区的呼声。| **dissenting voices** (=people expressing disagreement) 不满的声音 | **add/lend your voice etc** (=express your support for something) 对…表示声援，支持 *Carter lent his powerful voice to the call for disarmament.* 卡特积极响应裁军的呼吁。| **raise your voice against** (=oppose something publicly) 公开反对 *Not a voice was raised against the plan.* 没有一个人反对这项计划。| **make your voice heard** (=express your opinion so that people notice it) 发表意见〔让别人注意〕

6 speak with one voice if a group of people speak with one voice, they all express the same opinion 异口同声，一致地

7 ▶REPRESENTATIVE 代表◀ [singular] a person, organization, newspaper etc that expresses the opinions or wishes of a group of people 喉舌，代言人: *Martin Luther King had become the voice of the Civil Rights Movement.* 马丁·路德·金已成为民权运动的代言人。

8 the voice of reason/sanity/experience etc opinions or ideas that are reasonable, sensible, based on experience etc 合理的想法/明智的意见/经验之谈等: *"Marriage is a very risky business." "Ah, there speaks the voice of experience!"* "结婚是件冒险的事。""啊，这真是经验之谈呀！"

9 inner voice thoughts or feelings which you do not express but which seem to warn you or advise you 内心的想法[感觉]: *My inner voice told me to be cautious.* 我内心的感觉告诉我要小心谨慎。

10 active/passive voice *technical* the form of a verb that shows whether the subject of a sentence does an action or has an action done to it【术语】主动/被动语态

voice[2] *v* [T] **1** to tell people your opinions or feelings about a particular subject 表达，吐露: **voice opinions/doubts etc** *He voiced several objections to the plan.* 他对这项计划提出几点反对理由。**2** *technical* to produce a sound with a movement of the VOCAL CORDS as well as the breath【术语】把…发成浊音

Voice, The *trademark* a British newspaper especially for the black community【商标】《声音》〔英国专门面向黑人社团编印的一种报纸〕

voice box /'· ·/ *n* [C] *not technical* the part of your throat that you use to produce sounds when you speak; LARYNX【非术语】喉(头)

voiced /vɔɪst; vɔɪst/ *adj technical* voiced sounds are made using the VOCAL CORDS. For example /d/ and /g/ are voiced consonants【术语】(发)浊音的〈如/d/和/g/皆为浊辅音〉

voice·less /ˈvɔɪslɪs; ˈvɔɪsləs/ *adj technical* voiceless sounds are made without using the VOCAL CORDS. For example /p/ and /k/ are voiceless consonants【术语】(发)清音的〈如/p/和/k/为清辅音〉

voice mail /'· ·/ *n* [U] a system in which spoken messages are recorded onto a computer so that someone can listen to them later 语音信箱, 留言信箱

Voice of A·mer·i·ca, the /,· · ·'· · ·/ abbreviation 缩写为 VOA a US radio station which broadcasts news and other programmes to other countries 美国之音〔美国一广播电台, 向其他国家播放新闻等节目〕—see also 另见 the WORLD SERVICE

voice-o·ver /'· ·,··/ *n* [C] an explanation or remarks that are spoken on a television advertisement or film by someone who cannot be seen〔电视广告、电影的〕画外音, 解说

voice print /'· ·/ *n* [C] the sound of a particular person's voice recorded on a machine, which can be used to check who that person is〔某人嗓音的〕声纹; 声印

void[1] /vɔɪd; vɔɪd/ *adj* **1** *law* a contract or official agreement that is void is not legal and has no effect; NULL AND VOID【法律】〔合同或正式协议〕无效的, 没有法律效力的 **2 be void of** *formal* to completely lack something【正式】毫无…的, 缺乏…的: *Her eyes were void of all expression.* 她的眼睛空洞无神。

void[2] *n* [C usually singular 一般用单数] **1** a feeling of great sadness that you have when someone you love dies or when something is taken from you 空虚感; 孤寂感: *Their son's death left a painful void in their lives.* 儿子的死给他们的生活留下了痛苦的孤寂感。 **2** an empty area of space where nothing exists 空处, 空间: *the void between atoms* 原子之间的空隙 | *She looked over the cliff into the void.* 她从悬崖边上望下去, 下面一片虚空。 **3** a situation in which something important or interesting that previously existed is no longer present 空白, 空虚: *Many women re-enter the workforce after raising a family to fill a void in their lives.* 许多妇女把孩子养大后重新加入劳动大军, 以填补生活中的空虚。

void[3] *v* [T] **1** *law* to make a contract or agreement void so that it has no legal effect【法律】使〔契约或协议〕无效; 使作废 **2 void the bladder/bowels** *formal* to pass waste liquid or solid matter from your body【正式】排空膀胱/大肠

voi·là /vwɑˈlɑ; vwɑːˈlɑː/ *interjection French* used when suddenly showing something to someone【法】瞧!〔用于突然把某物展示给某人时〕: *Voilà! Your birthday cake!* 瞧! 你的生日蛋糕!

voile /vɔɪl; vɔɪl/ *n* [U] a very light almost transparent cloth made of cotton, wool, or silk 巴里纱〔一种用棉、毛或真丝织成的轻质近乎透明的薄纱〕

V

vol. the written abbreviation for 缩写 = VOLUME

vol·a·tile /ˈvɑlətḷ; ˈvɒlətaɪl/ *adj* **1** a volatile situation is likely to change suddenly and without much warning 易变的, 动荡不定的: *a volatile economic environment* 不稳定的经济环境 **2** someone who is volatile can suddenly become angry or violent 易激动的; 易发作的; 易怒的 **3** a volatile liquid or substance changes easily into a gas 易挥发的 —**volatility** /,vɑləˈtɪlətɪ; ,vɒləˈtɪlɨti/ *n* [U]

vol-au-vent /,vol o ˋvã; ,vɒl əʊ ˈvɒn/ *n* [C] *French* a small round piece of PASTRY that is filled with chicken, vegetables etc【法】〔一种以鸡肉、蔬菜等为馅的〕肉馅油酥饼

vol·can·ic /vɑlˋkænɪk; vɒlˈkænɪk/ *adj* **1** connected with or caused by a volcano 火山的; 由火山作用引起的: *black volcanic sand* 黑火山砂 **2** happening or reacting suddenly and violently 暴烈的, 猛烈的: *a man of volcanic passions* 性情暴烈的人

vol·ca·no /vɑlˋkeno; vɒlˈkeɪnəʊ/ *n plural* **volcanoes** *or* **volcanos** [C] a mountain with a large hole at the top, through which hot rocks, LAVA, and ash sometimes rise into the air from inside the earth 火山: *Pompeii was destroyed when the volcano erupted in 79AD.* 庞贝为公元79年的火山爆发所毁。| **active volcano** (=a volcano that may explode at any time) 活火山 | **dormant volcano** (=a volcano that is not active at present) 休眠火山 | **extinct volcano** (=a volcano that is no longer active) 死火山

vole /vol; vəʊl/ *n* [C] a small animal like a mouse with a short tail that lives in fields and woods and near rivers 田鼠

Vol·ga, the /ˈvɑlgə; ˈvɒlgə/ a river in Russia which flows into the Caspian Sea, and is the longest river in Europe 伏尔加河〔俄罗斯境内一河流, 注入里海, 是欧洲最长的河流〕

vo·li·tion /voˋlɪʃən; vəˈlɪʃən/ *n* [U] *formal* the power to choose or decide something without being forced to do it【正式】意志力; 决断: **of your own volition** (=because you want to do something, not because you are forced to do it) 出于某人自己的意志 *Helena left the company of her own volition.* 海伦娜自愿离开了公司。

vol·ley[1] /ˈvɑlɪ; ˈvɒli/ *n* [C] **1** a large number of shots fired from guns at the same time〔枪炮等的〕群射, 齐射: [+of] *a volley of bullets* 子弹齐射 **2** a lot of questions, insults, attacks etc that are all said or made at the same time〔质问、辱骂、攻击等的〕连发; 迸发: [+of] *a volley of abuse* 一阵辱骂 | *a volley of blows* 一顿狠揍 **3** a hit in TENNIS, a kick in football etc when the player hits or kicks the ball before it touches the ground〔网球着地前的〕截击, 拦击;〔足球落地前的〕截踢, 凌空球 —see picture on page A23 参见A23页图 **4** a lot of objects that are thrown through the air at the same time 齐发, 群掷: [+of] *a volley of stones* 一阵石头乱砸

volley[2] *v* **1** [I,T] to hit or kick a ball before it touches the ground, especially in TENNIS or football 截击(球); 截踢(球): *Ince volleyed the ball over the net.* 英斯凌空一抽, 球高出了球网。 **2** [I] if a large number of guns volley, they are all fired at the same time〔枪炮〕群射, 齐鸣

vol·ley·ball /ˈvɑlɪ,bɔl; ˈvɒlibɔːl/ *n* **1** [U] a game in which two teams hit a ball backwards and forwards over a high net with their hands and do not allow it to touch the ground 排球(运动) **2** [C] the ball used in this game 排球

volt /volt; vəʊlt/ *n* [C] *technical* a unit for measuring the force of an electric current【术语】伏特, 伏〔电压单位〕

volt·age /ˈvoltɪdʒ; ˈvəʊltɪdʒ/ *n* [C,U] *technical* electrical force measured in volts【术语】电压, 伏特数: *a high voltage fence* 通了高压电的围栏

Vol·taire /volˋtɛə; vɒlˈteə/ (1694-1778) a French writer and PHILOSOPHER who was one of the leaders of the ENLIGHTENMENT, and whose ideas influenced the French Revolution. He wrote essays on many subjects, but his best-known work is the story *Candide.* 伏尔泰〔(1694-1778), 法国作家、哲学家、启蒙运动领袖人物之一。其思想曾对法国大革命产生巨大影响。伏尔泰的作品涉猎广泛, 以小说《老实人》最为著名〕

volte-face /ˈvɑlt,fɑs; ,vɒlt ˈfæs/ *n* [C usually singular 一般用单数] *formal* a change to a completely opposite opinion or plan of action【正式】〔意见、行动计划等的〕完全改变, 大转变, 180度大转弯

volt·me·ter /ˈvolt,mitə; ˈvəʊlt,miːtə/ *n* [C] an instrument for measuring voltage 伏特计, 电压表

vol·u·ble /ˈvɑljəbḷ; ˈvɒljʊbəl/ *adj formal*【正式】**1** talking a lot 健谈的: *a voluble spokesman* 口若悬河的发言人 **2** a voluble speech, explanation etc uses a lot of words and is spoken quickly〔讲话等〕滔滔不绝的; 流利的: *She broke into voluble and perfect Italian.* 她突然说起一口流利而纯正的意大利语来。—**volubly** *adv* —**volubility** /,vɑljəˈbɪlɪtɪ; ,vɒljʊˈbɪlɨti/ *n* [U]

vol·ume /ˈvɑljəm; ˈvɒljuːm/ *n* 2

1 ►**SPACE FILLED** 充满的空间◄ [C,U] the amount of space that a substance or object contains or fills 容量; 体积; 容积: *The volume of the container measures 100,000 cubic metres.* 这个集装箱的容量是10万立方米。| *an instrument for measuring the volume of a gas* 测量气体体积的仪器

2 ►**AMOUNT** 数量◄ [C,U] the total amount of something, especially when it is large or increasing〔尤指巨大的或正在增加的〕量, 总量: *The volume of traffic on the roads has increased dramatically in recent years.* 近年来公路交通量急剧增加。| *the volume of trade* 贸易量

3 ►**SOUND** 声音◄ [U] the amount of sound produced by a television, radio etc 音量;(音)响度: *Can you turn the volume down on the stereo.* 把立体声音响的音量调小一点。

4 ►**BOOK** 书籍◄ **a)** [C] one of the books into which a very long book is divided〔书的〕卷, 册: *the M-Mon volume of the encyclopedia* 百科全书的M-Mon卷 **b)** [C] *formal* a book【正式】书籍: *a volume of poetry* 诗集 —see also 另见 **speak volumes** (SPEAK (11))

vo·lu·mi·nous /vəˋlumənəs; vəˈluːmɨnəs/ *adj formal*【正式】**1** a voluminous piece of clothing is very large and loose〔衣服〕宽大的, 宽松的: *a voluminous cloak* 宽大的斗篷 **2** voluminous books, documents etc are very long and contain a lot of detail〔书籍、文件等〕多卷的; 篇幅长的, 大部头的: *He took voluminous notes during the lecture.* 他在听课时做了大量笔记。 **3** a voluminous container is very large and can hold a lot of things〔容器〕大的; 容量大的: *a voluminous suitcase* 一个能装很多东西的手提箱

vol·un·ta·ry[1] /ˈvɑlən,tɛrɪ; ˈvɒləntəri/ *adj* **1 voluntary work/service etc** work etc that is done by people who do it because 3

they want to, and without expecting any money for it 义务工作/服务等: *When she retired she did a lot of voluntary work for the Red Cross.* 她退休后为红十字会做了大量的义务工作。| **on a voluntary basis** *Participants in the experiment took part on a voluntary basis.* 参加实验的人员都是自愿的。**2 voluntary organization/society/institution etc** an organization etc that is organized or supported by people who give their money, services etc because they want to and without expecting reward 志愿组织/团体/机构等: *a voluntary organization providing help for the elderly* 一个为老年人提供帮助的志愿组织 **3 voluntary worker/helper/assistant etc** someone who works without expecting or receiving payment 志愿人员/帮手/助手等 **4** done willingly and without being forced 自愿的, 志愿的; 自发的: *The suspect has given the police his voluntary cooperation.* 嫌疑犯自愿与警方合作。| *Workers are being encouraged to take voluntary redundancy.* 工人被鼓励自愿离职。—compare 比较 COMPULSORY **5** *technical* voluntary movements of your body are controlled by you【术语】〔身体活动〕自如的, 随意的 —opposite 反义词 INVOLUNTARY —**voluntarily** /ˌvɑlənˋtɛrılı; ˈvɒləntərˌli/ *adv*: *She wasn't fired – she left voluntarily.* 她不是被解雇的—— 她是自愿离职的。

CULTURAL NOTE 文化注释

Some British and American people spend a period of time doing voluntary work abroad for charities (CHARITY) such as VSO (=Voluntary Service Overseas), a British organization, or the Peace Corps, an American government organization, which help people in developing countries (DEVELOPING COUNTRY) in areas such as AGRICULTURE and education. Traditionally, many people used to do this work immediately after leaving university. VSO, especially, now prefers to use older people with more experience and skills. 有些英国人和美国人花一段时间去国外做志愿工作, 例如接受英国的海外志愿服务队或美国的政府组织和平队的派遣, 去帮助发展中国家的农业和教育事业等。传统上, 很多人通常大学一毕业就投身到志愿工作中。现在的组织, 特别是海外志愿服务队, 更乐意用年龄较长、有经验和技术的人来做志愿工作。

Some people, especially older people, do voluntary work in their own countries such as working in a charity shop. 有些人, 特别是年纪较大的人在国内做些志愿工作, 像在慈善商店做些服务等。

voluntary² *n* [C] a piece of music, usually for the ORGAN (2), written to be played in church〔教堂中的〕(风琴) 演奏曲

Voluntary Eu·tha·na·si·a So·ci·e·ty, the /ˌ····· ·····ˌ···/ an organization in the UK which aims to change the law that forbids helping seriously ill people to die if they wish to. There is a similar organization in the US called the Hemlock Society. 自愿安乐死协会〔英国一组织, 旨在修改禁止安乐死的法律, 为自愿选择安乐死的重症病人提供帮助。美国也有一类似组织, 称"毒芹协会"〕

Voluntary Ser·vice O·ver·seas /ˌ···· ·ˌ··ˈ·/ the full name of VSO 海外志愿服务社〔VSO的全称〕

vol·un·teer¹ /ˌvɑlənˋtır; ˌvɒlənˈtɪə/ *n* [C] **1** someone who does something without being paid, or who is willing to offer to help someone 志愿者, 自愿参加者, 愿做志愿人员者: *Most of the relief work was done by volunteers.* 许多救援工作是由志愿人员做的。| *I need some volunteers to clean up the kitchen.* 我需要几名志愿者来收拾一下厨房。**2** someone who offers to join the army, navy, or air force 志愿兵

volunteer² *v* **1** [I,T] to offer to do something without expecting any reward, usually something that other people do not want to do 自愿〔做某事〕; 自告奋勇, 自愿效劳: **volunteer to do sth** *The company volunteered to donate fifty trucks to help the war effort.* 公司主动捐献50辆卡车支援战事。| **[+for]** *Sidcup volunteered for guard duty.* 西德卡普自告奋勇去站岗值勤。| **volunteer your services/help/advice** *I volunteered my services as a teacher.* 我自愿去当老师。**2** [T] to tell someone something without being asked 自动说出〔某事〕: *Michael volunteered the information before I had a chance to ask.* 我还未来得及发问, 迈克尔就自动把情况说了。**3** [I] to offer to join the army, navy, or airforce 志愿服役, 志愿参军: *When war broke out, my father volunteered immediately.* 战争一爆发, 我父亲立即志愿从军。**4** [T] to say that someone else will do a job even though they may not want to 让…做…: **volunteer sb for sth** *Mum volunteered Dave for washing-up duties.* 妈妈让戴夫负责洗刷餐具。

Volunteers of A·mer·i·ca /·ˌ·· ·ˈ···/ a non-profit organization that helps people in the US who need it, for example children who have been treated badly by their parents, families that do not have enough money, people who do not have a home, and old people who are too weak to take care of themselves. It also gives some medical care and helps people get homes that are not too expensive. 美国志愿者协会〔美国一非赢利性组织。其宗旨是帮助需要帮助的人, 如受父母虐待的儿童、经济拮据的家庭、无家可归者、丧失自理能力的老人等。该组织还提供医疗服务, 帮助人们寻找廉价房〕

vo·lup·tu·a·ry /vəˋlʌptʃυˌɛrı; vəˈlʌptʃuəri/ *n* [C] *literary* someone who enjoys physical, especially sexual, pleasure and having expensive possessions【文】骄奢淫逸的人; 酒色之徒

vo·lup·tu·ous /vəˋlʌptʃυəs; vəˈlʌptʃuəs/ *adj* **1** a woman who is voluptuous has large breasts and a soft curved body〔女性〕妖娆的, 丰满的, 性感的 **2** expressing strong sexual feeling or sexual pleasure 色情的; 勾起情欲的: *a voluptuous gesture* 挑逗的姿势 **3** *literary* something that is voluptuous gives you pleasure because it looks, smells, or tastes good【文】令人愉悦的, 给感官以快感的: *the voluptuous fragrance of a summer garden* 夏季花园中散发出的令人心旷神怡的芬芳 —**voluptuously** *adv* —**voluptuousness** *n* [U]

vom·it¹ /ˋvɑmıt; ˈvɒmˌt/ *v* [I,T] to bring food or drink up from your stomach out through your mouth, because you are ill 呕吐; 呕出, 吐出 —see 见 SICK¹ (USAGE)

vomit² *n* [U] food or other substances that come up from your stomach and through your mouth when you vomit 呕吐物, 吐出物

Von Braun /vɑn ˋbraυn; vɒn ˈbraʊn/, **Wern·her** /ˋvɛrnə; ˈveənə/ (1912-77) a ROCKET engineer who was born in Germany and developed the V-2 flying bomb for the Nazis. After World War II he went to the US and worked for NASA on the Apollo Program to send spacecraft to the moon. 冯·布劳恩〔(1912-1977), 火箭工程师, 生于德国, 曾为纳粹德国研制出V-2型导弹。二战结束后前往美国航天局工作, 参与了将宇宙飞船送上月球的"阿波罗"计划〕

voo·doo /ˋvudu; ˈvuːduː/ *n* [U] magical beliefs and practices used as a form of religion, especially by people in Haiti〔尤指海地人信仰的〕伏都教 (巫术)

voodoo e·co·nom·ics /ˌ·· ··ˈ··/ *n* [U] *AmE* economic ideas that seem attractive but that do not work effectively over a period of time【美】华而不实的经济学 (观点)

vo·ra·cious /vɔˋreʃəs; vəˈreɪʃəs/ *adj* **1** eating or wanting large quantities of food 贪吃的; 食量大的: *Pigs are voracious feeders.* 猪的食量很大, 需要喂很多饲料。| **a voracious appetite** *Kids can have voracious appetites.* 小孩子会有大胃口。**2** extremely eager to read books, gain knowledge etc 求知欲极强的: *a voracious reader* 求知欲极强的读者 —**voraciously** *adv* —**voraciousness** *n* [U] —**voracity** /-ˋræsətı; -ˈræsˌti/ *n* [U]

vor·tex /ˋvɔrtɛks; ˈvɔːteks/ *n* [C] *literary*【文】**1** a mass of wind or water that spins rapidly and pulls things into its centre〔风或水形成的〕旋风; 旋涡 **2** [usually singular 一般用单数] a situation that has a powerful effect on people's lives and that influences their behaviour, even if they did not intend it to〔无法控制的对生活有巨大影响的〕形势, 处境: **[+of]** *a black vortex of paranoia* 妄想症的黑色旋涡

vo·ta·ry /ˋvotərı; ˈvəʊtəri/ *n* [C] *formal* someone who regularly practises a particular religion【正式】信徒, 崇拜者

vote¹ /vot; vəʊt/ *n* W3

1 ▶CHOICE 选择◀ [C] a choice or decision that you make by voting in an election or meeting 投票所作的选择[决定]: *The Democratic Party is counting on your vote.* 民主党期望您投他们的票。| **[+for/against]** *There were 402 votes for Mr Williams, and 372 against.* 402票支持威廉斯先生, 372票反对。| **cast your vote** (=vote in a political election)〔在政治性选举中〕投票 —see also 另见 CASTING VOTE

2 ▶ELECTION 选举◀ [C] an act of voting, when a group of people vote in order to decide or choose something 投票, 表决: *The results of the vote were surprising – 80% of workers favoured strike action.* 表决结果令人惊讶——80%的工人赞成罢工行动。| **take/have a vote (on)** *We couldn't decide who to give the prize to so we took a vote on it.* 我们无法决定谁应该得奖, 于是投票表决。| **put sth to the vote** (=decide something by voting) 把某事诉诸表决 *Let's put it to the vote. All those in favor raise your hands.* 让我们投票表决, 赞成的举手。

3 ▶RESULT 结果◀ [singular] the result of a vote 投票[表决]结果: *a very close vote* 票数很接近的表决结果 | *The motion was passed by a vote of 215 to 84.* 该动议以215票对84票通过。

4 ▶PAPER 纸◀ [C] the piece of paper which you use to make your vote 选票: *Party members were up all night counting the votes.* 党员们通宵清点选票。

5 ►NUMBER OF VOTES 得票数◄ [singular] the total number of votes made in an election or the total number of people who vote〔选举中的〕得票总数; 投票人数: *The Republicans increased their share of the vote.* 共和党在得票总数中所占的份额提高了。| *policies designed to win the African-American vote* (=all the votes of African-Americans) 旨在赢取非裔美国人选票的各项政策

6 the vote the right to vote in political elections〔政治上的〕选举权, 投票权: *In France women didn't get the vote until 1945.* 在法国, 妇女到 1945 年才获得选举权。

7 sth gets my vote *spoken* used to say that you are ready to support something【口】我支持某事: *Anything that will mean a better deal for our children gets my vote.* 凡对我们的子孙有好处的事我都赞成。

3 3 **vote²** *v*

1 ►MAKE A CHOICE 作出选择◄ [I,T] to show by marking a paper or raising your hand which person you want to elect or whether you support a particular plan 投票, 表决: *In 1918 British women got the right to vote.* 1918 年, 英国妇女获得了选举权。| **vote for sb** *I voted for the Labour candidate in the last election.* 我在上次选举中投票支持工党候选人。| **[+on]** *If we can't agree, we'll have to vote on it.* 意见如果不能统一的话, 我们就得投票表决。| **vote to do sth** *Congress voted to increase foreign aid by 10%.* 国会表决通过增加 10% 的对外援助。| **vote for/in favour of/against sth** *53% of Danes voted in favour of the Maastricht treaty.* 53% 的丹麦人投票赞成《马斯特里赫特条约》。| **vote sth ↔ down** (=defeat a plan, law etc by voting) 否决 | **vote sth ↔ through** (=approve a plan, law etc by voting) 表决通过; 投票赞成〔计划、法案等〕| **vote Democrat/Socialist/Republican etc** *I've voted Democrat all my life.* 我一生都在投民主党的票。

2 ►ELECT 选举◄ [T] to elect or dismiss someone by voting 选出, 选上; 使落选: **vote sb in/out** (=elect or dismiss someone from a position of power) 使某人当选/落选 *With policies like that he'll be voted out in the next election.* 执行这样的政策, 他在下次选举中非落选不可。| **vote sb into power/office/parliament etc** *Callaghan had been voted into office.* 卡拉汉获选担任公职。

3 ►PRIZE 奖励◄ [T] to choose someone or something for a particular prize by voting for them 投票评选: *'Schindler's List' was voted 'Film of the Year'.* 《辛德勒的名单》被选为"年度最佳电影"。

4 ►MONEY 钱款◄ [T] if a parliament, committee etc votes a sum of money for something, they decide by voting to provide money for that particular purpose〔议会、委员会等通过投票〕同意提供〔款项〕: *Parliament has voted £20 million extra funding for road improvements.* 国会投票通过另拨 2000 万英镑用于改善道路。

5 vote sth a success/the best etc if people vote something a success etc, they all agree that it is a success 一致认为某事物是成功/最好的等: *Tom's party was voted a great success by everyone there.* 在场的人都认为汤姆的聚会办得非常成功。

6 ►SUGGEST 建议◄ [T] *informal* to suggest something【非正式】提议: **[+that]** *I vote that we go to the movies.* 我提议一起去看电影。

7 vote with your feet to show that you do not support a decision or action by leaving a place or organization 以退席[退出组织]表示不支持〔某决定、行动等〕

vote of cen·sure /ˌ· · ˈ··/ *n* [C] a process in which members of parliament vote in order to blame the government for something〔国会议员对政府的〕不信任投票

vote of con·fi·dence /ˌ· · ˈ···/ *n* [C] **1** a formal process in which people vote in order to show that they support someone or something, especially the government〔尤指对政府的〕信任票: *a unanimous vote of confidence* 全体一致的信任票 **2** something that you do or say that shows you support someone and approve of their actions 赞同[支持]的表示

vote of no con·fi·dence /ˌ· · · ˈ···/ *n* [C] **1** a formal process in which people vote in order to show that they do not support someone or something, especially the government 不信任票, 不信任表决 **2** something that you do or say that shows that you do not support someone 不赞同[不支持]的表示

vote of thanks /ˌ· · ˈ·/ *n* **propose a vote of thanks** *especially BrE* to make a short formal speech in which you thank someone, especially at a public meeting or a formal dinner【尤英】〔尤指在公众集会或正式晚宴上〕致答谢辞, 鸣谢

vot·er /ˈvotɚ; ˈvəʊtə/ *n* [C] someone who votes or has the right to vote, especially in a political election〔尤指政治性选举中的〕选举人, 投票人, 选民; 有投票权的人: *The party's policies do not appeal to the voters.* 该党的政策不受选民欢迎。| *Tory voters* 投保守党票的选民 —see also 另见 FLOATING VOTER

voting booth /ˈ·· ·/ *n* [C] *AmE* an enclosed place where you can make your vote secretly【美】〔投票站里供秘密写选票用的〕投票亭, 写票处; POLLING BOOTH *BrE*【英】

voting ma·chine /ˈ·· ·ˌ·/ *n* [C] a machine that records votes as they are made 投票机, 选票计算机

vo·tive /ˈvotɪv; ˈvəʊtɪv/ *adj technical* given or done to a promise made to God or to a SAINT【术语】〔对上帝或圣徒〕谢恩的; 还愿的: *votive offerings* 谢恩奉献物, 还愿的奉献物

vouch /vautʃ; vaʊtʃ/ *v*

vouch for sb/sth *phr v* [T] **1** to say that you believe that someone will behave well and that you will be responsible for their behaviour, actions etc 为〔某人的行为等〕作担保: *I can vouch for my son, officer.* 我可以为儿子作保, 长官。**2** to say that you firmly believe that something is true or good because of your experience or knowledge of it 为〔某事〕作担保, 保证: *I'll vouch for the quality of the report. I read it last night.* 我为报告的质量作保, 我昨晚看过。

vouch·er /ˈvautʃɚ; ˈvaʊtʃə/ *n* [C] **1** a kind of ticket that can be used instead of money for a particular purpose 代金券, 凭证: *a travel voucher* 旅行代金券 —see also 另见 LUNCHEON VOUCHER **2** an official statement or RECEIPT that is given to someone to prove that their accounts are correct or that money has been paid 收据, 收条; 凭单 3

vouch·safe /vautʃˈsef; vaʊtʃˈseɪf/ *v* [T] *formal*【正式】**1** to offer, give, or tell something to someone in a way that shows you trust them 惠予, 赐予: *insights into the future vouchsafed by God* 上帝赐予的对未来的洞察力 **2** to make it certain that something will be safe 确保…的安全: *political arrangements that vouchsafe peace* 确保和平的政治性安排

vow¹ /vau; vaʊ/ *n* [C] a serious promise 誓言; 誓约: *marriage vows* 结婚誓言 | **vow to do sth** *a vow to avenge his brother's death* 为他死去的兄弟报仇的誓言 | **take/make a vow** *She made a vow never to tell anybody what she had heard.* 她起誓决不把听到的告诉任何人。| **keep/break a vow** (=do or not do what you promised) 信守/违反誓言 | **vow of silence** (=a promise made to God that you will never speak again)〔向上帝〕立誓保持沉默[缄口保密] *monks who take the vow of silence* 立沉默之誓的僧侣 | **under a vow of** (=having promised to do something) 发过誓要… *nuns under the vow of chastity* 立誓保持贞洁的修女

vow² *v* [T] **1** *especially literary* to make a serious promise to yourself or someone else【尤文】立誓, 起誓: **vow to do sth** *He vowed to kill his wife's lover.* 他发誓要杀死妻子的情人。| **vow (that)** *I vowed that I would never drink again.* 我发誓决不再喝酒了。**2** *formal* to make a religious promise that you will give something to God, the church etc【正式】〔向上帝、教会等〕立誓奉献

vow·el /ˈvauəl; ˈvaʊəl/ *n* [C] **1** one of the human speech sounds that you make by letting your breath flow out without closing any part of your mouth or throat 元音 **2** a letter of the alphabet used to represent a vowel. In English the vowels are a, e, i, o, u, and sometimes y. 元音字母〔英语的元音字母为 a, e, i, o, u, 有时也包括 y〕

vox pop /ˌvaks ˈpap; ˌvɒks ˈpɒp/ *n* [U] *BrE informal* opinions expressed by ordinary people when they are asked questions about a particular subject during a television, radio, or newspaper report【英, 非正式】〔电视、电台或报纸就某主题采访的〕普通民众的观点, 公众舆论; 街头民意调查

voy·age¹ /ˈvɔɪ-ɪdʒ; ˈvɔɪ-ɪdʒ/ *n* [C] a long journey in a ship〔乘船的长途〕航行: *The voyage from England to India used to take six months.* 过去从英国航行到印度要用六个月。

voyage² *v* [I] *literary* to make a long journey in a ship【文】航行, 航海 —see 见 TRAVEL (USAGE)

Voy·ag·er /ˈvɔɪ-ɪdʒɚ; ˈvɔɪ-ɪdʒə/ also 又作 **the Voyager Program** a US government space programme which, in 1977, sent two spaceships without people on board, called Voyager 1 and Voyager 2, to collect information about Jupiter, Saturn, Uranus, and Neptune 旅行者计划〔美国政府的一项太空计划。1977 年将"旅行者 1 号"和"旅行者 2 号"无人驾驶飞船送入太空, 收集有关木星、土星、天王星和海王星的信息〕

voyager *n* [C] *literary* someone who makes long and often dangerous journeys on the sea【文】航海者; 海上探险者

voy·eur /ˌvwaˈjɝ; vwɑːˈjɜː/ *n* [C] **1** someone who gets sexual pleasure from secretly watching other people's sexual activities 窥淫狂者, 窥淫癖者 **2** someone who enjoys watching other people's private behaviour or suffering 喜欢窥探别人隐私的人 —**voyeurism** *n* [U] —**voyeuristic** /ˌvwajəˈrɪstɪk; ˌvwɑːjəˈrɪstɪk◂/

adj —**voyeuristically** /-klɪ; -kli/ *adv*

VP /ˌvi ˋpi; ˌviː ˈpiː/ the abbreviation of 缩写= VICE PRESIDENT

vs /ˈvɜ·səs; ˈvɜːsəs/ a written abbreviation of 缩写= VERSUS

V sign /ˈvi ˌsaɪn; ˈviː saɪn/ *n* [C] **1** a sign meaning peace or victory made by holding up the first two fingers of your hand with the front of the hand facing forwards V字手势, 胜利[和平]手势〔手掌向外, 伸出食指及中指做成V字形〕**2** *BrE* a rude sign made by holding up the first two fingers of your hand with the back of your hand facing towards another person【英】V字轻蔑侮辱手势, 粗鲁[下流]的手势〔手背向外竖起食指及中指〕

VSO /ˌvi ɛs ˋo; ˌviː es ˈəʊ/ Voluntary Service Overseas; a British organization which sends people to developing countries for at least two years, to live and work there and to share their skills and knowledge with the local people 海外志愿服务社〔英国一组织, 派遣志愿者前往发展中国家工作、生活, 与当地居民交流技术和知识, 服务期至少两年〕

VT the written abbreviation of 缩写= VERMONT

Vul·can /ˈvʌlkən; ˈvʌlkən/ in Roman MYTHOLOGY , the god of fire and of making things from metal. In Greek mythology his name is Hephaestus. 伏尔甘〔罗马神话中的火与锻冶之神。希腊神话中称为赫菲斯托斯〕

vul·can·ize also 又作 **-ise** *BrE*【英】/ˈvʌlkənˌaɪz; ˈvʌlkənaɪz/ *v* [T] to make rubber stronger using a special chemical treatment〔通过化学处理〕使〔橡胶〕硫化; 把〔橡胶〕强化 —**vulcanization** /ˌvʌlkənaɪˋzeʃən; ˌvʌlkənaɪ-ˈzeɪʃən/ *n* [U]

vul·gar /ˈvʌlgɚ; ˈvʌlgə/ *adj* **1** remarks, jokes etc that are vulgar deal with sex in a very rude and offensive way〔言语、玩笑等〕低俗的, 卑下的 **2** impolite and showing bad manners 无礼的, 粗俗的, 粗野的: *vulgar habits* 粗鄙的习惯 **3** *especially BrE* not showing good judgment about what is beautiful or suitable【尤英】庸俗的, 低级的: *a vulgar display of wealth* 庸俗地炫耀财富 —**vulgarly** *adv*

vulgar frac·tion /ˌ‥ ˈ‥/ *n* [C] *BrE old-fashioned* a FRACTION that is written as one number above a line and one number below it, and not as a DECIMAL【英, 过时】普通分数〔以分数式而不是以小数点表示〕; COMMON FRACTION *AmE*【美】

vul·gar·i·ty /vʌlˋgærətɪ; vʌlˈgærɪ̈ti/ *n* **1** [U] the state or quality of being vulgar 庸俗, 粗俗, 粗鄙 **2 vulgarities** [plural] vulgar remarks, jokes etc 粗俗的话[玩笑等]

vul·gar·ize also 又作 **-ise** *BrE*【英】/ˈvʌlgəˌraɪz; ˈvʌlgəraɪz/ *v* [T] *formal* to spoil the quality or lower the standard of something that is good【正式】使庸俗化; 降低〔美好事物〕的水准 —**vulgarization** /ˌvʌlgəraɪˋzeʃən; ˌvʌlgəraɪˈzeɪʃən/ *n* [U]

Vul·gate, the /ˈvʌlget; ˈvʌlgeɪt/ *n* the Latin Bible commonly used in the Roman Catholic Church 拉丁文本《圣经》〔天主教过去普遍使用的文本〕

vul·ne·ra·ble /ˈvʌlnərəbl; ˈvʌlnərəbəl/ *adj* **1** someone who is vulnerable is easily harmed or hurt emotionally, physically, or morally 感情脆弱的; 易受伤的: *a vulnerable young child* 易受伤害的小孩 **2** a place, thing, or idea that is vulnerable is easy to attack 易受攻击[责难]的: [+to] *The fort was vulnerable to attack from the north.* 该堡垒易从北面受到攻击。| *a theory vulnerable to criticism* 易受批评的理论 —**vulnerably** *adv* —**vulnerability** /ˌvʌlnərəˋbɪlɪtɪ; ˌvʌlnərəˈbɪlɪ̈ti/ *n* [U]: *the vulnerability of airports to terrorist activity* 易受恐怖分子袭击的机场 W3

vul·ture /ˈvʌltʃɚ; ˈvʌltʃə/ *n* [C] **1** a large bird that eats dead animals 秃鹫 **2** someone who uses other people's troubles for their own advantage 压榨别人的人, 盘剥弱者的人, 残酷劫掠者

vul·va /ˈvʌlvə; ˈvʌlvə/ *n* [C] the outer part of a woman's sexual organs 女阴, 外阴

vy·ing /ˈvaɪ·ɪŋ; ˈvaɪ-ɪŋ/ the present participle of VIE

W,w

W, w /ˈdʌblju; ˈdʌbəljuː/ *plural* **W's, w's** *n* [C] **1** the 23rd letter of the English alphabet 英语字母表的第二十三个字母 **2** the written abbreviation of 缩写= WEST OR WESTERN **3** the written abbreviation of 缩写= WATT

W-2 /ˌdʌblju ˈtu; ˌdʌbəljuː ˈtuː/ also 又作 **W-2 form** /ˌ···ˈ·, ·/ a FORM (=official document) that employers in the US prepare each year for their workers, showing how much a worker has earned that year and how much tax has been taken out of their wages. The worker then sends this form with his or her income tax return to the IRS. W-2 表，雇员薪资税表〔美国雇主每年向员工提供的一份表格，显示该员工当年的工资总额和工资扣税情况。员工将该表及纳税单送交联邦税务局〕—compare 比较 P60

WA the written abbreviation of 缩写= WASHINGTON STATE

WAC /wæk; wæk/ **1** the Women's Army Corp; the women's part of the US Army（美国）陆军妇女军团 **2** a member of the Women's Army Corp in the US（美国）陆军妇女军团成员

wack·y /ˈwækɪ; ˈwæki/ *adj informal* silly in an exciting or amusing way【非正式】疯疯癫癫的；古怪的，荒唐的 —**wackiness** *n* [U]

wad¹ /wɑd; wɒd/ *n* [C] **1** a thick pile of pieces of paper or thin material〔纸或轻薄材料的〕一叠；一沓：*a wad of dollar bills* 一叠美钞 —see picture on page A7 参见 A7 页图 **2** a thick soft mass of material that has been pressed together〔压在一起的〕一团〔软材料〕：*a wad of gauze* 一团纱布 **3** a piece of tobacco that you hold in your mouth 一小块〔嚼用烟草〕

wad² *v*

wad sth ↔ **up** *phr v* [T] *AmE* to press something such as a piece of paper or cloth into a small tight ball【美】把〔纸或布等〕压成一团

wad·ding /ˈwɑdɪŋ; ˈwɒdɪŋ/ *n* [U] soft material used for packing or to protect a wound 软填料；〔医用〕敷料

wad·dle /ˈwɑdl̩; ˈwɒdl/ *v* [I] to walk with short steps, swinging from one side to another like a duck〔似鸭子般〕摇摇摆摆地走：**[+along/around etc]** *Julie came waddling up the path, eight months pregnant.* 朱莉挺着八个月的大肚子，一摇一摆地从路上走来。—**waddle** *n* [singular]

wade /wed; weɪd/ *v* [I+across/through,T] to walk through water that is not deep 蹚水，涉水

wade in *phr v* [I] *BrE informal* to interrupt someone or become involved in something in an annoying way【英，非正式】干涉，介入，插手：*I wish you wouldn't always wade in with your opinion.* 我希望你不要总是插进来提意见。

wade through sth *phr v* [T] to read or deal with a lot of boring papers or written work 吃力地阅读；费力地完成〔乏味的文件或文章〕：*Look at this pile of paperwork I have to wade through!* 瞧这一大堆烦人的文书，我必须把它完成！—see picture on page A24 参见 A24 页图

wad·er /ˈwedɚ; ˈweɪdə/ *n* [C] **1** a bird that walks around in water to find its food and has long legs and a long neck 涉禽 **2 waders** [plural] high rubber boots that you wear for walking in water〔涉水用的〕高统防水胶靴

wading bird /ˈ··, ·/ *n* [C] a WADER (1) 涉禽

wad·ing pool /ˈ·· ·/ *n* [C] *AmE* a PADDLING POOL【美】嬉水池

Waf /wæf; wæf/ *AmE informal* a woman serving in the US Air Force【美，非正式】（美国）空军女兵

wa·fer /ˈwefɚ; ˈweɪfə/ *n* [C] **1** a very thin BISCUIT (1) 威化饼干，薄脆饼 **2** a thin round piece of bread eaten with wine in the Christian religious ceremony of COMMUNION (2)〔基督教圣餐时与酒一起吃的〕圣饼

wafer-thin /ˌ·· ˈ·◂/ *adj* extremely thin 极薄的：*wafer-thin chocolates* 薄片巧克力

waf·fle¹ /ˈwɑfl̩; ˈwɒfəl/ *n* [C] **1** a thin flat cake, marked with a pattern of deep squares〔带四方深纹的〕华夫饼，奶蛋烘饼 **2** [U] *informal especially BrE* talk or writing that uses a lot of words but says nothing important【非正式，尤英】胡扯，冗长而空洞的话：*His exam answer was a load of old waffle.* 他的考试答卷简直是废话连篇。

waffle² *v* [I] *informal*【非正式】**1** also 又作 **waffle on** *especially BrE* to talk or write using a lot of words but without saying anything important【尤英】唠叨，废话，空话连篇：*Stop waffling and get to the point.* 别唠叨了，说正题吧。**2** *AmE informal* to be unable to decide what action to take【美，非正式】犹豫不决：**[+over]** *Karl waffles over every darn decision!* 卡尔在每一个该死的决定上都举棋不定！

waffle i·ron /ˈ·· ,··/ *n* [C] a piece of kitchen equipment used to cook waffles 华夫饼烤模

waf·fle·stomp·er /ˈwɑflˌstɑmpɚ; ˈwɒfəlˌstɒmpə/ *n* [C usually plural 一般用复数] *AmE* a type of very heavy walking boot【美】厚底旅行靴

waft /wɑft; wɑːft/ *v* [I always+adv/prep] to move gently through the air〔在空气中〕飘荡：**[+up/along/off etc]** *Cooking smells wafted up from downstairs.* 烧菜的气味从楼下飘了上来。

wag¹ /wæg; wæg/ *v* [I,T] **1** to shake your finger or head repeatedly, especially to show disapproval〔反复〕摇动（手指或头）〔尤指表示不赞同时〕：**wag your finger** *"You naughty girl!" Mom said, wagging her finger at me.* "你这个淘气的丫头！"妈妈对我摆了摆手指说道。**2** If a dog wags its tail, it moves it repeatedly from one side to the other〔狗〕摇（尾巴）**3 tongues wag** *informal* used to say that people are talking in a disapproving way about someone else's behaviour【非正式】〔对某人的行为〕议论纷纷：*You'll have to stop visiting that woman – tongues are starting to wag.* 你不要再到那个女人那了，有人开始说闲话了。

wag² *n* **1** [C usually singular 一般用单数] a wagging movement 摇动，摆动 **2** [C] *old-fashioned* someone who talks or does something in a clever and amusing way【过时】爱说笑[逗乐]的人：*Some wag had drawn a face on the wall.* 爱逗乐的人在墙上画了个脸形。—see also 另见 CHINWAG, WAGGISH

wage¹ /wedʒ; weɪdʒ/ *n* **1** [singular] also 又作 **wages** [plural] money you earn that is paid according to the number of hours, days, or weeks that you work〔按小时、日、周所计的〕工资，薪金：*The job's not very exciting, but he earns a good wage.* 工作无甚趣味，但他工资赚得不少。| **wage increase** also 又作 **wage rise** *BrE*【英】*The wage increases will come into effect in June.* 6月将开始加薪。| **daily/weekly etc wage** *a weekly wage of $250* 周薪 250 美元 | **wage levels/rates** (=fixed amounts of money paid for particular jobs)〔特定工作的固定〕工资级别/率 —compare 比较 SALARY —see 见 PAY² (USAGE) **2 a living wage** money you earn for work that is enough to pay for the basic things that you need to live 够基本生活的工资 **3 wage freeze** an action taken by a company, government etc to stop wages increasing〔公司、政府等的〕工资冻结 **4 wage claim** the amount of money demanded by workers as an increase in wages 增加工资的要求

wage² *v* [T] to be involved in a war against someone, or a fight against something 发动，进行〔战争、斗争〕：**wage war (on)** *The police are waging war on drug pushers in the city.* 警方正在市内开展一场打击毒贩的行动。| **wage a campaign/struggle/fight etc** *The struggle for political liberty waged throughout the 18th century.* 争取政治自由的斗争贯穿了整个 18 世纪。

wage-earn·er /ˈ· ,··/ *n* [C] **1** someone who works for wages, often someone who works with their hands〔常指从事体力劳动的〕工人，劳动者：*Both wage-earners and salaried officials were protected by the new regulations.* 劳动者和受薪的高级职员都得到了新规定的保护。**2** someone in a family who earns money for the rest of the family 家庭中赚钱的人

wage-pack·et /ˈ· ,··/ *n* [C] *BrE* an envelope that contains your wages【英】工资袋

wa·ger¹ /ˈwedʒɚ; ˈweɪdʒə/ *n* [C] *old-fashioned* an agreement in which you win or lose money according to the result of something such as a race; BET² (1)【过时】打赌

wager² *v* [T] *old-fashioned*【过时】**1** to agree to win or lose an amount of money on the result of something such as a race 押赌注，打赌：**wager sth on** *Stipes wagered all his money on an unknown horse.* 斯蒂普斯把他所有的钱都押在一匹不知名的马上。**2 I'll wager** used to say that you are so sure that something is true that you are willing to risk money on it 我敢打赌〔表示你肯定某事是真实的〕：*I'll wager that boy's never worked in his life!* 我敢打赌这男孩从没有工作过！

wag·gish /ˈwægɪʃ; ˈwægɪʃ/ *adj* a waggish person makes clever and amusing jokes, remarks etc 爱开玩笑的，诙谐的 —**waggishly** *adv* —**waggishness** *n* [U]

wag·gle /ˋwægl̩; ˈwægəl/ *v* [I,T] to move something up and down or from side to side with short quick movements（使）上下[左右]摇动[摆动]: *Can you waggle your ears?* 你的耳朵会动吗？ —**waggle** *n* [C]

Wag·ner /ˋwægnɚ; ˈwægnə/, **Ho·nus** /ˋhonəs; ˈhəʊnəs/ (1874-1955) a US BASEBALL player who became one of the first members of the baseball Hall of Fame in 1936. He was called 'the Flying Dutchman'. 瓦格纳〔(1874-1955)，美国棒球运动员，最早入选美国棒球名人堂的球员之一(1936年)，被誉为"飞翔的荷兰人"〕

Wag·ner, Richard /ˋvɑgnɚ; ˈvɑːgnə/ (1813-83) a German COMPOSER who is most famous for his long OPERAs, which include *Tristram and Isolde*, and especially his series of four operas based on German MYTHOLOGY, called the *Ring of the Nibelung*. His music is often in a very exciting, dramatic style. He started his own theatre at Bayreuth and his operas are still performed there every summer. 瓦格纳〔(1813-1883)，德国作曲家。他创作的《特里斯丹和绮瑟》等长歌剧十分有名，尤其是取材于德国神话的四部歌剧《尼伯龙根的指环》。瓦格纳的音乐通常振奋人心，充满戏剧色彩。他在拜罗伊特建有自己的剧院，每年夏天都会上演他的歌剧，至今依然如此〕 —**Wagnerian** *adj*

wag·on also 又作 **waggon** *BrE*【英】/ˋwægən; ˈwægən/ *n* [C] **1** a strong vehicle with four wheels, used for carrying heavy loads and usually pulled by horses〔一般由马拉的〕四轮运货车 **2** *BrE* a large open container pulled by a train, used for carrying goods【英】〔无顶的〕铁路货车 **3 be on the wagon** *informal* to not drink alcohol any more【非正式】戒酒 **4 fall off the wagon** *informal* to start drinking alcohol again after you have decided to stop【非正式】开酒戒，又喝起酒来 —see also 另见 PADDY WAGON

wagon train /ˋ‥ ˏ/ *n* [C] a long line of wagons and horses used by the people who moved to the West of America in the 19th century〔19 世纪向美国西部移民时用的〕马车队

wag·tail /ˋwægˌtel; ˈwægteɪl/ *n* [C] a small European bird that moves its tail quickly up and down when it walks 鹡鸰〔欧洲一种小鸟，行走时尾巴上下快速摆动〕

waif /wef; weɪf/ *n* [C] **1** someone who is pale and thin, especially a child, and looks as if they do not have a home〔苍白瘦弱的〕无家可归者〔尤指小孩〕: *a grubby little waif huddled by the door* 蜷缩在门旁的邋遢的流浪儿 | **waif-like** (=very thin) 很瘦的 *teenage girls trying to emulate waif-like fashion models* 仿效瘦骨嶙峋的时装模特儿的少女们 **2 waifs and strays** children or animals, who do not have a home 无家可归的人[动物]: *She loved cats, and would take any waifs and strays into her home.* 她喜欢猫，会把所有无家可归的猫都带回家去养着。

Wai·ki·ki /waɪˋkikɪ; waɪˈkiːki/ a beach in Hawaii near Honolulu, which is very popular with tourists 怀基基海滩〔夏威夷一海滩，近火奴鲁鲁，为旅游胜地〕

wail /wel; weɪl/ *v* **1** [T] to say something in a loud, sad, and complaining way 大声哭叫: *"But what shall I do?" Bernard wailed.* 伯纳德哭叫着说："那我怎么办呢？" **2** [I] to cry out with a long, high sound, especially because you are very sad or in pain〔尤指因悲伤或痛楚而〕恸哭，痛哭: **weeping and wailing** *weeping and wailing with grief* 悲痛地恸哭起来 **3** [I] to make a long, high sound 呼啸，哀鸣: *The wind wailed in the chimney.* 风在烟囱里呼啸。 —**wail** *n* [C]: *the wail of police sirens* 警笛的尖啸

Wailing Wall, the /ˌ‥ˈˑ/ a high stone wall in Jerusalem where Jews go to pray. It is the only remaining part of the ancient Temple of Jerusalem, which was destroyed in AD 70. 哭墙〔耶路撒冷的一道石砌高墙，为犹太人的祈祷场所。哭墙是古耶路撒冷神庙仅有的遗址，该神庙毁于公元 70 年〕

wain·scot /ˋwenskət; ˈweɪnskət/ *n* [C] **1** a SKIRTING BOARD 踢脚板，壁脚板; BASEBOARD *AmE*【美】 **2** also 又作 **wainscotting** a wooden covering, especially on the lower half of the walls of an old house〔旧式房子中墙壁下半部的〕墙裙，护墙板 —**wainscotted** *adj*

waist /west; weɪst/ *n* [C] **1** the narrow part in the middle of the human body 腰，腰部: *wearing a belt around his waist* 他腰间系着一根腰带 | **from the waist up/down** (=in the top or bottom half of your body) 上身/下身 *Lota was paralysed from the waist down.* 洛塔下身瘫痪。 | **stripped to the waist** (=not wearing any clothes on the top half of your body) 上身赤裸的 | **slim-waisted/narrow-waisted/thick-waisted etc** (=having a thin, thick etc waist) 苗条/纤细/粗大等的腰身 —see picture at 参见 BODY 图 **2** the part of a piece of clothing that goes around this part of your body〔衣服的〕腰身部分 **3** *technical* the middle part of a ship【术语】〔船的〕中部; 甲板中部

waist·band /ˋwestˌbænd; ˈweɪstbænd/ *n* [C] the part of a skirt, trousers etc that fastens around your waist 腰带，裤带，裙带 —see picture on page A17 参见 A17 页图

waist·coat /ˋwestˌkot; ˈweɪskəʊt/ *n* [C] *BrE* a piece of clothing without arms that you wear over a shirt【英】马甲，〔西服〕背心; VEST¹ (2) *AmE*【美】

waistcoat 马甲，背心

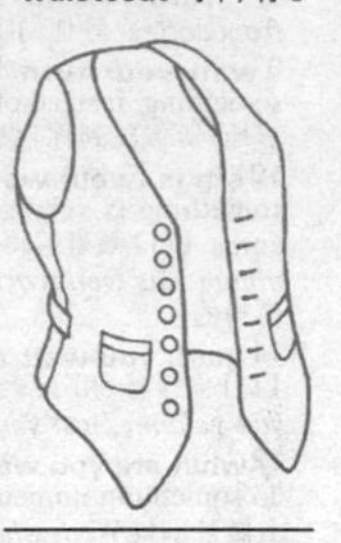

waist-deep /ˌ‥ˈ◂/ *adj, adv* deep enough to reach your waist 齐腰深的[地]: *waist-deep in muddy water* 在齐腰深的泥水中

waist-high /ˌ‥ˈ◂/ *adj, adv* high enough to reach your waist 齐腰高的[地]: *waist-high grass* 齐腰高的草

waist·line /ˋwestˌlaɪn; ˈweɪstlaɪn/ *n* **1** [singular] the amount you measure around the waist, especially used to judge how fat or thin you are 腰围: *a trim waistline* 苗条的腰身 | **watch your waistline** (=to be careful about what you eat so you do not get fat) 注意你的腰围，控制体重 **2** the position of the waist of a piece of clothing〔衣服的〕腰身部分

wait¹ /wet; weɪt/ *v* 1 1

1 ►DELAY/NOT START STH 延迟/未开始某事◄ [I] to not do something or go somewhere until something else happens, someone arrives etc 等，等候，等待: *Hurry up! Everyone's waiting.* 快点！大家在等着呢。| *Wait right here until I come back.* 就在这儿等，直到我回来。| **wait for sth/sb** *We had to wait over an hour for the bus.* 我们不得不花一个多小时等候公共汽车。| **wait until** *They'll just have to wait until I'm ready.* 他们得等到我准备好。| **wait for 3 hours/2 weeks etc** *Where have you been? I've been waiting for ages.* 你去哪里了？我等了好久。| **wait to do sth** *Are you waiting to use the phone?* 你在等着用电话吗？| **keep sb waiting** (=make someone wait, especially by arriving late)〔尤指迟到而〕使某人一直等候 *I'm sorry to have kept you waiting.* 我真抱歉让你一直等着。

2 ►EXPECT STH TO HAPPEN 期待某事发生◄ [I] to expect something to happen that has not happened yet 期待，盼望: *"Have you heard about the job?" "No, I'm still waiting."* "你听到那份工作的消息了吗？""没有，我一直在期待着呢。" | **wait for sth** *I'm still waiting for my test results.* 我还在等测验结果。| **wait for sb to do sth/wait for sth to happen** *I'm just waiting for him to realize how stupid he's been.* 我在等着他意识到自己有多么笨。

3 wait a minute/second/moment etc *spoken*【口】**a)** used to stop someone for a short time when they are leaving or starting to do something 等一下，慢着〔用于拖延某人离开或开始做某事〕: *Wait a second, I'll get my coat and come with you.* 等一等，我拿上大衣和你一起去。**b)** used to interrupt someone, especially because you do not agree with what they are saying 且慢〔用于打断别人的话，尤其是你反对的话〕: *Wait a minute! That's not what we agreed!* 且慢！我们同意的可不是那样！**c)** used when you suddenly remember or notice something 别忙〔用于突然想起或注意到某事〕: *Wait a moment, I'm sure I know her name.* 别忙，我肯定知道她的姓名。

4 I can't wait/I can hardly wait *informal*【非正式】**a)** used when you feel excited and impatient about something that is going to happen soon 我急着/等不及〔用于对即将发生的事感到兴奋和迫不及待〕: *We're going to Australia on Saturday – I can't wait!* 我们星期六去澳大利亚——我都等不及了！| **sb can't wait to do sth** *Tina can't wait to get home.* 蒂娜急着回家。| [**+for**] *I can't wait for my vacation.* 我迫不及待要放假。**b)** *spoken humorous* used to say that something seems likely to be very boring【口，幽默】我等不及了〔用于表示某事看来十分乏味〕: *A lecture on transformational grammar? I can hardly wait.* 有关转换语法的讲座？我可等不及了。

5 sth can/can't wait used to say that something is not, or is very urgent 某事不急[可以等着]/特急[刻不容缓]: *"What's so important? Can't it wait till tomorrow?" "No, it can't."* "什么事这么重要？不能等到明天吗？""不行，此事迫在眉睫。"

6 wait and see *especially spoken* used to say that someone should be patient because they will find out about something later【尤口】等着瞧〔用于叫某人耐心等待事情的结果〕: **sb will have to wait and see** *You'll have to wait and see what Father Christmas brings you.* 你们必须耐心等待，看看圣诞老人会给你们带来什么礼物。

7 wait until/till *spoken* used when you are excited about telling or showing someone something【口】等到…〔用于兴奋地告

诉某人某事或向某人展示某物〕: *Wait till you see Gaby's new house!* 等你看到加比的新家再说!

8 be waiting if something is waiting for you, it is ready for you to use, collect etc 等着〔表示某东西已准备好, 可供使用、提取等〕: *The report was typed up and waiting when they came back from coffee.* 等他们喝完咖啡回来, 报告已经打印好了。

9 wait your turn to stay calm until it is your turn to do something, instead of trying to move ahead of other people〔冷静地〕等候轮到你〔做某事〕

10 sth is (well) worth waiting for *spoken* used to say that something is very good, even though it takes a long time to come【口】某事值得等〔表示某事很好, 值得久等〕: *Their new album was well worth waiting for.* 他们的新唱片等待已久, 是值得的。

11 (just) you wait *spoken* used to warn or threaten someone【口】你等着〔用于警告或威胁某人〕: *I'll get you back for what you've done, just you wait.* 你等着, 我会跟你算账的。

12 what are you waiting for? *spoken* used to tell someone to do something immediately【口】你还在等什么?〔用于叫某人马上做某事〕: *Well, what are you waiting for? Go and apologize.* 唷, 你还在等什么呀? 道歉去。

13 what are we waiting for? *spoken* used to say in a cheerful way that you think everyone should start doing something immediately【口】我们还在等什么呀?〔高兴地表示你认为大家应立即做某事〕

14 wait for it *spoken*【口】**a)** used just before you tell someone something that is funny or surprising 且听这个〔用于表示要说的话有趣或使人吃惊〕: *Guess how much he won? Wait for it – $400,000!* 猜猜他赢了多少? 听着——40万美元! **b)** used to tell someone not to do something until the correct time because they seem very impatient to do it now〔用于告诉焦急的人〕等适当的时机到来再说

15 wait your chance/opportunity (to do sth) to wait until you have the best conditions to succeed in doing something 等待机遇/时机〔做某事〕: *Wilson was merely waiting his chance to get revenge.* 威尔逊只是在伺机报复。

16 be waiting in the wings to be ready to do something if it is necessary or if a suitable time comes 正时刻准备着〔做某事, 如果有需要或时机适当〕

17 wait on tables/wait at table *BrE formal*【英, 正式】, **wait tables** *AmE*【美】to serve food to people at their table in a restaurant〔在餐厅里〕侍候进餐

18 wait dinner/lunch etc (for sb) *AmE* to delay a meal until someone arrives【美】等〔某人〕吃晚饭/午饭: *Don't wait dinner for me, I'll be home late.* 别等我吃饭, 我要晚回家。

19 (play) a waiting game to do nothing deliberately and wait to see what other people do, in order to get an advantage for yourself 待机而动的策略

wait around also 又作 **wait about** *BrE*【英】*phr v* [I] to stay in the same place and do nothing while you are waiting for something to happen, someone to arrive etc〔无所事事地〕等待: *We waited around at the stage door to try and see the stars.* 我们在剧场后门等着, 想看看这些明星。

wait behind *phr v* [I] to stay somewhere after other people have left〔待他人走后〕留下来: *Paolo waited behind to speak to her alone.* 保罗留下来和她单独说话。

wait in *phr v* [I] *BrE* to stay at home and wait there for someone to arrive【英】在家等候〔某人到来〕: *I have to wait in for the repair man.* 我得在家等修理工来。

wait on sb/sth *phr v* [T] **1** to serve food to someone at their table, especially in a restaurant〔尤指在餐馆〕侍候〔客人〕进餐 **2** to wait for a particular event, piece of information etc, especially before doing something or making a decision〔尤指在做某事或决定前〕等待〔某事件或消息〕: *We're waiting on the blood test results.* 我们在等血液化验结果。**3 wait on sb hand and foot** *often humorous* to do everything for someone while they do nothing【常幽默】无微不至地侍候某人: *His wife waits on him hand and foot.* 他妻子侍候他, 无微不至。

wait sth ↔ **out** *phr v* [T] if you wait out an event or period or time, especially an unpleasant one, you wait for it to finish 耐心等待〔尤指讨厌的事件、时期或时间〕结束: *Let's find a place where we can wait out the storm.* 让我们找一个地方躲避暴风雨。

wait up *phr v* [I] **1** to wait for someone to return before you go to bed 等候着〔某人〕不睡: [+for] *Don't wait up for me – I'll be very late.* 不要熬夜等我, 我要很晚才回来。**2 Wait up!** *AmE* used to tell someone to stop, so that you can talk to them or go with them【美】〔叫别人〕停下片刻〔让自己赶上或跟他说话〕; 等一等!

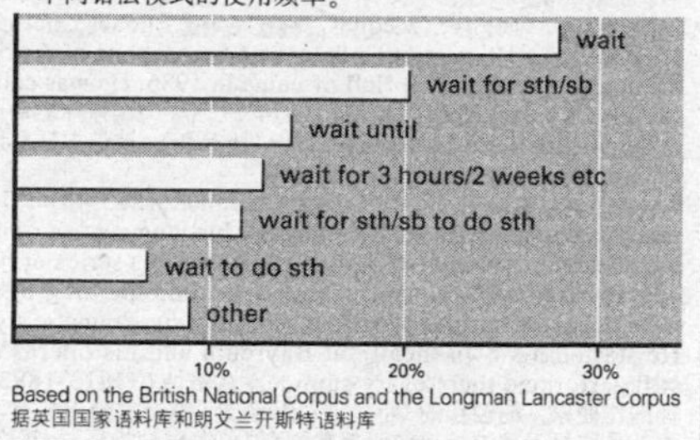

USAGE NOTE 用法说明: WAIT

WORD CHOICE 词语辨析: **wait for, await, wait, expect, look forward to**

If you **wait for** someone to come or for something to happen, you delay doing something or change what you are doing until they come or it happens. Often you do not do other things because you are **waiting**. wait for 指等候某人到来或某事发生, 表示你推迟做某事, 或改变正在做的工作直到某人到来或某事发生, 结果常常因等候而什么也没有做: *Why are you standing there? I'm waiting for John (to come).* 你为什么站在那儿? 我在等约翰(来)。| *I'm waiting to use that machine.* 我在等着用那台机器。**Await** is a much more formal word for **wait for**. await 比 wait for 正式得多。

If you **expect** someone or something, you are sure that the person will come or that the event will happen, but you do not necessarily change what you are doing now because of this. expect 指期待某人会来或某事会发生, 你肯定那人会来或那事会发生, 而你不必为此而改变正在做的事: *We're expecting a cold winter.* 我们预料会有一个寒冷的冬天。| *What kind of result are you expecting?* 你期待的是一种什么结局?

Waiting is something you do; **expecting** is a state of mind. waiting (等待) 是你在做的事; expecting (期待) 则是一种思想状态。

If you are expecting something good to happen and feel happy about it, you **look forward to** it 如果你期待某种好事发生, 并且为此而感到高兴, 适当的用语是 look forward to (盼望): *I'm looking forward to seeing him again.* 我盼望再次见到他。

GRAMMAR 语法

You **wait for** something (NOT *wait it*). But you **await** something (NOT *await for it*). 表示等待某事用 wait for it〔不用 wait it〕, 或用 await it〔不用 await for it〕。

wait² *n* [singular] a period of time in which you wait for something to happen, someone to arrive etc 等候[等待]的时间: [+for] *We then faced a six-month wait for the results to arrive.* 结果出来前, 我们要等六个月。—see also 另见 **lie in wait** (LIE¹ (6))

wait·er /ˈwetɚ; ˈweɪtə/ *n* [C] a man who serves food and drink at the tables in a restaurant〔餐馆的〕男服务员, 男侍应生 —see picture on page A15 参见 A15 页图

Waiting for God·ot /ˌwetɪŋ fɚ ˈgɑdo; ˌweɪtɪŋ fə ˈgɒdəʊ/ (1955) a play by the Irish writer Samuel Beckett about two men, Vladimir and Estragon, waiting for a third man, Godot, who never comes. The play is a typical example of the theatre of the absurd, and people use the phrase 'waiting for Godot' to describe a situation where they are waiting for something to happen but it probably never will.《等待戈多》〔(1955), 爱尔兰作家塞缪尔·贝克特的剧作。剧中主人公弗拉德米尔和埃斯特拉贡两人等待一个名叫戈多的男子, 但此人一直没有出现。该剧是荒诞派戏剧的代表作。后来人们就用"等待戈多"一词来形容等待一个不可能发生的奇迹〕: *I still haven't had my refund from the tax department – it's like waiting for Godot.* 我还没收到税务部门的退款, 就像等待戈多一样没有希望。

wait·ing list /ˈ· · ·/ *n* [C] a list of people who have asked for something but who must wait before they can have it 等候者名单〔等候所要得到事物者的名单〕: *a two-year waiting list* 一份要等两年的等候者名单

CULTURAL NOTE 文化注释

In the UK, newspapers often discuss the subject of 'NHS (=National Health Service) waiting lists', meaning lists of people who need a medical operation but cannot have it immediately. Politicians often promise to reduce waiting lists, but only rarely succeed in doing this. 英国的报纸常以"国民保健制度下的等候者名单"为主题进行讨论，这份名单所列的是那些需要手术治疗却不能得到即时治疗的病人。政治家常常许诺会减少等候时间，但一般成果寥寥。

waiting room /'· · ·/ *n* [C] a room for people to wait in, for example to see a doctor, take a train etc 等候室; 候诊室; 候车室

wait·ress /'wetrɪs; 'weɪtrɨs/ *n* [C] a woman who serves food and drink at the tables in a restaurant 〔餐馆的〕女服务员, 女侍应生 —see picture on page A15 参见 A15 页图

waive /wev; weɪv/ *v* [T] to state officially that a right, rule etc can be ignored, because at this time it is not useful or important 宣布放弃〔权利〕; 宣布取消〔规则〕: *She waived her right to a lawyer.* 她放弃了聘请律师的权利。

waiv·er /'wevɚ; 'weɪvə/ *n* [C] *technical* an official written statement saying that a right, claim etc can be waived【术语】弃权声明书

wake¹ /wek; weɪk/ *v past tense* **woke** /wok; wəʊk/ *or* **waked** *AmE*【美】*past participle* **woken** /'wokən; 'wəʊkən/ *or* **waked** *AmE*【美】[I,T] also 又作 **wake up** to stop sleeping, or to make someone stop sleeping 睡醒, 醒来; 唤醒, 弄醒: *James usually wakes up early.* 詹姆斯通常醒得早。| *I'll wake you up when it's time to leave.* 到要走的时候我会叫醒你。| *Try not to wake the baby.* 别把宝宝吵醒。

wake up *phr v* [I,T] **1** to start to listen or pay attention to something 开始听着, 开始注意: **Wake up!** (=give me your attention) 注意! *Wake up at the back there!* 后面的人注意! **2 wake up and smell the coffee** *AmE spoken* used to tell someone to recognize the truth or reality of something【美口】〔用于叫某人〕面对现实, 正视事实

wake (up) to *phr v* [T] **1** to experience something as you are waking up 醒来后发现: *Nancy woke to the sound of birds outside her window.* 南希醒来后听见窗外有鸟叫声。**2** to start to realize and understand a danger, an idea etc 开始觉察[认识]到〔危险、想法等〕: *It's time you woke up to the fact that it's a tough world out there.* 外面是冷酷的世界, 你该认识到这个事实了。

wake² *n* [C] **1 in the wake of** if something, especially something bad, happens in the wake of an event, it happens afterwards and usually as a result of it 〔尤指不好的事〕紧随…而来; 作为…的结果: *Famine followed in the wake of the drought.* 旱灾带来的是饥荒。**2 in sb's/sth's wake** behind or after someone or something 紧跟某人/某物后面: *The car left clouds of dust in its wake.* 汽车开过, 后面扬起阵阵灰尘。**3** the time before a funeral when friends and relatives meet to remember the dead person 〔葬礼前的〕守灵 **4** the track made behind a boat as it moves through the water 〔船开过后留下的〕航迹, 尾流

wake·ful /'wekfəl; 'weɪkfəl/ *adj* **1 a)** unable to sleep 不能入睡的, 失眠的: *lying wakeful in the hot night* 酷热的晚上躺着不能入睡 **b)** a wakeful period of time is one when you cannot sleep 失眠的〔时间〕**2** *formal* ready to do whatever is necessary【正式】戒备的, 警觉的 —**wakefulness** *n* [U]

wak·en /'wekən; 'weɪkən/ also 又作 **waken up** *v* [I,T] *formal* to wake, or to wake someone【正式】醒来; 唤醒: *She gently wakened the sleeping child.* 她轻轻地叫醒熟睡中的小孩。

wak·ey-wak·ey /,wekɪ 'wekɪ; ,weɪki 'weɪki/ *interjection BrE spoken* used to tell someone in a joking way to wake up【英口】醒醒〔用于以开玩笑形式唤醒某人〕

wak·ing /'wekɪŋ; 'weɪkɪŋ/ *adj* **waking hours/life/day etc** all the time when you are awake 醒着的时刻/生活/日子等: *How his face haunted her every waking moment!* 只要她一睁眼, 脑子里就满是他的音容笑貌!

Wal·den Pond /,wɔldn̩ 'pɑnd; ,wɔːldən 'pɒnd/ a small lake in Massachusetts in the US near the place where Henry David Thoreau lived and after which he named his book 'Walden, or Life in the Woods'. 瓦尔登湖〔美国马萨诸塞州的一个小湖。亨利·大卫·梭罗曾居住在该湖附近, 其作品《瓦尔登湖或林中生活》据此得名〕

Wal·dorf-As·to·ri·a, the /,wɔldɔrf æ'stɔrɪə; ,wɔːldɔːf æ'stɔːriə/ *trademark* a large, expensive hotel in New York City【商标】沃尔多夫—阿斯托里亚酒店〔纽约市一大型豪华酒店〕

Wales /welz; weɪlz/ a country in the United Kingdom, west of England, which was an independent country until it was brought under English rule in 1284. Population: 2,903,085 (2001). Capital: Cardiff. The country's Welsh name is Cymru. Traditionally, its main industries were farming, especially sheep farming and, in South Wales, coal mining. The mines have now all closed. The Welsh language is spoken by many people, especially in the north. The Welsh assembly gives the Welsh people more power to govern themselves while still being part of the UK. Some people, including the political party Plaid Cymru, want Wales to be an independent country. The national symbols of Wales are the LEEK, the DAFFODIL, and the red DRAGON. The PATRON SAINT is Saint David. 威尔士〔联合王国的组成部分, 东临英格兰, 1284 年起接受英格兰统治, 之前曾为独立国家。人口: 2,903,085 (2001), 首府: 加的夫。威尔士语称该国为 Cymru。传统支柱产业为农牧业, 尤以养羊业为主。南威尔士曾以采煤业为主, 但目前煤矿均已关闭。许多当地人尤其是北方人使用威尔士语。威尔士国民议会的成立给威尔士人赋予了更大的自治权, 但其仍为英国的一部分。包括威尔士党 (Plaid Cymru) 人在内的一些人支持威尔士独立。威尔士的民族标志为韭葱、黄水仙、红龙, 其主保圣人是圣大卫〕

Wales, the Prince of —see 见 PRINCE OF WALES

Wa·les·a /və'lɛsə; və'lesə/, **Lech** /lɛk; lek/ (1943-) the President of Poland from 1990 to 1995. He was leader of the Trade Union Solidarity during the 1980s and became popular in western countries for his opposition to Poland's Communist government. After losing the 1995 elections, Walesa became an ordinary citizen again. 瓦文萨〔(1943-), 1990 至 1995 年任波兰总统。20 世纪 80 年代曾担任团结工会领导人, 因反对波兰共产党政府受到西方国家欢迎。1995 年大选落败后, 他再度成为普通公民〕

walk¹ /wɔk; wɔːk/ *v*

1 ▶MOVE ALONG 往前走◀ [I] to move along putting one foot in front of the other 走, 行走: *We must have walked ten miles today.* 今天我们想必已经走了 10 英里。| [+along/around/up etc] *How long does it take to walk into town?* 进城要走多久? | *walk down the street* 走在街上 | **walk back/ home** *Marcus and I walked back through the park.* 我和马库斯穿过公园走回去。| **walk up to/walk over to** (=to go towards someone or something) 〔向某人或物〕走过去 *She just walked up to him and slapped his face.* 她走到他面前, 给了他一个耳光。—see picture on page A24 参见 A24 页图

2 ▶WALK ACROSS A PLACE 走过某处◀ [T] to walk in order to get somewhere, across a particular area or distance 〔为到某处而〕走过〔一个地方或一段距离〕: *I parked the car and walked the rest of the way.* 我停好汽车, 剩下的路是步行去的。

3 walk the dog to take a dog for a walk 遛狗: *Grandma's out walking the dog.* 祖母外出遛狗去了。

4 walk sb home/to school etc to walk somewhere with someone to make sure that they are safe 送某人回家/到学校等: *It's late – I'll walk you home.* 天色已晚, 我送你回家。

5 go walking to walk for pleasure and exercise, especially in the countryside 〔尤指在乡间〕散步, 徒步旅行: *Rhys and I went walking in Snowdonia last summer.* 去年夏天我和里斯在斯诺多尼亚徒步旅行。

6 walk it *spoken*【口】**a)** to make a journey by walking 徒步旅行: *If the last bus has gone, we'll have to walk it.* 如果末班车已过, 我们只得走回去了。**b)** *BrE* to succeed or win something easily【英】轻易取胜: *We thought it would be a tough match but in fact we walked it, winning 5–0.* 我们本以为这是一场硬仗, 但实际上我们以 5:0 轻易取胜。

7 walk free to leave a court of law without being punished or sent to prison 无罪释放: *the case of a teenage vandal who walked free from court* 一个故意破坏公物的少年被无罪释放的案件

8 walking pace the speed that you normally walk at 步速

9 walk tall to be proud and confident because you know that you have not done anything wrong 〔没有做坏事所以〕光明磊落, 理直气壮

10 walk on eggs/eggshells to treat someone vey carefully because they easily become very angry 〔对待易怒的人〕小心翼翼, 如履薄冰

11 ▶HEAVY OBJECT 重物◀ [T] to move a heavy object slowly by moving first one side and then the other 将〔重物〕一步一步地挪动

12 walk the plank a) to be forced to walk along a board laid over the side of the ship until you fall off into the sea 〔被迫〕走跳板〔即走在船舷边的跳板上, 直到掉进海里〕**b)** *AmE informal* to be dismissed from your job【美, 非正式】被解雇

13 walk on air to feel extremely happy 得意扬扬, 感到飘飘然

14 walk sb off their feet *BrE* to make someone tired by making them walk too far【英】使某人走得精疲力竭

W

walk away *phr v* [I +from] **1** to leave a bad situation, instead of trying to make it better 逃避〔困境〕: *You can't just walk away from 15 years of marriage!* 你不能就这样一走了之，放弃15年的婚姻！**2** to come out of an accident or very bad situation without being harmed 从〔事故或险情中〕平安脱身: *Miraculously both drivers walked away unscathed.* 两名司机奇迹般死里逃生，安然无恙。

walk away with sth *phr v* to win something easily 轻易赢得: *She knew all the answers and walked away with the prize.* 她知道所有的答案，轻而易举地赢得了奖品。

walk in *phr v* [I,T] **1** to enter a building or room especially unexpectedly or without being invited 突然[擅自]闯入: *You can't just walk in here whenever you feel like it!* 你不能就这样擅自闯入这里！| **walk in the door** *I walked in the door and caught him at it.* 我一进屋，撞见他在捣蛋。| **walk in off the street** (=visit someone such as a doctor without having previously arranged to see them) 未经预约拜访〔医生等〕*People can walk in off the street and get confidential pregnancy counselling.* 人们可以不经预约随时前来得到保密的妊娠咨询。**2** **walk in dirt/leaves etc** to make mud, leaves etc stick to the floor by walking over it when you have mud, leaves etc on your shoes〔屋里〕踩进泥巴/树叶等

walk in on sb *phr v* [T] to go into a place and interrupt someone who you did not expect to be there 进入〔某地〕出乎意料地撞上〔某人〕: *Arriving home early one day, she walked in on her husband and his mistress.* 一天她提早回家，撞上了丈夫和他的情妇。

walk into sth *phr v* [T] **1** to hit an object accidentally as you are walking along〔意外地〕撞着〔某物〕: **walk straight/right/bang etc into** *Zeke wasn't looking where he was going and walked straight into a tree.* 齐克走路不看路，径直撞到了树上。**2** if you walk into an unpleasant situation, you become involved in it without intending to〔无意地〕陷入〔尴尬局面〕**3** if you walk into a job, you get it very easily 轻易得到〔工作〕: *Nowadays you can't expect to leave university and walk into a job.* 如今你不能指望一出大学校门就轻易地得到一份工作。**4** to make yourself look stupid when you could easily have avoided it if you had been more careful〔由于不慎〕招致〔麻烦〕: **walk straight/right into** *You walked right into that one!* 那是你疏忽大意造成的！

walk off *phr v* [I] **1** to leave someone by walking away from them, especially in a rude or angry way〔尤指粗鲁或愤怒地〕离开〔某人〕: *Don't just walk off when I'm trying to talk to you!* 你别急着走，我想跟你说话！**2** [**walk** sth ↔ **off**] if you walk off an illness or unpleasant feeling, you go for a walk to make it go away 用散步来消除〔病痛或不快〕: *Let's go out – maybe I can walk off this headache.* 我们出去走走——或许我就不头痛了。| **walk off dinner/a meal etc** (=go for a walk so that your stomach feels less full) 走路帮助消化食物

walk off with sth *phr v* [T] to take or steal something, especially in a relaxed or confident way〔轻松或自信地〕拿走，偷走〔某物〕: *Thieves walked off with two million dollars' worth of jewellery.* 小偷毫不费力地偷走了价值200万美元的珠宝。| *Lottery winners can walk off with a cool £18 million.* 彩票中奖者能轻而易举地拿走足足1800万英镑。

W

walk over sb *phr v* [T] to treat someone badly by always making them do what you want them to do 刻薄[轻蔑]地对待〔某人〕: **walk all over sb** *It's terrible – she lets her kids just walk all over her.* 太可怕了——她就这样听任孩子们的摆布。

walk out *phr v* [I] **1** to go outside 走出去: [+into] *Payton walked out into the cold morning air.* 佩顿走了出去，走到清晨的寒冷空气中。**2** to leave a place suddenly, especially because you disapprove of something〔尤指由于反对某事而〕突然离开，退席: *Mike walked out after a row with one of his colleagues.* 与一名同事大吵之后迈克退席了。**3** to stop working as a protest 罢工〔以示抗议〕: *The electricians have walked out, and will stay out until their demands are met.* 电工举行罢工，并将坚持到他们的要求得到满足为止。**4** **walk out (with)** *old use* to have a romantic relationship with someone【旧】与…谈情说爱

walk out on sb/sth *phr v* [T] **1** to leave your husband, wife etc suddenly 突然遗弃〔丈夫、妻子等〕: *When she was three months pregnant, Pete walked out on her.* 她怀孕三个月时，皮特突然遗弃了她。**2** to stop doing something you have agreed to do or that you are responsible for 不履行〔答应了或有责任做的事〕: *"I never walk out on a deal," Dee said.* 迪伊说："我从不违背协议。"

walk sth ↔ **through** *phr v* [T] to practise something 排练: *Let's walk through scene two to see how long it takes.* 让我们排练第二场，看看需要多长时间。| **walk sb through sth** *I'll walk you through the procedure before you do it on your own.* 在你单独做之前，我将把步骤给你演示一下。

walk² *n* **1** [C] a journey that you make by walking, especially for exercise or enjoyment〔尤指为锻炼或消遣的〕步行；散步: *It's a long walk. Maybe we should get the bus.* 走着去很远，或许我们要搭乘公共汽车。| **go for a walk** *"What did you do yesterday?" "Nothing much – I went for a walk in the park."* "昨天你做了什么？""没做什么，只是到公园散散步。" | **take/have a walk** *She takes a short walk every day before breakfast.* 她每天早餐前都去散散步。| **take sb for a walk** *Why don't we take the kids for a walk?* 我们为什么不带孩子们去散步呢？| **walk to/through/across etc** *a short walk through the castle grounds* 穿过城堡的短途步行 | **long/short/five-mile/ten-minute etc walk** *I would put on heavy boots and go for long walks.* 我将穿上厚底靴作长途步行。**2** [C] a fixed ROUTE¹ (1) that you walk, especially through an attractive or interesting area 步行的路径〔尤指要经过胜地〕: *There are some particularly interesting walks to the north of the city.* 城市北部有一些特别有趣的散步场所。**3** [U] the way someone walks 步态: *You can often recognize people by their walk.* 你往往可以从走路的姿态辨认出一个人。**4** **take a walk** *especially AmE spoken* used to rudely tell someone to go away or to stop talking nonsense【尤美，口】走开〔用于粗鲁地叫某人离开或停止说废话〕，快走: *"Harry's here to see you." "Well, tell him to take a walk."* "哈里来看你了。""嗯，叫他滚吧。" —see also 另见 WALK OF LIFE, **sponsored walk** (SPONSORED)

walk·a·bout /ˈwɔkəˌbaʊt; ˈwɔːkəbaʊt/ *n* [C] **1** *BrE informal* an occasion when an important person walks through a crowd, talking informally to people【英，非正式】〔重要人物〕走入人群与他们闲聊: **go on a walkabout** *The Prince went on a walkabout near the war memorial.* 王子走进战争纪念碑附近的人群中和他们闲谈。**2** **go walkabout** *BrE spoken humorous* to disappear【英口，幽默】消失: *My watch seems to have gone walkabout again.* 我的手表看来又不见了。

walk·a·way /ˈwɔkəˌwe; ˈwɔːkəweɪ/ *n* [C] *AmE informal* an easy victory【美，非正式】轻易取得的胜利; WALKOVER *BrE*【英】

walk·er /ˈwɔkə; ˈwɔːkə/ *n* [C] **1** *especially BrE* someone who walks for pleasure or exercise; HIKER【尤英】〔散步或锻炼的〕步行者: *a keen hill-walker* 热衷于走山路的人 **2** **a fast/slow etc walker** someone who walks fast, slowly etc 走路走得快/慢等的人 **3** a piece of equipment for helping someone to walk; ZIMMER FRAME 助行架

Walker Cup, the /ˈ‥ ˌ‥, ˌ‥ ˈ‥/ a GOLF competition between two teams, one British and one American, of non-professional male golfers 沃克杯〔英美两支高尔夫球队之间的对抗赛。参赛者为非职业男性选手〕

walk·ies /ˈwɔkɪz; ˈwɔːkiz/ *n* [plural] *BrE spoken* used to tell a dog that you are going to take it for a walk【英口】散步〔对狗用语〕: *Come on, Shep! Walkies!* 来，谢普！散步去！

walk·ie-talk·ie /ˈwɔkɪˌtɔkɪ; ˌwɔːkiˈtɔːki/ *n* [C] one of a pair of radios that you can carry with you, and use to speak to the person who has the other radio 步话机，无线电对讲机

walk-in /ˈ‥ ˌ‥/ *adj* [only before noun 仅用于名词前] big enough for a person to walk inside 大得能容人走进的: *a walk-in closet* 步入式壁橱

walk·ing¹ /ˈwɔkɪŋ; ˈwɔːkɪŋ/ *n* [U] **1** *especially BrE* the activity or sport of going for walks, especially in the countryside; go hiking (HIKE¹ (1))【尤英】〔尤指在乡村的〕徒步旅行: **go walking** *We went walking near Cambridge last weekend.* 上周末我们在剑桥附近散步。**2** the sport of walking long distances as fast as you can without actually running 快步行走，竞走〔体育运动〕

walking² *adj* [only before noun 仅用于名词前] **1** **walking shoes/boots** shoes or boots that are strong and comfortable, because they are intended for walking long distances〔用于长途步行的〕轻便鞋/靴 —see picture at 参见 BOOT¹ 图 **2** **walking holiday/tour etc** *especially BrE* a holiday etc in which you walk a lot, especially in the countryside; hiking trip (HIKING)【尤英】〔尤指在乡村的〕徒步旅行的假日/游览等 **3** **walking dictionary/encyclopaedia** *humorous* someone who knows a lot, and always has the information that you want【幽默】活字典/百科全书〔形容博学的人〕**4** **walking disaster (area)** *humorous* someone who always drops things, has accidents, makes mistakes etc【幽默】冒失鬼〔形容经常丢三落四，发生事故、犯错等的人〕

walking pa·pers /ˈ‥ ˌ‥, ˌ‥ ˈ‥/ *n* [plural] **give sb their walking papers** *AmE* to tell someone that they must leave a place or a job【美】〔给某人的〕解雇通知书，辞退书 —see also 另见 **be given/get your marching orders** (MARCH¹ (5))

walking stick /ˈ· · ˌ/ *n* [C] **1** a stick that is used to support someone, especially an old person, while they walk〔尤指老人步行用的〕手杖，拐杖 —see picture at 参见 STICK[2] 图 **2** *AmE* a STICK INSECT【美】竹节虫

Walk·man /ˈwɔkmən; ˈwɔːkmən/ *n* [C] *trademark* a small CASSETTE PLAYER with HEADPHONES, that you carry with you so that you can listen to music; PERSONAL STEREO【商标】〔带耳机的〕随身听

walk of life /ˌ· · ˈ·/ *n* [C] the position in society someone has, especially the type of job they have〔尤指因工作性质决定的〕社会阶层: **from every walk of life/from all walks of life** *The club has members from every walk of life, from plumbers to doctors.* 该俱乐部的成员包括从管道工到医生的社会各阶层人士。

walk-on /ˈ· ·/ also 又作 **walk-on part** /ˈ· ·, ·/ *n* [C] a small acting part with no words to say in a play or film, or an actor who has a part like this〔戏剧或影片的〕跑龙套角色; 无台词的小角色

walk-out /ˈwɔkˌaut; ˈwɔːk-aʊt/ *n* [C] an occasion when people stop working or leave somewhere as a protest〔表示抗议的〕罢工; 退席，退会: **stage a walk-out** *The Irish delegation staged a walk-out in protest.* 爱尔兰代表退席以示抗议。—see also 另见 **walk out** (WALK[1])

walk·o·ver /ˈwɔkˌovɚ; ˈwɔːkˌəʊvə/ *n* [C] *informal* a very easy victory【非正式】轻易取得的胜利; WALKAWAY *AmE*【美】—see also 另见 **walk over** (WALK[1])

walk-up /ˈ· ·/ *n* [C] *AmE informal*【美，非正式】**1** a tall building with apartments in it that does not have an ELEVATOR (1) 无电梯的公寓大楼 **2** an apartment, office etc in a building like this 无电梯大楼里的公寓房间[办公室]

walk·way /ˈwɔkˌwe; ˈwɔːkweɪ/ *n* [C] an outside path, often above the ground, built to connect two parts of a building or two buildings〔连接建筑物两部分或两座建筑间的〕走道，人行通道: *a covered walkway* 有篷的人行通道

wall[1] /wɔl; wɔːl/ *n* [C]

1 ►AROUND AN AREA 围着一个区域◄ an upright flat structure made of stone or brick, that divides one area from another〔用石头或砖砌成、把区域分开的〕墙; 围墙: *The garden was surrounded by a high brick wall.* 一堵高高的砖墙把花园围起来。

2 ►IN A BUILDING 在建筑物中◄ one of the sides of a room or building〔房间或建筑物的〕墙壁: *We decided to paint the walls blue.* 我们决定把墙壁漆成蓝色。

3 ►TUBE/CONTAINER 管子/容器◄ the side of something hollow, such as a pipe or tube〔中空物如管子或管道的〕内壁，隔层: *The walls of the blood vessels had been damaged.* 血管壁已经受损。

4 wall of fire/water etc a tall mass of something such as fire or water, that prevents anything getting through〔阻止他物通过的高大〕火墙/水墙等: *A wall of fire was advancing through the forest.* 一道火墙在森林中蔓延开来。

5 wall of silence a situation in which nobody will tell you what you want to know〔你想知道某事却〕无人回应，沉默: *The police investigation was met with a wall of silence.* 警方的调查处处碰壁，没人配合。

6 go up the wall *BrE spoken* to become very angry【英口】非常恼火; 狂怒: *My mum went up the wall when I told her I wanted to leave school.* 我告诉妈妈我想辍学，她听了勃然大怒。

7 drive sb up the wall *spoken* to annoy someone very much【口】使某人非常恼火: *I wish she'd stop muttering – it drives me up the wall!* 我希望她不要再唠叨了——快把我逼疯了!

8 go to the wall *informal* if a company goes to the wall, it fails, especially because of financial difficulties【非正式】〔尤指公司因财政困难而〕破产，倒闭

9 these four walls *spoken* the room that you are in, especially considered as a private place【口】在屋里〔尤指私人地方〕; 私下里: *I don't want anything that I have said repeated outside these four walls.* 我不想我在这间屋里说的任何话传出去。

10 be climbing/crawling up the wall *informal to be* feeling extremely anxious, dissatisfied, and impatient, especially because you are waiting for something or cannot do something you want to do【非正式】〔尤指因等待某事或不能做某事而〕极度焦急，不满，不耐烦; 心烦意乱: *Last time I gave up smoking I was crawling up the wall within a few hours.* 上次我戒烟才几小时，便开始心烦意乱。

11 walls have ears used to warn people to be careful what they say, because other people, especially enemies, could be listening 隔墙有耳〔用于警告人们说话时要注意，以防备他人，尤指敌人听见〕

12 hit the wall *informal* to reach the point of greatest physical tiredness when doing a sport【非正式】运动时身体疲劳度达到极限 —see also 另见 **have your back to the wall** (BACK[2] (20)), **bang your head against a brick wall** (BANG[2] (5)), **the writing is on the wall** (WRITING (7)), OFF-THE-WALL

wall[2] *v*

wall sth ↔ **in** *phr v* [T] to surround an open area with walls 用墙围住: *They decided to wall the garden in.* 他们决定用墙把花园围起来。

wall sth ↔ **off** *phr v* [T] to keep one area or room separate from another, by building a wall 用墙〔把一个区域或房间〕隔开: *The control room is walled off by soundproof glass.* 控制室用隔音玻璃隔开。

wall sb/sth ↔ **up** *phr v* [T] **1** to fill in a doorway, window etc with bricks or stone 用砖石堵上〔通道、窗等〕: *The entrance had long since been walled up.* 入口处早就堵死了。**2** used to say that someone is a prisoner 监禁〔用于说某人是囚犯〕: *I can't bear the thought of her walled up in a cell.* 一想到她被关押在牢房里，我就无法忍受。

Wal·la·bies, the /ˈwɑləbiz; ˈwɒləbiːz/ Australia's international Rugby Union team 袋鼠队〔澳大利亚国际橄榄球联队〕

wal·la·by /ˈwɑləbɪ; ˈwɒləbi/ *n* [C] an Australian animal like a small KANGAROO 沙袋鼠〔澳大利亚的一种小体形袋鼠〕

Wallace /ˈwɑlɪs; ˈwɒlɪ̈s/, **George** (1919-98) a US politician in the Democratic Party who was Governor of Alabama for most of the period between 1963 and 1987. Many people consider him to be RACIST because he supported SEGREGATION. He was shot in 1972, when he was trying to be chosen to represent the Democratic Party in the election for President, and after that he had to use a WHEELCHAIR. 华莱士〔(1919-1998)，美国民主党政治家，1963 至 1987 年的大部分时间任亚拉巴马州州长。他因支持种族隔离被不少人指责为种族主义者，1972 年在竞选民主党总统候选人期间遭枪击，此后不得不以轮椅代步〕

Wallace, Sir William (1272-1305) a Scottish soldier and politician, who was a leader of the fight to keep Scotland independent of England. After being defeated in battle by the English king, Edward I, he was taken to London and hanged. In Scotland people regard him as a national hero. 华莱士〔(1272-1305)，苏格兰军人、政治家。他曾领导苏格兰为摆脱英格兰统治和争取独立而战。华莱士作战败给英王爱德华一世后，被押往伦敦处以绞刑。苏格兰人民尊其为民族英雄〕

Wallace and Grom·it /ˌwɑlɪs ənd ˈgrɑmɪt; ˌwɒlɪ̈s ənd ˈgrɒmɪ̈t/ *trademark* two characters in British CARTOON films made by Nick Park, which are extremely popular with both adults and children. Wallace is a man who is nice but rather stupid, who loves cheese, and who is always inventing new machines that do not work very well. Gromit, his dog, is extremely intelligent, and can read, fly a plane, and ride a MOTORCYCLE. Together they catch criminals.【商标】华莱士和格罗米特〔尼克·帕克拍摄的英国动画影片中的两个角色，颇受不同年龄的公众喜爱。华莱士是一个傻乎乎的好人，喜欢吃乳酪，总爱发明一些新机器，但却不大好用。格罗米特是他的宠物狗，聪明绝顶，识文断字，能驾飞机，会骑摩托。他俩同心协力将罪犯捉拿归案〕

wal·lah, walla /ˈwɑlɑ; ˈwɒlə/ *n* [C] *IndE, PakE* someone who does a particular kind of job or duty【印，巴】从事某种工作的人: *the medical wallahs* 医务工作者

wall·chart /ˈwɔltʃart; ˈwɔːltʃɑːt/ *n* [C] a large piece of paper with information on it that is fastened to a wall 挂图

walled /wɔld; wɔːld/ *adj* [only before noun 仅用于名词前] **walled garden/city/town etc** a garden etc that has a wall around it 有围墙的园子/城市/市镇等

Wal·ler /ˈwɑlɚ; ˈwɒlə/, **Fats** /fæts; fæts/ (1904-43) a US JAZZ piano player, songwriter, and band leader, famous for his humorous performances. His songs include *Honeysuckle Rose* and *Ain't Misbehavin'*. 沃勒〔(1904-1943)，美国爵士乐钢琴家、歌曲作家、乐队领队，以表演幽默风趣著称。其歌曲包括《忍冬玫瑰》和《并非无礼》〕

wal·let /ˈwɑlɪt; ˈwɒlɪ̈t/ *n* [C] **1** a small flat leather case that you carry in your pocket, for holding paper money etc〔装钞票等的〕钱包，皮夹子; BILLFOLD *AmE*【美】—compare 比较 PURSE[1] (2) —see picture at 参见 PURSE[1] 图 **2** a long leather case for official documents 公事包

wall-eyed /ˌ· ˈ·◄/ *adj AmE* having eyes that seem to point to the side, rather than straight forwards【美】斜视的

wall·flow·er /ˈwɔlˌflauɚ; ˈwɔːlˌflaʊə/ *n* [C] **1** *informal* someone at a party, dance etc who is not asked to dance or take part in the activities【非正式】"壁花"〔指在聚会、舞会等中没被邀请跳舞或参加活动的人〕**2** a sweet-smelling garden plant with yellow and red flowers 墙头花，桂竹香〔庭园植物，气味清香，开黄色和红色的花〕

wal·lop¹ /ˈwɑləp; ˈwɒləp/ *v* [T] *informal* to hit someone or something very hard【非正式】猛击〔某人或某物〕

wallop² *n* [C] *informal* a hard hit, especially with your hand【非正式】〔尤指用手〕狠揍

wal·lop·ing¹ /ˈwɑləpɪŋ; ˈwɒləpɪŋ/ *n spoken*【口】**give sb/get a walloping** to hit someone repeatedly as a punishment 给某人/遭到一顿痛打〔以示惩罚〕

walloping² *adj* [only before noun 仅用于名词前] **walloping great/big** *spoken* very big【口】非常大的: *a walloping great house in the country* 乡间一栋非常大的房子

wal·low¹ /ˈwɑlo; ˈwɒləʊ/ *v* [I] **1 wallow in self-pity/despair/defeat etc** to seem to enjoy being sad etc, especially because you get sympathy from other people 沉湎于自怜/绝望/失败等〔尤因为得到他人的同情〕: *Stop wallowing in self-pity, and do something positive.* 不要再自叹自怜，做点正经事吧。**2** if an animal wallows, it rolls around in mud, water etc for pleasure〔动物快乐地在泥、水等中〕打滚: *hippos wallowing in the mud* 在泥浆中打滚的河马 **3** if a ship or boat wallows, it moves with difficulty through a rough sea〔船舶在大浪中〕颠簸着前进

wallow² *n* **1 a wallow in sth** an act of wallowing in something 沉溺于某事: *She indulged in a wallow in self-pity.* 她老是爱顾影自怜。**2** [C] a place where animals go to wallow, especially in mud〔动物经常去打滚的〕泥沼

wall paint·ing /ˈ· ,··/ *n* [C] a picture that has been painted directly onto a wall, especially a FRESCO 壁画

wall·pa·per¹ /ˈwɔl,pepə; ˈwɔːl,peɪpə/ *n* [C,U] paper that you stick onto the walls of a room in order to decorate it 壁纸，墙纸

wallpaper² *v* [T] to put wallpaper onto the walls of a room 给〔房间〕糊墙纸

Wall Street /ˈ· ·/ *n* **1** a street in New York which is the most important financial centre in America 华尔街〔纽约市的一条街，是美国最重要的金融中心〕: *Wall Street jitters caused by the Gulf War* 海湾战争引起美国金融界的紧张不安 **2** the American STOCK MARKET 美国股票市场

Wall Street Crash, the /,· · ·ˈ·/ the sudden large fall in the value of company shares on the US Stock Exchange in October 1929. For about two years before this, the price of shares had risen very fast, and when people realized that companies were therefore worth more than their true value, they lost confidence. The severe fall that followed led directly to the Great Depression of the 1930s. 华尔街股市崩盘〔指 1929 年 10 月美国证券交易所上市公司股票价格突然大幅下跌。此前约两年时间内股价曾一路飙升，人们意识到公司股价超出了其实际价值，便丧失了信心。随之而来的股价暴跌直接导致了 20 世纪 30 年代的经济大萧条〕

Wall Street Jour·nal, The /,· · ˈ· ·/ a respected US daily newspaper, which is also sold in many other countries and which deals mainly with business and ECONOMICS《华尔街日报》〔美国一份备受推崇的日报，在其他许多国家也有销售，内容多涉及商务和经济〕—see also 另见 the FINANCIAL TIMES

wall-to-wall /,· · ˈ·◂/ *adj* **1** [only before noun 仅用于名词前] covering the whole floor 铺满整个地板的: *wall-to-wall carpeting* 铺满整个地板的地毯 **2** *informal* filling all the space or time available, especially in a way you do not like【非正式】〔尤指不情愿地〕占满所有空间[时间]的，无所不在的，无孔不入的: *wall-to-wall advertising on TV* 电视上没完没了的广告

wal·ly /ˈwɑlɪ; ˈwɒli/ *n* [C] *BrE informal* someone who behaves in a silly way【英，非正式】无能的人，笨蛋: *Stop being such a wally!* 别犯傻了！

wal·nut /ˈwɔl,nʌt; ˈwɔːlnʌt/ *n* **1** [C] a nut that you can eat, shaped like a human brain 胡桃，核桃: *coffee and walnut cake* 咖啡和核桃蛋糕 **2** [C] also 又作 **walnut tree** a tree that produces this type of nut 胡桃树 **3** [U] the wood from a walnut tree, often used to make furniture〔常用于制作家具的〕胡桃木

Wal·pole /ˈwɔlpol; ˈwɔːlpəʊl/, **Sir Rob·ert** (1676-1745) a British politician in the Whig party, who people usually regard as the first British Prime Minister. He held this position from 1721 to 1742. 沃波尔（(1676-1745)，英国辉格党政治家。后人普遍认为他是英国第一任首相，任期自 1721 至 1742 年）

wal·rus /ˈwɔlrəs; ˈwɔːlrəs/ *n* [C] a large sea animal with two long TUSKS (=like teeth) coming down from its head 海象

Walt Disney —see 见 Walt DISNEY

Walt Dis·ney World /,wɔlt ˈdɪznɪ ,wɜld; ,wɔːlt ˈdɪzni ,wɜːld/ *trademark* the official name for DisneyWorld【商标】沃尔特·迪斯尼世界〔迪斯尼世界的正式名称〕

Walter Mitty —see 见 Walter MITTY

Walting Ma·til·da /,wɔltsɪŋ məˈtɪldə; ,wɔːlsɪŋ məˈtɪldə/ a popular old Australian song which many Australians think of as their national song. It tells the story of a 'swagman' (=a worker who travels around the country carrying his possessions with him).《跳华尔兹舞的马蒂尔达》〔澳大利亚一首流行老歌。不少澳大利亚人视之为国歌。歌曲讲述了一个流浪者的故事〕

waltz¹ /wɔlts; wɔːls/ *n* [C] **1** a fairly slow dance with a strong regular beat 华尔兹舞 **2** a piece of music intended for this type of dance 华尔兹舞曲，圆舞曲: *a Strauss waltz* 施特劳斯圆舞曲

waltz² *v* **1** [I] to dance a waltz 跳华尔兹舞 **2** [I+adv/prep always] *informal* to walk somewhere calmly and confidently【非正式】神态自若地走: [**+in/into/up to**] *Jeff just waltzed up to the bar and helped himself to a drink.* 杰夫悠闲地走进酒吧，自斟自饮起来。

waltz off with sth *phr v* [T] *informal* to take something without permission or without realizing that you have done this【非正式】偷走；悄悄拿走: *Joe must have waltzed off with my jacket!* 肯定是乔偷走了我的外套！

waltz through sth *phr v* [T] *informal*【非正式】**waltz through an exam/test etc** to do an exam, test etc very well without any difficulty 轻而易举地通过考试/测验等

wam·pum /ˈwɑmpəm; ˈwɒmpəm/ *n* [U] **1** shells put into strings, belts etc, used in the past as money by Native Americans〔旧时北美印第安人作货币用的〕贝壳串[贝壳带] **2** *AmE informal* money【美，非正式】钱

wan /wɑn; wɒn/ *adj especially literary* looking pale, weak, or tired【尤文】苍白的；虚弱的；倦怠的: *She gave a wan smile.* 她惨淡地笑了一下。—**wanly** *adv*

wand /wɑnd; wɒnd/ *n* [C] **1** a thin stick you hold in your hand to do magic tricks〔表演魔术用的〕魔杖 **2** a tool that looks like a thin stick 细棒状工具: *a mascara wand* 染睫毛笔

wan·der¹ /ˈwɑndə; ˈwɒndə/ *v* (S3)

1 ►MOVE WITHOUT A DIRECTION 无目的地行进◄ [I,T] to move slowly across or around an area, without a clear direction or purpose〔在某地方〕徘徊；闲逛；漫步: **wander in/through/around etc** *I'll just wander around the mall for half an hour.* 我要在商场闲逛半个小时。| **wander sth** *Nomadic tribes wander these deserts.* 游牧民族在这些沙漠里四处流浪。

2 ►MOVE AWAY 离开◄ also 又作 **wander off** [I] to move away from where you are supposed to stay〔从应该逗留的地方〕离开: *Don't let any of the kids wander off.* 不要让任何一个小孩走散。

3 ►CHANGE THE SUBJECT 改变话题◄ [I] to start to talk about something not connected with the main subject that you were talking about before 离题: [**+from/off**] *Pastor Riker started to wander from the point.* 赖克牧师开始偏离话题了。

4 ►MIND/THOUGHTS 精神/注意力◄ [I] If your mind, thoughts etc wander, you no longer pay attention to something, especially because you are bored or worried〔精神、注意力等因厌倦或焦虑而〕不集中，走神: *I'm sorry, my mind was wandering. What did you say?* 对不起，我有点走神。刚才你说什么？

5 sb's mind is wandering used to say that someone has become unable to think clearly, especially because they are old〔尤因年老而〕头脑糊涂

6 ►ROAD/RIVER 道路/河流◄ [I] if a road or a river wanders somewhere, it does not go straight but in curves〔河流、道路等〕蜿蜒曲折: [**+through/across/along**] *The Missouri river wanders across several states.* 密苏里河蜿蜒曲折流经好几个州。—**wanderer** *n* [C]

wander² *n* [singular] a short relaxed walk 漫步: **go for/take a wander** *Let's take a wander down to the shops.* 我们溜达到商店去吧。

wan·der·ings /ˈwɑndərɪŋz; ˈwɒndərɪŋz/ *n* [plural] *literary* journeys to places where you do not stay for very long【文】〔在短暂停留处的〕漫游: *his wanderings through the Australian outback* 他在澳大利亚内地的漫游

wan·der·lust /ˈwɑndə,lʌst; ˈwɒndəlʌst/ *n* [singular, U] a strong desire to travel to different places〔想到不同地方去的〕旅游欲

wane¹ /wen; weɪn/ *v* [I] **1** if something such as power, influence, or a feeling wanes, it becomes gradually less strong or less important〔权力、影响或感觉〕逐渐减弱；逐渐变小: *My enthusiasm for the project was waning.* 我对这个计划的热情逐渐淡下去了。**2** when the moon wanes, you gradually see less of it〔月亮〕亏，缺 —compare 比较 WAX² (4)

wane² *n* **on the wane** becoming smaller, weaker, or less important 正在减小[减弱]，日渐衰败: *By the 5th century, the power of the Roman Empire was on the wane.* 到 5 世纪时，罗马帝国逐渐衰落。

wan·gle /ˈwæŋgl; ˈwæŋgəl/ *v* [T] *informal* to get something, or arrange for something to happen, by cleverly persuading or tricking someone【非正式】用巧计获得〔某物〕[办成〔某事〕]；哄

骗: **wangle sth out of sb** *In the end she wangled an invitation out of them.* 最终她施计从他们手中弄到了一张请帖。| **wangle it for sth to happen** *I managed to wangle it for us all to go.* 我设法使我们大家都去。| **wangle your way out of sth** (=get out of a difficult or unpleasant situation in this way) 用计谋摆脱某事〔困境或尴尬局面〕—**wangle** *n* [singular]

wank¹ /wæŋk; wæŋk/ *v* [I] *BrE taboo* to MASTURBATE【英讳】行手淫

wank² *n* [singular] *BrE taboo* an act of MASTURBATION【英讳】手淫

wank·er /ˈwæŋkə; ˈwæŋkə/ *n* [C] *BrE taboo* someone who you think is stupid or unpleasant【英讳】笨蛋; 讨厌的人

wan·na /ˈwɑnə; ˈwɒnə/ *spoken*【口】**1** a short form of 缩略式= want to **2** a short form of 缩略式= want a

wan·na·be /ˈwɑnəbɪ; ˈwɒnəbi/ *n* [C] *informal* someone who wants to be like someone famous or have money and power【非正式】仿效名人[富人]的人; 追逐名利者 —compare 比较 WOULD-BE

1 1 **want¹** /wɑnt; wɒnt/ *v* [not usually in progressive 一般不用进行式]

1 ▶DESIRE 渴望◀ [T] to have a desire for something 想要〔某物〕: *I want a drink.* 我想喝杯酒。| *What do you want for your birthday?* 你生日想要什么礼物? | **want to do sth** *Do you want to go to Kay's party?* 你想参加凯的聚会吗? | **want sb to do sth** *I don't want Linda to hear about this.* 我不想让琳达听到这事。| **want sth of sb** *formal* (=want someone to do something)【正式】想让某人做某事 *I wish I knew what he wanted of me.* 我希望我能知道他想要我做什么。

2 ▶NEED 需要◀ [T] to need something 需要〔某物〕: *Do you still want these magazines, or can I throw them out?* 你还需要这些杂志吗, 要不我就把它们扔掉了? | **want to do sth** *You only want to use a little glue.* 你只需要用一点胶水。| **want sth done** *I want that letter typed today.* 我要那封信在今天打好。| **what sb wants with sth** (=what someone needs something for) 某人想要某物〔做…〕*What do you want with a tool kit?* 你要工具箱干什么? | **want doing** *especially BrE informal* (=need to be done)【尤英, 非正式】需要做… *The carpet really wants cleaning.* 这块地毯真的需要清洗了。

3 ▶ASK FOR SB 要求见某人◀ [T] to ask for someone to come and talk to you, or to come to a particular place 要求〔某人〕到来; 要求与〔某人〕谈话; 要〔某人〕到某地来: *You're wanted on the phone.* 有你的电话。

4 ▶SHOULD 应该◀ [T] *spoken especially BrE* ought or should【口, 尤英】理应, 应该: **want to do sth** *You want to see a doctor about that cough.* 你应该找医生看一下咳嗽。

5 ▶LACK 缺少◀ [I,T] *formal* to suffer because you do not have something【正式】缺少〔某物〕〔因而受苦〕: *In many poorer countries, people still want basic food and shelter.* 在许多较贫困的国家, 人们仍然缺少基本的食物和住房。

6 want in/out *informal*【非正式】**a)** *especially AmE to* want to go in to or out of a place【尤美】想要进/出〔某处〕: *The cat wants out.* 这只猫要出去。**b)** to want to take part in a plan or stop being involved 想参加/退出〔计划〕: *If you want out, say so now.* 如果你想退出, 现在就说。—see also 另见 WANTED, WANTING, **waste not, want not** (WASTE² (7))

Frequencies of the verb **want** in spoken and written English 动词 want 在英语口语和书面语中的使用频率

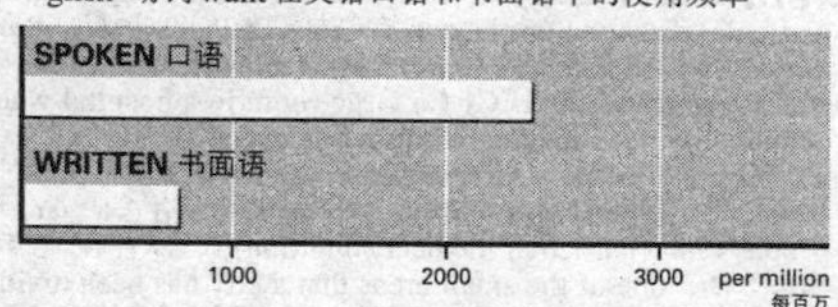

Based on the British National Corpus and the Longman Lancaster Corpus
据英国国家语料库和朗文兰开斯特语料库

This graph shows that the verb **want** is much more common in spoken English than in written English. This is because it used in a lot of common spoken phrases. 本图表显示, 动词 want 在英语口语中的使用频率远远高于书面语, 因为口语中很多常用短语是由 want 构成的。

want (*v*) **SPOKEN PHRASES**
含 want 的口语短语

7 I want/I don't want 我想要/我不想要: *I want a new coat.* 我想要一件新上衣。| *I don't want to go out tonight.* 今晚我不想出去。**8 what do you want?** used to ask, often in a slightly rude way, what someone wants you to give them, do for them etc 你想要什么?〔用于询问(有一点不客气)某人想要你给他什么或让你替他做什么等〕: *What do you want now? I'm busy.* 这会儿你想要什么?我忙着呢。| *What do you want – chocolate or vanilla?* 你想要什么, 巧克力还是香草冰淇淋? **9 do you want...?** used when offering something to someone 你想不想要…?〔用于给某人某物时〕: *Do you want a drink?* 你想喝杯酒吗? | *Do you want me to come with you?* 你想我和你一起去吗? **10 who wants...? a)** used to say that you do not like something, do not think that it is worth doing etc 谁想要…?〔表示你不喜欢某物, 认为某事不值得去做等〕: *Who wants to go to a noisy disco anyway?* 算了吧, 谁想去嘈杂的迪斯科舞厅! **b)** used when offering something to a group of people 谁想要…?〔用于给一群人某物时〕: *Who wants a cup of coffee?* 谁想来杯咖啡? **11 if you want** used when someone suggests doing something, to say that you will do it, although you do not especially want to 如果你想要的话〔用于表示自己会做对方建议的事, 虽然不太乐意〕: *"Hey, shall we go to the beach?" "If you want."* "嘿, 我们去海滨怎么样?" "如果你想去的话。" **12 I want you to do something** used to tell someone to do something 我想让你去做某事〔用于告诉某人做某事〕: *I want you to go and get me a newspaper.* 我想让你去拿一份报纸给我。**13 want...?** used when offering something to someone 要…好吗?〔用于给某人某物时〕: *Want a game of chess?* 想下盘棋吗? **14 what I want** used to explain or say exactly what it is that you want 我想要…〔用于确切解释或说明你想要的东西〕: *What I want is a car that's cheap and reliable.* 我想要的就是一辆既便宜又耐用的汽车。**15 all I want** used to say that you only want something simple or small, and you think it is fair to ask for it 我只想要〔用于索求简单或小的物品, 而且你认为提出的要求是合理的〕: *Look, all I want is a decent job. It's not much to ask for, is it?* 我只想要一份过得去的工作。这个要求不高, 不是吗? **16 you don't want** used to advise someone not to do something (你)不要…〔用于劝别人不要做某事〕: *You don't want to go there, it's much too crowded.* 你不要到那儿去, 太拥挤了。**17 I just wanted to say/know etc** used to politely say something, ask about something etc 我只想说/知道等〔用于彬彬有礼地说某事、探询某事等〕: *I just wanted to check that the meeting is still on next week.* 我只是想核实一下会议是否仍在下星期开。**18 it's/that's just what I (always) wanted** used to say that you like a present you have just been given very much 正是我所需要的〔用于表示你非常喜欢他人送的礼物〕

want for sth *phr v* [T] to not have something that you need 缺少〔所需之物〕: *Say what you like, my kids never wanted for anything.* 不管你怎么说, 我的孩子从来就什么都不缺。

want² *n*

1 ▶LACK 缺乏◀ [C,U] *formal* something that you need but do not have【正式】需要〔但缺乏〕的东西: **for want of sth** (=because of a lack of something) 因缺乏某物 *People often take casual jobs in catering for want of any alternative.* 人们常干承办宴席的临时工, 因为别无选择。| **satisfy a want** (=give someone what they need) 满足某人所需

2 ▶SITUATION WITHOUT FOOD/MONEY 缺乏食物/金钱的处境◀ [U] a situation in which you do not have enough food, money, clothes etc〔食品、金钱、衣服等的〕匮乏; 贫困: *They had lived all their lives in want.* 他们一辈子都生活在穷困之中。

3 for want of a better word/term/phrase used to say that there is no exact word to describe what you are talking about 没有更贴切的词语/术语/成语〔常表示词不达意〕: *a feeling that, for want of a better word, we call love* 那种感情太难以表达清楚, 我们称它为"爱情"

4 for want of anything better (to do) if you do something for want of anything better, you do it only because there is nothing else you want to do 既然没有更好的(办法做某事)

5 not for want of trying/asking etc used to say that you should have got what you wanted because you tried very hard or asked for it many times 并非没有尽力/请求等〔用于表示应该得到想要的东西, 因为曾努力尝试或多番请求〕: *Well, if he doesn't get the job it won't be for want of trying!* 好吧, 如果他得不到那份工作, 那并非是他没有尽力!

6 be in want of sth *formal* to need something【正式】需要某事物: *a creaking house, in want of repair* 房子嘎吱作响, 需要修葺

want ad /ˈ· ·/ *n* [C] *AmE* CLASSIFIED AD【美】分类广告

W

want·ed /ˈwɑntɪd; ˈwɒntɪd/ *adj* someone who is wanted is being looked for by the police 被警方追捕的，被通缉的：*He is wanted in connection with the murder of a teenage girl.* 他因涉嫌谋杀一名少女而被警方通缉。

want·ing /ˈwɑntɪŋ; ˈwɒntɪŋ/ *adj* [not before noun 不用于名词前] **1 be found wanting** proven not to be good enough for a particular purpose 证明不够标准；证明不够资格：*Traditional solutions had been tried and found wanting.* 尝试过传统的办法但发现行不通。**2 wanting in sth** *formal* not having enough of something【正式】某物不足；缺少某物：*wanting in grace and tact* 缺乏风度和机敏 **3** *formal* lacking or missing【正式】缺少的；找不到的：*A certain humanity is wanting in big cities.* 大城市少了一些人情味。

wan·ton /ˈwɑntən; ˈwɒntən/ *adj* **1** wanton cruelty, destruction etc deliberately harms someone or damages something for no reason〔残暴、破坏等〕恣意的，恶意的：*an act of wanton aggression* 肆无忌惮的侵略行为 **2** *old-fashioned* a wanton woman is considered immoral because she has sex with a lot of men【过时】〔妇女〕淫荡的 **3** *formal* uncontrolled【正式】不受拘束的：*wanton jungle growth* 生长繁茂的热带丛林 —**wantonly** *adv* —**wantonness** *n* [U]

Wap·ping /ˈwɑpɪŋ; ˈwɒpɪŋ/ part of the Docklands area of East London, which has been a centre of the British newspaper industry since the 1980s, when several newspapers moved their offices there from Fleet Street. 瓦平〔伦敦东部码头区的一部分。20世纪80年代起数家报社从舰队街迁至此地，使之成为英国报业中心〕

3 1 **war** /wɔr; wɔː/ *n*

1 ▶WAR IN GENERAL 一般意义上的战争◀ [U] fighting between two or more countries or opposing groups within a country, involving large numbers of soldiers and weapons〔两国或多国之间的〕战争；内战：*Cambodia has been ravaged by war for the past 20 years.* 在过去20年里，柬埔寨饱受战争的蹂躏。| **war breaks out** (=war begins) 战争爆发 *War broke out in September of 1939.* 1939年9月爆发了战争。| **be at war (with)** *In 1920 Poland and Russia were still at war.* 到1920年，波兰和俄国仍在交战。| **declare war (on sb)** (=announce publicly and officially that you are going to fight a war) 向(某人)宣战 | **go to war (with)** (=start to fight a war with another country) 与〔他国〕开战 | **wage war (on/against)** (=start and continue a war, especially for a long period)〔尤指长时期地〕与…进行战争 | **the outbreak of war** (=the start of fighting in a war) 战争的爆发

2 ▶A PARTICULAR WAR 某次战争◀ [C] a particular period of time when countries fight with soldiers and weapons 某段战争时期：*Do you remember the last war?* 你还记得上次战争吗？| **the Vietnam/Seven Years/First World etc War** *America's defeat in the Vietnam War* 美国在越战中的失败 | **[+with/against]** *Iran's seven year war with Iraq* 伊朗与伊拉克之间的七年战争 | **win/lose a war** *tactical errors that made France lose the war* 导致法国战败的战术性错误 | **fight a war** *Britain has fought two wars in Europe this century.* 本世纪英国在欧洲打过两场大仗。| **war between** *The war between England and France was to last another 50 years.* 英法两国之间的那场战争还将持续50年。| **a nuclear war** *Both countries wanted to avoid a nuclear war.* 两国都想避免一场核战争。| **a war hero** (=a brave soldier) 战斗英雄 | **a war veteran** (=a former soldier) 老兵，老战士，退伍军人

CULTURAL NOTE 文化注释

When British people talk about 'the war', they usually mean the Second World War. 英国人提到 the war 时，他们指的通常是第二次世界大战。

3 ▶AGAINST CRIME/DISEASE ETC 同犯罪/疾病等斗争◀ [C, U] a struggle over a long period of time to control something harmful〔为防止有害事物的蔓延而进行长时期的〕斗争：**[+against/on]** *the State's war on drugs* 国家针对毒品的斗争

4 ▶FOR POWER/CONTROL 为了权力/控制◀ [C,U] a situation in which a person or group is fighting for power, influence, or control〔人或团体为权力、影响、控制进行的〕斗争；竞争：*No one wants to start a trade war here.* 没有人想在这里开展一场贸易战。

5 This means war! *spoken humorous* used to say that you are ready to fight about something【口，幽默】这意味着战争！〔表示你已准备为某事物而斗争、争论〕

6 the war *especially BrE* the Second World War【尤英】第二次世界大战

7 between the wars the period between the First and Second World Wars 两次大战〔指第一次和第二次世界大战〕之间

8 look like you have been in the wars *BrE spoken* to look injured or damaged【英口】像是受了创伤或损伤 —see also 另见 CIVIL WAR, COLD WAR, PRICE WAR, PRISONER OF WAR, WAR OF ATTRITION, WAR OF NERVES, WAR OF WORDS, WARRING

This graph shows some of the words most commonly used with the noun **war**. 本图表所示为含有名词 war 的一些最常用词组。

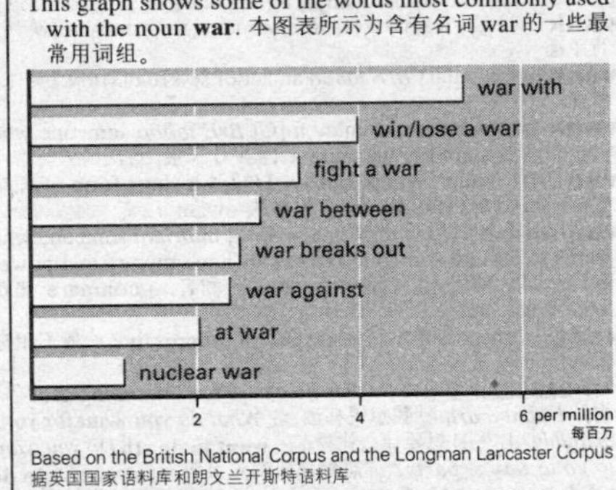

Based on the British National Corpus and the Longman Lancaster Corpus
据英国国家语料库和朗文兰开斯特语料库

War and Peace /ˌ· · ˈ·/ (1863-69) a NOVEL by the Russian writer Leo Tolstoy, set during the Napoleonic Wars and considered by many people to be one of the greatest novels ever written《战争与和平》〔(1863-1869)，俄国作家列夫·托尔斯泰所著长篇小说。该作品以拿破仑战争时期为背景，许多人认为它是有史以来最优秀的小说之一〕

War be·tween the States, the /ˌ· · · · ˈ·/ the American Civil War. This expression is used mainly by people in the South of the US. 州际之战〔指美国内战。此说法主要在美国南部各州使用〕

war·ble /ˈwɔrbl; ˈwɔːbəl/ *v* **1** [I] to sing with a high continuous but rapidly changing sound, the way a bird does 高声婉转地唱；〔鸟〕啭鸣 **2** [I, T] *humorous* to sing【幽默】唱：*Ned warbled a serenade.* 内德唱了一首小夜曲。

war·bler /ˈwɔrblɚ; ˈwɔːblə/ *n* [C] **1** a bird that can make musical sounds 鸣禽 **2** *humorous* a singer, especially one who does not sing very well【幽默】〔尤指唱得不好的〕歌手

war bride /ˈ· ·/ *n* [C] a woman who marries a foreign soldier who is in her country because there is a war 战时新娘〔指战时嫁给在自己国家作战的外国军人的妇女〕

war cab·i·net /ˈ· ˌ···/ *n* [C] a group of important British politicians who meet to make decisions during a war〔英国〕战时内阁

war chest /ˈ· ·/ *n* [C] *informal* the money that a government has available to spend on war【非正式】战争基金

war crime /ˈ· ·/ *n* [C] an illegal and cruel act done during a war 战争罪行 —**war criminal** *n* [C]

war cry /ˈ· ·/ *n* [C] a shout used by people fighting in a battle to show their courage and frighten the enemy〔作战时显示勇气和吓唬敌人的〕喊杀声 —see also 另见 BATTLE CRY

War Cry, The /ˈ· ·/ the weekly newspaper of the Salvation Army in the UK《救恩报》〔英国救世军组织创办的一份周报〕

-ward /wɚd; wəd/ *suffix* [in adjectives 构成形容词] towards a particular direction or place 朝特定方向[地方]：*our homeward journey* 我们归家的旅程 |*a downward movement* 向下的运动

ward¹ /wɔrd; wɔːd/ *n* [C] **1** a large room in a hospital where people who need medical treatment stay〔医院内的〕病房，病室：*She's in charge of three different wards.* 她负责三间不同的病房。| **maternity/general/ geriatric etc ward** (=a ward for people with a particular medical condition) 产科/普通/老年等病房 **2** *BrE* one of the small areas that a city has been divided into for the purpose of local elections【英】〔城市的〕选区 —compare 比较 CONSTITUENCY (2) **3** *law* someone, especially a child, who is under the legal protection of another person or of a law court【法律】受监护的人〔尤指儿童〕：*a ward of court* 受法院监护的人 3

ward² *v*

ward sth **off** *phr v* [T] to do something to prevent something such as an illness, danger, or attack from harming you 防止〔疾病、危险、攻击等〕，抵挡：*a spell to ward off evil spirits* 避邪的咒语

war dance /ˈ· ·/ *n* [C] a dance performed by tribes in preparation for battle or to celebrate a victory〔原始部落作战前或战后庆祝胜利跳的〕战舞

war·den /ˈwɔrdn; ˈwɔːdn/ *n* [C] **1** an official whose job is to make sure that rules are obeyed〔监督法规执行的〕监察员 **2** *AmE* the person in charge of a prison【美】监狱长; GOVERNOR (3) *BrE*【英】**3** *BrE* someone who takes care of a building and the people in it, for example a place such as a home for old people【英】〔建筑物的〕看守人; 监管员 —see also 另见 CHURCHWARDEN, GAME WARDEN, TRAFFIC WARDEN

ward·er /ˈwɔrdɚ; ˈwɔːdə/ *n* [C] *BrE* someone who works in a prison guarding the prisoners【英】监狱看守人

ward·ress /ˈwɔrdrɪs; ˈwɔːdrɪs/ *n* [C] *BrE* a woman who works in a prison guarding prisoners【英】监狱女看守

war·drobe /ˈwɔrdˌrob; ˈwɔːdrəʊb/ *n* **1** [C] *BrE* a piece of furniture like a large cupboard that you hang clothes in【英】大衣柜, 大衣橱; CLOSET¹ (2) *AmE*【美】**2** [C] the clothes that someone has〔某人拥有的〕服装: *Princess Diana requires an extensive wardrobe.* 戴安娜王妃需要大批的服装。**3** [singular] a department in a theatre, television company etc that deals with the clothes worn by actors on stage〔剧院、电视台等的〕戏装管理部门: **a wardrobe mistress** (=woman in charge of this department) 戏装女管理员

ward·room /ˈwɔrdˌrum; ˈwɔːdrʊm/ *n* [C] the space in a WARSHIP where the officers live and eat, except for the captain〔军舰上除舰长外的军官使用的〕军官起居室

-wards /wɚdz; wədz/ also 又作 **-ward** *especially AmE*【尤美】*suffix* [in adverbs 构成副词] towards a particular direction or place 向〔某方向或地方〕, 朝: *We're travelling northwards.* 我们向北方前进。| *The plane plunged earthwards.* 飞机朝地面俯冲。

-ware /wɛr; weə/ *suffix* [in U nouns 构成不可数名词] **1** articles made of a particular material, especially for use in the home〔尤指在家中使用的〕物品, 器皿: *glassware* (=glass bowls, glasses, etc) 玻璃器皿〔玻璃碗、玻璃杯等〕| *silverware* (=silver dishes, knives, etc) 银器; 银餐具〔银盘、银刀叉等〕**2** articles used in a particular place for the preparation or serving of food 制作或盛食物的用具: *ovenware* (=dishes for use in the OVEN) 烤箱用器皿 | *tableware* (=plates, glasses, knives, etc) 餐具〔盘、玻璃杯、刀等〕**3** things used in operating a computer〔用于操作电脑的〕…物件: *software* (=PROGRAMS) 软件 | *liveware* (=people who operate computers) 人件〔指操作电脑的人员〕

war ef·fort /ˈ· ˌ··/ *n* [singular] things done by all the people in a country to help when that country is at war〔全国人民的〕战备

ware·house /ˈwɛrˌhaus; ˈweəhaʊs/ *n* [C] a large building for storing large quantities of goods 仓库, 货栈

wares /wɛrz; weəz/ *n* [plural] things that are for sale, usually not in a shop〔一般不在商店内出售的〕商品, 货物: *the market trader's wares* 集市商贩出售的货物

war·fare /ˈwɔrˌfɛr; ˈwɔːfeə/ *n* [U] **1** a word meaning the activity of fighting in a war, used especially when talking about particular methods of fighting 战争状态〔尤指作战的方式〕: **nuclear/chemical/trench warfare** *the terrible prospect of large-scale nuclear warfare* 大规模核战争的可怕前景 | **guerrilla warfare** (=warfare by small groups of fighters in mountains, forests etc)〔山区、森林等里的〕游击战 **2** a continous struggle between groups, countries etc〔集团、国家等之间的〕斗争, 冲突: *political warfare* 政治 (宣传) 战 —see also 另见 **psychological warfare** (PSYCHOLOGICAL (3))

war game /ˈ· ˌ·/ *n* [C] **1** an activity in which soldiers fight an imaginary battle in order to test military plans 军事演习 **2** a game played by adults in which models of soldiers, guns, horses etc are moved around a table〔成人玩的〕战棋, 战争游戏〔有士兵、枪炮、战马等模型〕

war·head /ˈwɔrˌhɛd; ˈwɔːhed/ *n* [C] the explosive part at the front of a MISSILE (1) 导弹的弹头

War·hol /ˈwɔrˌhol; ˈwɔːhəʊl/, **An·dy** /ˈændɪ; ˈændi/ (1926-87) a US artist who had an important influence on modern art and music, especially in the 1960s. He is famous for his pictures in the POP art style, which were of ordinary objects such as the *Campbell's Soup Can*, or of famous people such as Marilyn Monroe. He also made films such as *The Chelsea Girls* (1966) and *Trash* (1970). His films, which usually dealt with sex and drugs, did not try to tell stories and the actors often invented their words as they spoke. 沃霍尔〔(1926-1987), 美国艺术家, 对现代音乐和艺术, 尤其是20世纪60年代的音乐和艺术产生了重要影响。沃霍尔以波普艺术风格的绘画作品著称, 主题为日常物品, 如《坎贝尔汤罐》, 或玛丽莲·梦露一类的名人。他还导演了《切尔西姑娘》(1966)、《垃圾》(1970) 等影片。其电影通常涉及性和吸毒问题, 不以讲述故事为目的。影片中的角色常常即兴创作台词〕

war·horse /ˈwɔrˌhɔrs; ˈwɔːhɔːs/ *n* [C] **1** *informal* a soldier or politician who has been in their job a long time, and enjoys dealing with all the difficulties involved in it【非正式】〔爱处理难题的〕老兵; 资深政治家 **2** a horse used in battle 军马, 战马

war·like /ˈwɔrˌlaɪk; ˈwɔːlaɪk/ *adj* **1** liking war and being skilful in it 好战的; 善战的: *a warlike nation* 好战的国家 **2** threatening war or attack 以战争相威胁的: *a warlike stance* 以战争相威胁的态度

war·lock /ˈwɔrˌlɑk; ˈwɔːlɒk/ *n* [C] a man who has magical powers, especially evil powers〔尤指有邪恶力量的〕男巫, 术士

war·lord /ˈwɔrlɔrd; ˈwɔːlɔːd/ *n* [C] a military leader, especially an unofficial one fighting against a government or king 军阀

warm¹ /wɔrm; wɔːm/ *adj*

1 ►**BE WARM** 温暖的◄ slightly hot, especially pleasantly 暖的, 温热的: *a warm bath* 温水浴 | *I hope we get some warmer weather soon.* 我希望天气很快就会回暖。| **keep sth warm** (=stop something from becoming cold) 防止某物变冷 *I've put your dinner in the oven to keep it warm.* 我把饭菜放进烤箱里保温。—see picture at 参见 HOT¹ 图表

2 ►**FEEL WARM** 感到暖和◄ feeling slightly hot, or making you feel this way〔感到〕暖和的, 温暖的: *Are you warm enough?* 你身上暖和吗? | **keep warm** (=wear enough clothes not to feel cold)〔穿足够的衣服以〕保暖, 不感到冷 *Make sure you keep warm!* 记得穿暖和点!

3 ►**CLOTHES/BUILDINGS** 衣服/建筑物◄ clothes or buildings that are warm can keep in heat or keep out cold〔衣服或建筑物〕保暖的, 防寒的: *Here, put on your nice warm coat.* 来, 穿上这件非常保暖的上衣。

4 ►**FRIENDLY** 友善的◄ friendly in a way that makes you feel comfortable 热情的, 热忱的: *a warm, reassuring smile* 热情而亲切的微笑 | **a warm welcome** *Please give a warm welcome to our special guest!* 请热烈欢迎我们的嘉宾!

5 ►**COLOUR** 色调◄ colours that are warm are red, yellow, orange, and similar colours〔红、黄、橙及类似颜色〕暖色调的

6 as warm as toast pleasantly warm 暖烘烘的

7 ►**CORRECT** 正确的◄ used especially in games to say that someone is near to guessing the correct answer or finding a hidden object〔尤指游戏中〕即将猜中〔答案〕的; 快要找到〔隐藏物〕的: *You're getting warmer.* 你快要猜中了。—opposite 反义词 COLD¹ (13)

8 make it/make things warm for sb *informal* to cause problems for someone in order to punish them【非正式】〔为惩罚而〕给某人出难题, 使某人为难

9 warm scent/trail a smell or path that has been made recently, which a hunter can easily follow〔猎人容易追寻的〕新近留下的气味/足迹

10 ►**ANGRY/EXCITED** 发怒的/激动的◄ *AmE* fairly angry or excited【美】怒气冲冲的; 相当激动的: *The atmosphere in the meeting grew warm.* 会议的气氛变得激烈起来。—**warmness** *n* [U]

warm² *v* also 又作 **warm up**

1 [T] to make someone or something warm or warmer 使某人[某物]暖和[更暖]: *Here, warm yourself by the fire.* 喂, 到炉火旁来取暖吧。**2** [I] to be heated 变热: [+**in**/ **by**/**on**] *There's some soup warming in the pot.* 锅里盛着汤, 正在热起来。

warm to sb/sth *phr v* [T] **1** to begin to like something, or someone you have just met 对〔刚接触的某物或某人〕有好感: *Bruce didn't warm to him as he had to Casey.* 布鲁斯对他不像对凯西那样有好感。**2** to become more eager or excited about something 对〔某物〕更加热心: **warm to a theme/subject/ topic etc** *The more she spoke, the more she warmed to her subject.* 这话题她越说越起劲。

warm up *phr v*

1 ►**MAKE WARM** 使温暖◄ [I,T] to become warm or to make someone or something warm 变暖; 使〔某人或某物〕暖和: **warm sb/sth ↔ up** *A brandy should warm you up.* 喝点白兰地你就会暖和起来。| *If you're ready for your dinner I'll warm it up.* 如果你准备吃饭, 我就把饭菜热一热。

2 ►**DO EXERCISES** 锻炼◄ [I] to do gentle physical exercises to prepare your body for dancing, sport etc〔舞蹈、运动前〕做准备活动: *The athletes are warming up before the race.* 运动员正在做赛前的热身运动。

3 ►**MACHINE/ENGINE** 机器/发动机◄ [I,T] if you warm up a machine or engine or it warms up, it becomes ready to work properly 预热〔使有效工作〕

4 ►**PARTY** 聚会◄ [I,T] if a party warms up, it starts to become enjoyable〔聚会〕热烈[兴奋]起来: *Don't go, things are just starting to warm up.* 别走, 一切刚开始热闹起来。

5 ►**BECOME CHEERFUL** 变得活跃◄ [I,T] to become cheerful, eager, and excited, or to make someone feel this way (使) 变得

活跃[激动, 兴奋]: **warm sb ↔ up** *He warmed up the audience by telling them a few jokes.* 他先说了几个笑话, 使观众的情绪兴奋起来。—see also 另见 **like death warmed up/over** (DEATH (9))

warm up to sth *phr v* [T] *AmE* to warm to someone or something【美】〔对刚接触的人或物〕产生好感

warm³ *n* **the warm** *especially BrE* a place that is warm【尤英】暖和的地方: *Come into the warm!* 到这暖和的地方来!

warm⁴ *adv* **wrap up warm** to put on enough clothes so that you do not feel cold 穿戴暖和〔以防寒〕

warm-blood·ed /ˌ·ˈ··◂/ *adj* animals that are warmblooded have a body temperature that remains fairly high whether the temperature around them is hot or cold〔动物〕温血的, 恒温的 —compare 比较 COLD-BLOODED

warmed o·ver /ˌ·ˈ··◂/ *adj AmE*【美】**1** food that is warmed over has been cooked before and then heated again for eating〔食物冷却后〕重新加热的 **2** an idea or argument that is warmed over has been used before and is not interesting or useful any more〔意见、论点〕重复的〔不再有趣或有用〕—see also 另见 **like death warmed up/over** (DEATH (9))

war me·mo·ri·al /ˈ· ·ˌ···/ *n* [C] a MONUMENT (1) put up to remind people of those killed in a war 战争[阵亡将士]纪念碑

> **CULTURAL NOTE 文化注释**
> In the UK, war memorials are often found in small towns and villages as well as larger cities. 在英国, 无论是大城市还是小城镇和乡村都可以见到战争纪念碑。

warm front /ˌ·ˈ·/ *n* [C] *technical* an expression used especially in weather reports meaning the front edge of a mass of warm air coming towards a place【术语】暖锋〔尤用于天气预报中〕

warm-heart·ed /ˌ·ˈ··◂/ *adj* friendly, kind, and always willing to help 友好的, 热心肠的: *a warm-hearted landlady* 热情的女房东 —compare 比较 COLD-HEARTED —**warm-heartedly** *adv* —**warm-heartedness** *n* [U]

warm·ing¹ /ˈwɔrmɪŋ; ˈwɔːmɪŋ/ *adj* making you feel pleasantly warm 使人感到暖热的: *a warming cup of cocoa* 一杯使人身上暖烘烘的热可可

warming² *n* [U] an act of making something warm or warmer 加温: **global warming** (=the increase in the temperature of the Earth's air) 地球气温变暖 *global warming caused by pollution* 污染引起的全球变暖

warming pan /ˈ··ˌ·/ *n* [C] a metal container with a long handle, used in the past to hold hot coals for warming beds〔旧时用来暖床的〕长柄炭炉; 暖床器

warm·ly /ˈwɔrmli; ˈwɔːmli/ *adv* **1** in a friendly way 友好地, 亲切地: *Teri greeted the visitor warmly.* 特里友好地迎接来客。**2** in a way that makes something or someone warm 使某物[某人]温暖: *Pat wrapped the baby up warmly.* 帕特把婴儿裹得暖暖的。| **dress warmly** (=so you do not become cold) 穿得暖 **3** eagerly 热切地: *"Do you like dancing?" "Love it," said Mary warmly.* "你喜欢跳舞吗?"玛丽热切地说: "喜欢。" **4** *AmE* slightly angrily【美】微怒地: *I may have spoken too warmly.* 我可能说话时带着点怒气。

war·mon·ger /ˈwɔrˌmʌŋgə; ˈwɔːˌmʌŋgə/ *n* [C] someone, especially a politician, who is eager to start a war to achieve an aim 战争贩子〔尤指热衷于发动战争的政客〕—**warmongering** *adj* —**warmongering** *n* [U]

warmth /wɔrmθ; wɔːmθ/ *n* [U] **1** a feeling of being warm 温暖: *the warmth of the sun* 太阳的温暖 **2** friendliness and happiness 友好; 热情: *the warmth of her smile* 她微笑中的热情

warm-up /ˈ· ·/ *n* [C] a set of gentle exercises you do to prepare your body for dancing, sport etc 热身〔跳舞、运动等前做的一套准备活动〕

S3 W2 **warn** /wɔrn; wɔːn/ *v* [I,T] **1** to tell someone that something bad or dangerous may happen, so that they can avoid it or prevent it 警告, 告诫; 提醒: *"Be careful, the rocks are slippery," Alex warned.* 亚历克斯提醒说: "小心, 岩石滑溜。" | **warn sb about** *I warned him about those stairs.* 我提醒他要注意那几级楼梯。| **warn (sb) of** *You were warned of the risks involved.* 请你注意所涉及的危险。| **warn sb not to do sth** *I warned you not to walk home alone.* 我告诫你不要独自走回家。| **warn sb (that)** *We warned them that there was a bull in the field.* 我们提醒他们, 田里有一头公牛。**2** to tell someone about something before it happens so that they are not worried or surprised by it 预先通知〔某人以免焦虑或惊讶〕: *Can you warn your mother you're going to be back late?* 你能否事先告诉你妈妈你准备晚点回去?

warn sb ↔ **against** sth *phr v* [T] to advise someone not to do something because it may have dangerous or unpleasant results〔因可能有危险或产生不良结果而〕告诫〔某人〕不要做〔某事〕: *Her financial adviser warned her against such a risky investment.* 她的财务顾问告诫她不要进行风险那么大的投资。| **warn sb against doing sth** *The police have warned tourists against going to remoter regions.* 警察告诫旅游者不要到边远地区去。

warn sb **off** *phr v* [T] **1** to tell someone to go away or not come near something, using threats〔用威胁手段〕警告〔某人〕离开[不要接近]〔某物〕: *The farmer waved his stick in the air to warn us off his land.* 农夫在空中挥动木杖警告我们离开他的田地。**2** to advise someone to go away or to avoid something 劝告〔某人〕走开[避开]〔某事〕: **warn sb off doing sth** *I tried to warn her off going out with him.* 我试着告诫过她不要与他交往。

Warner Bros /ˈwɔrnə ˌbrʌðəz; ˈwɔːnə ˌbrʌðəz/ *trademark* a US film company based in Hollywood, which has made many famous films and CARTOONS【商标】华纳兄弟影片公司〔美国一电影公司。总部设在好莱坞, 拍摄过许多著名影片和卡通片〕

warn·ing /ˈwɔrnɪŋ; ˈwɔːnɪŋ/ *n* **1** [C,U] something, especially a statement, that tells you that something bad, annoying, or dangerous might happen〔因可能发生某种不幸、讨厌或危险的事而发出的〕警告; 告诫: *the government health warning on packs of cigarettes* 香烟盒上的政府健康警告 | **warning against** *The police issued a warning against speeding.* 警察发出警告、不得超速行驶。| **warning of** *a warning of floods* 洪水警报 | **warning to sb** *a warning to pregnant women not to drink alcohol* 孕妇不要饮酒的警告 | **give a warning** *We were given no warning of possible delays at the airport.* 我们没有得到飞机可能误点的通告。| **a warning cry/sign/look etc** *Do not ignore warning signs such as tiredness and headaches.* 不要忽视诸如疲劳、头痛等警告性的征兆。| **without warning** *Without warning, the soldiers started firing into the crowd.* 没有发出警告, 士兵就向人群开枪了。| **advance warning** (=warning before something happens) 预先警告 **2** [C] a statement telling someone that if they continue to behave in an unsatisfactory way, they will be punished 通知〔告诉某人如继续他的不好行为, 将受到惩罚〕: **give a warning** *I'm giving you a final warning – don't be late again.* 我最后警告你一次 —— 不要再迟到了。**3 give fair warning** to tell someone about something long enough before it happens so that they can be ready 给予合理通知〔某事发生前先告诉某人, 让他有足够时间准备〕 S3 W2

war of at·tri·tion /ˌ· · ·ˈ··/ *n* [C] a struggle in which you harm your opponent in a lot of small ways, so that they become gradually weaker 消耗战

War of 1812, the /ˌwɔr əv ˌetin ˈtwɛlv; ˌwɔːr əv ˌeɪtiːn ˈtwelv/ a war between the US and the UK, which was fought from 1812 to 1815, and which was caused mainly by trade problems. During the war, British soldiers burned the White House and other buildings in Washington, D.C. 1812 年战争〔1812 至 1815 年美英两国主要由贸易问题引发的一场战争。战争期间, 英国军队焚毁了白宫及华盛顿特区的其他一些建筑物〕

War of In·de·pen·dence, the /ˌ· · · ·ˈ· ·/ the British name for the American Revolutionary War 美国独立战争〔英国对美国革命战争的称谓〕

war of nerves /ˌ· ·ˈ·/ *n* [C] an attempt to make an enemy worried, and to destroy their courage by threatening them, spreading false information etc 神经战, 心理战〔利用恐吓、散布假情报等手段, 使敌人忧虑并削弱对方战斗的意志〕

War of the Worlds, The /ˌ· · · ·ˈ·/ (1898) a NOVEL by H. G. Wells about an attack against Earth by creatures from Mars, which is one of the first great works of science FICTION. A radio play based on the book, made by Orson Welles in 1938, caused great fear and shock in the US, because many people thought that the events they heard on the radio were actually happening. 《世界大战》〔(1898), H.G.威尔斯所著的一部科幻小说, 讲述火星人攻击地球的故事, 堪称科幻小说最早的杰作。1938 年, 奥森·威尔斯根据这部小说改编而成的广播剧在美国引起了巨大恐慌, 许多人误以为收音机中收听到的事件是正在发生的真事〕

war of words /ˌ· ·ˈ·/ *n* [C] a public argument between politicians etc〔政治家等之间的〕论战, 口仗

warp¹ /wɔrp; wɔːp/ *v* **1** [I,T] to bend or twist and to be no longer in the correct shape, or to make something do this (使) 扭曲; (使) 变形: *The door's been warped or something, it won't close properly.* 门变了形或什么的, 关不严了。**2** to have a bad effect on someone so that they think strangely about things 使〔思想〕反常; 使有偏见: *Henry's view of women had been warped by a painful divorce.* 亨利痛苦的离异经历使他对妇女产生了偏见。

warp² *n* **1 the warp** *technical* the threads used in weaving cloth that go from the top to the bottom【术语】经纱〔织布中用的从上到下的线〕—compare 比较 WEFT **2** [singular] a part of some-

thing that is not straight or in the right shape〔某物的一部分〕弯曲; 变形 —see also 另见 TIME WARP

war paint /ˈ· ·/ *n* [U] **1** paint that some tribes put on their bodies and faces before going to war〔某些部落在打仗前〕涂在身上[脸上]的颜料 **2** *humorous* MAKE-UP (1)【幽默】化妆品: *Josie's just putting on her war paint.* 乔茜正在化妆。

war·path /ˈwɔr,pæθ; ˈwɔːpɑːθ/ *n informal*【非正式】**be on the warpath** to be angry and looking for someone to fight or punish 怒气冲冲地寻人打架, 寻衅

warped /wɔrpt; wɔːpt/ **1** someone who is warped has ideas or thoughts that most people think are unpleasant or not normal〔想法或思想〕怪诞的: *a warped mind* 怪诞的心态 | **have a warped sense of humour** (=think strange and unpleasant things are funny) 有怪异的幽默感 **2** something that is warped is bent or twisted so that it is not in the correct shape〔某物〕弯曲的; 变形的

war·rant[1] /ˈwɔrənt; ˈwɒrənt/ *n* **1** [C] written permission from a court of law allowing the police to take a particular action〔法院授权警方采取行动的〕令状: [**+for**] *The magistrate issued a warrant for his arrest.* 地方法官发出了对他的逮捕令。| **search warrant** (=permission to go into someone's house to look for something) 搜查令, 搜查证 —see also 另见 DEATH WARRANT **2** [U] *formal* good enough reason for doing something; JUSTIFICATION【正式】〔做某事的〕充分理由, 正常理由 —see also 另见 UNWARRANTED

warrant[2] *v* **1** [T] to be a good enough reason for something 使有充分理由: *This tiny crowd does not warrant such a large police presence.* 这一小群人, 没有理由出动这么多警察。**2** to promise that something is true; GUARANTEE[1] (1) 保证〔某物是真的〕 **3** [I,T] *old-fashioned* used to say that you are sure about something【过时】〔用于对某物表示〕肯定: *I'll warrant we won't see him again.* 我敢断言, 我们不会再见到他了。

warrant of·fic·er /ˈ· ·, ·ˌ· ·/ *n* [C] a middle rank in the army, air force, or US Navy〔陆军、空军〕准尉; 〔美国海军〕二级准尉 —see table on page C6 参见 C6 页附录

war·ran·ty /ˈwɔrəntɪ; ˈwɒrənti/ *n* [C] a written promise that a company makes to replace or fix a product if it breaks or does not work properly〔产品的〕保证书: *a five-year anticorrosion warranty* 五年的防腐保证书 —compare 比较 GUARANTEE[2] (3), SECURITY (4)

war·ren /ˈwɔrɪn; ˈwɒrən/ *n* [C] **1** the underground home of rabbits 野兔的地下洞穴 **2** a place with so many streets, rooms etc that it is difficult to know the correct way around it〔因街道、房间过多〕容易迷失的地方: *a warren of alleyways* 迷宫般的小胡同

Warren Re·port, the /ˈ· · ·,·/ an official US report about the murder of President John F. Kennedy. Earl Warren and a special committee, called the **Warren Commission**, studied the facts relating to Kennedy's murder and decided that the President was killed by a single person, and that there was no CONSPIRACY (=a secret plan involving several people). Many people, however, do not accept this decision, and believe that Kennedy's death was organized by political opponents《沃伦报告》〔关于约翰·F.肯尼迪总统遇刺案的一份美国官方报告。厄尔·沃伦及其领导的沃伦特别调查委员会在研究了与肯尼迪暗杀事件相关的事实之后, 认定总统遇刺纯属个人行为, 背后并无阴谋。然而, 许多人拒不接受这一结论, 认为肯尼迪之死是其政敌策划的阴谋〕

war·ring /ˈwɔrɪŋ; ˈwɔːrɪŋ/ *adj* [only before noun 仅用于名词前] at war or fighting each other 交战的, 敌对的: **warring factions** (=groups of people fighting each other) 交战的派别

war·ri·or /ˈwɔrɪɚ; ˈwɒriə/ *n* [C] a soldier or man experienced in fighting, especially in the past〔尤指昔日的〕武士, 战士, 勇士: *a noble warrior* 忠勇的战士

War·saw /ˈwɔrsɔ; ˈwɔːsɔː/ the capital city of Poland, on the River Vistula. Much of the city was destroyed in World War II, but many of the old buildings were rebuilt after the war. 华沙〔波兰首都, 位于维斯瓦河畔。该城在二战中几乎毁掉, 战后许多原有建筑得以重建〕

Warsaw Ghet·to, the /,· · ˈ· ·/ an area in the city of Warsaw in which almost half a million Jews were forced by the Nazis to live together during World War II, before they were taken to CONCENTRATION CAMPS, where most of them died. 华沙犹太人隔离区〔华沙市一区。二战期间, 约有50万名犹太人被纳粹驱逐到该区聚居, 然后再送进集中营, 其中大部分人惨死在集中营〕

Warsaw Pact, the /,· · ˈ·/ also 又作 **Warsaw Treaty Organization** /,· · ˈ· · · ·,· ·/ a group of countries in eastern Europe, including Bulgaria, Czechoslovakia, East Germany, Hungary, Poland, and the former Soviet Union, which was established in 1955 to oppose NATO during the Cold War. The Warsaw Pact ended in 1991. 华沙条约组织〔保加利亚、捷克斯洛伐克、东德、匈牙利、波兰等东欧国家和前苏联于1955年成立的一个组织。其目的是在冷战期间与北大西洋公约组织相抗衡。1991年, 华沙条约组织解体〕

war·ship /ˈwɔr,ʃɪp; ˈwɔː,ʃɪp/ *n* [C] a ship with guns that is used in a war 战舰, 军舰

Wars of the Ros·es, the /,· · · ˈ· ·/ the period of civil war in England (1455-85), between two parts of the English royal family, which each wanted its own leader to be king. One family was called Lancaster, and was represented by a red rose, and the other was called York, and was represented by a white rose. The Wars of the Roses ended at the battle of Bosworth Field. 玫瑰战争〔(1455-1485), 英格兰王室的两个家族为争夺王位而进行的一场内战。一方是由红玫瑰为族徽的兰开斯特家族, 另一方是以白玫瑰为标志的约克家族。玫瑰战争以博斯沃思原野战役而告终〕

wart /wɔrt; wɔːt/ *n* [C] **1** a small hard raised part on someone's skin〔皮肤上的〕肉赘, 疣 —see also 另见 VERRUCA **2 warts and all** *informal* including all the faults or unpleasant things【非正式】包括一切缺点: *Well, you married him – warts and all.* 好了, 你好歹已经嫁给他了。—**warty** *adj*

wart·hog /ˈwɔrt,hɑg; ˈwɔːthɒg/ *n* [C] an African wild pig with long front teeth that stick out of its mouth 疣猪〔非洲的一种野猪, 嘴上长着一对长长的獠牙〕

war·time /ˈwɔr,taɪm; ˈwɔːtaɪm/ *adj* happening or existing during the time when a country is at war 战时的: *a film set in wartime France* 一部以战时法国为背景的电影 —**wartime** *n* [U] —opposite 反义词 PEACETIME

war-torn /ˈ· ·/ *adj* [only before noun 仅用于名词前] a war-torn country, city etc is being destroyed by war, especially war between opposing groups from the same country 受战争蹂躏的〔国家、城市等, 尤指内战〕

War·wick·shire /ˈwɔrɪkʃɚ; ˈwɒrɪkʃə/ a COUNTY in west central England 沃里克郡〔英格兰中西部一郡〕

war wid·ow /ˈ· ,· ·/ *n* [C] a woman whose husband has been killed in a war 战争中失去丈夫的寡妇

war·y /ˈwɛrɪ; ˈweəri/ *adj* someone who is wary is careful because they think something might be dangerous or harmful〔人〕小心翼翼的, 谨慎的: **be wary of (doing) sth** *I'm a bit wary of driving in this fog.* 在这样的浓雾中开车, 我要小心一点。—**wariness** *n* [U] —**warily** *adv*: *"I want to ask you a favor." "What is it?" Mike said warily.* "我想请你帮个忙。" "什么事呀?"迈克小心翼翼地回答。

war zone /ˈ· ·/ *n* [C] an area where a war is being fought 战区; 交战地带

was /wəz; wəz; *strong* 强读 wɑz; wɒz/ the first and third person singular of the past tense of BE be的第一和第三人称单数过去式

Wash. the written abbreviation of 缩写= WASHINGTON

wash[1] /wɑʃ; wɒʃ/ *v* [S1] [W3]

1 ►WASH SOMETHING 洗某物◄ [T] to clean something using soap and water〔用肥皂和水〕洗, 洗涤: *I'm just going to wash my hands.* 我正准备去洗手。| *This shirt needs washing.* 这件衬衫该洗了。| **wash the dishes** *It's your turn to wash the dishes.* 轮到你洗餐具了。

2 ►WASH YOURSELF 洗澡◄ [I] to clean yourself with soap and water 洗澡: *Amy washed and went to bed.* 埃米洗过澡就睡觉去了。

3 ►FLOW 流动◄ [I always+adv/prep, T always+adv/prep] if a liquid or something carried by a liquid washes or is washed in a particular direction, it flows there〔液体向某方向〕流动; 〔某物被液体〕冲走, 冲刷: [**+against/away etc**] *The waves washed against the shore.* 浪涛拍打着海岸。| **wash sth away/against/down etc** *Floods had washed away the topsoil.* 洪水把表土冲掉了。| **wash ashore** (=be brought to the shore by waves)〔被浪〕冲上岸 *debris washed ashore by the tide* 被潮水冲上岸的碎片

4 sth doesn't/won't wash *spoken* used to say that you do not believe or accept someone's explanation, reason, attitude etc【口】不相信, 不接受〔某人的阐述、理由、态度等〕: *I'm sorry but all his charm just doesn't wash with me.* 对不起, 他的魅力我就是接受不了。

5 wash your hands of sth to refuse to be responsible for something anymore 对某事不愿再管: *I've washed my hands of the whole affair.* 整个事情我已经不再过问了。

6 wash your dirty linen in public to discuss something unpleasant or embarrassing in public 把丑事公开; 使家丑外扬

7 wash your mouth out! *spoken* used when someone has just sworn or said something rude, to tell them they should not have spoken that way【口】嘴巴干净点!〔用于告诫说了脏话的人〕

8 wash well/badly to be easy or difficult to clean using soap and water〔用肥皂和水〕耐洗/不耐洗: *Silk doesn't wash well.* 丝绸不耐洗。—see also 另见 **wash up**

wash sth ↔ **down** *phr v* [T] **1** to clean something large using a lot of water 用大量水冲洗〔大的物体〕: *Can you wash down the driveway?* 你能冲洗车道吗? **2** to drink something to help you swallow food or medicine〔借助饮料〕将〔食物或药物〕吞下: **wash sth down with sth** *steak and chips washed down with red wine* 一边吃牛排和炸薯条, 一边喝红葡萄酒

wash sth ↔ **off** *phr v* **1** [T] to clean dirt, dust etc from the surface of something with water〔用水将某物表面的污垢、尘埃等〕洗净 **2** [I] if a substance washes off, you can remove it from the surface of something by washing〔物质〕能从某物表面洗掉: *Will this paint wash off?* 这漆能洗掉吗?

wash sth ↔ **out** *phr v* **1** [T] to wash something quickly to get rid of the dirt in it 迅速洗净: *I'll just wash out my paint rags first.* 我要先把抹油漆的碎布洗干净。**2** [I] if a substance washes out, you can remove it from a material by washing it〔物质能从某材料上〕洗掉 **3 be washed out** if an event is washed out, it cannot continue because of rain〔因下雨〕使〔活动〕无法继续; 取消: *The summer fair was washed out by the English weather.* 英国夏季的雨使集市取消了。see also 另见 WASHED-OUT, WASHOUT

wash over sb *phr v* [T] if a feeling washes over you, you suddenly feel it very strongly〔感觉〕突然袭来: *A feeling of relief washed over her as the plane landed.* 飞机着陆时, 她如释重负。

wash up *phr v* **1** [I,T] *especially BrE* to wash plates, dishes, knives etc【尤英】洗餐具 —see also 另见 WASHING-UP —see picture at 参见 CLEAN² 图 **2** [I] *AmE* to wash your hands【美】洗手: *Go wash up before dinner.* 饭前去洗手。**3** [T **wash** sth ↔ **up**] if waves wash something up, they bring it to the shore〔波浪〕把〔某物〕冲到岸边: *His body was washed up the next morning.* 第二天早晨他的尸体被波浪冲到了岸边。—see also 另见 **wash ashore** (WASH¹ (3)), WASHED UP

USAGE NOTE 用法说明: WASH
GRAMMAR 语法
You do not usually use the expression **wash yourself** unless a special effort is needed 除非需要特别费劲, 通常不使用 wash yourself 这种表达方式: *He washed/had a wash, dressed, and fixed breakfast.* 他洗了澡, 穿好衣服, 然后准备早餐。| *Several children in the class still can't wash themselves.* 班上有几名小孩仍然不会自己洗澡。

wash² *n*
1 ►ACT OF CLEANING 洗◄ [C] an act of cleaning something using soap and water〔用肥皂和水的〕洗, 清洗: *Those drapes need a wash.* 这些布帘该洗了。| **have a wash** *I'll just have a quick wash before we go.* 走之前我赶紧洗一下澡。
2 in the wash waiting to be washed, being washed, or drying 待洗; 正在洗; 正在干: *Your blue shirt's in the wash – you'll have to wear another one.* 你的蓝衬衫正在洗——你得穿另一件衬衫。| **shrink/fade/get damaged etc in the wash** *I'm afraid your black sweater shrank in the wash.* 恐怕你的黑色毛线衫洗后会缩水。
3 it'll all come out in the wash *spoken* used to tell someone not to worry about a problem because it will be solved in the future【口】最后会得到圆满解决〔用于告诉某人不要为问题而担忧〕
4 ►BOAT 船◄ [singular, U] the movement of water caused by a passing boat〔船驶过后的〕尾流
5 ►SEA/RIVER 海/河◄ the wash of the movement or sound made by flowing water 水的流动[声音]: *the wash of the waves against the rocks* 浪涛冲击岩石的声音
6 ►SKIN 皮肤◄ [C] a liquid used to clean your skin 洗面乳; 沐浴液: *an anti-bacterial face wash* 抗菌洗面乳
7 ►COLOUR 颜料◄ [C] a very thin transparent layer of paint or colour 极薄的一层油漆[颜料]
8 ►CLOTHES 服装◄ [singular, U] *AmE* clothes that need to be washed, are being washed, or have just been washed【美】待洗[正在洗, 洗好了]的衣服; WASHING *BrE*【英】: **do the wash** (=wash dirty clothes) 洗衣服 | **hang the wash out** (=put it on the washing line)〔在晾衣绳上〕晾晒衣服
9 ►RIVER 河流◄ also 又作 **dry wash** [C] *AmE* a river in a desert that usually has no water in it【美】沙漠中一般干涸的河 **10** *n* [singular] the area of land that is sometimes covered by the sea 浅水滩 —see picture on page A12 参见 A12 页图

Wash, the a wide BAY (=an area of sea that curves inwards towards the land) on the east coast of England between Norfolk and Lincolnshire 沃什湾〔英格兰东部沿海一宽阔海湾, 位于诺福克郡和林肯郡之间〕

wash·a·ble /ˈwɑʃəbl; ˈwɒʃəbəl/ *adj* **1** something that is washable can be washed without being damaged 可洗的; 耐洗的: *washable cushion covers* 可洗的坐垫套 | **machine washable** *machine washable wool* 可机洗的羊毛织物 **2** paint, ink etc that is washable will come out of cloth when you wash it〔漆、墨水等〕洗后会掉色的

wash·ba·sin /ˈwɑʃˌbesn; ˈwɒʃˌbeɪsən/ *n* [C] *BrE* a container like a small SINK² used for washing your hands and face【英】(洗)脸盆

wash·board /ˈwɑʃˌbɔrd; ˈwɒʃbɔːd/ *n* [C] a piece of metal with a slightly rough surface, used in the past for rubbing clothes on when you are washing them〔旧时洗衣服用的〕搓板, 洗衣板

wash·cloth /ˈwɑʃˌklɔθ; ˈwɒʃklɒθ/ *n* [C] *AmE* a small square cloth used for washing your hands and face【美】〔洗脸、洗手用的〕毛巾; FACECLOTH *BrE*【英】

wash·day /ˈwɑʃˌde; ˈwɒʃdeɪ/ *n* [C,U] *old-fashioned* the day each week when you wash your clothes【过时】〔每星期固定的〕洗衣日

washed-out /ˌ·ˈ·◂/ *adj* **1** not brightly coloured any more usually as a result of being washed many times〔多次洗涤后〕退了色的: *a washed-out shade of blue* 退淡的蓝色 **2** feeling weak and looking unhealthy because you are very tired〔因疲劳而〕面色苍白的: *Debbie's looking a bit washed-out.* 黛比看上去脸色有点苍白。—see also 另见 **wash out** (WASH¹)

washed-up /ˌ·ˈ·◂/ *adj* if a person or an organization is washed-up, they will never be successful again〔人或组织〕彻底失败的; 不再有希望的: *washed-up ex-members of the Board* 不会再有建树的董事会前任成员 —see also 另见 **wash up** (WASH¹)

wash·er /ˈwɑʃɚ; ˈwɒʃə/ *n* [C] **1** a thin flat ring of plastic, metal, rubber etc that is put over a BOLT¹ (2) before the NUT¹ (2) is put on, or between two pipes, to make a tighter joint 垫圈〔塑料、金属、橡胶等做的扁环, 置于螺母和螺栓或两根管子之间, 使之接得更紧〕**2** *informal* a WASHING MACHINE【非正式】洗衣机

washer-dr·yer also 又作 **washer-drier** *BrE*【英】/ˌ··ˈ··/ *n* [C] a machine that washes and dries clothes 洗涤烘干两用洗衣机

wash·er·wom·an /ˈwɑʃɚˌwʊmən; ˈwɒʃəˌwʊmən/ *n* [C] a woman in the past whose job was to wash other people's clothes〔旧时的〕洗衣女工

wash·ing /ˈwɑʃɪŋ; ˈwɒʃɪŋ/ *n* [singular, U] *BrE* clothes that need to be washed, are being washed, or have just been washed【英】待洗[正在洗; 洗好了]的衣服; WASH² (8) *AmE*【美】: **do the washing** (=wash dirty clothes) 洗衣服 | **put the washing out** (=hang it on a washing line) 晾衣服 2

washing day /ˈ·· ·/ *n* [C] WASHDAY〔每周固定的〕洗衣日

washing line /ˈ·· ·/ *n* [C,U] *BrE* a piece of string stretched between two poles that you hang wet clothes on so that they become dry; CLOTHESLINE【英】晾衣绳

washing liq·uid /ˈ·· ˌ··/ *n* [C,U] soap in the form of a liquid used for washing clothes 洗衣液

washing ma·chine /ˈ·· ·ˌ·/ *n* [C] a machine for washing clothes 洗衣机 —see picture on page A10 参见 A10 页图

washing pow·der /ˈ·· ˌ··/ *n* [C,U] *BrE* soap in the form of a powder used for washing clothes【英】洗衣粉

washing so·da /ˈ·· ˌ··/ *n* [U] a chemical that is added to water to clean very dirty things 洗涤碱〔放入水中, 用来清洗很脏的东西〕

Washington /ˈwɔʃɪŋtən; ˈwɒʃɪŋtən/ **1** also 又作 **Washington, D.C., the District of Columbia, D.C.** the capital city of the US, on the Potomac River close to the country's east coast. Washington's many government buildings include the White House, and the Capitol, and the Supreme Court. It has no industry. D.C. stands for District of Columbia, meaning that Washington is a special area that governs itself and is not contained in any of the 50 states. 华盛顿哥伦比亚特区〔美国首都, 位于波托马克河畔, 邻近美国东海岸。白宫、国会大厦及联邦最高法院等政府大楼矗立于此, 区内没有工业。D.C. 代表哥伦比亚特区, 意指华盛顿为自治特区, 不隶属于 50 个州中的任何一个〕**2** the US president and his advisers in the White House 华盛顿〔指美国总统及白宫顾问〕: *Washington is expected to resist pressure to lift trade sanctions on Myanmar.* 华盛顿方面可望顶住压力, 取消对缅甸的贸易制裁。**3** also 又作 **Washington State** abbreviation 缩写为 **WA** a state in the northwestern US. Its largest cities are Seattle and Tacoma. 华盛顿州〔美国西北部一州。该州最大城市为西雅图和塔科马〕

Washington, Book·er /ˈbʊkɚ; ˈbʊkə/ **T.** (1856-1915) a US teacher whose parents had been SLAVES, who started the

Tuskegee Institute, one of the first US colleges for black people. He also wrote a book about his life called *Up from Slavery*. 华盛顿〔(1856-1915),美国教育家,出身奴隶家庭,创办了塔斯基吉学院。该学院为美国最早的黑人学院之一。著有自传《出身奴隶》〕

George Washington 乔治·华盛顿

Washington, George (1732-99) the first President of the US, from 1789 to 1797. Washington was a respected officer in the British army before he became commander of the COLONIAL armies during the American Revolutionary War. After the war he became the leader of the Constitutional Convention and influenced the states to officially accept the new Constitution of the United States. He was elected President of the US twice, but he refused to be president for a third time. 华盛顿〔(1732-1799),美国第一任总统,任期自1789至1797年。华盛顿曾是英国军队中一位深受推崇的军官,美国独立战争期间担任大陆军总司令。战后当选美国制宪会议主席,运用其影响力推动各州正式接受美国新宪法。他两度当选美国总统,但拒绝再次连任〕

CULTURAL NOTE 文化注释

Most people in the US know important historical facts about George Washington, such as that he was an important military leader in the American Revolutionary War against Britain; that he and his army suffered an extremely cold winter in Valley Forge; and that he became the first President of the US. 大多数美国人都知道乔治·华盛顿的一些重要历史事迹,例如他是美国独立战争时期的重要军事统帅,他和他的军队在福吉谷遭受了极度的严寒,还有后来他当上了美国第一任总统。

Most children in the US are told a story about Washington that shows he was an honest person. According to the story, when Washington was a boy, he chopped down a CHERRY tree with an AXE. Washington's father saw the tree, became angry, and asked Washington what had happened. Washington then replied "I cannot tell a lie" and admitted that he had cut down the tree. He is often called "the father of our country" and many tourists visit Mount Vernon, the home where he and his wife Martha lived in Virginia. His picture is on every US one-dollar BILL and every US QUARTER, and his birthday is celebrated every year on February 22nd as a public holiday called President's Day. 美国的很多孩子都听过一则讲述华盛顿诚实的故事。故事中说,在华盛顿还是个少年的时候,他用斧头砍倒了一株樱桃树。华盛顿的父亲发现树被砍之后大发雷霆,并质问华盛顿怎么回事。华盛顿回答说自己不能撒谎,然后承认是自己砍的。华盛顿常被称为"国父",很多游客都去拜访他和妻子玛莎在弗吉尼亚州芒特弗农的故居。他的头像被印在面值1元的美钞和面值25美分的硬币上。而他的生日,2月22日,被设立为公共假日来庆祝,叫做"总统日"。

Washington Mon·u·ment, the /,···'···/ a tall OBELISK (=stone structure) on the MALL (=park area) in Washington, D.C., which was built to show respect and admiration for George Washington, the first president of the US 华盛顿纪念碑〔位于华盛顿特区草地广场的一块高耸的方尖碑,为纪念美国首任总统乔治·华盛顿而建〕

washing-up /,··'·/ *n* [U] *BrE*【英】**1** the washing of plates, dishes, knives etc 洗餐具; dishes *AmE*【美】: **do the washing-up** *It's your turn to do the washing-up, Conrad.* 康拉德,轮到你来洗餐具了。**2** the dirty pans, plates, dishes, knives etc that have to be washed 待洗的餐具; dishes *AmE*【美】: *a pile of washing-up* 一堆要洗的餐具

washing-up liq·uid /,··'·,··/ *n* [U] *BrE* a liquid soap for washing plates, knives etc【英】〔洗餐具用的〕洗涤剂; DISHWASHING LIQUID *AmE*【美】—see picture on page A10 参见A10页图

wash·out /ˈwɑʃ,aʊt; ˈwɒʃ-aʊt/ *n* [C] *informal*【非正式】**1** a failure 失败: *The picnic was a total washout – nobody turned up!* 野餐彻底失败——没人来! **2** an occasion when heavy rain washes the soil away from a place〔大雨把泥土〕冲刷, 冲蚀 —see also 另见 **wash out** (WASH¹)

wash·room /ˈwɑʃ,rum; ˈwɒʃrʊm/ *n* [C] *AmE* a word meaning a room where you use the toilet, used to avoid saying this directly【美】厕所〔委婉用语〕

wash·stand /ˈwɑʃ,stænd; ˈwɒʃstænd/ *n* [C] a table in a bedroom used in the past for holding the things needed for washing your face〔旧时放在卧室中的〕脸盆架, 盥洗台

wash·tub /ˈwɑʃ,tʌb; ˈwɒʃtʌb/ *n* [C] a large bowl used in the past for washing clothes in〔旧时的〕洗衣盆

was·n't /ˈwɑznt; ˈwɒzənt/ the short form of 缩略式= 'was not': *Jason wasn't at the party.* 贾森没有出席聚会。

WASP /wɑsp; wɒsp/ *n* [C] *especially AmE* White Anglo-Saxon Protestant; an American whose family was originally from northern Europe and who is therefore considered to be part of the most powerful group in society【尤美】盎格鲁-撒克逊裔白人新教徒; 北欧裔美国人〔被看作属于社会上的高等阶层〕

wasp /wɑsp; wɒsp/ *n* [C] a thin black and yellow flying insect that can sting you 黄蜂

wasp·ish /ˈwɑspɪʃ; ˈwɒspɪʃ/ *adj* bad-tempered and cruel in the things that you say〔语言〕恶毒的, 尖酸刻薄的: *waspish remarks* 恶毒的评论 —**waspishly** *adv* —**waspishness** *n* [U]

was·sail /ˈwɑsel; ˈwɒseɪl/ *v* [I] *old use* to enjoy yourself eating and drinking at Christmas【旧】〔圣诞节时〕吃喝取乐 —**wassail** *n* [U]

wast /wəst; wɑst; *strong* 强读 wɑst; wɒst/ *v* **thou wast** *old use* you were【旧】你是〔第二人称单数过去式〕

wast·age /ˈwestɪdʒ; ˈweɪstɪdʒ/ *n* [U] **1 a)** the loss or destruction of something, especially in a way that is not useful or sensible 耗费〔尤指浪费〕; 损耗 **b)** the amount that is lost or destroyed 耗费量; 损耗量: *high levels of wastage in the fast-food industry* 快餐业的高消耗量 **2 natural wastage** *BrE* a reduction in the number of workers because of people leaving, retiring (RETIRE (1)) etc and not because they have lost their jobs【英】〔因离职、退休等造成的〕自然减员

waste¹ /west; weɪst/ *n* 

1 ►BAD USE 使用不当◄ [singular, U] things such as money or skills that should be used and are not, or that are not used effectively〔金钱或技能的〕浪费: *waste in government departments* 政府部门的浪费 | [+of] *Being unemployed is such a waste of your talents.* 失业简直是埋没了你的才能。

2 be a waste of time/money/effort etc to be not worth the time, money etc that you use because there is little or no result 完全是浪费时间/金钱/力气等: *We should never have gone – it was a total waste of time.* 我们真不该去——那是白费时间。

3 go to waste to be wasted 被浪费掉: *Don't let all this food go to waste.* 别让这些食物白白浪费掉。

4 ►UNWANTED MATERIALS 废料◄ [U] unwanted materials or substances that are left after you have used something〔使用某东西产生的〕废弃物: *It's a good idea to recycle household waste.* 回收利用家庭废弃物是个好主意。| **industrial/chemical etc waste** *Industrial waste has found its way into the water supply.* 工业废物已渗入到水源中了。

5 a waste of space *spoken* someone who has no good qualities【口】一无是处的人: *That woman is a complete waste of space!* 那个女人简直糟透了!

6 ►LAND 土地◄ [C usually plural 一般用复数] *especially literary* a large empty or useless area of land【尤文】大片荒地: *the icy wastes of Antarctica* 南极洲大片冰封的荒地 —see also 另见 WASTELAND

waste² *v* [T] 

1 ►NOT USE SENSIBLY 不理智地使用◄ to use more money, time, energy etc than you should, or use it in a way that is not useful or sensible 滥用; 浪费〔金钱、时间、精力等〕: *Leaving the heating on all the time wastes electricity.* 让暖气整天开着是浪费电力。| **waste sth on** *Don't waste your money on that junk!* 不要为那个破玩意儿浪费金钱!

2 waste your breath *spoken* to say something that has no effect【口】白费唇舌: *Don't try to reason with Paul – you're wasting your breath.* 不要跟保罗讲理了——你是白费唇舌。

W

3 waste no time (in) doing sth to do something as quickly as you can because it will help you〔因对自己有帮助而〕不失时机地做某事: *Sandy wasted no time in getting to know the boss's daughter.* 桑迪急切地想认识老板的女儿。
4 be wasted on sb if something is wasted on someone they are too stupid or unsuitable to be able to use or enjoy it〔某物〕浪费在某人身上〔因那人太笨或不会使用或欣赏〕: *Her words of advice were wasted on me.* 她的劝告对我不起任何作用。
5 be wasted in sth if someone is wasted in a job etc, they are not using all of their abilities〔工作等上〕才能没充分利用: *Hannah's wasted in that clerical job.* 汉娜干文书工作是大材小用。
6 ▶BECAUSE OF ILLNESS 因病◀ if an illness wastes someone, they become thinner and weaker〔疾病〕使〔身体〕消瘦, 使虚弱 —see also 另见 WASTED (3), WASTING
7 waste not, want not *spoken* used to say that if you use what you have carefully, you will not be left with nothing later【口】勤俭节约, 吃穿不愁
8 ▶HARM SB 伤害某人◀ *slang especially AmE* to kill someone, severely injure them, or defeat them【俚, 尤美】干掉某人, 废了某人〔指杀死、严重打伤或打败某人〕
waste away *phr v* [I] to gradually become thinner and weaker, usually because you are ill〔通常因有病而〕逐渐消瘦[衰弱]

3 **waste³** *adj* **1** waste materials, substances etc are unwanted because the good part of them has been removed〔材料、物资等〕废弃的, 无用的 **2** used for holding or carrying away materials and substances that are no longer wanted 盛废物的; 运走废物的: *a waste pipe* 排污管; 废气排放管 | *a waste tank* 垃圾箱 **3** waste land is empty or not fit to be used〔土地〕荒芜的; 无用的 —see also 另见 WASTE¹ (6), WASTELAND, **lay waste** (LAY² (8))

waste·bas·ket /ˈwestˌbæskɪt; ˈweɪstˌbɑːskɪt/ *n* [C] *especially AmE* a small container, usually indoors, into which you put unwanted paper etc【尤美】〔一般用于室内的〕废纸篓 —see picture at 参见 BASKET 图

wast·ed /ˈwestɪd; ˈweɪstɪd/ *adj* **1 a wasted journey/trip/phone-call etc** an action that is unsuccessful because it has no helpful result 无用的行程/旅游/电话等: *I'm sorry, you've had a wasted journey; Mr Newton isn't here.* 对不起, 让你白跑了一趟, 牛顿先生不在这里。**2** *slang* very drunk or affected by drugs【俚】烂醉的; 被毒品麻醉的 **3** very tired and weak-looking 疲劳的; 衰弱的

waste dis·pos·al /ˈ· ·ˌ··/ *n especially BrE*【尤英】**1** also 又作 **waste disposal un·it** /ˈ· ··ˌ··/ [C] a machine connected to the waste pipe of a kitchen SINK that cuts solid waste into small pieces 废物处理装置〔与厨房水槽废水管连接的机器, 可把厨房垃圾碾碎〕; GARBAGE DISPOSAL *AmE*【美】**2** [U] the process or system of getting rid of unwanted materials or substances 废物处理过程[系统]; DISPOSAL (1) *AmE*【美】: *the waste disposal plant* 废物处理厂

waste·ful /ˈwestfəl; ˈweɪstfəl/ *adj* using things such as money, energy, or work in a way that wastes them 挥霍的; 浪费的: *It's wasteful to throw so much away.* 扔掉这么多东西真是浪费。—**wastefully** *adv*: *Half the wood's energy is wastefully burned.* 燃烧的木材有一半能量白白地浪费了。—**wastefulness** *n* [U]

waste·land /ˈwestˌlænd; ˈweɪstlænd/ *n* [C,U] land that is empty, ugly, and not used for anything 不毛之地, 荒地: **an industrial wasteland** (=with empty, ruined old factories) 工业废址

W

Waste Land, The /ˌ· ˈ·/ (1922) a long poem by T.S. Eliot. It is written in a style that was new and unusual at that time, and it has had a great influence on modern poetry.《荒原》〔(1922), T.S.艾略特的长诗。其创作风格在当时新颖而奇特, 对现代诗歌产生了重大影响〕

waste pa·per /ˌ· ˈ··◂/ *n* [U] paper that has been thrown away, especially because it has already been used〔尤指用过的〕废纸

waste·pa·per bas·ket /ˈwestˌpepə ˈbæskɪt; ˌweɪstˈpeɪpə ˌbɑːskɪt/ *n* [C] a small container, usually indoors, into which you put unwanted paper etc 废纸篓 —see picture at 参见 BASKET 图

waste prod·uct /ˈ· ˌ··/ *n* [C] something useless, such as ASH or gas, that is produced in a process that produces something useful〔生产过程中产生的〕废物〈如灰烬、气体〉: *The waste products of combustion are fed into the car's exhaust.* 燃烧产生的废气输送入汽车排气管。

wast·er /ˈwestə; ˈweɪstə/ *n* [C] **1** someone who wastes their time, money etc in a stupid way 造成〔时间、金钱等〕浪费的人 **2 time-waster** someone or something that uses up too much time 浪费过多时间的人[物]: *Waiting in lines is such a time-waster.* 排队等候真是浪费时间。

wast·ing /ˈwestɪŋ; ˈweɪstɪŋ/ *adj* **wasting disease** a wasting disease is one that gradually makes you become thinner and weaker〔使人日益消瘦和虚弱的〕消耗性疾病

was·trel /ˈwestrəl; ˈweɪstrəl/ *n* [C] *literary* someone who wastes their time, money etc【文】浪费时间、金钱的人

watch¹ /wɑtʃ; wɒtʃ/ *v* 

1 ▶LOOK AT 看◀ [I,T] to look at and pay attention to something that is happening 观看, 注视: *Do you want to join in or just sit and watch?* 你是想加进来, 还是只坐在一旁观看呢? | **watch sb/sth** *Harriet watched the man with interest as he walked in.* 这个人走进来时, 哈丽雅特饶有兴味地看着他。| **watch sb do/doing sth** *Jack watched them slowly climb the wall.* 杰克看着他们慢慢地攀墙而上。| **watch television/a video/a film etc** *The Presidential debate was watched by over 10 million people.* 一千多万人(通过电视)观看了这场总统竞选辩论。| **watch what/how/when etc** *Watch how I do it.* 注意看我怎么做。—see picture at 参见 SEE¹ 图
2 ▶BE CAREFUL 小心◀ [T] to be careful with something 留心〔某事〕: **watch (that)** *Watch the milk doesn't boil over.* 当心不要让牛奶煮溢了。| **watch what/how/where etc** *Watch what you're doing with that knife!* 用那把刀时要当心! | **watch your weight** (=be careful not to get fat) 注意保持体重[不让发胖]
3 ▶LOOK AFTER 照顾◀ [T] to look after someone or something so that nothing bad happens to them 照顾〔某人或某物〕: *Can you watch the kids for a couple of hours tonight?* 今晚你能照看孩子几小时吗?
4 ▶SECRETLY 暗中◀ [T] to secretly watch a person or place 监视〔某人或某地〕; 看守: *I feel like I'm being watched.* 我感觉像是有人监视着我。
5 watch yourself to control how you behave or what you do 自我克制, 谨慎: *I have to watch myself when it comes to eating chocolate.* 说到吃巧克力, 我必须克制自己。
6 watch your step *informal* used to warn someone to be careful, especially about making someone angry【非正式】做事谨慎小心〔用于警告某人, 尤指不要惹怒他人〕: *You'd better watch your step or you'll be in trouble again.* 你最好小心谨慎一些, 否则又要自讨没趣。
7 watch the clock *informal* to keep checking to see if it is time to stop what you are doing, instead of doing it【非正式】老在看钟〔等待下班〕
8 watch this space *informal* an expression used especially in newspapers to tell people to wait because things are going to develop further【非正式】等待事态的发展〔尤用于报纸〕
9 watch the world go by to spend time looking at what is happening around you〔花时间〕观察周围发生的一切: *Bill likes to sit in the park and watch the world go by.* 比尔喜欢坐在公园里观察周围发生的事。
10 watch the time to make sure you know what time it is to avoid being late for something 留意时间〔以免耽误某事〕

Frequencies of the verb **watch** in spoken and written English 动词 watch 在英语口语和书面语中的使用频率

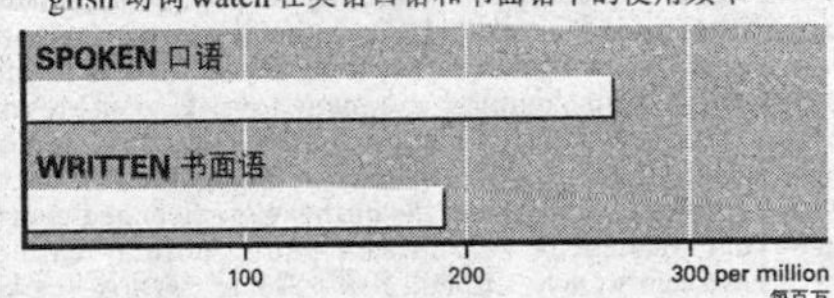

Based on the British National Corpus and the Longman Lancaster Corpus
据英国国家语料库和朗文兰开斯特语料库

This graph shows that the verb **watch** is more common in spoken English than in written English. This is because it is used in some common spoken phrases. 本图表显示, 动词 watch 在英语口语中的使用频率远远高于书面语, 因为口语中一些常用短语是由 watch 构成的。

watch (*v*) **SPOKEN PHRASES**
含 watch 的口语短语

11 watch it! a) used to tell someone to be more careful, especially in a dangerous situation〔尤指在危险情况下告诉某人〕小心! 留神!: *Watch it! You nearly knocked my head off with that ladder!* 小心点! 你差点让那把梯子砸开我的头了! **b)** used to threaten someone (给我)当心点!〔用于威胁某人〕: *Just watch it, right, or I'll get you!* 你可要当心点, 否则我就要给你颜色看! **12 watch yourself** used to warn someone to be careful not to hurt themselves, get into dan-

ger etc 当心〔告诫某人要小心, 不要受伤或陷入危险境地等〕: *Hey, watch yourself, that's very hot!* 嘿, 你要当心, 那东西很烫! **13 watch this/just watch** used to make someone watch you while you do something 留神〔用于使别人注意你正在做的事〕: *Watch this! I'm going to balance this bottle on my nose.* 看呀! 我要把这个瓶子在我鼻子上放稳。**14 you watch** used to tell someone to watch something because you know what is going to happen 你看〔用于告诉某人注意某事, 因为你知道将要发生什么事〕: *You watch. Every time she goes out he follows her.* 你看, 每次她一出去, 他就跟在她后面。**15 watch what you're doing** used to tell someone to do something more carefully 做某事要更小心: *Watch what you're doing! You're spilling it everywhere.* 做事小心点, 你洒得到处都是。**16 watch your mouth** used to tell someone rudely or angrily to be careful what they say 说话当心点〔用于粗鲁或愤怒地告诉某人要小心说话〕: *You'd better watch your mouth, young man!* 年轻人, 你说话该注意点!

watch for *phr v* [T] to wait and be ready for something 等待〔某事〕; 期待: *The prisoners watched for a chance to escape.* 犯人们等待逃跑的机会。

watch out *phr v* [I usually in imperative 一般用于祈使句] *spoken* used to tell someone to be careful【口】小心〔用于提醒某人〕: *Watch out! There's a car coming.* 注意! 有辆车开过来了。

watch out for sth/sb *phr v* [T] **1** to keep looking and waiting for someone or something 留意〔某人或某物〕: *Watch out for a tall man in a black hat.* 注意一个戴黑帽子的高个子男人。**2** to be careful of something 小心〔某事〕, 提防: *You have to watch out for fast traffic along here.* 当心这里来往的快速车辆。

watch over sb/sth *phr v* [T] to guard or take care of someone or something 看守, 照顾〔某人或某事〕: *a shepherd watching over his sheep* 照看羊群的牧羊人

S3 W3 **watch²** *n*

1 ▶CLOCK 计时器◀ [C] a small clock that you wear on your wrist or carry in your pocket 表, 手表; 怀表: *My watch has stopped.* 我的表停了。

2 ▶ACT OF WATCHING 注视◀ [singular, U] the act of watching something carefully in order to warn people of any danger 仔细注视〔一旦出现危险便警告他人〕, 监视: **keep watch** *I kept watch while the others slept.* 别人睡觉时我值班。

3 keep a (close) watch on a) to check a situation carefully so that you always know what is happening and are ready to deal with it 密切注视〔某情况, 以了解发生的事, 并准备处理〕: *UN forces are keeping a close watch on the area.* 联合国部队正密切注视着该地区的形势。**b)** to watch someone carefully, either because you think they may be doing something illegal, or in order to make sure they are safe 严密监视〔某人, 因认为他从事非法活动或为了保护他〕: *Police kept a 24-hour watch on the house.* 警方24小时严密监视着这座房子。

4 keep a watch out for to look carefully in order to try and find someone or something, while you are doing other things 做其他事时仔细留意, 以便找到〔某人或某物〕

5 be on the watch (for) to be looking and waiting for something that might happen or someone you might see 注意〔可能发生的事或可能看到的人〕: *You should always be on the watch for pickpockets.* 你应该随时注意提防扒手。

6 ▶PEOPLE 人们◀ [C] a group of people employed to guard or protect someone or something 警卫; 看守人

7 ▶GUARDING STH 看守某物◀ [C,U] a fixed period of the day or night when a group of people must look carefully for any signs of danger or attack 〔白天或夜间的〕值班时间: *the first watch* 第一班 | **be on watch** *Who's on watch tonight?* 今晚谁值班?

8 the watches of the night *poetical* a period of the night when you are awake【诗】夜晚醒着的时候

9 the (night) watch the group of policemen in former times who were responsible for keeping a town or city safe at night 〔昔日负责城镇夜间安全的〕巡夜警察 —see also 另见 NEIGHBOURHOOD WATCH

watch·band /ˈwɑtʃˌbænd; ˈwɒtʃbænd/ *n* [C] *AmE*【美】a WATCHSTRAP *BrE*【英】表带

watch·dog /ˈwɑtʃˌdɔg; ˈwɒtʃdɒg/ *n* [C] **1** a committee or person whose job is to make sure that companies do not do anything illegal or harmful 〔确保公司没有从事非法或有害活动的〕监察委员会; 监察人员: *a consumer watchdog* 保护消费者权益的监督员 **2** a dog used for guarding property 看门狗

watch·ful /ˈwɑtʃfəl; ˈwɒtʃfəl/ *adj* careful to notice what is happening, in case anything bad happens 留心的; 警惕的, 提防的: *watchful for any signs of activity* 随时注意活动的迹象 | **keep a watchful eye on** *Pam kept a watchful eye on the time.* 帕姆是个守时的人。—**watchfully** *adv* —**watchfulness** *n* [U]

watch·ing brief /ˈ· · ,·/ *n* [C] *law* instructions to a lawyer to watch a case that their client is not directly involved in【法律】让律师出庭旁听与委托人无直接关系的案件的委托书

watch·mak·er /ˈwɑtʃˌmekɚ; ˈwɒtʃˌmeɪkə/ *n* [C] someone who makes or repairs watches (WATCH² (1)) and clocks 钟表匠; 钟表制造[修理]工

watch·man /ˈwɑtʃmən; ˈwɒtʃmən/ *n* [C] *old-fashioned* someone whose job is to guard a building or place; SECURITY GUARD【过时】〔看守建筑物或一个地方的〕守门人; 警卫

watch·strap /ˈwɑtʃˌstræp; ˈwɒtʃstræp/ *n* [C] *BrE* a piece of leather or metal for fastening your watch to your wrist【英】〔皮革或金属的〕表带; WATCHBAND *AmE*【美】

watch·tow·er /ˈwɑtʃˌtauɚ; ˈwɒtʃˌtaʊə/ *n* [C] a high tower used for guarding a place, from which you can see things that are happening 岗楼, 瞭望塔

Watchtower, The a magazine produced by the religious group the Jehovah's Witnesses, who go to people's houses and try to persuade them to buy it《守望塔》〔宗教组织"耶和华见证会"编印的一份杂志。其成员登门游说人们购买此刊物〕

watch·word /ˈwɑtʃˌwɝd; ˈwɒtʃwɜːd/ *n* [singular] a word or phrase that explains what people should do in a particular situation 口号; 标语; 格言: *The watchword is caution.* 口号是"小心谨慎"。

wa·ter¹ /ˈwɔtɚ; ˈwɔːtə/ *n* [U] S3 W1

1 ▶LIQUID 液体◀ a) the clear colourless liquid that falls as rain, fills lakes and rivers, and is necessary for life to exist 水: *This reservoir supplies the whole city with water.* 这个水库供应全城的用水。| *The prisoners were given only bread and water.* 囚犯只获提供面包和水。| **seawater/bathwater/rainwater** (=a particular type of water) 海水/洗澡水/雨水 —see also 另见 FRESHWATER, SALTWATER **b)** the supply of water to homes, factories etc through pipes and TAPS 〔给家庭、工厂等的〕供水: **running water** (=water that flows, not kept in a container or pool) 自来水 *All rooms have hot and cold running water.* 每个房间都有冷热自来水供应。| **water shortage** (=a situation when there is not much water available) 缺水

2 ▶AREA OF WATER 水域◀ a) an area of water such as a lake, river etc 〔湖、河等的〕水域: *the water's edge* 水边 | *Denzel dived into the water and swam towards her.* 登泽尔跳入水中朝她游去。| **by water** (=by boat) 乘船; 由水路 *We can transport the goods by water.* 我们可以经水路运输货物。**b)** the surface of a lake, river etc 〔湖泊、河流等的〕水面: *What's that floating on the water?* 漂浮在水面上的是什么东西? | **underwater/under water** *a camera designed for use under water* 用于水下拍摄的照相机

3 waters [plural] **a)** the water in a particular lake, river etc 〔特定湖泊、河流等的〕水体: *the waters of the Amazon* 亚马孙河的河水 **b)** an area of sea near or belonging to a particular country 〔某国的〕领海, 海域: *the coastal waters of Alaska* 阿拉斯加近海水域 **c)** water containing minerals from a natural spring 矿泉水: **take the waters** (=drink the waters because you think it is good for your health) 〔为保健而〕喝矿泉水

4 keep your head above water *informal* to avoid trouble, especially because of lack of money【非正式】避免陷入困境〔尤指经济困境〕: *The firm is barely keeping its head above water.* 公司只不过在勉强维持。

5 be (like) water off a duck's back *informal* if advice, warnings, or rude remarks are like water off a duck's back to someone, they have no effect on them【非正式】〔忠告、警告、粗话等对某人〕毫无影响, 不起作用

6 be (all) water under the bridge *especially spoken* in the past, forgotten, and not worth worrying about【尤口】是过去[已忘记; 不值得担心]的事: *Look, it's all water under the bridge now. Let's leave it behind us.* 现在一切已成过去, 让我们把它忘记吧。

7 be all water under the bridge used to say that a situation has changed, especially over a long period of time or since a particular event 形势发生了变化〔尤指经过一段长时间或某特殊事件后〕

8 deep/murky/unknown etc waters a situation that is unfamiliar or dangerous 不熟悉[危险]的情况

9 waters break when a PREGNANT woman's waters break, liquid flows out of her body just before the baby is ready to be born 羊水破了〔孕妇即将生产〕

10 high/low water the highest or lowest level of the sea and some rivers; TIDE 〔海和一些河的〕涨潮/退潮

W

11 water on the brain/knee etc liquid that collects around the brain, knee etc as the result of a disease〔因疾病〕脑部/膝关节等的积水
12 make/pass water *formal* to URINATE【正式】小便
13 make water if a ship makes water, water gets inside it because of a LEAK² (1)〔因船漏而〕进水 —see also 另见 SODA WATER, TOILET WATER, **in deep water** (DEEP¹ (13)), **take to sth like a duck to water** (DUCK¹ (4)), **of the first water** (FIRST (30)), **like a fish out of water** (FISH¹ (3)), **not hold water** (HOLD¹ (41)), **get into hot water** (HOT¹ (8)), **muddy the waters** (MUDDY² (2)), **pour cold water on** (POUR (7)), **still waters run deep** (STILL² (5)), **test the water** (TEST² (7)), **tread water** (TREAD¹ (5))

water² *v*
1 ►PLANT/LAND 植物/土地◄ [T] to pour water on an area of land, a plant etc, especially in order to make things grow 给…浇水; 灌溉: *You must water the garden, it's very dry.* 你得给园子浇水, 太干了。
2 eyes water if your eyes water, tears (TEAR¹ (1)) come out of them because of cold weather, pain etc〔因天寒、疼痛等〕眼睛流泪: *Chopping onions always makes my eyes water.* 切洋葱总使我眼睛流泪。—see also 另见 MOUTH-WATERING, **make your mouth water** (MOUTH¹ (10))
3 ►ANIMAL 动物◄ [T] to give an animal water to drink 给〔牲畜〕饮水
4 ►BY RIVER 江河流经◄ [T usually passive 一般用被动态] *technical* if an area is watered by a river, the river flows through it and provides it with water【术语】〔江河〕流经并给〔某地区〕供水: *Colombia is watered by several rivers.* 有好几条江河流经哥伦比亚。
5 ►WEAKEN LIQUID 把液体稀释◄ [T] to add water to a drink in order to make it weaker than it should be 加水冲淡; 稀释: *Someone had been watering the beer.* 有人在啤酒里掺了水。
water sth ↔ **down** *phr v* [T usually passive 一般用被动态] **1** to make a statement, report etc less forceful by removing parts that may offend people〔删去声明或报告等中可能冒犯人的部分〕减弱〔其作用〕, 削弱 —see also 另见 WATERED-DOWN **2** to add water to a liquid, especially for dishonest reasons; DILUTE¹ (1) 往〔液体〕中掺水〔尤指出于不诚实的原因〕

Water Ba·bies, The /'‥ ,‥/ (1863) a book for children by Charles Kingsley about a young boy called Tom, who is a chimney-sweep. Tom falls into a river and magically changes into a 'water-baby', and he learns all about good and evil from the good and evil creatures under the water.《水孩儿》〔(1863), 查尔斯·金斯利的儿童小说, 讲述小男孩汤姆的故事。汤姆是一个烟囱清扫工, 有一次掉进河里, 神奇地变成了一个"水孩儿"。水中的生物善恶参半, 他从中学会了辨别善恶〕

wa·ter·bed /'wɔtə˞ˌbɛd; 'wɔːtəbed/ *n* [C] a bed made of rubber and filled with water 水床

water bird /'‥ ·/ *n* [C] a bird that swims or walks in water 水鸟, 水禽

water bis·cuit /'‥ ,‥/ *n* [C] a hard BISCUIT (1) made from flour and water 淡味硬饼干〔用水和面粉制成〕

wa·ter·borne /'wɔtə˞ˌbɔrn; 'wɔːtəbɔːn/ *adj* spread or carried by water 由水传播的; 由水运送的: *waterborne diseases such as cholera* 由水传播的疾病, 如霍乱

water bot·tle /'‥ ,‥/ *n* [C] **1** a bottle used for carrying drinking water 水瓶, 水壶 **2** a HOT-WATER BOTTLE 热水袋

water buf·fa·lo /'‥ ,‥‥/ *n* [C] a large black animal like a cow with long horns, used for pulling vehicles and farm equipment in Asia 水牛〔在亚洲地区用于拉车和耕地〕

water bug /'‥ ·/ *n* [C] *AmE informal* a small insect that lives in or on water【美, 非正式】水蝽, 划蝽

water butt /'‥ ·/ *n* [C] *especially BrE* a BARREL¹ (1) used for collecting rainwater【尤英】〔接雨水用的〕水桶

water can·non /'‥ ,‥/ *n* [C] a machine that sends out water at high pressure, used by police against crowds of people〔警察用于驱散人群的〕高压水炮

water chest·nut /'‥ ,‥/ *n* [C] a white fruit like a nut from a plant grown in water, used in Chinese cooking 荸荠

water clos·et /'‥ ,‥/ *n* [C] *old-fashioned* a wc (=a toilet)【过时】厕所

wa·ter·col·our /'wɔtə˞ˌkʌlə˞; 'wɔːtəˌkʌlə/ *n* **1** [C usually plural 一般用复数, U] paint that you mix with water and use for painting pictures 水彩颜料 **2** [C] a picture painted with watercolours 水彩画

wa·ter·course /'wɔtə˞ˌkɔrs; 'wɔːtəkɔːs/ *n* [C] **1** a passage with water flowing through it, that can be natural or built〔天然或人工的〕水道; 河道; 渠道 **2** a flow of water such as a river or underground stream 河; 地下河

wa·ter·cress /'wɔtə˞ˌkrɛs; 'wɔːtəkres/ *n* [U] a small plant with strong tasting green leaves that grows in water 水田芥〔水生植物, 叶辛辣〕

wa·tered-down /ˌ‥ '‥◂/ *adj* **1** a watered-down statement, plan etc is much weaker and less effective than a previous plan etc〔声明、计划等比原先〕减弱了的, 打了折扣的: *a watered-down version of the original* 削弱了的形式 **2** a watered-down drink, especially an alcoholic drink, has had water added to it, especially in order to cheat people〔尤指欺骗顾客而把酒〕用水稀释的; 冲淡了的

watered silk /ˌ‥ '·/ *n* [U] a silk that looks as if it is covered with shiny waves 波纹绸

wa·ter·fall /'wɔtə˞ˌfɔl; 'wɔːtəfɔːl/ *n* [C] water that falls straight down over a cliff or big rock 瀑布 —see picture on page A12 参见A12页图

Wa·ter·ford /'wɔtə˞fə˞d; 'wɔːtəfəd/ **1** a COUNTY in the southeast of the Republic of Ireland 沃特福德郡〔爱尔兰共和国东南部一郡〕 **2** the county town of Waterford 沃特福德〔沃特福德郡首府〕

Wa·ter·ford crys·tal /ˌ‥‥ '‥/ *trademark* a type of valuable glass, made into such things as wine glasses and vases, that is made from CRYSTAL (=a high quality type of glass) in Waterford in Ireland【商标】沃特福德水晶器皿〔用爱尔兰沃特福德出产的水晶制成的名贵水晶器皿, 如酒杯和花瓶等〕

water foun·tain /'‥ ,‥/ *n* [C] a DRINKING FOUNTAIN 喷泉式饮水器

wa·ter·fowl /'wɔtə˞ˌfaul; 'wɔːtəfaʊl/ *n plural* **waterfowl** [C, U] a bird that swims in water, such as a duck, GOOSE¹ (1) etc 水鸟, 水禽

wa·ter·front /'wɔtə˞ˌfrʌnt; 'wɔːtəfrʌnt/ *n* [C usually singular 一般用单数] a part of a town or an area of land that is next to the sea, a river etc〔城市的〕滨水地区; 水边土地

Wa·ter·gate /'wɔtə˞get; 'wɔːtəgeɪt/ also 又作 **the Watergate Affair** /'‥‥ ,·/ a famous political SCANDAL in the US in the early 1970s that caused President Nixon to leave his job before Congress could IMPEACH him (=charge him with a serious crime). It was discovered that Nixon had agreed to an attempt to obtain information about the Democratic Party's plans for the next election, by secretly going into their offices in the Watergate hotel in Washington D.C. Nixon later tried to prevent this information from being discovered. The Senate asked to hear recordings that Nixon had made of conversations in his office, but when they received them, parts of conversations seemed to have been deliberately removed. These recordings became known as the 'Watergate tapes'. The Watergate Affair shocked people in the US, and made them less willing to trust their political leaders. Because of these events, other political scandals are often given a name ending in '-gate', for example Irangate. 水门事件〔20世纪70年代初发生在美国的一宗臭名昭著的政治丑闻。这起事件致使尼克松总统在国会弹劾他之前自行辞职。经查证, 尼克松批准了一项为了解民主党下届总统选举计划而秘密潜入对方在华盛顿水门大厦办公室的行动。尼克松后来试图掩盖这一事实。参议员要求审听尼克松在办公室的谈话录音, 但录音的部分内容似乎被故意抹掉。这些录音被称作"水门录音带"。水门事件使美国人感到震惊, 从而对政治领袖的信任度开始下降。鉴于此, gate (门) 常被用在表示政治丑闻的词尾, 如 Irangate (伊朗门)〕

wa·ter·hole /'wɔtə˞ˌhol; 'wɔːtəhəʊl/ *n* [C] a small area of water in a dry country, where wild animals go to drink〔干旱地区野生动物饮水的〕水池, 水坑

water ice /'‥ ·/ *n* [C,U] *BrE* a SORBET【英】冰糕

wat·er·ing can /'‥‥ ·/ *n* [C] a container used for pouring water on garden plants, with a long tube at the front 洒水壶

watering hole /'‥‥ ·/ *n* [C] *humorous* a bar or other place where people go to drink alcohol【幽默】酒吧; 人们常去饮酒的地方: *a favorite watering-hole of Ernest Hemingway* 欧内斯特·海明威最喜欢去喝酒的地方

watering place /'‥‥ ·/ *n* [C] **1** a small area of water in a dry country, where wild animals go to drink〔干旱地区野生动物去饮水的〕小水池, 水坑 **2** a place with a spring of MINERAL WATER where people went in the past to be cured of various diseases; a SPA (1)〔昔日的〕矿泉疗养地

watering pot /'‥‥ ·/ *n* [C] *AmE* a watering can【美】洒水壶

water jump /'‥ ·/ *n* [C] an area of water that horses or runners have to jump over during a race or competition〔赛马中的〕水沟障碍;〔障碍赛跑中的〕水池

wa·ter·less /'wɔtə˞lɪs; 'wɔːtələs/ *adj* with no water for people or animals to drink 无水的; 干的

water lev·el /'‥ ,‥/ *n* [U] the height to which water has risen or fallen 水位, 水平面

water lil·y /ˈ· · ,·/ *n* [C] a plant that floats on the surface of water and has large white, yellow, or pink flowers 睡莲

wa·ter·line, the /ˈwɔtɚ,laɪn; ˈwɔːtəlaɪn/ *n* the level that water reaches on the side of a ship〔船的〕吃水线

wa·ter·logged /ˈwɔtɚ,lɑgd; ˈwɔːtəlɒgd/ *adj* **1** an area that is waterlogged is flooded with water and cannot be used〔地方〕水浸的, 水涝的 **2** a boat that is waterlogged is full of water and could soon sink〔船〕灌满水〔将沉〕的

Wa·ter·loo /,wɔtɚˈlu; ,wɔːtəˈluː◂/ **1** also 又作 **the Battle of Waterloo** an important battle fought in 1815 near Brussels, Belgium, in which the Duke of Wellington, leading the British and the Prussians, defeated Napoleon and the French. It was Napoleon's final defeat, and he never regained power after this. 滑铁卢战役〔1815年在比利时布鲁塞尔附近进行的一场重要战役。威灵顿公爵指挥下的英国和普鲁士联军击败了拿破仑指挥的法军, 这场战役标志着拿破仑的彻底失败, 此后他再也没能东山再起〕**2** one of the main railway stations in London, just south of the River Thames. Trains from Waterloo go to the south and southwest of England. 滑铁卢火车站〔伦敦市主要火车站之一, 位于泰晤士河以南。发自滑铁卢火车站的列车开往英格兰的南部和西南部〕**3 meet your Waterloo** to be finally defeated after a long period of success 遭遇滑铁卢〔指长期成功之后遭遇的灭顶之灾〕: *Despite widespread unpopularity, the party did not meet its Waterloo until the election of 1997.* 该党尽管普遍不得人心, 但直至1997年大选时才惨遭失败。

water main /ˈ· · ·/ *n* [C] a large underground pipe that carries the public supply of water to houses and other buildings〔地下的〕主输水管, 供水总管道

wa·ter·mark /ˈwɔtɚ,mɑrk; ˈwɔːtəmɑːk/ *n* [C] **1** a design that is put into paper and can only be seen when you hold it up to the light〔纸张上的〕水印(图案): *Banknotes have a watermark to prevent forgery.* 钞票上有水印图案以防伪造。**2 high/low watermark a)** a line showing the highest or lowest levels of the sea or a river〔海或河的〕高/低水位标志 **b)** a period of great success or failure 辉煌/低谷时期: *the high watermark of the Roman Empire* 罗马帝国的鼎盛时期

water mead·ow /ˈ· · ,· ·/ *n* [C] a field near a river, which is often flooded〔河边常被水淹的〕浸水草地

wa·ter·mel·on /ˈwɔtɚ,mɛlən; ˈwɔːtə,melən/ *n* [C,U] **1** a large round fruit with hard green skin, juicy red flesh, and a lot of black seeds 西瓜 —see picture on page A8 参见A8页图 **2 swallow a watermelon seed** *AmE informal* to become PREGNANT【美, 非正式】怀孕

water me·ter /ˈ· · ,· ·/ *n* [C] a piece of equipment that measures how much water is used 水表, 水量计

wa·ter·mill /ˈwɔtɚ,mɪl; ˈwɔːtə,mɪl/ *n* [C] a MILL[1] (1) that has a big wheel that is turned by the flow of water 水磨〔河水流动推动轮子转动〕

water moc·ca·sin /ˈ· · ,· · ·/ *n* [C] a poisonous North American snake that lives in water 棉口蛇, 水蝮蛇〔生活在北美洲水中的一种毒蛇〕

water pipe /ˈ· · ,·/ *n* [C] a pipe used for smoking tobacco, that consists of a long tube and a container of water; HOOKAH 水烟筒

water pis·tol /ˈ· · ,· ·/ *n* [C] a toy gun that shoots water 玩具水枪

water po·lo /ˈ· · ,· ·/ *n* [U] a game played by two teams of swimmers with a ball 水球运动

water pow·er /ˈ· · ,· ·/ *n* [U] power obtained from moving water, used to produce electricity or to make a machine work〔可发电或使机器运转的〕水力, 水能

wa·ter·proof[1] /ˈwɔtɚ`pruf; ˈwɔːtəpruːf/ *adj* waterproof clothing or material does not allow water to go through it〔衣服或材料〕防水的, 不透水的

waterproof[2] *n* [C usually plural 一般用复数] *BrE* a piece of clothing such as a coat, that prevents you from getting wet【英】防水层

water rat /ˈ· · ·/ *n* [C] a small animal like a large mouse that lives in holes near water and can swim〔生活在水边的〕水鼠

water-re·pel·lent /ˈ· · · ,· ·/ *adj* cloth or clothes that are water-repellent are specially treated with chemicals so that water runs off them〔织物或衣服经化学品处理而〕抗水的

water re·sis·tant /ˈ· · · ,· ·/ *adj* something that is water-resistant does not allow water to go through easily, but does not keep all water out 抗水的〔但不完全防水〕: *a watch that is water resistant to a depth of 50 metres* 一只防水深度50米的手表

wa·ter·shed /ˈwɔtɚ,ʃɛd; ˈwɔːtəʃed/ *n* [C] **1** an event or period when important changes or improvements happen in history or in someone's life〔在历史或人生中的〕转折点; 重要关头: [+in] *The 1932 election represented a watershed in American politics.* 1932年的选举是美国政治的转折点。—compare 比较 TURNING POINT **2 the (9 o'clock) watershed** *BrE* the time in the evening after which television programmes that are not suitable for children may be shown【英】〔晚上9点起成人电视节目可以播放的〕分水岭〔时间〕**3** the high land separating two river systems 分水岭, 分水线

wa·ter·side /ˈwɔtɚ,saɪd; ˈwɔːtəsaɪd/ *n* [singular] the edge of a lake, river etc 湖边; 河边; 水边 —**waterside** *adj*: *a waterside restaurant* 一家湖滨餐馆

water ski·ing /ˈ· · ,· ·/ *n* [U] a sport in which you SKI over water while being pulled by a boat 滑水运动, 水橇运动 —**water ski** *v* [I] —**water skier** *n* [C]

Waters, Muddy (1915-83) a US BLUES singer, songwriter, and GUITAR player, who greatly influenced many other singers of popular music 沃特斯〔(1915-1983), 美国布鲁斯歌手、词作家、吉他演奏家, 对许多流行音乐歌手产生过重大影响〕

water sof·ten·er /ˈ· · ,· · ·/ *n* **1** [U] a chemical used for removing unwanted minerals from water 软水剂 **2** [C] a piece of equipment used to do this 硬水软化器

water-sol·u·ble /ˈ· · ,· · ·/ *adj* a water-soluble substance becomes part of a liquid when mixed with water 能溶解于水的

water sports /ˈ· · ,·/ *n* [plural] sports played on or in water 水上运动

wa·ter·spout /ˈwɔtɚ,spaʊt; ˈwɔːtəspaʊt/ *n* [C] **1** a pipe that water flows through 喷水嘴 **2** a type of storm over the sea in which a violent circular wind pulls water into a tall twisting mass 水龙卷, 海龙卷 —compare 比较 TORNADO

water sup·ply /ˈ· · ·,·/ *n* [U] the water provided for a building or area, or the system of lakes, pipes etc through which it flows〔建筑物或地区的〕供水; 供水系统

water ta·ble /ˈ· · ,· ·/ *n* [C] the level below the surface of the ground where there is water 地下水位

wa·ter·tight /ˈwɔtɚ`taɪt; ˈwɔːtətaɪt/ *adj* **1** something that is watertight does not allow water to pass through it 不透水的, 水密的: *watertight boxes* 不透水的箱子 **2 watertight plan/case/argument etc** a plan etc that is made so carefully that there is no chance of any mistakes or problems 周密的计划/证据确凿的起诉/无懈可击的论据等: *The police can't do anything, he's got a watertight alibi.* 警方毫无办法, 他不在犯罪现场的申辩无懈可击。

water tow·er /ˈ· · ,· ·/ *n* [C] a very tall structure supporting a large container into which water is pumped in order to supply water to surrounding buildings〔自来水〕水塔

water va·pour *BrE*【英】, **water vapor** *AmE*【美】/ˈ· · ,· ·/ *n* [U] water in the form of gas in the air 水汽, 水蒸气

water vole /ˈ· · ·/ *n* [C] *BrE* a small animal like a large mouse that lives in holes near water and can swim; WATER RAT【英】水鼠

wa·ter·way /ˈwɔtɚ,we; ˈwɔːtəweɪ/ *n* [C] a river or CANAL (1) that boats travel on 水路, 航道: *inland waterways* 内河航道

wa·ter·wings /ˈwɔtɚ,wɪŋz; ˈwɔːtə,wɪŋz/ *n* [plural] two bags filled with air that are attached to your arms when you learn to swim〔学习游泳时套在两臂上的〕双翼形充气浮袋

wa·ter·works /ˈwɔtɚ,wɝks; ˈwɔːtəwɜːks/ *n* [plural] **1** the system of pipes and artificial lakes used to clean and store water before it is supplied to a town〔城镇的〕供水系统 **2 turn on the waterworks** *spoken* to start crying in order to get someone's sympathy【口】〔为赢得某人同情〕哭起来 **3** *informal or humorous* the system of organs and tubes inside your body that remove URINE (=liquid waste) from it【非正式或幽默】人体泌尿系统

wa·ter·y /ˈwɔtərɪ; ˈwɔːtəri/ *adj* **1** weak and pale in colour〔颜色〕淡的; 苍白的: *a watery sun* 淡淡的阳光 **2** full of water 充满水的: *a watery fluid* 含大量水分的液体 **3** related to water 与水有关的: *Watery gurgles came from the tank.* 从储水池传来水的汩汩声。**4** watery food or drink contains too much water and does not taste good〔食物或饮料〕稀薄的, 含水太多的: *watery soup* 稀汤 **5 a watery grave** *literary* if someone comes to a watery grave, they drown【文】葬身水底

Wat·ford /ˈwɑtfɚd; ˈwɒtfəd/ a small town on the northwestern edge of London 沃特福德〔伦敦西北边缘一小镇〕

Wat·ling Street /ˈwɑtlɪŋ ,strit; ˈwɒtlɪŋ ,striːt/ a long Roman road that started in Dover in the southeast of England, passed through London, and then went northwest to end near the modern town of Shrewsbury 华特灵大道〔以英格兰东南部多佛尔市为起点的一条漫长的罗马古道, 经伦敦往西北方向至现代城镇什鲁斯伯里附近〕

Wat·son /ˈwɑtsn; ˈwɒtsən/, **Dr** one of the main characters in Sir Arthur Conan Doyle's stories about Sherlock Holmes.

Watson is Holmes's friend and helps him in his work, but he is much less intelligent than Holmes. 华生医生〔阿瑟·柯南道尔爵士创作的夏洛克·福尔摩斯侦探故事中的主人公之一。华生是福尔摩斯的朋友和助手,但才智远在福尔摩斯之下〕

Watson, James (1928-) a US scientist who, together with Francis Crick, discovered the structure of DNA, the substance that carries GENETIC information in the cells of plants, animals and humans. They won a Nobel Prize for their work. 沃森〔(1928-),美国科学家,与弗朗西斯·克里克一同发现了脱氧核糖核酸的结构。脱氧核糖核酸是载有动植物及人类细胞基因信息的物质。两人因此分享诺贝尔奖〕

watt /wɑt; wɒt/ *n* [C] a measure of electrical power 瓦(特)〔电的功率单位〕

Watt, James (1736-1819) a British engineer who made important improvements to the steam engine. The measure of electrical power, the **watt**, is named after him. 瓦特〔(1736-1819),英国工程师,对蒸汽机作了重要改进。电功率的计量单位"瓦特"即以他的名字命名〕

watt·age /ˈwɑtɪdʒ; ˈwɒtɪdʒ/ *n* [singular, U] the power of a piece of electrical equipment measured in watts〔电器的〕瓦(特)数

wat·tle /ˈwɑtl; ˈwɒtl/ *n* [U] **1** a material used for making fences consisting of small sticks on a frame of rods〔用作篱笆的〕编条构架 **2** **wattle and daub** a mixture of this material and mud or clay used in the past to make the walls of houses〔旧时的〕抹灰篱笆墙,枝条泥巴墙 **3** a piece of red flesh that grows from the head or neck of a bird like the TURKEY (1)〔禽鸟,如火鸡头上或颈部的〕肉垂 **4** an Australian tree with small yellow flowers; ACACIA〔澳大利亚产的〕金合欢树

Waugh /wɔ; wɔː/, **Eve·lyn** /ˈivlɪn; ˈiːvlɪn/ (1903-66) a British writer who wrote NOVEL*s* about UPPER-CLASS English people in the period between World War I and World War II. His early books, such as *Decline and Fall*, are very funny SATIRE*s* on English upper-class society, but his later books, such as *Brideshead Revisited* are much more serious. 沃〔(1903-1966),英国作家。著有多部小说,以一战之后和二战之前的英国为背景,上流社会人士为题材。其早期作品如《衰落与瓦解》是针对英国上流社会的嘲弄之作,晚期作品如《旧地重游》则较为严肃〕

WAVE /wev; weɪv/ *informal* a woman who is a member of a US navy volunteer group【非正式】(美国海军)志愿紧急服役妇女队队员

Wave /wev; weɪv/ *n* [C] *AmE informal* a woman who is a member of a US navy VOLUNTEER[1] (2) group【美,非正式】〔美国海军〕志愿紧急服役妇女队队员

wave[1] /wev; weɪv/ *n*

1 ▶**ON THE SEA** 海上的◀[C] a line of raised water that moves across the surface of the sea 海浪,波涛: *Dee watched the waves breaking on the rocks.* 迪伊看着海浪拍打岩石。

2 ▶**OF YOUR HAND** 关于手的◀[C usually singular 一般用单数] a movement of your hand or arm from side to side 挥手;招手

3 ▶**OF LIGHT/SOUND** 关于光/声的◀[C] the form in which some types of energy such as light and sound move 光波,声波: *radio waves* 无线电波 —see also 另见 LONG WAVE, MEDIUM WAVE, SHORT WAVE

4 ▶**SUDDEN INCREASE** 激增◀[C] **a)** a sudden increase in a particular type of behaviour or activity, especially an unpleasant one〔尤指令人讨厌的行为或活动的〕突然增加,高潮: [**+of**] *a new wave of terrorist bombings* 一轮新的恐怖分子炸弹袭击的浪潮 | **crime wave** (=a sudden increase in crime) 犯罪率激增 **b)** a sudden increase in the number of people or things arriving at the same time 同时到达的人数[事物]激增: [**+of**] *a new wave of immigrants* 一股新的移民潮 **c)** a group of soldiers, aircraft etc that attack together 一批士兵[飞机]的同时攻击: [**+of**] *The next wave of troops went over the ridge.* 部队的下一波攻击越过山岭。**d)** a sudden strong feeling that spreads from one person to another 突发并互相影响的强烈情绪: [**+of**] *A wave of panic swept through the crowd.* 一阵恐慌情绪在人群中蔓延。

5 **in waves** if something happens in waves, a short period of activity is followed by a pause〔中间略有停顿的〕一阵一阵: *The pain swept over him in waves.* 一阵一阵的疼痛传遍他的全身。

6 ▶**OF HAIR** 头发的◀[C] a part of your hair that has an even curved shape〔头发的〕卷曲

7 **make waves** *informal* to cause problems【非正式】制造麻烦: *With so many jobs being cut, Parker didn't want to make waves.* 由于那么多工作被砍掉,帕克不想再制造麻烦。

8 **the waves** *literary* the ocean【文】大海

wave[2] *v*

1 ▶**HAND** 手◀[I,T] to move your hand or arm from side to side in order to greet someone or attract their attention 挥手〔问候〕,招手: *Toyah waved her hand regally.* 托亚威仪堂堂地挥手。| **wave to/at sb** *Tommy waved to us as he came across the field.* 汤米穿过田地时朝我们挥手。| **wave sth at sb** *Lee waved his fist at me angrily.* 李朝我愤怒地挥动着拳头。| **wave sth around/about** *BrE*【英】: *Stop waving your arms about.* 别挥动手臂了。| **wave sb goodbye/wave goodbye to sb** (=to say goodbye to someone by waving to them) 向某人挥手告别 *Wave bye-bye to Granny.* 向奶奶挥手告别。

2 ▶**SIGNAL** 信号◀[T always+adv/prep] to show someone where to go by waving your hand in that direction 对〔某人〕挥手以示方向: **wave sb through/on/away** *A guard waved me away from the fence.* 警卫挥手示意我离开围栏。

3 ▶**MAKE STH MOVE** 使某物移动◀[T] to hold something and move it from side to side 挥动〔某物〕: *The magician waved his wand and the door opened.* 魔术师一挥魔杖,门就开了。| **wave sth under/about/at etc** *Trudie waved a $50 bill under his nose.* 特鲁迪拿着一张50美元的钞票在他鼻子底下晃了晃。

4 ▶**MOVE SMOOTHLY** 平稳移动◀[I] to move smoothly up and down, or from side to side 上下起伏;左右摇晃: *flags waving in the wind* 迎风飘扬的旗帜

5 **wave sth goodbye** *informal* to be forced to accept that something you want will not happen【非正式】与某事挥别〔被迫接受不如意的结局〕: *A 3-0 defeat means United have waved their promotion chances goodbye.* 3:0的失败意味着联队失去了晋级的机会。

6 ▶**HAIR** 头发◀[I,T] if hair waves or is waved, it grows in loose curls (使)呈波浪形,(使)变曲

wave sth ↔ **aside** *phr v* [T] to refuse to accept someone's opinion or idea because you do not think it is important 对〔某人的意见、主意〕不屑一顾: *Nancy waved aside our objections.* 南希对我们的反对置之不理。

wave sb/sth ↔ **down** *phr v* [T] to signal to the driver of a car to stop by waving your arm at them 挥手示意停车

wave sb **off** *phr v* [T] to wave goodbye to someone as they leave〔某人离开时〕挥手告别

wave·band /ˈwevˌbænd; ˈweɪvbænd/ *n* [C] a set of radio waves of similar length which are used to broadcast radio programmes〔无线电的〕波段

wave·length /ˈwevˌlɛŋθ; ˈweɪvleŋθ/ *n* [C] **1** the size of a radio wave used to broadcast a radio signal〔无线电的〕波长 **2** the distance between two waves of energy such as sound or light〔声波、光波等的〕波长 **3** **be on the same wavelength/on a different wavelength** *informal* to have the same or different opinions and feelings as someone else【非正式】〔与其他人的观点、感情〕相投/不合: *We just aren't on the same wavelength when it comes to politics.* 说到政治,我们就意见不相近了。

wa·ver /ˈwevə; ˈweɪvə/ *v* [I] **1** to be or become weak and uncertain 减弱;动摇: *His voice wavered.* 他的声音变弱了。| **waver in sth** *Harris never wavered in his loyalty to the cause.* 哈里斯对事业的忠诚是坚定不移的。**2** to not make a decision because you have doubts 犹豫不决;踌躇: *wavering voters* 犹豫不决的选民 | **waver between (doing)** *Maya wavered between accepting and refusing his offer.* 是接受还是拒绝他的建议,马亚犹豫不决。**3** to move unsteadily first in one direction then in another 摇曳,摇摆: *reflections wavering in the water of the lake* 在湖水中摇曳的倒影 —**waverer** *n* [C]: *We must persuade the waverers to vote with us.* 必须说服犹豫不决的人投票支持我们。—**waveringly** *adv*

Waverley Novels /ˌ... ˈ../ thirty-two books and stories by the British writer Sir Walter Scott. The first book, *Waverley*, published in 1814, gave the series its name.《威弗利小说集》〔英国作家沃尔特·司各特爵士所著共32部小说和短篇故事的合集,以1814年出版的第一部小说《威弗利》命名〕

wav·y /ˈwevɪ; ˈweɪvi/ *adj* **1** wavy hair grows in waves〔头发〕鬈曲的 —see picture on page A6 参见A6页图 **2** a wavy line or edge has smooth curves in it 波形的,波纹的 —**waviness** *n* [U]

wax[1] /wæks; wæks/ *n* [U] **1** a solid material made out of fats or oils used to make CANDLE*s*, polish etc〔制造蜡烛、上光等用的〕蜡: *wax crayon* 蜡笔 **2** a natural sticky substance in your ears 耳垢 —see also 另见 BEESWAX

wax[2] *v*

1 ▶**FLOOR/FURNITURE** 地板/家具◀[T] to put a thin layer of wax on a floor or surface etc in order to polish it 给〔地板或表面等〕上蜡

2 ▶**MOON** 月亮◀[I] when the moon waxes, it grows larger〔月亮〕渐圆,渐满

3 **wax romantic/eloquent/lyrical etc** *literary* to speak in a romantic way【文】浪漫/滔滔不绝/热情奔放地说: *Mitch would wax eloquent on the subject of cars.* 说到汽车,米奇可以滔滔不绝。

4 wax and wane *literary* to increase and then decrease【文】兴衰, 荣枯

5 ▶LEGS 腿◀ [T] to put a thin layer of wax on your arms or legs in order to remove hairs〔在手臂或腿上〕涂蜡以去除体毛

waxed pa·per /ˌ·ˈ··/ also 又作 **wax·pa·per** /ˈwæksˌpepɚ; ˈwæksˌpeɪpə/ *n* [U] *AmE* paper with a thin layer of wax on used to wrap food【美】〔包食品的〕蜡纸; GREASEPROOF PAPER *BrE*【英】

wax·en /ˈwæksn̩; ˈwæksən/ *adj literary*【文】**1** pale and shiny like wax〔像蜡般〕苍白的; 光滑的 **2** made of or covered in wax 蜡制的; 涂蜡的

wax·work /ˈwæksˌwɝk; ˈwæksw3ːk/ *n* [C] **1 waxworks** *BrE*【英】**wax museum** *AmE*【美】a place where you pay to see models of famous people made of wax〔名人〕蜡像馆 **2** a model of a person made of wax 蜡像

wax·y /ˈwæksɪ; ˈwæksi/ *adj* **1** made of or covered in wax 蜡制的; 涂蜡的 **2** looking or feeling like wax 似蜡的; 感觉像蜡的: *waxy petals* 像蜡做的花瓣 —**waxiness** *n* [U]

S1 W1

way[1] /we; weɪ/ *n*

① METHOD 方法
② MANNER 方式
③ ROAD/PATH 道路/路线
④ DIRECTION 方向
⑤ DISTANCE 距离
⑥ TIME 时间
⑦ BEHAVIOUR 举止
⑧ ATTITUDE TO A SITUATION 对形势的态度
⑨ WHAT YOU WANT 想要的东西
⑩ PREVENT/BLOCK STH 妨碍/阻止某事
⑪ DEVELOPMENT/PROGRESS 发展/前进
⑫ SITUATION/CONDITION 情况/条件
⑬ MAKE WAY 让路
⑭ GIVE WAY 屈服
⑮ ON THE WAY 在途中
⑯ EITHER WAY 无论怎样
⑰ SPOKEN PHRASES 口语短语
⑱ OTHER MEANINGS 其他意思

① METHOD 方法

1 [C] a method of doing something〔做事的〕方法: *These vegetables can be cooked in several different ways.* 这些蔬菜可用几种不同的方法烹煮。| *At that time, the Pill was the easiest way of ensuring effective contraception.* 那时候口服避孕药是最简便有效的避孕方法。| *I've altered the way I teach science.* 我改变了我教自然科学的方法。| *I'll tell her in my own time and in my own way.* 我将在我方便的时候以我的方式告诉她。| **way of doing sth** *I've got no way of contacting him at all.* 我根本没有办法和他联系上。| **way to do sth** *What's the right way to say this in English?* 这句话英语该怎么说? | **way to go about sth** *I think you're going about this the wrong way.* 我觉得你这么做, 方法不对。

2 one way or another *spoken* using one of several possible methods, although you do not yet know which one【口】用某种方法〔虽然不知道用哪一种〕: *We'll find the money, one way or another.* 我们无论如何会想办法找到那笔钱。

3 ways and means special methods for doing something, especially something secret or illegal 特殊的办法〔尤指秘密或非法的〕: *There are ways and means of getting drugs in prison.* 在监狱内有特殊办法获得毒品。—see also 另见 WAYS AND MEANS COMMITTEE

4 way out/around a possible method of solving a problem or difficult situation 解决问题[困难]的办法: *I just can't see any way out of this mess.* 我真看不出有什么办法可摆脱这种困境。| *There's no way around it – we'll have to tell Mom.* 我们不得不告诉妈妈 —— 一点办法也没有。—see also 另见 WAY OUT, **take the easy way out** (EASY[1] (6))

5 way into television/publishing etc a possible method of getting a job in television etc, especially when this is difficult 进入电视界/出版界等的办法〔尤指不容易进入〕: *She thought that working in the box office might be a way into the theatre.* 她觉得在票房工作或许是进入戏剧界的一种途径。

② MANNER 方式

6 [C] a manner in which something can happen or be done, especially when there are several〔某事发生或做成的〕方式〔尤指有几种方式时〕: *I don't see it that way at all.* 我根本不那么看。| *Look at the way he's dressed!* 瞧他那副打扮! | *Not all birds of prey suffered in this way (by eating insecticide), but many did.* 并非所有猛禽都遭受这种不幸 (指食用了杀虫剂), 但有许多确实如此。| **in more ways than one** *spoken* (=in several ways)【口】不止一种方式 *This will benefit the company in more ways than one.* 这将在多方面对本公司有利。

7 that's no way to do sth *spoken* used to tell someone that they should not be doing something in a particular manner【口】不能用这种方式做某事: *That's no way to speak to your father!* 不能这样跟你父亲说话!

③ ROAD/PATH 道路/路线

8 [C] the road, path etc that you must follow in order to get to a particular place〔去某处的〕路, 道路: [+to] *Is this the way to Crouch End?* 到蹲尾区是走这条路吗? | **lose your way** *We lost our way in the forest.* 我们在森林里迷了路。| **know the way** *I hope Eric knows the way.* 我希望埃里克知道怎样走。

④ DIRECTION 方向

9 [C] a particular direction from where you are now〔特定的〕方向: *Which way is north?* 哪边是北? | *Walk this way.* 这边走。| *"Where's the lift?" "It's this way."* "电梯在哪儿?" "在这边。" | **show sb/lead the way** *Could you just show me the way?* 你能告诉我怎么走吗?

10 on sb's way in the direction that someone is going 在某人要去的路上, 顺路: *I'll give you a lift – it's on my way.* 你可以搭我的车 —— 我顺路。

11 out of sb's way not in the direction that someone is going 不在某人要去的路上, 不顺路: *You can't take me home – it's miles out of your way.* 你不能带我回家 —— 我家离你走的路线还很远呢。—see also 另见 OUT-OF-THE-WAY (1)

⑤ DISTANCE 距离

12 [singular] also 又作 **ways** *AmE informal* a distance, especially a long one【美, 非正式】路程〔尤指远距离〕: *We have a ways to go yet.* 我们还要走很远的路。| **a long way** *I was still a long way from home.* 我离家还很远。| **all this way** *It would be too bad to come all this way and not see them.* 从老远来却没有看见他们, 太不走运了。| **all the way down/across/through etc** (continuing for the full distance or length of something) 一直, 不停地 *Did you really swim all the way across?* 你真的是一直游过去的吗? | **way beyond** (=much further) 高得多; 远得多 *This achieves temperatures way beyond what is necessary.* 这样达到的温度比需要的高得多。

⑥ TIME 时间

13 [singular] a length of time, especially a long one〔尤指长的〕时段: *The two events were a long way apart.* 两次事件之间隔了很长时间。

⑦ BEHAVIOUR 举止

14 [C] a particular manner or style of behaving〔特殊的〕样子; 神态: *He had an annoying way of picking his nails.* 他剔指甲的样子让人讨厌。| *We all have our funny little ways.* 我们每个人都有些有趣的小动作。| **be (just) sb's way** *informal* (=be the way in which someone usually behaves, especially when this is unusual)【非正式】〔尤指某人不寻常的〕作风, 风格 *Oh, don't worry, that's just her way.* 噢, 别着急, 那正是她的风格。| **change/mend your ways** (=stop behaving badly)

W

改变作风〔停止错误的行为〕*Jamieson resolved to change his ways.* 贾米森决心改正。—see also 另见 **see the error of your ways** (ERROR (3))

⑧ **ATTITUDE TO A SITUATION** 对形势的态度

15 [C] one of the possible ways of thinking about a situation, or one of many parts of it 思考某情况的方法; 某情况的一方面: **in a way** *In a way, it's kind of nice to be working alone.* 在某种程度上讲, 独自一个人工作相当不错。| **in one way** *Well, in one way you're right, but it's not as simple as that.* 噢, 在某方面你是对的, 但是事情并非那么简单。| **in some ways** *In some ways, I'd rather he wasn't involved at all.* 从某些方面说, 我宁愿他根本没有牵涉进去。| **in no way** (=used to say that you should definitely not think about a situation in this way) 无论如何不, 决不〔用于表示你绝对不认同某观点〕*This should in no way be seen as a defeat.* 这绝对不能看做是一种挫折。

⑨ **WHAT YOU WANT** 想要的东西

16 get your (own) way to do what you want to, even though someone else wants something different 随心所欲〔虽然别人要求的不同〕: *You shouldn't let the children always get their own way.* 你不能总是让孩子想怎样就怎样。

17 if I had my way *spoken* used before telling someone how you think something should be done【口】如果由我来处理〔用于告诉某人你认为某事应怎样做〕: *Of course, if I had my way, they'd all be shot!* 当然, 要是由我来处理, 他们都该枪毙!

18 have it your own way! *spoken* used to tell someone in an annoyed way that you agree to what they want【口】按你的意思办吧!〔用于生气地表示同意某人的要求〕

19 go your own way to do what you want to do, make your own decisions etc 按自己的意愿行事

20 have your (wicked) way with sb *old-fashioned* to persuade someone to have sex with you【过时】劝某人与自己发生性关系

⑩ **PREVENT/BLOCK STH** 妨碍/阻止某事

21 be in the way/in sb's way to be in a place or position that prevents someone or something else from moving freely 挡住去路; 碍事: *There was a large truck blocking the way.* 有一辆大卡车挡在路上。| *Get out of my way!* 让开, 别挡我的路! | **[+of]** *Can you move that box? It's in the way of the door.* 你能搬开那只箱子吗? 它挡着进门的路。

22 get in the way of to prevent someone from doing something, or prevent something from happening 妨碍〔某人做某事〕; 阻止〔某事发生〕: *You mustn't let your social life get in the way of your studies.* 你不可以让社交生活影响你的学业。

23 not stand in sb's way to not try to stop someone from doing something they want to do 不阻止某人做想做的事: *If you want to leave home, I'm not going to stand in your way.* 如果你想离家过独立生活, 我不会阻止你的。

⑪ **DEVELOPMENT/PROGRESS** 发展/前进

24 have come a long way to have developed or changed a lot 进步[变化]很大: *Psychiatry has come a long way since the 1920s.* 自 20 世纪 20 年代以来, 精神病学进展很大。

25 have a long way to go to need to develop or change a lot in order to reach a particular standard〔为达到某标准〕仍有许多事要做: *Mac's still got a long way to go before he'll make a manager.* 要想当上经理, 马克仍有很长的路要走。

⑫ **SITUATION/CONDITION** 情况/条件

26 the way things are *spoken* used to describe the situation that you are in now【口】目前所处的情况: *The way things are at the moment, I don't think we're going to be able to go on vacation at all.* 根据目前的情况, 我认为我们不能休假了。

27 be in a bad way *BrE informal* to be very ill, injured, or upset【英, 非正式】病重, 严重受伤; 心烦意乱

⑬ **MAKE WAY** 让路

28 make way a) to move to one side so that someone or something can pass 给〔某人或某物〕让路〔以便其通过〕: **[+for]** *The crowd stepped aside to make way for the riders.* 人群避到一旁, 让路给骑马的人。**b)** to be removed so that something newer or better can take your place 让位〔给更新[更好]的事物〕: **[+for]** *Several houses were demolished to make way for the rail link.* 拆除了几栋房子, 好腾出地方来建铁路连接线。

29 make your way a) to move towards something, especially when this takes a long time 走向〔某物, 尤指要用一段长时间〕: *We made our way down the hill towards the town.* 我们下山朝城里走去。**b)** to slowly become successful in a particular job, activity, profession etc〔在工作、活动或职业中〕慢慢成功起来: *Gradually, Henderson began to make his way in politics.* 亨德森逐渐在政界有所建树。

30 make/find your own way *informal* to go somewhere without the other people in your group【非正式】独自一人去某处: *You'll have to make your own way to the pub.* 你得独自一个人去酒吧。

⑭ **GIVE WAY** 屈服

31 to break because of too much weight or pressure〔因重量或压力过多而〕坍塌; 垮掉: *The floor eventually gave way.* 地板最终塌了。

32 to have your place taken by something newer, better, or different 被〔更新、更好或不同的事物〕取代: **[+to]** *Steam trains finally gave way to electricity.* 蒸汽火车最终让位给电气火车。| *After a while my anger gave way to depression.* 过了一会儿, 我的怒气变成了沮丧。

33 to agree to do what someone else wants to do, instead of what you wanted to do 让步; 屈服: *Alison's too stubborn to give way.* 艾利森太固执己见, 决不让步。

34 *BrE* to allow vehicles to pass in front of you when you are driving【英】让其他车辆先行; YIELD¹ (5) *AmE*【美】: *You must give way to traffic coming from the right.* 你必须让右方驶来的车辆先行。

⑮ **ON THE WAY** 在途中

35 on your/the way (to) while travelling from one place to another 在途中: *Why don't you stop by our place on your way to Boston?* 在你去波士顿的途中, 何不顺道来我们这儿? | **on your way in/out/home etc** *Could you mail these letters on your way downtown?* 你在去城里的路上能把这几封信寄走吗?

36 be on the/its way to be arriving soon 即将到达: *There's a letter on its way to you.* 你很快会收到一封信。| *More changes are on the way.* 将会发生更多的变化。

37 be on your way *spoken* to be leaving one place in order to go somewhere else【口】离开〔某处〕去另外一些地方

38 be well on the way to to have almost finished changing from one state or situation to another, especially a better one〔尤指更好的改变〕行将完成: *The new building is well on the way to being finished.* 新大楼即将竣工。| *Jen is now well on the way to recovery.* 珍即将康复。

39 on/along the way while developing from one situation or part of your life to another 在〔生命中一个阶段到另一个阶段〕期间: *She had progressed smoothly through school and university, picking up several academic awards on the way.* 她顺利完成中学和大学学业, 因为成绩优异好几次获奖。

40 have a baby on the way *informal* to be PREGNANT【非正式】怀孕

⑯ **EITHER WAY** 无论怎样

41 either way *spoken* used to say that something will be the same, whichever of two possible choices you make【口】无论怎样〔用于表示有两个选择, 但不论选哪一个, 结果都一样〕: *Either way, it's going to be expensive.* 不管怎样, 都很费钱。

42 within two feet/ten years/one hour etc either way if a measurement is within two feet, ten years etc either way, it may be two feet etc more or less than the correct amount〔测量的误差〕在两英尺/十年/一小时等之内: *Your answer must be within a centimetre either way.* 答案的误差必须小于一厘米。

43 could go either way if a situation could go either way, both results are equally possible 两个结果都有可能: *The election could go either way.* 选举双方任何一方都可能获胜。

⑰ **SPOKEN PHRASES** 口语短语

44 by the way used before saying something that is not connected with the main subject you were talking about before 附带[顺便]说〔用于转入与刚才说的主题无关的事物〕: *By the way, have you seen my umbrella anywhere?* 顺便问问, 你在什么地方见过我的伞吗?

45 no way! a) used to say that you will definitely not do something 不!〔表示断然拒绝做某事〕: *"Can I borrow your car?" "No way!"* "我能借用你的汽车吗?" "不行!" | *No way am I going to help him.* 我决不去帮他。| **no way José!** (=used to emphasize that you will not do something) 绝对不做!〔用于强调〕**b)** *especially AmE* used to say that you do not believe something or are very surprised by it【尤美】不会吧; 不可能!〔表示

不相信或惊讶〕: *She's 45? No way!* 她45岁了?不会吧! **c)** used to say that something is not possible or cannot be done〔用于表示〕不可能〔完成某事〕: *There's no way we're going to get this finished on time.* 我们绝对不可能按时完成这项工作。

46 way out/over/across etc *AmE* a long distance out, over etc【美】离开〔某处〕一大段路程: *"Where's the meter?" "It's way the hell over there."* "停车计时收费器在哪儿?""在那边很远的地方。"

47 in a big way very much 十分; 大量地: *My little brother's into cars in a big way.* 我弟弟对汽车非常入迷。

48 by a long way by a large amount or difference 远远地; …得多: *He was the best in the group, by a long way.* 他是团队中最好最好的。

49 no two ways about it used to say that something is definitely true, especially something unpleasant〔尤指令人讨厌的事情〕就是这样, 千真万确

50 you can't have it both ways used to say that you cannot have the advantages from both of two different possible decisions or actions 你不能两全其美, 两者兼得: *You're either going to have to work harder or settle for lower grades – you can't have it both ways!* 你要么今后更加努力, 要么甘愿拿更低的分数 —— 你不可能两者兼得。

51 be with sb all the way to agree with someone completely 完全同意某人〔的意见〕: *I'm with you all the way on this salary issue, Joe.* 乔, 在工资这个问题上, 我完全同意你。

52 to my way of thinking used before telling someone your opinion 依我看; 我认为: *To my way of thinking, it ought to be banned altogether.* 我认为这应该全部取缔。

53 have sth in the way of to have particular amounts or types of something〔某物〕有一定的量〔种类〕: *They don't have much in the way of leisure facilities.* 他们没有多少休闲设施。

54 have a way of doing sth used to say that something usually happens in a particular way, especially when this is unpleasant or inconvenient〔尤指不愉快或不方便的事〕总是以某种形式发生: *These things have a way of turning up when you least expect them.* 这些事情总发生在我们最意料不到的时候。

55 get sth out of the way to finish, or deal with something, especially something difficult or unpleasant 完成〔处理〕某事〔尤指困难的或不愉快的事〕: *I'd rather have the interview in the morning and get it out of the way!* 我宁愿上午面试, 赶紧结束这件事!

56 every which way a) *BrE* every possible method【英】每一种可能的办法, 想尽办法: *We tried every which way we could think of, but it couldn't be done.* 我们绞尽脑汁, 但还是做不了。 **b)** *AmE* in all directions【美】四面八方, 到处: *When I came back there was popcorn flying every which way!* 当我回来的时候, 爆玉米花蹦得到处都是!

57 that's the way used to tell someone that they are doing something correctly or well, especially when you are showing them how 就这么做〔尤用于指导某人时, 告诉他做法正确〕: *Now bring your foot gently off the clutch – that's the way.* 现在把你的脚慢慢地移开离合器踏板 —— 对, 就这么做。

58 come sb's way if something comes your way, you get or experience it, especially unexpectedly or by chance〔某人〕得到〔经历〕某事〔尤指不期而遇或偶然的事情〕: *You must make the most of the opportunities that come your way.* 你必须充分利用碰到的机会。

59 way to go! *AmE* used to tell someone that they have done something very well, or achieved something special【美】干得好!〔用于赞赏某人做得不错或取得特别的成果〕

60 (that's/it's) always the way! used to say that things always happen in the way that is least convenient 总是这样!〔用于表示事情总是以让人感到最不方便的方式发生〕: *The train was delayed – always the way when you're in a hurry!* 火车误点了 —— 总是越急越误点!

61 across/over the way on the opposite side of the street 在〔路的〕对面: *They live across the way from us at number 23.* 他们住在我们对面的23号。

62 down your/London etc way in your area, the area of London etc 在你住的地区/在伦敦〔附近〕等

63 way out! *AmE* an expression meaning that something is very good or exciting, used especially in the 1970s【美】非常新奇〔时髦〕!〔尤用于20世纪70年代〕

64 get into the way of doing sth *BrE* to start to do something regularly【英】开始习惯于做某事: *I never got into the way of carrying my passport around with me.* 我不习惯随身带着护照。

65 go all the way (with sb) to have sex with someone〔与某人〕性交

⑱ OTHER MEANINGS 其他意思

66 lead the way a) to walk at the front of a group of people 引路, 带路: *We set off in single file with Lawrence leading the way.* 我们排成单列纵队出发, 由劳伦斯在前面带路。 **b)** to develop or discover something before other people 领先〔发明或发现〕, 带头: *a group that is leading the way in cancer research* 在癌症研究方面取得领先地位的一个小组

67 be under way a) to be happening or being done 正在发生; 在进行中: *Plans are under way for a new link road.* 建造一条新中继公路的计划正在进行之中。| **get under way** (=start happening) 开始发生〔进行〕*I'll wait till the campaign gets under way properly.* 我将等到活动顺利开展。| **be well under way** (=be definitely happening, and too late to stop or change) 进行已久〔太晚而无法停止或改变〕 *By the mid-sixties, the process of change was well under way.* 到60年代中期, 变革已成定局。 **b)** to be moving forwards 前进中: *The boat gave a lurch, and we were under way.* 船摇晃了一下, 然后我们开船了。

68 split sth two/three etc ways also 又作 **divide sth two/three etc ways** to divide something into two, three etc equal parts 将〔某物〕平分/分三等份: *We'll split the cost between us five ways.* 我们五个人平分费用。

69 by way of a) as a form of something, or instead of something 当做, 用作, 作为: *We had sandwiches by way of a meal.* 我们吃三明治, 算是一顿饭了。| *I'd just like to make a few comments by way of introduction.* 我想说几句作为开场白。 **b)** if you travel by way of a place, you go through it 经由〔某地〕, 经过: *We went by way of London.* 我们途经伦敦。

70 way around/round a particular order or position that something should be in〔某物属于某个〕次序〔位置〕: *Which way round does this skirt go?* 这条裙子该放在哪儿? | **right/wrong way around** *Make sure you get the slides the right way around.* 确保你放映的幻灯片次序正确。

71 know your way around to be familiar with a place, system, or organization 熟悉某个地点〔系统; 机构〕

72 have a way with to have a special ability to do something 有〔特殊〕能力〔做某事〕: *David seemed to have a way with children.* 戴维看来跟孩子打交道很有一手。

73 go out of your way to do sth to do something that you do not have to do and that involves making an effort 特地〔不怕麻烦〕做某事: *She went out of her way to be kind to the newcomer.* 她特意对新来的人示好。

74 go some way towards doing sth to help something to happen 有助于某事发生: *These donations will go some way towards repairing the damage.* 这些捐款将有助于弥补损失。

75 go your separate ways a) to start doing different things, having different interests etc, from someone you used to be friends with〔与朋友〕各走各路: *After leaving college, we went our separate ways.* 大学毕业以后, 我们就分道扬镳了。 **b)** to end a marriage or relationship 结束婚姻〔感情关系〕: *John and I have gone our separate ways now.* 我和约翰现在已经离婚。

76 keep out of sb's way to avoid someone 避开某人

77 in sb's own way used when you want to say that someone thinks, feels, or does something, although other people might think that they do not 其实, 实际上: *He seems harsh, I know, but in his own way he's quite caring.* 我知道, 他看上去严厉, 但实际上非常关心人。

78 Way used in the names of roads 大道〔用于道路名称〕: *Abercrombie Way* 阿伯克朗比大道

79 put sb in the way of (doing) sth *old-fashioned BrE* to give someone the opportunity to do or get something【过时, 英】给某人以〔做某事或得到某物〕的机会 —see also 另见 **in the family way** (FAMILY (6)), **go the way of all flesh** (FLESH[1] (10)), HALFWAY, **out of harm's way** (HARM[1] (6)), ONE-WAY, **the parting of the ways** (PARTING[1] (3)), **pave the way for** (PAVE (2)), **pay your way** (PAY[1] (12)), RIGHT OF WAY, **rub sb up the wrong way** (RUB[1] (9)), **see your way (clear) to** (SEE[1] (48)), TWO-WAY, **where there's a will there's a way** (WILL[2] (5))

S2 **way²** *adv* **1** by a large amount 大大地: **way above/below/out etc** *Her IQ is way above average.* 她的智商远远高于平均水平。| *Your guess was way out, he's actually thirty-eight.* 你猜得太离谱了, 他实际上是38岁。| **way back** (=a long time ago) 很久以前 *We first met way back in the 70s.* 我们早在70年代就初次见面了。 **2** very far 很远: **way ahead/behind/back** *American companies are way ahead when it comes to biotechnology.* 在生物技术方面, 美国公司遥遥领先。| **way off/a ways off** *AmE* (=far

from where you are)【美】离得很远 *Way off in the distance I could see snowcapped mountains.* 我能看到远处的高山，山峰白雪皑皑。| **way out in/past/beyond** (=far from the nearest town or from the point you mention)〔与最近的城镇或所提及的地点〕距离甚远 *O'Connell lives way out in the desert.* 奥康奈尔居住在遥远的沙漠里。**3** *AmE informal* very【美，非正式】非常，很: *"Hey, check out my new bike." "Way cool!"* "嘿，看看我的新自行车。""棒极了！"

way·far·er /ˈweˌfɛrə; ˈweɪˌfeərə/ *n* [C] *literary* a traveller who walks from one place to another【文】徒步旅行者 —**wayfaring** *adj* [only before noun 仅用于名词前]

way·lay /ˌweˈle; weɪˈleɪ/ *v past tense and past participle* **way·laid** /-ˈled; -ˈleɪd/ [T] to stop someone so that you can talk to them, rob them, or attack them〔为了说话而〕拦截〔某人〕; 拦路抢劫[伏击]

Wayne /wen; weɪn/, **John** (1907-79) a US film actor who was famous especially for appearing in WESTERNS (=films about the American west in the 19th century), such as *Stagecoach* (1939) and *True Grit* (1969). The characters he played were usually brave, strong, honest men who loved their country, and people think of him as representing typical American values. 韦恩〔(1907-1979)，美国电影演员，尤以出演《关山飞渡》(1939)、《大地惊雷》(1969)等西部片而著名。他扮演的角色通常勇敢、坚强、诚实并且爱国，被认为是典型的美国价值观的化身〕

way of life /ˌ· · ˈ·/ *n plural* **ways of life** [C] **1** the way someone lives, or the way people in a society usually live 生活方式: *The tribesmen's traditional way of life is under threat.* 部落人的传统生活方式受到了威胁。| **the American/British etc way of life** (=the life typical of Americans, British people etc) 美国人/英国人等〔典型〕的生活方式 **2** a job or interest that is so important that it affects everything you do 生活中重要的事情〔工作或兴趣〕: *Nursing isn't just a job; it's a whole way of life.* 护理不只是一份工作，而是生活的方方面面。

way out /ˌ· ˈ·/ *n* [C] *BrE*【英】**1** a door or a passage through which you can leave a building; EXIT〔建筑物的〕出口，太平门 **2** a way of getting away from a difficult or unpleasant situation 出路，摆脱困难的办法 —see also 另见 **take the easy way out** (EASY[1] (6)), **way out** (WAY[1] (4))

way-out /ˌ· ˈ·◂/ *adj informal* very modern, and unusual or strange【非正式】时髦的; 不寻常的; 新奇的: *I like jazz, but not the way-out stuff.* 我喜欢爵士音乐，但不喜欢出格的东西。

-ways /wez; weɪz/ *suffix* [in adverbs 构成副词] in a particular direction 朝…方向: *leaning sideways* (=leaning to the side) 向一侧倾斜

Ways and Means Com·mit·tee /ˌ· · ˈ· · ˌ·/ *n* [C] *AmE* a group of representatives in the government of a US state or in Congress who must find money for the government to spend【美】〔美国州政府、国会中负责税收、贸易政策等的〕岁入委员会

way·side /ˈweˌsaɪd; ˈweɪsaɪd/ *n* [singular] *literary* the side of a road or path【文】路边 —see also 另见 **fall by the wayside** (FALL[1] (23))

way sta·tion /ˈ· ˌ··/ *n* [C] *AmE* a place between the main stations of a railway where a train stops【美】〔火车停靠的〕小站

way·ward /ˈwewəd; ˈweɪwəd/ *adj* behaving in a way that is different from other people and that causes problems 怪僻的〔因而招致麻烦〕; 倔强的: *a wayward teenager* 任性的少年 —**waywardly** *adv* —**waywardness** *n* [U]

wa·zoo /wɑˈzu; wɑːˈzuː/ *n* [C] *AmE informal* your bottom【美，非正式】屁股

WBA /ˌdʌblju bi ˈe; ˌdʌbəljuː biː ˈeɪ/ World Boxing Association; one of the organizations responsible for controlling professional BOXING. A BOXER who holds a WBA title is described as a world CHAMPION. 世界拳击协会〔负责管理职业拳击赛事的组织之一。获得世界拳击协会冠军的拳击手被视为世界拳王〕

WBC, the /ˌdʌblju bi ˈsi; ˌdʌbəljuː biː ˈsiː/ World Boxing Council; one of the organizations responsible for controlling professional BOXING. It was formed in 1963. 世界拳击理事会〔负责管理职业拳击比赛的组织之一，成立于1963年〕

WBO, the /ˌdʌblju bi ˈo; ˌdʌbəljuː biː ˈəʊ/ World Boxing Organization; one of the organizations responsible for controlling professional BOXING. The WBO began in 1998. 世界拳击组织〔负责管理职业拳击比赛的组织之一，成立于1998年〕

WBU /ˌdʌblju bi ˈju; ˌdʌbəljuː biː ˈjuː/ World Boxing Union; one of the organizations responsible for controlling professional BOXING, although it is not as well known as the four main controlling organizations, the IBF, WBA, WBC and WBO. 世界拳击联盟〔负责管理职业拳击比赛的组织之一。其知名度次于四大拳击管理组织，即国际拳击联合会、世界拳击协会、世界拳击理事会和世界拳击组织〕

WC /ˌdʌblju ˈsi; ˌdʌbəljuː ˈsiː/ *n* [C] water closet; a word for toilet used especially on signs in public places 厕所〔尤用于公共厕所的标记〕

we /wɪ; wi; *strong* 强读 wi; wiː/ *pron* [used as the subject of a sentence 用作句子的主词] **1** I and one or more others 我们: *We were all amazed when we heard the news.* 我们听到这个消息都目瞪口呆。| *Shall we* (=you and I) *have a coffee, Ted?* 特德，我们喝杯咖啡好吗？| *Can we* (=I and the others) *go now, sir?* 先生，我们现在可以走吗？**2** *formal* used by a king or queen in official language to mean I【正式】寡人，朕〔国王或女王在正式场合的自称〕: *We are not amused.* 朕不觉得好笑。**3** used by a writer or a speaker to mean you (the reader or listener) and them 我们〔作者或说话人使用，指读者或听众和自己〕: *We saw in the previous chapter how this situation had arisen.* 在上一章里我们看到这种情况是怎样发生的。**4** used especially to children and people who are ill to mean you 我们〔尤用于与儿童或病人谈话，实际指对方〕: *And how are we feeling today, Mr Robson?* 罗布森先生，我们今天感觉如何？**5** *formal* people in general【正式】人，人类，人们: *Do we have the right to destroy the planet?* 人们有权利毁灭这个星球吗？

WEA, the /ˌdʌblju i ˈe; ˌdʌbəljuː iː ˈeɪ/ Workers' Educational Association; a British organization that arranges classes for adults, especially adults who started working at a young age and may not have had a good education 工人教育协会〔英国一成人教育机构，面向成人，尤其是参加工作较早且未曾接受过良好教育的成人安排培训课程〕

weak /wik; wiːk/ *adj*

1 ▶**PHYSICALLY** 身体上◀ not physically strong 虚弱的，不够强壮的: *The illness had left her feeling tired and weak.* 疾病使她感到疲惫而虚弱。| **[+with]** *Nina was weak with hunger.* 尼娜饿得没有气力。| **weak heart/bladder/eyes etc** (=that do not work properly) 衰弱的心脏/膀胱/眼睛等

2 ▶**CHARACTER** 性格◀ easily influenced by other people because you cannot make decisions by yourself 意志薄弱的; 无决断力的: *a weak and indecisive man* 软弱而优柔寡断的男人

3 ▶**NOT GOOD AT** 不精通◀ not having much ability or skill in a particular activity or subject〔在某活动或学科的能力、技能〕差的; 弱的: *a weak backhand* 差劲的反手击球 | **[+ at/in]** *Julie's always been weak in science.* 朱莉的理科总是弱项。

4 ▶**LEADERS/COUNTRIES/ORGANIZATIONS ETC** 领导人/国家/组织等◀ not having much power or influence 无权力的; 无影响力的: *weak trade unions* 无影响力的工会 | *a weak leader* 软弱的领导人

5 ▶**ARGUMENT/EXPLANATION/STORY ETC** 论据/阐述/描述等◀ not having the power to persuade or interest people 无说服力的; 不吸引人的: *The play was well-acted but the plot was weak.* 戏演得很好，但情节乏味。

6 ▶**INDUSTRY/COMPANY ETC** 工业/公司等◀ not successful financially〔金融上〕疲软的; 萧条的: *a weak economy* 不景气的经济 | *The pound was weak against the dollar.* 英镑对美元的汇率疲软。

7 ▶**BUILDINGS/OBJECTS** 建筑物/实物◀ unable to support a lot of weight 不牢固的: *a weak bridge* 不牢固的桥梁

8 ▶**DRINK/LIQUID** 饮料/液体◀ containing a lot of water or having little taste 稀薄的; 味淡的: *weak tea* 淡茶

9 ▶**LIGHT/SOUND** 光线/声音◀ difficult to see or hear 暗淡的; 微弱的: *a weak radio signal* 微弱的无线电信号

10 weak point/spot a part of something or of someone's character that can easily be attacked or criticized〔物〕薄弱环节;〔人〕弱点: **[+in]** *Agassi soon found the weak spots in Stich's game.* 阿加西很快发现了斯蒂克的花招存在的弱点。

11 weak at the knees not feeling well or strong, especially because you have had a sudden surprise or because you have seen someone you love〔尤指因突然受惊或遇见爱慕的人而〕两腿发软的: *His quick smile sent her weak at the knees.* 他闪露出的一丝笑容使她两腿酥软。

12 weak smile a slight smile, especially because you are not very happy〔尤指不很高兴而〕微微的一笑

13 a weak moment a time when you can be persuaded more easily than usual 意志薄弱的时刻: *David caught me at a weak moment and I lent him £10.* 戴维趁我心软的时候，让我借给了他10英镑。

14 weak in the head *informal* stupid or silly【非正式】愚蠢的; 头脑迟钝的

15 weak chin/jaw a weak chin or jaw is not very well developed and people often think it suggests a weak character 单薄的下巴〔常被认为是性格懦弱的象征〕

16 weak verb *technical* a verb that forms the past tense and past participle in a regular way【术语】弱动词, 规则变化的动词〔过去式和过去分词是规则形式的动词〕

17 weak consonant/syllable a weak CONSONANT or syllable is not emphasized 弱辅音/弱音节 —see also 另见 WEAKER SEX— **weakly** *adv*: *"I'm sorry," she said, smiling weakly.* "对不起," 她淡淡地一笑说。| *He sank down weakly on the sofa.* 他虚弱地瘫倒在沙发里。

weak·en /ˈwikən; ˈwiːkən/ *v*

1 ▶MAKE LESS POWERFUL 减弱◀ [I,T] to make someone or something less powerful or less important, or to become less powerful (使)〔某人或某物〕变弱; 削弱; 减弱: *Russia's influence on African affairs has weakened.* 俄罗斯对非洲事务的影响已经减弱。

2 ▶PHYSICALLY 体能上◀ [I,T often passive 常用被动态] to make someone lose their physical strength, or to become physically weak (使)〔某人〕虚弱, (使) 衰弱: *Julia was weakened by her long illness.* 朱莉亚长期生病, 身体衰弱。

3 ▶BUILDING/OBJECT 建筑物/实物◀ [T] to become less strong and less able to support a lot of weight 使不结实: *The explosion severely weakened the foundations of the house.* 爆炸使那座房屋的地基受到严重的毁坏。

4 weaken sb's determination/resolve to make someone less determined 动摇某人的决心[决定]: *The opposition she encountered did nothing to weaken her resolve.* 反对意见丝毫没有动摇她的决心。

5 ▶BECOME LESS CERTAIN 变得不肯定◀ [I] to become less determined, especially so that you change your opinion and accept someone else's (变得) 不坚决〔尤指改变自己的主张而听从别人〕; (变得) 犹豫: *I think Mum's weakening about us going to that party.* 我觉得妈妈心软下来了, 也许会让我们去参加聚会。

6 ▶MONEY 金钱◀ [I,T] if a particular country's money or a company's SHARE² (5) prices weaken or are weakened, their value is reduced (使)〔某国货币或公司股票的价格〕疲软

weak·er sex, the /ˈ· · ·, ·/ *n* an expression meaning women, that is now usually considered offensive 女性〔现在通常认为是冒犯用语〕

weak-kneed /, ˈ · ◂/ *adj informal* lacking courage and unable to make your own decisions【非正式】懦弱的; 缺乏决断力的

weak·ling /ˈwiklɪŋ; ˈwiːk-lɪŋ/ *n* [C] someone who is not physically strong 体格不强壮的人

3 **weak·ness** /ˈwiknɪs; ˈwiːknɪ̀s/ *n*

1 ▶PHYSICAL 身体的◀ [U] the state of being physically weak 虚弱, 衰弱, 不强壮: *weakness in the muscles* 肌肉软弱无力

2 ▶LACK OF DETERMINATION 缺乏决心◀ [U] lack of determination shown in someone's behaviour〔某人行为〕软弱; 懦弱: **sign of weakness** *Most people saw her sensitivity as a sign of weakness.* 多数人把她的敏感看作是懦弱的表现。

3 ▶LACK OF POWER 缺乏权力◀ [U] lack of power and influence 缺乏权力[影响力]: *the weakness of the Trade Union movement in post-Thatcher Britain* 后撒切尔时代的英国工会运动的衰落

4 ▶CHARACTER/DESIGN ETC 性格/设计等◀ [U] a fault in someone's character or in a system, organization, design etc〔性格或系统、组织、设计等的〕缺点, 弱点: *We spent two hours analyzing the team's strengths and weaknesses.* 我们花了两个小时分析队伍的强项和不足。| *a structural weakness in the aircraft* 飞机结构上的缺陷

5 ▶IDEA, PLAN ETC 想法、计划等◀ [C] a part of something that can easily be attacked or criticized 薄弱环节: [+in] *We finally found a weakness in their case.* 我们终于在他们的论据中找到了漏洞。

6 a weakness for sth if you have a weakness for something, you like it very much even though it may not be good for you〔对不太好事物的〕癖好, 嗜好: *Ryan's always had a weakness for fast cars.* 瑞安总是偏爱开快车。

weak-willed /, ˈ · ◂/ *adj* someone who is weak-willed cannot make decisions easily〔人〕优柔寡断的

weal /wil; wiːl/ *n* [C] a red swollen mark on the skin where someone has been hit〔皮肤上被打后的〕红肿, 伤痕

3 **wealth** /wɛlθ; welθ/ *n* **1** [U] a large amount of money and possessions 钱财, 财富: *The country's wealth comes from its oil.* 这个国家的财富来自石油。**2 a wealth of experience/knowledge/resources etc** a large number or amount of experience etc 丰富的经验/知识/资源等

wealth·y /ˈwɛlθɪ; ˈwelθi/ *adj* **1** having a lot of money, possessions etc, especially because your family has owned them for a long time 富裕的, 富有的: *wealthy landowners* 有钱的地主 **2 the wealthy** people who have a lot of money, possessions etc 有钱人, 富人

wean /win; wiːn/ *v* [I,T] to gradually stop feeding a baby or young animal on its mother's milk and start giving it ordinary food (使)〔婴儿或幼小动物〕断奶: *Some infants are weaned at six months.* 有些婴儿六个月时就断奶了。

wean sb **off** sth *phr v* [T] to make someone gradually stop doing something you disapprove of 使〔某人〕逐渐戒除〔做你不赞成的事〕: *I'm still trying to wean my daughter off sugary snacks.* 我仍在试图使女儿改掉吃甜点的习惯。

wean sb **on** sth *phr v* [T] **be weaned on** to be influenced by something from a very early age 从幼年起便受〔某物〕影响: *Like many of his generation, he was weaned on the Bible.* 跟许多同龄人一样, 他是在《圣经》的影响下长大的。

weap·on /ˈwɛpən; ˈwepən/ *n* [C] **1** something that you use to fight with, such as a knife, bomb, or gun 武器: *The crowd picked up sticks and bottles to use as weapons.* 群众捡起棍子和瓶子作为武器。| **lethal weapon** (=one that can kill) 致命的武器 **2** a type of behaviour, knowledge of a particular subject etc that you can use against someone when you are in a difficult situation〔身处困境时用来对付某人的〕手段: *The only weapon she could use against him was guilt.* 她用以对付他的唯一手段是唤起他的内疚。 2 2

weap·on·ry /ˈwɛpənrɪ; ˈwepənri/ *n* [U] a word meaning weapons, used especially when talking about particular types of weapons〔尤用于指某类〕武器: *nuclear weaponry* 核武器

wear¹ /wɛr; weə/ *v past tense* **wore** /wɔr; wɔː/ *past participle* **worn** /wɔrn; wɔːn/ 1 1

1 ▶ON YOUR BODY 在身上◀ [T] to have something such as clothes, shoes, or jewellery on your body 穿〔衣服、鞋子〕, 戴〔首饰〕: *I'm going to wear a black dress and my diamond earrings.* 我准备穿黑衣裙, 戴钻石耳环。| *Why aren't you wearing your glasses?* 你为什么不戴眼镜? | **wear a seatbelt** (=put it around yourself) 系上安全带 | **wear blue/black/red etc** *I rarely wear bright colors.* 我很少穿色彩艳丽的衣服。| **wear sth to a party/dance/ interview etc** *You can't wear jeans to the opera.* 你不能穿牛仔裤去歌剧院。

2 ▶HAIR 毛发◀ [T] to have your hair or BEARD in a particular style or shape 蓄〔须〕; 留〔发〕: *Fay wore her hair in a ponytail.* 费伊梳着马尾辫。

3 ▶BECOME DAMAGED 损坏◀ [I] to become thinner or weaker after continuous use〔经不断使用而〕磨损; 磨坏: *The stair carpet has worn in places.* 楼梯上的地毯很多处已磨损。

4 ▶HOLE 洞◀ [T] to change the shape or condition of something by using it a lot or gradually damaging it〔因长期使用而〕造成〔变形等〕: **wear a hole/groove/gap etc in sth** *You've worn a hole in these socks.* 你的袜子上已经磨出了一个洞。

5 wear well to remain in good condition without becoming broken or damaged after a period of time 经久耐用: *The concrete buildings of the 60s haven't worn well.* 60 年代的水泥楼房已显得破旧。

6 ▶EXPRESSION 表情◀ [T] to have a particular expression on your face 面露〔某种表情〕: **wear a frown/smile/grin** *Harry's face wore a broad grin.* 哈里的脸上挂着兴高采烈的笑容。

7 sth is wearing thin if an excuse, explanation, opinion etc is wearing thin, it has been used so often that you no longer believe or accept it〔借口、解释、意见等因使用过多而〕难以令人相信[接受]: *Neil says he has to work late again – I think that excuse is wearing thin.* 尼尔说他又得工作到很晚 —— 我觉得那个借口用得太多, 不可置信。

8 wear the trousers *BrE*【英】, **wear the pants** *AmE*【美】 *informal* to be the person in a family who makes the decisions【非正式】是一家之主

9 not wear sth *BrE spoken* used to say that you will not allow or accept something【英口】〔用于表示对某事情〕不能容忍: *Jane came home after 2 a.m. – I'm not wearing that.* 简凌晨两点多才回家 —— 我不能容忍这样。

10 wear your heart on your sleeve *informal* to show your true feelings openly【非正式】公开流露自己的感情—**wearable** *adj*

wear away *phr v* [I,T] to gradually damage something or make it get thinner or weaker by using it, rubbing it etc (使) 磨损; (使) 磨薄; (使) 磨掉: **wear sth ↔ away** *The cliff face is being worn away by the sea.* 海水逐渐把悬崖表面磨薄了。

wear down *phr v* **1** [I,T] to gradually become smaller or make something smaller, for example by rubbing it or using it a lot (使) 逐渐变小, 磨耗, 磨薄: *My shoes have worn down at the heel.* 我的鞋后跟已经磨薄了。**2** [T] to make someone physically weaker or less determined 削弱〔某人的〕体力[决心]: **wear sb ↔ down** *Haig's bullying was wearing me down.* 黑格的欺侮使我逐渐垮下来。

W

wear off *phr v* [I] **1** if pain or the effect of something wears off, it gradually stops〔疼痛或某种效果〕逐渐减少[消失]: *The effects of the anaesthetic were starting to wear off.* 麻醉剂的效果开始逐渐消退。**2 the novelty wears off** used to say that you stop feeling interested or excited about something because it is no longer new 新鲜感慢慢消失

wear on *phr v* [I] if time wears on, it passes very slowly, especially when you are waiting for something to happen〔时间〕慢慢地过去〔尤用于等待某事发生时〕: *As the night wore on there was still no news of the missing plane.* 长夜漫漫，仍然没有失踪飞机的消息。

wear out *phr v* [I,T] **1** to cause a lot of damage to something by using it a lot or for a long time so that it can no longer be used〔因过度或长期使用而〕磨损，用坏: *Damn! My camera batteries have worn out.* 该死的！我照相机里的电池已经没电了。| **wear sth ↔ out** *I've worn out the soles of my shoes.* 我的鞋底已经磨坏了。**2** to make someone feel extremely tired; EXHAUST¹ (1) 使〔某人〕精疲力竭: **wear sb ↔ out** *Two nights without sleep have worn me out.* 两夜没睡，我已疲惫不堪。| **wear yourself out** *The baby has stopped crying. I think he's worn himself out.* 宝宝不哭了，我想他是哭累了。—see also 另见 WORN OUT

wear² *n* **1** [U] damage caused by continuous use over a long period〔因长期使用而〕磨损；损坏: *The carpet is showing signs of wear.* 地毯已有磨损的痕迹了。**2** [U] the amount of use an object, piece of clothing etc has had, or the use you can expect to get from it〔物品、衣服等的〕耐用性，经久性: *Considering the wear it's had, your coat's in good condition.* 你的外套穿了那么久，看上去还过得去。| **have/get a lot of wear out of sth** *You'll get a lot of wear out of a canvas tent.* 帆布帐篷能使用很长时间。| **a lot of wear is left in sth** (=it is still useful or can still be worn) 仍然有用；还能穿 **3 sportswear/evening wear/childrens' wear etc** the clothes worn for a particular occasion or activity, or by a particular group of people 运动服/晚装/童装等: *a new range of casual wear* 新系列的休闲服 | *the menswear department* 男装部 | *footwear* (=shoes) 鞋 **4 wear and tear** the amount of damage you expect to be caused to furniture, cars, equipment etc when they are used for a long period of time〔家具、汽车、设备等使用了一段长时间后的〕损耗，磨损: **normal/everyday wear and tear** *The washer should last for ten years allowing for normal wear and tear.* 洗衣机在正常磨损的情况下可使用10年。—see also 另见 **the worse for wear** (WORSE¹ (8))

wear·er /ˋwɛrə; ˈweərə/ *n* [C] someone who wears a particular type of clothing, jewellery, etc〔服装、珠宝等的〕穿戴者，佩戴者: *Contact lens wearers often get red eyes.* 戴隐形眼镜的人常患红眼。

wear·ing /ˋwɛrɪŋ; ˈweərɪŋ/ *adj* making you feel tired or annoyed 使人疲倦的；令人厌烦的: *The constant arguments at home are very wearing.* 家里不断的争论真烦人。

wear·i·some /ˋwɪrɪsəm; ˈwɪərisəm/ *adj formal* making you feel bored, tired, or annoyed【正式】令人厌烦的；使人疲倦的；让人讨厌的: *a wearisome task* 乏味的任务

wear·y¹ /ˋwɪrɪ; ˈwɪəri/ *adj* **1** very tired, especially because you have been doing something for a long time〔尤指因长期做某事而〕筋疲力尽的，非常疲劳的: *I just feel weary – I wish I didn't have to work nights.* 我感到疲惫不堪——我希望不必挑灯夜战了。| *a weary smile* 疲倦的笑容 | **weary of doing sth** *I'm weary of arguing all the time.* 我对老是争辩感到厌倦。**2** *especially literary* making you very tired【尤文】令人厌倦的: *a long and weary march* 令人疲倦的长途步行 —**wearily** *adv*: *Alice sighed wearily.* 艾利斯疲倦地叹息。—**weariness** *n* [U]

weary² *v* [I,T] *formal* to become very tired or make someone very tired【正式】非常疲倦；令〔某人〕厌倦: *Amanda wouldn't admit how much the children wearied her.* 阿曼达不愿承认孩子们让她有多烦心。| **weary of doing** *Smoking is bad for you, as experts never weary of reminding us.* 专家不厌其烦地提醒我们，抽烟不利于健康。

wea·sel¹ /ˋwizl; ˈwiːzəl/ *n* [C] a small thin furry animal that kills and eats rats and birds 鼬，黄鼠狼

weasel² *v*

weasel out *phr v* [I] *informal* to avoid doing something you should do by using clever or dishonest excuses【非正式】逃避〔责任〕；〔狡猾地〕逃脱: [+of] *We made a deal and you can't weasel out of it.* 我们达成了协议，你不能借故反悔。

weasel word /ˈ‥ˌ·/ *n* [C] *informal* a word used instead of another word because it is less direct, honest, or clear【非正式】滑头话，狡辩之词

weath·er¹ /ˋwɛðə; ˈweðə/ *n* **1** [singular, U] the temperature and other conditions such as sun, rain, and wind 天气，气象: **the weather** *What was the weather like on your vacation?* 在你假期里的天气情况怎样？| **hot/wet/cold etc weather** *a spell of very dry weather* 一段非常干燥的天气 | **weather forecast** (=a report saying what the weather is expected to be like in the near future) 天气预报 | **weather permitting** (=if the weather is good enough) 如果天气好 *I'm playing golf this afternoon – weather permitting.* 天气好的话，我今天下午就去打高尔夫球。| **weather pattern** (=the way the weather usually is or changes over a long period of time)〔一段长时间的〕天气模式 | **weather map/chart** *The weather map shows a ridge of high pressure coming in from the Atlantic.* 气象图显示一股高气压正从大西洋到来。| **weather report** (=description of weather conditions on radio or television)〔电台或电视广播的〕气象报告 —see picture on page A13 参见A13页图 **2 the weather** *informal* the description of what the weather will be like in the near future, on radio, television, in newspapers etc【非正式】〔电台、电视广播或报纸刊登的〕天气预报: *I always watch the weather after the news.* 新闻之后我一定要看天气预报。**3 in all weathers** in all types of weather, even when it is very hot or cold 无论天气好坏: *There are homeless people sleeping on the streets in all weathers.* 不论什么天气都有无家可归的人露宿街头。**4 under the weather** *informal* slightly ill【非正式】身体不大舒服: *You look a bit under the weather.* 你看来身体不太好。**5 keep a weather eye on** to watch a situation carefully so that you notice anything unusual or unpleasant 密切注视，时刻警惕〔不寻常或令人不安的事情〕—see also 另见 **make heavy weather of sth** (HEAVY¹ (12))

weather² *v* **1** [I,T] if rock, wood etc weathers, or if wind, sun, rain etc weathers them, they change colour or shape over a period of time (使)〔岩石、木头等〕受风雨侵蚀: *a badly weathered statue* 一尊被风雨剥蚀得很厉害的雕像 **2** [T] to come through a very difficult situation safely 平安地渡过〔难关〕: **weather the storm** *Many small firms did not weather the storm of the recession.* 许多小公司经受不住经济衰退的冲击。

weath·er·board /ˋwɛðəˌbɔrd; ˈweðəbɔːd/ *n* **1** [U] *BrE* boards covering the outer walls of a house【英】〔房屋外墙上的〕护墙板，封檐板; CLAPBOARD *AmE*【美】**2** [C] a board or set of boards fixed across the bottom of a door, to prevent water from getting inside〔门底的〕防水板，挡雨板

weath·er·bound /ˋwɛðəˌbaund; ˈweðəbaʊnd/ *adj* unable to move or travel because of bad weather 因天气不好而受阻的

weather cen·tre *BrE*【英】, **weather bureau** *AmE*【美】/ˈ‥ˌ‥/ *n* [C] a place where information about the weather is collected and where reports are produced 气象中心，气象局

weath·er·cock /ˋwɛðəˌkak; ˈweðəkɒk/ *n* [C] a WEATHER VANE in the shape of a COCK¹ (1) 风标，风信鸡

weath·er·man /ˋwɛðəˌmæn; ˈweðəmæn/ *n* [C] a man on television or radio who tells you what the weather will be like〔电视台或电台的〕气象报告员

weath·er·per·son /ˋwɛðəˌpɜsn; ˈweðəpɜːsən/ *n* [C] someone on television or radio who tells you what the weather will be like〔电视台或电台的〕气象报告员

weath·er·proof /ˋwɛðəˋpruf; ˈweðəpruːf/ *adj* weatherproof clothing or material can keep out wind and rain〔衣物或材料〕防风雨的；不受气候影响的 —**weatherproof** *v* [T]

weather ship /ˈ‥ ·/ *n* [C] a ship at sea which reports on weather conditions〔海上的〕气象观测船

weather sta·tion /ˈ‥ˌ‥/ *n* [C] a place or building used for studying and recording weather conditions 气象站

weather strip /ˈ‥ ·/ *n* [C] a thin piece of plastic or other material put along the edge of a door or window to keep out cold air〔门、窗的〕挡风雨的密封条 —**weather stripping** *n* [U]

weather vane /ˈ‥ ·/ *n* [C] a metal thing fixed to the top of a building that blows around to show the direction the wind is coming from 风标

weave¹ /wiv; wiːv/ *v past tense* **wove** /wov; wəʊv/ *past participle* **woven** /ˋwovən; ˈwəʊvən/

1 ▶CLOTH 布◀ [I,T] to make threads into cloth by crossing them under and over each other on a LOOM¹, or to make cloth in this way 织；织〔布〕: *hand-woven scarves* 几条手织围巾

2 ▶MAKE STH 制造某物◀ [T] to make something by twisting pieces of something together 编，织: *traditional basket weaving* 传统的篮子编织 | **weave sth together** *Fir branches were woven together to make garlands.* 用冷杉树枝编成几个花环。

3 ▶STORY 故事◀ [T] to invent a complicated story or plan 编造〔故事或计划〕: *What I like is how he weaves elaborate plots.* 我喜欢他笔下精巧多变的布局。

4 get weaving *BrE spoken* used to tell someone to hurry up and start doing something【英口】赶快〔用于告诉某人赶快开始做某事〕

5 ►MOVE 移动◄ *past tense and past participle* **weaved** [I always+adv/prep, T always+adv/prep] to move somewhere by turning and changing direction a lot 迂回[穿插]行进: **[+through/across etc]** *cyclists weaving in and out of the traffic* 在车水马龙之中穿梭的骑车人 | **weave your way** *Cindy weaved her way through the crowd.* 辛迪在人群中穿插着往前走。

weave² *n* [C] the way in which a material is woven, and the pattern formed by this 织法; 编织式样: *a fine weave* 精织法

weav·er /ˈwivɚ; ˈwiːvə/ *n* [C] someone whose job is to weave cloth 织布工

web /wɛb; web/ *n* [C] **1** a net of thin threads made by a SPIDER to catch insects 蜘蛛网: **spin a web** (=make a web) 织网 —see also 另见 COBWEB —see picture at 参见 SPIDER 图 **2 a web of sth** a closely related set of things that can be very complicated 错综复杂的一套…: *a web of lies* 一套谎言 **3** pieces of skin that connect the toes of ducks and some other birds, and help them to swim well 〔鸭子等的〕蹼 **4 the web** the network of computers that forms the Internet 〔构成互联网的〕电脑网络

webbed /wɛbd; webd/ *adj* webbed feet or toes have skin between the toes 〔趾间〕有蹼的

web·bing /ˈwɛbɪŋ; ˈwebɪŋ/ *n* [U] strong woven material in narrow bands, used for supporting seats etc 〔支撑椅子等的〕结实的带状织物

web-foot·ed /ˌ·ˈ··◄/ *adj* also 又作 **web-toed** having toes that are joined by pieces of skin 有蹼足的

web off·set /ˌ·ˈ··/ *n* [U] a method of printing using one continuous roll of paper 卷筒纸胶印

Web·ster /ˈwɛbstɚ; ˈwebstə/, **Dan·iel** /ˈdænjəl; ˈdænjəl/ (1782-1852) a US politician who was Secretary of State from 1841 to1843 and from 1850 to 1852. He was also an important lawyer in the Supreme Court and was especially famous for his skill at public speaking. He strongly believed that the FEDERAL (=national) government was more important than the individual governments in each US state. 韦伯斯特〔(1782-1852)，美国政治家，1841至1843年、1850至1852年两度出任国务卿。他还是联邦最高法院举足轻重的律师，以擅长演说闻名。韦伯斯特坚信联邦政府的重要性是美国各州地方政府所不及的〕

Webster, Noah /ˈnoə; ˈnəʊə/ (1758-1843) a US LEXICOGRAPHER (=someone who writes dictionaries) who produced his famous *American Dictionary of the English Language* in 1828. His name is used for a series of dictionaries called Webster's dictionaries, which are the best-known English dictionaries produced in the US. 韦伯斯特〔(1758-1843)，美国词典编纂家。1828年编纂出版了著名的《美国英语词典》。韦氏系列词典即以他的名字冠名，是美国出版的最为著名的英语词典〕

Wed a written abbreviation of 缩写= WEDNESDAY

we'd /wid; wid; *strong* 强读 wid; wiːd/ **1** the short form of 缩略式= we had: *We'd better go now.* 我们最好现在就走。**2** the short form of 缩略式= we would: *We'd rather stay.* 我们宁愿留下来。

wed /wɛd; wed/ *v past tense and past participle* **wedded** or **wed** [I,T not in progressive 不用进行时] a word meaning to marry, used especially in literature or newspapers 娶; 嫁; 结婚〔尤用于文学或报刊中〕

wed·ded /ˈwɛdɪd; ˈwedɪd/ *adj* **1 sb's (lawful) wedded husband/wife** *formal* someone's legal husband or wife【正式】某人的(合法)丈夫/妻子 **2 be wedded to** to believe strongly in a particular idea or way of doing things 执著于〔某种思想或做法〕的, 坚持…的: *They're still very wedded to the idea of public ownership.* 他们仍然极力坚持公有制的思想。

S2 W3 **wed·ding** /ˈwɛdɪŋ; ˈwedɪŋ/ *n* [C] **1** a marriage ceremony, especially one with a religious service 〔尤指有宗教仪式的〕婚礼: **wedding present/reception/cake etc** *Careful with that vase! It was a wedding present.* 当心那只花瓶! 那是结婚礼物。**2 (hear the sound of) wedding bells** *spoken* used to say that you think it is likely that two people will get married【口】喜事要临门了〔用于表示认为两个人将要结婚〕: *I reckon it's wedding bells for Tony and Jane.* 我想托尼和简要结婚了。

wedding break·fast /ˈ·· ˌ··/ *n* [C usually singular 一般用单数] *BrE* a special meal after a wedding ceremony【英】婚礼后的喜宴, 婚宴

wedding chap·el /ˈ·· ˌ··/ *n* [C] a building used in the US for wedding ceremonies 〔美国〕婚礼教堂

wedding dress /ˈ·· ·/ also 又作 **wedding gown** *n* [C] a long white dress worn at a traditional wedding 婚纱

Wedding March, the /ˈ·· ·/ a piece of music that is traditionally played after a marriage ceremony when the BRIDE and GROOM start to walk down the AISLE (=a passage between rows of seats) of the church 婚礼进行曲〔婚礼结束新娘、新郎开始沿着教堂内的过道行走时按传统演奏的一首乐曲〕—see also 另见 HERE COMES THE BRIDE

wedding ring /ˈ·· ·/ *n* [C] a ring worn on the third finger of your left hand to show that you are married 结婚戒指

wedge¹ /wɛdʒ; wedʒ/ *n* [C] **1** a piece of wood, metal etc that has one thick edge and one pointed edge and is used especially for keeping a door open or for splitting wood 〔木头、金属等的〕楔子〔尤用于抵住门或劈开木头〕**2** a piece of food shaped like this 楔形〔食物〕: *a wedge of chocolate cake* 一块楔形的巧克力蛋糕 | *Garnish with lemon wedges.* 用楔形柠檬片装饰。**3 drive a wedge between** to make the relationship between two people or groups worse 造成〔两个人或团体〕之间的不和: *Their divorce has driven a wedge between the two families.* 他们的离婚导致了双方家庭的不和。—see also 另见 **the thin end of the wedge** (THIN¹ (11))

wedge² *v* **1** [T always+adv/prep] to force something firmly into a narrow space 把…挤入: **wedge sth behind/under/in etc** *Cloth wedged in the cracks failed to block out the drafts.* 塞到缝隙里的布挡不住风。| **wedged in** (=stuck in a small space) 挤入〔窄小的空间〕*I was wedged in between Tom and Amy on the back seat.* 在后座上我被夹在汤姆和埃米中间。**2 wedge sth open/shut** to put something under a door, window etc to make it stay open or shut 用楔子把某物〔门窗等〕抵住让它开着/关着

Wedg·wood /ˈwɛdʒˌwud; ˈwedʒwʊd/ *trademark* a type of fine CHINA, such as plates or bowls, made by the British company Wedgwood, which was established in the 18th century. Wedgwood china is often pale blue or pale green, with white designs or figures on it. The blue colour used in Wedgwood china is sometimes called **Wedgwood blue**.【商标】韦奇伍德瓷器〔指英国韦奇伍德公司出品的精致瓷器, 如瓷盘、瓷碗等。该公司成立于18世纪。韦奇伍德瓷器通常为浅蓝色或浅绿色, 饰以白色花纹或图案。韦奇伍德瓷器上的蓝色有时称为韦奇伍德蓝〕

wed·lock /ˈwɛdlɑk; ˈwedlɒk/ *n* [U] *old use*【旧】**1 born out of wedlock** if a child is born out of wedlock, its parents are not married when it is born 非婚生的 **2** the state of being married 已婚状态

Wednes·day /ˈwɛnzdɪ; ˈwenzdi/ written abbreviation 缩写为 **Wed** or 或 **Weds** *n* [C,U] the day between Tuesday and Thursday. In Britain, Wednesday is considered the third day of the week, and in the US it is considered the fourth day of the week 星期三〔在英国被看作是一星期的第三天, 在美国则被看作是一星期的第四天〕: *She'll arrive on Wednesday.* 她将于星期三到达。| *It happened Wednesday afternoon.* 这事发生在星期三下午。| *They left last Wednesday.* 他们是上星期三离开的。| **on Wednesdays** (=each Wednesday) 每星期三 *We play tennis on Wednesdays.* 我们每星期三打网球。| **a Wednesday** (=one of the Wednesdays of the year) 一年中的某个星期三 *My birthday's on a Wednesday this year.* 我今年的生日是一个星期三。| **the Wednesday** *BrE* (=the Wednesday of the week being mentioned)【英】〔话中所指的这个星期的〕星期三 *They're arriving on the Wednesday, and leaving just after Christmas.* 他们会在那周的星期三到, 过了圣诞节后就走。

Weds a written abbreviation of 缩写= WEDNESDAY

wee¹ /wi; wiː/ *adj* [usually before noun 一般用于名词前] **1** *ScotE or informal* very small【苏格兰或非正式】很小的: *a wee kitten* 小猫 **2 a wee bit** *informal* to a small degree【非正式】有些, 有点: *I'm a wee bit tired.* 我有点累了。**3 the wee (small) hours** *ScotE and AmE* the early hours of the morning, just after midnight【苏格兰和美】凌晨〔午夜后不久〕; SMALL HOURS *BrE*【英】

wee² *v* [I] *BrE spoken* a word meaning to pass water from your body, used by or to children; URINATE; WEE-WEE【英口】尿尿, 撒尿〔儿语〕—**wee** *n* [singular, U]: *Do you want a wee?* 你要尿尿吗?

weed¹ /wid; wiːd/ *n* **1** [C] a wild plant growing where it is not wanted and that prevents crops or garden flowers from growing properly 野草, 杂草, 莠草 **2** [U] a plant without flowers that grows on water in a large green floating mass 海藻, 水草 **3** [C] *BrE informal* someone who is weak【英, 非正式】孱弱的人: *Nigel's such a weed, isn't he?* 奈杰尔弱不禁风, 是不是啊? **4 the weed** *informal* cigarettes or tobacco【非正式】香烟; 烟草 **5** [U] *old-fashioned* CANNABIS【过时】大麻 **6 (widow's) weeds** *old use* black clothes worn by a woman whose husband has died【旧】〔寡妇穿的黑色〕丧服

weed² *v* [I,T] to remove unwanted plants from a garden or other place 除去杂草

weed sb/sth ↔ **out** *phr v* [T] to get rid of people or things that are not very good 淘汰〔不合格的人或物〕: *Unsuitable recruits were soon weeded out.* 不合格的新兵很快就遭淘汰了。

W

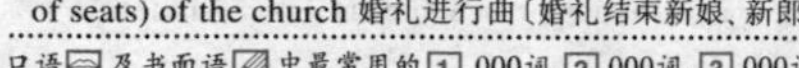
口语 及书面语 中最常用的 1 000词, 2 000词, 3 000词

weed·kil·ler /ˈwidˌkɪlɚ; ˈwiːdˌkɪlə/ *n* [C,U] poison used to kill unwanted plants 除草剂

weed·y /ˈwidɪ; ˈwiːdi/ *adj informal*【非正式】**1** full of unwanted wild plants 杂草丛生的 **2** *BrE* physically weak or having a weak character【英】瘦弱的; 懦弱的: *a weedy little man with glasses* 戴眼镜的小个子瘦男人

Wee Frees, the /ˌ· ˈ·/ a humorous name for the members of the Free Church of Scotland, a small Christian group with churches mainly in the Highlands of Scotland 独立教会会友, 自由教会教友〔对苏格兰独立[自由]教会教徒的谑称。该教派为小型基督教组织, 其教堂主要分布在苏格兰高地〕

1 1 **week** /wik; wiːk/ *n* [C] **1** a period of seven days and nights, usually measured in Britain from Monday to Sunday and in the US from Sunday to Saturday 星期, 周〔共七天, 在英国从星期一至星期日; 在美国从星期日至星期六〕: *The flight to Accra goes twice a week.* 飞往阿克拉的航班每星期两次。| *See you next week.* 下星期见。**2** any period of seven days and nights 连续七天, 一周: *The training program lasts three weeks.* 培训课程历时三周。**3** the part of the week when you go to work, usually from Monday to Friday; WORKING WEEK 工作周〔通常由星期一至星期五〕: *a 35-hour week* 每周工作 35 小时 | *I don't see her much during the week.* 在上班时间我不常见到她。**4 Monday week/Tuesday week etc** *BrE* a week after the day that is mentioned【英】星期一/星期二后一周等: *We're off to Spain Sunday week.* 我们星期日后一周去西班牙。**5 a week on Monday etc** *BrE*【英】, **a week from Monday etc** *AmE*【美】a week after the day that is mentioned 星期一后一周等: *The Reids are coming for dinner a week from Sunday.* 里兹一家星期日后一周来吃饭。| *Keith's coming home two weeks on Saturday.* 基思星期六后两周回家。**6 week after week** also 又作 **week in week out** *usually spoken* continuously for many weeks【一般口】连续几个星期, 一周又一周: *I just seem to do the same things week in week out.* 一周又一周, 我好像在反复做相同的工作。

> CULTURAL NOTE 文化注释
>
> Most people in Britain and the US work from Monday to Friday and work between 35 and 40 hours in total. 在英美, 大多数人从周一至周五上班, 每周总共工作35到40个小时。

week·day /ˈwikˌde; ˈwiːkdeɪ/ *n* [C] any day of the week except Saturday and Sunday 工作日〔星期一到星期五中某天〕

1 2 **week·end¹** /ˈwikˋɛnd; ˌwiːkˈend/ *n* [C] **1** Saturday and Sunday (and sometimes also Friday evening), especially when considered as time when you do not work 周末〔指星期六和星期日, 有时亦包括星期五晚上, 尤指不用工作的时间〕: *Are you doing anything nice this weekend?* 这个周末你有什么好的安排? | **a long weekend** (=Saturday and Sunday, and also Friday or Monday, or both) 长周末〔指星期六和星期日, 加上星期五及[或]下星期一〕 *We're going for a long weekend to EuroDisney.* 我们准备到欧洲迪斯尼去度一个长周末。| **at the weekend/at weekends** *BrE*【英】: *I never work at weekends.* 周末我从不工作。| **on the weekend/on weekends** *AmE*【美】: *What are you doing on the weekend?* 周末你准备干什么? | **weekend cottage/cabin etc** (=a place in the country where you spend your weekends) 周末度假村舍/小屋等 **2** a holiday from Friday evening until Sunday evening〔自星期五晚至星期日晚的〕周末假期: *You've won a weekend for two in Paris!* 你赢得周末到巴黎双人游的机会! —see also 另见 **dirty weekend** (DIRTY¹ (2))

weekend² *v* [I always+adv/prep] to spend the weekend somewhere〔到某处〕度周末: *We're weekending on the coast.* 我们正在海滨度周末。

week·end·er /ˈwikˋɛndɚ; ˌwiːkˈendə/ *n* [C] someone who spends time in a place only at weekends 外出度周末的人, 周末来客

week·long /ˈwikˌlɔŋ; ˈwiːklɒŋ/ *adj* [only before noun 仅用于名词前] continuing for a week 持续一周: *a weeklong seminar* 持续一周的研讨会

3 **week·ly¹** /ˈwiklɪ; ˈwiːkli/ *adj* happening once a week or every week 一周一次的, 每周的: *a weekly current affairs programme* 每周的时事节目 | *twice-weekly flights to Hong Kong* 每周两次飞往香港的航班 —**weekly** *adv*: *The magazine is published weekly.* 这本杂志是周刊。

weekly² *n* [C] a magazine that appears once a week 周刊: *a popular news weekly* 受欢迎的新闻周刊

week·night /ˈwikˌnaɪt; ˈwiːknaɪt/ *n* [C] any night apart from Saturday or Sunday 工作日夜晚〔星期一到星期五的某个夜晚〕

wee·nie /ˈwinɪ; ˈwiːni/ *n* [C] *AmE informal*【美, 非正式】**1** a type of SAUSAGE; a WIENER (1) 法兰克福香肠, 熏肉香肠: *a weenie roast* 法兰克福烤肠 **2** a word meaning someone who is weak, afraid, or stupid, used especially by children 胆小鬼, 笨蛋〔尤儿语〕

wee·ny /ˈwinɪ; ˈwiːni/ *BrE*【英】, **weensie** /ˈwinzɪ; ˈwiːnzi/ *AmE*【美】*adj spoken* extremely small【口】极小的 —see also 另见 TEENY WEENY

weep /wip; wiːp/ *v past tense and past participle* **wept** /wɛpt; wept/ **1** [I,T] *formal or literary* to cry, especially because you feel very sad【正式或文】〔尤因悲伤〕哭泣, 流泪: *James broke down and wept.* 詹姆斯控制不住感情, 哭了起来。| **weep bitterly** (=cry a lot) 大哭 **2 I could have wept** *spoken* used to say that you felt very disappointed about something【口】〔对某事〕大失所望: *I could have wept when we lost by one point.* 我们要是以一分之差落败, 我会大失所望的。**3** [I] if a wound weeps, liquid comes out of it〔伤口〕渗出液体 —**weep** *n* [singular]

weep·ie /ˈwipɪ; ˈwiːpi/ *n* [C] another spelling of WEEPY² weepy² 的另一种拼法

weep·ing /ˈwipɪŋ; ˈwiːpɪŋ/ *adj* **weeping willow/birch etc** a tree with branches that hang down towards the ground 垂柳/树枝低垂的白桦等

weep·y¹ /ˈwipɪ; ˈwiːpi/ *adj informal* tending to cry a lot【非正式】动不动就哭的, 眼泪汪汪的: *feeling emotionally exhausted and weepy* 觉得感情崩溃, 只想哭

weepy², **weepie** *n* [C] *informal* a film or story that seems to be deliberately intended to make you cry【非正式】催人泪下的电影〔或故事〕

wee·vil /ˈwivl̩; ˈwiːvəl/ *n* [C] a small insect that spoils grain, flour etc by eating it〔吃谷物、面粉等的〕象甲, 象鼻虫

wee-wee /ˈ· ·/ *v* [I] *spoken* a word meaning to pass water from your body, used by or to children; URINATE【口】尿尿, 撒尿〔儿语〕 —**wee-wee** *n* [singular, U]

Wee Wil·lie Win·kie /ˌwi ˌwɪlɪ ˋwɪŋkɪ; ˌwiː ˌwɪli ˈwɪŋki/ a character in a NURSERY RHYME (=an old song or poem for young children). 威·威利·威克〔一首童谣中的人物〕The rhyme goes 相关唱词为:

Wee Willie Winkie runs through the town,
Upstairs and downstairs in his nightgown.
威·威利·威克, 跑遍整个村镇,
上楼下楼上楼, 身穿睡衣闲逛。

weft /wɛft; weft/ *n* **the weft** *technical* the threads in a piece of cloth that are woven across the threads that go from top to bottom; WOOF²【术语】纬, 纬纱 —compare 比较 WARP² (1)

weigh /we; weɪ/ *v* 3

1 ►BE A PARTICULAR WEIGHT 有一定重量◄ [linking verb 连系动词] to have a particular weight 重(若干), 重量是…: *Our Christmas turkey weighed 16 pounds.* 我们的圣诞火鸡重 16 磅。| *How much do you weigh?* 你体重是多少?

2 ►MEASURE THE WEIGHT 测出重量◄ [T] to use a machine to find out what something or someone weighs 称…的重量: *Have you weighed yourself lately?* 你最近称过体重吗?

3 weigh a ton to be very heavy 非常重: *These books weigh a ton!* 这些书真重!

4 ►CONSIDER/COMPARE 斟酌/比较◄ [T] to consider something carefully so that you can make a decision about it 认真考虑〔某事〕; 权衡: *Tim weighed the alternatives in his mind.* 蒂姆在心里权衡着可能的选择。| **weigh sth against sth** *We have to weigh the costs of the new system against the benefits it will bring.* 我们在衡量新系统带来的好处时, 必须考虑到它的费用。—see also 另见 **weigh up** (WEIGH)

5 weigh your words to think very carefully about what you say because you do not want to say the wrong thing〔因不想说错话而〕字斟句酌, 推敲

6 ►INFLUENCE 影响◄ [I always+adv/prep] *formal* to influence a result or decision【正式】〔对结局或决定〕有影响: [**+with**] *Her evidence weighed quite strongly with the judge.* 法官非常重视她的证词。| **weigh against/in favour of** *a new argument that weighed heavily in Mark's favour* 对马克非常有利的新论据

7 weigh anchor to raise an ANCHOR and sail away 起锚; 启航

weigh sb/sth ↔ **down** *phr v* [T usually passive 一般用被动态] **1** to make someone or something bend or feel heavy under a load 使〔某人〕感到沉重; 压弯〔某物〕; 压下, 压倒: *Sally was weighed down with shopping bags.* 萨莉提着购物袋颇感费力。**2** to feel worried about a problem or difficulty〔因问题[困难]而〕感到焦虑: *a family weighed down with grief* 因悲伤而感到沮丧的家庭

weigh in *phr v* [I] **1** to have your weight tested before taking part in a fight or a horse race〔拳击手或骑师在赛前〕称体重 —see also 另见 WEIGH-IN **2 weigh in (with)** *informal* to add a remark to a discussion or an argument【非正式】〔讨论或争辩

时〕提出〔论点〕: *Each member weighed in with their own opinion.* 每个成员都提出了各自的观点。

weigh on sb/sth *phr v* [T] to make someone worried or give them problems 使〔某人〕烦恼; 使陷入困境: *Yvonne's responsibilities were beginning to weigh on her.* 伊冯娜承担的责任开始使她忧愁。| **weigh on sb's mind** *I'm sure there's something weighing on his mind.* 我敢肯定他有心事。| **weigh heavily** *responsibilities that weighed heavily on young shoulders* 在年轻人肩膀上压着的重担

weigh sth ↔ **out** *phr v* [T] to measure an amount of something by weight 称出〔某物的〕重量: *I watched as he weighed out half a pound of coffee beans and ground them up.* 我看着他称出半磅咖啡豆, 并将它磨碎。

weigh sb/sth **up** *phr v* [T] **1** to consider a choice carefully so that you can make a decision 仔细考虑, 权衡: *We're just weighing up the pros and cons of the two deals.* 我们正在仔细考虑两笔交易的利弊。**2** to form an opinion about someone by watching them, talking to them etc〔通过观察、谈话等〕评估〔某人〕: *I can't quite weigh Marilyn up.* 我弄不清玛丽莲的为人。

weigh·bridge /ˈweˌbrɪdʒ; ˈweɪˌbrɪdʒ/ *n* [C] a machine for weighing vehicles and their loads, with a flat area that you drive the vehicle onto〔称车辆及装载量的〕桥秤, 地秤, 地磅

weigh-in /ˈ· ·/ *n* [C usually singular 一般用单数] a check on the weight of a BOXER (1) or a JOCKEY[1] before a fight or a horse-race〔拳击手或骑师在赛前的〕称体重 —see also 另见 **weigh in** (WEIGH)

S1 W2 **weight[1]** /wet; weɪt/ *n*

1 ▶**WHAT SB/STH WEIGHS** 某人/某物的重量◀ [C,U] how heavy something is when measured by a particular system〔某物的〕重量: *The average weight of a baby at birth is just over seven pounds.* 婴儿出生时的平均重量仅仅高于七磅。

2 ▶**HOW FAT** 有多胖◀ [U] how heavy and especially how fat someone is〔某人的〕体重〔尤指肥胖〕: *A lot of teenage girls are obsessed about their weight.* 许多少女为体重所困扰。| **put on weight** (=get fatter) 身体变胖 | **lose weight** (=get thinner) 身体变瘦 | **watch your weight** (=be careful about what you eat so that you do not get fat) 注意节食减肥 | **have a weight problem** (=be too fat) 体重过重, 太胖 —see also 另见 OVERWEIGHT; UNDERWEIGHT

3 ▶**HEAVINESS** 重◀ [U] the fact of being heavy 重, 沉重: *The weight of her boots made it hard for Sue to run.* 休穿着沉重的靴子, 很难奔跑。| **under the weight of** (=supporting something heavy) 在…的重压下 *Karen staggered along under the weight of her backpack.* 卡伦背着沉重的背包, 蹒跚而行。

4 ▶**HEAVY THING** 重物◀ [C] something that is heavy 重东西: *Omar can't lift heavy weights because of his bad back.* 奥马尔因背部有毛病, 提不起重东西。

5 ▶**FOR MEASURING QUANTITIES** 测量分量◀ [C] a piece of metal weighing a particular amount that is balanced against something else to measure what it weighs 砝码; 秤砣

6 ▶**FOR EXERCISE** 用于锻炼◀ [C] a piece of metal that weighs a certain amount and is lifted by people who want bigger muscles or who are competing in lifting competitions 杠铃 —see also 另见 WEIGHTLIFTING

7 ▶**SYSTEM** 制度◀ [C,U] a system of standard measures of weight 重量单位制; 衡制: *metric weight* 公衡制 | *weights and measures* 度量衡

8 ▶**RESPONSIBILITY/WORRY** 责任/忧虑◀ [C] something that causes you a lot of worry 重压, 负担: [+on] *Since Jane's been sick, I've had to carry the full weight of running the school.* 自从简生病以来, 我不得不承担起管理学校的全部重任。

9 a weight off your mind something that solves a problem and makes you feel happier 除去心理负担: *Selling the house was a great weight off my mind.* 卖掉房子去掉了我心头的一块大石头。

10 ▶**IMPORTANCE** 重要性◀ [U] the influence or importance that something has when you are forming a judgment or opinions〔作出判断或形成意见时某物的〕影响; 重要性: *The weight of evidence against her led to her conviction.* 对她不利的重要证据致使她被定罪。| **carry weight** (=have influence) 有影响 *Una's opinion doesn't carry much weight around here.* 尤娜的意见在这里没有多少影响。| **add weight to** *His declining health added weight to the argument that the king should abdicate.* 国王身体日趋衰弱, 这更加证实了他应该退位的说法。| **attach weight to** (=think that something is important) 重视

11 throw your weight about/around *informal* to use your position of authority to tell people what to do in an unpleasant and unreasonable way【非正式】指手画脚; 滥用权势

12 throw your weight behind to use all your power and influence to support someone〔用权力和影响力〕支持〔某人〕: *The US has thrown its weight behind the new leader.* 美国利用其影响力支持这位新领导人。

13 pull your weight to do your full share of work 做好分内事: *Some people in the office hadn't been pulling their weight.* 办公室里有些人没有尽本分做好工作。

14 take the weight off your feet *spoken* used to tell someone to sit down【口】坐下: *Come in, take the weight off your feet.* 进来, 坐坐吧。

15 weight of numbers the combined strength, influence etc of a large group〔一个大群体〕联合起来的势力[影响]: *They are likely to win this battle through sheer weight of numbers.* 他们纯粹靠人多势众可能赢得这场战斗。

16 summer-weight/winter-weight a piece of clothing that is summer-weight or winter-weight, is made of material that is suitable for summer or winter 夏装/冬装〔用适合夏天或冬天穿的布料缝制〕

17 ▶**SCIENCE** 科学◀ [C,U] *technical* the amount of force with which an object is pulled down by GRAVITY (1)【术语】〔作用在物体上的〕重力 —see also 另见 **dead weight** (DEAD[1] (29))

weight[2] *v* [T] to add something heavy to something or put a weight on it, especially in order to keep it in place 加重量于〔某物, 以使稳固不动〕; 使变重: *fishing nets weighted with lead* 坠有铅锤的鱼网

weight·ed /ˈwetɪd; ˈweɪtɪ̈d/ *adj* **weighted in favour/against** producing conditions that are favourable or unfavourable to one particular group〔对某集团〕有利/不利的: [+against] *The voting system is weighted against the smaller parties.* 这种选举制度对小党派不利。| **weighted in favour of** *a pay increase heavily weighted in favour of the lower paid staff* 对低收入员工十分有利的加薪

weight·ing /ˈwetɪŋ; ˈweɪtɪŋ/ *n* [singular, U] *BrE* additional money that you get paid because of the high cost of living in a particular area【英】〔因居住在某个生活费用较高的地区而得到的〕额外津贴: *a London weighting* 伦敦地区的额外补贴

weight·less /ˈwetlɪs; ˈweɪtləs/ *adj* having no weight, especially when you are floating in space or water〔尤指在太空或水中〕失重的, 没有重量的 —**weightlessly** *adv* —**weightlessness** *n* [U]

weight·lift·ing /ˈwetˌlɪftɪŋ; ˈweɪtˌlɪftɪŋ/ *n* [U] **1** the sport of lifting specially shaped weights (WEIGHT[1] (6)) 举重运动 **2** also 又作 **weight training** *BrE* the activity of lifting specially shaped weights as a form of exercise【英】举重〔锻炼〕 —**weightlifter** *n* [C]

Weight Watch·ers /ˈ· ˌ··/ *trademark* an international organization that helps people who want to become thinner. Its members go to regular meetings, where they get advice about how to diet and where they all support each other and praise members who have succeeded in losing weight.【商标】体重控制协会〔专为减肥人士提供帮助的一国际组织。其成员定期参加会议, 听取节食建议, 相互支持, 并对减肥成功的会员予以表扬〕

weight·y /ˈwetɪ; ˈweɪti/ *adj* **1** important and serious 重要的; 严肃的: *weighty reasons for change* 改变的重要理由 **2** *especially literary* heavy【尤文】沉重的 —**weightily** *adv* —**weightiness** *n* [U]

Weill /vaɪl; vaɪl/, **Kurt** /kɝt; kɜːt/ (1900-50) a German COMPOSER, who wrote the music for *The Threepenny Opera*, for which Bertolt Brecht wrote the words 韦尔〔(1900-1950), 德国作曲家。他曾为《三便士歌剧》谱曲, 该剧的词作者为贝托尔特·布莱希特〕

Wei·mar /ˈvaɪmɑr; ˈvaɪmɑː/ a city in central Germany, where many important writers, such as Goethe and Schiller, lived in the 18th and 19th centuries 魏玛〔德国中部一城市。18、19 世纪时期, 歌德、席勒等许多著名作家在那里生活过〕

Wei·mar Re·pub·lic, the /ˈ·· ·ˌ··/ the first German republic, which was established in 1919 at a meeting in the city of Weimar. It faced difficult economic problems, including very high INFLATION, and ended when Hitler took control of the country in 1933. 魏玛共和国〔第一个德意志共和国, 1919 年在魏玛市召开的一次会议上成立。魏玛共和国成立后面临严重的经济问题, 其中包括恶性通货膨胀。1933 年希特勒统治德国后, 魏玛共和国宣告结束〕

weir /wɪr; wɪə/ *n* [C] **1** a low structure built across a river or stream to control the flow of water 拦河坝, 堰 **2** a wooden fence built across a stream to make a pool where you can catch fish 鱼梁〔溪流上用以捕鱼的木栅栏〕

weird /wɪrd; wɪəd/ *adj* **1** *informal* unusual and different from anything you have seen or heard before; BIZARRE【非正式】古怪的, 奇异的: *Mike's got a really weird sense of humour.* 迈克有 W2

一种实属怪异的幽默感。| **weird and wonderful** *Tom's full of weird and wonderful ideas.* 汤姆满脑子稀奇古怪的念头。**2** very strange, mysterious, or frightening 非常奇怪的; 神秘的; 可怕的: *A weird green glow lit the sky.* 神秘的绿光照亮了天空。—**weirdly** *adv*—**weirdness** *n* [U]

weird·o /ˈwɪrdo; ˈwɪədəʊ/ also 又作 **weird·ie** /ˈwɪrdɪ; ˈwɪədi/ *n* [C] *informal* someone who behaves strangely, wears unusual clothes etc【非正式】〔行为、衣着等〕怪异的人: *Jenny's going out with a real weirdo.* 珍妮正和一个十分古怪的人交往。

welch /wɛltʃ; welʃ/ *v* [I] another spelling of WELSH² welsh²的另一种拼法

S3 W2 **wel·come¹** /ˈwɛlkəm; ˈwelkəm/ *v* [T] **1** to say hello in a friendly way to someone who has just arrived 欢迎〔刚到达的人〕: *The Queen welcomed the President as he got off the plane.* 总统走下飞机, 女王上前迎接。**2** to accept an idea, suggestion etc happily 乐于接受〔某种思想、建议等〕: *Henri doesn't welcome intrusions into his privacy.* 亨利不希望有人干扰他的私生活。| *The college welcomes applications from people of all races.* 学院欢迎任何种族的人申请入学。**3 welcome sb/sth with open arms a)** to be very glad that someone has come 热情欢迎某人的到来 **b)** to be very happy to accept something 乐于接受某事

S2 W3 **welcome²** *adj* **1** someone who is welcome is gladly accepted in a place 〔某人〕受欢迎的: *I had the feeling I wasn't really welcome.* 我感觉到我其实不受欢迎。| **make sb welcome** (=make someone feel that you are pleased they have come) 使人感到受欢迎; 款待某人 **2** something that is welcome is pleasant and enjoyable, especially because it is just what you need or want 〔某物尤因正需要而〕令人愉悦的: *a welcome break from the pressures of work* 及时从工作压力中解脱出来的休息 | *A cup of tea would be very welcome.* 来杯茶非常不错。**3 be welcome to** *spoken* used to say that someone can have something if they want it, because you certainly do not want it【口】可以随意拥有〔某物, 因为说话者不需要〕: *If Rob wants that job he's welcome to it!* 罗布如果想要那份工作, 就请他随时来吧! **4 be welcome to do sth** *spoken* used to invite someone to do something if they would like to【口】可随意做某事〔用于邀请某人做某事〕: *You're welcome to stay for lunch.* 你就留下来吃午饭吧。**5 you're welcome!** *spoken, especially AmE* a polite way of replying to someone who has just thanked you for something【口, 尤美】不用谢; 别客气〔用于回答别人的感谢〕: *"Thanks for the coffee." "You're welcome."* "谢谢你的咖啡。""别客气。"

welcome³ *n* [C] **1** a greeting you give to someone when they arrive 欢迎, 迎接: *Mandela got a tremendous welcome at the airport.* 曼德拉在机场受到热烈欢迎。| **extend a welcome to** *formal* (=welcome someone)【正式】欢迎某人 **2 give sb/sth a warm welcome a)** to welcome someone in a very friendly way 热烈欢迎某人 **b)** to gladly accept an idea, suggestion etc 欣然接受〔意见、建议等〕 **3 outstay/overstay your welcome** to stay at someone's house longer than they want you to 因做客时间太久而不再受欢迎

welcome⁴ *interjection* **1** an expression of greeting to a guest or someone who has just arrived 欢迎〔用于对客人或刚刚到达的人表示欢迎〕: [+to] *Welcome to London!* 欢迎到伦敦来! | *Welcome back – it's good to see you again.* 欢迎归来——再次见到你很高兴。| **welcome home** (=used when someone has been away and returns home) 欢迎你回家 **2 welcome to the club** *spoken* used to make someone feel better when they are in a bad situation, by telling them you are already in that situation【口】彼此彼此〔用来安慰某人, 指大家都倒霉〕

welcome wag·on /ˈ··, ·ˈ/ *n* [C] *AmE* someone or something that welcomes someone who has just arrived in a new place【美】欢迎新来的人[物]: *The company is bringing out the welcome wagon for the new sales recruits.* 公司为新推销员举行迎新活动。

wel·com·ing /ˈwɛlkəmɪŋ; ˈwelkəmɪŋ/ *adj* a person or place that is welcoming makes you feel happy and relaxed when you meet them or arrive there 〔人或地方〕殷勤的, 亲切的; 赏心悦目的: *a welcoming smile* 亲切的微笑 | *The room was bright and welcoming.* 房间明亮如昼, 令人心旷神怡。| **welcoming committee/party** (=group of people who welcome someone) 欢迎委员会/迎宾会

weld¹ /wɛld; weld/ *v* **1** [I,T] to join metals by melting them and pressing them together when they are hot, or to be joined in this way 焊接〔金属〕, 熔接 **2** [T always+adv/prep] to join or unite people into a single, strong group 使〔人〕团结〔成一个强大集体〕: *A person of vision was needed to weld the various political factions together.* 需要一个有远见卓识的人把各个政治派别团结起来。—compare 比较 FORGE¹ (3), SOLDER²

weld² *n* [C] a joint that is made by welding two pieces of metal 焊接点[处]

weld·er /ˈwɛldɚ; ˈweldə/ *n* [C] someone whose job is to weld things 焊工

wel·fare /ˈwɛlˌfɛr; ˈwelfeə/ *n* [U] **1** health, comfort, and happiness; WELL-BEING 幸福, 健康; 福祉: *Our only concern is the children's welfare.* 我们唯一关心的是孩子的幸福。**2** help that is provided, especially by government organizations for people with social or financial problems 〔尤指政府机构提供的〕福利: *The company's welfare officer deals with employees' personal problems.* 公司负责福利的工作人员处理雇员的个人问题。| *welfare services* 福利机构 **3** *especially AmE* money paid by the government to people who are very poor, unemployed etc【尤美】〔政府对穷人、失业者等发放的〕救济金: **on welfare** *Most of the people in this neighborhood are on welfare.* 这住宅区的大多数人都领取福利救济金。—compare 比较 SOCIAL SECURITY S3 W2

welfare state /ˌ·· ˈ·/ *n* **1 the welfare state** a system by which the government provides money, free medical care etc for people who are unemployed or too old to work 福利制度 **2** [C] a country with such a system 福利国家

wel·far·is·m /ˈwɛlˌfɛrɪzm; ˈwelfeərɪzəm/ *n* [U] a way of life in which someone does not work, but accepts money from the government and makes no attempt to improve their situation 福利生活, 福利主义〔指一个人不工作而接受政府救济, 却不想改变这种状况〕

wel·kin /ˈwɛlkɪn; ˈwelkɪn/ *n poetical* the sky【诗】苍穹

we'll /wɪl; wil; *strong* 重读 wil; wiːl/ the short form of 缩略式= we will or 或 we shall

well¹ /wɛl; wel/ *adv comparative* 比较级 **better** *superlative* 最高级 **best** S1 W1

1 ►SATISFACTORILY 满意地◄ in a successful or satisfactory way 顺利地; 令人满意地: *Did you sleep well?* 你睡得好吗? | *James reads well for his age.* 对詹姆斯这个年龄来说, 他的阅读能力算不错了。| **fairly/moderately/pretty well** (=quite well) 不错/还可以/相当好 | **go well** (=happen in the way you planned or hoped) 成功〔与计划或期望的一样〕*I was really pleased that the concert had gone so well.* 音乐会办得如此成功, 我真高兴。

2 well-organized/well-educated etc organized, educated etc to a high standard 组织完善的/受过良好教育的等

3 do well a) to be successful, especially in work or business 〔尤指工作或生意〕成功: *Elizabeth's done well for herself – a well-paid job, a nice house and a sports car.* 伊丽莎白事业有成——高薪的工作、舒适的住房, 还有一辆跑车。**b)** if someone who has been ill is doing well, they are becoming healthy again 〔病人〕康复: *The operation was successful and the patient is doing well.* 手术成功, 病人正在康复中。

4 ►THOROUGHLY 彻底地◄ in a thorough way 彻底地, 充分地: *Mix the flour and butter well.* 把面粉和黄油搅拌好。

5 as well as in addition to something else 又, 也, 还: *They own a house in Provence as well as a villa in Spain.* 他们在普罗旺斯有一栋房子, 在西班牙还有一座别墅。| **as well as doing sth** *The organization encourages members to meet on a regular basis, as well as providing them with financial support.* 该机构鼓励成员经常聚会, 还给他们提供财政支持。

6 as well in addition to something or someone else 〔除某事或某人外〕还: *We're going to the cinema tonight, why don't you come along as well?* 我们今晚去看电影, 你为什么不一起去?

7 may/might/could well do/be sth used to say that something is likely to happen or is likely to be true 〔表示某事〕可能发生; 可能真实: *What you say may well be true.* 你说的或许是真实的。| *You could try the drugstore, but it may well be closed by now.* 你可以到药店去试试, 但是现在它可能关门了。

8 may/might/could (just) as well do sth a) *informal* used when you do not particularly want to do something but you decide to do it【非正式】〔做某事〕倒也无妨〔用于表示做不大想做的事〕: *I suppose we may as well get started.* 我想我们不妨开始吧。**b)** used to mean that another course of action would have an equally good result 倒不如…, 还是…较好〔用于表示另一个行动也可能产生相同的好结果〕: *The taxi was so slow, we might just as well have gone on the bus.* 出租车开得那么慢, 我们还不如乘公共汽车呢。

9 ►EMPHASIZING STH 强调某事◄ **a) well before/behind/down etc** a long way or a long time before, behind etc 〔很长一段时间或路程〕以前/以后等: *It was well after 12 o'clock when they arrived.* 12点过了好一阵子他们才到。| *Stand well back from the bonfire.* 站得离篝火远远的。**b) well pleased/well aware etc** very pleased etc 非常满意/充分了解等: *I'm well aware of the problems involved.* 我充分了解所涉及的问题。| *Pardoe was well pleased with his day's work.* 帕多对自己一天

的工作感到很满意。| **well worth (doing) sth** *The amphitheatre is well worth a visit.* 圆形露天竞技场很值得一看。**c)** [+adj] *BrE spoken* used to emphasize an adjective that describes how someone feels or what sort of situation they are in【英口】相当，很〔强调某人感情或所处形势的形容词〕: *Our boss came out of the meeting looking well fed-up.* 我们老板带着很厌倦的表情走出会场。**d) well and truly** completely 完全地: *I went out and got well and truly drunk.* 我到外面喝得酩酊大醉。

10 know full well to know or realize something very well〔对某事〕十分了解: *You know full well what I mean.* 你完全清楚我的意思。

11 speak/think well of to talk about someone in an approving way or to have a favourable opinion of them 称赞〔某人〕/重视〔某人〕: *Sue has always spoken well of you.* 休经常称赞你。

12 well done!/well played! used to praise someone when you think they have done something very well 干得好！真棒！〔用于赞扬某人做事做得好〕

13 be well in with *informal* to have a friendly relationship with someone, especially someone important【非正式】〔尤指同要人〕关系密切: *Paul's well in with the boss these days.* 保罗这段日子跟老板很要好。

14 be well out of *BrE spoken* to be lucky to no longer be involved in a particular situation【英口】幸而不受牵连; 幸而摆脱了: *She's well out of that marriage, her husband was a brute!* 她的婚姻幸好结束了，她丈夫是个恶棍！

15 be well up in/on *informal especially BrE* to know a lot about a particular subject【非正式，尤英】对〔某个科目〕非常熟悉: *Geoff's well up on the latest technological developments.* 杰夫对最新的科技发展了如指掌。

16 as well sb might/may used to say that there is a good reason for someone's feelings or reactions〔某人〕原该如此〔用于表示某人的感受或行为有充分的理由〕: *Marilyn looked guilty when she saw me, as well she might.* 玛丽莲见到我时显得感到内疚——本该如此。

17 do well by *informal* to treat someone generously【非正式】慷慨对待〔某人〕

well² *interjection*

1 ►EMPHASIZING STH 强调某事◄ used before a statement or question to emphasize it 好，嗯〔用在陈述或问题之前以示强调〕: *Well, I think it's a good idea, I don't care what anyone else says.* 好，我觉得这是一个好主意，我不在乎别人说什么。| *Well, all I can say is it's a bloody waste of taxpayer's money!* 是啊，我只能说，这是对纳税人的钱的极大浪费！| **well then** *"James doesn't want to come to the cinema with us." "Well then, let's go on our own."* "詹姆斯不想和我们一起去看电影。" "那么我们就自己去吧。"

2 ►PAUSING 停顿◄ used to pause or give yourself time to think before saying something 唔，噢〔用于停顿片刻或使自己在说某事前有时间考虑〕: *Mary's been a bit depressed and, well, I was worried she might do something stupid.* 玛丽有点沮丧，哦，我担心她也许会干什么傻事。| *Well, let's see now, I could book you in for an appointment next Thursday.* 嗯，我们看一下，我能给你预约在下星期四。| **well I mean** *Well, I mean the whole idea just sounds crazy to me.* 唉，我是说整个想法听起来真是不可思议。

3 ►ACCEPTING A SITUATION 接受某种局面◄ also 又作 **oh well** used to show that you accept a situation even though you feel disappointed or annoyed about it 好吧; 算了〔对不愉快的事表示接受〕: *Well, I did my best, I can't do any more than that.* 算了，我已经尽力，不能做得比这更好了。| *Oh well, we'll just have to cancel the holiday I suppose.* 唉，算了，我想我们不得不取消这次休假。

4 ►SHOWING SURPRISE 表示惊讶◄ also 又作 **well, well (,well)** used to express surprise or amusement 哎呀，哟〔表示惊讶或兴趣〕: *Well, so Steve's a senior manager now is he?* 哟，这么说史蒂夫现在是高级经理了？| *Well, well, well, I didn't think I'd see you here Sue.* 哎呀，哎呀，我没有想到在这里见到你，休。

5 ►SHOWING ANGER 表示生气◄ used to express anger or disapproval 嗯，嗳〔表示生气或不同意〕: *Well, you'd think at least she might have phoned to say she wasn't coming!* 嗯，本以为她至少会打电话来说她不来了！| **well honestly/well really** *"They were playing music next door until 4 a.m." "Well honestly, you'd think they'd show a bit more consideration."* "隔壁邻居播放音乐到凌晨4点。" "说实在的，本以为他们会顾及一下别人。"

6 ►FINAL REMARK 结束语◄ used to show that you are about to finish speaking or stop doing an activity 好了，好啦〔表示结束发言或停止做某事〕: *Well, that's all for today, I'll see you all tomorrow.* 好啦，今天就到此为止，我们明天见。

7 ►EXPRESSING DOUBT 表示怀疑◄ used to express doubt or the fact that you are not sure about something 哦〔表示怀疑或对某事并无把握〕: *"I reckon Mike Whelan is worth a place in the England side." "Well, he's not a very consistent player, is he?"* "我认为迈克·惠兰应该入选英格兰队。" "哦，他的状态不大稳定，对不？"

8 ►AGREEING 同意◄ **very well** used to show that you agree with or accept a suggestion, invitation etc 好吧〔表示同意或接受提议、邀请等〕: *"I think plain wallpaper would look better in this room." "Very well then, if you insist."* "我觉得这房间用素净的壁纸较好。" "好吧，如果你坚持的话。"

9 ►CONTINUING A STORY 接续故事◄ used to connect two parts of a story that you are telling people especially in order to make it seem more interesting 对了，于是〔用以接续所说的两部分，尤为使故事更有趣〕: *You know that couple I was telling you about the other day? Well, the police came round and arrested them both!* 你知道那天我告诉你的那对夫妻吗？对了，警察来过并把他俩都抓走了！

10 ►DEMANDING AN EXPLANATION 要求解释◄ **Well?** used to demand an explanation or answer when you are angry with someone 是吗？〔生某人气时，要求对方解释或回答〕: *Mrs Hawkins says she saw you hanging around the town centre with some of your mates last night. Well?* 霍金斯太太说她昨晚看见你和几个朋友在镇中心溜达，是不是呢？

Frequencies of the word **well** in spoken and written English
单词 well 在英语口语和书面语中的使用频率

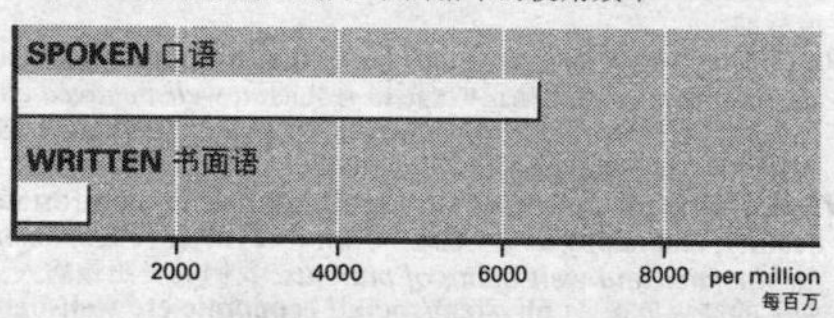

Based on the British National Corpus and the Longman Lancaster Corpus
据英国国家语料库和朗文兰开斯特语料库

This graph shows that **well** is much more common in spoken English than in written English. This is because it has several uses as an interjection in spoken English and is used in a lot of common spoken phrases. 本图表显示，单词well在英语口语中的使用频率远远高于书面语，因为作为感叹词，well在口语中有几种用法，并且口语中很多常用短语是由well构成的。

well³ *adj comparative* 比较级 **better** /ˈbetə; ˈbetə/ *superlative* 最高级 **best** /best; best/ **1** healthy 健康的: *"How are you?" "Very well thanks."* "你身体怎样？" "很好，多谢关心。"| **look/feel well** *You're looking well, the vacation obviously did you good.* 你看来气色不错，很明显，休假对你大有益处。| **get well soon** (=used to say that you hope someone soon feels better) 祝你早日恢复健康 **2 it is just as well (that)** *spoken* used to say that things have happened in a way that is fortunate or desirable【口】正好，幸好: *It's just as well I couldn't go to the funeral, I think I'd have found it too upsetting.* 幸好我不能去参加葬礼，我觉得葬礼太令人沮丧了。**3 it's/that's all very well but...** *spoken* used to say that you think something is not really satisfactory or acceptable, even if someone else thinks it is【口】…是好的，可是…〔表示对某事不真正满意或接受〕: *"They said Maria should go to bed and rest." "That's all very well but who's going to look after the children?"* "他们说玛丽亚应上床休息。" "好倒是好，可是谁去照料孩子呢？" **4 it might be as well** *spoken* used to give someone advice or make a helpful suggestion【口】最好…〔给某人劝告或提出有用的意见〕: *It might be as well to leave him on his own for a few hours.* 最好让他独自待上几个钟头。**5 that's/it's all well and good** *spoken especially BrE* used to say that you accept or approve of one part of a situation or thing but not of another part【口，尤英】固然好〔表示对某情况或事情部分接受或同意〕: *Going off on foreign holidays is all well and good but you've got to get back to reality sometime.* 到国外度假固然好，但日后你必须回到现实中来。**6 all is well/all is not well** *formal* used to say that a situation is satisfactory or not satisfactory【正式】〔情况〕令人满意/不满意: *All is not well with their marriage.* 他们的婚姻不美满。**7 all's well that ends well** used after a situation has ended in a satisfactory way 结果好就一切都好〔用于表示情况有令人满意的结果〕 **8** [not before noun 不用于名词前] *literary* happy and comfortable【文】满意的；舒服的: *We're very well where we are thank you.* 我们待的地方很不错，谢谢。

W

well⁴ *n* [C] **1** a deep hole in the ground from which people take water 井: *She lowered her bucket into the well.* 她把水桶放到井里。| **sink a well** (=dig a well) 掘井 **2** an OIL WELL 油井 **3** an enclosed space in a building which goes straight up and down and surrounds a lift, stairs etc〔建筑物中的〕电梯井道; 楼梯井 —see also 另见 STAIRWELL **4** *BrE* the space in front of a judge in a court of law【英】〔法庭中位于法官前面的〕律师席

well⁵ *v* also 又作 **well up** [I] *especially literary*【尤文】**1** if liquids well or well up, they start to flow〔液体〕涌溢, 开始流淌: *I felt tears well up in my eyes.* 我意识到泪水夺眶而出。**2** if feelings well or well up, they start to get stronger〔情绪〕变得强烈: *Anger welled up within him.* 他怒火中烧。

well-ad·just·ed /ˌ· ·ˈ··◂/ *adj* emotionally healthy and able to deal well with the problems of life 能适应环境的, 性格健全的

well-ad·vised /ˌ· ·ˈ·◂/ *adj* **you would be well-advised to do sth** used when you are strongly advising someone to do something that will help them avoid trouble 你应该做某事〔用于强烈忠告某人做某事, 以避免麻烦〕: *You would be well-advised to accept this settlement rather than go to court.* 你应该接受这种解决办法而不是对簿公堂。

well-ap·point·ed /ˌ· ·ˈ··◂/ *adj formal* a well-appointed house, hotel etc has very good furniture and equipment【正式】〔房屋、旅馆等〕设备完善的; 陈设齐全的

well-bal·anced /ˌ·ˈ··◂/ *adj* **1** a well-balanced meal or DIET¹ (1) contains all the things you need to keep you healthy〔饮食〕营养均衡的 **2** a well-balanced person is sensible and is not controlled by strong emotions; STABLE¹ (2)〔人〕理智的; 头脑清醒的

well-be·haved /ˌ· ·ˈ·◂/ *adj* behaving in a polite or socially acceptable way 行为端正的; 彬彬有礼的: *a well-behaved child* 行为端正的孩子 | *The crowd was noisy but well-behaved.* 这群人吵吵闹闹, 但行为还算规矩。

well-be·ing /ˌ·ˈ··/ *n* [U] a feeling of being comfortable, healthy, and happy 舒适; 健康; 幸福: [+of] *We are responsible for the care and well-being of patients.* 我们负责照顾病人, 为病人的健康负责。| **physical/social/ economic etc well-being** *the economic well-being of the country* 该国的经济繁荣 | **a sense of well-being** (=a feeling of being satisfied with your life) 生活幸福感

well-born /ˌ·ˈ·◂/ *adj formal* born into a rich or UPPER CLASS family【正式】出身优裕的; 出身高贵的

well-bred /ˌ·ˈ·◂/ *adj old-fashioned* very polite, behaving or speaking as if you come from a family of high social class【过时】有修养的, 有教养的: *the epitome of a well-bred Englishwoman who never shows her feelings* 感情含蓄、教养良好的英国淑女的典范

well-brought-up /ˌ· ·ˈ·◂/ *adj* a child who is well-brought-up has been taught to be polite and to behave well〔儿童〕从小受良好教育的

well-built /ˌ·ˈ·◂/ *adj* someone who is well-built is big and strong 体格健壮的, 结实的

well-cho·sen /ˌ·ˈ··◂/ *adj* carefully chosen 精心挑选的: **well-chosen words** (=suitable for a particular situation) 恰如其分的话语

well-con·nect·ed /ˌ· ·ˈ··◂/ *adj* knowing or being related to powerful and socially important people 与显贵人物有关系的, 和有社会地位的人有来往的

well-dis·posed /ˌ· ·ˈ·◂/ *adj* feeling friendly towards a person or positive about an idea or plan〔对人〕亲切的;〔对想法或计划〕表示赞同的: [+to/towards] *The management is not well-disposed towards technical innovation.* 资方对技术革新不予支持。

well-doc·u·ment·ed /ˌwɛl ˈdɑkjəmɛntɪd; ˌwelˈdɒkjʊmentɪ̣d/ *adj* well-documented events, behaviour etc definitely exist and people have written a lot about them〔确实存在的事件、行为等〕被大量记述的: *the well-documented problems faced by prisoners' families* 犯人家庭面对的被详细记录下来的问题

well-done /ˌ·ˈ·◂/ *adj* food that is well-done, especially meat, has been cooked thoroughly〔尤指肉〕熟透的, 煮透的 —compare 比较 RARE (2) —see also 另见 **well done!** (WELL¹ (12))

well-dressed /ˌ·ˈ·◂/ *adj* wearing attractive, fashionable, and usually expensive clothes 衣着考究的, 穿着入时的

well-earned /ˌ·ˈ·◂/ *adj* something that is well-earned is something you deserve because you have worked hard 应得的: *It's time for a well-earned rest.* 到应该有的休息时间了。

well-en·dowed /ˌ· ·ˈ·◂/ *adj informal or humorous*【非正式或幽默】**1** a woman who is well-endowed has large breasts〔妇女〕乳房大的 **2** a man who is well-endowed has a large PENIS (=sex organ)〔男人〕生殖器大的

Weller /ˈwɛlɚ; ˈwelə/, **Sam** a character in *The Pickwick Papers* by Charles Dickens. Sam is Mr Pickwick's servant, and when Mr Pickwick is sent to prison, Sam goes with him to look after him. 韦勒〔狄更斯小说《匹克威克外传》中一人物。萨姆·韦勒是匹克威克先生的侍从, 主人入狱期间, 他随侍左右〕

Welles /wɛlz; welz/, **Or·son** /ˈɔrsn̩; ˈɔːsən/ (1915-85) a US actor, film director, producer, and writer, famous especially for the film *Citizen Kane* (1941), which many people consider to be one of the greatest films ever made, and for his radio play *The War of the Worlds*, which in 1938 made thousands of people in the US believe that the Earth was really being attacked by creatures from Mars. Other films include *The Magnificent Ambersons* (1942) and *The Third Man* (1949). 韦尔斯〔(1915-1985), 美国演员、电影导演、制片人、作家, 尤以《公民凯恩》(1941) 一片闻名。该片被许多人认为是有史以来最出色的影片之一。他制作的广播剧《世界大战》1938 年播出时, 成千上万的美国人误以为地球真遭到了火星人攻击。其他影片有《安培逊大族》(1942) 和《第三者》(1949) 等〕

well-es·tab·lished /ˌ· ·ˈ··◂/ *adj* established for a long time and respected 久久享有盛誉的; 久负盛名的: *a well-established law firm* 久负盛名的律师事务所

well-fa·voured /ˌ·ˈ··◂/ *adj old-fashioned* good-looking【过时】好看的, 漂亮的 —compare 比较 ILL-FAVOURED

well-fed /ˌ·ˈ·◂/ *adj* regularly eating plenty of good healthy food, especially if this has made you a little fat 吃得好的; 胖胖的

well-found·ed /ˌ·ˈ··◂/ *adj* a belief, feeling etc that is well-founded is based on facts or good judgment〔信仰、感觉等〕有事实根据的; 基于准确判断的

well-groomed /ˌ·ˈ·◂/ *adj* having a very neat, clean appearance 穿戴整洁的: *a well-groomed businesswoman* 穿着整洁的女商人

well-ground·ed /ˌ·ˈ··◂/ *adj* **1 well-grounded in** fully trained in an activity or skill〔行动或技巧〕训练有素的: *The soldiers were well-grounded in survival skills.* 士兵们的求生技能熟练。**2** WELL-FOUNDED 有充分根据的: *well-grounded suspicions* 有凭有据的怀疑

well-heeled /ˌ·ˈ·◂/ *adj informal* rich and usually of a high social class【非正式】富裕的; 有社会地位的

well-hung /ˌ·ˈ·◂/ *adj informal or humorous* a man who is well-hung has a large PENIS (=sex organ)【非正式或幽默】〔男人〕阴茎很大的

wel·lie /ˈwɛlɪ; ˈweli/ *n* [C] *BrE informal* a wellington【英, 非正式】防水橡胶靴 —see also 另见 WELLY

well-in·formed /ˌ· ·ˈ·◂/ *adj* knowing a lot about a particular subject or about many subjects〔对某一问题〕非常熟悉的;〔在数门学科上〕知识渊博的: [+about] *They seemed to be remarkably well-informed about the royal family.* 他们似乎对皇室家庭的事情知之甚多。

Wel·ling·ton /ˈwɛlɪŋtən; ˈwelɪŋtən/ the capital city of New Zealand, on the North Island, the country's second-largest city and an important port. 惠灵顿〔新西兰首都, 位于北岛, 是该国第二大城市和主要港口〕

wellington also 又作 **wellington boot** /ˌ···ˈ·/ *n* [C] *BrE* a long rubber boot that stops your feet getting wet; RUBBER BOOT【英】长统橡胶雨靴, 防水橡胶靴 —see picture at 参见 BOOT¹ 图

Wellington, Duke of —see 见 the DUKE OF WELLINGTON

well-in·ten·tioned /ˌ· ·ˈ··◂/ *adj* trying to be helpful, but failing or actually making things worse 出于好心的〔但结果却不好〕: *well-intentioned grandparents who interfere between parents and children* 一片好心、在父母和孩子之间瞎掺和的祖父母

well-kept /ˌ·ˈ·◂/ *adj* **1** a well-kept building or garden is very well cared for and looks neat and clean〔建筑物或花园〕悉心照管的 **2** a well-kept secret is known only to a few people〔秘密〕严守的

well-known /ˌ·ˈ·◂/ *adj* known by a lot of people 众所周知的: *It's a well-known fact that smoking can cause lung cancer.* 众所周知, 抽烟会引起肺癌。| *This is probably their best-known song.* 这可能是他们最著名的歌曲。| [+for] *Mother Teresa is well-known for her work with the poor.* 特雷莎修女因为帮助穷人而闻名。—see 见 FAMOUS (USAGE)

well-man·nered /ˌ·ˈ··◂/ *adj* polite and having very good manners (MANNER (3)) 有礼貌的; 行为端正的: *the perfect well-mannered host* 完美无瑕、彬彬有礼的主人 —opposite 反义词 ILL-MANNERED

well-mean·ing /ˌ·ˈ··◂/ *adj* intending or intended to be helpful, but not succeeding 本意良好的, 好心好意的〔但不成功〕: *a well-meaning but misguided attempt to reconcile the couple*

出于好意想使夫妻言归于好但不明智的做法 —see also 另见 **he/she means well**(MEAN[1] (16))

well-meant/ˌ· ˈ·◂/ *adj* something you say or do that is well-meant is intended to be helpful, but does not have the result you intended〔说话或行动〕出于好意的〔但结果并不如意〕: *His comments were well-meant but a little tactless.* 他那番话是出于好意, 但有点儿直率了。—see also 另见 **he/she means well**(MEAN[1] (16))

well·ness /ˈwɛlnɪs; ˈwelnɨs/ *n* [U] *AmE* the state of being healthy【美】健康: *a wellness program to promote a healthy lifestyle* 提倡健康生活方式的健康计划

well-nigh/ˈ· ·/ *adv BrE formal or AmE* almost, but not quite【英, 正式或美】几乎, 近乎: *The company has existed for well-nigh 200 years.* 公司成立近 200 年了。| **well-nigh impossible** *Getting them to agree would be well-nigh impossible.* 使他们同意几乎不可能。

well-off/ˌ· ˈ·◂/ *adj comparative* 比较级 **better-off** *superlative* 最高级 **best-off** **1** having more money than many other people, or enough money to have a good standard of living 有钱的; 境遇好的: *The government claims that people are better off than they were five years ago.* 政府声称人民的生活比五年前改善了。**2** **well-off for** having plenty of something, or as much of it as you need〔某物〕充裕的, 有许多的: *We're well-off for supermarkets in this area.* 我们这个地区有许多超级市场。**3** **you don't know when you're well-off** *spoken* used to tell someone that they are more fortunate than they realize【口】你身在福中不知福 —opposite 反义词 BADLY-OFF

Well of Loneliness, The /ˌ· ·ˈ· ·· ·/ a NOVEL by British writer Radclyffe Hall about a LESBIAN relationship. It upset many people when it was published in 1928, and selling it was illegal for about 20 years.《孤独之井》〔英国作家拉德克利夫·霍尔的一部小说, 1928 年出版。其女同性恋题材遭到许多人反感, 销售遭禁约 20 年〕

well-oiled/ˌ· ˈ·◂/ *adj* **1** **a well-oiled machine** an organization or system that works very well〔机构或系统〕运作正常的 **2** *informal* drunk【非正式】喝醉的

well-paid/ˌ· ˈ·◂/ *adj* providing or receiving good wages 薪金优厚的, 高薪的: *a well-paid job* 高薪工作 | *well-paid managers* 薪金丰厚的经理

well-pre·served/ˌ· ·ˈ·◂/ *adj humorous* someone who is well-preserved still looks fairly young although they are getting old【幽默】〔人〕身体保养得好的; 不见老的

well-read/ˈwɛlˋrɛd; ˌwel ˈred◂/ *adj* having read many books and knowing a lot about different subjects 博览群书的; 知识渊博的

well-round·ed/ˌ· ˈ··◂/ *adj* **1** someone who is well-rounded has had a wide variety of experiences in life 生活阅历丰富的 **2** well-rounded education or experience of life is complete and varied〔教育或生活经验〕全面的, 多方面的: *She has a well-rounded background in management.* 她在管理方面有丰富的经验。**3** a woman who is well-rounded has a pleasantly curved figure; SHAPELY〔妇女的体型〕匀称的; 丰满的

Wells /wɛlz; welz/, **H.G.** (1866-1946) a British writer of NOVELS and political essays. His best-known works are his science FICTION novels such as *The Time Machine* and *The War of the Worlds.* 威尔斯〔(1866-1946), 英国小说家、政论家, 尤以科幻小说著称于世。代表作有《时间机器》和《世界大战》等〕

well-spok·en/ˌ· ˈ··◂/ *adj* speaking in a clear and polite way, and with an ACCENT (=way of pronouncing words) that is socially approved of 谈吐文雅的; 字正腔圆的

well-spring/ˈwɛlˌsprɪŋ; ˈwelˌsprɪŋ/ *n* [C +of] *literary* a never-ending supply of a personal quality【文】〔人的品性〕源源不断的供应, 源泉: *There was a wellspring of courage within her which she could continually draw upon.* 在她身上有不竭的勇气, 她能不断地从中汲取力量。

well-stacked /ˌ· ˈ·◂/ *adj informal or humorous* a woman who is well-stacked has very large breasts【非正式或幽默】乳房丰满的

well-stocked/ˌ· ˈ·◂/ *adj* having a large supply and variety of things 备货充足的; 贮货丰富的: *a well-stocked pantry* 备货充足的食品储藏室

well-thought-of/ˌ· ˈ· ·◂/ *adj* liked and admired by other people 受人喜欢的; 受人尊敬的: *Her work is well-thought-of in academic circles.* 她的工作在学术界受到普遍好评。

well-thought-out/ˌ· ˈ· ·◂/ *adj* carefully and thoroughly planned 缜密计划的; 精心设计的: *a well-thought-out strategy* 深思熟虑的策略

well-thumbed/ˌ· ˈ·◂/ *adj* a well-thumbed book, magazine etc has been used a lot〔书籍、杂志等〕翻旧了的, 常用的

well-timed/ˌ· ˈ·◂/ *adj* said or done at the most suitable moment 时机合适的; 及时的: *My arrival wasn't very well-timed.* 我来得不太是时候。

well-to-do/ˌ· · ˈ·◂/ *adj* **1** rich and with a high social position 富有的; 有地位的: *well-to-do families* 有钱人家 **2** **the well-to-do** people who are rich 富人

well-tried/ˌ· ˈ·◂/ *adj* **well-tried method/principle etc** a method or principle that has been used many times before and has always been successful 经反复验证、行之有效的方法/原理等

well-turned/ˌ· ˈ·◂/ *adj* a well-turned phrase or sentence is carefully expressed〔短语或句子〕措辞巧妙的

well-turned-out/ˌ· · ˈ·◂/ *adj* someone who is well-turned-out wears fashionable clothes and looks attractive 穿着入时的

well-versed/ˌ· ˈ·◂/ *adj* knowing a lot about something 精通的; 熟知的: [+in/on] *well-versed in matters of national security* 精通国家安全事务

well-wish·er /ˈ· ˌ· ·/ *n* [C] someone who does something to show that they admire someone and want them to succeed, be healthy etc 表示良好祝愿的人, 祝福者: *many messages of support from well-wishers* 来自祝福者表示支持的众多贺辞

well-wom·an/ˌ· ˈ· ·/ *adj* [only before noun 仅用于名词前] providing medical care and advice for women, to make sure that they stay healthy 妇女保健的: *a well-woman clinic* 妇女保健诊所

well-worn /ˌ· ˈ·◂/ *adj* **1** worn or used for a long time 穿旧了的; 使用了长时间的: *a well-worn jacket* 穿旧了的外衣 **2** a well-wom argument, phrase etc has been repeated so often that it is no longer interesting or effective〔理由、习语等〕陈腐的: *well-worn excuses* 陈腐的借口

wel·ly /ˈwɛlɪ; ˈweli/ *n* [C] *BrE infomal*【英, 非正式】**1** a WELLINGTON (=kind of boot) 防水橡胶靴 **2** **give it some welly!** *spoken* used to tell someone to put more effort into something they are doing【口】加油!努力干!

Welsh/wɛlʃ; welʃ/ *n* **1** [U] the original language of Wales 威尔士语 **2** **the Welsh** people from Wales 威尔士人 —**Welsh** *adj*

welsh, welch/wɛlʃ; welʃ/ *v* [I +on] *informal*【非正式】**1** to avoid paying money or your debts 赖账; 躲债 **2** to not do something you have promised to do for someone〔对某人〕食言: *He gave us his solemn word and then he welshed on us.* 他对我们信誓旦旦, 然后却反悔。

> **USAGE NOTE 用法说明: WELSH**
> POLITENESS 礼节
> Some Welsh people consider this verb to be offensive . 某些威尔士人认为这个动词具有冒犯性。

Welsh Assembly, the/ˌ· ˈ· · ·/ parliament for Wales which was established in 1999 and has the power to make laws in Wales. The leader of the parliament is the First Secretary, and its 60 members are called AMs – Assembly Members. They are elected by a system of PROPORTIONAL representation. 威尔士国民议会〔威尔士议会, 成立于 1999 年, 为威尔士立法机构。议会领导人称为首席大臣, 其 60 名成员按比例代表制选举产生, 称为 AM (议员)〕

Welsh dres·ser/ˌ· ˈ· ·/ *n* [C] *BrE* a piece of wooden furniture consisting of drawers and cupboards in the lower part and shelves on top【英】〔下部为抽屉和碗橱、上部为搁板的〕威尔士式餐具柜; HUTCH (2) *AmE*【美】

Welsh Na·tion·al·ist Par·ty, the —see 见 PLAID CYMRU

Welsh Of·fice, the/ˈ· · ·/ the British government department responsible for carrying out the government's policies (POLICY) in Wales. It is led by the **Secretary of State for Wales** who is a member of the British CABINET. 威尔士事务部〔英国一政府部门, 执行政府对威尔士的各项政策, 由英国内阁成员威尔士事务大臣负责〕

Welsh rare·bit/ˌwɛlʃ ˋrɛrbɪt; ˌwelʃ ˈreəbɪt/ also 又作 **Welsh rabbit**/ˌ· ˈ· ·/ *n* [C,U] a dish of cheese melted on bread 威尔士干酪烤面包

welt/wɛlt; welt/ *n* [C] **1** a raised mark on someone's skin where they have been hit〔被打后的〕肿块; 伤痕 **2** a piece of leather around the edge of a shoe, to which the top and bottom of the shoe are stitched〔鞋面和鞋底间的〕沿条, 贴边

wel·ter /ˈwɛltɚ; ˈweltə/ *n* **a welter of** a large and confusing number of different details, emotions etc〔细节〕杂乱无章;〔思绪〕起伏: *The researchers were inundated with a welter of information.* 研究人员陷入一大堆杂乱无章的资料之中。

W

wel·ter·weight /ˈwɛltɚ,wet; ˈweltəweɪt/ *n* [C] a BOXER (1) who is heavier than a LIGHTWEIGHT[1] (2) but lighter than a MIDDLEWEIGHT 次中量级拳击手

wench /wɛntʃ; wentʃ/ *n* [C] *old use or humorous* a girl or young woman, especially a servant【旧或幽默】姑娘，少妇〔尤指女仆〕

wend /wɛnd; wend/ *v* **wend your way** *especially literary* to move or travel slowly from one place to another【尤文】缓慢地走[移动]: *The procession wended its way through the streets.* 队伍缓缓地走过了街道。

Wen·dy /ˈwɛndɪ; ˈwendi/ one of the children visited by **Peter Pan** in the children's story *Peter Pan* by J.M. Barrie. The name Wendy was invented by Barrie. 温迪〔J.M.巴里的童话故事《彼得·潘》中彼得·潘拜访过的孩子之一。温迪这个名字是巴里杜撰的〕

wen·dy house /ˈwɛndɪ ˌhaʊs; ˈwendi ˌhaʊs/ *n* [C] *BrE* a small house for children to play in【英】儿童游戏屋; PLAY HOUSE *AmE*【美】

Wens·ley·dale /ˈwɛnzlɪdel; ˈwenzlideɪl/ *n* [U] a white cheese that does not have a very strong taste, originally from Yorkshire 文斯利代尔干酪〔原产约克郡，味道不是很浓〕

went /wɛnt; went/ the past tense of GO

We Plough the Fields and Scat·ter /ˌ· ˈ· ˌ· · ˈ··/ a hymn (=a song of praise to God) sung in the UK at harvest festivals.《我们耕田、撒种》〔英国一首在收获节吟唱的赞美诗〕It begins 开首为:

We plough the fields and scatter
The good seed on the land,
But it is fed and watered
By God's almighty hand ...
我们耕地播种，
良种撒于田间，
施肥浇水仰仗，
我主万能之手…

wept /wɛpt; wept/ the past tense and past participle of WEEP

we're /wɪr; wɪə/ the short form of 缩略式= we are

were /wɚ; wə; *strong* 重读 wɜ; wɜː/ *negative short form* 否定缩略式为 **weren't** /wɜnt; wɜːnt/ the past tense of BE

were·wolf /ˈwɪrˌwʊlf; ˈweəwʊlf/ *n* [C] a person who, in some stories, sometimes changes into a WOLF〔故事中的〕狼人，会变成狼的人

wert /wɜt; wɜːt/ *v* **thou wert** *old use* you were【旧】你是

We Shall O·ver·come /ˌ· ˈ· ˌ··ˈ·/ a protest song written in 1960 by Pete Seeger to an old traditional tune, which was especially popular during the civil rights movement in the US, when it was often sung by large crowds at meetings and on protest marches. It is still sung by groups of people who are fighting against unfair laws or unfair governments.《我们必将胜利》〔20世纪60年代由皮特·西格创作的一首抗议歌曲。歌曲采用一支传统老调，在美国民权运动时期非常流行，集会和抗议游行时常由大批群众高唱。现在，人们在抗议不公正法律或政府不公平行为时仍然高唱这首歌曲〕

Wes·ley /ˈwɛzlɪ; ˈwezli/, **John** (1703-91) an English religious leader who started a new type of Christianity called Methodism. He travelled around the country speaking to large numbers of people, and held his meetings outside rather than in churches. 卫斯理〔(1703-1791)，英国宗教领袖。他曾创立了一基督教派，名为循道公会，周游全国进行演说，在教堂之外的场所举行布道会〕

Wes·ley·an /ˈwɛzlɪən; ˈwezliən/ also 又作 **Methodist** *n* [C] a member of the Christian group established by John Wesley〔基督教〕循道公会教徒，卫斯理教派教徒 —**Wesleyan** *adj*: *a Wesleyan chapel* 卫斯理教派的小礼拜堂

Wes·sex /ˈwɛsɪks; ˈwesɪks/ an ancient Anglo-Saxon kingdom in the south and southwest of England, which continued until England became united in the 9th century. The writer Thomas Hardy used the name Wessex in his NOVEL*s* to mean the southwestern counties (COUNTY) of England, especially Dorset. 韦塞克斯〔古盎格鲁一撒克逊一王国。位于英格兰南部和西南部，9世纪英格兰统一后解体。托马斯·哈代在他的小说中用韦塞克斯一名指称英格兰的西南部各郡，尤指多塞特郡〕

West /wɛst; west/ *n* **the West 1** the western part of the world and the people that live there, especially Western Europe and North America 西方世界〔尤指西欧和北美〕**2** the western part of the US〔美国〕西部地区 —compare 比较 MIDWEST, WEST COAST

west[1] *n* [singular, U] **1** the direction towards which the sun goes down, and which is on the left of someone who is facing north 西，西面: **from/towards the west** *A strong wind was blowing from the west.* 一阵强风从西边吹来。| **to the west of** *Birmingham is to the west of Leicester.* 伯明翰位于莱斯特的西面。**2 the west** the western part of a country or area〔某国或地区的〕西部

west[2] *adj* [only before noun 仅用于名词前] **1** in the west or facing the west 在西方的; 朝西的: *the west door of the church* 教堂的西门 | *West Africa* 西非 **2** a west wind comes from the west〔风〕来自西面的

west[3] *adv* **1** towards the west 朝西，向西: *The room faces west.* 这房间朝西。**2 go west** *BrE old-fashioned humorous*【英，过时，幽默】**a)** to die 死，归西 **b)** to be damaged or ruined 坏了，完蛋了

West, the /wɛst; west/ **1** the western part of the world and the people that live there, especially Western Europe and North America 西方〔尤指西欧和北美〕**2** the western part of the US 美国西部

West, Mae /me; meɪ/ (1892-1980) a US film actress, famous for being sexually attractive, whose films include *She Done Him Wrong* (1933) and *I'm No Angel* (1933) 韦斯特〔(1892-1980)，美国电影演员，以性感迷人著称，出演过《侬本多情》(1933)和《我不是天使》(1933)等影片〕

West Bank, the /ˌ· ˈ·/ the land west of the Jordan River and the Dead Sea between Israel and Jordan, which the Israelis took control of in 1967 in the Arab-Israeli War, but which the Palestinian Arabs consider to be their land. Following the peace agreement of 1993, Israel began to remove its army from the West Bank. 约旦河西岸〔位于以色列和约旦之间、约旦河和死海以西的地区。1967年在阿以战争中被以色列人占领，但巴勒斯坦的阿拉伯人则认为该地区是他们的领土。1993年随着和平协议的签订，以色列人开始从约旦河西岸撤军〕

west·bound /ˈwɛstˌbaʊnd; ˈwestbaʊnd/ *adj* travelling or leading towards the west 向西行的

West Coast, the /ˌ· ˈ·/ *n* the western coastal states of the US〔美国〕西海岸

> **CULTURAL NOTE 文化注释**
>
> There are a lot of beaches, forests, and cliffs on the West Coast, and many people who live there are involved in outdoor sports, especially in California where the weather is often warm and sunny. The STEREOTYPE of people from the West Coast is that they do not accept traditional ideas and beliefs, because they prefer to develop their own opinions about religion, morals, and social behaviour. They also tend to wear comfortable, informal clothes such as SHORTS and T-SHIRT*s*. Another stereotype is that many people on the West Coast are concerned about nature and protecting the environment, and are known for eating HEALTH FOOD*s*, exercising a lot, and complaining about people who smoke. 美国西海岸有很多海滩、森林和悬崖峭壁。那里的很多人喜欢户外运动，特别是在气候温暖、阳光明媚的加利福尼亚州更是如此。西海岸人的典型形象是不接受传统的思想观念，对宗教、道德观和社会行为准则他们更愿意奉行自己的想法。他们往往穿舒适、随便的服装，如短裤、T恤衫之类。西海岸人给人的另外一个典型印象是，关注自然和保护环境，并且以吃健康食品、喜爱运动、抱怨别人吸烟而广为人知。

West Coun·try, the /ˈ· ˌ·· ·/ *n* the southwest part of England〔英格兰的〕西南部

West End, the /ˌ· ˈ·◂/ *n* the western part of central London where there are large shops, theatres, expensive hotels etc〔大商店、剧院、高级旅馆等集中的〕伦敦西区

west·er·ly /ˈwɛstəlɪ; ˈwestəli/ *adj* **1** towards or in the west 向西方的; 在西方的: *We set off in a westerly direction.* 我们出发往西去。**2** a westerly wind comes from the west〔风〕从西边吹来的

west·ern[1], Western /ˈwɛstɚn; ˈwestən/ *adj* from or connected with the west part of the world or of a country〔世界〕西方的;〔国家〕西部的: *The Russian ballet is making a tour of Western Europe.* 俄罗斯芭蕾舞团正在西欧巡回演出。

western[2] *n* [C] a film about life in the 19th century in the American West〔描写19世纪美国西部生活的〕西部电影

> **CULTURAL NOTE 文化注释**
>
> Western films often include GUNFIGHT*s* between good COWBOY*s* or SHERIFF*s* and bad cowboys who rob people, trains, or banks, and who CHEAT when playing cards and drink too much alcohol. The good cowboys often wear white hats, and the bad cowboys wear black hats. At the end of the film, the good cowboys win, making the town safe again. Most western films are not based on the facts of

what living in the American west was like. Instead, they show things in the way people imagine they were. 西部电影中常常有枪战场景, 交战的一方是好牛仔或城镇治安官; 另一方是那些抢劫他人、火车或银行的坏牛仔, 他们酒气熏天, 玩牌时使诈。好牛仔戴白帽子, 而坏牛仔戴黑帽子。在影片的结尾, 好牛仔赢了, 使城镇又恢复了安宁。大多数西部影片并不是取材于美国西部的真实生活, 相反, 它们展示的不过是人们想象中的西部景象。

Western Aus·tra·li·a /, · · · ˈ · · · / the largest state of Australia, in the west of the country, whose capital is Perth 西澳大利亚州〔澳大利亚面积最大的州, 位于该国的西部, 首府珀斯〕

Western Con·fe·rence, the /, · · ˈ · · / a group of professional BASKETBALL teams from the western part of the US, which play against one another. Together with the Eastern Conference, a similar group from the eastern US, these teams form the NBA. 西部联盟〔指美国西部地区的一批职业篮球队。各队之间进行比赛。美国东部也有一个类似团体, 名为"东部联盟"。西部联盟和东部联盟共同组成国家篮球协会〕

West·ern·er /ˈwɛstə·nə·; ˈwestənə/ *n* [C] **1** someone who lives in or comes from the western part of the world 西方人 **2** *AmE* someone who lives in or comes from the western part of the US 【美】〔美国的〕西部人

Western Europe /, · · ˈ · · / the western part of Europe or the countries in it, especially the ones that did not have Communist governments, such as France or the Netherlands 西欧〔指欧洲西部地区或该地区的国家, 尤指非共产党执政的国家, 如法国或荷兰〕

Western Front, the /, · · ˈ · / an area in northern France and Belgium where many battles of World War I were fought. The armies of the Allies (=Britain, France etc) and of Germany were based in TRENCH*es* (=long, deep holes in the ground) and suffered terrible conditions and great loss of life. 西线, 西部战线〔位于法国北部和比利时的一个地区。一战期间, 这里进行过多场战役, 协约国军队和德国军队躲避在战壕中, 作战条件恶劣, 人员伤亡惨重〕

Western Hemisphere, the /, · · ˈ · · / the half of the Earth that includes the Americas and the Caribbean 西半球〔包括美洲和加勒比海地区在内的半个地球〕

Western Isles, the /, · · ˈ · / a region in northwest Scotland consisting of the Outer Hebrides islands of Harris, Lewis, North and South Uist, and Barra. Its main town is Stornoway. 西部群岛区〔苏格兰西北部一行政区, 包括外赫布里底群岛的哈里斯、刘易斯、南北尤伊斯特及巴拉岛。主要城镇是斯托诺韦〕

west·ern·ize also 又作 **-ise** *BrE* 【英】/ˈwɛstə·ˌnaɪz; ˈwestənaɪz/ *v* [T] to bring customs, business methods etc that are typical of Europe and the US to other countries 使〔风俗、经营方式等〕西化 —**westernization** /ˌwɛstə·naɪˈzeʃən; ˌwestənaɪˈzeɪʃən/ *n* [U]

west·ern·ized also 又作 **-ised** *BrE* 【英】/ˈwɛstə·ˌnaɪzd; ˈwestənaɪzd/ *adj* copying the customs, behaviour etc typical of the US or Europe 〔风俗、行为等〕西化的

western medi·cine /, · · ˈ · · / *n* [U] the type of medical treatment that is standard in the WEST (1) 西方医学 —compare 比较 ALTERNATIVE MEDICINE

west·ern·most /ˈwɛstə·n,most; ˈwestənməʊst/ *adj* [no comparative 无比较级] furthest west 最西的

Western Sahara /, · · , · ˈ · / an area of northwest Africa, south of Morocco and east of Mauritania 西撒哈拉〔非洲西北一地区, 位于摩洛哥以南, 毛里塔尼亚以东〕

Western Sa·mo·a /, · · ˈ · · / the former name for Samoa 西萨摩亚〔萨摩亚的旧称〕

West Ger·ma·ny /, · ˈ · · / also 又作 **the Federal Republic of Germany** a former country in western Europe, between France and East Germany, whose capital city was Bonn. In 1949 Germany was split into two countries: the western part became West Germany or the Federal Republic of Germany, and the eastern part became East Germany or the German Democratic Republic, a communist country. The two countries joined together again in 1990 to become Germany, after the fall of the Berlin Wall. 西德〔原西欧一国家, 位于法国和东德之间, 首都波恩。1949年德国分裂成两个国家: 西部成为西德, 即德意志联邦共和国; 东部成为东德, 即德意志民主共和国, 为共产党执政国家。1990年柏林墙拆除后, 两国重新合并为统一的德国〕 —**West German** *n, adj*

West Gla·mor·gan /ˌwɛst gləˈmɔrgən; ˌwest gləˈmɔːgən/ a former COUNTY in South Wales which included the city of Swansea 西格拉摩根郡〔曾为南威尔士一郡, 包括斯旺西市〕

West Ham /, · ˈ · / a British football club from east London, officially called 'West Ham United' and informally called 'the Hammers' 西汉姆队〔英国伦敦东部一足球俱乐部, 正式名称为"西汉姆联队", 俗称"铁锤帮"〕

West In·di·an /, · ˈ · · · / *adj* from or connected with the West Indies 来自西印度群岛的; 与西印度群岛有关的

West In·dies, the /ˌwɛst ˈɪndɪz; ˌwest ˈɪndiz/ **1** the islands of the Caribbean Sea, between the southeast of the US and the north of South America, including the Bahamas, Cuba, Jamaica, Puerto Rico, Barbados, and Dominica 西印度群岛〔即加勒比海群岛, 位于美国东南部和南美北部之间, 包括巴哈马群岛、古巴、牙买加、波多黎各、巴巴多斯、多米尼加等〕 **2** an international CRICKET team made up of players from the islands of the West Indies that formerly belonged to the UK 西印度群岛国际板球队〔队员来自原英属西印度群岛〕

West·min·ster /ˈwɛstmɪnstə·; ˈwestmɪnstə/ **1** also 又作 **the City of Westminster** a BOROUGH (=a part of a city which is responsible for managing its own schools, roads etc) which contains a large part of west central London, including Westminster Abbey, the Houses of Parliament, and Buckingham Palace 威斯敏斯特〔伦敦一自治区, 包括伦敦市中心以西的大部分地区, 市内建筑有威斯敏斯特教堂、议会大厦、白金汉宫等〕 **2** the British Houses of Parliament 威斯敏斯特〔英国议会的别称〕: *Westminster was buzzing with anticipation today as MPs gathered for tonight's crucial vote.* 今天议员们聚集一堂, 晚上将有一轮重要的投票表决, 议会里人声嘈杂, 大家满怀期待。

Westminster Ab·bey /, · · · ˈ · · / a very large GOTHIC church in Westminster, London, first built in the 11th century. Almost all British kings and queens since William the Conqueror have been CROWN*ed* in the Abbey and many famous people are buried there. 威斯敏斯特教堂, 西敏寺〔位于伦敦市威斯敏斯特的一座大型哥特式教堂。始建于11世纪, 自征服者威廉起, 历代英国君主几乎都在这座教堂举行加冕典礼。许多名人去世后长眠于此〕

Westminster Ca·the·dral /, · · · · ˈ · · / the main Roman Catholic church in England and Wales, famous especially for its Byzantine design and stations of the Cross 威斯敏斯特天主教堂〔英格兰和威尔士的主要天主教堂, 尤以拜占庭式的设计及耶稣受难组图著称〕

West Point /, · ˈ · / another name for the United States Military Academy, where officers of the US Army are given a university education and trained 西点军校〔美国军事学院别称。美国军官在此接受大学教育和技能训练〕

West Side Sto·ry /, · · ˈ · · / a MUSICAL (=a play that uses singing and dancing to tell a story) by Leonard Bernstein, based on the play *Romeo and Juliet* by William Shakespeare, in which a boy and a girl in New York City fall in love, although they come from different GANG*s*, one of which consists of Puerto Rican people. The original stage musical, produced in 1957, was made into a successful film in 1961. 《西城故事》〔伦纳德·伯恩斯坦创作的一部音乐剧, 取材于威廉·莎士比亚的戏剧《罗密欧与朱丽叶》。剧中纽约市的一个男孩与一个女孩相爱了, 但两人来自不同的帮派, 其中一个帮派由波多黎各移民后裔组成。最初的舞台音乐剧于1957年推出, 1961年改编成一部优秀电影〕

West Sus·sex /, · ˈ · · / a COUNTY in southern England 西萨塞克斯郡〔英格兰南部一郡〕

West Vir·gin·i·a /, · · ˈ · · · / abbreviation 缩写为 **WV** a state in the eastern central US, that has many mountains. Its capital and largest city is Charleston, and its industries include coal, steel, and farming. 西弗吉尼亚州〔美国中东部一州, 多山。首府和最大城市是查尔斯顿, 产业包括煤矿业、钢铁工业和农业〕

west·ward /ˈwɛstwə·d; ˈwestwəd/ *adj* going towards the west 向[朝]西的 —**westward, westwards** *adv*

West York·shire /, · ˈ · · / a COUNTY in northeast England, whose main city is Leeds 西约克郡〔英格兰东北部一郡, 主要城市为利兹〕

wet¹ /wɛt; wet/ *adj*

1 ▶WATER/LIQUID 水/液体◀ covered in or full of liquid 湿的, 潮的: *wet grass* 湿草 | *My shirt's all wet!* 我的衬衫湿透了! | [+with] *His face was wet with sweat.* 他满脸汗水。| **get (sth) wet** *Try not to get your feet wet.* 尽量别把你的脚弄湿。| **wet through** (=completely wet) 湿透 | **soaking/sopping/dripping wet** (=extremely wet) 极湿的, 湿淋淋的 *soaking wet socks* 湿淋淋的袜子

2 ▶WEATHER 天气◀ rainy 多雨的, 下雨的: *wet weather* 下雨的天气 | *It's very wet outside.* 外面雨很大。

3 the wet a) rainy weather 雨天: *Come in out of the wet.* 快进来免得淋雨。**b)** wet ground 〔下雨后的〕湿地: *Don't trail your coat in the wet!* 别在湿地上拖着大衣!

W

4►PAINT/INK ETC 油漆/墨水等◄ not yet dry 未干的: *Careful, the paint's still wet.* 注意，油漆未干。

5►PERSON 人◄ **a)** *BrE informal* unable to make decisions or take firm actions【英，非正式】〔人〕犹豫不决的；软弱的: *Don't be so wet! Just tell them you don't want to go.* 别那么优柔寡断，就告诉他们你不想去。**b) be all wet** *AmE informal* to be completely wrong【美，非正式】大错特错

6 wet behind the ears *informal* very young and without much experience of life【非正式】过于年轻而没有经验的；乳臭未干的 —**wetly** *adv* —**wetness** *n* [U]

wet² *v past tense* **wet** *or* **wetted** [T] **1** to make something wet 把〔某物〕弄湿: *Wet your hair and apply the shampoo.* 弄湿头发，倒上洗发剂。**2** to make yourself, your clothes, or your bed wet because you pass water from your body by accident 尿湿；遗尿: **wet yourself** *I nearly wet myself I was so scared.* 我吓得几乎屁滚尿流。**3 wet your whistle** *old-fashioned* to have an alcoholic drink【过时】喝点酒

wet·back /ˈwɛtˌbæk; ˈwetbæk/ *n* [C] *AmE* an offensive word for someone from Mexico who has come to the US illegally【美】"湿背人"〔冒犯语，指由墨西哥进入美国的偷渡客〕

CULTURAL NOTE 文化注释

This expression comes from the fact that many Mexicans cross the Rio Grande River between the two countries in order to avoid IMMIGRATION officials at the border. 这个词的来源是，很多墨西哥人渡过两国交界的格兰德河来到美国，以回避移民官员在边境的审查。

wet bar /ˈ· ·/ *n* [C] *AmE* a small bar with equipment for making alcoholic drinks, in a house, hotel room etc【美】〔家庭、旅馆房间等附设的〕小酒吧

wet blan·ket /ˌ· ˈ··/ *n* [C] *informal* someone who tries to spoil other people's fun【非正式】扫兴的人，泼冷水的人

wet dream /ˌ· ˈ·/ *n* [C] a sexually exciting dream that a man has, resulting in an ORGASM 梦遗，梦中遗精

wet fish /ˌ· ˈ·/ *n* [U] *BrE* fresh uncooked fish that is on sale in a shop【英】〔商店出售的〕鲜鱼

We Three Kings /ˌ· · ˈ·/ a Christmas CAROL (=a traditional religious song) about the Three Kings or Wise Men who came from the East to visit the baby Jesus.《东方三圣》〔一圣诞歌曲。内容讲述东方三王或三贤哲朝拜圣婴耶稣的故事〕It begins 开首为:

We three kings of Orient are.
Bearing gifts we travel afar ...
三位贤哲来自东方，
携带礼物进献君王…

wet-look /ˈ· ·/ *adj* [only before noun 仅用于名词前] wet-look clothes have a shiny surface so that they look as if they are wet〔衣服〕表面闪光发亮的〔看起来像湿的一样〕

wet nurse /ˈ· ·/ *n* [C] *old use* a woman who is employed to give her breast milk to another woman's baby【旧】奶妈，乳母

wet-nurse *v* [T] to give someone too much care and attention as if they were a child 溺爱〔某人〕

wet suit 潜水服

wet suit /ˈ· ·/ *n* [C] a piece of clothing, usually made of rubber, that underwater swimmers wear to keep warm〔潜水者穿的〕保暖橡皮服；潜水服

wet·ting a·gent /ˈ··, ˌ··/ *n* [C] a chemical substance which, when spread on a solid surface, makes it hold liquid〔涂于固体表面、使其容易被液体润湿的〕润湿剂

wetting so·lu·tion /ˈ··, ·ˈ··/ *n* [C,U] a liquid used for storing contact lenses (CONTACT LENS) in, or for making them more comfortable to wear〔隐形眼镜用的〕护理液

we've /wɪv; wiv; *strong* 强读 wiv; wiːv/ the short form of 缩略式= we have

Wex·ford /ˈwɛksfəd; ˈweksfəd/ **1** a COUNTY in the southeast of the Republic of Ireland 韦克斯福德郡〔爱尔兰共和国东南部一郡〕**2** the county town of Wexford, where the **Wexford Festival**, an international festival of OPERA, takes place every autumn 韦克斯福德〔韦克斯福德郡首府。这里每年秋季举办国际歌剧节，名为韦克斯福德节〕

whack¹ /hwæk; wæk/ *v* [T] *informal*【非正式】**1** to hit someone or something hard 猛击，重击〔某人或某物〕: *Ow! You whacked me with your elbow!* 哎唷！你的胳膊肘撞到我！**2** *spoken* to put something somewhere【口】把〔某物〕置于某处: *Just whack it under the grill for a couple of minutes.* 就把它放在烤架下几分钟。

whack² *n* [C] *especially spoken*【尤口】**1** the act of hitting something hard or the noise this makes 重击（声）**2 have a whack at** to try to do something 试着做〔某事〕**3 do your whack** *BrE* to do a fair or equal share of a job or activity【英】做你应做的一份〔工作或活动〕: *I've done more than my whack of the driving – it's your turn.* 我已经开了好半天车 — 该轮到你了。**4 (the) full whack** *BrE* the full amount【英】总量，全额: *You don't have to pay full whack if you're unemployed.* 如果你没有工作，就不必付全部款额。**5 at/in one whack** *AmE* all on one occasion【美】一下子: *Steve lost $500 at one whack.* 史蒂夫一下子损失了500美元。**6 out of whack** *AmE* if a system, machine etc is out of whack, the parts are not working together correctly【美】〔系统、机器等〕有毛病，不正常

whacked /hwækt; wækt/ *adj* [not before noun 不用于名词前] *informal*【非正式】**1** also 又作 **whacked out** very tired 精疲力竭的 **2 whacked out** *AmE* behaving strangely, especially because of having too much alcohol or drugs【美】〔因醉酒、吸毒而〕行为怪异的

whack·ing /ˈhwækɪŋ; ˈwækɪŋ/ *adj* **whacking great** *BrE spoken* very big; WHOPPING【英口】巨大的，极大的: *We got a whacking great gas bill this morning.* 今天上午我们收到一张数额巨大的煤气账单。

whack·y /ˈhwækɪ; ˈwæki/ *adj* another spelling of WACKY wacky 的另一种拼法

whale 鲸

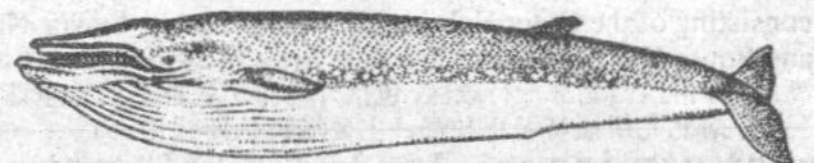

whale¹ /hwel; weɪl/ *n* [C] **1** a very large animal that lives in the sea and looks like a fish, but is actually a MAMMAL 鲸 **2 have a whale of a time** *informal* to enjoy yourself very much【非正式】玩得非常愉快

whale² *v* **whale into** *AmE* to start attacking someone【美】开始攻击〔某人〕

whale·bone /ˈhwelˌbon; ˈweɪlbəʊn/ *n* [U] a hard substance taken from the upper jaw of whales, used in the past for making women's clothes stiff〔旧时用以保持妇女衣服挺括的〕鲸须

whal·er /ˈhwelə; ˈweɪlə/ *n* [C] **1** someone who hunts whales 捕鲸者 **2** a boat which goes to hunt whales 捕鲸船

whal·ing /ˈhwelɪŋ; ˈweɪlɪŋ/ *n* [U] the activity of hunting whales 捕鲸（业）

wham /hwæm; wæm/ *interjection* **1** used to describe the sound of something suddenly hitting something else very hard 砰，嘭〔形容某物突然撞击他物的声音〕: *The car went wham into the wall.* 砰的一声，汽车撞到墙上。**2** used to express the idea that something very unexpected suddenly happens〔用于表示某事〕突如其来: *Life is going along nicely and then, wham, you lose your job.* 生活过得美满舒适，突然间，你失业了。

wham·my /ˈhwæmɪ; ˈwæmi/ *n* [C] **put the whammy on sb** to use magic powers to make someone have bad luck 用魔力使某人倒运 —see also 另见 DOUBLE WHAMMY

wharf /hwɔrf; wɔːf/ *n* [C] *plural* **wharfs** *or* **wharves** a place built on the edge of a sea or river, where ships can be tied up to load and unload goods〔起卸货物用的〕码头；停船处

Wharton /ˈwɔrtn; ˈwɔːtn/, **Edith** /ˈidɪθ; ˈiːdɪθ/ (1862-1937) a US writer of NOVELS, several of which have been made into films. Her novels include *The Age of Innocence*, *The House of Mirth*, and *Ethan Frome*. 华顿〔(1862-1937)，美国小说家。多部作品被改编成电影，其小说包括《纯真年代》、《欢乐之家》和《伊桑·弗罗姆》〕

S1 W1 **what¹** /hwɑt; wɒt/ *predeterminer, determiner, pron* **1** used when asking questions about a thing or person, or a kind of thing or person that you do not know anything about 什么〔用于疑问句，指某一或某种未知的事物或人〕: *What are you doing?* 你在做什么？| *What colour is the new carpet?* 新地毯是什么颜色的？| *"What do you do?" "I'm a teacher."* "你是干什么的？""我是教师。" | *What's your new boss like?* 你的新老板是个怎样的人？| *What do you mean, you want to spend Christmas alone?* 你是什么意思，你想一个人过圣诞节？**2** used especially in indirect questions to talk about things or information …的事情〔尤用于间接问句，指所说的事或信息〕: *I believe what he told me.* 我相信他对我说的话。| *Show me what you bought then.* 那么给我看看你买的东西。| *They're discussing what to do next.* 他们正在讨论下一步要做什么。| *I don't know what you think but if you ask me it's a waste of time.* 我不知道你怎么想，但是你如果问我，我认为那是浪费时间。| *She gave him what money she had.* (=all the money she had, although she did not have much) 她把她仅有的钱给了他。**3** *spoken* used at the beginning of a statement to emphasize what you are going to say【口】…的是…〔用在陈述句的开始，强调准备说的内容〕: *What that kid needs is some love and affection.* 那小孩需要的是关爱。| *What we'll do is leave a note for Mum to tell her we won't be back till late.* 我们要做的是给妈妈留一张便条，告诉她我们要很晚才回来。**4 what?** *spoken*【口】**a)** used to ask someone to repeat something they have just said because you didn't hear it properly 什么？〔因没有听清楚，要求对方重复所说的话〕: *"Have you got a pen I could borrow?" "What?"* "你有钢笔我可以借用一下吗？""你说什么？" **b)** used during conversations when you have heard someone talking to you and want to tell them to continue 什么？〔用于谈话中，希望对方继续说下去〕: *"Elaine!" "What?" "Are you coming?"* "伊莱恩！""什么？""你来吗？" **c)** used to show that you are surprised by what someone has said 真的？〔对他人所说的表示惊讶〕: *"My wallet's missing." "What?"* "我的钱包丢了。""真的吗？" **5** *spoken* used at the beginning of a sentence to show that you think something is very good, very bad etc【口】多么，何等〔用在句子的开头，表示某事很好或很坏等〕: *What a lovely day!* (=the weather is good) 多好的天气！| *What a horrible thing to do!* 做这种事真可怕！**6 what about...?** *spoken*【口】**a)** used to make a suggestion …怎么样？〔用于提出建议〕: *What about Czech for a holiday?* 到捷克度假去怎么样？| **what about doing** *What about going to a movie this evening?* 今晚去看电影怎么样？**b)** used to introduce a new person or thing into a conversation …怎么样？〔在交谈中说到新人或事〕: *What about Patrick? What's he doing nowadays?* 帕特里克怎么样？他现在在干什么？| *We've chosen the food, now, what about the wine?* 我们已经选了食品，那么，葡萄酒怎么办？**7 I tell you what** *spoken* used to make an offer or suggestion【口】我有个主意，你听我说〔用于提出建议或意见〕: *I tell you what, I'll give you £20 for it.* 你听我说，那件东西我给你20英镑。**8 guess what!** *spoken* used before telling someone some exciting or surprising news【口】猜猜发生了什么事！〔用于说出令人感到惊讶的事情前〕: *Guess what! Jane's getting married.* 猜猜发生什么事了！简要结婚了。**9 what (...) for?** *spoken*【口】**a)** why? 为什么？: *"She's decided to work part-time." "What for?"* "她决定去兼职。""为什么？" **b)** used to ask what purpose something has〔某物〕有何用？: *What's this gadget for?* 这个小玩意儿是干什么用的？**10** *spoken* used to give yourself time to think before guessing a number or amount【口】嗯，哦〔猜测数目或数量前给自己时间考虑〕: *You're looking at, what, about £4,000 for a decent second-hand car.* 一辆性能尚可的二手车得花你，嗯，大约4000英镑。**11 what's his/her/its name** also 又作 **what d'you call him/her/it** *spoken* used when talking about a person or thing whose name you cannot immediately remember【口】那个什么来着〔说到某人或某物时一时记不起名称〕: *The hospital have just got a, what d'you call it, er... a new scanner.* 医院刚买了一台新的叫什么来着，嗯…扫描仪。**12 (and) what's more** *spoken* used when adding something to what you have already said, especially when it is exciting or interesting【口】而且，更有甚者〔尤用于加上令人兴奋或有趣的一点〕: *These detergents are environmentally friendly, what's more, they're relatively cheap.* 这些洗涤剂有利环保，而且，价格还相对便宜。**13 what's what** *spoken* what a situation is really like as opposed to what people say it is like, or what they try and make you believe【口】事情的真相: *Shirley's been there before, she'll tell you what's what.* 雪莉以前到过那里，她会告诉你是怎么一回事。**14 what the hell/devil/blazes...?/what in God's name/heaven's name...?** *spoken* used to ask in an extremely angry or surprised way what is happening, what someone is doing etc【口】究竟什么…？到底什么…？〔用极生气或惊讶的口吻问〕: *What the hell do you think you're doing?* 你究竟认为自己在干什么？| *What in God's name will she think of next?* 接下来她到底会想到什么？**15 what the hell!** *spoken* used to say that you have decided to do something even though it is very expensive, difficult etc【口】管他呢！〔表示决定做某事，虽然昂贵、困难等〕: *Oh, what the hell! It's your birthday, let's have champagne!* 噢，管他呢！今天是你的生日，我们喝香槟酒吧！**16 ...or what?** *spoken* used to show that you are impatient when asking a question or because you think there is only one possible answer to the question【口】还是别的什么？〔发问时表示不耐烦或认为只有一个答案〕: *Are you coming then, or what?* 那么你是来还是不来？| *Is that work going to be finished by Friday or what?* 那工作会在星期五完成还是在别的什么时间完成？**17 so what?** *spoken* used to say that you do not care about something or to tell someone angrily that something does not concern them【口】那有什么了不起？〔对事情表示不关心或生气地告诉某人事情与他无关〕，那又怎样？: *"Your room looks a real mess Tracey." "So what?"* "特雷西，你房间看起来凌乱不堪。""那又怎么样？" **18 you what?** *spoken*【口】**a)** used to ask someone to repeat something they have just said, in a way people think is not polite 你说什么？〔用于让对方重复一遍，人们认为这样说不礼貌〕: *"Could you get the butter out of the fridge?" "You what?"* "请把黄油从冰箱里拿出来好吗？""你说什么？" **b)** used to show that you are surprised 你说什么？〔表示惊讶〕: *"I got the job!" "You what?"* "我获得那份工作啦！""你说什么？" **19 what if...** *spoken*【口】**a)** used to make a suggestion 如果…怎么样〔用于提出建议〕: *What if we go and see a film tomorrow night?* 我们明天晚上去看电影，你觉得怎么样？**b)** used to ask what will happen, usually if an unpleasant or frightening situation happens 如果…将会怎样〔用于问将会发生什么，通常是令人不快或惊恐的事〕: *What if we get burgled while we're on holiday?* 我们度假时，家里被盗怎么办？**20 ... and what have you** *spoken* used at the end of a list of things to mean other things of a similar kind【口】等等；这一类东西〔用于物品清单末尾，表示还有类似的东西〕: *The shelves were crammed with books, documents, and what have you.* 书架上塞满了书本、文件等一类东西。**21 have what it takes** *spoken* to have the right qualities or skills in order to succeed【口】具备成功的必要条件: *I reckon Jordi's got what it takes to be an international footballer.* 我认为乔迪已具备作为世界级足球运动员的条件。**22 what's with a)** *AmE spoken* used to ask a person or group of people who are behaving strangely or violently, why they are behaving in this way【美口】怎么啦〔用于询问某人或一群人为什么行为怪异或粗暴〕: *What's with you people?* 你们这些人怎么啦？**b)** used to ask the reason for something 怎么回事: *What's with the free sandwiches and beer?* 白吃三明治，白喝啤酒，是怎么回事？**23 what of it?** *spoken* used to say that you do not care about something or to tell someone angrily that something does not concern them【口】那又有什么关系？〔用于表示对事情不关心或生气地告诉某人事情与他无关〕: *"I hear you've just got a new car." "Yes, what of it?"* "我听说你刚买了辆新汽车。""是的，那又怎么样呢？" **24 now what?** *spoken* used to ask what is going to happen next, what you should do etc【口】下一步会怎样；下一步怎么办？

Frequencies of **what** in spoken and written English 英语口语和书面语中 what 的使用频率

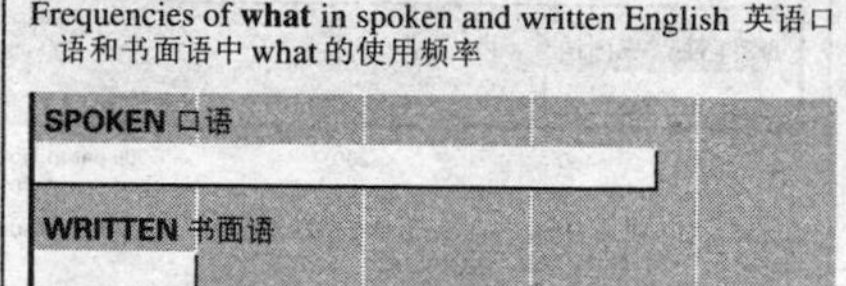

Based on the British National Corpus and the Longman Lancaster Corpus
据英国国家语料库和朗文兰开斯特语料库

This graph shows that **what** is much more common in spoken English than in written English. This is because it is used to ask questions, and it is used in a lot of common spoken phrases.
本图表显示，what 在英语口语中的使用频率远远高于书面语，因为该词经常用于问句中，而且口语中很多常用短语是由 what 构成的。

what² *adv* **1** used especially in questions to ask to what degree or in what way something matters 到什么程度；在哪方面〔尤用于问句〕: *What do you care about it?* (=I don't think you care at all) 你对这事恐怕没有什么要关心的吧？| *We may be a little late, but what does it matter?* 我们可能会晚到一会儿，但那有什么关系呢？**2 what with** *spoken* used to introduce a list of

reasons that have made something happen or have made someone feel a particular way【口】因为，由于〔用于列举引起某事或某种感受的原因〕: *What with neighbours, relatives, and friends there, the house was overflowing with people.* 由于有邻居、亲属及朋友在那里，房子里人满为患。

what·cha·ma·call·it /ˈwɑtʃəmə͵kɔlɪt; ˈwɒtʃəmə͵kɔːlɪt/ *n* [C] *spoken* a word you use when you cannot remember the name of something【口】叫什么东西来着〔忘记该东西的名称时用〕: *I've broken the whatchamacallit on my bag.* 我把袋子上的什么东西弄坏了。

1 1 **what·ev·er¹** /hwɑtˋɛvɚ; wɒtˈevə/ *determiner, pron* **1** any or all of the things that are wanted, needed, or possible 任何…的事物；什么…都: *Help yourself to whatever you want.* 尽请随意。| *Jake's dad told him he could have whatever he wanted for Christmas.* 杰克的爸爸告诉他圣诞节他想要什么礼物都行。**2** used to say that it is not important what happens, what you do etc because it does not change the situation 无论什么，不管什么: *Whatever I suggest, he always disagrees.* 无论我提什么建议，他总是不同意。| *The building must be saved whatever the cost.* 不论花多少钱，这座建筑物必须保留。| **whatever you do** *spoken*【口】: *Don't, whatever you do, let anyone see that letter.* 无论如何，你不要让任何人看那封信。**3** *spoken* used to say that you do not know the exact meaning or name of someone or something【口】…什么来着〔用于表示你不知道某人的姓名或某事的真正意思〕: *Why don't you invite Steve, or whatever he's called, to supper?* 你为什么不邀请那个叫史蒂夫还是什么的人来吃晚饭？**4 ... or whatever** *spoken* used after naming things on a list to mean other things of the same kind【口】任何类似的东西〔用于物品清单之后〕: *Anyone seen carrying boxes, bags, or whatever was stopped by the police.* 谁要是带盒子、袋子什么的，被警察看见了都得截查。| **... and whatever else** *Bring waterproof clothing, boots, and whatever else.* 带上防水衣、靴子，以及诸如此类的东西。**5** *spoken* used to show that you are angry or surprised when making a statement or asking a question【口】究竟是什么〔用于述说事情或提出问题时表示生气或惊讶〕: *Whatever can he mean?* 他能是什么意思？| **whatever next!** (=used to show surprise) 还要什么！〔表示惊讶〕*"Joan's learning Sanskrit." "Whatever next!"* "琼在学梵文。""她还要学什么！" **6** *spoken* used to tell someone that you do not care or are not interested when they ask you something【口】随便怎样，无所谓〔用于回答别人的问题，表示不感兴趣〕: *"Shall I call you tonight or tomorrow?" "Whatever."* "我是今晚还是明天打电话给你？""由你。" **7 whatever you say/whatever you think** *spoken* used to tell someone that you agree with them or will do what they want, often when you do not really agree or want to do it【口】随你说/想〔用于表示赞成，往往是勉强的赞成〕: *"I want to go camping, just for a change." "OK, whatever you say."* "我想去野营，只是想换换环境。""好，一切听你的。"

Frequencies of **whatever** in spoken and written English 英语口语和书面语中 whatever 的使用频率

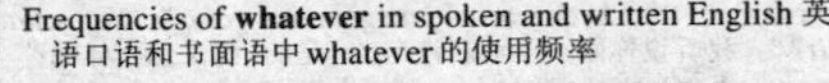

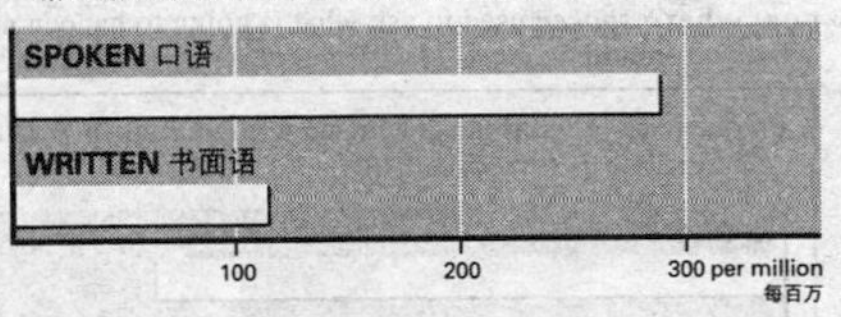

Based on the British National Corpus and the Longman Lancaster Corpus 据英国国家语料库和朗文兰开斯特语料库

This graph shows that **whatever** is more common in spoken English than in written English. This is because it is used in a lot of common spoken phrases. 本图表显示，whatever 在英语口语中的使用频率远远高于书面语，因为口语中很多常用短语是由 whatever 构成的。

whatever² *adv* used to emphasize a negative statement; WHATSOEVER 丝毫；任何〔用于强调否定句〕: *She gave no sign whatever of what she was thinking.* 她在想什么，毫无迹象可循。

whatever³ *adj* **1** of any possible kind 任何的: *I'll take whatever help I can get.* 我能得到什么帮助我都接受。**2** of some kind, but you are not sure what …什么样的〔但你不肯定是什么〕: *Ellen's refusing to come, for whatever reason.* 不知什么原因，埃伦不愿来了。

what·not /ˈhwɑt͵nɑt; ˈwɒtnɒt/ *n* **1 and whatnot** *spoken* an expression used at the end of a list of things when you do not want to give the names of everything【口】诸如此类的东西；等等〔用于物品清单末尾，不把物品一一列举时〕: *Put your bags, cases and whatnot in the back of the car.* 把你的袋子、盒子等诸如此类的东西放到汽车后座。**2** [C] a piece of furniture with shelves used especially in the 19th century to show small pretty objects〔19 世纪放小玩意儿的〕陈设架，古董架

whats·it /ˈhwɑtsɪt; ˈwɒtsɪ̥t/ *n* [C] *spoken* a word you use when you cannot think of the word you want【口】那个什么玩意儿〔指说不出名称的小东西〕: *Try and undo the screw to get the whatsit off.* 试着松开螺丝，把那个小玩意儿拆下来。

what·so·ev·er /͵hwɑtsoˋɛvɚ; ͵wɒtsəʊˈevə/ *adv* used to emphasize a negative statement; WHATEVER 丝毫〔用于强调否定句〕: 2
Political factors played no part whatsoever in this decision. 在这项决定中，政治因素丝毫没起作用。

What's On /͵ · ˈ·/ *trademark* a British magazine which gives details of all the films, plays, sports games, and other events and activities taking place in the current week or month. Many cities in the UK have a *What's On*.【商标】《娱乐天地》〔英国一杂志，详细介绍本周或当月的电影、戏剧、体育赛事等活动。英国许多城市均有当地的《娱乐天地》杂志〕

wheat /hwit; wiːt/ *n* [U] **1** the grain that bread is made from 小麦麦粒 **2** the plant that this grain grows on 小麦〔植物〕: *a field of wheat* 小麦地 **3 separate the wheat from the chaff** to choose the good and useful things or people and get rid of the others 分清好坏；去芜存菁

wheat·germ /ˈhwit͵dʒɝm; ˈwiːtdʒɜːm/ *n* [U] the centre of a grain of wheat 小麦胚芽

wheat·meal /ˈhwitmil; ˈwiːtmiːl/ *n* [U] *especially BrE* a brown flour made from whole grains of wheat【尤英】全麦面粉

whee /hwi; wiː/ *interjection* used by children to express happiness or excitement 哟；好啊〔儿童用以表示高兴或激动〕

whee·dle /ˈhwidl; ˈwiːdl/ *v* [I,T] to try to persuade someone by saying pleasant things which you do not mean 哄骗；〔用甜言蜜语〕骗取: *a wheedling voice* 哄骗的口吻 | **wheedle sb into doing sth** *He wheedled me into paying.* 他哄骗我让我付钱。| **wheedle sth from/out of sb** *She managed to wheedle an extra day's pay out of him.* 她用花言巧语从他那里多骗了一天的报酬。

wheel¹ /hwil; wiːl/ *n* [C] 2 3

1 ►ON A VEHICLE 车辆上的◄ [C] one of the round things under a car, bus, bicycle etc that turn when it moves〔汽车、公共汽车、自行车等的〕车轮 —see picture on page A2 参见 A2 页图

2 ►IN A MACHINE 机器上的◄ [C] a flat round part in a machine that turns round when the machine operates 机轮: *a gear wheel* 齿轮

3 ►FOR CONTROLLING A VEHICLE 用于控制车船等◄ [C] the piece of equipment in the shape of a wheel that you turn to make a car, ship etc move in a particular direction〔汽车等的〕方向盘；〔轮船等的〕舵轮: **at/behind the wheel** (=driving a car etc) 在驾驶〔汽车等〕| **take the wheel** (=drive instead of someone else) 替他人驾驶 —see also 另见 STEERING WHEEL

4 on wheels with wheels on the bottom 带轮的: *a table on wheels* 带轮的桌子

5 wheels/set of wheels *spoken* a car【口】汽车: *Like my new wheels?* 喜欢我的新车吗？

6 wheels within wheels *spoken* used to say that a situation is complicated and difficult to understand because it involves processes and decisions that you know nothing about【口】错综复杂的情况；复杂的形势 —see also 另见 **oil the wheels** (OIL² (2)), **put your shoulder to the wheel** (SHOULDER¹ (8)), **put a spoke in sb's wheel** (SPOKE² (2))

wheel² *v* **1** [T always+adv/prep] **a)** to push something that has wheels 推动〔带轮子的东西〕: **wheel sth out/down/into** *She wheeled her bike into the garage.* 她把自行车推到车库里。**b)** to move someone or something that is in an object with wheels, such as a WHEELCHAIR or a CART¹ (1) 用〔轮椅或手推车等〕运送〔某人或某物〕: *The nurse wheeled him into the ward.* 护士把他推进病房。**2** [I] if birds or planes wheel they fly around in circles〔鸟或飞机〕盘旋 **3** [I +around/round] to turn around suddenly 突然转身: *She wheeled around and started yelling at us.* 她突然转身，开始冲着我们大喊起来。**4 wheel and deal** to do a lot of complicated and sometimes slightly dishonest deals, especially in politics or business〔尤指在政治或商业上〕投机取巧；玩弄手段

wheel sb/sth ↔ **out** *phr v* [T] *informal* to publicly show someone or something, and use them to help you achieve something【非正式】〔为帮助自己达成某事而〕提出〔某人〕；推出〔某物〕: *The party always wheels out the same old celebrities whenever they need to raise money.* 每当需要募集资金的时候，该党总是推出这几位老名人。

wheel·bar·row /ˈhwil͵bæro; ˈwiːl͵bærəʊ/ *n* [C] a small CART[1] (1) that you use outdoors to carry things, with a single wheel and two handles 独轮手推车

wheel·base /ˈhwil͵bes; ˈwiːlbeɪs/ *n* [C] *technical* the distance between the front and back AXLES of a vehicle【术语】〔车辆前后轴的〕轴距

wheel·chair /ˈhwilˋtʃɛr; ˈwiːltʃeə/ *n* [C] a chair with wheels used by people who cannot walk 轮椅 —see picture at 参见 CHAIR[1] 图

wheel clamp /ˈ· ·/ *n* [C] a metal object that is fastened to the wheel of an illegally parked car 车轮锁夹〔锁住非法停放汽车的车轮的装置〕; DENVER BOOT *AmE*【美】—**wheel-clamp** *v* [T]

wheeled /hwild; wiːld/ *adj* having wheels 有轮子的

wheeler-deal·er /͵·· ˈ··/ *n* [C] someone who does a lot of complicated, often dishonest deals, especially in business or politics 善于投机取巧的人〔尤指在政治或商业上〕: *She was a real wheeler-dealer, sometimes loving the thrill of doing deals.* 她真是一个工于心计的人，有时觉得谈生意很带劲。

wheel·house /ˈhwil͵haʊs; ˈwiːlhaʊs/ *n* [C] the place on a ship where the CAPTAIN stands at the WHEEL[1] (3)〔船上的〕驾驶室，操舵室

wheel·ie /ˈhwilɪ; ˈwiːli/ *n* [C] **do a wheelie** *informal* to balance on the back wheel of a bicycle that you are riding【非正式】〔自行车前轮离地的〕后轮平衡特技

wheelie bin /ˈ··· ͵/ *n* [C] *BrE* a large container with wheels that you put household waste into【英】大型轮式垃圾箱〔放置家庭垃圾用〕

wheel·ing and deal·ing /͵·· · ˈ··/ *n* [U] activities that involve a lot of complicated and sometimes dishonest deals, especially in business or politics〔尤指在商业或政治上的〕投机取巧，耍手段

wheel·wright /ˈhwil͵raɪt; ˈwiːlraɪt/ *n* [C] someone who made and repaired the wooden wheels of vehicles pulled by horses in the past〔旧时〕制作或修理马车木轮的匠人

wheeze[1] /hwiz; wiːz/ *v* [I] to breathe with difficulty, making a whistling sound in your throat and chest 气喘吁吁，发出呼哧声

wheeze[2] *n* [C] **1** the act or sound of wheezing 气喘；气喘声 **2** *old-fashioned or humorous* a clever and amusing idea or plan【过时或幽默】巧妙的主意；把戏

wheez·y /ˈhwizɪ; ˈwiːzi/ *adj* wheezing or making a wheezing sound 气喘的；发出喘息声的: *You sound wheezy.* 你气喘吁吁。| *a wheezy cough* 呼哧呼哧的咳嗽 —**wheezily** *adv* —**wheeziness** *n* [U]

whelk /hwɛlk; welk/ *n* [C] a small sea animal that has a shell and can be eaten 蛾螺

whelp[1] /hwɛlp; welp/ *n* [C] a young animal, especially a dog or lion 幼兽〔尤指狗或狮的幼仔〕

whelp[2] *v* [I] *old-fashioned* if a dog or lion whelps, it gives birth【过时】〔狗或狮〕产仔

1 1 **when**[1] /hwɛn; wen/ *adv, conj* **1** at what time 什么时候: *When is Tara coming?* 塔拉什么时候来? | *Do you know when she will arrive?* 你知道她什么时候到吗? | *When did you hear about it?* 你什么时候听到这消息的? **2** at the time that 当…时候: *Things were different when I was young.* 我年轻的时候情况并不一样。| *The dog jumped up when he whistled.* 听到他的口哨声，狗跳了起来。| *When I give the signal, turn off the light.* 当我发出信号时，就关灯。| *When completed the tunnel will be the longest in the world.* 完工后，这隧道将是世界上最长的。**3 day/time/afternoon when** the day, time etc on or at which 那天/时/下午: *There are times when I wonder what you're talking about.* 有几次我不知道你在说什么。**4** considering that 考虑到: *Why do you want a new job when you've got such a good one already?* 既然你已经有了这么好的工作，为什么还要找新的工作? **5** even though or in spite of the fact that 虽然；尽管: *They kept digging when they must have known there was no hope.* 他们虽然明知没有希望，但还是在不停地挖。

when[2] *pron* **1 since when** used in questions to mean since what time 从什么时候〔用于问句〕: *Since when has it been any of your business what I do?* 从什么时候起我做的事和你有关系呢? **2** which time 那时: *next May, by when the new house should be finished* 明年5月，到那时新房子应该建成了

whence /hwɛns; wens/ *adv, pron old use* from where【旧】从哪里: *Whence came this man?* 这个人从哪儿来的? —compare 比较 WHITHER

2 3 **when·ev·er** /hwɛnˋɛvɚ; wenˈevə/ *adv, conj* **1** every time that a particular thing happens 每当: *Whenever we come here we see someone we know.* 我们每次来这儿都会见到熟人。| *If you feed a baby whenever he is hungry, you will have less difficulty with him later.* 每当婴儿饿的时候你就喂他，以后你就容易带他了。**2** at any time 任何时候: *I'd like to see you whenever it's convenient.* 在你方便的时候我想和你见面。**3** *spoken* used when it does not matter what time something happens, or when you do not know the exact time something happens【口】无论什么时候〔用于事情发生的时间并不重要或不确定时〕: *"Should I come over around six?" "Whenever."* "我6点左右来行吗?" "什么时候都行。"

where /hwɛr; weə/ *adv, conjunction* **1** at, to, or from a particular place or position 在哪里[某处]；往哪里[某处]；从哪里[某处]: *Where do you live?* 你住在哪里? | *I asked Lucy where she was going.* 我问露西她要去哪儿。| *Where are you going to put it?* 你会把它放到什么地方? | *Sit where you like.* 你爱坐哪儿就坐哪儿。—see 见 POSITION[1] (USAGE) **2** in, towards, or from a particular situation or at a particular point in a speech, argument etc〔发言、争论等〕在什么情况；在哪一点: *Now where was I? Oh yes, I was telling you about taking mother to the airport.* 我说到哪儿了? 哦，是的，我正告诉你我带着母亲去机场。| *Where will all this fighting and bloodshed end?* 这一切冲突、流血，结果会是什么样? **3** used at the beginning of a sentence in which the second part expresses the opposite, or something different from the first part〔用于句子开头，表示与第二部分的情况相反或不同〕: *Where most people saw nothing but a hardened criminal, Audrey saw a lonely and desperate man.* 许多人只看见一个冷酷无情的罪犯，但奥德丽却看到一个孤独而绝望的男人。 1 1

where·a·bouts[1] /͵hwɛrəˋbaʊts; ͵weərəˈbaʊts◂/ *adv spoken* used to ask in what general area something or someone is【口】在哪一带〔用于疑问句，不要求准确地点〕: *Whereabouts do you live?* 你住在哪一带?

where·a·bouts[2] /ˈhwɛrə͵baʊts; ˈweərəbaʊts/ *n* [U] the place or area where someone or something is〔某人或某物的〕去向；行踪: **sb's whereabouts** *His family refused to reveal his whereabouts.* 他的家人拒绝说出他的去向。| **the whereabouts of** *the whereabouts of the missing documents* 丢失文件的下落

where·as /hwɛrˋæz; weərˈæz/ *conj* **1** used to say that although something is true of one thing, it is not true of another 但是；却〔用于说某事不适用于所有情况〕: *Why are some cancers cured by chemotherapy alone, whereas others are unaffected by drugs?* 为什么有些癌症仅用化疗就能治愈，而有些用药物却不起作用呢? **2** *law* used at the beginning of an official document to mean because of a particular fact【法律】鉴于〔用于文件的开头〕 2 2

where·at /hwɛrˋæt; weərˈæt/ *conj formal*【正式】**1** used when something happens immediately after something else, or as a result of something happening; WHEREUPON 随即；于是 **2** at a particular place; WHERE (1) 在那里

where·by /hwɛrˋbaɪ; weəˈbaɪ/ *adv formal* by means of which or according to which【正式】由此；借以: *a law whereby the wearing of seat belts becomes compulsory* 强制系安全带的法律 3

where·fore /ˈhwɛr͵for; ˈweəfɔː/ *adv, conj old use*【旧】**1** used to ask why something has happened 为什么〔某事发生〕: *Wherefore comest thou?* 汝因何至此? **2** for that reason 为此，因此: *Skills are the art of doing, wherefore they must be taught by practical example.* 技能是实践的艺术，因此必须用实例来教。—see also 另见 **whys and wherefores** (WHY[3])

where·in /hwɛrˋɪn; weərˈɪn/ *adv, conj literary* in which place or part【文】在哪里；在哪方面: *the clay ovens wherein some farm wives still bake bread* 有些农妇仍然用来烘烤面包的泥灶 | *Wherein lies the difficulty?* 困难在哪儿?

where·of /hwɛrˋɑv; weərˈɒv/ *adv, conj old use* of which【旧】关于那个: *Theirs are the houses whereof I speak.* 我所说的是他们的房子。

where·on /hwɛrˋɑn; weərˈɒn/ *adv, conj old use* on which【旧】在那上面: *The sparrow flitted to the statue, whereon it perched.* 麻雀轻快地飞到塑像那里，在上面歇息。

where·so·ever /͵hwɛrsoˋɛvɚ; ͵weəsəʊˈevə/ *adv, conj literary* another word for WHEREVER【文】wherever的同义词

where·to /hwɛrˋtu; weəˈtuː/ *adv, conj old use* to which place【旧】向哪里

where·u·pon /͵hwɛrəˋpɑn; ͵weərəˈpɒn/ *conj* used when something happens immediately after something else, or as a result of something happening 马上；于是: *Molly banned her from the dining room, whereupon Bridget burst into tears.* 莫莉不准布丽奇特进饭厅，她于是大哭起来。

wher·ev·er /hwɛrˋɛvɚ; weərˈevə/ *adv* **1** to or at whatever place, position, or situation 无论去哪里；无论在任何地方；无论什么情况下: *If you could go wherever you wanted to in the world, where would you go?* 如果世界上任何地方你想去就能去的话，你会去哪儿? | *Sleep wherever you like.* 你爱睡哪儿都可以。| **... or wherever** (=used to emphasize that you are talking about 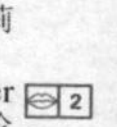

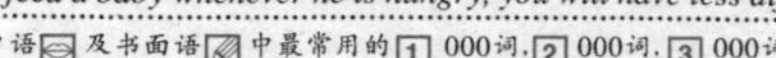

any place and not a specific place) 还是别的什么地方〔用于强调所述的不是一个特定的地方〕*There has been an increase in crime whether it be in Britain, France, Germany, or wherever.* 不论是在英国、法国、德国，还是别的什么地方，犯罪活动均有所增加。**2 wherever possible** when it is possible to do something 只要有可能〔做某事〕: *Wherever possible jobs are given to local people.* 只要有可能，工作都提供给当地人。**3** used at the beginning of a question to show surprise 究竟在哪儿〔用在问话前面，表示惊讶〕: *Wherever did you get that idea?* 那个念头你究竟是从哪儿来的? **4 wherever that may be** used to say that you do not know where a place or town is or have never heard of it〔表示不知道某地方或城镇的所在或从没有听说过〕: *Rita lives in Horwich now, wherever that may be.* 丽塔现在住在霍里奇，我不知道那个地方在哪儿。

where·with·al /ˈhwɛrwɪðˌɔl; ˈweəwɪðɔːl/ *n* **the wherewithal to do sth** the money you need in order to do something 做某事所需的金钱: *We don't have the wherewithal to pay for a big wedding.* 我们没有举行盛大婚礼所需的金钱。

whet /hwɛt; wet/ *v* [T] **1 whet sb's appetite (for sth)** if an experience whets your appetite for something, it increases your desire for it 引起某人(做某事)的欲望: *The trip to Paris has whetted my appetite for travel.* 巴黎之旅激起了我的旅游兴趣。**2** *literary* to make the edge of a blade sharp【文】〔将刃〕磨快

wheth·er /ˈhwɛðɚ; ˈweðə/ *conj* **1** used when talking about a choice you have to make or about two different possibilities 是否〔用于表示两种可能性中的选择〕: *He asked me whether she was coming.* 他问我她是否来。| *The decision whether to see her was mine alone.* 看不看她由我自己拿主意。| **whether or not** *I couldn't decide whether or not to go to the party.* 我拿不定主意参不参加这个聚会。**2** used to say that something definitely will or will not happen whatever the situation is 不管，不论〔用于表示无论发生哪种情况，某事肯定发生或不发生〕: *I'm sure we'll see each other again soon whether here or in New York.* 我深信我们不久会再见面的，不是在这里就是在纽约。| **whether... or not** *Whether you like it or not, you're going to have to face him one day.* 不管你乐意还是不乐意，总有一天你必须面对他。

USAGE NOTE 用法说明: WHETHER

GRAMMAR 语法

Whether and **if** are often used in similar contexts. However, **whether** is usually used for **if** when you also use the word **or** especially at the beginning of a sentence. whether 和 if 常用在相似的语境里。然而，在句子中与 or 连用，尤其在句子开头时，就常用 whether 代替 if。People say 人们常说: *Whether you see her or not, phone me later.* 不论你有没有见到她，过一会儿打电话给我。| *If you see her, phone me.* 如果你见到她，打电话给我。

If can usually be used instead of **whether** with clauses following some verbs and adjectives 与一些动词或形容词后面的从句连用时，if 通常替代 whether: *I wonder whether/if she can come.* 我不知道她是否能来。| *He wasn't sure whether/if he could come* (NOT 不用 *...whether could he come*). 他不敢肯定他是否能来。But you use **whether** (NOT **if**) before infinitives 但是，在不定式前用 whether (不用 if): *The question is whether to go or stay.* 问题是去还是留下。**Whether** is also used after prepositions. whether 也用在介词之后: *It depends on whether he's ready or not.* 这取决于他是否准备好了。It is also used after nouns 它也用在名词之后: *It's your decision whether you go or stay.* 去还是留要你自己拿主意。

You often use **whether** with **... or not** sentences, for example 常用whether…or not的句型, 如: *You're coming whether you like it or not.* 不管你乐意还是不乐意，你都要来。| *We have to decide whether or not to support this proposal.* 我们得决定是否支持这项提案。

SPELLING 拼法

Note the spelling is **whether** (NOT *weather*). *Weather* (=sunshine, snow etc) is a completely different word. 注意拼法是 whether 而不是 weather, weather (天气) 是完全不同的词。

whet·stone /ˈhwɛtˌston; ˈwetstəʊn/ *n* [C] a stone used to make the blade of cutting tools sharp 磨刀石

whew /hwju; hjuː/ *interjection* used when you are surprised, very hot, or feeling glad that something bad did not happen; PHEW 哟，唷，哎呀〔表示惊讶、感到炎热或高兴某种坏事竟然没有发生〕: *Whew, that man has some temper!* 唷，那个人的脾气真大!

whey /hwe; weɪ/ *n* [U] the watery liquid that is left after the solid part has been removed from sour milk〔酸牛奶中去掉凝乳部分后剩下的〕乳清

which /hwɪtʃ; wɪtʃ/ *determiner, pron* **1** used to ask or state what people or things you mean when a choice has to be made 哪一个；哪些〔用于选择疑问句中〕: *Which of these books is yours?* 这些书中哪本是你的? | *Ask him which one he wants.* 问问他想要哪一个。| *Karen comes from either Los Angeles or San Francisco, I can't remember which.* 卡伦不是来自洛杉矶就是来自旧金山，我记不清是哪个地方了。**2** used to show what specific thing or things you mean …的那个〔用于指明事物〕; …的那些: *Did you see the letter which came today?* 你看到今天来的那封信了吗? | *This is the book which I told you about.* 这就是我跟你说过的那本书。**3** used especially in written language after a COMMA, to add more information about a specific thing or things, or about the first part of the sentence〔尤用于书面语，放在逗号后，说明某物或句子开头部分〕: *The train, which takes only two hours, is quicker than the bus, which takes three.* 火车比公共汽车快，火车只用两小时，公共汽车却要三小时。| *The police arrived, after which the situation became calmer.* 警察到了，随后形势就平静下来。| **in which case** (=used to talk about a situation that you have just mentioned) 在那种情况下〔用于指刚提及的情况〕*She may have missed the train, in which case she won't arrive for another hour.* 她可能没有赶上火车，那样再过一个小时她也到不了。**4 which is which** used to say that you cannot tell the difference between two very similar people or things 谁是谁；哪个是哪个〔用于指无法区别两个相似的人或物〕: *They look so alike it's difficult to tell which is which.* 他们长得非常像，很难分清谁是谁。

USAGE NOTE 用法说明: WHICH

FORMALITY 正式程度

As subject of a relative clause which restricts the meaning of a noun, **that** is used more often than **which** in informal English. 在非正式英语中，限制名词含义的关系从句，用 that 作主语比用 which 作主语普遍: *the street market which/that is held near my house* 我家附近的集市

In informal or spoken English, you can often leave out **that** or **which**. For example, you are likely to say 在非正式或口头英语中，常可省略 that 或 which, 例如，可能会说: *Did you get the things you wanted?* 你拿到了想要的东西吗? rather than 而不说: *Did you get the things that/which you wanted?*

The form **to which** is very formal. to which 的形式极其正式: *He would lunch in one of the clubs to which he belonged.* 他参加了几家俱乐部，经常在其中一家吃中饭。You would more usually say 英语平常的说法是: *...one of the clubs (that) he belonged to.*

In relative clauses that add information but do not restrict the meaning of what comes before, you usually use **which**, especially after a comma 在补充信息但不限制先前的意思的关系从句中，尤其在逗号之后，通常用 which: *He's always really rude, which is why people tend to avoid him.* 他老是粗鲁不堪，所以人们总是躲着他。

Which? *trademark* a British magazine that tests products made by different companies and provides reports on them to help people decide which one to buy. There is a similar magazine in the US called Consumer Reports.【商标】《哪一个?》〔英国一杂志。该机构检测不同公司的产品，发布检测报告，帮助消费者作出选择。美国也有一类似杂志，名为《消费者报告》〕

which·ev·er /hwɪtʃˈɛvɚ; wɪtʃˈevə/ *determiner, pron* **1** used to say that it does not matter what thing you choose, what you do etc because it does not change the situation or someone's intention 无论哪个；无论哪些: *You can have whichever you like best.* 你可以拿你最喜欢的。| *Whichever way you look at it this is disastrous news for the shipping industry.* 无论你怎么看，对航运业而言，这是骇人听闻的消息。**2** used to talk about a specific thing, method etc …的那一个〔说及特定的事情、方法等〕: *I'll use whichever remedy the vet recommends.* 我将用兽医推荐的那一种治疗法。

whiff /hwɪf; wɪf/ *n* [C] **1** a very slight smell or something 一阵气味: [+of] *a whiff of garlic* 一股大蒜味儿 | **get/catch a whiff of** *As she walked past, I caught a whiff of her perfume.* 当她走过时，我闻到她身上的一股香水味儿。**2 a whiff of danger/adventure/freedom etc** a slight sign that something dangerous, exciting etc might happen 些微危险/冒险/自由等的迹象: *At the first whiff of trouble he was off like a shot.* 一有麻烦的迹象，他马上躲开了。

whif·fy /ˈhwɪfɪ; ˈwɪfi/ *adj BrE informal* having an unpleasant smell【英, 非正式】发出臭气的

Whig /hwɪg; wɪg/ *n* [C] a member of a British political party of the 18th and early 19th centuries which wanted to limit royal power, and later became the Liberal Party 辉格党党员〔辉格党是 18 世纪及 19 世纪初期英国的一个政党, 主张限制王室权力, 后成为自由党〕

while¹ /hwaɪl; waɪl/ *conjunction* **1** during the time that something is happening 当…时, 在…时: *They arrived while we were having dinner.* 他们来的时候, 我们正在吃饭。| *He got malaria while travelling in Africa.* 他在非洲旅行时患上了疟疾。**2** if something happens while something else is happening, it happens at the same time as it 与…同时(发生): *He was so tired he fell asleep while reading the newspaper.* 他疲惫不堪, 看着报纸就睡着了。**3** used to emphasize the difference between two situations, activities etc 却; 但是; 而〔用于强调两种情况、活动等之间的差别〕: *That region has plenty of natural resources while this one has none.* 那个地区自然资源丰富, 这个地区却一点也没有。**4** used to show that you partly agree with, or accept something but not completely 虽然, 尽管〔表示部分同意或接受某事〕: *While she is a likeable girl she can be extremely difficult to work with.* 她虽然是一个可爱的姑娘, 但有时很难与她共事。

while² *n* **a while** a period of time, especially a short one 一段时间, 〔尤指〕一会儿: *Can you wait a while or do you have to leave right now?* 你能等一会儿还是现在必须就走? | **a short/little while** *Bob's only been working here a short while.* 鲍勃在这里只工作了很短的一段时间。| **for a while** *He sat for a while, thinking about what Janice had said to him.* 他坐了一会儿, 思忖着贾妮丝跟他说过的话。| **quite a while** (=a fairly long time) 相当长的一段时间 | **all the while** (=all the time) 一直, 始终 —see also 另见 **once in a while** (ONCE¹ (8)), **it's worth your while** (WORTH¹ (5))

while³ *v* **while away the hours/evening/days etc** to spend time in a pleasant and lazy way 消磨时间/夜晚/日子等: *We whiled away the summer evenings talking and drinking wine.* 我们聊天、喝酒来打发夏日的夜晚。

While shep·herds watched their flocks by night /·, ·· , · ·, · ·ˈ/ the title and first line of a Christmas CAROL (=a traditional religious song)《牧人闻信》〔一首圣诞颂歌的曲名及首句唱词〕

whilst /hwaɪlst; waɪlst/ *conj especially BrE formal* WHILE¹【尤英, 正式】当…时; 与…同时; 却; 尽管

whim /hwɪm; wɪm/ *n* [C] a sudden feeling that you would like to do something or have something, especially when there is no particularly important or good reason 突发的念头, 一时的兴致: **on a whim** (=because of a whim) 兴之所至 *I went to visit her on a whim.* 我心血来潮就去看她了。| **at the whim of** *The palace decor kept changing at the whim of the princess.* 宫殿的装饰随着公主的心意不断更换。| **a passing whim** (=one that will soon be forgotten) 短暂的念头 | **sb's every whim** *I was spoiled. My every whim was catered to.* 我被宠坏了, 我的每一个怪念头都得到迎合。

whim·per /ˈhwɪmpɚ; ˈwɪmpə/ *v* [I] to make low crying sounds, or to speak in this way 呜咽, 啜泣; 抽噎地说: *The dog whimpered in the corner.* 那只狗在角落处呜咽地叫。| *"Okay," he managed to whimper.* 他啜泣着说: "好的。" —**whimper** *n* [C]

whim·si·cal /ˈhwɪmzɪkl; ˈwɪmzɪkəl/ *adj* unusual or strange and often amusing 古怪的; 异想天开的: *a whimsical smile* 古怪的笑 —**whimsically** /-klɪ; -kli/ *adv* —**whimsicality** /ˌhwɪmzəˈkælətɪ; ˌwɪmzɪˈkæləti/ *n* [U]

whim·sy /ˈhwɪmzɪ; ˈwɪmzi/ *n* **1** [U] a way of thinking or behaving that is unusual, strange, and often amusing 古怪〔而往往好笑的〕想法; 古怪[荒诞]行径 **2** [C] a strange idea or desire that does not seem to have any sensible purpose 离奇的想法, 怪念头: *This room, by some architectural whimsy, completely unbalanced the house.* 由于建筑上的一些奇思怪想, 这房间使整栋房屋完全失去了均衡感。

whine /hwaɪn; waɪn/ *v* [I] **1** to complain in a sad, annoying voice about something 哀诉; 嘀咕: *For goodness sake stop whining, it's not much further to go.* 千万不要抱怨了, 没有多少路要走了。| [+about] *Mark always seems to be whining about his job.* 马克好像总是对自己的工作埋怨个没完。**2** to make a long high sound because you are in pain or unhappy 〔因痛楚或不愉快而〕悲鸣, 哀叫: *a dog whining outside the door* 门外一条哀叫的狗 **3** if a machine whines, it makes a continuous high sound 〔机器〕发出嘎嘎响 —**whine** *n* [C]: *the whine of the plane's engine* 飞机发动机的嗡嗡声 —**whiner** *n* [C]

whinge /hwɪndʒ; wɪndʒ/ *v* [I] *BrE or AustrE* to keep complaining in an annoying way【英或澳】唠叨; 嘀咕: *Stop whingeing and get on with it!* 不要嘀嘀咕咕个没完, 继续干下去! —**whinge** *n* [C] —**whinger** *n* [C]: *People with genuine grievances are being dismissed as whingers.* 真正受委屈的人被当作发牢骚者解雇了。

whin·ny /ˈhwɪnɪ; ˈwɪni/ *v* [I] if a horse whinnies, it NEIGHS (=makes the sound that horses makes) quietly 〔马〕轻声嘶叫 —**whinny** *n* [C]

whip 鞭子

whip
鞭子

crop
短马鞭

whip¹ /hwɪp; wɪp/ *n* **1** [C] a long thin piece of rope or leather with a handle used for making animals move or punishing people 〔赶牲口或惩罚人用的〕鞭子: **crack a whip** (=make a loud noise with a whip) 甩响鞭 **2** [C] a member of the US Congress or the British Parliament who is responsible for making sure that the members of their party attend and vote 〔美国国会或英国议会中负责督导本党议员出席会议及投票的〕党鞭; 组织秘书; 政党的纪律委员 —see also 另见 CHIEF WHIP **3** [C] a written order sent to members of the US Congress or the British Parliament telling them when and how to vote 〔送交美国国会或英国议会议员有关投票事宜的〕书面通知 —see also 另见 TWO-LINE WHIP, THREE-LINE WHIP **4** **chocolate whip/strawberry whip etc** [C,U] *BrE* a sweet dish made from the white part of eggs and chocolate or fruit, beaten together to make a smooth, light mixture【英】〔蛋清、巧克力或水果搅拌而成的〕巧克力/草莓甜点等 —see also 另见 **crack the whip** (CRACK¹ (20)), **give sb a fair crack of the whip** (FAIR¹ (11))

whip², **whipped**, **whipping** *v* **1** [T] to hit someone with a whip 鞭打〔某人〕 **2** [I always+adv/prep] [T always+adv/prep] to move quickly and violently, or to make something do this 迅速[猛地]移动: [+across/around/past etc] *The wind whipped across the plain.* 风扫过平原。| **whip sth about/around** *The branches were being whipped about in the storm.* 树枝在狂风中四处摇曳。| **whip around/round** (=turn around quickly) 快速转身 *Suddenly, he whipped around and glared at them.* 突然之间, 他转过身来, 对着他们怒目而视。**3** [T always+adv/prep] to move or remove something with a quick sudden movement 突然移动[挪开]〔某物〕: [+away/off/out etc] *He whipped out a gun.* 他突然抽出枪来。**4** [T] also 又作 **whip up** to mix cream or the clear part of an egg very hard until it becomes stiff 搅打〔奶油或蛋清〕使成糊状 —see also 另见 WHISK¹, BEAT¹ (7) **5** **have the whip hand** to have power and control over someone 支配[控制]某人 **6** [T] to make a TOP¹ (25) spin by using a piece of string fixed to a stick 抽〔陀螺并使之转动〕 **7** [T] *BrE informal* to steal something【英, 非正式】偷走〔某物〕

whip through sth *phr v* [T] *informal especially BrE* to finish a job very quickly【非正式, 尤英】快速做完: *I can whip through all the cleaning in about half an hour.* 在大约半小时之内, 我能很快地把所有清洁工作做完。

whip up *phr v* [T] **1** **whip up support/anger/enthusiasm etc** to deliberately try to make people feel or react strongly 引发支持/煽起愤怒/激起热情等: *The rally was organised to whip up support for the independence campaign.* 组织群众集会以激起对独立运动的支持。| **whip up a crowd** *a speech designed to whip up the crowd* 意在鼓动民众的演讲 **2** [**whip** sth ↔ **up**] to quickly make something to eat 匆匆做好〔饭菜〕: *I just had time to whip up a light salad before I went out again.* 我在再次外出前正好有时间匆匆做一份清淡的沙拉。

whip·cord /ˈhwɪpˌkɔrd; ˈwɪpkɔːd/ *n* [U] **1** a strong type of CORD¹ (1) 鞭绳〔一种结实的细绳〕 **2** a strong woollen material 马裤呢

whip·lash /ˈhwɪpˌlæʃ; ˈwɪp-læʃ/ *n* [C,U] a neck injury caused when your head moves forward and back again suddenly and violently, especially in a car accident 鞭抽式损伤〔尤指汽车事故中颈椎过度屈伸损伤〕

whipped cream /ˌ· ˈ·/ *n* [U] cream that has been beaten until it is thick, eaten on sweet foods〔作为甜点食用的〕掼奶油

whip·per·snap·per /ˈhwɪpɚˌsnæpɚ; ˈwɪpəˌsnæpə/ *n* [C] *old-fashioned* a young person who is too confident and does not show enough respect to older people【过时】妄自尊大的年轻人，傲慢无礼的小子

whip·pet /ˈhwɪpɪt; ˈwɪpɪt/ *n* [C] a small thin racing dog like a GREYHOUND〔赛狗用的〕灵㹴

whip·ping /ˈhwɪpɪŋ; ˈwɪpɪŋ/ *n* [C usually singular 一般用单数] a punishment given to someone by whipping them; WHIP² (1)〔作为惩罚的〕鞭笞；鞭刑

whipping boy /ˈ·· ·/ *n* [singular] someone or something that is blamed for someone else's mistakes; SCAPEGOAT 代人受过者，替罪羊

whipping cream /ˈ·· ˌ·/ *n* [U] a type of cream that becomes very stiff when you beat it 可打稠制作掼奶油的奶油

whip·poor·will /ˌhwɪpɚˈwɪl; ˈwɪpʊəˌwɪl/ *n* [C] a small North American bird which makes a noise that sounds like its name 三声夜鹰〔一种产于北美洲的小鸟〕

whip·py /ˈhwɪpɪ; ˈwɪpi/ *adj* long, thin, and easy to bend 鞭子似的；易弯曲的

whip-round /ˈ· ·/ *n* **have a whip-round** *BrE informal* if a group of people have a whip-round, they all give some money so that they can buy something together【英，非正式】〔一群人〕凑钱〔买某物〕: *We're having a whip-round to get Sandy something for her birthday.* 我们正在凑钱买生日礼物送给桑迪。

Whip·snade /ˈhwɪpsned; ˈwɪpsneɪd/ an open-air zoo in Bedfordshire, southern England, where the animals are given a lot of freedom and are kept in natural surroundings 惠普斯奈德动物园〔英格兰南部贝德福德郡一露天动物园。园内动物享有很大自由，生活在自然环境中〕

whir /hwɝ; wɜː/ *v* [I] another spelling of WHIRR whirr 的另一种拼法

whirl¹ /hwɝl; wɜːl/ *v* **1** [I,T] to spin around very quickly, or to make something do this 急转；迅速旋转: **[+about/around/toward etc]** *The snowflakes whirled around as they fell to the ground.* 雪花打着转飘落到地面。| **whirl sth about/around/away etc** *Jim whirled the bike around.* 吉姆飞快地转着自行车。**2** [I] if your head is whirling, your mind is full of thoughts and ideas, and you feel very confused or excited 晕眩；〔思绪〕混乱

whirl² *n* [C usually singular 一般用单数] **1** a whirling movement 旋转，回旋: *a whirl of dust* 卷起的尘土 **2** **give sth a whirl** *informal* to try something that you are not sure you are going to like or be able to do【非正式】尝试〔不知道是否会喜欢或做得到的〕某事 **3** [singular] a lot of activity of a particular kind 接连不断的某类活动: *the mad social whirl around Christmas* 圣诞节期间纷乱繁忙的社交活动 **4** **be in a whirl** to feel very excited or confused about something〔对某事感到〕十分兴奋；一片混乱

whir·li·gig /ˈhwɝlɪˌgɪg; ˈwɜːlɪˌgɪg/ *n* [C] **1** a toy that spins; TOP¹ (25) 旋转式玩具；陀螺 **2** a MERRY-GO-ROUND (1) 旋转木马

whirl·pool /ˈhwɝlˌpul; ˈwɜːlpuːl/ *n* [C] a powerful current of water that spins around and can pull things down into it 旋涡

whirl·wind /ˈhwɝlˌwɪnd; ˈwɜːlˌwɪnd/ *n* [C] **1** an extremely strong wind that moves quickly with a circular movement, causing a lot of damage 旋风，龙卷风; TORNADO, TWISTER (2) *AmE*【美】**2** **a whirlwind romance/tour etc** something that happens much more quickly than usual 旋风式恋爱/旅行等〔指发生的速度很快〕**3** **a whirlwind of activity/emotions etc** a situation in which you experience a lot of different activities or emotions one after another 一连串的活动/激情等

whirr /hwɝ; wɜː/ **whirred, whirring** *v* [I] to make a fairly quiet, regular sound, like the sound of a bird or insect moving its wings very fast〔像鸟或昆虫快速拍动翅膀一样〕呼呼作响；啪啪作响: *Cameras whirred and reporters scribbled.* 照相机咔咔地响，记者匆匆地记录。—**whirr** *n* [C usually singular 一般用单数] —see picture on page A19 参见 A19 页图

whisk¹ /hwɪsk; wɪsk/ *v* [T] to mix liquid or soft things very quickly so that air is mixed in, especially with a fork or a whisk〔尤指用叉子或搅拌器〕搅打

whisk sb/sth ↔ **away** *phr v* [T] **1** to take or remove something very quickly 迅速拿开〔某物〕: *He whisked the letter away before I could read it.* 他没等我看就匆匆把信拿走了。**2** to take someone quickly away from a place 将〔某人〕急忙送离〔某地〕: *At the end of the concert the band was whisked away to a secret location.* 音乐会结束时，乐队被匆匆送往一个秘密场所。

whisk sb **off** *phr v* [T] to take someone quickly away from a place; whisk away 将〔某人〕急忙送离〔某地〕

whisk² *n* [C] **1** a small kitchen tool made of curved pieces of wire used for beating eggs, cream etc〔搅拌鸡蛋、奶油等的〕搅拌器 —see picture on page A11 参见 A11 页图 **2** [usually singular 一般用单数] a quick light sweeping movement 扫；拂，掸: **[+of]** *The cow brushed away the flies with a whisk of its tail.* 这头母牛甩动尾巴拂去苍蝇。

whisk broom /ˈ· ·/ *n* [C] *AmE* a small stiff BROOM (1) that you use to brush clothes【美】〔刷衣服用的〕掸帚；小笤帚

whis·ker /ˈhwɪskɚ; ˈwɪskə/ *n* [C] **1** one of the long, stiff hairs that grow near the mouth of a cat, mouse etc〔猫、老鼠等嘴边的〕须 **2** **whiskers** [plural] the hair that grows on a man's face〔男人的〕连鬓胡子，颊须，髯须 **3** **do sth by a whisker/come within a whisker** *informal* to only just fail or just manage to do something【非正式】做某事险些…: *We came within a whisker of defeat.* (=were almost defeated) 我们差点战败了。—**whiskery** *adj*

whis·key /ˈhwɪskɪ; ˈwɪski/ *n* [C,U] a strong alcoholic drink made in Ireland or the US from grain, or a glass of this〔爱尔兰或美国产的〕威士忌酒；一杯威士忌酒

whis·ky /ˈhwɪskɪ; ˈwɪski/ *n* [C,U] a strong alcoholic drink made in Scotland from grain such as BARLEY, or a glass of this〔苏格兰产的〕威士忌酒；一杯威士忌酒 3

whis·per¹ /ˈhwɪspɚ; ˈwɪspə/ *v* **1** [I,T] to speak or say something very quietly, using your breath rather than your voice 悄声说；低语；耳语: *What are you two whispering about over there?* 你们两人在那边嘀咕什么？| **whisper sth to sb** *James leaned over to whisper something to Michael.* 詹姆斯俯身跟迈克尔低声说了点什么。**2** [T+that] to say or suggest something privately or secretly〔私下或秘密地〕传说〔某事〕: *Some White House staff were whispering that the President was no longer in control.* 一些白宫职员在窃窃私语，说总统不再掌权了。 3

whisper² *n* [C] **1** a very quiet voice, when you are whispering 低语；耳语: **in a whisper** *"They're coming," he said in an excited whisper.* 他压低声音激动地说："他们来了。" **2** a piece of news or information that has not been officially announced; RUMOUR 传闻；谣言: *The first whisper of the redundancies came from the newspapers.* 最初的裁员消息来自报纸。| **[+that]** *I've heard a whisper that he's going to resign.* 我听到一个传闻，说他准备辞职。**3** **a whisper of wind/silk etc** *literary* a low soft sound made by wind etc【文】风/丝绸等轻柔的飒飒声

whis·per·ing cam·paign /ˈ···· ˌ·/ *n* [C] an attack on someone that is made by privately spreading criticism about them 造谣活动〔指私下散布谣言攻击某人〕

whist /hwɪst; wɪst/ *n* [U] a card game for four players in two pairs, in which each pair tries to win the most tricks (TRICK¹ (11))〔由四人组成两对对打的〕惠斯特纸牌戏

whist drive /ˈ· ·/ *n* [C] a meeting to play whist between several pairs of partners who change opponents 惠斯特纸牌戏比赛

whis·tle¹ /ˈhwɪsl; ˈwɪsəl/ *v*

1 ►**HIGH SOUND** 高声◄ [I,T] to make a high or musical sound by blowing air out through your lips 吹口哨；用口哨吹奏〔曲调〕: *Adam whistled happily as he walked along.* 亚当一边走一边愉快地吹着口哨。| **whistle a song/tune** *I heard this song on the radio and I've been whistling it all day.* 我在收音机里听过这首歌，然后整天用口哨吹它的曲调。| **whistle to sb** (=to get their attention) 向某人吹口哨〔以引起对方注意〕*Adrian whistled to them but they didn't seem to hear him.* 阿德里安向他们吹口哨，可他们似乎没有听见。

2 ►**USE A WHISTLE** 用哨子◄ [I] to make a high sound by blowing into a whistle 吹哨子: *The referee whistled and the game began.* 裁判哨声一响，比赛开始了。

3 ►**GO/MOVE FAST** 快速运动◄ [I always+adv/prep] to move quickly with a whistling sound 呼啸着行进: *Bullets and shells were whistling overhead.* 子弹和炮弹在头顶呼啸而过。

4 ►**STEAM TRAIN/KETTLE** 蒸汽火车/水壶◄ [I] to make a high sound when air or steam is forced through a small hole 鸣汽笛；响壶哨

5 ►**BIRD** 鸟◄ [I] to make a high, often musical sound〔鸟〕啭鸣

6 **whistle in the dark** *informal* to try to show that you are brave when really you are afraid【非正式】借吹口哨壮胆，故作镇定: *Her fine words had been so much whistling in the dark.* 她的豪言壮语都是虚张声势。

7 **you can whistle for it** *BrE spoken* used to tell someone that there is no chance of them getting what they have asked for【英口】空指望；一定得不到〔想要的东西〕

8 **not be whistling Dixie** *AmE spoken* to be saying something because it is true, not just because you wish it was true【美口】认真的〔表示某物是真的，并非出于个人愿望〕: *Hey, this is good – and I'm not just whistling Dixie.* 嘿，这个好——我不是闹着玩的。

whistle² *n* [C] **1** a small object that produces a high whistling sound when you blow into it 哨子: **blow a whistle** *Wait till the referee blows his whistle.* 等到裁判吹响哨子。—see also 另见 PENNY WHISTLE **2** a high sound made by blowing a whistle, by blowing air out through your lips, or when air or steam is forced through a small opening 口哨声; 哨子声; 汽笛声 —see also 另见 WOLF WHISTLE **3** the sound of something moving quickly through the air 呼啸声: *the whistle of the wind in the trees* 风吹过树林的呼啸声 —see also 另见 **blow the whistle on** (BLOW[1] (22)), **as clean as a whistle** (CLEAN[1] (19)), **wet your whistle** (WET[2] (3))

whistle·blow·er /ˈ· ·, ·ˈ/ *n* [C] someone who tells people in authority or the public about dishonest or illegal practices in business, government etc〔将企业、政府等中的欺诈或非法行为揭发出来的〕告发者, 告密者 —see also 另见 **blow the whistle on** (BLOW[1] (22)) —**whistle-blowing** *n* [U]

Whis·tler /ˈhwɪslɚ; ˈwɪslə/, **James Mc·Neill** /dʒemz məkˋnil; dʒeɪmz məkˈniːl/ (1834-1903) a US artist most famous for the picture known as *Whistler's Mother* 惠斯勒〔(1834-1903), 美国画家, 以作品《艺术家的母亲》闻名〕

whistle-stop /ˈ· · ·/ *n* [C] *AmE* a town where trains stop only if there are passengers who want to get on or off【美】〔遇有乘客想上、下火车才停的〕招呼站, 小站

whistle-stop tour /ˌ· · ˈ· ·/ *n* [C] a very quick trip around a place 短暂的旅行访问: *a whistle-stop tour of the United States* 对美国作短暂的旅行访问

Whit /hwɪt; wɪt/ *n* [C,U] *especially BrE* WHITSUN【尤英】圣灵降临节

whit *n* **not a whit** *old use* not at all【旧】一点不, 毫不

Whit·ak·er's Al·ma·nack /ˌhwɪtəkɚz ˈɔlmənæk; ˌwɪtəkəz ˈɔːlmənæk/ *trademark* a book produced every year in the UK since 1868, which provides useful information about the UK and its government, and about other countries【商标】《惠特克年鉴》〔英国自1868年起每年出版的年鉴, 提供有关英国、英国政府及其他国家的有用资料〕

S1 W1 **white¹** /hwaɪt; waɪt/ *adj* **1** having the colour of milk, salt or snow 白的; 白色的; 雪白的: *white paint* 白油漆 —see picture on page A5 参见A5页图 **2** looking pale, because of illness, strong emotion etc〔因疾病、感情激动等而面色〕苍白的; 无血色的: **white with anger/fear etc** *Her face was white with fear.* 她吓得脸色苍白。| **white as a sheet** (=extremely pale because you are frightened, ill etc)〔因惊慌、生病等〕面色苍白 **3 a)** belonging to a race with pale skin〔人〕白种的 **b)** of or for white people 白人的; 白人用的: *a white neighborhood* 白人居住区 **4** white coffee has milk or cream in it〔咖啡〕加牛奶[奶油]的 —opposite 反义词 BLACK[1] (3) **5** white wine is a very pale yellow or pale green colour〔白葡萄酒〕淡黄色的; 浅绿色的 —**whiteness** *n* [U]

S3 **white²** *n* **1** [U] the colour of milk, salt, and snow 白色 **2** [C] someone who belongs to a pale-skinned race 白种人, 白人: *The party got a lot of support from South Africa's whites.* 该政党得到众多南非白人的支持。**3** [C+of] the white part of your eye 眼白 **4** [C,U] the transparent part of an egg that surrounds the YOLK (=yellow part) 蛋清, 蛋白 **5 whites** [plural] **a)** white clothes, sheets etc, which are separated from dark colours when they are washed〔洗涤时要跟深色衣物分开的〕白色衣服[床单]等 **b)** *especially BrE* white clothes that are worn for some sports, such as TENNIS【尤英】〔做某些运动, 如打网球时穿的〕白色运动服

White, Pearl (1889-1938) a US actress who worked in silent films, for example being tied to a railway line by the VILLAIN when a train is coming. 怀特〔(1889-1938), 美国女演员。出演过无声电影, 比如在一部影片中有列火车就要驶来, 她被剧中的恶棍绑在铁轨上〕

White, Reg·gie /ˈrɛdʒɪ; ˈredʒi/ (1961-) a US football player who is famous for achieving the most SACKs in the NFL 怀特〔(1961-), 美式橄榄球运动员。他以在全国橄榄球联盟比赛中擒杀次数最多而著称〕

white ant /ˌ· ˈ·/ *n* [C] a TERMITE 白蚁

white·bait /ˈhwaɪtˌbet; ˈwaɪtbeɪt/ *n* [U] very young fish of several types, used as food 银鱼〔数种供食用的鱼类之幼鱼〕: *deep-fried whitebait* 油炸银鱼

white blood cell /ˌ· ˈ· · ·/ *n* [C] one of the cells in your blood which fights against infection; LEUCOCYTE 白细胞, 白血球 —compare 比较 RED BLOOD CELL

white·board /ˈhwaɪtˌbɔrd; ˈwaɪtbɔːd/ *n* [C] a large board with a white, smooth surface used in classrooms for writing on〔书写用的〕白板 —compare 比较 BLACKBOARD —see picture at 参见 BOARD[1] 图

white-bread /ˈ· ·/ *adj AmE informal* ordinary and traditional in your opinions and way of life【美, 非正式】〔意见和生活方式〕平淡无奇的, 恪守传统的; 典型白人中产阶级口味的: *a white-bread family* 典型白人中产阶级家庭

white·caps /ˈhwaɪtˌkæps; ˈwaɪtkæps/ *n* [plural] *AmE* WHITE HORSES【美】白浪

White Cliffs of Do·ver, the /ˌ· ˌ· · ˈ· ·/ **1** the white cliffs made of CHALK, which are the first part of England that you see when crossing the English Channel from France 多佛尔海峡的白色峭壁〔为白垩质悬崖, 是从法国穿越英吉利海峡抵达英国时最先映入眼帘的英国国土〕**2** a popular song sung by British singer Vera Lynn during World War II《多佛尔海峡的白色峭壁》〔二战期间英国歌手维拉·林恩演唱的一首流行歌曲〕

white-col·lar /ˌ· ˈ· ·◂/ *adj* **1** white-collar workers work in offices, banks etc as opposed to people who work in factories, mines etc〔在办公室、银行等工作的〕白领阶层的〔与在工厂、矿山等工作的人相比〕**2 white-collar crime** crimes involving white-collar workers, for example when someone secretly steals money from the organization they work for〔偷盗公款等〕白领犯罪 —compare 比较 BLUE-COLLAR, PINK-COLLAR

white cor·pus·cle /ˌ· ˈ· · ·/ *n* [C] a WHITE BLOOD CELL 白细胞, 白血球

white dwarf /ˌ· ˈ·/ *n* [C] *technical* a hot star, near the end of its life, that is more solid but less bright than the sun【术语】白矮星 —compare 比较 RED GIANT

white el·e·phant /ˌ· ˈ· · ·/ *n* [C] something that is completely useless, although it may have cost a lot of money 昂贵而无用的东西

white flag /ˌ· ˈ·/ *n* [C] a sign that you accept that you have been defeated〔投降用的〕白旗: **wave/show the white flag** (=accept defeat) 挥动/举起白旗〔投降〕*There was no question of the Republicans throwing in the towel or showing the white flag.* 共和党党员不会认输, 这是毫无疑问的。

white flour /ˌ· ˈ·/ *n* [U] wheat flour from which the BRAN (=outer layer) and WHEAT GERM (=inside seed) have been removed〔去掉麦麸及麦胚的〕精白面粉 —compare 比较 WHOLEMEAL

white goods /ˈ· ·/ *n* [plural] a word used especially in business meaning large pieces of equipment used in the home, for example washing machines and REFRIGERATORS 大型家用电器〔此词尤用于商业, 指洗衣机、冰箱等〕—compare 比较 BLACK GOODS

White·hall /ˈhwaɪtˌhɔl; ˈwaɪthɔːl/ *n* [U] **1** the British government, especially the government departments rather than parliament or the Prime Minister 英国政府〔尤指政府部门而不是议会或首相〕**2** the street in London where many of the government departments are 白厅〔英国很多政府部门所在的伦敦的一条街道〕

white heat /ˌ· ˈ·/ *n* [U] the very high temperature at which a metal turns white 白热〔金属变成白色的高温〕—see also 另见 WHITE-HOT

white hors·es /ˌ· ˈ· ·/ *n* [plural] *BrE* waves in the sea or on a lake that are white at the top【英】白浪; WHITECAPS *AmE*【美】

white-hot /ˌ· ˈ·◂/ *adj* white-hot metal is so hot that it shines white〔金属〕白热的

White House, the /ˈ· ·/ *n* **1** the President of the US and the people who advise him 美国总统〔及其顾问人员〕**2** the official home in Washington DC of the President of the US 白宫〔美国总统官邸, 在华盛顿特区〕

white knight /ˌ· ˈ·/ *n* [C] a person or company that puts money into a business in order to save it from being controlled by another company〔为某公司提供资金使其免受其他公司控制的〕白衣骑士; 救星, 救急的人[公司]

white-knuck·led /ˌ· ˈ· ·◂/ *adj* anxious or afraid 神经紧张的; 害怕的

white lead /ˌhwaɪt ˋlɛd; ˌwaɪt ˈled/ *n* [U] a poisonous compound of lead with CARBON (1) and oxygen, used in the past in house paint〔旧时用于油漆的〕铅白

white lie /ˌ· ˈ·/ *n* [C] *informal* a lie that you tell in order to avoid hurting someone's feelings【非正式】善意的谎话; 无伤大雅的谎言

white light·ning /ˌ· ˈ· ·/ *n* [U] *AmE slang* MOONSHINE (=illegal strong alcohol)【美俚】非法酿造的烈酒

white ma·gic /ˌ· ˈ· ·/ *n* [U] magic used for good purposes 善意的法术, 白法术, 白魔术 —compare 比较 BLACK MAGIC

white meat /ˈ· ·/ *n* [U] meat that is pale in colour, especially from some types of cooked bird, for example chicken 白肉〔尤指某些家禽煮熟的肉, 如鸡肉〕—compare 比较 RED MEAT

whit·en /ˈhwaɪtn̩; ˈwaɪtn/ *v* [I,T] to become more white, or to make something do this 使更白; 变白; 漂白; 刷白

whit·en·er /ˈhwaɪtnə; ˈwaɪtnə/ also 又作 **whit·en·ing** /ˈhwaɪtnɪŋ; ˈwaɪtnɪŋ/ *n* [C,U] a substance used to make something more white 增白剂

White Nile, the /,· ·ˈ/ a river which flows from Lake Victoria in East Africa to Khartoum in Sudan, where it joins the Blue Nile. Both rivers then become the Nile, which flows through Egypt to the Mediterranean Sea. 白尼罗河〔发源于东非维多利亚湖的一条河流，在苏丹喀土穆与青尼罗河交汇形成尼罗河，然后流经埃及，注入地中海〕

white noise /,· ˈ·/ *n* [U] noise coming from a radio or television which is turned on but not tuned (TUNE[2] (3)) to any programme 白噪声〔收音机或电视机没有调到有节目的频道而发出〕

white·out /ˈhwaɪt,aʊt; ˈwaɪtaʊt/ *n* **1** [C] weather conditions in which there is so much cloud or snow that you cannot see anything 乳白天空〔一种天气现象，因云或冰雪太多而使人眼花缭乱〕 **2** [U] *AmE* TIPP-EX【美】修正液，涂改液

White Pag·es, the /,· ˈ··/ *n* the white part of a telephone DIRECTORY in the US with the names, addresses, and phone numbers of people with telephones 白页电话簿〔美国的电话簿，刊登电话用户的姓名、地址和电话号码〕—compare 比较 YELLOW PAGES

White Pa·per /,· ˈ··/ *n* [C] an official report from the British government, explaining their ideas and plans concerning a particular subject before a new law is introduced 白皮书〔英国政府就某一问题在立法前所作的正式报告〕—compare 比较 GREEN PAPER

white pep·per /,· ˈ··/ *n* [U] a white powder made from the crushed inside of a PEPPERCORN which gives a slightly hot taste to food 白胡椒粉

White Rab·bit, the /,· ˈ··/ a character from *Alice's Adventures in Wonderland* by Lewis Carroll. He keeps looking at his watch because he is late, and disappearing down rabbit holes. 白兔〔刘易斯·卡罗尔所著《艾丽丝漫游奇境记》中的人物。故事中他因迟到而频频看表，并不时消失在兔子洞中〕—see also 另见 ALICE IN WONDERLAND

white sale /ˈ· ·/ *n* [C] *AmE* a period when sheets, TOWELS etc, are sold for a lower price【美】〔床单、毛巾等家用织物的〕削价销售期

white sauce /,· ˈ·/ *n* [C,U] a thick white liquid made of flour, milk, and butter which is sometimes eaten with meat and vegetables 白汁，白汁沙司〔用面粉、牛奶和黄油做成，有时拌着肉和蔬菜吃〕

white slav·e·ry /,· ˈ···/ *n* [U] *old-fashioned* the practice or business of taking girls to a foreign country and forcing them to be PROSTITUTES【过时】拐卖妇女到外国为娼

white space /,· ˈ·/ *n* [U] *AmE informal* free time【美，非正式】自由时间；闲暇时间

white spir·it /,· ˈ··/ *n* [U] *BrE* a chemical liquid made from petrol, used for making paint thinner, removing marks on clothes etc; TURPENTINE【英】〔稀释油漆等用的〕石油溶剂油

white su·prem·a·cy /,· ·ˈ···/ *n* [U] the belief that white people are better than other races and that other races should be kept at a lower social level 白人至上〔认为白人比其他人种优越，应把其他人种限制在社会低层的看法〕—**white supremacist** *n* [C]

white-tailed deer /,· ,· ˈ·/ *n* [C] a common North American DEER with a long tail that is partly white 白尾鹿，弗吉尼亚鹿〔产于北美，长尾巴部分呈白色〕

white-tie /,· ˈ·◂/ *adj* a white-tie social occasion is a very formal one at which the men wear white BOW TIES and tails (TAIL[1] (5b))〔非常正式的社交场合男士〕系白领结并穿燕尾服的 —compare 比较 BLACK-TIE

white trash /,· ˈ·/ *n* [U] *AmE informal* an insulting expression meaning white people who are poor and uneducated【美，非正式】穷苦白人〔冒犯语〕

white·wall /ˈhwaɪt,wɔl; ˈwaɪtwɔːl/ *n* [C] *AmE* a car tyre that has a wide white band on its side【美】胎壁上有宽阔白色环子的轮胎，白胎壁轮胎

white·wash[1] /ˈhwaɪt,waʃ; ˈwaɪtwɒʃ/ *n* **1** [C,U] a report or examination of events that hides the true facts about something so that the person who is responsible will not be punished 掩饰真相；粉饰 **2** [U] a white liquid mixture used especially for painting walls〔尤指刷墙用的〕石灰水 **3** [C] an easy win in sport〔在体育运动中〕轻而易举的胜利

whitewash[2] *v* [T] **1** to hide the true facts about a serious accident or illegal action 掩饰〔严重意外或非法行为的真相〕；粉饰 **2** to cover something with whitewash 用石灰水粉刷〔某物〕 **3** to defeat an opponent in sport easily〔在体育运动中〕轻松击败〔对手〕

white·wa·ter /,hwaɪtˈwɔtə; ,waɪtˈwɔːtə◂/ *n* [U] a part of a river that looks white because the water is running very quickly over rocks; RAPIDS〔河水撞击岩石后的〕浪花；湍流: *whitewater canoeing* 激流中划独木舟

white wed·ding /,· ˈ··/ *n* [C] a traditional wedding at which the woman being married wears a long white dress 新娘披白色婚纱的婚礼

whit·ey /ˈhwaɪtɪ; ˈwaɪti/ *n* [C,U] *AmE slang* an insulting word for a white person or white people in general, used especially by black people【美俚】白鬼〔尤用于黑人称白人〕

whith·er /ˈhwɪðə; ˈwɪðə/ *adv old use*【旧】**1** a word meaning 'to which', used when talking about places 去何处；往哪儿: *the place whither he went* 他去的那个地方 **2** a word meaning 'where' …的地方 **3** *formal* a word used to ask what the future of something will be or how it will develop【正式】向何处去〔用于问某事的未来或发展〕: *Whither European Union?* 欧洲联盟何去何从？—compare 比较 WHENCE

whit·ing /ˈhwaɪtɪŋ; ˈwaɪtɪŋ/ *n* [C] a black and silver fish that lives in the sea and can be eaten 牙鳕〔一种可食用的海鱼〕

whit·ish /ˈhwaɪtɪʃ; ˈwaɪtɪʃ/ *adj* almost white in colour 带白色的

Whit·man /ˈhwɪtmən; ˈwɪtmən/, **Walt** /wɔlt; wɔːlt/ (1819-92) a US writer who wrote poetry about the beauty of nature and the value of freedom. He is one of the greatest and most influential US poets, and his best-known work is *Leaves of Grass*. 惠特曼〔(1819-1892)，美国作家。其诗篇描写自然之瑰丽，颂扬自由之可贵。他是最伟大和最具影响力的美国诗人之一，代表作为《草叶集》〕

Whit Mon·day /,· ˈ··/ the day after Whit Sunday, which used to be a public holiday in the UK. There is now a holiday around the same time called the 'Spring Bank Holiday', but it is not always on Whit Monday. 圣灵降临节翌日〔过去曾为英国的公众假日。现在这一天前后另有一个假日，称"春季公共假日"，但日期并不完全重合〕

Whit·ney /ˈwɪtnɪ; ˈwɪtni/, **Mount** a mountain in California that is part of the Sierra Nevada line of mountains. 惠特尼山〔加利福尼亚州境内的一座山，为内华达山脉的一部分〕

Whit·sun /ˈhwɪtsn; ˈwɪtsən/ *n* [C,U] **1** also 又作 **Whit Sun·day** /,· ˈ··/ the seventh Sunday after Easter, when Christians celebrate the HOLY SPIRIT coming down from heaven; PENTECOST[2] 圣灵降临节〔复活节后第七个星期日〕 **2** also 又作 **Whit·sun·tide** /ˈhwɪtsən,taɪd; ˈwɪtsəntaɪd/ the period around Whitsun 圣灵降临周

Whit·ting·ton /ˈhwɪtɪŋtən; ˈwɪtɪŋtən/, **Dick** (?1385-1423) an English businessman who was Lord Mayor of London. Although he was a real person, there are also many stories about his life. According to old stories, he went to London with his cat when he was a young man because he believed 'the streets were paved with gold' (=he thought it was easy to become rich there.) At first he was very unsuccessful and decided to leave London. But as he was leaving, he thought he heard the words 'Turn again, Whittington, Lord Mayor of London' in the sound of the church bells. So he went back, and later became Lord Mayor of London three times. 惠廷顿〔(?1385-1423)，英国商人，曾任伦敦市长。尽管确有其人，但有关他的生平传说颇多。相传惠廷顿年轻时相信伦敦"遍地黄金"便带着猫去了伦敦。起初一事无成，打算离开时，他依稀听到教堂的钟声传来这样的话，"转回来，惠廷顿，伦敦市长大人。"于是，他抽身返回，后来三次担任伦敦市长〕

whit·tle /ˈhwɪtl; ˈwɪtl/ *v* [I,T] to cut a piece of wood into a particular shape by cutting off small pieces with a small knife 削〔木头〕

whittle sth **↔away** *phr v* [T] to gradually reduce the amount or value of something 削减，削弱: *centralizing measures that had whittled away the powers of local government* 削弱了地方政府权力的中央集权措施

whittle sth **↔down** *phr v* [T] to gradually make something smaller by taking parts away 逐渐减少，缩小: *I've whittled down the list of people from 30 to 16.* 我已经把名单上的人由30人减少到16人。

whizz[1] also 又作 **whiz** *especially AmE*【尤美】/hwɪz; wɪz/ *v* [I] **1** [always+adv/prep] *informal*【非正式】**a)** to move very quickly, often making a sound like something rushing through the air 嗖地飞驰: [+by/around/past] *Martin whizzed by us on his bicycle.* 马丁骑着自行车嗖的一声从我们身边经过。**b)** to do something very quickly 迅速地做完〔某事〕: *Let's just whizz through it one more time.* 让我们快速再干一遍。**2** *AmE spoken* to URINATE【美口】撒尿 —see also 另见 GEE WHIZ

whizz[2] also 又作 **whiz** *especially AmE*【尤美】*n* **1** [C] *informal* someone who is very fast, intelligent, or skilled in a particular activity【非正式】快手，高手，能人: *a whiz on the com-*

puter 电脑高手 **2** [singular] *AmE spoken* an act of urinating (URINATE)【美口】撒尿

whizz·bang, whizbang /ˌhwɪzˋbæŋ; ˌwɪzˈbæŋ/ *n* [C] *AmE informal* something that is noticed a lot because it is very good, loud, or fast【美, 非正式】非同寻常[引人注目]的东西: *a whizz-bang of a stereo* 引人注目的立体声音响

whizz-kid also 又作 **whizkid** *especially AmE*【尤美】/ˋhwɪzkɪd; ˈwɪzkɪd/ *n* [C] *informal* a young person who is very skilled or successful at something【非正式】神童; 年轻有为的人: *financial whizzkids in the City* 该市的年轻理财能手

WHO /ˌdʌbḷju etʃ ˋo; ˌdʌbəljuː eɪtʃ ˈəʊ/ the abbreviation of 缩写= the WORLD HEALTH ORGANIZATION

1 1 **who** /hu; huː/ *pron* **1** used in questions to ask what person or people 谁, 什么人〔用于问句〕: *Who's that woman over there?* 在那边的那个女人是谁? | *Did they find out who stole the money?* 他们查明是谁偷钱的了吗? | *Who did you stay with?* 你和谁住在一起? **2** used in a question or statement to show what person or people you are talking about …的人〔用于问句或陈述句, 指代提及的人〕: *Do you know the people who live over the road?* 你认识住在马路对面的人吗? | *A postman is a man who delivers letters.* 邮递员是送信的人。**3** used especially in written language after a COMMA, to add more information about a person or people 他, 她; 他们, 她们〔尤用于书面语, 置于逗号之后, 以提供更多关于某人的资料〕: *I discussed it with my brother, who is a lawyer.* 我和我弟弟商讨了此事, 他是律师。**4 who are you to...?** used to say that someone should not judge someone or something because they have faults themselves or do not have the necessary experience 你凭什么…?〔指某人不应提出批评, 因他本身也有缺点或没有所需的经验〕: *Who am I to say how you should bring up your kids; I don't have any.* 我凭什么告诉你应该如何养育孩子; 我一个孩子都没有。**5 who's who** the people within a particular organization or group and how important each person is, what their job is etc 谁是谁〔某组织或团体的人, 各人的地位、职位等〕: *I'm just getting to know who's who in the department.* 我正在了解这个部门每个人的情况。

USAGE NOTE 用法说明: WHO

FORMALITY 正式程度

Except in very formal English, **who** is used instead of **whom** as an object in all kinds of questions. 除了在非常正式的英语中, who 可替代 whom 在所有问句中用作宾语: *Who did you see?* 你看见了谁? | *I wonder who she married in the end.* 我想知道最终她和谁结婚。| *Who was she dancing with?* 她在和谁跳舞? Compare the much more formal 比较正式得多的英语: *With whom was she dancing?* 她在和谁跳舞?

The same is true when **who** is used in relative clauses that add information but do not restrict the meaning of the noun they follow, often after a comma. 在起补充说明而修饰限定作用的关系从句里, 一般也用who 替代 whom, 这时 who 常用在逗号之后: *This is Jed, who you haven't met before/who I work for* (=this is Jed, and I work for him). 这是杰德, 你以前没有见过他/他是我的老板。

In relative clauses that restrict the meaning of the noun, even **who** is rare as an object in informal or spoken English. Instead, **that** or nothing is used. 在非正式或口头英语中, 限制名词含义的关系从句的宾语, 连 who 也不常用, 一般用 that 或什么都不用: *I'm the person (that) you need to see/speak to* (NOT 不用 *which*). 我就是你需要见的人/你要跟某人谈话, 那人就是我。It would be very formal to say 极正式的说法: *... to whom you need to speak.* 你要与其谈话的…。However, **whom** must be used immediately after a preposition, and you can avoid this by rephrasing your sentence. 然而, whom 必须紧跟在介词之后, 改用其他措辞可避免这个现象。For example, instead of saying 例如, 与其说: *To whom are you sending that letter?* It is much more natural to say 不如改用较自然的说法: *Who are you sending that letter to?* 那封信你寄给谁?

You can also use **that** instead of **who** when it is the subject of a relative clause. who 作为关系从句的主语时, 也可用 that 替代: *I hate people who/that can't stop talking.* 我讨厌唠唠叨叨的人。

GRAMMAR 语法

You can use **who** or **that** when a word for a group of people like **family** or **team** is followed by a plural verb (N.B. this is only usual in British English). 当 family 或 team 等表示一群人的词后跟复数动词形式时, 可用 who 或 that (注意, 这种用法只常见于英国英语中): *a family who quarrel among themselves* 一个吵吵闹闹的家庭。When such words are followed by a singular verb, you usually use **which** or **that** 当这类词后跟单数动词形式时, 通常用 which 或 that: *a team which/that has won most of its games* 一支常胜的运动队

Who, Dr —see 见 DR WHO

whoa /hwo; wəʊ/ *interjection* a command given to a horse to make it stop 吁!〔用于吆喝马停下〕

who·dun·it, whodunnit /huˋdʌnɪt; ˌhuːˈdʌnɨt/ *n* [C] *informal* a book, film etc about a murder case, in which you do not find out who did the murder until the end【非正式】〔追查谁是凶手的〕侦探小说[影片]

who·ev·er /huˋɛvɚ; huːˈevə/ *pron* **1** used to say that it does not matter who does something, is in a particular place etc 不管是什么人; 无论是谁: *I'll take whoever wants to go.* 谁想去我就带谁去。| **... or whoever** (=used to emphasize that you are talking about anyone and not about a specific person) 随便谁〔用于强调所指是任何人〕 *You could ask Gary or Jane or whoever really.* 你可以问加里或简, 或随便谁都可以。**2** used to talk about a specific person or people〔用于指特定的人〕: *Whoever is responsible for this will be punished.* 对此事有责任的人将受到惩罚。**3** used at the beginning of a question to show surprise or anger 到底是谁, 究竟是谁〔置于问句开头, 表示惊讶或生气〕: *Whoever would do a thing like that to an old woman?* 究竟是谁会对一位老太太做出那样的事? **4 whoever she/he may be** used to say that you do not know who someone is〔表示你不知道某人是谁〕: *You've got a message from someone called Tony Gower, whoever he may be.* 一个名叫托尼·高尔的人给你一个口信, 但不清楚他究竟是什么人。 2

whole¹ /hol; həʊl/ *adj* **1** all of something; ENTIRE 全部的, 整个的: You *have your whole life ahead of you!* 你还年轻, 来日方长! | *His whole attitude bugs me.* 他的整个态度让我讨厌。| **the whole school/country/village etc** (=all the people in a school, country etc) 全校/全国/全村等(的人) *The whole school meets together once a week.* 全校师生每星期集会一次。| **the whole thing** (=everything about a situation) 事情的全部 *The whole thing just makes me sick.* 整个事件令我作呕。—see also 另见 **the whole of** (WHOLE² (1)) **2 a whole variety/series/range etc** used to emphasize that there are a lot of things of the same type 各种类/系列/范畴等〔用于强调同一类中包含很多东西〕: *a whole series of embarrassing defeats* 一连串令人尴尬的失败 **3** complete and not divided or broken into parts 完整的; 没有破碎的: *Place a whole onion inside the chicken.* 把整个洋葱放在鸡里。**4 the whole point (of)** an expression meaning the main idea or reason for something, used especially to emphasize this and make it completely clear〔某事的〕中心思想〔尤用于强调和阐明〕; 宗旨: *I thought the whole point of the meeting was to decide which offer to accept.* 我以为会议的目的是决定接受哪一种提议。**5 in the whole (wide) world** an expression meaning 'anywhere' or 'at all', used to emphasize a statement 普天之下〔用于强调陈述句〕: *You're my best friend in the whole wide world!* 世上只有你是我最好的朋友! **6 go the whole hog** *informal* to do something as completely or as well as you can, without any limits【非正式】彻底地干; 尽力而为: *I'm gonna go the whole hog and have a live band at the barbecue.* 我准备全力以赴, 在烧烤野餐上安排现场乐队表演。**7 go the whole nine yards** *AmE spoken* to continue doing something until it is completely done and everything has been settled, even if this is difficult【美口】〔事情虽然困难, 但仍〕全部完成 —see also 另见 WHOLLY, **a whole new ball game** (BALL GAME (3)), **the whole shebang** (SHEBANG), **the whole shooting match** (SHOOTING MATCH), —**wholeness** *n* [U] 1 1

whole² *n* **1 the whole of** all of something, especially something that is not a physical object 整个, 全部〔尤用于非实物〕: *The whole of the morning was wasted trying to find the documents.* 为了设法找到这些文件, 整个上午给浪费了。**2 on the whole** used to say that something is generally true 总的看来, 总体而言: *On the whole, life was much quieter after John left.* 总的说来, 自从约翰离开之后, 生活变得平静多了。**3 as a whole** used to say that all the parts of something are being considered 整个来看〔用于表示所有部分都已考虑〕: *This rule does not only apply to seniors, but to the school as a whole.* 这项规定不仅仅适用于毕业班的学生, 而是适用于全校。**4** [C usually singular 一般用单数] something that consists of a number of parts, but is considered as a single unit 整体〔某物包含数部分, 但被当作一个单位〕: *Two halves make a whole.* 两个一半构成全部。 3 2

whole·food /ˋholˌfud; ˈhəʊlfuːd/ *n* [C,U] food that is considered healthy because it is in a simple natural form〔没有加工的〕营养食品; 天然食品

whole-heart·ed /ˌ· ˈ··◂/ *adj* **whole-hearted support/approval/effort etc** involving all your feelings, interest etc 全力支持/衷心赞许/全力以赴等: *enjoying the whole-hearted support of both governments* 得到两国政府的全力支持 —**whole-heartedly** *adv*

whole·meal /ˈholˌmil; ˈhəʊlmiːl/ *adj BrE* wholemeal flour or bread uses all of the grain, including the outer layer【英】〔面粉或面包〕全麦的; WHOLE WHEAT *AmE*【美】

whole note /ˈ· ·/ *n* [C] *AmE* a musical note which continues for as long as two HALF NOTES【美】全音符; SEMIBREVE *BrE*【英】—see picture at 参见 MUSIC 图

whole num·ber /ˌ· ˈ··/ *n* [C] a number such as 0, 1, 2 etc or −1, −2 etc; INTEGER 整数

whole·sale[1] /ˈholˌsel; ˈhəʊlseɪl/ *n* [U] the business of selling goods in large quantities, especially at low prices 批发, 趸售 —compare 比较 RETAIL[1]

wholesale[2] *adj* **1** connected with the business of selling goods in large quantities, usually at low prices 批发的; 整批卖的: *a wholesale price* 批发价 **2** affecting almost everything or everyone, and often done without any concern for the results 大规模的〔常包含不考虑结果而做某事的意思〕: *There will be no wholesale changes but a gradual modernization.* 不会有大规模变化, 但会逐步现代化。—**wholesale** *adv*: *I can get it for you wholesale.* 我可以为你以批发价买它。

whole·sal·er /ˈholˌselə; ˈhəʊlˌseɪlə/ *n* [C] someone who sells goods wholesale 批发商: *This profit covers the wholesaler's overheads.* 这项利润够支付批发商的经常开支。

whole·some /ˈholsəm; ˈhəʊlsəm/ *adj* **1** likely to make you healthy 对健康有益的: *well-balanced wholesome meals* 营养均衡的保健餐 **2** considered to have a good moral effect 在道德上有益的: *games that are just good clean wholesome fun* 增进身心健康的娱乐活动 —**wholesomeness** *n* [U]

whole wheat /ˈ· ·◂/ *adj AmE* whole wheat flour etc uses all of the grain, including the outer layer【美】〔面粉等〕全麦的; WHOLEMEAL *BrE*【英】

who'll /hul; huːl/ the short form of 缩略式= who will

whol·ly /ˈholɪ; ˈhəʊl-li/ *adv* [often with negatives 常与否定词连用] *formal* completely【正式】完全地: *a wholly satisfactory solution* 完全满意的解决 | *This seems to me a not wholly convincing argument.* 我看来这不是一个令人十分信服的论据。

 **whom** /hum; huːm/ *pron* the object form of WHO, used especially in formal speech or writing 谁, 什么人〔who的宾格形式, 尤用于正式说话或书面语里〕: *a neighbour with whom I shared a garden* 与我共享花园的邻居 | *She brought with her three friends, none of whom I had ever met before.* 她带来三位朋友, 没有一位是我以前见过的。

whomp /hwɑmp; wɒmp/ *v* [T] *spoken*【口】**1** to hit someone very hard with your hand closed; PUNCH[1] (1) 用拳痛打〔某人〕 **2** to defeat another team easily 轻易地击败〔另一队〕

whoop /hup; wuːp/ *v* [I] **1** to shout loudly and happily 〔高兴地〕大叫, 欢呼 **2 whoop it up** *informal* to enjoy yourself very much, especially in a large group【非正式】〔尤指在一群人中〕玩得很痛快; 狂欢 —**whoop** *n* [C] *whoops of victory* 胜利的欢呼

whoop-de-do /ˌhup dɪ ˋdu; ˌwuːp diː ˈduː/ *n* [C] *AmE spoken* a noisy party or celebration【美口】喧闹的聚会[庆祝会]

whoo·pee[1] /ˈhwuˋpi; wʊˈpiː/ *interjection* a shout of happiness 哈哈! 好呀!〔高兴的喊叫〕

whoop·ee[2] /ˈhwʊpɪ; ˈwʊpi/ *n* **make whoopee a)** *BrE old-fashioned* to go out and enjoy yourself【英, 过时】〔外出〕狂欢作乐 **b)** *AmE old-fashioned* to have sex【美, 过时】性交

whoopee cush·ion /ˈ·· ˌ··/ *n* [C] a rubber CUSHION[1] (1) filled with air that makes a funny noise when you sit on it〔橡胶制, 坐在上面会发出声响的〕放屁坐垫

whoop·ing cough /ˈhupɪŋ ˌkɔf; ˈhuːpɪŋ kɒf/ *n* [U] an infectious disease that especially affects children, and makes them cough and have difficulty breathing 百日咳〔尤影响儿童的一种传染病〕

whoops /hups; wʊps/ *interjection* **1** used when someone has fallen, dropped something, or made a small mistake 哎哟〔某人跌倒、掉了东西或出小差错时用语〕: *Whoops! I nearly dropped it.* 哎哟! 我差点把它掉了。**2 whoops-a-daisy** used when someone, usually a child, falls down 起来吧, 没事啦!〔通常用于儿童摔倒时〕

whoosh[1] /hwʊʃ; wʊʃ/ *n* [C usually singular 一般用单数] a soft sound like air or water moving quickly 呼的一声, 嗖的一声: *a sudden whoosh of flame and then a big bang* 火苗突然呼的一声蹿了起来, 然后一声巨响

whoosh[2] *v* [I always+adv/prep] *informal* to move very fast with a soft rushing sound【非正式】〔呼呼地〕飞快移动

whop /hwɑp; wɒp/ *v* [T] *informal especially AmE* WHUP【非正式, 尤美】大获全胜

whop·per /ˈhwɑpə; ˈwɒpə/ *n* [C] *informal*【非正式】**1** something unusually big 庞然大物, 特大的东西: *The fish Mike caught was a real whopper!* 迈克捉到的这条鱼大得吓人! **2** a lie 谎话

whop·ping /ˈhwɑpɪŋ; ˈwɒpɪŋ/ also 又作 **whopping great** /ˈ·· ·/ *adj* [only before noun 仅用于名词前] *spoken* very large【口】极大的, 异常大的: *a whopping fee* 一笔巨额费用

who're /ˈhuə; ˈhuːə/ the short form of 缩略式= who are

whore /hɔr; hɔː/ *n* [C] **1** an offensive word for a woman who has sex for money; PROSTITUTE 妓女〔冒犯用词〕**2** *taboo* an offensive word for a woman who has many sexual partners【讳】淫妇

whore·house /ˈhɔrˌhaus; ˈhɔːhaʊs/ *n* [C] *informal* a place where men can pay to have sex; BROTHEL【非正式】妓院, 窑子

whor·ing /ˈhɔrɪŋ; ˈhɔːrɪŋ/ *n* [U] *old-fashioned* the activity of having sex with a PROSTITUTE【过时】嫖妓: *drinking, gambling and whoring* 吃喝嫖赌

whorl /hwɜl; wɜːl/ *n* [C] **1** a pattern made of a line that curls outwards in circles that get bigger and bigger 涡; 螺旋状 **2** a circular pattern of leaves or flowers on a stem〔茎部的叶或花的〕轮生体

who's /huz; huːz/ the short form of 缩略式= who is or 或 who has

 **whose** /huz; huːz/ *determiner, pron* **1** used to ask which person or people a particular thing belongs to〔用于问物品属于〕谁的: *Whose house is this?* 这是谁的房子? | *Whose is this car?* 这辆汽车是谁的? **2** used to show the relationship between a person or thing and something that belongs to that person or thing 他(们)的; 她(们)的; 它(们)的〔表示人与物间的关系〕: *That's the man whose house has burned down.* 就是那个男人的房子被烧毁了。| *a new laptop computer whose low cost will make it attractive to students* 新型可携式电脑价格低廉, 对学生有吸引力

who·so·ev·er /ˌhusoˋɛvə; ˌhuːsəʊˈevə/ *pron old use* WHOEVER (1)【旧】无论谁

Who's Who /ˌ· ˈ·/ *trademark* a book produced every year in the UK that contains an alphabetical list of famous and important people, such as politicians, writers, and entertainers, and provides information about their achievements, their families etc【商标】《名人录》〔英国每年出版一辑。按字母顺序收录政界、文学界、娱乐界名人、要人的名字, 并对其成就和家庭情况加以介绍〕: *In Who's Who, Mortimer lists his hobbies as gardening and listening to opera.* 莫蒂默在《名人录》中列举的业余爱好为园艺和听歌剧。

who've /huv; huːv/ the short form of 缩略式= who have

whup /hwʌp; wʌp/ *v* [T] *informal especially AmE* to defeat someone easily in a sport or fight【非正式, 尤美】〔在体育运动或拳击赛中〕大获全胜: *We whupped them!* 我们打败了他们!

why[1] /hwaɪ; waɪ/ *adv, conj* **1** for what reason 为什么: *Why do you say that?* 你为什么那么说? | *Why should we bother waiting any longer?* 我们为什么还要费工夫等下去? | *I can't think why he would do such a thing.* 我不明白他为什么做这种事。| **why ever...?** (=used to add force to a question) 究竟为什么…?〔用于加强问句语气〕*Why ever would he come specially to visit us?* 他究竟为什么专程来探望我们? **2 why not...? a)** used to make a suggestion 为什么不…?〔用于提出建议〕: *Why not make your own Christmas cards instead of buying them?* 你为什么不自己做圣诞贺卡而要去买呢? | *Why don't you contact Eric – he may be able to help?* 你为什么不与埃里克联络, 他也许可以给你提供帮助呢? **b)** used to show that you agree with a suggestion or idea 干嘛不?〔表示同意某建议或想法〕: *"It might be nice to see a film this afternoon." "Yes, why not?"* "今天下午去看电影也许不错。" "对, 是不错。" **3 why on earth...?** *spoken* used to ask in a surprised way why something has happened【口】到底为什么…?〔用于惊异地问某事为何发生〕: *But why on earth didn't you ask me to help?* 你到底为什么不叫我帮忙? **4 why the hell...?** *spoken* used to ask in a very angry way why something has happened【口】〔生气地问〕究竟为什么…?: *Why the hell did you buy it in the first place?* 你当初究竟为什么去买它? **5 why oh why...?** *spoken* used to show that you very much regret something you did【口】为什么要…?〔表示很后悔做了某事〕: *Why oh why did I say those horrible things?* 我为什么会那样胡言乱语? **6 why me/ her?** *spoken* used to ask why something has been done, given etc to you or someone else【口】为什么是我/她?: *Why me? Why can't someone else drive you?* 怎么是我呢? 为什么别人不能开车送你?

Frequencies of **why** in spoken and written English 英语口语和书面语中 why 的使用频率

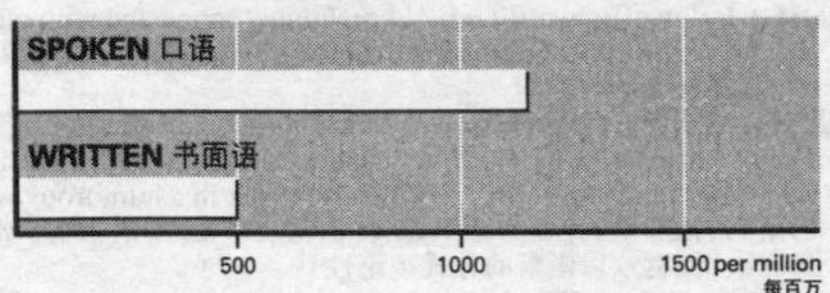

Based on the British National Corpus and the Longman Lancaster Corpus 据英国国家语料库和朗文兰开斯特语料库

This graph shows that **why** is much more common in spoken English than in written English. This is because it is used in questions and in some common spoken phrases. 本图表显示, why 在英语口语中的使用频率远远高于书面语, 因为该词经常用于疑问句中, 而且口语中一些常用短语是由 why 构成的。

why² *interjection especially AmE* used to show that you are surprised or annoyed【尤美】哎呀!嗨!〔表示惊讶或生气〕: *Why, where on earth can Don have got to!* 嗨, 唐究竟去了哪儿呢?

why³ *n* **the why(s) and the wherefore(s)** the reasons or explanations for something 缘故, 理由: *I'm not interested in the whys and the wherefores, just tell me what it will cost.* 我对前因后果不感兴趣, 就告诉我这东西要多少钱。

WI¹ /ˌdʌbḷju ˋaɪ; ˌdʌbəljuː ˈaɪ/ the abbreviation of 缩写= the WOMEN'S INSTITUTE

WI² the written abbreviation of 缩写= WISCONSIN

Wichita /ˋwɪtʃɪˌtɔ; ˈwɪtʃɪtɔː/ the largest city in the US state of Kansas. Wichita was on the Chisholm Trail, the main route used by COWBOY*s* moving cattle from Texas to the north of the US. Today the city is one of the main aircraft manufacturing centres in the US. 威奇托〔美国堪萨斯州最大城市, 位于奇泽姆牛车道沿线。过去, 牛仔们主要沿着这条线路把牛群从得克萨斯州赶往美国北部。如今, 该城是美国主要的飞机制造中心之一〕

wick /wɪk; wɪk/ *n* [C] **1** the piece of thread in a candle that burns when you light it 蜡烛芯 —see picture at 参见 CANDLE 图 **2** a long piece of material in an oil lamp that sucks up oil so that the lamp can burn〔油灯的〕灯芯 **3 get on sb's wick** *BrE spoken* to annoy someone【英口】激怒某人

wick·ed /ˋwɪkɪd; ˈwɪkɪ̵d/ *adj* **1** behaving in a way that is morally wrong; evil 邪恶的; 缺德的: *the wicked stepmother in 'Hansel and Gretel'* 《汉塞尔和格蕾特尔》中伤天害理的继母 **2** *informal* behaving badly in a way that is amusing; MISCHIEVOUS【非正式】淘气的; 恶作剧的: *Carl had a wicked grin on his face as he crept up behind Ellen.* 卡尔蹑手蹑脚地走到埃伦后面, 脸上现出调皮的笑容。**3** *spoken* very good; excellent【口】棒的; 极好的: *That's a wicked bike!* 这辆自行车真棒! —**wickedly** *adv* —**wickedness** *n* [U]

Wicked Witch of the West, the /ˌ‥ ‥ ‥ ˈ‥/ a character in the book and film *The Wizard of Oz*, who is evil and ugly, and can do magic 邪恶的西方女巫〔电影及同名小说《绿野仙踪》中的人物。该角色邪恶丑陋, 善施巫术〕

wick·er /ˋwɪkɚ; ˈwɪkə/ *adj* [only before noun 仅用于名词前] made from thin dry branches or REED*s* woven together 柳条[芦苇秆]编的: *a wicker basket* 柳条筐

wick·er·work /ˋwɪkɚˌwɝk; ˈwɪkəwɜːk/ *n* [U] objects made from wicker 柳条编制品

wick·et /ˋwɪkɪt; ˈwɪkɪ̵t/ *n* [C] one of two sets of three wooden sticks that are stuck in the ground in a game of CRICKET (2), which the BOWLER tries to hit with the ball〔板球的〕三柱门 —see also 另见 **be on a sticky wicket** (STICKY (9))

wicket gate /ˈ‥ ˌ·/ *n* [C] *old use* a small door or gate that is part of a larger one【旧】〔大门上的〕小门, 边门

wicket keep·er /ˈ‥ ˌ‥/ *n* [C] a player who stands behind the wicket in CRICKET (2)〔板球运动中的〕三柱门守门员

Wick·low /ˋwɪklo; ˈwɪkləʊ/ a COUNTY in the east of the Republic of Ireland 威克洛郡〔爱尔兰共和国东部一郡〕

1 1 **wide¹** /waɪd; waɪd/ *adj*

1 ▶DISTANCE 距离◀ a) measuring a large distance from one side to the other 宽的, 宽阔的: *a hat with a wide brim* 宽边帽子 —opposite 反义词 NARROW¹ (1) **b) five metres/two miles etc wide** measuring five metres etc from one side to the other 5米宽/两英里宽等: *The door's three feet wide.* 门3英尺宽。—see picture at 参见 THICK¹ 图

2 ▶VARIETY 种类◀ including or involving a large variety of different people, things, or situations〔包括或涉及的人、物或形势等〕广泛的; 范围大的; 广阔的: *a man with a wide experience of foreign affairs* 外交事务经验丰富的人 | **wide range/variety/selection etc** *We stock a wide range of furnishing materials.* 我们备有各种各样的装饰材料。

3 ▶IN MANY PLACES 在许多地方◀ [usually before noun 一般用于名词前] happening among many people or in many places 众多的; 广泛的〔发生于许多人中或地方的〕: *The Whitewater scandal received wide publicity.* 白水丑闻引起了公众广泛的关注。

4 wide difference/gap/variation etc a large and noticeable difference 巨大的差别/差距/变化等: *the ever-wider gap between the richest and poorest countries* 最富国与最穷国之间日益加大的差距

5 the wider issues/view/context etc the more general features of a situation, rather than the specific details 概貌/概观/概况等: *We also have a wider aim: the restoration of democracy.* 我们也有一个总目标: 恢复民主。

6 ▶EYES 眼睛◀ *especially literary* wide eyes are fully open, especially when someone is very surprised, excited, or frightened【尤文】〔眼睛〕睁大的〔尤指某人非常吃惊、兴奋或恐惧〕: *Her eyes grew wide in anticipation.* 她睁大着眼睛期待着。

7 give sb/sth a wide berth *especially BrE* to avoid someone or something【尤英】对某人/某物敬而远之

8 the big wide world *especially spoken* places outside the small familiar place where you live【尤口】〔在熟识的小天地以外的〕广阔世界: *Soon you'll leave school and go out into the big wide world.* 很快你就要离开学校, 进入社会。

9 nationwide/city-wide etc happening or existing all over the nation, city etc 全国的/全市的等: *a country-wide problem* 全国的问题 —see also 另见 WIDELY, WIDTH

USAGE NOTE 用法说明: WIDE

WORD CHOICE 词语辨析: **wide, broad, big, large, wide-ranging**

Wide is the most usual word to describe something that measures a long distance from one side to another. 形容宽的物体, wide 是最常用的词: *a wide road/lake/doorway/entrance/staircase* 宽阔的马路/湖面/门道/入口/楼梯。You also use **wide** to express how much something measures from side to side. wide 也可用来表示某物的宽度: *The gap was only a few inches wide.* 这条裂缝才几英寸宽。

Broad is often used about parts of the body. broad 常用于描述身体各个部位的宽度: *broad shoulders/hips* 宽肩膀/臀部 | *a broad nose/forehead.* 大鼻子/宽额头。**Broad** often suggests that something is wide in a good or attractive way. broad 常表示某物令人心旷神怡地"宽广"或"宽阔": *a broad sunny avenue running through the middle of the town* 穿过镇中心的一条宽阔明亮的大道

Sometimes you may need to think whether you really mean **wide** or **broad**, or just **big** or **large** (=wide in all directions) 有时需要考虑想表达的确切含意是wide 还是 broad, 是 big 还是 large (各个方向都宽): *a wide carpet/field* 宽地毯/宽广的田野 or 或 *a large carpet/field?* 大地毯/大片田野

Wide-ranging means covering a lot of different subjects or including a lot of different ideas. wide-ranging 意为"覆盖面大的; 广泛的": *a wide-ranging review/report/speech* 全面的回顾; 内容广泛的报告/讲话

wide² *adv* **1 a)** a door or window that is wide open is open as fully as it can be〔门或窗〕大开; 敞开 **b)** if someone's eyes or mouth are wide open, they are open as far as possible, especially when they are surprised〔尤指吃惊时嘴或眼〕张得很大地 **c)** if a competition, election etc is wide open, it is possible for anyone to succeed〔竞赛、选举等〕没有一个参赛者有必胜把握: *After Milan's win the championship is wide open.* 米兰获胜后, 不知鹿死谁手。**2** opening or spreading as much as possible 充分地张开: *The door opened a little wider.* 门开得再大一点。| **open/spread sth wide** *Spiro spread his arms wide in a welcoming gesture.* 斯皮罗伸开双臂, 做出欢迎的姿势。| **wide apart** *Sandy stood with his back to the fire, legs wide apart.* 桑迪背对着火, 双脚叉开站着。**3** not hitting the point you were aiming at 未击中目标: *One of the guards fired at us but the shot went wide.* 一名卫兵向我们开枪, 但打歪了。**4 wide awake** completely awake 毫无睡意, 完全醒着 —see also 另见 **far and wide** (FAR¹ (5)), **off the mark/wide of the mark** (MARK² (11))

wide-an·gle lens /ˌ· ‥ ˈ‥/ *n* [C] a camera LENS (2) that lets you take photographs with a wider view than normal〔照相机的〕广角镜

wide boy /ˈ· ·/ *n* [C] *BrE informal* a man who makes money in dishonest ways and uses it to buy expensive clothes, cars etc【英，非正式】〔用骗来的金钱购买昂贵衣物、汽车等的〕骗子：*Cockney wide boys trying to sell you something* 想卖东西给你的伦敦东区的骗子

wide-eyed /ˌ· ˈ·◂/ *adj, adv* **1** with your eyes wide open, especially because you are surprised or frightened〔尤因惊讶或恐惧而〕睁大着眼睛（地）**2** too willing to believe, accept, or admire things because you do not have much experience of life; NAIVE 天真的[地]，单纯的[地]

wide·ly /ˈwaɪdlɪ; ˈwaɪdli/ *adv* **1** in a lot of different places or by a lot of people 广泛地：*widely publicized events* 广为宣传的事件 | *an author who had travelled widely in the Far East* 一位游历过远东很多地方的作者 **2** varying to a large degree 差异很大：*The quality of the applicants varies widely.* 申请人的素质差异很大。**3** **widely read** **a)** read by a lot of people 读者众多的：*a widely read magazine* 一本读者众多的杂志 **b)** having read many different books 博览群书的：*She's very widely read.* 她博览群书。

wid·en /ˈwaɪdn̩; ˈwaɪdn/ *v* [I,T] **1** to become wider or make something wider（使）变宽：*They're widening the road.* 他们正在拓宽马路。**2** to become larger in degree or range, or make something do this（使）〔程度〕增加；（使）〔范围〕扩大：*The gap between income and expenditure has widened to 11%.* 收入和支出之间的差距扩大到了 11%。| *They are trying to widen the discussion to include environmental issues.* 他们正设法把这次讨论扩大到环境问题。—opposite 反义词 NARROW² (1)

wide-rang·ing /ˌ· ˈ· ·◂/ *adj* including a wide variety of subjects, things, or people 范围大的，广泛的：*a wide-ranging discussion* 内容广泛的讨论 | *wide-ranging proposals to improve the rail network* 改善铁路网的各种提议

wide·spread /ˈwaɪdˋsprɛd; ˈwaɪdspred/ *adj* existing or happening in many places or situations, or among many people 分布广的；广泛流传的：*the widespread use of chemicals in agriculture* 农业上化学品的广泛使用

wid·get /ˈwɪdʒɪt; ˈwɪdʒɪt/ *n* [C] **1** *spoken* a small piece of equipment that you do not know the name for【口】〔不知其名的〕小装置 **2** *informal* a word meaning an imaginary product that a company might produce【非正式】〔某公司的〕虚构产品：*Company A produces 6,000 widgets a month at a unit price of $0.33.* A 公司每月生产 6000 件产品，每件单价 0.33 美元。

wid·ow /ˈwɪdo; ˈwɪdəʊ/ *n* [C] **1** a woman whose husband has died and who has not married again 寡妇，遗孀：*Mr Castle's widow, Anne, described the sentence as 'obscene'.* 卡斯尔先生的遗孀安妮认为那句话"下流"。**2** **football widow/golf etc widow** *humorous* a woman whose husband spends all his free time watching football, playing golf etc【幽默】〔丈夫沉溺于足球、高尔夫球等而被冷落的〕足球/高尔夫球寡妇

wid·owed /ˈwɪdod; ˈwɪdəʊd/ *adj* having become a widow or widower 守寡的；成为鳏夫的：*She was widowed at the age of 25.* 她 25 岁时成了寡妇。

wid·ow·er /ˈwɪdəwɚ; ˈwɪdəʊə/ *n* [C] a man whose wife has died and who has not married again 鳏夫

wid·ow·hood /ˈwɪdoˌhʊd; ˈwɪdəʊhʊd/ *n* [U] the time when you are a widow 守寡，孀居

width /wɪdθ; wɪdθ/ *n* **1** [C,U] the distance from one side of something to the other〔从一边到另一边的〕宽度：*What's the width of the desk?* 这张书桌的宽度是多少？| **in width** *It's about 6 metres in width.* 它大约 6 米宽。—compare 比较 BREADTH, LENGTH —see picture at 参见 LENGTH 图 **2** [C] a piece of a material that has been measured and cut〔裁剪了的〕料子：*four widths of curtain material* 四幅窗帘布料子

wield /wild; wiːld/ *v* [T] **1** **wield power/influence/authority etc** to have a lot of power or influence, and be ready to use it 有权力/影响/权威等〔并随时使用〕：*The Church wields immense power in Ireland.* 在爱尔兰，教会具有很大的权力。**2** to hold a weapon or tool that you are going to use 拿起〔武器或工具〕：*She had her car windows smashed by a gang wielding baseball bats.* 一伙挥舞棒球球棒的人把她的汽车玻璃窗砸碎了。

wie·ner /ˈwinɚ; ˈwiːnə/ also 又作 **wie·nie, weenie** /ˈwinɪ; ˈwiːni/ *n* [C] *AmE*【美】**1** a type of SAUSAGE 法兰克福香肠 **2** *informal* someone who does something stupid【非正式】蠢人，傻瓜 **3** a word used by children meaning a PENIS 小鸡鸡〔儿童用语，指阴茎〕

Wie·sen·thal /ˈwizn̩tɑl; ˈwiːzəntɑːl/, **Simon** (1908-2005) a Jewish man who spent many years after World War II trying to catch Nazi officers so that they could be officially punished for their violent crimes against the Jews during the war 维森塔尔〔（1908-2005），犹太人。二战结束后，他用多年时间追捕纳粹军官，要他们为自己在战争期间对犹太人犯下的罪行伏法〕

wife /waɪf; waɪf/ *plural* **wives** /waɪvz; waɪvz/ *n* [C] the woman that a man is married to 妻子：*Have you met his wife?* 你见到他妻子了吗？

wife·ly /ˈwaɪflɪ; ˈwaɪfli/ *adj old-fashioned* connected with qualities that are supposed to be typical of a good wife【过时】贤慧的；具备好妻子美德的

Wife of Bath, the /ˌ· · ˈ·/ a character in the poem *The Canterbury Tales* by Geoffrey Chaucer. She has been married five times, and she enjoys talking about sex in a humorous way. 巴斯妇〔杰弗里·乔叟的诗作《坎特伯雷故事集》中的人物。她结过五次婚，喜欢以幽默的方式谈论性〕

wig /wɪg; wɪg/ *n* [C] artificial hair that you wear on your head 假发

wig·gle¹ /ˈwɪgl̩; ˈwɪgəl/ *v* [I,T] to move with small movements from side to side or up and down, or make something move like this〔动作较小地〕摆动；扭动：*Henry wiggled his toes.* 亨利扭动他的脚趾。

wiggle² *n* [C] **1** a small movement from side to side or up and down 摆动；扭动：*a wiggle of the hips* 屁股的扭动 **2** **get a wiggle on!** *AmE spoken* used to tell someone to do something more quickly【美口】赶快！赶紧！〔用于告诉某人更快地做某事〕

wig·gly /ˈwɪglɪ; ˈwɪgəli/ *adj informal* a wiggly line is one that has small curves in it; WAVY (2)【非正式】〔线〕波浪形的

Wight —see 见 ISLE OF WIGHT

wight /waɪt; waɪt/ *n* [C] *old use* a person【旧】人

wig·wam /ˈwɪgwɑm; ˈwɪgwæm/ *n* [C] a tall tent in which some Native Americans used to live〔北美印第安人居住的帐篷式〕棚屋

Wil·ber·force /ˈwɪlbɚfors; ˈwɪlbəfɔːs/, **William** (1759-1833) a British politician who is played an important part in stopping the British trade in SLAVES, and later stopping the practice of SLAVERY in all parts of the British Empire 威尔伯福斯〔（1759-1833），英国政治家。他先后为终止英国的奴隶贸易和大英帝国的奴隶制作出了重要贡献〕

wild¹ /waɪld; waɪld/ *adj*

1 ►**PLANTS/ANIMALS** 植物/动物◄ living in a natural state, not changed or controlled by humans 野生的；未经栽培的；未经驯化的：*wild flowers* 野花 | *a wild rabbit* 野兔 | **grow wild** *daffodils growing wild in the meadow* 草地上野生的黄水仙

2 ►**EMOTIONS** 感情◄ feeling or expressing strong uncontrolled emotions, especially anger, happiness, or excitement 感情强烈的〔尤指生气、高兴或激动〕：*wild laughter* 狂笑 | **[+with]** *wild with excitement* 兴奋不已

3 **go wild** **a)** to behave in a very excited way〔行为〕疯狂：*The crowd went wild as soon as Jackson stepped onto the stage.* 杰克逊一走上舞台，人群就骚动起来。**b)** to get very angry 狂怒

4 ►**CRAZY** 疯狂的◄ behaving in an uncontrolled, sometimes violent way〔行为〕凶悍的；疯狂的：*She's great fun, but a bit wild.* 她是一个有趣的人，但有点狂。| *Jack had a wild look in his eyes.* 杰克眼中流露出狂野的神色。

5 ►**ENJOYABLE** 有趣的◄ *informal* very enjoyable and exciting【非正式】十分有趣的；棒极了的：*That was a really wild party last night!* 昨晚的那个聚会真是棒极了！

6 **be wild about** to be very interested in or excited about something 对〔某物〕极喜爱；着了魔似的：*My son's wild about racing cars.* 我儿子对赛车如醉如痴。

7 ►**WITHOUT CAREFUL THOUGHT** 未经仔细考虑◄ done or said without much thought or care, or without knowing all the facts〔做事或说话〕轻率的；缺乏根据的：*wild accusations* 诬告 | **a wild guess** *I just made a wild guess and it turned out to be right.* 我只是胡乱猜测，结果却猜对了。

8 **run wild** **a)** if a garden or plant runs wild, it grows uncontrollably because no one is looking after it〔园子因没人照料〕荒芜；〔植物〕蔓长 **b)** if children run wild, they do what they like because they are not controlled by an adult〔孩子〕肆无忌惮，无法无天

9 **beyond your wildest dreams** beyond anything you imagined or hoped for 超出想象的：*an invention that was to change our lives beyond our wildest dreams* 一项超乎我们想象改变我们生活的发明

10 ►**WEATHER** 天气◄ violent and strong 猛烈的；狂暴的：*wild winds* 狂风

11 ►**CARD GAMES** 牌戏◄ a card that is wild can be used to represent any other card in a game〔纸牌〕百搭的 —see also 另见 WILD CARD (1) —**wildly** *adv*: *The crowd ran wildly through the streets.* 人群疯狂地在街道上跑。| *wildly inaccurate statements* 极不准确的话 —**wildness** *n* [U]

wild² *n* **1** **in the wild** in natural and free conditions, not kept or controlled by humans 处于野生状态：*There are very few pan-*

das living in the wild now. 现在只有极少数的大熊猫处于野生状态。**2 the wilds of Africa/Alaska etc** areas where there are no towns and not many people live 非洲/阿拉斯加州等的偏僻地区〔人烟稀少的地区〕

wild boar /ˌ· ˈ·/ *n* [C] a large wild pig with long hair〔长毛〕野猪

wild card /ˈ· ·/ *n* [C] **1** a playing card that can represent any other card〔纸牌游戏中的〕百搭牌 **2** *technical* a sign that can represent any letter in some computer commands【术语】〔电脑中的〕通配符 **3** someone that you do not know well, so that you cannot guess how they will behave in certain situations〔因不了解而〕无法猜度的人

wild·cat¹ /ˈwaɪldˌkæt; ˈwaɪldkæt/ *n* [C] a type of cat that looks similar to a large pet cat and lives in mountains, forests etc〔生活在山区、森林等的〕野猫

wildcat² *v* [I] *AmE* to look for oil in a place where nobody has found any yet【美】勘探〔石油〕—**wildcatter** *n* [C]

wildcat strike /ˌ·· ˈ·/ *n* [C] an occasion when people suddenly and unofficially stop working in order to protest about something 野猫式罢工〔指未经工会批准的突然罢工〕

Wilde /waɪld; waɪld/, **Oscar** (1854-1900) an Irish writer of poems, stories, and especially humorous plays. His works include the play *The Importance of Being Earnest* and the NOVEL *The Picture of Dorian Gray*. He was also famous for the clever and funny things he said in conversations. 王尔德〔(1854-1900),爱尔兰诗人、小说家、喜剧作家。作品包括剧本《认真的重要性》和小说《道林·格雷的肖像》。他还以谈吐机智、风趣著称〕

wil·de·beest /ˈwɪldəˌbist; ˈwɪldəbiːst/ *n* [C] a large Southern African animal with a tail and curved horns; GNU 牛羚,角马〔产于南非〕

Wild·er /ˈwaɪldə; ˈwaɪldə/, **Billy** (1906-2002) a US film DIRECTOR, who was born in Austria, who made both serious and humorous films, including *Sunset Boulevard* (1950) and *Some Like It Hot* (1959) 怀尔德〔(1906-2002),美国电影导演,生于奥地利。拍摄的影片既有严肃题材,又有幽默题材,包括《日落大道》(1950)和《热情如火》(1959)等〕

Wilder, Lau·ra In·galls /ˈlɔrə ˈɪŋglz; ˈlɔːrə ˈɪŋgəlz/ (1867-1957) a US writer who wrote a series of NOVELS for children known as the 'Little House' books, that are based on her life as a child in the Midwest, when her family were among the first white people to live there. 怀尔德〔(1867-1957),美国作家。著有儿童小说"小屋"系列,取材于其童年时代在美国中西部的生活经历。她的家人是最早移居到当地的白人〕

Wilder, Thorn·ton /ˈθɔrntən; ˈθɔːntən/ (1897-1975) a US writer famous especially for his plays *Our Town* and *The Skin of Our Teeth* 怀尔德〔(1897-1975),美国作家,尤以剧本《小城风光》和《千钧一发》闻名〕

wil·der·ness /ˈwɪldənɪs; ˈwɪldənəs/ *n* [C usually singular 一般用单数] **1** a large area of land that has never been developed or farmed 荒野,不毛之地: *a bleak wilderness of undrained marshes* 一片荒凉的未经排干的沼泽 **2** any place where there is no sign of people or their effect 杳无人烟的地方: *That garden is a wilderness.* 那个花园里一片荒芜。| *The south side of the city had become a lawless wilderness.* 这个城市的南部已成为法纪荡然的蛮荒地区。**3 in the wilderness** away from the centre of power and activity, especially political activity 离开权力和活动的中心;〔尤指政治上的〕在野状态: *his return to office after several years in the wilderness* 他在野数年后的再度掌权

wilderness a·re·a /ˈ··· ˌ···/ *n* [C] an area of public land in the US where no buildings or roads are allowed to be built〔美国不允许在内建房、筑路的〕公共莽原区

wild·fire /ˈwaɪldˌfaɪr; ˈwaɪldfaɪə/ *n* [U] —see 见 **spread like wildfire** (SPREAD¹ (3a))

wild·fowl /ˈwaɪldˌfaul; ˈwaɪldfaʊl/ *n* [plural] birds, especially ones that live near water〔尤指水边的〕野禽

wild-goose chase /ˌ·ˈ· ˌ·/ *n* [C] a situation where you are looking for something that does not exist or that you are very unlikely to find, so that you waste a lot of time 徒劳的寻找,白费气力的追寻

wild·life /ˈwaɪldˌlaɪf; ˈwaɪldlaɪf/ *n* [U] animals and plants growing in natural conditions 野生动植物: *a wildlife park* 野生动物园 | *studying the wildlife* 研究野生生物

wild rice /ˌ· ˈ·/ *n* [U] the seed of a type of grass that grows in parts of North America and China 菰米〔生长在北美部分地区和中国〕

Wild West, the /ˌ· ˈ·/ the western US, where many European settlers moved during the 19th century to establish new farms and new cities. 荒蛮西部,西大荒〔指美国西部地区。19世纪,大批欧洲移民在此定居,开辟农场,兴建城市〕

> **CULTURAL NOTE 文化注释**
>
> In the US, people think of the Wild West as being an exciting but violent place, where not many people obeyed the law. It is also seen as a place where people were able to be very independent. Films, stories, and television programmes about the Wild West usually have GUNFIGHTS between bad COWBOYS and the town's SHERIFF or good cowboys. These stories may not be based on fact, but they are how people imagine cowboys lived in the past. 美国人认为荒蛮西部是刺激但暴力猖獗的所在,法律对很多人毫无约束力。那里也被认为是人们能够非常独立自主的地方。有关荒蛮西部的电影、故事和电视剧通常会有枪战情景,坏牛仔一方与城镇治安官和好牛仔一方作战。这些故事可能并不基于真人真事,而是人们想象的过去西部牛仔的生活。

wiles /waɪlz; waɪlz/ *n* [plural] clever talk or tricks used to persuade someone to do what you want 花言巧语; 巧计: *She used all her wiles to coax a young man to help her escape.* 她用了各种花言巧语哄骗一个年轻人帮助她逃脱。

wil·ful *BrE*【英】, **willful** *AmE*【美】/ˈwɪlfəl; ˈwɪlfəl/ *adj* **1** continuing to do what you want, even after you have been told to stop 任性的; 固执的: *a wilful child* 任性的孩子 **2 wilful damage/disobedience/exaggeration etc** deliberate damage etc, when you know that what you are doing is wrong 故意损害/违抗/夸大其词等—**wilfully** *adv*—**wilfulness** *n* [U]

wi·li·ness /ˈwaɪlɪnɪs; ˈwaɪlinəs/ *n* [U] the quality of being WILY 诡计多端; 狡诈

will¹ /wɪl; wɪl/ [modal verb 情态动词] *v* **1** used to express the simple future tense 将,会,要〔用于表示简单将来式〕: *A meeting will be held next Tuesday at 3 p.m.* 下星期二下午3点将召开一个会议。| *What time will she arrive?* 她会什么时候到达? | *When will you be leaving for America?* 你准备什么时候起程去美国? **2** used to show that you are willing or ready to do something 愿; 要〔用于表示愿意、准备做某事〕: *I will come up and help you clear the attic in a moment.* 我马上来帮你清理顶楼。| *Alma won't come to the party I'm sure.* 我敢肯定阿尔玛不会参加这次聚会。| *Dr Weir will see you now.* 韦尔医生现在要给你看病了。**3** used to ask someone to do something 请…好吗〔用于请求某人做某事〕: *Will you phone me later?* 你过一会再给我打电话好吗? | *Shut the door will you?* 把门关上,好吗? **4** used to say what always happens in a particular situation or what is generally true 总是,惯于〔表示某事经常发生或总是如此〕: *Oil will float on water.* 油总是浮在水上。| *Accidents will happen.* 事故总是会发生的。**5** used like 'can' to show what is possible 能〔表示可能性〕: *This car will hold five people comfortably.* 这辆汽车能舒舒服服地坐五个人。**6** used like 'must' to show what you think is likely to be true 可能; 大概〔表示某事可能是真的〕: *That will be Tim coming home now.* 现在到家的大概是蒂姆。**7** used to order or tell someone angrily to do something 必须,一定〔气愤地命令某人做某事〕: *Will you two shut up for God's sake!* 天啊,你们俩住嘴! **8** used to offer something to someone or to invite them to do something 要不要〔提供某物给某人或邀请某人做某事〕: *Will you be staying the night?* 你在这里过夜好吗? **9** used to describe someone's habits, especially when you find them strange or annoying 老是〔用于描述某人的习性,尤指奇异或恼人的〕: *Trish will keep asking damn silly questions.* 特里斯老是不停地问一些十分愚蠢的问题。**10 I will** *spoken* used during a wedding ceremony to show that you agree formally to marry【口】〔婚礼时表示〕我愿意〔娶[嫁]〕

will² *n*

1 ▶DETERMINATION 决心◀ [C,U] determination to do something that you have decided to do, even if this is difficult 意志,毅力: *Children sometimes have very strong wills.* 孩子有时有很强的意志力。| **the will to live/fight/succeed etc** *The survivors never lost the will to live.* 幸存者从未丧失求生的意志。| **iron will** (=very strong determination) 钢铁般的意志 | **a battle/clash of wills** (=when two people who both have strong wills oppose each other) 意志的较量 —see also 另见 FREE WILL, STRONG-WILLED, WEAK-WILLED

2 ▶LEGAL DOCUMENT 法律文件◀ [C] a legal document that says who you want your money and property to be given to after you die 遗嘱: **make a will** *Have you made a will yet?* 你的遗嘱立好了吗? | **in sb's will** *My grandmother left me these jewels in her will.* 祖母在她的遗嘱中把这些首饰留给了我。

3 ▶WHAT SB WANTS 某人的意愿◀ [singular] what someone wants to happen in a particular situation〔某人的〕意愿,意旨: *I wish he'd stop trying to impose his will on others.* 我希望他不

要企图把自己的意愿强加于其他人。| *obedience to God's will* 服从上帝的意旨 | **against your will** *The prisoner was made to sign a confession against his will.* 犯人被强迫在供状上签了字。
4 with the best will in the world *spoken* used to say that something is not possible, however much you want to do it【口】不管用意是多么的好〔用于表示某事不可能〕: *With the best will in the world, I don't see what more I can do.* 尽管我煞费苦心,也不知道还能再做点什么。
5 where there's a will there's a way *spoken* used to say that if you really want to do something, you will find a way to succeed【口】有志者事竟成
6 at will whenever you want and in whatever way you want 随心所欲: *a terrifying creature that could change its shape at will* 一只可任意改变形状的可怕怪物
7 with a will in an eager and determined way 起劲地; 热情地; 诚心诚意

will³ *v* **1** [T] to try to make something happen by thinking about it very hard 设法用意志力驱使〔某事发生〕: **will sb to do sth** *She was willing herself not to cry.* 她极力使自己不要哭出来。**2** [T] to officially give something that you own to someone else after you die 立遗嘱把〔财产〕遗赠〔某人〕**3** [I,T] *old use* to want something to happen【旧】希望, 想要〔某事发生〕: *The King wills it.* 国王希望如此。

will·ful /ˈwɪlfəl; ˈwɪlfəl/ *adj* the American spelling of WILFUL wilful 的美式拼法

Wil·liam /ˈwɪljəm; ˈwɪljəm/, **Prince** (1982-) the elder son of Prince Charles and Diana, Princess of Wales. 威廉王子〔(1982-), 查尔斯王子与威尔士王妃戴安娜的长子〕

William I —see 见 WILLIAM THE CONQUEROR

William II /ˌwɪljəm ðə ˈsɛkənd; ˌwɪljəm ðə ˈsekənd/, **King** (?1056-1100) the king of England from 1087 until his death. He was sometimes called **William Rufus**. He was the son of William the Conqueror, and was killed in a hunting accident. 威廉二世〔(?1056-1100), 英格兰国王, 1087年即位直至去世, 有时也称为"红脸威廉"。他是征服者威廉之子, 在一次狩猎中意外身亡〕

William III —see 见 King WILLIAM OF ORANGE

William of Or·ange /ˌ· · · ˈ· ·/, **King** (1650-1702) the king of Britain and Ireland from 1689 until his death. He was also called **William III**. He was married to the daughter of King James II, and was asked by James's enemies to become king instead of him. William and his Protestant army beat James and his Catholic army at the Battle of the Boyne, and for this reason Protestants still admire him in Northern Ireland and sometimes call him 'King Billy'. William's wife, Queen Mary II, had equal power, and people usually talk about the reign of **William and Mary**. 奥兰治的威廉〔(1650-1702), 1689年就任不列颠及爱尔兰国王, 直至去世, 亦称威廉三世。因威廉娶了英王詹姆斯二世的女儿为妻, 詹姆斯的政敌提出立他为王。威廉率领其新教徒军队在博因河战役中击败了詹姆斯及其天主教徒军队。有鉴于此, 北爱尔兰的新教徒至今依然崇拜威廉, 有时称他为"比利国王"。威廉的妻子, 即女王玛丽二世, 和他共享王权。人们常称这一时期为"威廉与玛丽执政时期"〕

Wil·liams /ˈwɪljəmz; ˈwɪljəmz/, **Hank** (1923-53) a US country and western singer and songwriter, who greatly influenced the development of country and western music, and whose songs include *Your Cheatin' Heart* and *I'm So Lonesome I Could Cry* 威廉斯〔(1923-1953), 美国乡村和西部音乐歌手、词作家。他对乡村和西部音乐的发展产生过重大影响。歌曲包括《你的欺骗之心》和《我孤单得想要落泪》〕

W

Williams, Ralph Vaughan —see 见 Ralph VAUGHAN WILLIAMS

Williams, Tennessee /ˌtɛnəˈsi; ˌtenəˈsiː◂/ (1911-83) a US writer whose plays are mainly about the emotional problems of people living in the South of the US. His plays include *A Streetcar Named Desire*, *The Glass Menagerie*, and *Cat on a Hot Tin Roof.* 威廉斯〔(1911-1983), 美国作家。其剧作主要反映美国南方人的情感问题, 代表作有《欲望号街车》、《玻璃动物园》和《热铁皮屋顶上的猫》〕

Williams, William Carlos /ˈkɑrləs; ˈkɑːləs/ (1883-1963) a US poet and medical doctor who wrote mainly about ordinary life. His best known poems include *Paterson*. He also wrote plays and essays, and won a Pulitzer Prize in 1963 for *Pictures from Breughel.* 威廉斯〔(1883-1963), 美国诗人、医生。其作品主要描述普通人的生活。最著名的诗歌包括《佩特森》等。威廉斯还创作戏剧和散文, 并以《来自布吕格尔的图画》荣获1963年普利策奖〕

William the Con·quer·or /ˌ· · · ˈ· · ·/ (1027-87) the king of England from 1066 until his death. He was also called William I. William was the Duke of Normandy (in northern France), and became king of England by defeating King Harold at the Battle of Hastings in 1066. His arrival brought great changes in English society, and people see it as the end of the Anglo-Saxon period and the beginning of the Middle Ages. 征服者威廉〔(1027-1087), 1066年就任英格兰国王, 直至去世, 亦称威廉一世。威廉原是法国北部的诺曼底公爵, 1066年在黑斯廷斯战役中打败哈罗德国王, 成为英格兰国王。威廉的到来给英国社会带来巨变, 标志着盎格鲁－撒克逊时代的终结和中世纪的肇始〕

wil·lie /ˈwɪli; ˈwɪli/ *n informal*【非正式】**1 get the willies** to feel nervous or frightened 紧张不安; 心惊胆战 **2 give sb the willies** to make someone feel nervous or frightened 使某人紧张[害怕]: *It gives me the willies to even think about plastic surgery.* 一想到整形外科, 我就不寒而栗。**3** [C] another spelling of WILLY willy 的另一种拼法

will·ing /ˈwɪlɪŋ; ˈwɪlɪŋ/ *adj* **1 be willing (to do sth)** to be prepared to do something, or have no reason to not want to do it 乐意(做某事); 没有理由不想(做某事): *How much are they willing to pay?* 他们愿意付多少钱? | **quite/perfectly willing** *I told them I was perfectly willing to help.* 我告诉他们, 我非常愿意帮忙。**2 willing helper/worker etc** someone who is eager to help etc and does not have to be persuaded 热心的帮手/积极肯干的工人等: *60% of voters said they would willingly pay higher taxes for better health care.* 60%的选民表示, 为了得到更好的医疗保健, 他们乐意交纳更高的税款。—**willingly** *adv* —**willingness** *n* [U]  2 3

will o' the wisp /ˌ· · · ˈ·/ *n* [C usually singular 一般用单数] **1** a blue moving light that can be seen over wet ground at night 磷火; 鬼火 **2** someone that you can never completely depend on, or something that you can never achieve 捉摸不定的人; 实现不了的事

wil·low /ˈwɪlo; ˈwɪləʊ/ *n* [C,U] a type of tree that has long thin branches and grows near water, or the wood from this tree 柳树; 柳木

wil·low·y /ˈwɪləwɪ; ˈwɪləʊi/ *adj* tall, thin, and graceful 苗条的; 婀娜多姿的: *She was pale and willowy with the most amazing violet eyes.* 她脸色苍白、身材修长, 有一双惊人的蓝紫色眼睛。

will·pow·er /ˈwɪlˌpaʊɚ; ˈwɪlˌpaʊə/ *n* [U] the ability to control your mind and body in order to achieve something that you want to do 毅力; 意志力: *It took all his willpower to remain calm.* 他竭尽全力才能保持镇定。

wil·ly, willie /ˈwɪlɪ; ˈwɪli/ *n* [C] *BrE informal* a PENIS【英, 非正式】阴茎

willy-nil·ly /ˌwɪlɪ ˈnɪlɪ; ˌwili ˈnɪli/ *adv* if something happens willy-nilly, it happens whether you want it to or not 不管愿不愿意; 无论想不想要: *The Church is being forced, willy-nilly, to make clear its position on homosexuality.* 不管愿不愿意, 教会被迫表明对同性恋的立场。

Wil·son /ˈwɪlsn; ˈwɪlsən/, **Harold** (1916-95) a British politician in the Labour Party, who was Prime Minister from 1964 to 1970, and 1974 to 1976, when he gave up his position. He then became **Lord Wilson**. When he first became Prime Minister, people saw him as someone with modern ideas and an informal manner, who understood ordinary people, at a time when many politicians were very UPPER-CLASS and formal. The Open University was established by Harold Wilson. 威尔逊〔(1916-1995), 英国工党政治家, 1964至1970年、1974至1976年先后出任英国首相, 1976年辞职, 后受封为爵士。初任首相时, 公众普遍认为威尔逊具有现代理念、举止随和、了解百姓疾苦, 与当时普遍举止刻板、上流社会气息浓重的政客大不相同。开放大学就是哈罗德·威尔逊一手创立的〕

Wilson, Wood·row /ˈwʊdro; ˈwʊdrəʊ/ (1856-1924) a US politician in the Democratic Party who was President of the US from 1913 to 1921. During his time as president, the US became involved in World War I, women were given the right to vote, and PROHIBITION started. He also helped to establish the League of Nations. 威尔逊〔(1856-1924), 美国民主党政治家, 1913至1921年任美国总统。其任期内的大事有: 美国介入一战, 妇女获得选举权, 禁酒令实施。威尔逊还促成了国际联盟的建立〕

wilt¹ /wɪlt; wɪlt/ *v* [I] **1** if a plant wilts, it bends over because it is too dry or old〔植物〕枯萎; 凋谢 —see picture on page A18 参见A18页图 **2** *informal* to feel weak, tired, or upset, especially because you are too hot【非正式】〔因太热而〕萎靡不振[疲倦; 无精打采]

wilt² *v old use* **thou wilt** you will【旧】你将

Wilt·shire /ˈwɪltʃɚ; ˈwɪltʃə/ a COUNTY in southwest England, whose main towns are Trowbridge, Salisbury, and Swindon 威尔特郡〔英格兰西南部一郡。主要城镇有特罗布里奇、索尔兹伯里和斯温登〕

wil·y /ˈwaɪlɪ; ˈwaɪli/ *adj* clever at getting what you want, especially by tricking people 诡计多端的; 狡诈的: *a wily politician* 老奸巨猾的政客 —**wiliness** *n* [U]

Wim·ble·don /ˈwɪmbl̩dən; ˈwɪmbəldən/ a tennis competition that takes place every year in Wimbledon, south London, and is one of the most important international tennis events 温布尔登网球公开赛〔每年在伦敦南部的温布尔登举行，是最重要的国际网球赛事之一〕

wimp[1] /wɪmp; wɪmp/ *n* [C] *informal*【非正式】**1** someone who has a weak character and is afraid to do something difficult or unpleasant 懦弱无用的人: *Don't be such a wimp!* 别那么窝囊! **2** a man who is thin and physically weak 瘦弱的男人 —**wimpish, wimpy** *adj*

wimp[2] *v*

wimp out *phr v* [I] *spoken* to not do something that you intended to do, because you do not feel brave enough, strong enough etc【口】〔因缺乏勇气、力量等〕不敢做〔想做的事〕

wim·ple /ˈwɪmpl̩; ˈwɪmpəl/ *n* [C] a piece of cloth that a NUN wears over her head〔修女戴的〕头巾

Wim·sey /ˈwɪmzɪ; ˈwɪmzi/, **Lord Peter** the main character in the books by Dorothy L. Sayers. He is an English lord who is also a DETECTIVE, and he is very good at solving crimes. 温姆西〔多萝西·塞耶斯小说中的主人公。他是一位英国贵族，也是一位神探，破案手段高明〕

S1 W1 **win**[1] /wɪn; wɪn/ *v past tense and past participle* **won** /wʌn; wʌn/ *present participle* **winning**

1 ►COMPETITION/RACE 竞赛/比赛◄ [I,T] to be the best or first in a competition, game, election etc〔在竞赛、游戏、选举等中〕获胜，赢: *Who do you think will win the next election?* 你认为谁会在下一次竞选中获胜? | **win at sth** *I never win at cards.* 我玩纸牌从来赢不了。| **win by a mile/10 points etc** *We won by just one point.* 我们只赢了一分。| **win hands down** (=win very easily) 轻易获胜

2 ►PRIZE 奖; 奖品◄ [T] to get something as a prize for winning in a competition or game 赢得，获得〔奖品〕: *How does it feel to have won the gold medal?* 获得金牌的感觉如何? | *She won £160 on the lottery.* 她中彩券得了160英镑。

3 ►GET/ACHIEVE 取得/获得◄ [T] to get or achieve something that you want because of your efforts or abilities〔经努力或凭能力〕获得，博得〔某物〕: *Do you think he will win the Republican nomination?* 你认为他会获得共和党的提名吗? | **win sb sth** *Those tactics won't win them any votes.* 那些策略不会给他们赢得任何选票。| **win sb's approval/trust/love etc** *Proposals for an out-of-town shopping mall have won the approval of the city council.* 在城外建一座购物中心的提案得到市议会的批准。| **win sb's heart** (=make them love you) 赢得某人的爱情

4 you win *spoken* used to agree to what someone wants after you have tried to persuade them to do something else【口】听你的; 照你的做〔在试图说服某人后，表示同意他的要求〕: *OK, you win – we'll go to the movie.* 好，听你的——我们看电影去。

5 you can't win *spoken* used to say that there is no satisfactory way of dealing with a particular situation【口】没法子〔用于表示没有令人满意的方法处理某情况〕: *You can't win, can you? You either work late and upset Jenny, or go home and risk your job.* 你没有法子，是吧? 你要么工作到深夜，惹得珍妮不高兴; 要么冒着失业的危险回家去。

6 you can't win them all *spoken* used to show sympathy when someone has had a disappointing experience【口】你不可能事事都成功〔对某人失意表示同情〕

7 win the day to finally be successful in a discussion or argument; TRIUMPH[2]〔在讨论或争论中〕最终获得胜利: *Common sense won the day, and the development plans were dropped.* 常识最终获胜，发展规划取消了。—see also 另见 **win the toss** (TOSS[2] (3)), WINNER, WINNING

win sb ↔ **round/around** *phr v* [T] to win someone over 说服〔某人〕; 把〔某人〕争取过来

win sb/sth ↔ **back** *phr v* [T] to succeed in getting back something or someone that you had before 重新获得〔某物或某人〕，把…赢回来: *How can I win back her trust?* 我怎么能重新赢得她的信任?

win out *phr v* [I] to win through〔经历困难后〕终于成功

win sb ↔ **over** *phr v* [T] to get someone's support or friendship by persuading them or being nice to them〔通过劝说或示好以〕获得〔某人的支持或友谊〕，把〔某人〕争取过来: *We'll be working hard over the next ten days to win over the undecided voters.* 我们将在接下来的10天努力，把犹豫未决的选民争取过来。

win through *phr v* [I] to eventually succeed in spite of problems〔经历困难后〕终于成功: *As in most of his films, it's the good guys who win through in the end.* 正如在他的大多数电影里一样，好人最终获得胜利。

> **USAGE NOTE 用法说明: WIN**
>
> WORD CHOICE 词语辨析: **win, beat, defeat**
>
> You can **win** a game, race, competition, election etc (NOT **gain**). 在游戏、比赛、竞赛、选举中获胜的用词是 win（不用 gain）。After the event you can say 事后可以说 *I've won!* 我赢了! A country can **win** a battle or war (NOT **gain**). 一个国家赢得战役或战争用 win（不用 gain）。As a result you can also **win** a victory, championship, prize, scholarship, or a seat in the Senate. 于是赢得胜利〔锦标赛、奖品、奖学金、参议院议席〕也用 win。—see also 另见 GAIN (USAGE NOTE)
>
> When you win a game etc, you **beat** the other person or the other team or, more formally, you could say **defeat** 在运动比赛等中获胜，打败了其他人或其他队用 beat，较为正式地可以用defeat: *We beat their team by ten points.* (NOT 不用 *won*) 我们以10分的优势击败了他们的队。| *He beat all his opponents/rivals for the seat.* 他击败所有对手/敌手，获得这个席位。
>
> When a country wins a war it **defeats** its enemies (**beat** can be used informally) 一个国家在战争中获胜，就是打败了 (defeat) 它的敌人〔beat是非正式用语〕: *The Americans defeated the British in 1781.* 美国人在1781年打败了英国人。

win[2] *n* [C] a success or victory, especially in sport〔尤指在体育比赛中的〕胜利，赢: *We've had two wins so far this season.* 这个赛季开始以来，我们赢了两场。| [+over] *In the under-16 event England had their first win over Germany, by 2-1.* 在16岁以下的比赛项目中，英格兰队以2:1的成绩第一次战胜了德国队。—see also 另见 NO-WIN SITUATION W3

wince /wɪns; wɪns/ *v* [I] **1** to suddenly change the expression on your face as a reaction to something painful or upsetting 皱眉蹙眼〔因疼痛或不安导致面部表情突然改变〕: *Sandra winced as the dentist started to drill.* 牙医开始钻牙时，桑德拉皱眉蹙眼。**2** to suddenly feel very uncomfortable or embarrassed because of something that happens, something you remember etc〔因发生或记起某事等而突然〕感到不安; 畏缩: **wince at the thought/idea/memory** *I still wince at the thought of that terrible evening.* 一想起那可怕的夜晚，我仍然不寒而栗。—**wince** *n* [singular]

win·cey·ette /ˌwɪnsɪˈɛt; ˌwɪnsiˈet◂/ *n* [U] *BrE* light material with a soft surface, used especially for clothes you wear in bed; FLANNELETTE【英】〔尤指做睡衣的〕棉织薄法兰绒

winch[1] /wɪntʃ; wɪntʃ/ *n* [C] a machine with a rope or chain for lifting heavy objects 绞车; 起货机

winch[2] *v* [T always+adv/prep] to lift something or someone up using a winch 用绞车提（起）; 用起货机吊（起）: **winch sth out/from etc** *He was winched out of the sinking boat just in time.* 他被及时地从下沉的船中吊出来。

Win·ches·ter /ˈwɪntʃɛstɚ; ˈwɪntʃɪstə/ an ancient city in southern England, famous for its CATHEDRAL and for its PUBLIC SCHOOL (=a school that is paid for by the parents and not by the government), **Winchester College**. Winchester was England's capital city in the 9th and 10th centuries. 温切斯特〔英格兰南部一古城，以天主教堂和温切斯特公学著称于世。9世纪和10世纪，该城曾为英格兰王国的首都〕

wind[1] /wɪnd; wɪnd/ *n* S2 W2

1 ►AIR 空气◄ [C,U] moving air, especially when it moves strongly or quickly in a current 风: *a 70-mile-an-hour wind* 时速70英里的风 | *branches swaying in the wind* 枝条在风中摆舞 | **the wind blows** *A gentle wind was blowing through the trees.* 一阵微风吹过树林。| **strong/high winds** *The forecast is for strong winds and heavy rain.* 天气预报报道会出现狂风暴雨。| **a gust of wind** (=a short strong wind) 一阵强风 *A sudden gust of wind blew the door shut.* 突然一阵强风把门关上了。| **east/west/north/south wind** (=coming from the east etc) 东/西/北/南风 | **a gentle/soft/light wind** *A soft wind teased a tendril of her hair.* 和风拂动着她的一绺头发。| **a bitter/chill/biting wind** (=a very cold wind) 刺骨的寒风 | **the wind is up/gets up** (=blows more strongly) 风势渐大 | **the wind drops** (=blows less strongly) 风势渐弱 *We'll wait till the wind drops before we put the tent up.* 我们等风势减弱后再把帐篷支起来。—see also 另见 HEADWIND —see picture on page A13 参见A13页图

2 get/have wind of *informal* to hear or find out about something secret or private, especially if you learn it accidentally or unofficially【非正式】〔尤指偶然地或非正式地〕听到…的风声;

获得…的线索: *Jeremy, I don't want that reporter getting wind of this.* 杰里米，我不想让那名记者获得这方面的线索。

3 ▶BREATH 呼吸; 气息◀[U] your ability to breathe without difficulty〔正常〕呼吸能力: **get your wind (back)**(=be able to breathe normally again, for example after running)〔跑步等后〕恢复正常呼吸，喘过气来 | **knock the wind out of**(=hit someone in the stomach so that they cannot breathe for a moment)〔打[撞]某人的腹部〕使透不过气来 —see also 另见 SECOND WIND, WINDPIPE

4 take the wind out of sb's sails *informal* to make someone lose their confidence, especially by saying or doing something unexpected【非正式】〔尤指以意想不到的言语或行动〕使某人丧失信心

5 see which way the wind is blowing to find out what the situation is before you do something or make a decision〔做事或做决定前〕观望形势，看风向

6 be in the wind used to say that something is happening or going to happen, but not many people know what it is〔某事〕正在进行中; 即将发生〔但知道的人很少〕

7 the winds of change/freedom/public opinion etc events and changes that have started to happen and will have important effects, and that cannot be stopped〔有重要影响而不可遏止的〕〕改革/自由/舆论等的趋势

8 get the wind up/put the wind up sb *BrE informal* to become anxious or frightened, or to make someone feel this way【英，非正式】(使) 某人担惊受怕; (使) 某人受到惊吓: *The threat of legal action will be enough to put the wind up them.* 用法律行动作威胁足以使他们心惊胆战。

9 ▶IN YOUR STOMACH 在胃中◀[U] *BrE* the condition of having air or gas in your stomach, or the air or gas itself【英】肠胃气胀; 胃气，肠气; GAS *AmE*【美】: *I can't drink beer, it gives me wind.* 我不能喝啤酒，它会令我肠胃胀气。

10 the winds/the wind section all the musicians who play WIND INSTRUMENTS in a band〔乐队中的〕管乐部，管乐组

11 ▶TALK 交谈◀[U] *informal* useless talk that does not mean anything【非正式】空谈，空话 —see also 另见 WINDY, **break wind**(BREAK¹ (43)), **an ill wind (that blows nobody any good)** (ILL¹ (5)), **sail close to the wind**(SAIL¹ (6)), **a straw in the wind** (STRAW (4))

wind² /waɪnd; waɪnd/ *v past tense and past participle* **wound** /waʊnd; waʊnd/ **1** [I always+adv/prep, T always+adv/prep] to turn or twist something repeatedly, especially around something else〔尤指绕着他物〕缠绕，卷绕: **wind sth around/round** *Wind the wires around those pins there.* 把金属丝绕在那边的那些钉子上。| **wind sth forward/back** *Can you wind the video back a little way – I want to see that bit again.* 请你把录像往回倒一点，我想再看看那一小段。| [**+around/round**] *Make sure the thread winds evenly around the bobbin.* 确保线均匀地绕在线轴上。—see also 另见 REWIND **2** also 又作 **wind up** [T] to turn something such as a handle or part of a machine around and around, especially in order to make something move or start working〔为使某物移动或起动而〕摇动〔把手等〕，转动; 给〔机器〕上发条: *What time is it? I forgot to wind my watch.* 几点了？我忘记给表上发条了。| *It was one of those old gramophones that you have to wind up.* 那是一台手摇的老式唱机。| **wind sth down/up** *BrE*【英】: *Would you mind winding down the window?* 请把窗户摇下来好吗？**3** [I always+adv/prep] if a road, track, river etc winds, it has many smooth bends and is usually very long〔道路、轨道、河流等〕蜿蜒; 曲折前进: **wind (its way) through/along** *Highway 99 winds its way along the coast.* 99号公路沿着海岸弯弯曲曲地延伸。—see also 另见 WINDING

wind down *phr v* **1** [T **wind** sth ↔ **down**] to gradually reduce the work of a business or organization so that it can be closed down completely 使〔业务〕逐步结束; 使〔组织〕停止运作 —compare 比较 **wind up**(2) **2** [I] to rest and relax after a lot of hard work or excitement〔紧张工作或兴奋之后〕平静下来; 放松: *I find it difficult to wind down after a day at work.* 一天工作之后，我觉得很难让自己平静下来。

wind up *phr v* **1** [I, T **wind** sth ↔ **up**] bring an activity, meeting etc to an end (使)〔活动、会议等〕结束: *OK, just to wind up, could I summarize what we've decided?* 好了，该结束了，我来把我们的决定做个总结好吗？| *It's time to wind things up – I have a plane to catch.* 该结束了，我还得赶飞机。**2** [T **wind** sth ↔ **up**] to close down a company or organization 结束〔公司、机构〕: *Our operations in Jamaica are being wound up.* 我们在牙买加的业务正准备结束。—compare 比较 WIND DOWN¹ **3** [I, linking verb 连系动词] *informal* to unintentionally get into an unpleasant situation or place as a result of something you have done【非正式】〔无意间〕卷入; 牵涉到: [**+with/in/at etc**] *You know you're going to wind up in court over this.* 你知道你终归会因此对簿公堂。| **wind up doing** *I wound up wishing I'd never come.* 我最后真希望我从未来过。| **wind up drunk/dead/ill etc** *You keep driving like that and you'll wind up dead.* 你老是那样开车，到头来就得一命呜呼。**4** [T **wind** sb ↔ **up**] *BrE* to deliberately say or do something in order to annoy someone, especially because you enjoy annoying them【英】故意惹恼〔某人，尤因你喜欢这样做〕，愚弄: *Stupid! They're only winding you up.* 傻瓜！他们只是在拿你开心。—see also 另见 WOUND-UP

wind³ /waɪnd; waɪnd/ *n* [C] a bend or turn 弯曲; 转动: **give sth a wind** *Give that crank another wind, will you?* 你再摇一下那个曲柄，好吗？

wind⁴ /wɪnd; wɪnd/ *v* [T] to make someone have difficulty in breathing 使〔某人〕喘不过气: **be winded** *"Is he OK?" "Yeah, I think he's just winded."* "他没事吧？" "没事，我想他只不过是喘不过气来。"

wind·bag /ˈwɪnd͵bæg; ˈwɪndbæg/ *n* [C] *informal* someone who talks too much; GASBAG【非正式】夸夸其谈的人; 喋喋不休的人; 话匣子

wind·break /ˈwɪnd͵brek; ˈwɪndbreɪk/ *n* [C] a fence, line of trees, or wall that is intended to protect a place from the wind 挡风篱[墙]; 防风林

wind break·er /ˈwɪnd ͵brekɚ; ˈwɪnd ͵breɪkə/ *AmE*【美】, **windcheat·er** /ˈwɪnd͵tʃitɚ; ˈwɪnd͵tʃiːtə/ *BrE old-fashioned*【英，过时】*n* [C] a type of coat that is made specially to keep the wind out 风衣，防风夹克 —see picture at 参见 COAT¹ 图

wind chime /ˈwɪnd ͵tʃaɪm; ˈwɪnd tʃaɪm/ *n* [C] long thin pieces of metal or glass hanging together in a group that make musical sounds when the wind blows 风铃

wind·ed /ˈwɪndɪd; ˈwɪndɨd/ *adj* unable to breathe easily, because you have been running or you have been hit in the stomach〔因跑步或腹部被打而〕呼吸困难的，喘不过气的

Win·der·mere /ˈwɪndɚmɪr; ˈwɪndəmɪə/ one of the lakes in the Lake District, northwest England, which is the largest lake in England 温德米尔湖〔英格兰西北部湖区的湖泊之一，是英格兰最大的湖泊〕

wind·fall /ˈwɪnd͵fɔl; ˈwɪndfɔːl/ *n* [C] **1** an amount of money that you get unexpectedly 意外之财: *Jackpot pools winner Salters toasted his £2 million windfall at his Edinburgh home.* 累积奖金得主索特尔斯在爱丁堡的家中庆祝他获得200万英镑的横财。| **windfall gain/profit etc**(=high profits that you did not expect to make) 意外的巨大收获/巨额利润等 **2** a piece of fruit that has fallen off a tree 被风吹落的果实

Windhoek /ˈwɪndhuk; ˈwɪndhʊk/ the capital city of Namibia 温得和克〔纳米比亚首都〕

wind·ing /ˈwaɪndɪŋ; ˈwaɪndɪŋ/ *adj* having a twisting turning shape 弯曲的; 蜿蜒的: *a winding path* 弯弯曲曲的小路 —see also 另见 WIND² (3)

winding sheet /ˈwaɪndɪŋ ͵ʃit; ˈwaɪndɪŋ ʃiːt/ *n* [C] *old use* a SHROUD¹ (1)【旧】裹尸布

wind in·stru·ment /ˈwɪnd ͵ɪnstrəmənt; ˈwɪnd ͵ɪnstrɡmənt/ *n* [C] a musical instrument that you play by blowing through it 管乐器

The Wind in the Willows《杨柳风》

Wind in the Wil·lows, The /͵wɪnd ɪn ðə ˈwɪloz; ͵wɪnd ɪn ðə ˈwɪləʊz/ (1908) a famous book for children by Kenneth Grahame. It describes the adventures of a group of animals who talk and behave like humans, and the main characters include Mole and Ratty, who live on the river bank, and Toad of Toad Hall, who is very rich and lives in a large house.《杨柳风》〔(1908)，肯尼思·格雷厄姆的一部著名儿童小说，讲述一群动物

的冒险经历，它们言谈举止类似人类。主人公包括住在河岸上的鼹鼠和河鼠，还有蟾蜍府的蟾蜍先生，它非常富有，住在一幢大房子里〕

wind·jam·mer /ˈwɪnd,dʒæmɚ; ˈwɪnd,dʒæmə/ *n* [C] a large sailing ship of the type that was used for trade in the 19th century〔19 世纪从事贸易用的〕大帆船

wind·lass /ˈwɪndləs; ˈwɪndləs/ *n* [C] a machine for pulling or lifting heavy objects 绞车

wind·mill /ˈwɪnd,mɪl; ˈwɪnd,mɪl/ *n* [C] **1** a building or structure with parts that turn around in the wind, used for producing electrical power or crushing grain 风车；风力磨坊 **2** *BrE* a toy consisting of a stick with curved pieces of plastic at the end that turn around when they are blown【英】玩具风车；PINWHEEL *AmE*【美】

1 1 **win·dow** /ˈwɪndo; ˈwɪndəʊ/ *n* [C] **1** an opening in the wall of a building, car etc that lets in light and air, and is usually covered with glass〔建筑物、汽车等上的〕窗；窗户；橱窗：*Do you mind if I open the window?* 我开窗可以吗？| *looking at the Christmas displays in the shop windows* 观看橱窗里的圣诞陈列品 —see picture on page A2 参见 A2 页图 **2** one of the separate areas on a computer screen where different processes or PROGRAMS are operating〔电脑屏幕上显示不同程序正在操作的〕视窗 **3** a short period of time that is available for a particular activity〔某种活动能进行的〕短暂时限 **4 go out (of) the window** *informal* to disappear completely or no longer have any effect【非正式】完全消失；不起作用：*One glass of wine, and all my good intentions went out the window.* 一杯酒让我所有善意都白费了。**5 window of opportunity** a lucky opportunity to do something that you will not always be able to do 难逢的良机

window box /ˈ· · ,·/ *n* [C] a long narrow box in which you can grow plants outside your window〔狭长形的〕窗台花箱，窗口花坛

window clean·er /ˈ· · ,· ·/ *n* [C] someone whose job is to clean windows 窗户清洁工

> **CULTURAL NOTE 文化注释**
>
> In the UK, some people make jokes about window cleaners because they imagine that window cleaners see a lot of interesting and strange things while they are cleaning windows, especially women without any clothes on. 在英国，有些人爱拿窗户清洁工来开玩笑，因为他们浮想联翩地认为窗户清洁工在清洗窗户时能看到不少有趣和奇怪的事情，特别是能看到光着身子的女人。

window dress·er /ˈ· · ,· ·/ *n* [C] someone whose job is to arrange goods attractively in shop windows〔商店的〕橱窗设计[布置]人

window dress·ing /ˈ· · ,· ·/ *n* [U] **1** something that is intended to give people a favourable idea about your plans or activities, and to stop them seeing the true situation 粉饰门面；弄虚作假：*All these glossy pamphlets are just window dressing – the fact is that the new mall will ruin the environment.* 所有这些五光十色的小册子只不过是用来装饰门面而已，事实是新商场将破坏环境。**2** the art of arranging goods in a shop window so that they look attractive to customers〔商店的〕橱窗布置[装饰]术

win·dow·pane /ˈwɪndo,pen; ˈwɪndəʊpeɪn/ *n* [U] a single whole piece of glass in a window〔整块〕窗玻璃

Win·dows /ˈwɪndoz; ˈwɪndəʊz/ *n* [U] *trademark* a system produced by the Microsoft Corporation for organizing information on a personal computer, which can run several PROGRAMS in separate areas of the computer screen【商标】〔美国微软公司开发的〕视窗〔一种电脑操作系统〕

window seat /ˈ· · ,·/ *n* [C] **1** a seat next to the window on a bus, plane etc〔公共汽车、飞机等的〕靠窗座位 **2** a seat directly below a window〔指凸窗处的〕窗座

window shade /ˈ· · ,·/ *n* [C] *AmE* BLIND³ (1)【美】窗帘；遮帘

window-shopping /ˈ· · ,· ·/ *n* [U] the activity of looking at goods in shop windows without intending to buy them 浏览商店橱窗；逛街看商店橱窗〔不打算购物〕—**window-shopper** *n* [C]

win·dow·sill /ˈwɪndo,sɪl; ˈwɪndəʊ,sɪl/ *n* [C] a shelf fixed along the bottom of a window 窗台，窗沿 —see picture on page A4 参见 A4 页图

wind·pipe /ˈwɪnd,paɪp; ˈwɪndpaɪp/ *n* [C] the tube through which air passes from your mouth to your lungs 气管

wind·screen /ˈwɪnd,skrin; ˈwɪndskriːn/ *n* [C] *BrE* the large window at the front of a car, bus etc【英】〔汽车等前部的〕挡风玻璃；WINDSHIELD *AmE*【美】—see picture on page A2 参见 A2 页图

windscreen wip·er /ˈ· · ,· ·/ *n* [C] *BrE* a long thin piece of metal with a rubber edge that moves across a windscreen to remove rain【英】〔汽车挡风玻璃上的〕刮水器，雨刷；WINDSHIELD WIPER *AmE*【美】—see picture on page A2 参见 A2 页图

wind·shield /ˈwɪnd,ʃild; ˈwɪndʃiːld/ *n* [C] **1** *AmE* a windscreen【美】挡风玻璃 —see picture on page A2 参见 A2 页图 **2** a piece of glass or clear plastic fixed at the front of a MOTORCYCLE〔摩托车前面的〕挡风玻璃，透明挡风板

windshield wip·er /ˈ· · ,· ·/ *n* [C] *AmE* a windscreen wiper【美】〔汽车挡风玻璃上的〕刮水器，雨刷 —see picture on page A2 参见 A2 页图

wind·sock /ˈwɪnd,sɑk; ˈwɪndsɒk/ *n* [C] a tube of material fastened to a pole at airports to show the direction of the wind 风向袋，〔筒状〕风标

Wind·sor /ˈwɪnzɚ; ˈwɪnzə/ a town in southern England on the River Thames famous for its castle 温莎镇〔英格兰南部一小镇。位于泰晤士河畔，以当地的城堡著称〕

Windsor Cas·tle /,· · ˈ· ·/ one of the official homes of the British royal family, in the town of Windsor 温莎堡〔英国王室官方居所之一，位于温莎镇〕

Windsor Great Park /,· · ˈ· ,·/ the large park in which Windsor Castle stands 温莎大公园〔温莎堡所在的一座大型公园〕

Wind·sors, the /ˈwɪnzɚz; ˈwɪnzəz/ a name used especially by newspapers for the present British royal family, whose family name is Windsor 温莎〔尤为报界用来指当今英国王室，其姓氏为温莎〕

wind·storm /ˈwɪnd,stɔrm; ˈwɪndstɔːm/ *n* [C] a period of bad weather when there are strong winds but not much rain〔少雨的〕风暴

wind-surfing 帆板运动

wind·surf·ing /ˈwɪnd ,sɝfɪŋ; ˈwɪnd ,sɜːfɪŋ/ *n* [U] the sport of sailing across water by standing on a board and holding on to a large sail 帆板运动，风帆滑浪〔运动〕—**wind-surfer** *n* [C] —**wind-surf** *v* [I]

wind·swept /ˈwɪnd,swɛpt; ˈwɪndswept/ *adj* **1** a place that is windswept is often windy because there are not many trees or buildings to protect it〔地方〕迎风的；无遮挡的：*windswept moors* 当风的沼泽地 **2** hair, clothes etc that are windswept have been blown around by the wind〔头发、衣服等〕被风吹乱[散]的

wind tun·nel /ˈwɪnd ,tʌnl; ˈwɪnd ,tʌnl/ *n* [C] a large enclosed passage where aircraft are tested by forcing air past them〔测验飞机的〕风洞

wind tur·bine /ˈwɪnd ,tɝbɪn; ˈwɪnd ,tɜːbaɪn/ *n* [C] a modern WINDMILL (1) for providing electrical power 风力涡轮机；风力发电机

wind-up /ˈwaɪnd ʌp; ˈwaɪnd ʌp/ *n* [C] *BrE informal* something you say or do to deliberately make someone angry or worried【英，非正式】为了激怒人故意说的话[做的事]

wind·ward¹ /ˈwɪndwɚd; ˈwɪndwəd/ *adj, adv* **1** towards the direction from which the wind is blowing 迎风的[地]，向风的[地] **2** pointing towards the wind 顶风(的)：*the windward side of the boat* 船的迎风一边 —opposite 反义词 LEEWARD

windward² *n* [U] the place from which the wind is blowing 迎风面，向风面：*We sailed to windward across Oyster Bay.* 我们逆风航行，横渡奥伊斯特湾。

Windward Is·lands, the /ˈ· · ,· ·/ a group of islands in the Caribbean Sea, which includes Martinique, Grenada and St Lucia 向风群岛〔加勒比海一群岛，包括马提尼克岛、格林纳达岛、圣卢西亚岛〕

wind·y /ˈwɪndɪ; ˈwɪndi/ *adj* **1** with a lot of wind blowing 多风的，风大的：*It's too windy for a picnic.* 今天风太大，不适合野餐。**2** getting a lot of wind 当风的；受大风吹刮的：*a windy hill-* 3

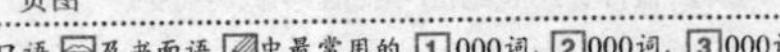
口语 及书面语 中最常用的 1000词，2000词，3000词

side 风很大的山坡 **3** windy talk is full of words that sound impressive but do not mean much 夸夸其谈的; 空话连篇的: *the politician's windy generalizations* 政客夸夸其谈的概括 —**windily** *adv* —**windiness** *n* [U]

Windy Cit·y, the /,·· '··/ an informal name for the US city of Chicago 风城〔美国芝加哥市的俗称〕

wine¹ /waɪn; waɪn/ *n* [C,U] **1** an alcoholic drink made from GRAPES, or a type of this drink 葡萄酒: *a glass of white wine* 一杯白葡萄酒 | *a delicious Californian wine* 醇香味美的加利福尼亚葡萄酒 **2** an alcoholic drink made from another fruit or plant 果酒: *elderflower wine* 接骨木果酒 **3 wine, women and song** *old-fashioned* a pleasant, enjoyable life of dancing, drinking etc【过时】醇酒、美人、情歌〔指纵情欢乐的生活〕, 声色犬马

wine² *v* [T] **wine and dine** to entertain someone well with a meal, wine etc 以酒宴款待: *Hawksworth wined and dined potential clients.* 霍克斯沃思设宴招揽客户。

wine bar /'· ·/ *n* [C] *BrE* a place that serves mainly wine and light meals【英】〔主要供应葡萄酒和小吃的〕酒吧

CULTURAL NOTE 文化注释

Wine bars are very different from pubs and usually aim to have a more fashionable image. They are popular especially with MIDDLE-CLASS professional men and women. 这种酒吧和小酒馆差别很大, 通常也以更为时尚的形象示人, 尤其受中产阶级职业男女的欢迎。

wine cool·er /'· ,··/ *n* [C] **1** *AmE* a drink made with wine, fruit juice, and water【美】果汁清凉酒〔由葡萄酒、果汁和水调配而成的饮料〕 **2** a special container that you put a bottle of wine into to make it cool 镇酒冰壶

wine vin·e·gar /,· '···/ *n* [U] a type of VINEGAR made from sour wine, used in cooking〔烹调用〕葡萄酒醋

wing¹ /wɪŋ; wɪŋ/ *n* [C]

1 ▶BIRDS 鸟类◀ a) one of the parts of a bird's or insect's body that it uses for flying〔鸟、昆虫的〕翅膀, 翼: *a butterfly with beautiful markings on its wings* 翅膀上有美丽花纹的蝴蝶 | **flap its wings** (=move them up and down) 拍动翅膀 *vultures circling overhead, lazily flapping their wings* 兀鹫缓缓地拍动双翅, 在头顶上盘旋 **b)** the meat on the wing bone of a chicken, duck etc, used as food〔用作食物的〕翅膀〈如鸡翅、鸭翅等〉: *spicy chicken wings* 香辣鸡翅

2 ▶PLANE 飞机◀ one of the large flat parts that stick out from the side of a plane and help to keep it in the air〔飞机的〕机翼 —see picture at 参见 AIRCRAFT 图

3 ▶BUILDING 建筑物◀ one of the parts of a large building, especially one that sticks out from the main part〔尤指建筑物的〕侧翼; 侧厅; 耳房, 厢房: *the east wing of the palace* 宫殿的东厢房 | *She works in the hospital's maternity wing.* 她在医院的妇产科工作。

4 ▶POLITICS 政治◀ a group within a political party or similar organization, whose members share particular opinions and aims, especially when these are different from those of most people in the organization〔观点与政党、组织中大多数人不一致的〕派别, 派〔系〕: *She's on the liberal wing of the Republican Party.* 她是共和党内的自由派。—see also 另见 LEFT WING, RIGHT WING

5 ▶SPORT 体育运动◀ a) someone who plays on the far left or far right of the field in games like football〔足球等运动中的〕边锋, 侧翼队员 **b)** the far left or right part of the field 运动场的边沿

6 ▶CAR 汽车◀ *BrE* the part of a car's body that covers the wheels【英】〔汽车的〕挡泥板, 翼子板; FENDER (2) *AmE*【美】—see picture on page A2 参见 A2 页图

7 take sb under your wing to give help and protection, especially to someone younger or less experienced 将某人置于自己的庇护下〔尤指对年轻或经验不足的人〕

8 (waiting) in the wings ready to take action or ready to be used when the time is right 准备行动〔只等待时机成熟〕; 随时可以使用: *There's a whole series of tax-cutting measures waiting in the wings.* 有一整套减税方案准备出台。

9 ▶THEATRE 剧场◀ the wings [plural] the parts at either side of a stage where the actors are hidden from view〔舞台的〕侧面

10 be on the wing *literary* if a bird is on the wing, it is flying【文】〔鸟〕在飞行中, 飞翔

11 take wing *literary* to fly away【文】飞走

12 get your wings to pass the necessary flying exams and become a pilot〔当飞行员前〕通过必要的飞行考试

wing² *v* **1** [I always+adv/prep] *especially literary* to fly【尤文】飞行, 飞: *a flock of geese winging down the coast from Iceland* 沿着冰岛海岸南飞的一群鹅 **2 wing its way a)** to fly 飞行, 飞: *planes winging their way to exotic destinations* 飞往充满异国情调的目的地的飞机 **b)** to be sent quickly from one place to another〔从一地〕快速送〔到另一地〕: *Our special first prize will soon be winging its way towards you.* 我们的特等头奖将很快地送给你。**3** [T] to wound a person or bird in the arm or wing 弄伤〔人的〕手臂; 打伤〔鸟的〕翅膀 **4 wing it** *AmE spoken* to do something without planning or preparation【美口】临时凑成; 即席而为: *I didn't have time to prepare for the meeting – I'll just have to wing it.* 这次会议我没有时间准备, 我只好见机行事。

wing chair /'· ·/ *n* [C] a comfortable chair that has a high back and pieces pointing forward on each side 翼状靠背扶手椅

wing col·lar /,· '··/ *n* [C] a type of shirt collar for men that is worn with very formal clothes〔男装礼服的衬衫的〕燕子领

wing com·mand·er /'· ·,··/ *n* a rank in the Royal Air Force〔英国皇家空军的〕空军中校 —see table on page C7 参见 C7 页附录

wing·ding /'wɪŋ,dɪŋ; 'wɪŋ,dɪŋ/ *n* [C] *AmE old-fashioned* a party【美, 过时】狂欢会; 热闹的聚会

winge /wɪndʒ; wɪndʒ/ *v* another spelling of WHINGE whinge 的另一种拼法

winged /wɪŋd; wɪŋd/ *adj* having wings 有翼的; 有翅膀的: *winged insects* 有翅的昆虫

wing·er /'wɪŋɚ; 'wɪŋə/ *n* [C] **1** a player in games such as football, whose position is on the far left or far right of the field〔足球运动等的〕边锋 —see also 另见 WING¹ (5) **2 right-winger/left-winger** someone who belongs to the RIGHT WING or LEFT WING² of a political group〔政治群体中的〕右翼分子/左翼分子

wing mir·ror /'· ,··/ *n* [C] a mirror fixed to the side of a car〔汽车的〕侧镜 —see picture on page A2 参见 A2 页图

wing nut /'· ·/ *n* [C] a NUT¹ (2) for fastening things, which has sides that stick out to make it easier to turn 蝶形螺母

wing·span /'wɪŋ,spæn; 'wɪŋspæn/ *n* [C] the distance from the end of one wing to the end of the other 翼展, 翼幅〔两翼展开时的宽度〕

wing·tip /'wɪŋtɪp; 'wɪŋtɪp/ *n* [C] **1** the point at the end of a bird's or a plane's wing〔鸟、飞机的〕翼尖, 翼梢 **2** *AmE* a type of man's shoe with a pattern of small holes on the toe【美】〔脚尖处有孔的〕拷花男皮鞋

wink¹ /wɪŋk; wɪŋk/ *v* **1** [I,T] to close and open one eye quickly, usually to communicate amusement or a secret message 眨〔一只眼〕, 使眼色〔常用于示意〕: [+at] *Joel winked at me, and I realized he was joking.* 乔尔向我眨眼示意, 我明白他是在开玩笑。**2** [I] to shine with a light that flashes on and off〔光〕闪烁, 明灭: *the winking lights of buoys out to sea* 海上的浮标发出的闪烁灯光

wink 眨〔一只眼〕

wink at sth *phr v* [T] to pretend not to notice something bad or illegal, in a way that suggests you approve of it 对〔坏事、非法的事〕睁一只眼闭一只眼, 假装没有看见

wink² *n* **1** [C] a quick opening and closing of your eye, usually as a signal between people 眨眼〔示意〕: *a conspiratorial wink* 诡秘地眨一下眼 **2 not get a wink of sleep/not sleep a wink** not be able to sleep at all 无法入睡 **3 tip sb the wink** to secretly warn someone about something or give them information 暗中警告某人[向某人透露消息] **4 quick as a wink** *AmE* very quickly【美】很快地 —see also 另见 FORTY WINKS, **a nod's as good as a wink** (NOD² (3))

wink·ers /'wɪŋkɚz; 'wɪŋkəz/ *n* [plural] *BrE informal* the small usually orange lights on a car that flash on the right or left to show that the car is turning【英, 非正式】〔汽车左右两边表示拐弯的橙色〕频闪信号灯, 方向指示灯; BLINKERS (3) *AmE*【美】

win·kle¹ /'wɪŋkl; 'wɪŋkəl/ *n* [C] a small sea animal that lives in a shell and is used for food〔可食用的〕蛾螺; 玉黍螺

winkle² *v*

winkle sth/sb ↔ **out** *phr v* [T] **1** to make someone leave somewhere 把〔某人〕赶出〔某地〕: *Government critics were winkled out of their positions of influence.* 批评政府的人士被解除了重要职位。**2** to discover something such as information 发现〔消息等〕: *Candy was very good at winkling out secrets.* 坎迪极善于刺探秘密。

Winkle, Rip Van —see 见 RIP VAN WINKLE

winkle pick·er /'·· ,··/ *n* [C usually plural 一般用复数] *BrE* a type of man's shoe with very pointed toes, popular in the 1950's【英】〔流行于 20 世纪 50 年代的〕男式尖头皮鞋

Win·ne·ba·go /ˌwɪnɪˋbego; ˌwɪnɪˈbeɪgəʊ/ *trademark* a type of CARAVAN sold in the US, which is often very large and comfortable【商标】温内巴戈〔在美国销售的一种旅行房车, 车身很大, 乘坐舒适〕

3 2 **win·ner** /ˋwɪnɚ; ˈwɪnə/ *n* [C] **1** a person or an animal that has won something 获胜者〔人或动物〕: *a Nobel prize winner* 诺贝尔奖得主 | *Sid backed a winner at this year's Derby.* 锡德下注买中了今年德比马赛中获胜的马。**2** *informal* someone or something that is likely to be very successful【非正式】可望成功的人[事]: *That idea's a real winner.* 那个主意的确好。| **be onto a winner** (=be selling, producing etc something that is very likely to be successful) 销售[生产]极有市场的物品

Win·nie the Pooh /ˌwɪnɪ ðə ˋpu; ˌwɪni ðə ˈpuː/ (1926) a famous book for children by A.A. Milne, about a boy called Christopher Robin and his TEDDY BEAR Winnie-the-Pooh, who is also called **Pooh** or **Pooh Bear**. Pooh is not very clever or brave, but he is very happy and helpful and has lots of friends, including Eeyore, Piglet, and Tigger. He likes inventing songs and poems and his favourite food is honey.《小熊维尼》〔(1926), A.A.米尔恩创作的童话, 讲述一个名叫克里斯托弗·罗宾的男孩子与他的玩具熊维尼(又称"噗噗熊")的故事。维尼既不太聪明, 也不太勇敢, 但十分快乐, 也乐于助人。它有许多朋友, 包括小驴依唷、小猪和跳跳虎。维尼喜欢编歌、作诗, 最爱吃蜂蜜〕

win·ning /ˋwɪnɪŋ; ˈwɪnɪŋ/ *adj* [only before noun 仅用于名词前] very pleasant and attractive in a way that makes everyone like you 可爱的; 迷人的: *a winning smile* 迷人的微笑

winning post /ˈ‥ ˌ·/ *n* [singular] *especially BrE* the place where a horse race ends【尤英】〔赛马的〕终点柱

win·nings /ˋwɪnɪŋz; ˈwɪnɪŋz/ *n* [plural] money that you win in a game or by betting (BET[1] (1))〔在比赛或打赌中〕赢得的钱

win·now /ˋwɪno; ˈwɪnəʊ/ *v* [T] to blow the CHAFF (=outer part) away from grain 簸去〔谷壳〕

wi·no /ˋwaɪno; ˈwaɪnəʊ/ *n* [C] *informal* someone who drinks a lot of cheap alcohol and lives on the streets【非正式】〔露宿街头的〕醉鬼, 酒鬼: *accosted by winos asking for money* 被酒鬼搭讪要钱

win·some /ˋwɪnsəm; ˈwɪnsəm/ *adj literary* pleasant and attractive, especially in a simple, direct way【文】迷人的; 令人喜欢的: *a winsome smile* 迷人的微笑

2 2 **win·ter**[1] /ˋwɪntɚ; ˈwɪntə/ *n* [C,U] the season after autumn and before spring 冬季, 冬天: *the cold Canadian winters* 加拿大寒冷的冬天 | *the winter of 1942* 1942年冬季 | **in (the) winter** *It usually snows here in winter.* 这儿冬天一般会下雪。| **winter coat/shoes etc** (=designed for cold weather) 冬衣/冬鞋等

winter[2] *v* [I always+adv/prep] to spend the winter somewhere〔在某处〕过冬: *Swallows winter in Africa or India.* 燕子在非洲或印度过冬。

win·ter·ize /ˋwɪntəraɪz; ˈwɪntəraɪz/ *v* [T] *AmE* to prepare your car, house etc for winter conditions【美】在〔汽车、房屋等〕内装御寒设备

winter sol·stice /ˌ‥ ˈ‥/ *n* [singular] the shortest day of the year in the Northern Hemisphere, usually around December 22nd 冬至〔在北半球, 一年中白昼最短的一天, 通常在12月22日左右〕

winter sports /ˌ‥ ˈ·/ *n* [plural] sports that take place on snow or ice, such as skiing (SKI[2]) 冬季运动〈例如滑雪〉

win·ter·time /ˋwɪntɚˌtaɪm; ˈwɪntətaɪm/ *n* [U] the winter season when the weather is cold 冬季; 冬天

win·try /ˋwɪntrɪ; ˈwɪntri/ also 又作 **win·ter·y** /ˋwɪntrɪ; ˈwɪntəri/ *adj* like winter, or typical of winter, especially because it is cold 冬天似的; 寒冷的: *a wintry night* 寒冬的晚上

3 **wipe**[1] /waɪp; waɪp/ *v*

1 ▶CLEAN/RUB 清理/擦◀ [T] **a)** to rub a surface with a cloth in order to remove dirt, liquid etc 擦, 拭, 揩: *I wiped the table with a damp cloth.* 我用一块湿布擦桌子。| **wipe your eyes** (=stop crying or remove tears from your face) 擦干眼泪, 停止哭泣 **b)** to clean something by rubbing it against a surface 擦干净〔某物〕: *She wiped her hands on the back of her jeans.* 她双手在牛仔裤后面抹了抹。

2 ▶REMOVE DIRT 去除污垢◀ [T always+adv/prep] to remove liquid, dirt, or marks by wiping 擦掉〔水、污垢、印迹等〕: *Wipe any dirt from round the cap before unscrewing it.* 把四周的尘土擦掉再把盖子拧开。| **wipe sth off/away from** *I'll just wipe all these crumbs off the table.* 我会把桌子上的面包屑擦掉。

3 ▶COMPUTER/TAPE 电脑/磁带◀ [T] to remove all the information that has been stored on a TAPE[1] (1a), VIDEO[1] (1,2), or computer DISK 抹掉〔磁带上的录音或录像、磁盘上的信息〕

4 ▶FORGET 忘却◀ [T] to try to forget an unhappy or upsetting experience 忘记; 抹掉〔不愉快或令人不安的经历〕: *I tried to wipe the whole experience from my mind.* 我设法忘记整个经历。

5 wipe the floor with *informal* to defeat someone completely in a competition or argument【非正式】〔在比赛、辩论中〕把〔某人〕打得大败

6 wipe the slate clean to agree to forget about mistakes or arguments that happened in the past 把以往的错误[争论]一笔勾销

7 wipe the smile/grin off sb's face *informal* to make someone less pleased or satisfied, especially because they are annoying you【非正式】使某人高兴不起来〔尤指因对方触怒了你〕: *Tell him how much it'll cost – that should wipe the smile off his face!* 告诉他要花多少钱, 那样他就笑不出来了!

8 wipe sth off the face of the earth/off the map to destroy something completely so that it no longer exists 彻底毁灭某物: *Another few years and this species could be wiped off the face of the earth.* 过不了几年, 这物种可能从地球上彻底消失。

9 ▶PLATES/CUPS ETC 盘子/杯子等◀ [I,T] *BrE* to dry plates, cups etc that have been washed【英】〔把洗过的碟子、杯子等〕擦干: *You wash, I'll wipe.* 你洗, 我来擦。

wipe sth ↔ **down** *phr v* [T] to completely clean a surface using a wet cloth〔用湿布把表面〕擦干净

wipe out *phr v* **1** [T **wipe** sb/sth ↔ **out**] to destroy, remove, or get rid of something completely 彻底毁灭〔某物〕, 勾销, 去除: *Half the population was wiped out by plague.* 鼠疫夺走了一半人的生命。**2** [T **wipe** sb ↔ **out**] *informal* to make you feel extremely tired【非正式】使疲惫不堪: *The heat had wiped us out.* 炎热使我们精疲力竭。—see also 另见 WIPED OUT **3** [I] *AmE* to fall or hit another object when driving a car, bicycle etc【美】〔开车、骑自行车时〕翻跌下来; 撞上某物

wipe sth ↔ **up** *phr v* [T] to remove liquid from a surface using a cloth〔用布〕揩干: *I hastily wiped up the milk I had spilled.* 我连忙把洒出来的牛奶擦干净。—see picture at 参见 CLEAN[2] 图

wipe[2] *n* [C] **1** a wiping movement with a cloth 擦, 拭, 揩: *An occasional wipe with a soft cloth will keep the surface shiny.* 时不时用软布擦一擦, 将使表面保持光亮。| **give sth a wipe** *Give the baby's nose a wipe, would you?* 擦擦这孩子的鼻子, 行吗? **2** a special piece of wet material that you use to clean something and then throw away〔用完即弃〕湿抹布: *antiseptic wipes* 抗菌抹布

wiped out /ˌ· ˈ·/ *adj* [not before noun 不用于名词前] *informal* extremely tired; EXHAUSTED (1)【非正式】疲惫不堪的

wip·er /ˋwaɪpɚ; ˈwaɪpə/ *n* [C] a WINDSCREEN WIPER or WINDSHIELD WIPER 挡风玻璃刮水器

wire[1] /waɪr; waɪə/ *n* **1** [U] thin metal in the form of a thread 金属丝[线]: *String wasn't strong enough, so we used wire.* 线不够结实, 所以我们用了金属丝。| *a wire fence* 金属丝网 **2** [C] a piece of metal like this, usually covered in plastic, used for taking electricity from one place to another 电线 **3 get your wires crossed** to become confused about what someone is saying because you think they are talking about something else 弄不清某人说的话; 误会 **4 right down to the wire** *informal* with very little time left before something must be finished or completed【非正式】〔完成某事的〕期限将近; 接近截止期 **5** [C] *AmE* a piece of electronic recording equipment, usually worn secretly on someone's clothes【美】窃听器〔一般秘密地戴在衣服上〕**6** [C] *AmE* a TELEGRAM【美】电报—see also 另见 LIVE WIRE, WIRY 3 3

wire[2] *v* [T] **1** also 又作 **wire up** to connect wires to something, especially in an electrical system 给〔电气系统的某物〕连上电线: *Check that the plug has been wired up properly.* 检查一下插头的电线是否已经接好。**2** to fasten two or more things together using wire 用金属丝把〔两件或两件以上的东西〕捆扎在一起: *The poles had all been wired together.* 已经用金属丝把杆子捆在一起了。**3** to send money electronically from one bank to another〔通过银行〕电汇〔钱〕**4** *AmE* to send a TELEGRAM to someone【美】〔给某人〕打电报 —see also 另见 WIRING

wire cut·ters /ˈ· ˌ‥/ *n* [plural] a special tool like very strong scissors, used for cutting wire 钢丝钳; 铁丝剪

wired /waɪrd; waɪəd/ *adj* **1** also 又作 **wired up** fitted with hidden electronic recording equipment for listening to people's conversations 装有窃听器的: *Careful what you say – the room could be wired.* 说话注意——房间里可能装有窃听器。**2** *AmE informal* very excited or nervous; TENSE[1] (1)【美, 非正式】极其兴奋的; 极其紧张的 **3** *AmE informal* very active and excited, because you have taken a drug【美, 非正式】〔因吸食毒品而致〕神经兴奋的

wire-haired /ˌ· ˈ·◂/ *adj* a wire-haired dog has fur that is stiff not soft〔狗〕粗毛的; 硬毛的: *a wire-haired terrier* 粗毛狐㹴

wire·less /ˋwaɪrlɪs; ˈwaɪələs/ *n* [C,U] *old-fashioned especially BrE* a radio【过时, 尤英】无线电收音机

wire net·ting /ˌ· ˈ· ·/ *n* [U] wires that have been woven together to form a net, used especially for fences 金属丝网；铁丝网〔尤用于篱笆〕

wire·tap /ˈwaɪrˌtæp; ˈwaɪətæp/ *v* [T] to secretly listen to other people's telephone conversations, by fixing something to the wires of their phone〔在某人的电话线路上〕搭线窃听 —**wiretap** *n* [C] —**wiretapping** *n* [U]

wire wool /ˌ· ˈ·/ *n* [U] a mass of very thin pieces of wire, used for cleaning pans〔洗锅盘用的〕钢丝绒

wir·ing /ˈwaɪrɪŋ; ˈwaɪərɪŋ/ *n* [singular] **1** the network of wires that form the electrical system in a building〔建筑物中〕供电系统的线路: *faulty wiring* 出毛病的线路 | *The wiring needs to be replaced.* 供电线路需要更换。**2** a length of wire that is used for making a network for electricity〔电气线路的〕配线；布线: *copper wiring* 铜线

Wir·ral, the /ˈwɪrəl; ˈwɪrəl/ an area between the River Dee and the River Mersey, near Liverpool in northwest England. It is a mainly MIDDLE CLASS area, and many of the people who live there work in Liverpool. 威勒尔区〔位于迪河与默西河之间一地区，近英格兰西北部的利物浦。居民多为中产阶级人士，其中许多人在利物浦上班〕

wir·y /ˈwaɪrɪ; ˈwaɪəri/ *adj* **1** someone who is wiry is thin but has strong muscles〔人〕瘦而结实的 **2** hair that is wiry is stiff and curly〔毛发〕硬而卷曲的 —**wiriness** *n* [U]

Wis·con·sin /wɪˈskɑnsɪn; wɪˈskɒnsɪ̩n/ abbreviation 缩写为 **WI** a state in the north central US, to the west of Lake Michigan. It is an important area for producing milk, cheese, and butter. 威斯康星州〔美国中北部一州，东濒密歇根湖，是重要的牛奶、乳酪和黄油产区〕

Wis·den /ˈwɪzdn̩; ˈwɪzdən/ also 又作 **Wisden's Cricketers' Almanack** *trademark* a book about CRICKET which is produced every year in the UK and which contains the results of all the important games, the SCOREs (=points won) of all the players etc【商标】《怀斯登板球年鉴》〔板球运动参考书。每年在英国出版一辑，记录当年所有重大赛事的结果及每位参赛球员的得分情况〕

wis·dom /ˈwɪzdəm; ˈwɪzdəm/ *n* [U] **1** good sense and judgment, based especially on your experience of life〔尤指基于生活阅历的〕智慧；明断: *a man of great wisdom* 才智卓越的人 | **question the wisdom of** *formal* (=say that you think something is not sensible)【正式】怀疑…是否明智 *I would question the wisdom of lending him such a large sum of money.* 借给他这么一大笔钱，我怀疑这是否明智。**2** knowledge gained over a long period of time through learning or experience 知识，学问: *the collected wisdom of many centuries* 许多世纪积累的知识 **3 received/conventional wisdom** a belief that is generally thought to be true 普遍的看法，传统的信念: *The received wisdom is that boys mature more slowly than girls.* 人们普遍认为男孩子比女孩子晚熟。**4 in his/her (infinite) wisdom** used to say jokingly that you do not understand why someone has decided to do something 以他/她(无限的)智慧〔含戏谑意味，表示不明白某人为何决定做某事〕: *The boss, in her infinite wisdom, has decided to reorganize the whole office yet again.* 老板无比英明，又决定重新安排整个办公室。

wisdom tooth /ˈ· · ·/ *n* [C] one of the four large teeth at the back of your mouth that do not grow until you are an adult 智齿，智牙 —see picture at 参见 TEETH 图

wise¹ /waɪz; waɪz/ *adj*

1 ▶DECISION/IDEA ETC 决定/意见等◀ wise decisions and judgements are based on good sense and experience; sensible〔决定和判断〕明智的；有才智的；有判断力的: *I think that would be a wise precaution.* 我觉得那会是一种明智的预防措施。| **be wise to do sth** *I think you were wise to leave when you did.* 我认为你当时就走很明智。

2 ▶PERSON 人◀ someone who is wise makes good decisions, gives good advice etc, especially because they have a lot of experience of life〔人因阅历丰富而〕英明的；有智慧的: *a wise old man* 睿智的老人 | **older and wiser** (=having learned from the experiences of life) 智慧随年龄增长而增加 | **wise in the ways of** *formal* (=knowing a lot about something)【正式】〔对某方面〕知识丰富的

3 get wise to/be wise to *informal* to realize that someone is being dishonest【非正式】知道，了解〔某人不诚实〕: *I've got wise to his little tricks now.* 现在我已经看透他的小把戏了。—see also 另见 **wise up** (WISE²)

4 be none the wiser *informal* to not understand something, even after it has been explained【非正式】〔解释后〕还是不明白，仍然不懂: *Charlie explained how the system works, but I'm still none the wiser.* 查利解释了系统是如何运作的，可是我还是不明白。

5 no-one will be any the wiser *spoken* used to say that no-one will find out about something bad someone has done【口】没有人会知道〔某人做了坏事〕: *Just put it back on the shelf, and no-one will be any the wiser.* 就把它放回架子上，没人会知道。

6 wise guy *informal especially AmE* an annoying person who thinks they know more than they really do【非正式，尤美】自作聪明的人: *OK, wise guy, shut up and listen for a minute!* 好了，万事通，你先别说，留神听一会儿！

7 act wise *AmE spoken* to speak or behave in a rude way【美口】说话[行为]粗鲁

8 be wise after the event to know how a mistake could have been avoided, after it has been made 事后聪明 —see also 另见 WISDOM, **sadder but wiser** (SAD (6)) —**wisely** *adv*: *Invest the money wisely.* 明智地投资这笔钱。| *He nodded wisely.* 他点点头，一副睿智的样子。

wise² *v*

wise up *phr v informal*【非正式】**1** [I] to realize the unpleasant truth about a situation 知道〔不愉快的真相〕，了解: *Wise up, Vic – he's cheating you!* 明白吗，维克，他是在骗你！**2** [T **wise sb up (to)**] *especially AmE* to make someone realize the unpleasant truth about a situation【尤美】使〔某人〕知道〔不愉快的真相〕

wise³ *n* **1 price-wise/time-wise etc** *especially spoken* concerning or connected with prices etc【尤口】(有关)价格/时间等: *Time-wise we're not doing too badly.* 时间方面我们做得还可以。**2 crosswise/lengthwise etc** in a direction across something, along the length of something etc 横向地/纵向地等: *Cut the carrots lengthwise.* 将胡萝卜纵向切开。**3** [singular] *old use* a way or manner【旧】方式；方法: *They are in no wise to blame.* 他们根本不该受到责备。—see also 另见 STREETWISE

wise·a·cre /ˈwaɪzˌekɚ; ˈwaɪzeɪkə/ *n* [C] *informal especially AmE* an annoying person who thinks they know more than they really do【非正式，尤美】自以为是的人，自作聪明的人

wise·crack /ˈwaɪzˌkræk; ˈwaɪzkræk/ *n* [C] a clever funny remark or reply 俏皮话；妙语 —**wisecrack** *v* [I]

wish¹ /wɪʃ; wɪʃ/ *v*

1 ▶WANT STH IMPOSSIBLE 希望不可能的事◀ [T] to want something to be true although you know it is either impossible or unlikely 希望〔不可能或可能性很小的事〕: **wish (that)** *I wish I didn't have to go to work today.* 但愿我今天不用上班。| **wish to goodness** *spoken* (=wish very much)【口】极其希望 *I wish to goodness they'd hurry up!* 我真希望他们能快点！

2 ▶WANT TO DO STH 想做某事◀ [I,T] *formal* to want to do something【正式】想做(某事): **wish to do sth** *I wish to make a complaint.* 我想投诉。| **if you wish** *You may leave now, if you wish.* 你想离开现在就可以离开。| **(just) as you wish** (=used to tell someone you will do what they want) 正如你愿意的〔告诉某人会按其意思做事〕 *"I'd like it ready by six." "Just as you wish, sir."* "我希望6点钟准备就绪。""先生，听您的。"

3 ▶HAPPINESS/LUCK ETC 幸福/幸运等◀ [T] to say that you hope someone will have good luck, a happy life etc 祝，祝愿〔某人好运、幸福等〕: **wish sb sth** *We wish you a Merry Christmas and a Happy New Year!* 我们祝你圣诞快乐、新年幸福！| *Wish me luck!* 祝我走运吧！| **wish sb well** (=hope that good things happen to someone) 祝福某人 *They wished me well in my new job.* 他们祝我新的工作一切顺利。

4 I don't wish to interfere/be nosy etc *spoken* used to show you are sorry if what you are going to say upsets or annoys someone【口】我无意干涉/多管闲事等〔如果将要说的话令某人不安或烦恼，用于道歉〕: *I don't wish to seem ungrateful, but it's not quite what I expected.* 我不想表现得不领情，可是那的确不是我期望的样子。

5 I (only) wish I knew *spoken* used to emphasize that you do not know something, and you wish you did know【口】我知道就好了〔用于强调不知道某事〕: *"Where on earth have they gone?" "I wish I knew!"* "他们到底去哪儿啦？""我知道就好了！"

6 I/you wish! *spoken* used to say that something is not true, but you wish it was【口】但愿如此！〔表示某事不是事实，但你希望是真的〕: *"Oh no, you're quite thin really." "I wish!"* "噢，不，你真的很瘦了。""真是瘦就好了！"

7 wouldn't wish sth on/upon sb *spoken* used to say that something is very unpleasant【口】不想某事发生在某人身上〔表示此事讨厌、可怕〕: *It's so painful, you wouldn't wish it on your worst enemy, honestly!* 太痛苦了，坦白说，就是你的死敌你也不愿他这样。

wish for sth *phr v* [T] **1 the best/nicest etc that you would wish for** used to emphasize that something is as good, nice etc as it could possibly be 最理想的: *It was as fine an afternoon as you could wish for.* 这个下午难得的晴朗。| *He had everything*

a child could possibly wish for. 他拥有一个孩子可能想得到的一切。**2** [I] to ask silently for something you want and hope that it will happen 默默期盼: *Her only hope now was to wish for a miracle.* 现在她的唯一希望是默默盼望有奇迹出现。

wish sth ↔ **away** *phr v* [T] to want something unpleasant to disappear, without doing anything about it 希望〔不愉快的事〕自行消失: *You can't just wish your problems away, you know!* 你知道，你不能一相情愿，希望问题自动解决！

USAGE NOTE 用法说明: WISH

WORD CHOICE 词语辨析: **wish, want**

In sentences where both can be used, **wish** sounds much more formal than **want**. 在两者都可以用的句子中，wish 比 want 正式得多。In a conversation you might say 在会话中可说: *I want to write to him but I don't know his address.* 我想给他写信，可是不知道他的地址。| *They want us to come to dinner.* 他们想要我们去吃晚饭。But speaking officially you might say 但正式场合则说: *You may leave if you wish.* 你想走就请便吧。You are more likely to see **wish** on official forms and notices. 在正式表格及通告中，会更多地用 wish。

GRAMMAR 语法

An infinitive after **wish, want,** or **hope** must always have *to* with it. wish, want 及 hope 后的不定式必须带 to: *I want/hope to see you soon.* (NOT 不用 *...want see you...*)我想/希望不久就见到你。| *I wish to speak* (NOT 不用 *wish speak*). 我想要发言。

Wish and **hope**, unlike **want**, are not used with a direct object. wish 和 hope 与 want 不同，不能与直接宾语连用: *Everybody wants a happy life* (NOT 不用 *wishes* or 或 *hopes*, but you could say 但可以说: *Everybody wishes to have a happy life/hopes for a happy life.* 每个人都想要/渴望过幸福的生活。)

Wish and **hope** (but NOT **want**) are both used with *that* clauses, but the verbs in them usually have to be in different tenses. wish 和 hope〔而不是 want〕均与 that 引导的从句连用，然而从句中的动词时态通常却不同: *I hope (that) you will be happy* (NOT 不用 *wish* or 或 *want*). 我希望你会幸福。| *I wish (that) you could be happy.* 我祝愿你幸福。(For the difference in meaning see 意思的差异见 **hope** WORD CHOICE) These are the main tenses used after **wish** 以下是用于 wish 后面的主要时态:

If you wish a particular situation existed at this moment, you use the past tense 如果希望此时某特定情况存在，使用过去时: *I wish I knew/had my own house.* 但愿我了解/拥有自己的房子。| *He wished it were Tuesday already.* 他但愿今天已经是星期二。In informal British English it is common to use *was* instead of *were* in sentences like the last, but in American English *was* would be considered incorrect here. 在非正式英国英语中，上句中的 were 通常可用 was 代替，但是在美国英语中，此处如果用 was，则被认为是不正确的。

If you wish a situation would exist in the future, you use *could* 如果希望某情景在未来出现，那就用could: *I wish I could have my own house* (NOT 不用 *I wish I'll have my own house* or 或 *I wish I would...* or 或 *I wish if I could...*). 我希望我能拥有自己的房子。

If you wish a situation had existed or something had happened in the past, you use the past perfect 如果希望某情况已经存在，或某事在过去已经发生，那就用过去完成时: *I wish I had been alive in the twenties.* 我希望生活在 20 世纪 20 年代。| *I wish I'd had a chance to talk to you before you left.* 我想在你离开前能有机会和你谈谈（可惜没有）。

If you wish something would happen at this moment or at some time in the future, you use **would** or **could** 如果希望某事在此时或将来某时发生，则用 would 或could: *I wish you could/would come* (*could*=but something is stopping you 但目前有事阻止你来; *would*=but you don't want to 会来，但你不想来). 我希望你能/会来。| *He wished the problem could be solved* (NOT 不用 *...problem be solved*). 他希望问题会得到解决。| *I wish you wouldn't go out every night.* 我希望你不要每天晚上都出去。

[S3] **wish²** *n* [C]

1 ▶DESIRE 愿望◀ a feeling of wanting to do something, or wanting something to happen 希望; 愿望: *It's important to respect the wishes of the patient.* 尊重病人的意愿极为重要。| **a wish to do sth** *She had expressed a wish to see the children.* 她表达了要见孩子们的愿望。

2 ▶THING YOU WANT 希望发生的事/想要的东西◀ something that you want to have or to happen 想要的东西; 希望发生的事: *She wanted a new bike for Christmas, and she got her wish.* 她想在圣诞节得到一辆新自行车，她如愿以偿了。| *the wishes of the majority* 大多数人的意愿 | **dearest/greatest wish** (=what you want most of all) 最想要的/最大的愿望 *His dearest wish was to become a father.* 他最大的愿望是当爸爸。| **sb's wish is granted/fulfilled** (=they get what they want) 某人如愿以偿 | **sb's wish comes true** (=they get what they want, especially in a surprising and unexpected way) 某人的愿望成真〔尤指通过令人吃惊或意想不到的途径〕| **last wish/dying wish** (=something that you say you want just before you die) 临终遗愿

3 against sb's wishes if you do something against someone's wishes, you do it even though you know they do not want you to〔做事〕违反某人的意愿: *She had left school against her mother's wishes.* 她违反母亲的愿望，辍学了。| **go against sb's wishes** (=do something against their wishes) 与某人的意愿相违

4 have no wish to do sth *formal* used to emphasize that you do not want or intend to do something【正式】无意做某事〔用于强调〕: *I have no wish to speak to her ever again.* 我再也不愿意跟她说话了。

5 best wishes a) used in cards to say that you hope someone will be happy 最好的祝愿〔贺卡中的祝词〕: *best wishes for your married life* 致以新婚最好的祝愿 **b)** used as a greeting at the end of a letter 祝好〔用于信件末尾的祝词〕

6 ▶SILENT REQUEST 默祷◀ a silent request for something to happen as if by magic 默祷，祈求; 许愿: **make a wish** *I closed my eyes and made a wish.* 我闭上眼睛许了个愿。

7 your wish is my command *especially humorous* used to say that you will do whatever someone asks you to do【尤幽默】悉听尊命

CULTURAL NOTE 文化注释

Making a wish 许愿

There are several customs in the US and the UK that involve making wishes, although people do not really believe that they can affect the future. In the US, people make a wish when they first see a star at night, and in the UK people say that you should make a wish when you see a SHOOTING STAR. People also make a wish after blowing out the CANDLE*s* on their BIRTHDAY cake. Some public places have FOUNTAIN*s* or WISHING WELL*s* and people make a wish as they throw a coin into the water. In the US, people think of a wish and then try to blow all the seeds off of a DANDELION (=a wild plant that has yellow flowers and then white balls of seeds), and say that their wish will come true if all the seeds come off in one blow. Another tradition for making a wish is to pull on a WISHBONE (=the small V-shaped bone in a cooked chicken). Two people each hold one of the ends of the bone and pull on it, and the person who pulls off the larger piece of bone makes a wish. Wishes are very important in stories, especially FAIRY TALE*s* such as 'Aladdin', which is about a boy who rubs a magic lamp, and a GENIE (=a magical spirit) comes out and allows him to make three wishes. 在英美有不少许愿的习俗，尽管人们并不是真的相信愿望能够影响未来。美国人看到夜晚的第一颗星星时许愿，而英国人说应该在看到流星的时候许愿。人们在吹灭生日蛋糕上的蜡烛后也会许愿。很多公共场所设有喷泉和许愿井，人们将一枚硬币投入水中并许下愿望。在美国，人们想好一个愿望之后尽力吹散蒲公英的种子，他们说如果一口气把所有的种子都吹掉了那么自己的愿望就能成真。另一个传统的许愿方式是拽许愿骨（一般是鸡的叉骨），两个人各执一端，拽下大块的人许下愿望。在故事中，许愿发挥的作用很大，特别是在童话中更是如此，例如《阿拉丁》就讲述了一个少年擦拭神灯，然后灯神就会出现并许诺实现他的三个愿望。

wish·bone /ˈwɪʃˌbon; ˈwɪʃbəʊn/ *n* [C] the breast bone from a cooked chicken etc, which two people pull apart to decide who will make a wish 叉骨，如愿骨〔煮熟的鸡等的胸骨，由两人同时拉扯，以决定由谁许愿〕

CULTURAL NOTE 文化注释

After the bird has been cooked, the ends of the wishbone are pulled apart by two people, and the one who gets the longer piece can make a wish. 禽类被烹煮后，两个人各执许愿骨的一端拽开，得到较长一块的人可以许下一个愿望。

wish·ful think·ing /ˌ‥ˈ‥/ *n* [U] the false belief that something will happen just because you want it to 如意算盘；痴心妄想

wish·ing well /ˈ‥ ˌ/ *n* [C] a WELL[4] (1) or pool of water that people throw coins into while making a wish〔投币许愿的〕许愿井

wish list /ˈ· ˌ/ *n* [C] *informal, especially AmE* all the things that you want in a particular situation【非正式，尤美】〔在某情况中的〕愿望清单

wish·y-wash·y /ˈwɪʃɪ ˌwɑʃɪ; ˈwɪʃi ˌwɒʃi/ *adj informal*【非正式】**1** a wishy-washy person does not have firm or clear ideas and seems unable to decide what they want〔人〕优柔寡断的；没有明确目标的：*a bunch of wishy-washy liberals* 一群没有清晰目标的自由主义者 **2** colours that are wishy-washy are pale, not strong or dark〔色彩〕淡的，弱的，浅的

wisp /wɪsp; wɪsp/ *n* [C] **1 wisp of hair/hay/grass etc** a thin piece of hair etc that is separate from the rest 一缕头发／一把干草／一束青草等：*A wisp of hair had escaped from under her hat.* 在她的帽子下面露出一缕头发。—see picture on page A7 参见A7页图 **2 wisp of smoke/cloud etc** a small thin line of smoke etc that rises upwards 一缕轻烟／一丝浮云等 —see also 另见 WILL O' THE WISP —**wispy** *adj*

wis·te·ri·a /wɪsˈtɪrɪə; wɪˈstɪəriə/ *n* [C,U] a climbing plant with purple or white flowers 紫藤〔一种攀缘植物，开紫色或白色花〕

wist·ful /ˈwɪstfəl; ˈwɪstfəl/ *adj* feeling rather sad and thoughtful, especially because of something that you would like but can no longer have〔尤指因心爱之物不复存在而〕惆怅的；思念的；依依不舍的：*wistful memories of her lost youth* 对她逝去青春的惆怅回忆 —**wistfully** *adv* —**wistfulness** *n* [U]

wit /wɪt; wɪt/ *n*

1 ▶AMUSING 娱人的◀ [U] the ability to say things that are clever and amusing〔说话〕机智风趣：*a woman of great wit and charm* 说话风趣、风韵动人的女人 | **quick/dry/sharp wit** *His sharp wit had them all smiling.* 他的机智诙谐使所有人笑得合不拢嘴。

2 ▶AMUSING PERSON 说话风趣的人◀ [C] someone who is able to say clever and funny things 说话风趣诙谐的人：*Oscar Wilde was a famous wit.* 奥斯卡·王尔德是著名的说话风趣的人。

3 wits [plural] your ability to think quickly and make the right decisions 机智：*It was a tricky situation – I had to use all my wits to extricate myself.* 形势微妙，我得费尽心机才能脱身。| **keep/have your wits about you** (=be ready to think quickly and do what is necessary in a difficult situation)〔在困难的情况下〕保持头脑清醒，随机应变

4 have the wit to do sth to be clever enough to know the right thing to do 足够明智，作出正确决定做某事

5 frighten/scare sb out of their wits *informal* to frighten someone very much【非正式】吓坏某人

6 at your wits' end very worried, because you have tried everything possible to solve a problem 智穷计尽，束手无策

7 not beyond the wit of *often humorous* not too difficult for someone to do【常幽默】有做某事的才智：*It's surely not beyond the wit of man to come up with a solution.* 人类要想出解决方法肯定没有困难。

8 to wit *old use* that is to say; NAMELY【旧】即，就是 —see also 另见 **a battle of wits** (BATTLE[1] (5)), HALF-WIT, **live by your wits** (LIVE[1] (9)), OUTWIT, QUICK-WITTED, WITTY —**witless** *adj*

witch 女巫，巫婆

witch /wɪtʃ; wɪtʃ/ *n* [C] **1** a woman who is supposed to have magic powers, especially to do bad things〔尤指做坏事的〕女巫，巫婆 **2** *informal* an insulting word for an old or unpleasant woman【非正式】丑老太婆〔恶语〕—see also 另见 BEWITCH

CULTURAL NOTE 文化注释

The STEREOTYPE of a witch is a very ugly old woman wearing a long black dress and a tall, black pointed hat. She usually has a black cat and rides through the air on a BROOMSTICK. Between the 14th and the 17th centuries people were very frightened of witches, and many women were killed because they were thought to be witches. People remember this happening especially in the town of Salem, in the US. There were many strange tests to see if someone was a witch, including things such as tying a heavy stone to someone and throwing them in a river or pond. If they FLOAT*ed*, they were thought to be a witch. 典型的巫婆是一个相貌丑陋的老女人，穿着长长的黑色衣服，戴着一顶黑色的高尖顶帽。她通常有一只黑猫陪伴，并骑在扫帚把上在空中飞舞。14至17世纪的人们很惧怕女巫，很多妇女被当成女巫处死。人们尤其对发生在美国塞勒姆的处决女巫的事记忆犹新。有很多奇怪的方法来甄别某人是否为女巫，例如，在人身上绑上一块重重的石头，然后将其投入河流或池塘。如果她们仍能漂浮，就可断定是女巫。

witch·craft /ˈwɪtʃˌkræft; ˈwɪtʃkrɑːft/ *n* [U] the use of magic to make things happen 巫术；魔法

witch-doc·tor /ˈ·ˌ‥/ *n* [C] a man who is believed to have magic powers and the ability to cure people of diseases, especially in some parts of Africa〔尤指非洲某些地区的〕巫医

witch-ha·zel /ˈ·ˌ‥/ *n* [C,U] a substance used for treating small wounds on the skin, or the tree that produces it〔用于治疗伤口的〕金缕梅酊剂；金缕梅（树）

witch-hunt /ˈ· ˌ/ *n* [C] a deliberate attempt, often based on false information, to find and punish people in a society or organization whose opinions are regarded as wrong or dangerous 迫害：*McCarthy's Communist witch-hunts* 麦卡锡对共产党人的政治迫害

witch·ing hour /ˈ‥ ˌ/ *n* [singular] *literary* the time, especially in the middle of the night, when strange or magic things are believed to happen【文】〔尤指夜半〕怪事发生的时刻

with /wɪð; wɪð/ *prep* **1** near someone or something, or in someone's presence 在〔某人或某物〕附近；与〔某人〕在一起：*I saw Bob in town with his girlfriend.* 我在城里看见鲍勃与他的女朋友在一起。| *Mix the powder with boiling water.* 用开水把粉末调和。**2** having, possessing, or showing a particular thing, quality or feeling 具有；带有；显出〔某物、某种特性或感情〕：*a book with a green cover* 一本有绿色封面的书 | *Jack beamed with pleasure when he heard the news.* 杰克在听到这消息后笑逐颜开。| **complete with** *The mixer comes complete with instructions and a guarantee.* 搅拌机带有使用说明书和保证书。**3** including 包括…在内：*With a tip, the meal cost $30.* 包括小费在内，这顿饭花了30美元。**4** by means of something or using it 用；以；借：*Eat your melon with a knife and fork.* 用刀、叉吃甜瓜。| *What will you buy with the money?* 你会用这笔钱买什么？**5** used to show the idea of filling, covering, or containing something〔表示填充、覆盖、含有的概念〕：*Her boots were covered with mud.* 她的靴子上满是污泥。| *Fill the bowl with sugar.* 把这个碗装满糖。**6** concerning, or in the case of 关于，对于，至于：*Be careful with that glass.* 小心那只玻璃杯。| *Britain's trade with Japan* 英国与日本之间的贸易 | *He's in love with you.* 他爱上了你。**7** supporting or liking someone or something 支持，赞同〔某人或某物〕：*Some opposition MPs voted with the Government.* 一些反对党的议员投票支持政府。| *You're either with me or against me.* 你要么支持我，要么反对我。**8** against or opposing someone 反对；与〔某人〕对立：*Stop fighting with your brother!* 不要和弟弟打架！| *We're competing with foreign businesses.* 我们在和外国公司竞争。**9** in the same direction as someone or something 与〔某人、某物〕方向一致：*We sailed with the wind.* 我们顺风航行。**10** at the same time or rate as something else 与〔某物〕同时；随着：*This wine improves with age.* 这种酒越陈越醇。**11** used when comparing two things or considering the relationship between them 与…相比；考虑到〔两物的关系〕：*Compared with other children of the same age, Robert's very tall.* 和同年龄的其他孩子相比，罗伯特长得很高。**12** used in some expressions to show that one person or thing separates from another〔用于表示〕分离：*Joan doesn't want to part with the money.* 琼不想花掉这笔钱。| *a complete break with tradition* 与传统彻底决裂 **13** in spite of 尽管；虽然：*With all his faults, I still like him.* 他尽管有许多缺点，仍然讨我喜欢。**14** because of or considering the fact of 因为；考虑到：*They were trembling with fear.* 他们吓得直发抖。| *With John away there's more room in the house.* 因为约翰不在，家里宽敞了一些。**15** used to express a strong wish or command〔用于表达强烈的愿望和命令〕：*Down with school!* 打倒学校！| *Off to bed with you!* 上床睡觉去！**16 with it** *informal*【非正式】**a)** dressing in fashionable clothes and knowing about new ideas 衣着时髦；熟悉新思想：*I can't get over how with it your mother is.* 你妈妈多么时髦，我感到惊讶极了！**b)** lively and able to understand things 生气勃勃的，机灵的：*I'm sorry I'm not feeling very with it today.* 对不起，我今天有点迟钝。—see also 另见 WITH-IT **17 with you**

informal【非正式】**a)** understanding someone's explanation about something 听懂某人的话: *I'm sorry, I'm not really with you; could you repeat what you just said.* 对不起，我没有听懂；请你重复一遍刚才所说的话。**b)** supporting someone by agreeing with what they say or do 支持，同意〔对人所说、所为〕: *I'm with Harry all the way on this one.* 在这一方面我一直完全支持哈里。**18 with that** also 又作 **at that** used to say that something happens immediately after something else 随即；接着: *He gave a little wave and with that he was gone.* 他轻轻地挥了一下手，随即就走了。

with·al /wɪð`ɔl; wɪð'ɔːl/ *adv old use* besides; together with this【旧】此外；而且；又

W2 **with·draw** /wɪð`drɔ; wɪð'drɔː/ *v past tense* **withdrew** /-`dru; -'druː/ *past participle* **withdrawn** /-`drɔn; -'drɔːn/

1 ▶MONEY 金钱◀ [T] to take money out of a bank account 提取〔银行存款〕: **withdraw sth from** *Liz withdrew $100 from her account.* 莉兹从她的账户上提取了100美元。

2 ▶TAKE AWAY 取走，拿走◀ [T] to remove something or take it away or take it back, often because of an official decision〔常因正式决定而〕撤回，撤销，收回: *a government decision to withdraw funding* 政府撤销的提供资金的决定 | *One of the minority parties had withdrawn its support for Chancellor Kohl.* 一个少数党已经不再支持科尔总理了。| **withdraw sth from** *She withdrew a document from her briefcase.* 她从公文包中取出一份文件。| **withdraw sth from sale/from the market** (=stop selling it) 从销售/市场中收回某物；停止销售 *The drug has been withdrawn from the market for further tests.* 该药已从市场上收回，以便做进一步的化验。

3 withdraw a remark/accusation to say that a remark that you made earlier was completely untrue; RETRACT 撤回评论/撤销指控: *The newspaper has agreed to withdraw its allegations.* 这家报社已同意撤回其指控。

4 ▶NOT TAKE PART 不参加◀ **a)** [I] to no longer take part in or belong to an organization 退出〔组织〕: **[+from]** *calls for Britain to withdraw from the European Union* 要求英国退出欧洲联盟的呼声 **b)** [I,T] to no longer take part in an activity, race etc, or to prevent someone from doing this (使)不参加〔活动、比赛等〕: **[+from]** *Injury forced Clare to withdraw from the event.* 克莱尔因伤被迫退出比赛。| **withdraw sth/sb from** *Ted withdrew his horse from the race.* 特德让他的马退出了这次比赛。

5 ▶LEAVE 离开◀ **a)** [I] to leave a place, especially in order to be alone or go somewhere quiet 离开〔尤指想独处或悄悄地去某处〕: *We withdrew to the garden for a private talk.* 我们退到花园里进行密谈。**b)** [I,T] if an army withdraws or is withdrawn, it leaves a place, especially in order to avoid defeat〔尤指军队避免战败而〕撤退

6 ▶STOP COMMUNICATING 停止交流◀ [I] to become quieter, less friendly, and more concerned about your own thoughts 变得冷漠；离群索居: **[+into/from]** *The little girl seemed to withdraw into a private world.* 小女孩看来要把自己封闭起来。

W3 **with·draw·al** /wɪð`drɔəl; wɪð'drɔːəl/ *n*

1 ▶MONEY 金钱◀ [C,U] the act of taking money from a bank account, or the amount you take out〔从银行账户中〕提款；提款额

2 ▶ARMY 军队◀ [C,U] the act of moving an army, weapons etc away from the area where they were fighting 撤军；撤退；撤回: **[+of/from]** *the withdrawal of all UN forces from the region* 所有联合国部队从该地区撤退

3 ▶REMOVAL/ENDING 移走/终结◀ [U] the removal or stopping of something such as support, an offer, or a service〔对支持、建议、服务等的〕取消，收回: **[+of]** *withdrawal of government aid* 取消政府的资助

4 ▶STOP TAKING PART 停止参与◀ [U] the act of no longer taking part in an activity or being a member of an organization 退出〔活动或组织〕: **[+from]** *Germany's withdrawal from the talks* 德国退出谈判

5 ▶DRUGS 毒品◀ [U] the period after you have given up a drug that you were dependent on, and the mental and physical effects that this process involves 脱瘾(过程)，戒毒: **withdrawal symptoms** (=the painful or unpleasant effects caused by withdrawal) 脱瘾症状〔因脱瘾而引起的痛苦或不适〕

6 ▶STATEMENT 陈述◀ [U] the act of saying that something you previously said was in fact untrue 取消，撤销: **[+of]** *the withdrawal of all allegations* 撤销的所有指控

with·drawn /wɪð`drɔn; wɪð'drɔːn/ *adj* very shy and quiet, and concerned only about your own thoughts 孤僻的；内向的；沉默寡言的

with·er /`wɪðɚ; 'wɪðə/ *v* also 又作 **wither away** [I,T] if plants wither they become drier and smaller and start to die〔植物〕枯萎，干枯

with·ered /`wɪðɚd; 'wɪðəd/ *adj* **1** a withered plant has become drier and smaller and is dead or dying〔植物〕枯萎的，干枯的 **2** a withered person looks thin and weak and old〔人〕枯槁的，憔悴的 **3** a withered arm or leg has not developed properly and is thin and weak〔胳膊或腿〕发育不全的；萎缩的

with·er·ing /`wɪðərɪŋ; 'wɪðərɪŋ/ *adj* **a withering look/remark etc** a look, remark etc that makes someone feel stupid, embarrassed, or lose confidence 咄咄逼人的眼色/尖刻的言语等: *She gave him a withering glance.* 她咄咄逼人地瞪了他一眼。—**witheringly** *adv*

with·ers /`wɪðɚz; 'wɪðəz/ *n* [plural] the highest part of a horse's back, above its shoulders 鬐甲〔马肩甲骨间隆起的部分〕—see picture at 参见 HORSE[1] 图

with·hold /wɪð`hold; wɪð'həʊld/ *v past tense and past participle* **withheld** /-`hɛld; -'held/ [T] **1** to refuse to let someone have something, especially until something else is done 拒绝给予〔尤指直至某事完成〕，扣留: *I withheld payment until they had completed the work.* 他们工作完成以后我才付钱。**2 withhold facts/evidence/information** to refuse to give information 隐瞒事实/证据/信息: *Ian was accused of withholding vital information from the police.* 伊恩被控向警方隐瞒关键情报。

with·hold·ing tax /·`·· ,·/ *n* [C,U] *AmE* money that is taken out of your wages as tax【美】〔工资中〕扣除的所得税

with·in /wɪð`ɪn; wɪð'ɪn/ *adv, prep* **1 a)** before a certain period of time has passed 在〔某时间过去〕前: *Ray left suddenly promising to be back within the hour.* 雷突然离开，他答应一小时内回来。**b)** during a certain period of time 在〔某段时间〕之内: *Her car has been broken into three times within a month.* 在一个月内，她的汽车被撬三次。| **within the space of ...** *Within the space of a year three of the town's biggest factories have closed down.* 在一年内，城里最大的厂家已有三家倒闭了。**2** inside a certain area and not beyond it 在…范围以内: *Children must remain within the school grounds during the lunch break.* 午饭时间孩子必须留在校园里。| **within 20 metres/50 kilometres/10 miles of etc** (=less than twenty metres, fifty kilometres etc from a particular place)〔离某地〕不出20米/50公里/10英里等 *We are now within two kilometres of the centre of Istanbul.* 我们现在离伊斯坦布尔市中心不到两公里。| **apply/enquire within** (=used on notices and advertisements especially when someone is trying to sell something) 入内面洽/查询〔通告和广告用语，尤指在出售物品时〕*Baby rabbits for sale. Enquire within.* 有小兔子出售，请入内洽询。**3** inside a society, organization, or group of people 在〔社会、组织或一群人〕里面: *There have been a lot of changes within the department since I joined.* 自我加入后，部门内发生了很多变化。| **from within** *an attempt to reform the system from within* 从内部改革体制的尝试 **4** according to particular limits or rules 在〔限制、规则〕之内: *We have to operate within a very tight budget.* 我们必须在极其严格的预算之内经营。| *This clause is no longer valid within the terms of the new settlement.* 在新协议的条款下，这条款不再有效。**5 within sight/earshot etc** if something is within sight, earshot etc you can see or hear it 在视线/听力等范围内 **6 within reach a)** near, so that people can get there without difficulty 在…附近，距离…不远: *We live within easy reach of the shops.* 我们住在离商店不远的地方。**b)** near enough to be picked up or touched when you stretch out your hand 伸手可及: *The key was hanging from a hook on the wall, just within my reach.* 钥匙挂在墙上的钩子上，我伸手就能够到。**7 a play within a play/a university within a university etc** a small place, thing etc which exists inside a bigger place or thing of the same kind 戏中戏/大学中大学等

with-it /`· ·/ *adj old-fashioned* fashionable and modern in the way that you dress, think etc【过时】〔衣着、思想等〕时髦的，时兴的 —see also 另见 **with it** (WITH)

with·out /wɪð`aut; wɪð'aʊt/ *adv, prep* **1** lacking something, especially something that is basic or necessary 缺乏；没有〔尤指基本或必要之物〕: *We had to survive without light or heating for a whole month.* 整个月没有照明、没有暖气，我们也得活下去。| **can't do without** (=unable to live or work without something) 没有〔某物〕无法生活[工作] *We can't do without hot water for too long.* 我们不能太长时间没有热水。**2** not doing or having something, or not showing a particular feeling, especially when it is considered normal or polite 不，不曾: *He had gone out without his parents' permission.* 他没经父母的同意便出去了。| **without doing** *How dare you do such a thing without consulting me?* 你没有和我商量，竟敢做这样的事？| **without so much as ...** (=used to say that someone does not do something that they should do) 连…也不；甚至于不〔用于表示某人没有做应做的事〕*Without so much as a word of thanks Bowen*

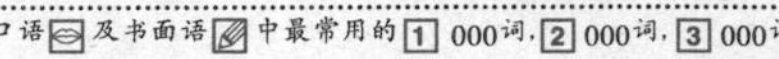

turned and went back into the office. 连一个谢字也不说，鲍恩转身回到了办公室。**3** not being with someone, or not having them to help you, especially someone you like or need 无〔某人，尤指喜欢或需要的人〕相伴[相助]: *She found it hard to face up to the prospect of life without Ken.* 没有肯，她觉得很难面对未来的生活。**4** if something happens without something unpleasant happening, it happens in a way that is pleasant or easy〔某事〕在没有〔不愉快事情〕的情况下〔发生〕: *I managed to get through the exam without too much trouble.* 在没太多困难的情况下我考试及格了。**5 without wanting to/without wishing to** used before a criticism, complaint, or other statement to make it less definite 不想/不愿意…〔用于批评、投诉或其他陈述之前，以示婉转〕: *Without wanting to sound too boastful, I think we have the best television programmes in the world.* 不想太吹牛，我觉得我们有世界上最精彩的电视节目。**6** *old use* outside【旧】在外面

with·stand /wɪθˋstænd; wɪðˈstænd/ *v past tense and past participle* **withstood** /-ˋstʊd; -ˈstʊd/ [T] **1** to be strong enough to remain unharmed by something such as great heat or cold, great pressure etc 耐受，承受〔酷热、严寒、高压等〕: *a type of desert bush that can withstand extremes of temperature* 一种能耐受温差悬殊的沙漠灌木 | **withstand the test of time** (=still be important, effective etc after a long time) 经得起时间的考验 *theories that have withstood the test of time* 经得起时间考验的理论 **2** to defend yourself against attack, and successfully oppose someone or something 抵挡；顶住: *withstanding a heroic doomed attack by six allied divisions* 顶住了盟军六个师注定失败的英勇进攻

wit·less /ˋwɪtlɪs; ˈwɪtləs/ *adj* **1** not very intelligent or sensible; silly 无才智的；愚蠢的: *if I catch the witless yobs who did this* 要是我抓住干这件事的愚蠢无赖 **2 scare sb witless** to make someone very frightened 把某人吓坏 —**witlessly** *adv* —**witlessness** *n* [U]

2 3 **wit·ness**[1] /ˋwɪtnɪs; ˈwɪtn̩s/ *n* **1** [C] someone who sees a crime or an accident and can describe what happened〔罪行或事故的〕目击者: *Police have appealed for witnesses to come forward.* 警方呼吁目击者作证。**2** [C] someone in a court of law who tells what they saw or what they know about a crime〔法庭上的〕证人: *One witness claimed to have seen the gun.* 一位证人声称曾见过这支枪。**3 bear witness** *formal* to show or prove that something is true or that something happened in the past【正式】证明〔某事是事实〕，证实〔过去的事〕: *The temples and theatres all bear witness to the city's former greatness.* 庙宇和剧场都证明了这个城市以前的辉煌。**4** [C] someone who is present when an official paper is signed and who signs it to prove this〔正式文件的签署的〕见证人，连署人: **witness to** *a witness to a will* 遗嘱的见证人 **5 be witness to** *formal* to be present when something happens, and watch it happening【正式】是…的目击者: *We were witness to the worst excesses of the military.* 我们目击了最恶劣的军事暴行。**6** [C,U] *AmE* a public statement of strong Christian belief, or someone who makes such a statement【美】见证〔表示笃信基督教的公开声明〕；见证人〔做这种见证的人〕

witness[2] *v* **1** [T] to see something happen, especially a crime or accident, because you are present when it happens 目击，亲眼看见〔尤指罪行或事故发生〕: *Police are appealing to any driver who may have witnessed the accident.* 警方正呼吁曾目睹这事故的司机协助。**2** [T] **a)** to experience important events or changes because you are there when they are happening 亲自经历〔重要事件或变迁〕: *We witnessed the break-up of the former Soviet Union.* 我们亲身经历了前苏联的解体。**b)** if a time or place witnesses an event, the event happens during that time or in that place 是发生〔某事件〕的时间[地点]: *The 1980s witnessed increasing unemployment throughout Europe.* 20世纪80年代是全欧洲失业日益加剧的年代。**3** [T] to be present when someone signs an official document, and sign it yourself to show this〔在正式文件上〕连署；在〔正式文件〕上签署作证: *Will you witness my signature?* 你愿意在我的签字旁连署吗？**4** [T] **a)** to be a sign or proof of something 表明；是〔某事〕的证明: *the rise in crime, as witnessed by our overcrowded prisons* 拥挤不堪的监狱证明犯罪的增多 **b)** used to give an example that proves something you have just mentioned〔用于给刚提及的事举例〕作证: *Poor school grades don't prove much – witness Dana's amazing success in business.* 学校成绩不好说明不了什么 —— 达纳惊人的经商成就即是明证。**5** [I] *AmE* to speak publicly about your strong Christian beliefs【美】见证〔公开表示笃信基督教〕

witness to sth *phr v* [T] to formally state that something is true or happened 证实；证明〔某事〕: *Her principal was called to witness to her good character.* 她的校长被传唤来证明她优良的品德。| **witness to doing sth** *The driver witnessed to having seen the man enter the building.* 司机作证说，他看到此人进入那栋建筑物。

witness box *BrE*【英】，**witness stand** *AmE*【美】/ˈ‥ ˌ/ *n* [C] the place in a court of law where a witness stands to answer questions〔法庭的〕证人席，证人台

wit·ter /ˋwɪtɚ; ˈwɪtə/ also 又作 **witter on** *v* [I] *informal* to talk a lot in a boring way or about something unimportant【非正式】絮叨；啰唆: **[+about]** *I'm sick of her wittering on about New Men.* 她絮叨新派男子的事我听得厌烦透了。

Witt·gen·stein /ˋvɪtgənʃtaɪn; ˈvɪtgənʃtaɪn/, **Lud·wig** /ˋlʊdwɪg; ˈlʊdvɪg/ (1889-1951) an Austrian PHILOSOPHER, who studied and taught at Cambridge in the UK. His interests included the relationship between language and the physical world, and his best known works are *Tractatus Logico-Philosophicus* and *Philosophical Investigations.* 维特根斯坦〔(1889-1951)，奥地利哲学家，曾在英国剑桥大学求学并任教。他关注语言与物质世界的关系问题，代表作有《逻辑哲学论》和《哲学研究》〕

wit·ti·cis·m /ˋwɪtəˌsɪzəm; ˈwɪtɪ̵sɪzəm/ *n* [C] a clever amusing remark 妙语；俏皮话；诙谐语

wizard 巫师，术士

wit·ty /ˋwɪtɪ; ˈwɪti/ *adj* using words in a clever and amusing way 说话风趣的；妙趣横生的: *a witty speaker* 讲话风趣的人 | *witty remarks* 妙语 —**wittily** *adv* —**wittiness** *n* [U]

wives /waɪvz; waɪvz/ the plural of WIFE

wiz·ard /ˋwɪzɚd; ˈwɪzəd/ *n* [C] **1** a man who is supposed to have magic powers 巫师，术士 **2** someone who is very good at something 能手，奇才: *a financial wizard* 理财能手 | **[+at]** *Ben's a real wizard at chess.* 本是十足的国际象棋能手。

CULTURAL NOTE 文化注释

A wizard is usually shown in stories as an old man with a pointed hat and a long CLOAK who uses a MAGIC WAND to do SPELL*s*. 故事中把巫师描述成一个戴尖帽、披长斗篷的老头，他用一根魔杖来施魔咒。

Wizard of Oz, The /ˌ‥ ˈ ˌ/ (1939) a very popular US MUSICAL (=a film that uses singing and dancing to tell a story), based on a children's book by L. Frank Baum. In the film Judy Garland appears as a girl called Dorothy who, with her dog Toto, is carried by a very powerful storm from the farm where she lives in Kansas to the magic land of Oz. There they travel along the Yellow Brick Road, meet the Scarecrow, the Cowardly Lion, and the Tin Man, and have many adventures before they meet the Wizard of Oz himself and finally get home. The film contains many well-known songs, including 'Over the Rainbow'. 《绿野仙踪》〔(1939)，一部颇受欢迎的美国音乐片，根据L.弗兰克·鲍姆的儿童小说改编。影片中朱迪·嘉兰饰演小女孩多萝西。一股强劲的暴风将多萝西和她的小狗托托从居住的堪萨斯农场上吹到了魔幻之地奥兹。她们沿着黄砖道行进，途中遇到稻草人、胆小狮和铁皮人，在经历种种磨难后终于见到了奥兹巫师，并回到了家中。影片中有不少家喻户晓的歌曲，如《在彩虹上》等〕

wiz·ard·ry /ˋwɪzɚdrɪ; ˈwɪzədri/ *n* [U] impressive ability at something or an impressive achievement 杰出的才能[成就]: *The best thing about the movie is the sheer wizardry of the special effects.* 电影中最精彩的部分是非凡的特技。

wiz·ened /ˋwɪzn̩d; ˈwɪzənd/ *adj* a wizened person, fruit etc is small and thin and has skin with a lot of lines and WRINKLES〔人、水果等〕干瘦的；干瘪的: *wizened old Frenchmen playing boules in the square* 在广场上玩滚木球游戏的干瘦的法国老人

wk the written abbreviation of 缩写= WEEK

woad /wod; wəʊd/ *n* [U] a blue DYE (=colouring substance) used in ancient times to colour people's bodies〔古代用以染身的〕靛蓝〔染料〕

wob·ble /ˋwɑbl̩; ˈwɒbəl/ *v* **1** [I,T] to move unsteadily from side to side, or make something do this 摇晃；使〔某物〕摇摆: *The pile of bricks wobbled and fell.* 一堆砖摇摇晃晃，然后倒了。| *His fat thighs wobbled as he ran along.* 他跑起步来，肥胖的大腿不住颤动。| **wobble sth** *Stop wobbling the table with your foot.* 别用脚把桌子弄得摇摇晃晃。**2** [I always+adv/prep] to go in a particular direction while moving unsteadily from

side to side 摇晃不稳〔朝某方向走〕: [+off/along/across etc] *Cindy wobbled along the street on her bike.* 辛迪在街上摇摇晃晃地骑着自行车。**3** *AmE* to be unsure whether to do something 【美】犹豫不决: *The President appeared to wobble over sending the troops in.* 对于是否出兵总统显得犹豫不决。—**wobble** *n* [C]

wob·bly[1] /ˈwɑblɪ; ˈwɒbli/ *adj* **1** moving unsteadily from side to side 摇摆的; 颤动的: *a wobbly table* 摇摇晃晃的桌子 **2** *informal* feeling weak and unable to keep your balance 【非正式】〔身体因虚弱而〕震颤的: *I've gone all wobbly – I think I'll sit down.* 我浑身乏力, 我想我要坐下来。**3** a wobbly voice is weak and shakes, especially when you feel frightened or upset 〔声音〕颤抖的〔尤因感到害怕或不安时〕

wobbly[2] *n* [C] *BrE informal* 【英, 非正式】 **throw a wobbly** to suddenly become very angry or frightened 勃然大怒; 大惊失色

Wo·be·gon, Lake —see 见 LAKE WOBEGON

Wode·house /ˈwʊdhaus; ˈwʊdhaʊs/, **P. G.** (1881-1975) a British writer who later moved to the US, who wrote many humorous NOVELs about UPPER CLASS English people. His best-known stories are about a rich and stupid young man called Bertie Wooster, who does not work and spends most of his time visiting other rich people. He depends on his clever servant Jeeves to get him out of trouble. 沃德豪斯〔(1881-1975), 英国作家, 后移居美国, 著有大量描写英国上层社会生活的喜剧小说。其最著名的系列小说描写一个名叫伯蒂·伍斯特的年轻富豪, 他迷迷糊糊, 游手好闲, 把大部分时间花在拜访其他有钱人上面, 靠着聪明的仆人吉夫斯摆脱了不少麻烦〕

Wo·den /ˈwodn̩; ˈwəʊdn/ the Anglo-Saxon name for Odin, the king of the gods. The word 'Wednesday' is based on his name. 沃登〔盎格鲁－萨克逊语中对众神之王奥丁的称呼。Wednesday (星期三) 一词源自他的名字〕

wodge /wɑdʒ; wɒdʒ/ *n* [C] *BrE informal* a thick, solid piece or large amount of something 【英, 非正式】〔某物的〕一大块; 大量: *a wodge of ten pound notes* 一大沓 10 英镑钞票

woe /wo; wəʊ/ *n* **1** [U] *literary* great sadness 【文】悲伤; 悲哀: *a tale of woe* 悲伤的故事 **2 woes** [plural] *formal* the problems and troubles affecting someone 【正式】困难; 难题: *They tend to blame all of Africa's woes on colonialism.* 他们倾向于把非洲的所有灾难归咎于殖民主义。**3 woe betide** *especially humorous* used to warn someone that there will be trouble if they do something 【尤幽默】将要遭殃〔用于警告某人做某事会有麻烦〕: *Woe betide anyone who smokes in our house!* 谁在我们房子里抽烟谁倒霉!

woe·be·gone /ˈwobɪˌgɔn; ˈwəʊbɪgɒn/ *adj especially literary* looking very sad 【尤文】愁眉苦脸的: *Her woebegone expression made him feel protective.* 她满脸愁容, 令他动了呵护之心。

woe·ful /ˈwofəl; ˈwəʊfəl/ *adj* **1** very bad or serious; DEPLORABLE 极坏的, 糟透的: *a woeful lack of information* 信息极其匮乏 **2** *literary* very sad; PATHETIC 【文】悲哀的; 可怜的: *The little girl looked up at him with woeful eyes.* 小女孩用忧郁的眼神仰望着他。—**woefully** *adv*: *woefully inadequate facilities* 设施严重不足

wog /wɑg; wɒg/ *n* [C] *BrE taboo* a very offensive word for a black person 【英讳】外国佬〔对黑人的冒犯语〕

wok /wɑk; wɒk/ *n* [C] a wide pan shaped like a bowl, used in Chinese cooking 〔烹调中国菜时用的〕铁锅; 镬子 —see picture at 参见 PAN[1] 图

woke /wok; wəʊk/ the past tense of WAKE[1]

wok·en /ˈwokən; ˈwəʊkən/ the past participle of WAKE[1]

wolds /woldz; wəʊldz/ *n* [plural] *BrE* a word for an area of hilly countryside, especially used in the names of places 【英】丘陵地区; 荒野〔尤用于地名〕: *the Yorkshire Wolds* 约克郡丘陵地区

wolf[1] /wʊlf; wʊlf/ *n plural* **wolves** /wʊlvz; wʊlvz/ [C] **1** a wild animal that looks like a large dog and lives and hunts in groups 狼: *a pack of wolves* 一群狼 **2 a wolf in sheep's clothing** someone who seems to be friendly but is in fact, unpleasant etc 披着羊皮的狼〔指伪装友善的人〕 **3 cry wolf** to keep asking for help that you do not really need, with the result that when you do need help people do not believe you 喊"狼来了"〔指人不断发假警报, 到真正需要帮忙时, 没有人相信〕: *Jurgen's cried wolf one too many times. I'm sick of it!* 朱尔根多次谎报情况, 我感到烦透了! **4 keep the wolf from the door** to earn just enough money to buy the basic things you need 勉强维持生计: *Between us, we earn just enough to keep the wolf from the door.* 我们一起赚的钱勉强够维持生计。—see also 另见 LONE WOLF —**wolfish** *adj*: *a wolfish grin* 狞笑

wolf[2] also 又作 **wolf down** *v* [T] *informal* to eat something very quickly, swallowing it in big pieces 【非正式】狼吞虎咽地吃

Wolfe /wʊlf; wʊlf/, **General James** (1727-59) a British general who died leading the army which took Quebec from the French and gave the British control of Canada 沃尔夫将军〔(1727-1759), 英国将军。他曾率领部队从法军手中夺回魁北克, 并使英国获得对加拿大的控制权, 自己在战斗中阵亡〕

wolf·hound /ˈwʊlfˌhaund; ˈwʊlfhaʊnd/ *n* [C] an extremely large dog 〔大〕狼狗

wol·fram /ˈwʊlfrəm; ˈwʊlfrəm/ *n* [U] TUNGSTEN 钨

wolf whis·tle /ˈ· ˌ··/ *n* [C] a way of whistling that men sometimes use to show that they think a woman is attractive 〔男人对美貌女子吹的〕挑逗口哨 —**wolf-whistle** *v* [I]

Woll·stone·craft /ˈwʊlstənkræft; ˈwʊlstənkrɑːft/, **Mary** (1759-97) a British writer who was one of the first FEMINISTs. In her book *A Vindication of the Rights of Women*, she wrote that women should have the same education and opportunities as men. She was the mother of Mary Shelley. 沃斯通克拉夫特〔(1759-1797), 英国作家, 最早的女权主义者之一。在其著作《女权的辩护》中, 她写到女性理应与男性接受相同的教育, 享有同等的机会。她是玛丽·雪莱的母亲〕

Wol·sey /ˈwʊlzɪ; ˈwʊlzi/, **Cardinal Thomas** (?1475-1530) an English CARDINAL (=a high-ranking Catholic priest) and politician who was very rich and powerful, but who lost power after failing to persuade the Pope to allow King Henry VIII to end his marriage to Catherine of Aragon 红衣主教托马斯·沃尔西〔(?1475-1530), 英国红衣主教、政治家。他曾经富可敌国, 权倾朝野, 但后来因未能说服教皇批准国王亨利八世与阿拉贡的凯瑟琳离婚而失势〕

wolves /wʊlvz; wʊlvz/ the plural of WOLF

Wo·mad /ˈwomæd; ˈwəʊmæd/ a music FESTIVAL, held for three days every year in fields near Reading in southern England, where people camp and many musicians from all over the world give performances 沃马德音乐节〔每年在英格兰南部雷丁附近的空地上举行的音乐节, 为期三天。有世界各地的许多音乐家前来献艺, 其间人们在那里搭帐篷居住〕

Woman *trademark* a British weekly magazine for women, especially popular with married women who have families 【商标】《妇女》〔英国一份女性周刊, 颇受婚育妇女的欢迎〕

wom·an /ˈwʊmən; ˈwʊmən/ *n plural* **women** /ˈwɪmɪn; ˈwɪmɪn/ 

1 ▶FEMALE 女性◀ [C] an adult female person 成年女子, 妇人: *I was talking to a woman I met on the flight.* 我正在和在飞机上相遇的一个女子交谈。| **married women** 已婚妇女 | **a woman priest/driver etc** *How long will it be until we have a woman President?* 需要多长时间我们才会有一位女总统? | **women's clothes/organization etc** *Kate works for a popular women's magazine.* 凯特在一家受欢迎的妇女杂志社工作。—see 见 MAN[1] (USAGE)

2 ▶FORM OF ADDRESS 称呼形式◀ *spoken* a rude way of addressing a woman when you are angry, annoyed etc 【口】婆娘〔生气、烦恼时对妇女的粗鲁称呼〕: *Pull yourself together, woman!* 振作起来, 你这个婆娘!

3 another woman/the other woman *informal* a woman that a man is having a sexual relationship with, even though he is married to someone else 【非正式】已婚男人的情人/情妇: *I'm sure he's got another woman.* 我敢肯定他有情妇。

4 ▶GENERAL TERM 一般用语◀ [singular] *formal* women in general 【正式】女人〔泛称〕: *A woman's work is never done.* 女人的工作永远干不完。

5 ▶PARTNER 伴侣◀ also 又作 **the old woman** [singular] *spoken* expressions meaning your girlfriend or wife, which many women find offensive 【口】女朋友; 老婆〔许多妇女认为这是冒犯语〕: *Did he bring his woman with him?* 他带老婆来了吗?

6 businesswoman/spokeswoman etc a woman who has a particular kind of job 女商人/女发言人等: *a spokeswoman for the charity* 慈善团体的女发言人

7 be your own woman to make your own decisions and be in charge of your own life, without depending on anyone else 独立自主; 不依赖他人

8 woman of easy virtue/woman of the night *old-fashioned* a PROSTITUTE[1] (1) 【过时】娼妓

9 ▶SERVANT 佣人◀ [C] a female servant or person who does works for you in your house 女佣; 女仆 —see also 另见 **make an honest woman of** (HONEST (8)), OLD WOMAN, **wine, women and song** (WINE[1] (3)), **be a man/woman of the world** (WORLD[1] (26))

wom·an·hood /ˈwʊmənˌhud; ˈwʊmənhʊd/ *n* [U] **1** the state of being a woman, not a man or a girl 女子成年〔的状态〕 **2** *formal* women in general 【正式】女人〔泛称〕—compare 比较 MANHOOD

wom·an·ish /ˈwʊmənɪʃ; ˈwʊmənɪʃ/ *adj* a womanish man looks or behaves in a way that is supposed to be typical of women 〔男人的外表或行为〕女人气的; 女人腔的

wom·an·izer also 又作 **-iser** *BrE*【英】/ˈwʊmən͵aɪzɚ; ˈwʊmənaɪzə/ *n* [C] a man who has sexual relationships with many different women 玩弄女性的男人 —**womanize** *v* [I] —**womanizing** *n* [U]

wom·an·kind /ˈwʊmənˋkaɪnd; ˈwʊmənkaɪnd/ *n* [U] women considered together as a group 女性, 妇女〔总称〕—compare 比较 MANKIND

wom·an·ly /ˈwʊmənlɪ; ˈwʊmənli/ *adj approving* behaving, dressing etc in a way that is thought to be typical of or suitable for a woman【褒】〔行为、衣着等〕有女子气质的; 女人特有的: *her soft womanly curves* 她的女性特有的曲线美 —**womanliness** *n* [U]

Woman's Hour /ˈ·· , ·/ a British radio programme broadcast on BBC Radio, which has news, interviews, and discussions on subjects considered to be of special interest to women《妇女时光》〔英国广播公司一档广播节目, 播出新闻、访谈以及论坛节目, 就妇女特别关注的话题展开讨论〕

Woman's Own /, ··ˈ·/ a British weekly magazine for women, especially popular with married women who have families【商标】《妇女界》〔英国一份女性周刊, 颇受婚育妇女的欢迎〕

womb /wum; wu:m/ *n* [C] the part of a female's body where her baby grows before it is born 子宫

wom·bat /ˈwɑmbæt; ˈwɒmbæt/ *n* [C] an Australian animal like a small bear whose babies live in a pocket of skin on its body 毛鼻袋熊〔产于澳大利亚〕

wom·en /ˈwɪmɪn; ˈwɪmɪn/ the plural of WOMAN

wom·en·folk /ˈwɪmɪn͵fok; ˈwɪmɪnfəʊk/ *n* [plural] all the women in a particular family or society〔某个家庭或社会中的〕(全体)妇女

Women in Love /, ··· ˈ·/ (1921) a NOVEL by D. H. Lawrence about two sisters, Ursula and Gudrun Brangwen, and their difficult relationships with men《恋爱中的女人》〔(1921), D.H. 劳伦斯所著的一部小说, 讲述布兰温两姐妹厄休拉和古德伦复杂的情感纠葛〕

Women's In·sti·tute, the /, ··ˈ···/ abbreviation 缩写为 **the WI** a British organization for women, especially women in country areas, who meet for social and educational activities 妇女协会〔英国一个为妇女, 尤其乡村妇女服务的团体, 组织各类社会活动和教育活动〕

wom·en's lib /, ··ˈ·/ also 又作 **women's lib·e·ra·tion** /, ·· ··ˈ··/ *n* [U] *old-fashioned* all the ideas, actions, and politics connected with giving women the same rights and opportunities as men【过时】妇女解放运动 —**women's libber** *n* [C]

CULTURAL NOTE 文化注释

Some people associate women's lib with the idea of women burning their BRA*s* to show that they are free, which some women did in the 1960s when the movement began. 有人将妇女解放运动与妇女烧掉胸罩的想法联系起来, 这是20世纪60年代妇女解放运动刚开始时一些妇女的行为, 她们这么做是为了展示她们有了自由。

women's move·ment /ˈ·· , ·ˈ/ *n* **the women's movement** all the women who are involved in the aim of improving the social, economic, and political position of women and of ending sexual DISCRIMINATION (1) 妇女(解放)运动, 女权运动

women's re·fuge /, ··ˈ··/ *n* [C] a special place where women and their children can go to escape being physically hurt by their husband, partner etc〔收容遭到丈夫、伴侣等虐待的妇女及其子女的〕妇女避难所

women's room /ˈ·· ·/ *n* [C] *especially AmE* a public TOILET (2) for women【尤美】女洗手间; 公共女厕所

won /wʌn; wʌn/ the past tense and past participle of WIN[1]

won·der[1] /ˈwʌndɚ; ˈwʌndə/ *v* [I,T] **1** to think about something that you are not sure about and try to guess what is true, what will happen etc〔对某事〕感到疑惑; 想要知道: **wonder who/what/how etc** *I wonder how James is getting on.* 我想知道詹姆斯的近况。| *What are they going to do now, I wonder?* 我想知道他们现在准备做什么。| **wonder if/whether/why** *I wonder if I'll recognize Philip after all these years.* 过了这些年, 我不知道是否还认得菲利普。| **it makes you wonder** *especially spoken*【尤口】: *Patrick's reaction made me wonder if he knew more than he'd told me.* 帕特里克的反应使我怀疑他是否只告诉我一部分。**2 I wonder if/whether** *spoken* used to ask politely for something【口】我不知道是否〔用于礼貌地询问某事〕: *I wonder if I might have a glass of water?* 我可不可以要一杯水? **3 I was wondering if/whether a)** *spoken* used to politely ask someone to help you【口】我想知道〔用于礼貌地请求帮助〕: *I was wondering if I could borrow your car?* 请问我能否借一下你的汽车? **b)** used to ask someone politely if they would like to do something 不知可不可以〔礼貌地请求他人做某事〕: *I was wondering if you'd like to come to dinner.* 不知道你是否愿意来吃晚饭。**4** [I,T] to feel surprised and unable to believe something〔对某事〕感到惊讶〔不能相信〕: **[+about/at]** *Sometimes I wonder about his behaviour.* 有时我对他的行为感到惊讶。| **[+how]** *I wonder how he dares to show his face after last night!* 昨晚之后他竟然还敢露面, 我觉得奇怪! | **I don't wonder** *BrE spoken* (=I am not surprised)【英口】我不觉得奇怪 *I don't wonder you're tired after the day you've had.* 你经过那样的一天之后感到疲乏, 我觉得很正常。| **I shouldn't wonder** *BrE spoken* (=I would not be surprised about something)【英口】我觉得不足为奇 *He'll come back soon enough, I shouldn't wonder.* 他会很快回来, 我对此一点也不觉得奇怪。**5** [I,T] to doubt or question whether something is true 怀疑〔某事的真实性〕: *"Is she serious?" "I wonder."* "她是认真的吗?" "我看不一定。" | **wonder if/whether** *Ken says such stupid things that I wonder if he's got any sense at all!* 肯说出这种蠢话来, 我不知道他究竟还有没有理智!

wonder[2] *n*

1 ▶ADMIRATION 赞赏◀ a) [U] a feeling of surprise and admiration for something very beautiful or new to you〔对漂亮或新事物的〕惊叹; 惊奇; 诧异: *The sight of the Taj Mahal filled us with wonder.* 看见泰姬陵, 我们充满了惊叹之情。**b)** [C] something that makes you feel surprise and admiration 奇事; 奇迹, 奇观: *technological wonders* 技术奇迹 | *the Seven Wonders of the World* 世界七大奇观

2 (it's) no wonder/small wonder/little wonder *especially spoken* used to say that you are not surprised by something【尤口】并不奇怪/不足为奇/十分自然: *No wonder you've got a headache, the amount you drank last night.* 昨晚你喝得太多, 头痛不足为怪。

3 ▶SURPRISING 惊讶◀ it's a wonder (that) *especially spoken* used to say that something is very surprising【尤口】令人惊奇的是: *It's a wonder Louise remembered to come, she's so scatty.* 真想不到路易丝那么健忘, 她居然记得。

4 do/work wonders to be very effective in solving a problem 创造奇迹/取得惊人成效

5 ▶CLEVER PERSON 聪明人◀ [singular] *BrE* someone who is clever at doing difficult things【英】奇才, 奇人: *Philip's a wonder, the way he manages on his own.* 菲利普真是奇才, 什么问题他都能独自解决。

6 wonders will never cease! *spoken humorous* used to show you are surprised and pleased about something【口, 幽默】真是无奇不有 —see also 另见 **chinless wonder** (CHINLESS (3)), **nine days' wonder** (NINE (3))

wonder[3] *adj* [only before noun 仅用于名词前] very good and effective 极好的; 灵验的: *a new wonder drug* 新的灵丹妙药

Wonder, Ste·vie /ˈstivɪ; ˈsti:vi/ (1950-) a US soul singer, songwriter, and piano player who was born blind. He started making records with the Motown record company when he was 12, and became one of the most successful popular musicians in the world. He is also famous for his political support for black people in the US and Africa. His songs include *Superstition* and *I Just Called To Say I Love You.* 汪德〔(1950-), 美国灵歌歌手、词作家、钢琴演奏家。先天双目失明, 12岁时即与摩城唱片公司合作录制唱片, 成为世界上最成功的流行乐音乐家之一。同时, 他因在政治上支持美国及非洲的黑人而著名。其歌曲包括《迷信》和《电话诉衷情》〕

Won·der·bra /ˈwʌndɚbrɑ; ˈwʌndəbrɑ:/ *trademark* a type of BRA that pushes a woman's breasts up so that they look larger【商标】魔术文胸〔一种胸罩, 能将女性的乳房托起, 从而显得更加丰满〕

Won·der·bread /ˈwʌndɚbrɛd; ˈwʌndəbred/ *trademark* a type of soft white bread which is sold in the US. It is sold in a plastic bag and is already cut into SLICE*s*, and is typically used for making SANDWICH*es*.【商标】神奇面包〔美国一种袋装销售的切片白面包, 质地松软, 通常用于制做三明治〕

won·der·ful /ˈwʌndɚfəl; ˈwʌndəfəl/ *adj* **1** making you feel very happy 令人高兴的; 使人愉快的: *We had a wonderful time in Spain.* 我们在西班牙过得极为愉快。**2** making you admire someone or something very much〔某人、某物〕令人惊叹的; 奇妙的: *It's wonderful what doctors can do nowadays.* 当今医生能做的着实令人称奇。—**wonderfully** *adv* 

won·der·ingly /ˈwʌndərɪŋlɪ; ˈwʌndərɪŋli/ *adv* in a way that shows admiration, surprise, and pleasure 惊叹地; 不可思议地; 令人高兴地

won·der·land /ˈwʌndɚ͵lænd; ˈwʌndəlænd/ *n* [U] an imaginary place in stories〔故事中的〕仙境, 奇境

won·der·ment /ˈwʌndɚmənt; ˈwʌndəmənt/ *n* [U] *literary* a feeling of pleasant surprise or admiration【文】惊叹; 惊奇

won·drous /ˈwʌndrəs; ˈwʌndrəs/ *adj poetical* good or impressive in a surprising way【诗】奇妙的; 令人惊叹的

won·ga /ˈwɑŋgə; ˈwɒŋgə/ *n* [U] *BrE slang* money【英俚】金钱

wonk /wɑŋk; wɒŋk/ *n* [C] *AmE informal* someone who works hard and is very serious【美, 非正式】用功而严肃的人: *policy wonks surrounding the President* 总统周围一本正经的政策专家

won·ky /ˈwɑŋki; ˈwɒŋki/ *adj BrE informal* unsteady or not straight or level【英, 非正式】不稳的; 歪斜的; 不平的: *a wonky table* 放不稳的桌子

won't /wont; wəʊnt/ the short form of 缩略式 = will not

wont¹ /wont; wəʊnt/ *n old-fashioned*【过时】**as is sb's wont** used to say that it is someone's habit to do something 就像某人惯常那样〔表示某人惯于做某事〕: *He spoke for too long, as is his wont.* 他说话总是这样长篇大论。

wont² *adj formal*【正式】**be wont to do sth** to be likely to do something 惯于做某事

wont·ed /ˈwʌntɪd; ˈwəʊntɪd/ *adj* [only before noun 仅用于名词前] *old-fashioned* usual【过时】通常的

woo /wu; wuː/ *v* [T] **1** to try to persuade someone to buy something from you, vote for you etc 努力说服〔顾客、选民等〕: *The politicians will be wooing the voters before the election.* 选举前政治家都尽力争取选民的支持。**2** *old-fashioned* to try to persuade a woman to love you and marry you【过时】〔向女子〕求爱; 求婚 —**wooer** *n* [C]

CULTURAL NOTE 文化注释

The TRADITIONAL and old-fashioned way for a man to woo a woman is for him to buy her flowers, chocolates, and other presents, to write love letters to her, and to take her to expensive restaurants. Many men (especially young men) no longer do this and some women (especially FEMINISTs) disapprove of this type of behaviour because they think that by behaving in this way men are not treating women as equals. 男人向女人求爱的传统老式的方法是买一束花、送巧克力和其他礼物, 或者是给她写情书、带她去高级饭店。很多男人(特别是年轻人)现在已经放弃了这些做法, 而且有些女人(特别是女权主义者)鄙视这种行为, 因为她们认为男人这样求爱是不公平地对待女人。

S2 W2 **wood** /wʊd; wʊd/ *n* **1** [C,U] the material that trees are made of 木; 木材; 木料: *Put some more wood on the fire.* 往火上再添些木柴。| *a polished wood floor* 擦得光亮的木地板 | **soft/hard wood** *Pine is a soft wood.* 松木是软质木材。**2** [C] also 又作 **the woods** a small forest 树林; 林地: *a walk in the woods* 在树林里散步 **3** [C] one of a set of four GOLF CLUBS with wooden heads 木头球杆〔杆头为木制的高尔夫球杆〕**4 not be out of the wood(s) yet** *informal* used to say that there are likely to be more difficulties before things improve【非正式】仍未脱离困[险]境: *It's been going well lately, but we're not totally out of the woods yet.* 情况最近有所好转, 但我们仍未完全摆脱困境。**5 not see the wood for the trees** to not notice what is important about something because you give too much of your attention to small details 见树不见林〔指着重细节而忽略重要部分〕—see also 另见 **dead wood** (DEAD¹ (30))

Wood, Grant (1892-1942) a US artist who painted the painting *American Gothic* 伍德〔(1892-1942), 美国画家, 画作有《美国哥特人》〕

Wood, Sir Henry (1869-1944) a British CONDUCTOR (=someone who directs a group of musicians) who started the Proms, a series of concerts which take place in London every summer 伍德爵士〔(1869-1944), 英国指挥家。首创了逍遥音乐会, 即每年夏天在伦敦举办的系列音乐会〕

Woods /wʊdz; wʊdz/, **Tiger** (1975-) a US GOLFER who, in 1997, became the youngest person ever to win the US Masters Tournament. In 2000 he won the US Open and The Open (in Britain). This made him the youngest player to have won all four Majors (=the two Opens, the US Masters, and the PGA). In 2001 he won the US Masters to complete a GRAND SLAM of holding all four major titles at the same time. 伍兹〔(1975-), 美国高尔夫球运动员, 1997年成为历史上最年轻的美国名人赛冠军。2000年, 他获得美国公开赛及英国公开赛冠军, 从而成为荣获过四大赛事(美国公开赛、英国公开赛、美国名人赛及美国职业高尔夫球协会锦标赛)冠军的最年轻的球员。2001年, 他再度在美国名人赛中折桂, 实现了同时拥有四大赛事冠军头衔的大满贯〕

wood·bine /ˈwʊdˌbaɪn; ˈwʊdbaɪn/ *n* [U] **1** *poetical* HONEYSUCKLE【诗】忍冬〔一种攀缘植物〕**2** *AmE* VIRGINIA CREEPER【美】五叶地锦

wood·block /ˈwʊdˌblɑk; ˈwʊdblɒk/ *n* [C] **1** a piece of wood with a shape cut on it, used for printing〔印刷用的〕木刻印版 **2** a block of wood used in making a floor〔铺地板用〕木板, 木块

wood·carv·ing /ˈwʊdkɑrvɪŋ; ˈwʊdkɑːvɪŋ/ *n* [C,U] the process of shaping wood with special tools, or a piece of art produced in this way 木雕; 木雕艺术品

wood·chuck /ˈwʊdˌtʃʌk; ˈwʊdtʃʌk/ *n* [C] a GROUNDHOG 土拨鼠

wood·cock /ˈwʊdˌkɑk; ˈwʊdkɒk/ *n* [C] a brown bird that lives in woods〔树林中的〕丘鹬

wood·craft /ˈwʊdˌkræft; ˈwʊdkrɑːft/ *n* [U] the practical knowledge of woods and forests 森林生活技巧; 森林知识

wood·cut /ˈwʊdˌkʌt; ˈwʊdkʌt/ *n* [C] **1** a picture that you make by pressing a shaped piece of wood and a colouring substance onto paper 木版画 **2** a WOODBLOCK (1) 木刻印版

wood·cut·ter /ˈwʊdˌkʌtɚ; ˈwʊdˌkʌtə/ *n* [C] someone whose job is to cut down trees in a forest 伐木者

wood·ed /ˈwʊdɪd; ˈwʊdɪd/ *adj* having woods or covered with trees 多树木的; 长满树木的: *densely wooded hills* 树木茂盛的山岗

wood·en /ˈwʊdn̩; ˈwʊdn/ *adj* **1** made of wood 木制的: *a wooden bench* 木头长凳 **2** not showing enough expression, emotion, or movement, especially when performing in public〔尤指公开表演时〕呆板的; 木讷的; 笨拙的: *a rather wooden performance* 相当呆板的表演 —**woodenly** *adv* —**woodenness** *n* [U] S3 W3

wooden-head·ed /ˌ‥ˈ‥◂/ *adj informal* stupid and slow to understand things【非正式】愚蠢的; 迟钝的

wooden spoon /ˌ‥ˈ·/ *n* [C] a large wooden spoon used in cooking〔烹调用的〕木匙 —see picture at 参见 SPOON¹ 图

wood·land /ˈwʊdˌlænd; ˈwʊdlənd/ also 又作 **woodlands** *plural n* [U] an area of land covered with trees 林地; 林区

wood·louse /ˈwʊdˌlaʊs; ˈwʊdlaʊs/ *n plural* **woodlice** /-laɪs; -laɪs/ [C] a small grey insect that lives under wood, stones etc〔生活在木头、石块等处的〕潮虫, 土鳖

wood·peck·er /ˈwʊdˌpɛkɚ; ˈwʊdˌpekə/ *n* [C] a bird with a long beak that it uses to make holes in trees 啄木鸟

wood·pile /ˈwʊdˌpaɪl; ˈwʊdpaɪl/ *n* [C] a pile of firewood 木柴堆

wood pulp /ˈ· ·/ *n* [U] wood crushed into a soft mass, used for making paper〔造纸用的〕木浆

wood·shed /ˈwʊdˌʃɛd; ˈwʊdʃed/ *n* [C] a place for storing wood for burning 柴棚, 木柴间

woods·man /ˈwʊdzmən; ˈwʊdzmən/ *n plural* **woodsmen** /-mən; -mən/ [C] someone who works in a forest cutting down trees etc 伐木人

Wood·stock /ˈwʊdstɑk; ˈwʊdstɒk/ a music FESTIVAL, held over three days in 1969 near the town of Woodstock in New York State, where about 500,000 young people went to see rock, pop, and folk singers and bands, such as Janis Joplin, Jimi Hendrix, Jefferson Airplane, and The Who. It is famous especially for the HIPPIEs who attended it, and people see it as a very typical example of the hippie culture. 伍德斯托克音乐节〔1969年在纽约州伍德斯托克镇附近举办的一次为期三天多的音乐节, 约有50万青年人前往观赏了摇滚、流行、民歌歌手及乐队的演出, 如贾尼斯·乔普林、吉米·亨德里克斯、"杰斐逊飞机"乐队、"谁人"乐队等。这次音乐节尤因嬉皮士的加入而著名, 一般认为它代表了典型的嬉皮士文化〕

wood·sy /ˈwʊdzɪ; ˈwʊdzi/ *n AmE informal* connected with the woods【美, 非正式】与树林有关的: *a woodsy smell* 树林的气味

wood·wind /ˈwʊdˌwɪnd; ˈwʊdˌwɪnd/ also 又作 **the woodwind** *n* [C,U] the group of musical instruments that you play by blowing and pressing keys (KEY² (3)) 木管乐器 —**woodwind** *adj*

wood·work /ˈwʊdˌwɝk; ˈwʊdwɜːk/ *n* [U] **1** *BrE*【英】, **wood·work·ing** /ˈwʊdˌwɝkɪŋ; ˈwʊdwɜːkɪŋ/ *AmE*【美】the skill or activity of making wooden objects 木工手艺; 木工活 **2** the parts of a house or room that are made of wood〔房屋或房间的〕木建部分: *The woodwork needs painting.* 木建部分需要油漆。**3 crawl/come out of the woodwork** if people you don't like crawl out of the woodwork, there suddenly seems to be a lot of them〔令你讨厌的人〕突然纷纷出现; 大群露面: *When they heard about the funeral, suddenly all our weird relatives came crawling out of the woodwork.* 当听到丧葬的事后, 我们所有奇怪的亲戚都突然跑了出来。

wood·worm /ˈwʊd͵wɝm; ˈwʊdwɜːm/ *n* [C] **1** a small insect that makes holes in wood 蛀木虫，木蠹 **2** [U] the damage that is caused to wood by this creature 蛀木虫害

wood·y /ˈwʊdɪ; ˈwʊdi/ *adj* **1** a plant that is woody has a stem like wood〔植物〕木茎的；木质的 **2** a woody area of land has a lot of trees growing on it〔地方〕树木茂盛的

woof[1] /wʊf; wʊf/ *interjection* a word used for describing the sound a dog makes 汪汪〔形容狗的吠声〕 —**woof** *v* [I] *informal*【非正式】

woof[2] /wuf; wuːf/ *n* [C] WEFT 纬纱，纬线

woof·er /ˈwʊfɚ; ˈwuːfə/ *n* [C] a LOUDSPEAKER (1) that produces deep sounds 低音喇叭，低音扬声器 —compare 比较 TWEETER

woof·ter /ˈwʊftɚ; ˈwʊftə/ *n* [C] *BrE slang* an offensive word for a man who speaks or behaves in a way that is considered typical of HOMOSEXUALS【英俚】〔因言谈举止被认为是〕同性恋的男子〔冒犯语〕

Wook·ey Hole /͵wʊkɪ ˋhol; ͵wʊki ˈhəʊl/ a place in southwest England that is popular with tourists, with a cave where, according to an old story, a WITCH (=a woman with magic powers) used to live 伍基洞〔英格兰西南部一旅游胜地，为一岩洞，相传洞中曾有女巫居住〕

wool /wʊl; wʊl/ *n* [U] **1** the soft thick hair that sheep and some goats have on their body 羊毛 **2** material made from wool 毛织物：*Is this coat wool?* 这件大衣是毛料的吗？| **wool jacket/carpet/blanket etc** *a pure wool skirt* 纯毛裙子 **3** thread made from wool that you use for knitting (KNIT[1] (1)) clothes 毛线，绒线 **4 pull the wool over sb's eyes** to deceive someone by not telling the truth 蒙骗某人 —see also 另见 COTTON WOOL, DYED-IN-THE-WOOL, WIRE WOOL

Woolf /wʊlf; wʊlf/, **Virginia** (1882-1941) a British writer and CRITIC who was an important member of the Bloomsbury Group and is admired by FEMINISTS. Her NOVELS, such as *To the Lighthouse* and *The Waves*, use the style called stream of consciousness. 吴尔夫（1882-1941），英国作家、评论家，布卢姆斯伯里派的重要成员，受到女权主义者的崇拜。其小说如《到灯塔去》及《海浪》均采用了意识流的创作风格〕

wool·len *BrE*【英】, **woolen** *AmE*【美】/ˈwʊlən; ˈwʊlən/ *adj* [only before noun 仅用于名词前] made of wool 羊毛制的，毛料的 —see picture on page A16 参见 A16 页图

wool·lens *BrE*【英】, **woolens** *AmE*【美】/ˈwʊlənz; ˈwʊlənz/ *n* [plural] clothes made from wool, especially wool that has been knitted (KNIT[1] (1)) 毛料衣服；〔尤指〕针织毛线衣 —see also 另见 WOOLLY[2]

wool·ly[1] *BrE*【英】, **wooly** *AmE*【美】/ˈwʊlɪ; ˈwʊli/ *adj* **1** made of or feeling like wool 羊毛制的；像羊毛的：*a woolly hat* 羊毛帽子 **2** not showing clear thinking〔思想〕不清楚的，混乱的：*a woolly argument* 思路混乱的论点 —**wooliness** *n* [U]

woolly[2] *n* [C usually plural 一般用复数] *BrE* a piece of clothing made of wool, especially wool that has been knitted (KNIT[1] (1))【英】毛料服装；〔尤指〕针织毛线衣：*winter woollies* 冬季毛衣

woolly-head·ed /͵‥ ˈ‥◂/ *adj* not able to think clearly 头脑糊涂的；思想混乱的

Woos·ter /ˈwʊstɚ; ˈwʊstə/, **Ber·tie** /ˈbɝtɪ; ˈbɜːti/ a character in the many humorous stories by P. G. Wodehouse. He is a rich, rather stupid UPPER CLASS English man, who depends on his servant Jeeves to get him out of trouble. 伍斯特〔P.G.沃德豪斯所著的众多幽默故事中的一个人物。他是个富有但十分愚蠢的英国上流社会青年，依靠仆人吉夫斯帮助自己摆脱困境〕

woo·zy /ˈwuzɪ; ˈwuːzi/ *adj informal* feeling weak and unsteady; DIZZY (1)【非正式】虚弱的；眩晕的

wop /wɑp; wɒp/ *n* [C] a very offensive word for someone who is Italian 意大利佬〔严重的冒犯语〕

Worces·ter /ˈwʊstɚ; ˈwʊstə/ a city in west central England, famous for its CHINA (=plates, cups etc made from baked clay) and for its CATHEDRAL 伍斯特〔英格兰中西部一城市，以瓷器及大教堂闻名〕

Worces·ter·shire /ˈwʊstɚʃɚ; ˈwʊstəʃə/ a COUNTY in southwest England 伍斯特郡〔英格兰西南部一郡〕

Word *trademark* a popular type of computer SOFTWARE used for word PROCESSING (=typing letters, reports etc and storing information), produced by the Microsoft Corporation【商标】Word 软件〔一款流行的计算机文字处理软件，由微软公司制作〕

word[1] /wɝd; wɜːd/ *n*

① LANGUAGE/STH YOU SAY OR WRITE 语言/所说或所写的东西
② TALK/DISCUSSION 谈话/讨论
③ INFORMATION/NEWS 信息/新闻
④ ORDER/DECISION 命令/决定
⑤ PROMISE 诺言
⑥ OTHER MEANINGS 其他意思

① LANGUAGE/STH YOU SAY OR WRITE 语言/所说或所写的东西

1 [C] the smallest unit of language that people can understand if it is said or written on its own〔最小的语言单位〕字；词；单词：*Write an essay of about five hundred words.* 写一篇大约五百字的文章。| *There were a lot of words in the film I couldn't understand.* 影片中有许多词我听不懂。| *It's not a word I often use.* 这不是我常用的词。| *I know the tune, but not the words.* 我熟悉曲调，但不知道歌词。| **a word for** (=a word that means) …意思的一个字 *"Casa" is the Italian word for house.* casa 是意大利语"房屋"的意思。| **sb's words** (=what someone says) 某人所言 *Those are the editor's words, not mine.* 那都是编辑的话，不是我的。| **in your own words** *Tell us exactly what happened in your own words.* 你自己对我们说，到底发生了什么事情。

2 not believe/hear/understand a word to not believe etc what someone says or writes〔对某人所说、所写〕一点都不相信/听不到/不了解：*He says he played in a jazz group, but I don't believe a word of it.* 他说他在一爵士乐队表演过，但我一点都不信。| *Stuart didn't understand a word of that stuff on genetics either.* 那些有关遗传学的东西，斯图尔特也一点儿都不懂。| *Can you speak up, we can't hear a word.* 你能大声点说吗，我们什么都听不见。

3 put your feelings into words to express what you want to say clearly 用语言表达感觉：*I'm not very good at putting my feelings into words, but I'll try to explain.* 我不善表达，但我会设法解释。

4 find the words to choose the words that express your feelings or ideas clearly 用恰当的语言表达：*She only wished she could find the words to express her affection for the old man.* 她只希望能用恰当的语言表达对这位老人的感情。

② TALK/DISCUSSION 谈话/讨论

5 have a word (with) *especially spoken* to talk to someone quickly, especially because you need their advice about something or you want to tell them to do something【尤口】与〔某人〕说几句话〔尤因要征求对方的意见或叫对方做事〕：*Could I have a word with you after the meeting?* 会后我们可否谈谈？| **have/exchange a few words** (=have a short conversation) 进行简短的谈话 | **have a quick/brief word (with)** (=have a short conversation) 简短交谈 *We managed to have a quick word before the others arrived.* 在其他人到来之前，我们谈了几句。

6 want a (little) word *spoken* to want to speak to someone, especially in order to criticize or warn them【口】想和某人谈话〔尤指批评或警告对方〕：*The boss wants a little word with you.* 老板要跟你谈一下。

7 a word/a few words a short talk for a particular purpose〔为某目的〕作简短交谈：**a word of advice/warning/encouragement etc** *Could you give the boys a few words of encouragement?* 你能鼓励男孩子们几句吗？

8 not say/breathe a word to not say anything about something to anyone because it is a secret〔因守秘密〕绝口不谈；坚守秘密：*Don't say a word about the party to Dad.* 不要跟父亲说聚会的事。

9 have/drop a word in sb's ear to say something to someone privately especially in order to arrange something that would otherwise have been difficult〔尤指为事情顺利进行〕秘密地告诉某人〔某事〕：*Don't worry – I've dropped a word in his ear – everything's settled.* 别担心，我已经和他通了气，一切都已安排妥当。

10 have/exchange words (with) an expression meaning to

quarrel, used to avoid saying this directly 与…吵架; 和…吵嘴〔委婉语〕: *I saw Gwen after the meeting. We had words.* 会后我见到格温, 我们吵了起来。

③ **INFORMATION/NEWS 信息/新闻**

11 [singular, U] a piece of news or a message 一则新闻[消息]: **word gets out/around** (=people hear about something) 消息传开; 人们听说 *If word of the Royal visit gets out, we'll have the press here in force.* 如果王室到访的消息传开, 这里就会有大批的记者。| **The word is (that)/word has it (that)** (=people are saying that) 人们都在说 *The word is that Ben is leaving after Christmas.* 大家都在说本圣诞节后离开。| **no word from** *There's been no word from Susan since July.* 自7月以来, 苏珊一点消息也没有。| **send/bring word** (=send or bring a message) 送来/带来消息 *The mayor sent word he'd be late.* 市长派人传话说, 他要晚来。| **spread/pass the word** (=tell other people the news) 传播消息

④ **ORDER/DECISION 命令/决定**

12 the last/final word a) the power to decide whether or how to do something〔做不做或如何做某事的〕最后决定权: *The final word rests with the board.* 最后决定取决于董事会。| **have the last/final word** *My boss has the final word on hiring staff.* 雇用员工问题, 我的老板说了算。**b)** the last statement or speech in a discussion or argument〔讨论、争论中〕最后的话: **have the last/final word** *Why must you always have the last word in any argument?* 为何什么争论最后都由你说了算?

13 [C usually singular 一般用单数] an order to do something〔做某事的〕命令: *On the word 'go' I want you to start running.* 一听到"起步", 我希望你马上起跑。| **give the word** *Captain Rix gave the word and we moved forward.* 里克斯船长发出命令, 我们向前航行。

⑤ **PROMISE 诺言**

14 my/sb's word a sincere promise 我的/某人的诺言: **give sb your word** (=promise someone very sincerely that you will do something)〔真诚地〕对某人保证〔会做某事〕| **keep your word** *Gail kept her word and returned all the money.* 盖尔履行了她的诺言, 把钱如数归还。| **be as good as your word** (=do exactly what you have promised to do) 按承诺行事, 践诺 | **a man of his word/woman of her word** (=a man or woman who does what they have promised to do) 一诺千金的人

15 take sb at their word to choose to believe what someone has said even though it is possible they do not mean it 相信某人的话〔尽管它不一定是真话〕: *Geoff said we could call him any time, so let's take him at his word.* 杰夫说我们随时可以找他, 所以我们姑且相信他吧。

16 take my word for it *spoken* used to say that someone should accept what you say as true【口】相信我的话〔用于告诉某人应该信任你〕: *The business is doing very well. You can take my word for it.* 买卖进展顺利。你可以相信我的话。

⑥ **OTHER MEANINGS 其他意思**

17 in other words used to introduce a simpler explanation or version of something you have said 换句话说, 也就是说〔用于较简单地解释刚才说的话〕: *In other words, the objective is to avoid losing.* 也就是说, 目的是要避免失败。| *The woman has stopped going through her monthly cycle, in other words she is pregnant.* 这位女士已经不来月经, 换句话说, 她怀孕了。

18 in a word used to introduce a very simple answer or explanation 总之; 一句话; 简言之〔用于引出十分简单的答案或解释〕: *"Did you enjoy the film?" "In a word – no."* "你喜欢这部电影吗?" "一句话, 不喜欢。"

19 in as many words/not in so many words in a clear direct way or not in a clear direct way 明确地/不直截了当地: *"Did Kathy say she liked him?" "Not in so many words."* "凯茜说过喜欢他吗?" "没有直说过。" | *Aunt Fay was angry and said so in as many words.* 费伊姑妈很气愤, 并且明确地这样说。

20 word for word a) in exactly the same words 逐字逐句: *The newspaper printed his speech more or less word for word.* 报纸几乎逐字逐句刊登了他的讲话。**b)** also 又作 **word by word** if you translate a piece of writing from a foreign language word for word, you translate the meaning of each single word rather than the meaning of a whole phrase or sentence 逐字〔翻译〕, 一字对一字〔地翻译〕

21 take the words (right) out of sb's mouth *spoken* if someone takes the words out of your mouth, they have just said what you were going to say【口】先说出某人想说的话

22 put words into sb's mouth *spoken* to suggest falsely that someone has said a particular thing【口】硬说某人说过某话〔事实上并没说过〕: *Will you stop putting words into my mouth – I never said I disliked the job.* 你不要信口开河, 我从未说过不喜欢这工作。

23 too silly/ridiculous/stupid etc for words *spoken* very silly, ridiculous etc【口】傻/荒谬/笨得难以言传

24 put in a (good) word for sb to praise someone or suggest them for a particular job 为某人说好话〔称赞某人或推荐他做某工作〕: *Can you put in a good word for me with the Marketing Manager?* 你能替我跟市场经理美言几句吗?

25 words fail me *spoken* used to say that you are so surprised, angry, or shocked that you do not know what to say【口】〔因惊讶、生气或震惊〕说不出话来; 不知说什么好: *I... words fail me.* 我…我不知说什么好。

26 (Upon) my word! *old-fashioned spoken* used to say you are very surprised because something unusual has happened【过时, 口】哎呀!〔表示吃惊, 因发生不寻常的事〕

27 tired/angry/pleased isn't the word for it *spoken* used to say you are extremely tired or angry etc【口】疲劳/生气/高兴得难以言表

28 the last word in comfort/luxury/elegance etc the most comfortable or luxurious etc thing of its type〔在同类型中〕最舒适/最奢华/最雅致等: *a kitchen that is the last word in luxury* 最奢华的厨房

29 by word of mouth if information or news comes to you by word of mouth, someone tells you instead of you reading about it or seeing an advertisement〔消息或新闻〕口传的; 口头的

30 never have a good word to say for sb *spoken* if you never have a good word to say for someone, you never praise them even if they do something well【口】从不说某人好话〔尽管他做得好〕

31 get a word in edgeways also 又作 **edgewise** *AmE*【美】*informal* to get a chance to speak【非正式】找到说话的机会, 插嘴: *Once Terry starts talking it's difficult to get a word in edgeways.* 特里一说起话来, 别人很难插嘴。

32 the Word (of God) the religious teachings in the Bible〔基督教〕《圣经》的教义

33 from the word go *spoken* from the beginning【口】从一开始: *Lena was against me from the word go.* 莉娜从一开始就跟我作对。—see also 另见 **eat your words** (EAT (8)), FOUR-LETTER WORD, **mark my words** (MARK[1] (9)), **not mince your words** (MINCE[1] (3)), **play on words** (PLAY[2] (8)), **say the word** (SAY[1] (28))

word² *v* [T] to use words that are carefully chosen in order to express something 用言语表达: *The final version was worded in general terms.* 最终版本采用概括的词语表达。

word blind·ness /ˈ· ˌ··/ *n* [U] DYSLEXIA 阅读困难症

word·ed /ˈwɝdɪd; ˈwɜːdɪ̈d/ *adj* **carefully/clearly strongly etc worded** using words that express an idea carefully or clearly 措辞严谨/清晰/激烈等: *a carefully worded question* 一个措辞严谨的问题

word·ing /ˈwɝdɪŋ; ˈwɜːdɪŋ/ *n* [U] the words and phrases used to express something 用词; 措辞: *the exact wording of the contract* 合同里的确切字眼

word·less /ˈwɝdlɪs; ˈwɜːdləs/ *adj* without words; silent 无话的; 默默无言的: *a wordless prayer* 默祷

Word·per·fect /ˌ· ˈ· ·/ *trademark* a popular type of computer SOFTWARE used for word PROCESSing, produced by the Canadian Corel company【商标】Wordperfect 软件, 完美文字处理软件〔一款流行的计算机文字处理软件, 由加拿大考尔勒公司制作〕

word-per·fect /ˌ· ˈ· ·/ *adj BrE* able to remember and say every word of something correctly【英】背得一字不错的: *She rehearsed her speech until she was word-perfect.* 她反复练习, 直到把讲稿背得滚瓜烂熟。

word-play /ˈ· ·/ *n* [U] making jokes by using words in a clever way 文字游戏; 俏皮话; 双关语

word pro·cess·or /ˈ· ˌ··/ *n* [C] a small computer used especially for writing letters or storing information 文字处理机〔一种小型电脑〕—**word processing** *n* [U] —see picture on page A14 参见 A14 页图

Words·worth /ˈwɝdzwɝθ; ˈwɜːdzwəθ/, **William** (1770-1850) a British Romantic poet whose poems are mainly about the beauty of nature. They often describe the countryside in the Lake District in northwest England, where he went to live in

W

the village of Grasmere with his sister, **Dorothy Wordsworth** (1771-1855), who was also a writer. His best-known book of poetry is *Lyrical Ballads*, which was written with Samuel Taylor Coleridge, and his most famous poems include *Daffodils* and *The Prelude*. 华兹华斯〔(1770-1850)，英国浪漫派诗人。其诗作大多描写自然之美。他曾与同为作家的妹妹多萝西·华兹华斯(1771-1855)一起在湖区的格拉斯米尔村居住，因此诗中不乏对英格兰西北部湖区乡间景色的描绘。华兹华斯最出名的诗集是与塞缪尔·泰勒·柯尔律治合作的《抒情歌谣集》，著名的诗作有《水仙》和《序曲》等〕

word·y /ˈwɝdɪ; ˈwɜːdi/ *adj* using too many formal words 话太多的；冗长的：*a wordy explanation* 冗长累赘的解释 —**wordily** *adv* —**wordiness***n* [U]

wore /wɔr; wɔː/ the past tense of WEAR[1]

work[1] /wɝk; wɜːk/ *v*

① DO A JOB 做工作
② USE YOUR TIME AND ENERGY TO DO STH 花时间及精力做某事
③ MATERIAL/SUBSTANCE 材料/物质
④ MACHINE 机器
⑤ PRODUCE RESULTS/BE SUCCESSFUL 产生结果/成功
⑥ MOVE 活动
⑦ OTHER MEANINGS 其他意思

① DO A JOB 做工作

1 [I] to do a job that you are paid for 做工作，劳动：*Harry is 78, and still working.* 哈里78岁了，仍在工作。| [**+for**] *David works for the BBC.* 戴维为英国广播公司工作。| **work as a secretary/builder etc** *She works as a management consultant for a design company.* 她为一家设计公司当管理顾问。| **work long hours/nights etc** *There's no way I'm working Sundays.* 星期天我决不会上班。

2 [I,T] to do the activities and duties that are part of your job 工作；从事职业：*Sally isn't working tomorrow.* 萨莉明天不工作。| *I'm tired of working ten-hour days.* 我讨厌每天工作10个小时。

3 ►HELP 帮助◄[**I +with**] if you work with someone or a group of people, your job involves trying to help them 与〔某人或群体〕一起工作〔职责包括帮助他们〕：*Jane works with deaf children.* 简帮助失聪儿童。

4 ►AREA 地区◄[T] to travel around a particular area as part of your job, especially in order to sell something 在〔某地区〕从事活动〔尤指兜售货品〕：*Markowitz works the Tri-State area.* 马科维茨在三州交界地区工作。

② USE YOUR TIME AND ENERGY TO DO STH 花时间及精力做某事

5 [I] to do an activity which needs time and effort, especially one that you want to do or that needs to be done 做事；劳动〔尤指你想做或需要做的事〕：*Dad's been working all day in the garden.* 爸爸一整天都在花园里做事。| *We had to work non-stop to get everything ready for the party.* 为使聚会一切准备就绪，我们不得不马不停蹄地工作。| [**+on**] *Whenever I get the time we go out to the camp and work on it.* 只要我有时间，我们就去营房工作。| [**+at**] *Juan's English isn't very good, but he works at it.* 胡安的英语不很好，但他很用功学习。

6 ►STUDY 学习◄[I] *BrE* to study a subject by reading books, doing exercises etc, especially in order to pass an exam【英】〔尤为通过考试而〕学习；做作业：*You'll have to work really hard if you want to pass your exams.* 你如果想通过考试，就必须非常刻苦地学习。

7 work sb hard [T] to make someone use a lot of time or effort when doing a job or activity 使某人努力工作[做某活动]：*The coach has been working us really hard this week.* 教练这星期使我们训练得很辛苦。

8 [I] to try continuously and patiently to achieve a particular thing〔持久坚定地〕努力：[**+for**] *a life spent working for peace and justice* 为和平与正义而奉献的一生 | **work to do sth** *We worked hard to persuade the French to attend the meeting.* 我们竭力说服法国参加会议。| **work tirelessly** (=work hard) 孜孜不倦地工作 *an organization that works tirelessly on behalf of the poor* 为穷人孜孜不倦工作的组织 | **work your passage** (=to work instead of paying for a journey) 打工以支付船费

③ MATERIAL/SUBSTANCE 材料/物质

9 [T] if you work a material such as metal, leather, or clay you cut, SEW, or shape it in order to make something 把〔金属、皮革、黏土等〕加工成〔某物〕；切割；缝合；制成…

10 [I] to use a particular material or substance in order to make something such as a picture, design, jewellery etc〔用特定材料、物质〕制作〔画、设计、珠宝饰物等〕：[**+in/with**] *a sculptor who works in steel* 用钢创作的雕刻家 | *a jeweller who works with silver* 打制银器的宝石匠

11 ►LAND/SOIL 田地/土壤◄[T] if you work the land or the soil, you do all the work necessary to grow crops on it 耕种

12 ►MINE 矿◄[T] if you work a mine you remove a substance such as coal, gold, or oil from it 开采〔煤、金、石油等〕

④ MACHINE 机器

13 a) [I] if a machine or piece of equipment works, it does what it is supposed to do 运转；活动：*The remote control doesn't work.* 遥控器失灵。| *Damn! The TV's not working again.* 该死！这台电视又坏了。**b)** [T] to make a complicated machine or piece of equipment do what it is supposed to do 操作〔复杂的机器〕；使用：*Does anyone know how to work the microwave?* 有谁知道如何使用微波炉？

⑤ PRODUCE RESULTS/BE SUCCESSFUL 产生结果/成功

14 [I] if a method, plan, or system works, it produces the results you want〔方法、计划或体制〕产生〔预想的〕效果：*What do you think of Jill's suggestion? Will it work?* 你觉得吉尔的建议怎么样？可行吗？| *The recipe works just as well if you use margarine instead of butter.* 食谱中用人造黄油代替天然黄油，效果一样。| *I told Mum I was too sick to go to school, but it didn't work.* 我对妈妈说我病得不能上学，但却不管用。

15 work like magic/like a charm if a plan, method, or trick works like magic or like a charm, it happens in exactly the way you planned it to happen〔计划、方法或把戏〕非常灵验/非常有效

16 ►ART/LITERATURE 艺术/文学◄if a painting, film, piece of writing etc works, it is successful artistically because it has the effect on you that its maker intended〔绘画、电影、作品等〕奏效：*I don't think the scene where the family is seated around the table really works, do you?* 我觉得全家围坐在桌子旁的场面不会真的产生效果，你说呢？

17 ►MEDICINE/TREATMENT 药物/治疗◄[I] if a medicine or medical treatment works, it has the physical effect you want it to have 起作用；有效：*The antibiotics will only work if you take them every day for ten days.* 这种抗生素只有连服10天才会产生疗效。

18 ►HAVE AN EFFECT 有效果◄[I always+adv/prep] if something such as a fact, situation, or system works in particular way, it has a particular effect on someone or something〔事实、情况或系统等对某人或事〕有特效：**work in sb's favour** (=help someone) 帮助某人；对某人有利 *The fact that you went to the same school should work in your favour.* 你上同一所学校，这个事实应该对你有利。| **work against sb** (=harm someone or cause them problems) 对某人不利 *Tax laws tend to work against small organizations.* 税法往往不利于小机构。

⑥ MOVE 活动

19 [I always+adv/prep,T always+adv/prep] to move into a particular state or position very gradually, either in a series of small movements or after a long time〔通过一连串小动作或长时间而〕逐步达到〔某情况或位置〕：*Slowly he worked the screwdriver into the crack.* 他慢慢地把螺丝刀插进缝隙。| **work (its way)**

loose *One of the screws must have worked loose.* 其中一颗螺丝肯定已经松了。

20 [I,T] if a part of your body works or you work it, it moves (使)〔身体某部分〕活动起来: **work sth** *He tried to work his face into a smile.* 他尽力装出笑脸。

21 **work your way** if you work your way somewhere, you go there slowly and with great effort 缓慢而费力地到达某处: *Although exhausted, he managed to work his way up the last few feet of rock.* 虽然疲惫不堪, 他还是努力爬上最后几英尺的山岩。

⑦ **OTHER MEANINGS** 其他意思

22 ▶**MIND/BRAIN** 智力/头脑◀ [I] if your mind or brain is working, you are thinking or trying to solve a problem 思考; 〔用头脑或智力〕解决〔问题〕

23 **work yourself into a state/rage/frenzy etc** to make yourself become very excited, upset or angry 使自己非常激动/愤怒/发狂等: *You could tell he was working himself into a panic about it.* 可见他正在为此惊惶失措。

24 **work wonders** to be surprisingly effective in dealing with a difficult problem or situation 〔处理困难或困境〕创奇迹; 取得惊人效果: *Try rubbing salt on it. It can work wonders with stains.* 试着在污垢上用盐搓, 这种方法十分有效。

25 **work it/things** *spoken* to make arrangements for something to happen, especially by acting in a clever or skilful way【口】〔尤指巧妙地安排〕使某事发生: *We should try and work it so that we can all go together.* 我们应该设法作出安排, 让大家都可以一起去。

26 **work your fingers to the bone** *informal* to work very hard【非正式】拼命干活; 努力工作

27 ▶**BEER/WINE** 啤酒/葡萄酒◀ [I] *technical* to FERMENT[1]【术语】发酵

28 ▶**CALCULATE** 计算◀ [T] *AmE formal* to calculate the answer to a mathematical problem【美, 正式】计算〔数学问题的答案〕; 算出

29 **work to rule** *BrE* to protest about a situation at work by doing your job slowly with the excuse that you must obey all the rules exactly【英】故意死抠规章而少干活; 按章工作

work sth ↔ **in** *phr v* [T] **1** to add one substance to another and mix them together in a very thorough way 〔在一种物质中加进另一种后〕掺和, 混合: **work sth into sth** *Work the butter into the flour with your fingers.* 用手指把黄油掺到面粉里。**2** to include something you want to say or do while you are doing or saying something else 〔说某话、做某事时〕插入〔某事〕: *Do you think you can work in a reference to our project?* 你觉得能顺带提一下我们的计划吗? | **work sth into sth** *The minister will try and work a visit to hospital into his schedule.* 部长会设法在他的日程安排中加进参观医院一项。

work sth ↔ **off** *phr v* [T] to try to get rid of a feeling such as anger, disappointment, or embarrassment, especially by being unpleasant to other people or behaving violently 〔尤指通过无礼地对待他人或行为粗暴来〕发泄〔怒气、沮丧、窘迫之情〕: *I'm sorry about all the yelling, it was Terry trying to work off his frustration.* 我为喊叫声表示歉意, 那是特里在发泄他的不满。

work on *phr v* [T] **1** [**work on** sth] to spend time making or fixing something 致力于: *Ken was working on some sets for an opera at the Met.* 肯正忙于为在大都会歌剧院演出的一部歌剧制作几台布景。| *I worked all night on that article.* 我通宵在写那篇文章。**2** to try continuously to influence someone or persuade them to do something 努力影响[说服]〔某人做某事〕: **work on sb to do sth** *My parents spent the weekend working on me to go on holiday with them.* 爸妈用了一个周末来说服我和他们一起度假去。

work out *phr v*

1 ▶**CALCULATE** 计算◀ [T **work** sth ↔ **out**] to calculate an answer, amount, price, or value 计算出〔答案、数量、价格、价值〕: *You can work out the answer by adding all the numbers.* 你把所有数加在一起就能算出答案了。| *See if you can work this bill out.* 看看你能不能把这份账单算出来。| **work out how much/how many etc** *We'll have to work out how much food we'll need for the party.* 我们必须算出这次聚会需要多少食物。

2 ▶**UNDERSTAND** 理解◀ *especially BrE*【尤英】[T **work** sth ↔ **out**] to think about something and manage to understand it 设法弄懂: *The plot is very complicated, it'll take you a while to work it out.* 情节极其复杂, 你要花一些时间才能弄明白。| **work sth out for yourself** *I'm not telling you the answer – work it out for yourself.* 我不告诉你答案, 你自己去弄明白。

3 [I, linking verb 连系动词+adj] if something works out at a particular amount, you calculate that it costs that amount 总计为〔某一费用〕: **work out at/to £10/$500 etc** *The bill works out at £15 each.* 账单算下来是每人 15 英镑。| **work out expensive/costly/cheap etc** (=be expensive or cheap) 算下来贵/费钱/便宜等 *If we go by taxi, it's going to work out very expensive.* 要是我们坐出租车去, 就要花不少钱。

4 ▶**PLAN** 计划◀ [T **work** sth ↔ **out**] to think carefully about how you are going to do something and plan a good way of doing it 精心制订出: *UN negotiators have worked out a set of compromise proposal.* 联合国谈判人员制订出一套折中方案。| **work out what/ where/how etc** *I haven't worked out who's going to look after the kids tonight.* 我还没有计划好让谁今晚去照料小孩。| **have it all worked out** (=have completely planned how you are going to do something) 计划周全 *Listen, I've got it all worked out. Here's what we should do.* 听着, 我已经计划好了。我们应该这么办。

5 ▶**GET BETTER** 好起来◀ [I,T] if a problem or complicated situation works out, it gradually gets better or gets solved 〔问题〕逐渐解决; 〔复杂情况〕逐渐化解: *Ken and Ella had loads of problems when they first got married, but things worked out in the end.* 肯和埃拉最初结婚时遇到大量问题, 但最终好了起来。| *I hope it all works out between Gina and Andy.* 我希望吉娜和安迪之间一切问题均会得到解决。| **work itself out** *I know you're not happy with things right now, but I'm sure everything will work itself out.* 我知道你现在诸事不如意, 但我相信一切问题都会自行解决。

6 ▶**HAPPEN** 发生◀ if a situation works out in a particular way, it happens in that way 按某种方式发生: **work out well/badly** *Financially, things have worked out very well for us.* 我们的经济情况很好。

7 **I can't work sb out** *spoken* an expression meaning you cannot understand someone's behaviour【口】我弄不懂某人〔指不理解某人的行为〕: *I can't work Geoff out, one day he's friendly the next day he ignores me completely.* 我对杰夫真是搞不明白, 他忽而对我友好, 忽而对我视同路人。

8 ▶**EXERCISE** 锻炼◀ [I] to make your body fit and strong, especially by doing a programme of exercises regularly 〔尤指定期〕锻炼; 健身: *He works out with weights twice a week.* 他每星期两天练举重健身。

9 **be worked out** if a mine is worked out, all the coal, gold etc has been removed from it 〔煤矿等〕采掘完

work sb **over** *phr v* [T] *informal* to hit someone hard and repeatedly all over their body【非正式】殴打; 狠狠地揍〔某人〕

work sb/sth ↔ **up** *phr v* **1** **work up enthusiasm/interest/courage etc** to become enthusiastic or interested etc 产生热情/兴趣/勇气等: *I'm trying to work up enough courage to go to the dentist.* 我努力鼓起勇气去看牙医。**2** **work up an appetite/thirst** to make yourself hungry or THIRSTY, especially by doing physical exercise or waiting a long time before you eat or drink 〔尤指做运动或长时间没饮食〕激起食欲/渴感: *You can work up a really big thirst playing tennis.* 打网球会令你十分口渴。**3** to make someone very angry, excited, or upset about something 使某人〔为某事〕感到气愤[激动; 不安]: **work yourself up** *Paula has worked herself up into a complete state about the exam.* 葆拉将自己调整到最佳状态去迎接考试。**4** to develop and improve a skill or a piece of writing 逐步培养〔技能〕; 逐步完善〔文章、作品〕: *Jack took notes which he would work up into a report later.* 杰克记下笔记, 稍后将整理成一份报告。

work up to sth *phr v* [T] to prepare yourself to do something that you do not want to do by gradually making yourself more and more determined to do it 逐渐下决心〔去做不想做的事〕: *I haven't told Carmela I don't want to go, I'm still working up to it.* 我还没有告诉卡梅拉我不想去, 我还在做心理准备。

S1 W1 **work²** *n*

1 [U] a job you are paid to do or an activity that you do regularly to earn money 工作; 职业: *My father started work when he was 14.* 我父亲 14 岁就开始工作了。| *The work is interesting and well paid.* 工作有趣, 报酬优厚。| *There isn't a lot of work at this time of the year.* 每年这个时候工作机会不多。| **be in work/out of work** (=have or not have a job) 有/没有工作 | **look for work/find work** *Anne left college a year ago and she's still looking for work.* 安妮一年前大学毕业, 但她仍在找工作。| *He eventually found work on a construction site.* 他最终找到了一份在建筑工地的工作。| **return to work** (=start work again after a long period of time) 〔经过长时间后〕重新工作 *Dawn didn't return to work until the kids had started school.* 直到孩子们开始上学, 唐才重新出去工作。| **after/before work** (=after

or before you start work each day) 每天工作之后/工作之前 | **sb's line of work** (=the kind of work someone does) 某人从事的行业 *In my line of work we use a lot of heavy equipment – back-hoes, things like that.* 在我从事的行当中，我们使用大量重型设备——反铲挖土机和诸如此类的机械。—see 见 JOB (USAGE)

2 ▶PLACE 地点◀ [U] a place where you do your job, which is not your home 工作地点; 办公室: *He left work at the usual time.* 他按平常时间下班。| *I'll see you at work tomorrow.* 明天上班见。| **be at work** (=be working at your job at a place which is not your home) 在工作的地方，在工作 *My Dad's at work.* 我爸爸上班去了。

3 ▶DUTIES 责任◀ [U] the duties and activities that are part of your job 差事; 职务: *What kind of work are you looking for?* 你要找什么样的工作? | *A large part of the work we do involves using computers.* 我们一大部分工作要使用电脑。| **secretarial/legal/bar etc work** *I've been working in the field for 6 years, and would like a chance at some museum work.* 我从事野外考察六年，我希望有机会去博物馆工作。| **voluntary work** (=work that you do not get paid for) 义务工作

4 ▶RESULT 成果◀ [U] something that you produce as a result of doing your job or doing an activity 工作成果; 产品: *Send a résumé and example of your work.* 请寄一份履历及你所做的样品。| **piece of work** *This report really is an excellent piece of work.* 这份报告真是一篇杰作。

5 ▶USEFUL ACTIVITY 有用的活动◀ [U] the act of doing something that needs to be done or that you want to do, or the time and effort needed to do it 做〔需要做; 希望做〕的事; 做事花的时间和力量: *Ted's done a lot of work on the car.* 特德在这辆汽车上花了很多功夫。| *The house must have taken a lot of work.* 在这房子上一定花了很多功夫。| *Come on – hard work never hurt anyone.* 加油，吃苦没坏处。| **get down to work** (=start doing work) 着手干，开始干 *We decided to watch TV for a while before getting down to work.* 着手工作前我们决定先看一会儿电视。

6 ▶STUDY 学习◀ [U] study or RESEARCH, especially for a particular purpose 〔尤指为某一目的进行的〕学习，研究: *He did his postgraduate work in Sociology.* 他研究生时学的是社会学。| *Limited work was carried out on subjects between the ages of 16 and 20.* 对16至20岁的对象所做的研究有限。

7 at work a) doing your job or a particular activity 在工作，在干活: *Danger – men at work.* 危险! 正在施工。**b)** having a particular influence or effect 有特别影响; 起特殊作用: *Listen to her voice, you can hear her operatic training at work.* 留意她的嗓音，你就能听出她的歌剧训练在起作用。

8 ▶BOOK/PAINTING/MUSIC 书/画/音乐◀ [C] something such as a book, play, painting, or piece of music produced by a writer, painter, or musician 著作; 〔艺术〕作品: *the Collected Works of Shakespeare* 莎士比亚全集 | *Thirty-five Old Master works will be on loan from the Met.* 35幅古典名画家的作品将从大都会艺术博物馆借来展出。

9 the (whole) works *spoken* everything 【口】所有的东西，全部: *"What would you like – eggs, bacon, sausages, fries?" "The works."* "你喜欢吃什么? 有鸡蛋、咸猪肉、香肠、炸马铃薯条。" "我全都要。"

10 nice work/quick work *spoken* used to praise someone for doing something well or quickly 【口】干得好/干得快〔用于称赞某人〕: *The last image flickered on the screen and I turned to Herb and said 'Nice work!'* 最后一个画面在屏幕上晃动的时候，我回过头去对赫布说: "干得好!"

11 works a) *old-fashioned* a building or group of buildings in which goods are produced in large quantities or an industrial process happens 【过时】工厂: **ironworks/gasworks/cement works** *The brick works closed last year.* 这家砖厂去年关闭了。**b)** the activity involved in building something on a large scale 〔大规模的建筑〕工程: **engineering works/irrigation works/roadworks** *the official in charge of the engineering works* 负责工程的官员

12 it's all in a day's work *spoken* used to say that you do not mind doing something even though it will give you more work than usual 【口】这是习以为常[家常便饭]〔用于表示不介意做某事，虽然这样会增加工作〕

13 sb will have his/her work cut out *informal* it will be very difficult for someone to do something 【非正式】某人会面临艰巨的任务: *Dad and Sam will have their work cut out for them trying to calm her down.* 爸爸和萨姆要让她安静下来，并不是容易的事。

14 the works the moving parts of a machine 〔机器的〕活动机件; 运转机构

15 [U] *technical* force multiplied by distance 【术语】功〔力乘以距离〕—see also 另见 CLERK OF WORKS, **do sb's dirty work** (DIRTY[1] (7)), **make short work of** (SHORT[1] (8)), PUBLIC WORKS

wor·ka·ble /ˈwɝkəbl; ˈwɜːkəbəl/ *adj* **1** a workable system, idea etc can be used in a practical and efficient way 〔系统、思想等〕可行的: *a workable timetable* 可行的时间表 **2** a substance that is workable can be shaped with your hands 〔物质〕可〔用手〕成形的; 可塑的: *workable clay for making pots* 制作盆罐的可塑黏土

work·a·day /ˈwɝkəˌde; ˈwɜːkədeɪ/ *adj* [only before noun 仅用于名词前] ordinary and not interesting 平凡的; 乏味的: *The views from the plateau are in stark contrast to the workaday cottages below.* 从高原极目眺望的景色与坡下面平淡无奇的村舍形成了鲜明的对比。

work·a·hol·ic /ˌwɝkəˈhɔlɪk; ˌwɜːkəˈhɒlɪk/ *n* [C] *informal* someone who cannot stop working, and does not have time for anything else 【非正式】醉心于工作的人，工作狂

work·bas·ket /ˈwɝkˌbæskɪt; ˈwɜːkˌbɑːskɪt/ *n* [C] a container for SEWING equipment 针线篮[筐]

work·bench /ˈwɝkˌbɛntʃ; ˈwɜːkbentʃ/ *n* [C] a strong table with a hard surface for working on with tools 工作台

work·book /ˈwɝkˌbʊk; ˈwɜːkbʊk/ *n* [C] a school book containing questions and exercises 〔包含问题与练习的〕作业本; 练习本

work·day /ˈwɝkˌde; ˈwɜːkdeɪ/ *n* the amount of time that you spend working in a day 工作日〔一天的工作时数〕: *a 10 hour workday* 10小时工作日

> **CULTURAL NOTE 文化注释**
>
> In Britain and the US, most people start work at about 9 o'clock and finish at about 5 o'clock. 在英国和美国，大多数人上午9点左右开始工作，下午5点左右下班。

worked up /ˌ·ˈ·/ *adj* [not before noun 不用于名词前] *informal* very upset or excited about something 【非正式】〔对某事〕非常不安的，激动的: [+about] *Don't get worked up about it! It was only a suggestion.* 别为此事激动! 这只是个建议。—see also 另见 **work up** (WORK[1])

work·er /ˈwɝkɚ; ˈwɜːkə/ *n* [C] **1** one of the people who work for an organization, business etc and are below the level of a manager 〔级别比管理人员低的〕工人，雇员: **factory/farm/office etc worker** *new health and safety regulations for factory workers* 关于工厂工人健康和安全的新条例 | **skilled/unskilled worker** (=someone who has or does not have special skills) 技术熟练的工人/非熟练工人 | **manual worker** (=someone who does physical work) 体力劳动者 **2 research/rescue etc worker** someone who works to achieve a particular purpose 研究/救援等人员: *Rescue workers worked all night to free the victims.* 救援人员整夜都在解救灾民。**3** someone who works very well or quickly 干练[勤快]的人: *Mavis is a real worker – she gets twice as much done as everyone else.* 梅维丝是个能干的人，她做的工作总是比别人多一倍。| **good/hard/quick etc worker** *Mike's always been a hard worker.* 迈克一直是个努力工作的人。**4 the workers** the members of the WORKING CLASS 工人阶级的成员: *the workers' revolution* 工人阶级革命 —see also 另见 SOCIAL WORKER

Workers' Ed·u·ca·tion·al As·so·ci·a·tion /ˌ·· ·····, ·····/ the full name of the WEA 〔英国〕工人教育协会〔WEA的全称〕

work eth·ic /ˈ· ˌ··/ *n* [singular, U] a belief in the moral value of work 职业道德: *the Protestant work ethic* 新教徒的职业道德

work ex·pe·ri·ence /ˈ· ·ˌ···/ *n* **1** the experience you have had of working in a particular type of job 〔某类工作的〕工作经验: *She's well qualified but has no relevant work experience.* 她资格完全够，但没有相关的工作经验。**2** *BrE* a period of time that a young person spends working in a particular place, as a form of training 【英】实习〔年轻人在某地工作一段时间作为培训的一部分〕

work·fare /ˈwɝkfɛr; ˈwɜːkfeə/ *n* [U] a system that requires unemployed people to work before they are given money for food, rent etc by the government 工作福利制〔要求失业者先从事某种工作，然后才能领取政府提供的救济金的制度〕

work·force /ˈwɝkˌfɔrs; ˈwɜːkfɔːs/ *n* [singular] all the people who work in a particular country, industry, or factory 〔国家、行业或工厂的〕全体从业人员，劳动力: *a workforce of 3,500 employees* 3500名雇员

work·horse /ˈwɝkˌhɔrs; ˈwɜːkhɔːs/ *n* [C] **1** someone who does most of the work, especially when it is hard or boring 吃苦耐劳的人 **2** a machine or vehicle that can be used to do a lot of work 重负荷机器[运输工具]: *a software program that is rapidly be-*

coming the architect's workhorse 很快成为建筑师挑大梁的软件程序

work·house /ˈwɝkˌhaʊs; ˈwɜːkhaʊs/ *n* [C] a building in Britain in the past where poor people lived〔英国昔日的〕济贫院，救贫院

CULTURAL NOTE 文化注释

Conditions in workhouses were very bad and people were very afraid of having to go there. People now think of workhouses in connection with the Victorians and with writers such as Charles Dickens who described what they were like in order to try and improve the situation of poor people. 救贫院的条件很差，人们对不得不去那里凑合生活感到害怕。现在人们由救贫院联想到维多利亚时代和查尔斯·狄更斯等作家，他们描写济贫院的目的是试图改善穷人的处境。

S1 W1 **work·ing**[1] /ˈwɝkɪŋ; ˈwɜːkɪŋ/ *adj* [only before noun 仅用于名词前]

1 ▶HAVING A JOB 有工作◀ **a)** having a job that you are paid for 有工作的；有职业的: *a working mother* 在职母亲 **b)** having a job that requires physical rather than intellectual skill 从事体力劳动的: *an ordinary working man* 普通工人

2 ▶CLOTHES 服装◀ working clothes are designed for people to work in rather than to look attractive 穿来工作的；工作上用的

3 ▶CONDITIONS/PRACTICES 环境/常规◀ working conditions or practices are the ones you have in your job 工作的〔环境或常规〕: *recent improvements in working conditions* 工作环境近来的改善

4 ▶HOURS 小时◀ your working hours are the period of time during the day when you are doing your job 上班时间的；工作时间的

5 **have a working knowledge of** to have enough knowledge of a system, foreign language etc to be able to use it, although your knowledge is limited〔对某系统、外语等〕知识足够的: *Gita has a working knowledge of Spanish and French.* 吉塔的西班牙语和法语还过得去。

6 ▶RELATIONSHIP 关系◀ a working relationship is the kind of relationship that two people have who work well together〔两人〕工作关系良好的: *The working relationship between Hodges and Bradley began to deteriorate.* 霍奇斯与布拉德利的工作关系开始恶化。

7 ▶MODEL 模型◀ a working model is one that has parts that move〔模型〕部件能活动的

8 ▶PARTS OF A MACHINE 机器部件◀ the working parts of a machine are the parts that move and operate the machine〔机器部件〕能运转的；用于操作的

9 **be in working order** to be working properly and not broken 正常地运转: **be in good/perfect working order** *The car was old, but the engine was still in good working order.* 汽车虽旧，但发动机仍能良好地运转。—see graph at 参见 ORDER[1] 图表

10 ▶THEORY/DEFINITION 理论/释义◀ a working theory or definition is not complete in every detail, but is good enough for you to use as a basis for studying something or doing a job〔研究某事或做事时〕可作为基础的

11 **working breakfast/lunch/dinner** a breakfast, lunch etc which is also a business meeting 工作早餐/午餐/晚餐

working[2] *n* 1 [singular] also 又作 **workings** the way something such as a system, piece of equipment, or organization works〔系统、设备、组织等的〕工作方式；运行方式: [+of] *the inside workings of the Reagan presidency* 里根担任总统期间政府内的工作方式 | *I shall never understand the workings of his mind.* 我永远搞不懂他在想什么。2 [C usually plural 一般用复数] a mine or part of a mine where soil has been dug out in order to remove metals or stone 矿坑；(矿内)工作区: *the workings of a long-disused quarry* 废弃已久的采石场的工作区

working cap·i·tal /ˌ‥ˈ‥‥/ *n* [U] the money that is available to be used for the costs of a business 运营资金[资本] —see also 另见 VENTURE CAPITAL

working class /ˌ‥ˈ‥◂/ *n* [singular] *especially BrE* the group of people in society who traditionally do physical work and do not have much money or power【尤英】工人[劳工]阶级 —compare 比较 LOWER CLASS, MIDDLE CLASS, UPPER CLASS —**working class** *adj*

working day /ˌ‥ˈ◂/ *n* [C] 1 the amount of time that you spend working in a day 一天的工作时间 2 a day when you have to work 工作日

working girl /ˈ‥ ˌ/ *n* [C] *old-fashioned*【过时】1 a word for a woman who has sex for money, used when you want to avoid saying this directly 娼妓〔委婉语〕2 a young woman who has a paid job 年轻职业女性

working group /ˈ‥ ˌ/ *n* [C] a committee that is established to examine a particular situation or problem and suggest ways of dealing with it 专题调查委员会，特别工作组

working life /ˌ‥ˈ/ *n* [C] the part of your adult life when you work 工作生涯: *Geoff spent all his working life in the same company.* 杰夫在同一家公司干了一辈子。

working ma·jor·i·ty /ˌ‥ ‥ˈ‥‥/ *n* [singular] *BrE* enough support in parliament for a government to continue making laws and ruling a country【英】〔议会中支持政府的〕有效的多数

working or·der /ˈ‥ ˌ‥/ *n* [U] **in working order** a system, machine etc that is in working order is working well, with no problems〔系统、机器等〕良好的工作状态，正常的运转状态

working pa·pers /ˈ‥ ˌ‥/ *n* [plural] an official document that you need in the US in order to get a job if you are young or were born in a different country〔美国未成年或在外国出生的居民受雇时必须持有的〕工作许可证

working par·ty /ˈ‥ ˌ‥/ *n* [C] *BrE* a WORKING GROUP【英】专题调查委员会

working prac·tices /ˈ‥ ˌ‥‥/ *n* [plural] the way in which things are usually done in your job 工作常规: *The changes in working practices are designed to increase efficiency.* 改变工作常规是为了提高效率。

work·ings /ˈwɝkɪŋz; ˈwɜːkɪŋz/ *n* [plural] 1 the way in which something works〔某事的〕工作方式: *I shall never understand the workings of his mind.* 我永远搞不懂他在想什么。2 the parts of a mine that have been dug out 矿坑

working week /ˌ‥ˈ/ *n* [C] the days when you do your job, usually between Monday and Friday 工作周，一周的工作日〔通常指星期一至星期五〕

work·load /ˈwɝkˌlod; ˈwɜːkləʊd/ *n* [C] the amount of work that a person or machine is expected to do〔人或机器的〕工作量，工作负荷: *Paul has a heavy workload at the moment.* 保罗目前的工作量很大。

work·man /ˈwɝkmən; ˈwɜːkmən/ *n* [C] someone who does physical work such as building, repairing things etc〔建筑、维修等的〕工匠；工人

work·man·like /ˈwɝkmənˌlaɪk; ˈwɜːkmənlaɪk/ *adj* a workmanlike piece of work has been done well and looks good 能工巧匠的；精巧细致的

work·man·ship /ˈwɝkmənˌʃɪp; ˈwɜːkmənʃɪp/ *n* [U] *formal* skill in making things, especially in a way that makes them look good【正式】〔尤指精细的〕工艺，手艺

work·mate /ˈwɝkˌmet; ˈwɜːkmeɪt/ *n* [C] someone you work with 同事，一起工作的人

work of art /ˌ‥ˈ/ *n plural* **works of art** [C] 1 a painting, SCULPTURE etc of very high quality〔绘画、雕刻等的〕艺术精品 2 *often humorous* something that is very attractive and skilfully made【常幽默】精致的东西: *That cake's a real work of art!* 那蛋糕简直是件艺术品！

workout 锻炼

work·out /ˈwɝkˌaʊt; ˈwɜːkaʊt/ *n* [C] a period of physical exercise, especially as training for a sport〔尤指运动的〕锻炼，训练 —see also 另见 **work out** (WORK[1])

work per·mit /ˈ‥ ˌ‥/ *n* [C] an official document that you need if you want to work in a foreign country〔在外国工作时所需的〕工作许可证

work·place /ˈwɝkˌples; ˈwɜːkpleɪs/ *n* [C] the room, building etc where you work 工作场所

work·room /ˈwɝkˌrum; ˈwɜːkrʊm/ *n* [C] a room that you work in 工作间，作业室

W

work·sheet /ˈwɝkˌʃit; ˈwɜːkʃiːt/ *n* [C] a piece of paper with questions, exercises etc for students〔印有问题、练习等的〕学生作业纸, 活页练习题

work·shop /ˈwɝkˌʃɑp; ˈwɜːkʃɒp/ *n* [C] **1** a room or building where tools and machines are used for making or repairing things 车间, 工场 **2** a meeting at which people try to improve their skills by discussing their experiences and doing practical exercises〔目的在提高技巧的〕研讨会, 研习班

work-shy /ˈ· ·/ *adj* someone who is work-shy tries to avoid working because they do not like it 不愿劳动的, 怕工作的

work·sta·tion /ˈwɝkˌsteʃən; ˈwɜːkˌsteɪʃən/ *n* [C] the part of an office where you work, where your desk, computer etc are〔办公室中设有办公桌、电脑等的〕工作区; 操作岗位 —see picture on page A14 参见 A14 页图

work·sur·face /ˈ· ˌ· ·/ also 又作 **work·top** /ˈwɝktɑp; ˈwɜːktɒp/ *n* [C] *especially BrE* a flat surface for working on, especially in a kitchen【尤英】〔尤指厨房的〕工作台; 操作台; COUNTER[1] (4) *AmE*【美】—see picture on page A10 参见 A10 页图

work-to-rule /ˌ· · ˈ·/ *n* [singular] a situation in which people in a particular job refuse to do any additional work as a protest〔死抠规章制度, 拒绝做额外工作的〕怠工, 按章工作 —see also 另见 **work to rule** (WORK[1] (29))

work·week /ˈwɝkˌwik; ˈwɜːkwiːk/ *n* [C] *AmE* the total amount of time that you spend working during a week【美】工作周, 一周的工作时间: *a 40 hour workweek* 40 小时工作周

world[1] /wɝld; wɜːld/ *n*

1 ►OUR PLANET/EVERYONE ON IT 地球/全人类◄ the world the planet we live on, and all the people, cities, and countries on it; the Earth 世界; 地球: *the world's tallest building* 世界上最高的建筑 | *Tuberculosis is still common in some parts of the world.* (肺)结核病在世界上某些地区仍很普遍。| *At that time China was the most powerful country in the world.* 在那时中国是世界上最强大的国家。| *The Press Association flashed the news to the world.* 英国国家新闻通讯社把消息迅速发往全世界。| **all over the world** (=everywhere in the world) 世界各地 *Delegates from all over the world will be at the conference.* 世界各地的代表都将参加这次会议。

2 in the world used to emphasize a statement you are making 究竟; 到底〔用于加强语气〕: **the happiest/most exciting etc ... in the world** *If she asked me to marry her I'd be the happiest man in the world.* 她如果让我娶她, 我便是世上最幸福的人。| **not have a care in the world** (=not be worried at all about anything) 无忧无虑 | **nothing in the world** (=nothing at all) 没有什么 *Nothing in the world can save them now.* 现在什么也救不了他们。| **have all the time in the world** (=have a lot of time so that you do not have to hurry) 有的是时间 *Don't worry, we've got all the time in the world.* 别急, 我们有的是时间。| **What/Who/Where/How etc in the world...?** (=used after what or who etc to emphasize a question in order to show that you are very surprised, annoyed, or angry) 究竟是什么/是谁/在哪儿/怎么样等〔用于问句, 表示惊讶、烦恼或生气〕*What in the world are you doing here at seven in the morning?* 早上 7 点你究竟在这儿干什么?

3 the outside world the people who live outside a particular place, country etc; especially when the people living in that place or country cannot meet them or talk to them〔在某地方、国家等以外的〕外面世界: *a jungle tribe who have no contact with the outside world* 和外面的世界没有接触的一个丛林部落

4 ►THE SOCIETY WE LIVE IN 我们生活的社会◄ the society that we live in and the kind of life we have 社会; 生活: *The world is being transformed by information technology.* 信息科技正在改变社会。| *Parents want a better world for their children.* 父母想给孩子们更好的生活。—see 见 LAND[1] (USAGE)

5 ►GROUP OF COUNTRIES 国家集团◄ the Western World/the industrialized world/the developing world etc a particular group of countries 西方世界/工业化国家/发展中国家等: *The British are among the biggest sugar consumers in the developed world.* 在发达国家中, 英国是食糖消费最多的国家之一。—see also 另见 THIRD WORLD

6 ►PERIOD IN HISTORY 历史上的时期◄ the Roman world/the Medieval world etc a particular period in history and the society and people of that time 古罗马时代/中世纪等: *the artistic, literary, and intellectual culture of the Roman World* 古罗马时代的艺术、文学及知识文化

7 ►AREA OF ACTIVITY/WORK 活动/工作的领域◄ [C usually singular 一般用单数] a particular area of activity or work, and the people who are involved in it〔人们活动或工作的〕领域; 界: *the world of politics* 政界 | *an influential figure in the business world* 在商界有影响力的人物 | *The show-business world was out in force at the Oscar ceremony.* 奥斯卡颁奖典礼上娱乐界人士云集。

8 ►SB'S LIFE 某人的生活◄ [C] the life a particular person or group of people lives, especially the things they do and the people they know〔某人或一群人的〕生活〔尤指他们做的事和认识的人〕; 生活经历: *the world of children* 孩子的世界 | *Dean's world was filled with music and laughter.* 迪安的生活充满了音乐和笑声。

9 in a world of your own *informal* if someone lives in a world of their own, they do not seem to notice what is happening around them and are more concerned with their own thoughts【非正式】活在自己的世界里: *I can't get through to that girl – she seems to be in a world of her own.* 我无法使那女孩听懂, 她似乎活在自己的世界里。

10 ►KIND OF PLACE/SITUATION 某类地方/情况◄ a particular kind of place or situation, especially one that someone describes or which you imagine〔尤指某人描述或想象的〕地方; 情景: *the nightmare world of Orwell's novel 1984* 奥威尔小说《一九八四》中的梦魇世界 | *Italy's mountains and lakes are a stunning world of peace and tranquillity.* 意大利的山脉和湖泊是无比优美的宁静。

11 the animal/plant/insect world animals etc considered as a group of living things with their own particular way of living or behaving 动物/植物/昆虫(世)界

12 ►PLACE LIKE THE EARTH 天体◄ [C] a place like the Earth in another part of the universe where other things may live〔可能有生物的〕天体, 星球: *strange creatures from another world* 从另一个星球来的奇异生物

13 be out of this world *informal* something that is out of this world is so good, enjoyable etc, it is unlike anything else you have ever experienced【非正式】好得不得了: *Tracy's new apartment is just out of this world.* 特雷西的新公寓好得不得了。

14 do sb a world of good *informal* if something does someone a world of good, it makes them feel much better【非正式】〔某事〕对某人有好处: *Why don't you go for a walk, it'll do you a world of good.* 你为什么不去散步, 那会对你大有好处。

15 be/feel on top of the world *informal* to feel extremely happy【非正式】快活之极

16 be/mean all the world to to be more important to you than anyone or anything else〔某人或某物〕对…最重要, 最可宝贵: *I'd hate to lose her – she means all the world to me.* 我不愿失去她, 她就是我的一切。

17 think the world of sb to love and respect someone very much 非常喜欢某人; 对某人很尊重: *Lee thinks the world of you – you know that.* 李非常喜欢你, 你是知道的。

18 see the world to travel to many different countries so that you can get a lot of different experiences 到各国旅游丰富阅历

19 the world over in every country or area of the world; everywhere 全世界, 世界各地: *It's the same the world over.* 天下皆同。| *Her books have delighted adults and children the world over.* 她的书受到全世界大人和小孩的喜爱。

20 move up/go up in the world to move into a higher social class 升到更高的社会地位; 发迹: *He's gone up in the world now – he's far too posh to talk to me.* 他发迹了, 派头大得不屑跟我说话。

21 go down/come down in the world to move down to a lower social class 落魄, 潦倒

22 there's a world of difference between used when saying that two things or situations are completely different and people should not expect them to be the same〔两物或两种情况〕有天渊之别: *There's a world of difference between enjoying cooking and doing it for a living.* 喜欢烹饪与为生计而烹饪有天壤之别。

23 be worlds apart/be a world apart people, beliefs, or ideas that are worlds apart are so completely different that there is almost nothing about them that is similar〔人、信念或想法〕完全不同: *Their political views are just worlds apart.* 他们的政治观点截然不同。

24 for all the world as if/like *literary* exactly as if or exactly like【文】活像; 完全像: *She sat reading her paper, looking for all the world as if nothing had happened.* 她坐着看报, 就像什么事都没有发生过一样。

25 not for the world if someone would not do a particular thing for the world, they would never do it whatever happened 决不, 无论如何也不: *I wouldn't hurt her for the world.* 我决不伤害她。

26 be a man/woman of the world to be someone who has had many experiences and is not easily shocked 阅历丰富的人, 老于世故的人: *Victor is a man of the world – I'm sure he'll understand.* 维克托阅历丰富, 我敢肯定他懂。

27 set the world on fire/alight *spoken* an expression meaning to have a big effect or be very successful, often used when you think someone or something has failed to do this【口】惊人之举; 非常成功〔常用于否定〕: *His last film didn't exactly set the world on fire.* 他的最后一部电影全然没有引起轰动。

28 set/put the world to rights to discuss or say how the world should be changed to make people's lives better 畅谈如何改善世界, 指点江山: *We were having a few beers and generally putting the world to rights.* 我们一边喝着啤酒, 一边大谈如何改造世界。

29 the next world/the world to come *literary* the place where people's souls are believed to go after they die【文】阴间; 冥府

30 not be long for this world to not be going to live much longer 不久于人世, 行将谢世

31 this world *literary* the state of being alive【文】人生, 今世: **depart/leave this world** (=die) 去世, 离开人世

32 bring a child into the world *formal*【正式】**a)** if a woman brings a child into the world she gives birth to it 生小孩 **b)** if a doctor brings a child into the world he helps the mother give birth〔医生〕接生

33 come into the world *literary* to be born【文】降生, 出世

34 the Michael Jacksons/Paul Smiths etc of this world *spoken* used when making a general comment about a particular kind of person【口】迈克尔·杰克逊/保罗·史密斯等一类人〔用于对某一类人作一般评论时〕: *The Frank Clarkes of this world are only interested in furthering their own careers.* 弗兰克·克拉克这类人只顾成就自己的事业。

35 the world is your oyster used to tell someone that there is no limit to the opportunities that they have 你前途无量, 前程似锦: *"If you've got a good education, the world is your oyster," my father used to say.* 父亲常说: "只要你有良好的教育, 在这个世界你就大有可为。"

36 workers/women etc of the world used when addressing all workers, women etc in a speech, book etc 工友们/各位女性朋友等〔发言、书中等称呼〕

37 ►NOT RELIGIOUS 不是宗教的◄ the world the way of life most people live rather than a spiritual way of life 尘世, 世俗: *monks who renounce the world* 厌弃尘世的修道士们 —see also 另见 **best of both worlds** (BEST[3] (5)), **dead to the world** (DEAD[1] (9)), NEW WORLD, OLD WORLD

world[2] *adj* [only before noun 仅用于名词前] **1** existing in or affecting the whole world 遍及[影响]全世界的: *The prospects for world peace are improving.* 世界和平的前景正在改善。| *the world recession of the early nineties* 90年代初的世界经济衰退 | **world champion/record etc** (=the best in the world, especially in a sport) 世界冠军/纪录等 *Hawthorn became Britain's first world champion.* 霍索恩成为英国第一个世界冠军得主。**2** important or powerful enough to influence or affect the whole world 重要[强大]得足以影响世界的: *Britain's attempts to remain a world power* 英国保持世界强国地位的企图 | *a world figure on the international stage* 国际舞台上举足轻重的人物

World Al·ma·nac /ˌ· ˈ··· / *trademark* a large book produced each year in the US, giving short accounts of the news that has happened during the year and also information on politics, history, sport, medicine, entertainment etc. Several different publishers produce a World Almanac.【商标】《世界年鉴》〔美国每年出版的一部大型参考书。该书刊载当年时事新闻简述, 也有政治、历史、体育、医学、娱乐等方面的信息。有数家出版商参与出版《世界年鉴》〕

World Bank, the /ˌ· ˈ·/ an organization that is part of the UN (United Nations), which lends money to poorer countries so that they can develop their farming, industry, and health and education systems. Its official name is the International Bank for Reconstruction and Development. 世界银行〔联合国一分支机构。其职能是向贫困国家提供贷款, 帮助其发展本国的工农业、医疗及教育体系。其正式名称是"国际复兴开发银行"〕

world-beat·er /ˈ· ˌ··/ *n* [C] someone or something that is the best at a particular activity 举世无双的人[物]; 天下无敌的人[物] —**world-beating** *adj*

world-class /ˌ· ˈ·◄/ *adj* among the best in the world 世界第一流水平的: *a world-class tennis champion* 世界级的网球冠军

World Coun·cil of Church·es, the /ˌ· ˌ·· · ˈ··/ an international Christian organization that encourages friendship and understanding among different Christian religious groups. It has more than 300 churches as members, and its main offices are in Geneva. 世界基督教协进会〔一国际性基督教组织。其宗旨是增进基督教不同派别的友谊和理解。已吸收了三百多个教派为会员, 总部设在日内瓦〕

World Cup, the /ˌ· ˈ·/ **1** the most important international competition in football (soccer), which is held every four years in a different country. Teams representing most countries in the world first play a series of games to decide which 32 teams will play in the World Cup event itself. These teams then play against each other until there are two teams left who play in the **World Cup Final** The winners receive a gold cup called the 'Jules Rimet Trophy' (before 1971) or FIFA World Cup. 世界杯〔最重要的国际性足球赛事, 每四年一次在一个不同的国家举行。世界上大部分国家都派出代表队参加一系列预选赛, 决出32支球队参加世界杯。这些球队相互角逐直至最后剩下两支球队进入世界杯决赛。胜出者获得名为"雷米特杯"(1971年以前)或"大力神杯"的金杯〕**2** a similar international competition in some other sports, such as CRICKET or RUGBY 世界杯〔与世界杯足球赛类似的其他体育项目的国际赛事, 如板球或橄榄球〕

world-fa·mous /ˌ· ˈ··◄/ *adj* known about by people all over the world 世界著名的, 举世闻名的: *a world-famous singer* 世界著名的歌唱家

World Health Or·ga·ni·za·tion, the /ˌ· ˈ· ····ˌ ·/ abbreviation 缩写为 **WHO** an international organization that is part of the UN (United Nations), which helps countries improve their people's health by giving medicines and providing information and education about diseases, IMMUNIZATION etc 世界卫生组织〔联合国下属一国际机构。其职责是向有关国家援助药品, 提供疾病及免疫等方面的信息和教育, 帮助这些国家改善国民的健康状况〕

world·ly /ˈwɜldlɪ; ˈwɜːldli/ *adj* [only before noun 仅用于名词前] **1 worldly goods** everything you own 财产 **2** having a lot of experience and knowledge about people and life 生活经验丰富的; 善于处世的: *Crystal was worldly but willing to take a risk.* 克丽丝特尔老成练达, 但愿意冒险。—opposite 反义词 UNWORLDLY **3** connected with ordinary daily life rather than spiritual or religious ideas; MUNDANE 尘世的, 世俗的 —**worldliness** *n* [U]

worldly-wise /ˌ·· ˈ·◄/ *adj* having a lot of experience and knowledge about life so that you are not easily shocked or deceived 老于世故的; 会处世的

world pow·er /ˌ· ˈ··/ *n* [C] a country that has a lot of power and influence in many parts of the world 世界强国

World Se·ries, the /ˌ· ˈ··◄/ a set of up to seven BASEBALL games played between two teams, the winner of the American League, and the winner of the National League. 世界职业棒球锦标赛〔指美国棒球联盟与全国棒球联盟的冠军队之间进行的全部七场比赛〕

World Ser·vice, the /ˌ· ˈ··/ part of the BBC which broadcasts radio programmes, especially news, to all parts of the world. Its official name is the BBC World Service. 国际广播电台〔英国广播公司的组成部分。该台向全世界播出各类广播节目, 特别是新闻节目。其正式名称为英国广播公司国际广播电台〕

world-shak·ing /ˈ· ˌ··/ *adj* extremely important and having a great effect 非常重要的; 震惊世界的: *a world-shaking announcement* 震惊世界的宣告

World Trade Cen·ter, the /ˌ· ˈ· ˌ··/ abbreviation 缩写为 **the WTC** a group of buildings in Manhattan, New York City, which included two very tall SKYSCRAPERS that were destroyed by TERRORISTS in 2001. Thousands of people were killed when the terrorists flew two planes directly into the buildings. 世界贸易中心〔纽约市曼哈顿区的一组建筑物, 其中包括两幢摩天大楼。2001年, 恐怖分子驾驶两架飞机撞向大楼, 大楼遭摧毁, 数千人丧生〕

World Trade Or·ga·ni·za·tion, the /ˌ· ˈ· ····ˌ ·/ abbreviation 缩写为 **the WTO** an international organization, established in 1995 and based in Geneva, that deals with the rules of trade between different nations, and encourages them to trade fairly 世界贸易组织〔一国际性组织。成立于1995年, 总部设在日内瓦, 负责制订国际贸易规则, 鼓励公平贸易〕

World War I /ˌwɜld wɔr ˈwʌn; ˌwɜːld wɔː ˈwʌn/ also 又作 **the First World War** (1914-1918) a war in Europe fought between France, the UK and its EMPIRE, Russia, and the US on one side ('the Allies'), and Germany, Austria-Hungary, and Turkey on the other side. The war started as a result of the murder in Sarajevo of the Archduke Franz Ferdinand, a member of the Austrian royal family. 第一次世界大战〔(1914-1918), 发生在欧洲的一场大战。交战一方为法国、大英帝国、俄国和美国(称"协约国"), 另一方为德国、奥匈帝国及土耳其。奥地利王室成员斐迪南大公在萨拉热窝遭谋杀成为此次大战的导火索〕

W

CULTURAL NOTE 文化注释

When the First World War started, it was not expected to continue for very long. Some British politicians used the phrase "it will all be over by Christmas". In fact, it continued for four years and at least 10 million people were killed. The war was fought in many different areas, but for British people the strongest image is of the "Western Front" in Belgium and northern France. The armies of each side on the Western Front lived in TRENCH*es* (=long, deep holes in the ground), with an area called 'no-man's land' between them. Many of the famous battles on the Western Front ended without either side gaining much land. The names of these battles, especially the Somme, Passchendaele, and Ypres, have come to represent the way that millions of young men were killed for no very good reason. For people from Australia and New Zealand, the battle of Gallipoli, where thousands of their soldiers were killed, is remembered with great sadness. 第一次世界大战刚打响的时候, 人们认为它不会持续太长时间。英国有些政客说出如下的话: "圣诞节之前战争就将全面结束。" 这场战争实际上持续了4年时间, 并且至少有1000万人在战争期间失去生命。战争在多个战场展开, 但英国人印象最深的是位于比利时和法国北部的"西线"。西线的双方军队都躲在战壕里, 他们中间是所谓的"无人地带"。西线的多次著名战斗都以双方谁也没占到太多便宜收场。这些战役的名字, 像索姆河战役、帕森达勒战役和伊普尔战役, 都成了成百上千万年轻人无辜而死的代名词。成千上万的澳大利亚和新西兰将士在加利波利战役中阵亡, 因此两国人怀着万分沉痛的心情回忆这场战役。

Chemical weapons World War I is also remembered for the use of CHEMICAL WEAPON*s* such as CHLORINE gas and MUSTARD GAS. After World War I, many countries signed an agreement that chemical weapons would not be used in wars in the future. 化学武器: 人们记住第一次世界大战还因为这次战争使用了化学武器, 像氯气和芥子气。一战结束后, 很多国家签署条约禁止化学武器在未来战争中使用。

Remembering the dead In the UK, people remember the dead of World War I and World War II on **Remembrance Day**, which is held on 11 November, the day of the ARMISTICE (=the agreement to stop fighting) at the end of World War I in 1918. There is a special ceremony at the CENOTAPH in London, and people wear a red paper POPPY (=a type of flower) to show their respect for those killed in the wars. In the US, there are no special ceremonies, but 11 November is a holiday called **Veterans Day**, when people remember the soldiers killed in fighting all the wars the US has been involved in. 纪念死难者: 英国人在荣军纪念日这天纪念两次世界大战的死难者, 即11月11日, 也就是1918年第一次世界大战停战的日子。在伦敦的阵亡将士纪念碑前举行特殊的仪式, 人们戴着纸做的红色罂粟花以表达对战争中死难者的敬仰。美国没有特别的纪念仪式, 但11月11日是个称作"退伍军人节"的假日, 人们在这一天纪念在美国参与的所有战争中牺牲的美国将士。

W

World War II /ˌwɜrld wɔr ˈtu; ˌwɜːld wɔː ˈtuː/ also 又作 **the Second World War** (1939-45) a war involving almost every major country in the world. On one side were the Allies (including the UK, France, and Poland, and after 1941 the US and the Soviet Union) and on the other side the Axis (including Germany, Japan, and Italy). The war was started by Adolf Hitler, the Nazi leader of Germany, who aimed to increase German power by attacking other countries and taking control of them. The war ended when Germany was defeated, and the US dropped NUCLEAR BOMB*s* on the Japanese cities of Hiroshima and Nagasaki. About 55 million people were killed in the war. 第二次世界大战〔(1939-1945), 一场几乎所有主要国家都卷入的战争。战争一方是同盟国 (包括英国、法国和波兰等, 美国和苏联1941年后参战), 另一方是轴心国 (包括德国、日本和意大利)。挑起战争的是纳粹德国的领袖阿道夫·希特勒, 他企图通过进攻并控制其他国家来增强德国的实力。随着德国战败, 美国在日本城市广岛、长崎投放了原子弹, 第二次世界大战结束。这场战争夺取了大约5500万人的生命〕

CULTURAL NOTE 文化注释

Despite the fact that many people were killed, British people often think of the war years with pride, because it was a time when people helped and supported each other, and worked together to defeat the enemy. People who were not soldiers did special jobs, often jobs that they enjoyed, such as working on farms. During the war, many things were not available to be bought in shops, such as goods from abroad and fresh foods. The government introduced a system called RATION*ing*, which limited the amount of food, petrol, clothes etc that people could have. When British people think of the Second World War, they also think of the BLITZ, when German planes dropped bombs on British cities, especially London, and many buildings were destroyed. People built AIR RAID SHELTER*s* (=places under the ground where they were safe from bombs) in their gardens or went to Underground stations or other places to be safe from the bombs. 尽管很多人死于战火, 英国人经常在忆起二战岁月时还是充满自豪, 因为那个时候人们互助互爱, 同仇敌忾。没当兵的人做一些特别的工作, 常是些他们喜欢做的工作, 例如耕种农场。战争期间, 很多东西都无法从商店中买到, 像进口产品和新鲜食物等。政府实行配给制度, 限制食品、汽油、衣物等的购买量。英国人想起二战的时候, 他们会想到闪电战, 即德国在英国城市, 尤其是伦敦上空投掷炸弹, 很多建筑物都因此损毁。人们在花园中挖防空洞或者躲到地铁车站或其他能避开炸弹的地方去。

In the US, ordinary people were not affected by the war as much as people were in the UK. The only direct attack on the US was by the Japanese at Pearl Harbor, which led the US to enter the war. American people tend to think of the war in connection to the HOLOCAUST, when millions of Jewish people and other people were killed by the NAZI*s* in CONCENTRATION CAMP*s*. 在美国, 普通百姓没有遭受英国民众那样的浩劫。日本偷袭珍珠港是唯一一次针对美国的直接打击, 这把美国拖入了战争。美国人常把二战与针对犹太人的大屠杀联系起来, 其中数百万犹太人以及其他人在集中营里死于纳粹分子之手。

world-wear·y /ˌ·ˈ··◂/ *adj* no longer finding life interesting or exciting 厌世的 —**world-weariness** *n* [U]

world-wide /ˈwɜrldˈwaɪd; ˌwɜːldˈwaɪd◂/ *adj, adv* everywhere in the world 遍及全世界的[地]; 在全世界: *cars with a worldwide reputation for reliability* 以性能可靠享誉世界的汽车

World Wide Fund for Na·ture, the /ˌ···ˌ··ˈ··/ abbreviation 缩写为 **WWF** an international CHARITY organization, formerly called the **World Wildlife Fund**, which supports CONSERVATION (=protection of wild plants, animals, and natural areas of land) 世界自然基金会〔一国际性慈善组织, 旧称"世界野生生物基金会", 以自然保护为宗旨〕

World Wide Web /ˌ··ˈ◂/ *n* [singular] the net work of computers that forms the Internet 万维网

worm¹ /wɜm; wɜːm/ *n* [C] **1** a long thin creature with no bones and no legs that lives in soil 蠕虫 **2** someone who you do not like or respect 讨厌的人; 可鄙的人 **3 have worms** to have PARASITES (=small creature that eats your food or your blood) in your body 患有寄生虫 **4 the worm turns** *literary* used to say that someone who is normally quiet and obedient will change if they really need to【文】沉默规矩的人〔被逼〕也反抗 —see also 另见 **can of worms** (CAN² (4))

worm² *v* [T] **1 worm your way into/through etc** to move through a small place or a crowd slowly, carefully, or with difficulty〔在小的地方或人群中〕缓慢[小心, 艰难]地前行: *They wormed their way through the crowd.* 他们好不容易慢慢地挤出人群。**2 worm your way into sb's affections/heart/confidence etc** to gradually make someone love or trust you, especially by being dishonest〔尤指通过欺诈手段〕渐渐获得某人的感情/欢心/信任等 **3 worm sth out of sb** to get information from someone who does not want to give it 从某人处套出消息 **4 worm your way out of (doing) sth** to avoid doing something that you have been asked to do by making an excuse that is dishonest but clever〔不诚实但巧妙地〕逃避做某事: *Steve has managed to worm his way out of going to the meeting.* 史蒂夫设法巧妙地逃了, 没去参加会议。**5** to give an animal medicine in order to remove PARASITE*s* (1) that live inside them 给〔动物用药〕驱寄生虫

worm-eat·en /ˈ·ˌ··/ *adj* **1** worm-eaten wood or fruit has holes in it because it has been eaten by worms〔木材或水果〕虫蛀的, 多蛀孔的 **2** old and damaged 陈旧的; 破损的 —see picture on page A18 参见 A18 页图

worm·hole /ˈwɜmˌhol; ˈwɜːmhəʊl/ *n* [C] a hole in a piece of wood etc made by a type of WORM¹ (1)〔木材等上的〕蛀洞, 虫孔

worm·wood /ˈwɜmˌwud; ˈwɜːmwʊd/ *n* [U] a plant with a bitter taste 苦艾〔一种植物〕

Wormwood Scrubs /,·· ˈ·/ also 又作 **The Scrubs** *informal* a prison in West London【非正式】沃姆伍德·斯科拉布斯监狱〔伦敦西部一监狱〕

worm·y /ˈwɜːmi; ˈwɜːmi/ *adj* full of worms (WORM[1] (1)) 满是虫的

worn[1] /wɔrn; wɔːn/ the past participle of WEAR[1]

worn[2] *adj* **1** a worn object is old and damaged〔物品〕陈旧的, 损坏的: *a worn patch on the carpet* 地毯上一小块磨破的地方 **2** someone who looks worn seems tired 疲倦的; 筋疲力尽的

worn out /,· ˈ·◂/ *adj* **1** very tired because you have been working hard〔因工作卖力而〕精疲力竭的: *You look worn-out!* 你看来精疲力竭! **2** too old or damaged to be used 破旧的; 不能再用的: *a pair of old worn out walking boots* 一双穿破了的旧步行靴

[2] [3] **wor·ried** /ˈwɜrɪd; ˈwʌrid/ *adj* **1** unhappy because you keep thinking about a problem, or are anxious about something 担心的, 焦虑的: *Don't look so worried – we'll find him.* 不要愁眉不展, 我们会找到他的。| **[+about]** *She's so worried about her exams.* 她很担心考试。| **worried that** *I was worried that we wouldn't have enough money.* 我担心我们的钱不够。| **get worried** *I got really worried when I saw a police car outside our house.* 看到警车停在我们屋外, 我真的胆战心惊。| **worried expression/look/frown etc** *Jim looked up with a slightly worried expression.* 吉姆略带愁容地抬头看。| **worried sick** *spoken* (=extremely worried)【口】非常担心 *Where on earth have you been? I was worried sick!* 你究竟到哪儿去了?我都急坏了! —see 见 NERVOUS (USAGE) **2 you had me worried** *spoken* used to say that someone made you feel confused or anxious because you did not properly understand what they said, or did not realize that it was a joke【口】你让我担心〔因为误解对方的话或不知道那是玩笑〕: *You had me worried there for a minute – I thought the house really had burnt down!* 你让我担心了一会儿, 我以为房子真的烧毁了! **3 I'm not worried** *spoken* used to say that you do not mind what happens【口】我无所谓〔用于表示你不在乎发生何事〕: *"Shall we go out or stay in?" "Oh, I'm not worried – whichever you want."* "我们是出去还是留在家里?" "噢, 我无所谓, 随你喜欢。" —**worriedly** *adv*

wor·ri·er /ˈwɜɪə; ˈwʌriə/ *n* [C] someone who often worries about things 经常担心的人, 经常发愁的人: *Her mother was a born worrier.* 她母亲天生杞人忧天。

wor·ri·some /ˈwɜɪsəm; ˈwʌrisəm/ *adj formal* making you anxious【正式】令人焦虑的: *a worrisome problem* 一个令人担心的问题

[1] [2] **wor·ry[1]** /ˈwɜɪ; ˈwʌri/ *v*

1 ▶BE ANXIOUS 担忧◀ [I] to be anxious or unhappy about something so that you think about it a lot 担心; 为…发愁: **[+about]** *You've really got no need to worry about your weight.* 你真的不必担心你的体重。| **worry that** *He's worried that he might lose his job.* 他担心他会失业。| **[+over]** *Dad worries over the slightest thing.* 爸爸会为一点点小事发愁。

2 don't worry *spoken*【口】**a)** used when you are trying to make someone feel less anxious 别担心〔用于安慰别人〕: *Don't worry, darling, Daddy's here.* 宝贝, 别怕, 爸爸在这儿。**b)** used to tell someone that they do not need to do something 不用费心〔用于告诉某人不用做某事〕: *Don't worry about sorting them out – I'll do it later.* 不用把它整理出来, 过一会儿我会做的。**c)** used to tell someone that you will definitely do something 别担心〔用于告诉某人你肯定会做某事〕: *Oh don't worry, I'll get my own back on him somehow!* 噢, 别担心, 我总会想办法向他报复的!

3 ▶MAKE SB ANXIOUS 使某人担忧◀ [T] to make someone feel anxious about something 使某人〔为某事而〕忧虑: *The recent changes in the Earth's climate are beginning to worry scientists.* 近来地球的气候变化使科学家开始担忧。| **worry sb that** *Doesn't it worry you that Sarah spends so much time away from home?* 萨拉整天往外跑, 你不担心吗? | **worry yourself** (=feel anxious, especially when there is no need to)〔尤指不必要的〕担心; 发愁

4 not to worry *BrE spoken* used to say that something is not important【英口】没关系〔用于指某事不重要〕: *Not to worry, we can always go another time.* 没关系, 我们总能找别的时间去。

5 nothing to worry about *spoken* used to tell someone that something is not as serious or difficult as they think【口】没什么可担心的: *It's just a routine check-up – nothing to worry about.* 这只是例行检查, 没什么可担心的。

6 have enough to worry about *spoken* used to say that someone already has a lot of problems or is very busy【口】已经够烦的: *I don't think we should tell Mum about this – she's got enough to worry about as it is.* 我不认为要把这事告诉妈妈, 事实上她已经够烦的了。

7 ▶ANNOY 烦恼◀ [T] to annoy someone 使〔某人〕恼怒: **worry sb with sth** *Stop worrying your grandfather with all those questions.* 不要再问这问那烦你爷爷了。

8 ▶ANIMAL 动物◀ [T] if a dog worries sheep, it tries to bite or kill them〔狗〕追咬〔杀〕〔羊〕

worry at sth/sb *phr v* [T] **1** if an animal worries at a bone or piece of meat, it bites and shakes it〔动物〕撕咬〔骨头或肉块〕 **2** if you worry at a problem, you think about it a lot in order to try and find a solution 设法解决〔问题〕: *Jez was never happy unless he was worrying at some problem.* 如果不在竭力思索解决某个问题的办法, 杰泽就会不高兴。

worry[2] *n* **1** [C] a problem that you are anxious about or are not sure how to deal with 令人忧心[不知如何处理]的问题: *My main worry is how the divorce will affect the kids.* 我主要担心的是离婚会对孩子产生什么影响。| *financial worries* 财务上的烦恼事 | **[+about]** *We've got no more worries about the schedule at the moment.* 我们现在不再为日程安排而担心了。| **be a worry to/for sb** *Money was always a big worry for us.* 金钱总是我们的一大烦恼。**2** [U] the feeling of being anxious about something 担心; 忧虑: *The missing child's parents were frantic with worry.* 失踪孩子的父母急得发疯。**3 no worries** *spoken* used to agree to what someone wants and to say that it will be no problem【口】没问题〔用于应允别人的要求〕: *Can you deliver on Thursday? Yeah, no worries, mate.* 星期四你能送去吗? 噢, 没有问题, 老兄。 [3]

worry beads /ˈ·· ·/ *n* [plural] small stones or wooden balls on a string that you move and turn in order to keep yourself calm 安神念珠, 解愁数珠

wor·ry·ing /ˈwɜɪɪŋ; ˈwʌri-ɪŋ/ *adj* **1** making you feel anxious 令人担心的; 使人发愁的: *a worrying development* 叫人忧虑的事态发展 **2 worrying time/week/year etc** a time etc when you have many problems 多烦恼的时刻/星期/年头等: *It's been a worrying few weeks for us all.* 这几个星期大家都忧心忡忡。—**worryingly** *adv*: *a worryingly high level of pollutants in the atmosphere* 令人担忧的大气中高含量的污染物 [3]

wor·ry·wart /ˈwɜɪ,wɔrt; ˈwʌriwɔːt/ *n* [C] *AmE informal* someone who worries about unimportant things【美, 非正式】〔为琐事〕自寻烦恼的人

worse[1] /wɜs; wɜːs/ *adj* **1** [the comparative of *bad* bad 的比较级] not as good as someone or something else, or more unpleasant or of a lower standard 更坏的; 更糟的; 更差的: *The meal couldn't have been much worse.* 这饭菜糟糕透了。| **worse than** *The weather was worse than last year.* 天气比去年更糟。| **there's nothing worse than** *spoken*【口】*There's nothing worse than being angry about something and knowing it's your own fault.* 为自己惹的祸生气, 没有比这更糟的了。| **a lot/much worse** *The traffic is much worse after five.* 5点之后交通情况会糟得多。| **get worse** *I didn't like the noise when I first came and it's got worse since then.* 初来时我就不喜欢这种噪声, 那以后变得越来越讨厌了。| **worse and worse** *Paul's manners seem to get worse and worse.* 保罗似乎越来越无礼了。| **make matters/things/it worse** (=make a bad or difficult situation even worse) 使情况更困难[更差] *I tried to help but I think I made things worse.* 我试图去帮忙, 但我觉得自己使事情变得更糟。**2** [comparative of *ill* ill 的比较级] more ill than before 病情更重的: *If she's worse in the morning, I'll call the doctor.* 她如果早上病情恶化的话, 我要去请医生来。| **get worse** *After the operation he got worse instead of better.* 手术后他不是越来越好, 而是越来越糟。**3 be none the worse for** to not have been harmed, or not be worse because of something 没有因〔某事物〕受伤害[变得更差]: *The children were out in the rain all afternoon, but seem none the worse for it.* 孩子们整个下午都在淋雨, 但是看来并没有怎么样。**4 worse luck** *spoken* used to say that you are disappointed or annoyed by something【口】真不幸〔因某事而感到沮丧或生气时用〕: *When we got there the car had already been sold, worse luck!* 我们到那里时汽车已经卖掉了, 真倒霉! **5 sb can/could do worse than do sth** *spoken* used to say that you think it is a good idea if someone does a particular thing【口】做某事是好主意: *You could do worse than buy a few bottles of the local wine.* 你买几瓶当地的葡萄酒是个好主意。**6 it could have been worse** *spoken* used to say that a bad situation has something good about it【口】可能会更糟〔用于指实际情况并不那么糟糕〕 **7 take a change/turn for the worse** to change and become worse 恶化 **8 the worse for wear** *informal* in poor condition, or very tired【非正式】破旧不堪的; 精疲力竭的: *The living room carpet is looking the worse for wear.* 起居室的地毯看起来破旧不堪。—compare 比较 BETTER[1] —see also 另见 **go from bad to worse** (BAD[1] (13))

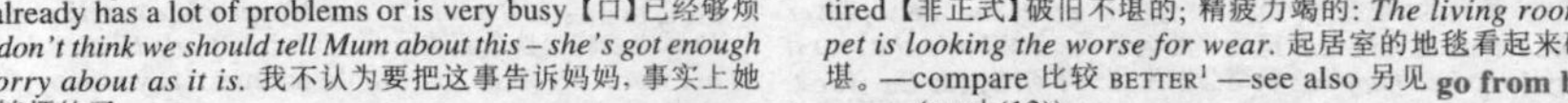

W

USAGE NOTE 用法说明: WORSE

GRAMMAR 语法

More and **most** are not used together with **worse** or **worst**. more 和 most 不与 worse 与 worst 连用: *Math is my worst subject* (NOT 不用 *my most worse/most worst subject*). 数学是我最差的科目。| *The situation is much worse than it was last week* (NOT 不用 *much more worse*). 形势比上周更糟。

Some people think that **worse** should not be used as an adverb meaning 'in a worse way'. 有人认为 worse 不应用作副词表示"更差", But in spoken English you will often hear 但在英语口语里却经常听到: *Because we're so short of time we're doing it worse than we should.* 因为时间太少, 我们做得比预期的还要差。You can avoid this problem by saying for example 为避免此类问题, 可以说: *...we're not doing it as well as we should.* …我们没有做得像预期的那样好。

Things *go/get bad,* but they *get worse.* 可以说事情 go bad 或 get bad (变坏), 但只可说事情 get worse (变得越来越坏)。

SPELLING 拼法

Remember the spellings: *even worse* is spelt with an 'e'; *the worst* with a 't'. 注意拼法: even worse 结尾是 e; 而 the worst 的结尾是 t。

worse² *n* [U] something worse 更差[坏]的事物: *We thought the situation was bad, but worse was to follow.* 我们以为形势不好, 但更糟的事还在后头。| **a change for the worse** (=a bad change) 变得更差[更坏] —compare 比较 BETTER³

worse³ *adv* [comparative of *badly* badly 的比较级] **1** in a more severe or serious way than before 更猛烈地; 更厉害地: *My head aches much worse than before.* 我头痛得比以前更厉害了。**2** to a lower standard or quality or less successfully 更差地; 更糟地; 更不成功地: *Dick scored worse than you in the test.* 迪克在测验中得的分数比你还差。

wors·en /ˈwɜ-sn̩; ˈwɜːsən/ *v* [I,T] to become worse or make something worse (使)变得更差; (使)恶化: *a worsening political situation* 日趋恶化的政治形势

worse off /,· ˈ·◂/ *adj* [not before noun 不用于名词前] **1** having less money than before or than someone else; poorer 比以前[别人]钱较少(的); 更贫穷: *The tax increases will leave us worse off.* 税收增加后我们赚的钱会更少。**2** in a worse situation than before or than someone else 形势比以前[别人]更糟: *The factories on the east bank of the river were even worse off as they had no direct link to the motorway.* 因为河东岸的工厂不直接与公路相连, 所以处境就更糟。

wor·ship¹ /ˈwɜ-ʃəp; ˈwɜːʃɪp/ *v* **worshipped, worshipping** also 又作 **worshiped, worshiping** *AmE* 【美】 **1** [I,T] to show respect and love for a god, especially by praying in a church, TEMPLE etc 敬奉(神)〔尤指在教堂、庙宇等祷告〕**2** [T] to admire and love someone very much 景仰; 十分喜爱: *She absolutely worships those children.* 她十分喜爱那些孩子。**3 worship the ground sb walks on** to admire or love someone so much that you cannot see their faults 拜倒在某人脚下〔以致看不到他的缺点〕—**worshipper** *n* [C]: *She was a regular worshipper at the Parish Church.* 她经常在教区教堂做礼拜。

worship² *n* [U] **1** a strong feeling of respect and love for a god〔对神的〕崇敬; 崇拜: *They bowed their heads in worship.* 他们低下头以示崇敬。**2** the activity of praying in a church, TEMPLE etc in order to show respect and love for a god〔在教堂、庙宇等祈祷以示对神的〕崇拜; 敬仰: **act of worship** (=religious service) 敬神仪式; 礼拜 | **house/place of worship** (=a church, temple etc)〔教堂、庙宇等〕崇拜的场所 **3** a strong feeling of love or admiration for someone or something, especially so that you cannot see their faults〔对某人或物的〕强烈崇拜〔尤指看不见其错误〕; 仰慕 —see also 另见 HERO WORSHIP **4 Your/His Worship** *BrE formal* used to address or talk about a public official such as a MAYOR or MAGISTRATE 【英, 正式】阁下〔对市长或地方法官等公务人员的称呼〕

wor·ship·ful /ˈwɜ-ʃəpfʊl; ˈwɜːʃɪpfəl/ *adj formal* showing respect or admiration for someone or something 【正式】尊敬的; 敬爱的

worst¹ /wɜ-st; wɜːst/ *adj* [the superlative of *bad* bad 的最高级] **1** [only before noun 仅用于名词前] worse than anything else of the same kind or worse than at any time before〔同类中或与以前比较〕最坏的; 最差的; 最糟的: *Ken is easily the worst player in the team.* 肯无疑是队里最差的运动员。| *What's the worst thing that could happen?* 最糟会发生什么事? | **by far the worst** *This is by far the worst book she's written.* 这无疑是她写的书中最差的一本。**2 be your own worst enemy** to continue to behave in a stupid or thoughtless way that harms you or stops you from becoming successful 自讨苦吃; 自己害自己 **3 come off worst** to lose a fight or argument〔在打架或争论中〕被击败

worst² *n* **1 the worst** the person, thing, situation, state, part etc that is worse than all others of the same kind or worse than at any time before〔同类中或与以前比较〕最坏的人[事, 形势, 国家, 部分等]: *None of them can play well, but Jane is the worst.* 他们中没有一个人打得好, 尤其是简打得最差。| **the worst of it** (=the worst part of something) …中最糟的 *I think we've done the worst of it.* 我觉得我们做得最不像样。| *The worst of it is, I can't let her know what's happening.* 最糟糕的是, 我不能让她知道发生了什么事。| **get/have the worst of it** *spoken* (=lose a fight or argument) 【口】〔在打架或争论中〕遭到失败 | **expect/fear the worst** (=expect the situation to have the worst possible result) 作最坏打算 *England play Brazil next week and I fear the worst.* 下星期英格兰队对巴西队, 我已作了最坏打算。| **at his/its etc worst** (=as bad as he or it can be) 在其最糟糕的时候 *You saw the garden at its worst, I'm afraid.* 恐怕你看到了花园最萧条时的情景。**2 at (the) worst** if things are as bad as they can be 在最坏的情况下: *Choosing the right software can be time-consuming at best and confusing or frustrating at worst.* 挑选合适的软件起码耗费时间, 最糟糕的是使人感到没有头绪且沮丧。**3 sb/sth can do their worst** used to say that you are not worried by the power of someone or something to harm you 某人/某物有什么手段尽管使出来〔用于表示不担心某人或物的力量对自己造成伤害〕: *All the wheat has been harvested, so the storm can do its worst.* 所有的小麦都已收割完毕, 暴风雨爱怎么样就怎么样吧。**4 if the worst comes to the worst** if the situation develops in the worst possible way 如果最坏的事情发生: *If the worst comes to the worst, we'll have to sell the car.* 如果遇上最坏的情况, 我们只得把汽车卖掉。

worst³ *adv* [the superlative of *badly* badly 的最高级] most badly 最坏地; 最糟地; 最差地: *Aid is being sent to the worst affected areas.* 援助物资正在送往受影响最严重的地区。| *the worst-dressed man in the office* 办公室里衣着最差的男人

worst⁴ *v* [T usually passive 一般用被动态] *old-fashioned* to defeat someone in a fight, competition, or argument 【过时】〔打架、比赛或争论中〕打败; 胜过〔某人〕

wor·sted /ˈwʊstɪd; ˈwʊstɪ̵d/ *n* [U] a type of cloth made from wool 毛料

worth¹ /wɜ-θ; wɜːθ/ *prep* **1 be worth** to have a value in money 值…钱: *How much is the ring worth?* 这个戒指值多少钱? | **be worth £10/ $500 etc** *The picture is worth about two thousand pounds.* 这幅画约值两千英镑。| **be worth a lot** *informal* (=be worth a lot of money) 【非正式】值许多钱 | **be worth nothing/not be worth anything** *I don't think my stereo is worth anything* 我觉得我的立体声唱机不值什么钱。| **be worth a fortune** *informal* (=be extremely valuable) 【非正式】非常有价值 *Now they've found oil the land must be worth a fortune.* 他们既然发现了石油, 这块土地肯定会价值连城。**2 be worth millions/a fortune** *informal* to be extremely rich 【非正式】极富有/极有钱: *The man who founded CNN must be worth a fortune.* 创办〔美国〕有线新闻网的那个人肯定极有钱。**3 be worth doing/reading/finding etc** to be something that will be useful and helpful if you do it or read it etc 值得做/阅读/寻找等: *a film worth seeing* 值得看的电影 | *It may be worth putting an advertisement in the local paper.* 也许值得在地方报纸上登广告。| **be worth it** *I didn't write to Louise, because I didn't think it was worth it.* 我没有给路易斯写信, 因为我觉得没有必要。**4 it's worth doing sth** used to say that someone should give the time or money needed to do something, because they will gain something useful 值得做某事: *It's worth taking your time when you visit the cathedral.* 值得花充分时间参观这座大教堂。| **it's worth the time/effort** *It's worth all the hard work you put in when you see so many happy children.* 你在看到那么多幸福的孩子时, 会觉得所有的辛劳都是值得的。| **it's worth it** *Have a medical every year, it's worth it.* 一年做一次体格检查, 是上算的。| **it's not worth it** *Don't get angry, it's not worth it.* 别生气了, 不值得。| **it's well worth doing sth/it** *It's well worth getting there an hour early, if you want a good seat.* 你如果想占一个好座位, 提前一个小时到那儿很有必要。**5 it's worth your/sb's while** *spoken* used to say that someone should give the time or money needed to do something, because they will gain something useful 【口】值得某人花时间[钱]一干: **it's worth your/sb's while to do sth** *It would be worth your while to talk to the editor.* 与那位编辑交谈会获益匪浅。| *I don't sell French books, it's not worth my while.* (=I would not make any money) 我不卖法文书, 划不来。**6 make it worth sb's while** *spoken* to offer

someone money if they agree to do something for you, especially something dishonest【口】酬谢某人〔尤因他为你干了不诚实的事〕, 给某人报酬: *Look, if you forget about the whole thing I'll make it worth your while.* 瞧, 要是你把所有事全忘了, 我会酬谢你的。**7 what's it worth?** *spoken humorous* used to ask someone how they will reward you if you do something for them【口, 幽默】会有什么好处?〔用于替别人做事时, 问对方会怎样酬谢自己〕 **8 for what it's worth** *spoken* used to say that you are not sure of the value or usefulness of what you are saying【口】不管价值如何〔用于表示自己的见解不一定对〕; 不管有没有用: *My suggestion – for what it's worth – is that we buy a bigger car.* 我的意见不一定对, 但我建议买一辆大点的汽车。**9 for all you are/he is etc worth** with as much effort as possible 竭尽全力: *Tom kept pulling away at the rope for all he was worth.* 汤姆不断地拼命扯绳子。**10 worth his/her salt** doing their job well or deserving respect 胜任的; 应受尊敬的: *No translator worth his salt would rely on a bilingual dictionary.* 没有哪一位称职的翻译工作时只靠一本双语辞典。**11 worth its/his/her weight in gold** very useful or valuable 非常有用[有价值]的

USAGE NOTE 用法说明: WORTH

WORD CHOICE 词语辨析: **worth, value**

Worth is common only after the verb **to be** and after words for amounts of something. worth 通常只用于 to be 及数量词之后, as in 如: *$100 worth of damage* 损失价值 100 美元 | *a week's worth of newspapers* 一个星期的报纸。As a noun it means the same as **value** but is a little old-fashioned and literary 作名词用时, worth 与 value 意思相同, 但略显过时及文气: *the value of life* (NOT 不用 the worth) 生命的价值。In an old story you might read 在旧故事中你可以读到: *a pearl of great worth* 一颗极有价值的珍珠

GRAMMAR 语法

be worth is often followed by the *-ing* form of a verb. be worth 后常跟动词的 -ing 形式: *Is it worth running such a risk?* (NOT 不用 *...worth to run...*) 冒这险值得吗? | *Niagara Falls is worth seeing.* (NOT 不用 *...to be seen*) 尼亚加拉瀑布值得一看。

be worth while may also be followed by the *-ing* form of a verb, or the infinitive. be worth while 也可以后接动词的 -ing 形式及不定式: *It'll be well worth while you coming/for you to come* (NOT 不用 *...worth while you come*). 你来是很值得的。

W3 **worth²** *n* **1** [U] value and importance, or value in money 价值; 用处: *Eliot's poems are of more lasting worth than the plays.* 艾略特的诗比他的剧本更有持久的价值。| *The balance sheet will not show the current worth of the company.* 资产负债表说明不了公司的当前资产价值。| **ten pounds'/$500 etc worth of sth** (=an amount of something worth ten pounds or $500) 值 10 英镑/500美元等的东西 *Dick cashed about a thousand pounds' worth of travellers cheques.* 迪克把约一千英镑的旅行支票兑换成了现金。| *$4,000 worth of camera equipment* 价值4000美元的照相器材 **2 ten minutes'/a week's etc worth of sth** something that takes ten minutes or a week to happen, do, or use 可维持[使用] 10 分钟/一星期等的某物; 需要 10 分钟/一星期等来完成的某物: *a quarter of an hour's worth of music* 持续 15 分钟的音乐 | *There's about a week's worth of work left.* 还剩下约一个星期的工作。

worth·less /ˈwɜːθlɪs; ˈwɜːθləs/ *adj* **1** having no value, importance, or use 无价值的; 没用处的: *a completely worthless exercise* 徒劳无功 **2** a worthless person has no good qualities or useful skills〔人〕一无是处的; 不中用的 —**worthlessly** *adv* —**worthlessness** *n* [U]

S3 **worth·while** /ˌwɜːθˋhwaɪl; ˌwɜːθˈwaɪl◂/ *adj* something worthwhile deserves the time, effort, or money you give to it 值得花时间[努力; 金钱]的: *I'd rather the money went to a worthwhile cause.* 我宁愿把钱花在有价值的事情上。

wor·thy¹ /ˈwɜːðɪ; ˈwɜːði/ *adj* **1** a worthy person, plan etc deserves respect or admiration because they have good qualities〔人因品行好而〕值得尊敬的; 值得赞赏的: *a worthy opponent* 值得钦佩的对手 **2 be worthy of** to deserve to be thought about or treated in a particular way 值得考虑的; 应用特殊方式对待的: [**+of**] *The plan is only worthy of our contempt.* 这计划一文不值。**3** having many good qualities but not very interesting or exciting 品质优良但乏味的

worthy² *n* [C] *formal* someone who is important and should be respected【正式】知名人士, 杰出人物: *Victorian worthies such as Ruskin* 维多利亚时代的重要人物, 如罗斯金

wot¹ /wɑt; wɒt/ *BrE* an informal spelling of WHAT【英】what 的非正式拼法

wot² *v* [I] *old use* to know【旧】知道; 了解

Wo·tan /ˈvotan; ˈvəʊtɑːn/ the German name for Odin, the king of the gods 佛坦, 沃顿〔众神之王奥丁的德文名〕

wotch·a /ˈwɑtʃə; ˈwɒtʃə/ *interjection BrE slang* hello【英俚】喂, 你好

would /wʊd; wʊd/ *v* [modal verb 情态动词] **1** used instead of 'will' to describe what someone has said, asked etc 将, 将会〔代替will, 转述他人已说或问的事〕: *They said they would meet us at 10:30 at the station.* 他们说他们会在 10 点 30 分在车站接我们。**2** used instead of 'will' with a past tense verb or to show what is likely or possible 将会〔用于动词过去式中代替 will 或表示可能〕: *What would you do if you won a million pounds?* 如果你赢了 100 万英镑, 你会做什么呢? | *He said there had been a serious accident, but wouldn't give any details.* 他说曾经发生一起严重的事故, 但不肯透露细节。**3** used to describe what someone used to do a lot or what used to happen a lot 老是, 总是〔用于表示经常做或发生的事〕: *When we worked in the same office, we would often have coffee together.* 我们过去在同一个办公室工作的时候, 经常一起喝咖啡。**4** used to show disapproval when talking about someone's annoying habits or behaviour 会〔谈论别人讨厌的习惯或行为时, 表示不同意〕: *You would go and spoil it, wouldn't you!* 你这样下去会把它弄坏的, 不是吗! **5 would rather** used to say that you would prefer to do or have one thing rather than another thing 宁愿, 宁可: *Which would you rather do, go to the cinema or go for a meal?* 你宁愿去看电影还是去吃饭? **6 would you...? a)** used to express a polite request 请…好吗?〔表示客气的请求〕: *Would you shut the window please?* 请把窗户关上, 好吗? **b)** used to express a polite offer or invitation …好吗?〔表示客气的提议或邀请〕: *Would you like to have a meal with us tomorrow evening?* 明晚你和我们一起吃饭好吗? **7 I would...** *spoken* used to tell someone what you think they should do in a particular situation【口】我会〔用于告诉他人在某情况下应如何做〕: *I would ring Joe and explain that you can't see him tomorrow.* 要是我就会给乔打电话, 解释明天不能去看他的理由。**8** used before verbs that express what you think, feel, or suppose, to make your opinion or feeling less definite〔用在表示意见、感受或推测的动词前, 使意思婉转〕: *I would imagine that the kids will stay with their grandparents.* 我猜想孩子们会与他们的祖父母在一起。**9 would that...** *literary* used to express a strong wish or desire【文】但愿…; 要是…多好〔表示强烈的愿望〕: *Would that we had seen her before she died.* 要是在她去世之前, 我们能见到她一面该有多好。

S1 W1

would-be /ˈ· ·/ *adj* **would-be actor/murderer etc** someone who hopes to have a particular job or intends to do a particular thing 想当演员的人/谋杀未遂的人等

would·n't /ˈwʊdn̩t; ˈwʊdnt/ the short form of 缩略式= would not

wouldst /wʊdst; wʊdst/ *old use* the second person singular of 'would'【旧】would 的第二人称单数

would've /ˈwʊdəv; ˈwʊdəv/ the short form of 缩略式= would have

wound¹ /waʊnd; waʊnd/ the past tense and past participle of WIND²

wound² /wund; wuːnd/ *n* [C] **1** an injury, especially a cut or hole made in your skin by a weapon such as a knife or a bullet 伤, 伤口, 创伤〔尤指刀伤、枪伤等〕: *A nurse cleaned and bandaged the wound.* 护士把伤口清洗包扎好。| *gunshot wounds* 枪伤 | **flesh wound** (=slight injury caused by a bullet touching your skin)〔子弹擦过而造成的〕轻伤, 皮肉之伤 **2** a feeling of emotional or mental pain that you get when someone says or does something unpleasant to you〔感情、心灵上的〕伤痛, 伤害: *the mental wounds caused by parental abuse* 遭父母虐待而引致的心灵伤害 | *a wound to my pride* 对我自尊心的伤害 **3 open old wounds** to remind someone of unpleasant things that happened in the past 揭旧疮疤 —see also 另见 **lick your wounds** (LICK¹ (6)), **rub salt into the wounds** (RUB¹ (7))

wound³ *v* [T] **1** to injure someone, especially by making a cut or hole in their skin using a knife, gun etc〔尤指用刀或枪等〕伤害〔某人〕: *Gunmen killed two people and wounded six others in an attack today.* 在今天的袭击中, 枪手打死了二人打伤了六人。**2** to make someone feel unhappy or upset 使〔某人〕不高兴[烦恼]: *a wounding remark* 伤人的话语

wound·ed /ˈwundɪd; ˈwuːndᵻd/ *adj* **1** injured by a weapon such as a gun or knife 受〔刀、枪等〕伤害的, 负伤的: *a wounded soldier* 受伤的士兵 | **mortally wounded** (=injured so badly that you will die) 受致命伤害的 **2** very upset because of something that someone has said or done 受〔言语或行为〕伤害的; 受损害

W

的: *wounded pride* 受到伤害的自尊心 **3 the wounded** people who have been injured, especially in a war〔尤指战争中的〕受伤者

Wounded Knee, Battle of /ˌ‥ ˈ ·/ the last important battle between the US army and the Native Americans, which took place at Wounded Knee Creek in South Dakota. US soldiers killed almost 200 Sioux people, including women and children, and the battle brought an end to the Indian Wars. 翁迪德尼之役〔美国军队与印第安人之间进行的最后一场重要战役, 发生在南达科他州的翁迪德尼河附近。美军杀死了约二百名苏族人, 其中包括妇女和儿童。此役给印第安战争画上了句号〕

wound up /ˈwaʊnd ˌʌp; ˌwaʊnd ˈʌp/ *adj* [not before noun 不用于名词前] anxious, worried, or excited 紧张[担忧; 激动]的: *I was too wound up to sleep.* 我焦虑不安得无法入睡。

wove /wov; wəʊv/ the past tense of WEAVE[1]

wov·en /ˈwovən; ˈwəʊvən/ the past participle of WEAVE[1]

wow[1] /waʊ; waʊ/ *interjection informal* used when you think something is impressive or surprising【非正式】呀!哇!〔表示赞叹或惊奇〕: *"Wow! Look at that car!"* "哇!看那辆车呀!"

wow[2] *v* [T] *informal* to make people admire you very much【非正式】使〔人们〕称赞: *Her performance wowed the critics.* 她的表演得到评论家的赞赏。

wow[3] *n* [singular] *informal* a great success【非正式】极大的成功

wow·ser, wowzer /ˈwaʊzə; ˈwaʊzə/ *n* [C] *AusE, NZE informal* someone who seems to stop you from having fun【澳, 新西兰, 非正式】让人扫兴的人

WP /ˌdʌbljʊ ˋpi; ˌdʌbəljuː ˈpiː/ the abbreviation of 缩写= WORD PROCESSOR

WPC /ˌdʌbljʊ pi ˋsi; ˌdʌbəljuː piː ˈsiː◂/ *n* [C] *BrE* Woman Police Constable; a female police officer【英】女警察

wpm /ˌdʌbljʊ pi ˋɛm; ˌdʌbəljuː piː ˈem/ words per minute 每分钟字数

WRAC, the /ræk; ræk/ the Women's Royal Army Corps; the women's part of the British Army (英国) 皇家陆军妇女队

wrack /ræk; ræk/ *n* [U] **1** a type of SEAWEED 海藻〔的一种〕**2** another spelling of RACK[2] rack[2] 的另一种拼法

WRAF, the /ræf; ræf/ the Women's Royal Air Force; the women's part of the British Royal Air Force (英国) 皇家空军妇女队

wraith /reθ; reɪθ/ *n* [C] *literary* a GHOST[1] (1) especially of someone who has just died【文】〔尤指刚去世者的〕阴魂, 幽灵; 新鬼

wran·gle[1] /ˈræŋgl; ˈræŋgəl/ *n* [C] a long and complicated argument〔长时间而复杂的〕争辩: *a damaging legal wrangle* 具损害性的法律纠纷 | *a bitter wrangle over imports* 在进口问题上的激烈争论

wrangle[2] *v* **1** [I] to argue with someone angrily for a long time〔长时间地〕吵架, 争论 **2** [T] *AmE informal* to gather together cows or horses from a large area【美, 非正式】放牧, 看管〔牛、马等〕

wran·gler /ˈræŋglə; ˈræŋglə/ *n* [C] *AmE informal* a COWBOY (1)【美, 非正式】牧人, 牛仔

Wran·glers /ˈræŋgləz; ˈræŋgləz/ *trademark* a type of jeans, made by a US company called Wrangler, which also produces other kinds of informal clothes【商标】威格牛仔裤〔美国威格公司生产的一款牛仔裤。该公司还生产其他类型的休闲服装〕: *a pair of Wranglers* 一条威格牛仔裤

wrap 包, 裹

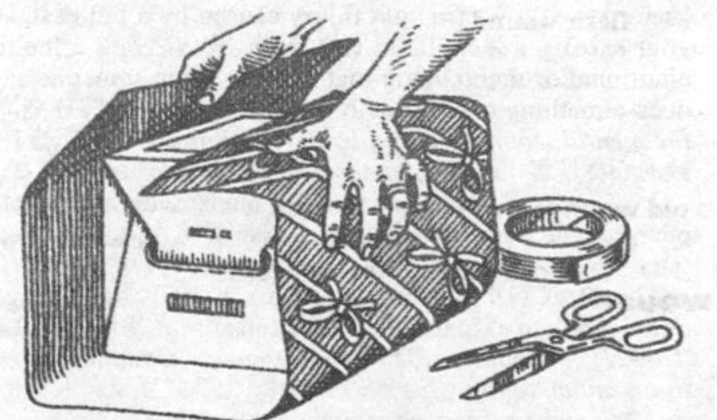

She wrapped the box in patterned paper.
她用有图案的纸把盒子包起来。

wrap[1] /ræp; ræp/ *v* [T] **1** to wind or fold cloth, paper etc around something〔用布、纸等〕包, 裹〔某物〕: *a present wrapped in shiny paper* 用闪光纸包着的一份礼物 | **wrap sth around sth/sb** *Ella wrapped a thick coat around her shoulders.* 埃拉在肩上围了一件厚外套。| **wrap sth/sb in sth** *Wrap the cake in tinfoil.* 用锡纸把蛋糕包起来。**2** if you wrap your arms, legs, fingers etc around something, you use them to hold it 用〔手臂、脚、手指等〕围住〔某物〕: *Chloe sat with her arms wrapped round her knees.* 克洛艾坐下来用双臂搂住膝盖。—see also 另见 **wrap sb in cotton wool** (COTTON WOOL (2))

wrap up *phr v* **1** [T **wrap** sth ↔ **up**] to completely cover something by folding paper, cloth etc around it〔用纸、布等〕包, 裹〔某物〕: *I haven't even wrapped my presents up yet!* 我甚至还没有把礼物包好呢! **2** [I] to put on warm clothes 穿得暖和: **wrap up warm/well** *Make sure you wrap up warm – it's freezing outside.* 你务必要穿暖和点, 外面冷极了。**3** [T **wrap** sth ↔ **up**] to finish or complete a job, meeting etc 完成; 结束〔工作、会议等〕: *The police will soon be wrapping up the investigation.* 警方将很快结束调查。**4 be wrapped up in your children/work etc** to give so much of your attention to your children, your work etc that you do not have time for anything else 全部精力放在小孩身上/工作中等 —see also 另见 **twist/wrap sb around your little finger** (FINGER[1] (13))

wrap[2] *n* **1** [C] a piece of thick cloth that you wear around your shoulders〔厚〕披肩, 围巾 **2** [U] *AmE* plastic used to cover food【美】〔食物的〕保鲜塑料薄膜 **3 keep sth under wraps** to keep something secret 保密; 隐藏 **4** [singular] the end of a day's filming〔一天的拍摄〕完成, 停机: *OK everybody, it's a wrap!* 好了, 各位, 今天就拍到这儿!

wrap-a·round /ˈ ‥ ˌ ·/ *adj* a wrap-around skirt is wound around your body with a double layer of cloth at the front〔裙子〕裹身的〔前面的部分交叠一起〕

wrap·per /ˈræpə; ˈræpə/ *n* [C] the piece of paper or plastic that covers something when it is sold〔货物的〕包装纸[塑料]: *a candy wrapper* 糖果包装纸

wrap·ping /ˈræpɪŋ; ˈræpɪŋ/ also 又作 **wrappings** *n* [C,U] cloth, paper, or plastic that is wrapped around something to protect it〔起保护作用的〕包装布; 包装纸; 包装塑料: *Torn Christmas wrapping littered the floor.* 撕破了的圣诞礼物包装纸扔得满地都是。

wrapping pa·per /ˈ ‥ ˌ ‥/ *n* [U] coloured paper that you use for wrapping presents〔礼物的〕彩色包装纸

wrap-up /ˈ · ·/ *n* [C] *AmE informal* a short report at the end of something, giving the main points again【美, 非正式】结论; 总结说明: *And finally here's a wrap-up of the six o'clock news.* 最后是6点新闻的摘要。

wrath /ræθ; rɒθ/ *n* [U] *formal* extreme anger【正式】愤怒, 狂怒: *fearing the wrath of God* 害怕上帝的震怒 **—wrathful** *adj* **—wrathfully** *adv*

wreak /rik; riːk/ *v past tense and past participle* **wreaked** also 又作 **wrought** /rɔt; rɔːt/ **wreak havoc/revenge** to cause a lot of damage, problems, and suffering 造成巨大破坏/施行报复: *A major power failure wreaked havoc in New York last night.* 昨晚纽约大停电引起了一片混乱。

wreath /riθ; riːθ/ *n* [C] **1** a circle made from leaves or flowers that you put on a grave or hang on the door at Christmas〔放在墓前或圣诞期间挂在门上的〕花圈, 花环 **2** a circle made from leaves that was given to someone in past times as an honour 花冠〔旧时荣誉的象征〕: *a laurel wreath* 桂冠

wreathe /rið; riːð/ *v literary*【文】**1 be wreathed in sth** to be surrounded by or covered in something 被…环绕[遮盖]: *The mountains were wreathed in mist.* 群山笼罩在雾中。**2 wreathed in smiles** looking very happy 笑容满面

wreck[1] /rɛk; rek/ *v* [T] **1** to completely spoil or destroy something such as a plan, relationship, or opportunity 破坏, 糟蹋〔计划、关系、机遇等〕: *I just hope the weather doesn't wreck our plans!* 我真希望天气不要破坏我们的计划! **2** to damage something such as a building, vehicle etc so badly that it cannot be repaired 使〔建筑、车辆等〕严重毁坏〔无法维修〕: *Hundreds of old buildings were wrecked by the earthquake.* 几百栋旧建筑在地震中遭到破坏。**3** [usually passive 一般用被动态] to destroy a ship, especially by hitting rocks in a storm〔尤指船只在风暴中触礁〕失事: *The ship was wrecked off the coast of Africa.* 那艘船在非洲海岸外失事了。

wreck[2] *n* [C] **1** a ship that has sunk or is so badly damaged that it cannot sail 沉船; 失事船: *the wreck of an old Spanish galleon* 古代西班牙大帆船的残骸 **2** something such as a car or plane that has been damaged very badly, especially in an accident〔尤指失事后汽车、飞机的〕残骸: *a plane wreck off the coast* 海岸外的飞机残骸 **3** [usually singular 一般用单数] *informal* someone who is very nervous, tired, or unhealthy【非正式】十分紧张[疲劳; 不健康]的人: *Look at me – I'm a complete wreck!*

看看我，我元气大伤了！| **nervous wreck** *Dean hated flying, and by the time we reached the airport he was a nervous wreck.* 迪安讨厌坐飞机，在我们到达机场时，他的神经快要崩溃了。**4** *AmE* an accident involving cars or other vehicles【美】〔涉及多辆车的〕交通事故: *The wreck caused a traffic jam three miles long.* 撞车事故使交通堵塞达3英里长。**5** *informal* something, especially a car, that is in a very bad condition【非正式】残破的东西〔尤指汽车〕: *Jo drives an old wreck of a Ford.* 乔开着一辆残破不堪的福特汽车。

wreck·age /ˈrɛkɪdʒ; ˈrekɪdʒ/ *n* [singular, U] **1** the parts of something such as a plane, ship, or building that are left after it has been destroyed in an accident〔飞机、船、建筑物被毁后的〕残骸: *sifting through the wreckage for survivors* 仔细地在残骸中寻找幸存者 **2** the destruction of someone's relationships, hopes, plans etc〔关系、希望、计划等的〕破坏，毁坏

wrecked /rɛkt; rekt/ *adj* [not before noun 不用于名词前] *informal*【非正式】**1** *BrE* very drunk【英】喝醉的，醉醺醺的 **2** extremely tired 疲惫不堪的

wreck·er /ˈrɛkɚ; ˈrekə/ *n* [C] **1** someone who destroys a relationship, plan, opportunity etc〔关系、计划、机遇等的〕破坏者: *a home wrecker* 破坏家庭的人 **2** *AmE* a vehicle used to move damaged cars or other vehicles【美】〔把损毁了的汽车拖走的〕拖吊车，救险车 **3** someone in past times who deliberately made ships hit rocks so that they could steal goods from them〔昔日〕毁船打劫者 **4** someone whose job is to save goods from ships that have been damaged〔工作〕打捞失事船货物的人

Wren a member of the WRNS（英国）皇家海军妇女服务队队员

wren /rɛn; ren/ *n* [C] a very small brown bird 鹪鹩〔一种褐色小鸟〕

Wren, Sir Chris·to·pher /ˈkrɪstəfɚ; ˈkrɪstəfə/ (1632-1723) an English ARCHITECT who built many churches in London, including Saint Paul's Cathedral, and other buildings in the UK, such as the Sheldonian Theatre in Oxford 雷恩爵士〔(1632-1723)，英国建筑师。他设计了伦敦市圣保罗大教堂等多座教堂和其他一些建筑，如牛津大学的谢尔登剧院等〕

wrench¹ /rɛntʃ; rentʃ/ *v* **1** [T always+adv/prep] to twist and pull something from its position using force 猛扭〔某物〕，猛拧，猛拉: **wrench sth away/free/off etc** *I managed to wrench the knife away from him.* 我设法从他那里把刀夺过来。**2** [T always+adv/prep] to use your strength to pull yourself away from someone who is holding you 挣脱〔某人〕: **wrench yourself away/free etc** *Tim struggled to wrench himself free from her grasp.* 蒂姆奋力挣脱她的搂抱。**3** [T] to twist a joint in your body suddenly and painfully 扭伤〔关节〕: *I wrenched my knee playing soccer.* 踢足球时，我扭伤了膝盖。

wrench² *n* **1** [singular] a strong feeling of sadness that you get when you leave a person or place that you love〔离别心爱的人或地方时的〕悲痛；离愁别绪: *Leaving Arizona for New York had been a terrible wrench.* 离开亚利桑那州到纽约是件痛苦的事。**2** [C usually singular 一般用单数] a twisting movement that pulls something violently 猛拧，猛扭，猛拉: *With one almighty wrench, the door opened.* 用力一拉，门开了。**3** [C] **a)** *AmE* a metal tool with a round end that fits over and turns nuts (NUT¹ (2))【美】扳手，扳钳; SPANNER *BrE*【英】**b)** *especially AmE* also 又作 **monkey wrench** a tool that you can use to hold or turn nuts (NUT¹ (2)) that are different sizes【尤美】活动扳手; adjustable spanner *BrE*【英】—see picture at 参见 TOOL¹ 图

wrest /rɛst; rest/ *v* [T always+adv/prep] *formal*【正式】**1** to take power or influence away from someone, especially when this is difficult 费力取走〔某人或权力或影响〕**2** to pull something away from someone violently 猛拉，抢夺: *I wrested the photograph from his grasp.* 我从他紧握着的手中把照片夺了过来。

wres·tle /ˈrɛsl; ˈresəl/ *v* **1** [I,T] to fight someone by holding onto them and pulling or pushing them 与〔某人〕摔跤；扭打: [+with] *The kids were wrestling with each other in the yard.* 孩子们在院子里扭打成一团。| **wrestle sb to the ground** (=make someone fall down by holding onto them and pushing them) 把某人摔倒在地上 **2** [I,T] to have difficulty controlling or holding something that is very large, heavy, or difficult to use 奋力控制[握住]〔很大、很重或很难使用的东西〕: [+with] *Daisy was wrestling with one of the larger boxes.* 黛西正努力搬动其中一个大箱子。**3** [I] to try to deal with or find a solution to a difficult problem 努力解决；绞尽脑汁: [+with] *I spent two hours wrestling with my maths homework.* 我花了两个小时绞尽脑汁地做数学作业。

wres·tler /ˈrɛslɚ; ˈreslə/ *n* [C] someone who wrestles as a sport 摔跤运动员，摔跤手

wres·tling /ˈrɛslɪŋ; ˈreslɪŋ/ *n* [U] a sport in which two people fight by holding onto each other and trying to make each other fall to the ground 摔跤（运动）

wretch /rɛtʃ; retʃ/ *n* [C] **1** someone that you feel sorry for 可怜的人: *The poor wretch had really suffered.* 那个可怜虫真吃足了苦头。**2** *often humorous* someone you are annoyed with【常幽默】淘气鬼；家伙: *You wretch! You've soaked my dress!* 你这家伙！把我的裙子弄得湿透了！**3** *literary* an evil person【文】恶棍，坏蛋

wretch·ed /ˈrɛtʃɪd; ˈretʃɨd/ *adj* **1** very unhappy or ill 极不愉快的；极不幸的: *I lay in bed feeling thoroughly wretched.* 我躺在床上，心情坏透了。**2** [only before noun 仅用于名词前] making you feel annoyed or angry 令人讨厌的；使人愤怒的: *What does the wretched woman want this time?* 这讨厌的女人，这次想要什么？**3** *literary* extremely bad or of very poor quality【文】恶劣的；质量低劣的: *wretched living conditions* 恶劣的生活条件 —**wretchedly** *adv* —**wretchedness** *n* [U]

wrig·gle¹ /ˈrɪgl; ˈrɪgəl/ *v* **1** [I] to twist from side to side with small quick movements 扭动；蠕动: *Stop wriggling and let me put your T-shirt on.* 别扭来扭去的，让我把T恤给你穿上。| [+under/through/into] *The hole was just deep enough for the dog to wriggle under the fence.* 篱笆下面的洞刚够深，狗扭动着身子就钻了出去。**2** [T] to make a part of your body move in this way 使〔身体某一部分〕扭动 —**wriggly** *adj*

wriggle out of sth *phr v* [T] to avoid doing something by using clever excuses 用计逃脱〔做某事〕；摆脱

wriggle² *n* [C] a wriggling movement 扭动；蠕动

-wright /raɪt; raɪt/ *suffix* [in nouns 构成名词] a maker of things of a particular kind〔某物的〕制作者: *wheelwright* (=someone who makes wheels) 车轮制造工匠 | *a playwright* (=someone who writes plays) 剧作家

Wright /raɪt; raɪt/**, Frank Lloyd** (1869-1959) a US ARCHITECT who most people regard as the most important US architect of the 20th century. He is famous for his use of modern materials and methods, in buildings such as the Guggenheim Museum in New York. 赖特〔(1869-1959)，美国建筑师。多数人认为他是20世纪美国最重要的建筑师。他使用现代建筑材料和方法设计了纽约古根海姆博物馆等建筑，并以此闻名〕

Wright, Richard (1908-1960) a black US writer of NOVELS and a CRITIC of American society and its treatment of black people. He is best known for *Black Boy* and *Native Son*. 赖特〔(1908-1960)，美国黑人小说家、评论家，抨击美国社会及其对黑人的不公正待遇。其作品以《黑孩子》和《土生子》最为著名〕

Wright Broth·ers, the /ˈ· ·, · ·/ two US brothers, **Orville Wright** (1871-1948) and **Wilbur Wright** (1867-1912), who built and flew the world's first plane in 1903, at Kitty Hawk in North Carolina 莱特兄弟〔指美国奥维尔·莱特(1871-1948)和威尔伯·莱特(1867-1912)两兄弟。1903年，他们设计并制造了世界上第一架飞机，并在北卡罗来纳州的基蒂霍克作首次飞行〕

wring /rɪŋ; rɪŋ/ *v past tense and past participle* **wrung** /rʌŋ; rʌŋ/ [T] **1** [always+adv/prep] to succeed in getting money, information, an agreement etc from someone, but only after a lot of effort〔经过很大努力从某人处〕逼取〔钱财、信息、协议等〕: **wring sth from sb/out of sb** *We finally succeeded in wringing a confession out of him.* 我们大费周折，终于使他招供。**2** also 又作 **wring out** to tightly twist a wet cloth or wet clothes in order to force out the water 把〔湿布或湿衣服〕拧干；绞出〔水〕**3** **wring your hands** to rub and twist your hands together because you are worried and upset〔因焦虑不安而〕绞紧双手 **4** **wring sth's neck** to kill something such as a chicken by twisting its neck 拧脖子以杀死某动物〈如小鸡〉**5** **I'll wring sb's neck** *spoken* used when someone has made you angry【口】〔生气时说〕我要拧断某人的脖子: *If you say that again I'll wring your neck!* 如果你再那样说，我会把你的脖子拧断！**6** **wringing wet** extremely wet 湿得能拧出水来的；湿淋淋的 **7** **wring sb's hand** to shake hands very firmly with someone 用力地握某人的手 **8** **wring your heart/soul** *literary* to make you feel very sorry for someone【文】〔为某人〕非常伤心

wring·er /ˈrɪŋɚ; ˈrɪŋə/ *n* [C] **1** a machine with two rollers (ROLLER (1)) that press the water from washed clothes when you turn a handle 滚筒式衣服绞干机 **2** **go through the wringer** *AmE informal* to have an upsetting experience【美，非正式】历经千辛万苦: *She's really been through the wringer since her husband died.* 丈夫去世之后，她受尽煎熬。

wrin·kle¹ /ˈrɪŋkl; ˈrɪŋkəl/ *n* [C] **1** a line on your face or skin that you get when you are old〔因年老而在脸、皮肤上出现的〕皱纹: *wrinkles around the eyes* 眼角的鱼尾纹 **2** a small untidy fold in a piece of clothing or paper〔布、纸上的〕皱褶 **3** **iron**

W

out the wrinkles to solve the small problems in something 解决小问题 **—wrinkly** *adj*

wrinkle² *v* **1** [I,T] if you wrinkle a piece of clothing or if it wrinkles, it gets small untidy folds in it（使）起皱纹;（使）皱起: *The trouble with linen is that it wrinkles so easily.* 亚麻布的毛病是太容易起褶。**2 wrinkle your nose/eyes/brow etc** to move part of your face so that there are wrinkles on or around it 皱起鼻子/眼睛/眉毛等

wrin·kled /ˈrɪŋkḷd; ˈrɪŋkəld/ *adj* skin, cloth, or paper that is wrinkled has lines or small untidy folds in it〔皮肤、布、纸〕有皱纹的; 有皱褶的

wrin·kly /ˈrɪŋklɪ; ˈrɪŋkli/ *n plural* **wrinklies** [C] *BrE informal* an impolite expression meaning someone who is old【英, 非正式】老东西, 老家伙〔不礼貌的表述〕

S3 **wrist** /rɪst; rɪst/ *n* [C] the joint between your hand and the lower part of your arm 腕（关节）—see picture at 参见 BODY 图

wrist·band /ˈrɪstˌbænd; ˈrɪstbænd/ *n* [C] **1** a band worn especially by tennis players around their wrists to keep their hands dry〔尤指网球员戴的保持双手干爽的〕腕套 **2** a band worn around your wrist, for example in a hospital 腕带〔例如在医院里用〕

wrist·watch /ˈrɪstˌwɑtʃ; ˈrɪstwɒtʃ/ *n* [C] a watch that you wear on your wrist 手表

writ¹ /rɪt; rɪt/ *n* [C] a document from a court that orders someone to do or not to do something〔法院的〕令状; 书面命令 —see also 另见 HOLY WRIT

writ² *adj* **writ large** *literary*【文】**a)** made clearer and easier to notice 显而易见 **b)** in a clearer and stronger form 更明显的; 更突出的: *The new evangelism is really old time religion writ large.* 新的福音派教义无非是旧教义的阐发。

S1 W1 **write** /raɪt; raɪt/ *v past tense* **wrote** /rot; rəʊt/ *past participle* **written** /ˈrɪtṇ; ˈrɪtn/

1 ►BOOK/ARTICLE ETC 书/文章等◄ a) [I,T] to produce a new book, poem song etc 写〔新书、诗歌等〕; 写作: *I can't come with you – I have an essay to write.* 我不能跟你一起去, 我要写一篇论文。| *a concerto written by Mozart* 莫扎特创作的协奏曲 | **write about** (=describe something) 描述 *The children are writing about their summer holidays.* 孩子在描述他们暑假的见闻。| **well/badly written** *The article's very well written.* 这篇文章写得棒极了。| **write a program** (=produce it on a computer) 编写〔电脑〕程序 *We're writing a program for a new spellchecker.* 我们正在编写一个新的拼写检查程序。**b)** [I] to be a writer of books, plays, articles etc 写作〔书、剧本、文章等〕, 创作: *"What do you do?" "I write."* "你是做什么的?" "我是作家。" | **[+for]** *Shaw started to write for the stage.* 肖开始写剧本。| **[+on]** *She writes on gardening for 'The Daily Telegraph'.* 她给《每日电讯报》撰写园艺方面的文章。

2 ►LETTER 信◄ [I,T] to write a letter to someone 写（信）: **[+to]** *Have you written to John yet?* 你给约翰写信了吗? | **write sb a letter** *I wrote her several letters, but she didn't reply.* 我给她写了几封信, 可是她没有回复。| **write sb** *AmE*【美】: *Steve wrote me about the wedding.* 史蒂夫写信告诉我婚礼的情况。| **write that** *The Ewings wrote that they might be able to visit us in the spring.* 尤因夫妇写信说, 他们也许春季能来看望我们。

3 ►WORDS 字◄ a) [I,T] to form letters or numbers with a pen or pencil〔用钢笔、铅笔〕书写; 写字: *Kerry could read and write when he was five.* 克里五岁时就能读书写字了。| *The price is written on the label.* 价格写在标签上。**b)** [I] if a pen or pencil writes, it works properly〔笔〕好写, 能写（字）: *What use is a pen that won't write?* 不能写字的笔有什么用?

4 ►CHEQUE/DOCUMENT ETC 支票/文件等◄ [T] also 又作 **write** sth ↔ **out** to write information on a cheque, form etc 填写〔支票、表格等〕: *Wouldn't it be easier if I just wrote a cheque for the lot?* 如果全部款项我用一张支票支付, 不是更方便吗?

5 have sth written all over your face to show very clearly what you are feeling or thinking 脸上明显表露出〔感受或思想〕: *He had guilt written all over his face.* 他一脸内疚。

6 nothing to write home about *informal* not particularly good or special【非正式】平平常常的; 没什么了不起的: *The hotel was good, but the food was nothing to write home about.* 这家酒店不错, 但饭菜不怎么样。

7 sb wrote the book on it *spoken* used to say that someone knows a lot about a subject【口】某人熟悉某方面的事: *Ask Harry about shark fishing, he wrote the book on it!* 问哈里去, 他精通钓鲨鱼之道!

write away for sth *phr v* [T] *AmE* to write to a company for something that has been advertised【美】写信索取〔已刊登广告的东西〕; 函购: *Write away for your free kitchen catalog today.* 请今天就来信索取免费厨房用具目录。

write back *phr v* [I] to answer someone's letter by sending them a letter 回信: *I sent them a card once, but they never wrote back.* 我给他们寄去一张贺卡, 但他们根本没有回信。

write sth ↔ **down** *phr v* [T] to write information, ideas etc on a piece of paper in order to remember them〔在纸上〕记下〔信息、想法等〕, 写下: *I wrote down the address in the back of my diary.* 我在日记背后写下地址。

write in *phr v* **1** [I] to write to an organization asking them for information or giving an opinion 给〔机构〕写信索取〔资料〕; 提供书面意见: *Hundreds of viewers have written in wanting to know the name of our signature tune.* 成百上千的观众写信来想知道我们节目主题曲的曲名。**2** [T **write** sb/sth ↔ **in**] *AmE*【美】to add someone's name to your BALLOT PAPER in order to vote for them 在选票上加进〔某人的名字, 以投他一票〕—see also 另见 WRITE-IN

write sth **into** sth *phr v* [T] to include something such as a rule or condition in a document, agreement etc 把〔规则、条件等〕写进〔文件、协议等〕: *I have to attend regular training sessions – it's written into my contract.* 我必须参加定期培训, 这已写入合同中。

write off *phr v* **1** [T **write** sb/sth ↔ **off**] to decide that someone or something is useless, unimportant, or a failure 认为〔某人[某事]〕不行[不重要; 失败]: **[+as]** *We've written the project off as a non-starter.* 我们已经认为该计划无望成功。**2** [T **write** sth ↔ **off**] to officially say that someone does not have to pay a debt〔正式〕勾销, 注销〔某人债款〕: *As part of the deal, all their debts were written off.* 作为交易的一部分, 他们的所有债务一笔勾销。**3** [I] to write to a company asking them to send you information on one of their products 向〔公司〕写信索取〔产品资料〕: **[+for]** *Are you going to write off for that free poster?* 你会写信索取那免费海报吗? **4** [T **write** sth ↔ **off**] *BrE* to damage a vehicle so badly that it can never be used again【英】使〔车辆〕报废; 毁掉 —see also 另见 WRITE-OFF

write sb/sth ↔ **out** *phr v* [T] **1** to write a list, report etc including all the necessary details 全部写出〔清单、报告等〕: *Write out exactly what happened and give it to your solicitor.* 如实写出发生了什么, 然后把它交给你的律师。**2** to write information on a cheque or a form 填写〔支票、表格〕: *She calmly wrote out a check for $500 and handed it to Will.* 她镇定地开出一张 500 美元的支票, 然后交给威尔。**3** to write something again in a better or more complete way 誊写, 抄写: *I'll write my essay out neatly and give it in tomorrow.* 我要把文章抄写整齐, 明天交上去。**4** to remove one of the characters from a regular radio or television programme 取消〔电台或电视长期节目中的角色〕

write sth ↔ **up** *phr v* [T] **1** to write a report, article etc using notes that you made earlier〔根据事前的笔记〕重新整理〔为报告、文章等〕: *I have to write up my report before the meeting.* 我必须在会议前把报告整理一下。**2** to write your opinion about a new book, play, or product for a newspaper, magazine etc〔替报刊等〕写文章评论〔新书、戏剧、产品〕—see also 另见 WRITE-UP

write-in /ˈ· ·/ *n* [C] *AmE* a vote you give to someone by writing their name on your BALLOT PAPER【美】选举人对非原定候选人所投的票

write-off /ˈ· ·/ *n* [C] **1** *BrE* a vehicle that has been so badly damaged that it can never be used again【英】报废的车: *The car was a complete write-off.* 那辆汽车彻底报废了。—see also 另见 **write off** (4) (WRITE) **2** an official agreement that someone does not have to pay a debt〔某人债款的〕注销, 勾销

writ·er /ˈraɪtɚ; ˈraɪtə/ *n* [C] someone who writes books, stories etc, especially as a job〔尤指职业〕作家; 作者: *a science-fiction writer* 科幻小说作家 | **[+on]** *a well-known writer on astrology* 著名的占星术作者 | **[+of]** *a writer of children's stories* 儿童故事撰稿人 S3 W2

writer's block /ˌ·· ˈ·/ *n* [U] the problem that a writer sometimes has of not being able to think of new ideas 作家一时文思不畅

writer's cramp /ˌ·· ˈ·/ *n* [U] a feeling of stiffness in your hand that you get after writing for a long time〔书写时间过长而引起的〕书写痉挛

write-up /ˈ· ·/ *n* [C] a written opinion about a new book, play, or product in a newspaper, magazine etc〔报刊上对新书、新剧或新产品的〕评论文章: *The play got a really good write-up in the press.* 这部戏剧大受新闻界的好评。

writhe /raɪð; raɪð/ *v* [I] **1** to twist your body from side to side violently, especially because you are suffering pain〔尤指因痛苦〕剧烈地扭动身体: **writhe in pain/agony** *He lay on the floor writhing in pain.* 他痛苦地在地上打滚。**2 writhe with anger/hate/shame etc** *literary* to feel very violent emotions of anger etc【文】感到极度愤怒/憎恶/羞耻等

writ·ing /ˈraɪtɪŋ; ˈraɪtɪŋ/ *n* [U] **1** words that have been written or printed〔书写、印刷的〕文字: *What does the writing on the back say?* 背面的文字讲些什么? **2 in writing** if you get something in writing, it is official proof of an agreement, promise etc〔协议、诺言等〕书面形式: **put sth in writing** *Could you put that in writing please?* 请你把它写下来好吗? **3** books, poems etc in general, especially those by a particular writer or about a particular subject〔尤指某作者或主题的〕著作; 作品: *Some of his most powerful writing is based on his childhood experiences.* 他有些最震慑人心的作品是根据儿时的经历写成的。**4** the activity of writing books, stories etc 写作; 著书: *In 1991 she retired from politics and took up writing as a career.* 1991年她退出政界, 开始写作。**5** the particular way that someone writes with a pen or pencil; HANDWRITING 字迹, 笔迹: *Your writing is very neat.* 你的笔迹很整齐。**6 writings** *plural* the books, stories etc that a particular person writes〔某人的〕著作〔书, 小说等〕: *Darwin's scientific writings* 达尔文的科学著作 **7 the writing is on the wall** used to say that it seems very likely that something will not exist much longer or someone will fail 厄运临头的预兆已经显露〔指某事物很可能即将消失或某人将失败〕: *The writing is on the wall for the old manufacturing industries.* 旧式制造业分明已经日薄西山, 江河日下了。

writing desk /ˈ‥ ·/ *n* [C] a desk with special places for pens, paper etc 书桌, 写字台

writing pa·per /ˈ‥ ,‥/ *n* [U] good quality paper that you use for writing letters〔优质〕信纸

writ·ten¹ /ˈrɪtn; ˈrɪtn/ the past participle of WRITE

written² *adj* [only before noun 仅用于名词前] **1** recorded in writing 书面的: **written agreement/reply etc** *You'll get a written report of my conclusions within ten days.* 10天之内你会收到我的结论的书面报告。**2 written test/exam** a test etc in which you have to write the answers 笔试 **3 the written word** *formal* writing as a way of expressing ideas, emotions etc【正式】〔表达思想、感情等的〕文字

WRNS, the /ˌdʌblju ɑr ɛn ˋɛs; ˌdʌbəljuː ɑːr en ˈes/ Women's Royal Naval Service; the women's part of the British Royal Navy (英国) 皇家海军妇女服务队

wrong¹ /rɔŋ; rɒŋ/ *adj*

1 ▶NOT CORRECT 不正确◀ saying, believing, or depending on something that is not correct 不正确的; 错误的: *Your calculations must be wrong.* 你肯定算错了。| **be wrong to think/say** *I'm sorry; I was wrong to assume that you wanted to go.* 对不起, 我误以为你想去。| **prove sb wrong** *I wish you'd stop trying to prove me wrong all the time.* 我希望你不要总想证明是我的错。

2 ▶NOT THE RIGHT ONE 不是正确的那个◀ not the one that you intended or the one that you should use 不对的, 弄错了的: *The letter was delivered to the wrong address.* 信寄错地址了。| *driving on the wrong side of the road* 在马路上开车逆行

3 ▶TELEPHONE 电话◀ wrong number used when you have telephoned the wrong person by mistake 拨错〔电话〕号码: *There's no-one called Julia here – I think you must have the wrong number.* 这儿没有叫朱莉娅的, 我想你肯定拨错号码了。

4 ▶NOT MORAL 不道德◀ not morally right or acceptable 不道德的; 不能接受的: **it is wrong to do sth** *You must have known it was wrong to take the money.* 你肯定知道偷钱是不对的。| **it is wrong that** *It's wrong that people should have to sleep on the streets.* 有人要露宿街头是无法接受的。—opposite 反义词 RIGHT¹ (6)

5 ▶NOT SUITABLE 不适合◀ not suitable for a particular purpose, situation, or person〔对某目的、情况或人〕不适合的: *It's the wrong time of year to be planning a holiday.* 计划一年中的这个时间去休假是不合适的。| [+for] *This is the wrong climate for growing grapes.* 这种气候不适合种植葡萄。

6 be the wrong way round/around a) to be in the wrong order〔次序〕颠倒, 相反: *These two paragraphs are the wrong way round.* 这两个段落顺序倒了。**b)** to be pointing in the wrong direction 方向不对: *You've got your T-shirt on the wrong way around.* 你的T恤穿反了。

7 be in the wrong place at the wrong time *spoken* to get involved in trouble without intending to【口】在错误的时间来到错误的地方〔指无意中落入困境〕

8 get on the wrong side of sb to do something that gives someone a bad opinion of you, so that they do not like or respect you in the future〔做某事〕冒犯某人, 招惹某人讨厌

9 get on the wrong side of the law to get into trouble with the police 与警方发生麻烦; 犯事

10 get off on the wrong foot to start a job, relationship etc badly by making a mistake that annoys people〔工作、关系等〕一开始就不顺利〔因犯错而使别人讨厌〕

11 take sth the wrong way to be offended by a remark because you have understood it wrongly 误解某句话〔因而感到不快〕

12 get the wrong end of the stick *informal* to understand a situation in completely the wrong way【非正式】完全误解形势

13 be on the wrong track/tack to have the wrong idea about a situation so that you are unlikely to get the result you want〔思考的〕方向错误/路子不对头

14 be from the wrong side of the tracks *AmE* to be from a poor part of a town or a poor part of society【美】来自贫民区, 来自下层社会

15 be on the wrong side of thirty/forty etc *informal* to be older than thirty etc【非正式】已过30/40岁等 —see also 另见 **get out of bed on the wrong side** (BED¹ (9))

Frequencies of the adjective **wrong** in spoken and written English 形容词wrong在英语口语和书面语中的使用频率

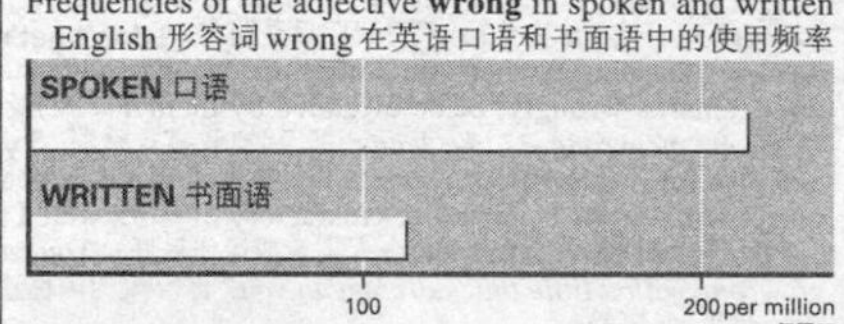

Based on the British National Corpus and the Longman Lancaster Corpus 据英国国家语料库和朗文兰开斯特语料库

This graph shows that the adjective **wrong** is much more common in spoken English than in written English. This is because it is used in some common spoken phrases. 本图表显示, 形容词wrong在英语口语中的使用频率远远高于书面语, 因为口语中一些常用短语是由wrong构成的。

wrong (*adj*) **SPOKEN PHRASES**
含wrong的口语短语

16 what's wrong? a) used to ask someone what problem they have, why they are unhappy etc 怎么啦?〔用于问别人有什么问题、为何不开心等〕: *"What's wrong?" "Oh, I'm just a bit worried about tomorrow."* "怎么啦?" "噢, 我对明天有点担心。" **b)** used to ask why something doesn't work 出了什么毛病?〔用于问为什么某物不运转〕: [+with] *What's wrong with this clock?* 这钟出什么毛病了? **c)** used to say that you think something is good, fair etc, and you do not understand why other people think it is not 有什么不可以?〔用于表示你认为某物很好、不错等, 但不明白为何别人的意见不同〕: [+with] *What's wrong with eating meat? I think it's natural.* 吃肉有什么不妥? 我觉得很正常。

17 there's something wrong used to say that there is a fault or problem with something〔用于表示某物〕有些毛病〔问题〕: *There's something wrong. The car won't start.* 有毛病了, 汽车发动不起来。| [+with] *There's something wrong with the phone, the line's dead.* 电话有毛病了, 线路不通。| **have sth wrong with** *She had to go home early – she's got something wrong with her back.* 她不得不早点回家, 她觉得背部不太舒服。

18 there's nothing wrong a) used to say that something has not got any faults or problems 没问题〔用于表示某物没毛病〕: *It's O.K. don't worry, there's nothing wrong.* 好了, 别担心, 没问题了。| [+with] *There's nothing wrong with the TV, it just wasn't plugged in.* 电视机没毛病, 只是没有插上插头。**b)** used to say that you do not think that something is bad or immoral 没有什么不对〔认为某事并非不好或不道德〕: [+with] *There's nothing wrong with drinking, as long as you know when to stop.* 只要适可而止, 喝酒并不是坏事。

19 correct me if I'm wrong used as a polite way of saying that you think what you are going to say is correct 如果错了请予纠正〔礼貌地表示自认为将要说的话是正确的〕: *Correct me if I'm wrong, but didn't you say you were going to do it?* 如果我错了, 请纠正, 你不是说过你准备做这事吗?

20 you're not wrong used to agree with someone 你没有错〔表示同意〕: *"This government is ruining the country!" "You're not wrong!"* "本届政府正在毁掉国家!" "说得一点都不错!"

W

wrong² *adv* **1** not in the correct way 错误地; 不正确地: *You've spelt my name wrong.* 你把我的名字拼写错了。| **do sth all wrong** (=in completely the wrong way) 事情完全做错了 *I asked him to sort those flies, but he's done it all wrong.* 我让他整理这些文 

件，可是他全做错了。**2 go wrong a)** to stop working properly 出毛病；出故障：*The television's gone wrong again.* 电视机又出毛病了。| **[+with]** *Something's gone wrong with my watch.* 我的手表出故障了。**b)** to make a mistake during a process so that you do not get the right result〔在过程中〕出错，弄错：**you can't go wrong** (=you are sure to succeed) 你不会出错 *Follow these instructions and you can't go wrong.* 按照操作指南去做，你就不会出错。**c)** to do something that makes a plan, relationship etc fail〔计划、关系等〕出现问题：*Thinking back on the marriage, I just don't know where we went wrong.* 回想起这段婚姻，我真不知道问题出在哪里。**3 get sth wrong** to make a mistake in the way you write, judge, or understand something 写错[误解；误会]某事：*This isn't it. We must have got the address wrong.* 不是这里，我们肯定把地址搞错了。| **get/have it all wrong** (=understand a situation in completely the wrong way) 完全误解[曲解] *No, no – you've got it all wrong! We're just friends!* 不，不是，你完全搞错了！我们只是朋友！**4 don't get me wrong** *spoken* used when you think someone may understand your remarks wrongly, or be offended by them【口】别误会：*Don't get me wrong – I like Jenny.* 别误会，我喜欢珍妮。**5 you can't go wrong (with sth)** *spoken* used to say that a particular object will always be suitable, satisfactory or work well【口】〔某物〕不会出问题〔总是合适、令人满意或运作良好〕：*You can't go wrong with a little black dress, can you?* 你穿短的黑色连衣裙不会错，是不是？

USAGE NOTE 用法说明：WRONG
COLLOCATION/GRAMMAR 搭配/语法

Many meanings of **wrong** only belong in particular phrases or structures that cannot be changed. wrong 的许多释义只用在特定的不能改变的短语或结构中。For example, if someone's health is bad, you can say something **is wrong with** them but not: *They are wrong* (which means not correct). 如某人身体欠佳，可以说 something is wrong with them，但不可以说 They are wrong（这是他们没做对的意思）。

You can **do something wrong** (=not in the correct way) but not **do a wrong thing** (though you can **do the wrong thing**). 犯错是 do something wrong 而不是 do a wrong thing（但可以说 do the wrong thing）。If you **do something wrong**, that does not mean there is something **wrong with you**. you do something wrong（犯错）和 there is something wrong with you（身体欠佳）不同：*He was angry with me but I hadn't done anything wrong.* 他生我的气了，但我没做什么错事。Note 注意 **...there was nothing wrong with me** (=I was not sick 我没生病).

Wrong used before a noun usually means 'not correct', 'not correctly chosen' or 'not suitable'. wrong用在名词前通常表示"不正确"，"选得不对"或"不合适"：*the wrong answer/key/furniture* 不正确的答案/钥匙选得不对/家具不合适。You would also say: *I can't find what is wrong/has gone wrong* (NOT *I can't find the wrong thing*) if you mean that something is not working 表示某物不运转时可以说：I can't find what is wrong/has gone wrong. 我找不出哪里有问题。(不用 I can't find the wrong thing) **Wrong** also means 'morally wrong', and is used in this way. wrong 也表示"不道德"并用于：*What you did was completely wrong* (NOT 不用 *You did wrong things/action*). 你做的事完全不道德。

Sometimes **bad** is a better word to use. You would call a day when everything **goes wrong** a *bad day* (NOT *a wrong day*). 有时选用单词 bad 较好。事事不顺利 (everything goes wrong) 的一天可以称作 a bad day（而不说 a wrong day）。If you **get things wrong** you make a lot of mistakes, and may get a *bad record* but not a *wrong record* (which means not correct). 如果做了很多错事 (get things wrong)，也许会有不良的记录（a bad record，但不说 a wrong record，这是"错误的记录"的意思）。

wrong³ *n* **1** [U] behaviour that is not morally right 坏事；邪恶：*He's too young to know right from wrong.* 他太年轻了，还不能辨别是非。| **sb can do no wrong** (=they are perfect) 某人不会做错事 *That man seems to think he can do no wrong.* 那个男人似乎认为自己不会做错事。**2** [C] an action, judgement, or situation that is unfair〔行为、判决、情形〕不公正：*The black population suffered countless wrongs at the hands of a racist regime.* 在种族主义政权统治下，黑人遭受了无尽的冤屈。| **right a wrong** (=bring justice to an unfair situation) 纠正错误；平反冤屈 **3 be in the wrong** to make a mistake or deserve the blame for something 犯错误；应负责任：*Which driver was in the wrong?* 是哪个司机出的错？**4 do sb wrong** *humorous* to treat someone badly and unfairly【幽默】冤枉某人；不公平地对待某人 **5 two wrongs don't make a right** *spoken* used to say that punishing someone will not make a bad situation right or fair【口】负负不能得正〔用于表示惩罚某人不能使坏情况变好或公平〕

wrong⁴ *v* [T] *formal* to treat or judge someone unfairly【正式】不公正地对待〔某人〕，冤枉：*I felt I had been grievously wronged.* 我感觉受到了极大的委屈。

wrong·do·ing /ˈrɔŋ̩duɪŋ; ˈrɒŋ̩duːɪŋ/ *n* [C,U] *formal* illegal or immoral behaviour【正式】不法行为；不道德行为；坏事 —**wrongdoer** *n*

wrong-foot /ˌrɔŋˈfʊt; ˌrɒŋˈfʊt/ *v* [T] to surprise and embarrass someone, especially by asking a question they did not expect 使大吃一惊；使仓皇失措〔尤指提出意想不到的问题〕

wrong·ful /ˈrɔŋfəl; ˈrɒŋfəl/ *adj* **wrongful arrest/conviction/dismissal etc** a wrongful arrest etc is unfair or illegal because you have done nothing wrong 不公正的逮捕/判决/解雇等：*She's threatening to sue her employers for wrongful dismissal.* 她扬言要控告雇主非法解雇。—**wrongfully** *adv*

wrong·head·ed /ˌrɔŋˈhɛdɪd; ˌrɒŋˈhedɪd◂/ *adj* based on or influenced by wrong ideas that you are not willing to change 坚持错误的；执迷不悟的 —**wrongheadedly** *adv*

wrong·ly /ˈrɔŋlɪ; ˈrɒŋli/ *adv* **1** incorrectly or in a way that is not based on facts 不正确地；错误地：*You're holding the racket wrongly.* 你球拍握得不对。| *Matthew was wrongly diagnosed as having a brain tumour.* 马修被误诊患有脑瘤。**2** in a way that is unfair or immoral 不公正地；不道德地：**wrongly convicted/imprisoned/accused/blamed** *Human rights organizations maintain that the men have been wrongly convicted.* 人权组织坚称这些人被错判了。**3** in a way that is not suitable or socially acceptable 不合适；普遍不接受：*I was wrongly dressed for a formal dinner.* 我的衣着不适合出席正式宴会。—see also 另见 **rightly or wrongly** (RIGHTLY)

wrote /rot; rəʊt/ the past tense of WRITE

wroth /rɔθ; rəʊθ/ *adj old use* angry【旧】发怒的

wrought i·ron /ˌrɔt ˈaɪɚn; ˌrɔːt ˈaɪən◂/ *n* [U] long thin pieces of iron formed into shapes to make gates, fences etc〔制作闸门、栅栏等的〕锻铁，熟铁

wrought-up /ˌ· ˈ·◂/ *adj* very nervous and excited 非常紧张的；极激动的

wrung /rʌŋ; rʌŋ/ the past tense and past participle of WRING

WRVS, the /ˌdʌbl̩ju ɑr vi ˈɛs; ˌdʌbəljuː ɑː viː ˈes/ the Women's Royal Voluntary Service; a British organization of women who help people who have difficulty taking care of themselves. The WRVS provides Meals on Wheels, a service which brings meals to people who cannot cook because they are very old or very ill. The women who work for the WRVS are VOLUNTEERS (=they are not paid for their work). 皇家妇女志愿服务队〔英国一妇女组织，旨在帮助无自理能力者。该组织提供"送饭上门"服务，将饭菜送到不能自理的老人或重症病人手中。该组织的妇女均为志愿者〕

wry /raɪ; raɪ/ *adj* [only before noun 仅用于名词前] showing a mixture of amusement and displeasure or disbelief 露出怪相的；苦笑的〔表示不悦或不相信〕：*He took a gulp of his Scotch and gave a wry smile at the injustices of the world.* 他喝了一大口苏格兰威士忌酒，对这个世界的不公平苦笑了一下。

wt the written abbreviation of 缩写= WEIGHT

WTC, the the abbreviation of 缩写= the WORLD TRADE CENTER

WTO, the /ˌdʌbl̩ju ti ˈo; ˌdʌbəljuː tiː ˈəʊ/ the abbreviation of 缩写= the WORLD TRADE ORGANIZATION

wun·der·kind /ˈwʌndɚkɪnd; ˈwʌndəkɪnd/ *n* [C] *German* a young person who is very successful【德】神童；非常成功的年轻人

wuss /wʊs; wʌs/ *n* [C] *AmE slang* someone who you think is weak because they are afraid to do something difficult or unpleasant【美俚】软弱无能的人

Wuth·er·ing Heights /ˌwʌðərɪŋ ˈhaɪts; ˌwʌðərɪŋ ˈhaɪts/ a NOVEL by the British writer Emily Brontë, one of the best-known books in English literature. It is a romantic and exciting story, set on the Yorkshire Moors, about the love between the two main characters, Catherine Earnshaw and Heathcliff.《呼啸山庄》〔英国作家埃米莉·勃朗特的一部小说，是英国文学中最为著名的作品之一。这是一个浪漫而又惊心动魄的故事，以约克郡漠泽为背景，讲述两个主人公凯瑟琳·厄恩肖与希思克利夫之间的爱情故事〕

WV the written abbreviation of 缩写= WEST VIRGINIA

W.Va. the written abbreviation of 缩写= WEST VIRGINIA

WWF, the /ˌdʌbl̩ju dʌbl̩ju ˈɛf; ˌdʌbəljuː dʌbəljuː ˈef/ the abbreviation of 缩写= the WORLD WIDE FUND FOR NATURE

WWI the written abbreviation of 缩写= WORLD WAR I

WWII the written abbreviation of 缩写= WORLD WAR II

WY the written abbreviation of 缩写= WYOMING

Wych·er·ley /ˈwɪtʃəlɪ; ˈwɪtʃəli/, **William** (1640-1716) an English Restoration COMEDY writer whose plays include *The Country Wife*. 威彻利〔(1640-1716)，英国王政复辟时期的喜剧作家，其剧作包括《乡下老婆》〕

Wyc·liffe /ˈwɪklɪf; ˈwɪklɪf/, **John** (?1328-84) an English THEOLOGIAN (=someone who studies religion and religious beliefs) who criticized the political and economic power of the Catholic Church. He also started the first complete translation of the Bible into English. 威克里夫〔(?1328-1384)，英国神学家。他曾对天主教会的政治及经济权力进行了抨击，还率先将《圣经》全文译成英文〕

Wy·eth /ˈwaɪəθ; ˈwaɪəθ/, **Andrew** (1917-2009) a US painter whose best-known painting is 'Christina's World'. His son **Jamie Wyeth** is also a painter. 韦思〔(1917-2009)，美国画家。最著名的画作是《克里斯蒂娜的世界》。其子杰米·韦思也是画家〕

Wy·nette /wɪˋnɛt; wɪˈnet/, **Tam·my** /ˋtæmɪ; ˈtæmi/ (1942-98) a US country and western singer whose songs include *D-I-V-O-R-C-E* and *Stand by your Man*, one of the most popular country and western songs ever made 怀尼特〔(1942-1998)，美国乡村音乐、西部音乐歌手。歌曲有《离婚》和《支持你的男人》。《支持你的男人》是有史以来最受欢迎的乡村音乐歌曲之一〕

Wyo. the written abbreviation of 缩写= WYOMING

Wy·o·ming /waɪˋomɪŋ; waɪˈəʊmɪŋ/ abbreviation 缩写为 **WY** a state in the Rocky Mountains in the northwestern US. Although it covers a large area, it has the smallest population of any state in the US. It produces minerals, BEEF, and wool. 怀俄明州〔美国西北部落基山区一州。该州面积广大，却是美国人口最少的州。出产矿物、牛肉和羊毛〕

WYSIWYG /ˋwɪzɪˌwɪg; ˈwɪziwɪg/ *n* [U] What You See Is What You Get; a word used in computing meaning what you see on the screen is exactly what will be printed 所见即所得〔电脑用语，指在屏幕上看见的与打印本丝毫不差〕

Wyss /waɪs; waɪs/, **Jo·hann** /ˈjohɑn; ˈjəʊhæn/ (1743-1818) a Swiss who wrote the very popular children's book *Swiss Family Robinson* 维斯〔(1743-1818)，瑞士人。著有畅销儿童读物《瑞士家庭鲁滨逊》〕

wy·vern /ˋwaɪvən; ˈwaɪvən/ *n* [C] an imaginary animal that has two legs and wings and looks like a DRAGON (1)〔想象中的〕双足飞龙

W

X,x

X[1], x /ɛks; eks/ *plural* **X's**, **x's** *n* [C] **1** the 24th letter of the English alphabet 英语字母表的第二十四个字母 **2** the number 10 in the system of ROMAN NUMERALS〔罗马数字〕十 **3** *technical* a letter used in mathematics to represent an unknown quantity or value【术语】〔数学中的〕未知数[量]: *if 3x=6, x=2.* 假设3x=6, 则 x=2。**4** a mark used to show that a written answer is wrong〔表示书面答案错误的符号〕**5** a mark used to show that you have chosen something on an official piece of paper, for example when voting〔表示选中的符号, 如选举时〕**6** a mark used instead of a signature by someone who cannot write〔不会写字的人用以代替签名的符号〕**7** a mark used to show a kiss, especially at the end of a letter〔表示亲吻的符号, 尤用于信末〕**8** a letter used to show that a film is not suitable for people under 18 X级〔电影的级别, 表示未满18岁者不宜观看〕**9** a letter used instead of someone or something's real name because you want to keep it secret or you do not know it〔用以代替不宜公开或不知其名的人或事物的名称〕: *At the trial, Ms X said that she had known the defendant for three years.* 在庭审中, X女士说她认识被告已有三年了。**10 X number of** used to say that there are a certain number of people or things when the exact number is not important X个〔用于说明有一些人或物, 而准确的数字并不重要〕**11 X marks the spot** used on maps in adventure stories to show that something is buried in a particular place〔地图上〕标有X的地点〔在探险故事中指埋有某物的地方〕

X[2] *v*

X out sth *phr v* [T] *AmE* to mark or remove a mistake in a piece of writing using an X【美】〔在一篇文章中〕用X符号标出[删去]〔错误〕; **cross out** (CROSS[1])

Xan·a·du /ˋzænədu; ˈzænəduː/ an imaginary place that is very beautiful. The name comes from a place in the poem *Kubla Khan* by Samuel Taylor Coleridge. 仙纳度, 世外桃源〔一个虚构的极其美丽的地方。此名出自塞缪尔·泰勒·柯尔律治的诗作《忽必烈汗》〕

X-cer·tif·i·cate /ˋɛks səˌtɪfɪkət; ˈeks səˌtɪfɪkət/ *adj* an X-certificate film is one that people under 18 are not allowed to see in Britain because it includes sex or violence〔电影〕X级的〔含有性或暴力内容, 在英国18岁以下者禁看〕—compare 比较 PG, R[2] (4), U (1)

X chro·mo·some /ˋɛks ˌkroməˌsom; ˈeks ˌkrəʊməsəʊm/ *n* [C] a type of CHROMOSOME that exists in pairs in female cells, and with a Y CHROMOSOME in male cells X染色体

xen·on /ˋzinɑn; ˈzenɒn/ *n* [U] a rare gas that is one of the chemical elements (ELEMENT (1)) 氙

xen·o·pho·bi·a /ˌzɛnəˋfobɪə; ˌzenəˈfəʊbiə/ *n* [U] extreme fear or dislike of people from other countries 对外国人的极度畏惧[憎恨], 恐外症—**xenophobic** *adj*

Xen·o·phon /ˋzɛnəfɑn; ˈzenəfən/ (?430-354 BC) a Greek HISTORIAN (=someone who writes books about history) and military leader whose best-known work, the *Anabasis*, describes a long journey by a Greek army through enemy land in western Asia. 色诺芬〔(公元前?430-前354), 希腊历史学家, 军事将领。他最著名的作品《远征记》讲述希腊军队长途跋涉穿越亚洲西部敌国领土的故事〕

Xe·rox /ˋzirɑks; ˈzɪərɒks/ *n* [C] *trademark* a copy of a piece of paper with writing or printing on it, made using a special machine; a kind of PHOTOCOPY[1]【商标】〔用静电复印法的〕复印本, 影印本 —**Xerox** *v* [T]

Xerox ma·chine /ˋ···, ·/ *n* [C] *trademark* a special electric machine used for making copies of written or printed material; a kind of PHOTOCOPIER【商标】〔静电〕复印机 —see picture on page A14 参见A14页图

Xer·xes /ˋzɝksiz; ˈzɜːksiːz/ (about 519-465 BC) a king of Persia who unsuccessfully tried to conquer Greece 薛西斯一世〔(公元前约519-前465), 波斯国王。他曾企图征服希腊, 但未获成功〕

X-Files, The /ˋɛks faɪlz; ˈeks faɪlz/ a popular US television science FICTION programme, also shown in the UK, whose main characters are two FBI agents who have many exciting and frightening adventures in their attempts to solve strange mysteries involving ALIENS (=creatures from other worlds) and other PARANORMAL events《X档案》〔美国一部广受喜爱的科幻电视剧, 也曾在英国播放。片中的主角是联邦调查局的两位探员, 为了解开外星人及其他超自然之谜共同经历了许多刺激而又恐怖的冒险奇遇〕

X-mas /ˋkrɪsməs; ˈkrɪsməs/ *n* [C,U] *informal* a word that means Christmas, often written on signs or cards【非正式】圣诞节〔常写于标志或贺卡上〕

X-rated /ˋɛks ˌretɪd; ˈeks ˌreɪtɪd/ *adj* an X-rated film is one that people under 18 are not allowed to see because it includes sex or violence〔电影〕X级的〔X级电影含有性或暴力内容, 18岁以下者禁看〕

X-ray[1] /ˋɛks ˋre; ˈeks reɪ/ *n* [C] **1** a beam of RADIATION (1) that can go through solid objects and is used for photographing the inside of the body X射线, X光 **2** a photograph of part of the body, taken in this way to see if anything is wrong X光片: *The X-ray showed that her leg was not broken.* X光片显示她的腿没有骨折。| *a chest X-ray* 胸部X光片, 胸透片 **3** a medical examination made using X-rays X光检查: *I had to go to hospital for an X-ray.* 我得去医院做X光检查。

X-ray[2] *v* [T] to photograph the inside of someone's body using X-rays 用X光拍照, 给…照X光: *The problem was only discovered when her lungs were X-rayed.* 她的肺部照了X光后才发现有问题。

xy·lo·phone /ˋzaɪləˌfon; ˈzaɪləfəʊn/ *n* [C] a musical instrument which consists of metal or wooden bars that you hit with a special stick to make sounds 木琴

Y, y

Y, y /waɪ; waɪ/ *plural* **Y's, y's** **1** the 25th letter of the English alphabet 英语字母表的第二十五个字母 **2 the Y** *AmE informal* the YMCA or the YWCA【美, 非正式】基督教青年会; 基督教女青年会

-y¹, -ey /ɪ; i/ *suffix* [in adjectives 构成形容词] **1** full of or covered with something 充满…的; 被…覆盖的: *dirty hands* (=covered with dirt) 脏手 | *a hairy chest* 多毛的胸膛 **2** tending to do something, or doing something 有…倾向的: *curly hair* (=hair that curls) 卷发 | *feeling sleepy* 感到困倦(欲睡)的 **3** like or typical of something 似…的: *a cold wintry day* (=typical of winter) 寒冷的冬日 | *his long, horsy face* (=he looks like a horse) 他那长长的马脸 **4** fond of or interested in something 热衷于…的, 爱好…的: *a horsy woman* (=who likes riding horses) 喜欢骑马的女人 **—ily** [in adverbs 构成副词] **—iness** [in nouns 构成名词]

-y² *suffix* [in nouns 构成名词] **1** also 又作 **-ie** used, especially when speaking to children, to make a word or name less formal, and often to show fondness〔尤用于对儿童说话时, 表示亲昵或喜爱〕: *Where's little Johnny?* (=John) 小约翰尼哪儿去了? | *my daddy* (=father) 我的爸爸 | *What a nice doggy!* (=dog) 多可爱的小狗啊! | *wellies* (=WELLINGTONs) 长统橡胶雨靴 **2** the action of doing something …动作; …行为: *the expiry date* (=date when something EXPIREs) 到期日

yacht 大型帆船; 大游艇

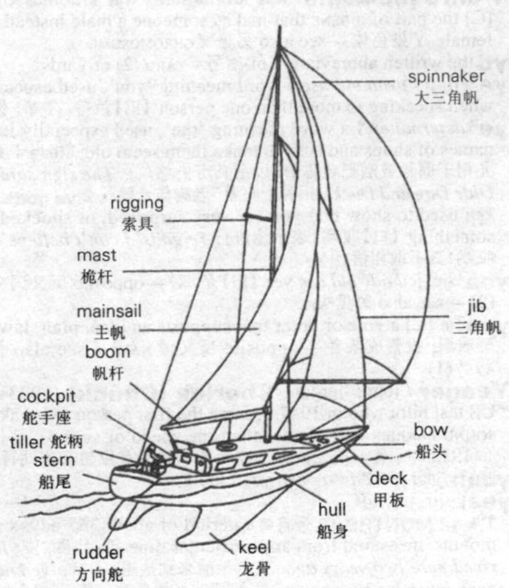

yacht /jɑt; jɒt/ *n* [C] a large sailing boat, especially one that you can sleep on〔尤指可在上面睡觉的〕大型帆船; 大游艇 —compare 比较 SAILING BOAT, SAIL BOAT

yacht·ing /ˈjɑtɪŋ; ˈjɒtɪŋ/ *n* [U] *especially BrE* sailing, travelling, or racing in a yacht【尤英】驾驶帆船[游艇]; 驾艇旅游; 帆船比赛 —compare 比较 SAILING

yachts·man /ˈjɑtsmən; ˈjɒtsmən/ *n* [C] someone who owns or sails a yacht 游艇主; 驾驶帆船[游艇]的人

yachts·wom·an /ˈjɑtsˌwʊmən; ˈjɒtswʊmən/ *n* [C] a woman who owns or sails a yacht 女游艇主; 驾驶帆船[游艇]的女子

ya·hoo /ˈjɑhu; jɑːˈhuː/ *n* [C] *old-fashioned* someone who is rough, noisy, or bad-mannered【过时】粗人, 吵闹粗鲁的人

Yahoo! *trademark* a type of SEARCH ENGINE (=a computer program used for searching for information on the Internet), which also provides other information such as news, city maps, and shopping【商标】雅虎〔一个搜索引擎, 同时提供新闻、市区地图、购物指南等信息〕

Yah·weh /ˈjɑwe; ˈjɑːweɪ/ *n* [singular] a Hebrew name for God 耶和华, 上帝〔希伯莱语〕

yak¹ /jæk; jæk/ *n* [C] an animal of central Asia that looks like a cow with long hair 牦牛〔产于中亚, 似牛但毛长〕

yak² *v* **yakked, yakking** [I] *informal* to talk continuously about things that are not very serious; CHATTER¹ (1)【非正式】喋喋不休地讲, 唠叨; 瞎扯

Yale /jel; jeɪl/ an old and respected US university, established in 1701 in New Haven, Connecticut. Yale is one of the Ivy League colleges. 耶鲁大学〔美国一所久负盛名的大学, 1701 年始建于康涅狄格州纽黑文。耶鲁大学是常春藤联合会大学之一〕

Yale lock /ˈ· ·/ also 又作 **Yale** *trademark* a type of lock often used on the main door of a house or building. Yale locks are very common in the UK and they have a special type of key.【商标】耶鲁锁〔用于房屋或建筑物大门上的一种锁。耶鲁锁在英国很常见, 配有一种特殊的钥匙〕

y'all /jɔl; jɔːl/ *pron AmE informal* a word meaning 'all of you', used mainly in the southern US states when speaking to more than one person【美, 非正式】你们大伙, 你们全都〔主要流行于美国南部〕: *Are y'all coming over for lunch?* 你们大伙都来吃午饭吗?

Yal·ta /ˈjɔltə; ˈjæltə/ **1** a port and city on the Black Sea in the Ukraine, popular with tourists 雅尔塔〔乌克兰境内濒临黑海的一座港口城市, 为旅游胜地〕 **2 the Yalta Conference** a meeting held at Yalta in 1945 between Churchill, Roosevelt, and Stalin, which greatly influenced the history of Europe after World War II. The three leaders discussed how to finish the war against Hitler's Germany, and how central and eastern Europe should be divided after the war. They also agreed to set up the United Nations. 雅尔塔会议〔丘吉尔、罗斯福和斯大林 1945 年在雅尔塔召开的一次会议。这次会议对二战后的欧洲历史进程产生了重大影响。三位领导人讨论了如何结束对希特勒德国的战争, 战后怎样分割中欧与东欧等问题。他们还就成立联合国一事达成协议〕

yam /jæm; jæm/ *n* [C] **1** a tropical climbing plant grown for its root, which is eaten as a vegetable 薯蓣, 山药 —see picture on page A9 参见 A9 页图 **2** *AmE* a type of SWEET POTATO【美】甘薯, 番薯

yam·mer /ˈjæmɚ; ˈjæmə/ also 又作 **yammer on** *v* [I] *BrE informal* to talk noisily and continuously【英, 非正式】〔不停地〕哇啦哇啦地大声说话: *a crowd of yammering aunts and cousins* 一群哇啦哇啦说个不停的姑婶和堂姐妹

yang /jæŋ; jæŋ/ *n* [U] the male principle in Chinese PHILOSOPHY which is active, light, positive and which combines with YIN (=the female principle) to influence everything in the world〔中国哲学概念中的〕阳

Yangôn a city which was the capital of Myanmar, formerly known as Rangoon 仰光〔缅甸一城市, 曾为该国首都, 旧称 Rangoon〕

Yangtze, the /ˈjæŋtsɪ; ˈjæŋtsi/ also 又作 **the Chang Jiang** the third longest river in the world, at 6,300 km or 3,915 miles long, and China's most important river 长江〔世界第三长河, 长约 6300 公里(即 3915 英里), 是中国最重要的河流〕

Yank /jæŋk; jæŋk/ *n* [C] *informal*【非正式】**1** a word meaning someone from the US, sometimes used in an insulting way by someone who is not American 美国人, 美国佬〔有时为侮辱性说法〕 **2** also 又作 **Yankee** *AmE* someone born or living in the northern, especially the northeastern, states of the US【美】美国北部各州的人, 北方佬

yank *v* [I,T] *informal* to suddenly pull something quickly and forcefully【非正式】猛拉, 使劲拉: **yank (on) sth** *John keeps yanking on my ponytail!* 约翰不停地拽我的马尾辫! | **yank sth out/back/open etc** *Keith yanked Robert out of his chair.* 基思一把将罗伯特从椅子里拉了出来。

Yan·kee /ˈjæŋkɪ; ˈjæŋki/ *n* [C] *informal*【非正式】**1** *AmE* someone born or living in the northern, especially the northeastern, states of the US【美】美国北部各州的人, 北方佬 **2** *especially BrE* someone from the US【尤英】美国人, 美国佬

Yankee Doo·dle /ˌ·· ˈ··/ a US song which first became popular with American soldiers during the American Revolutionary War and is now often sung by children.《扬基歌》〔美国

Y

一歌曲。最早由美国独立战争时期的美军士兵传唱，现常由儿童演唱〕It begins 曲首为:

Yankee Doodle went to town,
Riding on a pony;
Stuck a feather in his hat,
And called it macaroni.
扬基·杜德尔进城去，
骑着一匹小马驹，
帽上插根羽毛管，
他管这叫通心粉。

Yaoundé /jaun`de; ja:un`deɪ/ the capital city of Cameroon 雅温得〔喀麦隆首都〕

yap¹ /jæp; jæp/ *v* **yapped, yapping** [I] **1** if a small dog yaps, it BARKS (=makes short loud sounds) in an excited way〔小狗〕狂吠，汪汪乱叫 **2** to talk noisily without saying anything very important or serious 哇啦哇啦地说个不停；瞎扯: *Don't start yapping again.* 别再瞎扯了。

yap² *n* [C] the sound a small dog makes when it yaps〔小狗的〕狂吠声

2 2 **yard** /jard; ja:d/ *n* [C]

1 ▶ENCLOSED AREA 封闭地区◀ an enclosed area next to a building or group of buildings, used for a special purpose, activity, or business〔作专门用途、活动、交易的〕场所；围栏；工地: *a cattle yard* 牛[牲畜]栏 | *Their house is next to a builder's yard.* 他们的房子挨着一个建筑工地。

2 ▶MEASURE 尺度◀ written abbreviation 缩写为 **yd** a unit for measuring length, equal to 3 feet or 0.9144 metres 码〔长度单度，等于3英尺或0.9144米〕—see table on page C3 参见 C3 页附录

3 ▶GARDEN 园子◀ *AmE* the ground around a house, usually covered with grass【美】〔房子周围通常种满草的〕庭院；GARDEN¹ (1) *BrE*【英】: *backyard* 后院 | *Their front yard was full of kids playing tag.* 他们的前院有很多孩子在玩捉人游戏。—see also 另见 BACKYARD

4 prison/school yard an area outside a prison or school where prisoners or students go to do activities outdoors 监狱放风场/学校操场

5 ▶BACK OF HOUSE 宅子后部◀ *BrE* an enclosed area without grass at the back of a small house【英】后院

6 ▶SAILING 航行◀ *technical* a long pole that supports a square sail【术语】帆桁 —see also 另见 CHURCHYARD, FARMYARD, SHIPYARD

Yard, the *informal* a short form of Scotland Yard【非正式】苏格兰场〔Scotland Yard 的简称〕

yard·age /`jardɪdʒ; `ja:dɪdʒ/ *n technical*【术语】**1** [C,U] the size of something measured in yards or square yards 码数；平方码数: *a large yardage of sail* 码数很大的帆 **2** [U] the number of yards that a team or player moves forward in a game of American football〔美式橄榄球中〕将球向前推进的（总）码数

yard·arm /`jard,arm; `ja:d,a:m/ *n* [C] one of the ends of the pole that supports a square sail 帆桁的一端，桁端

yard·bird /`jard,bɝd; `ja:dbɜ:d/ *n* [C] *AmE slang*【美俚】**1** someone who is in prison, especially for a long time（老）囚犯，犯人 **2** someone who has just joined the army and has outdoor duties〔担当户外值勤等任务的〕入伍新兵

Yardie /`jardɪ; `ja:di/ *n* [C] **1** someone from the West Indies 亚迪人〔西印度群岛人〕**2** a member of an organized group of West Indian criminals 亚迪〔西印度群岛一有组织犯罪团伙成员〕

yard sale /`· ·/ *n* [C] *AmE* a sale of used things from someone's house that takes place in their YARD (3)【美】〔在自家院子进行的〕旧货出售 —compare 比较 GARAGE SALE

yard·stick /`jard,stɪk; `ja:d,stɪk/ *n* [C] **1** something that you compare another thing with, in order to judge how good or successful they are 衡量标准，评判尺度: [**+of/against**] *Is profit the only yardstick of success?* 利润是成功的唯一标准吗？**2** a special stick for measuring things that is exactly one YARD (2) long 码尺

Y

yar·mul·ke /`jarməlkə; `ja:mʊlkə/ *n* [C] a small circular cap worn by Jewish men 亚莫克便帽〔犹太男子戴的小圆帽〕

yarn /jarn; ja:n/ *n* **1** [U] *especially AmE* long thick thread, made of cotton or wool used to KNIT or make cloth【尤美】纱；线；毛线 **2** [C] *informal* a story of adventures, travels etc, usually made more exciting and interesting by adding things that never really happened【非正式】〔探险、旅行中的〕故事，奇谈: **spin a yarn** (=tell a long and often not completely true story)〔添油加醋地〕讲故事，胡诌 *The old captain would often spin us a yarn about life aboard ship.* 老船长经常给我们讲一些船上生活的奇闻轶事。

yash·mak /jæʃ`mæk; `jæʃmæk/ *n* [C] a piece of cloth that Muslim women wear across their faces〔穆斯林妇女所戴的〕面纱

yaw /jɔ; jɔ:/ *v* [I] *technical* if a ship, aircraft etc yaws it makes a turn away from its proper course【术语】〔船、飞机等〕偏航 —compare 比较 PITCH¹ (4), ROLL¹ (9) —**yaw** *n* [C,U]

yawl /jɔl; jɔ:l/ *n* [C] **1** a sailing boat with a main MAST (=pole) and sails and another small mast and sail close to the back 双桅帆船 **2** a small boat carried on a ship 船载小艇

yawn¹ /jɔn; jɔ:n/ *v* [I] **1** to open your mouth wide and breathe in deeply, usually because you are tired, or bored 打呵欠: *The boy stretched and yawned.* 那男孩伸懒腰打了个呵欠。**2** to be or become wide open 张得很大，张开: *a yawning hole* 口子很大的洞 | [**+open**] *The pit yawned open in front of them.* 深坑在他们面前裂开。| **yawning gap/gulf** *the yawning gap between training needs and training resources* 培训需求与培训资源之间的巨大差距

yawn 打呵欠

yawn² *n* **1** [C] an act of yawning 呵欠: **stifle a yawn** (=try to stop yawning) 忍住呵欠 *Kay shook her head and stifled a yawn.* 凯晃了晃脑袋，把呵欠压了回去。**2** [singular] *informal* someone or something that is boring【非正式】乏味的人[事物]: *The party was a big yawn.* 这次聚会乏味透了。

yaws /jɔz; jɔ:z/ *n* [U] a tropical skin disease 雅司病〔一种热带皮肤病〕

Y chro·mo·some /`waɪ ,kromə,som; `waɪ ,krəʊməsəʊm/ *n* [C] the part of a GENE that makes someone a male instead of a female Y染色体 —see also 另见 X CHROMOSOME

yd the written abbreviation of 缩写= YARD (2) or yards

ye¹ /ji; ji:/ *pron old use* a word meaning 'you', used especially when speaking to more than one person【旧】汝等，尔辈，你们

ye² *determiner* **1** a word meaning 'the', used especially in the names of shops and PUBs to make them seem old〔相当于 the，尤用于商号或酒吧名称中，以示其历史悠久〕: *The sign said 'Ye Olde Dog and Duck'.* 招牌上写着"老狗与老鸭"。**2 ye gods** *spoken* used to show that you are very surprised, or shocked, by something【口】哎哟〔表示惊讶〕: *Ye gods! I can't believe this.* 哎哟！真不敢相信。

yea¹ /je; jeɪ/ *adv old use* yes【旧】是，对 —opposite 反义词 NAY¹ (2) —see also 另见 AYE²

yea² *n* [C] a vote or voter that supports an idea, plan, law etc 赞成票；投赞成票者 —opposite 反义词 NAY² —see also 另见 AYE¹ (1)

Yeager /`jegn; `jeɪgə/, **Charles (Chuck)** (1923-) a US test pilot who in 1947 became the first person to break the SOUND BARRIER (=fly faster than the speed of sound). 耶格尔〔(1923-)，美国试飞员。1947年成为世界首位超音速飞行员〕

yeah /jɛə; jeə/ *adv spoken* yes【口】是，对

year /jɪr; jɪə/ *n* [C] 1 1 1

1 ▶12 MONTHS 12个月◀ a period of about 365 days or 12 months, measured from any particular time 年；年度；岁: *I arrived here two years ago.* 我两年前来到这里。| *We've known each other for over a year.* 我们彼此认识已逾一年。| *15 years old* 15岁 | *a three-year development* 三年的发展 | *a four-year-old child* 四岁的孩子 | **tax/fiscal/financial year** *The tax year begins in April.* 税收年度从4月份开始。| **school year** (=period during a year when students are in school, university etc) 学年

2 ▶JANUARY TO DECEMBER 一月至十二月◀ also 又作 **calendar year** a period of 365 or 366 days divided into 12 months beginning on January 1st and ending on December 31st 历年: *the year that Martin Luther King died* 马丁·路德·金遇害那年 | *Their lease expires at the end of the year.* 他们的租约到年底满期。| *1995 was a profitable year.* 1995年是个赢利年。| *the year 2000* 2000年 | **all (the) year round** (=during the whole year) 一年四季，一年到头

3 ▶MEASURE OF TIME 时间长度◀ *technical* a measure of time equal to 365 1/4 days, which is the amount of time it takes for the Earth to travel once around the sun【术语】年〔地球环绕太阳一周的时间〕

4 childhood/war/retirement etc years a particular period of time in someone's life or in history 童年/战争/退休等岁月: *He started writing poetry during his Harvard years.* 他是在念哈佛

期间开始写诗的。| *the boom years of the 1980's* 20世纪80年代的迅速发展时期

5 years a) *informal* many years【非正式】多年, 长久: **in/for years** *I haven't been there for years.* 我多年没去那里了。| *It's years since I rode a bike.* 我多年没骑自行车了。**b)** age, especially old age 年纪, 岁数〔尤指高龄〕: *Gramps is very active for a man of his years.* 从他的年龄来说, 格兰普斯算是很活跃了。| **getting on in years** (=no longer young) 年事渐高, 不再年轻 | **be 12/21 etc years of age** (=12/21 etc years old) 12/21岁等

6 year by year as each year passes 年年, 每年: *Year by year their business grew.* 他们的业务年年增长。

7 year after year continuously for many years 一年又一年, 年复一年: *It's always the same, year after year.* 一如既往, 年年如此。

8 never/not in a million years *spoken* used to say strongly that you will never do something【口】决不, 永不〔干某事〕: *I won't forgive him – never in a million years.* 我不原谅他, 永远也不。

9 first/second etc year *BrE* someone who is in their first etc year at school or university【英】〔中学或大学里的〕一年级/二年级等

CULTURAL NOTE 文化注释

There are thirteen years of education in UK schools. Children start school in 'Year 1' when they are about 5 years old. Their first year in SECONDARY SCHOOL when they are about 11, is 'Year 7', and they usually take their GCSE examinations in 'Year 11'. Students who remain in school after this can stay until 'Year 13', when they take their A level examinations. 英国的中小学教育共有13个学年。孩子们5岁左右上学, 即"第一学年"。学生11岁左右上中学, 即"第七学年"; 而到了"第十一学年"他们通常要参加普通中学教育证书考试。考试后仍能留在学校的学生一直学到"第十三学年", 这一年他们参加高级证书考试。— see Cultural Note at GRADE 见 GRADE 文化注释

10 put years on sb/take years off sb to make someone look or feel older or younger 使某人显得苍老/年轻: *Theresa's divorce has put years on her.* 特雷莎离婚后显老了。—see also 另见 **donkey's years** (DONKEY (3)), YEARLY

11 the year dot *BrE informal* a very long time ago【英, 非正式】很久以前: *Scientists have been involved in war since the year dot.* 很久以前, 科学家就卷入了战争。

year·book /ˈjɪrˌbʊk; ˈjɪəbʊk/ *n* [C] *AmE* a book printed once a year, especially by a school or college, with information and pictures about what happened there in the year just past【美】年鉴, 年刊

CULTURAL NOTE 文化注释

In the US, most students in HIGH SCHOOL buy a yearbook at the end of the school year. Yearbooks have pictures of every student in them, and pictures of sports teams, clubs, and different activities at the school. Friends sign their names in the yearbook, and close friends usually write long messages about the activities they did together over the year, and wish each other good luck in the future. Yearbooks are usually designed by a group of students, and sometimes SENIORS are allowed to design their own page or part of a page, in which they can have their photograph and special messages printed. 在美国, 大多数高中生在学年结束的时候都会买本年鉴。年鉴上有每名学生的照片, 此外还有运动队、俱乐部以及学校里各种不同活动的照片。朋友会在年鉴上签名, 而密友通常还会写上长长的一段, 记述在一年中共同参与的活动, 并互相留下良好的祝愿。年鉴通常是由一个学生群体共同设计, 有时允许高年级学生设计自己的页面或页面的一部分, 他们可以在上面印上自己的照片和特别留言。

year·ling /ˈjɪrlɪŋ; ˈjɪəlɪŋ/ *n* [C] an animal, especially a young horse, between one and two years old〔一周岁至两周岁之间的〕小动物;〔尤指〕小马驹

year·long /ˈjɪrˈlɔŋ; jɪəˈlɒŋ◂/ *adj* [only before noun 仅用于名词前] lasting for a year or all through the year 持续一年的, 整整一年的: *We store the apples so we have a yearlong supply.* 我们把苹果保存起来, 这样就全年不缺了。

year·ly /ˈjɪrlɪ; ˈjɪəli/ *adj* happening or appearing every year or once a year 每年(发生或出现)的; 一年一次[度]的: *a yearly pay award* 每年一次的奖金 | **3-yearly/5-yearly etc** (=every three years etc) 三年/五年等一次的 *a check-up at five-yearly intervals* 每隔五年一次的检查 —**yearly** *adv*: *We pay the fee yearly.* 我们按年付费。

yearn /jɝn; jɜːn/ *v* [I] *literary* to have a strong desire for something, especially something that is difficult or impossible to get【文】向往; 渴望: **yearn for sth** *Hannah yearned for a child.* 汉娜渴望有个孩子。| **yearn to do sth** *yearning to go home* 渴望回家

yearn·ing /ˈjɝnɪŋ; ˈjɜːnɪŋ/ *n* [C,U] a strong desire or feeling of wanting something 思慕, 向往: [**+for**] *an actor with a yearning for recognition* 渴望得到认同的演员 | **a yearning to do sth** *a yearning to travel* 渴望旅游

yeast /jist; jiːst/ *n* [U] a substance used for producing alcohol in beer and wine and for making bread rise 酵母; 发酵物 —**yeasty** *adj*: *a yeasty taste* 发酵的味道

yeast ex·tract /ˈ·,··/ *n* [U] a food made from yeast, used to make things taste better 酵母精

yeast in·fec·tion /ˈ·,··/ *n* [C] an infectious condition that affects the VAGINA in adult women; THRUSH (2) 念珠菌阴道炎

Yeats /jets; jeɪts/, **W.B.** (1865-1939) an Irish writer of poems and plays, whose early work is often based on old Irish stories. He is one of the most important Irish writers, and he won the Nobel Prize for Literature in 1923. 叶芝〔(1865-1939), 爱尔兰诗人、剧作家。早期作品常以古老的爱尔兰传说为蓝本。他是爱尔兰最重要的作家之一, 1923年获诺贝尔文学奖〕

yecch /jʌk; jʌk/ *interjection AmE slang* used to say that you think something is very unpleasant; YUCK【美俚】呸, 讨厌〔用于对某事表示强烈的厌恶〕

yell¹ /jɛl; jel/ *v* [I,T] **1** also 又作 **yell out** to shout or say something very loudly, especially because you are frightened, angry, or excited〔尤因恐惧、愤怒或激动而〕叫喊, 大嚷大叫: *The spectators yelled and cheered.* 观众又是喊叫又是欢呼。| [**+at**] *Don't you yell at me like that!* 别这样对我大喊大叫的! | *"Go, go!" he yelled out.* "走, 走!"他大声说。| **yell at sb to do sth** *They yelled at him to stop.* 他们朝他喊, 让他停下。**2** *spoken, especially AmE* to ask for help【口, 尤美】大声呼救: *If you need me just yell.* 需要我时就喊一声。

yell² *n* [C] **1** a loud shout 叫喊: **let out a yell** *Frank let out a yell and jumped away.* 弗兰克大叫一声跳开了。| **a yell of delight/triumph/warning etc** *He gave a yell of delight as the election results came in.* 选举结果出来后, 他高兴得大喊了一声。**2** *AmE* words or phrases that students and CHEERLEADERS shout to show support for their school, college etc【美】拉拉队的叫喊声

yel·low¹ /ˈjɛlo; ˈjeləʊ/ *adj* **1** having the colour of butter, gold, or the middle part of an egg 黄(色)的 —see picture on page A5 参见A5页图 **2** an offensive way of describing the skin colour of people from parts of Asia〔部分亚洲民族〕黄皮肤的〔冒犯说法〕**3** also 又作 **yellow-bellied** *informal* not brave; COWARDLY【非正式】胆小的, 卑怯的, 懦弱的 —**yellow** *n* [U] S2 W3

CULTURAL NOTE 文化注释

The colour yellow is often used to represent a lack of courage. 黄色常常用来代表缺乏勇气。

yellow² *v* [I,T] to become yellow or make something become yellow (使)变黄, (使)发黄: *The paper was yellowed with age.* 这纸因年久而变黄了。

yellow card /,·· ˈ·/ *n* [C] a yellow card held up by a football REFEREE¹ (1) to show that a player has done something wrong〔足球裁判对被罚球员出示的〕黄牌

yellow fe·ver /,·· ˈ··/ *n* [C] a dangerous tropical disease in which your skin turns slightly yellow 黄热病

yel·low·ham·mer /ˈjɛlo,hæmɚ; ˈjeləʊ,hæmə/ *n* [C] a small European bird with a yellow head 黄鹀〔欧洲的一种小鸟, 头部呈黄色〕

yellow line /,·· ˈ·/ *n* [C] a line of yellow paint along the edge of a street in Britain which means you can only park your car for a short time or at particular times 黄线〔英国街道边的黄色标线, 表示在某一时段内不得在此停车〕: **double yellow line** (=two lines of paint that mean you cannot park there) 双黄线〔表示禁止在此停车〕

Yellow Pag·es /,·· ˈ··/ *n* [singular] *trademark* the name of a book that contains the telephone numbers of businesses and organizations in an area, arranged according to the type of business they do【商标】黄页〔电话号码簿〕—compare 比较 WHITE PAGES

Yellow Riv·er, the /,·· ˈ··/ a long river in northern China, famous for the terrible floods which have caused many deaths and much damage, and the yellow SILT (=loose sand and soil) that it carries 黄河〔中国北部地区一条长河。该河曾泛滥成灾, 造成严重伤亡和破坏, 水中携带大量黄色泥沙〕

Y

Yel·low·stone Na·tion·al Park /ˌjɛloston ˌnæʃənḷ ˋpɑrk; ˌjeləʊstəʊn ˌnæʃənəl ˈpɑːk/ a large national park mostly in Wyoming, in the northwestern US, famous for its hot springs and GEYSERS (=natural springs of hot water that rise suddenly into the air), especially one called Old Faithful which many tourists come to see 黄石国家公园〔美国一大型国家公园。大部分位于该国西北部的怀俄明州境内, 园中的温泉和间歇喷泉十分有名, 尤其是"老忠实泉", 前来观赏者众多〕

yel·low·y /ˋjɛloɪ; ˈjeləʊi/ *adj* having a slight yellow colour 略带黄色的, 淡黄色的: *The cream was thick and yellowy.* 奶油很稠, 略带黄色。

yelp /jɛlp; jelp/ *v* [I] to make a short sharp high cry because of excitement, pain etc〔因兴奋、痛苦等而〕尖叫, 叫喊: *The dog ran up and down, yelping.* 狗来回跑着叫个不停。| *He yelped as his bare foot hit the box.* 他光脚踢在箱子上, 痛得大叫起来。**—yelp** *n* [C]: *Rose gave a yelp of dismay.* 罗丝沮丧地叫了一声。

Yem·en /ˋjɛmən; ˈjemən/ a country in southwest Asia, south of Saudi Arabia, which was formed in 1990 when the separate countries of North Yemen and South Yemen united. Population: 14,500,000 (1995). Capital: Sana'a. 也门〔亚洲西南部一国家, 位于沙特阿拉伯以南, 1990年由北也门和南也门统一而成。人口: 14,500,000 (1995), 首都: 萨那〕 **—Yemeni** *n, adj*

yen /jɛn; jen/ *n plural* **yen 1** [C] the standard unit of money in Japan 日圆 **2** [singular] a strong desire 渴望, 热望: **[+to/for]** *a yen to travel* 对旅游的渴望

yeo·man /ˋjomən; ˈjəʊmən/ *n plural* **yeomen** /-mən; -mən/ [C] **1** *BrE especially literary or old use* a farmer who owned and worked on his own land in former times【英, 尤文或旧】自耕农 **2** an officer in the US navy who often has secretarial duties〔美国海军〕文书军官

yeo·man·ry /ˋjomənrɪ; ˈjəʊmənri/ *n* **the yeomanry** *BrE literary* the people who owned and farmed their own land in the past【英, 文】〔过去的〕自耕农〔总称〕

yeoman ser·vice /ˌ‥ ˋ‥/ *n* [U] *BrE formal* long and loyal service, help and support【英, 正式】长期忠诚的服务〔帮助、支持〕

yer /jɚ; jə/ *determiner* used in writing as an informal way of saying 'your' 你的; 你们的〔书面语中your的非正式说法〕

Yerevan /ˌjɛrɪˋvæn; jeriˈvæn/ the capital city of Armenia 埃里温〔亚美尼亚首都〕

yes¹ /jɛs; jes/ *adv spoken*【口】**1** used as an answer to say that something is true, that you agree, that you want something, or that you are willing to do something 是, 是的〔表示同意或愿意〕: *"Is that real gold?" "Yes, it is."* "那是真金吗?" "是的。" | *"It was a great film." "Yes, it was."* "这是部很棒的电影。" "是的。" | *"Would you like a sandwich?" "Yes, please."* "来个三明治吧?" "好的。" | *"Can you help us on Saturday?" "Yes I think so."* "星期六能帮我们一下吗?" "行, 我想可以。" —opposite 反义词 NO **2** used as an answer to give permission 可以〔表示允许〕: *"Can I have a glass of water?" "Yes, of course."* "我可以喝杯水吗?" "当然可以。" | **say yes to (doing) sth** *I hope my parents will say yes to the party.* 我希望我父母会同意举行这个聚会。**3** used to politely show that you do not agree with all or some of what someone has said 是的, 不错〔礼貌地表示只部分同意〕: **yes but** *"We need a new car." "Yes, but where will we get the money?"* "我们需要一辆新车。" "是的, 可是从哪儿弄到钱呢?" **4** used to show that you have heard a request, call, command etc 好的; 什么〔用于表示听到请求、叫唤、命令等〕: *"Can you close the door, please?" "Yes, in a minute."* "请关上门好吗?" "好的, 马上就关。" | *"Michael!" "Yes?"* "迈克尔!" "什么事?" **5** used to ask someone what they want〔用于询问别人的需求〕: *Yes? Can I help you find something, madam?* 我能帮你找什么吗, 女士? **6 yes, yes** used to show annoyance when someone is talking to you and you do not want to listen 好的, 好的〔表示不耐烦〕: *"And don't forget to lock the door!" "Yes, yes ok."* "还有, 别忘了锁门!" "好的, 好的, 可以。" **7 yes and no** used to show that there is not one clear answer to a question 既是又不是〔表示难以明确答复〕: *"Did you have a good time?" "Well, yes and no. The lake was beautiful, but Craig and Jen fought the whole time."* "玩得好吗?" "嗨, 一言难尽。湖确实很美, 可是克雷格和珍整天吵架。" **8 yes/no question** a question to which you only answer yes or no 只用是或否回答的问题 —see also 另见 YEAH

yes² *n* [C] a vote, voter, or reply that agrees with an idea, plan, law etc 赞成票; 赞成者; 赞成: *five yeses and three nos* 五张赞成票, 三张反对票 **—yes** *adj: a yes vote* 一张赞成票

ye·shi·va, ye·shi·vah /jəˋʃivə; jəˈʃiːvə/ *n* a school for Jewish students, where they can train to become RABBIS (=religious leaders)〔培养拉比的〕犹太神学院; 犹太高等学校

yes-man /ˋjɛs ˌmæn; ˈjes mæn/ *n plural* **yes-men** /-ˌmɛn; -men/ [C] someone who always agrees with and obeys their employer, leader, etc in order to gain some advantage 唯唯诺诺的人, 遵命先生

yes·ter·day /ˋjɛstɚdɪ; ˈjestədi/ *n* **1** [U] the day before today 昨天, 昨日: *What did you do yesterday?* 昨天你干什么了? | *The day before yesterday was Monday.* 前天是星期一。| *He left yesterday afternoon.* 他昨天下午离开的。| *I'm looking for yesterday's paper.* 我在找昨天的报纸。—see picture at 参见 DAY 图 **2** [C] the recent past 近来, 最近: **yesterday's news** (=not new or modern and therefore no longer of any interest) 昨日新闻, 旧闻 *The voters won't care about the scandal – that's yesterday's news.* 选民才不会计较这种丑事呢——那已是旧闻啦。**3 I wasn't born yesterday** used to say that you cannot be easily deceived 我不是小孩子, 我不会轻易上当受骗: *Don't lie to me! Do you think I was born yesterday?* 别跟我撒谎! 你以为我是小孩子吗?

yes·ter·year /ˋjɛstɚˌjɪr; ˈjestəjɪə/ *n* **of yesteryear** *literary* from a time in the past【文】往昔的: *the familiar songs of yesteryear* 熟悉的老歌

yet¹ /jɛt; jet/ *adv* **1** [in questions or negatives 用于疑问句或否定句] until now or until a particular time (现在) 还; 至此, 迄今; 已经: *Has Edmund arrived yet?* 埃德蒙来了吗? | *The potatoes aren't quite ready yet.* 马铃薯还没做好呢。—see 见 JUST (USAGE) **2 as yet** an expression meaning until this moment, used in questions and negatives 到目前为止〔用于疑问句和否定句〕: *We've had no luck as yet.* 到目前为止, 我们运气还不太好。| *As yet, there's been no news.* 目前还没有消息。**3 not yet** an expression meaning not at the present time, used especially in the answer to questions 尚未, 仍未〔尤用于回答问题〕: *"Are you ready to leave?" "Not just yet."* "你准备走了吗?" "还没呢。" **4** but or in spite of something 但是, 而, 然而; 尽管: *a simple yet effective system* 简单而有效的系统 **5 months/weeks/ages yet** used to emphasize how long it will be before something happens or how long a situation will last 还早[远]着呢〔用于强调〕: *"When's your holiday?" "Oh, not for ages yet."* "什么时候去休假?" "噢, 不知何年何月呢。" **6** in the future, in spite of the way that things seem now 将来, 迟早: *We may win yet.* 我们迟早会赢的。| *The plan could yet succeed.* 这计划迟早会成功的。**7** even or still 更; 仍, 还: *yet another reason to be cautious* 再一个要谨慎的理由 | *a yet worse mistake* 一个更糟糕的错误 | **yet again** (=one more time after many others) 再一次 *I'm sorry to disturb you yet again.* 很抱歉再一次打扰你。**8** *formal* still【正式】仍然, 仍旧: *I have yet to hear Ray's version of what happened* (=I still have not heard it). 雷仍未对我描述所发生的事。

USAGE NOTE 用法说明: YET

FORMALITY 正式程度

Yet often comes either immediately after a negative word or at the end of a clause, but there is a difference of style. In a formal meeting you might hear yet 常用在否定词后或从句末尾, 但两者在文体上有差别。在正式会议中, 你或许会听到: *We do not yet know the answer.* 我们还不知道答案呢。In informal conversation you might say 在非正式对话中, 你可以说: *I don't know the answer yet* (NOT 不用 *I don't know yet the answer*). 我还不知道答案呢。

Yet may also be placed immediately after the verb where a clause follows. yet 也可直接用在动词与宾语从句之间: *I don't know yet whether she'll come or not.* 我还不知道她是否会来。

yet² *conjunction* used to introduce a statement that is surprising after what you have just said 但是, 可是, 然而〔连接句子, 表示含惊讶之义的转折〕: *It's only a little shop and yet it always has such lovely decorations.* 这只是一家小店铺, 然而它总是装饰得那么可爱。| *She's a funny girl, yet you can't help liking her.* 她是个古怪的姑娘, 然而你总禁不住会喜欢她。

yet·i /ˋjɛtɪ; ˈjeti/ *n* [C] a large hairy animal like a human which is supposed to live in the Himalayan mountains but many people do not believe exists 雪人〔传说生活在喜玛拉雅山上多毛的、形如人类的动物〕

Yev·tu·shen·ko /ˌjɛvtuˋʃɛŋko; jevtuːˈʃeŋkəʊ/, **Yev·ge·ny** /jɛvˋgenɪ; jevˈgeɪni/ (1933-) a Russian poet, some of whose works, such as *Babi Yar*, criticized Russian society and made him very unpopular with the Soviet government 叶夫图申科 (1933-), 俄罗斯诗人。因《娘子谷》等作品抨击俄国社会而为前苏联政府所不欢迎〕

yew /ju; juː/ *n* [C,U] a tree with dark green leaves and red berries, or the wood of this tree 紫杉树; 紫杉木

y-fronts /ˈwaɪ frʌnts; ˈwaɪ frʌnts/ *n* [plural] *BrE* men's underwear which has a part at the front shaped like an upside down Y【英】〔男用〕倒Y形内裤, 三角短裤

YHA, the /ˌwaɪ etʃ ˈe; ˌwaɪ eɪtʃ ˈeɪ/ the Youth Hostels Association; the British organization that runs youth HOSTELs in the UK, and is a member of the international organization that runs youth hostels in many other countries (英国) 青年旅舍协会〔国际青年旅舍组织成员。该组织在世界许多国家开办青年旅舍〕

yid /jɪd; jɪd/ *n* [C] *taboo* an extremely offensive word for a Jewish person【讳】犹太人〔极冒犯的用语〕

Yid·dish /ˈjɪdɪʃ; ˈjɪdɪʃ/ *n* [U] a language based on German used by Jewish people, especially those who are from eastern Europe 依地语, 意第绪语〔尤指东欧的犹太人使用的一种语言〕

yield¹ /jild; jiːld/ *v*

1 ▶CROPS/PROFITS 庄稼/利润◀ [T] to produce crops, profits etc 出产; 产生: *The land yielded a good wheat crop.* 这块地盛产小麦。| *Mining shares often yield a high level of return.* 矿业股常有很高的回报率。

2 ▶RESULT 结果◀ [T] to produce a result, answer, or a piece of information 得出〔结果等〕: *Careful analysis yielded the following conclusions.* 经仔细分析得出以下结论。

3 ▶AGREE 同意◀ [I,T] to agree to do something you do not want to do because you have been forced or persuaded to 服从, 被迫同意: [+to] *The hijackers refuse to yield to demands to release the passengers.* 劫机者拒不答应释放乘客的要求。

4 yield to your emotions/feelings to finally decide to do something because you cannot control your feelings any longer 屈从自己的感情/感觉

5 ▶TRAFFIC 交通◀ [I] *AmE* to allow other traffic on a bigger road to go first【美】让〔其他车或人〕先行, 让路; **give way** (WAY¹ (34)) *BrE*【英】

6 ▶GIVE UP FIGHTING 放弃战斗◀ [I] *literary* to stop fighting and accept defeat【文】投降, 屈服

7 ▶MOVE/BEND/BREAK 移动/弯曲/断裂◀ [I] to move, bend, or break because of physical force or pressure〔因外在力量或压力而〕移动, 弯曲, 断裂: *The door wouldn't yield despite all our efforts to move it.* 虽然我们竭尽全力, 这门就是挪不动。

8 ▶CHANGE 变换◀ [I] *formal* if one thing yields to another thing, this other thing replaces it【正式】让与: [+to] *Open spaces around town are yielding to huge hyper-stores.* 该镇周围的空地都让超级大商店给占了。

yield sth ↔**up** *phr v* [T] *literary* to show or give someone something that has been hidden for a long time or is very difficult to obtain【文】泄露, 揭示: *Little by little, the universe yields up its many secrets.* 宇宙一点一点地显露出许多秘密。

yield² *n* [C] the amount of profits, crops etc that you get 产量; 收益: *investments with high yields* 高收益的投资

yield·ing /ˈjildɪŋ; ˈjiːldɪŋ/ *adj* **1** a surface that is yielding is soft and will move or bend when you press it〔物体表面〕易变形的, 易弯曲的 **2** willing to agree with other people's wishes and letting them decide instead of you 柔顺的, 依从的: *She is too yielding when clients make demands on her time.* 她过于柔弱, 以致客户们能随意占用她的时间。**3 high/low yielding** producing a large or small amount of something such as crops 高/低产的

yin /jɪn; jɪn/ *n* [U] the female principle in Chinese PHILOSOPHY which is inactive, dark and negative, and which combines with YANG (=the male principle) to influence everything in the world〔中国哲学概念中的〕阴

yin and yang /ˌ· · ˈ·/ *n* [U] the ancient Chinese PHILOSOPHY which is based on the idea that everything in the Universe is formed and influenced by the combination of two forces called YIN and YANG〔中国古代哲学概念中的〕阴和阳

yip·pee /ˈjɪpi; jɪˈpiː/ *interjection* used when you are very pleased or excited about something 好啊〔表示欢欣的欢呼声〕

YMCA /ˌwaɪ ɛm si ˈe; ˌwaɪ em siː ˈeɪ/ *n* [singular] Young Men's Christian Association; an organization in many countries that provides places to stay and sports activities for young people 基督教青年会〔遍布许多国家的一个组织, 为青年人安排住宿和体育活动〕

yo /jo; jəʊ/ *interjection slang, especially AmE* used to greet someone or get their attention【俚, 尤美】唷〔用于招呼或唤起注意〕: *Yo dude! How's it goin'?* 唷, 老兄!日子过得怎样?

yob /jɑb; jɒb/ also 又作 **yob·bo** /ˈjɑbo; ˈjɒbəʊ/ *n* [C] *BrE*【英】**1** a rude, noisy, sometimes violent, young man 野小子, 粗鲁吵闹的年轻人 **2 yob culture/uniform/element etc** behaviour, clothes etc connected with yobs 野小子习气/服装/环境等—**yobbery** *n* [U]

yodel 用约德尔调唱(歌)

yo·del¹ /ˈjodəl; ˈjəʊdl/ *v* **yodelled, yodelling** *BrE*【英】, **yodeled, yodeling** *AmE*【美】[I,T] to sing while changing between your natural voice and a very high voice, traditionally done in the mountains of countries such as Switzerland and Austria 用约德尔调唱(歌)〔瑞士和奥地利山区人用真假嗓音互换的唱法〕—**yodeller** *n* [C]

yodel² *n* [C] a song or sound made by yodelling〔用真假嗓音互换唱法的〕约德尔唱法; 约德尔曲; 约德尔调

yo·ga /ˈjogə; ˈjəʊgə/ *n* [U] **1** a Hindu PHILOSOPHY in which you learn exercises to control your mind and body in order to try to achieve a union with God〔古印度哲学中的〕瑜伽 **2** a system of these exercises that helps you relax 瑜伽功

yog·hurt, yogurt /ˈjogɚt; ˈjɒgət/ *n* [C,U] a thick liquid food that tastes slightly sour and is made from milk, or an amount of this 酸奶; 酸乳酪 S3

yo·gi /ˈjogɪ; ˈjəʊgi/ *n* [C] someone who is very skilled at and has a lot of knowledge about yoga and who often teaches it to other people 瑜伽师, 教瑜伽者

Yogi Bear /ˌ· · ˈ·/ a US television CARTOON character who has been popular since the 1960s. Yogi is a clever bear who lives in Jellystone Park and, with his friend Boo-Boo, is always trying to steal food from the tourists there. 瑜伽熊〔20世纪60年代起流行的美国电视卡通形象。瑜伽熊是一只聪明的熊, 和朋友波波熊一起住在杰利斯通公园, 总是想方设法从游人那里偷东西吃〕

yog·urt /ˈjogɚt; ˈjɒgət/ *n* [C,U] another spelling of YOGHURT yoghurt 的另一种拼法

yoke¹ /jok; jəʊk/ *n* [C] **1** a wooden bar used for joining two animals, especially cattle, together in order to pull heavy loads 牛轭 **2** a frame fitted across someone's shoulders so that they can carry two equal loads〔挑东西用的〕轭状扁担 **3 the yoke of sth** *literary* something that restricts your freedom, making life hard or unpleasant【文】某事物的束缚[羁绊]: *the yoke of tradition* 传统的束缚 **4** a part of a skirt or shirt just below the waist or collar, from which the main piece of material hangs in folds〔女服的〕上衣抵肩; 裙腰

yoke² *v* [T+together/to] **1** to join two animals with a yoke〔用轭〕把〔牲口〕套在一起 **2** *literary* to bring two ideas or people together so that they work well with each other【文】使结合; 使匹配: *The poet's choice of metaphor cleverly yokes together two dissimilar things.* 诗人的比喻把两个不同的事物巧妙地连结在一起。

yokel 乡下佬, 土包子

yo·kel /ˈjokḷ; ˈjəʊkəl/ *n* [C] *humorous* someone who comes from the countryside, seems to be a little stupid, and does not know much about modern life, ideas etc【幽默】乡下佬, 土包子

Yo·ko·ha·ma /ˌjokoˈhɑmə; jəʊkəʊˈhɑːmə/ a city and port on Tokyo Bay, Japan 横滨〔日本东京湾一港口城市〕

yolk /jok; jəʊk/ *n* [C,U] the yellow part in the centre of an egg 蛋黄

Yom Kip·pur /ˌjom ˈkɪpɚ; ˌjɒm ˈkɪpə/ *n* [singular] the religious holiday when Jewish people do not eat, but pray to be forgiven for the things they have done wrong 赎罪日〔犹太教节日, 于此日禁食及作忏悔祈祷〕

yon·der /ˈjɑndɚ; ˈjɒndə/ also 又作 **yon** *adj, adv, determiner old use* used for telling someone which place or direction you

mean【旧】那边(的);在远处(的):*the fresh blooms on yonder tree* 那边树上新开的花

yonks /jɑŋks; jɒŋks/ *n* [U] *BrE spoken* a long time【英口】好久,很长一段时间:*It's yonks since we had a good night out.* 我们好久没出去玩通宵了。| **not do sth for yonks** *We haven't seen Tom and Jean for yonks.* 我们很久没看见汤姆和琼了。| **yonks ago** *We went to Blackpool once, yonks ago.* 我们很久以前到过布莱克浦一次。

yoo-hoo /ˌju ˋhu; ˌjuː ˈhuː/ *interjection informal* used to attract someone's attention when they are a long way from you【非正式】喂〔用于引起相距较远之人的注意〕

yore /jɔr; jɔː/ *n* **of yore** *literary* of a long time ago【文】从前,往昔,很久以前

Yor·ick /ˈjɔrɪk; ˈjɒrɪk/ a character in the play *Hamlet* by William Shakespeare. He was once the king's JESTER (=someone whose job was to entertain the King and make him laugh) but is now dead. Hamlet finds his SKULL and says "Alas! poor Yorick. I knew him, Horatio." 约里克〔威廉·莎士比亚剧作《哈姆雷特》中的一个人物。他曾为宫廷小丑,后来去世。哈姆雷特发现了他的头盖骨,叹道:"唉,可怜的约里克!霍拉旭,我可认得他。"〕

York /jɔrk; jɔːk/ an ancient city in North Yorkshire in northern England. York was originally a Roman city, and it is a popular place for tourists to visit because of its old city wall and its large CATHEDRAL, York Minster. 约克〔英格兰北部北约克郡一古城,曾为古罗马城市。凭借古城墙及宏伟的约克敏斯特大教堂而成为旅游胜地〕

York, Duke of —see 见 Prince ANDREW

York·shire /ˈjɔrkʃɚ; ˈjɔːkʃə/ an area and former COUNTY in northeast England, now divided into North, East, South and West Yorkshire. Yorkshire is partly very industrial, with large cities such as Leeds, Sheffield, and Bradford and, in the past, many coal mines. It also has large areas of beautiful, wild countryside, including the North York Moors and the Dales. 约克郡〔英格兰东北部一地区,原为一郡,现划分为北约克郡、东约克郡、南约克郡和西约克郡。约克郡的部分地区工业很发达,拥有如利兹、设菲尔德和布拉德福德等大城市,以前还有大量煤矿。约克郡境内有大片风景秀丽的乡村旷野,包括北约克郡漠泽及约克谷地〕

Yorkshire Moors, the /ˌ··ˈ·/ another name for the North York Moors, an area of high, open land in the former COUNTY of Yorkshire 约克郡漠泽〔北约克郡漠泽别称,是前约克郡辖区内一片地势高且开阔的地区〕

York·shire pud·ding /ˈjɔrkʃɚ ˋpudɪŋ; ˌjɔːkʃə ˈpʊdɪŋ/ *n* [C,U] a food made from flour, eggs and milk, eaten with meat in Britain〔英国的〕约克郡布丁

Yorkshire ter·ri·er /ˈjɔrkʃɚ ˋtɛrɪɚ; ˌjɔːkʃə ˈteriə/ *n* [C] a type of dog that is very small with long brown hair 约克郡㹴〔一种长着棕色长毛的小狗〕

York·town /ˈjɔrktaun; ˈjɔːktaʊn/ a town in Virginia, US, where the last battle of the American Revolutionary War and the final SURRENDER of the British to the Americans took place in 1781 约克敦〔美国弗吉尼亚州一城镇。1781年,美国独立战争中的最后一役在此进行,英军最后向美军投降〕

Yo·sem·i·te Na·tion·al Park /joˌsɛmətɪ ˌnæʃənḷ ˋpɑrk; jəʊˌsemɪ̧ti ˌnæʃənəl ˈpɑːk/ a national park in California, US, famous for its beautiful lakes, WATERFALLS, and large REDWOOD trees 约塞米蒂国家公园〔美国加利福尼亚州境内一国家公园,以拥有景色如画的湖泊、瀑布及高大的红杉木而闻名〕

you /ju; jə; *strong* 强读 ju; juː/ *pron* [used as a subject or an object 用作主语或宾语] **1** the person or people someone is speaking or writing to 你,你们:*You look nice, Sally.* 你看起来很好,萨莉。| *You must all listen carefully.* 你们必须仔细听着。| *I can see you.* 我能看见你。| *Did Robin give the money to you?* 罗宾把钱给你了吗? | *I told you this would happen.* 我告诉过你会发生这种事的。| *Only you can make this decision.* 只有你能作出这种决定。**2** people in general〔泛指〕任何人:*You have to be careful with people you don't know.* 对陌生人要小心。| *You can't learn to ride a horse by reading books about it.* 光看书谁也学不会骑马。**3** used with nouns or phrases when you are talking to or calling someone 你(这个),你们(这些)〔与名词或短语连用,与某人谈话或称呼某人时用〕:*You boys have got to learn to behave yourselves.* 你们这些男孩得学规矩点儿。| *You twit!* 你这个傻瓜! | *Hey, you over there! Get out of the way!* 喂,那边的人!走开!

you'd /jud; jəd; *strong* 强读 jud; juːd/ **1** the short form of 缩略式= 'you had' **2** the short form of 缩略式= 'you would'

you'll /jul; jəl; *strong* 强读 jul; juːl/ **1** the short form of 缩略式= 'you will' **2** the short form of 缩略式= 'you shall'

You'll Nev·er Walk A·lone /ˌ·,··,··ˈ·/ a song from the MUSICAL (= a play that uses singing and dancing to tell a story) *Carousel*, by Richard Rodgers and Oscar Hammerstein. In the UK it is often sung at football games.《你永远不会孤身而行》〔理查德·罗杰斯和奥斯卡·哈默斯坦合作的音乐剧《旋转木马》中的一首歌曲,在英国常在足球比赛中传唱〕

young¹ /jʌŋ; jʌŋ/ *adj* **1** not having lived for very long 年轻的;幼小的:*a young child* 幼儿 | *young seedlings* 幼苗 | *You're too young to learn to drive.* 你太小了,不能学开车。| **in your younger days** (=when you were young) 年轻时 *John was a great footballer in his younger days.* 约翰年轻时是个很棒的足球员。**2** not having existed for a long time 新建立的:*a young country* 新兴的国家 **3 young for your age** looking or behaving in a way that makes you seem as if you are younger than you really are 比实际年龄年轻 **4 young at heart** *approving* thinking and behaving as if you are young even though you are old【褒】(人老)心不老:*Arthur's 96, but he's still young at heart.* 阿瑟96岁了,但他仍然有一颗年轻的心。**5** seeming or looking younger than you are; YOUTHFUL 有青春活力的,朝气蓬勃的:*Rosie has a very young face.* 罗西有一张很青春的面孔。**6** designed or meant for young people 专为年轻人设计的:*That hat is too young for you.* 那种帽子是年轻人戴的,不适合你。

young² *n* **1 the young** young people considered as a group 年轻人〔总称〕**2** [plural] a group of young animals that belong to a particular mother or type of animal 幼小动物,崽,雏:*The lioness fought to protect her young.* 那头母狮为保护幼狮而搏斗。

Young, Brig·ham /ˈbrɪgəm; ˈbrɪgəm/ (1801-77) a US leader of the Mormon religion. In Illinois Mormons were being badly treated, and so they decided to move away. In 1847, Young led 5000 Mormons across the US to their new home in what later became the state of Utah, where they built Salt Lake City. 杨百翰〔(1801-1877),美国摩门教领袖。在当时的伊利诺伊州,摩门教徒因受到不公正待遇而决定迁移。1847年,杨百翰带领5000名摩门教徒长途跋涉来到新的居住地,也就是后来的犹他州,在那里兴建了盐湖城〕

Young, Cy /saɪ; saɪ/ (1867-1955) a BASEBALL player who was famous for his skill as a PITCHER. Every year the Cy Young Award is given to the best pitchers in the American League and the National League. 赛伊·扬〔(1867-1955),棒球运动员,以投球技巧闻名。"赛伊·扬奖"为颁发给美国棒球联盟及全国棒球联盟年度最佳投手的奖项〕

young·er /ˈjʌŋgɚ; ˈjʌŋgə/ *adj* **sb the younger** *old-fashioned* someone who has the same name as their mother or father【过时】小…〔与父或母同名者〕:*William Pitt the younger* 小威廉·皮特 —compare 比较 ELDER¹ (2b)

young la·dy /ˌ·ˈ··/ *n* [C] *old-fashioned*【过时】**1** a way of speaking to a young girl when you are angry 小姐〔生气时用语〕:*Now, listen to me, young lady!* 好了,听我说,小姐! **2** someone's GIRLFRIEND〔某人的〕女朋友

young man /ˌ·ˈ·/ *n* [C] *old-fashioned*【过时】**1** a way of speaking to a young boy when you are angry 年轻人〔生气时用语〕:*You'd better do as I tell you, young man.* 你最好照我说的做,年轻人。**2** someone's BOYFRIEND〔某人的〕男朋友

young mar·rieds /ˌ·ˈ··/ *n* [plural] *especially AmE* young people who have recently got married【尤美】新婚的年轻人

young of·fend·er /ˌ··ˈ··/ *n* [C] a criminal in Britain who is not an adult according to the law〔英国的〕青少年罪犯

Young Pre·tend·er, the /ˌ··ˈ··/ another name for Bonnie Prince Charlie 小王位觊觎者〔Bonnie Prince Charlie的别称〕

young·ster /ˈjʌŋstɚ; ˈjʌŋstə/ *n* [C] *old-fashioned* a young person【过时】年轻人

your /jʊr; jə; *strong* 强读 jur; jɔː/ *determiner* **1** belonging to or connected with the person or people someone is speaking to 你的;你们的:*Could you move your car?* 你能把你的车挪一下吗? | *That's your problem.* 那是你的问题。| *You must all come – and bring your husbands.* 你们都得来,还要带上你们的丈夫。| *It's your own fault if you've lost them.* 你如果丢了它们,就是你自己的错。**2** belonging to any person 任何人的:*If you are facing north, east is on your right.* 假如你面向北,你的右边就是东。**3** *informal* used when mentioning something that is a good example of a particular type of thing or quality【非正式】〔用于提及典型的某物或某种品质〕:*Your typical 60s pop group had 3 guitarists and a drummer.* 60年代典型的流行乐队有三个吉他手和一个鼓手。| *Where are your Georgie Bests in today's game?* 今天的比赛中,你们那乔治·贝斯特斯到哪里去了?

you're /jʊr; jə; *strong* 强读 jur; jɔː/ the short form of 缩略式= 'you are'

yours /jurz; jɔːz/ *pron* **1** belonging to or connected with the person or people someone is speaking to 你的(东西);你们的(东西):*This is our room, and yours* (=your room) *is just op-*

posite. 这是我们的房间，你们的在对面。| *My eyes are blue and yours are green.* 我的眼睛是蓝色的，你的是绿色的。| *Is Maria a friend of yours?* 玛丽娅是你的朋友吗? **2 be yours for the taking/asking** if something important, desirable etc is yours for the taking, you can easily obtain or achieve it 探囊可取，唾手可得: *If you want the job, it's yours for the taking.* 如果你想要这份工作，容易得很。**3 Yours faithfully/truly** used to end a formal letter that begins 'Dear Sir' or 'Dear Madam' 您忠诚的/您真诚的〔用于正式信函的结尾〕**4 Yours sincerely/Yours** used to end a less formal letter that begins 'Dear Mr. Graves', 'Dear Miss Hope' etc 你的真挚的〔用于不太正式的信函的结尾〕**5 yours truly** *informal* used to mean 'I', 'me', or 'myself'【非正式】我，我自己: *They all went out, leaving yours truly to clear up the mess.* 他们都出去了，留下我来收拾残局。

S1 W2 **your·self** /jur`sɛlf; jə'self/ *pron plural* **yourselves** /-`sɛlvz; -'selvz/ **1** the REFLEXIVE form of 'you' 你自己〔you的反身代词〕: *Mind you don't hurt yourself with those scissors.* 注意，别让剪刀伤了你自己。| *Go and buy yourself an ice-cream.* 去给你自己买个冰淇淋吧。**2** used as a stronger form of "you" 你亲自，你本人〔用以加强语气〕: *You yourself said he was a dead loss.* 是你自己说他输定了的。| *If you don't trust me you'd better go yourself.* 你如果不相信我，最好自己去。**3 not be/feel yourself** *informal* to be slightly ill, tired, or upset【非正式】有点不适[疲惫、烦恼]: *Of course I'll forgive you; I know you weren't yourself yesterday.* 我当然不会跟你计较，我知道你昨天有点儿烦。| *Are you all right? You don't seem yourself this morning.* 你没事吧?今天早上你好像不太舒服。**4 (all) by yourself a)** without anyone helping you 独力地，全靠你自己: *Can you put your shoes on all by yourself, Ben?* 你能自己穿上鞋吗，本? **b)** with no other people with you 独自地: *You can't go home by yourself in the dark.* 天黑你不能独自回家。—see 见 ALONE[1] (USAGE) **5 to yourself** if you have a room, time etc to yourself, it is your own and you do not have to share it with anyone 独自享有〔房间、时间等〕: *If you got there early you had the whole beach to yourself.* 你如果早点到达那里，整个沙滩都是你一人的天下了。| *It's nice to have an evening to yourself now and then.* 偶尔独自呆一晚上也很惬意。—see also 另见 DO-IT-YOURSELF, **keep sth to yourself** (KEEP[1])

S2 W2 **youth** /juθ; ju:θ/ *n plural* **youths** /juðz; ju:ðz/ **1** [U] the period of time when someone is young, especially the period between being a child and being fully grown 青少年时期: *Youth is a time when many people rebel against their parents.* 在青少年时期，许多人都会违拗自己的父母。| **in sb's youth** (=when they were young) 在某人年轻时 *In his youth, Jimmy was an idealist and a rebel.* 吉米年轻时是个理想主义者和叛逆者。**2** [C] a word meaning boy or young man, especially a TEENAGER, used especially when you disapprove of them (毛头) 小伙子〔尤用于贬义〕: *gangs of youths hanging about on street corners* 在街角闲荡的一群群小伙子 —see 见 CHILD (USAGE) **3** [also+plural verb *BrE* 英] young people considered as a group 青年人〔总称〕: *the courage of youth* 青年人的勇气 | **the youth of** *The youth of the country are being ignored by politicians.* 这个国家的年轻人不受政治家的重视。**4** [singular,U] the quality or state of being young 青春 (活力)，朝气: *a product that claims to restore youth and vitality to your skin* 一种声称可恢复肌肤青春活力的产品

youth club /'· ·/ *n* [C] a meeting place for young people where they can drink coffee, play games etc 青年俱乐部

youth cul·ture /'· ,··/ *n* [U] the interests and activities of young people, especially the music, films etc they enjoy 青年文化〔尤指年轻人感兴趣的音乐、电影等〕

youth·ful /`juθfəl; 'ju:θfəl/ *adj* **1** typical of or having qualities typical of youth 富于青春活力的; 朝气蓬勃的: *youthful enthusiasm* 年轻人特有的热情 | *She's over 50, but has a youthful complexion.* 她五十多岁了，但面容依然姣好。**2** young 年轻的; 青年的: *youthful soldiers* 年轻的士兵 —**youthfully** *adv* —**youthfulness** *n* [U]

youth hos·tel /'· ,··/ *n* [C] a place where people, especially young people who are travelling, can stay very cheaply for a short time 青年旅舍

youth hos·tel·ling /'· ,···/ *n* [U] *BrE* the activity of staying in youth hostels and walking or cycling between them【英】青年旅舍寄宿活动: **go youth hostelling** *I went youth hostelling in the Peak District.* 我到皮克区参加青年旅舍寄宿活动了。

Youth Train·ing /,· '··/ the full name of YT 青年职业培训〔YT的全称〕

you've /juv; jəv; *strong* 强读 juv; ju:v/ the short form of 缩略式= 'you have'

yowl /jaul; jaʊl/ *v* [I] to make a long loud cry, especially because you are sad or in pain〔尤指悲痛或疼痛时〕嚎叫; 惨叫: *A tomcat was yowling out on the lawn.* 一只公猫在草坪上哀叫。—**yowl** *n* [C]

yo-yo /`jo jo; 'jəʊ jəʊ/ *n* [C] a toy you hold in your hand made of two circular parts joined together that go up and down a string as you lift your hand up and down 摇摇，悠悠，溜溜球〔一种圆形玩具，可用绳索拉上拉下〕

Y·pres /`iprə; 'i:prə/ a town in southern Belgium where three great battles took place in World War I. Hundreds of thousands of soldiers died in these battles, but neither side gained much advantage. British soldiers called it Wipers. 伊普尔，又译伊珀尔〔比利时南部一镇。一战期间在此进行过三次重大战役，成千上万的士兵阵亡，但参战双方均未获得明显利益。英国士兵将该地称为 Wipers〕

yr *plural* **yrs** the written abbreviation of 缩写= YEAR

YT /,waɪ `ti; ,waɪ 'ti:/ Youth Training; a British government plan which is intended to provide training for young people to help them get jobs. British citizens who are between 16 and 18 must do YT if they are not students or do not have jobs, but they receive small payments while they are training. 青年职业培训计划〔英国政府的一项计划，旨在为青年人提供培训以帮助其就业。年龄在16至18岁之间的英国公民如果既非在校学生又无职业，就必须参加青年职业培训，培训期间只能得到低额工资〕

yu·an /ju`ɑn; jʊ'ɑ:n/ *n* [C] the standard unit of money in China 元〔中国货币单位〕

Yuc·a·tán /,jukə`tɑn; ,jʊkə'tɑ:n/ **1** also 又作 **the Yucatán Peninsula** a large PENINSULA (=a long, thin area of land with sea on three sides) in central America, between the Gulf of Mexico and the Caribbean Sea, which consists of Belize, North Guatemala, and part of Mexico. The Maya people came from this area, and there are several ancient Maya buildings there. 尤卡坦半岛〔中美洲一大半岛，位于墨西哥湾和加勒比海之间，由伯利兹、危地马拉北部及墨西哥部分地区构成。马雅人就来自这一地区，当地现仍保留有一些古马雅建筑遗迹〕**2** a Mexican state 尤卡坦州〔墨西哥一州〕

yuc·ca /`jʌkə; 'jʌkə/ *n* [C] a desert plant with long pointed leaves on a thick straight stem 丝兰 (属植物)

yuck, yuk /jʌk; jʌk/ *interjection informal* used to show that you think something is very unpleasant【非正式】呸! 啐! 讨厌!〔表示强烈的厌恶〕

yuck·y /`jʌkɪ; 'jʌki/ *adj informal* extremely unpleasant【非正式】令人极度厌恶的: *a yucky colour* 非常难看的颜色 | *The food was yucky.* 这食物令人厌恶。

Yu·go·sla·vi·a /,jugo`slavɪə; ,ju:gəʊ'slɑ:viə/ a former country in southeast Europe, between the 1920s and early 1990s, that was made up of six REPUBLICs: Slovenia, Croatia, Bosnia-Herzegovina, the former Yugoslav Republic of Macedonia, Serbia, and Montenegro 南斯拉夫〔曾经是欧洲东南部一国家，存在于20世纪20年代至90年代初期，由斯洛文尼亚、克罗地亚、波斯尼亚－黑塞哥维那、前南斯拉夫的马其顿共和国、塞尔维亚及黑山6个共和国组成〕—**Yugoslav** /`jugoslav; 'ju:gəʊslɑ:v/, **Yugoslavian** *n, adj* —see 见 FEDERAL REPUBLIC OF YUGOSLAVIA

yuk /jʌk; jʌk/ *interjection* another spelling of YUCK yuck 的另一种拼法

Yu·kon, the /`jukɑn; 'ju:kɒn/ **1** a territory in northwest Canada, where the Klondike Gold Rush took place in the 1890s 育空〔加拿大西北部一地区。19世纪90年代，这里曾掀起克朗代克淘金热〕**2** a river in the northwest of North America, flowing from the Yukon area, through Alaska, and into the Pacific Ocean 育空河〔北美洲西北部一河流，自育空地区流经阿拉斯加，注入太平洋〕

Yule /jul; ju:l/ *n old use* Christmas【旧】圣诞节

yule log /'· ·/ *n* [C] **1** a LOG of wood traditionally burnt on the evening before Christmas 圣诞柴〔圣诞前夜焚烧的大块木头〕**2** a chocolate cake shaped like a LOG and eaten at Christmas 形状像圣诞柴的巧克力蛋糕

Yule·tide /`jul,taɪd; 'ju:ltaɪd/ *n* [U] *poetical* Christmas【诗】圣诞节

yum·my /`jʌmɪ; 'jʌmi/ *adj informal* food that is yummy tastes very good【非正式】〔食物〕美味的，可口的

yup·pie, yuppy /`jʌpɪ; 'jʌpi/ *n* [C] a young person who seems to be only concerned with their job, making a lot of money, and spending it on expensive things 雅皮士〔只关心工作、有高收入并爱买高档物品的职业青年〕: *The Docklands area has been converted into smart flats for yuppies.* 船坞区已成了雅皮士聚居的时髦公寓区。

CULTURAL NOTE 文化注释

In Britain, most people think of yuppies as being young people who earn a lot of money without necessarily working very hard, usually on the financial markets in the City. They typically drive expensive cars, especially Porsches, and use car PHONES, PERSONAL ORGANIZERS and other modern expensive goods and are more concerned about enjoying their lifestyle than having a family or helping others in society. In the US, yuppies are thought of as being slightly older and as being insensitive, AMBITIOUS, and too interested in material goods. 在英国，大多数人认为雅皮士是一群高收入的年轻人，他们不需要太玩命工作就能挣很多钱，例如在伦敦的金融市场上套利。他们通常开着高级轿车，特别是像保时捷这样的汽车，使用汽车电话、个人备忘录和其他现代高档产品。他们更关注怎样享受生活，而不是建立家庭和帮助别人。在美国，雅皮士被认为是年龄稍大的一群人，他们比较冷漠，有进取心，过于关注物质产品。

YWCA /ˌwaɪ dʌbl̩ju si ˋe; ˌwaɪ dʌbəljuː siː ˈeɪ/ *n* [singular] Young Women's Christian Association; an organization in many countries that provides places to stay and sports activities for young people 基督教女青年会〔遍布许多国家的一个组织，为青年人安排住宿和体育活动〕

Z,z

Z, z /zi; zed/ *plural* **Z's, z's** or **Zs, zs** **1** the last letter of the English alphabet 英语字母表的最后一个字母 **2 Z's** *AmE informal* sleep【美, 非正式】睡觉: **catch/get some Z's** (=to sleep) 抓紧睡一会儿 *I think I'll go catch some Z's.* 我想我得抓紧睡一会儿去。

Zagreb /ˋzɑgrɛb; ˈzɑːgreb/ the capital city of Croatia 萨格勒布〔克罗地亚首都〕

Zaharias /zəˋhɛrɪəs; zəˈheəriəs/, **Mildred "Babe"** /ˋmɪldrɪd beb; ˈmɪldrɪd beɪb/ (1911-56) a US woman GOLFER and a gold medal winner for the JAVELIN and 100 metres HURDLES race in the 1932 Olympic Games. She was one of the greatest golfers of all time, winning the British championship and three US Opens in the 1940s and 1950s. 扎哈里亚斯〔(1911-1956), 绰号"芭比", 美国女高尔夫球手, 1932年洛杉矶奥运会女子标枪及100米跨栏金牌得主。她是当时最伟大的高尔夫球员之一, 曾在20世纪40、50年代获得英国锦标赛冠军和连续三届美国公开赛冠军〕

Zaïre /zəˋɪrə; zaɪˈɪə/ the former name of the Democratic Republic of Congo, a country in central Africa 扎伊尔〔刚果民主共和国旧称, 非洲中部一国家〕—**Zaïrean** *n, adj*

Zam·bezi, the /zæmˋbizɪ; zæmˈbiːzi/ also 又作 **the Zambesi** a large river in south central Africa. Victoria Falls and the Kariba Dam are both on the Zambezi. 赞比西河〔非洲中南部一条长河。沿河有维多利亚瀑布和卡里巴水坝〕

Zam·bi·a /ˋzæmbɪə; ˈzæmbiə/ a country in south central Africa, between Zimbabwe and the Democratic Republic of Congo. Population: 9,770,000 (2001). Capital: Lusaka. Zambia is rich in minerals, especially COPPER. Its former name, when it was ruled by Britain, was **Northern Rhodesia**. It became independent in 1964, and is a member of the British Commonwealth. 赞比亚〔非洲中南部一国家, 位于津巴布韦和刚果民主共和国之间。人口: 9,770,000 (2001), 首都: 卢萨卡。赞比亚矿产资源丰富, 尤其盛产铜矿。在英国统治时期称北罗得西亚。1964年独立, 为英联邦成员国〕—**Zambian** *n, adj*

za·ny /ˋzenɪ; ˈzeɪni/ *adj* crazy or unusual in a way that is amusing 滑稽的, 可笑的: *zany comedian Lenny Henry* 滑稽可笑的喜剧演员伦尼·亨利

Zan·zi·bar /ˋzænzɪbɑr; ˈzænzɪbɑː/ an island off the coast of East Africa which joined with Tanganyika in 1964 to form the new country of Tanzania 桑给巴尔岛〔东非近海一岛屿。1964年与坦噶尼喀组成新国家坦桑尼亚〕

zap[1] /zæp; zæp/ *v* **zapped, zapping** *informal*【非正式】**1** [T] to quickly attack or destroy something, especially in a computer game〔尤指在电子游戏中〕快速攻击, 摧毁: *You get 100 points for each plane you zap.* 每击落一架飞机你就能得100分。**2** [T always+ adv/prep, I always+adv/prep] to do something very quickly or go somewhere very quickly 迅速做〔某事〕; 迅速到达〔某地〕: **zap sth in/into** *He zapped the car into fourth gear and screeched off.* 他迅速把车挂上四挡, 然后呼啸而去。| [+past/through/along etc] *I'll have to zap through the work to make the deadline.* 我得赶在限期之前把这工作干完。**3** [T] *AmE informal* to cook something in a MICROWAVE[1] (1)【美, 非正式】用微波炉烹制〔食物〕

zap[2] *n* [U] *BrE informal* interest and excitement; ENERGY (1)【英, 非正式】趣味; 活力; 精力: *The advert needs a bit more zap.* 这广告需要再活泼一些。

Za·pa·ta, E·mi·li·a·no /ɛˌmilɪˋɑno; eˌmiːliˈɑːnəʊ/ (1879-1919) a Mexican REVOLUTIONARY, who led an army of native Mexicans against the government in an attempt to get back land that had been taken away from them. He was partly successful but was later murdered. The Zapata MOUSTACHE (=a type of moustache that curves down at the sides) is named after him. 萨帕塔〔(1879-1919), 墨西哥革命领袖。他曾带领由墨西哥土著组成的军队与政府对抗, 试图夺回被强占的土地。萨帕塔取得了一定胜利, 但后来遭人暗杀。萨帕塔式八字须是以他的名字命名的〕

Zap·pa /ˋzæpə; ˈzæpə/, **Frank** (1940-93) a US musician and singer who wrote many different types of music, including CLASSICAL music, but is famous for his ROCK music, which was always new and different, and which criticized American society and music of the 1960s and 1970s. His group was called **The Mothers of Invention**. 扎帕〔(1940-1993), 美国音乐家、歌唱家。他创作有许多不同风格的音乐作品, 其中包括古典音乐, 但以摇滚乐最为著名, 其摇滚乐通常新颖别致, 歌词抨击美国社会和20世纪60、70年代的音乐。他的乐队称作"发明之母"〕

zap·per /ˋzæpɚ; ˈzæpə/ *n* [C] *AmE informal*【美, 非正式】**1** a thing you use for changing channels (CHANNEL[1] (1)) on a television from a distance; REMOTE CONTROL (1)〔电视〕遥控器 **2** a piece of electrical equipment that attracts and kills insects 灭虫器

zap·py /ˋzæpɪ; ˈzæpi/ *adj BrE informal* interesting and exciting【英, 非正式】活泼有趣的, 生动的: *a zappy poster* 活泼有趣的海报

Zar·a·thus·tra /ˌzærəˋθustrə; ˌzærəˈθuːstrə/ —see 见 ZOROASTER

zeal /zil; ziːl/ *n* [U] eagerness to do something, especially to achieve a particular religious or political aim〔尤指实现宗教或政治目标的〕热情, 热忱: *revolutionary zeal* 革命热情

zeal·ot /ˋzɛlət; ˈzelət/ *n* [C] someone who has extremely strong beliefs, especially religious or political beliefs, and is too eager to make other people share them〔尤指政治或宗教信仰方面的〕热心者; 狂热者: *religious zealots* 宗教狂热分子 —**zealotry** *n* [U]

zeal·ous /ˋzɛləs; ˈzeləs/ *adj* extremely enthusiastic about something that you believe in very strongly and behaving in a way that shows this 热心[热情]的; 狂热的: *a zealous preacher* 热心的传教士 —**zealously** *adv* —**zealousness** *n* [U]

ze·bra /ˋzibrə; ˈziːbrə/ *n* [C] an animal that looks like a horse but has black and white lines all over its body 斑马

zebra cross·ing /ˌ‥ ˈ‥/ *n* [C] *BrE* a place marked with black and white lines where people who are walking can cross a road safely【英】斑马线; CROSSWALK *AmE*【美】—compare 比较 PELICAN CROSSING

zed /zɛd; zed/ *BrE*【英】, **zee** *AmE*【美】*n* [C] a way of writing the letter 'z' that shows how you pronounce it 字母Z〔读音的拼写形式〕

Zee·brug·ge /ˋzebrugə; zeɪˈbrʊgə/ a sea port in northern Belgium, where ferries (FERRY) arrive from Britain 泽布吕赫〔比利时北部一海港, 是英国渡轮的停靠港〕

zeit·geist /ˋzaɪtˌgaɪst; ˈzaɪtgaɪst/ *n* [singular] *German* the general spirit or feeling of a period in history, as shown by people's ideas and beliefs at the time【德】时代精神[思潮]

Zen /zɛn; zen/ *n* [U] a kind of Buddhism that is popular in Japan 禅宗〔日本佛教的一大宗派〕

zen·ith /ˋzinɪθ; ˈzenɪ̥θ/ *n* [C usually singular 一般用单数] **1** the most successful point in the development of something〔事物发展的〕顶点, 顶峰: **reach its zenith/be at its zenith** *Opera reached its zenith at the turn of the century.* 歌剧在世纪之交达到了巅峰。**2** the highest point that is reached by the sun or the moon in the sky 天顶〔太阳或月亮在天空中达到的最高点〕

zeph·yr /ˋzɛfɚ; ˈzefə/ *n* [C] *poetical* a soft gentle wind【诗】和风, 微风

zep·pe·lin /ˋzɛpəlɪn; ˈzepəlɪn/ *n* [C] a German AIRSHIP used in World War I 齐柏林飞艇〔第一次世界大战时的德国飞艇〕

Zer·matt /zɝˋmæt; ˈzɜːmæt/ a place in the Swiss Alps where people go skiing, and where the famous mountain the Matterhorn is 采尔马特〔位于瑞士阿尔卑斯山脉的滑雪胜地。著名的马特峰矗立于此〕

ze·ro[1] /ˋzɪro; ˈzɪərəʊ/ *n plural* **zeros** or **zeroes** *number*

1 ►NUMBER 数字◄ 0 零

2 ►MEASUREMENT 计量◄ the point between + and - on a scale for measuring something, or the lowest point on a scale that shows how much there is left of something〔刻度上的〕零点, 零位: *The petrol gauge was already at zero.* 汽油表已指示零位。

3 ►TEMPERATURE 温度◄ the point on the Celsius scale at which water freezes〔摄氏温度表上的〕零度: *It was five degrees below zero last night.* 昨晚零下5度。| *sub-zero temperatures* 零下的温度 —see also 另见 ABSOLUTE ZERO

4 ►NOTHING 全无◄ *informal* the lowest possible amount or level of something【非正式】〔某事物的〕最低点; 无, 没有: *'Today?' I said, my spirits sinking to zero.* "今天?"我说, 我的情绪降到了最低点。| *The kids showed zero interest in what I was saying.* 孩子们对我说的话一点儿都不感兴趣。

Z

5 zero growth/inflation/gravity no growth, INFLATION (1) etc at all 零增长/通货膨胀/重力: *The country is aiming at zero growth in its population by the year 2010.* 该国力争到2010年使其人口达到零增长。

zero² *v*

zero in on sb/sth *phr v* [T] **1** to direct all your attention towards a particular person or thing 全神贯注于…: *Hayley zeroed in on the toys, the minute she saw them.* 海莉一看见玩具就心无旁骛了。**2** to aim a gun towards something or someone 把〔枪炮等〕瞄准…

zero hour /ˈ‥ ·/ *n* [singular] the time when a military operation or an important event is planned to begin〔军事行动或重要事件的〕开始时刻; 进攻时间

zero-sum game /,‥ˈ· ,·/ *n* [singular] *AmE* a situation in which you receive as much money or advantages as you give away【美】得益与损失平衡的局面, 零和局面[游戏]: *Diplomatic negotiations often aim at a zero-sum game.* 外交谈判常常以得失平衡的局面为目标。

zest /zɛst; zest/ *n* **1** [U] eager interest and enjoyment 热心, 热情; 快乐: *zest for life* 对生活的热情 **2** [singular, U] the quality of being exciting and interesting 趣味性; 刺激性: *The danger of being caught added a certain zest to the affair.* 有被捉的危险为这件事增添了一些刺激性。**3** [U] the outer skin of an orange or LEMON (1), used in cooking〔烹调中用作香料的〕橙皮, 柠檬皮 —**zestful** *adj* —**zestfully** *adv*

Zeus /zus; zjuːs/ in Greek MYTHOLOGY, the king of the gods, and ruler of the universe. In Roman mythology his name is Jupiter. 宙斯〔希腊神话中的众神之王和宇宙之主宰。罗马神话中称朱庇特〕

Zieg·feld /ˈzɪgfɛld; ˈzɪgfeld/, **Flor·enz** /ˈflɔrəns; ˈflɒrəns/ (1869-1932) a US theatre producer who arranged a show every year from 1907 to 1931, called the **Ziegfeld Follies**. These shows contained singing, dancing, and jokes, and were famous for their beautiful dancers. 齐格飞〔(1869-1932), 美国戏剧制作人, 1907至1931年间每年组织上演一部《齐格飞大歌舞》。这些表演包括歌曲、舞蹈和笑话, 以剧中靓丽的舞蹈演员闻名〕

zig·zag¹ /ˈzɪgzæg; ˈzɪgzæg/ *n* [C] a pattern that looks like a line of z's joined together 之字形, Z字形: *a zigzag path along the cliff* 沿悬崖而下的之字形小路—see picture on page A16 参见A16页图

zigzag² *v* **zigzagged, zigzagging** [I] to move forward in sharp angles, first to the left and then to the right etc 作之字形行进, 曲折移动: *The path zigzagged down the hillside.* 小路沿着山坡弯弯曲曲而下。

zilch /zɪltʃ; zɪltʃ/ *n* [U] *informal* nothing at all【非正式】无; 零: *"How much money is left?" "Zilch."* "还剩多少钱?" "一分也没有了。"

zil·lion /ˈzɪljən; ˈzɪljən/ *n* [C] *informal* an extremely large number of something【非正式】极大的数目: **[+of]** *zillions of mosquitoes* 无数的蚊子

Zim·ba·bwe /zɪmˈbɑbwe; zɪmˈbɑːbwei/ a country in south central Africa, south of Zambia and north of South Africa. Population: 11,365,000 (2001). Capital: Harare. Zimbabwe was formerly called Rhodesia, and was ruled by the British from 1889. In 1965 its white government announced that it was independent but the British government regarded this as an illegal claim. Zimbabwe became officially independent, under a new mainly black government in 1980. Its main products include tobacco, cloth, and minerals. 津巴布韦〔非洲中南部一国家, 位于赞比亚以南和南非以北。人口: 11,365,000 (2001), 首都: 哈拉雷。津巴布韦1889年起受英国统治, 旧称罗得西亚。1965年, 该国白人政府宣布独立, 但英国政府称其为非法宣言。1980年, 津巴布韦在一个以黑人为主的新政府领导下正式独立。该国以出产烟草、布匹和矿物为主〕

zim·mer frame /ˈzɪmə frem; ˈzɪmə freɪm/ *n* [C] *BrE trademark* a metal frame that old or ill people use to help them walk【英, 商标】〔老人或病人用的〕齐默助行架; WALKER (3) *AmE*【美】

zinc /zɪŋk; zɪŋk/ *n* [U] a bluish-white metal, used to make BRASS and to cover and protect objects made of iron 锌

Zin·fan·del /ˈzɪnfəndɛl; ˈzɪnfəndel/ a type of rosé wine made in the US, especially in California 增芳德葡萄酒〔美国一种玫瑰葡萄酒, 尤产于加利福尼亚〕

zing¹ /zɪŋ; zɪŋ/ *n* [U] *informal* the quality of being full of energy or taste【非正式】精力, 活力; 味道: *Lemon juice adds zing to drinks and sorbets.* 柠檬汁为饮料和果汁冰水增添了风味。—**zingy** *adj*

zing² *v* [I always+adv/prep] *informal* to move quickly, making a whistling noise【非正式】嗖嗖地掠过: **[+past/off]** *The shots went zinging off the rocks.* 子弹嗖嗖地擦过岩石弹开。

Zi·on /ˈzaɪən; ˈzaɪən/ **1** a name given to Israel or to an imagined land where the Jewish people could live in peace, after many centuries of not having a land of their own 锡安, 理想之国〔指以色列或一虚构之地。许多世纪以来, 以色列人一直过着没有家园的生活, 锡安才是他们安居的地方〕**2** *literary* heaven【文】天堂 **3** in the Old Testament of the Bible, another name for Jerusalem 锡安〔《圣经·旧约》中耶路撒冷的别称〕

Zi·on·is·m /ˈzaɪən,ɪzəm; ˈzaɪənɪzəm/ *n* [U] support for the establishment and development of a state for the Jews in Israel 犹太复国主义 —**Zionist** *n* [C]

zip¹ /zɪp; zɪp/ *n* **1** [C] *BrE* two lines of small metal or plastic pieces that slide together to fasten a piece of clothing【英】拉链; ZIPPER *especially AmE*【尤美】: *The zip on my skirt had broken.* 我裙子上的拉链坏了。| **do up/undo your zip** (=close or open a piece of clothing using a zip) 拉上/拉开拉链 *Your zip's undone at the back.* 你背后的拉链开了。—see picture at 参见 FASTENER 图 **2** [U] *informal* if someone or something has zip, they can do something quickly and with a lot of energy【非正式】精力, 活力: *This car goes with a bit more zip than my last one.* 这辆车的速度比我上一辆要快些。**3** [singular] *AmE informal* nothing at all or zero【美, 非正式】全无; 零: *We beat them 10 to zip.* 我们以10比0赢了他们。| *"How much money have you got left?" "Zip!"* "你还剩多少钱?" "一分都不剩。"

zip² *v* **zipped, zipping 1** [T always+adv/prep] to open or shut something using a zip 用拉链拉开[拉上]: **[+in/inside]** *The money was safely zipped inside my jacket.* 钱在我的上衣内袋里, 有拉链安全保护。| **zip sth shut/open** *Olsen zipped the bag shut.* 奥尔森拉上了袋子的拉链。**2** [I always+adv/prep] *informal* to do something or go somewhere very quickly【非正式】快速地做某事[到某地]: **[+through/past/along etc]** *We zipped through customs in no time.* 我们很快通过了海关。**3 zip your lip** *AmE spoken* used to tell someone not to say anything about something, or to tell them to be quiet【美口】别开口: *You'd better zip your lip or you'll be in trouble!* 你最好别开口, 不然会有麻烦的!

zip up *phr v* [T] **1** **[zip** sth **↔ up]** to fasten a piece of clothing using a zip 用拉链拉上〔衣服〕: *Zip your jacket up – you'll get cold.* 把夹克的拉链拉上, 否则你会着凉的。—opposite 反义词 UNZIP **2** **[zip** sb **up]** to close the zip on a piece of clothing that someone else is wearing 拉上〔某人衣服〕的拉链: *"Could you zip me up please? I can't reach."* "帮我把拉链拉上好吗? 我够不着。"

zip code /ˈ· ·/ *n* [C] *AmE* a number that you put below the address on an envelope to help the post office deliver the mail more quickly【美】邮政编码; POSTCODE *BrE*【英】

zip·per /ˈzɪpɚ; ˈzɪpə/ *n* [C] *especially AmE* two lines of small metal or plastic pieces that slide together to fasten a piece of clothing【尤美】拉链; ZIP¹ (1) *BrE*【英】—see picture at 参见 FASTENER 图

zip·po /ˈzɪpo; ˈzɪpəʊ/ *n* [singular] *AmE informal* nothing at all or zero【美, 非正式】全无; 零

zit /zɪt; zɪt/ *n* [C] *informal* a spot on someone's skin; PIMPLE【非正式】丘疹

zith·er /ˈzɪðɚ; ˈzɪðə/ *n* [C] a musical instrument from Eastern Europe, played by pulling its wire strings with your fingers 齐特琴〔东欧的一种用手指弹拨的弦乐器〕

zo·di·ac /ˈzodɪ,æk; ˈzəʊdiæk/ *n* **the zodiac** an imaginary area through which the sun, moon, and PLANETS appear to travel, which some people believe influences our lives 黄道带〔指太阳、月亮及行星所构成的假想带〕: **sign of the zodiac** (=one of the twelve parts that this area is divided into) 黄道十二宫[星座]之一 *"Which sign of the zodiac were you born under?" "Leo."* "你的生日属于哪个星座?" "狮子座。" —see also 另见 HOROSCOPE —**zodiacal** /zoˈdaɪəkḷ; zəʊˈdaɪəkəl/ *adj*

CULTURAL NOTE 文化注释

The signs of the **zodiac** are used in **astrology**. The signs are: **Aquarius, Pisces, Aries, Taurus, Gemini, Cancer, Leo, Virgo, Libra, Scorpio, Sagittarius,** and **Capricorn.** 黄道十二宫图用于占星术中, 它们是: 宝瓶座, 双鱼座, 白羊座, 金牛座, 双子座, 巨蟹座, 狮子座, 室女座, 天秤座, 天蝎座, 人马座, 摩羯座。

Zo·la /ˈzolə; ˈzəʊlə/, **Em·ile** /ˈɛmil; ˈemiːl/ (1840-1902) a French writer of NOVELS who developed the style of literature called naturalism (=showing people and the world exactly as they really are) in novels such as *Nana* and *Germinal*, which describe life and society in a very detailed way, and are often about crime, murder, and people who are poor. He

Z

also supported Alfred Dreyfus, and criticized the people who had sent Dreyfus to prison, by writing the public letter *J'accuse*. 左拉〔(1840-1902), 法国小说家。著有《娜娜》、《萌芽》等小说, 倡导自然主义创作风格, 以深入、细腻的笔触描写社会生活, 内容常涉及犯罪、谋杀和穷苦百姓。他曾撰写公开信《我控诉》支持阿尔弗雷德·德雷福斯, 并抨击将德雷福斯送入监狱的人〕

zom·bie /ˋzɑmbɪ; ˈzɒmbi/ *n* [C] **1** *informal* someone who moves very slowly and does not seem to be thinking about what they are doing, especially because they are very tired【非正式】〔尤指因极度疲劳而〕行动呆板的人, 无精打采的人 **2** a dead person whose body is made to move by magic, according to some African and Caribbean religions〔非洲和加勒比海地区一些部族宗教信仰中的〕还魂尸, 僵尸, 行尸〔被巫术驱动的死尸〕

zon·al /ˋzonḷ; ˈzəʊnl/ *adj technical* connected with or arranged in zones【术语】区域性的; 分成区的; 划好范围的 —**zonally** *adv*

3 **zone** /zon; zəʊn/ *n* [C] a large area that is different from other areas around it in some way〔与周围地区有所不同的〕地区; 地带; 区域: *This is a no-parking zone.* 这是禁止泊车区。| *a nuclear-free zone* 无核区 | **danger zone** (=an area where it is dangerous to go) 危险地带 | **war/battle/combat zone** *The south side of the city has virtually become a war zone.* 该城的南边实际上已成为战区。| **pedestrian zone** (=an area where no cars are allowed) 步行区 | **residential/industrial/commercial etc zone** (=an area of a city that is used for a particular purpose, such as houses or shops) 居民/工业/商业区等 —see also 另见 **buffer zone** (BUFFER[1] (3)), EROGENOUS ZONE, **exclusion zone** (EXCLUSION (3)), TIME ZONE

zoned /zond; zəʊnd/ also 又作 **zoned out** *adj* [not before noun 不用于名词前] *AmE informal* unable to think clearly and quickly, especially because you are tired or ill【美, 非正式】〔尤因疲劳或患病而〕思维麻木的; 反应迟钝的

zon·ing /ˋzonɪŋ; ˈzəʊnɪŋ/ *n* [U] a system of choosing areas to be developed for particular purposes, such as houses or shops, when planning a town 分区制; 分区布局

zodiac 黄道十二宫图

Aquarius 宝瓶座
21 Jan-19 Feb
1月21日-2月19日

Pisces 双鱼座
20 Feb-20 Mar
2月20日-3月20日

Aries 白羊座
21 Mar-20 Apr
3月21日-4月20日

Taurus 金牛座
21 Apr-22 May
4月21日-5月22日

Gemini 双子座
23 May-21 Jun
5月23日-6月21日

Cancer 巨蟹座
22 Jun-22 Jul
6月22日-7月22日

Leo 狮子座
23 Jul-22 Aug
7月23日-8月22日

Virgo 室女座
23 Aug-22 Sept
8月23日-9月22日

Libra 天秤座
23 Sept-22 Oct
9月23日-10月22日

Scorpio 天蝎座
23 Oct-21 Nov
10月23日-11月21日

Sagittarius 人马座
22 Nov-22 Dec
11月22日-12月22日

Capricorn 摩羯座
23 Dec-20 Jan
12月23日-1月20日

zonked /zɑŋkt; zɒŋkt/ also 又作 **zonked out** *adj* [not before noun 不用于名词前] *informal* extremely tired; EXHAUSTED (1)【非正式】筋疲力尽的: *Paul was zonked after the conference in Amsterdam.* 保罗在阿姆斯特丹的会议后累得疲惫不堪。

zoo /zu; zuː/ *n* [C] a place, usually in a city, where animals of many kinds are kept so that people can go to look at them 动物园

zoo·keep·er /ˈ· ˌ· ·/ *n* [C] someone who looks after animals in a zoo 动物园饲养员

zo·ol·o·gist /zoˋɑlədʒɪst; zuːˈɒlədʒɪ̵st/ *n* [C] a scientist who studies animals and their behaviour 动物学家

zo·ol·o·gy /zoˋɑlədʒɪ; zuːˈɒlədʒi/ *n* [U] the scientific study of animals and their behaviour 动物学 —**zoological** /ˌzoəˋlɑdʒɪkḷ; ˌzuːəˈlɒdʒɪkəl◂/ *adj* —**zoologically** /-kḷɪ; -kli/ *adv*

zoom[1] /zum; zuːm/ *v* [I] *informal*【非正式】**1** [always+adv/prep] to go somewhere or do something very quickly 疾行; 快速做〔某事〕: [**+past/through/off etc**] *Brenda zoomed past on her Honda.* 布伦达骑着她的本田摩托车疾驰而过。| *The work was really easy and I was able to zoom through it in a couple of hours.* 这工作一点不难, 我用了两三个小时就干完了。**2** to increase suddenly and quickly 陡升, 激增: [**+to**] *Interest rates zoomed up to 20% in the late 80s.* 80年代后期, 利率急升至20%。

zoom in/out *phr v* [I] if a camera zooms in or out, it moves quickly between a picture that is close and detailed and one that is distant〔镜头〕拉近/推远: **zoom in on sth/sb** *The camera zoomed in on the child's face.* 摄影机向孩子的脸部推近。

zoom[2] *n* [singular] *informal* a sound made by a vehicle that is travelling fast【非正式】〔车辆快速行驶时发出的〕隆隆声

zoom lens /ˈ· ·, ·ˈ/ *n* [C] a camera LENS (2) that can change from a distant to a close view 可变焦距透镜, 变焦镜头 —see picture at 参见 CAMERA 图

zoot suit /ˋzut ˌsut; ˈzuːt suːt/ *n* [C] a suit that consists of wide trousers and a JACKET with wide shoulders, worn especially in the 1940s and 1950s 佐特装〔由宽肩夹克和宽大裤子组合的服装, 尤流行于20世纪40和50年代〕

Zor·o·as·ter /ˋzɔroæstɚ; ˌzɒrəʊˈæstə/ also 又作 **Zarathustra** (?628-?551 BC) a Persian religious teacher and PROPHET (=someone whom people believe has been sent by God to lead and teach them) who started a new religion called Zoroastrianism 琐罗亚斯德〔(公元前? 628-前? 551), 古代波斯宗教领袖和先知, 创立了一个新教派, 名为琐罗亚斯德教〕

Zor·o·as·tri·a·nis·m /ˌzɔroˋæstrɪənɪzəm; ˌzɒrəʊˈæstriənɪzəm/ *n* [U] an ancient religion from Persia (=modern Iran), whose followers believe that there is a continual battle between the forces of good (or light) and the forces of evil (or darkness), but that good will win in the end and humans must help this to happen. The religion is now practised by only a small number of people, most of whom are Parsees living in India. 琐罗亚斯德教, 祆教, 拜火教〔起源于古代波斯(今伊朗)的宗教。其信徒笃信善(或光明)与恶(或黑暗)这两股力量之间在不断地进行着较量, 但善最终会战胜恶, 人类必须要促成善的胜利。现在信奉这一宗教的人很少, 主要为居住在印度的帕西人〕 —**Zoroastrian** *adj*

Zor·ro /ˋzɔro; ˈzɒrəʊ/ a character in a series of old US films and television programmes who wore a black MASK, and protected people from crime 佐罗〔美国经典系列电影、电视连续剧中的一个角色。佐罗佩戴黑色面罩, 除暴安良〕

zuc·chi·ni /zuˋkinɪ; zʊˈkiːni/ *n* [C] *AmE* a small vegetable with a dark green skin, shaped like a short stick【美】小胡瓜, 绿皮密生西葫芦; COURGETTE *BrE*【英】—see picture on page A9 参见A9页图

Zu·lu /ˋzulu; ˈzuːluː/ *n* **1 the Zulu** a large tribe of people who live in South Africa〔南非的〕祖鲁族 **2** [C] a member of this tribe 祖鲁人 —**Zulu** *adj*

Zul·u·land /ˋzululænd; ˈzuːluːlænd/ an area in the northeastern part of South Africa which is the original home of the Zulu people. The area is now part of the South African province of Kwa Zulu Natal. 祖鲁兰〔南非东北部一地区, 是祖鲁人的原始聚居地, 现为南非夸祖卢纳塔尔省的一部分〕

Zü·rich /ˋzurɪk; ˈzʊərɪk/ a city in Switzerland which is an important international centre for banking 苏黎士〔瑞士一城市, 也是重要的国际银行业中心〕

zwie·back /ˋzwaɪbæk; ˈzwiːbæk/ *n* [U] *AmE* a kind of hard dry bread, often given to babies【美】〔常给婴儿食用的一种〕烤面包干 —compare 比较 RUSK *BrE*【英】

zy·de·co /ˋzaɪdəko; ˈzaɪdəkəʊ/ *n* [U] a kind of Cajun music 柴迪科舞曲

zy·gote /ˋzaɪgot; ˈzaɪgəʊt/ *n* [C] a cell that is formed when an egg is fertilized (FERTILIZE (1)) 受精卵

Z

Position and Direction 位置和方向

The prepositions below refer to the picture opposite.

下面的介词请参见右图。

"Good Afternoon Ladies and Gentlemen. Welcome to the 6th national cycle race.

女士们，先生们，下午好！欢迎观看第六届全国自行车大赛。

It's turning into quite a day! **All about/around** me people are leaning **over**① the barriers to get a good view of the race. Local residents are hanging **out**② of their windows, and **beyond** the spectators, traffic is **at**③ a standstill.

今天是个相当热闹的日子。我周围的人俯身探出护栏，以便看清楚这场比赛。当地的居民也都探身自家窗外。在观众那边，交通都停顿了。

The police are out in full force. There's a police motorbike **next to/beside/alongside**④ the cyclists, a policewoman leaning **on upon/against**⑤ the barriers, and a helicopter **overhead**⑥.

警察全体出动。一辆警用摩托车跟在选手旁边，一位女警察倚栏站立，一架直升机在空中盘旋着。

Not far **from** me, **in/among** the crowd I can see last year's champion with his daughter **on**⑦ his shoulders. And **off** to the right, there are a number of fans pushing their way **through**⑧ the crowd **to/towards** the front.

离我不远的人群中，我看见去年的冠军，他的肩上驮着他的女儿。在右边的护栏外，一群自行车赛迷正从人群中往前挤。

Across⑨ the finishing line **in** first place comes number thirty four. Directly **in front**⑩ of me photographers are trying to get shots of the winner, and just **below/beneath/underneath**⑪ me jubilant fans are cheering.

首先冲过终点线的是 34 号选手。在我的正前方，摄影师们正在抢拍冠军的照片；就在我的下方，兴高采烈的自行车赛迷正在欢呼雀跃。

On/to⑫ the left of the new champion, cycling **past** the photographers is number sixty one. Then, **behind**⑬ the leaders, **in** a red helmet is De Kosten **from** Belgium who is racing **towards/in the direction of** the finishing line. Chasing **after**⑭ him are numbers ninety two and a hundred and five, and at this very moment a small group of cyclists have just come **round**⑮ the corner **into** view.

在新冠军的左侧，61 号选手骑着车在摄影师前掠过。紧跟着这两位领先者后面的是戴着红头盔的比利时选手德·柯斯汀，他正向着终点线冲去。在他后面追赶的是 92 号和 105 号选手。就在此刻，一小群选手刚拐过那个街角，进入人们的视线。"

POLICE
6
3
15
2
4
14
13
11
1
12
10
81
34
FINISH
9
8
7
5
Jupiter

Car 汽车

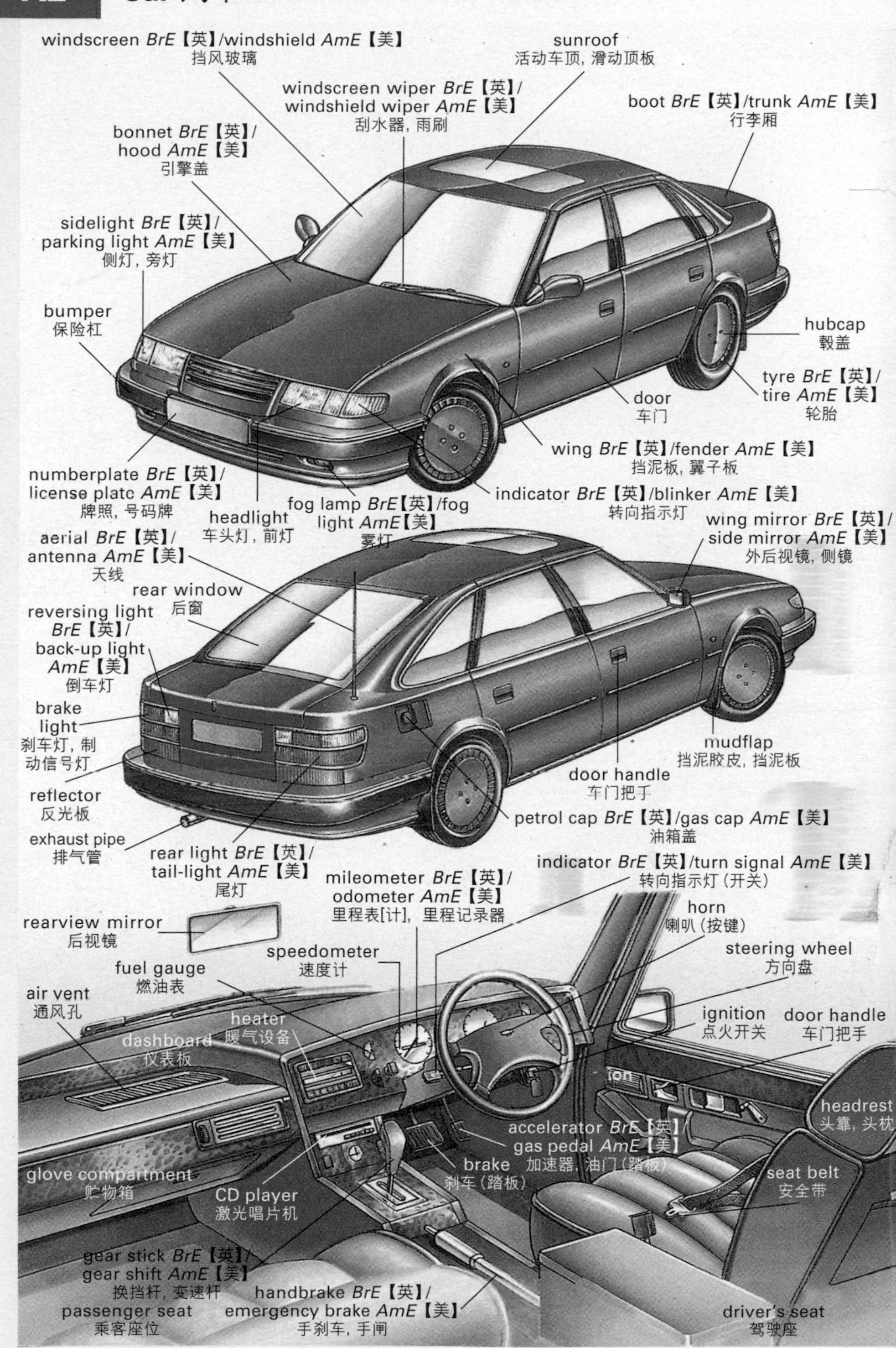
windscreen BrE【英】/windshield AmE【美】
挡风玻璃
sunroof
活动车顶，滑动顶板
windscreen wiper BrE【英】/
windshield wiper AmE【美】
刮水器，雨刷
boot BrE【英】/trunk AmE【美】
行李厢
bonnet BrE【英】/
hood AmE【美】
引擎盖
sidelight BrE【英】/
parking light AmE【美】
侧灯，旁灯
bumper
保险杠
hubcap
毂盖
tyre BrE【英】/
tire AmE【美】
轮胎
door
车门
wing BrE【英】/fender AmE【美】
挡泥板，翼子板
numberplate BrE【英】/
license plate AmE【美】
牌照，号码牌
headlight
车头灯，前灯
fog lamp BrE【英】/fog
light AmE【美】
雾灯
indicator BrE【英】/blinker AmE【美】
转向指示灯
wing mirror BrE【英】/
side mirror AmE【美】
外后视镜，侧镜
aerial BrE【英】/
antenna AmE【美】
天线
rear window
后窗
reversing light
BrE【英】/
back-up light
AmE【美】
倒车灯
brake
light
刹车灯，制
动信号灯
reflector
反光板
exhaust pipe
排气管
rear light BrE【英】/
tail-light AmE【美】
尾灯
mudflap
挡泥胶皮，挡泥板
door handle
车门把手
petrol cap BrE【英】/gas cap AmE【美】
油箱盖
indicator BrE【英】/turn signal AmE【美】
转向指示灯（开关）
mileometer BrE【英】/
odometer AmE【美】
里程表[计]，里程记录器
horn
喇叭（按键）
rearview mirror
后视镜
speedometer
速度计
steering wheel
方向盘
fuel gauge
燃油表
air vent
通风孔
heater
暖气设备
dashboard
仪表板
ignition
点火开关
door handle
车门把手
headrest
头靠，头枕
accelerator BrE【英】/
gas pedal AmE【美】
加速器，油门（踏板）
brake
刹车（踏板）
glove compartment
贮物箱
CD player
激光唱片机
seat belt
安全带
gear stick BrE【英】/
gear shift AmE【美】
换挡杆，变速杆
handbrake BrE【英】/
emergency brake AmE【美】
手刹车，手闸
passenger seat
乘客座位
driver's seat
驾驶座

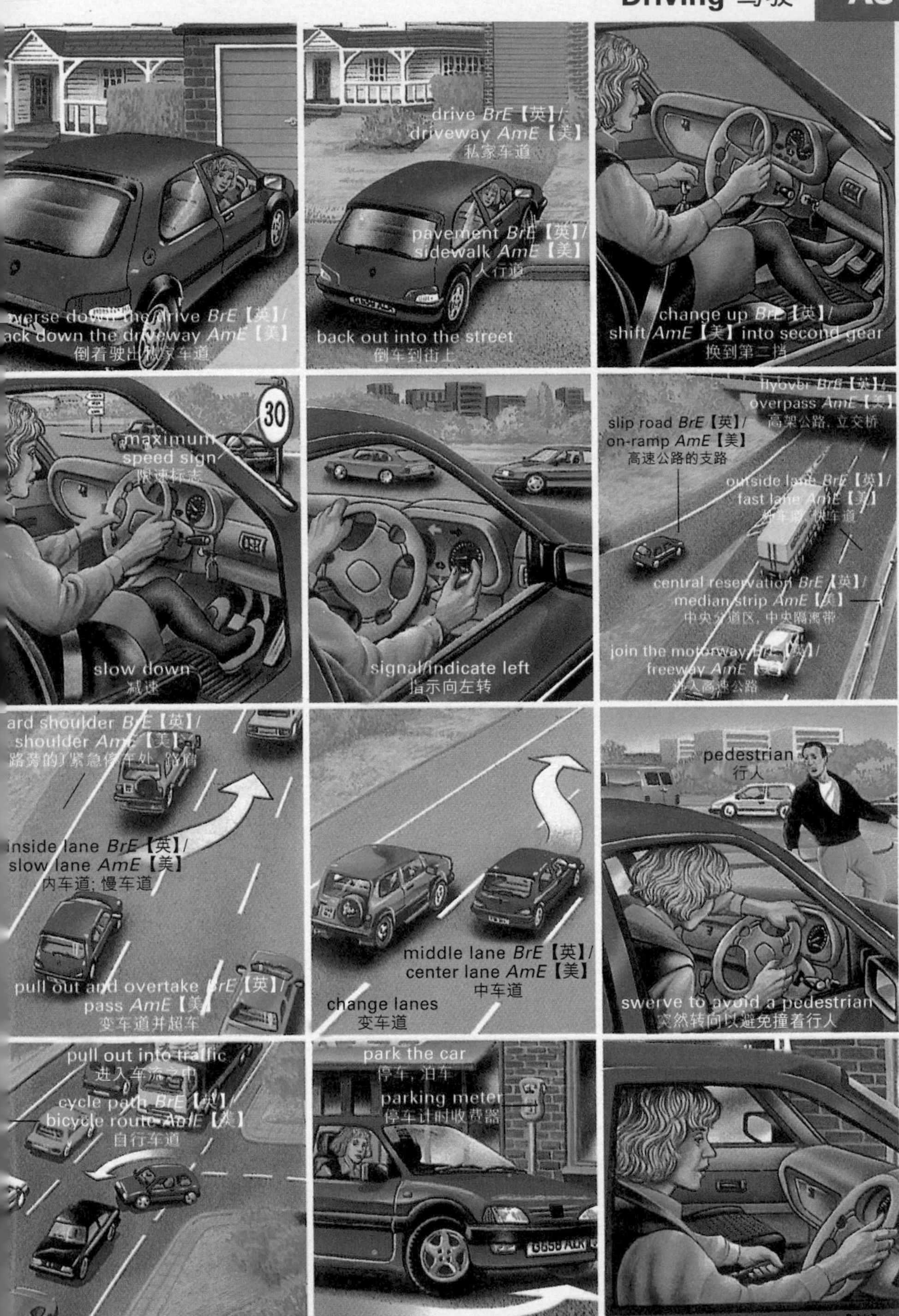
reverse down the drive BrE【英】/
back down the driveway AmE【美】
倒着驶出私家车道
drive BrE【英】/
driveway AmE【美】
私家车道
pavement BrE【英】/
sidewalk AmE【美】
人行道
back out into the street
倒车到街上
change up BrE【英】/
shift AmE【美】into second gear
换到第二档
maximum
speed sign
限速标志
30
slow down
减速
signal/indicate left
指示向左转
flyover BrE【英】/
overpass AmE【美】
高架公路，立交桥
slip road BrE【英】/
on-ramp AmE【美】
高速公路的支路
outside lane BrE【英】/
fast lane AmE【美】
外车道；快车道
central reservation BrE【英】/
median strip AmE【美】
中央分道区，中央隔离带
join the motorway BrE【英】/
freeway AmE【美】
并入高速公路
hard shoulder BrE【英】/
shoulder AmE【美】
路旁的紧急停车处，路肩
inside lane BrE【英】/
slow lane AmE【美】
内车道；慢车道
pull out and overtake BrE【英】/
pass AmE【美】
变车道并超车
middle lane BrE【英】/
center lane AmE【美】
中车道
change lanes
变车道
pedestrian
行人
swerve to avoid a pedestrian
突然转向以避免撞着行人
pull out into traffic
进入车流之中
cycle path BrE【英】/
bicycle route AmE【美】
自行车道
park the car
停车，泊车
parking meter
停车计时收费器
put on the handbrake BrE【英】/
emergency brake AmE【美】
使用手刹车[紧急刹车]

House 房屋

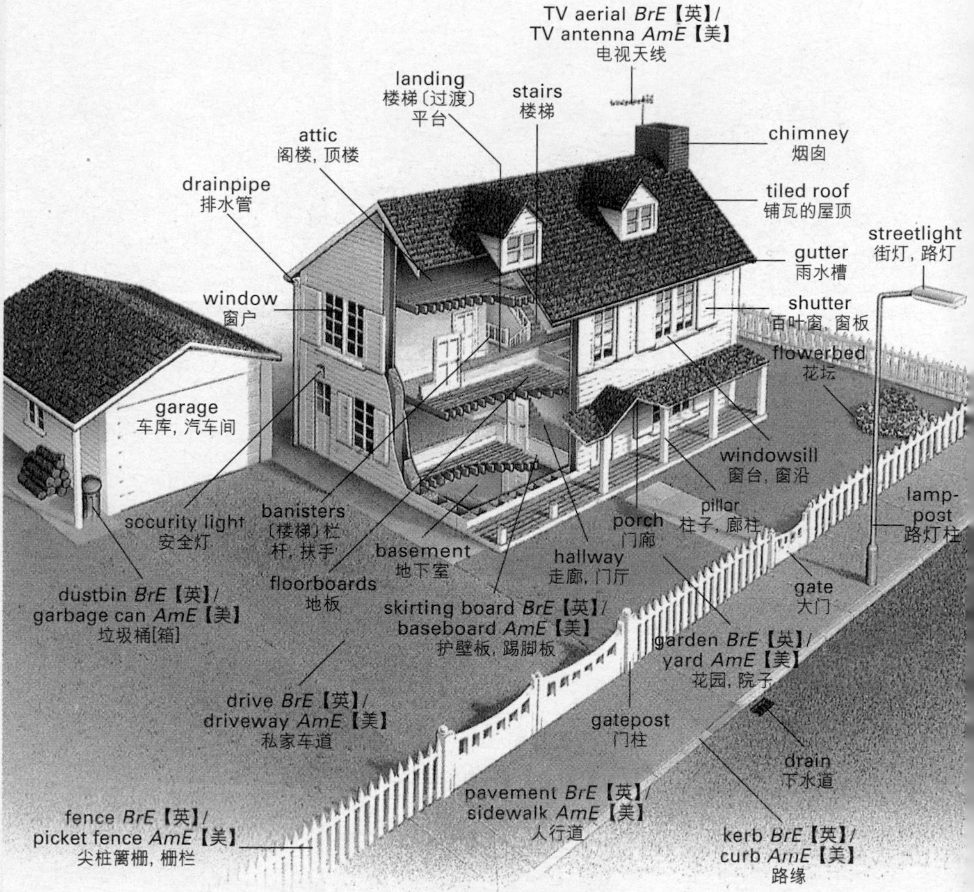

TV aerial BrE【英】/
TV antenna AmE【美】
电视天线
landing
楼梯〔过渡〕平台
stairs
楼梯
attic
阁楼, 顶楼
chimney
烟囱
drainpipe
排水管
tiled roof
铺瓦的屋顶
streetlight
街灯, 路灯
gutter
雨水槽
window
窗户
shutter
百叶窗, 窗板
flowerbed
花坛
garage
车库, 汽车间
windowsill
窗台, 窗沿
lamp-post
路灯柱
pillar
柱子, 廊柱
security light
安全灯
banisters
〔楼梯〕栏杆, 扶手
porch
门廊
basement
地下室
hallway
走廊, 门厅
gate
大门
dustbin BrE【英】/
garbage can AmE【美】
垃圾桶[箱]
floorboards
地板
skirting board BrE【英】/
baseboard AmE【美】
护壁板, 踢脚板
garden BrE【英】/
yard AmE【美】
花园, 院子
drive BrE【英】/
driveway AmE【美】
私家车道
gatepost
门柱
drain
下水道
pavement BrE【英】/
sidewalk AmE【美】
人行道
fence BrE【英】/
picket fence AmE【美】
尖桩篱栅, 栅栏
kerb BrE【英】/
curb AmE【美】
路缘

bungalow
平房
terraced houses BrE【英】/
row houses AmE【美】
排屋
semi-detached BrE【英】/
duplex AmE【美】
半独立式房屋, 毗联式住宅
ranch house
牧场式住宅
block of flats BrE【英】/
apartment building AmE【美】
公寓大楼

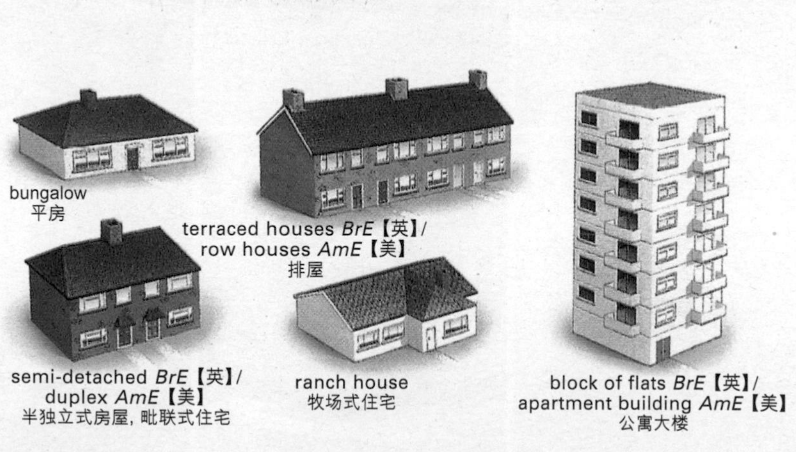

sky-blue
天蓝色
lime green
浅黄绿色
olive
黄绿色，橄榄色
jade
绿玉色，翡翠绿
violet
蓝紫色
beige
米黄色
poppy
深橘红色
scarlet
绯红色，猩红色，鲜红色
tan
棕黄色，黄褐色
golden
金色，金黄色
navy blue
深蓝色，藏青色
khaki
土黄色，黄褐色
bottle green
深绿色
russet
赤褐色
cream
奶油色，淡黄色
mustard
芥末黄；深黄色
turquoise
青绿色
royal blue
品蓝色
peach
桃红色
emerald
翠绿色
maroon
栗色，褐紫红色
lemon
淡黄色
burgundy
深（紫）红色
magenta
洋红色，品红色
rose
玫瑰红色
tangerine
橘红色
mauve
淡紫色
apricot
杏黄色
green
绿色
pink
粉红色
lilac
淡紫色
coffee
咖啡色
purple
紫色
buff
浅[暗]黄色，米色
red
红色
blue
蓝色
black
黑色
crimson
深红色
grey
灰色
white
白色
orange
橙色；橘黄色
brown
褐色，棕色
yellow
黄色
aquamarine
海蓝色，蓝绿色

Describing People 描写人物

Emma has long wavy gingery-brown hair, with a centre parting *BrE*/ center part *AmE*. She has freckles, hazel eyes and wears her hair pushed back behind her ears.
埃玛梳着姜棕色的波浪形长发，中间分缝。她脸上长有雀斑，眼睛是浅褐色的，头发梳到耳后。

Roald has short spiky fair hair. He's got thick bushy eyebrows, a five o'clock shadow and sideburns.
罗尔德有一头短而直立的金发。他的眉毛又粗又浓密，满脸胡子茬，还留了鬓角。

Kaori has straight shoulder-length hair, a side parting *BrE* /side part *AmE* and a short fringe *BrE* / short bangs *AmE*. She has dark brown eyes and high cheekbones.
考丽梳着齐肩的长直发，侧分缝，额前有短短的刘海儿。她的眼睛是深褐色的，颧骨很高。

Eduardo is clean-shaven with greying hair and a receding hairline. He has a small scar on his jaw and a dimple in his chin.
His wife, Nadia, has long straggly dark hair.
爱德华多胡子剃得干干净净，他的头发有些灰白，而且前发际线已经后移了。他的下颌处有一道小疤痕，下巴上有个小凹痕。
他的妻子纳迪娅梳着散乱的长黑发。

Sue has blonde hair with a wispy fringe. She has a beauty spot on her cheek and a pointed chin.
休的头发是金黄色的，稍留了一小绺刘海儿。她的脸颊上有一个美人痣，下巴尖尖的。

John is slightly tanned with wavy ginger hair and a roman nose. He has stubble, a double chin and wears half moon spectacles *BrE* / reading glasses *AmE*. Nick has lank auburn hair, a pale complexion, and is growing a goatee beard.
约翰晒得有些黑，鬈曲的头发是姜黄色的。他长着高鼻梁鹰钩鼻，蓄胡子茬，双下巴。他戴着半月形眼镜。尼克的头发又软又直，是红褐色的。他面色苍白，正在留起山羊胡子。

Adjectival Word Order 形容词词序

Quality 特征，特点	Size/Age/Shape 大小/年龄/形状	Colour 颜色	Origin 起源；来源	Made of 由什么制成的	Type/Usage 类型/用法	Noun 名词
beautiful 漂亮的	long 长的	brown 棕色的				hair 头发
	old 旧的		French 法国的			car 汽车
				metal 金属的	half moon 半月形的	spectacles 眼镜

bar of chocolate
一块巧克力
bar of soap
一块肥皂
hunk of cheese
一块干酪
chunk of rock
一大块岩石
rasher of bacon BrE【英】
一片熏猪肉
block of ice
一大块冰
cube of sugar
一块方糖
wad of banknotes BrE【英】/
bills AmE【美】一沓钞票
slab of concrete
混凝土板
clod of earth
土块, 泥块
slice of bread
一片面包
slice of cake
一块蛋糕
lump of butter
一块黄油
dollop of jam
一匙果酱
sheet of newspaper
一张报纸
pane of glass
一块玻璃
blob of paint
一滴油漆
trickle of rain
流淌下来的雨水
segment of orange
一瓣橙子
square of chocolate
一方块巧克力
pinch of salt
一撮盐
squirt of liquid
(喷出的) 少量液体
squeeze of lemon
(挤出的) 少许柠檬汁
dash of sauce
(滴进) 少许酱汁
drop of sauce
一滴酱汁
wisp of smoke
一缕烟
puff of perfume
(喷出的) 少许香水
crumb of cake
蛋糕屑
speck of dirt
一点污渍
grain of sand
沙粒
flake of paint
(剥落的) 一片油漆
shred of cloth
一小片碎布
chip of china
一块碎瓷片
splinter of wood
一片尖木片
sliver of glass
一片碎玻璃
scrap of paper
一小片碎纸

Fruit 水果

1 strawberries 草莓
2 cranberries 越橘
3 blackberries 黑莓
4 raspberries 山莓, 覆盆子
5 gooseberries 醋栗
6 grapes 葡萄
7 blueberries 蓝莓
8 loganberries 罗甘莓
9 oranges 柑橘, 橙
10 grapefruit 西柚, 葡萄柚
11 limes 酸橙
12 lemon 柠檬
13 clementines 克莱门氏小柑橘
14 cantaloup *BrE*【英】/cantaloupe *AmE*【美】罗马甜瓜, 皱皮香瓜
15 watermelon 西瓜
16 honeydew melon 白甜瓜, 蜜瓜
17 pineapple 菠萝
18 mango 芒果
19 coconuts 椰子
20 plantains 大蕉
21 bananas 香蕉
22 papaya 番木瓜
23 lychee 荔枝
24 passion fruit 西番莲果实
25 starfruit 杨桃
26 persimmons 柿子
27 quinces 榅桲
28 figs 无花果
29 peaches 桃子
30 nectarines 油桃
31 pears 梨
32 plums 李子
33 kiwi fruit 猕猴桃, 奇异果
34 cherries 樱桃
35 apricots 杏子
36 apples 苹果

1 garlic 蒜
2 leeks 韭葱
3 spring onions *BrE*【英】/green onions *AmE*【美】大葱
4 onions 洋葱
5 yam 薯蓣
6 sweet potato 红薯, 番薯
7 potatoes 马铃薯
8 Jerusalem artichoke 菊芋
9 cucumbers 黄瓜
10 marrow *BrE*【英】/ squash *AmE*【美】西葫芦
11 courgettes *BrE*【英】/ zucchini *AmE*【美】小胡瓜
12 pumpkin 南瓜
13 butter beans 利马豆
14 green beans 青菜豆, 嫩菜豆
15 broad beans 蚕豆
16 aduki beans 赤豆
17 peas 豌豆
18 kidney beans 菜豆, 四季豆
19 runner-beans 红花菜豆
20 beansprouts 豆芽
21 swede *BrE*【英】/ rutabaga *AmE*【美】芜菁甘蓝
22 beetroot *BrE*【英】/ beet *AmE*【美】甜菜(根)
23 white radish 白萝卜
24 ginger 姜
25 radishes 小萝卜
26 carrots 胡萝卜
27 parsnips 欧洲防风
28 turnips 芜菁
29 cabbage 卷心菜, 洋白菜
30 corn cobs 玉米(棒子)
31 chinese leaves *BrE*【英】/bok choy *AmE*【美】白菜
32 celery 芹菜
33 artichoke 洋蓟
34 okra 秋葵
35 asparagus 芦笋
36 cauliflower 花椰菜
37 lettuce 生菜
38 spinach 菠菜
39 red pepper 红辣椒
40 green pepper 青(甜)椒
41 broccoli 西兰花; 花茎甘蓝
42 aubergine *BrE*【英】/ egg plant *AmE*【美】茄子
43 mushrooms 蘑菇
44 tomatoes 番茄, 西红柿
45 brussels sprouts 球芽甘蓝(菜), 抱子甘蓝

Kitchen 厨房

tap BrE【英】/ faucet AmE【美】
水龙头
breadbin BrE【英】/
breadbox AmE【美】
面包箱
fire extinguisher
灭火器
cupboard
橱柜
washing-up liquid
BrE【英】/
dishwashing liquid
AmE【美】
洗涤剂
microwave
微波炉
fridge
电冰箱
cooker BrE【英】/
stove AmE【美】
炉灶
scouring pad
百洁布
sink
洗涤槽
draining
board
滴水板
funnel
漏斗
FRY
煎，炸
(electric) ring BrE【英】
burner AmE【美】
环形灶盘
oven glove
烤炉用的手套
BAKE
烘，焙
freezer
冷冻柜
dishwasher
洗碗机
washing
machine
洗衣机
ROAST
烤
oven
烤炉
kettle
（电）水壶
floor
地板
baking tray BrE
【英】/ cookie
sheet AmE【美】
烤盘，饼干烘制板
scales BrE【英】/ scale AmE【美】
磅秤
measuring jug
量壶
BURN
烤焦
fish slice BrE【英】/
spatula AmE【美】
（煎鱼）铲；锅铲
measuring
spoons
量匙
toaster
烤面包机
cake tin BrE【英】/
muffin tin AmE【美】
蛋糕烤盘；松饼烤盘
cloth
（桌）布
cutlery BrE【英】/
silverware AmE【美】
（西餐）餐具；银餐具
corkscrew
瓶塞钻
tin opener BrE【英】/
can opener AmE【美】
开罐器
food processor
食品加工器
drawer
抽屉
worktop BrE【英】/
counter AmE【美】
操作台
bin BrE【英】/ wastebas-
ket AmE【美】
垃圾桶
breadboard
切面包板
napkin
餐巾
tea towel BrE【英】/
dishcloth AmE【美】
茶巾；洗碗布

Verbs in the Kitchen 厨房中常用的动词

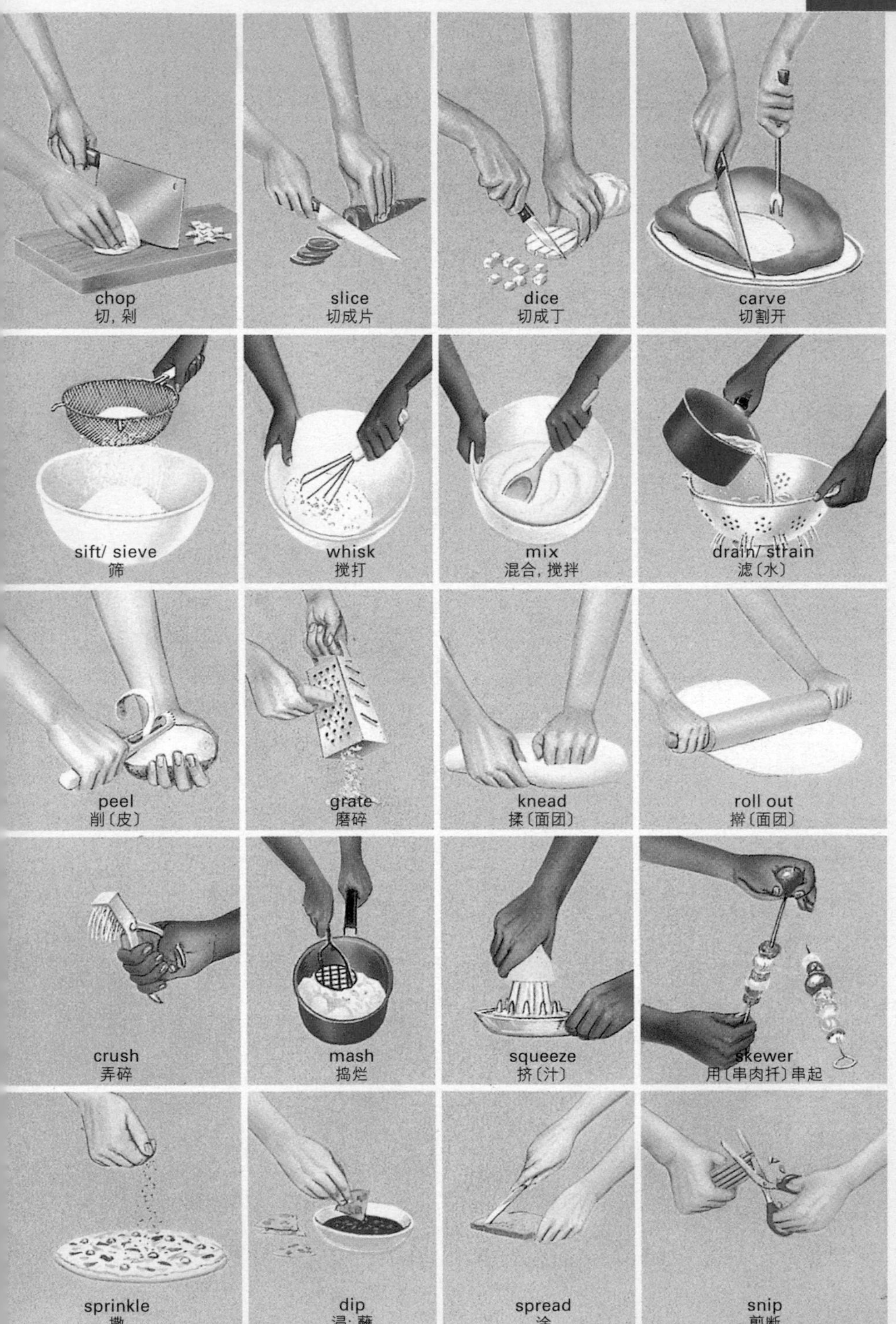

A12 Landscapes 风景地貌

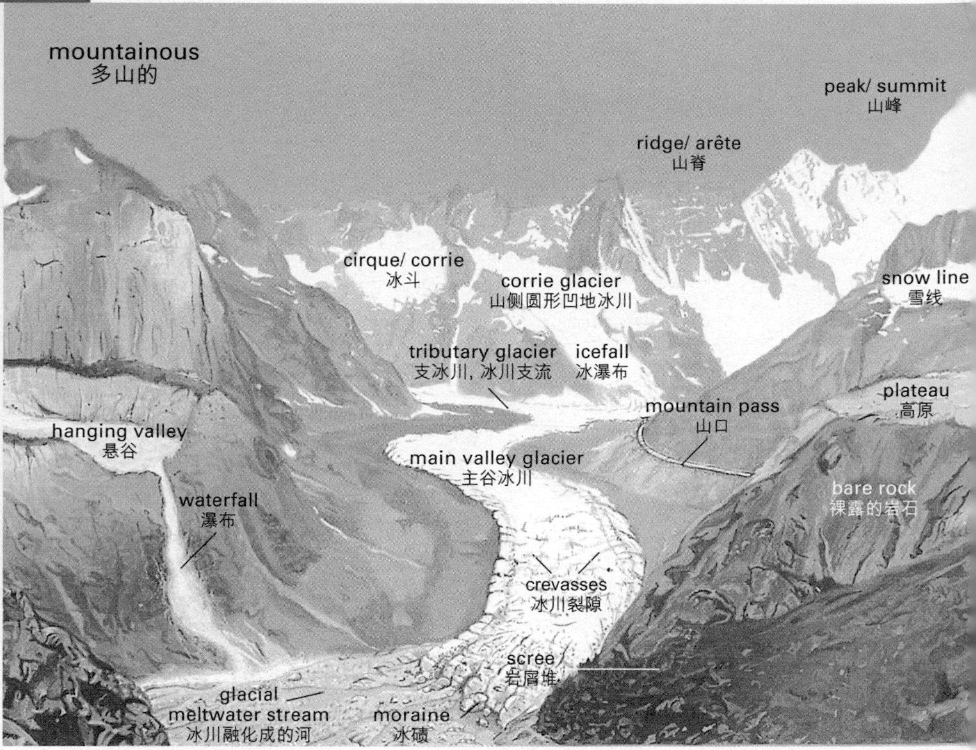

mountainous 多山的

peak/ summit 山峰
ridge/ arête 山脊
cirque/ corrie 冰斗
corrie glacier 山侧圆形凹地冰川
snow line 雪线
tributary glacier 支冰川，冰川支流
icefall 冰瀑布
plateau 高原
mountain pass 山口
hanging valley 悬谷
main valley glacier 主谷冰川
bare rock 裸露的岩石
waterfall 瀑布
crevasses 冰川裂隙
scree 岩屑堆
glacial meltwater stream 冰川融化成的河
moraine 冰碛

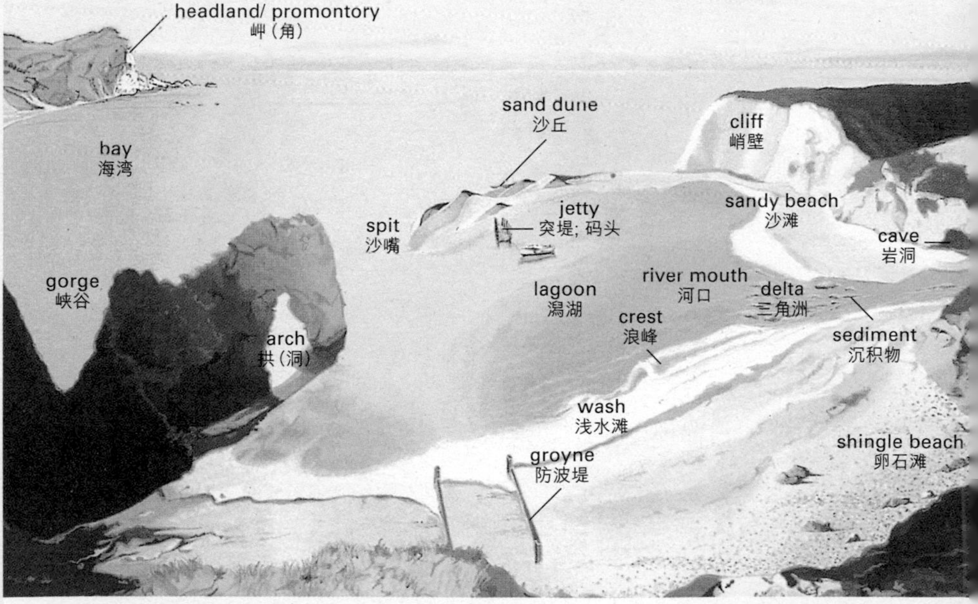

coastal 海岸的

headland/ promontory 岬（角）
sand dune 沙丘
cliff 峭壁
bay 海湾
jetty 突堤；码头
sandy beach 沙滩
spit 沙嘴
cave 岩洞
gorge 峡谷
lagoon 潟湖
river mouth 河口
delta 三角洲
crest 浪峰
sediment 沉积物
arch 拱（洞）
wash 浅水滩
shingle beach 卵石滩
groyne 防波堤

1 The car was stuck in a blizzard.
汽车被困在暴风雪中。

2 The sky was overcast and it had begun to sleet.
天空阴沉沉的，开始下雨夹雪。

3 We saw forked lightning as the storm got closer.
随着暴风雨临近，我们看到了叉状闪电。

4 The tree was blown down in a gale.
一阵大风把树吹倒了。

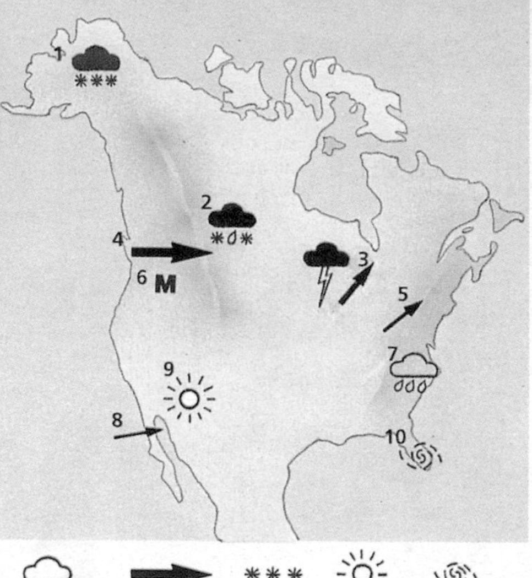

5 The wind was so blustery that leaves were blown from the trees.
狂风大作，树叶纷纷从树上吹落。

6 The mountains were veiled in mist.
群山被薄雾笼罩。

7 The downpour had caused a flood.
倾盆大雨引发了一场洪水。

8 Palm trees swayed in the breeze.
棕榈树在微风中摇曳。

9 Sun had baked the parched soil.
烈日把土壤晒得干裂。

10 The hurricane tore the roofs off the houses.
飓风把屋顶掀掉。

Office 办公室

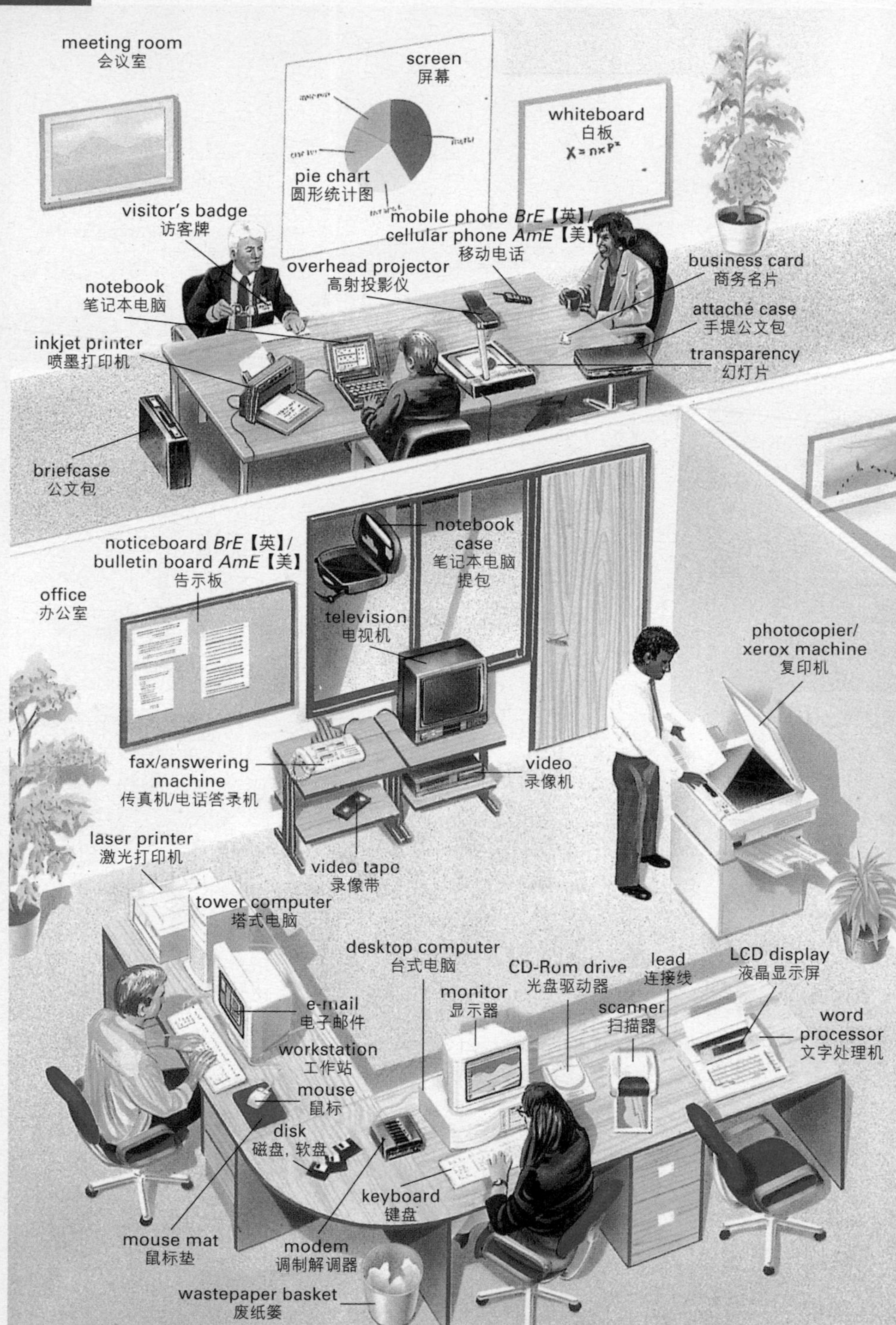
meeting room
会议室
screen
屏幕
whiteboard
白板
pie chart
圆形统计图
visitor's badge
访客牌
mobile phone *BrE*【英】/
cellular phone *AmE*【美】
移动电话
overhead projector
高射投影仪
business card
商务名片
notebook
笔记本电脑
attaché case
手提公文包
inkjet printer
喷墨打印机
transparency
幻灯片
briefcase
公文包
notebook case
笔记本电脑提包
noticeboard *BrE*【英】/
bulletin board *AmE*【美】
告示板
office
办公室
television
电视机
photocopier/
xerox machine
复印机
fax/answering machine
传真机/电话答录机
video
录像机
laser printer
激光打印机
video tape
录像带
tower computer
塔式电脑
desktop computer
台式电脑
CD-Rom drive
光盘驱动器
lead
连接线
LCD display
液晶显示屏
monitor
显示器
e-mail
电子邮件
scanner
扫描器
word processor
文字处理机
workstation
工作站
mouse
鼠标
disk
磁盘，软盘
keyboard
键盘
mouse mat
鼠标垫
modem
调制解调器
wastepaper basket
废纸篓

hat stand BrE【英】/coat stand AmE【美】
衣帽架
board
告示牌
SPECIALS
Rainbow
Trout.
coat rack
挂衣架
customer
顾客
POUR
倒（酒）
swing door
双开式弹簧门
waiter
男服务员
corkscrew
瓶塞钻
UNCORK
开酒瓶塞
maitre d'/
head waiter
服务员领班
SERVE
布菜
bow tie
蝶形领结
napkin/
serviette BrE【英】
餐巾
chef
厨师
FLAMBÉ
浇酒点燃后食用的（菜）
ashtray
烟灰缸
RESERVED
SEAT
坐
RESERVED
预订座
tablecloth
桌布
waitress
女服务员
espresso cup
蒸馏咖啡杯
dessert trolley BrE【英】/
dessert cart AmE【美】
甜点推车
TAKE THE
ORDER
记下（客人）
要点的菜
apron
围裙
crudités
生拌凉菜
menu
菜单
TIP
付小费
cheeseboard
干酪板
table mat
碗垫，盘垫
dip
调味酱
bill BrE【英】/
check AmE【美】
账单
cutlery/silverware AmE【美】
西餐具；银餐具

Patterns and Fabrics 图案和布料

button-down collar
〔有纽扣〕可扣住的衣领
single cuff
单式袖口
drawstring waistline
拉绳式腰围线
crew neck
圆式衣领
polo neck BrE【英】/
turtle neck AmE【美】
高圆领
double cuff
复式袖口
collarless/
granddad collar
无领领型
waistband
裙带
scooped neck
汤匙领
collar
领子
bow tie
蝶形领结
buttonhole
扣眼
seam
接缝
sleeve
袖子
neck
领口
open-necked shirt
开领衬衫
top pocket
上口袋
turtle neck BrE【英】/
mock turtle AmE【美】
半高领口
shirt
衬衫
cuff
袖口
v-neck
V字形领口
jacket
上衣
double-breasted jacket
双排扣外套
belt
皮带
waistcoat
马甲; 西服背心
cufflinks
袖扣
trousers
BrE【英】/
pants AmE
【美】
裤子
pleated skirt
百褶裙
pencil skirt
直筒长裙, 笔杆裙
single-breasted jacket
单排扣外套
straight skirt
直筒裙
hem
下摆
laces
鞋带
tights
裤袜
capped sleeves
罩肩袖
straight trousers
BrE【英】/ pants
AmE【美】
直筒裤
wrap-over skirt
折叠式裙
espadrille
帆布便鞋
long sleeves
长袖
flat shoe
平底鞋
high-heeled shoe
高跟鞋
flared trousers BrE【英】/
pants AmE【美】
喇叭裤
turn-ups BrE【英】/
cuffed pants AmE【美】
卷边裤
short sleeves
短袖
thick-soled shoe
厚底鞋

Adjectives 形容词: Broken 坏损的

buzz
嗡嗡声
clink
叮当声
crack
噼啪声
crackle
噼啪声
crash
碰撞声，砰的一声
crunch
嘎吱声
fizz
嘶嘶声
hiss
嘶嘶声
honk
喇叭声
jingle
叮当声
pop
砰[啪，噗]的一声
ring
钟[铃]声
rustle
沙沙作响
sizzle
滋滋声
snap
啪的一声
splash
溅泼声，飞溅声
squelch BrE【英】/
squish AmE【美】
咯吱声
tick
滴答声
tinkle
叮当声
whirr
呼呼[啪啪]作响

Physical Contact 身体接触 1

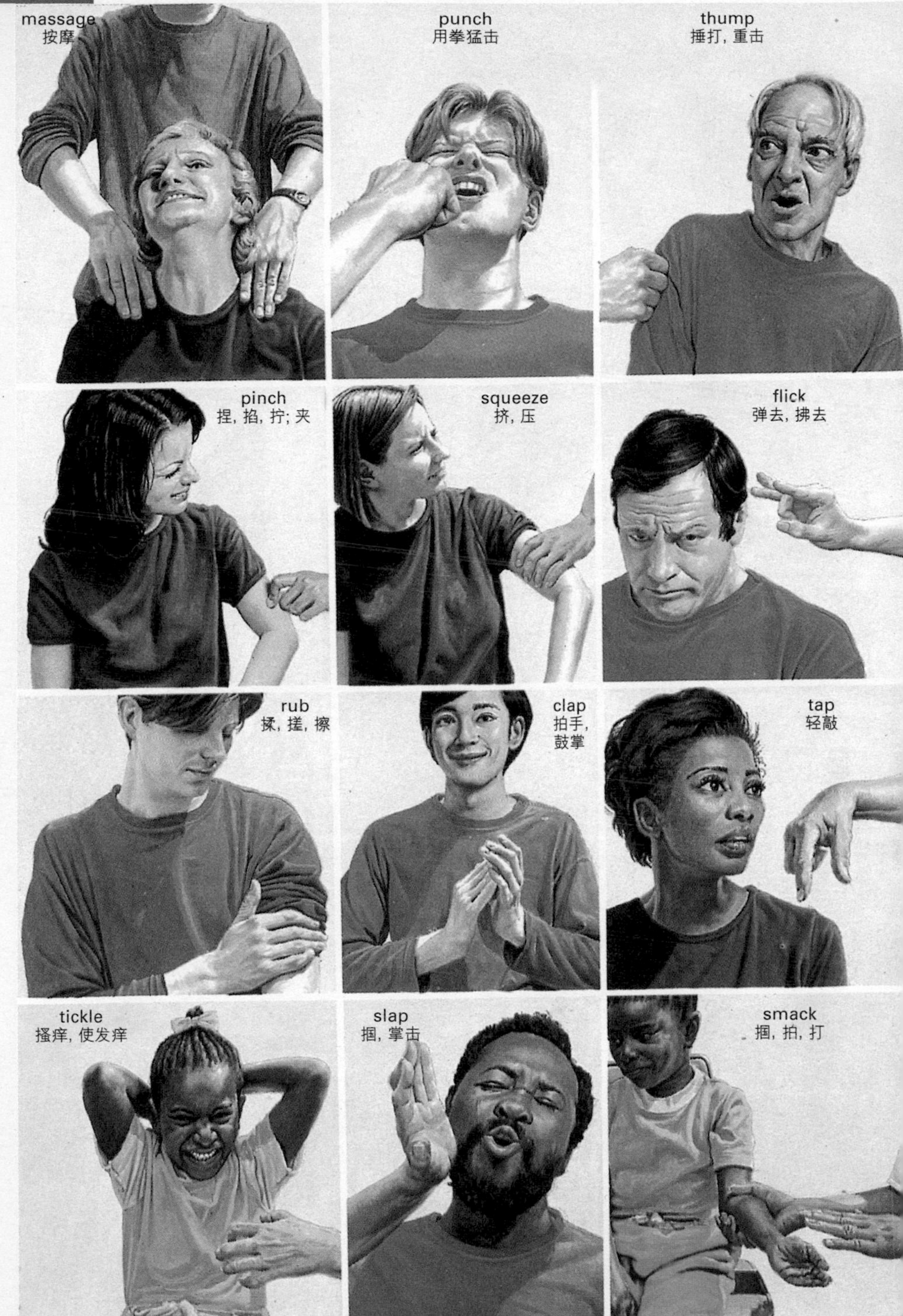

nudge
〔用肘〕轻推，轻碰

elbow
用肘推[挤]

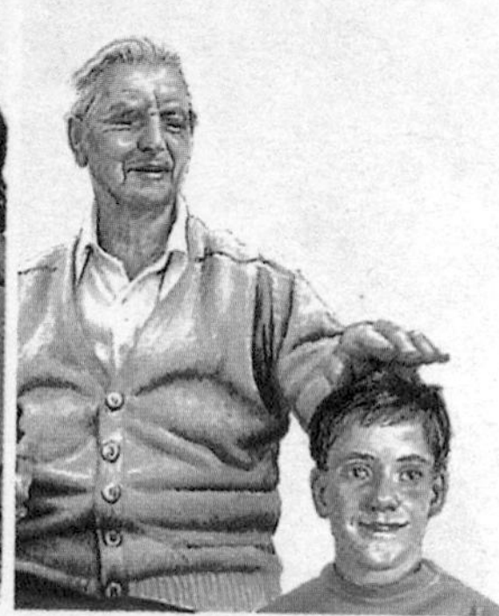
pat
轻拍

stroke
抚摸

hug
拥抱

cuddle
搂抱

feel
〔触〕摸

frisk
搜身

pull/drag
拖，拉

prod/poke
戳

push/shove
推

chop
砍，劈

Sports 体育运动 1

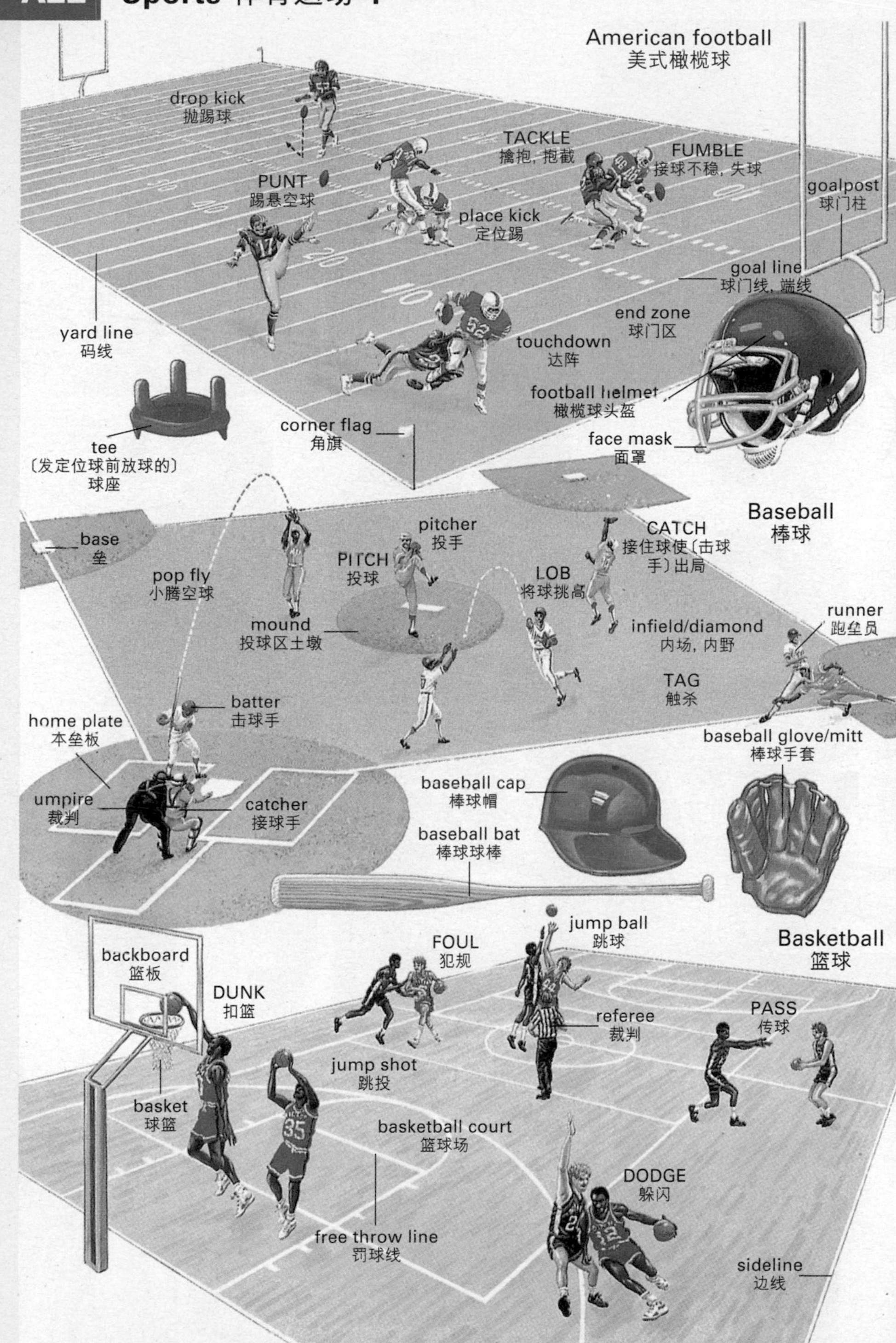

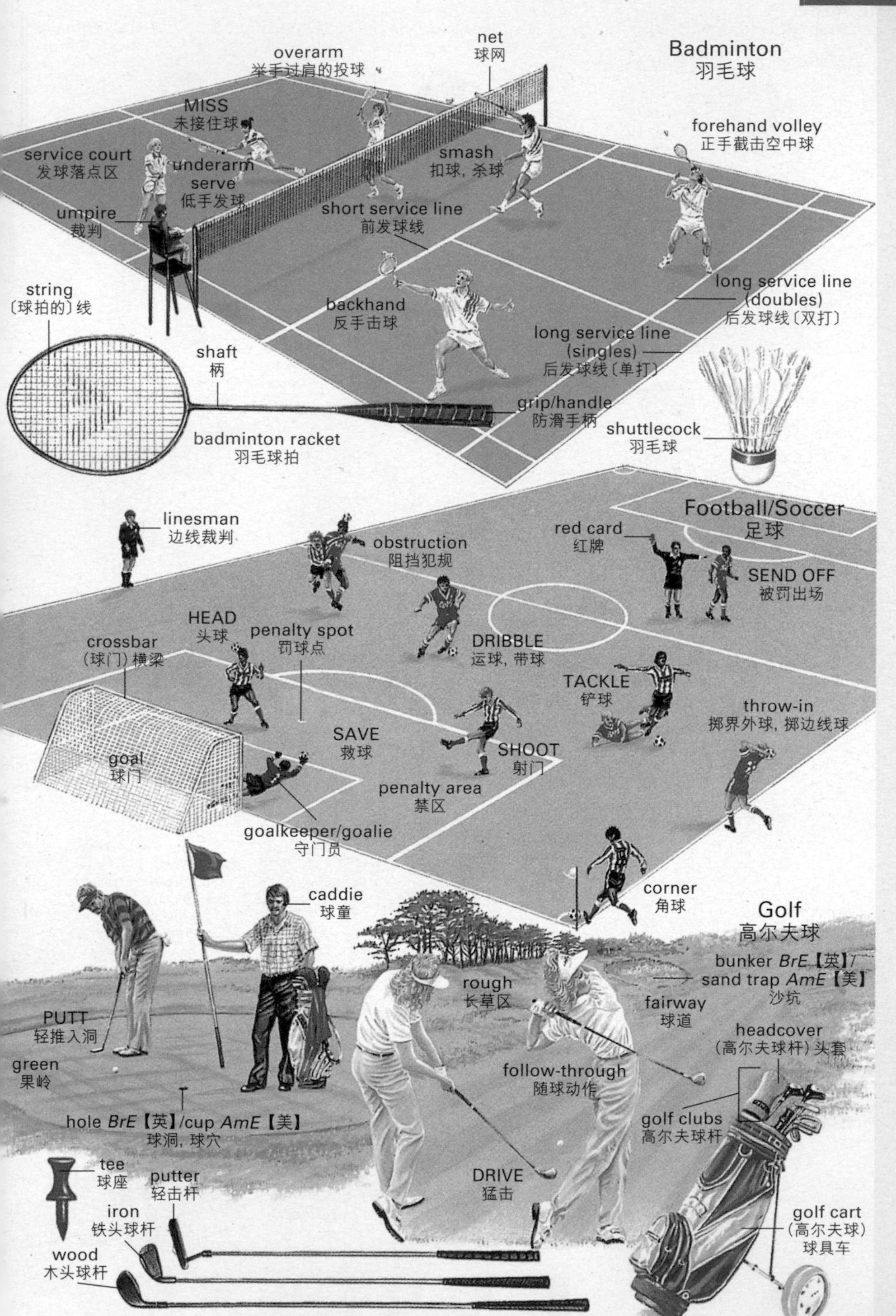
Badminton
羽毛球
overarm
举手过肩的投球
net
球网
MISS
未接住球
forehand volley
正手截击空中球
service court
发球落点区
underarm serve
低手发球
smash
扣球，杀球
umpire
裁判
short service line
前发球线
string
〔球拍的〕线
backhand
反手击球
long service line (doubles)
后发球线〔双打〕
long service line (singles)
后发球线〔单打〕
shaft
柄
grip/handle
防滑手柄
shuttlecock
羽毛球
badminton racket
羽毛球拍
Football/Soccer
足球
linesman
边线裁判
obstruction
阻挡犯规
red card
红牌
SEND OFF
被罚出场
HEAD
头球
penalty spot
罚球点
DRIBBLE
运球，带球
crossbar
〔球门〕横梁
TACKLE
铲球
throw-in
掷界外球，掷边线球
SAVE
救球
SHOOT
射门
goal
球门
penalty area
禁区
goalkeeper/goalie
守门员
corner
角球
caddie
球童
Golf
高尔夫球
bunker BrE【英】/
sand trap AmE【美】
沙坑
rough
长草区
fairway
球道
PUTT
轻推入洞
headcover
〔高尔夫球杆〕头套
green
果岭
follow-through
随球动作
hole BrE【英】/cup AmE【美】
球洞，球穴
golf clubs
高尔夫球杆
tee
球座
putter
轻击杆
DRIVE
猛击
iron
铁头球杆
golf cart
〔高尔夫球〕
球具车
wood
木头球杆

A24 Types of Walk 各种步姿

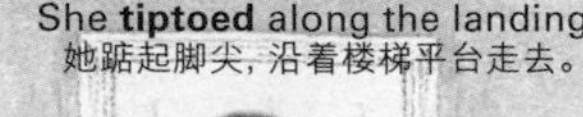

Liz **crept** upstairs trying not to wake her parents.
莉兹蹑手蹑脚地上楼，以免把父母吵醒。

She **tiptoed** along the landing.
她踮起脚尖，沿着楼梯平台走去。

Bob **edged** away from the guard.
鲍勃慢慢地从警卫旁
溜走。

Garcia **limped** off in agony.
加西亚十分痛苦地一瘸一拐地走开。

Granny **shuffled** across the room.
老奶奶拖着缓慢的步伐走过房间。

She **trudged** home with the shopping.
她提着买来的东西，步履艰难地走回家。

Sue **paddled** *BrE*【英】/ **waded** *AmE*【美】in the sea.
休在海里涉水玩。

The fisherman **waded** across the river.
那个钓鱼者蹚着水过河。

He **paced** up and down waiting for news.
他来回踱步等候消息。

The baby stood and **tottered** forwards.
小宝宝站了起来，摇摇晃晃地往前走。

He **staggered** under the weight of the box.
他在箱子的重压下步履蹒跚。

We took a **stroll** in the park.
我们在公园漫步。

...age Note: Addressing People 语言提示: 称呼

...you address people (What do you call them) when you want to talk to them? 当你想要同人说话...怎样称呼他们呢?

Talking to strangers 同陌生人说话

When talking to strangers there is often no special form of address in English. Usually, if you want to attract the attention of a stranger it is necessary to use phrases such as **Excuse me** 同陌生人说话, 英语中没有什么特定的称呼。在通常情况下, 如果想吸引陌生人的注意, 就要用 **Excuse me** (对不起) 一类的短语:

> **Excuse me!** *Can you tell me how to get to Oxford Street?*
> 对不起, 请问到牛津街怎么走?
>
> **Say!** (*AmE informal*) *Is it far to the subway from here?*
> 【美, 非正式】请问, 从这儿到地铁站远吗?

In British English **Sir** and **Madam** are too formal for most situations. They are used mostly to customers in shops, restaurants, etc. 在英式英语中, **Sir** (先生) 和 **Madam** (太太) 都太正式, 在大多数场合是不用的, 这两个词通常是商店、餐馆中店员对顾客的称呼:

> *Would you like your coffee now,* **Madam/Sir**?
> 太太 [先生], 现在上咖啡好吗?
>
> *Shall I wrap it for you,* **Madam/Sir**?
> 太太 [先生], 我替你把它包起来好吗?

In American English **Sir** and **Ma'am** are not as formal and are commonly used in conversations with strangers, especially with older people whose names you do not know 在美式英语中, **Sir** 和 **Ma'am** 并不那么正式, 经常用于同陌生人, 特别是同不知道其姓名的年长者的谈话中:

> *Please... to meet you,* **Ma'am**. 幸会, 太太。
>
> *Excuse me...* **Sir**. *Could you tell me the way to the nearest subway?*
> 对不起先生, 请问到最近的地铁车站怎么走?

...ames of occ...tions 职业名称

...tor and **nurse** ca... used as forms of address. **Doctor** 和 **nurse** 可用作称呼:

> *Can I have a word w...* **doctor**?
> ...生, 跟您说句话行吗?
>
> ...**rse**, *could I have a gl...ter?*
> ...请给我一杯水。

The nam... of a few other occupatio... porter and **waiter** are sometimes used as forms of address, t...gh some people consic... espe... is impolite. However, most names of occupations cannot be us... in this way. (Note, ...**acher** is not used as a form of address.) **porter** (搬运工) 和 **waitr...** (服务员) 等一些其他职业...于称呼, 不过有些人认为这样叫不礼貌。但大多数职

Language Note: Addressing People 语言提示

业名称是不能用作称呼的。(特别要注意的是, **teacher** (老师) 不能用作称呼。)

Special forms of address 特殊的称呼

There are some special forms of address that show respect to people, especially if they are in position of authority. These are used in formal situations 为了对某些人, 特别是对地位高的人表示尊敬, 可以用一些特殊的称呼。这些称呼都用于正式的场合:

Ladies and gentlemen (a formal opening of a speech)
女士们, 先生们〔讲话的正式开头〕

Your Excellency (to an ambassador) 阁下〔称呼大使〕

Your Highness (for a prince or princess)
殿下〔称呼王子或公主等〕

Mr/Madam President 总统阁下

Prime Minister 总理阁下

■ Talking to people you know 同认识的人说话

When you know people you can use their names. People's names can be used to attract their attention or to show that you are talking particularly to them. If you are friends, use their first name; if your relationship is more formal, use **Ms/Mr Smith** etc. 对于认识的人, 可以叫他们的姓名。叫姓名可用以引起对方注意, 或者表示是特地同他们说话。如果是朋友, 可以用名字; 如果关系是公务上的, 可用 **Ms/Mr Smith** (史密斯女士 [先生]) 等:

Mary, *could you help me with this box?*
玛丽, 帮我抬一下这箱子好吗?

What's your opinion, **Eric**? 埃里克, 你有什么意见?

Dr Davis, *could you tell us what the committee have decided?*
戴维斯博士, 你能告诉我们委员会作出了什么决定吗?

Sign here please, **Ms Burton**. 伯顿女士, 请把名字签在这里。

Note that **Ms**, **Miss**, **Mrs**, and **Mr** are not usually used alone in speech or writing but are followed by the family name 请注意, 在口语或书写中, **Ms**, **Miss**, **Mrs** 和 **Mr** 通常都不单独使用而是用在姓氏的前面, 如: **Ms Green** (格林女士), **Mrs Brown** (布朗太太), etc.等。

■ Talking to family or friends 同家人或朋友ddress. "Family" words most

Within a family or between friends there are many possible fmal)/auntie and uncle are etimes
commonly used by children talking to parents: **dad/dadd**auntie May | uncle Tom. 人或朋友
Father and **mother** are also used, but they are more form "亲昵"词语: **dad/daddy** ( ) | **mum/**
used alone as a form of address, but the name is of 是比较正式。**Aunt** (【正式】) /au le 和 **uncle**
之间有许多种可以使用的称呼方式。孩子们称呼父母) | **uncle Tom** (汤姆叔叔) 等。
mom (【美】) | **mummy** (【英】). **Father** 和 **moth**
有时单独用作称呼, 但常常在后面加上名字: **au**

um/mom (*AmE*) | **mum** (*BrE*).

Language Note: Addressing People 语言提示: 称呼

Many words can be used informally to express friendship or love 许多词语可以作为非正式用语用来表示友谊或爱情, such as 如 **darling/dear/honey** (*AmE*【美】)/**(my) love/sweetheart**, etc. 等: *Hurry up,* **darling**, *or we'll be late.* (快点, 亲爱的, 否则我们就要晚了。)

▶ Be careful! 注意!

There are many other forms of address which can be used between friends or strangers. However, many of these are limited in use. For example, **pal** and **mate** (*BrE*) can be used between strangers, but are usually only used by men talking to other men. 朋友之间或陌生人之间还有许多称呼, 但其中不少使用起来是有限制的。如 **pal** (老朋友) 和 **mate** (伙伴) (【英】) 可以用于陌生人之间, 但通常只在男人之间使用。

You will also hear such words as **darling**, **dear**, **honey**, and **love** used between strangers. In this case they do not, of course, express love, but are being used as informal forms of address. The use of these words is not general but depends on such things as the variety of English being spoken, the sex of speaker and hearer, and the social position of speaker and hearer. For example, in Britain a waiter or waitress might address a customer as **love**, but only in an informal restaurant or cafe, and never in an expensive restaurant. 你也会听到 **darling, dear, honey** 和 **love** (亲爱的) 这类词用于陌生人之间。在这种情况下, 这些词当然不表示爱情, 而只是作为一种非正式的称呼。这些词的使用并不普遍, 而且要取决于某些情况, 如所说英语的种类、说话人和听话人的性别以及他们的社会地位等。例如在英国, 一个服务员可以称呼顾客 **love**, 但只限于在非正规的餐馆或咖啡馆, 而从不会在高级餐馆中使用。

See also 另见 MISS², SIR

Language Note: Apologies 语言提示: 道歉语

Apologies can be very short and direct, or longer and more complex. When deciding which expressions are suitable for which situations, it is useful to ask certain questions. 道歉语可以非常简短而直截了当，也可以长一些、复杂一些。要决定哪些用语适合哪种情况，先问一些问题是有用的。

Considerations affecting choice of expression 影响选择不同用语的几种考虑

— How bad is the thing which has happened? If it is very bad, the apology will be stronger. 已经发生的事情坏到什么程度？如果非常坏，道歉的语气就应该重些。

— What is the relationship between the person who is apologizing (the speaker) and the person they are speaking to (the hearer)? If the hearer is in a position of authority, the apology may be stronger. 表示道歉的人（讲话人）和接受道歉的人（听话人）是什么关系？如果听话的人处于权威地位，道歉的语气可以重些。

— How responsible is the speaker for what has happened? If the speaker is really at fault, the apology will be stronger. 讲话人对已发生的事所负责任的程度如何？如果讲话人确有过错，道歉的语气要重些。

— Will the hearer immediately know the reason for the apology? If not, the speaker must make this clear. 听话人是否会当即明白道歉的原因？如果不明白，讲话人必须说清楚。

Quick apologies 简捷的道歉语

For something small (such as accidentally bumping into someone on a bus) 为一些小事情（如在公共汽车上偶然撞到了某人）：

apologies 道歉语	**responses** 答语
(I'm) sorry. 对不起。	*It's/That's all right.* 没关系。
Excuse me. (*AmE*【美】) 对不起。	*It's/That's OK.* (*informal*【非正式】) 没什么。
Pardon me. (*AmE*【美】) 请原谅。	*Don't worry.* (*informal*【非正式】)/*It's all right.*
I beg your pardon. (*formal*【正式】) 请你原谅。	(*informal*【非正式】) 没事（儿）；没关系。

For something bigger (such as spilling coffee all over someone's new clothes), it is usual to add a comment 为了大一些的事情（如把咖啡洒在某人的新衣服上），通常要多说一些客气话：

(Oh!) I'm sorry. （噢！）对不起。	*I didn't see you sitting there.* (explanation/excuse) 我没看见您坐在那儿。〔解释，辩白〕
	Are you all right? (expression of concern) 您没事儿吧？〔表示关心〕
	I'll fetch a cloth. (offer of help) 我去拿块布来。〔主动提出帮忙〕
	That was really clumsy of me. (self-criticism) 都是我笨手笨脚。〔自我批评，自责〕

Language Note: Apologies 语言提示: 道歉语

It is also possible to add words to make the apology stronger 也可以增加一些词语以加重道歉的语气:

I'm **really/awfully/so/terribly** (*BrE*【英】) *sorry*. 我确实［非常、很、极为］抱歉。

I **do** *beg your pardon.* (*BrE formal*【英, 正式】) 请多多原谅。

■ Explaining an apology 说清楚道歉的缘由

When apologizing for something which the hearer does not yet know about or may not remember, the speaker needs to explain what has happened, or remind the hearer of the situation. It is usual to add an explanation, excuse, offer of help, etc. 对于所道歉的事, 如果听话的人还不清楚, 或者可能已不记得, 说话的人就需要说明是什么事, 或让听话的人回想起当时的情况。常见的做法是作进一步的解释、说明缘由或主动提出给予帮助等:

John, about the meeting. I'm sorry I was late — I missed the bus. 约翰, 是开会的事。对不起, 我来迟了 —— 我没赶上公共汽车。

I really must apologize for my behaviour last night (*formal*【正式】). *I'm afraid I was in rather a bad mood.* 昨天晚上我太不对了, 实在对不起。当时我情绪不太好。

I've got something awful to tell you. I lost that book you lent me. I'm really sorry. I'll buy you another. 有件糟糕的事要告诉你, 我把你借给我的书弄丢了, 真对不起。我会买一本还你的。

I feel dreadful about what I said on the phone. I didn't really mean it, you know. 我觉得很不好受, 我在电话里说了那样的话, 你知道其实我并不是那个意思。

Note that, as in the last example, it is not always necessary to use any direct words of apology. 注意: 正像上面的最后一个例子, 并非总是要使用直接的道歉语。

■ Written and formal apologies 书面的和正式的道歉语

Formal apologies, especially in written form, are often marked by the use of the word **apology** or **apologize** 正式的, 特别是书面的道歉常以使用 **apology** 或 **apologize** 为标志:

I am writing to apologize for my absence from last week's meeting. I was unexpectedly held up at work and was not able to contact you. (*formal*【正式】) 我未能参加上周的会议, 谨此致歉。我因突然有公事而无法脱身, 故未能同你们联系。

British Rail wishes to/would like to apologize for the late running of this train. (*formal*【正式】) (announcement at a station or on a train) 本列车晚点, 英国铁路公司谨此表示歉意。〔火车站或列车上的通告〕

Please accept our (sincere) apologies for any inconvenience caused by the delay in delivery of your order. The goods have now been shipped to you. (*formal*【正式】) 您订购的货物我们未能按时交货, 对因此而造成的不便, 我们谨表示（诚挚的）歉意, 该批货物现已装运发给贵方。

See 参见 EXCUSE[1] (USAGE)

Language Note: Articles 语言提示：冠词

In English, it is often necessary to use an article in front of a noun. There are two kinds of article: the definite article **the**, and the indefinite article **a** or **an**. In order to speak or write English well, it is important to know how articles are used. When deciding whether or not to use an article and which kind of article to use, you should ask the following questions 在英语中，名词之前往往需要加冠词。冠词有两种：定冠词 **the** 和不定冠词 **a** 或 **an**。为了说好英语和写好英语，正确掌握冠词的用法具有重要意义。是否需要用冠词，是用定冠词还是用不定冠词，应考虑以下几个问题：

■ Is the noun countable or uncountable? 这个名词是可数名词还是不可数名词？

Singular countable nouns always need an article or another determiner like **my**, **this**, etc. Other nouns can sometimes be used alone. The chart below tells you which articles can be used with which type of noun 单数的可数名词前面总是需要有冠词或其他限定词，如 **my**, **this** 等，其他一些名词有时可以不加冠词。下表说明，哪种类型的名词可以用哪种冠词：

the	+	singular countable nouns 单数的可数名词	the bag, the apple
		plural countable nouns 复数的可数名词	the bags, the apples
		uncountable nouns 不可数名词	the water, the information
a/an	+	singular countable nouns 单数的可数名词	a bag, an apple
no article or **some** 不用冠词或用 **some**	+	plural countable nouns 复数的可数名词	(some) bags, (some) apples
		uncountable nouns 不可数名词	(some) water, (some) information

The dictionary shows you when nouns are countable [C] or uncountable [U]. (The nouns which have no letter after them are countable in all their meanings.) The examples below show how articles can be used with countable and uncountable nouns. 本辞典中的名词标明何时是可数名词 [C]，何时是不可数名词 [U]。(名词后面没有标明字母的，表示所有义项都是可数名词。) 下面的例句表明可数名词和不可数名词前冠词的用法：

countable/uncountable noun 可数 [不可数] 名词	**examples** 例句
butterfly [C] 蝴蝶	**The butterfly** *is an insect.* 蝴蝶是一种昆虫。 **The butterflies** *on that bush are very rare.* 灌木丛上那几只蝴蝶是非常罕见的。 *She caught* **a butterfly** *in her net.* 她用网捉到一只蝴蝶。 *There were* **some butterflies** *in the tree.* 树上有几只蝴蝶。 *The garden was full of* **butterflies**. 花园里到处都是蝴蝶。
egg[1] [C] 蛋	**The egg** *I found in the fridge was bad.* 我在冰箱里找到的蛋已经坏了。 **The eggs** *you bought last week have all been eaten.* 你上星期买的蛋都吃光了。 *I'd like* **an egg** *for tea.* 我在喝茶时想吃只蛋。 *Can you buy* **some eggs** *on your way home?* 你在回家的路上买些蛋好吗？ *He hates* **eggs**. 他讨厌吃蛋。
egg[2] [C] 〔作食物的〕蛋；鸡蛋	*He wiped* **the egg** *from round his mouth.* 他擦去嘴边的蛋。 *Would you like* **some** *scrambled* **egg** *with your toast?* 你要不要来点炒蛋和烤面包一起吃？ *The baby had* **egg** *all over her face.* 小宝宝吃得满脸都是蛋。
information [U] 信息，资料	**The information** *they gave us was wrong.* 他们给我们的信息是错误的。 *We'd like* **some information**, *please.* 请给我们一些资料。 *What we really need is* **information**. 我们真正需要的是信息。

Language Note: Articles 语言提示: 冠词

Note that most proper nouns, like **Susan**, **London**, and **Canada**, do not usually have an article: **Susan***'s coming through* **London** *next week, on her way to* **Canada**. However, **the** is usually used with rivers (**the Thames**), seas (**the Pacific**), groups of mountains (**the Andes**), deserts (**the Gobi Desert**), cinemas and theatres (**the Playhouse**), and hotels (**the Ritz Hotel**). It is also used with a few countries, especially those whose names contain a common countable noun, such as **the People's Republic of China**. 注意: 大多数专有名词如 **Susan** (苏珊), **London** (伦敦) 和 **Canada** (加拿大) 等通常都不用冠词: **Susan***'s coming through* **London** *next week, on her way to* **Canada**. (苏珊在去加拿大的途中, 下星期将经过伦敦。) 可是, 在表示下列事物的专有名词前通常要加 **the**: 河流 (**the Thames** 泰晤士河), 海洋 (**the Pacific** 太平洋), 山脉 (**the Andes** 安第斯山), 沙漠 (**the Gobi Desert** 戈壁沙漠), 电影院和戏院 (**the Playhouse** 普莱豪斯剧院), 旅馆 (**the Ritz Hotel** 里茨饭店)。一些国家的名称, 特别是其名称中含有普通可数名词的国家名称也要加 **the**, 如 **the People's Republic of China** (中华人民共和国)。

■ Are you talking about things and people in general? 所述及的事物和人是泛指的吗?

When nouns appear in general statements, they can be used with different articles, depending on whether they are countable or uncountable. 在一般陈述中出现的名词可以使用不同的冠词, 视其为可数名词或不可数名词而定。

In general statements, countable nouns can be used 在一般陈述中可数名词可以下列形式出现:

in the plural without an article 复数不加冠词:

> *Elephants have tusks.* 大象有象牙。| *I like elephants.* 我喜欢大象。

in the singular with **the** 单数用 **the**:

> *The elephant is a magnificent animal.* 大象是一种巨兽。| *He is studying the elephant in its natural habitat.* 他正在研究自然栖息地中的大象。

in the singular with **a/an** 单数用 **a/an**:

> *An elephant can live for a very long time.* 大象可以活很久。

Note that **a/an** can only be used in this way if the noun is the grammatical subject of the sentence. 注意: 如果名词是句子中的主语, **a/an** 只能这样用。

In general statements, uncountable nouns are always used 在一般陈述中, 不可数名词总是在以下情况中出现:

without an article 不用冠词:

> *Photography is a popular hobby.* 摄影是一种很流行的业余爱好。| *She's interested in photography.* 她对摄影很感兴趣。| *Water is essential to life.* 水是生命所必不可少的。

■ Are you talking about things and people in particular? 所述及的事物和人是特指的吗?

Nouns are more often used with a particular meaning. Particular meanings can be **definite** or **indefinite**, and they need different articles accordingly. 名词的使用, 更多的情况是带有特定的含义, 特定含义可以是限定的或不限定的, 因此便相应地要使用不同的冠词。

Language Note: Articles 语言提示：冠词

Definite 限定的

Both countable and uncountable nouns are definite in meaning when the speaker and the hearer know exactly which people or things are being referred to. For example, the definite article **the** is used 当说话人和听话人都明确地知道所说的人或事物所指为何时，可数名词或不可数名词在含义上都是限定的，例如，下列情况就需要使用定冠词 **the**:

when the noun has already been mentioned 当该名词已经被提到过:

> *I saw a man and a woman in the street.* **The man** *looked very cold.* 我在街上看见一个男人和一个女人，那个男人看起来很冷。| *I took her some paper and a pencil, but she said she didn't need* **the paper**. 我拿给她一些纸和一支铅笔，但是她说她不需要那些纸。

when it is clear from the situation which noun you mean 当在具体情景中已经清楚所指的名词是什么:

> *Can you pass me* **the salt** *please?* (=the salt on the table) 请把盐〔指餐桌上的盐瓶〕递给我好吗？| *I'm going to* **the market** *for some fruit.* (=the market I always go to) 我去市场〔指我常去的那个市场〕买些水果。

when the words following the noun explain exactly which noun you mean 当名词后面的词语确切地说明该名词指的是什么:

> *I've just spoken to* **the man from next door**. (=not just any man) 我刚刚同隔壁那个人〔非任何人〕说话。| **The information that you gave me** *was wrong.* (=not just any information) 你给我的信息〔非任何信息〕是错误的。

when the person or thing is the only one that exists 当所说的人或事物是唯一存在的:

> *I'm going to travel round* **the world**. (there is only one world) 我要环游世界。〔世界只有一个〕

Indefinite 非限定的

Nouns can also be used with a particular meaning without being definite. For example, in the sentence *I met* **a man** *in the street*, the speaker is talking about one particular man (not all men in general) but we do not know exactly which man. 名词还可以具体有所指而并不表示限定。例如，在"我在街上遇到一个人"这个句子里，说话人说的是一个特定的人（不是一般概念上所有的人），但是我们并不确切了解是哪一个人。

Singular countable nouns with an indefinite meaning are used with the indefinite article **a/an** 具有非限定意义的单数可数名词用不定冠词 **a/an**:

> *Would you like* **a cup** *of coffee?* 喝一杯咖啡好吗？
> *She's* **an engineer**. 她是一位工程师。

When their meaning is indefinite, plural countable nouns and uncountable nouns are used with **some** or **any**, or sometimes with no article 当不可数名词和复数的可数名词具有非限定意义时则用 **some** 或 **any**，或者有时不加冠词:

> *I think you owe me* **some money**. 我看你还欠我钱。
> *Have you got* **any money** *on you?* 你身上带着钱吗？
> *We need* **some matches**. 我们需要些火柴。
> *We haven't got* **any biscuits**. 我们没有饼干。
> *Would you like* **some coffee**? 你想喝咖啡吗？
> *Would you like* **coffee**, **tea**, *or* **orange juice**? 你想喝咖啡、茶、还是橙汁？

Language Note: Articles 语言提示: 冠词

■ Does the noun follow a special rule for the use of articles? 名词前面冠词的用法有特定的规律可循吗?

The dictionary will tell you if a noun is always used with a particular article. For example 本辞典会告诉你, 一个名词是否总是与一个特定的冠词相连用, 例如:

Nouns describing people or things which are considered to be the only ones of their kind are used with **the**. 表示人或事物的名词如果被认为是其同类中唯一的一个时用 **the**。

private sec·tor, the /ˌ‥ˈ‥◂/ *n* the industries and services in a country that are owned and run by private companies, and not by the state or government 私营企业: *pay increases in the private sector* 私营企业的工资增长 | *private sector employers* 私营企业的雇主 —compare 比较 PUBLIC SECTOR

Some nouns are used with different articles when they have different meanings. (The entry tells you that **French** in its third meaning is always used with **the** and is followed by a plural verb.) 某些名词随意义的不同而使用不同的冠词。(右侧词条表示, **French** 的第三义项总是用 **the**, 后接的动词为复数。)

French¹ /frɛntʃ; frentʃ/ *n* **1** the language of France, and some other countries 法语: *How do you ask for directions in French?* 你怎样用法语问路? **2** the language and literature of France as a subject of study 法国语言文学: *She's studying French at London University.* 她在伦敦大学学习法国语言文学。**3 the French** the people of France 法国人: *The French celebrate 14th July.* 法国人庆祝7月14日国庆节。

Some nouns are never used with **the** 某些名词从来不与 **the** 连用。

par·lia·ment /ˈpɑrləmənt; ˈpɑːləmənt/ *n* [C] **1** the group of people who are elected to make a country's laws and discuss important national affairs 议会, 国会 **2 Parliament** the main law-making institution in the United Kingdom, which consists of the HOUSE OF COMMONS and the HOUSE OF LORDS 英国议会〔由上议院和下议院组成〕: **enter Parliament/get into Parliament** (=be elected as a member of Parliament) 被选为议员

Nouns in some common expressions such as **do the housework** etc., use **the** 在诸如 **do the housework** (做家务) 等惯用语中, 名词前加 **the**。

house·work /ˈhausˌwɝk; ˈhaʊswɜːk/ *n* [U] work that you do to take care of a house such as washing, cleaning etc 家务 (劳动): *I spent all morning doing the housework.* 我整个上午都在做家务。

In some common expressions with prepositions such as **on foot**, **go home**, **go to hospital** (*BrE*【英】), **go to school**, **by plane**, **at noon**, the nouns do not use an article. (Note that the entry tells you if the use of the article is different in American and British English.) 某些带介词的常见用语, 如 **on foot** (步行), **go home** (回家), **go to hospital** (去医院看病), **go to school** (上学), **by plane** (乘飞机), **at noon** (中午) 等, 其中的名词不加冠词。(注意: 如果美国英语和英国英语中冠词用法不同, 词条中会有所标注。)

hos·pi·tal /ˈhɑspɪtḷ; ˈhɒspɪtl/ *n* [C,U] a large building where sick or injured people are looked after and receive medical treatment 医院: **in/to/from hospital** *BrE*【英】: *He's in hospital, recovering from an operation.* 他手术后正在医院里康复。| **in/to/from the hospital** *AmE*【美】*After the accident Jane was rushed to the hospital.* 事故发生后简被紧急送往医院。| **be admitted to (the) hospital** (=be brought into a hospital for treatment) 被收进医院 *A man has been admitted to hospital with gunshot wounds.* 一个受枪伤的男人被收进了医院。| **hospital bed** (=a place in a hospital for a sick person) 病床

When you look up a word in this dictionary, check the entry and read the examples to see whether there is any special information about the use of the article. 查阅本辞典时请注意词条及其例证中是否提供了关于冠词的特别说明。

See also 另见 A, AN, ANY, SOME; see 参见 THE (USAGE)

Language Note: Collocations 语言提示: 词语搭配

A collocation is a grouping of words which "naturally" go together through common usage. Unlike idioms, their meaning can usually be understood from the individual words. In order to speak natural English, you need to be familiar with collocations. You need to know, for example, that you say "a heavy smoker" because **heavy** (NOT **big**) collocates with **smoker**, and that you say "free of charge" because **free of** collocates with **charge** (NOT **cost**, **payment**, etc.). If you do not choose the right collocation, you will probably be understood but you will not sound natural. This dictionary will help you with the most common collocations.
词语搭配是指在日常应用中"自然地"组合在一起的一组词语。它们和习语有所不同, 其含义一般可通过单个词反映出来。为了说出地道的英语, 就必须熟悉词语搭配。例如你需要知道英语说 *a heavy smoker* (烟抽得很多的人), 而不能说 a big smoker, 因为 **heavy** 和 **smoker** 搭配; 又如英语说 *free of charge* (免费的), 而不说 free of cost 或 free of payment 等, 因为 **free of** 和 **charge** 搭配。你使用英语时如用错了搭配, 人家也许可以理解你的意思, 但你的英语听起来很不自然。本辞典为你指出最常见的词语搭配。

■ Common fixed collocations 常见的固定词语搭配

When you look up a word, read the examples carefully. Common collocations are shown in blue:
你在辞典中查阅一个词语时, 应仔细阅读其下的例子。常见的词语搭配都用蓝字印刷:

These entries show you that 右栏的词条中显示 **freak of nature** (畸形生物), **bring sth to a halt** (使停顿), **call a halt (to)** (停止), **keep the peace** (维护治安), and 和 **peace of mind** (安心) are all common collocations 都是常见的词语搭配。Note that you cannot change the word order in these phrases and that you cannot use other words even if they have similar meanings. 请注意, 这些词语搭配中的词语顺序是不能随便改动的; 此外, 词语搭配中的词不能用其他词取代, 即使其意义相同。We say 我们可以说 **call a halt** (NOT **stop**) **to**, **a freak** (NOT **monster**) **of nature** etc., 而不能说 call a stop to, 也不能说 a monster of nature 等。
Note that other examples in the entries show natural patterns of language. For example, 请注意右栏词条中有些例子是英语的自然表述模式, 例如 *a lasting peace* (持久的和平), and 和 *inner peace* (内心的平静) are all very common uses of the word peace, although they are not such strong collocations as those shown in blue. 这些都是 **peace** 一词最常见的用法, 虽然还不是那种能用蓝字印刷的固定搭配。

freak[1] /frik; friːk/ *n* [C] **1 bike/fitness/film etc freak** *informal* someone who is so interested in bikes, fitness etc that other people think they are strange or unusual【非正式】自行车迷/健美迷/电影迷等: *Carrot juice is a favourite with health-food freaks.* 胡萝卜汁是健康食品迷最爱喝的。**2** someone who looks very strange or behaves in a very unusual way 怪异的人: *Women who were good at physics used to be considered freaks.* 擅长物理学的女性过去常被看作怪人。**3** something in nature, such as a strangely-shaped plant or animal, that is very unusual 畸形生物: *One of the lambs was a freak – it had two tails.* 其中一只羔羊是畸形的——它有两条尾巴。| **a freak of nature** (=something physically strange or unusual) 畸形物; 怪异的事物 *By some freak of nature there was a snowstorm in June.* 天公作怪, 6月份竟然有暴风雪。**4 control freak** someone who always wants to control situations and other people 支配欲极强的人

halt[1] /hɔlt; hɔːlt/ *n* [singular] a stop or pause 停止, 停住; 暂停: **bring sth to a halt** (=make something stop moving or continuing) 使…停顿; 使…中止 *Heavy snowfalls brought traffic to a halt on the Brenner Pass.* 大雪使得布伦纳山口的交通陷于停顿。| *fuel shortages that have brought the industry to a grinding halt* 使该工业慢慢地停止生产的燃料短缺 | **call a halt (to)** (=officially stop an activity from continuing) 〔正式〕中止, 停止 *The IRA leadership has called a halt to its campaign of violence.* 爱尔兰共和军的领导层已经停止其暴力活动。

peace /pis; piːs/ *n*
1 ►NO WAR 没有战争◄ **a)** [U] a situation in which there is no war between countries or in a country 和平: **world peace** *a dangerous situation that threatens world peace* 威胁世界和平的危险局面 | **peace agreement/treaty etc** *the Geneva peace talks* 日内瓦和谈 | **be at peace with** *Germany has been at peace with France for fifty years.* 德国已与法国和平相处了五十年。**b)** [singular] a period of time in which there is no war 和平时期: *a lasting peace* 持久和平

Language Note: Collocations 语言提示：词语搭配

c) peace movement/campaign etc organized efforts to prevent war 和平运动

… … …

4 ►CALMNESS 平静，安宁◄ [U] a feeling of calmness and lack of worry and problems 平静，安宁：*the search for inner peace* 寻求内心的平静 | **peace of mind** (=to stop you from worrying) 心境的平静，安心 *Ann had to check the baby every few minutes for her own peace of mind.* 为使自己安心，安不得不每隔几分钟就查看一下婴儿。| **at peace with yourself** (=calm and happy) 平静而快乐 *Lynn never seems to be at peace with herself.* 琳恩好像永不会平静下来似的。**5** [U] a situation in which there is no quarrelling between people who live or work together 和睦〔相处〕：*peace and stability in industrial relations* 劳资关系的和睦稳定 | **keep the peace** (=stop people from quarrelling, fighting, or causing trouble) 维持治安

■ Collocating prepositions 与介词连用的搭配

When you look up a word, the entry will show you if there is a particular preposition which collocates with it. 你在本辞典中查阅一个词时，如果该词需与某一介词搭配，词条中会告诉你。

These entries show that you say
右栏的词条告诉你：

graduate (from)〔graduate 与 from 连用〕：
Jerry graduated from high school last year.
（杰里去年中学毕业。）

graduate³ *v* **1** [I] to obtain a degree, especially a first degree, from a college or university〔尤指以学士学位〕大学毕业：**[+from]** *Mitch graduated from Stanford with a degree in Law.* 米奇毕业于斯坦福大学，获法学学位。**2** [I] *AmE* to complete your education at HIGH SCHOOL【美】中学毕业：**[+from]** *Jerry graduated from high school last year.* 杰里去年中学毕业。**3 graduate (from sth) to** to start doing something that is bigger, better or more important〔从某处〕升级到：*Bob played college baseball but never graduated to the Majors.* 鲍勃在大学是棒球队队员，但从来没有升级加入职业棒球队。**4** [T] *especially AmE* to give a degree or DIPLOMA to someone who has completed a course【尤美】向〔毕业生〕授予学位[文凭]

gratitude (for)〔gratitude与 for 连用〕：
I didn't get a single word of gratitude for all my trouble.
（我没有听到一句对我的辛劳表示感谢的话。）

grat·i·tude /ˈgrætəˌtjud; ˈgrætɪ̯tjuːd/ *n* [U] the feeling of being grateful 感激（之情）：*Tears of gratitude filled her eyes.* 她的眼里充满感激的泪水。| *I couldn't adequately express my gratitude to Francis.* 我对弗朗西斯的感激之情难以言尽。| **[+for]** *I didn't get a single word of gratitude for all my trouble.* 我没有听到一句对我的辛劳表示感谢的话。| **deepest gratitude** (=very great gratitude) 万分的感激 —opposite 反义词 INGRATITUDE —see also 另见 **owe a debt of gratitude to sb** (DEBT (4))

harmful (to)〔harmful 与 to 连用〕：
chemicals that are harmful to the environment
（对环境有害的化学品）

harm·ful /ˈhɑrmfəl; ˈhɑːmfəl/ *adj* causing or likely to cause harm 有害的；致伤的：*the harmful effects of smoking* 吸烟的害处 | **[+to]** *chemicals that are harmful to the environment* 对环境有害的化学品 **—harmfully** *adv* **—harmfulness** *n* [U]

See 参见 LANGUAGE NOTES: **Idioms**, **Intensifying Adjectives**, **Make and Do**

Language Note: Criticism and Praise
语言提示: 批评和赞扬

Making criticisms 提出批评

Criticisms can be very short and direct, or they can be longer and more indirect. When deciding which expressions are suitable for which situations it is useful to ask certain questions. 批评可以简短而直截了当, 也可以较长且迂回曲折。在决定何种场合采取何种批评方式时, 先来考虑一些问题是有益的。

Considerations affecting choice of expression 在选择批评方式时的几种考虑

— How bad is the thing or action which is being criticized? How important is it to the speaker? 要批评的事情或行为, 其严重程度如何? 对说话人来说, 其重要程度如何?

— What is the relationship between the person who is making the criticism (the speaker) and the person who is being criticized (the hearer)? The more direct expressions, for example, are mostly used between friends or when the speaker is in a position of authority. 批评者和被批评者之间的关系如何? 举例来说, 直截了当的批评方式大多用于朋友之间或者批评者居于权威地位。

— Is the attitude of the speaker friendly or unfriendly? 批评者所持的态度是友善的还是不友善的?

Indirect criticism 迂回的批评

Indirect expressions are commonly used in order to be polite. These expressions usually avoid very strong words such as **bad**, **failure**, **dreadful**, etc., and often use negative forms such as, **not quite right** and **not very good**. They also use other ways of softening what is being said. 为了表示客气, 通常使用迂回的批评方式。迂回的批评方式常常避免使用像 **bad** (坏的, 拙劣的, 错误的)、**failure** (失败) 和 **dreadful** (糟透了的) 之类感情色彩强烈的词语, 而是代之以诸如 **not quite right** (不是很对) 和 **not very good** (不是很好) 之类的否定式, 或是使语气缓和的其他形式 (see 参见 LANGUAGE NOTE: **Tentativeness**):

That **doesn't look quite right** *to me, you know. Maybe you should try again.* (Friend to friend) 我觉得这样不是很对, 或许你应该再试一试。〔朋友对朋友〕

I'm afraid your last essay was **not quite** *up to standard.* (Teacher to pupil) 我看你最近写的一篇文章不大达标。〔老师对学生〕

Very often, speakers begin by saying something good about the person or thing they are going to criticize. 批评者往往会对所要批评的人事先说一些好话:

I love the colour, *but I wonder if the style is right for you.* (Friend to friend) 我喜欢这颜色, 但是我说不准这样式是不是适合你。〔朋友对朋友〕

The band's great, *but I'm not so sure about the singer.* (Friend criticizing a friend's choice of music) 乐队挺不错, 但歌手就不好说了。〔批评朋友对音乐的选择〕

Your written work has really improved, *but you still have a bit of a problem with your spelling.* (Teacher to pupil) 你的书面作业确有进步, 但你在拼写方面还有些问题。〔教师对小学生〕

Language Note: Criticism and Praise
语言提示: 批评和赞扬

Direct criticism 直截了当的批评

Direct expressions are sometimes used informally between members of the same family or between good friends. 一家人或好朋友之间有时可在非正式场合进行直截了当的批评:

You can't possibly wear that tie. It looks awful. (Wife to husband) 你无论如何也不能系那条领带, 难看极了。〔妻子对丈夫〕

Your room's an absolute mess; when are you going to clear it up? (Mother to daughter) 你的房间乱得不成样子, 你打算什么时候才清理?〔母亲对女儿〕

Direct expressions are also used when the speaker is in a position of authority. Here, the effect is usually unfriendly, especially if the language is formal. 如果批评者居于权威地位, 也可采用直截了当的批评方式。它给人的感觉常常是尖刻的, 尤其是在使用正式语言的情况下:

Your uniform's filthy. (Sergeant to soldier) 你的制服太脏。〔班长对兵士〕

There are a lot of typing errors in this report. (Boss to secretary) 这份报告有许多打字错误。〔经理对秘书〕

The exam results this year are appalling. (Teacher to class) 今年的考试成绩简直可怕。〔教师对全班学生〕

Giving praise 赞扬

Speakers usually feel that praise will be acceptable to the hearer, so praise can be given in a direct way. The hearer usually responds to the praise by thanking the speaker and often adds a comment. When responding, some people like to appear to disagree with the praise but this is not necessary in order to be polite. 说话人觉得赞扬的话通常都是人所爱听的, 因此也就有什么说什么, 不必拐弯抹角。受赞扬的人通常以向对方表示感谢应答外, 还要再说点什么。有的人喜欢表示一下似乎不同意所受到的赞扬, 但是这并不是表示客气所必需的:

praise 赞扬	**response 应答**
Well done!/That was great. 很不错!/好极了。	*Thank you./Thanks.* 谢谢你。/谢谢。
I love that dress. Is it new? 我喜欢这件衣服, 是新的吗?	*(Oh,) thank you. No, it's quite old, but I've always liked it.* (喔,) 谢谢你。不, 这衣服相当旧了, 但我一直都喜欢穿它。
That was a wonderful meal. 这顿饭好极了。	*Thank you. I'm glad you enjoyed it.* 谢谢你, 我很高兴你喜欢吃。
You're a great cook. 你的厨艺真不错。	*Well, I don't know about that but I enjoy cooking/I do my best.* 嗯, 我看还谈不上吧, 不过我喜欢做菜/尽力而为。
You've made a lot of progress this year. I'm very pleased with your performance. 你今年有不少进步, 我为你的表现感到十分高兴。	*Thank you.* 谢谢你。

Language Note: Criticism and Praise
语言提示: 批评和赞扬

► Be careful! 注意!

In informal English, expressions of praise are sometimes used sarcastically as a form of criticism. The situation or the speaker's tone of voice usually makes the meaning clear. Between friends, this kind of sarcasm is usually used in a friendly way, often as a joke. 在非正式英语中, 一些赞扬的言辞有时被用作挖苦的话来批评人。说话当时的具体情况和说话人的语调通常能表达这种用意。在朋友之间这种挖苦通常是很善意的, 而且时常是作为一种玩笑:

> *You're a regular Albert Einstein, Tom.* (Tom has done or said something stupid.) 你倒是个十足的爱因斯坦, 汤姆。〔汤姆做了什么傻事或说了什么傻话。〕
>
> *Well, that's what I call a miracle of organization!* (The speaker is complaining about bad organization.) 哟, 这组织工作做得真是顶呱呱!〔讲话者对组织工作太差表示不满。〕

In other situations, it usually shows that the speaker has a very unfriendly attitude. 在其他情况下, 通常表现说话人的态度很不友善。

> *Another brilliant performance, Mr Smith!* (The speaker is furious about Mr Smith's failure.) 又一个成就, 史密斯先生!〔说话人对史密斯先生的失败非常恼火。〕

See 参见 LANGUAGE NOTE : **Tentativeness**

Language Note: Gradable and Non-gradable Adjectives 可分等级和不可分等级的形容词

Gradable adjectives 可分等级的形容词

Most English adjectives are gradable. That is, their meaning can have different possible degrees of strength. They can therefore be used with adverbs which express these different degrees. Gradable adjectives can be divided into two kinds: scale adjectives and limit adjectives. 大多数英语形容词都是可分等级的。就是说它们的含义可以有不同的强度，这些形容词因而可与副词连用来表达这些不同的程度。可分等级的形容词又可分成两类: 程度形容词和极限形容词。

Scale adjectives 程度形容词

These are adjectives like **small**, **cold**, **expensive**, which can have many different degrees. They make up the biggest group of adjectives in English. 这类形容词，如 **small**, **cold**, **expensive** 等可以有不同程度，它们是英语形容词中最大的一类。

Scale adjectives can be used in comparative and superlative forms 程度形容词可有比较级和最高级形式:

He's happier than he used to be.
（他比过去更快乐。）

She's the strongest girl in the class.
（她是全班最有劲的女生。）

Scale adjectives can also be used with the following adverbs to express a high, medium, or small degree 程度形容词也可与下列副词连用来表达高、中或低级程度:

To express a high degree 表示高级程度

very, **extremely**, **incredibly**, **quite** (*AmE*【美】) etc. 等

That's a **very nice** *sweater you're wearing.*
（你穿的这件毛衣非常好看。）

New York's **extremely hot** *in July.*
（纽约在7月份非常热。）

To express a medium degree 表示中级程度

fairly, **pretty** (*informal*【非正式】), **quite**, **rather**

You don't need a coat. It's **quite warm** *outside.*
（你不需要穿外套，外面相当暖和。）

She's **rather a famous** *poet.*
（她是一名比较有名的诗人。）

To express a small degree (when you want to reduce the effect of the adjective)
表示低级程度〔当你想减弱某个形容词的效果时〕

slightly, **a little**, **a bit** (*informal*【非正式】)

I'm afraid the milk is **slightly sour**.
（我看牛奶有点发酸了。）

He was **a bit upset** *when you mentioned the accident.*
（你提起那次事故时，他有点不舒服。）

Language Note: Gradable and Non-gradable Adjectives 可分等级和不可分等级的形容词

Note that in American English **quite** can be used with scale adjectives to express a high degree. In British English it is used with scale adjectives to express only a medium degree. An American person, for example, would be pleased to be told that a new shirt was **quite nice**; but a British person might think that the speaker did not really like it very much. 请注意，在美国英语中 **quite** 与程度形容词连用可表示高级程度。但在英国英语中，它与程度形容词连用只表示中级程度。例如，如果你说某人的新衬衫 **quite nice**，美国人就会很高兴；但若他是英国人，就会觉得你其实不是很喜欢这件衣服。

(For a comparison of **fairly**, **quite**, and **rather**, see Usage Note at RATHER. 对 **fairly**, **quite** 和 **rather** 的比较，请参见 rather 的用法说明。)

Limit adjective 极限形容词

These are adjectives like **perfect**, **unique**, **impossible**, **worthless**, whose meaning already contains the idea of an absolute degree. These words are not usually used in comparative and superlative forms. Limit adjectives can be used with the following adverbs to express the "highest" or "close to the highest" degree 这类形容词，如 **perfect**, **unique**, **impossible**, **worthless** 等，其含义已包括了极度的意思，因此一般没有比较级和最高级形式。极限形容词可与以下副词连用来表达"最高的"或"接近最高的"程度：

To express the highest degree (the meaning is used to its limit)
表示最高程度〔词的含义已表达极限〕

absolutely, **completely**, **quite**, **totally**, **utterly**

That's **quite** *impossible.*
（那是完全不可能的。）

We were **absolutely** *speechless.*
（我们简直连一句话都说不出来。）

To express closeness to the highest degree
表示接近最高程度

almost, **nearly**, **practically**, **virtually**

The waiting room was **virtually empty**.
（候诊室里已几乎空无一人。）

It's **almost impossible** *to say.*
（要说出来几乎是不可能的。）

Some adjectives which have extreme meanings, such as **disgusting**, **amazed**, **terrified**, are usually used with "highest degree" adverbs 有些有极端含义的形容词，如 **disgusting**, **amazed**, **terrified** 等，一般都和"最高级"的副词连用，如：**absolutely disgusting**（讨厌之极）| **utterly amazed**（非常吃惊）| **completely terrified**（彻底受惊）。

Note, however, that they are not usually used with "closeness to the highest degree" adverbs, such as **almost** or **nearly**. 但请注意，这类形容词一般不和表示"接近最高级程度"的副词，如 **almost** 或 **nearly** 连用。

You can often express a meaning more strongly by using a limit adjective rather than a scale adjective. The choice of adverb depends on which type of adjective you use. 用极限形容词常常可以比程度形容词表达更强烈的意思。选用哪个副词完全要看你用的是哪一类的形容词。Compare 请比较：

Language Note: Gradable and Non-gradable Adjectives 可分等级和不可分等级的形容词

very good (很好)
incredibly tired (非常疲倦)
a bit difficult (有点困难)
absolutely marvellous (简直美妙之极)
totally exhausted (完全精疲力竭)
practically impossible (几乎不可能)

Note that some adjectives, like **empty**, **full**, **new**, can be treated as both scale and limit adjectives 请注意，有些形容词，如 **empty, full, new** 等，既可作程度形容词，也可作极限形容词：*Watch you don't spill that glass. It's* **very full**. (注意别洒了杯子里的东西，杯子装得很满。) | *There are no more seats — the theatre's* **completely full**. (没有座位了 — 剧场完全满座了。)

▶ Be careful! 注意！

Sometimes adjectives like **unique**, **perfect**, **identical**, whose meaning contains the idea of an absolute degree, are treated as scale adjectives 有些形容词，如 **unique**, **perfect**, **identical**, 虽然意思包含极度，但有时使用时仍按程度形容词处理：*It was* **rather a unique** *experience.* (那是一次比较独特的经历。) However, some people consider this use to be incorrect. 但也有人认为这种用法是不正确的。

■ Non-gradable adjectives 不可分等级的形容词

Adjectives are non-gradable if their meaning cannot have different degrees. For example, the adjective **atomic** is non-gradable because things (bombs, reactions, science, etc.) are either atomic or not atomic; there are no degrees in between. 形容词的意思如无不同程度之分当然就是不可分等级的形容词了。例如形容词 **atomic** (原子的) 就是不可分等级的，因为事物 (如炸弹、反应、科学等) 不是原子的，就是非原子的，它们之间不存在不同的程度。

Non-gradable adjectives are not usually used in comparative and superlative forms, and are not usually used with adverbs of degree. 不可分等级形容词一般无比较级和最高级，通常也不和表示程度的副词连用。

Here are some more examples of non-gradable adjectives 下面再举一些不可分等级形容词的例子：

American/British (and all nationality adjectives 以及一切表示国籍的形容词) (美国的/英国的)
biological (warfare etc.) (生物学的) 〈如细菌战等〉
electric (oven, fire, etc.) (电气的) 〈如电烤炉，电热炉等〉
medical (医学的)
monthly (每月的) (of newspapers etc. 指报纸等)
painted (着了色的)
polar (bear, region, etc.) (地极的) 〈如北极熊；极地等〉
previous (先前的)
southern (南方的)
stainless (steel etc.) (无污点的) 〈如不锈钢等〉

▶ Be careful! 注意！

Note that some non-gradable adjectives can sometimes be used with a special meaning and may then be gradable. Adjectives of nationality, for example, may be used to refer to a person's way of behaving. *He's very French* means "he seems or behaves very much like a typical French person". 有些不可分等级的形容词有时有特别的含义，在这种情况下就有可能成为可分等级的形容词。例如表示国籍的形容词可用来形容某人的行为举止：*He's very French* 表示"他看起来是个典型的法国人"或"他的行为、举止非常像法国人"。

See also 另见 NEARLY, UTTERLY, VIRTUALLY; see 参见 ALMOST (USAGE), RATHER (USAGE), and 以及 LANGUAGE NOTE: **Intensifying Adjectives**

Language Note: Idioms 语言提示: 习语

What is an idiom? 什么是习语?

An idiom is a fixed group of words with a special meaning which is different from the meanings of the individual words. 习语是一种具有特定含义的固定词组, 其含义不同于组成固定词组的每个单词的含义。

Idioms are usually fixed 习语通常都是固定的

Although certain small changes can be made in idiomatic expressions (see below: **Using idioms**) you cannot usually change the words, the word order, or the grammatical forms in the same way as you can change a non-idiomatic expression. 习语虽然可作某些小的变动 (见下文: **Using idioms** 习语的使用), 但通常不能像非习语词语那样改换其中的词、词序或语法形式。For example 如:

The answer's easy can be changed to *The answer's simple*. But in the expression *It's* **(as) easy as pie**, the word **simple** cannot be used. *The answer's easy* 可以改换成 *The answer's simple* (答案很容易), 但在 **It's (as) easy as pie** (容易之极) 中, 就不能改用 **simple**。

She likes cats and dogs can be changed to *She likes dogs and cats*. But in the expression *It's* **raining cats and dogs** (=raining hard), the word order is fixed. 句子 *She likes cats and dogs* (她喜爱猫和狗) 可以改换成 *She likes dogs and cats* (她喜爱狗和猫), 但在 **It's raining cats and dogs** (下倾盆大雨) 中, *cats and dogs* 的词序则是固定不变的。

He always delivers the goods can be a literal expression meaning, for example, "he always brings the goods to his customer's house". In this case, **the goods** can be replaced by a pronoun: *He always delivers them*, or the verb can be used in the passive form: *The goods* **are** *always* **delivered** *on time*. However, *He always* **delivers the goods** can also be a fixed idiomatic expression meaning "he always produces the desired results". When this expression is used as an idiom, no word changes are possible. 句子 *He always delivers the goods* 可以按其字面意思来理解, 即"他总是把货物送到顾客家中"。在这种情况下 the goods 可以用代词代替: *He always delivers them*, 动词也可以换用被动形式: *The goods are always* **delivered** *on time* (货物总是准时送出)。但 *He always* **delivers the goods** 也可以是习语, 意思是"他总是不负所望", 此时其中的词便不能改换。

Idioms have a special meaning 习语有特定的含义

Sometimes the meaning of an idiom can be guessed from the meaning of one of the words 有时习语的含义可以从其中的一个词猜测到:

to **rack your brains** (=to think hard; something to do with **brains**) (苦思冥想) 〔与 **brains** 有关〕

to live **in the lap of luxury** (=to live in a very luxurious way; something to do with **luxury**) (过奢侈生活) 〔与 **luxury** 有关〕

Usually, however, the meaning of an idiom is completely different from any of the separate words 然而, 通常习语的含义同构成词语的个别单词的含义全然不同:

She was **over the moon** *about her new job*. (=she was extremely happy) (她对她的新工作感到极为满意。)

The exam was a **piece of cake**. (=the exam was very easy) (考试非常容易。)

Sometimes an expression can have two meanings, one literal and one idiomatic. This happens most often when the idiomatic expression is based on a physical image 有时一个词语可以有两个含义。一个是字面意义, 另一个是习语含义。这通常出现在含人体形象的词语中:

Language Note: Idioms 语言提示: 习语

a slap in the face (=a physical blow to the face 一记耳光; an insult or action which seems to be aimed directly at somebody 侮辱; 打击)

to **keep your head above water** (=to prevent yourself sinking into the water 不要被水淹没; to be just able to live on your income; to be just able to go on with life, work, etc. 收入仅够糊口; 凑合着生活、工作等)

Recognizing idioms 习语的分辨

How do you recognize an idiom? It is sometimes difficult to know whether an expression is literal or idiomatic, so it is useful to remember some of the most common types of idioms. 怎样才能辨认出习语? 一个词语是表达字面意义或是习语含义, 有时很难分辨。因此记住某些最常见的习语类型就很有用了。

Pairs of words 成对词

touch-and-go 无把握的; 不确定的
high and dry (船) 搁浅; 陷入困境
stuff and nonsense 胡说八道
the birds and the bees 〔可告诉儿童的〕两性关系的基本常识

(Note that the word order in these pairs is fixed 注意成对词中的词序是固定的。)

Similes 明喻

(as) blind as a bat 眼睛完全看不见东西的
(as) large as life 与实物一般大小; 确确实实
(as) mad as a hatter 疯疯癫癫的
(as) old as the hills 非常古老的

Phrasal verbs 短语动词

chicken out of (sth.) 因害怕而退出〔某事〕
come across (sth. or sb.) 偶然碰上〔某人〕; 无意中发现〔某物〕
nod off 打瞌睡, 睡着
put up with (sth. or sb.) 忍受〔某事或某人〕

Actions which represent feelings 说明感情的动作

look down your nose (in scorn or dislike) 轻视, 瞧不起; 不喜欢
raise your eyebrows (in surprise, doubt, displeasure, or disapproval) 惊奇, 疑惑; 不悦; 不同意

These idioms can be used by themselves to express feelings even when the feeling is not stated. 上列习语本身就可用来表示一种感情, 即使这种感情没有明说出来。

For example 例如: *There were a lot of raised eyebrows at the news of the minister's dismissal* (大家对部长被免职的消息都非常惊讶) just means "everyone was very surprised". 这个例句中的习语就是表示"大家都很惊讶"。

Sayings 谚语

Many sayings are complete sentences. Remember, however, that sayings are not always given in full 许多谚语都是完整的句子。但请记住, 谚语在使用时有时是不完整的:

Language Note: Idioms 语言提示：习语

Well, **two's company** *I always say. What do you think, Mary?* (The speaker wants to be alone with someone and is asking the third person, Mary, to go away.)（嗯，我总是觉得"二人结伴"，玛丽，你觉得怎么样？）〔讲话的人想要单独与某人在一起，因此要求第三者玛丽走开。〕The full saying is 这句谚语的完整说法是：**Two's company, three's a crowd.**（二人结伴，三人不欢。）

Ring up the dentist and make an appointment now. **A stitch in time**, *you know.* (The speaker wants the hearer to go to the dentist immediately, before she gets bad toothache.)（现在就给牙医打电话约个门诊时间，你要知道"小洞不补"可不行啊。）〔讲话的人要对方在牙痛恶化之前立即去看牙医。〕The full saying is 这句谚语的完整说法是：**A stitch in time saves nine.**（小洞不补，大洞吃苦；一针不补，十针难缝。）

It's a bit of a **swings and roundabouts** *situation, I'm afraid.* (The speaker is discussing two possibilities which have equal advantages and disadvantages.)（我倒觉得现在的形势有点利弊各半。）〔讲话的人在讨论两种利弊参半的可能性。〕The full saying is 这句谚语的完整说法是：**What you gain on the swings you lose on the roundabouts.**（失之东隅，收之桑榆。）

Using idioms 习语的使用

Before using an idiom, ask yourself the following questions 使用习语时应注意以下问题：

How fixed is the expression? 词语的固定程度如何？

Sometimes certain parts of an idiom can be changed. 有时习语的某些部分是可以更换的。

Verbs, for example, can often be used in different forms. (Note, however, that they are rarely used in the passive form.) 例如动词可以用不同的形式。（注意：很少用被动形式。）

He **caught** *her eye.*（他吸引住她的视线。）| *Something***'s just caught** *my eye.*（有件东西正引起我的注意。）| **Catching** *the waiter's eye, he asked for the bill.*（他招呼男服务员，要求结账。）

In many expressions, it is possible to change the **subject pronoun** 许多词语的代词主格可以更换：

He *swallowed his pride.*（他暂时忍气吞声。）| **They** *swallowed their pride.*（他们暂时忍气吞声。）| **Janet** *swallowed her pride.*（珍妮特暂时忍气吞声。）

Someone can usually be replaced by other nouns or pronouns. **someone** 通常可以代之以其他名词或代词：

jog **someone's** *memory*（唤起某人的回忆）| *She jogged* **my** *memory.*（她唤起我的回忆。）| *This photograph might jog* **your** *memory.*（这张照片可能会唤起你的回忆。）

Remember, however, that most idioms are far more fixed than literal expressions, and many cannot be changed at all. 不过请记住，大多数习语较之一般按字面意思理解的词语更为固定，而且有许多是不能更换的。

Language Note: Idioms 语言提示: 习语

Is the style right for the situation? 文体与语境是否一致?

Many idiomatic expressions are informal or slang, and are only used in informal (usually spoken) language. 许多习语性词语是非正式文体或者俚语，只用于非正式语体（通常是口语）中。Compare 比较:

> *He said the wrong thing*（他说错了话）and 和 *He* **put his foot in it**. (*informal*【非正式】)（他把事情弄砸了。）
>
> *They all felt rather depressed*（他们都很消沉）and 和 *They were all* **down in the dumps**. (*informal*【非正式】)（他们全都灰溜溜的。）

Some expressions are pompous, literary, or old-fashioned, and are not often used in everyday language except, perhaps, as a joke 某些习语文体浮华，纯属文学用语或用法过时，因而除了作为开玩笑之外，不常用于日常语言中:

> **Gird up your loins!** *It's time to go home.* (humorous use of a literary idiom)（做好准备！该回家了。）〔文雅习语的幽默用法〕

You will find all the common English idioms in this dictionary. Look them up at the entry for the first main word in the idiom. Idioms are shown in blue at the end of an entry, and each idiom has its own number. 本辞典收录了全部常用英语习语。习语置于以其第一个中心词为词目的词条的末尾，用蓝字标出，有独立的义项序号。

See 参见 LANGUAGE NOTES: **Collocations**, **Phrasal Verbs**

Language Note: Intensifying Adjectives
语言提示: 强语势形容词

You can use many different adjectives to talk about large physical size: **big**, **large**, **enormous**, **huge**, **tall**, etc. But which adjectives can you use to intensify a noun (to express the idea of great degree or strength) when you are talking about something which is not physical? 有许多不同的形容词如 **big**, **large**, **enormous**, **huge**, **tall** 等可用来表示物体之大, 但是哪些形容词可用来表示非物体之大呢 (例如程度或力量之大)?

Below are some of the most common intensifying adjectives. Note that nouns can have different intensifying adjectives without really changing their meaning 下面是一些最常用的强语势形容词。请注意, 一些名词尽管换了不同的强语势形容词, 整个语义却是一样的:

> *a* **great/large** *quantity* (大量); *a* **big/bitter/great** *disappointment* (非常失望); *a* **big/definite/distinct/marked** *improvement* (显著的改进)

However, the choice of adjective depends on the noun; different nouns need different adjectives to intensify them. Below you will find some of the most common examples. 不过, 形容词的选择取决于名词, 不同的名词要由不同的形容词来加强语势, 以下是一些最常见的例子。

■ Great 重大的, 强烈的, 极大的

Great is used in front of uncountable nouns which express feelings or qualities 形容词 **great** 用于表示感情或性质的不可数名词的前面: *She takes* **great pride** *in her work*. (她对自己的工作感到很自豪。) | *His handling of the problem showed* **great sensitivity**. (他对这个问题的处理表明他非常敏锐。)

With uncountable nouns, **great** can be replaced by **a lot of** which is more informal, but very common. 当 **great** 与不可数名词连用时, 可以由更为非正式但又很通用的 **a lot of** 取代: *I have* **a lot of admiration** *for her.* (我对她极为钦佩。) | *It takes* **a lot of skill** *to pilot a plane.* (驾驶飞机需要有很娴熟的技能。)

When used with countable nouns, **great** is more formal than **big**. 当 **great** 与可数名词连用时, 它比 **big** 要正式得多: *a* **big/great surprise** (非常惊讶)

Great can often be replaced by stronger adjectives, such as **enormous**, **terrific** (*informal*【非正式】), and **tremendous**. 此外 **great** 常常可由更强烈的形容词如 **enormous**, **terrific** 和 **tremendous** 取代: **enormous enjoyment** (极大的乐趣) | **tremendous admiration** (不胜钦佩)

Great is commonly used with these nouns 通常 **great** 可与下列名词连用:

great admiration (非常钦佩)
great anger (大怒)
in great detail (很详细地)
(a) great disappointment (极失望)
great enjoyment (巨大的乐趣)
great excitement (非常激动)
a great failure (重大失败)
great fun (很好玩)
great happiness (极大的幸福)
great joy (大喜)
at great length (极为详细地)
a great mistake (*especially BrE*【尤英】) (重大错误)
a great number (of) (大量的…)
great power (强国)
great pride (非常自豪)
a great quantity (of) (大量的…)
great sensitivity (非常敏锐)
great skill (很高的技术)
great strength (巨大的力量)
great understanding (非常理解)
great wealth 巨大的财富

Language Note: Intensifying Adjectives
语言提示: 强语势形容词

■ Absolute 纯粹的, 完全的, 绝对的

Absolute, **complete**, **total**, and **utter** are used more frequently than **great** in front of words which express very strong feelings (such as **ecstasy** or **amazement**), or extreme situations, happenings, etc., especially bad ones (such as **chaos** or **disaster**). 形容词 **absolute, complete, total** 和 **utter** 较 **great** 更经常用于表示强烈感情的词 (如 **ecstasy** 或 **amazement**) 或者极端的 (尤指坏的) 情况、事端的词 (如 **chaos** 或 **disaster**) 的前面:

She stared at him in **utter amazement**. (她极惊讶地盯着他看。) | *The expedition was* **a total disaster**. (这次探险是一次巨大的灾难。)

In the examples below, **complete**, **total**, and **utter** could all be used in place of **absolute**. 在下列例句中, **absolute** 都可用 **complete**, **total** 和 **utter** 代替:

absolute agony (极大的痛苦)
absolute astonishment (非常惊讶)
absolute bliss (极大的幸福)
an absolute catastrophe (巨大的灾难)
absolute despair (完全的绝望)
absolute ecstasy (欣喜若狂)
absolute fury (狂怒)
an absolute idiot (十足的白痴)
absolute loathing (极端的厌恶)
absolute madness (极端的疯狂)

■ Big 大的, 重大的, 重要的

Big is mostly used when talking about physical size but it can also be used as an intensifying adjective. Note that it is not usually used with uncountable nouns. 形容词 **big** 最常用于形容物体之大, 但也可用作强语势形容词。但要注意它通常不与不可数名词连用:

a big decision (重大的决定)
a big disappointment (巨大的失望)
a big eater (=someone who eats a lot) (食量大的人)
a big improvement (重大的改善)
a big mistake (严重的错误)
a big surprise (巨大的惊喜)
a big spender (=someone who spends a lot) (花钱大手大脚的人)

■ Large 大的, 巨大的

Large is mostly used to express physical size. It is also commonly used with nouns which are connected with numbers or measurements, as in the examples below. Note that it is not usually used with uncountable nouns. 形容词 **large** 多数用来表示物体之大。它通常也同与数量或度量有关的名词连用, 其用例如下。要注意它通常不与不可数名词连用:

a large amount (大数额)
a large number (of) (大量的…)
a large population (众多的人口)
a large proportion (一大份)
a large quantity (大量)
a large scale (大规模)

Language Note: Intensifying Adjectives
语言提示: 强语势形容词

■ Deep/heavy/high/strong 非常的, 极度的, 深厚的/大量的, 狂暴的, 严重的/高度的, 很大的/强烈的, 烈性的

Deep, **heavy**, **high**, and **strong** are also commonly used as intensifying adjectives, as in these examples
形容词 **deep**, **heavy**, **high**, **strong** 通常也用作强语势形容词, 其用例如下:

deep

deep depression (极度的沮丧)	a deep feeling (=emotion) (深情)	in deep thought (在沉思中)
deep devotion (非常的忠诚)	(a) deep sleep (酣睡)	in deep trouble (陷入极困难的境地)

heavy

a heavy drinker (酒量大的人)	a heavy sleeper (睡得很沉的人)	heavy snow (大雪)
heavy rain (大雨)	a heavy smoker (吸很多烟的人)	heavy traffic (繁忙的交通)

high

high cost (高费用)	a high expectation (of) (对…的高期望)	high pressure (高压)
high density (高密度)	a high level (of) (高水平的…)	a high price (高价)
high energy (高能量)	a high opinion (of someone or something) (〔对某人或某事的〕高度评价)	high quality (高质量)
high esteem (高度尊敬)		high speed (高速)

strong

strong criticism (猛烈的批评)	a strong opinion (about something) (〔对某事的〕坚定的看法)	a strong smell (浓烈的气味)
a strong denial (强烈的否认)	a strong sense of (humour/fun etc.) (浓厚的〔幽默、风趣等〕感)	a strong taste (浓烈的味道)
a strong feeling (that) (=idea) 〔…的〕(强烈的想法)		

Language Note: Intensifying Adjectives
语言提示: 强语势形容词

■ Other intensifying adjectives 其他强语势形容词

The examples above show some of the most common intensifying adjectives, but many other adjectives are used to express the idea of great degree, size, or strength. When deciding which adjective to use, remember that it usually depends on the noun. Particular nouns need particular adjectives. 上面举到的例子是一些最常用的强语势形容词, 但是还有很多其他形容词可用来表示程度、规模或者强度的巨大。在考虑用哪个形容词时, 记住这通常都取决于被形容的名词, 特定的名词需要特定的形容词:

a **fierce/heated argument** (激烈的争论)
a **distinct/marked improvement** (显著的改进)
a **close connection** (紧密的联系)
a **hard worker** (勤劳的工人)

Note that different adjectives are used with different senses of a noun. 还要注意, 一个名词如有不同的意义, 与之连用的形容词也不同:

He has a very **high opinion** *of her work.* (=he thinks it is very good) (他认为她工作得很好。) | *She has* **strong opinions** *about politics.* (她对政治有明确、坚定的看法。)

See 参见 LANGUAGE NOTES: **Collocations**, **Gradable and Non-gradable Adjectives**

Language Note: Invitations and Offers
语言提示: 邀请和提议

Politeness in invitations 邀请时的礼貌问题

It is possible to use both direct and indirect expressions when giving invitations. When deciding which expressions are suitable, it is important to ask the question: Can the speaker assume that the invitation will be acceptable to the hearer? 在提出邀请时, 可使用直接表达的语句, 也可使用间接表达的语句。究竟何者为宜, 重要的是邀请者有无把握知道被邀请者是否接受邀请。

When it is not clear whether an invitation will be acceptable (for example, when the speaker does not know the hearer very well), it is often safer to use an indirect expression. This makes it possible for the hearer to refuse without creating an uncomfortable situation. 当不清楚邀请是否会被接受 (例如邀请人对被邀请者不是很了解) 时, 用间接表达的语句比较稳妥。这样, 被邀请者如果拒绝也不会出现任何不快:

Would you like some coffee? 您要喝点咖啡吗?

We were wondering if you'd like to come to dinner. 不知你是否愿来吃饭?

How about coming to the movies tonight? (*informal*【非正式】) 今天晚上来看电影怎么样?

Why don't you come and eat with us? (*informal*【非正式】) 何不过来和我们一起吃饭?

However, it is also polite to give invitations in a very direct way. This is possible whenever the speaker feels sure that the invitation will be to the hearer's advantage. 但是, 用很直接的方式提出邀请也是有礼貌的。当邀请者相信邀请是有利于对方时就可以用直接的方式:

Have a cup of tea. 请喝杯茶。

Help yourself. 请自便。

Come and see us next time you're in town. 下次到城里来时请来看看我们。

Try some of this cake. 尝一点这种蛋糕吧。

Politeness in offers 提议时的礼貌问题

If the speaker does not know whether an offer will be acceptable, especially if the speaker and the hearer do not know each other very well, it is usual to use an indirect expression. 假使说话人不知道对方是否愿意接受自己的提议, 特别是双方彼此不甚了解时, 通常都使用间接方式:

May I give you a hand with the dishes? 我来帮你洗餐具好吗?

Would you like me to bring any food to the party? 我要不要带些食品来参加聚会?

I was wondering whether you'd like me to check the figures with you. 我同你一起核对一下数字好吗?

However, speakers often feel that an offer will be to the advantage of the hearer, and so offers can be made in a polite way by using a direct form. 但是, 说话人常常感到自己的提议有利于对方, 因此可以有礼貌地用直接方式提出:

Language Note: Invitations and Offers
语言提示: 邀请和提议

I'll get you a taxi. 我帮你叫辆出租车。

Leave the dishes to me. 餐具留给我来洗。

Give me that heavy bag. 我来提那只沉的袋子。

(You must) phone me if you need any help. 需要帮忙时(你就)给我打电话。

▶ Be careful! 注意!

In some cases an indirect form should not be used. For example *Would you like me to pay for this?* may suggest that the speaker does not really want to pay. In this situation it is much better to say *I'll pay for this* or *Let me pay for this.* 在某些情况下,间接方式是不应该使用的,例如: *Would you like me to pay for this?*(我来付钱好吗?)可能表示说话的人并不真正想付钱。在这种情况下,最好用以下两种说法: *I'll pay for this.*(我来付钱。)或者: *Let me pay for this.*(让我来付钱吧。)

See also 另见 COULD, MAY; see 参见 LANGUAGE NOTES: **Politeness**, **Tentativeness**

Language Note: Make and Do 语言提示: make 和 do

Why do you **drive** a car but **ride** a bicycle, **do** your best but **make** a mistake, **give** a performance but **play** a part? There is often no real reason except that a particular noun needs a particular verb to express what is done to it. 为什么开汽车 (car) 的“开”用 **drive**, 而骑自行车 (bicycle) 的“骑”用 **ride**; 尽最大努力 (best) 的“尽”用 **do**, 而犯错误 (mistake) 的“犯”用 **make**; 做演出 (performance) 的“做”用 **give**, 而扮演角色 (part) 的“扮演”用 **play**? 这往往没有什么其他真正的理由, 唯一的理由是特定的名词需要特定的动词来表示所施予的动作。

In order to speak English well, it is important to know which nouns take **make** and which take **do**. There are some general rules to help you decide (see Usage Note at MAKE) but often it has to be learnt through practice. 为了说好英语, 懂得哪些名词要与 **make** 连用, 哪些名词要与 **do** 连用, 这是很重要的。有一些一般的规则可以帮助你作出选择 (参见 MAKE 词条的用法说明), 但往往还必须通过实践才能学会。

■ Some typical uses of make and do
make 和 do 的一些典型搭配

You can **make** 可与 **make** 搭配的名词

- an accusation 提出控告
- an arrangement 作安排
- an attempt 试图
- a change 加以改变
- a comment 加以评论
- a deal (*AmE*【美】) 做交易
- a decision 作出决定
- a demand 提出要求
- an effort 做出努力
- an estimate 做出估计
- a fuss 大惊小怪
- a gesture 做出姿态
- a guess (*BrE*【英】) 猜测
- an impression (on someone) (给某人) 留下印象
- a meal (=prepare a meal) 做饭
- a mistake 犯错误
- money 赚钱
- a movement 动一动
- a noise 发出响声
- an offer 提出帮助 [建议]
- progress 取得进步
- a promise 做出承诺
- a recommendation 加以推荐
- a remark 加以评论
- a request 提出要求
- a statement 发表声明

You can **do** 可与 **do** 搭配的名词

- your best 尽最大努力
- business (with someone) (与…) 做生意
- the cleaning 打扫
- a course (of study) 修读课程
- (some) damage 损坏
- a dance 跳舞
- a deal (*BrE*【英】) 做交易
- a degree (in engineering, etc.) 修读 (工程等) 学位
- the dishes/the washing-up (*BrE*【英】) 洗餐具
- your duty 尽你的责任
- (someone) a favour 给〔某人〕帮个忙
- the gardening 在园子里侍弄花草
- (someone) a good turn 做一件有利于 (某人) 的事
- harm 损害
- your homework 做你的家庭作业
- the housework 做家务
- the ironing 烫衣物
- a job 做工作
- research 进行研究
- the shopping 购物
- the washing/the wash (*AmE*【美】) 洗衣服
- (some) work 做 (些) 工作

■ Other verbs commonly used with particular nouns
通常与特定名词搭配的其他一些动词

Language Note: Make and Do 语言提示: make 和 do

You can **give** 可与 **give** 搭配的名词	You can **take** 可与 **take** 搭配的名词	You can **have** 可与 **have** 搭配的名词
(someone) a chance 给(某人)一个机会 a command 下指令 details 详细叙述 evidence 作证 information 提供信息 a party (*especially BrE*【尤英】) 举行聚会 a performance 举行演出 permission 准许 an opinion 提出看法 an order 下命令 a talk/speech/lecture 发表谈话; 做演讲; 讲课	action 采取行动 advantage (of something or someone) 利用(某事或某人) a bath (*especially AmE*【尤美】) 洗澡 a guess (*AmE*【美】) 猜猜 a look 看一看 an exam 参加考试 medicine 服药 notice (of something) 注意(某事) a photo 拍照片 a pill 服药丸 responsibility (for) 承担对…的责任 risks 冒险 a walk (*AmE*【美】) 去散步	an accident 出了事故 a bath (*especially BrE*【尤英】) 洗澡 a fit 大发脾气 a headache 头痛 an idea 想出个主意 an illness (flu etc.) 生病[患流感等] an interview 进行访谈 a look 看一看 a meal (= eat a meal) 吃饭 an operation (if you are ill) 〔病人〕接受手术 a party 举行聚会 a rest 休息 a thought 考虑

You can **play** 可与 **play** 搭配的名词	You can **perform** 可与 **perform** 搭配的名词
cards 打牌 a game 玩游戏 a musical instrument 演奏乐器 (some) music 演奏(某段)乐曲 a part 扮演角色; 起作用 a record (cassette, tape, etc.) 放唱片[卡式录音带、磁带等] a role 扮演角色; 起作用 a trick (on someone) 开(某人)玩笑 a tune 奏一曲	a duty 履行职责 a function 发挥功用 an operation (if you are a surgeon) 〔外科医生〕施行手术 a piece of music 演奏一首乐曲 a play 演出戏剧 a task 执行任务

■ Using more than one verb with a noun 用不同的动词与同一个名词搭配

Using different verbs with a similar meaning 用不同的动词表示相似的意义

Sometimes it is possible to use more than one verb with a noun to express a similar meaning, for example, you can **arrive at/come to/make/reach/take** a decision. Usually, however, the choice is limited. 有时，用不同的动词与同一个名词搭配以表示相似的意义是可能的。例如，**arrive at** a decision, **come to** a decision, **make** a decision, **reach** a decision 和 **take** a decision 都表示“作出决定”的意思。但通常这种可供选择的情况是有限的。

Language Note: Make and Do 语言提示: make 和 do

Using different verbs for different actions 用不同的动词表示不同的动作

Of course there are usually several different things which can be done to a noun and different verbs are used to describe these actions. 当然，对于同一个名词通常都可以施以不同的动作，因此就用不同的动词来描述这些动作。

Compare 比较:

You **sit** (*BrE*【英】)/**take** *an exam.* (if you are a student) 你参加考试。〔如果你是学生〕	*You* **drive** *a train.* (if you are the driver) 你开火车。〔如果你是司机〕
You **give/set** *an exam.* (if you are a teacher) 你主持考试[出试题]。〔如果你是教师〕	*You* **ride** (*AmE*【美】)/ **take** *a train.* (to travel from A to B) 你乘火车。〔由 A 地往 B 地〕
You **pass** *an exam.* (if you are successful) 你通过考试。〔如果你成功〕	*You* **catch** *a train.* (if you arrive on time) 你赶上火车。〔如果你及时到〕
You **fail** *an exam.* (if you are not successful) 你考试不及格。〔如果你不成功〕	*You* **miss** *a train.* (if you are too late) 你未赶上火车。〔如果你迟到太久〕

Using different verbs for different senses 用不同的动词表示不同的意义

If a noun has more than one sense, different verbs may be used for the different senses. 如果一个名词有若干语义，则可用不同的动词与之搭配以表示这些不同的语义。

Compare 比较:

He **played** *a trick on his brother.* (trick=a joke) 他跟他的兄弟开了个玩笑。 *She* **performed/did** *some tricks at the party.* (tricks=card tricks or magic tricks) 她在聚会上表演了一些魔术。	*He* **placed** *an order for some new office furniture.* (order=a list of things to be bought) 他订购了一些新的办公室家具。 *The captain* **gave** *orders to advance.* (orders=military commands) 连长下令前进。

When you look up a word in this dictionary, remember to read the examples! They will often help you to choose a verb to go with the noun. 查阅本辞典中的某个词时，记住要看一看例句！例句往往能帮助你选择可同某个名词搭配的动词。

See 参见 LANGUAGE NOTE: **Collocations**

Language Note: Modals 语言提示: 情态动词

Modal verbs are a small group of verbs which are used with other verbs to change their meaning in some way. The tables below show you some of the many meanings which can be expressed by the modal verbs: **can**, **could**, **may**, **might**, **must**, **need**, **ought**, **shall**, **should**, **will**, and **would**. The examples show you some of the ways in which these verbs are commonly used.
情态动词是指与其他动词连用而在某些方面改变其语义的一小组动词。下面几个表告诉你可以用情态动词 **can**, **could**, **may**, **might**, **must**, **need**, **ought**, **shall**, **should**, **will** 和 **would** 表示的某些语义。例句是告诉你这些情态动词通常的用法:

prediction of future events 对未来事件的预料	*He'll* (= **will**) *forget his umbrella if you don't remind him.* 如果你不提醒他,他会忘记拿雨伞的。 *What* **will** *it be like, living in the 21st century?* 21 世纪的生活会是什么样子? *We'll* (= **will/shall**) *all be dead in a hundred years.* 100年后我们全都死了。 *Stop crying! It* **won't** *make things any better, you know.* 别哭了! 你知道哭是一点用处也没有的。	**Shall** can be used with first person singular (**I**) and first person plural (**we**). However, it is less common than **will**, especially in American English. **shall** 可用于第一人称单数 (**I**) 和第一人称复数 (**we**), 但用得不如 **will** 多, 尤其是在美国英语中。
willingness, wish 意愿,希望	**Will/would** *you help me with my homework?* (request) 你帮我做作业好吗?〔请求〕 *No, I* **won't**. (refusal) 不, 不行。〔拒绝〕 *I'll* (=**will**) *do it for you if you like.* (offer) 如果你愿意, 我可以替你做。〔建议〕 **Shall I** *give you a hand with the dishes?* (*BrE*【英】) (offer) 我帮你洗餐具好吗?〔建议〕 **Shall we** *buy her a present?* (*BrE*【英】)(suggestion) 我们给她买件礼品吧?〔提议〕 *Did you ask him to the party?* **Will** *he come?* 你请了他来参加聚会吗? 他愿意来吗?	In British English, first person questions expressing willingness or wish use **shall** (**Shall I/we?** = Do you wish me/us to...?) 英国英语中表示意愿或希望的第一人称疑问句用 **shall**。First person statements use **will (I/we will)** 第一人称陈述句用 **will**。 Note that **shall** is not usually used in this way in American English. 请注意, 美国英语通常不这样用 **shall**。
ability 能力	*I* **can** *speak Chinese, but I* **can't** *write it.* 我会说汉语, 但我不会写。 *She* **could** *swim for miles when she was younger.* 她年轻时游泳能游好几英里。	**Could** is used to talk about ability, NOT about particular events which actually happened in the past. Verbs like **manage to** or **be able to** are used instead. **could** 用于表示能力, 而不是表示过去实际发生的具体事情。表示后一种情况则用 **manage to** 或 **be able to** 等: *She finally* **managed to** *pass the exam.* (她终于设法通过了考试。)
	Can/Could *you close the window, please?* (request) 请你把窗户关上好吗?〔请求〕	Polite requests are often made by appearing to ask about ability with **can** and **could**. 有礼貌的请求常常表现为用 **can** 和 **could** 询问对方有无这样做的能力。

Language Note: Modals 语言提示：情态动词

permission 允许	**Can/may** *I have another piece of cake, Dad?* (request) 爸爸，我可以再吃一块蛋糕吗？〔请求〕 *No, you* **can't**. *You'll make yourself sick.* 不可以，你会吃坏肚子的。 *Do you think I* **could** *leave early tonight?* (request) 今天晚上我可以早些离开吗？〔请求〕 *You* **can/may** *leave at 5.30 if you like.* 如果你愿意，你可以在5:30离开。 *I'm afraid you* **can't** *leave till you've finished that work.* 恐怕你要完成了那件工作才能走。 **Might** *I have a word with you?* (*BrE*【英】) (formal request) 我同你说句话可以吗？〔正式请求〕	**Can** is commonly used to ask for or give permission. **May** is more formal. 通常用 **can** 询问是否允许或表示允许，**may** 则是较为正式的词。 **Could** and **might** are used to ask for (NOT to give) permission. They are more tentative than **can**. **could** 和 **might** 用于询问是否允许，而不用于表示允许，较之 **can** 更具试探性。
unreality, hypothesis 不真实，假设	*I* **would** *love to travel round the world.* (if I had the chance) 我真愿环游世界（如果我有这个机会的话）。 *What* **would** *you do if you won a lot of money?* 如果你赢了许多钱，你会做什么呢？ *I* **wouldn't have** *gone, if I'd known he was going to be there.* 如果我当初知道他也要到那里去，我就不会去的。 **Would** *you like some tea (If I made some)?* (invitation)（如果我沏茶）你想喝点茶吗？〔邀请〕 **Should** *he protest* (if he protested), *what would you say?* (*formal*) 如果他抗议，你会说什么呢？〔正式〕	**Would** is commonly used in the main clause of conditional sentences to show that a situation is unreal or tentative. **would** 通常用于条件性句子的主句，表示非真实或不确定的情况。 Because it can express tentativeness, **would** is also used in polite invitations, offers, and requests. 由于 **would** 可以表示不确定性，因而也用于有礼貌的邀请、建议和请求。
possibility 可能性	*She* **may/might** *(not) go to Paris tomorrow.* 她明天可能（不）去巴黎。 *They* **may/might** *(not) be meeting her.* 他们可能（不）会见到她。 *Joe* **may have/might have** *missed the train.* 乔可能没赶上火车。 *Where* **can/could** *they be?* 他们可能在什么地方呢？ *You* **can't have** *forgotten my birthday!* 你不可能忘了我的生日吧！ *Learning English* **can** *be fun.* (=is sometimes fun) 学习英语可以是很有趣的。 *Don't touch that wire. It* **could** *be dangerous.* 别碰那根电线，可能有危险。 *They* **could have** *had an accident, I suppose.* 我猜想他们可能出了车祸。	**Could** suggests that something is less likely than **may** or **might**. **could** 所表示的可能性不及 **may** 或 **might** 大。 When it expresses possibility, **can** is most often used in question forms. **can** 在表示可能性时，多半用于疑问句: *What* **can have** *happened?*（可能发生了什么事呢?）However it is also used to express general possibility in sentences where its meaning is similar to "sometimes". 但是，如果 **can** 在句子中的语义近似 "sometimes"（有时），则 **can** 也可用于表示一般的可能性: *His behaviour* **can** *make us laugh.* (=sometimes makes us laugh)（他的举止有时会使我们发笑。） **Can't** and **can't have** are used to show that there is no possibility. (See **certainty** below) **can't** 和 **can't have** 用于表示没有可能性。(参见下面的 **certainty**)

Language Note: Modals 语言提示: 情态动词

certainty 肯定	*Joe* **must** *be at least 45.* (=I'm sure he's at least 45) 乔肯定至少有45岁了。 *No, he* **can't** *be over 40.* (=I'm sure he isn't over 40) 不, 他一定不会超过40岁。 *He* **must have** *graduated years ago.* (=I'm sure he graduated years ago) 他一定是多年以前毕业的。 *We* **can't have** *been at college together.* (=I'm sure we weren't at college together) 我们不可能是同一个时候上大学。 *They'***ll** *be back by now.* (=I'm sure they're back) 他们现在肯定已经回来了。 *No, they* **won't** *be there yet.* (=I'm sure they are not there yet) 不, 他们肯定还没有到那里。 *Mary* **will have** *arrived already.* (=I'm sure she's arrived already) 玛丽肯定早已到了。 *No, she* **won't have** *left home yet.* (=I'm sure she hasn't left home yet) 不, 她肯定还没有离开家。	**Must have** is the past form of **must** when it is used to express certainty. **must** 表示肯定时, 其过去式是 **must have**。 **Must** and **must have** express stronger certainty than **will** and **will have**. **must** 和 **must have** 所表示的肯定, 强于 **will** 和 **will have** 。 **Can't** and **can't have** express stronger certainty than **won't** and **won't have**. **can't** 和 **can't have** 所表示的肯定强于 **won't** 和 **won't have** 。
obligation, requirement 义务, 职责, 责任, 要求	*You* **must** *finish this job by tomorrow.* 你必须最迟在明天完成这一工作。 *I* **must** *phone my parents tonight.* 我今天晚上必须给我的父母打电话。 *He* **had to** *finish the job by the next day.* 他必须在次日前完成这一工作。 *You* **don't have to/don't need to/needn't** (*BrE*【英】) *do it until next week.* (=it is not necessary) 你现在不是一定要做那件事, 可以在下星期做。 *You* **must not** *smoke in the cinema.* (=it is forbidden) 你在电影院里是不可吸烟的。 *I* **didn't need to/didn't have to** *get up early this morning.* (=**a** the speaker did not get up early, or **b** the speaker did, in fact, get up early) **a** 我今天早晨不必早起〔说话人没有早起〕。或者 **b** 我今天早晨本来是没必要早起的〔说话人事实上已早起了〕。 *You* **needn't have** *bought me a present.* (*BrE*【英】) (=but you did buy a present) 你本来不必给我买礼物〔实际上你已经买了〕。	**Had to** is the past form of **must** when it is used to express obligation. **must** 在表示"必须"时, 过去式用 **had to**。 **Don't have to/don't need to/needn't** (*BrE*【英】) are used to show that there is no obligation. **Must not** is used to show that there is an obligation not to do something. **don't have to/don't need to/needn't** 表示"不必"、"无义务"。**must not** 则表示"有义务不做某事"。 The contracted forms **needn't** and **mustn't** are common in British English but rarely used in American English. 缩略形式 **needn't** 和 **mustn't** 在英国英语中用得很多, 但很少用于美国英语。

Language Note: Modals 语言提示：情态动词

desirability 可取性，应当，应该	*You* **should/ought to** *give up smoking.* (advice) 你应当戒烟。〔忠告〕 *We* **should/ought to** *go to that new Japanese restaurant sometime.* (suggestion) 我们应当找个时间去那家新开的日本餐馆。〔建议〕 *The farmers* **should have/ought to have** *been consulted.* (but they were not consulted) 本该找农场主们商量商量的。〔但没有商量〕 *You* **shouldn't/ought not to** *work so hard, you know.* 你知道，你是不应该工作得这样辛苦的。	The contracted form **oughtn't** is common in British English but rarely used in American English. 缩略形式 **oughtn't** 在英国英语中用得很多，但美国英语用得很少。

probability 或然性	*Their meeting* **should/ought to** *be over now.* (=I expect it is) 他们的会议现在该结束了。〔我估计结束了〕 *He* **should/ought to** *be home at 5 o'clock today.* (=I expect he will be) 他今天5点钟该到家了。〔我估计他会这样的〕 *They* **should have/ought to have** *received our letter by now.* (=I expect they have) 他们现在该已收到我们的信了。〔我估计他们已收到了〕	In this meaning **should** and **ought to** are not as strong as **will** and **must**. (See **certainty** above) **should** 和 **ought to** 在"或然性"的语义上较 **will** 和 **must** 弱。(参见上面的 **certainty**)

personal intention 个人的意向	*I'll* (= **will/shall**) *be back in a minute.* 我一会儿就回来。 *I* **won't/shan't** *ever speak to him again.* 我再也不(会)同他说话了。 *We* **will/shall** *overcome all difficulties.* 我们会克服一切困难。	**Shall** can be used with **I** and **we**, but is less common than **will**, especially in American English. **shall** 可用于 **I** 和 **we**，但用得不如 **will** 多，尤其是美国英语。

■ Grammatical behaviour of modal verbs 情态动词在语法上的特点

Grammatically, modal verbs behave in a different way from ordinary verbs. 在语法上，情态动词与普通动词是有区别的。

They have no **-s** in the third person singular. 情态动词的第三人称单数不加 **-s**。

Most modal verbs, except for **ought**, are followed by the infinitive of other verbs without **to**. 除了 **ought**，绝大多数情态动词后接不带 **to** 的其他动词的不定式。

Modal verbs have no infinitive or **-ing** form. They can be replaced by other expressions if necessary. 情态动词没有不定式或 **-ing** 形式，必要时可用其他词语代替：*I* **must** *work hard.* (我必须苦干。) | *I don't like* **having to** *work hard.* (我不喜欢非要苦干不可。)

They make questions and negative forms without using **do/did**. 情态动词不用 **do/did** 来构成疑问和否定形式：**May** *I see that?* (我可以看看那个东西吗?) | *You* **mustn't** *shout.* (你不应该喊叫。)

Language Note: Modals 语言提示: 情态动词

In British English **need** can be both a modal verb and an ordinary verb. As a modal, it is most often used in questions and negatives. (In American English it is not used as a modal.) 在英国英语中, **need** 可以是情态动词也可以是普通动词。作为情态动词, 它大多用于疑问句和否定句。(在美国英语中 **need** 不用作情态动词。)

Note that some modal verbs appear to have past tense forms (**could**, **should**, **might**), but these are not usually used with a past meaning. One exception is **could** which, when talking about ability, is used as a past form of **can**. 请注意, 某些情态动词好像有过去式 (**could**, **should**, **might**), 但是它们通常并不具有"过去"的语义。**could** 是个例外, 在表示能力时, 用作 **can** 的过去形式: *I* **could** *run a long way when I was younger.* (我年轻时能跑很长一段距离。)

Most modal verbs can be used in some of their meanings with a perfect infinitive to talk about the past. 大多数情态动词的某些语义可以与完成式不定式连用以表示过去的事情: ***I may have seen*** *him yesterday.* (我昨天可能见过他。) | *You* **should have told** *me last week.* (你本该上周告诉我的。) (See the Table for more examples. 更多的例子请参见表。)

In past indirect speech, the following modals usually change their form 下列情态动词在过去式的间接引语中通常要改变时态:

can	*"You* **can't** *leave until tomorrow."* "你明天才能离开。" *They said she* **couldn't** *leave until the next day.* 他们说她要到第二天才能离开。
may	*"They* **may** *have missed the bus."* "他们或许没有赶上公共汽车。" *He suggested that they* **might** *have missed the bus.* 他认为他们或许没有赶上公共汽车。
shall	"**Shall** *I post it?"* (*BrE*【英】) "我把这封信寄出去好吗?" *She asked if she* **should** *post the letter.* 她问她是否应把这封信寄出去。
will	*"**I'll** do that tomorrow."* "我明天做那件事。" *She said she* **would** *do it the next day.* 她说她第二天做那件事。

Other modals usually remain the same 其他情态动词通常保持不变:

She said she **would** *like some coffee.* 她说她想喝点咖啡。| *She told me I* **ought to** *stop smoking.* 她对我说, 我应当停止吸烟。| *He told me I* **must/had to** *work harder.* 他对我说, 我应该更加努力工作。

See 参见 CAN (USAGE), and 和 LANGUAGE NOTES: **Invitations and Offers**, **Requests**, **Tentativeness**

Language Note: Phrasal Verbs
语言提示: 短语动词

In this dictionary, a verb is considered to be a phrasal verb if it consists of two or more words. One of these words is always a verb; the other may be an adverb as in **throw away**, a preposition as in **look into**, or both an adverb and a preposition as in **put up with**. The meaning of a phrasal verb is often quite different from the meaning of the verb on its own. For example, **look into** (= investigate) and **look after** (= take care of) have quite separate meanings from **look**. In fact, many phrasal verbs are idiomatic.
在本辞典中, 一个动词如果包含两个或两个以上的词, 就被认为是短语动词。短语动词中有一个词一定是动词, 其余的可以是副词, 如 **throw away** 中的 **away**; 可以是介词, 如 **look into** 中的 **into**; 也可以是一个副词和一个介词, 如 **put up with** 中的 **up** 和 **with**。短语动词的词义常常同其中的动词本身的词义很不相同。例如, **look into** (调查) 和 **look after** (照管) 同 **look** 的词义就完全不一样。实际上许多短语动词都是习惯用语。(see 参见 Language Note: **Idioms**)

■ How are phrasal verbs listed? 短语动词是如何排列的?

Phrasal verbs are listed in alphabetical order underneath the entry for the main verb. They are marked *phr v*. In this sample entry **polish off** and **polish up** are phrasal verbs listed after the entry for **polish**.
短语动词放在主要动词词条之下, 按字母顺序排列, 以 *phr v* 表示。在本样条中, **polish off** 和 **polish up** 都是短语动词, 置于 **polish** 词条之下。

pol·ish¹ /ˈpɑlɪʃ; ˈpɒlɪʃ/ *v* [T] to make something smooth, bright, and shiny by rubbing it 擦亮, 擦光: *The floor had been polished to a satiny sheen.* 地板已被擦得光亮如缎。| *It was my duty to polish the silver on Saturdays.* 我的职责是每星期六把银器擦亮。—**polisher** *n* [C]: *an electric floor polisher* 电动地板磨光机[打蜡机] —**polishing** *n* [U] —see picture at 参见 CLEAN 图
polish sth ↔ **off** *phr v* [T] *informal* to finish food, work etc, quickly or easily【非正式】快速[轻易]做完〔工作等〕; 很快吃完〔食物〕: *At lunch, Rowan polished off six sandwiches!* 吃午饭时, 罗恩一转眼就吃掉了六份三文治!
polish sb ↔ **off** *phr v* [T] *AmE informal* to kill or defeat someone【美, 非正式】杀死〔某人〕; 击败〔某人〕: *Mather was polished off with a shotgun in another gangland killing.* 马瑟在另一次黑社会仇杀中被人用猎枪打死了。
polish sth ↔ **up** *phr v* [T] **1** to improve a skill or an ability by practising it〔通过练习〕提高, 改善〔技术、能力〕: *I need to polish up my Spanish before we go on vacation.* 我们去度假前, 我需要练习一下我的西班牙语。**2** to polish something 擦亮, 擦光

Sometimes the main verb of a phrasal verb is not used alone. In these cases, the verb is shown as a headword but has no entry of its own. The phrasal verb is listed immediately underneath the headword. This sample entry tells you that the verb **gad** is not used alone but only as part of the phrasal verb **gad about /around**.
有时, 一个短语动词中的主要动词不单独使用。在这种情况下, 本辞典中这类词作为词目出现, 但它本身不成其为词条, 短语动词紧列在该词目之下。右列样条显示, **gad** 不单独使用, 只用作短语动词 **gad about / around** 的一部分。

gad /gæd; gæd/ *v* **gadded, gadding**
gad about/around *phr v* [I] *informal* to go out and enjoy yourself, going to many different places, especially when you should be doing something else【非正式】闲荡, 外出寻乐〔尤指本应做点别的什么事〕: *While I'm at home cooking, he's gadding about with his friends.* 我在家做饭, 而他却在跟他的朋友一起寻乐。

Language Note: Phrasal Verbs
语言提示: 短语动词

Transitive or intransitive? 及物还是不及物?

Phrasal verbs, like all verbs, can be transitive or intransitive and are marked [T] or [I] accordingly. These sample entries show that **grow out of** is a transitive verb and **grow up** is an intransitive verb.
同所有动词一样, 短语动词也有及物与不及物之分, 因而分别标以 [T] 和 [I]。右列样条显示 **grow out of** 是及物短语动词, 而 **grow up** 是不及物短语动词。

grow out of sth *phr v* [T] **1** if a child grows out of clothes, they become too big to wear them〔小孩〕因长大而穿不进〔原来的衣服〕**2** if a child grows out of a habit, they stop doing it as they get older〔因年龄增长而〕戒除, 改掉〔原有的习惯〕: *She used to bite her nails but seems to have grown out of it.* 她过去经常咬指甲, 但现在似乎已经改掉了。**3** to develop from something small or simple into something bigger or more complicated 由〔小或简单的事〕发展成〔大或复杂的事〕: *The dispute grew out of an argument between a worker and the foreman.* 这场争执是从一名工人和工头的争论引发的。

grow up *phr v* [I] **1** develop from being a child to being an adult 长大成人: *What do you want to be when you grow up?* 你长大以后想当什么? | *I grew up on a farm.* 我是在农场里长大的。**2 grow up!** *spoken* used to tell someone to behave more like an adult, especially when they have been behaving in a silly way【口】要像个大人样!〔尤用于某人行为幼稚可笑之时〕**3** to start to exist and become bigger or more important 形成, 兴起, 发展: *Trading settlements grew up along the river.* 河的两岸形成了一些贸易区。

Position of the direct object 直接宾语的位置

When a phrasal verb is transitive, it is important to know where to put the direct object. Sometimes it comes after the adverb or preposition. This entry tells you that the direct object, which can be a person or a thing, is always placed after the complete phrasal verb **pick on**.
对于及物短语动词, 它的直接宾语放在什么位置是很重要的。右列词条显示, 直接宾语可以是人也可以是物, 而且永远置于整个短语动词 **pick on** 之后。

pick on sb/sth *phr v* [T] *spoken*【口】**1** to choose someone to do an unpleasant job or blame someone for something, especially unfairly 选中〔某人做不愉快的工作〕;〔尤指不公平地〕责备〔某人〕: *Why does the boss always pick on me?* 为什么老板总是跟我过不去? | *You big bully – pick on someone your own size!* 你这个恃强凌弱的大坏蛋—— 挑一个跟你个头一样大的人欺负呀! **2** to decide to choose someone or something 选中〔某人或某物〕: *First, pick on some daily task that you all share.* 首先, 挑选出某项你们都要分担的日常工作。

Sometimes the direct object can appear in either position. This is shown by the use of the symbol ↔. This entry tells you that you can say **Hand in** *your papers* or **Hand** *your papers* **in**.
有时直接宾语可放在整个短语动词之后, 也可以放在主要动词与介词或副词之间。符号 ↔ 就用于表示这种情况。右列词条显示, 既可以说 **Hand in** *your paper*, 也可以说 **Hand** *your paper* **in**.

hand sth ↔ **in** *phr v* [T] to give something to a person in authority 上交; 提交: *Hand your papers in at the end of the exam.* 考试结束后把试卷交上来。

Note, however, that with verbs of this type, when the direct object is a pronoun it MUST be put between the verb and the adverb or preposition.
但要注意, 如直接宾语是代词, 则必须置于主要动词与副词或介词之间。

Language Note: Phrasal Verbs
语言提示: 短语动词

Hand in *your papers* but **Hand** *them* **in**.
可以说 **Hand in** your paper, 但必须说 **Hand** them **in**。

They **knocked down** *the building* but *They* **knocked** *it* **down**.
可以说 **They knocked down** the building, 但必须说 **They knocked** it **down**。

Some transitive phrasal verbs can have more than one object. The dictionary will help you decide where to put these objects. This entry tells you that **put down to** has two objects; the first always follows the verb and the second always follows **to**.
某些及物短语动词可能有一个以上的宾语。本辞典可帮助读者确定这些宾语的位置。右列词条表示 **put down to** 有两个宾语, 第一个总是放在动词的后面, 第二个总是放在 **to** 的后面。

put sth **down to** sth *phr v* [T] **1** to explain the reason for something, especially when you are only guessing 把〔某事〕归因于: *I put Jane's moodiness down to the stress she was under.* 我把简的喜怒无常归因于她所承受的压力。**2 put it down to experience** used to tell someone not to feel too upset by failure, but to learn something useful from it 把它当作一次经验教训: *Everyone gets rejected from time to time; put it down to experience.* 每个人都偶尔会被拒绝, 把它当作一次经验教训吧。

Finally, note that some phrasal verbs can be both transitive and intransitive. This entry shows you that **join in** is one of these verbs. It also tells you that when it is transitive, the direct object comes after **in**.
最后请注意, 某些短语动词可以是及物的, 又可以是不及物的。右列词条表示 **join in** 就是这类动词。同时表示, 作为及物短语动词, 其直接宾语置于 **in** 的后面。

join in *phr v* [I,T] to take part in an activity as one of a group of people 参加〔活动〕; 加入进来: *Come on, Ian, join in! You can sing!* 伊恩, 你也来! 你会唱歌! | **join in the fun/party** *We couldn't wait to join in the fun.* 我们迫不及待地参加进去一起玩。

■ Passives 被动语态

In passive forms, phrasal verbs follow the usual pattern of word order with the subject coming in front of the main verb. 在被动形式中, 短语动词按通常的词序规律, 主语置于主要动词的前面。

When's this problem **going to be looked into**? 什么时候处理这个问题?

He says he'**s** *always* **being picked on** *by the boss.* 他说, 老板总是挑他的毛病。

Papers **must be handed in** *before the end of the week.* 作业必须在本周末以前交上来。

Her rudeness **was put down to** *her being so tired.* 她态度粗暴被解释为是由于劳累过度。

See 参见 LANGUAGE NOTES: **Idioms**, **Prepositions**

Language Note: Politeness 语言提示: 礼貌

In most societies there are particular ways of behaving and speaking which are considered to be polite, but these are not the same in all societies. Forms of behaviour and language which are considered to be polite in one society can sometimes seem strange, insincere, or even rude in another. When learning a new language, it is often necessary to learn new ways of expressing politeness.
在大多数社会里，都有一些被认为是有礼貌的特定的行为方式和说话方式，但这些礼貌言行并非在所有社会里都是一样的。有时候，在某一个社会里被认为是礼貌的言行在另一个社会里却会被看成是古怪的、虚伪的或者甚至是粗鲁的。学习一种新语言时，常常需要学习各种新的表达礼貌的方式。

Sometimes English expresses politeness in ways which are not commonly used in other languages 有时英语表示礼貌的方式在其他语言中并不普遍适用

For example, speakers of British English often use indirectness or tentativeness in order to be polite in situations where other languages are more direct. (Note also that speakers of American English tend to be more direct in similar situations.)
例如，讲英国英语的人常用间接的或试探性的口吻来表示礼貌，而其他语言在同样情景下则用较为直接的方式表示。（请注意，说美国英语的人在同样情景下倾向于用较为直接的方式。）

(See 参见 LANGUAGE NOTES: **Criticism and Praise**, **Invitations and Offers**, **Requests**, **Tentativeness**)

Another example is the way in which speakers of British English tend to say *Thank you* for small or unimportant things in situations where speakers of other languages would not consider this to be necessary. (Often, for example, when a shop assistant is giving change to a customer, both people will say *Thank you.* Speakers of American English do not usually do this.) On the other hand, in some situations it is possible in British English to make no reply when somebody thanks you, but in American English, as in some other languages, it is necessary to respond, for example by saying *You're welcome.*
另一个例子是：讲英国英语的人对一点点微不足道的小事也喜欢道一声 *Thank you*（谢谢你），而讲其他语言的人则往往会认为无此必要。（例如售货员找给顾客零钱时，双方都会说一声 *Thank you*。讲美国英语的人通常则没有这种客套。）另一方面，对于对方的道谢，在某些情景下，在英国英语中是不作什么表示的，但讲美国英语的人以及一些操其他语言的人则必须有所表示，例如说一声 *You're welcome*（不用谢）。

(See 参见 LANGUAGE NOTE: **Thanks**)

Sometimes English does not use forms of politeness which are common in other languages 有时英语不使用其他语言中普遍使用的礼貌形式

In some languages, for example, it is polite to respond to a compliment by refusing to accept it, and by saying something bad about yourself or the thing which has been complimented. In English, although it is possible to hesitate a little before accepting, it is usually considered impolite to reject a compliment too strongly.
例如，在某些语言中，对于对方的称赞或恭维都要客气一番，对自己或对方所恭维的事说点贬低的话。在英语中，尽管在接受称赞时可能要有一点犹豫，但通常太强烈的拒绝看作是不礼貌的。

(See 参见 LANGUAGE NOTE: **Criticism and Praise**)

Language Note: Politeness 语言提示: 礼貌

To take another example, in some societies it is necessary to use different forms of language according to the social position (superior, inferior, or equal) of the person you are speaking to. Although English has some special forms of address which are used in particular situations, there are no strict rules of language which depend only on the social relationship of the speaker and the hearer.
另一个例子是: 在某些社会里, 对不同社会地位 (上级、下级或同级) 的人说话, 使用不同的语言形式。英语虽然在特定的场合也有某些专门的称呼, 但并没有仅仅根据说话者和听话者双方社会关系而确定的严格的语言规则。

(See 参见 LANGUAGE NOTES: **Addressing People**, **Apologies**, **Criticism and Praise**, **Requests**)

Several of the Language Notes in this dictionary discuss ways of being polite in English. 本辞典有若干项语言提示都讨论英语中表达礼貌的方式。

See 参见 LANGUAGE NOTES: **Addressing People**, **Apologies**, **Criticism and Praise**, **Invitations and Offers**, **Requests**, **Tentativeness**, **Thanks**

Language Note: Prepositions 语言提示: 介词

A preposition is a word which is used to show the way in which other words are connected. Prepositions may be single words such as: **by**, **from**, **over**, **under**, or they may be more complex and composed of several words such as: **apart from**, **in front of**, **in spite of**, **instead of**. 介词是用来表示词与词之间的连接方式的词。介词可以是单个的词, 如 **by**, **from**, **over**, **under** 等, 也可以较为复杂, 由几个词组成, 如 **apart from**, **in front of**, **in spite of**, **instead of** 等。

Where are prepositions used? 介词用在什么地方?

Prepositions are usually followed by a noun or pronoun, a verb with **-ing**, or a **wh-** clause. In the following sentences **in** is a preposition. 介词通常后接名词, 代词, 带 **-ing** 的动词, 或者 **wh-** 从句, 下列例句中的 **in** 就是介词:

Write your name **in** *the book.* 在书本上写上你的名字。

This tea's too sweet. There's too much sugar **in** *it.* 这茶太甜了, 放的糖太多了。

There's absolutely no point **in** *complaining.* 埋怨是毫无意义的。

I'm very interested **in** *what you've just said.* 我对你刚才说的很感兴趣。

Note that prepositions are NOT used in front of infinitives or clauses beginning with **that**. 注意: 介词不用在带 to 的不定式或者以 **that** 开始的从句的前面:

I was astonished **at/by** *the news.* 这则新闻使我感到惊讶。

I was astonished to hear the news/to hear what she said. 我听到这条新闻 [她所说的话] 感到惊讶。

*I was astonished (***by** *the fact) that she had left her job.* 她辞职了, (这件事) 使我感到惊讶。

What do prepositions mean? 介词意味着什么?

Unlike some other languages, English makes frequent use of prepositions to express basic relationships between words. Relationships of time and place, for example, are usually expressed by the use of a preposition. 同某些其他语言不同, 英语经常用介词来表示词与词之间的关系。例如, 时间关系和地点关系通常就是用介词表示的:

I can see you **on Monday/in August/at 8 pm/for half an hour/during the holidays**, *etc.* 我可以在星期一见你/在8月份见你/在下午8点见你/同你谈半小时/在假日见你等。

I'll meet you **at school/in Rome/on the corner/outside the cinema/under the station clock**, *etc.* 我将在学校/罗马/街角/电影院外面/车站的钟下面等同你会面。

Language Note: Prepositions 语言提示: 介词

Prepositions are used to express many other different kinds of relationships, such as 介词还用来表示其他许多种不同的关系, 如:

reason 原因 — *I did it* **because of** *my father*/**for** *my mother*/**out of** *duty.* 我做这件事是因为我的父亲/为了我的母亲/出于责任心。

manner 方式 — *She spoke* **with** *a smile*/**in** *a soft voice.* 她微笑着/柔声地说话。

means 方法 — *I came* **by** *bus*/**on** *foot*/**in** *a taxi, etc.* 我乘公共汽车/步行/乘出租车等来。

reaction 反应 — *I was surprised* **at** *his attitude*/**by** *his refusal, etc.* 我对他的态度/他的拒绝等感到惊讶。

Note that a particular preposition can often be used to express more than one kind of relationship. For example, **by** can be used for the following relationships 注意: 一个特定的介词常可用来表示不止一种关系。例如, **by** 可以表示以下各种不同的关系:

time 时间 — **by** *next week* 最迟到下星期

place 地点 — **by** *the window* 在窗子旁边

means 方法 — **by** *working very hard* 通过非常努力地工作

The entries for prepositions in this dictionary will show you which relationships they can be used to express. 本辞典中的各个介词词条都会告诉你它们可用来表示什么样的关系。

■ Prepositions in fixed phrases 固定短语中的介词

Prepositions are often part of fixed phrases in phrasal verbs, collocations, and idioms. 介词常常是短语动词、搭配和习语等固定短语的一个组成部分。

Phrasal verbs 短语动词

Sometimes a combination of a verb and a preposition has its own particular meaning: **call on**, **look after**, **send for**. In this dictionary, these combinations are treated as phrasal verbs. They are listed as separate entries after the entry for the main verb. 有时一个动词和一个介词结合在一起具有其自身的特定含义: **call on**（拜访）, **look after**（照顾）, **send for**（派人去叫）。本辞典把这种短语作为短语动词处理。它们作为另列的词条排在主要动词条目的后面。

Collocating prepositions 起搭配作用的介词

Some nouns, verbs, and adjectives are often followed by particular prepositions: **example (of)**, **prohibit (from)**, **afraid (of)**. The prepositions which can be used with particular words are shown at the entries for these words. 某些名词、动词和形容词常常后接特定的介词, 如 **example (of)**（…的例子）, **prohibit (from)**（禁止做…）, **afraid (of)**（害怕…）。某个特定的词应与哪个介词连用, 在该特定词的条目下都有明确的指示。

Language Note: Prepositions 语言提示: 介词

Idioms and typical collocations 习语和典型搭配

Typical collocations (groups of words which "naturally" go together, through common usage) are shown in blue in the dictionary entries. These collocations often show a fixed use of prepositions. 典型搭配（指通过惯常使用而"自然地"结合在一起的词组）在本辞典的词条中以蓝字标出，这类搭配常常表示要固定使用某一介词，例如:

by the name of 名叫 | **beyond help** 无法帮助 | **be under an illusion** 存在幻想 | **in safe hands** 在稳妥可靠的人手中

■ Word order 词序

In some situations it is possible for a preposition to come at the end of a clause or sentence. This happens especially with **wh-** questions, relative clauses, exclamations, passives, and some infinitive clauses. 在某些情况下，介词可能被放在从句或句子的末尾，尤其是 **wh-** 问句、关系从句、感叹句、被动形式以及某些不定式从句常有这种情况:

Who are you speaking **to**? 你在跟谁讲话?

Is this the book you are interested **in**? 你感兴趣的是这本书吗?

What a mess we're **in**! 我们处于何等的混乱之中!

Don't worry. He's being looked **after**. 别担心，他有人照管。

She's really interesting to talk **to**. 同她谈话确实很有趣。

This use is very common in everyday informal English. Some people feel that in formal English it is better to avoid putting the prepositions at the end, by using sentences like this 在日常非正式英语中，这种用法很常见。有人认为在正式英语中最好避免把介词放在末尾，办法是使用类似这样的句子:

To whom *are you speaking?* 你在跟谁讲话?

Is this the book **in which** *you are interested?* 你感兴趣的是这本书吗?

However, sentences such as these can sometimes sound too formal, especially in spoken English. 不过，这样的句子有时听起来太正式，尤其在英语口语中。

See 参见 LANGUAGE NOTES: **Collocations**, **Phrasal Verbs**, **Words Followed by Prepositions**

Language Note: Questions 语言提示: 问句

Why do people ask questions? 人们为何要发问?

People usually ask questions because they want to know something; they are asking for information. There are, however, many other possible reasons for asking questions. The question form is made to do a lot of work in the English language. Look, for example, at the following question:
人们通常因为想知道某事而发问, 他们要求得到信息。然而, 发问还有许多其他原因。在英语中, 问句这种形式可以用来表达许多意思。例如, 请看下面这个问句:

> *How did you cook this fish?* 你是怎么烧这条鱼的?

This may simply mean, "I'd like to have the recipe" (the speaker is asking for information). On the other hand, it may also mean, "It's delicious" (the speaker wants to compliment the cook). However it may also mean, "It tastes awful" (the speaker is criticizing or complaining). Usually, the situation and the way in which the words are spoken will tell the hearer which meaning is the right one, and the reply will depend on the way in which the hearer has understood the meaning. Here are some possible replies to the question above:
这句话的意思可以是"我想知道它的烹饪方法"〔要求得到信息〕。又可以是"味道好极了"〔想恭维厨师〕。但也可以是"难吃极了"〔提出批评或抱怨〕。通常, 说话时的情景以及说话的语气和方式可以使人听出确切的语义, 而答复将取决于如何理解这问话的语义。以下是几种可能的回答:

> *Well, first I did X and then I did Y... .* (the cook is giving the recipe) 我先…, 然后…。〔厨师在说明烹饪方法〕
>
> *Oh! It's easy really.* (the cook has recognized the compliment) 啊! 做起来并不难。〔厨师接受恭维〕
>
> *Why? Don't you like it?* (the cook has recognized possible criticism) 噢, 你不爱吃? 〔厨师听出了对方可能在批评〕

Here is another question which can have several different meanings 下面的问句也有好几种不同的含义:

> *Can you feel a draught from that window?* 你感到有风从那窗户吹过来吗?

This may mean, "I think you are cold, and if you are, I'm going to close the window" (the speaker is offering to help). On the other hand, it may mean, "I'm feeling cold and I want you to close the window" (the speaker is asking the hearer to do something). It may also mean, "If you're as cold as I am, then, we should close the window, move to another room, etc." (the speaker is suggesting that they do something). It is, in fact, unlikely that this particular question is simply a request for information. Here are some possible replies:
这句话的含意可以是"我想你是觉得冷了, 如果是的话, 我就把窗户关上"〔想帮对方〕。又可以是"我觉得冷, 请你关一下窗户"〔请对方帮忙〕。也可以是"如果你同我一样觉得冷, 那我们就把窗户关起来, 或者到别的房间去等"〔建议他们俩采取措施〕。事实上这一特定的询问不会只是要求得到信息。以下是几种可能的回答:

> *No, I'm fine thanks.* (polite refusal of offer) 不, 我不冷, 谢谢。〔婉言谢绝帮助〕
>
> *Yes, it is a bit cold.* (polite acceptance of offer) 是的, 是有点冷。〔有礼貌地接受对方的帮助〕
>
> *Oh, are you cold? I'll close the window.* (response to request for action) 啊, 你觉得冷了? 我去把窗户关起来。〔回应对方要采取行动的要求〕
>
> *Yes. Should we move to another room?* (response to suggestion) 是的, 我们到别的房间去吧。〔回应对方的建议〕

Language Note: Questions 语言提示：问句

Below are just a few examples of the ways in which questions can be used in English. Note that some of the questions are directly related to the speaker's meaning. Others, like the examples above, are more indirect, and their meaning depends on the situation in which they are used. 下面只是可以使用问句的情况的一些举例。注意其中有些问句同说话人的用意是直接关联的。有些如以上所举各例则较为间接，其含意取决于使用时的情景。

Some ways in which questions can be used 可以使用问句的一些情况

when complaining or criticizing 表示不满或批评:

Can't you drive more quickly? (you're too slow) 你不能开快点吗？〔你开得太慢了〕

Have you washed your hands recently? (they look filthy) 你最近洗过手吗？〔手看起来很脏〕

Why did you paint it red? (I don't like it) 你为什么把它漆成红的？〔我不喜欢红的〕

Where on earth did you get that hat? (it looks awful) 你从哪里弄来这么一顶帽子？〔帽子太难看了〕

when introducing people 介绍:

Have you met/Do you know Mr Jones? 你见过［认识］琼斯先生吗？

Do you two know each other? 你们两位彼此相识吗？

when inviting 邀请:

Are you doing anything tomorrow night? (used to introduce an invitation) 明天晚上你有空吗？〔用于引出邀请〕

Would you like to come to a film on Friday? 你星期五想看场电影吗？

Why don't you come dancing with us? 你何不来同我们一起跳舞？

when offering 提供帮助:

Won't you have some more coffee? 再来点咖啡好吗？

Shall I give you a hand? 要我给你帮个忙吗？

Would you like me to help you carry that? 我帮你提这个东西好吗？

when ordering or instructing 指挥或指示:

Will you just roll up your sleeve? (doctor to patient) 请把袖子卷起来。〔医生对病人〕

Close the window, will you/would you? (the speaker is in a position of authority) 请把窗户关上。〔权位高的人〕

Will you listen to me for a minute? (the speaker is probably angry) 你听我说好不好？〔说话者可能生气了〕

Language Note: Questions 语言提示: 问句

when asking permission 请求同意:

Do you mind if I smoke? 你不介意我吸烟吧?

Can I come in? 我可以进来吗?

when requesting 提出要求:

Could you pass me the newspaper? 请把报纸递给我, 行吗?

Can you reach the salt? (please pass it to me) 你能拿到盐吗?〔请把它递给我〕

Have you got a minute? (I'd like to speak to you) 你现在有空吗?〔我想同你说点事〕

when suggesting 提出建议:

Why don't we have lunch before we go? 我们何不吃了午饭再去?

Have you tried doing it this way? 你试过用这种方式做吗?

How about asking Bill to the party? 请比尔参加聚会好不好?

when sympathizing 表示同情:

How are you feeling today? (after an illness) 你今天觉得怎么样?〔病后〕

Are you all right? (after a slight accident) 你没有事儿吧?〔轻微事故之后〕

when threatening 威吓:

Do you want a smack? (parent to naughty child) 你想挨巴掌吗?〔父母对顽童〕

How would you like a punch on the nose? 给你鼻子上来一拳怎么样?

Note that even when a question is used in an indirect way it is still a question and so it usually needs an answer. For example, the question, *Do you know Mr Jones?* requires the answer, *Yes* or *No*. If the answer is "Yes", then it is not necessary to continue the introduction. Similarly, the answer to the question, *Are you doing anything tomorrow night?* may be *Yes* or *No*. The speaker will only go on to invite the hearer if the answer is "No". 注意, 问句即使是以间接方式提问, 仍然是个问句, 因此通常需要回答。例如, 问句 *Do you know Mr Jones?* (你认识琼斯先生吗?) 就需要回答 *Yes* 或 *No* ("认识"或"不认识")。如果回答是 *Yes* (认识), 就没有必要继续介绍。同样, 问句 *Are you doing anything tomorrow night?* (你明天晚上有事吗?) 可以答 *Yes* 或 *No* ("有事"或"没有事")。如果对方答 *No* ("没有事"), 这时才可以提出邀请。

See 参见 LANGUAGE NOTES: **Apologies**, **Criticism and Praise**, **Invitations and Offers**, **Politeness**, **Requests**, **Tentativeness**, **Thanks**

Language Note: Requests 语言提示: 请求

■ Politeness in requests 提出请求时的礼貌问题

When you are asking someone to do something for you or trying to influence their actions, you can often show that you want to be polite by saying things in an indirect way. 在你请求别人为你做某事或者你企图影响他们的行为时，常常可以用间接的措辞来显示你想表示出有礼貌:

direct 直接	*Help me lift this box (please).* (请) 帮我提一下这箱子。 *(Please) will you help me lift this box?* (请) 帮我提一下这箱子好吗? *Could you help me lift this box (please)?* (请) 帮我提一下这箱子行吗? *Do you think you could possibly help me lift this box?* 想请您帮我提一下这箱子, 不知道可以吗?
indirect 间接	*I was wondering if you could possibly help me lift this box.* 不知是否可以请您帮我提一下这箱子。

Generally speaking, the more indirect the expression you use, the more polite you will seem. If you are too direct you may be considered rude. However, the more indirect expressions can sound "too polite" or in some cases pompous if they are used in the wrong situations. When deciding which expressions are suitable for which situations it is useful to ask certain questions. 一般地说，愈是间接的措辞愈是显得有礼貌，如果措辞太直接会被认为是粗鲁。但是如果很间接的措辞用在不当的场合，也会让人听起来"太客气"，或者在某种情况下显得"不实在"。在决定什么情况下使用什么措辞，考虑以下一些问题是有裨益的。

Considerations affecting choice of expression 选择措辞时的若干考虑

— What is the relationship between the person who is speaking (the speaker) and the person they are speaking to (the hearer)? The more direct expressions, for example, are mostly used between friends or when the speaker is in a position of authority. 说话人与听话人之间是什么关系? 例如，在朋友之间，或者说话人处于较高的地位，通常使用较为直接的措辞。

— How important is the action to the speaker? If the action is very important the speaker will probably use a more indirect expression. 请求对方做的事对说话人的重要性如何?如果很重要，说话人就可能使用较为间接的措辞。

— How much inconvenience will this action cause for the hearer? If, for example, the hearer is being asked to make a lot of effort or do something which they do not usually do, the speaker will probably use a more indirect expression. 该行为麻烦对方的程度如何?例如，如果是使人家颇为费事或是做平常不做的事，可能需要使用较为间接的措辞。

Here are some examples from spoken English which show how these considerations can affect the choice of expression 以下是英语口语中显示这类考虑如何影响措辞选择的一些例子:

polite indirectness 间接性措辞的礼貌程度		**request inconvenient or unusual** 所提的要求很麻烦或很不寻常	**speaker in authority** 说话人处于较高的地位	**hearer in authority** 听话人处于较高的地位
	Put your plate in the kitchen when you've finished eating. (Father to child) 吃完了把盘子放到厨房里去。〔父亲对孩子〕		■	
	I want you to stop talking and listen to me. (Teacher to class) 别说话了，听我讲。〔老师对全班学生〕		■	
	Give me a hand with this box, Joe. (Friend to friend) 乔，帮我提一下这个箱子。〔朋友之间〕			

Language Note: Requests 语言提示: 请求

polite indirectness 间接性措辞的礼貌程度		request inconvenient or unusual 所提的要求很麻烦或很不寻常	speaker in authority 说话人处于较高的地位	hearer in authority 听话人处于较高的地位
■	**Could you** *check these letters before I send them out Ms Wells?* (Employer to employee) 韦尔斯女士, 我发出这些信之前帮我检查一下好吗?〔雇主对雇员〕		■	
■	**Could you** *buy some more milk on your way home from work?* (Friend to friend) 你下班回家时再买点牛奶好吗?〔朋友之间〕			
■■	**Could you possibly** *explain that point again?* (Student to professor) 这个问题请您再解释一下好吗?〔学生对教授〕			■
■■	**Do you think you could possibly** *stay late to type these letters?* (Employer to employee) 下班后您可否多待些时候把这些信打出来?〔雇主对雇员〕	■	■	
■■■	**Could you** *spare a moment?* **We were wondering whether you would be able to** *advise us on a small problem.* (Junior manager to managing director) 耽误您一点时间, 有个小问题要向您请示, 不知道是不是可以?〔下级经理对总经理〕	■		■
■■■	**I was wondering if you could possibly** *lend me your car tomorrow.* (Friend to friend) 我想明天借用您的车, 不知道行不行。〔朋友之间〕	■		

▶ Be careful! 注意!

Choosing to use polite expressions which seem to be "too polite" for the situation will usually be seen as sarcasm. In the following examples the requests are not inconvenient or unusual, but the speaker is using indirect expressions to emphasize a feeling of annoyance with the hearer. 使用"太客气"的措辞通常被视为是有意讽刺挖苦。在以下数例中, 所要求的事并非很麻烦或不寻常, 但说话人使用间接措辞以强调对听话人的生气:

I was wondering, Tom, whether it might be possible for you to help do the dishes occasionally? (Friend to friend)
汤姆, 我想请您偶尔帮帮忙洗一洗餐具, 不知道是否可以?〔朋友之间〕

Mary, I wonder if I might ask you to turn your eyes in this direction? (Teacher to student)
玛丽, 我不知道是否可以请你把眼睛转向这边?〔老师对学生〕

Do you think it would be possible for you to refrain from smoking for five minutes? (Colleague to colleague)
不知道是否有可能请您停止吸烟五分钟?〔同事之间〕

See also 另见 COULD, MAY, POSSIBLY; see 参见 LANGUAGE NOTES: **Politeness**, **Tentativeness**

Language Note: Synonyms 语言提示: 同义词

You will often find that several words share a similar general meaning. But be careful — their meanings are nearly always different in one way or another. When comparing two words in the dictionary, look at the definitions and examples and any Usage Notes. Then ask yourself these questions 有时几个词在总的含义上相似。但是要注意: 它们的词义几乎经常不是在这方面就是在那方面多少有点不同。在对本辞典中的两个词进行比较时, 请注意看它们各自的释义和例证以及可能有的用法说明, 然后向自己提出以下问题:

■ Is the meaning exactly the same? 词义是否完全一样?

Compare 比较:

injure/wound 伤害

Both words can mean "to damage part of someone's body" but **wound** is used to suggest that there is a hole or tear in the skin, especially if this has been done on purpose with a weapon. 这两个词都表示"伤害某人身体的一部分", 但 **wound** 用于表示在皮肤上造成伤口, 尤指是有意使用武器造成的:

> *He was badly* **injured** *in a car crash.* 他在车祸中受了重伤。| *Two people were killed and forty* **wounded** *when fighting broke out late last night.* 昨天深夜开战, 有两人被打死, 40 人受伤。

kill 杀死/**murder** 谋杀

To **murder** means "to **kill**" but always has the additional meaning of "unlawfully and on purpose". to **murder** 意为"杀死", 但又总是含有"非法地和有意地"之义:

> *She was sent to prison for* **killing/murdering** *her brother.* 她因杀死[谋杀] 她的兄弟被送入监狱。| *Fifty people were* **killed** (NOT **murdered**) *on the roads last weekend.* 上周末, 有 50 人死于车祸〔不能用 **murdered**〕。

smell 气味 *n*/**stink** 恶臭 *n*

A **smell** can be good or bad but a **stink** is always a bad smell,especially a very strong one. 名词 **smell** 可以是好闻的气味也可以是不好闻的气味, 但 **stink** 总是指坏气味, 尤其是恶臭:

> *a* **smell** *of roses/of stale cooking* 玫瑰的香味/烧煮陈腐食物的气味 | *a* **stink** *of burning rubber* 燃烧橡胶的难闻气味

Sometimes the words are different in degree 有时各个词在程度上是有区别的

adore is a stronger word than **love**	**adore** (很喜欢) 比 **love** (喜欢) 强烈
astonishment is a stronger word than **surprise**	**astonishment** (惊讶) 比 **surprise** (惊奇) 强烈
filthy is a stronger word than **dirty**	**filthy** (污秽的) 比 **dirty** (脏的) 强烈
furious is a stronger word than **angry**	**furious** (狂怒的) 比 **angry** (愤怒的) 强烈
soaked is a stronger word than **wet**	**soaked** (湿透的) 比 **wet** (湿的) 强烈
terror is a stronger word than **fear**	**terror** (恐怖) 比 **fear** (害怕) 强烈

Language Note: Synonyms 语言提示: 同义词

Sometimes the words express a different attitude 有时各个词表示不同的态度

You can say someone is **slim** if they are thin and you like the way they look. If you think they are too thin, you might say they are **skinny** or, if you really want to be rude, **scrawny**. 如果某人瘦, 而你又认为瘦得好看, 就可以用 **slim**（苗条的）, 但如果你认为某人太瘦, 则可用 **skinny**（瘦削的）, 或者如果你确实想说得粗鲁一些, 则可用 **scrawny**（骨瘦如柴的）。

You say something is **newfangled** if you disapprove of it because it is too modern. If you do not feel disapproval you use words like **new** or **modern**. 如果你对某事物持否定态度, 认为它太新潮, 可用 **newfangled**（新奇花哨的）, 如不持否定态度, 则可用 **new** 或 **modern**（新式的）这一类词。

■ Are the words used in the same situations? 各个词用于同一语境吗?

Words with a similar meaning are often used in quite different situations. 具有相似含义的词往往用于相当不同的语境。

Sometimes the words have a different style 有时各个词有不同的风格

In these pairs, one of the words has a particular style which means that it is not usually used in an ordinary situation. 在以下各对词中, 其中的一个词具有一种特殊的风格, 这意味着该词通常不在一般的语境中使用。

Compare 比较:

brainy (*informal*【非正式】) 伶俐的/**intelligent** 聪明的
comely (*literary*【文】) 秀丽的/**beautiful** 美丽的
cop (*informal*【非正式】) 差人/**policeman** 警察
fag (*BrE slang*【英俚】) 烟卷儿/**cigarette** 香烟
kick the bucket (*humorous slang*【幽, 俚】) 翘辫子/**die** 死
pass away (*euphemism*【婉】) 逝世, 作古/**die** 死
seek (*formal or literary*【正式或文】) 寻觅/**look for** 寻找

Sometimes the words have a different register 有时候各个词有不同的语域:

Some words are normally used by specialists, such as doctors or scientists. Other people will use another word for the same thing 某些词是医生或科学家等专业人员所用的术语。同样一个事物, 其他人则用另外的词来表达:

Compare 比较:

bequeath (*formal*【正式】) 遗赠/**leave** (money etc. after death) 死后留下〔家产等〕
patella (*technical*【术语】) 髌〔骨〕/**kneecap** 膝盖骨

Sometimes the words belong to a different variety of English 有时各词分属不同地方的英语

Compare 比较:

crook (*AustrE informal*【澳, 非正式】)/**poorly** (*BrE informal*【英, 非正式】) 健康状况不佳的
elevator (*AmE*【美】)/**lift** (*BrE*【英】) 电梯
pavement (*BrE*【英】)/**sidewalk** (*AmE*【美】) 人行道

Language Note: Synonyms 语言提示: 同义词

■ Do the words have the same grammar? 这些词的语法搭配是一样的吗?

Sometimes words with a similar meaning are used in different grammatical patterns. 有时, 词义相似的词, 其语法搭配并不一样。

Compare 比较:

rob 抢劫/**steal** 盗窃

You **rob** a bank or **rob** somebody (of something) 动词 **rob** 可以后接机构 (to rob a bank 抢劫银行) 或人 (to rob somebody 抢劫某人), 抢走的东西则要置于 **of** 的后面:

> *He* **robbed** *the old couple (of all their savings).* 他抢了这对老夫妇 (的全部积蓄)。

You **steal** something (from somebody or from a place) 但 **steal** 后要接所盗窃的东西, 被盗窃的人或场所则要置于 **from** 的后面:

> *He* **stole** *a glass from the restaurant.* 他从这家餐馆偷了一个玻璃杯。| *She* **stole** *some money from her sister.* 她从她姐姐那里偷了一些钱。

answer *v*/**reply** *v* 回答

Answer can be both transitive and intransitive 动词 **answer** 可以是及物的也可以是不及物的:

> *I called him but he didn't* **answer**. 我叫他了, 但他没有回答。| *They never* **answer** *our letters.* 他们从来不回复我们的信。

Reply is always intransitive 而 **reply** 则总是不及物的:

> *I wrote to her but she didn't* **reply**. 我给她写了信, 但她没有回复。| *They never* **reply** *to our letters.* 他们从来不回复我们的信。

advise 劝告/**recommend** 建议

Both verbs can mean "to tell someone what you think should be done" but are followed by different verb patterns 这两个动词的意思都表示"告诉某人你认为应该做什么", 但是后面接的动词句型却不一样:

> *The doctor* **advised** *me to stay in bed.* 医生要我卧床。| *The doctor* **recommended** *that I (should) stay in bed.* 医生建议我 (应该) 卧床。

Notice that even when words appear to be synonyms they are rarely the same in all the ways discussed here. The entries in this dictionary will help you decide how they are different. 请注意: 当一些词看来是同义词时, 它们在以上所讨论的各个方面却极少是完全一致的, 本辞典的条目会帮助你认识它们的不一致之处。

See 参见 THIN (USAGE)

Language Note: Tentativeness 语言提示: 试探语气

In English, speakers often show politeness by being indirect and tentative. This is especially true in situations where there is a risk of causing offence. 在英语中, 说话人常常通过间接方式和用试探性的语气来表示礼貌, 这在有可能引起对方反感的情况下尤其如此。

There are many different ways of expressing tentativeness. One way is to use words which "soften" what is being said, making it less forceful and direct. 表示试探有许多种不同的方式。一种方式是使用某些词语使所说的话听起来"柔和"一些, 使之不那么强硬和直接。

Here are some common "softening words". 下面是一些常用的"柔和字眼"。

Maybe and **perhaps** are used **maybe 和 perhaps** 可用于以下场合:

— when making suggestions and recommendations 提出建议或忠告时:

Maybe *we should ask Liz for her opinion.* 也许我们应该征求一下莉兹的意见。

Perhaps *you ought to talk to John about it.* 也许你该同约翰谈谈这件事。

— when making a request 提出要求时:

Could you **perhaps** *just say a few words about your new project?* 或许你可以就你的新项目说几句话, 行吗?

Maybe *you could phone me later this week.* 或许你可以在本周晚些时候给我打个电话。

Perhaps *you'd like to let me know when you've finished.* 你做完时或许可以通知我一下。

— when expressing criticism 表示批评时:

It's a beautiful pink, but it's **perhaps** *a little bright for my taste.* 这种粉红色很漂亮, 不过从我的爱好来说, 似乎太鲜艳了一点。

Possibly is used **possibly** 可用于以下场合:

— mainly with can and could in requests 主要用于表示请求, 与 can 和 could 连用:

Could you **possibly** *write the report by tomorrow?* 您是否有可能至迟在明天写好报告?

Do you think I could **possibly** *borrow your bike?* 我借用一下你的自行车你看可以吗?

— but also when expressing criticism 但也可用于表示批评:

The food is wonderful but it's **possibly** *a little bit expensive.* 这食品味道好极了, 不过可能贵了一点。

Language Note: Tentativeness 语言提示：试探语气

Wonder is used wonder 可用于以下场合:

— when giving invitations 提出邀请时:

We were wondering *whether you'd like to come to dinner next week.* 我们正在想，不知道你下周能不能过来吃饭。

— when making suggestions and recommendations 提出建议或忠告:

I wonder *if we should go by train.* 不知道我们是否该乘火车去?
I wonder *if you'd find it easier to do it this way.* 不知道这样做你会不会觉得容易一些?

— when making requests 提出要求时:

I wonder *whether you could spare me a moment.* 不知道是不是可以打扰你一会儿?
We were wondering *if you could help us.* 不知道你能不能帮我们一下?

— when expressing criticism or disagreement 表示批评或不同意时:

It's a lovely dress but **I wonder** *if it's quite your colour.* 这衣服很漂亮，可我不知道颜色是不是十分适合你。
I wonder *whether these figures are quite right.* 我不知道这些数字是不是完全对。
Is that true, **I wonder**? 那是真的吗?我可不敢说。

Notice that the use of past tense forms (**I wondered**, **I was wondering**, etc.) makes the suggestion, request, etc. even more tentative. 注意: 使用过去时 (**I wondered**, **I was wondering** 等) 可以使建议、要求等更带试探的色彩。

Quite is used with negative forms quite 用于各种否定形式:

— when expressing disagreement or criticism 表示不同意或批评:

That's not **quite** *what I said, you know.* 恐怕我不完全是那样说的，你要知道。
Are you sure? That doesn't seem **quite** *right to me.* 你能肯定吗?我似乎觉得那并不完全对头。
I'm not **quite** *sure I agree with you there.* 我不敢完全肯定在那个问题上同你的看法一致。

Note that sometimes several softening words are used together, and this makes the suggestion, request, etc., even more tentative 注意: 有时若干柔和字眼可以连用，从而更加强了建议、要求等的试探语气:

I was wondering *whether I could* **possibly** *have the day off tomorrow.* 我在想，不知我明天请一天假行不行。
I wonder *whether it isn't* **perhaps** *a little bit too bright.* 我不知道这是否太鲜亮了一点。
It's a lovely sweater but I think **maybe** *it's not* **quite** *the right size for me.* 这毛衣很漂亮，但我看或许尺寸不怎么合我的身。

See also 另见 POSSIBLY, QUITE; see 参见 MAYBE (USAGE), and 和 LANGUAGE NOTE: **Politeness**

Language Note: Thanks 语言提示: 致谢

Expressions used to thank people can be very short and direct, or they can be longer and more complex. When deciding which expressions are suitable for which situations it is useful to ask certain questions. 用于对人表示感谢的词语可以很短而且直接, 也可以比较长而复杂。在考虑何种情况下使用何种词语时, 问几个问题是很有用的。

Considerations affecting choice of expression 涉及选择词语的种种考虑

— How important is the thing or the action for which the speaker is thanking the hearer? If it is very important to the speaker, the expression of thanks will be stronger. 说话人对听话人所要表示感谢的事物或行为, 其重要性如何? 如果对说话人很重要, 感谢的词语就要较为强烈。
— Is the action something which the hearer has to do or ought to do, or is it something unusual or special? If the hearer has done something unusual or special, the expression of thanks will be stronger. 这个行为是听话人所必须或应该做的, 抑或是一种不寻常的行为? 如果是后者, 感谢的词语就要较为强烈。
— Will the hearer immediately know the reason for the thanks? If not, the speaker must make this clear. 听话人是否会立即明白讲话人感谢他的原因? 如果不是这样, 讲话人就必须说清楚。

Quick thanks 简短的感谢语

When someone does something small for you which is part of normal polite behaviour, it is usual to say thank you. For instance, if a flight attendant brings you a meal, a friend holds the door open for you, a bank clerk gives you your money, or the person sitting next to you passes the salt, you should use a short expression of thanks. The examples below show the usual short forms of thanks and response. (Note that in British English it is not always necessary to respond.) 当有人出于正常的礼貌考虑为你做了一件小事时, 通常要表示感谢。例如, 空中小姐送来饭菜, 朋友为你开门, 银行职员把钱给你, 或者邻座的人递给你盐瓶, 你都应用简短的词语表示感谢。以下所列为常用的简短的感谢词语以及答语 (注意: 在英国英语中, 对于道谢并不是全都要回答的):

thanks 感谢语	**responses** 答语
Thank you. 谢谢你。 *Thanks.* 谢谢。	*You're welcome.* (*especially AmE*【尤美】) 别客气。 *That's all right.* 不用谢。 *That's OK.* (*informal*【非正式】) 没什么。 *No problem.* (*AmE informal*【美, 非正式】) 没问题。 *Not at all.* (*formal*【正式】) 用不着客气。

Stronger ways of thanking 较强烈的感谢方式

When someone gives you a present or does something special for you, it is usual to thank them in a stronger way. This can be done by making the expression stronger and adding a comment. (Note that the comment may come before or after the expression of thanks.) 当有人送给你礼物或者特地为你做了什么事情, 通常都要用较为强烈的方式表示感谢。做法是使用较为强烈的词语并加上说明 (注意: 说明的话可以在感谢词语之前, 也可以在之后):

Language Note: Thanks 语言提示: 致谢

stronger expressions 较强烈的词语	**comments** 说明
Thank you **very much**. 非常感谢。 *(Oh great!) Thanks* **a lot**. (*rather informal*【较非正式】) (嗬, 太好了!) 太感谢了。 **Many** *thanks*. (*rather formal*【较正式】) 甚为感谢。	*It's wonderful/just what I wanted.* (comment on a present) 好极了/正是我想要的。〔称赞礼物〕 *That's really kind of you.* 你真是太好了。| *You didn't have to, you know.* (comment on hearer's generosity) 你用不着这样破费呀。〔称赞对方的慷慨大方〕 *I don't know what I'd have done without you.* 我真不知道没有你该怎么办。| *I'd never have managed on my own.* (when someone has helped you to do something) 我自己是怎么也弄不成的。〔称赞对方帮你做了某事〕

■ Explaining 解释

When thanking someone for something which has already happened, the speaker needs to remind the hearer of the situation 为早已发生的某事感谢某人, 说话人需要提醒一下对方当时的情况:

Thank you for all your hard work last week. I don't think we could have managed without you. 谢谢你上周的大力帮忙。要是没有你, 我们是干不成的。

My mother was thrilled to get those flowers on her birthday. Thanks a lot — it was really thoughtful of you. 我母亲过生日那天收到那些花高兴极了。太谢谢你了 —— 你想得真周到。

It was very good of you to give Billy a lift home from school yesterday. Thank you. 你真好, 昨天比利放学时你让他搭你的车回家。谢谢你了。

We're really grateful for all your help while Arthur was ill. Thank you very much. 阿瑟生病期间幸亏你多方帮助, 我们非常感谢。

(Note that **grateful** is most often used when the hearer has helped the speaker in some way. It is not usually used when saying thank you for a present. 注意: **grateful** 通常用于感谢听者为说话人提供的某种帮忙, 一般不用于感谢对方赠送礼物。)

■ Written and formal thanks 书面和正式的感谢语

Written and formal expressions of thanks often refer directly to the action of thanking 书面和正式的感谢用语常常是开门见山的:

I am writing to thank you for… 本人来信是为了特意感谢您…

I am writing to say how grateful we are… 为向您表示我们感激之情, 本人现来函向您致意…

Please accept our (grateful) thanks… (*formal*【正式】) 请接受我们〔衷心〕的感谢…

We would like to thank you for your contribution (*formal*【正式】). 承蒙惠赐, 谨表谢忱。

We would like to express our gratitude for your cooperation. (*formal*【正式】) 承蒙台端合作, 特此致谢。

The management would like to express its gratitude to the following people for their work in the fund-raising campaign… (*formal*【正式】) 公司谨对在此次筹集资金活动中作出贡献之下列人员表示感谢…

Language Note: Words Followed by Prepositions
语言提示: 后接介词的词语

In English many nouns, verbs, and adjectives are commonly followed by prepositions. If you do not know whether to use a preposition with a particular word or if you are not sure which preposition to use, look up the word in this dictionary. At each entry, you will be given the prepositions which are commonly used with that word. These are printed in dark type before the definition and the examples. After you have found the preposition, go on to look at the examples; these will often show you how the prepositions are used. 英语中许多名词、动词和形容词通常都后接介词。如果你不知道某一个词是否与介词连用或不能肯定用哪一个介词，请在本辞典中查阅该词的词条，在每一个词条中你都能找到通常与该词连用的介词，这些介词用黑体排在释义和例证的前面，找到这个介词后再往下看例证，了解其用法。

Below are some sample entries for nouns, verbs, and adjectives. 下面是一些名词、动词和形容词词条的示例。

■ Prepositions with nouns 介词与名词连用

This entry tells you that in its second meaning **insight** can be used with the preposition **into**. 这个词条告诉你在第二个义项中 **insight** 可以与介词 **into** 连用。

in·sight /ˈɪnˌsaɪt; ˈɪnsaɪt/ *n* **1** [U] the ability to understand and realize what people or situations are really like 洞察力，眼光: *a woman of great insight* 一位极有眼光的妇女 **2** [C] a sudden clear understanding of something, especially something complicated〔尤指对复杂事情的〕顿悟，猛省: **[+into]** *The article gives us a real insight into the causes of the present economic crisis.* 这篇文章分析目前经济危机的原因，发人深省。

This entry tells you that in its first meaning **intrusion** can be used with **into**, **on** or **upon**. The examples show you that the prepositions are used with the same meaning. 本词条告诉你在第一个义项中 **intrusion** 可以与 **into**, **on** 或者 **upon** 连用。例证表示这几个介词用起来意思是一样的。

in·tru·sion /ɪnˋtruʒən; ɪnˈtruːʒən/ *n* [C,U] **1** an unwanted event or person in a situation that is private〔讨厌的事或人的〕干扰，侵扰: *She considered Pam's presence in the kitchen an intrusion.* 她认为帕姆待在厨房是一种干扰。| **[+into/on/upon]** *I resented this intrusion into my domestic affairs.* 我讨厌这种对我家事的干涉。**2** something that has an unwanted effect on a situation, on people's lives etc〔对某种情况、别人生活等的〕侵袭；打扰: *the intrusion of Western values on a culture that has existed for centuries* 西方价值观对一种已存在几百年的文化的侵袭

This entry shows you that in its first meaning **preparation** can be used with either **for** or **of**. The choice of preposition will depend on the meaning of the sentence in which the word is used. 这个词条向你显示，在第一个义项中 **preparation** 可以同 **for** 或者 **of** 连用。介词的选择取决于句子的语义。

prep·a·ra·tion /ˌprɛpəˋreʃən; ˌprepəˈreɪʃən/ *n* **1** [U] the act or process of preparing something 预备，准备: **[+for]** *Business training is a good preparation for any career.* 商业培训对任何职业都是良好的基础。| **[+of]** *Richard's currently involved in the preparation of the budget.* 理查德当前在忙于编制预算。| **in preparation for** (=in order to prepare for something) 为…作准备 *Justin had opened several bottles of wine in preparation for the party.* 贾斯廷已开了好几瓶葡萄酒为聚会作准备。| **be in preparation** (=being prepared) 在准备中 *Plans for the new school are now in preparation.* 建造新校舍的图样正在绘制之中。**2 preparations** [plural] arrangements for something that is going to happen 准备工作，筹备工作: **[+for]** *preparations for the Queen's visit* 女王访问的准备工作 | **make preparations** *The army is making preparations for a full-scale invasion.* 军队正在为全面侵略作准备。**3** [C] a medicine, COSMETIC etc 配制剂；药剂: *a new preparation for cleansing the skin* 清洁皮肤的新护肤剂

Language Note: Words Followed by Prepositions
语言提示: 后接介词的词语

■ Prepositions with verbs 介词与动词连用

This entry tells you that **compensate** is used with the preposition **for**. The example in its second meaning shows that you usually **compensate** somebody **for** something. 这个词条告诉你 **compensate** 与介词 **for** 连用。第二个义项中的例证说明用 **compensate** somebody **for** something 表示"为某事物赔偿给某人"。

com·pen·sate /ˋkɑmpən,set; ˈkɒmpənseɪt/ *v* **1** [I] to replace or balance something good that has been lost or is lacking, by providing or doing something equally good 弥补, 补偿: *Because my left eye is so weak, my right eye has to work harder to compensate.* 因为我左眼视力差, 右眼就要辛苦点来弥补一下。| **[+for]** *Her intelligence more than compensates for her lack of experience.* 她的才智过人, 因此虽然经验不足, 也游刃有余。**2** [I,T] to pay someone money because they have suffered injury, loss or damage 赔偿, 补偿: **compensate sb for sth** *The firm agreed to compensate its workers for their loss of earnings.* 公司同意补偿工人的收入损失。

This entry tells you that **joke** is used with the prepositions **about** and **with**. The first example shows that you joke **about** something. 这个词条告诉你, **joke** 与介词 **about** 和 **with** 连用。第一个例证说明 **joke about** something 用以表示"就某事开玩笑"。

joke² *v* [I] **1** to say things that are intended to be funny 开玩笑, 说笑话: **[+about/with]** *It's serious, Donny, don't joke about it!* 事情很严重, 唐尼, 别开玩笑了! **2 you're joking!/you must be joking!** *spoken* used to tell someone that what they are suggesting is so strange or silly that you cannot believe that they are serious【口】你(一定)是在开玩笑吧?〔用来表示某人说的话很奇怪或愚蠢, 你无法相信他们是认真的〕: *What! Buy a house on my salary? You must be joking!* 什么? 用我的薪水买房子? 你一定是在开玩笑吧? **3 only joking** *BrE spoken* used to say that you did not really mean what you just said【英口】只是说着玩的, 开个玩笑而已〔用来表示刚才所说并不是认真的〕: *Only joking, darling – I love you really!* 亲爱的, 只不过开个玩笑, 我真的很爱你! **4 joking apart/aside** *BrE* used before you say something serious after you have been joking【英】说正经的〔用来表示停止开玩笑, 开始说严肃的事〕: *Joking apart, she is a very talented painter.* 说正经的, 她真是一位很有才华的画家。—**jokingly** *adv*

This entry tells you that **progress** is used with the preposition **to**. The example shows that the preposition can be followed by a verb in the **-ing** form. 这个词条告诉你, **progress** 与介词 **to** 连用。例证说明 **to** 可以后接动词的 **-ing** 形式。

progress² /prəˋgrɛs; prəˈgres/ *v* [I] **1** to develop over a period of time and become something better or more complete 进步; 进展: *Work on the ship progressed quickly.* 轮船的建造进展迅速。| *I asked the nurse how my son was progressing.* 我向护士询问我儿子身体恢复得如何。| **[+to]** *Cindy has progressed to reading on her own.* 辛迪进步了, 开始自己阅读了。**2** if an activity or situation progresses, it continues to happen or develop gradually〔活动等〕继续进行; 逐步发展: *As the meeting progressed, Nina grew more and more bored.* 随着会议的进行, 尼娜越来越感到无聊。**3** to move forward slowly 缓慢行进: *Our taxi seemed to be progressing with agonizing slowness.* 我们的出租车仿佛以令人难以忍受的缓慢速度向前行驶。**4** to move on from doing one thing to doing another〔从做一件事〕转向〔做另一件事〕: **[+to]** *We started with a bottle of wine, and then progressed to whisky.* 我们先喝了一瓶葡萄酒, 之后便喝起了威士忌。—compare 比较 REGRESS

Language Note: Words Followed by Prepositions
语言提示: 后接介词的词语

■ Prepositions with adjectives 介词与形容词连用

This entry tells you that **desirous** is followed by the preposition **of**. 这个词条告诉你, **desirous** 后接介词 **of**。

de·sir·ous /dɪˋzaɪrəs; dɪˈzaɪərəs/ *adj formal* wanting something very much【正式】希望的, 渴望的: **[+of]** *No one had ever been so openly desirous of my attention.* 从未有人如此公开地表示过渴望引起我的注意。

This entry tells you that in its second meaning **immune** is used with the preposition **to**, but in its third meaning it is used with the preposition **from**. 这个词条告诉你, 在第二个义项中 **immune** 与介词 **to** 连用, 而在第三个义项中与介词 **from** 连用。

im·mune /ɪˋmjun; ɪˈmjuːn/ *adj* **1** someone who is immune to a particular disease cannot catch it〔对疾病〕有免疫力的 **2** not affected by something such as criticism, bad treatment etc 不受〔批评、虐待等〕影响的: **[+to]** *They're always so rude that I've almost become immune to it.* 他们总是如此粗暴无礼, 我都几乎习以为常了。**3** specially protected from something unpleasant 豁免的; 可免…的: **[+from]** *Peterson was told he would be immune from prosecution if he cooperated with the police.* 彼得森被告知, 如果他与警方合作, 就可免受起诉。

This entry tells you that when **impervious** means "not affected or influenced by something", it is used with the preposition **to**. Note that in its second meaning it is used without a preposition. 这个词条告诉你, 当 **impervious** 作"不受影响的"解时, 与介词 **to** 连用。请注意: 在第二个义项中 **impervious** 不与介词连用。

im·per·vi·ous /ɪmˋpɝvɪəs; ɪmˈpɜːviəs/ *adj* **1** not affected or influenced by something and seeming not to notice it 不受影响的; 无动于衷的: **[+to]** *Janet carried on reading, impervious to the row going on around her.* 珍妮特不受周围的嘈杂声影响, 继续看书。| *He seems to be impervious to criticism.* 他好像对批评毫不在乎。**2** not allowing anything to enter or pass through〔任何东西都〕不能进入的; 不能穿过的: *impervious volcanic rock* 不透水不透气的火山岩

■ Summary 总结

Some words can be followed by different prepositions without changing their meaning. 某些词可以后接不同的介词而含义不变。(see 参见 **Intrusion**)

Some words are followed by different prepositions according to their different meanings. 某些词按不同的含义后接不同的介词。(see 参见 **Immune**)

Some words can be followed by more than one prepositon, but these are used in different ways. 某些词可以后接一个以上的介词, 但是用法是各不相同的。(see 参见 **joke**, **preparation**)

Some words can be used either with or without a prepositon. 某些词可以与介词连用, 也可以不与介词连用。(see 参见 **prepared**)

Prepositions can be followed by verbs in the **-ing** form. They cannot be followed by infinitives. 介词可以后接 **-ing** 形式的动词, 但不可以后接不定式。(see 参见 **progress**)

■ Phrasal verbs 短语动词

The examples in this Language Note show words which can be used with a preposition but have a complete meaning in themselves. There are also many verbs where a word which looks like a preposition makes up part of the meaning, for example **come across** (=discover), **look into** (=investigate), etc. These are considered to be phrasal verbs and are listed in this dictionary as separate headwords in alphabetical order under the main verb. 本语言提示中所举的例证展示了可以和介词连用但本身具有完整语义的词。此外, 也有许多动词, 它们的构成中有像是介词的词, 这些词组成了部分语义, 如 **come across** (发现), **look into** (调查) 等, 这些动词称作短语动词, 本辞典把它们作为单独词条按字母顺序列在主要动词的下面。

See 参见 LANGUAGE NOTES: **Collocations**, **Phrasal Verbs**

Table 1 附录 1

Numbers 数字

How numbers are spoken 数字读法

Numbers over 20 20以上的数字

21	twenty-one
22	twenty-two
32	thirty-two
99	ninety-nine

Numbers over 100 100以上的数字

101	a/one hundred (and) one
121	a/one hundred (and) twenty-one
200	two hundred
232	two hundred (and) thirty-two
999	nine hundred (and) ninety-nine

Note: In British English the "and" is always used 注：在英国英语中总是用 and: *two hundred and thirty-two.* But in American English it is often left out 但在美国英语中 and 往往略去: *two hundred thirty-two.*

Numbers over 1000 1000以上的数字

1001	a/one thousand (and) one
1121	one thousand one hundred (and) twenty-one
2000	two thousand
2232	two thousand two hundred (and) thirty-two
9999	nine thousand nine hundred (and) ninety-nine

Ordinal numbers 序数

20th	twentieth
21st	twenty-first
25th	twenty-fifth
90th	ninetieth
99th	ninety-ninth
100th	hundredth
101st	hundred and first
225th	two hundred (and) twenty-fifth

Dates 日期

1066	ten sixty-six
1624	sixteen twenty-four
1900	nineteen hundred
1903	nineteen-oh-three
1987	nineteen eighty-seven
2000	the year two thousand
2001	two thousand (and) one
6 January, 1990	the sixth of January nineteen ninety
January 6, 1990	January (the) sixth nineteen ninety

Numbers and grammar 数字和语法

Numbers can be used as 数字可用作:

Determiners 限定词 *Five people were hurt in the accident.* 事故中有五人受了伤。| *the three largest companies in the US* 美国最大的三家公司 | *several hundred cars* 几百辆小汽车

Pronouns 代词 *We invited a lot of people but only twelve came/only twelve of them came.* 我们邀请了许多人，但是（他们中）只来了12个人。| *Do exercise five on page nine.* 做第9页上的练习5。

Nouns 名词 *Six can be divided by two and three.* 6可以被3和2整除[除尽]。| *Three twos make six.* 3乘2等于6。

What numbers represent 数字表示什么

Numbers are often used on their own to show:
单独使用的数字常用来表示:

Price 价格	*It costs eight seventy-five* (= 8 pounds 75 pence or 8 dollars 75 cents: £8.75 or $8.75). 这值8镑75便士 [8美元75美分]。
Time 时间	*We left at two twenty-five* (= 25 minutes after 2 o'clock). 我们在2点25分离开。
Age 年龄	*She's forty-six* (= 46 years old). 她46岁。| *He's in his sixties* (= between 60 and 69 years old). 他60多岁。
Size 尺寸	*This shirt is a thirty-eight* (= size 38). 这件衬衣是38号的。
Temperature 温度	*The temperature fell to minus fourteen* (= –14°). 温度降至零下14度。| *The temperature was in the mid-thirties* (= about 34–36°). 温度在35度上下。
The score in a game 比赛得分	*Becker won the first set six-three* (= by six games to three: 6–3). 贝克尔以6比3赢了第一盘。
Something marked with the stated number 标有某个数字的事物	*She played two nines and an eight* (= playing cards marked with these numbers). 她打出两张9和一张8。
A set or group of the stated number 组 [支等]	*The teacher divided us into fours* (= groups of 4). 老师把我们分成四人一组。| *You can buy cigarettes in tens or twenties* (= in packets containing 10 or 20). 你可以买10支或20支包装的香烟。

Roman numerals 罗马数字

I *(i)* = 1
II *(ii)* = 2
III *(iii)* = 3
IV *(iv)* = 4
V *(v)* = 5
VI *(vi)* = 6
IX *(ix)* = 9
X *(x)* = 10
XI *(xi)* = 11
XV *(xv)* = 15
XIX *(xix)* = 19
XX *(xx)* = 20
XL *(xl)* = 40
L *(l)* = 50
XC *(xc)* = 90
XCIX *(xcix)* = 99
C *(c)* = 100
D *(d)* = 500
CM *(cm)* = 900
M *(m)* = 1000

MCMXCIX = 1999
MDCCCI = 1801
MM = 2000

$\bar{\mathbf{X}}$ = 10 × 1,000 = 10,000
$\bar{\mathbf{C}}$ = 100 × 1,000 = 100,000
$\bar{\mathbf{M}}$ = 1,000 × 1,000 = 1,000,000

Table 2 附录 2

Weights and Measures 度量衡单位

The words in **dark type** are the ones that are most commonly used in general speech.
排成黑体词的为口语中最常用的单位。

METRIC 公制

Units of length 长度单位

	1 **millimetre** (毫米)	= 0.03937 inch (英寸)
10 mm	= 1 **centimetre** (厘米)	= 0.3937 inch (英寸)
10 cm	= 1 decimetre (分米)	= 3.937 inches (英寸)
10 dm	= 1 **metre** (米)	= 39.37 inches (英寸)
10 m	= 1 decametre (十米)	= 10.94 yards (码)
10 dam	= 1 hectometre (百米)	= 109.4 yards (码)
10 hm	= 1 **kilometre** (千米)	= 0.6214 mile (英里)

Units of weight 重量单位

	1 **milligram** (毫克)	= 0.015 grain (格令)
10 mg	= 1 centigram (厘克)	= 0.154 grain (格令)
10 cg	= 1 decigram (分克)	= 1.543 grains (格令)
10 dg	= 1 **gram** (克)	= 15.43 grains (格令) = 0.035 ounce (盎司)
10 g	= 1 decagram (十克)	= 0.353 ounce (盎司)
10 dag	= 1 hectogram (百克)	= 3.527 ounces (盎司)
10 hg	= 1 **kilogram** (千克)	= 2.205 pounds (磅)
1000 kg	= 1 **tonne** (公吨) (metric ton (公吨))	= 0.984 (long) ton (长吨)
		= 2204.62 pounds (磅)

Units of capacity 容量单位

	1 millilitre (毫升)	= 0.00176 pint (品脱)
10 ml	= 1 centilitre (厘升)	= 0.0176 pint (品脱)
10 cl	= 1 decilitre (分升)	= 0.176 pint (品脱)
10 dl	= 1 **litre** (升)	= 1.76 pints (品脱) = 0.22 UK gallon (加仑)
10 l	= 1 decalitre (十升)	= 2.20 gallons (加仑)
10 dal	= 1 hectolitre (百升)	= 22.0 gallons (加仑)
10 hl	= 1 kilolitre (千升)	= 220.0 gallons (加仑)

Square measure 面积单位

	1 square millimetre (平方毫米)	= 0.00155 square inch (平方英寸)
100 mm²	= 1 square centimetre (平方厘米)	= 0.1550 square inch (平方英寸)
100 cm²	= 0.01 square metre (平方米)	= 0.01196 square yard (平方码)
100 m²	= 1 are (公亩)	= 119.6 square yards (平方码)
100 ares	= 1 **hectare** (公顷)	= 2.471 acres (英亩)
100 ha	= 1 square kilometre (平方千米)	= 247.1 acres (英亩)

Cubic measure 体积单位

		1 cubic centimetre (立方厘米)	= 0.06102 cubic inch (立方英寸)
1000 cm^3	=	1 cubic decimetre (立方分米)	= 0.03532 cubic foot (立方英尺)
1000 dm^3	=	1 cubic metre (立方米)	= 1.308 cubic yards (立方码)

Circular measure 圆弧单位

	1 microradian (微弧度)	= 0.206 seconds (秒)
1000 μrad	= 1 milliradian (毫弧度)	= 3.437 minutes (分)
1000 mrad	= 1 radian (弧度)	= 57.296 degrees (度) = 180/π degrees (度)

Metric prefixes 公制词首

	Abbreviation 缩写	*Factor* 阶乘, 因子		*Abbreviation* 缩写	*Factor* 阶乘, 因子
tera- 太 (拉)	T	10^{12}	centi- 厘	c	10^{-2}
giga- 吉 (咖)	G	10^{9}	milli- 毫	m	10^{-3}
mega- 兆	M	10^{6}	micro- 微	μ	10^{-6}
kilo- 千	k	10^{3}	nano- 纳 (诺)	n	10^{-9}
hecto- 百	h	10^{2}	pico- 皮 (可)	p	10^{-12}
deca- 十	da	10^{1}	femto- 飞 (母托)	f	10^{-15}
deci- 分	d	10^{-1}	atto- 阿 (托)	a	10^{-18}

BRITISH AND AMERICAN 英、美制

Units of length 长度单位

	1 **inch** (英寸)	= 2.54 cm
12 inches (英寸)	= 1 **foot** (英尺)	= 0.3048 m
3 feet (英尺)	= 1 **yard** (码)	= 0.9144 m
$5^1/_2$ yards (码)	= 1 rod, pole, or perch (杆)	= 5.029 m
22 yards (码)	= 1 chain (链)	= 20.12 m
10 chains (链)	= 1 furlong (浪)	= 0.2012 km
8 furlongs (浪)	= 1 **mile** (英里)	= 1.609 km
6076.12 feet (英尺)	= 1 nautical mile (海里)	= 1852 m

Units of weight 重量单位

	1 grain (格令)	= 64.8 mg
	1 dram (打兰)	= 1.772 g
16 drams (打兰)	= 1 **ounce** (盎司)	= 28.35 g
16 ounces (盎司)	= 1 **pound** (磅)	= 0.4536 kg
14 pounds (磅)	= 1 stone (英石)	= 6.350 kg
2 stones (英石)	= 1 quarter (夸特)	= 12.70 kg
4 quarters (夸特)	= 1 (long) **hundredweight** (长担)	= 50.80 kg
20 hundredweight (英担)	= 1 (long) **ton** (长吨)	= 1.016 tonnes
100 pounds (磅)	= 1 (short) **hundredweight** (短担)	= 45.36 kg
2000 pounds (磅)	= 1 (short) **ton** (短吨)	= 0.9072 tonnes

The short hundredweight and ton are more common in the US.
美国多用短担和短吨。

Units of capacity 容量单位

	1 fluid ounce (液盎司)	= 28.41 cm^3
5 fluid ounces (液盎司)	= 1 gill (吉耳)	= 0.1421 dm^3
4 gills (吉耳)	= 1 **pint** (品脱)	= 0.5683 dm^3
2 pints (品脱)	= 1 **quart** (夸脱)	= 1.137 dm^3
4 quarts (夸脱)	= 1 (UK) **gallon** (英加仑)	= 4.546 dm^3
231 cubic inches (立方英寸)	= 1 (US) **gallon** (美加仑)	= 3.785 dm^3
8 gallons (加仑)	= 1 bushel (蒲式耳)	= 36.369 dm^3

Square measure 面积单位

	1 square inch (平方英寸)	= 645.16 mm^2
144 square inches (平方英寸)	= 1 square foot (平方英尺)	= 0.0929 m^2
9 square feet (平方英尺)	= 1 square yard (平方码)	= 0.8361 m^2
4840 square yards (平方码)	= 1 acre (英亩)	= 4047 m^2
640 acres (英亩)	= 1 square mile (平方英里)	= 259 ha

Cubic measure 体积单位

	1 cubic inch (立方英寸)	= 16.39 cm^3
1728 cubic inches (立方英寸)	= 1 cubic foot (立方英尺)	= 0.02832 m^3
		= 28.32 dm^3
27 cubic feet (立方英尺)	= 1 cubic yard (立方码)	= 0.7646 m^3
		= 764.6 dm^3

Circular measure 圆弧单位

	1 second (秒)	= 4.860 µrad
60 seconds (秒)	= 1 minute (分)	= 0.2909 µrad
60 minutes (分)	= 1 degree (度)	= 17.45 µrad
		= π /180 rad
45 degrees (度)	= 1 oxtant (八分之一圆)	= π /4 rad
60 degrees (度)	= 1 sextant (六分之一圆)	= π /3 rad
90 degrees (度)	= 1 quadrant (象限) or 或 1 right angle (直角)	= π /2 rad
360 degrees (度)	= 1 circle or 1 circumference (圆周)	= 2π rad
1 grade or gon (百分度)	= 1/100th of a right angle (百分之一直角)	= π /200 rad

US dry measure 美制干量单位

1 pint (品脱)	= 0.9689 UK pint (英品脱)	= 0.5506 dm^3
1 bushel (蒲式耳)	= 0.9689 UK bushel (英蒲式耳)	= 35.238 dm^3

US liquid measure 美制液量单位

1 fluid ounce (液盎司)	= 1.0408 UK fluid ounces (英液盎司)
	= 0.0296 dm^3
16 fluid ounces (液盎司)	= 1 pint (品脱) = 0.8327 UK pint (英品脱)
	= 0.4732 dm^3
8 pints (品脱)	= 1 gallon (加仑) = 0.8327 UK gallon (英加仑)
	= 3.7853 dm^3

Temperature 温度

°*Fahrenheit* (华氏) $= \left(\frac{9}{5} \times X°C\right) + 32$ °*Celsius* (摄氏) $= \frac{5}{9} \times \left(X°F - 32\right)$

Table 3 附录 3

Military Ranks 军衔

Royal Navy (英国)皇家海军	US Navy 美国海军
Admiral of the Fleet 海军元帅	Fleet Admiral 海军五星上将
Admiral 上将	Admiral 上将
Vice-Admiral 中将	Vice Admiral 中将
Rear-Admiral 少将	Rear Admiral 少将
Commodore 准将	Commodore 准将
Captain 上校	Captain 上校
Commander 中校	Commander 中校
Lieutenant-Commander 少校	Lieutenant Commander 少校
Lieutenant 上尉	Lieutenant 上尉
Sub-Lieutenant 中尉	Lieutenant Junior Grade 中尉
Midshipman 候补少尉	Ensign 少尉
–	Chief Warrant Officer 一级准尉
Fleet Chief Petty Officer 海军总上士	Warrant Officer 二级准尉
–	Master Chief Petty Officer 一级军士长
–	Senior Chief Petty Officer 二级军士长
Chief Petty Officer 上士	Chief Petty Officer 三级军士长
Petty Officer 军士	Petty Officer 1st Class 上士
–	Petty Officer 2nd Class 中士
Leading Seaman 上等水兵	Petty Officer 3rd Class 下士
Able Seaman 一等水兵	Seaman 一等兵
Ordinary Seaman 二等水兵	Seaman Apprentice 二等兵
Junior Seaman 水兵	Seaman Recruit 三等兵

British Army 英国陆军	US Army 美国陆军
Field-Marshal 陆军元帅	General of the Army 陆军五星上将
General 上将	General 上将
Lieutenant-General 中将	Lieutenant General 中将
Major-General 少将	Major General 少将
Brigadier 准将	Brigadier General 准将
Colonel 上校	Colonel 上校
Lieutenant-Colonel 中校	Lieutenant Colonel 中校
Major 少校	Major 少校
Captain 上尉	Captain 上尉
Lieutenant 中尉	1st Lieutenant 中尉
2nd Lieutenant 少尉	2nd Lieutenant 少尉
–	Chief Warrant Officer 一级准尉
Warrant Officer 1st Class 一级准尉	Warrant Officer 二级准尉
Warrant Officer 2nd Class 二级准尉	–
Staff Sergeant 上士	Sergeant Major 军士长
Sergeant 中士	Master Sergeant 一级军士长
–	1st Sergeant 二级军士长
–	Sergeant 1st Class 三级军士长
–	Staff Sergeant 上士
–	Sergeant 中士
Corporal 下士	Corporal 下士
Lance Corporal 一等兵	Private 1st Class 一等兵
Private 二等兵	Private 士兵

RAF (英国) 皇家空军	**USAF** 美国空军
Marshal of the Royal Air Force 空军元帅	General of the Airforce 空军五星上将
Air Chief Marshal 上将	General 上将
Air Marshal 中将	Lieutenant General 中将
Air Vice Marshal 少将	Major General 少将
Air Commodore 准将	Brigadier General 准将
Group Captain 上校	Colonel 上校
Wing Commander 中校	Lieutenant Colonel 中校
Squadron Leader 少校	Major 少校
Flight Lieutenant 上尉	Captain 上尉
Flying Officer 中尉	First Lieutenant 中尉
Pilot Officer 少尉	Second Lieutenant 少尉
–	Chief Warrant Officer 准尉
Warrant Officer 准尉	Chief Master Sergeant 一级军士长
–	Senior Master Sergeant 二级军士长
Flight Sergeant 上士	Master Sergeant 三级军士长
Chief Technician 总技术军士	Technical Sergeant 上士
Sergeant 中士	Staff Sergeant 中士
Corporal 下士	Airman 1st Class 一等兵
Junior Technician 初级技术军士	–
Senior Aircraftman 一等兵	Airman 2nd Class 二等兵
Leading Aircraftman 二等兵	Airman 3rd Class 三等兵
Aircraftman 新兵	Airman Basic 空军士兵

Royal Marines (英国) 皇家海军陆战队	**US Marine Corps** 美国海军陆战队
General 上将	General 上将
Lieutenant-General 中将	Lieutenant General 中将
Major-General 少将	Major General 少将
Brigadier 准将	Brigadier General 准将
Colonel 上校	Colonel 上校
Lieutenant-Colonel 中校	Lieutenant Colonel 中校
Major 少校	Major 少校
Captain 上尉	Captain 上尉
Lieutenant 中尉	1st Lieutenant 中尉
2nd Lieutenant 少尉	2nd Lieutenant 少尉
–	Chief Warrant Officer 一级准尉
Warrant Officer 1st Class 一级准尉	Warrant Officer 二级准尉
Warrant Officer 2nd Class 二级准尉	–
Colour Sergeant 上士	Sergeant Major 军士长
–	Master Gunnery Sergeant 一级军士长
Sergeant 中士	Master Sergeant 二级军士长
–	1st Sergeant 三级军士长
–	Gunnery Sergeant 枪炮军士
–	Staff Sergeant 上士
–	Sergeant 中士
Corporal 下士	Corporal 下士
–	Lance Corporal 准下士
Lance Corporal 一等兵	Private 1st Class 一等兵
Marine 士兵	Private 二等兵

Table 4 附录 4

Word Formation 构词法

In English there are many word beginnings (prefixes) and word endings (suffixes) that can be added to a word to change its meaning or its word class. The most common ones are shown here, with examples of how they are used in the process of word formation. Many more are listed in the dictionary. 在英语中有许多词头 [前缀] 和词尾 [后缀] 可加在一个词的前面或后面以改变其意义或词性。此处列出最常见的一些, 并附有它们在构词过程中如何使用的例证。更多的则列在本辞典的正文之中。

Verb formation 动词的构成

The endings **-ize** and **-ify** can be added to many nouns and adjectives to form verbs, like this 词尾 -ize 和 -ify 可加在许多名词和形容词之后构成动词, 如:

American		Americanize
legal	**-ize**	legalize
modern		modernize
popular		popularize

They want to make the factory more **modern**. *They want to* **modernize** *the factory.* 他们想让该工厂现代化。

beauty		beautify
liquid	**-ify**	liquefy
pure		purify
simple		simplify

These tablets make the water **pure**. *They* **purify** *the water.* 这些药片可以把水净化。

Adverb formation 副词的构成

The ending **-ly** can be added to most adjectives to form adverbs, like this 词尾 -ly 可加在大多数形容词之后构成副词, 如:

easy		easily
main	**-ly**	mainly
quick		quickly
stupid		stupidly

His behaviour was **stupid**. *He behaved* **stupidly**. 他表现得很愚蠢。

Noun formation 名词的构成

The endings **-er**, **-ment**, and **-ation** can be added to many verbs to form nouns, like this 词尾 -er, -ment 和 -ation 可加在许多动词之后构成名词, 如:

drive		driver
fasten	**-er**	fastener
open		opener
teach		teacher

John **drives** *a bus. He is a bus* **driver**. 约翰驾驶公共汽车。他是公共汽车司机。
A can **opener** *is a tool for* **opening** *cans.* 开罐器是开罐头的工具。

amaze		amazement
develop	**-ment**	development
pay		payment
retire		retirement

Children **develop** *very quickly. Their* **development** *is very quick.* 儿童发育得很快。

admire		admiration
associate	**-ation**	association
examine		examination
organize		organization

The doctor **examined** *me carefully. He gave me a careful* **examination**. 医生仔细地给我做了检查。

The endings **-ity** and **-ness** can be added to many adjectives to form nouns, like this 词尾 -ity 和 -ness 可加在许多形容词之后构成名词, 如:

cruel		cruelty
odd	**-ity**	oddity
pure	**-ty**	purity
stupid		stupidity

Don't be so **cruel**. *I hate* **cruelty**. 不要这么残忍。我讨厌残忍。

dark		darkness
deaf	**-ness**	deafness
happy		happiness
kind		kindness

It was very **dark**. *The* **darkness** *made it impossible to see.* 天色很黑。因天黑什么也看不见。

Adjective formation 形容词的构成

The endings **-y**, **-ic**, **-ical**, **-ful**, and **-less** can be added to many nouns to form adjectives, like this 词尾 -y, -ic, -ical, -ful 和 -less 可加在许多名词之后构成形容词，如:

bush dirt hair smell	**-y**	bushy dirty hairy smelly

There was an awful **smell** *in the room. The room was very* **smelly**. 房间里有一股难闻的气味。

atom biology grammar poetry	**-ic** **-ical**	atomic biological grammatical poetic

This book contains exercises on **grammar**. *It contains* **grammatical** *exercises.* 这本书里有一些语法练习。

pain hope care	**-ful**	painful hopeful careful

His broken leg caused him a lot of **pain**. *It was very* **painful**. 他的腿摔断了，很疼。

pain hope care	**-less**	painless hopeless careless

The operation didn't cause her any **pain**. *It was* **painless**. 手术没有使她感到疼痛。手术不疼。

The ending **-able** can be added to many verbs to form adjectives, like this 词尾 -able 可加在许多动词之后构成形容词，如:

wash love debate break	**-able**	washable lovable debatable breakable

You can **wash** *this coat. It's* **washable**. 你可以洗洗这件外套。它是可以洗的。

Opposites 反义词

The following prefixes can be used in front of many words to produce an opposite meaning. Note, however, that the words formed in this way are not always EXACT opposites and may have a slightly different meaning. 下列的词头可加在许多词之前以产生反义。然而要注意这样构成的词并不总是恰好反义的，而可能有稍稍不同的含义。

un-	happy fortunate wind block	unhappy unfortunate unwind unblock

I'm not very **happy**. *In fact I'm very* **unhappy**. 我不太高兴。事实上我很不高兴。

in- **im-** **il-** **ir-**	efficient possible literate regular	inefficient impossible illiterate irregular

It's just not **possible** *to do that. It's* **impossible**. 不可能那样做。这是不可能的。

dis-	agree approve honest	disagree disapprove dishonest

I don't **agree** *with everything you said. I* **disagree** *with the last part.* 我并不完全同意你的话。我不同意你说的最后一部分。

de-	centralize increase ascend inflate	decentralize decrease descend deflate

Increase *means to make or become larger in amount or number.* **Decrease** *means to make or become smaller in amount or number.* increase 意为(使)数量变大。decrease 意为(使)数量变小。

non-	sense payment resident conformist	nonsense nonpayment nonresident nonconformist

The hotel serves meals to **residents** (= people who are staying in the hotel) *only.* **Nonresidents** *are not allowed in.* 这家旅馆只为住宿的客人提供膳食。非住宿者不得入内。

Table 5 附录 5

The Verb "Be" 动词 be

present 现在式

		questions 疑问式	*negatives* 否定式
I	I am, I'm	am I?	I am not, I'm not, aren't I?
you	you are, you're	are you?	you are not, you're not, you aren't
she/he/it	she is, he's	is she/he/it?	it is not, he's not, she isn't
we/they	we are, they're	are we/they?	we are not, they're not, we aren't

present participle 现在分词: being

past 过去式

		questions 疑问式	*negatives* 否定式
I	I was	was I?	I was not, I wasn't
you	you were	were you?	you were not, you weren't
she/he/it	she was	was she/he/it?	she was not, it wasn't
we/they	we were	were we/they?	they were not, we weren't

past participle 过去分词: been

Table 6 附录 6

Irregular Verbs 不规则动词

verb 动词	past tense 过去式	past participle 过去分词
abide	abided, abode	abided
arise	arose	arisen
awake	awoke	awoken
be	*see Table 5* 见附录5	
bear	bore	borne
beat	beat	beaten
become	became	become
befall	befell	befallen
beget	begot (also 又作 begat *biblical*【圣经】)	begotten
begin	began	begun
behold	beheld	beheld
bend	bent	bent
bereave	bereft, bereaved	bereft, bereaved
beseech	besought, beseeched	besought, beseeched
beset	beset	beset
bestride	bestrode	bestridden
bet	bet, betted	bet, betted
betake	betook	betaken
bethink	bethought	bethought
bid	bade, bid	bid, bidden
bind	bound	bound
bite	bit	bitten
bleed	bled	bled
bless	blessed, blest	blessed, blest
blow	blew	blown
break	broke	broken
breed	bred	bred
bring	brought	brought
broadcast	broadcast	broadcast
browbeat	browbeat	browbeaten
build	built	built
burn	burned, burnt	burned, burnt
burst	burst	burst
bust	(*BrE*【英】) bust, (*especially AmE*【尤美】) busted	(*BrE*【英】) bust, (*especially AmE*【尤美】) busted
buy	bought	bought
can	*see dictionary entry* 见辞典内该条目	
cast	cast	cast
catch	caught	caught
chide	chided, chid	chided, chid, chidden
choose	chose	chosen
cleave	cleaved, cleft, clove	cleaved, cleft, cloven
cling	clung	clung
come	came	come
cost ①	cost	cost
could	*see dictionary entry* 见辞典内该条目	
creep	crept	crept
cut	cut	cut
deal	dealt /dɛlt; delt/	dealt

verb 动词	**past tense** 过去式	**past participle** 过去分词
dig	dug	dug
dive	dived, (*AmE*【美】) dove	dived
do	did	done
draw	drew	drawn
dream	dreamed, dreamt	dreamed, dreamt
drink	drank	drunk
drive	drove	driven
dwell	dwelt, dwelled	dwelt, dwelled
eat	ate	eaten
fall ②	fell	fallen
feed	fed	fed
feel	felt	felt
fight	fought	fought
find	found	found
flee	fled	fled
fling	flung	flung
fly	flew	flown
forbear	forbore	forborne
forbid	forbade	forbidden
forecast	forecast	forecast
foresee	foresaw	foreseen
foretell	foretold	foretold
forget	forgot	forgotten
forgive	forgave	forgiven
forego	forewent	foregone
forsake	forsook	forsaken
forswear	forswore	forsworn
freeze	froze	frozen
gainsay	gainsaid	gainsaid
get	got	got (also 又作 gotten *AmE*【美】)
gird	girded, girt	girded, girt
give	gave	given
go	went	gone
grind	ground	ground
grow	grew	grown
hamstring	hamstrung	hamstrung
hang	hung	hung
have	had	had
hear	heard	heard
heave	heaved, hove	heaved, hove
hew	hewed	hewn, hewed
hide	hid	hidden
hit	hit	hit
hold	held	held
hurt	hurt	hurt
input	inputted, input	inputted, input
inset	inset, insetted	inset, insetted
interbreed	interbred	interbred
interweave	interwove	interwoven
keep	kept	kept
kneel	knelt, (*especially AmE*【尤美】) kneeled	knelt, (*especially AmE*【尤美】) kneeled
knit	knitted, knit	knitted, knit
know	knew	known
lay ③	laid	laid
lead	led	led

verb 动词	**past tense** 过去式	**past participle** 过去分词
lean	leaned (also 又作 leant *especially BrE*【尤英】)	leaned (also 又作 leant *especially BrE*【尤英】)
leap	leapt, (*especially AmE*【尤美】) leaped	leapt, (*especially AmE*【尤美】) leaped
learn	learned, learnt	learned, learnt
leave	left	left
lend	lent	lent
let	let	let
lie ④	lay	lain
light	lit, lighted	lit, lighted
lose	lost	lost
make	made	made
may	*see dictionary entry* 见辞典内该条目	
mean	meant	meant
meet	met	met
might	*see dictionary entry* 见辞典内该条目	
miscast	miscast	miscast
mishear	misheard	misheard
mislay	mislaid	mislaid
mislead	misled	misled
misread	misread	misread
misspell	misspelt, misspelled	misspelt, misspelled
misspend	misspent	misspent
mistake	mistook	mistaken
misunderstand	misunderstood	misunderstood
mow	mowed	mown, mowed
outbid	outbid	outbid
outdo	outdid	outdone
outgrow	outgrew	outgrown
outride	outrode	outridden
outrun	outran	outrun
outsell	outsold	outsold
outshine	outshone	outshone
overbear	overbore	overborne
overcast	overcast	overcast
overcome	overcame	overcome
overdo	overdid	overdone
overdraw	overdrew	overdrawn
overeat	overate	overeaten
overhang	overhung	overhung
overhear	overheard	overheard
overlay	overlaid	overlaid
overload	overloaded	overloaded, overladen
overpay	overpaid	overpaid
override	overrode	overridden
overrun	overran	overrun
oversee	oversaw	overseen
oversell	oversold	oversold
overshoot	overshot	overshot
oversleep	overslept	overslept
overtake	overtook	overtaken
overthrow	overthrew	overthrown
partake	partook	partaken
pay	paid	paid
plead	pleaded, (*especially AmE*【尤美】) pled	pleaded, (*especially AmE*【尤美】) pled
pre-set	pre-set	pre-set

verb 动词	**past tense** 过去式	**past participle** 过去分词
proofread	proofread	proofread
prove	proved	proved (also 又作 proven *AmE*【美】)
put	put	put
quit	quit (also 又作 quitted *BrE*【英】)	quit (also 又作 quitted *BrE*【英】)
read	read /rɛd; red/	read /rɛd; red/
rebind	rebound	rebound
rebuild	rebuilt	rebuilt
recast	recast	recast
redo	redid	redone
relay	relaid	relaid
remake	remade	remade
rend	rent	rent
repay	repaid	repaid
rerun	reran	rerun
resell	resold	resold
reset	reset	reset
resit	resat	resat
retell	retold	retold
rethink	rethought	rethought
rewind	rewound	rewound
rewrite	rewrote	rewritten
rid	rid, ridded	rid
ride	rode	ridden
ring	rang	rung
rise	rose	risen
run	ran	run
saw	sawed	(*especially BrE*【尤英】) sawn, (*especially AmE*【尤美】) sawed
say	said	said
see ⑤	saw	seen
seek	sought	sought
sell	sold	sold
send	sent	sent
set	set	set
sew	sewed	sewn (also 又作 sewed *AmE*【美】)
shake	shook	shaken
shall	*see dictionary entry* 见辞典内该条目	
shear	sheared	shorn, sheared
shed	shed	shed
shine	shone	shone
shit	shit, shat	shit, shat
shoe	shod	shod
shoot	shot	shot
should	*see dictionary entry* 见辞典内该条目	
show	showed	shown
shrink	shrank	shrunk
shut	shut	shut
sing	sang	sung
sink	sank, sunk	sunk
sit	sat	sat
slay	slew	slain
sleep	slept	slept
slide	slid	slid
sling	slung	slung
slink	slunk	slunk
slit	slit	slit

verb 动词	**past tense** 过去式	**past participle** 过去分词
smell	(*especially BrE*【尤英】) smelt, (*especially AmE*【尤美】) smelled	(*especially BrE*【尤英】) smelt, (*especially AmE*【尤美】) smelled
smite	smote	smitten
sneak	sneaked (also 又作 snuck *AmE*【美】)	sneaked (also 又作 snuck *AmE*【美】)
sow	sowed	sown, sowed
speak	spoke	spoken
speed	sped, speeded	sped, speeded
spell	(*especially BrE*【尤英】) spelt, (*especially AmE*【尤美】) spelled	(*especially BrE*【尤英】) spelt, (*especially AmE*【尤美】) spelled
spend	spent	spent
spill	(*especially BrE*【尤英】) spilt, (*especially AmE*【尤美】) spilled	(*especially BrE*【尤英】) spilt, (*especially AmE*【尤美】) spilled
spin	spun	spun
spit	spat (also 又作 spit *AmE*【美】)	spat (also 又作 spit *AmE*【美】)
split	split	split
spoil	spoiled, spoilt	spoiled, spoilt
spoon-feed	spoon-fed	spoon-fed
spotlight	spotlighted, spotlit	spotlighted, spotlit
spread	spread	spread
spring	sprang (also 又作 sprung *AmE*【美】)	sprung
stand	stood	stood
steal	stole	stolen
stick	stuck	stuck
sting	stung	stung
stink	stank	stunk
strew	strewed	strewn, strewed
stride	strode	stridden
strike	struck	struck
string	strung	strung
strive	strove	striven
swear	swore	sworn
sweep	swept	swept
swell	swelled	swollen
swim	swam	swum
swing	swung	swung
take	took	taken
teach	taught	taught
tear	tore	torn
tell	told	told
think	thought	thought
thrive	thrived, throve	thrived
throw	threw	thrown
thrust	thrust	thrust
tread	trod	trodden
unbend	unbent	unbent
unbind	unbound	unbound
undergo	underwent	undergone
underlie	underlay	underlaid
undersell	undersold	undersold
understand	understood	understood
undertake	undertook	undertaken
underwrite	underwrote	underwritten
undo	undid	undone
unwind	unwound	unwound
uphold	upheld	upheld
upset	upset	upset

verb 动词	**past tense** 过去式	**past participle** 过去分词
wake	woke (also 又作 waked *AmE*【美】)	woken (also 又作 waked *AmE*【美】)
waylay	waylaid	waylaid
wear	wore	worn
weave	wove	woven
wed	wedded, wed	wedded, wed
weep	wept	wept
wet	wetted, wet	wetted, wet
will	*see dictionary entry* 见辞典内该条目	
win	won	won
wind ⑥ /waɪnd; waɪnd/	wound	wound
withdraw	withdrew	withdrawn
withhold	withheld	withheld
withstand	withstood	withstood
would	*see dictionary entry* 见辞典内该条目	
wreak	wreaked, wrought	wreaked, wrought
wring	wrung	wrung
write	wrote	written

注: ① 注意与规则动词 cost（估价）的不同: I've costed the work.（我已对工程估了价。）
② 汁意与规则动词 fell（砍伐）的不同: They've felled that tree.（他们已砍倒了那棵树。）
③ 注意现在式 lay (laid, laid) 不要与 lie (lay, lain) 的过去式混淆。
④ 注意与规则动词 lie（说谎）(lied, lied) 的不同: He lied to me.（他对我撒谎。）
⑤ 比较 see（看见）(saw, seen) 和 saw（锯）(sawed, sawn/sawed)。
⑥ 注意与规则动词 wind（使喘不过气）的不同: I was winded by the blow.（我被那拳打得喘不过气来。）

Table 7 附录 7

Geographical Names 地名

This list of geographical names is included to help advanced students in their reading of contemporary newspapers and magazines. 此地名表供高年级学生阅读当代报纸杂志使用。

Name 地名		Adjective 形容词
Afghanistan /æf`gænə,stæn; æf'gænɪ̩stɑːn/	阿富汗	Afghan /`æfgən; 'æfgæn/ *person* 人: Afghanistani /æf`gænə,stænɪ; æf,gænɪ̩'stɑːni/, Afghan
Africa /`æfrɪkə; 'æfrɪkə/	非洲	African /`æfrɪkən; 'æfrɪkən/
Alaska /ə`læskə; ə'læskə/	阿拉斯加	Alaskan /ə`læskən; ə'læskən/
Albania /æl`benɪə; æl'beɪniə/	阿尔巴尼亚	Albanian /æl`benɪən; æl'beɪniən/
Algeria /æl`dʒɪrɪə; æl'dʒɪəriə/	阿尔及利亚	Algerian /æl`dʒɪrɪən; æl'dʒɪəriən/
America /ə`mɛrɪkə; ə'merɪ̩kə/	美洲; 美国	American /ə`mɛrɪkən; ə'merɪ̩kən/
Andorra /æn`dɔrə; æn'dɔːrə/	安道尔	Andorran /æn`dɔrən; æn'dɔːrən/
Angola /æŋ`golə; æŋ'gəʊlə/	安哥拉	Angolan /æŋ`golən; æŋ'gəʊlən/
Antarctic /ænt`ɑrktɪk; æn'tɑːktɪk/	南极（地区）	Antarctic
Antigua /æn`tigə; æn'tiːgə/	安提瓜岛	Antiguan /æn`tigən; æn'tiːgən/
Arctic /`ɑrktɪk; 'ɑːktɪk/	北极（地区）	Arctic
Argentina /,ɑrdʒən`tinə; ,ɑːdʒən'tiːnə/	阿根廷	Argentinian /,ɑrdʒən`tɪnɪən; ,ɑːdʒən'tɪniən/
Armenia /ɑr`minɪə; ɑː'miːniə/	亚美尼亚	Armenian /ɑr`minɪən; ɑː'miːniən/
Asia /`eʃə; 'eɪʃə/	亚洲	Asian /`eʃən; 'eɪʃən/
Atlantic /ət`læntɪk; ət'læntɪk/	大西洋	Atlantic
Australia /ɔ`streljə; ɒ'streɪliə/	澳大利亚，澳洲	Australian /ɔ`streljən; ɒ'streɪliən/
Austria /`ɔstrɪə; 'ɒstriə/	奥地利	Austrian /`ɔstrɪən; 'ɒstriən/
Azerbaijan /,ɑzɚbaɪ`dʒɑn; ,æzəbaɪ'dʒɑːn/	阿塞拜疆	Azerbaijani /,ɑzɚbaɪ`dʒɑnɪ; ,æzəbaɪ'dʒɑːni◂/
Bahamas /bə`hɑməz; bə'hɑːməz/	巴哈马	Bahamian /bə`hemɪən; bə'heɪmiən/
Bahrain /bɑ`ren; bɑː'reɪn/	巴林	Bahraini /bɑ`renɪ; bɑː'reɪni/
Baltic /`bɔltɪk; 'bɔːltɪk/	波罗的海	Baltic
Bangladesh /`bæŋglə,dɛʃ; ,bæŋglə'deʃ/	孟加拉国	Bangladeshi *person* 人: Bangladeshi /`bæŋglə,dɛʃɪ; ,bæŋglə'deʃi/
Barbados /bɑr`bedoz; bɑː'beɪdɒs/	巴巴多斯	Barbadian /bɑr`bedɪən; bɑː'beɪdiən/
Belarus /,bjɛlə`rus; ,belə'ruːs/ (Belorussia) /,bɛlo`rʌʃə; ,beləʊ'rʌʃə/	白俄罗斯	Belorussian /,bɛlo`rʌʃən; ,beləʊ'rʌʃən/
Belgium /`bɛldʒɪəm; 'beldʒəm/	比利时	Belgian /`bɛldʒən; 'beldʒən/
Belize /bɛ`liz; bə'liːz/	伯利兹	Belizean /bɛ`lizɪən; bə'liːziən/
Benin /bə`nɪn; be'niːn/	贝宁	Beninese /,bɛnɪ`niz; ,benɪ'niːz◂/
Bermuda /bɚ`mjudə; bə'mjuːdə/	百慕大	Bermudan /bɚ`mjudn; bə'mjuːdn/
Bhutan /bu`tan; buː'tɑːn/	不丹	Bhutanese /,butə`niz; ,buːtə'niːz◂/
Bolivia /bə`lɪvɪə; bə'lɪviə/	玻利维亚	Bolivian /bə`lɪvɪən; bə'lɪviən/
Bosnia-Herzegovina /`bɑznɪə ,hɛtsəgo`vinə; ,bɒzniə ,hɜːtsəgəʊ'viːnə/	波斯尼亚和黑塞哥维那	Bosnian /`bɑznɪən; 'bɒzniən/
Botswana /bɑts`wɑnɑ; bɒt'swɑːnə/	博茨瓦纳	Tswana /`tswɑnə; 'tswɑːnə, 'swɑː-/ *person* 人: *sing.* 单数= Motswana /mɑt`swɑnə; mɒt'swɑːnə/ *pl.* 复数= Batswana /bæt`swɑnə; bæt'swɑːnə/

Name 地名		**Adjective** 形容词
Brazil /brə`zɪl; brə'zɪl/	巴西	Brazilian /brə`zɪljən; brə'zɪliən/
Brunei /bru`naɪ; 'bru:naɪ/	文莱	Bruneian /bru`naɪən; bru:'naɪən/
Bulgaria /bʌl`gɛrɪə; bʌl'geəriə/	保加利亚	Bulgarian /bʌl`gɛrɪən; bʌl'geəriən/
Burkina Faso /bur͵kinə `fæso; bɜ:͵ki:nə 'fæsəʊ/	布基纳法索	Burkina *person* 人: Burkinabe /͵burkinæ`be; ͵bɜ:ki:næ'beɪ/
Burma /`bɝmə; 'bɜ:mə/ former name of Myanmar	缅甸 〔Myanmar 的旧称〕	
Burundi /bə`rʌndɪ; bʊ'rʊndi/	布隆迪	Burundian /bə`rʌndɪən; bʊ'rʊndiən/
Cambodia /kæm`bodɪə; kæm'bəʊdiə/	柬埔寨	Cambodian /kæm`bodɪən; kæm'bəʊdiən/
Cameroon /͵kæmə`run; ͵kæmə'ru:n/	喀麦隆	Cameroonian /͵kæmə`runɪən; ͵kæmə'ru:niən◂/
Canada /`kænədə; 'kænədə/	加拿大	Canadian /kə`nedɪən; kə'neɪdiən/
Cape Verde /͵kep `vɝd; keɪp 'vɜ:d/	佛得角	Cape Verdean /͵kep`vɝdɪən; keɪp 'vɜ:diən/
Caribbean /͵kærə`biən; ͵kærɪ'bi:ən◂/	加勒比海	Caribbean
Cayman Islands /`kemən `aɪləndz; 'keɪmən ͵aɪləndz/	开曼群岛	Cayman Island /͵kemən `aɪlənd; ͵keɪmən 'aɪlənd◂/ *person* 人: Cayman Islander /͵kemən `aɪləndɚ; ͵keɪmən 'aɪləndə/
Central African Republic /͵sɛntrəl ͵æfrɪkən rɪ`pʌblɪk; ͵sentrəl ͵æfrɪkən rɪ'pʌblɪk/	中非共和国	
Chad /tʃæd; tʃæd/	乍得	Chadian /`tʃædɪən; 'tʃædiən/
Chile /`tʃɪlɪ; 'tʃɪli/	智利	Chilean /`tʃɪlɪən; 'tʃɪliən/
China /`tʃaɪnə; 'tʃaɪnə/	中国	Chinese /tʃaɪ`niz; ͵tʃaɪ'ni:z◂/
Colombia /kə`lʌmbɪə; kə'lʌmbiə/	哥伦比亚	Colombian /kə`lʌmbɪən; kə'lʌmbiən/
Congo /`kɑŋgo; 'kɒŋgəʊ/	刚果	Congolese /͵kɑŋgo`liz; ͵kɒŋgə'li:z◂/
Costa Rica /`kɑstə `rikə; ͵kɒstə 'ri:kə/	哥斯达黎加	Costa Rican /`kɑstə `rikṇ; ͵kɒstə 'ri:kən◂/
Croatia /kro`eʃə; krəʊ'eɪʃə/	克罗地亚	Croatian /kro`eʃən; krəʊ'eɪʃən/
Cuba /`kjubə; 'kju:bə/	古巴	Cuban /`kjubən; 'kju:bən/
Cyprus /`saɪprəs; 'saɪprəs/	塞浦路斯	Cypriot /`sɪprɪət; 'sɪpriət/
Czech Republic /͵tʃɛk rɪ`pʌblɪk; ͵tʃek rɪ'pʌblɪk/	捷克共和国	Czech /tʃɛk; tʃek/
Denmark /`dɛnmɑrk; 'denmɑ:k/	丹麦	Danish /`denɪʃ; 'deɪnɪʃ/ *person* 人: Dane /den; deɪn/
Djibouti /dʒɪ`butɪ; dʒɪ̵'bu:ti/	吉布提	Djiboutian /dʒə`butɪən; dʒɪ̵'bu:tiən/
Dominica /də`mɪnɪkə; ͵dɒmɪ̵'ni:kə/	多米尼克	Dominican /də`mɪnɪkən; ͵dɒmɪ̵'ni:kən◂/
Dominican Republic /də`mɪnɪkən rɪ`pʌblɪk; də͵mɪnɪkən rɪ'pʌblɪk/	多米尼加共和国	Dominican /də`mɪnɪkən; də'mɪnɪkən/
Ecuador /`ɛkwə͵dɔr; 'ekwədɔ:/	厄瓜多尔	Ecuadorian /͵ɛkwə`dɔrɪən; ͵ekwə'dɔ:riən◂/
Egypt /`idʒəpt; 'i:dʒɪpt/	埃及	Egyptian /ɪ`dʒɪpʃən; ɪ'dʒɪpʃən/
El Salvador /ɛl`sælvə͵dɔr; el 'sælvə͵dɔ:/	萨尔瓦多	Salvadorian /͵sælvə`dɔrɪən; ͵sælvə'dɔ:riən◂/
Equatorial Guinea /͵ikwə`torɪəl `gɪnɪ; ͵ekwətɔ:riəl 'gɪni/	赤道几内亚	Equatorial Guinean /͵ikwə`torɪəl `gɪnɪən; ͵ekwətɔ:riəl 'gɪniən/
Eritrea /͵ɛrɪ`triə; ͵erɪ'treɪə/	厄立特里亚	Eritrean /͵ɛrɪ`treən; ͵erɪ'treɪən◂/
Estonia /ɛ`stonɪə; e'stəʊniə/	爱沙尼亚	Estonian /ɛ`stonɪən; e'stəʊniən/
Ethiopia /͵iθɪ`opɪə; ͵i:θi'əʊpiə/	埃塞俄比亚	Ethiopian /͵iθɪ`opɪən; ͵i:θi'əʊpiən◂/
Europe /`jurəp; 'jʊərəp/	欧洲	European /͵jurə`piən; ͵jʊərə'pi:ən◂/
Fiji /`fidʒi; 'fi:dʒi:/	斐济	Fijian /fi`dʒiən; fi:'dʒi:ən/
Finland /`fɪnlənd; 'fɪnlənd/	芬兰	Finnish /`fɪnɪʃ; 'fɪnɪʃ/ *person* 人: Finn /fɪn; fɪn/
France /fræns; frɑ:ns/	法国	French /frɛntʃ; frentʃ/ *person* 人: *singular* 单数=Frenchman /`frɛntʃmən; 'frentʃmən/ (*feminine* 女性 -woman) /-͵wumən; -͵wʊmən/

Name 地名		Adjective 形容词
		plural 复数= Frenchmen /ˋfrɛntʃmən; ˈfrentʃmən/ *people* 人民: French
Gabon /gaˋbõ; gæˈbɒn/	加蓬	Gabonese /ˌgæbəˋniz; ˌgæbəˈniːz◂/
Gambia /ˋgæmbɪə; ˈgæmbiə/	冈比亚	Gambian /ˋgæmbɪən; ˈgæmbiən/
Georgia /ˋdʒɔrdʒə; ˈdʒɔːdʒə/	格鲁吉亚	Georgian /ˋdʒɔrdʒən; ˈdʒɔːdʒən/
Germany /ˋdʒɝmənɪ; ˈdʒɜːməni/	德国	German /ˋdʒɝmən; ˈdʒɜːmən◂/
Ghana /ˋgɑnə; ˈgɑːnə/	加纳	Ghanaian /gɑˋneɪən; gɑːˈneɪən/
Gibraltar /dʒɪˋbrɔltɚ; dʒɪˈbrɔːltə/	直布罗陀	Gibraltarian /dʒɪbrɔlˋtɛrɪən; ˌdʒɪbrɔːlˈteəriən/
Greece /gris; griːs/	希腊	Greek /grik; griːk/
Greenland /ˋgrinlənd; ˈgriːnlənd, -lænd/	格陵兰(岛)	Greenlandic /grinˋlændɪk; griːnˈlændɪk/ *person* 人: Greenlander /ˋgrinləndɚ; ˈgriːnləndə/
Grenada /grɪˋnedə; grəˈneɪdə/	格林纳达	Grenadian /grɪˋnedɪən; grəˈneɪdiən/
Guatemala /ˌgwɑtəˋmɑlə; ˌgwɑːtəˈmɑːlə/	危地马拉	Guatemalan /ˌgwɑtəˋmɑlən; ˌgwɑːtəˈmɑːlən◂/
Guiana /gɪˋɑnə; giˈɑːnə/	圭亚那(高原)	Guianan /gɪˋɑnən; giˈɑːnən/
Guinea /ˋgɪnɪ; ˈgɪni/	几内亚	Guinean /ˋgɪnɪən; ˈgɪniən/
Guinea-Bissau /ˌgɪnɪ bɪˋsau; ˌgɪni bɪˈsaʊ/	几内亚比绍	Guinea-Bissauan /ˌgɪnɪ bɪˋsauən; ˌgɪni bɪˈsaʊən/
Guyana /gaɪˋænə; gaɪˈænə/	圭亚那	Guyanese /gaɪæˋniz; ˌgaɪəˈniːz◂/
Haiti /ˋhetɪ; ˈheɪti/	海地	Haitian /ˋhetɪən; ˈheɪʃən/
Holland /ˋhɑlənd; ˈhɒlənd/ another name for 又作 The Netherlands	荷兰	Dutch /dʌtʃ; dʌtʃ/
Honduras /hɑnˋdurəs; hɒnˈdjʊərəs/	洪都拉斯	Honduran /hɑnˋdurən; hɒnˈdjʊərən/
Hungary /ˋhʌŋgrɪ; ˈhʌŋgəri/	匈牙利	Hungarian /hʌŋˋgɛrɪən; hʌŋˈgeəriən/
Iceland /ˋaɪslənd; ˈaɪslənd/	冰岛	Icelandic /aɪsˋlændɪk; aɪsˈlændɪk/ *person* 人: Icelander /ˋaɪsˌlændɚ; ˈaɪsləndə/
India /ˋɪndɪə; ˈɪndiə/	印度	Indian /ˋɪndɪən; ˈɪndiən/
Indonesia /ˌɪndoˋniʃə, -ʒə; ˌɪndəˈniːʒə, -ziə/	印度尼西亚	Indonesian /ˌɪndoˋniʃən, -zɪən; ˌɪndəˈniːʒən◂, -ziən◂/
Iran /ɪˋræn, iˋrɑn; ɪˈrɑːn, -æn/	伊朗	Iranian /ɪˋrenɪən; ɪˈreɪniən/
Iraq /ɪˋrɑk, ɪˋræk; ɪˈrɑːk, -æk/	伊拉克	Iraqi /ɪˋrɑkɪ; ɪˈrɑːki, -æki/
Irish Republic /ˌaɪrɪʃ rɪˋpʌblɪk; ˌaɪərɪʃ rɪˈpʌblɪk/	爱尔兰共和国	Irish /ˋaɪrɪʃ; ˈaɪərɪʃ/ *person* 人: *singular* 单数= Irishman /ˋaɪrɪʃmən; ˈaɪərɪʃmən/ (*feminine* 女性 -woman) /-ˌwʊmən; -ˌwʊmən/ *plural* 复数= Irishmen /ˋaɪrɪʃmən; ˈaɪərɪʃmən/ *people* 人民 : Irish
Israel /ˋɪzrɪəl; ˈɪzreɪl/	以色列	Israeli /ɪzˋrelɪ; ɪzˈreɪli/
Italy /ˋɪtḷɪ; ˈɪtəli/	意大利	Italian /ɪˋtæljən; ɪˈtæliən/
Ivory Coast /ˋaɪvərɪ kost; ˌaɪvəri ˈkəʊst/	象牙海岸	Ivorian /ˌaɪˋvɔrɪən; aɪˈvɔːriən/
Jamaica /dʒəˋmekə; dʒəˈmeɪkə/	牙买加	Jamaican /dʒəˋmekən; dʒəˈmeɪkən/
Japan /dʒəˋpæn; dʒəˈpæn/	日本	Japanese /ˌdʒæpəˋniz; ˌdʒæpəˈniːz◂/
Jordan /ˋdʒɔrdṇ; ˈdʒɔːdn/	约旦	Jordanian /dʒɔrˋdenɪən; dʒɔːˈdeɪniən/
Kazakhstan /ˌkɑzɑkˋstɑn; ˌkæzækˈstɑːn/	哈萨克斯坦	Kazakh /kəˋzæk; kəˈzæk, -ˈzɑːk/
Kenya /ˋkɛnjə, ˋkinjə; ˈkenjə, ˈkiː-/	肯尼亚	Kenyan /ˋkɛnjən, ˋkinjən; ˈkenjən, ˈkiː-/
Korea /kəˋriə; kəˈrɪə/, Democratic People's Republic of	朝鲜	North Korean /ˌnɔrθ kəˋriən; ˌnɔːθ kəˈrɪən/
Korea, Republic of	韩国	South Korean /ˌsauθ kəˋriən; ˌsaʊθ kəˈrɪən/
Kuwait /kuˋwaɪt; kʊˈweɪt/	科威特	Kuwaiti /kuˋwetɪ; kʊˈweɪti/
Laos /lauz; ˈlɑːɒs, laʊs/	老挝	Laotian /leˋoʃən; ˈlaʊʃən/
Latvia /ˋlætvɪə; ˈlætviə/	拉脱维亚	Latvian /ˋlætvɪən; ˈlætviən/
Lebanon /ˋlɛbənən; ˈlebənən/	黎巴嫩	Lebanese /ˌlɛbəˋniz; ˌlebəˈniːz◂/

Name 地名		**Adjective** 形容词
Lesotho /lə`sutu; lə'su:tu:/	莱索托	Sotho /`soto; 'su:tu:/ *person* 人: *singular* 单数= Mosotho /mə`sutu; mə'su:tu:/ *plural* 复数= Basotho /bə`sutu; bə'su:tu:/
Liberia /laɪ`bɪrɪə; laɪ'bɪəriə/	利比里亚	Liberian /laɪ`bɪrɪən; laɪ'bɪəriən/
Libya /`lɪbɪə; 'lɪbiə/	利比亚	Libyan /`lɪbɪən; 'lɪbiən/
Liechtenstein /`lɪktən,staɪn; 'lɪktənstaɪn/	列支敦士登	Liechtenstein *person* 人: Liechtensteiner /`lɪktən,staɪnɚ; 'lɪktənstaɪnə/
Lithuania /,lɪθju`enɪə; ,lɪθju'eɪniə/	立陶宛	Lithuanian /,lɪθju`enɪən; ,lɪθju'eɪniən◂/
Luxemburg /`lʌksəm,bɝg; 'lʌksəmbɜ:g/	卢森堡	Luxemburg *person* 人: Luxemburger /`lʌksəm,bɝgɚ; 'lʌksəmbɜ:gə/
Macedonia /,mæsə`donɪə; ,mæsɪ'dəʊniə/	马其顿	Macedonian /,mæsə`donɪən; ,mæsə'dəʊniən◂/
Madagascar /,mædə`gæskɚ; ,mædə'gæskə/	马达加斯加	Malagasy /,mælə`gæsɪ; ,mælə'gæsi◂/
Malawi /mɑ`lɑwi; mə'lɑ:wi/	马拉维	Malawian /mɑ`lɑwɪən; mə'lɑ:wiən/
Malaysia /mə`leʒə; mə'leɪziə/	马来西亚	Malaysian /mə`leʃən, -ʒən; mə'leɪziən/
Maldives /`mɔldivz; 'mɔ:ldi:vz/	马尔代夫	Maldivian /mɔl`dɪvɪən; mɔ:l'dɪviən/
Mali /`mɑlɪ; 'mɑ:li/	马里	Malian /`mɑlɪən; 'mɑ:liən/
Malta /`mɔltə; 'mɔ:ltə/	马耳他	Maltese /mɔl`tiz; ,mɔ:l'ti:z◂/
Marshall Islands /`mɑrʃəl ,aɪləndz; 'mɑ:ʃəl ,aɪləndz/	马绍尔群岛	Marshall Islander /`mɑrʃəl ,aɪləndɚ; ,mɑ:ʃəl 'aɪləndə/
Mauritania /,mɔrɪ`tenɪə; ,mɒrɪ'teɪniə/	毛里塔尼亚	Mauritanian /,mɔrɪ`tenɪən; ,mɒrɪ'teɪniən◂/
Mauritius /mɔ`rɪʃɪəs; mə'rɪʃəs, mɔ:-/	毛里求斯	Mauritian /mɔ`rɪʃɪən; mə'rɪʃən, mɔ:-/
Mediterranean /,mɛdətə`renɪən; ,medɪtə'reɪniən◂/	地中海	Mediterranean
Melanesia /,mɛlə`niʒə; ,melə'ni:ziə/	美拉尼西亚	Melanesian /,mɛlə`niʒən; ,melə'ni:ziən◂/
Mexico /`mɛksɪ,ko; 'meksɪkəʊ/	墨西哥	Mexican /`mɛksɪkən; 'meksɪkən/
Micronesia /,maɪkro`niʒə; ,maɪkrəʊ'ni:ziə/	密克罗尼西亚	Micronesian /,maɪkrə`niʒən; ,maɪkrəʊ'ni:ziən, -ʒən/
Moldova /mɑl`dovə; mɒl'dəʊvə/	摩尔多瓦	Moldovian /mɑl`dovɪən; mɒl'dəʊviən/
Monaco /`mɑnə,ko; 'mɒnəkəʊ/	摩纳哥	Monegasque /mɑnɪ`gæsk; ,mɒnɪ'gæsk◂/
Mongolia /mɑŋ`goljə; mɒŋ'gəʊliə/	蒙古	Mongolian /mɑŋ`golɪən; mɒŋ'gəʊliən/ *person* 人: Mongolian or 或 Mongol /`mɑŋgəl; 'mɒŋgɒl, -gəl/
Montserrat /,mɑntsə`ræt; ,mɒntse'ræt/	蒙特塞拉特岛	Montserratian /,mɑntsə`reʃən; ,mɒntse'reɪʃən◂/
Morocco /mə`rɑko; mə'rɒkəʊ/	摩洛哥	Moroccan /mə`rɑkən; mə'rɒkən/
Mozambique /,mozəm`bik; ,məʊzəm'bi:k/	莫桑比克	Mozambican /,mozəm`bikən; ,məʊzəm'bi:kən◂/
Myanmar /`mjænmɑr; 'mjænmɑ:/	缅甸	Burmese /bɝ`miz; ,bɜ:'mi:z◂/
Namibia /nə`mɪbɪə; nə'mɪbiə/	纳米比亚	Namibian /nə`mɪbɪən; nə'mɪbiən/
Nauru /nɑ`uru, nɑ`ru; nɑ:'u:ru:, nɑ:'ru:/	瑙鲁	Nauruan /,neɪə`ruən; nɑ:'u:ruən, nɑ:'ru:ən/
Nepal /nɪ`pɔl; nɪ'pɔ:l/	尼泊尔	Nepalese /,nɛpə`liz; ,nepə'li:z◂/
The Netherlands /ðə `nɛðɚləndz; ðə 'neðələndz/	荷兰	Dutch /dʌtʃ; dʌtʃ/ *person* 人: *singular* 单数= Dutchman /`dʌtʃmən; 'dʌtʃmən/ (*feminine* 女性 -woman) /-,wʊmən; -,wʊmən/ *plural* 复数= Dutchmen /`dʌtʃmən; 'dʌtʃmən/ *people* 人民：Dutch
New Zealand /nju`zilənd; nju:'zi:lənd/	新西兰	New Zealand, Maori /`maurɪ; 'maʊri/

Name 地名		Adjective 形容词
		person 人: New Zealander /nju `ziləndɚ; nju: 'zi:ləndə/
Nicaragua /ˌnɪkə`rɑgwə; ˌnɪkə'rægjuə/	尼加拉瓜	Nicaraguan /ˌnɪkə`rɑgwən; ˌnɪkə'rægjuən◂/
Niger /`naɪdʒɚ, ni`ʒɛə; 'naɪdʒə, ni:'ʒeə/	尼日尔	Nigerien /ni`ʒɛərɪən; ni:'ʒeəriən/
Nigeria /naɪ`dʒɪrɪə; naɪ'dʒɪəriə/	尼日利亚	Nigerian /naɪ`dʒɪrɪən; naɪ'dʒɪəriən/
Norway /`nɔrwe; 'nɔ:weɪ/	挪威	Norwegian /nɔr`widʒən; nɔ:'wi:dʒən/
Oman /o`mæn; əʊ'mɑ:n/	阿曼	Omani /o`mænɪ; əʊ'mɑ:ni/
Pacific /pə`sɪfɪk; pə'sɪfɪk/	太平洋	Pacific
Pakistan /ˌpɑkɪ`stɑn, ˌpækɪ`stæn; ˌpɑ:kɪ'stɑ:n, ˌpækɪ'stæn/	巴基斯坦	Pakistani /ˌpɑkɪ`stɑnɪ, ˌpækɪ`stɑnɪ; ˌpɑ:kɪ'stɑ:ni◂, ˌpæk-/
Palestine /`pæləsˌtaɪn; 'pæləstaɪn/	巴勒斯坦	Palestinian /ˌpæləs`tɪnɪən; ˌpælə'stɪniən/
Panama /ˌpænə`mɑ, `pænəˌmɑ; ˌpænə'mɑ:◂/	巴拿马	Panamanian /ˌpænə`menɪən; ˌpænə'meɪniən/
Papua New Guinea /ˌpæpjuə nju `gɪnɪ; ˌpæpuə nju: 'gɪni/	巴布亚新几内亚	Papuan /`pæpjuən; 'pæpuən/
Paraguay /`pærəˌgwe; 'pærəgwaɪ/	巴拉圭	Paraguayan /ˌpærə`gweən; ˌpærə'gwaɪən◂/
Persia /`pɝʒə; 'pɜ:ʃə, -ʒə/ former name of Iran	波斯〔伊朗的旧称〕	
Peru /pə`ru; pə'ru:/	秘鲁	Peruvian /pə`ruvɪən; pə'ru:viən/
Philippines /`fɪləˌpinz; 'fɪlᵻpi:nz/	菲律宾	Philippine /`fɪləˌpin; 'fɪlᵻpi:n/ *person* 人: Filipino /ˌfɪlə`pino; ˌfɪlᵻ'pi:nəʊ/
Poland /`polənd; 'pəʊlənd/	波兰	Polish /`polɪʃ; 'pəʊlɪʃ/ *person* 人: Pole /pol; pəʊl/
Polynesia /ˌpɑlə`niʒə; ˌpɒlɪ'ni:ziə/	波利尼西亚	Polynesian /ˌpɑlə`niʒən; ˌpɒlɪ'ni:ziən◂/
Portugal /`pɔrtʃəgl; 'pɔ:tʃʊgəl/	葡萄牙	Portuguese /`pɔrtʃəˌgiz; ˌpɔ:tʃʊ'gi:z◂/
Puerto Rico /ˌpwɛrtə`riko; ˌpwɜ:təʊ'ri:kəʊ/	波多黎各	Puerto Rican /ˌpwɛrtə`rikən; ˌpwɜ:təʊ'ri:kən/
Qatar /`kɑtɑr; kʌ'tɑ:/	卡塔尔	Qatari /`kɑtɑrɪ; kʌ'tɑ:ri/
Quebec /kwɪ`bɛk; kwɪ'bek/	魁北克	Quebecois /kwɪ`bɛkə; ˌkebe'kwɑ:/
Romania /ro`menjə; ru:'meɪniə/	罗马尼亚	Romanian /ro`menɪən; ru:'meɪniən/
Russia /`rʌʃə; 'rʌʃə/	俄罗斯	Russian /`rʌʃən; 'rʌʃən/
Rwanda /rʊ`ɑndə; ru'ændə/	卢旺达	Rwandan /rʊ`ɑndən; ru'ændən/
Saint Kitts-Nevis /sent ˌkɪts ənd `nivəs; sənt ˌkɪts ənd 'ni:vᵻs/	圣基茨和尼维斯	Kittitian /kə`tɪʃən; kᵻ'tɪʃən/ Nevisian /nə`vɪʒən; nᵻ'vɪziən/
Saint Lucia /sent `luʃə; sənt 'lu:ʃə/	圣卢西亚	Saint Lucian /sent `luʃən; sənt 'lu:ʃən/
Samoa /sə`moə; sə'məʊə/	萨摩亚	Samoan /sə`moən; sə'məʊən/
San Marino /sæn mə`rino; sæn mə'ri:nəʊ/	圣马利诺	Sanmarinese /ˌsænˌmærə`niz; ˌsænmærᵻ'ni:z/
São Tomé and Principe /ˌsaʊn təˌme ənd `prɪnsəpə; ˌsaʊn təˌmeɪ ənd 'prɪnsᵻpeɪ/	圣多美和普林西比	São Toméan /ˌsaʊn tə`meən; ˌsaʊn tə'meɪən/
Saudi Arabia /sə`udɪ ə`rebɪə; ˌsaʊdi ə'reɪbiə/	沙特阿拉伯	Saudi Arabian /sə`udɪ ə`rebɪən; ˌsaʊdi ə'reɪbiən/ *person* 人: Saudi or 或 Saudi Arabian
Senegal /ˌsɛnɪ`gɔl; ˌsenɪ'gɔ:l/	塞内加尔	Senegalese /ˌsɛnɪgə`liz; ˌsenɪgə'li:z◂/
Seychelles /se`ʃɛlz; seɪ'ʃelz/	塞舌尔	Seychellois /seʃɛl`wɑ; ˌseɪʃel'wɑ:◂/
Sierra Leone /sɪ`ɛrə lɪ`onɪ; siˌerə li'əʊn/	塞拉利昂	Sierra Leonean /sɪ`ɛrə lɪ`onɪən; siˌerə li'əʊniən/
Singapore /`sɪŋgəˌpor; ˌsɪŋə'pɔ:/	新加坡	Singaporean /ˌsɪŋgə`porɪən; ˌsɪŋə'pɔ:riən◂/
Slovak Republic /ˌslovɑk rɪ`pʌblɪk; ˌsləʊvæk rɪ'pʌblɪk/	斯洛伐克共和国	Slovak /`slovæk; 'sləʊvæk/
Slovenia /slo`vinɪə; sləʊ'vi:niə/	斯洛文尼亚	Slovene /slo`vɪn; 'sləʊvi:n/ *person* 人: Slovenian /slo`vinɪən; sləʊ'vi:niən/
Solomon Islands /`sɑləmən ˌaɪləndz; 'sɒləmən ˌaɪləndz/	所罗门群岛	Solomon Islander /ˌsɑləmən `aɪləndɚ; ˌsɒləmən 'aɪləndə/

Name 地名		**Adjective** 形容词
Somalia /sə`mɑlɪə; səʊ'mɑːliə/	索马里	Somali /so`mɑlɪ; səʊ'mɑːli/
South Africa /saʊθ `æfrɪkə; saʊθ 'æfrɪkə/	南非	South African /saʊθ `æfrɪkən; saʊθ 'æfrɪkən/
Spain /spen; speɪn/	西班牙	Spanish /`spænɪʃ; 'spænɪʃ/ *person* 人: Spaniard /`spænjɚd; 'spænjəd/
Sri Lanka /ˌsrɪ`læŋkə; sriː 'læŋkə/	斯里兰卡	Sri Lankan /ˌsrɪ `læŋkən; sriː 'læŋkən/
Sudan /su`dæn; sʊ'dæn, -'dɑːn/	苏丹	Sudanese /ˌsudə`niz; ˌsuːdə'niːz◂/
Surinam /ˌsurɪ`nɑm; ˌsʊərɪ̩'næm/	苏里南	Surinamese /ˌsurɪnɑ`mis; ˌsʊərɪ̩nə'miːz◂/ *person* 人: Surinamer /`surɪˌnæmɚ; ˌsʊərɪ̩'nɑːmə/
Swaziland /`swɑzɪˌlænd; 'swɑːzilænd/	斯威士兰	Swazi /`swɑzɪ; 'swɑːzi/
Sweden /`swidn̩; 'swiːdn/	瑞典	Swedish /`swidɪʃ; 'swiːdɪʃ/ *person* 人: Swede /swid; swiːd/
Switzerland /`swɪtsɚlənd; 'swɪtsələnd/	瑞士	Swiss /swɪs; swɪs/
Syria /`sɪrɪə; 'sɪriə/	叙利亚	Syrian /`sɪrɪən; 'sɪriən/
Tahiti /tɑ`hitɪ; tə'hiːti/	塔希提岛	Tahitian /tɑ`hitɪən; tə'hiːʃən/
Tajikistan /tɑˌdʒikɪ`stɑn; tɑːˌdʒiːkɪ'stɑːn/	塔吉克斯坦	Tajik /tɑ`dʒik; tɑː'dʒiːk/
Tanzania /ˌtænzə`niə; ˌtænzə'nɪə/	坦桑尼亚	Tanzanian /ˌtænzə`niən; ˌtænzə'nɪən◂/
Thailand /`taɪlənd; 'taɪlænd, -lənd/	泰国	Thai /taɪ; taɪ/
Timor, East /ˌist `timor; ˌiːst 'tiːmɔː/	东帝汶	Timorese /ˌtimo`rɪz; ˌtiːmɔː'riːz◂/
Togo /`togo; 'təʊgəʊ/	多哥	Togolese /ˌtogo`liz; ˌtəʊgə'liːz◂/
Tonga /`tɑŋgə; 'tɒŋgə/	汤加	Tongan /`tɑŋgən; 'tɒŋgən/
Trinidad and Tobago /`trɪnəˌdæd ənd tə`bego; ˌtrɪnɪdæd ən tə'beɪgəʊ/	特立尼达和多巴哥	Trinidadian /`trɪnəˌdædɪən; ˌtrɪnɪ̩'dædiən◂/ Tobagonian /ˌtobə`gonɪən; ˌtəʊbə'gəʊniən/
Tunisia /tju`nɪʃə; tjuː'nɪziə/	突尼斯	Tunisian /tju`nɪʃɪən; tjuː'nɪziən/
Turkey /`tɝkɪ; 'tɜːki/	土耳其	Turkish /`tɝkɪʃ; 'tɜːkɪʃ/ *person* 人: Turk /tɝk; tɜːk/
Turkmenistan /ˌtɝkmɛnɪ`stæn; ˌtɜːkmenɪ̩'stɑːn/	土库曼斯坦	Turkmen /`tɝkmɛn; 'tɜːkmən/
Uganda /ju`gændə; juː'gændə/	乌干达	Ugandan /ju`gændən; juː'gændən/
Ukraine /`jukren, ju`kren; juː'kreɪn/	乌克兰	Ukranian /ju`krenɪən; juː'kreɪniən/
United Arab Emirates /ju`naɪtɪd `ærəb ə`mɪrɪts; juːˌnaɪtɪ̩d ˌærəb 'emɪrɪ̩ts/	阿拉伯联合酋长国	Emirian /ə`mɪrɪən; e'mɪəriən/
United Kingdom of Great Britain and Northern Ireland /ju`naɪtɪd `kɪŋdəm əf gret ˌbrɪtən ənd ˌnɔrðɚn `aɪrlənd; juːˌnaɪtɪ̩d 'kɪŋdəm əv greɪt ˌbrɪtən ənd ˌnɔːðən 'aɪələnd/	大不列颠及北爱尔兰联合王国, 英国	British /`brɪtɪʃ; 'brɪtɪʃ/ *person* 人: Briton /`brɪtən; 'brɪtən/, *AmE*【美】Britisher /`brɪtɪʃɚ; 'brɪtɪʃə/ *people* 人民: British
England /`ɪŋglənd; 'ɪŋglənd/	英格兰	English /`ɪŋglɪʃ; 'ɪŋglɪʃ/ *person* 人: *singular* 单数= Englishman /`ɪŋglɪʃmən; 'ɪŋglɪʃmən/ (*feminine* 女性 -woman) /-ˌwumən; -ˌwʊmən/; *plural* 复数= Englishmen /`ɪŋglɪʃmən; 'ɪŋglɪʃmən/ *people* 人民: English
Scotland /`skɑtlənd; 'skɒtlənd/	苏格兰	Scottish /`skɑtɪʃ; 'skɒtɪʃ/ or 或 Scots /skɑts; skɒts/ *person* 人: *singular* 单数= Scot or 或 Scotsman /`skɑtsmən; 'skɒtsmən/ (*feminine* 女性 -woman) /-ˌwumən; -ˌwʊmən/; *plural* 复数= Scotsmen /`skɑtsmən; 'skɒtsmən/ *people* 人民 : Scots

Name 地名		**Adjective** 形容词
Wales /welz; weɪlz/	威尔士	Welsh /wɛlʃ; welʃ/ *person* 人: *singular* 单数= Welshman /ˋwɛlʃmən; ˈwelʃmən/ (*feminine* 女性 -woman) /-ˌwʊmən; -ˌwʊmən/; *plural* 复数= Welshmen /ˋwɛlʃmən; ˈwelʃmən/ *people* 人民: Welsh
United States /juˋnaɪtɪd ˌstets; juːˌnaɪtᵻd ˈsteɪts/	美利坚合众国, 美国	American /əˋmɛrɪkən; əˈmerᵻkən/, US *person* 人: American /əˋmɛrɪkən; əˈmerᵻkən/
Upper Volta /ˋʌpɚ ˋvɑltə; ˌʌpəˈvɒltə/ former name of Burkina Faso	上沃尔特〔布基纳法索的旧称〕	
Uruguay /ˋjʊrəˌgwe; ˈjʊərəgwaɪ/	乌拉圭	Uruguayan /ˌjurəˋgweən; ˌjʊərəˈgwaɪən◂/
Uzbekistan /uzˌbɛkɪˋstæn; ʊzˌbekᵻˈstɑːn/	乌兹别克斯坦	Uzbek /ˋʊzbɛk; ˈʊzbek/
Vanuatu /ˌvænuˋɑtu; ˌvænuˈɑːtuː/	瓦努阿图	Vanuatuan /ˌvænuˋɑtuən; ˌvænuˈɑːtuən/
Venezuela /ˌvɛnəˋzwilə; ˌvenᵻˈzweɪlə/	委内瑞拉	Venezuelan /ˌvɛnəˋzwilən; ˌvenᵻˈzweɪlən◂/
Vietnam /ˌviɛtˋnɑm; ˌvjetˈnæm/	越南	Vietnamese /viˌɛtnɑˋmiz; ˌvjetnəˈmiːz◂/
West Samoa /wɛst səˋmoə; ˌwest səˈməʊə/	西萨摩亚	Samoan /səˋmoən; səˈməʊən/
Yemen /ˋjɛmən; ˈjemən/	也门	Yemeni /ˋjɛmənɪ; ˈjeməni/
Zaire /zəˋirə; zaɪˈɪə/	扎伊尔	Zairean /ˌzəˋirən; zaɪˈɪəriən/
Zambia /ˋzæmbɪə; ˈzæmbiə/	赞比亚	Zambian /ˋzæmbɪən; ˈzæmbiən/
Zimbabwe /zɪmˋbɑbwe; zɪmˈbɑːbweɪ/	津巴布韦	Zimbabwean /zɪmˋbɑbweən; zɪmˈbɑːbweɪən/

Table 8 附录 8

The Longman Defining Vocabulary 朗文释义词汇

The Longman Defining Vocabulary of around 2,000 common words has been used to write all the definitions in this dictionary. The words in the Defining Vocabulary have been carefully chosen to ensure that the definitions are clear and easy to understand, and that the words used in explanations are easier than the words being defined. Words in the Defining Vocabulary have been checked to make sure that they are frequent in the Longman Corpus Network, and that they are used correctly by learners in the Longman Learner's Corpus. Over 200 students took part in tests for this new dictionary, to check that they understood the definitions and could find the correct translation in their own language for words used. 本辞典采用包含大约 2,000 个常用词的朗文释义词汇编写所有释义。这些词语都经过精心挑选，以保证释义清楚易懂，释义用词比被解释的词容易。释义词汇中的词都经过核对，以确保这些词都是朗文语料库网络中使用频率高的词，而且是朗文学习语料库中学习者正确使用的词。有 200 多名学生参加了这部新辞典的测试，以检查他们理解释义，及他们能否把释义词汇正确地译成母语。

We have also used a special computer program that checks every entry to make sure that words from outside the defining vocabulary have not been used. 我们还使用了专门的电脑程序核对每一个词条，以确保没有使用释义词汇以外的词。

The words listed below are the main forms which are used in definitions. However, there are other limits on which word forms and meanings may be used. 下表列出的词是释义中使用的主要形式。然而，在词形和可能使用的词义方面还有其他的限制.

Word meanings 词义

The definitions only use the most common and 'central' meanings of the words in the list. 释义词汇表中的词在释义时只取其最常用、最核心的词义。

Word classes 词类

For some words in the list, a word class label such as *n* or *adj* is shown. This means that this particular word is used in definitions only in the word class shown. So **anger**, for example, is used only as a noun and not as a verb. 释义词汇表中有些词标注了词类，如 *n, adj* 等，表示这个特定的词只以标注的词性用于释义。例如 anger 只用作名词，而不用作动词。

Phrasal verbs 短语动词

Phrasal verbs are not used in definitions, except for the ones included in the list. Other phrasal verbs which are common in English and could be formed from words in the Defining Vocabulary list (such as **put up with**) are not used. 除了释义词汇表中的短语动词外，本辞典在释义中不使用短语动词。其他在英语中常见的而且能从释义词汇表中的词构成的短语动词（如 put up with）一律不采用。

Prefixes and suffixes 前缀和后缀

Some words on the list may have prefixes (like **un-**) or suffixes (like **-ly**) added to them to make different word forms in the definition. The list of these affixes is included at the end of the Defining Vocabulary list. The forms which are common, or which change their meaning when a prefix or suffix is added, (such as **acceptable** and **agreement**) are included in the full list. 部分释义词汇表中的词可能会加上前缀（如 un-）或后缀（如 -ly）构成释义中不同的词形。这些词缀列成表附在释义词汇表之后。那些常见的形式，或加上词缀后意义有改变的词（如 acceptable 和 agreement），则列于释义词汇表之中。

Proper names 专有名词

The Defining Vocabulary does not include the names of actual places, nationalities, religions, and so on, which are occasionally mentioned in definitions. 释义词汇不包括实际地方、国籍、宗教等的名称，尽管释义中有时会提到这类词。

Words not in the Defining Vocabulary 释义词汇以外的词

It is sometimes necessary or helpful to use a word that is not in the Defining Vocabulary. These are shown in SMALL CAPITAL LETTERS, and sometimes followed by an explanation in brackets. 有时有必要使用释义词汇以外的词，这些词用小号大写字母表示，有时还附有解释（置于括号中）。

insider trad·ing /ˌ·ˌ··ˈ··/ also 又作 **insider dealing** *n* [U] illegal buying and selling of a company's shares (SHARE² (5)) involving the use of secret information known only by people connected with the company〔股票的〕内幕交易，内线交易〔指利用秘密的内幕消息非法买卖一家公司的股票〕

Sometimes a definition includes a word which has its own entry and definition very close by. This word is written in ordinary type, even if it is not in the defining vocabulary. For example 有时释义中包含一个本身的词条和释义就在附近的词, 这个词用普通字体书写, 即使它不在释义词汇之中。例如:

in·sin·u·a·tion /ɪnˌsɪnjuˈeʃən; ɪnˌsɪnjuˈeɪʃən/ *n* **1** [C] something that someone insinuates 影射, 暗示: *the insinuation that they did not know how to run their own business* 关于他们经营无方的暗示 **2** [U] the act of insinuating something 暗示, 暗指

The word **insinuate** is not in the special list of defining words, but its own definition is only one entry away, so it can be found very easily. insinuate 这个词不在这个专门的释义词汇表之中, 但它本身的释义只有一个词条之隔, 因此很容易就能查到。

Example sentences 例句

The example sentences in this dictionary are not written using only the Defining Vocabulary. They are based on corpus evidence, and show the ways in which a word or phrase is used in a natural, typical context. However, care has been taken to make sure that these examples are helpful to the student. Where necessary, changes have been made to sentences found on corpus, or new examples have been written, to show the uses found on corpus in a simpler form. 本辞典中的例句不限于使用释义词汇, 而是以语料库中的证据为基础, 说明词或短语在自然、典型的语境中是如何使用的。然而我们注意确保这些例句对学生是有帮助的。必要时我们对语料库中的句子进行了改写, 或编写了新的例句, 以较简单的形式表示某词在语料库中的用法。

A
abbreviation
ability
able
about
above *adv, prep*
abroad
absence
absent *adj*
accept
acceptable
accident
accidental
according (to)
account *n*
achieve
achievement
acid
across
act
action
active
activity
actor, actress
actual
actually
add
addition
additional
address
adjective
admiration
admire
admit
adult
advanced
advantage
adventure *n*
adverb
advertise
advertisement
advice
advise
affair
affect
afford
afraid
after *adv, conj, prep*
afternoon
afterwards
again
against
age *n*
ago
agree
agreement
ahead
aim
air *n*
aircraft
airport
alcohol
alive
all *adv, pron, determiner, predeterminer*
allow
almost
alone
along
alphabet
already
also
although
always
among
amount *n*
amuse
amusement
amusing
an
ancient *adj*
and
anger *n*
angle *n*
angry
animal
announce
annoy
annoying
another
answer
anxiety
anxious
any
anyone
anything
anywhere
apart
apartment
appear
appearance
apple
approval
approve
area
argue
argument
arm *n*
army
around
arrange
arrangement
arrival
arrive
art
article
artificial
as
as opposed to
ashamed
ask
asleep
association
at
atom
attack
attempt
attend
attention
attitude
attract
attractive
authority
autumn
available
average *adj, n*
avoid
awake *adj*
away *adv*
awkward

B
baby
back *adj, adv, n*
background
backward(s) *adv*
bad
bag *n*
bake *v*
balance
ball *n*
band *n*
bank *n*
bar *n*
base *n, v*
basic
basket
bath *n*
battle *n*
be
beach *n*
beak
beam *n*
bean
bear
beat
beautiful
beauty
because
become
bed
beer
before
begin
beginning
behave
behaviour
behind *adv, prep*
belief
believe
bell
belong
below
belt *n*
bend
beneath
beside(s)
best
better *adj, adv*
between
beyond *adj, adv*
bicycle *n*
big *adj*
bill
bird
birth
bit
bite
bitter *adj*
black *adj, n*
blade
blame
blind *adj*
block
blood
blow
blue
board *n*
boat
body
boil
bomb
bone *n*
book *n*
boot *n*
border *n*
bored
boring
born
borrow
both
bottle *n*
bottom *n*
bowl *n*
box *n*
boy
brain *n*
branch *n*
brave *adj*
bread
break *v*
breakfast *n*
breast
breath
breathe
breed
brick
bridge *n*
bright
bring
broad *adj*
broadcast *v*
brother
brown *adj, n*
brush
build *v*
building
bullet
burn
burst *v*
bury
bus
bush
business
busy
but *conj*
butter *n*
button *n*
buy *v*
by *prep*

C
cake *n*
calculate
call *v*
calm *adj*
camera
camp *n,v*
can
cap
capital
car
card
care
careful
careless
carriage
carry
case *n*
castle
cat
catch *v*
cattle
cause
ceiling
celebrate
cell
central
centre *n*
century
ceremony
certain *adj, determiner*
chain *n*
chair *n*
chance *n*
change
character
charge
chase *v*
cheap
cheat *v*
check
cheek *n*
cheerful
cheese
chemical
chemistry
cheque
chest
chicken
chief
child
children
chin
chocolate
choice *n*
choose
church *n*
cigarette
cinema
circle *n*
circular *adj*
citizen
city
claim *v*
class *n*
clay
clean *adj, v*
clear *adj, v*
clever
cliff
climb *v*
clock *n*
close *adj, adv, v*
cloth
clothes
clothing
cloud *n*
club *n*
coal
coast *n*
coat *n*
coffee
coin *n*
cold *adj, n*
collar *n*
collect *v*
college
colour
comb
combination
combine *v*
come
comfort
comfortable
command
committee
common *adj*
communicate
communication
company
compare *v*
comparison
compete
competition
competitor
complain
complaint
complete
completely
complicated
compound *n*
computer
concern *v*
concerning
concert
condition *n*
confidence
confident
confuse
confusing
connect
connection
conscious
consider
consist
contain
container
continue
continuous
contract *n*
control
conversation
cook *n,v*
copy
corn
corner *n*
correct *adj, v*
cost
cotton
cough
could
council *n*
count *v*
country *n*
countryside
courage
course *n*
court *n*
cover
cow *n*
crack *n, v*
crash *n, v*
crazy
cream *n*
creature
crime
criminal
criticism
criticize
crop *n*
cross *n, v*
crowd
cruel
crush *v*
cry
cup *n*
cupboard
cure

curl
current *n*
curtain *n*
curve
custom *n*
customer
cut
cycle *v*

D

daily *adj, adv*
damage
dance
danger
dangerous
dark
date *n*
daughter
day
dead *adj*
deal *n*
deal with
death
debt
decay
deceive
decide
decision
decorate
decoration
decrease
deep *adj*
defeat
defence
defend
definite
definitely
degree
delay
deliberate *adj*
deliberately
delicate
deliver
demand
department
depend
dependent
depth
describe
description
desert *n*
deserve
design
desirable
desire
desk
destroy
destruction
detail *n*
determination
determined
develop
dictionary
die *v*
difference
different
difficult
difficulty
dig *v*
dinner
direct
direction
dirt
dirty *adj*
disappoint
disappointing
discover
discovery
discuss
discussion
disease *n*
dish *n*
dismiss
distance
distant
divide
do *v*
doctor *n*
document *n*
dog *n*
dollar
door
double *adj, v, predeterminer*
doubt
down *adv, prep*
draw *v*
drawer
dream
dress *n, v*
drink
drive *n, v*
drop
drug *n*
drum *n*
drunk *past participle, adj*
dry
duck *n*
dull *adj*
during
dust *n*
duty

E

each
eager
ear
early
earn
earth *n*
east
eastern
easy *adj*
eat
economic
edge *n*
educate
educated
education
effect *n*
effective
effort
egg
eight
either
elbow
elect *v*
election
electric
electricity
electronic
else
embarrass
embarrassing
emotion
emphasize
employ *v*
employer
employment
empty *adj, v*
enclose
encourage
end
enemy
energy
engine
engineer *n*
enjoy
enjoyable
enjoyment
enough
enter
entertain
entertainment
entrance *n*
envelope
environment
equal *adj, n*
equipment
escape
especially
establish
even *adj, adv*
evening
event
ever
every
everyone
everything
everywhere
evil
exact *adj*
exactly
examination
examine
example
excellent
except *conj, prep*
exchange
excite
exciting
excuse
exercise
exist
existence
expect
expensive
experience
explain
explanation
explode
explosion
explosive
express *v*
expression
extreme *adj*
extremely
eye

F

face
fact
factory
fail *v*
failure
fair *adj*
fairly
faith
faithful *adj*
fall
false
familiar
family
famous
far
farm
farmer
fashion *n*
fashionable
fast *adj, adv*
fasten
fat
father *n*
fault *n*
favourable
favourite *adj*
fear *n*
feather *n*
feature *n*
feed *v*
feel *v*
feeling(s)
female
fence *n*
fever
few
field *n*
fifth
fight
figure *n*
fill *v*
film
final *adj*
finally
financial
find *v*
find out
fine *adj*
finger *n*
finish *v*
fire
firm *adj*
first *adj, determiner*
fish
fit *adj, v*
five
fix *v*
flag *n*
flame *n*
flash *n, v*
flat *adj*
flesh
flight
float *v*
flood
floor *n*
flour *n*
flow
flower *n*
fly *n, v*
fold
follow
fond
food
foot *n*
football
for *prep*
force
foreign
foreigner
forest *n*
forget
forgive
fork *n*
form
formal
former
fortunate
forward(s) *adv*
four(th)
frame *n*
free
freedom
freeze *v*
frequent *adj*
fresh
friend
friendly
frighten
frightening
from
front *adj, n*
fruit *n*
full *adj*
fun
funeral
funny
fur *n*
furniture
further *adj, adv*
future

G

gain *v*
game *n*
garage *n*
garden
gas *n*
gate
gather *v*
general *adj*
generally
generous
gentle
gentleman
get
gift
girl
give *v*
glad
glass *adj, n*
glue
go *v*
goat
god
gold
good
goodbye
goods
govern
government
graceful
gradual
grain
gram
grammar
grand *adj*
grandfather
grandmother
grandparent
grass *n*
grateful
grave *n*
great *adj*
green
greet
greeting
grey *adj, n*
ground *n*
group *n*
grow
growth
guard *v*
guess *v*
guest *n*
guide
guilty
gun *n*

H

habit
hair
half
hall
hammer *n*
hand *n*
handle
hang *v*
happen *v*
happy
hard
hardly
harm
harmful
hat
hate *v*
hatred
have
he
head *n*
health
healthy
hear
heart
heat
heaven
heavy *adj*
heel *n*
height
hello
help
helpful
her(s)
here
herself
hide *v*
high *adj, adv*
hill
him
himself
his
historical
history
hit
hold *v*
hole
holiday *n*
hollow *adj*
holy
home *adv, n*

honest
honour *n*
hook *n*
hope
hopeful
horn
horse *n*
hospital
hot *adj*
hotel
hour
house *n*
how *adv*
human
humorous
humour
hundred(th)
hungry
hunt *v*
hurry
hurt *v*
husband *n*

I

ice *n*
idea
if
ignore
ill *adj*
illegal
illness
image
imaginary
imagination
imagine
immediately
importance
important
impressive
improve
improvement
in *adv, prep*
include
including
income
increase
independent
indoor(s)
industrial
industry
infect
infection
infectious
influence *v*
inform
information
injure
injury
ink *n*
inner
insect
inside
instead
institution
instruction
instrument
insult *v*
insulting
insurance
insure
intelligence
intelligent
intend
intention
interest
interesting
international *adj*
interrupt
into
introduce
introduction
invent
invitation
invite *v*
involve
inwards
iron *adj, n*
island
it *pron*
its

J

jaw
jewel
jewellery
job
join
joint
joke
journey *n*
judge
judgement
juice
jump
just *adv*
justice

K

keen
keep *v*
key *n*
kick
kill *v*
kilo
kilogram
kilometre
kind
king
kiss
kitchen
knee *n*
kneel
knife *n*
knock *v*
knot
know *v*
knowledge

L

lack
lady
lake
lamb
lamp
land
language
large
last *adv, determiner*
late
lately
laugh
laughter
law
lawyer
lay *v*
layer *n*
lazy
lead *v*
leaf *n*
lean *v*
learn
least
leather
leave *v*
left
leg *n*
legal
lend
length *adv, pron, determiner*
less
lesson
let *v*
let go of
letter
level *adv, adj, n*
library
lid
lie
lie down
life
lift
light
like *prep, v*
likely
limit
line *n*
lion
lip
liquid
list *n*
listen *v*
literature
litre
little
live *v*
load
local *adj*
lock
lonely
long *adj, adv*
look
look after
look for
look sth up
loose *adj*
lord *n*
lose
loss
lot
loud
love
low *adj*
lower
loyal
loyalty
luck *n*
lucky
lung

M

machine *n*
machinery
magazine
magic
mail
main *adj*
make *v*
make into
make up *v*
male
man *n*
manage
manager
manner
many
map *n*
march *v*
mark
market *n*
marriage
married
marry
mass *n*
match
material *n*
mathematics
matter
may *v*
me
meal
mean *v*
meaning *n*
means
measure
measurement
meat
medical *adj*
medicine
meet *v*
meeting
melt
member
memory
mental
mention *v*
message
metal *n*
method
metre
middle
might *v*
mile
military *adj*
milk *n*
million(th)
mind
mine *n, pron*
mineral
minister *n*
minute *n*
mirror *n*
miss *v*
mist *n*
mistake *n*
mix *v*
mixture
model *n*
modern *adj*
moment
money
monkey *n*
month
moon *n*
moral *adj*
more
morning
most
mother *n*
motor *adj, n*
mountain
mouse
mouth *n*
move *v*
movement
much
mud
multiply
murder
muscle *n*
music
musician
must *v*
my
mysterious
mystery

N

nail
name
narrow *adj*
nasty
nation
national *adj*
natural *adj*
nature
navy
near *adj, adv, prep*
nearly
neat
necessary
neck
need
needle *n*
negative *adj*
neither
nerve *n*
nervous
net *n*
network *n*
never
new
news
newspaper
next *adj, adv*
nice
night
nine
ninth
no *adv, determiner*
noise *n*
none *pron*
nonsense
no one
nor
normal
north
northern
nose *n*
not
note *n*
nothing
notice
noticeable
noun
now
nowhere
number *n*
nurse
nut

O

obey
object *n*
obtain
occasion *n*
ocean
o'clock
of
off *adv, prep*
offence
offend
offensive *adj*
offer
office
officer
official
often
oil *n*
old
old-fashioned
on *adv, prep*
once *adv*
one
onion
only
only just
onto
open *adj, v*
operate
operation
opinion
opponent
opportunity
oppose
as opposed to
opposite
opposition
or
orange
order
ordinary
organ
organise
organization
origin
original
other
ought
our(s)
out *adj, adv*
outdoor(s)
outer
outside
over *adv, prep*
owe
own
owner
oxygen

P

pack *v*
package
page *n*
pain *n*
painful
paint
painting
pair *n*

pale *adj*
pan *n*
paper *n*
parallel *adj, n*
parent
park
parliament
part *n*
participle
particular *adj*
partly
partner *n*
party *n*
pass *v*
passage
passenger
past
path
patient *adj*
pattern *n*
pause
pay
payment
peace
peaceful
pen *n*
pence
pencil *n*
people *n*
pepper *n*
per cent
perfect *adj*
perform
performance
perhaps
period *n*
permanent
permission
person
personal
persuade
pet *n*
petrol
photograph
phrase *n*
physical *adj*
piano *n*
pick *v*
pick up
picture *n*
piece *n*
pig *n*
pile *n*
pilot *n*
pin
pink *adj, n*
pipe *n*
pity
place
plain *adj, n*
plan
plane *n*
plant
plastic
plate *n*
play
pleasant
please
pleased
pleasure *n*
plenty *pron*
plural
pocket *n*
poem
poet
poetry
point
pointed
poison
poisonous
pole *n*
police *n*
polish *v*
polite
political
politician
politics
pool *n*
poor
popular
population
port *n*
position *n*
positive
possess
possession
possible *adj*
possibly
possibility
post
pot *n*
potato
pound *n*
pour
powder *n*
power *n*
powerful
practical
practice
practise
praise
pray
prayer
prefer
preparation
prepare
present *adj, n*
preserve *v*
president
press *v*
pressure *n*
pretend
pretty *adj*
prevent
previous
price *n*
priest
prince
principle
print
prison
prisoner
private *adj*
prize *n*
probably *adv*
problem
process *n*
produce *v*
product
production
profession
profit *n*
programme
progress *n*
promise
pronounce
pronunciation
proof *n*
proper
property
proposal
protect
protection
protective
protest
proud
prove
provide
public
pull
pump
punish
punishment
pupil
pure
purple
purpose *n*
push
put

Q

quality
quantity
quarrel
quarter *n*
queen *n*
question
quick *adj*
quiet *adj, n*
quite

R

rabbit *n*
race
radio *n*
railway
rain
raise *v*
range *n*
rank *n*
rapid *adj*
rare
rat *n*
rate *n*
rather
raw
reach *v*
react
reaction
read *v*
ready *adj*
real
realize
really
reason
reasonable
receive
recent
recently
recognize
record *n, v*
red
reduce
reduction
refusal
refuse *v*
regard *v*
regular *adj*
related
relative
relation
relationship
relax
relaxing
religion
religious
remain
remark *n*
remember
remind
remove *v*
rent
repair
repeat *v*
replace
reply
report
represent
representative *n*
request *n*
respect
responsible
rest
restaurant
restrict
result
return *n, v*
reward
rice
rich
rid
ride
right *adj, adv, n*
ring *n*
rise
risk
river
road
rob
rock *n*
roll *v*
romantic *adj*
roof *n*
room *n*
root *n*
rope *n*
rose
rough *adj*
round *adj, adv, prep*
row
royal *adj*
rub *v*
rubber
rude
ruin *v*
rule
ruler
run
rush *v*

S

sad
safe *adj*
safety
sail
sale
salt *n*
same
sand *n*
satisfaction
satisfactory
satisfy
save *v*
say *v*
scale *n*
scatter *v*
scene
school *n*
science
scientific
scientist
scissors
screen *n*
screw
sea
search
season *n*
seat
second *adv, n, determiner*
secret
secretary
see *v*
seed *n*
seem
sell *v*
send
sense *n*
sensible
sensitive
sentence *n*
separate *adj, v*
series
serious
servant
serve
service *n*
set *n, v*
settle *v*
seven(th)
several
severe
sex *n*
sexual
shade
shadow *n*
shake
shall
shame *n*
shape
share
sharp *adj*
she
sheep
sheet
shelf
shell *n*
shelter
shine *v*
shiny
ship *n*
shirt
shock *n, v*
shocking
shoe *n*
shoot *v*
shop
shore *n*
short *adj*
shot *n*
should
shoulder *n*
shout
show *n, v*
shut
shy
sick *adj*
side *n*
sideways
sight *n*
sign
signal
silence *n*
silent
silk
silly
silver
similar
simple
since
sincere *adj*
sing
single *adj*
singular
sink *v*
sister
sit
situation
six(th)
size *n*
skilful
skill
skin *n*
skirt *n*
sky *n*
sleep
slide *v*
slight *adj*
slippery
slope
slow
small
smell
smile
smoke
smooth *adj*
snake *n*
snow
so
soap *n*
social *adj*
society
sock *n*
soft
soil *n*
soldier *n*
solid
solution
solve
some *pron, determiner*
somehow
someone
something
sometimes
somewhere
son
song
soon
sore *adj*
sorry

sort *n*
soul
sound *n, v*
soup
sour *adj*
south
southern
space *n*
speak
special *adj*
specific
speech
speed *n*
spell *v*
spend
spin *v*
spirit *n*
in spite of
split *v*
spoil *v*
spoon *n*
sport *n*
spot *n*
spread *v*
spring
square *adj, n*
stage *n*
stair
stamp
stand *v*
standard
star *n*
start
state
statement
station *n*
stay
steady *adj*
steal *v*
steam *n*
steel *n*
steep *adj*
stem *n*
step
stick
sticky
stiff *adj*
still *adj, adv*
sting
stitch
stomach *n*
stone *n*
stop
store
storm *n*
story
straight *adj, adv*
strange
stream *n*
street
strength
stretch *v*
strict
strike *v*

string *n*
strong
structure *n*
struggle
student
study
stupid
style *n*
subject *n*
substance
succeed
success
successful
such
suck *v*
sudden
suffer
sugar *n*
suggest
suit
suitable
sum *n*
summer
sun *n*
supply *n, v*
support *n, v*
suppose
sure *adj*
surface *n*
surprise
surprising
surround *v*
swallow *v*
swear
sweep *v*
sweet
swell *v*
swim
swing
sword
sympathetic
sympathy
system

T

table *n*
tail *n*
take *v*
talk
tall
taste
tax
taxi *n*
tea
teach
team *n*
tear
technical
telephone
television
tell
temper *n*
temperature
temporary

ten
tend
tendency
tennis
tense *n*
tent
terrible
test
than
thank
that *conj, pron, determiner*
the
theatre
their(s)
them
then *adv*
there
therefore
these
they
thick *adj*
thief
thin *adj*
thing
think *v*
third
this *pron, determiner*
thorough
those
though
thought
thousand(th)
thread *n*
threat
threaten
threatening
three
throat
through *adv, prep*
throw
thumb *n*
ticket *n*
tidy *adj, v*
tie
tight *adj*
time *n*
tired
tiring
title
to
tobacco
today
toe *n*
together
toilet
tomorrow
tongue
tonight
too
tool *n*
tooth
top *adj, n*

total *adj, n*
touch
tourist
towards
tower *n*
town
toy *n*
track *n*
trade *n*
traditional
traffic *n*
train
training
translate
transparent
trap
travel
treat *v*
treatment
tree
tribe
trick *n, v*
trip *n*
tropical
trouble
trousers
true *adj*
trust
truth
try *v*
tube
tune *n*
turn
twice
twist
two
type *n*
typical
tyre

U

ugly
under *prep*
understand
underwear
undo
unexpected
uniform *n*
union
unit
unite
universe
university
unless
until
unusual
up *adj, adv, prep*
upper
upright *adj, adv*
upset *v, adj*
upside down
upstairs *adj, adv*
urgent
us

use
useful
useless
usual

V

valley
valuable *adj*
value *n*
variety
various
vegetable
vehicle
verb
very *adv*
victory
view *n*
village
violence
violent
visit
voice *n*
vote
vowel

W

wages
waist
wait *v*
wake *v*
walk
wall *n*
want
war *n*
warm *adj, v*
warmth
warn
warning
wash
waste
watch
water
wave
way
we
weak
wealth
weapon
wear *v*
weather *n*
weave *v*
wedding
week
weekly *adj, adv*
weigh
weight *n*
welcome
well *adj, adv, n*
west
western *adj*
wet *adj*
what *predeterminer, determiner, pron*

whatever
wheat
wheel *n*
when *adv, conj*
whenever
where
whether
which
while *conj*
whip
whistle
white
who
whole
whose
why *adv, conj*
wide *adj, adv*
width
wife
wild *adj, adv*
will
willing
win *v*
wind
window
wine *n*
wing *n*
winter
wire *n*
wise *adj*
wish
with
within
without
woman
wood
wooden
wool
word *n*
work
world
worry
worse
worst
worth
would
wound
wrap *v*
wrist
write
wrong *adj, adv, n*

Y

year
yellow
yes
yet
you
young *adj*
your(s)

Z

zero

Prefixes and suffixes that can be used with words in the Defining Vocabulary
可以与释义词汇中的词连用的前缀和后缀

-able
-al
-ance
-ation
dis-
-ed
-ence
-er
-ful
-ic
-ical
im-
in-
-ing
-ion
ir-
-ish
-ity
-ive
-ize
-less
-ly
-ment
-ness
non-
re-
self
-th
un-
-y

出版人的话

● 新词是怎样收进辞典内的?

我们经常被问及一个词是如何收进辞典内的。这个问题尤其与新词有关, 因为, 正如艾奇逊教授在她的结束语中所指出的, 并不是所有新词都有用或都可以在语言中保存下来。《朗文当代英语大辞典》新词附录的编辑方针是, 只有根据本辞典的编纂者和出版人的判断, 那些极可能成为未来英语词汇宝库中一部分的新词才会被收入。

作出判断是否收入某个词有很大难处, 但我们的主要标准是: 收录的新词应在书面上至少使用过一次, 而在口语中应使用过数次, 而且其引文应至少出自三个不同的来源。但实际作出判断时情况往往更为复杂, 假如辞典编纂者认为某一词是新词, 尽管只能 (在口语或书面材料中) 找到一个出处, 也会从语言学角度对其作出判断。

● 新兴的词语

我们在"新词附录"中已收录那些现有的、但出于某些原因而开始得到更加广泛使用的词语。最明显的例子是已在美国英语中用了一段时间, 然后又开始在英国英语和英语的其他变体中使用的一些词语。例如, **farmer's market** (农贸市场) 和 **conjoined twins** (连体双胞胎) 已在美国英语中使用了一段时间, 但只是最近才开始用于英国英语。

还有一些类似的词语是首先在科学或其他专门领域通用, 然后出现在报刊文章中, 从而逐渐成为英语的一部分。

《朗文当代英语辞典在线》(http://www.ldoceonline.com) 是最新的朗文辞典。这是一部可在朗文和培生出版网站上免费使用或下载至所有万维网站使用的网上辞典。你还可以在进行文字处理或书写电子邮件时使用本辞典查找需要的词语。该辞典也是朗文辞典中最大的, 包含百科词条和许多既见于美国英语又见于英国英语辞典语料库中的词条。

英语词汇不断涌现

琼·艾奇逊

● 英语学习者为何需要新词

在英语中，词汇一直不断地涌现。报纸、电视、广播及近来的万维网上，不断冒出新的词语，成为数以万计的英语词汇中的新成员。一个受过教育的、以英语为母语的人（无论来自美国、英国、澳大利亚和其他以英语为主要交际语言的任何一个国家）至少掌握5万个英语单词，而这个数目仅为现有词汇量的一部分。母语为英语的人在13岁时就学会约2万个单词。[1] 理想情况下，英语学习者需要这个数量的词语去书写和谈论他们要讨论的各种话题。

但是，人们需要掌握哪些词语呢？这随着热点话题的变化而不断发生变化，新的词项（单词、词组或旧词新义）便会产生。英语学习者需要学习新加进英语中的这些词语，需了解它们的含义。达到这一目的的一个好方法是查阅一部在线辞典，如 Longman Dictionary of Contemporary English Online（朗文当代英语辞典在线）http://www.ldoceonline.com，因为这类辞典总会时时更新其收词。为了那些不方便上网的读者着想，《朗文当代英语大辞典》的编纂者和出版人编写了这个新词附录以帮助学习者掌握这些新词。

● 新词进入英语的三个途径

新词语进入英语主要有三个途径。第一，是从另一种语言、某地的方言或英语的另一变体借来的外来词（loanwords）。英语接受了来自多种不同语言的词语。来自美国英语的词语传播到英语的其他变体中已成为一种强烈的趋势。《朗文当代英语大辞典》的新词部分收录的词语许多在美国英语中已是人尽皆知，但对英国英语和世界其他地区的英语来说却是新词。

第二，是通过构词法（word formation）生成新词，即用原有的词语或原有词语中的一部分合起来造出新词，例如，chat room（（网上）聊天室）或change management（变动管理）。

第三，新词可以通过插入法（layering）生成，即一个现存的词语可以分解出不止一个词义。这就会造成所谓的多义性（polysemy）（一个词具有几个词义），例如campus这个词的新用法，可以指属于某大公司的土地和全部建筑（〔大公司的〕园区）：Microsoft's campus in Redmond, Washington（微软公司在华盛顿州雷德蒙德的园区）。

以下将讨论这三种途径。英语的词汇量一如既往地在不断扩大，这将会越来越明显，由于英语已经成为全球商贸往来和新技术所使用的语言，近年新词增加的速度和数量都很惊人。

1　历史上的外来词

与其他一些语言不同，英语从来没有设法阻止外来词语进入其词汇。英语中的外来词来自法语、拉丁语、希腊语、意大利语、西班牙语、汉语、日语、印地语，以及许多其他语言。这些外来的词语往往已失去外来词的色彩而成为英语词。

1066年，征服者威廉从法国的诺曼底入侵英格兰，法语开始成为代表权力和地位的语言。这在格洛斯特的罗伯特写于大约1300年的英国史中就清楚地表明了这一点。他说（根据翻译）：

所以，这块土地上的贵族（征服英格兰的法国人）的后裔始终坚持使用同一种语言（即法语）……因为一个人如果不通晓法语，就几乎不为人们所注意……但是，下层人民一直使用英语。[2]

在那一时期，大量法语词进入英语，尤其是与权力有关的词语，如duke（公爵）、duchess（公爵夫人或女公爵）、count（伯爵）、countess（伯爵夫人或女伯爵）；与官方有关的词语，如parliament（议会）、government（政府）；或与法律有关的词语，如accuse（控告）、attorney（律师）、crime（罪行）等。进入英语的另一些法语词有的与服装有关，如apparel（服饰）、dress（连衣裙）；有的与艺术有关，如music（音乐）、poem（诗歌）；有的与道德品质有关，如courtesy（谦恭有礼）、charity（仁慈，慈爱）等。

原有的英语词语在当时并不一定消失，它们会与新来的法语词一起存在，但用于更为普通的环境之中。例如，说英语的下等阶层仍然保留一些家畜的叫法，如cow（母牛）、sheep（绵羊）、swine（猪）等（都来自古英语）。与此同时，当指称这些家畜作食用的肉时，便采用它们的法语名称，如beef（牛肉）、mutton（羊肉）和pork（猪肉）等，因为富裕家庭和贵族家庭才经常吃肉。

拉丁语，作为教会的语言也扮演着重要的角色。在一些情况下，表示类似意义而来源于英语、法语和拉丁语的词并存，如表示“帮助”有help（英语）、aid（法语）和assistance（拉丁语），表示“书本”有book（英语）、volume（法语）和text（拉丁语）。

许多拉丁词语是在16世纪和17世纪进入英语的。它们主要是书面语的一部分，性质上往往涉及专门知识，如species（物种）、specimen（标本）、tedium（冗长）、squalor（肮脏）和antenna（触角，触须）等。有些拉丁词，如以上所举的几个例子直接以拉丁语形式进入英语，另一些则采用了英语的拼写方式，如history（历史，拉丁语为historia）、maturity（成熟，拉丁语为maturitas）、polite（礼貌的，拉丁语为politus）和scripture（经文，拉丁语为scriptura）。现在几乎没有人能看出history或polite这类词语是源于拉丁语。

17世纪，一些说英语的人开始对拉丁词大量涌入英语感到担心。伊丽莎白时代的剧作家本·琼森在他的戏剧《冒牌诗人》（1601）中嘲弄了这一趋势，剧中的一个角色脱口说出一连串词语，其中许多只是开玩笑的空话：

barmy froth, chilblained, clumsy, clutched, conscious, damp, defunct, fatuate, furibund, glibbery, incubus, inflate, lubrical, magnificate, oblatrant, obstupefact, prorumpted, puffy, quaking custard, reciprocal, retrograde, snarling gusts, snotteries, spurious, strenuous, turgidous, ventositous

但是，其中也有一些词是今天还在经常使用的，例如clumsy（笨手笨脚的，该词在琼森的时代居然是一个新词）、conscious（神志清醒的）、damp（潮湿的）、defunct（已死去的）、puffy（膨胀的）、reciprocal（相互的）、retrograde（后退的）、spurious（假的）、strenuous（干劲十足的）。

在17世纪，英语接触到欧洲其他主要语言，这可从以下的外来词反映出来，如借自法语的colonel（上校）、machine（机器）、cartridge（弹药筒）等，借自西班牙语的armada（舰队）、banana（香蕉）、galleon（西班牙大帆船）等，借自意大利语的ballot（选票）、carnival（狂欢节）、madrigal（牧歌）等。

2 来自其他语言的词语 — “外来词”

吸收外来词语的这种趋势仍然在继续。这些外来词来自众多不同的国家。但是，外来词并不是新词的主要来源。极大多数新词来自新技术领域，如计算机、互联网、生物科技、运动、娱乐、商业、社会变革等。然而，你会发现现有的一些外来词还有新的用法，如法语词 beaucoup 的新用法:

beaucoup *quantifier French spoken informal* a lot of or many【法口，非正式】许多，很多: *He makes beaucoup bucks* (=earns a lot of money) *in that job.* 他在那工作上挣了大把大把的钱。

来自印地语:

bindi *n* [C] a small amount of coloured powder or a piece of jewellery, usually in the shape of a round mark, that many Hindu people wear on their FOREHEAD*s* between their EYEBROW*s*. Bindis are worn for religious reasons and by women to show they are married, but now many women wear them to make themselves more attractive or fashionable.〔印度教女子加在两眉之间前额上的〕吉祥痣〔以前用于表示已婚，现在只是为了美观〕

许多来自其他语言的新词与食物有关，如 **latte**（拿铁，即牛奶咖啡，源自意大利语），**taqueria**（墨西哥食品快餐店，源自墨西哥西班牙语），以及 **radicchio**（菊苣，源自意大利语）。

源自美国英语的词语

美国英语的重要性与日俱增，这主要出于两个原因，一是美国在世界经济中所占的优势，这包括其作为计算机和互联网软件主要供应商的角色，二是美国通俗文化通过电影、电视和流行歌曲所起的影响。一些在美国已不是新词、但已得到全世界认同和广泛使用的词语被视为新词收录在《朗文当代英语大辞典》的新词附录中。例如，**majorly**（*slang* extremely【俚】极其，非常）在美国并不是一个新词，但已在全世界广泛使用，因而被收进了新词部分，并不再标明为美国英语。

当然，美国英语中出现的一些新词也收录进来，因为《朗文当代英语大辞典》除了收录英国英语外，也收录大量的美国英语，以及英语的其他变体。例如，新出现的 **somebody got game** 这个短语是美国英语口语中的一个习语，用以表示某人做某事十分熟练，尤指体育运动。另一个新词条为 **whassup**，这是一个美国俚语，源自‘What’s up?’（怎么啦?），尤其作为和熟人之间打招呼时的用语。

英国英语发展的一个重要趋势是采用来自美国英语的词，尤其来自工商业界、年轻一代的文化和黑人文化、流行音乐、计算机和互联网的词语，这一点在新词附录中有所反映。

但是，外来词（从其他语言汲取的词语）只是新词的一个来源。另一个来源，也是主要的来源，便是构词，接下来将讨论这一点。

3 新词

德国哲学家和语言学家洪堡于1836年指出:“一种语言的词汇绝不能看作是无生命的完全整体……词汇通过其构词能力会不断地生成和再生成”。[3] 这种“构词能力”可从两种途径进行探究。其一是探讨产生新词的生活领域。其二是研究构成新词的语言手段。

通过新词可以洞察某个时代广受关注的事物。例如，在 20 世纪初期创造了许多与交通运输有关的词: 汽车部件，如 accelerator（油门）; 与航空运输有关的词，如 air line（航线）、

airport（航空港）、air terminal（航站楼）等。此外，还增加了一些与现代家用电器有关的词，如 central heating（中央供暖），vacuum cleaner（吸尘器），当然，还有 radio（收音机）和 television（电视机）。

如今，在21世纪之初，与计算机和互联网有关的新词可能在数量上已超过所有其他来源的词语，例如：

cybersickness a feeling of illness caused by using a computer for long periods of time or being in a room with a lot of computers〔长期使用电脑或待在有很多电脑的房间中引致的〕电脑病

keypal someone with whom you regularly exchange E-MAIL 键盘友，网友：*If your daughter is interested in having a keypal next year, please have her get in touch.* 你的女儿如果来年有意结交网友的话，请让她同我联系。

screenager *informal* a young person who spends a lot of time using computers and the Internet【非正式】〔热衷于使用电脑和互联网的年轻人〕屏幕青少年

金融领域也产生了许多新词，如：

dead cat bounce *n* [C] *technical informal* a situation in which the price of SHARES rises a small amount after a large fall, sometimes before falling further【术语，非正式】"死猫"式反弹〔股票大跌后出现的轻微反弹〕

stealth tax *n* [C] *BrE informal* a tax that you pay on something that you buy rather than tax you pay directly to the government, and which you are less aware of paying than, for example, direct tax on your income【英，非正式】隐形税〔购物时含在商品里的一种税〕

有时，可由金融和计算机两个领域相结合产生新词，如：

dot-com *adj* [only before noun 仅用于名词前] *informal* relating to a person or company whose business is done using the Internet or involves the Internet【非正式】经营互联网业务的：*a dot-com company* 经营互联网业务的公司 | *dot-com millionaires* 经营互联网业务的大富翁

e-cash *n* [U] money that can be used to buy things on the Internet, but that does not exist in a physical form or belong to any particular country 电子现金

新事物的出现需要新的词语，其中许多来自科学、技术和商务活动，兹略举数例——有些来自计算机和互联网，如 **online auction**（网上拍卖），**PDA** 或 **personal digital assistant**（个人数码助理，掌上电脑），**access provider**（网络服务供应商），**animatronics**（电子动画学），**cookie**（"甜饼"，记录网站访问者的信息块），**MP3**（运动图像压缩标准第三层声音压缩文件）；有些来自医学和生物科学，如 **biologically engineered**（基因改良的，转基因的），**DNA profiling**（基因图测定），**genetically modified**（基因改良的，转基因的）；有些来自商务活动方面，如 **benchmark**（〔企业管理上〕以……为基准进行评定），**best practice**（最佳举措），**SOHO**（家庭办公室）等等。

4 构词过程

新词语并不都是全新的。其中大多数是由已有的一些成分构成的。同样的构词过程在全球各地都有发生，尽管每一种语言各有其特有的惯用构词方式。

首次启用的新词，通常置于引号（" "）之内，例如，在 The annual fee allows unlimited

entry to district parks for your dog for a year and a case of 100 "pooper-scoopers"中, pooper-scooper（长柄粪铲）是指铲除狗粪的一种工具。某个词被接受后，其引号最终会被舍弃。

i) 复合词 (Compounds)　　在英语中，**复合构词法**是整个20世纪最多产的构词方式。复合构词法包括简单地把两个词语放在一起，有时这两个词仍分开写。最近的例子有 **airport fiction**（机场小说，指在机场出售、供乘客在飞行途中阅读的消遣小说）和 **hot desk**（共用办公桌，指供不同工作人员在不同日子里轮换使用的同一张办公桌）。

有时候，两个部分组拼成单一的一个新词，如 **jobseeker**（求职者）和 **webhead**（网民，网络迷，指频繁并熟练使用互联网的人）。有时，这两个部分由连字符连结，如 **walk-in**（不用预约的），这是新近出现的一个形容词，用以指某个地方毋需预约即可自行前往，如用于 walk-in clinic（无需预约的诊所）。

ii) 词缀 (Affixes)　　添加词缀是构成新词的另一常见方式。词缀是一个词的附加部分，可加在其前面（前缀）或后面（后缀）。

在英语中，给已有的词加上一个词尾可产生许多新词。例如，给 brain（脑）一词的尾部加上后缀 -iac，即生成最近出现的新词 **brainiac**（【非正式，幽默】怪才，指整天思考高深问题、常无法与他人沟通的人: Electrical engineering is the perfect career for a brainiac like him. 电气工程是像他那样的怪才的理想职业）。这个词也用作形容词: The company is trying to change its brainiac image.（该公司试图改变其学究形象。）

许多新词通过添加后缀 -ization 而成，如 **dollarization**（美元化，指美国以外的国家不想用本国货币而想使用美元的情况）或 **globalization**（全球化，指世界各国的活动开始连成一体，尤因一些大公司在不同国家内开展贸易活动所致）。这实际上是把两个后缀连在一起，如第一个为 **globalize** 中的 -ize（即 global+-ize），然后再加上后缀 -ation。

另一个日常通用的后缀为 -land，如见于 **adland**（广告业，指围绕广告进行的整个业务活动）: Anything that grabs your attention is good in adland.（在广告业中，凡能吸引人们注意力的东西都是好东西。）和 **cyberland**（网络世界，指涉及互联网及其使用者的活动）。

前缀最近用得愈加广泛。cyber- 就是一个很好的例子，它已被用于构成一系列新词（该前缀原意为"电脑"，现在多含"使用互联网"之意）。例如，**cybercafé**（网吧）、**cybercrime**（网络犯罪）、**cyberforensics**（网络犯罪学）、**cyberfraud**（网络诈骗，指为了获取钱财和权力等利用网络诈骗他人的不法行为）、**cyberland**（网络世界）、**cyberporn**（网络色情，指显示在互联网上的色情图像、影片等）。

还有很多关于尺寸大小的前缀构成的新词，如 micro-, super- 和 multi- 等，如:

microbrewery *n* [C] a small company that makes only small qualities of beer, and often has a restaurant where its beer is served 小啤酒厂

microengineering *n* [U] the activity of designing structures and machines that are extremely small 微（型）工程

micromanage *v* [T] to organize and control all the details of other people's work in a way that they find annoying 微观管理〔指过分干预别人的工作〕: *Professors warned that students will suffer if the state legislature tries to micromanage public education.* 有教授警告说，如果州立法机关企图对公共教育实行微观管理，学生们将受害。

supersize *adj* [only before noun 仅用于名词前] *AmE* a supersize drink or meal in a FAST-FOOD restaurant is the largest size that the restaurant serves【美】〔快餐店提供的食物或饮料〕巨无霸式的，大份的

multi-tasking *n* [U] **1** a computer's ability to do more than one job at a time〔电脑的〕多任务处理（能力）**2** the ability to do different types of work at the same time 同时执行多项任务的能力

这些前缀大多意义清晰。后缀也可能有其意义, 如-ism是近年来有了更具体的含义的后缀, -ist也是如此。-ism的含义一度是相当"中性"的, 如pacifism（和平主义, 指认为一切战争和一切暴力都是错误的）。但-ism逐渐带上了贬义的色彩, 如ageism（歧视老人）指"人们因为年迈而受到的不公正的对待", 而持这种歧视态度的人就被称为 ageist（歧视老人者）。同样, **lookist**（*adj* 以貌取人的）是指不公正地仅凭某人的外表如胖瘦和衣着等决定好恶, 这样的作风被称为**lookism**（以貌取人主义）, 而持这种态度的人就被称作**lookist**（以貌取人者）。

iii)（词类）转化 (Conversion (change of word class))　这是一种构词方式, 有时会由此产生许多新词或新短语。词类转化是指某个词从一种词类（词性）转变成另一种词类, 这在当今英语中十分常见。对于没有很多词尾的语言, 利用词类转化过程很容易, 如 **to bookmark**（将名词用作动词）, 其含义为"（往文档中）标识〔网址, 方便下次浏览〕", 指保存互联网内的某个网页, 以便容易再找到它, **to ramp**（将名词用作动词）或**to ramp something up**的含义为"推高（公司股票价格）", 指想法子使人们相信某公司股票应值更多的钱; 又如**to sample**（将名词用作动词）的含义为"将……取样拼和", 指把取自激光唱盘或唱片中的小段乐曲用于新曲之中。

iv) 首字母缩略词和缩写（词） (Acronyms and Abbreviations)　词语的首字母缩略一直以来都有其重要性, 有些首字母缩略词和缩写（词）已广为人们所知和使用, 如墓碑和悼词用语RIP (Rest in Peace 愿他[她]安息吧) 或asap (as soon as possible 尽快) 等。有些首字母缩略词已被接受为完整的单词, 如 laser (light amplification by the stimulated emission of radiation 激光: 受激辐射式光频放大器), 像一个单词一样读作 /ˈlezɚ; ˈleɪzə/。近年来, 使用首字母缩略词和缩写（词）日趋频繁, 至少在青少年和年轻人当中是这样。这部分是因为手机虽然同样能发送信息, 但其屏幕空间又非常有限。因此, 缩写（词）构成的短信息愈来愈常见, 如**IMHO** (in my humble opinion 依鄙人之见) 和 **CUL** (see you later 一会儿见), 当然, 使用这类词要谨慎。有些缩写（词）容易引起混淆, 可作不同解释, 如**LOL**既可表示Lots of love（爱你）, 又可表示Laughing out loud（放声大笑）。

v) 混成词 (Blends)　两个词合成为一个词称为**混成词**（此术语现在比旧有的**portmanteau words**常用得多, 但后一术语有时仍用来描述这种现象）。

少数混成词已被人们接受为英语的一部分, 如brunch（早午餐）是由breakfast（早餐）和lunch（午餐）两词混合而成, 有些是故作幽默的, 例如:

netizen *n* [C] *slang* someone who uses the Internet, especially someone who uses it in a responsible way. This word comes from a combination of the words 'net', meaning 'the Internet', and 'citizen'.【俚】网民〔由net和citizen缩合而成〕: *China and India will soon have far larger numbers of netizens than any Western nation.* 中国和印度不久将会拥有大量网民, 数量远比任何一个西方国家多。

netiquette *n* [U] *informal* the commonly accepted rules for polite behaviour when communicating with other people on the Internet【非正式】网规, 网上礼仪: *Netiquette says that you don't use all capital letters in an e-mail, because that shows you are angry.* 网规说, 你在电子邮件中不得全部用大写字母, 因为那样做表示你在生气。

由 imagination（想象）和 engineer（工程师）构成 **imagineer**（点子大王，创意工程师）一词，指脑子中有许多新的主意并能把这些主意实践出来的人。

5 同层插入

然而新词并非一定是新的语词。一些现成的词可借着**同层插入**（layering）这一方式分出新的意义，如 **client**（客户机，指通过服务器在网上获得信息的电脑）或 **brother**（兄弟，黑人男子之间的互称）。同样地，**lurk**（潜水）现在不仅可指隐藏在矮树林中的可疑分子，也可指潜入 **chat room**（网上聊天室）中只是阅读信息而不发表意见的潜水者。

同层插入的另一类型是语词的含义"淡出"。事实上，如 **devastated** 新增的意义并未严重削弱原有的含义。The city was devastated（那座城市被彻底摧毁了）通常表示该城市遭到敌人或巨大的自然灾害（如火山）的破坏。但在 Peggy was devastated when her new hat got wet（佩吉因为她的新帽被淋湿了而极为不快）一句中，这里指的纯粹是一桩小事，所以只表示"佩吉极为不快"的意思。

● 结束语

可见，英语中不断有新词加入。那么英语是不是变得越来越庞大？是的，是这样。然而，词语并不总是永远存在下去的。当人们不使用某些词语，这些词语便会消亡。

那么，一个人怎么才能学好所有这些词语呢？办法只有一个，就是购买一本最新的词典。幸运的是，对于任何希望学好最新词汇以迎接21世纪的英语学习者，本版辞典已提供大量有用的词汇，足以使他们能充分面对21世纪的需要。

琼·艾奇逊（Jean Aitchison）是牛津大学鲁珀特·默多克语言与传播学讲座教授，著作颇丰，如《心里想的词语 —— 心智词汇导论》第二版，牛津：布莱克韦尔，1994年；《语言的变革：进步还是衰亡？》第三版，剑桥：剑桥大学出版社，2001年

1. "论语词的数目"，见琼·艾奇逊，《心里想的词语 —— 心智词汇导论》第二版，牛津：布莱克韦尔，1994。
2. 这段（英语）译文引自杰弗里·休斯，《英语词语的历史》，牛津：布莱克韦尔，2000，第110页。
3. 洪堡，《论语言》(1836)，彼得·希思（英）译，剑桥：剑桥大学出版社，1988，第93页。

A,a

abs /æbz; æbz/ *n* [plural]
informal the muscles on your ABDOMEN (=stomach)【非正式】腹肌: *exercises that improve your butt, legs, and abs* 改善臀部、腿部和腹部肌肉的锻炼

access pro·vid·er /ˈæksɛs prəˌvaɪdɚ; ˈækses prəˌvaɪdə/ *n* [C]
a company that provides the technical services that allow people to use the Internet, usually in exchange for a monthly payment; Internet Service Provider 网络服务供应商, 互联网服务供应商

acid jazz /ˌæsɪd ˋdʒæz; ˌæsɪ̡d ˈdʒæz/ *n* [U]
a type of popular music that combines features of many other kinds of music, especially JAZZ, HIP-HOP, and SOUL 迷幻爵士乐

acquaintance rape /əˋkwentəns ˌrep; əˈkweɪntəns ˌreɪp/ *n* [C,U]
a crime in which a person forces someone they know to have sex with them 熟人强奸: *The truth is acquaintance rape can occur at any time, no matter how long the two people have known each other.* 实际情况是任何时候都可能发生熟人强奸, 不管这两个人相互认识了多久。

ac·tu·als /ˋæktʃuəlz; ˈæktʃuəlz/ *n* [plural]
numbers that relate to something that has actually happened, rather than what was expected to happen, for example the sales of a particular product 实际数目: *Mobile phone operators had expected monthly usage of up to 250 minutes. Actuals are very different, at 100 minutes.* 移动电话运营商曾预计每个月通话量会达到250分钟, 实际数字则相差甚远, 只达到100分钟。

add-on /ˋæd ˌɑn; ˈæd ˌɒn/ *n* [C]
NEW MEANING
1 something extra that is added to an existing plan, agreement, or law etc〔计划、协议或法规等的〕附加内容: *The Senate's add-ons to the proposed budget are likely to cause controversy.* 参议院在预算案上添加的新内容看来会引起一番争议。**2** a product that is designed to be used with another product〔与其他产品配用的〕附件

ADHD /ˌe di etʃ ˋdi; ˌeɪ diː eɪtʃ ˈdiː/ *n* [U]
attention deficit hyperactivity disorder; a medical condition that especially affects children and causes them to be too active and unable to pay attention to anything for very long〔儿童〕注意缺陷障碍〔伴多动〕, 多动症, 过度活跃症

ad·hoc·ra·cy /ædˋhɑkrəsɪ; ædˈhɒkrəsi/ *n* [C]
a company or organization that does not have a formal structure or many rules. This word is often used to talk about new companies that make computer SOFTWARE, which do not operate in a traditional way. 没有成规的公司[组织]〔常指不按传统方式营运的电脑软件公司〕: *the emergence of adhocracies in the software engineering sector* 软件工程行业中出现的一些不守成规的公司

ad·land /ˋædlænd; ˈædlænd/ *n* [U]
the activity or business of advertising, considered as a whole 广告业: *Anything that grabs your attention is good in adland.* 在广告业中, 凡能吸引人们注意力的东西都是好东西。

adrenaline-charged /əˋdrɛnlɪn ˌtʃɑrdʒd; əˈdrenəlɪ̡n ˌtʃɑːdʒd/ *adj*
a game, film, activity etc that is adrenaline-charged is very exciting and possibly frightening〔游戏、影片、活动等〕非常刺激的; 惊心动魄的: *an adrenaline-charged movie starring Steven Seagal* 由史蒂文·西加尔主演的一部惊悚片

ADSL /ˌe di ɛs ˋɛl; ˌeɪ diː es ˈel/ *n* [U]
asymmetric digital subscriber line; a system that makes it possible for information, such as VIDEO images, to be sent to computers through telephone wires at a very high speed. The receiver is also able to send information back to the sender, but at a much slower speed. 非对称数位用户专线〔通过电话线上网的一种系统〕

ad·ver·to·ri·al /ˌædvɚˋtɔrɪəl; ˌædvəˈtɔːriəl/ *n* [C]
an advertisement in a newspaper or magazine that is made to look like a normal article. This word comes from a combination of the words 'ADVERT' and 'EDITORIAL'.〔报刊上的〕文章式广告, 社论式广告〔由advert 和 editorial 缩合而成〕

aer·i·a·list /ˋɛrɪəlɪst; ˈeəriəlɪ̡st/ *n* [C]
someone who goes down a mountain on SKI*s* and performs complicated jumps and turns in the air 高空滑雪杂技表演者, 高山花样滑雪者

AFAIK, afaik
a written abbreviation of 缩写= 'as far as I know', used in E-MAIL OR TEXT MESSAGE*s* on MOBILE PHONE*s* 据我所知〔电子邮件或手机短信用语〕

affinity card /əˋfɪnətɪ ˌkɑrd; əˈfɪnɪ̡ti ˌkɑːd/ *n* [C]
a type of CREDIT CARD, where an amount of money is given by the credit card company to a CHARITY every time the card is used 慈善信用卡〔这种卡每消费一次, 信用卡公司便会把其中一定数额的钱捐给慈善机构〕

af·flu·en·za /ˌæfluˋɛnzə; ˌæfluˈenzə/ *n* [U]
informal bad feelings such as shame or sadness that some people have when they suddenly become very rich. This word is a combination of the words 'AFFLUENCE' (=when you have a lot of money) and 'INFLUENZA' (=an illness which is like a very bad cold).【非正式】富贵病〔因暴富而产生羞耻或悲伤的情绪, 由 affluence 和 influenza 缩合而成〕

af·ter·mar·ket /ˋæftɚˌmɑrkɪt; ˈɑːftəˌmɑːkɪ̡t/ *n* [C] *BrE*
the market for the products that people buy after they have bought another related product, for example spare parts or additional pieces of equipment【英】零配件市场: *There is a large aftermarket for replacement car parts.* 有一个巨大的汽车配件市场。

age·ist /ˋedʒɪst; ˈeɪdʒɪ̡st/ *adj*
treating old people unfairly because of a belief that they are less important than younger people 歧视老人的: *The article seemed somewhat insensitive and ageist to me.* 在我看来, 这篇文章有点麻木不仁并带有歧视老人的味道。—**ageist** *n* [C] *She actually accused me of being an ageist.* 她实际上是在指责我歧视老人。

aggressive-growth /əˌgrɛsɪv ˋgroθ; əˌgresɪv ˈgrəʊθ◂/ *adj*
aggressive-growth fund a group of STOCK*s* that earns a lot of money very quickly because the stock price keeps rising 高增长基金, 积极成长型基金: *A retired couple looking for stability and minimal risk should not choose an aggressive-growth fund.* 期待稳定和低风险的退休夫妇不应该选择积极成长型基金。

a·git·pop /ˋædʒɪtˌpɑp; ˈædʒɪ̡tˌpɒp/ *n* [U] *BrE*
a type of popular music which has a political message and encourages people to get involved in political activities, such as improving working conditions for the poor and trying to stop big companies from being too powerful【英】鼓动音乐〔含有政治信息、鼓励人们参加政治活动的一种流行音乐〕: *an agitpop band* 鼓动音乐乐队

ag·ri·tour·ist /ˋægrɪˌturɪst; ˈægrɪˌtʊərɪ̡st/ *n* [C]
someone from a town or city who stays on a farm while they are on holiday 农业旅游观光者, 农家乐旅游者: *Agritourists enjoy country vacations; rural bed and breakfasts such as the Fieldstone Inn near Regina are popular destinations too.* 农业旅游观光者享受在乡村度假的乐趣, 诸如里贾纳附近的大卵石度假旅馆提供农村住宿和早餐, 也成了受欢迎的目的地。—**agritourism** *n* [U]

air /ɛr; eə/ *n*
NEW MEANING
get/catch some air *slang* to jump high off the ground, especially when playing BASKETBALL, SKI*ing*, or riding a

SKATEBOARD【俚】〔尤指篮球、滑雪等运动中〕弹跳得极高

air kiss 嘬唇示吻

air kiss /ˈɛr ˌkɪs; ˈeə ˌkɪs/ *n* [C]
humorous a way of greeting someone with a kiss that is near the side of their face, but that does not touch them【幽默】嘬唇示吻〔一种问候方式，嘴唇接近但并不接触对方的面颊〕**—air-kiss** *v* [I,T]: *As soon as Alice appeared, Beth rushed over, and the two women air-kissed.* 艾丽斯一出现，贝丝便跑了过去，两个女人嘬唇示吻。

airport fic·tion /ˈɛrpɔrt ˌfɪkʃən; ˈeəpɔːt ˌfɪkʃən/ *n* [U]
books, especially ones that are not very serious, that people buy at airports to read while they are travelling on planes 机场小说〔在机场出售、供乘客在飞行途中阅读的消遣小说〕

air quote /ˈɛr ˌkwot; ˈeə ˌkwəʊt/ *n* [C usually plural 一般用复数]
a movement that someone makes in the air with their fingers to show that what they are saying should be in QUOTATION MARKs, and that it should not be taken as their real opinion or their usual way of speaking 手势引号〔表示所说的话不是表达真正的意见或通常的说法〕: *Ryan used air quotes when he said the word 'band'.* 瑞安在说 band 一词时用了手势引号。| *"It was a 'dinner party'", he said, waving his fingers to make air quotes in that annoying way he has.* "这是一次 dinner party（宴会）。"他说着，并挥动手指做了个令人讨厌的引号动作。

air rage /ˈɛr ˌredʒ; ˈeə ˌreɪdʒ/ *n* [U]
violence and angry behaviour by a passenger on an aircraft towards other passengers or the people who work on the aircraft（飞机乘客）乘机暴怒，坐飞机闹事: *In another air rage incident, a flight to Spain was forced to land after a passenger threatened cabin staff when they refused to serve him more alcohol.* 在另一次空中闹事事件中，一名乘客由于乘务员拒绝再给他倒酒而作出恐吓，因此一架飞往西班牙的班机被迫降落。

airtime pro·vid·er /ˈɛrtaɪm prəˌvaɪdɚ; ˈeətaɪm prəˌvaɪdə/ *n* [C]
a company that provides the service that allows you to make and receive calls on a MOBILE PHONE 移动电话公司: *You may still receive invoices or statements from your airtime provider after you return the equipment.* 你在退还设备之后，仍可能会收到移动电话公司的发票或结算单。

al·co·pop /ˈælkoˌpɑp; ˈælkəʊˌpɒp/ *n* [C usually plural 一般用复数] *BrE*
a sweet drink with BUBBLEs which is sold in bottles and contains alcohol. Many people disapprove of these drinks because they think the makers want young people to buy them. This word comes from a combination of the words 'alcohol' and 'POP'.【英】泡泡甜酒〔含有酒精、起泡的甜饮料，由 alcohol 和 pop 缩合而成〕

A-list /ˈe lɪst; ˈeɪ lɪst/ *adj*
among the most popular or famous film stars, musicians etc 最受欢迎的；最著名的，一流的〔影星、音乐家等〕: *No doubt about it. A-list celebrities like Madonna really pull in the crowds to any music event.* 毫无疑问，像麦当娜那样的一流歌星在任何音乐演出中肯定会吸引许多观众。

all /ɔl; ɔːl/ *adv*
NEW MEANING
1 sb was all… *AmE spoken* used to report what someone said or did, when telling a story【美口】某人说[做]…: *He drove me somewhere once, and he was all, "I love this car – it's like a rocket!"* 有一次他开车把我带到一个地方，他说："我喜欢这辆车，它就像火箭一样！"
2 sb/sth is not all that *AmE slang* used to say that someone or something is not very attractive or desirable【美俚】某人/某物不怎么出色[吸引人]: *I don't know why you keep chasing her around – she's not all that.* 我不明白你为什么一直追求她——她并不怎么样。

all·fi·nanz /ɔlˈfaɪnæns; ɔːlˈfaɪnæns/ *n* [singular]
technical the combining of banking and insurance activities in one company【术语】银行保险综合业务，全金融业务: *Colonial is attempting to turn itself from a life insurance company into an allfinanz group.* 康联正设法由人寿保险公司转变为集银行、保险为一体的全金融业务集团。

al·lot·tee /əˌlɑˈti; əˌlɒˈtiː/ *n* [C]
technical a person or organization that is allowed to buy new SHAREs when they first become available【术语】可购买新股者，可认购新股的人[机构]

alpha geek /ˌælfə ˈgik; ˌælfə ˈgiːk/ *n* [C usually singular 一般用单数]
humorous the person who is the most skilful with computers in a group of people. This word comes from a combination of the words 'ALPHA MALE', which is a scientific word used about the most powerful male animal in a group, and 'GEEK', which means a person who is unfashionable and does not know how to behave in social situations【幽默】电脑高手[怪才]〔由 alpha male 和 geek 缩合而成〕: *Ask James – he's the alpha geek here.* 问詹姆斯吧，他是这儿的电脑高手。

alpha male /ˌælfə ˈmel, ˌælfə ˈmeɪl/ *n* [C usually singular 一般用单数]
humorous the man who has the most power and influence and the highest social position in a particular group. This phrase was first used by scientists to talk about groups of animals, especially monkeys and CHIMPANZEEs.【幽默】大哥大〔指群体中最有权势者。此短语最初由科学家用在猴子和黑猩猩等动物群体上〕

alternative life·style /ɔlˌtɝnətɪv ˈlaɪfstaɪl; ɔːlˌtɜːnətɪv ˈlaɪfstaɪl/ *n* [C]
the way that someone lives their life, including things such as the type of food they eat, where they live, or the way that they educate their children, when this is not the usual way that other people live 另类生活方式，非传统生活方式: *Some people say schools need to protect gay and lesbian students and teach tolerance of alternative lifestyles.* 有人主张学校应该保护同性恋学生，并教育学生对另类生活方式持宽容态度。

AM /ˌe ˈɛm; ˌeɪ ˈem/ *n* [C]
NEW MEANING
Assembly Member; a British politician who is one of the 60 members of the Welsh Assembly. The Welsh Assembly is the parliament for Wales.〔英国威尔士议会的〕议员

am·bi·sex·u·al /ˌæmbɪˈsɛkʃuəl; ˌæmbɪˈsekʃuəl/ also 又作 **ambi** *adj*
informal【非正式】**1** BISEXUAL 双性恋的；具有雌雄两性特征的 **2** suitable for either sex 适于两性的: *ambisexual fashion* 男女都能穿的时装

ambulance chas·er /ˈæmbjələns ˌtʃesɚ; ˈæmbjələns ˌtʃeɪsə/ *n* [C]
a lawyer who uses a lot of pressure to persuade someone who has been hurt in an accident to SUE other people or companies. The lawyer's main reason for doing this is in order to get part of the money if they win. This word is used by people who disapprove of this behaviour and the lawyers who do it. 怂恿事故受害者起诉以从中牟利的律师

amped /æmpt; æmpt/ *adj* [not before noun 不用于名词前] *slang*【俚】
1 if you are amped about something, you are very excited about it 对…痴迷的[兴奋的]: *"Did you hear about Jenny's party?" "Yeah, I'm totally amped about it."* "你听说过珍妮的晚会吗?" "听说了, 这次晚会太让我兴奋了!" **2** feeling extremely excited because you have taken an illegal drug〔在服食毒品后〕极度兴奋的

an·dro·pause /ˋændro͵pɔz; ˈændrəʊ͵pɔːz/ *n* [U]
the time when some men's bodies start producing less TESTOSTERONE (=a chemical substance produced in men's bodies) than before, and they have less energy and strength, usually around age 50 雄激素减少分泌, 男性更年期〔通常在50岁左右〕: *Andropause is easy to treat and to prevent with proper medical supervision.* 在适当的医疗指导下, 男性更年期不难防治。—**andropausal** *adj*: *There's no way of predicting who will experience andropausal symptoms.* 谁会出现男性更年期症状, 这是无法预料的。

an·i·ma·tron·ics /͵ænəməˋtrɑnɪks; ͵ænɪ̥məˈtrɒnɪks/ *n* [U]
the method or process of making or using moving models that look like real animals or people in films. This word comes from a combination of the words 'ANIMATE' and 'ELECTRONICS'. 电子动画制作术, 电子动画学〔由animate和electronics缩合而成〕

anorak /ˋænə͵ræk; ˈænəræk/ *n* [C] *BrE*
NEW MEANING
a boring person who is very interested in the unimportant details of a particular subject【英】〔纠缠于细枝末节的〕爱钻牛角尖的人: *1,200 anoraks have visited our website since 25th March.* 从3月25日以来, 已有1200个爱钻牛角尖的人浏览过我们的网站。| **anorak brigade** (=a group of anoraks) 专抠小问题的群体: *The anorak brigade certainly exist, but they tend to hide in the library for most of the year.* 的确有一批专抠小问题的人, 不过, 他们一年中大部分时间都往往躲在图书馆里。

an·tic·i·point·ment /æn͵tɪsəˋpɔɪntmənt; æn͵tɪsɪ̥ˈpɔɪntmənt/ *n* [U]
humorous a feeling of disappointment that you have when you see or read something for the first time and realize that it is not as good as you expected it to be. This word comes from a combination of the words 'ANTICIPATION' and 'DISAPPOINTMENT'.【幽默】期望落空, 大失所望〔由anticipation和disappointment缩合而成〕: *When you've heard too many good things about a film, it can become an anticipointment when you finally get to see it.* 你听说某部影片大获好评, 不过待你看过以后, 你可能会大失所望。

anti-dump·ing /͵æntɪ ˋdʌmpɪŋ; ͵ænti ˈdʌmpɪŋ/ *adj* [only before noun 仅用于名词前]
anti-dumping taxes or laws prevent people or companies from bringing foreign goods into the country and selling them at a very low price〔税, 法律〕反倾销的

an·ti·ox·i·dant /͵æntɪˋɑksədənt; ͵æntiˈɒksɪ̥dənt/ *n* [C]
a substance that helps to protect the body from CANCER by removing harmful substances from it 抗氧化剂: *Strawberries and spinach are full of antioxidants.* 草莓和菠菜含有丰富的抗氧化成分。| *antioxidant vitamins* 抗氧化的维生素

anti-spam /͵æntɪ ˋspæm; ͵ænti ˈspæm/ *adj*
anti-spam features/measures ways in which a computer PROGRAM finds and removes E-MAIL that someone does not want, for example advertisements sent by companies 清除垃圾邮件的性能/措施

anti-vi·rus soft·ware /͵æntɪ ˋvaɪrəs ͵sɔftwɛr; ͵ænti ˈvaɪərəs ͵sɒftweə/ also 又作 **anti-virus program** *n* [U]
a type of SOFTWARE that looks for and removes VIRUS*es* in programs and documents on your computer 杀毒软件: *You need to update your anti-virus software regularly.* 你需要定期升级自己的杀毒软件。

ap·plet /ˋæplət; ˈæplət/ *n* [C]
technical a computer program that is part of a larger program, and which performs a particular task. Applets are used, for example, to find documents on the Internet, WEBSITE*s* etc.【术语】小(应用)程序: *Java-based mini-programs known as applets are beginning to make their presence felt on the Internet.* 以Java语言编写的许多被称为小应用程序的微小程序开始在互联网上引起人们注意。

application ser·vice pro·vid·er /͵æpləkeʃən ˋsɝvɪs prə͵vaɪdɚ; ͵æplɪkeɪʃən ˈsɜːvɪ̥s prə͵vaɪdə/ *n* [C]
a company that supplies organized sets of computer SOFTWARE to other companies so that they can do business on the Internet 应用服务提供商

application soft·ware /æpləˋkeʃən ͵sɔftwɛr; æplɪˈkeɪʃən ͵sɒftweə/ *n* [U]
technical COMPUTER software that is designed for a particular use or user【术语】应用软件: *We need to ensure that the application software on both the PC and the Macintosh produces compatible files.* 我们需要确保这个应用软件能在个人电脑和苹果电脑上生成相互兼容的文件。

appraisal /əˋprezḷ; əˈpreɪzəl/ also 又作 **performance appraisal** *n* [C] *BrE*【英】
NEW MEANING
a meeting between an employer and a worker to discuss the quality of the worker's work and how well they do their job 绩效评估

aq·ua·e·ro·bics /ˋækwɛ͵robɪks; ˈækweə͵rəʊbɪks/ also 又作 **aqua-aerobics** /ˋækwə ɛ͵robɪks; ˈækwə eə͵rəʊbɪks/ *n* [U]
a type of physical exercise in which you stand in a SWIMMING POOL, usually with other people in a group, and move your arms and legs as music plays 水上韵律操

arcade game /ɑrˋked ͵gem; ɑːˈkeɪd ͵geɪm/ *n* [C]
a type of electronic game that was first popular in AMUSEMENT ARCADE*s* (=a place where you play games by putting coins in machines) in the early 1980s, but is now usually played on a computer (游戏机室)电子游戏, 街机游戏: *Play free classic arcade games right through your web browser!* 只需通过你的网页浏览器便可免费玩经典的电子游戏!

archive /ˋɑrkaɪv; ˈɑːkaɪv/ *v* [T]
technical to make a permanent copy of information held on a computer, or to store the original information so that it cannot be changed or lost【术语】将…存档: *CleanSweep will monitor your system for programs you don't often use and recommend that you archive them.* "清扫"(程序)会监测你的系统, 找出不常用程序, 并建议你把它们存档。—**archiving** *n* [U]: *electronic archiving systems* 电子储存系统

arm can·dy /ˋɑrm ͵kændɪ; ˈɑːm ͵kændi/ *n* [U]
a disapproving word for a very beautiful man or woman who goes with someone else of the opposite sex to parties and other events, but who is not having a sexual relationship with them〔充当派对等场合的伴侣, 但并无性关系的〕美女, 俊男〔贬义词〕: *Nora's acting as arm candy tonight.* 诺拉今晚充当女伴。

art ther·a·py /ˋɑrt ͵θɛrəpɪ; ˈɑːt ͵θerəpi/ *n* [U]
a treatment for mental or emotional problems in which you paint a picture, make a SCULPTURE etc and then examine the art you have made in order to understand your feelings and problems 艺(术)疗(法) —**art therapist** *n* [C]

as /əz; əz; *strong* 强读 æz; æz/ *conj*
NEW MEANING
as if! *slang* used as an answer to a suggestion that someone has made, to say that you think is untrue or wrong【俚】不对! 不是这样!: *"You're not still interested in Brad, are you?" "As if!"* (=no, I am not) "你不会对布拉德还感兴趣吧?" "才不会呢!"

ask /æsk; ɑːsk/ *n* [C]

1 a word meaning the lowest price that someone will sell STOCKS, SHARES etc for, used especially by people whose job is buying and selling shares etc 最低卖价〔股票市场术语〕: *When placing an ask, be sure to specify a price and a time limit.* 提出最低卖价时，一定要具体地说明价格和时限。**2 a big ask** a situation in a sports match when a team needs to get a lot of points in order to win〔体育比赛取胜所需的〕大比分: *Now they need to score twice in the last five minutes – it's a big ask.* 他们现在需要在最后5分钟内两次得分 —— 这可是个大比分。

ASP /ˌe ɛs ˋpi; ˌeɪ es ˈpiː/ *n* [C]
application service provider; a company that supplies organized sets of computer SOFTWARE to other companies so that they can do business on the Internet 应用服务提供商

assisted ar·e·a /əˌsɪstɪd ˋɛrɪə; əˌsɪstɪ̵d ˈeərɪə/ *n* [C]
in Britain, an area of the country that receives money from the government to help it develop, because many people in that area do not have jobs〔英国〕政府资助开发的地区

assisted-liv·ing fa·cil·i·ty /əˌsɪstɪd ˋlɪvɪŋ fəˌsɪlətɪ; əˌsɪstɪ̵d ˈlɪvɪŋ fəˌsɪlɪ̵ti/ *n* [C] *AmE*
a place where old or sick people can live, and where help and services such as medical care and social activities are provided【美】疗养院，护老院: *It's tough moving someone you love into an elder-care setting, such as a nursing home or an assisted-living facility.* 把你所爱的人迁入老年保健机构中去，如养老院或疗养所等，是令人难受的事。

assisted re·pro·duc·tion /əˌsɪstɪd riprəˋdʌkʃən; əˌsɪstɪ̵d riːprəˈdʌkʃən/ *n* [U]
medical methods that are used to help a woman and her partner have a baby 助孕（方法）

asylum seek·er /əˋsaɪləm ˌsikɚ; əˈsaɪləm ˌsiːkə/ *n* [C]
someone who has left their home country because of war or political problems and has gone to another country which they think is safer; REFUGEE 避难者；寻求政治庇护者: *Police officers are trained to understand the customs and culture of the asylum seekers and the political situation from which they have fled.* 警员接受训练以理解避难者的风俗习惯和文化背景，以及他们出逃国的政治形势。

ATM /ˌe ti ˋɛm; ˌeɪ tiː ˈem/ *n* [U]
NEW MEANING
technical asynchronous transfer mode; a way of sending writing, sound, or pictures very quickly over a computer network (=a system of computers that are connected to each other)【术语】异步传输[转移]模式

ATP /ˌe ti ˋpi; ˌeɪ tiː ˈpiː/ *n* [U] *BrE*
automatic train protection; a system that can be put into railway trains to prevent accidents by warning the driver when the train is too near another train, or when it goes past a signal where it is meant to stop【英】列车自动保护系统〔一种防止火车意外的预警系统〕

attachment /əˋtætʃmənt; əˈtætʃmənt/ *n*
NEW MEANING
1 [C,U] *law* a situation in which part of the money someone earns or money that is owed to them is taken by a court of law and used to pay their debts【法律】扣押偿债〔没收所得收入以抵偿欠他人之债〕**2** [C] a document, usually a file, that is sent with an E-MAIL message〔电子邮件的〕附件: *I'll send the spreadsheet as an attachment.* 我将把数据表以附件形式发送。**3** [C] *technical* a piece of paper fastened to a document such as an insurance agreement, which shows a special condition of the agreement【术语】〔保险契约等的〕附件，附款

attention def·i·cit hy·per·ac·tiv·i·ty dis·or·der /əˌtɛnʃən ˌdɛfəsɪt haɪpəræk`tɪvətɪ dɪsˌɔrdɚ; əˌtenʃən ˌdefɪ̵sɪ̵t haɪpərækˈtɪvɪ̵ti dɪsˌɔːdə/ *abbreviation* 缩写为 **ADHD** *n* [U]
a medical condition that especially affects children and causes them to be too active and unable to be quiet or pay attention to anything for very long〔儿童〕注意缺陷障碍〔伴多动〕，多动症，过度活跃症

au·thor·ing /ˋɔθərɪŋ; ˈɔːθərɪŋ/ *n* [U]
the activity of writing and designing WEBSITES 网站内容编写设计: *Here are a few tips on authoring and site design.* 这是关于网站内容编写设计的几条小提示。

aut·o·ma·gic·ally /ˌɔtəˋmædʒɪklɪ; ˌɔːtəˈmædʒɪkli/ *adv*
humorous very quickly and without much effort, in a way that seems to be happening by magic. This word is often used about computer PROGRAMS that can perform complicated operations very quickly. It comes from a combination of the words 'AUTOMATICALLY' and 'MAGICALLY'.【幽默】〔操作电脑〕快捷地，轻易地〔由automatically 和 magically 缩合而成〕: *If you press the return key, the date will be changed automagically.* 按一下回车键，日期就会马上改变。

automated cred·it trans·fer /ˌɔtəmetɪd ˋkrɛdɪt ˌtrænsfɚ; ˌɔːtəmeɪtɪ̵d ˈkredɪ̵t ˌtrænsfɜː/ *n* [C,U] *BrE*
a way of moving money into someone's bank account by computer, especially at regular times【英】〔尤指定期的〕自动转账: *The Government's decision to pay benefits by automated credit transfer and to computerise the Post Office network is going to make a huge difference.* 政府决定通过自动转账发放津贴并使邮政网络电脑化，工作效率将大有改观。

av·a·tar /ˋævətɑr; ˈævətɑː/ *n* [C]
technical a picture of a person or animal that represents you on a computer screen, for example in some CHAT ROOMS or when you are playing games over the Internet【术语】〔网络〕虚拟化身，虚拟角色，阿凡达: *Visitors to Alpha World can actually see each other, because each is given a virtual body or "avatar" that appears on screen.* 进入α世界的人可以相互看到对方，因为每个人有一个虚拟身体或"阿凡达"出现在屏幕上。

AVC /ˌe vi ˋsi; ˌeɪ viː ˈsiː/ *n* [C] *BrE*
additional voluntary contribution; an additional amount of money that a worker can put into their PENSION PLAN to make the amount of money grow faster【英】〔退休金计划中的〕自愿追加款，自愿额外供款: *Can I transfer my benefits from another pension scheme into my AVC account?* 我能不能把我另一个退休金计划中的金额转到我的自愿额外供款账户里呢？

AZT /ˌe zi ˋti; ˌeɪ zed ˈtiː/ *n* [U] *trademark*
a drug used by people with AIDS to slow down the progress of the disease【商标】齐多夫定，叠氮胸苷〔一种抗艾滋病药〕

B,b

B2B /ˌbi tu ˋbi; ˌbiː tuː ˈbiː/
the abbreviation for 缩写= BUSINESS TO BUSINESS

B2B2C /ˌbi tu ˌbi tu ˋsi; ˌbiː tuː ˌbiː tuː ˈsiː/
the written abbreviation of 缩写= 'business to business to consumer'; the selling of a product or service from a company to a customer with the help of a second company, usually on the Internet 公司对公司对客户〔通过另一家公司（通常在互联网上）向顾客售卖货品或提供服务〕

B2C /ˌbi tu ˋsi; ˌbiː tuː ˈsiː/
the written abbreviation of 缩写= 'business to consumer'; the selling of a product or service from a company directly to a customer, usually on the Internet 公司对客户〔直接（通常在互联网上）向顾客售卖货品或提供服务〕

B4
a written abbreviation of 缩写= 'before', used in E-MAIL or TEXT MESSAGES on MOBILE PHONES〔电子邮件和手机短信用语〕

babes /bebz; beɪbz/ *n* [plural]
a friendly way of addressing someone, especially some-

one you love 可人儿，宝贝儿：*You're going to have to cheer up, babes, or we're both going to get depressed.* 宝贝儿，你必须振作起来，要不然我们两个都会意志消沉。

back /bæk; bæk/ *n* [C] *AmE*

NEW MEANING

spoken **I've got your back** an expression meaning that you are willing to protect or help someone who is going to be in a dangerous or difficult situation【美口】我会帮你一把的

back·burn·er, backburner /ˌbæk ˋbɝnɚ; ˌbæk ˈbɜːnə/ *v* [T]

informal to delay doing something, because it does not need your attention immediately or because it is not as important as other things that you need to do immediately【非正式】暂时搁置：*Allison back-burnered her prestigious law career when she had a baby.* 艾莉森在生孩子后，暂时放下了自己如日中天的律师事业。| *The project has been back-burnered due to technical problems.* 这个项目由于技术问题被推迟了。—**back-burnering** *n* [U]

back·chan·nel /ˋbækˌtʃænḷ; ˈbækˌtʃænl/ *n* [C]

someone or something that passes information secretly or unofficially from one person to another 秘密（消息）渠道，非正规途径：*He may have served as a backchannel between ministers because he can be trusted to carry sensitive information.* 他可能充当了部长之间的秘密渠道，因为在传递敏感信息的事上，他是可信任的。| *back-channel diplomacy* 非正规渠道的外交

back office /ˌbæk ˋɔfɪs; ˌbæk ˈɒfɪs◂/ *n* [C]

the department of a bank or other financial institution that manages or organizes the work of the institution, but that does not deal with customers〔银行等〕内部办公室，后台部门 —**back-office** *adj* [only before noun 仅用于名词前]: *back-office operations* 内部运作

back sto·ry /ˋbæk ˌstɔrɪ; ˈbæk ˌstɔːri/ *n* [C]

the things that happened to a character in a book or film before the beginning of the story being told in the book or film〔书籍、影片等中故事开始之前的〕人物背景介绍：*The back story of why she hates her father is a bit too contrived.* 关于她为什么憎恨自己的父亲交待得有点牵强。

backup /ˋbækˌʌp; ˈbækʌp/ *n* [C usually singular 一般用单数]

a copy of a computer document, PROGRAM etc, which is made in case the original becomes lost or damaged 备份〔文件或程序等〕：*Don't forget to make a backup of any work you do.* 别忘了给自己做的所有工作留下备份。—**backup** *adj* [only before noun 仅用于名词前] *We keep backup copies of all files on the network.* 我们保留所有网络文件的备份。

back-up soft·ware /ˋbæk ʌp ˌsɔftwɛr; ˈbæk ʌp ˌsɒftweə/ *n* [U]

a type of computer SOFTWARE that makes copies of computer documents AUTOMATICALLY at regular times, to reduce the risk of losing documents that are stored on computers 自动备份软件

bad /bæd; bæd/ *n*

NEW MEANING

my bad! *AmE slang* used to say that you have made a mistake or that something is your fault【美俚】我错了！是我的错！

bad-ass /ˋbæd ˌæs; ˈbæd ˌæs/ *adj* [only before noun 仅用于名词前] *AmE slang*【美俚】

1 very good or impressive 顶呱呱的，印象深刻的：*This site is the best online magazine for bad-ass biker gear.* 这个网站是介绍顶级摩托车手装备的最佳在线杂志。**2** *approving* a bad-ass person is very determined and does not always obey rules【褒】意志坚决的，不盲从的：*Johnson plays this bad-ass cop named O'Riley.* 约翰逊扮演这个很倔的名叫奥赖利的警察。—**bad ass** *n* [C]: *Man, I think Steven Seagal rocks. The dude's just a total bad ass.* 老兄，我觉得史蒂文·西加尔真棒，这家伙倔劲十足。

bag² /bæg; bæg/ *v* [T]

NEW MEANING

informal to end an arrangement or agreement【非正式】终止〔安排或协议〕：*If the cable service doesn't live up to your expectations, bag it.* 如果有线服务不合你的期望，那就终止它吧。

bal·lis·tic /bəˋlɪstɪk; bəˈlɪstɪk/ *adj*

spoken【口】**go ballistic** to suddenly become very angry（突然）生气，发怒：*I couldn't believe it! She went ballistic just because there were peas in her pasta.* 我不敢相信！她仅仅因为面条中有豌豆而大发脾气。

bal·sam·ic vin·e·gar /bɔlˌsæmɪk ˋvɪnɪgɚ; bɔːlˌsæmɪk ˈvɪnɪgə/ *n* [U]

a type of VINEGAR that is dark brown and has a strong taste 香脂醋〔一种深棕色香醋〕

banc·as·sur·ance /ˋbæŋkəˌʃurəns; ˈbæŋkəˌʃʊərəns/ *n* [U]

the combining of banking and insurance activities in one organization 银行保险业

ban·di·ni /bænˋdinɪ; bænˈdiːni/ *n* [C]

a type of BIKINI that has a wide band of material for its top part and no STRAPS over the shoulders 班迪尼〔比基尼泳装的一种〕

band·width /ˋbændwɪdθ; ˈbændwɪdθ/ *n* [U]

technical the total amount of information that can be carried through a telephone wire, computer connection etc at one time【术语】〔标志网络传输速度的〕带宽，频宽：*Telecommunications equipment at the Milan office was replaced this year to increase capacity and bandwidth.* 米兰办事处的电信设备今年都更换过了，以增加容量和带宽。

bank /bæŋk; bæŋk/ *v*

NEW MEANING

be makin' bank *slang* to earn a lot of money for the work that you do【俚】挣大钱：*Check out Omar's new car. The brother must be makin' bank.* 看看奥马尔的新车，这位老兄肯定赚了大钱。

bank·roll·er /ˋbæŋkˌrolɚ; ˈbæŋkˌrəʊlə/ *n* [C]

someone who provides the money that a person or organization needs in order to do something, especially start a new business 融资者；〔尤指〕提供启动资金者

banner ad /ˋbænɚ ˌæd; ˈbænər ˌæd/ *n* [C]

an advertisement that appears across the top of a page on the Internet 网页标题广告，网页横额广告：*Part of the screen was taken up by a banner ad for NewsPage.* 屏幕上的一部分是新闻网页的标题广告。—**banner advertising** *n* [U]

bar-code hair·style /ˋbɑr kod ˌhɛrstaɪl; ˈbɑː kəʊd ˌheəstaɪl/ *n* [C]

humorous a hairstyle worn by some men who no longer have hair on the top of their head, in which they grow the hair on one side longer and COMB it over the top of their head. Some people believe that this style looks similar to a BAR CODE.【幽默】〔以遮掩秃顶的〕条形码式（男）发型

BASE jump·ing, base jumping /ˋbes ˌdʒʌmpɪŋ; ˈbeɪs ˌdʒʌmpɪŋ/ *n* [U]

a sport in which people jump off tall objects such as buildings, bridges, or cliffs, using a PARACHUTE. BASE jumping is illegal in many countries. BASE is an abbreviation for Building, Antenna, Span, Earth. 定点跳伞，高处跳伞〔从建筑物、桥梁、悬崖等上面跳下〕：*In BASE jumping, the parachute is opened anywhere between 1,000 and 200 feet above the ground.* 在定点跳伞运动中，降落伞在距离地面1000英尺到200英尺之间打开。—**BASE jump** *n* [C] —**BASE jumper** *n* [C]

bcc /ˌbi si ˋsi; ˌbiː siː ˈsiː/

blind carbon copy; used in an E-MAIL to show that you are sending someone a copy of a message that you have also sent to someone else, and that this person does not know that other people will receive the message〔电子邮件的〕密件抄送，暗抄；隐蔽副本，盲拷贝

BCNU
a written abbreviation of 缩写= 'be seeing you', used in E-MAIL or TEXT MESSAGEs on MOBILE PHONEs 再见〔电子邮件或手机短信用语〕

b-day /ˋbi de; ˈbiː deɪ/ *n* [C]
slang a BIRTHDAY【俚】生日: *Kevin Richardson's 29th b-day* 凯文·理查森的29周岁生日

bean count·er /ˋbin ˌkauntɚ; ˈbiːn ˌkaʊntə/ *n* [C]
informal someone whose job is to examine the cost of doing something, and who is concerned only with making a profit【非正式】〔一心只想赢利的〕成本核算员: *Since the bean counters took over the radio station, it's become a boring place to work.* 自从那些核数专家接管电台后, 在那个地方工作已变得枯燥乏味。

bear hug /ˋbɛr ˌhʌg; ˈbeə ˌhʌg/ *n* [C]
NEW MEANING
technical informal an offer to buy a company, in which more money is offered than the company is actually worth【术语, 非正式】〔对某公司的〕超值收购, 溢价收购

bear squeeze /ˋbɛr ˌskwiz; ˈbeə ˌskwiːz/ *n* [C]
technical a situation in which SHARE prices rise because people know that one group of people must buy the shares【术语】〔股票交易〕轧空头; 空头轧平; 空仓压力

beau·coup /ˋboku; ˈbəʊkuː/ *quantifier French spoken informal* a lot of or many【法口, 非正式】许多, 很多: *He makes beaucoup bucks* (=earns a lot of money) *in that job.* 他在那工作上挣了大把大把的钱。

bed-and-break·fast·ing /ˌbɛd ən ˋbrɛkfəstɪŋ; ˌbed ən ˈbrekfəstɪŋ/ *n* [U] *BrE*
technical informal an illegal situation in which someone sells SHAREs one day and buys them back the next day, in order to reduce the amount of CAPITAL GAINS TAX that they have to pay【英, 术语, 非正式】〔股票交易〕暮售朝购〔以减少所需缴付之资产增值税, 属非法行为〕

bed block·er /ˋbɛd ˌblɑkɚ; ˈbed blɒkə/ *n* [C] *BrE*
someone who has been ill but who is still in hospital because there is no one to look after them if they go home, and who is therefore using a bed that is needed for someone else who is more ill【英】赖病床者〔病已好而赖着不肯出院者〕

Bee·mer /ˋbimɚ; ˈbiːmə/ *n* [C]
informal a car made by BMW【非正式】宝马〔宝马公司制造的汽车〕

benchmark /ˋbɛntʃˌmɑrk; ˈbentʃmɑːk/ *v* [T]
to use a company's good performance as a standard by which to judge the performance of other companies of the same type〔企业管理上〕以…为基准进行评定: **benchmark sb/sth against sth** *British Steel is benchmarked against the best operations anywhere in the world.* 英国钢铁公司是以世界上最好的公司作为基准评定业绩。—**bench-marking** *n* [U]

ben·to box /ˋbɛnto ˌbɑks; ˈbentəʊ ˌbɒks/ *n* [C]
a box containing SUSHI or other Japanese food, which you can take to eat wherever you want〔盛装寿司等日式食品的〕便当盒

best /bɛst; best/ *adj BrE*
NEW MEANING
spoken informal favourite【英口, 非正式】最喜爱的: *What's your best band, or haven't you got a best at the moment?* 你最喜爱的是哪个乐队?你现在是不是还没有一个自己最喜欢的乐队?

best-ef·forts /ˌbɛst ˋɛfɚts; ˌbest ˈefəts/ *adj* [only before noun 仅用于名词前]
technical a best-efforts arrangement is one in which a bank agrees to sell another company's new SHAREs, but will not have to buy the shares itself if it cannot sell them【术语】〔发售新股中〕不作包销承诺的

best-of-breed, best of breed /ˌbɛst əv ˋbrid; ˌbest əv ˈbriːd/ *adj*
a best-of-breed computer system uses a combination of the best SOFTWARE from different companies rather than only using the software from one company〔计算机系统〕用最好的软件拼装的, 最佳品种的

best prac·tice /ˌbɛst ˋpræktɪs; ˌbest ˈpræktɪs/ *n* [C,U]
a description of the best way of performing a particular activity, especially in business, that can be used by other people or companies as a set of rules to follow 最佳做法, 最佳举措: *Management has proposed several steps to be adopted as best practice to bring the design and delivery processes closer together.* 管理层已就设计和生产过程紧密联系在一起的最佳措施提出若干建议。| *We are currently developing a number of best practices to help the Internet community enhance network security.* 目前我们正在研究若干最可行的方法, 以帮助互联网社区提高网络安全。

beta car·o·tene /ˌbetə ˋkærətin; ˌbiːtə ˈkærətiːn/ *n* [U]
a type of CAROTENE (=a substance found in vegetables such as CARROTs, which is important for good health) β胡萝卜素: *Are you taking beta carotene supplements?* 你在服用β胡萝卜素补充剂吗?

bev·vied up /ˌbɛvɪd ˋʌp; ˌbevid ˈʌp/ *adj* [not before noun 不用于名词前] *BrE*
informal drunk. This phrase comes from 'BEVVY' which is an informal word meaning BEVERAGE.【英, 非正式】喝醉的: **be bevvied up** *After a couple of hours everyone was so bevvied up that they didn't know what they were doing.* 几个小时后, 他们一个个都喝得醉醺醺的, 不知道自己在干什么。| **get bevvied up** *We're all going out tonight to get bevvied up.* 今天晚上我们都去喝他个一醉方休。

bidding war /ˋbɪdɪŋ ˌwɔr; ˈbɪdɪŋ ˌwɔː/ *n* [C]
a situation in which two or more people or organizations compete to buy something, for example a house or a company 竞价战: *She said she had expected a bidding war for the 5,000-square-foot home on Vargas Road.* 她说她已料到瓦尔加斯大道上那幢5000平方英尺的住房会引起一场竞价战。

big /bɪg; bɪg/ *v*
big sth **up** *phr v* [T] *BrE spoken informal* to spend a lot of money and enjoy yourself in a social situation, in a way that other people will notice【英口, 非正式】摆阔, 充大方

big air〔单板滑雪的〕空中技巧

big air /ˌbɪg ˋɛr; ˌbɪg ˈeə/ *n* [U]
a type of SNOWBOARDing in which people perform complicated jumps and turns in the air while going down a mountain〔单板滑雪的〕空中技巧: *After Saturday's big air competition, Christy says she's ready to come back next year.* 在星期六〔单板滑雪的〕空中技巧赛之后, 克丽丝蒂说她准备明年再来。

big·foot·ing /ˋbɪgˌfutɪŋ; ˈbɪgˌfʊtɪŋ/ *n* [U]
1 the practice of using your power or authority to take control of a situation from someone who is weaker than you 仗势压人, 以权压人 **2** a situation in which a large number of similar signals are sent at the same time from MOBILE PHONEs to a radio station so that it is difficult for the radio station to handle them〔对无线电通讯台的〕手机信息轰炸

big hair /ˌbɪg ˋhɛr; ˌbɪg ˈheə/ *n* [U]

informal a hair style in which someone's hair is high up above their head and wide at the sides, fashionable especially in the 1980s【非正式】蓬蓬头〔尤指20世纪80年代流行的一种发型〕: *Who's that woman with the big hair?* 那个留着蓬蓬头的女人是谁?

big hit·ter /ˌbɪg ˋhɪtɚ; ˌbɪg ˈhɪtə/ *n* [C]
someone who is very important and successful and who has a lot of influence 要人, 大亨: *For many years, Kenneth Clarke was one of the big hitters in the Conservative Party.* 许多年来, 肯尼思·克拉克一直是保守党内的大佬之一。

bike /baɪk; baɪk/ *v* [T]
to take something to someone by motorbike in order to get it there quickly 用摩托车带: **bike sth over/round** *We're late for our deadline. Can you bike the photos over to us?* 我们赶不上最后期限了, 你能用摩托车把那些照片捎过来吗?

bin·di /ˋbɪndɪ; ˈbɪndi/ *n* [C]
a small amount of coloured powder or a piece of jewellery, usually in the shape of a round mark, that many Hindu people wear on their FOREHEAD*s* between their EYEBROW*s*. Bindis are worn for religious reasons and by women to show they are married, but now many women wear them to make themselves more attractive or fashionable.〔印度教女子加在两眉之间前额上的〕吉祥痣〔以前用于表示已婚, 现在只是为了美观〕

bi·o·di·ver·si·ty /ˌbaɪodaɪˋvɝsətɪ; ˌbaɪəʊdaɪˈvɜːsɪ̤ti/ *n* [U]
technical the variety of plants and animals in a particular place【术语】〔某地的〕生物多样性: *One of our goals will be to involve local communities in biodiversity conservation.* 我们的目标之一是要让当地的社区参加保护生物多样性。

bi·o·eth·ics /ˌbaioˋɛθɪks; ˌbaɪəʊˈeθɪks/ *n* [U]
technical the study of whether some sciences, for example GENETIC ENGINEERING, are a good or bad thing for society【术语】生物伦理学

bi·o·in·for·ma·ti·cian /ˌbaɪoˌɪnfɚməˋtɪʃən; ˌbaɪəʊˌɪnfəməˈtɪʃən/ *n* [C]
someone who studies or works in BIOINFORMATICS 生物信息学〔研究〕者

bi·o·in·for·mat·ics /ˌbaɪoˌɪnfɔrˋmætɪks; ˌbaɪəʊˌɪnfɔːˈmætɪks/ *n* [U]
technical the use of computers to organize the large amounts of information produced in some kinds of science, for example GENETICS【术语】生物信息学

biologically en·gi·neered /baɪəˌlɑdʒɪkl̩ɪ ɛndʒəˋnɪrd; baɪəˌlɒdʒɪkli endʒɪ̤ˈnɪəd/ *adj*
another word for GENETICALLY MODIFIED genetically modified 的另一种说法

bi·o·nom·ics /ˌbaɪoˋnɑmɪks; ˌbaɪəʊˈnɒmɪks/ *n* [U]
technical a type of scientific study which compares economic systems to ECOSYSTEMS (=the living things in a particular area and how they relate to one another)【术语】生态经济学

bi·o·phar·ma·ceu·ti·cal /ˌbaɪoˌfɑrməˋsjutɪkl; ˌbaɪəʊˌfɑːməˈsjuːtɪkəl/ *adj* [only before noun 仅用于名词前]
technical relating to BIOTECHNOLOGY (=the use of living things to make drugs and chemicals) and PHARMACEUTICALS (= the development and production of drugs and medicines)【术语】生物制药的: *Not all biopharmaceutical companies make drugs themselves.* 不是所有生物制药公司都自制药物。

bi·ra·cial /ˌbaɪˋreʃəl; ˌbaɪˈreɪʃəl◂/ *adj*
if someone is biracial, he or she has parents who come from different races 双人种的, 双族裔的: *biracial children* 混血儿

birth /bɝθ; bɜːθ/ *v* [T]
literary to be the origin of something new; ORIGINATE【文】开创: *McMillan's 1992 novel birthed a new genre of contemporary fiction.* 麦克米伦1992年的长篇小说开创了当代小说的一种新体裁。

biz·jet /ˋbɪzdʒɛt; ˈbɪzdʒet/ *n* [C]
informal an aircraft used especially by business people【非正式】公务机, 商务人员专机

biz·zies /ˋbɪzɪz; ˈbɪziz/ *n* [plural] *BrE*
slang the police. This word is used especially in the city of Liverpool in north-west England.【英俚】警察〔尤用于利物浦〕: *I just hid in the corner until the bizzies had gone.* 我躲在角落里一直到警察离去。

black knight /ˌblæk ˋnaɪt; ˌblæk ˈnaɪt/ *n* [C]
a company that tries to take control of another company by offering to buy a lot of its SHARE*s* "黑骑士"〔通过购买另一公司大量股票从而对它加以控制的公司〕

blad·dered /ˋblædɚd; ˈblædəd/ *adj* [not before noun 不用于名词前] *BrE*
informal very drunk【英, 非正式】大醉的, 烂醉如泥的: **be bladdered** *Geoff was completely bladdered last night. He could hardly stand up.* 杰夫昨天夜里醉得一塌糊涂, 几乎站不起来。| **get bladdered** *He's down the pub getting bladdered.* 他到酒馆买醉去了。

blad·er /ˋbledɚ; ˈbleɪdə/ *n* [C]
informal someone who SKATES on ROLLERBLADES【非正式】轮滑者, 滚轴溜冰者, 滑旱冰者

blag·ger /ˋblægɚ; ˈblægə/ *n* [C] *BrE*
informal someone who gets something they want by lying to people in a clever way【英, 非正式】骗徒, 骗子

Blair·is·m /ˋblɛrɪzəm; ˈbleərɪzəm/ *n* [U] *BrE*
the political ideas of the British former PRIME MINISTER, Tony Blair, and his government【英】〔英国前首相〕布莱尔主义〔布莱尔及其政府所持的政治理念〕

Blair·ite /ˋblɛraɪt; ˈbleəraɪt/ *n* [C] *BrE*
someone who believes in the political ideas of the former British PRIME MINISTER, Tony Blair, and his government【英】布莱尔主义者 —**Blairite** *adj*

blame·storm·ing /ˋblemˌstɔrmɪŋ; ˈbleɪmˌstɔːmɪŋ/ *n* [U]
humorous the practice of sitting in a group and talking about why a particular job was not done properly, and deciding who was responsible for the failure. This word comes from a combination of the words 'BLAME' and 'BRAINSTORMING'.【幽默】〔为检讨某项目失败原因等而举行的〕追责风暴, 责任追究会〔由 blame 和 brainstorming 缩合而成〕

bleeding edge, the /ˌblidɪŋ ˋɛdʒ; ˌbliːdɪŋ ˈedʒ/ *n* [singular]
the most advanced stage or development of something. This expression developed from the phrase 'the cutting edge' and is used about things that are even newer, more advanced etc, especially related to computers. 尖端技术水平: **on the bleeding edge of sth** *developments on the bleeding edge of information technology* 信息科技尖端技术的发展 —**bleeding-edge** *adj* [only before noun 仅用于名词前]: *bleeding-edge applications* 尖端技术的应用

blended fam·i·ly /ˌblɛndɪd ˋfæməlɪ; ˌblendɪ̤d ˈfæməli/ *n* [C]
a family in which one or both parents have children from previous marriages living with the family 混合型家庭〔由夫妇及双方或其中一方在过去婚姻中所生子女组成的家庭〕: *Some experts had estimated that by the year 2000 there would be more blended families than intact biological families.* 一些专家估计, 到2000年混合型家庭将多于纯血缘的家庭。

bless /blɛs; bles/ *interjection BrE*
said to show that you think someone or something is very nice or loveable【英】棒极了!: *At that moment, a cute little dog came into the room. "Oh, bless," said Tamryn.* 就在那个时候, 一只可爱的小狗走进了房间。"呵, 好酷," 塔姆林说。

blind call /ˌblaɪnd ˋkɔl; ˌblaɪnd ˈkɔːl/ *n* [C]
another word for COLD CALL cold call 的另一种说法

blissed out /ˌblɪst ˋaʊt; ˌblɪst ˈaʊt/ *adj BrE*
informal extremely happy and relaxed, especially as a

result of using illegal drugs【英，非正式】〔尤指吸食毒品后〕感到极度欣喜和放松的: *a bunch of blissed out partygoers* 一群兴高采烈的聚会者 | *He just stood with a blissed out look on his face and danced.* 他带着极其轻松愉快的表情站了起来，跳起了舞。| *I felt really blissed out.* 我真的感到极度的快乐轻松。—**bliss out** *v* [I]: *I blissed out on ecstasy.* 我服了"狂喜"迷幻药后感到极度愉快轻松。

B-list /ˈbi ˌlɪst; ˈbiː ˌlɪst/ *adj*
among the group of film stars, musicians etc who are fairly famous or popular, but are not any of the most popular or famous〔影星、歌星等〕二流的，二线的: *The party was crowded by B-list personalities who could be relied on to turn up to any launch.* 这次晚会挤满了二流角色，这些人靠得住，什么样的推广活动，他们都会到场。

bloat·ware /ˈblotˌwɛr; ˈbləʊtweə/ *n* [U]
informal【非正式】**1** computer SOFTWARE that has many features that are not needed〔包含许多无用性能的〕大软件 **2** computer SOFTWARE that uses a large amount of the computer's MEMORY, and that is therefore not effective or useful〔因占用大量内存而效率降低的〕膨胀软件

blood /blʌd; blʌd/ *n*
NEW MEANING
blood on the carpet a situation where people have a very strong disagreement, with the result that something serious happens, such as someone losing his or her job〔造成严重后果的〕严重分歧

blood dop·ing /ˈblʌd ˌdopɪŋ; ˈblʌd ˌdəʊpɪŋ/ *n* [U]
the practice of removing red BLOOD CELLS from an ATHLETE'S body, preserving them for a period of time, and then putting them back before he or she competes in a sports event. Blood doping improves an athlete's performance and is illegal in most sports 血搀，违规输血〔从运动员体内抽出部分红血球，参赛前再注回其体内以提升运动员的成绩〕

blow /blo; bləʊ/ *n* [U]
NEW MEANING
slang the illegal drug COCAINE【俚】云雾〔指可卡因〕

blue·tooth /ˈblutuθ; ˈbluːtuːθ/ *n* [U]
trademark bluetooth technology allows electronic equipment to communicate by using radio, so that, for example, a computer and printer can work together without having a wire connecting them【商标】监牙（技术）〔代替专用连接电线的通用无线电连接〕

blunt /blʌnt; blʌnt/ *n* [C] *AmE*
slang a thick MARIJUANA cigarette that is made by taking the tobacco out of a CIGAR and filling the empty inner part with marijuana【美俚】大麻烟卷

BMP /ˌbi ɛm ˋpi; ˌbiː em ˈpiː/ *n* [C]
technical【术语】**1** basic multilingual plane 基本多语种平面 **2** bit mapped picture 位图

bo·de·ga /boˋdegə; bəʊˈdiːgə/ *n* [C] *Spanish*【西】
a small shop that sells food 小食品店

body warm·er /ˈbadɪ ˌwɔrmɚ; ˈbɒdi ˌwɔːmə/ *n* [C]
a piece of warm clothing without arms that you wear over a sweater or a shirt, especially when you are outside〔户外穿的〕背心，马甲: *a woolly fleece body warmer* 羊毛背心

boiler-room /ˈbɔɪlɚ ˌrum; ˈbɔɪlə ˌruːm/ also 又作 **boiler shop** *n* [C]
an organization that sells STOCKS, SHARES etc by telephone, often using dishonest or illegal methods of selling "锅炉房"式电话推销机构〔以欺诈方式通过电话推销股票等的非法组织〕: *boiler-room sales techniques* "锅炉房"式电话推销术

bolt-on /ˈbolt ˌan; ˈbəʊlt ˌɒn/ *adj*
bolt-on part/component/extra *especially BrE* something that is connected to the outside of a machine after it has been made, and is then part of the machine【尤英】可用螺栓固定的部分/部件/附件

bomb /bam; bɒm/ *n*
NEW MEANING
be the bomb *AmE slang* to be very good or exciting【美俚】极好的，轰动的: *That new Puff Daddy CD is the bomb.* 那张新出的吹牛老爹的CD非常轰动。

bone /bon; bəʊn/ *v* [T]
NEW MEANING
taboo to have sex with someone【讳】与〔某人〕性交

bonk·bust·er /ˈbaŋkˌbʌstɚ; ˈbɒŋkˌbʌstə/ *n* [C] *BrE humorous* a book or film which contains a lot of sex and which is very popular and successful, but which is not considered to have serious value as art. This word comes from a combination of the words 'bonk', which is a British slang word meaning 'to have sex', and 'BLOCKBUSTER'【英，幽默】风靡一时的性爱小说[电影]〔由bonk和blockbuster缩合而成〕: *She spent her holiday lying by the pool, reading the latest bonkbuster.* 她躺在游泳池边，阅读最新的性爱小说来消磨假日。—**bonkbuster** *adj*: *bonkbuster novels* 风靡一时的情欲小说

boob·ker·chief /ˈbubkɚˌtʃɪf; ˈbuːbkəˌtʃɨf/ *n* [C] *BrE informal* a piece of clothing for women that is made from a TRIANGLE-shaped piece of cloth that is fastened at the back, so that the arms and shoulders are not covered. This word is a combination of the words 'boobs', which is an informal word for a woman's BREASTS, and 'HANDKERCHIEF'.【英，非正式】胸兜，兜肚〔由boobs和handkerchief缩合而成〕

boogie board /ˈbugɪ ˌbɔrd; ˈbuːgi ˌbɔːd/ *n* [C]
an object that you lie on to ride on ocean waves, that is half the length of a SURFBOARD 卧式短冲浪板

bookmark¹ /ˈbʊkˌmark; ˈbʊkmaːk/ *n* [C]
NEW MEANING
a way of saving the address of a page on the Internet, so that you can find it again easily〔互联网上的〕书签

bookmark² /ˈbʊkˌmark; ˈbʊkmaːk/ *v* [T]
to save the address of a page on the Internet, so that you can find it again easily 标识〔网址，方便下次浏览〕，做书签

boom·er /ˈbumɚ; ˈbuːmə/ *n* [C]
a short form of 缩略式= BABY BOOMER

boot cut /ˈbut ˌkʌt; ˈbuːt ˌkʌt/ *adj*
boot cut trousers/jeans trousers or JEANS that are slightly wider at the bottom than at the knee so that you can wear boots with them 微喇裤/牛仔裤

bootstrap ac·qui·si·tion /ˈbutstræp ækwəˌzɪʃən; ˈbuːtstræp ækwɨˌzɪʃən/ *n* [C,U]
technical a way of buying a company over a period of time, in which you buy SHARES that you then use to borrow money. You then use this money to buy more shares until you own the company.【术语】渐进式收购，抵押式收购〔在一段时间内收购一家公司，先是通过购买股票，然后以股票作抵押借钱，再用借来的款项购买更多股票，直到控制该公司为止〕

boss key /ˈbɔs ˌki; ˈbɒs ˌkiː/ *n* [C]
a key on a computer keyboard that changes what is displayed on a screen. Boss keys are used by workers who are, for example, playing games or looking at WEB PAGES instead of working, when they hear their manager or BOSS coming close to them.〔电脑〕老板键，快速切换屏幕显示键

bot /bat; bɒt/ *n* [C]
technical a computer PROGRAM that performs the same operation many times in a row, for example, one that searches for information on the Internet as part of a SEARCH ENGINE【术语】机器人程序〔连续多次执行相同操作的电脑程序〕

Bo·tox¹ /ˈbotaks; ˈbəʊtɒks/ *n* [U]
trademark a substance that makes muscles relax, which can be INJECTED into the skin around someone's eyes to make the lines disappear and the skin look younger and more attractive【商标】保妥适肉毒毒素，毒杆菌素: *Botox injections for wrinkles* 用于去除皱纹的肉毒毒素注射剂

Botox² /ˋbotɑks; ˈbəʊtɒks/ *v* [T usually passive 一般用被动态]
trademark to use Botox to remove lines on your face【商标】使用保妥适去皱: *Getting Botoxed is pretty simple.* 使用保妥适去除脸上皱纹是很容易的。| *He Botoxed his forehead before the next film.* 他在演下一部影片前使用保妥适去掉前额的皱纹。

bottom fish·er /ˋbɑtəm ˏfɪʃɚ; ˈbɒtəm ˌfɪʃə/ *n* [C]
technical someone who buys companies, SHARES etc when their value is low, expecting the situation to improve later so that the companies etc increase in value【术语】趁低价时收购者

bounce /bauns; baʊns/ *v* also 又作 **bounce back**
NEW MEANING
1 [I,T] if an E-MAIL message that you send bounces or is bounced, it is AUTOMATICALLY returned to you because of a technical problem〔电子邮件〕自动退回, 弹回: *I tried to send you a message about half an hour ago, but it bounced back.* 半个小时前我试着给你发去了一个信息, 但是被自动退了回来。**2** [T] *informal* to force someone to leave a place, job, or organization, especially because they have done something wrong【非正式】迫使〔尤指犯错者〕去职, 把…从…中逐出: *That June, he bounced the other two leaders and named himself President.* 那年6月, 他迫使另外两名领袖下台, 并任命自己为总统。| **bounce sb from sth** *Taylor was bounced from the team for six weeks for assaulting his ex-girlfriend.* 泰勒因为侵犯前女友而被勒令离队六周。

boy band /ˋbɔɪ ˏbænd; ˈbɔɪ ˌbænd/ *n* [C]
a group of attractive young men who perform by singing and dancing, and who are especially popular with teenage girls 男孩乐队: *Christy's favorite boy band is Boyzone.* 克里斯蒂最喜爱的男孩乐队是"男孩地带"。

bps, BPS /ˏbi pi ˋɛs; ˌbiː piː ˈes/ *n* [U]
technical bits per second; a measurement of how fast a computer or MODEM can send or receive information【术语】每秒位元数, 位/秒, 比特/秒: *a 28,800 bps modem* 28,800位/秒的调制调解器

brain·i·ac /ˋbrenɪˏæk; ˈbreɪniæk/ *n* [C]
informal humorous someone who spends a lot of time studying and thinking about complicated ideas, but who is often unable to communicate with people in ordinary social situations【非正式, 幽默】怪才〔指整天思考高深问题、常无法与他人沟通的人〕: *Electrical engineering is the perfect career for a brainiac like him.* 电气工程是像他那样的怪才的理想职业。—**brainiac** *adj*: *The company is trying to change its brainiac image.* 该公司试图改变其学究形象。

branchless bank /ˏbræntʃlɪs ˋbæŋk; ˌbrɑːntʃləs ˈbæŋk/ *n* [C]
a bank that exists only on the Internet and which does not have a building that you can go to 网上银行

brand·ing /ˋbrændɪŋ; ˈbrændɪŋ/ *n* [U]
technical a practice in which a company gives a group of their products the same BRAND NAME. This is done to help the brand name become well known and to encourage people to buy new or different products that have the same brand.【术语】创品牌, 品牌打造

BRB, brb
a written abbreviation of 缩写= 'be right back', used by people communicating in CHAT ROOM*s* on the Internet 马上回来〔网上聊天室用语〕

breadboard /ˋbrɛdˏbɔrd; ˈbredbɔːd/ *n* [C]
NEW MEANING
technical a model of a CIRCUIT BOARD (=a piece of electronic equipment) that is used in order to test the design before it is produced【术语】实验电路板

break·beat /ˋbrekˏbit; ˈbreɪkbiːt/ *n* [U] *BrE*
a type of dance music which is popular in Britain, has a fast beat, and uses SAMPLES (=a small part of a song from a CD or record that is used in a new song)【英】霹雳舞曲, 碎拍音乐

breeder /ˋbridɚ; ˈbriːdə/ *n* [C]
NEW MEANING
an offensive word meaning HETEROSEXUAL, used by HOMOSEXUAL*s*, especially to talk about someone they do not like 配种人〔同性恋者称异性恋者的冒犯语〕

breeze /briz; briːz/ *v* [T]
NEW MEANING
to do very well in a test, a piece of written work etc, with very little effort 轻易地通过: *Don't bother studying for the English exam – you'll breeze it.* 不要为应付英语考试而头疼, 你会轻易通过的。

brilliant weap·on /ˋbrɪljənt ˏwɛpən; ˈbrɪljənt ˌwepən/ *n* [C]
a weapon that can find the object it is attacking without being guided by a computer 智能(化)武器

Brit·pop /ˋbrɪtpɑp; ˈbrɪtpɒp/ *n* [U]
a type of British popular music of the 1990s that often has tunes that are easy to remember, clever or interesting words, and is suitable for dancing. It is usually played by small bands with a drummer, one or two guitar players, and a singer. Well-known Britpop bands include Blur and Oasis.〔20世纪90年代流行的〕英式摇滚乐〔一种曲调易记, 歌词灵巧、有趣, 适合跳舞的音乐〕

broadband /ˋbrɔdˏbænd; ˈbrɔːdbænd/ *n* [U]
NEW MEANING
technical a system of connecting computers to the Internet and moving information, such as messages or pictures, at a very high speed【术语】宽(频)带 —**broadband** *adj* [only before noun 仅用于名词前]: *broadband communications* 宽带通信

broad mon·ey /ˋbrɔd ˏmʌnɪ; ˈbrɔːd ˌmʌni/ *n* [U]
technical cash and all other forms of money that cannot easily be turned into cash【术语】广义货币: *Broad money refers to money held both for transactions purposes and as a form of saving.* "广义货币"指的是既可用于交易又可用于储蓄的一种货币。

brother /ˋbrʌðɚ; ˈbrʌðə/ *n* [C]
NEW MEANING
slang a word meaning a black man, used especially by other black men【俚】兄弟〔黑人男子间互称〕

brown·field site /ˋbraunfild ˏsaɪt; ˈbraʊnfiːld ˌsaɪt/ *n* [C] *BrE*
a place, especially in a city, that is used for building homes, offices etc, where in the past there have already been buildings, industries etc【英】"棕色地带", 拆迁地, 重建区〔指城市中清除旧房后可用于建造新房的空地〕: *The government wants to raise the proportion of housing built on brownfield sites, rather than on unspoilt countryside.* 政府想提高在重建区而不是在未遭破坏的农村修建住房的比例。

brows·er /ˋbrauzɚ; ˈbraʊzə/ *n* [C]
a computer program that finds information on the Internet and shows it on your computer screen 浏览器: *a Web browser* 网页浏览器

bruschetta 盖浇吐司

bru·schet·ta /bruˋskɛtə; bruːˈsketə/ *n* [U]
bread that has been TOAST*ed* and has OLIVE OIL and usually vegetables, cheese etc on top of it〔上面浇有橄榄油、蔬菜、乳酪等的〕盖浇吐司, 意大利吐司

B-school /ˈbi ˌskul; ˈbiː ˌskuːl/ *n* [C]
a short form of 缩略式= BUSINESS SCHOOL

BTW, btw
a written abbreviation of 缩写= 'by the way', often used in E-MAIL or TEXT MESSAGEs on MOBILE PHONEs 顺便提一下〔电子邮件或手机短信用语〕

buffed /bʌft; bʌft/ *adj AmE*
spoken【美口】**1 get buffed** if you get buffed, you lift weights regularly so that your muscles will get bigger 练出肌肉块: *This is a beginner's guide to getting buffed and maintaining a complete physique.* 这本初学者指南教导读者如何锻炼肌肉和保持体形完美。**2** a buffed person has big strong muscles〔人〕肌肉发达的

buffer /ˈbʌfɚ; ˈbʌfə/ *v* [T]
if a computer buffers information, it holds it for a short while before using it. Computers buffer information when receiving VIDEO pictures over the Internet, for example, so that they have enough information to show the pictures smoothly and do not have to wait while more information arrives. 缓存〔信息〕

bug² /bʌg; bʌg/
bug sb **out** *phr v* [T] *informal* to annoy someone【非正式】使〔某人〕厌烦: *It really bugs me out how he's always talking about how much money he makes.* 他总在叨唠自己能挣多少钱，这真让我烦透了。

bull bars /ˈbul ˌbarz; ˈbʊl ˌbɑːz/ *n* [plural] *BrE*
a set of metal bars fixed to the front of a large vehicle such as a Jeep or Land Rover in order to protect it from damage【英】〔机动车的〕保险杠: *They fitted their 4×4 with bull bars.* 他们给自己的四轮驱动车装上了保险杠。**—bullbarred** *adj*: *bullbarred vehicles* 装有保险杠的车辆

bum /bʌm; bʌm/ *n*
NEW MEANING
bums on seats *BrE humorous* the number of people who go to a concert, play, or other performance. This expression is often used by people who disapprove of performances that are intended to attract as many people as possible, but that may not have a lot of serious artistic value【英，幽默】〔音乐会或其他演出活动的〕出席人数〔通常是艺术价值并不高但却想吸引更多人前来捧场的活动〕: *These managers just want to know what will put bums on seats.* 经理们只想知道如何能吸引人前来捧场。

bummed /bʌmd; bʌmd/ also 又作 **bummed out** *adj* [not before noun 不用于名词前]
informal especially spoken feeling sad or disappointed【非正式，尤口】悲伤的，沮丧的: *I was really bummed that I missed the game.* 我错过了这场比赛，感到十分失望。

bump /bʌmp; bʌmp/ *v*
NEW MEANING
1 [T] *informal* to move someone or something into a different class or group, or to move them out of a class or group altogether【非正式】把…移到〔另一个级别或群体〕，把…撵走 [挪走]: *Jeff was bumped to first class by American Airlines when he told them why he was flying back to Arizona.* 杰夫告诉了美国航空公司他要飞回亚利桑那的原因后，航空公司就安排他换到了头等舱。| *The flight was overbooked, and as Dad hadn't reconfirmed he was the first one to be bumped.* 这个航班超员预订，爸爸因为没有再确认机位，就成了第一个被挤掉的人。| **bump sb up/out of/from etc** *The reforms bumped many families off the state-provided healthcare list.* 这连串改革把许多家庭挤出了公费医疗名单。**2** to move a radio or television programme to a different time 将〔电台或电视节目〕改期播出: *The 'X Files' is moving from Friday to Sunday nights, and as a result, 'Married with Children' will be bumped from Sundays to Saturdays.*《X档案》由星期五改到星期天晚上播出，因此，《宝贝家庭》将从星期天挪到星期六播出。

bun /bʌn; bʌn/ *n plural* **buns**
NEW MEANING
informal humorous the part of your body that you sit on【非正式，幽默】屁股

bundle¹ /ˈbʌndl̩; ˈbʌndl/ *n* [C]
NEW MEANING
computer SOFTWARE and sometimes other equipment or services that are included with a new computer at little or no additional cost〔电脑〕捆绑式销售，附送: *Most computer makers include a bundle of useful software for you and the kids.* 许多电脑制造商随电脑附送一些对你和孩子们有用的软件。

bundle² /ˈbʌndl̩; ˈbʌndl/ *v* [T]
NEW MEANING
to include computer SOFTWARE or other services with a new computer at little or no extra cost〔销售电脑时〕捆绑销售，附送: **bundle sth with sth** *Microsoft can bundle Windows NT at discounted prices with its popular desktop application programs.* 微软打折销售流行的桌面应用软件时可附送视窗NT。

burn¹ /bɝn; bɜːn/ *v* [T]
NEW MEANING
if you burn a CD, you record music, images, or other information onto it, using special computer equipment 刻录，烧录〔盘片，光碟〕

burn rate /ˈbɝn ˌret; ˈbɜːn ˌreɪt/ *n* [U]
the rate at which a new company spends money when it is just starting, especially used of new Internet companies〔新互联网公司投入运作时〕花钱的速率

business-to-business /ˌbɪznɪs tə ˈbɪznɪs; ˌbɪznɪ̈s tə ˈbɪznɪ̈s/ *adj abbreviation* 缩写为 **B2B**
business-to-business advertising/commerce/marketing/transactions etc advertising or other business activities between different businesses, rather than between a business and ordinary people who are customers 商家对商家的广告/贸易/营销/交易等: *We hope to offer full business-to-business transactions over the Internet by next year.* 我们希望来年能通过互联网提供全面的商家对商家交易。| *business-to-business credit information* 商家之间的信贷信息

bust /bʌst; bʌst/ *v*
NEW MEANING
bust a move *AmE slang* to make unusual and impressive movements while dancing【美俚】跳出不同寻常的舞步
bust sb **not** *phr v* [T] *AmE slang* to strongly criticize someone【美俚】对…严加指责: *I busted him out for forgetting to pay me back.* 他忘了还我钱，我严责了他一顿。

bust·ed¹ /ˈbʌstɪd; ˈbʌstɪ̈d/ *adj* [not before noun 不用于名词前] *AmE*
informal caught doing something wrong and likely to be punished【美，非正式】被逮个正着的: *You guys are so busted!* 你们这些家伙可被逮个正着了！

busted² /ˈbʌstɪd; ˈbʌstɪ̈d/ *interjection AmE*
said when someone has been caught lying or doing something wrong【美】(这下)可(给)逮住了！

bust-up ac·qui·si·tion /ˈbʌst ʌp ækwəˌzɪʃən; ˈbʌst ʌp ækwɪ̈ˌzɪʃən/ *n* [C,U]
technical a situation in which a company gets a loan to buy another company by promising that it will sell the things the second company owns if it cannot pay back the loan【术语】二手抵押借贷，二手资产抵押

button-down /ˈbʌtn̩ ˌdaun; ˈbʌtn ˌdaʊn/ also 又作 **buttoned-down** *adj* [only before noun 仅用于名词前]
a button-down company or style is formal and traditional 循规蹈矩的；守旧的: *He didn't fit in with the button-down culture of his new boss.* 他不适应新老板那套循规蹈矩的做法。

buy² /baɪ; baɪ/ *n* [C usually singular 一般用单数,U]
NEW MEANING
an act of buying something, especially something illegal 购买，进货〔尤指私货〕: *A couple of guys were sit-*

ting behind me discussing some kind of buy. 坐在我后面的两个家伙正讨论要进点私货。

buy·back /ˋbaɪˌbæk; ˈbaɪbæk/ *n* [C,U]
an arrangement by which a person or company sells SHARES in a business and buys them back again later 回购〔股票〕: *Share buybacks are constrained by tight regulations.* 股票回购受到严格的条例限制。

buzzed-about /ˋbʌzd əˌbaʊt; ˈbʌzd əˌbaʊt/ *adj AmE informal* a buzzed-about film, book etc is one which a lot of people are talking about because it is new and interesting【美，非正式】多人谈论的: *It's one of the year's most buzzed-about movies.* 这是本年度最热门的电影之一。

BWL, bwl
a written abbreviation of 缩写= 'bursting with laughter', used in E-MAIL OT TEXT MESSAGES on MOBILE PHONES 笑死人了〔电子邮件或手机短信用语〕

C,c

C++ /ˌsi plʌs ˋplʌs; ˌsiː plʌs ˈplʌs/ *n* [U]
a computer language that is popular because it is useful for developing complicated computer PROGRAMS〔电脑的〕C++语言

C2C /ˌsi tu ˋsi; ˌsiː tuː ˈsiː/
the written abbreviation of 缩写= 'customer to customer'; the selling of a product or service from one customer to another, usually over the Internet, for example at an ONLINE AUCTION 客户对客户〔网上拍卖用语〕

ca·ble·cast /ˋkeblˌkæst; ˈkeɪbəlˌkɑːst/ *n* [C]
a show, film, sports event etc that is broadcast on a CABLE television station 有线电视广播: *The MTV Video Awards cablecast is almost as popular as the Grammy Awards.* 通过有线电视广播的音乐电视视频奖几乎和格莱美奖一样受欢迎。—**cablecast** *v* [T]

cable mo·dem /ˋkebl ˌmodɛm; ˈkeɪbəl ˌməʊdem/ *n* [C]
a MODEM (=a piece of equipment that allows information from one computer to be sent to another) that uses CABLE connections instead of telephone wires, and allows you to search the Internet very quickly 电缆调制解调器，缆线数据机: *Millions of people use cable modems at home for faster online access.* 数以百万计的人利用电缆调制解调器在家中以更快的速度上网。

cable-read·y /ˋkebl ˌrɛdɪ; ˈkeɪbəl ˌredi/ *adj*
a television that is cable-ready is able to receive CABLE TELEVISION signals directly without needing any special equipment〔电视〕能直接接收有线电视信号的

cache¹ /kæʃ; kæʃ/ *n* [C]
NEW MEANING
technical a special section of MEMORY in a computer that helps it work faster by storing information for a short time【术语】高速缓冲存储器，快取记忆体: *Every time a user requests a Web page, the provider's machine checks whether a copy is already stored in the cache.* 每当用户需要某个网页时，供应商的机器就会核查在高速缓冲存储器中是否已留有副本。| *In practice, cache memory can improve a computer's performance dramatically.* 高速缓冲存储器确能极大地改善电脑的性能。

cache² /kæʃ; kæʃ/ *v* [T]
NEW MEANING
technical to put information in a cache【术语】把资料存入高速缓冲存储器

café, **cafe** /kæˋfe; ˈkæfeɪ/ *n* [C]
NEW MEANING
a part of a WEBSITE which has general information about the website, discussion groups, a place to read or leave messages for other users etc〔网站的〕聊天茶座: *Only registered users may log on to the site's cafe.* 只有注册用户才可进入该网站的聊天茶座。

CALL /kɔl; kɔːl/ *n* [U]
computer-assisted language learning; the use of computers to help people learn foreign languages 电脑辅助外语学习

call cen·tre /ˋkɔl ˌsɛntɚ; ˈkɔːl ˌsentə/ *n* [C] *BrE*
an office where people answer customers' questions, make sales etc over the telephone【英】电话服务中心

caller di·splay /ˋkɔlɚ dɪˌsple; ˈkɔːlə dɪˌspleɪ/ *BrE*【英】, **caller ID** /ˋkɔlɚ aɪ ˌdi; ˈkɔːlər aɪ ˌdiː/ *AmE*【美】*n* [U]
a special service that uses a piece of equipment attached to your telephone to tell you the telephone number of the person who is calling 来电显示

call screen·ing /ˋkɔl ˌskrinɪŋ; ˈkɔːl ˌskriːnɪŋ/ *n* [U]
1 a special service that prevents particular people from calling you because their telephone number is on a list of telephone numbers from which you do not wish to receive calls 电话筛选服务（装置）**2** the practice of letting an ANSWERPHONE answer your telephone calls, and you then only talk to callers that you want to speak to 筛选式通话，来电过滤

call sens·ing u·nit /ˋkɔl sɛnsɪŋ ˌjunɪt; ˈkɔːl sensɪŋ ˌjuːnɨt/ *n* [C]
a piece of electronic equipment that tells Internet users when someone is trying to call them on the telephone〔上网时的〕来电提示装置

call·time /ˋkɔlˌtaɪm; ˈkɔːltaɪm/ *n* [U]
the amount of time that is available for the user of a MOBILE PHONE to make calls 呼叫时间，通话时间: *You get 20 minutes free calltime a day, but only after 7 p.m.* 每天你可以有20分钟免费通话时间，但这只能在晚上7点以后才行。

cam·i·ki·ni /ˋkæmɪˌkinɪ; ˈkæmɪˌkiːni/ *n* [C]
a type of BIKINI that has a top part that reaches down to the HIPS 卡米基尼〔比基尼的一种〕

campus /ˋkæmpəs; ˈkæmpəs/ *n* [C]
NEW MEANING
the land and buildings belonging to a large company〔大公司的〕园区〔包括土地和建筑物〕: *Microsoft's campus in Redmond, Washington* 微软公司在华盛顿州雷德蒙德的园区

candy /ˋkændɪ; ˈkændi/ *n*
NEW MEANING
mind/brain candy *informal* something that is entertaining or pleasant to look at, but which you do not approve of because you think it is not serious【非正式】使心情/脑子轻松的东西: *Most video games are just brain candy.* 大多数视频游戏只不过是放松脑子的玩意儿。—see also 另见 EYE CANDY, ARM CANDY

cannibalize /ˋkænəblˌaɪz; ˈkænɨbəlaɪz/ also 又作 **cannibalise** *BrE*【英】*v* [T]
NEW MEANING
technical if one of a company's new products cannibalizes an older one, the older product stops selling because people buy the new product instead【术语】淘汰〔旧产品〕，将…取而代之

canteen cul·ture /ˌkæntin ˋkʌltʃɚ; ˌkæntiːn ˈkʌltʃə/ *n* [U] *BrE*
old-fashioned and unfair behaviour and attitudes which some people think are typical of the police in Britain【英】〔警方的〕歧视性保守态度: *While the canteen culture flourishes, the police service will find it difficult to recruit and retain black officers.* 警察部门发现在歧视态度大行其道之时很难招募到和留住黑人警员。

can·yon·ing /ˋkænjənɪŋ; ˈkænjənɪŋ/ *n* [U]
a sport in which you walk and swim along a fast-moving river at the bottom of a CANYON (=a deep valley with very steep sides of rock) 溪降运动，探谷运动〔沿溪谷步行和游泳〕: *Canyoning continues to grow in popularity, especially in the US.* 溪降运动日益受到欢迎，尤其是在美国。| **go canyoning** *We're planning to go canyoning the weekend after next.* 我们计划在下下个周末进行溪降活动。

cap·let /ˈkæplɪt; ˈkæplɨt/ *n* [C]
a small smooth PILL (=solid piece of medicine) with a shape that is slightly longer and narrower than a TABLET (=a small round pill) 囊片〔较普通药片稍长且窄〕

carbon sink /ˈkɑrbən ˌsɪŋk; ˈkɑːbən ˌsɪŋk/ *n* [C]
a large area of forest that is believed to help the environment by taking in CARBON from the air as a way of reducing the effects of GLOBAL WARMING〔相信可通过吸收空气中的碳能减缓地球变暖的〕森林带，滤碳带

carbs /kɑrbz; kɑːbz/ *n* [U]
spoken informal foods such as rice, bread, and potatoes that contain CARBOHYDRATES【口，非正式】碳水化合物类食物：*Before a race, I make sure I eat plenty of carbs.* 赛跑之前，我一定要吃许多碳水化合物类的食物。

car·di·o /ˈkɑrdɪo; ˈkɑːdiəʊ/ *n* [U]
informal any type of exercise that makes the heart stronger and healthier, for example running【非正式】〔跑步等可使心脏强健的〕强心锻炼：*According to Max, the exhausting physical preparation – cardio, weight training, and kung fu – has changed him dramatically.* 按照马克斯的说法，消耗体力的赛前身体训练——强心锻炼、负重训练和"功夫"——令他脱胎换骨。

care in the com·mu·ni·ty /ˌkɛr ɪn ðə kəˈmjunətɪ; ˌkeər ɪn ðə kəˈmjuːnɨti/ *n* [U] *BrE*
the practice of helping and looking after people with mental problems in their homes, instead of making them stay in hospitals【英】社区护理（计划）：*Many people have fears about care in the community, but mental patients pose a far greater threat to themselves than to the public.* 许多人对社区护理感到恐惧，但是精神病患者对自己造成的威胁远大于对公众构成的威胁。

care·ware /ˈkɛrˌwɛr; ˈkeəweə/ *n* [U]
computer SOFTWARE that is free, although the people who wrote it ask you to give them some money if you use it 爱心软件〔一种共享软件〕

cargo pants /ˈkɑrgo ˌpænts; ˈkɑːgəʊ ˌpænts/ *n* [plural] also 又作 **cargoes**
big loose trousers with several large pockets 货船裤，船员裤〔有多个大口袋的宽松裤〕

car·o·tene /ˈkærətin; ˈkærətiːn/ *n* [C,U]
a chemical substance found in plants, such as CARROTs, that is important for good health and that might prevent CANCER 胡萝卜素：*Carotenes are found in orange and yellow vegetables.* 胡萝卜素存在于橙色和黄色蔬菜中。

carpetbagger /ˈkɑrpɪtˌbægə; ˈkɑːpɨtˌbægə/ *n* [C] *BrE*
NEW MEANING
someone who opens an account at a BUILDING SOCIETY because they think the building society will soon become a bank. When a building society becomes a bank, people who have accounts there receive money or SHAREs in the bank【英】在购房互助协会开立账户者

case /kes; keɪs/ *n*
NEW MEANING
be on the case *spoken* if someone says they are on the case, they are aware of a problem and are going to try to solve it【口】得悉问题并着手解决

cash ad·vance /ˈkæʃ ədˌvæns; ˈkæʃ ədˌvɑːns/ *n* [C]
money that you get from a bank, using a CREDIT CARD〔用信用卡〕取现金，透支：*It seems so easy to get a $100 cash advance every few days at a local ATM machine.* 每隔几天在当地的自动取款机透支100美元似乎不费什么事。

cash·back /ˈkæʃˌbæk; ˈkæʃbæk/ *n* [U] *BrE*【英】
1 a way of getting money at a shop when you use a DEBIT CARD to pay for the things you are buying, in which the shop gives you money which it takes from your bank account 购物支钱〔顾客用借记卡在商店购物时可顺便提取的现金〕：*I got £40 cashback.* 我购物时支取了40英镑现金。**2** a way of reducing the price of a car, piece of furniture etc where the seller says what the price is and offers to give a certain amount of money back to the person who buys it 现金回赠〔打折销售〕：*Price on the road – £8750. But on top of that, we'll give you £500 cashback.* 结清后可直接上路的车价是8750英镑，但除此之外，我们还会回赠你500英镑。

category kil·ler /ˈkætəgorɪ ˌkɪlə; ˈkætɨgəri ˌkɪlə/ *n* [C]
technical a very large company that has many stores in many cities, and that is able to offer low prices and therefore makes smaller stores go out of business【术语】品类杀手〔专营某类产品、以低价挤垮小店的大型连锁店〕

CBT /ˌsi bi ˋti; ˌsiː biː ˈtiː/ *n* [C]
1 an abbreviation for 缩写= computer-based testing; a way of taking standard tests such as the GRE on a computer 基于电脑的测试 **2** computer based training 电脑辅助培训：*OJ will provide full documentation and CBT software.* OJ会提供全套文本和电脑辅助培训软件。

CD burn·er /si ˋdi ˌbɝnə; siː ˈdiː ˌbɜːnə/ also 又作 **burner** *n* [C]
compact disc burner; a piece of computer equipment that records music, images, or other information onto a CD 光盘刻录设备，烧碟机

CD-R /ˌsi di ˋɑr; ˌsiː diː ˈɑː/ *n* [C]
compact disc recordable; a type of CD that you can record music, images, or other information onto, using special equipment on your computer. It can be recorded onto only once. 可刻录式光盘

CD-RW /ˌsi di ɑr ˋdʌbḷju; ˌsiː diː ɑː ˈdʌbəljuː/ *n* [C]
compact disc rewritable; a type of CD that you can record music, images, or other information onto, using special equipment on your computer. You can record onto it several times. 可擦写光盘，再写式光盘

cell /sɛl; sel/ *n* [C] *AmE*
NEW MEANING
a CELLULAR PHONE; a telephone that you can carry around with you, that works by using a network of radio stations to pass on signals【美】手机，蜂窝电话，移动电话；MOBILE *BrE*【英】：*Call me on my cell if you're running late.* 你要是晚了，就打我的手机。

cen·sor·ware /ˈsɛnsəˌwɛr; ˈsensəˌweə/ *n* [U]
a type of computer PROGRAM that can be used to stop someone from seeing certain WEBSITEs on their computer. This word comes from a combination of the words 'CENSOR' and 'SOFTWARE' and is used by people who do not approve of limiting the information that people can see on the Internet.〔阻止某人登录某些网站的〕审查软件〔由censor和software缩合而成〕

central /ˈsɛntrəl; ˈsentrəl/ *adj*
NEW MEANING
party/comedy etc central *informal* a place where something is happening a lot【非正式】经常聚会的地点：*Tim's house became party central for the band and their friends.* 蒂姆的房子成了乐队和朋友经常聚会的场所。| *This bulletin board serves as communications central* (=a common place to leave a message for someone) *for the campus.* 这个布告板成为校园内的联络中心。

ce·roc /sɪˋrɑk; sɨˈrɒk/ *n* [U]
a type of lively dance from France, similar to SALSA and JIVE 希洛克舞〔一种起源于法国，与萨尔萨舞和摇摆舞相似的轻快舞蹈〕

chad /tʃæd; tʃæd/ *n* [C,U]
small pieces of stiff paper that are produced when holes are made in cards, so that the cards can be ready by a computer or used in a machine〔卡片穿孔时产生的〕纸屑〔穿了孔的卡片可由电脑读取或可在机器上使用〕

chak·ra /ˈtʃɑkrə; ˈtʃʌkrə/ *n* [C]
one of the seven particular areas of the body which, according to some Asian medical practices, are important to consider when curing illness or disease 权轮〔某些亚洲医学认为对治疗疾病是重要的人体的七个特定部位之一〕

change man·age·ment /ˈtʃendʒ ˌmænɪdʒmənt; ˈtʃeɪndʒ ˌmænɪdʒmənt/ *n* [U]
the process of deciding which changes need to be made in a business or a computer system and how to make

them 变动管理: *A team of consultants was commissioned to investigate and report on the best current thinking and practice regarding change management.* 顾问组受托调查和报告关于变动管理的最新思维和推行情况。

channel /ˋtʃænl; ˈtʃænl/ *n* [C]
NEW MEANING
an electronic connection between two computers or other electronic equipment such as MODEMS, that information can travel along. A channel can be a physical object such as a CABLE or a particular radio FREQUENCY. 〔连接两台电脑或其他电子设备的〕信道, 通路

chat /tʃæt; tʃæt/ *v* [I]
NEW MEANING
to communicate with several people in a chat room on the Internet （网上）聊天

chat room /ˋtʃæt ˌrum; ˈtʃæt ˌruːm/ *n* [C]
a place on the Internet where you can write messages to other people and receive messages back from them immediately, so that you can have a conversation while you are ONLINE （网上）聊天室: *As well as offering access to the Internet, we have our own information centers and chat rooms.* 除了提供上网服务之外, 我们还有自己的信息中心和聊天室。

cheat² /tʃit; tʃiːt/ *n* [C]
NEW MEANING
a set of instructions given to a computer that make it easier for someone who is playing a computer game to win 〔玩电脑游戏时使用的〕作弊码

check card /ˋtʃɛk ˌkard; ˈtʃek ˌkɑːd/ *n* [C] *AmE*
a special plastic card, similar to a CREDIT CARD, that you can use to pay for things directly from your CHECKING ACCOUNT【美】支票卡

chill room /ˋtʃɪl ˌrum; ˈtʃɪl ˌruːm/ *n* [C]
1 a room in a bar, office etc where people go to play games, listen to music, watch television etc so that they can relax 〔酒吧、办公室等中的〕休闲室 **2** a WEBSITE or WEB PAGE that contains games, pictures, music etc and is designed for people who want to relax or have fun 休闲网站[页]

chud·dies /ˋtʃʌdɪz; ˈtʃʌdiz/ *n* [plural] *BrE slang humorous*【英俚, 幽默】**1** UNDERPANTS 衬裤, 内裤 **2 kiss my chuddies** a slightly insulting expression used to show that you do not respect someone or that you are angry with them. This expression was made popular in Britain by two characters on a television show who are TEENAGE boys and whose families originally came from South Asia. 亲亲我的内裤吧〔表示不尊重或恼怒对方, 稍带侮辱性〕

churn /tʃɝn; tʃɜːn/ *v* [I]
to change from one service provider such as a bank or telephone company to another because the second one offers better conditions 更换（服务商）: *The arrival of free Internet Service Providers in Europe caused Internet users to churn between ISPs much faster than was expected.* 免费互联网服务商抵达欧洲后, 互联网用户更换不同互联网服务商的速度出乎意料地快。—**churn** *n* [U]: *The mobile phone industry has experienced a high churn rate – typically between 18% and 24% of subscribers.* 移动电话业的用户流失率很高, 一般在18%至24%之间。

cin·e·phile /ˋsɪnɪˌfaɪl; ˈsɪnɪˌfaɪl/ *n* [C]
someone who likes films very much and considers them to be a form of art, not just entertainment 电影爱好者, 影迷: *My last boyfriend was a complete cinephile.* 我的上一位男友是个十足的影迷。

CJD /ˌsi dʒe ˋdi; ˌsiː dʒeɪ ˈdiː/ *n* [U]
the abbreviation of 缩写= CREUTZFELDT-JAKOB DISEASE

clam·dig·gers /ˋklæmˌdɪgɚz; ˈklæmˌdɪgəz/ *n* [plural]
a type of TROUSERS that fit closely and reach the middle of the lower leg 七分裤, 〔长及小腿肚的〕中长裤: *Shelly was wearing a pair of pink clamdiggers and a sleeveless blouse.* 谢利穿了一条粉红色的中长裤和一件无袖衬衫。

click·a·ble /ˋklɪkəbl; ˈklɪkəbəl/ *adj*
if a word or picture that you can see on a computer screen is clickable, it will connect you to more information when you CLICK on it. You click on something by pressing a button on a computer MOUSE. （用鼠标）可点击的

clicks and mor·tar /ˌklɪks ən ˋmɔrtɚ; ˌklɪks ən ˈmɔːtə/ *adj* [only before noun 仅用于名词前]
relating to a business that has both a store and a WEBSITE that customers can buy things from. Customers can often look at or try items in the store before they buy them from the website, or they can buy things on the website and return them to the store if they do not like what they have bought 两便的〔既有店铺又提供网上销售的〕: *Bellinger's new book shows how you can transform your company into a clicks-and-mortar business.* 贝林杰的新书会告诉你怎样把你的公司变成一个既有店铺又提供网上销售的虚实两便企业。—**clicks-and-mortar** *n* [C]

client /ˋklaɪənt; ˈklaɪənt/ *n* [C]
NEW MEANING
technical a computer on a network that receives information from a SERVER (=large powerful computer)【术语】客户机

client-serv·er, client server /ˌklaɪənt ˋsɝvɚ; ˌklaɪənt ˈsɜːvə◂/ *adj*
client-server network/technology/system etc a computer system in which CLIENTS (=small computers) are connected to a SERVER (=large powerful computer) and receive information from it 主从式网络/技术/系统等: *Client-server architecture usually links PCs to a database server, and most of the computing is done on the PC.* 主从式架构通常将个人电脑和数据服务器连接起来, 大多数数据处理在个人电脑上进行。

clip art /ˋklɪp ˌart; ˈklɪp ˌɑːt/ *n* [U]
images, photographs, or pictures that are stored on particular WEBSITES, which you can copy and use in your own computer documents. You can also buy collections of clip art on CD-ROM OR FLOPPY DISK. 〔网上的〕剪贴图片集, 图库

clipboard /ˋklɪpˌbɔrd; ˈklɪpˌbɔːd/ *n* [C]
NEW MEANING
a part of a computer's MEMORY that stores information when you are moving it from one document to another 剪贴板

clipper chip /ˋklɪpɚ ˌtʃɪp; ˈklɪpə ˌtʃɪp/ *n* [C] *AmE*
a special computer CHIP that can be put into a computer, MOBILE PHONE etc, which allows an organization such as a government to listen to or read private conversations made using these machines【美】〔电脑、手机等〕解密集成芯片

C-list /ˋsi ˌlɪst; ˈsiː ˌlɪst/ *adj*
among the group of film stars or people who appear on TV, but who are not really very famous or popular 〔影星等〕三流的: *You often see C-list, so-called celebrities, on the streets of London, just doing their shopping or going to a burger bar.* 伦敦的街上经常可以见到一些所谓名人的三流影星不是在购物, 就是在汉堡包店里进餐。

clock speed /ˋklɑk ˌspid; ˈklɒk ˌspiːd/ *n* [C usually singular 一般用单数]
technical a measurement of how quickly a computer's CPU (=main controlling part) can deal with instructions【术语】时钟速度〔计算中央处理器的运算速度〕: *The system I tested uses a chip with a clock speed of 1 gigahertz.* 我测试过的那个系统使用时钟速度为一千兆赫的芯片。

clone /klon; kləʊn/ *v* [T]
NEW MEANING
to copy the number of someone else's MOBILE PHONE onto a new CHIP and then use that number on a different telephone, so that the mobile phone's owner receives the telephone bill 烧机, 盗用他人手机号码

closure /ˋkloʒɚ; ˈkləʊʒə/ *n* [U]
NEW MEANING
a word used especially by PSYCHOLOGISTS to describe the

act of bringing an event or a period of time to an end, or the feeling that something has been completely dealt with 解脱〔尤为心理学家使用〕: *Funerals help give people a sense of closure.* 葬礼让人产生一种解脱的感觉。

club·land /ˋklʌbˏlænd; ˈklʌblænd/ *n* [U]
all the NIGHTCLUBs in an area, considered as a group and including the people who go to them and the performers that play in them 夜总会区, 夜总会〔总称〕: *They are one of clubland's favorite bands.* 他们是夜总会区最受欢迎的乐队之一。

cluster home /ˋklʌstɚ ˏhom; ˈklʌstə ˌhəʊm/ *n* [C] *BrE*
a house which is joined to other houses of the same kind to form a small group【英】密集型住宅, 住宅群

co-brand·ing /ˏko ˋbrændɪŋ; ˌkəʊ ˈbrændɪŋ/ *n* [U]
a practice in which two companies help each other to do business or sell products by using both company names, for example, having a particular bank inside a particular store〔两家公司〕品牌合用[共享]

co·coon·ing /kəˋkunɪŋ; kəˈkuːnɪŋ/ *n* [U] *AmE*
the practice of spending a lot of time in your own home because you feel comfortable and safe there【美】茧式生活, 茧居: *They produce extra-wide armchairs for people with serious cocooning in mind.* 他们为热衷于茧式生活者生产超宽扶手椅。

co·de·pend·en·cy /ˏkodɪˋpɛndənsɪ; ˌkəʊdɪˈpendənsi/ *n* [U]
when two people exist in a very close relationship and cannot leave it, because one of them needs to be looked after and the other one needs to be needed 互赖性 —**codependent** *n, adj*

cod·er /ˋkodɚ; ˈkəʊdə/ *n* [C]
informal a computer PROGRAMMER【非正式】程序设计员, 电脑程序编制员: *a coders' convention* 程序设计员规范

code-shar·ing /ˋkod ˏʃɛrɪŋ; ˈkəʊd ˌʃeərɪŋ/ *n* [U]
technical a practice in which two AIRLINE companies sell tickets together and use the same numbers for their flights【术语】共用班次, 航班共享

coe·li·ac dis·ease *especially BrE*【尤英】, **celiac disease** *AmE*【美】/ˋsilɪæk dɪˏziz; ˈsiːliæk dɪˌziːz/ *n* [U]
technical a disease caused by an ALLERGY to GLUTEN (=a substance in wheat flour)【术语】乳糜泻〔一种疾病〕

co-fund /ˏko ˋfʌnd; ˌkəʊ ˈfʌnd/ *v* [T]
if two organizations co-fund something, they pay for it together 为…共同提供资金: *The project is being co-funded by two California companies.* 这个项目由加州的两家公司共同提供资金。

cold call /ˏkold ˋkɔl; ˌkəʊld ˈkɔːl/ *v* [T]
to telephone someone you have never spoken to before and try to sell them a product or service〔推销员〕冒昧地给…打电话

cold fu·sion /ˏkold ˋfjuʒən; ˌkəʊld ˈfjuːʒən/ *n* [U]
a type of NUCLEAR FUSION (=the joining of the central parts of two atoms, which releases energy) that some scientists believe can occur at lower temperatures. Other scientists believe that nuclear fusion can only occur at temperatures of millions of degrees, and that cold fusion is not possible. 冷聚变

collateral /kəˋlætərəl; kəˈlætərəl/ *adj*
NEW MEANING
collateral damage a phrase meaning people who are hurt or property that is damaged as a result of war, although they are not the main TARGET. This phrase is used especially by the Army, Navy etc 附带损害: *Hitting any non-military targets would risk 'collateral damage' – which the US military does not want.* 攻击任何非军事目标都会冒殃及池鱼的风险, 这是美国军方不愿看到的。

color /ˋkʌlɚ; ˈkʌlə/ *v*
color me surprised/confused/embarrassed etc *AmE spoken informal* if you say color me surprised, confused etc, you mean that you are very surprised, confused etc by something【美口, 非正式】我太惊讶/迷惑/窘迫等: *"Color me amazed!" says prize winner Angela Harris.* 获奖者安杰拉·哈里斯说: "我真是大吃一惊!"

com·bats /ˋkɑmbæts; ˈkɒmbæts/ *n* [plural]
loose trousers, often with many pockets〔多口袋宽松式〕战斗裤: *She always wore combats, which were more fashionable than jeans.* 她老是穿着比牛仔裤更时髦的多口袋战斗裤。

commando /kəˋmændo; kəˈmɑːndəʊ/ *n*
NEW MEANING
go commando *AmE informal humorous* to not wear any underwear【美, 非正式, 幽默】没有穿内衣

com·min·gle /kəˋmɪŋgḷ; kɒˈmɪŋgəl/ *v*
1 *formal* [I,T] to mix together, or to make different things do this【正式】(使)混合, (使)掺和: *Many towns allow recyclable items to be commingled for collection in a single container.* 许多城镇允许将可循环利用的物品混放于一个容器内。**2** [T] if a bank, insurance company, or other financial organization commingles money, it mixes its own money with the money that belongs to one of its customers or to another part of the business, usually in an illegal way 挪用〔储户的钱款〕: *Southwest Securities faces charges that it commingled its own funds with customer funds.* 西南证券公司因把公司资金和顾客的钱款掺和在一起而面临控告。

comms /kɑmz; kɒmz/ *n* [plural] *BrE*
informal communications; used when talking about computer PROGRAMs that allow communication between different computers【英, 非正式】通信程序; communications software *AmE*【美】

community po·lic·ing /kəˏmjunətɪ pəˋlisɪŋ; kəˌmjuːnə̇ti pəˈliːsɪŋ/ *n* [U]
in Britain, a system in which the police and the people who live in an area work together to reduce crime 社区警务

comparison-shop /kəmˋpærəsn̩ ˏʃɑp; kəmˈpærə̇sən ˌʃɒp/ *v* [I]
to go to different shops in order to compare the prices of something, so that you can buy it at the cheapest possible price 货比三家, 比较价格进行购买 —**comparison shopping** *n* [U]

compassion fa·tigue /kəmˋpæʃən fəˏtig; kəmˈpæʃən fəˌtiːg/ *n* [U]
the feeling some people have that stops them caring a lot or giving money to CHARITY because they have seen too many reports or television programmes about DISASTERs 同情心疲乏: *Several speakers will offer advice on overcoming compassion fatigue.* 几名演讲人将就如何克服同情心疲乏提出建议。

com·po·nent·ize also 又作 **-ise** *BrE*【英】/kəmˋponəntaɪz; kəmˈpəʊnəntaɪz/ *v* [I,T]
to separate a system or machine into a number of smaller parts so that they can work together or work as part of another system or machine; used especially about computers and computer SOFTWARE 把…元件化〔把系统或机器分成较小的组件〕: *It is much easier to componentize your website before you design it.* 在设计之前把网站元件化要容易得多。

composed sal·ad /kəmˏpozd ˋsæləd; kəmˌpəʊzd ˈsæləd/ *n* [C] *AmE*
a SALAD that is arranged carefully on a plate, rather than mixed together【美】〔精心配放的〕花式沙拉

compress /kəmˋprɛs; kəmˈpres/ *v* [I,T]
NEW MEANING
to make a computer FILE smaller by using a special computer PROGRAM, which makes the file easier to store or send 压缩〔电脑文件〕

com·pu·ter·ate /kəmˋpjutərɪt; kəmˈpjuːtərə̇t/ *adj*
able to use a computer well 通晓电脑的, 擅长电脑操作的: *Students need to be computerate as well as literate.* 学生除了需要有读写能力外, 还要具备熟练操作电脑的能力。

con·fe·renc·ing /ˈkɑnfərənsɪŋ; ˈkɒnfərənsɪŋ/ *n*
video/telephone conferencing the use of VIDEO or telephone equipment that allows several people in different places to talk to each other at the same time 视频/电话会议

con·flic·ted /kənˋflɪktɪd; kənˈflɪktɨd/ *adj AmE*
be/feel conflicted to be confused about what choice to make, especially when the decision involves strong beliefs or opinions【美】思想挣扎, 难于抉择: *Neither Jane nor Neil feels conflicted about pursuing their careers while raising children.* 简和尼尔对抚养孩子和追求事业成功从没有感到难于抉择。

congestion charg·ing /kənˋdʒɛstʃən ˌtʃɑrdʒɪŋ; kənˈdʒestʃən ˌtʃɑːdʒɪŋ/ *n* [U]
a way of reducing traffic in city centres in Britain by charging drivers money to enter; ROAD PRICING〔英国的〕交通拥堵收费, 高峰期行车收费: *Plans to introduce congestion charging were dropped until after the election.* 高峰期行车收费的计划已被搁置, 直至选举过后。

conjoined twins /kənˌdʒɔɪnd ˋtwɪnz; kənˌdʒɔɪnd ˈtwɪnz/ *n* [plural]
two people who are born with their bodies joined to each other. This expression is used instead of SIAMESE TWINS, which some people consider to be offensive. 连体双胞胎

con·nect·ed·ness /kəˋnɛktɪdnɪs; kəˈnektɨdnɨs/ *n* [U]
1 the feeling people have that they are members of a group in society and that they share particular qualities with other members of that group 归属感, 联系: *Human beings have a need for both independence and connectedness.* 人既需要保持独立, 又需要与他人建立各种联系。 **2** the degree to which people are connected by electronic TECHNOLOGY such as the Internet and E-MAIL〔互联网等构成的人际〕联系: **[+between/with]** *Communication technology has increased the connectedness between physicians and patients.* 通讯技术加强了医师和病人之间的联系。

conspicuous /kənˋspɪkjuəs; kənˈspɪkjuəs/ *adj*
NEW MEANING
conspicuous consumption the act of buying a lot of things, especially expensive things that are not necessary, in order to IMPRESS other people and show them how rich you are 炫耀性消费: *Postwar Munich became rich, and flaunted it in expensive clothing and other forms of conspicuous consumption.* 战后的慕尼黑富了起来, 并以昂贵的服饰和其他形式的炫耀性消费向世人显示其财富。

content /ˋkɑntɛnt; ˈkɒntent/ *n* [U]
the information contained in a WEBSITE, considered separately from the software that makes the website work (网站) 内容: *The graphics are brilliant. It's just a shame the content is so poor.* 图像十分出色, 但内容如此贫乏, 实在可惜。

content pro·vid·er /ˋkɑntɛnt prəˌvaɪdɚ; ˈkɒntent prəˌvaɪdə/ *n* [C]
an organization or person that provides information on the Internet 网络内容提供者[商]

content site /ˋkɑntɛnt ˌsaɪt; ˈkɒntent ˌsaɪt/ *n* [C]
a WEBSITE that contains many pages of information on a particular subject 专题网站

contingent /kənˋtɪndʒənt; kənˈtɪndʒənt/ *adj AmE*【美】
NEW MEANING
1 contingent worker someone who is employed by a company for a fixed period of time, usually to do a particular piece of work 临时员工, 短期员工 **2 contingent job** a job that is limited to a fixed period of time, usually because the company does not want to continue to employ the person who does that job after the end of that particular job 临时工作

cookie /ˋkʊkɪ; ˈkʊki/ *n* [C]
NEW MEANING
technical information which a computer PROGRAM on the Internet leaves in your computer so that the program will recognize you when you use it again【术语】"甜饼"〔记录网站访问者的信息块, 以便下次使用时识别〕

cookie bust·er /ˋkʊkɪ ˌbʌstɚ; ˈkʊki ˌbʌstə/ *n* [C]
a computer PROGRAM that prevents a cookie from being placed on your computer's HARD DISK (=the part that permanently stores information), or removes one that is already there "甜饼"屏障, 信息块屏障

cool /kul; kuːl/ *adj*
NEW MEANING
be cool with sth *spoken informal* used to say that you agree with something or do not have a problem with it【口, 非正式】对…表示满意, 对…不持异议: *"Do you want to come over to my house and watch a video tonight?" "I'm cool with that."* "你想不想今晚来我家看影视录像?" "我很乐意。"

cop /kɑp; kɒp/ *v AmE*
NEW MEANING
slang【美俚】**1 cop an attitude** to behave in a way that is not nice, especially by showing that you think you are better or more intelligent than other people 摆架子 **2 cop a buzz** to feel the effects of taking illegal drugs or drinking alcohol〔吸毒或饮酒后〕产生快感

co-pay·ment, copayment /ˋkoˌpemənt; ˈkəʊˌpeɪmənt/ *n* [C]
a fairly small amount of money that you must pay a doctor in addition to the amount paid by your insurance company, if you have a particular type of health insurance〔病人在保险承担的费用之外所要支付的〕共付医疗费

copy /ˋkɑpɪ; ˈkɒpi/ *v*
copy sb **in** *phr v* [T] to send someone a copy of an E-MAIL message you are sending to someone else 给〔某人〕抄送: **[+on]** *Can you copy me in on the memo you're sending to Chris?* 你发给克里斯的便笺, 能否给我也抄送一份?

cop·y·left /ˋkɑpɪˌlɛft; ˈkɒpileft/ *n* [U]
the right to use something such as computer SOFTWARE without paying for it, as long as you do not try to sell it or stop other people from using it. This word was formed by changing the last part of the word 'COPYRIGHT'. 复制权, (软件) 通用许可证

core /kor; kɔː/ *adj*
core business/activity/product the business, activity etc that is the most important one for a company because it makes the most money〔某公司赚钱最多的〕核心业务/活动/产品: *The publishing company plans to sell its bookshops and concentrate on its core business.* 该出版公司打算把书店卖掉, 集中精力在核心业务上。

cor·po·rate·wear /ˋkɔrpərətˌwɛr; ˈkɔːpərətˌweə/ *n* [U]
clothes such as a SUIT and tie that are suitable for wearing to work in the offices of a large business 公司制服, 上班服

cos·me·ceu·ti·cal /ˌkɑzməˋsutɪkl; ˌkɒzməˈsjuːtɪkəl/ *n* [C]
a beauty product that contains special additional substances that are intended to improve the condition of your skin or health, almost like a medicine. This word comes from a combination of the words 'COSMETIC' and 'PHARMACEUTICAL'. 药用化妆品〔由 cosmetic 和 pharmaceutical 缩合而成〕

couch hop·ping /ˋkaʊtʃ ˌhɑpɪŋ; ˈkaʊtʃ ˌhɒpɪŋ/ *n* [U]
humorous the activity of staying at different people's homes and sleeping on their SOFAs when you do not have anywhere to live【幽默】到处借宿: *Well, I spent the next couple of weeks couch hopping and eventually ended up at Max's place.* 哦, 后来的几周我到处借宿, 最后住到马克斯那里。

counter¹ /ˋkaʊntɚ; ˈkaʊntə/ *n* [C]
NEW MEANING
a computer PROGRAM that counts the number of people that have used a WEBSITE〔统计进入网站人数的〕访客计数器

course·ware /ˋkɔrs͵wɛr; ˈkɔːs͵weə/ *n* [U]
computer SOFTWARE that is designed to be used for education 课(程软)件，教学软件

crack /kræk; kræk/ *v* [T]
NEW MEANING
informal to illegally copy computer SOFTWARE【非正式】非法复制〔电脑软件〕: *You can find out how to crack any kind of software on the web.* 你可以在网上找到任何一类软件的复制办法。

crack into sth *phr v* [T] to secretly enter someone else's computer system, especially in order to damage the system or steal the information stored on it 非法侵入〔电脑系统〕: *An Illinois teenager is accused of cracking into the company's network several times over the last several months.* 伊利诺伊州一名十几岁的孩子被控在最近几个月内几次非法侵入该公司的网络。

crack onto sb *phr v* [T] *slang* to try to start a sexual relationship with someone【俚】试图与〔某人〕发生性关系: *My best friend keeps trying to crack onto my boyfriend.* 我最要好的一个朋友一直在勾引我的男友。

crack ba·by /ˋkræk ͵bebɪ; ˈkræk ͵beɪbi/ *n* [C] *plural* **crack babies**
a baby that is born with medical and mental problems because his or her mother regularly smoked the illegal drug CRACK before the baby was born 可卡因婴儿

cracker /ˋkrækɚ; ˈkrækə/ *n* [C]
NEW MEANING
someone who illegally breaks into a computer system in order to steal information or stop the system from working properly 非法侵入电脑系统者，黑客: *Tough laws and security measures do little to deter computer crackers who steal company secrets or cause havoc by tapping into computer systems.* 严厉的法律和安全措施对阻止黑客非法入侵电脑系统窃取公司机密或制造混乱起不了多少作用。

crack·head /ˋkrækhɛd; ˈkrækhed/ *n* [C]
slang someone who uses the illegal drug CRACK【俚】吸食强效可卡因的人

crack house /ˋkræk ͵haus; ˈkræk ͵haʊs/ *n* [C]
a place where the illegal drug CRACK is sold, bought, and smoked 强效可卡因贩卖点

crank /kræŋk; kræŋk/ *n* [U] *AmE*
NEW MEANING
slang METHAMPHETAMINE (=an illegal drug)【美俚】甲基安非他明毒品

crash /kræʃ; kræʃ/ *v*
NEW MEANING
informal **crash and burn** if a business or company crashes and burns, it fails completely【非正式】彻底失败，倒闭: *Dozens of Internet startups have crashed and burned in the last two years.* 许多新成立的网络公司在最近两年内都垮了。

cream puff /͵krim ˋpʌf; ͵kriːm ˈpʌf/ *adj*
having a quality that is pretty and decorative 花哨的，装门面的，讲排场的: *Cream puff weddings, with the bride in a fancy white dress and the groom in a tuxedo, are as popular as ever.* 现时讲究排场的婚礼越来越流行，新娘穿着别致的白色婚纱，新郎穿着无尾晚礼服。

cre·den·tialed /krɪˋdɛnʃəld; krɪˈdenʃəld/ *adj*
someone who is credentialed is legally allowed to do a particular job, because they have done the right type of training 具有认证资格的: *a newly credentialed teacher* 一名新近取得认证资格的教师 | *Ask if the experts you're consulting online are appropriately credentialed.* 问问你在网上咨询的专家是否具有适当的认证资格。

Creutz·feldt-Jak·ob dis·ease /͵krɔɪtsfɛlt ˋjɑkob dɪ͵ziz; ͵krɔɪtsfelt ˈjækɒb dɪ͵ziːz/ *n* [U] *abbreviation* 缩写为 **CJD**
a very serious disease that kills people and that may be caused by eating BEEF that is affected by BSE 克罗伊茨费尔特－雅各布病，克－雅氏病〔可能与吃感染了疯牛病的牛肉有关〕

crib /krɪb; krɪb/ *n* [C] *AmE*
NEW MEANING
slang the place where someone lives【美俚】住所，窝: *I'm not at my crib, I'm at Jed's house.* 我不在自己的住所，我在杰迪家里。

crossover ve·hi·cle /ˋkrɔsovɚ ͵viɪkl; ˈkrɒsəʊvə ͵viːɪkəl/ *n* [C]
a vehicle that has some of the features of a car and some of the features of a larger vehicle such as a TRUCK 客货两用车

cross-sell·ing /͵krɔs ˋsɛlɪŋ; ͵krɒs ˈselɪŋ/ *n* [U]
a situation in which one company helps to sell another company's products by, for example, advertising the second company's products at the same time as its own 代卖，代销

cross-trad·ing /͵krɔs ˋtredɪŋ; ͵krɒs ˈtreɪdɪŋ/ *n* [U]
a way of buying and selling different CURRENCIES (=the type of money a country uses, for example the pound) in which people in one country buy or sell the money of a second country in exchange for the money of a third country 炒汇，交叉买卖外汇

cross-train·er /͵krɔs ˋtrenɚ; ͵krɒs ˈtreɪnə/ *n* [C usually plural 一般用复数]
a type of shoe that can be worn for playing different types of sports 多用途运动鞋

cross-train·ing /͵krɔs ˋtrenɪŋ; ͵krɒs ˈtreɪnɪŋ/ *n* [U]
1 the activity of training for more than one sport in the same period of time〔同时进行的〕多项运动训练: *Reebok makes shoes designed for aerobics, cross-training, walking, and running.* 锐步公司生产的鞋子适用于有氧体操、多项运动训练、散步和跑步。**2** the activity of learning different jobs in the same period of time〔同时进行的〕多项职业培训: *Cross-training is a vital part of job rotation.* 多项职业培训是职业轮换中关键的一环。— **cross-train** *v* [I]

cruis·ing /ˋkruzɪŋ; ˈkruːzɪŋ/ *n* [U]
the activity of walking or driving slowly around public places, looking for sexual partners 猎艳〔在公共场所寻觅性伴侣〕: **go cruising** *If you're thinking, "I don't want to go cruising in the park for a date," there is an alternative.* 如果你在想："我可不想在公园里蹓跶找约会的对象，"还有别的法子。

crush¹ /krʌʃ; krʌʃ/ *v* [T]

crush on sb *phr v* [T] *slang* to have a strong feeling of romantic love for someone that you are not already in a relationship with【俚】迷恋: *The guy I'd been crushing on for three years finally came into the diner where I work.* 我迷恋了三年的那个男子终于走进了我工作的小饭馆。

crush² /krʌʃ; krʌʃ/ *n* [C]
NEW MEANING
informal someone you have a CRUSH on (=have a strong feeling of romantic love for)【非正式】迷恋的对象: *"Who's that guy Elaine's talking to?" "Oh, he's just her latest crush."* "与伊莱恩交谈的那个男子是谁？""噢，他正是她最近迷恋的对象。"

crusty /ˋkrʌstɪ; ˈkrʌsti/ *n* [C] *BrE*
informal a young person without a job or permanent home who is very dirty【英，非正式】脏皮士，硬壳族〔无固定职业或居所的青年人〕

CU, cu
a short way of writing 'see you', used in E-MAIL or TEXT MESSAGES on MOBILE PHONES 再见〔"see you"的缩写，电子邮件和手机短信用语〕

cube farm /ˋkjub ͵fɑrm; ˈkjuːb ͵fɑːm/ *n* [C]
humorous a large office containing many rows of CUBICLES (=small areas with low walls around three sides)【幽默】办公农庄〔用矮身隔板分隔成许多小间的办公室〕

cuckoo egg /ˋkuku ͵ɛg; ˈkʊkuː ͵eg/ *n* [C]
a computer FILE which is designed to look like an MP3 music file but does not contain any music, and which is intended to confuse or annoy people who illegally trade

COPYRIGHT*ed* music on the Internet using services that provide recordings for free 杜鹃蛋〔一种酷似MP3标准音乐文件但却无音乐的反盗版电脑文件〕

cue² /kju; kjuː/ *v*

cue sth ↔ **up** *phr v* [T] to make a CASSETTE, VIDEO, or CD be exactly in the position you want it to be in, so that you can play something immediately when you are ready 将〔磁带、录像带或光盘〕调到〔要播放的位置〕: *The videotape's cued up and ready to go!* 录像带调好，可以播放了！

CUL, cul
a short way of writing 'see you later', used in E-MAIL or TEXT MESSAGES on MOBILE PHONES 一会儿见〔"see you later"的缩写，电子邮件或手机短信用语〕

customer-fac·ing /ˈkʌstəmɚ ˌfesɪŋ; ˈkʌstəmə ˌfeɪsɪŋ/ *adj*
in a company, the customer-facing workers are the people whose job involves them seeing and speaking to the customers 直接面对顾客的: *This course will prove invaluable for customer-facing staff and customer care personnel.* 这一课程将会对一线员工和客户服务员有极大的价值。

cybercafé 网吧

cy·ber·ca·fé, cyber cafe /ˈsaɪbɚkæˌfe; ˈsaɪbəˌkæfeɪ/ *n* [C]
a CAFÉ that has computers which are connected to the Internet for customers to use 网吧，网络咖啡馆

cy·ber·crime, cyber crime /ˈsaɪbɚˌkraɪm; ˈsaɪbəˌkraɪm/ *n* [C,U]
criminal activity that involves the use of computers or the Internet 网络犯罪

cy·ber·fo·ren·sics /ˈsaɪbɚfəˌrɛnsɪks; ˈsaɪbəfəˌrensɪks/ *n* [U]
the study of how computer crimes happen, especially ones involving the computer systems of large companies or organizations 网络犯罪学: *a new course to train law-enforcement officials in cyberforensics* 培训执法官员熟悉网络犯罪学的新教程

cy·ber·fraud /ˈsaɪbɚˌfrɔd; ˈsaɪbəˌfrɔːd/ *n* [U]
slang the illegal act of deceiving people on the Internet in order to gain money, power etc【俚】网络诈骗

cy·ber·kid·nap·per /ˈsaɪbɚˌkɪdnæpɚ; ˈsaɪbəˌkɪdnæpə/ *n* [C]
someone who gets to know people on the Internet, makes plans to meet them, and then KIDNAP*s* them (=takes them away illegally, usually by force) 网上绑架者

cy·ber·land /ˈsaɪbəˌlænd; ˈsaɪbəˌlænd/ *n* [U]
activity that involves the Internet and the people who use it 网络世界

cy·ber·porn /ˈsaɪbɚˌpɔrn; ˈsaɪbəˌpɔːn/ *n* [U]
slang sexual images, films etc shown on the Internet【俚】网络色情

cy·ber·sick·ness /ˈsaɪbɚˌsɪknɪs; ˈsaɪbəˌsɪknɪ̵s/ *n* [U]
a feeling of illness caused by using a computer for long periods of time or being in a room with a lot of computers〔长时间使用电脑或待在有很多电脑的房间中引致的〕电脑病

cy·ber·squat·ter /ˈsaɪbɚˌskwɑtɚ; ˈsaɪbəˌskwɒtə/ *n* [C]
someone who officially records the names of companies that they do not own or work for as DOMAIN NAME*s* on the Internet in order to try to sell these names to companies for profit〔网上〕抢注域名者，域名转售者

cy·ber·squat·ting /ˈsaɪbɚˌskwɑtɪŋ; ˈsaɪbəˌskwɒtɪŋ/ *n* [U]
the practice of officially recording the names of companies that you do not own or work for as DOMAIN NAME*s* on the Internet. People do this in order to try to sell the domain names at some time in the future for profit 抢注域名: *Many people think that cybersquatting should be made illegal.* 许多人认为应把抢注域名列为非法行为。

cy·ber·stalk·ing /ˈsaɪbɚˌstɔkɪŋ; ˈsaɪbəˌstɔːkɪŋ/ *n* [U]
the illegal use of the Internet, E-MAIL, or other electronic communication systems to follow someone or threaten them 网上骚扰: *The state's first cyberstalking laws went into effect a little over a year ago.* 这个州的第一部网上骚扰法生效才一年多。—**cyberstalker** *n* [C]

cy·ber·ter·ror·is·m /ˌsaɪbɚˈtɛrərɪzəm; ˌsaɪbəˈterərɪzəm/ *n* [U]
using the Internet to damage computer systems, especially for political purposes 网络恐怖主义: *I believe that cyberterrorism will emerge as one of the world's major post-Cold War security threats.* 我相信网络恐怖主义将成为冷战后对世界安全的主要威胁之一。

cy·ber·ter·ror·ist /ˌsaɪbɚˈtɛrərɪst; ˌsaɪbəˈterərɪ̵st/ *n* [C]
someone who uses the Internet to damage computer systems, especially for political purposes 网络恐怖分子: *Such a strategic attack, mounted by cyberterrorists, would shut down everything from power stations to air traffic control centres.* 网络恐怖分子发动的这类战略性攻击，将导致发电站、空中交通管制中心等全部瘫痪。

cy·ber·wid·ow /ˈsaɪbɚˌwɪdo; ˈsaɪbəˌwɪdəʊ/ *n* [C]
informal the wife of a man who spends a lot of time working or playing on his computer【非正式】网上寡妇〔在丈夫电脑上耗费大量时间的女人〕

cy·pher·punk /ˈsaɪfɚˌpʌŋk; ˈsaɪfəˌpʌŋk/ *n* [C]
NEW MEANING
someone who changes the information that they send from their computer into a form that can only be read by the people they send it to. Cypherpunks do this because they do not trust the government and people in authority and think that they will read this information. 网上朋客，网际浪人〔将资料加密传送，以防止政府等机构阅览〕—**cypherpunk** *adj* [only before a noun 仅用于名词前]: *the cypherpunk subculture* 网上朋客亚文化

D,d

damage con·trol /ˈdæmɪdʒ kənˌtrol; ˈdæmɪdʒ kənˌtrəʊl/ *n* [U]
an attempt to limit the bad effects of something 损害控制: *The call I received from Smith seemed to be an effort toward political damage control.* 史密斯给我打来电话，似乎是出于政治考虑，以防事件进一步恶化。| **do damage control** *Since the scandal broke, the Senator's staff have been busy doing damage control.* 自从这一丑闻传开以后，参议员一班人马一直忙于将该事件的不良影响控制在一定范围。

dashboard din·ing /ˈdæʃbɔrd ˌdaɪnɪŋ; ˈdæʃbɔːd ˌdaɪnɪŋ/ *n* [U]
humorous the practice of eating a meal while driving a car【幽默】〔驾驶中〕在仪表板上进餐: *Dashboard dining has become the breakfast norm in many cities in America.* 边开车边吃早餐已成为美国许多城里人的习惯。

data in·ter·change for·mat file /ˌdetə ˌɪntɚtʃendʒ ˈfɔrmæt ˌfaɪl; ˌdeɪtə ˌɪntətʃeɪndʒ ˈfɔːmæt ˌfaɪl/ *abbreviation* 缩写为 **DIF** *n* [C]

a computer file that allows you to take information from one PROGRAM and move it to a different program 信息交换格式文件

data min·ing /ˋdetə ˏmaɪnɪŋ; ˈdeɪtə ˌmaɪnɪŋ/ *n* [U]
the process of using a computer to examine large amounts of information about customers, in order to discover things about them that are not easily seen or noticed 数据开采, 数据剖析

dawg /dɔg; dɔːg/ *interjection*
slang used to emphasize how surprised, annoyed, or amused you are【俚】好家伙, 嗬〔表示惊讶、厌烦或开心等的感叹语〕: *Dawg, I wish I'd gotten a chance to do that.* 嗬, 我要是有机会那样做该多美呀!

daytime run·ning light /ˏdetaɪm ˋrʌnɪŋ ˏlaɪt; ˌdeɪtaɪm ˈrʌnɪŋ ˌlaɪt/ *AmE*【美】, **daytime running lamp** *BrE*【英】*n* [C]
one of two HEADLIGHT*s* (=the large lights at the front of a vehicle) that turn on at low power during the day so that it is easier for the vehicle to be seen 白天开的汽车前灯

day trad·ing /ˋde ˏtredɪŋ; ˈdeɪ ˌtreɪdɪŋ/ *n* [U]
the activity of using a computer to buy and sell SHARE*s* on the Internet, often buying and selling very quickly to make a profit out of small price changes〔股票交易〕当天炒卖 —**day trader** *n* [C]

dead cat bounce /ˏdɛd kæt ˋbaʊns; ˌded kæt ˈbaʊns/ *n* [C]
technical informal a situation in which the price of SHARE*s* rises a small amount after a large fall, sometimes before falling further【术语, 非正式】"死猫"式反弹〔股票大跌后出现的轻微反弹〕

dead tree e·di·tion /ˏdɛd ˋtri ɪˏdɪʃən; ˌded ˈtriː ɪˌdɪʃən/ *n* [C]
humorous a paper copy of a magazine or newspaper that is also published on the Internet【幽默】〔与电子版同时出版的〕印刷版, 印刷本: *I was sitting at my desk reading the dead tree edition of the Times when Josh walked in.* 乔希进来时, 我正坐在桌前读印刷版的《泰晤士报》。

de·bark /dɪˋbɑrk; dɪˈbɑːk/ *v* [I]
to DISEMBARK 下船, 上岸: [**+from**] *I remember how glad I felt debarking from a ship in Bremerhaven after six days on the ocean.* 我记得那次在海上航行了六天之后, 在不来梅港下船时我是多么的高兴。—**debarkation** *n* [U]

debt o·ver·hang /ˏdɛt ˋovɚhæŋ; ˌdet ˈəʊvəhæŋ/ *n* [U]
technical a situation in which a business or government has so much debt that it cannot make new INVESTMENT*s*【术语】债台高筑〔债务过多以致无法进行新的投资〕

decompress /ˏdikəmˋprɛs; ˌdiːkəmˈpres/ *v* [T]
NEW MEANING
technical to change the information in a computer document back into a form that can be easily read or used, when the information was stored on the computer in a special form that used less space on the computer's MEMORY【术语】解压缩: *Most Macintosh computers can decompress files automatically.* 大多数苹果电脑会自动为文件解压缩。

de·crypt /diˋkrɪpt; diːˈkrɪpt/ *v* [T]
to change a message or information on a computer back into a form that can be read, when someone has sent it to you in a type of computer CODE 解密; 破译: *Only certain employees will be able to decrypt sensitive documents.* 只有某些雇员可以对敏感文件解密。

de·cryp·tion /diˋkrɪpʃən; diːˈkrɪpʃən/ *n* [U]
the process of changing a message or information on a computer back into a form that can be read when it was in a type of computer code 解密: *decryption software* 解密软件

deep vein throm·bo·sis /ˏdip ven θrɑmˋbosɪs; ˌdiːp veɪn θrɒmˈbəʊsɪs/ *n, abbreviation* 缩写为 **DVT**
a serious illness which happens when a small amount of blood becomes very thick and causes the heart to stop beating properly. People think it can sometimes happen on long plane journeys, and it is also called 'economy class syndrome' in British English. 深静脉血栓塞〔英国英语中亦称"经济舱综合征"〕: *Deaths from DVT in passengers on long-haul flights are estimated at 2,000 per year.* 长途飞机乘客因深静脉血栓形成致死的估计每年有2000人。

def /dɛf; def/ *adj*
slang fashionable and attractive【俚】棒极的, 呱呱叫的: *Hey, check out that def car.* 嗨, 好好看看那部靓车。

de·friz·zer /diˋfrɪzɚ; diːˈfrɪzə/ *n* [C,U]
informal a substance that you put in your hair to make it less tightly curled【非正式】鬈发蓬松剂

de·gear·ing /diˋgɪrɪŋ; diːˈgɪərɪŋ/ *n* [U] *BrE*
DELEVERAGE【英】〔公司〕配股集资取代借贷

de·hir·ing /diˋhaɪrɪŋ; diːˈhaɪərɪŋ/ *n* [U] *AmE*
a situation in which a company stops employing people it no longer needs【美】解雇, 解聘

de·in·dus·tri·a·li·za·tion also 又作 **-isation** *BrE*【英】/ˏdiɪnˏdʌstrələˋzeʃən; ˌdiːɪnˌdʌstriəlaɪˈzeɪʃən/ *n* [U]
a situation in which there is less and less industry in an area or country 解除(某个地区或国家的)工业, 削减(某个地区或国家的)工业生产能力, 非工业化: *Britain's deindustrialization has meant more people are in service jobs.* 英国的非工业化意味着有更多人从事服务业工作。

de·lay·er·ing /diˋleərɪŋ; diːˈleɪərɪŋ/ *n* [U]
the act of reducing the levels of management in a company or organization (公司等的)管理架构精简

de·lev·er·age /diˋlɛvərɪdʒ; diːˈliːvərɪdʒ/ *n* [U]
technical a situation in which a company starts to get more of the money it needs by selling SHARE*s*, and less by borrowing【术语】〔公司〕配股集资取代借贷 —**deleverage** *v* [T]

demand man·age·ment /dɪˋmænd ˏmænɪdʒmənt; dɪˈmɑnd ˌmænɪdʒmənt/ *n* [U] *BrE*
a way of planning things such as new roads by trying to control the number of vehicles there will be, instead of always building new roads because the number of vehicles is always increasing【英】需求管理 —compare 比较 PREDICT AND PROVIDE

de·merge /diˋmɝdʒ; diːˈmɜːdʒ/ *v* [I,T]
technical to make one part of a large company into a separate company【术语】使分离, 拆分: *After the takeover, several subsidiary companies were demerged.* 收购之后, 有好几个子公司被分拆出去。

demo[1] /ˋdɛmo; ˈdeməʊ/ *n* [C]
NEW MEANING
a computer PROGRAM that shows what a new piece of SOFTWARE will be able to do when it is ready to be sold〔软件〕演示版: *Click here to download a demo of the new version of our personal finance software.* 点击这里下载我们个人理财软件新文本的演示版。

demo[2] /ˋdɛmo; ˈdeməʊ/ *v* [T]
informal to show or explain how something works or is done, especially new computer equipment; DEMONSTRATE【非正式】示范, 演示: *They're going to demo some of the new software at this year's Mac convention.* 他们准备在今年的苹果电脑大会上展示若干新软件。

demolition job /ˏdɛməˋlɪʃən ˏdʒɑb; ˌdeməˈlɪʃən ˌdʒɒb/ *n* [C]
1 an act of criticizing someone severely or telling other people things about them which may be unfair or untrue, in order to harm them or to cause people to have a bad opinion of them "拆台"行为, 诋毁行为: **do a demolition job on sb** *He accused opposition leaders of doing a demolition job on the President.* 他指责反对党领袖在诋毁总统。**2** an event, especially a sports event, in which one person or team is so strong that they defeat the opposition very severely〔体育比赛的〕大胜, (对手的)一败涂地: [**+against**] *Currie led the team with 55 points in the demolition job against Ireland.* 柯里率领该队以55分大败爱尔兰队。

dental dam /ˌdɛntḷ ˋdæm; ˌdentl 'dæm/ *n* [C]
a thin piece of rubber that a woman wears over her sex organs during ORAL SEX to protect herself or her partner from sexual diseases 牙障〔防止在口交中染上性病的薄橡皮〕

de·or·bit /diˋɔrbɪt; diː'ɔːbɪt/ *v* [I,T]
technical to make a SATELLITE (=a machine that has been sent into space) come back to Earth in a controlled way when it is no longer needed in space【术语】(使)脱离轨道: *The Russian government decided not to deorbit Mir.* 俄罗斯政府决定不让"和平"号返回地球。—**deorbit** *n* [C,U] *The crew is beginning final preparations for deorbit.* 全体人员开始作卫星脱离轨道返回地面的最后准备。

de·plane /diˋplen; diː'pleɪn/ *v* [I]
to get off a plane 下飞机

depleted u·ra·ni·um /dɪˋplitɪd juˋrenɪəm; dɪ'pliːtɪd jʊ'reɪniəm/ *abbreviation* 缩写为 **DU** *n* [U]
a very hard, slightly RADIOACTIVE metal that is used on the outside of some bullets and shells (SHELL[1] (2)) 贫铀

derm·a·ceu·ti·cal /ˌdɝməˋsutɪkḷ; ˌdɜːmə'sjuːtɪkəl/ *n* [C]
a substance that helps to improve the quality of someone's skin 护肤剂: *a privately owned company specializing in the development of dermaceutical products* 一家专门从事开发护肤产品的私营企业

de·sert·i·fi·ca·tion /dɪˌzɝtɪfiˋkeʃən; dɪˌzɜːtɪfɪ'keɪʃən/ *n* [U]
a process in which useful land, especially farm land, gradually becomes dry and useless, especially because too many bushes or trees have been cut down, or because too many farm animals have used the land 沙(漠)化

desk·fast /ˋdɛskfəst; 'deskfəst/ *n* [C usually singular 一般用单数] *AmE*
humorous breakfast that is eaten at someone's desk in an office【美, 幽默】办公桌早餐: *Hectic morning schedules mean that many families don't take time for breakfast. Some have a quick deskfast while others miss out altogether.* 忙乱的晨间安排意味着有许多家庭都抽不出时间用早餐, 一些人只得匆匆在办公桌吃早餐, 另一些人干脆不吃。

desk jock·ey /ˋdɛsk ˌdʒɑkɪ; 'desk ˌdʒɒki/ *n* [C]
informal someone who does all of their work at a desk or in an office【非正式】做文牍工作的人: *He's a desk jockey at a government agency in Detroit.* 他在底特律一个政府部门做文牍工作。

desktop charg·er /ˌdɛsktɑp ˋtʃɑrdʒɚ; ˌdesktɒp 'tʃɑːdʒə/ *n* [C]
a small piece of equipment that puts a new supply of electricity into the BATTERY of a MOBILE PHONE〔手机电池〕台式充电器, 座充

detail /ˋditel; 'diːteɪl/ *v* [T] *AmE*
NEW MEANING
to clean both the inside and outside of a car very thoroughly【美】全面清洗〔车辆〕—**detailing** *n* [U]

detox /ˋditɑks; 'diːtɒks/ *v* [I]
informal if someone detoxes, they are given special treatment at a hospital to help them stop drinking alcohol or taking drugs. This word is a short form of DETOXIFY.【非正式】戒除酒瘾[毒瘾]: *I detoxed in the hospital, and I've now been free of alcohol and drugs for 10 months – the longest I've ever been clean.* 我在医院里戒酒和戒毒, 现在我已10个月没有喝酒和吸毒了 —— 这是我戒酒、戒毒最长的一次。

development a·re·a /dɪˋvɛləpmənt ˌɛrɪə; dɪ'veləpmənt ˌeəriə/ *n* [C] *BrE*
an area of the country that the government tries to help by offering money, lower taxes etc to businesses that move to that area【英】开发区

dialogue box *BrE*【英】, **dialog box** *AmE*【美】/ˋdaɪəlɔg ˌbɑks; 'daɪəlɒg ˌbɒks/ *n* [C]
a box that appears on your computer screen when the PROGRAM you are using needs to ask you a question before it can continue to do something. You CLICK on one part of the box to give your answer. 对话框: *When the dialog box appears, click on 'OK.'* 出现对话框时, 就点击OK键。

dial-up /ˋdaɪəl ˌʌp; 'daɪəl ˌʌp/ *adj* [only before noun 仅用于名词前]
relating to a telephone line that is used to send information from one computer to another 拨号上网的: *a dial-up connection* 拨号连接 —**dialup** *n* [C]

diamond lane /ˋdaɪəmənd ˌlen; 'daɪəmənd ˌleɪn/ *n* [C] *AmE*
a special LANE (=area that you drive in) on a road that is marked with a diamond shape and can be used only by buses, taxis, and sometimes cars with more than one passenger【美】钻石车道: *a bus-only diamond lane* 公共汽车专用的钻石车道 | *Diamond lanes are meant to encourage car-pooling.* 钻石车道旨在鼓励合伙用车。

di·ge·rat·i /ˌdɪdʒəˋrɑtɪ; ˌdɪdʒə'rɑːti/ *n* [plural]
people who understand and use computers in a very skilful way. This word comes from a combination of the words 'DIGITAL' and 'LITERATI' (=people who know a lot about literature). 网上知识界, 电脑高手〔由digital和literati缩合而成〕: *the digerati who attended a software convention* 出席软件会议的电脑高手

di·gi·cam /ˋdɪdʒɪkæm; 'dɪdʒɪkæm/ *n* [C]
a type of camera that can store pictures as DIGITAL FILES which can be put into a computer, rather than on film 数字[数码]相机

digital age /ˋdɪdʒətḷ ˌedʒ; 'dɪdʒɪtl ˌeɪdʒ/ also 又作 **computer age** *n*
the Digital Age the time when computers become more common in a society and are used regularly in daily life to do ordinary activities. Most people believe the digital age has already begun. 数字[数码]时代

digital sig·na·ture /ˌdɪdʒətḷ ˋsɪgnətʃɚ; ˌdɪdʒɪtl 'sɪgnətʃə/ *n* [C]
information on an electronic message that proves who the person sending the message is 数字[数码]式签名, 数字[数码]标记

digital vid·e·o /ˌdɪdʒətḷ ˋvɪdɪo; ˌdɪdʒɪtl 'vɪdiəʊ/ *n* [U]
the process of recording pictures and sounds that are represented in the form of numbers, usually numbers in the BINARY system (=a system using the numbers 1 and 0), used especially in computing 数字视频, 数字显像, 数码录像

di·jo·naise /ˌdiʒəˋnez; ˌdiːʒɒ'neɪz/ *n* [U]
a mixture of a type of MAYONNAISE and MUSTARD that is eaten with some foods, especially meat or fish 第戎芥末蛋黄酱: *salmon with a dijonaise sauce* 用第戎芥末蛋黄酱调味的鲑鱼

direct de·pos·it /dəˌrɛkt dɪˋpɑzɪt; dɪˌrekt dɪ'pɒzɪt/ *v* [T]
to pay the money someone earns directly into their bank account 直接存入〔银行账户〕: *My pay is direct deposited on the 27th of each month.* 我的薪金是每月27日直接存入账户的。

direct-to-con·sum·er /dəˌrɛkt tə kənˋsumɚ; dɪˌrekt tə kən'sjuːmə/ *adj* [only before noun 仅用于名词前]
direct-to-consumer advertising is aimed at the customer who will buy the product, rather than at the shops that will sell them 直接面向消费者的: *Pharmaceutical advertising revenue is expected to soar 300%, reflecting a jump in direct-to-consumer advertising by drug companies.* 药品广告的收益可望上涨300%, 这反映了制药公司在直接面向消费者的广告支出激增。

director's cut /dəˋrɛktɚz ˌkʌt; dɪ'rektəz ˌkʌt/ *n* [C]
a film that contains all the parts that the DIRECTOR wanted to include, when the film was originally shown in cinemas without those parts〔未经剪辑的〕足本影片, 导演剪辑版: *The director's cut of The Godfather part III*

has nine minutes of film not included in the theatrical release.《教父》第三部的导演剪辑版有9分钟的片段未在剧院放映。

dirt-dish·er /ˋdɝt ˌdɪʃɚ; ˈdɜːt ˌdɪʃə/ *n* [C] *AmE informal* a DISHER【美，非正式】热衷于散布小道消息[内幕新闻]的人

dirty /ˋdɝtɪ; ˈdɜːti/ *adj*

NEW MEANING

a dirty sports event is one in which people competing in the event have illegally used drugs to improve their performance〔指体育比赛〕不正当的，使用违禁药物的：*Many people think that the race has been a dirty event for years.* 许多人认为这项赛跑多年来一直有人使用违禁药物。

dis also 又作 **diss** /dɪs; dɪs/ *v* **dissed, dissing** [T] *slang* another spelling of DISS; to make unfair and unkind remarks about someone【俚】诋毁，对…说无礼的话〔diss 的另一种拼法〕：*I feel bad for dissing him the way I did.* 我对自己曾蔑视他的做法感到歉疚。| *Quit dissing me.* 别再贬低我了。

disco bis·cuit /ˋdɪsko ˌbɪskɪt; ˈdɪskəʊ ˌbɪskɨt/ *n* [C] *BrE slang* the drug ECSTASY【英俚】"狂喜"迷幻药，摇头丸

dis·count·er /ˋdɪskauntɚ; ˈdɪskaʊntə/ *n* [C] a person or business that sells goods or services at lower prices than normal 廉价零售商[商店]

discretionary in·come /dɪˋskrɛʃənɛrɪ ˌɪnkʌm; dɪˈskreʃənəri ˌɪŋkʌm/ *n* [U] the money remaining from your income after your bills have been paid, which can be spent on things such as entertainment or holidays〔账款扣除后〕可随意支配的收入

dish /dɪʃ; dɪʃ/ *v* [I,T]

NEW MEANING

informal to give a lot of information about something or someone, especially something that would usually be secret or private, or to give someone a lot of information【非正式】传播，炒作〔内幕新闻等〕：**[+on]** *She's ready to dish on boys, beauty, and break-ups in her new column.* 她准备在她的新专栏中畅谈男人、美容以及分手等话题。

dish·er /ˋdɪʃɚ; ˈdɪʃə/ also 又作 **dirt-disher** *n* [C] *AmE informal* someone who enjoys telling other people a lot of GOSSIP (=information about other people's behaviour and private lives)【美，非正式】热衷于散布小道消息[内幕新闻]的人：*Women newspaper columnists have tended to play the role of the social commentator or the light-hearted Hollywood disher.* 报章专栏女作家往往扮演社会评论员或轻浮的好莱坞长舌妇的角色。

disrespect /ˌdɪsrɪˋspɛkt; ˌdɪsrɪˈspekt/ *v* [T] to say or do things that show a lack of respect for someone 对…不敬：*Hicks accused Williams of disrespecting him at a record company party.* 希克斯指责威廉斯在一次唱片公司举办的聚会上对他不敬。

DLL /ˌdi ɛl ˋɛl; ˌdiː el ˈel/ *n* dynamic link library; a collection of information in a computer file that is designed to be shared and used many times by many different programs〔计算机文件的〕动态链接库

DNA pro·fil·ing /ˌdi ɛn e ˋprofaɪlɪŋ; ˌdiː en eɪ ˈprəʊfaɪlɪŋ/ *n* [U] the act of examining the DNA found where a crime has happened and the DNA of people who may have done the crime, in order to find out who is responsible 基因图测定，DNA检测

do /du; duː/ *v*

NEW MEANING

do one! *BrE informal spoken* an impolite expression used to tell someone to go away【英，非正式，口】滚！滚蛋！

doc·u·soap, docusoap /ˋdakju ˌsop; ˈdɒkjʊ ˌsəʊp/ *n* [C] *BrE* a television programme that shows what happens in the daily lives of real people. This word comes from a combination of 'DOCUMENTARY' and 'SOAP OPERA'.【英】纪录片式肥皂剧〔由 documentary 和 soap opera 缩合而成〕

dog /dɔg; dɒg/ *v*

NEW MEANING

dog it *AmE informal* to not try as hard as you should in order to do something【美，非正式】〔工作中〕偷懒：*Quit dogging it and do your work.* 别吊儿郎当，好好干你的活。

d'oh /do; dəʊ/ *interjection* *spoken humorous* used when you have just realized that you have done or said something stupid【口，幽默】咳〔发现自己做了傻事或说了傻话后的感叹〕

dol·lar·iza·tion /ˌdalərəˋzeʃən; ˌdɒləraɪˈzeɪʃən/ *n* [U] *technical* a situation in which countries outside the US want to use the dollar rather than their own country's money【术语】美元化〔不用本国货币而用美元〕

dolphin-safe /ˋdalfɪn ˌsef; ˈdɒlfɨn ˌseɪf/ *adj* dolphin-safe fish is caught in a way that does not harm or kill DOLPHINS 不伤害海豚的：*I only buy dolphin-safe tuna.* 我只买那些在捕获中不会殃及海豚的金枪鱼。

domain name /dəˋmen ˌnem; dəˈmeɪn ˌneɪm/ *n* [C] a company's or organization's address on the Internet. A domain name is followed by an abbreviation which shows its type, for example .com for company, or its country of origin, for example .uk for the United Kingdom. 域名

domestic part·ner /dəˌmɛstɪk ˋpartnɚ; dəˌmestɪk ˈpɑːtnə/ *n* [C] *formal* someone who you live with and have a sexual relationship with, but who you are not married to【正式】家庭伴侣〔未婚而同居者〕：*The new law gave retirement and health benefits to the domestic partners of city employees.* 新的法律规定城市雇员的同居伴侣亦可享受退休津贴和医疗保健津贴。

done /dʌn; dʌn/ *adj*

NEW MEANING

be a done deal used to emphasize that something has been completed or that a final arrangement has been agreed（敲）定了的：*Despite the developer's claims, the mayor says the proposed hotel is not a done deal.* 尽管开发商说得很肯定，但是市长还是说计划中的宾馆并没有定案。

dope /dop; dəʊp/ *adj AmE slang* good or satisfactory【美俚】很棒的：*If we could be friends, that'd be dope.* 我们要是能成为朋友，那该有多棒啊。| *Eminem's dope new CD* 埃米内精彩的新激光唱片

dot-com also 又作 **dot.com, dot com** /ˌdat ˋkam; ˌdɒt ˈkɒm/ *adj* [only before noun 仅用于名词前] *informal* relating to a person or company whose business is done using the Internet or involves the Internet【非正式】经营互联网业务的：*a dot-com company* 经营互联网业务的公司 | *dot-com millionaires* 经营互联网业务的大富翁 **—dot-com** *n* [C]: *Several of the leading dot.coms saw their share prices slide yesterday.* 几家经营互联网业务的大公司看到它们的股票价格在昨天下挫。**—dot-com** *v* [T]: *We'll have to decide whether to dot-com our business.* 我们得决定要不要把业务发展至互联网上。

dot-com·mer also 又作 **dot.commer** /ˌdat ˋkamɚ; ˌdɒt ˈkɒmə/ *n* [C] people who work for or own a company whose business involves the Internet, especially people who earn a lot of money 网络公司工作人员[经营者]

doul·a /ˋdulə; ˈduːlə/ *n* [C] a woman whose job is helping new parents care for their babies 婴儿保姆〔帮助刚任父母亲者照料婴儿的妇女〕

down /daun; daʊn/ *adj*

NEW MEANING

be down with sb *slang spoken* to be friends with someone【俚，口】与某人关系密切

down·load /ˋdaʊnlod; ˈdaʊnləʊd/ *n* [C]
a computer FILE OR PROGRAM that has been moved from a large computer or the Internet to another computer 下载的电脑文件[程序]: *We've got reviews and downloads of the latest business software.* 我们有最新版本的商业软件的评论和下载文件。

down·load·a·ble /ˌdaʊnˋlodəbḷ; ˌdaʊnˈləʊdəbəl/ *adj*
if a computer PROGRAM OR FILE is downloadable, you are allowed to copy it from another computer onto your own computer 可下载的

downmarket /ˌdaʊnˋmɑrkɪt; ˌdaʊnˈmɑːkɨ̱t/ *adv BrE* 【英】
NEW MEANING
1 go/move downmarket to start buying or selling cheaper goods or services 进入[面向]〔针对低收入消费者的〕廉价商品市场, 低层次营销 **2 take sth downmarket** to change a product or service, so that it is cheaper and more popular 使…进入廉价商品市场, 使…转为低层次营销: *He was accused of taking the radio station downmarket in order to compete with commercial stations.* 他被指控为了与商业性电台竞争而把该无线电台转入低档次市场。

down·scale[1] /ˋdaʊnˌskel; ˈdaʊnskeɪl/ *adj AmE*
downscale goods or services are cheap and not of very good quality【美】低档的

downscale[2] /ˋdaʊnˌskel; ˈdaʊnskeɪl/ *v* [I,T] *AmE*
to sell or buy cheaper goods of lower quality【美】买卖低档次商品

down·shift /ˋdaʊnˌʃɪft; ˈdaʊnʃɪft/ *v* [I]
if someone downshifts, they choose to do a less important or difficult job, so that they do not have to worry about their work and have more time to enjoy their life 降格工作〔为过轻闲生活而改换次要或较容易的工作〕

down·time also 又作 **down time** /ˋdaʊnˌtaɪm; ˈdaʊntaɪm/ *n* [U]
NEW MEANING
informal a period of time when you have finished what you were doing, and you can relax or do something that you had not originally planned to do【非正式】不干活的时间, 空档期: *Often, during semesters, you have down time when you can do some exercise.* 学期中间往往会有一段空闲时间让你做一些运动。—**downtime** *adj*: *downtime activities for teachers* 教师的工余活动

dreads /drɛdz; dredz/ *n* [plural]
a short form of the word DREADLOCKS "骇人"型发绺〔dreadlocks的缩略式〕: *He'd bounce into the room, his little dreads flying, and drop his enormous bag with a bang.* 他总是蹦蹦跳跳地走进房间, 一头小巧的发绺飞扬着, 砰的一声把大袋子扔下。

drip ad·ver·tis·ing /ˋdrɪp ˌædvɚtaɪzɪŋ; ˈdrɪp ˌædvətaɪzɪŋ/ *n* [U]
technical a situation in which advertisements for a product or service are shown repeatedly over a long period of time【术语】长期重复播放的广告

drive-through de·liv·e·ry /ˌdraɪv θru dɪˋlɪvərɪ; ˌdraɪv θruː dɪˈlɪvəri/ *n* [C] *AmE*
a system of delivering babies used in some hospitals in which a woman spends only a very short period of time at the hospital after giving birth to a child【美】快速留院分娩

drop dead date /ˌdrɑp ˋdɛd ˌdet; ˌdrɒp ˈded ˌdeɪt/ *n* [C usually singular 一般用单数] *AmE*
NEW MEANING
informal a date by which you must have completed something, because after this date it is no longer worth doing【美, 非正式】最后期限

drum 'n' bass /ˌdrʌm ən ˋbes; ˌdrʌm ən ˈbeɪs/ *n* [U]
a type of popular music with a strong low beat that started in Britain in the 1990s 鼓点低音, 鼓打贝斯〔20世纪90年代在英国兴起的一种强节奏流行音乐〕

DSL /ˌdi ɛs ˋɛl; ˌdiː es ˈel/ *n* [C]
digital subscriber line; a telephone line that has special equipment which allows it to receive information from the Internet, or send information at very high speeds 数字用户线路, 数码用户专线: *the pros and cons of using a DSL connection to the Internet* 赞成和反对采用数字用户线路上网的理由

DU /ˌdi ˋju; ˌdiː ˈjuː/ *n* [U]
depleted uranium; a very hard slightly RADIO-ACTIVE metal that is used on the outside of some bullets and shells (SHELL[1] (2)) used by soldiers 贫铀

dual-band /ˌdjuəl ˋbænd; ˌdjuːəl ˈbænd/ *adj* [only before noun 仅用于名词前]
a dual-band MOBILE PHONE is able to work in at least two different countries, because it can receive two different sorts of signal〔手提电话〕双频段的

dub·by /ˋdʌbɪ; ˈdʌbi/ *adj BrE*
if a piece of music is dubby, it has some features that are typical of DUB (=a style of music from the West Indies) in which sounds are repeated like an ECHO【英】达布式的〔达布是西印度群岛流行的一种节奏重复的音乐〕

dumb /dʌm; dʌm/ *v*
dumb sth ↔ **down** [I,T] to present something such as news or information in a simple and attractive way without many details so that everyone can understand it. People who use this expression show that they disapprove of making complicated information too simple. 降低…的难度〔用于表示不同意把复杂的资料改得过分简单〕, 使简短易明: *Have history textbooks been dumbed down over the past decade?* 在过去10年期间, 历史课本是否改得过分简单了? —**dumbing down** *n* [U]

duvet day /duˋve ˌde; ˈduːveɪ ˌdeɪ/ *n* [C] *BrE*
a day when someone says that they are ill and does not go to work, even though they are not really ill【英】装病请假日: *Some employers nowadays are even happy to reward their staff with an unscheduled duvet day from time to time.* 近来一些雇主甚至乐于让雇员放不定期病假以作奖赏。

DVD /ˌdi vi ˋdi; ˌdiː viː ˈdiː/ *n* [C]
digital versatile disk or digital video disk; a type of COMPACT DISC that can have information, sound, and pictures on it and that has enough space for a full-length film 数字激光视盘, 数字多功能光盘, 数字影碟: *Every DVD player can also play standard audio CDs.* 所有数字影碟播放机也可播放标准的音频光盘。| *The film is now out on video and DVD.* 这部影片现在有录像带和DVD出售。

E,e

e-, E- /i; iː/ *prefix*
electronic; used before another word to mean something that is done on or involves the Internet 电子的, 网上的: *e-shopping* 网上购物 | *e-commerce* 电子商务

easter egg /ˋistɚ ˌɛg; ˈiːstər ˌeg/ *n* [C]
NEW MEANING
a secret message that is hidden in a computer PROGRAM, usually containing a funny message or the names of the people who wrote the program 复活节彩蛋〔电脑程序的隐藏内容, 一般包括有趣的内容或程序制作者的名字〕

e-book /ˋi bʊk; ˈiː bʊk/ also 又作 **electronic book** *n* [C]
a book that you read on a computer screen or on a special small computer that you can hold in your hands, and that is not printed on paper 电子书

e-busi·ness /ˋi ˌbɪznɪs; ˈiː ˌbɪznɨ̱s/ *n* [U]
electronic business; the activity of buying and selling goods and services and doing other business activities using a computer and the Internet 电子商务, 电子贸易

e-cash /ˋi ˌkæʃ; ˈiː ˌkæʃ/ *n* [U]
money that can be used to buy things on the Internet, but that does not exist in a physical form or belong to any particular country 电子现金

e-comm /ˈi ˌkɑm; ˈiː ˌkɒm/ *n* [U] *informal*【非正式】an abbreviation of 缩写= E-COMMERCE

e-com·merce /ˈi ˌkɑmɚs; ˈiː ˌkɒmɜːs/ *n* [U] electronic commerce; the activity of buying and selling goods and services and doing other business activities using a computer and the Internet; E-BUSINESS 电子商务: *e-commerce applications such as online ticketing and reservations* 网上购票和网上预订等电子商务应用系统

economy class syn·drome /ɪˈkɑnəmɪ klæs ˌsɪndrom; ɪˈkɒnəmi klɑːs ˌsɪndrəʊm/ *n* [U] *BrE* a serious illness which happens when a small amount of blood becomes very thick and causes the heart to stop beating properly. People believe that travelling in ECONOMY CLASS (=the cheapest seats) on long journeys in planes can cause this because passengers sit for a very long time and cannot move around very easily. The medical term is DEEP VEIN THROMBOSIS.【英】经济舱综合征〔其医学术语为"深静脉血栓塞"〕

e·co·pol·i·tics /ˈikoˌpɑlɪtɪks; ˈiːkəʊˌpɒlətɪks/ *n* [U] a type of political activity that is concerned with preserving and protecting the world's environment 生态政治学

e·co·tour·is·m /ˈikoˌtʊrɪzəm; ˈiːkəʊˌtʊərɪzəm/ *n* [U] the business of providing services for tourists who come to see beautiful places that are in danger of being harmed, so that people can earn money from the tourists rather than from activities that harm the environment. This word comes from a combination of the words 'ECOLOGY' and 'TOURISM'. 生态旅游（业）〔由 ecology 和 tourism 缩合而成〕: *Ecotourism generated new wealth in the north of Chile.* 生态旅游给智利北部创造了新的财富。

e-cur·ren·cy /ˈi ˌkɝənsɪ; ˈiː ˌkʌrənsi/ *n* [C] one of the types of money that can be used only on the Internet 电子货币

edge city /ˈɛdʒ ˌsɪtɪ; ˈedʒ ˌsɪti/ *n* [C] a SUBURB of a large city that has its own businesses, shops, offices etc, so that many of the people who used to live there while working in the large city now both live and work in the edge city〔兴建于大城市市郊的〕边缘城市

EDI /ˌi di ˈaɪ; ˌiː diː ˈaɪ/ electronic data interchange; a way for companies and banks to send information to each other by computer. Documents are sent in an agreed FORMAT so that the company receiving them can easily read them on their computer and print them out on paper. 电子数据交换

e-fit /ˈi ˌfɪt; ˈiː ˌfɪt/ *n* [C] *BrE* a picture, made by using a computer, of a person who the police think was responsible for a crime, which they show on television or the Internet in order to try and catch the person【英】〔嫌疑犯的〕电脑模拟画像

EFT /ˌi ɛf ˈti; ˌiː ef ˈtiː/ electronic funds transfer; the process by which money is moved from one bank account, business etc to another using only computer systems 电子资金转账[汇兑]

ego-surf·ing /ˈigo ˌsɝfɪŋ; ˈiːgəʊ ˌsɜːfɪŋ/ *n* [U] *humorous* the activity of searching for your name on the Internet in order to find out how many times it appears there【幽默】自我搜索, 自我冲浪〔找寻自己的名字在互联网上出现的次数〕

elder a·buse /ˈɛldɚ əˌbjuz; ˈeldər əˌbjuːz/ *n* [U] *especially AmE* cruel actions or remarks to an old person that harm them mentally or hurt them physically【尤美】对老人的虐待[凌辱]: *an agency that assists victims of elder abuse* 帮助受虐待老人的机构

el·der·care /ˈɛldɚˌkɛr; ˈeldə ˌkeə/ also 又作 **elder care** *n* [U] *especially AmE* the activity of looking after old people who cannot look after themselves properly, for example by making sure an old person gets good meals or medical care when they need it【尤美】老年保健: *More women than men have responsibility for elder care.* 妇女担负照料老人者要比男性多。—**elder care** *adj*: *an eldercare program* 老人保健计划 | *eldercare facilities* 老人保健设施

electronic bank·ing /ˌɛlɪkˈtrɑnɪk ˈbæŋkɪŋ; ˌelɪkˈtrɒnɪk ˈbæŋkɪŋ/ *n* [U] a service provided by banks that allows people to pay money from one account to another, pay bills etc using the Internet 电子银行业务

electronic cash /ˌɛlɪkˈtrɑnɪk ˈkæʃ; ˌelɪkˈtrɒnɪk ˈkæʃ/ *n* [U] money that can be used to buy things on the Internet, but that does not exist in a physical form or belong to any particular country 电子货币

electronic da·ta in·ter·change /ˌɛlɪkˈtrɑnɪk ˈdetə ˌɪntɚtʃendʒ; ˌelɪkˈtrɒnɪk ˈdeɪtə ˌɪntətʃeɪndʒ/ *abbreviation* 缩写为 **EDI** *n* [U] a way for companies and banks to send information to each other by using a computer. The information is sent in an agreed FORMAT so that the company receiving the documents can easily read them on their computer and print them out on paper. 电子数据交换: *software designed to facilitate Electronic Data Interchange* 旨在促进电子数据交换的软件

electronic funds trans·fer /ˌɛlɪkˈtrɑnɪk ˈfʌndz ˌtrænsfɝ; ˌelɪkˈtrɒnɪk ˈfʌndz ˌtrænsfɜː/ *abbreviation* 缩写为 **EFT** *n* [C,U] the process by which money is moved from one bank account, business etc to another using only computer systems 电子资金转账[汇兑]

electronic mon·ey /ˌɛlɪkˈtrɑnɪk ˈmʌnɪ; ˌelɪkˈtrɒnɪk ˈmʌni/ *n* [U] money that can be used to buy things on the Internet, but that does not exist in a physical form or belong to any particular country 电子货币

electronic or·ga·niz·er /ˌɛlɪkˈtrɑnɪk ˈɔrgənaɪzɚ; ˌelɪkˈtrɒnɪk ˈɔːgənaɪzə/ *n* [C] a small piece of electronic equipment that you can use to record addresses, telephone numbers, dates of meetings etc 电子记事簿

electronic pay·ment sys·tem /ˌɛlɪkˈtrɑnɪk ˈpemənt ˌsɪstəm; ˌelɪkˈtrɒnɪk ˈpeɪmənt ˌsɪstəm/ *n* [C] a system of paying or receiving money using the telephone or a computer and without using cash or cheques, for example DIRECT DEPOSIT 电子付款系统

electronic pub·lish·ing /ˌɛlɪkˈtrɑnɪk ˈpʌblɪʃɪŋ; ˌelɪkˈtrɒnɪk ˈpʌblɪʃɪŋ/ *n* [U] the business of producing books, magazines, or newspapers that are designed to be read using a computer 电子出版（业）

electronic sig·na·ture /ˌɛlɪkˈtrɑnɪk ˈsɪgnətʃɚ; ˌelɪkˈtrɒnɪk ˈsɪgnətʃə/ *n* —see 见 DIGITAL SIGNATURE

electronic tick·et·ing /ˌɛlɪkˈtrɑnɪk ˈtɪkɪtɪŋ; ˌelɪkˈtrɒnɪk ˈtɪkətɪŋ/ *n* [U] a service provided by airlines that allows people to buy their tickets on the Internet and usually does not give them tickets in the form of paper〔航空公司的〕网上购票（服务）

El Ni·ño /ɛl ˈninjo; el ˈniːnjəʊ/ *n* [singular, used without *the* 不与 the 连用] a condition that occurs every 3 to 7 years in which the surface of the Pacific Ocean becomes warmer near the West coast of South America, affecting the weather in many parts of the world and killing fish and other sea animals in that area 厄尔尼诺（现象）

e-mail, email /ˈi ˌmel; ˈiː ˌmeɪl/ *n* [C] NEW MEANING a message that is sent from one person to another electronically from one computer to another 电子邮件: *I'll send you an email when I know more about it.* 了解更多情况后我会给你发电子邮件。

e-mon·ey /ˈi ˌmʌnɪ; ˈiː ˌmʌni/ also 又作 **e-cash** *n* [U] money that can be used to buy things on the Internet,

but that does not exist in a physical form or belong to any particular country 电子货币

e·mo·ti·con /ɪˋmotɪkɑn; ɪˈməʊtɪkɒn/ *n* [C]
one of a set of special signs that is used to show an emotion in E-MAIL and on the Internet, often by making a picture. For example, the emoticon :-) looks like a smiling face when you look at it sideways and means that you have made a joke. This word comes from a combination of the words 'EMOTION' and 'ICON'. 〔电子邮件或互联网用符号表示的〕情感符〔由emotion和icon缩合而成〕

emotional in·tel·li·gence /ɪˌmoʃənḷ ɪnˋtɛlədʒəns; ɪˌməʊʃənəl ɪnˈteləd̥ʒəns/ *n* [U]
the skills and qualities that make you good at understanding people and knowing how they feel about a situation, as well as being good at solving problems 情感智力[智商]: *Emotional intelligence is a quality that employers are now looking for.* 情感智力是雇主目前寻求的(雇员应有的)一种品质。| *The course will help you increase your emotional intelligence.* 这个课程会帮助你提高自己的情感智力。

EMU /ˋimju, ˌi ɛm ˋju; ˈiːmjuː, ˌiː em ˈjuː/ *n* [U]
economic and monetary union or European monetary union; the use by many European Union countries of the same money, the Euro 经济与货币联盟, 欧洲货币联盟

-enabled /ɪnebḷd; ɪneɪbəld/ *suffix* [in adjectives 构成形容词]
Internet-enabled/Java-enabled etc a computer PROGRAM that is Internet-enabled, Java-enabled etc can be used with that program or includes it as one of its features 能上网的/能支援Java语言的等: *Find out more about our free Internet-enabled software.* 请进一步了解我们的免费可上网软件。

en·a·bler /ɪˋneblɚ; ɪˈneɪblə/ *n* [C]
someone who thinks they are helping someone else when actually they are preventing that person from improving their bad behaviour, for example because they deal with that person's problems instead of letting them deal with the problems on their own 代庖者, 纵容者: *Fletcher became his daughter's enabler by continuing to lend her money.* 弗莱彻继续借钱给女儿而成了她的纵容者。

en·crypt /ɪnˋkrɪpt; ɪnˈkrɪpt/ *v* [T]
to change information that has been written on a computer so that it is in a CODE, especially to prevent particular people from being able to read it 加密: *Users can click an on-screen button to encrypt an outgoing message.* 用户可点击屏幕键给要发送的信息加密。—**encryption** /ɪnˋkrɪpʃən; ɪnˈkrɪpʃən/ *n* [U] —**encrypted** *adj*

entry lev·el /ˋɛntrɪ ˌlɛvḷ; ˈentri ˌlevəl/ *adj* [only before noun 仅用于名词前]
entry level product/model/computer etc a product etc that is most suitable for people who do not have much money to spend or who do not have experience using that kind of product 入门级的产品/型号/电脑等

environmental im·pact as·sess·ment /ɪnˌvaɪrənmɛntḷ ˋɪmpækt əˌsɛsmənt; ɪnˌvaɪərənmentl ˈɪmpækt əˌsesmənt/ *n* [C]
NEW MEANING
an examination of the possible effects of a new building development or new road on the environment 环境影响评估: *A full environmental impact assessment will be required before any development within 25 miles of the coast.* 距海岸25英里内的任何开发项目都先要进行全面的环境影响评估。

environmental im·pact state·ment /ɪnˌvaɪrənmɛntḷ ˈɪmpækt ˌstetmənt; ɪnˌvaɪərənmentl ˈɪmpækt ˌsteɪtmənt/ *n* [C]
in the US, a report that explains what effects a new PROJECT, such as a building, will have on the environment. A company or organization must give this report to the government before the government will allow them to start the new project. 环境影响报告

EPROM /ˈiprɑm; ˈiːprɒm/ *n* [C]
electrically programmable read-only memory; a type of computer CHIP where the contents of the chip can be replaced or changed only by a special machine 电擦除可编程只读存储器

e-pub·lish·ing /ˈi ˌpʌblɪʃɪŋ; ˈiː ˌpʌblɪʃɪŋ/ *n* [U]
electronic publishing; the business of producing books, magazines, or newspapers that are designed to be read using a computer 电子出版(业): *"E-publishing is on the brink of acceptance but has to still fully develop into a common way to read," said Norris.* 诺里斯说:"电子出版差不多已得到认可,但它还需要充分发展成为普及的阅读方式才行。" —**e-publisher** *n* [C]

erectile dys·func·tion also 又作 **erectile disfunction** /ɪˌrɛktḷ dɪsˋfʌŋkʃən; ɪˌrektaɪl dɪsˈfʌŋkʃən/ *n* [U]
if a man has erectile dysfunction, he is unable to have sex because he cannot get an ERECTION 勃起功能障碍, 不举: *Regular exercise reduces a man's risk of erectile dysfunction.* 定期锻炼会减少男性患勃起功能障碍的风险。

e-res·u·me also 又作 **e-résumé** /ˈi ˌrɛzuˋme; ˈi ˌrezjʊmeɪ/ *n* [C]
an electronic written record of your education and previous jobs that you send to an employer over the Internet when you are looking for a new job 电子简历

e-sig·na·ture /ˈi ˌsɪgnətʃɚ; ˈi ˌsɪgnətʃə/ also 又作 **electronic signature** *n* [C]
a sort of CODE that is used in an electronic document in order to prove who was responsible for writing the document, so that the person who receives it can be sure who it is from. Some companies use e-signatures in their legal documents instead of written SIGNATURE*s* on paper. 电子签名

e-tail·er /ˈi ˌtelɚ; ˈiː ˌteɪlə/ *n* [C]
electronic retailer; a business that sells products or services on the Internet, instead of in a shop 网上零售商: *Some e-tailers need to improve their customer services.* 一些网上零售商需要改进对顾客的服务。—**e-tail** *n* [U]

ethical au·dit /ˌɛθɪkḷ ˋɔdɪt; ˌeθɪkəl ˈɔːdɪ̥t/ also 又作 **social audit** *n* [C]
an official examination of how well a company behaves, for example how it treats its employees, the environment etc 道德审计〔检查公司对雇员和环境的态度等〕

e-tick·et /ˈi ˌtɪkɪt; ˈiː ˌtɪkɪ̥t/ *n* [C]
electronic ticket; a ticket, especially a ticket for a plane journey, that is stored in a computer and is not given to the customer in the form of paper 电子票证; 电子机票

euro /ˈjuro; ˈjʊərəʊ/ *n* [C]
NEW MEANING
a CURRENCY that can be used in some countries of the EU, and that will become the only currency that those countries will use 欧元

Eu·ro·land /ˈjurolænd; ˈjʊərəʊlænd/ *n*
the countries in Europe who have started to use the Euro as a legal CURRENCY 欧元区

Eu·ro·scep·tic also 又作 **eurosceptic** *BrE* 【英】, **Euroskeptic** *AmE* 【美】/ˈjuroˌskɛptɪk; ˈjʊərəʊˌskeptɪk/ *n* [C]
someone, especially a politician, who believes that Britain should not become closely connected to the European Union 对欧盟有怀疑的人〔尤指认为英国不应与欧盟太亲密的政客〕—**eurosceptic** *adj*: *eurosceptic policies* 对欧盟持怀疑态度的政策

Eu·ro·trash /ˈjuroˌtræʃ; ˈjʊərəʊˌtræʃ/ *n* [U]
an insulting word for people from Europe who have a lot of money, wear fashionable clothes, and go to fashionable clubs and events, but who are considered lazy and too interested in their social lives "欧洲垃圾"〔对欧洲一些无所事事、太注重社交生活的富人的蔑称〕

Euro-zone /ˈjuro ˌzon; ˈjʊərəʊ ˌzəʊn/ *n* [singular]
the group of European countries that use the EURO as a standard unit of money 欧元区: *trade among the countries of the Euro-zone* 欧元区国家之间的贸易

eu·tha·nize /`juθənaɪz; 'juːðənaɪz/ also 又作 **eu·tha·nase** /-nez; -neɪz/ *BrE*【英】*v* [T]
to kill an animal in a painless way, usually because it is very sick or old 对〔动物〕施行无痛致死术，使〔动物〕安乐死: *The decision to euthanase a pet is one of the most heart-breaking anyone has to make.* 对宠物施行无痛致死术，对任何人来说都是最令人心碎的决定之一。

EVP /ˌi vi `pi; ˌiː viː 'piː/ *n*
Executive Vice-President; a very important job at the top of a large company or organization 执行副总裁: *George Werner has been named EVP for corporate affairs, effective from January 1, 2001.* 乔治·沃纳已被任命为处理公司事务的执行副总裁，该任命从2001年1月1日起生效。

ex·ec·u·ta·ry /ɪg`zɛkjuˌtɛrɪ; ɪg'zekjʊtəri/ *n* [C]
a secretary who works for an important person in a company, and who has more responsibility and a higher salary than secretaries usually have. This word comes from a combination of 'secretary' and 'EXECUTIVE'. 行政秘书〔由secretary和executive缩合而成〕: *An executary has to have the ability to make judgements and decisions when the executive is out of town.* 行政秘书必须具备主管不在时作出判断和决定的能力。

expansion card /ɪk`spænʃən ˌkɑrd; ɪk'spænʃən ˌkɑːd/ *n* [C]
a CIRCUIT BOARD that fits into a computer and makes it possible for the computer to do more things, for example play sounds or VIDEO pictures, or use a telephone line 〔计算机的〕扩充插件板[卡]，扩充卡，扩展卡

expansion slot /ɪk`spænʃən ˌslɑt; ɪk'spænʃən ˌslɒt/ *n* [C]
a place on a computer system CIRCUIT BOARD that can hold an EXPANSION CARD 〔计算机的〕扩充槽，扩展槽

export /ɪks`pɔrt; ɪk'spɔːt/ *v* [T]
NEW MEANING
to arrange information or the space on a computer DISK so that the information can be understood and used by a different computer PROGRAM 导出，输出〔资料〕

ex·tra·net /`ɛkstrənɛt; 'ekstrənet/ *n* [C]
a computer system in a company that allows better communication between the company and its customers by combining Internet and INTRANET systems, so that some customers can view some of the company's private information that is not normally available on the Internet 〔公司和客户之间的〕外联网

extreme /ɪk`strim; ɪk'striːm/ *adj*
NEW MEANING
1 [only before noun 仅用于名词前] **extreme sports/surfing/skiing etc** an extreme sport is one that is done in a way that has much more risk and so is more dangerous than an ordinary form of the sport 极限运动/冲浪/滑雪等: *Far from being crazy, people who do extreme sports are usually very in control, but love the excitement.* 参加极限运动的人绝不疯狂，他们通常很有自制，只是喜欢追求刺激而已。**2 extreme athlete/surfer/skier etc** someone who does extreme sports 极限运动员/冲浪者/滑雪者等: *Extreme surfers will ride waves that reach heights of more than fifty feet.* 极限冲浪者会在五十多英尺高的浪上滑行。

extreme fight·ing /ɪkˌstrim `faɪtɪŋ; ɪkˌstriːm 'faɪtɪŋ/ *n* [U]
a competition, similar to BOXING, in which two people are allowed to hit or kick each other and in which there are almost no rules. Extreme fighting is illegal in some countries, and in some parts of the US. 终极搏击，极限打斗: *Critics think extreme fighting should be banned completely.* 评论者认为终极搏击应该完全禁止。

eye can·dy /`aɪ ˌkændɪ; 'aɪ ˌkændi/ *n* [U]
informal someone who is attractive, but who you do not approve of because you think they have been chosen for something because of their appearance rather than their intelligence【非正式】中看不中用的人

e-zine /`i ˌzin; 'iː ˌziːn/ *n* [C]
a magazine that can be read on the Internet 电子杂志

F, f

face /fes; feɪs/ *n*
NEW MEANING
1 get in sb's face *AmE spoken* to annoy someone and try to tell them what to do【美口】啰唆: *She's the coach – you don't get in her face.* 她是教练，别当她的面啰唆个没完。**2 get out of my face** *AmE spoken* used to tell someone in an impolite way to go away because they are annoying you【美口】滚开，去你的 **3 in your face** *informal* behaviour, remarks etc that are in your face are very direct and often make people feel shocked or surprised【非正式】直截了当（地）；突如其来（地），出乎意料（地）: *Bingham has a very 'in your face' writing style.* 宾厄姆的作品有一种大胆直接的风格。

face time /`fes ˌtaɪm; 'feɪs ˌtaɪm/ *n* [U] *AmE*
1 time that you spend at your job because you want other people, especially your manager, to see you there, whether or not you are actually doing good work【美】为考勤作门面功夫: *Here we reward performance, not face time.* 我们这儿奖励的是工作表现，而不是门面功夫。**2** time that you spend talking to someone when you are with them, rather than on the telephone 面对面交谈的时间: *In return for his donation, he wanted face time with the President.* 他想与总统当面谈谈，作为捐赠的回报。

fac·toid /`fæktɔɪd; 'fæktɔɪd/ *n* [C]
a small interesting piece of information that is often not important 琐碎的新闻，有趣的资料: *This is actually one of those rare football factoids that's useful to know.* 事实上这是那种难得听到，但很有用的关于足球的小新闻。

fa·ji·ta /fə`hitə; fə'hiːtə/ *n* [C usually plural 一般用复数]
a TEX-MEX dish made with onions, peppers, and chicken or meat that are put in a TORTILLA 墨西哥铁板烧〔包含洋葱、辣椒以及鸡肉或其他肉的玉米粉圆饼〕

fallen an·gel /ˌfɔlən `endʒəl; ˌfɔːlən 'eɪndʒəl/ *n* [C]
informal something such as a STOCK that is not earning as much money as it did in the past【非正式】风光不再的东西〈如证券〉

FAQ, faq /fæk, ˌɛf e `kju; fæk, ˌef eɪ 'kjuː/ *n* [C usually plural 一般用复数]
frequently asked question(s); on WEBSITES, a list of questions that users often ask about the website, and answers to them 〔网站上的〕常见问题〔附答案〕

farmer's mar·ket /ˌfɑrməz `mɑrkɪt; ˌfɑːməz 'mɑːkɪt/ *n* [C]
a place where farmers bring their fruit and vegetables to sell directly to people in a town or city 农产品集贸市场，农贸市场

fash·ion·ist·a /ˌfæʃən`istə; ˌfæʃən'iːstə/ *n* [C]
informal someone who is very interested in fashion and who likes the very newest styles【非正式】超级时装迷，穿着非常时髦的人

fashion state·ment /`fæʃən ˌstetmənt; 'fæʃən ˌsteɪtmənt/ *n* [C]
something that you own, do, or wear that is considered new, exciting, or different, and is intended to make other people notice you and give them an idea of the kind of person you are 时尚炫耀，潮流象征: *Camouflage – the latest fashion statement.* 迷彩服——最新的时尚标志。| **make a fashion statement** *Mobile phones make a big fashion statement.* 手机现在成了热门的潮流象征。

fat /fæt; fæt/ *adj*
NEW MEANING
another spelling of PHAT; fashionable, attractive, or desirable 时尚的，精彩的，极好的〔phat的另一种拼法〕:

fat/phat beats (=music that sounds good) 精彩的音乐 *Check out these fat beats.* 听听这些精彩的音乐。

fat camp /ˋfæt ˌkæmp; ˈfæt ˌkæmp/ *n* [C]
a place where children go to lose weight and exercise, especially a place where they stay for several weeks〔儿童参加的〕减肥营

fat gram /ˋfæt ˌgræm; ˈfæt ˌgræm/ *n* [C usually plural 一般用复数]
a gram of fat in food〔食物中的〕脂肪克数: *Is it more important to count fat grams or calories when losing weight?* 减肥时计算食物中的脂肪克数重要还是卡路里重要?

fault·tol·er·ant /ˋfɔlt ˌtɑlərənt; ˈfɔːlt ˌtɒlərənt/ *adj*
fault-tolerant computer/machine a computer that continues working even if it has a fault or when there is a fault in a PROGRAM 容错电脑/机器

feel·bad fac·tor /ˋfilbæd ˌfæktɚ; ˈfiːlbæd ˌfæktə/ *n* [singular] *BrE*
an unfavourable economic situation in a country, which has a negative effect on people's attitudes. This expression developed from the phrase 'FEEL-GOOD FACTOR' and is used mainly in JOURNALISM.【英】令人担心的经济情况: *High house prices, low interest rates, and job insecurity all contribute to the feelbad factor.* 高房价、低利率和工作无保障都造成了令人担心的经济情况。

fence-mend·ing /ˋfɛns ˌmɛndɪŋ; ˈfens ˌmendɪŋ/ *adj* [only before noun 仅用于名词前]
fence-mending measures/talks/trip etc fence-mending trips, talks etc are between countries who have a disagreement about something, and are meant to try to improve relations between them 修复(友好)关系的措施/会谈/旅行等: *The Vice-President will be sent on a fence-mending trip throughout Latin America.* 副总统将被派往拉丁美洲作一次旨在修复关系的访问。| *The British Foreign Secretary will begin fence-mending talks with his Chinese counterpart on Tuesday.* 英国外务大臣将在星期二和中国外交部长进行一次修复关系的会谈。—**fence-mending** *n* [U]: *Behind the scenes, there are signs of a desire by Republicans and Democrats alike to engage in serious fence-mending.* 有迹象显示, 共和党和民主党私下里都有认真修复关系的愿望。

feng shui¹ /ˌfʌŋ ˋʃwe; ˌfʌŋ ˈʃweɪ/ *n* [U]
a Chinese system of organizing the furniture and other things in a house or building in a way that people believe will bring good luck and happiness 风水

feng shui² *v* [T]
feng shui a room/house etc to place the furniture and other things in a room or house in a particular position so that it is arranged according to the feng shui position 将房间/房子里的家具及物品按风水好的布局摆放

fire·wall /ˋfaɪrwɔl; ˈfaɪəwɔːl/ *n* [C]
1 a system that stops people who do not have permission looking at particular information on a computer, especially information on the Internet〔电脑系统的〕防火墙: *British Aerospace uses a firewall between its corporate network and the outside world.* 英国航空航天工业公司使用"防火墙"分隔公司的电脑网络和外界网络。
2 a system that is used by large financial or law companies to stop secret information being passed from one department to another〔金融公司或律师事务所阻止泄密的〕防火墙

fit /fɪt; fɪt/ *v* **fitted, fitting** [I] *BrE*
NEW MEANING
to have a SEIZURE (=a sudden condition in which someone cannot control the movements of their body)【英】痉挛发作: *The patient was still fitting.* 病人仍处于痉挛状态。—**fitting** *n* [U]: *Fitting continued for more than 5 minutes.* 痉挛持续时间超过了5分钟。

flack /flæk; flæk/ *n* [C] *AmE*
NEW MEANING
informal someone whose job is to represent an organization and answer questions about it, especially when something bad has happened【美, 非正式】代言人

flake /flek; fleɪk/ *v*
NEW MEANING
flake out *phr v* [I] *AmE spoken* to do something strange or forgetful, or to not do what you said you would do【美口】靠不住, 反复无常: **flake out on sb** *Kathy kind of flaked out on us today – said she couldn't take the stress.* 凯西今天临阵脱逃——她说她承受不了这种压力。

flame /flem; fleɪm/ *v* [T]
NEW MEANING
informal to send someone an angry or insulting message in an E-MAIL or on a BULLETIN BOARD【非正式】发送言辞愤怒的电子邮件; 在电子公告板上发布侮辱性信息: *I got flamed just for saying I thought Bruce Willis was cool!* 我只是说过我认为布鲁斯·威利斯很酷, 便收到了措辞愤怒的电子邮件! —**flame** *n* [C]

flash cam·paign /ˋflæʃ kæmˌpen; ˈflæʃ kæmˌpeɪn/ *n* [C]
a sudden large amount of activity such as a protest which starts quickly because information can be sent to a lot of people almost instantly by using the Internet〔网上煽动的〕闪速行动

flat·line /ˋflætˌlaɪn; ˈflætlaɪn/ *v* [I]
be flatlining to be at a low level or standard that is neither increasing nor decreasing. This word comes from the field of medicine, where doctors use special equipment to measure the beating of people's hearts. If the equipment shows a flat line, it means that the person's heart is not beating and they are dead or nearly dead. 呈现平线, 保持低水平, 不升不降〔原为医学用词, 人在死亡或临死时, 其心电图等呈现平线〕: *The Tories have been flatlining in the polls for the last three months.* 保守党在最近三个月的民意调查中的支持率一直处于低水平, 不升不跌。

flatpack 扁平组件

flat·pack /ˋflætˌpæk; ˈflætpæk/ *n* [C] *BrE*
a piece of furniture that is sold in pieces which are stored in a flat box so they are easy to carry. You put the piece of furniture together yourself at home【英】扁平(家具)组件: *flatpack furniture* 组合家具

fla·va /ˋflevʌ; ˈfleɪvʌ/ *n* [U]
slang flavour; an idea of what the typical qualities of something are【俚】特色

flex·ec·u·tive /flɛkˋsɛkjutɪv; flekˈsekjʊtɪv/ also 又作 **flex·ec** /ˋflɛksɛk; ˈfleksek/ *n* [C] *BrE*
a young, fashionable person who makes a lot of money, usually working in the computer or MEDIA industry, but who does not work in the usual way. For example, they often have more than one job, change jobs often, or spend a lot of time doing other things, such as travelling.【英】弹性行政人员〔通常为从事计算机或媒体行业的时尚青年, 他们收入甚丰, 而且工作方式灵活〕

float /flot; fləʊt/ *n* [C]
NEW MEANING
a time when you sit in a FLOTATION TANK in order to treat illness or injury, or to relax 浮桶盐水浴疗: *I experienced my first float last week and loved the total relaxation it provided.* 上周我第一次进行浮桶盐水浴疗, 就爱上了那种让人完全放松的感觉。

floating /ˋflotɪŋ; ˈfləʊtɪŋ/ *n* [U]
the activity of sitting in a FLOTATION TANK in order to relax, or to treat illness or injury 浮桶盐水浴疗: *Floating helped my recovery.* 盐水浴疗帮助我康复。

flotation tank /floˋteʃən ˌtæŋk; fləʊˈteɪʃən ˌtæŋk/ *n* [C]
a large container full of warm salty water, often with a cover on it to make it dark inside, that you float in so that you can relax, or to treat illness or injury 盐水浴疗浮桶: *When I first stepped into the flotation tank, I found myself a bit anxious and unsure.* 我第一次步入盐水浴疗浮桶时，感到有点担心和不知所措。

fly /flaɪ; flaɪ/ *adj*
NEW MEANING
slang very fashionable and attractive【俚】非常时尚迷人的: *Put on your flyest skirt for your Friday date.* 穿上你最时髦的裙子去赴星期五的约会。

fly·er·ing /ˋflaɪərɪŋ; ˈflaɪərɪŋ/ *n* [U]
the activity of fixing printed notices onto trees and buildings in order to advertise something such as a concert 张贴小广告

Flyover Coun·try /ˋflaɪovɚ ˌkʌntrɪ; ˈflaɪ-əʊvə ˌkʌntri/ *n* [U]
humorous the middle part of the US, which some people consider to be boring and which they only see when they are flying over it in a plane between the east and west coasts【幽默】飞越地区〔在飞机上看到的美国中部枯燥乏味的地区〕

food miles /ˋfud ˌmaɪlz; ˈfuːd ˌmaɪlz/ *n* [plural] *BrE*
an expression meaning the distance food has been moved by ship, plane, TRUCK, etc to get it to shops, used especially by people who think that it is better to eat food that has been produced near the area where you live rather than using a lot of energy to move it over long distances【英】〔食物运抵商店的〕食物运输距离: *We wanted to support the rural economy by encouraging village shops to stock fresh local produce and to cut down on food miles.* 我们想通过鼓励乡村商店采购本地新鲜的农产品和减少食物运输里程来支持农村的经济。

footprint /ˋfutˌprɪnt; ˈfʊtˌprɪnt/ *n* [C]
NEW MEANING
the amount of space on a desk that a computer fills 电脑基座所占面积: *These PCs have a 50% smaller footprint than older models.* 这些个人电脑的基座面积比旧款的小50%。

forklift up·grade /ˋfɔrklɪft ˌʌpgred; ˈfɔːklɪft ˌʌpgreɪd/ *n* [C]
an improvement to a computer system that involves buying a lot of expensive equipment rather than adding new SOFTWARE〔计算机的〕硬件升级: *This fix is convenient because it lets carriers add capacity or speed without going through a forklift upgrade.* 这次维修很方便，因为它让航空公司无需进行硬件升级便可提高容量和速度。

404 /ˌfɔr o ˋfɔr; ˌfɔːr əʊ ˈfɔː/ *adj* [not before noun 不用于名词前]
humorous someone who is 404 is stupid and unable to use computers or other complicated electronic equipment. This word comes from the usual message which appears on the Internet when a particular page you are searching for cannot be found.【幽默】电脑[电子设备]白痴〔源自无法找到网页时出现的信息〕

four-one-one also 又作 **411** /ˌfɔr wʌn ˋwʌn; ˌfɔː wʌn ˈwʌn/ *n*
the 411 (on sb/sth) *AmE slang* information or facts about someone or something. This word comes from the telephone number of the service, often called 'information', that you can call in the US in order to find out what someone's telephone number is.【美俚】〔关于某人或某物的〕资料，详情〔411 原为查询电话号码的服务台〕: *Here's the 411 on all the hottest bands on tour.* 这里有正在巡回演出的所有当红乐队的资料。

frac·tal /ˋfræktḷ; ˈfræktəl/ *n* [C]
technical a pattern, usually produced by a computer, that is made by repeating the same shape many times at smaller and smaller sizes【术语】分形〔由一个图形辗转缩小、重复产生的图形，一般用电脑制作〕—**fractal** *adj* [only before noun 仅用于名词前]: *fractal geometry* 分形几何(学)

fran·ken·food /ˋfræŋkənˌfud; ˈfræŋkənˌfuːd/ also 又作 **Fran·ken·stein foods** /ˋfræŋkənstaɪn ˌfudz; ˈfræŋkənstaɪn ˌfuːdz/ *n* [C usually plural 一般用复数]
informal a word meaning a food that has been produced by plants that were GENETICALLY MODIFIED, used when you disapprove of this process. This word is a combination of 'Frankenstein' (=the scientist who created a monster in the story by Mary Shelley) and 'food'.【非正式】转基因食品，恶魔食品〔带贬义，由 Frankenstein（科学怪人 —— 玛丽·雪莱小说中一名制造怪物的科学家）和 food 缩合而成〕

free rad·icals /ˌfri ˋrædɪkḷz; ˌfriː ˈrædɪkəlz/ *n* [plural]
atoms or groups of atoms that have at least one ELECTRON that does not form a pair with another electron, so that the atom joins with other atoms, causing chemical changes 自由基，游离基: *It is only recently that free radicals have been implicated in major diseases like cancer and heart disease.* 人们直到最近才知道自由基与癌症、心脏病等严重疾病有关。

freestyle[1] /ˋfriˌstaɪl; ˈfriːstaɪl/ *n* [C]
NEW MEANING
a RAP[2] (2) song in which the singer says words directly from their imagination, without planning or writing them first 即兴说唱歌曲

freestyle[2] /ˋfriˌstaɪl; ˈfriːstaɪl/ *v* [I,T]
to say the words of a RAP[2] (2) song directly from your imagination, without planning or writing them first 即兴地说唱: *Anderson began by freestyling a rap about his baby son.* 安德森一开始便即兴地说唱了一首关于他的小宝贝儿子的歌。

free-to-air /ˌfri tu ˋɛr; ˌfriː tʊ ˈeə/ *adj BrE*
free-to-air television or television programmes do not cost additional money to watch【英】〔电视节目〕不另外收费的: *The new channel will be free-to-air, funded by the licence fee.* 这个新设的频道将是不收费的，由电视许可证费提供资助。| *free-to-air television coverage of rugby league matches* 橄榄球联赛的免费电视转播

free·ware /ˋfriwɛr; ˈfriːweə/ *n* [U]
computer SOFTWARE that is given away free〔电脑的〕免费软件

fro-yo /ˋfrojo; ˈfrəʊjəʊ/ *n* [C]
a frozen sweet food made from YOGHURT. This word comes from a combination of the words 'FROZEN' and 'YOGHURT'. 冷冻酸奶〔由 frozen 和 yoghurt 缩合而成〕: *a strawberry fro-yo* 草莓冷冻酸奶

functional food /ˋfʌŋkʃənḷ ˌfud; ˈfʌŋkʃənəl ˌfuːd/ *n* [C,U]
food that contains special additional substances that are intended to have a good effect on your health 功能食品，保健食品

func·tion·al·ity /ˌfʌŋkʃənˋælətɪ; ˌfʌŋkʃəˈnælɪ̣ti/ *n* [U]
all of the operations that a computer is able to perform〔电脑的〕全部功能

fusion cui·sine /ˋfjuʒən kwɪˌzin; ˈfjuːʒən kwɪˌziːn/ also 又作 **fusion food** /ˋfjuʒən ˌfud; ˈfjuːʒən ˋfuːd/ *n* [U]
a style of cooking in which new dishes are developed which include foods from several different parts of the world, for example China and Mexico 融合烹饪法

future-o·ri·en·ted /ˌfjutʃɚ ˋɔrɪɛntɪd; ˌfjuːtʃər ˈɔːrientɪ̣d/ *adj*
giving a lot of time, effort, or attention to what is going to happen or needs to be done in the future 面向未来的: *future-oriented technology* 面向未来的技术 | *"Bavaria is open-minded and future-oriented, and is now among the strongest economic states in Europe," says Schmidt.*

施密特说:"巴伐利亚州思想开放,面向未来,现在已成为欧洲经济最强的地区之一。"

future-proof¹, futureproof /ˋfjutʃɚ ˌpruf; ˈfjuːtʃə ˌpruːf/ *v* [T]
to make or plan something in such a way that it will not become ineffective or unsuitable for use in the future 使〔某物〕不会过时: *Chairman Michael Cortese today announced dramatic plans to future-proof the company's network.* 迈克尔·科特斯主席今天宣布了宏大的计划,该计划将使公司的网络能应付未来的需要。

future-proof² /ˋfjutʃɚ ˌpruf; ˈfjuːtʃə ˌpruːf/ *adj*
if something is future-proof, it will not become ineffective or unsuitable for use in the future 不会过时的,不会失效的: *future-proof software* 不会过时的软件 | *future-proof technology* 经得起时间考验的技术

FWIW, fwiw
the written abbreviation of 缩写= 'for what it's worth', used in E-MAIL or TEXT MESSAGES on MOBILE PHONES, to mean that you are not sure of the value or usefulness of what you are saying 不论好坏,不管有没有用〔电子邮件或手机短信用语〕

FYI, fyi
the written abbreviation of 缩写= 'for your information', used especially in short business notes and E-MAILS, when you are telling someone something they need to know 供你参考〔尤作商业便笺和电子邮件用语〕

G,g

gag /gæg; gæg/ *v BrE*
NEW MEANING
slang【英俚】**1 be gagging to do sth/be gagging for sth** to be very eager to do or have something 急于干某事/拥有某物: *They were gagging to sign the contract.* 他们急于签订这份合同。**2 be gagging for it** used by a man to say he thinks a woman wants to have sex〔男人用语,指女人〕想干那个〔指发生性行为〕

game /gem; geɪm/ *n*
NEW MEANING
sb got game *AmE spoken informal* used to say that someone is very skilful at doing something, especially playing a sport【美口,非正式】某人做某事非常熟练〔尤指运动〕

gam·er /ˋgemɚ; ˈgeɪmə/ *n* [C]
1 *slang* someone who likes playing VIDEO GAMES, or who likes to play games in which they pretend to be a particular character【俚】玩电子游戏者,游戏玩家: *40,000 gamers have logged on each day since the site began.* 自那个网站开张以来,每天有4万名游戏玩家登入。**2** *AmE informal* a person who is very good at a sport, and can help a team to win games【美,非正式】〔帮助球队赢得胜利的〕优秀运动员,王牌运动员

gaming /ˋgemɪŋ; ˈgeɪmɪŋ/ *n* [U]
NEW MEANING
the activity of playing VIDEO GAMES 打电子游戏,打视频游戏: *Online gaming is becoming a huge business.* 在线游戏正成为一个庞大的产业。| *I've been involved in gaming for a long time.* 我迷上电子游戏有很长时间了。

gang·sta /ˋgæŋstʌ; ˈgæŋstʌ/ *n* [C] *AmE informal* someone who is a member of a GANG【美,非正式】帮派成员: *gangstas in South Central L.A.* 洛杉矶中南部的黑帮分子

gangsta rap /ˋgæŋstʌ ˌræp; ˈgæŋstʌ ˌræp/ *n* [U]
a type of RAP music with words about drugs, violence, and life in poor areas of cities〔以吸毒、暴力和贫民区生活为内容的〕冈斯特说唱乐,匪帮说唱乐 —**gangsta-rapper** *n* [C]

gap year /ˋgæp ˌjɪr; ˈgæp ˌjɪə/ *n* [C] *BrE*
a year between leaving school and going to university, which some young people use as an opportunity to travel, earn money, or get experience of working【英】休学年,空档年〔中学生毕业后上大学前旅游、打工等的一段时间〕: *Some students choose to work in high-tech industries during their gap year.* 一些学生选择在上大学前先去高科技产业工作一年。

garage /gəˋrɑʒ; ˈgærɑːʒ/ *n* [U]
NEW MEANING
a type of popular music played on electronic instruments, with a strong fast beat and singing 车库乐〔一种由电子乐器伴奏的、快节奏的、带吟咏的流行音乐〕: *a collection of the latest dance and garage hits* 最新流行的舞曲和车库乐集锦

gas·tro·pub /ˋgæstroˌpʌb; ˈgæstrəʊˌpʌb/ *n* [C] *BrE*
a PUB that is fashionable inside and that has good and expensive food. The word 'gastropub' comes from a combination of the words 'GASTRONOMY' (preparing and enjoying good food) and 'PUB'.【英】美食吧〔由gastronomy和pub缩合而成〕

gate¹ /get; geɪt/ *n*
NEW MEANING
right out of the gate immediately 立即: *The show bombed right out of the gate, and was canceled after two episodes.* 该节目一推出就砸锅了,播放了两集之后就被停播了。

gatekeeper /ˋgetˌkipɚ; ˈgeɪtˌkiːpə/ *n* [C]
NEW MEANING
1 someone in an organization who has a lot of influence over what products the organization buys, who it buys them from etc〔机构中对买入什么产品、向谁购买等有巨大影响力的〕把关人 **2** someone in an organization who tells customers or people with questions which people in the organization should be able to help them〔机构中转介顾客或查询人至有关负责人的〕引导员

gay pride /ˌge ˋpraɪd; ˌgeɪ ˈpraɪd/ *n* [U]
a political and social movement that encourages HOMOSEXUAL people not to keep the fact that they are homosexual a secret, and to be proud of themselves 同性恋者尊严: *a gay pride march* 提倡同性恋者尊严的游行

gay·dar /ˋgedɑr; ˈgeɪdɑː/ *n* [U] *AmE*
spoken humorous the ability to recognize that someone is HOMOSEXUAL. This word comes from a combination of the words 'GAY' and 'RADAR'.【美口,幽默】同性恋雷达〔指识别某人为同性恋者的能力,由gay和radar缩合而成〕

ga·zun·der /gəˋzʌndɚ; gəˈzʌndə/ *v* [T] *BrE*
be gazundered if you are gazundered, someone who has agreed to buy your house says that they will only buy it for less than the amount originally agreed【英】〔卖房时〕被压价

gender a·ware·ness /ˋdʒɛndɚ əˌwɛrnɪs; ˈdʒendər əˌweənɨs/ *n* [U]
if an employer or employee has gender awareness, they understand the differences between how men and women behave and are able to treat them both fairly and equally 性别意识〔能公平地对待不同性别〕

gender bi·as /ˋdʒɛndɚ ˌbaɪəs; ˈdʒendə ˌbaɪəs/ *n* [C,U]
if an employer or person has gender bias, they treat men and women differently in a way that is unfair 性别偏见[歧视]

Generation X /ˌdʒɛnəreʃən ˋɛks; ˌdʒenəreɪʃən ˈeks/ also 又作 **Gen-X** /dʒɛn ˋɛks; dʒen ˈeks/ *n* [U]
the group of people who are between about 20 and 35 years old 无名一代,X世代〔指大约在20至35岁之间的一代人〕: *the needs and attitudes of Generation X* 无名一代的需求和态度 —**Generation X-er** *n* [C] *Gen X-ers still attend more films than older age groups.* 无名一代的人比起老一辈人看的影片多。

genetically mod·i·fied /dʒəˌnɛtɪklɪ ˋmɑdɪfaɪd; dʒəˌnetɪkli ˈmɒdɨfaɪd/ also 又作 **genetically en·gin·eered** /dʒəˌnɛtɪklɪ ɛndʒəˋnɪrd; dʒəˌnetɪkli endʒɨˈnɪəd/ *adj*
genetically modified food or plants have had their GENETIC structure changed, especially so that they are not

affected by particular diseases or harmful insects 基因改良的，转基因的: *Consumers are worried by genetically modified products, and are becoming more interested in organic food.* 消费者对转基因食品不甚放心，而对有机食品越来越感兴趣。—**genetic modification** *n* [U]

ge·no·mic /dʒɪˋnomɪk; dʒɪˈnəʊmɪk/ *adj* *technical* relating to all the GENE*s* that are found in one type of living thing【术语】基因组的: *Researchers plan to use genomic information to develop drugs that specifically target the virus.* 研究人员计划利用基因组信息开发专门针对该病毒的药物。

gen·o·type /ˋdʒɛno͵taɪp; ˈdʒenəʊ͵taɪp/ *n* [C] all the GENE*s* that are found in one type of living thing 基因型

GHB /͵dʒi etʃ ˋbi; ͵dʒiː eɪtʃ ˈbiː/ *n* [U] an illegal chemical substance that is taken as a drug by some people, especially at parties and dance clubs 丙种羟基丁酸盐，迷奸药〔一种毒品〕

GIF /gɪf; gɪf/ *n* [C] *technical* graphics interchange format; a type of computer FILE that contains images and is used on the Internet【术语】图形交换格式（文件）

gig /gɪg; gɪg/ *n* [C]
NEW MEANING
informal a GIGABYTE; one billion BYTE*s* of information【非正式】吉字节，千兆字节〔即十亿位元组的信息〕

gimme /ˋgɪmɪ; ˈgɪmi/ *n* [C usually singular 一般用单数] *informal* something that is so easy to do or succeed at that you do not even have to try【非正式】轻而易举的事，轻易得到的东西: *The victory was a gimme for the New York Yankees.* 这场胜利对纽约扬基队来说简直轻而易举。

girl /gɝl; gɜːl/ *n*
NEW MEANING
(you) go girl! *AmE slang* used to encourage a girl or woman, or to say that you agree with what she is saying【美俚】加油！说得对！〔鼓励女孩或妇女，或表示同意她说的话〕

girl pow·er /ˋgɝl ͵paʊɚ; ˈgɜːl ͵paʊə/ *n* [U] **1** the idea that women should take control over their own lives or situations 女性自主思想 **2** the social or political influence that women have 女性权力〔即在社会和政治上的影响力〕

give /gɪv; gɪv/ *v*
NEW MEANING
give up *phr v* [T] **give it up (for sb)** to APPLAUD (=hit your open hands together) to show that you approve of someone or what they have done（给某人）鼓掌: *Come on everybody, let's give it up for George!* 各位，来，我们为乔治鼓掌！

global e·con·o·my /͵globḷ ɪˋkɑnəmɪ; ͵gləʊbəl ɪˈkɒnəmi/ *n* [singular] the economic activity of the world considered as a whole 全球经济

glo·bal·i·za·tion also 又作 **-isation** *BrE*【英】/͵globḷəˋzeʃən; ͵gləʊbəlaɪˈzeɪʃən/ *n* [U] the process by which countries all over the world become connected or similar, especially because large companies are doing business in many different countries 全球化: *the rapid globalization of the world economy* 世界经济的迅速全球一体化

glo·bal·ize also 又作 **-ise** *BrE*【英】/ˋglobḷaɪz; ˈgləʊbəlaɪz/ *v* [I,T] if a company, industry, or economy globalizes or is globalized, it has business activities all over the world, so that it is no longer dependent on the economic conditions in one country, but is affected by conditions all around the world 使全球化

glo·cal·i·za·tion /͵glokḷəˋzeʃən; ͵gləʊkəlaɪˈzeɪʃən/ *n* [U] the idea that companies should do business around the world, but use methods that are suitable for each particular country they work in 全球本地化〔指企业在全球做生意，但在每个国家都应使用适合当地情况的方法〕

GM /͵dʒi ˋɛm; ͵dʒiː ˈem/ *adj* [only before noun 仅用于名词前] *especially BrE* genetically modified; GM foods or plants have had their GENETIC structure changed, especially so that they are not affected by particular diseases or harmful insects【尤英】转基因的，基因改良的

GMO /͵dʒi ɛm ˋo; ͵dʒiː em ˈəʊ/ *n* [C] genetically modified organism; a plant or other living thing whose GENE*s* have been changed by scientists, especially in order to make it less likely to get diseases or be harmed by insects etc 转基因生物（体），基因改良生物（体）—**GMO** *adj* [only before noun 仅用于名词前]: *GMO crops* 转基因作物

go[1] /go; gəʊ/ *v*
NEW MEANING
don't (even) go there *spoken humorous* used to say that you do not want to talk or think about something【口，幽默】打住，别说了〔用于表示不想谈或回想某事〕: *"What if the two of you actually...?" "Don't even go there!"* "要是你们两个人真地…?" "不要再提了！"

go down *phr v* [I] *slang* to happen【俚】发生: *People still don't know what went down that night.* 人们仍然不知道那天夜里发生了什么。

go off on sb/sth *phr v* [T] *AmE* to show how angry you are at someone or about something by saying what you really think【美】直接表明对…有怒气: *Lisa called him a geek, so Brett just went off on her.* 莉萨称布雷特是个怪人，布雷特对她发火了。

go[2] /go; gəʊ/ *n*
NEW MEANING
sth is a go *AmE spoken* used to say that things are working correctly, or that you have permission to do something【美口】没问题: *I just got word from the boss, and the trip to London is a go.* 老板刚发了话，伦敦之行没问题。

God /gɑd; gɒd/ *n*
there is a God! *spoken humorous* said when someone is explaining that something really good happened to them at a time when they thought that their situation was very bad【口，幽默】真是老天帮忙！这倒不错！: *There was no-one interesting in the hotel, and then in walked four gorgeous, blond Swedish boys, and I thought "There is a God!"* 这饭店里没有一个让人感兴趣的人，后来进来了四个衣着华丽、白肤金发碧眼的瑞典小伙子，我想："这还不错！"

go-go fund /ˋgo go ͵fʌnd; ˈgəʊ gəʊ ͵fʌnd/ *n* [C] *informal* a company that makes INVESTMENT*s* that have a high risk, but also a chance of making large profits【非正式】以高风险博取高收益的投资公司

golden /ˋgoldṇ; ˈgəʊldən/ *adj*
NEW MEANING
sb is golden *AmE spoken informal* used to say that someone is in a very good situation【美口，非正式】某人形势大好了；某人交好运: *If the right editor looks at your article, you're golden.* 如果有位合适的编辑看到你的文章，那你就交好运了。

golden hand·cuffs /͵goldṇ ˋhændkʌfs; ͵gəʊldən ˈhændkʌfs/ *n* [plural] *informal* things such as a large SALARY or a good PENSION that make important employees want to continue working for an organization, rather than leave to work for a competing organization【非正式】金手铐〔雇主为拴住骨干职员而付给的高薪金或优厚的退休金〕

golden hel·lo /͵goldṇ həˋlo; ͵gəʊldən həˈləʊ/ *n* [C] *especially BrE* *informal* a large amount of money that is given to a new employee, in order to persuade them not to go to work for another organization【尤英，非正式】〔公司给新员工的〕丰厚见面礼: *In Britain, new maths and science teachers are being given golden hellos.* 在英国，新来的数学和自然科学教师都会得到丰厚的见面礼。

Gol·di·locks e·con·o·my /ˋgoldɪlaks ɪˏkanəmɪ; ˈgəʊldilɒks ɪˌkɒnəmi/ *n* [C] *BrE technical* an economy that is not growing too slowly or too fast【英, 术语】〔增长速度适中的〕温和(型)经济

good /gud; gʊd/ *adj*
NEW MEANING
it's all good *AmE spoken slang* used to say that a situation is good or acceptable, or that there is not a problem【美口, 俚】一切都没有问题: *Don't worry about it, man – it's all good.* 别担心, 老兄 —— 一切都挺好的。

gopher, GOPHER /ˋgofɚ; ˈgəʊfə/ *n* [U]
NEW MEANING
technical a computer PROGRAM that quickly collects information from many different places on the Internet. This word comes from 'GOFER' (=someone who carries messages or gets or takes things for their employer), which is a combination of the words 'go' and 'for'.【术语】信息鼠〔互联网上快速的信息查找程序, 由 go 和 for 缩合而成〕: *Gopher uses a series of menus to lead you to things of interest.* 信息鼠使用一系列选单让你找到感兴趣的东西。

GPS /ˌdʒi pi ˋɛs; ˌdʒiː piː ˈes/ *n* [C]
Global Positioning System; a system that uses radio signals from SATELLITE*s* to show your exact position on the Earth on a special piece of equipment, often used by the military or in cars and boats 全球(卫星)定位系统

grandfather /ˋgrændˏfaðɚ; ˈgrændˌfɑːðə/ *v* [T] *AmE* also 又作 **grandfather** sb/sth ↔ **in**
to give someone or something special permission to continue doing what they have been doing and not obey a new law or rule【美】使不受新法规约束: *Even though the new apartment owner banned pets, they grandfathered my cat so I could stay.* 尽管新的房东禁止养宠物, 但是他们破例让我养猫, 我因而能够住下来。

graphical us·er in·ter·face /ˌgræfɪkl̩ ˋjuzɚ ˏɪntɚfes; ˌgræfɪkəl ˈjuːzər ˌɪntəfeɪs/ *abbreviation* 缩写为 **GUI** *n* [C]
a way of showing and organizing information on a computer screen that is easy to use and understand 图形用户界面, 视窗系统

graphics card /ˋgræfɪks ˏkard; ˈgræfɪks ˌkɑːd/ also 又作 **graphics a·dapt·er** /ˋgræfɪks əˏdæptɚ; ˈgræfɪks əˌdæptə/, **video adapter** *n* [C]
a CIRCUIT BOARD that connects to a computer and allows the computer to show images, such as VIDEO images, on its screen〔电脑的〕图形卡, 图像适配卡, 显卡

graveyard mar·ket /ˋgrevjard ˏmarkɪt; ˈgreɪvjɑːd ˌmɑːkɪ̈t/ *n* [singular]
technical a situation on the STOCK MARKET in which a lot of SHARE*s* are being sold and the prices are becoming lower, but people do not want to buy shares until the situation improves, so that the people who own shares are losing money【术语】"墓地"市场〔指股票经过大幅抛售后, 股价下跌, 但买方仍然观望市场发展, 不买进股票, 因而对股票持有人造成损失〕

greed·head /ˋgridˏhɛd; ˈgriːdhed/ *n* [C]
slang someone who always wants more money, possessions etc【俚】财迷

green au·dit /ˌgrin ˋɔdɪt; ˌgriːn ˈɔːdɪt/ *n* [C]
an official examination of the effects of a company's activities on the environment 绿色审计, 绿色审查〔即审查公司活动对环境的影响〕: *Businesses in York are being asked to carry out a green audit, and to report by the end of the year.* 约克的各家企业被要求进行一次环保审查, 并在年底前交出报告。

green·ing /ˋgrinɪŋ; ˈgriːnɪŋ/ *n*
the greening of sth *informal* the process of making a person or organization be more concerned about environmental problems and what they can do to improve the environment【非正式】增强环保意识: *the greening of corporate America* 美国工商界环保意识的提升

green·mail /ˋgrinˏmel; ˈgriːnmeɪl/ *n* [U]
the practice of buying back SHARE*s* in your own company often for a very high price from someone who has bought them in order to try to take control of your company or the money paid to do this 绿票讹诈, 购股勒索〔指以溢价收买吞并者手上自己公司的股票〕; 付给绿票讹诈者的金钱: *He has a history of speculation in stocks and real estate and is known for his attempts at greenmail.* 他曾做过股票和房地产的投机买卖, 以绿票讹诈著名。

green·shoe /ˋgrinˏʃu; ˈgriːnʃuː/ *n* [U]
technical a situation in which all the SHARE*s* in a company that are being offered are sold, and then more stocks are also sold【术语】〔股票的〕增售, 绿鞋〔指发行的股票全部卖出后, 出售额外的股票〕

green shoots /ˌgrin ˋʃuts; ˌgriːn ˈʃuːts/ *n* [plural] *BrE*
NEW MEANING
an expression used to talk about the first signs of economic improvement during a RECESSION, used especially in newspapers【英】经济复苏的迹象〔尤用于报章〕

greige /greʒ; greɪʒ/ *n* [U]
a colour that is a mixture of grey and BEIGE (=a light brown colour) 灰褐色: *The shoes are available in black or greige.* 鞋子备有黑色和灰褐色以供选择。—**greige** *adj*

grey ec·on·o·my also 又作 **gray economy** *AmE*【美】/ˌgre ɪˋkanəmɪ; ˌgreɪ ɪˈkɒnəmi/ *n* [C]
business activity carried out by older people who have a lot of money because their children have left home and because they still work or they have a good PENSION 灰色经济〔指老人的经济活动〕

grey·ing usually 一般作 **graying** *AmE*【美】/ˋgre·ɪŋ; ˈgreɪ-ɪŋ/ *n*
the greying of sth the situation in which the average age of a population increases, so that there are more people who are old than there were in the past 老龄化, 人口老化: *the graying of America* 美国的老龄化

grey mar·ket, gray market *AmE*【美】/ˋgre ˏmarkɪt; ˈgreɪ ˌmɑːkɪ̈t/ *n* [C,U]
a situation in which people are buying and selling SHARE*s* just before they are officially made available to be sold for the first time 灰市〔股票在正式上市前的暗盘交易〕

grey pound /ˌgre ˋpaund; ˌgreɪ ˈpaʊnd/ *n* [singular] *BrE*
the money that older people have available to spend, especially after their children have grown up and left home【英】灰镑〔指老人的闲钱〕: *Although poverty amongst older people is a continuing concern, the power of the grey pound is growing as a proportion of the older community becomes increasingly affluent.* 虽然老年人的贫困现象一直让人关注, 但是随着老人社群日趋富裕, 灰镑的力量也日渐增大。

groov·er /ˋgruvɚ; ˈgruːvə/ *n* [C]
slang a musician, especially one who plays HOUSE music【俚】音乐家〔尤指豪斯音乐演奏者〕

ground·ed /ˋgraundɪd; ˈgraʊndɪ̈d/ *adj*
1 reasonable and in control of your emotions, even when this is difficult 沉得住气的 **2 keep sb grounded** to prevent someone, especially someone you have known for a long time, from thinking they are more important than they really are by treating them in the way you always have. This is used especially about the friends and family of people who have become famous. 防止某人自视过高

group·think /ˋgrupˏθɪŋk; ˈgruːpθɪŋk/ *n* [U]
the process through which bad decisions are made because too many people are involved in trying to reach it〔因人多而作出错误决定的〕集体思考: *What approaches to decision-making were used by the Kennedy administration during the Cuban Missile Crisis to avoid groupthink?* 肯尼迪政府在古巴导弹危机期间要作出决定时, 采取了哪些办法避免人多口杂而作出错误决定?

GTG
a written abbreviation of 缩写= 'got to go', used in E-MAIL or TEXT MESSAGEs on MOBILE PHONEs 该走了〔电子邮件和手机短信用语〕

GUI /ˌdʒi ju ˋaɪ, ˋguɪ; ˌdʒiː juː ˈaɪ, ˈguːi/ *n* [C]
graphical user interface; a way of showing and organizing information on a computer screen that is easy to use and understand 图形用户界面, 视窗系统

guilt /gɪlt; gɪlt/ *v*
guilt sb **into** sth *phr v* [T] *AmE informal* to try to make someone feel guilty, especially so they will do what you want【美, 非正式】设法使〔某人感到〕愧疚〔而做你希望他们做的事〕: **guilt sb into doing sth** *Her parents guilted her into not going to the concert.* 她的父母亲设法让她感到内疚而不去听音乐会。

guilt·ware /ˋgɪltˌwɛr; ˈgɪltweə/ *n* [U]
humorous a type of computer PROGRAM that is free but that contains a message describing how hard someone worked to write it, which is intended to make people feel that they should send some money to the person who wrote it. This word comes from a combination of the words 'GUILT' and 'SOFTWARE'.【幽默】负疚软件〔一种免费软件, 但里面附有描述编写者如何辛苦地编写它, 使用户感到内疚, 认为应该付钱给编写者, 由 guilt 和 software 缩合而成〕

gurn·ing /ˋgɝnɪŋ; ˈgɜːnɪŋ/ *n* [U]
informal the extremely happy expression on someone's face that shows that they have taken the illegal drug ECSTASY【非正式】〔吸食"狂喜"迷幻药者脸部呈现的〕陶醉感 —**gurn** *v* [I]

H,h

hack /hæk; hæk/ *v*
hack sb **off** *phr v* [T] *BrE* to make someone feel annoyed and angry【英】使生气: *He hacks people off sometimes, but he's good at what he does.* 他有时真让人生气, 但他做事情不错。

haemorrhage /ˋhɛmərɪdʒ; ˈhemərɪdʒ/ *BrE*【英】, **hemorrhage** *AmE*【美】*v* [T]
NEW MEANING
to lose a lot of something over a short period of time, such as money or jobs〔短期内〕大量流失: *The once prosperous automobile town has hemorrhaged manufacturing jobs over the last 15 years.* 这个一度繁荣的汽车城镇, 在过去 15 年间流失了大量的生产职位。

Hail Mary /ˌhel ˋmɛrɪ; ˌheɪl ˈmeəri/ *n* [C]
NEW MEANING
in American football, the act of throwing the ball as high and as far as you can, and hoping that a member of your team will catch it and gain some points〔美式橄榄球的〕扔高远球: *Bledsoe said he had thrown a dozen or so Hail Marys over his career.* 布莱索说, 在他的职业生涯中扔出过约十几个高远球。

half pipe /ˋhæf ˌpaɪp; ˈhɑːf ˌpaɪp/ *n* [C]
1 a CONCRETE structure which has a rounded bottom and sides and is used for SKATEBOARDING〔滑板运动的〕半圆形滑槽, U 形场地 **2** a structure which has a rounded bottom and sides, is made from snow, and is used for SNOWBOARDING〔单板滑雪运动中的〕半圆形雪槽

halo ef·fect /ˋhelo əˌfɛkt; ˈheɪləʊ ɪˌfekt/ *n* [C]
technical a situation in which people think a company is good because it is owned by or related to another company that is famous and important【术语】光环效应

handover /ˋhændˌovɚ; ˈhændəʊvə/ *n* [C,U]
the time when a MOBILE PHONE starts receiving signals from a different transmitter because the person using the phone has moved from one area to another〔移动电话〕越区切换

hand·set /ˋhændsɛt; ˈhændset/ *n* [C]
the part of a MOBILE PHONE that you hold in your hand〔移动电话〕手持机: *There's a 20% discount when you buy five handsets or more.* 购买 5 部或以上手机可打八折。

hands·free /ˌhændzˋfri; ˌhændzˈfriː/ *n* [C]
mobile phone equipment that allows you to speak to someone without having to hold the phone, either by having an EARPIECE or by having SPEAKERs in a car 免提移动电话装置〔用耳机或车上的话筒〕: *For just £19.99 this innovative handsfree features a microphone built into the earpiece.* 这种新颖的免提电话装置的特点是耳机上配有麦克风, 售价仅为 19.99 英镑。| *The A100 comes with a personal handsfree kit as well as slim and standard batteries.* A100 型号手机配有个人免提套件和标准电池及超薄电池。

handshake /ˋhændˌʃek; ˈhændˌʃeɪk/ *n* [C]
NEW MEANING
the sending of information from one computer to another computer, telling it that a connection has been made〔计算机之间的〕联络, 信号交换 —**handshaking** *n* [U]

ha·pa /ˋhɑpɑ; ˈhɑːpɑː/ *n* [C] *AmE*
informal an American who has some family members who originally came from Asia, and some family members who originally came from other places【美, 非正式】有亚裔血统的美国人: *Members of our club have had experiences in their lives that only other hapas can relate to.* 本俱乐部成员的经历只有亚裔美国人才能体会到。—**hapa** *adj*: *Kip explores issues related to hapa identity in his writing.* 基普的作品探讨了有关有亚裔血统美国人的身份问题。

happy-clap·py /ˋhæpɪ ˌklæpɪ; ˈhæpi ˌklæpi/ *adj BrE informal* related to a Christian church, where people sing, shout, show their emotions, and encourage other people to join their church. The word comes from a combination of 'happy' and 'CLAP'. It is sometimes used in a humorous way, and sometimes in a disapproving way【英, 非正式】〔与基督教有关的〕热情的〔有时用于幽默, 有时带贬义, 由 happy 和 clap 缩合而成〕: *happy-clappy Christians* 热情的基督徒 —**happy clappy** *n* [C]: *a retreat for travelling happy clappies* 给四处旅行的热情基督徒的静修所

hard-charg·ing /ˌhɑrd ˋtʃɑrdʒɪŋ; ˌhɑːd ˈtʃɑːdʒɪŋ/ *adj*
someone who is hard-charging has a very strong desire to succeed, even if it is difficult 渴望成功的: *Elfman has developed from a cute little girl into a glamorous, hard-charging corporate hotshot.* 埃尔芙曼已从一个可爱的小女孩长大成为公司里一个有魅力而事业心强的要人。

hard house /ˋhɑrd ˌhaʊs; ˈhɑːd ˌhaʊs/ *n* [U]
a type of HOUSE MUSIC that is fast and has a lot of energy〔节奏快, 力量强劲的〕硬豪斯音乐

hard·wire /ˋhɑrdˌwaɪr; ˈhɑːdwaɪə/ *v* [T] *AmE*
to be influenced in a harmful way by looking at or listening to something that becomes fixed in your memory【美】〔指坏影响〕深深植入, 根植: *Kids who listen to this kind of music are hardwiring garbage.* 听这类音乐的孩子脑子里灌满了垃圾。

harsh /hɑrʃ; hɑːʃ/ *v*
harsh on sb *phr v* [T] *AmE slang* to criticize someone or say things to them that are not true【美俚】〔以不正确的事〕批评, 指责: *Just quit harshing on me, will you?* 别老指责我了, 行吗?

harvesting strat·e·gy /ˋhɑrvɪstɪŋ ˌstrætədʒɪ; ˈhɑːvɪstɪŋ ˌstrætɪdʒi/ *n* [C,U]
a method for keeping as much profit as possible from a business or activity and spending as little as possible on it 开源节流策略

hate crime /ˋhet ˌkraɪm; ˈheɪt ˌkraɪm/ *n* [U]
a crime that is COMMIT*ted* against someone only because they belong to a particular race, religion etc〔因种族、宗教等的〕仇视性犯罪

HDL /ˌetʃ di ˋɛl; ˌeɪtʃ diː ˈel/ *n* [U] *technical* high-density lipoprotein; a type of CHOLESTEROL that is good for your health because it helps protect your body against heart disease by helping to get rid of fat in your arteries (=tubes that carry blood in your body)【术语】高密度脂蛋白: *People with high HDL ('good cholesterol') levels are less likely to have heart disease.* 高密度脂蛋白（好胆固醇）水平高的人通常不容易患上心脏病。—compare 比较 LDL

head game /ˋhɛd ˌgem; ˈhed ˌgeɪm/ *n* [C usually plural 一般用复数] *AmE* *informal* if you play head games with someone, you say or do things that you hope will make them show you what they really think or what their character is really like, in a way that confuses or annoys them【美, 非正式】〔使人显示真实性格或思想的〕智力游戏, 心理游戏: *Guys hate it when women play head games with them.* 男人讨厌女人跟他们玩心理游戏。

help screen /ˋhɛlp ˌskrin; ˈhelp ˌskriːn/ *n* [C] a screen that appears when you ask for help in using a computer program, showing extra information or advice〔电脑的〕帮助屏幕

hip /hɪp; hɪp/ *adj*
NEW MEANING
be hip to sth to understand and know about something, and not make mistakes about it 知晓某事; 对某事灵通: *It's a part of the city that is hip to ever-changing retail and entertainment trends.* 对不断变化的零售和娱乐潮流了如指掌是城市生活的一部分。

hip-hop /ˋhɪp ˌhɑp; ˈhɪp ˌhɒp/ *n* [U]
NEW MEANING
a type of popular CULTURE among young people in big cities, especially African Americans, which includes RAP music, dancing, and GRAFFITI art 嬉蹦文化〔美国大城市黑人青年的流行文化, 包括说唱乐、舞蹈、墙上涂鸦等〕

his·sy fit /ˋhɪsɪ ˌfɪt; ˈhɪsi ˌfɪt/ *n* [C] *informal* a sudden moment of unreasonable anger and annoyance; TANTRUM【非正式】无名火: **throw/have a hissy fit** *Williams threw a hissy fit when she decided her hotel room wasn't big enough.* 威廉斯认定自己的旅馆房间不够大时, 突然大发脾气。

hit /hɪt; hɪt/ *n* [C]
NEW MEANING
1 an occasion when someone uses a WEBSITE〔访问网站的〕点击（数）, 浏览次数: *Our site had 2,000 hits in the first month.* 我们的网站在第一个月的浏览次数是2000次。**2** a result of a computer search that you do for something on the Internet, a DATABASE etc〔在互联网、数据库等的〕检索结果, 命中目标: *You may get thousands of hits that are irrelevant to your question.* 你也许会得到数千条与你所提问题都不相干的检索结果。

ho /ho; həʊ/ *n* [C] *AmE* *slang*【美俚】**1** a PROSTITUTE 妓女 **2** an offensive word for a woman or girl who you do not respect because she is too willing to have sex with many different people 荡妇〔冒犯语〕

hold·out /ˋholdaut; ˈhəʊldaʊt/ *n* [C] a person or organization that does not do what many other similar people or organizations are doing 不随波逐流的人[机构]

home·girl /ˋhom ˌgɝl; ˈhəʊmgɜːl/ *n* [C] *AmE* *informal* a female HOMEY【美, 非正式】女老乡

home health aide /ˌhom ˋhɛlθ ˌed; ˌhəʊm ˈhelθ ˌeɪd/ *n* [C] *AmE* someone whose job is to help an old, sick, or DISABLED person in that person's home by cooking, cleaning, washing them, helping them get dressed etc, so that the person can continue to live in their own home rather than going to a hospital or NURSING HOME【美】〔照顾老弱病残的〕家庭护理员

home of·fice /ˌhom ˋɔfɪs; ˌhəʊm ˈɒfɪs/ *n* [C] a room in someone's home where that person works, which usually has equipment such as a computer, FAX MACHINE etc 家庭办公室

home·page also 又作 **home page** /ˋhom ˌpedʒ; ˈhəʊmpeɪdʒ/ *n* [C] the part of an Internet WEBSITE that has all the basic information about a person or organization, which you look at first and from which you can get to other parts of the website〔网站〕主页

home·stead·ing /ˋhom ˌstɛdɪŋ; ˈhəʊm ˌstedɪŋ/ *n* [U] *AmE* a situation in which people are given money so that they can improve the condition of their homes, especially in poor areas【美】〔尤指贫困地区的〕房屋津贴

hon·o·ree /ˌɑnəˋri; ˌɒnəˈriː/ *n* [C] someone who receives an honour or AWARD 获奖者: *Guests clapped and cheered for the honorees.* 来宾为获奖者鼓掌欢呼。

hood /hud; hʊd/ *n AmE*
NEW MEANING
slang a NEIGHBOURHOOD (=a small area of a town)【美俚】街坊, 邻近地区

hook /huk; hʊk/ *v*
NEW MEANING
hook sb **up with** sth *phr v* [T] to help someone get something that they need or want 帮助〔某人〕获得…: *Do you think you can hook me up with some tickets for the hockey game tonight?* 你看你能帮我拿到几张今晚曲棍球赛的入场券吗?

host² /host; həʊst/ *v* [T]
NEW MEANING
if an Internet company hosts a WEBSITE, it provides the computer equipment and technical knowledge needed to make the website work, but is not responsible for the information or ideas contained in it 主持, 托管〔网站〕: *The site is hosted by a small European access provider.* 网站是由欧洲一家小型网络服务商托管的。—**hosting** *n* [U]

hot desk /ˋhɑt ˌdɛsk; ˈhɒt ˌdesk/ *n* [C] *BrE* a desk which is used by different workers on different days, instead of by the same worker every day【英】共用办公桌

hot-desk·ing /ˌhɑt ˋdɛskɪŋ; ˌhɒt ˈdeskɪŋ/ *n* [U] *BrE* a situation in which people who work in an office do not have their own desks, but sit wherever a desk is not being used【英】办公桌共用（制）: *Hot-desking means that desks are never left unused when people are away from the office.* 办公桌共用制意味着在有人离开办公室时, 办公桌从来不会空着没人用。—**hot desk** *v* [I]: *The part-timers here have to hot desk.* 这里的兼职人员要共用办公桌。

hot link /ˋhɑt ˌlɪŋk; ˈhɒt ˌlɪŋk/ *n* [C] *informal* a HYPERTEXT LINK which allows you to move from one place in a computer document to another, or to a particular place in a different document, especially on the Internet【非正式】热[超文本]链接

hot spot /ˋhɑt ˌspɑt; ˈhɒt ˌspɒt/ *n* [C] a part of a computer screen that you can CLICK on to make other pictures, words etc appear 热点〔用鼠标点击可打开图像、文字等〕

hotty, hottie /ˋhɑtɪ; ˈhɒti/ *n* [C] *slang* someone who is sexually attractive【俚】性感者: *Jennifer's such a hotty.* 珍妮弗真是个性感女神。

house /haus; haʊs/ *n* [U]
NEW MEANING
house music, a type of dance music, usually with a fast beat, that is repeated in a very regular pattern. It is made using special electronic instruments, such as a SYNTHESIZER or by using a special computer PROGRAM. 豪斯音乐〔用电子合成器或电脑制成的快节拍舞曲〕

housing starts /ˋhauzɪŋ ˌstɑrts; ˈhaʊzɪŋ ˌstɑːts/ *n* [plural] *technical* the number of new houses, apartments etc on

which building work has started in a particular period of time【术语】〔某一时期的〕新屋动工数目

HOV lane /ˌetʃ o ˋvi len; ˌeɪtʃ əʊ ˈviː leɪn/ *n* [C] high-occupancy vehicle lane; a LANE on main roads that can only be used by vehicles carrying three or more passengers during the time of day when there is a lot of traffic 高容量车道〔交通繁忙时，只准载三人或以上的汽车使用的车道〕

HTH, hth a written abbreviation of 缩写= 'hope this helps', used in E-MAIL OR TEXT MESSAGES ON MOBILE PHONES when they have answered someone's question 希望能管用〔电子邮件或手机短信用语〕

HTML /ˌetʃ ti ɛm ˋɛl; ˌeɪtʃ tiː em ˈel/ *n* [U] hypertext markup language; a computer language used for producing pages of writing and pictures that can be put on the Internet 超文本标记语言: *There are three ways to produce HTML documents: write them yourself; use an HTML editor; or convert documents from other formats to HTML.* 有三种方式可制作超文本标记语言文件，一是自己编写，二是使用超文本标记语言编辑软件，三是将文件从其他格式转变成超文本标记语言格式。

http /ˌetʃ ti ti ˋpi; ˌeɪtʃ tiː tiː ˈpiː/ *n* [U] hypertext transfer protocol; a set of standards that controls how computer documents that are written in HTML connect to each other 超文本传输[传送]协议

huge /hjudʒ; hjuːdʒ/ *adj* *informal* very famous or successful【非正式】走红（的），成功的: *Trust me – this band is going to be huge next year.* 相信我好了，这乐队明年准会走红。

hype /haɪp; haɪp/ *v*
NEW MEANING
hype sb **up** *phr v* [T] to make someone feel excited 使〔某人〕兴奋

hy·per·ki·ne·tic /ˌhaɪpɚkɪˋnɛtɪk; ˌhaɪpəkɪˈnetɪk/ *adj* fast, exciting, and appearing to be uncontrolled 多动的，令人亢奋的: *the director's hyperkinetic new film about American football* 该导演一部反映美式橄榄球的令人亢奋的新片

hy·per·link /ˋhaɪpɚˌlɪŋk; ˈhaɪpəˌlɪŋk/ *n* [C] a word or picture in a WEBSITE or computer document that will take you to another page or document if you CLICK on it 超（文本）链接: *We should encourage hyperlinks to each others' webpages.* 我们应当鼓励彼此网页之间的超链接。

hy·per·text /ˋhaɪpɚˌtɛkst; ˈhaɪpəˌtekst/ *n* [U] written information on a computer screen that has words marked in colour or with a line underneath them, in order to allow you to move from one document to another very quickly. You use the computer's MOUSE TO CLICK on one of these words, and the information on the screen changes so that you see the new information〔计算机〕超（级）文本〔可以互访的文本网络〕: *Hypertext links take you directly from a listing of bestsellers on the home page to a particular book.* 超文本链接可以让你直接从主页的畅销书目录进入一本特定的书。

I, i

ice queen /ˋaɪs ˌkwin; ˈaɪs ˌkwiːn/ *n* [C] a word used to talk about an attractive woman who you think is unfriendly and behaves as though she does not care about other people 冷美人

IIRC, iirc a written abbreviation of 缩写= 'if I remember correctly', used in E-MAIL OR TEXT MESSAGES ON MOBILE PHONES 如果我没有记错的话〔电子邮件或手机短信用语〕

ill /ɪl; ɪl/ *adj*
NEW MEANING
slang very good【俚】很棒的，顶刮刮的: *Isn't Lucia Rijker the world's illest female boxer?* 露西娅·赖克不是世界上最棒的女拳击手吗？

IM /ˌaɪ ˋɛm; ˌaɪ ˈem/ *n* [U] instant messaging; a type of service available on the Internet that allows you to quickly exchange written messages with people that you know 即时信息

image ad·ver·tis·ing /ˋɪmɪdʒ ˌædvɚtaɪzɪŋ; ˈɪmɪdʒ ˌædvətaɪzɪŋ/ *n* [U] *technical* advertising that tries to make a connection between a particular product and a particular way of life, rather than telling you that the product is very good【术语】形象广告

image host·ing /ˋɪmɪdʒ ˌhostɪŋ; ˈɪmɪdʒ ˌhəʊstɪŋ/ *n* [U] the business of providing people with space on an Internet WEBPAGE, so that they can put pictures on this webpage to advertise products that they want to sell or exchange 图像托管: *image hosting for online auctions* 用作网上拍卖的图像托管 | *This image hosting service can be used to simply show off your collection.* 这个图像托管服务可以让你炫耀一下你的收藏品。

i·ma·gi·neer /ɪˌmædʒəˋnɪr; ɪˌmædʒ½ˈnɪə/ *n* [C] someone who has a lot of new ideas and who is able to use these ideas to do practical things. This word comes from a combination of the words 'imagination' and 'ENGINEER'. 点子大王，创意工程师〔由 imagination 和 engineer 缩合而成〕: *We're lucky to have great imagineers like Mr. Rose who are willing to apply their minds to the problem.* 我们幸好有罗斯先生那样的点子大王，他们乐意动脑子解决问题。—**imagineering** *n* [U]

im·a·ging /ˋɪmɪdʒɪŋ; ˈɪmɪdʒɪŋ/ *n* [U] a technical process in which pictures of the inside of someone's body are produced, especially for medical reasons〔尤用于医学目的的〕（体内器官）成像: *New imaging technologies mean that doctors are better able to screen for breast cancer.* 新的成像技术意味着医生能更容易检查出乳腺癌。

IMHO, imho a written abbreviation of 缩写= 'in my humble opinion', used in E-MAIL OR TEXT MESSAGES ON MOBILE PHONES 依鄙人之见〔电子邮件或手机短信用语〕

im·mu·no·ther·a·py /ˌɪmjunoˋθɛrəpɪ; ˌɪmjʊnəʊˈθerəpi/ *n* [U] a way of curing a disease by helping the body to produce the natural substances that protect it from the disease 免疫疗法

IMO, imo a written abbreviation of 缩写= 'in my opinion', used in E-MAIL OR TEXT MESSAGES ON MOBILE PHONES 依本人之见〔电子邮件或手机短信用语〕

I-mode phone /ˋaɪ mod ˌfon; ˈaɪ məʊd ˌfəʊn/ *n* [C] *trademark* a MOBILE PHONE (=a telephone that you can carry with you and use in any place) that has a small SCREEN which you can use for Internet and E-MAIL services【商标】移动互联网制式电话〔可上网和发送电子邮件的一种移动电话〕

in·box /ˋɪnbɑks; ˈɪnbɒks/ *n* [C] a place on a computer which stores the E-MAIL messages that you have received〔电子邮件的〕收件箱

in·cu·ba·tor /ˋɪnkjəˌbetɚ; ˈɪŋkjʊbeɪtə/ *n* [C]
NEW MEANING
an organization which helps new businesses develop by giving them office space, services, and equipment, and providing them with business and technical advice〔企业〕培育基地，孵化器: *a high-tech incubator on the East coast* 东海岸的高科技培育基地

index fund /ˋɪndɛks ˌfʌnd; ˈɪndeks ˌfʌnd/ also 又作 **tracker fund** *BrE*【英】*n* [C] *technical* an INVESTMENT that includes a combination of SHARES that are in a particular SHARE INDEX, and that earns money depending on the value of the shares in that index【术语】指数基金

industrial-strength /ɪnˌdʌstrɪəl ˋstrɛŋθ; ɪnˌdʌstriəl ˈstreŋθ/ *adj*
humorous an industrial-strength liquid is very strong【幽默】〔液体〕浓度高的, 有效的: *They served us industrial-strength coffee.* 他们给我们端出了浓咖啡。

infected /ɪnˋfɛktɪd; ɪnˈfektɪ̈d/ *adj*
NEW MEANING
if a computer or DISK is infected, the information in or on it has been changed or destroyed by a computer VIRUS〔受计算机病毒〕感染的

inflation-in·de·xed bond /ɪnˌfleʃən ɪndɛkst ˋbɑnd; ɪnˌfleʃən ɪndekst ˈbɒnd/ *n* [C]
technical a BOND sold by the government in which the amount paid in INTEREST goes up when the rate of INFLATION goes up【术语】通胀指数债券〔一种利率随通胀率调节的债券〕

information o·ver·load /ˌɪnfɚmeʃən ˋovɚlod; ˌɪnfəmeɪʃən ˈəʊvələʊd/ *n* [U]
a situation in which someone gets too much information at one time, for example on the Internet, and becomes tired and unable to think very carefully about any of it 信息超载: *The greater the amount of data we have access to, the greater the risk of information overload.* 我们可以获取的信息量越大, 信息超载的风险也越大。| *a workshop to help you cope with information overload* 帮助处理信息超载的工作室

ink /ɪŋk; ɪŋk/ *v* [T]
NEW MEANING
to make a document, agreement etc official and legal by writing your signature on it 签署〔文件、合约等〕: *Motorola and IBM have inked a deal.* 摩托罗拉和国际商业机器公司已签了合约。

in-line skate /ˌɪn laɪn ˋsket; ˌɪn laɪn ˈskeɪt/ *n* [C]
a special boot for ROLLER SKATING with a single row of wheels attached under it 滚轴轮滑鞋, 单排轮滑鞋

inner /ˋɪnɚ; ˈɪnə/ *adj*
NEW MEANING
sb's inner child the part of someone's character that still feels like a child even though they are an adult 某人内心的孩童性格: *Through therapy she has got in touch with her inner child.* 通过理疗, 她得以认识自我内心的孩童性格。

in·nit /ˋɪnɪt; ˈɪnɪt/ *interjection BrE*
slang said at the end of a statement or in reply to a statement to mean 'isn't it?'. This word is often used by someone to emphasize what they have just said rather than to ask for someone else's opinion.【英俚】可不是嘛!〔用于强调〕: *"Did you see the way Schumacher went past him?" "Innit."* "你看见舒马赫超过他时的那个帅劲吗?" "可不是嘛!"

instant mes·sag·ing /ˌɪnstənt ˋmɛsɪdʒɪŋ; ˌɪnstənt ˈmesɪdʒɪŋ/ *abbreviation* 缩写为 **IM** *n* [U]
a type of service available on the Internet that allows you to quickly exchange written messages with people that you know 即时信息: *The Internet's two main instant messaging services are both owned and run by AOL.* 互联网两大即时信息服务是由美国在线公司拥有和经营的。

in·sti·net /ˋɪnstɪnɛt; ˈɪnstɪnet/ *n* [U]
trademark an electronic network that allows people to buy and sell SHARES using a computer when a STOCK EXCHANGE is closed. Instinet is owned by Reuters.【商标】〔随时可进行股票买卖的〕瞬时网, 即时电子交易网

institutionalized ra·cis·m /ˌɪnstətjuʃənl̩aɪzd ˋresɪzəm; ˌɪnstɪ̈tjuːʃənəlaɪzd ˈreɪsɪzəm/ also 又作 **-ised** *BrE*【英】*n* [U]
racism that has become an established part of the normal behaviour and ideas of people in an organization 制度化的种族主义

interface /ˋɪntɚfes; ˈɪntəfeɪs/ *v* [I]
NEW MEANING
to have a conversation with someone, especially in a work-related situation or for example in a situation between a doctor and a PATIENT〔尤指工作场景下〕交谈: [+**with**] *How often does your job require you to interface with people from other departments?* 你的工作需要你和其他部门互通情况有多频繁?

in·ter·faith /ˌɪntɚˋfeθ; ˌɪntəˈfeɪθ◂/ *adj* [only before noun 仅用于名词前]
between or involving people of different religions 不同宗教信仰者(间)的: *an interfaith Thanksgiving service* 跨宗教信仰的感恩(祈祷)仪式

in·ter·gen·e·ra·tion·al /ˌɪntɚdʒɛnəˋreʃənl̩; ˌɪntədʒenəˈreɪʃənəl/ *adj*
between or involving people from different age groups 两代[多代]人之间的: *School officials say the intergenerational programs help both the children and the retired people.* 学校管理人员说, 跨世代计划对儿童和退休人员都有帮助。

in·ter·leu·kin /ˌɪntɚˋlukɪn; ˌɪntəˈluːkɪn/ *n* [C]
a type of PROTEIN (=a substance the body produces) that helps the body fight disease 白细胞介素

in·ter·mer·cial /ˌɪntɚˋmɝʃəl; ˌɪntəˈmɜːʃəl/ *n* [C]
advertisements that appear on the Internet. This word comes from a combination of the words 'Internet' and 'COMMERCIAL' (=a television advertisement). 网上(商业)广告〔由 Internet 和 commercial 缩合而成〕

Internet ac·cess com·pa·ny /ˌɪntɚnɛt ˋæksɛs ˌkʌmpənɪ; ˌɪntənet ˈækses ˌkʌmpəni/ *n* [C]
a company whose business is providing a service that allows computer users to find information on the Internet 互联网服务公司

Internet ac·count /ˋɪntɚnɛt əˌkaunt; ˈɪntənet əˌkaʊnt/ *n* [C]
an arrangement that you make with an ACCESS PROVIDER (=company that provides Internet services) that allows you to use the Internet from your computer, usually in exchange for a monthly payment 互联网账户: *How do I set up an Internet account?* 我怎样开一个互联网账户呢?

Internet bank·ing /ˋɪntɚnɛt ˌbæŋkɪŋ; ˈɪntənet ˌbæŋkɪŋ/ also 又作 **online banking** *n* [U]
a service provided by banks so that people can find out information about their bank account, pay bills etc using the Internet 网上银行(业务)

Internet pro·to·col /ˋɪntɚnɛt ˌprotəkɑl; ˈɪntənet ˌprəʊtəkɒl/ *abbreviation* 缩写为 **IP** *n* [C]
technical a set of rules that describe how and in what form electronic information should be sent on the Internet【术语】网际协议, 网络协议

Internet store·front /ˌɪntɚnɛt ˋstorfrʌnt; ˌɪntənet ˈstɔːfrʌnt/ also 又作 **storefront** *n* [C]
a WEBSITE that is used to sell products or services to the public 销售网站: *Now you can reach millions of potential customers with your own Internet storefront.* 你现在可通过自己的销售网站接触数以百万计的潜在客户。

in·ter·op·e·ra·bil·i·ty /ˌɪntɚˌɑpərəˋbɪlətɪ; ˌɪntərˌɒpərəˈbɪlɪ̈ti/ *n* [U]
technical the ability of different kinds of computer SOFTWARE or HARDWARE to work together or exchange information【术语】互操作性, 协同性, 通容性 —**interoperable** *adj* —**interoperate** *v* [I]

intolerance /ɪnˋtɑlərəns; ɪnˈtɒlərəns/ *n*
NEW MEANING
food/wheat/lactose etc intolerance if you have a food intolerance, you cannot DIGEST a type of food, or it makes you ill 食物/小麦/乳糖等的不耐受: *People with a lactose* (=a substance in milk) *intolerance often find yogurt easier to digest.* 乳糖耐受不良者常发现酸奶较易消化。

in·tra·net /ˋɪntrənɛt; ˈɪntrənet/ *n* [C]
a computer network used for exchanging or seeing information within a company, which works in the same way as the Internet〔企业内部的〕内联网: *Photographs of new employees appear on the company's intranet.* 新员工的相片出现在公司的内联网上。

in·tra·pre·neur /ˌɪntrəprəˋnɝ; ˌɪntrəprəˈnɜː/ *n* [C] someone who works for a large company and whose job is to develop new ideas or ways of doing business for that company. This word comes from a combination of 'INTRA-', which means 'within', and 'ENTREPRENEUR', which means 'a person who starts new businesses and takes risks in order to make money'. 内部企业家〔企业内进行创新性开发和营销的部门经理，由 intra- 和 entrepreneur 缩合而成〕—**intrapreneuring** *n* [U]

investment club /ɪnˋvɛstmənt ˌklʌb; ɪnˈvestmənt ˌklʌb/ *n* [C] a group of people who meet regularly to decide which INVESTMENTS to buy and sell together, with money that they all put into the group 投资俱乐部: *O'Hara belongs to an investment club in Detroit.* 奥哈拉是底特律一家投资俱乐部的会员。

IPO /ˌaɪ pi ˋo; ˌaɪ piː ˈəʊ/ *n* [C usually singular 一般用单数] *technical* initial public offering; an occasion when a company makes SHARES available for sale on the STOCK MARKET for the first time【术语】〔股票的〕首次公开发行，新股发行

ISA /ˋaɪsə; ˈaɪsə/ *n* [C] *BrE* individual savings account; an arrangement in Britain by which you can save money in a bank without paying tax on it【英】个人储蓄账户

ISDN /ˌaɪ ɛs di ˋɛn; ˌaɪ es diː ˈen/ *n* [U] *technical* Integrated Services Digital Network; a special telephone network through which computers can send information much faster than usual【术语】综合业务数字网: *an ISDN line* 综合业务数字网线路

ISP /ˌaɪ ɛs ˋpi; ˌaɪ es ˈpiː/ *n* [C] *technical* Internet service provider; a business that connects people's computers to the Internet【术语】互联网服务提供者[商]

issue[1] /ˋɪʃu; ˈɪʃuː/ *n*
NEW MEANING
have issues (with sb/sth) *informal* if you have issues with someone or something, you do not agree with or approve of them【非正式】(与某人/对某事)持不同看法: *I have a few issues with Marc.* 我与马克在一些问题上有不同看法。

It girl /ˋɪt ˌgɝl; ˈɪt ˌgɜːl/ *n* [C] *informal especially BrE* a young woman who is famous mainly because she is rich and beautiful, and whose photograph appears in a lot of magazines and newspapers【非正式，尤英】〔照片经常见诸报刊的〕款姐，名媛

iTV /ˌaɪ ti ˋvi; ˌaɪ tiː ˈviː/ *n* [U] interactive television; a type of television programme that allows people who are watching at home to answer questions or find out more information by using a computer or special electronic equipment 交互式电视，互动电视

J,j

jack /dʒæk; dʒæk/ *v* [T] *slang*【俚】a short form of 缩略式= CARJACK

jam /dʒæm; dʒæm/ *n* [C]
NEW MEANING
informal【非正式】**1** a song or piece of music, especially one by a RAP or ROCK group 即兴音乐〔一种摇滚或说唱乐〕: *a totally dope jam from Puff Daddy* 吹牛老爹一支劲道十足的即兴乐曲 **2 kick out the jams** to play ROCK MUSIC loudly and with a lot of energy or emotion 卖劲地演奏即兴音乐: *Make no mistake – these guys know how to kick out the jams.* 毫无疑问 —— 这几个家伙知道如何演奏即兴音乐。

jam·cam /ˋdʒæmkæm; ˈdʒæmkæm/ *n* [C] a camera that is connected to a WEBSITE that shows where the traffic is very bad〔与网站相连的〕交通堵塞情况摄录装置: *Remember you can always check out the jamcams on our website to avoid the worst of the traffic in the rush hour.* 记住，你可随时查看我们网站上的交通堵塞情况，以避开繁忙时间最糟的交通拥堵。

Jaws of Life, the /ˌdʒɔz əv ˋlaɪf; ˌdʒɔːz əv ˈlaɪf/ *n* [plural] *trademark* a tool used to make a hole in a car, TRUCK etc after an accident, so that the people inside can be taken out【商标】救生颚〔交通事故中在汽车上开洞救人用的装置〕

jelly /ˋdʒɛlɪ; ˈdʒeli/ *n*
NEW MEANING
1 jellies [plural] *BrE informal* amounts of a drug that makes you feel relaxed and sleepy, which some people use illegally【英，非正式】"果冻"〔一种镇静剂〕**2 jellies** [plural] shoes made of clear coloured plastic 透明彩色塑料鞋

jig·gy /ˋdʒɪgɪ; ˈdʒɪgi/ *adj* **get jiggy** *AmE slang* to dance with a lot of energy to popular music【美俚】〔随着流行音乐〕跳劲舞

JIT *adj* the written abbreviation for 缩写= JUST-IN-TIME

job lock /ˋdʒɑb ˌlɑk; ˈdʒɒb ˌlɒk/ *n* [C] *AmE informal* a situation in which you are afraid to leave your job because you will lose your medical insurance【美，非正式】〔因担心失去医疗保险而〕不愿离开工作岗位

job·seek·er /ˋdʒɑbˌsikɚ; ˈdʒɒbˌsiːkə/ *n* [C] *BrE* someone who is trying to find a job【英】求职者

job-seeker's al·low·ance /ˌdʒɑbsikɚz əˋlauəns; ˌdʒɒbsiːkəz əˈlaʊəns/ *n* [U] in Britain, money that the government pays to people who do not have a job but who are trying to get one〔在英国给失业者的〕求职者津贴

jock /dʒɑk; dʒɒk/ *n* [C]
NEW MEANING
informal a DISC JOCKEY【非正式】唱片节目主持人

joined-up /ˌdʒɔɪnd ˋʌp; ˌdʒɔɪnd ˈʌp◂/ *adj BrE* joined-up systems, institutions etc combine many different groups, ideas, or parts in a way that works well【英】联组的，联合的: **joined-up thinking/government** *the need for joined-up thinking between departments* 需要各部门集思广益 | *Partnerships are still not joined-up enough.* 合伙人之间还不够群策群力。| *Joined-up government offers great opportunities to deliver better services.* 联合政府缔造很多机会以提供更好的服务。

joint /dʒɔɪnt; dʒɔɪnt/ *n* [C]
NEW MEANING
slang a record or film that someone has made【俚】唱片；影片: *Cypress Hill released their latest studio joint earlier this year.* "墓园三人组"今年早些时候发行了他们最新录制的唱片。

jones /dʒonz; dʒəʊnz/ *n* **get your jones** *slang* to get or do something that you want or need very much【俚】如愿以偿: *I'm a total sushi addict – I have to get my jones at least once a week.* 我对寿司特别上瘾 —— 我每周至少要饱餐它一顿。

JPEG /ˋdʒe ˌpɛg; ˈdʒeɪ ˌpeg/ also 又作 **JPG** /ˌdʒe pi ˋdʒi; ˌdʒeɪ piː ˈdʒiː/ *n* [C] *technical* Joint Photographic Experts Group; a type of computer FILE used on the Internet that contains pictures, photographs, or other images【术语】联合图像专家组，静止图像压缩标准〔Joint Photographic Experts Group 的缩写〕

juice /dʒus; dʒuːs/ *n*
NEW MEANING
the juice information about people's private lives; GOSSIP 艳闻，逸闻: **[+about/on]** *Have you heard the juice about Maria and Tim?* 你听到关于玛丽亚和蒂姆的艳闻吗？

juiced /dʒust; dʒuːst/ also 又作 **juiced up** *adj* [not before noun 不用于名词前] *AmE*

NEW MEANING
informal excited【美, 非正式】兴奋的: *If I'm nervous and juiced up, I pitch better.* 我要是紧张兴奋的话, 我会把球投得更好。

jungle /ˋdʒʌŋgl; ˈdʒʌŋgəl/ *n* [U]
NEW MEANING
a type of popular British dance mucic that has a fast beat and useq SAMPLEs (=small parts of a song from a CD or record that are copied and used in a new song) 丛林音乐〔英国的一继流行舞乐, 节奏明快, 往往借用别的歌曲的节录〕: *Click here to download free jungle, drum and bass, and garage tracks.* 点击这里免费下载丛林音乐、鼓打贝斯和车库乐。—**junglist** *n* [C]

just-in-time /ˌdʒʌst ɪn ˋtaɪm; ˌdʒʌst ɪn ˈtaɪm/ *abbreviation* 缩写为 **BIT** *adj* [only before noun 仅用于名词前] *technical* if goods are produced or bought using a just-in-time system, they are produced or bought just before they are needed so that the company does not have to store things for a long time.【术语】〔货物〕适时按需制造的, 零库存的: *The firm is worried that delays could cause problems with their just-in-time manufacturing methods.* 这家公司担心那些延误会影响他们的适时生产安排。

K,k

key·pal /ˋkipæl; ˈkiːpæl/ *n* [C]
someone with whom you regularly exchange E-MAIL 键盘友, 网友: *If your daughter is interested in having a keypal next year, please have her get in touch.* 你的女儿如果来年有意结交网友的话, 请让她同我联系。

kick /kɪk; kɪk/ *v*
NEW MEANING
1 be kicking (it) *spoken* to be relaxing and having a good time【口】悠闲自得: *I was just kicking with my buddies.* 我正和朋友优哉游哉, 自得其乐。**2 be kicking it** *slang spoken* to be having a romantic relationship with someone【俚, 口】和…有一腿〔有男女关系〕: *My sources say that Blige was kicking it with Thomas while she was on tour.* 我得到的消息说布莱奇在旅游中和托马斯有一腿来着。

kiddie-cam /ˋkɪdɪ ˌkæm; ˈkɪdi ˌkæm/ *n* [C]
a camera that allows parents to see their child or children when the parents are somewhere else 观察儿童摄像机: *She stays connected to her kids through e-mail and watching them on day-care kiddie-cam over the Internet.* 她通过电子邮件和自己的孩子保持联系, 并通过日间托儿所的互联网摄像机观察他们的情况。

kid·ult /ˋkɪdʌlt; ˈkɪdʌlt/ *n* [C]
an adult who likes to play games or buy things that most people consider more suitable for children. This word comes from a combination of the words 'KID' and 'adult'. 喜欢儿童游戏[玩意儿]的成人〔由kid和adult缩合而成〕: *What is amazing is the size of the kidult population and the money they are willing to spend on products.* 让人感到惊讶的是竟有那么多的"大孩子"愿意花那么多钱在一些儿童玩意儿上面。

killer app /ˋkɪlɚ ˌæp; ˈkɪlər ˌæp/ also 又作 **killer ap·pli·ca·tion** /ˋkɪlɚ æpləˌkeʃən; ˈkɪlər æplɪˌkeʃən/ *n* [C]
a piece of computer SOFTWARE that many people want to buy, especially one that works so well on a particular type of machine that people also want to buy the machine "杀手"软件〔许多人想买的软件, 尤指在某类机器中运行良好, 使许多人想连带买下机器的软件〕

kite surf·ing /ˋkaɪt ˌsɝfɪŋ; ˈkaɪt ˌsɜːfɪŋ/ *n* [U]
the activity of moving across water on a SURFBOARD while holding a large KITE which is attached to strong strings 风筝冲浪

kluge /kludʒ; kluːdʒ/ *adj* [only before noun 仅用于名词前] *AmE*
slang a kluge solution to a computer problem is not a good or intelligent solution【美俚】〔解决电脑问题的办法〕不好使的, 不灵的

knowledge-based soft·ware /ˌnɑlɪdʒ best ˋsɔftwɛr; ˌnɒlɪdʒ beɪst ˈsɒftweə/ *n* [U]
technical SOFTWARE that learns while it works and is able to use this knowledge to find more effective ways of doing a particular job【术语】知识软件, 智能型软件

L,l

lad mag /ˋlæd ˌmæg; ˈlæd ˌmæg/ *n* [C] *BrE*
a magazine for young men that includes articles about sports and fashion, pictures of women without many clothes on, and some writing about problems and experiences of young men【英】少男杂志: *Sheena has been on the cover of almost all of the lad mags.* 希娜几乎当过所有少男杂志的封面女郎。

lad·dish /ˋlædɪʃ; ˈlædɪʃ/ *adj BrE*
a young man who is laddish likes spending time with other men, drinking alcohol and enjoying things like popular music and sport rather than being interested in CULTURE or intellectual things【英】有男子汉气概的; 粗放的: *People expect us to be a bit laddish, like the characters we play in the series.* 人们以为我们比较粗放, 像我们在系列片中扮演的角色那样。

lad·dis·m /ˋlædɪzəm; ˈlædɪzəm/ *n* [C] *BrE*
the attitudes and behaviour of some young men in Britain, who drink a lot of alcohol, are interested in sports, and think that women are less important than men【英】大男子作风, 大男子主义: *Experts in the U.K. blame the culture of laddism for boys' low test scores.* 英国的一些专家把男孩子测验成绩差归咎于大男子主义的文化。

la·dette /læˋdɛt; læˈdet/ *n* [C] *BrE*
humorous a young woman who likes to do some things that young men typically do, such as drinking alcohol in pubs and talking about sex and sports【英, 幽默】野丫头, 具男孩作风的女孩子

lai·ry /ˋlɛrɪ; ˈleəri/ *adj BrE*
slang behaving in a way that is very loud, or with too much confidence【英俚】嗓门大的, 大大咧咧的: *He's a bit lairy, your friend Mick.* 你的朋友米克多少有点大大咧咧的。

lap danc·ing /ˋlæp ˌdænsɪŋ; ˈlæp ˌdɑːnsɪŋ/ *n* [U]
dancing with sexy movements performed by a young woman who removes her clothes while sitting on a customer's LAP in a NIGHTCLUB 大腿艳舞 —**lap dancer** *n* [C]: *Carla, a single mother of two, says she can make more than three hundred dollars a night as a lap dancer.* 有两个孩子的单身母亲卡拉说, 她跳大腿舞, 一晚能挣三百多美元。—compare 比较 TABLE DANCING

large /lɑrdʒ; lɑːdʒ/ *v*
large it (up) *BrE slang* to enjoy yourself, especially in a way that involves drinking alcohol, dancing etc【英俚】自娱, 饮酒作乐: *Here's a picture of us larging it up in Brighton last summer.* 这是去年夏天我们在布赖顿欢宴的照片。

large-cap /ˋlɑrdʒ ˌkæp; ˈlɑːdʒ ˌkæp/ *n* [C]
a SHARE in a large company 大盘股, 大市值股票 —**large-cap** *adj*: *They put their money into some large-cap mutual funds.* 他们把钱投放在一些投资大市值股票的共同基金上。—opposite 反义词 SMALL-CAP

laser point·er /ˋlezɚ ˌpɔɪntɚ; ˈleɪzə ˌpɔɪntə/ *n* [C]
a small piece of equipment that produces a LASER BEAM (=powerful narrow beam of light) that you hold in your hand and use to point at things on a map, board etc so that other people will pay attention to them. Laser pointers are often used by teachers and people who are giving talks. 激光笔

lashed /læʃt; læʃt/ *adj* [not before noun 不用于名词前] *BrE slang* very drunk【英俚】醉醺醺的, 酩酊大醉的: **get lashed** *This might be my last chance to go out and get lashed with my mates.* 这可能是我和朋友们出去喝得酩酊大醉的最后一次机会。

lat·te /ˈlɑte; ˈlæteɪ/ *n* [C,U] coffee with hot milk in it, or a cup of this type of coffee 牛奶咖啡, 拿铁咖啡: *Jody was sipping a decaf latte.* 乔迪呷着脱咖啡因的牛奶咖啡。

launch /lɔntʃ; lɔːntʃ/ *v* [T]
NEW MEANING
to make a computer PROGRAM start 启动〔电脑程序〕: *Double-click on an icon to launch an application.* 双击图标启动应用程序。

LDL /ˌɛl di ˋɛl; ˌel diː ˈel/ *n* [C] *technical* low-density lipoprotein; a type of CHOLESTEROL that is bad for your health because it helps fat stay on the inside of your heart and blood VESSELS【术语】低密度脂蛋白: *Studies show that keeping your LDL ('bad cholesterol') levels below 160 can add years to your life.* 研究表明, 使低密度脂蛋白 (坏胆固醇) 水平保持在160以下可以延长寿命。—compare 比较 HDL

leap sec·ond /ˈlip ˌsɛkənd; ˈliːp ˌsekənd/ *n* [C] a second that is sometimes officially added to the last minute of a day, occurring at the end of June or at the end of December, to make the very accurate clocks that scientists use more exact 闰秒

LEP /lɛp; lep/ *adj* [only before noun 仅用于名词前] *AmE technical* limited English proficient; concerning someone whose first language is not English and who cannot communicate very well in English【美, 术语】英语不够熟练的: **LEP students** *The number of LEP students in the district has risen since 1993.* 1993年以来, 该区英语不够熟练的学生人数有所增加。

lep·tin /ˈlɛptɪn; ˈleptɪn/ *n* [U] a HORMONE that controls how much you weigh, how hungry you are, and how much energy you have. Scientists think that taking leptin might help fat people lose weight. 瘦蛋白, 瘦身素

LETS /lɛts; lets/ *n* [C] local exchange trading system; an arrangement among a group of people to exchange goods and services with each other instead of buying these things from a store 地区性交换式贸易系统: *the benefits of belonging to a LETS* 属于地区性交换式贸易系统的好处

let·ter·box·ing /ˈlɛtɚˌbɑksɪŋ; ˈletəˌbɒksɪŋ/ *n* [U] the practice of broadcasting a cinema film on television with black bands at the top and bottom of the television SCREEN so that the film will have the same DIMENSIONs as it did on a cinema screen〔电视上播电影时屏幕上下留下两条黑边的〕宽银幕式

leverage /ˈlɛvərɪdʒ; ˈliːvərɪdʒ/ *v* [T]
NEW MEANING
to use borrowed money to buy a particular company or INVESTMENT 举债投资, 贷杠: *They were extremely effective at capturing federal resources to leverage local development.* 他们极为懂得如何争取联邦贷款以投资当地经济。

lifetime /ˈlaɪfˌtaɪm; ˈlaɪftaɪm/ *n*
NEW MEANING
not in this lifetime *spoken* not at all; never【口】这辈子不行: *"Would you go out with him after he dropped you?" "Not in this lifetime."* "他甩了你之后你还会跟他交往吗?" "这辈子都不会。"

link /lɪŋk; lɪŋk/ *n* [C]
NEW MEANING
a special word or picture in an Internet document that you CLICK on to move quickly to another part of the same document or to another document 链接 (点): *Click on the link below to return to the home page.* 点击下面的链接返回主页。

lippy /ˈlɪpɪ; ˈlɪpi/ *n* [U] *BrE informal* LIPSTICK【英, 非正式】口红, 唇膏: *Wait a minute, I'll just put a bit of lippy on.* 等一会儿, 我涂一点口红就好。

lipstick les·bi·an /ˈlɪpstɪk ˌlɛzbɪən; ˈlɪpstɪk ˌlezbiən/ *n* [C] *informal* an offensive word for a LESBIAN who dresses in a typically female way and wears MAKE-UP, as opposed to one who dresses like a man【非正式】口红女同性恋〔扮演女性角色的女同性恋, 冒犯用语〕

list·serv /ˈlɪstˌsɝv; ˈlɪstˌsɜːv/ *n* [C] a computer PROGRAM that allows a group of people to send and receive E-MAIL to and from each other about a particular subject〔计算机的〕邮件清单管理程序

load fund /ˈlod ˌfʌnd; ˈləʊd ˌfʌnd/ *n* [C] an amount of money that you give a company and pay them to INVEST for you 投资于抽佣基金的钱款

lo·gy /ˈlɑgɪ; ˈlɒgi/ *adj slang* feeling as if you have no energy or no interest in doing anything; LETHARGIC【俚】懒洋洋的, 没有劲的: *You seem a bit logy today.* 你今天似乎有点没精打采。

LOL, lol a written abbreviation of 缩写= 'laughing out loud', used by people communicating in CHAT ROOMs on the Internet to say that they are laughing at something that someone else has written. LOL is also used at the end of informal letters, messages, meaning 'lots of love'. 放声大笑〔用于网上聊天室中〕; 爱你〔'lots of love' 的缩写, 用于非正式信件的结尾〕

look·ist /ˈlʊkɪst; ˈlʊkɪst/ *adj informal* unfairly deciding to like or not like someone by considering only the way they look, their weight, their clothes etc【非正式】以貌取人的: *It's time for women to stop making lookist remarks about each other and to start feeling good about their own bodies.* 妇女到了该停止互相评头品足, 而开始为各自的体态感到自豪的时候了。—**lookist** *n* [C] —**lookism** *n* [U]

low-rent /ˌlo ˋrɛnt; ˌləʊ ˈrent/ *adj* used to express disapproval of something that is not expensive or not good quality 质量低劣的, 廉价的〔有贬义〕

loyalty card /ˈlɔɪəltɪ ˌkɑrd; ˈlɔɪəlti ˌkɑːd/ *n* [C] a card given by a shop, SUPERMARKET etc that gives regular customers lower prices, money back on goods they buy etc〔商店、超市等发的〕忠诚卡: *The loyalty card offers a 5% discount on the store's own-brand goods.* 用忠诚卡购买商店自主品牌的商品可得到九五折。

LPG /ˌɛl pi ˋdʒi; ˌel piː ˈdʒiː/ also 又作 **LP gas** /ˌɛl pi ˋgæs; ˌel piː ˈgæs/ *n* [U] liquefied petroleum gas; a type of liquid FUEL that is burned to produce heat or power 液化石油气

LRP /ˌɛl ɑr ˋpi; ˌel ɑː ˈpiː/ *n* [U] *BrE* lead replacement petrol; a special type of PETROL that does not contain LEAD and is meant to be used in older cars which normally would require petrol containing lead【英】代铅汽油

lurk /lɝk; lɜːk/ *v* [I]
NEW MEANING
if you lurk in a CHAT ROOM on the Internet, you read what other people are writing to each other, but you do not write any messages to them 旁观〔阅读网上留言, 但不发表意见〕, 潜水: [+in] *I think it's sort of creepy how people lurk in chat rooms.* 我认为人们在聊天室里潜水有点令人毛骨悚然。—**lurker** *n* [C]

M,m

Maalox mo·ment /ˋmelɑks ˌmomənt; ˈmeɪlɒks ˌməʊmənt/ *n* [C usually singular 一般用单数] *AmE humorous* a short period when you suddenly become

extremely anxious or nervous and have pains in your stomach. Maalox is a trademark for a type of stomach medicine sold in the US. In television advertisements for this product, several people in STRESSFUL situations said, "I'm having a Maalox moment!" which meant that they needed to take some of this medicine to make them feel better.【美, 幽默】梅洛克斯症〔因极度紧张或担心而感到胃痛的一段时间, 此词来自梅洛克斯公司的胃药广告〕

mad /mæd; mæd/ *adj*
NEW MEANING
1 be mad for sb/sth *informal* if you are mad for someone or something, you are extremely interested in or attracted to them【非正式】对某人/某物着迷: *All the girls at school are mad for him.* 学校里的所有女孩都迷恋着他。**2 be mad for it** *BrE informal* if you are mad for it, you want to do something very much【英, 非正式】热衷[醉心]于

magnetic ink char·ac·ter rec·og·ni·tion /mæg͵nɛtɪk ͵ɪŋk `kærɪktɚ rɛkəg͵nɪʃən; mæg͵netɪk ͵ɪŋk 'kærɨktə rekəg͵nɪʃən/ *abbreviation* 缩写为 **MICR** *n* [U]
technical a system that recognizes printed letters of the alphabet, for example on a cheque or official document【术语】磁墨水字符识别

mail·bomb /`mel͵bɑm; 'meɪlbɒm/ *n* [C]
a large number of E-MAIL messages sent to the same computer, with the result that the computer has too much DATA and cannot work properly any more 电子邮件炸弹〔把大量电子邮件传送至某电脑, 使其因资料过多而无法正常运作〕

mailing list /`melɪŋ ͵lɪst; 'meɪlɪŋ ͵lɪst/ *n* [C]
NEW MEANING
a list of names and E-MAIL addresses kept on a computer so that you can send the same message to a group of people at the same time〔电脑上的〕邮件地址列表, 通讯名单

ma·jor·ly /`medʒɚlɪ; 'meɪdʒəli/ *adv*
slang extremely【俚】极其, 非常: *It's majorly cool.* 酷极了。| *She got majorly depressed after they broke up.* 两人分手之后, 她沮丧极了。

make·good /`mek͵gud; 'meɪkgʊd/ *n* [C usually plural 一般用复数]
an occasion when a television company has to broadcast an advertisement without being paid to do so, because the advertisement was not seen by as many people as the television company promised when it was first shown〔电视台因收看观众未达到事先承诺的人数而〕免费播放广告

makeover /`mek͵ovɚ; 'meɪkəʊvə/ *n* [C]
NEW MEANING
a process of changing the way a place looks 改建: *a kitchen makeover* 厨房改建

makeover TV /`mekovɚ ti ͵vi; 'meɪkəʊvə tiː ͵viː/ *n* [U]
television programmes in which skilled people help someone to improve the appearance of their house or garden 指导家居装修的电视节目

mall·rat /`mɔlræt; 'mɔːlræt/ *n* [C usually plural 一般用复数] *AmE*
informal a young person who goes to SHOPPING MALL*s* a lot in order to be with their friends, not to buy things【美, 非正式】商场逛客〔常在商场会友而不买东西的年轻人〕

man /mæn; mæn/ *n*
NEW MEANING
you the/da man! also 又作 **you're the man** *AmE slang* used to praise a man or boy for having done something well【美俚】做得好! 真棒!〔用以称赞男性〕

managed care pro·vid·er /͵mænɪdʒd `kɛr prə͵vaɪdɚ; ͵mænɪdʒd 'keə prə͵vaɪdə/ *n* [C] *AmE*
a doctor or hospital that provides medical services for people who have a type of health insurance that limits the amount or type of medical care they can receive【美】提供管理式护理的医生[医院]〔病人所接受的医疗服务在数量及种类上均有限制〕: *How can I change my managed care provider?* 我怎样才能换一家提供管理式护理的医院呢?

managed fund /͵mænɪdʒd `fʌnd; ͵mænɪdʒd 'fʌnd/ *n* [C]
technical a FUND (=group of INVESTMENTs) in which some of the investments are bought and sold in order to try to increase the value of the fund【术语】管理基金

ma·no a ma·no /͵mɑno ɑ `mɑno; ͵mænəʊ ɑː 'mænəʊ/ *adv*
with only two people involved; ONE-TO-ONE 一对一地: *Come on now – put your questions to the senator, mano a mano, by speaking to him online in real time.* 来吧, 把你的问题向参议员提出, 一对一地、实时地在网上跟他谈。| *He finally faced up to his father, mano a mano, telling him he was going to leave college.* 他终于鼓起勇气, 面对面告诉父亲自己打算从大学辍学。

ma·qui·la·do·ra /mɑ͵kilə`dorə; mæ͵kiːlə'dɔːrə/ *n* [C] *Spanish*
a factory in Mexico, especially one that is owned by a foreign company【西】〔尤指外资在墨西哥开设的〕保税加工厂

mashed /mæʃt; mæʃt/ *adj* [not before noun 不用于名词前] *BrE*
slang very drunk or strongly affected by drugs【英俚】烂醉的; 〔吸毒后〕迷迷糊糊的: *We got completely mashed last night.* 我们昨夜醉得一塌糊涂。

massive¹ /`mæsɪv; 'mæsɪv/ *n* [C] *BrE*
NEW MEANING
slang a group of friends from a particular place who share an interest in RAP, HIP-HOP, or HOUSE music, considered as a group【英俚】〔某地的说唱乐、豪斯乐等的〕乐迷团: *the Staines massive* 斯坦斯乐迷团

massive² /`mæsɪv; 'mæsɪv/ *adj BrE*
NEW MEANING
slang extremely good【英俚】棒极的, 顶呱呱的: *Listen to this. It's a massive song.* 听, 这歌棒极了。

mass vol·ume ver·ti·cal drink·ing /͵mæs ͵vɑljəm ͵vɝtɪkl̩ `drɪŋkɪŋ; ͵mæs ͵vɒljuːm ͵vɜːtɪkəl 'drɪŋkɪŋ/ *n* [U] *BrE*
technical an expression used by the British police to describe the way in which large numbers of young people drink large amounts of alcohol in bars that are so crowded that everyone is standing up【英, 术语】聚众站着酗酒〔英国警方用语, 指很多年轻人挤在酒吧里站着喝酒〕

max /mæks; mæks/ *v*
NEW MEANING
max sth ↔ **out** *phr v* [T] *AmE informal* to use all of something such as money or supplies so that there is none left【美, 非正式】把〔金钱、供应品等〕用光, 一点不剩: *We maxed out the credit card last weekend at Oakland Mall.* 上周末我们在奥克兰购物中心把信用卡的签账额用了个精光。

MBWA /͵ɛm bi ͵dʌbl̩jʊ `e; ͵em biː ͵dʌbəljuː 'eɪ/ *n* [U]
management by walking around; a way of managing people in a company in which the manager often walks around and speaks to workers in order to find out what they are doing〔公司的〕巡查式管理

MC /͵ɛm `si; ͵em 'siː/ *n* [C]
NEW MEANING
the person in a RAP group who holds the MICROPHONE and says the words to the songs 说唱乐队中手持麦克风吟唱的人 —**MC** *v* [I]: *He was MC'ing in clubs in the evening.* 他晚上在夜总会演唱说唱乐曲。

m-com·merce /`ɛm ͵kɑmɝs; 'em ͵kɒmɜːs/ *n* [U]
mobile commerce; the buying or selling of goods and services using a radio connection to the Internet, for example using a LAPTOP or MOBILE PHONE〔通过笔记本电脑或手机进行的〕移动商务

meat·space /`mit͵spes; 'miːtspeɪs/ *n* [U]
the real world of physical things and people, rather than

CYBERSPACE〔相对于网络的虚拟世界的〕现实（物质）世界，人肉世界：*I'm so pathetic that I'm updating my webpage at 8pm on a Friday night. I've apparently given up on having a life in meatspace.* 我太惨了，星期五晚上8点钟还在更新我的网页。我显然已经放弃了在现实世界的生活。

medal /ˋmɛdl; ˈmedl/ *v* **medalled, medalling** *BrE*【英】, **medaled, medaling** *AmE*【美】[I]
to win a MEDAL (=a prize) at the Olympic Games 赢得奥运奖牌：[**+in**] *Germany has the potential to medal at least four times in gymnastics this year.* 德国有潜力在本届奥运体操赛中取得至少四枚奖牌。

Med·i·gap /ˋmɛdɪˌgæp; ˈmedɪgæp/ *n* [U]
a system in the US by which people who have Medicaid pay money to a company so that they can receive additional medical care and services that they need〔美国的〕补充性医疗保险计划：*My mom has to pay high premiums every month for Medigap to cover prescription drugs.* 我妈妈每月得缴付高额的补充性医疗保险金以承担处方药物的费用。

meet-and-greet /ˌmit ən ˋgrit; ˌmiːt ən ˈgrit/ also 又作 **m and g** *n* [C]
1 an event that is organized for famous musicians, writers, artists etc to meet and talk to their FANS (=people who admire them)〔歌星、作家、艺术家等与他们的支持者的〕见面会：*There will be a meet-and-greet after the show.* 演出结束后将有一个观众见面会。**2** a service that sends people to greet and help a person or group when they arrive at an airport〔机场的〕接机（服务）**3** an event in which parents go to their children's school and meet the teachers and other people who work there〔家长与教师的〕见面会，家长会

memory hog /ˋmɛmərɪ ˌhɑg; ˈmeməri ˌhɒg/ *n* [C] *informal*【非正式】
1 a computer program that uses a lot of memory 占用大量内存的电脑程序 **2** someone who uses computer programs that use a lot of the power available, so that other people on the NETWORK have trouble using their programs〔电脑的〕高用量用户〔他们使用占用大量资源的程序，给其他的网络用户带来不便〕—**memory-hogging** *adj* [only before noun 仅用于名词前]

mental health day /ˌmɛntḷ ˋhɛlθ ˌde; ˌmentl ˈhelθ ˌdeɪ/ *n* [C] *AmE informal* a day when you do not go to work, in order to rest【美，非正式】歇工日，休息日

menu bar /ˋmɛnju ˌbɑr; ˈmenjuː ˌbɑː/ *n* [C]
a bar across the top of a computer SCREEN that contains several PULL-DOWN MENUS, for example 'File', 'View', 'Help' etc〔电脑显示屏上方的〕选项栏，菜单条：*Some applications in LEO don't have a menu bar.* 一些低轨道卫星的应用程序没有选项栏。

menu op·tion /ˋmɛnju ˌɑpʃən; ˈmenjuː ˌɒpʃən/ *n* [C]
one of the things you can choose in a PULL-DOWN MENU on a computer〔电脑的〕菜单选项

message¹ /ˋmɛsɪdʒ; ˈmesɪdʒ/ *n*
NEW MEANING
keep to the message an expression used especially by politicians which means that you should always emphasize your party's most important ideas when you are trying to gain people's support〔尤指政治人物〕坚持政党思想，不改初衷：*Don't confuse the voters. Keep to the message.* 别把投票的人搞糊涂了，还是坚守政党理念吧。—see also 另见 OFF-MESSAGE, ON-MESSAGE

message² /ˋmɛsɪdʒ; ˈmesɪdʒ/ *v* [T]
to send a message using electronic equipment, for example by E-MAIL〔用电子设备〕发信息〈如用电子邮件〉：*I messaged the ship's owner to let him know that everything was going well.* 我给船主发信息，让他知道一切都很顺利。

message board /ˋmɛsɪdʒ ˌbɔrd; ˈmesɪdʒ ˌbɔːd/ *n* [C]
a place on a WEBSITE where you can read or leave messages; ELECTRONIC BULLETIN BOARD 电子公告板，网上留言板：*Please read the healthnut.com message board guidelines before posting any messages.* 留言前请先阅读 healthnut.com〔关心健康网站〕电子公告板上的说明。

mes·sag·ing /ˋmɛsɪdʒɪŋ; ˈmesɪdʒɪŋ/ *n* [U]
the system or process of sending messages using electronic equipment〔通过电子设备进行的〕信息发送：*automated messaging* 自动信息发送 | *new technology to protect the privacy of electronic messaging and online commerce* 保护电子信息发送和网上贸易隐私的新技术

met·a·da·ta /ˋmɛtəˌdetə; ˈmetəˌdeɪtə/ *n* [U, plural]
information that describes what is contained in large computer DATABASES, for example who wrote the information, what it is for, and in what form it is stored 元数据，诠释资料

me-too /ˌmi ˋtu; ˌmiː ˈtuː/ *adj* [only before noun 仅用于名词前]
informal a me-too product is one that a company begins to sell after it has seen that other companies are successful with the same type of product【非正式】〔产品〕仿效出售的，跟风的

MICR /ˌɛm aɪ si ˋɑr; ˌem aɪ siː ˈɑː/ *n* [U]
magnetic ink character recognition; a system that recognizes printed letters of the alphabet, for example on a cheque or official document 磁墨水字符识别

mi·cro·brew /ˋmaɪkroˌbru; ˈmaɪkrəʊˌbruː/ *n* [C]
a type of beer that is produced by a company only in small quantities〔产量很少的〕微酿啤酒

mi·cro·brew·e·ry /ˋmaɪkroˌbruərɪ; ˈmaɪkrəʊˌbruːəri/ *n* [C]
a small company that makes only small quantities of beer, and often has a restaurant where its beer is served 小啤酒厂：*Hundreds of microbreweries across the country are making wonderful, full-flavoured beers.* 全国各地有数以百计的小啤酒厂在酿制可口味醇的啤酒。

mi·cro·en·gi·neer·ing /ˋmaɪkroɛndʒəˌnɪrɪŋ; ˈmaɪkrəʊendʒɪˌnɪərɪŋ/ *n* [U]
the activity of designing structures and machines that are extremely small 微（型）工程 —**microengineer** *n* [C]

mi·cro·fi·nance /ˋmaɪkrofəˌnæns; ˈmaɪkrəʊˌfaɪnæns/ *n* [U]
a system that allows people in poor countries to borrow small amounts of money to help them start a small business 小额创业贷款制度：*Small loans schemes can raise living standards, but microfinance should not be the only tool for poverty reduction, says a new report from the World Bank.* 世界银行的一份新报告指出，小额创业贷款计划能提高生活水平，但是小额融资不应该是扶贫的唯一办法。

mi·cro·loan /ˋmaɪkroˌlon; ˈmaɪkrəʊˌləʊn/ *n* [C]
a small amount of money that is lent by a government organization to people who want to start small businesses, especially in poor countries〔尤指在贫困国家由政府发放的〕小额创业贷款：*Write for a free brochure about the Microloan Program for Entrepreneurs.* 免费函索为创业者而设的小额贷款计划的简介。

mi·cro·man·age /ˋmaɪkroˌmænɪdʒ; ˈmaɪkrəʊˌmænɪdʒ/ *v* [T]
to organize and control all the details of other people's work in a way that they find annoying 微观管理〔指过分干预别人的工作〕：*Professors warned that students will suffer if the state legislature tries to micromanage public education.* 有教授警告说，如果州立法机关企图对公共教育实行微观管理，学生们将受害。

MIDI /ˋmɪdɪ; ˈmɪdi/ *n* [U]
technical musical instrument digital interface; a system that allows computers to communicate with electronic musical instruments【术语】"迷笛"，乐器数字接口〔电子乐器数码界面〕：*Unlike digital recordings, which can gobble up megabytes of disk space, MIDI files are relatively compact.* 有别于占据大量磁盘空间的数码唱片，迷笛档案比较紧凑。| *With this special software, you can hook up a MIDI keyboard to your computer, play a song,*

and record it. 借助这一专用软件，你可以把迷笛电子琴接到自己的电脑上，弹奏一首歌曲并把它录下来。

millennium bug /mə`lɛnɪəm ˏbʌg; mɪ'leniəm ˌbʌg/ *n* [singular]
the problem that some people believed would affect many computers which did not recognize the date when the year 2000 began 千年[禧]虫

Millennium Man /mə`lɛnɪəm ˏmæn; mɪ'leniəm ˌmæn/ *n* [C]
a man whose personal qualities and behaviour are considered to be very modern〔性格特点和行为都十分新潮的〕千年[禧]男人: *Just answer these five simple questions to find out if your man's a true Millennium Man.* 回答这五个简单的问题就可以知道你的男人是不是真正的"千禧男人"。

ming·ing /`mɪŋɪŋ; 'mɪŋɪŋ/ *adj BrE*
informal very ugly or very dirty【英，非正式】丑极的; 脏极的: *These toilets are minging.* 这些厕所脏透了。

mirror site /`mɪrɚ ˏsaɪt; 'mɪrə ˌsaɪt/ *n* [C]
a WEBSITE that is an exact copy of another one, but which is in a different place on the Internet. Mirror sites make it possible for more people to find and use the information, especially if the original website is busy and slow to use. 镜像网站〔其内容与另一网站完全相同〕

mission creep /`mɪʃən ˏkrip; 'mɪʃən ˌkriːp/ *n* [U] *AmE*
a series of gradual unplanned changes in the purpose or aim of what someone or an organization is trying to do, with the result that they do something different from what they originally planned to do【美】任务蠕变〔任务的目的随时间而逐渐变化〕: *The government has learned the lessons of the mission creep problem in Somalia, and would only expand the military's assignment in a careful, deliberate way.* 政府已从索马里的任务蠕变问题中汲取了教训，并将仔细谨慎地扩大军事任务范围。

mission state·ment /`mɪʃən ˏstetmənt; 'mɪʃən ˌsteɪtmənt/ *n*
personal mission statement a clear statement about what you want to achieve with your life 人生目标宣言, 个人目标陈述: *Use a personal mission statement to chart your career course.* 利用人生目标宣言来制定你的事业进程。

mo' /mo; məʊ/ *quantifier AmE*
spoken informal a short form of 缩略式 = MORE², used especially by people who listen to or perform RAP² (2) music【美口，非正式】更多〔尤为聆听或演奏说唱乐的人所使用〕: *It's just like Biggie says – mo' money means mo' problems.* 正如比吉所说，钞票越多，问题也越多。

mock·ney /`mɑknɪ; 'mɒkni/ *n* [U] *BrE*
a way of speaking English that is popular among fashionable people in London, England, which uses some sounds and words that are more typical of WORKING-CLASS speech. This word comes from a combination of the words 'MOCK', which means 'not real', and 'COCKNEY' which means a WORKING-CLASS person from the eastern part of London.【英】模仿伦敦劳工阶层人士的口音〔由 mock 和 cockney 缩合而成〕: *Jameson sings in this awful mockney accent.* 詹姆森用这种模仿伦敦乡音的怪声怪调唱歌。

mommy track /`mɑmɪ ˏtræk; 'mɒmi ˌtræk/ *n* [singular] *AmE*
informal a situation in which women with children have less opportunity to make large amounts of money or become very successful in their jobs, for example because they are not able to work as many hours as other people【美，非正式】妈咪轨道〔指母亲为了照顾孩子而损失挣大钱和晋升等的机会〕: *The mommy track unfairly penalizes women, especially in the developed countries.* 妈咪轨道使妇女受到不公平的待遇，这在发达国家尤为常见。

morph /mɔrf; mɔːf/ *v* [I,T]
to change, or to make something develop a new appearance or change into something else 变化，(使)变形: *The Sunnyvale computer animators morphed Woody Harrelson's face in the movie "Natural Born Killers."* 太阳谷电脑动画制作师让伍迪·哈勒尔森的脸在电影《天生杀人狂》中变了样子。| [+ into] *The Consumnes River flooded its banks and morphed into a giant sea that swamped homes and ranches.* 孔苏莫内斯河河水溢出河岸变成了一片汪洋，淹没了房屋和牧场。

mosh /mɑʃ; mɒʃ/ *v* [I]
slang to dance to ROCK music, especially at a concert, by jumping around and waving your arms in the air with a lot of energy【俚】〔随着摇滚乐〕狂舞: *Few albums offer as much food for thought or music for moshing as "The Gray Race".* 很少有唱片集能像《灰色一族》那样让人思考，让人随之狂舞。

mosh pit /`mɑʃ ˏpɪt; 'mɒʃ ˌpɪt/ *n* [C]
slang an area in front of the stage at a ROCK concert where people dance with a lot of energy. People sometimes jump off the stage and are caught by people in the mosh pit.【俚】〔摇滚乐音乐会的舞台前的〕狂舞区: *bands who appeal to shirtless, sweaty boys in the mosh pit* 吸引那些不穿衬衣、满身是汗在舞台前狂舞的小伙子的乐队

motor vot·er /`motɚ ˏvotɚ; 'məʊtə ˌvəʊtə/ *n* [U] *AmE*
a law which makes it easier for Americans to REGISTER to vote because they can do it at the same time and place where they get their DRIVER'S LICENSES. The official name of this law is the National Voter Registration Act.【美】汽车选民登记法〔美国法律，让人可以在取驾驶执照时进行选举登记〕

mountain board /`maʊntn̩ ˏbɔrd; 'maʊntɪn ˌbɔːd/ also 又作 **all-terrain board** *n* [C]
a long wide board made of plastic or wood, with four rubber wheels, which people use to travel down the sides of mountains for sport 山地滑板 —**mountain boarding** *n* [U] —**mountain boarder** *n* [C]

mouse potato 电脑迷

mouse po·ta·to /maus pə`teto; 'maʊs pə'teɪtəʊ/ *n plural* **mouse potatoes** [C]
informal someone who spends a lot of time playing on a computer. This word developed from the words 'COUCH POTATO' which means someone who spends a lot of time watching television.【非正式】电脑迷〔老泡在电脑前的人，由 couch potato (电视迷) 转化而来〕

mover /`muvɚ; 'muːvə/ *n* [C]
NEW MEANING
a company whose SHARES are being bought and sold in large quantities〔其股票被大批买卖的〕公司

MP3 /ˏɛm pi `θri; ˌem piː 'θriː/ *n* [C]
a type of computer FILE which contains music. MP3 files are COMPRESSED (=made smaller) so that they can more easily be sent from computer to computer using the Internet. MP3 文件，运动图像压缩标准第三层声音压缩文件〔一种压缩的音乐文件〕

MP3 play·er /ˏɛm pi `θri ˏpleɚ; ˌem piː 'θriː ˌpleɪə/ *n* [C]
a piece of electronic equipment or computer SOFTWARE that allows you to play and listen to MP3 FILES MP3 播放器[播放软件]

MPEG /`ɛm ˏpɛg; 'em ˌpeg/ *n* [U]

Motion Picture Expert Group; a way in which sound and VIDEO material can be presented on the Internet MPEG（运动图像压缩）标准〔一种网上音频及影像压缩技术〕

MRI /ˌɛm ɑr ˋaɪ; ˌem ɑːr ˈaɪ/ *n* [C,U]
technical magnetic resonance imaging; a way of producing a picture of the inside of your body without cutting it open, by using radio waves and strong MAGNETIC FIELDS【术语】磁共振成像〔一种检查人体内部器官的技术〕: *An MRI revealed a tear in the cartilage of his left knee.* 一张磁共振成像的片子显示他左膝的软骨撕裂了。

MSP /ˌɛm ɛs ˋpi; ˌem es ˈpiː/ *n* [C]
Member of the Scottish Parliament; a British politician who is a member of the Scottish Parliament 苏格兰议会议员

mullet /ˈmʌlɪt; ˈmʌl$\frac{1}{3}$t/ *n* [C usually singular 一般用单数] *BrE*
NEW MEANING
a hairstyle for men in which the hair on the sides and top of the head is short and the hair on the back of the head is long. This style was quite common in the 1980s but is now considered unfashionable.【英】胭脂鱼发型〔两侧及头顶短，后边长的一种男子发型，20世纪80年代颇为流行〕

multi-eth·nic, multiethnic /ˌmʌltɪ ˋɛθnɪk; ˌmʌlti ˈeθnɪk/ *adj*
1 involving or including people of several different ETHNIC types 多种族的: *multi-ethnic Britain* 多种族的英国 **2 multiethnic people** *AmE* people who have parents from different races【美】混血儿〔双亲来自不同种族的人〕

multi-play·er gam·ing, multiplayer gaming /ˌmʌltɪ pleɚ ˋgemɪŋ; ˌmʌlti pleɪə ˈgemɪŋ/ *n* [U]
the playing of computer games on the Internet by more than one person at the same time, using different computers 网上多人游戏

mul·ti·plex·er /ˈmʌltɪˌplɛksɚ; ˈmʌltiˌpleksə/ *n* [C]
technical a piece of computer equipment that is used to send several electrical signals using only one connection, especially with a MODEM【术语】多路转换器，复用器

mul·ti·plex·ing /ˈmʌltɪˌplɛksɪŋ; ˈmʌltiˌpleksɪŋ/ *n* [U]
technical a method used to send several electrical signals using only one connection, especially with a MODEM【术语】〔尤指通过调制解调器的〕多路传输: *Multiplexing is used to control such vehicle functions as lighting, automatic windows, and door locks.* 多路传输用于控制车辆的照明、自动窗和门锁等功能。**—multiplex** *v* [I,T]

mul·ti·skill·ing /ˈmʌltɪˌskɪlɪŋ; ˈmʌltiˌskɪlɪŋ/ *n* [U]
the improvement of workers' skills so that they can do many different types of things 多技能化: *There are several training options for multiskilling in engineering firms.* 工程公司有几套多技能化培训方案可供选择。

mul·ti·task, multi-task /ˈmʌltɪˌtæsk; ˈmʌltiˌtɑːsk/ *v* [I]
to do several things at the same time 同时执行多项任务: *The successful applicant for this job must be able to multitask.* 能同时执行多项任务的人才能成功申请到这个职位。**—multitasker** *n* [C]

multi-task·ing, multitasking /ˈmʌltɪ ˌtæskɪŋ; ˈmʌlti ˌtɑːskɪŋ/ *n* [U]
1 a computer's ability to do more than one job at a time〔计算机的〕多任务处理（能力）**2** the ability to do different types of work at the same time 同时执行多项任务的能力

music des·ti·na·tion /ˈmjuzɪk dɛstəˋneʃən; ˈmjuːzɪk dest$\frac{1}{3}$ˈneɪʃən/ *n* [C]
a type of WEBSITE on the Internet that has a lot of information about music and musicians, and through which you can buy music 音乐目的地〔介绍音乐知识并出售音乐产品的网站〕: *Clasica is the ultimate online music destination for classical music lovers.* Clasica是古典音乐爱好者的最佳网上音乐目的地。

mu·so /ˈmjuzo; ˈmjuːzəʊ/ *n* [C] *BrE*
informal someone who plays popular music or knows a lot about it【英，非正式】流行乐师[乐迷]: *He's not just another actor turned muso.* 他并非一般转做流行乐手的演员。| *To be a muso is a way of life.* 成为流行乐迷也是一种生活方式。

must /mʌst; mʌst/ *modal verb*
NEW MEANING
a must-see/must-do/must-read etc something that is so good, exciting, interesting etc that you think people should see it, do it, read it etc 必看/做/读等的事物: *Rowling's latest Harry Potter book is a must-read for the kids.* 罗琳最近的一部《哈利·波特》是孩子们必读的书。

N,n

nag·ware /ˈnægˌwɛr; ˈnægweə/ *n* [U]
humorous a type of computer PROGRAM that is available free but that contains a message reminding people who use it to send their name, address, and other information to the person or company that created it so that they can use this information. This word comes from a combination of the words 'NAG' and 'SOFTWARE'.【幽默】提醒软件〔可免费使用，但会提醒用户给开发者发送其姓名、地址等信息的一种软件。此词由nag和software缩合而成〕

name /nem; neɪm/ *v*
name and shame *BrE* to publicly say that a person or a company has been responsible for something illegal or has not achieved a particular standard, so that a lot of people will know about it【英】公之于众使臭名昭著[远扬] **—naming and shaming** *n* [U]: *The recent spate of naming and shaming of child-sex offenders has been severely criticized by the government.* 最近将大量对儿童进行性侵犯者的名字公之于世的做法已经受到政府的严厉批评。

nanny cam /ˈnænɪ ˌkæm; ˈnæni ˌkæm/ *n* [C]
a small hidden VIDEO CAMERA which allows parents who are away from home to watch or record how their children are being treated by the person who is taking care of them. This word is a combination of 'NANNY', meaning a woman who takes care of children in their own home, and 'cam', which is a short form of 'camera'. 保姆摄像机〔父母在外出时用于观察或摄录孩子被照顾的情况，由nanny和camera的缩略形式cam缩合而成〕

nan·o·tech·nol·o·gy /ˈnænotɛkˌnɑlədʒɪ; ˈnænəʊtekˌnɒlədʒi/ *n* [U]
technical an area of science which involves developing and making extremely small structures【术语】纳米技术

navigate /ˈnævəˌget; ˈnæv$\frac{1}{3}$geɪt/ *v* [I,T]
NEW MEANING
to find your way around on a particular WEBSITE, or to move from one website to another〔网站上〕导航，漫游: *It's considered the most popular browser to navigate the Internet.* 这被认为是最受大众欢迎的互联网导航浏览器。| *The magazine's website is slick and easy to navigate.* 该杂志的网站是第一流的，很容易导航浏览。

need-to-know /ˌnid tə ˋno; ˌniːd tə ˈnəʊ/ *adj*
on a need-to-know basis if information is given to people on a need-to-know basis, they are given only the details that they need at the time when they need them 在须知的基础上: *Access to the manufacturing process is on a strictly need-to-know basis.* 只有绝对必要时才可接触生产工序的内容。

negative eq·ui·ty /ˌnɛgətɪv ˋɛkwətɪ; ˌnegətɪv ˈekw$\frac{1}{3}$ti/ *n* [U] *BrE*
a situation in which someone's house is worth less than the amount of money they borrowed in order to buy it【英】〔抵押资产的〕负净值，负资产

net·iquette /ˋnɛtɪkɛt; ˈnetɪket/ *n* [U]
informal the commonly accepted rules for polite behaviour when communicating with other people on the Internet【非正式】网规, 网上礼仪: *Netiquette says that you don't use all capital letters in an e-mail, because that shows you are angry.* 网规说, 你在电子邮件中不得全部用大写字母, 因为那样做表示你在生气。

net·i·zen /ˋnɛtɪzn̩; ˈnetɪzən/ *n* [C]
slang someone who uses the Internet, especially someone who uses it in a responsible way. This word comes from a combination of the words 'net', meaning 'the Internet', and 'citizen'.【俚】网民〔由 net 和 citizen 缩合而成〕: *China and India will soon have far larger numbers of netizens than any Western nation.* 中国和印度不久将会拥有大量网民, 数量远比任何一个西方国家多。

net·pre·neur /ˋnɛtprəˌnɝ; ˈnetprəˌnɜː/ also 又作 **net·re·pre·neur** /ˌnɛtrəprəˋnɝ; ˌnetrəprəˈnɜːr/ *n* [C]
informal someone who has started an Internet business. This word comes from a combination of the words 'net', meaning 'the Internet', and 'ENTREPRENEUR', which means 'a person who starts new businesses'.【非正式】网络企业家〔由 net 和 entrepreneur 缩合而成〕

net·speak /ˋnɛtspik; ˈnetspiːk/ *n* [U]
the expressions, technical words, SLANG etc commonly used on the Internet 网络用语: *a glossary of netspeak terms* 网络用语汇编

neural com·pu·ter /ˌnjurəl kəmˈpjutɚ; ˌnjʊərəl kəmˈpjuːtə/ *n* [C]
a computer that is designed to operate in a way similar to the human brain〔运行方式与人脑相似的〕神经电脑 —**neural computing** *n* [U]

neu·ro·in·for·mat·ics /ˋnjurɔɪnfɚˌmætɪks; ˈnjʊərəʊɪnfəˌmætɪks/ *n* [U]
a scientific study which combines NEUROSCIENCE (=the study of the brain) and INFORMATION SCIENCE (=the collecting, storing, and arranging of information, especially using powerful computers) 神经信息学

new /nju; njuː/ *adj*

NEW MEANING

...is the new... *BrE* used to say that something is thought to be the new fashion that will replace an existing thing【英】时髦的: *Don't you know that vodka is the new water, my dear?* 我亲爱的, 你难道不知道喝伏特加是最时髦的吗? | *And grey is the new black! By which I mean – you can wear grey anywhere now and still be smart and fashionable.* 灰色取代黑色成了最时髦的颜色! 我的意思是现在你可以穿着灰色衣服到处走, 显得那么帅而入时。

New Age mu·sic /ˌnju ˋedʒ ˌmjuzɪk; ˌnjuː ˈeɪdʒ ˌmjuːzɪk/ also 又作 **New Age** *n*
a type of music that is intended to help you relax and feel calm 新世纪音乐

new·bie /ˋnjubɪ; ˈnjuːbi/ *n* [C]
informal someone who has just started doing something, especially using the Internet or computers【非正式】〔尤指互联网或电脑的〕新手, 新用户

new e·con·o·my /ˌnju ɪˋkɑnəmɪ; ˌnjuː ɪˈkɒnəmi/ *n* [singular]
an economic system that is based on computers and modern TECHNOLOGY, and is therefore dependent on educated workers〔基于计算机和现代技术的〕新经济: *As we move into a new economy, trade unions will have to reinvent themselves to stay relevant.* 我们进入了新经济, 工会必须重新塑造自己的角色才能与时俱进。| *a Washington conference on the New Economy* 讨论新经济的华盛顿会议 —**new economy** *adj: new economy methods* 新经济的办法

new lad /ˌnju ˋlæd; ˌnjuː ˈlæd/ *n* [C] *BrE*
a young man whose attitudes and behaviour are a reaction to those of the NEW MAN. New lads do not feel embarrassed about enjoying traditionally male activities such as drinking too much alcohol, playing or watching sports, making rude jokes, and looking at pictures of attractive women.【英】新男青年, 新派小子

new school /ˋnju ˏskul; ˈnjuː ˌskuːl/ *adj* [only before noun 仅用于名词前]
informal using new ideas in a type of music or art【非正式】新派的: *new school hip hop artists* 新派的嘻哈乐艺术家

news·group /ˋnjuzgrup; ˈnjuːzgruːp/ *n* [C]
a discussion group on the Internet, with a place where people with a shared interest can exchange messages〔网上的〕新闻组

new va·ri·ant CJD /ˌnju vɛrɪənt ˏsi dʒe ˋdi; ˌnjuː veərɪənt ˌsiː dʒeɪ ˈdiː/ *n* [U]
a deadly brain disease in humans that may be caused by eating BEEF that is affected by BSE 新变异型克－雅氏病, 新变种克－雅氏病

NiCad /ˋnɪkæd; ˈnɪkæd/ *n* [C]
the abbreviation of 缩写= nickel-cadmium; a type of BATTERY that can be used in cameras and small electronic equipment. NiCad batteries can be RECHARGED. 镍镉电池

NIH syn·drome /ˌɛn aɪ ˋetʃ ˏsɪndrom; ˌen aɪ ˈeɪtʃ ˌsɪndrəʊm/ *n*
the abbreviation of 缩写= NOT-INVENTED-HERE SYNDROME

NiMH *n*
the abbreviation of 缩写= nickel metal hydride; a type of BATTERY that can be used in cameras and small electronic equipment. Nickel metal hydride batteries can be RECHARGED. 镍氢电池

no-brain·er /ˌno ˋbrenɚ; ˌnəʊ ˈbreɪnə/ *n* [singular]
a decision that is easy, and that you do not need to think about, used when you want to emphasize that it is really very easy 无须费脑的事: *Joining the savings plan is a no-brainer. Just do it.* 参加储蓄计划一点也不费神, 参加吧。

no-frills /ˌno ˋfrɪlz; ˌnəʊ ˈfrɪlz◂/ *adj* [only before noun 仅用于名词前]
a no-frills product or service includes only basic features and is not of the highest possible quality 只提供必需品[服务]的, 无修饰的: *a no-frills airline* 只提供基本服务的航空公司 | *no-frills budget accommodation* 朴实无华的廉价膳宿

no-load fund /ˌno ˋlod ˏfʌnd; ˌnəʊ ˈləʊd ˌfʌnd/ *n* [C]
technical a FUND (=group of INVESTMENTs) that people can buy without having to pay any charges【术语】无负担基金, 免佣基金

non-tra·di·tion·al /ˌnɑn trəˋdɪʃənl̩; ˌnɒn trəˈdɪʃənəl/ *adj* [only before noun 仅用于名词前]
different from the way something happened or from what was considered typical in the past 非传统的, 另类的: *older, non-traditional university students* 年岁较大的非传统大学生 | *non-traditional workdays* 非传统的工作日

north /nɔrθ; nɔːθ/ *adv*

NEW MEANING

north of *AmE informal* if an amount is north of another amount, it is more than that amount【美, 非正式】〔数额〕比…大[多]: *To be a big player, a company must spend somewhere north of $500 million a year.* 一家公司若要成为行业里的龙头企业, 一年的支出肯定超过5亿美元。

not-in·vent·ed-here syn·drome /ˌnɑt ɪnˌvɛntɪd ˋhɪr ˏsɪndrom; ˌnɒt ɪnˌventɪd ˈhɪə ˌsɪndrəʊm/ *abbreviation* 缩写为 **NIH syndrome** *n* [U]
a situation in which people in one department of a company consider new products or ideas from other departments as threats, rather than using them to make the whole company more successful 拒绝创新症候群〔指某一部门的人视其他部门的新产品或创意为威胁而不加以采用, 使公司更成功〕

nu·tra·ceu·ti·cal /ˌnutrəˋsutɪkl̩; ˌnjuːtrəˈsjuːtɪkəl/ *n* [C]

a food or something added to food that is meant to have a good effect on health and that might help to prevent disease 保健食品, 营养食品: *a Canadian owned nutritional research company and manufacturer dedicated to setting new standards in the development of safe alternative nutraceuticals* 一家加拿大的营养研究和制造公司, 致力于为开发安全的替代性保健食品制定新标准

object /ˋɑbdʒɪkt; ˈɒbdʒɪkt/ *n* [C]
NEW MEANING
a combination of written information on a computer and instructions that act on the information, for example in the form of a document or a picture 对象, 信息单元: *object-oriented programming* 对象取向的程序设计 | *multimedia data objects* 多媒体数据对象

OCD /ˌo si ˋdi; ˌəʊ siː ˈdiː/ *n* [U]
obsessive compulsive disorder; a form of mental illness in which a person does the same thing again and again and cannot stop doing it, for example washing their hands many times a day 强迫症, 强迫性神经官能症〈例如洁癖〉

OCR /ˌo si ˋɑr; ˌəʊ siː ˈɑː/ *n* [U]
optical character recognition; computer software that recognizes letters of the alphabet, so that you can put paper documents onto a computer 光字符识别 (软件)

off-mes·sage /ˌɔf ˋmɛsɪdʒ; ˌɒf ˈmesɪdʒ◂/ *adj, adv*
a politician who is off-message says things that are different from the ideas and policies of the political party they belong to 与所属政党的思想[政策]不一致的: *I must be careful not to go off-message here!* 我必须小心不在这里背离党的政治策略!

OGM /ˌo dʒi ˋɛm; ˌəʊ dʒiː ˈem/ *n* [C]
outgoing message; the message that you record on your telephone and that people will hear if they telephone you and you do not answer the phone 表明已外出的电话留言

old e·con·o·my /ˋold ɪˌkɑnəmɪ; ˈəʊld ɪˌkɒnəmi/ *n* [singular]
an economic system that is based on older types of industry, such as steel, energy, and machinery 旧经济〔以钢铁、能源、机械工业等为基础的经济体系〕: *The view that Australia has an old economy is wrong.* 认为澳大利亚拥有旧经济的观点是错误的。| *Is the Old Economy really dead?* 旧经济真的寿终正寝了吗? — **old economy** *adj*: *old economy practices* 旧经济体系的惯例

old-growth /ˌold ˋgroθ; ˌəʊld ˈgrəʊθ◂/ *adj*
old-growth forest/trees/timber etc trees that have been growing in a place for a long time in an undisturbed way 原始林/古树/陈年木材等

old-school /ˌold ˋskul; ˌəʊld ˈskuːl◂/ *adj*
old-fashioned, or relating to ideas from the past 旧式的, 老派的: *Wyclef Jean shows off some old-school dance moves in his latest video.* 威克莱夫·琼在最近的录像中卖弄了几个老派的舞蹈动作。

O·les·tra /oˋlɛstrə; əʊˈlestrə/ *n* [U]
trademark an artificial substance that is similar to fat, but cannot be DIGESTed by your body. It is sometimes used to make foods such as ICE CREAM.【商标】奥利斯特拉人造脂肪〔一种脂肪的代替物〕

online auc·tion /ˌɑnlaɪn ˋɔkʃən; ˌɒnlaɪn ˈɔːkʃən/ *n* [C]
a type of WEBSITE in which you can sell things to the person who offers you the highest price 网上拍卖: *We are the premier online auction site with more items and categories than any other.* 我们是首屈一指的网上拍卖站, 拍卖的物品最多, 种类也最多。

online bank·ing /ˌɑnlaɪn ˋbæŋkɪŋ; ˌɒnlaɪn ˈbæŋkɪŋ/ also 又作 **Internet banking** *n* [U]
a service provided by banks so that people can find out information about their bank account, pay bills etc using the Internet 网上银行 (业务): *the growth of online banking* 网上银行业务的增长

on-mes·sage /ˌɑn ˋmɛsɪdʒ; ˌɒn ˈmesɪdʒ/ *adj, adv* [not before noun 不用于名词前]
a politician who is on-message says things that are in agreement with the ideas of his or her political party 与所属政党的思想[政策]一致的: *She is a loyal supporter of the Government, and is always on-message.* 她是政府的忠实支持者, 言论总是与政府的政策保持一致。| *MPs were given every incentive to stay on-message.* 下议院议员得到各方鼓励与所属政党的思想保持一致。

open /ˋopən; ˈəʊpən/ *v* [T]
NEW MEANING
to make a document or computer PROGRAM ready to use 打开, 启动〔文件或电脑程序〕: *Click on this icon to open your File Manager.* 点击这个图标打开文件管理器。

open-jaw fare /ˋopən dʒɔ ˌfɛr; ˈəʊpən dʒɔː ˌfeə/ *n* [C]
the price you pay to travel on a plane, train etc when this includes travel to a place and travel back from a different place〔回程路线不同的〕双程票价

optical char·ac·ter rec·og·ni·tion /ˌɑptɪkl̩ ˋkærɪktə rɛkəgˌnɪʃən; ˌɒptɪkəl ˈkærɪ̈ktə rekəgˌnɪʃən/ *abbreviation* 缩写为 **OCR** *n* [U]
technical computer software that recognizes letters of the alphabet, so that you can put paper documents onto a computer【术语】光字符识别 (软件)

or·gan·o·gram /ɔrˋgænəˌgræm; ɔːˈgænəˌgræm/ *n* [C]
a chart that shows the different ranks of the people working in an organization 组织系统图, 员工组织结构图

OTE /ˌo ti ˋi; ˌəʊ tiː ˈiː/ *n* [U] *BrE*
on target earnings; used in advertisements for jobs to say that the person will receive the complete pay only if he or she succeeds in doing as much work or selling as many things as the employer wants them to, and will get less pay if he or she doesn't【英】〔随工作业绩浮动的〕绩效收入

OTOH
a written abbreviation of 缩写= 'on the other hand', used in E-MAIL or TEXT MESSAGES on MOBILE PHONES 另一方面〔电子邮件或手机短信用语〕

outlet mall /ˋaʊtlɛt ˌmɔl; ˈaʊtlet ˌmɔːl/ *n* [C] *AmE*
a large specially built area which is usually outside but still near to a town or city, where there are a lot of shops that sell popular products for less than the usual price. Outlet malls sometimes sell clothes that are no longer fashionable or products that are slightly damaged.【美】近郊购物中心, 特价商品购物中心

o·ver·class /ˋovəˌklæs; ˈəʊvəˌklɑːs/ *n* [C]
a word meaning a group of people who are powerful, or rich, or have a lot of influence 上层阶层, 特权阶层

oxygen bar /ˋɑksədʒən ˌbɑr; ˈɒksɪ̈dʒən ˌbɑː/ *n* [C]
a bar where you pay to breathe pure oxygen, or oxygen that has a pleasant smell, so that you can relax and have more energy 氧吧

P,p

packet /ˋpækɪt; ˈpækɪ̈t/ *n* [C]
NEW MEANING
technical a unit of electronic information sent over a computer network. When information is sent from one computer to another, it is often separated into pieces called packets in order to make it travel more quickly.【术语】数据包, 信息包

packet sniff·er /ˋpækɪt ˌsnɪfɚ; ˈpækɪ̣t ˌsnɪfə/ *n* [C] *technical* a computer PROGRAM which helps a network to work well by checking PACKET*s* for problems【术语】数据[信息]包探测程序, 数据包嗅探器

page traf·fic /ˋpedʒ ˌtræfɪk; ˈpeɪdʒ ˌtræfɪk/ *n* [U] *technical* the number of people who read a particular page in a magazine, newspaper etc【术语】页面阅读量〔报纸、杂志某页的读者人数〕

pain /pen; peɪn/ *n*

NEW MEANING

feel no pain *informal* to be drunk【非正式】喝醉了: *We saw her coming out of the club. I asked her how she was and she said, "Oh, you know, feeling no pain."* 我们看到她从夜总会出来, 我便问她感觉怎么样, 她说, "哦, 你看, 我醉了。"

palm-sized /ˋpɑm ˌsaɪzd; ˈpɑːm ˌsaɪzd/ *adj*

palm-sized computer/PC/PDA a palm-sized computer, PC etc is small enough to fit in your hand 掌上电脑/个人电脑/个人数码助理

pants /pænts; pænts/ *adj* [not before noun 不用于名词前] *BrE*

slang extremely bad【英俚】极坏的, 糟透了的: *The film was pants.* 这部影片糟透了。

paradigm shift /ˋpærədaɪm ˌʃɪft; ˈpærədaɪm ˌʃɪft/ *n* [C]

an important change in which the usual way of thinking or doing something is replaced by another way of thinking or doing something 思考[做事]方式的重大改变, 根本变化

parallel da·ta que·ry /ˌpærəlɛl ˋdetə ˌkwɪrɪ; ˌpærəlel ˈdeɪtə ˌkwɪəri/ *n* [U]

a system on a computer that can deal with several problems, tasks etc at the same time 并行数据查询

parental leave /pəˌrɛntḷ ˋliv; pəˌrentl ˈliːv/ *n* [U] time that a parent is allowed to spend away from work with his or her baby 父母假, 照顾子女假

pash·mi·na /pæʃˋminə; pæʃˈmiːnə/ *n* [C] a piece of soft cloth that is worn by women around their shoulders 羊绒披肩

pay-as-you-go /ˌpe əz ju ˋgo; ˌpeɪ əz jə ˈgəʊ/ *adj* [only before noun 仅用于名词前]

a pay-as-you-go MOBILE PHONE or Internet service is one that you must pay for before you can use it. You use the service until the moment when the time you have used has cost the same as the amount of money you paid. 预付费的, 需先付费才能使用的〔移动电话、网上服务等〕

pay-per-view /ˌpe pɚ ˋvju; ˌpeɪ pə ˈvjuː/ *adj* [only before noun 仅用于名词前]

a pay-per-view television CHANNEL makes people pay for each programme they watch〔电视节目〕按次付费的 —**pay-per-view** *n* [U]: *The game is only being shown on pay-per-view.* 这场比赛只在按次付费节目中播出。

pay TV /ˋpe ti ˌvi; ˈpeɪ tiː ˌviː/ also 又作 **pay tel·e·vi·sion** /ˋpe ˌtɛləvɪʒən; ˈpeɪ ˌteḷ̣vɪʒən/ *n* [U] television CHANNEL*s* that you must pay to watch 付费电视

PC Card /ˌpi ˋsi ˌkɑrd; ˌpiː ˈsiː ˌkɑːd/ *n* [C] *trademark* Personal Computer Card; a small flat object which stores information that can be added to some computers【商标】PC卡, 个人电脑界面卡

PCP /ˌpi si ˋpi; ˌpiː siː ˈpiː/ *n* [C] *AmE*

NEW MEANING

primary care physician; a doctor you go to when you are ill, who may treat you or advise you to see a SPECIALIST (=a doctor who deals with a particular part of the body)【美】初级保健医师, 普通科医生

PCS /ˌpi si ˋɛs; ˌpiː siː ˈes/ *n* [U] personal communications service; a communication system that allows MOBILE PHONE*s* to communicate with each other 个人通信服务

PDA /ˌpi di ˋe; ˌpiː diː ˈeɪ/ *n* [C] personal digital assistant; a very small, light computer that you can carry with you, and that you use to store information such as telephone numbers, addresses, and APPOINTMENT*s*. Some personal digital assistants can send and receive E-MAIL, and connect to the Internet. 个人数码助理, 掌上电脑

PDF /ˌpi di ˋɛf; ˌpiː diː ˈef/ *n* [U] portable document format; a way of storing computer FILE*s* so that they can be easily read when they are moved from one computer to another 可移植文档格式, 可携式文件格式

pear-shaped /ˋpɛr ˌʃept; ˈpeə ˌʃeɪpt/ *adj*

NEW MEANING

go pear-shaped *BrE slang* if a situation goes pear-shaped, it fails completely or develops in a way that you do not want【英俚】一败涂地, 不如意: *I told him not to borrow so much money, but he wouldn't listen, and now it's all gone pear-shaped.* 我对他说过别借那么多钱, 可他就是不听, 现在什么都完了。

peep /pip; piːp/ *v* [T]

NEW MEANING

slang to look at something because it is interesting or attractive【俚】瞧, 观看: *On our website you can peep our video interview with R&B's newest supergroup.* 在我们的网站, 你可以观赏我们对节奏布鲁斯的最新超级乐队所进行的采访录像。

peer-to-peer /ˌpɪr tə ˋpɪr; ˌpɪə tə ˈpɪə/ also 又作 **P2P** /ˌpi tə ˋpi; ˌpiː tə ˈpiː/ *adj* [only before noun 仅用于名词前]

peer-to-peer architecture/network/technology etc a computer system etc in which all of the computers are connected to each other and they do not need a SERVER (=a main computer that controls all the others). Peer-to-peer networks are simpler and less expensive than CLIENT-SERVER NETWORKS, but they usually can only work well when a small number of computers are in the network〔计算机网络上〕对等的[点对点]架构/网络/技术等: *Setting up a peer-to-peer network is not difficult.* 建立对等网络并不困难。| *How will peer-to-peer technology be important to the average Internet user?* 对等技术对互联网一般用户有什么重要性?

performance en·han·cer /pɚˋfɔrməns ɪnˌhænsɚ; pəˈfɔːməns ɪnˌhɑːnsə/ also 又作 **enhancer** *n* [C] a drug used illegally by people competing in sports events to improve their performance 兴奋剂: *Officials will be testing for the performance enhancer EPO at this year's Olympic Games.* 今年奥运会上官员们将对兴奋剂EPO〔促红细胞生成素〕进行检测。—**performance-enhancing** *adj* [only before noun 仅用于名词前]: *performance-enhancing drugs* 兴奋剂类药物

personal com·mu·ni·ca·tor /ˋpɝsṇḷ kəˋmjunəketɚ; ˈpɜːsənəl kəˈmjuːnɪ̣keɪtə/ *n* [C] a small computer that you can carry with you and use to send, store, and receive FAX*ed*, spoken, or written messages 个人通信器

personal da·ta or·ga·niz·er /ˌpɝsṇḷ ˋdetə ˌɔrgənaɪzɚ; ˌpɜːsənəl ˈdeɪtə ˌɔːgənaɪzə/ *n* [C] a personal digital assistant 个人信息整理器, 个人数码助理

personal di·gi·tal as·sis·tant /ˌpɝsṇḷ ˌdɪdʒətḷ əˋsɪstənt; ˌpɜːsənəl ˌdɪdʒɪ̣tl əˈsɪstənt/ *abbreviation* 缩写为 **PDA** *n* [C]

a very small light computer that you can carry with you, and that you use to store information such as telephone numbers, addresses, and APPOINTMENT*s*. Some personal digital assistants can send and receive E-MAIL, and connect to the Internet 个人数码助理, 掌上电脑: *This site will help you choose the right PDA.* 本网站会帮助你挑选合适的掌上电脑。

personal electronic devices
个人电子器材

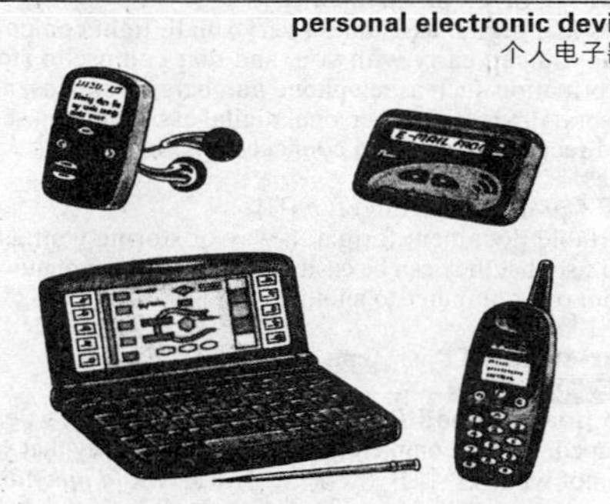

personal el·ec·tron·ic de·vice /ˌpɝsn̩l ɪlɛkˌtrɑnɪk dɪˋvaɪs; ˌpɜːsənəl ɪlekˌtrɒnɪk dɪˈvaɪs/ *n* [C]
a piece of electronic equipment, such as a LAPTOP computer or a MOBILE PHONE, that is small and easy to carry 个人电子器材

personal shop·per /ˌpɝsn̩l ˋʃɑpɚ; ˌpɜːsənəl ˈʃɒpə/ *n* [C]
someone whose job is to help people decide what to buy, or to go shopping for them 个人购物助理

personal train·er /ˌpɝsn̩l ˋtrenɚ; ˌpɜːsənəl ˈtreɪnə/ *n* [C]
someone whose job is to help people decide what type of exercise is best for them and show them how to do it 个人健身教练: *He works out every day with his personal trainer.* 他每天和自己的健身教练一起锻炼。

pet·a·flop /ˋpɛtəˌflɑp; ˈpetəˌflɒp/ *n* [C usually plural 一般用复数]
a unit that measures how fast a computer works. One petaflop is one million BILLION operations every second. 每秒10^{15}次〔浮点运算〕

PET scan /ˋpɛt ˌskæn; ˈpet ˌskæn/ *n* [C]
technical positron emission tomography scan; a type of medical test that can produce a picture of areas in your body where cells are very active, for example the brain or where a TUMOUR is growing【术语】正子造影〔一种医学扫描法〕: *Two people with different levels of intelligence were given PET scans to measure their brain activity while they worked on a difficult problem.* 两个智力水平不同的人接受了正子造影，测定他们在解决一道难题时的大脑活动情况。

phantom pro·mo·tion /ˌfæntəm prəˋmoʃən; ˌfæntəm prəˈməʊʃən/ *n* [C]
a move to a new job in the same company that does not pay better or include more responsibility than the previous job, even though it appears to〔职位的〕假晋升

phat /fæt; fæt/ also 又作 **phat-ass** /ˋfæt ˌæs; ˈfæt ˌæs/ *adj AmE*
slang fashionable, attractive, or desirable【美俚】时髦的，酷的，称心的: *a phat song* 流行的歌 | *These shoes are just so phat.* 这些鞋子真酷。

phe·nom /fɪˋnɑm; fɪˈnɒm/ *n* [C] *AmE*
informal someone who is unusual and impressive because they are very good or successful at something【美，非正式】杰出人才，奇才: *an 18-year-old tennis phenom* 一名18岁的网球奇才

phone sex /ˋfon ˌsɛks; ˈfəʊn ˌseks/ *n* [U]
the activity of talking with someone on the telephone about sex in order to become sexually excited 电话性爱: **have phone sex (with sb)** *She claimed the relationship consisted mainly of him calling her up to have phone sex.* 她声称同他的关系主要由他打电话来进行电话性爱。

phone tree /ˋfon ˌtri; ˈfəʊn ˌtriː/ *n* [C]
informal a list of all the telephone numbers of the people in an organization, the workers in a company etc, showing who should call whom if there is important information that everyone should know【非正式】电话树，员工通讯录

piece /pis; piːs/ *n* [C]
NEW MEANING
spoken humorous **sb's a (real) piece of work** used to say that someone behaves in an unusual or strange way, especially when this is annoying or difficult to deal with【口，幽默】某人真怪

piercing /ˋpɪrsɪŋ; ˈpɪəsɪŋ/ *n* [C,U]
the process of putting holes in different parts of your body, so that you can wear jewellery, or the holes produced in this way〔为悬挂珠宝饰物而在身体某个部位〕穿孔: *people with multiple piercings* 身上有多个穿孔的人

pik·ey /ˋpaɪkɪ; ˈpaɪki/ *n* [C] *BrE*
a disapproving word for someone who is uneducated and does not have much money【英】低教育及低收入人士〔含贬义〕

Pi·la·tes /pɪˋlɑtiz; pɪˈlɑːtiz/ *n* [U]
a type of exercise that is based on YOGA and dance, that you do with special equipment, that makes you push, pull, and stretch, so that your body moves more easily and becomes stronger 普拉提操〔瑜伽式健身操〕: *The YMCA is offering Pilates classes.* 基督教男青年会开办普拉提操课程。| *Pilates is offered in health clubs and independent studios.* 健身俱乐部和独立的排舞室都开设有普拉提操课程。

pink pound /ˌpɪŋk ˋpaʊnd; ˌpɪŋk ˈpaʊnd/ *n* [singular] *BrE*
the money that people who are HOMOSEXUAL have available to spend【英】〔代表同性恋者购买力的〕粉红英镑: *Companies are trying to attract the pink pound.* 各公司力图吸引粉红英镑。

pink slip par·ty /ˌpɪŋk ˋslɪp ˌpɑrtɪ; ˌpɪŋk ˈslɪp ˌpɑːti/ *n* [C] *AmE*
a meeting in a bar where people who have recently lost their jobs get together to talk to each other and help each other find a new job【美】〔酒吧中的〕新失业者聚会: *Judging by the general flow of conversation, most of the pink slip party attendees want to stay in the dot-com world.* 根据交谈中总的趋势，参加新失业者聚会的大多数人仍然想留在互联网这个行业里。

pix·el·at·ed, pixellated /ˋpɪksəletɪd; ˈpɪksəleɪtɪ̣d/ *adj*
consisting of PIXEL*s* (=small spots that combine to form a picture on a computer SCREEN) 像素化的: *pixelated photographs* 像素化照片

plateau /plæˋto; ˈplætəʊ/ *v* [I]
if something plateaus, it reaches and then stays at a particular level 达到并保持一定的水平: *The athletic footwear market has not yet plateaued.* 运动鞋市场还没有达到稳定的水平。

play /ple; pleɪ/ *v* [T]
NEW MEANING
to have a sexual relationship with someone and not tell them you are having other relationships at the same time 玩弄〔异性〕: *She went postal when she found out Jez has been playing her.* 她发现杰斯一直在玩弄自己之后真的发了火。

player /ˋpleɚ; ˈpleɪə/ *n* [C]
NEW MEANING
slang a man who is good at meeting women and persuading them to have sex with him【俚】玩弄女性者

pleath·er /ˋplɛðɚ; ˈpleðə/ *n* [U]
an artificial material that looks like leather and is used to make clothes 人造革: *a pleather jean jacket* 人造革牛仔夹克（衫）

PLS, pls
a written abbreviation of 缩写= 'please', used in E-MAIL or TEXT MESSAGE*s* on MOBILE PHONE*s* 请〔电子邮件和手机短信用语〕

plug and play /ˌplʌg ən ˋple; ˌplʌg ən ˈpleɪ/ *abbreviation* 缩写为 **PnP** *n* [U]
the ability of a computer and a new piece of equipment

to be used together as soon as they are connected〔新设备与计算机连接上〕即插即用

plug-in also 又作 **plugin** /ˋplʌg ɪn; ˈplʌg ɪn/ *n* [C]
a piece of computer SOFTWARE that can be used in addition to existing software in order to make particular PROGRAMS work properly 外加软件，插件

point /pɔɪnt; pɔɪnt/ *n*
NEW MEANING
be on point *slang spoken* used to say that someone is correct about something, or that you agree with what they have said【俚，口】说到点子上: *Your article in last month's issue about the rising cost of CDs was on point.* 你发表在上个月期刊上那篇关于激光唱片涨价的文章真是说到点子上了。

poison pill /ˌpɔɪzn̩ ˋpɪl; ˌpɔɪzən ˈpɪl/ *n* [C]
technical informal something in a company's financial or legal structure that is intended to make it difficult for another company to take control of it【术语，非正式】"毒丸"〔指公司为避免被兼并而给对方设置的障碍〕

pop /pɑp; pɒp/ *n BrE*
informal **take a pop at** to criticize someone in public【英，非正式】当众指责〔某人〕: *When you play for a Premiership football club, you expect people to take a pop at you now and again.* 当你为足球强队效力，你要准备时不时会有人指责你。

pop psy·chol·o·gy /ˌpɑp saɪˋkɑlədʒɪ; ˌpɒp saɪˈkɒlədʒi/ *n* [U]
ways of dealing with personal problems that are made popular on television or in books, but are not considered serious or suitable for every situation 大众心理学

port /pɔrt; pɔːt/ *v* [T]
to move SOFTWARE from one computer system to another 移植〔软件〕: *Can Windows applications be ported to Unix?* 能否把视窗应用软件移植到Unix系统上？

portable /ˋpɔrtəbl̩; ˈpɔːtəbəl/ *adj*
NEW MEANING
portable benefits health insurance, PENSION PLANS etc that workers can keep when they move from one job to another〔换工作时〕可转移的福利〈如医疗保险、退休金计划等〉

portal /ˋpɔrtl̩; ˈpɔːtl/ *n* [C]
NEW MEANING
a WEBSITE that helps you find other websites 门户网站

port·ing /ˋpɔrtɪŋ; ˈpɔːtɪŋ/ *n* [U]
the process of moving SOFTWARE or information from one computer system to another〔软件、信息等的〕移植: *Call in at your local store where a consultant will organise the porting of your mobile phone number to your new network.* 请与本地商店联系，那里有顾问会安排把你的手机号码移到你的新网络去。

posse /ˋpɑsɪ; ˈpɒsi/ *n* [C]
slang a group of friends from a particular place who share an interest in RAP, HIP-HOP, or HOUSE music, considered as a group【俚】〔同一个地区说唱乐等爱好者组成的〕帮派，哥儿们

post[1] /post; pəʊst/ also 又作 **posting** *n* [C]
NEW MEANING
a message sent to an Internet discussion group so that all members of these groups can read it〔在互联网上讨论区发布的〕帖子，留言: *It's amusing to read post after post criticizing the Prime Minister and his views.* 看到一则又一则批评首相及其观点的留言，实在有趣。| *In your last posting, you mentioned something about a new project.* 在上次的留言中，你提到了一个新项目。

post[2] /post; pəʊst/ *v* [T]
NEW MEANING
1 to officially record and announce information about a company's financial situation or a country's economy 公布〔公司财务或国家经济情况〕: *Golden West Financial Corp. posted a 25% gain in second-quarter net income.* 科尔登西部金融公司公布第二季度纯收益增长了25%。| *Shares fell after the government posted worse than expected figures on inflation.* 在政府公布了比预期还糟的通胀数字后，股票下跌了。**2** to put a message or computer document on the Internet so that other people can see it〔在互联网上〕发布〔电子公告〕: *Chris has already asked Matt to post those new flyers on Vivid's website.* 克里斯已要求马特在维维特的网站上发布那些新的广告传单。

postal /ˋpostl̩; ˈpəʊstl/ *adj*
NEW MEANING
go postal *AmE slang* to become very angry and behave in a violent way【美俚】怒不可遏

posting /ˋpostɪŋ; ˈpəʊstɪŋ/ also 又作 **post** *n* [C]
NEW MEANING
a message sent to an Internet discussion group so that all members of these groups can read it〔在互联网上讨论区发布的〕帖子，留言

post-mod·ern /ˌpost ˋmɑdən; ˌpəʊst ˈmɒdn◂/ *adj*
used to describe styles and attitudes that are IRONIC and that are not serious in the way they treat the ideas and beliefs that a lot of people have 后现代的: *They might be a bit young for post-modern, ironic stand-up comedy.* 要表演后现代讽刺滑稽说笑喜剧，他们也许还有点嫩。

POTS /pɑts; pɒts/ *n* [singular]
informal plain old telephone service; the ordinary form of telephone services, rather than newer services such as the Internet【非正式】普通电话服务

power /ˋpauə; ˈpaʊə/ *v*
power sth ↔ **up** *phr v* [T] to make a machine start working 启动，开动: *Never move a computer while it is powered up.* 电脑在操作时不可搬动。

power-brok·ing /ˋpauə ˌbrokɪŋ; ˈpaʊə ˌbrəʊkɪŋ/ *n* [U]
the use of political power or influence, sometimes in an unfair way 政治权力运用: *an article about Washington power-broking in the 1990s* 一篇关于华盛顿在20世纪90年代政坛角力的文章 —**power broker** *n* [C]

power-nap /ˋpauə ˌnæp; ˈpaʊə ˌnæp/ *n* [C]
a short sleep in the middle of the day that helps you to have more energy, do your job better, and make better decisions〔恢复精力的〕午间小睡: *A power-nap lasts no longer than 20 minutes.* 午间小睡一般不超过20分钟。—**power nap** *v* [I]: *Never power nap on your bed.* 不要在床上打盹。

power-shar·ing /ˋpauə ˌʃɛrɪŋ; ˈpaʊə ˌʃeərɪŋ/ *n* [U]
a situation in which two or more people or groups run a government together 权力分享〔两个以上的人[组织]共同执政〕—**power-sharing** *adj* [only before noun 仅用于名词前] *a power-sharing arrangement* 一种权力分享的安排

PPO /ˌpi pi ˋo; ˌpiː piː ˈəʊ/ *n* [U]
preferred provider organization; a type of health insurance in which people can go to any hospital or doctor, but the insurance company pays more to hospitals and doctors in their system than to those outside their system 优先提供者组织〔一种医疗保险〕

PPP /ˌpi pi ˋpi; ˌpiː piː ˈpiː/ *n*
1 *technical* point-to-point protocol; the information that your computer gives to an INTERNET SERVICE PROVIDER using the telephone line, so that you can connect your computer with them and use the Internet, send E-MAIL etc【术语】点对点协议 **2** [U] public-private partnership; a system of providing money for transport systems, hospitals, schools etc where the government pays some money and private INVESTORS provide the rest of the money 公私联营

prairie-dog·ging /ˋprɛrɪ ˌdɔgɪŋ; ˈpreəri ˌdɒgɪŋ/ *n* [U]
humorous the activity of standing up in an office CUBICLE in order to look over the top of the short walls to see what is happening in the rest of the office. This word comes from PRAIRIE DOG (=a small American animal that lives in a hole in the ground) and describes a similarity to the way this animal comes out of its hole and stands up on its back legs to look for danger.【幽默】〔办公室内〕隔着挡板站起来窥视

pre·but·tal /prɪ`bʌtḷ; prɪ'bʌtl/ *n* [C]
a statement that a politician makes saying that a criticism of them is false or unfair, before the criticism has been made〔针对政坛对手提出批评的〕预先驳斥: *Stark issued a prebuttal against his opponent's speech, even before the text was delivered to reporters.* 在对手连演讲词也未发放给记者前, 斯塔克已先发制人, 发表了反驳声明。

predatory lend·ing /ˌprɛdətorɪ `lɛndɪŋ; ˌpredətərɪ 'lendɪŋ/ *n* [U]
the use of unfair practices by banks, especially taking away people's homes, cars etc if they cannot pay back money they have borrowed 掠夺性贷款: *legislation designed to combat predatory lending* 针对掠夺性贷款的法规 **—predatory lender** *n* [C]

predict and pro·vide /prɪˌdɪkt ən prə`vaɪd; prɪˌdɪkt ən prə'vaɪd/ *n* [U] *BrE*
a way of planning things such as new roads by guessing the rate of increase in the number of vehicles using the roads, and building more roads to make sure there is enough space for all of them【英】超前规划〔基于未来需求量而作出规划〕—compare 比较 DEMAND MANAGEMENT

pre-loved /ˌpri `lʌvd; ˌpriː 'lʌvd/ *adj*
a pre-loved house, pet etc has already been owned by someone else; used especially in advertisements to suggest the previous owner cared strongly about the object, animal etc〔尤用于广告中, 表示房子、动物等〕曾被细心照料的: *The Animal Network helps place pre-loved pets with new pet guardians.* 动物网帮助失去关爱的宠物, 为它们找新的保护人。

premium rate /ˌprimɪəm `ret; ˌpriːmiəm 'reɪt◂/ *n*
premium rate number/line/service a telephone connection to a particular service or company that costs a lot more than the usual rate when you call it because the company you are calling takes some of the money that you pay for the call 高价电话号码/线路/服务〔致电某公司需付出高昂电话费, 因该公司从中图利〕: *Companies who advertise misleading job vacancies using premium rate telephone lines are now facing a total ban.* 刊登误导性求职广告的公司使用高价电话线路以从中图利的做法现正面临全面取缔。

prenuptial a·gree·ment /priˌnʌpʃəl ə`grimənt; priːˌnʌpʃəl ə'griːmənt/ also 又作 **prenup** /`prinʌp; 'priːnʌp/ *n* [C]
a legal document that is written before a man and a woman get married, in which they agree things such as how much money each will get if they DIVORCE 婚前协议

pre-owned /ˌpri `ond; ˌpriː 'əʊnd◂/ *adj*
if something that is for sale is pre-owned, it has been owned and used by someone else before; SECOND-HAND. People use this word when they want to make something not sound old 二手(货)的: *Pre-owned cars may still come with a warranty.* 二手车可能仍然有保修单。

pre-pay /`pri ˌpe; 'priː ˌpeɪ/ *adj* [only before noun 仅用于名词前]
pre-pay MOBILE PHONE systems make you pay before you use the service, rather than sending you a demand for money after you have been using the service〔移动电话〕预先付款的

pres·en·tee·is·m /ˌprɛzən`tiɪzəm; ˌprezən'tiːɪzəm/ *n* [U]
a situation when people spend a lot of time at work, even if they are ill or could take a holiday, because they want their employers to see that they are working very hard. This word developed from 'ABSENTEEISM', which means 'absences from work without a good reason'.〔为了讨好雇主的〕故意加班

pri·on /`praɪən; 'praɪən/ *n* [C]
a very small piece of PROTEIN that is thought to cause some infectious brain diseases such as BSE 朊病毒, 普利子〔据认为会引起疯牛病等一些传染性脑疾病〕

probs /prɑbz; prɒbz/ *n BrE*
spoken informal **no probs** used to say that you will be able to do something easily and with no problems【英口, 非正式】没问题: *Don't worry. We'll have it ready by six. No probs.* 别担心, 我们在6点之前就会准备好, 不成问题的。

product place·ment /`prɑdəkt ˌplesmənt; 'prɒdʌkt ˌpleɪsmənt/ *n* [U]
a form of advertising in which a company arranges for one or more of its products to appear in a television programme or a film 产品安插〔在电视节目或电影中使产品出现的一种广告形式〕: *Does product placement have an effect on sales?* 产品安插对销售起作用吗?

pro·fil·ing /`profaɪlɪŋ; 'prəʊfaɪlɪŋ/ *n* [U]
NEW MEANING
1 the way in which some police organizations stop people from particular races or other groups in society in order to ask them questions, search them etc, because they think that people in those groups are more likely to be involved in crimes or do bad things 种族[阶级]定性〔有些警察因认为某类人较可能会犯罪或做坏事而截查他们〕**2** the activity of collecting information about people that you wish to sell something to. Companies do this in order to make their ADVERTISING more effective. 顾客资料收集分析

prop² /prɑp; prɒp/ *n*
NEW MEANING
give props to sb also 又作 **give sb props** *AmE slang* to tell someone, or people in general, that someone has done something well or that you admire them【美俚】称赞某人: *I just want to give all you girls props for going out and showing you can be just as good as us guys.* 姑娘们, 你们出去并证明了你们和我们男孩一样出色, 我要向你们致敬。

proxy serv·er /`prɑksɪ ˌsɝvɚ; 'prɒksi ˌsɜːvə/ *n* [C]
technical a powerful computer which helps a SERVER (=main computer on a network) operate a computer network【术语】代理服务器

Pro·zac /`prozæk; 'prəʊzæk/ *n* [U]
trademark a type of drug used for treating DEPRESSION (=when you feel very unhappy) and ANXIETY (=when you feel very worried). Prozac makes people feel happier, but some doctors worry that people may take it instead of trying to deal with their problems.【商标】百忧解〔一种治疗情绪抑郁的药〕: **be on Prozac** *Ben's been on Prozac for over a year.* 本服用百忧解有一年多了。

psychic in·come /ˌsaɪkɪk `ɪnkʌm; ˌsaɪkɪk 'ɪŋkʌm/ *n* [U]
the feeling of satisfaction, power, importance etc that you get from your job 精神收益〈如工作上得到的满足感、权力等〉

pull·back /`pulbæk; 'pʊlbæk/ *n* [C]
1 the act of moving soldiers away from the area where they were fighting 撤兵: **[+from]** *The government is planning to implement a second pullback from the area.* 政府正计划从该地区第二次撤兵。**2** a reduction in the value, amount or level of something 缩小, 降低: *Don't be surprised if this spring or summer you see a significant pullback in the stock market.* 要是这个春季或夏季看到股票市场有明显的资金撤走, 不要感到惊讶。

pull-down men·u /`pul daun ˌmɛnju; 'pʊl daʊn ˌmenjuː/ *n* [C]
a list of things a computer PROGRAM can do. You make a pull-down menu appear on the computer SCREEN by CLICK*ing* on a special word with a MOUSE.〔电脑〕下拉式菜单

pull strat·e·gy /`pul ˌstrætədʒɪ; 'pʊl ˌstrætɪdʒi/ *n* [C,U]
a method of selling goods, in which a company uses advertising, letters etc to make people want the goods, so that people will ask for the goods at a store and the store will ask the company for the goods to be sold "拉顾客"促销法, 拉式策略〔公司利用广告、信件等推销商品, 有人向店铺查询, 店铺就向该公司取货售卖〕

pulse /pʌls; pʌls/ *v* [I,T]
NEW MEANING
to push a button on a FOOD PROCESSOR to make the machine go on and off regularly, rather than work continuously〔按动食品搅拌器上的按钮〕使有规律地开机[停机]: *Pulse several times until the mixture looks like oatmeal.* 将混合物用食品搅拌器有规律地搅拌几次直到它看上去像燕麦糊那样。

pump /pʌmp; pʌmp/ *v*
pump and dump the act of raising the price of STOCKs that are not worth very much money by buying a large amount of them when they are still cheap, and then selling them at a profit 先买后抛, 低买高沽, 推高出货〔通过大量买进股票引起涨价后再抛出〕

pump-prim·ing /ˋpʌmp ˏpraɪmɪŋ; ˈpʌmp ˌpraɪmɪŋ/ *n* [U]
the process of trying to help a business, industry, or economy to develop by giving it money〔帮助企业、行业或经济发展的〕注入性投资, 资金扶植

push strat·e·gy /ˋpʊʃ ˏstrætədʒɪ; ˈpʊʃ ˌstrætɪ̮dʒi/ *n* [C,U]
a method of selling goods in which a company tries to make stores want to have the goods, for example by selling them to the stores for a much lower price than usual〔公司吸引商店销售其商品的〕减价促销法, 推式策略

push tech·nol·o·gy /ˋpʊʃ tɛkˏnɑlədʒɪ; ˈpʊʃ tekˌnɒlədʒi/ *n* [U]
a system that allows information to be sent regularly over the Internet to people who have asked to receive it〔网上〕推送技术〔定期传送信息给要求收到该信息的人〕

pussy-whipped /ˋpʊsɪ ˏhwɪpt; ˈpʊsi ˌwɪpt/ *adj* [not before noun 不用于名词前] *AmE*
slang an offensive word used to describe a man who does whatever his GIRLFRIEND or wife wants him to do. This expression is used to criticize someone for allowing himself to be treated like this.【美俚】〔冒犯语〕怕老婆的, 受女人支配的

Q,q

QALY /ˏkju e ɛl ˋwaɪ; ˌkjuː eɪ el ˈwaɪ/ *n* [C]
technical quality adjusted life year; a way of measuring how much improvement in their health someone is likely to get as a result of having a particular type of medical treatment in the National Health Service in Britain【术语】〔英国国民保健制度中的〕疗效检查, 质量调整生命年

Q-rat·ing /ˋkju ˏretɪŋ; ˈkjuː ˌreɪtɪŋ/ *n* [C] *AmE*
a way of describing how well known by the public someone is【美】受欢迎程度, 知名度: *His Q-rating increased after he landed a role in a sit-com.* 他在情景喜剧中担任一个角色之后, 人气指数有所上升。

quad bike /ˋkwɑd ˏbaɪk; ˈkwɒd ˌbaɪk/ *n* [C] *BrE*
a small vehicle, similar to a MOTORCYCLE but with four wide wheels, usually ridden on rough paths or fields【英】四轮摩托车; FOUR WHEELER *AmE*【美】

queer·core /ˋkwɪrˏkɔr; ˈkwɪəˌkɔː/ *n* [U]
slang a type of loud fast music performed by musicians who are HOMOSEXUAL【俚】同志朋克核心〔一种由同性恋者演奏的强劲的音乐〕

quotient /ˋkwoʃənt; ˈkwəʊʃənt/ *n* [C]
NEW MEANING
the amount or degree of a quality, feeling etc in a person, thing, or situation 商〈如智商、情绪商数等〉, 指数: *Is all this healthy food supposed to increase my happiness quotient?* 是不是所有这些保健食品都会增加我的幸福指数?

R,r

race-bait·ing /ˋres ˏbetɪŋ; ˈreɪs ˌbeɪtɪŋ/ *n* [U]
the process of using pictures or words that make people afraid of or not trust people of another race, especially in order to gain a political advantage 种族挑拨: *The campaign has been marked by accusations of race-baiting.* 这次竞选因被指责带有种族挑拨成分而蒙上了污点。—**race-bait** *v* [I,T] —**race-baiter** *n* [C]

race card /ˋres ˏkɑrd; ˈreɪs ˌkɑːd/ *n*
NEW MEANING
play the race card if a politician plays the race card, he or she says or writes something which is unfair towards people from a different race, often to try and convince other people to vote for them 打种族牌: *But the leader of the opposition denied that he had been playing the race card, and insisted that his comments had been taken out of context.* 但反对党的领导人否认他在打种族牌, 并坚称他的评论被断章取义了。

rad /ræd; ræd/ *adj*
slang exciting or interesting【俚】顶呱呱的, 棒极的: *Have you guys seen Wendy's new place? It's so rad.* 你们几个见过温迪的新居没有? 棒极了。

ra·dic·chi·o /rəˋdikɪo; rəˈdɪkiəʊ/ *n* [U]
a type of plant used in SALADs that is red and has a bitter taste 菊苣〔做沙拉用的一种菜〕

-rage /redʒ; reɪdʒ/ *suffix* [in nouns 构成名词]
used to describe the particular situations in which people become extremely angry and violent. For example, road-rage is when someone becomes angry and violent because of something that happens while they are driving; air-rage happens when a passenger in a plane becomes angry and violent etc. 盛怒, 暴怒〔发作〕〈如 road-rage 路上驾车狂怒, air-rage 飞行途中狂怒等〉

rail trail /ˋrel ˏtrel; ˈreɪl ˌtreɪl/ *n* [C] *AmE*
a path that used to be a railway track but has been covered with a hard surface for people to walk, run, or ride bicycles on【美】〔铺设硬路面因而让人可以通行或骑车的〕铁轨路

ramp /ræmp; ræmp/ *v*
ramp sth ↔ **up** *phr v* [T] **1** to try to persuade people that a company's SHAREs are worth more than they really are 推高〔公司股票价格〕: *To ramp up a share price during a takeover bid is unacceptable.* 在出价收购期间推高股票的价格是不能接受的。**2** if a company ramps up an activity, it increases it 增加〔某种活动〕: *Producers can quickly ramp up production to prevent any shortages.* 制造商可以迅速增加生产以防止缺货。

rat /ræt; ræt/ *v*
rat sb **out** [T] *AmE informal* to be disloyal to someone, especially by telling a person in authority about something wrong that he or she has done【美, 非正式】背信弃义: *You can't rat out your teammates.* 你不可以出卖你的队友。

rat run /ˋræt ˏrʌn; ˈræt ˌrʌn/ *n* [C]
a small road, often with houses along it, which is used by drivers as a quicker way of going somewhere, instead of using a larger road which has more traffic 住宅区小路, 捷径

real /ˋriəl; rɪəl/ *adj*
NEW MEANING
keep it real *AmE spoken* used to tell someone to behave in an honest way and not pretend to be different from how they really are【美口】〔老实点〕别装蒜

reality check /rɪˋælətɪ ˏtʃɛk; riˈælɪ̮ti ˌtʃek/ *n* [C usually singular 一般用单数]
informal an occasion when you consider the facts of a situation, as opposed to what you would like or what you have imagined【非正式】面对现实: *It's time for a reality check. The Bears aren't as good a team as you think.* 该是面对现实的时候了, 熊队不像你想象的那么优秀。

reality soft·ware /rɪˋælətɪ ˏsɔftwɛr; riˈælɪ̮ti ˌsɒftweə/ *n* [U]
technical computer PROGRAMs that allow you to show

pictures on a screen that have height, depth, and length, so that you seem to see or be inside a real place【术语】现实仿真软件

re-chip /ˌri `tʃɪp; ˌriː ˈtʃɪp/ *v* [T] to put a new computer CHIP into a piece of electronic equipment such as a MOBILE PHONE or a computer games CONSOLE so that you can use SOFTWARE that you are not supposed to use, or use a service that you have not paid for 给…装上新的芯[晶]片

red goods /ˈrɛd ˌgudz; ˈred ˌgʊdz/ *n* [plural] goods such as food that people use quickly after buying them, and that do not make a lot of profit〔食品等低利润、消耗快的〕大路货, 消耗品

red-line /ˌrɛd `laɪn; ˌred ˈlaɪn◂/ *adj* **red-line issue** something that you want to do, or that you want to happen, and that you continue to want even when someone offers you something else instead; used especially when people are involved in political or business NEGOTIATIONS〔尤用于政治或商业谈判中〕坚持不懈追求的目标, 坚定的方针: *Keeping the pound is a red-line issue as far as this party is concerned.* 就该党而言, 继续使用英镑是其始终坚持的目标。

red-top /ˈrɛd ˌtɑp; ˈred ˌtɒp/ *n* [C] *BrE* *informal* a British newspaper that has its name in red at the top of the front page. Red tops have a lot of readers, but are not considered to be as serious as other newspapers.【英, 非正式】通俗小报〔因其头版顶端的报纸名称套红刊印而得名〕

re·for·mat /ri`fɔrmæt; riːˈfɔːmæt/ **reformatted, reformatting** *v* [T] if you reformat a document, you change the way it is organized or arranged, for example the amount of space between lines 使〔文件〕重新设置格式: *The books will be condensed and reformatted for electronic reading.* 这些书将被压缩并重新设计格式以供电子阅读。

re·home /ri`hom; riːˈhəʊm/ *v* [T] to arrange for a pet to have a new owner and home, especially a pet that has been looked after in a SHELTER 安排重新收养〔宠物〕, 为〔宠物〕找寻新家: *The kittens have been rehomed.* 小猫已经被重新收养。| *We thought it would be difficult to rehome a maimed animal.* 我们以为为伤残动物寻找新家会很困难。

rei·ki /ˈrekɪ; ˈreɪki/ *n* [U] a type of medicine of Japanese origin in which a person touches someone who has a mental or a physical illness in order to make them more healthy 灵气〔源自日本的一种接触疗法〕: *I can't come on Thursday. That's the night I see my reiki healer.* 我星期四来不了, 正好那天晚上我要看灵气医师。

re-look, relook /ri`luk; riːˈlʊk/ *v* [I+at] to consider something for a second time after you have already considered it 再考虑: *I think we should relook at John's proposal for car parking restrictions outside.* 我认为我们应重新考虑约翰提出的关于限制在户外停车的建议。—**relook** /ˈriluk; ˈriːlʊk/ *n* [C]: *The ministry ordered a relook at the contract.* 部长命令对该合同再作一次审查。

remote ac·cess /rɪˌmot `æksɛs; rɪˌməʊt ˈækses/ *n* [U] a system that allows you to use information on a computer that is far away from your computer〔电脑的〕远程存取, 远程访问

remote in·ter·ro·ga·tion /rɪˌmot ɪntɛrə`geʃən; rɪˌməʊt ɪnterəˈgeʃən/ *n* [U] the process of calling your own telephone when you are away from your home or office so that you can listen to messages that people have left on your ANSWERPHONE 远程电话留言查询

remote work·ing /rɪˌmot `wɝkɪŋ; rɪˌməʊt ˈwɜːkɪŋ/ *n* [U] a situation in which people do their work at home, using a computer that is connected to the computer system in an office 远程工作〔通过与办公室的电脑联网在家里工作〕

rep /rɛp; rep/ *v* *slang*【俚】**1** [T] to be someone's representative 代表〔某人〕: *It didn't take me long to realize that I wasn't very good with a camera, so I started repping other photographers.* 没有过多久我就意识到自己在摄影方面不太在行, 于是我就当起了其他摄影师的代表。**2** [I] to be proud of your beliefs, your nationality, your race etc, and to make your feelings obvious to other people 自豪

re·plat·form /ri`plætfɔrm; riːˈplætfɔːm/ *v* [T] *BrE*【英】**be replatformed** when a train is replatformed, passengers have to go to a different part of the station than usual in order to get on it 换站台 —**replatformed** *adj*: *The replatformed 19:47 to Leeds will now leave from platform six.* 19点47分开往利兹的火车将换到6号站台开车。

report /rɪ`port; rɪˈpɔːt/ *n* [C] *BrE*

NEW MEANING

someone who works for a particular manager【英】〔经理的〕下属: *Only Gordon's direct reports are attending the training course.* 只有戈登的直系下属在参加培训课程。

re·pur·pose /ri`pɝpəs; riːˈpɜːpəs/ *v* [T] if something such as equipment, a building, or a document is repurposed, it is used in a new way that is different from its original use, without having to be changed very much 改变用途: *We put a lot of material up on our website simply by repurposing our exising catalog and other content from our products.* 我们只是改变了一下现有的产品目录和其他内容, 就把大量的材料放上我们的网站上。

rescue rem·e·dy /ˈrɛskju ˌrɛmədɪ; ˈreskjuː ˌreməˌdi/ *n* [C] *BrE* an oil made from flowers that is used to make you feel calmer when you are not well or nervous【英】镇静药

retail ther·a·py /ˌritel `θɛrəpɪ; ˌriːteɪl ˈθerəpi/ *n* [U] *humorous* the act of buying things that you do not need when you are unhappy because you think it will make you feel better【幽默】购物疗法: *What you need is a bit of retail therapy!* 你需要接受一点购物治疗!

re·tro·vi·rus /ˈrɛtroˌvaɪrəs; ˈretrəʊˌvaɪərəs/ *n* [C] a VIRUS of a type that includes some cancer viruses and the AIDS virus, but that also has a quality that makes it useful for GENETIC ENGINEERING 逆转录病毒〔包含一些癌症病毒和艾滋病病毒的一种病毒, 用于基因工程中〕

re-up /ri `ʌp; riː ˈʌp/ *v* [I] *informal* to agree to work on something or for someone again, used especially about work in television, and film-making or sports【非正式】同意再次做…; 同意为…继续干〔尤指电视、电影制作或运动方面〕: *Several of the actors have agreed to re-up for a sequel to the movie.* 有几名演员已同意再为该部影片拍续集。

reverse en·gi·neering /rɪˌvɝs ɛndʒə`nɪrɪŋ; rɪˌvɜːs endʒəˈnɪərɪŋ/ *n* [U] *technical* a situation in which a product is examined to see how it is made, so that it can be copied【术语】逆向工程, 反向工程 —**reverse engineer** *v* [T]

revolving door /rɪˌvɑlvɪŋ `dor; rɪˌvɒlvɪŋ ˈdɔː/ *n* [singular]

NEW MEANING

1 used to say that the people involved in a situation, organization etc change often 人员流动频繁: *The park director position has been a revolving door for seven appointees.* 公园经理这个职位已经接二连三地换了七个人。**2** used to say that people return to a situation, position etc often, but usually for a different reason 旋转门〔指出于不同理由而屡次重返某场合或职位等〕: *This could mean that we end up with a revolving door Congress, in which former members return as lobbyists.* 这可能意味着我们的国会最后就成了一道旋转门, 一些前议员退下后又回来, 摇身一变成了从事院外活动的说客。

right·size /ˋraɪtsaɪz; ˈraɪtsaɪz/ *v* [I,T]
if a company or organization rightsizes, or if it rightsizes its operations, it reduces the number of people it employs in order to reduce costs. This word developed from 'DOWNSIZE', which has the same meaning, and is used to make the reduction in the number of workers sound good and sensible 缩小〔公司等的〕规模, 精简: *They have been given one year to rightsize their workforce.* 他们有一年时间精简职工人数。—**rightsizing** *n* [U]: *Many aerospace workers lost their jobs as a result of rightsizing.* 航空航天部门的许多工人因裁员而失去了工作。

ring·tone /ˋrɪŋton; ˈrɪŋtəʊn/ *n* [C]
the sound made by a telephone, especially a MOBILE PHONE, when someone is calling it〔电话, 尤指手机的〕铃声: *Select a personal ringtone for your mobile from over 700 great tunes, including pop, rock, TV and movies.* 请从包括流行音乐、摇滚乐、影视音乐等超过700种乐曲中给你的手机挑选一种个性化的铃声。

riot grrl also 又作 **riot girl** /ˋraɪət ˌgɝl; ˈraɪət ˌgɜːl/ *n* [C]
a young woman who believes that women should have the same rights and opportunities as men, especially one who uses music to express this belief in an angry and determined way 反叛女孩〔尤指通过用音乐等愤怒并坚决地表达其信仰的女权主义者〕

rip /rɪp; rɪp/ *v*
rip on sb/sth *phr v* [T] *AmE slang* to complain a lot about someone or something【美俚】抨击, 严厉批评: *Ginny's always ripping on her boss.* 金妮总是向老板发牢骚。

ripped /rɪpt; rɪpt/ *adj*
slang having large strong-looking muscles【俚】肌肉发达的: *Fisher's sculpted, ripped physique* 费希尔像雕塑一般健壮的体形 | *How can I get lean and ripped?* 我怎样才能既清瘦又结实呢?

Rit·a·lin /ˋrɪtḷɪn; ˈrɪtəlɪn/ *n* [U]
trademark a drug that is used to treat ATTENTION DEFICIT HYPERACTIVITY DISORDER (=a condition that causes people, especially children, to be too active and not able to pay attention for very long)【商标】利他林〔一种用于治疗儿童多动症的药物〕: *Zack's parents don't want to put him on Ritalin.* 扎克的父母不想让他服用利他林。

road pric·ing /ˋrod ˌpraɪsɪŋ; ˈrəʊd ˌpraɪsɪŋ/ *n* [U]
a system in which drivers have to pay to use the roads at particular times 道路收费(制度)〔在某些时段收费以缓和交通拥堵〕: *Road pricing could fund pollution reduction projects.* 道路收费能为减轻污染项目提供资金。| *road pricing schemes for congested cities* 针对交通拥堵城市的道路收费计划

road war·ri·or /ˋrod ˌwɔrɪɚ; ˈrəʊd ˌwɒriə/ *n* [C]
slang someone who uses computers, MOBILE PHONE*s*, PAGER*s* etc in a place other than their home or office【俚】道路勇士〔指经常在路上奔波并使用便携式电脑、手机、传呼机等的人〕

roam·ing /ˋromɪŋ; ˈrəʊmɪŋ/ *n* [U]
the process that a MOBILE PHONE uses when it is in a different country or region from usual, and has to connect to a different NETWORK (手机)漫游: *Our international roaming facility allows you to use 198 networks in 91 countries worldwide.* 我们的国际漫游功能能让你使用全球91个国家的198个网络。

rock¹ /rɑk; rɒk/ *n* [U]
NEW MEANING
1 a very pure form of the illegal drug COCAINE, that some people smoke for pleasure 石毒〔结晶体可卡因〕**2** [C] a small amount of this drug 少量石毒

rock² /rɑk; rɒk/ *v*
NEW MEANING
sb/sth rocks *slang* said to show that you strongly approve of someone or something【俚】某人/某物特别棒: *This band still rocks.* 这支乐队仍然很棒。

rocket sci·en·tist /ˋrɑkɪt ˌsaɪəntɪst; ˈrɒkɪ̆t ˌsaɪəntɪ̆st/ *n* [C]
informal【非正式】**1 it doesn't take a rocket scientist** said to emphasize that something is easy to do or understand 这不需要有高深学问: *It doesn't take a rocket scientist to work out that doubling productivity will improve profits.* 生产率加倍会提高利润, 这用不着学问高深的人也能想得到。**2** someone who is extremely clever and intelligent 特别聪明的人, 智力超常者: *Just cos my brother's a rocket scientist doesn't mean I know all the answers.* 我哥哥是天才并不等于我什么都懂。**3** someone working for a financial company who uses advanced mathematics to calculate what INVESTMENT*s* to make, to design new financial products etc 股市[投资]分析高手, 金融工程学家

rock 'n' roll /ˋrɑk ən ˋrol; ˌrɒk ən ˈrəʊl/ *n*
NEW MEANING
sth is the new rock 'n' roll *BrE* used to say that a particular activity has become very popular and fashionable and is being discussed a lot on television, in newspapers etc【英】某事是非常流行和热门的活动: *Hadn't Mark heard that cooking was the new rock 'n' roll?* 马克难道没有听说烹饪是新的热门活动吗?

rogue trad·er /ˌrog ˋtredɚ; ˌrəʊg ˈtreɪdə/ *n* [C]
a STOCKBROKER who takes a lot of risks without permission from the company he or she works for, and who sometimes loses a lot of money and tries to hide this 无赖交易人〔未经公司授权进行风险投资而造成巨大损失的证券经纪人〕: *The Bank says a rogue trader in New York secretly racked up $1.1 billion in losses over 11 years.* 该银行说纽约的一名违规交易人员在过去11年来私下累计造成了11亿美元的亏损。

roll /rol; rəʊl/ *v*
NEW MEANING
roll sth ↔ **out** to make a new product available for people to buy or use 推出〔新产品〕: *L'Oreal rolled out a line of skin-care products called Plenitude.* 欧莱雅公司推出了一系列称为"佛兰特"的护肤新产品。

roof·ies /ˋrufɪz; ˈruːfiz/ *n* [plural] *AmE*
slang an illegal drug that is sometimes used to make someone unconscious so they can be RAPE*d*【美俚】迷奸药〔一种令人失去知觉进而实施强奸的违禁药〕

ROTFL, rotfl
a written abbreviation of 缩写= 'rolling on the floor laughing', used by people communicating in CHAT ROOM*s* on the Internet to say that they are laughing very hard at something that someone else has written 笑死人了〔网上聊天室用语〕

rout·er /ˋrutɚ; ˈruːtə/ *n* [C]
technical a piece of electronic equipment that makes sending messages between different computers or between different networks easier and faster【术语】路由器

RTF /ˌɑr ti ˋɛf; ˌɑː tiː ˈef/ *n* [U]
technical Rich Text Format; a system used to arrange and show the information in computer documents【术语】丰富文本格式〔计算机文件的一种格式〕

RTM
the written abbreviation of 缩写= 'read the manual', used by people whose job is to answer questions from customers who have problems with computer SOFTWARE or other equipment, when they think a customer's question is stupid and the customer could have easily found the answer by reading the instructions for using the product 请读手册〔用于回答顾客有关软件等方面的问题〕

rur·ban /ˋrɝbən; ˈrɜːbən/ *adj*
happening or relating to areas on the edge of cities that are being developed and may soon become part of the city. This word is a combination of the words 'rural' meaning to do with the countryside, and 'urban' which means to do with towns. 发生在城乡结合地区的; 与城乡结合地区有关的: *rurban areas north of London* 伦敦北部城乡结合地区

S,s

SAD /ˌɛs e ˋdi, sæd; ˌes eɪ ˈdiː, sæd/ *n* [U]
seasonal affective disorder; a feeling of sadness and lack of energy that some people get in the winter because there is not enough light from the sun 季节性情感紊乱

safe /sef; seɪf/ *adj BrE*
NEW MEANING
slang used to say that something is fine and that there is no problem【英俚】不错的, 挺好的: *"How's your new boss?" "She's safe."* "你的新老板好吗?" "她挺好的。"

sal·a·ry·man /ˋsælərɪˌmæn; ˈsælərimæn/ *n plural* **salarymen** /-ˌmɛn; -men/ [C]
a man who works in an office, often for many hours each day, and receives a salary as payment, especially in Japan〔尤指日本的〕白领阶层人士

same-sex /ˌsem ˋsɛks; ˌseɪm ˈseks◂/ *adj*
same-sex marriage/relationship etc a marriage, relationship etc between two men or two women 同性婚姻/关系等

sample[1] /ˋsæmpl̩; ˈsɑːmpəl/ *n* [C]
NEW MEANING
a small part of a song from a CD or record that is used in a new song〔用于新乐曲中的〕节录乐曲, 选录乐曲: *Her latest album makes extensive use of samples from a wide range of acid jazz tracks.* 她最新的一张专辑广泛采用了迷幻爵士乐的节录乐曲。

sample[2] /ˋsæmpl̩; ˈsɑːmpəl/ *v* [T]
NEW MEANING
to use a small part of a song from a CD or record in a new song 将…节录[选录]: *His songs have often been sampled by other people.* 他的歌曲经常被他人节录。

sampler /ˋsæmplɚ; ˈsɑːmplə/ *n* [C]
NEW MEANING
a machine that can record sounds or music so that you can change them and use them for a new piece of music 音乐节录器

satellite /ˋsætl̩ˌaɪt; ˈsætl̩laɪt/ *v*
satellite sb **out** *phr v* to move a worker in a large company to an office or place of business that is smaller and separate from the company's main building 把〔大公司的职工〕派到分公司: *They've decided to satellite Melrose out.* 他们已决定把梅尔罗斯调到分公司去。

sat·u·rate /ˋsætʃərɪt; ˈsætʃərl̩t/ *n* [C,U]
a type of fat from meat or milk products that is thought to be less healthy than other kinds of fat from vegetables or fish; SATURATED FAT 饱和脂肪: *Choose a type of spread that's lower in saturates than butter.* 挑选一种饱和脂肪含量低于黄油的涂酱。

scal·a·bil·i·ty /ˌskeləˋbɪlətɪ; ˌskeɪləˈbɪll̩ti/ *n* [U]
a computer system's scalability is the degree to which it is able to grow and become more powerful as the number of people using it increases〔电脑系统的〕可缩放性, 可变比例性

SCART /skɑrt; skɑːt/ *n* [C]
a piece of equipment used in some countries to connect electrical equipment and transfer VIDEO and AUDIO signals from one piece of equipment to another, for example from a VIDEO RECORDER to a television〔连接录像和音响等设备的〕21针连接器: *a SCART cable* 21针连接器电缆

school run /ˋskul ˌrʌn; ˈskuːl ˌrʌn/ *n* [C usually singular 一般用单数] *BrE*
a time when parents drive their children to school in the morning or home from school in the afternoon【英】父母开车接送孩子上下学: **do the school run** *We hope to increase the safety of children who walk to school and cut the number of cars doing the school run.* 我们希望能提高学童步行上学的安全, 以减少父母接送的车辆。

schtick /ʃtɪk; ʃtɪk/ *n* [singular]
a typical quality or feature that someone, especially an entertainer, is famous for〔演员等的〕独特风格: *Eminem's whole schtick is being outrageous, so he gets to do whatever he wants to do.* 埃米纳姆的独特风格就是肆无忌惮, 所以他能做想做的任何事情。

scratch·card /ˋskrætʃˌkɑrd; ˈskrætʃkɑːd/ *n* [C] *BrE*
a small card you can buy which gives you a chance to win a prize. You rub off the surface of the card to find out whether you have won anything, for example by uncovering three SYMBOL*s* of the same type.【英】〔封蜡刮去后能显示中奖与否的〕刮刮卡

scratch·ing /ˋskrætʃɪŋ; ˈskrætʃɪŋ/ *n* [U]
a special type of sound used in RAP MUSIC, which is produced by pushing a RECORD backwards and forwards on a TURNTABLE with your hands〔说唱乐中使用的〕擦音

scratch·pad /ˋskrætʃˌpæd; ˈskrætʃpæd/ *n* [C]
a small screen on a MOBILE PHONE that lets you write short notes and stores them for you〔移动电话的〕手写屏幕

screen /skrin; skriːn/ *v*
NEW MEANING
screen (your) calls to find out who is calling you on the telephone, especially by using an ANSWERING MACHINE, so that you do not have to speak to someone you do not want to speak to 筛选来电

screen·a·ger /ˋskrinedʒɚ; ˈskriːneɪdʒə/ *n* [C]
informal a young person who spends a lot of time using computers and the Internet【非正式】〔热衷于使用电脑和互联网的〕屏幕青少年

screen dump /ˋskrin ˌdʌmp; ˈskriːn ˌdʌmp/ *n* [C]
a picture of everything that appears on a computer screen at a particular time, which can be saved and put into a computer document, for example to show how to use a computer PROGRAM 屏幕转储

scrunch·y, scrunchie /ˋskrʌntʃɪ; ˈskrʌntʃi/ *n* [C]
a small circular piece of rubber that is covered with cloth, used for holding hair together in a PONYTAIL〔扎头发的〕布包橡皮圈, 橡皮头绳

SCSI /ˋskʌzɪ; ˈskʌzi/ *n* [U]
small computer systems interface; something that helps a small computer work with another piece of electronic equipment, such as a PRINTER, especially when they are connected by wires 小型电脑系统界面, SCSI接口[端口]: *a SCSI port* SCSI接口, SCSI端口

scuz·zy /ˋskʌzɪ; ˈskʌzi/ *n* [C]
informal the usual pronunciation of SCSI. People sometimes also write 'scuzzy' to mean SCSI.【非正式】〔SCSI的通常发音, 有时也作为SCSI的书写形式〕: *What's the biggest scuzzy hard drive you have?* 你最大的SCSI接口[端口]硬盘是什么?

search en·gine /ˋsɝtʃ ˌɛndʒən; ˈsɜːtʃ ˌendʒl̩n/ *n* [C]
a computer PROGRAM that helps you find information on the Internet 搜索引擎: *You could try typing your query into another search engine.* 你可以试着把你的问题键入另一个搜索引擎。

seasonal af·fect·ive dis·or·der /ˌsizn̩əl əˌfɛktɪv dɪsˋɔrdɚ; ˌsiːzənəl əˌfektɪv dɪsˈɔːdə/ *abbreviation* 缩写为 **SAD** *n* [U]
a feeling of sadness and lack of energy that some people get in the winter because there is not enough light from the sun 季节性情感紊乱

sector fund /ˋsɛktɚ ˌfʌnd; ˈsektə ˌfʌnd/ *n* [C]
technical a type of INVESTMENT in which the money buys many different STOCK*s* in a particular area of the ECONOMY, such as electronics, health care etc【术语】行业型基金〔购入某一经济领域多种股票的投资方式〕

seed mon·ey /ˋsid ˌmʌnɪ; ˈsiːd ˌmʌni/ *n* [U]
the money needed to start a new business idea or project〔启动一项新事业的〕种子基金, 创业基金: *How much seed money will be needed to pay for the new factory?* 开办这个新厂需要多少种子基金?

seismic /ˋsaɪzmɪk; ˈsaɪzmɪk/ *adj*

NEW MEANING
very great, serious, or important 十分重大的: *seismic changes in international relations* 国际关系方面的重大改变

self·build, self-build /ˌsɛlfˋbɪld; ˌselfˈbɪld◂/ *n* [U]
the activity of building your own house rather than paying professional builders to do it for you 自己建房: *a selfbuild kit* 自己建房的全套工具 **—self-builder** *n* [C]

self-di·rec·ted /ˌsɛlf dəˋrɛktɪd; ˌself dʒˈrektɪd◂/ *adj* [only before noun 仅用于名词前] *AmE*
self-directed workers are responsible for organizing and judging their own work, rather than getting instructions from other people【美】自主的, 无需他人指示的

senior mo·ment /ˋsinjɚ ˌmomənt; ˈsiːniə ˌməʊmənt/ *n* [C usually singular 一般用单数] *AmE*
informal humorous a short period of time when you are unable to remember a fact or piece of information that you are sure you know or should know. This expression is related to the phrase 'senior citizen' which is a polite way of talking about an old person【美, 非正式, 幽默】老痴呆瞬间〔短时间出现遗忘, 由 senior citizen 衍生而来〕: **have a senior moment** *Oh, what's her name, the woman at the reception desk. Sorry, I'm having a senior moment.* 唉, 接待处的那位女士叫什么名字? 不好意思, 我一时头脑短路。

sensitivity train·ing /sɛnsəˋtɪvətɪ ˌtrenɪŋ; sensʒˈtɪvʒti ˌtreɪnɪŋ/ *n* [U]
training that teaches people to have more respect for people of different races, people who are DISABLED etc, especially as part of their job〔尊重其他种族的人、残疾人等的〕敏感训练

serial mo·nog·a·my /ˌsɪrɪəl məˋnɑgəmɪ; ˌsɪəriəl məˈnɒgəmi/ *n* [U]
the practice of having several romantic relationships in which you only have one sexual partner and do not see anyone else 系列单配偶制, 阶段性单配偶生活 **—serial monogamist** *n* [C]

ser·o·to·nin /ˌsɛrəˋtonɪn; ˌserəˈtəʊnɪn/ *n* [U]
technical a chemical in the body that helps carry messages from the brain and is believed to make you feel happy【术语】血清素, 5-羟色胺

server /ˋsɝvɚ; ˈsɜːvə/ *n* [C]
NEW MEANING
someone whose job is to bring you your food in a restaurant〔餐馆中的〕服务员, 侍者: *Our server told us about the day's specials.* 服务员给我们介绍了当天的特色菜。

server farm /ˋsɝvɚ ˌfɑrm; ˈsɜːvə ˌfɑːm/ *n* [C]
an office which has a large amount of computer equipment holding all the SOFTWARE and DATA for WEBSITE*s* 服务器农场, 服务器组群〔具有大量电脑软件和网址信息的电脑设备所在的办公室〕: *Massive server farms are beginning to cause problems for local jurisdictions that have to deal with the sudden increase in demand for power.* 大规模的服务器组群开始为地区管辖带来了问题, 管理当局不得不应付突然增加的电力需求。

set-a·side /ˋsɛt əˌsaɪd; ˈset əˌsaɪd/ *n* [C,U]
1 an amount of money that is kept so that it can be used for a special purpose; RESERVE 储备金 **2** *BrE* an arrangement in which a government pays farmers to leave part of their fields empty, to avoid producing too much of a crop and to keep prices of those crops higher【英】〔政府提供津贴让农户减少农作物产量以保持高价位的〕农田闲置措施 **3** in the US, an arrangement in which a local government helps small businesses to develop by making loans and other financial help available to them〔美国地方政府提供给小企业的〕信贷支持措施: *In 1976, Connecticut established one of the nation's first setaside programs.* 1976年, 康涅狄格州制定了小企业扶持计划, 这在全美国属于最早的一批。

set-top box /ˋsɛt tɑp ˌbɑks; ˈset tɒp ˌbɒks/ *n* [C] *BrE*
a piece of electronic equipment that is connected to your television to make it able to receive a different form of BROADCASTING, especially DIGITAL signals【英】机顶盒〔连接在电视机上尤用于接收数码信号的电子设备〕

sex tour·is·m /ˋsɛks ˌturɪzəm; ˈseks ˌtʊərɪzəm/ *n* [U]
the activity of travelling to other countries in order to have sex, especially sexual activities that are illegal in your own country 性旅游业, 色情旅游业: *Sex tourism is closely connected with child prostitution throughout the world.* 世界各地的色情旅游业都和童妓有着密切的关联。**—sex tourist** *n* [C]

sex work·er /ˋsɛks ˌwɝkɚ; ˈseks ˌwɜːkə/ *n* [C]
formal a polite expression for a PROSTITUTE【正式】性工作者〔娼妓的婉称〕

SGML /ˌɛs dʒi ɛm ˋɛl; ˌes dʒiː em ˈel/ *n* [U]
technical standard generalized markup language; a way of writing a document on a computer so that its structure is clear, and so that it can easily be read on a different computer system【术语】标准通用标记语言〔用这种计算机语言编写的文件结构清晰, 便于在其他计算机系统上阅读〕

shadow e·con·o·my /ˌʃædo ɪˋkɑnəmɪ; ˌʃædəʊ ɪˈkɒnəmi/ *n* [C]
technical business activities that are difficult for the authorities to find out about, for example because they are illegal【术语】影子经济, 地下经济〔往往属于非法〕

shake /ʃek; ʃeɪk/ *v*
NEW MEANING
shake down *phr v* [I] if a new situation or arrangement shakes down, people start to get used to it and it becomes more effective〔新情况或安排〕逐渐为人们所适应: *The restructure has shaken down, and staff are showing a new sense of purpose.* 这次改组已经为人们所适应, 全体员工表现出一种新的干劲。
NEW MEANING
shake out *phr v* **1** [I] if an organization or industry shakes out, it becomes calmer after a difficult period of time 恢复元气: *He'll look for bargains in a year or two, after the real estate market shakes out.* 一两年后, 等房地产市场恢复元气后, 他将设法买便宜货。**2** [T] **shake** sth ↔ **out** to change a situation by removing things from it that are not useful or that do not make a profit 淘汰, 剔除〔没有用或不赢利的东西〕: *As the airline industry shakes out all but the very fittest, catering companies could face serious troubles.* 随着航空业汰弱留强, 配餐公司有可能会面临重大困难。

shake·down /ˋʃekdaun; ˈʃeɪkdaʊn/ *n* [C]
1 a period of time when people start to get used to a new arrangement and it becomes more effective 适应调整期 **2** a period of time when prices are falling on a financial market〔金融市场的〕疲软时期

shark re·pel·lent /ˋʃɑrk rɪˌpɛlənt; ˈʃɑːk rɪˌpelənt/ *n* [C,U] *AmE*
informal an action that a company takes to make it less likely that another company will try to control it【美, 非正式】驱鲨行动〔反收购措施〕: *How could the adoption of a shark repellent affect a firm's long-term performance?* 采取驱鲨行动会如何影响一家公司的长期业绩呢?

shark watch·er /ˋʃɑrk ˌwɑtʃɚ; ˈʃɑːk ˌwɒtʃə/ *n* [C]
informal a company whose business is to discover that someone may be trying to take control of other companies, for example by buying a lot of SHARE*s*, and to give advice about what those companies should do【非正式】反收购侦探公司, 鲨鱼观察员

sharp /ʃɑrp; ʃɑːp/ *adj*
NEW MEANING
not be the sharpest knife in the drawer *BrE humorous* to be stupid or slow to learn or understand things【英, 幽默】迟钝的, 不机灵的: *Dave might not be the sharpest knife in the drawer, but he's a nice guy.* 戴夫也许不够机灵, 可是个好人。

shed·load /ˈʃɛdlod; ˈʃedləʊd/ *n*
shedloads of sth *BrE informal* a lot of something【英，非正式】一大堆，许许多多: *They've got shedloads of stuff for sale.* 他们有一大批东西要出售。

shock jock /ˈʃɑk ˌdʒɑk; ˈʃɒk ˌdʒɒk/ *n* [C] *especially AmE*
someone on a radio show who plays music and talks about subjects that offend many people【尤美】震撼骑师〔惊世骇俗、出言不逊的电台音乐节目主持人〕

short sell·ing /ˌʃɔrt ˈsɛlɪŋ; ˌʃɔːt ˈselɪŋ/ *n* [U]
the practice of selling SHARES, currencies (CURRENCY) etc immediately after buying them, and then buying them back again later when the price has become lower, in order to make a profit 卖空: *Critics of short selling say it can cause huge falls in prices.* 卖空的批评者说这会造成价格的暴跌。

shorty /ˈʃɔrtɪ; ˈʃɔːti/ *n* [C]
NEW MEANING
slang【俚】**1** a word meaning a woman, used especially by people who play or listen to HIP-HOP music 娘儿们〔嬉蹦音乐家、爱好者尤常用〕: *I love it when a shorty can hang out with me when I drink.* 我喜欢在喝酒时有个娘儿们陪在身边。**2** a word meaning a baby, used especially by people who play or listen to HIP-HOP music 娃娃〔嬉蹦音乐家、爱好者尤常用〕: *Shawna says she's gonna be having my shorty.* 肖娜说她怀了我的孩子。

shov·el·ware /ˈʃʌvl̩ˌwɛr; ˈʃʌvəlˌweə/ *n* [U]
information that first appears in printed form, for example in a book or newspaper, and then is put onto the Internet or CD-ROM without any new or interesting ways to look at or use the information 铲件〔指毫无新意的媒体产品，内容只是照搬印刷品〕: *Many of the educational software titles are nothing but shovelware.* 许多教育软件只是照搬书刊的内容而已。

shroud-wav·ing /ˈʃraud ˌwevɪŋ; ˈʃraʊd ˌweɪvɪŋ/ *n* [U] *BrE*
the practice of making warnings in public, especially by doctors or politicians, about the poor quality of medical care in the British National Health Service, in order to make the government provide more money for it【英】〔国民保健制度的〕状况恶化警告: *Complaints about the NHS tend to focus on the problems of hospitals' waiting lists and shroud-waving in response to spending controls.* 对（英国）国民保健制度的抱怨往往集中在各医院都有许多病人等待接受治疗，以及控制开支造成的医疗状况恶化等问题上。

sick build·ing syn·drome /ˌsɪk ˈbɪldɪŋ ˌsɪndrom; ˌsɪk ˈbɪldɪŋ ˌsɪndrəʊm/ *n* [U]
a situation in which chemicals and GERMS stay in an office building and make the people who work there feel ill 病楼综合征〔指办公楼内化学物质和病菌等积聚造成的不适〕: *Research has shown that a household fungus can contribute to sick building syndrome.* 研究表明室内真菌会引起病楼综合征。

side·bar /ˈsaɪdbɑr; ˈsaɪdbɑː/ *n* [C] *AmE*
law an occasion when the lawyers and the judge in a TRIAL discuss something without letting the JURY hear what they are saying【美，法律】〔法庭中不让陪审团听到的〕法官与律师的讨论

SIDS /sɪdz; sɪdz/ *n* [U] *AmE* SUDDEN INFANT DEATH SYNDROME【美】婴儿猝死综合征

sim card /ˈsɪm ˌkɑrd; ˈsɪm ˌkɑːd/ *n* [C]
a plastic card in a MOBILE PHONE that stores your personal information and allows you to use the phone〔手机上的〕用户识别卡

sin·gle·sit /ˈsɪŋgl̩ˌsɪt; ˈsɪŋgəlˌsɪt/ *n* [C] *BrE*
a house or apartment for a single person living on their own, rather than for a family【英】单身者住房[寓所]

sink /sɪŋk; sɪŋk/ *adj* [only before noun 仅用于名词前]
sink estate/school *BrE* a sink estate or school is in a very bad condition and there is little hope of improvement【英】残旧住宅区/学校: *Go to almost any city and you find sink estates where you get the feeling that the council hates the place and the people too.* 差不多到任何一个城市，你都会发现有残旧的住宅区，让你觉得那地方和那地方的人都遭市议会的嫌弃。

six-pack /ˈsɪks ˌpæk; ˈsɪks ˌpæk/ *n* [C]
humorous well-developed muscles that you can see on a man's stomach. This expression developed from the idea that these muscles look like a group of six CANs of beer or SOFT DRINK which are sold together, also called a six-pack【幽默】发达的腹肌: *Find out how to get a six-pack, or just a flat stomach, in six weeks.* 看看怎样能在六周内收平肚子，甚至锻炼出发达的肌肉。

skank /skæŋk; skæŋk/ *n* [C]
slang an offensive word for a woman who you have a bad opinion of, because she has sex with a lot of men【俚】骚婆娘〔冒犯用语〕—**skanky** *adj*

ski·jor·ing /ˈskiˌdʒɔrɪŋ; ˈskiːˌdʒɔːrɪŋ/ *n* [U]
a sport in which a SKIER is pulled over snow or ice by one or more dogs 狗拉滑雪: *long distance skijoring in Alaska* 在阿拉斯加的长途狗拉滑雪 —**skijor** *v* [I]

skin /skɪn; skɪn/ *n* [U]
NEW MEANING
the way particular information appears on a computer screen, especially when this can be changed quickly and easily〔软件、网站等的〕皮肤，界面，面板，外壳

skin art·ist /ˈskɪn ˌɑrtɪst; ˈskɪn ˌɑːtɪst/ also 又作 **skin de·sign·er** /ˈskɪn dɪˌzaɪnɚ; ˈskin dɪˌzaɪnə/ *n* [C]
someone who changes the way that a computer PROGRAM shows information on the screen to the user 软件界面设计师

skunk works /ˈskʌŋk ˌwɝks; ˈskʌŋk ˌwɜːks/ *n* [singular]
informal a part of a large company where a small group of workers try to develop new products in secret, within a shorter period of time than usual. This phrase comes from 'Skonk Works', the name of a place in an old American COMIC STRIP. Alcohol was illegally made at the 'Skonk Works'.【非正式】保密的开发部门〔本短语由旧时美国连环漫画中制造私酒的地方 Skonk Works 衍生而来〕: *A few companies have a skunk works where secret projects are funded in the hope that they will lead to new products in a couple of years.* 一些公司设有保密的开发部门，公司为那里的秘密研究项目提供资金，以期在两三年内研制出新产品。

sky /skaɪ; skaɪ/ *v* [I]
to jump higher than everyone else when you are playing BASKETBALL〔篮球赛中〕高跃〔于其他人之上〕

slam·min /ˈslæmɪn; ˈslæmɪn/ *adj, adv AmE*
slang very good【美俚】顶棒的[地]: *Man, we had a slammin time last night.* 老兄，我们昨天夜里玩得真高兴。

slap·head /ˈslæphɛd; ˈslæphed/ *n* [C] *BrE*
informal an impolite word for describing someone who is BALD (=has little or no hair on their head)【英，非正式】秃顶，光头〔非礼貌用语〕

slaugh·tered /ˈslɔtɚd; ˈslɔːtəd/ *adj* [not before noun 不用于名词前] *BrE*
informal very drunk【英，非正式】烂醉（如泥）的: **get slaughtered** *We all got completely slaughtered last night.* 昨天夜里我们全都喝得烂醉如泥。

smack /smæk; smæk/ *v* [T]
smack sb up *slang* to hit someone hard many times with your hand【俚】狠揍: *Don't make me come over there and smack you up.* 不要招惹我过来揍你一顿。

small-cap /ˌsmɔl ˈkæp; ˌsmɔːl ˈkæp◂/ *n* [C]
a SHARE in a small company 小盘股，小公司股票 —**small-cap** *adj*: *They poured their money into some small-cap mutual funds.* 他们把钱注入几个专门投资小盘股的互助基金。—opposite 反义词 LARGE-CAP

small of·fice/home of·fice /ˌsmɔl ˈɔfɪs ˈhom ˌɔfɪs; ˌsmɔːl ˈɒfɪs ˈhəʊm ˌɒfɪs/ *abbreviation* 缩写为 **SOHO** *n* [C]
a room in someone's home with electronic equipment

such as a computer and a FAX MACHINE, that is used as a place in which to work 家庭办公室

smil·ey /ˋsmaɪlɪ; ˈsmaɪli/ *n* [C]
a sign that looks like a face when you look at it sideways, for example :-), used in E-MAIL messages to show that you are happy or pleased about something 笑容符〈如 :-), 用于电子邮件中〉

smoothie /ˋsmuðɪ; ˈsmuːði/ *n* [C]
NEW MEANING
a thick drink made of fruit and fruit juices, and sometimes YOGHURT, that have been mixed together until they are smooth 思乐冰, 沙冰〔一种由水果、果汁、酸奶等混合制成的饮料〕

SMS /ˌɛs ɛm ˋɛs; ˌes em ˈes/ *n*
short messaging system or short message service; a feature on a MOBILE PHONE that allows a user to send or receive written messages〔手机的〕短信息服务

snap /snæp; snæp/ *v*
snap on sb *phr v* [T] *slang* to suddenly stop being able to control your temper and attack someone physically or with words【俚】对〔某人〕发脾气[大打出手, 大肆攻击]: *I've seen him snap on people just for looking at him.* 我看见过他仅仅因为人家看了他一眼就对他们大发脾气。

snarf /snɑrf; snɑːf/ also 又作 **snarf down** *v* [T]
informal to eat something very quickly, often in an untidy or noisy way【非正式】很快(出声)地吃: *Don't lie! I saw you snarfing down all those doughnuts!* 不要扯谎! 我看见你把所有的炸面圈一下子全吃光了。

snar·ky /ˋsnɑrkɪ; ˈsnɑːki/ *adj*
saying unkind and unpleasant things about other people 尖刻的: *If she's bothering you and you say something snarky, she'll know she's getting to you.* 如果她不断打扰你, 而你说了一些刻薄的话, 她就会知道她让你感到烦透了。

snip·ing /ˋsnaɪpɪŋ; ˈsnaɪpɪŋ/ *n* [U]
the practice of waiting until the final moments of an ONLINE AUCTION and then offering the highest price for the thing being sold 狙击〔网上拍卖中等到最后时刻出最高价格〕—**sniper** *n* [C] —**snipe** *v* [I,T]

so /so; səʊ/ *adv*
NEW MEANING
1 *AmE spoken* a word used especially by TEENAGE girls, before noun phrases and verbs, to emphasize what they are saying【美口】简直, 确实〔表示强调, 多为女孩用〕: **so not** *Orange is just so not the right color for Kari.* 橙色压根儿和卡里不相配。| *I have so messed up!* 我真的把事情弄得一团糟! **2** *spoken* used to say that a particular action, attitude, type of behaviour etc is typical of someone …型[式]的: *Jenna's hairstyle is so Lisa Bonet.* 詹娜的发型和莉萨·博内特一模一样。

sobriety check·point /səˋbraɪətɪ ˌtʃɛkpɔɪnt; səˈbraɪəti ˌtʃekpɔɪnt/ *n* [C]
a place in the road where the police stop vehicles, so that police can test drivers to see if they have drunk too much alcohol or used illegal drugs 醉酒驾驶检测站: *Officers will be conducting a sobriety checkpoint in the central Torrance area tomorrow.* 警察明天将在托兰斯中部地区设一个醉酒驾驶检测站。

soccer mom /ˋsɑkɚ ˌmɑm; ˈsɒkə ˌmɒm/ *n* [C] *AmE*
a mother who spends a lot of time driving her children to sports practice, music lessons etc, considered as a typical example of women from the middle to upper classes in US society【美】足球妈咪〔经常驱车带领孩子参加体育活动、音乐课等的母亲〕

social au·dit /ˌsoʃəl ˋɔdɪt; ˌsəʊʃəl ˈɔːdɪt/ also 又作 **ethical audit** *n* [C]
an official examination of how well a company behaves, for example how it treats its employees, the environment etc 社会[伦理]审计: *The social audit of Ben & Jerry's Ice Cream commends the company, which gives 7.5% of pre-tax profits to charity.* 对本－杰里冰激凌的社会审查表扬了该公司, 因为该公司将其税前利润的7.5%捐给了慈善事业。

social ex·clu·sion /ˌsoʃəl ɪkˋskluʒən; ˌsəʊʃəl ɪkˈskluːʒən/ *n* [U] *BrE*
the situation that results when people suffer the effects of a combination of problems such as unemployment, crime, and bad housing, and have very little chance of being able to improve their lives【英】遭社会排斥〔指遭遇失业、犯罪、住房差等问题并无法改善生活〕: *A number of proposals have been submitted to combat poverty and social exclusion.* 已提出了许多消除贫穷和社会排斥的建议。

soft /sɔft; sɒft/ *adj*
NEW MEANING
1 soft loan/credit money that is lent at a lower INTEREST RATE than usual, because it will be used, for example, for creating a business in an area where many people do not have jobs 优惠贷款/信贷 **2 soft money** money that is given to political parties, rather than directly to particular CANDIDATES, by people, companies, or organizations. The amount of money that can be given to political parties in this way is not restricted. 软性捐款〔指捐赠给竞选人所属政党而非本人的款项〕

SOHO /ˋsoho; ˈsəʊhəʊ/
small office/home office; a room in someone's home with electronic equipment such as a computer and a FAX MACHINE, that is used as a place in which to work 家庭办公室

solid /ˋsɑlɪd; ˈsɒlɪd/ *adj BrE*
NEW MEANING
slang【英俚】**1** used to say that something is good 了不起的 **2** used to say that something is very difficult 很难的: *I couldn't do any of the maths last night – it was solid.* 昨晚的数学题我一道也不会, 太难了。

sort /sɔrt; sɔːt/ *v* [T] *BrE*
NEW MEANING
usually spoken to deal with a situation so that all the problems are solved and everything is organized as it should be【英, 一般口】安排妥当: *Don't give me any more excuses. Just sort it!* 不要再找借口了, 把事情办妥!

sort·ed /ˋsɔrtɪd; ˈsɔːtʃd/ *adj* [not before noun 不用于名词前] *BrE*
spoken informal【英口, 非正式】**1** properly arranged or planned 安排有序的: *Good, that's your accommodation sorted.* 好, 那就是给你安排的住所。**2** provided with the things that you want 满足需要的: *"Can I get you anything?" "We're sorted, thanks."* "我要给你们拿什么东西来吗?" "我们什么都不缺, 谢谢。" | *"Did you manage to get a ticket for tonight?" "Sorted!"* "弄到今天晚上的票了吗?" "弄到了。" | **be sorted for** *Are you sorted for booze and something to smoke?* 你有喝的酒和吸的烟吗?

sound·card, sound card /ˋsaʊndˌkɑrd; ˈsaʊndˌkɑːd/ *n* [C]
a CIRCUIT BOARD that can be added to a computer so that it is able to produce sound〔电脑的〕声卡

SPAD /spæd; spæd/ *n* [C] *BrE*
signal passed at danger; a signal near a railway track that has been passed by a train when it should not have passed. If a signal is passed in this way, it could cause an accident or a dangerous situation on the railway line.【英】超越(铁道)危险信号

spam /spæm; spæm/ *n* [U]
E-MAIL messages that a computer user has not asked for and does not want to read, for example from someone who is advertising something 电子垃圾,〔网上的〕垃圾邮件: *You can filter out spam with special software.* 你可以用专门的软件把电子垃圾滤除。

spam·mer /ˋspæmɚ; ˈspæmə/ *n* [C]
a person or company that sends the same computer message to many different people who do not want to receive it, usually as a way of advertising something 垃圾

邮件发送者: *Some ISPs have cancelled contracts with spammers, but it's not easy.* 有些互联网服务商中止了与垃圾邮件发送者的合同，但是这样做并不容易。

species bar·ri·er /ˈspiʃɪz ˌbærɪɚ; ˈspiːʃiːz ˌbæriə/ *n* [singular]
a natural system which is believed to prevent diseases moving from one type of plant or animal to another. This expression is often used in relation to the cow disease BSE, which is believed to have crossed the species barrier and become the disease CJD in humans. 物种屏障〔防止其他物种被传染疾病的自然系统〕: **cross/jump the species barrier** *When and how the disease jumped the species barrier may never be known.* 这种疾病是在何时和以何种方式越过物种屏障，也许永远不得而知。

speed dial /ˈspid ˌdaɪəl; ˈspiːd ˌdaɪəl/ also 又作 **speed dialing** *n* [U]
a special feature on a telephone that lets you DIAL someone's telephone number very quickly by pressing just one button〔电话的〕快速拨号: *Does this phone have speed dial?* 这部电话有快速拨号功能吗? —**speed dial** *v* [I,T]

spider /ˈspaɪdɚ; ˈspaɪdə/ *n* [C]
NEW MEANING
a computer program that AUTOMATICALLY searches for WEB PAGE*s* on the Internet（网上）蜘蛛〔互联网上的网页自动搜索程序〕

sport-u·ti·li·ty ve·hi·cle /ˌspɔrt juˈtɪlətɪ ˌvikḷ; ˌspɔːt juːˈtɪləti ˌviːkəl/ *abbreviation* 缩写为 **SUV** *n* [C] *AmE*
a type of vehicle that is bigger than a car and is made for travelling over rough ground【美】运动型多用途车, 运动型多功能车, 越野车

spy·ware /ˈspaɪˌwɛr; ˈspaɪweə/ *n* [U]
computer SOFTWARE that secretly arrives onto someone's computer while they are using the Internet, which records information about which WEBSITE*s* they visit. This information is then used by advertising companies, who try to sell them products. 间谍软件: *Most net surfers probably have spyware embedded in their computers.* 大多数网民的电脑都可能被埋置了间谍软件。

squeegee merchants
耍赖擦车仔

squeegee mer·chant /ˈskwidʒi ˌmɝtʃənt; ˈskwiːdʒiː ˌmɜːtʃənt/ *n* [C] *BrE*
someone who uses water and a SQUEEGEE (=tool with a thin rubber blade and a short handle) to clean the front windows of cars that have stopped in traffic, and then asks the drivers for money, sometimes in a threatening way【英】耍赖擦车仔

stag /stæg; stæg/ *v past tense and past participle* **stagged** *present participle* **stagging** [T] *BrE*
stag an issue to buy SHARE*s* in a company in order to sell them quickly and make a profit【英】炒卖股票〔以求迅速获利〕

stakeholder /ˈstekˌholdɚ; ˈsteɪkˌhəʊldə/ *n* [C]
NEW MEANING
someone who is considered to be an important part of an organization or a society because they have responsibility in it and receive advantages from it〔某一组织或社团的〕利益攸关者, 利益共享者: *How can we encourage students to become stakeholders in the classroom?* 我们怎样才能激励学生在课堂上一起分担责任, 共享成果呢?

stakeholder e·con·o·my /ˈstekholdɚ ɪˌkɑnəmɪ; ˈsteɪkhəʊldər ɪˌkɒnəmi/ *n* [C] *BrE*
an economic system in a society that citizens feel they receive advantages from and have responsibilities to【英】利益共享经济: *The Prime Minister declared his intention to create a stakeholder economy involving all the people, not just a privileged few.* 首相宣布, 他打算建立的是全民的利益共享经济, 而不是仅仅为少数特权者服务。

stand-a·lone /ˈstænd əˌlon; ˈstænd əˌləʊn/ *adj*
NEW MEANING
a stand-alone company or business is one that is not part of a larger company〔公司或企业〕独立（经营）的

standby time /ˈstændbaɪ ˌtaɪm; ˈstændbaɪ ˌtaɪm/ *n* [U]
1 the time during which a person or a machine is available to work but is not able to work because they are waiting to be given a specific job to do〔人或机器的〕待命时间 **2** the period of time that passes while you wait for a computer to carry out a command or a request〔计算机执行指令时的〕等候时间

stand-up, standup /ˈstænd ˌʌp; ˈstænd ˌʌp/ *n* [C]
NEW MEANING
a COMEDIAN who does STAND-UP COMEDY (=tells jokes to an audience) 单人喜剧表演者[说笑演员]: *He's simply one of the best new standups around at the moment. Go see his show!* 他是目前最好的滑稽说笑新星之一, 去看他的演出吧!

start /stɑrt; stɑːt/ *n*
NEW MEANING
1 [C usually plural 一般用复数] a job that has just started, a business that has just been started, or someone who has just started a new job 新工作; 新商店; 新手: *The number of business starts plummeted 10.5% during the second half of the year.* 下半年开业的新店数目锐减了10.5%。| **new starts** *a training course for new starts* 新人培训课程 **2 housing starts** the number of new houses, apartments etc on which building work has started in a particular period of time〔某段时间内的〕新屋动工数目: *The number of housing starts was lower than expected last quarter.* 上季度新屋动工数目比预期的少。

start-up /ˈstɑrt ˌʌp; ˈstɑːt ˌʌp/ *n* [C]
a small new company whose work usually involves computers or the Internet 新成立的小公司〔常与电脑或互联网有关〕: *Jill works for an Internet start-up in San Jose.* 吉尔为圣何塞的一家新开的互联网公司工作。

stay-at-home /ˈste ət ˌhom; ˈsteɪ ət ˌhəʊm/ *adj*
stay-at-home mother/father etc a stay-at-home mother or father stays at home, usually to take care of their children, rather than working in an office, factory etc〔不去工作, 在家照顾孩子的〕家庭主妇/主夫等: *The study found that stay-at-home moms are no longer the majority in America.* 研究发现家庭主妇在美国已不再是大多数了。

stealth tax /ˈstɛlθ ˌtæks; ˈstelθ ˌtæks/ *n* [C] *BrE informal* a tax that you pay on something that you buy rather than tax you pay directly to the government, and which you are less aware of paying than, for example, direct tax on your income【英, 非正式】隐形税〔购物时含在商品里的一种税〕

steaming /ˈstimɪŋ; ˈstiːmɪŋ/ *n* [U]
a method of stealing in which a large group of young people go into a public place, surprise and scare the people there, and then rob them 聚众[结帮]行劫: *The success of steaming depends on surprise.* 结帮行劫是否得逞取决于出其不意。—**steamer** *n* [C] *Steamers waited until a member of staff opened a security door.* 结帮行劫者等候到一个职员把防盗门打开才动手。—**steaming** *adj*: *The steaming gangs are often in their early teens.* 聚众行劫的团伙经常是一些十三四岁的青少年。

stellar /ˋstɛlɚ; ˈstelə/ *adj*
NEW MEANING
go stellar *BrE informal* if a pop band, TV actor, etc goes stellar, they become very popular and famous【英，非正式】走红，受欢迎: *There's a stand-up comedian, and my sources tell me he is about to go stellar.* 有一个单人表演的喜剧演员，根据我的消息来源，他即将走红。

stem cell /ˋstɛm ˏsɛl; ˈstem ˌsel/ *n* [C]
technical a special type of cell in the body that can divide in order to form other types of cells that have particular qualities or purposes【术语】干细胞: *Research has now shown that stem cells are present in the adult brain and spinal cord.* 研究显示干细胞存在于成人的脑和脊髓中。

step aer·o·bics /ˋstɛp ɛˏrobɪks; ˈstep eəˌrəʊbɪks/ *n* [U]
a type of physical exercise in which you step on and off a small raised PLATFORM while doing movements with the upper part of your body 踏板健身操: *Which night is your step aerobics class?* 哪天晚上你上踏板健身操课？

sticky /ˋstɪkɪ; ˈstɪki/ *adj*
NEW MEANING
slang a WEBSITE that is sticky is interesting to the people looking at it and makes them want to look at it for a long period of time【俚】〔网站〕令人着迷的，有魅力的 —**stickiness** *n* [U]

stif·fy /ˋstɪfɪ; ˈstɪfi/ *n* [C]
taboo an ERECTION (1)【讳】〔阴茎的〕勃起

stock park·ing /ˋstɑk ˏpɑrkɪŋ; ˈstɒk ˌpɑːkɪŋ/ *n* [U]
a situation in which the owner of SHARES leaves them with another person or organization, usually in order to hide who really owns them 股票存托

stop-loss or·der /ˏstɑp ˋlɔs ˏɔrdɚ; ˌstɒp ˈlɒs ˌɔːdə/ *n* [C]
technical an arrangement in which the person who buys and sells your STOCKS for you agrees to buy or sell STOCKS when they reach a particular price【术语】〔指示经纪人在股价涨或落到某价位时立即买进或卖出的〕限价买卖指令，止损指令

straight-to-vid·e·o /ˏstret tə ˋvɪdɪo; ˌstreɪt tə ˈvɪdiəʊ/ *n* [C]
a film that is never shown in the cinema but that is available only on VIDEO 直接影像制品〔指未在电影院上映而直接制成录像带或光盘发行的影片〕

stream /strim; striːm/ *v* [T]
NEW MEANING
to play sound or VIDEO on your computer while it is being DOWNLOAD*ed* from the Internet, rather than saving it as a FILE and then playing it〔不下载直接从网上〕直流收看[收听]: *Click here to stream video from the Olympic Games.* 点击这里直流收看奥运会的录像。

stream·ing /ˋstrimɪŋ; ˈstriːmɪŋ/ *n* [U]
playing sound or VIDEO on your computer while it is being broadcast over the Internet instead of DOWNLOAD*ing* it and saving it into a FILE so that you can listen to it or watch it later〔网上的〕直流接收: **audio/video streaming** *Our service began with live audio streaming of radio programs.* 我们的服务以直流接收现场直播的电台节目开始。

stress /strɛs; stres/ *v* [T]
NEW MEANING
stress sb **out** *slang* to make someone so worried or nervous that they cannot relax【俚】使焦虑[紧张不安]: *Cathy's job really stresses her out.* 凯茜的工作着实使她焦虑不安。

stuff /stʌf; stʌf/ *n*
NEW MEANING
and stuff *spoken informal* used to say that there are other things similar to what you have just mentioned, but you are not going to say what they are【口，非正式】诸如此类的东西: *There's some very good music there, CD systems and stuff, and laser discs.* 那里有一些非常不错的音乐、激光唱片系统等东西，还有激光影碟。

style sheet /ˋstaɪl ˏʃit; ˈstaɪl ˌʃiːt/ *n* [C]
a set of instructions that specifies what the TYPEFACE and colours of an electronic document should be 样式单，格式页: *When the electronic newspaper comes with style sheets, we will be able to specify that headings are in the right type-style, so it will look like the printed paper.* 电子报纸附有样式页时，我们就能确定那标题的字体对不对，那样看起来会同印刷的报纸一样。

styl·ing /ˋstaɪlɪŋ; ˈstaɪlɪŋ/ also 又作 **sty·lin'** /ˋstaɪlɪn; ˈstaɪlɪn/ *adj* [not before noun 不用于名词前] *AmE slang* attractive and fashionable【美俚】时髦的，引人注目的: *If I had a car like this, I'd be stylin'.* 我要是有这样一辆车，那才神气呢。

STYS *especially BrE*
a written abbreviation of 缩写= 'speak to you soon', used in E-MAIL OR TEXT MESSAGE*s* on MOBILE PHONE*s*【尤英】很快与你通话〔电子邮件或手机短信用语〕

suck-up /ˋsʌk ˏʌp; ˈsʌk ˌʌp/ *n* [C] *AmE informal* someone who says or does nice things in order to make someone like them or get what they want【美，非正式】马屁精: *Nobody wants to seem like a suck-up.* 没有人希望被人看作马屁精。

Sudden In·fant Death Syn·drome /ˌsʌdn̩ ˏɪnfənt ˋdɛθ ˏsɪndrom; ˌsʌdn ˌɪnfənt ˈdeθ ˌsɪndrəʊm/ *abbreviation* 缩写为 **SIDS** *n* [U]
a situation in which a baby stops breathing and dies while it is sleeping, for no known reason 婴儿猝死综合征

suicide /ˋsuəˏsaɪd; ˈsuːɪsaɪd/ *n*
suicide by cop *humorous* an occasion in which someone who wants to kill himself or herself uses threatening behaviour towards a police officer so that the police officer kills the person in order to defend himself or herself【幽默】借警察之手自杀〔有人利用威胁警察的行为，令警察在自卫的情况下把他/她杀死，以达到自杀的目的〕

suit /sut; suːt/ *n* [C usually plural 一般用复数]
NEW MEANING
informal a man, especially a manager, who works in an office and who has to wear a suit when he is at work【非正式】〔上班时需穿套装的〕高级管理人员: *I bought myself a mobile phone and joined the other suits on the train to the City.* 我给自己买了一部手机，与其他穿得笔挺的高级职员一起上了进城的火车。

sunset in·dus·try /ˋsʌnsɛt ˏɪndəstrɪ; ˈsʌnset ˌɪndəstri/ *n* [C]
an industry that uses old equipment and methods, usually in an area that once had many industries like it, and that is becoming less successful 夕阳工业: *sunset industries such as steel* 诸如钢铁等夕阳工业

su·per·cat /ˋsupɚˏkæt; ˈsuːpəˌkæt/ *n* [C] *especially BrE*
a word meaning someone who earns a very large amount of money for running a company, especially a company that was previously owned by the government, used in newspapers to show disapproval【尤英】超级猫〔利用原先由政府拥有的公司来赚大钱的经营者，常用于报章，含贬义〕

su·per·size¹ /ˋsupɚˏsaɪz; ˈsuːpəˌsaɪz/ *adj* [only before noun 仅用于名词前] *AmE*
a supersize drink or meal in a FAST-FOOD restaurant is the largest size that the restaurant serves【美】〔快餐店提供的食物或饮料〕巨无霸式的，大份的: *Could I get a supersize fries with that?* 我能附带得到大份的薯条吗？

supersize² /ˋsupɚˏsaɪz; ˈsuːpəˌsaɪz/ *v* [T] *AmE*
to give someone a larger sized meal or drink in a FAST-FOOD restaurant【美】〔快餐店〕提供大份食物[饮料]: *Can I supersize that drink for you?* 那饮料我给你大份的好吗？

surround-sound, surround sound /səˋraʊnd ˏsaʊnd; səˈraʊnd ˌsaʊnd/ *n* [U]
a system of four or more SPEAKER*s* (=pieces of equipment that sound comes out of) used with films and television so that the sounds from the film seem to come from all directions 环绕立体声 —**surround-sound** *adj*

[only before noun 仅用于名词前]: *surround-sound speakers* 环绕立体声扬声器

SUV /ˌɛs ju ˋvi; ˌes juː ˈviː/ *n* [C] *AmE*
sport-utility vehicle; a type of vehicle that is bigger than a car and is made for travelling over rough ground【美】运动型多用途车, 运动型多功能车, 越野车

sweat eq·ui·ty /ˋswɛt ˌɛkwətɪ; ˈswet ˌekwətiˈ/ *n* [U] *AmE*
the amount of value that something gains as a result of a lot of work【美】血汗权益〔通过大量工作而获得的增值部分〕: *The volunteer work that parents put into the school system was calculated to be worth $2.2 million in sweat equity.* 当局计算出家长投入学校系统的义务工作共值 220 万美元。

sweet[1] /swit; swiːt/ *adj*
NEW MEANING
spoken **Sweet!** used to say that you think that something is very good【口】棒极了的: *"I got four tickets to the concert." "Sweet!"* "我弄到四张音乐会门票。""太棒了!"

swipe card /ˋswaɪp ˌkard; ˈswaɪp ˌkɑːd/ *n* [C]
a special plastic card that you slide through a machine in order to get into a building or open a door〔开门等的〕插卡, 刷卡

switch·ing /ˋswɪtʃɪŋ; ˈswɪtʃɪŋ/ *n* [U]
a system that allows information to be exchanged between different computer networks〔信息的〕交换 (系统), 转接

SWOT /swɑt; swɒt/ *n*
strengths, weaknesses, opportunities, threats; a system for examining the way a company is run or the way someone works, to see what the good and bad points are 态势分析, SWOT 分析〔公司或个人的情况分析, 包括优势、劣势、机会、威胁四个方面, 是 strengths, weaknesses, opportunities, threats 的首字母缩合〕

sync, synch /sɪŋk; sɪŋk/ *v*
sync up, synch up *phr v* [I,T] to arrange for two things to occur at the same time, or to occur at the same time, as arranged; SYNCHRONIZE 同步发生; 使…同步: *For some reason, I couldn't get the audio and video to synch up.* 由于某种原因, 我不能使音响和视频同步。

T,t

table danc·ing /ˋtebḷ ˌdænsɪŋ; ˈteɪbəl ˌdɑːnsɪŋ/ *n* [U]
dancing with sexy movements that is performed close to a customer's table in a restaurant or NIGHTCLUB 桌上舞〔饭店或夜总会中在靠近客人桌子的地方表演的一种色情舞蹈〕—compare 比较 LAP DANCING

T cell, T-cell /ˋti ˌsɛl; ˈtiː ˌsel/ *n* [C]
a type of WHITE BLOOD CELL that helps the body fight disease T 细胞〔一种白血球〕

Tae-Bo /ˌtaɪ ˋbo; ˌtaɪ ˈbəʊ/ *n* [U]
a type of exercise that combines dancing, kicking, and quick hand movements 太保操, 韵律搏击〔包括跳舞踢打等动作〕

tag /tæg; tæg/ *n* [C] *AmE*
NEW MEANING
someone's name or NICKNAME that they have painted on a wall, train etc illegally【美】涂鸦签名: *You can see the tags of young graffiti artists in railway yards in every major city of the world.* 全世界所有大城市的火车站里都可以看到年轻涂鸦艺术家的涂鸦签名。

tag·ging /ˋtægɪŋ; ˈtægɪŋ/ *n* [U] *AmE*
the crime of painting your name or NICKNAME (=a pretend name that you call yourself) on walls, trains etc【美】涂鸦签名 (罪行): *Tagging landed Torres in the Santa Clara County boys ranch for juvenile offenders for five months.* 托雷斯因为到处乱涂签名而被关进圣克拉拉县男少年劳教牧场五个月。| *These kids see the older boys going out and tagging, getting their names up, and they want to do it.* 这些小孩子见到那些大孩子出去把名字乱涂在墙上, 于是也想学样。—**tagger** *n* [C]: *California's most prolific tagger is suspected of spray-painting the name 'Chaka' at 10,000 locations from Los Angeles to San Francisco.* 人们怀疑加利福尼亚最多产的涂鸦者在从洛杉矶到旧金山的一万多处地点用油漆喷涂了"Chaka"这个名字。

talk /tɔk; tɔːk/ *v*
NEW MEANING
talk trash *AmE informal* to say impolite or offensive things to or about someone, especially to opponents in a sports competition【美, 非正式】〔尤指对比赛中的对手〕谩骂, 爆粗口: *Both teams talk trash on the basketball court.* 两队在篮球场上对骂了起来。

talk time /ˋtɔk ˌtaɪm; ˈtɔːk ˌtaɪm/ *n* [U]
the time when a MOBILE PHONE is being used to make or receive calls or messages〔手机的〕通话时间: *The rechargeable battery allows approximately 135 minutes of talk time.* 充电式电池能维持大约 135 分钟通话时间。

ta·mox·i·fen /təˋmɑksɪfɛn; təˈmɒksɪfen/ *n* [U]
trademark a drug that is used to treat breast cancer【商标】他莫昔芬, 三苯氧胺〔用于治疗乳腺癌〕

tank /tæŋk; tæŋk/ *n*
NEW MEANING
in the tank *AmE informal* failing and losing money【美, 非正式】失败赔钱: **be/go in the tank** *Sales can't keep going up, but that doesn't mean the industry is going in the tank.* 销售额不能保持增长的势头, 但这并不意味该行业失败赔钱。

tan·ki·ni /tæŋˋkinɪ; tæŋˈkiːni/ *n* [C]
a type of BIKINI that has a small shirt with no SLEEVES as its top part 坦基尼〔比基尼的一种〕: *Julie was wearing a stylish tankini and sandals.* 朱莉穿着一件挺时髦的坦基尼和一双凉鞋。

ta·que·ri·a /ˌtækəˋriə; ˌtækəˈrɪːə/ *n* [C] *Spanish*
an informal MEXICAN restaurant, especially in the southwest US【西】〔尤指美国西南部的〕墨西哥食品快餐店

tariff /ˋtærɪf; ˈtærɪf/ *n* [C] *BrE*
NEW MEANING
a list or system of prices which MOBILE PHONE companies charge for the different services they provide【英】〔手机分项服务〕收费表

task /tæsk; tɑːsk/ *v* [T]
to give someone the responsibility for doing something 分配〔某人〕任务: **be tasked with sth** *We were tasked with completing the job by the end of 2004.* 我们被指派在 2004 年底完成该项工作。

TAXOL, taxol /ˋtæksɔl; ˈtæksɒl/ *n* [U]
a drug made from the outer surface of a particular tree, that is used to treat CANCER of the ovaries (OVARY) 泰素〔又译紫杉酚, 是一种抗卵巢癌药物〕

team play·er /ˋtim ˌpleɚ; ˈtiːm ˌpleɪə/ *n* [C]
someone who works well as a member of a team, especially in business〔尤指生意上的〕合作伙伴, 具有团队精神的人: *He was a good businessman, but never a team player.* 他是一名出色的生意人, 但从来不是一个好的合作伙伴。

teaser ad /ˋtizɚ ˌæd; ˈtiːzər æd/ *n* [C]
an advertisement that is used to make people interested in a product, but that does not give very much information about the product, so that people will pay attention to more advertisements later 吊胃口广告〔这种广告先引起人们对产品的兴趣, 但不会给予很多资料, 借此吸引人们注意其后推出的更多广告〕

technical sup·port /ˌtɛknɪkḷ səˋport; ˌteknɪkəl səˈpɔːt/ also 又作 **tech support** /ˋtɛk səˌport; ˈtek səˌpɔːt/ *n* [U]
1 help or information that you receive to improve a computer program or system, make it continue working, or use it correctly〔计算机程序或系统的〕技术支持 **2** the department of a company that provides this type of help

技术支持服务部: *Maybe you'd better try calling tech support.* 或许你最好打电话去技术支持服务部。

tel·e·con·fe·rence¹ /ˋtɛlɪˌkɑnfərəns; ˈtelɪˌkɒnfərəns/ *n* [C]
a business meeting in which people in different places communicate by telephone, television etc 电视[电话]会议 —**teleconferencing** *n* [U]: *video teleconferencing equipment* 视频电话会议设备

teleconference² /ˋtɛlɪˌkɑnfərəns; ˈtelɪˌkɒnfərəns/ *v* [I]
to have a meeting with people who are not in the same place as you, and be able to see and talk to them by using special VIDEO equipment or computers and telephone lines 召开电视[电话]会议

telephone bank·ing /ˋtɛləfon ˌbæŋkɪŋ; ˈteləfəʊn ˌbæŋkɪŋ/ *n* [U]
a service provided by banks so that people can find out information about their bank account, pay bills etc by telephone rather than by going to a bank 电话银行服务

tel·e·port /ˋtɛlɪˌport; ˈtelɪˌpɔːt/ *v* [I,T]
a word used in SCIENCE FICTION meaning to move or move something from one place to another immediately by using special powers or a machine such as a computer〔科幻小说经常提到的〕远距离传送: *If you slay the dragon, you will be teleported to the palace.* 你如果杀死这条龙，就会通过远距离传送到达王宫。—**teleportation** /ˌtɛlɪporˋteʃən; ˌtelɪpɔːˈteɪʃən/ *n* [U]

tel·e·thon /ˋtɛlɪθɑn; ˈteləθɒn/ *n* [C]
a special television programme, usually lasting many hours, in which famous people provide entertainment and ask people to give money to CHARITY〔为募捐等举行的〕马拉松式电视节目

tel·e·van·ge·list /ˌtɛlɪˋvændʒəlɪst; ˌteləˈvændʒələst/ *n* [C]
someone who appears regularly on television to try to persuade people to become Christians, and often also asks people to give them money. This word comes from a combination of the words 'TELEVISION' and 'EVANGELIST'. 电视布道者〔由 television 和 evangelist 缩合而成〕: *With mass media now available, televangelists are already at work in Eastern Europe.* 电视布道者已经借助现有的大众传媒在东欧开展活动。—**televangelism** *n* [U]

ten·bag·ger /ˋtɛn ˌbægɚ; ˈten ˌbægə/ *n* [C]
informal a SHARE whose value becomes ten times as big as it was when you bought it【非正式】十倍股〔购进后增值十倍的股票〕

ter·a·byte /ˋtɛrəˌbaɪt; ˈterəˌbaɪt/ *n* [C]
a unit for measuring the amount of information a computer can store or use, equal to a TRILLION BYTE*s* 万亿字节，兆兆字节，太字节

ter·a·flop /ˋtɛrəflɑp; ˈterəflɒp/ *n* [C usually plural 一般用复数]
a unit that measures how fast a computer works. One teraflop is one TRILLION operations every second. 每秒万亿次浮点运算: *Two weeks ago the machine hit an astonishing speed of 1.8 teraflops, easily outdistancing the previous record holder.* 两周前这台机器达到了每秒1.8万亿次的惊人运算速度，轻易就把原先的记录保持者远远地抛在后面。

term /tɝm; tɜːm/ *v*
NEW MEANING
be termed out of office *AmE* to be forced to leave a political position because the law says that someone can be in that position for only a particular number of years【美】任期到便退职，届满即退: *Senator Jansen will be termed out of office next year.* 参议员詹森明年因任期已满将不得不离任。

test·deck /ˋtɛstdɛk; ˈtestdek/ *n* [C]
technical a computer PROGRAM that is used to check a small amount of information, which is then compared to the same work done by a person, to make sure the computer is operating correctly【术语】测试程序

tes·ti·ly·ing /ˋtɛstəˌlaɪ·ɪŋ; ˈtestəˌlaɪ-ɪŋ/ *n* [U]
the activity of saying things that are not true in a court of law. Some people believe that police officers do this in order to make sure that people who they think are guilty of a crime will go to prison, even if there is not enough proof. This word comes from a combination of 'TESTIFYING' and 'LYING'.〔警方在法庭审讯过程中〕弄虚作假〔由 testifying 和 lying 缩合而成〕

text /tɛkst; tekst/ *v*
—see 见 TEXT MESSAGE²

text mes·sage¹ /ˋtɛkst ˌmɛsɪdʒ; ˈtekst ˌmesɪdʒ/ *n* [C]
a written message that is sent or received on a MOBILE PHONE or PAGER〔手机或传呼机的〕短信(息)

text message² /ˋtɛkst ˌmɛsɪdʒ; ˈtekst ˌmesɪdʒ/ also 又作 **text** *v* [T]
to send someone a written message on a MOBILE PHONE or PAGER〔用手机或传呼机〕给…发送短信(息): *I'll text you as soon as I get the results.* 一有结果我就给你发短信。

them·self /ðəmˋsɛlf; ðəmˈself/ *pron*
spoken used when you are referring to one person, but you want to avoid saying 'himself' or 'herself' because you do not know the sex of the person. Many people think this use is incorrect【口】其人〔指"他"或"她"，因不知其性别时用，但许多人认为这种用法并不正确〕: *It makes me happy to help someone help themself.* 能帮助人自助让我感到高兴。

the·oph·yl·line /θɪˋɑfəlin; θiˈɒfəliːn/ *n* [U]
a drug similar to CAFFEINE that is used to treat heart and breathing problems 茶碱

ther·mo·bar·ic /ˌθɝmoˋbærɪk; ˌθɜːməʊˈbærɪk/ *adj*
thermobaric weapons make a lot of heat and pressure when they explode and kill people by damaging their lungs and other organs〔武器〕热压的，热冲击波的: *There's no doubt that US Marines will encounter thermobaric weapons on battlefields in the near future.* 毫无疑问，美国海军陆战队不久的将来会在战场上遭遇到热压武器。

third age, Third Age /ˌθɝd ˋedʒ; ˌθɜːd ˈeɪdʒ/ *n* [singular, U]
the part of your life when you are 55 or older. People sometimes say 'third age' instead of 'old age' to emphasize that in this time of life people can still be healthy and active.〔生命的〕第三年龄段〔55岁以上，婉指 old age(老年)〕: *Bob reinvented himself during third age, enjoying a new and different career.* 到了第三年龄段，鲍勃彻底改变自己，高兴地从事另一项新的事业。| *a magazine for people in the Third Age of life* 针对老年人的杂志 —**third age** *adj* [only before noun 仅用于名词前]: *third age professionals* 老年专业人员 —**third ager** *n* [C]: *university programmes for third agers* 为老年人而设的大学课程

thrash met·al /ˋθræʃ ˌmɛtḷ; ˈθræʃ ˌmetl/ *n* [U]
a type of loud fast music that combines features of PUNK and HEAVY METAL music 快节奏重金属摇滚乐〔综合朋克和重金属音乐特点的一种摇滚乐形式〕

thread /θrɛd; θred/ *n* [C]
NEW MEANING
a series of electronic messages concerning the same subject, written by members of an Internet discussion group〔网上讨论区涉及同一主题的〕一连串帖子: *I'd like to refer to something that was posted in an earlier thread.* 我想提一下早前的一连串帖子中说到的一件事。

three-peat /ˋθri ˌpit; ˈθriː ˌpiːt/ *n* [C] *AmE*
informal the act of winning a sports competition three times, one after the other. The word comes from a combination of the words 'three' and 'repeat'.【美，非正式】三连冠〔由 three 和 repeat 缩合而成〕: **pull off a three-peat** *Laura Davies is trying to become the first player to pull off a three-peat since Sandra Haynie.* 劳拉·戴维斯正力争成为继桑德拉·海尼之后第一个赢得三连冠的运动员。

thumbnail /ˋθʌmˌnel; ˈθʌmneɪl/ *n* [C]
NEW MEANING
a small picture on a computer screen of a document,

showing you what it will look like when you print it 缩略图〔网页上指甲大小的图块〕: *Click on the thumbnails to view a larger version of each image.* 点击缩略图，看一下每个图像的放大版本。

THX
a written abbreviation of 缩写= 'thanks', used in E-MAIL or TEXT MESSAGES on MOBILE PHONES 谢谢〔电子邮件或手机短信用语〕

tick /tɪk; tɪk/ *v*
tick down *phr v* [I] *technical* if the price of a financial SHARE, BOND product etc ticks down, its value decreases【术语】〔股票、债券等〕贬值: *Rates on 30-year mortgages ticked down last week.* 上周 30 年期抵押债券价格下跌。
tick up *phr v* [I] *technical* if the price of a financial SHARE, BOND product etc ticks up, its value increases〔股票、债券等〕升值;〔价格〕上扬: *Economists predict that oil prices will tick up again.* 经济学家预言石油价格将再次上扬。

tick·et·ing /ˋtɪkɪtɪŋ; ˈtɪkətɪŋ/ *n* [U]
the process or system of selling or printing tickets for planes, trains, concerts etc〔飞机、火车、音乐会等的〕售票系统，票务系统: *Most airlines are using electronic ticketing now.* 目前大多数航空公司都使用电子售票系统。

TIFF /tɪf; tɪf/ *n* [C]
technical Tag Image File Format; a type of computer FILE created by a SCANNER or DESKTOP PUBLISHING PROGRAM【术语】〔扫描仪或桌面出版系统中的〕标签图像文件格式

time-poor /ˋtaɪm ˌpʊr; ˈtaɪm ˌpʊə/ *adj BrE*
someone who is time-poor does not have very much free time because they work all day and often work in the evenings too【英】缺乏空闲时间的〔极为忙碌，由早忙到晚〕: *These young men, exceedingly rich, are time-poor because of their demanding jobs on the Stock Exchange.* 这些年轻人虽然十分富裕但却缺乏余暇时间，因为他们在证券交易所的工作十分忙碌。

tip·pee trad·ing /tɪˋpi ˌtedɪŋ; tɪˈpiː ˌtreɪdɪŋ/ *n* [U]
an illegal situation in which someone who receives secret information about a company, SHARES etc tells another person about it, and then that person uses the information to gain a financial advantage〔股票买卖等的〕内幕交易 —see also 另见 INSIDER TRADING

tip sheet /ˋtɪp ˌʃit; ˈtɪp ˌʃiːt/ *n* [C]
informal a newspaper that gives advice and information about which SHARES should be bought and sold【非正式】提供股市行情的报章: *a tip sheet for private investors* 面向私人投资者的股市行情报章

TLA /ˌti ɛl ˋe; ˌtiː el ˈeɪ/ *n* [C]
three-letter acronym; a combination of three letters, such as BTW or IMO, that are used as a short form of a phrase, especially on the Internet and in E-MAILS 三字母缩写词〔尤在互联网和电子邮件中使用〕

to-die-for /tə ˋdaɪ ˌfɔr; tə ˈdaɪ ˌfɔː/ *adj*
informal humorous extremely good or desirable【非正式，幽默】好得要命的，极合意的: *Betty's strawberry cheesecake is simply to-die-for.* 贝蒂的草莓干酪蛋糕美味极了! | *Their recently launched cosmetics line comes in to-die-for packaging of purple, orange, or red plastic.* 他们最近推出的化妆品系列采用了特酷的紫色、橙色和红色塑料包装。

toning ta·bles /ˋtonɪŋ ˌteblz; ˈtəʊnɪŋ ˌteɪbəlz/ *n* [plural]
a piece of equipment that you lie on and that moves your arms and legs up and down, which is supposed to make your muscles firmer 健身床

top /tɑp; tɒp/ *adj, interjection BrE*
NEW MEANING
spoken informal very good【英口，非正式】一流的: *I just love that man, he's a top guy.* 我就是爱那个男人，他是个出色的人。| *D'you like onion on your pizza? —Oh, top!* 你想在比萨饼上放点洋葱吗? —— 噢，那可棒极了!

Total Qual·i·ty Man·age·ment /ˌtotḷ ˋkwɑlətɪ ˌmænɪdʒmənt; ˌtəʊtl ˈkwɒləti ˌmænɪdʒmənt/ *abbreviation* 缩写为 **TQM** *n* [U]
a system for making sure that each department in an organization works in the most effective way and that the goods or services it produces are of the best quality possible 全面质量管理

tot·ty, tottie /ˋtɑtɪ; ˈtɒti/ *n* [C,U] *BrE*
slang an offensive word used by men to describe women who they think are sexually attractive【英俚】骚货〔男人形容女人的冒犯语〕

touch·y-feel·y /ˌtʌtʃɪ ˋfilɪ; ˌtʌtʃi ˈfiːli/ *adj*
informal expressing sympathy and care towards other people, often in a way that does not seem sincere, and using a lot of physical contact between people, such as HUGging【非正式】〔常指通过拥抱等身体接触，不太真诚地〕表示关爱的: *a touchy-feely afternoon talk show* 一个流于表面关怀的下午清谈节目 | *The whole atmosphere was getting a little too touchy-feely for me.* 整个气氛对我来说有点肉麻。

TQM /ˌti kju ˋɛm; ˌtiː kjuː ˈem/
abbreviation of 缩写= TOTAL QUALITY MANAGEMENT

tracker fund /ˋtrækɚ ˌfʌnd; ˈtrækə ˌfʌnd/ *n* [C] *BrE*
technical another name for an INDEX FUND: an INVESTMENT that includes a combination of SHARES that are in a particular SHARE INDEX, and that earns money depending on the value of the shares in that index【英，术语】指数基金

trance /træns; trɑːns/ *n* [U]
NEW MEANING
a type of popular electronic dance music with a fast beat and long continuous notes played on a SYNTHESIZER 迷幻音乐〔用电子音响合成器演奏的快节奏、连续长音符的电子舞曲〕

trans·gen·der /ˌtrænzˋdʒɛndɚ; ˌtrænzˈdʒendə/ also 又作 **transgendered** *adj* [only before noun 仅用于名词前]
a transgender person wants to be or look like a member of the opposite sex, especially by having a medical operation〔尤指通过手术〕变性的 —**transgender** *n* [C] —**transgenderism** *n* [U]

trans·gen·ic /ˌtrænsˋdʒɛnɪk; ˌtrænzˈdʒenɪk/ *adj*
technical having one or more GENES from a different type of animal or plant【术语】转基因的: *transgenic mice* 转基因老鼠

trash /træʃ; træʃ/ *v* [T]
NEW MEANING
informal to criticize someone or something severely【非正式】抨击: *Some of the people he trashed on the show are planning to sue.* 在电视节目中受到他抨击的人中有几个正打算起诉他。

trash talk·ing, trash-talking /ˋtræʃ ˌtɔkɪŋ; ˈtræʃ ˌtɔːkɪŋ/ *n* [U] *AmE*
rude or insulting language spoken by a member of a sports team to or about a member of another sports team, or the same kind of language spoken by sports FANS【美】〔运动员或球迷的〕侮辱性骂人行为: *Coaches say they want to take trash talking out of high school football.* 教练们说他们想杜绝学校足球赛中的骂人现象。—**trash talker** *n* [C]

trash·talk /ˋtræʃˌtɔk; ˈtræʃtɔːk/ *n* [U] *AmE*
informal things you say about someone that are not nice【美，非正式】侮辱性的话: *I'm not prepared to tolerate any trashtalk on court.* 我不会在法庭上容忍任何侮辱性的话。

trend-chas·ing, trend chasing /ˋtrɛnd ˌtʃezɪŋ; ˈtrend ˌtʃeɪzɪŋ/ *n* [U]
1 the act of copying what other people are doing or what is currently popular 赶时髦: *The music is complete, with no trend chasing or compromise.* 这首乐曲很完美，没有赶时髦或折中的倾向。**2** *technical* a way of INVESTING (=giving money to a company in order to get a profit) in which you watch how others are investing and copy them【术语】〔投资中的〕跟风: *trend-chasing among investors* 投资者中的跟风现象 —**trend-chaser** *n* [C]

trend·spot·ter /ˈtrɛnd,spɑtɚ; ˈtrend,spɒtə/ *n* [C] someone who notices and reports on new fashions, activities that people are starting to do, or the way a situation is developing 时尚[潮流]观察者

trey /tre; treɪ/ *n* [C] *AmE*
NEW MEANING
an action of throwing a basketball through the HOOP that is worth three points【美】〔篮球〕三分球

trial bal·loon /ˈtraɪəl bə,lun; ˈtraɪəl bə,luːn/ *n* [C] something that you do or say in order to see whether other people will accept something or not 试探性言行: *Senator Lott is floating trial balloons to test public opinion on the bill.* 参议员洛特正试探公众对该议案的看法。

tri-band /ˈtraɪ ,bænd; ˈtraɪ ,bænd/ *adj* a tri-band MOBILE PHONE is one that will work in the US and Canada as well as in Britain〔手机〕三频的〔可在美国、英国和加拿大使用〕

trickle /ˈtrɪkl̩; ˈtrɪkəl/ *v* [I]
NEW MEANING
trickle up *phr v* [I] if money trickles up, it tends to move from the poorest people to the richest people in a society, or from the poorest countries to the richest countries 资金向上滴流, 逆向滴流〔指金钱由穷人或穷国流向富人或富国〕

trip /trɪp; trɪp/ *v*
NEW MEANING
sb is tripping *AmE slang* used to say that you think someone is not thinking clearly or being reasonable【美俚】某人在犯糊涂: *Ken's tripping if he thinks I'm going to lend him $500.* 肯如果认为我会借给他500美元, 那是他脑子有病。

trol·leyed /ˈtrɑlɪd; ˈtrɒlid/ *adj* [not before noun 不用于名词前] *BrE slang* very drunk or affected by drugs【英俚】大醉的; 吸毒后迷迷糊糊的: *I'm a totally different person when I'm trolleyed.* 喝醉了的时候, 我会变成完全另外的一个人。

trophy wife /ˈtrofɪ ,waɪf; ˈtrəʊfi ,waɪf/ *n* [C] a young beautiful woman who is married to a rich and successful man〔富人的〕年轻貌美的妻子: *The resort was full of doctors and lawyers with their trophy wives.* 度假胜地到处可见有娇妻作伴的医生和律师。

trouser /ˈtraʊzɚ; ˈtraʊzə/ *v* [T] *BrE informal* to take and keep a large amount of money, usually dishonestly【英, 非正式】把〔钱〕占为己有: *It's true that he trousered several hundred thousand pounds, but his dishonesty went far beyond that.* 不错, 他是把几十万镑的钱占为己有, 但是, 他的不诚实行为远不止此。

trust·a·fari·an /,trʌstəˈfɛrɪən; ,trʌstəˈfeəriən/ *n* [C] *BrE informal* a young man or woman who has very rich parents and who usually lives in a rich area, but who dresses and acts like someone from a much poorer background【英, 非正式】〔衣着、举止〕像穷人的富家子女

'tude /tud; tjuːd/ *n* [U] *AmE slang* an attitude, style, type of behaviour etc that shows you have the confidence to do unusual and exciting things without caring what other people think; attitude【美俚】自信, 神气: **with 'tude** *Atlanta is definitely a city with 'tude.* 亚特兰大确实是一座神气十足的城市。

turn·ta·blist /ˈtɝn,teblɪst; ˈtɜːn,teɪbləst/ *n* [C] *informal* a DEEJAY who plays recorded music at parties or dances, and who mixes together parts of different records to form new music【非正式】〔聚会或舞会上的〕混合音乐唱片骑师

TV-14 /,ti vi fɔrˈtin; ,tiː viː fɔːˈtiːn/ *adj* used in the US to show that a television programme is not suitable for children under the age of 14〔美国电视节目〕14岁以下儿童不宜的

TV-G /,ti vi ˈdʒi; ,tiː viː ˈdʒiː/ *adj* used in the US to show that a television programme is suitable for people of all ages, including children〔美国电视节目〕各年龄组皆宜的

TV-M /,ti vi ˈɛm; ,tiː viː ˈem/ *adj* used in the US to show that a television programme is not suitable for people under the age of 17〔美国电视节目〕适于17岁以上成人观看的

TV-PG /,ti vi pi ˈdʒi; ,tiː viː piː ˈdʒiː/ *adj* used in the US to show that a television programme may include parts that are not suitable for young children to see〔美国电视节目〕含有部分儿童不宜的

TV-Y/,ti vi ˈwaɪ; ,tiː viː ˈwaɪ/ *adj* used in the US to show that a television programme is suitable for children〔美国电视节目〕适于儿童观看的

TV-Y7 /,ti vi waɪ ˈsɛvən; ,tiː viː waɪ ˈsevən/ *adj* used in the US to show that a television programme is not suitable for children under the age of seven〔美国电视节目〕七岁以下儿童不宜的

tween /twin; twiːn/ also 又作 **tween·ag·er** /ˈtwinedʒɚ; ˈtwiːneɪdʒə/ *n* [C] children who are 11 or 12 years old; PRE-TEENS 十一二岁的儿童: *The study found that tweens – not older teenagers – fight most often with their parents.* 研究显示, 十一二岁的儿童〔而不是更大的少年〕和父母吵得最多。

24/7 /,twɛntɪ,fɔr ˈsɛvən; ,twentifɔː ˈsevən/ *adv slang* twenty-four hours a day, seven days a week; all the time【俚】一天二十四小时, 一周七天; 每时每刻, 不间断地: *I can't stop thinking about her 24/7.* 我忍不住时时都在想她。—**24/7** *adj*: *a 24/7 call center* 每周七天二十四小时电话服务中心

twen·ty·some·thing /ˈtwɛntɪ,sʌmθɪŋ; ˈtwenti,sʌmθɪŋ/ *n* [C] someone who is between the ages of 20 and 29 二十多岁的人: *A crowd of twentysomethings were gathered outside the club.* 俱乐部外面聚了一群二十多岁的男女青年。

U,u

ultimate fight·ing /,ʌltəmɪt ˈfaɪtɪŋ; ,ʌltəmət ˈfaɪtɪŋ/ also 又作 **extreme fighting** *n* [U] a competition, similar to BOXING, in which two people are allowed to hit or kick each other and in which there are almost no rules. Ultimate fighting is not illegal in some countries, and in some parts of the US.〔类似拳击的〕极限格斗, 极限搏击

un·plugged /ʌnˈplʌgd; ʌnˈplʌgd/ *adj, adv* if a group of musicians performs unplugged, they perform without electric instruments〔音乐演奏〕不用电子乐器的[地], 不插电的[地]

unzip /ʌnˈzɪp; ,ʌnˈzɪp/ *v* [T]
NEW MEANING
to change a computer FILE back to its normal size so that you can use it, after it has been made to take up less space 给〔计算机文件〕解压缩

up /ʌp; ʌp/ *adj*
NEW MEANING
be up for sth *spoken* to be willing to do something that someone invites you to do with them【口】心甘情愿地做某事: *John wanted to see a movie last night, but I just wasn't up for it.* 约翰昨晚想去看电影, 可是我恰好没有心思去。| **be up for doing sth** *I might be up for having a drink later.* 我也许晚些时候会乐意去喝上一杯。

up·draft /ˈʌp,dræft; ˈʌpdrɑːft/ *n* [C] a situation in which prices, SHARES etc go up, or when business becomes better〔价格、股票等〕上扬;〔生意〕看好

up·load¹ /ˈʌp,lod; ˈʌpləʊd/ *v* [I,T] if information, a computer PROGRAM etc uploads, or if you upload it, you move it from a small computer to a computer network so that many people can see it or use it 上传, 上载〔由终端输入中央电脑〕: *I was trying to upload something to an electronic bulletin board but crashed the system.* 我想上传资料到电子告示牌上, 但却

把系统弄坏了。| *It might take a while for this to upload.* 把这些资料上传也许需要一些时间。

upload² /ˈʌpˌlod; ˈʌpləʊd/ *n* [C]
information, computer PROGRAMs etc that have been uploaded, or the process of uploading them 上传的信息[程序]; 上传: *You can receive regular e-mail updates of new uploads.* 你可以定期收到最新上传内容的电子邮件。| *tips on handling file uploads* 上传文件的操作提示

up·skill·ing /ˈʌpˌskɪlɪŋ; ˈʌpˌskɪlɪŋ/ *n* [U]
improving the skills of workers, usually through training, so that they will be better at their jobs 通过培训提高工人技能

up·tick /ˈʌpˌtɪk; ˈʌptɪk/ *n* [C]
an increase or improvement in the level of something 提高; 上升: [**+in**] *We have had an uptick in sales this year.* 我们本年度的销售额有所上升。

up·time /ˈʌpˌtaɪm; ˈʌptaɪm/ *n* [U]
the period of time when a computer is working normally and is able to be used〔电脑的〕正常运行时间, 可使用时间: *Some customers need 99% or better uptime from their mainframe computers.* 一些顾客需要他们的主电脑能有 99% 或更长的正常运行时间。

URL /ˌju ɑr ˈɛl; ˌjuː ɑːr ˈel/ *n* [C]
uniform resource locator; a description of where a particular computer FILE can be found, especially on the Internet. Internet URLs usually begin with http://. 统一资源定位地址〔如互联网的统一资源定位地址常以 http:// 开头〕

USB /ˌju ɛs ˈbi; ˌjuː es ˈbiː/ *n* [C]
universal serial bus; a way of connecting equipment such as a MOUSE and printer to a computer using wires so that all the equipment can work together 通用串行总线, 通用序列埠: *Many USB devices come with their own built-in cable.* 许多带通用串行总线接口的设备都有内置连线。

user fee /ˈjuzɚ ˌfi; ˈjuːzə ˌfiː/ *n* [C]
NEW MEANING
an amount of money someone pays for a service on the Internet〔上网〕用户费

user name /ˈjuzɚ ˌnem; ˈjuːzə ˌneɪm/ also 又作 **user ID** /ˈjuzɚ aɪ ˌdi; ˈjuːzər aɪ ˌdiː/ *n* [C]
a name or special word that proves who you are and allows you to enter a computer system or use the Internet. Usually, this name and PASSWORD must be entered into the computer before you are allowed to use the computer or the Internet 用户名: *Please enter your user name and password and click 'OK'.* 请输入你的用户名和密码, 然后点击"确认"。| *The computer keeps saying my user name is invalid.* 电脑反复显示我的用户名无效。

USP /ˌju ɛs ˈpi; ˌjuː es ˈpiː/ *n* [C]
unique selling proposition; a feature of a product that makes it different from other similar products, and therefore more attractive to people who might buy it 商品特色, 卖点: *Your business needs to have a USP.* 你的企业需要有经营特色。

V,v

value-ad·ded re·sell·er /ˌvælju ædɪd riˈsɛlɚ; ˌvæljuː ædɪ̣d riˈselə/ *abbreviation* 缩写为 **VAR** *n* [C]
a person or company who sells goods, especially computers, after combining them with other products or services, in order to increase their value〔尤指电脑的〕增值分销商

vanilla /vəˈnɪlə; vəˈnɪlə/ also 又作 **plain vanilla** *adj*
NEW MEANING
very basic and having no special features 基本的, 普普通通的, 没有特色的: *Their vanilla model is priced at just under five hundred dollars.* 他们的基本型号的价格仅在 500 美元以下。| *The company produces plain vanilla computer chips.* 该公司生产普通的电脑芯片。

va·pour·ware *BrE*【英】, **vaporware** *AmE*【美】/ˈvepɚˌwɛr; ˈveɪpəweə/ *n* [U]
humorous a new type of computer product that has been advertised but is not finished or available to buy yet. This word comes from a combination of the words 'VAPOUR', which means a mass of small drops of liquid floating in the air, and 'HARDWARE' or 'SOFTWARE'.【幽默】朦胧件, 雾件〔指已进行广告宣传但尚未上市的电脑新产品, 由 vapour 和 hardware 或 software 缩合而成〕

VAR /ˌvi e ˈɑr; ˌviː eɪ ˈɑː/ *n* [C]
abbreviation of 缩写= VALUE-ADDED RESELLER

V-chip /ˈvi ˌtʃɪp; ˈviː ˌtʃɪp/ *n* [C]
an electronic CHIP in a television that allows parents to prevent their children from watching programmes that are violent or have sex in them V 芯[晶]片〔一种可装入电视机内用以阻断暴力或色情节目的电子芯片〕

vCJD /ˌvi si dʒe ˈdi; ˌviː siː dʒeɪ ˈdiː/ *n* [U]
new variant Creutzfeldt-Jacob Disease; a human form of the deadly brain disease BSE 新变异型克－雅氏病, 人类疯牛症: *Early symptoms of vCJD may include memory loss and difficulty walking.* 变异克－雅氏病的早期症状包括丧失记忆和行走困难。

veg·e·ta·tive /ˈvɛdʒəˌtetɪv; ˈvedʒɪ̣tətɪv/ *adj*
a vegetative state a condition in which you cannot think or move because your brain has been damaged in an accident 植物人状态

vertical ex·pan·sion /ˌvɝtɪkḷ ɪkˈspænʃən; ˌvɜːtɪkəl ɪkˈspænʃən/ *n* [U]
technical a situation in which a company starts to do some of the business activities that were done in the past by companies that supplied it with goods or services, or by its customers【术语】纵向扩展, 抢行〔开始经营过去由供应商或客户提供的业务〕

Vi·ag·ra /vaɪˈægrə; vaɪˈægrə/ *n* [U]
trademark a drug that helps men have an ERECTION (1)【商标】万艾可, 伟哥〔一种治疗男性阳痿的药〕

vid·e·o·card /ˈvɪdɪoˌkɑrd; ˈvɪdiəʊˌkɑːd/ *n* [C]
a CIRCUIT BOARD (=piece of electronic equipment carrying electrical signals) that can be added to a computer so that it is able to show moving pictures〔电脑的〕视频卡, 显示卡

video on de·mand /ˌvɪdɪo ɑn dɪˈmænd; ˌvɪdiəʊ ɒn dɪˈmɑːnd/ *n* [U]
a service available on the Internet that allows you to choose and watch recordings of television programmes or films that have been stored as computer FILEs〔网上〕视频点播 (服务)

viral mar·ket·ing /ˌvaɪrəl ˈmɑrkɪtɪŋ; ˌvaɪərəl ˈmɑːkɪ̣tɪŋ/ *n* [U]
a type of advertising used by Internet companies in which computer users receive and send out advertising messages or images through E-MAIL without being aware that they are doing this. This kind of marketing is named after the computer VIRUS, which spreads rapidly among computer users.〔互联网公司进行的〕病毒式营销 (手法): *You can reach more potential customers by using viral marketing techniques.* 利用病毒式营销, 你可以接触到更多潜在的客户。

virgin /ˈvɝdʒɪn; ˈvɜːdʒɪ̣n/ *n* [U]
NEW MEANING
spoken humorous someone who has never done a particular activity【口, 幽默】生手, 新手: *Even computer virgins should be able to quickly learn how to use this software.* 就连电脑新手也能很快地学会如何使这款软件。

virtual /ˈvɝtʃuəl; ˈvɜːtʃuəl/ *adj* [only before noun 仅用于名词前]
NEW MEANING
relating to something that is made, done, seen etc on a computer, rather than in the real world〔电脑〕虚拟的: *The website allows you to take a virtual tour of the campus.* 该网站能让你对校园作一次虚拟游览。

virtual ad·ver·ti·sing /ˌvɝtʃuəl ˋædvɚtaɪzɪŋ; ˌvɜːtʃuəl ˈædvətaɪzɪŋ/ *n* [U]
advertising that is added to a television programme of a sports event, and which uses SPECIAL EFFECTS so that only the people who are watching the event on television can see it 虚拟广告〔以特技效果放在电视播映的体育比赛节目中，只有收看该节目的观众才能看到〕

virtual cash /ˌvɝtʃuəl ˋkæʃ; ˌvɜːtʃuəl ˈkæʃ/ *n* [U]
money that is used to pay for something that you buy on the Internet, using a CREDIT CARD〔网上购物使用的〕虚拟现金

virtual com·mu·ni·ty /ˌvɝtʃuəl kəˋmjunətɪ; ˌvɜːtʃuəl kəˈmjuːnəti/ also 又作 **community** *n* [C]
a group of people who use the Internet to discuss things with each other and share ideas about a particular subject or common interest 虚拟社区〔指在网上讨论共同主题的一群人〕: *a list of online music communities* 在线音乐虚拟社区清单

virtually /ˋvɝtʃuəlɪ; ˈvɜːtʃuəli/ *adv*
NEW MEANING
on a computer, rather than in the real world〔电脑〕虚拟地: *Both articles were virtually published on the Internet before appearing in the magazine.* 两篇文章都是先在网上发表，然后才刊登在杂志上。

virtual of·fice /ˌvɝtʃuəl ˋɔfɪs; ˌvɜːtʃuəl ˈɒfəs/ *n* [C]
a situation in which a company's workers do not go to an office to work, but instead use computers that are connected to the Internet to work and communicate with each other from different places 虚拟办公室: *Does the virtual office equal freedom or isolation?* 虚拟办公室意味着自由还是隔绝呢?

virus /ˋvaɪrəs; ˈvaɪərəs/ *n* [C]
a PROGRAM that sends a large number of annoying messages to many people's MOBILE PHONES in an uncontrolled way〔移动电话的〕病毒

visit /ˋvɪzɪt; ˈvɪzət/ *v* [T]
NEW MEANING
to go to a WEBSITE on the Internet 访问〔网站〕: *Over 1,000 people visit our site every week.* 每个星期有千余人访问我们的网站。—**visitor** *n* [C]

visitation /ˌvɪzəˋteʃən; ˌvɪzəˈteɪʃən/ *n* [C,U]
NEW MEANING
law in a situation where parents are DIVORCE*d*, an occasion when one parent is allowed to spend time with their children who are living with the other parent, or the right to do this【法律】〔离婚夫妇对跟另一方生活的子女的〕探视: *visitation rights* 探视权

VOD /ˌvi o ˋdi; ˌviː əʊ ˈdiː/ *n* [U]
video on demand; a special service that lets television viewers pay to watch particular films at whatever time they choose to watch them 视频点播（服务），自选电视（节目）

voice jail /ˋvɔɪs ˌdʒel; ˈvɔɪs ˌdʒeɪl/ *n* [U]
humorous a telephone system that contains recorded messages giving you information or instructions, and that requires you to make different choices by pressing buttons on your telephone. This expression comes from a combination of the words 'voice mail' and 'jail' because some people find it annoying not to be able to speak to a real person on these systems.【幽默】电话语音提示系统〔由voice mail和jail缩合而成〕: *When the caller lost in voice jail is a potential customer, your company risks losing a sale.* 如果对电话语音提示搞不清楚的来电者是潜在的顾客，贵公司就有可能失去一笔生意。

voice mail·box /ˋvɔɪs ˌmelbɑks; ˈvɔɪs ˌmeɪlbɒks/ *n* [C]
a system in which telephone messages are recorded onto a computer so that someone can listen to them later 语音信箱，留言信箱: *To access your voice mailbox, dial 3882.* 要进入你的语音信箱，请拨打3882。

voyeur TV /vwɑˋjɝ ti ˌvi; vwɑːˈjɜː tiː ˌviː/ *n* [U]
television programmes that show a group of ordinary people who have been chosen to be recorded while doing things in their daily lives, without a planned SCRIPT. Some people disapprove of this type of programme because they do not think it is right to watch other people's private lives. 纪实电视节目，窥视电视节目

VR /ˌvi ˋɑr; ˌviː ˈɑː/
the abbreviation of 缩写= VIRTUAL REALITY

vulture cap·i·tal·ist /ˋvʌltʃɚ ˌkæpətl̩ɪst; ˈvʌltʃə ˌkæpətl̩ɪst/ *n* [C]
someone who INVEST*s* money in a new business but then takes control of the business, usually in an unfair way 秃鹰资本家，敌意收购资本家〔投资新企业，然后通常以不公正的手法取得控制权的人〕

vulture fund /ˋvʌltʃɚ ˌfʌnd; ˈvʌltʃə ˌfʌnd/ *n* [C]
technical informal a company that INVEST*s* in companies that are having difficulties, in order to gain control of them【术语，非正式】秃鹰基金，敌意收购基金〔为取得控制权而投入的资金〕

W,w

wack /wæk; wæk/ *adj*
slang very bad【俚】低劣的，极差的: *Man, that is just so wack.* 老兄，那真是太差劲了。

wack·o /ˋwæko; ˈwækəʊ/ *n* [C]
informal someone who is crazy or behaves in a strange way【非正式】疯癫的人；古怪的人

wait·ron /ˋwetrən; ˈweɪtrən/ *n* [C]
humorous a WAITER or WAITRESS【幽默】侍者，服务员

wake /wek; weɪk/ *v*
NEW MEANING
wake up and smell the coffee *spoken* used to tell someone that they should realize what is really happening in a situation【口】面对现实

wake-up call /ˋwek ʌp ˌkɔl; ˈweɪk ʌp ˌkɔːl/ *n* [C usually singular 一般用单数]
an experience or event that shocks you and makes you realize that something bad is happening and that changes must be made 警钟: *Maybe the results of his medical exam will give Dad the wake-up call he needs to start living a healthier lifestyle.* 爸爸的体检结果也许会给他敲响警钟，使他认识到需要开始以一种较健康的方式生活。

walk-in /ˋwɔk ˌɪn; ˈwɔːk ˌɪn/ *adj* [only before noun 仅用于名词前]
NEW MEANING
walk-in business/clinic/centre etc a business, doctor's office etc that you can use or go to without an APPOINTMENT (=an arrangement to be somewhere or meet someone at an agreed time or place)〔不用预约的〕即时业务/诊所/中心等

walking bus /ˋwɔkɪŋ ˌbʌs; ˈwɔːkɪŋ ˌbʌs/ *n* [C] *BrE*
a group of children who walk to or from school together, with other children and their parents joining the group at different places along the way【英】步行巴士〔一起走路上学或放学的孩子和他们的父母〕

walk·through /ˋwɔkˌθru; ˈwɔːkθruː/ *n* [C]
written instructions that tell you all the details of how you should play a VIDEO GAME〔电脑游戏的〕通关方法，攻略: [+for] *The site has a collection of hints, cheats and walkthroughs for PC games.* 网站上有一系列关于个人电脑游戏的提示、作弊码和通关方法。| *the official walkthrough for Tomb Raider*《古墓丽影》的官方攻略

WAP /wæp; wæp/ *n* [U]
wireless application protocol; a system that uses radio waves to allow electronic equipment that is not physically attached to a computer, for example a MOBILE PHONE, to use the Internet 无线应用协议〔一种通信制式〕

WAP-en·a·bled /ˋwæp ɪnˌebl̩d; ˈwæp ɪnˌeɪbəld/ *adj*
a WAP-enabled MOBILE PHONE can receive written information from the Internet on a small screen that is part of the phone〔手机〕可支持无线应用协议[上网]的

war chest /ˋwɔr ˏtʃɛst; ˈwɔː ˌtʃest/ *n* [C]
the money that a government has available to solve a problem〔政府的〕应急基金: *The government's huge war chest could be used to improve transport in time for the election.* 政府庞大的应急基金在选举前可及时用于改善交通状况。

was·a·bi /ˋwɑsəbɪ; ˈwɒsəbi/ *n* [U]
a green strong-tasting Japanese food, which is added to SUSHI and other food in small amounts in order to make it taste hotter 辣根, 绿芥末〔一种日本调味料〕

was·sup /wɑˋsʌp; wɒˈsʌp/ *interjection*
slang another spelling of WHASSUP【俚】whassup的另一种拼法

water cool·er /ˋwɔtɚ ˏkulɚ; ˈwɔːtə ˌkuːlə/ *n* [C]
1 a machine that you can get a cup of drinking water from 饮水器 **2 water cooler gossip** conversation about other people's behaviour or private lives that happens in offices when people meet each other by the water cooler〔人们在办公室饮水器旁说的〕闲话

WAV /ˏdʌbḷju e ˋvi; ˌdʌbəljuː eɪ ˈviː/ *n* [U]
technical waveform audio; a type of computer FILE that contains sound【术语】波形音频〔一种包含声音的计算机文件〕

web brows·er /ˋwɛb ˏbraʊzɚ; ˈweb ˌbraʊzə/ *n* [C]
a BROWSER; a computer PROGRAM that finds information on the Internet and shows it on your computer screen 网络浏览器

web·cam /ˋwɛbˏkæm; ˈwebkæm/ *n* [C]
a special camera that films events and broadcasts them on a WEBSITE as they happen 网络摄影机

web·cast[1] /ˋwɛbˏkæst; ˈwebkɑːst/ *n* [C]
a programme that is broadcast on the Internet 网络播放节目: *Visitors to our website can download tomorrow night's webcast for free.* 进入我们网站的访客可免费下载明晚的网络播放节目。

webcast[2] /ˋwɛbˏkæst; ˈwebkɑːst/ *v* [I,T]
to broadcast an event on the Internet, at the time the event happens 网络(实时)播放: *Various local news sites plan to webcast each of the mayoral debates.* 各个地区的新闻网站计划通过网络播放每场市长竞选辩论。

web·cast·ing /ˋwɛbˏkæstɪŋ; ˈwebˌkɑːstɪŋ/ *n* [U]
the use of the Internet to send information, especially news or entertainment, to many people at the same time 网上实时播放〔尤指新闻和娱乐活动〕

web de·sign·er /ˋwɛb dɪˏzaɪnɚ; ˈweb dɪˌzaɪnə/ *n* [C]
someone who designs WEBSITEs, especially websites for businesses or organizations 网站设计师

web·head /ˋwɛbˏhɛd; ˈwebhed/ *n* [C]
informal someone who uses the Internet a lot, especially in a skilful way【非正式】〔尤指熟练使用互联网的〕网民, 网络迷

web·log /ˋwɛbˏlɔg; ˈweblɒg/ also 又作 **blog** *n* [C]
a WEBSITE that contains a list of LINKs (=connections) that allow you to go to other websites, and a short description of those sites〔可连接其他网站并有其简介的〕网站信息中心: *Jay's Picks remains one of the most popular weblogs on the Internet.* "杰伊精选"一直是互联网上最受欢迎的网站信息中心之一。

web·mast·er /ˋwɛbˏmæstɚ; ˈwebˌmɑːstə/ *n* [C]
someone who organizes a WEBSITE and makes sure it keeps working properly 网站管理[维护]员, 网管

web·page /ˋwɛbˏpedʒ; ˈwebpeɪdʒ/ *n* [C]
all the information that you can see in one section of a website. You have to CLICK on a button to go to another webpage on the same website. 网页

web ring /ˋwɛb ˏrɪŋ; ˈweb ˌrɪŋ/ *n* [C]
a group of similar WEBSITEs which are connected to each other by LINKs to make it easy for people to find a lot of information on a particular subject on the Internet 网圈, 网站联盟: *a classical music web ring* 古典音乐网圈

web·site /ˋwɛbˏsaɪt; ˈwebsaɪt/ *n* [C]
a set of FILEs on a computer that people can read over the Internet using a BROWSER 网站; 网址: *Nearly all publishers have their own websites now.* 现在差不多所有出版社都有自己的网站。

web·zine /ˋwɛbˏzin; ˈwebziːn/ *n* [C]
a collection of articles, stories, and pictures that you can see and read on the Internet, but is not printed onto paper or sold in stores 网络杂志

wet sales /ˋwɛt ˏselz; ˈwet ˌseɪlz/ *n* [plural] *BrE technical* the money that a restaurant, bar etc makes from the sale of alcoholic drinks【英, 术语】售酒精饮料所得: *Most of the pub's money is made in wet sales.* 酒吧的钱大多数是靠售卖酒精饮料赚来的。

whack /hwæk; wæk/ *v* [T] *AmE*
slang to murder someone, especially in connection with MAFIA activities【美俚】谋杀〔尤与黑手党活动有关〕: *O'Neill learned that the New Yorkers were planning to whack him.* 奥尼尔得知"纽约帮"在计划干掉他。— **whack** *n* [C]

whas·sup /wɑˋsʌp; wɒˈsʌp/ *interjection*
slang a word meaning 'hello', used especially as a greeting to someone you know very well【俚】喂; 你好〔对熟人的一种问候语〕

what /hwɑt; wɒt/ *pron*
NEW MEANING
what's up with that? *AmE spoken* used to say that you do not understand a situation or think it is unreasonable【美口】那是怎么回事?〔用于表示不明白某情形或认为那是不合理的〕: *The college is raising tuition by 20% – what's up with that?* 学院要把学费提高 20% —— 那是怎么回事?

whip·saw /ˋhwɪpsɔ; ˈwɪpsɔː/ *v* [T]
technical informal【术语, 非正式】**be whipsawed** if money that people have used to buy SHAREs, or people who have bought shares are whipsawed, they are trapped in a STOCK MARKET where prices are falling and rising very quickly, and it is difficult to say what might happen〔股票买卖中〕被套牢

white flight /ˋhwaɪt ˏflaɪt; ˈwaɪt ˌflaɪt/ *n* [U] *AmE*
a situation in which white people move away from an area or send their children to private schools in order to avoid being near people who are not white【美】白人迁移〔以逃避非白种人〕

white hat hack·er /ˏhwaɪt hæt ˋhækɚ; ˌwaɪt hæt ˈhækə/ *n* [C]
a computer HACKER who has been hired by a company to help protect its computer system. This word comes from the tradition in old Western films for the good people to wear white hats, while the bad people wore black hats. Computer HACKERs are usually considered to do harmful things to computer systems, but white hat hackers use their skills to do helpful things. 白帽黑客〔公司雇用以保护自己电脑系统的网络高手, 源于西部影片中的好人多戴白帽子〕—**white hat hacking** *n* [U]

white van man /ˋhwaɪt væn ˏmæn; ˈwaɪt væn ˌmæn/ *n* [C] *BrE*
informal humorous a word used to talk about a man who drives a white VAN, especially for delivering goods to places in towns or cities, in an AGGRESSIVE and dangerous way【英, 非正式, 幽默】白色飞车手〔指驾驶白色货车、开车鲁莽的司机〕

wig·ger /ˋwɪgɚ; ˈwɪgə/ *n* [C]
slang humorous a white person who speaks and acts like a black person who is interested in, for example, HIP HOP music and culture【俚, 幽默】〔谈话举止像黑人的〕白人嬉蹦族

windfall tax /ˋwɪndfɔl ˏtæks; ˈwɪndfɔːl ˌtæks/ *n* [C]
in Britain, an additional amount of tax that the government sometimes takes from a company that has suddenly earned a large amount of money that it did not expect to earn 意外利润税〔英国政府对企业意外获得的大额收入征收的税项〕

win·ning·est /ˈwɪnɪŋɪst; ˈwɪnɪŋɪst/ *adj AmE slang* **the winningest team/pitcher/coach etc (in sth)** used in news reports of sporting events to describe the team, player etc that has won the most games【美俚】〔赢得比赛最多的〕获胜场次最多的球队/投手/教练等〔新闻报道用语〕: *Smith became the winningest coach in college basketball history.* 史密斯成了大学篮球赛历史上获胜场次最多的球队教练。

win-win /ˌwɪn ˈwɪn; ˌwɪn ˈwɪn◂/ *adj* [only before noun 仅用于名词前]
a win-win situation, strategy, approach etc is one that will end well for everyone involved in it 双赢的: *It's a win-win situation all around.* 这在各个方面都是一种双赢局面。—**win-win** *n* [C]: *The agreement is a win-win for everyone.* 这项协议对大家来说都是双赢。

WIP /ˌdʌbljʊ aɪ ˈpi; ˌdʌbəljuː aɪ ˈpiː/ *n*
work in progress or work in process; work that is being done 进行中的工作, 正在办的事

wireless com·mu·ni·ca·tions /ˌwaɪrlɪs kəmjunəˈkeʃənz; ˌwaɪələs kəmjuːnɪˈkeɪʃənz/ *n* [plural]
a system of sending and receiving electronic signals that does not use electrical or telephone wires, for example the system used by MOBILE PHONES 无线通信

word /wɝd; wɜːd/ *n*
NEW MEANING
word! *AmE slang* used to say that you understand or agree with what someone has just said【美俚】一句话! 没说的!〔表示明白或赞成某人刚才说的话〕

work·flow /ˈwɝkˌflo; ˈwɜːkfləʊ/ *n* [U]
the way that a particular PROJECT is organized by a company, including which part of a project someone is going to do, and when they are supposed to do it 工作流程

WORM /wɝm; wɜːm/ *n* [C]
write once, read many; a CD on which information can be stored only once, but seen or used many times 一写多读(光盘)

worthy /ˈwɝðɪ; ˈwɜːði/ *adj*
NEW MEANING
I'm/We're not worthy *spoken humorous* used to say that you consider it a great honour to be with someone because they are famous, or much more skilful at doing something than you are【口, 幽默】我/我们深感荣幸

wrap /ræp; ræp/ *n* [C]
NEW MEANING
a type of SANDWICH made with thin bread which is rolled around meat, vegetables etc〔用薄面包裹着肉、菜等的〕面卷饼

wraparounds 贴面式太阳镜

wrap·a·rounds /ˈræpəˌraundz; ˈræpəˌraʊndz/ *n* [plural]
a type of SUNGLASSES curved in such a way that they fit close to your face, from one ear to the other 围裹式墨镜, 贴面式太阳镜

wreckage /ˈrɛkɪdʒ; ˈrekɪdʒ/ *n* [U]
NEW MEANING
a word used in news reports meaning a business activity, company etc that has failed or is likely to fail〔生意、公司等的〕失败, 破产〔新闻报道用语〕

WRT
a written abbreviation of 缩写= 'with regard to', used in E-MAIL or by people communicating in CHAT ROOMs on the Internet 关于…, 就…而言〔电子邮件和网上聊天室用语〕

X /ɛks; eks/ *n* [U] *AmE*
NEW MEANING
slang the illegal drug ECSTACY【美俚】"狂喜"迷幻药, 摇头丸

xen·o·trans·plant /ˌzɛnoˈtrænsplænt; ˌzenəʊˈtrænsplɑːnt/ *n*
1 [C,U] the operation of putting an organ, piece of skin etc from an animal into a person's body 异种器官移植术, 动物器官人体移植术: *Doctors in Mississippi performed the world's first heart xenotransplant.* 密西西比州的医生完成了世界上第一例异种心脏移植。**2** [C] the organ that is moved in this type of operation 异种移植的器官 —**xenotransplant** *v* [T] —**xenotransplanted** *adj*: *xenotransplanted organs* 异种移植的器官

xen·o·trans·plan·ta·tion /ˌzɛnoˌtrænsplænˈteʃən; ˌzenəʊˌtrænsplɑːnˈteɪʃən/ *n* [U]
the practice of putting organs or other body parts from animals into people's bodies 异种器官移植术: *health risks related to xenotransplantation* 异种器官移植给健康带来的风险

XML /ˌɛks ɛm ˈɛl; ˌeks em ˈel/ *n* [U]
technical extensible markup language; a way of writing a document on a computer so that its structure is clear, and so that it can easily be read on a different computer system【术语】可扩展标记语言

Y2K /ˌwaɪ tu ˈke; ˌwaɪ tuː ˈkeɪ/
the abbreviation of 缩写= 'year two thousand', used especially to talk about problems that some people believed would affect many computers which did not recognize the date when the year 2000 began 公元2000年〔尤在谈到千年虫问题时使用〕: *Click here for a guide to the essential Y2K resources on the Internet.* 点击此处可找到互联网上2000年的重要资料的指南。

yad·a yad·a yad·a, yadda yadda yadda /ˌjædə jædə ˈjædə; ˌjædə jædə ˈjædə/ *AmE*
spoken said when you do not want to give a lot of detailed information, because it is boring or because the person you are talking to already knows it【美口】如此这般〔不想提供详细资料时用, 因为内容沉闷或听者已经知道那事〕: *I started talking to her and – yada yada yada – it turns out she's from New York too.* 我开始跟她谈话, 说了半天, 结果发现她也是纽约人。

Yard·ie /ˈjɑrdɪ; ˈjɑːdi/ *n* [C] *BrE*【英】
1 someone from the West Indies 西印度群岛人 **2** a member of an organized group of West Indian criminals 亚迪(帮成员)〔西印度群岛一个犯罪组织的成员〕

yoof /juf; juːf/ *adj* [only before noun 仅用于名词前] *BrE humorous* relating to young people; YOUTH【英, 幽默】青年人的, 青年的: *a yoof magazine* 年轻人的杂志 —**yoof** *n* [U] *today's yoof* 今日的年轻人

yup·pi·fy /ˈjʌpəfaɪ; ˈjʌpɪfaɪ/ *v* [T usually passive 一般用被动态]
humorous to improve the buildings in an area, or to open expensive restaurants, shops etc so that rich young people want to live in the buildings or use the restaurants etc. This word comes from the noun YUPPIE which is used to talk about young people in professional jobs with a high

income that they enjoy spending.【幽默】〔建筑物、昂贵的餐厅等〕使雅皮士化〔源自名词yuppie雅皮士，指高收入、崇尚消费的专业人士〕: *The restaurant's yuppified interior was done in colors like teal and mauve.* 该饭馆雅皮士化的内部装修是以蓝绿和淡紫等作为主色。

Z,z

zap /zæp; zæp/ *v* [I,T]
NEW MEANING
to change the CHANNEL on a television, using a remote control (=something that allows you to control a television without touching it)〔使用遥控器〕换〔电视〕频道: *Dave just sat there, zapping through all 70-plus channels.* 戴夫就坐在那里，用遥控器把70多个频道全部扫视了一遍。

zero tol·e·rance /ˌzɪro ˋtɑlərəns; ˌzɪərəʊ ˈtɒlərəns/ *n* [U]
a way of dealing with crime in which every person who breaks the law, even in a very small way, is punished as severely as possible 零容忍，零宽容〔指对各种违法行为，不论轻重，一律严惩，绝不容忍的做法〕: *The policy of zero tolerance has been proved effective in inner-city areas.* 零容忍政策证明了在旧城区十分有效。

zine, 'zine /zin; ziːn/ *n* [C]
a small magazine, usually about things such as popular music, fashion etc, that is written and printed by people who are not professional writers〔由业余人士编印的〕同好杂志

zip file /ˋzɪp ˌfaɪl; ˈzɪp ˌfaɪl/ *n* [C]
technical a computer file in which the information is COMPRESS*ed* (=made smaller) so that it uses less space【术语】〔计算机的〕压缩文件[文档]

IELTS Vocabulary
雅思常考词汇

IELTS是International English Language Testing System的缩写，即国际英语水平测试（又称雅思），由英国文化协会联同英国一些大学及澳洲教育机构等制订，是国际认可的英语水平测试之一。由于其资格得到很多大学及企业的认可，近年吸引了不少人士报考。

IELTS的考试内容分四部分，包括听力、会话、阅读及写作，考试时间共两小时四十五分钟。每部分考试除有独立分数外，亦有总分数。成绩共分九级，级数愈高，表示英语能力水平愈高。以考大学为例，一般要考到第六级合格才有机会被大学录取。目前已超过150个国家可提供IELTS考试。

词汇在IELTS考试中占有重要的位置，附录所挑选的都是以往IELTS考卷中经常出现的词汇。由于考试内容不断更新变化，本附录仅供各考生参考，不足之处，恳请原谅。

A, a

abandon¹ *v* **1** 抛弃，遗弃〔某人〕**2** 离弃，逃离〔某地方或交通工具等〕**3** 放弃，中止 **4** 放弃〔信仰或原则〕**5 abandon yourself to** 沉湎于，放纵〔感情〕**6 abandon ship** 〔由于船在下沉而〕弃船（逃生）—**abandonment** *n*

abandon² *n* **with gay/wild abandon** 尽情；放纵

abnormal *adj* 不正常的，反常的；变态的

absorb *v* **1 ►LIQUID** 液体◄ 吸收〔液体〕**2 ►INFORMATION** 信息◄ 理解，掌握 **3 ►INTEREST** 兴趣◄ 吸引〔某人〕，使专心 **4 ►BECOME PART OF** 成为…的一部分◄ 并入；吞并 **5 ►MONEY/TIME ETC** 金钱/时间等◄ 消耗，花去 **6 ►FORCE** 力◄ 消减，缓冲 **7 ►LIGHT/HEAT/ENERGY** 光/热/能◄ 吸收

abstract¹ *adj* **1** 纯理论上的，纯概念的 **2** 抽象的 **3**〔艺术〕抽象派的

abstract² *n* **1 in the abstract** 抽象地，从理论上说 **2** 摘要，梗概 **3** 抽象派作品

abstract³ *v* **1** 摘录，节录 **2** 转移开

academic¹ *adj* **1** 学术的 **2** 学术上的；理论上的 **3** 不合实际的，理论的 **4** 学业（成绩）优秀的 —**academically** *adv*

academic² *n* 大学教师

accelerate *v* **1** 加快，加速 **2**（使）加快；（使）提前 —反义词 DECELERATE

access¹ *n* **1** 入口；进入 **2** 途径 **3** 进入权；使用权 **4 have access to** 有权接触〔机密等〕**5** 探视权 **6 have access to a phone/a computer etc** 附近有电话/电脑等可供使用 **7 gain/get access (to)** 到达〔某地〕；见到〔某人或某物〕

access² *v* 存取〔尤指电脑数据〕

accommodate *v* **1** 容纳 **2** 为…提供住处[工作场所] **3** 迎合；迁就 **4**（使）适应；（使）顺应 **5** 宽限；通融

accompany *v* **1** 陪伴，陪同 **2** 为…伴奏 **3** 伴随 **4** 附有，带有，配有

accomplish *v* 完成〔任务等〕，取得〔成功〕

account¹ *n* **1 ►DESCRIPTION** 描述◄ **a)** 报道，叙述，描写 **b)** 详尽的科学描述 **2 ►AT A BANK** 在银行◄ 账户 **3 take account of sth/take sth into account** 把…考虑在内 **4 on account of** 因为，由于 **5 accounts a)** 账目 **b)** 会计部 **6 on account** 赊账 **7 ►WITH A SHOP** 与商店◄ 赊购账 **8 ►BILL** 账单◄ 账单 **9 ►ARRANGEMENT TO SELL GOODS** 售货安排◄ 客户 **10 by/from all accounts** 根据各方面所说 **11 on my/his etc account** 为了我/他等的缘故 **12 on your own account** 靠自己；为自己 **13 on no account/not on any account** 决不 **14 by your own account** 据某人自己所说 **15 on that account/on this account** 考虑到那种/这种情况 **16 give a good/poor account of yourself** 表现好/表现差 **17 bring/call sb to account** 责令某人对…作出解释 **18 put/turn sth to good account** 充分利用某物 **19 of no account/of little account** 不重要，没关系 **20 of some account** 相当重要

account² *v*
  account for sth *phr v* **1** 是…的原因 **2** 对…作出〔满意的〕解释 **3** 占…〔比例〕**4** 说明…在何处 **5 there's no accounting for taste** 人各有所好

accumulate *v* **1** 积累，积聚 **2** 大量聚积 —**accumulation** *n*

accurate *adj* **1**〔资料、报道、描述等〕准确的 **2**〔测量、计算、记录等〕精确的，无差错的 **3**〔仪器〕精密的 **4**〔射击、投掷等〕准确的 —**accurately** *adv*

accustom *v* 使…习惯于

achieve *v* **1** 实现；取得；达到 **2** 获得成功 —**achievable** *adj*

acknowledge *v* **1 ►ADMIT** 承认◄ 承认；供认 **2 be acknowledged as** 被公认为是… **3 ►ACCEPT SB'S AUTHORITY** 承认某人的权威◄ 承认〔政府、法庭、领袖等〕的合法性 **4 ►LETTER/MESSAGE ETC** 信/口信等◄ 确认〔收悉〕**5 ►SHOW THANKS FOR** 表示感谢◄〔公开〕表示感谢 **6 ►SHOW YOU NOTICE SB** 表明注意到某人◄ 打招呼，理会

acquaintance *n* **1** 相识〔但不很熟〕的人；泛泛之交 **2 make sb's acquaintance** 结识某人 **3 of your acquaintance** 你认识的〔人〕**4** 所知；了解 **5 on further/closer acquaintance** 进一步了解

acquire *v* **1** 购得，得到〔尤指昂贵的或难以得到的东西〕**2** 掌握，获得〔知识、技能等〕**3 acquire a taste for** 慢慢喜欢上 **4 be an acquired taste** 是后来喜欢上的东西 **5** 以不正当的方式获得[占有]

adapt *v* 1（使）适应，（使）适合 2 改造，改装 3 **be well adapted to** 特别适应 4 改编
address[1] *n* 1 地址 2 讲话，演说 3〔电脑的〕位址，地址 4 **form/style/mode of address** 称呼方式/风格/语气
address[2] *v* 1 在〔信封、包裹等〕上写姓名和地址 2 向…讲话 3 **address a meeting/crowd/conference etc** 在会上/对人群/在大会上等发表演说 4 称呼 5 探讨〔如何处理问题〕
adequate *adj* 1 适当的，足够的，充分的 2 可以胜任的 3 差强人意的，过得去的 —**adequately** *adv* —**adequacy** *n*
adjust *v* 1 调整，调节 2 适应；使适合
administer *v* 1 管理，治理 2 执行，实施 3 给予，用〔药等〕
admire *v* 1 钦佩，赞美，羡慕 2 欣赏，观赏 3 **admire sb from afar** 暗自仰慕 —**admiring** *adj* —**admiringly** *adv*
admit *v* 1 承认，赞同 2 **admit to** 承认〔做错了事，犯了罪〕3 允许…进入 4 允许加入，接纳 5 **be admitted to hospital** 被送进医院 6 **admit defeat**〔中途〕承认失败，认输 7 **an admitted alcoholic/atheist etc** 自认的酒鬼/无神论者等
admit of sth *phr v* 容许有
adolescence *n* 青春期
adopt *v* 1 ►**CHILD** 孩子◄ 收养，领养 2 **adopt an approach/strategy/policy** 采用某方法/战略/政策 3 ►**STYLE/MANNER** 风格/方式◄ 采取，采用 4 ►**ACCEPT A SUGGESTION** 接受建议◄〔尤指通过表决〕正式批准；认可；接受 5 **adopt a name/country** 选定姓名/国家 6 ►**ELECTION** 选举◄ 提名…为候选人
adore *v* 1 敬慕，爱慕 2 非常喜欢
advance[1] *n* 1 **in advance** 预先，提前 2 ►**DEVELOPMENT/IMPROVEMENT** 发展/改进◄ 进步，进展 3 ►**FORWARD MOVEMENT** 向前的移动◄ 前进 4 ►**MONEY** 金钱◄ 预付款 5 **advances**〔对异性的〕挑逗，勾引 6 ►**INCREASE** 增加◄ 上涨，攀升
advance[2] *v* 1 ►**MOVE** 运动◄〔尤指缓慢而坚定地〕前进，推进 2 ►**DEVELOP** 发展◄ 进展 3 **advance a plan/idea/proposal etc** 提出计划/看法/建议等 4 ►**MONEY** 金钱◄ 预支 5 **advance a cause/your interests/your career etc** 拓展事业/兴趣/职业生涯等 6 ►**PRICE** 价格◄〔价格、价值〕上涨 7 ►**CHANGE TIME** 改变时间◄ 提前 8 ►**FILM/CLOCK** 电影/钟表◄ 进〔片〕；往前拨〔钟表〕
advance[3] *adj* 1 **advance planning/warning/booking etc** 预先的计划/警告/订票[订座]等 2 **advance party/team**〔提前到某地为活动做准备的〕先行组
advantage *n* 1 ►**THAT HELPS YOU** 有利于你的◄ 有利条件，优势 2 **take advantage of sb**〔不公正地〕利用某人，占某人的便宜 3 **take advantage of sth**〔巧妙地〕利用某物 4 ►**STH GOOD** 好事物◄ 好处，优点，利益 5 **to good advantage** 表现出优点地，有利地 6 ►**TENNIS** 网球◄ X 占先，X 领先一分〔终局前平分后先得一分〕
adventure *n* 冒险（经历）
advertise *v* 1（为…）做广告（宣传）2 登广告招聘；做广告宣传〔某一活动等〕3 宣扬〔不宜公开的事〕—**advertiser** *n*
affect *v* 1 影响 2 [一般用被动态] 使某人产生强烈的感情，使感动 3 故作姿态，假装
agenda *n* 1〔会议的〕议程 2 **be on the agenda**〔事项〕待办；待讨论 3 话题，议题
aid[1] *n* 1 援助，救助 2 帮助 3 辅助性工具 4 **what's this in aid of?** 这有什么用途？这样做是什么用意？
aid[2] *v* 1 帮助，援助 2 **aid and abet** 协助和教唆，伙同…作案，与…同谋
alarm[1] *n* 1 惊恐，惊慌 2 警报器 3 **sound/raise the alarm** 发出警报 4 闹钟
alarm[2] *v* 使恐慌[不安，焦虑]
alcohol *n* 1 含酒精的饮品，酒 2 酒精，乙醇
alien[1] *adj* 1 外国的；异族的 2 截然不同的；非常怪异的 3 外星人的
alien[2] *n* 1 外侨，侨民 2 外星人
allowance *n* 1〔定期或出于特殊原因而给予的〕津贴，补助 2 允许量，限额 3〔收入的〕免税额 4 零用钱 5 **make allowances** 体谅，顾及 6 **make (an) allowance for** 考虑到
alter *v* 1 使变化，改变 2 使改动，更改〔把衣服加长、加宽等〕3 阉割〔猫或狗〕
amateur[1] *adj* 1 业余（爱好）的，非职业的 2 外行的，生手的
amateur[2] *n* 业余爱好者
amaze *v* 使大为惊奇，使惊愕
ambition *n* 1 抱负，雄心；野心 2 愿望，志向
amend *v* 修改，修订[法律或文件]
ample *adj* 1 充足的，充裕的 2 **ample bosom/figure/torso etc** 宽阔的胸膛/丰满的体形/魁梧的身材等 —**amply** *adv*
amuse *v* 1 使开心，逗笑 2 给…提供娱乐[消遣]
analyse【英】, **analyze**【美】*v* 1 分析 2 对…进行精神分析
ancestor *n* 1 祖先，祖宗 2〔现代机器、车辆等的〕原型 —**ancestral** *adj*
ancient[1] *adj* 1 古代的 2 古老的，年代久远的 3 老掉牙的，老的
ancient[2] *n* **the ancients** 古人〔尤指古希腊及古罗马人〕
announce *v* 1 宣布，通告，公布于众 2 大声宣布 3〔尤指在机场或火车站〕广播 4〔在电视或电台〕主持〔节目〕
annoy *v* 使烦恼，烦扰，打搅
annual[1] *adj* 1 一年一度的，每年的 2 按年度计算的 —**annually** *adv*
annual[2] *n* 1 一年生植物；一季生植物 2 年刊，年报，年鉴〔尤指儿童年册〕
anticipation *n* 预期，预料，期望
anxiety *n* 1 焦虑，不安，担心 2 使人焦虑的事情 3 渴望
apologize *v* 道歉，谢罪
apparatus *n* 1 设备，仪器，装置，器械，用具 2 机制
apparent *adj* 1 显而易见的；明白的 2 显得…的，表面上的
appeal[1] *n* 1 恳求；呼吁 2 感染力，吸引力 3 上诉
appeal[2] *v* 1 恳请，恳求；呼吁 2 **appeal to sb** 吸引

某人 3（提出）上诉 4 **appeal to sb's better nature/sense of honour/sense of justice etc** 呼唤某人的良知/荣誉感/正义感等

appearance *n* 1 ▶**WAY SB/STH LOOKS** 外貌◀ 外表；外观 2 ▶**STH NEW** 新事物◀ 出现，呈现 3 ▶**ARRIVAL** 到达◀〔出其不意的〕到来，出现 4 ▶**PLAY/FILM/CONCERT ETC** 戏剧/电影/音乐会等◀ 登台，表演 5 **keep up appearances** 维持面子；装门面 6 **for appearances' sake/for the sake of appearances** 为了面子关系 7 **put in an appearance/make an appearance** 露一下面 8 ▶**LAW COURT/MEETING** 法庭/会议◀ 出庭；出席

appetite *n* 1 胃口，食欲 2 欲望；喜爱

applaud *v* 1（为…）鼓掌 2 称赞，赞许

apply *v* 1 ▶**REQUEST PERMISSION/A JOB** 请求准许/求职◀ 申请 2 ▶**USE STH** 使用某物◀ 使用，应用，运用 3 ▶**AFFECT STH** 影响某事物◀ 适用于〔某人、某种情况〕；有效 4 **apply yourself** 致力于，专心于 5 ▶**MAKE STH WORK** 使某物起作用◀ 使…起作用 6 ▶**SPREAD PAINT/LIQUID ETC** 涂油漆/液体等◀ 涂，敷 7 **apply force/pressure** 用力/施压 8 ▶**USE A WORD** 用某词◀ 使用〔某个单词或名称〕

appointment *n* 1 约定，预约 2 任命，委任 3 **by appointment** 按约定，按事先确定的时间 4 委任的工作[职位] 5 **by appointment to the Queen** 经女王御准〔可向王室出售商品或提供服务〕

appreciate *v* 1 欣赏；赏识；鉴赏 2 感激 3 完全理解，明白 4 增值 —反义词 DEPRECIATE

approach[1] *v* 1 ▶**MOVE TOWARDS** 向…移动◀ 走近；靠近；接近 2 ▶**ASK** 请求◀ 接洽，交涉 3 ▶**FUTURE EVENT** 未来事件◀ 临近 4 ▶**ALMOST REACH STH** 几乎到…◀ 接近 5 ▶**DEAL WITH** 对付◀ 对付，处理

approach[2] *n* 1 方法；步骤 2 靠近；接近；临近 3 通路，入口 4 要求 5 **the approach of...** 的来临[临近]

appropriate[1] *adj* 恰当的；合适的 —反义词 INAPPROPRIATE —**appropriately** *adv* —**appropriateness** *n*

appropriate[2] *v* 1 挪用；占用；盗用 2 拨出〔款项〕

approve *v* 1 批准；认可 2 赞成，同意

approximate[1] *adj* 大致的，大约的，大概的 —**approximately** *adv*

approximate[2] *v* 1 接近 2 近似

arise *v* 1 发生 2 由…引起 3 **when the need arises/should the need arise** 如果有必要 4 起床；起立；起来 5 出现，呈现 6 起来〔表示觉醒〕

arouse *v* 1 **arouse interest/expectations etc** 引起兴趣/期望等 2 **arouse anger/fear/dislike etc** 激起愤怒/恐惧/讨厌等 3 激起…的性欲 4 唤醒

artificial *adj* 1 人造的，人工的 2 假的，仿造的 3 虚假的，不真挚的，矫揉造作的 4 人为的 —**artificially** *adv* —**artificiality** *n*

ascend *v* 1 上升，升高 2 攀登，爬 3 上升，向上 4 **ascend the throne** 登上王位，登基 5 **in ascending order** 按升序排列 —反义词 DESCEND

aspect *n* 1 方面 2 朝向，方位 3 面貌，外观，神态 4〔动词的〕体

assemble *v* 1 集合，聚集 2 收集；召集 3 组装，装配

assign *v* 1 分配，分派，指派〔任务〕 2 订出，确定〔时间或期限〕 3 把〔财产、设备等〕转让与

assist[1] *v* 1 帮助，协助 2 使做…变得更容易

assist[2] *n*〔体育项目中的〕助攻

associate[1] *v* 1 **associate sb/sth with** 把某人/某事物与…联系起来 2 **be associated (with)** 与…有关，与…有瓜葛 3 **associate with sb** 与〔他人不赞同的〕人交往[合伙，结交]

associate[2] *n* 1 同事；（生意）伙伴 2 准学位证书持有者

associate[3] *adj* **associate member/director/head etc** 非正式会员/副主任/副主管等

assorted *adj* 各种各样的

assume *v* 1 假定，假设 2 **assume control/power/responsibilities etc** 开始控制/掌权/承担责任等 3 **assume a manner/air/expression etc** 装出…的态度/样子/表情等 4 呈现出，出现为 5 以…为先决条件，预先假定

assure *v* 1 向…保证，使确信，让…放心 2 **be assured of** 有信心，有把握 3 确保，提供保证

atmosphere *n* 1 **the atmosphere** 大气（层） 2〔室内的〕空气 3 气氛，环境

atom *n* 1 原子 2 一点儿

attach *v* 1 ▶**CONNECT** 连接◀ 系；绑；贴；固定；连接；附上 2 ▶**LIKE** 喜欢◀ **be attached to** 喜欢，依恋 3 **attach importance/significance etc** 重视，认为…很重要 4 **attach blame** 与…有牵连 5 ▶**FEELING/QUALITY** 感觉/质量◀ **be attached to** 与…联系起来 6 ▶**ORGANIZATION/COMPANY** 组织/公司◀ **be attached to sth a)**〔尤指短期地〕为…工作 **b)** 附属于…，属于…的一个分支

attack[1] *n* 1 ▶**VIOLENCE AGAINST SB** 针对某人的暴力行为◀ 暴力事件，打斗 2 ▶**IN A WAR** 在战争中◀ 进攻，袭击，攻击 3 ▶**CRITICISM** 批评◀ 抨击，攻击，非难，责骂 4 ▶**ACTIONS TO STOP STH** 阻止某事的行动◀〔对体制、法律等的〕处理，解决 5 ▶**ILLNESS** 疾病◀ 突然发作 6 ▶**SPORT** 体育◀ **a)** 进攻 **b)** 进攻队员 7 **an attack of fear/panic/anxiety etc** 一阵恐惧/惊慌/焦虑等

attack[2] *v* 1 ▶**ATTACK SOMEONE** 攻击某人◀ 袭击，殴打 2 ▶**IN A WAR** 在战争中◀ 进攻，攻击，袭击 3 ▶**CRITICIZE** 批评◀ 抨击，攻击，责难 4 ▶**SPORT** 体育◀ 进攻 5 ▶**BEGIN DOING** 开始做◀ 着手处理，投入 6 ▶**DISEASE** 疾病◀ 给…造成伤害；侵袭，侵蚀

attain *v* 1 达到，获得，赢得 2 达到，涨到 —**attainable** *adj*

attempt[1] *n* 1 努力，尝试，企图〔尤指较难的事情〕 2 **an attempt on sb's life** 企图谋杀某人〔尤指名人或重要人物〕

attempt[2] *v* 试图，尝试，企图

attend *v* 1 参加，出席，到场 2 上〔学〕，去〔教堂〕 3 陪伴，伴随…而至 4 看护，照料

attend to sb/sth *phr v* 1 处理，料理〔生意或个人事务〕 2〔在商店或饭店〕照顾，接待〔顾客〕

attitude *n* 1 态度，心态；感觉 2 姿态 3 我行我素的打扮

attract *v* 1 吸引，引起〔兴趣、关注等〕 2 **be attracted to** 喜爱，为…所吸引 3 吸引；引诱 4 招引；吸引

audience *n* **1** 听众; 观众 **2** 〔某节目的〕固定观众[听众]〔人数〕 **3** 谒见, 觐见, 正式拜会

authority *n* **1** ►**POWER** 权力◄ 权力, 权威, 威信 **2 the authorities** 当局, 官方; 当权者 **3** ►**ORGANIZATION** 组织◄ 公共事业机构 **4 I have it on good authority** 我完全相信 **5** ►**EXPERT** 专家◄ 权威人士, 大师, 泰斗 **6** ►**PERMISSION** 允许◄ 〔正式的〕许可, 授权

automatic¹ *adj* **1** 自动的, 自动化的 **2** 必然发生的 **3** 不自觉的, 无意识的, 不假思索的

automatic² *n* **1** 自动武器 **2** 自动汽车, 有自动变速器的汽车

available *adj* **1** 可获得的; 可用的 **2** 有暇的, 可接待客人的 **3** 未婚的; 没有伴侣的 —**availability** *n*

average¹ *adj* **1** 平均(数)的 **2** 中等的, 适中的 **3** 平常的, 普通的 **4** 不好不坏的, 一般的

average² *n* **1** 平均数 **2 on average** 平均来看 **3** 平均水平

average³ *v* **1** 平均做; 平均是 **2** 算出…的平均数

average out *phr v* **1** 算出…的平均数 **2** 达到平均量

aware *adj* **1** 意识到的, 明白的, 知道的 **2** 注意到的, 察觉到的 **3** 有…意识的 **4 so/as far as I am aware** 就我所知

awkward *adj* **1** 尴尬的, 为难的 **2** 不方便的 **3** 笨拙的, 不灵活的; 别扭的 **4** 难用的, 不好操作的 **5** 难相处的, 不好应付的 —**awkwardly** *adv* —**awkwardness** *n*

B, b

badge *n* **1** 徽章, 证章; 标记, 象征 **2** 〔佩戴在身上以显示官职的〕徽章〈如警徽〉 **3** 〔给童子军等的〕布制徽章 **4 badge of office** 职位标识物

balance¹ *n* **1** ►**STEADY** 稳定的◄ 平衡 **2** ►**EQUALITY** 均等◄ 均衡, 均势, 平衡 — 反义词 IMBALANCE **3 on balance** 全面考虑之后, 权衡利弊, 总的说来 **4 off balance a)** 没站稳的, 失去平衡的 **b)** 吃惊的, 糊涂的 **5 the balance of evidence/probability etc** 从各方面的证据/可能性等来看 **6** ►**FOR WEIGHING** 用于称重量◄ 天平, 秤 **7** ►**BANK** 银行◄ 余数, 余额, 差额, 结余 **8** ►**THE REST** 其余的◄ 剩余(部分) **9** ►**OPPOSITE FORCE** 相反的力◄ 平衡力; 制衡作用; 抵消因素 **10 be/hang in the balance** 悬而未决 **11 tip/swing the balance** 影响事态的结果

balance² *v* **1** ►**KEEP STEADY** 保持稳定◄ (使)平稳, (使)保持平衡 **2** ►**BE EQUAL TO** 等于◄ (使)〔重量、数量、重要性等〕均衡, 相抵, 相等 **3** ►**GO WELL WITH** 与…相配◄ 使〔两种相反的效果〕适中 **4** ►**KEEP STH EQUAL** 保持某物均衡◄ 平衡好, 处理好 **5** ►**THINK ABOUT** 思考◄ 权衡, 斟酌, 比较 **6 balance the books/budget** 使收支平衡

ban¹ *n* 禁止, 禁令

ban² *v* 禁止, 取缔

band¹ *n* **1** ►**MUSIC** 音乐◄ 〔尤指演奏流行音乐的〕乐队, 乐团 **2** ►**GROUP OF PEOPLE** 人群◄ 一伙, 一群, 一帮 **3** ►**PIECE OF MATERIAL** 材料◄ 系物的带子; 箍带 **4** ►**PATTERN** 图形◄ 条纹 **5 tax/income/age etc band** 税收/收入/年龄等范围 **6** ►**RADIO** 无线电◄ 波段, 频带

band² *v* 给…加上条纹边框, 给…镶边

band together *phr v* 团结起来, 联手

bar¹ *n* **1** ►**PLACE TO DRINK IN** 饮酒场所◄ **a)** 酒吧 **b)** 酒吧间 **2** ►**PLACE TO BUY DRINK** 买饮料处◄ 出售酒的柜台 **3 coffee/snack/salad etc bar** 咖啡店/小吃店/沙拉自助柜台等 **4** ►**BLOCK OF STH** 一块东西◄ 条, 棒, 根 **5** ►**PIECE OF METAL/WOOD** 金属/木头◄ 〔门, 窗等的〕闩; 横木; 阻碍物 **6** ►**MUSIC** 音乐◄ 〔乐曲中的〕一小节 **7 a bar to (doing) sth** 做某事的障碍 **8** ►**GROUP OF LAWYERS** 律师◄ **a) the bar** 〔有资格出庭处理诉讼案件的〕大律师 **b)** 律师界, 律师业 **9 be called to the bar a)** 成为大律师 **b)** 成为律师 **10** ►**PILE OF SAND/STONES** 沙/石堆◄ 〔港口入口处的〕沙洲; 暗礁 **11** ►**COLOUR/LIGHT** 颜色/光◄ 线条, 条纹, 带 **12** ►**UNIFORMS** 制服◄ 〔军服上的〕军阶杠; 绶带 **13** ►**HEATER** 加热器◄ 〔电暖气的〕电热线[片] **14 behind bars** 在狱中

bar² *v* **1** 闩上, 闩住〔门、窗〕 **2** 摒除, 排挤于…之外; 阻止 **3** 阻止通行; 阻挡, 阻拦

bar³ *prep* **1** 除了…以外 **2 bar none** 无人可比

bare¹ *adj* **1** ►**WITHOUT CLOTHES** 未穿衣服◄ 赤裸的 **2** ►**LAND/TREES** 土地/树木◄ 叶子全落的; 光秃秃的 **3** ►**ROOMS** 房间◄ 空的, 无装饰的 **4 the bare facts/truth** 暴露无遗的事实/赤裸裸的真相 **5** ►**SMALLEST AMOUNT NECESSARY** 最少必需量◄ 仅有的, 勉强的, 最低限度的 **6 the bare bones** 梗概 **7 lay sth bare a)** 显示出某事物, 使某事物暴露 **b)** 揭露, 揭发 **8 with your bare hands** 赤手空拳 —**bareness** *n*

bare² *v* **1** 使暴露, 使赤裸, 露出 **2 bare your soul** 敞开心扉, 剖白心事, 诉说真情, 披肝沥胆

bargain¹ *n* **1** 便宜货, 廉价货 **2** 协议; 交易 **3 into the bargain** 此外, 外加, 而且 **4 make the best of a bad bargain** 困难时尽力而为; 善处逆境, 随遇而安 —**bargainer** *n*

bargain² *v* 讲价钱, 讨价还价; 洽谈(交易)条件

bargain for sth *phr v* 考虑到, 估计到, 预料到

bark¹ *v* **1** 〔狗等动物〕吠, 叫 **2** 大声嚷, 吼叫 **3 bark up the wrong tree** 打错了主意; 认错了目标 **4 bark at the moon** 狂犬吠月, 徒劳无功; 杞人忧天 **5** 擦破〔皮〕

bark² *n* **1** 狗叫声 **2** 树皮 **3** 响声; 吼叫声 **4 sb's bark is worse than their bite** 嘴巴凶, 心不狠 **5** 三桅[四桅, 五桅]帆船

barren *adj* **1** 贫瘠的, 荒芜的 **2** 〔妇女或雌性动物〕不孕的, 不生育的 **3** 不结果实的, 不结籽的 **4** 无用的; 无效果的

barrier *n* **1** 障碍物; 栅栏; 关卡 **2** 〔阻止或妨碍人们做事的〕障碍 **3** 屏障 **4 the 10 second/40% etc barrier** 〔难以超越的〕10秒/40%等难关

battle¹ *n* **1** ►**BETWEEN ARMIES** 军队之间◄ 战斗, 战役〔尤指大型战争中的局部〕 **2** ►**BETWEEN OPPONENTS** 对手之间◄ 较量, 竞争, 争夺 **3** ►**ATTEMPT** 试图◄ 奋斗, 抗争 **4 be half the battle** 成

功了一半, 胜利大有希望 **5 a battle of wits** 智慧的较量 **6 do battle (with)** 与…争论[斗争] **7 the battle of the sexes** 男女之间权力的竞争

battle² *v* **1** 与…斗争, 与…搏斗 **2 battle it out** 决出胜负 **3** 参战; 与…作战

beam¹ *n* **1 ►LIGHT 光◄ a)** 光束, 光线 **b)** 束, 柱 **2 ►WOOD/METAL 木头/金属◄** 梁, 横梁 **3 ►SMILE 微笑◄** 喜色, 笑容 **4 off (the) beam** 不正确的, 错误的, 不对头的 **5 ►SPORT 体育◄** 〔体操〕平衡木 **6 ►SHIP 船◄** 船宽

beam² *v* **1** 笑, 眉开眼笑 **2** 向…发送〔信号〕 **3** 发光; 发热, 发射

bear¹ *v* **1 can't bear a)** 忍受不了 **b)** 接受不了…的事实 **2 bear in mind (that)** 记住; 考虑到 **3 ►BE BRAVE 勇敢◄** 忍受, 忍耐, 经受住 **4 bear the costs/burden/expense etc** 承担费用/负担/开支等 **5 bear responsibility/the blame etc** 承担责任/应受责备等 **6 ►SUPPORT 支持◄** 支撑〔重量〕 **7 doesn't bear thinking about** 不堪设想 **8 bear a resemblance/relation etc to** 与…相似/与…有关等 **9 bear the strain/pressure etc** 承受压力等 **10 bear the brunt of** 首当其冲 **11 bear (sb) a grudge** 对〔某人〕怀恨在心 **12 bear fruit a)** 〔尤指计划、决定等长时间之后〕有了成果; 成功了 **b)** 〔果树〕结果 **13 ►SHOW SIGNS OF 显出…的迹象◄** 显示; 具有, 带有〔标记或特征〕 **14 not bear examination/inspection etc** 经受不住检查/审查等 **15 bring influence/pressure etc to bear (on)** 〔对…〕施加压力; 敦促 **16 bear witness to** 证明, 作证 **17 bear right/left** 向右/左转 **18 ►BABY 婴儿◄** 生育 **19 bear yourself** 表现; 保持某种举止 **20 ►CARRY 携带◄** 运送; 携带; 传运 **21 ►WIND/WATER 风/水◄** 吹动; 传送 **22 ►SIGN/MARK 记号/标记◄** 带有〔标记〕 **23 ►NAME/TITLE 姓名/头衔◄** 具有, 拥有〔名字或头衔〕 **24 bear sb no malice/ill will etc** 对某人没有恶意/敌意等

bear down *phr v* **1 bear down on** 向…逼近; 冲向 **2** 使劲推; 使劲压下 **3** 压倒; 征服; 打败

bear on/upon sth *phr v* 与…有联系, 与…有关

bear sb/sth **out** *phr v* 为…作证, 证实, 支持〔某种说法〕

bear up *phr v* 支持住, 撑下去; 不气馁

bear with sb/sth *phr v* **1 bear with me** 耐心等待; 别着急 **2** 容忍, 忍耐

bear² *n* **1** 熊 **2** 〔股市或期货〕看跌的人 **3** 粗暴鲁莽的人, 脾气暴躁的人 **4 be like a bear with a sore head** 脾气暴躁

behaviour *n* **1** 举止, 行为 **2 be on your best behaviour** 尽可能好地表现; 尽量行为检点 **3** 性能; 特点; 活动 **—behavioural** *adj* **—behaviourally** *adv*

bend¹ *v* **1 ►MOVE YOUR BODY 挪动身体◄** 俯身; 弯腰 **2 ►CURVE 曲线◄ a)** 使弯曲 **b)** 呈弯形; 变弯曲 **3 bend the rules** 放宽规则; 通融 **4 bend over backwards (to do sth)** 竭尽全力〔做某事〕 **5 bend sb's ear** 和某人谈心〔尤指谈令人烦恼的事〕 **6 on bended knee a)** 努力劝说; 恳求 **b)** 跪着 **7 bend your mind/efforts/thoughts etc to** 集中全力于…, 专心致志于…

bend² *n* **1** 〔尤指道路或河流的〕弯曲处 **2** 〔身体的〕弯曲〔动作〕 **3 the bends** 潜水夫病, 潜函病, 减压病〔潜水员浮出水面过快引致的一种令人非常疼痛的病〕 **4 drive sb round the bend** 惹恼某人 **5 be/go round the bend** 发疯

beneficial *adj* 有益的, 有利的, 有用的 **—beneficially** *adv*

bewilder *v* 使迷惑; 使昏乱

bind¹ *v* **1 ►TIE/FASTEN 束/缚◄ a)** 捆, 绑 **b)** 〔用布或带子〕束紧; 捆扎 **2 ►UNITE 联合◄** 把…紧紧联系在一起; 使关系密切 **3 ►STICK TOGETHER 粘起来◄** 〔使〕黏合; 〔使〕凝结 **4 ►RESTRICT 限制◄** 约束; 使负有义务 **5 ►STITCH 缝◄** 给…加上饰边; 给…镶边 **6 ►BOOK 书◄** 装订

bind² *n* **a bind** 窘境, 困境

bite¹ *v* **1 ►WITH YOUR TEETH 用牙◄** 咬 **2 ►INSECT/SNAKE 虫/蛇◄** 〔昆虫〕叮, 蜇; 〔蛇〕咬伤 **3 ►FISH 鱼◄** 吞饵, 上钩 **4 ►NOT SLIP 不滑◄** 抓紧; 卡紧; 咬住 **5 ►HAVE AN EFFECT 有效◄** 达到预期的〔坏〕效果 **6 bite your tongue** 强忍住不说 **7 bite the dust a)** 死亡; 失败; 被击败 **b)** 完全不好用; 报废 **8 bite the bullet** 咬紧牙关忍受痛苦, 勇敢地面对 **9 bite sb's head off** 发火; 蛮横粗暴地说话[回答] **10 bite off more than you can chew** 试图承担力所不及的事 **11 he/she won't bite** 不必怕他/她〔尤指权威人士〕 **12 what's biting you/her etc?** 什么事烦扰着你/她等? 愁什么呢? **13 once bitten twice shy** 一次吃亏, 二次小心; 一朝被蛇咬, 十年怕井绳 **14 bite the hand that feeds you** 恩将仇报; 以怨报德 **15 be bitten by the bug/craze etc** 热衷于, 迷上

bite back *phr v* **1** 强忍着不说出来 **2** 回嘴; 反唇相讥

bite into sth *phr v* 咬进; 陷进; 砍入

bite² *n* **1 ►WITH YOUR TEETH 用牙◄** 咬〔的动作〕 **2 ►WOUND 伤◄** 被咬[叮, 蜇]的伤口 **3 a bite (to eat)** 量少的一餐 **4 ►COLD 冷◄** 冷意, 寒意 **5 ►TASTE 味道◄** 辛辣; 苦涩 **6 ►EFFECTIVENESS 效果◄** 〔演说或文章的〕犀利; 有说服力 **7 ►FISH 鱼◄** 吞饵; 上钩 **8 bite-size/bite-sized** 很小的, 一口大小的 **9 another bite/a second bite at the cherry** 第二次机会

blame¹ *v* **1** 责怪, 指摘; 把…归咎于 **2 don't blame me** 不要怪我〔用于劝告某人不要做某事〕 **3 I don't blame you/them etc** 我理解某人的做法 **4 only have yourself to blame** 只能怪你自己 **5** 批评; 责难

blame² *n* 〔对错误或坏事应负的〕责任

blank¹ *adj* **1** 无表情的; 漠然的; 不感兴趣的 **2** 无字迹的; 空白的 **3 go blank a)** 脑子突然一片空白, 怎么也想不起来 **b)** 〔屏幕等〕一片空白 **—blankly** *adv* **—blankness** *n*

blank² *n* **1** 空白处 **2 my mind's a blank** 脑子里一片空白, 怎么也想不起来 **3** 〔有火药而无弹头的〕空弹 **—blankness** *n*

blank³ *v* **1** 突然记不起, 脑子突然一片空白 **2** 不理睬

blank sth ↔ **out** *phr v* **1** 涂掉, 删去 **2** 〔尤指故意地〕全部忘记

blaze¹ *v* **1** 熊熊燃烧 **2** 发光, 照亮 **3** 快速而连续地射击 **4 blaze a trail** 做开路先锋, 起先导作用 **5 be blazed across/all over** 使广为人知地刊登

blaze² *n* **1** ▶**FIRE** 火◀ **a)** 火焰; 烈火 **b)** 危险的大火 **2** ▶**LIGHT/COLOUR** 光/颜色◀〔光线、色彩等的〕光辉, 闪耀; 五彩缤纷 **3** ▶**GUNS** 枪炮◀ 急促而连续的射击 **4 a blaze of anger/hatred/passion etc** 突发的怒气/仇恨/激情等 **5 in a blaze of glory/publicity etc** 在盛赞/公众瞩目之下等 **6 what the blazes/who the blazes etc** 到底在搞什么/是谁等〔用于加强问题的语气, 表示厌烦〕 **7 like blazes** 尽可能地 **8 go to blazes** 滚开 **9** ▶**MARK** 记号◀〔尤指马鼻上的一条〕白斑

bless *v* **1 be blessed with** 有幸得到, 被赋予 **2** 祈求上帝祝福[保佑], 求神赐福于 **3** 使神圣; 视…为圣物; 赞颂 **4 bless you! a)** 长命百岁!〔别人打喷嚏时说〕 **b)** 谢谢〔某人〕 **5 bless him/her etc** 真不错; 干得好〔表示喜欢或满意〕 **6 bless my soul/I'll be blessed!** 我的天哪!〔表示吃惊〕

block¹ *n* **1** ▶**SOLID MASS** 固体◀ 一大块〈如木、石等通常有直切边的坚硬物体〉 **2** ▶**STREET/STREETS** 街◀ **a)** 街段 **b)** 街区 **3** ▶**LARGE BUILDING** 大楼◀ 栋, 座, 幢 **4** ▶**QUANTITY OF THINGS** 数量◀ 一组, 一批, 一套, 一叠 **5 block booking/voting** 成批购买/集体投票 **6** ▶**UNABLE TO THINK** 不能思考◀ 阻滞 **7** ▶**STOPPING MOVEMENT** 阻止行动◀ 障碍物, 堵塞物 **8 the block**〔昔时的〕断头台 **9 lay/put your head on the block** 冒着败坏自己名声的危险 **10** ▶**SPORT** 体育◀ 拦挡〔动作〕 **11** ▶**INFORMATION** 信息◀ 信息组〔指磁带或磁盘上储存信息的物理单位〕 **12** ▶**PRINTING** 印刷◀ 印版, 版垫, 衬版, 木印板 **13** ▶**LAND** 土地◀ 一大片土地

block² *v* **1** 阻挡, 堵塞 **2** 阻止, 妨碍, 阻挠 **3** 挡住〔视线〕 **4 block sb's way** 挡住某人的去路 **5** 限制使用〔某国货币〕

block sth ↔ in/out *phr v* 草拟; 画…的简略图

block sth ↔ off *phr v* 封闭, 封锁〔道路〕

block sth ↔ out 1 挡〔光〕 **2** 不去想

bloom¹ *n* **1** 花 **2 in (full) bloom**〔花朵〕盛开, 怒放 **3**〔葡萄或李子等水果表面的一层〕粉霜, 粉衣 **4 the bloom of youth/love etc** 豆蔻年华; 全盛时期

bloom² *v* **1** 开花; 〔花〕盛开 **2** 精神焕发; 兴旺

blot¹ *v* **1**〔用软纸或布等〕吸干 **2 blot your copybook** 玷污自己的名声

blot sth ↔ out *phr v* 把…遮住, 遮盖; 涂去; 隐藏

blot sth ↔ up *phr v*〔用软布或纸张等〕擦干, 吸干

blot² *n* **1** 污点, 污渍 **2** 破坏了某地方景致的东西〈如楼房等〉 **3**〔尤指名誉的〕污点, 瑕疵

blow¹ *v* **1** ▶**WIND MOVING** 风移动◀〔风〕吹, 刮 **2** ▶**WIND MOVING STH** 风吹动某物◀ 吹动; 刮走 **3** ▶**AIR FROM YOUR MOUTH** 嘴里呼出的空气◀ 吹气; 喷气 **4** ▶**MAKE A NOISE** 弄出声响◀ 吹奏; (使)鸣响 **5** ▶**VIOLENCE** 暴力◀ 炸毁, 摧毁 **6** ▶**LOSE MONEY** 损失金钱◀ 乱花, 挥霍 **7** ▶**LOSE AN OPPORTUNITY** 失去机会◀ 失掉, 断送 **8** ▶**SURPRISE/ANNOYANCE** 惊讶/烦恼◀ **blow/blow me/blow that etc** 真没料到; 糟糕〔表示惊讶、烦恼或决心〕 **9** ▶**MAKE A SHAPE** 造成某形状◀ 吹制 **10 blow sth (up) out of all proportion** 小题大作; 夸大 **11** ▶**LEAVE** 离开◀ **blow town** 匆忙离开 **12** ▶**ELECTRICITY STOPS** 电力中断◀〔保险丝〕烧断 **13** ▶**TYRE** 轮胎◀ 爆裂, (使)破裂 **14** ▶**MAKE A SECRET KNOWN** 泄密◀ 泄露〔秘密〕 **15 blow hot and cold** (对…)反复无常, 忽冷忽热, 摇摆不定 **16 blow sb a kiss** 给某人一个飞吻 **17 blow your mind** 使惊喜, 使吃惊 **18 blow your nose** 擤鼻涕 **19 blow sth sky-high a)** 粉碎; 使破灭 **b)** 把…炸得粉碎, 彻底摧毁 **20 blow your top/stack** 勃然大怒, 大发雷霆 **21 blow your own trumpet/horn** 自吹自擂, 自夸 **22 blow the whistle on**〔向有关当局或公众〕揭发〔错事〕, 揭露 **23 blow a gasket/fuse** 大怒, 暴跳如雷

blow away *phr v* **1** 枪杀 **2**〔尤指在比赛中〕彻底战胜〔某人〕 **3**〔尤指用某人羡慕的东西〕使大为惊讶

blow down *phr v* 吹倒, 刮倒

blow in *phr v* 突然到来

blow sb/sth off *phr v* 视〔某人或某事〕不重要, 不重视, 轻视

blow out *phr v* **1** 吹灭; 熄灭 **2**〔车胎〕爆裂 **3 blow itself out**〔风暴〕停止 **4 a)** 轻而易举地战胜 **b)** 失约; 失信于〔某人〕 **5**〔油井或气井〕井喷

blow over *phr v* **1** 刮倒 **2**〔暴风雨等〕停止, 平息; 过去 **3**〔重要性〕消失; 被遗忘

blow up *phr v* **1** 炸毁, (使)炸得粉碎 **2** 给…充气, 打气 **3** 放大〔照片〕 **4**〔恶劣天气〕来临 **5**〔形势、争论等〕变得严峻 **6** 大发雷霆

blow² *n* **1** ▶**HARD HIT** 重击◀ 重击 **2** ▶**BAD EFFECT** 坏效果◀〔对信心、成功的可能性等的〕打击 **3** ▶**UNHAPPY EVENT** 不幸事件◀ 突然的打击; 不幸 **4** ▶**BLOWING** 吹◀〔指动作〕吹 **5 come to blows** 打起来 **6 soften/cushion the blow** 缓和…的打击 **7** ▶**WIND** 风◀ 劲风; 风暴

blunt¹ *adj* **1** 钝的, 不锋利的, 不尖的 —反义词 SHARP **2**〔说话〕不客气的, 直言不讳的, 耿直的 —**bluntness** *n*

blunt² *v* **1** 减弱 **2** 把〔铅笔尖或刀〕弄钝

boast¹ *v* **1** 夸口, 夸耀, 吹嘘 **2**〔地方、物体或机构〕拥有〔好的事物或特征〕—**boaster** *n*

boast² *n* **1** 引以为豪的事物 **2 no idle boast** 绝非吹牛

boil¹ *v* **1** 使达到沸点, 煮沸, 烧开 **2** (使)〔容器里的液体〕沸腾 **3**〔用开水〕煮〔食物〕 **4**〔用高温水〕洗〔衣服〕

boil away *phr v* 煮干, 汽化

boil down *phr v* **1** 煮稠, 浓缩 **2** 压缩〔资料等〕

boil down to sth *phr v* 相当于, 归结为

boil over *phr v* **1** 沸腾而溢出 **2**〔局面或感情〕控制不住

boil up *phr v* **1** 发展到危险程度 **2** 把…加热, 煮沸

boil² *n* **1 the boil** 煮沸; 沸腾 **2** 疖子, 疔 **3 go off the boil** 生疏了

bold *adj* **1** ▶**PERSON/ACTION** 人/行动◀ 果敢的, 冒险的, 无畏的 **2** ▶**MANNER/APPEARANCE** 举止/外貌◀ 唐突的, 冒失的, 鲁莽的, 放肆的 **3** ▶**COLOURS/SHAPES** 颜色/形状◀ 醒目的, 显眼的, 轮廓清晰的 **4** ▶**LINES/WRITING** 线条/书写◀ 粗线条的; 粗大醒目的 **5 in bold (type)**〔印刷〕用黑体字排印

的 **6 make so bold as to do sth** 冒昧，胆敢 **7 if I may be so bold** 恕我冒昧地问 —**boldly** *adv* —**boldness** *n*

bond¹ *n* **1** ►**MONEY** 钱◄ 债券，证券，公债 **2** ►**UNITE** 团结◄〔因共同利益或感情而使人连系起来的〕纽带，维系，连结物，关系 **3 bonds a)** 枷锁，桎梏，限制人自由的东西 **b)** 镣铐，绳索 **4** ►**GLUE** 胶（水）◄ 结合，黏合 **5** ►**CHEMISTRY** 化学◄ 化学键 **6** 契约，盟约 **7 my word is my bond** 我说的话（像契约一样）可靠，我一定会履行诺言 **8 in/out of bond**〔进口货物〕存入关栈中以待完税/已完税出关

bond² *v* **1**〔尤指用胶水〕黏合 **2**〔与某人〕培养一种特殊的关系 **3**〔把货物〕存入关栈[保税仓库]中

bonus *n* **1** 奖金；红利；特别津贴 **2** 没有预料到的好事 **3 no-claims bonus** 未索赔鼓励金〔一种汽车保险优惠〕

boom¹ *n* **1** ►**INCREASE IN BUSINESS** 业务增加◄〔生意〕繁荣，兴旺，景气 **2** ►**WHEN STH IS POPULAR** 某事物流行之时◄ 流行时期 **3** ►**SOUND** 声音◄ 隆隆声 **4** ►**LONG POLE** 长杆子◄ **a)** 帆的下桁，帆杆 **b)**〔装卸货物时用的〕吊杆，起重臂 **c)**〔一端挂照相机或麦克风的〕活动支架，吊杆 **5** ►**ON A RIVER** 在河上◄〔横拦于河面以阻止物件漂走的〕挡栅，水栅

boom² *v* **1 a)** 发低沉的声音，隆隆作响 **b)** 用洪亮而低沉的声音说 **2**〔商业、贸易等〕繁荣；〔城镇等〕兴起；迅速发展 —**booming** *adj*

boost¹ *v* **1** 增加，提高，促进 **2 boost sb's confidence/morale/ego** 增强某人的自信心/士气/自尊 **3** 吹捧，大肆宣传 **4** 向上推起，托一把

boost² *n* **1** 激励，鼓舞；增加，改进 **2**〔火箭、电器等的〕动力增强，助推 **3 give sb a boost (up)** 推起，托某人一把

border¹ *n* **1** 国界，边境，边界；边境地区 **2** 边，边饰 **3** 草地的边缘部分，〔花园等边缘狭长的〕绿化带

border² *v* **1** 形成…的边界，毗邻 **2** 与…接壤

border on sth *phr v* 近似，接近

bore¹ the past tense of BEAR¹

bore² *v* **1**〔尤指以无聊的长话〕使〔人〕厌烦 **2** 钻（孔），开凿，挖（洞） **3**〔令人不安地〕盯住看

bore³ *n* **1**〔尤指因过多谈论自己而〕令人厌烦的人 **2** 令人厌烦的事 **3 12-bore/small bore etc**〔枪〕12毫米口径/小口径等 **4** 钻孔，井眼

bother¹ *v* **1** ►**MAKE AN EFFORT** 作出努力◄ 费心，尽力〔做某事〕，因…操心 **2** ►**WORRY** 担心◄（使）担心，（使）苦恼 **3** ►**ANNOY** 使恼怒◄ 打扰，烦扰 **4 can't/couldn't be bothered** 不想费神[没有心思]去做某事 **5 not bothered** 无所谓，不在意 **6 sorry to bother you** 对不起打扰你一下 **7** ►**FRIGHTEN** 吓唬◄ 骚扰；恐吓 **8 hot and bothered**〔尤指不必要地〕心急火燎的 **9 not bother yourself/not bother your head** 不为…操心[伤脑筋] **10 bother it/them etc** 真讨厌〔表示厌烦〕

bother² *n* **1** 麻烦，不便；忧虑；烦恼的事 **2** 难对付的事[人]

bother³ *interjection* 真烦人！真讨厌！〔表示有些恼火〕

boundary *n* **1** ►**EDGE** 边◄ 分界线，边界 **2** ►**WALL/FENCE** 墙/篱笆◄ 界限，范围 **3** ►**LIMIT** 限制◄ 限度，界限 **4** ►**BETWEEN FEELINGS/QUALITIES ETC** 感情/特质等之间◄ 分野 **5 push back the boundaries (of)** 扩展…的领域 **6** ►**CRICKET** 板球◄ 球场边界线；击球超过边界线得分

bow¹ *v* **1** 鞠躬，躬身行礼 **2** 躬身向前看〔尤指为靠近些看〕 **3 be bowed (under sth)**〔被背上重物〕压得躬着身子 **4 bow and scrape**〔对人〕卑躬屈膝，点头哈腰

bow down *phr v* **1** 深度躬身致敬 **2 bow down to sb** 向某人屈服；屈从于某人

bow out *phr v* **1**（从…）退出，退场；辞职 **2** 不守信用，背信弃义

bow to sb/sth *phr v* 向…让步，屈服于

bow² *n* **1** 鞠躬 **2** 船头 **3 take a bow**〔表演结束时〕谢幕

bow³ *n* **1** 弓 **2** 蝴蝶结 **3**〔弦乐器的〕弓 **4 bow legs** 弓形腿，罗圈腿

bow⁴ *v* **1** 弯曲，弯成弓形 **2** 用弓拉奏〔乐曲〕

brag *v* 自夸，吹嘘

branch¹ *n* **1** ►**ON A TREE** 树上◄ 树枝 **2** ►**IN A LOCAL AREA** 在当地◄ 分行；分支机构 **3** ►**OF AN ORGANIZATION** 某机构的◄〔政府或机构的〕部门 **4** ►**OF A SUBJECT** 某学科的◄ 分科 **5** ►**OF A FAMILY** 某家族的◄〔家族中的〕一支，分支 **6** ►**SMALLER PART** 较小的部分◄ 分支；支线；支流

branch² *v* 分支；分岔

branch off *phr v* **1** 分岔；分支；分道 **2** 离开主路[干线]，走入岔道 **3** 岔开〔话题〕

branch out *phr v* 扩大〔兴趣、活动〕范围，开辟新的领域

breed¹ *v* **1**〔动物〕繁殖，下崽，下蛋 **2** 育种，饲养繁殖；培植；改良（品种） **3** 引起；酿成，招致〔一般指不良之事〕 **4 breed like rabbits** 生太多的孩子

breed² *n* **1**〔尤指人工培育的动植物〕品种 **2**〔人或物的〕某种类型

brief¹ *adj* **1** ►**TIME** 时间◄ 短时间的；短暂的 **2 have a brief word** 说几句话 **3 be brief** 长话短说 **4** ►**SPEECH/LETTER** 演讲/信◄ 简洁的，简明的 **5 in brief a)** 简而言之；简单地说 **b)** 粗略地，梗概地 **6** 唐突无礼的；〔说话〕草率的 **7** ►**CLOTHES** 衣服◄ 短的，暴露的

brief² *n* **1** 简短命令，工作指示 **2** 案情摘要，案情简介 **3 briefs** 贴身短内裤，三角裤

brief³ *v* 作简单的指示；为…提供信息

bruise¹ *n* **1** 青淤，伤痕，擦伤 **2**〔水果的〕擦痕，碰伤

bruise² *v* **1**（使）碰伤，擦伤，（使）成淤伤 **2**（使）〔水果〕碰伤，擦伤 —**bruising** *n*

bud¹ *n* **1** 芽；苞；蓓蕾 **2** 老兄；喂

bud² *v* 发芽，长出花蕾，含苞

bud·get¹ *n* **1** 预算 **2** 政府预算案

budget² *v* **1**〔精心地〕制定预算；按预算来安排（开支） **2**（为…）作出安排

budget³ *adj* 经济的，特价的，便宜的

bump¹ *v* **1** 猛碰，撞 **2**〔车辆〕颠簸而行

bump into sb *phr v* 巧遇，邂逅，碰见

bump sb ↔ **off** *phr v* 杀死〔某人〕

bump sth ↔ **up** *phr v* 突然大幅度提高，增加

bump² *n* **1**〔撞击造成的〕肿块 **2** 隆起之处 **3**〔汽

车〕碰撞 4 砰然一声; 撞击声

bunch¹ *n* 1 **bunch of flowers/keys/grapes etc** 一束花/一串钥匙/一串葡萄等 2〔人〕一群, 一伙 3 **the pick of the bunch** 佼佼者 4 大量 5 **in bunches**〔把头发分在两边〕扎成两束 6 **thanks a bunch** 多谢了〔玩笑说法, 表示毫无感激之意〕

bunch² *v* 1 聚成堆[群] 2 绷紧〔身体的一部分〕3 将〔东西〕绑成一束 4 使起褶

burst¹ *v* 1 ►**BREAK OPEN** 裂开◄ (使)破裂;(使)爆裂;(使)胀破;(使)爆炸 2 **bursting with** 充满 3 ►**MOVE SUDDENLY** 突然移动◄ 冲, 闯, 突然出现 4 **burst open** 突然开了 5 **be bursting to do sth** 迫不及待要做某事 6 **be bursting with pride/confidence/energy etc** 充满自豪/自信/精力等 7 **be bursting**〔大小便〕憋不住了 8 **full to bursting**〔吃得〕太饱 9 **bursting at the seams** 胀满

burst in on/upon sb/sth *phr v* 突然闯入, 打扰; 突然插嘴

burst into sth *phr v* 1 突然…起来〔尤指哭、笑、唱等〕2 **burst into flames** 突然起火〔尤指火势失去控制〕

burst out *phr v* 1 **burst out laughing/crying etc** 突然大笑/大哭等 2 突然说出

burst² *n* 1 破裂, 爆炸; 喷出; 裂口 2 **a burst of sth** a) 突然用力, 加速 b) 突发的响声 c) 情感的突然爆发

C, c

calculate *v* 1 计算, 核算 2 估算, 估计 3 **be calculated to do sth** 旨在, 用意在于; 打算; 适于(做)…

calculate on sth *phr v* 指望, 期望

candidate *n* 1 候选人; 候补人 2 应考人, 投考者 3 极有可能有某结局的人[群体、观点等]

capacity *n* 1 容量, 容积; 容纳力 2 能力, 才能 3 职位; 地位; 身份; 职责 4〔工厂、公司、机器等的〕产量, 生产力

capital¹ *n* 1 ►**CITY** 城市◄ 首都; 首府; 省会 2 ►**FINANCIAL** 金融的◄ 资本, 资金 3 ►**LETTER** 字母◄ 大写字母 4 ►**CENTRE OF ACTIVITY** 活动中心◄〔工商业及其他活动的〕中心 5 **make capital out of** 利用…, 从…中捞一把[获益] 6 ►**BUILDING** 建筑物◄ 柱头, 柱顶

capital² *adj* 1 **capital letter** 大写字母 2 **capital offence/crime** 可处死刑的罪 3 极好的

career¹ *n* 1 职业, 事业 2 **career soldier/teacher etc** 职业士兵/教师等 3 生涯; (一段)工作经历, 履历

career² *v*〔常指失控地〕猛冲

carve *v* 1 把〔熟肉〕切成小块; 从〔熟肉上〕割下薄片 2 雕, 刻; 把〔木、石等〕雕成〔某物〕3 刻〔图形或字母〕

carve sth ↔ **out** *phr v* **carve out a career/niche/reputation etc** 开创出事业/谋得合适的职位/赢得名声

carve sb/sth ↔ **up** *phr v* 1 瓜分, 分割 2 快速超车, 快速切入别人的行车线

category *n* 类别, 种类, 范畴

caution¹ *n* 1 小心, 谨慎, 慎重 2 **word/note of caution** 警示, 警告〔某人小心〕3 **throw/fling/cast caution to the winds** 不顾一切/鲁莽行事 4〔给犯了轻罪的人的〕正式(口头)警告, 训诫 5 滑稽有趣的人

caution² *v* 1 警告, 告诫, 提醒 2 给某人正式警告

cease¹ *v* 停止, 终止, 结束

cease² *n* **without cease** 不停地, 持续地

celebrate *v* 1 庆祝 2〔口头或书面〕赞扬, 赞美, 歌颂 3 主持〔宗教仪式, 尤指弥撒〕

ceremony *n* 1 典礼, 仪式 2 礼仪, 礼节 3 **without ceremony** 随意地; 无礼地

certainty *n* 1 确定[确实]的事; 必然会发生的事 2 确实(性), 确信, 确知

certify *v* 1〔尤指经过某种检验〕证明, 证实, 核证 2 给〔某人〕颁发(完成专业培训的)合格证书[文凭] 3 正式证明〔某人〕有精神病

chain¹ *n* 1 ►**JOINED RINGS** 连接在一起的环◄ 链子, 链条 2 **chain of events/circumstances etc** 一系列[一连串]的事件/情况等 3 ►**SHOPS/HOTELS** 商店/旅馆◄ 连锁店, 连锁集团 4 ►**CONNECTED LINE** 连接线◄ 连成一行的人; 山脉; 群岛 5 ►**PRISONER** 囚犯◄ **chains**〔锁住囚犯四肢的〕镣铐, 锁链 6 ►**BUYING A HOUSE** 购房◄〔先卖旧房再买新房的〕链式购房法, 连环购房链 7 ►**MEASURE** 度量◄ 链〔旧时的长度单位〕

chain² *v* 1〔尤指为防逃跑或被盗而〕锁在一起, 拴住, 束缚 2 **be chained to something** 受到〔责任〕的束缚

challenge¹ *n* 1 ►**STH DIFFICULT** 棘手的事◄ 挑战, 具有挑战性的事物, 考验〔某人〕能力的事物 2 ►**QUESTIONING OF RIGHTNESS** 对公正性的质疑◄〔对某事的正确性、合法性等的〕质疑 3 ►**INVITATION TO COMPETE** 挑战◄ 挑战,〔比赛等的〕提议 4 ►**A DEMAND TO STOP** 停止的命令◄ 喝停盘问 5 ►**IN LAW** 法律方面◄〔开庭前律师〕反对某人任陪审团成员的声明

challenge² *v* 1 质疑〔某事的正确性、合法性等〕, 对…表示怀疑 2 向…挑战; 邀请〔某人〕比赛 3 考验…的技术[能力]; 激发; 激励 4 喝停盘问〔某人的身份、意图等〕5〔开审前在选定陪审员时〕对(某候选陪审员)表示反对 —**challenger** *n*

chamber *n* 1〔人体内或某些机器中的〕室, 腔 2 作特殊用途的房间〔尤指令人不快者〕3 大会议室, 会议厅 4〔美国〕参[众]议院;〔英国〕上[下]议院 5 私人房间, 寝室 6 **chambers**〔大律师或法官的〕办公室; 事务所 7 枪膛, 炮膛

champion¹ *n* 1〔尤指体育比赛中的〕冠军, 第一名 2 **champion of**〔为某目标或原则如某群人的权利而奋斗的〕斗士

champion² *v* 公开为〔某目标或原则〕而斗争; 维护

channel¹ *n* 1 ►**TELEVISION** 电视◄ 频道 2 ►**RADIO** 广播◄〔发送和接收无线电信号的〕波段 3 ►**SYSTEM OF INFORMATION** 信息系统◄ 又作 **channels**〔传递或获得信息的〕途径; 手段; 渠道 4 ►**FOR WATER** 水◄ 管道; 水渠, 水沟 5 ►**SEA/RIVER** 海洋/河流◄ a) 海峡 b) 航道 6 ►**IN A SURFACE** 在表面◄〔在表面形成的〕槽, 沟 7 ►**WAY TO**

EXPRESS YOURSELF 表达方式◀〔表达思想、感情或发泄情绪的〕方式, 渠道, 途径

channel[2] *v* **1** 把〔钱或精力等〕导向〔某一特定目的〕; 引导 **2** 在〔某物上〕形成槽 **3**〔透过管道〕输送〔水等〕

character *n* **1** ▶**ALL SB'S QUALITIES** 某人所有的品质◀〔某人的〕个性, 性格, 气质 **2** ▶**QUALITIES OF STH** 某物的特征◀〔某物或某地的〕特色, 特点 **3** ▶**INTERESTING QUALITY** 有趣的特点◀〔使某人或某物特别或有趣的〕特征 **4** ▶**MORAL STRENGTH** 道德力量◀ 人格, 好的品质, 品性 **5** ▶**PERSON** 人物◀ **a)**〔书、剧本、电影等中的〕人物, 角色 **b)** 人;〔尤指〕怪人 **c) be a character** 是个人物〔指其人有趣或不同寻常〕**6** ▶**REPUTATION** 声誉◀ 名誉, 名声, 声誉 **7** ▶**LETTER/SIGN** 字母/符号◀〔书写、印刷或电脑的〕字; 字体; 符号

charge[1] *n* **1** ▶**PRICE** 价格◀ 费用, 价钱 **2** ▶**CONTROL** 控制◀ **a) be in charge (of)** 负责…, 掌管… **b) put sb in charge (of)** 让…全权负责 **c) take charge (of)** 控制, 掌管〔局面、组织或人〕**3** ▶**RESPONSIBILITY/CARE FOR** 责任/照料◀ **a) be in/under sb's charge** 由…照料[照顾] **b)** 被照顾的人 **4** ▶**THAT SB IS GUILTY** 某人有罪◀ 指控, 控告, 罪名 **5** ▶**BLAME** 责备◀〔书面或口头的〕指责, 批评, 责备 **6** ▶**ATTACK** 进攻◀〔士兵或野生动物等〕猛烈的攻击 **7** ▶**ELECTRICAL FORCE** 电力◀ 电荷; 电量 **8** ▶**EXPLOSIVE** 爆炸物◀〔一定量的〕炸药 **9** ▶**STRENGTH OF FEELINGS** 感情的力量◀〔感情的〕力量; 感染力 **10 get a charge out of sth** 从〔某事〕得到快乐[刺激、兴奋] **11** ▶**AN ORDER TO DO STH** 命令◀ 命令, 指示, 吩咐

charge[2] *v* **1** ▶**MONEY** 钱◀ **a)** (向…)收费; 开价 **b) charge sth to sb's account** 把某物记在某人的账上 **c)** 用信用卡付账 **2** ▶**RUSH/ATTACK** 冲击/攻击◀ **a)** 进攻, 冲锋; 冲向 **b)** 快步走向[跑向] **3** ▶**WITH A CRIME** 有罪◀ 控告; 指控 **4** ▶**BLAME SB** 指责某人◀〔公开〕指责, 责备 **5** ▶**ELECTRICITY** 电◀ (使)充电 **6** ▶**ORDER SB** 命令某人◀ 吩咐, 命令 **7** ▶**GUN** 枪◀ 给〔枪〕装子弹 **8** ▶**GLASS** 杯子◀ 斟满〔杯〕

charity *n* **1** 救济(金), 施舍(物) **2** 慈善机构, 慈善团体 **3** 宽容, 宽厚, 宽大 **4 charity begins at home** 慈善始于家庭, 施舍先及亲友

charm[1] *n* **1** 魅力, 魔力, 吸引力; 可爱之处 **2** 魔法; 咒语 **3**〔装在手链、手镯上表示吉祥的〕小装饰品; 护身符 **4 work like a charm** 完全[迅速]地奏效

charm[2] *v* **1** 迷住, 吸引 **2** 向…施魔法, 用魔法控制 **3 have/lead a charmed life** 总是幸运, 总能逢凶化吉 —**charmed** *adj*

chart[1] *n* **1** 图表, 图 **2** 地图; 〔尤指〕海图, 航海图 **3 the charts**〔流行歌曲每周〕排行榜

chart[2] *v* **1** 给…制图; 记述 **2** 绘制…的地图[海图]; 把〔途经路线〕绘入地图[海图]

chase[1] *v* **1** ▶**FOLLOW** 跟随◀ 追逐, 追赶; 追捕 **2** ▶**HURRY** 赶快◀ 急忙赶往 **3** ▶**TRY TO GET STH** 试图得到某物◀ 努力赢得, 设法获得 **4** ▶**MAN/WOMAN** 男人/女人◀ 追求, 求爱 **5** ▶**METAL** 金属◀ 镂刻, 雕镂〔金属制品〕**6 chase the dragon** 吸食海洛因

chase sb/sth ↔ **up** *phr v* **1** 提醒某人〔实践诺言〕**2** 加速…的发生进程, 催促

chase[2] *n* **1** 追逐, 追赶; 追捕 **2 give chase** 追逐〔某人或某物〕

check[1] *v* **1** ▶**FIND OUT** 发现◀ 检查, 核对, 查验 **2** ▶**ASK SB** 询问某人◀ 询问; 征求同意; 核实 **3** ▶**NOT DO STH** 不做某事◀ 克制〔自己〕; 停止[阻止]〔自己〕做〔某事〕**4** ▶**STOP STH** 停止某事◀ 阻碍, 制止; 抑制 **5** ▶**MAKE A MARK** 做标记◀ 给〔答案、清单的项目等〕打勾 **6** ▶**BAGS/CASES ETC** 袋子/箱子等◀ 托运〔行李〕; 接受托运〔行李〕

check in *phr v* **1**〔在旅馆〕登记办理入住手续;〔在机场〕办理登机手续 **2**〔到图书馆〕归还〔图书〕

check sth ↔ **off** *phr v* 在〔处理过或核对过的项目后〕打勾

check out *phr v* **1** ▶**MAKE SURE** 确定◀ **a)** 调查, 检查, 核实, 查证 **b)** 证实是对的, 得到证实, 查证无误的 **2** ▶**LOOK AT SB/STH** 看某人/物◀〔因某人或物有趣或吸引人而〕盯着看 **3** ▶**GET INFORMATION** 获得资料◀ 了解…的情况 **4** ▶**TEST STH** 检测某物◀ 检测〔某物〕**5** ▶**HOTEL** 旅馆◀ 办理退房手续, 结账退房 **6** ▶**BOOKS** 书籍◀〔从图书馆〕借出〔书〕

check sth ↔ **over** *phr v* **1** 检查; 查看 **2** 体检, 健康检查

check up on sb *phr v*〔尤指秘密地〕调查, 查核〔某人〕

check on sb *phr v* 检查; 查看〔某人是否安全等〕

check[2] *n* **1** ▶**ON SAFETY/CORRECTNESS/TRUTH ETC** 安全/正确/真实等◀〔以确保某物安全、正确、真实等的〕检查; 查核 **2 keep a check (on sb/sth)** 监视; 监听 **3 run/do a check** 进行检查[调查] **4** ▶**A CONTROL ON STH** 控制某事◀ 制止(手段), 抑制(手段), 控制 **5** ▶**PATTERN** 图案◀〔尤指布料上的〕方格图案 **6** ▶**FROM YOUR BANK** 从银行◀ 支票 **7** ▶**IN A RESTAURANT** 在餐馆◀ 账单 **8** ▶**FOR YOUR COAT/BAG** 衣物/袋子◀ **a) coat check/hat check**〔餐馆、剧院等的〕衣帽寄存处 **b)** 存放单, 寄存物品的凭证 **9** ▶**MARK** 记号◀〔表示答案正确或某事项已处理的〕勾号 **10** ▶**CHESS** 国际象棋◀〔国际象棋中〕被"将军"的局面〔王棋处于被攻击的位置上〕

cherish *v* [一般用被动态] **1** 珍爱, 珍惜, 钟爱 **2** 视为珍贵[重要]

chill[1] *v* **1** (使)冷却, (使)变冷 **2** [一般用被动态] 使〔某人〕感到很冷 **3**〔尤指以残忍和暴力的手段〕使…不寒而栗, 使…寒心 **4** 使失望; 使〔热情〕冷却

chill out *phr v* 完全放松, 不紧张

chill[2] *n* **1** 寒冷, 寒气 **2** 害怕; 心寒 **3** 小感冒, 轻微发烧 **4** 不友好, 冷漠, 冷淡

chill[3] *adj* 寒冷的, 寒气袭人的

chop[1] *v* **1** ▶**CUT STH** 切某物◀ 又作 **chop up** 将〔食物、木材等〕切碎; 劈开 **2** ▶**REDUCE STH** 减少某物◀〔大幅度〕削减 **3** ▶**SWING A TOOL** 挥舞工具◀〔用斧头等〕砍, 劈 **4** ▶**MAKE A PATH** 开路◀ 开路, 辟路 **5 chop and change** 不停地改变主意; 变化无常 **6** ▶**HIT STH** 打中某物◀〔用手向下〕砸

chop sth ↔ **down** *phr v*〔用斧头等利器〕砍倒, 伐倒

chop sth ↔ off *phr v* 〔用斧等〕砍掉, 砍断

chop² *n* **1** ►**MEAT** 肉◄〔羊、猪等〕带骨的肉块 **2 get the chop a)** 被辞退, 被解雇 **b)** 被中止; 被削减 **3 be for the chop** 很可能停止[关闭] **4** ►**WITH YOUR HAND** 用手◄ 掌劈〔尤用掌侧〕 **5** ►**WITH A TOOL** 用工具◄〔用斧头等利器〕砍, 劈 **6 the chops** 颚, 下巴

chore *n* **1** 家庭杂务; 日常琐碎工作 **2** 令人厌烦的工作

circulate *v* **1** (使) 循环 **2** 流传; 传播; 散布 **3** 发送; 传播 **4** 〔在聚会上〕到处走动, 来回周旋 —**circulatory** *adj*

circumstance *n* **1 circumstances** 情况, 情形 **2 under/in no circumstances** 决不, 无论如何都不 **3 under/in the circumstances** 在这种情况下, 情形既然如此 **4** 无法控制的因素; 环境; 境遇 **5 live in reduced circumstances** 财政状况不佳, 经济拮据 **6 pomp and circumstance** 盛大隆重的场面

cite *v* **1** 引证, 援引 **2** 引用, 引述 **3** 传召; 传讯〔到法院〕 **4** 传唤 **5** 嘉奖; 表扬, 表彰

civil *adj* **1** 公民的; 民间的 **2** 普通公民的; 平民的; 民用的; 非军事的 **3** 民事的 **4** 客气的; 文明的; 有礼貌的

claim¹ *v* **1** 声称; 断言; 主张 **2** 索赔; 索取 **3** 认领; 要求; 索取〔应得的权利或财物〕 **4** 夺去, 夺走〔生命〕 **5** 值得; 需要〔花时间或精力〕

claim² *n* **1** ►**MONEY** 金钱◄ **a)** 〔根据权利而提出的〕要求, 索款 **b)** 索赔金额 **2** ►**STATEMENT** 声明◄ 声称; 断言; 主张 **3** ►**FOR PRAISE/RESPECT ETC** 用于表扬/尊敬等◄ 应得的权利[资格] **4** ►**TO OWN OR TAKE SOMETHING** 拥有或拿某物◄ 所有权 **5 lay claim to sth** 声称对某物拥有所有权 **6 stake your claim** 声称对…拥有所有权〔尤指当别人也同时作出相同的声明〕 **7 claim to fame** 出名的原因〔常为戏谑说法, 一般指实际上并不怎么重要的东西〕 **8 have a claim on sb** 有权得到〔某人的〕注意; 有权占用〔某人的〕时间 **9** ►**LAND** 土地◄ 要求得到的东西〈如含有矿产的土地〉

clarify *v* 澄清, 讲清楚, 阐明 —**clarification** *n*

classify *v* **1** 〔依据某系统〕将…分类 **2** 把…归入一类[一个等级] —**classifiable** *adj*

climate *n* **1** 〔某一时期社会上的〕风气, 思潮; 趋势 **2** 气候 **3** 气候带, 地带

cling *v* **1** 〔尤指感觉不安全而〕紧紧抓住[抱住] **2** 缠着; 黏着 **3** 挨近, 贴近; 依附

cling to sth *phr v* 坚持, 忠于

coarse *adj* **1** 粗的, 粗糙的 **2** 粗线条构成的; 粗的 **3** 粗俗的; 猥亵的; 粗鲁的 **coarsely** *adv* —**coarseness** *n*

code¹ *n* **1** ►**BEHAVIOUR** 行为◄ 行为准则; 道德规范 **2** ►**RULES/LAWS** 规章/法律◄ 法典, 法规 **3 code of practice** 行业规则 **4** ►**SECRET MESSAGE** 秘密信息◄ 密码; 代码; 代号 **5** ►**SIGNS GIVING INFORMATION** 信息符号◄编码, 编号, 标记 **6** ►**TELEPHONES** 电话◄ 又作 **dialling code, STD code** 长途电话区号 **7** ►**COMPUTERS** 电脑◄〔电脑的〕编码 **8** ►**SOUNDS/SIGNALS** 声音/信号◄〔电报等发出的〕电码

code² *v* **1** 把…编码[编号] **2** 把…编成密码 **3 colour code** 颜色编码 —**coded** *adj*

collective¹ *adj* 集体的; 共同的; 共有的

collective² *n* **1** 集体企业[农庄]人员 **2** 集体经营的企业[农庄]

colossal *adj* 巨大的, 庞大的 —**colossally** *adv*

combine¹ *v* **1** (使) 结合; (使) 组合 **2** (使) 化合, (使) 组合, 调和 **3** 同时做〔两件完全不同的事〕 **4** (使) 联合〔以达成某项目〕; 合并

combine² *n* **1** 又作 **combine harvester** 联合收割机 **2** 〔为某一目的而组成的〕联盟, 联合 (体)

comedy *n* **1** 喜剧 **2** 喜剧性, 喜剧成分; 幽默

comfort¹ *n* **1** ►**EMOTIONAL** 情感的◄ 安慰, 慰藉 **2** ►**PHYSICAL** 身体的◄ 舒适感, 满足感 **3** ►**MONEY/POSSESSIONS** 钱/财产◄ 舒适, 安逸 **4 comforts** 使生活舒适之物; 奢侈品 **5** ►**SB/STH THAT HELPS** 有用的人/物◄ 安慰者; 慰藉物 **6 too close/near etc for comfort** 〔因危险而〕使人忧虑[不快, 不适]的事情 **7 cold/small comfort** 不起作用的安慰 —**comfortless** *adj*

comfort² *v* 安慰, 慰问 —**comforting** *adj* —**comfortingly** *adv*

commemorate *v* 庆祝, 为…举行纪念活动 —**commemorative** *adj*

comment¹ *n* **1** 意见, 评论 **2** 〔对某人所说或所做事情的〕批评; 议论 **3 be a comment on** 是〔反映事物不足之处的〕标志, 特征

comment² *v* 评论; 发表意见

commerce *n* **1** 买卖, 贸易; 商务; 商业 **2** 联系; 交流

commit *v* **1** ►**CRIME** 罪行◄ 犯〔错误、罪行〕 **2** ►**SAY THAT SB WILL DO STH** 保证某人会做某事◄ 使承担义务, 作出保证 **3 commit yourself** 答应, 承诺 **4** ►**MONEY/TIME** 金钱/时间◄ 拨出…供使用, 调拨 **5** ►**PRISON/HOSPITAL** 监狱/医院◄ 把…关进监狱[医院], 监禁 **6 commit sth to memory** 牢记某事 **7 commit sth to paper** 写下某事

commodity *n* **1** 商品 **2** 有用的性质; 有用的东西

commonplace¹ *adj* 平常的; 平凡的; 不足为奇的

commonplace² *n* **1** 平常的事, 司空见惯的事 **2 the commonplace** 一般, 没有特色, 单调乏味

communicate *v* **1** ►**EXPRESS** 表达◄ 表达, 传达〔思想、感情〕 **2** ►**EXCHANGE INFORMATION** 交流信息◄〔用符号等〕与〔他人〕交流信息; 交谈 **3** ►**CONTACT** 联系◄〔尤指用电话、书信等〕与他人联系 **4** ►**UNDERSTAND** 理解◄ 沟通〔思想、情感〕 **5** ►**ROOMS** 房间◄〔不同房间或楼房的不同部分〕互通, 相连 **6** ►**DISEASE** 疾病◄ [一般用被动态]〔疾病〕传染

community *n* **1** ►**PEOPLE** 人们◄〔住同一地的人所构成的〕社区 **2** ►**PARTICULAR GROUP** 特定团体◄ **sense of community** 社区归属感〔居住在同一地的人们所有的一种归属感〕 **3** 〔由同国籍、同宗教等构成的〕群体; 社区 **4 the community** 社会; 公众 **5** ►**PLANTS/ANIMALS** 植物/动物◄ 群落〔生长或生活在同一环境中的植物或动物群〕

compact¹ *adj* **1** 小巧便携的 **2** 小而紧凑的 **3** 紧密的; 密集的 **4** 矮小结实的, 壮实的 **5** 简洁的 —**compactly** *adv* —**compactness** *n*

compact² *n* 1〔内有镜子的〕女式化妆粉盒 2 小型汽车 3〔人与人、国与国之间的〕协定

compact³ *v*〔将柔软或由小块组成的物质〕压紧, 压实 —**compacted** *adj*

companion *n* 1 同伴; 同行者 2 构成一对的两件物品中的一件 3 伴侣〔尤指受雇陪一位老人一起生活或旅行的人, 尤为女子〕4 手册, 指南〔用于书名〕

compare¹ *v* 1 ►**SIMILAR/DIFFERENT** 类似的/不同的◄ 比较 2 **compared to/with**〔尺寸、质量、数量〕与…相比 3 ►**LIKE/EQUALLY GOOD** 像/同样好◄〔表示某物、某人与另一物、另一人〕相像或一样好, 一样大等 4 **does not compare** 不能相比 5 ►**BETTER/WORSE** 较好/较糟◄〔在某方面〕比〔某人/某物〕好[差] 6 **compare notes**〔两人对所做过的事〕交换意见

compare² *n* **beyond/without compare** 无可比拟; 无可匹配

compensate *v* 1 弥补, 补偿 2 赔偿, 补偿

complex¹ *adj* 1 复杂的〔指由许多密切联系的部分或过程构成的〕2 难以理解的, 难处理的; 复杂的 3〔词、句〕复合的

complex² *n* 1 综合楼群〔由众多大楼或一座主楼和诸多辅楼组成〕2 情结, 夸大的情绪反应 3 **a complex of roads/regulations etc** 纵横交织的道路网/纷繁芜杂的条例等

complicated *adj* 1 难懂的; 难处理的 2 结构复杂的

component *n*〔机器或系统的〕零件; 成分; 组成部分

compose *v* 1 **be composed of** 由…组成 2 组成, 构成 3 作曲 4 **compose a letter/poem/speech etc** 写信/诗/讲稿等 5 **compose your thoughts/features** 镇静心情/使外表平静 6〔为达到特殊效果而〕为〔绘画、照片场景〕构图

compound¹ *n* 1 化合物 2 由两件或更多事情, 两种或更多情况结合造成的局势 3 四周有篱笆或围墙的建筑群 4 复合名词; 复合形容词

compound² *adj* 1 **compound eye/leaf etc** 复眼/复叶等 2 **compound noun/adjective** 复合名词/复合形容词

compound³ *v* 1 使恶化, 加重 2 使混合; 使合成; 使化合 3 以复利计算支付〔利息〕

compute *v* 计算〔结果、答案、总数等〕

conceal *v* 1 隐匿, 隐藏 2 隐藏真实感情; 隐瞒真相 —**concealment** *n*

concentrate¹ *v* 1 专注, 专心; 集中注意力 2 **be concentrated on/in/around etc** 集中于; 汇集于 3 使…头脑清醒 4 浓缩〔液体〕

concentrate sth ↔ **on** *phr v* 把注意力集中于, 全神贯注于

concentrate² *n* 浓缩物; 浓缩液

concern¹ *n* 1 ►**WORRY** 担忧◄ a) 担心的事, 关切的事 b) 忧虑; 担心 2 **be of concern (to sb)** 令〔某人〕感到担心的; 是〔某人〕所关心的 3 与某人有关的事, 对某人重要的事 4 ►**FEELING FOR SB** 对某人的情感◄ 关心; 关怀 5 **sb's concern** 由某人负责的事 6 **not sb's concern/none of sb's concern** 某人不感兴趣的事; 与某人无关的事 7 ►**BUSINESS** 企业◄ 企业; 公司

concern² *v* 1〔活动、情况、规则等〕对…有影响; 与…相关 2 [不用被动态] 使忧虑, 使担心 3 [不用被动态]〔故事、书、报告等〕与…有关, 关于 4 **concern yourself with/about sth** 关心, 担心 5 **to whom it may concern**〔写在正式信函开头的一句套话, 用于写信人不知道收信人的姓名时〕

concise *adj* 简洁的; 简明的 —**concisely** *adv* —**conciseness** 又作 **concision** *n*

conclude *v* 1 作出结论, 断定 2 完成, 结束 3〔以做某事或讲某话来〕结束〔会议或演说〕4 **conclude an agreement/treaty/contract etc** 达成协议/缔结条约/签订合同等

concrete¹ *adj* 1 混凝土的 2 有真凭实据的 3 具体的 —**concretely** *adv*

concrete² *n* 混凝土

concrete³ *v* 用混凝土浇筑[覆盖]〔小路、墙等〕

conduct¹ *v* 1 **conduct a survey/experiment/inquiry etc**〔尤指为获取信息或证实某事时〕进行调查/实验/调查研究等 2 ►**MUSIC** 音乐◄ 指挥 3 ►**ELECTRICITY/HEAT** 电/热◄ 传导 4 ►**SHOW SB STH** 带某人参观◄ 带领某人参观某地 5 **conduct yourself** 行为, 表现〔尤指人们借此作出评判〕

conduct² *n* 1〔社会、职业等〕行为举止 2〔某项生意、活动的〕组织安排; 管理; 经营

conference *n* 1 会议〔指很多人参加讨论重要事宜的大型会议, 尤指历时数天的会议〕2 少数人参加的私下会议 3〔运动〕联合会

confirm *v* 1 证实, 证明 2 使〔想法、感觉〕巩固, 更坚定, 加强 3 证实 4 肯定, 确认〔安排、日期等〕5 **be confirmed** 行坚信典礼〔从而正式成为基督教会成员〕

conflict¹ *n* 1〔意见等〕冲突, 相左 2〔在对立的需要或影响之间选择的〕矛盾, 冲突 3 战斗; 战争 4 矛盾心理 5 **conflict of interest/interests** a) 利益冲突 b)〔不同人之间的〕利益冲突

conflict² *v* 矛盾, 冲突, 抵触

confront *v* 1 以暴力相威胁 2 勇敢地面对; 正视 3 [一般用被动态] 突然面临 4 对质, 当面对证

confuse *v* 1 使困惑; 把〔某人〕弄糊涂 2〔把人、物或想法〕混淆, 弄错 3 **confuse the issue/matter/argument etc** 使问题/事情/争论等更加难以弄清或处理

congratulate *v* 1 祝贺, 向…道喜 2 **congratulate yourself (on)** 为自己高兴, 感到自豪 —**congratulation** *n* —**congratulatory** *adj*

congress *n* 1 代表大会 2 国会; 议会 3 **Congress**〔由参议院和众议院组成的〕美国国会 —**congressional** *adj*

conquer *v* 1 征服 2 击败, 战胜 3 克服; 制伏 4 成功登上〔从未有人攀登过的山顶〕5〔在某地〕大获成功 —**conqueror** *n* —**conquering** *adj*

conscious *adj* 1 注意到的; 意识到的 2 清醒的 3 **a conscious effort/decision/attempt etc** 特意作出的努力/决定/尝试等 4 **safety-conscious/fashion-conscious etc** 特别注意安全的/十分关注时尚的等 —反义词 UNCONSCIOUS —**consciously** *adv*

consent¹ *n* 1 许可, 允许 2 同意, 赞同 3 **with one consent** 全体一致同意

consent² *v* 同意, 允许

consequence *n* **1** 后果 **2 as a consequence (of sth)/in consequence (of sth)** 因为; 由于 **3 of little/no/any consequence** 不重要的/无足轻重的

conservative[1] *adj* **1 Conservative**〔英国〕保守党的 **2** 因循守旧的, 不喜欢变化的 **3**〔式样、口味等〕不时兴的, 传统的 **4 a conservative estimate/guess** 保守的估计/猜测 **—conservatively** *adv*

conservative[2] *n* **1 Conservative** 英国保守党的支持者; 保守党党员 **2** 因循守旧者, 保守者

considerable *adj* 相当大的〔尤指大到足以产生某种影响的程度〕

consist *v*

consist in sth *phr v* 在于, 决定于

consist of sth *phr v* 由…组成, 由…构成

constant[1] *adj* **1** 始终如一的, 恒久不变的 **2** 持续不断的, 经常发生的 **3** 忠实的, 忠诚的

constant[2] *n* **1** 常数, 恒量 **2** 不变的事; 恒定的事物

consult *v* **1** 咨询; 请教 **2** 取得〔某人〕的允许; 与〔某人〕商量共同决定 **3** 查阅

consume *v* **1** 消耗; 消费 **2 time-consuming** 耗费时间的 **3** 吃; 喝 **4 consumed with** 被〔某种情感〕所折磨 **5**〔大火〕(彻底) 烧毁

contact[1] *n* **1 ►COMMUNICATION 交流◄** 联系, 联络; 交往 **2 ►TOUCH 触摸◄** 接触 **3 come into contact with sb** 会见某人 **4 ►PERSON WHO CAN HELP 能提供帮助的人◄**〔能提供帮助或建议的〕熟人 **5 ►SITUATION/PROBLEM 局势/问题◄**〔处理某种局面或问题的〕经验 **6 point of contact a)** 联系点; 联系人 **b)** 联系点; 接合点 **7 ►ELECTRICAL PART 电路元件◄**〔电路的〕触点; 接头 **8 ►EYES 眼睛◄** 隐形眼镜

contact[2] *v*〔写信、打电话〕联系〔某人〕

contact[3] *adj* **1**〔电话号码或地址〕可供联系的 **2**〔炸药或化学物质〕凭接触起作用的

contain *v* **1** 包含; 容纳; 装盛 **2** 克制〔强烈的感情〕**3** 抑制, 控制 **4** 包围〔图形或角〕

contemporary[1] *adj* **1** 当代的 **2** 发生[存在]于同一时代的

contemporary[2] *n* 同时代的人; 同辈

content[1] *n* **1 contents a)** 容纳的东西 **b)**〔书、信等的〕内容 **2** 含量 **3**〔演讲或文章的〕内容

content[2] *adj* **1** 满意的, 满足的 **2 not content with** 对…不满足

content[3] *n* **1** 满意, 满足 **2 do sth to your heart's content** 尽情[心满意足]地做某事

content[4] *v* **1 content yourself with sth** 使自己满足[甘心]于某事 **2** 使满意; 使满足

contest[1] *n* **1** 比赛, 竞赛 **2** 竞争, 争夺, 角逐 **3 no contest** 轻易获胜, 轻取

contest[2] *v* **1** 对…提出质疑; 抗辩 **2** 竞争, 争夺, 角逐

contract[1] *n* **1** 契约; 合同 **2 subject to contract**〔达成协议但还〕须签订合约 **3** 刺杀协议

contract[2] *v* **1** 缩小; 收缩; 缩短 **2** 感染〔疾病〕, 患〔病〕**3 contract to do sth** 签合同做… **4 contract a marriage/alliance etc** 订立婚约/盟约等

contract in *phr v* 同意参与; 订约加入

contract out *phr v* **1** 把〔工作等〕承包出去 **2** 同意不加入〔退休金计划等〕

contrary[1] *n* **1 on the contrary** 正相反, 恰恰相反〔用于表示强烈不赞同别人刚说的话〕**2 to the contrary** 意思相反; 完全不同 **3 the contrary** 相反; 反面; 对立面

contrary[2] *adj* **1** 相反的, 相对的 **2** 故意作对的, 对抗的 **3 contrary to** 与…相反〔用于表示与别人观点相反的事实〕**4**〔天气〕不作美的, 不合人意的 **—contrariness** *n*

contrast[1] *n* **1** 差异, 差别 **2 in contrast/by contrast** 与…相反/相比之下 **3** 对照物, 明显的对比物 **4**〔绘画、照片中颜色、明暗的〕反差 **5**〔电视画面的〕对比度, 衬度

contrast[2] *v* **1** 使成对比, 使成对照 **2** 形成对照; 对比之下现出区别

contribute *v* **1** 捐献; 捐助; 出一分钱; 出一分力 **2 contribute to sth** 对某事起促成作用 **3**〔给报纸、杂志等〕撰稿; 投稿

convenience *n* **1** 方便, 便利; 合宜 **2**〔个人的〕便利; 自在, 舒适 **3 at your earliest convenience** 尽快〔常用于书信〕**4** 便利措施; 带来方便的装置 **5** 又作 **public convenience** 公共厕所 **6 a marriage of convenience** 基于利害关系的婚姻

convey *v* **1** 传达; 表达〔想法、感情〕**2** 传递〔信息〕; 传送; 传播 **3** 传送〔物件〕; 输送; 运送 **4** 把〔财产〕让与; 转让

convince *v* **1** 使确信; 使信服 **2** 说服, 劝服

cooperate 又作 **co-operate 1** 合作, 协作 **2** 配合; 协助

cope[1] *v* **1**〔成功地〕应付, 对付 **2**〔机器或系统〕能处理; 能应付

cope[2] *n*〔教士在特别日子穿的〕长袍, 法衣

core[1] *n* **1 ►FRUIT 水果◄**〔苹果等的〕果核 **2 ►CENTRAL PART 中心部分◄**〔事物的〕核心, 最重要部分 **3 core values/beliefs/concerns** 最重要的标准/最重要的信仰/最关心的问题 **4 ►PEOPLE 人们◄**〔组织的〕核心成员 **5 to the core** 十分地; 彻底地 **6 ►PLANETS 行星◄** 地心; 〔天体的〕核心 **7 ►NUCLEAR REACTOR 核反应堆◄**〔核反应堆的〕活性区

core[2] *v* 去掉〔水果〕的果核

corporation *n* **1** 大型公司; 大企业; 企业集团 **2** 市镇当局; 市议会 **3 corporation tax** 公司(利润)税

correspond *v* **1** 符合; 相一致 **2** 相类似, 相当 **3** 通信

cosmetic *adj* **1** 装门面的; 表面的 **2** 化妆的; 美容的

cosmopolitan[1] *adj* **1**〔某地的人〕来自世界各地的 **2**〔人〕见识广的; 〔信仰、意见等〕兼容并包的

cosmopolitan[2] *n* 游历四方的人; 四海为家的人

costume *n* **1**〔代表某一特定地方或历史时期的〕服装 **2** 化装服; 戏装 **3** 游泳衣, 泳装

counter[1] *n* **1 ►SHOP 商店◄** 柜台 **2 over the counter**〔买药〕不用处方 **3 under the counter** 秘密地, 暗地里〔通常违法地〕**4 ►KITCHEN 厨房◄**〔尤指厨房中的〕操作台面, 工作台 **5 ►GAME 游戏◄** 筹码 **6 ►EQUIPMENT 装备◄** 计算器, 计数器 **7 ►ACTION AGAINST STH 反对◄** 制止; 反驳

counter[2] *v* **1** 反驳, 反对 **2** 抵消; 对抗; 制止

counter³ *adv* 相反地 —**counter** *adj*
courteous *adj* 有礼貌的 —反义词 DISCOURTEOUS —**courteously** *adv* —**courteousness** *n*
coverage *n* **1** 新闻报道 **2** 保险范围，保险项目 **3** 课程内容；一堂课的内容
crack¹ *v* **1** ►**BREAK** 断裂◄（使）破裂；（使）裂开 **2** ►**LOUD SOUND** 响声◄（使）发爆裂声 **3** ►**HIT STH** 击撞某物◄ 重击 **4** ►**HIT SB** 击打某人◄ 重击〔某人〕 **5** ►**LOSE CONTROL** 失控◄ 又作 **crack up**〔因受大压力而〕失去控制；崩溃 **6** ►**MENTALLY ILL** 精神病◄ 又作 **crack up**（使）发疯，（使）神经错乱 **7** ►**VOICE** 声音◄〔声音〕变嘶哑 **8** ►**NERVE** 神经◄ 失去勇气 **9** ►**EGG/NUT** 蛋/坚果◄ 打开，砸开〔鸡蛋、坚果等〕的壳 **10** ►**STEAL** 偷◄ 非法地打开；撬开〔保险柜盗窃〕 **11** ►**SOLVE** 解决◄ 解决〔难题〕；破解〔密码〕 **12** ►**STOP CRIME/ENEMY** 制止犯罪/敌人◄ 消灭〔敌人〕；制止〔敌人做的事〕 **13 crack it** 成功 **14 crack a deal**〔尤指费力地〕达成协议；做成买卖 **15 crack a joke** 说笑话 **16 crack a smile** 转怒为喜；破涕为笑 **17 crack open a bottle** 打开一瓶酒 **18 not all/everything it's cracked up to be** 不如人们所说的那样好；名不副实 **19 get cracking** 抓紧时间 **20 crack the whip** 逼手下人努力工作
crack down *phr v*〔对…〕采取严厉措施；制裁；镇压
crack on *phr v* 继续努力
crack up *phr v* **1**（使）捧腹大笑 **2** 吃不消，精神垮掉
crack² *n* **1** ►**THIN SPACE** 狭窄的空间◄ 裂缝，缝隙 **2** ►**BREAK** 断裂◄ 裂痕，裂口 **3** ►**PROBLEM** 问题◄ 瑕疵，缺点 **4** ►**SOUND** 声音◄ 爆裂声，噼啪声 **5** ►**JOKE/REMARK** 玩笑/话语◄ 俏皮话；粗鲁的话 **6** ►**CHANCE TO DO STH** 机遇◄ 试图，尝试 **7 a crack on the head** 脑袋上挨了一下 **8 a crack in sb's voice**〔尤指因情绪激动而引起的〕嗓音的变化 **9 crack of dawn** 大清早，黎明 **10** ►**DRUG** 毒品◄ 强效可卡因 **11 good crack** 一群人友好的交谈；尽兴的谈话 **12 what's the crack?** 发生什么事了？最近发生了什么事？
crack³ *adj* **1** 第一流的；受过良好训练的 **2 crack shot** 神枪手
cradle¹ *n* **1** ►**BED** 床◄ 摇篮 **2 the cradle of** …的发源地；…的策源地 **3 from/in the cradle** 从/在婴儿[幼年]时期 **4 from the cradle to the grave** 一辈子，从生到死 **5**〔空中作业用的〕吊架，吊篮 **6**〔电话的〕听筒架，叉簧
cradle² *v* 轻轻地抱着
craft¹ *n* **1 a)** 小船 **b)** 飞机，飞行器，航空器；航天器 **2**〔尤指传统的手工〕工艺；手艺 **3** 行业，职业 **4** 诡计，手腕
craft² *v* [一般用被动态] 手工制作，精制
crash¹ *v* **1** ►**CAR/PLANE ETC** 汽车/飞机等◄（使）〔飞机、汽车等〕坠毁；撞坏 **2** ►**HIT STH/SB HARD** 重击某物/某人◄〔哗啦啦地〕猛撞，猛击 **3** ►**MAKE A LOUD NOISE** 发出巨响◄ 发出巨响 **4** ►**SLEEP** 睡觉◄ 又作 **crash out a)**〔尤指由于很疲倦〕很快入睡 **b)**〔尤指事先没有准备而留在别人家里〕过夜 **5** ►**COMPUTER** 电脑◄〔电脑〕瘫痪 **6** ►**FINANCIAL** 金融◄〔股票〕狂跌 **7** ►**PARTY** 聚会◄ 不请自来〔参加聚会〕 **8 crashing bore** 令人厌烦的人
crash² *n* **1**〔汽车的〕撞车事故；〔飞机的〕失事 **2** 突然发出的巨响；〔东西倒下、打破等时发出的〕碰撞声 **3**〔电脑或电脑系统的〕瘫痪，失效，死机 **4**〔股票的〕狂跌
create *v* **1** 创造；创建 **2** 发明；创作 **3 create sb/sth** 封爵；任命；授予 **4** 大喊大叫；大发雷霆
credit¹ *n* **1** ►**DELAYED PAYMENT** 推迟付款◄ 赊购 **2** ►**PRAISE** 赞扬◄ 赞扬；赞许 **3 be a credit to sb/sth** 又作 **do sb/sth credit** 为…增光 **4 have sth to your credit** 成功 **5 be in credit**〔银行账户中〕有存款 **6** ►**FILM** 电影◄ **the credits**〔影片或电视节目的〕演员和摄制人员名单 **7 on the credit side** 好的方面；正面 **8** ►**UNIVERSITY** 大学◄ 学分 **9** ►**TRUE/CORRECT** 真的/正确的◄ 信任
credit² *v* **1** 信任；相信 **2** 把钱存入〔账户〕 **3 credit sb with sth** 相信某人有优点[做了好事] **4 be credited to** 归功于…；…是某事发生的原因
creep¹ *v* **1** 悄悄地小心行进 **2** 爬行，匍匐 **3** 渐渐侵入，逐渐融进 **4**〔植物〕攀缘，蔓生 **5**〔雾、云等〕弥漫 **6** 卑躬屈膝，巴结奉承 **7 sb/sth makes my flesh creep** 某人/某事物使我不舒服[恐惧]
creep up on sb/sth *phr v* **1** 蹑手蹑脚在后面走〔而吓人一跳〕 **2**〔感情或观点〕渐渐变强 **3** 不知不觉中到来
creep² *n* **1** 极讨厌的人 **2** 献媚者；奴颜婢膝的人 **3 give sb the creeps**〔人或地方〕使某人毛骨悚然[紧张]
crime *n* **1** ►**CRIME IN GENERAL** 犯罪◄〔泛指〕违法犯罪活动 **2** ►**A PARTICULAR CRIME** 罪行◄ 罪，罪行 **3 it's a crime**（这么做是）不道德的 **4 crime against humanity** 违反人性的罪行 **5 crime of passion** 情杀罪；桃色案件 **6 crime doesn't pay** 违法犯罪是没有好处的
cripple¹ *n* **1** 跛子；手臂残废者〔侮辱用语〕 **2 emotional cripple** 感情残废〔指不能处理自己或他人的感情的人〕
cripple² *v* **1** 使〔手臂或腿〕受伤致残 **2** 严重损坏[削弱] —**crippled** *adj* —**crippling** *adj*
crisis *n* **1**〔尤指政治、经济等〕危机；紧要关头 **2**〔个人的〕危急之际 **3**〔重病的〕转折点 **4 crisis management** 应付危机[困境]的技巧；危机[困境]处理过程 **5 crisis of confidence** 信任危机
crude¹ *adj* **1** 粗俗的，粗野的；粗鲁的 **2** 粗制的 **3**〔石油、橡胶等〕天然的，未加提炼的 **4** 粗糙的；未加修饰的；简陋的 **5 in crude terms** 简单地说 —**crudely** *adv* —**crudity** 又作 **crudeness** *n*
crude² 又作 **crude oil** *n* 原油
crush¹ *v* **1** 压碎，压坏，压扁 **2** 捣碎，弄碎，粉碎 **3 crush a rebellion/uprising/revolt etc** 平定叛乱/起义/反叛等 **4 crush sb's hopes/enthusiasm/confidence etc** 毁灭某人的希望/热情/信心等 **5** 使非常伤心；使震惊
crush up *phr v* 挤，塞，挤入
crush² *n* **1** 拥挤的人群 **2**〔尤指对年龄比自己大者的〕迷恋 **3 orange/lemon etc crush** 橙汁/柠檬汁等
cure¹ *v* **1** 治愈〔病人〕 **2** 治愈，治好〔疾病〕 **3** 解决〔问题〕；改善〔困境〕 **4**〔用晒、熏、腌等方法〕保存〔食

品、烟草等〕

cure² *n* **1** 药, 药剂; 疗法 **2** 对策 **3** 治愈 **4 take the cure** 进行矿泉治疗

curious *adj* **1** 好奇的, 好打听的 —反义词 INCURIOUS **2** 稀奇古怪的 —**curiously** *adv*

curl¹ *n* **1** 鬈发 **2** 卷曲物, 螺旋状物 **3 a curl of your lip/mouth** 撇嘴〔表示不赞同〕

curl² *v* **1** 盘绕, 缠绕 **2** (使)弯曲 **3**〔表示反对〕撇〔嘴〕**4 make your hair curl**〔故事、经历等〕使人毛骨悚然, 使…战栗

curl up *phr v* **1** 蜷缩 **2** 卷曲 **3** 弯曲着上升, 螺旋着上升

current¹ *adj* 现时的, 当前的, 现行的 —**currently** *adv*

current² *n* **1** 流; 水流 **2** 电流

curse¹ *v* **1** 咒骂 **2**〔嘴上或心里〕臭骂 **3** 诅咒

curse² *n* **1** 骂人话 **2** 诅咒, 咒语 **3** 祸因, 祸根 **4 the curse** 月经

cushion¹ *n* **1** 垫子 **2** 垫形物, 起垫子作用的东西; 缓冲物 **3** 起缓解作用的东西; 防备不时之需的积蓄〔尤指金钱〕**4**〔台球桌的〕橡皮边, 弹性衬边

cushion² *v* **1** 缓冲 **2** 减轻〔令人不愉快的〕效果

custom *n* **1** 风俗, 习惯, 传统 **2** 日常习惯 **3**〔经常性的〕惠顾, 光顾 **4 customs** 海关

cycle¹ *n* **1** 循环 **2** 自行车; 摩托车 **3** 周期 **4**〔表现同一重大事件的〕组歌, 组诗

cycle² *v* 骑自行车

D, d

damage¹ *n* **1** ►**PHYSICAL HARM** 对物体或身体的损害◄〔对某物、某人造成的〕损害 **2** ►**EMOTIONAL HARM** 情感上受到的伤害◄〔对一个人感情或心理造成的〕伤害 **3** ►**BAD EFFECT** 不好的影响◄ 坏影响 **4** ►**MONEY** 钱◄ 损害赔偿金 **5 the damage is done** 已造成的伤害无法挽回 **6 what's the damage?** 要花多少钱? **7 damage limitation** 损失控制, 降低损失

damage² *v* **1** 损害, 损坏, 损伤〔某物或某人的身体部位〕**2**〔对某物或某人〕有不好的影响 —**damaging** *adj*

damp¹ *adj* **1** 潮湿的 **2 damp squib** 未达到预期效果而使人失望的事; 湿水爆竹 —**damply** *adv*

damp² *n* 潮湿的部分[地方]

damp³ *v* 减低〔声响〕

damp sth ↔ **down** *phr v* **1**〔常指用盖灰的方法〕封〔火〕, 减弱〔火势〕**2** 抑制〔感情〕

dash¹ *v* **1** 猛冲 **2** 猛击, 撞击 **3 dash sb's hopes** 使某人的希望破灭, 让某人失望 **4 (I) must dash/(I) have to dash** (我)得赶紧走了 **5 dash it (all)!** 讨厌!〔表示有些厌烦、生气〕**6**〔波浪或大雨猛烈地〕撞击, 冲击

dash off *phr v* **1** 匆匆地离开 **2** 匆匆地写[画]〔某物〕

dash² *n*

1 ►**LINE** 线条◄ 破折号 **2 make a dash for** 猛冲, 飞奔 **3** ►**SMALL AMOUNT** 少量◄ 少许, 少量〔液体或其他物质〕**4 a mad dash** 急奔, 狂冲 **5** ►**SOUND** 声音◄〔用莫尔斯电码发报时用的〕长音; 光的一长闪 **6** ►**CAR** 汽车◄〔汽车的〕仪表板 **7** ►**STYLE** 风范◄〔如士兵般的〕帅劲, 精力, 干劲; 勇气 **8 cut a dash**〔尤指穿着〕有气派, 精神, 漂亮

date¹ *n* **1** 日期, 日子 **2** 日子〔特定的某一天〕**3 at a later date** 晚些时候〔将来的某个时间〕**4 to date** 迄今, 至今, 到目前为止 **5 a)**〔恋人之间的〕约会 **b)** 约会对象 **6 make a date** 约好时间 **7** 椰枣, 海枣

date² *v* **1**〔在某物上〕写上[印上]日期 **2** 鉴定〔古书、古画、古建筑等的〕年代 **3**〔衣物、艺术等〕过时 **4**〔谈恋爱〕与…约会 **5** 显示〔某人〕老了

date from 又作 **date back to** *phr v* 自…存在至今, 追溯到…年代

dawn¹ *n* **1** 黎明, 破晓 **2 the dawn of civilization/time etc** 文明/时代等的开端 **3 a false down** 假曙光〔指虚幻的好迹象〕

dawn² *v* **1** 破晓, 天亮 **2** 开始 **3** 开始明白, 第一次想起〔某种感觉或想法〕

dawn on sb *phr v* [不用被动态] 开始明白〔某个事实〕, 醒悟

debate¹ *n* **1** 讨论, 辩论 **2**〔就某一个话题进行的〕正式讨论 **3 be open to debate** 又作 **be a matter for debate**〔某种观点〕可以进行讨论的 **4 under debate** 正在讨论[辩论]中

debate² *v* **1**〔正式地〕讨论, 辩论 **2**〔作出决定前〕反复考虑, 斟酌 —**debater** *n*

decay¹ *v* **1** (使)腐烂; (使)变坏 **2**〔可以指建筑物、结构或地区等的状况〕变坏, 破败 **3**〔传统观念、道德、标准等〕失去影响力, 衰败, 衰落

decay² *n* **1** 腐烂, 朽烂 **2** 腐烂部分, 腐蚀部分 **3**〔观念、信仰、社会组织或政治组织等的〕衰退, 衰败 **4**〔经济上的〕成功到贫穷的转变, 衰退 **5**〔疏于管理而造成建筑物和大楼的〕逐渐毁坏

deceive *v* **1** 欺骗 **2 deceive yourself** 自欺欺人 **3 are my eyes deceiving me?** 我是不是看错了? 是不是我眼花了?〔表示非常惊讶〕—**deceiver** *n*

decent *adj* **1** 可接受的, 相当好的, 像样的 **2**〔待人〕公平的; 和善的 **3** 正派的, 规矩的 **4** 穿着得体的, 不暴露太多的 —反义词 INDECENT **5 a decent burial funeral** 体面的葬礼 —**decently** *adv*

declare *v* **1** ►**STATE OFFICIALLY** 正式宣布◄ 宣布, 声明 **2 declare war (on sb) a)** 对〔某人、某国〕宣战 **b)** 向〔不好的事〕宣战 **3** ►**SAY WHAT YOU THINK/FEEL** 说出所想/感觉到的◄ 声称, 宣称 **4** ►**MONEY/PROPERTY ETC** 金钱/财产等◄ 申报〔收入、财产等〕**5 declare an interest** 宣布和…有关系 **6 declare bankruptcy** 宣告破产 **7** ►**SURPRISE** 惊奇◄ **(Well) I declare!** 嘿! 真怪了!〔用于表示惊奇〕—**declarable** *adj*

declare against sb/sth *phr v* 声明反对

declare for sb/sth *phr v* 声明赞成

decline¹ *n* 减少, 削减

decline² *v* **1** ►**BECOME LESS** 变少◄ 减少, 下降, 衰退 **2** ►**BECOME WORSE** 变糟◄〔质量〕越来越差 **3** ►**SAY NO** 说不◄ 拒绝, 谢绝 **4** ►**REFUSE** 拒绝◄ 拒绝〔做某事〕**5 sb's declining years** 某人的晚年, 残生 **6** ►**GRAMMAR** 语法◄ **a)** 变格, 词形变化〔根据名词、代词或形容词在句中的作用, 作主语、宾语或

其他成分〕**b)** 使〔名词等〕词形变化, 使变格

decorate *v* **1** 装修 **2** 装饰, 布置, 美化 **3** 授予…勋章[奖章] —**decorating** *n*

decrease¹ *v* (使)变小, (使)减少 — 反义词 INCREASE —**decreasing** *adj*

decrease² *n* 减少; 减少的数量

dedicate *v* **1 a)** 把〔作品等〕献给〔某人〕**b)** 用…命名〔建筑物, 以表达崇敬之情〕**2 dedicate yourself/your life to sth** 献身于/把一生献给某事

defeat¹ *n* **1** 失败 **2** 战胜, 击败

defeat² *v* **1**〔在战争、竞争、比赛等中〕战胜, 打败 **2** 把〔某人〕难住 **3** 使…失败

defect¹ *n* 缺陷, 瑕疵

defect² *v* 背叛, 叛变, 投敌, 变节 —**defector** *n* —**defection** *n*

defend *v* **1** 保护, 保卫 **2** 捍卫, 维护 **3** 为…辩护, 为…辩白, 为…辩解 **4**〔在比赛中〕防守, 防卫 **5 defend a title/championship**〔冠军〕卫冕 **6**〔律师〕为〔被指控犯罪者〕辩护

define *v* **1** 阐明, 说明 **2** 给…下定义, 解释 **3** 标明…界限, 显出…轮廓 **4** 是…的特征, 界定 —**definable** *adj*

delay¹ *n* **1** 延误的时间, 耽搁的时间 **2** 延误, 耽搁 **3** 推迟〔某事没有按时发生或开始〕

delay² *v* **1** 推迟, 延期〔做某事〕**2** [常用被动态] 耽误, 耽搁 —**delayed** *adj*

delegate¹ *n* 代表

delegate² *v* **1** 授权, 委托权限 **2** 委派〔某人〕做〔某项工作〕; 委任〔某人〕做代表

delete *v* 删除, 删掉

deliberate¹ *adj* **1** 故意的, 有意的, 蓄意的 **2**〔讲话、思想或行动〕沉着的, 从容不迫的 —**deliberateness** *n*

deliberate² *v* 仔细考虑

delicate *adj*
1 ▶EASILY DAMAGED 容易受损的◀ 易坏的, 易碎的, 脆弱的 **2 ▶NEEDING SENSITIVITY 需要敏感性的◀** 微妙的, 需要谨慎处理的 **3 ▶PERSON 人◀**〔人〕容易生病的; 娇弱的 **4 ▶PART OF THE BODY 身体的一部分◀** 优美的, 优雅的 **5 ▶SKILFULLY MADE 制作精巧的◀** 精巧的, 精致的, 精美的 **6 ▶TASTE/SMELL/COLOUR 味道/气味/颜色◀** 柔和的, 清淡的, 淡雅的 —**delicately** *adv*

delicious *adj* **1** 美味的, 可口的; 芳香的 **2** 宜人的, 令人愉快的

deliver *v* **1 ▶TAKE STH SOMEWHERE 把某物带到某处◀** 把〔货物、信件等〕送往〔某处〕**2 deliver a speech/lecture/talk etc** 发言/授课/讲话等 **3 ▶DO STH YOU SHOULD DO 做应该做的事◀** 不负所望, 做该做的事 **4 ▶BABY 婴儿◀** 给…接生; 帮助〔产妇〕分娩 **5 deliver a blow/shock etc to** 给予〔某人〕打击/使〔某人〕震惊等 **6 deliver a verdict/judgment/ruling etc** 作出裁决/判断/裁定等 **7 ▶PERSON 人◀** 把〔某人〕交出; 把〔某人〕送到…手中 **8 ▶VOTES 投票◀**〔在竞选中〕为…拉票 **9 ▶MAKE SB FREE OF 解脱某人◀** 解救, 解脱〔某人〕—**deliverer** *n*

deliver sth **up** *phr v* [常用被动态] 把〔某物〕移交给〔某人〕

demand¹ *n* **1 ▶FIRM REQUEST 坚决要求◀** 要求, 请求 **2 demands** 困难的[烦人的、累人的]事情 **3 ▶GOODS/SERVICES 货物/服务◀** 需求 **4 by popular demand** 应公众要求 **5 on demand** 见票即付

demand² *v* **1**〔坚决〕要求〔尤其是别人不想给的东西〕**2** 询问, 质问; 命令 **3** 需要〔时间、精力、技能等〕

demonstrate *v* **1** 证明, 论证, 证实 **2** 示范, 演示 **3**〔为公开抗议某事〕游行示威 **4** 展示, 表露出〔某种技能、品质或能力〕

dense *adj* **1 ▶CLOSE TOGETHER 挨在一起◀** 茂密的, 密集的, 稠密的 **2 ▶SMOKE/MIST 烟/雾◀** 浓密的, 不易看透[呼吸]的 **3 ▶STUPID 愚蠢的◀** 迟钝的, 愚蠢的 **4 ▶WRITING 写作◀**〔写的东西〕不易懂的 **5 ▶SUBSTANCE 物质◀** 密度大的 —**densely** *adv* —**denseness** *n*

deny *v* **1 ▶SAY STH IS UNTRUE 说某事不是事实◀** 否认, 否定 **2 ▶NOT ALLOW 不允许◀** [常用被动态] 不允许〔某人拥有某物或做某事〕**3 there's no denying** 无可否认, 不容否认 **4 ▶PRINCIPLES/BELIEFS 原则/信仰◀** 背弃, 抛弃 **5 ▶FEELINGS 感情◀** 拒绝承认 **6 deny yourself**〔尤指出于道德或宗教原因〕克制自己, 自制

depart *v* **1** 离开〔尤指动身去旅行〕, 启程, 上路 **2 depart this life** 去世, 故去, 离开人间

depart from sth *phr v* 背离, 违反, 不同于〔常规等〕

depend *v* **it/that depends** 那得看情况

depend on/upon *phr v* **1** 依靠, 依赖 **2** 信赖, 相信 **3** 取决于…, 视…而定

deposit¹ *n* **1 ▶SUM OF MONEY 金额◀**〔购屋、买车、度假等的〕定金, 头款, 首期 **2 ▶RENT 租用◀**〔租用东西的〕押金, 保证金 **3 ▶BANK 银行◀** 存款 **4 ▶SOIL/MINERALS 土壤/矿物质◀** 矿床 **5 ▶LAYER 层◀** 沉积物, 沉积层 **6 ▶ELECTION 选举◀** 选举保证金〔在英国参加政治选举的候选人付的保证金, 如果候选人得到足够的选票, 保证金将发还给他〕

deposit² *v* **1** 把〔某物〕放在〔某地〕**2** 沉积 **3** 将〔钱等贵重物品〕存入〔银行或其他安全的地方〕

depress *v* **1** 使忧愁, 使抑郁 **2** 使不能正常运转, 使不活跃, 使不景气 **3** 按下, 压下, 推下〔尤指机器的一部分〕**4** 减少, 降低〔价格或工资〕

deprive *v*

deprive sb **of** sth *phr v* [常用被动态] 剥夺

deputy *n* **1**〔经理的〕副手;〔经理不在时负责工作的〕代理人 **2**〔某些国家如法国的〕下议院议员 **3** 美国县治安官的助理

descend *v* **1** 下来, 下降 —反义词 ASCEND **2**〔黑暗、夜幕等〕降临 **3 in descending order** 降序排列〔按照从大到小或从最重要的到最次要的顺序排列〕

descend from sth *phr v* **1** 从〔过去的东西〕继承下来, 传下来 **2 be descended from sb** 为某人的后裔

descend on/upon sb/sth *phr v* **1** 使感觉到 **2** 突然造访

descend to sth *phr v* 自降身份到…, 堕落到…

describe *v* **1** 描述, 描写, 叙述, 形容 **2**〔用手在空中〕画出〔某种形状〕

desert¹ *n* **1** 沙漠, 荒漠 **2** 荒凉的地方

desert² *v* **1** 遗弃，抛弃，离弃 **2** 舍弃，离开〔某地〕 **3** 丧失，失去〔感觉、品质〕 **4** 擅自离开〔军队〕

deserve *v* **1** 应得，应受到〔奖赏或惩罚〕 **2 deserve consideration/attention etc**〔建议、观点、计划〕值得考虑/注意等 **3 deserve a medal** 应奖赏一枚勋章〔表示欣赏某人应付某种局面或处理某个问题的方式〕

design¹ *n* **1** ►**ARRANGEMENT OF PARTS** 各部分的安排◄ 设计〔包括其外观及运作方式等〕 **2** ►**PATTERN** 图案◄ 装饰图案 **3** ►**DRAWING PLANS** 绘制图表◄ 设计术，制图术 **4** ►**DRAWN PLAN** 绘制的图纸◄ 设计图，图样，图纸 **5** ►**INTENTION** 意图◄〔头脑中的〕计划 **6 have designs on sb** 对某人居心不良〔想和某人发生性关系〕 **7 have designs on sth** 企图将某物据为己有〔尤指可以带来钱财的东西〕

design² *v* **1** 设计 **2** [一般用被动态]〔为某种特定目的〕计划，设计

desire¹ *v* **1** 想要，希望 **2 leave a lot to be desired** 不够好，仍有许多有待提高之处〔表明某事做得不如期望的好〕 **3** 想和〔某人〕发生性关系 —**desired** *adj*

desire² *n* **1** 渴望；欲望 **2 sb's heart's desire** 某人内心的渴望 **3** 肉欲，性欲

despair¹ *n* **1** 绝望 **2 the despair of sb** 令某人绝望的人[事]

despair² *v* 绝望，感到无望

desperate *adj* **1**〔由于处在绝境而〕拼命的，不顾一切的 **2** 非常需要的，极其需要的 **3**〔局势、情形等〕危急的，严峻的 **4**〔在危急时刻〕孤注一掷的

destroy *v* **1** 破坏，毁掉，摧毁 **2** 杀死〔动物，尤因其生病或产生危险〕 **3 destroy sb** 毁掉某人

detach *v* **1** 拆下，分开，拆开，卸下 **2 detach yourself** 使自己超然物外

detail¹ *n* **1** 细节，详情 **2 details** 详细情况，详细资料 **3**〔军队中的〕特遣队，小分队

detail² *v* **1** 详述 **2 detail sb to do sth** 指派某人〔尤指士兵〕做某事

detect *v* 发现，察觉〔尤指不易察觉到的事物〕 —**detectable** *adj*

devote *v* **1 devote time/effort/money etc to** 为…付出时间/努力/金钱等 **2 devote yourself to** 献身于…，专心致力于…

diagnose *v* 判断；诊断

diagram *n* 图解，图表，示意图 —**diagrammatic** *adj* —**diagrammatically** *adv*

dialect *n* 方言，地方话，土语

diameter *n* 直径

dictate¹ *v* **1** 口授，让〔某人〕听写 **2** 命令，强制规定，指定 **3** 支配；影响；决定

dictate² *n* 命令，规定，指示

diet¹ *n* **1** ►**KIND OF FOOD** 食物种类◄ 日常饮食 **2** ►**TO GET THIN** 减肥◄ 节食 **3** ►**FOR HEALTH** 为了健康◄〔基于健康考虑的〕饮食限制，规定饮食 **4 a diet of** 多得令人生厌的 **5** ►**MEETING** 会议◄〔讨论政治或宗教问题的正式〕会议

diet² *v*〔为减肥而〕节食，限食，按规定进食

differ *v* **1**〔在质量、特征等上〕不同于，不一样，有区别 **2** 有异议，〔意见〕有分歧 **3 agree to differ** 承认意见分歧，保留不同意见 **4 I beg to differ** 恕我不能同意，恕我不能赞同

digest¹ *v* **1** 消化〔食物〕 **2** 理解，领悟，消化〔尤指大量新或难以理解的信息〕

digest² *n* 摘要，概要，文摘

dignity *n* **1** 庄重，尊贵，尊严，体面 **2** 庄严，端庄 **3 be beneath your dignity** 有失身份，有失体面 **4 stand on your dignity** 要求受到礼遇，摆架子 **5** 高位，显职

diligent *adj* 勤奋的，勤勉的 —**diligently** *adv* —**diligence** *n*

dim¹ *adj* **1** ►**DARK** 暗◄ 阴暗的，昏暗的 **2** ►**SHAPE** 形状◄ 朦胧的，隐约的 **3** ►**EYES** 眼睛◄ 视力不好的，弱视的 **4 dim recollection/awareness etc** 模糊的记忆/意识等 **5** ►**FUTURE CHANCES** 未来的机会◄〔未来成功的机会或可能〕暗淡的，不乐观的 **6 in the dim and distant past** 很久以前 **7 take a dim view of** 不赞成〔某事〕 **8** ►**UNINTELLIGENT** 不聪明的◄ 愚笨的 —**dimly** *adv* —**dimness** *n*

dim² *v* **1**（使）变暗淡，（使）变得不亮 **2**〔感觉等〕变弱，〔质量等〕下降 **3 dim your headlights/lights**〔尤其当对面有车开来的时候〕使汽车前灯灯光变暗

dimension *n* **1**〔形势的〕方面，部分 **2**〔空间的〕量度，维度〈如长度、高度等〉 **3 dimensions a)** 大小，尺寸，规模〔尤指某物的长、宽、高〕 **b)**〔问题的〕严重程度

diminish *v* **1**（使）减少，（使）减小 **2** 削弱，贬低〔重要性、价值〕 **3 diminishing returns** 收益递减，报酬递减

dip¹ *v* **1** 蘸，浸 **2** 下降，下落 **3 dip your headlights/lights** 降低汽车前灯角度〔尤其当对面有车开来时〕 **4** 让〔动物〕洗药浴〔灭虫〕

dip into sth *phr v* **1** 翻阅，浏览〔书或杂志等〕 **2** 动用〔存款〕 **3** 把手伸进〔袋里或盒子里，为了把里面的东西掏出来〕

dip² *n* **1** ►**SWIM** 游泳◄〔为时较短的〕游泳 **2** ►**DECREASE** 下降◄〔某物数量上轻微的〕减少下降 **3** ►**IN A SURFACE** 在表面◄ 凹陷 **4** ►**FOOD** 食物◄〔用来蘸食物吃的〕调味酱汁 **5** ►**FOR ANIMALS** 动物用的◄〔给动物洗浴用的〕药浴液〔以便杀虫〕 **6** ►**PERSON** 人◄ 傻瓜，笨蛋

diplomatic *adj* **1** 外交的 **2** 世故的，圆滑的 —**diplomatically** *adv*

dlsable *v* **1** [常用被动态] 使丧失能力，使残废 **2** 故意毁坏〔机器设备〕，使无法使用 —**disablement** *n*

disadvantage *n* 不利条件，劣势

disaster *n* **1** 灾难，灾祸〈如水灾、暴风雨、意外事故等〉 **2** 彻底的失败

discipline¹ *n* **1** 纪律，纪律状况 **2**〔思想或行为的〕训练，磨练 **3** 克制能力 **4** 处罚，惩处，处分 **5**〔大学里学习的〕专业，科目

discipline² *v* **1** 训练，管教 **2 discipline yourself (to do sth)** 严格要求自己，约束自己〔去做某事〕 **3** 惩处〔某人〕

disclose *v* **1**〔尤指在被隐瞒后〕透露，揭露，泄露；公开〔某事〕 **2**〔把盖在某物上的东西去掉以〕显露；揭开

discourage *v* **1**（设法）阻止，打消…的念头 **2** 使灰心，使泄气 —反义词 ENCOURAGE

discriminate *v* **1** 区别，辨别 **2** 不公正地区别对待〔某人〕；歧视

dismay¹ *n* 忧虑; 失望; 沮丧; 恐慌
dismay² *v* 使〔某人〕担忧[失望、伤心]
dismiss *v* **1** ►**IDEA 观点**◄ 拒绝考虑〔某人的观点、意见等〕 **2** ►**JOB 工作**◄ 解雇, 开除 **3** ►**SEND AWAY 打发走**◄ 把〔某人〕打发走; 让〔某人〕离开; 解散 **4** ►**IN A COURT 在法庭上**◄ 驳回, 不受理〔案子〕 **5** ►**SPORT 体育运动**◄ 〔板球比赛中〕迫使〔对方击球员或球队〕退场
disorder *n* **1** 混乱; 凌乱; 杂乱; 无秩序 **2** 动乱; 暴乱; 骚乱 **3** 〔身体机能的〕失调; 功能紊乱
dispatch¹ 又作 **despatch**【英】*v* **1** 派遣; 发送 **2** 故意杀死〔人或动物〕 **3** 办完〔全部事情〕
dispatch² 又作 **despatch**【英】*n* **1** 〔在军官或政府官员之间传递的〕公文, 急件 **2** 〔由身在另一城市或国家的记者发给报刊的〕报道, 电讯 **3 with dispatch** 利落地, 迅速地 **4** 派遣, 发送
display¹ *n* **1** ►**ATTRACTIVE ARRANGEMENT 吸引人的布置**◄〔物品的〕展示, 陈列 **2** ►**PERFORMANCE 表演**◄〔为了娱乐人们而进行的〕公开表演 **3 be on display** 被展示, 被陈列 **4 display of affection/temper/loyalty etc** 爱慕/脾气/忠诚等的流露 **5** ►**EQUIPMENT 设备**◄ 显示器
display² *v* **1** 展示, 陈列 **2** 显示, 显露〔某种情感、态度、才能等〕 **3** 显示〔信息等〕
dispose *v* 安排, 编排, 处理, 支配〔事物〕
dispose of sth *phr v* **1** 处置, 处理〔尤指难以处理的东西〕 **2** 成功地处理问题, 解决问题 **3** 战胜, 打败〔对手〕
dispose sb **to** sth *phr v* [一般用于被动态] 使〔某人〕较倾向于
dispute¹ *n* **1** ►**SERIOUS DISAGREEMENT 严重分歧**◄ 争吵; 争端 **2 be beyond dispute** 无可争辩; 确定无疑 **3 be in/under dispute** 处在争论中; 有争议 **4 be in dispute (with sb)** 〔与某人或某个群体〕有分歧 **5 be open to dispute** 不确定的; 有争议的
dispute² *v* **1** 对〔某事〕表示异议; 辩驳 **2** 与〔某人〕争辩, 争论, 争执; 有分歧 **3** 〔与其他国家、群体等〕争夺〔土地〕
disregard¹ *v* 忽视; 轻视; 无视; 不顾
disregard² *n* 忽视; 轻视; 无视
dissolve *v* **1** ►**STH SOLID 固体物**◄ **a)** 〔固体〕溶解 **b)** 使〔固体〕溶解 **2 dissolve into laughter/tears** 开始哈哈大笑/泪流满面 **3** ►**BECOME WEAKER 变弱**◄ 变弱, 消失 **4** ►**PARLIAMENT 议会**◄〔在大选前〕正式解散〔议会〕 **5** ►**MARRIAGE/BUSINESS/ORGANIZATION 婚姻/商务/组织**◄ [一般用被动态] 解除〔婚姻关系〕; 取消〔商务安排〕; 解散〔组织〕
distinct *adj* **1** 明显不同的; 不同种类的 **2 as distinct from** 与…有所区别〔用于表示强调你在谈论的是某一事物〕 **3** 清晰的, 清楚的, 明显的 **4** 〔指可能性、感觉、特征等〕确实存在的; 确实重要的; 不容忽视的
distinguish *v* **1** 区别, 辨别 **2** 辨清〔某物的轮廓〕; 分清〔某种声音〕 **3** 使有别于; 使有特色 **4 distinguish yourself** 表现突出
distort *v* **1** 歪曲〔事实、陈述、观点等〕 **2** 使变形; 使失真; 使反常 —**distorted** *adj* —**distortion** *n*
distract *v* 分散〔某人的〕注意力; 使〔某人〕分心 —**distracting** *adj*
distress¹ *n* **1** ►**EXTREME WORRY 极度忧虑**◄ 极度忧虑; 苦恼 **2** ►**PAIN 疼痛**◄ 身体上的痛苦, 剧痛 **3** ►**LACK OF MONEY/FOOD 缺少钱/食物**◄ 贫困; 困苦 **4 distress signal** 求救信号 **5 be in distress** 〔船只、飞机等〕处于险境, 遇险
distress² *v* 使伤心, 使不安, 使忧虑
distribute *v* **1** 〔尤指有计划地〕分发, 分配, 分送 **2** 提供, 配送〔货物〕 **3** 分享〔财富或权力〕 **4** 散布; 分布; 撒; 播
district *n* **1** 地区; 区域 **2** 行政区
disturb *v* **1** ►**INTERRUPT 打扰**◄ 干扰, 打扰, 使中断 **2** ►**WORRY 忧虑**◄ 使焦虑, 使惊讶 **3** ►**MOVE 移动**◄ 挪动, 移动, 改变〔某物的〕位置 **4 do not disturb** 请勿打扰〔挂在门上的牌子〕 **5 disturb the peace** 扰乱治安
dizzy *adj* **1** 〔因旋转或生病而〕头晕目眩的 **2 the dizzy heights** 令人眩晕的高处〔指重要的职位〕 **3** 粗心大意的; 心不在焉的; 糊涂健忘的 **4 dizzy height/peak** 令人头晕的高度/顶峰 —**dizzily** *adv* —**dizziness** *n*
document¹ *n* 文件; 公文
document² *v* 〔通过记述、拍电影或拍照片的方式来〕记载
domestic¹ *adj* **1** ►**WITHIN ONE COUNTRY 国内的**◄ 国内的; 本国的 **2** ►**USED AT HOME 家用的**◄ 家中使用的, 家用的 **3** ►**ABOUT FAMILY AND HOME 关于家庭的**◄ 涉及家庭关系和生活的; 家事的 **4** ►**PERSON 人**◄ 喜爱操持家务的, 善于烹饪、清洁等家务的 **5** ►**ANIMAL 动物**◄ 驯养的; 家养的 —**domestically** *adv*
domestic² *n* 仆人, 佣人
donate *v* **1** 捐赠, 捐献〔尤指钱〕 **2 donate blood** 捐血, 献血
double¹ *adj* **1** ►**OF TWO PARTS 两部分的**◄ 成对的, 成双的 **2 double l/s/9 etc** 两个 l/s/9 等〔用在拼写单词或告诉某人某个数字时, 表示应该重复某个字母或数字〕 **3** ►**TWICE AS BIG 两倍大**◄ 双倍的, 两倍的 **4** ►**FOR TWO PEOPLE 双人的**◄ 供两人使用的 **5** ►**WITH TWO DIFFERENT USES 双重用途的**◄ 有两种用途的, 双重的 **6** ►**DECEIVING 欺诈的**◄ 两面派的, 表里不一的; 欺诈的 **7** ►**FLOWER 花**◄ 双瓣的; 重瓣的
double² *n* **1** ►**TWICE THE SIZE 两倍**◄ 两倍, 双倍(的量、数) **2** ►**SIMILAR PERSON 相似的人**◄ 极为相似的人 **3** ►**IN FILMS 在电影中**◄ 替身演员 **4 at the double**【英】, **on the double**【美】飞快地, 快步地 **5** ►**TENNIS 网球**◄ **doubles** 双打 **6 double or nothing**【美】, **double or quits**【英】〔下注的一种方式〕要么赢双倍, 要么输得精光; 一赌决输赢 **7** ►**IN RACING 在比赛中**◄ 复式押注〔下注于两场比赛, 第一场若赢将自动转押到第二场上〕 **8** ►**A THROW 投掷**◄〔投镖游戏中的〕投中加倍记分圈 **9** ►**A HIT 击打**◄〔棒球的〕二垒打
double³ *v* **1** (使)加倍 **2** 把某物对折 **3** 〔棒球比赛中〕击出二垒打 **4 double your fists** 握紧拳头〔准备打斗〕
double as sb/sth *phr v* 兼任, 兼作
double back *phr v* 原路折回
double up *phr v* **1** 〔笑、痛得〕弯下腰; 使…直不

起身 2〔尤指卧室的〕共用

double⁴ *adv* **1 see double**〔因眼睛有问题〕看到重影 **2 be bent double** 弯得很厉害 **3 fold sth double** 将某物对折〔使其比以前厚一倍〕

double⁵ *predeterminer* 是…两倍那么多

doze *v* 小睡, 打瞌睡, 打盹儿 —**doze** *n*

doze off *phr v*〔尤指在无意的情况下〕打盹, 打瞌睡

draft¹ *n* **1** ▶**UNFINISHED FORM** 未完成的形式◀ 草稿; 草图; 草案 **2** ▶**ARMY** 军队◀ **the draft a)** 征兵, 征募 **b)** 被征入伍者 **3** ▶**MONEY** 钱◀ 汇票 **4** ▶**SPORTS** 体育运动◀〔美国一些职业球队〕从大学选拔队员的制度 **5** ▶**COLD AIR/DRINKS** 冷空气/饮料◀ draught 的美式拼法

draft² *v* **1** 起草, 草拟〔计划、信件、报告等〕**2**〔战时〕征召〔某人〕入伍; 征募

dramatic *adj* **1** 给人深刻印象的; 突然的; 惊人的 **2** 激动人心的 **3** 戏剧的 **4** 夸张的; 像演戏似的 —**dramatically** *adv*

drift¹ *v* **1** 飘移; 漂流 **2**〔毫无计划或漫无目的地〕漂泊 **3 drift into sth** 不知不觉进入某种状况 **4**〔指雪、沙等受风〕吹积 **5 let sth drift** 听任某事发展下去, 听之任之

drift apart *phr v*〔人们之间的关系逐渐地〕疏远

drift off *phr v* 慢慢入睡

drift² *n* **1** ▶**SNOW** 雪◀〔风吹积成的〕雪堆, 沙堆 **2** ▶**SHIP** 船◀ 偏移, 偏离 **3** ▶**GENERAL MEANING** 大意◀ **the drift**〔话语的〕大意, 要旨 **4** ▶**CHANGE** 变化◀〔情形、意见等的〕渐变; 趋势 **5** ▶**MOVEMENT OF PEOPLE** 人口流动◀〔大量人口缓慢、无计划的〕流动

drill¹ *n* **1** ▶**TOOL** 工具◀ 钻; 钻床; 钻机 **2** ▶**WAY OF LEARNING** 学习方法◀ 练习; 训练 **3 fire/emergency drill** 消防/应急演习 **4** ▶**MILITARY TRAINING** 军事训练◀ 军事操练 **5** ▶**CLOTH** 布◀ 粗斜纹布 **6 the drill** 正确的步骤; 程序 **7** ▶**SEEDS** 种子◀ **a)** 条播机 **b)** 条播的一排种子

drill² *v* **1**〔用钻〕钻孔, 打眼 **2** 教〔某人〕反复练习 **3** 训练, 操练 **4** 条播〔种子〕

drill sth **into sb** *phr v* 向某人灌输〔某事〕

drip¹ *v* **1** 滴水, 漏水 **2** (使) 滴下; 沥下 **3 be dripping with jewels/diamonds etc** 浑身戴满了珠宝/钻石等

drip² *n* **1** 滴水声; 滴落 **2** 液滴 **3** 滴注器 **4** 怯懦无趣的人, 平庸乏味者

drown *v* **1** (使) 淹死, (使) 溺毙 **2** 又作 **drown out**〔用声音〕淹没 **3** 把〔某物〕浸泡在〔液体〕中 **4 drown your sorrows** 借酒浇愁

dual *adj* **dual nationality/controls/purpose etc** 双重国籍/控制/目的等 —**duality** *n*

due¹ *adj* **1 be due** 预定, 预期 **2 due to** 由于, 因为 **3** ▶**OWED** 欠下◀ 欠下的, 应给的 **4** ▶**MONEY** 钱◀ 应付的, 到期的 **5 with (all) due respect** 恕我冒昧〔用以礼貌地反对某人或批评某人〕**6 in due course** 在适当[一定]的时候 **7** ▶**PROPER** 适当的◀ 适当的, 适宜的

due² *n* **1 give sb his/her due** 给予某人应有的承认〔用于批评某人时〕**2 dues** 会(员)费 **3 your/his etc due** 某人应得的钱物[权益]

due³ *adv* **due north/south/east/west** 正北/正南/正东/正西

dull¹ *adj* **1** ▶**BORING** 乏味的◀ 无趣的, 枯燥的; 沉闷的; 无聊的 **2 never a dull moment** 绝不会有沉闷无聊之时 **3** ▶**COLOUR/LIGHT** 颜色/光◀ 暗淡的, 不鲜明的 **4** ▶**SOUND** 声音◀ 不清楚的, 沉闷的 **5** ▶**PAIN** 疼痛◀ 隐约的, 不明显的 **6** ▶**WEATHER** 天气◀ 阴沉的, 昏暗的 **7** ▶**NOT INTELLIGENT** 不聪明的◀ 迟钝的; 愚笨的 **8** ▶**KNIFE/BLADE** 刀/刃◀ 不锋利的, 钝的 **9** ▶**TRADE** 贸易◀ 萧条的, 不景气的 —**dully** *adv* —**dullness** *n*

dull² *v* 使〔疼痛、感觉等〕不明显, 使不清楚

dumb *adj* **1**〔指人〕哑巴的, 不能说话的〔有些人认为此词具有冒犯性〕**2** 愚蠢的 **3**〔因愤怒、惊讶、震惊等而〕说不出话的 **4 dumb animals/beasts** 不会说话的动物, 哑巴牲口〔用于强调动物不会说话, 但人们常虐待它们〕—**dumbly** *adv* —**dumbness** *n*

dump¹ *v* **1** ▶**PUT STH SOMEWHERE** 将某物放置某处◀ 乱放, 乱堆, 乱扔 **2** ▶**GET RID OF** 丢弃◀ 抛弃〔某人〕; 丢弃, 扔掉〔某物〕**3** ▶**SELL GOODS** 出售货物◀〔向国外〕廉价倾销〔货物〕**4** ▶**COPY INFORMATION** 复制信息◀ 转储; 转存; 转出〔将存储在电脑中的资料转存到磁盘或磁带中〕**5 dumping ground** 把想摆脱掉的人送往的地方; 垃圾倾倒场

dump on sb *phr v* **1**〔不公正地〕诋毁, 贬低 **2** 向〔某人〕倾诉〔所有的问题〕

dump² *n* **1** ▶**WASTE** 废品◀ 垃圾堆, 垃圾场, 废品堆 **2** ▶**WEAPONS** 武器◀ 军需品存放处; 军需品 **3** ▶**UNPLEASANT PLACE** 讨厌的地方◀ 脏乱的居住之地 **4 down in the dumps** 伤心的, 对生活失去兴趣的 **5** ▶**COMPUTER** 电脑◀ 转储, 转存, 转出

duplicate¹ *n* **1** 复制品 **2 in duplicate** 一式两份 —**duplicate** *adj*

duplicate² *v* **1** 复制 **2**〔成功地〕重复 —**duplication** *n*

durable *adj* **1** 耐用的 **2** 持久的 —**durably** *adv* —**durability** *n*

dusk *n* 黄昏, 傍晚

duty *n* **1** ▶**STH YOU HAVE TO DO** 应做的事情◀〔道德上或法律上的〕义务, 责任 **2** ▶**PART OF YOUR JOB** 职责的一部分◀〔工作或社会方面的〕职责, 义务 **3 be on/off duty** 值班[勤]/下班[不值勤] **4** ▶**TAX** 税◀〔购物缴纳的〕税 **5 do duty as/for sth** 用以充当/代替某物

dwarf¹ *n* **1** 小矮人〔虚构的人物〕**2** 矮子, 侏儒〔一些人认为此词对身材矮小者带有侮辱性〕

dwarf² *adj*〔植物或动物等〕矮小的

dwarf³ *v* [一般用被动态]〔因自身巨大而〕使…显得矮小; 使…相形见绌

dwell *v*〔在某一地方〕居住

dwell on/upon sth *phr v* 老是想着; 唠叨〔令人不愉快的事情〕

E, e

edible *adj* 可以食用的

elegant *adj* **1** 高雅的, 优美的 **2**〔想法或计划〕巧

妙的，简洁的 —**elegantly** *adv* —**elegance** *n*

eligible *adj* **1** 合格的；有资格的 **2**〔作为婚姻对象〕理想的，合适的— **eligibility** *n*

eliminate *v* **1** 消除，根除 **2** [一般用被动态] 淘汰 **3** 消灭；铲除

embark *v* 上船；装船；使上船；装载 —反义词 DISEMBARK —**embarkation** *n*

embark on/upon sth *phr v* 开始，着手〔尤指新的、有难度且费时的事〕

embarrass *v* **1**〔尤指在社交场合〕使尴尬，使窘迫 **2** 为〔政府、政治组织或政治人物〕出难题；使…陷入困境

embrace[1] *v* **1** 抱，拥抱 **2** 包括，涉及 **3** 欣然接受，采纳 **4**〔开始〕信奉；皈依

embrace[2] *n* 拥抱

emerge *v* **1** 浮现，出现 **2** 显露，暴露 **3**〔从困境中〕摆脱出来，出头 **4** 开始被人所知；兴起 —**emergence** *n*

eminent *adj*〔指人〕杰出的，显赫的

emit *v* **1** 散发〔热、光、气等〕**2** 发出〔声响〕

emphasize *v* 又作 **-ise**【英】强调，着重

employ[1] *v* **1** 雇用 **2** 使用，运用 **3 be employed in doing sth** 花时间做某事；忙于做某事

employ[2] *n* **in sb's employ** 受雇于某人，为某人工作

enclose *v* **1** 随信附上，随信装入 **2** [常用被动态]〔用篱笆或围墙〕围起来

encounter[1] *v* **1** 遇到，遭遇〔问题、困难、反对〕**2** 偶然碰到〔某人〕；突然遇到〔某事〕

encounter[2] *n* **1** 相遇，邂逅 **2** 遭遇战；冲突

encyclopedia 又作 **encyclopaedia**【英】*n* 百科全书；〔某一学科的〕专科全书，大全

endanger *v* 使处于险境；危及

endeavour[1]【英】**endeavor**【美】*v* 努力；奋力

endeavour[2]【英】**endeavor**【美】*n* 尝试；努力

energetic *adj* 充满活力的，精力充沛的—**energetically** *adv*

enforce *v* **1** 执行〔法律〕，实施 **2**〔强迫〕实行；把…强加于 —**enforceable** *adj* —**enforcement** *n*

engage *v* **1** 吸引〔某人的兴趣〕**2** 安排雇用，聘请 **3**（使）〔机器〕啮合，接合 —反义词 DISENGAGE **4** 开始与〔敌人〕交战

engage in *phr v* **1** 参加；参与 **2 engage sb in conversation** 与某人攀谈；使某人加入谈话中

enlighten *v* 指导，教导；启迪 —**enlightening** *adj*

enormous *adj*〔尺寸、数量〕巨大的，庞大的 —**enormously** *adv* —**enormousness** *n*

enrich *v* **1** 使丰富，充实；富集，强化 **2** 使〔某人〕更富裕 —**enrichment** *n*

enrol【英】**enroll**【美】*v* 招（生），吸收（成员）；注册（学习） —**enrolment** *n*

ensure *v* 确保，保证

enterprise *n* **1**〔尤指与人合作的〕大型而复杂的工作 **2** 创业能力，开创能力 **3** 企业，公司；组织 **4** 创立和经营小企业（的行为）

entertain *v* **1** 招待，款待，请客 **2** 使〔某人〕快乐；使〔某人〕有兴趣 **3 entertain an idea/hope/doubt etc** 怀有想法/希望/疑惑等

enthusiasm *n* **1** 热情，热忱 **2** 热衷的活动；热爱的事物

entitle *v* **1** 给予〔某人获得某物或做某事的〕权利 **2 be entitled sth** 给〔书、剧等〕命名，起名 **3 be entitled to do something** 有权选择做某些事情

environment *n* **1** 环境，周围状况 **2 the environment** 自然环境

equip *v* **1** 装备，配备 **2** 使有准备，使能够〔做某事〕

equivalent[1] *adj* 等同的，等价的，相当的 —**equivalently** *adv* —**equivalence** *n*

equivalent[2] *n* 等同物；等价物；对应物

erase *v* **1** 删除〔电脑文件〕；抹去〔磁带录音〕**2** 擦掉；抹去〔痕迹或文字〕**3** 消除，消灭 **4 erase sth from your mind/memory** 忘却〔坏事〕

erect[1] *adj* **1** 直立的，垂直的 **2**〔阴茎〕勃起的；〔乳头〕挺起的 —**erectly** *adv* —**erectness** *n*

erect[2] *v* **1** 建造，建立 **2** 搭建，竖起 **3** 创建，确立〔体系或制度〕

essence *n* **1** 本质，实质；要素 **2** 香精，精油 **3 in essence** 本质上，实质上 **4 speed/time is of the essence** 速度/时间是至关重要的

establish *v* **1** 建立，设立 **2** 证实，确定 **3** 使被接受；使得到承认 **4 establish links/contacts/trust etc** 建立关系/联系/信任等

esteem[1] *n* 尊敬，敬重

esteem[2] *v* **1** 尊敬，尊重 **2 esteem it an honour/favour/pleasure etc** 将某事物看做一种荣耀/恩惠/乐趣等 **3 esteem someone worthy/reliable etc** 认为某人值得信赖/可靠等

estimate[1] *n* **1** 估计，估算 **2** 估价，报价

estimate[2] *v* 估计，估算 —**estimated** *adj* —**estimator** *n*

evaluate *v* 评估，评价

evolve *v*（使）逐步发展；（使）逐渐演变

exceed *v* **1** 超过，超出〔尤指超过一固定值〕**2** 超越〔政府或法律规定的范围〕

excel *v* 优于，擅长，胜过他人

exclude *v* **1**〔故意〕不包括；把…排除在外 **2** 不准…参与〔某事〕；不准…进入 **3** 排斥〔某人〕；不理睬〔某人〕**4** 认为…不可能；排除…的可能性 — 反义词 INCLUDE

execute *v* **1**〔尤指依法〕将…处死 **2** 实行；执行；履行 **3** 完成，表演〔高难动作〕**4** 确保〔遗嘱〕得到执行 **5** 创作〔绘画等艺术作品〕

exhaust[1] *v* **1** 使精疲力竭 **2** 用完，耗尽 **3 exhaust a subject/topic etc** 详尽无遗地论述某主题/话题等

exhaust[2] *n* **1** 排气管 **2**〔引擎排出的〕废气

expand *v* **1**（使）扩大；增加 **2** 增加〔活动量〕；扩展〔活动范围〕**3** 扩展（业务）**4** 变得更自信[友善] **expand on/upon** sth *phr v* 详述，进一步说明

expire *v* **1**〔正式文件等〕到期，过期，失效 **2**〔任期〕届满 **3** 死亡

explode *v* **1** ►**BURST** 爆炸◄（使）爆炸 **2** ►**GET ANGRY** 发怒◄ 勃然大怒；变得危险 **3** ►**PROVE FALSE** 证明错误◄ 戳穿，破除 **4** ►**GET BIGGER** 变大◄ 急剧增长，激增 **5** ►**MAKE A LOUD NOISE** 发出巨响◄ 爆响，发出巨大声音 **6** ►**MOVE SUDDENLY** 突然移动◄ 迸发，突发

explore *v* **1** 勘查，考察〔某地区〕**2** 检查，探讨

expose *v* 1 ▶**SHOW** 显示◀ 显露, 暴露 2 ▶**TO STH DANGEROUS** 遇到危险之物◀ 使暴露于〔险境〕, 使置身于〔危险〕当中 3 ▶**TELL THE TRUTH** 讲真话◀ 揭露, 揭发 4 ▶**SEE/EXPERIENCE** 看/体验◀ 使接触〔学习新事物〕 5 ▶**PHOTOGRAPH** 照片◀ 使曝光 6 ▶**FEELINGS** 感受◀ 显露〔情感〕 7 **expose yourself** 〔由于病态心理而在公共场所〕裸露性器官

extend *v* 1 ▶**CONTINUE** 继续◀ 延伸, 伸展 2 ▶**MAKE STH BIGGER** 使某物增大◀ 扩大; 延长〔建筑或道路等〕 3 ▶**HAPPEN/EXIST** 发生/存在◀ 延续, 持续 4 ▶**TIME** 时间◀ 延长, 推延〔期限〕 5 ▶**CONTROL/INFLUENCE** 控制/影响◀ 延伸, 扩大 6 ▶**OFFER HELP/THANKS** 提供帮助/表示感谢◀ 提供, 给予, 表示 7 ▶**ARMS/LEGS ETC** 手臂/腿等◀ 伸开, 舒展 8 ▶**STRENGTH/INTELLIGENCE** 力量/智力◀ 使竭尽全力

exterminate *v* 灭绝, 根除 —**exterminator** *n* —**extermination** *n*

external *adj* 1 外面的; 外部的 2 来自外部的, 外来的 3 外国的 4 来自学校[大学]之外的, 外来的 5 **external ear/gill/genitals etc** 〔动物长在身体〕外部的耳朵/鳃/生殖器等 —反义词 INTERNAL —**externally** *adv*

extinct *adj* 1 灭绝的, 绝种的 2〔信仰或风俗〕已废弃的 3〔火山〕死的, 不再活跃的

extinguish *v* 1 熄灭〔火、光〕 2 使〔想法或感情〕破灭; 使消亡

extract[1] *v* 1 取出, 拔出 2 采掘; 提炼 3 灵巧地取出, 抽出 4 套出〔信息〕; 逼问; 索得〔钱财〕

extract[2] *n* 1 摘录; 选段 2 提炼物, 提取物

extravagant *adj* 1〔花钱〕浪费的, 无必要的 2 **extravagant with sth** 大手大脚, 过度使用[浪费]某物 3 豪华的; 铺张的 4 过度的; 越轨的 —**extravagantly** *adv* —**extravagance** *n*

F, f

fabulous *adj* 1 极好的; 绝妙的 2 巨额的; 巨大的 3 神话寓言中的, 传说中的

facilitate *v* 使容易, 使便利; 有助于 —**facilitation** *n*

faculty *n* 1 天赋, 能力 2 才能, 技能 3〔大学的〕系, 部, 院 4 **the faculty**〔大学的〕全体教员

fade *v* 1 逐渐消失 2〔使〕退色; 〔使〕失去光泽 3 又作 **fade away**〔身体〕变得虚弱 4〔运动队〕水准下降

fade sth ◻ **in** *phr v* 使〔画面〕淡出, 渐显; 使〔声音〕渐强 —**fade-in** *n*

fade sth ◻ **out** *phr v* 使〔画面〕淡入, 渐隐; 使〔声音〕渐弱 —**fade-out** *n*

faint[1] *adj* 1〔指看、听、嗅等〕不清楚的, 模糊的 2 **a faint hope/chance/feeling etc** 很小的希望/机会/感觉等 3〔因生病、疲倦或饥饿而〕虚弱的 4 **not have the faintest idea**〔对某事〕根本不知道, 一无所知 —**faintly** *adv* —**faintness** *n*

faint[2] *v* 1 晕倒, 昏厥 2 **I nearly/almost fainted** 我差点昏过去〔表示很惊讶〕

faint[3] *n* 昏厥

faith *n* 1 ▶**TRUST/BELIEF IN SB/STH** 信任/相信某人/某物◀ 信念; 信任; 信心 2 ▶**RELIGION** 宗教◀ a) 对上帝的信仰; 宗教信仰 b) 宗教 3 **break faith with** 背弃; 背信, 不信守; 脱离 4 **keep faith with** 恪守对…的信仰; 信守; 不背弃 5 **good faith** 真诚, 诚意, 诚信 6 **an act of faith** 信赖某人的行为[表示]

fake[1] *n* 1 赝品, 假货 2 骗子, 冒充者, 假冒者

fake[2] *adj* 1 伪造的, 假的 2 冒充的, 假冒的

fake[3] *v* 1 仿造; 捏造, 伪造 2 假装, 伪装 3〔比赛中〕做(…的)假动作

fake sb **out** *phr v* 故意欺骗〔某人〕

familiar[1] *adj* 1 ▶**EASY TO RECOGNIZE** 容易辨认的◀ 熟悉的 2 **be familiar with** 通晓, 熟悉 3 ▶**PLACE/SITUATION** 地方/状况◀ 熟悉的 4 ▶**COMMON** 普通的◀ 常见的, 普通的 5 **be on familiar terms with** 和…交情很好, 和…关系友好 6 ▶**TOO FRIENDLY** 过分友好的◀ 故作亲密的, 过分亲昵的 7 ▶**INFORMAL STYLE** 非正式文体◀ 非正式的; 随和的

familiar[2] *n* 1〔与女巫共居的〕妖兽, 妖精 2 **familiars** 密友, 伴侣

fantastic *adj* 1 极好的, 吸引人的, 有趣的 2 太好了 3〔数量〕极大的 4〔计划、建议等〕不现实的, 异想天开的 5〔故事、生物或场所等〕奇异的, 荒唐的, 古怪的 —**fantastically** *adv*

fascinate *v* 迷住, 吸引; 使…着迷

fashion[1] *n* 1〔衣服、头发等的〕流行式样; 〔行为等的〕时髦; 时尚 2 时装; 时尚 3 时装业; 时装研究 4 **in a... fashion** 以…方式 5 **after a fashion** 不很好, 马马虎虎, 勉强凑合 6 **after the fashion of** 像〔某人〕的风格, 模仿 7 **like it's going out of fashion** 大量地吃[喝, 用] 8 **fashion victim** 盲目赶时髦的人; 穿戴只图时髦而不管是否合适的人

fashion[2] *v* 1〔用手或几件工具〕制作, 把…做成〔…形状〕 2 [一般用被动态] 影响; 形成, 塑造

fasten *v* 1 ▶**CLOTHES/BAG ETC** 衣服/袋子等◀ 又作 **fasten up** —反义词 UNFASTEN a) 扣牢; 系牢, 缚紧; 把拉链拉好 b) 扣牢; 钩住; 系牢; 钉牢 2 ▶**WINDOW/GATE ETC** 窗子/大门等◀ a) 把〔窗、门等〕关住 —反义词 UNFASTEN b) 扣牢, 关紧 3 ▶**FIX STH TO STH** 将某物固定在某物上◀〔尤指用胶带、别针等〕贴; 固定; 钉 4 **fasten your teeth/legs/arms etc** 用牙齿咬住/用双腿夹住/用双臂抱住等 5 **fasten your eyes on** 注视着, 盯着 6 **fasten your attention on** 集中注意力于; 认真地考虑 7 **fasten blame on** 责怪, 指责, 怪罪〔常为不公正地〕

fasten on/upon sth *phr v* 迅速决定〔采用某一主意或方法〕

fasten onto sb *phr v* 缠住, 纠缠

fatal *adj* 1 致命的 2 灾难性的, 毁灭性的

favourite[1]【英】, **favorite**【美】 *adj* 1 最喜欢的 2 **favourite son** 受家乡人欢迎的政治家、运动员等

favourite[2]【英】, **favorite**【美】*n* 1 最喜爱的东西 2 受宠的人, 宠儿 3 最有希望获胜的马[选手等]; 最被看好的竞赛者

feasible *adj*〔计划、想法或方法〕可行的, 可实行的, 行得通的 —**feasibly** *adv* —**feasibility** *n*

feat *n* 业绩, 功绩, 壮举

feature[1] *n* **1** 特点, 特征, 特色 **2**〔报纸或杂志上的〕特写〈报道〉**3** 面貌的一部分〈如眼、鼻等〉; 面貌〈特征〉; 五官 **4** 影片, 故事片, 正片

feature[2] *v* **1**〔在电影、杂志、表演等中〕介绍, 特载; 特别推出; 以…为主要内容 **2** 是…的特色 **3** 以…为特色〔尤用于广告〕**4** 展示〔某种产品〕, 为…做广告 **5** 放映〔电影〕; 上演〔戏剧〕

fiction *n* **1** 小说 —反义词 NON-FICTION **2** 虚构的事, 想象的事

fierce *adj* **1** 凶猛的; 凶狠的 **2**〔感情〕强烈的; 愤怒的 **3** 猛烈的; 激烈的 **4** 极度的, 极端的 **5 something fierce** 极其强烈, 很厉害 —**fiercely** *adv* —**fierceness** *n*

finite *adj* **1** 有限的; 有限制的 —反义词 INFINITE **2** 限定的〔动词的限定形式能显示出具体的时态或主语, 例如 "am","was"和"are", 但 "being" 和 "been" 是动词的非限定形式〕

flash[1] *v* **1 ►SHINE 发光◄**〈使〉闪光, 闪亮 **2 ►MOVE QUICKLY 迅速移动◄** 飞驰, 掠过 **3 ►SHOW STH QUICKLY 快速亮出某物◄** 亮出〔随即收起〕**4 ►MEMORIES/IMAGES 记忆/印象◄** 闪现 **5 ►TIME 时间◄** 一闪而过, 飞逝 **6 ►PICTURES 图片◄**〔在电视或电影中〕闪现 **7 ►EYES 眼睛◄**〔尤指由于突如其来的感情而〕闪耀, 发亮 **8 ►NEWS/INFORMATION 新闻/消息◄**〔通过收音机、计算机或卫星〕迅速播出; 传送 **9 flash a smile/glance/look etc at sb** 对某人一笑/一瞥/一看等 **10 ►SEX ORGANS 性器官◄**〔男子〕当众暴露性器官, 露阴 **11 your life flashes before your eyes**〔尤指处于极度危险或临终时〕平生之事都闪现在眼前

flash sth **around** *phr v* 炫耀〔金钱〕

flash[2] *n* **1 ►LIGHT 光◄**〔一闪而后消失的〕闪光 **2 ►CAMERA 照相机◄** 闪光灯 **3 in a flash/like a flash/quick as a flash** 一会儿, 马上 **4 flash of brilliance/inspiration/intuition/anger** 才华/灵感/直觉/怒气的闪现 **5 ►BRIGHT COLOUR/STH SHINY 艳丽的颜色/闪亮的东西◄** 闪现物; 惹人注目的东西 **6 ►LOOK 看◄** 一瞥 **7 ►SIGNAL 信号◄**〔信号灯的〕闪亮 **8 a flash in the pan** 昙花一现 **9 ►MILITARY 军队的◄**〔军装上的〕肩章

flash[3] *adj* **1** 闪现的, 突发的, 短暂的 **2** 奢华的, 华丽的 **3** 爱炫耀的

flatter *v* **1** 奉承, 讨好, 向…谄媚 **2 be flattered**〔因被喜欢或看重而〕感到荣幸[高兴] **3** 使形象胜过〔本人〕**4 flatter yourself** 自以为是, 自鸣得意

flavour[1]【英】**flavor**【美】*n* **1** 味, 味道 **2** 任何滋味, 味道 **3** 特色, 特点 **4** 特色; 情调; 风味 **5 flavour of the month** 当前最受欢迎的思想[人物、风格等]

flavour[2]【英】**flavor**【美】*v* 加味于…, 使更有…味道

flaw *n* **1** 瑕疵, 缺点 **2**〔论点、计划或思想中的〕错误, 缺陷 **3**〔性格上的〕缺点

flee *v* 逃, 逃走

flexible *adj* **1** 灵活的, 可变通的 —反义词 INFLEXIBLE **2** 易弯曲的, 有弹性的 —**flexibly** *adv*

float[1] *v* **1 ►ON WATER 在水上◄ a)** 浮; 漂 **b)** 使浮起 **2 ►IN THE AIR 在空中◄** 飘浮 **3 ►MUSIC/SOUNDS/SMELLS ETC 音乐/声音/气味等◄**〔声音、气味等〕飘 **4 ►MONEY 货币◄**〈使〉浮动 **5 ►SUGGEST 建议◄**〔尤指为了解人们的想法而〕提出〔建议或计划〕**6 ►COMPANY 公司◄** 首次发行〔股票〕**7 ►CHEQUE 支票◄** 开〔空头支票〕**8 ►MOVE GRACEFULLY 优雅地走动◄** 飘然移动 **9 ►NO DEFINITE PURPOSE 无明确目的◄** 不断改变; 游荡 —**floater** *n*

float[2] *n* **1**〔游行时用的〕彩车 **2** 浮有冰激凌的饮料 **3**〔尤指钓鱼用的〕漂浮物; 鱼漂, 浮子 **4**〔游泳时用的〕救生衣; 救生圈 **5**〔商店的〕备用零钱

flock[1] *n* **1** 畜群; 鸟群 **2**〔同类型的〕一大群人 **3**〔经常到某位牧师所属教堂礼拜的〕全体教徒[会众] **4**〔填充垫子的〕絮屑, 毛棉填料 **5** 又作 **flocking**〔供在墙纸、窗帘等表面制作图案的〕植绒材料; 柔软贴料

flock[2] *v* 成群结队; 蜂拥而至

flourish[1] *v* **1** 生长茂盛 **2** 繁荣, 兴旺, 成功 **3**〔为引起注意〕挥动〔手中的东西〕

flourish[2] *n* **1 with a flourish** 用引人注意的动作, 挥舞 **2** 不必要的装饰; 过分华丽的词藻 **3**〔手写花体字的〕花饰 **4**〔尤指重要人物进场时演奏的〕响亮的乐曲

flush[1] *n* **1**〔尤指因尴尬、生病或激动而引起的〕脸红, 潮红 **2 a flush of pride/embarrassment etc** 一阵自豪感/尴尬等 **3 the first flush of youth/success etc** 首次感到充满青春活力的/首次感到成功的〈一阵〉喜悦等 **4**〔纸牌戏中的〕同花牌 **5**〔马桶里的〕冲洗装置 **6**〔用水〕冲洗, 冲水

flush[2] *v* **1**〔用水〕冲洗〔马桶〕;〔马桶〕被冲洗 **2** 脸红,〔脸〕发红 **3** 又作 **flush out**〔用水或其他液体〕冲洗, 冲出 **4** 使〔某人〕离开隐蔽之处

flush[3] *adj* **1** 在同一平面上的, 齐平的 **2** 突然很有钱的, 暴富的

flush[4] *adv* 齐平地

forbid *v* **1** 不许, 禁止 **2 God/Heaven forbid** 但愿不会发生这样的事 **3** 阻止; 妨碍, 使〔某人〕不可能做某事

forgive *v* **1** 原谅; 宽恕; 饶恕 **2 forgive me** 请原谅, 对不起 **3 sb could be forgiven for thinking/wondering/believing etc sth** 某人认为…/想知道…/相信…等, 那是可以理解的

foundation *n* **1 ►BUILDING 建筑物◄** 又作 **foundations** 地基, 基础 **2 ►BASIC IDEA 基本的思想◄** 基础; 根据; 基本原理 **3 ►ORGANIZATION 组织◄** 基金会 **4 ►ESTABLISHMENT 建立◄** 建立; 创办 **5 lay/provide the foundation(s) for** 为…打下基础 **6 be without foundation/have no foundation** 没有根据 **7 ►SKIN 皮肤◄**〔与肤色相同的、化妆时打底用的〕粉底霜 **8 shake/rock sth to its foundations** 从根本上动摇某物; 动摇…的基础

fraction *n* **1** 少量; 一点儿 **2**〔数学上的〕分数; 小数

framework *n* **1**〔建筑物、车辆、物体的〕构架, 框架, 结构 **2** 体系, 体制; 参照标准; 准则 **3 social/political/legal etc framework** 社会/政治/法律等的结构[制度]

freeze[1] *v* **1 ►LIQUID 液体◄**〈使〉结冰, 凝固 **2 ►EARTH 土地◄**〈使〉冻硬;〈使〉封冻 **3 ►MACHINE/ENGINE 机器/发动机◄** 又作 **freeze up**〈使〉冻住;〈使〉冻到不能正常运转 **4 ►FOOD 食品◄** 冷藏, 冷冻; 适合冷藏 **5 it's freezing** 太冷了 **6 ►FEEL**

COLD 感到寒冷◀ 感到很冷, 冻僵 7 ▶WAGES/PRICES 工资/价格◀ (使)冻结〔在某种水平上〕 8 ▶MONEY/PROPERTY 钱/财产◀ 冻结〔存款、财产〕 9 ▶STOP MOVING 停止移动◀ 突然停止; 呆住 10 **freeze to death** 冷死, 冻死

freeze sb **out** *phr v* 〔通过刁难或用冷淡的态度等〕不让〔某人〕参加; 把〔某人〕排除在外

freeze over *phr v* 表面结冰, 封冻

freeze² *n* 1〔工资、价格等的〕冻结 2〔活动〕停止 3 严寒期 4〔尤指夜间的〕短时间的天寒地冻

freight¹ *n* 1〔船、火车或飞机运载的〕货物; 货运 2 货运列车; 集装箱列车

freight² *v* 〔用飞机、轮船或火车〕运送, 托运〔货物〕

frustrate *v* 1 使恼怒, 使灰心丧气 2 挫败; 阻挠

fundamental¹ *adj* 1 根本的; 基本的; 基础的 2 必不可少的; 十分重要的

fundamental² *n* 基本原理; 基本规则

furious *adj* 1 狂怒的, 暴怒的 2 猛烈的, 强烈的, 激烈的 —**furiously** *adv*

furnish *v* 1 为〔房屋或房间〕配备家具 2 供应, 提供 —**furnished** *adj*

G, g

gale *n* 1 大风 2 **a gale/gales of laughter** 〔突发的〕一阵大笑声/阵阵大笑声

gamble¹ *v* 1 赌博 2 投机, 冒险 —**gambler** *n*

gamble sth ↔ **away** *phr v* 赌输掉

gamble² *n* 冒险, 碰运气

gang¹ *n* 1〔常聚在一起闹事打斗的〕一帮年轻人 2 一群合伙作案的罪犯 3 一群朋友〔尤指年轻人〕 4〔干体力活的〕一群工人, 一群囚犯

gang² *v*

gang up on sb *phr v* 合伙打击[反对]

gap *n* 1 ▶A SPACE 间隔◀ 缺口, 裂缝 2 ▶DIFFERENCE 差别◀ 差距; 差额; 差别 3 ▶STH MISSING 缺少的东西◀ 空白, 缺漏 4 ▶IN A MOUNTAIN 在山里◀ 山峡, 山口 5 ▶IN TIME 在时间上◀ 间隙 6 **gap in the market** 市场空白〔开发销售一种尚无人开发的产品的机会〕

garbage *n* 1 垃圾 2 蠢话, 废话, 愚蠢的看法 3 **garbage in, garbage out** 〔电脑运算中〕错进, 错出〔用来表示若将垃圾信息输入电脑, 所输出的也是垃圾〕

garment *n* 〔一件〕衣服

gather¹ *v* 1 ▶COME TOGETHER 聚集◀ 聚集, 集合 2 ▶KNOW/THINK 了解/思考◀ 推断, 推测, 知道, 认为 3 ▶COLLECT 收集◀ a) 搜集, 采集 b) 收集〔信息、主意等〕 4 **gather speed/force** 加快速度/加大力量 5 **gather dust** 闲置 6 **gather momentum** a) 增加动量[速度] b) 势头日益增强 7 ▶CLOTH 布◀ a) 给…打褶裥 b) 拉近 8 **gather yourself/gather your strength** 〔为某事, 尤指难事〕做好准备 9 ▶CLOUDS 云朵◀ 积聚 10 **the gathering darkness/dusk/shadows etc** 黄昏时分 11 **gather sb to you/gather sb up** 拥抱, 抱住

gather sth ↔ **in** *phr v* 收〔庄稼〕

gather sth ↔ **together/up** *phr v* 集拢, 合拢

gather² *n* 褶裥

gay¹ *adj* 1 同性恋的 2 鲜艳的 3 快乐的, 兴奋的 4 **with gay abandon** 任意地, 纵情地, 放纵地 —**gayness** *n*

gay² *n* 〔尤指男〕同性恋者

gaze¹ *v* 〔尤指无意识地〕凝视, 盯着看

gaze² *n* 凝视, 注视

gem *n* 1 宝石, 珠宝 2 精品 3 难能可贵的人, 非常有用的人

generalize 又作 **-ise**【英】*v* 1 笼统地表达, 概括地论述 2 概括, 归纳 3 推广, 扩大〔原则、论述或规律的〕应用范围

generate *v* 1 产生, 创造 2 **generate excitement/interest/ill-feeling** 〔在一大群人之中〕引起兴奋/兴趣/敌意 3 产生〔热能、电能或其他能量〕

genius *n* 1 天才, 天赋 2 有天才的人, 天才 3 **have a genius for (doing) sth** 有(做)某事的天才 4〔某一群体的人、某个时期等的〕特征

genuine *adj* 1〔感情、欲望等〕真诚的 2〔物品〕真正的 3 真心实意的 4 **the genuine article** 〔某类型的人或物中〕真正的代表 —**genuinely** *adv* —**genuineness** *n*

gesture¹ *n* 1 手势, 姿势 2 表示, 姿态 —**gestural** *adj*

gesture² *v* 用手势示意

gigantic *adj* 巨大的, 庞大的 —**gigantically** *adv*

glance¹ *v* 1 一瞥, 看一眼 2 快速阅读 3 闪耀, 闪光

glance off *phr v* 擦过, 掠过

glance² *n* 1 一瞥, 很快的一看 2 **at a glance** 看一眼便知道 3 **at first glance** 乍一看, 最初看到时

glare¹ *v* 1 怒目而视 2 发出刺眼的强光

glare² *n* 1 刺眼的强光 2 怒视 3 **the glare of publicity** 众目睽睽

glide¹ *v* 滑行, 滑动

glide² *n* 1 滑行, 滑动 2 滑音, 延音 3 滑音

global *adj* 1 全球的, 世界的 2 全面的, 整体的 —**globally** *adv*

glorious *adj* 1 辉煌的, 光荣的, 荣耀的 2 壮丽的, 吸引人的 3 极其愉快的, 极好的 4 **glorious day/summer/weather** 晴朗的一天/美好的夏季/宜人的天气 —**gloriously** *adv*

glow¹ *n* 1〔尤指没有火焰的燃烧物发出的〕光亮, 光辉 2〔尤指红色和橙色的〕鲜艳 3〔运动后或兴奋时脸部或身体出现的〕红润光泽 4 **a glow of pleasure/satisfaction/happiness etc** 极大的愉快/满足/幸福等

glow² *v* 1 发出柔和稳定的光 2〔无焰地〕发光生热 3〔由于运动或强烈情感〕面部[身体]发红[发热] 4 **glow with pride/pleasure/triumph etc** 出于自豪/愉快/胜利等容光焕发

glue¹ *n* 胶, 胶水

glue² *v* 1 胶合, 黏合, 粘贴 2 **be glued to** 盯着眼看, 审视 3 **glued to the spot** 〔由于惊恐或极感兴趣而〕动弹不得的

goal *n* 1 目标, 目的 2〔足球、曲棍球等〕得分 3 球门

govern *v* 1 管理, 统治〔国家〕 2〔规则、原则等〕规定, 管制, 制约 3〔语法中〕支配〔另一词, 决定该词应具有何种形式〕 4 抑制, 控制〔强烈或危险的感情〕

grab¹ *v* 1 ▶WITH YOUR HAND 用手◀ 攫取, 抓住

2 ►**FOOD/SLEEP** 食品/睡◄〔因忙碌而〕赶紧, 抓紧〔吃或睡〕3 ►**GET STH FOR YOURSELF** 为自己获取某物◄〔尤指通过不公平手段〕霸占, 捞取, 强夺 4 **how does sth grab you?** 你对某事是否有兴趣? 5 **grab a chance/opportunity** 抓住机会

grab at *phr v* 1〔迅速伸手〕抓住 2 抓住〔机会〕

grab² *n* 1 **make a grab for/at**〔猛然去〕抓 2 **be up for grabs**〔工作、奖金、机会等〕人人都可以争取得到的, 供争夺的 3 抓具, 抓斗挖土机

graceful *adj* 1〔动作, 线条〕优美的, 雅致的 2 优雅得体的, 体面的 —**gracefully** *adv* —**gracefulness** *n*

gradual *adj* 1 逐渐的, 逐步的 2〔坡〕缓的, 不陡的 —**gradualness** *n*

graduate¹ *n* 1〔尤指完成学士学位课程的〕大学毕业生 2 毕业生

graduate² *adj* 1 攻读硕士[博士]研究生的 2 研究生〔课程〕的

graduate³ *v* 1〔尤指以学士学位〕大学毕业 2 中学毕业 3 **graduate (from sth) to**〔从某处〕升级到 4 向〔毕业生〕授予学位[文凭]

grant¹ *n*〔政府发给的〕补助金

grant² *v* 1 给予, 准予〔尤指官方授权〕2 承认〔确有某事, 但不影响自己的看法〕3 **take it for granted (that)** 想当然地认为 4 **take sb/sth for granted** 视某人/某事为当然〔因而对其从不特别关注或感谢〕

grasp¹ *v* 1 抓牢, 握紧 2 理解, 领会〔尤指复杂的意思〕3 **grasp a chance/opportunity**〔急切地〕抓住机会 4 **grasp the nettle** 果断地处理棘手问题

grasp at sth *phr v* 1 急切尝试利用〔一次机会〕2 企图抓住

grasp² *n* 1 抓, 握 2〔对复杂概念或棘手状况的〕理解力 3 力所能及; 把握; 掌握 4 控制, 权力

gratitude *n* 感激〔之情〕—反义词 INGRATITUDE

grave¹ *n* 1 坟墓 2 **the grave** 死亡 3 **sb would turn/spin in their grave** 某人于九泉之下不得安宁〔表示某人在九泉之下也不会赞成〕

grave² *adj* 1 严重的; 令人担忧的 2〔由于发生重大事情, 表情或说话〕严肃的 —**gravely** *adv*

grave³ *adj* 有沉[抑]音符〔法语等语言中加在字母之上表示发音的符号〕的

greedy *adj* 1 贪吃的, 贪喝的 2〔对金钱、财产等〕贪婪的, 渴望的 —**greedily** *adv* —**greediness** *n*

greet *v* 1 问候, 迎接, 招呼 2 对〔某事〕作出反应 3 最先映入〔某人〕的眼帘; 传入〔某人〕的耳中

grief *n* 1 极度悲伤〔尤指因所爱之人去世而感受的悲痛〕2 伤心事, 不幸 3 **good grief!** 哎哟!〔用于略感惊讶或气恼之时〕4 **come to grief** 失败;〔在事故中〕受损; 被毁 5 **give sb grief** 数落[责备]某人

grind¹ *v* 1 ►**INTO SMALL PIECES** 变成碎末◄ **a)** 又作 **grind up** 把〔玉米、咖啡豆等〕碾碎, 磨成粉末 **b)**〔用机器将食物, 尤指肉〕绞碎 2 ►**SMOOTH/SHARP** 光滑的/锋利的◄ 磨光, 磨利 3 ►**PRESS STH DOWN** 向下挤压某物◄ 用力旋转地挤压 4 **grind your teeth** 把牙齿磨得嘎嘎响 5 **grind to a halt a)**〔车辆〕慢慢停下来 **b)**〔国家、组织或进程〕逐渐停顿, 慢慢瘫痪 6 **grind the faces of the poor** 压榨穷人

grind sb ↔ **down** *phr v* 长期欺压某人〔使其达到绝望地步〕

grind on *phr v* 令人厌烦地长期持续

grind sth ↔ **out** *phr v* 大量撰写, 大量提供〔信息、文字或音乐作品等〕

grind² *n* 1 令人疲劳[厌倦]的苦事 2 埋头学习[死读书]的学生

gross¹ *adj* 1 ►**TOTAL** 总共的◄ **a)**〔扣去税或成本之前〕总的, 毛的 **b)** 毛重的 2 **gross negligence/misconduct/injustice etc** 明显的过失/行为不端/不公平等 3 ►**RUDE** 粗鲁的◄〔行为〕极端粗鲁的, 完全不能接受的 4 ►**NASTY** 令人厌恶的◄ 看上去[想起来]令人厌恶的 5 ►**FAT** 胖的◄ 太胖而难看的 —**grossly** *adv* —**grossness** *n*

gross² *adv* **earn £20,000/$30,000 etc gross** 税前收入20,000英镑/30,000美元等

gross³ *v* 获得…的总利润[毛利, 税前收入]

gross sb **out** *phr v* 但愿某人没看过[听过]〔如此恶劣的事情〕

guarantee¹ *v* 1 ►**PROMISE STH WILL HAPPEN** 许诺某事会发生◄ 担保, 保证 2 ►**A PRODUCT** 产品◄ 保修; 包换 3 ►**LEGAL** 法律上的◄ 保证付款 4 ►**MAKE STH CERTAIN** 确保某事◄ 保证〔某事必然发生〕5 ►**CERTAIN TO DO STH** 肯定做某事◄ **be guaranteed to do sth** 肯定会以某种方式行事[工作, 发生] 6 ►**PROTECT** 保护◄ **guarantee sth against**〔为免受伤害或损毁〕提供完全的保护

guarantee² *n* 1 保修单; 包换单 2〔某事必将办到或发生的〕正式而坚定的承诺 3 **a)** 担保〔尤指为保证还债而作的担保〕**b)**〔尤指对债务的〕担保物; 抵押品

guardian *n* 1 监护人 2〔尤指某种制度或道德准则的〕维护者, 保卫者

guilt *n* 1 内疚, 自责 2 犯罪 3 责任, 罪责 4 **guilt trip** 负疚感

gust¹ *n* 1 一阵狂风 2 突发的一阵怒气、兴奋等

gust² *v*〔狂风〕一阵阵劲吹

H, h

habitual *adj* 1 已成习惯的 2 习惯(性)的, 惯常的 —**habitually** *adv*

hail¹ *n* 1 雹, 冰雹 2 **a hail of bullets/stones** 一阵弹雨/一阵像雹子般袭来的石块 3 **a hail of criticism/abuse** 连珠炮般的批评/辱骂

hail² *v* 呼喊; 大声招呼

hail sb/sth as sth *phr v* [常用被动态] 把…称作, 把…誉为

hail from sth *phr v* [不用被动态] 出生地是, 来自

halt¹ *n* 停止, 停住; 暂停

halt² *v* 1 停下, 停止 2 **halt!**〔口令〕站住! 立定! 3 阻止

hamper¹ *v* 阻碍, 妨碍; 牵制

hamper² *n* 1〔用于携带食品的〕有盖儿的篮子 2〔放置待洗脏衣物的〕洗衣筐

handle¹ *v* 1 ►**DEAL WITH STH** 处理某事◄ **a)** 应付〔困难局面〕, 处理〔难题〕**b)** 处理 2 ►**DEAL WITH SB** 应付某人◄ 对待, 应付〔某人〕3 ►**HOLD** 拿◄ 触; 摸; 碰; 拿 4 ►**CONTROL WITH YOUR HANDS** 用

手操纵◀ a) 操纵, 操作〔车辆、工具等〕 **b) handle well/ badly etc** 容易/不易操纵 5 ▶**IN CHARGE OF** 负责◀ 负责 6 ▶**MACHINES/SYSTEMS** 机器/系统◀ 处理〔一定数量的工作、人员等〕 7 ▶**BUY/SELL** 买/卖◀ 经销; 买卖; 处理

handle² *n* 1 把手 2 柄 3 **get a handle on** 开始理解, 了解〔某人、某形势等〕 4 民用波段无线电用户的呼号

harbour¹【英】, **harbor**【美】*n* 港口, 港湾, 海港

harbour²【英】, **harbor**【美】*v* 1 窝藏, 包庇〔罪犯〕 2 怀有〔不好的想法、恐惧等〕

harmony *n* 1〔音乐中的〕和声 2 **be in harmony with**〔思想、感情等的〕和睦, 一致, 融洽 3 **live/work in (perfect) harmony** 一起生活/工作得(十分)融洽 4 和谐, 协调

hatch¹ *v* 1 又作 **hatch out**〔蛋〕孵化 2 又作 **hatch out**〔幼禽等〕孵出, 破壳而出 3 **hatch a plot/plan/deal etc** 秘密策划阴谋/计划/交易等

hatch² *n* 1〔船、飞机上的〕舱口; 舱门 2 又作 **hatchway**〔墙、地板上的〕开口, 活板门 3 孵蛋

haul¹ *v* 1 拖, 拉 2 **haul sb over the coals** 狠狠责备, 训斥 3〔用车辆〕运送〔货物〕 4 **haul yourself up/out of etc a)** 提高〔社会地位〕; 取胜 **b)** 起来; 走出 5 **haul off and hit/punch sb** 重击 6 **haul ass** 赶快

haul sb up *phr v* [一般用被动态] 传讯, 把…拉上法庭

haul² *n* 1〔一大批〕赃物, 走私物品 2 **long/slow haul** 耗时费力的事 3 一网的捕鱼量

haunt¹ *v* 1〔鬼魂〕经常出没于… 2 缠扰, 烦扰; 萦绕在…心头 3〔长期〕给〔某人〕带来麻烦

haunt² *n*〔某人〕常去的地方

hazard¹ *n* 1 危险; 隐患; 会造成危害的事物 2〔不可避免的〕风险

hazard² *v* 1 斗胆提出; 大胆猜测 2 冒…的风险

heal *v* 1 又作 **heal up**〔伤口或折断的骨〕长好, 愈合 2 医治; 治愈 3 **heal the wounds/breach/divisions** 治愈创伤/弥补裂痕/消除分歧

heal over *phr v* 1〔伤口或破损的皮肤〕愈合, 痊愈 2 忘掉过去的争吵, 重新和好

heap¹ *n* 1〔大而杂乱的〕堆 2 **heaps of** 大量, 许多 3 破旧的汽车 4 **fall/collapse in a heap** 瘫倒/动弹不了 5 **be struck/knocked all of a heap** 被突然惊呆, 被弄得慌作一团

heap² *v* 1 又作 **heap up**〔杂乱地〕堆积, 堆放 2 **be heaped with**〔盘子〕堆满〔食物〕 3 **heap praises/insults etc on** 极力称赞/百般侮辱等

hearing *n* 1 听觉 2 听证会; 审讯; 聆讯 3 **give sb a (fair) hearing** 给某人一个(公平的)解释机会 4 **in/within sb's hearing** 在某人听力所及的范围内

heighten *v* 加强, 增加

herd¹ *n* 1〔同一种类并一同栖息的〕兽群 2 **the herd**〔易受人支配的〕民众, 老百姓, 芸芸众生

herd² *v* 1〔尤指粗暴地〕(使)集合在一起 2 放牧

hesitate *v* 1 犹豫, 踌躇, 迟疑(不决) 2 **hesitate to do sth** 不愿做某事, 对…有顾虑 —**hesitatingly** *adv*

hesitation *n* 踌躇, 犹豫, 迟疑(不决)

hike¹ *n* 1〔在山区或乡间的〕徒步旅行, 远足 2〔价格、工资、税率等的〕大幅度上升 3 **take a hike** 滚开!

hike² *v* 1 徒步旅行, 远足 2 又作 **hike sth ↔ up** *phr v*〔大幅度〕提高〔价格、税款、服务费等〕

hike sth ↔ up 1 提起, 拉起〔衣服〕 2 大幅度提高

hinder *v* 阻碍, 妨碍, 阻止

hint¹ *n* 1 暗示 2 (细微的)迹象; 少许, 微量 3 有益的建议[指点]

hint² *v* 暗示, 示意

historic *adj* 1 有重大历史意义的, 历史性的 2 有历史记载的

hollow¹ *adj* 1 空(心)的, 中空的 2 **hollow face/eyes etc** 凹陷的脸颊/双眼等 3〔声音〕空洞的, 低沉的 4〔感情、语言〕虚假的, 无诚意的 5 **hollow laugh/voice etc** 干巴巴的笑声/声音等 —**hollowly** *adv* —**hollowness** *n*

hollow² *n* 浅坑, 凹陷处

hollow³ *v*

hollow sth ↔ out *phr v* 把…挖空[掏空], 使成中空

holy *adj* 1 (有关)上帝[宗教]的, 神圣的 2 虔诚的 3 **holy cow/cats/shit/mackerel etc** 大啊! 上帝呀!〔表示惊讶、赞美或恐惧〕 4 **a holy terror** 捣蛋鬼, 顽皮的小孩

honest *adj* 1 ▶**CHARACTER** 人品◀ 诚实的, 正直的 2 ▶**STATEMENT/ANSWER ETC** 讲话/回答等◀ 坦诚的, 直率的, 不隐瞒真相的 3 **to be honest** 说实话, 老实说 4 **honest!** 真的! 不骗你! 5 **honest to God** 确实, 千真万确 6 ▶**WORK** 工作◀ 用正当手段的, 努力认真的 7 ▶**ORDINARY/GOOD PEOPLE** 普通的/好人◀ 诚实的; 规矩的 8 **make an honest woman (out) of** 因…已怀孕而娶她为妻

honesty *n* 1 诚实, 正直; 坦诚 2 **in all honesty** 说实话

hook¹ *n* 1 ▶**FOR HANGING THINGS ON** 用来挂东西◀ 挂钩, 吊钩 2 ▶**FOR CATCHING FISH** 用来钓鱼◀ 鱼钩, 钓钩 3 **by hook or by crook** 千方百计地, 下定决心地 4 **let/get sb off the hook** 让/帮某人脱离困境 5 **leave/take the phone off the hook**〔因不想接听电话而〕摘下电话听筒 6 ▶**WAY OF HITTING SB** 拳击方法◀〔拳击中的〕钩拳 7 **hook, line, and sinker** 完全地, 无保留地〔相信谎言〕 8 ▶**A TUNE** 曲调◀ 曲调中易记的部分

hook² *v* 1 ▶**FISH** 鱼◀〔用钩〕钓鱼 2 ▶**FASTEN** 固定◀ 吊, 挂; 把…固定住 3 ▶**BEND YOUR FINGER/ARM ETC** 弯起手指/手臂等◀ 把〔手指、手臂或腿〕屈起〔以拉动或抱住某物〕 4 ▶**ATTRACT** 吸引◀ 勾引; 吸引

hook sth ↔ up *phr v*〔电器〕连接, 接通

hook up with *phr v* **a)** 跟…结交 **b)** 挂钩〔指与某个组织合作〕

hop¹ *v* 1 ▶**JUMP** 跳跃◀〔人〕单足蹦跳 2〔鸟、昆虫、小动物〕(快速小步)跳跃 3 跳上[跳下]〔车辆〕 4 **hop a plane/bus/train etc**〔尤指突然决定〕乘搭〔飞机、公共汽车、火车等〕 5 **hop it!** 走开! 滚开! 6 **hopping mad** 非常生气, 暴跳如雷

hop² *n* 1 **keep sb on the hop** 让某人十分忙碌 2 **catch sb on the hop** 使某人措手不及 3 ▶**JUMP** 跳跃◀〔小步〕跳跃, 蹦跳 4 ▶**PLANT** 植物◀ 忽布, 啤酒花〔用来酿制啤酒〕 5 ▶**FLIGHT** 飞行◀ 短程飞

行 6 ►**DANCE** 跳舞◄ 舞会

horizon *n* **1** **the horizon** 地平线 **2** **horizons**〔思想、知识、经验的〕范围，界限；眼界 **3** **be on the horizon** 将要发生

horrible *adj* **1** 可怕的，吓人的，令人恐惧的 **2** 糟糕的，令人不快的，极讨厌的 **3** 粗鲁的，不友好的 —**horribly** *adv*

hospitality *n* 好客，殷勤

host[1] *n* **1** ►**AT A PARTY** 在聚会上◄ 东道主，主人 **2** ►**ON TELEVISION** 电视中◄ 节目主持人 **3** ►**COUNTRY/GOVERNMENT** 国家/政府◄ 主办者，东道国 **4** **a (whole) host of** 大量，许多 **5** ►**IN CHURCH** 在教堂里◄ **the Host**〔圣餐仪式中的〕圣饼 **6** ►**ANIMAL/PLANT** 动物/植物◄ 寄主，宿主〔寄生物所寄生的动物或植物〕 **7** ►**ARMY** 军队◄ 部队 **8** 旅馆老板

host[2] *v* **1** 主办，作…的东道主 **2** 做〔广播或电视的〕节目主持人

hostile *adj* **1** 怀有敌意的，敌对的，不友善的 **2** 强烈反对的 **3** 敌人的，敌方的 **4** **hostile environment** 逆境，艰苦的条件

hover *v* **1**〔鸟、昆虫〕盘旋；〔直升机〕悬停 **2**〔等待或拿不定主意时〕徘徊；走来走去 **3** 不确定，摇摆不定

hug[1] *v* **1** 热烈地拥抱〔某人〕 **2** 抱住〔某物〕 **3** 靠近[紧挨]…走 **4** **hug yourself with joy/delight etc** 沾沾自喜

hug[2] *n* 拥抱，紧抱

humble[1] *adj* **1**〔地位〕卑微的，低下的 **2** 谦虚的，谦卑的 —反义词 PROUD **3** **my humble apologies** 是我错〔一种不太认真的口气〕 **4** **in my humble opinion** 敝人以为，依我愚见〔略带幽默的说法〕 **5** 简单而实用的 **6** **eat humble pie**〔低声下气地〕承认错误；赔礼道歉 **7** **your humble servant** 您卑微的仆人；卑职；愚〔旧时信末的自谦词〕 —**humbly** *adv*

humble[2] *v* **1** **be humbled** 使谦卑，使感到自惭 **2**〔轻易〕击败〔强敌〕 **3** **humble yourself** 做出谦恭的姿态；不耻下问；勇于认错 —**humbling** *adj*

humidity *n* **1** 湿度；湿气 **2** 闷热潮湿的空气[天气]

hygiene *n* **1** 卫生（学）；保健（学） **2** 个人卫生

I, i

ideal[1] *adj* **1** 理想的，最好的 **2** 想象的；理想中的〔世界、职业、制度等〕

ideal[2] *n* **1**〔希望实现的〕理想 **2** 完美典型〔想象中完美的事物〕

identical *adj* 完全相同的 —**identically** *adv*

identify *v* **1** 认出〔某人或某物〕，识别 **2** 确定；发现 **3** 表明[显示]身份

identify with *phr v* **1** 与〔某人〕在感情上认同，与〔某人〕有同感 **2** **be identified with** 与〔政治派别等〕关系紧密 **3** 将〔某物〕等同于〔某物〕

idle[1] *adj* **1** 不工作的；空闲的 **2** 懒惰的 **3** 不认真的；漫无目的的 **4** **the idle rich** 不用工作的富人

idle[2] *v* **1** 虚度时间，闲混，无所事事 **2**（使）〔发动机低速地〕空转 **3**〔尤指暂时〕使〔工厂〕闲置；使〔工人〕闲着

idle sth ↔ **away** *phr v* 虚度〔光阴〕，消磨〔时间〕

ignorant *adj* **1** 无知的，没有学识的，愚昧的 **2** 因无知而产生的 **3** 粗鲁的，不礼貌的

illusion *n* **1**〔尤指对自己的〕幻觉，幻想 **2** 假象，错觉

illustrate *v* **1** 举例说明〔某事物〕 **2** 作为例证说明〔事实〕 **3** [一般用被动态]〔给书籍、文章等〕制作插图

image *n* **1** ►**PUBLIC OPINION** 公众舆论◄〔某人、组织、产品等的〕形象 **2** ►**IDEA IN MIND** 脑海中的想法◄〔脑海中对某人或某物的〕印象，形象 **3** ►**PICTURE/WHAT YOU SEE** 图像/所见的东西◄ **a)**〔镜子或照相机镜头中的〕映像 **b)**〔电视机、电脑屏幕上或银幕上的〕图像 **c)**〔尤指用木头或石头雕刻成的人或物的形状〕塑像，雕像 **4** ►**DESCRIPTION** 描绘◄〔修辞中的〕比喻 **5** **be the (very/living/spitting) image of** 酷似〔某人或某物〕 **6** **in the image of** 与…同形

imitate *v* **1**〔认为是好的而〕仿效〔某物〕 **2** 模仿〔某人的行为、说话、动作等，尤指引人发笑的模仿〕 —**imitator** *n*

immense *adj* 巨大的

immigrate *v*〔为定居而从外国〕移入

impose *v* **1** **impose a ban/tax/fine etc (on)**〔正式〕实施禁令/征收税款/惩收罚款等 **2** **impose a burden/strain etc (on/upon)** 增加负担/压力等 **3**〔将想法、信仰〕强加于〔某人〕 **4** 麻烦〔别人〕

impress[1] *v* **1** 令人称羡，使留下深刻印象 **2** 使〔某人〕了解〔某事的〕重要性 **3** 把〔某物〕压入〔柔软的平面〕；压印；盖〔印〕于

impress[2] *n* 印记；压痕

improve *v* **1** 改善，改进 **2** 变得更好

improve on/upon sth *phr v* 改进，做得比…更好，超过

incident *n* **1**〔尤指不平常的〕事件 **2**〔导致争论的〕严重[暴力]事件

inclination *n* **1** ►**DESIRE** 欲望◄ 意向；倾向 **2** ►**TENDENCY** 趋势◄〔思想或行为的〕倾向 **3** **inclination of the head** 点头 **4** ►**SLOPE** 斜面◄ 斜坡；斜度

incorporate *v* 把〔某物〕并入，包含；吸收 —**incorporation** *n*

incur *v* **1**〔因自己的举动而〕招致〔不愉快的事〕，招惹，遭受 **2** **incur expenses** 招致花费

index[1] *n* **1**〔书后人名、题目等的〕索引 **2**〔用于图书馆等处的〕卡片索引 **3**〔用于判断或量度水平的〕标志 **4**〔用于比较今昔价格、费用等的〕指数

index[2] *v* **1** 为〔某物〕编索引 **2** 使〔工资、养老金等〕与物价指数挂钩 —**indexation** *n*

indicate *v* **1** ►**FACTS** 事实◄ 表明；表示 **2** ►**POINT AT** 指向◄ 指，指着〔以引起注意〕 **3** ►**YOUR WISHES/INTENTIONS** 希望/意愿◄〔说或做某事〕表明〔意向等〕 **4** ►**A SIGN FOR** 为…的标志◄ 标志着；代表 **5** ►**IN A CAR** 在汽车里◄〔用指示车灯或手势〕指示〔转弯方向〕 **6** ►**TREATMENT** 治疗◄ **be indicated** 显示有…的需要

individual[1] *adj* **1** 单独的，个别的 **2** 个人的，供一

个人的 **3**〔风格、做事方式等〕独特的，与众不同的

individual² *n* **1** 个人，个体 **2** 有自己的思想、感情和观念的人 **3** 有某种特点的人〔尤指在某些方面与众不同的人〕

induce *v* **1** 劝诱〔某人做某事，尤指不好的事〕，诱导 **2**〔用药物〕为〔产妇〕引产 **3** 诱发〔某种身体反应〕

industrious *adj* 勤劳的，勤奋的 **—industriously** *adv* **—industriousness** *n*

inevitable *adj* **1** 必然发生的，难以避免的 **2 the inevitable** 不可避免的事情 **3** 照例必有的 **—inevitability** *n*

infant¹ *n* **1** 幼儿，婴儿 **2 infants**〔英国学校里四至八岁的〕学童 **3 infant school/teacher/class etc**〔英国为四至八岁儿童设立的〕儿童学校/教师/班级等

infant² *adj*〔公司、组织等〕刚成立的，初创的

infect *v* **1** 传染〔疾病给人〕 **2**〔以病菌等〕污染〔食物、水、空气等〕 **3**〔情绪等〕感染〔别人〕，使〔人〕受影响

infer *v*〔根据其他资料〕推断，推定

inferior¹ *adj* **1**〔质量、价值、技能等〕差的，次的 **2** 低级别的，下级的 **—inferiority** *n*

inferior² *n* 下级，下属，部下

inflation *n* **1** 物价上涨（率），通货膨胀（率） **2** 充气

influence¹ *n* **1** 影响 **2** 有影响的人[物] **3 under the influence** 喝醉了

influence² *v* 影响，起作用

informative *adj* 资料丰富的；增进知识的 **—informatively** *adv* **—informativeness** *n*

inhabit *v*〔动物或人〕居住于〔某地〕 **—inhabitable** *adj*

inhabitant *n* 居民

inherit *v* **1** 继承〔遗产〕 **2** 承担〔他人过去错误造成的问题〕 **3** 遗传得到〔父母的性格、外貌〕 **4** 接收〔别人不再需要的东西〕

inhibit *v* **1** 抑制，约束 **2** 使羞于，使怯于

initiate¹ *v* **1** 开始实施〔重要的事，如官方程序或新计划〕；发起 **2** 向〔某人〕传授专门知识[技巧] **3**〔通过特殊仪式〕使〔某人〕加入〔组织、俱乐部、社团等〕

initiate² *n* 被吸纳加入某组织并授以诀窍的人

inject *v* **1**〔向体内〕注射〔液体，尤指药液〕 **2** 增加〔气氛、兴趣等〕 **3** 投入〔更多的资金、设备等〕

injury *n* **1**〔对身体的〕伤害，损害 **2**〔因事故或攻击造成的〕人身伤害 **3 do yourself an injury**〔意外地〕自我伤害

innocent¹ *adj* **1** 无罪的 **2 innocent victims/bystanders/ people etc**〔战争或犯罪行为〕无辜的受害者/旁观者/人们等 **3** 不带恶意的 **4** 天真无邪的，阅世不深的 **—innocently** *adv*

innocent² *n* 涉世不深的人

innovation *n* **1** 新观念，新方法，新发明 **2** 革新；创新

innumerable *adj* 不可胜数的

inquire, enquire *v* **1** 询问，打听 **2 inquire within** 详情请入内查询〔用于商店橱窗内的告示，意思是你若进入店内，可得知更多情况〕 **—inquirer** *n*

inquire after sb/sth *phr v* 问候，问好

inquire into sth *phr v* 查问，查究，调查

inquire sth **of** sb *phr v* 向〔某人〕询问

insert¹ *v* **1** 插入，放进 **2**〔在文件或文稿中〕加入，加进

insert² *n* **1**〔夹在报刊中的〕插页广告 **2** 插入物

insist *v* **1** 坚持宣称，坚决认为 **2** 坚持主张，坚决要求，一定要 **3 if you insist** 如果你一定要这样〔用来对你并不真正想做的事表示同意〕

insist on sth *phr v* **1** 认为〔某事〕非常重要〔并坚持得到它〕 **2** 坚持做〔尤指麻烦或令人讨厌的事〕

inspect *v* **1** 仔细检查；检验 **2** 视察；检阅

inspire *v* **1** 鼓舞，激励 **2** 使〔某人〕产生〔某种感情或反应〕，激起，唤起 **3** 给〔某人〕创作灵感 **4** 吸气

install, instal *v* **1** 安装〔设备〕，设置 **2**〔尤指通过特别仪式〕正式任命，使正式就职 **3 install yourself in/at etc** 把自己安顿在〔某地逗留很长一段时间〕，安置

instance¹ *n* **1 for instance** 例如 **2**〔特定情况的〕例子，实例 **3 at sb's instance** 应某人的请求 **4 in the first instance**〔一连串行动的〕第一步，首先

instance² *v* 举…为例

instinct *n* 本能；直觉；天性

institute¹ *n* 学院；研究院，研究所

institute² *v* 制定〔制度、规则等〕；提起〔诉讼〕

instruct *v* **1** 命令；指示 **2** 教授，指导 **3** [一般用被动态] 通知 **4** 聘请〔律师〕出庭

instrument *n* **1 ►TOOL 工具◄**〔指用来进行细致工作的〕器械，器具 **2 ►MUSIC 音乐◄** 乐器 **3 ►FOR MEASURING 测量◄** 仪器，仪表 **4 ►METHOD 方法◄** 制度；方法；法律 **5 ►DOCUMENT 文件◄** 法律文件 **6 instrument of fate/God** 受命运/上帝摆布的人[物] **7 instrument of torture** 刑具

intellectual¹ *adj* **1** 智力的；需用脑力的 **2** 有知识的，受过良好教育的 **—intellectually** *adv* **—intellectualize** *v*

intellectual² *n* 知识分子

intelligence *n* **1 a)** 智力；理解力 **b)** 聪颖；聪明 **2 a)** 情报，谍报 **b)** 情报机构；谍报人员

intend *v* **1** 计划，打算，想要 **2 be intended for sb/sth** 是为…而准备的；专供…使用的 **3 intended target/victim/destination etc** 预期的目标/被害人/目的地等

intention *n* 意图，目的；打算

interfere *v* 介入；干涉；干预

interfere with sth/sb *phr v* **1** 妨碍，阻止 **2** 干扰〔广播或电视播送〕 **3** 对〔儿童〕性侵犯

interior¹ *n* **1** 内部 —反义词 EXTERIOR **2 the interior** 内地，腹地 **3 Minister/Department of the Interior** 内政部长/内政部

interior² *adj* 内部的，里面的；室内的 —反义词 EXTERIOR

intermediate *adj* **1** 中间的，居中的 **2** 中级程度的，中等水平的

interpret *v* **1** 把〔某人的行为或某一事件〕理解为；解释为 **2** 口译 **3** 解释，阐释 **4**〔表演者根据自己对戏剧、音乐等的感受或理解来〕表演，演绎；体现

interrupt *v* **1** 打断〔某人的〕讲话；中断〔某人的〕行动；打扰 **2** 使〔过程、活动〕暂时停止 **3** 中断〔直线、平面、风景等的连续性〕 **—interruption** *n*

intersection *n* **1**〔尤指两条道路的〕交叉口，十字路口；〔线的〕交点 **2** 横断；交叉

interval *n* **1**〔两件事情、两种活动等之间的〕间隔，间歇 **2 sunny/bright intervals**〔阴雨天中的〕短暂晴朗 **3 at weekly/20 minute etc intervals** 每周/每20分钟等 **4 at regular intervals a)** 每隔一定时间 **b)**〔物件〕按相同间距〔摆放〕**5**〔戏剧、音乐会等〕幕间休息 **6** 音程

interview¹ *n* **1**〔求职、入学等的〕面试，面谈 **2**〔报纸、杂志、电视的〕采访，访谈 **3**〔与提问者的〕正式晤谈，接见，会见

interview² *v* **1** 对〔求职者、学校考生等〕进行面试 **2** 采访〔名人〕**3** 向〔某人〕正式提问

intimate¹ *adj* **1 ►FRIENDS 朋友◄** 亲密的 **2 ►PRIVATE 私人的◄** 隐私的，个人的 **3 an intimate knowledge of sth**〔因细心研究或经验丰富而〕精通某事 **4 ►RESTAURANT/MEAL/PLACE 饭店/餐饮/地方◄** 幽静亲切的〔因此使人感觉舒服的〕**5 ►CONNECTION 关联◄ intimate link/connection etc**〔两者间的〕密切联系 **6 ►SEXUAL 性的◄ a)** 与性有关的 **b) be intimate with** 与…发生性关系 —**intimately** *adv*

intimate² *v* 暗示；提示

intimate³ *n* 知己，密友，至交

introduce *v* **1 ►WHEN PEOPLE MEET 人们相遇时◄** 介绍，引见；使相互认识 **2 ►MAKE STH HAPPEN/EXIST 使某事物发生/存在◄** 引进〔变革、计划、制度等〕，实施；推行 **3 ►BRING TO A PLACE 带到某地◄** 首次引入〔某物〕，使传入 **4 ►NEW EXPERIENCE 新经历◄ introduce sb to sth** 使某人初次尝试某物 **5 ►TELEVISION/RADIO 电视/广播◄**〔在电视或广播节目开始时为节目〕作开场白 **6 ►BE THE START OF 为…的开始◄**〔某事的发生〕作为[标志着]〔一个时期或变化的〕开始 **7 ►LAW 法律◄**〔尤指在英国议会，将一项新法律〕提交讨论 **8 ►PUT STH INTO 把某物放入◄** 小心地把〔某物〕放入〔另一物里〕

invaluable *adj* 极有价值的

invent *v* **1** 发明；创造 **2** 捏造，编造〔观点、故事，一般用来欺骗别人〕；虚构

invest *v* **1** 投资；入股 **2** 投入〔大量时间、精力等以成就某事〕

 invest in sth *phr v* **1** 买进〔以便高价卖出赚钱〕**2** 买〔对自己有用的东西〕

 invest sb/sth **with** sth *phr v* [常用被动态] **1** 授权给 **2** 使似乎具有〔某种特性或品质〕

investigate *v* **1** 查明〔犯罪、事故或科学问题等的真相〕；调查；审查 **2**〔由于可能牵涉犯罪而〕调查〔某人〕

invite¹ *v* **1** 邀请 **2**〔礼貌地〕请求〔某人做某事〕**3**〔尤指无意地〕招致〔麻烦或批评等不好的事〕；引诱

 invite sb **along** *phr v*〔去某地时〕邀请〔某人〕同往

 invite sb **back** *phr v*〔在与某人一同外出之后〕再邀请他到自己的住处

 invite sb **in** *phr v* 邀请〔某人〕进屋

 invite sb **over** *phr v* 邀请〔某人〕来家里〔通常是请他喝酒或吃饭〕

invite² *n*〔聚会、吃饭等的〕邀请

involve *v* **1** 包含〔必要的部分或结果〕，包括，需要 **2** 涉及；影响 **3**〔邀请或允许某人〕参与 **4 involve yourself** 积极参与

isolate *v* **1** 孤立〔国家或政治团体等〕**2** 分离〔物质、疾病等以作研究〕**3** 分离〔观点、单词、问题等〕**4**〔在社会、团体中〕使〔某人〕孤立 **5** 使某地与其他地方隔离 **6** 把〔某人，尤指病人〕与其他人隔离

issue¹ *n*

1 ►SUBJECT/PROBLEM 话题/问题◄ 问题；议题 **2 ►MAGAZINE 杂志◄**〔杂志、报纸的〕期；号 **3 at issue** 问题的焦点 **4 take issue with**〔向某人对某事〕提出异议 **5 make an issue (out) of sth** 挑起争端〔尤指对方认为是小题大作〕**6 ►SET OF THINGS FOR SALE 待售之物◄**〔新股票或邮票的〕发行 **7 ►ACT OF GIVING STH 给予某物◄**〔正式〕发给；分配 **8 die without issue** 死后无嗣

issue² *v* **1** 发表〔声明〕；颁布；发出〔命令、警告等〕**2** 分给〔团体中每个成员〕；配发 **3** 正式发行〔新邮票、硬币、股票等〕

 issue forth *phr v*〔从某处〕发出

 issue from *phr v*〔尤指声音或液体〕来自，产生于

J, j

jam¹ *n* **1** 果酱 **2** 拥挤；堵塞 **3 be in a jam** 处于困境 **4 jams**〔长及膝盖以上的〕彩色短裤 **5 jam tomorrow** 许而不与的好东西〔指对耐心的人来说美好的事物总会到来〕

jam² *v* **1 ►PUSH HARD 用力推◄** 用力推挤，塞进〔将许多物件塞进一个小处所〕**2 ►MACHINE 机器◄** 又作 **jam up**（使）卡住；（使）发生故障 **3 ►BLOCK 堵塞◄** 又作 **jam up**〔人、车〕堵塞〔某地〕**4 ►MUSIC 音乐◄** 未经练习的非正式演奏，即兴演奏 **5 jam on the brakes** 猛踩刹车 **6 jam the switchboard** 使电话线路堵塞 **7 ►RADIO 无线电◄** 干扰〔无线电广播或其他电子信号〕**8 sb is jamming** 某人干得好

jar¹ *n* **1**〔用来盛果酱、蜂蜜等的玻璃〕广口瓶 **2** 一广口瓶所装之量 **3**〔两物碰撞引起的〕震动；突然的痛楚 **4**〔过去用来盛食物或饮料、用黏土或石头等制成的〕坛，罐 **5** 一杯啤酒

jar² *v* **1** 撞伤〔身体的一部分〕**2**（使）〔某物〕震动；相撞 **3** 又作 **jar on** 令〔人〕略感不快[不舒服] **4** 不和谐，不相配 —**jarring** *adj*

jealous *adj* **1** 嫉妒的，妒忌的 **2** 吃醋的 **3 jealous of**〔因对某物引以自豪而〕珍惜的；小心守护的—**jealously** *adv*

jog¹ *v* **1**〔尤指为锻炼身体而〕慢跑 **2**〔非故意〕轻碰，轻推 **3 jog sb's memory** 使某人记起某事

 jog along *phr v* 如常进行，照旧继续

jog² *n* **1**〔尤指为锻炼身体而进行的〕慢跑 **2**〔意外地〕轻碰，轻推

joint¹ *adj* **1** 共享的；共有的；共同的 **2 joint effort** 共同努力 **3 joint venture** 合资经营项目；合资企业 **4 joint resolution**〔由美国国会众议院和参议院两院同意并经总统签署的〕共同决议 —**jointly** *adv*

joint² *n* **1** 骨关节 **2**〔供烹调的〕一大块肉〔一般带有骨头〕**3**〔两个物体或部分的〕接合处；汇合处 **4 out**

of joint a)〔骨〕脱臼, 脱节 b)〔系统、组织的〕混乱, 不协调 5 廉价酒馆[俱乐部、餐厅] 6〔含有大麻的〕香烟

joint³ *v* 把〔肉〕切成大块

journal *n* 1〔供专业人士或具有某种兴趣的人读的〕期刊, 杂志 2 日记; 日志

journey¹ *n* 1〔尤指长途的〕旅行, 旅程 2 历程, 过程

journey² *v* 旅行

judgment 又作 judgement【英】*n* 1 ►OPINION 看法◄〔认真思考后的〕意见; 看法; 评价 2 ►ABILITY TO DECIDE 决断力◄ 判断力 3 ►LAW 法律◄〔法官或法庭的〕审判, 判决 4 **against your better judgment**〔做某事〕违心的; 明知是不对的 5 **a judgment** 报应; 天谴 6 **sit in judgment over sb** 对某人的行为进行批评〔尤指不公正的批评〕 7 **judgment call** 裁判员的判决〔指由于没有固定的规章可循而必须自行作出的决定〕

junction *n*〔公路、铁轨等的〕联接点, 汇合处, 交叉口

jungle *n* 1 热带丛林 2〔堆满东西的〕杂乱的地方 3〔尤因竞争者众多〕难以成功的局面

junior¹ *adj* 1〔在组织或行业中〕级别[职位]低的 —反义词 SENIOR 2 **be junior to sb**〔级别〕低于某人

junior² *n* 1 **be two/five/ten etc years sb's junior** 比某人小两岁/五岁/十岁等 2 低级职位的人 3 小学生 4〔四年制大学或高中的〕三年级学生 5〔指自己的〕儿子

junk¹ *n* 1 废旧杂物 2 中国平底帆船 3 毒品〔尤指海洛因〕 4〔多热量、少营养的〕劣质[垃圾]食物

junk² *v* 丢掉〔废旧物品〕

justice *n* 1 正义; 公正; 合理 —反义词 INJUSTICE 2 司法制度; 审判; 法律制裁 3 **bring sb to justice** 将犯人缉拿归案 4 **justice has been done/served** 正义得以伸张 5 **do justice to sb/sth** 又作 **do sb/sth justice** 公平对待某人/某物; 充分展现某人/某物的最佳素质 6 **do yourself justice**〔在考试等中〕充分发挥自己的能力 7 又作 **Justice** a) 法官 b)〔高等法院的〕法官的头衔 8 正确; 公正

justify *v* 1 证明〔别人认为不合理的事〕有道理; 为…辩护 2 **justify yourself (to sb)**（向某人）为自己辩护 3 是…的正当理由

juvenile *adj* 1 少年的 2 幼稚的, 年幼无知的 —**juvenile** *n*

K, k

keen¹ *adj* 1 ►INTERESTED/EAGER 感兴趣的/渴望的◄ 热衷的, 渴望的, 热切的 2 ►ATTRACTED 着迷的◄ **be keen on sb** 对某人十分着迷 3 ►CLEVER 聪明的◄ 头脑敏捷的 4 ►COMPETITION 竞争◄ **keen competition** 激烈的竞争 5 ►SIGHT/SMELL/HEARING 视觉/嗅觉/听觉◄ 灵敏的, 敏锐的 6 ►SHARP 锋利的◄〔刀、刃〕锋利的 7 ►WIND 风◄〔风〕刺骨的 8 **keen as mustard** a) 极其渴望的 b) 非常聪颖的 —**keenly** *adv* —**keenness** *n*

keen² *v*〔为死者〕哀号, 哀歌, 唱挽歌

kneel 又作 **kneel down** *v* 跪着, 跪下

knit *v* 1 又作 **knit up**〔用毛线和两根编织针〕编织, 针织 2 织平针 3 使〔人、物或想法〕紧密结合 4〔折骨〕愈合 5 **knit your brows** 紧皱眉头〔表示忧虑、思索等〕 —**knitter** *n*

knob *n* 1 球形把手; 旋钮 2 **a knob of** 一小块 3 阴茎 4 **with (brass) knobs on** 更是那样〔尤为小孩反唇相讥时用语〕

knot¹ *n* 1 ►TIED STRING 绑好的绳◄〔绳索、布条、线等两端打成的〕结 2 ►HAIR 毛发◄ a) 绞成一团的头发[线等] b) 发髻, 圆髻 3 ►SHIP'S SPEED 船速◄ 节〔即1853米/小时, 船和飞机的速度单位〕 4 ►PEOPLE 人◄〔站在一起的〕一小群人 5 ►HARD MASS 硬结◄ 硬结, 隆起（物） 6 ►WOOD 木头◄〔木材上枝与干分离处的〕节, 节疤 7 **a knot in your stomach/throat etc**〔恐惧或生气等强烈情绪导致的〕心窝揪紧/喉咙哽住等

knot² *v* 1 使打结, 使缠结 2 a)（使）〔头发、线〕绞缠 b) **knot your hair** 把头发梳理成一个圆髻 3（使）〔肌肉〕暴突,（使）〔身体某部分〕紧揪

knowledgeable *adj* 有知识的; 博学的 —**knowledgeably** *adv*

L, l

label¹ *n* 1 标签, 标记 2 唱片公司名 3〔用以描述人、组织或事物的〕称号, 外号, 绰号;〔以不公平或不正确的称号给人扣上的〕帽子

label² *v* 1 贴标签于; 用标签标明 2〔用称号、外号、绰号〕描述〔某人或某物〕; 给…扣帽子

lame¹ *adj* 1 瘸的, 跛的 2〔解释或借口〕无说服力的, 站不住脚的 3 **lame duck** 跛足鸭〔遭遇困难需要帮助的人或企业等〕 4 **lame duck president/administration etc** 任期即将结束的总统/政府等 —**lameness** *n*

lame² *v* [一般用被动态] 使〔人或动物〕跛[瘸]; 使残废

landscape¹ *n* 1〔陆上的〕风景, 景致, 景色 2 风景照, 风景画 3 风景绘画, 山水绘画 4 **the political/intellectual etc landscape** 政治/知识界的概貌 5 横向格式

landscape² *v* [常用被动态] 用园艺美化〔公园、花园等〕

lane *n* 1〔尤指乡间的〕小道; 小巷; 胡同; 里弄 2 车道, 行车线 3 …巷〔用于路名〕 4 跑道; 泳道 5〔船舶或飞机的〕航线, 航道

launch¹ *v* 1 ►START STH 开始做某事◄ 发动, 发起, 开始进行 2 ►PRODUCT 产品◄ 把〔新产品、新书等〕投放市场, 出版, 发行 3 ►BOAT 船◄ 将〔船或舰〕下水 4 ►SKY/SPACE 天空/太空◄ 发射〔武器或航天器〕 5 **launch yourself forwards/up/from etc**〔用力〕扑向前/跃起/从…扑过去等

launch into sth *phr v* 突然开始〔描述、叙述、抨击〕

launch out *phr v* 开始, 着手〔新事情, 尤指有风险的事〕

launch² *n* 1〔新产品的〕投放市场;〔新书的〕发行 2 游艇, 汽艇

layer¹ *n* **1**〔覆盖的〕层 **2**〔物质的〕层 **3**〔组织、系统、思想等的〕层次 **4 multi-layered/single-layered etc** 多/单层等的

layer² *v* **1** 铺一层…; 把…堆成层 **2** 把〔头发〕分层剪短

leaflet¹ *n* 散页印刷品; 传单; 广告单张

leaflet² *v* (向…) 散发传单

leak¹ *v* **1** (使) 漏; (使) 渗 **2**〔气体、液体〕漏出 **3** 泄露〔秘密给报纸、电视台等〕 **4 leak like a sieve** 漏得很厉害

leak out *phr v* 泄露

leak² *n* **1** 漏洞, 裂缝 **2 a gas/oil/water leak** 煤气/油/水的泄漏 **3**〔向报纸、电视台等的〕透露秘密 **4 take/have a leak** 小便, 撒尿

legal *adj* **1** 法律允许的, 合法的, 法定的 **2** (有关) 法律的 **3 take legal action/proceedings** 采取法律行动/提起法律诉讼 —反义词 ILLEGAL

legend *n* **1** 传说, 传奇 (故事) **2** 民间传说 **3**〔某领域中的〕传奇式人物 **4 a)**〔牌匾等上的〕镌刻文字, 铭文 **b)**〔图片、地图等的〕文字说明, 图例

liable *adj* **1 be liable to do sth** 易于〔做某事〕, 倾向于…的 **2** 有赔偿责任的 **3** 易出问题的, 易得病的 **4** 可能受处罚的, 可能承担有法律义务的

Liberal *n*〔英国前〕自由党支持者[党员], 自由民主党支持者[党员] —**Liberal** *adj*

liberal¹ *adj* **1** 心胸宽阔的, 尊重别人想法[意见; 感情]的 **2** (思想) 开放的, 支持[主张]变革的 **3** 丰富的, 充足的 **4** 慷慨大方的 **5** 不拘一格的, 不拘泥字面的 **6 liberal education** 通才教育

liberal² *n* 开明人士

licence【英】, **license**【美】*n* **1 ►DOCUMENT** 文件◄ 许可证, 执照, 证书 **2 ►FREEDOM** 自由◄ **a)**〔行动、言论的〕自由, 不受拘束 **b)** 放纵, 淫荡 **3 artistic/poetic licence** 艺术/诗的破格[奔放], 打破常规 **4 ►RIGHT TO DO STH** 做某事的权利◄ 许可, 特许 **5 under licence** 获许可〔出售、生产等〕

linguist *n* **1** 研究并通晓几种外语的人 **2** 语言学家

link¹ *v* **1 be linked** 有联系, 有关联 **2** 联系〔电脑、广播系统等, 使电子信息能在它们之间传递〕, 连接 **3** 把〔两个或以上的事物〕联系在一起 **4**〔某事或情况〕和…有联系; 由…引起 **5** 连接〔另一处〕 **6 link arms** 挽着手臂

link up *phr v* 连接; 联系

link² *n* **1** 关联〔指两种事物或思想的因果〕 **2**〔人、国家、组织等之间的〕联系, 关系 **3**〔链的〕一环 **4 rail/road/telephone link** 铁路/公路/电话线连接 **5 link in the chain** 过程中的一环 **6 weak link**〔计划中的〕薄弱环节;〔一队中的〕最弱的队员

literacy *n* **1** 有读写能力, 有文化 **2 computer literacy** 使用电脑的能力

literature *n* **1** 文学 (作品) **2**〔作为学科研究的〕文学 **3**〔某一学科的〕著述, 文献资料 **4**〔促销商品或提供信息的〕印刷品; 宣传品

litter¹ *n* **1**〔扔在公共场所的〕垃圾, 废弃物 **2** 一窝〔小狗、小猫等〕 **3 cat/kitty litter** 猫砂〔特殊物质的颗粒, 放在容器中供猫便溺用〕 **4**〔家畜睡觉用的〕褥草 **5 a litter of** 杂乱的一堆 **6**〔旧时载重要人物的〕轿

litter² *v* **1** 又作 **litter up**〔在某处〕乱丢东西; 把〔某处〕弄乱 **2 be littered with** 充满〔某物〕 **3**〔在公共场所〕乱扔〔废弃物〕 **4**〔狗、猫等动物〕产仔

locality *n* 地区

locate *v* **1** 找出〔某物〕的准确位置 **2 be located in/by/near etc** 位于[坐落在]…/…边上/…附近等 **3** 将〔公司等〕设立〔在某处〕

lodge¹ *v* **1 ►STAY SOMEWHERE** 暂住在某处◄ 租住, 寄宿, 寄住 **2 lodge a complaint/protest/appeal etc** 提出控告/抗议/上诉等 **3 ►BE STUCK** 卡住◄ [一般用被动态] (使) 卡住, (使) 固定在…里 **4 ►PUT SB SOMEWHERE** 安排某人住在某处◄ 供…寄住; 给…找寄住处〔通常要付钱〕 **5 ►IN A SAFE PLACE** 在安全的地方◄ 把〔某物〕存放〔在正规的地方〕

lodge² *n* **1**〔乡村大宅院中的〕小屋, 侧屋 **2**〔建筑物的〕门房, 管理员室 **3**〔乡村或山间供猎人、滑雪者等使用的〕小屋, 小舍 **4 a)** 共济会的分会 **b)** 共济会分会集会处 **5**〔河狸的〕洞穴 **6** 山区旅馆 **7**〔印第安人居住的〕棚屋

logic *n* **1** 逻辑学 **2** 推理方法 **3** 合乎逻辑的道理; 合理的想法 **4**〔电脑的〕逻辑

loyal *adj*〔对…〕忠贞的, 忠实的, 忠诚的 —**loyally** *adv*

luxurious *adj* 奢华的, 华丽的, 舒适的 —**luxuriously** *adv* —**luxuriousness** *n*

M, m

magnet *n* **1** 磁铁; 磁石, 吸铁石 **2** 有吸引力的人[地方]

magnify *v* **1** 放大 **2** 夸张, 夸大 **3** 使〔问题〕加重 **4** 赞美〔上帝〕 —**magnifier** *n*

maiden¹ *n* 少女; 姑娘

maiden² *adj* **1 maiden flight/voyage**〔飞机或船的〕首次飞行/航行 **2 maiden speech**〔在议会中的〕首次演说

maintain *v* **1 ►MAKE STH CONTINUE** 使某事继续◄ 保持; 维持 **2 ►LEVEL/RATE** 水平/速度◄ 保持〔水平或速度〕 **3 ►MACHINE/BUILDING** 机器/建筑物◄ 维修; 保养〔机器、建筑物等〕 **4 maintain your silence/opposition etc** 保持沉默/坚持反对意见等 **5 ►SAY** 说◄ 断言〔某事〕属实; 坚持说… **6 ►MONEY/FOOD** 金钱/食物◄ 供养; 赡养 **7 maintain life** 维持〔动植物等的〕生命

majesty *n* **1 Your/Her/His Majesty** 陛下〔对国王或女王的称呼〕 **2** 雄伟, 壮丽; 庄严; 崇高

majority *n* **1** 多数, 大多数〔人或物〕 **2 be in the majority** 构成多数, 占多数 **3** 超过的票数〔选举中获胜党或个人所得票数与其他政党或候选人所得票数之间的差额〕 **4** 成年; 法定年龄 —反义词 MINORITY

manifest¹ *v* **1** 显示, 表明, 表露〔感情、态度等〕 **2 manifest itself** 显现, 显露

manifest² *adj* 显而易见的, 明显的 —**manifestly** *adv*

manual¹ *adj* **1** 手的; 手工的 **2** 用手操作的; 用手做的; 靠人工的 —**manually** *adv*

manual² *n* **1**〔机器的〕说明书, 使用手册 **2 on**

manual〔机器〕手工操作的, 手动的

manufacture¹ *v* **1**〔用机器大量〕制造, 生产 **2**〔人体〕生成 **3** 编造〔虚假情况、借口等〕

manufacture² *n* **1**〔大量商品的〕制造 **2 manufactures**〔用机器大批量制造的〕商品

manuscript *n* **1** 手稿; 底稿 **2** 手抄本, 手写本

margin *n* **1** 页边的空白, 页边, 白边 **2**〔选举或竞赛中胜方或负方在选票、时间或距离上的〕差数 **3**〔成本与售价间的〕差额, 利润, 赚头 **4 on the margin(s)** 处于〔社会、集团或活动〕的边缘 **5 margin of error** 误差幅度, 误差值 **6**〔森林、岛屿或其他区域的〕边缘

marine *adj* **1** 海洋的 **2** 船舶的; 海军的

marvel¹ *v*〔尤指对某人的行为〕感到惊讶, 钦佩

marvel² *n* 十分有用[灵巧]的物[人]

massive *adj* **1** 大而重的, 厚重的 **2** 巨大的; 强大的, 强烈的; 极具破坏力的

material¹ *n* **1** 料子, 衣料, 布料 **2** 材料, 原料〈如木材、塑料、金属等〉 **3** 又作 **materials** 材料 **4**〔用于书本、电影等中的〕素材 **5 officer material/executive material etc** 军官/管理人员等的料〔指适合做军官/管理人员等〕

material² *adj* **1** 物质上的, 非精神上的 **2** 物质的, 实体的, 有形的 **3** 重要的, 须予以考虑的 **4** 重大并有显著影响的

mature¹ *adj* **1 ►SENSIBLE 理智的◄**〔小孩或年轻人举止〕成熟的, 理智的, 明白事理的 —反义词 IMMATURE **2 ►FULLY GROWN 成年的◄** 成年的; 成熟的 **3 ►WINE/CHEESE ETC 酒/干酪等◄** 制成的; 已酿成的 **4 ►OLDER 较老的◄** 不再年轻的; 中年的〔礼貌或幽默的说法〕 **5 ►NOVEL/PAINTING ETC 小说/油画等◄** 成熟的; 技巧娴熟的; 老练的 **6 on mature reflection/consideration** 经过仔细考虑 **7 ►FINANCIAL 金融的◄**〔债券或保单〕到期应付的 —**maturely** *adv*

mature² *v* **matured, maturing 1** 变成熟; 完全长成 **2** 变理智;〔举止〕变成熟 **3**〔使〕〔干酪、葡萄酒、威士忌酒等〕制成,〔使〕酿成;〔使〕酿熟 **4**〔债券或保单〕到期

maximum¹ *adj* 最大量的, 最大限度的, 最大值的

maximum² *n*〔可能或可允许的〕最大量, 最大值

medium¹ *adj* **1**〔大小、高矮等〕中等的; 中号的 **2 medium brown/blue etc** 中等色调的褐色/监色等

medium² *n* **1** 传播媒介〈如报纸、电视等〉 **2**〔尤指作家或艺术家表达思想的〕方法, 手段; 艺术形式 **3 medium of instruction** 教学语言 **4 medium of exchange** 交换媒介〔指金钱或其他的支付方法〕 **5** 培养基 **6** 媒质, 媒介物; 传导体

medium³ *n* 灵媒, 巫师, 招魂者

merchandise¹ *n* 商品〔尤指在商店陈列供出售的货物〕

merchandise² *v*〔用广告等方式〕推销〔商品或服务〕

mercy *n* **1**〔对自己有权力支配的人所表示的〕仁慈, 宽容, 怜悯 **2 it's a mercy** 幸运的是, 幸亏〔用于表示更糟的情况得以避免总算是幸运〕 **3 at the mercy of** 任凭…的摆布〔而无力保护自己〕 **4 leave sb to sb's (tender) mercies** 任凭某人受他人折磨[摆布] **5 be thankful/grateful for small mercies** 庆幸一种坏的情况还没有到更糟糕的地步 **6 mercy flight/mission etc** 救援飞行/任务等 **7 throw yourself on sb's mercy** 恳求某人帮忙[宽恕]

merit¹ *n* **1** 长处, 优点 —反义词 DEMERIT **2**〔使某物受赞扬或赞美的〕优秀品质 **3 judge sth on its (own) merits** 就某物自身的品质对其作出判断〔不考虑其他因素〕

merit² *v* 应得到, 值得

microscope *n* **1** 显微镜 **2 put sth under the microscope** 认真仔细地检查某物

might¹ *modal verb* **1** 也许, 可能, 大概 **2** 也许, 可能; 可以〔may 的过去式〕 **3** 可以〔用于提建议〕 **4 a)** 可以〔用于礼貌地请求允许做某事〕 **b) might I say/ask/add etc** 我可否说/问/补充等〔用于礼貌地提供更多信息、问问题、插话等〕 **5** 应该, 本该〔表示说话人因某人还没做某事而生气或惊奇〕 **6 I might have known/guessed etc** 我早该知道/猜到等〔表示对某种情况不感到吃惊〕 **7 might well** 很可能, 极有可能 **8 might (just) as well** 最好还是…, 还是…为好, 倒不如… **9 might...but...** 也许…但是…〔表示尽管某人所说是事实, 但与其似乎非常不同的事也真实〕 **10** 能, 会〔以表示原因〕 **11**〔用于客气地询问〕

might² *n* **1** 力量; 威力; 权力 **2 might is right**【英】, **might makes right**【美】强权就是公理

migrate *v* **1**〔鸟或兽〕迁徙, 移栖 **2**〔尤指为找工作〕移居; 迁移

mimic¹ *v* **1** 模仿〔某人的言行, 尤指为了逗乐〕, 学…的样子 **2** 学…的样子; 模拟 **3**〔动物为保护自己〕伪装成〔另一事物〕—**mimicry** *n*

mimic² *n* **1**〔模仿名人言行的〕喜剧演员, 小丑 **2** 善于模仿的人[动物]

mimic³ *adj* **1** 拟态的 **2** 模仿的, 模拟的

minor¹ *adj* **1**〔尤指与其他事物相比〕小的; 不很重要的; 不很严重的 —反义词 MAJOR **2**〔音乐〕小调的; 小音阶的

minor² *n* **1** 未成年人 **2**〔大学中的〕辅修科目 **3 the minors**〔美国棒球的〕小联盟; 小企业, 小公司; 小机构[组织]

minor³ *v*

minor in sth *phr v*〔大学里〕辅修〔某课程〕—反义词 MAJOR³

minute¹ *n* **1 ►TIME 时间◄** 分, 分钟 **2 at the last minute** 在最后一刻; 在紧要关头 **3 by the minute** 又作 **every minute, minute by minute** 每过一分钟; 越来越 **4 love/enjoy/hate etc every minute of** 特别喜欢/尽情享受/极其憎恨〔某物〕等 **5 within minutes** 片刻后, 转瞬间 **6 ►MEETING 会议◄ minutes** 会议记录, 议事录 **7 ►NOTE ON A REPORT 报告记录◄** 简短的批示; 备忘录 **8 ►MATHEMATICS 数学◄** 分〔角的计量单位, 即 1/60 度〕 **9 a minute** 一会儿, 片刻 **10 in a minute** 很快, 立刻, 马上 **11 wait a minute/just a minute/hold on a minute/hang on a minute a)** 稍等片刻 **b)** 且慢 **12 any minute now** 随时, 马上, 在任何时刻 **13 have you got a minute?**【英】, **do you have a minute?**【美】能耽误你一点时间吗? **14 one minute a)** 一会儿〔表示情况突然变化〕 **b)** 稍等一会儿 **15 the minute sb does sth** 某人一做某事就… **16 the next minute** 马上, 立刻, 紧接着 **17 not think/believe**

etc for one minute 一点也不认为/相信等 **18 this minute** 立刻，马上〔用于叫人马上做某事，常带有怒意〕

minute² *adj* **1** 极小的 **2** 非常仔细的，极详细的 —**minutely** *adv* —**minuteness** *n*

minute³ *v* 将…记入议事录[会议记录]

miracle *n* **1** 意外的奇事，不可思议的事；奇迹 **2**〔神创造的〕奇迹 **3 miracle cure/drug** 有奇效的疗法/药物 **4 work/perform miracles** 创造奇迹；有奇效 **5 a miracle of engineering/design etc** 工程学/设计等上的奇迹

mirror¹ *n* **1** 镜子 **2 a mirror of** 清楚地反映…的东西

mirror² *v* **1** 反映〔情况、事实、信念等〕**2** 与…十分相似；与…完全一样

miserable *adj* **1** 极不愉快的，痛苦的 **2** 总是不高兴[不满意]的；总是抱怨的 **3** 令人不愉快的；令人不舒服的，使人难受的 **4** 质量极差的；数量极少的 —**miserably** *adv*

mission *n* **1** ►**AIRFORCE/ARMY ETC 空军/陆军等**◄ 任务，使命 **2** ►**GOVERNMENT/GROUP 政府/团体**◄ 代表团，工作团；外交使团 **3** ►**JOB 工作**◄〔尤指给予被派遣人员的〕重要任务，使命 **4** ►**DUTY 职责**◄ 职责，天职；使命 **5** ►**RELIGION 宗教**◄ **a)**〔在国外进行基督教的〕传教，布道 **b)** 布道所用的建筑物 **6 mission accomplished** 任务已完成

mock¹ *v* **1** 嘲笑，讥笑，嘲弄；〔以模仿〕取笑 **2** 使无效；使失败，挫败 —**mocker** *n* —**mockingly** *adv*

mock sth ↔ **up** *phr v*〔照原尺寸〕模仿，仿制

mock² *adj* **1** 非真实的；模拟的 **2 mock surprise/horror/indignation etc** 假装的吃惊/害怕/愤怒等〔尤指开玩笑〕**3 mock Tudor/Georgian** 仿都铎/乔治王朝建筑风格的

mock³ *n* **1 mocks** 模拟考试 **2 make mock of** 嘲笑；嘲弄

mode *n* **1** 方式，方法，做法 **2**〔机器的〕运行方式；状态，模式 **3 be in work mode/holiday mode etc** 思想上处于工作状态/休假状态等 **4 be the mode** 流行，时髦 **5**〔音乐的〕调式

moderate¹ *adj* **1** 中等的，适度的 **2** 不极端的，温和的；稳健的 **3** 有节制的，不过分的

moderate² *v* **1**（使）和缓；（使）减轻；节制，克制 **2** 做调解人；做考试监督员；做〔比赛等〕主持人

moderate³ *n* 持温和观点的人，温和派人士

modest *adj* **1** 谦虚的，谦逊的，谦恭的 **2** 不太大的；不很贵的 **3** 羞怯的，腼腆的；忸怩的 **4**〔衣服〕庄重的 —**modestly** *adv*

modify *v* **1**〔略微地〕修改，更改；改进，改造 **2**〔形容词、副词等〕修饰〔另一词〕

moist *adj* 潮湿的，微湿的，湿润的 —**moistness** *n*

monitor¹ *v* **1** 监视；监测，检测；监督 **2** 监听

monitor² *n* **1** 监视器 **2**〔电脑的〕显示器 **3**〔人体内部〕检测监视仪，监护仪 **4**〔学校的〕班长，级长，值勤生 **5**〔外国电台的〕监听员

monstrous *adj* **1** 极端错误的；非常不道德的；极不公正的 **2** 巨大而丑陋的 —**monstrously** *adv*

monument *n* **1** 纪念碑，纪念塔，纪念馆 **2** 遗迹，遗址，名胜古迹 **3 be a monument to** 是…的例证[见证]

morality *n* **1** 道德；道德观 **2** 道德性；道义性；正当性 **3** 道德体系；道德规范 —反义词 IMMORALITY

motion¹ *n* **1** ►**MOVEMENT 移动**◄ 动；运动；移动 **2** ►**MOVING YOUR HEAD OR HAND 动头或手**◄〔手或头的〕示意动作；手势；姿势 **3** ►**SUGGESTION AT A MEETING 会议上的建议**◄ 提议，动议 **4 in motion** 运动中的 **5 go through the motions** 装样子，做姿态，敷衍塞责地做 **6 set/put sth in motion** 使某事开始 **7 in slow motion** 以慢动作，慢速地 **8** ►**BOWELS 肠**◄ 排便〔此词尤为医护人员所用〕

motion² *v* 用手势示意

motivate *v* **1** 激发，激励，促动 **2** [常用被动态] 为…的动机

motto *n* **1** 箴言，格言，座右铭 **2**〔圣诞彩包爆竹中印在纸片上的〕俏皮话，妙语

mount¹ *v* **1** ►**INCREASE 增加**◄ 渐渐增加，增长〔尤指朝着使情况更糟的方向〕**2 mount a campaign/attack/exhibition etc** 发起战役/发动进攻/举办展览等 **3** ►**HORSE/BICYCLE 马/自行车**◄ 骑上，跨上 —反义词 DISMOUNT **4** ►**CLIMB STAIRS 爬楼梯**◄ 走上，爬上，登上 **5 be mounted to/on** 被固定在…上 **6** ►**PICTURE 图画**◄ 裱贴〔图画或照片〕**7** ►**SEX 性**◄〔雄性动物〕趴到〔雌性动物〕身上交配 **8 mount guard (over)** 担任警卫；站岗

mount up *phr v*〔规模或数量〕逐渐增加，增长

mount² *n* **1 Mount** …山，…峰〔山名的一部分〕**2** 被乘骑的马，坐骑 **3** 山，山岳

muffle *v* [一般用被动态] **1** 使〔声音〕减弱[低沉] **2** 又作 **muffle up**〔用保暖的衣物〕裹住

multiply *v* **1**（使）大大增加 **2** 乘，乘以 **3** 繁殖

murmur¹ *v* **1** 小声说，咕哝 **2**〔向朋友和同事〕私下抱怨，发牢骚 **3** 发出轻柔的声音 —**murmuring** *n*

murmur² *n* **1** 轻轻的谈话声，低语声 **2**〔尤指向朋友和同事的〕私下的抱怨，怨言，咕哝 **3**〔溪流、风等发出的〕细声，轻柔的声音 **4**〔心脏的〕杂音

muscular *adj* **1** 肌肉发达的；强壮的 **2** 肌肉的；影响肌肉的 —**muscularly** *adv* —**muscularity** *n*

mushroom¹ *n* 蘑菇

mushroom² *v* **1** 快速成长；迅速发展 **2**〔在空中〕呈蘑菇状扩散

mute¹ *adj* **1** 缄默的，不说话的；拒绝说话的 **2** 不会说话的，哑的 **3**〔语音中〕不发音的 —**mutely** *adv* —**muteness** *n*

mute² *v* **1** 使〔声音〕减弱 **2** 使〔乐器〕听起来柔和些，使〔乐器声音〕弱化

mute³ *n* **1**〔乐器上的〕弱音器 **2** 哑巴

mutual *adj* **1 mutual respect/hatred/support** 相互尊重/仇恨/支持 **2 mutual friend/interest** 共同的朋友/兴趣 **3 mutual admiration society** 相互吹捧 —**mutuality** *n*

myth *n* **1**〔许多人相信但不真实的〕荒诞传说，无根据的观念 **2**〔古代的〕神话 **3** 神话故事

N, n

naive *adj* 无经验的，幼稚的，天真的 —**naively** *adv* —**naivety** 又作 **naiveté** *n*

naked *adj* **1** 裸体的, 赤条条的 **2 with the naked eye** 凭肉眼 **3 naked sword/light/flame etc** 无鞘剑/无罩灯/没有遮挡的火焰等 **4 naked truth/self-interest/aggression etc** 明摆着的事实/明显的私利/赤裸裸的侵略等 **—nakedly** *adv* **—nakedness** *n*

narrate *v* 讲〔故事〕; 叙述, 描述

naughty *adj* **1**〔孩子〕淘气的, 顽皮的; 没有规矩的; 不听话的 **2**〔开玩笑地说成年人〕不听话的; 不守规矩的 **3 naughty jokes/magazines/pictures etc** 黄色笑话/杂志/图片等 **—naughtily** *adv* **—naughtiness** *n*

navigable *adj*〔水域〕可通航的, 可航行的 **—navigability** *n*

navigation *n* **1** 航行学; 航海术; 航空术 **2** 航行; 航海; 航空 **3**〔船或飞机的〕航行 **—navigational** *adj*

neglect¹ *v* **1** 疏于照料; 疏忽 **2** 忽视; 忽略 **3 neglect to do sth** 没有做某事

neglect² *n* **1** 忽视; 疏忽; 忽略 **2** 被忽略的状况

negotiate *v* **1**〔尤指商业或政治〕谈判, 协商 **2** 顺利通过 **—negotiator** *n*

nerve¹ *n* **1 ►FEELINGS 情绪◄ nerves** 焦虑; 紧张 **2 get on sb's nerves** 烦扰某人, 使人心烦不安 **3 ►COURAGE 勇气◄** 镇定; 勇气; 意志力 **4 have a nerve** 厚颜无耻; 放肆 **5 ►BODY PART 身体部分◄** 神经 **6 hit/touch a raw nerve**〔尤指无心地〕触到敏感话题; 触到痛处

nerve² *v* **nerve yourself** 鼓起勇气

nightmare *n* **1** 噩梦, 梦魇 **2** 不愉快的[可怕的]经历 **3** 可能发生的恐怖事件 **—nightmarish** *adj*

nobility *n* **1 the nobility** 贵族(阶层) **2** 崇高, 高贵

notable *adj* 显要的; 显著的; 值得注意的

notify *v*〔正式地〕通知, 告知

notorious *adj* 臭名远扬的, 声名狼藉的 **—notoriously** *adv*

novelty *n* **1** 新奇的事物 **2** 新颖; 新奇性 **3** 新颖小巧而价廉的物品

novice *n* **1** 新手, 生手; 初学者 **2** 见习修道士; 见习修女

nuisance *n* **1** 讨厌或麻烦的人[事物, 情况] **2** 妨害公共利益的行为 **3 nuisance value** 给对手造成麻烦的价值, 阻扰[骚扰]作用

numerous *adj* 许多的, 很多的

nutrition *n* 营养(作用); 滋养 **—nutritional** *adj* **—nutritionally** *adv*

O, o

obedient *adj* **1** 服从的, 顺从的, 听话的 **2 your obedient servant** 您恭顺的仆人〔正式信尾用语〕—反义词 DISOBEDIENT **—obediently** *adv*

objection *n* **1** 反对, 不赞成; 异议 **2** 反对的原因

oblige *v* **1** [一般用被动态] 使〔某人〕非做…不可, 迫使; 责成 **2** 帮忙; 答应〔某人的〕请求 **3 I'd be obliged if** 多谢〔请别人帮忙时的客气话〕 **4 (I'm) much obliged (to you)** (我)非常感谢(你)〔用于有礼貌地向某人致谢〕

obscure¹ *adj* **1** 无名的; 微贱的 **2** 难理解的, 晦涩的 **—obscurely** *adv*

obscure² *v* **1** 搞混, 使难理解 **2** 遮蔽, 使朦胧; 使听不清

observe *v* **1** 看到, 注意到 **2** 观察, 监视, 观测 **3** 遵守, 奉行〔法律、协议或习俗〕 **4** 评述, 评论, 说 **5 closely observed**〔戏剧、人物等〕与现实生活非常相似的, 逼真的

obstacle *n* **1** 障碍, 阻碍, 妨碍 **2** 障碍物

obstruct *v* **1** 阻塞, 堵塞〔道路、通道等〕 **2** 阻挠, 妨碍, 阻止

obtain *v* **1**〔尤指通过自身的努力、技能或工作等〕获得, 得到 **2**〔情况、系统、规则等〕继续存在, 通用

occurrence *n* **1** 发生的事, 事件 **2**〔事件的〕发生, 出现

odour【英】, **odor**【美】*n* **1** 气味;〔尤指〕臭气 **2 be in bad odour (with)** 不得宠; 不受(…的)青睐[欢迎]

officious *adj* 爱发号施令的, 好管闲事的 **—officiously** *adv* **—officiousness** *n*

offspring *n* **1**〔某人的〕子女, 子孙, 后代 **2**〔动物的〕崽

omit *v* **1** 省去, 略去, 删去; 遗漏 **2 omit to do sth** 忘记做某事; 故意不做某事

opponent *n* **1**〔竞争、比赛等的〕对手, 敌手 **2** 反对者

oppress *v* [常用被动态] **1** 压迫, 压制 **2** 使压抑, 使烦恼

optimistic *adj* **1** 乐观的; 乐观主义的 **2**〔对未来〕(过于)有信心的, (过分)乐观的 **—optimistically** *adv* —反义词 PESSIMISTIC

orbit¹ *v* 环绕…轨道运行

orbit² *n* **1**〔环绕地球或太阳等运行的〕轨道 **2** 势力范围

organism *n* **1** 生物, 有机体 **2** 有机组织[体系]

originate *v* **1** 发源; 开始; 起因 **2** 创始; 创造; 发起

ornament¹ *n* **1** 装饰品, 点缀物, 饰物, 摆设 **2** 装饰, 点缀 **3 be an ornament to** 给…增加光彩[重要性、美丽]

ornament² *v* **be ornamented with** 用…装饰, 装饰有…

outweigh *v* 比…更重要; 比…更有价值

oversee *v* 监管, 监察, 监督

P, p

pacific *adj* **1** 平静的, 安宁的; 爱好和平的 **2** 求和的, 和解的; 息事宁人的 **—pacifically** *adv*

painstaking *adj* 小心的; 费尽心思的; 精心的 **—painstakingly** *adv*

panic¹ *n* **1** 惶恐, 惊恐, 惊慌 **2** 大恐慌 **3** 忙乱, 慌乱 **4 press/push the panic button** 惊慌失措, 在紧急情况下慌乱行事 **5 panic stations** 紧急慌乱的状态, 惊慌

panic² *v* (使)恐慌, (使)惊慌失措

paraphrase¹ *v*〔把书面或口头的文字以简短、清晰的方式〕意译, 释义; 改述

paraphrase[2] *n*〔对一段口头或书面文字的〕意译, 释义; 改述

partial *adj* 1 部分的, 不完全的 2 **be partial to sth** 特别喜欢某物, 偏爱某物 3 偏向一方的, 偏袒的, 不公平的 —反义词 IMPARTIAL

participate *v* 参加, 参与

particle *n* 1 微粒, 粒子 2 **not a particle of truth/evidence etc** 没有一点真实性/证据等 3〔语法中的〕小品词, 虚词〈如连词、介词〉

passion *n* 1 强烈的情感, 激情〔尤指性爱、愤怒或对某种思想、原则的信念〕2 对…的强烈爱好, 热爱 3 **the Passion** 耶稣的受难 —**passionless** *adj*

passive[1] *adj* 1 被动的; 消极的; 顺从的 2〔动词或句子〕被动式[态]的 —**passively** *adv* —**passiveness, passivity** *n*

passive[2] *n* **the passive**〔动词的〕被动式; 被动语态〈如句子 'The ball was kicked by the boy.' 中的 'was kicked'〉

pastime *n* 消遣; 娱乐

peculiar *adj* 1 奇怪的; 异常的; 乖僻的 2 **be peculiar to**〔某人、某地方或某情况所〕特有的 3〔行为〕怪癖的; 有点疯狂的 4 **feel peculiar** 感到有点不舒服

penalty *n* 1〔因违反法律、规则或合约而受到的〕惩罚, 处罚 2〔行为或处境所造成的〕不利结果; 苦恼 3〔体育运动中对犯规者的〕处罚 4〔足球中因一方犯规而给予对方的〕罚球

pension[1] *n* 养老金; 退休金; 抚恤金

pension[2] *v*

pension sb/sth ↔ **off** 1〔尤指由于年老或疾病而〕发给〔某人〕养老金使其(提早)退休 2〔因太旧或不再有用而〕丢弃某物

performance *n* 1 **a)** 表演; 演出; 演奏 **b)**〔戏剧、音乐等的〕表演, 演出 2 **a)** 履行, 执行 **b)**〔工作或活动中的〕表现 3〔汽车或机器的〕性能 4 **a) a performance** 费时费力的事 **b)**〔带有愤怒叫喊的〕糟糕的行为[举止]

periodical *n* 期刊, 杂志

permanent[1] *adj* 长久的; 永久的, 永恒的 —**permanently** *adv*

permanent[2] *n*〔用化学剂的〕烫发

permissible *adj*〔根据法律或规定〕允许的, 许可的, 准许的 —**permissibly** *adv*

persevere *v* 坚忍不拔, 坚持不懈 —**persevering** *adj*

persist *v* 1 坚持; 执意 2 继续存在[发生]

personality *n* 1 个性; 性格 2〔使某人有趣、友好、受人喜爱的〕品质; 个性 3〔因常出现在报纸、电视等上而知名的〕名人 4 **personalities** 人身攻击, 诽谤 5〔地方或事物的〕特色

personnel *n* 1〔公司、组织或军队等中的〕全体人员; 员工, 全体职员 2 人事部门

perspective *n* 1〔思考问题的〕角度; 观点; 想法 2〔对事物的〕合理判断, 正确认识 3 透视(画)法; 透视效果, 透视感 4〔尤指由近而远的〕景, 远景

persuade *v* 1 说服; 劝服 2 使相信, 使信服

pessimistic *adj* 悲观的; 悲观主义的 —反义词 OPTIMISTIC —**pessimistically** *adv*

phenomenon *n* 1〔尤指因不理解而加以研究的〕现象 2 非凡的人[事物]; 奇才; 奇迹

philosophy *n* 1 哲学 2〔以哲学为基础的〕思想体系; 哲学体系 3 人生哲学; 生活[工作]准则

picturesque *adj* 1〔某个地方〕美丽的, 风景如画的 2〔语言〕生动的, 形象化的, 绘声绘色的 3〔人的外表或行为〕奇特的, 独特的, 不同寻常的 —**picturesquely** *adv* —**picturesqueness** *n*

plateau *n* 1 高原 2 平稳时期, 稳定状态; 停滞时期

plea *n* 1 恳求, 请求 2〔法庭上所作的〕答辩, 辩护, 抗辩 3 借口, 托词, 口实

plight[1] *n*〔坏的、严重的或悲伤的〕境况, 困境, 苦境

plight[2] *v* **plight your troth** 答应结婚, 订婚

plunge[1] *v* 1 (使)突然向前倒下[跌落] 2〔价格、价值等〕暴跌, 骤降 3〔船〕猛烈地颠簸

plunge in *phr v*〔迅速而自信地〕开始谈论[做]〔某事〕

plunge into *phr v* 1 **plunge sth into sth** 把某物投[插, 刺]入某物中 2 **plunge sb/sth into sth** 使某人/某物陷入[遭受]某种情况 3 **plunge into sth** 突然[仓促]地开始做某事

plunge[2] *n* 1 **take the plunge**〔尤指经过拖延或踌躇之后〕最终决定做某事, 决定冒险一试 2 ►**DOWNWARD MOVEMENT** 向下移动◄ 突降; 俯冲 3 ►**INTO WATER** 进入水中◄ 跳水;〔短时间的〕游泳 4 ►**DECREASE** 降低◄〔财产、股票等价值的〕暴跌, 骤降

polish[1] *v* 擦亮, 擦光 —**polisher** *n* —**polishing** *n*

polish sth ↔ **off** *phr v* 快速[轻易]做完〔工作等〕; 很快吃完〔食物〕

polish sb ↔ **off** *phr v* 杀死〔某人〕; 击败〔某人〕

polish sth ↔ **up** *phr v* 1〔通过练习〕提高, 改善〔技术、能力〕2 擦亮, 擦光

polish[2] *n* 1 上光剂; 擦光剂; 上光蜡; 鞋油; 亮漆 2 优美, 高雅, 精致, 完善 3〔因摩擦而产生的〕光亮的表面 4 擦亮, 磨光

popularity *n* 流行, 普及, 受欢迎; 声望

possession *n* 1 ►**STH YOU OWN** 个人拥有的东西◄ 所有物; 财产, 财物 2 ►**STATE OF HAVING STH** 拥有某物的状态◄ 拥有, 持有, 占有〔尤指贵重物品、资料等〕3 **take possession of sth** 拥有[占有]某物, 拿到某物 4 ►**DRUGS/GUN** 毒品/枪支◄〔毒品或枪支的〕私藏, 持有, 管有 5 ►**COUNTRY** 国家◄ 领地, 属地, 殖民地 6 ►**BALL** 球◄〔一些体育运动中对球的〕控制 7 ►**AMERICAN FOOTBALL** 美式足球◄〔进攻一方球队的〕控球时间 8 ►**EVIL SPIRITS** 魔鬼◄ 鬼魂附体, 着魔 9 **in (full) possession of your faculties/senses** 神智[头脑](非常)清醒 10 **possession is nine-tenths of the law** 现实占有, 败一胜九〔实际占有者在财产诉讼中十有九胜〕

postpone *v* 使〔事件、行动等〕延期, 延迟, 推迟 —**postponement** *n*

potent *adj* 1 有效力的, 效力大的; 有影响力的 2 强有力的, 有威力的; 有说服力的 —**potently** *adv*

potential[1] *adj* 潜在的, 可能的

potential[2] *n* 1 可能性, 潜在性 2 潜力, 潜能 3 电势, 电位, 电压

precaution *n* 预防措施

precedent *n* **1**〔可援引的〕先例；判例 **2** 先例，前例 **3** 惯例

preference *n* **1**〔两者之中〕较喜欢的东西；偏爱，偏好 **2**〔一组东西中〕最喜欢的东西，偏爱的事物 **3 give/show preference to** 偏爱…；给予…优先权；流露出对…的偏爱 **4 in preference to** 优先于…

prejudice[1] *n* **1** 偏见，成见；歧视 **2 to the prejudice of** 对…不利；有损于 **3 without prejudice**〔对…〕没有不利；无损〔于〕

prejudice[2] *v* **1** 使有偏见，使有成见；使不公正地偏向 **2** 损害，不利于

preliminary[1] *adj* 初步的；预备的

preliminary[2] *n* **1** 初步行动，准备工作 **2 the preliminaries** 预赛，预试

prescription *n* **1** 处方，药方 **2**〔医生开的〕处方药；治疗方法 **3 on prescription** 凭处方的，根据药方的 **4** 解救方法，诀窍 **5** 开处方，开药；指示疗法

presence *n* **1** 出席；到场；存在 —反义词 ABSENCE **2 in sb's presence** 在某人面前，当着某人的面 **3** 仪态，风度；风采 **4**〔某国在外国的〕势力；〔部队或警察的〕驻扎；存在 **5**〔看不见的〕灵气，鬼怪 **6 make your presence felt** 使周围的人感到你的重要

presentation *n* **1** ►**PROOF** 证据◄ 提出；出示 **2** ►**APPEARANCE** 外貌◄ 讲述，描绘；外观，外貌 **3** ►**PRESENT PRIZE** 颁奖◄ 授予，颁发 **4** ►**TALK** 讲话◄ 报告；〔新产品的〕介绍；〔观点的〕陈述，说明 **5** ►**PERFORMANCE** 表演◄ 表演，演出 **6** ►**BABY** 婴儿◄〔胎儿的〕先露位置，产位 —**presentational** *adj*

preserve[1] *v* **1** 维护，保护；保存〔使免受破坏〕 **2** 腌制；保存〔食物〕 **3** 保持，维持 —**preservable** *adj*

preserve[2] *n* **1** 果酱 **2**〔某群体〕独有[专有]的活动 **3** 私人渔猎区

press[1] *n* **1** ►**NEWS** 新闻◄ **a)** 又作 **the press**〔报纸、电台、电视台的〕记者们；新闻界 **b)**〔报纸、电台、电视台的〕新闻报道 **2 get/be given a bad press** 受到舆论界的批评 **3 get/be given a good press** 受到舆论界的好评 **4** ►**PRINTING** 印刷◄ **a)** 出版社 **b)** 又作 **printing press** 印刷机 **5 trouser/flower/wine press** 裤子熨烫机/压花器/葡萄榨汁机 **6** ►**PUSH** 推◄ 按，揿 **7 go to press** 付印，开印 **8** ►**CROWD** 人群◄ 拥挤的人群

press[2] *v* **1** ►**AGAINST STH** 靠着某物◄ 按；压 **2** ►**BUTTON** 按钮◄ 按，揿 **3** ►**CLOTHES** 衣服◄ 熨平〔衣物〕 **4** ►**CROWD** 人群◄ 拥挤着移动，挤着走 **5** ►**PERSUADE** 劝说◄ 极力劝说，敦促，催促 **6** ►**FOR JUICE** 为取得果汁◄ 挤取，榨取 **7** ►**MAKE STH FLAT** 使某物平整◄ 把…压平[压扁] **8** ►**HOLD SB/STH CLOSE** 抱紧某人/某物◄ 使紧贴；紧抱，紧握 **9 press sb's hand/arm** 紧握某人的手/手臂〔表示友好、同情等〕 **10 press charges** 提出诉讼 **11** ►**CLAIM/STATEMENT** 声称/声明◄ 坚持，竭力要求 **12 press sb/sth into service**〔因意外问题而〕将就使用[暂用]某人/某物 **13 press sth home a)** 把某物推入[压入，按入，塞入]适当的位置 **b)** 重复[强调]某事物〔以使人们记住它〕 **14 press home your advantage** 尽量利用优势大获成功 **15 press the flesh** 与许多人握手 **16** ►**RECORD** 唱片◄ 压制〔唱片〕

press (sb) **for** sth *phr v* 敦促，催促；迫切要求；努力取得

press on *phr v* **1** 又作 **press ahead** 继续坚定做某事〔尤指工作〕 **2** 硬给，强迫〔某人〕接受〔某物〕

prestige *n* **1** 威望，声望，威信 **2 prestige car/position/neighbourhood etc** 气派的汽车/令人羡慕的职位/气派的住宅区等

presume *v* **1**〔没有证据地〕相信，认为；推测 **2** 认定，视为，推定〔尤用于法律〕 **3** 冒昧做某事，放肆，擅作主张 **4** 意味着，以…为先决条件

presume on/upon sth *phr v* 滥用，不正当地利用〔某种关系、某人的好心〕

prevail *v* **1**〔信念、风俗等〕盛行，流行 **2**〔某人或其观点〕获胜；占优势，占上风

prevail on/upon sb *phr v* 劝说，说服〔某人〕

primitive[1] *adj* **1** 原始的，远古的 **2**〔人类或动植物〕原始的；早期的 **3** 简陋的，粗糙的，简单的 **4** 过时的，老式的，简陋的，不舒适的 —**primitively** *adv* —**primitiveness** *n*

primitive[2] *n* **1** 原始人 **2** 原始派画家 **3** 文艺复兴时期以前的画家[雕塑家]

principal[1] *adj* 最重要的，首要的；主要的

principal[2] *n* **1** 本金；资本 **2**〔中小学的〕校长 **3**〔大学、学院或中小学的〕校长 **4**〔戏剧、音乐等演出的〕主角，主要演员 **5**〔代理关系中的〕委托人，本人，被代理人

principle *n* **1** ►**MORAL RULE** 道德准则◄ **a)** 道德，操守，准则，为人之道 **b)**〔行为的〕准则，规范 **2** ►**RULES OF A PROCESS** 某个过程的规则◄ **a)** 原理 **b) principles** 基本原理 **3** ►**BELIEF** 信念◄ 原则；信念 **4 man/woman of principle** 正直的男人/女人，是非分明的人 **5 in principle a)** 按道理，在理论上 **b)** 原则上，基本上，大体上

privacy *n* **1** 隐居；独处；清静 **2** 隐私

privilege *n* **1**〔特定个人或群体的〕特权 **2**〔某些有权有势者的〕特权，特别待遇 **3** 荣幸 **4** 言行自由权，〔尤指〕议员〔言行不受惩罚〕权

proceed *v* **1** 继续进行，继续做 **2 proceed to do sth** 接着做某事〔尤指令人讨厌或惊奇的事〕 **3**〔向某一方向〕前进，移动

proceed against sb *phr v* 起诉〔某人〕，对〔某人〕提起诉讼

proceed from sth *phr v* [不用被动态] 源于某物，出自

productivity *n* 生产力；生产率，生产效率

professional[1] *adj* **1** ►**JOB** 工作◄ 职业的，专业的 **2** ►**WELL TRAINED** 受过良好训练的◄ 专业的，内行的 **3** ►**PAID** 有报酬的◄ 职业性的；专业的；非业余的 **4** ►**TEAM/EVENT** 球队/比赛项目◄ 由职业人员参加的；职业性的 **5 professional person/man/woman etc** 专业人员；专家 **6 a professional liar/complainer etc** 撒谎过多的人/抱怨过多的人等 **7 professional foul**〔体育运动中的〕故意犯规

professional[2] *n* **1** 把〔别人通常作为消遣的活动〕作为职业的人，专门职业者；职业选手 **2** 专业人士，专家 **3** 技术精湛经验丰富的人，内行 **4 tennis/golf/swimming etc professional**〔私人俱乐部的〕网球/高尔夫球/游泳等教练

proficiency *n* 熟练；精通

profound *adj* **1**〔感情〕强烈的; 深切的; 严肃的 **2**〔影响〕深刻的, 极大的 **3** 知识渊博的; 见解深刻的 **4** 深的; 深处的 **5** 完全的 —**profoundly** *adv*

prohibit *v* **1**〔以法令、规则等〕禁止 **2** 使不可能, 阻止

project¹ *n* **1** 项目; 工程; 计划; 规划 **2**〔学校的〕课题, 研究项目 **3** 又作 **the projects** 低收入人群住宅区

project² *v* **1** ►**CALCULATE** 计算◄ 预计, 推断 **2** ►**STICK OUT** 突出◄ 凸出, 突出 **3** ►**FILM** 电影◄ 放映; 投射 **4** ►**YOURSELF** 你自己◄ 使别人对自己有某种看法, 使〔自己的特点〕呈现, 表现〔自己〕 **5** ►**FEELING** 感情◄ 想象〔他人〕具有〔本人的思想感情〕; 把〔自己的感情〕投射给别人 **6** ►**PLAN** 计划◄ **be projected** 计划, 预定 **7** ►**THROW** 扔, 投◄ 投掷, 发射 **8** ►**PICTURE** 图画◄ **a)** 做〔立体物的〕投影图 **b)** 用投影法制作地图 **9 project yourself into the future/past etc** 设想自己身处将来/过去等 **10 project your voice** 放大声音〔使大厅或大房间的每个人都能听见〕

prolong *v* **1** 延长〔感觉、活动等〕, 拉长, 拖长 **2 prolong the agony** 延长痛苦〔拖延告诉某人他很想知道的事情〕

prominent *adj* **1** 著名的; 卓越的, 杰出的; 重要的 **2** 突出的, 凸出的 **3 a prominent place/position** 突出的[显著的, 显眼的]位置

promising *adj* 大有希望的, 很有前途的 —**promisingly** *adv*

promote *v* **1** 促进, 增进 **2** [一般用被动态] 擢升, 提升, 晋升〔某人〕 —反义词 DEMOTE **3** 促销, 推销〔货物〕; 推广〔产品〕 **4** 负责筹办, 主办〔大型活动〕〈如音乐会或体育比赛〉 **5** 倡议; 提倡 **6 be promoted**〔运动队〕被升级 —反义词 RELEGATE

prompt¹ *v* **1** 促使; 激励 **2** 引起, 激起〔某人说或做某事〕 **3** 为〔说话者〕提示 **4** 为〔演员〕提示台词

prompt² *adj* **1** 迅速的; 立刻的; 及时的 **2** 准时的 —**promptly** *adv* —**promptness** *n*

prompt³ *adv* 准时

prompt⁴ *n* **1**〔给演员的〕提词, 提白 **2**〔电脑屏幕上的〕提示〔显示电脑已完成某项操作, 准备进入下一项〕

propel *v* 推动; 推进; 驱动

property *n* **1** 所有物; 资产, 财产 **2** 房产; 地产; 房地产 **3**〔尤指律师或房地产经纪人所指的〕房产, 建筑, 房子; 地产, 房地产 **4** 特性, 性质; 属性 **5** 所有权; 财产权

prophet *n* **1**〔基督教、犹太教、伊斯兰教的〕先知 **2 the Prophet**〔伊斯兰教的创始人〕穆罕默德 **3 the Prophets** 犹太教诸先知〔其著作构成《圣经·旧约》的一部分〕,《先知书》的作者们;《先知书》 **4 prophet of doom/disaster** 预言厄运/灾难的人 **5**〔新观念、新思想的〕提倡者, 首倡者, 倡导者

prospect¹ *n* **1**〔成功的〕可能性; 机会 **2** 可能的事情, 很可能发生的事情; 前景 **3 prospects** 将来成功的机会, 前途, 前程 **4** 有前途的人[工作, 计划] **5**〔尤指从高处看到的〕景象, 开阔的景观, 景色 **6 in prospect** 即将可能发生的

prospect² *v* 勘探, 勘察〔以寻找金、银、石油等矿藏〕

prosper *v* **1** 成功; 兴旺, 发达, 繁荣 **2** 健康成长, 顺利发展, 蓬勃发展 **3** 使成功, 使繁荣

proverb *n* 谚语, 格言

provision¹ *n* **1** 供应, 供给, 提供 **2 make provision for** 为…作好准备, 为…预先采取措施 **3 provisions**〔尤指为旅行储备的〕粮食, 食物 **4**〔协议或法律中的〕规定, 条款, 条件

provision² *v*〔尤指为旅行〕提供大量的食品和其他供应品

publicity *n* **1**〔报纸、电视等对某人或某物的〕关注 **2** 宣传, 推广

punctual *adj* 准时的, 守时的, 如期的 —**punctually** *adv* —**punctuality** *n*

purity *n* 纯; 纯洁; 洁净; 纯正; 纯粹 — 反义词 IMPURITY

pursuit *n* **1** 追求 **2** 追赶, 追踪 **3** 花很多时间做的事情; 工作; 嗜好, 消遣; 追求

Q, q

qualification *n* **1** 合格证明 **2** 资历, 资格; 技能条件 **3** 限制; 限定性条件 **4** 取得〔参赛或就业〕资格

queue¹ *n* **1**〔人或车辆为等候而排的〕队, 行列 **2** 队列〔电脑必须按一定顺序处理的一系列工作〕

queue² *v* 排队〔等候〕

quiz¹ *n* **1** 问答比赛, 智力竞赛 **2** 小测验, 小考

quiz² *v* 查问, 盘问

R, r

radiate *v* **1** 辐射〔光或热〕;〔向四面八方〕发射 **2** 流露, 显示〔感情、态度等〕 **3** 从中心散开

radius *n* **1**〔圆的〕半径 **2 within a 10 mile/200 metre etc radius** 在10英里/200米等的半径范围内 **3** 半径〔线〕 **4** 桡骨

rage¹ *n* **1** 盛怒, 狂怒 **2 be (all) the rage** 流行, 时髦 **3 a rage for** 最时髦的东西, 时新式样, 时尚

rage² *v* **1**〔战斗、争论〕激烈进行,〔风暴〕狂吹 **2** 大怒, 发脾气

ragged *adj* **1** ►**CLOTHES** 衣服◄ 又作 **raggedy** 破旧的 **2** ►**PEOPLE** 人◄ 衣衫褴褛的 **3** ►**UNEVEN** 不平的◄ 又作 **raggedy**〔边缘〕参差不齐的 **4** ►**TIRED** 疲倦的◄ 疲乏的 **5** ►**PERFORMANCE** 表演◄〔表演、呼喊声等〕不协调的, 不齐的 **6 be on the ragged edge** 极度疲惫; 惴惴不安 —**raggedly** *adv* —**raggedness** *n*

raid¹ *n* **1** 突袭, 袭击 **2**〔警察进行的〕突击搜查 **3**〔对银行等处的〕抢劫, 打劫 **4**〔某公司〕大量购买另一家公司的股票以获得其控制权的企图

raid² *v* **1**〔警察〕突然搜查 **2** 武装突袭 **3** 抢劫, 洗劫 —**raider** *n*

random *adj* **1** 随意的, 任意的, 随机的 **2 at random** 任意地, 随便地 —**randomly** *adv* —**randomness** *n*

rash¹ *adj* 急躁的, 鲁莽的, 草率的 —**rashly** *adv* —

rashness *n*

rash² *n* **1** 皮疹 **2 a rash of** 大量的〔指一下子出现的令人不快的事件、变化等〕

ratio *n*〔两个数量之间的〕比, 比例, 比率

raw¹ *adj* **1** ►**FOOD** 食品◄ 生的, 未烧煮的 **2** ►**INFORMATION** 信息◄ **raw data/statistics etc** 原始数据/统计数字等 **3** ►**SKIN** 皮肤◄ 又红又痛的, 刺痛的 **4** ►**MATERIALS** 材料◄〔棉、糖、羊毛等〕天然状态的, 未经过处理加工的 **5** ►**NOT EXPERIENCED** 没有经验的◄ 没有经验的, 未经过充足训练的 **6 touch/hit a raw nerve**〔说话〕触及某人痛处 **7 get a raw deal** 受到不公正的待遇 **8** ►**WEATHER** 天气◄ 湿冷的 **9** ►**EMOTIONS/QUALITIES** 情感/素质◄ 强烈的, 自然的〔但未经充分琢磨或约束〕**10** ►**LANGUAGE** 语言◄ 下流的, 粗俗的 **11** ►**DESCRIPTIONS** 描述◄ 不加掩饰的 —**rawness** *n*

raw² *n* **1 life/nature in the raw** 未开化的生活/原始的自然状态 **2 in the raw** 裸体的 **3 catch/touch sb on the raw**〔说话或做事〕触及某人的痛处

react *v* **1** 反应 **2** 产生化学反应 **3**〔因服某种药品、食用某种食物而〕产生不良反应

react against sth *phr v* 反抗

realistic *adj* **1** 现实的, 实际的 —反义词 UNREALISTIC **2**〔图画、模型、戏剧等〕逼真的, 栩栩如生的

reap *v* **1** 收割 **2 reap the benefit/reward/profit (of)** 受益/得到回报/获利 —**reaper** *n*

rear¹ *n* **1 the rear** 后部, 后面, 背部 **2** 臀部 **3 bring up the rear** 殿后

rear² *v* **1** 养育, 抚养; 饲养 **2** 又作 **rear up**〔动物〕用后腿站起 **3 be reared on**〔小时候〕总是吃〔某种食物〕; 看〔某类书〕; 玩〔某类游戏〕**4 rear its ugly head**〔问题、困境〕冒头, 出现

rear³ *adj* 后部的, 后面的

reassure *v* 使安心, 使放心, 安慰

recall¹ *v* **1** ►**REMEMBER STH** 记起某事◄ 回忆, 回想 **2** ►**PERSON** 人◄ 召回 **3** ►**PRODUCT** 产品◄ 收回〔有问题的产品〕**4** ►**ON A COMPUTER** 在电脑上◄〔在电脑屏幕上〕重新调出〔信息〕, 检索 **5** ►**BE SIMILAR TO** 相似◄〔由于酷似而〕使回忆起 —**recallable** *adj*

recall² *n* **1** 记忆力 **2** 召回 **3 beyond/past recall** 无法回忆的, 记不起来的

recede *v* **1**〔景物、声音〕逐渐远去以至消失 **2**〔记忆〕变模糊;〔感情〕逐渐淡漠;〔可能性〕逐渐消失 **3**〔水〕退, 退去 **4**〔头发〕从前额开始向后脱落 **5 receding chin** 向后收缩的下巴

recipe *n* **1** 烹饪法; 食谱 **2 be a recipe for** 是…的秘诀[窍门]; 很可能是造成…的原因

recital *n* **1** 演奏会; 演唱会; 朗诵会〔一般由一个人表演〕**2**〔一连串事件的〕叙述, 口头描述

reckon *v* **1** 认为, 以为 **2** 估算, 估计 **3** 认为〔某人或物〕是… **4** 计算

reckon sth ↔ **in** *phr v* 把…计算在内

reckon on sth *phr v* 指望

reckon sth ↔ **up** *phr v* 把…加起来, 计算…的总数

reckon with sb/sth *phr v* **1 not reckon with** 没有考虑到 **2 sb/sth to be reckoned with** 必须认真考虑[对待]的某人/某事 **3 have sb/sth to reckon with** 必须对付某人/某事

reckon without sb/sth *phr v* 没有考虑到; 对…不加考虑

recognize 又作 **-ise**【英】*v* **1** 认出, 认识; 辨认出 **2** 正式承认, 认可 **3 be recognized as** 得到承认, 被公认为 **4**〔往往勉强地〕接受, 承认; 明白 **5** 表扬; 表彰; 嘉奖 —**recognizable** *adj* —**recognizably** *adv*

recollect *v* 记起; 想起

recommend *v* **1** 劝告; 建议 **2** 推荐, 介绍 **3 sth has much/little/nothing to recommend it** 某物有很多/少有/没有可取之处

recreation *n* 娱乐, 消遣 —**recreational** *adj*

reel¹ *n* **1 a)** 卷轴, 卷筒; 卷盘; 绕线轮 **b)** 一卷〔之量〕**2**〔一部影片的〕一盘 **3** 里尔舞〔一种轻快的苏格兰或爱尔兰舞〕; 里尔舞曲

reel² *v* **1** 又作 **reel back**〔尤指遭受打击或震惊而〕站立不稳 **2** 震惊; 迷惑 **3**〔感觉〕晕眩, 天旋地转 **4** 卷, 绕 **5** 蹒跚

reel sth ↔ **off** *phr v* 滔滔不绝地重复

reference *n* **1** 提及, 谈到 **2** 查阅, 查看 **3 with reference to** 关于〔尤用于公函〕**4 a)** 推荐信, 介绍信 **b)** 推荐人, 介绍人 **5 a)** 出处; 参考书目 **b)**〔书籍或地图等中的〕参照号, 参照符号

refine *v* **1**〔慢慢地、微小地〕改进; 完善 **2** 净化; 提炼

reflect *v* **1** 反射〔光、热、声或影像等〕**2** 显示, 反映 **3** 仔细思考; 表达意见

reflect on/upon *phr v* 给某人对…的评价造成〔尤指不利的〕影响

reform¹ *v* **1** 改进, 改革 **2** 改过, 改造

reform² *n* 改进, 改革

refreshing *adj* **1** 消除疲劳的, 提神的; 清凉的 **2** 令人耳目一新的 —**refreshingly** *adv*

refund¹ *n* 退款

refund² *v* 退还; 偿还〔尤指因对所购货物或服务不满意〕

refuse¹ *v* **1** 拒绝〔做某事〕**2** 不接受, 谢绝〔别人给的东西〕**3** 拒绝把…给…

refuse² *n* 废料, 废物

register¹ *n* **1** ►**OFFICIAL LIST** 正式名单◄ 名册 **2** ►**OFFICIAL BOOK** 正式的簿/册◄ 登记簿 **3** ►**MUSIC** 音乐◄〔人声或乐器的〕音域 **4** ►**LANGUAGE STYLE** 语言风格◄ 语域 **5** ►**BUSINESS MACHINE** 商用机器◄ 现金出纳机 **6** ►**HEATING CONTROL** 加热控制装置◄〔加热或冷却系统中控制气流的〕调风器, 节气门

register² *v* **1** ►**ON A LIST** 记入名单◄ **a)** 记录, 登记 **b)**〔旅馆入住〕登记;〔课程〕注册 **2** ►**SHOW A FEELING** 表示感情◄ 流露[表达]感情 **3** ►**STATE YOUR OPINION** 发表意见◄ 正式表达, 说明 **4** ►**REALIZE** 意识到◄ 受到注意; 注意到, 意识到 **5** ►**MEASUREMENT** 度量◄〔仪器〕显示, 记录 **6** ►**MAIL** 邮件◄ 以挂号寄送

reinforce *v* **1** 加强〔信心、信念、感觉等〕**2** 加强, 加固〔建筑、结构、衣物等〕**3** 增援, 加强…的力量〔尤指军队〕

reject¹ *v* **1** ►**OFFER/SUGGESTION** 提议/建议◄ 拒绝〔接受〕**2** ►**NOT EMPLOY** 不雇用◄ 拒绝〔雇用、录取〕**3** ►**PRODUCT** 产品◄〔因质量不好而〕废

弃 4 ▶**BELIEF** 信念◀ 摒弃 5 ▶**ORGAN** 器官◀ 排斥〔移植器官〕6 ▶**NOT LOVED** 不受关爱的◀ 冷落 —**rejection** *n*

reject[2] *n* 次品, 废品

relate *v* 1 把…联系起来, 证明…有关联; 有关联 2 讲述 3 认同, 理解〔别人的问题、处境等〕

relate to sb/sth *phr v* 1 有关, 涉及 2 与…直接相关 3 和睦相处; 认同 4 认同, 产生共鸣

relax *v* 1 ▶**REST** 休息◀ (使)放松, (使)轻松 2 ▶**LOOSEN** 放松◀ 使〔身体部位〕松弛, 放松 3 **relax your hold/grip** a) 松开手 b) 放宽 4 **relax rules/controls/regulations etc** 放宽规定/控制/管制等 5 **relax your vigilance/concentration etc** 放松警惕/使注意力松懈等

release[1] *v* 1 ▶**LET SB FREE** 释放某人◀ 释放, 放出 2 ▶**STOP HOLDING** 松手◀ 松开, 放开〔某物〕3 ▶**MAKE PUBLIC** 公布◀ 公开发表, 发布 4 ▶**MACHINERY** 机器◀ 放开, 松开 5 ▶**FEELINGS** 感情◀ 表达; 发泄 6 ▶**FILM/RECORD** 电影/唱片◀ 发行; 上映 7 ▶**CHEMICAL** 化学品◀ 释放 8 ▶**FROM A DUTY** 从职务中◀ 解除〔职务或工作〕; 解脱 9 ▶**WEAPON** 武器◀ 发射, 投〔弹〕

release[2] *n* 1 ▶**FROM PRISON** 从狱中◀ 释放 2 ▶**FEELINGS** 感情◀ a) 流露, 表达 b) 解脱, 摆脱 3 ▶**RECORD/FILM** 唱片/电影◀ 新唱片; 新电影 4 **on (general) release**〔电影、唱片等〕已经上映[发行] 5 ▶**OFFICIAL STATEMENT** 正式声明◀〔发布的〕正式声明 6 ▶**CHEMICALS** 化学品◀ 释放 7 ▶**MAKING STH AVAILABLE** 供应某物◀ 发布, 发行 8 ▶**ON A MACHINE** 在机器上◀ 释放装置, 松脱装置

relevant *adj* 有关的, 切题的 —反义词 IRRELEVANT —**relevance** 又作 **relevancy** *n* —**relevantly** *adv*

reliable *adj* 可信赖的, 可靠的 —反义词 UNRELIABLE —**reliably** *adv* —**reliability** *n*

relief *n* 1 ▶**COMFORT** 安慰◀〔因恐惧、忧虑或痛苦的解除而感到的〕安慰 2 ▶**REDUCTION OF PAIN** 减少疼痛◀〔疼痛或不快的〕减轻; 缓解 3 ▶**HELP** 帮助◀ 救济品 4 ▶**MONEY** 金钱◀ 救济金 5 ▶**REPLACE SB** 替换某人◀ 接班[替班]的人 6 **the relief of** …的解围, …的解救 7 ▶**DECORATION** 装饰◀ 浮雕, 浮雕品 8 ▶**STICKING OUT** 凸出◀ **in relief** 凸出 9 **stand out in bold/stark/sharp relief** 与周围形成鲜明的反差; 非常突出 10 **light/comic relief**〔严肃的电影、书或情景中作为调剂的〕轻松/滑稽场面 11 ▶**MAP** 地图◀ **in relief** 用地势图表示

religious *adj* 1 宗教的 2 笃信宗教的; 虔诚的

reluctant *adj* 勉强的, 不愿的 —**reluctance** *n* —**reluctantly** *adv*

remedy[1] *n* 1 补救(法) 2 药物; 治疗物 3 **beyond/past/without remedy** 不可救药的; 无法挽回的

remedy[2] *v* 补救; 纠正; 改善

remind *v* 1 使想起; 提醒 2 使〔某人〕想起 3 **Don't remind me** 别跟我提这事〔某人提到使你尴尬或不快的事情时诙谐的说法〕4 **let me remind you/may I remind you** 让我提醒你〔用于加强警告或批评的语气〕

remind sb **of** sb/sth *phr v* 使〔某人〕想起〔相似之人或物〕

remote[1] *adj* 1 遥远的 2 偏僻的, 偏远的 3 很不相同的 4 **a remote chance/possibility** 渺茫的希望/微乎其微的可能性 5 不友善的, 冷淡的 6 **not have the remotest idea** 一无所知 —**remoteness** *n*

remote[2] *n* 遥控

renovate *v* 修复; 装修; 整修 —**renovation** *n*

replace *v* 1 取代, 接替 2 替换, 调换 3 更换 4 把…放回原处 —**replaceable** *adj*

represent *v* 1 ▶**SPEAK FOR SB** 代表某人说话◀ a) 代表 b) 表达〔某团体的情感、意见等〕2 **be represented**〔某团体〕由〔某人〕代表出席 3 **represent an improvement/an obstacle/a challenge etc** 应视为进步/障碍/挑战等〔用于表示某事有某些特质〕4 ▶**GOVERNMENT** 政府◀ 当〔某地区〕的议员[其他立法机构的成员] 5 ▶**A SIGN** 标志◀〔尤指在地图上或平面图里的〕象征, 表示 6 ▶**SHOW STH** 展现某物◀ 用图画[雕塑]表示, 描绘, 雕出 7 **represent yourself as** 佯称自己是… 8 **represent sb as** 把某人描写为…

reproach[1] *n* 1 责备, 指责, 责怪 2 责备的话 3 **a reproach to** 耻辱; 不名誉

reproach[2] *v* 1 责备, 怪责〔表示失望但不含怒气〕2 **reproach yourself** 自责

reputation *n* 1 名誉, 名望 2 **live up to your reputation** 名不虚传, 不负盛名 3 **live up to its reputation**〔行为〕与名声相符

rescue[1] *v* 拯救, 解救; 救援 —**rescuer** *n*

rescue[2] *n* 救援, 营救

resemblance *n*〔尤指样子〕相似, 类似

reservoir *n* 1 水库, 蓄水池 2 储藏, 积蓄 3 储液器

reside *v* 居住

reside in sth/sb *phr v* [不用被动态] 1 存在于 2 又作 **reside within** sth/sb〔权力、权利等〕属于

resignation *n* 1 辞职; 辞呈 2 听从, 顺从

resist *v* 1 抗拒, 对抗 2 反抗, 抵抗 3 忍住〔拥有某东西的欲望〕, 按捺 4 抵挡; 保持原状; 不受…的损害 5 **resist arrest** 拒捕 —**resistable** *adj*

resolution *n* 1 ▶**DECISION** 决定◀ 决议, 决定 2 ▶**SOLUTION** 解决◀ 解决 3 ▶**DETERMINATION** 决心◀ 坚决, 坚定, 决心 4 ▶**PROMISE** 诺言◀〔做事的〕决心 5 ▶**CLEARNESS** 清晰◀〔电视、照相机、显微镜的〕清晰度, 分辨率

response *n* 1 反应 2 回答 3〔宗教仪式上会众同牧师〕轮流应答[吟唱]的祈祷文

responsible *adj* 1 ▶**GUILTY** 有罪的◀〔对事故、错误、罪行等〕负有责任的, 应承担责任的 2 ▶**IN CHARGE OF** 负责◀〔对某人、某事〕负责的 3 **responsible job/position/post** 要职 4 ▶**SENSIBLE** 明智的◀ 可信赖的, 可靠的 —反义词 IRRESPONSIBLE 5 **be responsible to** 对〔某人〕负责 6 ▶**CAUSE** 起因◀ 作为原由的

restore *v* 1 ▶**FORMER SITUATION** 以前的状态◀ 恢复 2 **restore hope/confidence/calm etc** 恢复希望/信心/镇静等 3 **restore order** 恢复秩序 4 ▶**REPAIR** 修理◀ 修复 5 ▶**GIVE STH BACK** 归还某物◀ 归还 6 **restore sb's sight/hearing etc** 恢复某人的视力/听力等 7 ▶**BRING BACK A LAW** 恢复法律◀ 恢复, 重新采用〔法律、税收、权利等〕8 **restore sb to power/the throne** 使某人重新掌权/恢复王位

restrain *v* 1 阻止, 抑制〔某人做有害或愚蠢的事〕 2 控制, 限制〔趋于增长的东西〕

restrict *v* 1 ▶**SIZE/AMOUNT/RANGE** 体积/数量/范围◀ 限制; 控制 2 ▶**MOVEMENT/ACTIVITY** 运动/活动◀ 约束, 限制〔行动、活动〕 3 **restrict yourself to** 限制自己…

result[1] *n* 1 ▶**HAPPENING BECAUSE OF STH** 因为某事而发生◀ 结果, 后果 2 ▶**SPORTS/ELECTIONS** 体育运动/选举◀〔比赛〕成绩, 比分;〔选举的〕结果 3 ▶**SCIENTIFIC TESTS** 科学测试◀〔科学研究、测试的〕结果 4 ▶**EXAMINATIONS** 考试◀ 成绩 5 ▶**SUCCESS** 成功◀ **results** 成效 6 ▶**BUSINESS** 生意◀ **results** 〔年度〕业绩 7 **get a result** 〔在体育比赛中〕赢, 取胜

result[2] *v*〔因…〕产生, 发生;〔由…而〕造成

result in sth *phr v* [不用被动态] 导致, 造成

resume[1] *v* 1〔中断之后〕继续 2〔活动或过程〕重新开始 3 **resume your seat/place/position** 回到座位/原地/原职位

resume[2], **résumé** *n* 1〔文章或讲话等的〕梗概, 摘要 2 个人简历

retreat[1] *v* 1 ▶**MOVE BACK** 后退◀ **a)**〔因恐惧或尴尬而〕后退, 退却 **b)**〔水、雪、土地〕范围缩小 2 ▶**OF AN ARMY** 军队◀ 撤退 3 ▶**CHANGE YOUR MIND** 改变主意◀〔承诺、立场等〕撤回 4 ▶**TO A QUIET PLACE** 到僻静处◀ 去宁静、安全的地方 5 **retreat into yourself/your thoughts etc** 陷入沉思

retreat[2] *n* 1 ▶**MOVEMENT BACK** 后退◀ 后退, 退却, 躲避 2 ▶**CHANGE OF INTENTION** 改变意图◀〔承诺的〕撤回,〔立场的〕改变, 放弃 3 ▶**OF AN ARMY** 军队◀ 撤退 —反义词 ADVANCE 4 ▶**PLACE** 地方◀ 静养所, 静居所 5 ▶**THOUGHT AND PRAYER** 冥想与祈祷◀〔宗教的〕静修(期)

reveal *v* 1 展现, 显露 2 揭示, 揭露, 泄露

revenge[1] *n* 1 报复, 报仇 2 **get your revenge** 雪耻〔指在比赛中战胜曾击败自己的对手〕—**revengeful** *adj*

revenge[2] *v* **revenge yourself on/be revenged on** 向…报仇

reverse[1] *v* 1 ▶**CHANGE STH** 改变某事物◀ 推翻, 撤销 2 ▶**CAR** 汽车◀ 倒车 3 ▶**CHANGE THE ORDER** 改变顺序◀ 颠倒〔通常的次序〕 4 ▶**TURN STH OVER** 翻转某物◀ 翻转 5 **reverse the charges** 〔电话〕由受话方付款 —**reversible** *adj* —**reversibility** *n*

reverse[2] *n* 1 ▶**THE OPPOSITE** 相反◀ **the reverse** 正相反 2 **go into reverse** 逆转 3 ▶**IN A CAR** 在汽车里◀ 倒车挡 4 ▶**A DEFEAT** 失败◀ 失败; 挫折 5 ▶**OTHER SIDE** 另一面◀ 背面 6 ▶**OF A COIN** 硬币◀ 背面

reverse[3] *adj* 1 **reverse order/procedure/process etc** 相反的顺序/程序/过程等 2 **the reverse side** 反面, 背面

ridiculous *adj* 愚蠢的; 荒唐的, 可笑的 —**ridiculously** *adv* —**ridiculousness** *n*

rim[1] *n* 1〔圆形物的〕外缘, 边缘, 边 2 **gold-rimmed/red-rimmed etc** 金框/红框的等 —**rimless** *adj*

rim[2] *v* 环绕〔边缘〕

ripe *adj* 1〔水果、庄稼〕成熟的 —反义词 UNRIPE 2 **be ripe for** 适宜…,〔尤指变革等〕条件成熟 3 **the time is ripe (for)** (…的)时机已经成熟 4 **ripe old age** 很大年纪 5〔干酪〕熟透的 6〔气味〕浓烈难闻的 7〔语言〕粗俗有趣的 —**ripeness** *n*

risk[1] *n* 1 ▶**POSSIBILITY OF BAD RESULT** 不良后果的可能性◀ 危险性, 风险 2 **take a risk** 冒险 3 **at risk** 处境危险 4 **run a risk** 冒险 5 **at the risk of doing sth** 冒着…的危险 6 **at your own risk** 自担风险, 责任自负 7 ▶**CAUSE OF DANGER** 危险的起因◀ 可能造成伤害[危险]的事[人] 8 ▶**INSURANCE/BUSINESS** 保险/商业◀〔按其风险评估的〕保险对象; 贷款对象

risk[2] *v* 1 使遭受〔失去、毁坏或伤害〕的危险 2 担…风险, 冒…的危险 3 冒险做〔某事, 其结果是危险或令人讨厌的〕

rival[1] *n* 1 对手, 竞争者 2 匹敌者, 可相比的东西

rival[2] *v* 与…匹敌[媲美]

roar[1] *v* 1 吼叫, 呼啸 2 咆哮, 大声喊叫 3 又作 **roar with laughter** 哄笑, 大笑, 狂笑 4〔车辆〕轰鸣着疾驶

roar[2] *n* 1 吼叫声, 咆哮声 2〔机器〕轰鸣声;〔风〕呼啸声

robust *adj* 1 强健的, 健壮的 2〔东西〕结实的, 坚固的 3〔系统、组织等〕健全的, 稳固的 4〔行为或说话〕强硬的, 坚定的 —**robustly** *adv* —**robustness** *n*

romantic[1] *adj* 1 ▶**SHOWING LOVE** 表现感情的◀ 多情的 2 ▶**CONNECTED WITH LOVE** 与爱情有关的◀ 浪漫的, 风流的 3 ▶**BEAUTIFUL** 美丽的◀ 富于浪漫色彩的; 充满传奇色彩的 4 ▶**NOT PRACTICAL** 不实际的◀ 不切实际的, 耽于幻想的, 空想的 5 ▶**STORY/FILM** 故事/电影◀ 关于爱情的, 浪漫的 6 **Romantic art/literature etc** 浪漫主义的艺术/文学等 —**romantically** *adv*

romantic[2] *n* 1 富于浪漫气息的人 2 爱幻想的人, 浪漫主义者 3 又作 **Romantic** 浪漫主义作家[画家等]

rotate *v* 1 (使)旋转, 转动 2 (使)轮流做…, 轮换 3 轮种, 轮作

rouse *v* 1 **rouse sb (from their sleep/slumbers)** 〔艰难地把某人从熟睡中〕唤醒 2 激励〔某人做某事, 尤其在他很疲倦或不愿意做时〕, 使振奋 3 激起〔希望、恐惧等〕

route[1] *n* 1〔尤指经常使用, 可在地图上显示的〕路线 2〔交通工具常用的〕路线 3〔做事或达到特定结果的〕途径, 方法 4 **Route 66, 54 etc** 〔美国〕66[54]号等公路

route[2] *v* 按特定路线发送〔东西或人〕

routine[1] *n* 1 惯例, 常规 2〔表演的〕一套固定舞步, 舞蹈动作 3〔输入电脑的〕程序 —**routinize** *v*

routine[2] *adj* 1 **routine questions/examination/visit etc** 例行问题/检查/访问等 2 一般的, 平淡的, 乏味的

row *n* 1 一排, 一行, 一列 2〔剧院或电影院里的〕一排座位 3 **three/four etc times in a row** 连续三/四次等 4 **go for a row** 去划船

ruin[1] *v* 1〔完全地〕毁坏, 毁掉 2 使破产 —**ruined** *adj*

ruin² *n* 1 破产; 垮台; 身败名裂 2 **be the ruin of** 使…破产[身体垮掉, 名誉扫地等] 3 又作 **ruins** 倒塌的建筑物, 废墟 4 **the ruins of** 〔组织、体制或思想〕的残余部分 5 **be/lie in ruins a)** 〔建筑物〕倾塌了的, 破败不堪的 **b)** 〔人的生命、希望、计划或组织有严重困难, 无法继续而〕垮掉的 6 **go to ruin** 又作 **fall into ruin** 〔某物因缺乏照料而〕衰落, 败落

rumour【英】, **rumor**【美】*n* 流言, 谣言, 谣传

rural *adj* 1 农村的, 乡村的, 田园的 2 像农村的; 使人想起农村的 — 反义词 URBAN

rust¹ *n* 1 锈, 铁锈 2 〔植物的〕锈病

rust² *v* (使)生锈

rust away *phr v* 因生锈而慢慢烂掉

S, s

sacred *adj* 1 神的, 宗教(性)的 2 受崇敬的, 神圣的 3 极重要的〔尤指在他人看来有点愚蠢〕 4 **is nothing sacred?** 怎么能这样呢?〔表示在贵重物品或重要事物受到损害时的惊讶〕 —**sacredly** *adv* —**sacredness** *n*

sacrifice¹ *n* 1 牺牲 2 献祭〔尤指从前在宗教仪式中把动物或人杀死作祭品〕 3 祭品, 供品 4 **the final/supreme sacrifice** 牺牲自己的生命, 捐躯

sacrifice² *v* 1 牺牲, 献出 2 献祭; 以…作祭品

safeguard¹ *v* 保护, 保卫〔某物〕

safeguard² *n* 保障条款; 保护措施

salute¹ *v* 1 (向…)行军礼, (向…)致敬 2 〔尤指公开地〕赞扬, 颂扬 3 〔以挥手等〕向〔某人〕打招呼, 致意

salute² *n* 1 〔通常指士兵向军官的〕敬礼, 致敬 2 〔向要人致敬的〕鸣礼炮(仪式) 3 〔以挥手、点头等动作表示的〕打招呼, 致意

sane *adj* 1 心智健全的, 神智正常的 — 反义词 INSANE 2 明智的, 清醒的 3 **keep sb sane** 不让某人担忧 —**sanely** *adv*

sanitary *adj* 1 有关卫生的, 与健康有关的 2 清洁的; 于健康无害的 — 反义词 INSANITARY

scan¹ *v* 1 细看, 审视, 查找 2 又作 **scan through** 粗略地看, 浏览, 快读 3 〔用电磁波等〕扫描 4 〔用雷达或声纳〕搜索, 寻找, 探测 5 **a)** 〔诗〕符合格律 **b)** 找出[标出]〔诗或诗句的〕格律

scan² *n* 1 细查, 审视 2 扫描(检查) 3 〔胎儿的〕扫描影像

scar¹ *n* 1 (伤)疤 2 〔精神上的〕创伤 3 疤痕, 伤痕 4 悬崖, 峭壁, 陡岩坡

scar² *v* 1 **be scarred** 留下伤痕[疤痕] 2 使〔精神上〕受创伤 3 又作 **scar over** 结疤, 留下伤疤

scarce¹ *adj* 1 不足的, 缺乏的 2 **make yourself scarce** 〔为避免麻烦等〕离开; 溜走

scarce² *adv* 几乎不[没有]; 仅仅

scatter *v* 1 撒 2 (使)分散, 驱散, (使)散开〔尤指为逃离危险〕 3 **be scattered to the four winds** 东零西散

scene *n* 1 ►**PLAY/FILM** 戏剧/电影◄ **a)** 〔戏剧中的〕一场 **b)** 〔电影、书等中的〕场景, 场面 2 ►**VIEW/PICTURE** 风景/图画◄ 〔某地方或图画中的〕景色 3 ►**ACCIDENT/CRIME** 事故/罪行◄ 〔事故或罪行的〕发生地点, 现场 4 **the gay/fashion/political etc scene** 同性恋的天地/时装界/政治领域等 5 ►**ARGUMENT** 争辩◄ 〔在公开场合的〕争吵, 吵嘴 6 ►**SITUATION** 情景◄ 情景, 景象 7 **bad scene** 困境 8 **not your scene** 并非某人喜爱的事物, 不合口味的东西 9 **behind the scenes** 秘密地, 在幕后 10 **set the scene a)** 〔为…〕提供条件 **b)** 〔在讲故事前〕叙述背景 11 **be/come on the scene** 出现, 到来; 参与, 卷进

scent¹ *n* 1 香味 2 〔动物或人的〕臭气, 臭迹 3 **throw/put sb off the scent** 〔给某人错误信息〕使某人失去线索 4 香水

scent² *v* 1 〔动物〕嗅出…的气味 2 **scent fear/danger/victory etc** 觉察到恐怖/危险/胜利等的气息

scheme¹ *n* 1 计划, 规划, 方案〔指正式计划, 如教育、培训等〕 2 阴谋, 诡计 3 〔用于组织资料等的〕系统, 体系, 组合 4 **be in the scheme of things** 按事物的一般规律, 在一般格局中

scheme² *v* 搞阴谋, 密谋, 策划 —**schemer** *n*

scold¹ *v* 责骂, 斥责〔某人, 尤指小孩〕—**scolding** *n*

scold² *n* 爱埋怨指责的女人

script *n* 1 〔演讲的〕原稿, 讲稿; 戏剧[电影]剧本 2 〔一种语言的〕全套字母, 字母表 3 〔考生的〕笔试答卷, 考卷 4 笔迹, 手迹〔尤指英语中字母连写的手写体〕

secondary *adj* 1 **secondary education/schooling/teaching etc** 中等教育/教学〔指对 11 岁至 16 岁孩子的教育〕 2 第二的, 次要的 3 从属的, 继发(性)的 —**secondarily** *adv*

secure¹ *v* 1 〔尤指经过努力而〕获得, 永久得到〔某物〕 2 使安全, 保护…〔免受攻击、伤害或损失〕 3 缚牢, 系紧, 将〔某物〕固定 4 向〔债权人〕提供保证〔偿还债务〕, 为〔借款〕作保

secure² *adj* 1 ►**PERMANENT/CERTAIN** 永久的/确定的◄ 稳固的, 可靠的, 稳定的 2 ►**SAFE PLACE** 安全的地方◄ **a)** 锁牢的; 关紧的 **b)** 安全的, 受保护的 3 ►**SAFE FEELING** 安全感◄ 安心的, 无恐惧的, 感到安全的 4 ►**CONFIDENT** 有信心的◄ **a)** 〔对自己和自己的能力〕有自信的 — 反义词 INSECURE **b)** 有保障的, 没有顾虑的 5 ►**FIRMLY FIXED** 牢固的◄ 固定住的, 系牢的, 缚紧的

seize *v* 1 〔突然猛烈地〕抓取, 攫取 2 〔用武力〕夺取, 占领, 抢去 3 没收〔毒品、武器等非法物品〕, 收缴〔物品〕 4 **seize a chance/opportunity (with both hands)** 抓住机会/机遇 5 **be seized with terror/desire etc** 突然感到恐惧/受到欲望支配等 6 抓获, 捕获

seize on/upon sth *phr v* 抓住, 利用〔借口等〕

seize up *phr v* **a)** 〔发动机或机器部件在运转中因缺油等〕卡住, 停止运转 **b)** 〔背等身体部位〕突然僵痛

select¹ *v* 〔经过认真思考〕挑选, 选择, 选拔

select² *adj* 1 挑选出的, 精选的 2 仅限于少数富人居住[参观, 使用]的, 专用的, 高级的, 奢华的

senior¹ *adj* 1 年长的 2 〔地位或级别〕较高的

senior² *n* 1 **be two/five/ten etc years sb's senior** 比某人大二岁/五岁/十岁 —反义词 JUNIOR 2 〔中学或大学〕最高年级的学生, 毕业班学生 3 老年人

sensible *adj* 1 明智的, 合理的, 实际的 2 **sensible**

clothes/shoes 实用的衣服/鞋子 **3 sensible of sth** 感知某事, 察觉到某事 **4** 可感觉到的, 明显的 —**sensibly** *adv*

sensitive *adj* **1** ►**UNDERSTANDING PEOPLE** 理解别人◄ 能理解〔别人的感情和问题〕的 —反义词 INSENSITIVE **2** ►**EASILY OFFENDED** 容易生气的◄〔感情〕易受伤害的, 神经过敏的 **3** ►**COLD/PAIN ETC** 冷/疼痛等◄〔尤对疼痛〕易感受的, 敏感的 **4** ►**ART/MUSIC ETC** 艺术/音乐等◄〔对文学艺术〕感受力强的, 有表现能力的 **5** ►**SITUATIONS/SUBJECTS** 情况/问题◄〔情况、问题等〕需小心处理的, 敏感的, 可能触怒人的 **6** ►**HEAT/LIGHT ETC** 热/光等◄〔对光、热等的变化〕能准确计量的, 灵敏度高的 —**sensitively** *adv* —**sensitivity** 又作 **sensitiveness** *n*

sequence *n* **1**〔通常导致某种结果的〕一连串相关事件[行动] **2**〔事件或行动发生的〕顺序, 先后次序 **3**〔电影中描述同一主题或动作的〕连续镜头; 一段情节;〔故事的〕片段

series *n* **1** 连续发生的同类事件; 系列 **2**〔相互联系并有特定结果的〕系列(事件) **3**〔电视、广播等的〕系列片; 系列节目 **4**〔有计划的〕系列活动 **5 in series**〔电器的〕串联

session *n* **1** 会期;〔某团体从事某项活动的〕集会〔时间〕 **2** 正式会议;〔法院的〕(一次)开庭;〔议会的〕(一次)会议 **3 sessions a)** 简易法庭 **b)** 季审法庭

severe *adj* **1** ►**VERY BAD** 非常糟◄ 严重的, 剧烈的 **2** ►**WEATHER** 天气◄ 严酷的; 恶劣的; 极热[冷, 干]的 **3** ►**STRICT** 严格的◄〔人〕严格的, 严厉的, 苛刻的 **4** ►**EXTREME** 极度的◄〔批评、惩罚等〕极其严厉的 **5** ►**UNFRIENDLY** 不友好的◄ 不赞成的; 不友好的 **6** ►**PLAIN** 朴素的◄ 朴素的; 简洁的; 不加装饰的 —**severity** *n*

shallow[1] *adj* **1** 浅的, 不深的 **2**〔对问题的理解等〕肤浅的, 浅薄的 **3 shallow breathing** 浅呼吸〔吸入少量空气〕 —**shallowly** *adv* —**shallowness** *n*

shallow[2] *v* 变浅

shed[1] *n* **1** 棚屋, 小屋, 小库房〔通常为简陋小木房, 尤用于存放杂物〕 **2**〔用作车间、停放大型车辆或存放机器等的〕棚式建筑物

shed[2] *v* **1** ►**LIGHT** 光线◄〔灯〕发出〔光线〕; 照亮, 照射 **2** ►**DROP/FALL OFF** 落下◄ **a)** 落下, 使〔某物〕脱落 **b)**〔动物或植物〕使〔外皮、毛发、叶子等〕蜕下, 脱落, 剥落 **3** ►**GET RID OF** 去掉◄ 去掉〔不需要或不想要的东西〕 **4 shed light on**〔通过提供新信息等〕使〔某事物〕清楚些[易于理解] **5** ►**WATER** 水◄〔表面〕排掉, 不沾〔水〕 **6 shed blood** 流血〔尤指战争或打斗中的杀戮或伤害〕 **7 shed tears** 流泪 **8 shed its load**〔车辆不经意〕掉落〔所载货物〕

shift[1] *v* **1** ►**MOVE** 移动◄ **a)** (使)移动〔地点、位置〕, (使)转移 **b)** 移动; 搬动〔尤指提起来搬〕 **2 shift attention/emphasis/focus** 转移注意力/重点/中心 **3** ►**COSTS/SPENDING** 费用/开支◄ 转嫁, 转给 **4** ►**OPINIONS** 意见◄ 改变〔意见、信仰, 尤指政治方面〕 **5 shift the blame/responsibility** 推卸责任 **6** ►**DIRT/MARKS** 污垢/痕迹◄ 除去〔表面或衣服上的污迹〕 **7** ►**IN A CAR** 在汽车中◄ 换挡, 调挡

shift[2] *n* **1**〔想法、做法等的〕改变 **2 a)**〔工作人员在工厂、医院等轮值工作的〕当班时间 **b)** 轮班工人 **3 a)** 宽松直筒式家常女服 **b)** 裙式女内衣 **4**〔电脑、打字机上的〕大写字母转换键 **5** 手段, 计谋

shiver[1] *v*〔因寒冷或害怕而〕颤抖, 哆嗦, 发抖

shiver[2] *n* **1**〔因寒冷或恐惧引起身体的〕颤抖, 发抖 **2 give you the shivers** 使人打寒战[害怕] **3 send shivers (up and) down your spine** 使人脊骨发凉, 令人毛骨悚然; 令人兴奋 **4 shivers** 碎片, 破片

shower[1] *n* **1** ►**FOR WASHING IN** 洗澡用◄ 淋浴用的喷头, 淋浴器 **2** ►**ACT OF WASHING** 洗澡◄ 淋浴 **3** ►**RAIN** 雨◄〔短时间的〕降雨, 阵雨; 降雪 **4** ►**THINGS IN THE AIR** 空中的东西◄〔许多细小而轻的东西的〕大量洒落或出现 **5** ►**PARTY** 聚会◄〔为将要结婚或分娩的女子举行的〕送礼会 **6** ►**PEOPLE** 人◄ 一群笨[懒]人

shower[2] *v* **1** 洗淋浴 **2** (使)〔大量细而轻的东西〕洒落 **3** 给〔某人〕大量东西

shrink[1] *v* **1** (使)缩小, (使)收缩 **2**〔数量、体积或价值〕变小, 减少, 缩小 **3**〔因恐惧而〕退缩, 畏缩

shrink from sth *phr v* 避免做, 不愿做〔困难或不愉快的事〕

shrink[2] *n* 精神分析学家; 精神科医生

sigh[1] *v* **1**〔尤指因厌烦、失望、疲倦等〕叹气, 叹息 **2**〔风〕呼啸, 呜咽 **3 sigh for sth** 思念, 惋惜

sigh[2] *n* 叹气; 叹息

significant *adj* **1** 重要的, 重大的, 影响深远的 **2** 相当数量的, 影响明显的 **3**〔眼神、微笑等〕表示某种意义的, 有特殊含义的

similarity *n* **1** 类似, 相似 **2** 类似之点, 相似之处

simplify *v* 使简易, 使简明, 简化 —**simplified** *adj* —**simplification** *n*

sin[1] *n* **1**〔冒犯上帝或宗教法规的〕罪, 罪恶, 罪孽 **2** 过错, 罪过 **3 live in sin**〔未婚男女〕同居, 姘居 **4 as miserable/ugly/guilty as sin** 非常不愉快/难看/内疚 **5 for my sins** 自作自受, 活该, 该死 —**sinless** *adj*

sin[2] *v* **1** 违反上帝的戒律, 违犯教规 **2 be more sinned against than sinning** 人负我甚于我负人; 受到超过应得的惩罚

sincere *adj* **1**〔感情等〕由衷的, 真诚的, 真心实意的 **2**〔人〕诚实的, 不虚伪的, 诚恳的 —反义词 INSINCERE

situated *adj* **1 be situated** 位于…的, 坐落在…的 **2 be well/badly situated** 境况良好/处境困难

skeleton *n* **1** ►**BONES** 骨◄ **a)**〔人体或动物的〕全副骨骼 **b)**〔医学研究用的〕骷髅, 骨架; 骨架模型 **2** ►**MAIN PART** 主要部分◄ 骨架, 框架; 梗概, 纲要 **3** ►**THIN** 瘦的◄ 骨瘦如柴的人[动物] **4 a skeleton in the cupboard/closet** 不可外扬的家丑, 隐私, 秘密 **5 skeleton staff/service** 最基本的人员/服务

sketch[1] *n* **1** 素描, 速写; 草图 **2**〔舞台、电视等上的〕滑稽短剧 **3** 短篇描写, 随笔; 简介, 梗概

sketch[2] *v* (给…)写生, (给…)画素描

sketch in sth *phr v* 补充〔内容〕

sketch sth ↔ **out** *phr v* 概述; 草拟

skim *v* **1** 从液体表面撇去〔漂浮的油脂或固体物质〕 **2**〔为掌握大意的〕略读, 浏览 **3** 飞快掠过, 擦过 **4 skim stones/pebbles etc**〔用石子等在水面〕打水漂 **5**〔为逃税而〕瞒报〔收入〕; 非法捞到〔钱〕

skim sb ↔ **off** *phr v* 挖走〔最优秀的人〕; 选取〔精

华〕;〔通过瞒报而〕捞走〔大部分的钱〕

skip[1] *v* **1** ►**MOVEMENT 动**◄ 蹦跳着走 **2** ►**NOT DO STH 不做某事**◄ 不做〔本来常做或应做的事〕 **3** ►**NOT DEAL WITH 不处理**◄ 略过, 跳过, 遗漏 **4** ►**CHANGE SUBJECTS 换主题**◄ 不按次序地改变话题, 随意跳动 **5** 又作 **skip rope** 跳绳 **6 skip town/skip the country** 逃出城/国境 **7 skip it!** 〔生气地说〕别再提这件事了! **8 skip rocks/stones** 〔用石子〕打水漂 **9 skip a year/grade** 〔在学校〕跳级 **10 sb's heart skips a beat** 心跳停一下〔用于表示非常兴奋、惊讶或害怕〕

skip out 又作 **skip off** 偷偷离开, 秘密逃走

skip[2] *n* **1** 轻跳, 蹦跳 **2** 〔用来清理砖、木等沉重废料的〕废料桶

slack[1] *adj* **1** 懒散的, 懈怠的, 马虎的 **2** 〔生意〕萧条的, 清淡的 **3** 〔绳子等〕不(拉)紧的, 松弛的 —**slackly** *adv* —**slackness** *n*

slack[2] *n* **1** 闲置的资源〈如不需要的资金、场地、人力等〉 **2 take up the slack a)** 把绳子拉紧 **b)** 接替别人停下的工作 **3** 〔绳子、绳结等的〕松弛, 不紧 **4 slacks** 宽松长裤, 便裤 **5** 煤屑

slack[3] 又作 **slack off** *v* 放松, 松劲, 懈怠

slam[1] *v* **1** ►**DOOR/GATE 门/大门**◄ (使)砰地关上, 使劲关闭 **2** ►**PUT STH SOMEWHERE 放东西**◄ 砰地放下, 使劲放下 **3 slam on the brakes** 猛踩刹车 **4** ►**CRITICIZE STH 批评某事**◄ 猛烈抨击〔报刊用语〕 **5 slam the door in sb's face a)** 用力关门不让某人进入, 让某人吃闭门羹 **b)** 〔粗鲁地〕拒绝会见某人; 拒绝与某人谈话

slam into sth *phr v* 〔车等因速度太快而〕撞到…

slam[2] *n* 砰的关门声; 〔门〕砰的关上

slender *adj* **1** 细长而优美的, 修长的; 苗条的; 纤细的 **2** 微少的, 微薄的, 不足的 —**slenderness** *n*

slice[1] *n* **1** 片, 薄片, 切片 **2** 〔指好东西的〕份儿, 部分 **3** 〔用于分菜或铲起食物的〕小铲子, 锅铲 **4 a)** 〔网球、高尔夫球等的〕削球, 斜切球, 侧旋球 **b)** 削球打法, 斜切球打法 **5 a slice of life** 〔电影、书等中的〕如实地反映生活的一个侧面, 现实生活的片段

slice[2] *v* **1** 又作 **slice up** 把…切成薄片 **2** 〔干净利落地〕切, 割, 切开, 割破 **3** (使)轻松迅速地划过〔水面等〕; (使)轻快地穿过〔空中等〕 **4** 〔打网球、高尔夫球等时〕削〔球〕, 斜切〔球〕, 打〔侧旋球〕 **5 any way you slice it** 无论你怎样考虑这个问题

slice sth ↔ **off** *phr v* 〔一刀〕切下, 〔一刀〕割去

slide[1] *v* **1** (使)滑动 **2** (使)悄悄移动, 偷偷溜走 **3** 〔价格等〕下滑, 降低 **4 let sth slide** 〔对某事〕听其自然, 任其恶化, 放任不管

slide[2] *n* **1** ►**FOR CHILDREN 儿童用的**◄ 〔儿童游戏用的〕滑梯 **2** ►**FOR HAIR 用于头发**◄ 小发夹 **3** ►**MOVEMENT 移动**◄ 滑动, 打滑 **4** ►**PICTURE 图片**◄ 幻灯片 **5** ►**PRICE/AMOUNT 价格/数量**◄ 滑落, 跌落, 下降 **6** ►**IN SCIENCE 在科学上**◄ 〔显微镜用的〕载(物)玻(璃)片 **7** ►**MUSIC 音乐**◄ 〔机器或乐器的〕滑动部件〈如长号的U字形伸缩管〉 **8** ►**EARTH/SNOW 土/雪**◄ 〔土、石、雪等的〕崩落, 崩塌

slim[1] *adj* **1** 苗条的, 修长的 **2 slim chance/hopes etc** 〔机会、希望等〕微小的, 渺茫的 **3** 非常薄[少]的

slim[2] *v* **1** 〔通过节食、加强运动等〕减肥 **2** 又作 **slim down** (使)减少, 缩小; 裁减 —**slimmer** *n*

slippery *adj* **1** 〔因湿或有油脂〕滑的, 滑溜的 **2** 滑头的, 不可信赖的 **3 be on the slippery slope** 〔恶习等〕无法克制以至后果严重 —**slipperiness** *n*

slogan *n* 口号, 标语

smash[1] *v* **1** 打破, 打碎, (使)粉碎 **2** (使)猛撞, 猛击, 猛掷 **3** 击溃, 击毁; 消灭 **4** 〔在网球等运动中〕杀〔球〕, 猛扣〔球〕

smash sth ↔ **down** *phr v* 击倒〔门、墙等〕

smash sth ↔ **in** *phr v* 将〔某物〕撞出窟窿

smash sth ↔ **up** *phr v* 〔故意〕撞毁, 打碎

smash[2] *n* **1** 撞碎声, 破碎声 **2** 〔网球等的〕杀球, 扣球 **3** 严重的交通事故, 车祸

snatch[1] *v* **1** 抢, 强夺, 攫取 **2** 抓住〔机会〕, 抓紧〔时间〕 **3** 抓走, 抢去, 夺走

snatch at sth *phr v* 伸手试图抓住[攫取]

snatch[2] *n* **1 a snatch of conversation/music/song etc** 谈话/音乐/歌曲等的片段 **2 in snatches** 断断续续地 **3** 抓, 抢, 夺

soar *v* **1** ►**AMOUNTS/PRICES ETC 数量/价格等**◄ 猛增, 骤升 **2** ►**IN THE SKY 在天上**◄ **a)** 高飞, 翱翔 **b)** 急速升高 **3** ►**SPIRITS/HOPES 情绪/希望**◄ 高涨, 腾飞 **4** ►**LOOK TALL 显得很高**◄ 耸立, 屹立 —**soaring** *adj*

social[1] *adj* **1** ►**SOCIETY 社会**◄ 社会的, 有关社会的 **2** ►**RANK 地位**◄ 社会地位[阶层]的 **3** ►**MEETING PEOPLE 与人交往**◄ 社交的, 交际的 **4** ►**WITH FRIENDS 和朋友在一起**◄ 交谊的, 联谊的 **5** ►**ANIMALS 动物**◄ 群居的, 合群的 —**socially** *adv*

social[2] *n* 社交聚会; 联谊会; 教友联谊会

sophisticated *adj* **1** 老于世故的; 有判断力的; 有鉴赏力的 **2** 〔机器、系统、方法等〕复杂的, 精密的, 高级的, 尖端的 **3** 富有经验的, 老练的; 精通的 —**sophistication** *n*

sorrow[1] *n* **1** 悲伤, 悲痛 **2** 引起悲伤的事, 不幸 **3 more in sorrow than in anger** 〔对某事〕悲哀多于愤怒

sorrow[2] *v* 感到[表示]悲伤

sound *adj* **1** ►**WELL-JUDGED 判断正确的**◄ 明智的, 合理的, 正确的 —反义词 UNSOUND **2** ►**PERSON 人**◄ 有判断力的, 见地高的 —反义词 UNSOUND **3** ►**THOROUGH 彻底的**◄ 完全的, 彻底的 **4** ►**IN GOOD CONDITION 状况良好的**◄ 完好的, 无损的 **5** ►**HEALTHY 健康的**◄ 〔生理或心理上〕健康的 **6** ►**SLEEP 睡觉**◄ 酣的, 深沉的, 平静的 **7** ►**PUNISHMENT 惩罚**◄ 严厉的, 沉重的 —**soundness** *n*

souvenir *n* 纪念品, 纪念物

spacious *adj* 宽敞的, 广阔的; 广大的 —**spaciously** *adv* —**spaciousness** *n*

span[1] *n* **1** 〔注意力、生命等持续的〕时间 **2** 〔两个日期或两件事之间的〕时距, 期间 **3** 〔桥梁、拱门等的〕跨距; 墩距 **4** 〔从一端到另一端的〕全长

span[2] *v* **1** 〔时间〕持续, 延伸 **2** 〔空间、地域〕跨越, 包括 **3** 〔桥梁〕跨越〔水面〕, 横跨

specialize 又作 **-ise** 【英】 *v* 专门研究, 专门从事, 专攻 —**specialization** *n*

species *n* 〔动植物的〕物种, 种

specimen *n* **1** 样品, 样本, 标本 **2** 实例, 范例 **3** 某

种类型的人, 家伙

sphere *n* **1** 球, 球形, 球体 **2**〔活动、工作、知识等的〕范围, 领域 **3 sphere of influence** 势力范围, 影响所及的范围

spill¹ *v* **1**(使)溢出, (使)泼出, (使)洒落 **2**〔人群〕涌出 **3 spill the beans** 泄露秘密, 走漏风声 **4 spill your guts**〔尤指因心情不好〕把自己知道的一切和盘托出 **5 spill blood** 杀人; 伤人

spill over *phr v*〔问题或坏情况〕蔓延, 扩散

spill² *n* **1** 洒出, 溢出; 洒出量, 溢出量 **2**〔用于点灯、生火等的〕木片; 纸捻 **3**〔从马、自行车等上的〕摔下

spiritual¹ *adj* **1** 精神(上)的, 心灵的 **2** 宗教(上)的 **3 spiritual home** 精神家园, 精神归宿〔指一个自己能认同其思想和态度的地方〕**—spiritually** *adv*

spiritual² *n* 灵歌〔一种原为美国黑人唱的宗教歌曲〕

spoil *v* **1 ▶RUIN STH** 毁掉某物◀ 损坏, 糟蹋, 破坏 **2 ▶FOOD** 食物◀〔开始〕变坏, 变质; 腐败 **3 ▶CHILD** 小孩◀ 宠坏, 惯坏, 溺爱〔小孩〕**4 ▶TREAT KINDLY** 体贴地对待◀ 无微不至地关心; 过分地照顾, 纵容 **5 ▶VOTING PAPER** 选票◀〔因划票不符合规定〕使〔选票〕成废票 **6 be spoiling for a fight/argument** 一心想打架/吵架

sponsor¹ *n* **1**〔出资举办表演、广播、体育比赛等以在其中做广告的〕赞助者, 赞助商 **2** 慈善募捐活动的赞助者 **3** 担保人, 保证人 **4** 提案人; 发起者, 倡议者 **5** 教父; 教母

sponsor² *v* **1** 赞助, 资助〔体育比赛、演出等〕**2** 赞助〔某人的慈善募捐活动〕**3** 倡议〔法案〕; 支持〔法案〕

spot¹ *n* **1 ▶PLACE** 地方◀〔尤指休闲的〕地点, 场所 **2 ▶AREA** 面积◀ (圆)点, 斑点 **3 ▶MARK** 痕迹◀ 污渍, 斑点 **4 on the spot** 立即, 马上; 当场 **5 be on the spot** 在现场 **6 ▶MARK ON SKIN** 皮肤上的斑点◀ **a)**〔皮肤上的〕红斑 **b)**〔尤指脸上红色的〕丘疹; 粉刺 **7 ▶POSITION** 地位◀〔在比赛、电视节目等中的〕地位, 位置 **8 run/dance/hop etc on the spot** 原地跑步/跳舞/跳跃等 **9 weak spot a)** 弱点, 不足(之处) **b)**〔对某物的〕特别喜爱, 偏爱 **10 put sb on the spot**〔故意〕使某人处于难堪地位 **11 in a spot** 处于困难境地 **12 bright spot** 亮点, 困境中使人高兴的事 **13 a spot of** 一点点 **14 ▶ON CLOTH** 在布上面◀ **spots**〔指布上的〕圆点图案, 斑点 **15 spots of rain** 几滴雨 **16 ▶LIGHT** 灯◀ 聚光灯 **17 five-spot/ten-spot etc** 一张5美元/10美元等的钞票 **18 ▶ADVERTISEMENT** 广告◀ 广告插播〔尤指为政客做的广播或电视短广告〕

spot² *v* **1 ▶NOTICE** 注意到◀ 看出, 认出; 找出 **2 ▶RECOGNIZE** 辨认出◀ 发现, 辨认出〔某人或某事的特性〕**3 be spotted**〔表面〕有斑点, 有污渍 **4 ▶GAME** 比赛◀〔在比赛中〕让〔对手〕

spot³ *adj* 现货的; 现付(款)的

spouse *n* 配偶〔指丈夫或妻子〕

spray¹ *v* **1** 喷 **2**〔液体或碎屑〕飞溅出来 **3 spray (sb/sth with) bullets** (向某人/某物)开枪扫射

spray² *n* **1 ▶LIQUID** 液体◀ 喷雾液体 **2 ▶A CAN** 一罐◀ 喷雾罐, 喷雾器 **3 ▶FROM THE SEA** 海上来的◀ 浪花, 水花 **4 ▶BRANCH** 树枝◀〔装饰用的〕小树枝 **5 ▶FLOWERS/JEWELS** 花朵/珠宝◀ 带花〔镶有珠宝〕的枝状饰物 **6 a spray of bullets/dust etc** 一阵枪弹/灰尘等

spring¹ *n* **1 ▶SEASON** 季节◀ 春天, 春季 **2 ▶BED/CARS ETC** 床/汽车等◀ **a)** 弹簧; 发条 **b)** 弹性, 弹力 **3 ▶WATER** 水◀ 泉, 泉源 **4 with a spring in your step** 步伐轻快 **5 ▶SUDDEN JUMP** 突然一跳◀ 跳, 跳跃

spring² *v* **1 ▶MOVE SUDDENLY** 突然移动◀ 跳, 跳跃, 跳起 **2 ▶EXPRESSION/TEARS** 表情/眼泪◀〔在脸上或眼中〕突然出现, 冒出 **3 ▶MOVE BACK** 复原◀ 弹回原处, 反弹 **4 spring to mind** 马上想到 **5 spring into action** 又作 **spring to life** 突然活跃起来 **6 spring into existence** 突然出现 **7 spring open/shut** 突然打开/合上 **8 spring a trap a)**〔动物〕触发捕捉器〔而被捉〕**b)** 诱使某人说出[干]某事 **9 spring a leak**〔船或容器〕出现裂缝〔开始漏水〕**10 spring to sb's defence** 迅速为某人辩护 **11 spring to attention**〔士兵〕霍然立正 **12 spring a surprise** 使突然发生, 使大吃一惊 **13 ▶PRISON** 监狱◀ 帮助〔某人〕越狱

spring from *phr v* **1** 由…引起 **2 where did you/she etc spring from?** 你/她等是从哪儿冒出来的?〔用于表示惊讶〕

spring sth **on** sb *phr v* 向〔某人〕突然说〔某事, 令人惊讶或震惊〕

spring up *phr v* 突然出现

squeeze¹ *v* **1** 压; 挤; 捏; 榨 **2** 压出; 挤出; 榨出〔液体〕**3**(使)挤进; 塞入 **4 squeeze sth out of sb** 强迫某人说出某事 **5 squeeze sb out (of sth)**〔通过吸引某人的顾客〕将某人挤出(某行业) **6**〔在很忙的时候〕设法安排〔做某事〕**7 squeeze in/into/through** 侥幸成功; 险胜; 勉强通过〔考试〕**8** 紧缩〔公司或机构的〕资金; 使…经济拮据

squeeze² *n* **1 a (tight) squeeze** 拥挤; 密集 **2** 紧捏; 紧握; 挤压 **3 a squeeze of lemon/lime etc** 挤出微量的柠檬汁/酸橙汁等 **4 a squeeze** 拮据; 紧缩 **5 put the squeeze on sb** 试图说服某人 **6 your/her/his main squeeze** 你/她/他的男[女]朋友

stabilize 又作 **-ise**【英】*v*(使)稳固;(使)稳定 **—stabilization** *n*

stable¹ *adj* **1** 稳定的; 安定的; 不变的 **2** 平静的; 稳重的 **3**〔物质〕稳定的, 不易分解[变化]的 — 反义词 UNSTABLE **—stably** *adv*

stable² *n* **1** 马厩, 马房 **2** 牲口棚 **3 a)**〔一位马主或驯马师所拥有的〕一群赛马 **b)**〔在同一家公司工作或受同一教练训练的〕一群人 **4 shut/close the stable door after the horse has bolted** 贼去关门

stable³ *v* 置〔马〕于马厩

stage¹ *n* **1 ▶TIME/STATE** 时间/状态◀ 时期; 阶段 **2 ▶THEATRE** 戏院◀ 舞台 **3 ▶ACTING** 表演◀ **the stage** 舞台生涯; 戏剧表演 **4 take centre stage/be at the centre of the stage** 成为大家注意的中心; 非常重要 **5 ▶PLACE** 地方◀〔重大事件发生的〕地点, 场所 **6 set the stage for** 为…作准备; 使…成为可能 **7 he's/she's going through a stage** 他/她正在经历成长阶段〔指某些年轻人过了这个阶段后, 很快就会改变不良或者奇怪的行为〕

stage² *v* 举办; 举行

stain¹ *v* **1** 染污, 沾污; 留下难以清除的污迹 **2** 给〔某

物, 尤指木制品〕染色[着色] **3 stain sb's name/honour/reputation etc** 玷污某人的名誉

stain² *n* **1**〔尤指液体造成的〕污迹, 污点 **2**〔尤指木材的〕着色剂, 染色剂 **3 a stain on sb's character/reputation etc** 某人性格/名声等上的污点

standard¹ *n* **1 ▶LEVEL OF QUALITY 质量水平◀** 水平; 水准; 标准 **2 ▶COMPARING 比较◀** 标准; 规范; 规格 **3 ▶MORAL RULE 道德准则◀** 道德标准; 道德准则 **4 ▶MEASUREMENT 计量, 测量◀**〔重量、纯度、价值等的〕标准, 基准 **5 ▶SONG 歌曲◀**〔很多歌星演唱过的〕流行歌曲 **6 ▶FLAG 旗◀** 仪式用旗帜 **7 ▶MILITARY POLE 军队旗杆◀**〔旧时军队的〕军旗旗杆

standard² *adj* **1** 正常的; 普通的; 普遍接受的 **2**〔形状、大小、质量等〕规则的; 标准的 **3**〔某一学科的书、作品、作者等〕公认为标准的; 有权威的 **4 standard English/spelling/pronunciation etc** 标准英语/拼法/发音等

stare¹ *v* **1** 凝视; 盯着看 **2 be staring sb in the face a)** 非常清楚而容易看见; 明显的 **b)** 看来无法避免

stare sb **out**【英】, **stare** sb **down**【美】*phr v* 盯得〔某人〕不敢再对视

stare² *n* 盯视; 凝视

stationary *adj* 不(移)动的; 静止的

statue *n* 雕像; 塑像

status *n* **1**〔人、组织、国家等的〕法律地位; 身份, 状况 **2 a)** 社会地位; 专业资格; 职位 **b)** 重要地位; 重要身份 **3**〔尤指争论、讨论等的〕状态; 状况

steer¹ *v* **1 ▶CAR/BOAT ETC 汽车/船等◀** 操纵〔车、船的行驶方向〕; 驾驶〔车、船等〕 **2 ▶CHANGE SB/STH 改变某人/某物◀** 引导, 指导, 带领〔某人的行为〕 **3 ▶BE IN CHARGE OF 负责◀** 掌管, 控制;〔尤指在困难时期〕带领…渡过 **4 ▶GUIDE SB TO A PLACE 引领某人到某处◀** 带领, 引导〔尤指用手轻推某人的背或肩等〕 **5 steer clear (of)** 避开; 从…脱身 **6 steer a middle course** 选择一条中间路线, 不走极端

steer² *n*〔阉过的〕小公牛

stereotype¹ *n* 模式化的思想[形象]; 老一套; 旧框框 —**stereotypical** *adj*

stereotype² *v* [一般用被动态] 对…有老一套看法; 把…模式化 —**stereotyping** *n* —**stereotyped** *adj*

stir¹ *v* **1 ▶MIX 混合◀** 搅, 搅拌, 搅动 **2 ▶FEELINGS 感情◀ a)** 激发, 激起〔强烈的感情〕, 引起〔强烈的反应〕 **b)**〔感情〕激起, 唤起, 挑起 **3 ▶MOVE SLIGHTLY 微动◀ a)**〔睡觉时〕轻轻地移动[挪动] **b)** 微微地动 **4 ▶DO STH 做某事◀** 激发, 激励〔某人做某事〕 **5 ▶CAUSE TROUBLE 导致麻烦◀**〔通过散布谣言〕搬弄是非, 挑拨 **6 ▶MAKE STH MOVE 使某物移动◀** 使轻轻地移动

stir sth ↔ **up** *phr v* **1** 惹起〔麻烦〕, 挑起〔争吵〕 **2** 搅起, 搅动, 使扬起

stir² *n* **1** 搅拌, 搅动 **2** 激动[烦恼]的感觉

straightforward *adj* **1** 诚实的, 坦率的, 老实的 **2** 简单的, 易懂的 **3** 无条件限制的, 明确的 —**straightforwardly** *adv* —**straightforwardness** *n*

strategy *n* **1**〔战争中的〕战略; 战略学 **2**〔为实现某目标, 尤指为战胜对手而制定的〕行动计划; 计谋, 策略 **3** 战略, 策略

strengthen *v* **1 ▶FEELING/BELIEF/RELATIONSHIP 感情/信仰/关系◀** (使)变强, 加强; 使更坚固 **2 ▶TEAM/ARMY ETC 团队/军队等◀** 增强〔某组织或军队等的〕实力 **3 ▶MONEY 钱◀**〔货币〕增值; 增加〔货币的〕价值 **4 ▶FINANCIAL SITUATION 财政状况◀** 增强, 改善〔某国或公司的财政状况〕 **5 ▶STRUCTURE 结构◀** 加固 **6 ▶PROOF/REASON 证据/理由◀** 为…提供更有力的理由[证据] **7 ▶WIND/CURRENT 风/水流◀** 加强, 增大

stress¹ *n* **1** 压力; 忧虑; 紧张 **2** 应力 **3** 强调; 重要性 **4** 重音, 重读;〔音乐中的〕加强

stress² *v* **1** 强调, 着重 **2** 重读

stretch¹ *v* **1 ▶MAKE STH BIGGER/LOOSER 使某物更大/更松◀ a)** (使)变大; (使)变松; 拉长 **b)** 可伸展, 可延伸, 有弹性 **2 ▶ARM/BODY 手臂/身体◀** 伸开, 张开, 伸展〔肢体〕 **3 ▶MAKE STH TIGHT 使某物变紧◀** 拉紧, 拽紧 **4 ▶IN SPACE 在空间上◀** 延伸, 绵延 **5 ▶IN TIME 在时间上◀** 延续, 延伸 **6 ▶RULE/LIMIT 规则/限制◀** 放宽规则[限制] **7 stretch sb's patience/credulity etc** 使某人难以忍受/相信等 **8 ▶ABILITIES 能力◀** 使〔某人〕施展才华 **9 be stretched (to the limit)** 手头拮据, 没有足够的钱[日用品] **10 stretch the truth** 夸大事实, 言过其实 **11 not stretch to sth** 买不起某物, 支付不起某物的费用 **12 stretch your legs**〔尤指久坐后〕伸伸腿; 散散步 —**stretchable** *adj*

stretch out *phr v* **1** 躺下〔睡觉或休息〕 **2** 伸出, 伸开〔手、脚等〕

stretch² *n* **1 ▶LENGTH OF LAND/WATER 一片地域/水域◀**〔尤指长而窄的〕一片地域; 一片水域 **2 ▶TIME 时间◀** 连续的一段时间 **3 ▶BODY 身体◀** 伸展动作;〔肢体的〕伸展, 伸开, 张开 **4 ▶MATERIAL 材料◀** 伸展性, 弹性 **5 not by any stretch of the imagination** 无论怎样想象都不〔表示某事怎么想象或推想也不可能是真实的〕 **6 ▶JAIL 监狱◀** 服刑期, 徒刑 **7 at full stretch a)** 全力以赴, 竭尽所能 **b)** 身体[肢体]伸直

strict *adj* **1** 严格的, 严厉的 **2**〔命令、规则〕必须严格遵守的 **3** 严谨的; 精确的, 确凿的 **4 strict Muslim/vegetarian etc** 不折不扣的穆斯林/素食者等 —**strictness** *n*

stride¹ *v* 迈大步走, 大踏步走

stride² *n* **1 ▶WALKING 走, 步行◀** 大步, 阔步 **2 ▶PATTERN OF STEPS 步态◀** 步法, 步态 **3 ▶IMPROVEMENT 改进◀**进步, 进展, 发展 **4 get into your stride**【英】, **hit your stride**【美】〔做某工作〕开始上轨道, 驾轻就熟 **5 take sth in your stride** 从容地对付 **6 put sb off their stride** 使某人分心 **7 (match sb) stride for stride** (设法与某人)并驾齐驱 **8 without breaking stride** 不加停顿地; 心平气和地 **9 strides** 裤子

striking *adj* **1** 惊人的, 显著的 **2** 吸引人的, 惹人注目的 —**strikingly** *adv*

strip¹ *v* **1 ▶TAKE OFF CLOTHES 脱衣服◀** 又作 **strip off** 脱去(…的)衣服 **2 ▶REMOVE A LAYER 除去一层◀** 剥去, 除去 **3 strip sb of sth**〔作为惩

罚〕剥夺某人的头衔、财产或权力 **4 ►ENGINES/EQUIPMENT 发动机/设备◄** 又作 **strip down** 拆卸〔发动机或设备以进行清理或检修〕 **5 ►BUILDING/SHIP 建筑物/轮船◄** 搬走〔建筑物、轮船、汽车等中的〕所有东西，搬空

strip sth ↔ **away** *phr v* 逐渐摆脱〔习惯、风俗等〕

strip² *n* **1** 条，狭条状物〈如纸、布料等〉 **2** 狭长的一块土地 **3 do a strip** 表演脱衣舞 **4** 〔沿途有许多商店、餐馆等的〕公路 **5** 〔运动队穿的某种颜色的〕运动服，队服 **6** 连环漫画

strive *v* 〔为获得某物而〕努力，奋斗

stroke¹ *n* **1 ►ILLNESS 疾病◄** 卒中，脑卒中；中风 **2 ►SWIMMING/ROWING 游泳/划船◄ a)** 〔游泳或划船的〕一次划水 **b)** 〔游泳的〕游法；〔划船的〕划法 **c)** 〔指挥划桨速度的〕尾桨手，领桨手 **3 a) at a/one stroke** 一举，一下子 **b) a bold stroke** 勇敢的行动 **4 ►A HIT 击，打◄** 一击，一抽 **5 on the stroke of seven/nine etc** 在 7 点整/9 点整等 **6 ►CLOCK/BELL 时钟/铃◄** 〔时钟、铃等报时的〕一次鸣响，敲击声 **7 a stroke of luck/fortune** 一桩意外的幸事/运气 **8 a stroke of lightning** 〔尤指击中某物的〕闪电的一击 **9 a stroke of genius/inspiration etc** 聪明之举/绝妙的主意等 **10 ►SPORT 体育运动◄** 〔网球、高尔夫球、板球等的〕击球；一击，一抽 **11 ►A MOVEMENT OF YOUR HAND 手的动作◄** 轻抚，抚摸 **12 ►PEN/BRUSH 钢笔/毛笔◄ a)** 〔钢笔或毛笔的〕一挥，挥笔动作 **b)** 一笔，一画；笔画 **13 with/at a stroke of the pen** 大笔一挥〔签字〕 **14 not do a stroke (of work)** 什么（工作）也不做 **15 put sb off their stroke** 使某人分心 **16 ►IN NUMBERS 在数字中◄** 斜线（号）

stroke² *v* **1** 轻抚，抚摸 **2** 用手轻轻地移动〔某物〕

subjective *adj* **1** 主观的 —反义词 OBJECTIVE **2** 主观想象的，只存在于想象之中的 **3** 〔文法中〕主词的，主语的 —**subjectively** *adv* —**subjectivity** *n*

submit *v* **1** 顺从，服从；屈从 **2** 呈送，提交，呈递〔计划等〕 **3** 同意服从[遵守] **4** 建议，主张

subsequent *adj* 随后的，继…之后的

substitute¹ *n* **1** 代替者；替补队员[演员] **2** 代替物，替代品 **3 be no substitute for sth** 没有…那样好，不如…称心

substitute² *v* **1** 用〔新的或不同的事物〕代替 **2** 替代，顶替；替换

subtract *v* 减去，减掉

sufficient *adj* 足够的，充足的 —反义词 INSUFFICIENT

summary¹ *n* 总结，摘要，概要

summary² *adj* 立即的；速决的〔未顾及惯常的程序、规定等〕 —**summarily** *adv*

summit *n* **1** 山顶 **2** 首脑会议，最高级会议，峰会 **3 the summit of** …的顶峰，…的极点

superior¹ *adj* **1** 职位[级别]更高的；上级的 **2** 更好的；更强的；更有效的 **3** 质量上乘的，优质的〔尤用于广告〕 **4** 有优越感的，高傲的，傲慢的 **5** 上面的，上部的 **6 Mother Superior** 女修道院院长

superior² *n* 上级，上司，长官

supervise *v* 监督；管理；指导 —**supervisor** *n* —**supervisory** *adj*

supplementary *adj* 补充的，增补的，附加的

suppose¹ *v* **1 be supposed to do sth a)** 被期望做某事；应该做某事 **b)** 本应，本该〔用于表示某事本应发生而没有发生〕 **2 be supposed to be sth** 被相信是…，被认为… **3** 认为，料想，猜想，假定 **4** 假定，预期；以…为条件 **5 I suppose a)** 我想，我认为〔用于认为某事真实，但不敢肯定〕 **b)** 我想〔尤用于表示勉强同意某人做某事〕 **c)** 我猜想〔用于表示猜测〕 **d)** 我看〔用于生气地表示预料某事真实〕 **e)** 恐怕〔用于表示某事很可能真实，虽然自己希望并非如此〕 **6 suppose/supposing** 假设，假定〔用于要某人设想如果某情况存在会发生什么事〕 **7 I don't suppose (that) a)** 〔用于很礼貌地提出要求〕 **b)** 我以为不会〔用于表示某事不大可能发生〕 **8 who/what etc do you suppose** 你认为是谁/什么… **9 what's that supposed to mean?** 这是什么意思?〔用于表示对某人刚说的话感到恼火〕

suppose² *conjunction* **1** 假设，假定〔用于假设某事发生后带来的后果〕 **2** 〔用于提出建议〕

supreme *adj* **1** 〔权力、地位、重要性或影响力〕最高的，至高无上的 **2** 〔程度〕最大的，极度的 **3 make the supreme sacrifice** 为国捐躯；〔为原则等〕牺牲

surpass *v* **1** 超过；胜过 **2 surpass yourself** 超越自己〔表示比自己过去做得更好，但常用于开玩笑，表示做得很差〕

surplus¹ *n* **1** 剩余，过剩；剩余额，多余的量 **2** 盈余；顺差

surplus² *adj* **1** 过剩的，剩余的，多余的 **2 be surplus to requirements** 不再需要

survey¹ *n* **1** 调查 **2** 〔尤指为购房者所做的〕房屋鉴定[查勘] **3** 〔绘制地图前对某地的〕勘测，测量，测绘 **4** 〔对某一专题或形势的〕概论，概述

survey² *v* **1** [常用被动态] 调查 **2** 〔尤指为形成某种意见而〕审视，仔细考虑 **3** 〔尤指为购房者〕鉴定〔房屋〕 **4** 测量，勘测，勘定

survive *v* **1** 〔经历事故、战争或疾病后〕活下来，幸存；幸免于难 **2** 经历〔困难和危险后〕仍然存在；保存下来 **3** 从〔困难中〕挺过来；挣扎着过下去 **4 survive on** 〔靠很少钱〕继续维持生活 **5** 比〔尤指亲人〕活得更长，比〔某人〕长寿

suspect¹ *v* **1** 猜想，怀疑，觉得〔尤指坏事〕可能是事实 **2** 怀疑〔某人〕有罪，认为〔某人〕有嫌疑 **3** 不信任，不相信；怀疑…的真实性

suspect² *n* 〔犯罪〕嫌疑人，可疑分子

suspect³ *adj* **1** 可疑的；不可信任的；不可靠的 **2** 〔包裹、货物等〕可疑的

suspend *v* **1** 暂停，中止 **2** 〔尤指因违反纪律〕使…暂时停学[停职] **3** 悬，挂，吊 **4 suspend judgment** 暂不作出判断 **5 be suspended in** 悬浮在

suspicious *adj* **1** 怀疑的，猜疑的 **2** 可疑的，引起怀疑的 **3** 感到怀疑的，认为有问题的

swarm¹ *n* **1** 移动中的一群昆虫；〔尤指〕蜂群 **2** 〔迅速移动的〕人群

swarm² *v* **1** 成群结队地移动，蜂拥，涌往 **2** 〔蜜蜂〕成群飞离蜂巢寻觅新巢

swarm with sb/sth *phr v* 挤满〔移动的人群或动物〕

sway¹ *v* **1** （使）摇摆，（使）摆动，（使）摇晃 **2** [常用被动态] 影响〔某人〕；使改变看法

sway² *n* **1** 摇摆，摆动，摇晃 **2** 影响力；支配；统治

swear *v* 1 ▶**OFFENSIVE LANGUAGE** 无礼的语言◀〔尤指因生气〕诅咒, 咒骂, 用粗话骂人 2 ▶**SERIOUS PROMISE** 严肃的许诺◀ 起誓保证 3 ▶**PUBLIC PROMISE** 公开承诺◀〔尤指在法庭上〕宣誓, 起誓 4 ▶**STATE THE TRUTH** 说真话或实话◀ 保证〔自己说的是真话〕, 郑重说明 5 **swear sb to secrecy/silence** 使某人发誓保守秘密

swear by sth *phr v* 极其信赖

swear sb ↔ **in** *phr v* [一般用被动态] 1 使〔某人〕宣誓就职 2 使〔某人〕在法庭宣誓

swear off sth *phr v* 承诺终止〔某种不良行为〕

swear to *phr v* **not swear to (doing) sth** 不能保证〔某事〕属实

sweep¹ *v* 1 ▶**CLEAN STH** 把…弄干净◀ 扫, 打扫, 清扫 2 ▶**PUSH STH SOMEWHERE** 把某物推到某处◀ a) 扫去, 拂去, 清除 b) 卷走; 冲走; 移去; 刮走 3 ▶**CROWD** 人群◀ 迅速地移动; 冲过 4 ▶**PERSON** 人◀ 昂首阔步地走 5 ▶**WIND/WAVES ETC** 风/浪等◀〔风、浪、风暴等迅速猛烈地〕扫过, 掠过〔某地〕 6 ▶**IDEA/FEELING** 思想/感情◀ 风行; (在…)迅速传播 7 **sweep sb along/away** a)〔人群〕拥着某人向前 b)〔感情、思想〕令某人着迷; 使某人深受影响 8 **sweep to victory/power** 大获全胜/一举掌权 9 **sweep the board**〔尤指轻易地〕大获全胜, 囊括全部奖项 10 ▶**FORM A CURVE** 形成曲线◀ 蜿蜒; 延伸 11 ▶**LOOK** 看◀〔目光等〕扫视 12 **sweep sb off their feet** 把某人一下子迷住, 使某人神魂颠倒 13 **sweep sth under the carpet** 又作 **sweep sth under the rug** 掩盖某事〔尤指错事〕

sweep sth ↔ **aside** *phr v* 拒不理会, 无视

sweep sth ↔ **away** *phr v* 1 扫除; 消灭; 摧毁 2 **be swept away by** 深受…感染, 被…打动

sweep sth ↔ **back** *phr v* 把〔头发〕梳向后面, 向后掠〔头发〕

sweep up *phr v* 1 打扫, 清扫 2 一下抱起〔某人〕 3 **sweep sb's hair up** 把某人的头发梳到后面

sweep² *n* 1 挥动 2 打扫, 清扫 3 **the sweep of** a) 长而弯曲的一段〔土地〕; 连绵弯曲的地带 b)〔思想、作品等的〕广度, 范围 4〔大面积的〕搜索, 搜查; 扫荡 5 **sweeps** 赌金全赢制 6 烟囱清洁工

swell¹ *v* 1 ▶**PART OF YOUR BODY** 身体部位◀ 又作 **swell up** 肿, 肿胀 2 ▶**PEOPLE** 人◀〔数量〕逐渐增加, 增多, 增大 3 ▶**SOUND** 声音◀〔声音〕增强, 变响亮 4 ▶**SHAPE** 形状◀ 又作 **swell (sth ↔) out** (使)鼓起, (使)隆起 5 **swell with pride/anger etc** 扬扬得意/怒气冲冲等 6 ▶**SEA** 海◀ 波涛汹涌

swell² *n* 1 海面的起伏, 浪涌 2〔尤指音乐〕音量逐渐增强 3 膨胀; 鼓起; 隆起 4 时髦人物; 头面人物, 要人

swell³ *adj* 极好的, 第一流的

swift¹ *adj* 1 迅速的; 立刻的 2 (能)迅速移动的; 速度非常快的 3 **be swift to do sth** 迅速做某事, 立刻做某事 —**swiftly** *adv* —**swiftness** *n*

swift² *n* 雨燕

switch¹ *v* 1〔常指突然地〕转换, 转变, 改变 2〔秘密地〕换掉, 替换 3〔与同事〕调换上班时间, 调班 4〔用开关〕改变〔机器的运转〕, 转换

switch off *phr v* 1〔用开关〕关掉, 关上 2 不听; 对…不加理睬[注意]

switch on *phr v*〔用开关〕开, 打开

switch over *phr v* 1〔方法、产品等〕完全改变, 完全转变 2 转换〔电台或电视频道〕

switch² *n* 1〔电灯、收音机、机器等的〕开关; 电闸 2 骤变, 突变 3 **make the switch**〔偷偷地〕调换, 掉包 4 细软的枝条

symbolize 又作 **-ise**【英】*v* 1 象征, 是…的象征 2 用符号代表, 用象征物表示 —**symbolization** *n*

sympathetic *adj* 1 同情的; 有同情心的 2〔对某目的或计划〕赞成的, 支持的 3 合意的; 合适的 4 **sympathetic figure/character**〔书、戏剧等中〕令人喜爱的人物/角色 —**sympathetically** *adv*

symposium *n* 1 专题研讨会; 讨论会 2 专题论文集

symptom *n* 1 症状 2〔严重问题存在的〕征兆, 征候

systematic *adj* 有系统的, 有条理的, 仔细周到的 —**systematically** *adv*

T, t

tailor¹ *n*〔为男顾客量体裁衣的〕裁缝

tailor² *v* **tailor sth to your needs/requirements** 根据特定需要制作…

talent *n* 1 天资, 天赋; 才能 2 有才能的人, 天才, 才子 3 性感的人, 尤物

tame¹ *adj* 1 平淡的; 枯燥乏味的; 令人失望的 2〔动物〕驯服的; 由人驯养的 —**tamely** *adv* —**tameness** *n*

tame² *v* 1 制服, 控制; 驾驭 2 驯服〔野生动物〕, 使驯化

tap¹ *n* 1 ▶**WATER/GAS** 水/煤气◀〔水、煤气等管道或容器的〕龙头, 阀门 2 ▶**BARREL** 桶◀〔桶的〕塞子 3 ▶**A LIGHT HIT** 轻轻的敲击◀〔尤指为了引起某人注意而对某物的〕轻轻敲击, 轻叩, 轻拍 4 **on tap** a) 可随时取用[使用]的 b)〔桶装啤酒〕可随时旋开旋塞供饮用的 5 ▶**DANCING** 跳舞◀ 又作 **tap dancing** 踢踏舞 6 ▶**TELEPHONE** 电话◀ 电话窃听 7 ▶**TUNE** 乐调◀ **taps**〔军营里的〕熄灯号;〔军队的〕葬礼号

tap² *v* 1 ▶**HAND OR FOOT** 手或脚◀〔用手或脚〕轻敲, 轻叩, 轻拍 2 ▶**ENERGY** 能源◀ 又作 **tap into** 发掘, 开发〔能源或电力〕 3 ▶**IDEAS** 思想◀ 又作 **tap into** 利用, 采用〔思想、经验、知识等〕 4 ▶**TELEPHONE** 电话◀ 电话窃听 5 ▶**TREE** 树木◀ 在〔树干〕上凿孔以取其液汁 6 **tap sb for sth** 从某人处弄到钱

tap sth ↔ **in** *phr v* 把〔信息、数据等〕敲入[键入, 输入]〔电脑、电话等〕

target¹ *n* 1 ▶**OBJECT OF ATTACK** 攻击对象◀〔有意攻击的〕目标; 攻击对象 2 ▶**AN AIM** 目标◀ 想要达到的结果〈如总数、时限等〉; 想要实现的目标; 指标 3 ▶**SHOOTING** 射击◀〔射击的〕靶子 4 **target group/area/audience etc** 特别针对的群体/领域/听众等 5 **be the target of criticism/complaints etc** 成为批评/抱怨等的对象

target² *v* 1 对…瞄准, 把…当做靶子 2 以…为目标

[对象] **3** 把…选作目标

technique *n* **1** 技巧; 手法 **2** 技术水平; 技能

tedious *adj* 枯燥乏味的; 冗长的 **—tediously** *adv* **—tediousness** *n*

temperate *adj* **1 temperate climate/region** 温和的气候; 温带地区 **2** 〔行为〕温和的, 心平气和的; 自我节制的

temporary *adj* **1** 暂时的, 临时的 **2** 短期的, 短暂的 **—temporariness** *n* **—temporarily** *adv*

temptation *n* **1** 引诱, 诱惑 **2** 很有诱惑力的东西

tenant *n* 房客; 租户

tendency *n* **1** 〔发育、思想、行为等的〕倾向 **2 artistic/alcoholic etc tendencies** 艺术的气质/酗酒的危险等 **3** 趋势, 趋向 **4** 〔政党内部观点往往较为极端的〕激进派

tender¹ *adj* **1 ▶MEAT/VEGETABLES 肉食/蔬菜◀** 嫩的; 软的; 易炖烂的〔尤指烹饪恰到好处〕— 反义词 TOUGH **2 ▶PART OF YOUR BODY 身体的某一部分◀** 疼痛的, 一触即痛的 **3 ▶GENTLE 温柔的◀** 温柔的; 体贴入微的; 慈爱的 **4 tender loving care** 体贴入微的关怀 **5 tender blossoms/plants etc** 娇弱的花朵/幼嫩的植株等 **6 tender age** 年幼时期; 未成熟时期 **—tenderly** *adv* **—tenderness** *n*

tender² *n* **1** 投标(书) **2** 〔来往于岸边和大船之间运送人员或补给品的〕驳运船; 补给船; 交通艇 **3** 〔蒸汽火车的〕煤水车

tender³ *v* **1** 投标〔承办某事〕 **2** 递呈, 呈交; 提出 **3** 付款, 偿还

tension *n* **1 ▶NERVOUS FEELING 紧张感觉◀** 紧张; 焦虑; 焦急 **2 ▶NO TRUST 不信任◀** 〔人与人、国家与国家之间的〕紧张关系, 紧张局势 **3 ▶DIFFERENT INFLUENCES 不同的影响力◀** 〔需求、势力或影响力间的〕冲突; 紧张状况 **4 ▶TIGHTNESS 绷紧◀** 〔电线、绳子、肌肉等的〕拉紧, 绷紧 **5 ▶FORCE 力量◀** 张力, 拉力

term¹ *n* ① **ONE WAY OF REGARDING SOMETHING** 看待某事的一种方式 **1 in financial/artistic/psychological etc terms** 就金融/艺术/心理学等而言 **2 in terms of** 在…方面, 从…方面来说; 根据…来解释 **3 in sb's terms** 在某人看来, 根据某人的观点 **4 in real terms** 〔价格或费用的〕实际变化情况 ② **WORDS/LANGUAGE** 字词/语言 **5 ▶WORD/EXPRESSION 字词/词组◀** 专门名词; 术语 **6 a term of abuse/endearment etc** 骂人的词/表示爱意的词 **7 in glowing terms/in strong terms** 以十分赞许的口吻/以强烈的措辞 **8 in no uncertain terms** 〔通常带着怒气〕直截了当地 ③ **PERIOD OF TIME** 时段 **9 ▶SCHOOL/UNIVERSITY 中小学/大学◀** 学期〔一学年分为三学期〕 **10 in the long/short/medium term** 就长期/短期/中期而言 **11 ▶TIME IN A JOB 工作的时间◀** 〔当选重要政府职务的〕任期, 期限 **12 prison/jail term etc** 服刑期限 **13 ▶BUSINESS 商务◀** 〔合同等的〕有效期限 **14 ▶END OF BUSINESS AGREEMENT 商务协议的终止◀** 〔商务协议的〕终止期 **15 ▶HAVING A BABY 生孩子◀** 分娩期, 足月(分娩) ④ **CONDITIONS/AGREEMENT** 条件/协议 **16 ▶CONDITIONS 条件◀ terms a)** 〔协议、合同或法律文件的〕条款 **b)** 付款条件; 购买[出售]条件 **17 on your (own) terms** 按照自己的条件 **18 terms of reference** 〔对某一官方委员会或报告的〕授权范围; 研究事项 ⑤ **RELATIONSHIP** 关系 **19 be on good/bad terms** 关系好/关系不好 **20 be on speaking terms** 〔尤指吵架后〕关系好, 友好地相互说话 ⑥ **OTHER SENSES** 其他意思 **21 come to terms with sth** 与…妥协, 对…让步; 接受〔不愉快的事〕 **22 on equal terms/on the same terms** 在平等的条件下/在相同的条件下 **23 be thinking/talking in terms of** 正考虑做某事; 正打算做某事 **24 ▶NUMBER/SIGN 数字/符号◀** 〔数学运算中的〕项

term² *v* [一般用被动态] 把…称为, 把…叫做

terminate *v* (使)结束, (使)终止

terrific *adj* **1** 极好的, 极棒的; 非常愉快的 **2** 〔尺寸或程度〕极其巨大的, 大得惊人的

territory *n* **1 ▶GOVERNMENT LAND 政府土地◀** 领土, 版图, 领地 **2 ▶TYPE OF LAND 某一类土地◀** 〔某种特定的〕地区, 地方 **3 US Territory** 〔美国的〕属地 **4 ▶EXPERIENCE 经验◀** 〔经验或知识的〕领域 **5 ▶ANIMAL 动物◀** 〔兽类、鸟类等的〕地盘, 领域 **6 ▶BUSINESS 商务◀** 〔商务活动、尤指商业销售的〕地区 **7 come/go with the territory** 在某种工作、情况中难免碰到的事

testify *v* **1** 〔尤指在法庭上〕作证 **2** 证明, 证实 **3** 作见证〔指基督徒向人诉说上帝的恩典〕

theft *n* **1** 盗窃罪 **2** 偷窃, 偷盗

theme *n* **1** 主题 **2** 主调; 主旋律 **3** 〔为某一特定学科写作的〕作文, 短论文 **4 theme music/song/tune** 主题音乐/主题歌/主调

theoretical 又作 **theoretic** *adj* **1** 〔科学〕理论的 **2** 理论上的; 推想的, 臆测的

thesis *n* **1** 论文〔指大学的高级学位论文, 如文学硕士论文或哲学博士论文〕 **2** 〔设法解释某事的〕论点

thoughtful *adj* **1** 认真思考的, 沉思的; 若有所思的 **2** 想得周到的; 体贴的, 关心的 **—thoughtfully** *adv* **—thoughtfulness** *n*

threaten *v* **1** 威胁, 恐吓〔某人〕 **2** 威胁到; 危害到 **3** 〔不利的事〕将要发生; 〔某事〕可能引起〔不利的后果〕

thrift *n* 节省, 节俭

timber *n* **1** 木材, 原木; 〔可作木材的〕树木 **2** 〔尤指构成房屋主要结构的〕栋木, 大梁 **3 timber!** 倒啦! 避开! 〔用来警告人们所伐树木快要倒下〕

timely *adj* 适时的, 及时的

toil¹ *v* **1** 又作 **toil away** 长时间地苦干, 辛苦劳作 **2** 吃力地慢行, 跋涉

toil² *n* **1** 长时间的辛苦劳作 **2 the toils of** 困境; 困惑; 迷惑

tolerance *n* **1** 忍受, 容忍; 宽容 **2** 〔痛苦、困难等的〕忍受程度, 忍耐力 **3** 〔某物在大小、重量等方面的〕公差〔偏离公差则不能正常工作〕

toss¹ *v* **1 ▶THROW 扔◀** 扔, 掷, 抛〔尤指轻快地抛较轻的东西〕 **2 ▶MOVE 移动◀** (使)动来动去; (使)翻转不停 **3 ▶THROW A FLAT OBJECT 抛扔扁平的物体◀** 把〔扁平的物体〕抛向空中使其翻转落下 **4 ▶A COIN 硬币◀** 又作 **toss up** 把(硬币)抛向空中〔以决定某事〕 **5 ▶IN COOKING 烹调过程中◀** 〔在液体中〕摇晃, 搅拌〔食物〕 **6 toss your head** 把头

往后一仰〔表示气愤〕**7 toss your cookies** 呕吐

toss off *phr v* **1** 轻而易举地完成〔某事〕**2** 将…一饮而尽 **3** 手淫

toss[2] *n* **1** 抛硬币〔决定某事〕**2** 猛一仰头 **3 win/lose the toss** 〔在比赛等开始时〕抛硬币赢了/输了 **4** 〔轻轻的〕抛，扔，投 **5 not give a toss** 根本不在乎

tournament *n* **1 tennis/chess/badminton etc tournament** 网球/国际象棋/羽毛球等锦标赛 **2** 〔中世纪的〕骑士比武大会

trace[1] *v* **1** ►**FIND SB/STH** 发现某人/某物◄ 仔细找寻 **2** ►**ORIGINS** 来源◄ 追溯；追查 **3** ►**HISTORY/DEVELOPMENT** 历史/发展◄ 研究…的历史；探索…的发展；追寻…的轨迹 **4** ►**COPY** 誊写◄〔用透明纸在图上〕描摹，描绘 **5** ►**DRAW** 勾画◄〔用手指或脚趾在物体表面〕画〔线〕；留下〔印迹〕**6 trace a call** 〔利用特殊的电子设备〕追查打电话的人 —**traceable** *adj*

trace[2] *n* **1** ►**SIGN OF STH** 某物的迹象◄ 踪迹，痕迹，迹象 **2** ►**SMALL AMOUNT** 小量◄ 微量；痕量 **3** ►**TELEPHONE** 电话◄〔利用特殊电子设备对电话的〕追查，追踪 **4** ►**INFORMATION RECORDED** 记录的信息◄〔记录电信号的机器在屏幕或纸上作的〕描记线 **5 kick over the traces** 挣脱羁绊，摆脱约束 **6** ►**CART/CARRIAGE** 大车/马车◄〔大车或马车上的〕挽绳

track[1] *n* **1** ►**ROAD** 道路◄〔路面粗糙不平的、可行车的〕小道，窄路 **2** ►**PATH** 小径◄〔尤指经常行走踩出来的〕小路，小径 **3** ►**FOR RACING** 用于比赛◄ 跑道 **4** ►**RAILWAY** 铁路◄〔铁路的〕轨道，铁路线 **5 tracks** 〔人、兽等的〕足迹，痕迹；〔车辆的〕轨迹，车辙 **6 be on the right/wrong track** 思路正确/错误 **7** ►**MUSIC/SONG** 音乐/歌曲◄〔唱片、录音带或CD上的〕一首歌；一支曲子 **8 keep/lose track of** 掌握/失去…的线索；了解/不了解…的动态 **9 stop (dead) in your tracks** 〔尤指因惊吓而〕突然停下 **10 cover/hide your tracks** 掩盖/隐匿自己的行踪[活动] **11 be on the track of** 追踪，追寻 **12** ►**SPORT** 体育运动◄ **a)** 径赛运动 **b)** 田径运动 **13 I'd better make tracks** 我得马上离开〔尤指自己并不想离开〕 **14** ►**DIRECTION** 方向◄〔物体移动的〕方向；行动路线 **15** ►**ON A VEHICLE** 交通工具上◄〔车辆的〕履带 **16** ►**FOR RECORDING** 录音用的◄〔录音带的〕音轨，磁迹 **17 be on track** 有可能获得〔想要的结果〕**18 get off the track** 偏离正题，离题

track[2] *v* **1** ►**SEARCH** 搜寻◄ 追踪，跟踪 **2** ►**AIRCRAFT/SHIP** 飞行器/轮船◄〔用雷达〕跟踪〔飞机或轮船〕**3** ►**CAMERA** 摄像机◄〔电影或电视摄像机〕跟踪摄影，移动摄影 **4** ►**RECORD** 唱片◄〔唱针在唱片纹道中〕移动 **5** ►**SCHOOL** 学校◄ 把〔学生〕按能力分组 **6** ►**MARK** 印迹◄ 留下…的足印 —**tracker** *n*

track sb/sth ↔ **down** *phr v* 追踪到；追查到

tradition *n* **1 a)** 传统 **b)** 传统信仰；传统习俗 **2** 传统方式，惯例，老规矩 **3 be in the tradition of** 沿袭…的传统

tragedy *n* **1** 悲剧性事件，惨剧，惨案 **2** 〔因浪费、失去或伤害而造成的〕不幸；遗憾 **3 a)** 悲剧作品 **b)** 悲剧〔文学类别之一〕

trail[1] *v* **1** 拖，拉；拖在后面 **2** 又作 **trail along** 〔尤指因疲倦或厌烦〕慢腾腾地走（在后面）**3** 〔体育比赛、竞赛或选举中〕落后于 **4** 跟踪，追踪

trail away/off *phr v* 〔说话的声音〕逐渐变小，减弱

trail[2] *n* **1 be on sb's trail** 跟踪，追踪〔某人〕**2 while the trail is still hot** 〔某人〕刚离开〔就随后追赶〕**3** 〔人或动物的〕足迹，踪迹；嗅迹 **4** 小路，小径 **5 trail of blood/dust etc** 血迹/尘土等的痕迹 **6 a trail of broken hearts/unpaid bills etc** 〔某人留下的〕一串破碎的心/一大摞未支付的账单等

trait *n* 〔人性格中的〕特性，品质

tramp[1] *n* **1** 流浪者，游民 **2** （长途）跋涉 **3** 荡妇 **4 the tramp of** …沉重的脚步声

tramp[2] *v* 用重重的脚步走（过）

transfer[1] *v* **1** ►**PERSON** 人◄ 转移（地方）；调动（工作）〔尤指在同一机构中〕**2** ►**THING/ACTIVITY** 东西/活动◄ 搬运；迁移 **3** ►**MONEY** 钱◄ 把〔钱〕转到另一账户上 **4 transfer your affection/loyalty etc** 移情于别人/转而支持别人等 **5** ►**PROPERTY** 财产◄ 把〔财产〕转让给另一人 **6 transfer power/responsibility/control (to)** 转让权力/责任/控制权（给…）**7** ►**PLANE** 飞机◄ 转机；转乘，改乘 **8** ►**RECORDING** 录音◄ 录制，转录〔信息、音乐等，如从录音带转换成光碟〕—**transferable** *adj*

transfer[2] *n* **1 a)** 〔地点的〕转移；〔工作的〕调动 **b)** 已调动的人；已转移的东西 **2 transfer of power** 权力的转让[过渡] **3** 〔可粘贴或印制的〕图画，图案 **4** 〔公共汽车、火车等的〕转乘票证

transform *v* 使改观，使变形；使转化 —**transformable** *adj*

translate *v* **1** 翻译，把〔话语或文字〕译成〔另一种语言〕**2** （被）翻译 **3** 把…变成另一种形状，转化为… —**translatable** *adj*

transmit *v* **1** 发送，播送，播放〔电子信号、信息等〕**2** 传送，传递，传播 **3** 传播〔声音或光〕

transplant[1] *v* **1** 移植，移栽〔植物〕**2** 移植〔器官、皮肤等〕**3** 搬运，搬迁，迁移 —**transplantation** *n*

transplant[2] *n* **1** 〔器官、皮肤等〕移植（手术）**2** 移植的器官，移植物

transport[1] *n* **1** 〔旅客或货物的〕运输，运送 **2** 交通工具，运输途径 **3** 运输（过程）；运输（业务） **4** 〔运送士兵或供给品的〕运输船；运输机 **5 be in a transport of delight/joy etc** 感到非常高兴/快乐等

transport[2] *v* **1** 运输，运送〔货物、人等〕**2 be transported back/into etc** 〔想象中〕被带回到/被带入〔另一地点或时间等〕**3** 〔旧时〕流放，放逐〔犯人〕**4 be transported with delight/joy etc** 欣喜若狂，喜不自胜 —**transportable** *adj*

trap[1] *n* **1** ►**FOR ANIMALS** 用于动物的◄〔捕捉动物的〕夹子，罗网，陷阱 **2** ►**BAD SITUATION** 恶劣的处境◄ 圈套；困境 **3** ►**CLEVER TRICK** 聪明的计策◄ 计谋，策略；陷阱 **4 fall into the trap of doing sth** 做〔某事〕不明智 **5 keep your trap shut** 不把…说出去，不泄密 **6 shut your trap!** 闭上你的嘴！**7** ►**VEHICLE** 车辆◄ 双轮轻便马车 **8** ►**SPORT** 体育运动◄〔高尔夫球场的〕沙坑 **9** ►**DOG RACE** 赛狗◄〔赛狗开始时放狗出笼的〕围栏

trap[2] *v* **1** ►**IN A DANGEROUS PLACE** 在危险的地点◄ [一般用被动态] 困住，关住；使陷于危险中 **2**

►**IN A BAD SITUATION** 在恶劣的处境中◄ **be trapped** 使陷于困境 3 ►**ANIMAL** 动物◄ 用陷阱捕猎〔兽或鸟〕 4 ►**CATCH SB** 抓住某人◄ 把〔某人〕困住〔以便捕捉〕; 使陷入罗网 5 ►**TRICK SB** 欺骗某人◄ 诱骗, 诱使 6 ►**CRUSH** 压扁◄ 被夹住; 被压扁 7 ►**GAS/WATER ETC** 气/水等◄ 把〔气、水等〕储存; 留存

treasure¹ *n* 1 金银财宝, 宝藏 2 珍宝, 珍品 3 很有用的人, 得力帮手

treasure² *v* 珍藏, 珍惜, 珍视

treatise *n* 专著, 专题论文

treatment *n* 1 ►**MEDICAL** 医学的◄ 治疗; 疗法 2 ►**BEHAVIOUR TOWARDS SB** 对待某人的行为◄ 对待(方式), 待遇 3 ►**OF A SUBJECT** 有关某一主题◄〔针对某一主题的〕讨论, 论述 4 ►**CLEAN/PROTECT** 清理/保护◄ 处理〔指清理、保护等的过程〕

treaty *n* 1〔国家或政府间的〕条约 2〔尤指为了购房, 两人之间签订的〕协议, 协定

tremble *v* 1〔尤指因难受或受到惊吓而〕颤抖, 发抖, 战栗 2〔轻微地〕摇晃, 震颤 3〔说话声〕紧张, 发抖 4 焦虑, 担忧; 担惊受怕 —**tremble** *n* —**trembly** *adj*

tremendous *adj* 1 巨大的; 极快的; 强有力的 2 极好的, 特棒的

trend *n* 1 趋势, 趋向, 倾向, 动向 2 **set the trend** 开创潮流

trial¹ *n* 1 ►**COURT** 法庭◄ 审判, 审理 2 ►**TEST** 试验◄ **a)** 试验, 试用 **b)** 试验期, 试用期 3 **by trial and error** 反复试验〔以得出最佳效果〕 4 ►**WORRY/ANNOY** 焦虑/厌烦◄ **be a trial (to)**〔令某人〕焦虑[厌烦] 5 **trials and tribulations** 艰难困苦 6 ►**SPORTS** 体育运动◄ **trials** 预赛, 选拔赛

trial² *v*〔全面彻底地〕测试, 试验, 试用

trick¹ *n* 1 ►**DECEIVING SB** 欺骗某人◄ 骗局, 花招, 诡计 2 **dirty/rotten/mean trick** 下流的/无耻的/卑鄙的诡计 3 ►**JOKE** 玩笑◄ 恶作剧 4 **do the trick** 奏效, 达到预期效果 5 ►**CLEVER METHOD** 巧妙办法◄ 诀窍; 技巧, 技法 6 **use every trick in the book** 使出各种绝招, 使出浑身解数 7 **sb can teach/show you a trick or two**〔某人〕可以教你一两招,〔某人〕比你懂得多 8 **be up to your (old) tricks** 耍(老)花招 9 ►**MAGIC** 魔术◄ 戏法, 把戏 10 **a trick of the light** 灯光引起的错觉 11 ►**CARDS** 纸牌◄〔纸牌游戏中出的或赢的〕一圈牌, 一墩牌 12 ►**HABIT** 习惯◄ **have a trick of doing sth** 有〔使用某句口头禅或以特别的方式活动脸部或身体〕的习惯 13 **never miss a trick** 对所发生的事无所不晓; 了如指掌 14 **how's tricks?** 近来如何?〔寒暄语〕 15 **turn a trick** 卖淫

trick² *v* 1 欺骗, 诱骗, 哄骗 2 **be tricked out with/in** 装饰, 打扮

trick³ *adj* 1 **trick photography** 特技摄影 2 **trick question** 看似容易其实困难的问题 3 **trick knee/ankle etc** 软弱无力会突然撑不住的膝关节/脚踝骨等

trifle¹ *n* 1 **a trifle** 有点儿, 稍稍 2 琐碎事; 无价值的东西 3 蛋糕甜食〔一种由蛋糕、水果、果冻、牛奶蛋糊、奶油等层层构成的冷甜食〕

trifle² *v*

trifle with sb/sth *phr v* 轻视, 小看, 随便对待

trivial *adj* 1 微不足道的, 没有什么价值的 2 普通的, 平常的 —**trivially** *adv*

trunk *n* 1 树干 2〔汽车后部的〕行李箱 3 象鼻 4 **trunks** 男式游泳裤 5〔人体的〕躯干 6 大箱子, 大旅行箱

trustworthy *adj* 值得信赖的, 可靠的 —**trustworthiness** *n*

tuition *n* 1〔尤指学生人数不多的〕教学, 讲课 2 学费

twilight *n* 1 暮色, 黄昏的天色 2 黄昏时分, 薄暮时分 3〔人生的〕暮年时期 4 **twilight world** 朦胧世界; 阴暗世界

twin¹ *n* 双胞胎中的一个

twin² *adj* 1 **twin problems/goals etc** 两个同时出现、密切相关的问题/目标等 2 **twin beds/engines etc** 成对的(单人)床/双引擎等

twin³ *v* [一般用被动态]〔不同国家的两个类似城市〕结为姐妹城市

twinkle¹ *v* 1 闪烁, 闪耀 2〔眼睛〕闪闪发光 3 **in the twinkling of an eye** 转眼间, 瞬间, 霎时

twinkle² *n* 1 **a twinkle in your eye** 眼睛里闪烁着愉悦的光芒 2 **when you were just a twinkle in your father's eye** 在你还未出世的时候 3 闪烁的光

typical *adj* 1 典型的, 有代表性的 2 表现出个性的, 一向如此的 3 **typical!** 老是这样!〔表示气愤〕

U, u

undergo *v* [不用被动态] 经历, 经受; 遭受

undertake *v* 1 着手做; 承担, 接受 2 **undertake to do sth** 答应做某事; 同意做某事

unfold *v* 1 展开, 打开, 摊开〔卷着的东西〕 2〔故事、计划等〕逐渐明确; 逐渐呈现; 展示

uniform¹ *n* 1〔警察、军人等穿的〕制服 2 **be in uniform a)** 穿着制服 **b)** 做一名军人, 当兵

uniform² *adj* 全部相同的, 一致的 —**uniformly** *adv*

unify *v* 1 统一〔国家、组织等〕, 使成一体 2 使相同, 使一致

unique *adj* 1 独一无二的; 独特的 2 极好的; 难得的, 不同寻常的; 特别的 —**uniquely** *adv* —**uniqueness** *n*

universal *adj* 1 全体(做)的, 一致的 2 普遍的, 一般的 3 通用的; 万能的 —**universally** *adv* —**universality** *n*

update¹ *v* 1 为…提供最新信息; 更新 2 使现代化

update² *n* 最新消息

uphold *v* 1 支持, 维护〔法规、制度或原则〕 2〔法庭〕维持〔原判〕 —**upholder** *n*

urban *adj* 城市的, 都市的

urgent *adj* 1 紧急的, 急迫的, 需迅速处理的 2 强求的; 急切的 —**urgency** *n* —**urgently** *adv*

utensil *n* 器皿, 用具〔尤指烹调用具〕

utmost¹ *adj* **the utmost importance/respect/care etc** 极度的重要/尊敬/关心等

utmost² *n* 1 极度, 极限, 最大可能 2 **do your utmost** 竭尽全力

utterly *adv* 完全地, 十足地

V, v

vacant *adj* **1** 〔座位、房屋等〕空的, 未被占用的 **2** 〔工作或职位〕空缺的 **3 vacant expression/smile/stare etc** 茫然的表情/微笑/凝视等 **4 situations vacant** 〔报纸上的〕招聘栏 **—vacantly** *adv*

vacuum¹ *n* **1** 真空 **2** 失落感; 空虚(感) **3 in a vacuum** 在真空状态中; 与外界隔绝 **4** 真空吸尘器

vacuum² *v* 用真空吸尘器打扫

vague *adj* **1** 含糊的, 不明确的, 不清楚的 **2 have a vague idea/feeling/recollection etc that** 隐约地想到/感到/忆起等 **3** 模糊不清的 **—vagueness** *n*

vain *adj* **1** 自负的, 自视过高的 **2 in vain** 徒劳, 无结果 **3 vain attempt/hope/effort etc** 徒劳的尝试/希望/努力等 **4 vain threat/promise etc** 空洞的威胁/承诺等 **5 take sb's name in vain** 〔趁其不在场而〕轻慢地谈论某人 **6 take the Lord's name in vain** 亵渎上帝之名 **—vainly** *adv*

vanish *v* **1** 突然不见, 消失〔尤指以一种不易解释的方式〕 **2** 灭绝 **3 do a vanishing act** 突然消失〔尤指当有人在寻找你时〕

vapour 【英】, **vapor** 【美】 *n* **1** 蒸汽, 水汽, 〔某种液体的〕蒸气 **2 the vapours** 突然眩晕感 **—vaporous** *adj*

variation *n* **1** 〔数量或形式的〕变化, 变动 **2** 〔做事方式的〕变更 **3** 〔音乐中的〕变奏(曲)

vast *adj* **1** 巨大的, 广大的, 广阔的 **2 the vast majority/bulk of** …的绝大多数 **—vastness** *n*

vehicle *n* **1** 运载工具; 车辆 **2 vehicle for (doing) sth** 媒介(物); 用作…的工具

versatile *adj* **1** 多才多艺的 **2** 有多种用途的, 多功能的, 万用的 **—versatility** *n*

version *n* **1** 〔同一种物件稍有不同的〕样式, 型号; 复制件, 变体 **2** 〔某人对某一事件作出的〕描述; 说法, 讲法 **3** 〔依据书、音乐等稍作改编的戏剧、电影、音乐等的〕版本; 改编本 **4 an English/Japanese/Spanish version** 英文/日文/西班牙文译本

vessel *n* **1** 船; 舰 **2** 〔盛液体用的〕容器, 器皿 **3** 〔人体的〕血管; 脉管; 〔植物的〕导管

victim *n* **1** 受害者; 牺牲者 **2** 〔恶劣情况的〕受灾者; 〔疾病的〕患者 **3** 牺牲品 **4 be a victim of its own success** 因成功而反受其害 **5 sacrificial victim** 献祭用的人[牲畜], 牺牲品 **6 fashion/style victim** 盲目追求时尚者

victory *n* **1** 胜利, 成功, 赢 —反义词 DEFEAT **2 be a victory for common sense** 常理获胜, 不偏不倚的裁决

vigorous *adj* **1** 强有力的; 积极的 **2 a vigorous opponent/defender etc** 顽强的反对者/捍卫者等 **3** 强健的, 精力旺盛的 **—vigorously** *adv*

violate *v* **1** 违背, 违反; 侵犯 **2** 〔用暴力〕挖掘〔坟墓〕; 强行进入〔圣地〕; 亵渎 **3 violate the peace/privacy of** 破坏…的和平/惊扰…的独处 **4** 强奸 **—violator** *n*

virtue *n* **1** 善; 德 —反义词 VICE **2** 美德; 德行 **3** 优点, 长处 **4 by/in virtue of** 凭借; 由于, 因为 **5 make a virtue of necessity** 爽爽快快[心甘情愿]地做非做不可的事

visible *adj* **1** 看得见的; 可见的 **2** 〔影响〕明显的; 显然的; 可察觉的 **3** 〔经常在电视上、报纸上等〕露面的

vital *adj* **1** 极其重要的, 必不可少的 **2** 有生命力的; 充满活力的, 生机勃勃的 **3** 维持生命所必需的

vivid *adj* **1** 〔记忆、梦境、描述等〕生动的; 逼真的; 清晰的 **2 vivid imagination** 活跃的想象力 **3** 〔色彩、图案〕鲜艳的; 鲜明的 **—vividly** *adv* **—vividness** *n*

vocational *adj* **vocational training/guidance/course etc** 职业培训/指导/课程等

voluntary¹ *adj* **1 voluntary work/service etc** 义务工作/服务等 **2 voluntary organization/society/institution etc** 志愿组织/团体/机构等 **3 voluntary worker/helper/assistant etc** 志愿人员/帮手/助手等 **4** 自愿的, 志愿的; 自发的 **5** 〔身体活动〕自如的, 随意的 —反义词 INVOLUNTARY **—voluntarily** *adv*

voluntary² *n* 〔教堂中的〕(风琴)演奏曲

voyage¹ *n* 〔乘船的长途〕航行

voyage² *v* 航行, 航海

W, w

wander¹ *v* **1 ►MOVE WITHOUT A DIRECTION 无目的的行进◄** 〔在某地方〕徘徊; 闲逛; 漫步 **2 ►MOVE AWAY 离开◄** 又作 **wander off** 〔从应该逗留的地方〕离开 **3 ►CHANGE THE SUBJECT 改变话题◄** 离题 **4 ►MIND/THOUGHTS 精神/注意力◄** 〔精神、注意力等因厌倦或焦虑而〕不集中, 走神 **5 sb's mind is wandering** 〔尤因年老而〕头脑糊涂 **6 ►ROAD/RIVER 道路/河流◄** 〔河流、道路等〕蜿蜒曲折 **—wanderer** *n*

wander² *n* 漫步

ward¹ *n* **1** 〔医院内的〕病房, 病室 **2** 〔城市的〕选区 **3** 受监护的人〔尤指儿童〕

ward² *v*

ward sth off *phr v* 防止〔疾病、危险、攻击等〕, 抵挡

weave¹ *v* **1 ►CLOTH 布◄** 织; 织〔布〕 **2 ►MAKE STH 制造某物◄** 编, 织 **3 ►STORY 故事◄** 编造〔故事或计划〕 **4 get weaving** 赶快〔用于告诉某人赶快开始做某事〕 **5 ►MOVE 移动◄** 迂回[穿插]行进

weave² *n* 织法; 编织式样

weight¹ *n* **1 ►WHAT SB/STH WEIGHS 某人/某物的重量◄** 〔某物的〕重量 **2 ►HOW FAT 有多胖◄** 〔某人的〕体重〔尤指肥胖〕 **3 ►HEAVINESS 重◄** 重 **4 ►HEAVY THING 重物◄** 重东西 **5 ►FOR MEASURING QUANTITIES 测量分量◄** 砝码, 秤砣 **6 ►FOR EXERCISE 用于锻炼◄** 杠铃 **7 ►SYSTEM 制度◄** 重量单位制; 衡制 **8 ►RESPONSIBILITY/WORRY 责任/忧虑◄** 重压, 负担 **9 a weight off your mind** 除去心理负担 **10 ►IMPORTANCE 重要性◄** 〔作出判断或形成意见时对某物的〕影响; 重要性 **11 throw your weight about/around** 指手画脚; 滥用权势 **12 throw your weight behind** 〔用权力和影响力〕支持〔某人〕 **13 pull your weight** 做

好分内事 **14 take the weight off your feet** 坐下 **15 weight of numbers**〔一个大群体〕联合起来的势力[影响] **16 summer-weight/winter-weight** 夏服/冬装〔用适合夏天或冬天穿的布料缝制〕 **17 ►SCIENCE** 科学◄〔作用在物体上的〕重力

weight² *v* 加重量于〔某物, 以使稳固不动〕, 使变重

wholesome *adj* **1** 对健康有益的 **2** 在道德上有益的 —**wholesomeness** *n*

wicked *adj* **1** 邪恶的; 缺德的 **2** 淘气的; 恶作剧的 **3** 棒的; 极好的 —**wickedly** *adv* —**wickedness** *n*

wilderness *n* **1** 荒野, 不毛之地 **2** 杳无人烟的地方 **3 in the wilderness** 离开权力和活动的中心;〔尤指政治上的〕在野状态

wit *n* **1 ►AMUSING** 娱人的◄〔说话〕机智风趣 **2 ►AMUSING PERSON** 说话风趣的人◄ 说话风趣诙谐的人 **3 wits** 机智 **4 have the wit to do sth** 足够明智, 作出正确决定〔做某事〕 **5 frighten/scare sb out of their wits** 吓坏某人 **6 at your wits' end** 智穷计尽, 束手无策 **7 not beyond the wit of** 有做某事的才智 **8 to wit** 即, 就是 —**witless** *adj*

withdraw *v* **1 ►MONEY** 金钱◄ 提取〔银行存款〕 **2 ►TAKE AWAY** 取走, 拿走◄〔常因正方决定而〕撤回, 撤销, 收回 **3 withdraw a remark/accusation** 撤回评论/撤销指控 **4 ►NOT TAKE PART** 不参加◄ **a)** 退出〔组织〕 **b)**〔使〕不参加〔活动、比赛等〕 **5 ►LEAVE** 离开◄ **a)** 离开〔尤指想独处或悄悄地去某处〕 **b)**〔尤指军队避免战败而〕撤退 **6 ►STOP COMMUNICATING** 停止交流◄ 变得冷漠; 离群索居

withstand *v* **1** 耐受, 承受〔酷热、严寒、高压等〕 **2** 抵挡; 顶住

witness¹ *n* **1**〔罪行或事故的〕目击者 **2**〔法庭上的〕证人 **3 bear witness** 证明〔某事是事实〕, 证实〔过去的事〕 **4**〔正式文件的签署的〕见证人, 连署人 **5 be witness to** 是…的目击者 **6** 见证〔表示笃信基督教的公开声明〕; 见证人〔作这种见证的人〕

witness² *v* **1** 目击, 亲眼看见〔尤指罪行或事故发生〕 **2 a)** 亲自经历〔重要事件或变迁〕 **b)** 是发生〔某事件〕的时间[地点] **3**〔在正式文件上〕连署; 在〔正式文件〕上签署作证 **4 a)** 表明; 是〔某事〕的证明 **b)**〔用于给刚提及的事举例〕作证 **5** 见证〔公开表示笃信基督教〕

witness to sth *phr v* 证实; 证明〔某事〕

worship¹ *v* **1** 敬奉〔神〕〔尤指在教堂、庙宇等祷告〕 **2** 景仰; 十分喜爱 **3 worship the ground sb walks on** 拜倒在某人脚下〔以致看不到他的缺点〕 —**worshipper** *n*

worship² *n* **1**〔对神的〕崇敬; 崇拜 **2**〔在教堂、庙宇等祈祷以示对神的〕崇拜; 敬仰 **3**〔对某人或物的〕强烈崇拜〔尤指看不见其错误〕; 仰慕 **4 Your/His Worship** 阁下〔对市长或地方法官等公务人员的称呼〕

wreck¹ *v* **1** 破坏, 糟蹋〔计划、关系、机遇等〕 **2** 使〔建筑、车辆等〕严重毁坏〔无法维修〕 **3** [一般用被动态]〔尤指船只在风暴中触礁〕失事

wreck² *n* **1** 沉船; 失事船 **2**〔尤指失事后汽车、飞机的〕残骸 **3** 十分紧张[疲累; 不健康]的人 **4**〔涉及多辆车的〕交通事故 **5** 残破的东西〔尤指汽车〕

Y, y Z,z

yield¹ *v* **1 ►CROPS/PROFITS** 庄稼/利润◄ 出产; 产生 **2 ►RESULT** 结果◄ 得出〔结果等〕 **3 ►AGREE** 同意◄ 服从, 被迫同意 **4 yield to your emotions/feelings** 屈从自己的感情/感觉 **5 ►TRAFFIC** 交通◄ 让〔其他车或人〕先行, 让路 **6 ►GIVE UP FIGHTING** 放弃战斗◄ 投降, 屈服 **7 ►MOVE/BEND/BREAK** 移动/弯曲/断裂◄〔因外在力量或压力而〕移动; 弯曲; 断裂 **8 ►CHANGE** 变换◄ 让与

yield sth ↔ **up** *phr v* 泄露, 揭示

yield² *n* 产量; 收益

zone *n*〔与周围地区有所不同的〕地区; 地带; 区域

The British Isles 不列颠群岛

The British Isles are made up of The United Kingdom (England, Scotland, Wales, and Northern Ireland) and the Republic of Ireland. 不列颠群岛由英国(英格兰、苏格兰、威尔士及北爱尔兰)和爱尔兰共和国组成。

THE UNITED KINGDOM 英国
capital city: London 首都: 伦敦
money: pounds sterling 货币: 英镑

SCOTLAND 苏格兰
capital city: Edinburgh 首府: 爱丁堡
patron saint: Saint Andrew 主保圣人: 圣安得烈
languages:
English, Scottish, Gaelic 语言: 英语, 苏格兰英语, 盖尔语

NORTHERN IRELAND 北爱尔兰
capital city: Belfast 首府: 贝尔法斯特
patron saint: Saint Patrick 主保圣人: 圣帕特里克
languages:
English, Irish, Gaelic 语言: 英语, 爱尔兰语, 盖尔语

Shetland Islands 设得兰群岛
Orkney Islands 奥克尼群岛
Hebrides 赫布里底群岛
SCOTLAND 苏格兰
Skye 斯凯岛
Inverness 因弗内斯
Aberdeen 阿伯丁
Loch Ness Monster 尼斯湖水怪
Ben Nevis 本尼维斯山
whisky 威士忌

Atlantic Ocean 大西洋
North Sea 北海
Glasgow 格拉斯哥
Edinburgh 爱丁堡
Londonderry 伦敦德里
Newcastle-upon-Tyne 泰恩河畔纽卡斯尔
NORTHERN IRELAND 北爱尔兰
THE UNITED KINGDOM 英国
Belfast 贝尔法斯特
ENGLAND 英格兰
Isle of Man 马恩岛
爱尔兰海 Irish Sea
Leeds 利兹
York 约克
Guinness 健力士啤酒
Blackpool 布莱克浦
Manchester 曼彻斯特
Liverpool 利物浦
Sheffield 设菲尔德
Dublin 都柏林
Anglesey 安格尔西
Snowdon 斯诺登山
Nottingham 诺丁汉
REPUBLIC OF IRELAND 爱尔兰共和国
伯明翰 Birmingham
Shakespeare 莎士比亚
Stratford-on-Avon❶
Cambridge 剑桥
James Joyce 詹姆斯·乔伊斯
WALES 威尔士
Cork 科克
Shamrock 三叶草
卡菲利城堡 *Caerphilly Castle*
Oxford 牛津
Big Ben 大本钟
Swansea 斯旺西
Bristol❷
London 伦敦
Cardiff 加的夫
Bath 巴斯
Dover 多佛尔
Brighton 布赖顿
Exeter 埃克塞特
Stonehenge 巨石阵
Isle of Wight 怀特岛
Channel Tunnel 海峡隧道
Newquay 纽基
Plymouth 普利茅斯
Isles of Scilly 锡利群岛
CORNWALL 康沃尔半岛
English Channel 英吉利海峡
Guernsey 根西岛
Jersey 泽西岛
0 150 miles 英里
0 250 km 千米

❶ 埃文河畔斯特拉特福
❷ 布里斯托尔

REPUBLIC OF IRELAND 爱尔兰共和国
capital city: Dublin 首都: 都柏林
patron saint: Saint Patrick 主保圣人: 圣帕特里克
languages:
English, Irish, Gaelic 语言: 英语, 爱尔兰语, 盖尔语

ENGLAND 英格兰
capital city: London 首府: 伦敦
patron saint: Saint George 主保圣人: 圣乔治
language:
English 语言: 英语

WALES 威尔士
capital city: Cardiff 首府: 加的夫
patron saint: Saint David 主保圣人: 圣大卫
languages:
English, Welsh 语言: 英语, 威尔士语

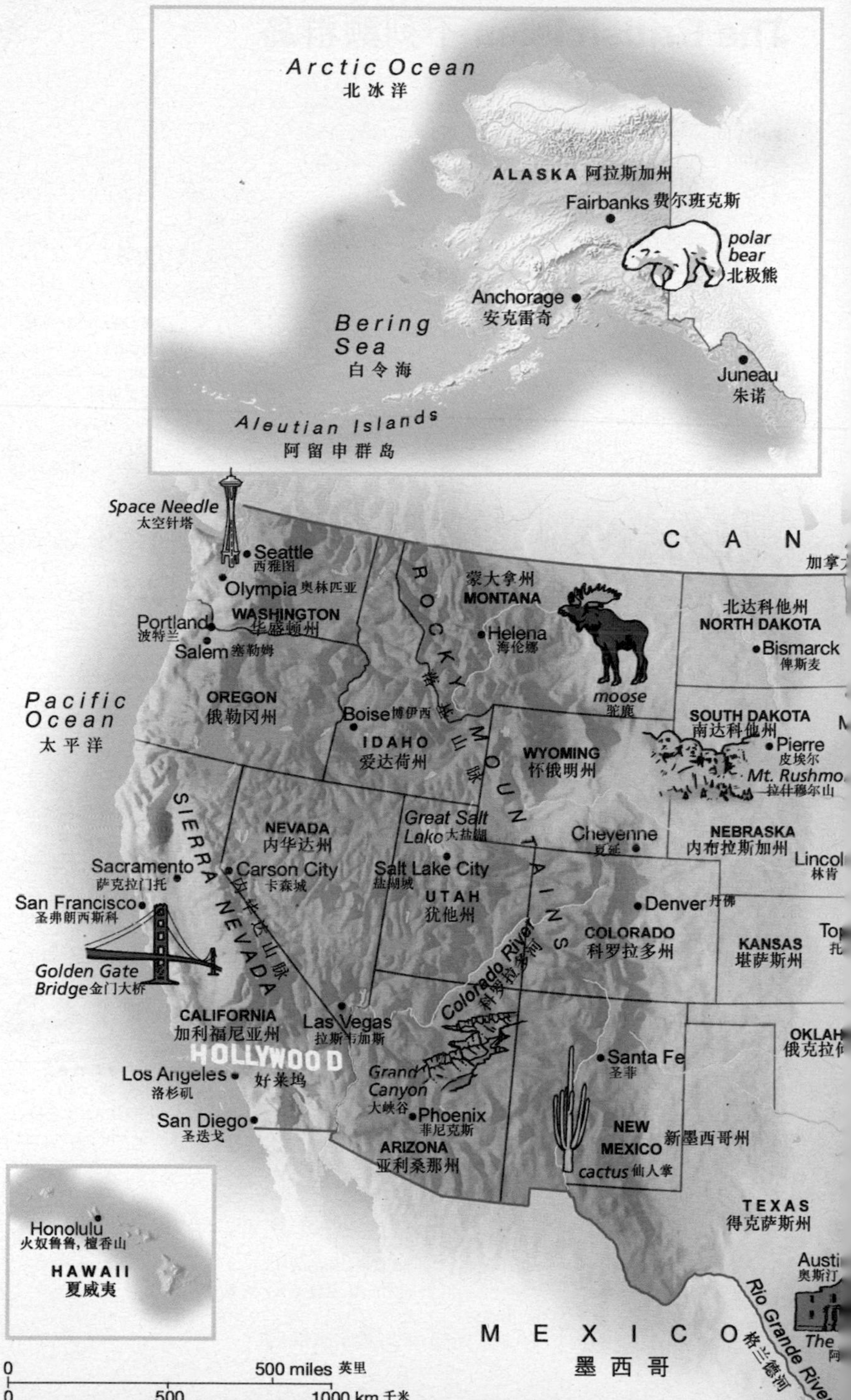
Arctic Ocean
北冰洋
ALASKA 阿拉斯加州
Fairbanks 费尔班克斯
polar bear 北极熊
Anchorage 安克雷奇
Bering Sea
白令海
Juneau
朱诺
Aleutian Islands
阿留申群岛
Space Needle
太空针塔
Seattle
西雅图
Olympia 奥林匹亚
WASHINGTON
华盛顿州
Portland
波特兰
Salem 塞勒姆
Pacific Ocean
太平洋
OREGON
俄勒冈州
Boise 博伊西
IDAHO
爱达荷州
蒙大拿州
MONTANA
Helena
海伦娜
moose
驼鹿
ROCKY MOUNTAINS
落基山脉
C A N
加拿大
北达科他州
NORTH DAKOTA
Bismarck
俾斯麦
SOUTH DAKOTA
南达科他州
Pierre
皮埃尔
Mt. Rushmore
拉什莫尔山
WYOMING
怀俄明州
Cheyenne
夏延
NEBRASKA
内布拉斯加州
Lincoln
林肯
SIERRA NEVADA
内华达山脉
NEVADA
内华达州
Carson City
卡森城
Sacramento
萨克拉门托
San Francisco
圣弗朗西斯科
Golden Gate Bridge 金门大桥
Great Salt Lake 大盐湖
Salt Lake City
盐湖城
UTAH
犹他州
Denver 丹佛
COLORADO
科罗拉多州
KANSAS
堪萨斯州
Colorado River
科罗拉多河
CALIFORNIA
加利福尼亚州
Las Vegas
拉斯韦加斯
HOLLYWOOD
好莱坞
Los Angeles
洛杉矶
San Diego
圣迭戈
Grand Canyon
大峡谷
Phoenix
菲尼克斯
ARIZONA
亚利桑那州
Santa Fe
圣菲
NEW MEXICO 新墨西哥州
cactus 仙人掌
OKLAHOMA
俄克拉何马州
TEXAS
得克萨斯州
Austin
奥斯汀
Honolulu
火奴鲁鲁, 檀香山
HAWAII
夏威夷
MEXICO
墨西哥
Rio Grande River
格兰德河
0
500 miles 英里
0
500
1000 km 千米

The United States of America 美利坚合众国

The United States of America is a very large country which is divided into 50 separate states. There are many different types of weather and land, with desert in the southwest near Mexico and snowy mountains in Alaska (the most northern part). New York is the biggest city in the US, but the capital city, where the President lives, is Washington, D.C. Native Americans lived in America for a long time before large numbers of people came from Europe to live there. 美国是一个很大的国家，共分成50个州。美国的气候和地形变化多样，在临近墨西哥的西南部有沙漠，在（最北端的）阿拉斯加州有白雪皑皑的群山。纽约是全美最大的城市，但首都却设在华盛顿特区，总统就住在这里。在大批的欧洲移民涌入美国定居之前，美国印第安人已经在这片大陆上繁衍生息了很长时间。

The United States is the world's richest and most industrial country. Most of the industries are in the northeastern part of the country, particularly in the area around the Great Lakes. 美国是世界上最富裕，也是工业化程度最高的国家。多数工业位于该国的东北部，特别是位于五大湖区域。

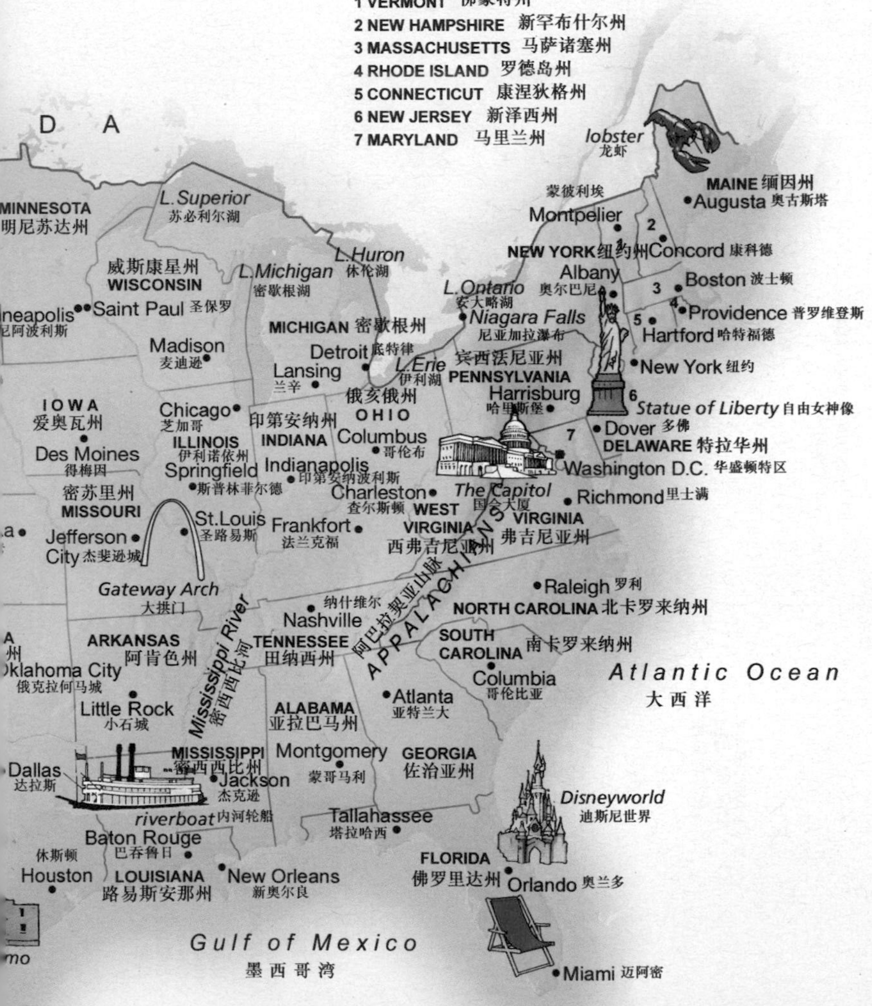

Central London
伦敦市中心
KING'S CROSS ST.PANCRAS STATIONS 国王十字路口站 圣潘克拉斯站
Regent's Park 摄政公园
EUSTON STATION 尤斯顿站
BRITISH MUSEUM 大英博物馆
MARYLEBONE STATION 马里尔伯恩站
Madame Tussaud's 图索德夫人蜡像馆
圣保罗大教堂 ST PAUL'S CATHEDRAL
LIVERPOOL STREET STATION 利物浦街站
SWISS RE BUILDING 瑞士再保险总部
Baker Street 贝克街
NELSON'S COLUMN AT TRAFALGAR SQUARE 特拉法尔加广场的纳尔逊纪念柱
PADDINGTON STATION 帕丁顿站
牛津街 Oxford Street
Oxford 牛津广场 Circus
Soho 苏豪区
Covent Garden 科文特加登
Fleet st 舰队街
TOWER OF LONDON 伦敦塔
Bayswater Road 贝斯沃特路
MARBLE ARCH 大理石拱门
EROS AT PICCADILLY CIRCUS 皮卡迪利广场的爱神厄洛斯雕像
National Gallery 国家美术馆
LONDON EYE 伦敦巨眼摩天轮
TATE MODERN 塔特美术馆
RIVER THAMES 泰晤士河
Hyde Park 海德公园
皮卡迪利街 Piccadilly
Green Park 绿色公园
The Mall 林荫道
St. James's Park 圣詹姆斯公园
WATERLOO STATION 滑铁卢站
LONDON BRIDGE STATION 伦敦桥站
TOWER BRIDGE 塔桥
N
ROYAL ALBERT HALL 皇家艾伯特大厅
Harrods 哈罗兹百货商店
HOUSES OF PARLIAMENT 议会大厦
BUCKINGHAM PALACE 白金汉宫
VICTORIA STATION 维多利亚站
Natural History Museum 自然历史博物馆
Victoria and Albert Museum 维多利亚和阿尔伯特博物馆
RIVER THAMES 泰晤士河

Central New York City 纽约市中心
NEW JERSEY
新泽西
HUDSON RIVER
哈得孙河
Lincoln Tunnel
林肯隧道
Holland Tunnel
荷兰隧道
Upper West Side
上西部
LINCOLN CENTER FOR THE PERFORMING ARTS
林肯表演艺术中心
大都会艺术博物馆
METROPOLITAN MUSEUM OF ART
GUGGENHEIM MUSEUM
古根海姆博物馆
中央公园
Central Park
Upper East Side
上东部
RCA BUILDING AT ROCKEFELLER CENTER
洛克菲勒中心的RCA大厦
5th Avenue
第五大道
Madison Avenue
麦迪逊大街
CHRYSLER BUILDING
克莱斯勒大厦
Queensboro Bridge
昆斯伯罗桥
Times Square
时代广场
Avenue of the Americas (6th Avenue)
美洲大道（第六大道）
Broadway
百老汇
Grand Central Station
中央车站
QUEENS
昆斯区
Madison Square Garden
麦迪逊广场花园
EMPIRE STATE BUILDING
帝国大厦
UNITED NATIONS HEADQUARTERS
联合国总部
Queens Midtown Tunnel
昆斯一米德敦隧道
Chelsea
切尔西
Madison Square Park
麦迪逊广场公园
Greenwich Village
格林尼治村
MANHATTAN
曼哈顿区
East Village
东村
East River Park
东河公园
Soho
苏豪区
Little Italy
小意大利
Lower East Side
下东部
Tribeca
特里贝卡
Chinatown
唐人街
EAST RIVER
东河
Manhattan Bridge
曼哈顿桥
World Financial Center
世界金融中心
Ground Zero
归零地
NEW YORK STOCK EXCHANGE
纽约证券交易所
BROOKLYN BRIDGE
布鲁克林桥
Wall Street
华尔街
Battery Park
炮台公园
BROOKLYN
布鲁克林区
Brooklyn Battery Tunnel
布鲁克林一炮台隧道
ELLIS ISLAND
埃利斯岛
GOVERNORS ISLAND
加弗纳斯岛
STATUE OF LIBERTY
自由女神像
LIBERTY ISLAND
自由女神岛
N

Colours and Their Associations
各种颜色及联想意义

In all cultures, different colours have different associations. Here are the associations that different colours have for British and American people. 在各种文化中，不同的颜色给人不同的联想。英美人对不同的颜色会产生下述这些联想。

Red 红色

Red warns of danger. The expression **red alert** is used to warn of a sudden and very dangerous situation. The expression **like a red rag to a bull** means that something is likely to make someone very angry and cause them to react violently. People imagine that the devil is red. Red heart shapes and red roses are used to represent romantic love. Red clothes, and lips and fingernails that are painted red are often associated with sexual desire. Red is thought to be an exciting colour; the expression **paint the town red** means to go out at night to bars, clubs etc and have a very good time. In politics, red is used to represent COMMUNISM and SOCIALISM. In the UK the LABOUR PARTY is represented by a red rose. If someone is **red in the face**, they are very embarrassed. It is traditional to welcome a king, queen, or president to a place by having a **red carpet** for them to walk on. 红色是对危险的警告。短语red alert（红色警报）用来警示突如其来而且十分凶险的境况。短语like a red rag to a bull（像红布之于公牛）的意思是某事物很可能会让某人雷霆大怒，并激起他们的剧烈反应。人们把恶魔想象成红色。红心形状和红玫瑰表示爱情。红衣、朱唇和红指甲通常与性欲相联系。红色被认为是一种让人兴奋的色彩，而短语paint the town red（将城镇刷成红色）指夜间出入于酒吧、夜总会等场合，玩到尽兴。政治上的红色代表共产主义和社会主义。在英国，工党的象征是一朵红玫瑰。如果某人red in the face（脸红），就说明他异常尴尬。国王、女王或总统造访某地，传统的欢迎方式是让他们走红地毯。

Blue 蓝色

In the US and UK it is very common for clothes to be blue. NAVY BLUE (=very dark blue) is a common colour for UNIFORMS such as those worn by sailors and the police, and formal clothes worn for work: *a navy blue suit*. In the UK, blue is the colour of the CONSERVATIVE PARTY. There is a joke that old ladies who support this party have a **blue rinse**, which means that they have their white or grey hair dyed a pale blue colour. The expression **blue-collar** is used to talk about social class. A blue-collar worker works in a factory, repairs machines etc (compare WHITE-COLLAR). Blue is connected with coldness. If you say that someone is **blue with cold**, you mean that they are very cold. Pale blue is associated with baby boys, who are traditionally dressed in this colour. Today many parents avoid dressing their boys in blue because they think that it strengthens sexual STEREOTYPEs. People who belong to royal families are said to be **blue-blooded** (=to have blue blood). This suggests that they are special, and different from ordinary people, who have red blood. 在美国和英国，蓝色的衣服极为常见。制服通常为深蓝色（navy blue），例如水手和警察穿的制服。另外上班穿的正装通常也是深蓝色：navy blue suit 深蓝色的套装。在英国，蓝色是保守党的代表色。有则笑话说支持该党的老太太将自己灰白的头发染成淡蓝色（即blue rinse）。短语blue-collar（蓝领）在谈及社会阶级时使用，蓝领工人指的是在工厂中做工或修理机器的那些人（比较WHITE-COLLAR）。蓝色与寒冷相联系，说某人blue with cold，意思是他被冻得青紫。浅蓝色常让人想到男婴，传统上他们正是穿这种颜色的衣服。现在很多父母回避给自己的男孩子穿浅蓝色衣服，因为他们认为这样会强化性别印记。王室成员常被人说成是blue-blooded（蓝血的），这暗示了他们的卓尔不群，与那些流淌着红色血液的普通民众区别开来。

Purple 紫色

Purple is associated with kings and queens and Roman EMPERORS, and in the past, these were the only people who were allowed to wear purple clothes. It is also connected with the pope. **Purple prose** is a piece of writing that has a grand style. If someone is **purple with rage** or **purple in the face**, they are extremely angry. 紫色与国王、女王和罗马皇帝相联系，过去只有他们可以穿紫色衣服。紫色还与教皇有关。purple prose 指一种风格华丽的散文。如果说某人purple with rage或purple in the face（脸气得发紫），意思是他们极度愤怒。

Green 绿色

British and American people think of green as the colour

that represents nature. If you describe a place as green, you mean that it is covered with grass or trees: *green fields*. The **green belt** is an area of land around a city where building is not allowed, in order to protect fields and woods. Green is the national colour of Ireland, also known as the EMERALD ISLE because of its many green fields. Green also means 'connected with the environment'. **Green issues** are ideas about the environment that are discussed in parliament, newspapers etc. In Britain and some other countries there is a political party called **the Green Party** which is chiefly interested in Green issues. Products that are described as green are thought to cause less harm to the environment than other products. Green is used to describe someone who is young and lacks experience in a job. Green represents jealousy. If you are **green with envy**, you are very jealous of someone who has something that you want. The expression **green-eyed monster** is used to mean sexual jealousy. If someone's face is green, they look pale and unhealthy, especially because they are about to VOMIT. 英美人认为绿色是代表自然的颜色。如果把某地描述成绿色的，说明此地植被繁茂，绿树成荫，绿草如茵：green fields 绿色的田野。绿化带（green belt）是为保护田野和树林而在城市周边设立的区域，其中不允许有建筑物。绿色是爱尔兰的民族色，因为岛上绿野遍布，所以爱尔兰也被称为“绿宝石岛”。绿色还意味着“与环境有关”。green issues（绿色问题）指议会和报纸等讨论的、有关环境的观点。英国及其他一些国家都有绿党（the Green Party），其兴趣点主要是环境问题。较之其他产品，绿色产品一般被认为能给环境带来较少的危害。绿色还被用来描述那些年轻和缺乏工作经验的人。绿色代表着妒忌，说某人 green with envy，就是说他特别眼红别人手里的东西。短语 green-eyed monster（绿眼怪）指在男女关系上争风吃醋。说某人脸色发绿，意思是他们脸色苍白得不健康，特别是描述他们快要呕吐时的脸色。

Grey *BrE*【英】, Gray *AmE*【美】灰色

In the US and UK, grey is connected with being dull and boring. It is, however, also a common colour for both men's and women's clothes. A **grey day** is an unpleasant one because the sky is full of grey clouds. Grey is connected with old people, and is used in expressions such as the **grey vote** (=the support of old people in an election) and the **grey pound** (=the money that older people have available to spend). 在美国和英国，灰色与单调乏味相联系。然而，灰色确是男装和女装的常用颜色。grey day 指天空乌云密布、天气不佳的一天。灰色与老年人相联系，并被用到 grey vote（指选举中老年选民的投票）和 grey pound（指年纪较大的人手中可用于消费的钱）等短语中。

Black 黑色

In the US and UK, black is a very popular colour for clothes of all types, and especially formal clothes. It is typically worn at funerals to show respect and sadness. Black clothes are often worn to social occasions in the evening, when women sometimes wear a **little black dress** (=a simple, short, black dress with no SLEEVEs, that is acceptable at most social occasions that happen in the evening or at night) and men sometimes wear a black DINNER JACKET. Black is associated with death and evil. WITCHes (=women thought to have magic powers that they use to do bad things) are thought to wear black and to have black cats. **Black magic** is believed to be magic that uses the power of the devil for evil purposes. The **black sheep** of a family is a member of a family who chooses to live his or her life in a way that is different from the other members, and that they disapprove of. 在美国和英国，黑色是所有款式的服装都会选用的流行色，正装更是惯于选用黑色。出席葬礼的人常穿黑色，以表达敬重和哀悼。在晚间的社交场合上，穿黑色衣服很常见。女士有时穿一件黑色无袖短裙（little black dress），男士则穿黑色无尾礼服。黑色常让人联想到死亡和邪恶。人们认为女巫穿黑衣，有黑猫相伴。巫术（black magic）被认为是借助魔鬼的力量来达成邪恶的目的。black sheep 指活法不同于家人的人，他们的活法被认为有辱家门。

White 白色

In the UK and US, white is associated with purity and VIRGINITY (=the condition of never having had sex). Traditionally, women wear long white dresses when they get married. White is also associated with moral goodness. People imagine that the Christian god and his ANGELS (=spirits that live with god and have white wings) wear white, and that HEAVEN (=believed by Christians to be the home of god, where good Christians go when they die) is a place where there are many white clouds. If someone's face looks as **white as a sheet**, they are pale because they are ill or very frightened. A **white flag** is traditionally used by people fighting in a battle, to show they SURRENDER (=accept that they have been defeated). The expression **white-collar** is used to talk about social class. A white-collar worker works in an office, bank etc (compare BLUE-COLLAR). 在英美，白色与纯洁和童贞相关。传统上，女子结婚时穿长长的白色婚纱。白色还让人联想到道德高尚。人们想象基督教的

上帝和天使都身着白衣，而天堂里也是白云飘飘的景象。如果说某人的脸 white as a sheet，意思是他们因生病或惊吓而面色惨白。白旗（white flag）是战争中投降的符号。短语 white-collar（白领）在言及社会阶层时使用，白领的工作地点是办公室、银行等（比较 BLUE-COLLAR）。

Pink 粉色

In the UK and US, pink is thought of as a pretty colour that is worn by women and girls. Pale pink is associated with baby girls, who are traditionally dressed in this colour. Today many parents avoid dressing their girls in pink because they think that it strengthens sexual STEREOTYPES. Pink is also connected with HOMOSEXUAL men, and is used in expressions such as the **pink pound** (=the money that homosexual men have available to spend). 在英国和美国，粉色被认为是一种漂亮的颜色，妇女和姑娘穿粉色衣服。淡粉色常让人联想到女婴，她们传统上会穿淡粉色衣服。现在很多父母回避给自己的女儿穿淡粉色，因为他们认为这样会强化性别印记。粉色还与男同性恋相联系，并被用在 pink pound（男同性恋手中可用于消费的钱）等短语中。

Decades 年代

The Fifties 50 年代

British and American people typically think of the 1950s as a time when people obeyed the law and respected authority, and when the idea of having sex without being married was fairly shocking. The British ECONOMY had been severely damaged by WORLD WAR II, and during the 1950s it improved only gradually. Many of the countries of the British EMPIRE became independent during the 1950s. The SUEZ CRISIS in 1956 made British people realize that their country was no longer a world power (=a country that has power in many parts of the world). The new world powers were the US and the Soviet Union. 英美人一般认为在20世纪50年代人们遵守法律和尊重权威，而不结婚就发生性行为是骇人听闻的。英国经济受到二战的严重破坏，在整个50年代它只是慢慢得到改善。大英帝国旗下的很多国家也在50年代纷纷独立。1956年的苏伊士运河危机让英国人意识到自己的国家已经不是一个世界强国了，新的世界强国是美国和苏联。

In the 1950s, youth culture changed a lot in the US. TEENAGERS began to have a separate culture from their parents. They listened to a new type of music, ROCK 'N' ROLL, played by people such as Bill HALEY and Elvis PRESLEY, which quickly became popular with young people around the world. The US became much more wealthy in the 1950s. Many people could afford to buy big cars and electrical equipment for their homes, and it is thought of as a time when American people were very hopeful about the future. 20世纪50年代的美国，年轻人文化发生了显著变化。青少年的文化与其父辈的文化有了分化。他们听新派的音乐——摇滚乐，这些由比尔·哈利、埃尔维斯·普雷斯利等人演唱的音乐受到年轻人的欢迎，迅速传遍全世界。在20世纪50年代美国变得愈加富裕，很多人有钱买得起大汽车和家用电器。这一时期的美国人被认为对未来满怀希望。

The Sixties 60 年代

The 1960s became known as the SWINGING SIXTIES and is thought of as a time when young people had a lot of

fun. The UK economy improved, and Britain became a very fashionable place, especially Liverpool, the home of the BEATLES, and London, where the most fashionable clothes were designed. Long hair for men became very fashionable, and for women, the miniskirt was very popular. 20世纪60年代以"时髦放纵的60年代"而为人所知，被认为是年轻人寻欢作乐的年代。英国的经济状况得到改善。此时的英国也成了时尚之地，特别是在诞生了甲壳虫乐队的利物浦和设计出最时尚衣服的伦敦。男子蓄长发非常时髦，而女子穿超短裙也异常流行。

When people in the US and UK think of the 1960s, they think of a time of great social change, when young people in many western countries began developing a new set of values and opinions that were very differ-

ent from the traditional ones their parents had. They began to take part in political protests against the VIETNAM WAR, and NUCLEAR WEAPONS. Young people known as HIPPIES began using drugs such as LSD for pleasure and the introduction of the PILL gave people much more sexual freedom. The music and clothes also expressed the new ways of thinking. In 1963 the people of the US were deeply shocked when President KENNEDY was shot dead. In 1969 the American ASTRONAUT Neil ARMSTRONG became the first man to walk on the moon. 英美人想起20世纪60年代，他们就会想到这个时期社会的巨大变迁，西方国家的年轻人开始形成一套与其父辈相去甚远的价值观念。他们开始投入到反对越南战争和核武器的政治抗议运动中。称为"嬉皮士"的年轻人开始用起迷幻药之类的毒品，而避孕药丸的出现给了人们更多的性自由。音乐和服饰也展示了新的思维方式。1963年肯尼迪总统的遇刺身亡使美国人大为震惊。1969年，美国宇航员内尔·阿姆斯特朗成为第一个踏上月球的人。

The Seventies 70年代

People in the US and UK generally think of the seventies as a time of bad style, when people wore FLARES (=trousers that become wider below the knee), PLATFORM SHOES (=shoes with very thick soles), and clothes made of artificial material such as NYLON. People decorated their homes in brown, orange, and purple. WALLPAPER with a strong pattern was popular. 英美人一般认为20世纪70年代是时尚风格被糟蹋的年代。那时人们穿喇叭裤、厚底鞋和尼龙等人造材料做成的衣服。人们用棕色、橙色和紫色来装饰房子，印有强烈视觉冲击图案的墙纸非常流行。

When people think of seventies popular music, they think of DISCO music. In the mid-seventies older people were shocked by a new type of youth culture and music, PUNK. When people in the US think of the 1970s, they think of the WATERGATE SCANDAL which forced President NIXON to stop being the president in 1974. People in the UK think of the 1970s as a time when TRADE UNIONS were very powerful. In 1979 the Labour government lost a general election after a 'WINTER OF DISCONTENT' when there were many STRIKES. 对于70年代的流行音乐，人们想到的是迪斯科音乐。70年代中期上了年纪的人对在年轻人中间流行的新派的朋克文化和音乐感到震惊。美国人想到70年代，他们会记起导致尼克松总统1974年下台的水门丑闻。英国人对70年代的印象是那时的工会势力很大。1979年在罢工盛行的"不满的冬天"之后，工党政府输掉了大选。

The Eighties 80年代

During the 1980s, the UK and the US had RIGHT-WING governments led by Margaret THATCHER and Ronald REAGAN. They encouraged people to be successful in business, and reduced the amount of help given to poor people. The aim was to make people more SELF-SUFFICIENT and less dependent on the state. The eighties was a time when a lot of people became very concerned with making money, and they did not care much about poorer people. Leaders of large corporations received increasingly large salaries while the wages of their workers grew much more slowly. Young people working on the stock market or in banks earned huge sums of money. 20世纪80年代的英国和美国分别是由玛格丽特·撒切尔和罗纳德·里根领导的右翼政府执政。他们鼓励人们在商业上获取成功，而削减对穷人的补给。目标是促使人民自力更生和降低对政府的依赖。80年代是

很多人一门心思只顾赚钱的时期，他们对穷人并不十分关心。大公司领导的薪水愈来愈高，而工人的工资却增长缓慢。在证券市场和银行从业的年轻人挣得大笔金钱。

In their homes, people typically had WALLPAPER, bed covers, curtains etc all in the same pattern; or they chose a MINIMALIST style in black and white with very simple furniture. It was in the eighties that it first became fashionable to CONVERT old warehouses in city centres into flats for people to live in. The eighties was also the decade when President GORBACHEV brought about great changes in the Soviet Union and greatly improved relations with the countries of the West. The BERLIN WALL was taken down in 1989, and by 1990 the COLD WAR had ended. 人们一般用相同图案的墙纸、窗帘和被罩来装点房子，他们或者选择尽可能简单的黑白装饰风格，其中家具非常简单。将城市中心的旧仓库改造成公寓供人居住正是在 80 年代开始流行。也是在 80 年代，戈尔巴乔夫总统使苏联发生了巨变并大大改善与西方国家的关系。柏林墙 1989 年被推倒，而到了 1990 年冷战也已经结束。

The Nineties 90 年代

In both the US and UK, the RIGHT-WING governments of the 1980s lost power, and were replaced by governments whose ideas were less extreme. Bill CLINTON became US President in 1993, and Tony BLAIR became Prime Minister of the UK in 1997. The nineties became known as the 'caring, sharing nineties', because it is thought that people were less concerned with making money, and more concerned about other people and the environment than they were in the 1980s. Diana, Princess of Wales, who died in 1997, was extremely popular because she was thought to be very caring, and to represent nineties values. 英美两国 80 年代的右翼政府纷纷下台，取而代之的是不那么极端的政府。1993 年比尔·克林顿就任美国总统，托尼·布莱尔 1997 年当上英国首相。90 年代以“关心、分享的 90 年代”为人所知，因为人们被认为已经不像 80 年代那样只关心赚钱了，而是把目光更多地投向他人和周围的环境。威尔士王妃戴安娜受到人们的热烈爱戴，因为她被认为充满爱心，代表着

90 年代的价值观。她于 1997 年仙逝。

Popular music included GRUNGE in the early 1990s, and BRITPOP in the late 1990s. Dance music (=music produced from electronic sounds usually with a fast beat) was popular through the whole of the nineties, especially with young people in CLUBS (=places where you go to dance at night) or at RAVES (=large parties in empty buildings). It became common for young people in clubs to take illegal drugs, especially ECSTASY. 流行音乐有 90 年代早期的垃圾乐和 90 年代晚期的不列颠流行乐。快节奏的电子舞曲在整个 90 年代都很流行，特别是受到夜总会和狂欢聚会中年轻人的喜爱。去夜总会的年轻人吸食毒品开始常见，特别是吸食“狂喜”迷幻药。

Christmas 圣诞节

Christmas is the most important festival in the US and the UK, and takes place on and around December 25th. Although it is a CHRISTIAN holiday, when the birth of JESUS is celebrated, people who are not Christian also celebrate Christmas as an occasion to give presents and spend time with their families. 圣诞节是英美最重要的节日，时间在12月25日前后。尽管圣诞节是个庆祝耶稣诞辰的基督教假日，非基督徒同样会欢度圣诞节，他们借此场合馈赠礼物及陪伴家人。

Before Christmas Day 圣诞日之前

Christmas shopping 圣诞购物

People traditionally buy presents for their friends and family for Christmas, and in the weeks before Christmas the shops are very busy. Many shops and stores decorate their buildings with lights and CHRISTMAS TREES, and pictures of things like HOLLY, and some big stores and malls also have a special area decorated like Santa's home, called SANTA'S GROTTO, where children can meet Santa and tell him what presents they want. Although many people enjoy Christmas shopping, some people complain that the holiday is too COMMERCIAL (=concerned with spending money and making a profit), and that the real purpose of Christmas should be about remembering the story of Jesus' birth and being kind to other people. 人们在圣诞节有买礼物送给朋友和家人的传统，而商店在节前的几周也是顾客满堂。很多商店和商场用彩色灯泡、圣诞树和绘有冬青树枝等的图片装点建筑。大的商场和购物中心还专门辟出一片地方布置成圣诞老人屋（Santa's Grotto），孩子们可以去那里见圣诞老人并告诉他自己想要什么礼物。尽管有很多人享受在过圣诞节时逛街购物，还是有人抱怨说假日过于商业化，说圣诞节的真正初衷应该是铭记耶稣出生的故事和善待他人。

Christmas cards 圣诞贺卡

People also send CHRISTMAS CARDS to their friends in order to say Merry Christmas or Happy Christmas (*BrE*). Christmas cards usually have pictures relating to Christmas traditions and winter, such as Christmas trees, HOLLY, snowmen, and SANTA CLAUS. Cards with religious messages usually show pictures of the NATIVITY (=the birth of Christ). 人们还给朋友送贺卡，以恭祝"圣诞快乐！"（Merry Christmas, Happy Christmas【英】）。圣诞贺卡上通常绘有与圣诞节传统和冬季有关的图片，例如圣诞树、冬青树枝、雪人和圣诞老人。含有宗教内容的贺卡通常绘有耶稣诞生图。

Christmas carols 圣诞颂歌

During the Christmas period there are many performances of CAROLS (=special religious Christmas songs). They are sung in church as part of a religious ceremony, and schools have special concerts in which their students sing carols. People sometimes **go carol singing** (*BrE*) or **go caroling** (*AmE*), which means they sing carols outside in a large group, especially outside people's houses, and collect money for CHARITY (=money given to help people who are poor, sick etc). 圣诞节期间有很多场唱颂歌的表演。在教堂中唱圣诞颂歌是宗教仪式的一部分。学校会举办学生圣诞颂歌演唱的专场音乐会。人们有时走出家门

加入一大群人中唱圣诞颂歌(go carol singing【英】, go caroling【美】), 特别是到人家的房子外面唱, 以此来为慈善事业募捐。

Christmas decorations 圣诞装饰

Many people decorate their homes for Christmas. Most people buy a Christmas tree, which they put small lights and decorations on. Some people also buy plants with bright red leaves called POINSETTIAs, and hang branches of MISTLETOE above their doors. There is a tradition that if you are **under the mistletoe** with someone else, you have to kiss them. In the UK, people hang shiny, brightly coloured decorations made of paper from the ceiling or along the walls inside their homes. Some people both in the UK and the US put small lights along the edges of their windows, the roof, and the main door of their houses. And many people decorate their front doors with a WREATH (=a circle made of green leaves). 很多人为过圣诞节而把房子装点一番。多数人会买一株圣诞树, 在上面悬挂彩色小灯泡和其他装饰。有些人买来长着鲜红色叶子的植物圣诞红, 并且在门上悬挂槲寄生的小树枝。一项传统是如果你与别人一同站在槲寄生小树枝下, 你就要亲他。在英国, 人们在家里从天花板上或者沿着墙壁悬挂纸制的、颜色鲜亮的装饰物。在英国和美国有些人在窗框、屋顶以及房子的大门上挂上彩色小灯泡。还有很多人用一个绿叶编成的环来装饰房子的正门。

Parties 聚会

In the UK most offices have a Christmas party. The stereotype of the office party is an event where everyone drinks too much and people say things to their boss that they would never say at any other time. 在英国, 办公室大都举行一场圣诞节聚会。在典型的办公室圣诞节聚会上, 每个人都会饮过量的酒, 人们向老板吐露自己在其他时候都不会说出的话。

Christmas food 圣诞食品

People usually eat more food and drink more alcohol at Christmas than at other times of the year. In the US, people eat CHRISTMAS COOKIES, special cookies that are baked at home. Traditional British food includes CHRISTMAS CAKE and MINCE PIEs. 人们通常在圣诞节大吃大喝, 这是一年中的其他时候所没有过的。在美国, 人们享用圣诞甜饼, 这是家里特别烘制的甜饼。英国传统的圣诞节食品包括圣诞蛋糕和肉馅饼。

Christmas Eve – December 24th 圣诞前夕——12月24日

The day before Christmas Day is known as CHRISTMAS EVE. Some people go to church to a special service called MIDNIGHT MASS (*BrE*) or **Christmas Eve service** (*AmE*). Other people have a drink with their friends. Children get very excited on Christmas Eve because they believe that Santa Claus will come down the CHIMNEY of their house in the night and put presents in the CHRISTMAS STOCKING (=a special bag shaped like a large sock) at the end of their bed or on the MANTELPIECE. They leave a glass of SHERRY (=a type of strong wine) and a mince pie, a small sweet PIE filled with RAISINs, apples, and SPICEs, for Santa. 圣诞日之前的一天称为圣诞前夕。有人去教堂做一次特别的礼拜, 叫做午夜弥撒(Midnight Mass【英】)或圣诞前夕礼拜(Christmas Eve service【美】)。其他人则会和朋友们喝上几杯。孩子们在圣诞前夕十分兴奋, 因为他们相信圣诞老人会顺着家里房子的烟囱爬下, 然后把礼物放到挂在床头或壁炉架上的圣诞袜里。他们留给圣诞老人一杯雪利酒和一块百果馅饼, 即用葡萄干、苹果和调料做成的小甜馅饼。

Christmas Day – December 25th 圣诞日——12月25日

Christmas Day is a public holiday and people spend the day with their families. They open their presents and then have a special meal called CHRISTMAS DINNER. This is typically TURKEY with potatoes and other

vegetables, usually CARROTs and SPROUTs. In the UK, this is followed by CHRISTMAS PUDDING. At the start of the meal, British people usually pull a CHRISTMAS CRACKER (=a brightly coloured paper tube that makes a small explosion when you pull it apart, and that contains a small toy, a paper hat, and a joke). 圣诞日是一个公共假日，这一天人们和家人一起欢度节日。他们拆开收到的礼物，然后享用一顿特别的圣诞大餐，通常包含火鸡、土豆以及胡萝卜、豆芽等蔬菜。在英国，用餐之后还食用圣诞布丁。圣诞大餐开始的时候，英国人通常会拉响一个圣诞爆竹（它是一个颜色鲜艳的纸筒，拉开的一瞬会有轻微的爆炸声响起，内盛一个小玩具、一个小纸帽和一则笑话）。

After Christmas Day 圣诞日次日

Many stores have special SALEs (=a period of time when goods can be bought cheaper) on the day after Christmas. In the UK, these used to be called the **January sales** because they did not start until January, but now they start straight after Christmas. 圣诞节的第二天很多商场都推出特卖活动。在英国这被称为“一月大甩卖”，因为在过去只有到了1月份才推出这种特卖，但是现在圣诞日次日商场就会推出这种活动。

In the UK, the day after Christmas Day is called BOXING DAY, and is also a public holiday. It is called Boxing Day because in the past it was the day when rich people gave their servants a present of money known as a 'Christmas box'. There are a lot of sporting events on Boxing Day. 在英国，圣诞日次日叫做“节礼日”，也是一个公共假日。之所以叫“节礼日”，是因为在过去有钱人常给他们的仆人送节礼，即一份称作Christmas box的钱。在节礼日这天有很多体育比赛举行。

TWELFTH NIGHT is 6th January, twelve days after Christmas, and is the day when people take down their decorations and remove their Christmas trees. 1月6日是主显节前夕，即圣诞日之后的第十二天。这一天人们拆掉圣诞装饰并将圣诞树移走。

Education 教育

In the US, children must go to school from the age of 5 or 6 to between the ages of 14 and 16, depending on the law in the state where they live. In the UK, all children have to go to school between the ages of 5 and 16. In some parts of the UK, PRESCHOOL or NURSERY Education is provided by the local government for children aged 3 and 4. In the US, parents have to pay for nursery education. 美国孩子从5或6岁至14或16岁期间必须就学接受教育，这取决于其所居住州的法律。英国孩子必须接受学校教育的年龄是5到16岁。在英国的一些地区，地方政府为3岁和4岁的儿童提供学前教育或幼儿园教育。美国父母要为子女的幼儿园教育付费。

State and Private Schools 公立学校和私立学校

In both the US and the UK, most children go to schools that are provided by the government. In the US these are known as public schools, and in the UK they are known as STATE SCHOOLs. 在美国和英国，大多数孩子都是去政府设立的学校上学。这些公立学校在美国称为public school，在英国称为state school。

In the UK, some children go to schools that their parents pay for. These are called private schools, but the most famous ones, such as ETON, HARROW, WINCHESTER, and RUGBY, are called PUBLIC SCHOOLs. Public schools are often BOARDING SCHOOLs, where students live as well as study. Some British people think that children at public schools get a better education than children at state schools. 在英国，有些孩子上自费学校。这些学校叫做私立学校，但最著名的私立学校却称为“公学”，如伊顿公学、哈罗公学、温切斯特公学和拉格比公学。公学通常是寄宿制学校，即学生不仅在学校中学习，还要住在那里。有些英国人认为孩子上公学比上公立学校能接受更好的教育。

Some children in the US also go to schools that their parents pay for, which are called PRIVATE SCHOOLs. Private schools in the US are often run by church groups, when they are known as PAROCHIAL SCHOOLs, but there are private schools, especially on the East Coast, that are considered to be very good, such as the **Hotchkiss School**, **Andover Academy**, and **Choate Rosemary Hall**. 美国也有些孩子去自费学校读书，这些学校称作私立学校。美国的私立学校通常由教会团体开办，因此称作教会学校。但是也有一些被认为质量极佳的私立学校，特别是在东海岸，例如霍奇基斯学校、安多弗私立中学和乔特－罗斯玛丽·霍尔学校。

Subjects 课程

In the US, national, state, and local governments decide what subjects will be taught in the schools, so children in different states and even within the same state may be taught slightly different things. Most schools, however, teach very similar subjects. 在美国，联邦、州和地方政府决定在学校中可以教授哪些课程，所以不同的州，即便是同一个州的学生学的东西都可能会有些微差别。但大多数学校的课程都差别不大。

In England and Wales the subjects taught in schools are listed in the NATIONAL CURRICULUM, which was introduced in 1988, and lists in detail the subjects that all children must study. Children are tested at the ages of 7, 11, 14, and 16 to see if they have reached a particular level of achievement in those subjects. The National Curriculum does not apply in Scotland, where each school decides what subjects it will teach. 在英格兰和威尔士，学校教授的课程由1988年颁布的全国统一课程表列明，其中详细列出所有孩子都必修的学科。7、11、14和16岁的孩子要参加测试，以检查他们是否已经达到某一特定的学业程度。全国统一课程表在苏格兰并不适用，那里的每个学校自行决定教授什么课程。

Some British schools have prayers and religious teaching, but US public schools are not allowed to include prayers or to teach particular religious beliefs. 有些英国学校设有祈祷仪式和宗教教育，但美国的公立学校不允许有祈祷仪式和传授特别的宗教信仰。

Examinations 考试

In the US, students do not take national examinations as the British do. Students in HIGH SCHOOL usually take examinations in the subjects they are studying at the end of each SEMESTER, and their marks in their courses are based partly on these examinations and partly on other tests, HOMEWORK, and work done in class. The marks a student gets in his or her courses are added together, and then divided by the number of classes the student has taken to produce the student's GRADE POINT AVERAGE, or **G.P.A.** The highest G.P.A. possible is 4.0, which is equal to getting an A in every class. 和英国不同，美国的学生并不参加全国性的考试。高中生在每个学期期末参加所学习的学科的相关考试，学科的学分部分基于这些考试，另外取决于其他测试、家庭作业以及课堂表现。各科学分相加然后除以学生所修课程的总数，这样就算出学生的平均分（Grade Point Average或GPA）。最高平均分可能达到4.0，这相当于每门课程都拿到A。

Students who have passed enough courses GRADUATE from high school at the end of the twelfth grade, and receive a HIGH SCHOOL DIPLOMA from their school at a graduation ceremony which is held at the end of the school year. American students who want to go to university must take a test called the SAT or another test called the **ACT**, and some universities ask students to take tests in several subjects as well. Students give their test scores, G.P.A., and a record of their other achievements to a university when they apply to go to that university. 通过足够多的课程的学生在念到12年级时从高中毕业，并在学年末的毕业典礼上被授予高中毕业文凭。美国打算上大学的学生必须参加学业能力倾向考试(SAT)或美国大专院校测试(ACT)，有些大学还要求学生参加几门课程的测试。向大学提出入学申请时，学生会提交自己的测试分数、平均分和其他方面成绩的记录。

At age 16, students in England and Wales take GCSE examinations in subjects that they have been studying for two years. The GCSE examinations involve a final examination as well as CONTINUOUS ASSESSMENT, a way of judging a student's level of achievement by looking at their **coursework** (=work that they do during the course). The marks students get in their examinations help them decide which subjects to study for A-LEVEL, if they are not planning to leave school. Students who take A-levels study for two years and take A/S level exams after the first year, and A2 level exams at the end of the second year. Universities select their students on the basis of the A-level results. In order to go to a good university and study a popular subject such as medicine or English, students usually need to get grade A or B in all their A-levels. For less popular subjects, they do not need to achieve such high grades. 英格兰和威尔士的学生在16岁时参加普通中等教育证书考试(GCSE)，考试范围是他们过去两年学习的学科。普通中等证书考试包括终结考试和连续性评估，后者参考学生平时的作业完成情况来评估其学业成绩。如果学生想继续留校学习，这个考试成绩有助于学生决定为参加高级程度考试(A-level)要修习哪些学科。参加高级程度考试的学生要学习两年，第一年结束时参加高级补充程度会考(A/S level)，第二年结束时参加第二阶段的高级程度会考(A2 level)。大学根据高级程度考试的分数来录取学生。要上好的大学或学习医学、英语等热门专业，学生在所有的高级程度考试中通常成绩都要达到A或B。对于不那么热门的专业，学生并不需要取得如此高的分数。

Social Events and Ceremonies 社会活动和仪式

In US high schools there is a formal ceremony for graduation (=when the students have completed their high school education). Students wear a special hat and a gown (=a long, loose piece of clothing worn for special ceremonies) and receive their DIPLOMA. The student who has earned the highest grades in his/her courses all through the high school and who therefore has the highest G.P.A. in the class is the class VALEDICTORIAN. The valedictorian usually gives a speech at the graduation ceremony, and in smaller towns his/her photograph may be printed in the local newspaper. 美国的高中有正式的毕业典礼。学生头戴特别的帽子，身着长袍，获授文凭。整个高中阶段在所有学科上获得最高分数的学生，亦即班级中平均分最高的学生就是班级的毕业生代表。毕业生代表通常要在毕业典礼上发言，小城镇中的毕业生代表的照片还会登上当地报纸。

Sports events, especially football, are very popular in US schools, and CHEERLEADERs lead the students in supporting the school teams. There are often dances, plays, and musical events organized and performed by the students. At the end of the last year of high school there is a special formal dance, often held at a hotel, called a PROM. Most students buy a YEARBOOK each year and their friends write messages in it and sign it. 体育运动，特别是橄榄球运动，在美国的学校中非常受欢迎，学生们在拉拉队的带领下为校队加油。还有不少学生组织和表演的舞会、戏剧和音乐演出。高中最后一学年结束的时候有一场特别的舞会，通常在酒店中举行，叫做prom(班级舞会)。大多数学生每年都买一本学校年鉴，并让好友在上面签名留言。

In the UK, schools often have dances, plays, and musical events, and many students play sports. In many schools the SPORTS DAY and the school FETE are important events. 在英国，学校通常有舞会、戏剧和音乐演出，参加体育运动的学生也很多。在很多学校，运动会和学校游乐会都是学校的大事。

Universities 大学

In the US, students usually study at college for four years, although some students take five years to finish their DEGREE. Students usually choose one main subject to study, which is called their MAJOR, and often choose to study one other subject, called a MINOR. If you major in a subject, you study it as your major subject: *Karen majored in music.* Students must also take classes in other subjects. Some universities are partly paid for by state governments, but even students at these universities must pay a lot of money for their education. Most students work PART-TIME while they are studying, to pay for their living costs. Many borrow money which they begin to pay back after they GRADUATE (=successfully complete their course), and it sometimes takes many years to pay it back. 在美国，学生在大学中通常学习四年，尽管有些学生五年才完成学位。学生通常选择一个主要学科来学习，称之为专业，并且通常还选择一个辅修科目。如果学生选择了一个学科，就把它当作自己的主攻专业来学习：Karen majored in music. 卡伦学习的专业是音乐。学生还要上其他学科的课程。有些大学的经费部分由州政府支付，但学生即便是在这样的大学中学习也要交不少钱。大多数学生边学习边做兼职工作，以此挣生活费。很多学生贷款上学，毕业后开始偿还，

有时需要多年才能还清。

In England and Wales university courses usually last for three years, and students typically study either one subject, or two subjects that are related. In Scotland the university system is different, and courses usually continue for four years. In the UK, students take out STUDENT LOANS, which means that they borrow money from a bank to pay for their living costs, and often have large debts by the time they finish their course. Some students from poor families receive a GRANT from the government to help pay for their living costs. Since 1999, students have had to pay TUITION FEES. Originally, these were £1000 a year, but from 2005, universities can charge as much as £3,000 a year for tuition fees. The fees mean that students have to borrow even more money, so the government introduced a system which means students pay the money back gradually, after they have left university, and only after their income goes over £15,000 a year. 在英格兰和威尔士，大学课程通常持续三年，学生一般修一个学科或修两个相近的学科。苏格兰的大学体系有所不同，课程通常有四年。在英国，学生可以申请学生贷款，即从银行借钱来偿付生活费用，这样他们在上完大学后往往背上一大笔债。有些家庭贫困的学生可以领到政府的助学金来支付生活费用。从1999年开始学生必须要缴纳学费。过去学费是1000英镑，但从2005年起，大学可以收取多达3000英镑的学费。这些费用意味着学生要借更多的钱，因此政府推出一项制度，允许学生在离校后并且年收入超过15000英镑的前提下分步偿还贷款。

class 年级	UK school 英国学校	age 年龄	US school 美国学校	class 年级
	nursery school, playgroup, or 托儿所，幼儿游戏组或	3	nursery school (optional) 托儿所（非强制教育）	
	kindergarten (optional) 幼儿园（非强制教育）	4		
reception class 学前班	infant school 幼儿学校	5	kindergarten 幼儿园	
year 1 一年级		6		first grade 一年级
year 2 二年级		7		second grade 二年级
year 3 三年级	junior school, primary school 小学	8	elementary school**/grade school 小学	third grade 三年级
year 4 四年级		9		fourth grade 四年级
year 5 五年级		10		fifth grade 五年级
year 6 六年级		11		sixth grade 六年级
year 7 七年级	secondary school 中学	12	junior high school 初中	seventh grade 七年级
year 8 八年级		13		eighth grade 八年级
year 9 九年级		14		ninth grade (freshman) 九年级
year 10 十年级		15		tenth grade (sophomore) 十年级
year 11 十一年级		16		eleventh grade (junior) 十一年级
year 12 十二年级	technical college, sixth form college* 工学院，预科学校	17		twelfth grade (senior) 十二年级
year 13 十三年级		18		freshman 大学一年级
first year (fresher) 大学一年级	university 大学	19	college 大学	sophomore 大学二年级
second year 大学二年级		20		junior 大学三年级
third/final year 大学三年级		21		senior 大学四年级
postgraduate 研究生	university 大学	22	graduate school 研究生院	
		23		

* Some areas do not have sixth form colleges, and students continue to study for a further two years in the sixth form of their secondary school instead. 有些地区没有预科学校，那里的学生就在中学的六年级之后再继续学习两年时间。

** In some areas children go to elementary school up to grade 5, and then go to middle school for grades 6, 7, and 8. They then go to high school for grades 9, 10, 11, and 12. 在有些地区儿童在小学上到五年级，然后到初中上六年级、七年级和八年级。他们然后再到高中上九年级、十年级、十一年级和十二年级。

Multiculturalism 文化多样性

Multiculturalism in the UK 英国的文化多样性

Ethnic Diversity in the UK 英国的种族多样性

The traditional image of the United Kingdom is of a country with a mainly white population. Although white people make up over 90% of the UK population, there are also many other groups living in Britain, who make up nearly 10% of the population. The largest ETHNIC group is Asian, and they are over 4% of the population. Included in this group are people from India, Pakistan, and Bangladesh. The other main ethnic groups are Afro-Caribbean, African, Arabic, and Chinese. 英国给人的传统印象是一个主要由白种人构成的国家。尽管白种人占英国总人口的90% 以上，还是有许多其他族群的人生活在英国，占到总人口的近 10%。人数最多的是亚洲族群，占英国人口的4% 以上。归入这一族群的是来自印度、巴基斯坦和孟加拉国的人。其他主要的族群有非裔加勒比人、非洲黑人、阿拉伯人和华人。

There are approximately 4.5 million non-white people living in Britain, and about 80% live in large cities in England. Most live in London, Manchester, Birmingham or Leeds, or in areas close to these cities. In London, almost 30% of the population are Asian and black. 大约有 450 万的非白色人种生活在英国，而其中的80% 生活在英格兰的大城市中。大多数人居住在伦敦、曼切斯特、伯明翰和利兹，或者生活在靠近这些城市的区域。几乎 30% 的伦敦人口都是亚洲人和黑人。

Immigrants arriving in Britain on the *Empire Windrush* (1950s)
移民乘“帝国疾风号”轮船到达英国（20 世纪 50 年代）

Immigration to the UK 英国的移民

Immigration to the UK increased greatly after World War II. During the 1950s, the country was still rebuilding its economy after the war. It needed workers for the factories, and for the hospitals of the new National Health Service. Immigrants were encouraged to come to Britain to take up these jobs. Many came from Ireland and from countries that were part of the former British Empire, especially the West Indies, India, and Pakistan. Immigrants from these Commonwealth countries held a British passport and had the right to British citizenship. At first, they were considered to be different and not everyone welcomed them. In the 1970s, a law was passed which made it illegal to treat black people differently from anyone else. 第二次世界大战后移民英国的人口激增。在 20 世纪 50 年代，英国还处于战后经济恢复重建阶段，不仅需要产业工人，还需要新的国民保健计划中医院的服务人员。当时鼓励移民去英国从事这些工作。很多移民来自爱尔兰和前大英帝国旗下的国家，特别是西印度群岛、印度和巴基斯坦。这些英联邦国家的移民拥有英国的护照和获取英国公民身份的权利。最初这些移民被视为异类，并不是每个人都欢迎他们的到来。70 年代通过了一项法律规定歧视黑人是非法的。

Now, 50 years later, the children and grandchildren of the earlier immigrants are well-established members of British society. 50 年之后的今天，早期移民的子孙已

经成为英国社会实实在在的成员了。

Britain is a member of the EU, and citizens of other EU countries are allowed to live and work in the UK. In 2004, ten new countries joined the EU. These were mostly countries that were formerly part of communist Eastern Europe. People from countries such as Poland and the Czech Republic have come to live and work in Britain. 英国是欧盟的成员国，所以允许欧盟其他成员国的公民到英国生活和工作。2004 年又有 10 个国家加入欧盟。这些国家大部分是以前东欧共产主义阵营中的国家。波兰和捷克共和国等国家的人也来到英国生活和工作。

Food 食品

Britain's taste in food has changed over the last 30 years. In place of the food that used to be typical of British cooking, it is possible to eat a wide variety of foods from around the world. 英国的饮食口味在过去的 30 年中发生了变化。取代过去典型的英式菜肴的是可以吃到的来自世界各地种类繁多的食品。

Indian food is especially popular and there are Indian and Chinese restaurants in almost every town and city. Two of the UK's most popular Indian dishes, Balti and Chicken Tikka Masala, are not eaten in India. They were created by Indian cooks in Britain who wanted to make dishes that people in the UK would like. Areas with a lot of Balti restaurants, such as Brick Lane in London, are very popular with local people and with tourists. 印度饭菜尤其受青睐，几乎每个小镇和城市都有印度餐馆和中餐馆。英国最火的两样印度菜肴，巴尔蒂菜和泰特拉齐妮鸡在印度并没有。这两样菜是印度厨师的创意，想以此来迎合英国人的口味。巴尔蒂菜餐馆林立的区域，例如伦敦的布里克巷，大受当地人和游客的欢迎。

Chinese food is also very popular. London, Manchester, and Birmingham all have areas in the centre of the cities that are called Chinatown, where there are many Chinese restaurants and shops, and where many Chinese people live. 中餐也很风行。伦敦、曼切斯特和伯明翰的市中心都有叫做唐人街的地方，那里有很多中餐馆和商店，同时也是很多华人的居住区。

Religious Faith and Religious Holidays 宗教信仰和宗教假日

The UK is officially a Christian country, and the Queen is head of the Church of England. However, in British schools, children are taught about other religious faiths, and people living in the UK have the legal right to believe in any religion without being criticized or punished. About 70% of British people consider themselves to be Christian. Other religious groups make up a further 15% of the population, and they include Muslims, Hindus, Sikhs, Jews, and Buddhists. In the 2001 census, about 15% of British people said they did not believe in any religion at all. 英国是一个正统的基督教国家，女王是英国国教会的领袖。然而英国的学校也把其他的宗教信仰宣讲给学生。法律规定英国人有信仰任何宗教而不受指摘或惩罚的权利。大约 70% 的英国人认为自己是基督徒。其他宗教群体占到总人口的 15%，其中包括穆斯林、印度教徒、锡克教徒、犹太教徒和佛教徒。2001 年的人口普查表明，有 15% 的英国人声明自己不信仰任何宗教。

The main Christian festivals – Easter and Christmas – are public holidays in the UK, and many non-Christians celebrate Christmas, though not in a religious way. British people are becoming more familiar with non-Christian religious festivals. Many will have heard of the Muslim festivals of Eid ul-Fitr and Eid ul-Adha. Hindus living in Britain celebrate the religious festival of Diwali with fireworks during October and November. 主要的基督教节日复活节和圣诞节在英国是公共假日，很多非基督徒同样会庆祝圣诞节，尽管不是以宗教的方式来庆祝。英国人对非基督教的宗教节日也越来越熟悉，很多人都听说过开斋节和宰牲节两个穆斯林的节日。10 月和 11 月份，英国的印度教徒以燃放烟火的方式来庆祝其宗教节日排灯节。

Festivals 节日

On the last Sunday and Monday in August, there is a big festival in Notting Hill in London. It started as quite a small event in 1959, and was organized by people from the West Indies as a Caribbean street festival. Over the years, it has grown in size, and now over one million people come to the Carnival every year. It is a huge multiracial event, and it is now the biggest street festival in Europe. 在 8 月份的最后一个周日和周一，伦敦的诺丁山地区有一个大的节庆。1959 年这还是一个小活动，它由来自西印度群岛的人组织，是一个加勒比人的街头狂欢节。多年过去，它的范围已经变大，现在每年有超过一百万的人来此狂欢。这是一个盛大的多种族的节庆，是欧洲最大的街头狂欢节。

Ethnic Diversity in the USA 美国的种族多样性

Americans come from all parts of the world. White Americans still make up the majority of the US population (about 75%). In 2000, blacks or African Americans were about 12% of the population, Asians and Pacific Islanders nearly 4%, and American Indians and Alaska Natives were about 1%. About 8% were of mixed race or other races. A separate category counts Hispanics as 13% of the population – Hispanics are people from Latin American countries, who could be of any race. 美国人来自世界各地。白种人仍然占据美国人口的绝大部分（约75%）。2000 年，非洲裔美国黑人占美国人口的 12%，来自亚洲和太平洋岛国的人占到 4%，美国印第安人和阿拉斯加州土著居民占 1%。有 8% 是混血人口和其

他种族的人口。另一项分类统计出拉美裔占到美国人口的13%，他们来自拉丁美洲国家，种族不一。

Over half the African Americans live in cities, compared to around 80% of non-Hispanic whites who live outside the major cities. And although the whole country is becoming more mixed, over half of blacks live in the South, about half of all Hispanics live in Texas and California, and about half of all Asians and Pacific Islanders live in the western United States. In California and Hawaii, whites make up less than half of the population. 超过半数的非洲裔美国人生活在城市里，与之形成对比的是约有80%的非拉美裔白种人住在大城市之外。尽管整个国家人口居住地愈来愈混杂，还是有一半以上的黑人生活在南方，拉美裔人口中约一半生活在得克萨斯州和加利福尼亚州，约有一半的亚裔和来自太平洋岛国的人居住在美国西部。在加利福尼亚和夏威夷，白种人不到总人口的一半。

Immigration to the United States 美国的移民

Native Americans (or American Indians) had lived in the area we now call the United States for many thousands of years before the first Europeans arrived. Between 1492 and 1880 most immigrants came from Britain, Ireland, and northern Europe. Immigrants from China also began arriving in the 1800s. From 1880 to 1930, there was a huge growth in immigration to the US. The largest groups during this period came from southern and eastern Europe. Today, the largest groups of immigrants come from Mexico, the Philippines, and other parts of Latin America and Asia. The United States still accepts more immigrants each year than any other country in the world. 在第一批欧洲人来到现在称之为美国的这片大陆之前，美国土著（或称美国印第安人）已经在这里生活了几千年的时间。1492到1880年之间，大多数移民来自英国、爱尔兰和北欧。在19世纪初，中国的移民也抵达这里。从1880年到1930年，登陆美国的移民激增，这一阶段最大的移民群体来自南欧和东欧。今天最主要的移民来自墨西哥、菲律宾和拉丁美洲及亚洲的其他地区。美国每年接纳的移民数量都超过世界任何其他国家。

Civil Rights 民权

Relations between the various ethnic groups in the United States have often been difficult. European settlers fought against and killed Native Americans on many occasions. They forced Africans to come to America as slaves, and even after slavery ended in the 1860s, whites continued to treat African Americans unfairly. In many parts of the country, blacks had to go to separate schools, eat in separate restaurants, and sit at the back of public buses. Jews and sometimes Roman Catholics were kept out of many clubs and neighbourhoods. And people of one race were not allowed to marry people from other races. 美国不同种族间的关系通常比较难相处。过去的欧洲定居者曾多次与印第安人作战并屠杀他们。他们强迫非洲人来到美国当奴隶，虽然奴隶制在19世纪60年代已经瓦解，白种人仍然不公平地对待黑人。在美国的很多地方，黑人要到不同的学校上学，到不同的餐馆吃饭，此外乘坐公交车时要坐在车的后部。犹太人和一些天主教徒被排挤在很多俱乐部和社区之外。不同种族之间也不准通婚。

The Civil Rights Movement of the 1950s and '60s tried to change the situation. The Supreme Court ruled that public schools must allow children of all races to attend. Immigration laws were changed. And the government passed other laws that made it illegal to treat people differently because of their race. 20世纪50、60年代的民权运动试图改变这种状况。最高法院裁定公立学校必须接纳所有种族的儿童入学。移民法也做了修改。政府通过其他法律禁止因为种族原因而歧视他人。

Religion, Holidays, and Festivals 宗教，假日和节日

Many of the first Europeans came to America to escape countries where they could not practise their religion freely. The US Constitution guarantees freedom of religion, and there is no official religion. About 77% of Americans consider themselves Christian. Jews make up 1.3% of the population, and Muslims, Buddhists, and Hindus about 0.5% each. A growing number of Americans (about 14%) do not claim any religion. 因为无法坚持自己的宗教信仰，很多早期的欧洲移民才逃离原来的国家。美国宪法保证宗教信仰自由，在美国也没有一种官方宗教。77%的美国人认为自己是基督徒。犹太人占人口的1.3%，穆斯林、佛教徒和印度教徒各占约0.5%。宣称自己不信仰任何宗教的美国人在逐渐增多（约14%）。

Most national public holidays in the United States are not connected to one particular religious or ethnic group. One exception to this is Christmas, which is an important Christian holiday, but which is celebrated by many non-Christians in a nonreligious way. Around the same time of year as Christmas, Jews celebrate Hanukkah, and some African Americans celebrate Kwanzaa, a festival that includes elements of Christmas, Hanukkah, and African traditions. 美国大

多数的全国公共假日与特别的宗教或种族并无联系。一个例外是圣诞节，这是一个重要的基督教假日，很多非基督徒也以非宗教的方式来庆贺这个节日。在圣诞节前后的相近时间里，犹太人庆祝献殿节，有些非洲裔美国人庆祝宽扎文化节，它是一个兼具圣诞节、献殿节和非洲传统的节日。

Music and Food 音乐和饮食

nachos
辣味乳酪玉米面

Chinese food
中餐

When people think about American food, they often imagine large portions of meat and potatoes, fried food, or fast food. But this is not the only food that Americans eat. The many immigrants who have come to the US have brought their native food with them, and ethnic food is very popular. Even very small towns will have Chinese, Mexican, and Italian restaurants. In large cities, you can find any kind of food you want. 人们想到美国饮食的时候，他们经常想到大份量的肉食和土豆、油炸食品或快餐。但美国人并非只吃这些。很多移民美国的人也把自己家乡的食物带到了美国，因此民族饮食非常受欢迎。即便在很小的城镇都能找到中餐馆、墨西哥餐馆或意大利餐馆。在大城市想吃的东西应有尽有。

Different ethnic groups have also added to American musical culture. Salsa music and dance was introduced by Puerto Ricans and Cubans. And African-Americans are responsible for the creation of jazz, rhythm and blues, rap, hip-hop and other music and fashion trends that have become popular around the world. 不同的种族也为美国的音乐文化带来了影响。萨尔萨舞曲是波多黎各人和古巴人传到美国的。爵士乐、节奏布鲁斯、说唱乐、嬉蹦乐和其他音乐，以及其他在全世界都很受追捧的音乐和时尚流行趋势的创立要归功于非洲裔美国人。

Festivals 节日

New Year 新年

New Year's Eve – 31st December 除夕: 12月31日

New Year's Day – 1st January 元旦: 1月1日

People celebrate the start of the new year by going to parties on New Year's Eve. When midnight comes they say "Happy New Year" to each other, kiss each other, and sing a song called AULD LANG SYNE. The New Year is seen as a time when people try to change their lives, for example by promising to stop smoking or to take more exercise. These promises are called **New Year's resolutions**. 除夕那天，人们参加聚会，庆祝新年的开始。午夜时分，人们互祝新年快乐，彼此亲吻，唱一首叫做《友谊地久天长》的歌曲。人们把新年看成改变生活的时机，如承诺戒烟或加强锻炼，这些承诺叫做新年决心。

Groundhog Day 土拨鼠日

2nd February 2月2日

According to US tradition, this is the first day of the year that the GROUNDHOG (=a small animal with brown fur that lives in holes in the ground) comes out of its hole. If it sees its shadow, there will be six more weeks of winter; if it does not, good weather will come early. 依照美国传统，2月2日是当年土拨鼠出洞的第一天。如果土拨鼠能看到自己的影子，冬季将再持续六个星期；如果不能，则好天气会早早来到。

Presidents' Day 总统日

the third Monday in February 2月的第三个星期一

A holiday in the US to remember the BIRTHDAY*s* of George WASHINGTON and Abraham LINCOLN. 这是一个美国节日，纪念乔治·华盛顿和亚伯拉罕·林肯的诞辰。

Valentine's Day 情人节，圣瓦伦丁节

February 14th 2月14日

A day when people celebrate romantic love, and send cards or give red roses or chocolates to the person they love. Traditionally a Valentine's card is not signed by the person who sends it, so the person who receives it has to guess who it is from. 这一天，人们为爱情而庆祝，向爱人赠送贺卡、红玫瑰或巧克力。传统的做法是，贺卡上不写名字，收到贺卡的人得猜卡片是谁送的。

Mardi Gras 狂欢节，肥美的星期二

A CARNIVAL held in New Orleans, Louisiana, in the days before LENT. There is drinking, dancing, entertainment, and a PARADE (=a public celebration when musical bands and people dressed in special clothes move along the street in decorated vehicles). 这是美国路易斯安那州新奥尔良在大斋期之前举行的一个狂欢节，人们饮酒，跳舞，娱乐，参加游行。

Shrove Tuesday, also Pancake Day *BrE* 【英】忏悔星期二，又称薄煎饼日

In the UK this is a day when people eat PANCAKE*s* (=very thin, flat, round cakes made by frying (FRY) a mixture of butter, flour, and eggs). It is the last day before LENT, a period of forty days when, in the past, Christians ate only simple food. People used up all their milk, butter, and eggs on Shrove Tuesday because they were not allowed to eat them during Lent. 英国人在这一天吃薄煎饼。第二天就是大斋期，过去基督徒在为期40天的大斋期里只吃简单的食物。人们在忏悔星期二吃掉所有的牛奶、黄油和鸡蛋，因为大斋期就不能再吃了。

St Patrick's Day 圣帕特里克节

17th March 3月17日

The national day of Ireland, that is also celebrated by Irish people in the UK and US, when people wear green clothes, dye flowers green, and go to the PUB and drink GUINNESS. 这是爱尔兰的国庆节，英美两国的爱尔兰人也庆祝这一节日。节日期间，人们穿上绿衣服，把花朵染成

绿色，去酒吧喝健力士黑啤。

Palm Sunday 棕榈主日

the Sunday before Easter 复活节前的星期日

The day when Christians celebrate JESUS' arrival in Jerusalem, when PALM leaves were spread on the ground for his DONKEY to walk on. 这一天人们庆祝耶稣进入耶路撒冷，当时人们把棕榈树叶铺在地上让他的驴从上面走。

Easter 复活节

Good Friday – the Friday before Easter 受难节：复活节前的星期五

This is the day when Christians remember the CRUCIFIXION of Christ. It is a public holiday in the UK, and people eat HOT-CROSS BUNS on this day. 这天人们纪念耶稣被钉在十字架上。受难节是英国的公众节日，这一天要吃十字面包。

Easter Sunday – March or April 复活节星期日：3月或4月

The day when Christians celebrate the RESURRECTION of Christ. People give each other EASTER EGG*s* and EASTER BASKET*s*. In the US, children believe that these are brought by the EASTER BUNNY. 当天基督徒纪念耶稣复活。人们互赠复活节彩蛋和复活节篮子，美国儿童认为这些东西是复活节兔子带来的。

Mother's Day, also Mothering Sunday 母亲节，又称拜望双亲节

the fourth Sunday in Lent 大斋期的第四个星期日

A day in the UK when people give presents and cards to their mother. Mothers are often taken out for lunch, and usually do not have to do the work they normally do. Mother's Day in the US is later in the year. 英国人在这一天送礼物和贺卡给自己的母亲。母亲常被儿女带出去吃午餐，并且通常不用做日常家务。美国的母亲节略晚一些。

April Fools' Day 愚人节

1st April 4月1日

In the US and UK, a day when people and newspapers, radio programmes etc play tricks on people by making them believe something that is not true. One of the most famous April Fools' tricks in the UK was when a serious DOCUMENTARY programme on television called Panorama showed trees in Italy that had SPAGHETTI growing on them. 英美人在这一天编造谎话让别人信以为真，报纸和电台节目也搞此类恶作剧。英国最有名的愚人节恶作剧是：当时一个叫做《全景》的严肃的纪实类电视节目播放了一些意大利树木的画面，树上长着细面条。

May Day 五一劳动节；五朔节

1st May 5月1日

In the past, this was the day when people welcomed the arrival of spring by dancing around a MAYPOLE. The first Monday in May is a public holiday in the UK. May Day is connected with workers and LEFT-WING political parties. 人们过去在这一天围绕五月柱跳舞，迎接春天的到来。五月的第一个星期一在英国是公共节日。五一劳动节与工人及左翼政党有关。

Mother's Day 母亲节

the second Sunday in May 5月的第二个星期日

A day in the US when people give presents and cards to their mother. Mother's Day in the UK is earlier in the year. 美国人在当天送礼物和贺卡给自己的母亲。英国的母亲节略早一些。

Memorial Day 阵亡将士纪念日

the last Monday in May 5月的最后一个星期一

A holiday in the US to remember soldiers killed in wars —see also VETERANS DAY. In the UK, the last Monday in May is also a bank holiday, called late May bank holiday. 这是一个美国节日，纪念在战争中阵亡的将士（另见 VETERANS DAY）。5月的最后一个星期一在英国也是一个银行假日，叫做5月末银行假日。

Flag Day 国旗日

14th June 6月14日

A day when US people fly the US flag, remembering the day in 1777 when the STARS AND STRIPES (=the US flag) was officially accepted and first used. 美国人在

当天升国旗，纪念1777年的这一天星条旗被正式定为美国国旗并投入使用。

Father's Day 父亲节

the third Sunday in June 6月的第三个星期日

A day in the US and UK when people give presents and cards to their father. 英美人送礼物和贺卡给自己父亲的节日。

Battle of the Boyne 博因河战役纪念日

the Monday nearest to 12th July 距7月12日最近的星期一

A bank holiday in Northern Ireland, when PROTESTANT*s* celebrate a battle in 1690 when King WILLIAM III of England defeated JAMES II, a Catholic and the former King of Britain. The ORANGEMEN (=members of a society of Protestants in Northern Ireland) march through the streets. 这一天在北爱尔兰是银行假日，新教徒庆祝1690年英格兰国王威廉三世在战役中击败天主教徒、前英国国王詹姆斯二世。橙带党党员走上街头游行庆祝节日。

Fourth of July, also Independence Day 美国独立日

4th July 7月4日

A national holiday when the people of the US celebrate their independence from England in 1776 with PARADE*s*, PICNIC*s*, and FIREWORK*s*. 这是美国的全国性节日，美国人在这一天游行、野餐、放烟火，庆祝1776年脱离英格兰取得独立。

August Bank Holiday 8月银行假日

the last Monday in August 8月的最后一个星期一

A holiday in the UK, when people have a final celebration before the end of summer. There are many outdoor events held on this weekend, such as the NOTTING HILL CARNIVAL. 英国节日，英国人在夏季结束前举行最后的庆祝，该节日所在的周末有很多户外庆祝活动，如诺丁山狂欢节。

Labor Day 劳工节

the first Monday in September 9月的第一个星期一

A national holiday in the US. It was originally held to show support for workers, but now many people celebrate it as the end of summer with PICNIC*s* and BARBECUE*s*. 这是美国的全国性节日，最初设立是为了支持工人，但现在很多人把该节日当作夏季之末来庆祝，举行野餐和烧烤。

Columbus Day 哥伦布节

12th October 10月12日

A public holiday in many US states, to celebrate the discovery of America by Christopher COLUMBUS. 这在美国的很多州都是公众节日，庆祝克里斯托弗·哥伦布发现美洲。

Halloween 万圣节

31st October 10月31日

The day when, in the past, people believed that the spirits of dead people appeared. Especially in the US, children celebrate Halloween by dressing up as WITCH*es*, GHOST*s* etc and going TRICK OR TREAT*ing*. They knock on people's doors, and people give them sweets and small presents. 过去人们相信死者的亡灵会在这一天出现。孩子们装扮成巫师、鬼魂，玩“请吃糖还是想遭殃”的游戏来庆祝这一节日，在美国尤其如此。他们敲开住户房门，人们会给他们糖果或小礼物。

The Mexican Day of the Dead 墨西哥亡灵节

2nd November 11月2日

A festival in Mexico and parts of the US where there are many Mexicans, when the spirits of dead people are believed to come back to visit their families. The families offer them gifts of food, flowers, and toys. There is music and dancing, and children play with toy SKELETON*s*. 墨西哥和墨西哥人聚集的美国部分地区庆贺这一节日。人们相信这一天死者的亡灵会回来拜访他们的家人，死者家属为亡灵提供食物、花朵、玩具等礼物。人们奏乐、跳舞，孩子则拿玩具骷髅玩耍。

Armistice Day 停战纪念日

11th November 11月11日

The day when people remember the end of WORLD WAR I. In the US this is known as **Veterans Day**, and people remember the men and women who have fought in all the wars that the US has been involved in. At 11 in the morning, (the eleventh hour of the eleventh day of the

eleventh month) people are silent for two minutes to show respect for those who died in the wars of the 20th and 21st centuries. 人们在这一天纪念第一次世界大战结束。在美国该节日称退伍军人节，人们缅怀美国所卷入的战争中参战的男女。11 月 11 日上午 11 点，人们默哀两分钟，以示对 20 世纪和 21 世纪的战争死难者的尊敬。

Election Day 选举日

The first Tuesday after the first Monday in November in even years (2004, 2006, 2008 etc) is the day in the US when national elections are held. In some states this is a public holiday. 偶数年份 11 月第一个星期一后的星期二是美国举行全国大选的日子，这一天在一些州是公众假日。

Remembrance Sunday 荣军纪念星期日

the Sunday nearest to Armistice Day 距停战纪念日最近的星期日

In the UK, people wear red paper POPPIES in the days leading up to Remembrance Sunday. Poppies are especially SYMBOLIC because they grew in the fields in Flanders where many British soldiers died in World War I. On Remembrance Sunday there are special ceremonies all over the UK. At the main ceremony in London, the King or Queen lays a WREATH at the CENOTAPH in Whitehall. 节前几天，英国人佩戴红色的纸制罂粟花。罂粟生长在佛兰德的田野，一战时很多英国士兵于此丧命，因此罂粟尤具象征意义。荣军纪念星期日这一天，英国全国举行特别仪式。在伦敦的主仪式上，国王或女王为白厅街的纪念碑敬献花圈。

Guy Fawkes' Night, Bonfire Night 盖伊·福克斯之夜

5th November 11 月 5 日

In the UK, a day when people light BONFIREs and let off FIREWORKS. Traditionally this is done to remember the time when Guy FAWKES failed in an attempt to destroy the HOUSES OF PARLIAMENT with GUNPOWDER in 1605. 英国人在这一天点燃篝火，燃放烟火。传统上这样做是为了纪念 1605 年盖伊·福克斯炸毁议会大厦的企图被挫败。

Thanksgiving 感恩节

the fourth Thursday in November 11 月的第四个星期四

A national holiday in the US when people remember how, in the 17th century, Native Americans helped English people who had come to live in America by showing them how to grow local crops. People usually spend Thanksgiving with their families, and have a special meal of TURKEY and PUMPKIN PIE. 这在美国是一个全国性的节日，纪念 17 世纪时美洲原住民教英格兰移民如何种植当地农作物。美国人一般和家人一起过感恩节，吃火鸡、南瓜饼等特别的食物。

Christmas 圣诞节

Christmas Eve – 24th December 平安夜: 12 月 24 日

Christmas Day – 25th December 圣诞节: 12 月 25 日

Boxing Day *BrE*【英】**– 26th December** 节礼日: 12 月 26 日

Christmas is the most important FESTIVAL of the year. It is the birthday of Jesus Christ, but is also celebrated by people who are not Christians. People have a holiday from school and work, give each other presents, and decorate their homes. Children believe that presents are brought to them by SANTA CLAUS on the night of Christmas Eve. On Christmas Day families have a special meal together. 圣诞节是一年中最重要的节日，这是耶稣基督的诞辰，但不信基督教的人也过圣诞。人们不用去上学或上班，互赠礼物，装点房屋。孩子们相信，礼物是圣诞老人在平安夜带给他们的。圣诞节那天，一家人一起吃顿特别的晚餐。

The festivals and special days mentioned above are all either Christian or non religious. Many British and US citizens belong to other religions which have their own special days. 以上所列为基督教徒或不信宗教者的节日或纪念日，很多相信其他宗教的英美人有自己的特殊节日。

Government 政府

Government in the US 美国政府

There are three levels of government in the US – FEDERAL, state, and local. All of these are elected by the people of the country. 美国政府分三级：联邦政府、州政府和地方政府。政府官员均由国民选举产生。

Federal government 联邦政府

The federal government is the national government of the US. The CONSTITUTION OF THE UNITED STATES limits the power of the federal government to defence, FOREIGN AFFAIRS, printing money, controlling trade and relations between the states, and protecting HUMAN RIGHTS. The federal government is made up of CONGRESS, the PRESIDENT, and the SUPREME COURT. 联邦政府是美国的国家政府，美国宪法规定，联邦政府的权限为国防、外交、货币印制、管理各州间贸易及各种关系，以及保护人权。联邦政府由国会、总统和联邦最高法院组成。

Congress 国会

Congress is the institution that makes laws, and is made up of the HOUSE OF REPRESENTATIVES and the SENATE. The house of representatives has 435 members called **Representatives** or **Congressmen** and **Congresswomen**, who are elected by the people of a state to represent that state. The number of Representatives for each state depends on the size of the population of the state, and each state has at least one Representative. The Senate has 100 members called **Senators**, who are elected by their state. Each state has two Senators. Congress decides whether a BILL (=a suggested new law) becomes law. If both the Senate and House of Representatives agree to a law, the President is asked to agree. The President can VETO a bill (=refuse to allow it), but Congress can still make it a law if two-thirds of the members of each house agree to it. 国会为立法结构，由众议院和参议院组成。众议院有435名议员，称众议员，由各州选民选举产生，代表该州。各州众议员的数量取决于该州人口数，每州至少有一名众议员。参议院有100名议员，称参议员，由议员所在的州选举产生，每州有两个参议员。国会决定是否通过议案，使之成为法律。若参众两院一致同意通过议案，则会征求总统同意。总统可拒绝签署议案，但若参众两院均有三分之二的议员同意通过议案，国会仍可使之成为法律。

State government 州政府

State government has the greatest influence over people's daily lives. Each state has its own written CONSTITUTION (=set of fixed laws) and has different laws. There are sometimes great differences in law between the different states, concerning things such as property, crime, health, and education. The highest elected official of each state is the **Governor**. Each state also has one or two elected institutions that make laws, known as **state legislatures**, whose members represent the different parts of the state. 州政府对人们的日常生活影响最大。每个州都有自己的成文宪法和不同的法律。在财产、犯罪、卫生、教育等方面，各州的法律有时差别很大。各州由选举产生的最高长官是州长，每个州另有一个或两个选举产生的机构，负责制定法律，称州议会。州议会的议员代表本州不同地区。

Local government 地方政府

The organizations that are responsible for local government in the US are called **town** or **city** or **county councils**. They make laws that affect a town, city, or COUNTY. These laws concern things such as traffic, when and where alcohol can be sold, and keeping animals. The highest elected official of a town or city is usually the MAYOR. 美国负责地方政府的机构叫做镇议会、市议会或县议会，负责制定针对本镇、本市或本县的法律，涉及的方面有交通、何时何地可以卖酒、饲养动物等。镇或市选举产生的最高长官一般为镇长、市长或县长。

The Law and the Constitution 法律和宪法

Every law at every level of government must be in agreement with the United States Constitution. Any citizen who thinks that he or she has not been given their rights under the law may take their case to a court of law, and through all the courts in the system up to the Supreme Court if necessary. Any law which is found by the court to be UNCONSTITUTIONAL (=not in agreement with the constitution) cannot remain law. For more information see Law on page A23. 各级政府的法律必须符合美国宪法。美国公民若认为自己没有得到法律赋予的权利，就可以向法庭起诉，必要时可以逐级上诉，直至最高法院。一旦法庭认定某项法律违反宪法，该法律即告废止。更多内容请见F31页的“法律”部分。

Government in the UK 英国政府

National government 国家政府

The centre of government in the UK is Parliament, which makes all the important laws for the country. Parliament is made up of the HOUSE OF COMMONS, the HOUSE OF LORDS (known together as the HOUSES OF PARLIAMENT) and the Queen or King. The Houses of Parliament are in a part of London called WESTMINSTER, and the word Westminster is often used to mean Parliament. 英国政府的中心是议会，负责制定英国所有重要的法律。英国议会由下议院和上议院（合称议会上下两院）与女王或国王构成。议会两院位于伦敦威斯敏斯特，该地经常用来指代议会。

The House of Commons, also known as the Commons, is more powerful than the House of Lords. It has 650 members who have been elected by the people of the UK, called MEMBERS OF PARLIAMENT or MP*s*, each representing a CONSTITUENCY (=an area of land and the people who live in it). 下议院比上议院权力大。下议院的650名议员由英国国民选举产生，称议会议员，每名议员代表一个选区。

The House of Lords, also known as the Lords, is made up of HEREDITARY PEER*s* and LIFE PEER*s*. They are not elected. Until 2002, all hereditary peers were allowed to vote in the Lords, but now only 92 may do so. These 92 are chosen by a vote among all hereditary peers. All life peers can vote in the Lords. Hereditary peers are members of the aristocracy, and have titles such as Duke or Viscount which they take on the death of their father. Life peers are given their title as a reward for their good work, and they cannot pass the title on to their children. Although their titles are officially given to them by the Queen, most of them are suggested by a committee and have the approval of the Prime Minister. 上议院由世袭贵族和终身贵族组成，非由选举产生。2002年前，所有世袭贵族都有上议院的投票权，但现在只有世袭贵族中选出的92名代表有此权利。终身贵族都有上议院的投票权。世袭贵族隶属贵族阶层，享有公爵、子爵等头衔，父死子继。终身贵族因其成就获得头衔，头衔不可继承。头衔虽由女王正式授予，但大多由委员会提名，并经首相同意。

The government brings BILLS (=suggested new laws) to the House of Commons, where they are discussed by MP*s*. The bills then go to the House of Lords. The House of Lords can suggest changes to a bill, but does not have the power to stop it from becoming law. When the bills come back to the Commons, MPS vote on them, and if they are PASS*ed* (=if the MPs vote for them) they are signed by the Queen or King and become Acts of Parliament, which means that they become part of British law. 政府将议案提交下议院。下议员讨论后，议案呈交上议院。上议院可对议案提出修改意见，但无权否决议案。议案返回下议院后，下议员就议案投票，若投票通过，则由女王或国王签署议案，议案成为议会的法令，即成为英国法律的一部分。

Devolution for Scotland and Wales 对苏格兰和威尔士的放权

In 1997, the people of Scotland and Wales voted for DEVOLUTION, and now have their own separate parliaments, called the Scottish Parliament and the Welsh Assembly. The UK government in Westminster continues to deal with things such as foreign affairs, defence, and immigration, but the Scottish Parliament and Welsh Assembly deal with things such as health, education, transport, and the environment. Scotland has had a separate legal and educational system for a long time. 1997年，苏格兰人和威尔士人就权利下放投票，现已拥有独立的议会，称为苏格兰议会和威尔士议会。位于威斯敏斯特的英国政府仍负责处理外交、国防、移民等事务，但卫生、教育、交通、环境等问题则由苏格兰议会和威尔士议会处理。苏格兰早就有了独立的司法和教育体系。

Local government 地方政府

The organizations that are responsible for local government in the UK are called COUNCIL*s*. Their main job is to provide local services such as schools, libraries, and the Fire Service. They are also responsible for the local environment, and take rubbish from people's houses and clean the streets. 英国负责地方政府事务的机构叫做地方议会，主要职责是为本地提供学校、图书馆、消防等地方公共服务，也负责保护地区环境、清理垃圾、打扫街道。

Councils are given an amount of money each year by the national government, and also get money from local taxes. Local councils are elected by people who live in that area. The people who are elected, known as COUNCILLOR*s*, usually represent one of the national political parties, but are often elected because of their policies (POLICY) on local issues. Councils can make small laws known as BYLAW*s*, which only apply in their area. For example, councils decide which streets people can park their cars on, and how much parking FINE*s* (=money paid as a punishment for parking illegally) should be. 地方议会的财政来自国家政府的每年拨款和地方税收。地方议会由当地居民选举产生，当选者称地方议会议员，通常是某个全国性政党的成员，但其当选往往是由于其针对当地事务的施政方针。地方议会可以制定一些不太重要的地方法规，如规定哪些街道可以停车、违法停车罚款应是多少等。

Government of the European Union 欧盟政府

The 27 members of the EU (European Union) are: Belgium, France, Germany, Italy, Luxemburg, the Netherlands, the UK, Denmark, the Republic of Ireland, Greece, Spain, Portugal, Austria, Finland, Sweden, Cyprus, the Czech Republic, Estonia, Hungary, Latvia,

Lithuania, Malta, Poland, Slovakia, Slovenia, Romania and Bulgaria. 欧盟 27 个成员国是：比利时、法国、德国、意大利、卢森堡、荷兰、英国、丹麦、爱尔兰、希腊、西班牙、葡萄牙、奥地利、芬兰、瑞典、塞浦路斯、捷克共和国、爱沙尼亚、匈牙利、拉脱维亚、立陶宛、马耳他、波兰、斯洛伐克、斯洛文尼亚、罗马尼亚和保加利亚。

Laws made by the EU apply across all of the member countries. These laws typically concern things such as trade, CONSUMER PROTECTION, the environment, and money given to certain industries or certain places in Europe to help with economic development. The EU is made up of three institutions – the **European Commission**, the **European Parliament**, and the **Council of the European Union**, informally known as the **Council of Ministers**. The European Parliament is the only one of these that is elected by the people of the member countries. 欧盟制定的法律适用于所有成员国，主要涉及贸易、消费者保护、环境、拨款扶植某些行业或某些地区经济发展等方面。欧盟由欧洲执委会、欧洲议会和部长理事会三个机构组成，其中只有欧洲议会由成员国国民选举产生。

The European Commission is a group of 27 politicians known as **Commissioners**. The Commission is changed every five years. The governments of the member countries suggest the politicians who they want to become Commissioners, and then the European Parliament decides whether to accept them. 欧洲执委会由 27 名官员组成，称为委员，每五年改选一次。欧盟成员国推荐委员竞选人，欧洲议会决定是否通过。

The European Parliament meets in Strasbourg in France, but most of its committees meet in Brussels, and the word Brussels is often used to mean the EU. The European Parliament currently has 736 members called EURO-MPs or MEPs, who are elected every 5 years. The European Parliament has the power to get rid of the Commission by a VOTE OF NO CONFIDENCE, although this has never happened. The European Parliament has much less power and influence over people's daily lives than the national governments, but its power has increased since the SINGLE EUROPEAN ACT in 1986 and the MAASTRICHT TREATY in 1992. Its powers cannot be increased any further without the agreement of all of the member countries. 欧洲议会的会议地点在法国的斯特拉斯堡，但其委员会大多在布鲁塞尔开会，这样布鲁塞尔一词常用来指代欧盟。欧洲议会现有 736 名议员，称欧洲议会议员，每五年改选一次。欧洲议会有权投不信任票解散欧洲执委会，但从未行使此权利。相比各国政府，欧洲议会在人们日常生活方面的权力和影响要小得多，但自从 1986 年《单一欧洲法案》和 1992 年《马斯特里赫特条约》通过以后，欧洲议会有了更大的权力。非经所有成员国同意，欧洲议会不得继续扩大其权力。

The European Commission make proposals for new laws, which are then sent to the European Parliament, where they are discussed and changes are suggested. The proposals are then discussed by the Council of Ministers. If the European Parliament does not agree with the changes made by the Council of Ministers, it has the power to VETO (=refuse to allow) a proposal. 欧洲执委会提议制定新的法律，提案然后送交欧洲议会，由后者审议并提出修改意见，然后交部长理事会审议。欧洲议会若不同意部长理事会作出的修改，有权否决提案。

The Single Currency 单一货币

In 2002, the Euro became the official currency in most of the 15 states that then formed the EU, replacing the different currencies that had existed in those countries. The UK, Denmark, and Sweden did not switch to the Euro but kept their own currencies, though they may start using the Euro at a later date. 2002 年，欧元取代当时欧盟 15 国中大多数国家的原有货币成为官方货币，英国、丹麦和瑞典未加入欧元区，仍保留原有货币，但将来可能会采用欧元这一货币。

Holidays 假期

Paid holiday 带薪假期

Paid holiday is time that you are allowed to spend away from work, but are still paid for. Most people in the US get 2 weeks paid VACATION a year, unless they have worked somewhere for a long time, when they may get 3 or 4 weeks. In the UK most people have 4 or 5 weeks paid holiday each year. In addition, there are 8 days in the UK which are public holidays and 13 in the US. These public holidays are known as **bank holidays** in the UK. Many of these are on a Monday, giving people a **long weekend**, also called a **three-day weekend** (*AmE*【美】), and a **bank holiday weekend** (*BrE*【英】). 带薪假期指虽休假但薪水照发的假期。美国人每年的带薪假期大多有两周，工作时间长的则可能有三周或四周。英国人每年的带薪假期大多有四或五周。此外，英国每年有八天公共假日，美国有 13 天。在英国，这种假期叫做银行假日。很多公共假期都在星期一，这样就可以休一个长周末，美国称三天周末，英国称银行假日周末。

In the UK so many people drive to another part of the country on bank holiday weekends that there are terrible TRAFFIC JAMs (=lines of cars which cannot move). 银行假日周末，很多英国人驾车出游，交通堵塞十分严重。

Popular holiday places for Americans 美国人钟爱的度假地

Within the US, the NATIONAL PARKs such as the GRAND CANYON, YOSEMITE, and YELLOWSTONE are popular places to go on vacation. Young people may go walking or camping in the mountains. Many people have RVs (=a large vehicle with cooking equipment, beds etc) to stay in. If they are in a car they might stay in MOTELs while they are on the journey. DISNEYLAND and DISNEYWORLD are very popular. People also go skiing (SKI) in the ROCKY MOUNTAINS. 在美国，大峡谷、约瑟米蒂、黄石等国家公园是人们度假爱去的地方。年轻人会去山间远足或露营。很多人有活动房车，可以住在里面。有车的美国人旅行时会住汽车旅馆。迪斯尼乐园和迪斯尼世界很受欢迎。人们还会去落基山脉滑雪。

It is also very common to use vacations to visit relatives who live in states that are far away. Some children go to SUMMER CAMP for several weeks during the summer vacation from school, where they do special activities such as sports and CRAFTs (=making things from wood, cloth etc). 利用假期探访远方亲戚也很普遍。有些孩子在暑假里参加几个星期的夏令营，那里他们可以参加一些特别的活动，如体育运动和手工。

When Americans want to relax in the sun, they usually go to Florida, Hawaii, Mexico, or the Caribbean. They sometimes go to Europe for CULTURE, for example to see art and historic buildings. But travelling outside the US is not very typical, and it is believed that only about 20% of Americans have a passport. 美国人想享受阳光时，通常会去佛罗里达、夏威夷、墨西哥或加勒比海。有时美国人去欧洲体验那里的文化，如观看艺术品、探访古迹。不过，美国人出国旅游并不普遍，据信只有 20% 的美国人持有护照。

Popular holiday places for British people 英国人钟爱的度假地

In the past, British people spent their holidays at the SEASIDE (=a place by the sea) in towns such as SKEGNESS or BOURNEMOUTH. Today, however, many people prefer to go abroad on holiday, especially to somewhere warm. Many British people go to southern Europe, for example to the Greek islands. Spain and the Spanish islands of MAJORCA and IBIZA are also very popular. Ibiza is famous for its NIGHTCLUBs, and is especially popular with young

people. 过去，英国人去斯凯格内斯或伯恩茅斯等海滨城镇度假。不过，现在很多人更喜欢出国度假，尤其是去温暖的地方。很多英国人去南欧，如希腊群岛。西班牙和西班牙的马略卡岛、伊维萨岛等地也很受欢迎。伊维萨岛以夜总会闻名，尤受年轻人喜爱。

When British people go on holiday abroad, they often go on a PACKAGE HOLIDAY (=a holiday arranged by a company that includes travel, the hotel, and sometimes meals, all for a fixed price). These have made travelling abroad easier and cheaper, and today many people go to places that are very far away, such as Thailand, Tunisia, and India. 英国人出国度假常选择包价旅游，这样比较方便和省钱。现在很多人去很远的地方，如泰国、突尼斯和印度。

People who stay in the UK for their holidays often go to the country, especially to walk, in places like SCOTLAND, WALES, or the LAKE DISTRICT. 在国内度假的英国人常去苏格兰、威尔士和湖区等地的乡村，尤其是去那里远足。

Law 法律

According to the law of both the US and UK, people are considered to be innocent until proven guilty. This means that if someone is accused (ACCUSE) of a crime, they cannot be punished until it has been **proved beyond reasonable** doubt that they are guilty. If someone is **found guilty** by a court (=the court decides that they are guilty), they can sometimes ask for permission to APPEAL to a higher court in the hope that it will change the decision. 依照英美法律，某人未经证明有罪即是无辜的。也就是说，如果有人受到犯罪指控，必须证明他确实有罪才能实施惩罚。如法庭判决某人有罪，此人有时可申请向上一级法院上诉，以期改判。

Criminal Law in the US 美国的刑法

The US has two separate court systems, state courts and federal courts. State courts are used when someone has done something against the laws or CONSTITUTION of a particular state. Federal courts deal with cases that concern the laws and constitution of the United States as a whole. Federal courts also hear cases where the US government is one of the sides involved. Serious crimes can be tried (TRY) in either state courts or federal courts depending on the situation. 美国有两级法院，即州法院和联邦法院。州法院审理触犯本州法律或宪法的案件，联邦法院审理触犯美国联邦法律或宪法的案件，也审理美国政府为当事方的案件。情节严重的犯罪案件视其情况归州法院或联邦法院审理。

After someone is ARREST*ed*, a judge, or in some cases a GRAND JURY made up of between 16 and 23 ordinary men and women, decides whether they should go to TRIAL. If there is enough EVIDENCE, the **accused** goes to court, and is asked, 'Do you **plead guilty** or **not guilty**', meaning 'do you admit that you committed the crime, or do you say that you did not do it?'. If they say that they are not guilty, they are sent to trial in either a State Court or County Court, or in federal cases, a District Court. There they are tried by a judge and a JURY of 6 or 12. If the accused is **found guilty**, they may have the right to appeal to a higher court, as shown below. 嫌犯被捕后，法官（或某些情况下由16到23名普通人组成的大陪审团）决定是否起诉。若证据充分，嫌犯出庭，被要求回答是否认罪。若嫌犯不认罪，则交州法院或县法院审理，涉及联邦法律或宪法的则交联邦地方法院，由法官及六人或十二人陪审团作出审理。嫌犯若被判有罪，有权向上一级法院上诉，详见下文。

The highest court in the US is the **Supreme Court**. It deals with appeals from lower courts and in some cases from the State Supreme Court. It is made up of a **Chief Justice** and eight justices who are chosen by the President. The Supreme Court decides which cases it will hear. 美国的最高一级法院是最高法院，审理下级法院（有的情况下是州最高法院）移交的上诉案件。最高法院有一名首席法官和八名法官，均由总统任命。最高法院决定受理哪些案件。

The Appeals System in the US 美国的上诉程序

The diagram shows the courts in order of importance with arrows representing the appeals system. 下表所示为按重要性排序的各级法院，箭头表示上诉程序。

Federal Courts 联邦法院	**State Courts 州法院**
Supreme Court 最高法院	Appellate Court 上诉法院
▲	▲
Court of Appeals 上诉法院	State Supreme Court 州最高法院
▲	▲
District Court 联邦地方法院	State/County Court 州/县法院

Criminal Law in England and Wales 英格兰和威尔士的刑法

When someone is arrested, the Crown Prosecution Service (CPS), a government organization, decides whether there is enough evidence for the case to go to court. If there is enough evidence and the case is serious, the accused is sent to a Crown Court for a trial with a judge and a jury of 12 people. If the VERDICT (=decision) of the jury is that the accused is guilty, the judge decides the SENTENCE (=punishment). If there is enough evidence and the crime is a less serious, the case is heard in a **Magistrates' Court**. If someone is found guilty in the Crown Court, but thinks that this was wrongly decided, they can take their case to the Court of Appeal (Criminal Division) to be heard by a judge, as shown in the diagram below. 嫌犯被逮捕后，刑事检察院（属政府机构）裁定提出起诉的证据是否充分。若证据充分，案情严重，嫌犯则移交刑事法院，由法官和12人陪审团作出审理。如陪审团认定罪名成立，则由法官宣判罪刑。若证据充分，案情不太严重，则由治安法院审理。若刑事法院判决罪名成立，嫌犯不服判决，可向上诉法院（刑事庭）上诉，由一名法官审理，如下表所示。

The Appeals System in England and Wales 英格兰和威尔士的上诉程序

The diagram shows the courts in order of importance, with arrows representing the appeals system. 下表所

示为按重要性排序的各级法院，箭头表示上诉程序。

Criminal Courts in England and Wales

英格兰和威尔士的刑事法庭

House of Lords 上议院

⬆

Court of Appeal (Criminal Division) 上诉法院（刑事庭）

⬆

Crown Court 刑事法院

⬆

Magistrates' Court 治安法院

Criminal Law in Scotland 苏格兰的刑法

Scotland has a separate court system. After someone is arrested, an official called the **procurator fiscal** decides whether there is enough evidence for a trial. If there is enough evidence and the crime is a very serious one, the accused is sent to a **High Court of Justiciary**, to be tried by a judge and jury. In Scotland there are 15 people on a jury. If the crime is a less serious one, the case is heard in a **Sheriff Court**. The sheriff is a trained lawyer who acts as a judge. Appeals from the Sheriff's Court go to the High Court of Justiciary. 苏格兰有一个独立的司法体系。嫌犯被捕后，由地方检察官决定是否有充分的证据起诉。若证据充分，案情十分严重，嫌犯移交高等司法官法院，由法官和陪审团审理。苏格兰的陪审团由 15 人组成。若案情不十分严重，则由郡法院审理。郡长是受过培训的律师，充当法官。不服郡法院判决可向高等司法官法院上诉。

The Death Penalty 死刑

The DEATH PENALTY is the punishment of death, for very serious crimes such as murder. The UK has not had the death penalty since 1965, and many people think that it is morally wrong, although some people would like to bring it back. In the US, some states have the death penalty. 严重的犯罪案件，如谋杀，可判处死刑。1965 年英国废除了死刑，很多人认为死刑是不道德的，但也有人想恢复死刑。美国的一些州有死刑。

Pubs 小酒馆

Pubs are an important part of British life. Even very small villages nearly always have a pub. People often go to the pub for a drink in the evenings and at weekends, and have one pub near their home that they go to regularly, known as their **local**. In the past, women did not go to pubs, but today it is quite normal for women to go into pubs. According to the law, you must be 18 years old before you can drink alcohol in a pub. Children are not usually allowed into pubs, although some pubs, usually ones that serve food, let parents bring their children. 小酒馆是英国人生活的重要部分。就算很小的村子差不多也有一家小酒馆。傍晚或周末，英国人常去酒馆喝一杯，通常有一个离家近、经常去的酒馆，叫做local。过去，女性不去小酒馆，但现在女性去小酒馆已很常见。法律规定，去小酒馆喝酒须年满18岁。儿童一般不许进小酒馆，但也有一些小酒馆允许家长带孩子入内，这些酒馆通常提供食物。

The people in a pub 小酒馆里的各色人等

landlady – a woman who runs a pub 女店主
landlord – a man who runs a pub 男店主
barmaid – a woman who serves drinks in a pub 女服务员
barman – a man who serves drinks in a pub 男服务员
the barstaff – the barmaids and barmen 服务员（总称）
the locals/regulars – the customers who go to the same pub regularly 小酒馆常客

Drinks 酒类

Pubs serve beer and wine and SPIRITS (=strong alcoholic drinks such as GIN, VODKA, and WHISKY). People go up to the bar to be served – the barstaff do not come to your table to ask what you want. 小酒馆提供啤酒、葡萄酒和烈性酒（如杜松子酒、伏特加和威士忌）。人们到吧台要酒，服务员不会到顾客桌前问顾客喝什么酒。—see also Cultural Note at BEER 另见 BEER 文化注释。

Many pubs serve food, especially at lunch time. Since the 1980s, it has become much more common for pubs to serve food in the evenings too. The quality of food in pubs is much better than it was in the past, when all you could buy was CRISPS (=very thin pieces of potato cooked in oil and eaten cold) and PEANUTS. 很多小酒馆也提供食物，午餐时间尤其如此。20世纪80年代以后，小酒馆晚餐时提供食物也已经常见得多了。过去小酒馆只卖薯条和花生，现在的食物品类已大为改观。

Opening times 营业时间

Pubs are usually open from 11:00 am to 11:00 pm. At around 10:50 pm the landlady or landlord rings a bell and shouts **'last orders'** (=buy your last drinks), then at 11:00 rings the bell again and shouts **'time'** (=no more drinks will be served, and people should finish their drinks and go home). According to the law, the barstaff must stop serving drinks at 11:00 pm. The customers then have 10 minutes to finish their drinks, known as **drinking up time**, and another 10 minutes to leave the pub. **After-hours drinking** (=drinking after this time) is illegal. If the landlady or landlord does not obey these laws, their licence (=official permission to sell alcoholic drinks) could be taken away from them. 小酒馆的营业时间一般从上午11点到晚上11点。晚上10点50左右，店主会打铃，叫道："最后一次要酒了！"11点时会再次打铃，叫道："关门时间到！"法律规定，晚上11点以后服务员不能卖酒。接着，顾客得在十分钟之内喝完杯中酒，这段时间叫做"干杯时间"，接着的十分钟内离开小酒馆。过了这个时间饮酒是违法的。如果店主违反法律，可能会被吊销卖酒许可证。

Pub names 小酒馆店名

Pubs have names such as *The King's Arms*, *The Red Lion*, *The White Horse*, or *The Rose and Crown*. There is often a sign outside the pub showing the name with a picture. 小酒馆常起的名字有“御用武器”、“红狮”、“白马”、“玫瑰与皇冠”等。小酒馆外常有招牌，上有店名和图画。

Entertainment 娱乐活动

Pubs often have games for people to play, such as POOL and DARTs. Some pubs organize a **pub quiz**. The customers form teams and someone calls out questions on subjects such as sport, history, popular music, or films. In the UK many important football matches are broadcast on SATELLITE television, and many people go to the pub to watch the matches on a big screen. 小酒馆里常有一些游戏可以玩，如台球和飞镖。有的小酒馆组织问答比赛，顾客组队，有人提出体育、历史、流行音乐、电影等方面的题目。在英国，很多重要足球赛事是通过卫星电视转播的，很多人去小酒馆通过大屏幕电视观看比赛。

Shakespeare 莎士比亚

Shakespeare the man 莎士比亚其人

William Shakespeare is the most famous writer in the English language, and many people think he is also the best ever writer in English. 威廉·莎士比亚是最著名的英语作家，很多人认为他也是有史以来最出色的英语作家。

He lived from 1564 until 1616, and for most of his life, Elizabeth I was Queen. These were dangerous and exciting times in England. In 1588, the ships of the Spanish Armada tried to attack England, and were beaten back by the small English ships that went out to fight them in the English Channel. During Shakespeare's time, new theatres were being built, especially in London. One theatre, the Globe, is especially associated with Shakespeare. It burned down in 1613, but in 1997 a new Globe theatre was built near the exact site. 莎士比亚的生活年代是1564年到1616年，其间多在伊丽莎白一世治下。这是英格兰一段危险而又刺激的时期。1588年，西班牙无敌舰队试图进攻英格兰，英格兰小型舰队在英吉利海峡迎战，击退了敌军。在莎士比亚的时代，伦敦等地兴建了一些新剧院，其中一家叫做"寰球"的剧院与莎士比亚的关系尤其紧密。1613年该剧院毁于火灾，但1997年在原址附近重建了一个新的"寰球"剧院。

the Globe Theatre "寰球"剧院

Shakespeare came to London from Stratford-upon-Avon, in Warwickshire, where he was born and brought up. He became a member of a group of actors called the Lord Chamberlain's Men, and wrote several plays which they performed. After the Queen died in 1603, the new King, James I, ordered them to change their name to The King's Men. We do not know the exact date when Shakespeare was born, but we do know he was christened on April 26th, 1564. So his birthday is now celebrated on April 23rd. This is a good day to celebrate England's greatest writer, as it is also St George's Day (St George is the Patron Saint of England). On the weekend closest to April 23rd, people from all over the world come to Stratford, and there are many special events, including a parade through the streets. April 23rd is also the day when he died, in 1616. 莎士比亚在沃里克郡埃文河畔斯特拉特福出生和长大。来到伦敦后，他加入了一个叫做"宫务大臣供奉"的演员团体，写了几个剧本以供演出。1603年女王去世后，新王詹姆斯一世命令该团体改名为"国王供奉"。我们不清楚莎士比亚出生的确切日期，但可以肯定，他在1564年4月26日受洗，因此4月23日成了他的出生纪念日。在这一天庆祝这位英格兰最伟大作家的确很好，因为当天是圣乔治节（圣乔治是英格兰的主保圣人）。距离4月23日最近的周末，世界各地的人来到斯特拉特福。有很多纪念活动，如上街列队游行。1616年莎士比亚逝世，也是在4月23日。

Shakespeare the writer 作家莎士比亚

Shakespeare wrote poems, sonnets, and three sorts of plays: tragedies, comedies, and histories. In **tragedies**, the main character is always responsible for a terrible event, usually without intending to. In Shakespeare's tragedies, a lot of people die. The most famous tragedies are *Hamlet*, *Macbeth*, *Romeo and Juliet*, and *Othello*. The **comedies** are not so serious, and usually have a happy ending. In some of them, the plots include women dressing up as men, which was considered very funny in the 17th century because women were not allowed to be actors, and the parts for women were played by boys. So boys had to pretend they were women pretending to be men! The **histories** tell the story of English Kings. One of the interesting things about the histories is that although they are about people who had been dead for a long time, Shakespeare was often making a point about people or politics in his own lifetime. 莎士比亚创作了诗歌、十四行诗和三类戏剧：悲剧、喜剧和历史剧。悲剧中的可怕

事件总是由主角造成的，通常是无心使然。在莎士比亚的悲剧中，很多人死于非命。他最著名的悲剧有《哈姆雷特》、《麦克白》、《罗密欧与朱丽叶》和《奥赛罗》。喜剧不那么严肃，通常有个圆满的结局。一些喜剧中有女扮男装的情节，这在17世纪被认为是十分滑稽的，因为当时女人不能当演员，女性角色由男孩扮演，因此男孩得装成是假扮男子的女人。历史剧讲述英格兰国王的故事，让人感兴趣的一点是，尽管这些剧作说的是早已作古的人，莎士比亚却影射了当时的人物和政治。

Many of Shakespeare's plays have been used as the basis for famous films, such as *West Side Story* (1961), a musical film about two gangs in New York who are always fighting each other, which is based on *Romeo and Juliet*. The science fiction film *Forbidden Planet* (1956), based on *The Tempest*, is another. The Japanese director, Akira Kurosawa, has made films based on *Macbeth* and on *King Lear*. All these films use Shakespeare's plots to tell a modern story. Other films have been made of Shakespeare's plays, including *Gamlet* (1964), a version of *Hamlet* in Russian which is considered to be one of the best films of a Shakespeare play ever made. In 1944, Laurence Olivier's film of *Henry V* was deliberately made in order to tell the story of English courage and to encourage British people during World War II. 莎士比亚的很多戏剧为一些著名电影提供了素材，如讲述纽约两大黑帮仇杀的音乐剧电影《西区故事》(1961)取材于《罗密欧与朱丽叶》，科幻电影《惑星历险》(1956)取材于《暴风雨》。日本导演黑泽明曾取材《麦克白》和《李尔王》拍摄电影。这些电影都用莎剧的情节讲述当代的故事。还有一些电影改编自莎士比亚的戏剧，如1964年的《伽姆雷特》即是《哈姆雷特》的俄语版本，被认为是改编得最好的莎剧电影之一。1944年，劳伦斯·奥利弗特意拍摄了电影《亨利五世》，讲述英国人勇气的故事，激励二战中的英国人。

And in theatres all over the world, Shakespeare's plays are still regularly performed. Even after 400 years, we are still discovering that Shakespeare has a lot to say to us. 莎士比亚的戏剧仍在世界各地的剧院里定期上演。即便时间已经过去了400年，莎士比亚仍能带给我们很多启示。

Shakespeare's Plays 莎士比亚戏剧

Shakespeare wrote over 40 plays, and some of the most famous are listed below. 莎士比亚创作四十多部戏剧，下面是一些知名之作。

Tragedies 悲剧

1595 Romeo and Juliet《罗密欧与朱丽叶》

Romeo and Juliet is a story about the power of young love. Romeo and Juliet, whose families hate each other, are prepared to do anything to be together. The strength of young feeling is also shown in the violent battles between the young men of the two families, who are prepared to die for their honour. Romeo and Juliet suffer because of these unreasonable attitudes. These attitudes lead to the deaths of many characters, and of Romeo and Juliet. 《罗密欧与朱丽叶》讲述年轻人爱情的力量。罗密欧与朱丽叶所属的家族互相敌视，但两人却不惜一切想要结合。年轻人情感的力量也表现在两大家族青年的暴力冲突上，他们准备为捍卫荣誉而死。因为这些不理性的态度，罗密欧与朱丽叶深受其害。很多角色因此身亡，包括罗密欧与朱丽叶在内。

1601 Hamlet《哈姆雷特》

Hamlet is Prince of Denmark and his father, the king, has been murdered by his uncle. Only Hamlet knows that his father's death was murder. His uncle becomes king, and marries Hamlet's mother. Hamlet swears to his dead father that he will take revenge. The play deals with Hamlet's doubts and suffering as he tries to deal

with his situation and to carry out his promise. He thinks of killing himself, and he behaves very strangely and violently. In the last scene, he kills an old friend in a fight, and Hamlet and his mother and uncle also die. 哈姆雷特是丹麦王子，他的父王被他叔叔谋杀，只有哈姆雷特知道父亲是被害身亡的。他的叔叔继承王位，娶了哈姆雷特的母亲。哈姆雷特对父亲亡灵发誓，一定要复仇。剧本刻画了哈姆雷特试图处理问题、实现承诺时的动摇和痛苦。他想过自杀，他举止古怪，行为暴烈。最后一幕，他在战斗中杀死了一个老友，哈姆雷特、他的母亲和叔叔也纷纷殒命。

1604 Othello《奥赛罗》

Othello is a play about jealousy and how it can destroy people's judgment and their love for each other. It is also the study of an evil person, in the character of Iago. Othello is a great general, who loves his wife Desdemona, and Iago is an officer serving him. Iago hates Othello and wants to destroy him. He makes Othello think that Desdemona has a lover, although she has not. Othello is almost mad with doubt and sadness. Finally he believes Iago and he kills his young wife before killing himself.《奥赛罗》一剧讲述嫉妒如何摧毁人的判断力和爱情，也刻画了一个邪恶的角色伊阿古。奥赛罗是位了不起的将军，深爱着妻子苔丝狄蒙娜。伊阿古是奥赛罗手下的军官，他仇恨奥赛罗，想毁掉他。他让奥赛罗误以为苔丝狄蒙娜出轨。奥赛罗被怀疑和悲伤折磨得几乎发疯。最后，他信了伊阿古的话，杀死了年轻的妻子，然后自杀。

1606 Macbeth《麦克白》

Macbeth is a play about the desire for power and the evil that can result from this. Macbeth believes that he will one day be King of Scotland, and he does not want to wait. His wife, Lady Macbeth, encourages him, and he murders the present King, Duncan. Macbeth becomes King, but he commits further murders because he is afraid people will find out he killed Duncan. Macbeth and his wife have extremely guilty feelings, which lead Lady Macbeth to madness, and Macbeth to the belief that life has no meaning. In the end, Macbeth is killed by Macduff, whose family he had murdered.《麦克白》讲述权力欲及其带来的罪恶。麦克白相信，有一天他将成为苏格兰国王，他不想等了。他的妻子麦克白夫人，怂恿他杀死了现任国王邓肯。麦克白登基后，生怕他谋害邓肯的行为败露，杀了更多的人。麦克白夫妇陷入深深的内疚，麦克白夫人最终发疯，麦克白悲观厌世。最后，麦克白被马克杜夫杀死，而他曾经谋杀过马克杜夫的家人。

Comedies 喜剧

1596 A Midsummer Night's Dream《仲夏夜之梦》

A Midsummer Night's Dream is a play about love and magic. In a wood near Athens, we meet Oberon and Titania, the King and Queen of the fairies, and Oberon's servant, Puck. Puck uses his magic to make the other characters in the play fall in love with all the wrong people. This leads to some very amusing situations. The most famous of these is when Titania falls in love with Bottom, a young actor who is wearing a donkey's head at the time. The play ends happily: the magic has gone and all the right couples are together.《仲夏夜之梦》讲述爱情和魔法。雅典附近的一处树林里，生活着奥布朗和提泰妮娅，童话里的仙王和仙后，以及奥布朗的仆人迫克。迫克施展魔法，让剧中其他人物都爱错了人，引发了一些令人捧腹的场景，最著名的一幕是提泰妮娅爱上了波顿——一个由青年演员戴着驴头演出的角色。该剧有个圆满的结局：魔法消失，有情人皆成眷属。

Histories 历史剧

1591 King Richard III《理查三世》

Richard III enjoys being evil. He even murders his own brother and nephews, the two little princes, in order to become king. But the play is not about the desire for power. Richard cannot be happy, so he wants to make others unhappy too, and to destroy the peace of the country. An army of rebels meets his army at Bosworth Field. Richard's horse is killed under him and he dies

calling for another one: "A horse! a horse! my kingdom for a horse!" 理查三世喜欢作恶，为了取得王位，他甚至杀害了自己的亲哥哥和侄子——两位小王子。但该剧与权力欲无关。理查三世郁郁寡欢，所以他想让别人也不快乐，想破坏国家的安定。他率军在博斯沃斯与叛军相遇，坐骑被杀，他死前央求人再给他一匹马："给我匹马，我愿意用王位换一匹马！"

Famous sayings 著名台词

Shakespeare was very clever with words. A lot of lines from his plays are very famous. For example, "O Romeo, Romeo! Wherefore art thou Romeo?" which Juliet says when she is standing on her balcony. Everyone knows this line, and where it comes from. But there are lots of sayings in English which people use all the time without realizing that they come from Shakespeare. 莎士比亚擅长写名言隽语，剧中很多台词都很有名。例如"噢，罗密欧，罗密欧！为什么偏偏是罗密欧。"这是朱丽叶站在阳台上说的话。这句话及其出处尽人皆知，但也有很多英语中的常用语人们并不知道来自莎士比亚。

All that glitters is not gold is a common saying. It means that some things are simply not as good as they seem to be at first. Shakespeare actually wrote *All that glisters is not gold* (*in the Merchant of Venice*).
发光的不一定是金子。
这句话人们经常说，意思是说有的东西并不像初看起来那样好。莎士比亚的原句是 All that glisters is not gold（出自《威尼斯商人》）。

It stinks to high heaven.
People say this if something smells horrible. The expression began with Shakespeare, when Hamlet's uncle admits to himself that he has done something dreadful by killing his brother. He says *O my offence is rank, it smells to heaven.*
臭气冲天。
闻到臭味时人们经常这么说。该句缘自莎士比亚——哈姆雷特的叔叔自认杀死兄长是可怕的罪行，他说："哦，我罪行滔天，臭不可闻。"

Why then, the world's mine oyster.
From *The Merry Wives of Windsor*. These days, when people say "the world's your oyster" they mean that you can do or achieve anything you want to.
为什么不？这世界就是我的囊中物。
出自《温莎的风流娘儿们》，现在当人们表示你能心想事成，就说："这世界就是你的囊中物。"

There are more things in heaven and earth, Horatio, than are dreamed of in your philosophy.
From *Hamlet*. People often say "there are more things in heaven and earth" to mean that we cannot think of everything that might happen or that might exist. This is what Hamlet was saying when he was telling his friend Horatio that he really had seen the ghost of his father.
天下之大，无奇不有，霍拉旭，你那一套理论做梦都想不到。
出自《哈姆雷特》。人们常说："天下之大，无奇不有"表示可能发生或可能存在的事物我们未必想象得到。这句话是哈姆雷特说的，当时他对自己的朋友霍拉旭说他的确见到了父亲的亡灵。

Is this a dagger which I see before me ...?
From *Macbeth*. Another saying that people use humorously. People sometimes hold an object up and say, for example, "Is this a saucepan which I see before me?" or "Is this a ticket which I see before me?"
我面前这东西是把匕首吗？
出自《麦克白》。这句话人们也常幽默地加以运用。比如，有时人们会举着一个东西，问："我面前这东西是炖锅吗？"或"我面前这东西是一张票吗？"

Parting is such sweet sorrow.
From *Romeo and Juliet*. People sometimes say this when they are saying goodbye. They usually mean it slightly humorously.
离别如此甜蜜，又如此忧伤。
出自《罗密欧与朱丽叶》，有时人们分别时这样说，通常略带戏谑。

To be, or not to be, that is the question.
This is Hamlet, beginning his most famous speech, and thinking about killing himself. People sometimes use this quote with a different verb, usually humorously. For example, if someone is trying to decide whether to use their car or take a train for a journey, they might say "To drive, or not to drive?"
活，还是不活，这是问题所在。
这是哈姆雷特考虑自杀时著名独白中的第一句。有时人们把这句话换一个动词，通常表示幽默。例如，某人想决定开车还是坐火车旅行，他们会说："开车，还是不开车？"

A pound of flesh.
People often talk about "demanding a pound of flesh" when they mean they want what is owed to them. This comes from the *Merchant of Venice*. Antonio has had to borrow money from Shylock. If he doesn't pay the money back on time, then he has to give up a pound

of his flesh. Of course, he can't pay it back, and so Shylock demands his pound of flesh.

一磅肉。

人们想要回自己的东西时经常说："要一磅肉"。该句出自《威尼斯商人》，安东尼奥被迫向夏洛克借钱，如果到期不还，就得让人割下身上的一磅肉。他当然还不起，所以夏洛克要他的一磅肉。

There's method in his/her madness is a common saying in English. People say it when talking about strange behaviour which they realize has a proper purpose. It comes from *Hamlet* again, where he says *Though this be madness, yet there is method in't.*

疯狂自有疯狂的道理。

这句话在英语中很常用，经常表示古怪的行为也有正当的原因。该句也出自《哈姆雷特》，剧中他说："这确实是疯狂，但自有道理。"

A horse! a horse! my kingdom for a horse!

From *Richard III*. During the Battle of Bosworth Field, Richard loses his horse and is desperate for another one, so offers his entire kingdom in exchange for it. It's another Shakespeare line which people sometimes use humorously, saying things like "A drink, a drink! My kingdom for a drink!"

"给我匹马，我愿意用王位换一匹马！"

出自《理查三世》。博斯沃斯之战中，理查三世失去坐骑，急切想要另一匹马，因此宁愿拿整个王国来换。这句话有时也用来表示戏谑，比如说："给我杯酒，我愿意拿王位换一杯酒！"

You have to be cruel to be kind.

It means that sometimes you have to do something that someone else does not like, but which will eventually be good for them. Originally, this came from *Hamlet*, when he said: *I must be cruel only to be kind.*

要做善人，先得心狠。

意思是说，有时你不得不做一些别人不喜欢的事，但最终这些事会对他们有益。该句出自《哈姆雷特》，剧中他说："要做善人，我先得心狠。"

Weddings 婚礼

In the UK people get married either in a church or a REGISTER OFFICE (=a local government building). In the US people often get married in a house, a park, a hotel, or WEDDING CHAPEL, as well as in a church. The traditional wedding, called a **white wedding** as the bride wears a white dress, takes place in a church. People who are not religious often choose to have a traditional wedding. 英国人在教堂或婚姻登记处结婚，美国人的婚礼地点除教堂外，也可以在家里、公园、酒店、或婚礼小教堂。传统婚礼叫做“白色婚礼”，在教堂举办，新娘穿白色长裙。无宗教信仰的人经常选择传统婚礼。

The main people at a wedding 婚礼的主角

The BRIDE is the woman who is getting married. Traditionally, she wears a long white dress and a VEIL, and carries a BOUQUET of flowers. She also wears **something old, something new, something borrowed, and something blue** to bring her luck. The BRIDEGROOM (also called the **groom**) is the man who is getting married. He wears a SUIT, or sometimes a TUXEDO in the US, or a MORNING SUIT in the UK. The BRIDESMAIDs are usually female friends of the bride, or her sisters or cousins, and they usually wear long dresses and carry flowers. The BEST MAN is a male friend of the groom. 依照传统，新娘穿白色长裙，戴面纱，手持花束，也会穿旧衣服、新衣服、借来的衣服或者蓝色衣服以求好运。新郎穿礼服，美国新郎有时穿燕尾晚礼服，英国新郎有时穿晨礼服。伴娘通常是新娘的女伴、姐妹或堂[表]姐妹，常着长裙，手持鲜花。伴郎是新郎的男伴。

Before the ceremony 婚礼前

It is considered bad luck if the bridegroom sees the bride on the morning of the wedding. The bridegroom arrives first at the church and waits at the ALTAR with the best man. The best man is responsible for bringing the WEDDING RING, and there are many jokes about him losing or forgetting it. The bride arrives at the church in a car with her father. There are often jokes about the bride being late, and the groom being very nervous as he waits and worries that she may not be coming. 新郎婚礼当天早上见到新娘被认为是不吉利的。新郎先到教堂，与伴郎在祭坛前等候。伴郎负责携带婚戒，有很多关于伴郎丢失或忘带婚戒的笑话。新娘和她的父亲乘车来到教堂，常有笑话讲，新娘迟到，新郎惴惴不安，唯恐新娘不来了。

The ceremony 婚礼仪式

It is traditional for the bride's father to **give her away** (=to walk to the front of the church with her and formally give permission for her to marry). The bride and her father walk slowly up the AISLE (=the central passage) and the bridesmaids follow. When the bride and bridegroom are together at the altar, the priest begins the wedding service. He or she asks if there is anyone present who knows of any legal reason why the couple should not get married, and says, 'Speak now, or for ever hold your peace.' Then the bride and groom **exchange the traditional vows**. It is sometimes possible to change the vows or even write your own. A typical example of a wedding vow might be: *"I, Jane Smith, take thee, David Jones, to be my lawful wedded husband, to have and to hold from this day forth, for better, for worse, for richer, for poorer, in sickness and in health, to love and to cherish, forsaking all others, until death do us part."* 传统做法是，新娘的父亲把新娘交到新郎手上。新娘父女沿过道缓缓走上前去，伴娘跟在后面。新娘和新郎在祭坛前会面时，神甫[牧师]开始婚礼仪式。他[她]询问在场的人是否有合法的理由反对这门婚事，说道：“要么现在说出来，要么永远不要说。”然后新郎和新娘互相立誓，誓约有时会有改动，甚至是自己写的。结婚誓言常为：“我，简·史密斯，嫁与你，戴维·琼斯为妻，缔结合法婚姻。自今日起，无论是好是坏、是富是贫、有恙无恙，珍重爱护，唯此一人，相伴终生，至死不渝。”

The couple then give each other a gold ring and say *"With this ring I thee wed"* (=with this ring I marry you). At the end of the ceremony, the priest says *"I pronounce you man and wife"*, which means that they are officially married. The husband and wife then sign the REGISTER (=the official record of their marriage). 接着新婚夫妇交换金戒指，说：“你我结为夫妇，有此婚戒为证。”婚礼最后，神甫[牧师]说：“我宣布，你们结为夫妇。”表示新人正式成婚。接下来新郎和新娘在注册簿上签字。

After the ceremony 婚礼仪式后

Outside the church the friends of the bride and groom throw CONFETTI (=small pieces of coloured paper) or rice over them. A photographer takes the **wedding photographs**. 教堂外，新人的朋友向他们抛撒五彩纸屑或大米，摄影师为他们照相。

The bride and groom and the guests then go to the RECEPTION, which is a special meal and a party to celebrate the wedding. During the meal the bride and groom cut the WEDDING CAKE together. In the US they feed each other a small piece, and it is traditional for them to try and make a mess on each other's faces. At the end of the meal there are speeches made by the bride's father, the groom, and the best man. Before the reception ends, the bride and groom drive away to a hotel to spend their WEDDING NIGHT, before beginning their honeymoon (=a holiday taken by people who have just got married). The car that the couple drive away in has usually been decorated by their friends. Before she leaves, the bride throws her bouquet to her friends. According to custom, the girl or woman who catches it will be the next one to get married. 然后，新人和宾客参加婚宴，新人一起切结婚蛋糕。美国新人常互相喂一口蛋糕，按传统，他们会用蛋糕把对方的脸涂花。婚宴临近结束时，由新娘的父亲、新郎和伴郎致词。婚宴结束前，新人驾车去酒店度过新婚之夜，然后开始蜜月。新人开的车常由朋友装饰过。新人离场前，新娘把手中花束抛给她的朋友。根据传统说法，接到花束的女人会成为下一个新娘。

Landmarks in British History and American History 英美大事记

Landmarks in British History 英国大事记

The Battle of Hastings in 1066 was the last time England was successfully invaded. King Harold was killed in the battle, and two months later, on Christmas Day, William of Normandy was crowned King in Westminster Abbey. 1066年的黑斯廷斯战役是英格兰最后一次被征服。国王哈罗德阵亡，两个月后的圣诞节，诺曼底公爵威廉在威斯敏斯特教堂登基称王。

In 1215, a group of Barons took control of London in protest at the way King John was ruling the country. King John agreed to limit his royal powers by signing the Magna Carta, and the Barons allowed him to remain as king. 1215年，一群男爵占领了伦敦，抗议英王约翰的统治方式。约翰同意签署《大宪章》，对王权作出限制，男爵们允许他保留王位。

When the Black Death came to England in the 14th century, dead bodies had to be taken away and buried as quickly as possible. Men would come through the streets shouting "Bring out your dead". 14世纪，黑死病传到英格兰，尸体必须尽快运走并掩埋，人们沿街叫道："把家里的死人抬出来。"

In 1588, the Spanish sent an Armada of 122 ships – or galleons – to invade England. They were beaten back by Sir Francis Drake and his fleet of 66 much smaller ships. The Spanish had to go back to Spain round the top of Scotland as their way back was blocked, and they lost many ships in storms. 1588年，西班牙派出拥有122艘大型军舰的无敌舰队入侵英格兰，被弗朗西斯·德雷克爵士率领66艘小得多的军舰击退。因为退路被切断，西班牙人被迫绕道苏格兰北部，很多军舰在风暴中沉没。

Landmarks in American History
美国大事记

The Great Fire of London began in a baker's shop in Pudding Lane in 1666. As many as over 13,000 houses, 89 churches were destroyed, including the original St Paul's Cathedral. 1666年的伦敦大火是由普丁巷一家面包房失火引起的。超过1.3万间房屋、89所教堂毁于大火，包括古老的圣保罗大教堂。

Native Americans had lived on the North American continent for thousands of years before the first Europeans arrived in 1492. 1492年第一批欧洲人来到美洲，此前美洲原住民已在北美大陆生活了数千年。

The Industrial Revolution brought about a huge change in the way people lived. Many workers came from the countryside to work in factories in towns and cities. 工业革命极大地改变了人们的生活。很多工人从乡村来到城镇的工厂里工作。

The Pilgrim Fathers arrived in North America in 1620, and built a town which they called Plymouth – the same name as the town in England where they had started their journey. 1620年清教徒前辈移民来到北美，建立了第一个城镇，起名普利茅斯，与他们从英格兰启程离开的城镇同名。

July 4th is celebrated throughout the United States as Independence Day. It is the date when 13 states signed the Declaration of Independence from Britain in 1776. 7月4日称为“独立日”，美国举国庆祝。1776年的这一天，13个州签署了脱离英国统治的《独立宣言》。

Between 1892 and 1924, more than 20 million immigrants came to the United States through Ellis Island in New York. 1892年到1924年，两千多万移民通过纽约的埃利斯岛来到美国。

The Civil War, from 1861 to 1865, was fought between 11 states of the North and 11 states of the South. Over half a million people died in the war. The result was victory for the North and the end of slavery in the United States. 1861年至1865年的美国内战在北部11州与南部11州之间展开，五十多万人死于战争。最终北部获胜，美国的奴隶制从此废除。

During the 1960s, the civil rights movement demanded equal rights for African Americans. In August 1963, over 250,000 people from all over the country took part in the March on Washington. After the march, the leaders went to talk to President John F. Kennedy in the White House. A year later, the Civil Rights Act made it illegal to discriminate against people because of their colour. 20世纪60年代，美国爆发了争取非洲裔美国人平等权利的民权运动。1963年8月，超过25万人从全国各地来到华盛顿参加游行。游行后，民权领袖来到白宫，与总统约翰·F.肯尼迪谈判。一年后，《公民权利法案》规定，因肤色而歧视他人是违法的。

图书在版编目(CIP)数据

朗文当代英语大辞典:英英·英汉双解:新版/(英)梅厄(Mayor,M.)主编;王立弟等译.—北京:商务印书馆,2011

ISBN 978-7-100-06738-6

Ⅰ.①朗… Ⅱ.①梅… ②王… Ⅲ.①英语—双解词典 ②双解词典—英、汉 Ⅳ.①H316

中国版本图书馆 CIP 数据核字(2009)第 133418 号

LǍNGWÉN DĀNGDÀI YĪNGYǓ DÀCÍDIǍN

朗文当代英语大辞典

(英英·英汉双解)

新 版

出版:商务印书馆
(北京王府井大街 36 号 邮政编码 100710)
培生教育出版亚洲有限公司
(香港鲗鱼涌英皇道 979 号太古坊康和大厦 18 楼)
中国内地总发行:商务印书馆
中国香港、澳门、台湾地区以及世界其他各地
总发行:培生教育出版亚洲有限公司
印刷:北京中科印刷有限公司
ISBN 978-7-100-06738-6

2004 年 6 月第 1 版　开本 880×1230 1/32
2011 年 10 月第 2 版　印张 78⅛ 插页 1
2011 年 10 月北京第 6 次印刷　印数 50 000 册

定价:138.00 元

Grammar Codes 语法代号表

[C] countable: a noun that can be counted and has a plural form 可数名词, 即可以计数并有复数形式的名词: *We planted an orange* **tree**. 我们种了一棵橘子树。| *Children love to climb* **trees**. 小孩喜欢爬树。

[U] uncountable: a noun that cannot be counted and has no plural form 不可数名词, 即不可以计数, 也没有复数形式的名词: *the* **peace** *of the May afternoon* 5月下午的平静 | *a blade of* **grass** 草的叶片

[I] intransitive: a verb that has no direct object 不及物动词, 即没有直接宾语的动词: *I'm sure I can* **cope**. 我肯定能应付。| *Our food supplies soon* **ran out**. 我们的食物很快就吃完了。

[T] transitive: a verb that is followed by a direct object, that can be either a noun phrase or a clause 及物动词, 即后面跟直接宾语 (既可以是名词短语, 也可以是从句) 的动词: *I* **like** *swimming, playing tennis, and things like that.* 我喜欢游泳、打网球等诸如此类的事情。| *I* **hope** *I'm not disturbing you.* 我希望没有打扰你。| *We never* **found out** *her real name.* 我们始终没有弄清楚她的真名。

[singular] a noun that is used only in the singular, and that has no plural form 单数名词, 即只用单数而没有复数形式的名词: *She gets in such a* **fuss** *before people come to dinner.* 有人来吃饭以前, 她总是如此小题大做。| *the distant* **hum** *of traffic* 远处车辆的嘈杂声

[plural] a noun that is used only with a plural verb or pronoun, and that has no singular form 复数名词, 即只与复数动词或代(名)词连用的名词, 没有单数形式: *electrical* **goods** 电器商品 | *My* **spirits** *sank when I saw the mess.* 看到乱七八糟的情况, 我的情绪一下子低落了。

[linking verb] a verb that is followed by a noun or adjective complement, that refers to the subject of the verb 连系动词, 即后面跟说明动词的主语的名词或形容词补语: *Her skin* **felt** *cold and rough.* 她的皮肤摸上去又冷又粗糙。| *We* **were** *hungry.* 我们饿了。| *The weather* **became** *warmer.* 天气变暖了。

[always + adv/prep] shows that a verb must be followed by an adverb or a prepositional phrase 这个代号表示某一动词后面必须跟副词或介词短语: *The door suddenly* **flew** *open.* 门突然开了。| *Sandra* **flounced** *out of the room.* 桑德拉猛然从房间里走出来。

[not in progressive] shows that a verb is not used in the progressive form, that is, the -ing form after be 这个代号表示某一动词不能用于进行时, 即不能用be + -ing 的形式: *I* **hate** *housework.* 我讨厌做家务。(not 不能说 *I am hating housework.*) | *Who* **knows** *the answer?* 谁知道答案?

[no comparative] shows that an adjective is not used in the comparative or superlative form, that is, not with -er and -est, or with more and most 这个代号表示某一形容词不能用于比较级或最高级, 即不能与-er [-est] 或 more [most] 连用: *She needs* **proper** *medical attention.* 她需要接受妥善治疗。

[only before noun] shows that an adjective can only be used before a noun 这个代号表示某一形容词只能用于名词前: *the* **final** *episode of "Prime Suspect"*《头号嫌疑犯》的最后一集 | *the* **main** *points of her speech* 她演讲的要点

[not before noun] shows that an adjective cannot be used before a noun 这个代号表示某一形容词不能用于名词前: *Quiet! The baby is* **asleep**. 安静点! 宝宝在睡觉。

[only after noun] shows that an adjective is only used immediately after a noun 这个代号表示某一形容词只能紧跟在名词之后: *There are bargains* **galore** *in the sales.* 大减价中有大量的特价商品出售。

[sentence adverb] shows that an adverb modifies a whole sentence 这个代号表示某一副词修饰整个句子: **Apparently** *they've run out of tickets.* 显然, 他们没有票了。

[+ adj/adv] shows an adverb of degree 这个代号表示程度副词: *She plays the violin* **remarkably** *well for a child of her age.* 就她这个年纪的孩子而言, 她拉小提琴拉得特别好。| *You look* **absolutely** *fantastic in that dress.* 你穿那件连衣裙绝对好看。

[also + plural verb *BrE*] shows that a group noun can take a plural verb in British English 这个代号表示某一集合名词在英国英语中可以用复数动词: *The* **committee** *have decided to raise membership fees for next year.* 委员会决定增加明年的会员费。

[+ **between**] [+ **about**] shows that a word is followed by a particular preposition 这种代号表示某个词后面跟特定的介词: *I'm trying to* **decide** *between the green and the blue. Now are you* **certain** *about that?* 我想在绿色与蓝色之间作出选择。你现在对此肯定吗?

decide that shows that a word can be followed by a clause beginning with that 这种形式表示某个词后面可以跟以that引导的从句: *It* **was decided** *that four hospitals should be closed.* 决定要关闭四家医院。

sure (that) shows that a word can be followed by a clause beginning with that, or the word 'that' can be left out 这种形式表示某个词后面可以跟以that引导的从句, 但that

英汉双解版工作人员名单

语言部分 Language

主审
Chief Reviser
- 汪榕培 Wang Rongpei

审订
Revisers
- 区 铁 Ou Hong
- 杨枕旦 Yang Zhendan
- 陈德彰 Chen Dezhang
- 夏祖煃 Xia Zukui

翻译
Translators
- 王立弟 Wang Lidi
- 王峻岩 Wang Junyan
- 王逢鑫 Wang Fengxin
- 李红梅 Li Hongmei
- 李景峰 Li Jingfeng
- 杨信彰 Yang Xinzhang
- 杨镇明 Yang Zhenming
- 吴建平 Wu Jianping
- 宋志平 Song Zhiping
- 张显奎 Zhang Xiankui
- 陈永培 Chen Yongpei
- 陈 凯 Chen Kai
- 柯克尔 Ke Ke'er
- 龚少瑜 Gong Shaoyu
- 常晨光 Chang Chenguang
- 梁卫红 Liang Weihong
- 韩 红 Han Hong
- 蔡关平 Cai Guanping
- 霍庆文 Huo Qingwen
- 戴瑞亮 Dai Ruiliang
- 杨枕旦（新词） Yang Zhendan

文化部分 Culture

审订
Reviser
- 徐式谷 Xu Shigu

文化词条翻译
Translator of Cultural Entries
- 李瑞林 Li Ruilin

文化注释和文化特写翻译
Translators of Cultural Notes and Features
- 刘 彤 Liu Tong
- 邢三洲 Xing Sanzhou

	培生教育出版亚洲有限公司	商务印书馆
出版人 **Publishers**	黄 娴 Isa Wong	于殿利 Yu Dianli
策划编辑 **Managing Editors**	王伟文 Wong Wai Man	黄希玲 Huang Xiling
责任编辑 **Executive Editors**	谢福荣 Floyd Xie	邢三洲 Xing Sanzhou
编辑 **Editors**	梁 路 John Liang	方 铭 Fang Ming; 顾晓军 Gu Xiaojun; 李 君 Li Jun; 刘军怀 Liu Junhuai; 刘 彤 Liu Tong; 罗平岩 Luo Pingyan; 郄一帆 Qie Yifan; 许晓娟 Xu Xiaojuan; 杨 冀 Yang Ji; 杨子辉 Yang Zihui; 张显奎 Zhang Xiankui; 赵景纯 Zhao Jingchun; 周治淮 Zhou Zhihuai
校对 **Proofreaders**	张瑾之 Kitty Zhang	商务印书馆校对科 The Commercial Press (Beijing) Proofreading Team
封面设计 **Graphic Designers**	梁兆康 Leung Siu Hong	李有良 Li Youliang
排版 **Pagemaking**	姚 琍 Judy Yao; 张 慧 Amy Zhang; 王 莹 Annie Wang	

Pronunciation Table 发音表

Consonants 辅音/子音

K.K.	IPA	KEY WORD 范例
p	p	pen
b	b	back
t	t	ten
d	d	day
k	k	key
g	ɡ	get
f	f	fat
v	v	view
θ	θ	thing
ð	ð	then
s	s	soon
z	z	zero
ʃ	ʃ	ship
ʒ	ʒ	pleasure
h	h	hot
x	x	loch
tʃ	tʃ	cheer
dʒ	dʒ	jump
m	m	sum
n	n	sun
ŋ	ŋ	sung
w	w	wet
l	l	let
r	r	red
j	j	yet

Vowels 元音/母音

	K.K.	IPA	KEY WORD 范例
short 短音	ɪ	ɪ	bit
	ɛ	e	bed
	æ	æ	cat
	ɑ	ɒ	pot
	ʌ	ʌ	but
	ʊ	ʊ	put
	ə	ə	about
	ɪ	i	happy
	ʊ	u	actuality
long 长音	i	iː	sheep
	ɑ	ɑː	father
	ɔ	ɔː	four
	u	uː	boot
	ɝ	ɜː	bird
diphthongs 双元音	e	eɪ	make
	aɪ	aɪ	lie
	ɔɪ	ɔɪ	boy
	o	əʊ	note
	aʊ	aʊ	now
	ɪr	ɪə	rear
	ɛr	eə	hair
	ʊr	ʊə	sure
	ʊə	uə	actual
	jɚ	iə	peculiar

Special signs 特别符号

; 此符号之左边为 K.K. 音标 *，右边为 IPA 音标 * *。K.K. 音标所标示的是美国音; IPA 音标所标示的是英国音。

/ˋ/, /ˈ/ 表示主重音。

/ˏ/, /ˌ/ 表示次重音。

/◂/ 表示重音转移。

/ɪ̵/ 表示有些人以 /ɪ/ 发音，有些人以 /ə/ 发音。

/ʊ̵/ 表示有些人以 /ʊ/ 发音, 有些人以 /ə/ 发音。

/ə/ 表示 /ə/ 可发音可不发音。

* K.K. 音标是由美国两位语言学家 John S. Kenyon 和 Thomas A. Knott 共同研究出来的，故取二人姓氏第一个字母而简称为 K.K. 音标。其特点是按照一般的美国读法标音。

* * 本辞典所用的 IPA 音标是英国 Jones 音标的最新修订形式。

关于读音的更多信息, 参见第 xvi 页

Chronology

1932 The Bonus Riot in Washington
15,000,000 jobless
Election of FDR
Rumors of revolution

1933 Collapse of the nation's banks
FDR's Hundred Days
Back from the brink

1934 J. Edgar Hoover and *Famous Funnies*
Black blizzards
Dr. Townsend, Father Coughlin, and Huey Long

1935 The Second Hundred Days
The birth of swing music
The rise of John L. Lewis
The Supreme Court challenges FDR

1936 The Liberty League: "Save the Constitution!"
Gone With the Wind
FDR routs Landon and the *Literary Digest*

1937 The Supreme Court "pack" plan
Birth of Congress's conservative coalition
Sit-down strikes in Detroit
Japanese sink the U.S.S. *Panay*
Isolationism at its peak

1938 Munich and H. V. Kaltenborn
New England hurricane
Orson Welles's Martian broadcast

1939 New York World's Fair
World War II starts. Lindbergh: "Keep out!"

1940 The Fall of France
America First; "God Bless America"
Einstein writes FDR a letter
Willkie vs. the Champ

1941 House Bill 1776: Lend-Lease
Nazi sub torpedoes the *Reuben James*
CCNY dismisses Bertrand Russell
Marian Anderson sings at the Lincoln Memorial
Pearl Harbor: "This is no drill"

1942 Retreat in the Pacific; Midway; Guadalcanal
GIs invade North Africa
At home: "I'll Walk Alone"
The ordeal of the Issei and Nisei

1943 Salerno, Cassino, and Tarawa
At home: Frank Sinatra and Henry J. Kaiser

1944 Anzio, Normandy, the Bulge
Saipan and Leyte Gulf

1945 Iwo Jima and Okinawa
The U.N. Charter
FDR dies; Truman is President
V-E Day
Hiroshima and Nagasaki
V-J Day

1946 Postwar inflation and strikes
"Wanna-go-home" riots
Churchill uses "Iron Curtain" in Missouri

1947 The Truman Doctrine and the Marshall Plan
A New Look in fashions

1948 The Kinsey Report
The Berlin airlift
Dixiecrats and Henry Wallace's Progressives
Truman beats Dewey

1949 William J. Levitt's first Levittown
First report of flying saucers
TV: Gorgeous George and skating derbies
China becomes Red China
Russia has the Bomb

1950 The conviction of Alger Hiss
The rise of Joe McCarthy
War in Korea; Inchon; Red China attacks

1951 Direct Distance Dialing starts
The Great Debate
MacArthur is relieved
The age of Mickey Spillane
The silent generation emerges
TV replaces radio as popular entertainment
Kefauver crime hearings

1952 The hydrogen bomb
Scandals shake Truman administration
Nixon's "Checkers" speech
Ike beats Stevenson, who is "too old to cry"

1953 Massive retaliation; bigger bang for a buck
Stalin dies; peace in Korea
The death of Taft

1954 *McCall's* coins "togetherness"
The Bricker amendment
The Army-McCarthy hearings

Contents

目 录

Appendices 附录

Features 文化特写

Preface

英 文 版 序

The *Longman Dictionary of English Language and Culture* is aimed at teachers and advanced students of English who need to understand not just difficult general words of English, such as *dysfunctional* or *accede*, but also the thousands of references to places, people, events, products, and institutions that they meet when they read newspapers or novels, or when they hear spoken language, for example, in films.

Not being able to understand these references has always made it difficult for students of English from other cultures to understand exactly what the author or speaker means. This Dictionary aims to enable those students to see more deeply into the culture of native speakers of English by giving not only a brief definition to explain what the person or thing is, but also by describing the connotations of the term. For example, if British people refer to the **M25** you may be able to deduce from the context that this is a big important road in the UK, but the Dictionary tells you what it is famous for to British people – being very slow because of traffic jams.

This New Edition contains a full dictionary with 80,000 general language words and phrases, but also with 15,000 cultural references in addition. These range from literary figures and artists to popular culture and celebrities, from **Enid Blyton** and **Shakespeare** to **the Beatles**. In this edition, we have also increased the coverage of American culture substantially and you can now find more entries for American institutions, celebrities and products, such as the **Grammy Awards** and **Hershey's Kisses**.

Happy users of the previous editions of this book have written to us to express their satisfaction with a book that provides the kind of information rarely found in other reference titles. We hope that users of this New Edition will find it just as useful, if not more so!

Michael Mayor
Editorial Director – Longman Dictionaries

To Our Readers

致 读 者

培生朗文和词典出版的关系，可谓源远流长。塞缪尔·约翰逊博士(Dr Samuel Johnson，1709-1784)，在英国是家喻户晓的名字。他花了九年时间独力编成A Dictionary of the English Language，被誉为现代英语词典之父。时至今日，国内外词典专家仍习惯于称呼这本词典为《约翰逊词典》。1755年，朗文出版了这本英语词典界的开山之作。

20世纪二三十年代，世界经历了第一轮英语热，英语学习人数与日俱增，人们开始不满足于使用那些原本为英国学生编写的英语词典。母语学习者和外语学习者对语言工具书的要求有着显著差异。那些专门为外国学习者编写、解决英语学习困难和障碍的词典，我们称之为英语学习词典。由迈克尔·韦斯特(Michael West)和詹姆斯·恩迪科特(James Endicott)合力编写的《新方法英语词典》(A New Method English Dictionary)，便是世界上第一本英语学习词典，于1935年由朗文出版，后经多次修订重印，历久常新。

20世纪六七十年代，新兴工业国经济起飞，世界又经历了第二轮英语热，英语学习从广度向深度发展，高阶英语学习者要求有更多、更好、更新的词典供选择。培生适时推出了Longman Dictionary of Contemporary English，自1978年出版至今，广受读者欢迎。语言离不开文化，能说一口流利的英语，不可能不对英美文化有较为深入的了解，否则英语理解难免欠准确，表达难免不到位。语言是硬功夫，文化是软知识，要“软硬兼施”、“文武兼备”，英语学习才能事半功倍，尤其对于高阶英语学习者而言。

培生有见及此，于1992年推出Longman Dictionary of English Language and Culture，以高阶英语学习者所需要的语文条目为基础，增加15,000条英美文化条目，全面介绍历史、地理、政治、艺术以至流行文化等方面的知识。以Grand Central Station为例，读者从字面上看得出来它是一个大火车站，去过美国的还可能知道它是纽约的重要交通枢纽，但是未必人人晓得美国人常用以比喻人多嘈杂拥挤的地方，如: Our house was like Grand Central Station last night! 我家昨晚简直就像中央大火车站！

北京商务印书馆独具只眼，了解到中国市场缺乏而中国读者需要这么一本“兼备”的词典，于2004年与培生合作，在中国内地推出Longman Dictionary of English Language and Culture的英汉双解版，取名为《朗文当代英语大辞典》。事过七年，时代有所转变，语言有所更新，而该词典仍然独一无二，是市面上唯一的高阶程度、语言与文化兼备的英语学习词典。

我们很高兴与商务印书馆一道，为中国广大读者呈献新一版的《朗文当代英语大辞典》，进一步帮助高阶英语学习者认识当代的英语及英美文化。

培生教育出版亚洲有限公司

2011年4月

Expert's Preface

专 家 序 言

孔子曰:“工欲善其事,必先利其器。”学习语言必须要有好词典,好词典可以让我们深入地了解语言,熟练地使用语言。词典可以规范语言,净化语言,丰富语言,传播语言,就此而言,词典也是文化积累、文化建设、文化传承的重要工具。

我上大学期间,虽然偶尔也查查全本(unabridged)词典,但查的、翻的、背的最多的还是学习词典。大学毕业时,我的两本学习词典已经散了页。记得其中的一本是1978年初英文版的《朗文当代高级英语辞典》。这部词典对单词的释义中包含着很多语法因素,有利于学习者在学单词的同时,学习与单词有关的语法。词典中不仅注明名词是可数的还是不可数的,动词是及物的还是不及物的,而且还注明不同名词、动词、形容词后面应该跟随的搭配成分是介词、副词、动词不定式、that从句,还是wh-词等等。这样,学习者很容易学会语法规则,而且还会在不经意之中总结出一些语法规律。这种“双重描述”(double articulation)构成了一个非常实用的语法解释系统。

我们手头的这部《朗文当代英语大辞典》(英英·英汉双解,新版)(Longman Dictionary of English Language and Culture (English-Chinese) *New Edition*)除具备学习词典的特色外,又增加了大量文化内容,将语言与文化紧密地结合起来。按照汉语习惯,只收录词语的为“词典”,不止收录词语的为“辞典”,所以我们看到的是一部真正的“大辞典”。在这部最新版的“大辞典”里,有560多项“文化注释”(CULTURAL NOTE),对词汇做文化意义上的延伸和阐释。同时,还有全新彩页的文化特写(Features)。这些与语言特色紧密结合的文化特色对学习者大有裨益。

当然,新版的语言特色也愈加鲜明。新版继承“双重描述”的传统,愈加注重词语搭配,提供数千处搭配实例。而与之相关的“用法说明”(USAGE NOTE)也全面改写,详细讲解词语间的细微区别和词语的正确用法。作为学习词典一以贯之的特色,这部辞典的所有释义均用英语中最常用的2000个单词撰写而成,以利于学习者的阅读。作为延伸阅读,辞典还提供了24页彩页、58页语言提示、30页附录,为读者指点迷津。

朗文词典也是最早的计算机化词典——不是一般的机读词典,而是基于数据库、可以对语言材料进行计算机分析的计算机化词典。词典编纂在今天已经不是个体劳动,甚至也不是一般的团队作业。一部优秀词典凝聚着大批各领域专家的心血,同时也仰仗数字化语料库这一现代化工具。《朗文当代英语大辞典》的新版基于朗文语料库网络(Longman Corpus Network),对旧版作了全面修订。新版标注出口语及书面语中最常用的1000词、2000词、3000词,这一非常体贴学习者的做法也显示出数据库的实力。辞典还根据数据库的资料注明absolutely和actually之类的词在口语中远比在书面语中常用。一共设置了150个这样的词汇使用频率表,对词汇在口语和书面语中的使用频率进行图解,这为读者进行选择提供了很大方便。

朗文拥有悠久的英语词典出版传统,是英语词典业的巨擘,如今又与中国最好的辞书出版社商务印书馆合作,推出这本语言与文化相结合的《朗文当代英语大辞典》(新版),以满足中文环境下学习英文的需要。这两家出版社的合作可以说是珠联璧合，一家提供最好的英文词典，另一家则提供最好的汉化服务。辞典中译文准确、规范、通畅。对于学习者而言，有时并不需要参考中译文，但是，对于一些名词，特别是一些专用名词，在费力阅读了英文解释之后还不甚了了之时，看一眼简单明了、准确规范的汉译，马上就会有豁然开朗的感觉。辞典的中译文对于翻译工作者来说也时有启发。

《朗文当代英语大辞典》是一部十分全面的词典，不仅适合于狭义的学习者，也适合于广义的学习者，可以满足学习英语、进行翻译、一般阅读、从事教学等种种需要。如果对语言和文化感兴趣，那么阅读这部辞典就是一种乐趣。通过阅读，就会发现一个单词居然会有这么丰富的意义，这么灵活的用法，这么微妙的联想；几个单词居然会有如此灵活、如此美妙、如此给力的搭配；而所谓文化，必须依靠语言才能丰富多彩。读词典也是学语言和文化的最好方法。

中国文化的繁荣一直都获益于对外开放。学习《朗文当代英语大辞典》之类的好词典，也有益于丰富中国语言和文化。我们在汉语词典的编纂和出版上，也应该赶超世界先进水平。30年前，吕叔湘先生曾经感叹过，法国的"词典两万多种，我们不知道出到了两千种没有，相形之下实在是难为情"。这种情况今天虽已有所改善，但还是不尽如人意。我们虽有质量极高的精品词典，例如《汉语大词典》、《现代汉语词典》、《辞源》、《辞海》等等，但相对于世界很多语言的词典而言，品种较为单一，数量也比较少，而且含金量高的品牌更少，更新的速度缓慢。随着汉语的国际推广，我们也需要像朗文词典一样的汉语学习者词典。我们需要比吕叔湘先生主编的《现代汉语八百词》规模更大、质量更高的汉语学习者词典。相信随着中国文化建设的进步，随着我们现代语言学研究、语法学研究的进步，随着海量的汉语语料库的建设，我们也会有更多种类、更多系列、更多一线品牌的汉语词典。

《朗文当代英语大辞典》值得拥有。一旦拥有，就会开卷有益，帮我们学习和工作，给我们以乐趣，说不定还会让我们思考。

程朝翔

2011年2月

程朝翔，北京大学外国语学院院长、北京大学英语系教授、中国外国文学学会英语文学分会会长。主要研究方向为英美戏剧与电影、比较戏剧、外语教育等。

Explanatory Chart

图 示

ar·du·ous /ˋɑrdʒuəs; ˈɑːdjuəs/ *adj* involving a lot of strength and effort 费力的, 艰巨的: *an arduous journey through the mountains* 艰难的山区旅行 **—arduously** *adv* **—arduousness** *n* [U]

读音用国际音标标注（前为美式 K.K. 音标，后为英式 IPA 音标）。

am·ber /ˋæmbɚ; ˈæmbə/ *n* [U] **1** a yellowish brown colour 琥珀色 **2** a yellowish brown substance used to make jewellery 琥珀 **—amber** *adj*

词类 —— 动词、名词、形容词、介词等等 —— 均用斜体字标出。

a·bode[1] /əˋbod; əˈbəʊd/ *n* [C] *formal or humorous* someone's home【正式或幽默】住所: *Welcome to my humble abode.* 欢迎光临寒舍。| **of no fixed abode** (=having no permanent home) 居无定所

abode[2] the past tense of ABIDE

拼写相同但属于不同词类的词汇当作同形词处理，分列词条。

an·nu·al[1] /ˋænjuəl; ˈænjuəl/ *adj* **1** happening once a year 一年一度的, 每年的: *an annual conference* 年会 **2** based on or calculated over a period of one year 按年度计算的: *Steel output reached an annual figure of one million tons.* 钢的年产量达到 100 万吨。**—annually** *adv*

如果一个词有一个以上意义，每项词义均用黑体数字标出。

ar·dour *BrE*【英】, **ardor** *AmE*【美】/ˋɑrdɚ; ˈɑːdə/ *n* [U] **1** very strong positive feelings 激情, 热诚: *They sang with real ardour.* 他们唱得很有激情。**2** *literary* strong feelings of love【文】炽热的爱情

如果一个词可以用两种不同方法拼写，两种拼法均列出。

a·bra·sive[1] /əˋbresɪv; əˈbreɪsɪv/ *adj* **1** seeming rude or unkind in the way you behave towards people because you say what you think very directly 生硬的; 粗鲁的: *a rather abrasive manner* 相当粗鲁的举止

词义均用约 2000 个朗文释义词汇解释，语言简洁易明。

ar·cher /ˋɑrtʃɚ; ˈɑːtʃə/ *n* [C] someone who shoots ARROWS (1) from a BOW[3] (1) 射箭运动员; 弓箭手

不在释义词汇范围内的词均用小号大写字母列出。

an·noy·ing /əˋnɔɪ-ɪŋ; əˈnɔɪ-ɪŋ/ *adj* making you feel slightly angry 令人心烦的: *an annoying habit of interrupting* 打断他人讲话的令人恼火的习惯 | *The annoying thing is he's usually right.* 令人气恼的是, 他通常都是对的。| **it's annoying that** *It's annoying that we didn't know about this before.* 令人恼火的是, 我们事先并不知道。**—annoyingly** *adv*: *annoyingly small portions* 量少得让人恼火

实用而自然的例子均以源自朗文语料库网络的资料为根据。

am·biv·a·lent /æmˋbɪvələnt; æmˈbɪvələnt/ *adj* not sure whether you want or like something or not〔心情〕矛盾的: *Her feelings about getting married are distinctly ambivalent.* 她显然对是否要结婚感到矛盾。**—ambivalence** *n* [U] **—ambivalently** *adv*

派生词列于原词之后，其词义与原词相近。

ad·here /ədˋhɪr; ədˈhɪə/ *v formal* [I+to] to stick firmly to something【正式】黏附, 附着

adhere to sth *phr v* [T] *formal* to continue to behave according to a particular rule, agreement, or belief【正式】坚持; 信守: *adhere to your principles* 坚持原则 | *adhere to the regulations* 遵守规定

短语动词直接在其主要动词的词条后列出。

after ef·fect /ˈ‥ ·,·/ *n* [C usually plural 一般用复数] an unpleasant effect that remains for a long time after the condition or event that caused it 后效; 后作用; 副作用; 后遗效应: *the after-effects of his illness* 他这种病的后遗症

复合词作为词目列出，标有重音模式。

au·ber·gine /ˋobɚ,ʒin; ˈəʊbəʒiːn/ *n* [C,U] *BrE* a large dark purple vegetable【英】紫茄子; EGGPLANT *AmE*【美】—see picture on page A9 参见 A9 页图

英国英语和美国英语用词均列出。

abandon[2] *n* [U] **with gay/wild abandon** in a careless or uncontrolled way without thinking or caring about what you are doing 尽情; 放纵: *The kids hurled pieces of wood on the fire with gay abandon.* 孩子们不管不顾地把木块往火上扔。

短语与习语均列出，并附其意义。

at·trib·u·ta·ble /ə`trɪbjutəbḷ; ə'trɪbjʊtəbəl/ *adj* [not before noun 不用于名词前] likely to be caused by something 可归因于…的: **[+to]** *Death was attributable to gunshot wounds.* 死因可能是枪伤。

ab·hor /əb`hɔr; əb'hɔː/ *v* **abhorred, abhorring** [T not in progressive 不用进行时] *formal* to hate a kind of behaviour or way of thinking, especially because you think it is morally wrong【正式】厌恶, 憎恶: *Some genuinely abhorred slavery, others were simply convinced by the economic arguments against it.* 有些人真正厌恶奴隶制, 而另一些人只是出于经济上的理由才反对奴隶制的。

an·noyed /ə`nɔɪd; ə'nɔɪd/ *adj* slightly angry 烦恼[略感生气]的: *I'll be annoyed if we don't finish by eight.* 如果我们8点还未完成, 我会很懊恼。| **[+with]** *She was annoyed with Duncan for forgetting to phone.* 邓肯忘了打电话使她气恼。| **[+about/by]** *He was annoyed by her apparent indifference.* 她看起来很冷淡, 这让他很恼火。| **be annoyed that** *Mr Davies was annoyed that the books were missing.* 那些书不见了, 戴维斯先生很懊恼。

ar·gu·ment /`ɑrgjəmənt; 'ɑːgjʊmənt/ *n* **1** [C] a situation in which two or more people disagree, often angrily 争论, 争辩, 争吵: **[+with]** *an argument with my husband* 跟我丈夫争吵 | **[+about/over]** *The argument seemed to be about who was going to take the cat to the vet.* 争论似乎是关于由谁带猫去看兽医。| **have an argument** *They were having an argument about the children.* 他们为孩子的事争吵。| **get into an argument** *I got into an argument with the other driver.* 我和另一位司机吵了起来。| **win/lose an argument** *He lost his argument with the doctor.* 他说不过医生。| **heated argument** (=very angry argument) 激烈的争论

ab·sorb /əb`sɔrb; əb'sɔːb/ *v* [T]

1 ▶LIQUID 液体◀ if something absorbs a liquid, it takes the liquid into itself from the surface or space around it 吸收〔液体〕: *Plants absorb nutrients from the soil.* 植物从土壤中吸收养分。

2 ▶INFORMATION 信息◀ to read or hear a large amount of new information and understand it 理解, 掌握: *I haven't really had time to absorb everything that he said.* 我还真没有时间弄懂他说的一切。

3 ▶INTEREST 兴趣◀ to interest someone very much 吸引〔某人〕, 使专心: **be absorbed in** *Judith lay on the settee, absorbed in her book.* 朱迪丝躺在沙发椅上专心致志地看书。| **absorb sb's attention** *The video was totally absorbing the children's attention.* 录像完全吸引了孩子们的注意力。

ap·pend /ə`pɛnd; ə'pend/ *v* [T+to] *formal* to add something to a piece of writing【正式】附加, 增补

ante- /æntɪ; æntɪ/ *prefix* before 在…以前: *to antedate* (=be earlier than something) 先于, 早于 | *antenatal* (=before birth) 出生前的 —compare 比较 ANTI-, POST-, PRE-

an·te[1] /`æntɪ; 'ænti/ *n* **up/raise the ante** to increase your demands or try to get more things from a situation, even though this involves more risks 加赌注 —see also 另见 PENNY ANTE

a·rise /ə`raɪz; ə'raɪz/ *v past tense* **arose** /ə`roz; ə'rəʊz/ *past participle* **arisen** /ə`rɪzṇ; ə'rɪzən/ [I]

语法信息置于方括号内，或在例子前用黑体字标示。

经常一起使用的单词用黑体字标出，并附例子或解释。

较长词条里的指示标记帮助你找到所需要的词义。

某单词用于何种情景及词源方面的信息均用斜体字标出。

"互见"标签提示参见其他单词、短语、图画及用法说明等。

不规则动词的各种形式及不规则名词的复数形式均列出。

Guide to the Dictionary

本辞典使用方法简介

Contents 目录

1 How to find the word you are looking for 如何查出你要寻找的词

本辞典的词汇按字母顺序排列。

1.1 Compound words 复合词

复合词由两个或两个以上的词组成, 具有固定形式和特殊意义, 例如 front man (发言人) 和 front line (前线)。这些复合词多数作为独立的词目列出 (参见第 1.6 节短语与习语)。复合词像普通单词一样按字母顺序排列, 其两个部分之间的空格或连字符均不计算在内。

front·al
frontal sys·tem
front-and-center
front bench
front·bench·er
front door
fron·tier

1.2 Phrasal verbs 短语动词

多个单词组成的动词, 例如 give up 或 put off, 按字母顺序直接列在其主要动词的词条后。例如:

face[2] *v* [T]
  face sb ↔ **down**
  face up to sth
  face sb **with** sth
face card

1.3 Derived words without definition 不附释义的派生词

有些单词通过添加后缀派生而成, 故无需释义。例如 gracefully 和 gracefulness 均派生自 graceful, 而其意义即由原主要单词意义加上后缀意义组合而成。这些派生词在其源词的词条末尾列出。

grace·ful /ˋgresfəl; ˈgreɪsfəl/ *adj* **1** moving in a smooth and attractive way, or having an attractive shape〔动作、线条〕优美的, 雅致的: *a slim graceful figure* 修长而优美的身材 **2** behaving in a polite and pleasant way 优雅得体的, 体面的: *a graceful apology* 得体的道歉 —**gracefully** *adv*: *When I am no longer needed, I shall retire gracefully.* 当不再需要我的时候, 我将体面地退休。—**gracefulness** *n* [U]

在此例中, gracefully 意为'以优美的方式'或'得体地', 而 gracefulness 意为'优美'或'得体'。

1.4 Homographs 同形异义词

同形异义词是指拼写相同, 但在其他方面有差异的单词, 这些单词在辞典里以独立的词条列出。在本辞典中, 不同词类的单词作同形异义词处理。

face[1] /fes; feɪs/ *n* [C]
1 ▶FRONT OF YOUR HEAD 头部的正面◀ the front part of the head from the chin to the forehead 脸, 面部: *She has such a pretty face.* 她有那么美的一张脸。| *Bob's face was covered in cuts and bruises.* 鲍勃的脸上满是划痕与擦伤。| **a sea of faces** (=a lot of faces seen together) 许许多多的脸 *The Principal looked down from the platform at the sea of faces below.* 校长从讲台上看着下面数不清的脸。—see picture at 参见 HEAD[1] 图
face[2] *v* [T]
1 ▶DIFFICULT SITUATION 困难的局面◀ if you face a difficult situation or if it faces you, you must deal with it 面临, 面对: *The President faces the difficult task of putting the economy back on its feet.* 总统面对着恢复经济的艰巨任务。| *McManus is facing the biggest challenge of his career.* 麦克马纳斯正面临着职业生涯中的最大挑战。| **be faced with/by** *I was faced with the awful job of breaking the news to the girl's family.* 我面临着向女孩的家人报告这一消息的可怕任务。

同形异义词排列顺序取决于其常用程度。face 用作名词的频率比用作动词为多, 因此名词 face 的词条列在前面。

词类和拼写相同、而读音不同的单词, 以分开的词目列出。例如名词 row (=a line 排, 行) 和 row (=an argument 争吵), 因为读音不同, 而分列为不同词目。

如果两个单词拼写形式相同, 而其中一个以大写字母开头, 并具有完全不同的意义, 例如形容词 catholic 和 Catholic, 也分列为不同词目。

某个名词的复数形式具有独自的意义时, 通常当作该名词的一个义项列出:

blue[2] *n* **1** [C,U] the colour that is blue 蓝色: *the rich greens and blues of the tapestry* 挂毯浓艳的蓝绿色调 | *She nearly always dresses in blue.* 她几乎总穿蓝色衣服。**2 blues** [plural] a slow sad style of music that came from the southern US 布鲁斯音乐〔起源于美国南方的一种缓慢、忧郁的乐曲〕: *a blues singer* 布鲁斯歌手 —see also 另见 RHYTHM AND BLUES **3 the blues** [plural] *informal* feelings of sadness【非正式】忧郁, 沮丧: *Don't be surprised if you get the blues for a while after your baby is born.* 如果你在生完孩子后出现暂时的忧郁, 你不必感到惊讶。

但如果某个单词的复数形式比其单数形式重要, 而且有多层意义时, 则作为独立的词目列出。因此, goods 作为一个词条, 与名词 good 分列。

1.5 Other types of headwords 其他类型的词目

缩略语及 dis- 一类的前缀或 -able 一类的后缀, 均作为词目独立列出。

不同的拼写形式会放在词目后, 也会作为词目另条列出, 并指引你查找主要词条。

in·quire, enquire /ɪnˋkwaɪr; ɪnˈkwaɪə/ *v* [I,T] **1** to ask someone for information 询问, 打听: *"Are you getting married?" the television interviewer inquired.* "你准备结婚了吗?"电视采访记者问道。
en·quire /ɪnˋkwaɪr; ɪnˈkwaɪə/ *v* [I,T] *especially BrE*【尤英】another spelling of INQUIRE inquire 的另一种拼法

单词的不规则屈折变化形式在其主要形式的词条下列出, 并作为独立的词目列出, 引导你查找主要词条。

have[1] /v, əv, həv; v, əv, həv; *strong* 强读 hæv; hæv/ *auxiliary verb past tense* **had** /əd, həd; d, əd, həd; *strong* 强读 hæd; hæd/ *third person singular present tense* **has** /əz, həz; z, əz, həz; *strong* 强读 hæz; hæz/ *negative short forms* 否定缩略式为 **haven't** /ˋhævn̩t; ˈhævənt/, **hadn't** /ˋhædn̩t; ˈhædnt/, **hasn't** /ˋhæzn̩t; ˈhæzənt/
had /əd, həd; d; əd, həd; *strong* 强读 hæd; hæd/ **1** the past tense and past participle of HAVE

1.6 Phrases and idioms 短语与习语

有些单词经常用于特定的短语里, 而本辞典的一个重要特色是将这些短语作为独立的义项处理。例如:

face[1] /fes; feɪs/ *n* [C]
17 sb's face doesn't fit used to say that someone is not the right kind of person for a particular group,

organization etc 某人不适合〔某个群体、组织等〕

18 put a brave face (on) to make an effort to behave in a happy cheerful way when you are upset or disappointed〔虽然烦恼、失望等但〕装作若无其事的样子: *He was shattered, though he put on a brave face.* 他大为震惊, 尽管他装作若无其事的样子。

19 set your face against *especially BrE* to be very determined that something should not happen【尤英】沉下脸反对, 坚决反对

有些复合词因为是习语, 也按此处理。如 big deal 作为 big 的一个词义来处理。

短语与习语通常在该短语或习语的第一个主要单词下列出 (即不列在 the, to, something 或 be 这类词下), 所以 have egg on your face 的释义列在 egg 下, 而不在 face 下。但在 face 条下查找, 也会在该词条末尾找到这个短语的相互参照说明, 告诉你在何处找到其释义。

face[1] /fes; feɪs/ *n* [C]
—see also 另见 **have egg on your face** (EGG[1] (4)), **fly in the face of** (FLY[1] (28))

2. Understanding meaning 理解词义

2.1 Words with more than one meaning 多义词

一个单词具有一个以上词义时, 每项词义都有一个编号, 并根据对我们的口语和书面语语料的分析, 最常用的词义列在最前。

a·chieve·ment /əˋtʃivmənt; əˈtʃiːvmənt/ *n* **1** [C] something important that you succeed in doing by your own efforts 成绩, 成就: *Winning three gold medals is a remarkable achievement.* 赢得三枚金牌是个了不起的成绩。| **no mean achievement/quite an achievement** (=a very impressive achievement) 了不起的成绩 **2** [U] the act of achieving something 实现; 完成; 达到: *the achievement of economic stability* 经济稳定的实现 | **sense of achievement** (=a feeling of pride when you succeed in doing something difficult) 成就感 *You get a wonderful sense of achievement when you reach the top.* 当你到达最高处时, 你会有一种绝妙的成就感。

本辞典根据对大量的口头英语和书面英语语料的分析, 标出单词或短语的使用频率。

短语如包含该单词并具有独特意义, 则作为独立的义项列出, 并按其使用频率顺序排列。例如:

look·out /ˋlʊk,aut; ˈlʊk-aʊt/ *n*

1 be on the lookout for to watch a place or situation continuously in order to find something you want or to be ready for problems or opportunities 监视, 留神观察: *Police were on the lookout for anyone behaving suspiciously.* 警察随时注意可疑的人。| *We're always on the lookout for new business opportunities.* 我们随时留意新的商机。

2 keep a lookout to keep watching carefully for something or someone, especially for danger 密切注视〔尤指危险〕: **keep a sharp/special lookout** *When you're driving keep a sharp lookout for cyclists.* 驾驶时要特别注意骑自行车的人。

3 ►PERSON 人◄ [C] someone whose duty is to watch carefully for something, especially danger 监视者, 守望者: *A lookout reported an enemy plane approaching.* 监视哨报告说一架敌机正在飞近。

4 ►PLACE 地方◄ [C] a place for a lookout to watch from 哨所, 瞭望台: *a coastguard lookout on the clifftop* 海边悬崖顶上的哨所

5 it's your/their own lookout *BrE spoken* used to say that what someone has chosen to do is their own problem or risk, and no one else's【英口】那是你们/他们自己的事〔与别人不相干〕: *If he wants to ruin his health with all these drugs, that's his own lookout.* 如果他要用所有这些毒品毁掉自己的健康, 那是他自己的事。

6 be a poor/bad lookout for sb *BrE spoken* used to say that something bad or unsatisfactory is likely to happen【英口】对某人不是件好事, 事情不妙: *It'll be a poor lookout for James if she finds that letter.* 如果她发现那封信, 詹姆斯就惨了。

这表示 lookout 的最常见用法是用于短语 be on the lookout for 之中 。

2.2 Definitions 释义

本辞典的所有释义均用由大约 2000 个常用词构成的"朗文释义词汇"写成, 文字清晰简洁。这些释义所用的词汇列于本辞典末尾的附录 8, 该附录准确地说明了如何使用这些单词。

2.3 Examples 例子

本辞典大部分释义后均列有例子, 说明该词用法。

例子有的是短语, 有的是完整的句子, 均用斜体字标示:

clear instructions 清楚的指示 | *You must never do that again. Is that clear?* 不许你再那样做, 明白吗?

本辞典的所有例子均以"朗文语料库网络"的口语和书面语语料内容为基础。有些例子直接选自语料库; 有些例子略有改动, 去掉了艰深的词; 有些例子专门为该词条编写。不管什么情况, 例子均精心挑选, 有助于说明该单词或短语的一般用法。

例子还可以用来说明该单词的语法, 以及示范该单词如何与其他词语一起使用 (即词语搭配) 。

be clear on *The rules are quite clear on the point.* 在这一点上各项规定都明白易懂。| **clear to sb** *Is all this clear to you?* 你全都明白了吗?

2.4 Collocations 词语搭配

本辞典的一个重要目的是清楚地说明一个单词的搭配, 即经常与该单词一起使用的其他词语。词语搭配用蓝色字标示出, 其后括号里有简短的释义或例子, 或两者都有。

make yourself clear (=express something well) 表达清楚 *To make yourself clear without using facial expressions can be very difficult.* 很难不借助面部表情而清楚地表达自己。| **get sth clear** *Let's get one thing clear; you have my whole-hearted support.* 你要明白一件事, 我全力支持你。

这些词语搭配按使用频率顺序列出, 最重要的搭配列在最前面。

2.5 Finding the meaning you want – Signposts 查出你需要的词义 —— 指示标记

在有多项释义的词条里, 我们加上了"指示标记", 以便快速查出需要的合适释义。这些指示标记在释义前用大写字母标出, 并且只用"朗文释义词汇"中的单词编写。

bridge[1] /brɪdʒ; brɪdʒ/ *n* [C]

1 ►OVER A RIVER/ROAD ETC 在河/路等的上方◄ a structure built over a river, road etc, that allows people or vehicles to cross from one side to the other 桥, 桥梁

2 ►CONNECTION 连接◄ something that provides a

connection between two things; LINK[2] (1)〔事物之间的〕桥梁, 纽带, 联系: *The training programme is seen as a bridge between school and work.* 该培训计划被视为学校与工作之间的桥梁。
3 ▶SHIP 船◀ the raised part of a ship from which the officers control it 船桥, 舰桥, 驾驶台
4 ▶CARD GAME 纸牌戏◀ [U] a card game for four players who play in pairs 桥牌
5 the bridge of your nose the bony upper part of your nose between your eyes 鼻梁
6 ▶PAIR OF GLASSES 眼镜◀ the part of a pair of glasses that rests on the bridge of your nose〔眼镜的〕鼻托, 鼻梁架 —see picture at 参见 GLASS[1] 图
7 ▶MUSICAL INSTRUMENT 乐器◀ a small piece of wood under the strings of a VIOLIN or GUITAR, used to keep them in position〔弦乐器的〕弦柱, 弦马, 琴马
8 ▶FOR TEETH 用于牙齿的◀ a small piece of metal for keeping false teeth in place〔假牙上的〕齿桥 —see also 另见 **build bridges** (BUILD[1] (7)), **burn your bridges** (BURN[1] (22)), **cross that bridge when you come to it** (CROSS[1] (8)), **be (all) water under the bridge** (WATER[1] (7))

指示标记为单词或短语, 可以引导你查到合适的词义。它可能是一个同义词、一个简短的释义, 或一个动词的典型主语或宾语。

2.6 Long entries with menus 附项目单的长词条

在一些较长的词条里, 紧密相关的词义列在一起或成为一个段落。而词条开头的项目单列出各分段标题, 便于找到所需词义的部分。这些词义均另起一行开始, 为方便查找, 往往还有指示标记。请看单词 run 和 way 的分段方式作为参考。

2.7 Showing words with similar and opposite meanings 标示词义相似和相反的单词

有时, 标出同义词, 即与该词具有相同意义或几乎相同意义的单词, 是很有用的。同义词在释义之后列出, 例如:

im·ma·te·ri·al /ˌɪməˈtɪrɪəl; ˌɪməˈtɪəriəl◂/ *adj* **1** not important in a particular situation; IRRELEVANT 无关紧要的; 不相关的: *The causes of the problem are immaterial now – we need solutions.* 问题的原因现在已无关紧要, 我们需要的是解决方法。**2** *formal* not having a real physical form【正式】非实体的, 无形的

具有相似意义或相似形式的单词标 'compare 比较' 用于提示, 也列出有用的反义词。

i·ma·gi·na·ry /ɪˈmædʒəˌnɛrɪ; ɪˈmædʒənəri/ *adj* not real, but produced from pictures or ideas in your mind 想象的, 虚构的: *All the characters in this book are imaginary.* 本书人物纯属虚构。—compare 比较 IMAGINATIVE

im·mod·est /ɪˈmɑdɪst; ɪˈmɒdəst/ *adj* **1** having a very high opinion of yourself and your abilities, and not embarrassed about telling people how clever you are etc 骄傲的, 不谦虚的 —opposite 反义词 MODEST (1) **2** *old-fashioned* behaviour or clothes that are immodest may embarrass or offend people because they do not follow the usual social rules concerning sexual behaviour【过时】〔行为或衣着〕不端庄的, 不正派的; 下流的, 有伤风化的 —**immodestly** *adv* —**immodesty** *n* [U]

3 Frequency 使用频率

你已看到本辞典是按使用频率排列的。一个单词的使用频率最高的意义首先列出, 而同形异义词也按照使用频率顺序标出。一个单词的每一义项, 说明语法和词语搭配的例子, 也均按使用频率顺序排列。我们对使用频率的所有判断是根据对语料库资料的分析得出来的。这种组织编排原则提供了英语的重要信息, 而且有助于学生学习。

对一些重要的单词, 提供图表对使用频率做进一步说明。一些图表说明某个单词在英语口语中比在书面语中使用频繁得多, 而另一些图表则比较具有相同意义的单词, 说明哪个单词在书面语中使用得多, 哪个单词在口语中使用得多。还有些图表说明某个单词在其每项最常用的搭配或语法句型中的使用频率, 另外一些图表则简要说明了英国英语与美国英语的差异。

本辞典还对培生朗文所能得到的所有语料库资料用电脑进行了分析, 在这一基础上说明哪些单词是使用得最频繁的词汇。符号S1、S2和S3分别表示一个单词属于英语口语中前1000、前2000和前3000个使用得最频繁的词汇。符号W1、W2和W3则相应表示一个单词属于英语书面语中前1000、前2000和前3000个使用得最频繁的词汇。单词的标记是S1、S2还是W1、W2等, 乃根据其在美国英语与英国英语中的使用频率而综合计算出来的。

4 Grammar 语法

本辞典包含大量有关各单词的语法信息, 包括每个词目所属的词类 —— 名词、动词、形容词等, 以及词汇屈折变化的信息 —— 即过去时态、复数、比较级以及其他形式的变化。此外, 对单词的句法也有详尽的说明 —— 该单词与其他单词结合而组成的各种句型。

4.1 Word classes 词类

词类(或'词性')是这样标示的:

il·lo·gi·cal /ɪˈlɑdʒɪkl; ɪˈlɒdʒɪkəl/ *adj* **1** not sensible or reasonable 不合理的, 悖理的: *erratic and illogical behaviour* 古怪、乖戾的行为 —opposite 反义词 LOGICAL (1) **2** not based on the principles of LOGIC 不合逻辑的: *an illogical conclusion* 荒谬的结论 —**illogically** /-klɪ; -kli/ *adv* —**illogicality** /ɪˌlɑdʒɪˈkælətɪ; ɪˌlɒdʒəˈkæləti/ *n* [U]

这意味着 illogical 是形容词。其派生形式也标示了词类: illogically 是副词, 而 illogicality 是名词。

本辞典所使用的词类为:

word class 词类	**example 例子**
adj (adjective) 形容词	a **fast** car, **straight** lines, **amazing** speed, **frequent** trains
adv (adverb) 副词	smiling **happily**; put it **away**; **frankly**, I'm not bothered
auxiliary verb 助动词	be, have
conjunction 连词	and, but
determiner 限定词	this, which
interjection 感叹词	damn, wow
modal verb 情态动词	must, can, should

n (noun) 名词	car, rabbit, president, dignity, excuse
number 数词	five, ninth
phr v (phrasal verb) 短语动词	put off, shut up, take over
predeterminer 前置限定词	all, both
prefix 前缀	dis-, centi-
prep (preposition) 介词	in, after, to
pron (pronoun) 代(名)词	he, theirs, us
quantifier 数量词	many, several
suffix 后缀	-ity, -ness
v (verb) 动词	go, send, indicate

4.2 Inflections 屈折变化

屈折变化是单词根据其在句子里的语法作用而产生的形式变化。大部分单词的屈折变化是有规律可循的。例如:大部分名词加 -s 或 -es 构成复数形式,大部分动词加 -ed 构成过去式形式。除非有可能引起混淆,或规则变化的发音有难度,本辞典一般不列出这些规则的屈折变化形式。

不规则的屈折变化形式则一律列出,直接放在词类后面,用蓝色字标出,例如:

cri·sis /ˋkraɪsɪs; ˈkraɪsɨs/ *n plural* **crises** /-siz; -siːz/ [C, U]

eat /it; iːt/ *v past tense* **ate** /et; eɪt/ *past participle* **eaten** /ˋitn̩; ˈiːtn/

good¹ /gʊd; gʊd/ *adj comparative* 比较级 **better** /ˋbɛtɚ; ˈbetə/ *superlative* 最高级 **best** /bɛst; best/

不规则屈折变化形式还按本身的字母顺序作为词目列出,引导你去查找主词:

ate /et; eɪt/ the past tense of EAT

列出的屈折变化还包括:

在过去式和 -ing 形式中需双写字母的动词:

hug¹ /hʌg; hʌg/ *v* **hugged, hugging** [T]

以 -y 结尾的动词:

car·ry¹ /ˋkærɪ; ˈkæri/ *v* **carried, carrying**

以 -y 结尾的形容词:

dirt·y¹ /ˋdɝtɪ; ˈdɜːti/ *adj* **dirtier, dirtiest**

本辞典后从 C10 页开始,有不规则动词表列出所有不规则变化的动词。

4.3 Syntax – verbs 句法 —— 动词

动词的基本用法在方括号内说明:

代号 [I] (不及物) 和 [T] (及物) 表示该动词有宾语还是没有宾语。

hard·en /ˋhɑrdn̩; ˈhɑːdn/ *v* **1** [I,T] to become firm or stiff, or to make something firm or stiff (使) 变硬; (使) 坚固; (使) 硬化: *Make sure you give the paint enough time to dry and harden.* 你一定要让油漆有足够的时间干透和变硬。**2** [I] to become more strict and determined and less sympathetic 变得更坚定; 变得冷酷无情: *Opposition to the military regime has hardened since the massacres.* 大屠杀后,反对军政府的力量更强硬了。| *a hardening of attitudes* 态度变得强硬 | *His face hardened.* 他的脸沉了下来。—compare 比较 SOFTEN (4) **3** [T] if an experience hardens someone, it makes them stronger and more able to deal with difficult or unpleasant situations 使变得坚强, 使更有忍耐力

代号 [linking verb 连系动词] 的意思是该动词表示其前后的事物是同样的事,或是对前面事物的描述。

look¹ /lʊk; lʊk/ *v*
3 ►SEEM 看似◄ [linking verb 连系动词] to seem to be something, especially by having a particular appearance 看上去, 看起来: *How do I look in this dress?* 我穿这件连衣裙看起来怎样? | **look like** *The intruder was holding what looked like a shotgun.* 闯入者手里握着看似猎枪一样的东西。| **look as if** *You look as if you haven't slept all night.* 你看上去似乎整夜没有睡觉。

be² *v* **1** [linking verb 连系动词] used to show that someone or something is the same as the subject〔表示某人或某事与主语相同〕: *It's me.* 是我。| *Lack of money is our biggest problem.* 缺钱是我们最大的问题。| *If I were you, I shouldn't do it.* 如果我是你,我就不会这样做。

方括号也可能给出该动词用法的限制,包括 [not in progressive 不用进行时]:

pre·fer /prɪˋfɝ; prɪˈfɜː/ *v* **preferred, preferring** [T not in progressive 不用进行时] **1** to like someone or something more than someone or something else 更喜欢:

[I always+adv/prep]:

am·ble /ˋæmbl̩; ˈæmbəl/ *v* [I always+adv/prep] to walk in a slow relaxed way 漫步: [**+along/across etc**] *The old man came out and ambled over for a chat.* 老人出来了,从容地走过去聊天。—**amble** *n* [singular]

不可以只说 he ambled, 需加上 along 或 towards me 一类的词或短语。

[usually in passive 一般用被动态]:

carpet² *v* [T] **1** [usually in passive 一般用被动态] to cover a floor with carpet 在…上铺地毯: *a carpeted corridor* 铺有地毯的走廊 **2** *informal especially BrE* to blame someone for something they have done; REPRIMAND【非正式, 尤英】斥责, 责备, 责骂 **3 carpeted with grass/flowers etc** *literary* covered with a thick layer of grass etc【文】覆盖着一层厚厚的草/花等

[not in passive 不用被动态]:

concern² *v* [T] **1** if an activity, situation, rule etc concerns you, it affects you or involves you〔活动、情况、规则等〕对…有影响; 与…相关: *The tax changes will concern large corporations rather than small businesses.* 税收上的变化影响到的是大公司而不是小企业。**2** [not in passive 不用被动态] to make someone feel worried or upset 使忧虑, 使担心: *The fact that she spends so much time on her own really concerns me.* 她很多时间都是一人独处,这真让我担心。**3** [not in passive 不用被动态] if a story, book, report etc concerns someone or something, it is about them〔故事、书、报

告等〕与…有关, 关于: *This article concerns a man who was wrongly imprisoned.* 这篇文章写的是一个被冤枉而入狱的人。**4 concern yourself with/about sth** to become involved in something because you are interested in it or because it worries you 关心, 担心: *More and more people are concerning themselves with environmental problems.* 越来越多的人关心起环境问题。**5 to whom it may concern** an expression written at the beginning of a formal letter when you do not know the name of the person you want to communicate with 敬启者〔写在正式信函开头的一句套话, 用于写信人不知道收信人的姓名时〕—see also 另见 CONCERNED

如果提供的基本信息适用于单词的所有意义, 该信息会列在词目后; 如果该信息只适用于单词的某个义项, 则该信息会列在该义项的序号之后。

动词其他用法的信息会在例子中显示出来。典型的结构用蓝色字表示, 后接例子。

4 decide in favour of/decide against a) to choose or not choose someone or something 选择/不选择〔某人或某物〕: *After long discussion they decided in favour of the younger candidate.* 经过长时间的讨论, 他们决定选那个年轻些的候选人。**b)** if a judge or JURY (1) decides in favour of someone or against someone, they say in court that someone is guilty or not guilty 作出有利于/不利于〔某人的〕裁决: *The jury decided in favour of the plaintiff.* 陪审团作出了有利于原告的裁决。

这些例子按使用频率顺序列出, 将最常用的结构列在最前面。

4.4 Phrasal verbs 短语动词

对于短语动词而言, 其介词是否既可以放在宾语前面, 也可以放在其后, 或者只能放在宾语前面或后面, 是非常重要的。介词既可放于宾语之前, 又可放于宾语之后, 这一点在本辞典里用双向箭头"↔"表示。

hand² *v* [T]

hand sth ↔ **out** *phr v* [T] **1** to give something to each member of a group of people; DISTRIBUTE 分发, 散发: *Could you start handing these books out.* 请你把这些书分发出去吧。**2 hand out advice** to give advice, even if people do not want to hear it 出主意 —see also 另见 HANDOUT

hammer² *v*

hammer out sth *phr v* [T] to decide on an agreement, contract etc after a lot of discussion and disagreement 〔经详细的讨论及争议后〕得出〔协议、解决办法等〕: *The UN is trying to force the warring factions to get together and hammer out a solution.* 联合国正在试图拉拢各敌对派系一起寻求解决问题的方案。

这词条表示你可以说 hand the books out, 或者说 hand out the books, 但是说 hammer an agreement out 则是不正确的。

4.5 Syntax – nouns 句法 — 名词

方括号内提供的语法信息, 表示名词或其某个义项是可数的 (如 a pen, three pens), 或是不可数的 (如 honour, daylight)。

hab·i·ta·tion /ˌhæbəˈteʃən; ˌhæbɪ̌ˈteɪʃən/ *n formal* 【正式】**1 unfit for human habitation** a building that is unfit for human habitation is not safe or healthy for people to live in 不适合人类居住, 不适宜住人 **2** [U] the act of living in a place 居住: *There was no sign of habitation as far as the eye could see.* 放眼望去, 看不到有人居住的迹象。**3** [C] a house or place to live in 住宅, 住处

hes·i·ta·tion /ˌhɛzəˈteʃən; ˌhezɪ̌ˈteɪʃən/ *n* [C,U] the action of hesitating 踌躇, 犹豫, 迟疑 (不决): *After some hesitation one of them began to speak.* 犹豫了一会儿之后, 其中一个人开口了。| **have no hesitation in** *I would have no hesitation in declining the post.* 我会毫不犹豫地拒绝这个职位。| **after/without a moment's hesitation** *Without a moment's hesitation she kissed him.* 她毫不犹豫地亲吻了他。

如果某个名词或其某个义项总是单数, 或总是复数, 也在方括号内标明。

hard right /ˌ· ˈ·◂/ *n* [singular] the part of a political party that believes strongly in RIGHT WING political ideas 极右派

high heels /ˌ· ˈ·/ *n* [plural] women's shoes with high heels 高跟鞋 —**high-heeled** *adj* —see picture on page A17 参见 A17 页图

如果名词后通常跟某个介词或某几个介词, 这在说明该名词的例子前用蓝色字表示。某个名词后的典型结构也在例子前用蓝色字表示出来。

hope² *n* [U]

5 ▶CHANCE 机会◀ [C,U] a chance of succeeding or of something good happening 机会, 可能性: **[+of]** *There was no hope of escape.* 没有逃脱的希望了。| **hope that** *There is some hope that we'll find a solution to our problems.* 我们还有一点希望能找到解决问题的方法。

4.6 Syntax – adjectives and adverbs 句法 — 形容词与副词

形容词或副词用法的信息在方括号内说明, 包括:

[only before noun 仅用于名词前]:

ac·tu·al /ˈæktʃuəl; ˈæktʃuəl/ *adj* [only before noun 仅用于名词前] **1** real, especially as compared with what is believed, expected or intended 实际的, 现实的: *a big difference between the opinion polls and the actual election results* 民意测验和实际选举结果的巨大差异 | *I'm not joking. Those were his actual words.* 我不是开玩笑, 那都是他的原话。| **in actual fact** (=really) 实际上 *In actual fact, there is not much evidence to support these allegations.* 事实上, 没有多少证据支持这些指控。

[only after noun 仅用于名词后]:

ga·lore /gəˈlɔr; gəˈlɔː/ *adj* [only after noun 仅用于名词后] in large amounts or numbers 大量的, 许多的: *There are bargains galore in the sales this year.* 今年的大减价期间有许多便宜货。

[not before noun 不用于名词前]:

ad·vi·sab·le /ədˈvaɪzəbḷ; ədˈvaɪzəbəl/ *adj* [not before noun 不用于名词前] something that is advisable should be done in order to avoid problems or risks 可取的; 明智的: *For heavy smokers, regular medical checks are advisable.* 抽烟很多的人最好定期进行健康检查。| **it is advisable to do sth** *It is advisable to disconnect the computer before you open it up.* 拆开电脑之前, 最好先切断电源。—**advisability** /ədˌvaɪzəˈbɪlətɪ; ədˌvaɪzəˈbɪlɪ̌ti/ *n* [U]

[no comparative 无比较级]:

ef·fec·tive /əˈfɛktɪv; ɪˈfektɪv/ *adj* **1** producing the result that was wanted or intended 产生预期效果的; 有效的: *The ads were simple, but remarkably effective.* 这些广告很简单, 但效果出奇的好。**2** impressive or interesting enough to be noticed 引人注意的; 醒目的: *an* *effective use of colour* 使用引人注目的颜色 **3** [no comparative 无比较级] if a law, agreement, or system becomes effective, it officially starts〔法律、协议或制度等〕生效的: *The cut in interest rates is effective from Monday.* 从星期一起利率下调正式生效。**4** [no comparative 无比较级] real rather than what is officially intended or generally believed 实际的, 事实上的: *The rebels are in effective control of the city.* 反叛者实际上已控制了城市。—**effectiveness** *n* [U]

[+adj/adv]:

in·creas·ing·ly /ɪn`krisɪŋlɪ; ɪn'kriːsɪŋli/ *adv* more and more all the time [+adj/adv] 不断增加地, 越来越多地: *The classes at the college have become increasingly full over the past five years.* 在过去的五年中, 这所学院的各班级越来越满。[sentence adverb 句子副词]: *Increasingly, it is the industrial power of Japan and South East Asia that dominates world markets.* 主宰世界市场的是日本和东南亚的工业实力 —— 这一情况日益明显。

[sentence adverb 句子副词]:

hap·pi·ly /`hæpɪlɪ; 'hæpɪli/ *adv* **1** in a happy way 高兴地, 快乐地: *a happily married couple* 一对幸福的夫妇 **2** [sentence adverb 句子副词] fortunately 幸运地: *Happily, his injuries were not serious.* 幸好, 他的伤并不严重。**3** very willingly 很乐意地: *I'd happily go for you.* 我很乐意为你去一趟。

[sentence adverb 句子副词] 这一语法信息表示 happily 在这个义项上用以修饰全句。

某个形容词后的介词或结构在例子前用蓝色字表示出来。

hope·ful[1] /`hopfəl; 'həʊpfəl/ *adj* **1** believing that what you hope for is likely to happen 抱有希望的, 抱乐观态度的: [**+about**] *Everyone's feeling pretty hopeful about the future.* 人人都对未来充满希望。| **hopeful that** *We're hopeful that the team will be fit for next Saturday's game.* 我们有信心球队能以良好的状态参加下星期六的比赛。| **be hopeful of doing sth** *BrE*【英】 *The police are hopeful of finding more clues to the murder.* 警方有望找到更多有关这宗谋杀案的线索。

4.7 Very infrequent words 极不常用的单词

对学生很可能不需要使用的极不常用的单词, 只列出基本的语法信息, 不再举例。

5. Information on register and usage 语域和用法方面的信息

5.1 Indicating register 表示语域

有些单词和义项后提供了它们很可能用于何种情景的信息。这种信息在词目后或在义项序号后, 用斜体标出。

clobber[2] *n* [U] *informal especially BrE* someone's possessions, especially their clothes【非正式, 尤英】随身带的东西; 衣物: *Don't forget all your clobber if you're staying the night.* 如果在外面过夜, 别忘了带衣服。| **fishing/swimming/football clobber etc** (=clothes and equipment needed for a particular activity) 渔具/泳衣/足球衣物

ab·ne·ga·tion /ˌæbnɪ`geʃən; ˌæbnɪ'geɪʃən/ *n* [U] *formal* the act of not allowing yourself to have or do something that you want【正式】自制, 克己

a·blu·tions /əb`ljuʃənz; ə'bluːʃənz/ *n* [plural] *formal or humorous* the things that you do to make yourself clean, such as washing yourself, cleaning your teeth etc【正式或幽默】沐浴; 漱洗

【俚】(俚语) 或【讳】(讳忌语), 尤其是讳忌语, 表示即使在非正式场合也需谨慎使用。

【文】(文学用语)、【诗】(诗歌用语)、【术语】(技术用语)、【旧】(老式用语) 或【过时】(过时用语), 表示人们在讲话或写作中不常用。

5.2 Spoken words and phrases 口语单词与短语

【口】(口语) 标志表示某短语通常用于讲话而不用于书面。

24 that's life *spoken* used when you are disappointed or upset that something has happened but realize that you must accept it【口】生活就是这样〔表示无奈地接受令人失望或生气之事〕: *Oh well, that's life!* 算了, 生活就是这样!

由于朗文语料库网络中既有口语语料, 又有书面语语料, 所以我们能够提供大量这类信息。有些重要单词有图表来说明其在口头英语中的使用频率比在书面英语中高多少。某些这样的单词, 例如 bet, 有特设的"口语短语"方框或段落加以说明。

5.3 Usage notes 用法说明

本辞典有英语特殊用法方面的说明。这些用法说明列在有关的主要单词的词条后面。该项用法说明涉及的其他单词在各自词条下有相互参照的指示。

6. Pronunciation 发音

每个单词后用美式 K.K. 音标和国际音标 (IPA) 标注发音, 两种音标用分号 (;) 隔开。K.K. 音标列在前面; 国际音标列在后面。所用符号列在本辞典的发音表中。可替代的音标在逗号之后列出。如果该音标只有部分不同, 则只标出不同的部分, 用连字符标出其在单词中的位置。

a·ber·rant /æb`ɛrənt; 'æbərənt/ *adj formal* not usual or normal【正式】异常的; 脱离常规的: *aberrant behaviour* 异常行为

ab·duct /æb`dʌkt; əb'dʌkt/ *v* [T] to take someone away by force; KIDNAP 劫持, 绑架; 诱拐: *Police suspect she was abducted late last night.* 警方怀疑她昨天深夜被绑架了。—**abductor** *n* [C] —**abduction** /æb`dʌkʃən; əb'dʌkʃən/ *n* [C,U]

由某个单词有规则地派生而成、并列在该单词后不附释义的大多数单词, 其发音即为其主词加上后缀的发音。这种情况不标注音标, 其他情况则注有音标。

6.1 Compound words 复合词

带空格或连字符的复合词, 一般不标注完整的音标。这是因为其中每个单词都有自己的词条, 词条处都标注了音标。但这类复合词都标有重音模式, 一个音节用一个圆点代替, 标在上方和下方的重音符号分别表示主重音和次重音。

aircraft car·ri·er /'· ·, ··· / *n* [C] a type of ship that has a large flat surface that planes fly from 航空母舰

有些复合词 (如 plate glass) 或一些单词 (如 independent), 如果直接用在名词前时 (如 plate glass window 或 independent observer), 则只有一个主重音 (重音模式中第一个位置)。在这种情况下, 表示重音转移的符号 /◂/ 会标在复合词的重音模式后面:

plate glass /ˌ· ˈ·◂/ *n* [U] big pieces of glass made in large thick sheets for use especially in shop windows 〔尤用于商店橱窗的〕厚玻璃板，平板玻璃

或在单词的音标后面：

in·de·pen·dent /ˌɪndɪˈpɛndənt; ˌɪndɪˈpendənt◂/ *adj*

7. British and American English 英国英语与美国英语

参与本辞典编纂工作的词条撰稿人有英国人也有美国人，因此本辞典收录了大量的英国英语与美国英语。释义正文是用英国英语写的，但实例有英国英语也有美国英语。单词的英国英语形式和美国英语形式在发音和拼写方面的差异都列出标明。仅出现在英国英语的单词、单词的义项、语法结构、短语和词语搭配标有 *BrE*【英】，而仅存在于美国英语的上述内容则标有 *AmE*【美】。更常用于英国英语的标有 *especially BrE*【尤英】，而更常用于美国英语的标有 *especially AmE*【尤美】。

7.1 Pronunciation and spelling differences 发音与拼写的差异

英国英语和美国英语中拼写不同的单词，两种拼写方式均列出并注音。

cen·tre[1] *BrE*【英】, **center** *AmE*【美】/ˈsɛntɚ; ˈsentə/ *n* **1 ▶MIDDLE** 中间◀ [C] the middle of a space, area, or object, especially the exact middle 〔空间、地域或物体的〕(正)中间，中心(点)：*Draw a line through the centre of the circle.* 画一条线通过那个圆的圆心。| *Tony only likes chocolates with soft centres.* 托尼只爱吃软夹心巧克力。| [+of] *There was an enormous oak table in the center of the room.* 房间中央有一张巨大的橡木桌子。

cen·ter /ˈsɛntɚ; ˈsentə/ *n, v* the American spelling of CENTRE centre 的美式拼法

如果某词在英国英语或美国英语中有时拼写方式不同于主词，该拼写方式列在"also 又作"之后。

jail[1] also 又作 **gaol** *BrE*【英】/dʒel; dʒeɪl/ *n* [C,U] a place where criminals are kept as part of their punishment, or where people who have been charged with a crime are kept before they are judged in a law court; PRISON (1) 监狱

有些动词在英国英语中其过去式与 -ing 形式末字母要双写，而在美国英语中却不需要。这时两种拼写均列出并标明：

label[2] *v* **labelled, labelling** *BrE*【英】, **labeled, labeling** *AmE*【美】[T]

7.2 Words and meanings – British and American differences 单词与词义 —— 英国英语和美国英语的差异

有时，英国英语和美国英语使用完全不同的单词来表示相同的事物。在这种情况下，英国英语单词的词条释义后面标出其美国英语的同义词，反之亦然。

el·e·va·tor /ˈɛləˌvetɚ; ˈeləveɪtə/ *n* [C] **1** *AmE* a machine that takes people and goods from one level to another in a building【美】电梯; LIFT[2] (1) *BrE*【英】**2** a machine with a moving belt and containers, used for lifting grain and liquids, or for taking things off ships 〔运送粮食、液体或卸船的〕升降机，起卸机

有时，一个英国英语的单词在美国英语中没有对等词，或者该对等词很少使用。这样的单词仅标上【英】或【美】：

airing cup·board /ˈ· · ˌ· ·/ *n* [C] *BrE* a warm cupboard in a house where sheets and clean clothes are kept【英】〔储存被单、衣服的〕烘柜

air·head /ˈɛrˌhɛd; ˈeəhed/ *n* [C] *slang especially AmE* someone who is stupid【俚，尤美】傻瓜，笨蛋

如果单词的某义项仅存在于英国英语或美国英语，会于该义项序号后加以标明：

home·ly /ˈhomlɪ; ˈhəʊmli/ *adj* **1** *BrE* simple and ordinary in a way that makes you feel comfortable【英】朴实无华的；家常的：*The cottage had a warm, homely feel.* 那间小屋给人一种温馨的感觉。**2** *AmE* people or faces that are homely are unattractive or ugly【美】相貌平庸的；丑陋的：*I've never seen such a homely dog in my life!* 我这辈子从未见过如此难看的狗！

7.3 Differences in grammar 语法差异

有些单词仅在英国英语或美国英语后跟某个特定的介词或结构，这些差异均予标明。

一种差异是：像 government 或 class 这类集合名词在英国英语里可以用复数动词，但在美国英语里却不行。对于这类重要的单词，这种差异均给予说明并标示出来：

gov·ern·ment /ˈgʌvɚnmənt; ˈgʌvənmənt/ *n* **1** also 又作 **Government** [C] the group of people who govern a country or state 政府：*The new military government does not have popular support.* 新上台的军人政府没有得到广泛的支持。| [also+plural verb *BrE* 英] *The Government are planning further cuts in public spending.* 政府正计划进一步削减公共支出。

7.4 Differences in phrases and collocations 短语与词语搭配的差异

英国英语与美国英语的一个重要差异是两者各有丰富的习语。有些单词在这两种英语之一有典型的搭配，而在另一种英语中却没有。仅在英国英语或美国英语中出现的短语和搭配均标示如下。

jack[2] *v*

jack sb **around** *phr v* [T] *AmE slang* to waste someone's time by deliberately making things difficult for them【美俚】故意刁难〔某人〕以浪费其时间：*Stop jacking me around and make up your mind!* 别浪费我的时间了，拿定主意吧！

jack sth ↔ **in** *phr v* [T] *BrE informal* to stop doing something【英，非正式】停止做：*I'd love to jack in my job and go live in the Bahamas.* 我很愿意辞去工作，去巴哈马居住。

8. Culture 文化

8.1 Cultural entries 文化词条

本辞典收录人名、地名、政治、历史、文学、艺术、流行文化等文化词条，提供详尽的百科信息。

8.2 Cultural notes 文化注释

文化注释详细说明某个单词在以英语为母语的人心里的联想意义。有时这些联想与古老的说法或传说有关，有些与流传的故事有关，有些则与历史事件或政治事件有关，有些还与英国人和美国人生活的某个方面有关。文化注释位于单词的释义和例证的后面：

Cal·i·for·ni·a /ˌkælɪˈfɔrnɪə; ˌkæl̩ˈfɔːniə/ abbreviation 缩写为 **CA** a state in the southwest of the US, next to the Pacific Ocean, whose main cities include San Francisco and Los Angeles 加利福尼亚〔美国西南部一州。濒临太平洋，主要城市有圣弗朗西斯科和洛杉矶〕

CULTURAL NOTE 文化注释

When British and American people think of California, they often think of beaches, warm sunny weather, and SURF*ing*. The state, especially northern California, is often considered to be more LIBERAL than other states in the US, but it has also elected RIGHT-WING politicians such as Ronald Reagan and Arnold Schwarzenegger as GOVERNOR. In the 1960s, San Francisco was a centre of the HIPPY movement which supported LEFT-WING politics and had RADICAL ideas about changing society. At the University of California, Berkeley, there were many protests against the Vietnam War. California is known as a place where people like to follow the latest fashions in LIFESTYLE, and where people want to stay physically fit and look young. 英美人想到加利福尼亚，常会想到海滩、温暖晴朗的天气和冲浪运动。加利福尼亚，尤其是该州北部常被认为比美国其他各州更为思想开放，但一些右翼政界人士，如罗纳德·里根和阿诺德·施瓦辛格也被选为州长。20世纪60年代，圣弗朗西斯科成为嬉皮士运动的中心。嬉皮士运动支持左翼政治，持激进的观点，试图改良社会。在加利福尼亚大学伯克利分校，曾有很多反对越战的抗议活动。加利福尼亚以人们热衷追逐最新潮流闻名，当地人都想保持体型健美，外表年轻。

8.3 Features 文化特写

本辞典中的文化特写部分是为提供英美某些方面的文化资料而特别编写的。文化特写作为插页彩色印刷。

本辞典所使用的符号说明

1. 本辞典英语原文所使用的各种符号可以参见辞典的 Explanatory Chart (图示) 或 Grammar Codes (语法代号表); 如涉及语音的符号, 请参见 Pronunciation Table (发音表)。

2. 本辞典的中文译文也使用了几种不同的符号, 它们的形式和所表示的含义如下:

   (1) 鱼尾括号【 】: 用于标示原文的说明性略语之中译, 如: *derog*【贬】等。详情请参见 Short Forms and Labels (缩略语和说明性略语)。

   (2) 六角括号〔 〕: 表示 ① 括号内为解释性、限定性的文字;
   ② 某些动词的宾语的位置, 例如: **bale²** to tie something such as paper or hay into a large block 把〔纸、干草等〕绑成一大捆

   (3) 三角括号〈 〉: 用于举例, 如: **obeisance** 敬礼〈如鞠躬〉。

   (4) 圆括号 ( ): 表示 ① 括号内文字可省略;
   ② 括号内文字有及无两种情况兼可。

   (5) 方括号 [ ]: 表示和括号前面的文字可相互替代, 例如: **aerogramme** 航空邮简[笺]。

   (6) 等号 = : 表示 ① 词目与等号后的词同义;
   ② 词目的详细释义可参见等号后的词的释义。

Acknowledgements

鸣 谢

Editorial Director
Michael Mayor

Senior Publisher
Laurence Delacroix

Managing Editor
Stephen Bullon

Editor
Michael Murphy

Lexicographers
Daniel Barron
Elizabeth Beizai
Karen Cleveland-Marwick
Stephen Handorf
Martin Stark
Rebecca Campbell
Michael Janes
Joanna Leigh
Clare Vickers
Donald Watt

Research
David Hallworth

Project Manager
Alan Savill

Production Manager
Clive McKeough

Computational Linguist
Allan Ørsnes

Production Editor
Paola Rocchetti

Project and Database Administrator
Denise McKeough

Technical Support Manager
Trevor Satchell

Network Administrator
Kim Lee-Amies

Pronunciation Editor
Dinah Jackson

Proofreaders
Sandra Anderson
Isabel Griffiths
Carole Murphy
Ruth Hillmore
Jane Horwood
Ruth Noble
Daphne Trotter

Features
Stephen Bullon
Stephen Handorf
Michael Murphy
Joanna Leigh
Cindy Leaney

Keyboarders
Denise McKeough
Pauline Savill
Janine Trainor

Design
Mick Harris

Picture Research
Sue Donoghue
Sandra Hilsdon
Hilary Luckcock
Lisa Wren

Artwork
Bob Harvey (Pennant Illustration)
Chris Rothero (Beehive Illustration)
Martin Sanders (Beehive Illustration)
Tony Wilkins

Photo Acknowledgements

The Publishers are grateful to the following for their permission to reproduce copyright photographs: **Alamy**/Jiri Rezac for F33 left. **Alamy**/Photofusion Picture Library for F23 top left. **Alamy**/Robert Mullan for F33 right. **Alamy**/Stock Connection Blue for F13 left. **Alamy**/The Photolibrary Wales for F29 right. **Corbis**/Adam Woolfitt for F12 bottom right. **Corbis**/Ariel Skelley for F24. **Corbis**/Bettmann for F9 right. **Corbis**/Catherine Karnow for F6 left. **Corbis**/Chuck Savage for F18 left. **Corbis**/Jose Luis Pelaez, Inc. for F20. **Corbis**/Ken Skalski for F10 right. **Corbis**/Marco Cristofori for F11 right. **Corbis**/Philip Gould for F22 top right. **Corbis**/Richard Cummins for F12 left. **Corbis**/Robbie Jack for F36 and F37 top left. **Corbis**/Rolf Konow/Sygma for F37 bottom left. **Getty Images** for F6 right. **Getty Images**/Hulton Archive/Keystone/Stringer for F18 right. **Getty Images**/Popperfoto for F10 left and F9 left. **Getty Images**/Stone/Rick Rusing for F41. **Getty Images**/The Image Bank/Andrea Pistolesi for F35 bottom left. **Hemera Technologies** for F12 top right, F13 right, F14 left, F21, F22 bottom right, F22 left, F23 bottom left, F25, F29 left and F7 right. **Photolibrary**/Warwick Kent for F7 left. **Punchstock**/Corbis for F8 left.

朗文当代英语大辞典

(英英·英汉双解)

新版

(简化汉字版)

出版前言

本辞典由商务印书馆与培生教育出版亚洲有限公司合作出版，是我馆于2004年在内地出版发行的《朗文当代英语大辞典》(Longman Dictionary of English Language and Culture) 简化汉字本的修订版。

语言与文化密不可分。本辞典针对中高级英语学习者，共收单词及短语近10万条，含1.5万余文化词条，涵盖历史、地理、文学、艺术、教育、流行文化等领域，是一本百科全书式的英语学习辞典。

新版继承和保留了旧版的诸多优点，如释义简明，使用最常用的2000个单词撰写释义，浅显易懂；例证典型，全部例证来自语料库，突出语词的实用性；注重词语搭配的学习，提供数千处搭配示例，方便读者查阅研习等。较之旧版，新版内容有以下特色：(一) 收词英美并重。基于朗文语料库网络 (Longman Corpus Network)，特别在文化类词目的选择上对旧版作了全面修订，增加了美国文化内容的比重。(二) 重视语言的文体差异。标示出口语和书面语中最常用的1000词、2000词和3000词。(三) 设置"词汇使用频率表"。基于统计数据设置的150多个"词汇使用频率表"，对词汇在口语和书面语中的使用情况作详细解说。(四) "用法说明"全面改写。讲解词语间的细微区别，示意语言的正确用法。

本辞典出版前，经培生教育出版亚洲有限公司同意，我们对原书在文字上作了一些技术处理，以便更符合内地读者的使用习惯。辞典编辑工作繁复琐碎，疏漏之处在所难免，尚祈广大读者不吝指正为感。

商务印书馆辞书研究中心

2011年6月

此扉页用含有商务印书馆注册商标的水印防伪纸印制，有这种扉页的《朗文当代英语大辞典》（英英·英汉双解，新版）是正版图书。请注意识别。

当代英语大辞典

（英英·英汉双解）

新版

New Edition

ONGMAN Dictionary of English Language and Culture

(English-Chinese)

语言部分

主审：汪榕培

翻译：王立弟等

文化部分

审定：徐式谷

翻译：李瑞林等

商務印書館

The Commercial Press

PEARSON

Longman朗文